EXCEEDING EXPECTATIONS:

A USER'S GUIDE TO IMPLEMENTING BRAIN RESEARCH IN THE CLASSROOM

by Susan J. Kovalik
and
Karen D. Olsen

THIRD EDITION

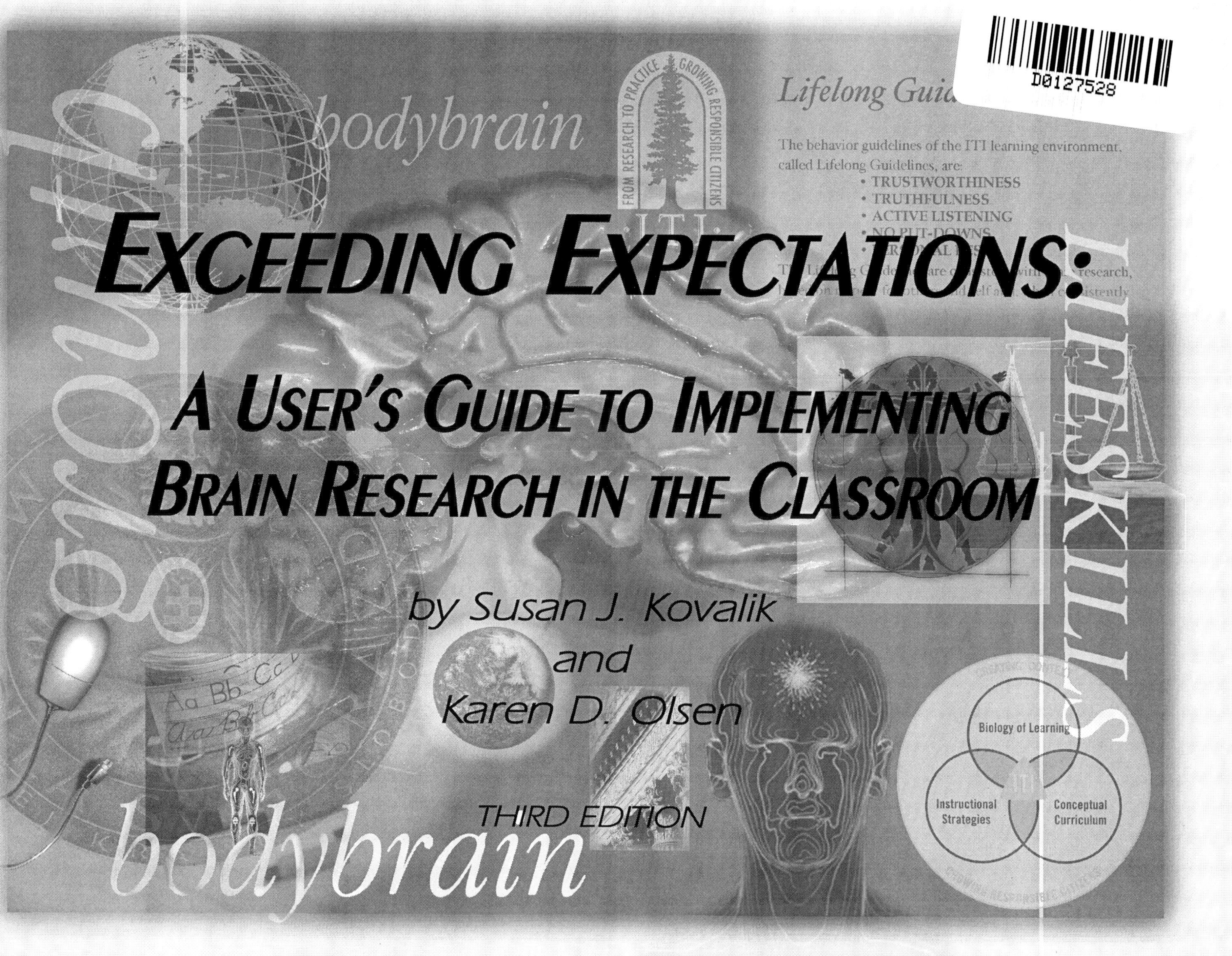

Exceeding Expectations:

A User's Guide to Implementing Brain Research in the Classroom

Third Edition

by Susan J. Kovalik and Karen D. Olsen

Edited by Kathleen Wolgemuth
Graphics & Illustrations by Lanitta Jaye Delk

Published by Susan Kovalik & Associates, Inc.
www.kovalik.com

Distributed by Books for Educators, Inc.
33506 10th Place S
Federal Way, WA 98003-6306
888/777-9827
E-mail: books4@oz.net
www.books4educ.com

ISBN # 1-878631-85-3

Printed in the United States of America

Dedication

For educators everywhere

who understand that it takes courage, integrity, and perseverance

to bring the very best of what we know to all children.

Susan J. Kovalik

Acknowledgements

The very least you can do in
your life is to figure out what
you hope for.
And the most you can do is
live inside that hope.

—Barbara Kingsolver

The "hope" of Susan Kovalik and Associates is to facilitate learning communities that are dynamic environments for teaching and learning, providing multiple opportunities for meaningful content, which will enable students to become responsible and informed citizens.

The associates of Susan Kovalik and Associates, all classroom teachers or administrators, are responsible for the training and coaching of thousands of educators in the United States and around the world. They are on the road at least 50% of the year, guiding and supporting educators who are committed to creating true learning communities. Their contributions to the development of the ITI model are many and varied:

Karen Olsen, who has held the intellectual conscience and integrity of the ITI model since 1987. She is author, co-author, or contributing editor of all our publications.

Ann Ross, who believed that ITI could work in middle schools, no matter what the neighborhood, and who wrote, with Karen D. Olsen, the first ITI middle school book for the ITI model.

Patty Harrington who patiently helped us understand the need to build a sense of community in the classroom as a means of improving academic learning.

Kari Kling, whose initiative and perseverance produced the ITI math book, *It's Not About Math, It's About Life,* and *The Only Being-There Experience Guide Students Ever Need: Connect Learning, Trips, Kids, and School.*

Judy Eacker, whose talent and spirit gave the LIFESKILLS a voice through song and a sensitive ear to the needs of students and teachers. Judy also orchestrated the *Sign On* video at the Colorado School of the Deaf so that everyone can learn to teach and use the Lifelong Guidelines & LIFESKILLS in American Sign Language.

Dean Tannewitz, who leads with wisdom and intention, building community wherever she goes and inspiring schools to go the distance toward success.

Sue Pearson, whose efforts and commitment produced the LIFESKILL book, *Tools For Citizenship and Life: Using the ITI Lifelong Guidelines and LIFESKILLS in Your Classroom.*

Nicole Miller, whose enlightened teaching in an inner city middle school is documented in the video, *ITI in the Urban Middle School*. Now CEO of Susan Kovalik and Associates, she brings wisdom, vision, and a burning conviction that all students can succeed.

Linda Jordan, who co-developed an exceptional teacher training program to provide graduating college students with the ITI tools to succeed.

Jill Hay, who as a special education supervisor adopted a class and taught one day a week for a year to understand firsthand the power of the ITI model for special education students and thus provide better leadership through staff development.

Cathy Frederick, a comprehensive staff development coordinator who is now Executive Director of Susan Kovalik and Associates. She has been instrumental with aiding school districts in their overall three-year plans and helping them select grants to further fund their growth.

To the associates who are no longer on the road but have influenced the model: Jo Gusman, Barbara Pedersen, Robert Ellingsen, Martha Kaufeldt, Ventura Lopez, Jacque Melin, Sally Johnson, Pattie Mills, Joy Raboli, Kathy Theuer, Jane McGeehan, and Sister Patt Walsh.

None of this is possible without the support of the people back home. A big thank you to all the families out there who realize the power of knowledge and commitment and who share those they love with other people's children.

Also, a heartfelt thank you to the people who answer the phone at Susan Kovalik & Associates and make it all happen.

To all the teachers who have worked with us during model teaching weeks and summer institutes, thank you for enriching the model through your enthusiasm, talents, and insights. Multiple schools and entire school districts all over the country have caught the vision of the ITI model and have joined the quest for excellence in their state: Alaska, Arizona, California, Colorado, Florida, Georgia, Indiana, Iowa, Kansas, Kentucky, Michigan, Minnesota, Missouri, Nevada, New Jersey, New York, North Carolina, North Dakota, Ohio, Oklahoma, Oregon, Pennsylvania, South Carolina, Tennessee, Texas, Utah, Virginia, Washington, and Wisconsin.

Thousands of students and teachers go to school each day excited by the possibilities. Each of you, in countless ways during untold hours, has contributed to that possibility.

Thank you isn't a big enough phrase, but I do thank each of you for allowing me to "live inside my hope." For in the end,

We will conserve only what we love.
We will love only what we understand.
We will understand only what we are taught.

Baba Dioum

Table of Contents

Preface

"This is a "must read" book for every educator who would like practical methods for applying brain research. Throughout the world, international and national schools are using the ITI conceptual framework to develop responsible citizens. The ITI model is applicable to any classroom and applies well to all cultures. At our K-12 school in Kobe, Japan we have found that the nomenclature is easy to teach to children of all nationalities. LIFESKILLS are the cornerstone for our program of character/values education and parents are able to understand the concepts and reinforce these values at home. But more important, the ITI model gives our multinational teaching staff common language to use in their professional day-to-day life."

—David Ottaviano, Ed.D.
Headmaster, Canadian Academy
Kobe, Japan

"If there were just one book that I could buy to be a more effective teacher, it would be *Exceeding Expectations.* This book is an effective coach for the first year teacher as well as for me, a 20-year teacher. The explanations and examples make the ITI model clear and understandable. I found "meat" in every section of every chapter.

The book is elegantly written—no wasted words—just clear, precise, beautiful language. The personal examples of Karen Olsen helped me to understand the model more completely even though I have been implementing ITI over eight years now. I also appreciate the research and the sources provided at the end of each chapter, many of which have a short overview that gives you an idea of what that book is all about and its usefulness to you.

Exceeding Expectations goes beyond being a step-by-step guide for ITI; it is a guide book for effective teaching for all teachers of all experience levels. I still don't know how the authors accomplished this task but they did. This is an award-winning book if I've ever seen one."

—Barbara Norris, 6th Grade Teacher
Florida

This book is a labor of love. It represents a lifetime of thinking and teaching and it holds forth the hope that we will find the political will to use brain research to transform our schools and, in so doing, transform our world. It is heartening to hear from those implementing ITI that this hope is taking wing and that, in ways big and small, ITI is contributing to making the world a better place. We invite you to join with us.

The Authors

Introduction

Origins of the ITI Model

As a new sixth grade teacher, I worked my intuition overtime to come up with the best ways to teach my students. As an Italian, that meant providing plenty of enthusiasm, exuberant gestures, laughs, hugs, and food. My formula worked; my students loved school and loved learning. Then I became a K-6 science teacher for 1,200 students. To my basic Italian instructional strategies, I added lots of hands-on-of-real-things—your basic nightmare for a custodian and for the music teacher with whom I shared space. Snakes, rats, chickens, you name it. More good results with kids. Then one day the custodian told me he had seen a notice for a new job opening—teacher for the gifted and talented (GT). He told me I should apply! Whether it was because he had noticed the enthusiasm of my students or hoped longingly for a more traditional science teacher with fewer critters and exploratory items, I'll never know. But I took his suggestion. My work with GT students led me to giving workshops, in the course of which I was noticed by a talent scout for an organization that sponsored conferences across the country. Fully convinced that we needed to save students from the boredom and tedium of textbooks and worksheets—so why not start with the gifted!—I hit the road.

As I'd promised my three teenage children that I would take each of them on the road with me for a week, I soon found myself in Indiana with my youngest son, Marshall. The GT coordinator, our dinner hostess, was very enthusiastic about her mission, effusive about the needs and achievements of GT students. As the testimonials rolled on, my son spun his corner-fold napkin to make a loop and pretended to hang himself, gagging for added effect. As I stared in disbelief at my son's rudeness, I was further shocked as he burst out: "Do you really believe that the only students who want a good teacher and something interesting to learn are the ones that score high on a one-hour test?" In response our dinner hostess said he seemed a little hostile. "Yes," he said, "my brother and sister [who were in a GT program] get all the good teachers and I get the leftovers. And no one ever asked me what I wanted."

Marshall was right. Every kid deserves a good teacher. I left the field of gifted education and turned my attention to learning for all students.

The most important lessons in life often come from our own family experiences.

Three years later, Marshall came home from high school in January of his senior year and said to me, "I know what you believe and I know what you stand for, but I'm quitting school. Before you say anything, you go sit in my classes for a day. If, at the end of the day, you can look me in the eye and tell me that six more months of this will really enhance who I am as a person, then we'll talk about it." After sitting through his classes, I could not look him in the eye and say, "Yes, it would." Marshall left school.

Marshall was right again.

My quest for answers intensified. I scoured bookstores for books about learning and happened upon Leslie Hart's *Human Brain and Human Learning* in 1983. At last . . . an explanation about how the brain learns from a scientific perspective. New doors began to open. To my wonderment, many of my earlier intuitions about instructional strategies and curriculum development were confirmed by brain research. I was ecstatic! I began to analyze my teaching strategies. They worked not because I was an extroverted Italian but because they allowed students' brains to work the way they naturally work; the strategies were, as Hart coined the term, "brain-compatible." In fact, anyone could learn the techniques and they worked for all students—not just GT, not just reluctant learners, but all students. The ITI model was born.

Over the past 18 years, the ITI model has continued to evolve to stay current with emerging brain research and the ongoing efforts by my associates and I and ITI teachers across the country to develop the best possible curricular and instructional practices to translate brain research into practical applications.

The ITI model reflects another side of my family experience, that of the political activism of my parents, Malcolm and Josephine Jafferies. They imprinted on me early in life that the purpose of an educated life is citizenship—active participation in our democratic processes.

On behalf of all the Marshalls out there who want, and deserve, good teachers and something interesting to learn and in deep gratitude for my parents who modeled citizenship, knowing how precious and fragile a democratic society is, I welcome you to the ITI model.

Susan J. Kovalik
January, 2005
Covington, Washington

Overview of the ITI Model

The ITI model has two main goals:

- To create participating citizens, willing and able to engage in our democratic processes to improve life now and for future generations
- To help educators translate current brain research into practical strategies for the classroom and schoolwide

Pursuing one goal without the other is an empty activity. The world has urgent problems to solve and we have children waiting to learn and grow and hoping to have meaningful work to do.

The ITI model is based in current brain research. Our knowledge of how the human brain learns—the biology of learning—informs us about what's worth teaching as we develop curriculum and instructional strategies that will work best.

Few will be surprised by the core concepts of brain research presented in this book; they ring true with our intuitions. We believe that schools of the 21st century must develop curriculum and instructional strategies illuminated by brain research, not by educational tradition and habit.

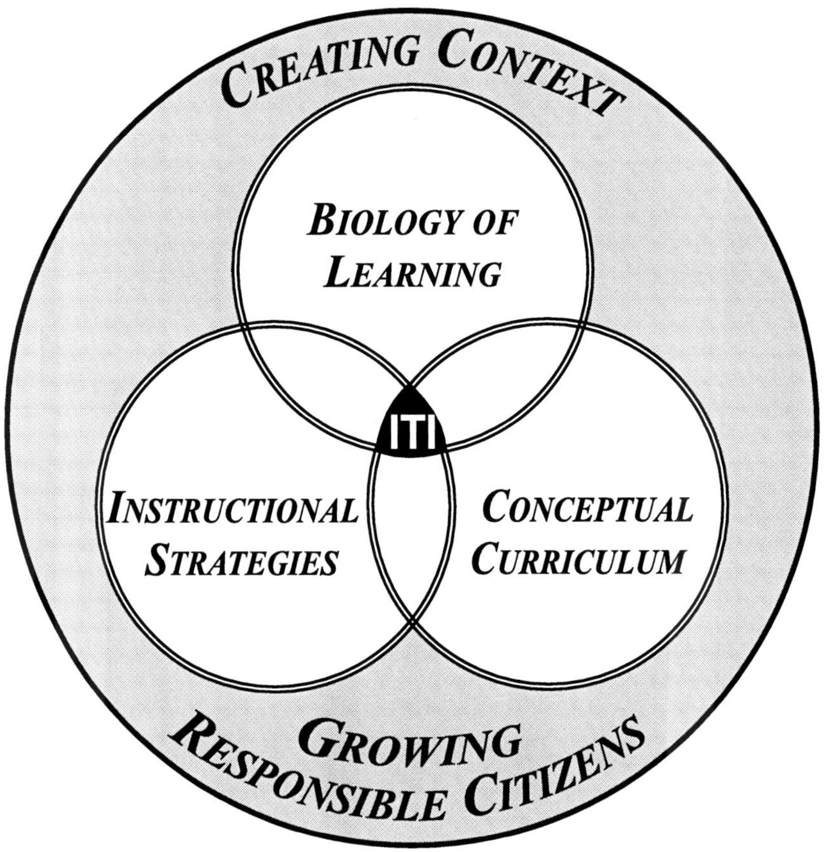

Brain Biology — The Four ITI Learning Principles

The ITI model is based on four basic principles from brain research, each of which is discussed in Part A, Chapters 1-5:

1. ***Intelligence*** is a function of experience (see Chapter 1)

2. Learning is an inseparable partnership between ***brain*** and ***body*** (see Chapter 2)
   - –Emotion is the gatekeeper to learning and performance
   - –Movement enhances learning

3. There are ***multiple intelligences*** or ways of solving problems and/or producing products (see Chapter 3)

4. Learning is a ***two-step process***:
   - –Step one: Making meaning through pattern seeking (see Chapter 4)
   - –Step two: Developing a mental program for using what we understand and wiring it into long-term memory (see Chapter 5)

The Nine Bodybrain-Compatible Elements of Curriculum Development and Instruction

The bodybrain-compatible elements of the ITI model are the primary ways of translating brain research into action in the classroom. These nine elements are:

- ***Absence of Threat/ Nurturing Reflective Thinking***
- ***Meaningful Content***
- ***Movement***
- ***Enriched Environment***
- ***Choices***
- ***Adequate Time***
- ***Collaboration***
- ***Immediate Feedback***
- ***Mastery/Application***

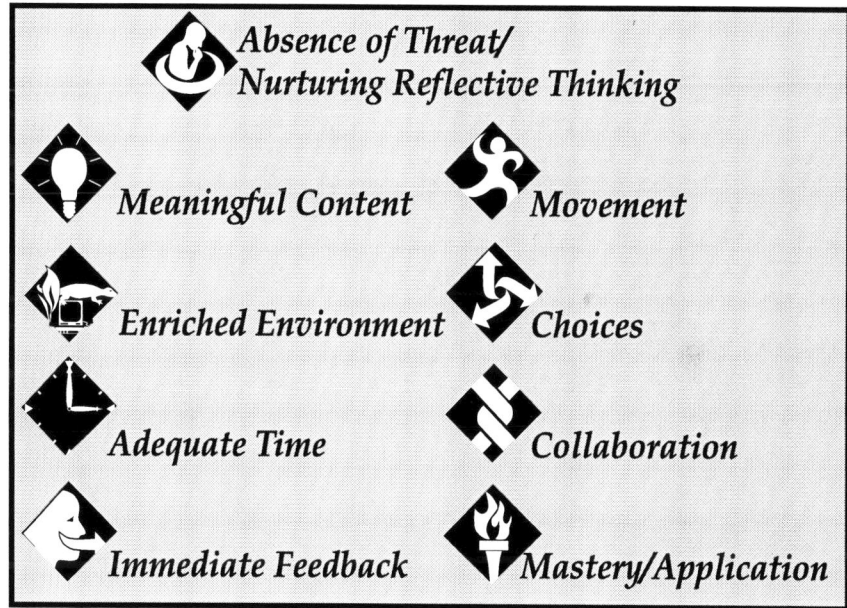

These nine bodybrain-compatible elements appear at the back of each of the six chapters dealing with an ITI Learning Principle (see Chapters 1-5). This intermix of theory and practical applications—the Learning Principles with the Bodybrain-Compatible Elements—is illustrated on the next page. The concentric circles represent the brain research concepts; the pie wedges represent the bodybrain-compatible elements.

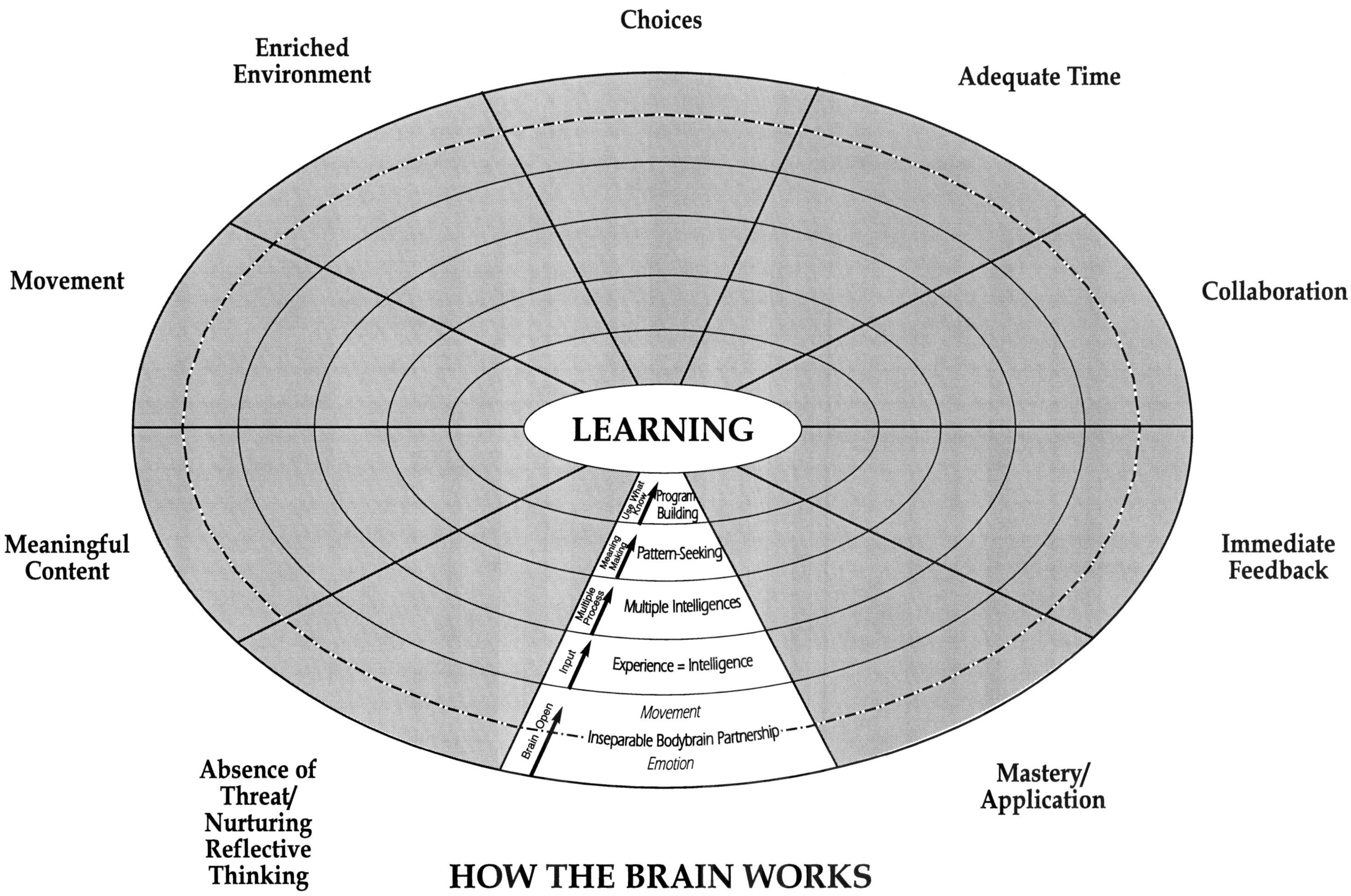
Choices
Enriched Environment
Adequate Time
Movement
Collaboration
LEARNING
Use What Know
Program Building
Meaning Making
Pattern-Seeking
Multiple Process
Multiple Intelligences
Input
Experience = Intelligence
Brain Open
Movement
Inseparable Bodybrain Partnership
Emotion
Meaningful Content
Immediate Feedback
Absence of Threat/ Nurturing Reflective Thinking
Mastery/ Application

HOW THE BRAIN WORKS

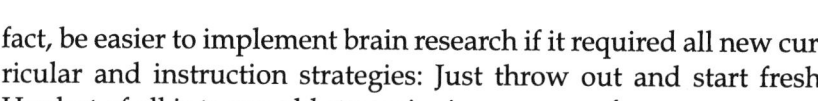

Toward Bodybrain-Compatible Teaching/Learning

Although little about the five ITI Learning Principles from brain research and their relationship to the nine bodybrain-compatible elements may surprise you, implementing them in the face of a system that is brain-antagonistic in so many ways is indeed a challenge.

Coherence, Not Piecemeal. Achieving bodybrain-compatibility for your students is not the result of following a check list. The concepts from brain research cannot be implemented by a few simple strategies. Effective implementation will only come through full understanding of the brain research and the richness of its implications. As you study each of the ITI Learning Principles in Chapters 1-6, do ask yourself, "So what?" What does this mean to my students? What does this suggest that I change about my classroom? What does it mean to base my teaching in brain research rather than traditional practices?

Implementing ITI is not a piecemeal affair in which one picks and chooses what to implement. Perhaps the most important thing to say about brain research and its implementation is this: ***If even one of the bodybrain-compatible elements is not in place, the learning environment is not bodybrain-compatible.***

Old Yet New. It is important to recognize that the curricular and instructional strategies described in the ITI model are not new. Good teachers have implemented them over the years but did so intuitively. However, intuition alone is insufficient when putting together a coherent, comprehensive approach to curriculum and instruction for a schoolwide program improvement effort.

Basing our improvement efforts on brain research requires us to use old tools differently and for new purposes. It would, in fact, be easier to implement brain research if it required all new curricular and instruction strategies: Just throw out and start fresh. Hardest of all is to use old strategies in new ways for new purposes.

What makes this so hard is that it's extremely difficult to maintain a clear vision of old tools used anew when one lives in an old structure with its old pictures, old habits, and old vocabulary with its old ideas. Before we know it, we're back where we started. And old tools used in old ways will not produce the results for students that we desire. But when old tools are used in new ways, with the purpose of translating brain research into action, you will be amazed at the changes in student behavior, attitudes, and test scores. You'll also find yourself enjoying teaching more than you ever thought possible.

The Balance Between Curriculum and Instruction

The ITI model is perhaps best known as a curriculum development model with its integrated yearlong theme structure, yet it is first and foremost a means of translating brain research into practical classroom applications. Experience has taught us that creating a bodybrain-compatible teaching/learning environment is a necessary prerequisite before we can move on to more traditional aspects of curriculum development. Once these environmental and classroom leadership/management elements are in place, the curriculum development aspects of the ITI model can then come to the forefront.

How to Use This Book

This is not a book to be read from cover to cover in one swoop. It is designed to be read in stages over three-to-five years. These stages, which follow the *ITI Classroom Stages of Implementation,* describe how to implement the ITI model from before school begins through full implementation of a brain research-based integrated thematic instruction model. The stages are:

- Stage 1: Getting Started.
  - Before the first day of school (Stage 1.1)
  - The first day of school and beyond (Stage 1.2)
  - What to accomplish before moving on to the next stage (1.3)
- Stage 2: First Steps to Integrating Curriculum
- Stages 3-5: Working Toward Total Integration in a Fully Bodybrain-Compatible Learning Environment

Note the symbols along the right. They mark the pages for each part of the book as described below.

Part A is your touchstone. Read it and re-read it until you feel you have a grasp of the vision it forecasts. Revisit it each time you begin a new part of the book.

Read **Part B** when you're ready to begin implementing Stage 1*—what to do before school starts, what to do the first day of school (includes an outline and lesson plan for the first day of school) and beyond, and what to accomplish before moving on to Stage 2.

Once you have your bodybrain-compatible learning environment firmly in place (which typically takes a year of concerted effort), review Part A and read **Part C.** Part C explains how to begin integrating curriculum, your first step in Stage 2.

Part D describes how to work toward total integration as described in Implementation Stage 3. Stage 3 assumes that you have mastered the environmental and instructional strategies of previous stages. Before you begin, review Part A, the summary of brain research. It is essential for the stage.

Part E explains how to achieve full integration of curriculum through Stages 4-5 of the ITI Classroom Stages of Implementation. This section includes a discussion of further integration and creating a micro-community.

Part F discusses tools for living with change. Read it when you begin implementing Stage 1.2. Revisit it as you begin planning for each subsequent stage.

As you use this book, notice that we have provided quick graphic references for you. Every page carries one of the distinguishing symbols above, quickly identifying where you are. Also, the first page of each part can be quickly located by looking for the gray stripe along the right edge of the book.

As you read through Parts A and B, keep in mind the curriculum development structures for the ITI model that appear on the next page. **Key points** are what you want students to understand (concepts, significant knowledge, and skills) and **inquiries** are what you want students to be able to do with what they understand. You should be familiar with them from the very beginning of your journey into the ITI model.

> ### Key Points
> *Key points answer the question: "What do we want students to understand?"*
>
> ### Inquiries
> *Inquiries answer the question: "What do we want students to do with what they understand?"*

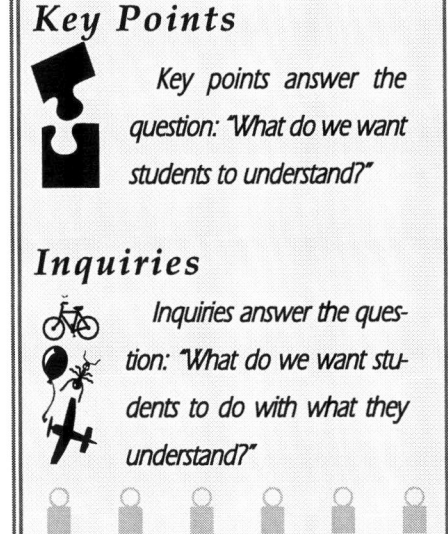

Examples of *key points are accompanied by a strip of puzzle pieces* along the left margin, symbolic of the brain's pattern-seeking processes as it attempts to make meaning of its surroundings. *Inquiries are accompanied by a strip of action elements* along the left margin, symbolic of the brain's drive to use what it understands through doing-taking action, applying what is being learned in order to become wired into long-term memory such as that requested in the inquiries.

Thank you for joining us.

* See *ITI Classroom Stages of Implementation* by Karen D. Olsen. Available through Books for Educators.

Part A

Brain Research

And Its Practical Application

Brain Research and the ITI Model

The ITI model starts with brain research to determine best practice—everything from curriculum development to instructional strategies, classroom assessment of student progress to evaluating student achievement program-wide, classroom and school design to budgeting.

The challenges facing students, teachers, and administrators are greater than ever before and are not likely to be solved until we change our ways of thinking about learning and teaching. As Einstein commented: "Problems can't be solved by the same thinking that created them." This is the 21st century. Traditional ways of teaching and the habits of mind that go with them must give way to using best knowledge.

Bodybrain Biology

In 1990, President George Bush proclaimed the final years of the 20th century as the Decade of the Brain. As we enter the 21st century, our public and private school systems still struggle to come to terms with how brain research should be used as a basis for reform efforts. We believe that a significant part of the resistance to using brain research stems from piecemeal views of brain research findings. Teachers need and deserve a comprehensive view of brain research that includes practical applications to the classroom. For others, the source of resistance comes from an awareness that what brain research is telling us suggests a rigorous need to change our 150+ year old practices, a degree of change that may seem overwhelming or outside our level of commitment.

The purpose of Part A is to describe the four learning principles from brain research that provide a biological base for a comprehensive view of the instructional strategies and curriculum development needed to improve students learning. Embedded in the four concepts is a discussion of the nine bodybrain-compatible elements of the ITI model that translate brain research insights into practical, everyday applications in the classroom and school.

Four Learning Principles from Brain Research

Although the enormous complexity of the brain and the dizzying, science fiction-like capabilities of today's research technologies can make for heavy treading when reading brain research studies, descriptions of how the human brain learns can be expressed in relatively simple conceptual terms. And although we may not know as much as we will, we certainly know enough to get started.

> *"Most school practice arises from tradition, ritual, and the context within which schools are conducted. Only during this century has scientific learning theory had an influence and then only in a minor way. The school is a kind of subculture in which are preserved the relics of former times, with a few practices added or subtracted because of contemporary thought."*
>
> *Foshay*

The learning principles outlined here are, we believe, fundamental to establishing a working theory of human learning for the 21st century. Corroborated by researchers studying the human brain from many different avenues, they provide a powerful template for making decisions about curriculum and instruction and other issues for systemic rethinking of American education.

These four principles defined here are discussed in Chapters 1 through 5. Each chapter describes how the nine bodybrain-compatible elements of the ITI model are used to translate each of these brain principles into practical, and powerful, classroom applications. The bodybrain-compatible elements are described in each chapter in Part A in the order of their power to implement that particular learning principle.

The Four ITI Learning Principles About How the Human Brain Learns Are:

- ***Intelligence as a function of experience***[1]

Learning is the result of real, observable physiological growth in the brain[1] that occurs as a result of sensory input and the processing, organizing, and pruning it promotes. Genetics is not the immutable determiner of intelligence it is generally believed to be; although it sets parameters, experiences with high levels of sensory input can significantly increase development of one's potential.

- ***Learning is an inseparable partnership between the brain and body***[2]

—Emotion is the gatekeeper to learning and performance

Much of the information processed in the brain comes from "information substances" produced throughout the body, many of which are the "molecules of emotion" that drive attention which in turn drives learning and memory.

—Movement enhances learning

The movement centers of the brain also help sequence our thoughts.

- ***There are multiple intelligences***[3]

We have not one, generic intelligence but at least seven,[4] each of which operates from a different part of our brain. As defined by Howard Gardner, intelligence is "a problem-solving and/or product-producing capability."[5]

- ***Learning is a two-step process:***[6]

Step One—The brain makes meaning through pattern seeking. As it does so, it is not logical or sequential. **Step one of learning** *is the extraction, from confusion, of meaningful patterns.*[7]

Step Two—Most information we use is embedded in **programs**, a planned sequence to accomplish a purpose or goal; information not embedded in programs is generally unretrievable and thus unusable. **Step two of learning** *is the acquisition of a mental program.*[8]

Notes

1 Recommended first book to read is *Magic Trees of the Mind: How to Nurture Your Child's Intelligence, Creativity, and Healthy Emotions from Birth Through Adolescence* by Marion Diamond (New York: Penguin, 1998).

2 Recommended first books to read are *Molecules of Emotion: Why We Feel the Way We Feel* by Candace Pert (New York: Touchstone, 1997) and *Smart Moves: Why Learning Is Not All in Your Head* by Carla Hannaford (Alexander, NC: Great Ocean Publishers, 1995).

3 Recommended first book to read is *Multiple Intelligences in the Classroom* by Thomas Armstrong (Alexandria, VA: ASCD, 2000).

4 Howard Gardner originally proposed seven intelligences. To qualify, each intelligence had to meet many criteria. Key for us was that the intelligence operated from a different part of the brain. Recently, Gardner has proposed an eighth candidate, the naturalist, that he explores quite thoroughly (see *Intelligence Reframed: Multiple Intelligences for the 21st Century*, Chapter 4). However, the naturalist intelligence does not appear to operate from a distinct part of the brain and, even more troublesome for us, its description parallels general functions of the brain as a whole as described by Leslie Hart, pattern seeking, and by Elkhonon Goldberg (*The Executive Brain: Frontal Lobes and the Civilized Mind. Oxford: University Press, 2001*) and others (notably Nobel Prize-winning psychologist Herbert Simon). Another reason we do not address the naturalist intelligence here is that it would add yet another issue for teachers to tussle with, one we feel is best addressed under ITI Learning Principle #4, the first step in learning: pattern seeking.

5 This definition of intelligence was developed by Howard Gardner in the early 1980s. See *Frames of Mind: The Theory of Multiple Intelligences*. He has updated and expanded that definition: "A biopsychological potential to process information that can be activated in a cultural setting to solve problems or create products that are of value in a culture." (See *Intelligence Reframed: Multiple Intelligences for the 21st Century*. New York: Basic Books, 1999, page 33-34.) Says Gardner, "Although we all receive these intelligences as part of our birthright, no two people have exactly the same intelligences in the same combinations. After all, intelligences arise from the combination of a person's genetic heritage and life conditions in a given culture and era." (*Intelligence Reframed*, p. 45.)

6 Recommended first book to read is *Human Brain and Human Learning* by Leslie A. Hart (Covington, WA: Books For Educators, Inc., 1999).

7 This definition of step one of learning comes from the work of Leslie Hart, *Human Brain and Human Learning*, p. 127.

8 This definition of step two of learning comes from the work of Leslie Hart, *Human Brain and Human Learning*, p. 161.

Chapter 1: Intelligence* As a Function of Experience

Learning is the result of real, observable physiological growth in the brain[1] that occurs as a result of sensory input and the processing, organizing, and pruning it promotes. The richer the sensory input, the greater the physiological growth in the brain and thus the greater the learning that will be wired into long-term memory. This factor is the important issue in the great nature versus nurture debate about intelligence. It now appears that there is plenty of scientific evidence to establish the power of both. Genetics was once thought to be an immutable determiner of intelligence—what you were born with was what you would end up with. Not so, but it does set parameters, a range of potential. However, within those parameters, experiences matter greatly. An undeveloped potential is just that, an undeveloped brain capable of less intelligent behaviors. It is our responsibility as educators to provide the kinds and amounts of sensory input that will ensure that each child's brain is developed to the full range of its potential.

The work of Marian Diamond, UC Berkeley, Reuven Feurstein, Israel, and many others refutes the long-held beliefs that intelligence is a genetically fixed, singular quality. Feurstein and his associates have even gone so far as to stipulate that "Genetics is no barrier to learning."[3] Marian Diamond's work[4] shows that an enriched environment results in measurable physiological growth in the brain. In short, if we know how the brain learns—what happens physiologically when learning occurs—we can assist a learner to create new "hardwiring" in the brain to carry new learnings. Intelligence, the capability to solve problems and create products, is significantly influenced by environment and experience. For example, most "gifted" students in our programs for the gifted and talented are not "gifted" as in the realm of such people as Einstein, Mozart, David Packard, Eleanor Roosevelt, Steve Wozniak, Sacajawea, or Maria Montessori. Rather, they are advantaged; they are students whose parents provided an enriched environment which nurtured a physiological development of neural networks which became long-term memory of knowledge and skills and greatly expanded vocabulary.

ITI Learning Principles

- *Intelligence as a function of experience*
- *Inseparable bodybrain partnership*
  - *—emotion as gatekeeper*
  - *—movement to enhance learning*
- *Multiple intelligences*
- *Learning as a two-step process*

* In the ITI model, we use Howard Gardner's definition of intelligence—"a problem-solving and/or product-producing capability."[2]

An enriched environment spurs brain growth; a sterile and/or hostile environment retards mental growth and can even lead to a decline in capacity. Here is the story.

The Biology of Learning

Due to fantastic advances in technology such as PET scans, MRI, and fMRI, our understanding of how learning takes place has radically expanded in the past two decades. While the story is fantastically more complex than we need to delve into here, a simplified accounting of the biology of learning provides, we believe, valuable images that can help teachers enhance student learning. "Just what does go on in there?" is a question of undeniable human curiosity. The answer are critical to improving teaching and learning. As Leslie Hart says, "Although we don't know as much as we may and will, we know sufficient to change our ways."[5] And we can do so without taking "a bridge too far."[6]

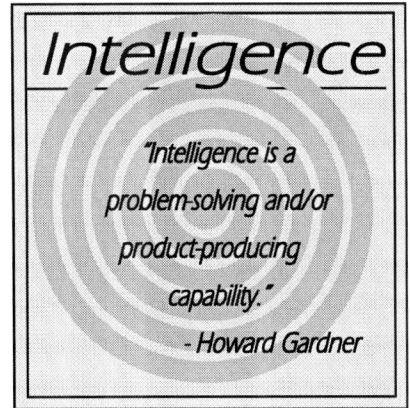

> **Intelligence**
>
> *"Intelligence is a problem-solving and/or product-producing capability."*
> *- Howard Gardner*

An Old Paradigm: Genetics Versus Environment

In the midst of our deep discouragement over our failures to deliver on the promise that all students can learn, it is easy to fall victim to the old belief that genetics sets intelligence and capability in an immutable way. Today what we know about the genetics versus environment debate is summed up beautifully by Dr. John Ratey: "We are not prisoners of our genes or our environment. Poverty, alienation, drugs, hormonal imbalances, and depression don't dictate failure. Wealth, acceptance, vegetables, and exercise don't guarantee success. Our own free will may be the strongest force directing the development of our brains, and therefore our lives. . . . the brain [child and adult] is both plastic and resilient, and always eager to learn. ***Experiences, thoughts, actions, and emotions actually change the structure of our brains.***"[7] As Ratey says, everything affects brain development and development is a lifelong process. The challenge of educators and parents is to provide the best possible environment for learning—one in which experiences are powerful enough (engaging sensory input, the subject of this chapter), thinking is reflective and analytical not just reactive, actions/movement are used to enhance learning, and emotions open the door to learning and performance (the subject of Chapter 2).

When standing before a group of 30-35 students, we must believe in our hearts and know without a shadow of a doubt in our minds that all students can learn, that all students can succeed and that, with help from brain research and this book, that it is in everyone of us to make such learning happen.

The Basic Building Blocks of Learning

The basic building blocks of learning are: neurons, brain organization, and information substances.

Neurons, Dendrites, and Axons

There are, by conservative estimate, 100 billion brain cells (neurons). Each neuron has one axon and as many as 100,000 dendrites. The resulting intertwining forms 100 trillion *constantly changing* connections. There are more possible ways to connect the brain's neurons than there are atoms in the universe.[8]

How neurons organize themselves and how they connect with each other results in the outward manifestations of learning and the quality we call intelligence. For example, the graphic below illustrates the increase in complexity of dendrites and axons from birth to age two. As a result, the brain becomes measurably denser and heavier (during infancy, the overall size of the skull increases as well, reaching full size by age five).

Growth in complexity of neurons from birth to age two

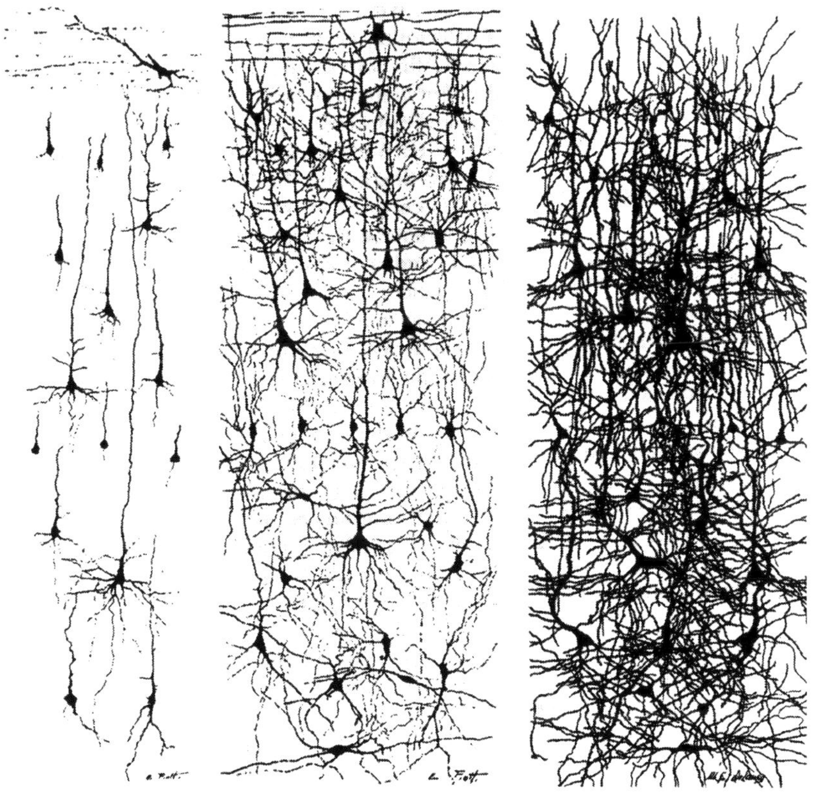

At birth | At 6 months | At 24 months

Source: *Magic Trees of the Mind: How to Nurture Your Child's Intelligence, Creativity, and Healthy Emotions from Birth Through Adolescence* by Marian Diamond, Ph.D., and Janet Hopson, pp. 106-107.

Such growth—multiple branching of the dendrites, myelination of axons, enlargement of synapses and overall size of the neurons—is the brain's response to rich sensory input from an enriched environment. In contrast, sterile, boring environments not only result in significantly less growth but in actual shrinking of existing dendrites. A period of drastically reduced enrichment, even as short as four days, can result in measurable shrinkage of dendrites.[9] "Use it or lose it"[10] is a universally acknowledged premise among neuroscientists and is powerful advice when it comes to growing and maintaining a healthy brain. Parents and educators alike, take heed. Your job is to help children (and fellow adults) grow dendrites[11] and to nurture continued use of what is grown.

Exactly how learning occurs is still a mystery, hidden at the molecular level. But the story is rapidly unfolding. In simple terms, there are two ways that neurons in the brain communicate with each other. The means of communication that has been understood for decades is an electrical-chemical process. The sending neuron transmits an electrical signal down its axon to its tip which is very close to the bulbous ending on the dendritic spines of the receiving cell. Chemical messengers, neurotransmitters, travel from the axon to the dendrite across the synaptic gap. If the information is compelling enough[12] to the receiving neuron, it in turn will spark an electrical transmission down its axon to the dendrites of another cell and on and on until the communication is complete, all at the rate of up to a billion times a second.[13] This means of communication carries the bulk of academic learning, particularly symbolic and abstract content, but is heavily influenced by emotion. (See the discussion of information substances in Chapter 2)

Enrichment Theory. The story of neurons, axons, and dendrites and how to make them develop and grow leads us to the new field of brain enrichment pioneered by Dr. Marian Diamond. The kinds of questions such researchers ask are closely akin to those that educators raise with the timeless question, "How can I best help Johnny learn X (math or geography or spelling)?" Dr. Diamond suggests that the question "How can I help Johnny?" should be rephrased: "How do I best stimulate Johnny's brain to make it grow, to increase the number and strength of connections being made, and to "hard-wire" learning into long-term memory?"

In short, learning is the result of actual physical growth in the brain. To talk about learning is to talk about the physiology of the brain and how to enhance its physical growth and thus learning. According to Dr. Diamond, a number of physiological changes occur when the brain is immersed in an enriched environment:[14]

1. Dendritic spines grow, change shape, or shrink as we experience the world. Neurons grow larger. The brain becomes denser and heavier. Therefore, choose the types of input that will produce the greatest physiological change in the brain.

2. The stimulation of an enriched environment results in significant physiological change in the brain—as much as 20% compared to brains in sterile, boring environments.

3. There is a correlation between brain structure and what we do in life—what we spend time doing and not doing.[15] In other words, how we spend our time—what we ask our brain to do on a daily basis—actually alters its physical structure. Vast amounts of time spent on television and/or video games (4-6 hours daily) wires the brain to do television and video games and does not wire the brain for other things such as physical exploration or high facility for initiating and processing language. If students cannot do what you expect of them, such as learn phonics, take time to build the neural wiring and structures that will enable them to do what is expected of them.

4. Much of the increase in the physical size of the brain (at birth, the brain is one quarter of its eventual adult size) is due to myelination, a process by which fatty tissue forms around the axons of frequently-firing neurons which act like rubber insulation on electrical cords. This allows for speedier and more reliable transmission of electrical impulses thus improving communication among neurons. While much of this process occurs with the unfolding maturation of the brain,[16] much can be deliberately enhanced through ample practice in using the knowledge or skill being learned, particularly in real-world settings which allow for rich sensory input and feedback. See Chapters 4 and 5 for a discussion of developing mental programs.

Communication of Neurons Across the Synaptic Gap

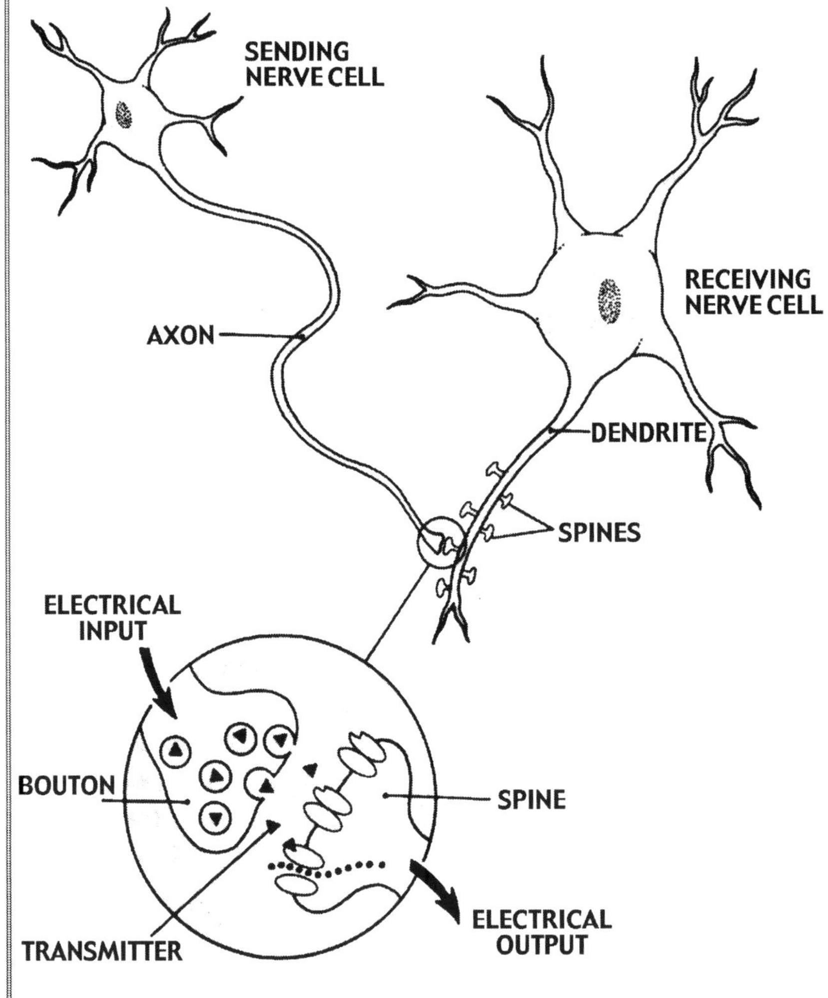

Source: *Magic Trees of the Mind: How to Nurture Your Child's Intelligence, Creativity, and Healthy Emotions from Birth Through Adolescence* by Marian Diamond, Ph.D., and Janet Hopson, p. 26.

5. Use it or lose it is a maxim for all ages—birth through old age. "Brains don't just steadily make more and more connections. Instead, they grow many more connections than they need and then get rid of those that are not used. It turns out that deleting old connections is just as important as adding new ones."[17]

Implications: If learning is the result of such physiological changes, then the question for teachers becomes: What should the classroom teacher do to maximize growth in the brain? The answers aren't mysterious or complicated yet they fly in the face of our traditional curricular tools and instructional processes.

1. Eliminate or drastically reduce low-sensory input materials and processes such as textbooks, worksheets, and working in isolation. Provide large amounts of sensory input from *being there* experiences in the real world. Remember, dittos don't make dendrites!

2. Demanding performance when the requisite wiring is not in place is akin to keeping the high jump bar over someone's head when he/she doesn't have the physical skills for jumping it at waist height. In track sports, this would be instantly recognized as both cruel and a foolish waste of time.

3. Design curriculum and instructional strategies that encourage practice and mastery in real-world situations, rather than aiming at quick quiz responses that usually stop short of ability to recognize content and don't demand students understand and and are able to use it. Using knowledge and skills in real-world applications greatly increases development and maintenance of neural connections.

Brain Organization

Our understanding of how the brain organizes itself is currently undergoing a major paradigm shift. In the 1980s and early 1990s, our view was that the brain was modular, that different parts of the brain control different abilities and these parts (or modules) operate independently. In this view, words and their meaning were stored in certain places and that functions such as vision and hearing were operated by specific, different parts of the brain.[18]

In contrast, the gradiental/distributive view of the brain holds that different aspects of word meaning are stored close to the sensory and motor areas that participated in acquiring information about these objects.[19] For instance, naming animals activates the left occipital areas (name plus picture) whereas naming tools activates the left premotor regions in charge of right-hand movements (name plus movement when using the tool). For further discussion of the gradiental/distributive view of the brain, see pages 4.2-4.3.

This is exciting stuff! It provides hard brain science to back up what teachers know from working with students. Learning the meanings of 20 vocabulary words a week, when presented for straight memorization, is harder for students to learn and remember than those same 20 words used in real-world conversation at a *being there* location. Inviting the brain to associate words meanings in multiple locations in the brain makes the learning and recall easier, faster, and increases the number of memory "hooks" that can be used to recall.

Information Substances

The description of neurons, dendrites, and axons described in pages 1.3-1.5 has been bedrock knowledge for some decades. Recently, however, the story has expanded quite dramatically. In short, it seems that the Greeks were on to something 2,000 years ago when they emphasized the importance of educating and training both mind and body.

Another means of communication among neurons, and one that interconnects the entire body, is wholly chemical. These chemicals, often called "information substances"[20] include transmitters, peptides, hormones, factors, and protein ligands. They carry information throughout the body. Some of these substances are created in other organs in the body but, wherever they are produced and wherever else they are received (the heart and respiratory center are major "hot spots"), all are received by neurons in the brain. See the discussion of information substances in Chapter 2.

Translating Brain Research into Action Using the Nine Bodybrain-Compatible Elements

Intelligence as a function of experience—active, full-bodied participation in the world—presents a very different picture of learning than the traditional one based on seat time with students quietly working in rows and credits earned for specified hours of lecture and reading of assigned textbooks. Curriculum content cannot be inserted into students' heads but must be assembled by each student through his/her sensory system. Admittedly this is not a tidy or orderly process as it differs dramatically with the uniqueness of each and every brain. Nor are there any guarantees. The major lesson for teachers is that the only way to achieve uniform results is to radically vary the sensory input, giving each student what he/she needs to develop accurate and comprehensive understandings and then learn to apply what they understand.

Bodybrain-Compatible Elements

- *Enriched Environment*
- *Meaningful Content*
- *Collaboration*
- *Movement*
- *Choices*
- *Adequate Time*
- *Immediate Feedback*
- *Mastery*
- *Absence of Threat / Nurturing Reflective Thinking*

The ITI model presents nine ways to translate brain research into action in the classroom and school. Each of the nine bodybrain-compatible elements is discussed in the order of their power to translate this body of brain research—intelligence as a function of experience—into practical strategies in the classroom.

Enriched Environment

Our window on the world is far more powerful than conventional thinking indicates. Human beings have at least 19 senses, not five.[21] And, not surprisingly, there is a direct correlation between the number of senses activated and the amount and locations of brain activity. Quite simply, the greater the range of sensory input, the greater the physiological activity and growth in the brain. The result is more learning and a greater likelihood that such learning will be retained in long-term memory.

While the names of some of these senses may seem foreign, your use of them is not. Consider this story for example, a childhood memory of co-author Karen Olsen that is as vivid today as it was almost half a century ago.

An Example of Vivid Memory Based on High Sensory Input

Age eight, with her older brother, engaged in the thoroughly hopeless but intriguing task of attempting to dam up the creek south of the family home; sunshine on their backs, reflections dancing on the water; bare feet scrunching in the pebbly gravel and gooey mud; the tepid, slow-moving water with darting minnows disturbed by rearranging of rocks and the shovels full of smelly mud; the sweat from their efforts dripping down their faces; their laughter rippling across the creek; her brother's nearness; his patience with a little sister who "never stayed home like the other girls did" ...the lessons of that day, the wonder of the creek, the beauty of family relationships.

Such moments of acute sensory awareness stay with us always.[22] To see examples of what information each of the 19 senses processed, see the chart on the following page.

An enriched environment is a learning environment that focuses sensory input—through all 19 senses—on the concept or skill to be learned. Maximizing sensory input is a fundamental ITI goal when developing curriculum and planning instructional strategies for a number of reasons. First, input through the senses is the brain's only way to bring in information from the outside world; there are no short cuts. Second, large amounts of sensory input enable students to grasp the concepts/information accurately and completely, thereby eliminating misunderstandings. Third, large amounts of sensory input is what causes physiological changes in the brain, resulting in the phenomena of learning.

Lesson Planning for the 19 Senses

A fundamental ITI goal when developing curriculum and planning instructional strategies is to maximize sensory input focusing on the concepts and skills to be taught. When lesson planning, the 19 senses can be grouped into six categories or kinds of input to consider.

The 19 senses activated by each of these kinds of input are illustrated on pages 1.10 and 1.12.

The two kinds of input **least used** in classrooms, *being there* and *immersion,* provide the **most sensory input.** Conversely, the two ***most commonly used,*** *secondhand* and *symbolic,* provide the ***least sensory input.*** The definitions of these six kinds of input and the senses they feed are described on pages 1.12 and 1.13.

In the typical classroom, 90 percent of the input consists of secondhand and symbolic input and most hands-on experience comes from manipulating representational items. In the ITI classroom, the goal is to flip those percentages so that 90 percent of the sensory input during initial learning (meaning-making and practicing how to use what is learned in real-world ways) is from *being there* and immersion experiences and 10 percent from hands-on experience with the real thing.

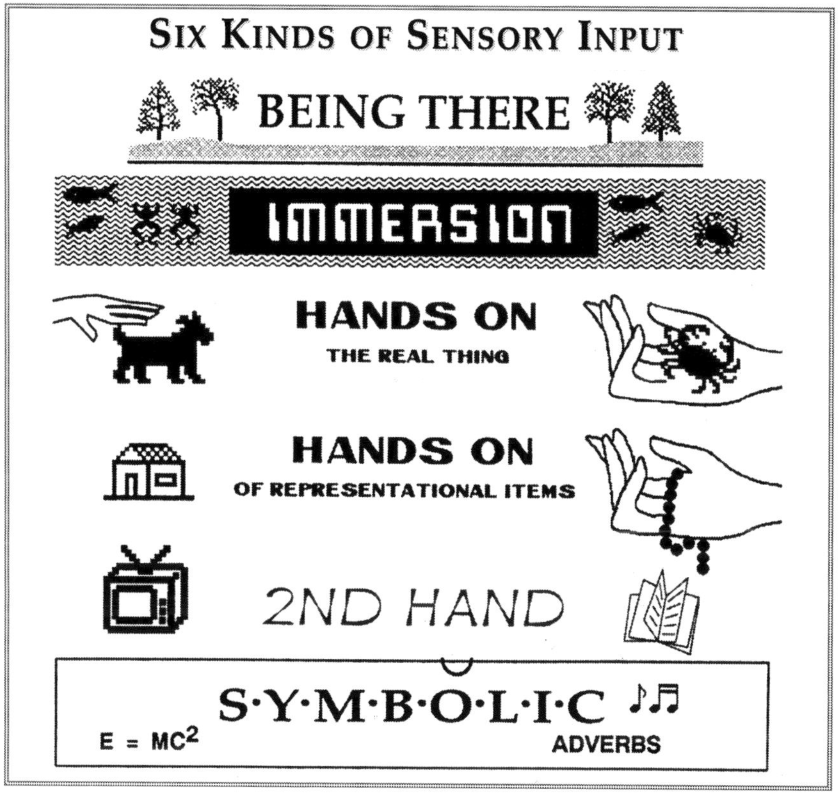

Secondhand input—principally reading, Internet, and video—is then a useful way to extend what has been learned through *being there* experiences supplemented with immersion, and hands-on experiences with the real thing.[23]

If this information seems disturbing and too impossible to be true, think back to an attempt to learn something "from scratch" that was fraught with difficulties and failures. For co-author Karen Olsen, it was her first experience trying to "learn" computers. This is her story: A colleague and his wife offered computer literacy classes in their home (at the time, they had more computers in their spare bedroom for such a class than the local university did). I was

The 19 Senses

SENSES	KIND OF INPUT	EXAMPLES OF SENSORY INPUT FROM STORY
Sight	Visible light	Reflections dancing on the water; darting minnows, dams breaking, etc.
Hearing	Vibrations in the air	Laughter, gravel scrunching; mud sucking; rocks clashing,splashing
Touch	Tactile contact	Bare feet scrunching in the pebbly gravel; tepid, slow-moving water
Taste	Chemical molecular	Sweat dripping down their faces; an occasional splash of creek water
Smell	Olfactory molecular	Smelly mud
Balance	Kinesthetic geotropic	Keeping balance wading in the deep gravel; moving rocks/mud
Vestibular	Repetitious movement	Re-arranging rocks and shoveling smelly mud
Temperature	Molecular motion	Warm summer day
Pain	Nociception	Thankfully, none!
Eidetic imagery	Neuroelectrical image retention	The vivid picture of the scene and its details
Magnetic	Ferromagnetic orientation	The location of the creek—south of the family home
Infrared	Long electromagnetic waves	The warmth and power of the sun's rays
Ultraviolet	Short electromagnetic waves	The warmth and power of the sun's rays
Ionic	Airborne ionic charge	The refreshing feeling from being around water
Vomeronasal	Pheromonic sensing	Primal sense of smell—body odors, sweat, rotting vegetation
Proximal	Physical closeness	The nearness of the brother
Electrical	Surface charge	The humidity of the creek eliminated any perceivable static electricity
Barometric	Atmospheric pressure	The steady, unchanging atmospheric pressure of a calm summer day
Geogravimetric	Sensing mass differences	Density (weight to mass) of material—pebbly gravel versus gooey mud

thrilled at the opportunity, paid my $30 and sat in the front row. Her instructor-friend dove right into "what goes on inside the box." "Wow," I thought, "If I understood how things work, program writing, never mind word processing, would be a piece of cake. This is the class for me!"

The story that unfolded boggled my mind. Whoever thought up this stuff in the first place? If I didn't understand something, I raised my hand and kept it there until I got an explanation I understood. The night was fascinating. I left the class thrilled to my toes! It was, after all, quite understandable conceptually despite its sci-fi veneer.

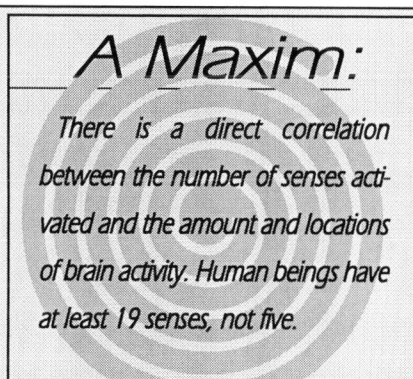

> **A Maxim:**
>
> *There is a direct correlation between the number of senses activated and the amount and locations of brain activity. Human beings have at least 19 senses, not five.*

The next morning, my mother, whom I tried to talk into coming with me during her visit, asked reasonably enough, "Well, what did you learn last night?"

"Holy moley, Mom! You should have come. You would've loved it. It was our kind of workshop. He explained what goes on inside the box. It was fabulous!"

"Oh," she said, "just what does go on in there?"

"Well, when you plug it in and turn it on, it . . . ah, er."

Egad, how is it possible? I couldn't remember a thing except that I remembered that I understood it at the time. But nothing else stuck in my brain. Two things conspired against my getting the information into long-term memory. First, I had no prior experience with what goes on inside the black box, no mental post office box address for the information. Second, the only sensory input for this new learning was auditory and thus provided no context to help learn about the goings on in the box. Consequently, the information evaporated from my short-term memory during the night.

Remember, there is no such thing as bypassing the sensory system; it is the bodybrain partnership's[24] way of taking in information. We cannot expect to set aside millions of years of evolution in favor of our traditional textbooks, lectures, and worksheets. Again, the moral of the story here is that dittos don't make dendrites!

Even in the area of language arts, sensory input is essential. For example, success in creative writing and poetry, even much of descriptive narrative, depends heavily upon sensory input and reflecting those experiences in words in order to evoke similar feelings and thoughts in the reader. Revisit co-author Karen Olsen's half-century-old memory of playing with her brother in a creek (see page 1.9). It is a vivid descriptive narrative, the stuff from which poetry is written. Interestingly, she wrote this description over 10 years ago, a quick, off the cuff reminiscence. Now, looking back and comparing it to each of the 19 senses, it is startling to see that the fullness of the memory relied on input from each and every sense.

There are many lessons here for teachers. If you want vivid creative writing, edge-to-edge painting with real detail, deep understanding of concepts, and accurate use of skills, to name but a few areas of learning, we must provide students with full sensory input. *Being there* experiences—visits to real-life locations—is the most powerful way to do so.

For example, choose a favorite work of fiction, such as Pat Conroy's *Prince of Tides*, a short story by Hemingway, a poem you memorized long ago and still recall. Analyze it against the 19 senses. If it is powerful enough to make you feel like you're there, looking at or participating in the scene, you're reading language encoded by all 19 senses or piggybacking on input that was. Once the high levels of sensory input have worked their magic, secondhand and symbolic input "makes sense" and can support learning.

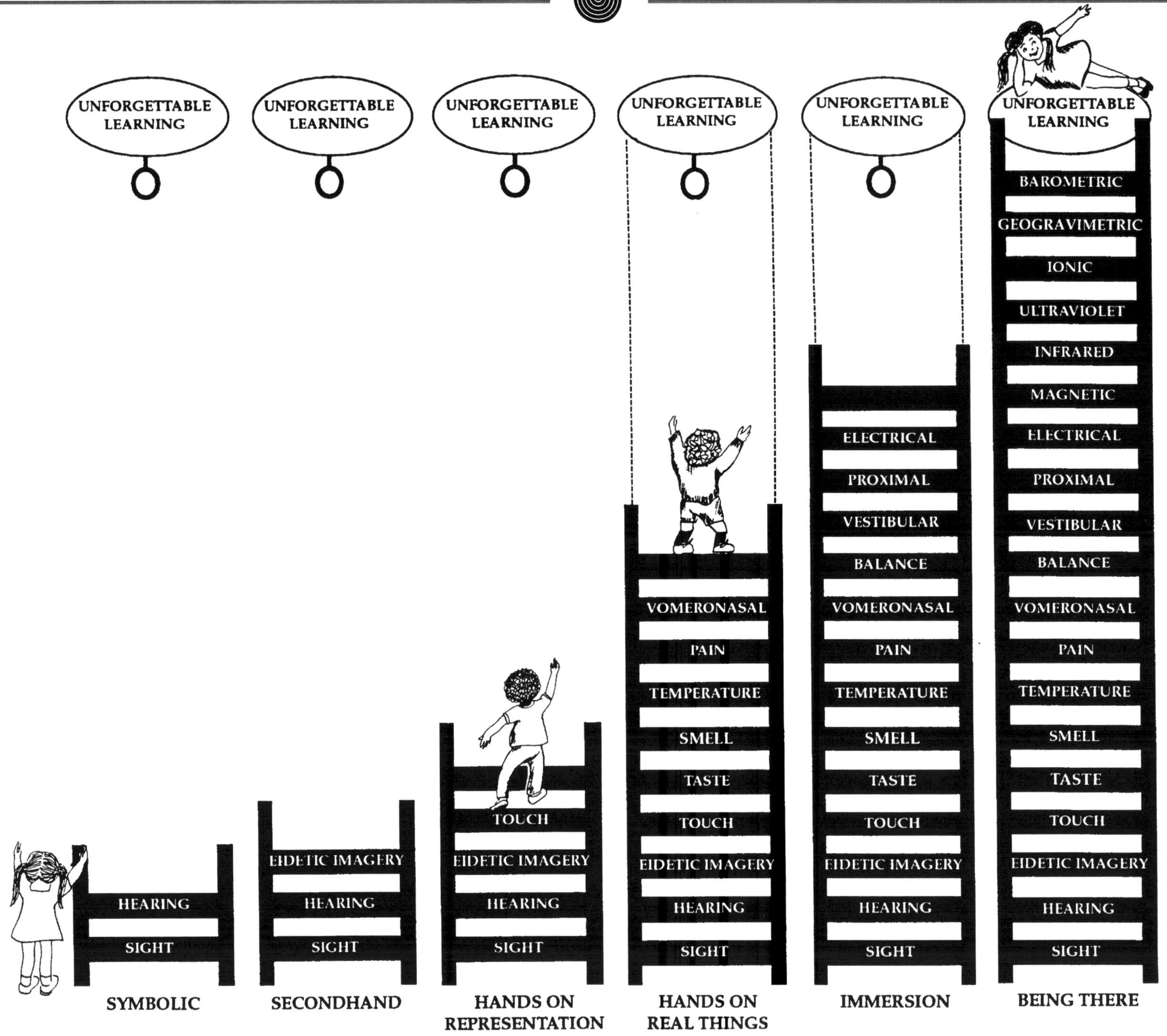
UNFORGETTABLE LEARNING
UNFORGETTABLE LEARNING
UNFORGETTABLE LEARNING
UNFORGETTABLE LEARNING
UNFORGETTABLE LEARNING
UNFORGETTABLE LEARNING
HEARING
SIGHT
SYMBOLIC
EIDETIC IMAGERY
HEARING
SIGHT
SECONDHAND
TOUCH
EIDETIC IMAGERY
HEARING
SIGHT
HANDS ON REPRESENTATION
VOMERONASAL
PAIN
TEMPERATURE
SMELL
TASTE
TOUCH
EIDETIC IMAGERY
HEARING
SIGHT
HANDS ON REAL THINGS
ELECTRICAL
PROXIMAL
VESTIBULAR
BALANCE
VOMERONASAL
PAIN
TEMPERATURE
SMELL
TASTE
TOUCH
EIDETIC IMAGERY
HEARING
SIGHT
IMMERSION
BAROMETRIC
GEOGRAVIMETRIC
IONIC
ULTRAVIOLET
INFRARED
MAGNETIC
ELECTRICAL
PROXIMAL
VESTIBULAR
BALANCE
VOMERONASAL
PAIN
TEMPERATURE
SMELL
TASTE
TOUCH
EIDETIC IMAGERY
HEARING
SIGHT
BEING THERE

Being there input occurs when real things are studied in their real-world context, such as a pond, lake or wetlands area, a mall, a factory, or a neighbor's backyard—literally "*being there*." All 19 senses are activated, producing maximum electrical and chemical activity in the brain. Input is rich, varied, and plentiful.

Immersion input replicates the real world context of the *being there* experience in the classroom as fully as possible. For example, if a pond is the *being there* site, a classroom pond (a child's swimming pool with a black plastic drape) is created with as many real pond critters and plants as possible. The classroom itself is then made to look like a pond with the water line slightly above the teacher's head when standing. Blue film covers the windows to simulate the water line of the pond. Replicas of animals and plants at the water's edge and underwater cover the walls. The tape deck plays water sounds and pond animal sounds. At least 100 books and other printed materials about ponds, and other multi-media resources fill the room. Models and pictures of pond animals and plants are available for close analysis and exploration. The environment provides input for 13 of the 19 senses.

Hands-on of the real thing provides input through examination of real world things but without the context of *being there* or *immersion*. In the case of the pond, there would be frogs and polliwogs, cattails, and so forth for students to handle and examine closely, engaging 9 of the 19 senses.

Hands-on of representational items provides input from models of real things such as plastic frogs and polliwogs. Without the context of *being there* or *immersion* or the experience of the real items, hands-on of representational items elicits response from only 4 of the 19 senses. Such limited sensory input provides limited brain activation and thus limits pattern-seeking capabilities for many learners. Program-building opportunities are all very limited because real world applications are so difficult to create with only representational items.

Secondhand input can be found in books, computers, videotapes, and other multi-media presentations which can activate only sight, hearing, and eidetic imagery. Such limited input makes pattern-seeking difficult and provides no opportunities for program-building.

Symbolic is the most difficult input to process. Fewer than 20 percent of students can learn well through this type of input which includes such things as mathematical sentences and parts of speech. High linguistic and spatial intelligence is needed to make use of symbolic input, plus prior *being there* experiences related to the new learnings.

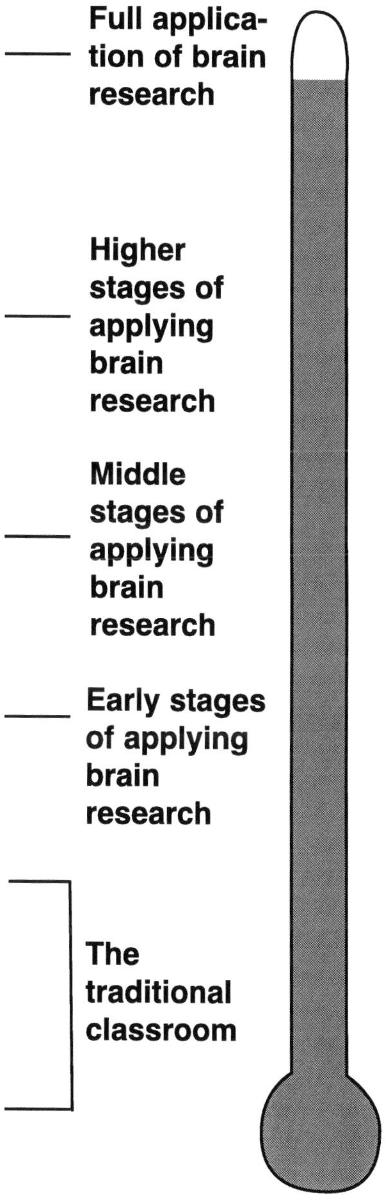

USING *ENRICHED ENVIRONMENT* TO ENHANCE DEVELOPMENT OF INTELLIGENCE

Curriculum Development

- Base curriculum planning at the classroom level on *being there* interactions with the real world. Provide them as early in the study of a concept or skill as possible. Then, revisit the location often and go again at the end of study as a means to assess students' ability to apply what they understand and whether the concepts and skills have been wired into long-term memory.
- Based on the *being there* experience, develop lots of group and individual inquiries* that provide opportunities for solving problems and producing real products, including social/political action projects.
- Take time to access prior experiences of students. Tapping existing memory gives a "post office" address in the brain making new learning more efficient and giving the teacher an opportunity to detect and correct misconceptions.
- Develop inquiries for "homework" which ask the student to apply the information/skill in settings relevant to the student's life (home, neighborhood, friends' interests, hobbies and workplaces of parents, extended family, family friends).

* Inquiries, or activities, are a key structure for developing curriculum in the ITI model. Inquiries provide opportunities to practice using the concepts and/or skills of the key points. For a discussion of inquiries and key points, see Chapters 15 and 14.

USING *ENRICHED ENVIRONMENT* TO ENHANCE DEVELOPMENT OF INTELLIGENCE

Instructional Strategies

- Make the classroom a complete immersion experience reflecting the *being there* location upon which your curriculum is based.
- Have at least 100 resources (print and nonprint) related to the current topic of student available in the room—real things, models, diagrams, blueprints, sketches, and art objects, as well as the traditional sources such as books, magazines, multimedia, including the Internet.
- Invite guest speakers who are experts on the topics of interest to the classroom.
- Take away all materials—posters, bulletin boards, books, displays, models, etc.—not directly related to the key points and inquiries of the current monthly component or weekly topic.

Meaningful Content

No one—student or teacher—gets up in the morning and says, "Oh, boy, I hope this day is boring!" Quite the opposite; children and adults dread boredom. For the brain, it is the straight-line equivalent of a heart monitor showing no heartbeat . . . death by multiple paper cuts. So what makes content meaningful? For the most part, it is real-life context, richness of sensory input, and relevance to the learner that produces an emotional response of "I care." Context means that the concept to be studied is placed in real-life settings that are experienceable by students. Richness means that the learning experience provides sensory input for all 19 senses. Please note, however, that richness and clutter are the antithesis of each other.

Using the Context of Real Life

Providing input through real-life contexts is important for several reasons:

- The amount and variety of sensory input (discussed in pages 1.9-1.13)
- Demonstration of how and why concepts and skills are used
- Reminding students of previous related experiences and illustrating future possibilities (work or interest)
- Overcoming inequities
- Correcting misconceptions
- Providing a base for second language acquisition

Demonstration of How and Why Concepts and Skills Are Used. Since its inception in the early 1800s, America's public education system has relied on textbooks to convey learning. If students stumbled, no worries. High dropout rates weren't a public concern for over 100 years. After all, there were plenty of jobs that didn't require the ability to read and write and apprenticeships, entry to various fields, were common.

Today, however, the ability to read and write is critical to virtually every job for men and women. We simply must find ways to teach all students to high levels of reading proficiency and writing skills. The key to doing so is massive sensory input.

The need for sensory input as the starting point for learning is well illustrated by the following. As the saying goes, 80 percent of reading comprehension is based on prior knowledge.

> "*Cayard* forced *America* to the left, filling its sails with 'dirty air,' then tacked into a right-hand shift. . . .That proved to be the wrong side. *America,* flying its carbon fiber/liquid crystal main and headsails, found more pressure on the left. *Cayard* did not initiate a tacking duel until *Il Moro* got headed nearly a mile down the leg. . . . *Cayard* did not initiate a jibbing duel to improve his position heading downwind and instead opted for a more straight-line approach to the finish."[25]

We can assume this paragraph has something to do with sailing and we could answer questions such as these:

1. What kind of air filled America's sail?
2. What kind of sail did America have?
3. How far down the leg did Il Moro get before Cayard initiated a tacking duel?
4. What strategy to the finish did Cayard use?

Does answering these questions about Cayard and America really mean you understand what is happening in this race or, even more importantly, could you participate in the race yourself? For over 99 percent of us, the answer is no. Why? Because we have never been sailing. We lack *being there* experiences from which concepts are developed. This passage could be understood with teacher explanation and the use of a dictionary but arrival at a level of comprehension needed to read and understand other short descriptions of sailing would likely not occur.

This statement bears repeating: Understanding of concepts, as opposed to memorizing factoids, requires large amounts of sensory- based input; the best source of sensory input (richness and variety) comes from *being there* experiences in real-world settings (see the sensory input ladders on page 1.12). Sensory experience is not a luxury; it is a prerequisite for understanding.

The moral to this story is that it is possible to be an A student because you are a good reader yet not really understand what you've read. Most standardized tests of content, such as science and social studies, are tests of reading ability, not of mastery of content.

Reminding Students of Previous Related Experiences and Illustrating Future Possibilities. Connecting to prior, related experiences is particularly crucial when learning something new. First, it provides a post office box (column of cells) in the brain ready to receive and process related concepts/skills. Second, it heightens emotional response. "This relates to something I already care about."

Students can only dream to the limits of their awareness. *Being there* experiences open new doors and fire off emotions that make the bodybrain attend more carefully and fully to the concepts and skills to be learned. (See Chapter 2 for a discussion of molecules of emotion.)

Overcoming Inequities. Providing students with real-life context for learning is especially critical if students have no prior experience (or no successful experience) with the concept or skill to be learned. The only way to overcome the disparity of experiences that students bring to the classroom is to provide the sensory input that leads to concept development through *being there* and immersion experiences. If we were truly committed to leveling the playing field for students, we would focus time and resources on those subjects that allow us to overcome gaps in students' prior experiences most quickly. Sound hard to do? Not at all.

The subject area in which the gaps among students can most readily be overcome is science, a subject that begs for *being there* experiences, immersion, and hands-on of the real thing. Within minutes, enough sensory input can be provided that students can all be on equal footing.

The subject area in which the gaps among students is the greatest and takes the most time and work to bridge is language arts. Why? Because it trades primarily in second-hand input and symbolic input.

Where does a traditional schedule allocate the most time? Language arts. The least time, science.

If we were serious about learning for all students, we would base our integrated themes in science because most science, particularly at elementary grades, is directly experienceable through the 19 senses.

Correcting Misconceptions. If students hold misconceptions, massive amounts of sensory input is needed to rewire the brain.[26] For example the graduating Harvard students and their faculty, when asked to explain the reasons for the seasons, still applied the "the stove is hot" experiences of their childhood—things are hotter the closer you get (to a hot stove and the earth to the sun in summer) and colder the farther away you get—despite all high school and college courses in between.[27] Lessons about the earth's orbit being round rather than highly elliptical that were based primarily upon secondhand information—lecture and textbooks in high school and university—failed to provide the necessary sensory input to override learning from their infancy about hot objects.

Second Language Acquisition. Sensory experience is also crucial to the learning of a second language because many words do not translate from one language to another as interchangeable pieces.

For example, Eskimos have many words for snow; English but a few. Would one of those English words fully convey the conditions of today's snow those native to the Arctic Circle? Probably not. Similarly, the Slovak language has one word for sad, pensive, melancholy, wistful, reflective.[28]

Words are not learned in isolation; they are learned in context, in real-world settings which contribute to the specific meaning of a word. Without this contextual backdrop, learning a second language is emotionless and flat and difficult.

Learning in the ITI Model: A New Definition

Based on the brain research discussed so far, learning is defined in the ITI model as:

Sensory input from being there
EXPERIENCE → CONCEPT → LANGUAGE → APPLICATION TO REAL WORLD → LONG-TERM MEMORY

In other words, powerful, bodybrain-compatible learning for students occurs when high levels of sensory input from *being there* experiences are processed by the pattern-seeking brain to construct meaning which can be expressed by language (the attachment of a word to this new understanding). Having language then makes possible further exploration and application (program building for long-term retention and use). The brain readily learns (makes meaning) and applies (builds a program for using) information learned in this sequence.

Please note: This paradigm of learning is especially important for second language acquisition.

In contrast, conventional schooling relies heavily on lecture and reading (textbooks/worksheets, Internet, and other secondhand explanations). Beginning with and staying focused on language or vocabulary—definitions of things and processes, whether via lecture or reading—works only when students have had prior experience with what is being discussed or have unusually high linguistic skills. Although such an approach may, and often does, result in high test scores for highly verbal students, it fails to enable students to apply knowledge and skills. The remarkable lack of transfer to long-term memory as represented by the fading ink in the graphic below.

LANGUAGE → → → CONCEPT → → → APPLICATION

School As Counter Balance

Every child's brain is unique; a portion of this uniqueness comes from genetic wiring, much is shaped by environment. According to Jane Healy, in her book *Endangered Minds: Why Our Children Don't Think,* "Experience—what children do every day, the ways in which they think and respond to the world, what they learn, and the stimuli to which they decide to pay attention—shapes their brains. Not only does it change the ways in which the brain is used (functional change), but it also causes physical alterations (structural change) in neural wiring systems."[29] What is taken in by the senses makes for profound differences in the structure of the brain. In short, the brain of Video Kid is quite different in structure than that of the Child of Print (the child whose parents have immersed him/her in books, stories, conversation, etc.).

The differences between Video Kid and Child of Print are profound from the teacher's point of view. Whereas Child of Print comes to school with a "well-muscled" left hemisphere and language center, Video Kid, on the other hand, arrives with a Joe Puny left hemisphere and undeveloped language capacity (albeit an active right hemisphere and visually-oriented brain). In the "use it or lose it" environment of the brain, connections form and rapidly die. If Video Kid watches television an average of 130 minutes seven days a week but spends less than four minutes a day on reading,[32] it is clear that Video Kid's preparation is not only highly language-deficient but, in fact, such a daily diet is also very language-antagonistic in terms of developing needed neural networking for language processing. Numerous studies suggest that the brains of spectators, however rich the visual images, are no different from those brains which live in impoverished environments.[33] In other words, if there is no active involvement, there is minimal activity in the brain.

It is not our purpose here to catalog the impact on the modern brain of TV, computers, and other visual, non-interactive technologies.[34] We intend only to make the point that many of today's students come with very little direct experience of the real world and thus with minimal conceptual understanding of what makes the world work. Accompanying this deficit is minimal language development; without receptive and expressive language capability, the seven scientific thinking processes[33] are simply not possible. Thinking demands language; according to Healy, "language is the scaffolding for thought."[35]

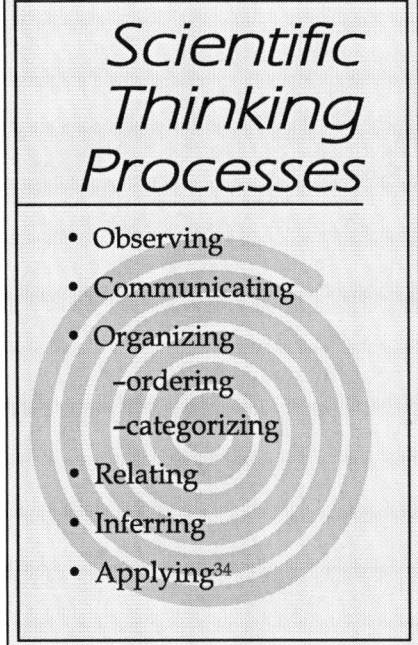

Scientific Thinking Processes

- Observing
- Communicating
- Organizing
  - -ordering
  - -categorizing
- Relating
- Inferring
- Applying[34]

In the past we could assume that students came to school with a wide range of experience of the real world and the concepts and language that come with such experience. After all, a working farm was a virtual gold mine of real life experience—animal husbandry, crops of all kinds, the economics of supply and demand, problem-solving spurred by equipment that breaks down in a remote field, and the geometry and mathematics involved in building fences and new buildings. City kids who were a part of the street markets and who had family members living in different neighborhoods had a range of firsthand experiences as well—economics, supply and demand, varied forms of transportation. Consequently, schools of the past could use a wide range of "secondhand" sources during instruction—books, textbooks, workbooks, worksheets, dittos, pictures, models, and, more recently, videos, the internet, etc.—because children came to school possessing a rich tapestry of real experiences to build upon and learning continued apace.

Today's students, on the other hand, come with scant experience with the real world and the concepts and language that accompany them because in many areas of the U.S. it is not considered safe to be out exploring the neighborhood. These students arrive at school ill-equipped to learn from our "secondhand" sources. As 80% of reading comprehension is based on prior knowledge, one can only take from a book what one brings to the book. Books can expand our knowledge but cannot create it from scratch. According to Frank Smith, "Much of today's school failure results from academic expectations for which students' brains were not prepared—but which were bulldozed into them anyway. Deficits in everything from grammar to geography may be caused by teaching that bypasses the kind of instruction that could help children conceptually come to grips with the subject at hand."[36]

USING *MEANINGFUL CONTENT* TO ENHANCE DEVELOPMENT OF INTELLIGENCE

Curriculum Development

- State curriculum as concepts and base them in real-world locations, situations, and events.
- Ensure that curriculum is age-appropriate—comprehensible to the student given his/her stage of brain development.
- When planning your curriculum and daily lessons, find out what prior experiences students have had. What concepts and skills do they already understand and can apply? Don't assume that students have the necessary conceptual building blocks from prior experience to understand what your curriculum is about. Investing the time to get to know each student pays big dividends.
- Be alert to misconceptions. To correct them, provide massive amounts of sensory input.

USING *MEANINGFUL CONTENT* TO ENHANCE DEVELOPMENT OF INTELLIGENCE

Instructional Strategies

- Provide *being there* interactions with the real world—people, processes, things. Allow students to explore beyond what you envision in order to construct their own meaning-understandings that are accurate, complete, and comprehensive.
- Base second language acquisition on *being there* and immersion experiences which convey the fullness of what the words of the new language mean.
- Use cooperative learning strategies that encourage students to connect prior knowledge with the new.

Collaboration

Research provides a very compelling endorsement of the power of collaboration to increase learning, improve the quality of products, and make the work/learning environment more pleasant and productive. The research over the past 50 years is conclusive.[37]

Also, from a brain perspective, Leslie Hart, *Human Brain and Human Learning, Updated,* talks about the need for great quantities of input to the brain which collaboration helps provide. Frank Smith, in *Insult to Intelligence: The Bureaucratic Invasion of Our Classrooms,* lists opportunity for manipulation of information as one of the key ingredients for learning. Active learning processes result in active brains. Collaboration is not just a bow to the social needs of students, it is a vital way of enhancing academic learning.

Full understanding of what is being learned and the ability to apply it in real-life settings—creative problem solving and flexible use of what is learned—depends upon ample opportunity to manipulate information in our heads, to test it, expand it, connect it with prior learnings. Collaborating with others allows us to examine our own thinking while expanding our knowledge base. According to both authors, one teacher facing a classroom of thirty brains, each with very different ways of learning, is insufficient to the task. Collaboration—students teaching each other and providing a sounding board for each other—is an essential classroom structure in a bodybrain-compatible learning environment.

Powerful rationales for collaboration come also from business. In 1989, the U.S. Department of Labor released its commission report entitled, *Investing In People.* An entire chapter was devoted to what education needs to do in order to improve the quality of the American work force. This is one of their observations:

> "Business can make additional contributions by providing schools with the information that they need to develop course content and instructional methods that meet the current and emerging needs of the work place. Increasingly, employees will have to work in cooperative groups, be able to make decisions about production problems and processes, and develop the ability to acquire new skills and behavior on the job. We urge schools to adjust their instructional methods to match more closely the situation students will later face in the work place."

The requisite skills for running one's own business are and have always been problem-solving, decision-making, and the ability to communicate with peers and adults—be it farmer, homemaker, inventor, engineer, or a businessman (even as a shoeshine boy or delivery girl). However, with the growth of huge, multi-national corporations and large bureaucracies, a significant portion of our population are now employees, not entrepreneurs. Thus, significant numbers of students are growing up in homes where the work of the parents or other adults is not known to them and the standards of successful business (such as the drive to master skills and provide quality customer service) are rarely modeled with a sense of consequence to the survival of the business or to one's personal reputation in the community. Collaboration in the classroom over real problems to be solved and real products to be created goes a long way to filling in that experiential gap for students.

Life

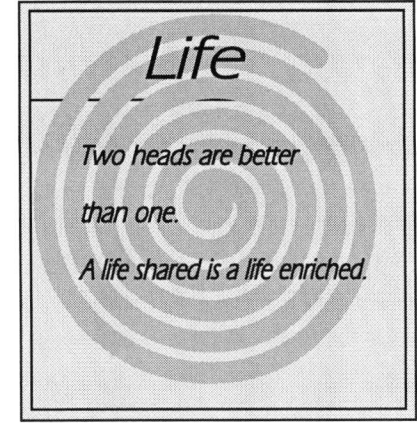

Two heads are better than one.

A life shared is a life enriched.

As previously cited, collaboration increases understanding and improves quality of output. And this brings us back to the classroom. Collaboration dramatically increases opportunities for the bodybrain partnership to play an active rather than passive role in learning thus spurring physiological change in the brain. It is an essential instructional strategy for the classroom and should be used daily. Do note, however, that collaboration needs to be balanced with times for reflective thinking (see Chapter 2).

USING *COLLABORATION* TO ENHANCE DEVELOPMENT OF INTELLIGENCE

Curriculum Development

- The content for good collaboration should be:
  1) A challenge that no one group member working alone can do. Thus, genuine inclusion of all is a must rather than a sociological nicety.[38]
  2) Reflective of real life and engage the 19 senses.
- The content of inquiries assigned for collaborative work should include social/personal skills as well as curriculum content.
- In the ITI model, collaborative groups are called Learning Clubs.[39] The goal of collaborative tasks should always be increased achievement and higher quality products. Collaboration is a means to an end (learning), not an end in itself. Never use collaboration as a social event. If you want to have a party or allow chatting to fill in an odd moment or two, have the party or allow chatting in pairs. Collaboration should be viewed by students as genuine work, serious study. The value of the work should be obvious to all during collaborative work.

USING *COLLABORATION* TO ENHANCE DEVELOPMENT OF INTELLIGENCE

Instructional Strategies

- Change the composition of the Learning Clubs monthly or at least every six weeks. Getting to know others well accelerates learning, prevents cliques, and increases opportunities to practice applying the Lifelong Guidelines and LIFESKILLS.* Changing group members gives an opportunity for a fresh start for students who get off on the wrong foot with their first Learning Club group. Learning how to get to know others, and be comfortable doing so, is a critical personal/social skill.
- In addition to the ongoing class family group, create groups for skills and interests.

  Skill groups—short-term, ad hoc groups for studying specific skills or concepts among which students shift from group to group as mastery is attained

  Interest groups—opportunities to share/work on a topic of special interest
- The two primary purposes of collaboration are to:
  1) Enhance achievement by increasing input to the bodybrain learning partnership and increasing emotional engagement and opportunities to apply what is learned and 2) Equalize social status in the classroom. .

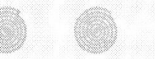

* The Lifelong Guidelines and LIFESKILLS are the behaviors guiding both students and adults. They form the basis for creating a sense of community and for ongoing classroom leadership and management. See Chapters 9 and 10.

Movement

It's humbling to think that our amazing, science fiction-like technology of the 21st century has finally reached a level that it can tell us what the Greeks knew 2,500 years ago. The body and mind are a partnership affair—you can't develop one without the other. They are in fact a single operating system. What took us so long?

The Greeks understood this partnership through observation of the human condition and applied it to the education of their young. We now know from scientific fact that it's true yet seem resistant to applying the implications to our schools and homes. But, I'm getting ahead of myself. For an explanation of the brain research behind movement as a tool for enhancing learning, see Chapter 2. For our purposes here, three things are key:

- Movement is fundamental to the very existence of a brain. In fact, only an organism that moves from place to place even requires a brain.[40]
- The entire front half of the brain is devoted to organizing action, both physical and mental. "Higher" brain functions have evolved from movement and still depend on it.[41]
- Movement is crucial to every brain function, including memory, emotion, language, and learning.[42]

This being the case, it is obvious that having students sit quietly in rows is a worst case scenario for the brain. What it needs is active participation from its partner, the body. In contrast, *being there* experiences are tailored made for the bodybrain partnership. There is action, emotion, and plenty of raw material for cognitive processes.

USING *MOVEMENT* TO ENHANCE DEVELOPMENT OF INTELLIGENCE

Curriculum Development

- Add to your key points an example of how the concept is used so the movement inherent in using the concept is part of the brain's encoding. Do the same with skill key points unless the use of the skill is obvious. Whenever possible, point out applications of the key point that affect students now at home, school, their favorite mall, etc., not just down the road later in life.
- Base your inquiries in *being there* locations. Make them action oriented, requiring that a problem typical of that location be solved or a product needed or sold at that location be produced.
- Code your inquiries according to the multiple intelligences as a way of reminding yourself how well you are including movement. Make sure you develop plenty of inquiries for bodily-kinesthetic, musical, spatial, and interpersonal intelligences, all of which emphasize movement.

USING *MOVEMENT* TO ENHANCE DEVELOPMENT OF INTELLIGENCE

Instructional Strategies

- During direct instruction, illustrate using hands-on of the real thing
- When selecting inquiries for whole class, group, or individual work, assign those that include movement first. Assign linguistic inquiries (e.g., write a paragraph or essay, make a list, look up in the dictionary, write a poem or lyrics for a rap song) only after students have developed a full and accurate understanding of the concept or skill and are able to apply what they understand. In fact, as a rule of thumb, assign last those inquiries that are wholly linguistic.
- Use movement throughout the day to:
  - –Reset emotions (to energize or to slow the pace as needed)
  - –Pique interest by illustrating how things are used
  - –Use the body to do memorable simulations (such as make the shapes of the letter of the alphabet, mimic animal movements, perform plays, skits, and hand signs, and so forth)

Choices

The most mind-numbing quality of bureaucracy is its assembly line sameness. Common sense and brain research to the contrary, "the system" is based on the misguided assumption that the same input (textbook and lecture) will produce the same learning, that the same equals equity, that the same equals fairness, and that because of the misbehavior of a few, all must be restricted from an activity or punished with a blanket treatment.

In reality, nothing could be more unfair than giving two very different brains—and no two brains are alike—the same input and expecting the outcome to be the same. It's not only unfair, it's cruel. If we want the same learning outcomes from different brains, we must provide different input to each—whatever each brain needs to arrive at the standard end point. And given the huge differences in prior experiences, intelligence strengths, personality preferences, and brain processes, reliance on the textbook and lecture are patently ridiculous.

Choices

In reality, nothing could be more unfair than giving two very different brains—and no two brains are alike—the same input and expecting the outcome to be the same. It's not only unfair, it's cruel.

To some, however, the idea of offering choices to students (and teachers) may seem like warmed-over "Do your own thing" from the 60s. Somehow offering alternatives is viewed as antithetical to high standards or the notion of core curriculum for all. Some might believe that having choices is fluff or, more to the point, that it runs against the grain of having clear standards and high expectations: one can't just go around doing what one wants all the time; learning after all is serious business and therefore should be expected to hurt a little.

But in reality, offering students choices—ones well crafted/selected by the teacher—has enormous power to enhance learning. In addition to its many positive emotional effects, having choices allows students to select the kind of input that they most need in order to understand and apply concepts and skills. Although this demands that teachers develop a rich variety of inquiries in the short run, in the long run it's much more time and energy efficient because it significantly reduces the amount of re-teaching and remedial teaching needed when initial instruction fails.

The choices to be offered vary greatly due to age, ability to stay focused on the task, and experience with making and sticking with decisions.

For example, for the young learner, choice can be as simple as chalk versus crayon or paint and the number of options need to be limited to two or three. Although learning to speak and write standard English is not an item of choice for an educated person, the content of essays could and should take into account student interests. Also, students who have never been to the ocean, need more time exploring tidepools and more time discussing what they find than students who frequently visit the ocean. First timers would also benefit from construction projects creating an immersion experience of the tidepools while the frequent visitor might be ready to move to secondhand resources at the library.

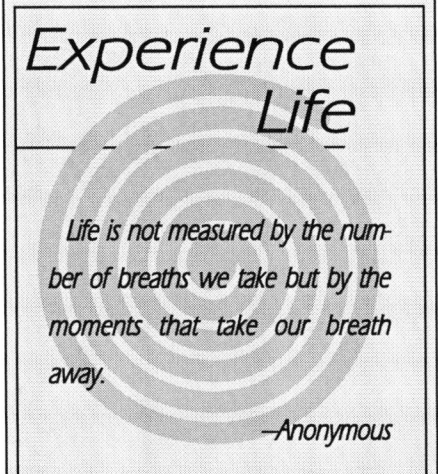

> **Experience Life**
>
> *Life is not measured by the number of breaths we take but by the moments that take our breath away.*
>
> —Anonymous

The truth is that offering choices is essential if one's goal is mastery and application of concepts and skills, not to mention creating lifelong learners who possess a passion for learning.

USING *CHOICES* TO ENHANCE DEVELOPMENT OF INTELLIGENCE

Curriculum Development

- Develop at least 5-10 inquiries for every key point.
  - Design some for whole class work, some for collaborative choice, and some for individual choice.
  - Make sure that you build in choice based on the multiple intelligences and Bloom's taxonomy (see Chapter 3) plus personality preferences (see Chapter 6).
  - Make them action-oriented requiring students to apply concepts and skills to real-life problems and products.
- Encourage students, after teaching them the format, to write their own inquiries. Select those you think will provide the best application and practice of concepts and skills.

Instructional Strategies

- During meaning-making/gaining an understanding of concepts and skills, invite students to select inquiries that rely on intelligences in which the student is strong; during practice applying what is understood, encourage students to select inquiries requiring intelligences that they wish to strengthen.
- Provide opportunities for students to tutor each other. Looking for ways to explain and demonstrate what we understand to another person increases our mental processing and creates new " Aha's."

Adequate Time

It was Albert Einstein who said that man invented the concept of time and has spent the rest of his life being controlled by it! It seems all the more true today when technology has literally added 20 percent to our work week, mainly because we take on larger and larger undertakings due to the fabled promise of assistance from our technological helpers—computers, fax machines, cellular telephones, and instantaneous worldwide communication.

In addition, knowledge continues to accumulate daily at an ever-expanding rate. As it does so, it is more essential than ever that we constantly reevaluate what we believe students should know in order to become contributing members of society. As higher expectations—state standards, benchmarks, tests, etc.—wind their political course, too often the result is more of the same—more dates, more facts, more definitions, more homework.

> **Adequate Time**
>
> *To everything there is a season, and a time for every purpose under heaven.*

We need to reduce the number of standards by writing them conceptually so they can take us deeper into meaningful content which in turn allows students to immerse themselves in understanding and learning to use what they understand in real-world ways. Skills likewise should be grouped into meaningful wholes. Until then, we need to pull the standards, however fragmented they might be, into real-world settings that can help give them a sense of coherence, relevance, and importance. *Being there* experiences provide a powerful glue. Both understanding and learning to use what we understand require time for the brain to engage and make those mysterious physiological changes that result in long-term memory.

USING *ADEQUATE TIME* TO ENHANCE DEVELOPMENT OF INTELLIGENCE

Curriculum Development

- Reduce the number of things to be learned by teasing out the underlying concepts and presenting them in meaningful chunks. Once students understand the concept, additional related knowledge can be learned much more easily. As Frank Smith says, "Understanding takes care of learning." Learning then becomes nearly effortless and automatic.
- Clarify in your own mind exactly what you want students to understand and then what you want them to do with it. Factoids can then easily be left behind.

Instructional Strategies

- Before you begin planning the sensory input students will need, carefully assess the extent of their prior experience and knowledge relevant to the concept or skill. Then allocate the time needed for *being there, immersion,* and *hands-on of the real thing* in the initial time block so students move beyond recognition to understanding. For subsequent instruction and inquiries, make sure students can complete their work without interruption. Long-term projects are the exception but even then adequate blocks of time should be allocated to allow students to "get into it" and make satisfying progress.
- Teach students to manage their time and to recognize plateau points in their work—natural breaking points at which a pause would be productive rather than disruptive.
- Make time for reflecting on what was accomplished—individually and as a group.

Simply put, physical growth—of the body or of the brain—requires time. Time to explore, time to reflect, time to act, time to evaluate, time to try again and again until we get it right, until we master the concept or skill to be learned. And, clearly, the amount of time needed varies wildly from brain to brain depending on the amount of prior knowledge relevant to the current task, the brain's processing preferences, personal likes and passions, and so forth.

To understand the power of this brain-compatible element, it might be helpful to apply it to our own lives first. For example, how many of us would sit down to complete our income taxes on a short weekend, knowing that the task will take at least three to four days of uninterrupted work to figure it out and then get it computed? Or, how many of us are eager to take a two-hour task out of our in-basket when we don't have a two-hour time block and we know that, with interruptions, it will end up taking us six hours? How many of us jump into learning a new software program at work because we don't have the needed chunk of time? Answer: a very rare few.

Similarly, how many of our students refuse to engage in a learning task when they feel certain that they won't have enough time to complete it successfully? In too many classrooms the clock is the commander. Ten minutes for recess, 40 minutes for language arts, 20 minutes for P.E., 35 minutes for music. What percentage of misbehavior and acting out has its roots in the frustration that comes from knowing time is inadequate and failure a certainty? Just a guess, more than half.

Adequate time is a critical element for successful learning and performance. We must begin to value learning more highly than bureaucracy's demand for lock step schedules.

Immediate Feedback

Immediate feedback is a necessary element in the learning environment—both for pattern seeking and for program building (see Chapter 1). In all learning environments except the school, it is present in abundance. Consider, for example, when children first begin to talk. Each time they say something incorrectly, we immediately give them the correct word, usage, and pronunciation. Imagine letting all their mistakes pile up during the week and correcting them on Friday!

Or, think back to the time you learned to drive a car. Feedback was instantaneous and continuous. If you returned home with no dents and no tickets, your parents knew you had a fairly successful time! Similarly, when learning to play a game or sport or beginning a hobby, feedback is built in, immediate, and continuous. In such cases, the learning materials or the conditions themselves provided the immediate feedback, or your fellow adventurer interpreted your progress toward mastery. This is a far cry from the classroom setting where students must press for information with the often asked questions: "Is this right, teacher?" "Teacher, is this the way it's supposed to be?"

Frank Smith, in *Insult to Intelligence: The Bureaucratic Invasion of Our Classrooms*,[43] states that learning does not require coercion or irrelevant reward. Learning is its own reward. Feedback that tells us we have succeeded at a learning task produces a burst of neurotransmitters, producing a "chemical high" that is readily observable in the spark in a child's eye as the " aha" registers.

The more immediate, intrinsic, and unambiguous the feedback, the faster and more accurate the learning. For example, learning to ride a bike. If you don't get the balance right, you hit the ground. Ambiguous? Not! In contrast, taking an essay test that will be graded and returned next week (and that is fast as essay exams go!) or doing all the odd number problems for math homework and getting a response from the teacher hours or days after the task is done violates all the important rules for learning. By then, the brain either learned it wrong or didn't learn it at all.

Few worksheets or dittos provide feedback that is self-correcting or intrinsic. As a consequence, children feel rudderless, confused, powerless, dependent on someone else, and either anxious or bored. Hardly the characteristics of a bodybrain-compatible learning environment. Without immediate feedback, learning is seriously impeded and students are left to tug at their teacher's shirt sleeve to ask, "Teacher, teacher, is this right?"

USING *IMMEDIATE FEEDBACK* TO ENHANCE DEVELOPMENT OF INTELLIGENCE

Curriculum Development

- Re-evaluate the starting point of your curriculum content. Shift the point of view of your curriculum content from disciplines to a need to understand the real world: locations, events, settings. "Disciplines" are an artifact of Western culture's way of talking about the world, a classic example of the parts not adding up to the whole. Start with the whole—the real world and *being there* experiences that offer intrinsic feedback rather than external (teacher or expert) feedback. Focus on doing, on applying concepts and skills in productive ways.
- Design action-oriented inquiries whose tasks provide natural, real-world feedback as the students progress carry out the inquiry.
- Teach students how to use/adapt the 3Cs of assessment and other self-assessment tools. The 3Cs are: correct, complete, and comprehensive (see Chapter 17).

USING *IMMEDIATE FEEDBACK* TO ENHANCE DEVELOPMENT OF INTELLIGENCE

Instructional Strategies

- Teach students to identify what they will need before they begin a learning task—what LIFESKILLS, prerequisite skills and knowledge, and how to tell if they are being successful at coming to an accurate understanding of and ways to apply concepts and skills. Model/Teach them to use self-talk to help them when they feel confused, bogged down, or discouraged.
- Help sensitize students to the feedback built into the real world; help them learn to direct self-talk to guide reflection on their own work and thus develop confidence in their own ability to provide feedback for themselves.
- Increase the number of "teachers" by organizing students into Learning Clubs; empower them to provide feedback. Also, eliminate tracking (students are equally unable to help each other), create multi-age classrooms (at least three grade levels is ideal), and arrange for cross-age tutoring.
- Limit your direct instruction to 16 minutes or less; during inquiry work, circulate among the students to give them immediate feedback individually and as a group.
- Allow sufficient time for students to be thoughtful about what they're doing and the progress they're making.
- Teach them to use simple, self-constructed or teacher-made rubrics by which they can assess their progress. Often just asking a self-assessment question helps guide learning.

Mastery

One of the greatest frustrations for teachers is "I taught them but they didn't learn." What happened?

In the ITI model, mastery means completion of both steps in the new definition of learning (see Chapters 4 and 5); it means being able to apply what is understood in real-world ways and practicing how to use that skill or knowledge until it becomes wired into long-term memory. .

Mastery in the ITI model does not mean achieving adult-level expertise; it means acquiring competence at understanding and using concepts and skills at a level appropriate for a child at his/her age.

The goal of mastery is achieving competence at navigating through life. This is in stark contrast to accepting a score of 80 percent or higher on a quiz or standardized test as proof of "learning," an unacceptable outcome for the billions we spend on education and testing.

A Dash of Common Sense

To assess mastery/competence in the ITI classroom, we recommend asking two common sense questions:

"What do you want students to understand?" and

"What do you want them to do with it?"

These two questions parallel the two-step definition of learning used in the ITI model.

The Caines, in their book *Making Connections: Teaching and the Human Brain,* suggest four relevant and useful indicators to guide your evaluation:[44]

- The ability to use the language of the discipline or subject in complex situations and in social interaction
- The ability to perform appropriately in unanticipated situations
- The ability to solve real problems using the skills and concepts
- The ability to show, explain, or teach the idea or skill to another person who has a real need to know

These guidelines are imminently genuine and authentic; they also require both *being there* experiences and real-world practice using concepts and skills before the assessment process begins. For a discussion of learning to the level of mastery as a two-step process, see Chapters 4 and 5.

USING *MASTERY* TO ENHANCE DEVELOPMENT OF INTELLIGENCE

Curriculum Development

- Make sure what you're asking students to understand and be able to do is genuinely useful in the real world. Eliminate factoids* and always provide examples of uses for concepts and skills beyond the school walls.

- Base your curriculum in real-life locations. Use the real-world standards of mastery inherent in the roles of those who work/use the location. What concepts and skills from your curriculum must these people understand and be able to use? To what levels?

Instructional Strategies

- Help students tune in to the real-world standards that apply to what you are teaching. Eliminate any double standards—this is good enough for school but would get you fired on the job.
- Encourage students to question. "What is this good for?" "So what?" "Why is this important for me to know and be able to do?" Be prepared to answer such questions.

* When developing curriculum, there is no bigger enemy than factoids. They kill student interest killers, elicit little emotion to assist the learning process, and aren't memorable. They therefore are difficult hard to record in long-term memory. For example, Columbus sailed in 1492.

Absence of Threat/Nurturing Reflective Thinking

In simple terms, fear limits exploration. Threat—real or perceived—significantly restricts, if not eliminates, students' ability to fully engage in the learning process. To explore the new and different and to be open to new ideas requires confidence that one is in a safe environment, one in which mistakes and difficulty in understanding/doing something are considered just part of learning, not an opportunity for sarcasm and put-downs.

Building intelligence—the capability to solve problems and produce products—requires exuberant and curiosity-driven exploration, full focus on the learning at hand, maximum activation of the senses and bodybrain partnership. For this, absence of threat is an absolute must, a prerequisite for reaching the mental state of reflective thinking.

For a fuller discussion of the role of emotion as a gatekeeper to learning and performance, see Chapter 2.

USING *ABSENCE OF THREAT/ NURTURING REFLECTIVE THINKING* TO ENHANCE DEVELOPMENT OF INTELLIGENCE

Curriculum Development

- Know your students. Make sure that your curriculum is age-appropriate and thus understandable to them. Nothing tears down students' sense of confidence faster than knowing that they don't understand what is going on.
- Develop, and begin with, inquiries that help students bring forward any prior experiences related to the key point.

Instructional Strategies

- Help students make connections between what they are now studying and their lives now—at school, at home, wherever they go. If you can't find a connection, don't waste your students' and your time teaching it. The world is full of urgent things for students to learn—for their safety, their health, their well-being, not to mention their future capacity to succeed at work and family life and be a contributing member of society.
- Provide a good mix of collaborative time and intrapersonal time, stimulation and time to be reflective.
- Provide immediate feedback in order to keep self-doubt and frustration at a minimum.

Notes

1 For an extraordinary look at this physiological growth in the brain, see Diane Sawyer, "Your Child's Brain," *ABC News Prime Time* (January 25, 1995).

2 This definition of intelligence, developed by Howard Gardner, is the most useful definition for the classroom that we have found. See *Frames of Mind: Theory of Multiple Intelligences* (New York: Basic Books, Inc., 1985), x and *Intelligence Reframed* (New York: Basic Books, Inc., 1999), 44. For other models of intelligence, see David Perkins and Strauss.

3 Reuven Feurstein is an eminent cognitive psychologist, known for his groundbreaking research in cognitive mediation and practice. He has established the principle that "all children can learn" while working with culturally deprived, retarded, and autistic children. Professor Feurstein developed a classroom curriculum designed to build the cognitive functions of students diagnosed by others as incapable of learning. His program, Instrumental Enrichment, provides students with the concepts, skills, strategies, operations, and techniques necessary to become independent thinkers.

4 Marian Diamond, author of several books on the brain, has been a Professor of Anatomy at Berkeley for over thirty years and was director of the University's Lawrence Hall of Science from 1990 to 1996. She is a pioneer brain researcher who has conducted numerous lines of research into the effect of the environment and hormones on the forebrain. She also has investigated structural changes in the cerebral cortex induced by an enriched environment and structural changes in the cerebral cortex as influenced by sex steroid hormones.

5 Leslie A. Hart, *Human Brain and Human Learning* (Covington, WA: Books for Educators, Inc., 1999), 87.

6 John Bruner, in his article, "A Bridge Too Far" (*Educational Researcher,* August, 1997) has challenged that a jump from brain research to classroom application is too far a leap, that we don't have grounds for doing so, that we should, instead, base educational practice on the work of cognitive psychologists (he being one). While his cautionary tale is important—education is infamous for its leaps to unfounded fads—there are brain research findings that have been confirmed and reconfirmed over the past twenty years. The concepts resonate with our intuitions and experiences, personal and professional. Furthermore, the curriculum development and instructional strategies recommended to translate them into action are not "new." They are proven strategies from the fields of psychology, sociology, and education. See page 18.

7 John J. Ratey, *A User's Guide to the Brain: Perception, Attention, and the Four Theaters of the Brain* (New York: Pantheon Books, 2001), 18.

8 Ratey, *User's Guide to the Brain*, 20.

9 Marian Diamond observed the impact of boredom on young and adolescent rats: "A boring environment had a more powerful thinning effect on the cortex than an exciting environment had on cortex thickening. Young rats are obviously very susceptible to losing mental ground when not challenged, and that shrinkage shows up after just four days. In rodent teenagers, at least, the shrinkage can begin to be reversed again after four days of enrichment." Given the number of parallels between the effects of enrichment and boredom on the brains of rats and humans that have proven true, this is quite disturbing. Among many things, it should cause us to reexamine the school calendar. It would appear that the traditional agrarian calendar with three months of summer vacation works strongly against those who most depend upon the public schools for learning. See *Magic Trees of the Mind: How to Nurture Your Child's Intelligence, Creativity, and Healthy Emotions from Birth Through Adolescence.* (New York: A Dutton Book, 1998).

10 "Use it or lose it" is more than a catchy phrase or metaphor. It applies to the brain "directly and literally." See Elkhonon Goldberg, *The Executive Brain: Frontal Lobes and the Civilized Mind* (Oxford: University Press, 2001), 209.

11 For a powerful, electrifying image of how dendrites grow and connect in the brain, see Diane Sawyer, "Your Child's Brain," *ABC News Prime Time* (January 25, 1995).

12 William Calvin, author of *How Brains Think: Evolving Intelligence, Then and Now,* talks about competing choruses, each singing its own message or answer and trying to get others neurons to agree. The chorus best able to recruit neighboring neurons into singing its song determines which competing message wins out. An example of this is when we "can't make up our mind." Choice A or B, is it a cheetah or a leopard? (Conversations with William H. Calvin, January, 1997, Covington, Washington.)

13 Marian Diamond and Janet Hopson, *Magic Trees of the Mind: How to Nurture Your Child's Intelligence, Creativity, and Healthy Emotions from Birth Through Adolescence* (New York: Penguin, 1998), 26.

14 Diamond and Hopson, *Magic Trees of the Mind*, 26.

15 Jane Healy, *Endangered Minds: Why Children Don't Think – and What We Can Do About It* (New York: Simon & Schuster, 1990).

16 Diamond and Hopson, *Magic Trees of the Mind*, 26.

17 Another method of organization is pruning, the result of a chemical wash of neurons that are not connected. The synapses that carry the most messages get stronger and survive, while weaker synaptic connections are cut out. Experience determines which connections will be strengthened and which will

be pruned: connections that have been activated most frequently get preserved. Between about age ten and puberty, the brain will ruthlessly destroy its weakest connections, preserving only those that experience has shown to be useful. See A. Gopnik, A. Meltzoff, and Patricia Kuhl, *The Scientist in the Crib: Minds, Brains, and How Children Learn* (New York: William Morrow and Company, 1999), 186-187. Also see Ratey, *User's Guide to the Brain*, 24-26. See Ibid., 19-26 for an electrifying description of how the fetal brain forms, connects, organizes, prunes, and operates.

18 Elkhonon Goldberg, *The Executive Brain: Frontal Lobes and the Civilized Mind* (Oxford: University Press, 2001), 209.

19 Goldberg, *Executive Brain*, 65.

20 Candace Pert, *Molecules of Emotion: Why You Feel the Way You Feel* (New York: Scribner, 1997), 179.

21 Our first introduction to the existence of at least 19 senses came from Bob Samples, *Open Mind, Whole Mind* (CA: Jalmar Press, 1987). See also Robert Rivlin and Karen Gravelle, *Deciphering Your Senses* (New York: Simon and Schuster, 1984). There is an interesting history here. Robert Rivlin and Karen Gravelle present the scientific evidence underpinning the 19 senses and give a historical perspective explaining why the mistaken notion of the five senses has persisted for so many centuries despite scientific evidence to the contrary. ". . . according to the Medieval philosopher Cornelius Agrippa, arguing Plato's philosophy, 'Divinity is annexed to the mind, the mind to the intellect, the intellect to the intention, the intention to the imagination, the imagination to the senses, and the senses at last to things. For this is the bond and continuity of nature.'"

"It used to be so simple. There were five senses and they created a picture of the world inside your head. But new ways of probing the brain are transforming this view of sensory perception. For starters, we have far more than five senses; the consensus is that there are at least 21." *New Scientist*, (New York: Shnell Publishing Co. Inc., January 29, 2005).

"There was, in fact, a divine relationship between the senses and the world they sensed. And, like many things in God's divine plan for the universe, the senses were seen to occur in fives—a prime number with considerable symbolic significance. How convenient, then, to think of the body as having five senses, corresponding roughly to the sensory organs (eyes, ears, nose, tongue, and skin). That the skin could feel both temperature and touch, to say nothing of pain, was somehow conveniently overlooked in order to align the essential unity of the human body with a metaphysical plan of the universe; to say we had eight or eighteen senses simply wouldn't do" (Rivlin and Gravelle, *Deciphering Your Senses*, 15).

22 The power of the 19 senses is easily verified by our own experiences. Simply ask yourself to remember your most vivid memory from childhood. Analyze the scene in your mind's eye. You will discover input from most, if not all, of the 19 senses.

23 One can't overstress the importance of full sensory input through *being there* experiences in building the necessary neural wiring for understanding the concepts involved. Once understanding through sensory input and prior experience is brought together, secondhand input allows the learner to extend and expand learning.

24 Candace Pert's pioneering research (discovery of the opiate receptor, 1972) on how the chemicals inside our bodies form a dynamic information network, linking mind and body, is revolutionary. By establishing the biomolecular basis for our emotions, Pert has come to the brilliant conclusion that it is our emotions and their biological components that establish the crucial link between mind and body. This does not repudiate modern medicine's gains; rather her findings complement existing techniques by offering a new, scientific understanding of the power of our minds and our feelings to affect our health,

well being, and learning.

25 *USA Today,* May 13, 1992, 9.

26 Hart, *Human Brain and Human Learning,* 18.

27 A good example of the weakness of this approach is illustrated by the video, *A Private Universe.* Interviewers ask Harvard University graduates in their caps and gowns the answer to this question: "Explain the reasons for the seasons." Over 80 percent of the randomly selected students and faculty—despite their middle school and university science classes—give the "stove is hot" theory, i.e., in the summer the earth is much closer to the sun and is therefore hotter. In fact, the earth's orbit is nearly round; distance from the sun is not a factor. This despite the amount of formal teaching received—varying from none to classes in advanced planetary motion—yet another example of the power of the *being there* experience over secondhand information! The toddler's experience with hot stoves prevails.

Therefore, meaningfulness for elementary students must begin with firsthand, *being there,* here and now experiences. They provide the mental scaffolding for the words which represent the concepts and definitions of things they have experienced. The number of "experiences" must continuously increase so that students will have a basis for relating and applying new information.

28 Patty Harrington, associate of Susan Kovalik & Associates, Inc., trained teachers in the Slovak Republic through translators in the late 1990s. In response to a particular event, she asked if they felt pensive, melancholy, sad, blue, or lonely. To her surprise, the translator used the same Slovak word each time. The Slovak language had only one word for all of those shades of meaning.

29 Healy, *Endangered Minds,* 50-51.

30 Ibid., 23. (A study of "typical" fifth graders by Dr. Bernice Cullinan, New York University. Ninety percent read four minutes or less per day. Cullinan concludes that "our society is becoming increasingly aliterate." She defines "aliterate" as a person who knows how to read but who doesn't choose to read. Such an aliterate "is not much better off than an illiterate, a person who cannot read at all.")

31 Ibid., 72.

32 Jane Healy, *Failure to Connect: How Computers Affect Our Children's Minds—And What We Can Do About It* (New York: Simon & Schuster, 1998), 110.

33 Susan J. Kovalik & Karen Olsen, *Kid's Eye View of Science* (Covington, WA: Books For Educators, Inc., 1994).

34 Larry Lowery, "Scientific Thinking Processes," *California State Science Curriculum Framework,* 1986.

35 Healy, *Endangered Minds,* 69.

36 Frank Smith, *Insult to Intelligence: The Bureaucratic Invasion of Our Classrooms* (New York: Arbor House, 1986).

37 There are many collections of data about the power of collaboration to improve learning and performance. The *Handbook of Research on Improving Student Achievement, Second Edition,* cites over two dozen studies beginning in 1985 (Gordon Cawelti, Editor (Arlington, Virginia: Educational Research Service, 1999), 159). Robert J. Marzano, in *Classroom Instruction That Works: Research-Based Strategies for Increasing Student Achievement,* summarizes nine synthesis studies on collaboration, from 1987-1996 (Alexandria, VA: ASCD, 2001) 86-87. An author who makes important connections to curriculum development for collaborative work is Elizabeth Cohen; see *Designing Groupwork: Strategies for the Heterogeneous Classroom* (New York: Teachers College Press, 1994).

38 This sage advice comes from Elizabeth Cohen. She provides the best guidance for developing curriculum for collaborative

tasks that we have found to date. See *Designing Groupwork,* Chapter 5.

39 Learning Clubs is a term used by Frank Smith who describes the glue of "clubs" in real life. For example, when we join a golf club, our sense of belonging propels us to learn what others in our club know—golf, the style of dress of the members, stock market, etc. See Smith, *Insult to Intelligence.*

40 Ratey, *A User's Guide to the Brain,* 37.

41 Ibid., 150, 148.

42 Ibid., 148.

43 Smith, *Insult to Intelligence.,* 29-30.

44 Renata and Geoffrey Caine, *Making Connections: Teaching and Human Brain* (California: Addison-Wesley, 1994), 103.

Chapter 2: The Inseparable Bodybrain Partnership — Emotion and Movement

There are two aspects of the bodybrain partnership that are critical to the classroom:

- Emotion—the gatekeeper to learning and performance. In the words of Dr. Robert Sylwester, "Emotion drives attention which drives learning, memory, problem solving, and just about everything else."[1] The role of the limbic system, highly interconnected with all parts of the brain and thought to be the core of emotion, has been studied for more than 50 years. Researchers now believe that most of the brain systems, including the limbic system, participate in emotion and its connection to cognition. A second biological system of emotion was discovered in the 1990s. This chemical system operates through the body, making an inseparable bodybrain partnership.[2]

- Movement to enhance learning—in many respects the mobility of the body grows the brain[3] and the motion centers in the brain are responsible for sequencing thought.[4] This area of brain research is changing our perception of brain development and processing. At one level it is absolutely astonishing; at another, it resonates with our intuition. The implications here for classroom life are enormous.

Emotion As Gatekeeper to Learning and Performance

> **ITI Learning Principles**
>
> - *Intelligence as a function of experience*
> - ***Inseparable bodybrain partnership—***
>   ***—Emotion as gatekeeper to learning and performance*** *and*
>   ***—Movement to enhance learning***
> - *Multiple intelligences*
> - *Learning as a two-step process*

Given the Western world's love affair with science and technology, with their underpinnings of rational, logical thought, investigating the biological basis of emotion has been slow in coming. But once begun, brain research in this area has exploded, especially in the last 15 years of the 20th century and early 21st century. Today we must talk in terms of a bodybrain partnership, an inseparable partnership running parallel complementary information systems. One system is a combination of electrical and chemical, one wholly chemical.

Years of Research: Learning from Fear

One of the earliest attempts to analyze the role of emotion in brain function emerged from Dr. Paul MacLean's work at National Institute for Health in the 1950s. In describing the basic functions of the various structures of the brain, MacLean was the first to make clear that emotions significantly affect brain functions and thus learning, memory, and behavior. However, MacLean mistakenly perpetuated the assumption that we mostly operate from our cerebral cortex, known for its logic and rational thinking and home of academic learning, and only occasionally downshifted into our limbic system. Now we know that emotions are a function of the entire bodybrain partnership and are with us all of the time. Emotions, in fact, filter incoming sensory input, modulating what the cerebral cortex attends to, processes, and stores in long term memory. Emotions truly are the gatekeeper to learning and performance.

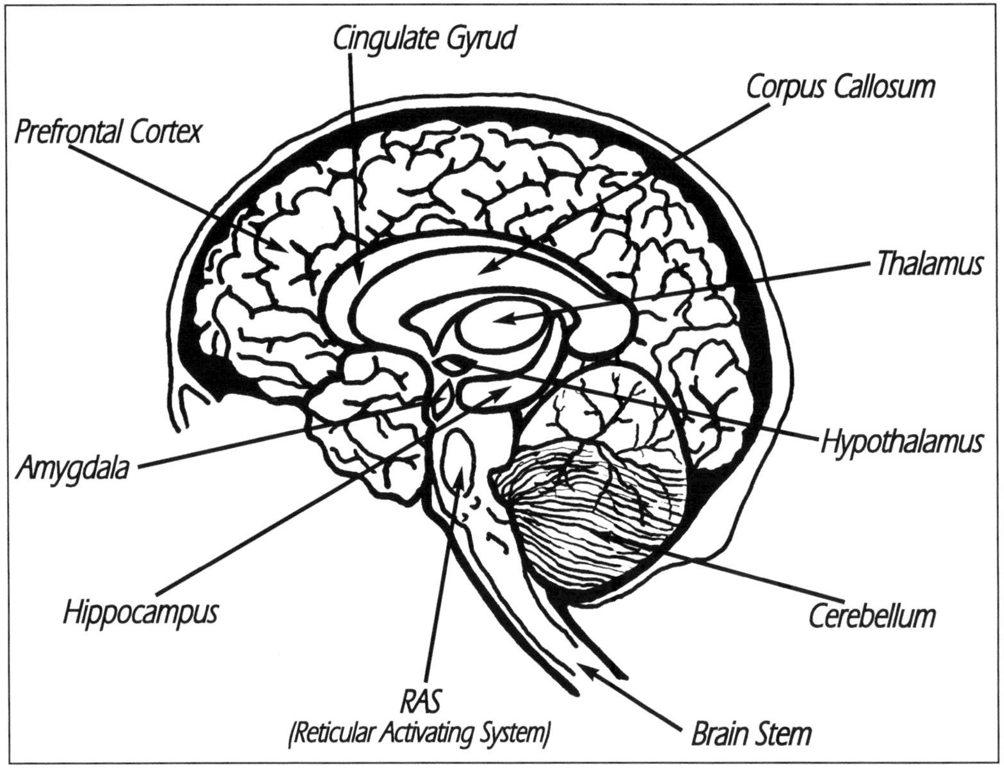

As researchers explore the brain and its responses to emotion, they are discovering how enormously complex the brain is. Because fear is essential to survival and was easier to study, it has been studied more than any other emotion.

So what did researchers find? Somewhat to our surprise, we have discovered that emotions are processed throughout the entire brain and all of its structures—particularly the interconnected structures of the amygdala, hippocampus, thalamus, hypothalamus, and cingulate gyrus, an area once referred to as the "limbic system."

How Emotion Affects Learning

What happens in our brains when emotionally charged sensory data comes in? A great deal. Here's how:[5]

- The walnut-sized thalamus, located in the center of the brain, receives, sorts, and forwards almost all input from the sensory organs. It is the relay station for all of the 19+ senses, except the olfactory or sense of smell, which goes directly to the cortex. Some sensory information from the thalamus travels to the amygdala, which is essential to decoding certain emotions, particularly those related to potential dangers in the environment.
- The almond-shaped amygdala is located close to the hippocampus, in the frontal portion of the temporal lobe. Sensory information arrives at the amygdala via either the

short, fast, but imprecise route directly from the thalamus or the long, slow, precise route from the various sensory cortexes. Information coming to the amygdala directly from the thalamus arrives very quickly and helps us prepare for potential danger before we even know exactly what it is. After receiving the information from the thalamus, the amygdala sends signals to the hypothalamus, informing it of potential danger.

- The hypothalamus, a pecan-sized structure below the thalamus, unleashes a host of chemicals that raise blood pressure, increase heart rate, release fat into the blood stream and in many other ways prepare the body to fight, flight, or freeze. This rapid automatic response often means the difference between life and death.
- The hippocampus, Greek for "seahorse" because of its shape, seems to be primarily responsible for helping form and find long-term memories which are actually stored elsewhere in the cerebral cortex.
- The cingulate gyrus, located on top of the corpus callosum that connects the two hemispheres of the brain, helps resolve ambiguous situations. The cingulate gyrus reviews incoming sensory data from the 19+ senses and determines whether the data has emotional significance. It then coordinates the retrieval and analysis of memories about previous similar situations and relays information to the prefrontal cortex for a decision about what to do.

The prefrontal cortex acts like the CEO of the brain, coordinating and integrating almost all basic brain functions. Unlike most other animals that can primarily react to sensory input, humans have a large prefrontal cortex that permits proactive behavior that anticipates and prepares for challenges. When there is sufficient time, it is the prefrontal cortex that analyzes possible choices and makes the decision as to the best action for the bodybrain to take.[4]

Sensory information sent directly from the thalamus to the amygdala and then on to the hypothalamus for the appropriate fight, flight, or freeze response helps get us out of danger fast. Information sent via the long, slow, precise route from the sensory cortex to the amygdala arrives after the brain has had a chance to process the input and decide if it really is threatening. The prefrontal cortex also seems to be involved in the final phase of confronting a danger, where, after the initial automatic, emotional reaction, with input from the cingulated gyrus, the brain must react and choose the course of action to move us out of the dangerous situation. The connections between the prefrontal cortex and the amygdala help the amygdala store additional information such as perceptions of sight and sound to create an automatic response the next time a similar dangerous situation is perceived. Meantime, our memory immediately stores details of where we are, what we are doing, who we are with, what we are feeling, and when this is happening in the hippocampus.

The connections between prefrontal cortex and amygdala are also involved with anxiety. At times the prefrontal cortex can gain some control over anxiety, but at other times our creative prefrontal cortex generates anxiety through imagination of failure or presence of dangers that do not actually exist. When students are anxious or fearful for either real or imagined reasons, the amygdala may begin its automatic response and hijack the thinking, reasoning prefrontal cortex.[6] The only learning that takes place during this time is the amygdala's recognition of another potential danger to add to its list of automatic responses to remove the body from danger. Reflective thinking and long-term learning do not take place during times of real or perceived threat.

Emotions in the Classroom

It is clear that emotion does drive attention. Goldberg suggests that the prefrontal cortex becomes particularly active during emotional experiences. "The function of the prefrontal cortex is to calculate "what is good for the organism," more than to calculate what is true" in an abstract, dispassionate sense."[7] Engaging the prefrontal cortex in determining what is good for the organism seems to be critical for the formation of new cognitive routines and patterns so that learning can take place.

Providing opportunities for full sensory input through study trips or *being there* experiences allows students to look for novel solutions to problems or situations and take in sensory data from a variety of sources. The brain is constantly scanning the environment for patterns in the form of sensory data. This sensory data is stored throughout the brain and is then available to help form neural connections as further learning takes place. However, we can not take in all of the sensory information available to us. If you focus your attention on listening, you will become aware of sounds that you hadn't heard before. If you focus your attention on feeling, you will become aware of your clothes as they touch your body. If every bit of the sensory data available to us came into the brain all at once, we would suffer sensory overload. The brainstem, the thalamus, and the sensory cortex together form the RAS or reticular activating system. The RAS acts somewhat like a dimmer switch or volume control to filter the amount of sensory input that makes it to our cortex. Important data that we are paying attention to makes it past the filter to the cortex where the patterns are manipulated, processed, combined with other future learnings, and turned into programs and long-term memories.[8]

In ITI classrooms, teachers greet students at the door to welcome them back to class and take their emotional temperature, providing a time for students who are anxious or fearful to have a short conversation with the teacher to help center and focus themselves. When classrooms are safe and free from threats, the thalamus allows life to go on in a "normal" pattern and learning is possible. Providing relevant and meaningful curriculum that students can experience both emotionally and cognitively encourages involvement of the prefrontal cortex and helps it to determine what is good for the organism and can be moved to long-term storage. Lack of engagement often happens when information and skills are broken down into small discrete parts that do not allow students to see patterns and search for novel solutions. Using instructional strategies that tap the power of emotion such as collaborative learning, simulations, music, and drama enable students to engage more systems in their brains and make learning powerful and memorable.

Testing can be a scary time for students—and teachers. Practicing deep breathing, movement activities such as those found in *Brain Gym*[9], and using the steps of *Freeze Frame*[10] can help students cope with anxiety. When students can't remember the answer to a question, they need to allow their hippocampus time to retrieve the information. Knowing that by breathing deeply and calming themselves, they can refocus their brains and "find" the answer will give them the confidence they need to do their best.

So it would seem that the structures of the brain make learning and performance an emotionally driven function. As summarized by Dr. Robert Sylwester, "Emotions drive attention which drives learning, memory, problem-solving and just about everything else."[11] But there's more to the story. The groundbreaking work now done on the chemical origins and operations of emotions by Dr. Candace Pert and others in the past 20 years suggests that there is a chemical information system used by the brain that parallels the electrical-chemical synaptic gap system. These chemicals, according to Pert are the "molecules of emotion."[12] Collectively referred to as "information substances," they are, as Paul Harvey would say, the rest of the story begun in Chapter 1. In effect, we learn through the cooperative interaction of multiple systems of the brain and body working together as an inseparable unit.

Information Substances: The Rest of the Story

Just as Paul Harvey's "The Rest of the Story" adds a stunning twist that makes us view the earlier part of the story differently, so it is with brain research. For 100 years, scientists have understood the basic electrical-chemical building blocks of learning in the brain: nerve cells (neurons) grow dendrites (structures that receive information from other neurons) and axons (structures that send information to other neurons). Electrical impulses travel down the axon, turn into chemical messengers that jump (actually float across) the tiny gap (synapse) to the dendrites of the next neuron. Although there were many mysteries yet to be understood, such as how this all results in learning and memories, the basic explanation still holds true. During the 1950s, structures in the brain that process emotion were discovered; over the next 30 years, it became clear that emotion has a powerful impact on learning. Dr. Robert Sylwester's summary is no exaggeration: Emotion drives our attention, what we attend to determines what we perceive and thus drives learning, memory, problem-solving, behavior, and on and on.[13]

The neurotransmitters in the brain responsible for the synaptic leap, discussed at some length in Chapter 1, are but one category of "information substances" found throughout the body and brain that carry out the process we call learning. Likewise, the limbic system is only one source of "emotional messages" in the bodybrain partnership. The term "information substances" was coined initially by Francis Schmitt, elder statesman of neuroscience from the Massachusetts Institute of Technology, to describe a variety of transmitters, peptides, hormones, factors, and protein ligands that make up a second system. In this system, chemical information substances travel the extracellular fluids circulating throughout the body to reach their specific receptors, receptors on cells located not just in the brain but throughout the body.[14]

This second system parallels the conventional model of neuronal circuitry with its dendrites, axons, and synaptic leaps. Some neuroscientists now speculate that less than two percent of neuronal communication actually occurs at the synapse.[15] Less than two percent! Most of the information received by a neuron is taken in by the receptors at the cell's surface. And no wonder. The number of receptors on a neuron is staggering; current estimates are tens of thousands to a million plus per neuron.[16] That's a lot of potential for conversation! It would appear that the ability to perceive understandable patterns and learn from them is so important to survival that it cannot be posited only in one place or with one method of communication—not just one part of the neuron (at the synaptic gap) nor just in the brain. The entire body is involved.[17]

So just what are these "information substances" and what is their role in learning? These molecules, or ligands, are the basic units of a language used by cells throughout the organism to communicate across systems such as the endocrine, neurological, gastrointestinal, and even the immune system. As they travel, they inform, regulate, and synchronize.[18] Peptides are the largest category of information substances; one kind or another is produced in every cell in the body, not just by cells in the brain. Furthermore, every peptide now known to be produced within the body has receptors in the brain, thus qualifying each peptide to be considered a "neuropeptide." This means that the body talks to the brain, giving it information that alters its messages back to the body and vice versa.

According to Dr. John Ratey, "We are learning that emotions are the rules of multiple brain and body systems that are distributed over the whole person. We cannot separate emotion from cognition or cognition from the body."[19]

The Molecules of Emotion: The effect of such "conversations" on the organism is to change physical activity cell by cell and as a total organism, *"including behavior and even mood – the closest word to emotion in the lexicon of hard science."*[20] Examples of outward manifestation of such inner "conversations" include a "gut feeling" about something; a first impression of someone as untrustworthy; a physical restlessness that something is wrong before you can put your finger on it; a spark in the eye that says, "I get it even though I can't yet explain it"; a passion for one's hobby; deep love for the beauty of nature; the contentment of a quiet hour spent with a special friend. As was foreseen by the now virtually abandoned triune brain theory,[21] core limbic brain structures such as the amygdala, hippocampus, and hypothalamus—which were long believed to be involved in emotional behavior—contain a whopping percent of the various neuropeptide receptors studied to date, perhaps as high as 85 to 95 percent.[16] Now add to that the startling finding that several of the key emotion molecules such as endorphins can be found in single-cell animals as well as on up the evolutionary trail. Peptides, it appears, have been carrying information since before there were brains, leading researchers such as Antonio Damasio to assert that "emotion is the highest part of our mindbody survival kit."[23] One of their key roles is to tell the brain what's worth attending to and the "attitude" with which one attends. Again, as so nicely summarized by Dr. Robert Sylwester, "Emotion drives attention and attention drives learning and memory, problem solving, and just about everything else."

Emotion As Filter. Another important piece of this new view of learning as a bodybrain partnership is the discovery that there are other locations in the body where high concentrations of almost every neuropeptide receptor exist. One example is the dorsal horn (the back side of the spinal cord) which is the first synapse with the nervous system where all somatosensory information is processed. In fact, in virtually all locations where information from the five senses—sight, sound, taste, smell, and touch—enter the nervous system, there are high concentrations of neuropeptide receptors. Such regions, called nodal points or hot spots, seem to be designed so that they can be accessed and modulated by almost all neuropeptides as they go about their job of processing information, prioritizing it, and biasing it to cause unique neurophysiological changes. Thus, peptides filter the input of our experiences, significantly altering our perception of reality and the input selected and allowed in during any learning situation.[24] According to Dr. Candace Pert, author of *Molecules of Emotion: Why You Feel the Way You Feel,* "Emotions and bodily sensations are thus intricately intertwined, in a bidirectional network in which each can alter the other. Usually this process takes place at an unconscious level but it can also surface into consciousness under certain conditions or be brought into consciousness by intention."[25]

Implications: In summary, this wholly chemical system of learning, that parallels the electrical-chemical system of neurons, dendrites, axons, and synapses as described in Chapter 1, expands our definition of learning in multiple ways. We now know that:

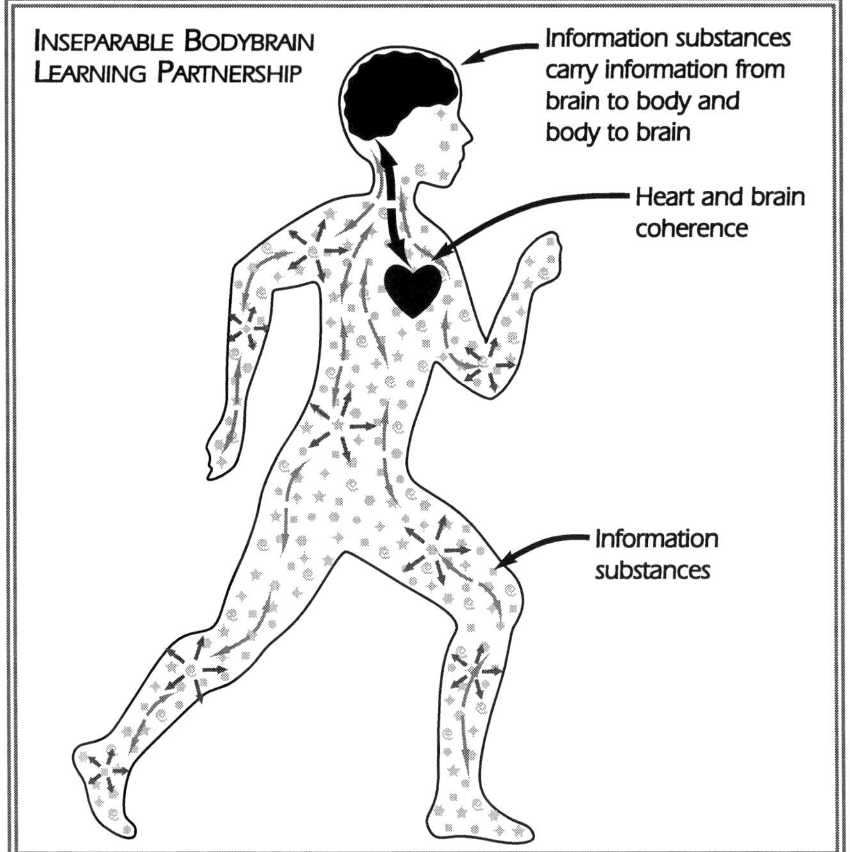

1) The body and brain form an inseparable learning partnership. Each sends messages out to the other which alters the messages that are sent back. Most sensory input (if not all) is filtered through/modulated by our emotions which direct our attention. What we attend to then drives learning, problem solving, and memory. Conversely, if we do not attend, learning and memory cannot occur.

2) Therefore, the environment of the body is critical—the physical surroundings and the quality of interrelationships of those in it (student to student and student-adult). Consequently, implementation of the ITI model begins with ensuring that the classroom and schoolwide environment enhance rather than impede students' abilities to focus on the learning at hand. Two essential aspects are an absence of threat (real and perceived) and the creation of a sense of community. [26] See Part B, Chapters 8-10.

Movement to Enhance Learning

The Western world's view of the brain is that it is rational, logical, ruler of all; the body in this scheme has been primarily viewed as merely the vehicle that carried the brain from one cerebral task to another. And, if it was good looking and athletic to boot, so much the better! Now, however, it is clear that there is no hierarchy, no separation between the body and the brain. What the Greeks knew 2,000 years ago is being confirmed by today's high tech brain research—if you want the best performance from your brain, tune the body and brain together.

During the 1980s and 1990s, the popular press has extolled and sold the virtues of physical fitness as a means increasing mental sharpness and reducing stress, to overall health and well-being. But the story now emerging from brain research is amazing. As Carla Hannaford is fond of saying, "The body grows the brain."[27] Indeed, animals that don't move, don't have a brain. And those like the sea squirt that move early in its life cycle, later reabsorb their brain when they permanently affix themselves to a stationary object.[28]

What Brain Research Is Telling Us

The brain research into the relationship between movement and cognition is nothing less than startling. The major findings that we believe are key for classroom teachers are:

- Movement is fundamental to the very existence of a brain. Only an organism that moves from place to place requires a brain.[29]
- The entire front half of the brain—the newest in evolutionary terms—is devoted to organizing action, both physical and mental.[30] "Higher" brain functions have evolved from movement and still depend on it.
- Movement is crucial to every brain function including planning and executing plans, memory, emotion, language, and learning.[31]
- The ability to mimic, one of young human's most powerful avenues for learning, is movement based.

Movement Is Fundamental. Only an organism that moves from place to place even requires a brain.[32] This is not a casual link! The brain and body are an inseparable partnership. As Dr. John Ratey points out, "What the brain communicates to the body depends largely on what messages the body is sending to the brain. Together they collaborate for the good of the whole organism."[33] In classroom life, this means that the body and brain are always talking and working together. When one partner is shut down, told to sit still and not move, the functioning of the other partner is deeply affected.

As we think about the traditions of the educational system we inherited, we can't help but marvel at how far off the mark some of its features are. Children sitting quietly in rows, not moving, not talking. What a recipe for failure to learn!

This suggests that the pendulum swings in school reform over the past century may have failed not because they were inherently flawed but because throughout those reforms the bodybrain partnership remained divided and thus ineffective at learning.

Half of the Entire Brain Is Devoted to Organizing Action. This is another powerful message for teachers. Half the brain! And the newest, most powerful parts of the brain at that. The frontal cortex learns, routinizes, and processes motor and mental functions in parallel. Movement, then, becomes inextricably tied to cognition.[34]

This feature of the physiology of the brain underscores the importance of defining learning as a two-step process: understanding and then ***using*** what is understood. It turns out that the brain *expects* to use what it understands.

Movement Is Crucial to Every Brain Function. Although our Olympic-level athletes have discovered the impressive power of the brain to improve the performance of its partner, the brain, we in the U.S. are slow to acknowledge reciprocal power of the body on the brain. According to Ratey, "our physical movements can directly influence our ability to learn, think, and remember. Evidence is mounting that each person's capacity to master new and remember old information is improved by biological changes in the brain brought on by new activity."[35]

What does this all mean for the classroom teacher? Nothing short of a revolutionary shift in our view of our students as learners. What this means is that the bodybrain partnership perceives, processes, and stores in long-term memory concepts and skills in terms of their usability and usefulness. Not useable (who cares?), not useful (relevant now), then, not worth learning. We must reframe what we teach and why we teach it. Learning not for the sake of learning but for the sake of using what we learn—for our own lives and as contributing citizens.

Ideally, the resources spent on textbooks, workbooks, blackline masters, and copy paper and machines should be redirected to *being there* experiences. Knowing how concepts and skills are *used* in the real world greatly enhance building long-term memories.

Mimicry. Startling research is emerging that suggests the presence of "mirror neurons," a subset of movement-related neurons in premotor cortex area [36] that buzz away when we watch someone do something that interests us. Whether these neurons merely assist us to understand or to mirror gestures or actions is still uncertain. Some researchers such as Ramachandran believe that mirror neurons play a bigger role than is generally appreciated. Ramachandran believes that not only are they the missing link between gesture and language but they help explain human learning, ingenuity, and culture in general. "Language, imitative learning, and mind reading, seemingly unrelated human developments, may all be shown to be linked through these intriguing nerve cells."[71]

Translating Brain Research into Action Using the Nine Bodybrain-Compatible Elements

Bodybrain-Compatible Elements

- *Absence of Threat/Nurturing Reflective Thinking*
- *Movement*
- *Collaboration*
- *Meaningful Content*
- *Choices*
- *Enriched Environment*
- *Adequate Time*
- *Immediate Feedback*
- *Mastery*

The ITI model presents nine ways to translate brain research into action in the classroom and school. Each of the nine is described here. They are discussed in the order of their power to translate this area of brain research—the bodybrain partnership—into practical strategies in the classroom.

Absence of Threat/Nurturing Reflective Thinking

Given the primacy of emotions to drive attention and thus memory, problem-solving, and virtually every other aspect of learning and performance, the number one job of a teacher is creating and maintaining an environment free from threat. Once this is in place, that environment must also actively nurture reflective thinking. These two qualities form the heart and soul of bodybrain-compatibility and are at the very heart of the ITI model. They are also the beginning point of implementation and the ongoing touchstone of ITI. Once created, they cannot be ignored but must receive consistent, on-going, **daily** attention from teacher and students.

Creating Absence of Threat

When creating absence of threat, it is important to consider two truisms:

- Like beauty, what constitutes threat—even perceived threat—is in the eye of the beholder. What is threatening to one person may not be considered threatening to another. However, that does not minimize the sense of perceived threat held by that person. Its affect on the functions of the bodybrain partnership are profound.
- Absence of threat does not mean absence of consequences. Misbehavior and failure to complete work have consequences in the real world and so should they in the classroom. What matters is fairness, consequences appropriate to the nature of the infraction, and emotional consistency of those who apply the consequences.

For some traditionalists, a little bit of threat is often considered a good thing,—"keeps 'um on their toes"and "shows them who's in charge." But, as Dr. John Ratey points out, the excess mental noise that goes on in the brain as a result of dealing with threat and stresses "can make it difficult to perceive what's going on, overloading other circuits of attention, memory, learning, cognition, emotional stability, or any other brain function." In effect, the system goes into information overload, which is precisely what can happen when highly anxious people take tests. "They will look at a test question and literally not see certain words, which causes them to misinterpret it and give the wrong answer. They may even miss seeing entire questions on the page. Their brains are so busy dealing with the noise that the visual channels in the brain aren't open to perceive accurately. *Our brains are not infinite.* They run out of space, run out of gas, as it were. If the brain is busy trying to filter uncomfortable and frustrating noise, worries, or other concerns, there is less 'brain stuff' available for perceiving.[38] There are many aspects of our traditional curriculum and instructional strategies that are threatening to students and cause excess mental noise.

Curriculum and Threat. Curricular aspects that have a strong bodybrain-antagonistic effect include:

- Boring when too hard or too easy
- Difficult to understand if no perceivable relevance to their life; humiliating when they can't get it; source of acting out
- Frustrating because content is not understandable—the material is not age appropriate and/or is composed of factoids

> **Absence of Threat**
>
> *Absence of threat does not mean absence of challenge or lack of consequences for misbehavior or bad choices. It does mean lack of real and perceived threat to physical and emotional safety.*

USING *ABSENCE OF THREAT* TO ENHANCE THE BODYBRAIN PARTNERSHIP

Instructional Strategies

- Use the Lifelong Guidelines and LIFESKILLS full-time (see Chapters 7, 9, 10). Ask guest experts to share which Guidelines/LIFESKILLS are used in the workplace.
- Ensure full membership in a community—the class family—plus being in relationship with the teacher.
- Use daily agendas and written procedures (see Chapters 7 and 8).
- Provide active, purposeful body movement in the classroom every hour to re-focus (release energy or re-energize as needed) the brain and body using activities that are an extension of what is being studied.
- Eliminate all pull-out programs except for short-term, urgent interventions.

Instructional Strategies and Threat. Instructional strategies that have a strong bodybrain-antagonistic effect include:

- Low standards for cleanliness, maintenance, and decor (lower than for most other public and private settings)
- Lack of community building
- Lack of personal relationship between teacher and students
- Poor leadership—students uncertain about what's happening and why or what will happen next
- Restricting body movement in the classroom, limited to recess, lunch, and P.E.

USING *ABSENCE OF THREAT* TO ENHANCE THE BODYBRAIN PARTNERSHIP

Curriculum Development

- Teach students about the power of emotion to enhance or impede learning and performance; present this through both formal introductory lesson and through ongoing pre- and post-lesson processing
- Teach students the personal and social skills they need to succeed with their peers and teachers.
- Eliminate fear of failure by ensuring that content is age appropriate, and thus understandable, and that inquiries are doable given current skill levels and the option to choose inquiries based on intelligence(s) of strength.
- Base curriculum in *being there* locations that are kid-grabbers, ones that require that they do something and actively participate in. Study trips that are "look and listen" experiences don't readily engage the emotions.
- State curriculum as concepts; include how the concept is/can be used in the students' world.
- Allow students to make choices—among inquiries (how they learn required curriculum), about social/political action projects, yearlong projects, and other study tasks as appropriate.

- Adherence to rigid time lines, inadequate time to complete tasks
- Threat of bad grades (potential negative consequences from teacher, parent, and fellow students)

An environment with absence of threat is fundamental to learning and a prerequisite for reflective thinking.

Nurturing Reflective Thinking

The ability—and the inclination—to think reflectively is an invaluable habit of mind. It lowers stress, improves learning and decision making, and enhances performance. In learning situations, reflective thinking allows students to move from "So what?" to "How can I use this now and in the future?" Without such automatic questioning, learning will be on the surface in the short run and will probably fail to trigger the brain's decision to store learning in long-term memory.

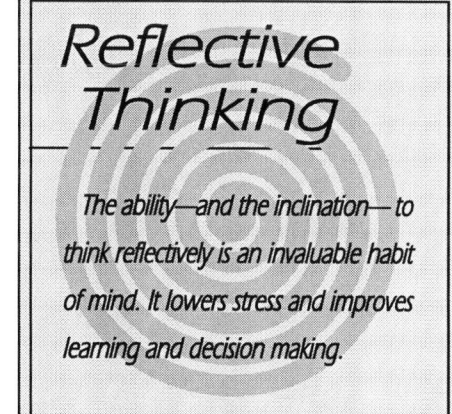

> **Reflective Thinking**
>
> *The ability—and the inclination—to think reflectively is an invaluable habit of mind. It lowers stress and improves learning and decision making.*

While reflective thinking may seem a vague or elusive term[39], each of us can recall times when we were so immersed in something that we lost track of time and external distractions stayed at bay. Mihaly Csikszentmihalyi (pronounced CHICK-sent-me-high-ee) provides a wonderful description of the state of mind that is home to reflective thinking, a state he calls "flow experience."[40] This state of mind is attained in exceptional moments when we find ourself totally and completely immersed in a place where our heart, mind, and will are simultaneously interacting and to the point that outside distractions are not able to penetrate. This metaphor of "flow" is one that we have experienced and can reflect upon as some of the best times of our lives. It is also a state of mind ideal for learning because engagement is extremely high and learning seems effortless.

Reflective Thinking As an Act of Discipline. Reflective thinking doesn't just happen automatically. It is an act of either conscious discipline or habit of mind. We must first slow down,[41] clear away distractions, focus our thoughts on what we're learning and doing and why, and use self-talk to guide our thinking when puzzled or stuck.

Second, to be reflective is a choice, a decision that can be made only by the learner. No teacher can hammer thoughtfulness into a student; it must come from within. The Greek/Latin base for the word educate means "to draw forth." As part of drawing forth, we need to set up conditions that nurture reflective thinking. Most importantly, we must model it and then provide ample opportunities for students to develop and practice it.

Impact of the Physical Environment. Humans beings are, as alertness to ensure survival demands, extremely sensitive to their environment. Children are even more so than adults. The ongoing impact of the physical environment of the classroom is extremely powerful. If you doubt this, think of your favorite environment, the one that relaxes you yet you remain alert and aware, fully enjoying your time there. Be that Yosemite Falls or your favorite five-star hotel, you know what an impact it has on your emotions and mental processing. In contrast, think of the environment that has the opposite effect on you—perhaps the teachers' lounge at your school with its machines and their fumes, messy coffee station, and old, uncomfortable furniture. Or, maybe it's the drab, dirty, crowded vehicle licensing office with its long lines and no place to sit while you wait; and, when your turn comes up you feel pressed to complete your tasks and so you hurry through, only half engaged in the tasks at hand. Or, maybe it's parts of your own aging school . . . the cafeteria/gym with stained ceiling tiles, unremitting, high-decibel

USING *REFLECTIVE THINKING* TO ENHANCE THE BODYBRAIN PARTNERSHIP

Curriculum Development

- Teach students how to redirect themselves when things get in the way of their learning, for example, when any of the four psychological needs identified by William Glasser are not in place (belonging, fun, power, and freedom).[42]
- Teach students simple techniques, such as Freeze Frame, [43] for bringing themselves to a reflective state of mind.
- Teach students how to direct their own learning—a foundational building block for becoming lifelong learners—by allowing them to exercise self-direction when appropriate. For example, choice of inquiries and helping develop inquiries, selecting their role to play in social/political action projects, and conducting a yearlong research project on a topic of their own choosing.

noises (no sound dampener). Wherever this is, it's a place you dread going to and a cloud of gloom settles over you every time you even think about having to go there.

If any of this rings a bell with you, you already know that one's physical environment strongly affects one's ability to slip into a reflective state of mind and stay there. So it should come as no surprise that your first steps—even before school begins—is to address the physical environment of your classroom. At a minimum, it should be:

- Healthful—clean, well lighted, pleasant smelling, and free from harmful chemicals and allergens
- Aesthetically pleasing—calming colors and music, living plants, well organized, and comfortable furniture
- Uncluttered yet reflects what is being learned

An environment that meets these benchmarks eliminates competing sensory input to the learning at hand from within and from out-

USING *REFLECTIVE THINKING* TO ENHANCE THE BODYBRAIN PARTNERSHIP

Instructional Strategies

- Ensure that the physical environment is healthful, aesthetically pleasing, and uncluttered (see Chapter 7).
- Offer rich input from *being there,* immersion, and hands-on-of-real-things so students can construct meaning rather than have to rely on attempts to memorize as a coping strategy.
- Provide adequate time for group and independent exploration.
- Be readily available to refocus, reenergize, and redirect students; during student work time, keep circulating through the classroom taking advantage of the teachable moment and building a personal relationship with each student.
- Balance time for collaborative learning with personal time for applying skills and knowledge to individual interests, exploring related ideas, and reflect on what one is learning and how it could be used now and in the future (vocations and hobbies).
- Institute a mastery-based instruction with a pass/not-yet passed accountability system coupled with in-class and cross-age tutoring as needed until each student achieves mastery of the concepts of the curriculum.

side of the body thus making it easier for students to focus on what they're learning and to reflect on how and when and why they can use the concepts and skills they are studying. Without this reflective time, school is a blur and seems largely unrelated to their life. This is especially true in departmentalized settings.

Movement

With a nod to classical education, primarily the Greek tradition of training body and mind in a mutually supportive partnership, American education has long required physical education. Unfortunately, in practice P.E. is primarily training in sports, particularly competitive team sports such as football, baseball, basketball, with purported mental and character carry over bonuses.

Given what we know today, competitive sports should be extracurricular and P.E. should be renamed "movement to enhance learning" and become the province of the classroom teacher. In other words, we should teach students how to enhance their ability to learn through movement of their body.

Why? Memory of knowledge and skills also records the emotional state of the learner at the time the learning took place. If the emotion was negative and unpleasant, we prefer to suppress the content as well as the emotion. Statements such as, "I hate reading" or "I hate math" are really someone's way of saying, "Every time I think of reading or math, I feel bad. I remember the frustration and humiliation, feeling stupid and feeling like an outcast."

How many of us know people who know how to read but choose not to? They choose not to because there are so many negative memories. This suggests that teachers battle not only for the minds of their students (getting knowledge and skills into long-term memory) but also for their hearts (wanting to use what they have learned and doing so of their own volition).

Why do we bring this up under a discussion about the importance of movement and emotion? Because movement is the quickest and most reliable way to add fun to the moment. Movement resets our emotional state. It provides opportunities for wiggly students to let off steam, tired students to get reenergized. When movement is planned as an extension or application of the concepts or skills being learned, additional parts of the brain wake up and content gets encoded in additional areas of the brain.

For the teacher searching for the key to his/her students' minds and hearts, eureka! You have found it.

USING *MOVEMENT* TO ENHANCE THE BODYBRAIN PARTNERSHIP

Curriculum Development

- Use movement as an extension or application of content rather than as a separate activity.
- Invite students to help you plan movement sequences that will help the class master concepts and skills.
- Teach students the skills for reading and using body language effectively. For example, miming, role playing, acting, public speaking, and dancing.
- The curriculum addresses movement both as a content itself (e.g., teaching students of the importance of movement in learning and positive emotional states) and as a means of enhancing academic learning (e.g., using the body to explore through the 19 senses and using the body to role play, react, and so forth).

Remember, movement in this context means using the bodybrain partnership fully and joyously to learn the concepts and skills of the curriculum—science, social studies, art, language arts, science, and technology. Movement for sports, the traditional view of P.E., is not included in this discussion.

USING *MOVEMENT* TO ENHANCE THE BODYBRAIN PARTNERSHIP

Instructional Strategies

- Use movement every hour. Whenever possible, make it an extension of the concepts or skills being studied. However, movement to reset emotions and prepare the bodybrain for a change of pace is also worthwhile.
- Add music and singing to your movement sequences. Melody, rhythm, rhyme, and words add fun and increase retention.
- Include these movement sequences during celebrations of learning,[44] parent nights, and cross-age tutoring.
- List the movement activities you currently use. Identify which contribute to learning curriculum content and which are "sponge activities," worthwhile ways to use up small amounts of time while waiting for the next event or scheduled activities to begin. Add to your list as needed.

Collaboration

Almost all learning occurs in a social context. From birth we are genetically wired to connect with others[45] and to learn through imitating others—be it learning to speak, the rules and strategies of a playground game of Red Rover or organized sports, or etiquette at a community BBQ. We are social animals; collaborating isn't something we do, it is who we are and the context in which we live. Over the millennium, collaboration has often meant the difference between life and death. The John Wayne mythology of the Old West—of individualism writ large— runs counter to what really goes on in rural living, then and now. Collaboration, with few exceptions, has always increased the likelihood of success. However, like most social skills, collaborating—with family, friends, and in the workplace—must be learned, through modeling and practice. Done poorly, it is a lifelong source of emotional upset. Done well, it is the key to satisfaction and success throughout one's life.

Building Collaboration

The three stages[46] of building a Learning Club in the ITI model are:

- *Developing a sense of inclusion/belonging*
- *Creating common ground*
- *Taking action*

The jury has weighed in on this instructional strategy. Its power to improve the learning environment and increase academic learning is indisputable.[47] In short, learning how and when to collaborate is essential to our emotional health, our capacity to learn, and our performance levels throughout life. In the classroom, skills and knowledge that help students keep their emotional state geared to learning are precursors to the rest of the curriculum.

USING *COLLABORATION* TO ENHANCE THE BODYBRAIN PARTNERSHIP

Curriculum Development

- Have students analyze historical events and literature for where collaboration, or lack of, was key in changing the course of national/world events and human lives.
- Make sure that the curriculum content of collaborative work is specifically designed for collaboration, not just putting students together to answer questions at the back of the chapter. An appropriate task for collaborative work is one that the brightest student can't do alone; every member of the group is needed to be successful. Otherwise, collaborative work negatively reinforces low social status for middle and lower achieving students and the brightest students end up doing all the work.[48]
- Have students review the content of the Lifelong Guidelines/LIFESKILLS they will most need to be successful at their task and make decisions about how they will apply it to their work.
- At every being there location, have students focus on the most important Lifelong Guidelines/LIFESKILLS needed to be an informed participant at that location and those needed to be an employee there.
- Whenever feasible, require content-related movement during collaborative work.

USING *COLLABORATION* TO ENHANCE THE BODYBRAIN PARTNERSHIP

Instructional Strategies

- Keep in mind that collaboration has but two critical goals: increasing achievement and equalizing social status in the classroom (raising status of all to that of equal peer among peers).[49]
- Insist that students consistently use the Lifelong Guidelines/LIFESKILLS; no exceptions. As the adult in charge, you must ensure that the classroom environment is free from threat at all times.
- To equalize social status in groups, rotate the role of group leader frequently and equally. If you think that a lower achieving student will have difficulty with the content of a task which will then impede his/her leadership role, work with the student in advance so that he/she can carry out the leadership role successfully and thus grow in social status.[50]
- Reflective thinking: After they are finished with each collaborative task, have students analyze how well they utilized the Lifelong Guidelines/LIFESKILLS, how they felt about the process of working together, how they could have improved both process and product, and, very importantly, what they learned about their personal and social skills for working together. How will they put that knowledge into action during the next collaborative work session.
- Convene class meetings at least once a day.
- Read student-written acknowledgments from the Acknowledgments Box at least once a day.

The instructional strategies to implement collaboration, usually referred to as cooperative learning, are well known and proven. Three excellent resources are *Designing Groupwork: Strategies for the Heterogeneous Classroom* by Elizabeth Cohen for research and practical curriculum and instructional strategies, *Cooperative Learning, All Grades* by Spencer Kagan, and *TRIBES: A New Way of Thinking and Being Together* by Jeanne Gibbs. In addition to these, the ITI model recommends numerous curriculum development and instructional strategies to ensure that students' collaborative work is consistent with what we now know about emotions as gatekeeper to learning and performance.

Meaningful Content

"You can lead a horse to water but you can't make him drink" is an old rural proverb that is equally true in the city and especially true in the classroom. Horses drink water only when they're thirsty. Students drink in what they find meaningful to them. Meaningfulness starts with an emotional reaction and continues with the "aha" experience that makes the eyes dance.

Renata and Geoffrey Caine describe the role of emotion and passion in learning in their description of what they call "natural thinking knowledge, " a combination of "felt meaning" and "deep meaning." "Felt meaning," is that "aha" response that occurs when something we've been trying to learn suddenly clicks into place and we "get it." It begins as "an unarticulated general sense of relationship and culminates in the 'aha' experience that accompanies insight."[51] According to the Caines, "such insight is much more important in education than is memorization."[52]

The second concept is "deep meaning," defined by the Caines as ". . . whatever drives us and governs our sense of purpose."[53] It includes all the instincts embedded in our reptilian brains, our needs for social relationships and an emotionally rich life, and our intellectual and spiritual needs.[54] These drives are sources of individual meaning, what people live for, and they are meaningful and drive our inner engines whether they are articulated or not and even whether or not we are conscious of them.[53] The important thing for us here is that ". . . people access passion when deep meanings are engaged." Deep meanings, therefore, ". . . provide a sense of direction because they govern what people look for and what they are willing to do, whether in sports, computing, music, finance, or writing poetry, or teaching. And, in part, deep meanings are a source of the energy that people are capable of bringing to bear on a task or activity."[56]

According to the Caines, when information, felt meaning and deep meaning come together, the result is "natural knowledge," knowledge so much a part of us that we refer to it as "second nature."[57] For example, "I love cars. I can't walk through a parking lot without diagnosing motors from the sounds they make. Fixing problems is second nature to me." With natural knowledge, "the learner has acquired a felt meaning for the subject or concept or procedure so that new information and procedures fit together. In addition, there is a sufficient connection with the learner's interests or deep meanings so that the information and procedures are personally relevant."[58]

Clearly, "natural knowledge" is arrived at by young children—outside of school and without the benefit of worksheets. What draws them on is the emotion of belonging to various "clubs"[59] (family, neighborhood play group, scouts club, school Learning Club, etc.) and through the exuberance of their natural search for meaning to their "why" questions begun as two year-olds.[60] Emotion and meaningfulness go hand in hand. You can't have a decision of meaningfulness without an emotional hook—something that grabs attention and elicits a strong desire to know more.

USING *MEANINGFUL CONTENT* TO ENHANCE THE BODYBRAIN PARTNERSHIP

Curriculum Development

- When selecting *being there* locations, look for ones that:
  - Are innately appealing to your students and will generate high levels of emotion
  - Students will consider useful to know about (from their perspective, of course)
  - Offer a high level of interaction and participation ("doing" raises emotional responses).
- Restate your curriculum as concepts rather than as lists of factoids (dates, definitions, etc.). Because concepts are generalizable to other situations, you will be more likely to intersect with students' existing areas of felt meaning and deep meaning.
- Develop inquiries allowing children to follow their natural curiosity—their whys and wherefores—when applying the skill and knowledge you want them to master.
- Allow students to participate in curriculum development so they can build in ways of using knowledge and skills that most interest them; invite them to write inquiries and then you select those you think are the best use of students' time.

USING *MEANINGFUL CONTENT* TO ENHANCE THE BODYBRAIN PARTNERSHIP

Instructional Strategies

- Build in "doing"—a natural blend of body and brain working in partnership which always produces more neurotransmitters that excite learning than sitting at one's desk.
- Utilize the power of membership in the Learning Club and classroom to expand and deepen what students find meaningful.
- Bring resource people to the classroom that students can respect and admire—the experts, the everyday heroes.
- Be passionate about what you teach! Show your love of learning, model the excitement and joy of being a lifelong learner.

Choices

As every parent quickly learns, offering a two-year old a choice of A or B—do what I've asked or go to time out—significantly defuses a potential power struggle and improves the child's attitude toward the task chosen. The same is true in the classroom. Giving students a choice of inquiry A or inquiry B—often makes the difference between sloppy work performed with indifference or a project given one's personal best. Yet despite our experience and common sense, in schools we too often succumb to the law of bureaucracies: mind-numbing insistence on assembly-line sameness. We must leave behind the foolish insistence that the same input (textbook and lectures) will produce the same learning outcomes, that same equals equity and fairness, that misbehavior of a few should result in all receiving the same punishment regardless of circumstances. In our opinion, public education's worst, and most deadly, enemy is bureaucracy.

Offering choices is a frontal assault against the bureaucratic mentality of sameness and control and a huge emotional boost for the bodybrain partnership. Offering students choice strengthens their commitment to learn because:

- Having choices allows students to design their own path between too hard (leading to failure) and too easy (leading to boredom). It also allows them to alternate between intelligences of strength and those they are working on.
- The higher the level of interest, the higher the level of motivation and commitment to learn, and thus the higher the level of neurotransmitters generated to assist the learning process.
- The power to choose gives students a measure of power and control over their own learning, perquisites for emotional stability[61] and becoming a lifelong learner.
- Having choices increases the likelihood of students' success in learning skills and knowledge and wiring them into long-term memory.

In many ways, having choice makes learning easier. As Frank Smith points out, thinking is made easy and effective when two fundamental requirements are met: 1) we understand what we are thinking about; and 2) the brain itself is in charge, in control of its own affairs, going about its own business.[62] "Thinking," he points out, "becomes difficult and inefficient when the brain loses

USING *CHOICES* TO ENHANCE THE BODYBRAIN PARTNERSHIP

Curriculum Development

- Develop inquiries which offer real choice rather than more of the same; this is particularly important for the practice and mastery of skills (reading, writing, speaking, and mathematics). Do so by building on the multiple intelligences and using real-life situations. Also make sure there are inquiries for Learning Club work and for individual exploration as well as for whole class assignment.
- Develop a sufficient number of inquiries to allow for real choice. For example, being assigned one's choice of three out of 12 rather than three out of four is real choice. However, it takes time to up students' capacity to handle choice. Start small and build upward as quickly as you can.
- Invite students, from third grade and up, to develop their own inquiries from which you as teacher select the best. Learning to pose our own questions is more important to lifelong learning than being able to answer someone else's questions. Encourage students to apply the concepts and knowledge of your curriculum to areas of their personal interest.

control, when what we try to think about is contrived . . . it throws the brain out of gear. Something that in less forced circumstances might be thought about with ease becomes an obstacle, a blurred focus of contrary purposes, aggravated often by frustration and irritation." "The most difficult kind of thinking is that which is imposed on us by someone else. . ."[63]

USING *CHOICES* TO ENHANCE THE BODYBRAIN PARTNERSHIP

Instructional Strategies

- Begin offering choices on a small scale. Start with a choice of two and set a time limit for the decision, after which you will make the choice for them.
- Shift your role from "sage on the stage" to "guide on the side" as quickly as you can. Nothing interrupts the deep state of reflective thinking called "flow" more completely than someone cutting across your thoughts; nothing kills exploration faster than someone giving the answer or obvious clues. In the ITI model, more teacher time and energy is spent developing, organizing, and orchestrating learning than "teaching" through direct instruction, controlling students and events, and adhering to a rigid schedule.
- Provide choice through activities, all of which you deem equally effective to help students learn the agreed upon curriculum for your school. Do so whenever possible. Be open to thoughtful proposals from students; always ask them how their proposal will ensure that they learn concepts X and skill Y (those in the key points) that is part of your curriculum. Help them monitor their progress. Learning to "know when you know" and "know when you don't know" is essential to becoming a successful lifelong learner.

Enriched Environment

Given the choice of spending a day in a five-star hotel or in an old, ramshackle, filthy, chaotic, house on the corner of the busiest street in the city, which would you choose? Or, a day at Disney World/Epcot or at the nearby strip mall? In which environments would you smile the most, in which would time seem to pass quickly and without your notice? Clearly, the environments that were planned for you with your best interests in mind. Not only that, but the creators of such environments used the very best scientific research available at the time about the impact of color, interior design.

USING *ENRICHED ENVIRONMENT* TO ENHANCE THE BODYBRAIN PARTNERSHIP

Curriculum Development

- Plan for role models/experts.
- Create an immersion wall(s) that best simulates the real thing.
- Add hands-on-of-the-real-thing items, models, posters, videos, computer software, books, and so forth that directly support your key points and inquiries.
- Provide an area of the room for movement that will enhance learning the key points and wiring those skills and knowledge into long-term memory.

USING *ENRICHED ENVIRONMENT* TO ENHANCE THE BODYBRAIN PARTNERSHIP

Instructional Strategies

- Revisit the *being there* location, each time digging for greater understanding of how the conceptual and significant knowledge key points of your curriculum are used in real life.

- Request that your guest speakers/experts bring as many hands on and immersion items as possible. Work with them in advance to create scenarios for role playing, problem solving, and groupwork assignments. Emphasize *how to use* the knowledge and skills in as realistic a setting as possible.

Adequate Time

Lack of time is our society's number one cause of anxiety and stress. It starts early when infants must awake according to the family schedule instead of their own internal time clock. In school, our rigid schedules ensure that most children will fail to finish the initial task or, if speedy, run out of time on the second task. Or, and equally nightmarish for children, is too much time with nothing engaging to do and thus boredom sets in. The "baby bear" experience of time being "just right" is exceedingly rare. Few children learn good time-management skills because time is not under their control nor are most of the elements important to the task.

The more important completion of a task is to us, the greater the stress, anxiety, and frustration—all elements that add up to perceived threat. Consequently, many students unconsciously withdraw their commitment to completion with high standards as a way of protecting themselves against high levels of emotional upheaval. In effect, our rigid schedules train students to not care, to be surface thinkers and mediocre performers. In most secondary systems, the departmentalized learning environments of junior and senior high fit such trained behavior perfectly and continue to further shape attitudes and behaviors that run counter to becoming effective lifelong learners.

USING *ADEQUATE TIME* TO ENHANCE THE BODYBRAIN PARTNERSHIP

Curriculum Development

- When writing inquiries, keep in mind the time frames in which you will have students use them, e.g., all morning or all afternoon, for an hour before the schoolwide assembly, the 30 minutes before the bus arrives for your *being there* experience, and so forth. If the inquiry requires more time than the schedule permits, even after using maximum flexibility, think through natural breaking points in advance.

- Teach students useful ways to organize their work and related materials. Help them find a balance between efficiently organized for tasks and their personality preferences, e.g., judging versus perceiving.[64] An optimum balance here will do much to reduce threat and enhance reflective thinking now and for the rest of their lives.

- Embrace "less is more." Make it your number one goal for the year. Teach conceptually rather than "covering" all the chapters of a textbook.

USING *ADEQUATE TIME* TO ENHANCE THE BODYBRAIN PARTNERSHIP

Instructional Strategies

- Develop, with student input, written procedures for what to do when they finish their assignment early. Include "looking back" questions—questions that help them evaluate whether the information has reached their long-term memory, introspections about how they might use such information in the future, and other questions that help students realize that their learning is for them, not for the teacher or the grade point or other external audiences or purposes.
- Create an agenda every day and use it throughout the day to organize your time and your students'.
- Teach students time management skills through modeling, mini-lessons during teachable moments, and through reflective thinking questions before, during, and after collaborative work and individual assignments, especially those lasting over multiple days. Give students genuine control over relevant elements of their work so that they can realistically practice effective time management.
- Model good time management practices and "talk out loud" as you think your way out of time crunch dilemmas and your stress reactions to them.

Immediate Feedback

Immediate feedback that tells us if we're on track or not is one of the greatest sources of motivation. Lingering on with a task that we suspect we're doing "all wrong" and therefore will have to do over again and, worse, makes us feel stupid in the process, is a recipe for giving up, not caring, not wanting to try again.

Another motivation killer is having to rely on external sources for our feedback, especially a control figure such as one's classroom teacher. The older students get, the more they, like we adults, begin to resent being dependent on someone else and powerless.

In just these two examples, it is clear that inadequate feedback produces highly charged negative emotions. It is critical that teachers master this late phase in the learning process; otherwise, all earlier efforts are in vain. In contrast, feedback that tells us we have succeeded at a learning task produces a burst of neurotransmitters, producing a "chemical high" that is readily observable in the spark in a child's eye as the "Aha" registers. As Frank Smith points out in *Insult to Intelligence: The Bureaucratic Invasion of Our Classrooms,* learning does not require coercion or irrelevant reward. Learning—driven by immediate feedback—is its own reward.

USING *IMMEDIATE FEEDBACK* TO ENHANCE THE BODYBRAIN PARTNERSHIP

Curriculum Development

- When developing an inquiry, make it clear and specific enough that students can judge for themselves whether they've completed it correctly, completely, and comprehensively. Use real world standards of performance whenever possible.
- Base the inquiries on real world settings and situations. The less abstract the assignment, the more likely students are to have a sense of what high standards are.

Instructional Strategies

- Select materials from the real world that have feedback built in naturally.
- Utilize peer review and feedback systems.
- Help students develop their own rubrics for judging their work.

Mastery

The emotional side of mastery is the foundation of positive self-concept, of seeing ourselves as a competent person, capable of handling whatever life puts in front of us. Such positive, learning-enhancing emotions are the life blood of the lifelong learner and, in the short run, they make the classroom sizzle with excitement and love of learning. The bodybrain partnership lives here—using what we understand, putting to use what we know and can do in ways **we** value.

Just as successful implementation of a mental program is its own reward, accompanied by feelings of accomplishment and increased satisfaction, having to abort a mental program that doesn't work is emotionally unsettling because it leaves us unsure of what to do next and decreases our sense of self confidence.[65] In other words, the brain has its own built in means of evaluating whether we've achieved mastery. The brain knows the difference between scoring 100% on a quiz versus being capable of performing something needed and valued in the real world.

USING *MASTERY* TO CREATE ABSENCE OF THREAT AND ENHANCE REFLECTIVE THINKING

Curriculum Development

- When developing an inquiry, make it clear and specific enough that students can judge for themselves whether they've completed it correctly, completely, and comprehensively. Use real world standards of performance whenever possible.
- Base the inquiries on real world settings and situations. The less abstract the assignment, the more likely students are to have a sense of what high standards are.
- Encourage students to write their own inquiries applying what they understand to problems and situations important to them. Make sure they state what actions would convince them they have mastered the knowledge or skill in the inquiry.

Instructional Strategies

- Select materials from the real world that have feedback built in naturally.
- Utilize peer review and feedback systems.
- Help students develop their own rubrics for judging their work. Whenever possible, reinforce their efforts to assess themselves in realistic ways.

Notes

1 Robert Sylwester has synthesized a good deal of research into a very useful and memorable phrase: "Emotion drives attention, attention drives learning/memory/problem-solving/just about everything else." Quoted in an unpublished paper entitled "The Role of the Arts in Brain Development and Maintenance." See also *A Celebration of Neurons: An Educator's Guide to the Human Brain* (Alexandria, VA: ASCD, 1995), especially Chapter 4.

2 Candace Pert, *Molecules of Emotion: Why You Feel the Way You Feel* (New York: Scribner, 1997).

3 Conversations with Carla Hannaford, Summer Institutes sponsored by Susan Kovalik & Associates, summer, 1999. See also *Smart Moves: Why Learning Is Not All in Your Head* (Alexander, North Carolina: Great Ocean, 1995).

4 John J. Ratey, A *User's Guide to the Brain: Perception, Attention, and the Four Theaters of the Brain* (New York: Pantheon Books, 2001).

5 Robert Sylwester, *How to Explain a Brain* (Thousand Oaks, CA: Corwin Press, 2005), 160-161, 18, 85-86, 82, 46, 69-70.

6 Synthesized from information found under the topic of "Emotions and the Brain" on the Web site titled, "The Brain from Top to Bottom," located at http://www.thebrain.mcgill.ca/flash/index_i.html. Material on the Web site was developed by Bruno Dubuc in conjunction with Douglas Hospital Research Center in Quebec and the Canadian Institutes of Health Research: Institute of Neurosciences, Mental Health and Addiction. Hosted by McGill University, all material on the Web site is free of copyright.

7 Elkhonon Goldberg, *The Wisdom Paradox: How your Mind Can Grow Stronger As Your Brain Grows Older.* (New York: Gotham Books, 2005), 229.

8 Patricia Wolfe, *Brain Matters: Translating Research into Classroom Practice*. (Alexandria, VA: ASCD, 2001), 76– 86.

9 Isabel Cohen and Marcelle Goldsmith, *Hands On: How to Use Brain Gym in the Classroom* (Ventura, CA: Edu Kinesthetics, 2002).

10 Doc Childre, *Freeze Frame* (Boulder Creek, CA: Planetary Publications, 1995).

11 Sylwester, *Celebration of Neurons*.

12 Pert, *Molecules of Emotion*, Chapters 1 and 7.

13 Sylwester, *Celebration of Neurons*.

14 Pert, *Molecules of Emotion*, 139.

15 Ibid.

16 Conversations with Dr. Candace Pert, Best of the Best Invitational sponsored by Susan Kovalik & Associates, Tukwila, Washington, May, 1998.

17 An amazing but still mysterious discovery is the presence of cells through the digestive track—from mouth to anus—that are identical to neurons in the brain. Dr. Candace Pert and other scientists wonder aloud if these cells may be the source of our "gut feelings."

18 Pert, *Molecules of Emotion*, 26-27.

19 Ratey, *User's Guide to the Brain*, 223.

20 Pert, *Molecules of Emotion*, 38.

21 Joseph LeDoux, "The Emotional Brain," presentation at Emotional Intelligence, Education, and the Brain: A Symposium, Chicago, IL, December 5, 1997. See also *The Emotional Brain: The Mysterious Underpinnings of Emotional Life* (New York: Simon and Schuster, 1996).

Given the typical time lag between findings within the brain research community and education, it will likely be some years into the 21st century before reference to the triune brain is abandoned and new ways of talking about, and implementing, the power of emotion in the bodybrain partnership are developed and put into widespread use.

22 Pert, *Molecules of Emotion*, 133.

23 Antonio Damasio, "Thinking about Emotion," presentation at "Emotional Intelligence, Education, and the Brain: A Symposium," Chicago, IL, December 5, 1997. See also *Descartes' Error: Emotion, Reason, and the Human Brain,* (New York: G. P. Putnam Sons, 1994).

24 Pert, *Molecules of Emotion*, 141-142. Somasensory refers to any bodily sensations or feelings, whether it is the touch of another's hand on our skin or sensations arising from the movement of our own organs as they carry on our bodily processes.

25 Ibid., 142.

26 There are many useful definitions of community that can be readily and powerfully applied to the classroom. In *Creating Community Anywhere*, Carolyn Shaffer and Kristin Anundsen define community as "a dynamic whole that emerges when a group of people participate in common practice, depend on one another, make decisions together, identify themselves as part of something larger, and commit over the long term to their own, one another's and the group's well-being." (See *Creating Community Anywhere* (New York: Putnam's Son, 1993), 10.)

27 Carla Hannaford, presentation at Summer Institute sponsored by Susan Kovalik & Associates, 2000.

28 Ratey, *User's Guide to the Brain*, 156.

29 Ibid.

30 Ibid., 150, 148.

31 Ibid., 148.

32 Ibid., 156.

33 Ibid., 159.

34 Ibid., 158.

35 Ibid.

36 William Calvin, "The Mind's Big Bang and Mirroring," unpublished manuscript, Seattle: University of Washington, 2000.

37 Alison Motluk, writing in *New Scientist Magazine,* January 27, 2001. For further reading, see "Mirror Neurons and Imitation Learning As the Driving Force Behind 'the Great Leap Forward' in Human Evolution" by V. S. Ramachandran at www.edge.org/documents/archives/edge69.html; Victorio Gallese and Alvin Goodman, "Mirror Neurons and the Simulation Theory of Mind-Reading" in *Trends in Cognitive Sciences, Vol. 2* (1998), 493; and Giacomo Rizzolatti and Michael Arbib, "Language Within Our Grasp" in *Trends in Neurosciences, Vol. 21* (1998), 188.

38 Ratey, *User's Guide to the Brain*, 61-62.

39 There are many terms for an established, on-going performance review process. "Metacognition" is used by Costa and Garmston in their peer coaching model. "Thinking about thinking" is used by Caine and Caine. Jeanne Gibbs uses the phrase "processing the process." Following through on brain research findings, we use the term "reflective thinking."

Warnings against the unexamined life are as old as Socrates: "The unexamined life is not worth living." Because there are so many personal and social skills that need to be honed for successful group work, we recommend that the you make reflective thinking a regular part of your classroom life—before, during, and after groupwork on a daily basis.

40 Mihaly Csikszentmihalyi provides a useful definition for assessing engagement for learning. He identifies several necessary ingredients: See *Flow: The Psychology of Optimal Experience* (New York: Harper Row, 1990), 74-75.

41 Part of "slowing down" is allowing the brain and heart to come into coherence. See Doc Childre and Howard Martin with Donna Beech, *The HeartMath Solution* (San Francisco: HarperSan Francisco, 2000). This fascinating book opens new windows on the relationship between brain and heart, a connection not considered important by neuroscience until very recently.

42 We are mistaken if we believe that discipline, dropouts, and drugs are what is wrong with today's schools; they are merely symptoms of a much larger underlying problem: far too many capable students make little or no effort to learn. In the landmark book *Control Theory in the Classroom* by William Glasser, MD (New York: Harper & Row Publishers, Inc., 1986), a new and powerful explanation of how we behave explains why this problem exists and how we can begin to solve it through learning teams.

43 See Doc Childre, *Freeze Frame: A Scientifically Proven Technique for Clear Decision Making and Improved Health* (Boulder Creek, CA: Planetary Publications, 1998). The well known HeartMath Freeze Frame technique shows how to manage thoughts and emotions in the moment by applying five simple steps, which enhances performance and creativity.

44 For a description of Celebrations of Learning, an important instructional strategy in the ITI model, see Chapter 15.

45 See YMCA of the USA, Dartmouth Medical School, and Institute for American Values, *Hardwired to Connect: A New Scientific Case for Authoritative Communities* (New York: Institute for American Values, 2003), and the work of Sigurd Zielke.

46 Our own experiences as social beings tells us that there are levels of knowing others, levels of trust we are willing to ascribe to another, degrees of intimacy we allow at different stages of getting to know someone. These levels are described in different ways by gurus of group building, sociologists, and psychologists. Tuckman, in 1965, described three stages as forming, storming,

and norming, the result of which is performing (see "Reconsidering Group Process in Challenge Education: Paradigmatic Shifts" by Don DeGraaf and Jeff Ashby).

Chapter 3: The Multiple Intelligences

As any parent with two or more children knows, children's brains are different—in how they process experiences and information, in their talents and challenges, in their likes and dislikes, and more. So, if even the same gene pool can and does produce enormous variations, imagine the range of differences in a classroom of 30 students. However hard some schools may seek homogeneity by sorting students according to age, IQ number, achievement levels, and so forth, teachers will always face a group of students whose brains are more different than alike. For handling such dizzying differences among learners, Howard Gardner's theory of multiple intelligences[1] is, in our opinion, one of the most powerful and practical areas of brain research to apply in the classroom. His first gift to us is an imminent common sense and intuitive definition of intelligence: ". . . a problem-solving and/or product-producing capability."[2]

Gardner's work not only sheds light on how and why students approach learning differently but also points toward very practical strategies for dealing with such differences in ways that can significantly improve the classroom learning environment and curriculum for all—for each student and also the teacher.

This chapter describes each of the multiple intelligences and discusses specific—and practical—ways to use them when developing curriculum and selecting instructional strategies.

Gardner's Theory of Multiple Intelligences

> **ITI Learning Principles**
>
> - *Intelligence as a function of experience*
> - *Inseparable bodybrain partnership—emotion as gatekeeper to learning and performance and movement to enhance learning*
> - ***Multiple intelligences***
> - *Learning as a two-step process*

Since the 1980s, our definition of intelligence has changed dramatically. We used to be told that intelligence was a singular, general characteristic set by genetics—people were either across-the-board smart or not so smart. Of course, all of this was determined by a paper-pencil test that distilled human capability down to a single number, an intelligence quotient or IQ number. And, clearly, to have an IQ of 120 was far more desirable than 100.

Nature Versus Nurture

The current, broad-based view of intelligence refutes the belief that intelligence, however defined, is immutably set by genetics, that what you were born with is what you will end up with. Although genes do play a significant role, experiences from conception to death also shape intelligence. As science and our own common sense and personal and professional experiences tell us, lots of practice solving real problems and creating products of value in the real world does increase capacity to do so. In the ITI model, we call this increase in capacity to make connections in order to solve ever more complex problems and create more resourceful and valuable products ***an increase in intelligence***.

> **Intelligence**
>
> *"Intelligence is a problem-solving and/or product-producing capability."*
>
> *Howard Gardner*

For example, co-author Karen Olsen, having decided at age five that what she would do with her life was become a teacher, hoped desperately to become a vocal music teacher. Her genetic gifts, however, did not include perfect pitch or even an ear that would allow her to play anything but a fixed-pitch instrument such as a piano. Yet, through her thousands of hours of practice, double and triple what students with innate musical talent spent, she did succeed in significantly increasing her musical intelligence—her problem-solving and product-producing capability in music. However, her product, holding her own in eight-part harmony, was accomplished through compensating measures—using the feel of the vibration in her throat (if it was "off," she knew she had either the wrong note or poor tone; in either case, stop for a bar and then pick up again). But she also knew she would never be able to rise to the level of excellence that those with inborn musical intelligence could achieve quite easily. Nor could she rise to a level of adequacy to train and direct musical groups. She therefore switched her teaching career to language arts, an area of innate gifts.

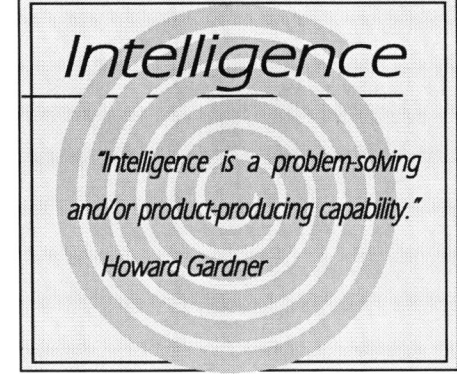

The decision to abandon music was deeply disappointing but an important lesson to Karen as a future educator. Even though she couldn't hit the pinnacle of music performance, there wasn't a moment of her musical experiences—singing with community and church groups and as a music minor in college—that she doesn't cherish to this day. Although painful, the lesson she learned is that the purpose of public education ought to be that of assisting students to develop all of Howard Gardner's intelligences. Our goal should be giving students options in life—options which make life rich and deeply satisfying both vocationally and avocationally.

Karen's story is not uncommon. Parents everywhere have watched their children struggle and triumph, embracing a vocation or hobby challenging to them or pursuing another area that they find easier to develop. In effect, each of us has our own experiences and observation of the nature-nurture debate and will readily recognize it in discussion in the first five chapters of this book. As the "nature-nurture" debate rages on,[3] becoming more hotly contested with each passing decade, most observers believe it's a roughly 50-50 proposition.

We believe that it is the responsibility of every teacher to develop curriculum and select instructional strategies that will enable every student to develop all his/her intelligences, to become Renaissance citizens, capable of rendering informed decisions in the voting booth, developing rich relationships within family and community, and nurturing a wide range of interests and skills by which to earn an adequate living and pursue a satisfying life richly lived.

The Theory of Multiple Intelligences

Gardner's definition of intelligence is an infinitely practical as well as theoretical way to look at human potential and behavior across cultures. As he developed his theory of multiple intelligence, he used several criteria:[4]

- Each intelligence had to be relatively independent of the others, with its own timetable for development, peak growth, and the like.
- Each had to operate from a different part of the brain.
- Each had to be valued in cultures around the world.

Multiple Intelligences Versus Modalities

To grasp the power of Gardner's theory of multiple intelligences, one must make a distinction between how students take in information (the visual, auditory, tactile, and kinesthetic modalities) versus how students process information inside their brains in order to first make meaning of the input and then use it to act upon the world. Remember that these intelligences are sets of problem-solving and product-producing skills/knowledge, not merely gateways through which information passes to reach the brain. Do not equate modalities with Gardner's intelligences.[5]

The Multiple Intelligences Defined

According to Gardner, intelligence "... entails a set of problem-solving skills, enabling the individual to resolve genuine problems or difficulties that he or she encounters and, when appropriate, to create an effective product; it also entails the potential for finding or creating problems, thereby laying the groundwork for the acquisition of new knowledge."[6]

And although each intelligence is a distinct entity meeting his research requirements, Gardner acknowledges that "... only the blend of intelligences in an individual makes possible the solving of problems and the creation of products of significance."[7] And, very importantly, an individual's intellectual gifts in one area cannot be inferred from his/her capacities in another.[8] For example, high mathematical ability doesn't necessarily mean the student will also be reading above grade level.

In his first book published in 1983, *Frames of Mind: The Theory of Multiple Intelligences,* Gardner identified seven intelligences. In the 1990s, he added an eighth intelligence, naturalist, and discusses a basis for two others—existential and spiritual.[9]

The following brief descriptions of the original seven intelligences, plus the naturalist intelligence, will provide curriculum designers and classroom teachers alike with beginning outlines for restructuring curriculum for the classroom. The task is a significant one because most of today's curriculum addresses only two of the multiple intelligences—logical-mathematical and linguistic—yet all seven are needed to succeed in life.

From core curriculum standards to homework assignments to extra credit work, we must ensure that our curriculum speaks to all learners, not just those high in linguistic and logical-mathematical intelligences.

Also, the multiple intelligences should be woven into our lesson planning and instructional strategies. During direct instruction we should make sure that we use all the intelligences, not just linguistic and logical-mathematical. And all other choices of strategies should selected with the goal of including all the intelligences.

The Multiple Intelligences

As you read this definition of the multiple intelligences, keep in mind real-life examples, such as the occupations of your extended family and friends, the intense interests and capabilities of students you've known over the years. After reading each one, jot down the name of at least three people you know well who typify that problem-solving and/or product-producing capability. You'll find you already know a great deal about these intelligences. Although considered "theoretical" in science, they seem more like common sense in real life.

Logical-mathematical

Linguistic

Spatial

Bodily-kinesthetic

Musical

Intrapersonal

Interpersonal

Naturalist

Logical-Mathematical Intelligence—primarily left hemisphere, front and back of both sides of the brain

This problem-solving and/or product-producing capability is the home of science and math. The core function of this intelligence is the interaction with the world of objects—ordering and reordering them, assessing their quantity, comprehending numerical symbols, appreciating the meaning of signs referring to numerical operations, and understanding the underlying quantities and operations themselves.[10]

Children high in logical-mathematical intelligence:

- Compute arithmetic problems quickly in their head
- Enjoy using computers
- Ask questions such as, "Where does the universe end?" "What happens after we die?" and "When did time begin?"
- Play chess, checkers, or other strategy games, and win
- Reason things out logically and clearly
- Revise experiments to test out things they don't understand
- Spend time working on logic puzzles such as Rubik's Cube[11]

This intelligence appears early and the most productive work is done by age forty if not by age thirty. The basis for all logical-mathematical forms of intelligence springs from the handling of objects; later these processes become internalized ("done in one's head"). One proceeds from objects to statements, from actions to the relations among actions, from the realm of the sensorimotor to the realm of pure abstraction—ultimately to the heights of logic and science.

The classical description of the development of this intelligence, the home of science and math, is that by Piaget. His work remains an accurate description of the development of logical-mathematical intelligence. However, his work does not describe development of the other intelligences.

Linguistic Intelligence—predominantly left hemisphere—temporal and frontal lobes

Linguistic competence is the most widely and most democratically shared across the human species. As Gardner says, "one could not hope to proceed with any efficacy in the world without considerable command of phonology, syntax, semantics, and pragmatics."[12]

The core operations of language, used with special clarity, include sensitivity to the following: the meaning of words; the order among words, such as using the rules of grammar, and on carefully selected occasions, choosing to violate them; the sound, rhythm, inflection, and meter of words; and the different functions of language— its potential to excite, convince, stimulate, convey information, or simply to please.

The major uses of linguistic intelligence:

- Rhetoric—the ability to use language to convince others of a course of action
- Mnemonics—a tool to help one remember information
- Explanation—the ability to use oral and written language to teach and learn
- Metalinguistic analysis— the use of language to reflect upon language, to explain its own activities[13]

Without question, high linguistic intelligence is over 80 percent of the formula for success in traditional schooling. Without it, schooling is painful and frustrating to students and the failure rate is obscenely high despite their competence in the other intelligences. Current brain research makes clear that there are many ways of knowing, of taking in information about the world. The most powerful of these is not through reading or lecture, but rather, through full sensory input from the real world.

Children strong in linguistic intelligence:

- Like to write
- Spin tall tales or tell jokes and stories
- Have a good memory for names, places, dates, or trivia
- Enjoy reading books in their spare time
- Appreciate nonsense rhymes and tongue twisters; typically spell words accurately and easily
- Enjoy crossword puzzles or games such as Scrabble or anagrams[14]

Spatial Intelligence–predominantly right hemisphere

The core operations of this intelligence depend on the ability to image. It also involves the capacity to perceive the visual world accurately, perform transformations and modifications upon one's initial perceptions, and recreate aspects of one's visual experience, even in the absence of relevant physical stimuli. This intelligence should be arrayed against and considered equal in importance to linguistic intelligence. Loosely put, *the mind's link to language is through pictures, not sound.* This intelligence is as critical as linguistic intelligence because the two are the principal sources of information storage and solving problems.[15]

Spatial intelligence is a collection of related skills. The images produced in the brain are helpful aids to thinking; some researchers have gone even further, considering visual and spatial imagery a primary source of thought.[16]

For many of the world's famous scientists, their most fundamental insights were derived from spatial models rather than from mathematical lines of reasoning. Einstein once commented: "The words of the language, as they are written and spoken, do not play any role in my mechanisms of thought. The psychical entities which seem to serve as elements in thought are certain signs and more or less clear images which can be voluntarily reproduced or combined. . . . The above mentioned elements are, in my case, of visual and some muscular type."[17] Examples of imaging as a primary source of thought are Darwin and the "tree of life," Freud and the unconscious as submerged like an iceberg, and John Dalton's view of the atom as a tiny solar system.

It is important to note that spatial intelligence should not be equated with the visual sensory modality. Even people who are blind from birth can develop spatial intelligence without direct access to the visual world.

A keenly developed spatial intelligence is not only an invaluable asset in our daily lives but is also essential for understanding the application of what is learned in school.[18] This is particularly true in areas where the elements are abstract and unseen (microscopic in size or invisible physical science areas such as the forces of gravity, electricity/magnets, etc.).

Children strong in spatial intelligence:

- Visualize while reading
- Spend free time engaged in art activities
- Report clear visual images when thinking about something
- Easily read maps, charts, and diagrams
- Draw accurate representations of people or things
- Like it when you show movies, slides, or photographs
- Enjoy doing jigsaw puzzles or mazes
- Daydream a lot[19]

Bodily-Kinesthetic Intelligence—tendency for left hemisphere dominance in right-handed people, right hemisphere dominance in left-handed people

Characteristic of this intelligence is the ability to use one's body in highly differentiated and skilled ways for expressive as well as goal-directed purposes, such as the mime, actor, athlete, and tradesman. This intelligence also brings the capacity to work deftly with objects, both those that involve the fine motor movements of one's bodily motions and the capacity to handle objects skillfully.[20]

Not only is the body an instrument for acting on knowledge, to a degree greater than previously understood, the body is also an active partner in learning (see Chapter 2).

Children strong in bodily-kinesthetic intelligence:

- Use body language to communicate thoughts and emotions
- Do well in sports and recreational hobbies requiring physical skill and effort
- Move, twitch, tap, or fidget while sitting in a chair
- Engage in physical activities such as swimming, biking, hiking, or skateboarding
- Need to touch people when they talk to them
- Enjoy scary amusement rides
- Demonstrate skill in a craft like woodworking, sewing, or carving
- Cleverly mimic other people's gestures, mannerisms, or behaviors[21]
- Easily remembers information when given movement cuing systems. For example, the algorithm for long division could be expressed as: first you divide (clap-clap), multiply (tap crossed hands twice), subtract (outward slicing movement of both hands twice), and then bring it down (two hands pulling imaginary pipe down as if chinning yourself). (See *I Can Divide And Conquer* video and companion book by Martha Kaufeldt, available through Books For Educators. See back of this book.)

Involving the rest of the body in any learning event increases the neural activity of the brain, activates the motor areas of the brain which assist in sequencing thought, increases the positive flow of epinephrine which aids transfer from short-term memory to long-term memory, and releases positive molecules of emotion.

Recent research, reported convincingly by both Elkhonon Goldberg and John Ratey, reveals that movement plays a critical role in learning and life and may not be as separate a function as first suggested by Howard Gardner. In *The Executive Brain: Frontal Lobes and the Civilized Mind,* Goldberg states that various features of cortical representations of objects and of word meanings denoting objects "are stored close to the sensory and motor areas that participated in acquiring information about these objects."[22] Furthermore, it is the motor part of the brain that sequences our thoughts. Ratey, in *A User's Guide to the Brain: Perception, Attention, and the Four Theaters of the Brain,* states that "movement is crucial to every other brain function, including memory, emotion, language, and learning . . . our 'higher' brain functions have evolved from movement and still depend on it." He goes on to say that "Motor function is as crucial to some forms of cognition as it is to physical movement. It is equally crucial to behavior, because behavior is the acting out of movements prescribed by cognition. If we can better understand movement, we can better understand thoughts, words, and deeds."[23]

Musical Intelligence—primarily right hemisphere

This intelligence is the most separate from the other intelligences and is the earliest to appear. For individuals high in this intelligence, composing and performing at age five, as Mozart did, is not unusual. It makes itself known as early as age three. Core functions include pitch, melody, rhythm, timber (tone), and pattern.

Students who are unusually high in musical intelligence and relatively low in linguistic intelligence will use their musical intelligence skills to "translate" language into rhythmic patterns. An example of this type of student is the one whose body begins to jive and tap the instant the teacher begins to speak, stopping the second the teacher stops talking, restarting with the next burst of speech—all in rhythm with the teacher's words. Content in rhyme can be readily absorbed by these students while the same information in an uninspiring lecture or in the stilted prose of a science textbook can be completely indigestible. Monotone speakers have particularly deadening effects on highly musical students.[24]

Musically gifted children:

- Play a musical instrument and/or sing
- Remember melodies of songs
- Tell you when a musical note is off-key
- Say they need to have music on in order to study
- Collect records or tapes
- Sing songs to themselves
- Keep time rhythmically to music; hum and drum[25]

Intrapersonal and Interpersonal Intelligences

Both intrapersonal and interpersonal intelligence are far more diverse and culturally dependent than the other intelligences.

Extreme circumstances such as times of war, subjugation, famine, disaster in general, recession/depression, life or death situations, and death itself greatly affect the expression of these intelligences. All of these circumstances make demands for action that most people don't practice. They are one-time or seldom experienced happenings. Yet the cultural beliefs and premises held by society demand that we respond to these events and express ourself in certain ways, depending upon locale, age, status in the community, etc. In short, these are problem-solving situations requiring problem-solving intelligences. Although not so dramatic, daily living demands the same kinds of problem-solving from us.

Intrapersonal Intelligence involves the examination and knowledge of one's own feelings, the "sense of self"—the balance struck by every individual and every culture between the prompting of inner feelings and the pressures of others.

The core capacity of intrapersonal intelligences is access to one's own "feeling life"—the range of our emotions; our capacity to instantly discriminate among these feelings and, eventually, to label them, to draw upon them as a means of understanding and guiding our behavior.[26]

At its advanced level, intrapersonal knowledge allows one to detect and to symbolize complex and highly differentiated sets of feelings, e.g., the novelist who can write introspectively about feelings, the patient or therapist who comes to attain a deep knowledge of his own inner world of feelings, the wise elder who draws upon his/her own wealth of inner experiences in order to advise members of the community.

Children strong in intrapersonal intelligence:

- Display a sense of independence or a strong will
- React with strong opinions when controversial topics are being discussed
- Seem to live in their own private, inner world
- Like to be alone to pursue some personal interest, hobby, or project
- Seem to have a deep sense of self-confidence
- March to the beat of a different drummer in their style of dress, their behavior, or their general attitude
- Motivate themselves to do well on independent study projects[27]

Interpersonal Intelligence involves looking outward toward the behavior, feelings, and motivations of others.

The core capacity of interpersonal intelligence is the ability to notice and make distinctions among other individuals and, in particular, among their moods, temperaments, motivations, and intentions.[28]

In an advanced form, interpersonal knowledge permits a skilled adult to read the intentions and desires of many other individuals—even when those have been hidden. This intelligence also permits us to act upon such knowledge, such as when influencing a group of disparate individuals to behave along desired lines; it's what we call leadership. We see highly developed forms of interpersonal intelligence in political and religious leaders (a Mahatma Gandhi or a John Fitzgerald Kennedy), in skilled parents and teachers, and in individuals enrolled in the helping professions, be they therapists, counselors, or concerned friends.

Interpersonally gifted children:

- Have a lot of friends
- Socialize a great deal at school or around the neighborhood
- Read people's intentions and motives
- Get involved in after-school group activities
- Serve as the "family mediator" when disputes arise
- Enjoy playing group games with other children
- Have a lot of empathy for others[29]

Naturalist Intelligence—allows people to distinguish among, classify, and use features of the environment.[30]

Howard Gardner suggests that this intelligence develops on its own in most children, " . . . particularly those who have a chance to spend time out of doors—in both rural and urban/suburban settings. The real trick is to maintain it, in the face of different pressures in school."[31] The naturalist pays attention to flora and fauna, noticing critical distinctions. Charles Darwin exemplifies the keen observation, curiosity, and awareness of patterns essential for strength in this intelligence. In a farming or hunting culture, persons strong in the naturalist intelligence are highly valued to ensure the group's continued success.

Placed in a culturally diverse environment, the naturalist picks up on characteristic patterns of speech, movement, dress, and the like with the result that he can both recognize group members and choose to conform and fit into the setting. People who move easily from mainstream to minority cultural environments are strong in naturalist intelligence.

Children who are talented naturalists:

- Ask many questions about their environment
- Delight in large collections of natural objects, e.g., insect collection
- Enjoy scouting or similar activity allowing them to pursue an interest at their own pace
- Stay intensely involved in an activity, not wanting to stop
- Are sensitive to patterns in the environment such as at the lake, in the woods, on the street, and in the classroom
- See structure and order where others see only noise or random elements[32]

A Message to Teachers

The multiple intelligences identify important ways for students to solve problems and produce products, each of which operates from a different part of the brain. If students are having difficulty learning a concept or skill, provide inquiries which call on the intelligence(s) of their strength. Later, when their understanding is solid and they're practicing how to use concepts or skills in order to wire them into long-term memory, teachers should provide inquiries which call on other intelligences. This wide input and processing not only helps cement long-term memory but strengthens students' problem-solving and product-producing capabilities in all areas of intelligence.

Do the activities within each category strike a familiar chord? They should. Each of us is born with all of these intelligences but we tend to develop those valued by our culture (home, school, church, community). It is the goal of the ITI classroom to make sure that all intelligences are developed and used on a daily basis.

Translating Brain Research into Action Using the Nine Bodybrain-Compatible Elements

The multiple intelligences are a major curriculum development tool in the ITI model. They are key when developing inquiries because they help the teacher build in choices and meaningfulness for students. (See Chapter 18.) They also serve as a check list for the teacher when creating an enriched environment.

Bodybrain-Compatible Elements

- *Choices*
- *Meaningful Content*
- *Enriched Environment*
- *Adequate Time*
- *Absence of Threat/Nurturing Reflective Thinking*
- *Collaboration*
- *Immediate Feedback*
- *Mastery*
- *Movement*

Choices

Choice based on variety just for the sake of variety is a one-way ticket to hard work for teachers and an investment with minimal return for students. Choice must be purposeful—specifically planned ways to provide input and/or apply concepts and skills that will enable each student to achieve at high levels.

USING *CHOICES* TO ENHANCE DEVELOPMENT OF THE MULTIPLE INTELLIGENCES

Curriculum Development

- Teach the theory of multiple intelligences to your students. Help them distinguish between the intelligences as ways of thinking to solve problems/produce products versus a subject content of the same name, such as music or language arts. For example, writing lyrics for a song is not necessarily using one's musical intelligence; it's likely just another linguistic activity. But figuring out how to use music composition skills as a study technique (to go from Ds to As in college) is a way of using musical intelligence to solve problems and produce products.[33] Also, doing arithmetic, carrying out the mechanics of a long division problem, is not the same as thinking mathematically to solve a problem in your environment. *The intelligences are a way of thinking, not a subject, not an entry way to the sensory system.*
- For every key point, develop at least 5-12 inquiries; ensure that there are two or more for each of the following intelligences: spatial, musical, bodily-kinesthetic, and mathematical intelligences. Then check that interpersonal and intrapersonal intelligence are addressed among the above five. Also check that inquiries address Bloom's taxonomy (see Chapter 17) and the way we take in information (see personality preferences, Chapter 6).
- Encourage students to write inquiries for themselves and for the class. Select those you think will provide the best application and practice of concepts and skills for students.

USING *CHOICES* TO ENHANCE DEVELOPMENT OF THE MULTIPLE INTELLIGENCES

Instructional Strategies

- Have students identify their strongest intelligences and those they would like to strengthen. Have them set goals and strategies for developing their intelligences on a weekly basis.
- Prepare resource people to talk about how they use the multiple intelligence most critical to their area of expertise. Prep them for such questions from students as: "When did you first know you had this capability?" "How did you build it when you were a student?" "What other occupations could you have chosen using this intelligence?"
  Explore these same issues with people at your *being there* locations.
- Teach students to observe how fellow Learning Club members use their intelligences. After every collaborative task, have students (individually and as a group) reflect on what they have learned from each other about using the intelligence(s) needed to successfully complete their work.
- Model respecting different ways of learning, solving problems, and producing products.
- When planning direct instruction and its immediate follow up, build in all of the first seven intelligences.
- Make the multiple intelligences a daily focus of your teaching. It is probably your most powerful means to empower students as learners now and throughout their lives.

Meaningful Content

Have you ever sat in a class and thought to yourself, "Why am I struggling so? This stuff can't be this hard. What's going on here?" If so, you were probably responding to a learning environment that didn't allow you to use your intelligence(s) of strength thus crippling your ability to learn. The moral of the story here is that much of meaningfulness is a function of how we go about learning rather than any innate quality of the concept or skill to be learned. For example, high interpersonal-intelligence people will happily absorb all kinds of concepts and skills if allowed to process them interpersonally. The same content approached intrapersonally may hold little interest and meaning to them. Likewise, study of the physics of sound waves may hold little interest to someone high in musical intelligence but low in logical/mathematical intelligence until he/she is allowed to apply the concepts to sound waves of various orchestral instruments from tuba to piccolo, bass viola to violin, piano to guitar.

Frank Smith, in *Insult to Intelligence: The Bureaucratic Invasion of Our Classrooms*, makes the point that when meaning is reached, "learning" occurs automatically and simultaneously.[34] The learner is always asking, What does this situation/information mean to me? How can I use it? How does it affect me now and in my future? "Making sense of the everyday world in relation to ourselves, our needs (physical, emotional, mental), and motivations (interests and need for fun in our lives) is our greatest concern and motivator."[35] According to Hart, "How much is learned by rote is a direct function of time and effort. But when the learning is meaningful we learn much faster and without effort."[36]

USING *MEANINGFUL CONTENT* TO ENHANCE DEVELOPMENT OF THE MULTIPLE INTELLIGENCES

Curriculum Development

- Help students discover and track their own intelligences.
- Know your students. Create curriculum that builds on their strengths while they are attempting to understand something new and learning how to apply it. During practice to cement such learning into long-term memory, encourage students to stretch using intelligences that aren't as well developed.
- The easiest way to respond to the fact that every brain is unique and therefore processes information, solves problems, and produces products differently is to ensure that your inquiries offer a range of mental engagement. For example, create inquiries that invite use of those intelligences that are most developed in students and also some that invite students to use their least developed intelligences. The goal is to create Renaissance minds, competent, flexible, powerful.

USING *MEANINGFUL CONTENT* TO ENHANCE DEVELOPMENT OF THE MULTIPLE INTELLIGENCES

Instructional Strategies

- Ask students what it would take to make the concept or skill to be learned meaningful to them. Know that each student's brain is different and that they will therefore process differently. Commit yourself to providing the kinds of input that they need to arrive at your levels of expectation.
- During direct instruction, provide input for all the intelligences; this increases students' understanding of the concept/skill and the perception of relevance.
- Provide opportunities for students to reflect on how well they're developing all of their intelligences.
- When students are reading literature, studying famous people, or attending a career day, have students analyze the intelligences most critical to that person and/or task.
- Until you have developed a mental program for engaging and supervising students in developing their multiple intelligences, create a class graph that allows you to track the intelligences required by the inquiries that students complete. Be ready to encourage students to stretch themselves.

Enriched Environment

The brain can't learn new things or make connections among previously learned concepts and skills without new input—a problem to be solved or a product to be made that forces us to "reshuffle the deck" of new sensory input. Thus, the elements we select to make learning come alive for students are crucial. In addition to taking into account the six kinds of input—with special emphasis on *being there* locations, *immersion*, and *hands on of the real thing*—we also need to take into account if and how that input will encourage and challenge the multiple intelligences. (For a discussion of levels of input, see Chapter 1.)

There are many examples of apparent fit that, once examined closely, don't accomplish the desired result. For example, a study trip to a grocery store would, on the surface, seem to address bodily-kinesthetic intelligence. But if the visit is a look-see-listen event, the body is walking and standing but not necessarily involved in solving problems or producing products. Similarly, a presentation by a visiting artist may challenge spatial intelligence or the visit may only be a linguistic experience on the topic of art.

Keep in mind that Gardner's theory of multiple intelligences is about how the brain solves problems and makes products. An enriched environment, therefore, must provide the substance for such thoughts and projects. Thus, the input must invite—even demand—action. An enriched environment is a purposeful environment that walks the tight rope between enough to activate the multiple intelligences and too much that results in clutter.

USING *ENRICHED ENVIRONMENT* TO ENHANCE DEVELOPMENT OF THE MULTIPLE INTELLIGENCES

Curriculum Development

- Check the power of every item you bring into your classroom to encourage solving a problem or producing products relating to your curriculum. Eye appeal is nice, interesting is nice, but the important questions are: "Does it invite problem solving? Will it play an integral role in producing a product?" If not, don't bring it into the classroom; your space is too limited. If yes, keep it and use it to build your curriculum, especially to design engaging inquiries.

Instructional Strategies

- Select *being there* locations that call upon and/or illustrate all the intelligences.
- Replicate/Simulate in your classroom the important elements of the *being there* location. If your replication/simulation is a mirror of the location, all the intelligences will be included automatically because real life is integrated and rich in its problems to be solved.
- Analyze hands-on-of-the-real-thing items; make sure their use (as a group) addresses all of the intelligences.
- Realize that what you find acceptable or endearing may have very opposite effects on some students due to their different strengths. Base your classroom decor and music on carefully researched principles of interior design and musicality, not on personal preferences.

Adequate Time

Solving problems and producing products are a far cry from rote memorizing; they require thinking and reflecting, searching for and understanding connections among prior and current learnings—all of which takes time.

Each of us can recall a time when we were deeply immersed in something and then were interrupted. Not only do we immediately feel irritated—a sense of loss—but when we can again return to the task, the enjoyment is gone. Worse, it takes some time before we are able to figure out where we were in our thinking process. Inadequate time causes tremendous stress and kills motivation for all of us.

For teachers, inadequate time is lethal. Many a worthwhile and widely-supported school improvement effort has died a premature death because of inadequate time to plan together, study together, prepare together, and implement together. In fact, without time, "together does not and cannot happen."

For students strong in logical-mathematical intelligence, inadequate time to complete a project or come to a logical breaking point is intolerable.

When learning—especially when learning the skills and attitudes for becoming a lifelong learner and developing intelligences that are not our strengths—it is important to remember that the race is not to the swift but to the thorough. Working with the multiple intelligences is not just a means to an end but a worthy goal in its own right because of the long-term benefits.

USING *ADEQUATE TIME* TO ENHANCE DEVELOPMENT OF THE MULTIPLE INTELLIGENCES

Curriculum Development

- Always remember, developing an intelligence is not about getting the right answer but about practicing new ways of thinking to solve problems and produce products and becoming more proficient in doing so. This takes time—lots of time and lots of practice. Always have more inquiries on hand than you think you'll need.
- Help students understand the importance of developing all of their intelligences so that they will challenge themselves to do so.
- Assign practice in applying concepts or skills to real-world situations through homework. Use class time the next day to process what students learned about their intelligences. What they learn about themselves as a learner is far more useful over a lifetime than memorizing any one concept.
- Encourage students who need more practice to use spare time during the school day and at home to complete inquiries. Invite them to develop their own inquiries to practice with.

USING *ADEQUATE TIME* TO ENHANCE DEVELOPMENT OF THE MULTIPLE INTELLIGENCES

Instructional Strategies

- Be flexible; reduce or eliminate "regular schedules" with their specified time blocks.
- Let students' interests and excitement lead them. Learning to learn, learning how to steer one's own learning takes time.
- Provide adequate wait time; let students mull and stew and benefit from self-talk or dialogue with Learning Club members before you accept an answer to your question. Make answering a question an adventure in reflective thinking rather than a competition to be first.
- If students are to work at developing all their intelligences, create an environment that encourages students to slow down so they can talk their way through their work, shifting from strengths to weaknesses and weaknesses to strengths, comfort level to extreme challenge and back again. Allow students to tell you if they need more time and then alter the schedule accordingly.
- Plan direct instruction that uses all intelligences. Alternate short periods of direct instruction (maximum of 11-16 minutes) with inquiries that invite the use of several different intelligences.

Absence of Threat/Nurturing Reflective Thinking

In Chapter 1 we made the case that absence of threat is a prerequisite for but not the same as reflective thinking. Reflective thinking assumes absence of threat but requires that we are allowed to think and solve problems and produce products thinking the way we think best, that is, using our dominant intelligences. It also requires, however, that we have multiple ways to tackle a problem so that we can have many avenues to pursue, not just one approach.

Absence of Threat. Stress in all its forms, including threat (real or perceived), almost always makes us retreat to more familiar territory, coping strategies, and habits of mind. For example, when under stress, we tend to revert to old eating habits and styles of interacting with others. In the classroom, this translates into reverting to our problem-solving/product-producing strengths. If linguistic intelligence is not our strength and we are confronted with a paper-pencil test situation we believe we will fail, we are likely to revert to our strong intelligence. If that is interpersonal, we are likely to begin talking with our neighbor; if bodily-kinesthetic, moving about. Neither strategy assists in successful test taking.

Traveling the multiple intelligences is a balancing act between using our dominant strengths when content and situations are challenging versus learning to stretch ourselves to build our problem-solving/product-producing strategies and approaches. The most effective learners and performers are those who can, and are willing to, dance between the two. Again, our goal in public education ought to be the creation of Renaissance people, the Leonard da Vincis and everyday geniuses of the 21st century.

Reflective Thinking. According to Einstein, "Imagination is more important than knowledge." His greatest insights came when he was in a dreamlike state, another kind of reflective thinking.

This is an important awareness. Nose to the grindstone, never taking time to look up or rethink what one is doing is a recipe for pain and inefficiency. Advances in thinking come from seeing with new eyes, an aha! preceded by a quiet moment of introspection and/or undirected, free-flowing thought.

The key here is to use your classroom leadership to create frequent times for students to work quietly on their own, developing their intrapersonal intelligence and helping them learn to use it to guide their problem solving and product producing efforts.

USING *ABSENCE OF THREAT AND NURTURING REFLECTIVE THINKING* TO ENHANCE DEVELOPMENT OF THE MULTIPLE INTELLIGENCES

Curriculum Development

- Teach students the theory of multiple intelligences. Have them assess their strengths and areas yet to be developed. Develop key points and inquiries just as you would for science or social studies.
- Make sure that the inquiries for each key point address all of the first seven intelligences. (For a discussion of each of the kinds of key points and inquiries, key curriculum structures in the ITI model, see Chapters 14 and 15.)
- When selecting inquiries for whole class use, select first those that use the greatest sensory input and manipulation of the information or skill, e.g., inquiries designed for bodily-kinesthetic and interpersonal intelligences and that are application-based. Select last those that are linguistic, especially those based on the knowledge and comprehension levels of Bloom's Taxonomy (see Chapter 17).
- Invite students to write inquiries that they consider a stretch for themselves, inquiries that require them to use an intelligence they want/need to develop.

USING *ABSENCE OF THREAT AND NURTURING REFLECTIVE THINKING* TO ENHANCE DEVELOPMENT OF THE MULTIPLE INTELLIGENCES

Instructional Strategies

- Create classroom procedures for instituting daily time periods for intrapersonal time. They are an important part of classroom leadership. For more information about procedures, see Chapter 8.
- Provide time for and model using intrapersonal time; orchestrate conditions that encourage reflective thinking.
- Invite students to reflect on their progress in developing one or two intelligences they don't normally use.
- Use reflective thinking questions after collaborative learning to ensure that students see the value of multiple intelligences, e.g., "Which intelligences did we use/could have used to complete this task?"
- During intrapersonal time, invite and encourage students to choose the inquiry they will work on or write their own.
- Involve students in writing inquiries they believe will best help them stay engaged and learn best.

Collaboration

When it comes to teaching students how to develop and use the first seven intelligences, collaboration is your most powerful tool. Why? Because a Learning Club composed of students with strengths in different intelligence provides ongoing modeling of how each intelligence operates and contributes to a more effective result. And since imitation is a core learning strategy of all children, daily modeling of an intelligence by someone they like and respect is very powerful indeed. Understanding how the different intelligences work is a first step toward appreciating intellectual differences rather than being intimidated by them or feeling superior about them.

Likewise, collaboration among staff produces better products when differences are acknowledged and consciously used to achieve a better result.

USING *COLLABORATION* TO ENHANCE DEVELOPMENT OF THE MULTIPLE INTELLIGENCES

Curriculum Development

- Make sure that the content of each inquiry assigned for collaborative work requires several intelligences, not just linguistic, so that no one student by him/herself can do it.[37] This ensures that each student must contribute and thus each intelligence is demonstrated to be important to successfully completing the task.
- Ensure a balance of inquiries using interpersonal (collaborative work) and intrapersonal (working alone) intelligences.
- Consider the match between the intelligences required by an inquiry and the intelligence strengths of the student assigned to be the leader of the group for that task. Develop additional inquiries if needed so that each student leader can be successful as leader as well as learner.

USING *COLLABORATION* TO ENHANCE DEVELOPMENT OF THE MULTIPLE INTELLIGENCES

Instructional Strategies

- When establishing the membership of your collaborative groups, called Learning Clubs in the ITI model, use problem-solving/product-producing strengths as a major criteria. In your groups of four to five students,[38] do your best to have strengths in at least four intelligences represented.

- Whenever students work on a group inquiry, have them analyze what intelligences they will most need to complete the assigned inquiry. This will alert students not strong in that intelligence to tune into that mode of solving problems or producing products. Similarly, during reflective thinking after a collaborative task, have students analyze how they used/didn't use the multiple intelligences as they worked together. (Reflective thinking is an important strategy for maximizing learning in group settings—both of subject content and ability to work together as a group.)

- Have students analyze what intelligence the frequent group roles require, e.g., recorder, leader, materials gatherer. Encourage them to observe how specific roles and intelligences make the group successful.

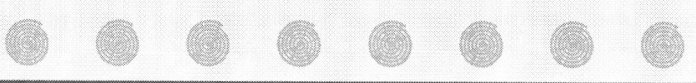

Immediate Feedback

Each intelligence has its own built-in ways of thinking, e.g., shifting immediately to mindmapping information or creating a mathematical formula to show relationships, reading the directions first or "playing with it" first to figure it out. To learn new ways of thinking, immediate feedback is essential. The issue here is not about getting the right answer but about actually thinking differently. After-the-fact feedback is therefore useless. What is needed is "in-flight" assessments and adjustments. External feedback from teachers and fellow Learning Club members is therefore invaluable.

However, since external feedback is not always available, in the long run students must learn to expand their capacity for self-talk, a key factor in intrapersonal intelligence. Self-talk can provide a running dialogue for students. It can ask pertinent questions to guide the next attempt at solving the problem or get around a production problem to complete a project.

For example, co-author Karen Olsen has learned to rely on self-talk a great deal when writing a book. When writer's block appears, the self-talk begins. "Now, why am I stuck on this? Is it the content I'm hung up on or how to express it? Are my examples only linguistic or have I provided pictures of how it would look in the classroom (spatial input) and ways students could act on this idea (bodily-kinesthetic)?" And the internal dialogue continues. Are some of my questions hard to answer? You bet! Musical intelligence is my low suit still and interpersonal isn't my first preference but the beat goes on. Problem solving even for a linguistic task such as writing a book is greatly enhanced by use of all of the intelligences.

Lifelong learners and effective performers learn to use intrapersonal intelligence to redirect use of all the other intelligences. In effect, conscious use of the intrapersonal intelligence is a way to provide ourselves instant and ongoing feedback.

USING *IMMEDIATE FEEDBACK* TO ENHANCE DEVELOPMENT OF THE MULTIPLE INTELLIGENCES

Curriculum Development

- Structure inquiries so that the materials used and/or the processes required provide intrinsic feedback, i.e., the student can determine on his/her own whether his/her effort worked (solved the problem) or the product meets expected standards (real-world work standards)
- Include in group inquiries reflective thinking questions that invite students to reflect on:
  - Which of the multiple intelligences, and what combinations of them, they used to complete their inquiry
  - How did they use these intelligences (give examples)
  - How well they used those intelligences
  - What they learned about the strengths of the group and how well the group modeled each intelligence
  - What each member learned about his/her ability to use each of the intelligences.
- Consider student misbehavior an indicator of curricular weaknesses. Analyze the intelligence students are using to create their product called misbehavior. They may be telling you that they need more inquiries using this intelligence.

USING *IMMEDIATE FEEDBACK* TO ENHANCE DEVELOPMENT OF THE MULTIPLE INTELLIGENCES

Instructional Strategies

- Use of rubrics which invite students to ask themselves questions about their work—a "guided practice" of intrapersonal intelligence
- After reflecting thinking after a collaborative task, invite students to record their thoughts in their journals. Have them create a section of their journals called "Me and My Shadow" or "Are You Listening?" and record how they used self-talk to increase their power as a learner.
- Use student misbehavior as an indicator of limited range of instructional strategies, especially during direct instruction. Analyze the intelligence students are using to create their product called misbehavior. They are telling you that you need to utilize that intelligence during instructional time—direct instruction for the class as well as during one-on-one explanations.
- Find someone to provide immediate feedback to you about how well you provide immediate feedback to your students (and other issues you may choose).

Mastery

In the ITI model, the focus of mastery is one's ability to apply concepts and skills in real-life settings in accordance with real world standards and expectations. Rote memory therefore is a small piece of success in the ITI model—a means to an end but not valued as an end in itself. It is the ability to use what is understood, not just repeat it back, that is valued.

Clearly, the ability to use what is understood requires facility in handling a wide range of circumstances and tools. The best way to acquire this flexibility and expertise is to develop the capacity to solve problems and produce products in each of the multiple intelligences. Until then, allow students to demonstrate what they understand using their strengths rather than their weaknesses and to practice what they know in various ways until the new information becomes stored in long-term memory.

USING *MASTERY* TO ENHANCE DEVELOPMENT OF THE MULTIPLE INTELLIGENCES

Curriculum Development

- When developing ways to determine student mastery—tests, rubrics for self-assessment and group feedback, and so forth—avoid only paper-pencil tools. Require ability to use concepts and skills in real world ways; instead of multiple choice answers to a single question, offer students their choice of assessment options based on spatial, bodily-kinesthetic, musical, and logical-mathematical intelligences which require students to "do" something, not just talk.

USING *MASTERY* TO ENHANCE DEVELOPMENT OF THE MULTIPLE INTELLIGENCES

Instructional Strategies

- Have students manipulate information in a variety of ways that can lead to mastery.
- Model how to use the different intelligences to assess a product or a problem-solving process.
- Help students develop a sense of "knowing when they know" and "knowing when they don't know." If a little knowledge is a dangerous thing, a person with a little knowledge who perceives it to be a lot is a detriment to himself and to others. For example, the on-line investors who lose their retirement nest egg because they failed to recognize what they didn't know about investing. Or, meetings with people who hog the agenda yet have no grasp of the extent of their ignorance on the topic (but nonetheless were adamant in their opinions)—a nightmare in a democratic society when citizens gather together to solve a problem!
- Provide time for students to reflect in their journals about how they can tell if they know enough about a topic to make decisions responsibly and when they need to gather more information
- Provide models of quality products so students can see what mastery looks like.
- Involve students in designing portfolios that demonstrate mastery.

Movement

The multiple intelligences are rarely used in isolation—one at a time. Almost any real-world task requires a rich mixture of intelligences. *Being there* experiences are especially effective in making us move about and use a combination of intelligences. In such active learning situations, movement and bodily-kinesthetic intelligence meld together. Thus, if you plan explorations of *being there* locations, you will automatically engage both movement and bodily-kinesthetic intelligence. Our only word of advice is this: Assign authentic action. Avoid that which is contrived.

USING *MOVEMENT* TO ENHANCE DEVELOPMENT OF THE MULTIPLE INTELLIGENCES

Curriculum Development

- Remember that bodily-kinesthetic intelligence is a problem-solving and product-producing capability. Inquiries should offer important problems to be solved and worthwhile products to be produced. Anything less is a waste of time and insulting to students. Always ask yourself, "If I were the age of my students, would I find this task worthy of my time? Would the task help me understand that concept or skill or learn to apply it? Would the task help me remember the concept or skill 10 years from now?
- Think movement, think action, think doing something worthwhile while practicing how to use key points.

USING *MOVEMENT* TO ENHANCE DEVELOPMENT OF THE MULTIPLE INTELLIGENCES

Instructional Strategies

- Because the motor areas of the brain sequence thinking, the more students ***do*** things with what they know, the more solid the learning. Add movement to every possible aspect of your instructional processes—from direct instruction to independent study and everything in between.[39]
- Design inquiries that ask students, in Learning Clubs or in pairs, to create movements as mnemonics for applying and remembering the concept or skill of a skill point.
- Develop an active cross-age tutoring or buddy program that invites your students to demonstrate what they know to younger students. The tutor/buddy rule: Demonstrate, don't tell.

Notes

1 Howard Gardner's theory of intelligence is widely received and well ensconced; it is also our choice for the ITI model because it can be easily applied in the classroom and with great power. However, Dr. Robert Sylwester points out that Gardner's theory isn't the only credible theory of multiple intelligences. He believes that the work of David Perkins and Robert Sternberg (see below) is also intriguing and useful, fitting well with ITI and the brain functions explored by Elkhonon Goldberg (see Chapter 4).

David Perkins defines intelligence as "knowing one's way around" seven realms of human experience: dispositional, challenge, tool, technical, field, situational, and contextual. See *Outsmarting IQ: The Emerging Science of Learnable Intelligence.* (Free Press, 1995).

Robert Sternberg's triarchic brain model identifies three intelligences: creative, analytic, and practical. Sylwester sees close parallels between these intelligences and the capabilities of the principal brain, especially the frontal lobes: 1) the ability to develop a useful solution to a novel challenge, 2) the ability to develop effective cognitive routines to use when confronted by familiar challenges, and 3) the ability to anticipate the motives, intentions, and behaviors of others. See *Successful Intelligence.*

The views of Dr. Robert Sylwester about this area are taken from discussions based on his August 4, 2003 letter to the authors.

2 We use Gardner's work because it rings with our experiences with children and adults and because it so readily lends itself to practical applications when developing curriculum and selecting instructional strategies. See *Frames of Mind: The Theory of Multiple Intelligences* (New York: Basic Books, Inc., 1985).

3 For fascinating accounts of the interacting of genes and environment, see Richard Restak, MD, *The New Brain: How the Modern Age is Rewiring Your Mind* (Emmaus, PA: Rodale Inc., 2003).

4 For a description of the criteria used by Gardner to define an area of intelligence, see *Frames of Mind.*

5 According to Howard Gardner, "Intelligences are not equivalent to sensory systems" (*Frames of Mind*, 68). The theory of multiple intelligences expands and replaces our previous understandings of sensory input, such as the modalities. Such frames of reference were based upon observing *from the outside,* variations in student learning behavior and then, based on such observations, making assumptions about how students learn.

In contrast, current research into how the human brain learns—the focus of this book—is based on high-tech observations *of the inside* of the brain as it is operating. These observations about what the brain is actually doing as it thinks and learns then allow us to determine what educational practices will assist the brain to do its job most naturally and thus most powerfully.

This difference is critical because although you may find considerable overlap in recommended instructional strategies for modalities and multiple intelligences, implementation of each of those instructional strategies must differ in subtle but powerful ways because the whys and whats behind what you are trying to achieve are different. In simple terms, modalities focus on instructional approaches and materials that provide input through different pathways to the brain—kinesthetic, taste, and smell as well as visual and auditory. In contrast, multiple intelligences focus on how the brain processes information once it gets to the brain—how it uses what it learns to solve problems and/or produce products. The difference is between the route through which input arrives versus ways of processing and thinking about what comes in.

6 Gardner, *Frames of Mind*, 60-61.

7 Ibid., x.

8 Ibid., xiii.

9 Since his initial work in the 1980s, Gardner has considered evidence for three additional intelligences: naturalist, spiritual, and existential. See Chapters 4 and 5, *Intelligence Reframed: Multiple Intelligences for the 21st Century* by Howard Gardner (New York: Basic Books, 1999). The naturalist intelligence is considered the strongest candidate so far. However, as you read through this chapter and Chapters 9 and 10 about how to develop curriculum in the ITI model, you will notice that we do not utilize the naturalist intelligence. There are several reasons: Gardner himself states that the naturalist intelligence develops on its own in most children. We believe that well constructed *being there* experiences, along with teaching the scientific thinking processes, will provide ample practice in observing, classifying, and using features of the environment. Also, it is our contention that Gardner's comment that the "pattern-recognizing talents of artists, poets, social scientists, and natural scientists are all built on the fundamental perceptual skills of naturalist intelligence" is incorrect. In our opinion, "pattern-recognition" as described in Chapter 4 is a **general function of the entire brain**, not just that of the naturalist intelligence. This is consistent with the fact that Gardner does not assign the function of naturalist intelligence to a particular region of the brain as he does the first seven intelligences. In effect, the naturalist intelligence does not meet Gardner's initial criteria for identifying distinct intelligences.

Howard Gardner's definition of intelligence is an extremely useful alternative to the standard I.Q. number. See *Frames of Mind*, x.

10 Gardner, *Frames of Mind*, Chapter 7.

11 Thomas Armstrong, *In Their Own Way* (New York: Tarcher Press, 1987).

12 Gardner, *Frames of Mind*, Chapter 5.

13 Ibid., Chapter 5.

14 Armstrong, *In Their Own Way*, 20.

15 Gardner, *Frames of Mind*, 177.

16 Armstrong, *In Their Own Way*, 18.

17 Gardner, *Frames of Mind*, 190.

18 For a teacher-friendly tool for strengthening spatial intelligence, the best resource we have found is Nanci Bell, *Visualizing and Verbalizing for Improved Language Comprehension: A Teacher's Manual* (CA: Academy of Reading, 1987).

19 Armstrong, *In Their Own Way*, 21.

20 Gardner, *Frames of Mind*, Chapter 9.

21 Armstrong, *In Their Own Way*, 23.

22 Elkhonon Goldberg, *The Executive Brain: Frontal Lobes and the Civilized Mind* (Oxford: Oxford University Press, 2001), 65-66.

23 John Ratey, *A User's Guide to the Brain: Perception, Attention, and the Four Theaters of the Brain* (New York: Pantheon Books, 2001), 48 (Chapter 4).

24 Gardner, *Frames of Mind*, Chapter 6.

25 Armstrong, *In Their Own Way*, 22.

26 Gardner, *Frames of Mind*, Chapter 10.

27 Armstrong, *In Their Own Way*, 24.

28 Gardner, *Frames of Mind*, Chapter 10.

29 Armstrong, *In Their Own Way*, 23-24.

30 For reasons discussed in footnote 9, we do not use the naturalist intelligence in our curriculum work for the ITI model.

31 E.F. Shores, "Howard Gardner on the Eighth Intelligence: Seeing the Natural World," *Dimensions of Early Childhood* (Summer, 1995), 5-7.

32 Shores, "Howard Gardner," 5-7.

33 Co-author Karen Olsen interviewed a young man who had given up on college—frustration and low grades. After touring with a band for several years, he returned to college. Determined to succeed, and armed with information about Gardner's multiple intelligences, he began to figure out ways to use his considerable musical talent as study aids. For classes with a lot of details and definitions, he would first choose a letter or word representing each element and then compose a short melody using those letters/words. Before long, he was composing and singing his way to high grades—consistently As and B+s.

34 Frank Smith, *Insult to Intelligence: The Bureaucratic Invasion of Our Classrooms* (New Hampshire: Heinemann, 1986), 62.

35 Susan Kovalik, *Integrated Thematic Instruction: The Model.* (Kent, WA: Susan Kovalik & Associates, 1992), 14.

36 Hart, *Human Brain and Human Learning*, 67.

37 This sage advice comes from Elizabeth Cohen. She provides the best guidance for developing curriculum for collaborative tasks that we have found to date. See Elizabeth Cohen, *Designing Groupwork: Strategies for the Heterogeneous Classroom, Second Edition* (New York: Teachers College Press, 1994).

38 Learning Clubs with three to four members are an ideal size (see Robert J. Marzano et al, *Classroom Instruction That Works: Research-Based Strategies for Increasinsg Student Achievement*, 88). However, if students have never worked collaboratively before, you will likely need to start with groups of two and work up to five. This could take days or months depending on the personal and social skills of your students. The Lifelong Guidelines and LIFESKILLS are a crucial tool for teaching students how to work together. And, don't be dismayed if you must begin with a group of one. Start where your students are.

39 This recent area of brain research is critical to educators. More than any other area we know of, it explains why traditional classrooms, with their "sit quietly and work on your own" assignments, produce such minimal results. For more information, see *A User's Guide to the Brain: Perception, Attention, and the Four Theaters of the Brain* by John Ratey, especially Chapter 4, and *The Executive Brain: Frontal Lobes and the Civilized Mind* by Elkhonon Goldberg, especially 65-66.

Notes to Myself

Chapter 4: Pattern Seeking—Step One of Learning

A New Definition of Learning

Recent brain research is revolutionizing teaching by revealing how we learn. Leslie Hart, a pioneer in synthesizing and applying brain research to education, defines learning as a two-step process.[1]

> **Learning Is a Two-Step Process**
>
> - Detecting and understanding patterns—a process through which our brain creates meaning
> - Developing meaningful mental programs to use what is understood and to store it in long-term memory—the capacity to use what is understood, first with assistance and then almost automatically

Hart's definition of learning is much more stringent than is what is currently used. In his view, students must not only be able to detect and understand patterns but also to use use them, first with guidance in familiar settings and then in varying situations on one's own until the ability to use the knowledge or skill is readily at hand, almost automatic.

> **ITI Learning Principles**
>
> - *Intelligence as a function of experience*
> - *Bodybrain partnership—emotion as gatekeeper to learning and performance* ***and*** *movement to enhance learning*
> - *Multiple intelligences*
> - ***Learning as a two-step process***
>   - ***—pattern seeking/meaning making***
>   - *—program building/wiring for long-term memory*

This definition of learning carries us far beyond that assumed by makers of standardized tests. The typical multiple choice and true/false questions can be answered based on a faint ring of familiarity of one answer over another. "Choice B rings a bell. . . ." "Hmm, that statement doesn't sound familiar, so it must be false. . . ." The test takers don't even have to understand the content.

And step two of learning—being able to use what is understood and then to apply it until it becomes stored in long-term memory—isn't even considered by test makers.

Does it shock you that we spend billions of dollars on standardized testing based on ever-increasing state and federal standards but don't care whether learning can be be applied or will last beyond the exam? We hope so. We hope it will motivate you and your school to sit down and seriously apply brain research in all your program improvement efforts. A beginning point in your deliberations is to adopt a definition of learning that all can work toward. Hart's two-step definition is the most useful and useable we have found. And, 20 years after he proposed it, there is even more convincing evidence from brain research to substantiate it.

The Gradiental/Distributive View of the Brain

As introduced in Chapter 4, the gradiental/distributive theory of brain function is now overlaying the modular theory of the brain. The modular theory viewed the brain as storing word meanings as separate, compact modules separate from the cerebral representation of the real physical world they denote—a view now still accepted as true but not complete.

The newly emerging gradiental/distributive view of the brain suggests that the brain—especially in contextually rich, meaningful, real-lifelike settings—is extremely active and more integrated than the modular theory first envisioned. Activity shifts over time as the new learnings are used and committed to long-term memory. As seen in the graphic on the right, the frontal lobe is active when the cognitive task is new (the brain is naive), row (a). Frontal activation drops with task familiarization, row (b). The frontal lobes become partially activated again when a somewhat different or novel task is introduced (similar to a known one but not identical to it). These right to left, front to back, and top to bottom shifts illustrate the widespread involvement of the brain in learning and the significant physiological activity and growth/change that is the process of learning, a process unique to each brain with a timeline that cannot be dictated by bureaucratic needs.

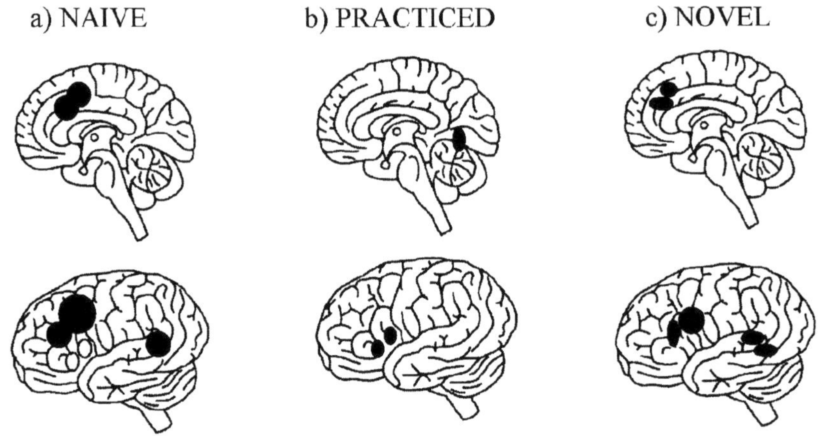

Source: *The Executive Brain* by Elkhonon Goldberg, page 70. [Adapted from M. E. Raichle, J. A. Fiez, T. O. Videen, A. M. MacLeod, J. V. Pardo, P. T. Fox, S. E. Petersen, "Practice-related changes is human brain functional anatomy during nonmotor learning," *Cerebral Cortex* vol. 4, no. 1 (1994)].

In classroom terms, the gradiental/distributive view of the brain explains why boredom is deadly (little or no brain activity occurs) and why rote memorization, when absent a sense of how the knowledge/skill is used, frequently produces little long-term memory (little happens inside the brain).

Brain Organization and the ITI Definition of Learning

Perhaps the most fascinating aspect of Goldberg's gradiental model with its shifts from right to left frontal, from front to back, and neocortex to older structures is that it provides a physiological explanation for Leslie Hart's definition of learning as a two-step process (see graphic in next column). To assist teachers in planning curriculum and instructional strategies, we have broken each of those steps into two phases. The correspondence of the two views is striking.

New definition of learning	*Brain activity when learning something new*
▪ Step One: Pattern-Seeking	
Identifying patterns....................................	Primarily right frontal lobes shifting to
Making meaning/understanding................	Primarily left frontal lobes
▪ Step Two: Program-Building	
Able to use learning with support.............	Shift from front toward back of brain
Ability to use the learning becomes automatic and part of long-term memory.......	Shift to back and lower/older brain structures

Admittedly, these are broad brush strokes but knowing that different parts of the brain must be engaged to move learning from an initial "Aha" to long-term memory of how to *use* the knowledge or skill gives us a larger view of learning. It allows us to key in to what sensory and motor input students need, what practice *using* the knowledge or skill will move the learning from new to practiced, and the time it takes to make those physiological shifts in the brain. Suddenly, "covering" content and relying on paper-pencil tests to indicate mastery can be seen as the useless strategies that they are.

This chapter addresses the first step of learning—identifying patterns and making meaning of them, the shift from right to left in the frontal lobes. Chapter 5 addresses step two of learning.

The Most Notable Characteristic of the Human Brain

The most notable characteristic of the human brain is its phenomenal penchant for seeking and detecting patterns. In his book, *Human Brain and Human Learning*, Leslie A. Hart stipulates that no part of the human brain is naturally logical while it is learning,"[2] i.e., making meaning. (This is distinguished from its ability to use information already learned in a "logical" or sequential way if the situation so requires.) Instead, the brain learns by sifting through massive amounts of input that is arriving simultaneously from all the senses, processing thousands of bits of information per minute. Obviously, such information is processed in a multi-path, multi-modal way with the brain attending to changes in the pattern of incoming data.

> *"The brain detects, constructs, and elaborates patterns as a basic, built-in, natural function. It does not have to be taught or motivated to do so, any more than the heart needs to be instructed or coaxed to pump blood. In fact, efforts to teach or motivate the pattern detection, however well meant, may have inhibiting and negative effects."*
>
> *Leslie A. Hart*

The simultaneity of its processing makes patterns obvious while processing along one avenue at a time, however speedily, would produce no "aha," no sense of an overall picture whatsoever. Imagine if the brain processed only one set of information at a time, e.g., first vision, then hearing, then bodily-kinesthetic, etc. Like the three blind men, recognizing an elephant would, at best, be an extremely time consuming and laborious task.

Pattern seeking progresses along a continuum: detection, identification, and understanding.

What Is a Pattern?

Hart defines a pattern as:

> "An entity, such as an object, action, procedure, situation, relationship or **system**, which may be recognized by substantial consistency in the **clues** it presents to a brain, which is a pattern-detecting apparatus. The more powerful a brain, the more complex, finer, and subtle patterns it can detect. Except for certain **species wisdom** patterns, each human must learn to recognize the patterns of all matters dealt with, storing the **learning** in the brain. Pattern recognition tells what is being dealt with, permitting selection of the most appropriate program in brain storage to deal with it. The brain tolerates much variation in patterns (we recognize the letter *a* in many shapes, sizes, colors, etc.) because it operates on the basis of **probability**, not on digital or logic principles. Recognition of **patterns** accounts largely for what is called insight, and facilitates transfer of learning to new situations or needs, which may be called creativity."[3]

Examples of patterns include those shown in the graphic in the next column.

As the brain attempts to make sense out of the chaos which surrounds each of us, it constantly searches for patterns that can impose meaning on the input received. Its "aha" arise from detection of a recognizable (from the learner's perspective) pattern or patterns. This pattern detection propensity is seen in the operation of each of the senses. The ear registers every sound wave within its perceivable frequency but it attends only to those that provide a meaningful pattern. Sounds of traffic or workshop chatter are ignored and only the presenter's voice is tuned in or noted as a pattern to attend to. Similarly, the eye recognizes a chair; be it a three-legged milking stool, a church pew, or the more common no-frills

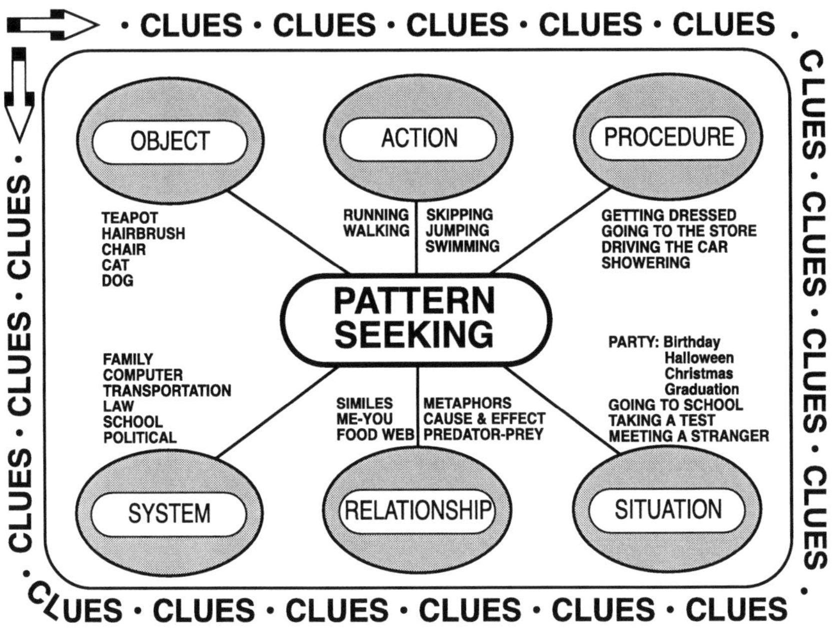

chair at the kitchen table; it does so by looking for the pattern or **collection of attributes** necessary for something to be a chair when one wants to sit down.

From the time we are born until we die, the brain takes in these patterns as they present themselves, sorting and categorizing in an attempt to make sense out of our complex world. Learning takes place when the brain sorts out patterns using past experiences to make sense out of new input the brain receives.

According to Hart, the first step in learning is ". . . the extraction, from confusion, of meaningful patterns." In real-life settings, information comes at the learner in a way that can best be described as rich, random, and even chaotic.[4] Over the millenniums, the brain has perfected learning within such an environment.

This pattern-detecting aspect of the brain can be clearly seen in the brain's mastery of one of its biggest accomplishments: learning the mother language. Watch mothers just home from the hospital with their newborns (or even listen to them talk to their child in utero!). Mothers know how to teach language. They do not "dumb down" their language to the infant to single syllable communications. Instead, mothers discuss the everyday happenings of life and share their hopes and dreams for their little one—"When you grow up, you'll go to Stanford and become an astronaut. You'd like that very much, I think. Very, very exciting occupation." "Yikes, there are so many choices at this grocery store. Which brand was it that we tried last week that was so good?" "Come, it's time to toss in a load of laundry; we'll do the whites first with hot water." Why do mothers do this? Because it works. Because every noun and verb in the English dictionary (and in our curriculum) is a pattern. Each has attributes that distinguish one word from another. The more experience with the attributes, the finer the patterns so that choosing among words such as pensive and melancholy is not a random choice but a decisive match with someone's emotions at the moment.

Such a barrage of sounds coming at the child in real-life fashion would at first seem a hopeless environment in which to master language. But an environment similar to the one previously mentioned—rich, random, even chaotic—gives large amounts of input to the child, and thus provides his or her mind with the opportunity to search for patterns. As educators, we have been carefully and logically taught that such an environment would make the task of learning a language impossible. Consequently, we teach English as a second language logically and carefully, "This is a pen. What is this? This is a ______." Unfortunately, the human brain does not learn well from such logical, tidy, greatly restricted input because it is so antagonistic to the learning methods the brain has perfected over the ages.

In short, the mind is genetically designed to learn from the natural complexities of the natural world. To the extent that schools oversimplify, or make logical, or restrict the world's natural complexity is the extent to which schools inhibit the natural workings of the mind and restrict a student's ability to learn. In contrast, input from the real world engages all of the senses. Logical, sequential curricula are highly brain-antagonistic. Comments Hart, "Perhaps there is no idea about human learning harder to accept for people familiar with classrooms and schools than this: that *the ideal of neat, orderly, closely-planned, sequentially logical teaching will, in practice with young students, guarantee severe learning failure for most.*"[5] A common mistake of the public schools is stripping down the input to a small amount of content, all analyzed and dissected into small bits, so that the "right" answer seems inescapable. This does not work. Patterns are the building blocks of meaning, the heart of curriculum development.

Learning: Step One

Pattern-matching is inherently pleasing because that is what our minds are designed [or programmed] for. . . . Quite apart from anything the teacher does. . . the student, being human, is a pattern-finder and a pattern-maker. Possibly the greatest obstacle to our making use of this not very startling principle is our ingrained notion that education is the acquisition and mastery of new material. What we "teach" and they do not "learn" is the "material."

—David B. Bronson[6]

Stripping a learning situation of its real-life richness also robs the child's mind of the possibility of perceiving patterns and thus making sense of what is in front of him/her. Ironically, we do this consistently with students who need special help. If they are slow, conventional wisdom has dictated that the task be broken into smaller and smaller pieces. We've now achieved pieces that are so small and so "easy"—only one item to focus on—that there is no longer any pattern to perceive. Consequently, Chapter 1 students with their finely-chopped, oversimplified diet say "I don't get it" which confirms to us that they are "slow." However, most Chapter 1 students are adept learners from real-world input. They come to us having learned their mother tongue and a wide range of skills for coping with life. Consider the immigrant child who is the translator for the entire family, the urban child with street savvy, the migrant child with flexibility and resourcefulness to figure out each new setting from town to town.

The amazing flexibility of the brain in its pattern seeking is apparent in its ability to recognize the pattern of the letter *a*; we recognize it amid an amazing range of fonts, sizes, shapes, positions. This speed and flexibility can occur because the brain naturally works on a probabilistic basis. The brain does not add up, for example, all the parts of a cat until all parts are perceived and accounted for: four legs, a tail, fur, meows, purrs, etc. Rather, the mind "jumps to the conclusion" that the pattern "cat" applies when only one or a few characteristics have been noted. While this jumping to conclusions sometimes gets us in trouble, it is crucial to rapid completion of myriad actions minute by minute. The rapid reader, for example, does not see every letter before deciding what the word is. Context clues or the mere outline of the word are used, in probabilistic fashion, to jump to conclusions.

In the example of our infant learning its mother tongue, language pours around the child for hours and hours a day. The more input, the more readily the child learns. The first patterns perceived are those that are most meaningful—the child's name and then the name of mom and dad. Patterns are at first quite gross, i.e., "Dadda" means any man in trousers. Over time, with continued rich input and immediate feedback, the patterns become more and more refined until, finally, the educated adult ends up with a vocabulary of 10,000-plus words with subtle shades of meaning and the ability to use them with considerable precision.

The entire structure of language is based on pattern. For example, plurals mostly end in *s* except for mice, moose, fish, etc. Past tense ends with *ed*. Words ending in *ing* are a real thrill for most children. When they first grasp the *ing* pattern, everything is jumping, leaping, hitting, running, and so forth for several days until another pattern of language gets discovered. Every noun and verb in our language reflects a pattern.

Pattern-seeking is the brain's way of striving to extract meaning from the thousands of bits of input pouring into the brain each minute through the 19 senses. And, very importantly, what is one learner's pattern is another learner's hodgepodge. This is to say, we cannot predict what any one particular child will perceive as a pattern because so much depends upon prior knowledge, the existing neural networking of the brain used to process the input, and the context in which the learning takes place.

However, if the input is rich and varied, all learners can arrive at an understanding of the pattern to be learned.

The First Fundamental of Learning: Making Meaning*

Over 80 years ago, for example, Aldous Huxley remarked that "What emerges most strikingly from recent scientific developments is that perception is not a passive reception of material from the outside world; it is an active process of selection and imposing of patterns."[7]

The findings Huxley referred to were well known in fields more scientifically oriented than education then and that are thoroughly established now. Brain researchers of the 1990s accept this as a given.[8] We do not have to look far for confirmation—our own daily experience tells us most convincingly that the brain has this ability and has it to an astounding degree.

Examples from Personal Experience

Imagine that you are attending a sporting event. People by the thousands stream by as you find your seats. The merest glance tells you they are all strangers. But now you see two figures that immediately seem familiar and in a moment you have identified them as former neighbors, Francine and Peter. Somehow, your brain has picked them out of this vast crowd; somehow it has separated them from all the other people you know so that you can identify them and greet them warmly by name. There is no question that our human brain can do this—usually effortlessly. (If we simply look at what we all can do, we begin to glimpse the enormous powers of the brain.)

* The text in this font, from here through page 4.10, indicates excerpts from *Human Brain and Human Learning* by Leslie A. Hart. (Covington, Washington: Books for Educators, 1999). Used by written permission of the publisher.

The feat is even more impressive because you haven't seen these friends for three years, didn't expect to run into them here. Both are wearing clothes you have never seen them in. Francine has a new hair style, Peter wears sunglasses that partly hide his features. Yet, you recognized them as familiar while they were still 50 feet away.

Clearly, the recognition does not stem from any logical process. You did not check Francine's height in inches or Peter's weight in kilos. You put no measure to their middle finger bones, Bertillon fashion,[9] nor did you use a color-comparison guide to determine the shade of skin and hair. While Peter has a distinctive walking movement and Francine an animated manner, trying to measure or describe these exactly would be an impossible task. Let us grasp firmly the clear fact that your brain does not work that way but that it did quickly and accurately accomplish recognition and identification by some other means.

Nor was this an isolated, unusual phenomenon. If I were to display a teakettle, a paint brush, a handsaw, a necklace, a bunch of carrots, a pencil sharpener, a violin, a telephone, a sweater, a microscope, a toothbrush, a slice of Swiss cheese . . . you would recognize and name each in the same effortless way. You were plainly not born knowing these objects, so this recognition has been learned at some time between birth and the present.

We are so used to looking at something and immediately knowing what it is that we come to think of the process as automatic. Comparisons of eye and camera may also mislead us. A camera can't recognize anything; our brain can, using not only vision but also hearing, smell, touch, and other aspects of our senses.

When we are exposed to something quite unfamiliar, we simply do not see it in any meaningful way. To look inside some complex machine, for example, we may see only a confusion of forms. In a museum, observing some fossilized remains of various ancient animals, we may see only vague shapes, in contrast to what the curator sees. I often dramatize this in workshops by showing a newspaper in Arabic or Chinese. The participants see only squiggles that a moment later they are hopelessly unable to reproduce—although a person knowing the language would see headlines and news, information at a glance.

If we place a teakettle before a month-old infant, the baby will regard it with momentary interest but plainly have no notion of what it is. As adults we can see a vessel, a handle, and a spout; the baby can see none of this arrangement, only edges, shapes, and surfaces.

Even if the teakettle were made of unfamiliar materials or shaped like an elephant, we would recognize it as a teakettle. Any familiar item, from a paint brush to a necklace,would be identifiable. Moderate differences do not bother us a bit.

Examples from Classroom Life

Consider, for instance, the 20 different forms of the letter a that appear below. Despite the range of shapes they cover, we have no difficulty seeing any one as a. We could, of course, carry this recognition much

further, to letters of many larger sizes, in different colors, formed of lights or dots, put into three-dimensional materials, tilted, laid on the floor, or seen on the side of a moving vehicle. Even holding just to typefaces available for printing, there are literally thousands of alphabets; handwritten, drawn, or printed forms add thousands more. There is no letter a, only a pattern we conventionally call a.

In the same sense, teakettle, paintbrush, carrots, violin, and the rest are patterns. Our knowledge of the pattern is what enables us to say what object is what. But we are by no means limited to hard, visual patterns. We can detect and learn patterns far more subtle or complex. In time, adults normally become quite familiar with such patterns as cat, city park, affection, boss, fraction, racial bigotry, jealousy, or adventurousness.

Just how the brain detects and recognizes patterns cannot be easily or quickly explained. Yet, it is an astoundingly powerful, subtle, living computer with billions of neurons at its command. We do know in a general way that the brain detects characteristics or features and also relationships among these features.

The lower-case letter a, for example, may consist of a hook facing left which may take a variety of forms,

connected to a more or less round enclosure form.

The relationship between these shapes has a key role. If the hook were 20 centimeters tall and the enclosure only a millimeter high, one might have much difficulty seeing it as an a. On the other hand, there is a different pattern for small a that lacks the hook altogether that we can

readily learn to accept as an alternate. It is illogical to have two forms but, as we have seen, logic is the least of the human brain's concerns.

Key Factors in Pattern Seeking

When looking at the brain as a seeker of patterns, consider five key factors: Use of clues and cues, use of multiple sensory input and prior experience, sensitivity to negative clues, categorizing down through patterns within patterns, and using probability.

Use of Clues and Cues

Our brain's ability to detect and identify patterns is impressive for its flexibility. We can be certain about our identification of something without needing to perceive most or even many of its features and relationships. With experience, in fact, we normally become extremely expert in using clues (sometimes the term cues is used in the same sense) to make very rapid judgments. We would not be able to read at all if we had to study all the features of letters. The capable reader goes much further and uses clues for whole words and even phrases.[10]

Use of Multiple Sensory Input and Prior Experience

In practice our pattern-detecting ability depends on clues from vision, hearing, touch, or other senses, on behavior and relationships, and/or on the situation. In short, the ability to detect and recognize patterns depends heavily on our experience, on what we bring to the act of pattern detection and recognition. The more that experience tells us what we are likely to be looking at, or dealing with, the less detailed, feature-type information we need to jump to a probably correct conclusion.

Sensitivity to Negative Clues

One reason we can rely on little information is the sensitivity of the brain to negative clues. When clues do not fit together rapidly within a pattern, or when one or more are jarringly strange or contradictory, our pattern-detecting apparatus quickly senses something wrong. Suppose that I am going to the house of people I have visited a couple of times before, on a dark suburban street where house numbers are hard to find. As I walk toward what seems to be the house, I come to a flagstone walk. It "doesn't feel right," prompting me to retreat and try the house next door. Or, perhaps another day I identify an all-black bird as a Brewer's blackbird. When I see a flash of color on the wing, I must revise my identification to "red-winged blackbird."

Patterns Within Patterns: Categorizing Down

In the example of recognizing friends Francine and Peter, only a yes/no kind of decision was involved—they were or were not those individuals. But more common is the detection and recognition of patterns within patterns, which leads to finer and finer discriminations, a process called categorizing down, a most important aspect of learning. For example, we can detect the pattern "animal," then categorize it down to "dog," and then to "Afghan hound." Or, observing a number of people at a gathering, we may categorize further by noting that the people are festively dressed, a "party," and then on seeing a cake with candles, conclude it's a "birthday party."

But we must note that a person from a country where birthday cakes are not a custom would not be prepared to interpret that clue the way we so easily do. Again, what the observer brings to the recognition act—in terms of prior relevant experience and previously acquired knowledge—plays a critical part. (It is startling to observe that in conventional teaching this absolutely fundamental principle is largely ignored.)

In small children, the process of enlarging pattern detection and extending and refining categorizing-down chains is often clearly observable. A girl just starting to talk may say "Daddy!" while pointing to any man who comes into sight—we gather she is using daddy in the sense of man.

A little later, guided by such feedback as "No, that is not Daddy—Daddy is at his office," the child may point to any man who comes into the home, whether young cousin or elderly grandfather, as daddy. With further feedback, categories gradually get straightened out and daddy is used to mean only one person. It may take much longer for the child to become clear on the fact that her friend also has a daddy (and some years to grasp the relationship). It may take still more time to be able to categorize surely from people to males, to relatives and friends, neighbors, policeman, mailman, Mr. Jackson (who lives next door), as well as boys, girls, and many other subtle relationships.[11]

It seems apparent that the brain must have some kind of organizational process that enables humans to rapidly categorize down patterns as they are detected, so that they can be identified quickly.

Matching. The principle of matching is well understood. In simplest terms, one receives an input from outside the brain—for example, visual input that comes from a door. Inside the brain, stored, is a pattern, door.[12] If the current input and the stored pattern pretty well match, recognition occurs. Looking in the night sky, one may see any one of several patterns that match up with stored patterns for moon. Hearing some sound waves that compose a certain pattern, we recognize it as the word scarecrow, since it fairly well fits our stored pattern for scarecrow. The matches do not have to be precise—another principle, probability, applies. This permits us to recognize "scarecrow" whether spoken by a child in a thin, high voice or by a man or woman in other pitches, and despite various pronunciations. The brain searches for a probable match. (If this were not so, we would all have a terrible time trying to read English, with its frequently weird spellings!)

Parallel Processing. But to operate effectively, the brain cannot afford to search sequentially through tens of thousands of stored patterns to find the match. It seems likely that patterns are grouped in categories within hierarchies, or layers, much as mail is addressed (reading from the bottom up and right to left):

The country (USA).

The state (Connecticut).

The city or town (Bethel).

The street (Maple Avenue).

The house number (628).

The person in that house (Mr. or Mrs.)

This method, we know, quite efficiently makes a match between the letter and one out of more than 250 million inhabitants. If the address (the input) is a little wrong, the letter may still be delivered but if the error is large, no match can be made, no delivery can occur.

Experimental studies suggest that the brain does not usually need as many as six steps to categorize down. (That investigation is beyond the scope of this book.) Nor is the brain limited to one linear chain of categorizing down (such as that illustrated above in addressing a letter). It can employ many such chains simultaneously, as we have noted. This "parallel processing" enormously speeds recognition. It's like having l,000 clerks sorting the mail rather than just one.

Using Probability . . . Jumping to Conclusions

A variety of studies indicate that the brain naturally works on a probabilistic basis. The brain skillfully jumps to conclusions! It isn't an adding machine that must reach a correct total. For example, seeing a creature that has four legs, a tail, fur, and barks at a friend's home, we jump to the conclusion that the pattern "dog" applies. Why not "cat"? Because we pick up negative clues: Cats don't bark and ordinarily don't come aggressively to the door when a stranger enters. Why isn't it a monkey? Because the relationship of limbs is different. The situation also gives clues; we expect to find a dog in a home. If we visited a zoo, however, and found this same animal exhibited in a cage, we would assume it was not a dog but some similar creature. Our experience tells us that dogs are not displayed this way.

The Brain—A Master at Extracting Meaning from Confusion

This is the process of learning that Frank Smith and others aptly call "making sense of the world."[13] The ability that even infants have to gradually sort out an extremely complex, changing world is nothing short of astounding. And it's natural. But even more surprising still is that we learn from input presented in a completely random, fortuitous fashion—unplanned, accidental, unordered, uncontrolled, the polar opposite of didactic classroom teaching.

Consider, for example, the sorting-out problem a child has to grasp for such patterns as dessert, pie, and cake. Since a great variety of dishes may constitute dessert, the child must extract the idea that meals have a sequence (program) and dessert is the last course. He or she must also learn that dessert does not mean a particular dish, or even a tight group or class of dishes. Pie presents few problems to an adult with years of experience to draw on but, to a toddler, an open pumpkin pie, a crusted blueberry pie, and a lemon pie heaped with meringue topping present little in common. Or does pie mean round, the most obvious feature? Unfortunately many desserts are round, particularly cakes—which vary from pie-like cheesecake, to coffee cake, to layered birthday cake elaborately iced and decorated.

While adults and older siblings may provide gentle, casual, and almost incidental corrective feedback when the child calls a pie a cake or doesn't regard a fruit dish as dessert and cries in frustration, it would be most unusual for anything resembling teaching or instruction to deal with dessert, pie, and cake as subjects. Yet in a few years, from this confused, random exposure and experience, the child has extracted the patterns, gradually coming to see which features and relationships have significance in which settings, and which can be ignored. Frequently, however, the child extracts a pattern that sooner or later has to be revised in the light of new information. For example, everything if let go falls—until someone presents a gas-filled balloon. Children often find the need to revise something disturbing. The world keeps proving more complicated, with more exceptions, than they had previously thought. Adults have a similar problem; in time, they may become less flexible, cling to old ideas, refuse to revise, and even try to avoid the input that forces the contradiction. "Nonsense . . . that's crazy . . . I won't listen . . . don't bother me!"

Even more amazing is the obvious ability of preschool children to extract rules about language from the quite random speech they hear about them and engage in. We hear such expressions as sheeps and deers, plurals plainly not picked up from adults or older children. The added s makes unmistakably clear that the small child has extracted a general rule for plurals—end with the s sound—and is applying it even to what will later be learned as special exceptions. In the same way, most youngsters will use such constructions as "Tommy hitted me," or "I falled down," showing that they have extracted the pattern of past tense and the use of the ed sound, again even where there are common exceptions. Yet it would be absurd to expect a three- or four-year-old to explain plural or past tense.[14]

These familiar experiences and others like them are so prevalent that we cannot reasonably doubt that all of us, at whatever age, do extract patterns from the quite random, confused mass of input we are exposed to in the course of normal living. Nor can it be easily denied that the great bulk of practical knowledge we have and use to get along in the world is acquired in this way.

A Word About Rote Memory. The great bulk of general learning occurs through extracting meaningful patterns from confusion. The only other important method is via rote memory. But while "pure" rote learning—straight memorization—appears to suffice, as in the case of learning the alphabet in sequence, even rote learning is greatly helped by detecting the patterns involved where patterns clearly exist, as in the multiplication tables. Or consider the marching band, very much a rote activity. If the patterns in the music and in the maneuvers are understood, learning can be far faster and surer.

In Summary

In embracing a new definition of learning, it is important that we recognize a new view of the brain:

- The brain is by nature a magnificent pattern-detecting apparatus, even in the early years.
- Pattern detection and identification involve both features and relationships, processes that are greatly speeded up by the use of clues and a categorizing down procedure. (i.e., round ears or barks . . . not a house cat).
- Negative clues play an essential role.
- The brain uses clues in a probabilistic fashion, not by digital "adding up" of clues.
- Pattern recognition depends heavily on the experience one brings to a situation.
- Children must often revise the patterns they have extracted, to accommodate new experience.

Translating Brain Research into Action Using the Nine Bodybrain-Compatible Elements

Pattern seeking is the bodybrain partnership's way of making meaning of our world. The early phase of this process is detecting the existence of a pattern and then, through more experience with the concept or skill, coming to understand that pattern by exploring it and its uses to make sure that we understand it correctly and fully. The nine bodybrain-compatible elements will help you help your students to perceive and understand patterns in the curriculum and in their lives.

Although memorization does have a role in learning, it should have a minor one. As Frank Smith and Leslie Hart both affirm, *understanding takes care of learning.* ***Things that are understood and used are readily retained in long-term memory.*** Memorization is generally used as a teaching/learning tool only when there is no discernible meaning to the learner such as the order of the alphabet or when fast, automatic repetition is needed as with the multiplication tables.

Bodybrain-Compatible Elements

- *Meaningful Content*
- *Movement*
- *Enriched Environment*
- *Adequate Time*
- *Immediate Feedback*
- *Mastery*
- *Absence of Threat/ Nurturing Reflective Thinking*
- *Choices*
- *Collaboration*

The most critical job for a teacher is making learning meaningful for students. That being the case, teachers must go about curriculum development and choosing instructional strategies with a primary goal in mind: enhancing students' capacity to perceive and understand patterns.

The bodybrain-compatible elements in this chapter are discussed in the following order: meaningful content, movement, enriched environment, adequate time, immediate feedback, mastery, absence of threat/nurturing reflective thinking, choices, and collaboration.

Meaningful Content

Meaningfulness, like beauty, is in the eye of the beholder. But there are several things that teachers can do to increase the likelihood that students will perceive something as meaningful.

State Key Points As Concepts, Not Factoids

First, state what is to be learned as concepts (or significant knowledge directly linked to and necessary to support the concepts) rather than as factoids. Factoids have few attributes that give a sense of pattern. For example, "In 1492, Columbus sailed the ocean blue." Although catchy and cute, there is little for the brain to work on in terms of meaningfulness. This is a statement that only rote learning could lock into long-term memory.[15]

On the other hand, a concept is a rich collection of attributes that can provide a sense of pattern. For example: "Interactions among animals and plants to meet the need for food within a habitat are called a 'food chain' or 'food web'."

Rote memory is not needed here. In this conceptual statement, virtually every noun and verb is a pattern, each of which, with the possible exception of "habitat," is a pattern already familiar to students. Prior experience that can be pulled forward to help the students learn new content is a powerful ally. Furthermore, this concept allows students to place the information in a context they care about, e.g, their family and/or classroom pet(s), their favorite zoo animal, a local endangered animal, and so forth. (For a discussion of key points, see Chapter 14.)

Place Inquiries in Real-World Contexts

Second, for concepts or skills with which students have little or no prior experience, place the concept or skill to be learned in a real-world context. Develop inquiries that ask students to use the concept or skill in real-life situations. This heightens the sense of usefulness, an important trigger for the brain in transferring information to long-term memory.

For example: "A system is a collection of things and processes (and often people) that interact to perform some function. To study a system, one must define its boundaries." In this conceptual key point, every noun and verb is a pattern with which students are familiar. But, when put together in the above sentence, students may initially have no idea what is meant. However, when the concept is illustrated using first a bicycle and then one's school (transportation system, food system, classroom system and so on), the pattern becomes memorably clear and readily transferrable.

Similarly, few high school sophomores are innately interested in geometry but there are many who would be interested to learn how it applies to taking the best angle to run down and tackle a ball carrier, reading a map, driving a car, plotting the correct angle for a pool shot, and so forth.

Be Realistic

Third, when under the pressure of ever higher expectations, be realistic. Don't assume that because a concept is assigned to your grade level, it can be made understandable to students at your grade level. Some patterns require simultaneous attention to numerous variables before the intended pattern can emerge. Many such ideas must be considered age-inappropriate.[16] For example, the chemical processes of photosynthesis for sixth graders, tectonic plate movement as a cause of earthquakes for third graders. For more information about age-appropriateness, see *Thinking and Learning: Matching: Matching Developmental Stages with Curriculum and Instruction* by Lawrence F. Lowery.

Input Is Essential for Pattern Development

In Hart's view of learning, *input* is a key factor. "Input is critically important in any kind of learning situation, whoever the learner and whatever is to be learned. The process of learning is the extraction, from confusion, of meaningful patterns. Input is *the raw material* of that confusion, what is perceived through the senses by the individual that bears on that particular pattern in any way."[17]

By way of example, Hart recounts how a suburban teenager might go about learning the concept of *city*:[18]

> "Think of a 13-year-old suburban male who as yet has no clear concept of what is meant by city, although his teachers, his texts, and other sources have often presented that term. It easily can seem incredible to adults that children or adults less experienced in some specific area do not grasp a pattern that is already so familiar to those who already understand it. Once we have done the pattern extraction—a gradual process—and melded the concept into our collection of patterns, it seems so obvious that we have trouble putting ourselves into the brain of someone who has not acquired that pattern!
>
> But how could this 13-year-old come to understand the main connotations of city? If he is told in school that a city is a place where many people live close together, he may fail to see why his suburb (or at least those denser parts of it) is not a city. If he has contact with commuters, he may assume that city means Boston or St. Louis or Los Angeles, or whatever city his community is near. If

he visits that city occasionally, he may be impressed by traffic, noise, many stores, busy sidewalks, bridges, tall buildings, apartments, or development houses—yet a visit to another city may present quite different features, such as zoo, museum, or historic places. Going to the downtown part of a nearby suburb may impress him as being to a city, since he experiences crowded sidewalks, many stores, movie houses, considerable dirt, and apparent crowding—yet if he refers to this place, technically a village, as city he may be corrected or receive some negative feedback, such as being tolerantly laughed at.

It seems simple enough to tell him what city means. But it isn't simple, when we get down to trying it. A dictionary may say something like "a closely settled place of significant size," or "a chartered, incorporated municipality," but such definitions simply introduce new questions. With little effort, the boy can learn by rote a "right answer" to give in school but that hardly amounts to pattern extraction. It may function more as a cover-up answer to conceal uncertainty or lack of insight. The distress of teachers who by accident discover that students able to give "correct" answers actually don't understand the topic at all has long been familiar. Most adults, too, experience chastening moments when by some circumstance they discover that conventional right answers are like thin ice over a deep lake of ignorance or misconception. From personal and professional experience, educators have long been aware that "telling" methods can prove extremely ineffective in instruction.[19] Despite much evidence to the contrary, they are heavily used in conventional teaching."

The bottom line here according to Hart is that "words fail to convey much meaning except as the hearer already has experience and extracted patterns that give meaning to the words. Consider two statements. A stock broker: "If you sell a security to establish a loss, you just wait 30 days to buy it back or it will be viewed as a wash sale but the waiting period doesn't apply to gains." Or, a musician, "Since the B-flat clarinet is a transposing instrument, the note you play from the written music will actually sound a full tone lower." These are perfectly understandable statements if we bring prior experience to bear.

We must accept that words convey only limited meaning and that if our students lack relevant prior experience, we must rely on input from the real setting. Hearing speech intelligibly demands bringing information to the situation.[20] Even in social conversation, a comment or question off the subject usually produces a "Huh?" response until the new topic is settled on.

As Hart says, "While input via telling or lecture may be the most common and usually the easiest to provide in the classroom, it can prove ludicrously ineffective, even in supposedly simple situations."[21] The best environment for detecting and understanding patterns is to see them in their real-world context.

The power of real-world examples can't be overestimated. For example, the idea of 3/4 becomes clear only when it is recognized and used in multiple contexts such as the following:

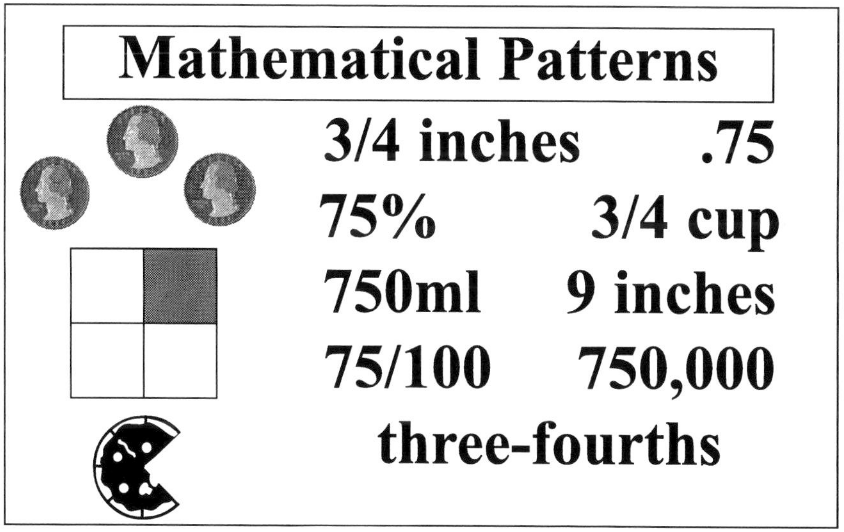
Mathematical Patterns
3/4 inches
.75
75%
3/4 cup
750ml
9 inches
75/100
750,000
three-fourths

USING *MEANINGFUL CONTENT* TO ENHANCE PATTERN SEEKING

Curriculum Development

- Because meaningfulness is in the eyes of the beholder, expect that your students' perceptions of what is meaningful will likely differ from yours. Thus, don't expect to start where you want students to end up. In other words, if a concept is substantive, don't begin teaching it in the form you want them to remember it, e.g., E=mc2. If you do, you will force students into memorization as a coping strategy rather than allowing them to construct their own understandings. Therefore, make sure that your curriculum has starting points that can reasonably bridge students' prior experience/knowledge to current sensory input to understanding the concept or skill. For example, include in the statement of the key point examples of settings or uses that students can recognize from their daily experiences. Include common objects as examples such as a multi-speed bicycle to evoke students' prior knowledge about chains (only as strong as its weakest link, potential to connect to multiple gears large and small) as a precursor to learning about the food chain/web.

- Teach students to become aware of how they know what they know. Help them become conscious of how their brain seeks patterns in an attempt to create meaning. Also help them avoid "jumping to conclusions" based on a couple of clues that may be true but not key by becoming sensitive to negative clues. Create activities such as playing a modified version of the old TV game show, "I Can Name That Tune in . . . Notes." Instead of notes, use the attributes of a concept or skill.

USING *MEANINGFUL CONTENT* TO ENHANCE PATTERN SEEKING

Instructional Strategies

- Ensure massive amounts of sensory input through all 19 senses. Schedule frequent *being there* field studies—early in students' study of the concepts/skills described in the key points, at the end, and in between.

- Make the classroom a complete immersion experience for the *being there* location your curriculum is based on.

- Invite guest speakers that will present their experiences using *hands on of the real thing*. Insist that students include examples of their concepts/skills from their experiences.

- Deliberately use collaboration as a way of increasing input and use of concepts and skills.

- Have at least 100 resources related to the current topic of study available in the room—real things, models, diagrams, blueprints, sketches, and art objects, as well as books, magazines, multimedia, and the Internet.

- Use analytical tools that help students key in on important attributes of a concept or skill. For example, T-charts that compare what something is and what it is not, Venn diagrams that compare similarities and differences between two items, and organizers that help students identify prior related experience (KWL charts that identify what we now think we know, want to know, and, afterwards, what we learned). For young children, dot-to-dot puzzles are useful to help them reveal visual attributes of things such as a frog or butterfly. (For more information on these organizers, see pp. 21.13 - 21.15 and 22.8 - 22.9)

Movement

Seeing firsthand how concepts and skills are used in real-world settings provides the richest possible environment for learning, especially when learning something new. Why? Because things in use have movement and motion to them. Who, what, why, and how are all attention-getting patterns. When the who becomes "I," patterns become richer, more engaging.

Furthermore, as discussed in Chapter 2, movement activates different areas of the brain and body, thus increasing the likelihood of retrieval later on. Many believe that some forms of memory, especially those associated with high emotional states, are stored in the body; others that movements of the body awaken memories that were being used when the memory was wired into long-term memory. In either case, the lesson for classroom teachers is that we *must* make the process of learning about concepts and skills mirror the ways those concepts and skills are used in real-world settings.

USING *MOVEMENT* TO ENHANCE PATTERN SEEKING

Curriculum Development

- Before you begin to write key points and inquiries, go experience how the concepts and skills are *used* in the real world. Practice them and the movements inherent in them until you have mastered them. Then, look around for other settings these same skills are used in, particularly settings/locations that students experience, e.g., a mall, home, school, neighborhood. Your curriculum should require the *use* of concepts and skills.

USING *MOVEMENT* TO ENHANCE PATTERN SEEKING

Curriculum Development (continued)

- Make your curriculum an experience in ***doing***, not just reading about or hearing about.
  - Include in the statement of the key point examples of settings or uses that students can recognize from their daily experiences.
  - State your key points conceptually; eliminate factoids.
  - Develop inquiries that require application of concepts and skills to students' prior experiences and to other real-life situations so that students can readily understand what the concept/ skill is, why it's important, and how and when to use it.
- Develop, and involve students in developing, movements to mimic or act out the key attributes of the patterns within the concept or skill you are teaching. Include these in your direct instruction and in inquiries.
- When writing inquiries, first develop those that address bodily-kinesthetic intelligence and Bloom's taxonomy levels of application and analysis.
- When writing inquiries for linguistic intelligence, add movement through music, dance, rhythm (such as rap), and bodily-kinesthetic mnemonics.
- When developing immersion experiences, include role playing of the actions of people working and conducting commerce at your *being there* locations. Go for richness; focus on the most important attributes of the patterns of the concepts/skills in the key point.

USING *MOVEMENT* TO ENHANCE PATTERN SEEKING

Instructional Strategies

- In direct instruction, always address the questions of a journalist – who, what, when, where, how, and why in the real world – for the concept or skill you are teaching. Emphasize the how and why – the movement of how used and why.
- When selecting inquiries to follow up on direct instruction, lead with bodily-kinesthetic inquiries and those spatial and musical inquiries that call for movement. As with young children, the first step in understanding and using what we learn is often through mimicking.
- Because the movement centers of the brain are also responsible for sequencing thought, encourage students to create and use movements that mimic the sequence, steps, or actions of the concept/skill when in use. For example, reenactments of events or processes (a famous historical event such as the Boston Tea Party or the blood/oxygen flow through heart and lungs), miming (the travails of the Westward Movement), bodily movements that mimic shapes or actions (letters of the alphabet or a butterfly emerging from its cocoon), and hand jives (to represent the steps in computing a long division problem).

Enriched Environment

The pattern-seeking penchant of the brain is in diametric opposition to the assumptions underlying our traditional curriculum – its structure and content. Several erroneous assumptions are:

- Small, isolated pieces automatically add up to large pictures of real life
- The small, isolated pieces provide focus for the brain, making them easier to learn, especially for slow or limited ability students
- Study of "subjects" explains the world to students

When these small pieces are presented through the sparse sensory input of lecture and textbooks/worksheets, pattern-seeking is paralyzed for lack of input and learning grinds to a halt.

> **Sensory Input**
>
> *In reality, nothing could be more unfair than giving two very different brains—and no two brains are alike—the same input and expecting the outcome to be the same. It's not only unfair, it's cruel.*

Consequently, conceptual curriculum in an enriched environment is not a luxury, it is a necessity. Pattern seeking is only possible when there is sufficient sensory input for the learner's brain to sift for patterns. And, very importantly, prior experience, existing mental wiring, and temperament guarantee that what one student sees as a pattern will remain invisible or a tangle of confusion to another. Thus, "Different Strokes for Different Folks" is more than that title of a TV sitcom. In the realm of the brain, it is utter truth. An enriched environment – *being there experiences, immersion, and hands on of the real thing* – provides something for everyone, ensuring that every student can succeed in understanding the concept or skill at hand. ***When input for a concept or skill is rich and varied, all learners can arrive at an understanding of the pattern to be learned.***

USING *ENRICHED ENVIRONMENT* TO ENHANCE PATTERN SEEKING

Curriculum Development

- Knowing there is a fine line between an enriched environment and a cluttered environment, make sure you have finished writing your key points and inquiries before you begin to gather resources to create an enriched environment. Once you know exactly what you want your students to understand and how you will have them use what they understand, be selective. Remove input about other topics from the room. Then, for each key point and inquiry, plan your input in descending order: first being there, then immersion, then hands on of the real thing, and so on. If possible, eliminate hands on of representational items in favor of the above three kinds of input. Include secondhand and symbolic input last; plan to use them during the latter stages of Step One of Learning—Pattern-Seeking.

USING *ENRICHED ENVIRONMENT* TO ENHANCE PATTERN SEEKING

Instructional Strategies

- Select materials and other resources appropriate to the lesson that provide contrasting points of view so that the attributes of issues become clear through their comparison with each other, such as that of the polluter and of the family whose child developed cancer, land use through the eyes of the cattleman and the farmer.
- Include resource people, preferably from the *being there* locations upon which your curriculum is based. Work with them in advance so they understand what students have done prior to their coming and what new input would be most valuable.
- Use student-generated role playing and skits as formats for students to demonstrate the attributes of a concept/skill they are learning to use. Follow up these presentations with a discussion of what attributes of the concept/skill were demonstrated. Add any new ones to KWL chart and correct any misconceptions.

Adequate Time

Just as every brain is different, so is each student's approach to detecting patterns and making meaning. So, too, is the amount of time needed.

Factors that directly affect the amount of time students need to detect patterns and construct their own meaning are:

- Prior experience
- Whether the concept/skill is studied in its real-life context
- The kind and amount of input involves an intelligence of strength (see discussion of the multiple intelligences in Chapter 3)
- The wiring of the learner's brain

Regardless of why a student may need more time, the critical point is that we must provide it. To close the grade book on a student because he/she didn't master something in the allotted time is discrimination of the worst kind. The implicit message is that if you aren't like everyone else, you will be cut off and abandoned. In such an environment the focus is not on mastery but on the lock-step demands of bureaucracy.

In the ITI classroom, the "grade book" is held open until the end of the year. Demonstration of mastery the last day of school is as good as mastery the first day the key point is studied.

But we're getting ahead of ourselves here. Step One of Learning is pattern-seeking, constructing meaning, *understanding* the concept or skill described in the key point.

USING *ADEQUATE TIME* TO ENHANCE PATTERN SEEKING

Curriculum Development

- Review the curriculum you have planned for your monthly components and weekly topics. Do you have more than students can come to understand and learn to apply, not just get 80% on a pop quiz? If so, start cutting back. Be realistic! Resist the political pressures to "cover" what looks good (for more information about monthly components and weekly topics, see Chapter 18).
- To help you cut back, use the principle of "selective abandonment." Put at the end of your curriculum those things you believe are least important for students to understand and be able to apply. Chief among these are factoids that won't affect their lives five or ten years from now. Then, if you run out of time—and who doesn't!—you will have given students the gift of what will most serve them later in life.
- Create time by stating your curriculum as conceptually as possible and using examples of how that concept is used in contexts that students experience in their daily life. For example, science is everywhere around us and is directly experienceable; the fundamental concepts in social studies have their parallel wherever people congregate. (However, concepts in social studies are not as hands on as science; also, for young children, because they've grown up with something doesn't mean it's any easier to see than water is for a fish.)

USING *ADEQUATE TIME* TO ENHANCE PATTERN SEEKING

Instructional Strategies

- Just as there is a silent period before vocalization when learning another language, so there is a quiet period when students are learning a new concept or skill. Don't rush through such silences or periods of delayed responses. Allow students time intrapersonally to observe and sift through what they already know and how this new concept/skill relates to what they already understand and can do (the patterns and the interrelationships among the patterns). Allow them time to explore the patterns involved and to arrive at their own understandings—about how things work, what makes things tick, why they might be important to them. Allow time for personal exploration through sketching or diagramming/graphing/mindmapping the patterns they see and how they interrelate with other patterns. Allow interpersonal time to try out what they understand, to correct and/or add to what they understand with nonjudgmental, supportive peers. Only then ask for personal performances that will be "graded" or critiqued by an audience. New understandings are not layered into the brain as separate things; they are integrated into prior understandings or patterns.

- Take time to plan for and effectively teach a concept or skill the first time. Effective first teaching is a huge time saver but you must invest time up front.

USING *ADEQUATE TIME* TO ENHANCE PATTERN SEEKING

Instructional Strategies (continued)

- Deep understanding comes from identifying attributes of things and their uses and coming to understanding interrelationships among them. Such mental work requires rewiring and new wiring—physiological tasks of the brain that require time and processing of new input. This requires time.

- Revisit the *being there* location at least once or twice between the initial and culminating visits. Assign inquiries to be completed, including adding to their KWL chart and answering questions such as "How do you know that _______?" and "Where else would you find this occurring and why?"

Immediate Feedback

Leslie Hart points out that the most difficult thing for a brain to do is unlearn something. We're all familiar with this one. Is it *maintanence* or *maintainence* or *maintenance?*And every time we have to spell the word, all three choices pop up with competing intensity? Why? Because each time they simultaneously come to mind as options, the wiring of the three is equally reinforced. Or, how about the < and > signs. Is the number off the pointed end the smaller? Or does it depend on the order in which you say them? Or, hang it, I don't know! And you have trouble learning it because the confusion is wired in just as strongly as the right answer each time you try to recall which of the options is the correct one.

The number one purpose of immediate feedback is to prevent this kind of mental sputtering. Give feedback to students before they begin to practice something incorrectly or incompletely. Immediate feedback helps ensure that students come to a full and accurate understanding of a skill or concept—that they discover the critical attributes and understand how they fit together. This is especially important when students begin to integrate new experiences with prior learnings. For example, the videotape *A Private Universe*[22] provides an astounding example of how childhood experiences with heat (the closer you get, the hotter it becomes) override lecture and textbook. As the interviews with graduating Harvard students illustrate, even course work in advanced planetary motion can fail to dispel the assumption put together in childhood—that summers are hot because the earth gets closer to the sun.

The recent emphasis on effective first teaching and ensuring that students learn something correctly and thoroughly the first time is right on track.

USING *IMMEDIATE FEEDBACK* TO ENHANCE PATTERN SEEKING

Curriculum Development Guidelines

- Build checking for accuracy of understanding and performance—by Learning Club, partners, and self—into inquiries.
- Develop inquiries that require students to develop and use their own internal voice as they go through the two steps in learning—asking questions, checking their understanding, insisting upon looking for ways a concept or skill can be used in the real world, and so forth.
- Include in inquiries the criteria to be used in assessing performance or where such criteria exist.
- If students' understanding or performance is inaccurate, incomplete, or not yet wired into long-term memory, provide additional inquiries applying the same concept or skill until mastery occurs. Invite students who have reached an accurate and complete understanding of the concept or skill to write additional inquiries that might help create an "aha" for classmates. Have students review each other's inquiries using the 3Cs of Assessment (see pp. 16.6-16.7) as they are developing them and immediately upon their completion.
- Use the language of pattern-seeking and program-building in inquiries so that students may assess their understanding and performance along the continuum of learning as a two-step process—pattern seeking to make meaning and program building to use what they understand.

USING *IMMEDIATE FEEDBACK* TO ENHANCE PATTERN SEEKING

Instructional Strategies

- Develop a repertoire of ways you can provide students with immediate feedback and use them often:
  - Brief "talk with your neighbor" breaks during presentations to reflect on a question or check for understanding about something just presented
  - "Walk abouts"—opportunities to observe/listen/ask questions as students work collaborative
  - Journal writing assignments asking students to reflect on what they've just learned and how they might use it in their lives now and in the future
  - Self-check procedures of many kinds, such as rubrics, answer sheets, self-developed criteria
  - Creating tasks to be completed while visiting resource person is still available to give feedback.
- Develop a repertoire of ways classmates can provide each other with immediate feedback and use them often:
  - Use of rubrics by Learning Club members and study partners to check each other's work immediately (thereby eliminating overnight grading by teachers)
  - "Think-pair-share," reflective thinking (before and after an activity), and other similar cooperative learning strategies[23]
  - Peer review and assessment; cross-age buddies.
- Develop opportunities for immediate feedback outside the classroom and use them frequently through:
  - Developing legitimate audiences who hold real-world expectations for work by students
  - Using inquiries during *being there* study trips that require students to compare notes and check for accuracy.

Mastery

Given the ITI definition of learning as a two-step process—pattern-seeking for understanding and program-building for using what we understand—mastery must also be examined in these two steps because the ability to use what is understood begins with and builds upon how correct, complete, and comprehensive that understanding is.

When we become expert in a field, we know when we don't know something. When new to a field, a little bit of knowledge seems like great stuff and we often launch off with false certainty that we can do something. This is the source of the expression, "Taking off half cocked" or "Hell bent for leather" or "He's going fast to nowhere" and so forth. We've all been there. We thought we understood what to do and how to do it but once we got into it, disaster struck! We were humbled into an awareness that we knew only a fraction of what we needed to know.

Mastery, a Habit of Mind

Checking for mastery of understanding, the equivalent of looking before leaping, is an important habit of mind for students to develop. And it comes with two corner stones: a notable lack of arrogance that we know all that needs to be known and the self-confidence that we are capable of learning what we need to know.

Teachers nurture these two qualities by providing body-brain-compatible learning experiences. Arrogance about surface knowledge is counteracted by providing curriculum that explores concepts in depth and demands high levels of skill performance. Confidence in ability to learn blossoms in an atmosphere of success at learning—an environment that has high but appropriate expectations, that grades on mastered/not yet mastered, that provides plenty of learning support from both teacher and peers, and that holds the grade book open for mastery any time during the school year.

High But Appropriate Expectations

The clamor for higher expectations is a double-edged sword. Without question, the contribution of K-12 schooling to students' pool of knowledge and skills is inexcusably low. Yet the raising of the bar often results in state standards written by politicians, not educators. The results would be laughable if not so detrimental to students. For example, state curriculum standards from a southeastern state expects third graders to grasp an introduction to atomic fusion. Another led second graders to ponder the Preamble of the Constitution of the United States.

We cannot expect mastery of understanding of things that students' brains are incapable of processing due to the stage of their development—development that unfolds with age. Understandable curriculum—as compared to memorizable curriculum—is a must if we are to expect mastery. (For a discussion of age-appropriateness, see Appendix C.)

USING *MASTERY* TO ENHANCE PATTERN SEEKING

Curriculum Development Guidelines

- Make sure that the curriculum you present to students is in fact "getable" or understandable by children their age. If not, mastery is not possible. (If in doubt, see *Thinking and Learning: Matching Developmental Stages with Curriculum and Instruction* by Larry Lowery.)
- Embed the curriculum in *being there* experiences, preferably at real-life locations where people work and conduct commerce or where mother nature is at her most undisturbed. Make these experiences action-oriented rather than look and hear events. Seeing concepts and skills used by real people in real life settings makes recognition of patterns and their attributes much easier for students. It also increases motivation to learn and master.
- Include observation skills in your curriculum and teach students the verbal skills to report to themselves and others what they are witnessing. For example, see the discussion about using structure words to help students wire their brains for more effective language processing and comprehension in *Visualizing and Verbalizing for Improved Language Comprehension* by Nanci Bell. Better observation leads to more accurate and complete identification of the attributes of a thing, action, concept, or skill and thus a more comprehensive and in-depth degree of understanding.

USING *MASTERY* TO ENHANCE PATTERN SEEKING

Instructional Strategies

- Front load initial instruction with a wide variety of sensory input—*being there,* immersion, and hands-on-of-the-real thing. Stop frequently to provide students opportunities to experience and share observations; check frequently for accuracy and completeness of understanding.

- Have students use visual organizers for notetaking, such as KWL (*w*hat students know before you start, what they *w*ant to know, and later what they have *l*earned), mindmaps to show multiple relationships, Venn diagrams to compare attributes, and so forth, rather than the standard outline format. Have students compare their notes within their Learning Club, checking for accuracy and completeness, and resolving any differences in pattern-seeking before you move on. If more than one group has the same difference in understanding, bring the issue to the whole class. Tease out what previous learnings are interfering with correct understanding of the current concept or skill and then reteach by giving correct information about both prior and current concepts/skills. Then, recheck for understanding. Ask students, grades three and up, to write inquiries that would help them understand the differences between prior and current concepts. Select the best ones and allow students to choose which one or two they will complete.

Absence of Threat/Nurturing Reflective Thinking

The complaint du jour of 21st century living seems to be "I'm too busy to think." We're too busy to do anything but react. For fight-flight circumstances, this is workable. But not for academic learning.

Our classroom environments must not only be safe, they must also show students how to slow themselves down enough to be reflective. Why? Because pattern recognition depends heavily upon bringing together prior experiences with current input. To do so, students must be able to take time to put together several possible lines of inquiry rather than blurting out a guess. This requires uninterrupted time for sustained reflection.

USING *REFLECTIVE THINKING* TO ENHANCE PATTERN SEEKING

Curriculum Development

- Teach students the elements of Mihaly Csikszentmihalyi's "flow" experience[24] as applied to optimal learning. Help students recognize how to adjust their state of mind and/or learning environment so that they are in the best possible frame of mind for learning and remembering.
- Allow students to propose alternative ways of approaching a concept or skill that "makes more sense to them" and choice of additional situations for applying what they are learning, e.g., Freeze Frame.

USING *REFLECTIVE THINKING* TO ENHANCE PATTERN SEEKING

Instructional Strategies

- During whole-class instruction
  - –Eliminate distractions
  - –Provide a peaceful yet businesslike atmosphere with background music, non-vocal with 50-60 beats per minute
  - –Provide wait time
  - –Allow students to volunteer an answer rather than worry about being called on
  - –Provide reflective time before journal writing.
- During collaborative work
  - –Build in time for students to jot down their own thoughts before joining a brainstorming or discussion session
  - –Teach group leaders to insist on wait time when questions are posed to the group
  - –Use collaborative strategies such as think-pair-share and three-before-me.
- Provide a range of individual performance formats such as individual study projects, inquiries for personal choice, and journal writing.
- Invite students to learn to nurture the environmental elements that produce their own "flow" experiences.

Choices

Unless our goal is blind uniformity of both process and outcome, there is no justifiable reason for insisting on only one way of doing something. For example, we teach and accept only one algorithm (a mathematical term for pattern) for multiplication when there are more than 16 that do the job just as well. And likewise for long division, addition, and on and on.

As each brain is wired differently due to genetics, environment, and prior experiences, we should allow students to choose the patterns for solving a problem that work best for them while still producing accurate answers and useful products. Demanding that a brain operate in a specific way is the quickest way to frustration and a major disruption to reflective thinking.

USING *CHOICES* TO ENHANCE PATTERN SEEKING

Curriculum Guidelines

- Teach students that there are usually multiple ways to go about solving problems. Provide several examples and then let them devise others. Once you determine that the child has a pattern that they prefer—and that unfailingly produces correct answers—stop teaching other ways/patterns, even if they are the traditional ones.[25] Accept their method/pattern if it consistently gives them correct answers. As the saying goes, "If it ain't broke, don't fix it." Examples include many areas of mathematics such as multiplication, division, subtraction, addition, and percentages and areas of language arts such as decoding and spelling.

USING *CHOICES* TO ENHANCE PATTERN SEEKING

Instructional Strategies

- The world outside of school doesn't offer simplistic options such as true or false, *a* or *b*. Encourage students to begin to develop their own alternatives. When only one option is presented and not well understood, students must resort to memorization. When several patterns are examined and are understood well enough to make a choice among them, students needn't resort to memorization; learning is effortless, absorbed in the act of making meaning.
- When teaching a concept or skill, always illustrate several ways it can be used and give several examples of what it is not. Such attributes assist pattern seeking and meaning making by clarifying the pattern and making it more specific. Also, the fuller their sense of the pattern, the more likely they are to recognize it in their prior experiences.

Collaboration

A close-knit collaborative group such as a Learning Club is an ideal medium for pattern seeking. If you have constructed your Learning Clubs to ensure a range of intelligences (see Chapter 3), personality preferences (see Appendix C), and interests, then you have supplied your students with a veritable gold mine of patterns. Working closely with people representing such diversity in ways of thinking, organizing, carrying out tasks, and so forth opens a whole new vista on life—with new patterns come new possibilities. Collaboration is a powerful way to enrich the mental life of your students. It also encourages students to sharpen their strengths and learn the value of enhancing their undeveloped areas.

USING *COLLABORATION* TO ENHANCE PATTERN SEEKING

Curriculum Guidelines

- Teach students to look for patterns. Model it in your questioning strategies and when leading approaches to solving problems and producing products.
- Teach them the patterns in thinking and behavior in the multiple intelligences, personality preferences, and their own habits of mind.

Instructional Strategies

- Ask students to use reflective thinking frequently by having them discuss if and how their Learning Club's process helped them learn the content and reach social and personal goals in the process. Companion questions include what they have learned from answering these questions and what they could have done differently to make their group process more effective.
  Also ask such questions of the class as a whole; have students reflect, verbally and in their journals, on what they've learned.
- Incorporate the terms "patterns" and "attributes of a pattern" into your direct instruction and assessment questions. Help make students aware of the pattern-seeking operation of their brain.

Notes

1 With each succeeding book he wrote about how the brain learns, Leslie Hart continued synthesizing his conceptualization of the two fundamental brain concepts: pattern detection, addressed in this chapter, and program building, described in Chapter 6. His initial definition was simple and to the point:

> The process of learning is the extraction, from confusion, of meaningful patterns
>
> **and**
>
> Learning is the acquisition of useful programs.

The revised edition of his book takes yet another step forward, defining learning as a two-step process—step one involves input, step two involves output. Each step is in turn divided into two stages.

- Part one : **Input stage: Pattern detection** consists of first identifying or recognizing the pattern and, secondly, making meaning of the pattern including its relationship to other patterns.

and

- Part two: **Output stage: Program building** consists of learning to apply what is learned, at first experimentally and consciously, and then, after practice and wiring it up into long-term memory, applying what is learned with the almost automatic ease and skill of the expert.

This conceptualization of learning is an extremely important contribution to the field of learning because it is comprehensive enough to cover the wide range of practicalities that teachers, administrators, and parents face on a daily basis—from establishing curriculum to instruction to assessment.

For example, if we use Hart's two-step definition of learning when we examine current standardized testing instruments, we see that the ubiquitous multiple choice and true-false items call for no more than identification of a pattern (this choice *sounds* more familiar than that choice). *Understanding* the pattern is not necessary. Knowing how to use the information is well beyond the scope of the test and long-term memory of how to use it isn't even an issue.

This fuller, more comprehensive view of learning provides a set of lenses for examining all issues of curriculum, instruction, and assessment. It also provides a useful perspective when considering resource allocation and the success of improvement efforts.

See Leslie A. Hart, *Human Brain and Human Learning, Updated* (Covington, Washington: Books for Educators, 1999).

This shift from understanding (pattern seeking) to program building is reflected in Elkhonon Goldberg's discussion of learning as a "transition from novelty to routinization [right brain to left brain] . . . the universal cycle of our inner world." He describes a "cognitive continuum, a gradient." See Elkhonon Goldberg, *The Executive Brain: Frontal Lobes and the Civilized Mind* (Oxford: Oxford University Press, 2001), xii and 44. According to Goldberg, "At an early stage of every learning process the organism is faced with 'novelty,' and the end stage of the learning process can be thought of as 'routinization', " the result of the emergence of an effective solution(s). (See page 44.) This shift of the locus of cognitive control from the right to the left hemisphere occurs on many time scales: from minutes to hours to years and decades. (See page 52.)

Also, Herbert Simon, Nobel Prize-winning psychologist, believes that learning involves the accumulation of easy-to-recognize patterns of all kinds. See Herbert Simon, *The Sciences of the Artificial* (Cambridge, MA: MIT Press, 1996).

Regarding Hart's stipulation that programs, once learned, can be run off almost automatically, Goldberg adds: "The majority of our mental processes are effortless and automatic, conducted, as it were, on autopilot. By contrast, the effortful and consciously controlled cognitive tasks represent only a minor portion of our mental life." (*The Executive Brain*, 54).

Pattern recognition is described in Goldberg's new book, *The Wisdom Paradox* (85). By "pattern recognition" we mean the organism's ability to recognize a new object or a new problem as a member of an already familiar class of objects or problems. The capacity for pattern recognition is fundamental to our mental world. Without this ability, every object and every problem would be a totally de novo encounter and we would be unable to bring any of our prior experience to bear on how we deal with these objects or problems.

2 Hart, *Human Brain and Human Learning*, 133.

3 Ibid., 387.

4 Ibid., 147.

See Diane Ackerman, *An Alchemy of the Mind*, (New York: Scribner, 2004), 54–55. The brain is a pattern-mad supposing machine. It maps the known world. Given just a little stimuli it predicts the probable. When information abounds, it recognizes familiar patterns and acts with conviction. If there's not much for the senses to report, the brain imagines the rest.

Pattern pleases us, rewards a mind seduced and yet exhausted by complexity. We crave pattern and, not surprisingly, find it all around us, in petals, sand dunes, pinecones, and contrails. We imagine it when we look at clouds and driftwood; we create and leave it everywhere like tracks.

5 Hart, *Human Brain and Human Learning*, 142.

6 Quoted by David B. Brown in "Towards a Communication Theory," *Teachers College Record*, May 1977, 453.

7 See *The Human Situation* (Lectures at Santa Barbara, 1959), Pierro Ferrucci, ed. (New York: Harper & Row), 173. Also compare George A. Kelley, *A Theory of Personality* (New York: W. W. Norton, 1963): "Man looks at his world through transparent patterns or templates which he creates and then attempts to fit over the realities of which the world is composed" (17).

8 That the brain learns by detecting patterns among incoming sensory data has been amply confirmed by numerous brain researchers since Hart first published *Human Brain and Human Learning* in 1983. See Stanley I. Greenspan with Beryl Lieff Benderly, *The Growth of the Mind and the Endangered Origins of Intelligence* (New York: Addison-Wesley Publishing Company, 1997), 114 and Candace B. Pert, *Molecules of Emotion: Why You Feel the Way You Feel* (New York: Scribner, 1997), 147; John J. Ratey, *A User's Guide to the Brain: Perception, Attention, and the Four Theaters of the Brain* (New York: Pantheon Books, 2001); and Elkohon Goldberg, *Wisdom Paradox*.

From Goldberg's new book, *The Wisdom Paradox: How Your Mind Can Grow Stronger as Your Brain Grows Older*, 88, we already know the capacity for pattern formation and pattern recognition is not unique to humans. It is shared by every other species capable of learning. What sets us apart as humans is the powerful capacity for transmitting the repertoire of theses patterns from individual to individual and from generation to generation through culture.

9 Alphonse Bertillon (1853-1914) devised an elaborate system for positively identifying individuals in spite of their variety. It was intended primarily for criminal justice purposes. Later, fingerprinting proved far simpler but the system is still used by physical anthropologists.

10 John B. Carroll, speaking of the mature reader, suggests that it may be true, "astounding as it may seem, that reading is based upon a capability of instantly recognizing thousands or even tens of thousands of individual word patterns, almost as if words were Chinese characters not structured by an alphabetic principle." See *Theories of Learning and Instruction, 63d Yearbook of the National Society for the Study of Education* (Chicago: University

of Chicago Press, 1964), 341. For actual use of Chinese, see Paul Rozin and others, "American Children with Reading Problems Can Easily Learn to Read English Represented by Chinese Characters," in *Psycholinguistics and Reading*, Frank Smith, ed. (New York: Holt, Rinehart and Winston, 1973), Chapter 9.

We learn attributes of the neocortex memory from Jeff Hawkins, *On Intelligence*, (New York: Times Books, Henry Holt and Co., 2004), 69. The neocortex is not like a computer, parallel or otherwise. Instead of computing answers to problems the neocortex uses stored memories to solve problems and produce behavior. There are four attributes of neocortical memory:

• The noecortex stores sequences of patterns. You cannot tell me everything that happened all at once, no matter how quickly you or I listen. It is because the story is stored in your head in a sequential fashion and can only be recalled in the same sequence.

• The neocortex recalls patterns auto-associatively. An auto-associative memory system is one that can recall complete patterns when given only partial or distorted inputs. Inputs to the brain auto-associatively link to themselves, filling in the present, and auto-associatively link to what normally follows next. We call this chain of memories *thought*, and although its path is not deterministic, we are not fully in control of it either.

• The noecortex stores patterns in an Invariant form. Your brain holds an internal pattern. Memories are stored in a form that captures the essence of relationships, not the details of the moment. When you see, feel, or hear something, the cortex takes the detailed, highly specific input and converts it to an invariant form that is stored in memory. It is the invariant form of each new input pattern that it gets compared to. (The face of a long time friend, how to start a car, how you recognize a song, etc.)

• The neocortex stores patterns in a hierarchy. Rarely are the functions clearly delineated. Functionally they are arranged in a branching hierarchy. The lowest of the functional regions, the primary sensory areas, are where sensory information first arrives in the cortex. (44–45, 47)

You hear sound, see light, and feel pressure, but inside your brain there isn't any fundamental difference between these types of information. An action potential is an action potential. These momentary spikes are identical regardless of what originally caused them. All your brain knows is patterns. Your perceptions and knowledge about the world are built from these patterns. There's no light inside your head. It's dark in there. There's no sound entering your brain either. It's quiet inside. In fact, the brain is the only part of your body that has no senses itself. (56)

11 Much can be learned about the process of learning by observing how young children build their vocabulary and the knowledge of the world that that vocabulary represents. In going about this prodigious feat, children make great use of categorizing down. If something is at first not understandable, children, if unguided, rarely resort to repeated attempts at memorization of the original input or memorization of a definition. Instead, they move on, gulping in massive amounts of new input until they hit upon a kind of input that finally provides a recognizable pattern, triggering the "aha" response.

12 Just because the brain has stored a pattern for "door" does not mean that it has stored all of the attributes of the pattern called door in a single location. A truly startling quality of the brain is that it can access bits of information stored in different locations and array it to make sense, and do so with astonishing speed.

13 See Frank Smith, *Comprehension and Learning* (New York: Holt, Rinehart and Winston, 1975), 1. The "make sense" concept has been widely discussed by many brain researchers. Harry J. Jerison, for example, suggests that reality is "a creation of the brain, a model of a possible world that makes sense of the mass of information that reaches us through our various sensory (including motor feedback) systems." See *The Human Brain* (Englewood Cliffs, N. J.: Prentice Hall, 1977), 54.

14 This stage of language acquisition is familiar to many parents, teachers, and others who have contact with children. It has been

discussed by many psycholinguists. See, for example, James Britton, *The Teaching of English, 76th Yearbook of the National Society for the Study of Education* (Chicago: University of Chicago Press, 1977), 11.

15 Rote memory should be kept to a minimum; instead, focus on reaching an understanding via pattern seeking/meaning making. However, when rote memorization is necessary, use CUE—an acronym from the ITI model representing three methods which help ensure that students will remember. ***C*** stands for creative, such as use of skits or role playing or writing lyrics to a familiar tune. ***U*** stands for useful, such as having students make a connection to how a concept or skill is used in their lives. ***E*** stands for emotional, making an unforgettable emotional impact on students through the fun and adventure of a study trip, the sadness when animals die in oil spills, or the joy and deep satisfaction of making a contribution to others.

16 For a description of what makes concepts or skills age-appropriate, see Lawrence F. Lowery, *Thinking and Learning: Matching Developmental Stages with Curriculum and Instruction* (University of California, Berkeley, professor, Graduate School of Education and member of the board of directors for the Lawrence Hall of Science). Dr. Lowery also served as principal investigator for the FOSS project (Full Option Science Systems), developed under the auspices of the National Science Foundation and for the Equals Project (math for girls).

17 Hart, *Human Brain and Human Learning*, 223.

18 Ibid., 141-142.

19 The ITI Model expresses this concept by contrasting the typical input of the traditional classroom life (*second hand* and *symbolic*) and the input needed for fully brain-compatible learning (primarily *being there* and *immersion* when used as follow up to *being there*). The difference in the amount of sensory input, and thus learning, is enormous. Sensory input from *being there* and *immersion* experiences are especially important when learning something new. See Chapter 1.

20 Scientists investigating speech and listening to language have produced an impressive body of knowledge, much of it long established. Yet, apparently, it is all but unknown to most educators, who commonly refer to "auditory" and "listening" skills and similar ideas far off the mark. For an excellent discussion, see George A. Miller, *Language and Speech* (San Francisco: W. H. Freeman and Co., 1981), especially Chapter 6.

21 Hart, *Human Brain and Human Learning*, 134.

22 *A Private Universe* is a fascinating video illustrating the power of concepts generated by full sensory input as a child to override adult learning limited to lecture and reading. Harvard graduates are interviewed in their caps and gowns. The question "What makes for the seasons?" is answered the same by liberal arts students and those with science backgrounds, even including a course in advanced planetary motion—the earth gets closer to the sun in the summer (thus hotter) and farther away in the winter (and thus colder).

23 See *Cooperative Learning* by Spencer Kagan (San Clemente, CA: Kagan, 1994) and Kagan's *Smart Cards*.

24 See Mihaly Csikszentmilhalyi, *Flow: The Psychology of Optimal Experienc*e (New York: Harper, 1990).

25 The authors believe that our reading and math reforms have failed over the years because we have continue to insist that there is only one way to teach all students instead of finding a best way for individual students. For example, children that learn to read at age four and who can read and spell years ahead of their grade level, have discovered their own patterns for decoding and spelling. It is a disservice to inflict the standard phonics lessons on them. Doing so usually slows down their reading speed and often also diminishes their enjoyment of reading without providing any benefits. The more unconscious their system of pattern seeking, the more space they have in their conscious mental processing to deal with comprehension. On the other hand, students who haven't detected patterns for decoding that work do need

the standard phonics lessons. Pattern identification and understanding is as unique as each child's brain. And, it is far more powerful than our brief lessons can ever be. So, observe your students' pattern-seeking processes and outcome carefully. Complement them rather than force them.

Chapter 5: Program Building-Step Two of Learning

Our behavior, and that of our fellow human beings, has long been one of life's greater mysteries. Behavior—its building blocks and why specific building blocks are chosen at any one moment in time—must be understood if we are to create schools that foster real learning.

LEARNING IS A TWO-STEP PROCESS

- Detecting and understanding patterns—a process through which our brain creates meaning
- Developing meaningful mental programs to use what is understood and to store it in long-term memory—the capacity to use what is understood, first with assistance and then almost automatically

According to Hart, the key to understanding behavior is "the realization that we act very largely by programs . . . a fixed sequence for accomplishing some intended objective." In other words, to carry on activities, one must constantly select a program from among those stored in the brain and put it to use.[1]

Hart defines a *program* as:

"A sequence of steps or actions, intended to achieve some GOAL, which once built is stored in the brain and 'run off' repeatedly whenever needed to achieve the same goal, is perceived by the person. A program may be short, for example giving a nod to indicate 'yes,' or long, as in playing a piece on the piano which requires thousands of steps. A long program usually involves a series of shorter subprograms, and many parallel variations that permit choice to meet conditions of use. Many such programs are needed, for instance to open different kinds of doors by pushing, pulling, turning, thumbing a button or lever, and so on. Language requires many thousands of programs, to utter each

ITI Learning Principles

- *Intelligence as a function of experience*
- *Bodybrain partnership —emotion as gatekeeper to learning and performance—movement and cognition*
- *Multiple intelligences*
- ***Learning as a two-step process***
  - *—pattern seeking/meaning making*
  - ***—program building***

word, type it, write it in longhand, print it, and so forth. Frequently used programs acquire an 'automatic' quality: they can be used, once selected, without thinking, as when one puts on a shirt. Typically, a program is CONSCIOUSLY selected, then run off at a subconscious level. In general, humans operate by selecting and implementing programs one after another throughout waking hours."[2]

To understand the power of Hart's statements, consider some everyday examples. Simple ones are such things as a procedure for putting on one's shoes. There are the "right-foot-first" people and the "good heavens, no—the left first" folks. Same with putting on a coat. For high good humor, watch someone in a restaurant offering to help another with their coat. Of course the assistant offers the coat in the manner that he or she would put it on—from the left, high up near the shoulder while the recipient turns to receive the coat low from the right and the awkwardness ensues.

Or, how about the shower? Your favored hand grabs the soap and that soap knows just what to do. Zip! You're done with the shower. But, if for some temporary reason that hand can't get wet, the soap no longer remembers what to do. The result is much fumbling about, a shower that takes much longer, and the feeling of not being quite as clean and refreshed as usual. You can almost hear your mother's voice asking, "Did you wash behind your ears?"

For another example, think how many of us have driven miles with absolutely no recall of the journey. A little scary! Or, after being reassigned to a new school, we find ourselves one morning in the parking lot of our former school. How did that happen!

As John Ratey points out in his book, *A User's Guide to the Brain: Perception, Attention, and the Four Theaters of the Brain*, skill acquisition recruits more cortical neurons to master the skill; then, as the skill becomes more automatic, less of the recruited cortex is used and the function is delegated to lower parts of the brain. "Thus, the brain has a tremendous ability to compensate and rewire with practice."[3]

This shift from full attention to identifying patterns to automatic use of what is learned was outlined in Chapter 4. It is repeated here for your ready reference because it helps explain the journey from the first "Aha" to unconscious use of knowledge and skills.

The Gradiental/Distributive View of the Brain

As introduced in Chapter 4, and repeated here for your convenience, the gradiental/distributive theory of brain function is now replacing the modular theory of the brain. The modular theory viewed the brain as storing word meanings as separate, compact modules separate from the cerebral representation of the real physical world they denote—a view much more consistent with traditional views of learning the disciplines than the new gradiental/distributive view of the brain.

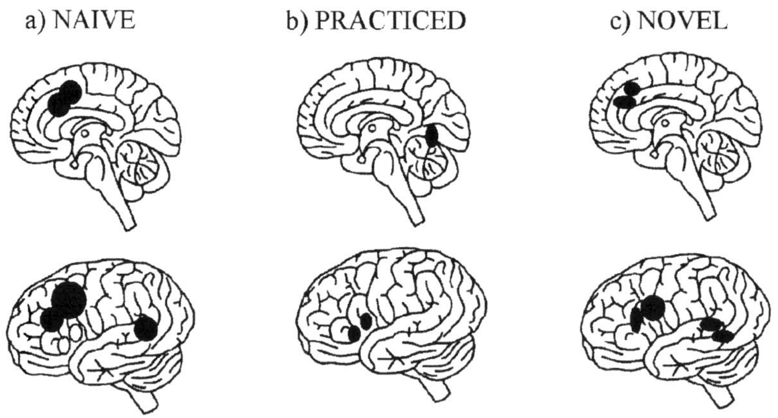

Source: *The Executive Brain* by Elkhonon Goldberg, page 70. [Adapted from M. E. Raichle, J. A. Fiez, T. O. Videen, A. M. MacLeod, J. V. Pardo, P. T. Fox, S. E. Petersen, "Practice-related changes is human brain functional anatomy during nonmotor learning," *Cerebral Cortex* vol. 4, no. 1 (1994)].Source: *The Executive Brain* by Elkhonon Goldberg, page 70. [Adapted from M. E. Raichle, J. A. Fiez, T. O. Videen, A. M. MacLeod, J. V. Pardo, P. T. Fox, S. E. Petersen, "Practice-related changes is human brain functional anatomy during nonmotor learning," *Cerebral Cortex* vol. 4, no. 1 (1994)].

ACADEMICS
Calendar: semesters. *Degree:* bachelor's.
Library: Clifton M. Miller Library.

STUDENT LIFE
Housing options: on-campus residence required through sophomore year; coed, men-only, women-only, special housing for students with disabilities. Campus housing is university owned. Freshman campus housing is guaranteed.

Activities and organizations: drama/theater group, student-run newspaper, radio station, choral group, Presidential Fellows, Dance Club, Habitat for Humanity, Peer Mentor, Animal Impact Club, national fraternities, national sororities.

Athletics Member NCAA. All Division III.

Campus security: 24-hour emergency response devices and patrols, student patrols, late-night transport/escort service, controlled dormitory access, LiveSafe mobile app.

Student services: health clinic, personal/psychological counseling.

COSTS & FINANCIAL AID
Costs (2018–19) ***Comprehensive fee:*** $59,420 includes full-time tuition ($45,888), mandatory fees ($1118), and room and board ($12,414). Part-time tuition: $1912 per credit hour. Part-time tuition and fees vary according to course load. No tuition increase for student's term of enrollment. ***College room only:*** $6000. Room and board charges vary according to board plan, housing facility, and location. ***Payment plans:*** tuition prepayment, installment.

Financial Aid Of all full-time matriculated undergraduates who enrolled in 2018, 1,056 applied for aid, 925 were judged to have need, 301 had their need fully met. 220 Federal Work-Study jobs (averaging $1696). In 2018, 334 non-need-based awards were made. ***Average percent of need met:*** 85. ***Average financial aid package:*** $35,342. ***Average need-based loan:*** $4434. ***Average need-based gift aid:*** $32,185. ***Average non-need-based aid:*** $19,595. ***Average indebtedness upon graduation:*** $32,767.

APPLYING
Standardized Tests *Required:* SAT or ACT (for admission).

Options: electronic application, early admission, early decision, early action, deferred entrance.

Required: essay or personal statement, high school transcript, 1 letter of recommendation. ***Required for some:*** interview. ***Recommended:*** interview.

CONTACT
Washington College, 300 Washington Avenue, Chestertown, MD 21620. *Phone:* 410-778-7700. *Toll-free phone:* 800-422-1782. *Fax:* 410-778-7287. *E-mail:* wc_admissions@washcoll.edu.

Yeshiva College of the Nation's Capital

Silver Spring, Maryland

http://www.yeshiva.edu/

CONTACT
Yeshiva College of the Nation's Capital, 1216 Arcola Avenue, Silver Spring, MD 20902.

MASSACHUSETTS

American International College

Springfield, Massachusetts

http://www.aic.edu/

- **Independent** comprehensive, founded 1885
- **Urban** 58-acre campus
- **Endowment** $15.0 million
- **Coed**
- **Minimally difficult** entrance level

FACULTY
Student/faculty ratio: 18:1.

ACADEMICS
Calendar: semesters. *Degrees:* associate, bachelor's, master's, doctoral, post-master's, and postbachelor's certificates.
Library: James J. Shea Sr. Library. *Books:* 56,511 (physical), 179,160 (digital/electronic); *Serial titles:* 183 (physical), 962 (digital/electronic); *Databases:* 64. Weekly public service hours: 100; students can reserve study rooms.

STUDENT LIFE
Housing options: on-campus residence required through sophomore year; coed, women-only. Campus housing is university owned. Freshman campus housing is guaranteed.

Activities and organizations: drama/theater group, student-run newspaper, choral group, Student Activities Committee, Model Congress, PRIDE (Persons Ready in Defense of Ebony), Student Government, School newspaper.

Athletics Member NCAA. All Division II except ice hockey (Division I), rugby (Division I).

Campus security: 24-hour emergency response devices and patrols, late-night transport/escort service, controlled dormitory access.

Student services: health clinic, personal/psychological counseling, veterans affairs office.

COSTS & FINANCIAL AID
Costs (2018–19) ***Comprehensive fee:*** $49,780 includes full-time tuition ($35,680) and room and board ($14,100). Full-time tuition and fees vary according to course load and program. Part-time tuition: $735 per credit hour. Part-time tuition and fees vary according to course load. ***Required fees:*** $30 per term part-time. ***College room only:*** $7140. Room and board charges vary according to board plan and housing facility.

Financial Aid Of all full-time matriculated undergraduates who enrolled in 2013, 1,394 applied for aid, 1,333 were judged to have need, 159 had their need fully met. 466 Federal Work-Study jobs (averaging $640). 161 state and other part-time jobs (averaging $1190). ***Average percent of need met:*** 70. ***Average financial aid package:*** $23,969. ***Average need-based loan:*** $4133. ***Average need-based gift aid:*** $19,916. ***Average indebtedness upon graduation:*** $35,587.

APPLYING
Options: electronic application, deferred entrance.

Required: high school transcript. ***Recommended:*** essay or personal statement, 1 letter of recommendation.

CONTACT
Mr. Jonathan Scully, Director of Undergraduate Admissions, American International College, 1000 State Street, Springfield, MA 01109-3189. *Phone:* 413-205-3270. *Toll-free phone:* 800-242-3142. *Fax:* 413-205-3051. *E-mail:* jonathan.scully@aic.edu.

Amherst College

Amherst, Massachusetts

http://www.amherst.edu/

- **Independent** 4-year, founded 1821
- **Small-town** 1020-acre campus
- **Coed**
- **Most difficult** entrance level

FACULTY
Student/faculty ratio: 8:1.

ACADEMICS
Calendar: semesters. *Degree:* bachelor's.
Library: Robert Frost Library plus 3 others.

STUDENT LIFE
Housing options: on-campus residence required for freshman year; coed, women-only, cooperative, special housing for students with disabilities. Campus housing is university owned. Freshman campus housing is guaranteed.

Activities and organizations: drama/theater group, student-run newspaper, radio station, choral group, Association of Amherst Students, Black Students Union, Student Publications (e.g., Amherst Student, Indicator), A Capella Groups (e.g., Zumbye's, Bluestockings), Amherst Dance.

Athletics Member NCAA. All Division III.

Campus security: 24-hour emergency response devices and patrols, late-night transport/escort service, controlled dormitory access.

Student services: health clinic, personal/psychological counseling, women's center.

COSTS & FINANCIAL AID

Costs (2018–19) ***Comprehensive fee:*** $71,166 includes full-time tuition ($55,520), mandatory fees ($906), and room and board ($14,740). ***College room only:*** $7990.

Financial Aid Of all full-time matriculated undergraduates who enrolled in 2018, 1,230 applied for aid, 1,084 were judged to have need, 1,084 had their need fully met. 880 Federal Work-Study jobs (averaging $1546). 194 state and other part-time jobs (averaging $1702). ***Average percent of need met:*** 100. ***Average financial aid package:*** $55,908. ***Average need-based loan:*** $449. ***Average need-based gift aid:*** $54,715. ***Average indebtedness upon graduation:*** $13,710.

APPLYING

Standardized Tests *Required:* SAT or ACT (for admission).

Options: electronic application, early admission, early decision, deferred entrance.

Application fee: $65.

Required: essay or personal statement, high school transcript, 3 letters of recommendation, Amherst College Supplement.

CONTACT

Katharine L. Fretwell, Dean of Admission and Financial Aid, Amherst College, PO Box 5000, Amherst, MA 01002-5000. *Phone:* 413-542-2328. *Fax:* 413-542-2040. *E-mail:* admission@amherst.edu.

Anna Maria College

Paxton, Massachusetts

http://www.annamaria.edu/

CONTACT

Mr. Peter Miller, Dean of Admissions and Financial Aid, Anna Maria College, 50 Sunset Lane, Paxton, MA 01612. *Phone:* 508-849-3586. *Fax:* 508-849-3362. *E-mail:* admissions@annamaria.edu.

★ Assumption College

Worcester, Massachusetts

http://www.assumption.edu/

- **Independent Roman Catholic** comprehensive, founded 1904
- **Suburban** 180-acre campus with easy access to Boston
- **Endowment** $109.7 million
- **Coed** 1,938 undergraduate students, 99% full-time, 57% women, 43% men
- **Moderately difficult** entrance level, 81% of applicants were admitted

UNDERGRAD STUDENTS

1,917 full-time, 21 part-time. Students come from 30 states and territories; 14 other countries; 35% are from out of state; 5% Black or African American, non-Hispanic/Latino; 8% Hispanic/Latino; 3% Asian, non-Hispanic/Latino; 0.1% Native Hawaiian or other Pacific Islander, non-Hispanic/Latino; 0.1% American Indian or Alaska Native, non-Hispanic/Latino; 2% Two or more races, non-Hispanic/Latino; 4% Race/ethnicity unknown; 2% international; 1% transferred in; 84% live on campus.

Freshmen:

Admission: 4,178 applied, 3,387 admitted, 553 enrolled. ***Average high school GPA:*** 3.3. ***Test scores:*** SAT evidence-based reading and writing scores over 500: 93%; SAT math scores over 500: 96%; ACT scores over 18: 100%; SAT evidence-based reading and writing scores over 600: 43%; SAT math scores over 600: 35%; ACT scores over 24: 76%; SAT evidence-based reading and writing scores over 700: 6%; SAT math scores over 700: 4%; ACT scores over 30: 14%.

Retention: 83% of full-time freshmen returned.

FACULTY

Total: 336, 40% full-time, 52% with terminal degrees.

Student/faculty ratio: 11:1.

ACADEMICS

Calendar: semesters. *Degrees:* bachelor's, master's, post-master's, and postbachelor's certificates.

ROTC: Army (c), Air Force (c).

Unusual degree programs: engineering with University of Notre Dame; Washington University at St. Louis; forestry with Duke University; special education; rehabilitation counseling; Heritage Studies (Regis College); law (Duquesne University); law (Western New England College); law (Vermont Law School).

Computers: 361 computers/terminals and 2,476 ports are available on campus for general student use. Students can access the following: campus intranet, computer help desk, free student e-mail accounts, online (class) grades, online (class) registration, online (class) schedules. Campuswide network is available. 100% of college-owned or -operated housing units are wired for high-speed Internet access. Wireless service is available via entire campus.

Library: Emmanuel d'Alzon Library. *Books:* 119,254 (physical), 155,116 (digital/electronic); *Serial titles:* 1,915 (physical), 43,143 (digital/electronic); *Databases:* 75. Weekly public service hours: 102; students can reserve study rooms.

STUDENT LIFE

Housing options: coed, women-only, special housing for students with disabilities. Campus housing is university owned. Freshman campus housing is guaranteed.

Activities and organizations: drama/theater group, student-run newspaper, television station, choral group, Volunteer center, Campus Activities Board, Student Government, Campus Ministry, intramural sports.

Athletics Member NCAA. All Division II. ***Intercollegiate sports:*** baseball M, basketball M(s)/W(s), cheerleading M(c)/W(c), cross-country running M/W, equestrian sports M(c)/W(c), field hockey W, football M, golf M, ice hockey M, lacrosse M/W, rowing W, soccer M/W, softball W, swimming and diving M(c)/W, tennis M/W, track and field M/W, ultimate Frisbee M(c)/W(c), volleyball M(c)/W. ***Intramural sports:*** basketball M/W, football M/W, ice hockey M/W, sand volleyball M/W, soccer M/W, softball M/W, swimming and diving M/W, table tennis M/W, volleyball M/W.

Campus security: 24-hour emergency response devices and patrols, student patrols, late-night transport/escort service, controlled dormitory access, front gate security, well-lit pathways.

Student services: health clinic, personal/psychological counseling.

COSTS & FINANCIAL AID

Costs (2019–20) ***Comprehensive fee:*** $55,444 includes full-time tuition ($41,516), mandatory fees ($800), and room and board ($13,128). Part-time tuition: $1384 per credit hour. ***College room only:*** $8310.

Financial Aid Of all full-time matriculated undergraduates who enrolled in 2018, 1,601 applied for aid, 1,425 were judged to have need, 400 had their need fully met. 415 Federal Work-Study jobs (averaging $1497). In 2018, 423 non-need-based awards were made. ***Average percent of need met:*** 77. ***Average financial aid package:*** $27,598. ***Average need-based loan:*** $4372. ***Average need-based gift aid:*** $23,728. ***Average non-need-based aid:*** $16,575.

APPLYING

Options: electronic application, early decision, early action, deferred entrance.

Application fee: $50.

Required: essay or personal statement, high school transcript, 1 letter of recommendation. ***Recommended:*** interview.

Application deadlines: 2/15 (freshmen), 7/1 (transfers).

Early decision deadline: 11/1.

Notification: continuous (freshmen), continuous (transfers), 12/8 (early decision).

CONTACT

Dr. Robert Mirabile, Vice President for Enrollment Management, Assumption College, 500 Salisbury Street, Worcester, MA 01609-1296. *Phone:* 508-767-7286. *Toll-free phone:* 866-477-7776. *Fax:* 508-799-4412. *E-mail:* r.mirabile@assumption.edu.

See next page for display ad and page 974 for the College Close-Up.

Babson College

Wellesley, Massachusetts

http://www.babson.edu/

- **Independent** comprehensive, founded 1919
- **Suburban** 370-acre campus with easy access to Boston
- **Endowment** $348.6 million
- **Coed** 2,361 undergraduate students, 100% full-time, 48% women, 52% men
- **Very difficult** entrance level, 24% of applicants were admitted

UNDERGRAD STUDENTS

2,361 full-time. Students come from 49 states and territories; 80 other countries; 76% are from out of state; 4% Black or African American, non-Hispanic/Latino; 11% Hispanic/Latino; 12% Asian, non-Hispanic/Latino; 0.1% Native Hawaiian or other Pacific Islander, non-Hispanic/Latino; 0.1% American Indian or Alaska Native, non-Hispanic/Latino; 2% Two or more races, non-Hispanic/Latino; 5% Race/ethnicity unknown; 28% international; 2% transferred in; 79% live on campus.

Freshmen:

Admission: 6,383 applied, 1,558 admitted, 539 enrolled. ***Test scores:*** SAT evidence-based reading and writing scores over 500: 99%; SAT math scores over 500: 100%; ACT scores over 18: 100%; SAT evidence-based reading and writing scores over 600: 89%; SAT math scores over 600: 93%; ACT scores over 24: 98%; SAT evidence-based reading and writing scores over 700: 20%; SAT math scores over 700: 55%; ACT scores over 30: 53%.

Retention: 94% of full-time freshmen returned.

FACULTY

Total: 263, 68% full-time, 74% with terminal degrees.

Student/faculty ratio: 11:1.

ACADEMICS

Calendar: semesters. *Degrees:* bachelor's, master's, and postbachelor's certificates.

Special study options: advanced placement credit, freshman honors college, honors programs, independent study, internships, off-campus study, services for LD students, student-designed majors, study abroad, summer session for credit. ***ROTC:*** Army (c).

Computers: Students can access the following: campus intranet, computer help desk, free student e-mail accounts, online (class) grades, online (class) registration, online (class) schedules. Campuswide network is available. Wireless service is available via entire campus.

Library: Horn Library plus 1 other.

STUDENT LIFE

Housing options: on-campus residence required for freshman year; coed, men-only, special housing for students with disabilities. Campus housing is university owned. Freshman campus housing is guaranteed.

Activities and organizations: drama/theater group, student-run newspaper, radio station, choral group, national fraternities, national sororities.

Athletics Member NCAA. All Division III except skiing (downhill) (Division II). ***Intercollegiate sports:*** baseball M, basketball M/W, cheerleading W(c), cross-country running M/W, field hockey W, golf M, ice hockey M/W(c), lacrosse M/W, rugby M(c)/W(c), skiing (downhill) M/W, soccer M/W, softball W, swimming and diving M/W, tennis M/W, track and field M/W, volleyball W. ***Intramural sports:*** basketball M/W, football M, ice hockey M/W, racquetball M/W, soccer M/W, softball M/W, squash M/W, tennis M/W, ultimate Frisbee M/W, volleyball M/W, wrestling M(c).

Campus security: 24-hour emergency response devices and patrols, late-night transport/escort service, controlled dormitory access.

Student services: health clinic, personal/psychological counseling, women's center.

COSTS & FINANCIAL AID

Costs (2019–20) ***Comprehensive fee:*** $69,384 includes full-time tuition ($52,608) and room and board ($16,776).

Financial Aid Of all full-time matriculated undergraduates who enrolled in 2018, 1,043 applied for aid, 970 were judged to have need, 610 had their need fully met. In 2018, 155 non-need-based awards were made. ***Average percent of need met:*** 99. ***Average financial aid package:***

$44,121. ***Average need-based loan:*** $4586. ***Average need-based gift aid:*** $41,446. ***Average non-need-based aid:*** $15,826. ***Average indebtedness upon graduation:*** $37,866. ***Financial aid deadline:*** 2/1.

APPLYING
Standardized Tests *Required:* SAT or ACT (for admission). *Recommended:* TOEFL or IELTS for non-native English speakers.

Options: electronic application, early decision, early action, deferred entrance.

Application fee: $75.

Required: essay or personal statement, high school transcript, 2 letters of recommendation. ***Recommended:*** interview.

Application deadlines: 1/3 (freshmen), 3/15 (transfers).

Early decision deadline: 11/1 (for plan 1), 1/2 (for plan 2).

Notification: 4/1 (freshmen), 5/15 (transfers), 12/15 (early decision).

CONTACT
Mrs. Christina Hamilton, Associate Director of Undergraduate Admission, Babson College, Lunder Undergraduate Admission Center, Babson Park, MA 02457-0310. *Phone:* 781-239-5522. *Toll-free phone:* 800-488-3696. *Fax:* 781-239-4135. *E-mail:* ugradadmission@babson.edu.

Bard College at Simon's Rock

Great Barrington, Massachusetts

http://www.simons-rock.edu/

CONTACT
Chandra Joos deKoven, Director of Admissions, Bard College at Simon's Rock, 84 Alford Road, Great Barrington, MA 01230-9702. *Phone:* 800-235-7186. *Toll-free phone:* 800-235-7186. *Fax:* 413-541-0081. *E-mail:* admit@simons-rock.edu.

Bay Path University

Longmeadow, Massachusetts

http://www.baypath.edu/

- **Independent** comprehensive, founded 1897
- **Suburban** 48-acre campus with easy access to Hartford, CT and Boston, MA
- **Endowment** $41.5 million
- **Undergraduate: women only; graduate: coed**
- **Moderately difficult** entrance level

FACULTY
Student/faculty ratio: 13:1.

ACADEMICS
Calendar: semesters. *Degrees:* certificates, associate, bachelor's, master's, doctoral, post-master's, and postbachelor's certificates.
Library: Hatch Library. *Books:* 52,565 (physical), 408,000 (digital/electronic); *Serial titles:* 80 (physical), 55,000 (digital/electronic); *Databases:* 110. Weekly public service hours: 86; students can reserve study rooms.

STUDENT LIFE
Housing options: women-only. Campus housing is university owned. Freshman campus housing is guaranteed.

Activities and organizations: drama/theater group, choral group, Habitat for Humanity, Tactical Team, Wellness Wildcats, Women of Culture, Alliance Club.

Athletics Member NCAA. All Division III.

Campus security: 24-hour emergency response devices and patrols, late-night transport/escort service, controlled dormitory access.

Student services: health clinic, personal/psychological counseling.

FINANCIAL AID
Financial Aid Of all full-time matriculated undergraduates who enrolled in 2018, 600 applied for aid, 573 were judged to have need, 51 had their need fully met. In 2018, 44 non-need-based awards were made. ***Average percent of need met:*** 73. ***Average financial aid package:*** $27,453. ***Average need-based loan:*** $4281. ***Average need-based gift aid:*** $22,595. ***Average non-need-based aid:*** $14,402. ***Average indebtedness upon graduation:*** $41,594.

APPLYING
Options: electronic application, early action, deferred entrance.

Required for some: essay or personal statement, high school transcript, interview. ***Recommended:*** minimum 2.0 GPA, interview.

CONTACT
Dawn Bryden, Dean of Traditional Undergraduate Enrollment and Admissions, Bay Path University, 588 Longmeadow Street, Longmeadow, MA 01106-2292. *Phone:* 413-565-1235. *Toll-free phone:* 800-782-7284 Ext. 1331. *E-mail:* dbryden@baypath.edu.

Bay State College

Boston, Massachusetts

http://www.baystate.edu/

CONTACT
Kimberly Odusami, Director of Admissions, Bay State College, 122 Commonwealth Avenue, Boston, MA 02116. *Phone:* 617-217-9186. *Toll-free phone:* 800-81-LEARN. *E-mail:* admissions@baystate.edu.

Becker College

Worcester, Massachusetts

http://www.becker.edu/

- **Independent** comprehensive, founded 1784
- **Urban** 100-acre campus with easy access to Boston, MA; Providence, RI; Hartford, CT
- **Coed**
- **Moderately difficult** entrance level

FACULTY
Student/faculty ratio: 14:1.

ACADEMICS
Calendar: semesters. *Degrees:* certificates, associate, bachelor's, and master's (also includes Leicester, MA small town campus).
Library: Ruska Library plus 1 other. *Books:* 14,869 (physical), 46,845 (digital/electronic); *Serial titles:* 15 (physical), 74 (digital/electronic); *Databases:* 68. Weekly public service hours: 168; study areas open 24 hours, 5–7 days a week; students can reserve study rooms.

STUDENT LIFE
Housing options: coed. Campus housing is university owned and leased by the school.

Activities and organizations: drama/theater group, student-run newspaper, choral group, Campus Activities Board (CAB), Animal Health Club/Pre-Veterinary Club, International Game Developers Association (IGDA), Dance Club, Marine Wildlife Conversation Club.

Campus security: 24-hour emergency response devices and patrols, late-night transport/escort service, controlled dormitory access.

Student services: health clinic, personal/psychological counseling.

COSTS & FINANCIAL AID
Costs (2018–19) ***One-time required fee:*** $275. ***Comprehensive fee:*** $53,000 includes full-time tuition ($35,600), mandatory fees ($3600), and room and board ($13,800). Full-time tuition and fees vary according to class time, course load, and program. Part-time tuition: $1483 per credit. Part-time tuition and fees vary according to class time, course load, and program. ***Room and board:*** Room and board charges vary according to housing facility.

Financial Aid Of all full-time matriculated undergraduates who enrolled in 2017, 888 applied for aid, 833 were judged to have need, 3 had their need fully met. 183 Federal Work-Study jobs (averaging $1300). In 2017, 146 non-need-based awards were made. ***Average percent of need met:*** 55. ***Average financial aid package:*** $25,324. ***Average need-based loan:*** $4266. ***Average need-based gift aid:*** $18,368. ***Average non-need-based aid:*** $15,715.

APPLYING
Standardized Tests *Required:* SAT or ACT (for admission).

Options: electronic application, early admission, early decision, early action.

Required: high school transcript, minimum 2.0 GPA. ***Recommended:*** essay or personal statement, letters of recommendation, interview.

CONTACT
Mr. Michael Perron, Dean of Admissions, Becker College, 61 Sever Street, Worcester, MA 01609. *Phone:* 508-373-9400. *Toll-free phone:* 877-5BECKER. *Fax:* 508-890-1500. *E-mail:* admissions@becker.edu.

Benjamin Franklin Institute of Technology

Boston, Massachusetts

http://www.bfit.edu/

CONTACT
Ms. Brittainy Johnson, Associate Director of Admissions, Benjamin Franklin Institute of Technology, Boston, MA 02116. *Phone:* 617-423-4630 Ext. 122. *Toll-free phone:* 877-400-BFIT. *Fax:* 617-482-3706. *E-mail:* bjohnson@bfit.edu.

★ Bentley University

Waltham, Massachusetts

http://www.bentley.edu/

- **Independent** comprehensive, founded 1917
- **Suburban** 163-acre campus with easy access to Boston
- **Endowment** $289.6 million
- **Coed** 4,253 undergraduate students, 98% full-time, 40% women, 60% men
- **Very difficult** entrance level, 43% of applicants were admitted

UNDERGRAD STUDENTS
4,185 full-time, 68 part-time. Students come from 44 states and territories; 76 other countries; 58% are from out of state; 4% Black or African American, non-Hispanic/Latino; 7% Hispanic/Latino; 8% Asian, non-Hispanic/Latino; 0.1% Native Hawaiian or other Pacific Islander, non-Hispanic/Latino; 2% Two or more races, non-Hispanic/Latino; 4% Race/ethnicity unknown; 16% international; 2% transferred in; 78% live on campus.

Freshmen:
Admission: 9,252 applied, 3,998 admitted, 1,014 enrolled. ***Test scores:*** SAT evidence-based reading and writing scores over 500: 100%; SAT math scores over 500: 99%; ACT scores over 18: 100%; SAT evidence-based reading and writing scores over 600: 82%; SAT math scores over 600: 89%; ACT scores over 24: 94%; SAT evidence-based reading and writing scores over 700: 17%; SAT math scores over 700: 42%; ACT scores over 30: 55%.

Retention: 93% of full-time freshmen returned.

FACULTY
Total: 463, 63% full-time, 72% with terminal degrees.

Student/faculty ratio: 11:1.

ACADEMICS
Calendar: semesters. *Degrees:* bachelor's, master's, doctoral, post-master's, and postbachelor's certificates.

Special study options: advanced placement credit, double majors, English as a second language, honors programs, independent study, internships, off-campus study, part-time degree program, services for LD students, study abroad, summer session for credit.

Computers: 4,620 computers/terminals and 10,752 ports are available on campus for general student use. Students can access the following: campus intranet, computer help desk, free student e-mail accounts, online (class) grades, online (class) registration, online (class) schedules, grade checking; online admission; blackboard; resume review; student employment; interlibary loan; free software. Campuswide network is available. 100% of college-owned or -operated housing units are wired for high-speed Internet access. Wireless service is available via entire campus.

Library: Bentley Library. *Books:* 184,868 (physical), 217,175 (digital/electronic); *Serial titles:* 2,781 (physical), 116,336 (digital/electronic); *Databases:* 144. Weekly public service hours: 110; students can reserve study rooms.

STUDENT LIFE
Housing options: coed, special housing for students with disabilities. Campus housing is university owned. Freshman campus housing is guaranteed.

Activities and organizations: drama/theater group, student-run newspaper, radio station, choral group, South Asian Student Association, Campus Activities Board, Delta Sigma Pi, Bentley Investment Group, National Association of Black Accountants, national fraternities, national sororities.

Athletics Member NCAA. All Division II except ice hockey (Division I). ***Intercollegiate sports:*** baseball M, basketball M(s)/W(s), cross-country running M/W, field hockey W, football M, golf M, ice hockey M(s), lacrosse M/W, soccer M/W, softball W, swimming and diving M/W, tennis M/W, track and field M/W, volleyball W. ***Intramural sports:*** basketball M/W, cheerleading M(c)/W(c), equestrian sports M(c)/W(c), ice hockey M(c)/W(c), rugby M(c)/W(c), sailing M(c)/W(c), soccer M/W, softball M/W, triathlon M(c)/W(c), ultimate Frisbee M/W, volleyball M/W.

Campus security: 24-hour emergency response devices and patrols, late-night transport/escort service, controlled dormitory access.

Student services: health clinic, personal/psychological counseling, women's center.

COSTS & FINANCIAL AID
Costs (2019–20) ***Comprehensive fee:*** $68,790 includes full-time tuition ($50,060), mandatory fees ($1770), and room and board ($16,960). ***College room only:*** $10,290.

Financial Aid Of all full-time matriculated undergraduates who enrolled in 2017, 2,453 applied for aid, 1,823 were judged to have need, 689 had their need fully met. 942 Federal Work-Study jobs (averaging $1877). 838 state and other part-time jobs (averaging $1656). In 2017, 1013 non-need-based awards were made. ***Average percent of need met:*** 92. ***Average financial aid package:*** $37,680. ***Average need-based loan:*** $4839. ***Average need-based gift aid:*** $32,947. ***Average non-need-based aid:*** $10,128. ***Average indebtedness upon graduation:*** $30,997. ***Financial aid deadline:*** 11/15.

APPLYING
Standardized Tests *Required:* SAT or ACT (for admission), TOEFL or IELTS is required for non-native English speakers (for admission).

Options: electronic application, early admission, early decision, deferred entrance.

Application fee: $75.

Required: essay or personal statement, high school transcript, 2 letters of recommendation. ***Recommended:*** interview.

Application deadlines: 1/7 (freshmen), 1/7 (out-of-state freshmen).

Early decision deadline: 11/15.

Notification: 3/31 (freshmen), 3/31 (out-of-state freshmen), continuous (transfers), 12/21 (early decision).

CONTACT
Mario Silva-Rosa, Director of Undergraduate Admissions, Bentley University, 175 Forest Street, Waltham, MA 02452-4705. *Phone:* 781-891-2244. *Toll-free phone:* 800-523-2354. *E-mail:* ugadmission@bentley.edu.

See next page for display ad and page 978 for the College Close-Up.

Berklee College of Music

Boston, Massachusetts

http://www.berklee.edu/

CONTACT
Mr. Damien Bracken, Director of Admissions, Berklee College of Music, 1140 Boylston Street, Boston, MA 02215-3693. *Phone:* 617-747-2222. *Toll-free phone:* 800-BERKLEE. *Fax:* 617-747-2047. *E-mail:* admissions@berklee.edu.

A ★ indicates that the school has detailed information with a Premium Profile on Petersons.com.

Boston Architectural College

Boston, Massachusetts

http://www.the-bac.edu/

- **Independent** comprehensive, founded 1889
- **Urban** 1-acre campus with easy access to Boston
- **Endowment** $10.1 million
- **Coed**
- **Noncompetitive** entrance level

FACULTY

Student/faculty ratio: 4:1.

ACADEMICS

Calendar: semesters. *Degrees:* certificates, bachelor's, and master's. **Library:** Shaw and Stone Library. *Books:* 42,224 (physical), 117,108 (digital/electronic); *Serial titles:* 613 (physical), 313,728 (digital/electronic); *Databases:* 73. Weekly public service hours: 71.

STUDENT LIFE

Housing options: college housing not available.

Activities and organizations: Student Government Association, Student American Society of Landscape Architects, BAC Interior Design Society (IIDA and ASID), National Organization of Minority Architecture Students (NOMAS), American Institute of Architectural Students.

Campus security: 24-hour emergency response devices and patrols, late-night transport/escort service, electronically operated building access, closed-circuit TV systems.

Student services: personal/psychological counseling, legal services.

COSTS & FINANCIAL AID

Costs (2018–19) ***Tuition:*** $21,144 full-time, $1762 per credit hour part-time. Full-time tuition and fees vary according to course load and program. Part-time tuition and fees vary according to course load and program. ***Required fees:*** $750 full-time, $225 per term part-time.

Financial Aid Of all full-time matriculated undergraduates who enrolled in 2016, 98 applied for aid, 93 were judged to have need, 1 had their need fully met. 18 Federal Work-Study jobs (averaging $2915). In 2016, 9 non-need-based awards were made. ***Average percent of need met:*** 33. ***Average financial aid package:*** $11,472. ***Average need-based loan:*** $5643. ***Average need-based gift aid:*** $6941. ***Average non-need-based aid:*** $2740.

APPLYING

Options: electronic application.

Required: essay or personal statement, high school transcript, resumé and creative exercise. ***Recommended:*** interview.

CONTACT

Ms. Meredith Spinnato, Director of Admission Office, Boston Architectural College, 320 Newbury Street, Boston, MA 02115-2795. *Phone:* 617-585-0123. *Fax:* 617-585-0121. *E-mail:* admissions@the-bac.edu.

Boston Baptist College

Boston, Massachusetts

http://www.boston.edu/

CONTACT

Mrs. Kim Melton, Director of Admissions, Boston Baptist College, 950 Metropolitan Avenue, Boston, MA 02136. *Phone:* 617-364-3510 Ext. 233. *Toll-free phone:* 888-235-2014. *Fax:* 617-399-8220. *E-mail:* kmelton@boston.edu.

Boston College

Chestnut Hill, Massachusetts

http://www.bc.edu/

- **Independent Roman Catholic (Jesuit)** university, founded 1863
- **Suburban** 227-acre campus with easy access to Boston
- **Endowment** $2.6 billion
- **Coed** 9,377 undergraduate students, 100% full-time, 53% women, 47% men
- **Very difficult** entrance level, 28% of applicants were admitted

UNDERGRAD STUDENTS
9,377 full-time. Students come from 54 states and territories; 68 other countries; 72% are from out of state; 4% Black or African American, non-Hispanic/Latino; 11% Hispanic/Latino; 10% Asian, non-Hispanic/Latino; 3% Two or more races, non-Hispanic/Latino; 4% Race/ethnicity unknown; 8% international; 2% transferred in; 84% live on campus.

Freshmen:
Admission: 31,084 applied, 8,669 admitted, 2,326 enrolled. ***Test scores:*** SAT evidence-based reading and writing scores over 500: 99%; SAT math scores over 500: 99%; ACT scores over 18: 100%; SAT evidence-based reading and writing scores over 600: 92%; SAT math scores over 600: 91%; ACT scores over 24: 98%; SAT evidence-based reading and writing scores over 700: 47%; SAT math scores over 700: 64%; ACT scores over 30: 87%.

Retention: 95% of full-time freshmen returned.

FACULTY
Total: 1,664, 50% full-time, 90% with terminal degrees.

Student/faculty ratio: 12:1.

ACADEMICS
Calendar: semesters. *Degrees:* certificates, bachelor's, master's, doctoral, and post-master's certificates (also offers continuing education program with significant enrollment not reflected in profile).

Special study options: accelerated degree program, advanced placement credit, double majors, honors programs, independent study, internships, off-campus study, part-time degree program, services for LD students, student-designed majors, study abroad, summer session for credit. ***ROTC:*** Army (c), Navy (c), Air Force (c).

Computers: 1,000 computers/terminals are available on campus for general student use. Students can access the following: campus intranet, computer help desk, free student e-mail accounts, online (class) grades, online (class) registration, online (class) schedules. Campuswide network is available. 100% of college-owned or -operated housing units are wired for high-speed Internet access. Wireless service is available via entire campus.

Library: O'Neill Library plus 8 others. *Books:* 3.3 million (physical), 875,636 (digital/electronic); *Serial titles:* 3,545 (physical), 44,846 (digital/electronic). Study areas open 24 hours, 5–7 days a week; students can reserve study rooms.

STUDENT LIFE
Housing options: coed, women-only. Campus housing is university owned. Freshman campus housing is guaranteed.

Activities and organizations: drama/theater group, student-run newspaper, radio and television station, choral group, marching band, UGBC and individual School Senates, Asian Caucus, Appalachia Volunteers, Dance Marathon, 4Boston.

Athletics Member NCAA. All Division I except football (Division I-A). ***Intercollegiate sports:*** baseball M(s), basketball M(s)/W(s), cheerleading M(c)/W(c), crew W(s), cross-country running M(s)/W(s), fencing M/W, field hockey W(s), golf M(s)/W(s)(c), ice hockey M(s)/W(s), lacrosse W(s), sailing M/W, skiing (downhill) M(c)/W, soccer M(s)/W(s), softball W(s), swimming and diving M(s)/W(s), tennis M(s)/W(s), track and field M(s)/W(s), volleyball W(s). ***Intramural sports:*** badminton M/W, basketball M(c)/W(c), crew M(c), cross-country running M(c)/W(c), equestrian sports M(c)/W(c), fencing W(c), golf M(c)/W(c), ice hockey M/W, lacrosse M(c)/W(c), racquetball M/W, rugby M(c)/W(c), soccer M(c)/W(c), softball M/W, squash M/W, tennis M/W, track and field M(c)/W(c), ultimate Frisbee M(c)/W(c), volleyball M(c)/W, water polo M(c)/W(c).

Campus security: 24-hour emergency response devices and patrols, late-night transport/escort service, controlled dormitory access.

Student services: health clinic, personal/psychological counseling, women's center.

FINANCIAL AID
Financial Aid Of all full-time matriculated undergraduates who enrolled in 2017, 4,317 applied for aid, 3,837 were judged to have need, 3,837 had their need fully met. In 2017, 223 non-need-based awards were made. ***Average percent of need met:*** 100. ***Average financial aid package:*** $44,099. ***Average need-based loan:*** $4489. ***Average need-based gift aid:*** $40,290. ***Average non-need-based aid:*** $22,464. ***Average indebtedness upon graduation:*** $20,915.

APPLYING
Standardized Tests *Required:* SAT or ACT (for admission).

Options: electronic application, early admission, early decision, deferred entrance.

Application fee: $80.

Required: essay or personal statement, high school transcript, 2 letters of recommendation.

Application deadlines: 1/1 (freshmen), 3/15 (transfers).

Early decision deadline: 11/1 (for plan 1), 1/1 (for plan 2).

Notification: 4/1 (freshmen), 6/15 (transfers), 12/15 (early decision plan 1), 2/15 (early decision plan 2).

CONTACT
Mr. Grant M. Gosselin, Director of Undergraduate Admission, Boston College, 140 Commonwealth Avenue, Chestnut Hill, MA 02467-3800. *Phone:* 617-552-3100. *Toll-free phone:* 800-360-2522. *Fax:* 617-552-0798.

See page 980 for the College Close-Up.

Boston University

Boston, Massachusetts

http://www.bu.edu/

- **Independent** university, founded 1839
- **Urban** 169-acre campus with easy access to Boston
- **Endowment** $2.2 billion
- **Coed** 18,515 undergraduate students, 94% full-time, 60% women, 40% men
- **Very difficult** entrance level, 22% of applicants were admitted

UNDERGRAD STUDENTS
17,396 full-time, 1,119 part-time. Students come from 52 states and territories; 121 other countries; 72% are from out of state; 4% Black or African American, non-Hispanic/Latino; 11% Hispanic/Latino; 15% Asian, non-Hispanic/Latino; 0.1% Native Hawaiian or other Pacific Islander, non-Hispanic/Latino; 4% Two or more races, non-Hispanic/Latino; 8% Race/ethnicity unknown; 21% international; 4% transferred in; 75% live on campus.

Freshmen:
Admission: 64,481 applied, 14,247 admitted, 3,612 enrolled. ***Average high school GPA:*** 3.7. ***Test scores:*** SAT evidence-based reading and writing scores over 500: 100%; SAT math scores over 500: 100%; ACT scores over 18: 100%; SAT evidence-based reading and writing scores over 600: 95%; SAT math scores over 600: 97%; ACT scores over 24: 99%; SAT evidence-based reading and writing scores over 700: 42%; SAT math scores over 700: 69%; ACT scores over 30: 76%.

Retention: 94% of full-time freshmen returned.

FACULTY
Total: 2,665, 70% full-time, 63% with terminal degrees.

Student/faculty ratio: 10:1.

ACADEMICS
Calendar: semesters. *Degrees:* certificates, bachelor's, master's, doctoral, post-master's, and postbachelor's certificates.

Special study options: accelerated degree program, adult/continuing education programs, advanced placement credit, cooperative education, distance learning, double majors, English as a second language, freshman honors college, honors programs, independent study, internships, off-campus study, part-time degree program, services for LD students, student-designed majors, study abroad, summer session for credit. ***ROTC:*** Army (b), Navy (b), Air Force (b).

Computers: 250 computers/terminals and 1,650 ports are available on campus for general student use. Students can access the following: campus intranet, computer help desk, free student e-mail accounts, online (class) grades, online (class) registration, online (class) schedules, research and educational networks. Campuswide network is available. 100% of college-owned or -operated housing units are wired for high-speed Internet access. Wireless service is available via classrooms, computer labs, dorm rooms, libraries, student centers.

Library: Mugar Memorial Library plus 20 others. *Books:* 1.2 million (physical), 2.1 million (digital/electronic); *Serial titles:* 248,885

(physical), 111,406 (digital/electronic); *Databases:* 721. Weekly public service hours: 123; students can reserve study rooms.

STUDENT LIFE

Housing options: on-campus residence required for freshman year; coed, women-only, cooperative, special housing for students with disabilities. Campus housing is university owned. Freshman campus housing is guaranteed.

Activities and organizations: drama/theater group, student-run newspaper, radio and television station, choral group, marching band, performing and Acappella groups, cultural organizations, service organizations, Student Government, residence hall associations, national fraternities, national sororities.

Athletics Member NCAA. All Division I. ***Intercollegiate sports:*** badminton M(c)/W(c), baseball M(c), basketball M(s)/W(s), cheerleading M(c)/W(c), crew M(s)/W(s), cross-country running M(s)/W(s), equestrian sports M(c)/W(c), fencing M(c)/W(c), field hockey W(s), golf M(c)/W(s), gymnastics M(c)/W(c), ice hockey M(s)/W(s), lacrosse M(s)/W(s), rowing M(s)/W(s), rugby M(c)/W(c), sailing M(c)/W(c), skiing (downhill) M(c)/W(c), soccer M(s)/W(s), softball W(s), squash M(c)/W(c), swimming and diving M(s)/W(s), table tennis M(c)/W(c), tennis M/W(s), track and field M(s)/W(s), triathlon M(c)/W(c), ultimate Frisbee M(c)/W(c), volleyball M(c)/W(c), water polo M(c)/W(c). ***Intramural sports:*** basketball M/W, football M/W, ice hockey M(c)/W(c), rowing M(c)/W(c), soccer M(c)/W(c), softball M/W, volleyball M/W.

Campus security: 24-hour emergency response devices and patrols, late-night transport/escort service, controlled dormitory access.

Student services: health clinic, personal/psychological counseling, women's center, veterans affairs office.

COSTS & FINANCIAL AID

Costs (2019–20) ***Comprehensive fee:*** $72,052 includes full-time tuition ($54,720), mandatory fees ($1172), and room and board ($16,160). Part-time tuition: $1710 per credit. ***Required fees:*** $60 part-time. ***College room only:*** $10,680. ***Payment plan:*** tuition prepayment.

Financial Aid Of all full-time matriculated undergraduates who enrolled in 2018, 8,626 applied for aid, 7,066 were judged to have need, 1,694 had their need fully met. 3,158 Federal Work-Study jobs (averaging $2241). In 2018, 1087 non-need-based awards were made. ***Average percent of need met:*** 84. ***Average financial aid package:*** $43,571. ***Average need-based loan:*** $3372. ***Average need-based gift aid:*** $38,201. ***Average non-need-based aid:*** $25,298. ***Average indebtedness upon graduation:*** $42,976. ***Financial aid deadline:*** 1/6.

APPLYING

Standardized Tests *Required for some:* SAT or ACT (for admission), SAT Subject Tests (for admission).

Options: electronic application, early admission, early decision, deferred entrance.

Application fee: $80.

Required: essay or personal statement, high school transcript, 2 letters of recommendation. ***Required for some:*** interview, audition, portfolio.

Application deadlines: 1/6 (freshmen), 3/1 (transfers).

Early decision deadline: 11/1 (for plan 1), 1/6 (for plan 2).

Notification: 4/1 (freshmen), continuous until 6/1 (transfers), 12/15 (early decision plan 1), 2/7 (early decision plan 2).

CONTACT

Ms. Kelly A. Walter, Associate Vice President for Enrollment and Dean of Admissions, Boston University, 233 Bay State Road, Boston, MA 02215. *Phone:* 617-353-2300. *E-mail:* admissions@bu.edu.

See this page for display ad and page 982 for the College Close-Up.

Brandeis University

Waltham, Massachusetts

http://www.brandeis.edu/

- **Independent** university, founded 1948
- **Suburban** 235-acre campus with easy access to Boston
- **Endowment** $1.0 billion
- **Coed** 3,639 undergraduate students, 99% full-time, 61% women, 39% men
- **Most difficult** entrance level, 31% of applicants were admitted

UNDERGRAD STUDENTS
3,619 full-time, 20 part-time. Students come from 49 states and territories; 56 other countries; 70% are from out of state; 5% Black or African American, non-Hispanic/Latino; 8% Hispanic/Latino; 14% Asian, non-Hispanic/Latino; 0.2% Native Hawaiian or other Pacific Islander, non-Hispanic/Latino; 0.1% American Indian or Alaska Native, non-Hispanic/Latino; 3% Two or more races, non-Hispanic/Latino; 3% Race/ethnicity unknown; 20% international; 0.9% transferred in; 76% live on campus.

Freshmen:
Admission: 11,798 applied, 3,675 admitted, 895 enrolled. ***Average high school GPA:*** 3.8. ***Test scores:*** SAT evidence-based reading and writing scores over 500: 99%; SAT math scores over 500: 98%; ACT scores over 18: 100%; SAT evidence-based reading and writing scores over 600: 91%; SAT math scores over 600: 86%; ACT scores over 24: 98%; SAT evidence-based reading and writing scores over 700: 38%; SAT math scores over 700: 60%; ACT scores over 30: 75%.

Retention: 92% of full-time freshmen returned.

FACULTY
Total: 541, 68% full-time, 82% with terminal degrees.

Student/faculty ratio: 10:1.

ACADEMICS
Calendar: semesters. *Degrees:* bachelor's, master's, doctoral, and post-master's certificates.

Special study options: advanced placement credit, double majors, independent study, internships, off-campus study, services for LD students, student-designed majors, study abroad, summer session for credit. ***ROTC:*** Army (c), Air Force (c).

Unusual degree programs: 3-2 engineering with Columbia University.

Computers: 130 computers/terminals are available on campus for general student use. Students can access the following: computer help desk, free student e-mail accounts, online (class) grades, online (class) registration, online (class) schedules, educational software. Campuswide network is available. 100% of college-owned or -operated housing units are wired for high-speed Internet access. Wireless service is available via entire campus.

Library: Brandeis Library plus 1 other. *Books:* 1.0 million (physical), 1.1 million (digital/electronic); *Serial titles:* 11,941 (physical), 37,330 (digital/electronic); *Databases:* 445. Students can reserve study rooms.

STUDENT LIFE
Housing options: on-campus residence required for freshman year; coed, special housing for students with disabilities. Campus housing is university owned. Freshman campus housing is guaranteed.

Activities and organizations: drama/theater group, student-run newspaper, radio and television station, choral group, Waltham Group, Undergraduate Theater Collective, Mountain Club, Student Union, BEMCo - student EMTs.

Athletics Member NCAA. All Division III. ***Intercollegiate sports:*** baseball M, basketball M/W, cross-country running M/W, fencing M/W, soccer M/W, softball W, swimming and diving M/W, tennis M/W, track and field M/W, volleyball W. ***Intramural sports:*** archery M(c)/W(c), badminton M/W, cheerleading M(c)/W(c), crew M(c)/W(c), equestrian sports M(c)/W(c), fencing W(c), gymnastics M(c)/W(c), lacrosse W(c), rugby M(c)/W(c), sailing M(c)/W(c), skiing (downhill) M(c)/W(c), soccer M/W, softball M/W, squash M(c)/W(c), table tennis M(c)/W(c), ultimate Frisbee M(c)/W(c), volleyball M(c), water polo M/W.

Campus security: 24-hour emergency response devices and patrols, late-night transport/escort service, controlled dormitory access.

Student services: health clinic, personal/psychological counseling, women's center.

COSTS & FINANCIAL AID
Costs (2019–20) ***Comprehensive fee:*** $73,641 includes full-time tuition ($55,340), mandatory fees ($2221), and room and board ($16,080). Part-time tuition: $1729 per credit. ***Required fees:*** $2221 per year part-time.

Financial Aid Of all full-time matriculated undergraduates who enrolled in 2017, 1,941 applied for aid, 1,707 were judged to have need, 1,050 had their need fully met. 338 Federal Work-Study jobs (averaging $2532). 15 state and other part-time jobs (averaging $2930). In 2017, 465 non-need-based awards were made. ***Average percent of need met:*** 94. ***Average financial aid package:*** $45,125. ***Average need-based loan:*** $4770. ***Average need-based gift aid:*** $40,634. ***Average non-need-based aid:*** $14,776. ***Average indebtedness upon graduation:*** $29,785. ***Financial aid deadline:*** 1/1.

APPLYING
Standardized Tests *Required:* SAT or ACT (for admission).

Options: electronic application, early admission, early decision, deferred entrance.

Application fee: $80.

Required: essay or personal statement, high school transcript, 1 letter of recommendation. ***Recommended:*** interview.

Application deadlines: 1/1 (freshmen), 4/1 (transfers).

Early decision deadline: 11/1 (for plan 1), 1/1 (for plan 2).

Notification: 4/1 (freshmen), 5/25 (transfers), 12/15 (early decision plan 1), 2/1 (early decision plan 2).

CONTACT
Jennifer Walker, Dean of Admissions & Financial Aid, Brandeis University, 415 South Street, PO Box 549110, Waltham, MA 02454-9110. *Phone:* 781-736-3500. *Toll-free phone:* 800-622-0622. *Fax:* 781-736-3536. *E-mail:* admissions@brandeis.edu.

Bridgewater State University

Bridgewater, Massachusetts

http://www.bridgew.edu/

- **State-supported** comprehensive, founded 1840, part of Massachusetts Department of Higher Education
- **Suburban** 278-acre campus with easy access to Boston
- **Endowment** $41.6 million
- **Coed** 9,504 undergraduate students, 83% full-time, 59% women, 41% men
- **Moderately difficult** entrance level, 90% of applicants were admitted

UNDERGRAD STUDENTS
7,877 full-time, 1,627 part-time. Students come from 28 states and territories; 34 other countries; 4% are from out of state; 9% Black or African American, non-Hispanic/Latino; 7% Hispanic/Latino; 2% Asian, non-Hispanic/Latino; 0.1% Native Hawaiian or other Pacific Islander, non-Hispanic/Latino; 0.1% American Indian or Alaska Native, non-Hispanic/Latino; 5% Two or more races, non-Hispanic/Latino; 1% Race/ethnicity unknown; 0.5% international; 11% transferred in; 40% live on campus.

Freshmen:
Admission: 6,806 applied, 6,135 admitted, 1,518 enrolled. ***Average high school GPA:*** 3.1. ***Test scores:*** SAT evidence-based reading and writing scores over 500: 76%; SAT math scores over 500: 73%; ACT scores over 18: 92%; SAT evidence-based reading and writing scores over 600: 20%; SAT math scores over 600: 14%; ACT scores over 24: 31%; SAT evidence-based reading and writing scores over 700: 1%; SAT math scores over 700: 1%; ACT scores over 30: 6%.

Retention: 78% of full-time freshmen returned.

FACULTY
Total: 789, 45% full-time, 62% with terminal degrees.

Student/faculty ratio: 19:1.

ACADEMICS
Calendar: semesters. *Degrees:* bachelor's, master's, post-master's, and postbachelor's certificates.

Special study options: academic remediation for entering students, accelerated degree program, adult/continuing education programs, advanced placement credit, distance learning, double majors, English as a second language, honors programs, independent study, internships, off-campus study, part-time degree program, services for LD students, study abroad, summer session for credit. ***ROTC:*** Army (c), Air Force (c).

Computers: 780 computers/terminals and 20 ports are available on campus for general student use. Students can access the following: campus intranet, computer help desk, free student e-mail accounts, online (class) grades, online (class) registration, online (class) schedules, student account information, application software. Campuswide network is available. 100% of college-owned or -operated housing units are wired for

high-speed Internet access. Wireless service is available via entire campus.
Library: Clement C. Maxwell Library. *Books:* 214,839 (physical), 54,656 (digital/electronic); *Serial titles:* 2,287 (physical), 31,407 (digital/electronic); *Databases:* 205. Weekly public service hours: 93.

STUDENT LIFE
Housing options: coed, special housing for students with disabilities. Campus housing is university owned. Freshman applicants given priority for college housing.

Activities and organizations: drama/theater group, student-run newspaper, radio station, choral group, BSU Chapter of the Student Education Association of Massachusetts, Residence Hall Association, Best Buddies, Alpha Sigma Tau Sorority, Delta Phi Epsilon Sorority, national fraternities, national sororities.

Athletics Member NCAA. All Division III. ***Intercollegiate sports:*** baseball M, basketball M/W, cross-country running M/W, field hockey W, football M, lacrosse W, soccer M/W, softball W, swimming and diving M/W, tennis M/W, track and field M/W, volleyball W, wrestling M. ***Intramural sports:*** basketball M/W, cheerleading W(c), equestrian sports W(c), football M/W, ice hockey M(c), lacrosse M(c), rugby W(c), soccer M/W, softball M/W, ultimate Frisbee M(c)/W(c), volleyball M/W.

Campus security: 24-hour emergency response devices and patrols, late-night transport/escort service, controlled dormitory access.

Student services: health clinic, personal/psychological counseling, veterans affairs office.

COSTS & FINANCIAL AID
Costs (2019–20) ***Tuition:*** state resident $910 full-time, $38 per credit hour part-time; nonresident $7050 full-time, $294 per credit hour part-time. ***Required fees:*** $9457 full-time, $387 per credit hour part-time. ***Room and board:*** $12,750; room only: $8400.

Financial Aid Of all full-time matriculated undergraduates who enrolled in 2017, 7,107 applied for aid, 5,703 were judged to have need, 754 had their need fully met. In 2017, 16 non-need-based awards were made. ***Average financial aid package:*** $8446. ***Average need-based loan:*** $3735. ***Average need-based gift aid:*** $6037. ***Average non-need-based aid:*** $5724. ***Average indebtedness upon graduation:*** $31,349.

APPLYING
Standardized Tests *Recommended:* SAT (for admission).

Options: electronic application, early action, deferred entrance.

Application fee: $50.

Application deadlines: 2/15 (freshmen), 2/15 (transfers), 11/15 (early action).

Notification: continuous until 4/15 (freshmen), continuous until 4/15 (transfers).

CONTACT
Mr. Gregg Meyer, Dean of University Admissions, Bridgewater State University, Gates House, 40 Cedar Street, Bridgewater, MA 02325. *Phone:* 508-531-1237. *Fax:* 508-531-1746. *E-mail:* admission@bridgew.edu.

Cambridge College
Boston, Massachusetts
http://www.cambridgecollege.edu/

CONTACT
Denise Haile, Director of Admissions, Cambridge College, 1000 Massachusetts Avenue, Cambridge, MA 02138-5304. *Phone:* 800-877-4725. *Toll-free phone:* 800-877-4723. *Fax:* 617-349-3561. *E-mail:* denise.haile@cambridgecollege.edu.

Clark University
Worcester, Massachusetts
http://www.clarku.edu/

- **Independent** university, founded 1887
- **Urban** 50-acre campus with easy access to Boston
- **Endowment** $436.9 million
- **Coed** 2,304 undergraduate students, 98% full-time, 61% women, 39% men
- **Moderately difficult** entrance level, 59% of applicants were admitted

UNDERGRAD STUDENTS
2,263 full-time, 41 part-time. Students come from 43 states and territories; 56 other countries; 61% are from out of state; 4% Black or African American, non-Hispanic/Latino; 9% Hispanic/Latino; 8% Asian, non-Hispanic/Latino; 3% Two or more races, non-Hispanic/Latino; 6% Race/ethnicity unknown; 12% international; 2% transferred in; 66% live on campus.

Freshmen:
Admission: 7,687 applied, 4,565 admitted, 582 enrolled. ***Average high school GPA:*** 3.7. ***Test scores:*** SAT evidence-based reading and writing scores over 500: 98%; SAT math scores over 500: 99%; ACT scores over 18: 101%; SAT evidence-based reading and writing scores over 600: 79%; SAT math scores over 600: 72%; ACT scores over 24: 91%; SAT evidence-based reading and writing scores over 700: 26%; SAT math scores over 700: 23%; ACT scores over 30: 51%.

Retention: 87% of full-time freshmen returned.

FACULTY
Total: 298, 69% full-time, 96% with terminal degrees.

Student/faculty ratio: 9:1.

ACADEMICS
Calendar: semesters. *Degrees:* bachelor's, master's, doctoral, and post-master's certificates.

Special study options: accelerated degree program, adult/continuing education programs, advanced placement credit, distance learning, double majors, English as a second language, honors programs, independent study, internships, off-campus study, part-time degree program, services for LD students, student-designed majors, study abroad, summer session for credit. ***ROTC:*** Army (c), Air Force (c).

Unusual degree programs: 3-2 business administration; engineering with Columbia University; environmental studies, international development, community planning, biology, biochemistry, chemistry, physics, economics, history, communications, public administration, geographic information systems.

Computers: Students can access the following: campus intranet, computer help desk, free student e-mail accounts, online (class) grades, online (class) registration, online (class) schedules, online course support. Campuswide network is available. 100% of college-owned or -operated housing units are wired for high-speed Internet access. Wireless service is available via entire campus.
Library: Robert Hutchings Goddard Library plus 8 others. Students can reserve study rooms.

STUDENT LIFE
Housing options: on-campus residence required through sophomore year; coed, women-only, special housing for students with disabilities. Campus housing is university owned. Freshman campus housing is guaranteed.

Activities and organizations: drama/theater group, student-run newspaper, radio and television station, choral group, marching band, International Students Association, Science Fiction People of Clark, Outing Club, Hillel, Clark Musical Theater.

Athletics Member NCAA, NAIA. All NCAA Division III. ***Intercollegiate sports:*** baseball M, basketball M/W, crew M/W, cross-country running M/W, field hockey W, lacrosse M/W, soccer M/W, softball W, swimming and diving M/W, tennis M/W, volleyball W. ***Intramural sports:*** basketball M/W, equestrian sports W(c), ice hockey M(c), lacrosse W(c), racquetball M/W, soccer M(c)/W, softball M/W, tennis M(c)/W(c), ultimate Frisbee M(c)/W(c), volleyball M(c)/W(c), water polo M/W.

Campus security: 24-hour emergency response devices and patrols, student patrols, late-night transport/escort service, controlled dormitory access.

Student services: health clinic, personal/psychological counseling, women's center.

COSTS & FINANCIAL AID

Costs (2019–20) ***Comprehensive fee:*** $56,680 includes full-time tuition ($46,850), mandatory fees ($350), and room and board ($9480). Part-time tuition: $1464 per unit. ***Payment plan:*** tuition prepayment.

Financial Aid Of all full-time matriculated undergraduates who enrolled in 2018, 1,765 applied for aid, 1,337 were judged to have need, 611 had their need fully met. In 2018, 665 non-need-based awards were made. ***Average percent of need met:*** 90. ***Average financial aid package:*** $32,377. ***Average need-based loan:*** $4007. ***Average need-based gift aid:*** $26,462. ***Average non-need-based aid:*** $17,384. ***Average indebtedness upon graduation:*** $32,318. ***Financial aid deadline:*** 2/1.

APPLYING

Options: electronic application, early admission, early decision, early action, deferred entrance.

Application fee: $60.

Required: essay or personal statement, high school transcript, 2 letters of recommendation. ***Recommended:*** interview.

Application deadlines: 1/15 (freshmen), 5/1 (transfers), 11/1 (early action).

Early decision deadline: 11/1 (for plan 1), 1/15 (for plan 2).

Notification: 4/1 (freshmen), 6/1 (transfers), 12/15 (early decision plan 1), 2/15 (early decision plan 2), 1/15 (early action).

CONTACT

Ms. Meredith Twombly, Vice President of Admissions and Financial Aid, Clark University, Admissions House, 950 Main Street, Worcester, MA 01610. *Phone:* 508-793-7431. *Toll-free phone:* 800-GO-CLARK. *Fax:* 508-793-8821. *E-mail:* admissions@clarku.edu.

College of the Holy Cross

Worcester, Massachusetts

http://www.holycross.edu/

- **Independent Roman Catholic (Jesuit)** 4-year, founded 1843
- **Suburban** 174-acre campus with easy access to Boston
- **Endowment** $783.2 million
- **Coed** 3,128 undergraduate students, 99% full-time, 52% women, 48% men
- **Very difficult** entrance level, 38% of applicants were admitted

UNDERGRAD STUDENTS

3,102 full-time, 26 part-time. Students come from 50 states and territories; 24 other countries; 58% are from out of state; 4% Black or African American, non-Hispanic/Latino; 10% Hispanic/Latino; 4% Asian, non-Hispanic/Latino; 0.1% Native Hawaiian or other Pacific Islander, non-Hispanic/Latino; 0.1% American Indian or Alaska Native, non-Hispanic/Latino; 3% Two or more races, non-Hispanic/Latino; 3% Race/ethnicity unknown; 3% international; 0.5% transferred in; 90% live on campus.

Freshmen:

Admission: 7,054 applied, 2,681 admitted, 868 enrolled. ***Test scores:*** SAT evidence-based reading and writing scores over 500: 100%; SAT math scores over 500: 100%; ACT scores over 18: 100%; SAT evidence-based reading and writing scores over 600: 94%; SAT math scores over 600: 91%; ACT scores over 24: 98%; SAT evidence-based reading and writing scores over 700: 34%; SAT math scores over 700: 37%; ACT scores over 30: 56%.

Retention: 95% of full-time freshmen returned.

FACULTY

Total: 328, 88% full-time, 92% with terminal degrees.

Student/faculty ratio: 10:1.

ACADEMICS

Calendar: semesters. *Degree:* bachelor's.

Special study options: accelerated degree program, advanced placement credit, double majors, honors programs, independent study, internships, off-campus study, services for LD students, student-designed majors, study abroad, summer session for credit. ***ROTC:*** Army (c), Navy (b), Air Force (c).

Unusual degree programs: 3-2 engineering with Columbia University.

Computers: 298 computers/terminals are available on campus for general student use. Students can access the following: computer help desk, free student e-mail accounts, online (class) grades, online (class) registration. Campuswide network is available. 100% of college-owned or -operated housing units are wired for high-speed Internet access. Wireless service is available via entire campus.

Library: Dinand Library plus 4 others. *Books:* 651,508 (physical), 292,776 (digital/electronic); *Serial titles:* 441 (physical), 24,739 (digital/electronic); *Databases:* 312. Study areas open 24 hours, 5–7 days a week; students can reserve study rooms.

STUDENT LIFE

Housing options: on-campus residence required through sophomore year; coed, special housing for students with disabilities. Campus housing is university owned. Freshman campus housing is guaranteed.

Activities and organizations: drama/theater group, student-run newspaper, radio station, choral group, marching band, SPUD (community service organization), choral and music groups, Campus Activities Board, Student Government Association, Purple Key Society.

Athletics Member NCAA. All Division I except football (Division I-AA). ***Intercollegiate sports:*** baseball M, basketball M(s)/W(s), crew M/W(s), cross-country running M/W(s), field hockey W(s), golf M/W, ice hockey M(s)/W, lacrosse M(s)/W(s), soccer M(s)/W(s), softball W(s), swimming and diving M/W(s), tennis M/W, track and field M/W(s), volleyball W(s). ***Intramural sports:*** baseball M(c), basketball M(c)/W(c), equestrian sports M(c)/W(c), fencing W(c), field hockey W(c), football M/W, golf M(c)/W(c), ice hockey M(c)/W(c), lacrosse M(c)/W(c), rugby M(c)/W(c), sailing M(c)/W(c), skiing (downhill) M(c)/W(c), soccer M(c)/W(c), softball M/W, swimming and diving M(c)/W(c), tennis M(c)/W(c), ultimate Frisbee M(c)/W(c), volleyball M(c)/W(c), water polo M/W.

Campus security: 24-hour emergency response devices and patrols, late-night transport/escort service, controlled dormitory access.

Student services: health clinic, personal/psychological counseling.

COSTS & FINANCIAL AID

Costs (2019–20) ***Comprehensive fee:*** $69,810 includes full-time tuition ($54,050), mandatory fees ($690), and room and board ($15,070). ***College room only:*** $8250.

Financial Aid Of all full-time matriculated undergraduates who enrolled in 2018, 2,022 applied for aid, 1,642 were judged to have need, 1,642 had their need fully met. In 2018, 70 non-need-based awards were made. ***Average percent of need met:*** 100. ***Average financial aid package:*** $40,533. ***Average need-based loan:*** $4490. ***Average need-based gift aid:*** $37,537. ***Average non-need-based aid:*** $24,694. ***Average indebtedness upon graduation:*** $25,260. ***Financial aid deadline:*** 1/15.

APPLYING

Options: electronic application, early admission, early decision, deferred entrance.

Application fee: $60.

Required: essay or personal statement, high school transcript, 2 letters of recommendation. ***Recommended:*** interview.

Application deadlines: 1/15 (freshmen), 4/1 (transfers).

Early decision deadline: 12/15.

Notification: 4/1 (freshmen), continuous (transfers), rolling (early decision).

CONTACT

Ms. Ann McDermott, Director of Admissions, College of the Holy Cross, 1 College Street, Worcester, MA 01610-2395. *Phone:* 508-793-2443. *Toll-free phone:* 800-442-2421. *Fax:* 508-793-3888. *E-mail:* admissions@holycross.edu.

Curry College

Milton, Massachusetts

http://www.curry.edu/

- **Independent** comprehensive, founded 1879
- **Suburban** 131-acre campus with easy access to Boston
- **Endowment** $99.4 million
- **Coed** 2,356 undergraduate students, 84% full-time, 58% women, 42% men
- **Moderately difficult** entrance level, 93% of applicants were admitted

UNDERGRAD STUDENTS
1,989 full-time, 367 part-time. Students come from 29 states and territories; 21 other countries; 26% are from out of state; 12% Black or African American, non-Hispanic/Latino; 8% Hispanic/Latino; 3% Asian, non-Hispanic/Latino; 0.2% Native Hawaiian or other Pacific Islander, non-Hispanic/Latino; 0.3% American Indian or Alaska Native, non-Hispanic/Latino; 3% Two or more races, non-Hispanic/Latino; 8% Race/ethnicity unknown; 2% international; 3% transferred in; 83% live on campus.

Freshmen:
Admission: 5,733 applied, 5,315 admitted, 581 enrolled. ***Average high school GPA:*** 3.0. ***Test scores:*** SAT evidence-based reading and writing scores over 500: 65%; SAT math scores over 500: 58%; ACT scores over 18: 81%; SAT evidence-based reading and writing scores over 600: 10%; SAT math scores over 600: 7%; ACT scores over 24: 20%.

Retention: 68% of full-time freshmen returned.

FACULTY
Total: 361, 36% full-time, 32% with terminal degrees.

Student/faculty ratio: 13:1.

ACADEMICS
Calendar: semesters. *Degrees:* bachelor's, master's, and post-master's certificates.

Special study options: academic remediation for entering students, accelerated degree program, adult/continuing education programs, advanced placement credit, double majors, English as a second language, honors programs, independent study, internships, off-campus study, part-time degree program, services for LD students, student-designed majors, study abroad, summer session for credit. ***ROTC:*** Army (c).

Unusual degree programs: 3-2 business administration; education.

Computers: 245 computers/terminals and 2,500 ports are available on campus for general student use. Students can access the following: campus intranet, computer help desk, free student e-mail accounts, online (class) grades, online (class) registration, online (class) schedules. Campuswide network is available. 100% of college-owned or -operated housing units are wired for high-speed Internet access. Wireless service is available via entire campus.

Library: Levin Library. *Books:* 71,564 (physical), 141,518 (digital/electronic); *Serial titles:* 66 (physical), 109,694 (digital/electronic); *Databases:* 101. Weekly public service hours: 98; students can reserve study rooms.

STUDENT LIFE
Housing options: coed, men-only, women-only. Campus housing is university owned.

Activities and organizations: drama/theater group, student-run newspaper, radio and television station, choral group, Students Entertainment and Events (SEE), Black Student Union (BSU), Latino Student Union (LSU), Multicultural Student Union (MSU), Student Government Association (SGA).

Athletics Member NCAA. All Division III. ***Intercollegiate sports:*** baseball M, basketball M/W, cross-country running W, equestrian sports M(c)/W(c), football M, ice hockey M/W(c), lacrosse M/W, rugby M(c), soccer M/W, softball W, tennis M/W, volleyball W. ***Intramural sports:*** badminton M/W, basketball M/W, bowling M/W, cheerleading M(c)/W(c), field hockey W, golf M(c)/W(c), skiing (downhill) M(c)/W(c), soccer M/W, softball M/W, tennis M/W, ultimate Frisbee M/W, volleyball M.

Campus security: 24-hour emergency response devices and patrols, late-night transport/escort service, controlled dormitory access, campus safety office.

Student services: health clinic, personal/psychological counseling.

COSTS & FINANCIAL AID
Costs (2019–20) ***One-time required fee:*** $360. ***Comprehensive fee:*** $57,210 includes full-time tuition ($38,950), mandatory fees ($1920), and room and board ($16,340). Part-time tuition: $1248 per credit. ***College room only:*** $8780.

Financial Aid Of all full-time matriculated undergraduates who enrolled in 2017, 1,632 applied for aid, 1,586 were judged to have need, 185 had their need fully met. 923 Federal Work-Study jobs (averaging $2338). In 2017, 379 non-need-based awards were made. ***Average percent of need met:*** 69. ***Average financial aid package:*** $28,668. ***Average need-based loan:*** $4394. ***Average need-based gift aid:*** $24,285. ***Average non-need-based aid:*** $16,232. ***Average indebtedness upon graduation:*** $45,947.

APPLYING
Standardized Tests *Required for some:* SAT or ACT (for admission), TOEFL for international applicants whose native language is not English.

Options: electronic application, early admission, early action, deferred entrance.

Application fee: $50.

Required: essay or personal statement, high school transcript, minimum 2.0 GPA, 1 letter of recommendation, Common Application Supplement and Program for Advancement of Learning (PAL), Cognitive and Achievement Testing for PAL. ***Required for some:*** interview.

Notification: continuous (freshmen), continuous (transfers).

CONTACT
Mr. Keith Robichaud, Associate Vice President and Dean of Admission, Curry College, 1071 Blue Hill Avenue, Milton, MA 02186. *Phone:* 617-333-2210. *Toll-free phone:* 800-669-0686. *Fax:* 617-333-2114. *E-mail:* curryadm@curry.edu.

Dean College
Franklin, Massachusetts
http://www.dean.edu/

- **Independent** 4-year, founded 1865
- **Suburban** 100-acre campus with easy access to Boston, MA and Providence, RI
- **Endowment** $47.1 million
- **Coed** 1,323 undergraduate students, 87% full-time, 52% women, 48% men
- **Moderately difficult** entrance level, 83% of applicants were admitted

UNDERGRAD STUDENTS
1,152 full-time, 171 part-time. Students come from 35 states and territories; 19 other countries; 44% are from out of state; 13% Black or African American, non-Hispanic/Latino; 10% Hispanic/Latino; 1% Asian, non-Hispanic/Latino; 0.2% Native Hawaiian or other Pacific Islander, non-Hispanic/Latino; 0.4% American Indian or Alaska Native, non-Hispanic/Latino; 4% Two or more races, non-Hispanic/Latino; 11% Race/ethnicity unknown; 4% international; 3% transferred in; 90% live on campus.

Freshmen:
Admission: 4,854 applied, 4,022 admitted, 475 enrolled. ***Average high school GPA:*** 2.8. ***Test scores:*** SAT evidence-based reading and writing scores over 500: 58%; SAT math scores over 500: 55%; ACT scores over 18: 76%; SAT evidence-based reading and writing scores over 600: 14%; SAT math scores over 600: 8%; ACT scores over 24: 15%; SAT evidence-based reading and writing scores over 700: 2%; SAT math scores over 700: 1%.

Retention: 70% of full-time freshmen returned.

FACULTY
Total: 150, 19% full-time.

Student/faculty ratio: 17:1.

ACADEMICS
Calendar: semesters. *Degrees:* certificates, associate, and bachelor's.

Special study options: accelerated degree program, adult/continuing education programs, advanced placement credit, distance learning, double majors, English as a second language, honors programs, independent study, internships, off-campus study, part-time degree program, services for LD students, student-designed majors, study abroad, summer session for credit.

Computers: 36 computers/terminals are available on campus for general student use. Students can access the following: campus intranet, computer help desk, free student e-mail accounts, online (class) grades, online (class) registration, online (class) schedules. Campuswide network is available. Wireless service is available via entire campus.

Library: E. Ross Anderson Library. *Books:* 35,672 (physical), 49,661 (digital/electronic); *Serial titles:* 100,000 (digital/electronic); *Databases:* 42. Weekly public service hours: 77.

STUDENT LIFE

Housing options: on-campus residence required through senior year; coed, men-only, women-only. Campus housing is university owned. Freshman campus housing is guaranteed.

Activities and organizations: drama/theater group, student-run radio and television station, choral group, National Society of Leadership and Success, Student Activities Committee, Residence Hall Association, International Student Association, Dean Community Outreach.

Athletics Member NCAA, USCAA. All Division III. ***Intercollegiate sports:*** baseball M, basketball M/W, cross-country running M/W, field hockey W, football M, golf M, lacrosse M/W, soccer M/W, softball W, volleyball M/W. ***Intramural sports:*** badminton M/W, basketball M/W, rock climbing M/W, sand volleyball M/W, table tennis M/W, volleyball M/W.

Campus security: 24-hour emergency response devices and patrols, student patrols, late-night transport/escort service, controlled dormitory access.

Student services: health clinic, personal/psychological counseling.

COSTS & FINANCIAL AID

Costs (2019–20) ***One-time required fee:*** $300. ***Comprehensive fee:*** $57,672 includes full-time tuition ($40,214), mandatory fees ($200), and room and board ($17,258). Part-time tuition: $365 per credit hour. ***Required fees:*** $25 per term part-time. ***College room only:*** $10,900.

Financial Aid Of all full-time matriculated undergraduates who enrolled in 2017, 947 applied for aid, 876 were judged to have need, 99 had their need fully met. In 2017, 265 non-need-based awards were made. ***Average percent of need met:*** 61. ***Average financial aid package:*** $27,345. ***Average need-based loan:*** $3926. ***Average need-based gift aid:*** $7605. ***Average non-need-based aid:*** $14,464. ***Average indebtedness upon graduation:*** $48,717.

APPLYING

Options: electronic application, early admission, early action, deferred entrance.

Required: high school transcript. ***Required for some:*** audition for performing arts majors. ***Recommended:*** essay or personal statement, minimum 2.0 GPA, 1 letter of recommendation, interview.

Application deadlines: rolling (freshmen), rolling (transfers), 12/1 (early action).

Notification: continuous (freshmen), 1/15 (early action).

CONTACT

Iris P. Godes, Associate Vice President of Enrollment/Dean of Admissions, Dean College, 99 Main Street, Franklin, MA 02038. *Phone:* 508-541-1508. *Toll-free phone:* 877-TRY-DEAN. *Fax:* 508-541-8726. *E-mail:* igodes@dean.edu.

See below for display ad and page 998 for the College Close-Up.

Eastern Nazarene College

Quincy, Massachusetts

http://www.enc.edu/

- **Independent** comprehensive, founded 1900, affiliated with Church of the Nazarene
- **Urban** 17-acre campus with easy access to Boston
- **Coed**
- **Moderately difficult** entrance level

ACADEMICS

Calendar: semesters. *Degrees:* associate, bachelor's, and master's.
Library: Nease Library. *Books:* 113,825 (physical), 314,187 (digital/electronic); *Serial titles:* 748 (physical), 295,387 (digital/electronic); *Databases:* 90. Weekly public service hours: 95; study areas open 24 hours, 5–7 days a week; students can reserve study rooms.

STUDENT LIFE

Housing options: on-campus residence required through senior year; men-only, women-only, special housing for students with disabilities. Campus housing is university owned. Freshman campus housing is guaranteed.

Activities and organizations: drama/theater group, student-run newspaper, choral group, Gospel Choir, A cappella Choir, Germantown Tutoring, ALANA, Spirit Team.

Athletics Member NCAA. All Division III.

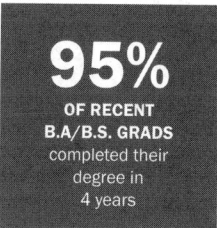

Campus security: 24-hour emergency response devices and patrols, student patrols, late-night transport/escort service, controlled dormitory access.

Student services: health clinic, personal/psychological counseling.

COSTS & FINANCIAL AID

Costs (2018–19) ***Comprehensive fee:*** $35,222 includes full-time tuition ($24,698), mandatory fees ($900), and room and board ($9624). Full-time tuition and fees vary according to class time, course load, degree level, location, program, and reciprocity agreements. Part-time tuition: $1338 per credit hour. Part-time tuition and fees vary according to class time, degree level, location, program, and reciprocity agreements. ***Room and board:*** Room and board charges vary according to board plan and housing facility.

Financial Aid Of all full-time matriculated undergraduates who enrolled in 2014, 761 applied for aid, 395 were judged to have need, 128 had their need fully met. 40 Federal Work-Study jobs (averaging $2500). In 2014, 67 non-need-based awards were made. ***Average percent of need met:*** 80. ***Average financial aid package:*** $29,431. ***Average need-based loan:*** $8837. ***Average need-based gift aid:*** $17,673. ***Average non-need-based aid:*** $13,644. ***Average indebtedness upon graduation:*** $25,251.

APPLYING

Standardized Tests *Required:* SAT or ACT (for admission).

Options: electronic application, early admission, deferred entrance.

Required: high school transcript, minimum 2.0 GPA, 1 letter of recommendation. ***Recommended:*** essay or personal statement, minimum 3.0 GPA, 2 letters of recommendation, interview.

CONTACT

Ms. Ashley Rudeen, Assistant Director of Admission/International DSO, Eastern Nazarene College, 23 East Elm Avenue, Quincy, MA 02170. *Phone:* 617-745-3861. *Toll-free phone:* 800-88-ENC88. *Fax:* 617-745-3992. *E-mail:* ashley.rudeen@enc.edu.

Elms College

Chicopee, Massachusetts

http://www.elms.edu/

- **Independent Roman Catholic** comprehensive, founded 1928
- **Suburban** 32-acre campus
- **Coed**
- **Moderately difficult** entrance level

FACULTY

Student/faculty ratio: 12:1.

ACADEMICS

Calendar: semesters. *Degrees:* associate, bachelor's, master's, doctoral, post-master's, and postbachelor's certificates.
Library: Alumnae Library.

STUDENT LIFE

Housing options: coed, women-only. Campus housing is university owned. Freshman campus housing is guaranteed.

Activities and organizations: choral group.

Athletics Member NCAA. All Division III.

Campus security: 24-hour emergency response devices and patrols, controlled dormitory access.

Student services: health clinic, personal/psychological counseling.

COSTS & FINANCIAL AID

Costs (2018–19) ***Comprehensive fee:*** $48,894 includes full-time tuition ($34,114), mandatory fees ($1674), and room and board ($13,106). Part-time tuition: $691 per credit hour. Part-time tuition and fees vary according to location and program. ***Room and board:*** Room and board charges vary according to board plan.

Financial Aid Of all full-time matriculated undergraduates who enrolled in 2018, 927 applied for aid, 878 were judged to have need, 64 had their need fully met. 93 Federal Work-Study jobs (averaging $1198). In 2018, 69 non-need-based awards were made. ***Average percent of need met:*** 62. ***Average financial aid package:*** $22,241. ***Average need-based loan:*** $4530. ***Average need-based gift aid:*** $18,973. ***Average non-need-based aid:*** $14,843. ***Average indebtedness upon graduation:*** $37,206.

APPLYING

Standardized Tests *Required:* SAT or ACT (for admission).

Options: early admission, deferred entrance.

Required: essay or personal statement, high school transcript, 2 letters of recommendation. ***Recommended:*** interview.

CONTACT

Mr. Joseph Wagner, Director of Admissions, Elms College, Chicopee, MA 01013-2839. *Phone:* 413-592-3189. *Toll-free phone:* 800-255-ELMS. *Fax:* 413-594-2781. *E-mail:* admissions@elms.edu.

★ Emerson College

Boston, Massachusetts

http://www.emerson.edu/

- **Independent** comprehensive, founded 1880
- **Urban** campus with easy access to Boston, MA
- **Endowment** $171.6 million
- **Coed** 3,855 undergraduate students, 98% full-time, 60% women, 40% men
- **Very difficult** entrance level, 36% of applicants were admitted

UNDERGRAD STUDENTS

3,779 full-time, 76 part-time. 78% are from out of state; 3% Black or African American, non-Hispanic/Latino; 13% Hispanic/Latino; 5% Asian, non-Hispanic/Latino; 0.1% Native Hawaiian or other Pacific Islander, non-Hispanic/Latino; 0.1% American Indian or Alaska Native, non-Hispanic/Latino; 4% Two or more races, non-Hispanic/Latino; 2% Race/ethnicity unknown; 11% international; 5% transferred in; 52% live on campus.

Freshmen:

Admission: 12,941 applied, 4,612 admitted, 923 enrolled. ***Average high school GPA:*** 3.7. ***Test scores:*** SAT evidence-based reading and writing scores over 500: 100%; SAT math scores over 500: 97%; ACT scores over 18: 100%; SAT evidence-based reading and writing scores over 600: 84%; SAT math scores over 600: 69%; ACT scores over 24: 95%; SAT evidence-based reading and writing scores over 700: 24%; SAT math scores over 700: 25%; ACT scores over 30: 41%.

Retention: 87% of full-time freshmen returned.

FACULTY

Total: 459, 45% full-time, 56% with terminal degrees.

Student/faculty ratio: 13:1.

ACADEMICS

Calendar: semesters. *Degrees:* certificates, bachelor's, master's, and doctoral.

Special study options: adult/continuing education programs, advanced placement credit, double majors, honors programs, independent study, internships, off-campus study, part-time degree program, services for LD students, student-designed majors, study abroad, summer session for credit.

Computers: 480 computers/terminals and 1,900 ports are available on campus for general student use. Students can access the following: computer help desk, free student e-mail accounts, online (class) grades, online (class) registration, online (class) schedules. Campuswide network is available. 100% of college-owned or -operated housing units are wired for high-speed Internet access. Wireless service is available via entire campus.

Library: Iwasaki Library plus 1 other. *Books:* 336,669 (physical), 2,484 (digital/electronic); *Serial titles:* 67,760 (digital/electronic); *Databases:* 125. Weekly public service hours: 93; students can reserve study rooms.

STUDENT LIFE

Housing options: on-campus residence required through junior year; coed. Campus housing is university owned. Freshman campus housing is guaranteed.

Activities and organizations: drama/theater group, student-run newspaper, radio and television station, choral group, EIV (Emerson Independent Video), National Broadcasting Society (student chapter), SPEC (Screenwriting), Entertainment Monthly (entertainment news), Emerson International (international student group), national fraternities, national sororities.

Athletics Member NCAA. All Division III. ***Intercollegiate sports:*** baseball M, basketball M/W, cross-country running M/W, golf M(c), lacrosse M/W, soccer M/W, softball W, tennis M/W, track and field W, volleyball M/W. ***Intramural sports:*** basketball M/W, soccer M/W, volleyball M/W.

Campus security: 24-hour emergency response devices and patrols, late-night transport/escort service, controlled dormitory access.

Student services: health clinic, personal/psychological counseling.

COSTS & FINANCIAL AID

Costs (2019–20) ***Comprehensive fee:*** $67,128 includes full-time tuition ($47,856), mandatory fees ($872), and room and board ($18,400).

Financial Aid Of all full-time matriculated undergraduates who enrolled in 2018, 2,428 applied for aid, 2,050 were judged to have need, 161 had their need fully met. In 2018, 593 non-need-based awards were made. ***Average percent of need met:*** 49. ***Average financial aid package:*** $23,479. ***Average need-based loan:*** $4551. ***Average need-based gift aid:*** $20,114. ***Average non-need-based aid:*** $13,850. ***Average indebtedness upon graduation:*** $23,653. ***Financial aid deadline:*** 2/1.

APPLYING

Options: electronic application, early admission, early action, deferred entrance.

Application fee: $65.

Required: essay or personal statement, high school transcript, 1 letter of recommendation. ***Required for some:*** interview.

Application deadlines: 1/15 (freshmen), 3/15 (transfers), 11/1 (early action).

Notification: continuous until 4/1 (freshmen), continuous until 5/1 (transfers), 12/15 (early action).

CONTACT

Mr. Michael Lynch, Director of Undergraduate Admission, Emerson College, 120 Boylston Street, Boston, MA 02116-4624. *Phone:* 617-824-8600. *Fax:* 617-824-8609. *E-mail:* admission@emerson.edu.

See this page for display ad and page 1008 for the College Close-Up.

Emmanuel College

Boston, Massachusetts

http://www.emmanuel.edu/

- **Independent Roman Catholic** comprehensive, founded 1919
- **Urban** 17-acre campus
- **Endowment** $137.3 million
- **Coed** 2,089 undergraduate students, 93% full-time, 75% women, 25% men
- 77% of applicants were admitted

UNDERGRAD STUDENTS

1,935 full-time, 154 part-time. Students come from 34 states and territories; 53 other countries; 40% are from out of state; 6% Black or African American, non-Hispanic/Latino; 11% Hispanic/Latino; 4% Asian, non-Hispanic/Latino; 0.2% American Indian or Alaska Native, non-Hispanic/Latino; 3% Two or more races, non-Hispanic/Latino; 8% Race/ethnicity unknown; 1% international; 2% transferred in; 72% live on campus.

Freshmen:

Admission: 5,770 applied, 4,443 admitted, 596 enrolled. ***Average high school GPA:*** 3.7. ***Test scores:*** SAT evidence-based reading and writing scores over 500: 98%; SAT math scores over 500: 92%; ACT scores over 18: 97%; SAT evidence-based reading and writing scores over 600: 55%; SAT math scores over 600: 41%; ACT scores over 24: 76%; SAT evidence-based reading and writing scores over 700: 7%; SAT math scores over 700: 6%; ACT scores over 30: 8%.

Retention: 78% of full-time freshmen returned.

FACULTY

Total: 199, 47% full-time, 71% with terminal degrees.

Student/faculty ratio: 13:1.

ACADEMICS

Calendar: semesters. *Degrees:* bachelor's, master's, post-master's, and postbachelor's certificates.

Special study options: advanced placement credit, distance learning, double majors, honors programs, independent study, internships, off-campus study, part-time degree program, services for LD students, student-designed majors, study abroad, summer session for credit. ***ROTC:*** Army (c).

Computers: 284 computers/terminals are available on campus for general student use. Students can access the following: campus intranet, computer help desk, free student e-mail accounts, online (class) grades, online (class) registration, online (class) schedules. Campuswide network is available. 100% of college-owned or -operated housing units are wired for high-speed Internet access. Wireless service is available via entire campus.

Library: Cardinal Cushing Library/Learning Commons. *Books:* 63,542 (physical), 191,776 (digital/electronic); *Serial titles:* 70 (physical), 2,855 (digital/electronic); *Databases:* 61. Weekly public service hours: 108; students can reserve study rooms.

STUDENT LIFE

Housing options: coed. Campus housing is university owned and leased by the school. Freshman campus housing is guaranteed.

Activities and organizations: drama/theater group, student-run newspaper, radio station, choral group, Student Government Association, Biology Club, Emmanuel College Programming Team, Black Student Union, EMS Club.

Athletics Member NCAA. All Division III. ***Intercollegiate sports:*** basketball M/W, cross-country running M/W, golf M, lacrosse M/W, soccer M/W, softball W, track and field M/W, volleyball M/W. ***Intramural sports:*** baseball M(c), field hockey W(c), ultimate Frisbee M(c)/W(c).

Campus security: 24-hour emergency response devices and patrols, late-night transport/escort service, controlled dormitory access.

Student services: health clinic, personal/psychological counseling.

COSTS & FINANCIAL AID

Costs (2019–20) ***One-time required fee:*** $350. ***Comprehensive fee:*** $56,892 includes full-time tuition ($41,028), mandatory fees ($420), and room and board ($15,444). Part-time tuition: $1282 per credit hour.

Financial Aid Of all full-time matriculated undergraduates who enrolled in 2018, 1,671 applied for aid, 1,546 were judged to have need, 539 had their need fully met. 538 Federal Work-Study jobs (averaging $1972). In 2018, 343 non-need-based awards were made. ***Average percent of need met:*** 72. ***Average financial aid package:*** $31,268. ***Average need-based loan:*** $4218. ***Average need-based gift aid:*** $27,158. ***Average non-need-based aid:*** $17,387.

APPLYING

Options: electronic application, early admission, early action, deferred entrance.

Application fee: $60.

Required: essay or personal statement, high school transcript, 2 letters of recommendation. ***Recommended:*** interview.

Application deadlines: 2/15 (freshmen), 4/1 (transfers), 11/1 (early action).

Notification: continuous until 1/15 (freshmen), 5/1 (transfers), 12/15 (early action).

CONTACT

Ms. Sandra Robbins, Dean for Enrollment, Emmanuel College, Admission Office, 400 The Fenway, Boston, MA 02115. *Phone:* 617-735-9715. *Fax:* 617-735-9801. *E-mail:* enroll@emmanuel.edu.

Endicott College

Beverly, Massachusetts

http://www.endicott.edu/

- **Independent** comprehensive, founded 1939
- **Suburban** 235-acre campus with easy access to Boston
- **Endowment** $88.7 million
- **Coed** 3,385 undergraduate students, 89% full-time, 62% women, 38% men
- **Moderately difficult** entrance level, 80% of applicants were admitted

UNDERGRAD STUDENTS

3,029 full-time, 356 part-time. Students come from 33 states and territories; 37 other countries; 50% are from out of state; 2% Black or African American, non-Hispanic/Latino; 5% Hispanic/Latino; 1% Asian, non-Hispanic/Latino; 0.1% Native Hawaiian or other Pacific Islander, non-Hispanic/Latino; 0.2% American Indian or Alaska Native, non-Hispanic/Latino; 2% Two or more races, non-Hispanic/Latino; 10% Race/ethnicity unknown; 2% international; 4% transferred in; 91% live on campus.

Freshmen:

Admission: 3,598 applied, 2,896 admitted, 764 enrolled. ***Average high school GPA:*** 3.4. ***Test scores:*** SAT evidence-based reading and writing scores over 500: 93%; SAT math scores over 500: 90%; ACT scores over 18: 96%; SAT evidence-based reading and writing scores over 600: 42%; SAT math scores over 600: 34%; ACT scores over 24: 51%; SAT evidence-based reading and writing scores over 700: 3%; SAT math scores over 700: 4%; ACT scores over 30: 8%.

Retention: 83% of full-time freshmen returned.

FACULTY

Total: 581, 19% full-time, 41% with terminal degrees.

Student/faculty ratio: 14:1.

ACADEMICS

Calendar: semesters. *Degrees:* certificates, associate, bachelor's, master's, doctoral, post-master's, and postbachelor's certificates.

Special study options: accelerated degree program, adult/continuing education programs, advanced placement credit, cooperative education, distance learning, double majors, English as a second language, honors programs, independent study, internships, off-campus study, part-time degree program, services for LD students, student-designed majors, study abroad, summer session for credit. ***ROTC:*** Army (c).

Computers: 285 computers/terminals are available on campus for general student use. Students can access the following: campus intranet, computer help desk, free student e-mail accounts, online (class) grades, online (class) registration, online (class) schedules. Campuswide network is available. 100% of college-owned or -operated housing units are wired for high-speed Internet access. Wireless service is available via entire campus.

Library: Diane M. Halle Library. *Books:* 112,262 (physical), 176,762 (digital/electronic); *Serial titles:* 47 (physical), 145,447 (digital/electronic); *Databases:* 175. Weekly public service hours: 97; students can reserve study rooms.

STUDENT LIFE

Housing options: coed, women-only, special housing for students with disabilities. Campus housing is university owned. Freshman campus housing is guaranteed.

Activities and organizations: drama/theater group, student-run newspaper, radio and television station, choral group.

Athletics Member NCAA. All Division III. ***Intercollegiate sports:*** baseball M, basketball M/W, cheerleading W(c), crew M(c)/W(c), cross-country running M/W, equestrian sports M/W, field hockey W, football M, golf M, ice hockey M/W, lacrosse M/W, rowing M(c)/W(c), rugby M(c)/W(c), soccer M/W, softball W, tennis M/W, track and field W, volleyball M/W. ***Intramural sports:*** basketball M/W, football M/W, ice hockey M/W, soccer M/W, softball M/W, ultimate Frisbee M/W, volleyball M/W.

Campus security: 24-hour emergency response devices and patrols, student patrols, late-night transport/escort service, controlled dormitory access.

Student services: health clinic, personal/psychological counseling, veterans affairs office.

COSTS & FINANCIAL AID

Costs (2019–20) ***Comprehensive fee:*** $49,664 includes full-time tuition ($33,304), mandatory fees ($700), and room and board ($15,660). Part-time tuition: $1024 per credit hour. ***College room only:*** $10,794. ***Payment plan:*** tuition prepayment.

Financial Aid Of all full-time matriculated undergraduates who enrolled in 2018, 2,293 applied for aid, 1,886 were judged to have need, 203 had their need fully met. 818 Federal Work-Study jobs (averaging $2000). In 2018, 751 non-need-based awards were made. ***Average percent of need met:*** 65. ***Average financial aid package:*** $21,861. ***Average need-based loan:*** $4450. ***Average need-based gift aid:*** $16,796. ***Average non-need-based aid:*** $10,078. ***Average indebtedness upon graduation:*** $46,269.

APPLYING
Standardized Tests *Required for some:* SAT or ACT (for admission).
Options: electronic application.
Application fee: $50.
Required: essay or personal statement, high school transcript, minimum 2.5 GPA, 1 letter of recommendation. ***Recommended:*** interview.
Application deadlines: 2/15 (freshmen), 3/15 (transfers).
Notification: continuous (freshmen), continuous (transfers).

CONTACT
Mr. Evan Lipp, Vice President of Admission and Financial Aid, Endicott College, 376 Hale Street, Beverly, MA 01915. *Phone:* 978-232-2005. *Toll-free phone:* 800-325-1114. *Fax:* 978-232-2520. *E-mail:* admissio@endicott.edu.

Fisher College

Boston, Massachusetts

http://www.fisher.edu/

- **Independent** comprehensive, founded 1903
- **Urban** 1-acre campus with easy access to Boston
- **Endowment** $34.0 million
- **Coed**
- 66% of applicants were admitted

FACULTY
Student/faculty ratio: 16:1.

ACADEMICS
Calendar: semesters. *Degrees:* certificates, associate, bachelor's, and master's.
Library: Fisher College Library. *Books:* 23,902 (physical), 105,119 (digital/electronic); *Serial titles:* 40 (physical); *Databases:* 104. Weekly public service hours: 72; study areas open 24 hours, 5–7 days a week; students can reserve study rooms.

STUDENT LIFE
Housing options: coed, women-only. Campus housing is university owned and leased by the school.
Activities and organizations: drama/theater group, choral group, National Society of Leadership and Success (NSLS), Psychology Club, Criminal Justice Club, Fashion Club, Multi-Cultural Club.
Athletics Member NAIA.
Campus security: 24-hour emergency response devices and patrols, student patrols, controlled dormitory access.
Student services: health clinic, personal/psychological counseling, women's center.

COSTS & FINANCIAL AID
Costs (2018–19) ***Comprehensive fee:*** $47,310 includes full-time tuition ($30,389), mandatory fees ($995), and room and board ($15,926). Part-time tuition: $1172 per course. Part-time tuition and fees vary according to course load. ***Required fees:*** $95 per course part-time. ***Room and board:*** Room and board charges vary according to housing facility.
Financial Aid Of all full-time matriculated undergraduates who enrolled in 2018, 561 applied for aid, 542 were judged to have need. 98 Federal Work-Study jobs (averaging $1527). In 2018, 91 non-need-based awards were made. ***Average financial aid package:*** $28,235. ***Average need-based loan:*** $4365. ***Average need-based gift aid:*** $14,785. ***Average non-need-based aid:*** $14,251. ***Average indebtedness upon graduation:*** $12,724.

APPLYING
Standardized Tests *Required for some:* SAT or ACT (for admission).
Options: electronic application.
Application fee: $50.
Required: high school transcript. ***Required for some:*** essay or personal statement, interview. ***Recommended:*** minimum 2.0 GPA.

CONTACT
Mr. Robert Melaragni, Vice President of Enrollment Management, Fisher College, Boston, MA 02116. *Phone:* 617-236-8818. *Fax:* 617-236-5473. *E-mail:* admissions@fisher.edu.

Fitchburg State University

Fitchburg, Massachusetts

http://www.fitchburgstate.edu/

- **State-supported** comprehensive, founded 1894, part of Massachusetts Public Higher Education System
- **Suburban** 78-acre campus with easy access to Boston
- **Endowment** $20.0 million
- **Coed** 4,164 undergraduate students, 80% full-time, 53% women, 47% men
- **Moderately difficult** entrance level, 87% of applicants were admitted

UNDERGRAD STUDENTS
3,320 full-time, 844 part-time. Students come from 26 states and territories; 5 other countries; 8% are from out of state; 11% Black or African American, non-Hispanic/Latino; 12% Hispanic/Latino; 2% Asian, non-Hispanic/Latino; 0.1% American Indian or Alaska Native, non-Hispanic/Latino; 3% Two or more races, non-Hispanic/Latino; 3% Race/ethnicity unknown; 0.3% international; 9% transferred in; 39% live on campus.

Freshmen:
Admission: 3,234 applied, 2,810 admitted, 715 enrolled. ***Average high school GPA:*** 3.1. ***Test scores:*** SAT evidence-based reading and writing scores over 500: 77%; SAT math scores over 500: 76%; ACT scores over 18: 90%; SAT evidence-based reading and writing scores over 600: 19%; SAT math scores over 600: 14%; ACT scores over 24: 33%; SAT evidence-based reading and writing scores over 700: 2%; SAT math scores over 700: 1%; ACT scores over 30: 5%.
Retention: 73% of full-time freshmen returned.

FACULTY
Total: 318, 66% full-time.
Student/faculty ratio: 13:1.

ACADEMICS
Calendar: semesters. *Degrees:* certificates, bachelor's, master's, post-master's, and postbachelor's certificates.
Special study options: academic remediation for entering students, accelerated degree program, adult/continuing education programs, advanced placement credit, distance learning, double majors, honors programs, independent study, internships, off-campus study, part-time degree program, services for LD students, student-designed majors, study abroad, summer session for credit. ***ROTC:*** Army (b).
Computers: 500 computers/terminals are available on campus for general student use. Students can access the following: computer help desk, free student e-mail accounts, online (class) grades, online (class) registration, online (class) schedules. Campuswide network is available. 100% of college-owned or -operated housing units are wired for high-speed Internet access. Wireless service is available via entire campus.
Library: Amelia V. Galucci-Cirio Library. *Books:* 222,517 (physical); *Databases:* 150. Weekly public service hours: 77.

STUDENT LIFE
Housing options: coed, special housing for students with disabilities. Campus housing is university owned. Freshman applicants given priority for college housing.
Activities and organizations: drama/theater group, student-run newspaper, radio station, choral group, Student Government Association, Dance Club, Activities Board, Greek Council, MASSPIRG, national fraternities, national sororities.
Athletics Member NCAA. All Division III. ***Intercollegiate sports:*** baseball M, basketball M/W, cross-country running M/W, field hockey W, football M, ice hockey M, lacrosse W, soccer M/W, softball W, track and field M/W. ***Intramural sports:*** basketball M/W, football M/W, racquetball M/W, soccer M/W, softball M/W, swimming and diving M/W, table tennis M/W, ultimate Frisbee M/W, volleyball M/W, water polo M/W.
Campus security: 24-hour emergency response devices and patrols, student patrols, late-night transport/escort service, controlled dormitory access.
Student services: health clinic, personal/psychological counseling.

COSTS & FINANCIAL AID
Costs (2018–19) ***Tuition:*** state resident $970 full-time, $40 per credit hour part-time; nonresident $7050 full-time, $294 per credit hour part-

time. Full-time tuition and fees vary according to class time and reciprocity agreements. Part-time tuition and fees vary according to class time and reciprocity agreements. ***Required fees:*** $9385 full-time, $391 per credit hour part-time. ***Room and board:*** $11,073; room only: $7583. Room and board charges vary according to board plan and housing facility. ***Payment plan:*** installment. ***Waivers:*** senior citizens and employees or children of employees.

Financial Aid Of all full-time matriculated undergraduates who enrolled in 2017, 2,949 applied for aid, 2,396 were judged to have need. 227 Federal Work-Study jobs (averaging $1737). In 2017, 153 non-need-based awards were made. ***Average percent of need met:*** 75. ***Average financial aid package:*** $11,376. ***Average need-based loan:*** $4421. ***Average need-based gift aid:*** $6907. ***Average non-need-based aid:*** $1310. ***Average indebtedness upon graduation:*** $27,377.

APPLYING

Standardized Tests *Recommended:* SAT or ACT (for admission), SAT and SAT Subject Tests or ACT (for admission).

Options: electronic application, deferred entrance.

Application fee: $50.

Required: essay or personal statement, high school transcript, minimum 2.0 GPA, 16 core courses.

Application deadlines: rolling (freshmen), rolling (transfers).

Notification: continuous (freshmen), continuous (transfers).

CONTACT

Jinawa McNeil, Director of Admissions, Fitchburg State University, 160 Pearl Street, Fitchburg, MA 01420-2697. *Phone:* 978-665-3140. *Toll-free phone:* 800-705-9692. *Fax:* 978-665-4540. *E-mail:* admissions@fitchburgstate.edu.

Framingham State University

Framingham, Massachusetts

http://www.framingham.edu/

- **State-supported** comprehensive, founded 1839, part of Massachusetts Public Higher Education System
- **Suburban** 77-acre campus with easy access to Boston
- **Endowment** $41.8 million
- **Coed** 3,937 undergraduate students, 87% full-time, 58% women, 42% men
- **Moderately difficult** entrance level, 73% of applicants were admitted

UNDERGRAD STUDENTS

3,421 full-time, 516 part-time. Students come from 12 other countries; 7% are from out of state; 12% Black or African American, non-Hispanic/Latino; 16% Hispanic/Latino; 3% Asian, non-Hispanic/Latino; 0.1% American Indian or Alaska Native, non-Hispanic/Latino; 4% Two or more races, non-Hispanic/Latino; 0.7% Race/ethnicity unknown; 0.4% international; 9% transferred in; 47% live on campus.

Freshmen:

Admission: 5,706 applied, 4,182 admitted, 767 enrolled. ***Average high school GPA:*** 3.0. ***Test scores:*** SAT evidence-based reading and writing scores over 500: 67%; SAT math scores over 500: 67%; ACT scores over 18: 79%; SAT evidence-based reading and writing scores over 600: 18%; SAT math scores over 600: 13%; ACT scores over 24: 22%; SAT evidence-based reading and writing scores over 700: 1%.

Retention: 70% of full-time freshmen returned.

FACULTY

Total: 327, 61% full-time, 73% with terminal degrees.

Student/faculty ratio: 14:1.

ACADEMICS

Calendar: semesters. *Degrees:* bachelor's, master's, and postbachelor's certificates.

Special study options: advanced placement credit, cooperative education, distance learning, double majors, English as a second language, honors programs, independent study, internships, off-campus study, part-time degree program, services for LD students, student-designed majors, study abroad, summer session for credit.

Computers: 216 computers/terminals and 3,500 ports are available on campus for general student use. Students can access the following: free student e-mail accounts, online (class) grades, online (class) registration, online (class) schedules. Campuswide network is available. 100% of college-owned or -operated housing units are wired for high-speed Internet access. Wireless service is available via entire campus.

Library: Henry Whittemore Library. *Books:* 156,090 (physical), 28,774 (digital/electronic); *Serial titles:* 120 (physical); *Databases:* 65. Weekly public service hours: 100.

STUDENT LIFE

Housing options: coed, women-only, special housing for students with disabilities. Campus housing is university owned. Freshman applicants given priority for college housing.

Activities and organizations: drama/theater group, student-run newspaper, radio station, choral group, Dance Club, Student Union Activities Board, Gatepost (student newspaper), Student Government Association, Hilltop Players (theater group).

Athletics Member NCAA. All Division III. ***Intercollegiate sports:*** baseball M, basketball M/W, cross-country running M/W, field hockey W, football M, ice hockey M, lacrosse W, soccer M/W, softball W, track and field W, volleyball W. ***Intramural sports:*** basketball M/W, cheerleading W(c), football M/W, golf M/W, lacrosse M(c), rugby M(c)/W(c), soccer M/W, volleyball M/W, weight lifting M/W.

Campus security: 24-hour emergency response devices and patrols, student patrols, late-night transport/escort service, controlled dormitory access.

Student services: health clinic, personal/psychological counseling, legal services, veterans affairs office.

COSTS & FINANCIAL AID

Costs (2019–20) ***Tuition:*** state resident $970 full-time, $162 per course part-time; nonresident $7050 full-time, $1175 per course part-time. ***Required fees:*** $9365 full-time, $1561 per course part-time. ***Room and board:*** $11,820. ***Payment plan:*** tuition prepayment.

Financial Aid Of all full-time matriculated undergraduates who enrolled in 2016, 2,498 applied for aid, 1,971 were judged to have need, 682 had their need fully met. In 2016, 218 non-need-based awards were made. ***Average percent of need met:*** 60. ***Average financial aid package:*** $9800. ***Average need-based loan:*** $5150. ***Average need-based gift aid:*** $4600. ***Average non-need-based aid:*** $2100. ***Average indebtedness upon graduation:*** $30,781.

APPLYING

Standardized Tests *Required:* SAT or ACT (for admission).

Options: electronic application, early action, deferred entrance.

Application fee: $50.

Required: high school transcript, minimum 2.0 GPA, minimum of 16 college preparatory courses in specified areas. ***Recommended:*** minimum 3.0 GPA.

Application deadlines: 2/15 (freshmen), 11/15 (early action).

Notification: continuous (freshmen), continuous (transfers).

CONTACT

Ms. Shayna Eddy, Associate Dean of Admissions, Framingham State University, 100 State Street, PO Box 9101, Framingham, MA 01701-9101. *Phone:* 508-626-4500. *Fax:* 508-626-4017. *E-mail:* admissions@framingham.edu.

Franklin W. Olin College of Engineering

Needham, Massachusetts

http://www.olin.edu/

- **Independent** 4-year, founded 1997
- **Suburban** 75-acre campus with easy access to Boston
- **Endowment** $384.3 million
- **Coed** 390 undergraduate students, 89% full-time, 50% women, 50% men
- **Most difficult** entrance level, 16% of applicants were admitted

UNDERGRAD STUDENTS

347 full-time, 43 part-time. Students come from 43 states and territories; 7 other countries; 89% are from out of state; 2% Black or African American, non-Hispanic/Latino; 9% Hispanic/Latino; 13% Asian, non-Hispanic/Latino; 7% Two or more races, non-Hispanic/Latino; 14%

Race/ethnicity unknown; 11% international; 0.8% transferred in; 100% live on campus.

Freshmen:
Admission: 878 applied, 138 admitted, 84 enrolled. ***Average high school GPA:*** 3.9. ***Test scores:*** SAT evidence-based reading and writing scores over 500: 100%; SAT math scores over 500: 100%; ACT scores over 18: 100%; SAT evidence-based reading and writing scores over 600: 100%; SAT math scores over 600: 100%; ACT scores over 24: 100%; SAT evidence-based reading and writing scores over 700: 82%; SAT math scores over 700: 100%; ACT scores over 30: 98%.

Retention: 100% of full-time freshmen returned.

FACULTY
Total: 58, 72% full-time, 83% with terminal degrees.

Student/faculty ratio: 8:1.

ACADEMICS
Calendar: semesters. *Degree:* bachelor's.

Special study options: independent study, internships, off-campus study, services for LD students, student-designed majors, study abroad.

Computers: 2,364 ports are available on campus for general student use. Students can access the following: campus intranet, computer help desk, free student e-mail accounts, online (class) grades, online (class) registration, online (class) schedules. Campuswide network is available. 100% of college-owned or -operated housing units are wired for high-speed Internet access. Wireless service is available via entire campus.
Library: Franklin W. Olin Library. *Books:* 24,500 (physical), 414,224 (digital/electronic); *Serial titles:* 35 (physical), 159,537 (digital/electronic); *Databases:* 112. Study areas open 24 hours, 5–7 days a week; students can reserve study rooms.

STUDENT LIFE
Housing options: on-campus residence required through senior year; coed, special housing for students with disabilities. Campus housing is university owned. Freshman campus housing is guaranteed.

Activities and organizations: drama/theater group, student-run newspaper, choral group, Council of Olin Representatives, Stay Late and Create, Support, Encourage and Recognize Volunteerism (SERV), Mini Baja, Olin Fire Arts Club.

Athletics ***Intercollegiate sports:*** soccer M(c)/W(c), ultimate Frisbee M(c)/W(c). ***Intramural sports:*** basketball M/W, softball M/W, volleyball M/W.

Campus security: 24-hour emergency response devices and patrols, controlled dormitory access.

Student services: health clinic, personal/psychological counseling.

COSTS & FINANCIAL AID
Costs (2019–20) ***One-time required fee:*** $2656. ***Comprehensive fee:*** $69,716 includes full-time tuition ($52,164), mandatory fees ($680), and room and board ($16,872). Part-time tuition: $1630 per credit hour.

Financial Aid Of all full-time matriculated undergraduates who enrolled in 2018, 184 applied for aid, 153 were judged to have need, 153 had their need fully met. In 2018, 191 non-need-based awards were made. ***Average percent of need met:*** 100. ***Average financial aid package:*** $49,873. ***Average need-based loan:*** $3216. ***Average need-based gift aid:*** $48,507. ***Average non-need-based aid:*** $24,734. ***Average indebtedness upon graduation:*** $20,480.

APPLYING
Standardized Tests *Required:* SAT or ACT (for admission).

Options: electronic application, deferred entrance.

Application fee: $85.

Required: essay or personal statement, high school transcript, 3 letters of recommendation, interview.

Notification: 4/1 (freshmen).

CONTACT
Ms. Emily Roper-Doten, Dean of Admission and Financial Aid, Franklin W. Olin College of Engineering, 1000 Olin Way, Needham, MA 02492-1200. *Phone:* 781-292-2222. *Fax:* 781-292-2210. *E-mail:* emily.roper-doten@olin.edu.

Gordon College

Wenham, Massachusetts

http://www.gordon.edu/

- **Independent nondenominational** comprehensive, founded 1889
- **Suburban** 485-acre campus with easy access to Boston
- **Endowment** $56.8 million
- **Coed** 1,618 undergraduate students, 96% full-time, 63% women, 37% men
- **Moderately difficult** entrance level, 75% of applicants were admitted

UNDERGRAD STUDENTS
1,555 full-time, 63 part-time. Students come from 44 states and territories; 48 other countries; 67% are from out of state; 5% Black or African American, non-Hispanic/Latino; 9% Hispanic/Latino; 5% Asian, non-Hispanic/Latino; 0.1% American Indian or Alaska Native, non-Hispanic/Latino; 3% Two or more races, non-Hispanic/Latino; 2% Race/ethnicity unknown; 9% international; 2% transferred in; 89% live on campus.

Freshmen:
Admission: 3,062 applied, 2,311 admitted, 432 enrolled. ***Average high school GPA:*** 3.6. ***Test scores:*** SAT evidence-based reading and writing scores over 500: 89%; SAT math scores over 500: 81%; ACT scores over 18: 97%; SAT evidence-based reading and writing scores over 600: 53%; SAT math scores over 600: 37%; ACT scores over 24: 71%; SAT evidence-based reading and writing scores over 700: 12%; SAT math scores over 700: 7%; ACT scores over 30: 28%.

Retention: 83% of full-time freshmen returned.

FACULTY
Total: 243, 38% full-time, 32% with terminal degrees.

Student/faculty ratio: 11:1.

ACADEMICS
Calendar: semesters. *Degrees:* bachelor's and master's.

Special study options: advanced placement credit, cooperative education, double majors, honors programs, independent study, internships, off-campus study, part-time degree program, services for LD students, student-designed majors, study abroad, summer session for credit. ***ROTC:*** Army (c), Air Force (c).

Unusual degree programs: 3-2 engineering with University of Southern California; nursing with Curry College.

Computers: 100 computers/terminals and 10 ports are available on campus for general student use. Students can access the following: campus intranet, computer help desk, free student e-mail accounts, online (class) grades, online (class) registration, online (class) schedules. Campuswide network is available. 100% of college-owned or -operated housing units are wired for high-speed Internet access. Wireless service is available via entire campus.
Library: Jenks Learning Resource Center. *Books:* 131,441 (physical), 199,117 (digital/electronic); *Serial titles:* 1,849 (physical). Weekly public service hours: 103; students can reserve study rooms.

STUDENT LIFE
Housing options: coed, men-only, women-only, special housing for students with disabilities. Campus housing is university owned. Freshman campus housing is guaranteed.

Activities and organizations: drama/theater group, student-run newspaper, radio station, choral group, Student Government Association, Student ministries and volunteer programs, Diverse music ensembles, Intramural sports, Short-term missions.

Athletics Member NCAA. All Division III. ***Intercollegiate sports:*** baseball M, basketball M/W, cross-country running M/W, field hockey W, lacrosse M/W, soccer M/W, softball W, swimming and diving M/W, tennis M/W, track and field M/W, volleyball W. ***Intramural sports:*** badminton M/W, basketball M/W, football M/W, racquetball M/W, rowing M(c)/W(c), soccer M/W, triathlon M/W, volleyball M/W, water polo M/W.

Campus security: 24-hour emergency response devices and patrols, late-night transport/escort service, controlled dormitory access.

Student services: health clinic, personal/psychological counseling.

COSTS & FINANCIAL AID
Costs (2019–20) ***Comprehensive fee:*** $49,900 includes full-time tuition ($37,000), mandatory fees ($1650), and room and board ($11,250). Part-

time tuition: $925 per credit. ***College room only:*** $7100.

Financial Aid Of all full-time matriculated undergraduates who enrolled in 2018, 1,211 applied for aid, 1,034 were judged to have need, 218 had their need fully met. 648 Federal Work-Study jobs (averaging $585). In 2018, 493 non-need-based awards were made. ***Average percent of need met:*** 74. ***Average financial aid package:*** $27,298. ***Average need-based loan:*** $4330. ***Average need-based gift aid:*** $22,802. ***Average non-need-based aid:*** $17,276. ***Average indebtedness upon graduation:*** $39,930.

APPLYING
Standardized Tests *Required:* SAT or ACT (for admission).

Options: electronic application, early admission, early action, deferred entrance.

Application fee: $50.

Required: essay or personal statement, high school transcript, 1 letter of recommendation, interview, pastoral recommendation and statement of Christian faith. ***Recommended:*** minimum 3.0 GPA.

Application deadlines: rolling (out-of-state freshmen), rolling (transfers).

Notification: continuous until 8/15 (freshmen), continuous (out-of-state freshmen), continuous (transfers).

CONTACT
Miss June Bodoni, Associate Vice President for Enrollment, Gordon College, 255 Grapevine Road, Wenham, MA 01984. *Phone:* 978-867-4218. *Toll-free phone:* 866-464-6736. *Fax:* 978-867-4682. *E-mail:* admissions@gordon.edu.

Hampshire College

Amherst, Massachusetts

http://www.hampshire.edu/

- **Independent** 4-year, founded 1965
- **Small-town** 800-acre campus
- **Endowment** $48.5 million
- **Coed**
- **Moderately difficult** entrance level

FACULTY
Student/faculty ratio: 10:1.

ACADEMICS
Calendar: semesters. *Degree:* bachelor's.
Library: Harold F. Johnson Library. *Books:* 125,971 (physical), 194,919 (digital/electronic); *Serial titles:* 753 (physical), 37,716 (digital/electronic); *Databases:* 133. Weekly public service hours: 102; study areas open 24 hours, 5–7 days a week; students can reserve study rooms.

STUDENT LIFE
Housing options: on-campus residence required through senior year; coed, men-only, women-only, special housing for students with disabilities. Campus housing is university owned. Freshman campus housing is guaranteed.

Activities and organizations: drama/theater group, student-run newspaper, radio station, choral group, Red Scare Frisbee, Queer Community Alliance, Excalibur (fantasy/role playing), Sports Coop, Circus Folks Unite.

Athletics Member USCAA.

Campus security: 24-hour emergency response devices and patrols.

Student services: health clinic, personal/psychological counseling, women's center.

COSTS & FINANCIAL AID
Costs (2018–19) ***Comprehensive fee:*** $63,636 includes full-time tuition ($50,030) and room and board ($13,606). ***College room only:*** $8520. Room and board charges vary according to board plan.

Financial Aid Of all full-time matriculated undergraduates who enrolled in 2018, 930 applied for aid, 818 were judged to have need, 141 had their need fully met. In 2018, 305 non-need-based awards were made. ***Average percent of need met:*** 93. ***Average financial aid package:*** $44,032. ***Average need-based loan:*** $4482. ***Average need-based gift aid:*** $37,225. ***Average non-need-based aid:*** $12,368. ***Average indebtedness upon graduation:*** $28,150. ***Financial aid deadline:*** 1/15.

APPLYING
Options: electronic application, early admission, early decision, early action, deferred entrance.

Required: essay or personal statement, high school transcript, 1 letter of recommendation. ***Recommended:*** interview.

CONTACT
Hampshire College, 893 West Street, Amherst, MA 01002. *Phone:* 413-559-5752. *Toll-free phone:* 877-937-4267. *E-mail:* admissions@hampshire.edu.

Harvard University

Cambridge, Massachusetts

http://www.harvard.edu/

- **Independent** university, founded 1636
- **Urban** 380-acre campus with easy access to Boston
- **Endowment** $39.2 billion
- **Coed** 6,788 undergraduate students, 100% full-time, 49% women, 51% men
- **Most difficult** entrance level, 5% of applicants were admitted

UNDERGRAD STUDENTS
6,785 full-time, 3 part-time. Students come from 56 states and territories; 106 other countries; 84% are from out of state; 8% Black or African American, non-Hispanic/Latino; 11% Hispanic/Latino; 20% Asian, non-Hispanic/Latino; 0.2% American Indian or Alaska Native, non-Hispanic/Latino; 7% Two or more races, non-Hispanic/Latino; 2% Race/ethnicity unknown; 13% international; 0.2% transferred in; 97% live on campus.

Freshmen:
Admission: 39,506 applied, 2,037 admitted, 1,652 enrolled. ***Average high school GPA:*** 4.2. ***Test scores:*** SAT evidence-based reading and writing scores over 500: 100%; SAT math scores over 500: 100%; ACT scores over 18: 100%; SAT evidence-based reading and writing scores over 600: 99%; SAT math scores over 600: 99%; ACT scores over 24: 100%; SAT evidence-based reading and writing scores over 700: 85%; SAT math scores over 700: 88%; ACT scores over 30: 95%.

Retention: 98% of full-time freshmen returned.

FACULTY
Total: 1,154, 85% full-time, 85% with terminal degrees.

Student/faculty ratio: 6:1.

ACADEMICS
Calendar: semesters. *Degrees:* bachelor's, master's, and doctoral.

Special study options: accelerated degree program, advanced placement credit, double majors, honors programs, independent study, internships, off-campus study, services for LD students, student-designed majors, study abroad, summer session for credit. ***ROTC:*** Army (b), Navy (b), Air Force (b).

Computers: 605 computers/terminals are available on campus for general student use. Students can access the following: computer help desk, free student e-mail accounts, online (class) grades, online (class) registration, online (class) schedules. Campuswide network is available. 100% of college-owned or -operated housing units are wired for high-speed Internet access. Wireless service is available via entire campus.
Library: Widener Library.

STUDENT LIFE
Housing options: on-campus residence required for freshman year; coed, cooperative, special housing for students with disabilities. Campus housing is university owned. Freshman campus housing is guaranteed.

Activities and organizations: drama/theater group, student-run newspaper, radio and television station, choral group, marching band, Phillips Brooks House Association, Asian-American Association, International Relations Council, Harvard Crimson (newspaper), Harvard/Radcliffe Chorus.

Athletics Member NCAA. All Division I except football (Division I-AA). ***Intercollegiate sports:*** baseball M, basketball M/W, crew M/W, cross-country running M/W, fencing M/W, field hockey W, golf M/W(c), ice hockey M/W, lacrosse M/W, rugby W, sailing M/W, skiing (cross-country) M/W, skiing (downhill) M(c)/W, soccer M/W, softball W, squash M/W, swimming and diving M/W, tennis M/W, track and field M/W, volleyball

M/W, water polo M/W, wrestling M. ***Intramural sports:*** archery M(c)/W(c), badminton M(c)/W(c), baseball M(c), basketball M/W, bowling M(c)/W(c), cheerleading M(c)/W(c), cross-country running M/W, fencing M/W(c), field hockey W, golf M(c)/W(c), gymnastics M(c)/W(c), ice hockey M/W, lacrosse M(c)/W(c), rugby M(c), skiing (cross-country) M(c)/W(c), skiing (downhill) M(c)/W(c), soccer M/W, squash M/W, swimming and diving M/W, table tennis M/W, tennis M/W, ultimate Frisbee M/W, volleyball M/W, water polo M(c)/W(c), weight lifting M(c)/W(c), wrestling M(c)/W(c).

Campus security: 24-hour emergency response devices and patrols, late-night transport/escort service, controlled dormitory access, required and optional safety courses.

Student services: health clinic, personal/psychological counseling, women's center.

COSTS & FINANCIAL AID

Costs (2018–19) ***Comprehensive fee:*** $67,580 includes full-time tuition ($46,340), mandatory fees ($4080), and room and board ($17,160). ***College room only:*** $10,609. ***Payment plans:*** tuition prepayment, installment.

Financial Aid Of all full-time matriculated undergraduates who enrolled in 2017, 3,973 applied for aid, 3,661 were judged to have need, 3,661 had their need fully met. 919 Federal Work-Study jobs (averaging $2805). 2,136 state and other part-time jobs (averaging $2871). In 2017, 13 non-need-based awards were made. ***Average percent of need met:*** 100. ***Average financial aid package:*** $56,820. ***Average need-based loan:*** $4406. ***Average need-based gift aid:*** $54,001. ***Average non-need-based aid:*** $15,730. ***Average indebtedness upon graduation:*** $13,372.

APPLYING

Standardized Tests *Required:* SAT or ACT (for admission), SAT Subject Tests (for admission).

Options: electronic application, early admission, early action, deferred entrance.

Application fee: $75.

Required: essay or personal statement, high school transcript. ***Recommended:*** 2 letters of recommendation, interview.

Application deadlines: 1/1 (freshmen), 3/1 (transfers).

Notification: 4/1 (freshmen), 6/15 (transfers).

CONTACT

Dr. William R. Fitzsimmons, Dean of Admissions and Financial Aid, Harvard University, Cambridge, MA 02138. *Phone:* 617-495-1551. *E-mail:* college@harvard.edu.

Hellenic College

Brookline, Massachusetts

http://www.hchc.edu/

CONTACT

Mr. Gregory Floor, Director of Admissions, Hellenic College, 50 Goddard Avenue, Brookline, MA 02445-7496. *Phone:* 617-850-1285. *Toll-free phone:* 866-424-2338. *Fax:* 617-850-1460. *E-mail:* admissions@hchc.edu.

Hult International Business School

Cambridge, Massachusetts

http://www.hult.edu/

CONTACT

Hult International Business School, 1 Education Street, Cambridge, MA 02141.

Lasell College

Newton, Massachusetts

http://www.lasell.edu/

- **Independent** comprehensive, founded 1851
- **Suburban** 53-acre campus with easy access to Boston
- **Endowment** $41.4 million
- **Coed** 1,674 undergraduate students, 97% full-time, 64% women, 36% men
- **Moderately difficult** entrance level, 80% of applicants were admitted

UNDERGRAD STUDENTS

1,624 full-time, 50 part-time. Students come from 28 states and territories; 22 other countries; 40% are from out of state; 7% Black or African American, non-Hispanic/Latino; 10% Hispanic/Latino; 2% Asian, non-Hispanic/Latino; 0.1% Native Hawaiian or other Pacific Islander, non-Hispanic/Latino; 0.1% American Indian or Alaska Native, non-Hispanic/Latino; 2% Two or more races, non-Hispanic/Latino; 6% Race/ethnicity unknown; 6% international; 9% transferred in; 73% live on campus.

Freshmen:

Admission: 3,180 applied, 2,537 admitted, 381 enrolled. ***Average high school GPA:*** 3.0. ***Test scores:*** SAT evidence-based reading and writing scores over 500: 76%; SAT math scores over 500: 73%; ACT scores over 18: 62%; SAT evidence-based reading and writing scores over 600: 22%; SAT math scores over 600: 15%; ACT scores over 24: 34%; SAT evidence-based reading and writing scores over 700: 1%; SAT math scores over 700: 2%.

Retention: 68% of full-time freshmen returned.

FACULTY

Total: 248, 34% full-time, 52% with terminal degrees.

Student/faculty ratio: 13:1.

ACADEMICS

Calendar: semesters. *Degrees:* bachelor's and master's.

Special study options: accelerated degree program, advanced placement credit, cooperative education, distance learning, double majors, English as a second language, honors programs, independent study, internships, off-campus study, part-time degree program, services for LD students, student-designed majors, study abroad, summer session for credit.

Unusual degree programs: 3-2 business administration with Lasell College; communication, sport management.

Computers: 219 computers/terminals are available on campus for general student use. Students can access the following: campus intranet, computer help desk, free student e-mail accounts, online (class) grades, online (class) registration, online (class) schedules, online tutoring. Campuswide network is available. 100% of college-owned or -operated housing units are wired for high-speed Internet access. Wireless service is available via entire campus.

Library: Brennan Library. *Books:* 35,093 (physical), 59,782 (digital/electronic); *Serial titles:* 63 (physical), 113,658 (digital/electronic); *Databases:* 88. Weekly public service hours: 83; students can reserve study rooms.

STUDENT LIFE

Housing options: coed, women-only, special housing for students with disabilities. Campus housing is university owned. Freshman campus housing is guaranteed.

Activities and organizations: drama/theater group, student-run newspaper, radio station, choral group, 19851 Chronicle, Campus Activities Board, Hope for Humanity, Lasell College Drama Club, Lasell College Radio (Marathon Monday).

Athletics Member NCAA. All Division III. ***Intercollegiate sports:*** baseball M, basketball M/W, cross-country running M/W, field hockey W, lacrosse M/W, soccer M/W, softball W, track and field M/W, volleyball M/W. ***Intramural sports:*** basketball M/W, cheerleading M(c)/W(c), crew M(c)/W(c), rugby M(c)/W(c), skiing (downhill) M(c)/W(c), tennis M(c)/W(c), ultimate Frisbee M(c).

Campus security: 24-hour emergency response devices and patrols, late-night transport/escort service, controlled dormitory access.

Student services: health clinic, personal/psychological counseling.

COSTS & FINANCIAL AID

Costs (2019–20) ***Comprehensive fee:*** $53,000 includes full-time tuition ($35,700), mandatory fees ($1300), and room and board ($16,000). Part-time tuition: $1155 per credit hour. ***Required fees:*** $325 per term part-time.

Financial Aid Of all full-time matriculated undergraduates who enrolled in 2018, 1,394 applied for aid, 1,318 were judged to have need, 176 had their need fully met. In 2018, 238 non-need-based awards were made. ***Average percent of need met:*** 52. ***Average financial aid package:*** $28,800. ***Average need-based loan:*** $3589. ***Average need-based gift aid:***

$25,300. ***Average non-need-based aid:*** $12,600. ***Average indebtedness upon graduation:*** $41,476.

APPLYING
Standardized Tests *Required for some:* SAT or ACT (for admission).

Options: electronic application, early action, deferred entrance.

Application fee: $40.

Required: essay or personal statement, high school transcript, 2 letters of recommendation, college preparatory program. ***Recommended:*** interview.

Application deadlines: rolling (freshmen), rolling (transfers), 11/15 (early action).

Notification: continuous (transfers).

CONTACT
Dean James Tweed, Dean of Undergraduate Admission, Lasell College, 1844 Commonwealth Avenue, Newton, MA 02466. *Phone:* 617-243-2225. *Toll-free phone:* 888-LASELL-4. *Fax:* 617-243-2380. *E-mail:* info@lasell.edu.

Lesley University
Cambridge, Massachusetts
http://www.lesley.edu/

- **Independent** comprehensive, founded 1909
- **Urban** campus with easy access to Boston
- **Coed, primarily women** 2,208 undergraduate students, 77% full-time, 79% women, 21% men
- 76% of applicants were admitted

UNDERGRAD STUDENTS
1,699 full-time, 509 part-time. 33% are from out of state; 7% Black or African American, non-Hispanic/Latino; 15% Hispanic/Latino; 5% Asian, non-Hispanic/Latino; 0.2% American Indian or Alaska Native, non-Hispanic/Latino; 4% Two or more races, non-Hispanic/Latino; 4% Race/ethnicity unknown; 4% international; 6% transferred in; 43% live on campus.

Freshmen:
Admission: 3,171 applied, 2,401 admitted, 378 enrolled. ***Average high school GPA:*** 3.2. ***Test scores:*** SAT evidence-based reading and writing scores over 500: 89%; SAT math scores over 500: 79%; ACT scores over 18: 94%; SAT evidence-based reading and writing scores over 600: 45%; SAT math scores over 600: 21%; ACT scores over 24: 62%; SAT evidence-based reading and writing scores over 700: 6%; SAT math scores over 700: 1%; ACT scores over 30: 15%.

Retention: 80% of full-time freshmen returned.

FACULTY
Total: 665, 22% full-time, 35% with terminal degrees.

Student/faculty ratio: 12:1.

ACADEMICS
Calendar: semesters. *Degrees:* certificates, associate, bachelor's, master's, doctoral, post-master's, and postbachelor's certificates.

Special study options: academic remediation for entering students, accelerated degree program, adult/continuing education programs, advanced placement credit, distance learning, double majors, freshman honors college, honors programs, independent study, internships, off-campus study, part-time degree program, services for LD students, student-designed majors, study abroad, summer session for credit.

Computers: Students can access the following: free student e-mail accounts, online (class) registration. Campuswide network is available. Wireless service is available via classrooms, student centers.
Library: Sherrill Library.

STUDENT LIFE
Housing options: coed, women-only. Campus housing is university owned and leased by the school. Freshman applicants given priority for college housing.

Activities and organizations: drama/theater group, student-run newspaper, choral group.

Athletics Member NCAA. All Division III except baseball (Division II). ***Intercollegiate sports:*** baseball M, basketball M/W, cross-country running M/W, soccer M/W, softball W, volleyball M/W. ***Intramural sports:*** swimming and diving M/W, tennis M.

Campus security: 24-hour emergency response devices and patrols, late-night transport/escort service, controlled dormitory access.

Student services: health clinic, personal/psychological counseling.

COSTS & FINANCIAL AID
Costs (2019–20) ***Comprehensive fee:*** $44,730 includes full-time tuition ($28,500) and room and board ($16,230). Part-time tuition: $920 per credit hour. ***College room only:*** $9830.

Financial Aid Of all full-time matriculated undergraduates who enrolled in 2018, 1,321 applied for aid, 1,176 were judged to have need, 134 had their need fully met. In 2018, 467 non-need-based awards were made. ***Average percent of need met:*** 70. ***Average financial aid package:*** $17,832. ***Average need-based loan:*** $4475. ***Average need-based gift aid:*** $13,073. ***Average non-need-based aid:*** $10,957. ***Average indebtedness upon graduation:*** $23,000.

APPLYING
Standardized Tests *Required for some:* SAT or ACT (for admission).

Options: electronic application, early action, deferred entrance.

Required: essay or personal statement, high school transcript. ***Recommended:*** interview.

Notification: continuous until 1/15 (freshmen), continuous (transfers), rolling (early action).

CONTACT
Ms. Deborah Kocar, Director of Admissions, Lesley University, 29 Everett Street, Cambridge, MA 02138-2790. *Phone:* 617-349-8800. *Toll-free phone:* 800-999-1959 Ext. 8800. *Fax:* 617-349-8810. *E-mail:* lcadmissions@lesley.edu.

Massachusetts College of Art and Design
Boston, Massachusetts
http://www.massart.edu/

- **State-supported** comprehensive, founded 1873, part of Massachusetts Public Higher Education System
- **Urban** 5-acre campus
- **Endowment** $16.0 million
- **Coed**
- **Moderately difficult** entrance level

FACULTY
Student/faculty ratio: 9:1.

ACADEMICS
Calendar: semesters. *Degrees:* certificates, bachelor's, master's, and postbachelor's certificates.
Library: Morton R. Godine Library. *Books:* 106,885 (physical), 173,498 (digital/electronic); *Databases:* 75.

STUDENT LIFE
Housing options: coed. Campus housing is university owned. Freshman campus housing is guaranteed.

Activities and organizations: drama/theater group, student-run newspaper, radio and television station, choral group, International Students' Club, Design Research Unit, Spectrum, film society, Event Works.

Campus security: 24-hour emergency response devices and patrols, late-night transport/escort service, controlled dormitory access, security lighting, self-defense workshops.

Student services: health clinic, personal/psychological counseling, women's center.

COSTS & FINANCIAL AID
Costs (2018–19) ***Tuition:*** state resident $13,200 full-time; nonresident $36,400 full-time. ***Room and board:*** $13,500. Room and board charges vary according to board plan and housing facility.

Financial Aid Of all full-time matriculated undergraduates who enrolled in 2018, 1,314 applied for aid, 1,079 were judged to have need. In 2018, 443 non-need-based awards were made. ***Average financial aid package:*** $7948. ***Average need-based loan:*** $4286. ***Average need-based gift aid:*** $7086. ***Average non-need-based aid:*** $4880. ***Average indebtedness upon graduation:*** $26,792.

APPLYING

Options: electronic application, early action, deferred entrance.

Application fee: $70.

Required: essay or personal statement, high school transcript, 2 letters of recommendation, portfolio of 15-20 pieces of artwork completed in the last 2 years. ***Recommended:*** minimum 3.0 GPA.

CONTACT

Lauren Wilshusen, Massachusetts College of Art and Design, 621 Huntington Avenue, Boston, MA 02115. *Phone:* 617-879-7222. *Fax:* 617-879-7250. *E-mail:* admissions@massart.edu.

Massachusetts College of Liberal Arts

North Adams, Massachusetts

http://www.mcla.edu/

- **State-supported** comprehensive, founded 1894, part of Massachusetts State University System
- **Small-town** 105-acre campus with easy access to Albany-Schenectady-Troy New York Metro Area
- **Coed** 1,277 undergraduate students, 87% full-time, 62% women, 38% men
- **Moderately difficult** entrance level, 74% of applicants were admitted

UNDERGRAD STUDENTS

1,109 full-time, 168 part-time. 25% are from out of state; 8% Black or African American, non-Hispanic/Latino; 10% Hispanic/Latino; 2% Asian, non-Hispanic/Latino; 0.1% Native Hawaiian or other Pacific Islander, non-Hispanic/Latino; 0.3% American Indian or Alaska Native, non-Hispanic/Latino; 3% Two or more races, non-Hispanic/Latino; 4% Race/ethnicity unknown; 0.5% international; 9% transferred in; 58% live on campus.

Freshmen:

Admission: 1,931 applied, 1,423 admitted, 262 enrolled. ***Average high school GPA:*** 3.2. ***Test scores:*** SAT evidence-based reading and writing scores over 500: 77%; SAT math scores over 500: 71%; ACT scores over 18: 82%; SAT evidence-based reading and writing scores over 600: 28%; SAT math scores over 600: 19%; ACT scores over 24: 27%; SAT evidence-based reading and writing scores over 700: 3%; SAT math scores over 700: 2%; ACT scores over 30: 9%.

Retention: 70% of full-time freshmen returned.

FACULTY

Total: 172, 52% full-time.

Student/faculty ratio: 12:1.

ACADEMICS

Calendar: semesters. *Degrees:* certificates, bachelor's, master's, post-master's, and postbachelor's certificates.

Special study options: academic remediation for entering students, accelerated degree program, adult/continuing education programs, advanced placement credit, cooperative education, distance learning, double majors, honors programs, independent study, internships, off-campus study, part-time degree program, services for LD students, student-designed majors, study abroad, summer session for credit.

Unusual degree programs: 3-2 engineering with University of Massachusetts Amherst; podiatric medicine with the New York School of Podiatric Medicine.

Computers: 140 computers/terminals are available on campus for general student use. Students can access the following: campus intranet, computer help desk, free student e-mail accounts, online (class) grades, online (class) registration, online (class) schedules. Campuswide network is available. 100% of college-owned or -operated housing units are wired for high-speed Internet access. Wireless service is available via entire campus.

Library: Eugene L. Freel Library. *Books:* 125,000 (physical), 229,000 (digital/electronic); *Serial titles:* 1,000 (physical), 43,000 (digital/electronic); *Databases:* 82.

STUDENT LIFE

Housing options: on-campus residence required through junior year; coed, special housing for students with disabilities. Campus housing is university owned. Freshman campus housing is guaranteed.

Activities and organizations: drama/theater group, student-run newspaper, radio and television station, choral group, Student Activities Council, Student Government Association, The Beacon (Student Newspaper), Harlequin-Musical Theatre Company, Dance Company.

Athletics Member NCAA. All Division III. ***Intercollegiate sports:*** baseball M, basketball M/W, cross-country running M/W, golf M, lacrosse W, soccer M/W, softball W, tennis M/W, volleyball W. ***Intramural sports:*** basketball M/W, cheerleading W(c), equestrian sports M/W, football M/W, golf M/W, lacrosse M(c), racquetball M/W, rugby M(c)/W(c), skiing (cross-country) M/W, skiing (downhill) M/W, soccer M/W, softball M/W, squash M/W, tennis M/W, ultimate Frisbee M/W, volleyball M/W.

Campus security: 24-hour emergency response devices and patrols, late-night transport/escort service, controlled dormitory access.

Student services: health clinic, personal/psychological counseling, women's center, veterans affairs office.

COSTS & FINANCIAL AID

Costs (2018–19) ***Tuition:*** state resident $1030 full-time, $43 per credit part-time; nonresident $9975 full-time, $416 per credit part-time. Full-time tuition and fees vary according to reciprocity agreements. Part-time tuition and fees vary according to course load and reciprocity agreements. ***Required fees:*** $9529 full-time, $323 per credit part-time. ***Room and board:*** $10,980. Room and board charges vary according to board plan and housing facility. ***Payment plan:*** installment. ***Waivers:*** senior citizens and employees or children of employees.

Financial Aid Of all full-time matriculated undergraduates who enrolled in 2018, 1,043 applied for aid, 871 were judged to have need, 685 had their need fully met. In 2018, 106 non-need-based awards were made. ***Average percent of need met:*** 79. ***Average financial aid package:*** $16,322. ***Average need-based loan:*** $3716. ***Average need-based gift aid:*** $7705. ***Average non-need-based aid:*** $3204. ***Average indebtedness upon graduation:*** $30,212.

APPLYING

Standardized Tests *Required:* SAT or ACT (for admission).

Options: electronic application, early admission, early action, deferred entrance.

Required: essay or personal statement, high school transcript, minimum 3.0 GPA, 1 letter of recommendation. ***Required for some:*** interview, sliding scale applies (GPA and SAT) if below 3.0.

Application deadlines: rolling (freshmen), rolling (transfers).

Notification: continuous (freshmen), continuous (transfers), 12/15 (early action).

CONTACT

Ms. Kayla Hollins, Associate Director of Admission, Massachusetts College of Liberal Arts, 375 Church Street, North Adams, MA 01247. *Phone:* 413-662-5410. *Toll-free phone:* 800-989-MCLA. *E-mail:* kayla.kollins@mcla.edu.

Massachusetts Institute of Technology

Cambridge, Massachusetts

http://www.mit.edu/

- **Independent** university, founded 1861
- **Urban** 166-acre campus with easy access to Boston
- **Endowment** $16.4 billion
- **Coed** 4,602 undergraduate students, 99% full-time, 46% women, 54% men
- **Most difficult** entrance level, 7% of applicants were admitted

UNDERGRAD STUDENTS

4,557 full-time, 45 part-time. 91% are from out of state; 6% Black or African American, non-Hispanic/Latino; 15% Hispanic/Latino; 28% Asian, non-Hispanic/Latino; 0.1% American Indian or Alaska Native, non-Hispanic/Latino; 7% Two or more races, non-Hispanic/Latino; 2% Race/ethnicity unknown; 10% international; 0.5% transferred in; 92% live on campus.

Freshmen:
Admission: 20,247 applied, 1,452 admitted, 1,114 enrolled. ***Test scores:*** SAT evidence-based reading and writing scores over 500: 100%; SAT math scores over 500: 100%; ACT scores over 18: 100%; SAT evidence-based reading and writing scores over 600: 100%; SAT math scores over 600: 100%; ACT scores over 24: 100%; SAT evidence-based reading and writing scores over 700: 87%; SAT math scores over 700: 100%; ACT scores over 30: 99%.
Retention: 99% of full-time freshmen returned.

FACULTY
Total: 1,617, 81% full-time, 88% with terminal degrees.
Student/faculty ratio: 3:1.

ACADEMICS
Calendar: 4-1-4. *Degrees:* bachelor's, master's, and doctoral.
Special study options: advanced placement credit, cooperative education, double majors, English as a second language, independent study, internships, off-campus study, services for LD students, study abroad. ***ROTC:*** Army (b), Navy (b), Air Force (b).
Computers: 1,050 computers/terminals and 50,000 ports are available on campus for general student use. Students can access the following: campus intranet, computer help desk, free student e-mail accounts, online (class) grades, online (class) registration, online (class) schedules. Campuswide network is available. 100% of college-owned or -operated housing units are wired for high-speed Internet access. Wireless service is available via entire campus.
Library: MIT Libraries plus 5 others. *Books:* 1.3 million (physical), 758,981 (digital/electronic); *Serial titles:* 50,139 (physical), 58,996 (digital/electronic); *Databases:* 336. Weekly public service hours: 95; study areas open 24 hours, 5–7 days a week; students can reserve study rooms.

STUDENT LIFE
Housing options: on-campus residence required for freshman year; coed, women-only, cooperative, special housing for students with disabilities. Campus housing is university owned. Freshman campus housing is guaranteed.
Activities and organizations: drama/theater group, student-run newspaper, radio and television station, choral group, marching band, Educational Studies Program, Dance Troupe, Science Fiction Society, The Tech (student newspaper), Anime Club, national fraternities, national sororities.
Athletics Member NCAA. All Division III except men's and women's crew (Division I), men's and women's rowing (Division I). ***Intercollegiate sports:*** baseball M, basketball M/W, crew M/W, cross-country running M/W, fencing M/W, field hockey W, football M, lacrosse M/W, riflery M/W, rowing M/W, sailing M/W, soccer M/W, softball W, squash M, swimming and diving M/W, tennis M/W, track and field M/W, volleyball M/W, water polo M. ***Intramural sports:*** archery M(c)/W(c), badminton M/W, basketball M/W, cheerleading M(c)/W(c), crew M(c)/W(c), golf M(c)/W(c), gymnastics M(c)/W(c), ice hockey M/W, rowing M(c)/W(c), rugby M(c)/W(c), soccer M/W, softball M/W, table tennis M/W, tennis M/W, triathlon M(c)/W(c), ultimate Frisbee M/W, volleyball M/W, water polo M/W, wrestling M(c).
Campus security: 24-hour emergency response devices and patrols, late-night transport/escort service, controlled dormitory access.
Student services: health clinic, personal/psychological counseling.

COSTS & FINANCIAL AID
Costs (2019–20) ***Comprehensive fee:*** $70,180 includes full-time tuition ($53,450), mandatory fees ($340), and room and board ($16,390). ***Required fees:*** $830 per credit hour part-time. ***College room only:*** $10,430.
Financial Aid Of all full-time matriculated undergraduates who enrolled in 2017, 2,947 applied for aid, 2,652 were judged to have need, 2,650 had their need fully met. 436 Federal Work-Study jobs (averaging $2957). 1,437 state and other part-time jobs (averaging $2835). ***Average percent of need met:*** 100. ***Average financial aid package:*** $50,292. ***Average need-based loan:*** $2959. ***Average need-based gift aid:*** $48,562. ***Average indebtedness upon graduation:*** $22,696. ***Financial aid deadline:*** 2/15.

APPLYING
Standardized Tests *Required:* SAT or ACT (for admission), SAT Subject Tests (for admission).
Options: electronic application, early admission, early action, deferred entrance.
Application fee: $75.
Required: essay or personal statement, high school transcript, 2 letters of recommendation. ***Recommended:*** interview.
Application deadlines: 1/1 (freshmen), 3/15 (transfers), 11/1 (early action).
Notification: 3/20 (freshmen), 5/1 (transfers), 12/20 (early action).

CONTACT
Stuart Schmill, Dean of Admissions, Massachusetts Institute of Technology, 77 Massachusetts Avenue, Cambridge, MA 02139-4307. *Phone:* 617-253-3400. *Fax:* 617-258-8304. *E-mail:* admissions@mit.edu.

Massachusetts Maritime Academy

Buzzards Bay, Massachusetts

http://www.maritime.edu/

- **State-supported** comprehensive, founded 1891, part of Massachusetts State University System
- **Small-town** 54-acre campus with easy access to Boston, Providence
- **Coed** 1,709 undergraduate students, 94% full-time, 14% women, 86% men
- **Moderately difficult** entrance level, 89% of applicants were admitted

UNDERGRAD STUDENTS
1,614 full-time, 95 part-time. 19% are from out of state; 1% Black or African American, non-Hispanic/Latino; 4% Hispanic/Latino; 1% Asian, non-Hispanic/Latino; 0.1% American Indian or Alaska Native, non-Hispanic/Latino; 2% Two or more races, non-Hispanic/Latino; 4% Race/ethnicity unknown; 0.6% international; 2% transferred in; 97% live on campus.

Freshmen:
Admission: 758 applied, 675 admitted, 399 enrolled. ***Average high school GPA:*** 3.2. ***Test scores:*** SAT evidence-based reading and writing scores over 500: 85%; SAT math scores over 500: 89%; ACT scores over 18: 88%; SAT evidence-based reading and writing scores over 600: 30%; SAT math scores over 600: 28%; ACT scores over 24: 55%; SAT evidence-based reading and writing scores over 700: 2%; SAT math scores over 700: 1%; ACT scores over 30: 7%.
Retention: 86% of full-time freshmen returned.

FACULTY
Total: 141, 62% full-time, 45% with terminal degrees.
Student/faculty ratio: 16:1.

ACADEMICS
Calendar: 4-1-4 plus sea term. *Degrees:* bachelor's and master's.
Special study options: advanced placement credit, cooperative education, distance learning, double majors, independent study, internships, off-campus study, part-time degree program, services for LD students, study abroad, summer session for credit. ***ROTC:*** Army (c).
Computers: 130 computers/terminals and 1,800 ports are available on campus for general student use. Students can access the following: computer help desk, free student e-mail accounts, online (class) grades, online (class) registration, online (class) schedules, course-supported e-learning. Campuswide network is available. 100% of college-owned or -operated housing units are wired for high-speed Internet access. Wireless service is available via entire campus.
Library: American Bureau of Shipping Information Commons plus 1 other. *Databases:* 124.

STUDENT LIFE
Housing options: on-campus residence required through senior year; coed. Campus housing is university owned and leased by the school. Freshman campus housing is guaranteed.
Activities and organizations: drama/theater group, marching band, Student Government, Intramurals, Regimental Leadership, Band/Honor Guard, NCAA Division 3 Athletics.
Athletics Member NCAA. All Division III. ***Intercollegiate sports:*** baseball M, crew M/W, cross-country running M/W, football M, lacrosse M/W, rowing M, sailing M/W, soccer M/W, softball W, track and field M/W, volleyball W. ***Intramural sports:*** basketball M/W, bowling

M(c)/W(c), equestrian sports M(c)/W(c), football M/W, golf M(c)/W(c), ice hockey M(c)/W(c), lacrosse M(c)/W(c), rock climbing M(c)/W(c), rugby M(c)/W(c), soccer M/W, softball M/W, swimming and diving M(c)/W(c), weight lifting M(c)/W(c), wrestling M(c)/W(c).

Campus security: 24-hour emergency response devices and patrols, late-night transport/escort service, controlled dormitory access.

Student services: health clinic, personal/psychological counseling, women's center, veterans affairs office.

COSTS & FINANCIAL AID

Costs (2018–19) ***Tuition:*** state resident $1782 full-time, $74 per credit part-time; nonresident $18,160 full-time, $757 per credit part-time. Full-time tuition and fees vary according to reciprocity agreements. Part-time tuition and fees vary according to course load and reciprocity agreements. ***Required fees:*** $7946 full-time, $320 per credit part-time. ***Room and board:*** $12,675; room only: $7560. ***Payment plan:*** installment. ***Waivers:*** employees or children of employees.

Financial Aid Of all full-time matriculated undergraduates who enrolled in 2018, 1,228 applied for aid, 922 were judged to have need, 393 had their need fully met. 409 Federal Work-Study jobs (averaging $1483). In 2018, 135 non-need-based awards were made. ***Average percent of need met:*** 71. ***Average financial aid package:*** $13,236. ***Average need-based loan:*** $4002. ***Average need-based gift aid:*** $8576. ***Average non-need-based aid:*** $3990. ***Average indebtedness upon graduation:*** $37,414.

APPLYING

Standardized Tests *Required:* SAT or ACT (for admission).

Options: electronic application, early action, deferred entrance.

Application fee: $50.

Required: essay or personal statement, high school transcript, minimum 2.0 GPA, 2 letters of recommendation, minimum college GPA 2.5 if transferring 12-23 credits, minimum college GPA 2.0 for more than 24 transferable credits. ***Recommended:*** interview.

Application deadlines: rolling (freshmen), rolling (transfers), 11/1 (early action).

Notification: continuous (freshmen), continuous (transfers), 12/31 (early action).

CONTACT

Mr. Joshua Tefft, Director of Admissions, Massachusetts Maritime Academy, 101 Academy Drive, Flanagan Hall, Buzzards Bay, MA 02532. *Phone:* 508-830-6687. *Toll-free phone:* 800-544-3411. *E-mail:* jtefft@maritime.edu.

MCPHS University

Boston, Massachusetts

http://www.mcphs.edu/

- **Independent** university, founded 1823
- **Urban** 3-acre campus
- **Endowment** $847.8 million
- **Coed**
- 84% of applicants were admitted

ACADEMICS

Calendar: semesters. *Degrees:* certificates, bachelor's, master's, doctoral, post-master's, and postbachelor's certificates.
Library: Henrietta DeBenedictis Library plus 2 others.

STUDENT LIFE

Housing options: coed, special housing for students with disabilities. Campus housing is university owned, leased by the school and is provided by a third party. Freshman campus housing is guaranteed.

Activities and organizations: drama/theater group, student-run newspaper, choral group, Residence Hall Council, Vietnamese Student Association, Student Government Association, Campus Activities Board, Student Indian Organization, national fraternities.

Campus security: 24-hour emergency response devices and patrols, late-night transport/escort service, controlled dormitory access, electronically operated academic area entrances, security guards at entrance.

Student services: health clinic, personal/psychological counseling.

COSTS & FINANCIAL AID

Costs (2018–19) ***Comprehensive fee:*** $49,105 includes full-time tuition ($31,600), mandatory fees ($1105), and room and board ($16,400). Full-time tuition and fees vary according to course load, degree level, location, program, and student level. ***College room only:*** $13,126. Room and board charges vary according to board plan, housing facility, and location.

Financial Aid Of all full-time matriculated undergraduates who enrolled in 2017, 2,640 applied for aid, 2,467 were judged to have need, 834 had their need fully met. In 2017, 885 non-need-based awards were made. ***Average percent of need met:*** 21. ***Average financial aid package:*** $8116. ***Average need-based loan:*** $2941. ***Average need-based gift aid:*** $5748. ***Average non-need-based aid:*** $6122. ***Average indebtedness upon graduation:*** $58,012.

APPLYING

Standardized Tests *Required:* SAT or ACT (for admission).

Options: electronic application, early action, deferred entrance.

Required: essay or personal statement, 1 letter of recommendation. ***Required for some:*** high school transcript, interview.

CONTACT

Giselle Colon, Visit Concierge, MCPHS University, 179 Longwood Avenue, Boston, MA 02115. *Phone:* 617-732-2744. *Fax:* 617-732-2118. *E-mail:* admissions@mcphs.edu.

Merrimack College

North Andover, Massachusetts

http://www.merrimack.edu/

- **Independent Roman Catholic** comprehensive, founded 1947
- **Suburban** 220-acre campus with easy access to Boston
- **Endowment** $58.5 million
- **Coed** 3,726 undergraduate students, 96% full-time, 50% women, 50% men
- **Moderately difficult** entrance level, 83% of applicants were admitted

UNDERGRAD STUDENTS

3,587 full-time, 139 part-time. Students come from 33 states and territories; 28 other countries; 29% are from out of state; 3% Black or African American, non-Hispanic/Latino; 7% Hispanic/Latino; 2% Asian, non-Hispanic/Latino; 0.1% Native Hawaiian or other Pacific Islander, non-Hispanic/Latino; 2% Two or more races, non-Hispanic/Latino; 7% Race/ethnicity unknown; 2% international; 2% transferred in; 71% live on campus.

Freshmen:

Admission: 8,668 applied, 7,174 admitted, 1,123 enrolled. ***Average high school GPA:*** 3.2.

Retention: 85% of full-time freshmen returned.

FACULTY

Total: 451, 44% full-time.

Student/faculty ratio: 14:1.

ACADEMICS

Calendar: semesters. *Degrees:* bachelor's, master's, and post-master's certificates.

Special study options: academic remediation for entering students, accelerated degree program, adult/continuing education programs, advanced placement credit, cooperative education, double majors, honors programs, independent study, internships, off-campus study, part-time degree program, services for LD students, student-designed majors, study abroad, summer session for credit. ***ROTC:*** Air Force (c).

Computers: Students can access the following: campus intranet, computer help desk, free student e-mail accounts, online (class) grades, online (class) registration, online (class) schedules. Campuswide network is available. 100% of college-owned or -operated housing units are wired for high-speed Internet access. Wireless service is available via entire campus.

Library: McQuade Library. *Books:* 90,940 (physical), 179,938 (digital/electronic); *Serial titles:* 56 (physical), 155,880 (digital/electronic); *Databases:* 231.

STUDENT LIFE
Housing options: coed, special housing for students with disabilities. Campus housing is university owned and leased by the school. Freshman campus housing is guaranteed.

Activities and organizations: drama/theater group, student-run newspaper, radio and television station, choral group, Onstagers, Live to Give (Relay for Life), Zeta Tau Alpha, WMCK, Young Athletes Program/Special Olympics, national fraternities, national sororities.

Athletics Member NCAA. All Division II except men's and women's ice hockey (Division I). ***Intercollegiate sports:*** baseball M(s), basketball M(s)/W(s), crew W(s), cross-country running M(s)/W(s), field hockey W(s), football M(s), golf W(s), ice hockey M(s)/W(s), lacrosse M(s)/W(s), rowing W(s), soccer M(s)/W(s), softball W(s), swimming and diving W(s), tennis M(s)/W(s), track and field M(s)/W(s), volleyball W(s). ***Intramural sports:*** badminton M/W, baseball M(c), basketball M(c)/W, cheerleading W(c), cross-country running M(c)/W(c), field hockey W(c), golf M(c), gymnastics W(c), ice hockey M(c)/W(c), lacrosse M(c)/W(c), rugby M(c)/W(c), soccer M(c)/W, softball M/W(c), track and field M(c)/W(c), ultimate Frisbee M(c)/W(c), volleyball M/W.

Campus security: 24-hour emergency response devices and patrols, late-night transport/escort service, controlled dormitory access.

Student services: health clinic, personal/psychological counseling.

COSTS & FINANCIAL AID
Costs (2018–19) ***Comprehensive fee:*** $58,150 includes full-time tuition ($39,330), mandatory fees ($2370), and room and board ($16,450). Full-time tuition and fees vary according to degree level. Part-time tuition: $1415 per credit. Part-time tuition and fees vary according to class time, course load, and degree level. ***Room and board:*** Room and board charges vary according to board plan and housing facility. ***Payment plan:*** installment. ***Waivers:*** senior citizens and employees or children of employees.

Financial Aid Of all full-time matriculated undergraduates who enrolled in 2018, 2,897 applied for aid, 2,551 were judged to have need, 355 had their need fully met. In 2018, 826 non-need-based awards were made. ***Average percent of need met:*** 65. ***Average financial aid package:*** $25,192. ***Average need-based loan:*** $4330. ***Average need-based gift aid:*** $21,647. ***Average non-need-based aid:*** $14,507.

APPLYING
Options: electronic application, early admission, early decision, early action, deferred entrance.

Required: essay or personal statement, high school transcript, 1 letter of recommendation, first quarter senior grades. ***Recommended:*** interview.

Application deadlines: 2/15 (freshmen), 8/25 (transfers), 1/15 (early action).

Early decision deadline: 11/15.

Notification: continuous until 3/15 (freshmen), continuous (transfers), 12/15 (early decision), 2/15 (early action).

CONTACT
Darren Conine, Associate Vice President of Admission, Merrimack College, 315 Turnpike Street, North Andover, MA 01845-5800. *Phone:* 978-837-5154. *Fax:* 978-837-5133. *E-mail:* conined@merrimack.edu.

Montserrat College of Art
Beverly, Massachusetts
http://www.montserrat.edu/

CONTACT
Mr. Jeffrey Newell, Director of Admissions, Montserrat College of Art, 23 Essex Street, Beverly, MA 01915. *Phone:* 978-921-4242 Ext. 1152. *Toll-free phone:* 800-836-0487. *Fax:* 978-921-4241. *E-mail:* jeffrey.newell@montserrat.edu.

Mount Holyoke College
South Hadley, Massachusetts
http://www.mtholyoke.edu/

- **Independent** comprehensive, founded 1837
- **Small-town** 800-acre campus with easy access to Springfield
- **Endowment** $729.4 million
- **Women only**
- **Very difficult** entrance level

FACULTY
Student/faculty ratio: 9:1.

ACADEMICS
Calendar: semesters. *Degrees:* bachelor's, master's, and postbachelor's certificates.
Library: Williston Memorial Library plus 2 others. *Books:* 662,010 (physical), 853,290 (digital/electronic); *Serial titles:* 603 (physical), 8,098 (digital/electronic); *Databases:* 227. Weekly public service hours: 115; students can reserve study rooms.

STUDENT LIFE
Housing options: on-campus residence required through senior year; women-only, special housing for students with disabilities. Campus housing is university owned. Freshman campus housing is guaranteed.

Activities and organizations: drama/theater group, student-run newspaper, radio station, choral group, Student Government Association, C.A.U.S.E. (Creating Awareness and Unity for Social Equality), MHC Outing Club, Mount Holyoke Symphony Orchestra, Mount Holyoke News.

Athletics Member NCAA. All Division III.

Campus security: 24-hour emergency response devices and patrols, student patrols, late-night transport/escort service, controlled dormitory access, police officers on-campus.

Student services: health clinic, personal/psychological counseling.

COSTS & FINANCIAL AID
Costs (2018–19) ***Comprehensive fee:*** $64,658 includes full-time tuition ($49,780), mandatory fees ($218), and room and board ($14,660). ***College room only:*** $7160.

Financial Aid Of all full-time matriculated undergraduates who enrolled in 2018, 1,528 applied for aid, 1,360 were judged to have need, 1,360 had their need fully met. 811 Federal Work-Study jobs (averaging $2229). 264 state and other part-time jobs (averaging $2258). In 2018, 292 non-need-based awards were made. ***Average percent of need met:*** 100. ***Average financial aid package:*** $40,576. ***Average need-based loan:*** $4284. ***Average need-based gift aid:*** $35,275. ***Average non-need-based aid:*** $22,092. ***Average indebtedness upon graduation:*** $25,538. ***Financial aid deadline:*** 2/1.

APPLYING
Options: electronic application, early admission, early decision, deferred entrance.

Application fee: $60.

Required: essay or personal statement, high school transcript, 2 letters of recommendation. ***Recommended:*** interview.

CONTACT
Ms. Gail Berson, Vice President of Enrollment and Dean of Admission, Mount Holyoke College, Office of Admission, South Hadley, MA 01075. *Phone:* 413-538-2023. *Fax:* 413-538-2409. *E-mail:* admission@mtholyoke.edu.

New England College of Business and Finance
Boston, Massachusetts
http://necb.edu/

CONTACT
New England College of Business and Finance, 10 High Street, Suite 204, Boston, MA 02111-2645. *Phone:* 617-951-2350 Ext. 6912. *Toll-free phone:* 800-997-1673.

New England Conservatory of Music
Boston, Massachusetts
http://necmusic.edu/

CONTACT
New England Conservatory of Music, 290 Huntington Avenue, Boston, MA 02115-5000. *Phone:* 617-585-1103.

Nichols College
Dudley, Massachusetts
http://www.nichols.edu/

- **Independent** comprehensive, founded 1815
- **Small-town** 250-acre campus with easy access to Boston
- **Endowment** $15.4 million
- **Coed** 1,322 undergraduate students, 93% full-time, 38% women, 62% men
- **Minimally difficult** entrance level, 82% of applicants were admitted

UNDERGRAD STUDENTS
1,224 full-time, 98 part-time. Students come from 23 states and territories; 15 other countries; 40% are from out of state; 7% Black or African American, non-Hispanic/Latino; 8% Hispanic/Latino; 1% Asian, non-Hispanic/Latino; 0.1% Native Hawaiian or other Pacific Islander, non-Hispanic/Latino; 0.2% American Indian or Alaska Native, non-Hispanic/Latino; 3% Two or more races, non-Hispanic/Latino; 0.2% Race/ethnicity unknown; 2% international; 16% transferred in; 77% live on campus.

Freshmen:
Admission: 2,435 applied, 2,003 admitted, 355 enrolled. ***Average high school GPA:*** 3.0. ***Test scores:*** SAT evidence-based reading and writing scores over 500: 63%; SAT math scores over 500: 64%; ACT scores over 18: 83%; SAT evidence-based reading and writing scores over 600: 13%; SAT math scores over 600: 14%; ACT scores over 24: 26%; SAT math scores over 700: 1%; ACT scores over 30: 7%.
Retention: 74% of full-time freshmen returned.

FACULTY
Total: 137, 37% full-time, 25% with terminal degrees.
Student/faculty ratio: 17:1.

ACADEMICS
Calendar: semesters. *Degrees:* bachelor's and master's.
Special study options: accelerated degree program, adult/continuing education programs, advanced placement credit, cooperative education, distance learning, double majors, honors programs, independent study, internships, off-campus study, part-time degree program, services for LD students, study abroad, summer session for credit.
Unusual degree programs: 3-2 business administration.
Computers: 154 computers/terminals are available on campus for general student use. Students can access the following: campus intranet, computer help desk, free student e-mail accounts, online (class) grades, online (class) registration, online (class) schedules. Campuswide network is available. 100% of college-owned or -operated housing units are wired for high-speed Internet access. Wireless service is available via entire campus.
Library: Conant Library. *Books:* 27,627 (physical), 150,177 (digital/electronic); *Serial titles:* 42 (physical); *Databases:* 35. Weekly public service hours: 102; study areas open 24 hours, 5–7 days a week; students can reserve study rooms.

STUDENT LIFE
Housing options: coed, men-only, women-only, special housing for students with disabilities. Campus housing is university owned. Freshman campus housing is guaranteed.
Activities and organizations: student-run radio station, Campus Activities Board, Institute for Women's Leadership, Student Government Association, Student Athletic Advisory Council, Student Alumni Association.
Athletics Member NCAA. All Division III. ***Intercollegiate sports:*** baseball M, basketball M/W, cheerleading M(c)/W(c), cross-country running M/W, field hockey W, football M, golf M, ice hockey M/W, lacrosse M/W, rugby M(c)/W(c), soccer M/W, softball W, tennis M/W, track and field M/W, volleyball M/W. ***Intramural sports:*** baseball M, basketball M/W, bowling M/W, football M/W, ice hockey M(c)/W(c), racquetball M(c)/W(c), rock climbing M/W, sand volleyball M/W, skiing (downhill) M/W, soccer M/W, volleyball M/W.
Campus security: 24-hour emergency response devices and patrols, student patrols, late-night transport/escort service, controlled dormitory access.
Student services: health clinic, personal/psychological counseling, women's center.

COSTS & FINANCIAL AID
Costs (2019–20) ***Comprehensive fee:*** $49,965 includes full-time tuition ($34,615), mandatory fees ($1100), and room and board ($14,250). Part-time tuition: $1130 per credit.
Financial Aid Of all full-time matriculated undergraduates who enrolled in 2018, 1,066 applied for aid, 974 were judged to have need, 183 had their need fully met. 224 Federal Work-Study jobs (averaging $2436). In 2018, 240 non-need-based awards were made. ***Average percent of need met:*** 78. ***Average financial aid package:*** $26,857. ***Average need-based loan:*** $3765. ***Average need-based gift aid:*** $18,861. ***Average non-need-based aid:*** $18,916. ***Average indebtedness upon graduation:*** $34,873.

APPLYING
Standardized Tests *Required for some:* SAT or ACT (for admission).
Options: electronic application, early action, deferred entrance.
Required: essay or personal statement, high school transcript, 1 letter of recommendation. ***Required for some:*** interview. ***Recommended:*** 2 letters of recommendation.
Application deadlines: rolling (freshmen), rolling (out-of-state freshmen), rolling (transfers).
Notification: continuous (out-of-state freshmen), continuous (transfers).

CONTACT
Mr. Paul Brower, Assistant Dean for Enrollment, Nichols College, 129 Center Road, Dudley, MA 01571. *Phone:* 508-213-2371. *Toll-free phone:* 800-470-3379. *E-mail:* paul.brower@nichols.edu.

★ Northeastern University
Boston, Massachusetts
http://www.northeastern.edu/

- **Independent** university, founded 1898
- **Urban** 73-acre campus
- **Coed**
- **Very difficult** entrance level

FACULTY
Student/faculty ratio: 14:1.

ACADEMICS
Calendar: semesters. *Degrees:* bachelor's, master's, doctoral, and post-master's certificates.
Library: Snell Library plus 3 others. *Books:* 530,566 (physical), 589,334 (digital/electronic). Study areas open 24 hours, 5–7 days a week; students can reserve study rooms.

STUDENT LIFE
Housing options: on-campus residence required through sophomore year; coed. Campus housing is university owned and leased by the school. Freshman campus housing is guaranteed.
Activities and organizations: drama/theater group, student-run newspaper, radio and television station, choral group, Student Government Association, Council for University Programs, Resident Student Association, Downhillers Ski and Snowboard Club, Northeastern University Huskiers and Outing Club, national fraternities, national sororities.
Athletics Member NCAA. All Division I.
Campus security: 24-hour emergency response devices and patrols, student patrols, late-night transport/escort service, controlled dormitory access, public safety website.
Student services: health clinic, personal/psychological counseling, veterans affairs office.

A ★ indicates that the school has detailed information with a Premium Profile on Petersons.com.

COSTS & FINANCIAL AID
Costs (2018–19) ***Comprehensive fee:*** $67,792 includes full-time tuition ($50,450), mandatory fees ($1072), and room and board ($16,270). ***Room and board:*** Room and board charges vary according to board plan and housing facility.

Financial Aid Of all full-time matriculated undergraduates who enrolled in 2018, 8,705 applied for aid, 5,836 were judged to have need, 2,849 had their need fully met. In 2018, 4896 non-need-based awards were made. ***Average percent of need met:*** 87. ***Average financial aid package:*** $30,981. ***Average need-based loan:*** $4255. ***Average need-based gift aid:*** $27,457. ***Average non-need-based aid:*** $13,707.

APPLYING
Standardized Tests *Required:* SAT or ACT (for admission).

Options: electronic application, early admission, early decision, early action, deferred entrance.

Application fee: $75.

CONTACT
Northeastern University, 360 Huntington Avenue, Boston, MA 02115. *Phone:* 617-373-2200. *E-mail:* admissions@northeastern.edu.

See below for display ad and page 1060 for the College Close-Up.

Northpoint Bible College
Haverhill, Massachusetts
http://northpoint.edu/

CONTACT
Helen Brouillette, Admissions Director, Northpoint Bible College, 320 South Main Street, Haverhill, MA 01835. *Phone:* 800-356-4014. *Toll-free phone:* 800-356-4014. *E-mail:* admissions@zbc.edu.

Pine Manor College
Chestnut Hill, Massachusetts
http://www.pmc.edu/

- **Independent** comprehensive, founded 1911
- **Suburban** 50-acre campus
- **Endowment** $11.0 million
- **Coed**
- **Moderately difficult** entrance level

FACULTY
Student/faculty ratio: 8:1.

ACADEMICS
Calendar: semesters. *Degrees:* associate, bachelor's, and master's.
Library: Annenberg Library plus 1 other. *Books:* 63,939 (physical), 46,446 (digital/electronic); *Serial titles:* 38 (physical), 8 (digital/electronic); *Databases:* 43. Weekly public service hours: 73; students can reserve study rooms.

STUDENT LIFE
Housing options: coed. Campus housing is university owned.

Activities and organizations: drama/theater group, student-run newspaper, radio station, choral group, African American, Latina, Asian, Native American and All (ALANA), Community Service Committee, International Student Club, The Model UN, Student Government Association (SGA).

Athletics Member NCAA. All Division III.

Campus security: 24-hour emergency response devices and patrols, student patrols, late-night transport/escort service, controlled dormitory access.

Student services: health clinic, personal/psychological counseling, women's center.

COSTS & FINANCIAL AID
Costs (2018–19) ***Comprehensive fee:*** $45,706 includes full-time tuition ($30,666), mandatory fees ($1210), and room and board ($13,830). Full-time tuition and fees vary according to course load. Part-time tuition: $955 per credit hour. Part-time tuition and fees vary according to course load.

Required fees: $1000 per year part-time. ***Room and board:*** Room and board charges vary according to housing facility.

Financial Aid Of all full-time matriculated undergraduates who enrolled in 2017, 259 applied for aid, 259 were judged to have need, 15 had their need fully met. 213 Federal Work-Study jobs (averaging $836). In 2017, 17 non-need-based awards were made. ***Average percent of need met:*** 75. ***Average financial aid package:*** $30,777. ***Average need-based loan:*** $4086. ***Average need-based gift aid:*** $24,971. ***Average non-need-based aid:*** $17,545. ***Average indebtedness upon graduation:*** $34,970.

APPLYING

Options: electronic application, deferred entrance.

Application fee: $25.

Required: essay or personal statement, high school transcript, letters of recommendation. ***Recommended:*** minimum 2.0 GPA, interview.

CONTACT

Pine Manor College, 400 Heath Street, Chestnut Hill, MA 02467. *Phone:* 617-731-7107. *Toll-free phone:* 800-762-1357.

Regis College

Weston, Massachusetts

http://www.regiscollege.edu/

CONTACT

Dr. Laura Bertonazzi, Dean of Undergraduate Enrollment and Retention, Regis College, 235 Wellesley Street, Weston, MA 02493. *Phone:* 781-768-7060. *Toll-free phone:* 866-438-7344. *Fax:* 781-768-7060. *E-mail:* admission@regiscollege.edu.

Salem State University

Salem, Massachusetts

http://www.salemstate.edu/

CONTACT

Dr. Mary Dunn, Assistant Dean for Undergraduate Admissions, Salem State University, 352 Lafayette Street, Salem, MA 01970. *Phone:* 978-542-6202. *Fax:* 978-542-6893. *E-mail:* admissions@salemstate.edu.

Simmons University

Boston, Massachusetts

http://www.simmons.edu/

- **Independent** university, founded 1899
- **Urban** 12-acre campus with easy access to Boston
- **Endowment** $188.2 million
- **Undergraduate: women only; graduate: coed**
- **Moderately difficult** entrance level

FACULTY

Student/faculty ratio: 12:1.

ACADEMICS

Calendar: semesters. *Degrees:* bachelor's, master's, doctoral, and post-master's certificates.

Library: Beatley Library. *Books:* 154,852 (physical), 37,362 (digital/electronic); *Serial titles:* 13 (physical), 278,000 (digital/electronic); *Databases:* 137. Weekly public service hours: 105; students can reserve study rooms.

STUDENT LIFE

Housing options: on-campus residence required for freshman year; coed, women-only. Campus housing is university owned. Freshman applicants given priority for college housing.

Activities and organizations: drama/theater group, student-run newspaper, radio station, choral group, Simmons College Dance Company, Student Government Association, Simmons Student Nursing Association, Sexuality Women and Gender (SWAG), Class Councils (2018, 2019, 2020, 2021).

Athletics Member NCAA. All Division III.

Campus security: 24-hour emergency response devices and patrols, late-night transport/escort service, controlled dormitory access.

Student services: health clinic, personal/psychological counseling, women's center.

COSTS & FINANCIAL AID

Costs (2018–19) ***Comprehensive fee:*** $56,000 includes full-time tuition ($39,660), mandatory fees ($1140), and room and board ($15,200). Full-time tuition and fees vary according to course load and program. Part-time tuition: $1360 per credit hour. Part-time tuition and fees vary according to course load and program. ***Required fees:*** $260 per term part-time. ***Room and board:*** Room and board charges vary according to board plan and location.

Financial Aid Of all full-time matriculated undergraduates who enrolled in 2018, 1,335 applied for aid, 1,232 were judged to have need, 176 had their need fully met. 815 Federal Work-Study jobs (averaging $2406). In 2018, 352 non-need-based awards were made. ***Average percent of need met:*** 77. ***Average financial aid package:*** $33,067. ***Average need-based loan:*** $4140. ***Average need-based gift aid:*** $29,480. ***Average non-need-based aid:*** $20,297. ***Average indebtedness upon graduation:*** $35,670.

APPLYING

Standardized Tests *Required:* SAT or ACT (for admission).

Options: electronic application, early action, deferred entrance.

Application fee: $55.

Required: essay or personal statement, high school transcript, 2 letters of recommendation. ***Recommended:*** minimum 3.0 GPA, interview.

CONTACT

Danielle Navarro, Senior Associate Director of Admission, Simmons University, 300 The Fenway, Boston, MA 02115. *Phone:* 617-521-2512. *Toll-free phone:* 800-345-8468. *Fax:* 617-521-3190. *E-mail:* danielle.navarro@simmons.edu.

Smith College

Northampton, Massachusetts

http://www.smith.edu/

- **Independent** comprehensive, founded 1871
- **Small-town** 147-acre campus with easy access to Hartford
- **Undergraduate: women only; graduate: coed**
- **Very difficult** entrance level

ACADEMICS

Calendar: semesters. *Degrees:* bachelor's, master's, doctoral, post-master's, and postbachelor's certificates.

Library: Neilson Library.

STUDENT LIFE

Housing options: on-campus residence required through senior year; women-only, cooperative. Campus housing is university owned. Freshman campus housing is guaranteed.

Activities and organizations: drama/theater group, student-run newspaper, radio and television station, choral group.

Athletics Member NCAA. All Division III.

Campus security: 24-hour emergency response devices and patrols, late-night transport/escort service, self-defense workshops, emergency telephones, programs in crime and sexual assault prevention.

COSTS & FINANCIAL AID

Costs (2018–19) ***Comprehensive fee:*** $69,924 includes full-time tuition ($52,120), mandatory fees ($284), and room and board ($17,520). Part-time tuition: $1630 per credit hour. ***College room only:*** $8800. ***Payment plans:*** tuition prepayment, installment.

Financial Aid Of all full-time matriculated undergraduates who enrolled in 2018, 1,749 applied for aid, 1,513 were judged to have need, 1,513 had their need fully met. In 2018, 189 non-need-based awards were made. ***Average percent of need met:*** 100. ***Average financial aid package:*** $53,790. ***Average need-based loan:*** $4305. ***Average need-based gift aid:*** $52,924. ***Average non-need-based aid:*** $17,119. ***Average indebtedness upon graduation:*** $22,083. ***Financial aid deadline:*** 1/25.

APPLYING

Standardized Tests *Required for some:* SAT or ACT (for admission).

Options: electronic application, early admission, early decision, deferred entrance.

Required: essay or personal statement, high school transcript, 3 letters of recommendation. ***Recommended:*** interview.

CONTACT
Ms. Debra Shaver, Dean of Admissions, Smith College, 7 College Lane, Northampton, MA 01063. *Phone:* 413-585-2500. *Toll-free phone:* 800-383-3232. *Fax:* 413-585-2527. *E-mail:* admission@smith.edu.

★ Springfield College
Springfield, Massachusetts
http://www.springfield.edu/

CONTACT
Richard K. Veres, Director of Undergraduate Admissions, Springfield College, 263 Alden Street, Springfield, MA 01109. *Phone:* 413-748-3136. *Toll-free phone:* 800-343-1257. *Fax:* 413-748-3694. *E-mail:* admissions@spfldcol.edu.

Stonehill College
Easton, Massachusetts
http://www.stonehill.edu/

- **Independent Roman Catholic** comprehensive, founded 1948
- **Suburban** 384-acre campus with easy access to Boston
- **Endowment** $211.4 million
- **Coed** 2,535 undergraduate students, 99% full-time, 60% women, 40% men
- **Very difficult** entrance level, 70% of applicants were admitted

UNDERGRAD STUDENTS
2,513 full-time, 22 part-time. Students come from 36 states and territories; 14 other countries; 36% are from out of state; 4% Black or African American, non-Hispanic/Latino; 5% Hispanic/Latino; 2% Asian, non-Hispanic/Latino; 0.1% American Indian or Alaska Native, non-Hispanic/Latino; 2% Two or more races, non-Hispanic/Latino; 2% Race/ethnicity unknown; 0.8% international; 2% transferred in; 86% live on campus.

Freshmen:
Admission: 6,609 applied, 4,598 admitted, 650 enrolled. ***Average high school GPA:*** 3.4. ***Test scores:*** SAT evidence-based reading and writing scores over 500: 94%; SAT math scores over 500: 91%; ACT scores over 18: 97%; SAT evidence-based reading and writing scores over 600: 46%; SAT math scores over 600: 45%; ACT scores over 24: 69%; SAT evidence-based reading and writing scores over 700: 6%; SAT math scores over 700: 6%; ACT scores over 30: 18%.

Retention: 87% of full-time freshmen returned.

FACULTY
Total: 280, 61% full-time, 70% with terminal degrees.

Student/faculty ratio: 12:1.

ACADEMICS
Calendar: semesters. *Degrees:* bachelor's and master's.

Special study options: advanced placement credit, double majors, honors programs, independent study, internships, off-campus study, part-time degree program, services for LD students, student-designed majors, study abroad, summer session for credit. ***ROTC:*** Army (b).

Unusual degree programs: 3-2 engineering with University of Notre Dame, Indiana.

Computers: 407 computers/terminals and 300 ports are available on campus for general student use. Students can access the following: campus intranet, computer help desk, free student e-mail accounts, online (class) grades, online (class) registration, online (class) schedules, Learning Management System, online degree evaluation/planning, add funds to ID, use at off campus locations, housing contracts and room lottery, financial aid awards, time sheets and payments for campus jobs, ebill. Campuswide network is available. 100% of college-owned or -operated housing units are wired for high-speed Internet access. Wireless service is available via entire campus.

Library: MacPhaidin Library plus 2 others. *Books:* 163,838 (physical), 302,839 (digital/electronic); *Serial titles:* 3,788 (physical), 79,489 (digital/electronic); *Databases:* 67. Weekly public service hours: 110; students can reserve study rooms.

STUDENT LIFE
Housing options: coed, women-only, special housing for students with disabilities. Campus housing is university owned.

Activities and organizations: drama/theater group, student-run newspaper, radio station, choral group, Community Engagement, Recreation/Intramural Sports Teams, Dance Club, Student Government Association, Financial Management Association.

Athletics Member NCAA. All Division II except golf (Division I). ***Intercollegiate sports:*** baseball M(s), basketball M(s)/W(s), cheerleading M(c)/W(c), cross-country running M(s)/W(s), equestrian sports W, field hockey W(s), football M(s), golf M(c)/W(s), ice hockey M, lacrosse M(c)/W(s), rugby M(c)/W(c), soccer M(s)/W(s), softball W(s), tennis M(s)/W(s), track and field M(s)/W(s), ultimate Frisbee M(c)/W(c), volleyball M(c)/W(s). ***Intramural sports:*** basketball M/W, fencing W, field hockey M/W(c), ice hockey M(c)/W(c), soccer M/W, softball M/W, table tennis M/W, tennis M/W, ultimate Frisbee M/W, volleyball M/W(c).

Campus security: 24-hour emergency response devices and patrols, late-night transport/escort service, controlled dormitory access, restricted access on weekends.

Student services: health clinic, personal/psychological counseling.

COSTS & FINANCIAL AID
Costs (2018–19) ***Comprehensive fee:*** $58,746 includes full-time tuition ($42,746) and room and board ($16,000). Part-time tuition: $1425 per credit hour. Part-time tuition and fees vary according to course load. ***College room only:*** $9992. ***Payment plans:*** tuition prepayment, installment. ***Waivers:*** employees or children of employees.

Financial Aid Of all full-time matriculated undergraduates who enrolled in 2018, 1,852 applied for aid, 1,556 were judged to have need, 777 had their need fully met. In 2018, 862 non-need-based awards were made. ***Average percent of need met:*** 89. ***Average financial aid package:*** $31,132. ***Average need-based loan:*** $4533. ***Average need-based gift aid:*** $25,513. ***Average non-need-based aid:*** $19,418. ***Average indebtedness upon graduation:*** $36,502.

APPLYING
Options: electronic application, early decision, early action, deferred entrance.

Application fee: $60.

Required: essay or personal statement, high school transcript, 2 letters of recommendation. ***Recommended:*** interview.

Application deadlines: 1/15 (freshmen), 4/1 (transfers).

Early decision deadline: 12/1.

Notification: 3/15 (freshmen), continuous until 5/31 (transfers), 12/31 (early decision).

CONTACT
Mr. Joseph P. Dacey, Dean of Admission, Stonehill College, 320 Washington Street, Easton, MA 02357. *Phone:* 508-565-1373. *Fax:* 508-565-1545. *E-mail:* admission@stonehill.edu.

Suffolk University
Boston, Massachusetts
http://www.suffolk.edu/

- **Independent** comprehensive, founded 1906
- **Urban** 2-acre campus with easy access to Boston, MA
- **Endowment** $231.7 million
- **Coed**
- **Moderately difficult** entrance level

FACULTY
Student/faculty ratio: 13:1.

ACADEMICS
Calendar: semesters. *Degrees:* certificates, diplomas, associate, bachelor's, master's, doctoral, post-master's, and postbachelor's certificates (doctoral degree in law).
Library: Mildred Sawyer Library plus 3 others. *Books:* 128,945 (physical), 249,567 (digital/electronic); *Serial titles:* 307 (physical), 65,782 (digital/electronic); *Databases:* 174. Weekly public service hours: 103; students can reserve study rooms.

STUDENT LIFE
Housing options: coed. Campus housing is university owned. Freshman applicants given priority for college housing.

Activities and organizations: drama/theater group, student-run newspaper, radio and television station, choral group, Student Government Association, Program Committee, Suffolk Free Radio, Black Student Union, Journey Leadership Program, national fraternities, national sororities.

Athletics Member NCAA. All Division III.

Campus security: 24-hour emergency response devices, late-night transport/escort service, controlled dormitory access.

Student services: health clinic, personal/psychological counseling, women's center.

COSTS & FINANCIAL AID
Costs (2018–19) ***One-time required fee:*** $240. ***Comprehensive fee:*** $56,412 includes full-time tuition ($38,420), mandatory fees ($146), and room and board ($17,846). Full-time tuition and fees vary according to course level and reciprocity agreements. Part-time tuition: $1130 per credit hour. Part-time tuition and fees vary according to course level, course load, and reciprocity agreements. ***Required fees:*** $19 per term part-time. ***College room only:*** $14,484. Room and board charges vary according to board plan and housing facility. ***Payment plans:*** installment, deferred payment.

Financial Aid Of all full-time matriculated undergraduates who enrolled in 2018, 3,245 applied for aid, 2,994 were judged to have need, 336 had their need fully met. 736 Federal Work-Study jobs (averaging $2362). 609 state and other part-time jobs (averaging $3540). In 2018, 1576 non-need-based awards were made. ***Average percent of need met:*** 67. ***Average financial aid package:*** $27,407. ***Average need-based loan:*** $4529. ***Average need-based gift aid:*** $9324. ***Average non-need-based aid:*** $14,335. ***Average indebtedness upon graduation:*** $25,639. ***Financial aid deadline:*** 6/30.

APPLYING
Options: electronic application, early action, deferred entrance.

Application fee: $50.

Required: essay or personal statement, high school transcript, 2 letters of recommendation. ***Required for some:*** interview.

CONTACT
Ms. Donna Grand Pre, Assistant Vice President/Director Undergraduate Admissions, Suffolk University, 8 Ashburton Place, Boston, MA 02108. *Phone:* 617-573-8460. *Toll-free phone:* 800-6-SUFFOLK. *Fax:* 617-742-4291. *E-mail:* admission@suffolk.edu.

Tufts University

Medford, Massachusetts

http://www.tufts.edu/

- **Independent** university, founded 1852
- **Suburban** 150-acre campus with easy access to Boston
- **Coed**
- **Most difficult** entrance level

FACULTY
Student/faculty ratio: 9:1.

ACADEMICS
Calendar: semesters. *Degrees:* certificates, bachelor's, master's, doctoral, post-master's, and postbachelor's certificates.
Library: Tisch Library plus 3 others. *Books:* 1.3 million (physical), 432,877 (digital/electronic); *Serial titles:* 1,012 (physical); *Databases:* 83,216. Weekly public service hours: 110; students can reserve study rooms.

STUDENT LIFE
Housing options: on-campus residence required through sophomore year; coed, women-only, special housing for students with disabilities. Campus housing is university owned. Freshman campus housing is guaranteed.

Activities and organizations: drama/theater group, student-run newspaper, radio and television station, choral group, Leonard Carmichael Society (community service), Tufts Dance Collective, intramural sports, Tufts Daily (newspaper), Tufts Mountain Club, national fraternities, national sororities.

Athletics Member NCAA. All Division III.

Campus security: 24-hour emergency response devices and patrols, late-night transport/escort service, controlled dormitory access, security lighting, call boxes to campus police.

Student services: health clinic, personal/psychological counseling, women's center, legal services.

COSTS & FINANCIAL AID
Costs (2018–19) ***Comprehensive fee:*** $70,942 includes full-time tuition ($55,172), mandatory fees ($1210), and room and board ($14,560). Part-time tuition: $2298 per credit hour. ***College room only:*** $7934. Room and board charges vary according to board plan. ***Payment plans:*** tuition prepayment, installment.

Financial Aid Of all full-time matriculated undergraduates who enrolled in 2018, 2,393 applied for aid, 2,065 were judged to have need, 1,993 had their need fully met. 2,073 Federal Work-Study jobs (averaging $1769). 193 state and other part-time jobs (averaging $1900). In 2018, 157 non-need-based awards were made. ***Average percent of need met:*** 98. ***Average financial aid package:*** $47,195. ***Average need-based loan:*** $2925. ***Average need-based gift aid:*** $45,887. ***Average non-need-based aid:*** $5400. ***Average indebtedness upon graduation:*** $28,014. ***Financial aid deadline:*** 2/1.

APPLYING
Standardized Tests *Required:* SAT or ACT (for admission). *Required for some:* art portfolio in lieu of Subject Tests for applicants to the School of Museum of Fine Arts.

Options: electronic application, early admission, early decision, deferred entrance.

Application fee: $75.

Required: essay or personal statement, high school transcript, 2 letters of recommendation, Common Application or Coalition Application or QuestBridge Application, the Tufts Supplement. ***Recommended:*** interview.

CONTACT
Office of Undergraduate Admissions, Tufts University, Bendetson Hall, Medford, MA 02155. *Phone:* 617-627-3170. *Fax:* 617-627-3860. *E-mail:* undergraduate.admissions@tufts.edu.

University of Massachusetts Amherst

Amherst, Massachusetts

http://www.umass.edu/

- **State-supported** university, founded 1863, part of University of Massachusetts
- **Small-town** 1463-acre campus with easy access to Springfield, MA and Hartford, CT
- **Endowment** $347.0 million
- **Coed** 23,515 undergraduate students, 93% full-time, 50% women, 50% men
- **Moderately difficult** entrance level, 60% of applicants were admitted

UNDERGRAD STUDENTS
21,784 full-time, 1,731 part-time. Students come from 49 states and territories; 81 other countries; 18% are from out of state; 5% Black or African American, non-Hispanic/Latino; 7% Hispanic/Latino; 10% Asian, non-Hispanic/Latino; 0.1% Native Hawaiian or other Pacific Islander, non-Hispanic/Latino; 0.1% American Indian or Alaska Native, non-Hispanic/Latino; 3% Two or more races, non-Hispanic/Latino; 6% Race/ethnicity unknown; 7% international; 5% transferred in; 62% live on campus.

Freshmen:
Admission: 41,612 applied, 24,911 admitted, 5,047 enrolled. ***Average high school GPA:*** 3.9. ***Test scores:*** SAT evidence-based reading and writing scores over 500: 99%; SAT math scores over 500: 99%; ACT scores over 18: 100%; SAT evidence-based reading and writing scores over 600: 77%; SAT math scores over 600: 78%; ACT scores over 24: 91%; SAT evidence-based reading and writing scores over 700: 17%; SAT math scores over 700: 32%; ACT scores over 30: 40%.

Retention: 91% of full-time freshmen returned.

FACULTY
Total: 1,745, 81% full-time, 89% with terminal degrees.

Student/faculty ratio: 17:1.

ACADEMICS

Calendar: semesters. *Degrees:* certificates, associate, bachelor's, master's, doctoral, post-master's, and postbachelor's certificates.

Special study options: accelerated degree program, adult/continuing education programs, advanced placement credit, cooperative education, distance learning, double majors, English as a second language, freshman honors college, honors programs, independent study, internships, off-campus study, part-time degree program, services for LD students, student-designed majors, study abroad, summer session for credit. ***ROTC:*** Army (b), Air Force (b).

Computers: 539 computers/terminals and 430 ports are available on campus for general student use. Students can access the following: computer help desk, free student e-mail accounts, online (class) grades, online (class) registration, online (class) schedules, online housing assignments, bill payment, Learning Management System, file storage, Web hosting, blogs. Campuswide network is available. 100% of college-owned or -operated housing units are wired for high-speed Internet access. Wireless service is available via entire campus.

Library: W. E. B. Du Bois Library plus 1 other. *Books:* 2.8 million (physical), 1.6 million (digital/electronic); *Serial titles:* 2,297 (physical), 126,215 (digital/electronic); *Databases:* 558. Weekly public service hours: 142; study areas open 24 hours, 5–7 days a week; students can reserve study rooms.

STUDENT LIFE

Housing options: on-campus residence required for freshman year; coed, special housing for students with disabilities. Campus housing is university owned. Freshman campus housing is guaranteed.

Activities and organizations: drama/theater group, student-run newspaper, radio and television station, choral group, marching band, Minutemen Marching Band, Ski and Board Club, Outing Club, University Programming Council, Student Government Association, national fraternities, national sororities.

Athletics Member NCAA. All Division I except football (Division I-A). ***Intercollegiate sports:*** baseball M(s), basketball M(s)/W(s), cheerleading W, crew W(s), cross-country running M(s)/W(s), field hockey W(s), ice hockey M(s), lacrosse M(s)/W(s), soccer M(s)/W(s), softball W(s), swimming and diving M(s)/W(s), tennis W(s), track and field M(s)/W(s). ***Intramural sports:*** badminton M/W, baseball M(c), basketball M/W, crew M(c), equestrian sports M(c)/W(c), fencing M(c)/W(c), field hockey W(c), football M/W, golf M(c)/W(c), gymnastics W(c), ice hockey M(c)/W(c), lacrosse M(c)/W(c), racquetball M/W, rugby M(c)/W(c), sailing M(c)/W(c), sand volleyball M/W, skiing (downhill) M(c)/W(c), soccer M(c)/W(c), softball W(c), swimming and diving M(c)/W(c), table tennis M(c)/W, tennis M(c)/W(c), triathlon M(c)/W(c), ultimate Frisbee M(c)/W(c), volleyball M(c)/W(c), water polo M(c)/W(c), wrestling M(c)/W(c).

Campus security: 24-hour emergency response devices and patrols, student patrols, late-night transport/escort service, controlled dormitory access.

Student services: health clinic, personal/psychological counseling, women's center, legal services, veterans affairs office.

COSTS & FINANCIAL AID

Costs (2018–19) ***One-time required fee:*** $185. ***Tuition:*** state resident $15,406 full-time, $5395 per term part-time; nonresident $34,089 full-time, $12,036 per term part-time. Full-time tuition and fees vary according to class time, location, program, reciprocity agreements, and student level. Part-time tuition and fees vary according to class time, course load, location, program, reciprocity agreements, and student level. ***Required fees:*** $481 full-time, $241 per term part-time. ***Room and board:*** $13,202; room only: $7068. Room and board charges vary according to board plan and housing facility. ***Payment plan:*** installment. ***Waivers:*** senior citizens and employees or children of employees.

Financial Aid Of all full-time matriculated undergraduates who enrolled in 2017, 16,889 applied for aid, 12,294 were judged to have need, 1,479 had their need fully met. 1,663 Federal Work-Study jobs (averaging $1508). In 2017, 4919 non-need-based awards were made. ***Average percent of need met:*** 83. ***Average financial aid package:*** $18,382. ***Average need-based loan:*** $4630. ***Average need-based gift aid:*** $11,176. ***Average non-need-based aid:*** $5220. ***Average indebtedness upon graduation:*** $31,897.

APPLYING

Standardized Tests *Required:* SAT or ACT (for admission).

Options: electronic application, early action, deferred entrance.

Application fee: $80.

Required: essay or personal statement, high school transcript, 1 letter of recommendation.

Application deadlines: 1/15 (freshmen), 4/15 (transfers), 11/1 (early action).

Notification: continuous (freshmen), continuous (transfers), 12/15 (early action).

CONTACT

Dr. James Roche, Vice Provost of Enrollment Management, University of Massachusetts Amherst, 255 Whitmore, Amherst, MA 01003. *Phone:* 413-545-0222. *Fax:* 413-545-4312. *E-mail:* mail@admissions.umass.edu.

University of Massachusetts Boston

Boston, Massachusetts

http://www.umb.edu/

- **State-supported** university, founded 1964, part of University of Massachusetts
- **Urban** 120-acre campus
- **Endowment** $74.4 million
- **Coed** 12,714 undergraduate students, 79% full-time, 54% women, 46% men
- **Moderately difficult** entrance level, 78% of applicants were admitted

UNDERGRAD STUDENTS

10,017 full-time, 2,697 part-time. 5% are from out of state; 17% Black or African American, non-Hispanic/Latino; 17% Hispanic/Latino; 14% Asian, non-Hispanic/Latino; 0.1% American Indian or Alaska Native, non-Hispanic/Latino; 3% Two or more races, non-Hispanic/Latino; 5% Race/ethnicity unknown; 11% international; 10% transferred in; 9% live on campus.

Freshmen:

Admission: 11,907 applied, 9,241 admitted, 2,315 enrolled. ***Average high school GPA:*** 3.3. ***Test scores:*** SAT evidence-based reading and writing scores over 500: 77%; SAT math scores over 500: 86%; ACT scores over 18: 92%; SAT evidence-based reading and writing scores over 600: 32%; SAT math scores over 600: 30%; ACT scores over 24: 48%; SAT evidence-based reading and writing scores over 700: 3%; SAT math scores over 700: 5%; ACT scores over 30: 6%.

Retention: 76% of full-time freshmen returned.

FACULTY

Total: 1,163, 62% full-time, 65% with terminal degrees.

Student/faculty ratio: 17:1.

ACADEMICS

Calendar: semesters. *Degrees:* certificates, bachelor's, master's, doctoral, post-master's, and postbachelor's certificates.

Special study options: academic remediation for entering students, accelerated degree program, adult/continuing education programs, advanced placement credit, cooperative education, distance learning, double majors, English as a second language, freshman honors college, honors programs, independent study, internships, off-campus study, part-time degree program, services for LD students, student-designed majors, study abroad, summer session for credit. ***ROTC:*** Army (c), Navy (c), Air Force (c).

Computers: 350 computers/terminals are available on campus for general student use. Students can access the following: computer help desk, free student e-mail accounts, online (class) grades, online (class) registration, online (class) schedules. Campuswide network is available. Wireless service is available via entire campus.

Library: Joseph P. Healey Library. *Books:* 459,163 (physical), 547,086 (digital/electronic); *Databases:* 124.

STUDENT LIFE

Housing options: college housing not available; coed.

Activities and organizations: drama/theater group, student-run newspaper, radio station, choral group, Student Arts and Events Council,

Haitian Student Association, Golden Key Honor Society, Campus Kitchens, Mass Media.

Athletics Member NCAA. All Division III. ***Intercollegiate sports:*** baseball M, basketball M/W, cross-country running M/W, ice hockey M/W, lacrosse M, soccer M/W, softball W, tennis M/W, track and field M/W, volleyball W. ***Intramural sports:*** basketball M/W, bowling M/W, football M, golf M/W, racquetball M/W, soccer M/W, softball M/W, volleyball M/W.

Campus security: 24-hour emergency response devices and patrols, late-night transport/escort service, crime prevention program, bicycle patrols.

Student services: health clinic, personal/psychological counseling, women's center, veterans affairs office.

COSTS & FINANCIAL AID

Costs (2018–19) ***Tuition:*** state resident $13,841 full-time, $577 per credit hour part-time; nonresident $33,640 full-time, $1402 per credit hour part-time. Full-time tuition and fees vary according to program. Part-time tuition and fees vary according to program. ***Required fees:*** $326 full-time, $14 per credit hour part-time.

Financial Aid Of all full-time matriculated undergraduates who enrolled in 2017, 7,205 applied for aid, 6,461 were judged to have need, 1,282 had their need fully met. In 2017, 608 non-need-based awards were made. ***Average percent of need met:*** 86. ***Average financial aid package:*** $16,480. ***Average need-based loan:*** $5002. ***Average need-based gift aid:*** $10,032. ***Average non-need-based aid:*** $8270. ***Average indebtedness upon graduation:*** $27,109.

APPLYING

Standardized Tests *Required for some:* SAT or ACT (for admission).

Options: electronic application, early admission, early action, deferred entrance.

Application fee: $60.

Required: high school transcript, minimum 2.5 GPA, 1 letter of recommendation. ***Required for some:*** essay or personal statement, minimum 2.8 GPA.

Notification: continuous until 4/30 (freshmen).

CONTACT

Mr. Corey Ford, Director of Undergraduate Admissions, University of Massachusetts Boston, 100 Morrissey Boulevard, Boston, MA 02125-3393. *Phone:* 617-287-6100. *Fax:* 617-287-5999. *E-mail:* enrollment.info@umb.edu.

University of Massachusetts Dartmouth

North Dartmouth, Massachusetts

http://www.umassd.edu/

- **State-supported** university, founded 1895, part of University of Massachusetts
- **Suburban** 710-acre campus with easy access to Boston, Providence
- **Endowment** $56.4 million
- **Coed** 6,841 undergraduate students, 86% full-time, 49% women, 51% men
- **Moderately difficult** entrance level, 78% of applicants were admitted

UNDERGRAD STUDENTS

5,895 full-time, 946 part-time. Students come from 38 states and territories; 39 other countries; 9% are from out of state; 16% Black or African American, non-Hispanic/Latino; 10% Hispanic/Latino; 4% Asian, non-Hispanic/Latino; 0.2% American Indian or Alaska Native, non-Hispanic/Latino; 4% Two or more races, non-Hispanic/Latino; 4% Race/ethnicity unknown; 2% international; 11% transferred in; 52% live on campus.

Freshmen:

Admission: 8,697 applied, 6,744 admitted, 1,421 enrolled. ***Average high school GPA:*** 3.3. ***Test scores:*** SAT evidence-based reading and writing scores over 500: 73%; SAT math scores over 500: 75%; ACT scores over 18: 85%; SAT evidence-based reading and writing scores over 600: 25%; SAT math scores over 600: 21%; ACT scores over 24: 45%; SAT evidence-based reading and writing scores over 700: 2%; SAT math scores over 700: 2%; ACT scores over 30: 7%.

Retention: 71% of full-time freshmen returned.

FACULTY

Total: 584, 69% full-time, 71% with terminal degrees.

Student/faculty ratio: 16:1.

ACADEMICS

Calendar: semesters. *Degrees:* certificates, bachelor's, master's, doctoral, post-master's, and postbachelor's certificates.

Special study options: academic remediation for entering students, accelerated degree program, advanced placement credit, cooperative education, distance learning, double majors, English as a second language, honors programs, independent study, internships, off-campus study, part-time degree program, services for LD students, student-designed majors, study abroad, summer session for credit. ***ROTC:*** Army (c).

Unusual degree programs: 3-2 engineering; nursing.

Computers: 400 computers/terminals and 27,000 ports are available on campus for general student use. Students can access the following: campus intranet, computer help desk, free student e-mail accounts, online (class) grades, online (class) registration, online (class) schedules. Campuswide network is available. 100% of college-owned or -operated housing units are wired for high-speed Internet access. Wireless service is available via entire campus.

Library: Claire T. Carney Library. *Books:* 242,682 (physical), 80,828 (digital/electronic); *Serial titles:* 1,348 (physical), 110,141 (digital/electronic); *Databases:* 142. Students can reserve study rooms.

STUDENT LIFE

Housing options: coed, special housing for students with disabilities. Campus housing is university owned.

Activities and organizations: drama/theater group, student-run newspaper, choral group, Outdoor Club, Ski and Snowboard Club, 20 Cent Fiction, Relay for Life, American Red Cross, national fraternities, national sororities.

Athletics Member NCAA. All Division III. ***Intercollegiate sports:*** baseball M, basketball M/W, cross-country running M/W, equestrian sports W, field hockey W, football M, golf M, ice hockey M, lacrosse M/W, sailing W, soccer M/W, softball W, swimming and diving M/W, tennis M/W, track and field M/W, volleyball W. ***Intramural sports:*** badminton M/W, basketball M/W, football M/W, rugby M(c)/W(c), skiing (downhill) M(c)/W(c), soccer M/W, softball M/W, tennis M/W, triathlon M/W, ultimate Frisbee M/W, volleyball M/W, water polo M/W.

Campus security: 24-hour emergency response devices and patrols, student patrols, late-night transport/escort service, controlled dormitory access.

Student services: health clinic, personal/psychological counseling, women's center.

COSTS & FINANCIAL AID

Costs (2018–19) ***One-time required fee:*** $100. ***Tuition:*** state resident $13,496 full-time, $562 per credit part-time; nonresident $28,716 full-time, $1197 per credit part-time. Full-time tuition and fees vary according to class time, program, and reciprocity agreements. Part-time tuition and fees vary according to class time, course load, program, and reciprocity agreements. ***Required fees:*** $425 full-time, $27 per credit part-time. ***Room and board:*** $13,582; room only: $4982. Room and board charges vary according to board plan and housing facility. ***Payment plan:*** installment. ***Waivers:*** senior citizens and employees or children of employees.

Financial Aid Of all full-time matriculated undergraduates who enrolled in 2017, 5,042 applied for aid, 4,293 were judged to have need, 1,458 had their need fully met. 2,092 Federal Work-Study jobs (averaging $1427). In 2017, 557 non-need-based awards were made. ***Average percent of need met:*** 83. ***Average financial aid package:*** $17,361. ***Average need-based loan:*** $8707. ***Average need-based gift aid:*** $10,432. ***Average non-need-based aid:*** $4489. ***Average indebtedness upon graduation:*** $29,000. ***Financial aid deadline:*** 6/30.

APPLYING

Standardized Tests *Required:* SAT or ACT (for admission).

Options: electronic application, early admission, early action, deferred entrance.

Application fee: $60.

Required: high school transcript, minimum 2.0 GPA. ***Recommended:*** essay or personal statement, 1 letter of recommendation.

Application deadlines: rolling (freshmen), rolling (out-of-state freshmen), rolling (transfers), rolling (early action).

Notification: continuous (freshmen), continuous (out-of-state freshmen), continuous (transfers), rolling (early action).

CONTACT

Ms. Hanan Khamis, Director of Admissions, University of Massachusetts Dartmouth, 285 Old Westport Road, North Dartmouth, MA 02747-2300. *Phone:* 508-999-8605. *Fax:* 508-999-8755. *E-mail:* admissions@umassd.edu.

★ University of Massachusetts Lowell

Lowell, Massachusetts

http://www.uml.edu/

- **State-supported** university, founded 1894, part of University of Massachusetts
- **Urban** 100-acre campus with easy access to Boston
- **Endowment** $91.7 million
- **Coed** 14,005 undergraduate students, 76% full-time, 39% women, 61% men
- **Moderately difficult** entrance level, 72% of applicants were admitted

UNDERGRAD STUDENTS

10,651 full-time, 3,354 part-time. Students come from 51 states and territories; 64 other countries; 8% are from out of state; 6% Black or African American, non-Hispanic/Latino; 11% Hispanic/Latino; 11% Asian, non-Hispanic/Latino; 0.0% Native Hawaiian or other Pacific Islander, non-Hispanic/Latino; 0.1% American Indian or Alaska Native, non-Hispanic/Latino; 3% Two or more races, non-Hispanic/Latino; 5% Race/ethnicity unknown; 4% international; 8% transferred in; 61% live on campus.

Freshmen:

Admission: 12,117 applied, 8,688 admitted, 2,083 enrolled. ***Average high school GPA:*** 3.6. ***Test scores:*** SAT evidence-based reading and writing scores over 500: 98%; SAT math scores over 500: 99%; ACT scores over 18: 99%; SAT evidence-based reading and writing scores over 600: 57%; SAT math scores over 600: 63%; ACT scores over 24: 80%; SAT evidence-based reading and writing scores over 700: 8%; SAT math scores over 700: 16%; ACT scores over 30: 23%.

Retention: 85% of full-time freshmen returned.

FACULTY

Total: 1,110, 57% full-time, 70% with terminal degrees.

Student/faculty ratio: 17:1.

ACADEMICS

Calendar: semesters. *Degrees:* certificates, associate, bachelor's, master's, doctoral, post-master's, and postbachelor's certificates.

Special study options: accelerated degree program, adult/continuing education programs, advanced placement credit, cooperative education, distance learning, double majors, honors programs, independent study, internships, off-campus study, part-time degree program, services for LD students, study abroad, summer session for credit. ***ROTC:*** Army (b), Air Force (b).

Computers: 2,145 computers/terminals and 4,100 ports are available on campus for general student use. Students can access the following: campus intranet, computer help desk, free student e-mail accounts, online (class) grades, online (class) registration, online (class) schedules. Campuswide network is available. 100% of college-owned or -operated housing units are wired for high-speed Internet access. Wireless service is available via entire campus.

Library: O'Leary Library and Learning Commons plus 2 others. *Books:* 224,700 (physical), 192,900 (digital/electronic); *Serial titles:* 5,641 (physical), 127,540 (digital/electronic); *Databases:* 180. Weekly public service hours: 118; students can reserve study rooms.

STUDENT LIFE

Housing options: coed. Campus housing is university owned and leased by the school.

Activities and organizations: drama/theater group, student-run newspaper, radio station, choral group, marching band, Student Government Association, Recreational Sports Clubs, Association of Students of African Origin, WUML (radio station), Campus Activities Programming Association, national fraternities, national sororities.

Athletics Member NCAA. All Division I. ***Intercollegiate sports:*** baseball M(s), basketball M(s)/W(s), cross-country running M(s)/W(s), field hockey W(s), ice hockey M(s), lacrosse M(s)/W(s), soccer M(s)/W(s), softball W(s), track and field M(s)/W(s). ***Intramural sports:*** badminton M/W, baseball M(c), basketball M/W, cheerleading M(c)/W(c), cross-country running M/W, fencing W(c), football M/W, golf M(c)/W(c), ice hockey M/W, lacrosse M(c)/W(c), racquetball M/W, rowing M(c)/W(c), rugby M(c)/W(c), skiing (cross-country) M(c)/W(c), skiing (downhill) M(c)/W(c), soccer M/W, softball M/W, squash M/W, swimming and diving M(c)/W(c), table tennis M/W, tennis M/W, track and field M(c)/W(c), triathlon M/W, ultimate Frisbee M/W, volleyball M/W.

Campus security: 24-hour emergency response devices and patrols, controlled dormitory access, police and security patrols.

Student services: health clinic, personal/psychological counseling, veterans affairs office.

COSTS & FINANCIAL AID

Costs (2018–19) ***Tuition:*** state resident $14,710 full-time, $613 per credit hour part-time; nonresident $32,357 full-time, $1348 per credit hour part-time. Part-time tuition and fees vary according to course load. ***Required fees:*** $470 full-time, $20 per credit hour part-time. ***Room and board:*** $12,748; room only: $8400. Room and board charges vary according to board plan and housing facility. ***Payment plan:*** installment. ***Waivers:*** senior citizens and employees or children of employees.

Financial Aid Of all full-time matriculated undergraduates who enrolled in 2016, 8,053 applied for aid, 6,115 were judged to have need, 2,604 had their need fully met. In 2016, 1595 non-need-based awards were made. ***Average percent of need met:*** 89. ***Average financial aid package:*** $15,884. ***Average need-based loan:*** $4350. ***Average need-based gift aid:*** $9151. ***Average non-need-based aid:*** $6877. ***Average indebtedness upon graduation:*** $32,744.

APPLYING

Standardized Tests *Required:* SAT or ACT (for admission). *Required for some:* short answer questions for No Test option.

Options: electronic application, early action, deferred entrance.

Application fee: $60.

Required: essay or personal statement, high school transcript, minimum 3.0 GPA, 1 letter of recommendation. ***Required for some:*** audition for music students, art portfolio for art majors, three additional short answer questions for No Test option.

Application deadlines: 2/1 (freshmen), 8/15 (transfers), 11/1 (early action).

Notification: 3/10 (freshmen), continuous (transfers), 12/10 (early action).

CONTACT

Ms. Kerri Johnston, Dean of Enrollment Management, University of Massachusetts Lowell, 1 University Avenue, Lowell, MA 01854. *Phone:* 978-934-3948. *Fax:* 978-934-3086. *E-mail:* kerri_johnston@uml.edu.

Wellesley College

Wellesley, Massachusetts

http://www.wellesley.edu/

- **Independent** 4-year, founded 1870
- **Suburban** 500-acre campus with easy access to Boston
- **Endowment** $1.9 billion
- **Women only**
- **Most difficult** entrance level

FACULTY

Student/faculty ratio: 7:1.

ACADEMICS

Calendar: semesters. *Degrees:* bachelor's (double bachelor's degree with Massachusetts Institute of Technology).

Library: Margaret Clapp Library plus 5 others. *Books:* 717,924 (physical), 770,553 (digital/electronic); *Serial titles:* 319,932 (physical), 94,450 (digital/electronic). Students can reserve study rooms.

STUDENT LIFE
Housing options: women-only, cooperative. Campus housing is university owned. Freshman campus housing is guaranteed.

Activities and organizations: drama/theater group, student-run newspaper, radio and television station, choral group, Student Government, community service organizations, cultural clubs, societies, theater groups.

Athletics Member NCAA. All Division III.

Campus security: 24-hour emergency response devices and patrols, late-night transport/escort service, controlled dormitory access.

Student services: health clinic, personal/psychological counseling, women's center.

COSTS & FINANCIAL AID
Costs (2018–19) ***Comprehensive fee:*** $70,200 includes full-time tuition ($53,408), mandatory fees ($324), and room and board ($16,468). Part-time tuition: $6676 per course. Part-time tuition and fees vary according to course load. ***Required fees:*** $41 per course part-time. ***College room only:*** $8468. ***Payment plans:*** tuition prepayment, installment.

Financial Aid Of all full-time matriculated undergraduates who enrolled in 2018, 1,501 applied for aid, 1,335 were judged to have need, 1,335 had their need fully met. ***Average percent of need met:*** 100. ***Average financial aid package:*** $53,776. ***Average need-based loan:*** $2416. ***Average need-based gift aid:*** $50,752. ***Average indebtedness upon graduation:*** $16,122.

APPLYING
Standardized Tests *Required:* SAT or ACT (for admission).

Options: electronic application, early admission, early decision, deferred entrance.

Required: essay or personal statement, high school transcript, 3 letters of recommendation, first senior marking period grades and mid-year report. ***Required for some:*** interview. ***Recommended:*** interview.

CONTACT
Ms. Grace Cheng, Director of Admission, Wellesley College, 106 Central Street, Wellesley, MA 02481. *Phone:* 781-283-2270. *Fax:* 781-283-3678. *E-mail:* admission@wellesley.edu.

★ Wentworth Institute of Technology

Boston, Massachusetts

http://www.wit.edu/

- **Independent** comprehensive, founded 1904
- **Urban** 31-acre campus with easy access to Boston, MA
- **Endowment** $94.1 million
- **Coed**
- **Moderately difficult** entrance level

FACULTY
Student/faculty ratio: 17:1.

ACADEMICS
Calendar: semesters for freshmen and sophomores, trimesters for juniors and seniors. *Degrees:* certificates, associate, bachelor's, and master's.
Library: Douglas D. Schumann Library & Learning Commons plus 1 other. *Books:* 51,754 (physical), 244,116 (digital/electronic); *Serial titles:* 210 (physical), 77,225 (digital/electronic); *Databases:* 75. Weekly public service hours: 100.

STUDENT LIFE
Housing options: on-campus residence required through sophomore year; coed. Campus housing is university owned. Freshman campus housing is guaranteed.

Activities and organizations: student-run radio station, Intramural Sports, Wentworth Events Board, Multicultural Student Association, Phi Sigma Pi, Major Particular Professional Student Associations.

Athletics Member NCAA. All Division III.

Campus security: 24-hour emergency response devices and patrols, student patrols, late-night transport/escort service, controlled dormitory access.

Student services: health clinic, personal/psychological counseling, women's center.

COSTS & FINANCIAL AID
Costs (2018–19) ***Comprehensive fee:*** $48,140 includes full-time tuition ($33,950) and room and board ($14,190). Full-time tuition and fees vary according to class time, course load, and program. Part-time tuition: $1060 per credit hour. Part-time tuition and fees vary according to class time, course load, and program. ***College room only:*** $11,090. Room and board charges vary according to board plan and housing facility.

Financial Aid Of all full-time matriculated undergraduates who enrolled in 2018, 3,760 applied for aid, 2,715 were judged to have need, 232 had their need fully met. 926 Federal Work-Study jobs (averaging $1590). 821 state and other part-time jobs (averaging $1780). In 2018, 937 non-need-based awards were made. ***Average percent of need met:*** 53. ***Average financial aid package:*** $20,615. ***Average need-based loan:*** $4376. ***Average need-based gift aid:*** $14,308. ***Average non-need-based aid:*** $10,547. ***Average indebtedness upon graduation:*** $41,429.

APPLYING
Standardized Tests *Required:* SAT or ACT (for admission).

Options: electronic application, deferred entrance.

Application fee: $50.

Required: essay or personal statement, high school transcript, 1 letter of recommendation. ***Recommended:*** minimum 2.0 GPA, interview.

CONTACT
Ms. Amy Dufour, Senior Associate Director of Admissions, Wentworth Institute of Technology, 550 Huntington Avenue, Boston, MA 02115. *Phone:* 617-989-4116. *Toll-free phone:* 800-556-0610. *Fax:* 617-989-4010. *E-mail:* dufoura@wit.edu.

Western New England University

Springfield, Massachusetts

http://www.wne.edu/

- **Independent** university, founded 1919
- **Suburban** 215-acre campus
- **Endowment** $73.0 million
- **Coed**
- **Moderately difficult** entrance level

FACULTY
Student/faculty ratio: 12:1.

ACADEMICS
Calendar: semesters. *Degrees:* certificates, associate, bachelor's, master's, doctoral, and postbachelor's certificates.
Library: D'Amour Library plus 1 other. *Books:* 106,500 (physical), 31,912 (digital/electronic); *Serial titles:* 46 (physical), 109,440 (digital/electronic); *Databases:* 128. Weekly public service hours: 97; study areas open 24 hours, 5–7 days a week.

STUDENT LIFE
Housing options: coed, special housing for students with disabilities. Campus housing is university owned. Freshman campus housing is guaranteed.

Activities and organizations: drama/theater group, student-run newspaper, radio and television station, choral group, Student Senate, Residence Hall Association, Campus Activities Board, student radio station, The Westerner (student newspaper).

Athletics Member NCAA. All Division III.

Campus security: 24-hour emergency response devices and patrols, student patrols, late-night transport/escort service, controlled dormitory access, security cameras.

Student services: health clinic, personal/psychological counseling.

COSTS & FINANCIAL AID
Costs (2018–19) ***Comprehensive fee:*** $50,394 includes full-time tuition ($34,338), mandatory fees ($2466), and room and board ($13,590). Full-time tuition and fees vary according to course load and program. Part-time tuition: $647 per credit. Part-time tuition and fees vary according to course load and program. ***Room and board:*** Room and board charges vary according to board plan and housing facility. ***Payment plans:*** tuition prepayment, installment.

Financial Aid Of all full-time matriculated undergraduates who enrolled in 2018, 2,260 applied for aid, 2,060 were judged to have need, 291 had their need fully met. 1,050 Federal Work-Study jobs (averaging $1805). In

A ★ indicates that the school has detailed information with a Premium Profile on Petersons.com.

2018, 486 non-need-based awards were made. ***Average percent of need met:*** 73. ***Average financial aid package:*** $26,824. ***Average need-based loan:*** $4340. ***Average need-based gift aid:*** $21,856. ***Average non-need-based aid:*** $16,360. ***Average indebtedness upon graduation:*** $46,591.

APPLYING
Standardized Tests *Required for some:* SAT or ACT (for admission).

Options: electronic application, early admission, deferred entrance.

Application fee: $40.

Required: high school transcript, 1 letter of recommendation. ***Recommended:*** essay or personal statement, interview.

CONTACT
Mr. Bryan Gross, Vice President for Enrollment Management, Western New England University, 1215 Wilbraham Road, Springfield, MA 01119. *Phone:* 413-782-1321. *Toll-free phone:* 800-325-1122 Ext. 1321. *Fax:* 413-782-1777. *E-mail:* learn@wne.edu.

Westfield State University

Westfield, Massachusetts

http://www.westfield.ma.edu/

- **State-supported** comprehensive, founded 1839, part of Massachusetts Public Higher Education System
- **Suburban** 256-acre campus
- **Endowment** $5.5 million
- **Coed**
- **Moderately difficult** entrance level

FACULTY
Student/faculty ratio: 16:1.

ACADEMICS
Calendar: semesters. *Degrees:* bachelor's, master's, and postbachelor's certificates.
Library: Governor Joseph B. Ely Library. *Books:* 129,289 (physical), 160,388 (digital/electronic); *Serial titles:* 5,137 (physical), 25,808 (digital/electronic); *Databases:* 138. Weekly public service hours: 92; students can reserve study rooms.

STUDENT LIFE
Housing options: coed, special housing for students with disabilities. Campus housing is university owned. Freshman applicants given priority for college housing.

Activities and organizations: drama/theater group, student-run newspaper, radio and television station, choral group, Student National Education Association, Student Government Association, Campus Activities Board, The Dance Company, Multicultural Student Association.

Athletics Member NCAA. All Division III.

Campus security: 24-hour emergency response devices and patrols, student patrols, late-night transport/escort service, controlled dormitory access.

Student services: health clinic, personal/psychological counseling, legal services, veterans affairs office.

COSTS & FINANCIAL AID
Costs (2018–19) ***Tuition:*** state resident $970 full-time, $315 per credit hour part-time; nonresident $7050 full-time, $315 per credit hour part-time. Full-time tuition and fees vary according to program and reciprocity agreements. Part-time tuition and fees vary according to course load. ***Required fees:*** $9459 full-time, $75 per term part-time. ***Room and board:*** $10,948. Room and board charges vary according to board plan and housing facility.

Financial Aid Of all full-time matriculated undergraduates who enrolled in 2017, 4,205 applied for aid, 3,138 were judged to have need, 283 had their need fully met. 278 Federal Work-Study jobs (averaging $1754). In 2017, 67 non-need-based awards were made. ***Average percent of need met:*** 59. ***Average financial aid package:*** $9008. ***Average need-based loan:*** $4216. ***Average need-based gift aid:*** $8379. ***Average non-need-based aid:*** $3303. ***Average indebtedness upon graduation:*** $29,050.

APPLYING
Standardized Tests *Required:* SAT or ACT (for admission).

Options: electronic application, deferred entrance.

Application fee: $50.

Required: high school transcript, minimum 3.0 GPA. ***Required for some:*** interview, audition for music majors, portfolio for art majors, essay and interview for nursing majors, sliding scale minimum high school GPA using SAT/ACT scores for GPAs between 2.0 and 3.0.

CONTACT
Dr. Kelly Hart, Director of Admissions, Westfield State University, 333 Western Avenue, Westfield, MA 01002. *Phone:* 413-572-5218. *Fax:* 413-572-0520. *E-mail:* admission@westfield.ma.edu.

Wheaton College

Norton, Massachusetts

http://www.wheatoncollege.edu/

- **Independent** 4-year, founded 1834
- **Suburban** 478-acre campus with easy access to Boston, MA
- **Endowment** $211.9 million
- **Coed** 1,760 undergraduate students, 99% full-time, 61% women, 39% men
- **Very difficult** entrance level, 70% of applicants were admitted

UNDERGRAD STUDENTS
1,751 full-time, 9 part-time. Students come from 39 states and territories; 67 other countries; 61% are from out of state; 5% Black or African American, non-Hispanic/Latino; 8% Hispanic/Latino; 5% Asian, non-Hispanic/Latino; 0.2% American Indian or Alaska Native, non-Hispanic/Latino; 4% Two or more races, non-Hispanic/Latino; 2% Race/ethnicity unknown; 10% international; 0.9% transferred in; 96% live on campus.

Freshmen:
Admission: 3,674 applied, 2,566 admitted, 496 enrolled. ***Average high school GPA:*** 3.4. ***Test scores:*** SAT evidence-based reading and writing scores over 500: 97%; SAT math scores over 500: 98%; ACT scores over 18: 98%; SAT evidence-based reading and writing scores over 600: 77%; SAT math scores over 600: 64%; ACT scores over 24: 94%; SAT evidence-based reading and writing scores over 700: 16%; SAT math scores over 700: 14%; ACT scores over 30: 49%.

Retention: 87% of full-time freshmen returned.

FACULTY
Total: 185, 71% full-time, 85% with terminal degrees.

Student/faculty ratio: 10:1.

ACADEMICS
Calendar: semesters. *Degree:* bachelor's.

Special study options: accelerated degree program, advanced placement credit, cooperative education, double majors, honors programs, independent study, internships, off-campus study, services for LD students, student-designed majors, study abroad, summer session for credit. ***ROTC:*** Army (c).

Computers: 196 computers/terminals are available on campus for general student use. Students can access the following: campus intranet, computer help desk, free student e-mail accounts, online (class) grades, online (class) registration, online (class) schedules, assistive technology, online software training, media equipment loan program. Campuswide network is available. 100% of college-owned or -operated housing units are wired for high-speed Internet access. Wireless service is available via entire campus.
Library: Madeleine Clark Wallace Library. *Books:* 297,992 (physical), 167,919 (digital/electronic); *Serial titles:* 4,504 (physical), 33,166 (digital/electronic); *Databases:* 157. Weekly public service hours: 114; students can reserve study rooms.

STUDENT LIFE
Housing options: coed, women-only, special housing for students with disabilities. Campus housing is university owned. Freshman campus housing is guaranteed.

Activities and organizations: drama/theater group, student-run newspaper, radio station, choral group, Student Government Association, Performance Groups (a capella, dance and improv), Black Student Association (BSA), Programming Activities Council, Feminist Association of Wheaton (FAW).

Athletics Member NCAA. All Division III. ***Intercollegiate sports:*** baseball M, basketball M/W, cross-country running M/W, field hockey W, lacrosse M/W, soccer M/W, softball W, swimming and diving M/W, tennis M/W, track and field M/W, volleyball W. ***Intramural sports:*** archery M(c)/W(c), basketball M/W, cheerleading M(c)/W(c), equestrian sports M(c)/W(c), fencing M(c)/W(c), football M/W, golf M/W, ice hockey M(c)/W(c), rugby M(c)/W(c), soccer M/W, tennis M(c)/W(c), ultimate Frisbee M(c)/W(c), volleyball M/W.

Campus security: 24-hour emergency response devices and patrols, student patrols, late-night transport/escort service, controlled dormitory access.

Student services: health clinic, personal/psychological counseling.

COSTS & FINANCIAL AID

Costs (2019–20) ***One-time required fee:*** $50. ***Comprehensive fee:*** $68,364 includes full-time tuition ($54,118), mandatory fees ($350), and room and board ($13,896). Part-time tuition: $6764 per course. ***College room only:*** $7412.

Financial Aid Of all full-time matriculated undergraduates who enrolled in 2018, 1,337 applied for aid, 1,225 were judged to have need, 278 had their need fully met. 624 Federal Work-Study jobs (averaging $1900). 367 state and other part-time jobs (averaging $1780). In 2018, 476 non-need-based awards were made. ***Average percent of need met:*** 87. ***Average financial aid package:*** $43,984. ***Average need-based loan:*** $4450. ***Average need-based gift aid:*** $38,800. ***Average non-need-based aid:*** $20,826. ***Average indebtedness upon graduation:*** $34,830. ***Financial aid deadline:*** 2/1.

APPLYING

Options: electronic application, early admission, early decision, early action, deferred entrance.

Application fee: $60.

Required: essay or personal statement, high school transcript, 2 letters of recommendation. ***Recommended:*** interview.

Application deadlines: 1/1 (freshmen), 1/1 (out-of-state freshmen), 5/1 (transfers), 11/1 (early action).

Early decision deadline: 11/1 (for plan 1), 1/1 (for plan 2).

Notification: 3/31 (freshmen), 3/31 (out-of-state freshmen), continuous (transfers), 12/3 (early decision plan 1), 2/1 (early decision plan 2), 1/15 (early action).

CONTACT

Chris Hooker-Haring, Interim Vice President of Enrollment, Wheaton College, 26 East Main Street, Norton, MA 02766. *Phone:* 508-286-8251. *Toll-free phone:* 800-394-6003. *Fax:* 508-286-8271. *E-mail:* admission@wheatoncollege.edu.

William James College

Newton, Massachusetts

http://www.williamjames.edu/

- **Independent** upper-level, founded 1974
- **Suburban** campus with easy access to Boston, Mass.
- **Coed, primarily women** 14 undergraduate students, 71% women, 29% men

UNDERGRAD STUDENTS

14 part-time. 14% Black or African American, non-Hispanic/Latino; 14% Hispanic/Latino; 7% American Indian or Alaska Native, non-Hispanic/Latino; 7% Race/ethnicity unknown.

FACULTY

Total: 7, 14% full-time.

ACADEMICS

Calendar: semesters. *Degrees:* certificates, bachelor's, master's, doctoral, and post-master's certificates.

CONTACT

Mario Murga, Director of Admissions, William James College, One Wells Avenue, Newton, MA 02459. *Phone:* 617-564-9376. *Toll-free phone:* 888-664-MSPP. *E-mail:* admissions@williamjames.edu.

Williams College

Williamstown, Massachusetts

http://www.williams.edu/

- **Independent** comprehensive, founded 1793
- **Small-town** 450-acre campus with easy access to Albany NY
- **Endowment** $2.8 billion
- **Coed** 2,073 undergraduate students, 97% full-time, 48% women, 52% men
- **Most difficult** entrance level, 13% of applicants were admitted

UNDERGRAD STUDENTS

2,020 full-time, 53 part-time. Students come from 45 states and territories; 90 other countries; 86% are from out of state; 8% Black or African American, non-Hispanic/Latino; 13% Hispanic/Latino; 13% Asian, non-Hispanic/Latino; 0.1% American Indian or Alaska Native, non-Hispanic/Latino; 5% Two or more races, non-Hispanic/Latino; 3% Race/ethnicity unknown; 8% international; 0.2% transferred in; 93% live on campus.

Freshmen:

Admission: 9,560 applied, 1,240 admitted, 533 enrolled. ***Test scores:*** SAT evidence-based reading and writing scores over 500: 100%; SAT math scores over 500: 100%; ACT scores over 18: 100%; SAT evidence-based reading and writing scores over 600: 99%; SAT math scores over 600: 97%; ACT scores over 24: 100%; SAT evidence-based reading and writing scores over 700: 80%; SAT math scores over 700: 76%; ACT scores over 30: 91%.

Retention: 99% of full-time freshmen returned.

FACULTY

Total: 357, 83% full-time, 93% with terminal degrees.

Student/faculty ratio: 7:1.

ACADEMICS

Calendar: 4-1-4. *Degrees:* bachelor's and master's.

Special study options: double majors, independent study, internships, off-campus study, services for LD students, student-designed majors, study abroad. ***ROTC:*** Air Force (c).

Unusual degree programs: 3-2 engineering with Columbia University, Dartmouth College.

Computers: 1,000 computers/terminals are available on campus for general student use. Students can access the following: computer help desk, free student e-mail accounts, online (class) grades, online (class) registration, online (class) schedules. Campuswide network is available. 100% of college-owned or -operated housing units are wired for high-speed Internet access. Wireless service is available via entire campus.

Library: Sawyer Library plus 2 others. *Books:* 1.0 million (physical); *Serial titles:* 737 (physical), 90,227 (digital/electronic). Weekly public service hours: 118; study areas open 24 hours, 5–7 days a week; students can reserve study rooms.

STUDENT LIFE

Housing options: on-campus residence required through junior year; coed, cooperative, special housing for students with disabilities. Campus housing is university owned. Freshman campus housing is guaranteed.

Activities and organizations: drama/theater group, student-run newspaper, radio station, choral group, marching band.

Athletics Member NCAA. All Division III except golf (Division II), men's and women's skiing (cross-country) (Division I), skiing (downhill) (Division I). ***Intercollegiate sports:*** badminton M(c)/W(c), baseball M, basketball M/W, crew M/W, cross-country running M/W, equestrian sports M(c)/W(c), fencing M(c)/W(c), field hockey W, football M, golf M/W, ice hockey M/W, lacrosse M/W, rugby M(c)/W(c), sailing M(c)/W(c), skiing (cross-country) M/W, skiing (downhill) M(c)/W, soccer M/W, softball W, squash M/W, swimming and diving M/W, tennis M/W, track and field M/W, ultimate Frisbee M(c)/W(c), volleyball M(c)/W, water polo M(c)/W(c), wrestling M. ***Intramural sports:*** basketball M/W, bowling M(c)/W(c), gymnastics M/W, ice hockey M/W, skiing (cross-country) M/W, skiing (downhill) M/W, soccer M/W, softball M/W, tennis M(c)/W(c), ultimate Frisbee M(c)/W(c), volleyball M/W, water polo M/W.

Campus security: 24-hour emergency response devices and patrols, student patrols, late-night transport/escort service, controlled dormitory access.

Student services: health clinic, personal/psychological counseling.

COSTS & FINANCIAL AID

Costs (2019–20) ***Comprehensive fee:*** $72,270 includes full-time tuition ($56,970), mandatory fees ($310), and room and board ($14,990). ***College room only:*** $7600.

Financial Aid Of all full-time matriculated undergraduates who enrolled in 2018, 1,165 applied for aid, 1,043 were judged to have need, 1,043 had their need fully met. ***Average percent of need met:*** 100. ***Average financial aid package:*** $58,728. ***Average need-based loan:*** $2970. ***Average need-based gift aid:*** $55,621. ***Average indebtedness upon graduation:*** $15,496. ***Financial aid deadline:*** 1/15.

APPLYING

Standardized Tests *Required:* SAT or ACT (for admission).

Options: electronic application, early admission, early decision, deferred entrance.

Application fee: $65.

Required: essay or personal statement, high school transcript, 2 letters of recommendation.

Application deadlines: 1/1 (freshmen), 3/1 (transfers).

Early decision deadline: 11/15.

Notification: 4/7 (freshmen), 4/15 (transfers), 12/15 (early decision).

CONTACT

Sulgi Lim, Director of Admission, Williams College, 995 Main Street, Williamstown, MA 01267. *Phone:* 413-597-2211. *Fax:* 413-597-4052. *E-mail:* admission@williams.edu.

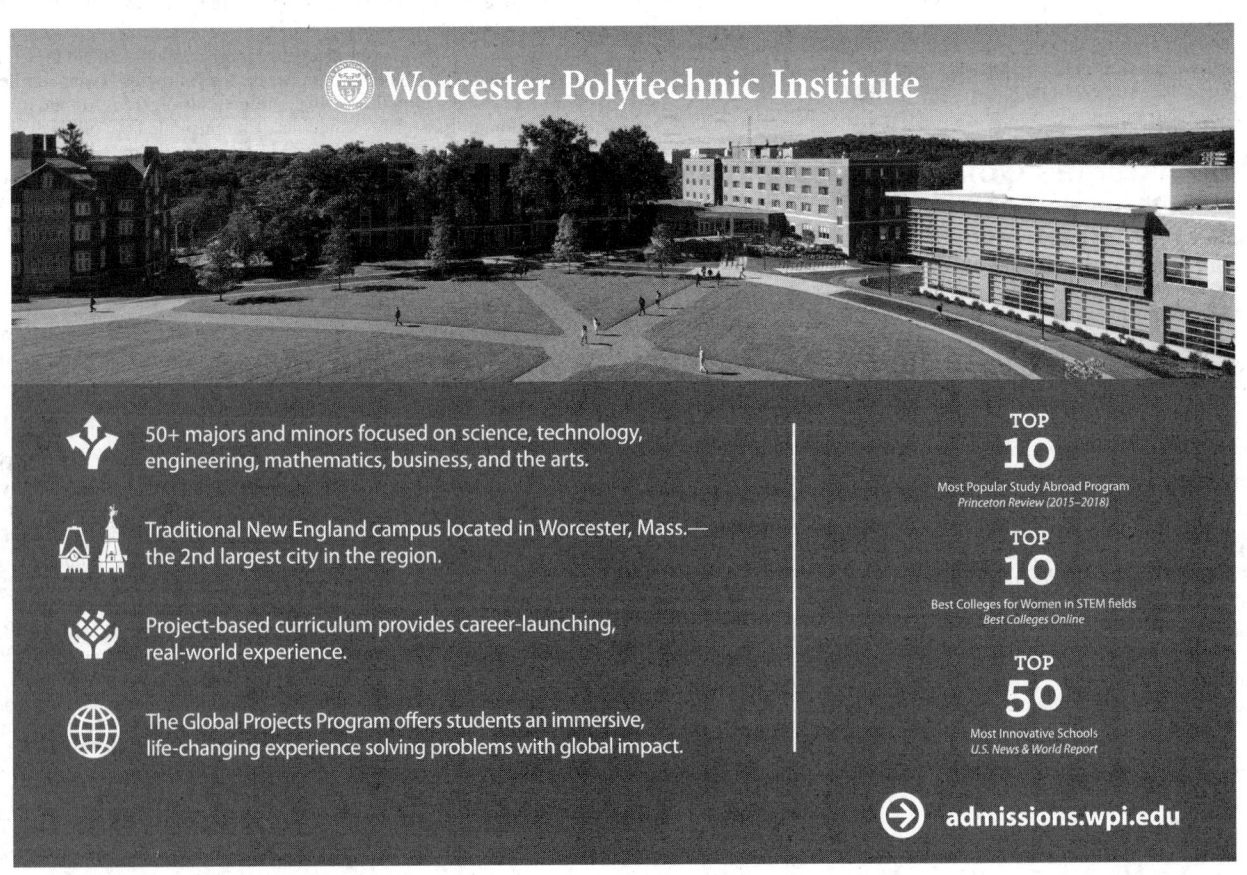

★ Worcester Polytechnic Institute
Worcester, Massachusetts
http://www.wpi.edu/

- **Independent** university, founded 1865
- **Suburban** 95-acre campus with easy access to Boston
- **Endowment** $519.6 million
- **Coed** 4,668 undergraduate students, 97% full-time, 38% women, 62% men
- **Very difficult** entrance level, 42% of applicants were admitted

UNDERGRAD STUDENTS

4,527 full-time, 141 part-time. Students come from 44 states and territories; 66 other countries; 55% are from out of state; 3% Black or African American, non-Hispanic/Latino; 9% Hispanic/Latino; 5% Asian, non-Hispanic/Latino; 0.3% American Indian or Alaska Native, non-Hispanic/Latino; 2% Two or more races, non-Hispanic/Latino; 8% Race/ethnicity unknown; 9% international; 0.8% transferred in; 49% live on campus.

Freshmen:

Admission: 10,584 applied, 4,402 admitted, 1,276 enrolled. ***Average high school GPA:*** 3.9. ***Test scores:*** SAT evidence-based reading and writing scores over 500: 100%; SAT math scores over 500: 100%; ACT scores over 18: 100%; SAT evidence-based reading and writing scores over 600: 90%; SAT math scores over 600: 97%; ACT scores over 24: 99%; SAT evidence-based reading and writing scores over 700: 32%; SAT math scores over 700: 61%; ACT scores over 30: 71%.

Retention: 96% of full-time freshmen returned.

FACULTY

Total: 508, 83% full-time, 81% with terminal degrees.

Student/faculty ratio: 13:1.

ACADEMICS

Calendar: 4 7-week terms. *Degrees:* bachelor's, master's, doctoral, and postbachelor's certificates.

Special study options: accelerated degree program, advanced placement credit, cooperative education, distance learning, double majors, English as a second language, independent study, internships, off-campus study, part-time degree program, services for LD students, student-designed majors, study abroad, summer session for credit. ***ROTC:*** Army (b), Navy (c), Air Force (b).

Computers: 860 computers/terminals and 800 ports are available on campus for general student use. Students can access the following: campus intranet, computer help desk, free student e-mail accounts, online (class) grades, online (class) registration, online (class) schedules, online course content. Campuswide network is available. 100% of college-owned or -operated housing units are wired for high-speed Internet access. Wireless service is available via entire campus.

Library: George C. Gordon Library plus 1 other. *Books:* 192,701 (physical), 750,858 (digital/electronic); *Serial titles:* 5,371 (physical), 143,312 (digital/electronic); *Databases:* 215. Weekly public service hours: 107; students can reserve study rooms.

STUDENT LIFE

Housing options: coed, special housing for students with disabilities. Campus housing is university owned. Freshman campus housing is guaranteed.

Activities and organizations: drama/theater group, student-run newspaper, radio station, choral group, Student Government Association, Panhellenic, Interfraternity Council, Intramural and Club Sports, Music Association, national fraternities, national sororities.

Athletics Member NCAA. All Division III. ***Intercollegiate sports:*** baseball M, basketball M/W, crew M/W, cross-country running M/W, field hockey W, football M, soccer M/W, softball W, swimming and diving M/W, track and field M/W, volleyball W, wrestling M. ***Intramural sports:*** badminton M(c)/W(c), basketball M/W, cheerleading M(c)/W(c), fencing M(c)/W(c), football M, golf M(c)/W(c), ice hockey M(c)/W(c), lacrosse M(c)/W(c), rugby M(c)/W(c), sailing M(c)/W(c), skiing (downhill) M(c)/W(c), soccer M/W, squash M(c)/W(c), table tennis M(c)/W(c), tennis M(c)/W(c), ultimate Frisbee M(c)/W(c), volleyball M/W, water polo M(c)/W(c), wrestling M(c).

Campus security: 24-hour emergency response devices and patrols, student patrols, late-night transport/escort service, controlled dormitory access.

Student services: health clinic, personal/psychological counseling.

COSTS & FINANCIAL AID

Costs (2018–19) ***One-time required fee:*** $200. ***Comprehensive fee:*** $65,304 includes full-time tuition ($49,860), mandatory fees ($670), and room and board ($14,774). Part-time tuition: $1385 per credit hour. Part-time tuition and fees vary according to course load. ***College room only:*** $8440. Room and board charges vary according to board plan and housing facility. ***Payment plans:*** tuition prepayment, installment, deferred payment. ***Waivers:*** employees or children of employees.

Financial Aid Of all full-time matriculated undergraduates who enrolled in 2017, 3,085 applied for aid, 2,582 were judged to have need, 1,170 had their need fully met. 413 Federal Work-Study jobs (averaging $1352). In 2017, 1584 non-need-based awards were made. ***Average percent of need met:*** 78. ***Average financial aid package:*** $36,730. ***Average need-based loan:*** $2414. ***Average need-based gift aid:*** $23,502. ***Average non-need-based aid:*** $16,237.

APPLYING

Standardized Tests *Required for some:* IELTS or TOEFL.

Options: electronic application, early admission, early action, deferred entrance.

Application fee: $65.

Required: essay or personal statement, high school transcript, 2 letters of recommendation. ***Required for some:*** interview.

Application deadlines: 2/1 (freshmen), 4/15 (transfers), 1/1 (early action).

Notification: 4/1 (freshmen), continuous (transfers), 2/1 (early action).

CONTACT

Jennifer Cluett, Director of Undergraduate Admissions, Worcester Polytechnic Institute, 100 Institute Road, Worcester, MA 01609-2280. *Phone:* 508-831-5286. *Fax:* 508-831-5875. *E-mail:* admissions@wpi.edu.

See previous page for display ad and page 1164 for the College Close-Up.

Worcester State University

Worcester, Massachusetts

http://www.worcester.edu/

- **State-supported** comprehensive, founded 1874, part of Massachusetts Public Higher Education System
- **Urban** 58-acre campus with easy access to Boston
- **Endowment** $17.4 million
- **Coed** 5,380 undergraduate students, 77% full-time, 60% women, 40% men
- **Moderately difficult** entrance level, 78% of applicants were admitted

UNDERGRAD STUDENTS

4,164 full-time, 1,216 part-time. Students come from 23 states and territories; 22 other countries; 4% are from out of state; 9% Black or African American, non-Hispanic/Latino; 13% Hispanic/Latino; 5% Asian, non-Hispanic/Latino; 0.1% Native Hawaiian or other Pacific Islander, non-Hispanic/Latino; 0.4% American Indian or Alaska Native, non-Hispanic/Latino; 3% Two or more races, non-Hispanic/Latino; 4% Race/ethnicity unknown; 1% international; 10% transferred in; 31% live on campus.

Freshmen:

Admission: 4,076 applied, 3,173 admitted, 891 enrolled. ***Average high school GPA:*** 3.3. ***Test scores:*** SAT evidence-based reading and writing scores over 500: 81%; SAT math scores over 500: 82%; ACT scores over 18: 95%; SAT evidence-based reading and writing scores over 600: 28%; SAT math scores over 600: 23%; ACT scores over 24: 54%; SAT evidence-based reading and writing scores over 700: 2%; SAT math scores over 700: 3%; ACT scores over 30: 5%.

Retention: 79% of full-time freshmen returned.

FACULTY

Total: 465, 45% full-time, 51% with terminal degrees.

Student/faculty ratio: 17:1.

ACADEMICS

Calendar: semesters. *Degrees:* bachelor's, master's, post-master's, and postbachelor's certificates.

Special study options: academic remediation for entering students, accelerated degree program, adult/continuing education programs, advanced placement credit, distance learning, double majors, English as a second language, honors programs, independent study, internships, off-campus study, part-time degree program, services for LD students, student-designed majors, study abroad, summer session for credit. ***ROTC:*** Army (c), Navy (c), Air Force (c).

Computers: Students can access the following: campus intranet, computer help desk, free student e-mail accounts, online (class) grades, online (class) registration, online (class) schedules. Campuswide network is available. 100% of college-owned or -operated housing units are wired for high-speed Internet access. Wireless service is available via entire campus.

Library: Learning Resource Center. *Books:* 128,798 (physical), 1.6 million (digital/electronic); *Serial titles:* 202 (physical), 144,391 (digital/electronic); *Databases:* 273. Weekly public service hours: 100.

STUDENT LIFE

Housing options: coed, men-only, women-only, special housing for students with disabilities. Campus housing is university owned.

Activities and organizations: drama/theater group, student-run radio and television station, choral group, Senate, SEC (Student Events Committee), TWA (Third World Alliance), WSCW (radio station), Dance Company/Club.

Athletics Member NCAA. All Division III except golf (Division II). ***Intercollegiate sports:*** baseball M, basketball M/W, cross-country running M/W, field hockey W, football M, golf M/W, ice hockey M, lacrosse W, soccer M/W, softball W, tennis W, track and field M/W, volleyball W. ***Intramural sports:*** basketball M/W, cheerleading M/W, equestrian sports M/W, lacrosse M/W.

Campus security: 24-hour emergency response devices and patrols, late-night transport/escort service, controlled dormitory access, well-lit campus, limited access to campus at night.

Student services: health clinic, personal/psychological counseling, veterans affairs office.

COSTS & FINANCIAL AID
Costs (2018–19) ***Tuition:*** state resident $970 full-time, $40 per credit hour part-time; nonresident $7050 full-time, $294 per credit hour part-time. Full-time tuition and fees vary according to class time, course load, degree level, and reciprocity agreements. Part-time tuition and fees vary according to class time, course load, degree level, and reciprocity agreements. ***Required fees:*** $9191 full-time, $383 per credit hour part-time. ***Room and board:*** $12,262; room only: $8428. Room and board charges vary according to board plan and housing facility. ***Payment plan:*** installment. ***Waivers:*** senior citizens and employees or children of employees.

Financial Aid Of all full-time matriculated undergraduates who enrolled in 2017, 3,536 applied for aid, 2,653 were judged to have need, 860 had their need fully met. In 2017, 111 non-need-based awards were made. ***Average percent of need met:*** 77. ***Average financial aid package:*** $15,173. ***Average need-based loan:*** $3029. ***Average need-based gift aid:*** $5149. ***Average non-need-based aid:*** $3051. ***Average indebtedness upon graduation:*** $28,759. ***Financial aid deadline:*** 5/1.

APPLYING
Standardized Tests *Required for some:* SAT or ACT (for admission).

Options: electronic application, early action, deferred entrance.

Application fee: $50.

Required: high school transcript, minimum 2.0 GPA. ***Required for some:*** essay or personal statement.

Application deadlines: rolling (transfers), 11/15 (early action).

Notification: 1/2 (freshmen), continuous (transfers).

CONTACT
Mr. Joseph DiCarlo, Director of Admissions, Worcester State University, 486 Chandler Street, Worcester, MA 01602-2597. *Phone:* 508-929-8040. *Fax:* 508-929-8183. *E-mail:* joseph.dicarlo@worcester.edu.

MICHIGAN

Adrian College

Adrian, Michigan

http://www.adrian.edu/

CONTACT
Mr. Frank Hribar, Vice President for Enrollment, Adrian College, 110 S. Madison Street, Adrian, MI 49221. *Phone:* 800-877-2246. *Toll-free phone:* 800-877-2246. *Fax:* 517-264-3331. *E-mail:* admissions@adrian.edu.

Albion College

Albion, Michigan

http://www.albion.edu/

- **Independent Methodist** 4-year, founded 1835
- **Small-town** 574-acre campus with easy access to Detroit
- **Endowment** $173.6 million
- **Coed** 1,533 undergraduate students, 98% full-time, 54% women, 46% men
- 68% of applicants were admitted

UNDERGRAD STUDENTS
1,509 full-time, 24 part-time. Students come from 31 states and territories; 11 other countries; 26% are from out of state; 15% Black or African American, non-Hispanic/Latino; 10% Hispanic/Latino; 2% Asian, non-Hispanic/Latino; 0.3% American Indian or Alaska Native, non-Hispanic/Latino; 3% Two or more races, non-Hispanic/Latino; 5% Race/ethnicity unknown; 2% international; 2% transferred in; 95% live on campus.

Freshmen:
Admission: 4,226 applied, 2,884 admitted, 428 enrolled. ***Average high school GPA:*** 3.5. ***Test scores:*** SAT evidence-based reading and writing scores over 500: 83%; SAT math scores over 500: 79%; ACT scores over 18: 99%; SAT evidence-based reading and writing scores over 600: 34%; SAT math scores over 600: 29%; ACT scores over 24: 46%; SAT evidence-based reading and writing scores over 700: 7%; SAT math scores over 700: 6%; ACT scores over 30: 8%.

Retention: 75% of full-time freshmen returned.

FACULTY
Total: 168, 70% full-time, 79% with terminal degrees.

Student/faculty ratio: 12:1.

ACADEMICS
Calendar: semesters. *Degree:* bachelor's.

Special study options: advanced placement credit, distance learning, double majors, honors programs, independent study, internships, off-campus study, part-time degree program, services for LD students, student-designed majors, study abroad, summer session for credit. ***ROTC:*** Army (c).

Unusual degree programs: 3-2 engineering with Columbia University, University of Michigan, Case Western Reserve University, Michigan Technological University; forestry with Duke University School of the Environment; nursing with Oakland University.

Computers: 250 computers/terminals and 1,217 ports are available on campus for general student use. Students can access the following: computer help desk, free student e-mail accounts, online (class) grades, online (class) registration, online (class) schedules, online student account and financial aid. Campuswide network is available. 100% of college-owned or -operated housing units are wired for high-speed Internet access. Wireless service is available via entire campus.
Library: Stockwell Mudd Libraries. *Books:* 345,123 (physical), 292,100 (digital/electronic); *Serial titles:* 752 (physical), 77,172 (digital/electronic); *Databases:* 205. Weekly public service hours: 110.

STUDENT LIFE
Housing options: on-campus residence required through senior year; coed, men-only, women-only. Campus housing is university owned. Freshman campus housing is guaranteed.

Activities and organizations: drama/theater group, student-run newspaper, radio station, choral group, marching band, Greek Life (Fraternities and Sororities), Student Senate (Student Government), Union Board (programming Board), Student Volunteer Bureau, Umbrella, national fraternities, national sororities.

Athletics Member NCAA. All Division III except golf (Division II). ***Intercollegiate sports:*** baseball M, basketball M/W, cross-country running M/W, equestrian sports M/W, football M, golf M/W, lacrosse M/W, soccer M/W, softball W, swimming and diving M/W, tennis M/W, track and field M/W, volleyball W. ***Intramural sports:*** basketball M/W, cheerleading M(c)/W(c), ice hockey M(c)/W(c), racquetball M/W, rugby M/W, sailing M(c)/W(c), skiing (downhill) M(c)/W(c), soccer M/W, softball M/W, swimming and diving M/W, tennis M/W, ultimate Frisbee M/W, volleyball M/W, water polo M(c)/W(c).

Campus security: 24-hour emergency response devices and patrols, late-night transport/escort service, controlled dormitory access.

Student services: health clinic, personal/psychological counseling, women's center.

COSTS & FINANCIAL AID
Costs (2019–20) ***One-time required fee:*** $185. ***Comprehensive fee:*** $60,470 includes full-time tuition ($47,570), mandatory fees ($520), and room and board ($12,380). ***College room only:*** $6080.

Financial Aid Of all full-time matriculated undergraduates who enrolled in 2018, 1,284 applied for aid, 1,206 were judged to have need, 222 had their need fully met. 333 Federal Work-Study jobs (averaging $1504). 185 state and other part-time jobs (averaging $1699). In 2018, 303 non-need-based awards were made. ***Average percent of need met:*** 88. ***Average financial aid package:*** $43,146. ***Average need-based loan:*** $4706. ***Average need-based gift aid:*** $38,416. ***Average non-need-based aid:*** $27,150. ***Average indebtedness upon graduation:*** $40,347.

APPLYING
Standardized Tests *Required:* SAT or ACT (for admission).

Options: electronic application, early admission, early action, deferred entrance.

Required: high school transcript, 1 letter of recommendation. ***Recommended:*** essay or personal statement, interview.

Application deadlines: rolling (freshmen), 8/15 (transfers), 12/1 (early action).

Notification: continuous until 10/15 (freshmen), continuous until 8/15 (transfers), 11/1 (early action).

CONTACT
Shar Sanders, Admissions Assistant, Albion College, 611 E. Porter Street, Albion, MI 49224. *Phone:* 517-629-0466. *Toll-free phone:* 800-858-6770. *Fax:* 517-629-0569. *E-mail:* ssanders@albion.edu.

Alma College

Alma, Michigan

http://www.alma.edu/

- **Independent Presbyterian** 4-year, founded 1886
- **Small-town** 128-acre campus with easy access to Lansing
- **Endowment** $120.2 million
- **Coed**
- **Moderately difficult** entrance level

FACULTY
Student/faculty ratio: 12:1.

ACADEMICS
Calendar: 4-4-1. *Degree:* bachelor's.
Library: Kerhl Building-Monteith Library. *Books:* 245,135 (physical), 150,135 (digital/electronic); *Serial titles:* 1,000 (physical). Weekly public service hours: 100; students can reserve study rooms.

STUDENT LIFE
Housing options: on-campus residence required through senior year; coed, special housing for students with disabilities. Campus housing is university owned. Freshman campus housing is guaranteed.

Activities and organizations: drama/theater group, student-run newspaper, choral group, marching band, Alma Ambassadors, Alma College Union Board, Alma College Otaku Gamers (ACOG), Student Congress, Alpha Phi Omega, national fraternities, national sororities.

Athletics Member NCAA. All Division III.

Campus security: 24-hour emergency response devices, late-night transport/escort service, controlled dormitory access.

Student services: health clinic, personal/psychological counseling.

COSTS & FINANCIAL AID
Costs (2018–19) ***Comprehensive fee:*** $51,256 includes full-time tuition ($39,998), mandatory fees ($260), and room and board ($10,998). Part-time tuition: $1195 per credit hour. Part-time tuition and fees vary according to course load. ***Room and board:*** Room and board charges vary according to board plan and housing facility. ***Payment plans:*** installment, deferred payment.

Financial Aid Of all full-time matriculated undergraduates who enrolled in 2018, 1,272 applied for aid, 1,170 were judged to have need, 131 had their need fully met. 690 Federal Work-Study jobs (averaging $1200). In 2018, 211 non-need-based awards were made. ***Average percent of need met:*** 71. ***Average financial aid package:*** $30,376. ***Average need-based loan:*** $4527. ***Average need-based gift aid:*** $29,329. ***Average non-need-based aid:*** $22,924. ***Average indebtedness upon graduation:*** $39,081.

APPLYING
Standardized Tests *Required:* SAT or ACT (for admission).

Options: electronic application.

Application fee: $25.

Required: essay or personal statement, high school transcript. ***Required for some:*** interview.

CONTACT
Craig Aimar, Director of Admissions, Alma College, 614 W. Superior Street, Alma, MI 48801-1599. *Phone:* 800-321-2562. *Toll-free phone:* 800-321-ALMA. *E-mail:* admissions@alma.edu.

Andrews University

Berrien Springs, Michigan

http://www.andrews.edu/

- **Independent Seventh-day Adventist** university, founded 1874
- **Small-town** 1650-acre campus
- **Endowment** $53.1 million
- **Coed**
- **Moderately difficult** entrance level

FACULTY
Student/faculty ratio: 10:1.

ACADEMICS
Calendar: semesters. *Degrees:* certificates, associate, bachelor's, master's, doctoral, post-master's, and postbachelor's certificates.
Library: James White Library plus 2 others. *Books:* 950,014 (physical), 394,023 (digital/electronic); *Serial titles:* 1,229 (physical), 198,545 (digital/electronic); *Databases:* 187.

STUDENT LIFE
Housing options: on-campus residence required through senior year; men-only, women-only. Campus housing is university owned. Freshman campus housing is guaranteed.

Activities and organizations: drama/theater group, student-run newspaper, radio station, choral group.

Campus security: 24-hour emergency response devices and patrols, controlled dormitory access.

Student services: health clinic, personal/psychological counseling.

COSTS & FINANCIAL AID
Costs (2018–19) ***Comprehensive fee:*** $38,366 includes full-time tuition ($28,272), mandatory fees ($1016), and room and board ($9078). Full-time tuition and fees vary according to course load. Part-time tuition: $1178 per credit hour. Part-time tuition and fees vary according to course load. ***Required fees:*** $124 per term part-time. ***College room only:*** $4778. Room and board charges vary according to board plan.

Financial Aid Of all full-time matriculated undergraduates who enrolled in 2018, 854 applied for aid, 777 were judged to have need, 141 had their need fully met. 525 Federal Work-Study jobs (averaging $767). In 2018, 568 non-need-based awards were made. ***Average percent of need met:*** 86. ***Average financial aid package:*** $31,065. ***Average need-based loan:*** $4224. ***Average need-based gift aid:*** $6794. ***Average non-need-based aid:*** $13,715. ***Average indebtedness upon graduation:*** $33,456.

APPLYING
Standardized Tests *Required:* SAT or ACT (for admission).

Options: electronic application, deferred entrance.

Application fee: $30.

Required: high school transcript, minimum 2.3 GPA, 2 letters of recommendation.

CONTACT
Elivette Diaz, Undergraduate Admissions Coordinator, Andrews University, Berrien Springs, MI 49104. *Phone:* 800-253-2874. *Toll-free phone:* 800-253-2874. *Fax:* 269-471-3228. *E-mail:* enroll@andrews.edu.

★ Aquinas College

Grand Rapids, Michigan

http://www.aquinas.edu/

- **Independent Roman Catholic** comprehensive, founded 1886
- **Suburban** 117-acre campus with easy access to Grand Rapids
- **Endowment** $40.8 million
- **Coed**
- **Moderately difficult** entrance level

FACULTY
Student/faculty ratio: 12:1.

ACADEMICS
Calendar: semesters. *Degrees:* associate, bachelor's, and master's.
Library: Grace Hauenstein Library plus 1 other. *Books:* 85,348 (physical), 196,003 (digital/electronic); *Serial titles:* 231 (physical); *Databases:* 85. Weekly public service hours: 90; students can reserve study rooms.

STUDENT LIFE

Housing options: on-campus residence required through junior year; coed. Campus housing is university owned. Freshman campus housing is guaranteed.

Activities and organizations: drama/theater group, student-run newspaper, radio station, choral group, Community Senate Programming Board, The Saint (newspaper), Insignis Honors Group, Community Action Volunteers of Aquinas (CAVA), Residence Hall Association.

Athletics Member NAIA.

Campus security: 24-hour emergency response devices and patrols, student patrols, late-night transport/escort service, controlled dormitory access.

Student services: health clinic, personal/psychological counseling, women's center, veterans affairs office.

COSTS & FINANCIAL AID

Costs (2018–19) ***Comprehensive fee:*** $41,906 includes full-time tuition ($31,976), mandatory fees ($598), and room and board ($9332). Full-time tuition and fees vary according to course load. Part-time tuition: $498 per credit hour. Part-time tuition and fees vary according to course load. ***Required fees:*** $60 per term part-time. ***College room only:*** $4376. Room and board charges vary according to board plan and housing facility. ***Payment plans:*** installment, deferred payment.

Financial Aid Of all full-time matriculated undergraduates who enrolled in 2018, 1,078 applied for aid, 974 were judged to have need, 220 had their need fully met. 130 Federal Work-Study jobs (averaging $994). In 2018, 196 non-need-based awards were made. ***Average percent of need met:*** 77. ***Average financial aid package:*** $25,507. ***Average need-based loan:*** $2623. ***Average need-based gift aid:*** $22,884. ***Average non-need-based aid:*** $16,633. ***Average indebtedness upon graduation:*** $32,204.

APPLYING

Standardized Tests *Required:* SAT or ACT (for admission).

Options: electronic application, deferred entrance.

Required: high school transcript, minimum 2.5 GPA. ***Required for some:*** essay or personal statement, interview.

CONTACT

Ms. Rebecca Roberts, Admissions Office Applications Specialist, Aquinas College, 1700 Fulton Street E., Grand Rapids, MI 49506-1801. *Phone:* 616-632-2900. *Toll-free phone:* 800-678-9593. *Fax:* 616-732-4469. *E-mail:* admissions@aquinas.edu.

See below for display ad and page 972 for the College Close-Up.

Baker College

Flint, Michigan

http://www.baker.edu/

CONTACT

Mr. Mark Heaton, System Marketing/Admission, Baker College, 1050 West Bristol Road, Flint, MI 48507-5508. *Phone:* 810-766-4280. *Toll-free phone:* 800-964-4299. *Fax:* 810-766-4279. *E-mail:* mark.heaton@baker.edu.

Calvin College

Grand Rapids, Michigan

http://www.calvin.edu/

- **Independent Christian Reformed** comprehensive, founded 1876
- **Suburban** 400-acre campus with easy access to Grand Rapids, MI
- **Endowment** $160.8 million
- **Coed** 3,625 undergraduate students, 94% full-time, 53% women, 47% men
- **Moderately difficult** entrance level, 79% of applicants were admitted

UNDERGRAD STUDENTS

3,417 full-time, 208 part-time. Students come from 46 states and territories; 64 other countries; 42% are from out of state; 3% Black or African American, non-Hispanic/Latino; 5% Hispanic/Latino; 5% Asian, non-Hispanic/Latino; 0.1% American Indian or Alaska Native, non-Hispanic/Latino; 3% Two or more races, non-Hispanic/Latino; 2% Race/ethnicity unknown; 12% international; 2% transferred in; 58% live on campus.

Freshmen:
Admission: 3,847 applied, 3,038 admitted, 842 enrolled. ***Average high school GPA:*** 3.8. ***Test scores:*** SAT evidence-based reading and writing scores over 500: 96%; SAT math scores over 500: 96%; ACT scores over 18: 99%; SAT evidence-based reading and writing scores over 600: 66%; SAT math scores over 600: 65%; ACT scores over 24: 78%; SAT evidence-based reading and writing scores over 700: 18%; SAT math scores over 700: 23%; ACT scores over 30: 32%.

Retention: 87% of full-time freshmen returned.

FACULTY
Total: 339, 68% full-time, 71% with terminal degrees.

Student/faculty ratio: 13:1.

ACADEMICS
Calendar: 4-1-4. *Degrees:* certificates, associate, bachelor's, and master's.

Special study options: academic remediation for entering students, accelerated degree program, advanced placement credit, distance learning, double majors, honors programs, independent study, internships, off-campus study, part-time degree program, services for LD students, student-designed majors, study abroad, summer session for credit. ***ROTC:*** Army (c).

Unusual degree programs: 3-2 occupational therapy with Washington University in St. Louis.

Computers: 1,025 computers/terminals and 2,656 ports are available on campus for general student use. Students can access the following: campus intranet, computer help desk, free student e-mail accounts, online (class) grades, online (class) registration, online (class) schedules. Campuswide network is available. 100% of college-owned or -operated housing units are wired for high-speed Internet access. Wireless service is available via classrooms, computer centers, computer labs, dorm rooms, learning centers, libraries, student centers.
Library: Hekman Library. *Books:* 524,139 (physical), 381,981 (digital/electronic); *Serial titles:* 6,139 (physical), 36,320 (digital/electronic); *Databases:* 120. Weekly public service hours: 90; students can reserve study rooms.

STUDENT LIFE
Housing options: on-campus residence required through sophomore year; men-only, women-only. Campus housing is university owned. Freshman campus housing is guaranteed.

Activities and organizations: drama/theater group, student-run newspaper, choral group, Dance Guild, Pre-Health Professionals, Calvin Outdoor Recreation, National Student Speech, Language, and Hearing Association, African Students Association.

Athletics Member NCAA. All Division III except ice hockey (Division I). ***Intercollegiate sports:*** baseball M, basketball M/W, cross-country running M/W, equestrian sports M(c)/W(c), golf M/W, ice hockey M, lacrosse M/W, rugby M(c)/W(c), soccer M/W, softball W, swimming and diving M/W, tennis M/W, track and field M/W, triathlon W, ultimate Frisbee M(c)/W(c), volleyball M(c)/W. ***Intramural sports:*** badminton M/W, basketball M/W, cross-country running M/W, football M/W, golf M/W, racquetball M/W, rock climbing M/W, rowing M(c)/W(c), sand volleyball M/W, skiing (downhill) M/W(c), soccer M/W, softball M/W, swimming and diving M/W, table tennis M/W, tennis M/W, track and field M/W, volleyball M/W, water polo M/W.

Campus security: 24-hour emergency response devices and patrols, student patrols, late-night transport/escort service, controlled dormitory access.

Student services: health clinic, personal/psychological counseling.

COSTS & FINANCIAL AID
Costs (2019–20) ***Comprehensive fee:*** $46,900 includes full-time tuition ($36,100), mandatory fees ($200), and room and board ($10,600). Part-time tuition: $867 per credit hour.

Financial Aid Of all full-time matriculated undergraduates who enrolled in 2018, 2,776 applied for aid, 2,047 were judged to have need, 406 had their need fully met. 713 Federal Work-Study jobs (averaging $1597). In 2018, 1289 non-need-based awards were made. ***Average percent of need met:*** 73. ***Average financial aid package:*** $24,606. ***Average need-based loan:*** $5936. ***Average need-based gift aid:*** $18,797. ***Average non-need-based aid:*** $13,011. ***Average indebtedness upon graduation:*** $29,768.

APPLYING
Standardized Tests *Required:* SAT or ACT (for admission), or CLT (for admission).

Options: electronic application, deferred entrance.

Application fee: $35.

Required: essay or personal statement, high school transcript, 1 letter of recommendation. ***Recommended:*** interview.

Application deadlines: 8/15 (freshmen), 8/15 (out-of-state freshmen), rolling (transfers).

Notification: continuous (freshmen).

CONTACT
Ms. Robin Wait, Associate Director of Admissions, Calvin College, 3201 Burton Street, SE, Grand Rapids, MI 49546. *Phone:* 616-526-6106. *Toll-free phone:* 800-688-0122. *Fax:* 616-526-6777. *E-mail:* admissions@calvin.edu.

Central Michigan University
Mount Pleasant, Michigan
http://www.cmich.edu/

- **State-supported** university, founded 1892
- **Small-town** 854-acre campus
- **Endowment** $130.7 million
- **Coed** 16,432 undergraduate students, 87% full-time, 58% women, 42% men
- **Moderately difficult** entrance level, 69% of applicants were admitted

UNDERGRAD STUDENTS
14,270 full-time, 2,162 part-time. Students come from 53 states and territories; 61 other countries; 7% are from out of state; 9% Black or African American, non-Hispanic/Latino; 5% Hispanic/Latino; 1% Asian, non-Hispanic/Latino; 0.8% American Indian or Alaska Native, non-Hispanic/Latino; 4% Two or more races, non-Hispanic/Latino; 1% Race/ethnicity unknown; 3% international; 6% transferred in; 36% live on campus.

Freshmen:
Admission: 17,858 applied, 12,293 admitted, 2,732 enrolled. ***Average high school GPA:*** 3.4. ***Test scores:*** SAT evidence-based reading and writing scores over 500: 80%; SAT math scores over 500: 75%; ACT scores over 18: 89%; SAT evidence-based reading and writing scores over 600: 32%; SAT math scores over 600: 24%; ACT scores over 24: 45%; SAT evidence-based reading and writing scores over 700: 4%; SAT math scores over 700: 4%; ACT scores over 30: 10%.

Retention: 77% of full-time freshmen returned.

FACULTY
Total: 1,218, 62% full-time, 67% with terminal degrees.

Student/faculty ratio: 20:1.

ACADEMICS
Calendar: semesters. *Degrees:* bachelor's, master's, doctoral, post-master's, and postbachelor's certificates.

ROTC: Army (b), Air Force (c).

Computers: 490 computers/terminals and 26,902 ports are available on campus for general student use. Students can access the following: campus intranet, computer help desk, free student e-mail accounts, online (class) grades, online (class) registration, online (class) schedules, learning management system. Campuswide network is available. 100% of college-owned or -operated housing units are wired for high-speed Internet access. Wireless service is available via entire campus.
Library: Charles V. Park Library. *Books:* 895,460 (physical), 709,885 (digital/electronic); *Serial titles:* 2,156 (physical), 114,678 (digital/electronic); *Databases:* 336. Weekly public service hours: 101; students can reserve study rooms.

STUDENT LIFE
Housing options: on-campus residence required for freshman year; coed, special housing for students with disabilities. Campus housing is university owned. Freshman campus housing is guaranteed.

Activities and organizations: drama/theater group, student-run newspaper, radio and television station, choral group, marching band, national fraternities, national sororities.

Athletics Member NCAA. All Division I except football (Division I-A). ***Intercollegiate sports:*** baseball M(s), basketball M(s)/W(s), cross-country running M(s)/W(s), field hockey W(s), golf W(s), gymnastics W(s), lacrosse W(s), soccer W(s), softball W(s), track and field M(s)/W(s), volleyball W(s), wrestling M(s). ***Intramural sports:*** baseball M(c), basketball M/W, bowling M/W, cross-country running M(c)/W(c), equestrian sports M(c)/W(c), football M/W, golf M(c)/W(c), ice hockey M(c)/W(c), lacrosse M(c)/W(c), racquetball M/W, rugby M(c)/W(c), skiing (downhill) M(c)/W(c), soccer M/W, softball M/W, swimming and diving M(c)/W(c), table tennis M/W, tennis M/W, track and field M(c)/W(c), triathlon M(c)/W(c), ultimate Frisbee M(c)/W(c), volleyball M/W, water polo M(c)/W(c), weight lifting M/W, wrestling M/W.

Campus security: 24-hour emergency response devices and patrols, late-night transport/escort service, controlled dormitory access.

Student services: health clinic, personal/psychological counseling, women's center, veterans affairs office.

COSTS & FINANCIAL AID

Costs (2018–19) ***Tuition:*** state resident $12,510 full-time, $417 per credit hour part-time; nonresident $23,670 full-time, $789 per credit hour part-time. Full-time tuition and fees vary according to location. Part-time tuition and fees vary according to location. ***Room and board:*** $9736; room only: $4868. Room and board charges vary according to board plan and housing facility. ***Payment plan:*** installment. ***Waivers:*** children of alumni, senior citizens, and employees or children of employees.

Financial Aid Of all full-time matriculated undergraduates who enrolled in 2017, 12,106 applied for aid, 9,559 were judged to have need, 4,678 had their need fully met. 665 Federal Work-Study jobs (averaging $1898). 429 state and other part-time jobs (averaging $1812). In 2017, 2238 non-need-based awards were made. ***Average percent of need met:*** 80. ***Average financial aid package:*** $14,041. ***Average need-based loan:*** $7112. ***Average need-based gift aid:*** $7344. ***Average non-need-based aid:*** $6071. ***Average indebtedness upon graduation:*** $32,453.

APPLYING

Standardized Tests *Required:* SAT or ACT (for admission).

Options: electronic application, early admission, early action, deferred entrance.

Application fee: $35.

Required: high school transcript. ***Required for some:*** essay or personal statement, interview.

Application deadlines: rolling (freshmen), rolling (transfers), 5/1 (early action).

Notification: continuous (freshmen), continuous (transfers), 5/8 (early action).

CONTACT

Dr. Lee Furbeck, Director, Undergraduate Admissions, Central Michigan University, 1200 South Franklin Street, Mount Pleasant, MI 48859. *Phone:* 989-774-2446. *Toll-free phone:* 888-292-5366. *E-mail:* furbe1l@cmich.edu.

Chamberlain College of Nursing

Troy, Michigan

http://www.chamberlain.edu/

CONTACT

Chamberlain College of Nursing, 200 Kirts Boulevard, Troy, MI 48084. *Toll-free phone:* 877-751-5783.

Cleary University

Howell, Michigan

http://www.cleary.edu/

CONTACT

Eric Brown, Director of Admissions, Cleary University, 3750 Cleary Drive, Howell, MI 48843. *Phone:* 800-686-1883. *Toll-free phone:* 800-686-1883. *Fax:* 517-338-5075. *E-mail:* admissions@cleary.edu.

College for Creative Studies

Detroit, Michigan

http://www.collegeforcreativestudies.edu/

CONTACT

Office of Admissions, College for Creative Studies, 201 East Kirby, Detroit, MI 48202-4034. *Phone:* 800-952-2787. *Toll-free phone:* 800-952-ARTS. *Fax:* 313-872-2739. *E-mail:* admissions@collegeforcreativestudies.edu.

Compass College of Cinematic Arts

Grand Rapids, Michigan

http://www.compass.edu/

- **Independent** 4-year
- **Urban** campus
- **Coed**
- **Minimally difficult** entrance level

ACADEMICS

Degrees: associate and bachelor's.

APPLYING

Standardized Tests *Recommended:* SAT or ACT (for admission).

Required: essay or personal statement, high school transcript, minimum 2.0 GPA, 2 letters of recommendation, interview, Portfolio of 2 film pieces and 2 non-film pieces.

CONTACT

Compass College of Cinematic Arts, 41 Sheldon Boulevard SE, Grand Rapids, MI 49503.

Concordia University Ann Arbor

Ann Arbor, Michigan

http://www.cuaa.edu/

CONTACT

Mr. Ben Limback, Director of Admissions, Concordia University Ann Arbor, 4090 Geddes Road, Ann Arbor, MI 48105-2797. *Phone:* 734-995-7311. *Toll-free phone:* 877-995-7520 (in-state); 877-955-7520 (out-of-state). *Fax:* 734-995-4610. *E-mail:* admissions@cuaa.edu.

Cornerstone University

Grand Rapids, Michigan

http://www.cornerstone.edu/

- **Independent nondenominational** comprehensive, founded 1941
- **Suburban** 132-acre campus with easy access to Grand Rapids
- **Endowment** $9.2 million
- **Coed**
- **Minimally difficult** entrance level

FACULTY

Student/faculty ratio: 15:1.

ACADEMICS

Calendar: semesters. *Degrees:* diplomas, associate, bachelor's, master's, and doctoral.

Library: Miller Library. *Books:* 102,008 (physical), 198,380 (digital/electronic); *Serial titles:* 522 (physical), 46,267 (digital/electronic); *Databases:* 176. Weekly public service hours: 85; students can reserve study rooms.

STUDENT LIFE

Housing options: on-campus residence required through junior year; men-only, women-only, special housing for students with disabilities. Campus housing is university owned. Freshman campus housing is guaranteed.

Activities and organizations: drama/theater group, choral group, Student Government, Student Education Association, Intramural Sports, Student Activities Council, International Justice Mission.

Athletics Member NAIA.

Campus security: 24-hour emergency response devices and patrols, student patrols, late-night transport/escort service, controlled dormitory access.

Student services: health clinic, personal/psychological counseling.

COSTS & FINANCIAL AID
Costs (2018–19) ***Comprehensive fee:*** $33,800 includes full-time tuition ($24,500) and room and board ($9300). Full-time tuition and fees vary according to course load and reciprocity agreements. Part-time tuition: $942 per credit hour. Part-time tuition and fees vary according to course load. ***Room and board:*** Room and board charges vary according to board plan and housing facility.

Financial Aid Of all full-time matriculated undergraduates who enrolled in 2017, 904 applied for aid, 841 were judged to have need, 110 had their need fully met. 183 Federal Work-Study jobs (averaging $941). In 2017, 209 non-need-based awards were made. ***Average percent of need met:*** 70. ***Average financial aid package:*** $21,975. ***Average need-based loan:*** $4154. ***Average need-based gift aid:*** $17,455. ***Average non-need-based aid:*** $10,381. ***Average indebtedness upon graduation:*** $33,729.

APPLYING
Standardized Tests *Required:* SAT or ACT (for admission).

Options: electronic application.

Required: essay or personal statement, high school transcript, minimum 2.5 GPA, 1 letter of recommendation, pastoral letter.

CONTACT
Mrs. Lisa Link, Office of Admissions, Cornerstone University, 1001 East Beltline Avenue, NE, Grand Rapids, MI 49525. *Phone:* 616-222-1426. *Toll-free phone:* 800-787-9778. *Fax:* 616-222-1418. *E-mail:* admissions@cornerstone.edu.

Davenport University

Grand Rapids, Michigan

http://www.davenport.edu/

- **Independent** comprehensive, founded 1866
- **Suburban** 77-acre campus with easy access to Grand Rapids
- **Endowment** $26.0 million
- **Coed** 5,166 undergraduate students, 49% full-time, 55% women, 45% men
- **Minimally difficult** entrance level, 89% of applicants were admitted

UNDERGRAD STUDENTS
2,518 full-time, 2,648 part-time. Students come from 30 states and territories; 20 other countries; 2% are from out of state; 13% Black or African American, non-Hispanic/Latino; 6% Hispanic/Latino; 3% Asian, non-Hispanic/Latino; 0.2% Native Hawaiian or other Pacific Islander, non-Hispanic/Latino; 0.6% American Indian or Alaska Native, non-Hispanic/Latino; 3% Two or more races, non-Hispanic/Latino; 8% Race/ethnicity unknown; 3% international; 6% live on campus.

Freshmen:
Admission: 2,184 applied, 1,951 admitted, 646 enrolled. ***Average high school GPA:*** 3.2.

Retention: 73% of full-time freshmen returned.

FACULTY
Total: 678, 21% full-time, 33% with terminal degrees.

Student/faculty ratio: 12:1.

ACADEMICS
Calendar: semesters. *Degrees:* certificates, diplomas, associate, bachelor's, master's, post-master's, and postbachelor's certificates.

Special study options: academic remediation for entering students, accelerated degree program, adult/continuing education programs, advanced placement credit, cooperative education, distance learning, English as a second language, independent study, internships, part-time degree program, services for LD students, study abroad, summer session for credit. ***ROTC:*** Army (c).

Computers: 3,098 computers/terminals and 315 ports are available on campus for general student use. Students can access the following: campus intranet, computer help desk, free student e-mail accounts, online (class) grades, online (class) registration, online (class) schedules. Campuswide network is available. 100% of college-owned or -operated housing units are wired for high-speed Internet access. Wireless service is available via entire campus.

Library: Margaret D. Sneden Library Information Commons plus 3 others. Students can reserve study rooms.

STUDENT LIFE
Housing options: coed. Campus housing is university owned. Freshman applicants given priority for college housing.

Activities and organizations: marching band, Business Professionals of America, Delta Epsilon Chi, Student Government, Health Occupations Students of America, Connect.

Athletics Member NAIA. ***Intercollegiate sports:*** baseball M(s), basketball M(s)/W(s), bowling M(s)/W(s), cheerleading W(s), cross-country running M(s)/W(s), football M(s), golf M(s)/W(s), ice hockey M(s)/W(s), lacrosse M(s)/W(s), rugby M(s)/W(s), soccer M(s)/W(s), softball M(s)/W(s), tennis M(s)/W(s), track and field M(s)/W(s), volleyball W(s), wrestling M(s).

Campus security: 24-hour emergency response devices and patrols, late-night transport/escort service, controlled dormitory access.

Student services: personal/psychological counseling.

COSTS
Costs (2018–19) ***Tuition:*** $17,544 full-time, $731 per credit hour part-time. Full-time tuition and fees vary according to location and program. Part-time tuition and fees vary according to location and program. ***Required fees:*** $700 full-time, $350 per term part-time. ***Room only:*** Room and board charges vary according to board plan and housing facility. ***Payment plan:*** installment. ***Waivers:*** employees or children of employees.

APPLYING
Standardized Tests *Recommended:* SAT (for admission), ACT (for admission).

Options: electronic application, deferred entrance.

Application fee: $25.

Required: high school transcript. ***Recommended:*** interview.

Application deadlines: rolling (freshmen), rolling (transfers).

Notification: continuous (freshmen), continuous (transfers).

CONTACT
Ms. David Lawrence, Executive Director of Admissions, Davenport University, 6191 Kraft Avenue SE, Grand Rapids, MI 49512. *Phone:* 616-451-3511. *Toll-free phone:* 800-686-1600 (in-state); 866-686-1600 (out-of-state). *Fax:* 616-732-1145. *E-mail:* david.lawrence@davenport.edu.

Eastern Michigan University

Ypsilanti, Michigan

http://www.emich.edu/

- **State-supported** comprehensive, founded 1849
- **Suburban** 460-acre campus with easy access to Detroit
- **Endowment** $67.2 million
- **Coed**
- **Moderately difficult** entrance level

FACULTY
Student/faculty ratio: 17:1.

ACADEMICS
Calendar: semesters. *Degrees:* bachelor's, master's, doctoral, post-master's, and postbachelor's certificates.
Library: Bruce T. Halle Library.

STUDENT LIFE
Housing options: on-campus residence required through sophomore year; coed, special housing for students with disabilities. Campus housing is university owned.

Activities and organizations: drama/theater group, student-run newspaper, radio and television station, choral group, marching band, International Student Association, Golden Key International Honor Society, Psychology Club, Indian Student Association, GREEN (Gathering Resources to Educate about our Environment and Nature), national fraternities, national sororities.

Athletics Member NCAA. All Division I except football (Division I-A).

Campus security: 24-hour emergency response devices and patrols, student patrols, late-night transport/escort service, controlled dormitory access, bicycle patrols, local police in dormitories, self-defense education, lighted pathways, bike lock lease program.

Student services: health clinic, personal/psychological counseling, women's center, legal services.

FINANCIAL AID

Financial Aid Of all full-time matriculated undergraduates who enrolled in 2017, 10,070 applied for aid, 8,564 were judged to have need, 292 had their need fully met. 523 Federal Work-Study jobs (averaging $2222). In 2017, 2210 non-need-based awards were made. ***Average percent of need met:*** 44. ***Average financial aid package:*** $10,283. ***Average need-based loan:*** $6097. ***Average need-based gift aid:*** $6259. ***Average non-need-based aid:*** $5588. ***Average indebtedness upon graduation:*** $29,213.

APPLYING

Standardized Tests *Required:* SAT or ACT (for admission).

Options: electronic application, deferred entrance.

Application fee: $35.

Required: high school transcript, minimum 2.0 GPA. ***Required for some:*** 1 letter of recommendation, interview.

CONTACT

Eastern Michigan University, Ypsilanti, MI 48197. *Phone:* 734-487-3060. *Toll-free phone:* 800-GO TO EMU.

Ferris State University

Big Rapids, Michigan

http://www.ferris.edu/

- **State-supported** comprehensive, founded 1884
- **Small-town** 941-acre campus with easy access to Grand Rapids
- **Endowment** $73.8 million
- **Coed**
- **Minimally difficult** entrance level

FACULTY

Student/faculty ratio: 16:1.

ACADEMICS

Calendar: semesters. *Degrees:* certificates, associate, bachelor's, master's, doctoral, and postbachelor's certificates.

Library: Ferris Library for Information, Technology and Education. *Books:* 267,897 (physical), 214,655 (digital/electronic); *Serial titles:* 161 (physical), 160,936 (digital/electronic); *Databases:* 183. Weekly public service hours: 93; study areas open 24 hours, 5–7 days a week; students can reserve study rooms.

STUDENT LIFE

Housing options: on-campus residence required for freshman year; coed, special housing for students with disabilities. Campus housing is university owned. Freshman campus housing is guaranteed.

Activities and organizations: drama/theater group, student-run newspaper, radio and television station, choral group, Student American Dental Hygiene Association, Pre-Pharm D, American Pharmacist Association, Student Nurses Association, American Marketing Association, national fraternities, national sororities.

Athletics Member NCAA. All Division II.

Campus security: 24-hour emergency response devices, student patrols, late-night transport/escort service, controlled dormitory access.

Student services: health clinic, personal/psychological counseling, veterans affairs office.

COSTS & FINANCIAL AID

Costs (2018–19) ***Tuition:*** state resident $12,630 full-time, $421 per credit hour part-time; nonresident $12,630 full-time, $421 per credit hour part-time. Full-time tuition and fees vary according to location, program, and student level. Part-time tuition and fees vary according to location and student level. ***Room and board:*** $9894. Room and board charges vary according to board plan and housing facility.

Financial Aid Of all full-time matriculated undergraduates who enrolled in 2018, 7,738 applied for aid, 5,879 were judged to have need, 1,029 had their need fully met. 417 Federal Work-Study jobs (averaging $2770). 237 state and other part-time jobs (averaging $2010). In 2018, 1205 non-need-based awards were made. ***Average percent of need met:*** 68. ***Average financial aid package:*** $11,820. ***Average need-based loan:*** $4110. ***Average need-based gift aid:*** $5260. ***Average non-need-based aid:*** $4200. ***Average indebtedness upon graduation:*** $36,530.

APPLYING

Standardized Tests *Required for some:* SAT or ACT (for admission).

Options: electronic application.

Required: high school transcript, minimum 2.5 GPA. ***Required for some:*** essay or personal statement, interview.

CONTACT

Mr. Jason Daday, Associate Director of Admissions, Ferris State University, 1201 South State Street, CSS 201, Big Rapids, MI 49307-2742. *Phone:* 231-591-3106. *Toll-free phone:* 800-433-7747. *Fax:* 231-591-2242. *E-mail:* dadayja@ferris.edu.

Finlandia University

Hancock, Michigan

http://www.finlandia.edu/

CONTACT

Martin Kinard, Finlandia University, 601 Quincy Street, Hancock, MI 49930. *Phone:* 906-487-7352. *Toll-free phone:* 877-202-5491. *Fax:* 906-487-7383. *E-mail:* admissions@finlandia.edu.

Grace Bible College

Grand Rapids, Michigan

http://www.gbcol.edu/

CONTACT

Mr. Kevin Gilliam, Director of Enrollment, Grace Bible College, 1101 Aldon Street, SW, PO Box 910, Grand Rapids, MI 49509. *Phone:* 616-538-2330 Ext. 239. *Toll-free phone:* 800-968-1887. *Fax:* 616-538-0599. *E-mail:* gbc@gbcol.edu.

Grand Valley State University

Allendale, Michigan

http://www.gvsu.edu/

- **State-supported** comprehensive, founded 1960
- **Small-town** 1391-acre campus with easy access to Grand Rapids
- **Endowment** $126.8 million
- **Coed** 21,680 undergraduate students, 89% full-time, 59% women, 41% men
- **Moderately difficult** entrance level, 83% of applicants were admitted

UNDERGRAD STUDENTS

19,233 full-time, 2,447 part-time. Students come from 47 states and territories; 73 other countries; 7% are from out of state; 5% Black or African American, non-Hispanic/Latino; 6% Hispanic/Latino; 2% Asian, non-Hispanic/Latino; 0.1% Native Hawaiian or other Pacific Islander, non-Hispanic/Latino; 0.3% American Indian or Alaska Native, non-Hispanic/Latino; 4% Two or more races, non-Hispanic/Latino; 0.3% Race/ethnicity unknown; 1% international; 7% transferred in; 29% live on campus.

Freshmen:

Admission: 17,133 applied, 14,178 admitted, 4,312 enrolled. ***Average high school GPA:*** 3.6. ***Test scores:*** SAT evidence-based reading and writing scores over 500: 90%; SAT math scores over 500: 85%; ACT scores over 18: 97%; SAT evidence-based reading and writing scores over 600: 40%; SAT math scores over 600: 31%; ACT scores over 24: 53%; SAT evidence-based reading and writing scores over 700: 5%; SAT math scores over 700: 5%; ACT scores over 30: 10%.

Retention: 85% of full-time freshmen returned.

FACULTY

Total: 1,783, 67% full-time, 56% with terminal degrees.

Student/faculty ratio: 17:1.

ACADEMICS

Calendar: semesters. *Degrees:* certificates, bachelor's, master's, doctoral, post-master's, and postbachelor's certificates.

Special study options: academic remediation for entering students, accelerated degree program, adult/continuing education programs, advanced placement credit, cooperative education, distance learning, double majors, English as a second language, freshman honors college, honors programs, independent study, internships, part-time degree program, services for LD students, study abroad, summer session for credit.

Computers: 2,600 computers/terminals are available on campus for general student use. Students can access the following: campus intranet, computer help desk, free student e-mail accounts, online (class) grades, online (class) registration, online (class) schedules, transcript, degree audit, credit card payments. Campuswide network is available. 100% of college-owned or -operated housing units are wired for high-speed Internet access. Wireless service is available via entire campus.

Library: Mary Idema Pew Library Learning and Information Commons plus 5 others. *Books:* 567,197 (physical), 1.0 million (digital/electronic). Students can reserve study rooms.

STUDENT LIFE

Housing options: coed. Campus housing is university owned. Freshman campus housing is guaranteed.

Activities and organizations: drama/theater group, student-run newspaper, radio and television station, choral group, marching band, Habitat for Humanity, Alternative Breaks, Hospitality and tourism Management Club, Dance Troupe, Colleges Against Cancer, national fraternities, national sororities.

Athletics Member NCAA. All Division II except golf (Division I). ***Intercollegiate sports:*** baseball M(s), basketball M(s)/W(s), cheerleading M(c)/W(c), crew M(c)/W(c), cross-country running M(s)/W(s), football M(s), golf M(s)/W(s), ice hockey M/W, lacrosse M(c)/W, rowing M/W, rugby M(c)/W(c), sailing M(c)/W(c), skiing (downhill) W(c), soccer M(c)/W(s), softball W(s), swimming and diving M(s)/W(s), tennis M(s)/W(s), track and field M(s)/W(s), volleyball M(c)/W(s), water polo M(c)/W(c), wrestling M(c). ***Intramural sports:*** archery M/W, basketball M/W, bowling M/W, cheerleading M/W, crew M/W, cross-country running M/W, fencing M/W, field hockey M/W, football M, golf M/W, gymnastics M/W, lacrosse M/W, racquetball M/W, skiing (cross-country) M/W, skiing (downhill) M/W, soccer M/W, softball M/W, squash M/W, swimming and diving M/W, tennis M/W, volleyball M/W, water polo M/W, weight lifting M/W, wrestling M.

Campus security: 24-hour emergency response devices and patrols, student patrols, late-night transport/escort service, controlled dormitory access.

Student services: health clinic, personal/psychological counseling, women's center.

COSTS & FINANCIAL AID

Costs (2018–19) ***Tuition:*** state resident $12,484 full-time, $521 per credit hour part-time; nonresident $17,762 full-time, $742 per credit hour part-time. Full-time tuition and fees vary according to course level, course load, program, and student level. Part-time tuition and fees vary according to course level, course load, program, and student level. ***Room and board:*** $8690; room only: $4345. Room and board charges vary according to board plan and housing facility. ***Payment plans:*** installment, deferred payment. ***Waivers:*** employees or children of employees.

Financial Aid Of all full-time matriculated undergraduates who enrolled in 2018, 15,629 applied for aid, 11,264 were judged to have need, 2,017 had their need fully met. 1,240 Federal Work-Study jobs (averaging $2882). In 2018, 3524 non-need-based awards were made. ***Average percent of need met:*** 66. ***Average financial aid package:*** $10,404. ***Average need-based loan:*** $4243. ***Average need-based gift aid:*** $7747. ***Average non-need-based aid:*** $3933. ***Average indebtedness upon graduation:*** $28,415.

APPLYING

Standardized Tests *Required:* SAT or ACT (for admission).

Options: electronic application.

Application fee: $30.

Required: high school transcript. ***Required for some:*** essay or personal statement, interview.

Notification: 5/1 (freshmen), continuous (transfers).

CONTACT

Ms. Jodi Chycinski, Director of Admissions, Grand Valley State University, 1 Campus Drive, Allendale, MI 49401. *Phone:* 616-331-2025. *Toll-free phone:* 800-748-0246. *Fax:* 616-331-2000. *E-mail:* go2gvsu@gvsu.edu.

Great Lakes Christian College

Lansing, Michigan

http://www.glcc.edu/

CONTACT

Mrs. Judy Carter, Admissions Office Manager, Great Lakes Christian College, 6211 West Willow Highway, Lansing, MI 48917-1299. *Phone:* 517-321-0242 Ext. 221. *Toll-free phone:* 800-YES-GLCC. *Fax:* 517-321-5902. *E-mail:* jcarter@glcc.edu.

★ Hillsdale College

Hillsdale, Michigan

http://www.hillsdale.edu/

- **Independent** comprehensive, founded 1844
- **Small-town** 400-acre campus
- **Endowment** $597.9 million
- **Coed** 1,468 undergraduate students, 98% full-time, 48% women, 52% men
- **Most difficult** entrance level, 36% of applicants were admitted

UNDERGRAD STUDENTS

1,434 full-time, 34 part-time. Students come from 51 states and territories; 12 other countries; 67% are from out of state; 100% Race/ethnicity unknown; 1% transferred in; 66% live on campus.

Freshmen:

Admission: 2,209 applied, 795 admitted, 341 enrolled. ***Average high school GPA:*** 3.9. ***Test scores:*** SAT evidence-based reading and writing scores over 500: 100%; SAT math scores over 500: 99%; ACT scores over 18: 100%; SAT evidence-based reading and writing scores over 600: 95%; SAT math scores over 600: 84%; ACT scores over 24: 99%; SAT evidence-based reading and writing scores over 700: 51%; SAT math scores over 700: 37%; ACT scores over 30: 67%.

Retention: 91% of full-time freshmen returned.

FACULTY

Total: 227, 63% full-time.

Student/faculty ratio: 10:1.

ACADEMICS

Calendar: semesters. *Degrees:* bachelor's, master's, and doctoral.

Special study options: advanced placement credit, double majors, honors programs, independent study, internships, off-campus study, part-time degree program, student-designed majors, study abroad, summer session for credit.

Unusual degree programs: 3-2 engineering.

Computers: 359 computers/terminals and 1 port are available on campus for general student use. Students can access the following: campus intranet, computer help desk, free student e-mail accounts, online (class) grades, online (class) registration, online (class) schedules. Campuswide network is available. 100% of college-owned or -operated housing units are wired for high-speed Internet access. Wireless service is available via entire campus.

Library: Michael Alex Mossey Library. *Books:* 275,174 (physical), 2.0 million (digital/electronic); *Serial titles:* 570 (physical), 30,000 (digital/electronic); *Databases:* 235.

STUDENT LIFE

Housing options: on-campus residence required through sophomore year; men-only, women-only, cooperative. Campus housing is university owned. Freshman campus housing is guaranteed.

Activities and organizations: drama/theater group, student-run newspaper, radio station, choral group, GOAL Volunteer Program, Greek Life, College Republicans, Intervarsity, Students for Life, national fraternities, national sororities.

Athletics Member NCAA. All Division II. ***Intercollegiate sports:*** archery M(c)/W(c), baseball M(s), basketball M(s)/W(s), cheerleading W(c), crew

M(c)/W(c), cross-country running M(s)/W(s), equestrian sports M(c)/W(c), football M(s), golf M(s), riflery M(c)/W(c), rugby M(c), sailing M(c)/W(c), soccer M(c)/W(c), softball W(s), swimming and diving W(s), tennis M(s)/W(s), track and field M(s)/W(s), volleyball M(c)/W(s). ***Intramural sports:*** basketball M/W, football M/W, golf M/W, rock climbing M/W, soccer M/W, table tennis M/W, volleyball M/W, water polo M/W.

Campus security: 24-hour emergency response devices and patrols, student patrols, late-night transport/escort service, controlled dormitory access.

Student services: health clinic, personal/psychological counseling.

COSTS & FINANCIAL AID

Costs (2018–19) ***One-time required fee:*** $325. ***Comprehensive fee:*** $38,578 includes full-time tuition ($26,300), mandatory fees ($1278), and room and board ($11,000). Full-time tuition and fees vary according to degree level. Part-time tuition: $1050 per credit hour. Part-time tuition and fees vary according to degree level. ***Required fees:*** $85 per credit hour part-time, $1278 per year part-time. ***College room only:*** $5440. Room and board charges vary according to board plan and housing facility. ***Payment plan:*** installment. ***Waivers:*** children of alumni and employees or children of employees.

Financial Aid Of all full-time matriculated undergraduates who enrolled in 2018, 779 applied for aid, 761 were judged to have need, 275 had their need fully met. In 2018, 655 non-need-based awards were made. ***Average percent of need met:*** 65. ***Average financial aid package:*** $18,932. ***Average need-based loan:*** $5919. ***Average need-based gift aid:*** $7915. ***Average non-need-based aid:*** $17,717. ***Average indebtedness upon graduation:*** $32,199.

APPLYING

Standardized Tests *Required:* SAT or ACT (for admission).

Options: electronic application, early admission, early decision.

Application fee: $35.

Required: essay or personal statement, high school transcript, 2 letters of recommendation. ***Recommended:*** minimum 3.5 GPA, interview, campus visit, college prep courses.

Application deadlines: 4/1 (freshmen), 4/1 (out-of-state freshmen), 4/1 (transfers).

Early decision deadline: 11/1.

Notification: continuous (freshmen), continuous (out-of-state freshmen), continuous (transfers), 12/1 (early decision).

CONTACT

Mr. Douglas Banbury, Vice President Admissions, Hillsdale College, 33 East College Street, Hillsdale, MI 49242-1298. *Phone:* 517-607-2327. *Fax:* 517-607-2223. *E-mail:* admissions@hillsdale.edu.

See below for display ad and page 1020 for the College Close-Up.

Hope College

Holland, Michigan

http://www.hope.edu/

- **Independent** 4-year, founded 1866, affiliated with Reformed Church in America
- **Suburban** 91-acre campus with easy access to Grand Rapids
- **Endowment** $208.0 million
- **Coed**
- **Moderately difficult** entrance level

FACULTY

Student/faculty ratio: 11:1.

ACADEMICS

Calendar: semesters. *Degree:* bachelor's.

Library: Van Wylen Library plus 2 others. *Books:* 247,002 (physical), 242,414 (digital/electronic); *Serial titles:* 2,530 (physical), 41,509 (digital/electronic); *Databases:* 166. Weekly public service hours: 96.

STUDENT LIFE

Housing options: on-campus residence required through junior year; coed, men-only, women-only, special housing for students with disabilities. Campus housing is university owned and leased by the school. Freshman campus housing is guaranteed.

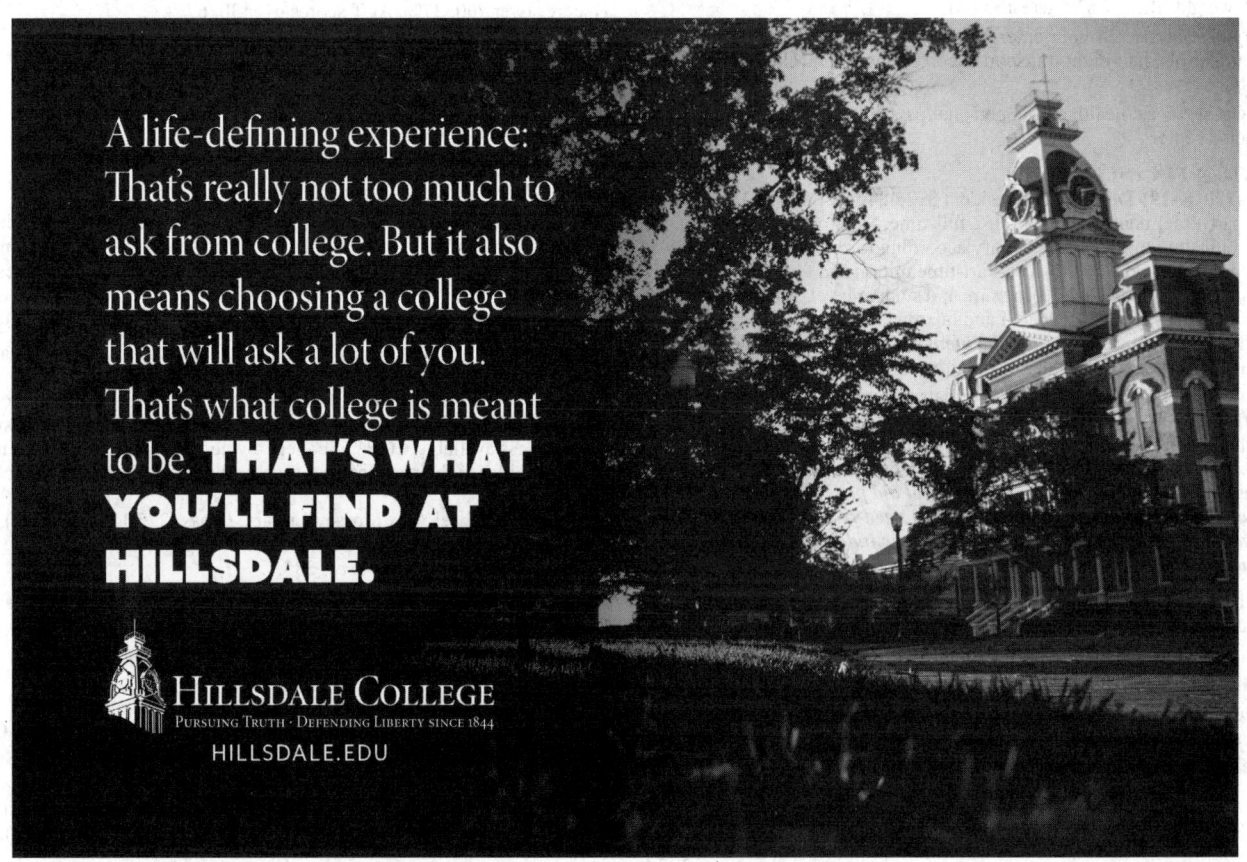

Activities and organizations: drama/theater group, student-run newspaper, radio station, choral group, Social Activities Committee,

Greek Life, Dance Marathon, Hockey Club, Relay for Life, national fraternities, national sororities.

Athletics Member NCAA. All Division III.

Campus security: 24-hour emergency response devices and patrols, late-night transport/escort service, controlled dormitory access.

Student services: health clinic, personal/psychological counseling.

COSTS & FINANCIAL AID

Costs (2018–19) ***Comprehensive fee:*** $44,320 includes full-time tuition ($33,700), mandatory fees ($310), and room and board ($10,310). Part-time tuition and fees vary according to course load and program. ***College room only:*** $4730. Room and board charges vary according to board plan.

Financial Aid Of all full-time matriculated undergraduates who enrolled in 2018, 2,102 applied for aid, 1,698 were judged to have need, 497 had their need fully met. 123 Federal Work-Study jobs (averaging $2616). 577 state and other part-time jobs (averaging $1226). In 2018, 888 non-need-based awards were made. ***Average percent of need met:*** 80. ***Average financial aid package:*** $27,356. ***Average need-based loan:*** $4376. ***Average need-based gift aid:*** $21,627. ***Average non-need-based aid:*** $9415. ***Average indebtedness upon graduation:*** $35,635.

APPLYING

Standardized Tests *Required:* SAT or ACT (for admission).

Options: electronic application, early admission, deferred entrance.

Application fee: $35.

Required: essay or personal statement, high school transcript. ***Required for some:*** 1 letter of recommendation. ***Recommended:*** interview.

CONTACT

Admissions Office, Hope College, 69 East 10th Street, PO Box 9000, Holland, MI 49422-9000. *Phone:* 616-395-7850. *Toll-free phone:* 800-968-7850. *E-mail:* admissions@hope.edu.

Kalamazoo College

Kalamazoo, Michigan

http://www.kzoo.edu/

- **Independent** 4-year, founded 1833, affiliated with American Baptist Churches in the U.S.A.
- **Urban** 60-acre campus with easy access to Grand Rapids
- **Endowment** $227.0 million
- **Coed** 1,467 undergraduate students, 99% full-time, 57% women, 43% men
- **Very difficult** entrance level, 73% of applicants were admitted

UNDERGRAD STUDENTS

1,457 full-time, 10 part-time. 33% are from out of state; 8% Black or African American, non-Hispanic/Latino; 14% Hispanic/Latino; 7% Asian, non-Hispanic/Latino; 0.1% American Indian or Alaska Native, non-Hispanic/Latino; 4% Two or more races, non-Hispanic/Latino; 3% Race/ethnicity unknown; 6% international; 1% transferred in; 60% live on campus.

Freshmen:

Admission: 3,371 applied, 2,454 admitted, 408 enrolled. ***Average high school GPA:*** 3.8. ***Test scores:*** SAT evidence-based reading and writing scores over 500: 96%; SAT math scores over 500: 94%; ACT scores over 18: 97%; SAT evidence-based reading and writing scores over 600: 74%; SAT math scores over 600: 58%; ACT scores over 24: 80%; SAT evidence-based reading and writing scores over 700: 23%; SAT math scores over 700: 22%; ACT scores over 30: 33%.

Retention: 22% of full-time freshmen returned.

FACULTY

Total: 141, 74% full-time, 88% with terminal degrees.

Student/faculty ratio: 13:1.

ACADEMICS

Calendar: quarters. *Degree:* bachelor's.

Special study options: advanced placement credit, double majors, independent study, internships, off-campus study, services for LD students, student-designed majors, study abroad. ***ROTC:*** Army (c).

Unusual degree programs: 3-2 engineering with University of Michigan, Washington University in St. Louis.

Computers: 250 computers/terminals are available on campus for general student use. Students can access the following: campus intranet, computer help desk, free student e-mail accounts, online (class) grades, online (class) registration, online (class) schedules, residential computer consultant. Campuswide network is available. 100% of college-owned or -operated housing units are wired for high-speed Internet access. Wireless service is available via entire campus.

Library: Upjohn Library Commons. *Books:* 272,425 (physical), 162,857 (digital/electronic); *Serial titles:* 2,660 (physical), 176,641 (digital/electronic); *Databases:* 517. Weekly public service hours: 114.

STUDENT LIFE

Housing options: on-campus residence required through junior year; coed. Campus housing is university owned. Freshman campus housing is guaranteed.

Activities and organizations: drama/theater group, student-run newspaper, radio station, choral group, Cirque du K, A cappella groups, Food Recovery Network, Women of Color, Swing Club.

Athletics Member NCAA. All Division III. ***Intercollegiate sports:*** baseball M, basketball M/W, cross-country running M/W, football M, golf M/W, lacrosse M/W, soccer M/W, softball W, swimming and diving M/W, tennis M/W, volleyball W. ***Intramural sports:*** badminton M/W, basketball M/W, cheerleading M(c)/W(c), lacrosse M(c)/W(c), racquetball M/W, soccer M/W, softball M/W, table tennis M/W, tennis M/W, ultimate Frisbee M(c)/W(c), volleyball M/W.

Campus security: 24-hour emergency response devices and patrols, late-night transport/escort service, controlled dormitory access.

Student services: health clinic, personal/psychological counseling.

COSTS & FINANCIAL AID

Costs (2019–20) ***Comprehensive fee:*** $60,546 includes full-time tuition ($50,046), mandatory fees ($366), and room and board ($10,134). ***College room only:*** $4929.

Financial Aid Of all full-time matriculated undergraduates who enrolled in 2018, 1,142 applied for aid, 1,016 were judged to have need, 363 had their need fully met. In 2018, 380 non-need-based awards were made. ***Average percent of need met:*** 91. ***Average financial aid package:*** $42,134. ***Average need-based loan:*** $4300. ***Average need-based gift aid:*** $34,817. ***Average non-need-based aid:*** $25,196. ***Average indebtedness upon graduation:*** $32,226.

APPLYING

Options: electronic application, early decision, early action, deferred entrance.

Required: essay or personal statement, high school transcript, 2 letters of recommendation. ***Recommended:*** minimum 3.0 GPA, interview.

Application deadlines: 1/15 (freshmen), 5/1 (transfers).

Early decision deadline: 11/1.

Notification: 4/1 (freshmen), 5/15 (transfers), 12/1 (early decision).

CONTACT

Gabriela Lovell, Records Assistant, Kalamazoo College, 1200 Academy Street, Kalamazoo, MI 49006. *Phone:* 269-337-5759. *Toll-free phone:* 800-253-3602. *Fax:* 269-552-5083. *E-mail:* gabriela.lovell@kzoo.edu.

★ Kettering University

Flint, Michigan

http://www.kettering.edu/

- **Independent** comprehensive, founded 1919
- **Urban** 85-acre campus with easy access to Detroit
- **Endowment** $81.3 million
- **Coed**
- **Very difficult** entrance level

FACULTY

Student/faculty ratio: 15:1.

ACADEMICS

Calendar: semesters (11 weeks of full-time study plus 12 weeks of paid co-op experience per semester). *Degrees:* bachelor's and master's.

Library: Kettering University Library.

STUDENT LIFE
Housing options: on-campus residence required for freshman year; coed, men-only, women-only, special housing for students with disabilities. Campus housing is university owned and is provided by a third party. Freshman campus housing is guaranteed.

Activities and organizations: student-run newspaper, radio station, choral group, Student Government, Dance Club, Firebirds, Outdoors Club, International Club, national fraternities, national sororities.

Campus security: 24-hour emergency response devices and patrols, late-night transport/escort service, controlled dormitory access, security card access to all campus buildings 24/7 except the campus center main entrance which is secure 11pm-7am.

Student services: health clinic, personal/psychological counseling, women's center.

COSTS & FINANCIAL AID
Costs (2018–19) ***Comprehensive fee:*** $51,730 includes full-time tuition ($43,490) and room and board ($8240). Part-time tuition: $1459 per credit hour. ***College room only:*** $5000.

Financial Aid Of all full-time matriculated undergraduates who enrolled in 2018, 1,423 applied for aid, 1,297 were judged to have need, 138 had their need fully met. In 2018, 490 non-need-based awards were made. ***Average percent of need met:*** 63. ***Average financial aid package:*** $22,631. ***Average need-based loan:*** $4517. ***Average need-based gift aid:*** $18,588. ***Average non-need-based aid:*** $16,048.

APPLYING
Standardized Tests *Required:* SAT or ACT (for admission).

Options: electronic application, early action, deferred entrance.

Required: high school transcript. ***Required for some:*** essay or personal statement. ***Recommended:*** minimum 3.0 GPA, interview.

CONTACT
Mr. Kip Darcy, Vice President of Marketing, Communications and Enrollment, Kettering University, 1700 University Avenue, Flint, MI 48504-6214. *Phone:* 810-762-9511. *Toll-free phone:* 800-955-4464 Ext. 7865 (in-state); 800-955-4464 (out-of-state). *Fax:* 810-762-9837. *E-mail:* kdarcy@kettering.edu.

Kuyper College

Grand Rapids, Michigan

http://www.kuyper.edu/

- **Independent Christian** 4-year, founded 1939
- **Suburban** 34-acre campus with easy access to Grand Rapids
- **Coed** 160 undergraduate students, 81% full-time, 62% women, 38% men
- **Moderately difficult** entrance level, 68% of applicants were admitted

UNDERGRAD STUDENTS
130 full-time, 30 part-time. Students come from 10 states and territories; 8 other countries; 8% are from out of state; 3% Black or African American, non-Hispanic/Latino; 3% Hispanic/Latino; 4% Asian, non-Hispanic/Latino; 0.6% American Indian or Alaska Native, non-Hispanic/Latino; 3% Two or more races, non-Hispanic/Latino; 10% Race/ethnicity unknown; 6% international; 9% transferred in; 42% live on campus.

Freshmen:
Admission: 119 applied, 81 admitted, 30 enrolled. ***Average high school GPA:*** 3.0. ***Test scores:*** SAT evidence-based reading and writing scores over 500: 50%; SAT math scores over 500: 41%; ACT scores over 18: 67%; SAT evidence-based reading and writing scores over 600: 18%; SAT math scores over 600: 9%; ACT scores over 24: 34%; SAT evidence-based reading and writing scores over 700: 4%.

Retention: 75% of full-time freshmen returned.

FACULTY
Total: 24, 33% full-time, 38% with terminal degrees.

Student/faculty ratio: 12:1.

ACADEMICS
Calendar: semesters. *Degrees:* certificates, associate, bachelor's, and master's.

Special study options: academic remediation for entering students, advanced placement credit, cooperative education, double majors, independent study, internships, off-campus study, part-time degree program, services for LD students, student-designed majors, study abroad, summer session for credit. ***ROTC:*** Army (c).

Computers: 70 computers/terminals and 70 ports are available on campus for general student use. Students can access the following: campus intranet, computer help desk, free student e-mail accounts, online (class) grades, online (class) registration, online (class) schedules. Campuswide network is available. 100% of college-owned or -operated housing units are wired for high-speed Internet access. Wireless service is available via entire campus.
Library: Zondervan Library plus 1 other. *Books:* 78,702 (physical), 14,199 (digital/electronic); *Databases:* 101. Weekly public service hours: 72; students can reserve study rooms.

STUDENT LIFE
Housing options: on-campus residence required through sophomore year; coed. Campus housing is university owned. Freshman campus housing is guaranteed.

Activities and organizations: drama/theater group, choral group, intramurals, Student Activities Club, Helping and Nurturing During Service, Yearbook, Roots.

Athletics ***Intramural sports:*** basketball M/W, soccer M/W, softball M/W, table tennis M/W, ultimate Frisbee M/W, volleyball M/W.

Campus security: 24-hour emergency response devices, student patrols, late-night transport/escort service, controlled dormitory access.

Student services: health clinic, personal/psychological counseling.

COSTS & FINANCIAL AID
Costs (2018–19) ***Comprehensive fee:*** $29,274 includes full-time tuition ($21,314), mandatory fees ($675), and room and board ($7285). Full-time tuition and fees vary according to course load and reciprocity agreements. Part-time tuition: $950 per credit hour. Part-time tuition and fees vary according to course load and reciprocity agreements. ***Required fees:*** $335 per year part-time. ***Room and board:*** Room and board charges vary according to board plan, housing facility, and student level. ***Payment plans:*** installment, deferred payment. ***Waivers:*** employees or children of employees.

Financial Aid Of all full-time matriculated undergraduates who enrolled in 2017, 121 applied for aid, 110 were judged to have need, 5 had their need fully met. In 2017, 2 non-need-based awards were made. ***Average percent of need met:*** 70. ***Average financial aid package:*** $17,268. ***Average need-based loan:*** $7344. ***Average need-based gift aid:*** $17,268. ***Average non-need-based aid:*** $11,750. ***Average indebtedness upon graduation:*** $25,555.

APPLYING
Standardized Tests *Required:* SAT or ACT (for admission).

Options: electronic application, deferred entrance.

Required: essay or personal statement, high school transcript, minimum 2.3 GPA. ***Recommended:*** interview.

Application deadlines: rolling (freshmen), rolling (transfers).

Notification: continuous (freshmen), continuous (transfers).

CONTACT
Ken Capisciolto, Vice President of Development, Kuyper College, 3333 East Beltline, NE, Grand Rapids, MI 49525-9749. *Phone:* 616-988-3676. *Fax:* 616-222-3045. *E-mail:* admissions@kuyper.edu.

Lake Superior State University

Sault Sainte Marie, Michigan

http://www.lssu.edu/

CONTACT
Lake Superior State University, 650 West Easterday Avenue, Sault Sainte Marie, MI 49783. *Phone:* 906-635-2231. *Toll-free phone:* 888-800-LSSU Ext. 2231.

Lawrence Technological University

Southfield, Michigan

http://www.ltu.edu/

- **Independent** university, founded 1932
- **Suburban** 107-acre campus with easy access to Detroit
- **Endowment** $50.4 million
- **Coed** 2,172 undergraduate students, 78% full-time, 26% women, 74% men
- **Moderately difficult** entrance level, 78% of applicants were admitted

UNDERGRAD STUDENTS

1,693 full-time, 479 part-time. Students come from 38 states and territories; 36 other countries; 9% are from out of state; 8% Black or African American, non-Hispanic/Latino; 3% Hispanic/Latino; 3% Asian, non-Hispanic/Latino; 0.2% American Indian or Alaska Native, non-Hispanic/Latino; 2% Two or more races, non-Hispanic/Latino; 10% Race/ethnicity unknown; 12% international; 7% transferred in; 39% live on campus.

Freshmen:

Admission: 2,347 applied, 1,826 admitted, 387 enrolled. ***Average high school GPA:*** 3.4. ***Test scores:*** SAT evidence-based reading and writing scores over 500: 82%; SAT math scores over 500: 86%; ACT scores over 18: 100%; SAT evidence-based reading and writing scores over 600: 41%; SAT math scores over 600: 47%; ACT scores over 24: 67%; SAT evidence-based reading and writing scores over 700: 5%; SAT math scores over 700: 11%; ACT scores over 30: 17%.

Retention: 81% of full-time freshmen returned.

FACULTY

Total: 352, 34% full-time, 47% with terminal degrees.

Student/faculty ratio: 11:1.

ACADEMICS

Calendar: semesters. *Degrees:* certificates, associate, bachelor's, master's, doctoral, and postbachelor's certificates.

Special study options: academic remediation for entering students, accelerated degree program, adult/continuing education programs, advanced placement credit, cooperative education, distance learning, double majors, English as a second language, honors programs, independent study, internships, off-campus study, part-time degree program, services for LD students, study abroad, summer session for credit. ***ROTC:*** Army (c).

Computers: 1,887 computers/terminals and 3,618 ports are available on campus for general student use. Students can access the following: campus intranet, computer help desk, free student e-mail accounts, online (class) grades, online (class) registration, online (class) schedules, degree audit, Canvas/Blackboard, Banner (student information), personal websites, document collection, Handshake, Placement, Mapworks advising. Campuswide network is available. 100% of college-owned or -operated housing units are wired for high-speed Internet access. Wireless service is available via entire campus.

Library: Lawrence Technological University Library plus 1 other. *Books:* 54,776 (physical), 427,400 (digital/electronic); *Serial titles:* 51,210 (digital/electronic); *Databases:* 171. Weekly public service hours: 73; students can reserve study rooms.

STUDENT LIFE

Housing options: coed, special housing for students with disabilities. Campus housing is university owned and is provided by a third party. Freshman applicants given priority for college housing.

Activities and organizations: drama/theater group, student-run newspaper, American Institute of Architecture Students, American Society of Mechanical Engineers, Sigma Phi Epsilon, American Society of Civil Engineers, Student Government, national fraternities, national sororities.

Athletics Member NAIA. ***Intercollegiate sports:*** baseball M(s), basketball M(s)/W(s), bowling M(s)/W(s), cross-country running M(s)/W(s), football M(s), golf M(s), ice hockey M, lacrosse M(s)/W(s), soccer M(s)/W(s), softball W(s), tennis M(s)/W(s), volleyball M(s)/W(s). ***Intramural sports:*** badminton M/W, basketball M/W, golf M/W, ice hockey M(c), racquetball M/W, skiing (downhill) M/W, soccer M/W, softball M/W, table tennis M/W, tennis M/W, track and field M(c)/W(c), ultimate Frisbee M(c)/W(c), volleyball M/W.

Campus security: 24-hour emergency response devices and patrols, late-night transport/escort service, controlled dormitory access.

Student services: personal/psychological counseling, veterans affairs office.

COSTS & FINANCIAL AID

Costs (2018–19) ***Comprehensive fee:*** $43,520 includes full-time tuition ($32,370), mandatory fees ($1200), and room and board ($9950). Full-time tuition and fees vary according to course level, degree level, location, program, and student level. Part-time tuition: $1079 per credit hour. Part-time tuition and fees vary according to course level, degree level, location, program, and student level. ***College room only:*** $7050. Room and board charges vary according to board plan and housing facility. ***Payment plan:*** installment. ***Waivers:*** employees or children of employees.

Financial Aid Of all full-time matriculated undergraduates who enrolled in 2017, 1,418 applied for aid, 1,056 were judged to have need, 164 had their need fully met. In 2017, 318 non-need-based awards were made. ***Average percent of need met:*** 70. ***Average financial aid package:*** $25,476. ***Average need-based loan:*** $6940. ***Average need-based gift aid:*** $15,285. ***Average non-need-based aid:*** $15,496. ***Average indebtedness upon graduation:*** $32,735.

APPLYING

Standardized Tests *Required:* SAT or ACT (for admission).

Options: electronic application, deferred entrance.

Application fee: $30.

Required: high school transcript, minimum 2.5 GPA. ***Required for some:*** essay or personal statement, minimum 2.8 GPA, 1 letter of recommendation, interview.

Notification: continuous until 8/26 (freshmen), continuous until 8/26 (transfers).

CONTACT

Jane Rohrback, Director of Admissions, Lawrence Technological University, 21000 West Ten Mile Road, Southfield, MI 48075. *Phone:* 248-204-3160. *Toll-free phone:* 800-225-5588. *Fax:* 248-204-2228. *E-mail:* admissions@ltu.edu.

Madonna University

Livonia, Michigan

http://www.madonna.edu/

- **Independent Roman Catholic** comprehensive, founded 1947
- **Suburban** 85-acre campus with easy access to Detroit
- **Endowment** $41.1 million
- **Coed** 2,440 undergraduate students, 59% full-time, 65% women, 35% men
- **Moderately difficult** entrance level, 78% of applicants were admitted

UNDERGRAD STUDENTS

1,431 full-time, 1,009 part-time. Students come from 20 states and territories; 5 other countries; 2% are from out of state; 11% Black or African American, non-Hispanic/Latino; 4% Hispanic/Latino; 2% Asian, non-Hispanic/Latino; 0.2% Native Hawaiian or other Pacific Islander, non-Hispanic/Latino; 0.1% American Indian or Alaska Native, non-Hispanic/Latino; 3% Two or more races, non-Hispanic/Latino; ####% Race/ethnicity unknown; 13% international; 20% transferred in; 12% live on campus.

Freshmen:

Admission: 985 applied, 771 admitted, 220 enrolled. ***Average high school GPA:*** 3.3. ***Test scores:*** SAT evidence-based reading and writing scores over 500: 70%; SAT math scores over 500: 66%; ACT scores over 18: 85%; SAT evidence-based reading and writing scores over 600: 23%; SAT math scores over 600: 18%; ACT scores over 24: 34%; SAT evidence-based reading and writing scores over 700: 2%; SAT math scores over 700: 3%.

Retention: 76% of full-time freshmen returned.

FACULTY

Total: 324, 31% full-time, 38% with terminal degrees.

Student/faculty ratio: 13:1.

ACADEMICS
Calendar: semesters. *Degrees:* certificates, associate, bachelor's, master's, doctoral, post-master's, and postbachelor's certificates.

Special study options: accelerated degree program, adult/continuing education programs, advanced placement credit, cooperative education, distance learning, double majors, English as a second language, independent study, internships, off-campus study, part-time degree program, services for LD students, student-designed majors, study abroad, summer session for credit. ***ROTC:*** Army (c).

Computers: 205 computers/terminals and 205 ports are available on campus for general student use. Students can access the following: campus intranet, computer help desk, free student e-mail accounts, online (class) grades, online (class) registration, online (class) schedules, online payments, online statements, online unofficial transcripts. Campuswide network is available. 100% of college-owned or -operated housing units are wired for high-speed Internet access. Wireless service is available via classrooms, computer labs, dorm rooms, learning centers, libraries, student centers.
Library: Madonna University Library. *Books:* 71,562 (physical), 181,927 (digital/electronic); *Serial titles:* 190 (physical), 70,781 (digital/electronic); *Databases:* 130. Weekly public service hours: 100; students can reserve study rooms.

STUDENT LIFE
Housing options: men-only, women-only. Campus housing is university owned. Freshman campus housing is guaranteed.

Activities and organizations: drama/theater group, student-run newspaper, radio and television station, choral group, Campus Ministry, Madonna University Nursing Student Association, Broadcast and Film Club, Society of Future Teachers, Michigan Blood Club.

Athletics Member NAIA. ***Intercollegiate sports:*** baseball M(s), basketball M(s)/W(s), bowling M(s)/W(s), cross-country running M(s)/W(s), football M(s), golf M(s)/W(s), lacrosse M(s)/W(s), soccer M(s)/W(s), softball W(s), track and field M(s)/W(s), volleyball W(s). ***Intramural sports:*** basketball M/W.

Campus security: 24-hour emergency response devices and patrols, late-night transport/escort service, controlled dormitory access.

Student services: personal/psychological counseling.

COSTS & FINANCIAL AID
Costs (2019–20) ***Comprehensive fee:*** $34,550 includes full-time tuition ($23,100) and room and board ($11,450). Part-time tuition: $770 per credit hour. ***College room only:*** $5500.

Financial Aid Of all full-time matriculated undergraduates who enrolled in 2007, 862 applied for aid, 698 were judged to have need, 122 had their need fully met. In 2007, 172 non-need-based awards were made. ***Average percent of need met:*** 56. ***Average financial aid package:*** $7396. ***Average need-based loan:*** $3862. ***Average need-based gift aid:*** $4508. ***Average non-need-based aid:*** $2427.

APPLYING
Standardized Tests *Required:* SAT or ACT (for admission).

Options: electronic application, early decision, deferred entrance.

Required for some: essay or personal statement, high school transcript, 2 letters of recommendation, Music performance and dance majors require auditions before selection to the program.. ***Recommended:*** minimum 2.8 GPA.

Application deadlines: rolling (freshmen), rolling (out-of-state freshmen), rolling (transfers).

Early decision deadline: 12/1.

Notification: continuous (freshmen), continuous (out-of-state freshmen), continuous (transfers), 1/15 (early decision).

CONTACT
Mr. Mark A. Schroeder, Director of Undergraduate Admissions, Madonna University, 36600 Schoolcraft Road, Livonia, MI 48150-1173. *Phone:* 734-432-5339. *Toll-free phone:* 800-852-4951. *Fax:* 734-432-5424. *E-mail:* mschroeder@madonna.edu.

Michigan State University
East Lansing, Michigan
http://www.msu.edu/

- **State-supported** university, founded 1855
- **Suburban** 5192-acre campus with easy access to Detroit
- **Endowment** $3.3 billion
- **Coed** 39,423 undergraduate students, 91% full-time, 51% women, 49% men
- **Moderately difficult** entrance level, 78% of applicants were admitted

UNDERGRAD STUDENTS
35,744 full-time, 3,679 part-time. Students come from 54 states and territories; 104 other countries; 14% are from out of state; 7% Black or African American, non-Hispanic/Latino; 5% Hispanic/Latino; 6% Asian, non-Hispanic/Latino; 0.1% Native Hawaiian or other Pacific Islander, non-Hispanic/Latino; 0.2% American Indian or Alaska Native, non-Hispanic/Latino; 3% Two or more races, non-Hispanic/Latino; 0.7% Race/ethnicity unknown; 10% international; 4% transferred in; 39% live on campus.

Freshmen:
Admission: 33,129 applied, 25,733 admitted, 8,688 enrolled. ***Average high school GPA:*** 3.7. ***Test scores:*** SAT evidence-based reading and writing scores over 500: 94%; SAT math scores over 500: 93%; ACT scores over 18: 97%; SAT evidence-based reading and writing scores over 600: 57%; SAT math scores over 600: 54%; ACT scores over 24: 73%; SAT evidence-based reading and writing scores over 700: 9%; SAT math scores over 700: 16%; ACT scores over 30: 20%.

Retention: 92% of full-time freshmen returned.

FACULTY
Total: 2,926, 87% full-time, 86% with terminal degrees.

Student/faculty ratio: 16:1.

ACADEMICS
Calendar: semesters. *Degrees:* certificates, bachelor's, master's, doctoral, and post-master's certificates.

Special study options: academic remediation for entering students, accelerated degree program, adult/continuing education programs, advanced placement credit, cooperative education, distance learning, double majors, English as a second language, freshman honors college, honors programs, independent study, internships, off-campus study, part-time degree program, services for LD students, student-designed majors, study abroad, summer session for credit. ***ROTC:*** Army (b), Air Force (b).

Unusual degree programs: 3-2 engineering.

Computers: Students can access the following: campus intranet, computer help desk, free student e-mail accounts, online (class) grades, online (class) registration, online (class) schedules. Campuswide network is available. 100% of college-owned or -operated housing units are wired for high-speed Internet access. Wireless service is available via classrooms, computer centers, computer labs, dorm rooms, learning centers, libraries, student centers.
Library: Main Library plus 2 others. *Books:* 3.6 million (physical), 3.0 million (digital/electronic); *Serial titles:* 136,425 (physical), 194,857 (digital/electronic). Weekly public service hours: 142.

STUDENT LIFE
Housing options: on-campus residence required for freshman year; coed, women-only, cooperative, special housing for students with disabilities. Campus housing is university owned. Freshman campus housing is guaranteed.

Activities and organizations: drama/theater group, student-run newspaper, radio and television station, choral group, marching band, national fraternities, national sororities.

Athletics Member NCAA. All Division I except football (Division I-A). ***Intercollegiate sports:*** baseball M(s), basketball M(s)/W(s), cheerleading M/W, crew M(c)/W(s), cross-country running M(s)/W(s), equestrian sports M(c)/W(c), fencing M(c)/W(c), field hockey W(s), golf M(s)/W(s)(c), gymnastics W(s), ice hockey M(s)/W(c), lacrosse M(c)/W(c), rowing M(c)/W(s), rugby M(c)/W(c), sailing M(c)/W(c), soccer M(s)/W(s), softball W(s), swimming and diving M(s)/W(s), table tennis M(c)/W(c), tennis M(s)/W(s), track and field M(s)/W(s), volleyball M(c)/W(s), water polo M(c)/W(c), wrestling M(s). ***Intramural sports:*** baseball M(c), basketball M/W, cheerleading W(c), crew M(c)/W(c), football M/W, ice hockey M/W, racquetball M/W, riflery M/W, rowing M(c)/W(c), rugby M(c)/W(c), sand volleyball M/W, soccer M(c)/W(c), softball M/W, squash M/W, table tennis M/W, tennis M/W, ultimate Frisbee M(c)/W(c), volleyball M/W, water polo M/W.

Campus security: 24-hour emergency response devices and patrols, late-night transport/escort service, controlled dormitory access.

Student services: health clinic, personal/psychological counseling, women's center, legal services, veterans affairs office.

COSTS & FINANCIAL AID
Costs (2018–19) ***Tuition:*** state resident $14,460 full-time, $482 per credit hour part-time; nonresident $39,765 full-time, $1326 per credit hour part-time. Full-time tuition and fees vary according to course load, program, and student level. Part-time tuition and fees vary according to course load, program, and student level. ***Room and board:*** $10,322; room only: $4292. Room and board charges vary according to board plan and housing facility. ***Payment plan:*** deferred payment. ***Waivers:*** employees or children of employees.

Financial Aid Of all full-time matriculated undergraduates who enrolled in 2018, 22,531 applied for aid, 16,867 were judged to have need, 1,956 had their need fully met. 1,625 Federal Work-Study jobs (averaging $2180). In 2018, 3013 non-need-based awards were made. ***Average percent of need met:*** 56. ***Average financial aid package:*** $15,505. ***Average need-based loan:*** $4027. ***Average need-based gift aid:*** $10,508. ***Average non-need-based aid:*** $9464. ***Average indebtedness upon graduation:*** $31,736.

APPLYING
Standardized Tests *Required:* SAT or ACT (for admission).

Options: electronic application, early action, deferred entrance.

Application fee: $65.

Required: essay or personal statement, high school transcript.

Application deadlines: rolling (freshmen), rolling (out-of-state freshmen), rolling (transfers).

Notification: continuous (freshmen), continuous (out-of-state freshmen), continuous (transfers).

CONTACT
John M Ambrose, Senior Associate Director of Admissions, Michigan State University, 250 Administration Building, East Lansing, MI 48824. *Phone:* 517-355-8332. *Fax:* 517-353-1647. *E-mail:* admis@msu.edu.

Michigan Technological University
Houghton, Michigan
http://www.mtu.edu/

- **State-supported** university, founded 1885
- **Small-town** 925-acre campus
- **Endowment** $106.4 million
- **Coed**
- **Moderately difficult** entrance level

FACULTY
Student/faculty ratio: 12:1.

ACADEMICS
Calendar: semesters. *Degrees:* certificates, associate, bachelor's, master's, doctoral, and postbachelor's certificates.
Library: J. R. Van Pelt and John and Ruanne Opie Library. *Books:* 362,342 (physical), 142,603 (digital/electronic); *Serial titles:* 14,050 (physical), 124,764 (digital/electronic); *Databases:* 347. Weekly public service hours: 105; study areas open 24 hours, 5–7 days a week; students can reserve study rooms.

STUDENT LIFE
Housing options: on-campus residence required for freshman year; coed, special housing for students with disabilities. Campus housing is university owned. Freshman campus housing is guaranteed.

Activities and organizations: drama/theater group, student-run newspaper, radio station, choral group, Indian Students Association, Society of Women Engineers, Huskies Pep Band, Fishing Club, WMTU, national fraternities, national sororities.

Athletics Member NCAA. All Division II except ice hockey (Division I).

Campus security: 24-hour emergency response devices and patrols, late-night transport/escort service, controlled dormitory access.

Student services: health clinic, personal/psychological counseling, women's center, veterans affairs office.

COSTS & FINANCIAL AID
Costs (2018–19) ***Tuition:*** state resident $15,346 full-time, $579 per credit hour part-time; nonresident $33,426 full-time, $1238 per credit hour part-time. Full-time tuition and fees vary according to program and student level. Part-time tuition and fees vary according to course load, program, and student level. ***Required fees:*** $300 full-time, $150 per term part-time. ***Room and board:*** $10,756; room only: $5982. Room and board charges vary according to board plan and housing facility. ***Payment plans:*** installment, deferred payment.

Financial Aid Of all full-time matriculated undergraduates who enrolled in 2018, 4,371 applied for aid, 3,577 were judged to have need, 583 had their need fully met. 170 Federal Work-Study jobs (averaging $1569). In 2018, 1376 non-need-based awards were made. ***Average percent of need met:*** 70. ***Average financial aid package:*** $15,585. ***Average need-based loan:*** $4288. ***Average need-based gift aid:*** $7840. ***Average non-need-based aid:*** $5804. ***Average indebtedness upon graduation:*** $36,502.

APPLYING
Standardized Tests *Required:* SAT or ACT (for admission).

Options: electronic application, deferred entrance.

Required: high school transcript. ***Required for some:*** essay or personal statement, examples of creative work for some majors in Visual and Performing Arts Department. ***Recommended:*** minimum 2.8 GPA.

CONTACT
Ms. Allison Carter, Director of Admissions, Michigan Technological University, 1400 Townsend Drive, Houghton, MI 49931-1295. *Phone:* 906-487-2335. *Toll-free phone:* 888-MTU-1885. *Fax:* 906-487-2125. *E-mail:* mtu4u@mtu.edu.

Northern Michigan University
Marquette, Michigan
http://www.nmu.edu/

- **State-supported** comprehensive, founded 1899
- **Small-town** 360-acre campus
- **Coed**
- 74% of applicants were admitted

FACULTY
Student/faculty ratio: 20:1.

ACADEMICS
Calendar: semesters. *Degrees:* certificates, associate, bachelor's, master's, doctoral, post-master's, and postbachelor's certificates.
Library: Lydia M. Olson Library.

STUDENT LIFE
Housing options: on-campus residence required through sophomore year; coed, men-only, women-only, special housing for students with disabilities. Campus housing is university owned. Freshman campus housing is guaranteed.

Activities and organizations: drama/theater group, student-run newspaper, radio and television station, choral group, marching band, national fraternities, national sororities.

Athletics Member NCAA. All Division II.

Campus security: 24-hour emergency response devices and patrols, student patrols, late-night transport/escort service, controlled dormitory access.

Student services: health clinic, personal/psychological counseling, veterans affairs office.

COSTS & FINANCIAL AID
Costs (2018–19) ***One-time required fee:*** $254. ***Tuition:*** state resident $9984 full-time, $427 per credit hour part-time; nonresident $15,864 full-time, $661 per credit hour part-time. Full-time tuition and fees vary according to student level. Part-time tuition and fees vary according to student level. ***Required fees:*** $745 full-time, $118 per term part-time. ***Room and board:*** $10,666; room only: $5692. Room and board charges vary according to board plan, housing facility, and student level. ***Payment plans:*** installment, deferred payment.

Financial Aid Of all full-time matriculated undergraduates who enrolled in 2017, 5,028 applied for aid, 4,249 were judged to have need, 531 had their need fully met. 589 Federal Work-Study jobs (averaging $1799). In 2017, 474 non-need-based awards were made. ***Average percent of need met:*** 61. ***Average financial aid package:*** $11,189. ***Average need-based loan:*** $4288. ***Average need-based gift aid:*** $4786. ***Average non-need-based aid:*** $3097. ***Average indebtedness upon graduation:*** $30,459.

APPLYING
Standardized Tests *Required:* SAT or ACT (for admission).

Options: electronic application, deferred entrance.

Application fee: $35.

Required: high school transcript.

CONTACT
Ms. Gerri Daniels, Director of Admissions, Northern Michigan University, 1401 Presque Isle Avenue, Marquette, MI 49855. *Phone:* 906-227-2650. *Toll-free phone:* 800-682-9797. *Fax:* 906-227-1747. *E-mail:* admissions@nmu.edu.

Northwestern Michigan College

Traverse City, Michigan

http://www.nmc.edu/

CONTACT
Catheryn Claerhout, Director of Admissions, Northwestern Michigan College, 1701 E. Front Street, Traverse City, MI 49686. *Phone:* 231-995-1034. *Toll-free phone:* 800-748-0566. *E-mail:* c.claerhout@nmc.edu.

Northwood University, Michigan Campus

Midland, Michigan

http://www.northwood.edu/

- **Independent** comprehensive, founded 1959
- **Small-town** 468-acre campus
- **Endowment** $99.5 million
- **Coed** 1,245 undergraduate students, 95% full-time, 34% women, 66% men
- **Moderately difficult** entrance level, 68% of applicants were admitted

UNDERGRAD STUDENTS
1,178 full-time, 67 part-time. Students come from 27 states and territories; 22 other countries; 12% are from out of state; 6% Black or African American, non-Hispanic/Latino; 4% Hispanic/Latino; 0.4% Asian, non-Hispanic/Latino; 0.1% Native Hawaiian or other Pacific Islander, non-Hispanic/Latino; 0.1% American Indian or Alaska Native, non-Hispanic/Latino; 3% Two or more races, non-Hispanic/Latino; 8% Race/ethnicity unknown; 6% international; 10% transferred in; 43% live on campus.

Freshmen:
Admission: 1,445 applied, 976 admitted, 263 enrolled. ***Average high school GPA:*** 3.3. ***Test scores:*** SAT evidence-based reading and writing scores over 500: 75%; SAT math scores over 500: 76%; ACT scores over 18: 86%; SAT evidence-based reading and writing scores over 600: 22%; SAT math scores over 600: 21%; ACT scores over 24: 34%; SAT evidence-based reading and writing scores over 700: 1%; SAT math scores over 700: 1%.

Retention: 78% of full-time freshmen returned.

FACULTY
Total: 141, 35% full-time, 39% with terminal degrees.

Student/faculty ratio: 20:1.

ACADEMICS
Calendar: semesters. *Degrees:* associate, bachelor's, and master's.

Special study options: academic remediation for entering students, accelerated degree program, adult/continuing education programs, advanced placement credit, cooperative education, distance learning, double majors, English as a second language, external degree program, honors programs, internships, off-campus study, part-time degree program, services for LD students, study abroad, summer session for credit.

Computers: 215 computers/terminals are available on campus for general student use. Students can access the following: campus intranet, computer help desk, free student e-mail accounts, online (class) grades, online (class) registration, online (class) schedules. Campuswide network is available. 100% of college-owned or -operated housing units are wired for high-speed Internet access. Wireless service is available via entire campus.

Library: Strosacker Library. *Books:* 30,504 (physical); *Databases:* 26. Weekly public service hours: 89; students can reserve study rooms.

STUDENT LIFE
Housing options: on-campus residence required for freshman year; coed, men-only, women-only, special housing for students with disabilities. Campus housing is university owned. Freshman campus housing is guaranteed.

Activities and organizations: drama/theater group, student-run newspaper, Student Government Association, intramural sports/club sports, United Way, Northwood University International Auto Show (NUTAS), Student Alumni Network, national fraternities, national sororities.

Athletics Member NCAA. All Division II. ***Intercollegiate sports:*** baseball M(s), basketball M(s)/W(s), cross-country running M(s)/W(s), football M(s), golf M(s)/W(s), soccer M(s)/W(s), softball W(s), tennis M(s)/W(s), track and field M(s)/W(s), volleyball W(s). ***Intramural sports:*** badminton M/W, baseball M, basketball M(c)/W, cheerleading W(c), football M, ice hockey M(c), lacrosse M(c), soccer M/W, softball M/W, table tennis M/W, tennis M/W, ultimate Frisbee M/W, volleyball M/W.

Campus security: 24-hour emergency response devices and patrols, late-night transport/escort service, controlled dormitory access.

Student services: health clinic, personal/psychological counseling.

COSTS & FINANCIAL AID
Costs (2018–19) ***Comprehensive fee:*** $37,540 includes full-time tuition ($25,710), mandatory fees ($1350), and room and board ($10,480). Full-time tuition and fees vary according to course load and location. Part-time tuition: $989 per credit hour. Part-time tuition and fees vary according to course load and location. ***College room only:*** $5460. Room and board charges vary according to board plan. ***Payment plan:*** installment. ***Waivers:*** employees or children of employees.

Financial Aid Of all full-time matriculated undergraduates who enrolled in 2017, 950 applied for aid, 831 were judged to have need, 178 had their need fully met. 136 Federal Work-Study jobs (averaging $1531). In 2017, 241 non-need-based awards were made. ***Average percent of need met:*** 63. ***Average financial aid package:*** $18,932. ***Average need-based loan:*** $4422. ***Average need-based gift aid:*** $6001. ***Average non-need-based aid:*** $7541. ***Average indebtedness upon graduation:*** $31,992.

APPLYING
Standardized Tests *Required:* SAT or ACT (for admission).

Options: electronic application, early admission, deferred entrance.

Application fee: $30.

Required: essay or personal statement, high school transcript, minimum 2.0 GPA. ***Recommended:*** 1 letter of recommendation, interview.

Notification: continuous (freshmen), continuous (out-of-state freshmen), continuous (transfers).

CONTACT
Miss Heidi Schall, Director of Admissions, Northwood University, Michigan Campus, 4000 Whiting Drive, Midland, MI 48640. *Phone:* 989-837-4342. *Toll-free phone:* 800-457-7878. *Fax:* 989-837-4490. *E-mail:* miadmit@northwood.edu.

Oakland University

Rochester, Michigan

http://www.oakland.edu/

- **State-supported** university, founded 1957
- **Suburban** 1444-acre campus with easy access to Detroit
- **Endowment** $87.1 million
- **Coed**
- **Moderately difficult** entrance level

FACULTY
Student/faculty ratio: 21:1.

ACADEMICS
Calendar: semesters. *Degrees:* bachelor's, master's, doctoral, post-master's, and postbachelor's certificates.
Library: Kresge Library plus 1 other. *Books:* 499,352 (physical), 648,059 (digital/electronic); *Serial titles:* 3,674 (physical), 59,485 (digital/electronic); *Databases:* 234. Weekly public service hours: 168; study areas open 24 hours, 5–7 days a week; students can reserve study rooms.

STUDENT LIFE
Housing options: coed, cooperative, special housing for students with disabilities. Campus housing is university owned. Freshman applicants given priority for college housing.

Activities and organizations: drama/theater group, student-run newspaper, radio and television station, choral group, Alternative Break, Beta Alpha Psi, Grizz Gang, Meadow Brook Ball Committee, Student Program Board, national fraternities, national sororities.

Athletics Member NCAA. All Division I.

Campus security: 24-hour emergency response devices and patrols, student patrols, late-night transport/escort service, controlled dormitory access, state certified police officers, security lighting, extensive camera system, self-defense/alcohol abuse classes.

Student services: health clinic, personal/psychological counseling, veterans affairs office.

FINANCIAL AID
Financial Aid Of all full-time matriculated undergraduates who enrolled in 2016, 9,753 applied for aid, 8,044 were judged to have need, 714 had their need fully met. In 2016, 1917 non-need-based awards were made. ***Average percent of need met:*** 71. ***Average financial aid package:*** $14,056. ***Average need-based loan:*** $4031. ***Average need-based gift aid:*** $6138. ***Average non-need-based aid:*** $4864. ***Average indebtedness upon graduation:*** $26,968.

APPLYING
Standardized Tests *Required:* SAT or ACT (for admission).

Options: electronic application, deferred entrance.

Required: high school transcript, minimum 2.5 GPA. ***Required for some:*** interview, audition for music, theatre, and dance.

CONTACT
Oakland University, 201 Meadow Brook Road, Rochester, MI 48309-4401. *Toll-free phone:* 800-OAK-UNIV.

Olivet College
Olivet, Michigan
http://www.olivetcollege.edu/

CONTACT
Admissions, Olivet College, 320 S. Main Street, Olivet, MI 49076. *Phone:* 800-456-7189. *Toll-free phone:* 800-456-7189. *E-mail:* admissions@olivetcollege.edu.

Rochester College
Rochester Hills, Michigan
http://www.rc.edu/

- **Independent** comprehensive, founded 1959, affiliated with Church of Christ
- **Suburban** 81-acre campus with easy access to Detroit
- **Coed** 1,065 undergraduate students, 65% full-time, 63% women, 37% men
- **Minimally difficult** entrance level, 100% of applicants were admitted

UNDERGRAD STUDENTS
697 full-time, 368 part-time. Students come from 21 states and territories; 5 other countries; 3% are from out of state; 16% Black or African American, non-Hispanic/Latino; 2% Hispanic/Latino; 1% Asian, non-Hispanic/Latino; 0.5% American Indian or Alaska Native, non-Hispanic/Latino; 2% Two or more races, non-Hispanic/Latino; 6% Race/ethnicity unknown; 2% international; 12% transferred in; 24% live on campus.

Freshmen:
Admission: 361 applied, 361 admitted, 139 enrolled.
Retention: 66% of full-time freshmen returned.

FACULTY
Total: 167, 23% full-time, 31% with terminal degrees.
Student/faculty ratio: 6:1.

ACADEMICS
Calendar: semesters. *Degrees:* associate, bachelor's, and master's.

Special study options: academic remediation for entering students, accelerated degree program, adult/continuing education programs, advanced placement credit, distance learning, double majors, external degree program, independent study, internships, off-campus study, part-time degree program, study abroad, summer session for credit.

Computers: 40 computers/terminals and 40 ports are available on campus for general student use. Students can access the following: campus intranet, computer help desk, free student e-mail accounts, online (class) grades, online (class) registration, online (class) schedules. Campuswide network is available. 100% of college-owned or -operated housing units are wired for high-speed Internet access.
Library: Ennis and Nancy Ham Library. *Books:* 46,238 (physical), 9,510 (digital/electronic); *Serial titles:* 37 (physical), 30,672 (digital/electronic); *Databases:* 74. Weekly public service hours: 69.

STUDENT LIFE
Housing options: on-campus residence required through sophomore year; men-only, women-only, special housing for students with disabilities. Campus housing is university owned. Freshman campus housing is guaranteed.

Activities and organizations: drama/theater group, student-run newspaper, choral group, Theatre, Shield Magazine and Shield Online, Image, Student Government.

Athletics Member NAIA. ***Intercollegiate sports:*** baseball M(s), basketball M(s)/W(s), bowling M(s)/W(s), cheerleading M(s)/W(s), cross-country running M(s)/W(s), golf M(s)/W(s), ice hockey M, lacrosse W(s), soccer M(s)/W(s), softball W(s), track and field M(s)/W(s), volleyball W(s), wrestling M(s). ***Intramural sports:*** basketball M/W, football M/W, volleyball M/W.

Campus security: 24-hour emergency response devices, late-night transport/escort service, controlled dormitory access.

Student services: personal/psychological counseling.

COSTS
Costs (2019–20) ***Comprehensive fee:*** $32,576 includes full-time tuition ($23,996) and room and board ($8580). Part-time tuition: $730 per semester hour.

APPLYING
Standardized Tests *Required:* SAT or ACT (for admission). *Recommended:* SAT (for admission).

Options: electronic application, early admission, deferred entrance.

Required: high school transcript, minimum 2.3 GPA. ***Required for some:*** essay or personal statement, interview.

Application deadlines: rolling (freshmen), rolling (out-of-state freshmen), rolling (transfers).

Notification: continuous (freshmen), continuous (out-of-state freshmen), continuous (transfers).

CONTACT
Mr. Scott Samuels, Vice President, Rochester College, 800 West Avon Road, Rochester Hills, MI 48307. *Phone:* 248-218-2123. *Toll-free phone:* 800-521-6010. *E-mail:* ssamuels@rc.edu.

Sacred Heart Major Seminary
Detroit, Michigan
http://www.shms.edu/

CONTACT
Fr. Michael Byrnes, Vice Rector, Sacred Heart Major Seminary, 2701 Chicago Boulevard, Detroit, MI 48206. *Phone:* 313-883-8552. *Fax:* 313-868-6400.

Saginaw Valley State University

University Center, Michigan

http://www.svsu.edu/

- **State-supported** comprehensive, founded 1963
- **Small-town** 782-acre campus
- **Endowment** $76.5 million
- **Coed** 7,739 undergraduate students, 84% full-time, 60% women, 40% men
- **Moderately difficult** entrance level, 77% of applicants were admitted

UNDERGRAD STUDENTS

6,483 full-time, 1,256 part-time. Students come from 27 states and territories; 36 other countries; 2% are from out of state; 8% Black or African American, non-Hispanic/Latino; 5% Hispanic/Latino; 0.8% Asian, non-Hispanic/Latino; 0.2% American Indian or Alaska Native, non-Hispanic/Latino; 3% Two or more races, non-Hispanic/Latino; 3% Race/ethnicity unknown; 6% international; 6% transferred in; 31% live on campus.

Freshmen:

Admission: 7,329 applied, 5,672 admitted, 1,576 enrolled. ***Average high school GPA:*** 3.4. ***Test scores:*** SAT evidence-based reading and writing scores over 500: 76%; SAT math scores over 500: 73%; ACT scores over 18: 86%; SAT evidence-based reading and writing scores over 600: 28%; SAT math scores over 600: 22%; ACT scores over 24: 43%; SAT evidence-based reading and writing scores over 700: 3%; SAT math scores over 700: 3%; ACT scores over 30: 5%.

Retention: 77% of full-time freshmen returned.

FACULTY

Total: 721, 40% full-time.

Student/faculty ratio: 17:1.

ACADEMICS

Calendar: semesters plus summer session. *Degrees:* bachelor's, master's, doctoral, and post-master's certificates.

Special study options: academic remediation for entering students, accelerated degree program, adult/continuing education programs, advanced placement credit, cooperative education, distance learning, double majors, English as a second language, honors programs, independent study, internships, part-time degree program, services for LD students, student-designed majors, study abroad, summer session for credit.

Computers: 424 computers/terminals are available on campus for general student use. Students can access the following: computer help desk, free student e-mail accounts, online (class) grades, online (class) registration, online (class) schedules. Campuswide network is available. 100% of college-owned or -operated housing units are wired for high-speed Internet access. Wireless service is available via entire campus.
Library: Zahnow Library. *Books:* 217,900 (physical), 107,479 (digital/electronic); *Serial titles:* 127 (physical), 50,164 (digital/electronic); *Databases:* 63. Weekly public service hours: 92.

STUDENT LIFE

Housing options: coed, special housing for students with disabilities. Campus housing is university owned. Freshman applicants given priority for college housing.
Activities and organizations: drama/theater group, student-run newspaper, radio station, choral group, marching band, His House Christian Fellowship, Criminal Justice Society, Delta Sigma Pi, Alpha Phi Omega, International Students Club, national fraternities, national sororities.

Athletics Member NCAA. All Division II. ***Intercollegiate sports:*** baseball M(s), basketball M(s)/W(s), bowling M(c)/W(c), cheerleading M(c)/W(c), cross-country running M(s)/W(s), equestrian sports M(c)/W(c), football M(s), golf M(s), gymnastics M(c)/W(c), ice hockey M(c)/W(c), lacrosse M(c)/W(c), rugby M(c)/W(c), soccer M(s)/W(s), softball W(s), swimming and diving M(s)/W(s), tennis M(c)/W(s), track and field M(s)/W(s), volleyball W(s), wrestling M(c). ***Intramural sports:*** badminton M/W, basketball M/W, football M/W, golf M/W, ice hockey M/W, racquetball M/W, soccer M/W, softball M/W, table tennis M/W, tennis M/W, volleyball M/W, water polo M/W.

Campus security: 24-hour emergency response devices and patrols, student patrols, late-night transport/escort service, controlled dormitory access, Sexual Assault Prevention Program.

Student services: health clinic, personal/psychological counseling, veterans affairs office.

COSTS & FINANCIAL AID

Costs (2018–19) ***Tuition:*** state resident $9870 full-time, $329 per credit hour part-time; nonresident $23,777 full-time, $793 per credit hour part-time. Full-time tuition and fees vary according to course level, degree level, location, and program. Part-time tuition and fees vary according to course level, degree level, location, and program. ***Required fees:*** $438 full-time, $15 per credit hour part-time. ***Room and board:*** $10,186; room only: $4380. Room and board charges vary according to board plan and housing facility. ***Payment plan:*** installment. ***Waivers:*** employees or children of employees.

Financial Aid Of all full-time matriculated undergraduates who enrolled in 2018, 5,104 applied for aid, 4,335 were judged to have need. In 2018, 1203 non-need-based awards were made. ***Average need-based gift aid:*** $7255. ***Average non-need-based aid:*** $8441. ***Average indebtedness upon graduation:*** $28,865.

APPLYING

Standardized Tests *Required:* SAT or ACT (for admission).

Options: electronic application, deferred entrance.

Application fee: $30.

Required: high school transcript, minimum 2.5 GPA.

Application deadlines: rolling (freshmen), rolling (transfers).

Notification: continuous (freshmen), continuous (transfers).

CONTACT

Jennifer Pahl, Director of Admissions, Saginaw Valley State University, 7400 Bay Road, University Center, MI 48710-0001. *Phone:* 989-964-4200. *Toll-free phone:* 800-968-9500. *Fax:* 989-790-0180. *E-mail:* admissions@svsu.edu.

Schoolcraft College

Livonia, Michigan

http://www.schoolcraft.edu/

- **District-supported** primarily 2-year, founded 1961, part of Michigan Department of Education
- **Suburban** campus with easy access to Detroit
- **Coed**
- **Noncompetitive** entrance level

FACULTY

Student/faculty ratio: 23:1.

ACADEMICS

Calendar: semesters. *Degrees:* certificates, associate, and bachelor's.
Library: Bradner Library plus 1 other. *Books:* 67,778 (physical), 74,201 (digital/electronic); *Databases:* 147. Students can reserve study rooms.

STUDENT LIFE

Housing options: college housing not available.

Activities and organizations: drama/theater group, student-run newspaper, choral group, Phi Theta Kappa, The Schoolcraft Connection Newspaper, Student Activities Board, Project Playhem Gaming Club, Otaku Anime Japanese Animation Club.

Athletics Member NJCAA.

Campus security: 24-hour emergency response devices and patrols, late-night transport/escort service.

Student services: health clinic, personal/psychological counseling, women's center, veterans affairs office.

COSTS & FINANCIAL AID

Costs (2018–19) ***Tuition:*** area resident $3450 full-time, $115 per credit hour part-time; state resident $4980 full-time, $166 per credit hour part-time; nonresident $7350 full-time, $245 per credit hour part-time. ***Required fees:*** $952 full-time, $23 per credit hour part-time, $43 per term part-time. ***Payment plans:*** installment, deferred payment.

Financial Aid Of all full-time matriculated undergraduates who enrolled in 2017, 124 Federal Work-Study jobs (averaging $4000).

APPLYING

Options: electronic application, early admission, deferred entrance.

Required for some: high school transcript. ***Recommended:*** high school transcript.

CONTACT

Ms. Lisa Bushaw, Director of Admissions, Schoolcraft College, 18600 Haggerty Road, Livonia, MI 48152-2696. *Phone:* 734-462-4683. *E-mail:* admissions@schoolcraft.edu.

Siena Heights University

Adrian, Michigan

http://www.sienaheights.edu/

CONTACT

Ms. Trudy Mohre, Director of Admissions, Siena Heights University, 1247 East Siena Heights Drive, Adrian, MI 49221. *Phone:* 517-264-7185. *Toll-free phone:* 800-521-0009. *E-mail:* tmohre@sienaheights.edu.

Spring Arbor University

Spring Arbor, Michigan

http://www.arbor.edu/

CONTACT

Office of Admissions, Spring Arbor University, 106 East Main Street, Spring Arbor, MI 49283-9799. *Phone:* 517-750-1200 Ext. 1468. *Toll-free phone:* 800-968-0011. *Fax:* 517-750-6620. *E-mail:* admissions@arbor.edu.

University of Detroit Mercy

Detroit, Michigan

http://www.udmercy.edu/

- **Independent Roman Catholic (Jesuit)** university, founded 1877
- **Urban** 70-acre campus with easy access to Detroit, MI
- **Endowment** $43.9 million
- **Coed** 2,880 undergraduate students, 87% full-time, 62% women, 38% men
- **Moderately difficult** entrance level, 83% of applicants were admitted

UNDERGRAD STUDENTS

2,494 full-time, 386 part-time. 6% are from out of state; 13% Black or African American, non-Hispanic/Latino; 6% Hispanic/Latino; 6% Asian, non-Hispanic/Latino; 0.1% Native Hawaiian or other Pacific Islander, non-Hispanic/Latino; 0.5% American Indian or Alaska Native, non-Hispanic/Latino; 2% Two or more races, non-Hispanic/Latino; 4% Race/ethnicity unknown; 8% international; 8% transferred in; 30% live on campus.

Freshmen:

Admission: 3,760 applied, 3,120 admitted, 583 enrolled. ***Average high school GPA:*** 3.6. ***Test scores:*** SAT evidence-based reading and writing scores over 500: 88%; SAT math scores over 500: 88%; ACT scores over 18: 98%; SAT evidence-based reading and writing scores over 600: 33%; SAT math scores over 600: 34%; ACT scores over 24: 58%; SAT evidence-based reading and writing scores over 700: 4%; SAT math scores over 700: 9%; ACT scores over 30: 11%.

Retention: 83% of full-time freshmen returned.

FACULTY

Total: 770, 44% full-time, 74% with terminal degrees.

Student/faculty ratio: 10:1.

ACADEMICS

Calendar: semesters. *Degrees:* certificates, diplomas, bachelor's, master's, doctoral, post-master's, and postbachelor's certificates.

Special study options: academic remediation for entering students, accelerated degree program, advanced placement credit, cooperative education, distance learning, double majors, English as a second language, honors programs, independent study, internships, off-campus study, part-time degree program, services for LD students, study abroad, summer session for credit.

Computers: 157 computers/terminals are available on campus for general student use. Students can access the following: campus intranet, computer help desk, free student e-mail accounts, online (class) grades, online (class) registration, online (class) schedules. Campuswide network is available. 100% of college-owned or -operated housing units are wired for high-speed Internet access. Wireless service is available via entire campus.

Library: McNichols Campus Library. *Books:* 468,257 (physical), 175,312 (digital/electronic); *Serial titles:* 107,735 (digital/electronic); *Databases:* 84. Weekly public service hours: 80.

STUDENT LIFE

Housing options: coed. Campus housing is university owned. Freshman campus housing is guaranteed.

Activities and organizations: drama/theater group, student-run newspaper, radio station, choral group, Alpha Phi Omega, Biology Club, Chemistry Club, Pre-Dentistry Club, Greek Organizations - NPC, NIC, and NPHC, national fraternities, national sororities.

Athletics Member NCAA. All Division I. ***Intercollegiate sports:*** basketball M(s)/W(s), cross-country running M(s)/W(s), fencing M(s)/W(s), golf M(s)/W(s)(c), lacrosse M(s)/W(s), soccer M(s)/W(s), softball W(s), tennis M(s)/W(s), track and field M(s)/W(s). ***Intramural sports:*** basketball M/W, cheerleading M/W, soccer M/W, table tennis M/W, volleyball M/W.

Campus security: 24-hour emergency response devices and patrols, student patrols, late-night transport/escort service.

Student services: health clinic, personal/psychological counseling.

COSTS & FINANCIAL AID

Costs (2019–20) ***Comprehensive fee:*** $38,620 includes full-time tuition ($28,840) and room and board ($9780). Part-time tuition: $1080 per credit hour.

Financial Aid Of all full-time matriculated undergraduates who enrolled in 2018, 2,013 applied for aid, 1,605 were judged to have need, 151 had their need fully met. In 2018, 750 non-need-based awards were made. ***Average percent of need met:*** 66. ***Average financial aid package:*** $21,954. ***Average need-based loan:*** $3832. ***Average need-based gift aid:*** $16,938. ***Average non-need-based aid:*** $11,184. ***Average indebtedness upon graduation:*** $44,180.

APPLYING

Standardized Tests *Required:* SAT or ACT (for admission).

Options: electronic application, early decision, deferred entrance.

Required: essay or personal statement, high school transcript, minimum 2.5 GPA. ***Recommended:*** 1 letter of recommendation, interview.

Application deadlines: rolling (freshmen), rolling (transfers).

Notification: continuous (freshmen), continuous (transfers).

CONTACT

Deborah Stieffel, Vice President for Enrollment Management and Student Affairs, University of Detroit Mercy, 4001 West McNichols Road, Detroit, MI 48221. *Phone:* 313-993-1245. *Toll-free phone:* 800-635-5020. *Fax:* 313-993-3326. *E-mail:* admissions@udmercy.edu.

University of Michigan

Ann Arbor, Michigan

http://www.umich.edu/

- **State-supported** university, founded 1817
- **Urban** 3207-acre campus with easy access to Detroit
- **Endowment** $11.7 billion
- **Coed** 30,318 undergraduate students, 96% full-time, 50% women, 50% men
- **Very difficult** entrance level, 23% of applicants were admitted

UNDERGRAD STUDENTS

29,245 full-time, 1,073 part-time. Students come from 54 states and territories; 92 other countries; 41% are from out of state; 4% Black or African American, non-Hispanic/Latino; 6% Hispanic/Latino; 15% Asian, non-Hispanic/Latino; 0.0% Native Hawaiian or other Pacific Islander, non-Hispanic/Latino; 0.1% American Indian or Alaska Native, non-Hispanic/Latino; 4% Two or more races, non-Hispanic/Latino; 5% Race/ethnicity unknown; 7% international; 4% transferred in; 31% live on campus.

Freshmen:
Admission: 64,917 applied, 14,818 admitted, 6,695 enrolled. ***Average high school GPA:*** 3.9. ***Test scores:*** SAT evidence-based reading and writing scores over 500: 100%; SAT math scores over 500: 100%; ACT scores over 18: 100%; SAT evidence-based reading and writing scores over 600: 94%; SAT math scores over 600: 91%; ACT scores over 24: 97%; SAT evidence-based reading and writing scores over 700: 55%; SAT math scores over 700: 66%; ACT scores over 30: 80%.

Retention: 97% of full-time freshmen returned.

FACULTY
Total: 3,527, 82% full-time, 88% with terminal degrees.

Student/faculty ratio: 15:1.

ACADEMICS
Calendar: trimesters. *Degrees:* bachelor's, master's, doctoral, post-master's, and postbachelor's certificates.

Special study options: accelerated degree program, adult/continuing education programs, advanced placement credit, cooperative education, distance learning, double majors, English as a second language, external degree program, honors programs, independent study, internships, off-campus study, part-time degree program, services for LD students, student-designed majors, study abroad, summer session for credit. ***ROTC:*** Army (b), Navy (b), Air Force (b).

Unusual degree programs: 3-2 business administration; engineering.

Computers: 4,000 computers/terminals are available on campus for general student use. Students can access the following: campus intranet, computer help desk, free student e-mail accounts, online (class) grades, online (class) registration, online (class) schedules, file storage, personal Web pages, printing. Campuswide network is available. 100% of college-owned or -operated housing units are wired for high-speed Internet access. Wireless service is available via entire campus.
Library: Shapiro Undergraduate Library plus 9 others. *Books:* 12.0 million (physical), 3.7 million (digital/electronic); *Serial titles:* 320,457 (physical), 221,979 (digital/electronic); *Databases:* 4,091. Weekly public service hours: 168; study areas open 24 hours, 5–7 days a week; students can reserve study rooms.

STUDENT LIFE
Housing options: coed, women-only, cooperative. Campus housing is university owned. Freshman campus housing is guaranteed.

Activities and organizations: drama/theater group, student-run newspaper, radio and television station, choral group, marching band, Hillel Society, K-Grams (Kids'; Program), M-Powered Entrepreneurial Club, Dance Marathon, Alternative Spring Break, national fraternities, national sororities.

Athletics Member NCAA. All Division I except football (Division I-AA). ***Intercollegiate sports:*** baseball M(s), basketball M(s)/W(s), cheerleading M(s)(c)/W(s)(c), crew M(c)/W(s), cross-country running M(s)/W(s), fencing M(c)/W(c), field hockey W(s), golf M(s)/W(s)(c), gymnastics M(s)/W(s), ice hockey M(s), lacrosse M(s)/W(s), riflery M(c)/W(c), rowing M(c), rugby M(c)/W(c), sailing M(c)/W(c), soccer M(s)/W(s), softball W(s), swimming and diving M(s)/W(s), table tennis M(c)/W(c), tennis M(s)/W(s), track and field M(s)/W(s), triathlon M(c), ultimate Frisbee M(c)/W(c), volleyball M(c)/W(s), water polo M(c)/W(s), wrestling M(s). ***Intramural sports:*** badminton M/W, baseball M(c), basketball M/W, cross-country running M(c)/W(c), fencing W, field hockey M, gymnastics W(c), ice hockey M(c)/W(c), lacrosse W(c), racquetball M/W, sand volleyball M/W, soccer M(c)/W(c), softball W(c), squash M/W, swimming and diving M/W(c), table tennis M/W, tennis M(c)/W(c), track and field M/W, ultimate Frisbee M/W, volleyball M/W, wrestling M(c).

Campus security: 24-hour emergency response devices and patrols, student patrols, late-night transport/escort service, controlled dormitory access.

Student services: health clinic, personal/psychological counseling, women's center, legal services, veterans affairs office.

COSTS & FINANCIAL AID
Costs (2019–20) ***Tuition:*** state resident $14,934 full-time; nonresident $49,022 full-time. ***Required fees:*** $328 full-time. ***Room and board:*** $11,534.

Financial Aid Of all full-time matriculated undergraduates who enrolled in 2017, 15,167 applied for aid, 11,229 were judged to have need, 8,481 had their need fully met. 5,480 Federal Work-Study jobs (averaging $2744). In 2017, 3135 non-need-based awards were made. ***Average percent of need met:*** 93. ***Average financial aid package:*** $27,695. ***Average need-based loan:*** $5104. ***Average need-based gift aid:*** $20,108. ***Average non-need-based aid:*** $5569. ***Average indebtedness upon graduation:*** $27,224. ***Financial aid deadline:*** 3/31.

APPLYING
Standardized Tests *Required:* SAT or ACT (for admission). *Required for some:* SAT Subject Tests (for admission).

Options: electronic application, early action, deferred entrance.

Application fee: $75.

Required: essay or personal statement, high school transcript, 1 letter of recommendation. ***Required for some:*** interview, audition for School of Music, Theatre and Dance; portfolio for School of Art and Design.

Application deadlines: 2/1 (freshmen), 2/1 (out-of-state freshmen), 2/1 (transfers), 11/1 (early action).

Notification: continuous (freshmen), continuous (transfers), 12/24 (early action).

CONTACT
Ms. Erica Sanders, Director, Office of Undergraduate Admissions, University of Michigan, Ann Arbor, MI 48109. *Phone:* 734-764-7433. *Fax:* 734-936-0740. *E-mail:* yale@umich.edu.

University of Michigan–Dearborn
Dearborn, Michigan
http://www.umdearborn.edu/

- **State-supported** comprehensive, founded 1959, part of University of Michigan System
- **Suburban** 202-acre campus with easy access to Detroit
- **Coed** 7,185 undergraduate students, 73% full-time, 46% women, 54% men
- **Moderately difficult** entrance level, 78% of applicants were admitted

UNDERGRAD STUDENTS
5,238 full-time, 1,947 part-time. Students come from 20 states and territories; 26 other countries; 3% are from out of state; 8% Black or African American, non-Hispanic/Latino; 6% Hispanic/Latino; 8% Asian, non-Hispanic/Latino; 0.1% Native Hawaiian or other Pacific Islander, non-Hispanic/Latino; 0.3% American Indian or Alaska Native, non-Hispanic/Latino; 3% Two or more races, non-Hispanic/Latino; 2% Race/ethnicity unknown; 2% international; 10% transferred in.

Freshmen:
Admission: 7,669 applied, 5,962 admitted, 1,093 enrolled. ***Average high school GPA:*** 3.6. ***Test scores:*** SAT evidence-based reading and writing scores over 500: 91%; SAT math scores over 500: 90%; ACT scores over 18: 98%; SAT evidence-based reading and writing scores over 600: 47%; SAT math scores over 600: 45%; ACT scores over 24: 62%; SAT evidence-based reading and writing scores over 700: 8%; SAT math scores over 700: 13%; ACT scores over 30: 22%.

Retention: 78% of full-time freshmen returned.

FACULTY
Total: 546, 65% full-time, 74% with terminal degrees.

Student/faculty ratio: 17:1.

ACADEMICS
Calendar: semesters. *Degrees:* certificates, bachelor's, master's, doctoral, and postbachelor's certificates.

Special study options: academic remediation for entering students, adult/continuing education programs, advanced placement credit, cooperative education, distance learning, double majors, English as a second language, honors programs, independent study, internships, off-campus study, part-time degree program, services for LD students, student-designed majors, study abroad, summer session for credit. ***ROTC:*** Army (b), Navy (c), Air Force (b).

Computers: 1,060 computers/terminals are available on campus for general student use. Students can access the following: campus intranet, computer help desk, free student e-mail accounts, online (class) grades, online (class) registration, online (class) schedules, tuition and application payments accepted online. Campuswide network is available. Wireless service is available via entire campus.

Library: Mardigian Library. *Books:* 189,907 (physical), 662,503 (digital/electronic); *Serial titles:* 387 (physical), 103,160 (digital/electronic); *Databases:* 795. Weekly public service hours: 95; students can reserve study rooms.

STUDENT LIFE
Housing options: college housing not available.

Activities and organizations: student-run newspaper, radio and television station, national fraternities, national sororities.

Athletics Member NAIA. ***Intercollegiate sports:*** baseball M(s), basketball M(s)/W(s), cross-country running M(s)/W(s), lacrosse M(s), soccer M(s)/W(s), softball W(s), volleyball W(s). ***Intramural sports:*** basketball M/W, cheerleading M(c)/W(c), ice hockey M(c), soccer M/W, tennis M(c)/W(c), volleyball M/W, wrestling M(c)/W(c).

Campus security: 24-hour emergency response devices and patrols, late-night transport/escort service.

Student services: personal/psychological counseling, women's center, veterans affairs office.

FINANCIAL AID
Financial Aid Of all full-time matriculated undergraduates who enrolled in 2017, 3,985 applied for aid, 3,501 were judged to have need, 298 had their need fully met. 216 Federal Work-Study jobs (averaging $2510). 702 state and other part-time jobs (averaging $4040). In 2017, 685 non-need-based awards were made. ***Average percent of need met:*** 72. ***Average financial aid package:*** $11,399. ***Average need-based loan:*** $4346. ***Average need-based gift aid:*** $7379. ***Average non-need-based aid:*** $5444. ***Average indebtedness upon graduation:*** $25,909.

APPLYING
Standardized Tests *Required:* SAT or ACT (for admission).

Options: electronic application, deferred entrance.

Required: high school transcript. ***Recommended:*** minimum 2.5 GPA.

Application deadlines: rolling (freshmen), rolling (transfers).

Notification: continuous (freshmen), continuous (transfers).

CONTACT
Ms. Deb Peffer, Director of Admissions and Orientation, University of Michigan–Dearborn, 4901 Evergreen Road, Room 1145 UC, Dearborn, MI 48128-1491. *Phone:* 313-593-5100. *Fax:* 313-436-9167. *E-mail:* umd-admissions@umich.edu.

University of Michigan–Flint
Flint, Michigan
http://www.umflint.edu/

- **State-supported** comprehensive, founded 1956, part of University of Michigan System
- **Urban** 76-acre campus with easy access to Detroit, Lansing
- **Endowment** $106.3 million
- **Coed**
- **Moderately difficult** entrance level

FACULTY
Student/faculty ratio: 13:1.

ACADEMICS
Calendar: semesters. *Degrees:* bachelor's, master's, doctoral, post-master's, and postbachelor's certificates.

Library: Frances Willson Thompson Library plus 1 other. *Books:* 251,483 (physical), 981,065 (digital/electronic); *Serial titles:* 1,862 (physical), 163,338 (digital/electronic); *Databases:* 1,387. Weekly public service hours: 96; students can reserve study rooms.

STUDENT LIFE
Housing options: coed. Campus housing is university owned.

Activities and organizations: drama/theater group, student-run newspaper, choral group, Fraternity and Sorority Life, National Society for Leadership and Success, Psychology Club, Baccalaureate Student Nurses Organization, Student Nurse Practitioner Association, national fraternities, national sororities.

Campus security: 24-hour emergency response devices and patrols, student patrols, late-night transport/escort service, controlled dormitory access.

Student services: personal/psychological counseling, women's center, veterans affairs office.

COSTS & FINANCIAL AID
Costs (2018–19) ***Tuition:*** state resident $11,388 full-time, $450 per credit hour part-time; nonresident $22,146 full-time, $895 per credit hour part-time. Full-time tuition and fees vary according to course level, course load, degree level, program, and student level. Part-time tuition and fees vary according to course level, course load, degree level, program, and student level. ***Required fees:*** $432 full-time, $216 per term part-time. ***Room and board:*** $8769; room only: $5709. Room and board charges vary according to housing facility.

Financial Aid Of all full-time matriculated undergraduates who enrolled in 2017, 3,130 applied for aid, 2,793 were judged to have need, 72 had their need fully met. 159 Federal Work-Study jobs (averaging $1823). In 2017, 144 non-need-based awards were made. ***Average percent of need met:*** 69. ***Average financial aid package:*** $12,867. ***Average need-based loan:*** $4552. ***Average need-based gift aid:*** $6912. ***Average non-need-based aid:*** $4017. ***Average indebtedness upon graduation:*** $29,386.

APPLYING
Standardized Tests *Required:* SAT or ACT (for admission).

Options: electronic application, deferred entrance.

Application fee: $30.

Required: high school transcript, minimum 2.7 GPA.

CONTACT
Ms. Karen Cuzydlo, Admissions Senior Associate Director, University of Michigan–Flint, 303 East Kearsley Street, 245 University Pavilion, Flint, MI 48502. *Phone:* 810-762-3300. *Toll-free phone:* 800-942-5636. *Fax:* 810-762-3272. *E-mail:* admissions@umflint.edu.

Walsh College of Accountancy and Business Administration
Troy, Michigan
http://www.walshcollege.edu/

- **Independent** upper-level, founded 1922
- **Suburban** 29-acre campus with easy access to Detroit
- **Endowment** $8.4 million
- **Coed**
- **Noncompetitive** entrance level

FACULTY
Student/faculty ratio: 15:1.

ACADEMICS
Calendar: 4 11-week semesters. *Degrees:* bachelor's, master's, and postbachelor's certificates.

Library: Vollbrecht Library plus 1 other. *Books:* 27,985 (physical), 18,425 (digital/electronic); *Serial titles:* 2,262 (physical), 71,676 (digital/electronic); *Databases:* 79. Weekly public service hours: 113.

STUDENT LIFE
Housing options: college housing not available.

Activities and organizations: Delta Mu Delta, Accounting and Taxation Student Organization, International Student Organization, MBA Association, Walsh College Marketing Association.

Campus security: 24-hour emergency response devices.

Student services: veterans affairs office.

APPLYING
Options: electronic application, deferred entrance.

Application fee: $35.

CONTACT
Walsh College of Accountancy and Business Administration, 3838 Livernois Road, Troy, MI 48083. *Phone:* 248-823-1610. *Toll-free phone:* 800-925-7401.

Wayne State University

Detroit, Michigan

http://www.wayne.edu/

- **State-supported** university, founded 1868
- **Urban** 195-acre campus with easy access to Detroit
- **Endowment** $366.7 million
- **Coed**
- **Moderately difficult** entrance level

FACULTY
Student/faculty ratio: 16:1.

ACADEMICS
Calendar: semesters. *Degrees:* certificates, bachelor's, master's, doctoral, post-master's, and postbachelor's certificates.
Library: David Adamany Undergraduate Library plus 5 others. *Books:* 1.7 million (physical), 1.1 million (digital/electronic); *Serial titles:* 60,832 (physical), 112,521 (digital/electronic); *Databases:* 700. Weekly public service hours: 138; study areas open 24 hours, 5–7 days a week.

STUDENT LIFE
Housing options: coed, special housing for students with disabilities. Campus housing is university owned. Freshman applicants given priority for college housing.
Activities and organizations: drama/theater group, student-run newspaper, radio station, choral group, marching band, national fraternities, national sororities.
Athletics Member NCAA. All Division II.
Campus security: 24-hour emergency response devices and patrols, late-night transport/escort service, controlled dormitory access, VIN etching, bike patrol, safety and defense classes, K-9 unit, victim assistance, confidential tip line.
Student services: health clinic, personal/psychological counseling, legal services, veterans affairs office.

FINANCIAL AID
Financial Aid Of all full-time matriculated undergraduates who enrolled in 2017, 9,975 applied for aid, 8,889 were judged to have need, 378 had their need fully met. In 2017, 2138 non-need-based awards were made. ***Average percent of need met:*** 50. ***Average financial aid package:*** $11,281. ***Average need-based loan:*** $4167. ***Average need-based gift aid:*** $7129. ***Average non-need-based aid:*** $5283. ***Average indebtedness upon graduation:*** $28,004. ***Financial aid deadline:*** 6/30.

APPLYING
Standardized Tests *Required:* SAT or ACT (for admission).
Options: electronic application, deferred entrance.
Application fee: $25.
Required: high school transcript.

CONTACT
Ms. Ericka M. Jackson, Director of Undergraduate Admissions, Wayne State University, 42 West Warren, Office of Undergraduate Admissions, Detroit 48202. *Phone:* 313-577-2100. *Toll-free phone:* 877-WSU-INFO. *E-mail:* admissions@wayne.edu.

Western Michigan University

Kalamazoo, Michigan

http://www.wmich.edu/

- **State-supported** university, founded 1903
- **Urban** 1289-acre campus
- **Endowment** $386.6 million
- **Coed**
- **Moderately difficult** entrance level

FACULTY
Student/faculty ratio: 17:1.

ACADEMICS
Calendar: semesters. *Degrees:* certificates, bachelor's, master's, doctoral, post-master's, and postbachelor's certificates.
Library: Waldo Library plus 4 others. *Books:* 1.8 million (physical), 661,724 (digital/electronic); *Serial titles:* 936 (physical), 80,141 (digital/electronic); *Databases:* 638. Weekly public service hours: 106; students can reserve study rooms.

STUDENT LIFE
Housing options: coed, men-only, women-only, special housing for students with disabilities. Campus housing is university owned. Freshman campus housing is guaranteed.
Activities and organizations: drama/theater group, student-run newspaper, radio station, choral group, marching band, Campus Activities Board, Western Student Association, Young Black Male Support Network, Drive Safe Kalamazoo, Alternative Spring Break, national fraternities, national sororities.
Athletics Member NCAA. All Division I except football (Division I-A).
Campus security: 24-hour emergency response devices and patrols, student patrols, late-night transport/escort service, controlled dormitory access, residence hall security system, engravers for identification of items, free bicycle registration.
Student services: health clinic, personal/psychological counseling, women's center, veterans affairs office.

COSTS & FINANCIAL AID
Costs (2018–19) ***Tuition:*** state resident $11,560 full-time, $464 per credit hour part-time; nonresident $14,450 full-time, $579 per credit hour part-time. Full-time tuition and fees vary according to course load, location, program, reciprocity agreements, and student level. Part-time tuition and fees vary according to course load, location, program, reciprocity agreements, and student level. ***Required fees:*** $923 full-time, $259 per term part-time. ***Room and board:*** $10,143; room only: $5231. Room and board charges vary according to board plan and housing facility.
Financial Aid Of all full-time matriculated undergraduates who enrolled in 2017, 11,365 applied for aid, 6,652 were judged to have need, 86 had their need fully met. In 2017, 1483 non-need-based awards were made. ***Average percent of need met:*** 72. ***Average financial aid package:*** $13,512. ***Average need-based loan:*** $4047. ***Average need-based gift aid:*** $3100. ***Average non-need-based aid:*** $5556. ***Average indebtedness upon graduation:*** $47,755.

APPLYING
Standardized Tests *Required:* SAT or ACT (for admission).
Options: electronic application.
Application fee: $40.
Required: high school transcript, minimum 2.5 GPA.

CONTACT
Western Michigan University, 1903 West Michigan Avenue, Kalamazoo, MI 49008. *Phone:* 269-387-2000. *E-mail:* ask-wmu@wmich.edu.

Yeshiva Beth Yehuda–Yeshiva Gedolah of Greater Detroit

Oak Park, Michigan

CONTACT
Rabbi P. Rushnawitz, Director, Yeshiva Beth Yehuda–Yeshiva Gedolah of Greater Detroit, 24600 Greenfield, Oak Park, MI 48237-1544.

MINNESOTA

Academy College

Bloomington, Minnesota

http://www.academycollege.edu/

- **Proprietary** 4-year, founded 1936
- **Urban** campus
- **Coed**
- **Noncompetitive** entrance level

FACULTY
Student/faculty ratio: 8:1.

ACADEMICS
Calendar: quarters. *Degrees:* diplomas, associate, and bachelor's.

Library: Learning Resource Center plus 1 other.

STUDENT LIFE
Housing options: college housing not available.

FINANCIAL AID
Financial Aid Of all full-time matriculated undergraduates who enrolled in 2017, 31 applied for aid, 31 were judged to have need.

APPLYING
Options: electronic application, early admission, deferred entrance.

Application fee: $40.

Required: high school transcript, interview.

CONTACT
Mr. Andrew Scoblionko, Director of Admissions, Academy College, 1600 W. 82nd Street, Suite 100, Bloomington, MN 55431. *Phone:* 952-851-0066. *Toll-free phone:* 800-292-9149. *Fax:* 952-851-0094. *E-mail:* admissions@academycollege.edu.

Argosy University, Twin Cities

Eagan, Minnesota

http://www.argosy.edu/locations/twin-cities/

CONTACT
Argosy University, Twin Cities, 1515 Central Parkway, Eagan, MN 55121. *Phone:* 651-846-2882. *Toll-free phone:* 888-844-2004.

Augsburg University

Minneapolis, Minnesota

http://www.augsburg.edu/

- **Independent Lutheran** comprehensive, founded 1869
- **Urban** 23-acre campus with easy access to Minneapolis-St. Paul
- **Coed**
- **Moderately difficult** entrance level

FACULTY
Student/faculty ratio: 13:1.

ACADEMICS
Calendar: semesters for undergraduate programs; trimesters for graduate programs and weekend college. *Degrees:* certificates, bachelor's, master's, doctoral, and postbachelor's certificates.
Library: James G. Lindell Library. Students can reserve study rooms.

STUDENT LIFE
Housing options: coed, special housing for students with disabilities. Campus housing is university owned. Freshman applicants given priority for college housing.

Activities and organizations: drama/theater group, student-run newspaper, radio station, choral group, Pan-Afrikan Student Union, Augsburg Business Organization, Queer Pride Alliance, Students for Racial Justice, Augsburg Asian Student Association.

Athletics Member NCAA. All Division III.

Campus security: 24-hour emergency response devices and patrols, student patrols, late-night transport/escort service, controlled dormitory access.

Student services: health clinic, personal/psychological counseling, women's center, veterans affairs office.

COSTS & FINANCIAL AID
Costs (2018–19) ***Comprehensive fee:*** $49,080 includes full-time tuition ($38,150), mandatory fees ($650), and room and board ($10,280). Full-time tuition and fees vary according to class time and location. Part-time tuition: $1192 per credit hour. Part-time tuition and fees vary according to class time and location. ***Required fees:*** $175 per term part-time. ***College room only:*** $5350. Room and board charges vary according to board plan and housing facility.

Financial Aid Of all full-time matriculated undergraduates who enrolled in 2017, 1,754 applied for aid, 1,643 were judged to have need, 230 had their need fully met. In 2017, 358 non-need-based awards were made. ***Average percent of need met:*** 74. ***Average financial aid package:*** $31,895. ***Average need-based loan:*** $4977. ***Average need-based gift aid:*** $25,758. ***Average non-need-based aid:*** $16,546. ***Average indebtedness upon graduation:*** $40,097.

APPLYING
Standardized Tests *Required:* SAT or ACT (for admission).

Options: electronic application, deferred entrance.

Required: essay or personal statement, high school transcript, 1 letter of recommendation, letter of recommendation from an academic teacher. ***Recommended:*** minimum 2.8 GPA, interview.

CONTACT
Ms. Keri VanOverschelde, Admissions Operations Program Director, Augsburg University, 2211 Riverside Avenue, Minneapolis, MN 55454-1351. *Phone:* 612-330-1001. *Toll-free phone:* 800-788-5678. *E-mail:* vanovers@augsburg.edu.

Bemidji State University

Bemidji, Minnesota

http://www.bemidjistate.edu/

- **State-supported** comprehensive, founded 1919, part of Minnesota State Colleges and Universities System
- **Small-town** 89-acre campus
- **Coed**
- **Moderately difficult** entrance level

FACULTY
Student/faculty ratio: 21:1.

ACADEMICS
Calendar: semesters. *Degrees:* certificates, associate, bachelor's, master's, and postbachelor's certificates.
Library: A. C. Clark Library.

STUDENT LIFE
Housing options: coed, special housing for students with disabilities. Campus housing is university owned. Freshman applicants given priority for college housing.

Athletics Member NCAA. All Division II except men's and women's ice hockey (Division I).

Campus security: 24-hour emergency response devices and patrols, late-night transport/escort service, controlled dormitory access.

COSTS & FINANCIAL AID
Costs (2018–19) ***Tuition:*** state resident $7630 full-time, $266 per credit part-time; nonresident $7630 full-time, $266 per credit part-time. ***Required fees:*** $1066 full-time, $18 per credit part-time. ***Room and board:*** $8408.

Financial Aid Of all full-time matriculated undergraduates who enrolled in 2017, 2,755 applied for aid, 2,136 were judged to have need, 351 had their need fully met. 238 Federal Work-Study jobs (averaging $2055). 193 state and other part-time jobs (averaging $2083). In 2017, 567 non-need-based awards were made. ***Average percent of need met:*** 59. ***Average financial aid package:*** $9533. ***Average need-based loan:*** $3995. ***Average need-based gift aid:*** $5929. ***Average non-need-based aid:*** $10,469.

APPLYING
Standardized Tests *Required:* SAT or ACT (for admission).

Options: electronic application, early action, deferred entrance.

Application fee: $20.

Required: high school transcript. ***Required for some:*** essay or personal statement, interview.

CONTACT
Bemidji State University, 1500 Birchmont Drive, NE, Bemidji, MN 56601-2699. *Phone:* 218-755-2040. *Toll-free phone:* 800-475-2001.

Bethany Global University

Bloomington, Minnesota

http://www.bethanygu.edu/

CONTACT
Bethany Global University, 6820 Auto Club Road, Suite C, Bloomington, MN 55438. *Toll-free phone:* 800-323-3417.

Bethany Lutheran College

Mankato, Minnesota

http://www.blc.edu/

- **Independent Lutheran** 4-year, founded 1927
- **Small-town** 50-acre campus with easy access to Minneapolis-St. Paul
- **Endowment** $43.3 million
- **Coed** 739 undergraduate students, 80% full-time, 52% women, 48% men
- **Moderately difficult** entrance level, 78% of applicants were admitted

UNDERGRAD STUDENTS

593 full-time, 146 part-time. Students come from 25 states and territories; 19 other countries; 24% are from out of state; 3% Black or African American, non-Hispanic/Latino; 4% Hispanic/Latino; 2% Asian, non-Hispanic/Latino; 2% Two or more races, non-Hispanic/Latino; 2% Race/ethnicity unknown; 10% international; 7% transferred in; 72% live on campus.

Freshmen:

Admission: 497 applied, 387 admitted, 176 enrolled. ***Average high school GPA:*** 3.4. ***Test scores:*** ACT scores over 18: 93%; ACT scores over 24: 37%; ACT scores over 30: 7%.

Retention: 80% of full-time freshmen returned.

FACULTY

Total: 69, 59% full-time, 36% with terminal degrees.

Student/faculty ratio: 9:1.

ACADEMICS

Calendar: semesters. *Degree:* certificates and bachelor's.

Special study options: academic remediation for entering students, adult/continuing education programs, advanced placement credit, cooperative education, distance learning, double majors, English as a second language, independent study, internships, services for LD students, student-designed majors, study abroad, summer session for credit. ***ROTC:*** Army (c).

Computers: 100 computers/terminals and 400 ports are available on campus for general student use. Students can access the following: campus intranet, computer help desk, free student e-mail accounts, online (class) grades, online (class) registration, online (class) schedules. Campuswide network is available. 100% of college-owned or -operated housing units are wired for high-speed Internet access. Wireless service is available via entire campus.

Library: Memorial Library plus 1 other. *Books:* 65,787 (physical), 27,706 (digital/electronic); *Serial titles:* 649 (physical), 224 (digital/electronic); *Databases:* 90. Weekly public service hours: 88.

STUDENT LIFE

Housing options: on-campus residence required through sophomore year; men-only, women-only. Campus housing is university owned. Freshman campus housing is guaranteed.

Activities and organizations: drama/theater group, student-run newspaper, choral group, Bethany Activities Committee, Student Senate, Scholastic Leadership Society, PAMA (Promoting Awareness, spurring Motivation, and encouraging Action), Bethany Society of Royal Scientists.

Athletics Member NCAA. All Division III except golf (Division II). ***Intercollegiate sports:*** baseball M, basketball M/W, cross-country running M/W, golf M/W, soccer M/W, softball W, tennis M/W, track and field M/W, volleyball W. ***Intramural sports:*** basketball M/W, football M/W, racquetball M/W, sand volleyball M/W, soccer M/W, volleyball M/W.

Campus security: 24-hour emergency response devices and patrols, late-night transport/escort service, controlled dormitory access.

Student services: health clinic, personal/psychological counseling.

COSTS & FINANCIAL AID

Costs (2019–20) ***One-time required fee:*** $130. ***Comprehensive fee:*** $36,170 includes full-time tuition ($27,400), mandatory fees ($680), and room and board ($8090). Part-time tuition: $1155. ***Required fees:*** $340 per term part-time.

Financial Aid Of all full-time matriculated undergraduates who enrolled in 2017, 447 applied for aid, 416 were judged to have need, 76 had their need fully met. 24 Federal Work-Study jobs (averaging $1621). 293 state and other part-time jobs (averaging $1063). In 2017, 63 non-need-based awards were made. ***Average percent of need met:*** 84. ***Average financial aid package:*** $22,460. ***Average need-based loan:*** $4662. ***Average need-based gift aid:*** $18,202. ***Average non-need-based aid:*** $10,190. ***Average indebtedness upon graduation:*** $36,911.

APPLYING

Standardized Tests *Required:* SAT or ACT (for admission).

Options: electronic application.

Required: high school transcript, minimum 2.4 GPA. ***Required for some:*** interview. ***Recommended:*** essay or personal statement, minimum 3.2 GPA, interview.

Application deadlines: 7/1 (freshmen), 7/1 (out-of-state freshmen), 7/1 (transfers).

Notification: continuous (freshmen), continuous (out-of-state freshmen), continuous (transfers).

CONTACT

Mr. Jeffrey Lemke, Vice President of Admissions and Enrollment Management, Bethany Lutheran College, 700 Luther Drive, Mankato, MN 56001. *Phone:* 507-344-7000 Ext. 373. *Toll-free phone:* 800-944-3066. *Fax:* 507-344-7376. *E-mail:* jeff.lemke@blc.edu.

★ Bethel University

St. Paul, Minnesota

http://www.bethel.edu/

- **Independent** comprehensive, founded 1871, affiliated with Baptist General Conference
- **Suburban** 289-acre campus with easy access to Minneapolis-St. Paul
- **Endowment** $47.9 million
- **Coed** 2,857 undergraduate students, 85% full-time, 62% women, 38% men
- **Moderately difficult** entrance level, 71% of applicants were admitted

UNDERGRAD STUDENTS

2,417 full-time, 440 part-time. Students come from 37 states and territories; 10 other countries; 21% are from out of state; 5% Black or African American, non-Hispanic/Latino; 5% Hispanic/Latino; 4% Asian, non-Hispanic/Latino; 0.1% Native Hawaiian or other Pacific Islander, non-Hispanic/Latino; 0.4% American Indian or Alaska Native, non-Hispanic/Latino; 4% Two or more races, non-Hispanic/Latino; 3% Race/ethnicity unknown; 0.8% international; 3% transferred in; 66% live on campus.

Freshmen:

Admission: 2,184 applied, 1,540 admitted, 613 enrolled. ***Average high school GPA:*** 3.6. ***Test scores:*** ACT scores over 18: 95%; ACT scores over 24: 60%; ACT scores over 30: 14%.

Retention: 85% of full-time freshmen returned.

FACULTY

Total: 287, 59% full-time, 60% with terminal degrees.

Student/faculty ratio: 11:1.

ACADEMICS

Calendar: 4-1-4. *Degrees:* associate, bachelor's, master's, doctoral, post-master's, and postbachelor's certificates.

Special study options: academic remediation for entering students, adult/continuing education programs, advanced placement credit, distance learning, double majors, honors programs, independent study, internships, off-campus study, part-time degree program, services for LD students, student-designed majors, study abroad, summer session for credit. ***ROTC:*** Army (c), Air Force (c).

Computers: 203 computers/terminals are available on campus for general student use. Students can access the following: campus intranet, computer help desk, free student e-mail accounts, online (class) grades, online (class) registration, online (class) schedules. Campuswide network is available. 100% of college-owned or -operated housing units are wired for high-speed Internet access. Wireless service is available via classrooms, computer centers, computer labs, dorm rooms, learning centers, libraries, student centers.

Library: Bethel University Library plus 1 other. *Books:* 131,467 (physical), 207,567 (digital/electronic); *Serial titles:* 748 (physical), 56,439 (digital/electronic); *Databases:* 126. Weekly public service hours: 96; students can reserve study rooms.

STUDENT LIFE
Housing options: on-campus residence required through sophomore year; special housing for students with disabilities. Campus housing is university owned. Freshman campus housing is guaranteed.

Activities and organizations: drama/theater group, student-run newspaper, radio station, choral group, Bethel Student Government, Bethel Business and Economics Association, Bethel Rec Sports, Welcome Week.

Athletics Member NCAA. All Division III. ***Intercollegiate sports:*** baseball M, basketball M/W, cross-country running M/W, football M, golf M/W, ice hockey M/W, soccer M/W, softball W, tennis M/W, track and field M/W, volleyball M(c)/W. ***Intramural sports:*** basketball M/W, football M, lacrosse M(c)/W(c), rugby M(c), volleyball M(c)/W.

Campus security: 24-hour emergency response devices and patrols, student patrols, late-night transport/escort service, controlled dormitory access, video surveillance for residence halls, academic buildings, and parking lots.

Student services: health clinic, personal/psychological counseling.

COSTS & FINANCIAL AID
Costs (2019–20) ***Comprehensive fee:*** $49,240 includes full-time tuition ($38,300), mandatory fees ($160), and room and board ($10,780). Part-time tuition: $1600 per credit. ***College room only:*** $5900. ***Payment plan:*** tuition prepayment.

Financial Aid Of all full-time matriculated undergraduates who enrolled in 2018, 1,978 applied for aid, 1,699 were judged to have need, 361 had their need fully met. In 2018, 519 non-need-based awards were made. ***Average percent of need met:*** 83. ***Average financial aid package:*** $30,734. ***Average need-based loan:*** $3909. ***Average need-based gift aid:*** $24,362. ***Average non-need-based aid:*** $15,382. ***Average indebtedness upon graduation:*** $37,883.

APPLYING
Standardized Tests *Required:* SAT or ACT (for admission).

Options: electronic application, early admission.

Required: essay or personal statement, high school transcript, rank in upper 50% of high school class. ***Required for some:*** 2 letters of recommendation. ***Recommended:*** minimum 2.5 GPA, interview.

Application deadlines: rolling (freshmen), rolling (transfers).

Notification: continuous (freshmen), continuous (transfers).

CONTACT
Mr. Bret Hyder, Director of Admissions, College of Arts and Sciences, Bethel University, 3900 Bethel Drive, St. Paul, MN 55112-6999. *Phone:* 651-638-6242. *Toll-free phone:* 800-255-8706 Ext. 6242. *Fax:* 651-635-1490. *E-mail:* undergrad-admissions@bethel.edu.

Bethlehem College & Seminary

Minneapolis, Minnesota

http://www.bcsmn.edu/

CONTACT
Bethlehem College & Seminary, 720 13th Avenue South, Minneapolis, MN 55415.

Capella University

Minneapolis, Minnesota

http://www.capella.edu/

CONTACT
Enrollment Services, Capella University, 225 South Sixth Street, Capella Tower, 9th Floor, Minneapolis, MN 55402. *Phone:* 866-283-7921. *Toll-free phone:* 866-283-7921. *Fax:* 612-977-5060. *E-mail:* info@capella.edu.

Carleton College

Northfield, Minnesota

http://www.carleton.edu/

- **Independent** 4-year, founded 1866
- **Small-town** 955-acre campus with easy access to Minneapolis-St. Paul
- **Endowment** $828.2 million
- **Coed**
- **Very difficult** entrance level

FACULTY
Student/faculty ratio: 9:1.

ACADEMICS
Calendar: 3 courses for each of three terms. *Degree:* bachelor's.
Library: Laurence McKinley Gould Library plus 1 other. *Books:* 499,801 (physical), 640,539 (digital/electronic); *Serial titles:* 82,879 (digital/electronic); *Databases:* 31,508. Weekly public service hours: 118.

STUDENT LIFE
Housing options: on-campus residence required through senior year; coed, special housing for students with disabilities. Campus housing is university owned. Freshman campus housing is guaranteed.

Activities and organizations: drama/theater group, student-run newspaper, radio station, choral group, CANOE (Carleton Association of Nature and Outdoor Enthusiasts), Farm Club, Ebony II, WHIMS (Women in Math and Science), Amnesty International.

Athletics Member NCAA. All Division III.

Campus security: 24-hour emergency response devices and patrols, student patrols, late-night transport/escort service, controlled dormitory access, Emergency Notification Service (cell phone text and email alerts).

Student services: health clinic, personal/psychological counseling, women's center.

COSTS & FINANCIAL AID
Costs (2018–19) ***Comprehensive fee:*** $68,844 includes full-time tuition ($54,438), mandatory fees ($321), and room and board ($14,085). ***College room only:*** $7398. Room and board charges vary according to board plan.

Financial Aid Of all full-time matriculated undergraduates who enrolled in 2017, 1,762 applied for aid, 1,134 were judged to have need, 1,134 had their need fully met. 388 Federal Work-Study jobs (averaging $2646). 1,342 state and other part-time jobs (averaging $2730). In 2017, 153 non-need-based awards were made. ***Average percent of need met:*** 100. ***Average financial aid package:*** $49,658. ***Average need-based loan:*** $5214. ***Average need-based gift aid:*** $42,350. ***Average non-need-based aid:*** $4727. ***Average indebtedness upon graduation:*** $21,020. ***Financial aid deadline:*** 1/15.

APPLYING
Standardized Tests *Required:* SAT or ACT (for admission). *Recommended:* SAT Subject Tests (for admission).

Options: electronic application, early admission, early decision, deferred entrance.

Application fee: $30.

Required: essay or personal statement, high school transcript, 2 letters of recommendation, Common Application Supplement. ***Recommended:*** interview.

CONTACT
Carleton College, One North College Street, Northfield, MN 55057-4001. *Phone:* 507-222-4190. *Toll-free phone:* 800-995-2275.

College of Saint Benedict

Saint Joseph, Minnesota

http://www.csbsju.edu/

- **Independent Roman Catholic** 4-year, founded 1913
- **Small-town** 300-acre campus with easy access to Minneapolis-St. Paul
- **Endowment** $78.1 million
- **Women only** 1,782 undergraduate students, 99% full-time
- **Moderately difficult** entrance level, 83% of applicants were admitted

UNDERGRAD STUDENTS
1,764 full-time, 18 part-time. Students come from 31 states and territories; 9 other countries; 17% are from out of state; 3% Black or African

American, non-Hispanic/Latino; 8% Hispanic/Latino; 5% Asian, non-Hispanic/Latino; 0.1% Native Hawaiian or other Pacific Islander, non-Hispanic/Latino; 0.7% American Indian or Alaska Native, non-Hispanic/Latino; 4% international; 0.7% transferred in; 93% live on campus.

Freshmen:
Admission: 1,931 applied, 1,610 admitted, 437 enrolled. ***Average high school GPA:*** 3.7. ***Test scores:*** SAT evidence-based reading and writing scores over 500: 76%; SAT math scores over 500: 74%; ACT scores over 18: 98%; SAT evidence-based reading and writing scores over 600: 31%; SAT math scores over 600: 24%; ACT scores over 24: 59%; SAT evidence-based reading and writing scores over 700: 5%; SAT math scores over 700: 7%; ACT scores over 30: 12%.

Retention: 89% of full-time freshmen returned.

FACULTY
Total: 169, 83% full-time, 83% with terminal degrees.

Student/faculty ratio: 12:1.

ACADEMICS
Calendar: semesters. *Degrees:* bachelor's (coordinate with Saint John's University for men).

Special study options: advanced placement credit, double majors, English as a second language, honors programs, independent study, internships, off-campus study, services for LD students, student-designed majors, study abroad. ***ROTC:*** Army (c).

Computers: 248 computers/terminals and 4,600 ports are available on campus for general student use. Students can access the following: campus intranet, computer help desk, free student e-mail accounts, online (class) grades, online (class) registration, online (class) schedules, online student accounts. 100% of college-owned or -operated housing units are wired for high-speed Internet access. Wireless service is available via entire campus.

Library: Clemens Library plus 2 others. *Books:* 659,802 (physical), 741,067 (digital/electronic); *Serial titles:* 798 (physical), 35,878 (digital/electronic); *Databases:* 226. Weekly public service hours: 104; students can reserve study rooms.

STUDENT LIFE
Housing options: on-campus residence required through senior year; women-only, special housing for students with disabilities. Campus housing is university owned. Freshman campus housing is guaranteed.

Activities and organizations: drama/theater group, student-run newspaper, radio and television station, choral group, Joint Events Council, Outdoor Leadership Center, Magis Ministries, Enactus, Archipelago Caribbean Association.

Athletics Member NCAA. All Division III except golf (Division II). ***Intercollegiate sports:*** basketball W, crew W(c), cross-country running W, golf W, ice hockey W, lacrosse W(c), rugby W(c), skiing (cross-country) W(c), soccer W, softball W, swimming and diving W, tennis W, track and field W, ultimate Frisbee W(c), volleyball W. ***Intramural sports:*** badminton W, basketball W, football W, racquetball W, soccer W, softball W, tennis W, volleyball W.

Campus security: 24-hour emergency response devices and patrols, student patrols, late-night transport/escort service, controlled dormitory access.

Student services: health clinic, personal/psychological counseling, women's center.

COSTS & FINANCIAL AID
Costs (2018–19) ***Comprehensive fee:*** $56,168 includes full-time tuition ($44,184), mandatory fees ($1080), and room and board ($10,904). Part-time tuition: $1841 per credit hour. Part-time tuition and fees vary according to course load. ***College room only:*** $5356. Room and board charges vary according to board plan and housing facility. ***Payment plan:*** installment. ***Waivers:*** employees or children of employees.

Financial Aid Of all full-time matriculated undergraduates who enrolled in 2018, 1,494 applied for aid, 1,330 were judged to have need, 390 had their need fully met. 322 Federal Work-Study jobs (averaging $2701). 1,020 state and other part-time jobs (averaging $3075). In 2018, 437 non-need-based awards were made. ***Average percent of need met:*** 88. ***Average financial aid package:*** $38,456. ***Average need-based loan:*** $4520. ***Average need-based gift aid:*** $31,926. ***Average non-need-based aid:*** $20,503. ***Average indebtedness upon graduation:*** $41,336.

APPLYING
Standardized Tests *Required:* SAT or ACT (for admission).

Options: electronic application, early action, deferred entrance.

Required: high school transcript, college preparatory program. ***Recommended:*** minimum 3.0 GPA.

Application deadlines: rolling (transfers), 12/15 (early action).

Notification: continuous until 10/1 (freshmen), continuous (transfers), 1/15 (early action).

CONTACT
Ms. Karen Backes, Dean of Admissions, College of Saint Benedict, PO Box 7155, Collegeville, MN 56321-7155. *Phone:* 320-363-5055. *Toll-free phone:* 800-544-1489. *Fax:* 320-363-5650. *E-mail:* admissions@csbsju.edu.

The College of St. Scholastica

Duluth, Minnesota

http://www.css.edu/

- **Independent** comprehensive, founded 1912, affiliated with Roman Catholic Church
- **Suburban** 186-acre campus
- **Endowment** $89.6 million
- **Coed** 2,479 undergraduate students, 83% full-time, 71% women, 29% men
- **Moderately difficult** entrance level, 66% of applicants were admitted

UNDERGRAD STUDENTS
2,062 full-time, 417 part-time. Students come from 49 states and territories; 20 other countries; 13% are from out of state; 3% Black or African American, non-Hispanic/Latino; 4% Hispanic/Latino; 3% Asian, non-Hispanic/Latino; 0.8% American Indian or Alaska Native, non-Hispanic/Latino; 3% Two or more races, non-Hispanic/Latino; 0.4% Race/ethnicity unknown; 2% international; 15% transferred in; 51% live on campus.

Freshmen:
Admission: 3,808 applied, 2,520 admitted, 397 enrolled. ***Average high school GPA:*** 3.5. ***Test scores:*** SAT evidence-based reading and writing scores over 500: 85%; SAT math scores over 500: 84%; ACT scores over 18: 95%; SAT evidence-based reading and writing scores over 600: 40%; SAT math scores over 600: 37%; ACT scores over 24: 44%; SAT evidence-based reading and writing scores over 700: 10%; SAT math scores over 700: 5%; ACT scores over 30: 6%.

Retention: 80% of full-time freshmen returned.

FACULTY
Total: 407, 51% full-time, 50% with terminal degrees.

Student/faculty ratio: 14:1.

ACADEMICS
Calendar: semesters. *Degrees:* certificates, bachelor's, master's, doctoral, post-master's, and postbachelor's certificates.

Special study options: accelerated degree program, adult/continuing education programs, advanced placement credit, distance learning, double majors, honors programs, independent study, internships, off-campus study, part-time degree program, services for LD students, student-designed majors, study abroad, summer session for credit. ***ROTC:*** Air Force (c).

Unusual degree programs: 3-2 occupational therapy.

Computers: 614 computers/terminals are available on campus for general student use. Students can access the following: campus intranet, computer help desk, free student e-mail accounts, online (class) grades, online (class) registration, online (class) schedules, student account information, transcripts. Campuswide network is available. 100% of college-owned or -operated housing units are wired for high-speed Internet access. Wireless service is available via entire campus.

Library: College of St. Scholastica Library. *Books:* 110,578 (physical), 10,442 (digital/electronic); *Serial titles:* 122 (physical), 208 (digital/electronic); *Databases:* 227. Weekly public service hours: 91.

STUDENT LIFE
Housing options: on-campus residence required through sophomore year; coed, special housing for students with disabilities. Campus housing is university owned. Freshman applicants given priority for college housing.

Activities and organizations: drama/theater group, student-run newspaper, television station, choral group, Campus Activity Board, InterVarsity, Habitat for Humanity, SHIMA, Volunteers Involved Through Action.

Athletics Member NCAA. All Division III except golf (Division II). ***Intercollegiate sports:*** baseball M, basketball M/W, cross-country running M/W, football M, golf M/W, ice hockey M/W, skiing (cross-country) M/W, soccer M/W, softball W, tennis M/W, track and field M/W, volleyball W. ***Intramural sports:*** basketball M/W, football M/W, soccer M/W, tennis M/W, volleyball M/W.

Campus security: 24-hour emergency response devices and patrols, late-night transport/escort service, controlled dormitory access, student door monitor at night.

Student services: health clinic, personal/psychological counseling, veterans affairs office.

COSTS & FINANCIAL AID

Costs (2019–20) ***Comprehensive fee:*** $48,370 includes full-time tuition ($37,622), mandatory fees ($660), and room and board ($10,088). Part-time tuition: $1175 per credit. ***College room only:*** $5602.

Financial Aid Of all full-time matriculated undergraduates who enrolled in 2018, 1,834 applied for aid, 1,671 were judged to have need, 356 had their need fully met. In 2018, 148 non-need-based awards were made. ***Average percent of need met:*** 74. ***Average financial aid package:*** $26,816. ***Average need-based loan:*** $4433. ***Average need-based gift aid:*** $7825. ***Average non-need-based aid:*** $17,517. ***Average indebtedness upon graduation:*** $42,183.

APPLYING

Options: electronic application, deferred entrance.

Application deadlines: rolling (freshmen), rolling (transfers).

Notification: continuous (freshmen), continuous (transfers).

CONTACT

Bryan Karl, Director, Undergraduate Admissions, The College of St. Scholastica, 1200 Kenwood Avenue, Duluth, MN 55811-4199. *Phone:* 218-723-6044. *Toll-free phone:* 800-249-6412. *E-mail:* bkarl@css.edu.

Concordia College

Moorhead, Minnesota

http://www.concordiacollege.edu/

CONTACT

Ms. Carola Thorson, Executive Director of Admissions and Scholarships, Concordia College, 901 8th Street South, Moorhead, MN 56562. *Phone:* 218-299-3004. *Toll-free phone:* 800-699-9897. *Fax:* 218-299-4720. *E-mail:* cthorson@cord.edu.

Concordia University, St. Paul

St. Paul, Minnesota

http://www.csp.edu/

- **Independent** comprehensive, founded 1893, affiliated with Lutheran Church–Missouri Synod
- **Urban** 37-acre campus with easy access to Minneapolis-St. Paul
- **Endowment** $48.3 million
- **Coed**
- **Minimally difficult** entrance level

FACULTY

Student/faculty ratio: 18:1.

ACADEMICS

Calendar: semesters. *Degrees:* certificates, associate, bachelor's, master's, doctoral, post-master's, and postbachelor's certificates.

Library: Library Technology Center. *Books:* 108,345 (physical), 226,902 (digital/electronic); *Serial titles:* 917 (physical), 98,931 (digital/electronic); *Databases:* 178. Weekly public service hours: 74; students can reserve study rooms.

STUDENT LIFE

Housing options: on-campus residence required for freshman year; coed, men-only, women-only, special housing for students with disabilities. Campus housing is university owned. Freshman campus housing is guaranteed.

Activities and organizations: drama/theater group, student-run newspaper, choral group, Southeast Asian Student Organization, United Minds of Joint Action.

Athletics Member NCAA. All Division II.

Campus security: 24-hour emergency response devices and patrols, student patrols, late-night transport/escort service, controlled dormitory access.

Student services: personal/psychological counseling, veterans affairs office.

COSTS & FINANCIAL AID

Costs (2018–19) ***Comprehensive fee:*** $31,775 includes full-time tuition ($22,775) and room and board ($9000). Full-time tuition and fees vary according to degree level and program. Part-time tuition: $600 per credit. Part-time tuition and fees vary according to course load, degree level, and program. ***Room and board:*** Room and board charges vary according to board plan and housing facility.

Financial Aid Of all full-time matriculated undergraduates who enrolled in 2018, 1,377 applied for aid, 1,177 were judged to have need, 110 had their need fully met. 111 Federal Work-Study jobs (averaging $2376). 453 state and other part-time jobs (averaging $2572). In 2018, 159 non-need-based awards were made. ***Average percent of need met:*** 58. ***Average financial aid package:*** $15,543. ***Average need-based loan:*** $4420. ***Average need-based gift aid:*** $11,139. ***Average non-need-based aid:*** $5077. ***Average indebtedness upon graduation:*** $36,686.

APPLYING

Standardized Tests *Required:* SAT or ACT (for admission).

Options: electronic application, early admission, deferred entrance.

Required: high school transcript, 2 letters of recommendation. ***Required for some:*** essay or personal statement. ***Recommended:*** minimum 2.0 GPA.

CONTACT

Ms. Leah Martin, Director of Traditional Admission, Concordia University, St. Paul, 1282 Concordia Avenue, St. Paul, MN 55104-5494. *Phone:* 651-641-8230. *Toll-free phone:* 800-333-4705. *Fax:* 651-603-6320. *E-mail:* admission@csp.edu.

Crown College

St. Bonifacius, Minnesota

http://www.crown.edu/

CONTACT

Mr. Bret Hyder, Assistant Director of Admissions, Crown College, 8700 College View Drive, St. Bonifacius, MN 55375-9001. *Phone:* 952-446-4142. *Toll-free phone:* 800-68-CROWN. *Fax:* 952-446-4149. *E-mail:* admissions@crown.edu.

Dunwoody College of Technology

Minneapolis, Minnesota

http://www.dunwoody.edu/

- **Independent** primarily 2-year, founded 1914
- **Urban** 11-acre campus with easy access to Minneapolis-St. Paul
- **Endowment** $22.6 million
- **Coed, primarily men** 1,305 undergraduate students, 81% full-time, 17% women, 83% men
- **Minimally difficult** entrance level, 62% of applicants were admitted

UNDERGRAD STUDENTS

1,053 full-time, 252 part-time. Students come from 3 other countries; 3% are from out of state; 5% Black or African American, non-Hispanic/Latino; 3% Hispanic/Latino; 7% Asian, non-Hispanic/Latino; 0.3% American Indian or Alaska Native, non-Hispanic/Latino; 6% Two or more races, non-Hispanic/Latino; 9% Race/ethnicity unknown; 0.2% international; 18% transferred in; 1% live on campus.

Freshmen:

Admission: 614 applied, 380 admitted, 217 enrolled. ***Average high school GPA:*** 2.7.

Retention: 100% of full-time freshmen returned.

FACULTY
Total: 155, 57% full-time, 17% with terminal degrees.
Student/faculty ratio: 10:1.

ACADEMICS
Calendar: semesters. *Degrees:* certificates, associate, and bachelor's.
Special study options: academic remediation for entering students, adult/continuing education programs, cooperative education, distance learning, independent study, internships, study abroad, summer session for credit.
Computers: 300 computers/terminals and 1,000 ports are available on campus for general student use. Students can access the following: campus intranet, computer help desk, free student e-mail accounts, online (class) grades, online (class) registration, online (class) schedules. Campuswide network is available. Wireless service is available via entire campus.
Library: Learning Resource Center plus 1 other. *Books:* 8,000 (physical), 188,153 (digital/electronic); *Serial titles:* 136 (physical); *Databases:* 26. Weekly public service hours: 55.

STUDENT LIFE
Housing options: college housing not available; coed.
Activities and organizations: Phi Theta Kappa, Historic Green, Dunwoody Motorsports Club, Architectural Institute of America Student Chapter, Professional Association for Design.
Campus security: 24-hour emergency response devices, late-night transport/escort service.
Student services: women's center.

COSTS & FINANCIAL AID
Costs (2019–20) ***Comprehensive fee:*** $28,753 includes full-time tuition ($21,394), mandatory fees ($1725), and room and board ($5634).
Financial Aid Of all full-time matriculated undergraduates who enrolled in 2017, 1,138 applied for aid, 993 were judged to have need, 45 had their need fully met. 19 Federal Work-Study jobs (averaging $4404). 28 state and other part-time jobs (averaging $5039). In 2017, 31 non-need-based awards were made. ***Average percent of need met:*** 42. ***Average financial aid package:*** $11,383. ***Average need-based loan:*** $3726. ***Average need-based gift aid:*** $9228. ***Average non-need-based aid:*** $1960.

APPLYING
Standardized Tests *Required for some:* ACT (for admission).
Options: electronic application.
Application fee: $50.
Required: interview. ***Required for some:*** 1 letter of recommendation, ACT scores and Resumes. ***Recommended:*** minimum 2.5 GPA.
Application deadlines: rolling (freshmen), rolling (transfers).
Notification: continuous (freshmen), continuous (transfers).

CONTACT
Kelly O'Brien, Director of Admissions, Dunwoody College of Technology, 818 Dunwoody Boulevard, Minneapolis, MN 55403. *Phone:* 612-381-3302. *Toll-free phone:* 800-292-4625. *Fax:* 612-677-3131. *E-mail:* kobrien@dunwoody.edu.

Gustavus Adolphus College

St. Peter, Minnesota

http://www.gustavus.edu/

- **Independent** 4-year, founded 1862, affiliated with Evangelical Lutheran Church in America
- **Small-town** 340-acre campus with easy access to Minneapolis-St. Paul
- **Endowment** $166.8 million
- **Coed**
- **Very difficult** entrance level

FACULTY
Student/faculty ratio: 11:1.

ACADEMICS
Calendar: 4-1-4. *Degree:* bachelor's.
Library: Folke Bernadotte Memorial Library. *Books:* 326,681 (physical), 53,368 (digital/electronic); *Serial titles:* 1,126 (physical); *Databases:* 108. Students can reserve study rooms.

STUDENT LIFE
Housing options: on-campus residence required through senior year; coed, special housing for students with disabilities. Campus housing is university owned. Freshman campus housing is guaranteed.
Activities and organizations: drama/theater group, student-run newspaper, radio and television station, choral group, Proclaim, Big Partner/Little Partner, Study Buddies, I am...We are, Pound Pals, national fraternities, national sororities.
Athletics Member NCAA. All Division III.
Campus security: 24-hour emergency response devices and patrols, late-night transport/escort service, controlled dormitory access.
Student services: health clinic, personal/psychological counseling, women's center.

COSTS & FINANCIAL AID
Costs (2018–19) ***One-time required fee:*** $490. ***Comprehensive fee:*** $55,010 includes full-time tuition ($44,900), mandatory fees ($200), and room and board ($9910). Part-time tuition: $7680 per course. ***College room only:*** $6300. Room and board charges vary according to board plan and housing facility. ***Payment plans:*** tuition prepayment, installment.
Financial Aid Of all full-time matriculated undergraduates who enrolled in 2018, 1,769 applied for aid, 1,589 were judged to have need, 654 had their need fully met. In 2018, 615 non-need-based awards were made. ***Average percent of need met:*** 93. ***Average financial aid package:*** $41,099. ***Average need-based loan:*** $3234. ***Average need-based gift aid:*** $35,807. ***Average non-need-based aid:*** $25,484. ***Average indebtedness upon graduation:*** $34,655. ***Financial aid deadline:*** 4/15.

APPLYING
Options: electronic application, early admission, early action, deferred entrance.
Required: essay or personal statement, high school transcript, 1 letter of recommendation. ***Recommended:*** interview.

CONTACT
Mr. Richard Aune, Vice President for Enrollment Management, Gustavus Adolphus College, 800 West College Avenue, St. Peter, MN 56082-1498. *Phone:* 507-933-7676. *Toll-free phone:* 800-GUSTAVU(S). *Fax:* 507-933-7474. *E-mail:* admission@gac.edu.

Hamline University

St. Paul, Minnesota

http://www.hamline.edu/

- **Independent** comprehensive, founded 1854, affiliated with United Methodist Church
- **Urban** 60-acre campus with easy access to Minneapolis-St. Paul
- **Coed** 2,106 undergraduate students, 96% full-time, 62% women, 38% men
- **Moderately difficult** entrance level, 67% of applicants were admitted

UNDERGRAD STUDENTS
2,028 full-time, 78 part-time. Students come from 35 states and territories; 34 other countries; 18% are from out of state; 9% Black or African American, non-Hispanic/Latino; 9% Hispanic/Latino; 7% Asian, non-Hispanic/Latino; 0.2% American Indian or Alaska Native, non-Hispanic/Latino; 6% Two or more races, non-Hispanic/Latino; 3% Race/ethnicity unknown; 0.9% international; 6% transferred in; 38% live on campus.

Freshmen:
Admission: 4,794 applied, 3,219 admitted, 538 enrolled. ***Average high school GPA:*** 3.5. ***Test scores:*** SAT evidence-based reading and writing scores over 500: 88%; SAT math scores over 500: 96%; ACT scores over 18: 94%; SAT evidence-based reading and writing scores over 600: 53%; SAT math scores over 600: 39%; ACT scores over 24: 49%; SAT evidence-based reading and writing scores over 700: 10%; SAT math scores over 700: 4%; ACT scores over 30: 12%.
Retention: 74% of full-time freshmen returned.

FACULTY
Total: 290, 52% full-time, 55% with terminal degrees.
Student/faculty ratio: 13:1.

ACADEMICS
Calendar: 4-1-4. *Degrees:* certificates, bachelor's, master's, doctoral, post-master's, and postbachelor's certificates.

Special study options: advanced placement credit, distance learning, double majors, English as a second language, honors programs, independent study, internships, off-campus study, part-time degree program, services for LD students, student-designed majors, study abroad, summer session for credit. ***ROTC:*** Army (c), Air Force (c).

Computers: 300 computers/terminals are available on campus for general student use. Students can access the following: campus intranet, computer help desk, free student e-mail accounts, online (class) grades, online (class) registration, online (class) schedules. Campuswide network is available. 99% of college-owned or -operated housing units are wired for high-speed Internet access. Wireless service is available via entire campus.

Library: Bush Library. *Books:* 125,914 (physical), 476,812 (digital/electronic); *Serial titles:* 807 (physical), 67,981 (digital/electronic); *Databases:* 113. Students can reserve study rooms.

STUDENT LIFE
Housing options: coed, special housing for students with disabilities. Campus housing is university owned. Freshman campus housing is guaranteed.

Activities and organizations: drama/theater group, student-run newspaper, radio and television station, choral group, Hamline Undergraduate Student Congress (HUSC), Hamline University Programming Board (HUPB), Black Student Collective (BSC), Feed Your Brain Campaign (FYB), Asian Pacific American Coalition (APAC), national fraternities, national sororities.

Athletics Member NCAA. All Division III. ***Intercollegiate sports:*** baseball M, basketball M/W, cross-country running M/W, football M, gymnastics W, ice hockey M/W, lacrosse W, soccer M/W, softball W, swimming and diving M/W, tennis M/W, track and field M/W, volleyball W. ***Intramural sports:*** badminton M/W, basketball M/W, football M/W, racquetball M/W, rock climbing M(c)/W(c), soccer M/W, ultimate Frisbee M/W, volleyball M/W.

Campus security: 24-hour emergency response devices and patrols, student patrols, late-night transport/escort service, controlled dormitory access.

Student services: health clinic, personal/psychological counseling, women's center, veterans affairs office.

COSTS & FINANCIAL AID
Costs (2019–20) ***Comprehensive fee:*** $53,366 includes full-time tuition ($41,734), mandatory fees ($1040), and room and board ($10,592). Part-time tuition: $1304 per credit hour. ***Required fees:*** $806 per year part-time. ***College room only:*** $5150.

Financial Aid Of all full-time matriculated undergraduates who enrolled in 2017, 1,865 applied for aid, 1,743 were judged to have need, 285 had their need fully met. In 2017, 294 non-need-based awards were made. ***Average percent of need met:*** 79. ***Average financial aid package:*** $30,738. ***Average need-based loan:*** $4664. ***Average need-based gift aid:*** $24,708. ***Average non-need-based aid:*** $17,525. ***Average indebtedness upon graduation:*** $33,341.

APPLYING
Standardized Tests *Required:* SAT or ACT (for admission).

Options: electronic application, early admission, early decision, early action, deferred entrance.

Required: essay or personal statement, high school transcript. ***Recommended:*** 1 letter of recommendation, interview.

Application deadlines: rolling (freshmen), rolling (out-of-state freshmen), rolling (transfers), 12/1 (early action).

Early decision deadline: 11/1.

Notification: continuous (freshmen), continuous (out-of-state freshmen), continuous (transfers), 11/15 (early decision), rolling (early action).

CONTACT
Ms. Mai Nhia Xiong-Chan, Director, Undergraduate Admissions, Hamline University, 1536 Hewitt Avenue, St. Paul, MN 55104-1284. *Phone:* 651-523-2207. *Toll-free phone:* 800-753-9753. *E-mail:* admission@hamline.edu.

Herzing University
Minneapolis, Minnesota
http://www.herzing.edu/minneapolis

CONTACT
Ms. Shelly Larson, Director of Admissions, Herzing University, 5700 West Broadway, Minneapolis, MN 55428. *Phone:* 763-231-3155. *Toll-free phone:* 800-596-0724. *Fax:* 763-535-9205. *E-mail:* info@mpls.herzing.edu.

Macalester College
St. Paul, Minnesota
http://www.macalester.edu/

- **Independent** 4-year, founded 1874
- **Urban** 53-acre campus
- **Endowment** $767.5 million
- **Coed** 2,174 undergraduate students, 98% full-time, 60% women, 40% men
- **Very difficult** entrance level, 41% of applicants were admitted

UNDERGRAD STUDENTS
2,140 full-time, 34 part-time. Students come from 54 states and territories; 96 other countries; 82% are from out of state; 3% Black or African American, non-Hispanic/Latino; 8% Hispanic/Latino; 8% Asian, non-Hispanic/Latino; 0.2% American Indian or Alaska Native, non-Hispanic/Latino; 6% Two or more races, non-Hispanic/Latino; 0.3% Race/ethnicity unknown; 16% international; 0.1% transferred in; 72% live on campus.

Freshmen:
Admission: 5,985 applied, 2,468 admitted, 621 enrolled. ***Test scores:*** SAT evidence-based reading and writing scores over 500: 100%; SAT math scores over 500: 100%; ACT scores over 18: 100%; SAT evidence-based reading and writing scores over 600: 96%; SAT math scores over 600: 93%; ACT scores over 24: 98%; SAT evidence-based reading and writing scores over 700: 48%; SAT math scores over 700: 56%; ACT scores over 30: 68%.
Retention: 96% of full-time freshmen returned.

FACULTY
Total: 264, 71% full-time, 75% with terminal degrees.

Student/faculty ratio: 10:1.

ACADEMICS
Calendar: semesters. *Degree:* bachelor's.

Special study options: advanced placement credit, double majors, honors programs, independent study, internships, off-campus study, part-time degree program, services for LD students, student-designed majors, study abroad, summer session for credit. ***ROTC:*** Army (c), Navy (c), Air Force (c).

Computers: 375 computers/terminals and 2,600 ports are available on campus for general student use. Students can access the following: campus intranet, computer help desk, free student e-mail accounts, online (class) grades, online (class) registration, online (class) schedules, wireless networking, free printing, specialized tools, 3D printing, scanning, A/V equipment checkout (cameras, microphones, etc.). Campuswide network is available. 100% of college-owned or -operated housing units are wired for high-speed Internet access. Wireless service is available via entire campus.

Library: DeWitt Wallace Library. *Books:* 326,620 (physical), 179,946 (digital/electronic); *Serial titles:* 2,412 (physical), 76,659 (digital/electronic); *Databases:* 202. Weekly public service hours: 109; study areas open 24 hours, 5–7 days a week; students can reserve study rooms.

STUDENT LIFE
Housing options: on-campus residence required through sophomore year; coed, men-only, women-only, cooperative. Campus housing is university owned. Freshman campus housing is guaranteed.

Activities and organizations: drama/theater group, student-run newspaper, radio station, choral group, Program Board, WMCN - Macalester College Radio, The Mac Weekly, Outing Club, Climbing Club.

Athletics Member NCAA. All Division III. ***Intercollegiate sports:*** baseball M, basketball M/W, crew M(c)/W(c), cross-country running M/W, football M, golf M/W, ice hockey M(c)/W(c), lacrosse W(c), rugby M(c)/W(c), skiing (cross-country) M(c)/W(c), soccer M/W, softball W, swimming and diving M/W, tennis M/W, track and field M/W, ultimate Frisbee M(c)/W(c), volleyball M(c)/W, water polo M(c)/W. ***Intramural sports:*** badminton M/W, basketball M/W, racquetball M/W, soccer M/W, softball M/W, table tennis M/W, tennis M(c)/W(c), ultimate Frisbee M/W, volleyball M/W.

Campus security: 24-hour emergency response devices and patrols, late-night transport/escort service, controlled dormitory access.

Student services: health clinic, personal/psychological counseling.

COSTS & FINANCIAL AID

Costs (2019–20) ***Comprehensive fee:*** $68,884 includes full-time tuition ($56,062), mandatory fees ($230), and room and board ($12,592). Part-time tuition: $1752 per credit. ***College room only:*** $6762.

Financial Aid Of all full-time matriculated undergraduates who enrolled in 2018, 1,557 applied for aid, 1,444 were judged to have need, 909 had their need fully met. In 2018, 272 non-need-based awards were made. ***Average percent of need met:*** 100. ***Average financial aid package:*** $47,763. ***Average need-based loan:*** $4911. ***Average need-based gift aid:*** $40,870. ***Average non-need-based aid:*** $15,251. ***Average indebtedness upon graduation:*** $24,880.

APPLYING

Standardized Tests *Required:* SAT or ACT (for admission).

Options: electronic application, early admission, early decision, deferred entrance.

Application fee: $40.

Required: essay or personal statement, high school transcript, 2 letters of recommendation. ***Recommended:*** interview.

Application deadlines: 1/15 (freshmen), 4/15 (transfers).

Early decision deadline: 11/15 (for plan 1), 1/1 (for plan 2).

Notification: 3/30 (freshmen), 5/15 (transfers), 12/15 (early decision plan 1), 2/1 (early decision plan 2).

CONTACT

Mr. Jeff Allen, Vice President of Admissions and Financial Aid, Macalester College, 1600 Grand Avenue, St. Paul, MN 55105-1899. *Phone:* 651-696-6357. *Toll-free phone:* 800-231-7974. *Fax:* 651-696-6724. *E-mail:* admissions@macalester.edu.

Martin Luther College

New Ulm, Minnesota

http://www.mlc-wels.edu/

- **Independent** comprehensive, founded 1995, affiliated with Wisconsin Evangelical Lutheran Synod
- **Small-town** 50-acre campus
- **Coed** 885 undergraduate students, 85% full-time, 51% women, 49% men
- **Moderately difficult** entrance level, 89% of applicants were admitted

UNDERGRAD STUDENTS

751 full-time, 134 part-time. 82% are from out of state; 1% Black or African American, non-Hispanic/Latino; 2% Hispanic/Latino; 0.7% Asian, non-Hispanic/Latino; 0.2% Native Hawaiian or other Pacific Islander, non-Hispanic/Latino; 0.1% American Indian or Alaska Native, non-Hispanic/Latino; 1% Two or more races, non-Hispanic/Latino; 2% international; 2% transferred in; 91% live on campus.

Freshmen:

Admission: 270 applied, 241 admitted, 195 enrolled. ***Average high school GPA:*** 3.5. ***Test scores:*** ACT scores over 18: 96%; ACT scores over 24: 58%; ACT scores over 30: 13%.

Retention: 85% of full-time freshmen returned.

FACULTY

Total: 79, 70% full-time, 35% with terminal degrees.

Student/faculty ratio: 12:1.

ACADEMICS

Calendar: semesters. *Degrees:* certificates, diplomas, bachelor's, and master's.

Special study options: advanced placement credit, distance learning, double majors, summer session for credit.

Computers: Campuswide network is available.

Library: Martin Luther College Library.

STUDENT LIFE

Housing options: on-campus residence required for freshman year; men-only, women-only, special housing for students with disabilities. Campus housing is university owned. Freshman campus housing is guaranteed.

Activities and organizations: drama/theater group, choral group.

Athletics Member NCAA, NAIA. All NCAA Division III except golf (Division II). ***Intercollegiate sports:*** baseball M, basketball M/W, cross-country running M/W, football M, golf M/W, soccer M/W, softball W, tennis M/W, track and field M/W, volleyball W. ***Intramural sports:*** badminton M/W, basketball M/W, bowling M/W, football M, soccer M/W, softball M/W, tennis M/W, volleyball M/W.

Student services: health clinic, personal/psychological counseling.

COSTS & FINANCIAL AID

Costs (2019–20) ***Comprehensive fee:*** $22,130 includes full-time tuition ($15,870) and room and board ($6260).

Financial Aid Of all full-time matriculated undergraduates who enrolled in 2017, 618 applied for aid, 552 were judged to have need, 83 had their need fully met. In 2017, 93 non-need-based awards were made. ***Average percent of need met:*** 72. ***Average financial aid package:*** $12,766. ***Average need-based loan:*** $4595. ***Average need-based gift aid:*** $8402. ***Average non-need-based aid:*** $3331. ***Average indebtedness upon graduation:*** $27,116. ***Financial aid deadline:*** 4/15.

APPLYING

Standardized Tests *Required:* SAT or ACT (for admission).

Options: deferred entrance.

Required: high school transcript, minimum 2.0 GPA.

CONTACT

Mark Stein, Director of Admissions, Martin Luther College, 1995 Luther Court, New Ulm, MN 56073. *Phone:* 507-354-8221 Ext. 360. *Toll-free phone:* 877-MLC-1995. *Fax:* 507-354-8225. *E-mail:* steinma@mlc-wels.edu.

Metropolitan State University

St. Paul, Minnesota

http://www.metrostate.edu/

CONTACT

Mr. Daryl Johnson, Director, Metropolitan State University, 700 East 7th Street, St. Paul, MN 55106. *Phone:* 651-793-1227. *Fax:* 651-793-1546. *E-mail:* daryl.johnson@metrostate.edu.

Minneapolis College of Art and Design

Minneapolis, Minnesota

http://www.mcad.edu/

- **Independent** comprehensive, founded 1886
- **Urban** 3-acre campus
- **Endowment** $47.9 million
- **Coed**
- **Moderately difficult** entrance level

FACULTY

Student/faculty ratio: 10:1.

ACADEMICS

Calendar: semesters. *Degrees:* bachelor's and master's.

Library: MCAD Library. *Books:* 50,000 (physical), 145,000 (digital/electronic); *Serial titles:* 329 (physical); *Databases:* 8.

STUDENT LIFE

Housing options: coed. Campus housing is university owned. Freshman applicants given priority for college housing.

Activities and organizations: Peoples Library, Black Artist Student Union, Animation Study Group, Comic Club, Kinda Midnight Movies Club.

Campus security: 24-hour emergency response devices and patrols, late-night transport/escort service, controlled dormitory access.

Student services: personal/psychological counseling.

COSTS & FINANCIAL AID

Costs (2018–19) ***Tuition:*** $38,670 full-time, $1612 per credit hour part-time. Part-time tuition and fees vary according to course load. ***Required fees:*** $450 full-time, $225 per term part-time. ***Room only:*** $5610. Room and board charges vary according to housing facility.

Financial Aid Of all full-time matriculated undergraduates who enrolled in 2014, 546 applied for aid, 490 were judged to have need, 54 had their need fully met. In 2014, 112 non-need-based awards were made. ***Average percent of need met:*** 68. ***Average financial aid package:*** $22,825. ***Average need-based loan:*** $4747. ***Average need-based gift aid:*** $17,718. ***Average non-need-based aid:*** $11,165. ***Average indebtedness upon graduation:*** $33,400. ***Financial aid deadline:*** 4/1.

APPLYING

Standardized Tests *Required for some:* SAT or ACT (for admission).

Options: electronic application, early action.

Application fee: $50.

Required: essay or personal statement, high school transcript. ***Recommended:*** interview.

CONTACT

Minneapolis College of Art and Design, 2501 Stevens Avenue, Minneapolis, MN 55404-4347. *Phone:* 612-874-3764. *Toll-free phone:* 800-874-6223.

Minnesota State University Mankato

Mankato, Minnesota

http://mankato.mnsu.edu/

CONTACT

Office of Admissions, Minnesota State University Mankato, 122 Taylor Center, Mankato, MN 56001. *Phone:* 507-389-1822. *Toll-free phone:* 800-722-0544. *Fax:* 507-389-1511. *E-mail:* admissions@mnsu.edu.

Minnesota State University Moorhead

Moorhead, Minnesota

http://www.mnstate.edu/

- **State-supported** comprehensive, founded 1885, part of Minnesota State Colleges and Universities System
- **Urban** 119-acre campus
- **Endowment** $24.5 million
- **Coed** 4,828 undergraduate students, 81% full-time, 61% women, 39% men
- **Moderately difficult** entrance level, 60% of applicants were admitted

UNDERGRAD STUDENTS

3,895 full-time, 933 part-time. Students come from 35 states and territories; 46 other countries; 33% are from out of state; 4% Black or African American, non-Hispanic/Latino; 3% Hispanic/Latino; 2% Asian, non-Hispanic/Latino; 0.1% Native Hawaiian or other Pacific Islander, non-Hispanic/Latino; 0.6% American Indian or Alaska Native, non-Hispanic/Latino; 4% Two or more races, non-Hispanic/Latino; 1% Race/ethnicity unknown; 6% international; 8% transferred in; 25% live on campus.

Freshmen:

Admission: 4,204 applied, 2,533 admitted, 795 enrolled. ***Average high school GPA:*** 3.4. ***Test scores:*** ACT scores over 18: 94%; ACT scores over 24: 35%; ACT scores over 30: 4%.

Retention: 72% of full-time freshmen returned.

FACULTY

Total: 309, 71% full-time, 74% with terminal degrees.

Student/faculty ratio: 19:1.

ACADEMICS

Calendar: semesters. *Degrees:* certificates, bachelor's, master's, doctoral, post-master's, and postbachelor's certificates.

Special study options: academic remediation for entering students, adult/continuing education programs, advanced placement credit, distance learning, double majors, English as a second language, honors programs, independent study, internships, off-campus study, part-time degree program, services for LD students, student-designed majors, study abroad, summer session for credit. ***ROTC:*** Army (c), Air Force (c).

Computers: 1,500 computers/terminals are available on campus for general student use. Students can access the following: computer help desk, free student e-mail accounts, online (class) grades, online (class) registration, online (class) schedules. Campuswide network is available. 100% of college-owned or -operated housing units are wired for high-speed Internet access. Wireless service is available via entire campus.

Library: Livingston Lord Library plus 1 other. *Books:* 326,187 (physical), 20,401 (digital/electronic); *Serial titles:* 1,634 (physical), 18,041 (digital/electronic); *Databases:* 84. Weekly public service hours: 79.

STUDENT LIFE

Housing options: coed, special housing for students with disabilities. Campus housing is university owned. Freshman campus housing is guaranteed.

Activities and organizations: drama/theater group, student-run newspaper, radio and television station, choral group, NSSLHA / Collegiate SERTOMA, Cinethusiasts, Student Council for Exceptional Children, Education Minnesota Student Program, National Society of Leadership and Success, national fraternities, national sororities.

Athletics Member NCAA. All Division II except golf (Division I). ***Intercollegiate sports:*** basketball M(s)/W(s), cheerleading M/W, cross-country running M(s)/W(s), football M(s), golf W(s), soccer M(c)/W(s), softball W(s), swimming and diving W(s), tennis M(c)/W(s), track and field M(s)/W(s), volleyball M(c)/W(s), wrestling M(s). ***Intramural sports:*** badminton M/W, baseball M(c), basketball M/W, fencing M(c)/W(c), football M/W, ice hockey M(c)/W(c), rock climbing M(c)/W(c), rugby M(c), soccer M/W, softball M/W, tennis M/W, ultimate Frisbee M/W, volleyball M/W, weight lifting M(c)/W(c).

Campus security: 24-hour emergency response devices and patrols, student patrols, late-night transport/escort service, controlled dormitory access.

Student services: health clinic, personal/psychological counseling, women's center, veterans affairs office.

COSTS & FINANCIAL AID

Costs (2018–19) ***One-time required fee:*** $90. ***Tuition:*** state resident $7410 full-time, $239 per credit hour part-time; nonresident $14,820 full-time, $478 per credit hour part-time. Full-time tuition and fees vary according to course load and reciprocity agreements. Part-time tuition and fees vary according to reciprocity agreements. ***Required fees:*** $1162 full-time, $48 per credit hour part-time, $581 per term part-time. ***Room and board:*** $9280; room only: $5950. Room and board charges vary according to board plan and housing facility. ***Payment plan:*** installment. ***Waivers:*** senior citizens and employees or children of employees.

Financial Aid Of all full-time matriculated undergraduates who enrolled in 2018, 3,137 applied for aid, 2,389 were judged to have need. 160 Federal Work-Study jobs (averaging $2631). 171 state and other part-time jobs (averaging $2367). ***Average financial aid package:*** $3284. ***Average need-based loan:*** $4007. ***Average need-based gift aid:*** $2974. ***Average indebtedness upon graduation:*** $32,713.

APPLYING

Standardized Tests *Required:* SAT or ACT (for admission). *Recommended:* ACT (for admission).

Options: electronic application, deferred entrance.

Application fee: $20.

Required: high school transcript.

Application deadlines: rolling (freshmen), rolling (out-of-state freshmen), rolling (transfers).

Notification: continuous (freshmen), continuous (out-of-state freshmen), continuous (transfers).

CONTACT

Ms. Brenda Amenson-Hill, Vice President of Enrollment Management & Student Affairs, Minnesota State University Moorhead, 1104 7th Avenue South, Moorhead, MN 56563. *Phone:* 218-477-2200. *Toll-free phone:* 800-593-7246. *E-mail:* brenda.amensonhill@mnstate.edu.

National American University
Bloomington, Minnesota
http://www.national.edu/

CONTACT
Ms. Jennifer Michaelson, Admissions Assistant, National American University, 321 Kansas City Street, Rapid City, SD 57201. *Phone:* 605-394-4827. *Toll-free phone:* 866-628-6387. *E-mail:* jmichaelson@national.edu.

National American University
Brooklyn Center, Minnesota
http://www.national.edu/

CONTACT
Admissions Office, National American University, 6200 Shingle Creek Parkway, Suite 130, Brooklyn Center, MN 55430. *Toll-free phone:* 866-628-6387.

National American University
Burnsville, Minnesota
http://www.national.edu/

CONTACT
National American University, 513 West Travelers Trail, Burnsville, MN 55337. *Toll-free phone:* 866-628-6387.

National American University
Roseville, Minnesota
http://www.national.edu/

CONTACT
Mr. Steve Grunlan, Director of Admissions, National American University, 1550 West Highway 36, Roseville, MN 55113. *Phone:* 651-644-1265. *Toll-free phone:* 866-628-6387.

North Central University
Minneapolis, Minnesota
http://www.northcentral.edu/

CONTACT
Ms. Sigi Shawa, Assistant Director, North Central University, 910 Elliot Avenue, Minneapolis, MN 55404-1322. *Phone:* 612-343-4460. *Toll-free phone:* 800-289-6222. *Fax:* 612-343-4146. *E-mail:* admissions@northcentral.edu.

Oak Hills Christian College
Bemidji, Minnesota
http://www.oakhills.edu/

CONTACT
Shelly Fast, Assistant Director of Admissions, Oak Hills Christian College, 1600 Oak Hills Road SW, Bemidji, MN 56601. *Phone:* 218-751-8670 Ext. 1285. *Toll-free phone:* 888-751-8670 Ext. 1285. *Fax:* 218-751-8825. *E-mail:* admissions@oakhills.edu.

Rasmussen College Blaine
Blaine, Minnesota
http://www.rasmussen.edu/

CONTACT
Ms. Susan Hammerstrom, Director of Admissions, Rasmussen College Blaine, 3629 95th Avenue NE, Blaine, MN 55014. *Phone:* 763-795-4720. *Toll-free phone:* 888-549-6755. *E-mail:* susan.hammerstrom@rasmussen.edu.

Rasmussen College Bloomington
Bloomington, Minnesota
http://www.rasmussen.edu/

- **Proprietary** 4-year, founded 1904, part of Rasmussen College System
- **Suburban** campus with easy access to Minneapolis-St. Paul
- **Coed**
- **Minimally difficult** entrance level

FACULTY
Student/faculty ratio: 22:1.

ACADEMICS
Calendar: quarters. *Degrees:* certificates, diplomas, associate, bachelor's, and postbachelor's certificates.
Library: Rasmussen College Library - Bloomington.

STUDENT LIFE
Housing options: college housing not available.

FINANCIAL AID
Financial Aid Of all full-time matriculated undergraduates who enrolled in 2017, 3 state and other part-time jobs (averaging $4338).

APPLYING
Standardized Tests *Required:* institutional exam (for admission).
Options: electronic application, early admission, deferred entrance.
Required: high school transcript, minimum 2.0 GPA. ***Required for some:*** interview.

CONTACT
Dwayne Bertotto, Vice President of Admissions and Student Experience, Rasmussen College Bloomington, 8300 Norman Center Drive, Suite 300, Bloomington, MN 55437. *Phone:* 952-806-3958. *Toll-free phone:* 888-549-6755. *E-mail:* dwayne.bertotto@rasmussen.edu.

Rasmussen College Brooklyn Park
Brooklyn Park, Minnesota
http://www.rasmussen.edu/

- **Proprietary** 4-year, part of Rasmussen College System
- **Suburban** campus with easy access to Minneapolis-St. Paul
- **Coed**
- **Minimally difficult** entrance level

FACULTY
Student/faculty ratio: 22:1.

ACADEMICS
Calendar: quarters. *Degrees:* certificates, diplomas, associate, and bachelor's.
Library: Rasmussen College Library - Brooklyn Park.

STUDENT LIFE
Housing options: college housing not available.

APPLYING
Standardized Tests *Required:* institutional exam (for admission).
Options: electronic application, early admission, deferred entrance.
Required: high school transcript, minimum 2.0 GPA. ***Required for some:*** interview.

CONTACT
Dwayne Bertotto, Vice President of Admissions and Student Experience, Rasmussen College Brooklyn Park, 8300 Norman Center Drive, Suite 300, Bloomington, MN 55437. *Phone:* 952-806-3958. *Toll-free phone:* 888-549-6755. *E-mail:* dwayne.bertotto@rasmussen.edu.

Rasmussen College Eagan
Eagan, Minnesota
http://www.rasmussen.edu/

- **Proprietary** 4-year, founded 1904, part of Rasmussen College System
- **Suburban** campus with easy access to Minneapolis-St. Paul
- **Coed**
- **Minimally difficult** entrance level

FACULTY
Student/faculty ratio: 22:1.

ACADEMICS
Calendar: quarters. *Degrees:* certificates, diplomas, associate, bachelor's, and postbachelor's certificates.
Library: Rasmussen College Library - Eagan.

STUDENT LIFE
Housing options: college housing not available.

APPLYING
Standardized Tests *Required:* institutional exam (for admission).

Options: electronic application, early admission, deferred entrance.

Required: high school transcript, minimum 2.0 GPA. ***Required for some:*** interview.

CONTACT
Mr. Dwayne Bertotto, Vice President of Admissions and Student Experience, Rasmussen College Eagan, 8300 Norman Center Drive, Suite 300, Bloomington, MN 55437. *Phone:* 952-806-3958. *Toll-free phone:* 888-549-6755. *E-mail:* dwayne.bertotto@rasmussen.edu.

Rasmussen College Lake Elmo/Woodbury

Lake Elmo, Minnesota

http://www.rasmussen.edu/

CONTACT
Ms. Susan Hammerstrom, Director of Admissions, Rasmussen College Lake Elmo/Woodbury, 8565 Eagle Point Circle, Lake Elmo, MN 55042. *Phone:* 651-259-6600. *Toll-free phone:* 888-549-6755. *E-mail:* susan.hammerstrom@rasmussen.edu.

Rasmussen College Mankato

Mankato, Minnesota

http://www.rasmussen.edu/

- **Proprietary** 4-year, founded 1904, part of Rasmussen College System
- **Suburban** campus with easy access to Minneapolis-St. Paul
- **Coed**
- **Minimally difficult** entrance level

FACULTY
Student/faculty ratio: 22:1.

ACADEMICS
Calendar: quarters. *Degrees:* certificates, diplomas, associate, bachelor's, and postbachelor's certificates.
Library: Rasmussen College Library - Mankato.

STUDENT LIFE
Housing options: college housing not available.

FINANCIAL AID
Financial Aid Of all full-time matriculated undergraduates who enrolled in 2017, 15 Federal Work-Study jobs (averaging $4000). 13 state and other part-time jobs (averaging $4000).

APPLYING
Standardized Tests *Required:* institutional exam (for admission).

Options: electronic application, early admission, deferred entrance.

Required: high school transcript, minimum 2.0 GPA. ***Required for some:*** interview.

CONTACT
Mr. Dwayne Bertotto, Vice President of Admissions and Student Experience, Rasmussen College Mankato, 1400 Madison Avenue, Mankato, MN 56001. *Phone:* 952-806-3958. *Toll-free phone:* 888-549-6755. *E-mail:* dwayne.bertto@rasmussen.edu.

Rasmussen College Moorhead

Moorhead, Minnesota

http://www.rasmussen.edu/

CONTACT
Ms. Susan Hammerstrom, Director of Admissions, Rasmussen College Moorhead, 1250 29th Avenue South, Moorhead, MN 56560. *Phone:* 218-304-6200. *Toll-free phone:* 888-549-6755. *E-mail:* susan.hammerstrom@rasmussen.edu.

Rasmussen College St. Cloud

St. Cloud, Minnesota

http://www.rasmussen.edu/

- **Proprietary** 4-year, founded 1904, part of Rasmussen College System
- **Suburban** campus
- **Coed**
- **Minimally difficult** entrance level

FACULTY
Student/faculty ratio: 22:1.

ACADEMICS
Calendar: quarters. *Degrees:* certificates, diplomas, associate, bachelor's, and postbachelor's certificates.
Library: Rasmussen College Library - St. Cloud.

STUDENT LIFE
Housing options: college housing not available.

FINANCIAL AID
Financial Aid Of all full-time matriculated undergraduates who enrolled in 2017, 34 Federal Work-Study jobs (averaging $866). 51 state and other part-time jobs (averaging $700).

APPLYING
Standardized Tests *Required:* institutional exam (for admission).

Options: electronic application, early admission, deferred entrance.

Required: high school transcript, minimum 2.0 GPA. ***Required for some:*** interview.

CONTACT
Dwayne Bertotto, Vice President of Admissions and Student Experience, Rasmussen College St. Cloud, 8300 Norman Center Drive, Suite 300, Bloomington, MN 55437. *Phone:* 952-806-3958. *Toll-free phone:* 888-549-6755. *E-mail:* dwayne.bertotto@rasmussen.edu.

St. Catherine University

St. Paul, Minnesota

http://www.stkate.edu/

- **Independent Roman Catholic** comprehensive, founded 1905
- **Urban** 110-acre campus with easy access to Minneapolis-St. Paul
- **Undergraduate: women only; graduate: coed**
- **Moderately difficult** entrance level

FACULTY
Student/faculty ratio: 10:1.

ACADEMICS
Calendar: 4-1-4. *Degrees:* certificates, associate, bachelor's, master's, doctoral, and postbachelor's certificates.
Library: St. Catherine Library.

STUDENT LIFE
Housing options: women-only. Campus housing is university owned. Freshman campus housing is guaranteed.

Activities and organizations: drama/theater group, student-run newspaper, radio station, choral group.

Athletics Member NCAA. All Division III.

Campus security: 24-hour emergency response devices and patrols, student patrols, late-night transport/escort service, controlled dormitory access.

COSTS & FINANCIAL AID
Costs (2018–19) ***Comprehensive fee:*** $51,523 includes full-time tuition ($41,504), mandatory fees ($759), and room and board ($9260). Full-time

tuition and fees vary according to degree level. Part-time tuition: $1297 per credit hour. Part-time tuition and fees vary according to degree level. ***Required fees:*** $322 per term part-time. ***Room and board:*** Room and board charges vary according to board plan and housing facility.

Financial Aid Of all full-time matriculated undergraduates who enrolled in 2018, 1,708 applied for aid, 1,443 were judged to have need, 413 had their need fully met. In 2018, 243 non-need-based awards were made. ***Average percent of need met:*** 90. ***Average financial aid package:*** $37,551. ***Average need-based loan:*** $4551. ***Average need-based gift aid:*** $9304. ***Average non-need-based aid:*** $19,833. ***Average indebtedness upon graduation:*** $34,567.

APPLYING

Standardized Tests *Required:* SAT or ACT (for admission).

Options: deferred entrance.

Required: high school transcript, 1 letter of recommendation. ***Required for some:*** essay or personal statement, interview. ***Recommended:*** interview.

CONTACT

Associate Director of Admission and Financial Aid, St. Catherine University, 2004 Randolph Avenue, St. Paul, MN 55105. *Phone:* 651-690-6047. *Toll-free phone:* 800-945-4599. *E-mail:* stkate@stkate.edu.

St. Cloud State University

St. Cloud, Minnesota

http://www.stcloudstate.edu/

CONTACT

Ms. Amber Schultz, Assistant Vice President for Admissions, Marketing, and Recruitment, St. Cloud State University, 720 4th Avenue South, AS 115, St. Cloud, MN 56301-4498. *Phone:* 320-308-3870. *Toll-free phone:* 877-654-7278. *Fax:* 320-308-2243. *E-mail:* scsu4u@stcloudstate.edu.

Saint John's University

Collegeville, Minnesota

http://www.csbsju.edu/

- **Independent Roman Catholic** comprehensive, founded 1857
- **Rural** 2500-acre campus with easy access to Minneapolis-St. Paul
- **Endowment** $196.8 million
- **Undergraduate: men only; graduate: coed** 1,667 undergraduate students, 99% full-time, 100% men
- **Moderately difficult** entrance level, 80% of applicants were admitted

UNDERGRAD STUDENTS

1,646 full-time, 21 part-time. Students come from 37 states and territories; 13 other countries; 20% are from out of state; 5% Black or African American, non-Hispanic/Latino; 8% Hispanic/Latino; 3% Asian, non-Hispanic/Latino; 0.3% Native Hawaiian or other Pacific Islander, non-Hispanic/Latino; 0.7% American Indian or Alaska Native, non-Hispanic/Latino; 0.1% Two or more races, non-Hispanic/Latino; 5% international; 1% transferred in; 88% live on campus.

Freshmen:

Admission: 1,552 applied, 1,241 admitted, 398 enrolled. ***Average high school GPA:*** 3.5. ***Test scores:*** SAT evidence-based reading and writing scores over 500: 73%; SAT math scores over 500: 82%; ACT scores over 18: 98%; SAT evidence-based reading and writing scores over 600: 37%; SAT math scores over 600: 37%; ACT scores over 24: 62%; SAT evidence-based reading and writing scores over 700: 8%; SAT math scores over 700: 8%; ACT scores over 30: 15%.

Retention: 87% of full-time freshmen returned.

FACULTY

Total: 157, 83% full-time, 76% with terminal degrees.

Student/faculty ratio: 12:1.

ACADEMICS

Calendar: semesters. *Degrees:* bachelor's and master's (coordinate with College of Saint Benedict for women).

Special study options: advanced placement credit, double majors, English as a second language, honors programs, independent study, internships, off-campus study, services for LD students, student-designed majors, study abroad. ***ROTC:*** Army (b).

Computers: 248 computers/terminals and 4,600 ports are available on campus for general student use. Students can access the following: campus intranet, computer help desk, free student e-mail accounts, online (class) grades, online (class) registration, online (class) schedules, online student accounts. Campuswide network is available. 100% of college-owned or -operated housing units are wired for high-speed Internet access. Wireless service is available via entire campus.

Library: Alcuin Library plus 2 others. *Books:* 659,802 (physical), 741,067 (digital/electronic); *Serial titles:* 798 (physical), 35,878 (digital/electronic); *Databases:* 226. Weekly public service hours: 104; students can reserve study rooms.

STUDENT LIFE

Housing options: on-campus residence required through senior year; men-only, special housing for students with disabilities. Campus housing is university owned. Freshman campus housing is guaranteed.

Activities and organizations: drama/theater group, student-run newspaper, radio and television station, choral group, Joint Events Council, Outdoor Leadership Center, Magis Ministries, Enactus, Archipelago Caribbean Association.

Athletics Member NCAA. All Division III. ***Intercollegiate sports:*** baseball M, basketball M, crew M(c), cross-country running M, football M, golf M, ice hockey M, lacrosse M(c), riflery M(c), rugby M(c), skiing (cross-country) M(c), soccer M, swimming and diving M, tennis M, track and field M, ultimate Frisbee M(c), volleyball M(c), water polo M(c), wrestling M. ***Intramural sports:*** basketball M, football M, racquetball M, soccer M, softball M, ultimate Frisbee M, volleyball M.

Campus security: 24-hour emergency response devices and patrols, student patrols, late-night transport/escort service, controlled dormitory access.

Student services: health clinic, personal/psychological counseling.

COSTS & FINANCIAL AID

Costs (2018–19) ***Comprehensive fee:*** $55,309 includes full-time tuition ($44,184), mandatory fees ($806), and room and board ($10,319). Part-time tuition: $1841 per credit hour. Part-time tuition and fees vary according to course load. ***College room only:*** $5171. Room and board charges vary according to board plan and housing facility. ***Payment plan:*** installment. ***Waivers:*** employees or children of employees.

Financial Aid Of all full-time matriculated undergraduates who enrolled in 2018, 1,296 applied for aid, 1,129 were judged to have need, 376 had their need fully met. 205 Federal Work-Study jobs (averaging $3400). 821 state and other part-time jobs (averaging $3400). In 2018, 403 non-need-based awards were made. ***Average percent of need met:*** 89. ***Average financial aid package:*** $35,626. ***Average need-based loan:*** $4434. ***Average need-based gift aid:*** $30,964. ***Average non-need-based aid:*** $17,970. ***Average indebtedness upon graduation:*** $39,531.

APPLYING

Standardized Tests *Required:* SAT or ACT (for admission).

Options: electronic application, early action, deferred entrance.

Required: high school transcript, college preparatory program. ***Recommended:*** minimum 3.0 GPA.

Application deadlines: rolling (transfers), 12/15 (early action).

Notification: continuous (transfers), 1/15 (early action).

CONTACT

Mr. Matt Beirne, Director of Admission, Saint John's University, PO Box 7155, Collegeville, MN 56321-7155. *Phone:* 320-363-5060. *Toll-free phone:* 800-544-1489. *Fax:* 320-363-3206. *E-mail:* admissions@csbsju.edu.

Saint Mary's University of Minnesota

Winona, Minnesota

http://www.smumn.edu/

- **Independent Roman Catholic** comprehensive, founded 1912
- **Small-town** 350-acre campus
- **Coed** 1,442 undergraduate students, 78% full-time, 57% women, 43% men
- **Moderately difficult** entrance level, 92% of applicants were admitted

UNDERGRAD STUDENTS
1,118 full-time, 324 part-time. Students come from 33 states and territories; 18 other countries; 48% are from out of state; 9% Black or African American, non-Hispanic/Latino; 8% Hispanic/Latino; 3% Asian, non-Hispanic/Latino; 0.1% Native Hawaiian or other Pacific Islander, non-Hispanic/Latino; 0.4% American Indian or Alaska Native, non-Hispanic/Latino; 0.4% Two or more races, non-Hispanic/Latino; 8% Race/ethnicity unknown; 3% international; 7% transferred in; 85% live on campus.

Freshmen:
Admission: 1,641 applied, 1,502 admitted, 306 enrolled. ***Average high school GPA:*** 3.4. ***Test scores:*** SAT evidence-based reading and writing scores over 500: 80%; SAT math scores over 500: 87%; ACT scores over 18: 98%; SAT evidence-based reading and writing scores over 600: 33%; SAT math scores over 600: 31%; ACT scores over 24: 44%; SAT evidence-based reading and writing scores over 700: 4%; ACT scores over 30: 8%.

Retention: 82% of full-time freshmen returned.

FACULTY
Total: 524, 19% full-time, 48% with terminal degrees.

Student/faculty ratio: 18:1.

ACADEMICS
Calendar: semesters. *Degrees:* certificates, diplomas, bachelor's, master's, doctoral, post-master's, and postbachelor's certificates.

Special study options: academic remediation for entering students, accelerated degree program, adult/continuing education programs, advanced placement credit, cooperative education, distance learning, double majors, English as a second language, honors programs, independent study, internships, off-campus study, part-time degree program, services for LD students, student-designed majors, study abroad, summer session for credit. ***ROTC:*** Army (c).

Computers: 200 computers/terminals and 50 ports are available on campus for general student use. Students can access the following: campus intranet, computer help desk, free student e-mail accounts, online (class) grades, online (class) registration, online (class) schedules. Campuswide network is available. 100% of college-owned or -operated housing units are wired for high-speed Internet access. Wireless service is available via computer centers, computer labs, dorm rooms, libraries, student centers.

Library: Fitzgerald Library plus 1 other. *Books:* 210,639 (physical), 10,144 (digital/electronic); *Serial titles:* 169 (physical), 82,154 (digital/electronic); *Databases:* 77. Weekly public service hours: 97; students can reserve study rooms.

STUDENT LIFE
Housing options: on-campus residence required through sophomore year; coed, men-only, women-only, special housing for students with disabilities. Campus housing is university owned. Freshman campus housing is guaranteed.

Activities and organizations: drama/theater group, student-run newspaper, radio station, choral group, Student Activity Committee, PR Business Club, Serving Others United in Love (Soul) - Mission Trips, Colleges Against Cancer, Club Hockey, national fraternities, national sororities.

Athletics Member NCAA. All Division III except golf (Division II). ***Intercollegiate sports:*** baseball M, basketball M/W, cross-country running M/W, golf M/W, ice hockey M/W, soccer M/W, softball W, swimming and diving M/W, tennis M/W, track and field M/W, volleyball W. ***Intramural sports:*** basketball M/W, cheerleading W(c), fencing M(c)/W, field hockey M/W(c), football M/W, ice hockey M, lacrosse M(c)/W(c), rugby M(c), skiing (downhill) M(c)/W(c), soccer M/W, softball M/W, tennis M/W, ultimate Frisbee M/W, volleyball M/W, water polo M(c)/W(c).

Campus security: 24-hour emergency response devices and patrols, late-night transport/escort service, controlled dormitory access.

Student services: health clinic, personal/psychological counseling.

COSTS & FINANCIAL AID
Costs (2019–20) ***Comprehensive fee:*** $45,940 includes full-time tuition ($36,050), mandatory fees ($540), and room and board ($9350). Part-time tuition: $1200 per credit. ***College room only:*** $5230.

Financial Aid Of all full-time matriculated undergraduates who enrolled in 2018, 885 applied for aid, 804 were judged to have need, 182 had their need fully met. In 2018, 266 non-need-based awards were made. ***Average percent of need met:*** 73. ***Average financial aid package:*** $27,072. ***Average need-based loan:*** $3595. ***Average need-based gift aid:*** $24,428. ***Average non-need-based aid:*** $20,068. ***Average indebtedness upon graduation:*** $34,917.

APPLYING
Standardized Tests *Required:* SAT or ACT (for admission).

Options: electronic application, early admission, deferred entrance.

Application fee: $25.

Required: essay or personal statement, high school transcript, minimum 2.5 GPA. ***Required for some:*** interview. ***Recommended:*** 2 letters of recommendation.

Notification: continuous (freshmen), continuous (transfers).

CONTACT
Mr. Dan Meyer, Vice President for Enrollment, Saint Mary's University of Minnesota, 700 Terrace Heights, Winona, MN 55987. *Phone:* 507-457-1700. *Toll-free phone:* 800-635-5987. *Fax:* 507-457-1722. *E-mail:* dmeyer@smumn.edu.

St. Olaf College

Northfield, Minnesota

http://www.stolaf.edu/

- **Independent Lutheran** 4-year, founded 1874
- **Small-town** 300-acre campus with easy access to Minneapolis-St. Paul
- **Endowment** $536.1 million
- **Coed** 3,048 undergraduate students, 99% full-time, 57% women, 43% men
- **Very difficult** entrance level, 50% of applicants were admitted

UNDERGRAD STUDENTS
3,023 full-time, 25 part-time. Students come from 49 states and territories; 85 other countries; 53% are from out of state; 3% Black or African American, non-Hispanic/Latino; 7% Hispanic/Latino; 7% Asian, non-Hispanic/Latino; 0.1% Native Hawaiian or other Pacific Islander, non-Hispanic/Latino; 4% Two or more races, non-Hispanic/Latino; 0.9% Race/ethnicity unknown; 10% international; 1% transferred in; 95% live on campus.

Freshmen:
Admission: 5,496 applied, 2,743 admitted, 809 enrolled. ***Average high school GPA:*** 3.7. ***Test scores:*** SAT evidence-based reading and writing scores over 500: 97%; SAT math scores over 500: 97%; ACT scores over 18: 99%; SAT evidence-based reading and writing scores over 600: 76%; SAT math scores over 600: 74%; ACT scores over 24: 86%; SAT evidence-based reading and writing scores over 700: 27%; SAT math scores over 700: 34%; ACT scores over 30: 44%.

Retention: 91% of full-time freshmen returned.

FACULTY
Total: 326, 64% full-time, 81% with terminal degrees.

Student/faculty ratio: 12:1.

ACADEMICS
Calendar: 4-1-4. *Degree:* bachelor's.

Special study options: advanced placement credit, double majors, English as a second language, independent study, internships, off-campus study, part-time degree program, services for LD students, student-designed majors, study abroad, summer session for credit.

Unusual degree programs: 3-2 engineering with Washington University in St. Louis.

Computers: 840 computers/terminals and 3,300 ports are available on campus for general student use. Students can access the following: campus intranet, computer help desk, free student e-mail accounts, online (class) grades, online (class) registration, online (class) schedules. Campuswide network is available. 100% of college-owned or -operated housing units are wired for high-speed Internet access. Wireless service is available via entire campus.

Library: Rolvaag Memorial Library plus 1 other. *Books:* 610,051 (physical), 606,055 (digital/electronic); *Serial titles:* 3,347 (physical), 119,677 (digital/electronic); *Databases:* 349. Weekly public service hours: 112.

STUDENT LIFE
Housing options: on-campus residence required through senior year; coed, special housing for students with disabilities. Campus housing is university owned. Freshman campus housing is guaranteed.

Activities and organizations: drama/theater group, student-run newspaper, radio station, choral group, Student Government Association, Ultimate Frisbee Teams, Ole Spring Relief, Alpha Phi Omega, SARN: Sexual Assault Resource Network.

Athletics Member NCAA. All Division III except golf (Division II), skiing (downhill) (Division II). ***Intercollegiate sports:*** baseball M, basketball M/W, cross-country running M/W, football M, golf M/W, ice hockey M/W, skiing (cross-country) M/W, skiing (downhill) M/W, soccer M/W, softball W, swimming and diving M/W, tennis M/W, track and field M/W, volleyball W, wrestling M. ***Intramural sports:*** badminton M(c)/W(c), basketball M/W, bowling M/W, crew M(c)/W(c), equestrian sports M(c)/W(c), football M/W, ice hockey M(c), lacrosse M(c)/W(c), rowing M(c)/W(c), rugby M(c)/W(c), sand volleyball M/W, soccer M/W, softball M/W, table tennis M/W, tennis M/W, triathlon M/W, ultimate Frisbee M/W, volleyball M(c)/W, water polo M/W.

Campus security: 24-hour emergency response devices and patrols, late-night transport/escort service, controlled dormitory access.

Student services: health clinic, personal/psychological counseling.

COSTS & FINANCIAL AID
Costs (2018–19) ***Comprehensive fee:*** $53,040 includes full-time tuition ($47,840) and room and board ($5200). Part-time tuition: $5980 per course. Part-time tuition and fees vary according to course load. ***College room only:*** $5650. Room and board charges vary according to board plan. ***Payment plan:*** installment. ***Waivers:*** senior citizens and employees or children of employees.

Financial Aid Of all full-time matriculated undergraduates who enrolled in 2018, 2,401 applied for aid, 2,254 were judged to have need, 1,705 had their need fully met. In 2018, 634 non-need-based awards were made. ***Average percent of need met:*** 95. ***Average financial aid package:*** $42,091. ***Average need-based loan:*** $4373. ***Average need-based gift aid:*** $35,236. ***Average non-need-based aid:*** $17,160. ***Average indebtedness upon graduation:*** $29,907. ***Financial aid deadline:*** 3/1.

APPLYING
Standardized Tests *Required:* SAT or ACT (for admission).

Options: electronic application, early decision, deferred entrance.

Required: essay or personal statement, high school transcript, 1 letter of recommendation. ***Recommended:*** 2 letters of recommendation, interview.

Application deadlines: 1/15 (freshmen), 4/1 (transfers).

Early decision deadline: 11/15.

Notification: 3/20 (freshmen), 5/1 (transfers), 12/15 (early decision).

CONTACT
Dave Wagner, Director of Admissions, St. Olaf College, 1520 St. Olaf Avenue, Northfield, MN 55057. *Phone:* 507-786-3025. *Toll-free phone:* 800-800-3025. *Fax:* 507-786-3832. *E-mail:* admissions@stolaf.edu.

Southwest Minnesota State University

Marshall, Minnesota

http://www.smsu.edu/

CONTACT
Mr. Andrew Hlubeck, Director of Admissions, Southwest Minnesota State University, 1501 State Street, Marshall, MN 56258. *Phone:* 507-537-6286. *Toll-free phone:* 800-642-0684. *Fax:* 507-537-7145. *E-mail:* andrew.hlubek@smsu.edu.

University of Minnesota, Crookston

Crookston, Minnesota

http://www.umcrookston.edu/

- **State-supported** 4-year, founded 1966, part of University of Minnesota System
- **Rural** 237-acre campus
- **Endowment** $15.2 million
- **Coed**
- **Minimally difficult** entrance level

FACULTY
Student/faculty ratio: 16:1.

ACADEMICS
Calendar: semesters. *Degree:* bachelor's.
Library: UMC Library. *Books:* 47,423 (physical), 336,375 (digital/electronic); *Serial titles:* 412 (physical), 8,500 (digital/electronic); *Databases:* 152. Weekly public service hours: 76.

STUDENT LIFE
Housing options: coed, special housing for students with disabilities. Campus housing is university owned. Freshman applicants given priority for college housing.

Activities and organizations: drama/theater group, choral group, National Society for Leadership and Success, Archery Club, Crookston Futbol Club, Choir, Student Athletic Advisory Council, national fraternities.

Athletics Member NCAA. All Division II.

Campus security: 24-hour emergency response devices, student patrols, controlled dormitory access.

Student services: health clinic, personal/psychological counseling, women's center.

FINANCIAL AID
Financial Aid Of all full-time matriculated undergraduates who enrolled in 2018, 939 applied for aid, 787 were judged to have need, 146 had their need fully met. In 2018, 92 non-need-based awards were made. ***Average percent of need met:*** 73. ***Average financial aid package:*** $12,358. ***Average need-based loan:*** $4106. ***Average need-based gift aid:*** $9540. ***Average non-need-based aid:*** $2328. ***Average indebtedness upon graduation:*** $28,291.

APPLYING
Standardized Tests *Required:* SAT or ACT (for admission). *Recommended:* ACT (for admission).

Options: electronic application, deferred entrance.

Application fee: $30.

Required: high school transcript, minimum 2.0 GPA, minimum ACT composite score of 21 or SAT of 980.

CONTACT
Michelle Christopherson, Director of Admissions, University of Minnesota, Crookston, 2900 University Avenue, Crookston, MN 56716-5001. *Phone:* 218-281-8679. *Toll-free phone:* 800-862-6466. *E-mail:* mchristo@crk.umn.edu.

University of Minnesota, Duluth

Duluth, Minnesota

http://www.d.umn.edu/

- **State-supported** comprehensive, founded 1947, part of University of Minnesota System
- **Suburban** 250-acre campus
- **Endowment** $170.8 million
- **Coed** 9,977 undergraduate students, 88% full-time, 48% women, 52% men
- **Moderately difficult** entrance level, 74% of applicants were admitted

UNDERGRAD STUDENTS
8,799 full-time, 1,178 part-time. Students come from 38 states and territories; 35 other countries; 12% are from out of state; 2% Black or African American, non-Hispanic/Latino; 3% Hispanic/Latino; 4% Asian, non-Hispanic/Latino; 0.1% Native Hawaiian or other Pacific Islander, non-Hispanic/Latino; 0.5% American Indian or Alaska Native, non-Hispanic/Latino; 3% Two or more races, non-Hispanic/Latino; 9%

Race/ethnicity unknown; 2% international; 4% transferred in; 33% live on campus.

Freshmen:
Admission: 9,204 applied, 6,843 admitted, 2,221 enrolled. ***Average high school GPA:*** 3.6. ***Test scores:*** SAT evidence-based reading and writing scores over 500: 101%; SAT math scores over 500: 97%; ACT scores over 18: 98%; SAT evidence-based reading and writing scores over 600: 57%; SAT math scores over 600: 53%; ACT scores over 24: 53%; SAT evidence-based reading and writing scores over 700: 12%; SAT math scores over 700: 23%; ACT scores over 30: 9%.

Retention: 79% of full-time freshmen returned.

FACULTY
Total: 599, 82% full-time, 67% with terminal degrees.

Student/faculty ratio: 18:1.

ACADEMICS
Calendar: semesters. *Degrees:* certificates, bachelor's, master's, doctoral, and postbachelor's certificates.

Special study options: academic remediation for entering students, adult/continuing education programs, advanced placement credit, distance learning, double majors, English as a second language, honors programs, independent study, internships, off-campus study, part-time degree program, services for LD students, student-designed majors, study abroad, summer session for credit. ***ROTC:*** Air Force (b).

Computers: 548 computers/terminals are available on campus for general student use. Students can access the following: campus intranet, computer help desk, free student e-mail accounts, online (class) grades, online (class) registration, online (class) schedules. Campuswide network is available. 100% of college-owned or -operated housing units are wired for high-speed Internet access. Wireless service is available via entire campus.

Library: Kathryn A. Martin Library. *Books:* 319,423 (physical), 611,335 (digital/electronic); *Serial titles:* 7,397 (physical), 130,550 (digital/electronic); *Databases:* 150. Weekly public service hours: 94; students can reserve study rooms.

STUDENT LIFE
Housing options: coed, men-only, women-only, special housing for students with disabilities. Campus housing is university owned. Freshman applicants given priority for college housing.

Activities and organizations: drama/theater group, student-run newspaper, radio station, choral group, marching band, UMD Student Association, Newman Catholic Campus Ministries, Panhellenic Council, Coloring Club, Rod and Gun Club at UMD, national fraternities, national sororities.

Athletics Member NCAA. All Division II except men's and women's ice hockey (Division I). ***Intercollegiate sports:*** badminton M(c)/W(c), baseball M(s), basketball M(s)/W(s), cheerleading W(c), cross-country running M(s)/W(s), football M(s), ice hockey M(s)/W(s), lacrosse M(s)(c)/W(s)(c), rugby M(c)/W(c), skiing (downhill) W(c), soccer M(c)/W(s), softball W(s), tennis W(s), track and field M/W, volleyball M(c)/W(s), water polo W. ***Intramural sports:*** badminton M/W, basketball M/W, bowling M/W, football M/W, golf M/W, ice hockey M/W, rock climbing M(c)/W(c), rowing M(c)/W(c), soccer M/W, softball M/W, swimming and diving M(c)/W(c), table tennis M(c)/W(c), tennis W, ultimate Frisbee M(c)/W(c), volleyball M/W, water polo M(c)/W(c), wrestling M(c).

Campus security: 24-hour emergency response devices and patrols, late-night transport/escort service.

Student services: health clinic, personal/psychological counseling, women's center, veterans affairs office.

COSTS & FINANCIAL AID
Costs (2018–19) ***Tuition:*** state resident $12,016 full-time, $462 per credit hour part-time; nonresident $17,134 full-time, $659 per credit hour part-time. Full-time tuition and fees vary according to course load, program, and reciprocity agreements. Part-time tuition and fees vary according to course load, program, and reciprocity agreements. ***Required fees:*** $1351 full-time. ***Room and board:*** $7760; room only: $3668. Room and board charges vary according to board plan and housing facility. ***Payment plan:*** installment. ***Waivers:*** children of alumni and employees or children of employees.

Financial Aid Of all full-time matriculated undergraduates who enrolled in 2017, 7,108 applied for aid, 5,070 were judged to have need, 1,527 had their need fully met. 496 Federal Work-Study jobs (averaging $1354). 1,566 state and other part-time jobs (averaging $664). In 2017, 1327 non-need-based awards were made. ***Average percent of need met:*** 75. ***Average financial aid package:*** $13,159. ***Average need-based loan:*** $6769. ***Average need-based gift aid:*** $8195. ***Average non-need-based aid:*** $2259. ***Average indebtedness upon graduation:*** $29,910.

APPLYING
Standardized Tests *Required:* SAT or ACT (for admission).

Options: electronic application.

Application fee: $40.

Required: high school transcript. ***Required for some:*** interview. ***Recommended:*** essay or personal statement.

Application deadlines: 6/15 (freshmen), 6/15 (out-of-state freshmen), 6/15 (transfers).

Notification: continuous until 9/15 (freshmen), continuous until 9/15 (out-of-state freshmen), continuous (transfers).

CONTACT
Mr. Scott Schulz, Director of Undergraduate Recruitment, University of Minnesota, Duluth, 1049 University Drive, Duluth, MN 55812-2496. *Phone:* 218-726-7171. *Toll-free phone:* 800-232-1339. *Fax:* 218-726-7040. *E-mail:* sschulz1@d.umn.edu.

University of Minnesota, Morris

Morris, Minnesota

http://www.morris.umn.edu/

- **State-supported** 4-year, founded 1959, part of University of Minnesota System
- **Rural** 130-acre campus
- **Endowment** $15.4 million
- **Coed** 1,554 undergraduate students, 94% full-time, 57% women, 43% men
- **Moderately difficult** entrance level, 63% of applicants were admitted

UNDERGRAD STUDENTS
1,463 full-time, 91 part-time. Students come from 32 states and territories; 23 other countries; 17% are from out of state; 2% Black or African American, non-Hispanic/Latino; 5% Hispanic/Latino; 3% Asian, non-Hispanic/Latino; 8% American Indian or Alaska Native, non-Hispanic/Latino; 13% Two or more races, non-Hispanic/Latino; 0.5% Race/ethnicity unknown; 11% international; 5% transferred in; 52% live on campus.

Freshmen:
Admission: 3,139 applied, 1,971 admitted, 370 enrolled. ***Average high school GPA:*** 3.6. ***Test scores:*** SAT evidence-based reading and writing scores over 500: 81%; SAT math scores over 500: 95%; ACT scores over 18: 97%; SAT evidence-based reading and writing scores over 600: 43%; SAT math scores over 600: 67%; ACT scores over 24: 58%; SAT evidence-based reading and writing scores over 700: 19%; SAT math scores over 700: 24%; ACT scores over 30: 14%.

Retention: 77% of full-time freshmen returned.

FACULTY
Total: 158, 79% full-time, 82% with terminal degrees.

Student/faculty ratio: 11:1.

ACADEMICS
Calendar: semesters. *Degree:* bachelor's.

Special study options: advanced placement credit, distance learning, double majors, English as a second language, freshman honors college, honors programs, independent study, internships, off-campus study, part-time degree program, services for LD students, student-designed majors, study abroad, summer session for credit.

Unusual degree programs: 3-2 engineering with University of Minnesota, Twin Cities Campus.

Computers: 350 computers/terminals and 548 ports are available on campus for general student use. Students can access the following: campus intranet, computer help desk, free student e-mail accounts, online (class) grades, online (class) registration, online (class) schedules.

Campuswide network is available. 100% of college-owned or -operated housing units are wired for high-speed Internet access. Wireless service is available via classrooms, computer labs, dorm rooms, learning centers, libraries, student centers.
Library: Rodney A. Briggs Library plus 1 other. *Books:* 218,848 (physical), 800,000 (digital/electronic); *Serial titles:* 140 (physical), 121,380 (digital/electronic); *Databases:* 112. Weekly public service hours: 99.

STUDENT LIFE
Housing options: coed, special housing for students with disabilities. Campus housing is university owned. Freshman campus housing is guaranteed.

Activities and organizations: drama/theater group, student-run newspaper, radio station, choral group, Student Radio Station, Inter-Varsity Christian Fellowship, Jazz Ensemble/Concert Choir, Big Friend, Little Friend, Student Newspaper.

Athletics Member NCAA. All Division III except golf (Division II). ***Intercollegiate sports:*** baseball M, basketball M/W, cross-country running M/W, football M, golf M/W, soccer M/W, softball W, swimming and diving W, tennis M/W, track and field M/W, volleyball W. ***Intramural sports:*** baseball M/W, basketball M/W, bowling M/W, cheerleading M(c)/W(c), equestrian sports M(c)/W(c), fencing M(c), field hockey W(c), football M/W, racquetball M(c)/W(c), rugby M(c)/W(c), sand volleyball M/W, skiing (cross-country) M/W, soccer M(c)/W(c), softball M/W, swimming and diving M(c)/W(c), table tennis M/W, triathlon M(c)/W(c), ultimate Frisbee M(c)/W(c), volleyball M/W, weight lifting M(c)/W(c).

Campus security: 24-hour emergency response devices and patrols, late-night transport/escort service, controlled dormitory access.

Student services: health clinic, personal/psychological counseling, women's center, legal services, veterans affairs office.

COSTS & FINANCIAL AID
Costs (2018–19) ***Tuition:*** state resident $12,142 full-time, $467 per credit hour part-time; nonresident $14,170 full-time, $545 per credit hour part-time. Full-time tuition and fees vary according to reciprocity agreements. Part-time tuition and fees vary according to course load and reciprocity agreements. ***Required fees:*** $1172 full-time. ***Room and board:*** $8342; room only: $3942. Room and board charges vary according to board plan and housing facility. ***Payment plan:*** installment. ***Waivers:*** senior citizens and employees or children of employees.

Financial Aid Of all full-time matriculated undergraduates who enrolled in 2016, 1,256 applied for aid, 1,019 were judged to have need, 257 had their need fully met. 307 Federal Work-Study jobs (averaging $1317). 96 state and other part-time jobs (averaging $1515). In 2016, 188 non-need-based awards were made. ***Average percent of need met:*** 75. ***Average financial aid package:*** $12,633. ***Average need-based loan:*** $3730. ***Average need-based gift aid:*** $10,095. ***Average non-need-based aid:*** $4187. ***Average indebtedness upon graduation:*** $25,732.

APPLYING
Standardized Tests *Required:* SAT or ACT (for admission).

Options: electronic application, deferred entrance.

Application fee: $35.

Required: high school transcript. ***Required for some:*** essay or personal statement, 1 letter of recommendation, interview.

Application deadlines: 8/1 (freshmen), 5/1 (transfers).

Notification: continuous (freshmen), continuous (transfers).

CONTACT
Jennifer Zych-Herrmann, Director of Admissions, University of Minnesota, Morris, 600 East 4th Street, Morris, MN 56267-2134. *Phone:* 320-539-6035 Ext. 6035. *Toll-free phone:* 888-866-3382.

University of Minnesota Rochester

Rochester, Minnesota

http://www.r.umn.edu/

CONTACT
University of Minnesota Rochester, 111 South Broadway, Suite 300, Rochester, MN 55904.

University of Minnesota, Twin Cities Campus

Minneapolis, Minnesota

http://www.twin-cities.umn.edu/

- **State-supported** university, founded 1851, part of University of Minnesota System
- **Urban** 2000-acre campus with easy access to Minneapolis-St. Paul
- **Coed** 34,633 undergraduate students, 87% full-time, 53% women, 47% men
- **Moderately difficult** entrance level, 52% of applicants were admitted

UNDERGRAD STUDENTS
30,001 full-time, 4,632 part-time. Students come from 51 states and territories; 98 other countries; 28% are from out of state; 5% Black or African American, non-Hispanic/Latino; 4% Hispanic/Latino; 10% Asian, non-Hispanic/Latino; 0.1% Native Hawaiian or other Pacific Islander, non-Hispanic/Latino; 0.3% American Indian or Alaska Native, non-Hispanic/Latino; 4% Two or more races, non-Hispanic/Latino; 1% Race/ethnicity unknown; 8% international; 6% transferred in; 22% live on campus.

Freshmen:
Admission: 43,444 applied, 22,525 admitted, 5,977 enrolled. ***Test scores:*** SAT evidence-based reading and writing scores over 500: 99%; SAT math scores over 500: 99%; ACT scores over 18: 99%; SAT evidence-based reading and writing scores over 600: 85%; SAT math scores over 600: 89%; ACT scores over 24: 90%; SAT evidence-based reading and writing scores over 700: 36%; SAT math scores over 700: 60%; ACT scores over 30: 39%.

Retention: 93% of full-time freshmen returned.

FACULTY
Total: 3,785, 69% full-time, 69% with terminal degrees.

Student/faculty ratio: 17:1.

ACADEMICS
Calendar: semesters. *Degrees:* certificates, diplomas, bachelor's, master's, doctoral, post-master's, and postbachelor's certificates.

Special study options: academic remediation for entering students, accelerated degree program, adult/continuing education programs, advanced placement credit, cooperative education, distance learning, double majors, English as a second language, external degree program, freshman honors college, honors programs, independent study, internships, off-campus study, part-time degree program, services for LD students, student-designed majors, study abroad, summer session for credit. ***ROTC:*** Army (b), Navy (b), Air Force (b).

Computers: Students can access the following: computer help desk, free student e-mail accounts, online (class) grades, online (class) registration, online (class) schedules. Campuswide network is available. Wireless service is available via entire campus.
Library: Wilson Library plus 17 others. *Books:* 4.1 million (physical), 1.2 million (digital/electronic); *Serial titles:* 153,056 (physical), 290,349 (digital/electronic); *Databases:* 947. Students can reserve study rooms.

STUDENT LIFE
Housing options: coed, cooperative, special housing for students with disabilities. Campus housing is university owned. Freshman campus housing is guaranteed.

Activities and organizations: drama/theater group, student-run newspaper, radio and television station, choral group, marching band, Student Government, national fraternities, national sororities.

Athletics Member NCAA. All Division I except football (Division I-A). ***Intercollegiate sports:*** baseball M(s), basketball M(s)/W(s), cross-country running M(s)/W(s), golf M(s)/W(s)(c), gymnastics M(s)/W(s), ice hockey M(s)/W(s), soccer W(s), softball W(s), swimming and diving M(s)/W(s), tennis M(s)/W(s), track and field M(s)/W(s), volleyball W(s), wrestling M(s). ***Intramural sports:*** baseball M/W, basketball M/W, bowling M/W, crew M/W, football M/W, golf M/W, ice hockey M/W, rugby M/W, skiing (cross-country) M/W, skiing (downhill) M/W, soccer M/W, softball M/W, tennis M/W, volleyball M/W, water polo M/W, wrestling M/W.

Campus security: 24-hour emergency response devices and patrols, student patrols, late-night transport/escort service, controlled dormitory access.

Student services: health clinic, personal/psychological counseling, women's center, legal services, veterans affairs office.

COSTS & FINANCIAL AID
Costs (2018–19) ***Tuition:*** state resident $13,058 full-time, $502 per credit part-time; nonresident $28,736 full-time, $933 per credit part-time. Full-time tuition and fees vary according to program and reciprocity agreements. Part-time tuition and fees vary according to course load, program, and reciprocity agreements. ***Required fees:*** $1635 full-time. ***Room and board:*** $10,312; room only: $5922. Room and board charges vary according to board plan, housing facility, and location. ***Payment plan:*** installment. ***Waivers:*** senior citizens.

Financial Aid Of all full-time matriculated undergraduates who enrolled in 2018, 19,792 applied for aid, 13,945 were judged to have need, 3,004 had their need fully met. In 2018, 2376 non-need-based awards were made. ***Average percent of need met:*** 72. ***Average financial aid package:*** $13,482. ***Average need-based loan:*** $4370. ***Average need-based gift aid:*** $10,672. ***Average non-need-based aid:*** $4923. ***Average indebtedness upon graduation:*** $26,262.

APPLYING
Standardized Tests *Required:* SAT or ACT (for admission).

Options: electronic application, early admission, deferred entrance.

Application fee: $55.

Required: high school transcript. ***Recommended:*** minimum 2.0 GPA.

Application deadlines: rolling (freshmen), rolling (out-of-state freshmen), rolling (transfers).

Notification: continuous (freshmen), continuous (out-of-state freshmen), continuous (transfers).

CONTACT
Heidi Meyer, Executive Director of Admissions, University of Minnesota, Twin Cities Campus, 240 Williamson, Minneapolis, MN 55455-0213. *Phone:* 612-625-2008. *Toll-free phone:* 800-752-1000. *Fax:* 612-626-1693. *E-mail:* admissions@tc.umn.edu.

University of Northwestern–St. Paul

St. Paul, Minnesota

http://www.unwsp.edu/

- **Independent nondenominational** comprehensive, founded 1902
- **Suburban** 107-acre campus with easy access to Minneapolis-St. Paul
- **Endowment** $17.9 million
- **Coed** 3,443 undergraduate students, 61% full-time, 62% women, 38% men
- **Moderately difficult** entrance level, 90% of applicants were admitted

UNDERGRAD STUDENTS
2,097 full-time, 1,346 part-time. Students come from 32 states and territories; 9 other countries; 22% are from out of state; 4% Black or African American, non-Hispanic/Latino; 6% Hispanic/Latino; 4% Asian, non-Hispanic/Latino; 0.3% American Indian or Alaska Native, non-Hispanic/Latino; 4% Two or more races, non-Hispanic/Latino; 2% Race/ethnicity unknown; 0.8% international; 5% transferred in; 56% live on campus.

Freshmen:
Admission: 930 applied, 840 admitted, 283 enrolled. ***Average high school GPA:*** 3.5. ***Test scores:*** SAT evidence-based reading and writing scores over 500: 80%; SAT math scores over 500: 90%; ACT scores over 18: 95%; SAT evidence-based reading and writing scores over 600: 43%; SAT math scores over 600: 37%; ACT scores over 24: 54%; SAT evidence-based reading and writing scores over 700: 17%; SAT math scores over 700: 3%; ACT scores over 30: 12%.

Retention: 79% of full-time freshmen returned.

FACULTY
Total: 313, 26% full-time, 52% with terminal degrees.

Student/faculty ratio: 18:1.

ACADEMICS
Calendar: semesters. *Degrees:* certificates, associate, bachelor's, master's, and postbachelor's certificates.

Special study options: academic remediation for entering students, adult/continuing education programs, advanced placement credit, distance learning, double majors, honors programs, independent study, internships, off-campus study, part-time degree program, services for LD students, student-designed majors, study abroad, summer session for credit. ***ROTC:*** Army (c), Air Force (c).

Unusual degree programs: 3-2 BA/MDiv in Pastoral Ministry.

Computers: 200 computers/terminals and 1,350 ports are available on campus for general student use. Students can access the following: campus intranet, computer help desk, free student e-mail accounts, online (class) grades, online (class) registration, online (class) schedules, network file space, personal web site, integrated student portal, b/w and color printing, virtual labs. Campuswide network is available. 100% of college-owned or -operated housing units are wired for high-speed Internet access. Wireless service is available via classrooms, computer centers, computer labs, dorm rooms, learning centers, libraries, student centers.

Library: Berntsen Resource Center. *Books:* 87,336 (physical), 377,241 (digital/electronic); *Serial titles:* 408 (physical), 49,850 (digital/electronic); *Databases:* 102.

STUDENT LIFE
Housing options: on-campus residence required through junior year; coed, men-only, women-only, special housing for students with disabilities. Campus housing is university owned. Freshman campus housing is guaranteed.

Activities and organizations: drama/theater group, student-run newspaper, radio and television station, choral group, Northwestern Student Association (student government), The Gathering (religious group), Student Missions Fellowship, Guardian Angels, Outreach Ministries.

Athletics Member NCAA, NCCAA. All NCAA Division III. ***Intercollegiate sports:*** baseball M, basketball M/W, cross-country running M/W, football M, golf M/W, ice hockey M(c), lacrosse M/W, soccer M/W, softball W, tennis M/W, track and field M/W, volleyball M(c)/W. ***Intramural sports:*** basketball M/W, football M/W, softball M/W, table tennis M/W, tennis M/W, ultimate Frisbee M/W, volleyball M/W.

Campus security: 24-hour emergency response devices and patrols, late-night transport/escort service, controlled dormitory access.

Student services: health clinic, personal/psychological counseling.

COSTS & FINANCIAL AID
Costs (2019–20) ***Comprehensive fee:*** $41,870 includes full-time tuition ($31,580), mandatory fees ($630), and room and board ($9660). Part-time tuition: $1345 per credit. ***College room only:*** $5810.

Financial Aid Of all full-time matriculated undergraduates who enrolled in 2017, 1,425 applied for aid, 1,266 were judged to have need, 114 had their need fully met. 217 Federal Work-Study jobs (averaging $1196). 253 state and other part-time jobs (averaging $1946). In 2017, 300 non-need-based awards were made. ***Average percent of need met:*** 69. ***Average financial aid package:*** $22,024. ***Average need-based loan:*** $4868. ***Average need-based gift aid:*** $17,076. ***Average non-need-based aid:*** $10,180. ***Average indebtedness upon graduation:*** $45,485. ***Financial aid deadline:*** 8/1.

APPLYING
Standardized Tests *Required:* SAT or ACT (for admission).

Options: electronic application, early admission, early action, deferred entrance.

Application fee: $25.

Required: essay or personal statement, high school transcript, minimum 2.0 GPA, 2 letters of recommendation, lifestyle agreement, statement of Christian faith. ***Required for some:*** interview. ***Recommended:*** minimum 3.0 GPA.

Application deadlines: 8/1 (freshmen), 8/1 (out-of-state freshmen), 8/1 (transfers), rolling (early action).

Notification: continuous (freshmen), continuous (out-of-state freshmen), continuous (transfers), rolling (early action).

CONTACT
Mr. Micheal R. Moroney, Vice President for Enrollment Management, University of Northwestern–St. Paul, 3003 Snelling Avenue North, St. Paul, MN 55113-1598. *Phone:* 651-631-5482. *Toll-free phone:* 800-827-6827. *Fax:* 651-631-5680. *E-mail:* mrmoroney@unwsp.edu.

University of St. Thomas

St. Paul, Minnesota

http://www.stthomas.edu/

- **Independent Roman Catholic** university, founded 1885
- **Urban** 78-acre campus with easy access to Minneapolis-St. Paul
- **Endowment** $494.0 million
- **Coed** 6,395 undergraduate students, 96% full-time, 47% women, 53% men
- **Moderately difficult** entrance level, 82% of applicants were admitted

UNDERGRAD STUDENTS

6,162 full-time, 233 part-time. 3% Black or African American, non-Hispanic/Latino; 5% Hispanic/Latino; 4% Asian, non-Hispanic/Latino; 0.2% American Indian or Alaska Native, non-Hispanic/Latino; 3% Two or more races, non-Hispanic/Latino; 4% Race/ethnicity unknown; 3% international; 3% transferred in; 40% live on campus.

Freshmen:

Admission: 6,819 applied, 5,583 admitted, 1,823 enrolled. ***Average high school GPA:*** 3.6. ***Test scores:*** SAT evidence-based reading and writing scores over 500: 97%; SAT math scores over 500: 94%; ACT scores over 18: 100%; SAT evidence-based reading and writing scores over 600: 63%; SAT math scores over 600: 62%; ACT scores over 24: 75%; SAT evidence-based reading and writing scores over 700: 16%; SAT math scores over 700: 30%; ACT scores over 30: 19%.

Retention: 86% of full-time freshmen returned.

FACULTY

Total: 826, 55% full-time, 66% with terminal degrees.

Student/faculty ratio: 14:1.

ACADEMICS

Calendar: 4-1-4. *Degrees:* certificates, associate, bachelor's, master's, doctoral, post-master's, and postbachelor's certificates.

Special study options: accelerated degree program, advanced placement credit, cooperative education, distance learning, double majors, English as a second language, honors programs, independent study, internships, off-campus study, part-time degree program, services for LD students, student-designed majors, study abroad, summer session for credit. ***ROTC:*** Army (c), Navy (c), Air Force (b).

Computers: Students can access the following: campus intranet, computer help desk, free student e-mail accounts, online (class) grades, online (class) registration, online (class) schedules. Campuswide network is available. 100% of college-owned or -operated housing units are wired for high-speed Internet access. Wireless service is available via entire campus.

Library: O'Shaughnessy-Frey Library plus 7 others. *Books:* 399,594 (physical), 1.2 million (digital/electronic); *Serial titles:* 1,701 (physical), 76,726 (digital/electronic); *Databases:* 308. Students can reserve study rooms.

STUDENT LIFE

Housing options: coed, men-only, women-only, special housing for students with disabilities. Campus housing is university owned. Freshman applicants given priority for college housing.

Activities and organizations: drama/theater group, student-run newspaper, radio and television station, choral group.

Athletics Member NCAA. All Division III except golf (Division II). ***Intercollegiate sports:*** baseball M, basketball M/W, cross-country running M/W, football M, golf M/W, ice hockey M/W, lacrosse M(c)/W(c), soccer M/W, softball W, swimming and diving M/W, tennis M/W, volleyball W. ***Intramural sports:*** badminton M/W, basketball M/W, crew M(c)/W(c), golf M/W, racquetball M/W, sailing M(c)/W, skiing (downhill) M(c)/W(c), soccer M/W, table tennis M/W, tennis M/W, track and field M(c)/W(c), volleyball M/W.

Campus security: 24-hour emergency response devices and patrols, late-night transport/escort service, controlled dormitory access.

Student services: health clinic, personal/psychological counseling, women's center, veterans affairs office.

COSTS & FINANCIAL AID

Costs (2019–20) ***Comprehensive fee:*** $56,942 includes full-time tuition ($44,780), mandatory fees ($1000), and room and board ($11,162). ***College room only:*** $6812.

Financial Aid Of all full-time matriculated undergraduates who enrolled in 2018, 4,323 applied for aid, 3,475 were judged to have need, 302 had their need fully met. 1,048 Federal Work-Study jobs (averaging $3119). 867 state and other part-time jobs (averaging $3087). In 2018, 752 non-need-based awards were made. ***Average percent of need met:*** 86. ***Average financial aid package:*** $29,751. ***Average need-based loan:*** $8238. ***Average need-based gift aid:*** $23,085. ***Average non-need-based aid:*** $21,057. ***Average indebtedness upon graduation:*** $40,983.

APPLYING

Standardized Tests *Required:* SAT or ACT (for admission).

Options: electronic application, early action, deferred entrance.

Required: essay or personal statement, high school transcript. ***Recommended:*** interview.

Application deadlines: rolling (freshmen), rolling (transfers).

Notification: continuous (freshmen), continuous (transfers).

CONTACT

University of St. Thomas, 2115 Summit Avenue, St. Paul, MN 55105-1096. *Toll-free phone:* 800-328-6819.

Walden University

Minneapolis, Minnesota

http://www.waldenu.edu/

CONTACT

Walden University, 100 Washington South, Suite 900, Minneapolis, MN 55401. *Toll-free phone:* 866-492-5336.

Winona State University

Winona, Minnesota

http://www.winona.edu/

- **State-supported** comprehensive, founded 1858, part of Minnesota State Colleges and Universities System
- **Small-town** 125-acre campus with easy access to Minneapolis-St.Paul
- **Endowment** $22.6 million
- **Coed**
- **Moderately difficult** entrance level

FACULTY

Student/faculty ratio: 18:1.

ACADEMICS

Calendar: semesters. *Degrees:* associate, bachelor's, master's, doctoral, post-master's, and postbachelor's certificates.

Library: Darrel W. Krueger Library. *Books:* 242,347 (physical), 59,498 (digital/electronic); *Serial titles:* 2,097 (physical), 34,000 (digital/electronic); *Databases:* 138. Weekly public service hours: 99; students can reserve study rooms.

STUDENT LIFE

Housing options: coed, men-only, women-only, special housing for students with disabilities. Campus housing is university owned and leased by the school. Freshman campus housing is guaranteed.

Activities and organizations: drama/theater group, student-run newspaper, radio station, choral group, University Program Activities Committee, Student Senate, Residence Hall Association, Inter Varsity, national fraternities, national sororities.

Athletics Member NCAA. All Division II except gymnastics (Division III).

Campus security: 24-hour emergency response devices and patrols, student patrols, late-night transport/escort service, controlled dormitory access, security cameras.

Student services: health clinic, personal/psychological counseling.

COSTS & FINANCIAL AID

Costs (2018–19) ***Tuition:*** state resident $7377 full-time, $244 per credit hour part-time; nonresident $13,298 full-time, $443 per credit hour part-time. Full-time tuition and fees vary according to location, program, and reciprocity agreements. Part-time tuition and fees vary according to course load, location, program, and reciprocity agreements. ***Required fees:*** $2049 full-time, $41 per credit hour part-time, $485 per term part-time. ***Room and board:*** $8746; room only: $5750. Room and board charges vary according to board plan, housing facility, and location.

Financial Aid Of all full-time matriculated undergraduates who enrolled in 2017, 5,240 applied for aid, 3,826 were judged to have need, 409 had their need fully met. In 2017, 877 non-need-based awards were made. ***Average percent of need met:*** 53. ***Average financial aid package:*** $5458. ***Average need-based loan:*** $3918. ***Average need-based gift aid:*** $6107. ***Average non-need-based aid:*** $3379. ***Average indebtedness upon graduation:*** $35,434.

APPLYING

Standardized Tests *Required:* SAT or ACT (for admission).

Options: electronic application, deferred entrance.

Application fee: $20.

Required: high school transcript, 16 high school preparation requirements and either minimum composite ACT of 21 with top two-thirds of high school class rank or minimum cumulative GPA of 2.75 or, minimum composite ACT of 18 with either top half of high school class rank or minimum cumulative high school GPA of 3.0.

CONTACT

Brian Jicinsky, Director of Admissions, Winona State University, 175 West Mark Street, Winona, MN 55987. *Phone:* 507-457-5100. *Toll-free phone:* 800-DIAL WSU. *Fax:* 507-457-5620. *E-mail:* admissions@winona.edu.

MISSISSIPPI

Alcorn State University

Lorman, Mississippi

http://www.alcorn.edu/

- **State-supported** comprehensive, founded 1871, part of Mississippi Institutions of Higher Learning
- **Rural** 1756-acre campus
- **Endowment** $17.3 million
- **Coed**
- **Moderately difficult** entrance level

FACULTY

Student/faculty ratio: 19:1.

ACADEMICS

Calendar: semesters. *Degrees:* associate, bachelor's, master's, and post-master's certificates.

Library: John Dewey Boyd Library plus 1 other. *Books:* 412,321 (physical), 441,114 (digital/electronic); *Serial titles:* 312 (physical), 75,805 (digital/electronic); *Databases:* 91. Weekly public service hours: 88; study areas open 24 hours, 5–7 days a week; students can reserve study rooms.

STUDENT LIFE

Housing options: men-only, women-only. Campus housing is university owned. Freshman campus housing is guaranteed.

Activities and organizations: drama/theater group, student-run newspaper, radio and television station, choral group, marching band, marching band, Gospel Choir, inter-faith choir, national fraternities, national sororities.

Athletics Member NCAA. All Division I.

Campus security: 24-hour emergency response devices and patrols, late-night transport/escort service, controlled dormitory access.

Student services: health clinic, personal/psychological counseling.

COSTS & FINANCIAL AID

Costs (2018–19) ***Tuition:*** state resident $7084 full-time, $592 per credit hour part-time; nonresident $7084 full-time, $592 per credit hour part-time. Full-time tuition and fees vary according to course load. Part-time tuition and fees vary according to course load. ***Room and board:*** $10,374; room only: $7078. Room and board charges vary according to board plan and housing facility.

Financial Aid Of all full-time matriculated undergraduates who enrolled in 2018, 1,236 applied for aid, 1,108 were judged to have need, 241 had their need fully met. In 2018, 936 non-need-based awards were made. ***Average percent of need met:*** 78. ***Average financial aid package:*** $7342. ***Average need-based loan:*** $6404. ***Average need-based gift aid:*** $3028. ***Average non-need-based aid:*** $5149. ***Average indebtedness upon graduation:*** $33,766.

APPLYING

Standardized Tests *Required:* SAT or ACT (for admission).

Options: electronic application, deferred entrance.

Required: high school transcript, minimum 2.0 GPA.

CONTACT

Mrs. Kantangelia Tenner, Director of Admissions, Alcorn State University, 1000 ASU Drive, #300, Alcorn State, MS 39096-7500. *Phone:* 601-877-6147. *Toll-free phone:* 800-222-6790. *Fax:* 601-877-6347. *E-mail:* ksampson@alcorn.edu.

Belhaven University

Jackson, Mississippi

http://www.belhaven.edu/

- **Independent Presbyterian** comprehensive, founded 1883
- **Urban** 46-acre campus
- **Endowment** $5.6 million
- **Coed**
- **Moderately difficult** entrance level

FACULTY

Student/faculty ratio: 15:1.

ACADEMICS

Calendar: semesters. *Degrees:* certificates, associate, bachelor's, master's, doctoral, and postbachelor's certificates.

Library: Warren A. Hood Library plus 1 other. *Books:* 42,425 (physical), 106,114 (digital/electronic); *Serial titles:* 160 (physical), 75,718 (digital/electronic); *Databases:* 96. Weekly public service hours: 104.

STUDENT LIFE

Housing options: men-only, women-only. Campus housing is university owned. Freshman campus housing is guaranteed.

Activities and organizations: drama/theater group, student-run newspaper, choral group, marching band, Belhaven Activities Team, Fellowship of Christian Athletes, Reformed University Fellowship, Phi Beta Lambda, Belhaven University New Music Society.

Athletics Member NCAA. All Division III.

Campus security: 24-hour emergency response devices and patrols, late-night transport/escort service, controlled dormitory access.

Student services: health clinic, personal/psychological counseling.

COSTS & FINANCIAL AID

Costs (2018–19) ***Comprehensive fee:*** $33,800 includes full-time tuition ($24,950), mandatory fees ($350), and room and board ($8500). Full-time tuition and fees vary according to location and program. Part-time tuition: $425 per credit hour. Part-time tuition and fees vary according to course load, location, and program. ***Required fees:*** $25 per credit hour part-time. ***Room and board:*** Room and board charges vary according to housing facility.

Financial Aid Of all full-time matriculated undergraduates who enrolled in 2017, 1,102 applied for aid, 968 were judged to have need, 88 had their need fully met. In 2017, 168 non-need-based awards were made. ***Average percent of need met:*** 65. ***Average financial aid package:*** $16,092. ***Average need-based loan:*** $3999. ***Average need-based gift aid:*** $11,243. ***Average non-need-based aid:*** $10,963. ***Average indebtedness upon graduation:*** $8654.

APPLYING

Standardized Tests *Required:* SAT or ACT (for admission).

Options: electronic application, early admission, deferred entrance.

Application fee: $25.

Required: high school transcript, minimum 2.0 GPA, 1 letter of recommendation. ***Required for some:*** essay or personal statement, interview.

CONTACT

Ms. Suzanne T. Sullivan, Assistant Vice President for Traditional and Online Admissions, Belhaven University, 1500 Peachtree Street, Jackson, MS 39202. *Phone:* 601-968-5940. *Toll-free phone:* 800-960-5940. *Fax:* 601-968-8946. *E-mail:* admission@belhaven.edu.

Blue Mountain College
Blue Mountain, Mississippi
http://www.bmc.edu/

- **Independent Southern Baptist** comprehensive, founded 1873
- **Rural** 190-acre campus with easy access to Memphis
- **Endowment** $15.6 million
- **Coed**
- **Moderately difficult** entrance level

FACULTY
Student/faculty ratio: 14:1.

ACADEMICS
Calendar: semesters. *Degrees:* bachelor's and master's.
Library: Guyton Library plus 1 other. *Books:* 41,725 (physical), 35,897 (digital/electronic); *Serial titles:* 143 (physical); *Databases:* 24. Weekly public service hours: 70.

STUDENT LIFE
Housing options: men-only, women-only. Campus housing is university owned.

Activities and organizations: drama/theater group, student-run newspaper, choral group, marching band, Baptist Student Union, Student Body Association, Intramural Association, Ministerial Association, Mississippi Association of Educators/Student Program.

Athletics Member NAIA.

Campus security: 24-hour emergency response devices and patrols, controlled dormitory access.

Student services: veterans affairs office.

COSTS & FINANCIAL AID
Costs (2018–19) ***Comprehensive fee:*** $19,054 includes full-time tuition ($10,690), mandatory fees ($1894), and room and board ($6470). Full-time tuition and fees vary according to course load, degree level, and program. Part-time tuition: $356 per semester hour. Part-time tuition and fees vary according to course load, degree level, and program. ***Required fees:*** $54 per semester hour part-time. ***Room and board:*** Room and board charges vary according to housing facility and location. ***Payment plans:*** installment, deferred payment.

Financial Aid Of all full-time matriculated undergraduates who enrolled in 2017, 526 applied for aid, 449 were judged to have need, 87 had their need fully met. In 2017, 39 non-need-based awards were made. ***Average percent of need met:*** 67. ***Average financial aid package:*** $11,919. ***Average need-based loan:*** $3581. ***Average need-based gift aid:*** $9950. ***Average non-need-based aid:*** $5966. ***Average indebtedness upon graduation:*** $19,084.

APPLYING
Standardized Tests *Required:* SAT or ACT (for admission).

Options: electronic application, early decision, deferred entrance.

Required for some: high school transcript. ***Recommended:*** minimum 2.0 GPA.

CONTACT
Mr. Lynn Gibson, Vice President for Enrollment Services, Blue Mountain College, PO Box 160, Blue Mountain, MS 38610-0160. *Phone:* 662-685-4771 Ext. 176. *Toll-free phone:* 800-235-0136. *Fax:* 662-685-4776. *E-mail:* lgibson@bmc.edu.

Delta State University
Cleveland, Mississippi
http://www.deltastate.edu/

- **State-supported** comprehensive, founded 1924, part of Mississippi Institutions of Higher Learning
- **Small-town** 332-acre campus
- **Endowment** $32.9 million
- **Coed** 3,075 undergraduate students, 65% full-time, 59% women, 41% men
- **Noncompetitive** entrance level, 85% of applicants were admitted

UNDERGRAD STUDENTS
1,989 full-time, 1,086 part-time. Students come from 31 states and territories; 47 other countries; 17% are from out of state; 28% Black or African American, non-Hispanic/Latino; 3% Hispanic/Latino; 1% Asian, non-Hispanic/Latino; 0.1% Native Hawaiian or other Pacific Islander, non-Hispanic/Latino; 0.2% American Indian or Alaska Native, non-Hispanic/Latino; 1% Two or more races, non-Hispanic/Latino; 0.9% Race/ethnicity unknown; 4% international; 14% transferred in; 39% live on campus.

Freshmen:
Admission: 905 applied, 771 admitted, 290 enrolled. ***Average high school GPA:*** 3.4. ***Test scores:*** SAT evidence-based reading and writing scores over 500: 64%; SAT math scores over 500: 68%; ACT scores over 18: 84%; SAT evidence-based reading and writing scores over 600: 14%; SAT math scores over 600: 27%; ACT scores over 24: 27%; ACT scores over 30: 4%.
Retention: 67% of full-time freshmen returned.

FACULTY
Total: 275, 57% full-time, 53% with terminal degrees.
Student/faculty ratio: 14:1.

ACADEMICS
Calendar: semesters. *Degrees:* certificates, bachelor's, master's, doctoral, and post-master's certificates.

Special study options: academic remediation for entering students, adult/continuing education programs, advanced placement credit, cooperative education, distance learning, double majors, freshman honors college, honors programs, independent study, internships, part-time degree program, services for LD students, summer session for credit.

Computers: Students can access the following: campus intranet, computer help desk, free student e-mail accounts, online (class) grades, online (class) registration, online (class) schedules. Campuswide network is available. 100% of college-owned or -operated housing units are wired for high-speed Internet access. Wireless service is available via entire campus.

Library: Roberts-LaForge Library plus 1 other. *Books:* 326,317 (physical), 72,046 (digital/electronic); *Serial titles:* 1,174 (physical), 25,014 (digital/electronic); *Databases:* 83. Weekly public service hours: 75.

STUDENT LIFE
Housing options: on-campus residence required for freshman year; coed, men-only, women-only, special housing for students with disabilities. Campus housing is university owned. Freshman campus housing is guaranteed.

Activities and organizations: drama/theater group, student-run newspaper, choral group, marching band, Student Government Association, Okra Patch, Baptist Student Union, Union Program Council, Wesley Foundation, national fraternities, national sororities.

Athletics Member NCAA. All Division II. ***Intercollegiate sports:*** baseball M(s), basketball M(s)/W(s), cross-country running W(s), football M(s), golf M(s), soccer M(s)/W(s), softball W(s), swimming and diving M(s)/W(s), tennis M(s)/W(s). ***Intramural sports:*** archery M/W, badminton M/W, basketball M/W, bowling M/W, football M/W, golf M/W, softball M/W, table tennis M/W, tennis M/W, track and field M/W, ultimate Frisbee M/W, volleyball M/W.

Campus security: 24-hour emergency response devices and patrols, late-night transport/escort service, controlled dormitory access.

Student services: health clinic, personal/psychological counseling.

COSTS & FINANCIAL AID
Costs (2018–19) ***Tuition:*** state resident $7076 full-time, $295 per credit hour part-time; nonresident $7076 full-time, $295 per credit hour part-time. Full-time tuition and fees vary according to course load. Part-time tuition and fees vary according to course load. ***Required fees:*** $170 full-time, $7 per credit hour part-time. ***Room and board:*** $7722; room only: $4442. Room and board charges vary according to board plan and housing facility. ***Payment plan:*** installment. ***Waivers:*** senior citizens and employees or children of employees.

Financial Aid Of all full-time matriculated undergraduates who enrolled in 2017, 1,851 applied for aid, 1,372 were judged to have need. 269 Federal Work-Study jobs (averaging $1510). In 2017, 337 non-need-based awards were made. ***Average financial aid package:*** $10,320. ***Average need-based loan:*** $4135. ***Average need-based gift aid:*** $5321. ***Average non-need-based aid:*** $4297.

APPLYING
Standardized Tests *Required:* ACT (for admission), SAT or ACT (for admission).

Options: electronic application, deferred entrance.

Application fee: $25.

Required: minimum 2.0 GPA. ***Required for some:*** high school transcript, interview for art, music majors.

Application deadlines: rolling (freshmen), rolling (transfers), 4/15 (early action).

Notification: continuous (freshmen), continuous (transfers).

CONTACT
Mr. Merritt Dain, Director of Admissions, Delta State University, 1003 West Sunflower Road, Kent Wyatt Hall, Office of Admissions, Cleveland, MS 38733. *Phone:* 662-846-4020. *Toll-free phone:* 800-468-6378. *E-mail:* admissions@deltastate.edu.

Jackson State University
Jackson, Mississippi
http://www.jsums.edu/

- **State-supported** university, founded 1877, part of Mississippi Institutions of Higher Learning
- **Urban** 250-acre campus
- **Coed** 5,331 undergraduate students, 91% full-time, 64% women, 36% men
- **Minimally difficult** entrance level, 69% of applicants were admitted

UNDERGRAD STUDENTS
4,840 full-time, 491 part-time. Students come from 58 other countries; 30% are from out of state; 92% Black or African American, non-Hispanic/Latino; 0.8% Hispanic/Latino; 0.2% Asian, non-Hispanic/Latino; 0.3% American Indian or Alaska Native, non-Hispanic/Latino; 2% Two or more races, non-Hispanic/Latino; 2% international; 8% transferred in; 41% live on campus.

Freshmen:
Admission: 7,680 applied, 5,294 admitted, 831 enrolled. ***Average high school GPA:*** 3.1. ***Test scores:*** ACT scores over 18: 67%; ACT scores over 24: 17%; ACT scores over 30: 1%.

Retention: 53% of full-time freshmen returned.

FACULTY
Total: 527, 66% full-time, 81% with terminal degrees.

Student/faculty ratio: 17:1.

ACADEMICS
Calendar: semesters. *Degrees:* bachelor's, master's, doctoral, and post-master's certificates.

Special study options: academic remediation for entering students, accelerated degree program, adult/continuing education programs, advanced placement credit, cooperative education, distance learning, double majors, English as a second language, honors programs, independent study, internships, off-campus study, part-time degree program, services for LD students, study abroad, summer session for credit. ***ROTC:*** Army (b), Air Force (b).

Computers: 2,000 computers/terminals are available on campus for general student use. Students can access the following: computer help desk, free student e-mail accounts, online (class) grades, online (class) registration, online (class) schedules. Campuswide network is available. 100% of college-owned or -operated housing units are wired for high-speed Internet access. Wireless service is available via entire campus. **Library:** H. T. Sampson Library plus 4 others. *Books:* 374,387 (digital/electronic); *Serial titles:* 317,232 (digital/electronic); *Databases:* 70.

STUDENT LIFE
Housing options: coed, men-only, women-only, special housing for students with disabilities. Campus housing is university owned and leased by the school. Freshman applicants given priority for college housing.

Activities and organizations: drama/theater group, student-run newspaper, choral group, marching band, Student Government Association, Sonic Boom of the South, MADDRAMA, Interfaith, NAACP, national fraternities, national sororities.

Athletics Member NCAA. All Division I except football (Division I-AA). ***Intercollegiate sports:*** baseball M(s), basketball M(s)/W(s), bowling W(s), cheerleading M/W, cross-country running M(s)/W(s), golf M(s)/W(s)(c), soccer W(s), softball W(s), tennis M(s)/W(s), track and field M(s)/W(s), volleyball W(s). ***Intramural sports:*** basketball M/W, football M/W, softball M/W, volleyball M/W.

Campus security: 24-hour emergency response devices and patrols, controlled dormitory access.

Student services: health clinic, personal/psychological counseling, veterans affairs office.

COSTS & FINANCIAL AID
Costs (2018–19) ***Tuition:*** state resident $7876 full-time, $329 per hour part-time; nonresident $19,104 full-time, $797 per hour part-time. Full-time tuition and fees vary according to course level, course load, degree level, and student level. Part-time tuition and fees vary according to course level, degree level, and student level. ***Required fees:*** $70 full-time. ***Room and board:*** $9552; room only: $5784. Room and board charges vary according to housing facility. ***Payment plan:*** installment. ***Waivers:*** children of alumni and employees or children of employees.

Financial Aid Of all full-time matriculated undergraduates who enrolled in 2017, 5,548 applied for aid, 5,036 were judged to have need, 453 had their need fully met. 1,104 Federal Work-Study jobs (averaging $2097). In 2017, 141 non-need-based awards were made. ***Average percent of need met:*** 51. ***Average financial aid package:*** $11,286. ***Average need-based loan:*** $4200. ***Average need-based gift aid:*** $5179. ***Average non-need-based aid:*** $9903. ***Average indebtedness upon graduation:*** $29,864.

APPLYING
Standardized Tests *Required:* SAT or ACT (for admission).

Options: electronic application.

Required: high school transcript, immunization record, minimum ACT Composite score of 16.

Application deadlines: rolling (transfers), rolling (early action).

Notification: continuous (freshmen), continuous (transfers).

CONTACT
Ms. Keiona Miller, Assistant Director of Undergraduate Recruitment, Jackson State University, PO Box 18389, 1400 John R. Lynch Street, Jackson, MS 39217. *Phone:* 601-979-2914. *Toll-free phone:* 800-848-6817. *Fax:* 601-979-2914. *E-mail:* keiona.miller@jsums.edu.

Millsaps College
Jackson, Mississippi
http://www.millsaps.edu/

- **Independent United Methodist** comprehensive, founded 1890
- **Urban** 100-acre campus
- **Endowment** $100.8 million
- **Coed** 798 undergraduate students, 99% full-time, 52% women, 48% men
- **Moderately difficult** entrance level, 59% of applicants were admitted

UNDERGRAD STUDENTS
790 full-time, 8 part-time. 55% are from out of state; 20% Black or African American, non-Hispanic/Latino; 5% Hispanic/Latino; 4% Asian, non-Hispanic/Latino; 1% American Indian or Alaska Native, non-Hispanic/Latino; 2% Race/ethnicity unknown; 5% international; 2% transferred in; 89% live on campus.

Freshmen:
Admission: 4,161 applied, 2,468 admitted, 244 enrolled. ***Average high school GPA:*** 3.7. ***Test scores:*** SAT evidence-based reading and writing scores over 500: 96%; SAT math scores over 500: 96%; ACT scores over 18: 100%; SAT evidence-based reading and writing scores over 600: 47%; SAT math scores over 600: 36%; ACT scores over 24: 59%; SAT evidence-based reading and writing scores over 700: 9%; SAT math scores over 700: 11%; ACT scores over 30: 19%.

Retention: 79% of full-time freshmen returned.

FACULTY
Total: 111, 74% full-time, 77% with terminal degrees.

Student/faculty ratio: 9:1.

ACADEMICS
Calendar: semesters. *Degrees:* bachelor's and master's.

Special study options: accelerated degree program, advanced placement credit, double majors, honors programs, independent study, internships, off-campus study, part-time degree program, services for LD students, student-designed majors, study abroad, summer session for credit. ***ROTC:*** Army (c), Air Force (c).

Unusual degree programs: 3-2 engineering with Auburn University, Columbia University, Vanderbilt University; nursing with University of Mississippi Medical Center, Vanderbilt University.

Computers: 150 computers/terminals are available on campus for general student use. Students can access the following: campus intranet, computer help desk, free student e-mail accounts, online (class) grades, online (class) registration, online (class) schedules, online transcripts. Campuswide network is available. 100% of college-owned or -operated housing units are wired for high-speed Internet access. Wireless service is available via entire campus.
Library: Millsaps-Wilson Library.

STUDENT LIFE
Housing options: on-campus residence required through sophomore year; coed, men-only, women-only, special housing for students with disabilities. Campus housing is university owned. Freshman campus housing is guaranteed.

Activities and organizations: drama/theater group, student-run newspaper, choral group, Campus Ministry Team, Student Body Association, SAPS (Campus Programming Board), Inter-fraternity/Panhellenic Councils, intramural sports, national fraternities, national sororities.

Athletics Member NCAA. All Division III except golf (Division II). ***Intercollegiate sports:*** baseball M, basketball M/W, cross-country running M/W, football M, golf M/W, lacrosse M/W, soccer M/W, softball W, tennis M/W, track and field M/W, volleyball W. ***Intramural sports:*** basketball M/W, cheerleading W(c), fencing M(c), field hockey W(c), football M/W, lacrosse W(c), soccer M/W, softball M/W, swimming and diving M(c)/W(c), ultimate Frisbee M(c)/W(c), volleyball M/W.

Campus security: 24-hour emergency response devices and patrols, student patrols, late-night transport/escort service, controlled dormitory access.

Student services: health clinic, personal/psychological counseling.

COSTS & FINANCIAL AID
Costs (2019–20) ***Comprehensive fee:*** $55,524 includes full-time tuition ($38,600), mandatory fees ($2714), and room and board ($14,210). Part-time tuition: $1190 per semester hour. ***College room only:*** $7950.

Financial Aid Of all full-time matriculated undergraduates who enrolled in 2017, 625 applied for aid, 552 were judged to have need, 125 had their need fully met. In 2017, 231 non-need-based awards were made. ***Average percent of need met:*** 78. ***Average financial aid package:*** $35,745. ***Average need-based loan:*** $4434. ***Average need-based gift aid:*** $29,435. ***Average non-need-based aid:*** $25,900. ***Average indebtedness upon graduation:*** $34,619.

APPLYING
Standardized Tests *Required:* SAT or ACT (for admission).

Options: electronic application, early admission, early action, deferred entrance.

Required: essay or personal statement, high school transcript, minimum 2.5 GPA, 1 letter of recommendation, secondary school report. ***Required for some:*** interview.

Application deadlines: 2/1 (freshmen), rolling (out-of-state freshmen), 7/1 (transfers), 11/15 (early action).

Notification: continuous until 3/15 (freshmen), continuous (out-of-state freshmen), continuous until 3/15 (transfers), 1/15 (early action).

CONTACT
Dr. Robert Alexander, Vice President of Enrollment and Communications, Millsaps College, 1701 North State Street, Jackson, MS 39210-0001. *Phone:* 601-974-1050. *Toll-free phone:* 800-352-1050. *Fax:* 601-974-1059. *E-mail:* admissions@millsaps.edu.

Mississippi College
Clinton, Mississippi
http://www.mc.edu/

CONTACT
Mr. William Kyle Brantley, Director of Admissions, Mississippi College, Box 4026, 200 South Capitol Street, Clinton, MS 39058-0001. *Phone:* 601-925-7634. *Toll-free phone:* 800-738-1236. *Fax:* 601-925-3950. *E-mail:* enrollment-services@mc.edu.

Mississippi State University
Mississippi State, Mississippi
http://www.msstate.edu/

- **State-supported** university, founded 1878, part of Mississippi Institutions of Higher Learning
- **Small-town** 4200-acre campus
- **Endowment** $472.0 million
- **Coed**
- **Moderately difficult** entrance level

FACULTY
Student/faculty ratio: 20:1.

ACADEMICS
Calendar: semesters. *Degrees:* associate, bachelor's, master's, doctoral, and post-master's certificates.
Library: Mitchell Memorial Library plus 2 others. *Books:* 257,296 (physical), 56,456 (digital/electronic); *Serial titles:* 1,646 (physical), 231,031 (digital/electronic); *Databases:* 185. Weekly public service hours: 110; students can reserve study rooms.

STUDENT LIFE
Housing options: on-campus residence required for freshman year; coed, men-only, women-only, special housing for students with disabilities. Campus housing is university owned. Freshman applicants given priority for college housing.

Activities and organizations: drama/theater group, student-run newspaper, radio and television station, choral group, marching band, Student Association, Black Student Alliance, Residence Hall Association, Fashion Board, Campus Activities Board, national fraternities, national sororities.

Athletics Member NCAA. All Division I except football (Division I-A).

Campus security: 24-hour emergency response devices and patrols, late-night transport/escort service, controlled dormitory access, bicycle patrols, crime prevention program, RAD program, general law enforcement services.

Student services: health clinic, personal/psychological counseling, veterans affairs office.

COSTS & FINANCIAL AID
Costs (2018–19) ***One-time required fee:*** $55. ***Tuition:*** state resident $8450 full-time, $361 per credit hour part-time; nonresident $23,140 full-time, $969 per credit hour part-time. Full-time tuition and fees vary according to degree level, location, and reciprocity agreements. Part-time tuition and fees vary according to course load, degree level, location, and reciprocity agreements. ***Required fees:*** $110 full-time. ***Room and board:*** $9764; room only: $5983. Room and board charges vary according to board plan, housing facility, and student level. ***Payment plans:*** tuition prepayment, installment.

Financial Aid Of all full-time matriculated undergraduates who enrolled in 2017, 12,575 applied for aid, 10,880 were judged to have need, 2,195 had their need fully met. 434 Federal Work-Study jobs (averaging $3719). In 2017, 3717 non-need-based awards were made. ***Average percent of need met:*** 56. ***Average financial aid package:*** $14,124. ***Average need-based loan:*** $3754. ***Average need-based gift aid:*** $6477. ***Average non-need-based aid:*** $4499. ***Average indebtedness upon graduation:*** $31,438.

APPLYING
Standardized Tests *Required:* SAT or ACT (for admission).

Options: electronic application.

Application fee: $40.

Required: high school transcript, minimum 2.0 GPA.

CONTACT
Ms. Lori Ball, Director of Undergraduate Admissions, Mississippi State University, PO Box 6334, Mississippi State, MS 39762. *Phone:* 662-325-2224. *Fax:* 662-325-1MSU. *E-mail:* admit@msstate.edu.

Mississippi University for Women
Columbus, Mississippi
http://www.muw.edu/

CONTACT
Mississippi University for Women, 1100 College Street, MUW-1600, Columbus, MS 39701-9998. *Phone:* 662-329-7106. *Toll-free phone:* 877-GO 2 THE W.

Mississippi Valley State University
Itta Bena, Mississippi
http://www.mvsu.edu/

CONTACT
Mississippi Valley State University, 14000 Highway 82 West, Itta Bena, MS 38941-1400. *Phone:* 662-254-3345. *Toll-free phone:* 800-844-6885.

Rust College
Holly Springs, Mississippi
http://www.rustcollege.edu/

- **Independent United Methodist** 4-year, founded 1866
- **Small-town** 126-acre campus with easy access to Memphis
- **Endowment** $41.7 million
- **Coed**
- **Minimally difficult** entrance level

FACULTY
Student/faculty ratio: 20:1.

ACADEMICS
Calendar: semesters. *Degrees:* associate and bachelor's.
Library: Leontyne Price Library. *Books:* 126,854 (physical), 438 (digital/electronic); *Serial titles:* 279 (physical); *Databases:* 6. Weekly public service hours: 90; students can reserve study rooms.

STUDENT LIFE
Housing options: on-campus residence required for freshman year; men-only, women-only. Campus housing is university owned. Freshman campus housing is guaranteed.

Activities and organizations: drama/theater group, student-run radio and television station, choral group, marching band, National Sororities, National Fraternities, Choral Group, Television Station, Radio Station, national fraternities, national sororities.

Athletics Member NCAA. All Division III.

Campus security: 24-hour emergency response devices and patrols, controlled dormitory access.

Student services: health clinic, women's center.

COSTS & FINANCIAL AID
Costs (2018–19) ***Comprehensive fee:*** $14,200 includes full-time tuition ($9900) and room and board ($4300). Full-time tuition and fees vary according to course load. Part-time tuition: $421 per credit hour. Part-time tuition and fees vary according to course load.

Financial Aid Of all full-time matriculated undergraduates who enrolled in 2004, 806 applied for aid, 806 were judged to have need, 481 had their need fully met. 492 Federal Work-Study jobs (averaging $714). 189 state and other part-time jobs (averaging $546). In 2004, 112 non-need-based awards were made. ***Average percent of need met:*** 60. ***Average financial aid package:*** $5067. ***Average need-based loan:*** $2158. ***Average need-based gift aid:*** $4281. ***Average non-need-based aid:*** $2795. ***Average indebtedness upon graduation:*** $9314.

APPLYING
Standardized Tests *Required:* ACT (for admission).

Application fee: $10.

Required: high school transcript, minimum 2.5 GPA, 2 letters of recommendation.

CONTACT
Mr. Braque Talley, Dean of Enrollment, Rust College, 150 Rust Avenue, Holly Springs, MS 38635-2328. *Phone:* 601-252-8000 Ext. 4059. *Toll-free phone:* 888-886-8492 Ext. 4065. *Fax:* 662-252-8895. *E-mail:* btalley@rustcollege.edu.

Southeastern Baptist College
Laurel, Mississippi
http://www.southeasternbaptist.edu/

CONTACT
Mrs. Emma Bond, Director of Admissions, Southeastern Baptist College, 4229 Highway 15 North, Laurel, MS 39440-1096. *Phone:* 601-426-6346.

Strayer University–Jackson Campus
Jackson, Mississippi
http://www.strayer.edu/mississippi/jackson/

CONTACT
Strayer University–Jackson Campus, 460 Briarwood Drive, Suite 200, Jackson, MS 39206. *Toll-free phone:* 888-311-0355.

Tougaloo College
Tougaloo, Mississippi
http://www.tougaloo.edu/

CONTACT
Dr. Juno Jacobs, Director of Admissions, Tougaloo College, 500 West County Line Road, Tougaloo, MS 39174. *Phone:* 601-977-7765. *Toll-free phone:* 888-42GALOO. *Fax:* 601-977-4501. *E-mail:* jjacobs@tougaloo.edu.

University of Mississippi
Oxford, Mississippi
http://www.olemiss.edu/

- **State-supported** university, founded 1844, part of Mississippi Institutions of Higher Learning
- **Small-town** 34,977-acre campus with easy access to Memphis
- **Endowment** $670.6 million
- **Coed**
- **Moderately difficult** entrance level

FACULTY
Student/faculty ratio: 18:1.

ACADEMICS
Calendar: semesters. *Degrees:* bachelor's, master's, doctoral, post-master's, and postbachelor's certificates.
Library: J. D. Williams Library plus 1 other. *Books:* 3.3 million (physical), 814,143 (digital/electronic); *Serial titles:* 39,667 (physical), 135,210 (digital/electronic); *Databases:* 389. Weekly public service hours: 109.

STUDENT LIFE
Housing options: on-campus residence required for freshman year; men-only, women-only. Campus housing is university owned, leased by the school and is provided by a third party. Freshman campus housing is guaranteed.

Activities and organizations: drama/theater group, student-run newspaper, radio and television station, choral group, marching band, Associated Student Body, Gospel Choir, sport clubs, Black Student Union, Student Programming Board, national fraternities, national sororities.

Athletics Member NCAA. All Division I except football (Division I-A).

Campus security: 24-hour emergency response devices and patrols, late-night transport/escort service, controlled dormitory access, crime prevention programs.

Student services: health clinic, personal/psychological counseling, women's center, veterans affairs office.

FINANCIAL AID
Financial Aid Of all full-time matriculated undergraduates who enrolled in 2017, 11,048 applied for aid, 8,498 were judged to have need, 1,131

had their need fully met. 382 Federal Work-Study jobs (averaging $1229). In 2017, 4466 non-need-based awards were made. ***Average percent of need met:*** 74. ***Average financial aid package:*** $11,150. ***Average need-based loan:*** $4707. ***Average need-based gift aid:*** $9883. ***Average non-need-based aid:*** $9830. ***Average indebtedness upon graduation:*** $31,086.

APPLYING
Standardized Tests *Required:* SAT or ACT (for admission).
Options: electronic application, deferred entrance.
Required: high school transcript, minimum 2.0 GPA.

CONTACT
Ms. Martina Brewer, Associate Director of Admissions, University of Mississippi, 128 Martindale Student Services Center, University, MS 38677. *Phone:* 662-915-7226. *Toll-free phone:* 800-653-6477. *Fax:* 662-915-5869. *E-mail:* admissions@olemiss.edu.

University of Mississippi Medical Center

Jackson, Mississippi

http://www.umc.edu/

CONTACT
Ms. Barbara Westerfield, Director of Student Records and Registrar, University of Mississippi Medical Center, 2500 North State Street, Jackson, MS 39216-4505. *Phone:* 601-984-1080. *Fax:* 601-984-1079.

University of Southern Mississippi

Hattiesburg, Mississippi

http://www.usm.edu/

- **State-supported** university, founded 1910, part of Mississippi Institutions of Higher Learning
- **Suburban** 1090-acre campus
- **Endowment** $82.7 million
- **Coed**
- **Moderately difficult** entrance level

FACULTY
Student/faculty ratio: 17:1.

ACADEMICS
Calendar: semesters. *Degrees:* certificates, bachelor's, master's, doctoral, post-master's, and postbachelor's certificates.
Library: Cook Memorial Library plus 4 others. *Books:* 1.4 million (physical), 331,932 (digital/electronic); *Serial titles:* 27,243 (physical), 118,798 (digital/electronic); *Databases:* 200. Weekly public service hours: 117; students can reserve study rooms.

STUDENT LIFE
Housing options: men-only, women-only, special housing for students with disabilities. Campus housing is university owned. Freshman applicants given priority for college housing.
Activities and organizations: drama/theater group, student-run newspaper, radio station, choral group, marching band, national fraternities, national sororities.
Athletics Member NCAA. All Division I.
Campus security: 24-hour emergency response devices and patrols, late-night transport/escort service, controlled dormitory access.
Student services: health clinic, personal/psychological counseling, women's center, legal services, veterans affairs office.

COSTS & FINANCIAL AID
Costs (2018–19) ***Tuition:*** state resident $8108 full-time, $338 per credit hour part-time; nonresident $10,108 full-time. Part-time tuition and fees vary according to course load and degree level. ***Room and board:*** $10,638; room only: $6598. Room and board charges vary according to board plan and housing facility.
Financial Aid Of all full-time matriculated undergraduates who enrolled in 2017, 8,733 applied for aid, 7,674 were judged to have need, 1,698 had their need fully met. In 2017, 702 non-need-based awards were made. ***Average percent of need met:*** 68. ***Average financial aid package:*** $10,728. ***Average need-based loan:*** $4365. ***Average need-based gift aid:*** $5705. ***Average non-need-based aid:*** $6075. ***Average indebtedness upon graduation:*** $28,068.

APPLYING
Standardized Tests *Required:* SAT or ACT (for admission).
Options: electronic application, early admission.
Application fee: $40.
Required: minimum 2.0 GPA. ***Required for some:*** high school transcript, statement of good standing from prior institutions, college transcripts.

CONTACT
University of Southern Mississippi, 118 College Drive, Hattiesburg, MS 39406-0001. *Phone:* 601-266-5000.

William Carey University

Hattiesburg, Mississippi

http://www.wmcarey.edu/

CONTACT
Mr. William N. Curry, Dean of Enrollment Management, William Carey University, 710 William Carey Parkway, Hattiesburg, MS 39401. *Phone:* 601-318-6051. *Toll-free phone:* 800-962-5991. *Fax:* 601-318-6154. *E-mail:* admissions@wmcarey.edu.

MISSOURI

American Business & Technology University

Saint Joseph, Missouri

http://www.abtu.edu/

CONTACT
Richard Lingle, Lead Admission Coordinator, American Business & Technology University, 1018 West St.Maartens Drive, Saint Joseph, MO 64506. *Phone:* 800-908-9329 Ext. 13. *Toll-free phone:* 800-804-1388. *E-mail:* ricahrd@acot.edu.

Avila University

Kansas City, Missouri

http://www.avila.edu/

- **Independent Roman Catholic** comprehensive, founded 1916
- **Suburban** 50-acre campus
- **Endowment** $10.8 million
- **Coed** 1,246 undergraduate students, 84% full-time, 60% women, 40% men
- **Minimally difficult** entrance level, 41% of applicants were admitted

UNDERGRAD STUDENTS
1,042 full-time, 204 part-time. Students come from 29 states and territories; 17 other countries; 33% are from out of state; 23% Black or African American, non-Hispanic/Latino; 10% Hispanic/Latino; 2% Asian, non-Hispanic/Latino; 0.5% Native Hawaiian or other Pacific Islander, non-Hispanic/Latino; 0.5% American Indian or Alaska Native, non-Hispanic/Latino; 3% Two or more races, non-Hispanic/Latino; 9% international; 11% transferred in; 31% live on campus.

Freshmen:
Admission: 2,302 applied, 946 admitted, 168 enrolled. ***Average high school GPA:*** 3.2. ***Test scores:*** SAT evidence-based reading and writing scores over 500: 75%; SAT math scores over 500: 87%; ACT scores over 18: 94%; SAT evidence-based reading and writing scores over 600: 8%; SAT math scores over 600: 8%; ACT scores over 24: 23%; ACT scores over 30: 3%.
Retention: 68% of full-time freshmen returned.

FACULTY
Total: 238, 31% full-time, 49% with terminal degrees.
Student/faculty ratio: 13:1.

ACADEMICS
Calendar: semesters. *Degrees:* bachelor's, master's, and postbachelor's certificates.

Special study options: academic remediation for entering students, accelerated degree program, adult/continuing education programs, advanced placement credit, cooperative education, distance learning, double majors, English as a second language, independent study, internships, off-campus study, part-time degree program, services for LD students, study abroad, summer session for credit. ***ROTC:*** Army (c).

Unusual degree programs: 3-2 occupational therapy, physical therapy, law with Rockhurst University, University of Missouri–Kansas City.

Computers: 141 computers/terminals and 225 ports are available on campus for general student use. Students can access the following: campus intranet, computer help desk, free student e-mail accounts, online (class) grades, online (class) registration, online (class) schedules, laptop checkout through library. Campuswide network is available. 100% of college-owned or -operated housing units are wired for high-speed Internet access. Wireless service is available via entire campus.
Library: Hooley-Bundshu Library plus 1 other. *Books:* 39,963 (physical), 309,288 (digital/electronic); *Serial titles:* 205 (physical), 389,497 (digital/electronic); *Databases:* 72. Weekly public service hours: 91; students can reserve study rooms.

STUDENT LIFE
Housing options: on-campus residence required through sophomore year; coed, men-only, women-only. Campus housing is university owned. Freshman campus housing is guaranteed.

Activities and organizations: drama/theater group, student-run newspaper, choral group, Avila Ambassadors, Avila Student Nurses Association, Campus Ministries, Saudi Arabian Student Association, Avila University Theatre Company.

Athletics Member NAIA. ***Intercollegiate sports:*** baseball M(s), basketball M(s)/W(s), cheerleading W(s), cross-country running M(s)/W(s), football M(s), golf M(s), soccer M(s)/W(s), softball W(s), track and field M(s)/W(s), volleyball W(s). ***Intramural sports:*** bowling M/W, table tennis M/W.

Campus security: 24-hour emergency response devices and patrols, student patrols, late-night transport/escort service, controlled dormitory access.

Student services: health clinic, personal/psychological counseling.

COSTS & FINANCIAL AID
Costs (2019–20) ***Comprehensive fee:*** $27,500 includes full-time tuition ($20,500) and room and board ($7000). Part-time tuition: $778 per credit hour. No tuition increase for student's term of enrollment. ***College room only:*** $3400.

Financial Aid Of all full-time matriculated undergraduates who enrolled in 2008, 1,927 applied for aid, 1,852 were judged to have need, 1,846 had their need fully met. 161 Federal Work-Study jobs (averaging $903). 55 state and other part-time jobs (averaging $885). In 2008, 60 non-need-based awards were made. ***Average percent of need met:*** 35. ***Average financial aid package:*** $12,976. ***Average need-based loan:*** $5465. ***Average need-based gift aid:*** $7854. ***Average non-need-based aid:*** $9152. ***Average indebtedness upon graduation:*** $16,508.

APPLYING
Standardized Tests *Required:* SAT or ACT (for admission).

Options: electronic application, early admission.

Required: high school transcript, minimum 2.5 GPA, secondary school report. ***Required for some:*** essay or personal statement. ***Recommended:*** interview.

Notification: 8/15 (freshmen), 8/15 (transfers).

CONTACT
Josh Parisse, Director of Undergraduate Admissions, Avila University, 11901 Wornall Road, Kansas City, MO 64145. *Phone:* 816-501-2400. *Toll-free phone:* 800-GO-AVILA. *Fax:* 816-501-2453. *E-mail:* josh.parisse@avila.edu.

Baptist Bible College
Springfield, Missouri
http://www.gobbc.edu/

CONTACT
Mr. Terry Allcorn, Director of Admissions, Baptist Bible College, 628 East Kearney Street, Springfield, MO 65803-3498. *Phone:* 417-268-6000. *Toll-free phone:* 800-228-5754. *Fax:* 417-268-6694.

Bryan University
Springfield, Missouri
http://www.bryanu.edu/

CONTACT
Bryan University, 4255 South Nature Center Way, Springfield, MO 65804. *Toll-free phone:* 855-566-0650.

Calvary University
Kansas City, Missouri
http://www.calvary.edu/

- **Independent nondenominational** comprehensive, founded 1932
- **Suburban** 55-acre campus with easy access to Kansas City
- **Endowment** $1.2 million
- **Coed**
- **Noncompetitive** entrance level

FACULTY
Student/faculty ratio: 7:1.

ACADEMICS
Calendar: semesters. *Degrees:* certificates, associate, bachelor's, and master's.
Library: Hilda Kroeker Library. *Books:* 41,841 (physical), 420 (digital/electronic); *Serial titles:* 268 (physical); *Databases:* 4.

STUDENT LIFE
Housing options: men-only, women-only. Campus housing is university owned. Freshman campus housing is guaranteed.

Activities and organizations: drama/theater group, choral group, Missions Encounter, Masterworks (Fine Arts).

Athletics Member NCCAA.

Campus security: 24-hour emergency response devices and patrols, late-night transport/escort service, controlled dormitory access, night patrols by trained security personnel, monitored closed circuit cameras.

Student services: personal/psychological counseling.

COSTS & FINANCIAL AID
Costs (2018–19) ***One-time required fee:*** $100. ***Comprehensive fee:*** $19,387 includes full-time tuition ($10,276), mandatory fees ($876), and room and board ($8235). Full-time tuition and fees vary according to location and program. Part-time tuition: $367 per credit hour. Part-time tuition and fees vary according to location and program. ***Required fees:*** $63 per credit hour part-time, $438 per term part-time. ***College room only:*** $3900. Room and board charges vary according to board plan and housing facility.

Financial Aid Of all full-time matriculated undergraduates who enrolled in 2016, 101 applied for aid, 95 were judged to have need, 7 had their need fully met. 8 Federal Work-Study jobs (averaging $1687). In 2016, 4 non-need-based awards were made. ***Average percent of need met:*** 66. ***Average financial aid package:*** $12,774. ***Average need-based loan:*** $4265. ***Average need-based gift aid:*** $5694. ***Average non-need-based aid:*** $2543. ***Average indebtedness upon graduation:*** $19,246.

APPLYING
Standardized Tests *Required:* SAT or ACT (for admission).

Options: electronic application.

Required: essay or personal statement, minimum 2.0 GPA, 2 letters of recommendation. ***Required for some:*** high school transcript. ***Recommended:*** interview.

CONTACT
Ms. Ann Rogers, Admissions Secretary, Calvary University, 15800 Calvary Road, Kansas City, MO 64147-1341. *Phone:* 816-322-0110 Ext. 1323. *Toll-free phone:* 800-326-3960. *Fax:* 816-331-4474. *E-mail:* ann.rogers@cavalry.edu.

Central Christian College of the Bible

Moberly, Missouri

http://www.cccb.edu/

CONTACT
Mr. Aaron Merritt, Director of Admissions, Central Christian College of the Bible, 911 Urbandale Drive East, Moberly, MO 65270-1997. *Phone:* 660-263-3900. *Toll-free phone:* 888-263-3900. *Fax:* 660-263-3936. *E-mail:* admissions@cccb.edu.

Central Methodist University

Fayette, Missouri

http://www.centralmethodist.edu/

- **Independent Methodist** comprehensive, founded 1854
- **Small-town** 80-acre campus
- **Endowment** $45.5 million
- **Coed**
- **Moderately difficult** entrance level

FACULTY
Student/faculty ratio: 12:1.

ACADEMICS
Calendar: semesters. *Degrees:* associate, bachelor's, and master's.
Library: Smiley Library. *Books:* 67,581 (physical), 127,545 (digital/electronic); *Serial titles:* 96 (physical), 38,528 (digital/electronic); *Databases:* 35. Students can reserve study rooms.

STUDENT LIFE
Housing options: on-campus residence required through senior year; coed, men-only, women-only. Campus housing is university owned. Freshman applicants given priority for college housing.

Activities and organizations: drama/theater group, student-run newspaper, radio and television station, choral group, marching band, Student Government Association, Enactus, Alpha Phi Omega, Beta Beta Beta, Campus Ministries, national fraternities, national sororities.

Athletics Member NAIA.

Campus security: 24-hour emergency response devices, late-night transport/escort service, controlled dormitory access.

Student services: health clinic, personal/psychological counseling.

COSTS & FINANCIAL AID
Costs (2018–19) ***One-time required fee:*** $100. ***Comprehensive fee:*** $32,360 includes full-time tuition ($23,650), mandatory fees ($770), and room and board ($7940). Full-time tuition and fees vary according to program and reciprocity agreements. Part-time tuition: $210 per credit hour. Part-time tuition and fees vary according to course load and program. ***Required fees:*** $31 per credit hour part-time. ***College room only:*** $3890. Room and board charges vary according to board plan and housing facility.

Financial Aid Of all full-time matriculated undergraduates who enrolled in 2018, 991 applied for aid, 911 were judged to have need, 170 had their need fully met. In 2018, 150 non-need-based awards were made. ***Average percent of need met:*** 75. ***Average financial aid package:*** $21,258. ***Average need-based loan:*** $4047. ***Average need-based gift aid:*** $5810. ***Average non-need-based aid:*** $13,979. ***Average indebtedness upon graduation:*** $30,798.

APPLYING
Standardized Tests *Required:* SAT or ACT (for admission).

Options: electronic application, deferred entrance.

Required: high school transcript, minimum 2.5 GPA. ***Required for some:*** 2 letters of recommendation.

CONTACT
Central Methodist University, 411 Central Methodist Square, Fayette, MO 65248-1198. *Toll-free phone:* 888-CMU-1854 (in-state); 877-CMU-1854 (out-of-state).

Chamberlain College of Nursing

St. Louis, Missouri

http://www.chamberlain.edu/

CONTACT
Admissions, Chamberlain College of Nursing, 11830 Westline Industrial Drive, Suite 106, St. Louis, MO 63146. *Phone:* 314-991-6200. *Toll-free phone:* 877-751-5783.

City Vision University

Kansas City, Missouri

http://www.cityvision.edu/

CONTACT
Mrs. Nancy Young, Director of Admissions, City Vision University, 3101 Troost Avenue, Suite 200, Kansas City, MO 64109-1845. *Phone:* 816-960-2008 Ext. 3. *Fax:* 816-256-8471. *E-mail:* newstudents@cityvision.edu.

College of the Ozarks

Point Lookout, Missouri

http://www.cofo.edu/

- **Independent Presbyterian** 4-year, founded 1906
- **Rural** 1000-acre campus
- **Endowment** $509.1 million
- **Coed** 1,565 undergraduate students, 98% full-time, 55% women, 45% men
- **Moderately difficult** entrance level, 12% of applicants were admitted

UNDERGRAD STUDENTS
1,533 full-time, 32 part-time. Students come from 33 states and territories; 20 other countries; 25% are from out of state; 0.6% Black or African American, non-Hispanic/Latino; 3% Hispanic/Latino; 0.8% Asian, non-Hispanic/Latino; 0.2% Native Hawaiian or other Pacific Islander, non-Hispanic/Latino; 0.4% American Indian or Alaska Native, non-Hispanic/Latino; 2% Two or more races, non-Hispanic/Latino; 3% Race/ethnicity unknown; 2% international; 2% transferred in; 90% live on campus.

Freshmen:
Admission: 2,874 applied, 331 admitted, 314 enrolled. ***Average high school GPA:*** 3.8. ***Test scores:*** SAT evidence-based reading and writing scores over 500: 100%; SAT math scores over 500: 89%; ACT scores over 18: 97%; SAT evidence-based reading and writing scores over 600: 83%; SAT math scores over 600: 50%; ACT scores over 24: 47%; SAT evidence-based reading and writing scores over 700: 11%; SAT math scores over 700: 6%; ACT scores over 30: 6%.

Retention: 75% of full-time freshmen returned.

FACULTY
Total: 133, 69% full-time, 45% with terminal degrees.

Student/faculty ratio: 14:1.

ACADEMICS
Calendar: semesters. *Degree:* bachelor's.

Special study options: academic remediation for entering students, advanced placement credit, double majors, English as a second language, independent study, internships, off-campus study, services for LD students, student-designed majors, summer session for credit.

Computers: 402 computers/terminals and 1,771 ports are available on campus for general student use. Students can access the following: campus intranet, computer help desk, free student e-mail accounts, online (class) grades, online (class) registration, online (class) schedules. Campuswide network is available. 100% of college-owned or -operated housing units are wired for high-speed Internet access. Wireless service is available via classrooms, dorm rooms, libraries, student centers.
Library: Lyons Memorial Library. *Books:* 96,874 (physical), 500,000 (digital/electronic); *Serial titles:* 77 (physical), 52,500 (digital/electronic); *Databases:* 52. Weekly public service hours: 80.

STUDENT LIFE
Housing options: on-campus residence required through senior year; men-only, women-only. Campus housing is university owned.

Activities and organizations: drama/theater group, student-run newspaper, radio station, choral group, Young Americans for Freedom, Chi Alpha, Baptist Student Union, Agriculture Club, FCA.

Athletics Member NCAA, NAIA. All NCAA Division II. ***Intercollegiate sports:*** baseball M(s), basketball M(s)/W(s), cheerleading M/W, cross-country running M/W, golf M/W, track and field M/W, volleyball W(s). ***Intramural sports:*** basketball M/W, football M/W, racquetball M/W, softball M/W, volleyball M/W.

Campus security: 24-hour emergency response devices and patrols, student patrols, late-night transport/escort service, controlled dormitory access, front gate closed 6 pm to 5 am, security checks cars for proper credentials for entry.

Student services: health clinic, personal/psychological counseling.

COSTS & FINANCIAL AID

Costs (2019–20) ***Comprehensive fee:*** includes mandatory fees ($460) and room and board ($7600). Part-time tuition: $310 per credit hour. ***Required fees:*** $230 per term part-time. ***College room only:*** $3800.

Financial Aid Of all full-time matriculated undergraduates who enrolled in 2016, 1,531 applied for aid, 1,366 were judged to have need. ***Average percent of need met:*** 83. ***Average financial aid package:*** $18,500. ***Average need-based gift aid:*** $14,188. ***Average non-need-based aid:*** $14,346.

APPLYING

Standardized Tests *Required:* SAT or ACT (for admission). *Recommended:* ACT (for admission).

Options: electronic application.

Required: high school transcript, 2 letters of recommendation, interview, medical history, financial statement. ***Recommended:*** minimum 3.0 GPA.

Application deadlines: 12/31 (freshmen), 12/31 (out-of-state freshmen), 12/31 (transfers).

Notification: continuous (freshmen), 1/15 (out-of-state freshmen), continuous (transfers).

CONTACT

Mrs. Kim Williams, Admissions Secretary, College of the Ozarks, PO Box 17, Point Lookout, MO 65726. *Phone:* 417-690-2636. *Toll-free phone:* 800-222-0525. *Fax:* 417-335-2618. *E-mail:* admissions@cofo.edu.

Columbia College

Columbia, Missouri

http://www.ccis.edu/

- **Independent** comprehensive, founded 1851, affiliated with Christian Church (Disciples of Christ)
- **Urban** 33-acre campus with easy access to St. Louis and Kansas City
- **Endowment** $171.7 million
- **Coed** 1,023 undergraduate students, 85% full-time, 56% women, 44% men
- **Minimally difficult** entrance level, 48% of applicants were admitted

UNDERGRAD STUDENTS

865 full-time, 158 part-time. Students come from 28 states and territories; 30 other countries; 12% are from out of state; 4% Black or African American, non-Hispanic/Latino; 4% Hispanic/Latino; 0.7% Asian, non-Hispanic/Latino; 0.1% Native Hawaiian or other Pacific Islander, non-Hispanic/Latino; 0.3% American Indian or Alaska Native, non-Hispanic/Latino; 6% Two or more races, non-Hispanic/Latino; 3% Race/ethnicity unknown; 7% international; 12% transferred in; 37% live on campus.

Freshmen:

Admission: 1,796 applied, 870 admitted, 146 enrolled. ***Average high school GPA:*** 3.6. ***Test scores:*** SAT evidence-based reading and writing scores over 500: 64%; SAT math scores over 500: 80%; ACT scores over 18: 97%; SAT evidence-based reading and writing scores over 600: 34%; SAT math scores over 600: 35%; ACT scores over 24: 48%; SAT math scores over 700: 10%; ACT scores over 30: 9%.

Retention: 71% of full-time freshmen returned.

FACULTY

Total: 150, 49% full-time, 53% with terminal degrees.

Student/faculty ratio: 11:1.

ACADEMICS

Calendar: semesters. *Degrees:* certificates, associate, bachelor's, and master's (offers continuing education program with significant enrollment not reflected in profile).

Special study options: adult/continuing education programs, advanced placement credit, cooperative education, distance learning, double majors, English as a second language, honors programs, independent study, internships, off-campus study, part-time degree program, services for LD students, student-designed majors, study abroad, summer session for credit. ***ROTC:*** Army (c), Navy (c), Air Force (c).

Unusual degree programs: 3-2 nursing; education.

Computers: 220 computers/terminals and 1,000 ports are available on campus for general student use. Students can access the following: campus intranet, computer help desk, free student e-mail accounts, online (class) grades, online (class) registration, online (class) schedules. Campuswide network is available. 100% of college-owned or -operated housing units are wired for high-speed Internet access. Wireless service is available via entire campus.

Library: J. W. and Lois Stafford Library. *Books:* 61,752 (physical), 225,968 (digital/electronic); *Serial titles:* 104 (physical), 63,429 (digital/electronic); *Databases:* 70. Weekly public service hours: 94; students can reserve study rooms.

STUDENT LIFE

Housing options: on-campus residence required through sophomore year; coed, women-only, special housing for students with disabilities. Campus housing is university owned and leased by the school. Freshman campus housing is guaranteed.

Activities and organizations: drama/theater group, choral group, International Club, Honor Student Association, Black Student Coalition, Pre-Healthcare Professionals, Commited and Serving Together.

Athletics Member NAIA. ***Intercollegiate sports:*** baseball M(s), basketball M(s)/W(s), bowling W(s), cross-country running M(s)/W(s), golf M(s)/W(s), lacrosse M(s), soccer M(s)/W(s), softball W(s), track and field M(s)/W(s), volleyball W(s). ***Intramural sports:*** badminton M/W, basketball M/W, football M/W, sand volleyball M/W, soccer M/W, softball M/W, table tennis M(c)/W(c), volleyball M/W.

Campus security: 24-hour emergency response devices and patrols, late-night transport/escort service, controlled dormitory access, building monitor patrols off-campus site.

Student services: health clinic, personal/psychological counseling, veterans affairs office.

COSTS & FINANCIAL AID

Costs (2018–19) ***Comprehensive fee:*** $30,512 includes full-time tuition ($22,704) and room and board ($7808). Full-time tuition and fees vary according to class time, course load, program, reciprocity agreements, and student level. Part-time tuition: $487 per credit hour. Part-time tuition and fees vary according to class time, course load, location, and reciprocity agreements. No tuition increase for student's term of enrollment. ***College room only:*** $4674. Room and board charges vary according to housing facility. ***Payment plans:*** installment, deferred payment. ***Waivers:*** children of alumni, senior citizens, and employees or children of employees.

Financial Aid Of all full-time matriculated undergraduates who enrolled in 2017, 690 applied for aid, 625 were judged to have need, 102 had their need fully met. In 2017, 100 non-need-based awards were made. ***Average percent of need met:*** 62. ***Average financial aid package:*** $16,589. ***Average need-based loan:*** $3764. ***Average need-based gift aid:*** $5378. ***Average non-need-based aid:*** $9057. ***Average indebtedness upon graduation:*** $22,159.

APPLYING

Standardized Tests *Required:* SAT or ACT (for admission).

Options: electronic application, deferred entrance.

Required: high school transcript, minimum 2.5 GPA. ***Required for some:*** essay or personal statement, interview.

Notification: continuous (freshmen), continuous (transfers).

CONTACT

Stephanie Johnson, Associate Vice President, Recruiting & Admissions, Columbia College, 1001 Rogers Street, Columbia, MO 65216-0002. *Phone:* 573-875-7352. *Toll-free phone:* 800-231-2391. *Fax:* 573-875-7506. *E-mail:* admissions@ccis.edu.

Conception Seminary College

Conception, Missouri

http://www.conception.edu/

- **Independent Roman Catholic** 4-year, founded 1886
- **Rural** 30-acre campus
- **Men only**
- **Noncompetitive** entrance level

FACULTY
Student/faculty ratio: 4:1.

ACADEMICS
Calendar: semesters. *Degrees:* bachelor's and postbachelor's certificates.
Library: Conception Seminary College Library.

STUDENT LIFE
Housing options: on-campus residence required through senior year; men-only. Campus housing is university owned.

Activities and organizations: drama/theater group, choral group, national fraternities.

Campus security: 24-hour emergency response devices.

Student services: health clinic, personal/psychological counseling.

COSTS & FINANCIAL AID
Costs (2018–19) ***Comprehensive fee:*** $34,385 includes full-time tuition ($21,326), mandatory fees ($250), and room and board ($12,809). Part-time tuition: $200 per credit hour. ***College room only:*** $5358.

Financial Aid Of all full-time matriculated undergraduates who enrolled in 2016, 35 applied for aid, 24 were judged to have need, 1 had their need fully met. 20 Federal Work-Study jobs (averaging $876). 34 state and other part-time jobs (averaging $977). In 2016, 22 non-need-based awards were made. ***Average percent of need met:*** 90. ***Average financial aid package:*** $30,220. ***Average need-based loan:*** $4941. ***Average need-based gift aid:*** $6347. ***Average non-need-based aid:*** $2016. ***Average indebtedness upon graduation:*** $31,817.

APPLYING
Standardized Tests *Required:* SAT or ACT (for admission).

Options: early admission, deferred entrance.

Required: essay or personal statement, high school transcript, minimum 2.0 GPA, 2 letters of recommendation, church certificate, medical history.

CONTACT
Mrs. Jeanette Schieber, Director of Admissions, Conception Seminary College, 37174 State Highway VV, Conception, MO 64433. *Phone:* 660-944-2886. *Fax:* 660-944-2829. *E-mail:* admissions@conception.edu.

Cottey College

Nevada, Missouri

http://www.cottey.edu/

- **Independent** primarily 2-year, founded 1884
- **Small-town** 51-acre campus
- **Endowment** $108.8 million
- **Women only**
- **Moderately difficult** entrance level

FACULTY
Student/faculty ratio: 7:1.

ACADEMICS
Calendar: semesters. *Degrees:* associate and bachelor's.
Library: Blanche Skiff Ross Memorial Library plus 1 other. Weekly public service hours: 88.

STUDENT LIFE
Housing options: women-only. Campus housing is university owned.

Activities and organizations: drama/theater group, choral group, Inter-Society, Golden Key, French Club, Student Government, Global Citizens.

Athletics Member NJCAA.

Campus security: 24-hour emergency response devices and patrols, late-night transport/escort service, controlled dormitory access.

Student services: health clinic, personal/psychological counseling.

COSTS & FINANCIAL AID
Costs (2018–19) ***Comprehensive fee:*** $28,850 includes full-time tuition ($19,900), mandatory fees ($1250), and room and board ($7700). Part-time tuition: $125 per credit hour. Part-time tuition and fees vary according to course load. ***Required fees:*** $22 per credit hour part-time, $88 per term part-time. ***College room only:*** $4200. Room and board charges vary according to housing facility.

Financial Aid Of all full-time matriculated undergraduates who enrolled in 2017, 208 applied for aid, 190 were judged to have need, 65 had their need fully met. 26 Federal Work-Study jobs (averaging $1943). 141 state and other part-time jobs (averaging $1913). In 2017, 69 non-need-based awards were made. ***Average percent of need met:*** 84. ***Average financial aid package:*** $20,618. ***Average need-based loan:*** $3234. ***Average need-based gift aid:*** $16,932. ***Average non-need-based aid:*** $14,736. ***Average indebtedness upon graduation:*** $20,406.

APPLYING
Standardized Tests *Required:* SAT or ACT (for admission). *Required for some:* TOEFL, IELTS.

Options: electronic application, early admission, deferred entrance.

Application fee: $20.

Required: essay or personal statement, high school transcript, 1 letter of recommendation. ***Recommended:*** minimum 2.6 GPA, interview.

CONTACT
Mrs. Angela Moore, Enrollment Office, Cottey College, 1000 West Austin Boulevard, Nevada, MO 64772. *Phone:* 417-667-8181. *Toll-free phone:* 888-526-8839. *Fax:* 417-667-8103. *E-mail:* amoore@cottey.edu.

Cox College

Springfield, Missouri

http://www.coxcollege.edu/

CONTACT
Cox College, 1423 North Jefferson, Springfield, MO 65802. *Phone:* 417-269-3083. *Toll-free phone:* 866-898-5355.

Culver-Stockton College

Canton, Missouri

http://www.culver.edu/

- **Independent** comprehensive, founded 1853, affiliated with Christian Church (Disciples of Christ)
- **Rural** 143-acre campus
- **Endowment** $24.8 million
- **Coed** 1,022 undergraduate students, 90% full-time, 49% women, 51% men
- **Moderately difficult** entrance level, 46% of applicants were admitted

UNDERGRAD STUDENTS
919 full-time, 103 part-time. Students come from 39 states and territories; 18 other countries; 45% are from out of state; 13% Black or African American, non-Hispanic/Latino; 5% Hispanic/Latino; 0.5% Asian, non-Hispanic/Latino; 0.1% Native Hawaiian or other Pacific Islander, non-Hispanic/Latino; 0.5% American Indian or Alaska Native, non-Hispanic/Latino; 3% Two or more races, non-Hispanic/Latino; 0.2% Race/ethnicity unknown; 5% international; 4% transferred in; 74% live on campus.

Freshmen:
Admission: 4,784 applied, 2,220 admitted, 288 enrolled. ***Average high school GPA:*** 3.2. ***Test scores:*** SAT evidence-based reading and writing scores over 500: 64%; SAT math scores over 500: 66%; ACT scores over 18: 85%; SAT evidence-based reading and writing scores over 600: 18%; SAT math scores over 600: 13%; ACT scores over 24: 19%; SAT evidence-based reading and writing scores over 700: 2%; ACT scores over 30: 3%.

Retention: 67% of full-time freshmen returned.

FACULTY
Total: 102, 52% full-time, 40% with terminal degrees.

Student/faculty ratio: 15:1.

ACADEMICS
Calendar: semesters. *Degrees:* bachelor's and master's.

Special study options: academic remediation for entering students, accelerated degree program, adult/continuing education programs, advanced placement credit, distance learning, double majors, honors programs, independent study, internships, part-time degree program, services for LD students, student-designed majors, study abroad, summer session for credit.

Unusual degree programs: 3-2 occupational therapy with Washington University in St. Louis, Athletic Training.

Computers: 100 computers/terminals and 50 ports are available on campus for general student use. Students can access the following: campus intranet, computer help desk, free student e-mail accounts, online (class) grades, online (class) registration, online (class) schedules. Campuswide network is available. 100% of college-owned or -operated housing units are wired for high-speed Internet access. Wireless service is available via entire campus.

Library: Carl Johann Memorial Library. *Books:* 106,810 (physical), 368,101 (digital/electronic); *Serial titles:* 755 (physical), 229,284 (digital/electronic); *Databases:* 26. Weekly public service hours: 65; students can reserve study rooms.

STUDENT LIFE

Housing options: on-campus residence required through senior year; coed, men-only, women-only. Campus housing is university owned. Freshman campus housing is guaranteed.

Activities and organizations: drama/theater group, student-run newspaper, radio and television station, choral group, Campus Programming Council (CPC), The Black Student Union (BSU), Student Government Association (SGA), Health Outreach Peer Educators (HOPE), Institute of Management Accountants (IMA), national fraternities, national sororities.

Athletics Member NAIA. ***Intercollegiate sports:*** baseball M(s), basketball M(s)/W(s), bowling M(s)/W(s), cheerleading M(s)/W(s), cross-country running M(s)/W(s), football M(s), golf M(s)/W(s), soccer M(s)/W(s), softball W(s), track and field M(s)/W(s), volleyball M(s)/W(s). ***Intramural sports:*** baseball M/W, basketball M/W, football M/W, soccer M/W, softball M/W, volleyball M/W.

Campus security: 24-hour emergency response devices and patrols, late-night transport/escort service, controlled dormitory access.

Student services: personal/psychological counseling.

COSTS & FINANCIAL AID

Costs (2019–20) ***One-time required fee:*** $210. ***Comprehensive fee:*** $35,900 includes full-time tuition ($26,780), mandatory fees ($425), and room and board ($8695). Part-time tuition: $610 per credit hour. ***Required fees:*** $18 per credit hour part-time. ***College room only:*** $3895.

Financial Aid Of all full-time matriculated undergraduates who enrolled in 2017, 851 applied for aid, 789 were judged to have need, 130 had their need fully met. 72 Federal Work-Study jobs (averaging $1146). 383 state and other part-time jobs (averaging $1117). In 2017, 153 non-need-based awards were made. ***Average percent of need met:*** 72. ***Average financial aid package:*** $21,033. ***Average need-based loan:*** $4259. ***Average need-based gift aid:*** $17,185. ***Average non-need-based aid:*** $9964. ***Average indebtedness upon graduation:*** $29,105. ***Financial aid deadline:*** 6/1.

APPLYING

Standardized Tests *Required:* SAT or ACT (for admission).

Options: electronic application, deferred entrance.

Required: high school transcript, minimum 2.0 GPA. ***Recommended:*** essay or personal statement, 1 letter of recommendation, interview.

Application deadlines: rolling (freshmen), rolling (transfers).

Notification: continuous (freshmen), continuous (transfers).

CONTACT

Erica Mitchell, Interim Director of Admission, Culver-Stockton College, One College Hill, Canton, MO 63435-1299. *Phone:* 573-288-6331. *Toll-free phone:* 800-537-1883. *Fax:* 573-288-6618. *E-mail:* admission@culver.edu.

DeVry University–Kansas City Campus

Kansas City, Missouri

http://www.devry.edu/

CONTACT

Admissions Office, DeVry University–Kansas City Campus, 11224 Holmes Road, Kansas City, MO 64131. *Phone:* 816-943-7300. *Toll-free phone:* 866-338-7934.

Drury University

Springfield, Missouri

http://www.drury.edu/

- **Independent** comprehensive, founded 1873
- **Urban** 90-acre campus
- **Endowment** $97.5 million
- **Coed** 1,489 undergraduate students, 98% full-time, 58% women, 42% men
- **Moderately difficult** entrance level, 73% of applicants were admitted

UNDERGRAD STUDENTS

1,462 full-time, 27 part-time. Students come from 33 states and territories; 57 other countries; 25% are from out of state; 3% Black or African American, non-Hispanic/Latino; 2% Hispanic/Latino; 1% Asian, non-Hispanic/Latino; 0.2% Native Hawaiian or other Pacific Islander, non-Hispanic/Latino; 1% American Indian or Alaska Native, non-Hispanic/Latino; 4% Two or more races, non-Hispanic/Latino; 7% international; 6% transferred in; 61% live on campus.

Freshmen:

Admission: 1,575 applied, 1,149 admitted, 377 enrolled. ***Average high school GPA:*** 3.8. ***Test scores:*** ACT scores over 18: 99%; ACT scores over 24: 65%; ACT scores over 30: 19%.

Retention: 83% of full-time freshmen returned.

FACULTY

Total: 141, 79% full-time, 75% with terminal degrees.

Student/faculty ratio: 13:1.

ACADEMICS

Calendar: semesters. *Degrees:* bachelor's and master's (also offers evening program with significant enrollment not reflected in profile).

Special study options: academic remediation for entering students, accelerated degree program, adult/continuing education programs, advanced placement credit, cooperative education, distance learning, double majors, English as a second language, freshman honors college, honors programs, independent study, internships, off-campus study, part-time degree program, services for LD students, student-designed majors, study abroad, summer session for credit.

Unusual degree programs: 3-2 engineering with Washington University in St. Louis; international management with American Graduate School of International Management, occupational therapy with Washington University in St. Louis.

Computers: 385 computers/terminals are available on campus for general student use. Students can access the following: campus intranet, computer help desk, free student e-mail accounts, online (class) grades, online (class) registration, online (class) schedules, digital imaging lab, online bill payment/student information. Campuswide network is available. 100% of college-owned or -operated housing units are wired for high-speed Internet access. Wireless service is available via entire campus.

Library: F. W. Olin Library plus 1 other. *Books:* 154,247 (physical), 234,110 (digital/electronic); *Serial titles:* 354 (digital/electronic); *Databases:* 44. Weekly public service hours: 92; students can reserve study rooms.

STUDENT LIFE

Housing options: on-campus residence required through junior year; coed, men-only, women-only. Campus housing is university owned and leased by the school. Freshman campus housing is guaranteed.

Activities and organizations: drama/theater group, student-run newspaper, radio and television station, choral group, Drury Volunteer Corps (DVC), International Student Association, Fanthers, Drury Allies, Commuter Student Association, national fraternities, national sororities.

Athletics Member NCAA. All Division II. ***Intercollegiate sports:*** baseball M(s), basketball M(s)/W(s), cheerleading M(s)/W(s), cross-country running M(s)/W(s), golf M(s)/W(s), riflery M/W, soccer M(s)/W(s), softball W(s), swimming and diving M(s)/W(s), tennis M(s)/W(s), track and field M(s)/W(s), triathlon W(s), volleyball W(s), wrestling M(s). ***Intramural sports:*** basketball M/W, bowling M(c)/W(c), football M/W, ice hockey M(c), soccer M/W, softball M/W, ultimate Frisbee M(c)/W(c), volleyball M/W.

Campus security: 24-hour emergency response devices and patrols, student patrols, late-night transport/escort service, controlled dormitory access.

Student services: health clinic, personal/psychological counseling, veterans affairs office.

COSTS & FINANCIAL AID

Costs (2019–20) ***One-time required fee:*** $150. ***Comprehensive fee:*** $38,561 includes full-time tuition ($28,500), mandatory fees ($1015), and room and board ($9046). Part-time tuition: $959 per credit hour. ***Required fees:*** $180 part-time. ***College room only:*** $5830.

Financial Aid Of all full-time matriculated undergraduates who enrolled in 2018, 1,124 applied for aid, 986 were judged to have need, 217 had their need fully met. 133 Federal Work-Study jobs (averaging $2491). In 2018, 444 non-need-based awards were made. ***Average percent of need met:*** 76. ***Average financial aid package:*** $23,196. ***Average need-based loan:*** $4261. ***Average need-based gift aid:*** $19,430. ***Average non-need-based aid:*** $11,480. ***Average indebtedness upon graduation:*** $35,202.

APPLYING

Standardized Tests *Required:* SAT or ACT (for admission).

Options: electronic application, deferred entrance.

Required: essay or personal statement, high school transcript, minimum 2.7 GPA, 1 letter of recommendation. ***Recommended:*** interview.

Application deadlines: rolling (freshmen), rolling (transfers).

Notification: continuous (freshmen), continuous (transfers).

CONTACT

Mr. Kevin Kropf, Executive Vice President for Enrollment Management, Drury University, 900 North Benton Avenue, Springfield, MO 65802. *Phone:* 417-873-7205. *Toll-free phone:* 800-922-2274. *Fax:* 417-866-3873. *E-mail:* druryad@drury.edu.

Evangel University

Springfield, Missouri

http://www.evangel.edu/

- **Independent** comprehensive, founded 1955, affiliated with Assemblies of God
- **Urban** 80-acre campus
- **Coed**
- **Moderately difficult** entrance level

FACULTY

Student/faculty ratio: 14:1.

ACADEMICS

Calendar: semesters. *Degrees:* associate, bachelor's, master's, and doctoral.

Library: Claude Kendrick Library.

STUDENT LIFE

Housing options: on-campus residence required through senior year; coed, men-only, women-only. Campus housing is university owned.

Activities and organizations: drama/theater group, student-run newspaper, radio and television station, choral group, marching band, Activities Board, student government, CrossWalk Student Ministries, Honor Societies, Music Ensembles.

Athletics Member NAIA.

Campus security: 24-hour emergency response devices and patrols, student patrols, late-night transport/escort service, controlled dormitory access.

Student services: health clinic, personal/psychological counseling.

COSTS & FINANCIAL AID

Costs (2018–19) ***Tuition:*** $22,146 full-time, $896 per credit hour part-time. Full-time tuition and fees vary according to course load. Part-time tuition and fees vary according to course load. ***Required fees:*** $1275 full-time. ***Room only:*** $4304. Room and board charges vary according to board plan.

Financial Aid Of all full-time matriculated undergraduates who enrolled in 2017, 1,393 applied for aid, 1,241 were judged to have need, 175 had their need fully met. 965 Federal Work-Study jobs (averaging $1872). In 2017, 180 non-need-based awards were made. ***Average percent of need met:*** 74. ***Average financial aid package:*** $19,362. ***Average need-based loan:*** $4765. ***Average need-based gift aid:*** $14,087. ***Average non-need-based aid:*** $8843. ***Average indebtedness upon graduation:*** $36,024.

APPLYING

Standardized Tests *Required:* SAT or ACT (for admission).

Options: electronic application, deferred entrance.

Required: essay or personal statement, high school transcript, interview. ***Recommended:*** minimum 2.0 GPA.

CONTACT

Evangel University, 1111 North Glenstone, Springfield, MO 65802. *Phone:* 417-865-2811 Ext. 7205. *Toll-free phone:* 800-382-6435. *Fax:* 417-865-9599. *E-mail:* admissions@evangel.edu.

Fontbonne University

St. Louis, Missouri

http://www.fontbonne.edu/

CONTACT

Mr. Michelle Palumbo, Associate Vice President of Undergraduate Admissions, Fontbonne University, 6800 Wydown Boulevard, St. Louis, MO 63105. *Phone:* 314-889-1400. *Toll-free phone:* 800-205-5862. *Fax:* 314-889-1451. *E-mail:* fbyou@fontbonne.edu.

Global University

Springfield, Missouri

http://www.globaluniversity.edu/

CONTACT

Rev. Todd Waggoner, Enrollment and International Student Services Director, Global University, 1211 South Glenstone Avenue, Springfield, MO 65804. *Phone:* 417-862-9533 Ext. 2335. *Toll-free phone:* 800-443-1083. *Fax:* 417-863-9621. *E-mail:* twaggoner@globaluniversity.edu.

Goldfarb School of Nursing at Barnes-Jewish College

St. Louis, Missouri

http://www.barnesjewishcollege.edu/

- **Independent** comprehensive, founded 1902
- **Urban** 2-acre campus with easy access to St. Louis, Missouri
- **Endowment** $25.2 million
- **Coed, primarily women**
- **Moderately difficult** entrance level

FACULTY

Student/faculty ratio: 11:1.

ACADEMICS

Calendar: trimesters. *Degrees:* bachelor's, master's, doctoral, and post-master's certificates.

Library: Goldfarb School of Nursing Library plus 2 others. *Books:* 1,100 (physical), 20,000 (digital/electronic); *Serial titles:* 62 (digital/electronic); *Databases:* 14.

STUDENT LIFE

Housing options: college housing not available.

Activities and organizations: student-run newspaper, Student Nurses Association, Student Council, GSON Men Excelling in Nursing, Veterans and Supporters Together.

Campus security: 24-hour patrols, late-night transport/escort service.

Student services: personal/psychological counseling, legal services, veterans affairs office.

COSTS & FINANCIAL AID
Costs (2018–19) ***Tuition:*** $20,020 full-time, $770 per credit hour part-time. Full-time tuition and fees vary according to course load and degree level. Part-time tuition and fees vary according to course load and degree level. ***Required fees:*** $1320 full-time, $615 per term part-time.

Financial Aid Of all full-time matriculated undergraduates who enrolled in 2018, 492 applied for aid, 466 were judged to have need. 19 Federal Work-Study jobs (averaging $31,557). In 2018, 4 non-need-based awards were made. ***Average financial aid package:*** $4648. ***Average need-based loan:*** $4598. ***Average need-based gift aid:*** $3646. ***Average non-need-based aid:*** $6000.

APPLYING
Options: electronic application, deferred entrance.

Application fee: $50.

CONTACT
Goldfarb School of Nursing at Barnes-Jewish College, 4483 Duncan Avenue, St. Louis, MO 63110. *Phone:* 314-362-9155. *Toll-free phone:* 800-832-9009.

Graceland University
Independence, Missouri
http://www.graceland.edu/

CONTACT
Admissions, Graceland University, 1401 West Truman Road, Independence, MO 64050-3434. *Phone:* 816-833-0524. *Toll-free phone:* 866-GRACELAND. *E-mail:* gic@graceland.edu.

Hannibal-LaGrange University
Hannibal, Missouri
http://www.hlg.edu/

- **Independent Southern Baptist** comprehensive, founded 1858
- **Small-town** 110-acre campus
- **Endowment** $8.4 million
- **Coed**
- **Minimally difficult** entrance level

FACULTY
Student/faculty ratio: 14:1.

ACADEMICS
Calendar: semesters. *Degrees:* certificates, associate, bachelor's, and master's.
Library: Roland Library plus 1 other. *Books:* 113,238 (physical), 11,053 (digital/electronic); *Databases:* 77. Students can reserve study rooms.

STUDENT LIFE
Housing options: on-campus residence required through junior year; men-only, women-only. Campus housing is university owned. Freshman applicants given priority for college housing.

Activities and organizations: drama/theater group, student-run newspaper, choral group, Phi Beta Lambda, Student Nursing Association, Student Teachers Organization, Phi Beta Delta, Alpha Tau Beta.

Athletics Member NAIA.

Campus security: 24-hour emergency response devices and patrols, student patrols, late-night transport/escort service, controlled dormitory access, camera surveillance, alert system.

COSTS & FINANCIAL AID
Costs (2018–19) ***One-time required fee:*** $150. ***Comprehensive fee:*** $30,858 includes full-time tuition ($21,450), mandatory fees ($1300), and room and board ($8108). Full-time tuition and fees vary according to course load, degree level, location, program, and student level. Part-time tuition: $715 per credit hour. Part-time tuition and fees vary according to course load, degree level, location, program, and student level. ***Required fees:*** $325 per term part-time. ***Room and board:*** Room and board charges vary according to housing facility.

Financial Aid Of all full-time matriculated undergraduates who enrolled in 2017, 80 Federal Work-Study jobs (averaging $750).

APPLYING
Standardized Tests *Required:* SAT or ACT (for admission).

Options: electronic application, early admission, deferred entrance.

Application fee: $25.

Required: high school transcript, minimum 2.0 GPA.

CONTACT
Dr. Ray Carty, Vice President for Enrollment Management, Hannibal-LaGrange University, 2800 Palmyra Road, Hannibal, MO 63401-1999. *Phone:* 573-629-3094. *Toll-free phone:* 800-HLG-1119. *E-mail:* admissions@hlg.edu.

Harris-Stowe State University
St. Louis, Missouri
http://www.hssu.edu/

- **State-supported** 4-year, founded 1857, part of Missouri Coordinating Board for Higher Education
- **Urban** 22-acre campus with easy access to St. Louis
- **Coed**
- **Noncompetitive** entrance level

FACULTY
Student/faculty ratio: 16:1.

ACADEMICS
Calendar: semesters. *Degree:* certificates and bachelor's.
Library: AT&T Library and Technology Center plus 1 other.

STUDENT LIFE
Housing options: coed. Campus housing is university owned. Freshman applicants given priority for college housing.

Activities and organizations: drama/theater group, choral group, Drama Club, Concert chorale, Student Government Association, Multicultural Council, Student Ambassadors, national fraternities, national sororities.

Athletics Member NAIA.

Campus security: 24-hour emergency response devices and patrols, late-night transport/escort service, controlled dormitory access.

Student services: health clinic, personal/psychological counseling.

COSTS & FINANCIAL AID
Costs (2018–19) ***Tuition:*** state resident $4944 full-time, $206 per credit hour part-time; nonresident $9576 full-time, $399 per credit hour part-time. Full-time tuition and fees vary according to course load. ***Required fees:*** $444 full-time, $222 per term part-time. ***Room and board:*** $9491; room only: $6741. Room and board charges vary according to housing facility.

Financial Aid ***Average financial aid package:*** $7027.

APPLYING
Standardized Tests *Required:* SAT or ACT (for admission).

Options: electronic application, early admission, deferred entrance.

Application fee: $20.

Required: high school transcript.

CONTACT
Dr. Chauvette McElmurry-Green, Registrar, Harris-Stowe State University, 3026 Laclede Avenue, St. Louis, MO 63103. *Phone:* 314-340-3300. *Fax:* 314-340-3555. *E-mail:* admissions@hssu.edu.

Kansas City Art Institute
Kansas City, Missouri
http://www.kcai.edu/

- **Independent** 4-year, founded 1885
- **Urban** 18-acre campus with easy access to Kansas City, MO
- **Coed**
- **Moderately difficult** entrance level

FACULTY
Student/faculty ratio: 9:1.

ACADEMICS
Calendar: semesters. *Degree:* certificates and bachelor's.
Library: Jannes Library. Weekly public service hours: 84; students can reserve study rooms.

STUDENT LIFE
Housing options: on-campus residence required for freshman year; coed. Campus housing is university owned. Freshman applicants given priority for college housing.

Activities and organizations: student-run radio station.

Campus security: 24-hour emergency response devices and patrols, late-night transport/escort service, controlled dormitory access.

Student services: personal/psychological counseling.

COSTS & FINANCIAL AID
Costs (2018–19) ***Comprehensive fee:*** $48,800 includes full-time tuition ($37,900), mandatory fees ($500), and room and board ($10,400). Full-time tuition and fees vary according to reciprocity agreements. Part-time tuition: $1510 per credit hour. Part-time tuition and fees vary according to reciprocity agreements.

Financial Aid Of all full-time matriculated undergraduates who enrolled in 2018, 603 applied for aid, 561 were judged to have need, 97 had their need fully met. In 2018, 98 non-need-based awards were made. ***Average percent of need met:*** 67. ***Average financial aid package:*** $26,872. ***Average need-based loan:*** $4234. ***Average need-based gift aid:*** $23,056. ***Average non-need-based aid:*** $18,583. ***Average indebtedness upon graduation:*** $37,096.

APPLYING
Standardized Tests *Required:* SAT or ACT (for admission). *Required for some:* TOEFL.

Options: electronic application, early admission, deferred entrance.

Application fee: $45.

Required: essay or personal statement, high school transcript, 1 letter of recommendation, portfolio. ***Recommended:*** minimum 2.5 GPA, interview.

CONTACT
Mr. Gerald Valet, Director of Admission Technology, Kansas City Art Institute, 4415 Warwick Boulevard, Kansas City, MO 64111-1874. *Phone:* 816-474-5224. *Toll-free phone:* 800-522-5224. *Fax:* 816-802-3309. *E-mail:* admiss@kcai.edu.

Lincoln University

Jefferson City, Missouri

http://www.lincolnu.edu/

- **State-supported** comprehensive, founded 1866
- **Small-town** 174-acre campus
- **Endowment** $1.6 million
- **Coed**
- **Noncompetitive** entrance level

FACULTY
Student/faculty ratio: 17:1.

ACADEMICS
Calendar: semesters. *Degrees:* associate, bachelor's, master's, and postbachelor's certificates.
Library: Inman E. Page Library. *Books:* 99,126 (physical), 197,476 (digital/electronic); *Serial titles:* 1,194 (physical), 19,000 (digital/electronic); *Databases:* 39. Weekly public service hours: 88.

STUDENT LIFE
Housing options: on-campus residence required through sophomore year; coed, men-only, women-only. Campus housing is university owned.

Activities and organizations: student-run newspaper, choral group, marching band, Student Government Association (SGA), Lincoln University Band, Alpha Kappa Mu, Army ROTC, International Student Association, national fraternities, national sororities.

Athletics Member NCAA. All Division II except golf (Division I).

Campus security: 24-hour emergency response devices and patrols, student patrols, late-night transport/escort service, controlled dormitory access, Rape Aggression Defense class upon request, Operation ID, timely warnings, text message safety alerts, Webpage with helpful tips.

Student services: health clinic, personal/psychological counseling, women's center, veterans affairs office.

COSTS & FINANCIAL AID
Costs (2018–19) ***Tuition:*** state resident $6270 full-time, $209 per credit hour part-time; nonresident $12,810 full-time, $427 per credit hour part-time. Full-time tuition and fees vary according to course load, location, and reciprocity agreements. Part-time tuition and fees vary according to course load, location, and reciprocity agreements. ***Required fees:*** $1362 full-time, $10 per credit hour part-time, $381 per term part-time. ***Room and board:*** $7068; room only: $3618. Room and board charges vary according to board plan and housing facility. ***Payment plans:*** installment, deferred payment.

Financial Aid Of all full-time matriculated undergraduates who enrolled in 2018, 1,039 applied for aid, 920 were judged to have need, 48 had their need fully met. 207 Federal Work-Study jobs (averaging $1006). 47 state and other part-time jobs (averaging $2581). In 2018, 8 non-need-based awards were made. ***Average percent of need met:*** 71. ***Average financial aid package:*** $9953. ***Average need-based loan:*** $4375. ***Average need-based gift aid:*** $6155. ***Average non-need-based aid:*** $3276. ***Average indebtedness upon graduation:*** $30,827.

APPLYING
Standardized Tests *Required:* SAT or ACT (for admission).

Options: electronic application, deferred entrance.

Required: high school transcript. ***Required for some:*** minimum 2.0 GPA.

CONTACT
Liz Morrow, Director of Admissions/Registrar, Lincoln University, Office of Admissions, 820 Chestnut Street, B-7 Young Hall, Jefferson City, MO 65101. *Phone:* 573-681-5102. *Fax:* 573-681-5889. *E-mail:* admissions@lincolnu.edu.

Lindenwood University

St. Charles, Missouri

http://www.lindenwood.edu/

- **Independent Presbyterian** comprehensive, founded 1827
- **Suburban** 285-acre campus with easy access to St. Louis
- **Endowment** $160.3 million
- **Coed** 6,529 undergraduate students, 91% full-time, 54% women, 46% men
- **Moderately difficult** entrance level, 88% of applicants were admitted

UNDERGRAD STUDENTS
5,969 full-time, 560 part-time. Students come from 48 states and territories; 86 other countries; 40% are from out of state; 13% Black or African American, non-Hispanic/Latino; 5% Hispanic/Latino; 0.9% Asian, non-Hispanic/Latino; 0.5% Native Hawaiian or other Pacific Islander, non-Hispanic/Latino; 0.3% American Indian or Alaska Native, non-Hispanic/Latino; 3% Two or more races, non-Hispanic/Latino; 11% Race/ethnicity unknown; 12% international; 11% transferred in; 55% live on campus.

Freshmen:
Admission: 3,416 applied, 3,010 admitted, 1,063 enrolled. ***Average high school GPA:*** 3.3. ***Test scores:*** SAT evidence-based reading and writing scores over 500: 78%; SAT math scores over 500: 78%; ACT scores over 18: 93%; SAT evidence-based reading and writing scores over 600: 21%; SAT math scores over 600: 19%; ACT scores over 24: 35%; SAT evidence-based reading and writing scores over 700: 1%; SAT math scores over 700: 1%; ACT scores over 30: 4%.

Retention: 70% of full-time freshmen returned.

FACULTY
Total: 1,223, 23% full-time, 51% with terminal degrees.

Student/faculty ratio: 13:1.

ACADEMICS
Calendar: 4-1-4 for daytime programs; quarters and trimesters for evening programs. *Degrees:* bachelor's, master's, doctoral, post-master's, and postbachelor's certificates.

Special study options: academic remediation for entering students, accelerated degree program, adult/continuing education programs, advanced placement credit, distance learning, double majors, English as a second language, external degree program, freshman honors college, honors programs, independent study, internships, off-campus study, part-time degree program, services for LD students, student-designed majors, study abroad, summer session for credit. ***ROTC:*** Army (c), Air Force (c).

Unusual degree programs: 3-2 engineering with University of Missouri–Columbia, University of Missouri–St. Louis, Washington University in St. Louis; nursing with Golfarb School of Nursing at Barnes-Jewish College.

Computers: 231 computers/terminals are available on campus for general student use. Students can access the following: campus intranet, computer help desk, free student e-mail accounts, online (class) grades, online (class) registration, online (class) schedules. Campuswide network is available. 100% of college-owned or -operated housing units are wired for high-speed Internet access. Wireless service is available via classrooms, computer centers, computer labs, dorm rooms, learning centers, libraries, student centers.

Library: Library and Academic Resource Center plus 1 other. *Books:* 74,836 (physical), 278,834 (digital/electronic); *Serial titles:* 193 (physical), 97 (digital/electronic); *Databases:* 141. Students can reserve study rooms.

STUDENT LIFE
Housing options: coed, men-only, women-only, special housing for students with disabilities. Campus housing is university owned and leased by the school. Freshman applicants given priority for college housing.

Activities and organizations: drama/theater group, student-run newspaper, radio and television station, choral group, marching band, Kappa Delta Pi, Athletes in Action, Black Student Union, Lindenwood Gender Sexualities Alliance, Psychology Interest Club, national fraternities, national sororities.

Athletics Member NCAA, NAIA, USCAA. All NCAA Division II except golf (Division I). ***Intercollegiate sports:*** baseball M(s), basketball M(s)/W(s), bowling M(s)/W(s), cheerleading M(s)/W(s), cross-country running M(s)/W(s), field hockey W(s), football M(s), golf M(s)/W(s), gymnastics W(s), ice hockey M(s)/W(s), lacrosse M(s)/W(s), riflery M(s)/W(s), rugby M(s)/W(s), soccer M(s)/W(s), softball W(s), swimming and diving M(s)/W(s), tennis M(s)/W(s), track and field M(s)/W(s), volleyball M(s)/W(s), water polo M(s)/W(s), weight lifting M(s)/W(s), wrestling M(s)/W(s). ***Intramural sports:*** basketball M/W, sand volleyball M/W, soccer M/W, softball M/W, volleyball M/W.

Campus security: 24-hour emergency response devices and patrols, late-night transport/escort service, controlled dormitory access.

Student services: health clinic, personal/psychological counseling, veterans affairs office.

COSTS & FINANCIAL AID
Costs (2019–20) ***Comprehensive fee:*** $27,300 includes full-time tuition ($18,000), mandatory fees ($100), and room and board ($9200). Part-time tuition: $495 per credit hour.

Financial Aid Of all full-time matriculated undergraduates who enrolled in 2018, 4,556 applied for aid, 3,803 were judged to have need, 592 had their need fully met. 178 Federal Work-Study jobs (averaging $2820). In 2018, 823 non-need-based awards were made. ***Average percent of need met:*** 57. ***Average financial aid package:*** $14,800. ***Average need-based loan:*** $4465. ***Average need-based gift aid:*** $8953. ***Average non-need-based aid:*** $8077. ***Average indebtedness upon graduation:*** $33,611.

APPLYING
Standardized Tests *Required for some:* SAT or ACT (for admission).

Options: electronic application, deferred entrance.

Required: minimum 2.5 GPA, personal resumé indicating community service, youth leadership, clubs, organizations, and non-academic experience. ***Required for some:*** essay or personal statement, high school transcript. ***Recommended:*** 3 letters of recommendation, interview.

Application deadlines: rolling (freshmen), rolling (transfers).

Notification: continuous (freshmen), continuous (transfers).

CONTACT
Kara Schilli, Director of University Admissions, Lindenwood University, 209 South Kings Highway, St. Charles, MO 63301. *Phone:* 636-949-4369. *Fax:* 636-949-4989. *E-mail:* KSchilli@lindenwood.edu.

Logan University
Chesterfield, Missouri
http://www.logan.edu/

- **Independent** upper-level, founded 1935
- **Suburban** 112-acre campus with easy access to St. Louis
- **Endowment** $15.6 million
- **Coed**
- 100% of applicants were admitted

FACULTY
Student/faculty ratio: 9:1.

ACADEMICS
Calendar: trimesters. *Degrees:* bachelor's, master's, and doctoral.

Library: Learning Resources Center. *Books:* 11,773 (physical), 3,679 (digital/electronic); *Serial titles:* 23 (physical), 64 (digital/electronic); *Databases:* 94. Weekly public service hours: 84.

STUDENT LIFE
Housing options: college housing not available.

Activities and organizations: Chiropractic on Purpose, SOT Club, Rehab2Performance, Family Wellness, Gonstead Club, national fraternities, national sororities.

Campus security: 24-hour patrols, late-night transport/escort service.

Student services: health clinic, personal/psychological counseling.

COSTS & FINANCIAL AID
Costs (2018–19) ***Tuition:*** $8250 full-time, $275 per credit hour part-time. Full-time tuition and fees vary according to course load, degree level, and program. Part-time tuition and fees vary according to course load, degree level, and program. ***Required fees:*** $100 full-time, $50 per term part-time.

Financial Aid Of all full-time matriculated undergraduates who enrolled in 2017, 46 applied for aid, 46 were judged to have need, 1 had their need fully met. ***Average percent of need met:*** 43. ***Average financial aid package:*** $11,002. ***Average need-based loan:*** $2818. ***Average need-based gift aid:*** $5525.

APPLYING
Options: electronic application.

Application fee: $25.

Required: minimum cumulative 2.0 GPA for transfer students.

CONTACT
Ms. Natach Douglas, Director of Admissions, Logan University, 1851 Schoettler Road, Chesterfield, MO 63017. *Phone:* 636-227-2100 Ext. 1718. *Toll-free phone:* 800-533-9210. *Fax:* 636-207-2425. *E-mail:* admissions@logan.edu.

Maryville University of Saint Louis
St. Louis, Missouri
http://www.maryville.edu/

- **Independent** university, founded 1872
- **Suburban** 130-acre campus with easy access to St. Louis
- **Endowment** $55.2 million
- **Coed** 3,678 undergraduate students, 71% full-time, 66% women, 34% men
- **Moderately difficult** entrance level, 95% of applicants were admitted

UNDERGRAD STUDENTS
2,594 full-time, 1,084 part-time. Students come from 46 states and territories; 45 other countries; 31% are from out of state; 10% Black or African American, non-Hispanic/Latino; 5% Hispanic/Latino; 3% Asian, non-Hispanic/Latino; 0.1% Native Hawaiian or other Pacific Islander, non-Hispanic/Latino; 0.5% American Indian or Alaska Native, non-Hispanic/Latino; 3% Two or more races, non-Hispanic/Latino; 4% Race/ethnicity unknown; 4% international; 19% transferred in; 26% live on campus.

Freshmen:
Admission: 2,074 applied, 1,960 admitted, 668 enrolled. ***Average high school GPA:*** 3.6.

Retention: 86% of full-time freshmen returned.

FACULTY
Total: 824, 19% full-time.

Student/faculty ratio: 14:1.

ACADEMICS
Calendar: semesters. *Degrees:* bachelor's, master's, doctoral, post-master's, and postbachelor's certificates.

Special study options: accelerated degree program, adult/continuing education programs, advanced placement credit, cooperative education, distance learning, double majors, English as a second language, external degree program, honors programs, independent study, internships, off-campus study, part-time degree program, services for LD students, study abroad, summer session for credit. ***ROTC:*** Army (c).

Unusual degree programs: 3-2 business administration; engineering with Washington University in St. Louis; social work with Saint Louis University; education.

Computers: 563 computers/terminals are available on campus for general student use. Students can access the following: campus intranet, computer help desk, free student e-mail accounts, online (class) grades, online (class) registration, online (class) schedules, specialized software, university catalog. Campuswide network is available. 100% of college-owned or -operated housing units are wired for high-speed Internet access. Wireless service is available via entire campus.

Library: University Library. *Books:* 57,027 (physical), 252,154 (digital/electronic); *Serial titles:* 78,331 (digital/electronic); *Databases:* 138. Weekly public service hours: 103; study areas open 24 hours, 5–7 days a week.

STUDENT LIFE
Housing options: coed. Campus housing is university owned.

Activities and organizations: drama/theater group, student-run newspaper, choral group, Campus Activities Board, Physical Therapy Club, Student Nurses Association, Community Service Club, Green Maryville Student Association.

Athletics Member NCAA. All Division II. ***Intercollegiate sports:*** baseball M(s), basketball M(s)/W(s), bowling W(s), cross-country running M(s)/W(s), golf M(s)/W(s), lacrosse M(s)/W(s), soccer M(s)/W(s), softball W(s), swimming and diving M(s)/W(s), tennis M(s)/W(s), track and field M(s)/W(s), volleyball W(s), wrestling M(s). ***Intramural sports:*** basketball M/W, cheerleading M/W, lacrosse M/W, rugby M, soccer M/W, softball W, table tennis M/W, tennis M/W, ultimate Frisbee M/W, volleyball M/W.

Campus security: 24-hour emergency response devices and patrols, late-night transport/escort service, controlled dormitory access, video security system in residence halls, self-defense and education programs.

Student services: health clinic, personal/psychological counseling.

COSTS & FINANCIAL AID
Costs (2019–20) ***Comprehensive fee:*** $38,558 includes full-time tuition ($26,070), mandatory fees ($2400), and room and board ($10,088). Part-time tuition: $781 per credit hour. ***Required fees:*** $450 part-time.

Financial Aid Of all full-time matriculated undergraduates who enrolled in 2018, 1,972 applied for aid, 1,763 were judged to have need, 262 had their need fully met. 427 Federal Work-Study jobs (averaging $1119). 123 state and other part-time jobs (averaging $3239). In 2018, 693 non-need-based awards were made. ***Average percent of need met:*** 65. ***Average financial aid package:*** $21,040. ***Average need-based loan:*** $3721. ***Average need-based gift aid:*** $16,518. ***Average non-need-based aid:*** $15,947. ***Average indebtedness upon graduation:*** $28,361.

APPLYING
Options: electronic application, deferred entrance.

Required: high school transcript, minimum 2.5 GPA. ***Required for some:*** essay or personal statement, interview, audition, portfolio.

Application deadlines: rolling (out-of-state freshmen), rolling (transfers).

Notification: continuous (freshmen), continuous (out-of-state freshmen), continuous (transfers).

CONTACT
Ms. Shani Lenore-Jenkins, Associate Vice President of Enrollment, Maryville University of Saint Louis, 650 Maryville University Drive, St. Louis, MO 63141-7299. *Phone:* 314-529-9350. *Toll-free phone:* 800-627-9855. *Fax:* 314-529-9927. *E-mail:* admissions@maryville.edu.

Metro Business College
Cape Girardeau, Missouri
http://www.metrobusinesscollege.edu/

CONTACT
Ms. Kyla Evans, Admissions Director, Metro Business College, 1732 North Kingshighway, Cape Girardeau, MO 63701. *Phone:* 573-334-9181. *Toll-free phone:* 888-206-4545. *Fax:* 573-334-0617.

Midwest University
Wentzville, Missouri
http://www.midwest.edu/

CONTACT
Jeoung H. Ham, Registrar/Director of Admissions, Midwest University, 851 Parr Road, Wentzville, MO 63385. *Phone:* 636-327-4645. *Fax:* 636-327-4715. *E-mail:* usa@midwest.edu.

Missouri Baptist University
St. Louis, Missouri
http://www.mobap.edu/

- **Independent Southern Baptist** comprehensive, founded 1964
- **Suburban** 65-acre campus with easy access to St. Louis
- **Coed** 4,413 undergraduate students, 33% full-time, 61% women, 39% men
- **Moderately difficult** entrance level, 52% of applicants were admitted

UNDERGRAD STUDENTS
1,469 full-time, 2,944 part-time. Students come from 37 states and territories; 20 other countries; 25% are from out of state; 6% Black or African American, non-Hispanic/Latino; 1% Hispanic/Latino; 2% Asian, non-Hispanic/Latino; 0.2% Native Hawaiian or other Pacific Islander, non-Hispanic/Latino; 1% American Indian or Alaska Native, non-Hispanic/Latino; 1% Two or more races, non-Hispanic/Latino; 24% Race/ethnicity unknown; 1% international; 8% transferred in; 28% live on campus.

Freshmen:
Admission: 807 applied, 422 admitted, 249 enrolled. ***Average high school GPA:*** 3.2. ***Test scores:*** SAT evidence-based reading and writing scores over 500: 68%; SAT math scores over 500: 56%; SAT evidence-based reading and writing scores over 600: 10%; SAT math scores over 600: 5%; SAT evidence-based reading and writing scores over 700: 2%.

Retention: 70% of full-time freshmen returned.

FACULTY
Total: 528, 14% full-time, 38% with terminal degrees.

Student/faculty ratio: 19:1.

ACADEMICS
Calendar: semesters. *Degrees:* certificates, associate, bachelor's, master's, doctoral, post-master's, and postbachelor's certificates.

Special study options: academic remediation for entering students, accelerated degree program, adult/continuing education programs, advanced placement credit, distance learning, double majors, honors programs, independent study, internships, off-campus study, part-time degree program, services for LD students, student-designed majors, study abroad, summer session for credit. ***ROTC:*** Army (c).

Computers: 100 computers/terminals are available on campus for general student use. Students can access the following: campus intranet, computer help desk, free student e-mail accounts, online (class) grades, online (class) registration, online (class) schedules. Campuswide network is available. 100% of college-owned or -operated housing units are wired for high-speed Internet access. Wireless service is available via entire campus.

Library: Jung-Kellogg Library. *Books:* 48,169 (physical), 222,044 (digital/electronic); *Serial titles:* 512 (physical), 104 (digital/electronic); *Databases:* 92. Weekly public service hours: 76.

STUDENT LIFE
Housing options: men-only, women-only, special housing for students with disabilities. Campus housing is university owned. Freshman applicants given priority for college housing.

Activities and organizations: drama/theater group, student-run radio station, choral group, Enactus: Students in Free Enterprise, Amp Ministries, Student Missouri State Teacher's Association, Gamma Delta Sigma, Ministerial Alliance, national fraternities, national sororities.

Athletics Member NAIA. ***Intercollegiate sports:*** baseball M(s), basketball M(s)/W(s), bowling M(s)(c)/W(s)(c), cheerleading M(s)/W(s), cross-country running M(s)/W(s), football M(s), golf M(s), lacrosse M(s)(c)/W(s)(c), soccer M(s)/W(s), softball W(s), tennis M(s)/W(s), track and field M(s)/W(s), volleyball M(s)/W(s), wrestling M(s)/W(s). ***Intramural sports:*** basketball M/W, bowling M/W, football M/W, soccer M/W, softball M/W, volleyball M/W.

Campus security: 24-hour emergency response devices and patrols, late-night transport/escort service, controlled dormitory access.

Student services: health clinic, personal/psychological counseling.

COSTS & FINANCIAL AID

Costs (2019–20) ***Comprehensive fee:*** $37,290 includes full-time tuition ($26,860), mandatory fees ($1360), and room and board ($9070). Part-time tuition: $929 per credit hour. ***Required fees:*** $29 per credit hour part-time.

Financial Aid Of all full-time matriculated undergraduates who enrolled in 2018, 1,275 applied for aid, 1,138 were judged to have need, 348 had their need fully met. 559 Federal Work-Study jobs (averaging $2296). In 2018, 56 non-need-based awards were made. ***Average financial aid package:*** $19,674. ***Average need-based loan:*** $4522. ***Average need-based gift aid:*** $5570. ***Average non-need-based aid:*** $7477. ***Average indebtedness upon graduation:*** $25,089.

APPLYING

Standardized Tests *Required:* SAT or ACT (for admission).

Options: electronic application.

Application fee: $35.

Required: high school transcript, minimum 2.0 GPA, 1 letter of recommendation.

Application deadlines: rolling (freshmen), rolling (transfers).

Notification: continuous (freshmen), continuous (transfers).

CONTACT

Mrs. Cynthia Sutton, Director of Admissions, Missouri Baptist University, One College Park Drive, St. Louis, MO 63141-8660. *Phone:* 877-434-1115. *Toll-free phone:* 877-434-1115 Ext. 2290. *Fax:* 314-434-7596. *E-mail:* admissions@mobap.edu.

Missouri Southern State University

Joplin, Missouri

http://www.mssu.edu/

CONTACT

Mr. Derek Skaggs, Director of Enrollment Services, Missouri Southern State University, 3950 East Newman Road, Hearnes 106B, Joplin, MO 64801-1595. *Phone:* 417-625-9537. *Toll-free phone:* 866-818-MSSU. *Fax:* 417-659-4429. *E-mail:* admissions@mssu.edu.

Missouri State University

Springfield, Missouri

http://www.missouristate.edu/

- **State-supported** comprehensive, founded 1905
- **Suburban** 225-acre campus
- **Coed**
- **Moderately difficult** entrance level

FACULTY

Student/faculty ratio: 21:1.

ACADEMICS

Calendar: semesters. *Degrees:* certificates, bachelor's, master's, doctoral, post-master's, and postbachelor's certificates.

Library: Meyer Library.

STUDENT LIFE

Housing options: on-campus residence required for freshman year; coed, special housing for students with disabilities. Campus housing is university owned. Freshman campus housing is guaranteed.

Activities and organizations: drama/theater group, student-run newspaper, radio and television station, choral group, marching band, Residence Hall Association, Campus Ministries, Fraternity and Sorority Life, Student Government Association, Student Activities Council, national fraternities, national sororities.

Athletics Member NCAA. All Division I except football (Division I-AA).

Campus security: 24-hour emergency response devices and patrols, late-night transport/escort service, controlled dormitory access, on-campus police substation.

Student services: health clinic, personal/psychological counseling, legal services.

COSTS & FINANCIAL AID

Costs (2018–19) ***Tuition:*** state resident $6360 full-time, $212 per credit hour part-time; nonresident $14,310 full-time, $477 per credit hour part-time. Full-time tuition and fees vary according to course level, course load, and program. Part-time tuition and fees vary according to course level, course load, and program. ***Required fees:*** $1016 full-time. ***Room and board:*** $8755. Room and board charges vary according to board plan, housing facility, and location.

Financial Aid Of all full-time matriculated undergraduates who enrolled in 2018, 11,681 applied for aid, 8,876 were judged to have need, 1,356 had their need fully met. In 2018, 1923 non-need-based awards were made. ***Average percent of need met:*** 67. ***Average financial aid package:*** $11,600. ***Average need-based loan:*** $4101. ***Average need-based gift aid:*** $6067. ***Average non-need-based aid:*** $3243. ***Average indebtedness upon graduation:*** $25,196.

APPLYING

Standardized Tests *Required:* SAT or ACT (for admission).

Options: electronic application.

Application fee: $35.

Required: high school transcript. ***Required for some:*** essay or personal statement, interview.

CONTACT

Mr. Andrew Wright, Director of Admissions, Missouri State University, 901 South National Avenue, Springfield, MO 65897. *Phone:* 417-836-5517. *Toll-free phone:* 800-492-7900. *Fax:* 417-836-5137. *E-mail:* info@missouristate.edu.

Missouri University of Science and Technology

Rolla, Missouri

http://www.mst.edu/

- **State-supported** university, founded 1870, part of University of Missouri System
- **Small-town** 284-acre campus
- **Endowment** $160.2 million
- **Coed**
- **Very difficult** entrance level

FACULTY

Student/faculty ratio: 20:1.

ACADEMICS

Calendar: semesters. *Degrees:* bachelor's, master's, doctoral, and postbachelor's certificates.

Library: Curtis Laws Wilson Library. *Books:* 305,834 (physical), 447,868 (digital/electronic); *Serial titles:* 14,178 (physical), 79,586 (digital/electronic); *Databases:* 180. Weekly public service hours: 112; students can reserve study rooms.

STUDENT LIFE

Housing options: on-campus residence required through sophomore year; coed, cooperative, special housing for students with disabilities. Campus housing is university owned and leased by the school. Freshman campus housing is guaranteed.

Activities and organizations: drama/theater group, student-run newspaper, radio station, choral group, marching band, Academic Organizations, Honor Society, Special Interest Group, Greek Organizations, Recreational and Sports Club, national fraternities, national sororities.

Athletics Member NCAA. All Division II.

Campus security: 24-hour emergency response devices and patrols, student patrols, late-night transport/escort service, controlled dormitory access, crime prevention programs.

Student services: health clinic, personal/psychological counseling, women's center, veterans affairs office.

COSTS & FINANCIAL AID
Costs (2018–19) ***Tuition:*** state resident $8460 full-time, $282 per credit hour part-time; nonresident $26,322 full-time, $877 per credit hour part-time. Full-time tuition and fees vary according to course load, degree level, program, and student level. Part-time tuition and fees vary according to course load, degree level, program, and student level. ***Room and board:*** $10,094. Room and board charges vary according to board plan, housing facility, and location.

Financial Aid Of all full-time matriculated undergraduates who enrolled in 2016, 3,567 applied for aid, 3,537 were judged to have need, 1,065 had their need fully met. In 2016, 696 non-need-based awards were made. ***Average percent of need met:*** 48. ***Average financial aid package:*** $15,065. ***Average need-based loan:*** $7584. ***Average need-based gift aid:*** $7978. ***Average non-need-based aid:*** $5550. ***Average indebtedness upon graduation:*** $27,500.

APPLYING
Standardized Tests *Required:* SAT or ACT (for admission). *Recommended:* ACT (for admission).

Options: electronic application, deferred entrance.

Application fee: $50.

Required: high school transcript. ***Required for some:*** essay or personal statement, interview.

CONTACT
Ms. Lynn Stichnote, Admissions Office, Missouri University of Science and Technology, 300 West 13th Street, 106 Parker Hall, Rolla, MO 65409. *Phone:* 573-341-4075. *Toll-free phone:* 800-522-0938. *Fax:* 573-341-4082. *E-mail:* admissions@mst.edu.

Missouri Valley College

Marshall, Missouri

http://www.moval.edu/

- **Independent** comprehensive, founded 1889, affiliated with Presbyterian Church
- **Small-town** 140-acre campus with easy access to Kansas City
- **Coed**
- **Minimally difficult** entrance level

FACULTY
Student/faculty ratio: 14:1.

ACADEMICS
Calendar: semesters plus 2 summer sessions. *Degrees:* associate, bachelor's, and master's.
Library: Murrell Memorial Library plus 1 other. *Databases:* 37.

STUDENT LIFE
Housing options: men-only, women-only. Campus housing is university owned. Freshman campus housing is guaranteed.

Activities and organizations: drama/theater group, student-run newspaper, radio and television station, choral group, national fraternities, national sororities.

Athletics Member NAIA.

Campus security: 24-hour emergency response devices, student patrols, late-night transport/escort service, evening to 4 am patrol by trained security personnel.

Student services: health clinic, personal/psychological counseling.

COSTS & FINANCIAL AID
Costs (2018–19) ***Comprehensive fee:*** $29,750 includes full-time tuition ($19,300), mandatory fees ($1300), and room and board ($9150). Full-time tuition and fees vary according to program. Part-time tuition: $350 per credit hour. Part-time tuition and fees vary according to program. ***College room only:*** $4850. Room and board charges vary according to board plan, gender, housing facility, location, and student level. ***Payment plans:*** tuition prepayment, installment.

Financial Aid Of all full-time matriculated undergraduates who enrolled in 2017, 1,041 applied for aid, 998 were judged to have need, 17 had their need fully met. In 2017, 20 non-need-based awards were made. ***Average percent of need met:*** 54. ***Average financial aid package:*** $19,215. ***Average need-based loan:*** $3850. ***Average need-based gift aid:*** $6659. ***Average non-need-based aid:*** $7272. ***Average indebtedness upon graduation:*** $36,349.

APPLYING
Standardized Tests *Required:* SAT or ACT (for admission).

Options: electronic application, early admission, deferred entrance.

Required: high school transcript. ***Required for some:*** essay or personal statement, 3 letters of recommendation, interview. ***Recommended:*** minimum 2.0 GPA, interview.

CONTACT
Ms. Jessica Green, Admissions and Student Visit Coordinator, Missouri Valley College, 500 East College, Marshall, MO 65340-3197. *Phone:* 660-831-4114. *Fax:* 660-831-4233. *E-mail:* admissions@moval.edu.

Missouri Western State University

St. Joseph, Missouri

http://www.missouriwestern.edu/

- **State-supported** comprehensive, founded 1915
- **Suburban** 744-acre campus with easy access to Kansas City
- **Coed**
- **Noncompetitive** entrance level

FACULTY
Student/faculty ratio: 17:1.

ACADEMICS
Calendar: semesters. *Degrees:* certificates, associate, bachelor's, master's, and postbachelor's certificates.
Library: Missouri Western State University Library. *Books:* 166,649 (physical), 215,083 (digital/electronic); *Serial titles:* 1,585 (physical), 57,298 (digital/electronic); *Databases:* 65.

STUDENT LIFE
Housing options: on-campus residence required for freshman year; coed, special housing for students with disabilities. Campus housing is university owned.

Activities and organizations: drama/theater group, student-run newspaper, television station, choral group, marching band, national fraternities, national sororities.

Athletics Member NCAA. All Division II.

Campus security: 24-hour patrols, student patrols, late-night transport/escort service, controlled dormitory access.

Student services: health clinic, personal/psychological counseling, women's center.

COSTS & FINANCIAL AID
Costs (2018–19) ***Tuition:*** state resident $6191 full-time, $206 per credit hour part-time; nonresident $12,782 full-time, $426 per credit hour part-time. Full-time tuition and fees vary according to course load, location, and program. Part-time tuition and fees vary according to course load, location, and program. ***Required fees:*** $718 full-time, $99 per credit hour part-time. ***Room and board:*** $8348; room only: $4690. Room and board charges vary according to board plan and housing facility.

Financial Aid Of all full-time matriculated undergraduates who enrolled in 2018, 285 Federal Work-Study jobs (averaging $1632). 629 state and other part-time jobs (averaging $1722).

APPLYING
Standardized Tests *Required:* SAT or ACT (for admission).

Options: electronic application.

Required: high school transcript.

CONTACT
Mrs. Jamie Sweiger, Assistant Director of Admissions, Missouri Western State University, 4525 Downs Drive, St. Joseph, MO 64507-2294. *Phone:* 816-271-4183. *Toll-free phone:* 800-662-7041. *E-mail:* admission@missouriwestern.edu.

National American University

Independence, Missouri

http://www.national.edu/

CONTACT

National American University, 3620 Arowhead Avenue, Independence, MO 64057. *Toll-free phone:* 866-628-1288.

National American University

Kansas City, Missouri

http://www.national.edu/

CONTACT

Admissions Office, National American University, 7490 Northwest 87th Street, Kansas City, MO 64153. *Phone:* 816-412-5500. *Toll-free phone:* 866-628-1288. *E-mail:* zradmissions@national.edu.

National American University

Lee's Summit, Missouri

http://www.national.edu/

CONTACT

National American University, 401 NW Murray Road, Lee's Summit, MO 64081. *Toll-free phone:* 866-628-1288.

Northwest Missouri State University

Maryville, Missouri

http://www.nwmissouri.edu/

- **State-supported** comprehensive, founded 1905, part of Missouri Coordinating Board for Higher Education
- **Small-town** 370-acre campus with easy access to Kansas City
- **Endowment** $29.8 million
- **Coed** 5,654 undergraduate students, 87% full-time, 57% women, 43% men
- **Moderately difficult** entrance level, 79% of applicants were admitted

UNDERGRAD STUDENTS

4,928 full-time, 726 part-time. Students come from 34 states and territories; 30 other countries; 32% are from out of state; 6% Black or African American, non-Hispanic/Latino; 4% Hispanic/Latino; 0.8% Asian, non-Hispanic/Latino; 0.1% Native Hawaiian or other Pacific Islander, non-Hispanic/Latino; 0.3% American Indian or Alaska Native, non-Hispanic/Latino; 4% Two or more races, non-Hispanic/Latino; 0.9% Race/ethnicity unknown; 3% international; 6% transferred in; 33% live on campus.

Freshmen:

Admission: 6,048 applied, 4,788 admitted, 1,329 enrolled. ***Average high school GPA:*** 3.4. ***Test scores:*** SAT evidence-based reading and writing scores over 500: 72%; SAT math scores over 500: 76%; ACT scores over 18: 91%; SAT evidence-based reading and writing scores over 600: 24%; SAT math scores over 600: 26%; ACT scores over 24: 32%; SAT evidence-based reading and writing scores over 700: 4%; SAT math scores over 700: 4%; ACT scores over 30: 4%.

Retention: 78% of full-time freshmen returned.

FACULTY

Total: 324, 74% full-time, 58% with terminal degrees.

Student/faculty ratio: 21:1.

ACADEMICS

Calendar: trimesters. *Degrees:* certificates, bachelor's, master's, post-master's, and postbachelor's certificates.

Special study options: academic remediation for entering students, advanced placement credit, distance learning, double majors, honors programs, independent study, internships, off-campus study, part-time degree program, services for LD students, study abroad, summer session for credit.

Computers: 260 computers/terminals and 1,145 ports are available on campus for general student use. Students can access the following: campus intranet, computer help desk, free student e-mail accounts, online (class) grades, online (class) registration, online (class) schedules, online courses with library and databases. Campuswide network is available. 100% of college-owned or -operated housing units are wired for high-speed Internet access. Wireless service is available via classrooms, computer centers, computer labs, dorm rooms, learning centers, libraries, student centers.

Library: Owens Library. *Books:* 165,794 (physical), 213,591 (digital/electronic). Weekly public service hours: 95; students can reserve study rooms.

STUDENT LIFE

Housing options: on-campus residence required for freshman year; coed, cooperative, special housing for students with disabilities. Campus housing is university owned. Freshman campus housing is guaranteed.

Activities and organizations: drama/theater group, student-run newspaper, radio and television station, choral group, marching band, Indian Student Association, ACM, National Society of Leadership and Success, Student Senate, Resident Hall Association (RHA), national fraternities, national sororities.

Athletics Member NCAA. All Division II except golf (Division I). ***Intercollegiate sports:*** baseball M, basketball M(s)/W(s), cheerleading M(s)/W(s), cross-country running M/W, football M(s), golf W, soccer W, softball W, tennis M(s)/W(s), track and field M(s)/W(s), volleyball W(s). ***Intramural sports:*** badminton M/W, basketball M/W, cross-country running M/W, football M/W, golf M/W, racquetball M/W, riflery M(c)/W(c), sand volleyball M/W, soccer M(c)/W(c), softball W, table tennis M/W, tennis M/W, track and field M/W, ultimate Frisbee M(c)/W(c), volleyball M/W, weight lifting M(c)/W(c), wrestling M(c).

Campus security: 24-hour emergency response devices and patrols, student patrols, late-night transport/escort service, controlled dormitory access.

Student services: health clinic, personal/psychological counseling, women's center, veterans affairs office.

COSTS & FINANCIAL AID

Costs (2018–19) ***Tuition:*** state resident $5702 full-time, $190 per credit hour part-time; nonresident $12,355 full-time, $412 per credit hour part-time. Full-time tuition and fees vary according to course load, location, program, and reciprocity agreements. Part-time tuition and fees vary according to course load and location. ***Required fees:*** $4103 full-time, $137 per credit hour part-time. ***Room and board:*** $10,016; room only: $6356. Room and board charges vary according to board plan and housing facility. ***Payment plans:*** installment, deferred payment. ***Waivers:*** senior citizens and employees or children of employees.

Financial Aid Of all full-time matriculated undergraduates who enrolled in 2017, 4,024 applied for aid, 3,242 were judged to have need, 1,323 had their need fully met. 410 Federal Work-Study jobs (averaging $1217). 1,061 state and other part-time jobs (averaging $1622). In 2017, 432 non-need-based awards were made. ***Average percent of need met:*** 60. ***Average financial aid package:*** $9815. ***Average need-based loan:*** $3938. ***Average need-based gift aid:*** $6163. ***Average non-need-based aid:*** $2841. ***Average indebtedness upon graduation:*** $36,117.

APPLYING

Standardized Tests *Required:* SAT or ACT (for admission).

Options: electronic application, deferred entrance.

Application fee: $25.

Required: high school transcript, minimum 2.0 GPA, minimum SAT score of 980 or ACT Composite of 21. ***Required for some:*** interview.

Application deadlines: rolling (freshmen), rolling (transfers).

Notification: continuous (freshmen), continuous (transfers).

CONTACT

Mrs. Tammi Grow, Associate Director of Admissions, Northwest Missouri State University, 800 University Drive, Maryville, MO 64468-6001. *Phone:* 660-562-1146. *Toll-free phone:* 800-633-1175. *Fax:* 660-562-1337. *E-mail:* admissions@nwmissouri.edu.

Ozark Christian College
Joplin, Missouri
http://www.occ.edu/

CONTACT
Mr. Bob Witte, Executive Director of Admissions, Ozark Christian College, 1111 North Main Street, Joplin, MO 64801-4804. *Phone:* 417-624-2518. *Toll-free phone:* 800-299-4622. *Fax:* 417-624-0090. *E-mail:* occadmin@occ.edu.

Park University
Parkville, Missouri
http://www.park.edu/

CONTACT
Mr. Eric Blair, Director of Undergraduate Admissions, Park University, 8700 NW River Park Drive, Campus Box 1, Parkville, MO 64152. *Phone:* 816-584-6858. *Toll-free phone:* 800-745-7275. *Fax:* 816-741-4462. *E-mail:* admissions@mail.park.edu.

Purdue University Global
St. Louis, Missouri
http://www.purdueglobal.edu/

CONTACT
Purdue University Global, 1807 Park 270 Drive, St. Louis, MO 63146.

Ranken Technical College
St. Louis, Missouri
http://www.ranken.edu/

CONTACT
Ranken Technical College, 4431 Finney Avenue, St. Louis, MO 63113. *Phone:* 314-371-0233 Ext. 4811. *Toll-free phone:* 866-4-RANKEN.

Research College of Nursing
Kansas City, Missouri
http://www.researchcollege.edu/

- **Independent** comprehensive, founded 1980, part of Rockhurst University
- **Urban** 66-acre campus with easy access to Kansas City
- **Coed, primarily women**
- **Moderately difficult** entrance level

FACULTY
Student/faculty ratio: 7:1.

ACADEMICS
Calendar: semesters. *Degrees:* bachelor's, master's, and post-master's certificates (bachelor's degree offered jointly with Rockhurst College).
Library: Greenlease Library.

STUDENT LIFE
Housing options: coed, men-only, women-only. Campus housing is university owned. Freshman campus housing is guaranteed.

Activities and organizations: drama/theater group, student-run newspaper, radio station, choral group, national fraternities, national sororities.

Athletics Member NCAA. All Division II.

Campus security: 24-hour emergency response devices and patrols, late-night transport/escort service, controlled dormitory access.

Student services: health clinic, personal/psychological counseling.

COSTS & FINANCIAL AID
Costs (2018–19) ***One-time required fee:*** $150. ***Comprehensive fee:*** $47,840 includes full-time tuition ($36,800), mandatory fees ($950), and room and board ($10,090). Part-time tuition: $1228 per credit hour. Part-time tuition and fees vary according to class time. ***Required fees:*** $35 per credit hour part-time. ***College room only:*** $6240. Room and board charges vary according to board plan, housing facility, and location. ***Payment plans:*** installment, deferred payment.

Financial Aid Of all full-time matriculated undergraduates who enrolled in 2015, 138 applied for aid, 102 were judged to have need, 52 had their need fully met. In 2015, 162 non-need-based awards were made. ***Average percent of need met:*** 78. ***Average financial aid package:*** $28,500. ***Average need-based loan:*** $5500. ***Average need-based gift aid:*** $9200. ***Average non-need-based aid:*** $34,800.

APPLYING
Standardized Tests *Required:* SAT or ACT (for admission).

Options: electronic application, deferred entrance.

Required: high school transcript, 1 letter of recommendation. ***Recommended:*** minimum 2.8 GPA, interview.

CONTACT
Mr. Kyle Johnson, Director of Admission, Research College of Nursing, 1100 Rockhurst Road, Kansas City, MO 64110. *Phone:* 816-501-4000. *E-mail:* kyle.johnson@rockhurst.edu.

Rockhurst University
Kansas City, Missouri
http://www.rockhurst.edu/

- **Independent Roman Catholic (Jesuit)** comprehensive, founded 1910
- **Urban** 35-acre campus
- **Endowment** $35.7 million
- **Coed**
- **Moderately difficult** entrance level

FACULTY
Student/faculty ratio: 13:1.

ACADEMICS
Calendar: semesters. *Degrees:* certificates, bachelor's, master's, doctoral, and postbachelor's certificates.
Library: Greenlease Library. *Books:* 112,979 (physical), 180,624 (digital/electronic); *Serial titles:* 798 (physical), 103,252 (digital/electronic); *Databases:* 110. Weekly public service hours: 85.

STUDENT LIFE
Housing options: on-campus residence required through sophomore year; coed, men-only, women-only, special housing for students with disabilities. Campus housing is university owned. Freshman campus housing is guaranteed.

Activities and organizations: drama/theater group, student-run newspaper, choral group, Student Activities Board, Student Senate, Voices for Justice, Panhellenic Sororities, IFC Fraternities, national fraternities, national sororities.

Athletics Member NCAA. All Division II.

Campus security: 24-hour emergency response devices and patrols, late-night transport/escort service, controlled dormitory access, closed-circuit TV monitors.

Student services: health clinic, personal/psychological counseling.

COSTS & FINANCIAL AID
Costs (2018–19) ***Comprehensive fee:*** $47,160 includes full-time tuition ($36,800), mandatory fees ($790), and room and board ($9570). Full-time tuition and fees vary according to class time and course load. Part-time tuition: $614 per credit hour. Part-time tuition and fees vary according to class time and course load. ***Required fees:*** $25 per credit hour part-time. ***College room only:*** $6240. Room and board charges vary according to board plan and housing facility. ***Payment plans:*** installment, deferred payment.

Financial Aid Of all full-time matriculated undergraduates who enrolled in 2016, 1,393 applied for aid, 973 were judged to have need, 268 had their need fully met. In 2016, 224 non-need-based awards were made. ***Average percent of need met:*** 84. ***Average financial aid package:*** $29,079. ***Average need-based loan:*** $4115. ***Average need-based gift aid:*** $23,642. ***Average non-need-based aid:*** $20,682. ***Average indebtedness upon graduation:*** $26,198.

APPLYING
Standardized Tests *Required:* SAT or ACT (for admission).

Options: electronic application, deferred entrance.

Required: high school transcript, minimum 2.0 GPA, 1 letter of recommendation. ***Required for some:*** essay or personal statement, interview.

CONTACT
Kyle Johnson, Director of Freshman Admissions, Rockhurst University, 1100 Rockhurst Road, Kansas City, MO 64110-2561. *Phone:* 816-501-4100. *Toll-free phone:* 800-842-6776. *Fax:* 816-501-4142. *E-mail:* admission@rockhurst.edu.

Saint Louis Christian College
Florissant, Missouri
http://www.stlchristian.edu/

CONTACT
Bob Farrar, Admissions Director, Saint Louis Christian College, 1360 Grandview Drive, Florissant, MO 63033. *Phone:* 314-837-6777 Ext. 1314. *Toll-free phone:* 800-887-SLCC. *E-mail:* bfarrar@stlchristian.edu.

St. Louis College of Health Careers
Fenton, Missouri
http://www.slchc.com/

CONTACT
St. Louis College of Health Careers, 1297 North Highway Drive, Fenton, MO 63026. *Toll-free phone:* 866-529-2070.

★ St. Louis College of Pharmacy
St. Louis, Missouri
http://www.stlcop.edu/

- **Independent** comprehensive, founded 1864
- **Urban** 9-acre campus with easy access to St. Louis
- **Endowment** $137.2 million
- **Coed**
- **Moderately difficult** entrance level

FACULTY
Student/faculty ratio: 8:1.

ACADEMICS
Calendar: semesters. *Degree:* bachelor's and doctoral.
Library: O. J. Cloughly Alumni Library. *Books:* 14,941 (physical), 180,979 (digital/electronic); *Serial titles:* 445 (physical), 43,334 (digital/electronic); *Databases:* 62. Weekly public service hours: 101; study areas open 24 hours, 5–7 days a week; students can reserve study rooms.

STUDENT LIFE
Housing options: on-campus residence required through junior year; coed, special housing for students with disabilities. Campus housing is university owned. Freshman applicants given priority for college housing.

Activities and organizations: drama/theater group, student-run newspaper, choral group, Student Government Association, Student Pharmacist Association, International Student Association, Women's Health Interest Group, Student Alumni Association, national fraternities, national sororities.

Athletics Member NAIA.

Campus security: 24-hour emergency response devices and patrols, late-night transport/escort service, controlled dormitory access.

Student services: personal/psychological counseling.

COSTS & FINANCIAL AID
Costs (2018–19) ***Comprehensive fee:*** $41,900 includes full-time tuition ($28,451), mandatory fees ($1530), and room and board ($11,919). Full-time tuition and fees vary according to degree level, program, and student level. Part-time tuition: $948 per credit hour. ***Required fees:*** $1530 per year part-time. ***College room only:*** $6489. Room and board charges vary according to board plan and housing facility.

Financial Aid Of all full-time matriculated undergraduates who enrolled in 2017, 375 applied for aid, 346 were judged to have need, 45 had their need fully met. 124 Federal Work-Study jobs (averaging $1088). In 2017, 58 non-need-based awards were made. ***Average percent of need met:*** 51. ***Average financial aid package:*** $18,922. ***Average need-based loan:*** $6054. ***Average need-based gift aid:*** $13,967. ***Average non-need-based aid:*** $13,294.

APPLYING
Standardized Tests *Required:* SAT or ACT (for admission).

Options: electronic application, early admission, early decision, early action, deferred entrance.

Application fee: $55.

Required: essay or personal statement, high school transcript, minimum 3.0 GPA, 3 letters of recommendation, letter of reference from science teacher. ***Required for some:*** interview.

CONTACT
Mrs. Connie Horrall, Admissions Processing Coordinator, St. Louis College of Pharmacy, 4588 Parkview Place, St. Louis, MO 63110-1088. *Phone:* 314-446-8328. *Toll-free phone:* 800-278-5267. *Fax:* 314-446-8310. *E-mail:* connie.horrall@stlcop.edu.

Saint Louis University
St. Louis, Missouri
http://www.slu.edu/

- **Independent Roman Catholic (Jesuit)** university, founded 1818
- **Urban** 282-acre campus
- **Coed** 7,167 undergraduate students, 92% full-time, 60% women, 40% men
- **Very difficult** entrance level, 58% of applicants were admitted

UNDERGRAD STUDENTS
6,560 full-time, 607 part-time. 59% are from out of state; 6% Black or African American, non-Hispanic/Latino; 6% Hispanic/Latino; 11% Asian, non-Hispanic/Latino; 0.1% American Indian or Alaska Native, non-Hispanic/Latino; 3% Two or more races, non-Hispanic/Latino; 1% Race/ethnicity unknown; 5% international; 5% transferred in; 53% live on campus.

Freshmen:
Admission: 15,120 applied, 8,698 admitted, 1,517 enrolled. ***Average high school GPA:*** 3.9. ***Test scores:*** SAT evidence-based reading and writing scores over 500: 97%; SAT math scores over 500: 98%; ACT scores over 18: 99%; SAT evidence-based reading and writing scores over 600: 74%; SAT math scores over 600: 70%; ACT scores over 24: 88%; SAT evidence-based reading and writing scores over 700: 17%; SAT math scores over 700: 24%; ACT scores over 30: 40%.

Retention: 90% of full-time freshmen returned.

FACULTY
Total: 1,166, 60% full-time, 67% with terminal degrees.
Student/faculty ratio: 9:1.

ACADEMICS
Calendar: semesters. *Degrees:* certificates, bachelor's, master's, doctoral, post-master's, and postbachelor's certificates.

Special study options: academic remediation for entering students, accelerated degree program, adult/continuing education programs, advanced placement credit, cooperative education, distance learning, double majors, English as a second language, honors programs, independent study, internships, part-time degree program, services for LD students, student-designed majors, study abroad, summer session for credit. ***ROTC:*** Army (c), Air Force (b).

Computers: Students can access the following: campus intranet, computer help desk, free student e-mail accounts, online (class) grades, online (class) registration, online (class) schedules. Campuswide network is available. 100% of college-owned or -operated housing units are wired for high-speed Internet access. Wireless service is available via entire campus.

Library: Pius XII Memorial Library plus 2 others. Study areas open 24 hours, 5–7 days a week; students can reserve study rooms.

STUDENT LIFE
Housing options: on-campus residence required through sophomore year; coed, special housing for students with disabilities. Campus housing is university owned. Freshman campus housing is guaranteed.

A ★ indicates that the school has detailed information with a Premium Profile on Petersons.com.

Activities and organizations: drama/theater group, student-run newspaper, radio and television station, choral group, national fraternities, national sororities.

Athletics Member NCAA. All Division I. ***Intercollegiate sports:*** badminton M(c)/W(c), baseball M(s), basketball M(s)/W(s), bowling M(c)/W(c), crew M(c)/W(c), cross-country running M(s)/W(s), equestrian sports M(c)/W(c), fencing M(c)/W(c), field hockey W(s), golf M(c), ice hockey M(c), lacrosse M(c)/W(c), racquetball M(c)/W(c), rugby M(c), soccer M(s)/W(s), softball W(s), swimming and diving M(s)/W(s), table tennis M(c)/W(c), tennis M(s)/W(s), track and field M(s)/W(s), ultimate Frisbee M(c)/W(c), volleyball M(c)/W(s), water polo M(c)/W(c). ***Intramural sports:*** badminton M/W, basketball M/W, bowling M/W, football M/W, golf M/W, racquetball M/W, sand volleyball M/W, soccer M/W, softball M/W, squash M/W, table tennis M/W, triathlon M/W, ultimate Frisbee M/W, volleyball M/W.

Campus security: 24-hour emergency response devices and patrols, late-night transport/escort service, controlled dormitory access.

Student services: health clinic, personal/psychological counseling, veterans affairs office.

COSTS & FINANCIAL AID

Costs (2019–20) ***One-time required fee:*** $200. ***Comprehensive fee:*** $58,024 includes full-time tuition ($44,700), mandatory fees ($724), and room and board ($12,600). Part-time tuition: $1560 per credit. ***Required fees:*** $240 part-time.

Financial Aid Of all full-time matriculated undergraduates who enrolled in 2018, 4,487 applied for aid, 3,844 were judged to have need, 813 had their need fully met. In 2018, 2124 non-need-based awards were made. ***Average percent of need met:*** 76. ***Average financial aid package:*** $33,452. ***Average need-based loan:*** $4240. ***Average need-based gift aid:*** $27,223. ***Average non-need-based aid:*** $18,995. ***Average indebtedness upon graduation:*** $34,413.

APPLYING

Standardized Tests *Required:* SAT or ACT (for admission).

Options: electronic application, early admission, deferred entrance.

Required: essay or personal statement, high school transcript. ***Recommended:*** 2 letters of recommendation, interview, Health exam.

Application deadlines: rolling (freshmen), rolling (out-of-state freshmen), rolling (transfers).

Notification: continuous (freshmen), continuous (out-of-state freshmen), continuous (transfers).

CONTACT

Jean M. Cox, Assistant Vice President and Dean of Admissions, Saint Louis University, One N. Grand Boulevard, DuBourg Hall, St. Louis, MO 63103. *Phone:* 314-977-2500. *Toll-free phone:* 800-758-3678. *Fax:* 314-977-7136. *E-mail:* admission@slu.edu.

Saint Luke's College of Health Sciences

Kansas City, Missouri

http://www.saintlukescollege.edu/

CONTACT

Mrs. Jennifer Wright, Student Services Associate, Saint Luke's College of Health Sciences, 624 Westport Road, Kansas City, MO 64111. *Phone:* 816-932-8629. *Fax:* 816-932-9064.

Southeast Missouri State University

Cape Girardeau, Missouri

http://www.semo.edu/

- **State-supported** comprehensive, founded 1873, part of Missouri Coordinating Board for Higher Education
- **Small-town** 400-acre campus
- **Endowment** $79.0 million
- **Coed** 10,041 undergraduate students, 73% full-time, 59% women, 41% men
- **Moderately difficult** entrance level, 84% of applicants were admitted

UNDERGRAD STUDENTS

7,296 full-time, 2,745 part-time. Students come from 43 states and territories; 56 other countries; 21% are from out of state; 8% Black or African American, non-Hispanic/Latino; 2% Hispanic/Latino; 1% Asian, non-Hispanic/Latino; 0.2% American Indian or Alaska Native, non-Hispanic/Latino; 2% Two or more races, non-Hispanic/Latino; 1% Race/ethnicity unknown; 5% international; 5% transferred in; 34% live on campus.

Freshmen:

Admission: 4,638 applied, 3,883 admitted, 1,573 enrolled. ***Average high school GPA:*** 3.5. ***Test scores:*** ACT scores over 18: 94%; ACT scores over 24: 36%; ACT scores over 30: 5%.

Retention: 74% of full-time freshmen returned.

FACULTY

Total: 555, 71% full-time, 61% with terminal degrees.

Student/faculty ratio: 20:1.

ACADEMICS

Calendar: semesters. *Degrees:* certificates, associate, bachelor's, master's, post-master's, and postbachelor's certificates.

Special study options: academic remediation for entering students, accelerated degree program, adult/continuing education programs, advanced placement credit, distance learning, double majors, English as a second language, honors programs, independent study, internships, off-campus study, part-time degree program, services for LD students, student-designed majors, study abroad, summer session for credit. ***ROTC:*** Air Force (b).

Computers: 1,550 computers/terminals are available on campus for general student use. Students can access the following: campus intranet, computer help desk, free student e-mail accounts, online (class) grades, online (class) registration, online (class) schedules. Campuswide network is available. 100% of college-owned or -operated housing units are wired for high-speed Internet access. Wireless service is available via classrooms, computer centers, computer labs, dorm rooms, learning centers, libraries, student centers.

Library: Kent Library. *Books:* 380,006 (physical), 263,780 (digital/electronic); *Serial titles:* 4,163 (physical), 58,594 (digital/electronic); *Databases:* 159. Weekly public service hours: 92.

STUDENT LIFE

Housing options: on-campus residence required through sophomore year; coed, special housing for students with disabilities. Campus housing is university owned. Freshman campus housing is guaranteed.

Activities and organizations: drama/theater group, student-run newspaper, radio and television station, choral group, marching band, Student Government, Student Activities Council, Greek Life, Residence Hall Association, International Students Association, national fraternities, national sororities.

Athletics Member NCAA. All Division I. ***Intercollegiate sports:*** baseball M(s), basketball M(s)/W(s), cheerleading M(s)/W(s), cross-country running M(s)/W(s), football M(s), gymnastics W(s), soccer W(s), softball W(s), tennis W(s), track and field M(s)/W(s), volleyball W(s). ***Intramural sports:*** archery M, basketball M/W, bowling M/W, equestrian sports M(c)/W(c), fencing M, field hockey W, football M/W, lacrosse M, riflery M/W, rock climbing M/W, rugby M/W, soccer M/W, softball M/W, table tennis M/W, tennis M/W, ultimate Frisbee M/W, volleyball M/W, weight lifting M/W.

Campus security: 24-hour emergency response devices and patrols, late-night transport/escort service, controlled dormitory access.

Student services: health clinic, personal/psychological counseling, veterans affairs office.

COSTS & FINANCIAL AID

Costs (2018–19) ***Tuition:*** state resident $6254 full-time, $208 per credit hour part-time; nonresident $11,991 full-time, $400 per credit hour part-time. Full-time tuition and fees vary according to course load and location. Part-time tuition and fees vary according to course load and location. ***Required fees:*** $1164 full-time, $39 per credit hour part-time. ***Room and board:*** $8935. Room and board charges vary according to board plan and housing facility. ***Payment plans:*** installment, deferred payment. ***Waivers:*** senior citizens and employees or children of employees.

Financial Aid Of all full-time matriculated undergraduates who enrolled in 2017, 6,174 applied for aid, 4,938 were judged to have need, 712 had their need fully met. 226 Federal Work-Study jobs (averaging $1426). 1,695 state and other part-time jobs (averaging $2044). In 2017, 1330 non-need-based awards were made. ***Average percent of need met:*** 59. ***Average financial aid package:*** $9586. ***Average need-based loan:*** $4208. ***Average need-based gift aid:*** $6582. ***Average non-need-based aid:*** $4655. ***Average indebtedness upon graduation:*** $27,318.

APPLYING
Standardized Tests *Required for some:* SAT or ACT (for admission).

Options: electronic application, deferred entrance.

Application fee: $30.

Required: high school transcript, minimum 2.0 GPA.

Application deadlines: 7/1 (freshmen), rolling (out-of-state freshmen), 7/1 (transfers).

Notification: 9/1 (freshmen), continuous until 9/1 (transfers).

CONTACT
Ms. Lenell Hahn, Director of Admissions, Southeast Missouri State University, One University Plaza, Cape Girardeau, MO 63701-4799. *Phone:* 573-651-2539. *Fax:* 573-651-5936. *E-mail:* lhahn@semo.edu.

Southwest Baptist University

Bolivar, Missouri

http://www.sbuniv.edu/

- **Independent Southern Baptist** comprehensive, founded 1878
- **Small-town** 152-acre campus
- **Endowment** $26.4 million
- **Coed** 2,663 undergraduate students, 67% full-time, 63% women, 37% men
- **Moderately difficult** entrance level, 71% of applicants were admitted

UNDERGRAD STUDENTS
1,780 full-time, 883 part-time. Students come from 34 states and territories; 16 other countries; 21% are from out of state; 4% Black or African American, non-Hispanic/Latino; 3% Hispanic/Latino; 0.7% Asian, non-Hispanic/Latino; 0.2% Native Hawaiian or other Pacific Islander, non-Hispanic/Latino; 0.8% American Indian or Alaska Native, non-Hispanic/Latino; 0.9% Two or more races, non-Hispanic/Latino; 21% Race/ethnicity unknown; 1% international; 8% transferred in; 50% live on campus.

Freshmen:
Admission: 1,946 applied, 1,373 admitted, 448 enrolled. ***Average high school GPA:*** 3.5. ***Test scores:*** SAT evidence-based reading and writing scores over 500: 79%; SAT math scores over 500: 74%; ACT scores over 18: 84%; SAT evidence-based reading and writing scores over 600: 29%; SAT math scores over 600: 27%; ACT scores over 24: 41%; SAT math scores over 700: 3%; ACT scores over 30: 10%.

Retention: 71% of full-time freshmen returned.

FACULTY
Total: 310, 50% full-time, 32% with terminal degrees.

Student/faculty ratio: 11:1.

ACADEMICS
Calendar: 4-1-4. *Degrees:* associate, bachelor's, master's, doctoral, and post-master's certificates.

Special study options: academic remediation for entering students, advanced placement credit, cooperative education, distance learning, double majors, honors programs, independent study, internships, off-campus study, part-time degree program, services for LD students, student-designed majors, study abroad, summer session for credit. ***ROTC:*** Army (c).

Unusual degree programs: 3-2 engineering with Missouri University of Science and Technology.

Computers: 351 computers/terminals are available on campus for general student use. Students can access the following: campus intranet, computer help desk, free student e-mail accounts, online (class) grades, online (class) registration, online (class) schedules. Campuswide network is available. 100% of college-owned or -operated housing units are wired for high-speed Internet access. Wireless service is available via entire campus.

Library: Harriett K. Hutchens Library. Weekly public service hours: 85; students can reserve study rooms.

STUDENT LIFE
Housing options: on-campus residence required through junior year; men-only, women-only, special housing for students with disabilities. Campus housing is university owned. Freshman campus housing is guaranteed.

Activities and organizations: drama/theater group, student-run newspaper, choral group, Enactus, Student Government Association, Fellowship of Christian Athletes, Student Missouri State Teachers Association, PSY CHI.

Athletics Member NCAA. All Division II except golf (Division I). ***Intercollegiate sports:*** baseball M(s), basketball M(s)/W(s), cheerleading M(s)/W(s), cross-country running M(s)/W(s), football M(s), golf M(s)/W(s), soccer M(s)/W(s), softball W(s), tennis M(s)/W(s), track and field M(s)/W(s), volleyball W(s). ***Intramural sports:*** basketball M/W, fencing M/W, football M/W, racquetball M/W, rock climbing M/W, sand volleyball M/W, soccer M/W, softball M/W, table tennis M/W, volleyball M/W.

Campus security: 24-hour emergency response devices and patrols, controlled dormitory access.

Student services: health clinic, personal/psychological counseling.

COSTS & FINANCIAL AID
Costs (2019–20) ***Comprehensive fee:*** $32,330 includes full-time tuition ($23,600), mandatory fees ($910), and room and board ($7820). Part-time tuition: $865 per credit hour. ***College room only:*** $3400.

Financial Aid ***Average indebtedness upon graduation:*** $29,429.

APPLYING
Standardized Tests *Required:* SAT or ACT (for admission).

Options: electronic application.

Application fee: $30.

Required: high school transcript, minimum 2.5 GPA. ***Required for some:*** 3 letters of recommendation. ***Recommended:*** essay or personal statement, interview.

Application deadlines: rolling (freshmen), rolling (transfers).

Notification: continuous (freshmen), continuous (transfers).

CONTACT
Mrs. Becky Van Stavern, Director of Admissions, Southwest Baptist University, 1600 University Avenue, Bolivar, MO 65613-2597. *Phone:* 417-328-1815. *Toll-free phone:* 800-526-5859. *Fax:* 417-328-1808. *E-mail:* bvanstavern@sbuniv.edu.

Stephens College

Columbia, Missouri

http://www.stephens.edu/

CONTACT
Tiffany Goalder, Director of Undergraduate Admissions, Stephens College, 1200 East Broadway, Box 2121, Columbia, MO 65215-0002. *Phone:* 573-876-7239. *Toll-free phone:* 800-876-7207. *Fax:* 573-876-7237. *E-mail:* apply@stephens.edu.

Stevens–The Institute of Business & Arts

St. Louis, Missouri

http://www.siba.edu/

- **Proprietary** 4-year, founded 1947
- **Urban** campus
- **Coed**
- **Moderately difficult** entrance level

FACULTY
Student/faculty ratio: 9:1.

ACADEMICS
Calendar: quarters. *Degrees:* associate and bachelor's.

Library: St. Louis Public Library.

STUDENT LIFE

Housing options: college housing not available.

Activities and organizations: Student Government.

Campus security: late-night transport/escort service, 24-hour controlled entrances.

COSTS

Costs (2018–19) ***Tuition:*** $12,720 full-time, $265 per credit hour part-time. Full-time tuition and fees vary according to course load and program. Part-time tuition and fees vary according to course load and program. No tuition increase for student's term of enrollment. ***Required fees:*** $600 full-time, $200 per term part-time.

APPLYING

Standardized Tests *Required for some:* SAT or ACT (for admission).

Options: electronic application, early admission, deferred entrance.

Application fee: $25.

Required: essay or personal statement, high school transcript, interview.

CONTACT

Sara Dorn, Director of Admissions, Stevens–The Institute of Business & Arts, 1521 Washington Avenue, St. Louis, MO 63103. *Phone:* 314-421-0949 Ext. 1118. *Toll-free phone:* 800-871-0949. *Fax:* 314-421-0304. *E-mail:* admission@siba.edu.

Truman State University

Kirksville, Missouri

http://www.truman.edu/

- **State-supported** comprehensive, founded 1867
- **Small-town** 140-acre campus
- **Endowment** $49.1 million
- **Coed** 5,504 undergraduate students, 87% full-time, 59% women, 41% men
- **Moderately difficult** entrance level, 65% of applicants were admitted

UNDERGRAD STUDENTS

4,771 full-time, 733 part-time. Students come from 40 states and territories; 48 other countries; 16% are from out of state; 4% Black or African American, non-Hispanic/Latino; 3% Hispanic/Latino; 3% Asian, non-Hispanic/Latino; 0.1% Native Hawaiian or other Pacific Islander, non-Hispanic/Latino; 0.3% American Indian or Alaska Native, non-Hispanic/Latino; 4% Two or more races, non-Hispanic/Latino; 1% Race/ethnicity unknown; 7% international; 2% transferred in; 40% live on campus.

Freshmen:

Admission: 4,568 applied, 2,983 admitted, 1,100 enrolled. ***Average high school GPA:*** 3.8. ***Test scores:*** SAT evidence-based reading and writing scores over 500: 91%; SAT math scores over 500: 86%; ACT scores over 18: 100%; SAT evidence-based reading and writing scores over 600: 59%; SAT math scores over 600: 52%; ACT scores over 24: 82%; SAT evidence-based reading and writing scores over 700: 16%; SAT math scores over 700: 24%; ACT scores over 30: 28%.

Retention: 84% of full-time freshmen returned.

FACULTY

Total: 370, 81% full-time, 75% with terminal degrees.

Student/faculty ratio: 16:1.

ACADEMICS

Calendar: semesters. *Degrees:* bachelor's and master's.

Special study options: accelerated degree program, advanced placement credit, cooperative education, double majors, honors programs, independent study, internships, off-campus study, part-time degree program, services for LD students, student-designed majors, study abroad, summer session for credit. ***ROTC:*** Army (b).

Unusual degree programs: 3-2 engineering with Missouri University of Science and Technology; University of Missouri, Columbia; chiropractic with Logan University.

Computers: 1,056 computers/terminals and 3,690 ports are available on campus for general student use. Students can access the following: campus intranet, computer help desk, free student e-mail accounts, online (class) grades, online (class) registration, online (class) schedules. Campuswide network is available. 100% of college-owned or -operated housing units are wired for high-speed Internet access. Wireless service is available via entire campus.

Library: Pickler Memorial Library. *Books:* 495,980 (physical), 388,874 (digital/electronic); *Serial titles:* 355 (physical), 2,407 (digital/electronic); *Databases:* 107. Weekly public service hours: 105; students can reserve study rooms.

STUDENT LIFE

Housing options: on-campus residence required for freshman year; coed, special housing for students with disabilities. Campus housing is university owned. Freshman campus housing is guaranteed.

Activities and organizations: drama/theater group, student-run newspaper, radio and television station, choral group, marching band, Alpha Phi Omega (co-ed service fraternity), Nursing Students Association, Alpha Sigma Gamma (service sorority), Beta Beta Beta (biology honors), National Society of Collegiate Scholars, national fraternities, national sororities.

Athletics Member NCAA. All Division II. ***Intercollegiate sports:*** baseball M(s), basketball M(s)/W(s), bowling M(c)/W(c), cheerleading M(c)/W(c), cross-country running M(s)/W(s), equestrian sports M(c)/W(c), football M(s), golf W(s), lacrosse W(c), riflery M(c)/W(c), rock climbing M(c)/W(c), rugby M(c)/W(c), soccer M(s)/W(s), softball W(s), swimming and diving M/W(s), tennis M(s)/W(s), track and field M(s)/W(s), ultimate Frisbee M(c)/W(c), volleyball M(c)/W(s), weight lifting M(c)/W(c), wrestling M(s). ***Intramural sports:*** badminton M/W, basketball M/W, cross-country running M/W, football M/W, skiing (cross-country) M(c)/W(c), skiing (downhill) M(c)/W(c), soccer M/W, softball M/W, swimming and diving M/W, table tennis M/W, tennis M/W, track and field M/W, ultimate Frisbee M/W, volleyball M/W.

Campus security: 24-hour emergency response devices and patrols, student patrols, late-night transport/escort service, controlled dormitory access.

Student services: health clinic, personal/psychological counseling, women's center.

COSTS & FINANCIAL AID

Costs (2019–20) ***Room and board:*** $9012; room only: $5848.

Financial Aid Of all full-time matriculated undergraduates who enrolled in 2017, 3,685 applied for aid, 2,712 were judged to have need, 935 had their need fully met. 415 Federal Work-Study jobs (averaging $1807). 993 state and other part-time jobs (averaging $734). In 2017, 1880 non-need-based awards were made. ***Average percent of need met:*** 82. ***Average financial aid package:*** $12,546. ***Average need-based loan:*** $4248. ***Average need-based gift aid:*** $7846. ***Average non-need-based aid:*** $6238. ***Average indebtedness upon graduation:*** $24,938.

APPLYING

Options: electronic application, deferred entrance.

Required: essay or personal statement, high school transcript. ***Recommended:*** minimum 3.0 GPA, interview, activities list/resume.

Application deadlines: rolling (freshmen), rolling (transfers).

Notification: continuous (freshmen), continuous (transfers).

CONTACT

Dawn Howd, Associate Director of Admission, Truman State University, Ruth Towne Museum and Visitors Center, 100 East Normal Avenue, Kirksville, MO 63501-4221. *Phone:* 660-785-4114. *Toll-free phone:* 800-892-7792. *Fax:* 660-785-7456. *E-mail:* dhowd@truman.edu.

University of Central Missouri

Warrensburg, Missouri

http://www.ucmo.edu/

- **State-supported** comprehensive, founded 1871
- **Small-town** 1561-acre campus with easy access to Kansas City
- **Coed**
- **Moderately difficult** entrance level

FACULTY

Student/faculty ratio: 18:1.

ACADEMICS
Calendar: semesters. *Degrees:* certificates, bachelor's, master's, post-master's, and postbachelor's certificates.
Library: James C. Kirkpatrick Library plus 1 other. *Books:* 499,982 (physical), 268,431 (digital/electronic); *Serial titles:* 1,579 (physical), 89,008 (digital/electronic); *Databases:* 97. Weekly public service hours: 96; students can reserve study rooms.

STUDENT LIFE
Housing options: on-campus residence required through sophomore year; coed, women-only, special housing for students with disabilities. Campus housing is university owned. Freshman campus housing is guaranteed.

Activities and organizations: drama/theater group, student-run newspaper, radio and television station, choral group, marching band, Roaring Red (Student Booster Club), Greek Organization, Campus Christian House, BSU (Baptist Student Union), International Student Organization, national fraternities, national sororities.

Athletics Member NCAA. All Division II.

Campus security: 24-hour emergency response devices and patrols, student patrols, late-night transport/escort service, controlled dormitory access, canine patrol.

Student services: health clinic, personal/psychological counseling, women's center, veterans affairs office.

COSTS & FINANCIAL AID
Costs (2018–19) ***Tuition:*** state resident $6770 full-time, $226 per credit hour part-time; nonresident $13,539 full-time, $451 per credit hour part-time. Full-time tuition and fees vary according to course load and location. Part-time tuition and fees vary according to location. ***Required fees:*** $903 full-time, $30 per credit hour part-time. ***Room and board:*** $8766; room only: $5502. Room and board charges vary according to board plan, housing facility, and student level. ***Payment plans:*** installment, deferred payment.

Financial Aid Of all full-time matriculated undergraduates who enrolled in 2016, 4,949 applied for aid, 3,701 were judged to have need, 355 had their need fully met. 87 Federal Work-Study jobs (averaging $1522). 1,690 state and other part-time jobs (averaging $1931). In 2016, 1728 non-need-based awards were made. ***Average percent of need met:*** 62. ***Average financial aid package:*** $8622. ***Average need-based gift aid:*** $2833. ***Average non-need-based aid:*** $3474. ***Average indebtedness upon graduation:*** $27,481.

APPLYING
Standardized Tests *Required:* SAT or ACT (for admission).

Options: electronic application, deferred entrance.

Application fee: $30.

Required: high school transcript, rank in upper two-thirds of high school class.

CONTACT
Mr. J. D. Gragg, Director of Admissions, University of Central Missouri, 1400 Ward Edwards, Warrensburg, MO 64093. *Phone:* 660-543-4290. *Toll-free phone:* 800-729-8266. *Fax:* 660-543-8517. *E-mail:* admit@ucmo.edu.

University of Missouri
Columbia, Missouri
http://www.missouri.edu/

- **State-supported** university, founded 1839, part of University of Missouri System
- **Suburban** 1262-acre campus
- **Endowment** $1.0 billion
- **Coed** 22,503 undergraduate students, 92% full-time, 52% women, 48% men
- **Moderately difficult** entrance level, 78% of applicants were admitted

UNDERGRAD STUDENTS
20,720 full-time, 1,783 part-time. Students come from 49 states and territories; 72 other countries; 20% are from out of state; 0.2% Black or African American, non-Hispanic/Latino; 5% Hispanic/Latino; 78% Asian, non-Hispanic/Latino; 8% American Indian or Alaska Native, non-Hispanic/Latino; 4% Two or more races, non-Hispanic/Latino; 0.7% Race/ethnicity unknown; 3% international; 4% transferred in; 21% live on campus.

Freshmen:
Admission: 18,948 applied, 14,750 admitted, 4,673 enrolled. ***Test scores:*** SAT evidence-based reading and writing scores over 500: 95%; SAT math scores over 500: 93%; ACT scores over 18: 100%; SAT evidence-based reading and writing scores over 600: 53%; SAT math scores over 600: 46%; ACT scores over 24: 70%; SAT evidence-based reading and writing scores over 700: 9%; SAT math scores over 700: 11%; ACT scores over 30: 21%.
Retention: 87% of full-time freshmen returned.

FACULTY
Total: 1,326, 95% full-time, 90% with terminal degrees.

Student/faculty ratio: 18:1.

ACADEMICS
Calendar: semesters. *Degrees:* bachelor's, master's, doctoral, post-master's, and postbachelor's certificates.

Special study options: accelerated degree program, adult/continuing education programs, advanced placement credit, cooperative education, distance learning, double majors, English as a second language, external degree program, freshman honors college, honors programs, independent study, internships, off-campus study, part-time degree program, services for LD students, student-designed majors, study abroad, summer session for credit. ***ROTC:*** Army (b), Navy (b), Air Force (b).

Unusual degree programs: 3-2 accountancy, occupational therapy.

Computers: 1,200 computers/terminals are available on campus for general student use. Students can access the following: computer help desk, free student e-mail accounts, online (class) grades, online (class) registration, online (class) schedules. Campuswide network is available. 99% of college-owned or -operated housing units are wired for high-speed Internet access. Wireless service is available via entire campus.
Library: Ellis Library plus 9 others. *Books:* 2.1 million (physical), 953,740 (digital/electronic); *Serial titles:* 87,432 (physical), 94,920 (digital/electronic); *Databases:* 60. Students can reserve study rooms.

STUDENT LIFE
Housing options: on-campus residence required for freshman year; coed, men-only, women-only, special housing for students with disabilities. Campus housing is university owned. Freshman campus housing is guaranteed.

Activities and organizations: drama/theater group, student-run newspaper, radio and television station, choral group, marching band, Alpha Kappa Psi Professional Business Fraternity (Academic), Pre-Medical Society (Academic), Alpha Phi Omega (Service), Mizzou Global Medical Training (Service), UM Investment Group (Academic), national fraternities, national sororities.

Athletics Member NCAA. All Division I except football (Division I-A). ***Intercollegiate sports:*** baseball M(s), basketball M(s)/W(s), cheerleading M/W, cross-country running M(s)/W(s), golf M(s)/W(s), gymnastics W(s), soccer W(s), softball W(s), swimming and diving M(s)/W(s), tennis W(s), track and field M(s)/W(s), volleyball W(s), wrestling M(s). ***Intramural sports:*** archery M(c)/W(c), badminton W(c), baseball M(c), basketball M(c)/W(c), bowling M(c)/W(c), cheerleading M(c)/W(c), crew M(c)/W(c), fencing M(c)/W(c), field hockey W(c), golf M(c)/W(c), gymnastics M(c)/W(c), ice hockey M(c)/W(c), lacrosse M(c)/W(c), racquetball M(c)/W(c), riflery M(c)/W(c), rock climbing M(c)/W(c), rugby M(c)/W(c), sand volleyball M/W, soccer M(c)/W(c), softball M(c)/W(c), swimming and diving M(c)/W(c), tennis M(c)/W(c), triathlon M(c)/W(c), ultimate Frisbee M(c)/W(c), volleyball M(c)/W(c), water polo M(c)/W(c), weight lifting M(c)/W(c).

Campus security: 24-hour emergency response devices and patrols, late-night transport/escort service, controlled dormitory access.

Student services: health clinic, personal/psychological counseling, women's center, legal services, veterans affairs office.

COSTS & FINANCIAL AID
Costs (2018–19) ***Tuition:*** state resident $8591 full-time, $288 per credit hour part-time; nonresident $25,707 full-time, $857 per credit hour part-time. Full-time tuition and fees vary according to course load, program, and reciprocity agreements. Part-time tuition and fees vary according to course load, program, and reciprocity agreements. ***Required fees:*** $1335 full-time, $32 per credit hour part-time. ***Room and board:*** $10,380; room only: $6620. Room and board charges vary according to board plan and housing facility. ***Payment plan:*** installment. ***Waivers:*** senior citizens and

employees or children of employees.

Financial Aid Of all full-time matriculated undergraduates who enrolled in 2017, 14,461 applied for aid, 10,634 were judged to have need, 1,448 had their need fully met. In 2017, 4050 non-need-based awards were made. ***Average percent of need met:*** 60. ***Average financial aid package:*** $12,070. ***Average need-based loan:*** $5091. ***Average need-based gift aid:*** $10,146. ***Average non-need-based aid:*** $6338. ***Average indebtedness upon graduation:*** $27,364.

APPLYING

Standardized Tests *Required:* SAT or ACT (for admission). *Recommended:* SAT (for admission), ACT (for admission).

Options: electronic application, deferred entrance.

Application fee: $55.

Required: high school transcript, specific high school curriculum.

Application deadlines: rolling (freshmen), rolling (out-of-state freshmen), rolling (transfers).

Notification: continuous (freshmen), continuous (out-of-state freshmen), continuous (transfers).

CONTACT

Mr. Charles May, Director of Admissions, University of Missouri, 230 Jesse Hall, Columbia, MO 65211. *Phone:* 573-882-7786. *Toll-free phone:* 800-225-6075. *Fax:* 573-882-7887. *E-mail:* mu4u@missouri.edu.

University of Missouri–Kansas City

Kansas City, Missouri

http://www.umkc.edu/

CONTACT

Ms. Tamera Byland, Director of Admissions, University of Missouri–Kansas City, Office of Admissions, 5100 Rockhill Road, Kansas City, MO 64110-2499. *Phone:* 816-235-1111. *Toll-free phone:* 800-775-8652. *Fax:* 816-235-5544. *E-mail:* admit@umkc.edu.

University of Missouri–St. Louis

St. Louis, Missouri

http://www.umsl.edu/

- **State-supported** university, founded 1963, part of University of Missouri System
- **Suburban** 350-acre campus with easy access to St. Louis
- **Endowment** $83.5 million
- **Coed**
- **Moderately difficult** entrance level

FACULTY

Student/faculty ratio: 18:1.

ACADEMICS

Calendar: semesters. *Degrees:* bachelor's, master's, doctoral, post-master's, and postbachelor's certificates.

Library: Thomas Jefferson Library plus 1 other. *Books:* 1.3 million (physical), 206,616 (digital/electronic); *Serial titles:* 990 (physical), 1,295 (digital/electronic); *Databases:* 195. Weekly public service hours: 82; students can reserve study rooms.

STUDENT LIFE

Housing options: coed, men-only, women-only, special housing for students with disabilities. Campus housing is university owned and is provided by a third party.

Activities and organizations: drama/theater group, student-run newspaper, radio station, choral group, Student Government Association, Associated Black Collegians, Pierre laclede Honors College Student Association, Residence Hall Association, UMSL Radio Station, national fraternities, national sororities.

Athletics Member NCAA. All Division II.

Campus security: 24-hour emergency response devices and patrols, late-night transport/escort service, controlled dormitory access, criminal investigations.

Student services: health clinic, personal/psychological counseling, women's center, veterans affairs office.

COSTS & FINANCIAL AID

Costs (2018–19) ***Tuition:*** state resident $350 per credit hour part-time; nonresident $930 per credit hour part-time. Full-time tuition and fees vary according to course level, course load, location, program, and reciprocity agreements. Part-time tuition and fees vary according to course level, course load, location, program, and reciprocity agreements. ***Room and board:*** Room and board charges vary according to board plan and housing facility.

Financial Aid Of all full-time matriculated undergraduates who enrolled in 2018, 4,174 applied for aid, 3,666 were judged to have need, 353 had their need fully met. 107 Federal Work-Study jobs (averaging $4655). In 2018, 255 non-need-based awards were made. ***Average percent of need met:*** 61. ***Average financial aid package:*** $11,595. ***Average need-based loan:*** $4423. ***Average need-based gift aid:*** $8451. ***Average non-need-based aid:*** $5167. ***Average indebtedness upon graduation:*** $25,110.

APPLYING

Standardized Tests *Required:* SAT or ACT (for admission).

Options: electronic application.

Application fee: $35.

Required: high school transcript, minimum 2.0 GPA, CBHE core requirements. ***Required for some:*** essay or personal statement, 2 letters of recommendation, interview.

CONTACT

Mr. Andrew L. Griffin, Dean of Admissions, University of Missouri–St. Louis, 351 Millennium Student Center, One University Boulevard, St. Louis, MO 63121-4400. *Phone:* 314-516-6941. *Toll-free phone:* 888-GO2-UMSL (in-state); 888-GO2-USML (out-of-state). *Fax:* 314-516-5310. *E-mail:* askdrew@umsl.edu.

Washington University in St. Louis

St. Louis, Missouri

http://www.wustl.edu/

- **Independent** university, founded 1853
- **Urban** 169-acre campus with easy access to St. Louis
- **Endowment** $7.7 billion
- **Coed** 7,751 undergraduate students, 92% full-time, 53% women, 47% men
- **Most difficult** entrance level, 15% of applicants were admitted

UNDERGRAD STUDENTS

7,146 full-time, 605 part-time. Students come from 53 states and territories; 50 other countries; 90% are from out of state; 9% Black or African American, non-Hispanic/Latino; 9% Hispanic/Latino; 16% Asian, non-Hispanic/Latino; 0.1% Native Hawaiian or other Pacific Islander, non-Hispanic/Latino; 5% Two or more races, non-Hispanic/Latino; 2% Race/ethnicity unknown; 7% international; 1% transferred in; 74% live on campus.

Freshmen:

Admission: 31,320 applied, 4,708 admitted, 1,797 enrolled. ***Average high school GPA:*** 4.2. ***Test scores:*** SAT evidence-based reading and writing scores over 500: 100%; SAT math scores over 500: 100%; ACT scores over 18: 100%; SAT evidence-based reading and writing scores over 600: 100%; SAT math scores over 600: 99%; ACT scores over 24: 100%; SAT evidence-based reading and writing scores over 700: 86%; SAT math scores over 700: 93%; ACT scores over 30: 94%.

Retention: 97% of full-time freshmen returned.

FACULTY

Total: 1,466, 67% full-time.

Student/faculty ratio: 8:1.

ACADEMICS

Calendar: semesters. *Degrees:* certificates, bachelor's, master's, doctoral, post-master's, and postbachelor's certificates.

Special study options: accelerated degree program, adult/continuing education programs, advanced placement credit, cooperative education, double majors, English as a second language, independent study, internships, off-campus study, part-time degree program, services for LD students, student-designed majors, study abroad, summer session for credit. ***ROTC:*** Army (b), Air Force (c).

Unusual degree programs: 3-2 business administration; engineering; social work; art, occupational therapy, physical therapy.

Computers: 2,500 computers/terminals and 3,500 ports are available on campus for general student use. Students can access the following: campus intranet, computer help desk, free student e-mail accounts, online (class) grades, online (class) registration, online (class) schedules. Campuswide network is available. 95% of college-owned or -operated housing units are wired for high-speed Internet access. Wireless service is available via classrooms, computer centers, computer labs, dorm rooms, learning centers, libraries, student centers.

Library: John M. Olin Library plus 12 others. *Books:* 2.8 million (physical), 2.0 million (digital/electronic); *Serial titles:* 704 (physical), 170,031 (digital/electronic); *Databases:* 955. Weekly public service hours: 120; study areas open 24 hours, 5–7 days a week; students can reserve study rooms.

STUDENT LIFE

Housing options: on-campus residence required for freshman year; coed, men-only, women-only, cooperative. Campus housing is university owned. Freshman campus housing is guaranteed.

Activities and organizations: drama/theater group, student-run newspaper, radio and television station, choral group, Campus Kitchen, KWUR - Campus Radio Station, Culinary Arts, Catholic Student Union, Ashoka, national fraternities, national sororities.

Athletics Member NCAA. All Division III except golf (Division II). ***Intercollegiate sports:*** archery M(c)/W(c), badminton M(c)/W(c), baseball M, basketball M/W, cross-country running M/W, equestrian sports M(c)/W(c), fencing M(c)/W(c), field hockey W(c), football M, golf M(c)/W, gymnastics M(c)/W(c), ice hockey M(c), lacrosse M(c)/W(c), rock climbing M(c)/W(c), rowing M(c)/W(c), rugby M(c)/W(c), sailing M(c)/W(c), soccer M/W, softball W, squash M(c)/W(c), swimming and diving M/W, table tennis M(c)/W(c), tennis M/W, track and field M/W, triathlon M(c)/W(c), ultimate Frisbee M(c)/W(c), volleyball M(c)/W, water polo M(c)/W(c), weight lifting M(c)/W(c), wrestling M(c). ***Intramural sports:*** archery M/W, badminton M/W, baseball M(c), basketball M(c)/W(c), bowling M/W, cross-country running M(c)/W(c), football M/W, golf M/W(c), racquetball M/W, sand volleyball M/W, soccer M(c)/W(c), softball M/W(c), squash M/W, swimming and diving M(c)/W(c), table tennis M/W, tennis M(c)/W(c), track and field M/W, ultimate Frisbee M/W, volleyball M/W(c), water polo M/W, weight lifting M/W.

Campus security: 24-hour emergency response devices and patrols, student patrols, late-night transport/escort service, controlled dormitory access.

Student services: health clinic, personal/psychological counseling, veterans affairs office.

COSTS & FINANCIAL AID

Costs (2019–20) ***Comprehensive fee:*** $72,192 includes full-time tuition ($54,250), mandatory fees ($1042), and room and board ($16,900). ***College room only:*** $11,650. ***Payment plan:*** tuition prepayment.

Financial Aid Of all full-time matriculated undergraduates who enrolled in 2018, 3,292 applied for aid, 2,971 were judged to have need, 2,943 had their need fully met. 1,386 Federal Work-Study jobs (averaging $2294). In 2018, 441 non-need-based awards were made. ***Average percent of need met:*** 100. ***Average financial aid package:*** $50,010. ***Average need-based loan:*** $4219. ***Average need-based gift aid:*** $47,335. ***Average non-need-based aid:*** $4323. ***Average indebtedness upon graduation:*** $22,555. ***Financial aid deadline:*** 2/1.

APPLYING

Standardized Tests *Required:* SAT or ACT (for admission).

Options: electronic application, early admission, early decision, deferred entrance.

Application fee: $75.

Required: essay or personal statement, high school transcript, 2 letters of recommendation. ***Required for some:*** portfolio for the College of Art and the College of Architecture. ***Recommended:*** minimum 3.5 GPA.

Application deadlines: 1/2 (freshmen), 3/1 (transfers).

Early decision deadline: 11/1 (for plan 1), 1/2 (for plan 2).

Notification: 4/1 (freshmen), 5/1 (transfers), 12/15 (early decision plan 1), 2/15 (early decision plan 2).

CONTACT

Mr. Kyle Strothmann, Senior Associate Director, Washington University in St. Louis, Campus Box 1089, One Brookings Drive, St. Louis, MO 63130-4899. *Phone:* 314-935-6000. *Toll-free phone:* 800-638-0700. *Fax:* 314-935-4290. *E-mail:* admissions@wustl.edu.

Webster University

St. Louis, Missouri

http://www.webster.edu/

- **Independent** comprehensive, founded 1915
- **Suburban** 47-acre campus with easy access to St. Louis
- **Coed**
- **Moderately difficult** entrance level

FACULTY

Student/faculty ratio: 9:1.

ACADEMICS

Calendar: semesters. *Degrees:* certificates, bachelor's, master's, doctoral, post-master's, and postbachelor's certificates.

Library: Emerson Library. Study areas open 24 hours, 5–7 days a week; students can reserve study rooms.

STUDENT LIFE

Housing options: on-campus residence required through sophomore year; coed, special housing for students with disabilities. Campus housing is university owned and leased by the school. Freshman applicants given priority for college housing.

Activities and organizations: drama/theater group, student-run newspaper, radio and television station, choral group, national sororities.

Athletics Member NCAA. All Division III.

Campus security: 24-hour emergency response devices and patrols, student patrols, late-night transport/escort service, controlled dormitory access.

Student services: health clinic, personal/psychological counseling, veterans affairs office.

COSTS & FINANCIAL AID

Costs (2018–19) ***One-time required fee:*** $125. ***Comprehensive fee:*** $38,950 includes full-time tuition ($27,700), mandatory fees ($200), and room and board ($11,050). Full-time tuition and fees vary according to program. Part-time tuition: $710 per credit hour. ***College room only:*** $6050. Room and board charges vary according to board plan and housing facility.

Financial Aid Of all full-time matriculated undergraduates who enrolled in 2017, 1,846 applied for aid, 1,500 were judged to have need, 283 had their need fully met. 1,291 Federal Work-Study jobs (averaging $2738). In 2017, 122 non-need-based awards were made. ***Average percent of need met:*** 63. ***Average financial aid package:*** $23,727. ***Average need-based loan:*** $4629. ***Average need-based gift aid:*** $8574. ***Average non-need-based aid:*** $13,621. ***Average indebtedness upon graduation:*** $29,867.

APPLYING

Standardized Tests *Required:* SAT or ACT (for admission).

Options: electronic application, early admission, deferred entrance.

Application fee: $35.

Required: essay or personal statement, high school transcript, minimum 2.5 GPA, 1 letter of recommendation. ***Required for some:*** interview, audition, portfolio review, and/or interview. ***Recommended:*** minimum 3.0 GPA.

CONTACT

Webster University, 470 East Lockwood Avenue, St. Louis, MO 63119-3194. *Phone:* 314-246-7910. *Toll-free phone:* 800-753-6765.

Westminster College

Fulton, Missouri

http://www.westminster-mo.edu/

CONTACT

Robert Andrews, Vice President and Dean of Enrollment Management, Westminster College, 501 Westminster Avenue, Fulton, MO 65251-1299. *Phone:* 573-592-5251. *Toll-free phone:* 800-475-3361. *Fax:* 573-592-5255. *E-mail:* admissions@westminster-mo.edu.

William Jewell College

Liberty, Missouri

http://www.jewell.edu/

- **Independent** comprehensive, founded 1849
- **Suburban** 200-acre campus with easy access to Kansas City
- **Endowment** $63.8 million
- **Coed** 803 undergraduate students, 97% full-time, 55% women, 45% men
- **Moderately difficult** entrance level, 46% of applicants were admitted

UNDERGRAD STUDENTS
779 full-time, 24 part-time. Students come from 30 states and territories; 19 other countries; 38% are from out of state; 5% Black or African American, non-Hispanic/Latino; 6% Hispanic/Latino; 1% Asian, non-Hispanic/Latino; 0.4% Native Hawaiian or other Pacific Islander, non-Hispanic/Latino; 0.1% American Indian or Alaska Native, non-Hispanic/Latino; 4% Two or more races, non-Hispanic/Latino; 2% Race/ethnicity unknown; 3% international; 5% transferred in; 85% live on campus.

Freshmen:
Admission: 1,316 applied, 605 admitted, 167 enrolled. ***Average high school GPA:*** 3.6. ***Test scores:*** SAT evidence-based reading and writing scores over 500: 86%; SAT math scores over 500: 90%; ACT scores over 18: 98%; SAT evidence-based reading and writing scores over 600: 38%; SAT math scores over 600: 44%; ACT scores over 24: 64%; SAT evidence-based reading and writing scores over 700: 10%; SAT math scores over 700: 8%; ACT scores over 30: 19%.

Retention: 73% of full-time freshmen returned.

FACULTY
Total: 96, 72% full-time, 68% with terminal degrees.

Student/faculty ratio: 10:1.

ACADEMICS
Calendar: semesters. *Degrees:* bachelor's, master's, and postbachelor's certificates (also offers evening program with significant enrollment not reflected in profile).

Special study options: accelerated degree program, advanced placement credit, cooperative education, distance learning, double majors, English as a second language, honors programs, independent study, internships, off-campus study, services for LD students, student-designed majors, study abroad, summer session for credit. ***ROTC:*** Army (c).

Unusual degree programs: 3-2 engineering with Washington University in St. Louis, University of Kansas, Vanderbilt University, Columbia University, Missouri University of Science and Technology; forestry with Duke University; occupational therapy with Washington University in St. Louis.

Computers: 25 computers/terminals and 900 ports are available on campus for general student use. Students can access the following: campus intranet, computer help desk, free student e-mail accounts, online (class) grades, online (class) registration, online (class) schedules, all students provided with an iPad and support service. Campuswide network is available. 100% of college-owned or -operated housing units are wired for high-speed Internet access. Wireless service is available via entire campus.

Library: Charles F. Curry Library. *Books:* 129,403 (physical), 364,504 (digital/electronic); *Serial titles:* 71 (physical), 57,096 (digital/electronic); *Databases:* 63. Weekly public service hours: 90; study areas open 24 hours, 5–7 days a week; students can reserve study rooms.

STUDENT LIFE
Housing options: on-campus residence required through senior year; coed, men-only, women-only, special housing for students with disabilities. Campus housing is university owned. Freshman campus housing is guaranteed.

Activities and organizations: drama/theater group, student-run newspaper, choral group, College Union Activities, Intramurals, Mosaic, Student Senate, Black Student Association, national fraternities, national sororities.

Athletics Member NCAA. All Division II. ***Intercollegiate sports:*** baseball M(s), basketball M(s)/W(s), cheerleading M(s)/W(s), cross-country running M(s)/W(s), football M(s), golf M(s), soccer M(s)/W(s), softball W(s), swimming and diving M(s)/W(s), tennis M(s)/W(s), track and field M(s)/W(s), volleyball W(s). ***Intramural sports:*** basketball M/W, racquetball M/W, sand volleyball M/W, soccer M/W, softball M/W, tennis M/W, ultimate Frisbee M/W, volleyball M/W.

Campus security: 24-hour emergency response devices and patrols, late-night transport/escort service, controlled dormitory access.

Student services: health clinic, personal/psychological counseling.

COSTS & FINANCIAL AID
Costs (2019–20) ***Comprehensive fee:*** $44,580 includes full-time tuition ($33,500), mandatory fees ($950), and room and board ($10,130). Part-time tuition: $980 per credit.

Financial Aid Of all full-time matriculated undergraduates who enrolled in 2018, 597 applied for aid, 503 were judged to have need, 153 had their need fully met. In 2018, 104 non-need-based awards were made. ***Average percent of need met:*** 85. ***Average financial aid package:*** $31,003. ***Average need-based loan:*** $4447. ***Average need-based gift aid:*** $25,967. ***Average non-need-based aid:*** $20,506. ***Average indebtedness upon graduation:*** $32,917.

APPLYING
Standardized Tests *Recommended:* SAT or ACT (for admission).

Options: electronic application, deferred entrance.

Required: essay or personal statement, high school transcript. ***Required for some:*** interview.

Application deadlines: rolling (freshmen), rolling (transfers).

Notification: 11/1 (freshmen), continuous (transfers).

CONTACT
Mr. Brian Haines, Director of Admission Services, William Jewell College, 500 College Hill, Liberty, MO 64068. *Phone:* 816-415-7871. *Toll-free phone:* 888-2JEWELL. *Fax:* 816-415-5040. *E-mail:* hainesb@william.jewell.edu.

William Woods University

Fulton, Missouri

http://www.williamwoods.edu/

- **Independent** comprehensive, founded 1870, affiliated with Christian Church (Disciples of Christ)
- **Small-town** 200-acre campus with easy access to St. Louis, Kansas City
- **Endowment** $18.5 million
- **Coed**
- **Moderately difficult** entrance level

FACULTY
Student/faculty ratio: 16:1.

ACADEMICS
Calendar: semesters. *Degrees:* associate, bachelor's, master's, doctoral, and post-master's certificates.
Library: Dulany Library. *Books:* 75,506 (physical), 274,700 (digital/electronic); *Serial titles:* 821 (physical), 122,059 (digital/electronic); *Databases:* 57. Weekly public service hours: 87; students can reserve study rooms.

STUDENT LIFE
Housing options: on-campus residence required through senior year; coed, men-only, women-only, special housing for students with disabilities. Campus housing is university owned. Freshman campus housing is guaranteed.

Activities and organizations: drama/theater group, student-run radio station, choral group, DECA, Students of Social Work, Campus Activities Board, Hands Up , Campus Crusade for Christ, national fraternities, national sororities.

Athletics Member NAIA.

Campus security: 24-hour emergency response devices and patrols, late-night transport/escort service, controlled dormitory access.

Student services: health clinic, personal/psychological counseling, veterans affairs office.

COSTS & FINANCIAL AID
Costs (2018–19) ***Comprehensive fee:*** $33,885 includes full-time tuition ($23,230), mandatory fees ($955), and room and board ($9700). Full-time tuition and fees vary according to course load and program. Part-time tuition: $425 per credit hour. Part-time tuition and fees vary according to course load and program. ***Required fees:*** $75 per term part-time. ***College***

room only: $5050. Room and board charges vary according to board plan and housing facility.

Financial Aid Of all full-time matriculated undergraduates who enrolled in 2018, 602 applied for aid, 543 were judged to have need, 76 had their need fully met. In 2018, 53 non-need-based awards were made. ***Average percent of need met:*** 70. ***Average financial aid package:*** $18,567. ***Average need-based loan:*** $8730. ***Average need-based gift aid:*** $16,233. ***Average non-need-based aid:*** $10,452. ***Average indebtedness upon graduation:*** $33,704.

APPLYING

Standardized Tests *Required:* SAT or ACT (for admission).

Options: electronic application, deferred entrance.

Required: high school transcript, minimum 2.5 GPA, 16 hours college preparatory units.

CONTACT

Mrs. Ashley Sundin, Admissions Office Coordinator, William Woods University, One University Avenue, Fulton, MO 65251. *Phone:* 573-592-4400. *Toll-free phone:* 800-995-3159 Ext. 4221. *Fax:* 573-592-1146. *E-mail:* ashley.sundin@williamwoods.edu.

MONTANA

Carroll College

Helena, Montana

http://www.carroll.edu/

- **Independent Roman Catholic** 4-year, founded 1909
- **Small-town** 61-acre campus
- **Endowment** $36.0 million
- **Coed**
- **Moderately difficult** entrance level

FACULTY

Student/faculty ratio: 12:1.

ACADEMICS

Calendar: semesters. *Degrees:* certificates, associate, and bachelor's.
Library: Corette Library plus 1 other. *Books:* 76,993 (physical), 230,000 (digital/electronic); *Databases:* 79. Study areas open 24 hours, 5–7 days a week; students can reserve study rooms.

STUDENT LIFE

Housing options: on-campus residence required through sophomore year; coed. Campus housing is university owned. Freshman campus housing is guaranteed.

Activities and organizations: drama/theater group, student-run newspaper, radio station, choral group, Student Government, Carroll Outreach Team, Carroll Adventure and Mountaineering Program, Up 'Til Dawn, Engineers Without Borders.

Athletics Member NAIA.

Campus security: 24-hour emergency response devices, late-night transport/escort service, controlled dormitory access.

Student services: health clinic, personal/psychological counseling.

COSTS & FINANCIAL AID

Costs (2018–19) ***Comprehensive fee:*** $45,466 includes full-time tuition ($34,506), mandatory fees ($980), and room and board ($9980). Full-time tuition and fees vary according to program. Part-time tuition: $1438 per credit hour. Part-time tuition and fees vary according to program. ***Required fees:*** $245 per year part-time. ***Room and board:*** Room and board charges vary according to board plan.

Financial Aid Of all full-time matriculated undergraduates who enrolled in 2017, 975 applied for aid, 840 were judged to have need, 202 had their need fully met. In 2017, 407 non-need-based awards were made. ***Average percent of need met:*** 78. ***Average financial aid package:*** $26,678. ***Average need-based loan:*** $4723. ***Average need-based gift aid:*** $21,060. ***Average non-need-based aid:*** $14,949. ***Average indebtedness upon graduation:*** $30,794.

APPLYING

Standardized Tests *Required:* SAT or ACT (for admission). *Required for some:* SAT Subject Tests (for admission).

Options: electronic application, deferred entrance.

Application fee: $35.

Required: essay or personal statement, high school transcript. ***Required for some:*** interview. ***Recommended:*** interview.

CONTACT

Director of Admission, Carroll College, 1601 North Benton Avenue, Helena, MT 59625-0002. *Phone:* 406-447-4384. *Toll-free phone:* 800-992-3648. *E-mail:* admission@carroll.edu.

Montana Bible College

Bozeman, Montana

http://www.montanabiblecollege.edu/

- **Independent Christian** 4-year
- **Urban** campus
- **Coed**

ACADEMICS

Calendar: semesters. *Degree:* certificates and bachelor's.
Library: Gail Horton Library plus 1 other.

STUDENT LIFE

Housing options: Campus housing is university owned.

COSTS

Costs (2018–19) ***Tuition:*** $7680 full-time, $240 per credit hour part-time. Full-time tuition and fees vary according to location. Part-time tuition and fees vary according to course load and location. ***Required fees:*** $600 full-time. ***Room only:*** $3200. Room and board charges vary according to housing facility.

APPLYING

Standardized Tests *Required:* SAT or ACT (for admission).

Options: electronic application.

Required: essay or personal statement, 4 letters of recommendation. ***Required for some:*** high school transcript, college transcript.

CONTACT

Montana Bible College, 3625 South 19th Avenue, Bozeman, MT 59718. *Toll-free phone:* 888-462-2463.

Montana State University

Bozeman, Montana

http://www.montana.edu/

CONTACT

Ms. Ronda Russell, Director of Admissions, Montana State University, PO Box 172190, Bozeman, MT 59717-2190. *Phone:* 406-994-2452. *Toll-free phone:* 888-MSU-CATS. *Fax:* 406-994-1923. *E-mail:* admissions@montana.edu.

Montana State University Billings

Billings, Montana

http://www.msubillings.edu/

- **State-supported** comprehensive, founded 1927, part of Montana University System
- **Urban** 92-acre campus
- **Endowment** $24.7 million
- **Coed**
- **Minimally difficult** entrance level

FACULTY

Student/faculty ratio: 14:1.

ACADEMICS

Calendar: semesters. *Degrees:* certificates, associate, bachelor's, and master's.
Library: Montana State University Billings Library plus 2 others. *Books:* 138,650 (physical), 351,351 (digital/electronic); *Serial titles:* 1,368 (physical), 669,204 (digital/electronic); *Databases:* 170. Weekly public service hours: 82; students can reserve study rooms.

STUDENT LIFE
Housing options: on-campus residence required for freshman year; coed, special housing for students with disabilities. Campus housing is university owned. Freshman applicants given priority for college housing.

Activities and organizations: drama/theater group, student-run newspaper, radio station, choral group, Intervarsity Christian Fellowship, Accounting Club, HEROES, Multicultural Club, Art Student League.

Athletics Member NCAA. All Division II.

Campus security: 24-hour emergency response devices and patrols, late-night transport/escort service, controlled dormitory access.

Student services: health clinic, personal/psychological counseling, women's center, legal services.

COSTS & FINANCIAL AID
Costs (2018–19) ***Tuition:*** state resident $4485 full-time, $187 per credit hour part-time; nonresident $17,678 full-time, $737 per credit hour part-time. Full-time tuition and fees vary according to course load, location, and program. Part-time tuition and fees vary according to course load, location, and program. ***Required fees:*** $1436 full-time. ***Room and board:*** $8186; room only: $4450. Room and board charges vary according to board plan and housing facility.

Financial Aid Of all full-time matriculated undergraduates who enrolled in 2016, 1,848 applied for aid, 1,473 were judged to have need, 487 had their need fully met. In 2016, 149 non-need-based awards were made. ***Average percent of need met:*** 75. ***Average financial aid package:*** $10,006. ***Average need-based loan:*** $6113. ***Average need-based gift aid:*** $4468. ***Average non-need-based aid:*** $2625. ***Average indebtedness upon graduation:*** $26,780.

APPLYING
Standardized Tests *Required for some:* SAT or ACT (for admission).

Options: electronic application.

Application fee: $30.

Required: high school transcript.

CONTACT
Ms. Tammi Watson, Associate Director of Admissions, Montana State University Billings, 1500 University Drive, Billings, MT 59101. *Phone:* 406-657-2158. *Toll-free phone:* 800-565-6782. *Fax:* 406-657-2302. *E-mail:* tammi.watson@msubillings.edu.

Montana State University–Northern

Havre, Montana

http://www.msun.edu/

CONTACT
Montana State University–Northern, PO Box 7751, Havre, MT 59501-7751. *Phone:* 406-265-3704. *Toll-free phone:* 800-662-6132.

Montana Tech of The University of Montana

Butte, Montana

http://www.mtech.edu/

- **State-supported** comprehensive, founded 1895, part of Montana University System
- **Small-town** 56-acre campus
- **Endowment** $32.9 million
- **Coed**
- **Moderately difficult** entrance level

FACULTY
Student/faculty ratio: 13:1.

ACADEMICS
Calendar: semesters. *Degrees:* certificates, diplomas, associate, bachelor's, master's, doctoral, and postbachelor's certificates.
Library: Montana Tech Library. *Books:* 80,864 (physical), 91,830 (digital/electronic); *Serial titles:* 1,859 (physical), 67,191 (digital/electronic); *Databases:* 148. Weekly public service hours: 80; students can reserve study rooms.

STUDENT LIFE
Housing options: on-campus residence required for freshman year; coed, special housing for students with disabilities. Campus housing is university owned. Freshman campus housing is guaranteed.

Activities and organizations: student-run newspaper, radio station, choral group, Circle K, Ski/Snowboard Club, BSU, Hockey Club, Dance Club.

Athletics Member NAIA.

Campus security: 24-hour patrols, controlled dormitory access.

Student services: health clinic, personal/psychological counseling.

COSTS & FINANCIAL AID
Costs (2018–19) ***Tuition:*** state resident $5707 full-time, $238 per credit part-time; nonresident $20,870 full-time, $886 per credit part-time. Full-time tuition and fees vary according to course load, degree level, location, and program. Part-time tuition and fees vary according to course load, degree level, location, and program. ***Required fees:*** $1704 full-time, $69 per credit part-time. ***Room and board:*** $9828; room only: $4366. Room and board charges vary according to board plan.

Financial Aid Of all full-time matriculated undergraduates who enrolled in 2017, 1,328 applied for aid, 1,006 were judged to have need, 142 had their need fully met. In 2017, 298 non-need-based awards were made. ***Average percent of need met:*** 62. ***Average financial aid package:*** $10,983. ***Average need-based loan:*** $3986. ***Average need-based gift aid:*** $5763. ***Average non-need-based aid:*** $3684. ***Average indebtedness upon graduation:*** $22,444.

APPLYING
Standardized Tests *Required:* SAT or ACT (for admission).

Options: electronic application, deferred entrance.

Application fee: $30.

Required: high school transcript, proof of immunization. ***Required for some:*** minimum 2.5 GPA.

CONTACT
Stephanie Crowe, Montana Tech of The University of Montana, 1300 West Park Street, Butte, MT 59701-8997. *Phone:* 406-496-4568. *Toll-free phone:* 800-445-TECH. *Fax:* 406-496-4705. *E-mail:* scrowe@mtech.edu.

Rocky Mountain College

Billings, Montana

http://www.rocky.edu/

- **Independent interdenominational** comprehensive, founded 1878
- **Suburban** 60-acre campus
- **Endowment** $30.9 million
- **Coed** 897 undergraduate students, 97% full-time, 49% women, 51% men
- **Moderately difficult** entrance level, 58% of applicants were admitted

UNDERGRAD STUDENTS
867 full-time, 30 part-time. Students come from 43 states and territories; 16 other countries; 47% are from out of state; 3% Black or African American, non-Hispanic/Latino; 6% Hispanic/Latino; 0.6% Asian, non-Hispanic/Latino; 0.7% Native Hawaiian or other Pacific Islander, non-Hispanic/Latino; 2% American Indian or Alaska Native, non-Hispanic/Latino; 5% Two or more races, non-Hispanic/Latino; 2% Race/ethnicity unknown; 4% international; 5% transferred in; 51% live on campus.

Freshmen:
Admission: 1,521 applied, 889 admitted, 252 enrolled. ***Average high school GPA:*** 3.4. ***Test scores:*** SAT evidence-based reading and writing scores over 500: 73%; SAT math scores over 500: 81%; ACT scores over 18: 93%; SAT evidence-based reading and writing scores over 600: 17%; SAT math scores over 600: 22%; ACT scores over 24: 37%; ACT scores over 30: 4%.

Retention: 67% of full-time freshmen returned.

FACULTY
Total: 112, 57% full-time, 60% with terminal degrees.

Student/faculty ratio: 11:1.

ACADEMICS
Calendar: semesters. *Degrees:* associate, bachelor's, master's, and doctoral.

Special study options: academic remediation for entering students, accelerated degree program, adult/continuing education programs, advanced placement credit, double majors, English as a second language, honors programs, independent study, internships, off-campus study, part-time degree program, services for LD students, student-designed majors, study abroad, summer session for credit. ***ROTC:*** Army (c).

Unusual degree programs: 3-2 accountancy.

Computers: 113 computers/terminals are available on campus for general student use. Students can access the following: campus intranet, free student e-mail accounts, online (class) grades, online (class) registration, online (class) schedules. Campuswide network is available. 100% of college-owned or -operated housing units are wired for high-speed Internet access. Wireless service is available via entire campus.
Library: Paul M. Adams Memorial Library. *Books:* 46,877 (physical), 172,956 (digital/electronic); *Serial titles:* 379 (physical), 92,127 (digital/electronic); *Databases:* 119. Weekly public service hours: 89.

STUDENT LIFE
Housing options: on-campus residence required through sophomore year; coed, special housing for students with disabilities. Campus housing is university owned. Freshman campus housing is guaranteed.

Activities and organizations: drama/theater group, student-run newspaper, choral group, Outdoor Recreation, Enactus, Flight Team/Club, Environmental Club, InterVarsity Christian Fellowship.

Athletics Member NAIA. ***Intercollegiate sports:*** basketball M(s)/W(s), cheerleading M(s)/W(s), cross-country running M(s)/W(s), equestrian sports M(c)/W(c), football M(s), golf M(s)/W(s), skiing (downhill) M(s)/W(s), soccer M(s)/W(s), track and field M(s)/W(s), volleyball W(s). ***Intramural sports:*** basketball M/W, fencing M(c)/W(c), football M/W, golf M/W, ice hockey M(c)/W(c), racquetball M/W, rock climbing M/W, skiing (downhill) M/W, soccer M/W, softball M/W, swimming and diving M/W, table tennis M/W, ultimate Frisbee M/W, volleyball M/W, weight lifting M(c)/W(c), wrestling M(c)/W(c).

Campus security: 24-hour emergency response devices, student patrols, late-night transport/escort service, controlled dormitory access.

Student services: health clinic, personal/psychological counseling, veterans affairs office.

COSTS & FINANCIAL AID
Costs (2019–20) *Comprehensive fee:* $38,004 includes full-time tuition ($28,962), mandatory fees ($590), and room and board ($8452). Part-time tuition: $1207 per credit. ***Required fees:*** $190 part-time. ***College room only:*** $4140.

Financial Aid Of all full-time matriculated undergraduates who enrolled in 2018, 730 applied for aid, 670 were judged to have need, 139 had their need fully met. 329 Federal Work-Study jobs (averaging $402). 160 state and other part-time jobs (averaging $927). In 2018, 33 non-need-based awards were made. ***Average percent of need met:*** 73. ***Average financial aid package:*** $24,815. ***Average need-based loan:*** $4018. ***Average need-based gift aid:*** $20,271. ***Average non-need-based aid:*** $12,688. ***Average indebtedness upon graduation:*** $32,435.

APPLYING
Standardized Tests *Required:* SAT or ACT (for admission).

Options: electronic application, deferred entrance.

Application fee: $35.

Required: high school transcript, minimum 2.5 GPA. ***Required for some:*** essay or personal statement, 2 letters of recommendation, interview.

Application deadlines: rolling (freshmen), rolling (transfers).

Notification: continuous (freshmen), continuous (transfers).

CONTACT
Austin Mapston, Dean for Enrollment Services, Rocky Mountain College, 1511 Poly Drive, Billings, MT 59102. *Phone:* 406-657-1026. *Toll-free phone:* 800-877-6259. *Fax:* 406-259-9751. *E-mail:* admissions@rocky.edu.

Salish Kootenai College

Pablo, Montana

http://www.skc.edu/

CONTACT
Ms. Jackie Moran, Admissions Officer, Salish Kootenai College, PO Box 70, Pablo, MT 59855-0117. *Phone:* 406-275-4866. *Fax:* 406-275-4810. *E-mail:* jackie_moran@skc.edu.

University of Montana

Missoula, Montana

http://www.umt.edu/

- **State-supported** university, founded 1893, part of Montana University System
- **Urban** 220-acre campus
- **Endowment** $166.4 million
- **Coed**
- **Moderately difficult** entrance level

FACULTY
Student/faculty ratio: 17:1.

ACADEMICS
Calendar: semesters. *Degrees:* certificates, associate, bachelor's, master's, doctoral, post-master's, and postbachelor's certificates.
Library: Maureen and Mike Mansfield Library plus 2 others. *Books:* 139,763 (physical), 602,331 (digital/electronic); *Serial titles:* 15,019 (physical), 62,294 (digital/electronic); *Databases:* 202. Students can reserve study rooms.

STUDENT LIFE
Housing options: on-campus residence required for freshman year; coed, men-only, women-only, special housing for students with disabilities. Campus housing is university owned. Freshman campus housing is guaranteed.

Activities and organizations: drama/theater group, student-run newspaper, radio station, choral group, marching band, national fraternities, national sororities.

Athletics Member NCAA. All Division I except football (Division I-AA).

Campus security: 24-hour emergency response devices and patrols, student patrols, late-night transport/escort service, controlled dormitory access.

Student services: health clinic, personal/psychological counseling, women's center, legal services, veterans affairs office.

COSTS & FINANCIAL AID
Costs (2018–19) *Tuition:* state resident $5347 full-time, $223 per credit hour part-time; nonresident $23,062 full-time, $961 per credit hour part-time. Full-time tuition and fees vary according to degree level, location, program, reciprocity agreements, and student level. Part-time tuition and fees vary according to course load, degree level, location, and student level. ***Required fees:*** $1897 full-time, $115 per credit hour part-time. ***Room and board:*** $9544. Room and board charges vary according to board plan and housing facility.

Financial Aid Of all full-time matriculated undergraduates who enrolled in 2018, 5,013 applied for aid, 4,022 were judged to have need, 382 had their need fully met. In 2018, 1258 non-need-based awards were made. ***Average percent of need met:*** 60. ***Average financial aid package:*** $11,663. ***Average need-based loan:*** $4207. ***Average need-based gift aid:*** $4771. ***Average non-need-based aid:*** $4845. ***Average indebtedness upon graduation:*** $28,157.

APPLYING
Standardized Tests *Required:* SAT or ACT (for admission).

Options: electronic application, early admission, deferred entrance.

Application fee: $36.

Required: high school transcript, minimum 2.5 GPA.

CONTACT
University of Montana, Missoula, MT 59812-0002. *Phone:* 406-243-6266. *Toll-free phone:* 800-462-8636. *Fax:* 406-243-5711. *E-mail:* admiss@umontana.edu.

The University of Montana Western

Dillon, Montana

http://www.umwestern.edu/

- **State-supported** 4-year, founded 1893, part of Montana University System
- **Small-town** 30-acre campus
- **Endowment** $5.1 million
- **Coed**
- **Minimally difficult** entrance level

FACULTY
Student/faculty ratio: 17:1.

ACADEMICS
Calendar: semesters. *Degrees:* certificates, associate, and bachelor's.
Library: Lucy Carson Memorial Library. *Books:* 76,813 (physical), 697,448 (digital/electronic); *Serial titles:* 97 (physical); *Databases:* 146. Weekly public service hours: 85; students can reserve study rooms.

STUDENT LIFE
Housing options: on-campus residence required for freshman year; coed, men-only, women-only, special housing for students with disabilities. Campus housing is university owned. Freshman campus housing is guaranteed.

Activities and organizations: drama/theater group, student-run radio station, choral group, Biology Club, Rodeo Club, YoungLife Club, Education Club, Social Club.

Athletics Member NAIA.

Campus security: 24-hour emergency response devices and patrols, student patrols, late-night transport/escort service.

Student services: health clinic, personal/psychological counseling, veterans affairs office.

COSTS & FINANCIAL AID
Costs (2018–19) ***Tuition:*** state resident $4523 full-time; nonresident $15,913 full-time. Full-time tuition and fees vary according to course load, location, program, reciprocity agreements, and student level. Part-time tuition and fees vary according to course load, location, program, reciprocity agreements, and student level. ***Required fees:*** $1194 full-time. ***Room and board:*** $8090; room only: $3290. Room and board charges vary according to housing facility. ***Payment plans:*** installment, deferred payment.

Financial Aid Of all full-time matriculated undergraduates who enrolled in 2017, 1,064 applied for aid, 931 were judged to have need. In 2017, 13 non-need-based awards were made. ***Average percent of need met:*** 16. ***Average financial aid package:*** $3756. ***Average need-based loan:*** $4058. ***Average need-based gift aid:*** $3382. ***Average non-need-based aid:*** $990.

APPLYING
Standardized Tests *Required:* SAT or ACT (for admission).

Options: electronic application, deferred entrance.

Application fee: $30.

Required: high school transcript, MMR immunization record.

CONTACT
Mrs. Janet Jones, Admissions Evaluator, The University of Montana Western, 710 South Atlantic, Dillon, MT 59725. *Phone:* 406-683-7331. *Toll-free phone:* 877-683-7331. *E-mail:* janet.jones@umwestern.edu.

University of Providence

Great Falls, Montana

http://www.uprovidence.edu/

- **Independent Roman Catholic** comprehensive, founded 1932
- **Urban** 40-acre campus
- **Coed** 877 undergraduate students, 52% full-time, 66% women, 34% men
- **Noncompetitive** entrance level, 72% of applicants were admitted

UNDERGRAD STUDENTS
453 full-time, 424 part-time. 65% are from out of state; 4% Black or African American, non-Hispanic/Latino; 3% Hispanic/Latino; 4% Asian, non-Hispanic/Latino; 0.4% Native Hawaiian or other Pacific Islander, non-Hispanic/Latino; 1% American Indian or Alaska Native, non-Hispanic/Latino; 13% Race/ethnicity unknown; 17% transferred in; 30% live on campus.

Freshmen:
Admission: 845 applied, 610 admitted, 141 enrolled. ***Average high school GPA:*** 3.2. ***Test scores:*** SAT evidence-based reading and writing scores over 500: 67%; SAT math scores over 500: 70%; ACT scores over 18: 84%; SAT math scores over 600: 30%; ACT scores over 24: 33%; ACT scores over 30: 2%.

Retention: 52% of full-time freshmen returned.

FACULTY
Total: 127, 43% full-time, 43% with terminal degrees.
Student/faculty ratio: 10:1.

ACADEMICS
Calendar: semesters. *Degrees:* certificates, associate, bachelor's, and master's.

Special study options: adult/continuing education programs, part-time degree program.

Computers: Students can access the following: campus intranet, computer help desk, free student e-mail accounts, online (class) grades, online (class) registration, online (class) schedules. Campuswide network is available. Wireless service is available via classrooms, computer centers, computer labs, dorm rooms, learning centers, libraries, student centers.

Library: University of Great Falls Library.

STUDENT LIFE
Housing options: on-campus residence required through sophomore year; coed. Campus housing is university owned and leased by the school. Freshman campus housing is guaranteed.

Athletics Member NAIA. ***Intercollegiate sports:*** basketball M(s)/W(s), cheerleading M(s)/W(s), cross-country running M/W, equestrian sports M(s)/W(s), golf M(s), soccer M(s)/W(s), softball W, track and field M(s)/W(s), volleyball W(s), wrestling M(s). ***Intramural sports:*** basketball M/W, equestrian sports M/W(c), football M/W, golf M/W, skiing (downhill) M/W, soccer M/W, softball W, table tennis M/W, track and field M/W, ultimate Frisbee M/W, volleyball M/W, wrestling M.

Campus security: 24-hour emergency response devices and patrols, late-night transport/escort service, controlled dormitory access.

COSTS & FINANCIAL AID
Costs (2019–20) ***Comprehensive fee:*** $35,770 includes full-time tuition ($25,692), mandatory fees ($200), and room and board ($9878). Part-time tuition: $838. ***College room only:*** $5350.

Financial Aid Of all full-time matriculated undergraduates who enrolled in 2018, 398 applied for aid, 332 were judged to have need, 11 had their need fully met. In 2018, 50 non-need-based awards were made. ***Average percent of need met:*** 68. ***Average financial aid package:*** $21,431. ***Average need-based loan:*** $3702. ***Average need-based gift aid:*** $10,921. ***Average non-need-based aid:*** $7383. ***Average indebtedness upon graduation:*** $26,723.

APPLYING
Standardized Tests *Required:* SAT or ACT (for admission). *Recommended:* SAT and SAT Subject Tests or ACT (for admission), SAT Subject Tests (for admission).

Options: electronic application, early admission, deferred entrance.

Application fee: $35.

Required: high school transcript. ***Recommended:*** essay or personal statement, interview.

Notification: continuous (freshmen), continuous (transfers).

CONTACT
Melanie Houge, Assistant Director of Admissions, University of Providence, 1301 20th Street South, Great Falls, MT 59405. *Phone:* 406-791-5202 Ext. 5211. *Toll-free phone:* 800-856-9544. *Fax:* 406-791-5209. *E-mail:* admissions@uprovidence.edu.

NEBRASKA

Bellevue University

Bellevue, Nebraska

http://www.bellevue.edu/

CONTACT

Nick Baker, Director of Undergraduate Enrollment, Bellevue University, 1000 Galvin Road South, Bellevue, NE 68005-3098. *Phone:* 402-557-7250. *Toll-free phone:* 800-756-7920. *E-mail:* nick.baker@bellevue.edu.

Bryan College of Health Sciences

Lincoln, Nebraska

http://www.bryanhealthcollege.edu/

- **Independent** comprehensive
- **Coed**
- 52% of applicants were admitted

ACADEMICS

Degrees: associate, bachelor's, and master's.

COSTS

Costs (2018–19) ***One-time required fee:*** $175. ***Tuition:*** $17,370 full-time, $579 per credit hour part-time. Full-time tuition and fees vary according to course load. Part-time tuition and fees vary according to course load. ***Required fees:*** $1050 full-time. ***Payment plans:*** installment, deferred payment.

APPLYING

Standardized Tests *Required:* SAT or ACT (for admission).

Options: electronic application.

Required: high school transcript, 2 letters of recommendation. ***Required for some:*** essay or personal statement, minimum 2.8 GPA, interview.

CONTACT

Bryan College of Health Sciences, 1535 South 52nd Street, Lincoln, NE 68506.

Chadron State College

Chadron, Nebraska

http://www.csc.edu/

CONTACT

Ms. Tena Cook, Director of Admissions, Chadron State College, 1000 Main Street, Chadron, NE 69337-2690. *Phone:* 308-432-6263. *Toll-free phone:* 800-242-3766. *Fax:* 308-432-6229. *E-mail:* inquire@csc.edu.

Clarkson College

Omaha, Nebraska

http://www.clarksoncollege.edu/

CONTACT

Clarkson College, 101 South 42nd Street, Omaha, NE 68131-2739. *Phone:* 402-552-3100. *Toll-free phone:* 800-647-5500.

College of Saint Mary

Omaha, Nebraska

http://www.csm.edu/

- **Independent Roman Catholic** comprehensive, founded 1923
- **Urban** 25-acre campus
- **Endowment** $19.8 million
- **Women only** 861 undergraduate students, 92% full-time
- **Minimally difficult** entrance level, 52% of applicants were admitted

UNDERGRAD STUDENTS

794 full-time, 67 part-time. Students come from 34 states and territories; 11 other countries; 24% are from out of state; 8% Black or African American, non-Hispanic/Latino; 12% Hispanic/Latino; 3% Asian, non-Hispanic/Latino; 0.4% Native Hawaiian or other Pacific Islander, non-Hispanic/Latino; 0.7% American Indian or Alaska Native, non-Hispanic/Latino; 6% Two or more races, non-Hispanic/Latino; 0.9% international; 17% transferred in; 25% live on campus.

Freshmen:

Admission: 428 applied, 223 admitted, 119 enrolled. ***Average high school GPA:*** 3.5. ***Test scores:*** ACT scores over 18: 97%; ACT scores over 24: 38%; ACT scores over 30: 2%.

Retention: 78% of full-time freshmen returned.

FACULTY

Total: 193, 37% full-time, 47% with terminal degrees.

Student/faculty ratio: 10:1.

ACADEMICS

Calendar: semesters. *Degrees:* certificates, associate, bachelor's, master's, doctoral, and postbachelor's certificates.

Special study options: academic remediation for entering students, accelerated degree program, advanced placement credit, distance learning, double majors, honors programs, independent study, internships, part-time degree program, services for LD students, study abroad, summer session for credit. ***ROTC:*** Army (c), Air Force (c).

Computers: 215 computers/terminals and 320 ports are available on campus for general student use. Students can access the following: campus intranet, computer help desk, free student e-mail accounts, online (class) grades, online (class) registration, online (class) schedules. Campuswide network is available. 100% of college-owned or -operated housing units are wired for high-speed Internet access. Wireless service is available via entire campus.

Library: College of Saint Mary Library. *Books:* 57,458 (physical), 23,434 (digital/electronic); *Serial titles:* 32 (physical), 108 (digital/electronic); *Databases:* 30. Weekly public service hours: 81; study areas open 24 hours, 5–7 days a week.

STUDENT LIFE

Housing options: on-campus residence required through sophomore year; women-only. Campus housing is university owned. Freshman campus housing is guaranteed.

Activities and organizations: drama/theater group, choral group, Residence Hall Council, Campus Activities Board, Student Education Association of Nebraska, Student Occupational Therapy Club, Student Nurses Association.

Athletics Member NAIA. ***Intercollegiate sports:*** basketball W(s), bowling W(s), cross-country running W(s), golf W(s), soccer W(s), softball W(s), swimming and diving W(s), tennis W(s), track and field W(s), volleyball W(s). ***Intramural sports:*** soccer W.

Campus security: 24-hour emergency response devices and patrols, late-night transport/escort service, controlled dormitory access.

Student services: health clinic, personal/psychological counseling.

COSTS & FINANCIAL AID

Costs (2019–20) ***Comprehensive fee:*** $28,600 includes full-time tuition ($20,750) and room and board ($7850). Part-time tuition: $765 per credit.

Financial Aid Of all full-time matriculated undergraduates who enrolled in 2018, 696 applied for aid, 624 were judged to have need, 61 had their need fully met. 165 Federal Work-Study jobs (averaging $2847). 12 state and other part-time jobs (averaging $7183). In 2018, 144 non-need-based awards were made. ***Average percent of need met:*** 59. ***Average financial aid package:*** $15,650. ***Average need-based loan:*** $4916. ***Average need-based gift aid:*** $10,532. ***Average non-need-based aid:*** $9508. ***Average indebtedness upon graduation:*** $36,309.

APPLYING

Standardized Tests *Required:* SAT or ACT (for admission). *Required for some:* ACT (for admission).

Options: electronic application.

Application fee: $30.

Required: high school transcript, minimum 2.0 GPA. ***Required for some:*** essay or personal statement, 3 letters of recommendation, interview.

Application deadlines: rolling (freshmen), rolling (transfers).

Notification: continuous (freshmen), continuous (transfers).

CONTACT

Ms. Sara Hanson, Vice President for Enrollment Services, College of Saint Mary, 7000 Mercy Road, Omaha, NE 68106. *Phone:* 402-399-2350. *Toll-free phone:* 800-926-5534. *Fax:* 402-399-2412. *E-mail:* shanson@csm.edu.

Concordia University, Nebraska

Seward, Nebraska

http://www.cune.edu/

- **Independent** comprehensive, founded 1894, affiliated with Lutheran Church–Missouri Synod
- **Small-town** 120-acre campus with easy access to Omaha
- **Endowment** $51.0 million
- **Coed**
- **Moderately difficult** entrance level

FACULTY
Student/faculty ratio: 14:1.

ACADEMICS
Calendar: 4-4-1. *Degrees:* bachelor's and master's.
Library: Link Library plus 1 other. *Books:* 124,354 (physical), 38,136 (digital/electronic); *Serial titles:* 711 (physical), 82 (digital/electronic); *Databases:* 22. Weekly public service hours: 89; students can reserve study rooms.

STUDENT LIFE
Housing options: on-campus residence required through junior year; men-only, women-only, special housing for students with disabilities. Campus housing is university owned. Freshman campus housing is guaranteed.

Activities and organizations: drama/theater group, student-run newspaper, choral group, Student Activities Council, Musical Groups, Curtain/Drama Club, Student Senate, Concordia Youth Ministry.

Athletics Member NAIA.

Campus security: 24-hour emergency response devices and patrols, controlled dormitory access.

Student services: health clinic, personal/psychological counseling.

COSTS & FINANCIAL AID
Costs (2018–19) ***Comprehensive fee:*** $40,690 includes full-time tuition ($31,620), mandatory fees ($600), and room and board ($8470). Part-time tuition: $925 per credit hour. ***Required fees:*** $150 per term part-time. ***College room only:*** $3570. Room and board charges vary according to board plan and housing facility.

Financial Aid Of all full-time matriculated undergraduates who enrolled in 2017, 1,057 applied for aid, 943 were judged to have need, 244 had their need fully met. In 2017, 97 non-need-based awards were made. ***Average percent of need met:*** 82. ***Average financial aid package:*** $25,229. ***Average need-based loan:*** $4392. ***Average need-based gift aid:*** $20,584. ***Average non-need-based aid:*** $16,989. ***Average indebtedness upon graduation:*** $27,722.

APPLYING
Standardized Tests *Required:* SAT or ACT (for admission).

Options: electronic application, deferred entrance.

Required: high school transcript. ***Required for some:*** essay or personal statement, 2 letters of recommendation.

CONTACT
Mr. Aaron W. Roberts, Director of Undergraduate Admissions, Concordia University, Nebraska, 800 North Columbia Avenue, Seward, NE 68434-1556. *Phone:* 800-535-5494 Ext. 7233. *Toll-free phone:* 800-535-5494. *Fax:* 402-643-4073. *E-mail:* admiss@cune.edu.

Creative Center

Omaha, Nebraska

http://www.creativecenter.edu/

- **Proprietary** 4-year, founded 1993
- **Urban** 2-acre campus with easy access to Omaha
- **Coed** 39 undergraduate students, 97% full-time, 77% women, 23% men

UNDERGRAD STUDENTS
38 full-time, 1 part-time.

Freshmen:
Admission: 13 enrolled.

FACULTY
Total: 11, 18% full-time, 27% with terminal degrees.
Student/faculty ratio: 10:1.

ACADEMICS
Calendar: semesters. *Degrees:* associate and bachelor's.

Special study options: accelerated degree program, advanced placement credit, part-time degree program, services for LD students.

Computers: 8 computers/terminals are available on campus for general student use. Students can access the following: campus intranet, computer help desk, all students own a laptop computer as part of tuition and fees. Campuswide network is available. Wireless service is available via entire campus.
Library: Student Library plus 1 other.

STUDENT LIFE
Housing options: college housing not available.

COSTS
Costs (2019–20) ***One-time required fee:*** $2800. ***Tuition:*** $25,600 full-time, $2560 per course part-time. ***Required fees:*** $2055 full-time, $200 per course part-time.

APPLYING
Application fee: $100.

Required: essay or personal statement, high school transcript, 1 letter of recommendation, interview, portfolio. ***Recommended:*** minimum 2.0 GPA.

Application deadlines: rolling (freshmen), rolling (out-of-state freshmen), rolling (transfers).

Notification: continuous (freshmen), continuous (out-of-state freshmen), continuous (transfers).

CONTACT
Mr. Richard Caldwell, Director of Admissions, Creative Center, 10850 Emmet Street, Omaha, NE 68164. *Phone:* 402-898-1000 Ext. 216. *Toll-free phone:* 888-898-1789. *Fax:* 402-898-1301. *E-mail:* rich_c@creativecenter.edu.

Creighton University

Omaha, Nebraska

http://www.creighton.edu/

- **Independent Roman Catholic (Jesuit)** university, founded 1878
- **Urban** 139-acre campus with easy access to Omaha
- **Endowment** $568.8 million
- **Coed** 4,446 undergraduate students, 97% full-time, 57% women, 43% men
- **Moderately difficult** entrance level, 71% of applicants were admitted

UNDERGRAD STUDENTS
4,291 full-time, 155 part-time. Students come from 50 states and territories; 31 other countries; 78% are from out of state; 2% Black or African American, non-Hispanic/Latino; 8% Hispanic/Latino; 9% Asian, non-Hispanic/Latino; 0.5% Native Hawaiian or other Pacific Islander, non-Hispanic/Latino; 0.4% American Indian or Alaska Native, non-Hispanic/Latino; 5% Two or more races, non-Hispanic/Latino; 0.1% Race/ethnicity unknown; 2% international; 0.7% transferred in; 55% live on campus.

Freshmen:
Admission: 10,112 applied, 7,224 admitted, 1,155 enrolled. ***Average high school GPA:*** 3.7. ***Test scores:*** SAT evidence-based reading and writing scores over 500: 98%; SAT math scores over 500: 96%; ACT scores over 18: 100%; SAT evidence-based reading and writing scores over 600: 67%; SAT math scores over 600: 63%; ACT scores over 24: 81%; SAT evidence-based reading and writing scores over 700: 14%; SAT math scores over 700: 18%; ACT scores over 30: 27%.
Retention: 89% of full-time freshmen returned.

FACULTY
Total: 912, 64% full-time, 79% with terminal degrees.
Student/faculty ratio: 11:1.

ACADEMICS
Calendar: semesters. *Degrees:* certificates, associate, bachelor's, master's, doctoral, post-master's, and postbachelor's certificates.

Special study options: accelerated degree program, adult/continuing education programs, advanced placement credit, distance learning, double majors, English as a second language, honors programs, independent study, internships, off-campus study, part-time degree program, services for LD students, study abroad, summer session for credit. ***ROTC:*** Army (b), Air Force (c).

Computers: 565 computers/terminals are available on campus for general student use. Students can access the following: campus intranet, computer help desk, free student e-mail accounts, online (class) grades, online (class) registration, online (class) schedules, financial aid information. Campuswide network is available. 100% of college-owned or -operated housing units are wired for high-speed Internet access. Wireless service is available via entire campus.

Library: Reinert Alumni Memorial Library plus 2 others. Study areas open 24 hours, 5–7 days a week.

STUDENT LIFE

Housing options: on-campus residence required through sophomore year; coed, special housing for students with disabilities. Campus housing is university owned. Freshman campus housing is guaranteed.

Activities and organizations: drama/theater group, student-run newspaper, radio station, choral group, Birdcage, Hui O Hawaii, Pre-Med Society, Partners Against Cancer, American Pharmacists Association Academy of Student Pharmacist, national fraternities, national sororities.

Athletics Member NCAA. All Division I. ***Intercollegiate sports:*** baseball M(s), basketball M(s)/W(s), crew W(s), cross-country running M(s)/W(s), golf M(s)/W(s)(c), soccer M(s)/W(s), softball W(s), tennis M(s)/W(s), volleyball W(s). ***Intramural sports:*** archery M/W, badminton M(c)/W(c), basketball M/W, crew M(c), football M/W, golf M/W, ice hockey M(c), lacrosse M(c)/W(c), racquetball M/W, rugby M(c), skiing (downhill) M(c)/W(c), soccer M/W, softball M/W, table tennis M/W, tennis M/W, ultimate Frisbee M/W, volleyball M/W.

Campus security: 24-hour emergency response devices and patrols, student patrols, late-night transport/escort service, controlled dormitory access.

Student services: health clinic, personal/psychological counseling, women's center, veterans affairs office.

COSTS & FINANCIAL AID

Costs (2019–20) ***Comprehensive fee:*** $52,674 includes full-time tuition ($39,630), mandatory fees ($1770), and room and board ($11,274). Part-time tuition: $1240 per credit hour. ***Required fees:*** $175 per term part-time.

Financial Aid Of all full-time matriculated undergraduates who enrolled in 2018, 2,882 applied for aid, 2,286 were judged to have need, 618 had their need fully met. 855 Federal Work-Study jobs (averaging $2175). In 2018, 1734 non-need-based awards were made. ***Average percent of need met:*** 78. ***Average financial aid package:*** $28,830. ***Average need-based loan:*** $6014. ***Average need-based gift aid:*** $22,423. ***Average non-need-based aid:*** $17,229. ***Average indebtedness upon graduation:*** $37,973.

APPLYING

Standardized Tests *Required:* SAT or ACT (for admission).

Options: electronic application, early action, deferred entrance.

Application fee: $40.

Required: essay or personal statement, high school transcript, 1 letter of recommendation. ***Recommended:*** minimum 3.0 GPA.

Application deadlines: 2/15 (freshmen), 8/1 (transfers), 11/1 (early action).

Notification: continuous (freshmen), continuous (transfers), rolling (early action).

CONTACT

Ms. Sarah Richardson, Director of Admissions and Scholarships, Creighton University, 2500 California Plaza, Omaha, NE 68178-0001. *Phone:* 402-280-2703. *Toll-free phone:* 800-282-5835. *Fax:* 402-280-2685. *E-mail:* admissions@creighton.edu.

Doane University

Crete, Nebraska

http://www.doane.edu/

- **Independent** comprehensive, founded 1872, affiliated with United Church of Christ
- **Small-town** 300-acre campus with easy access to Omaha
- **Endowment** $112.9 million
- **Coed**
- 65% of applicants were admitted

FACULTY

Student/faculty ratio: 11:1.

ACADEMICS

Calendar: 4-1-4. *Degrees:* bachelor's, master's, doctoral, and post-master's certificates (non-traditional undergraduate programs and graduate programs offered at Lincoln campus).

Library: Perkins Library plus 1 other. Study areas open 24 hours, 5–7 days a week; students can reserve study rooms.

STUDENT LIFE

Housing options: on-campus residence required through senior year; coed, women-only. Campus housing is university owned. Freshman campus housing is guaranteed.

Activities and organizations: drama/theater group, student-run newspaper, radio and television station, choral group, marching band, Student Activities Council, Hansen Leadership Program, band/choir, Doane Ambassadors, Doane Art League.

Athletics Member NAIA.

Campus security: 24-hour emergency response devices and patrols, student patrols, late-night transport/escort service, controlled dormitory access, evening patrols by trained security personnel.

Student services: health clinic, personal/psychological counseling.

COSTS & FINANCIAL AID

Costs (2018–19) ***Comprehensive fee:*** $43,200 includes full-time tuition ($33,000), mandatory fees ($800), and room and board ($9400). Full-time tuition and fees vary according to location. Part-time tuition: $1100 per credit hour. Part-time tuition and fees vary according to course load and location. ***Room and board:*** Room and board charges vary according to board plan, housing facility, and location.

Financial Aid Of all full-time matriculated undergraduates who enrolled in 2018, 840 applied for aid, 749 were judged to have need, 238 had their need fully met. In 2018, 69 non-need-based awards were made. ***Average percent of need met:*** 86. ***Average financial aid package:*** $25,910. ***Average need-based loan:*** $4447. ***Average need-based gift aid:*** $22,116. ***Average non-need-based aid:*** $17,801. ***Average indebtedness upon graduation:*** $33,933.

APPLYING

Standardized Tests *Required:* SAT or ACT (for admission).

Options: electronic application.

Required: high school transcript, 2 letters of recommendation. ***Required for some:*** interview. ***Recommended:*** minimum 2.0 GPA.

CONTACT

Mr. Kyle McMurray, Director of Admission, Doane University, 1014 Boswell Avenue, Crete, NE 68333. *Phone:* 402-826-8222. *Toll-free phone:* 800-333-6263. *E-mail:* kyle.mcmurray@doane.edu.

Hastings College

Hastings, Nebraska

http://www.hastings.edu/

CONTACT

Mr. Chris Schukei, Director of Admissions, Hastings College, 710 North Turner Avenue, Hastings, NE 68901-7621. *Phone:* 402-461-7341. *Toll-free phone:* 800-532-7642. *Fax:* 402-461-7490. *E-mail:* cschukei@hastings.edu.

Midland University

Fremont, Nebraska

http://www.midlandu.edu/

CONTACT
Danielle Oliver, Associate Director of Admissions, Midland University, Fremont, NE 68025-4200. *Phone:* 402-941-6501. *Toll-free phone:* 800-642-8382 Ext. 6501. *E-mail:* oliver@midlandu.edu.

National American University

Bellevue, Nebraska

http://www.national.edu/

CONTACT
National American University, 3604 Summit Plaza Drive, Bellevue, NE 68123.

Nebraska Christian College of Hope International University

Papillion, Nebraska

http://www.nechristian.edu/

- **Independent** comprehensive, founded 1944, affiliated with Christian Churches and Churches of Christ
- **Small-town** 85-acre campus with easy access to Omaha, NE
- **Endowment** $1.3 million
- **Coed**
- 44% of applicants were admitted

FACULTY
Student/faculty ratio: 12:1.

ACADEMICS
Calendar: semesters. *Degrees:* certificates, associate, bachelor's, master's, and postbachelor's certificates.
Library: Swedberg Library.

STUDENT LIFE
Housing options: on-campus residence required through junior year; men-only, women-only. Campus housing is university owned. Freshman campus housing is guaranteed.

Activities and organizations: choral group, Global Gospel Group, Running Club, Minority Students Organization, Spiritual Life Group, Writing Club.

Athletics Member NCCAA.

Campus security: student patrols, controlled dormitory access.

COSTS & FINANCIAL AID
Costs (2018–19) ***Comprehensive fee:*** $26,685 includes full-time tuition ($17,350), mandatory fees ($315), and room and board ($9020). Full-time tuition and fees vary according to course load. Part-time tuition: $760 per credit hour. Part-time tuition and fees vary according to course load. ***Required fees:*** $315 per year part-time. ***College room only:*** $5100. Room and board charges vary according to board plan and housing facility.

Financial Aid Of all full-time matriculated undergraduates who enrolled in 2018, 87 applied for aid, 79 were judged to have need, 12 had their need fully met. In 2018, 9 non-need-based awards were made. ***Average percent of need met:*** 27. ***Average financial aid package:*** $9329. ***Average need-based loan:*** $2545. ***Average need-based gift aid:*** $7119. ***Average non-need-based aid:*** $4930. ***Average indebtedness upon graduation:*** $16,843.

APPLYING
Standardized Tests *Required:* ACT (for admission).

Application fee: $40.

Required: essay or personal statement, high school transcript, 2 letters of recommendation. ***Required for some:*** interview, minimum ACT score of 18 for recent high school graduates.

CONTACT
Mr. D. J. Perkey, Associate Director of Admissions, Nebraska Christian College of Hope International University, 12550 S. 114th Street, Papillion, NE 68046. *Phone:* 402-935-9439. *E-mail:* dj.parkey@nechristian.edu.

Nebraska Methodist College

Omaha, Nebraska

http://www.methodistcollege.edu/

- **Independent** comprehensive, founded 1891, affiliated with United Methodist Church
- **Urban** 8-acre campus
- **Coed** 795 undergraduate students, 53% full-time, 90% women, 10% men
- **Moderately difficult** entrance level, 91% of applicants were admitted

UNDERGRAD STUDENTS
419 full-time, 376 part-time. Students come from 17 states and territories; 5 other countries; 14% are from out of state; 4% Black or African American, non-Hispanic/Latino; 6% Hispanic/Latino; 2% Asian, non-Hispanic/Latino; 0.1% Native Hawaiian or other Pacific Islander, non-Hispanic/Latino; 0.3% American Indian or Alaska Native, non-Hispanic/Latino; 3% Two or more races, non-Hispanic/Latino; 2% Race/ethnicity unknown; 0.1% international; 19% transferred in; 10% live on campus.

Freshmen:
Admission: 86 applied, 78 admitted, 51 enrolled. ***Average high school GPA:*** 3.5. ***Test scores:*** ACT scores over 18: 96%; ACT scores over 24: 31%.
Retention: 81% of full-time freshmen returned.

FACULTY
Total: 67, 93% full-time, 30% with terminal degrees.
Student/faculty ratio: 12:1.

ACADEMICS
Calendar: semesters. *Degrees:* certificates, associate, bachelor's, master's, doctoral, post-master's, and postbachelor's certificates.

Special study options: academic remediation for entering students, accelerated degree program, adult/continuing education programs, advanced placement credit, cooperative education, distance learning, external degree program, independent study, services for LD students, summer session for credit. ***ROTC:*** Air Force (c).

Computers: 50 computers/terminals and 25 ports are available on campus for general student use. Students can access the following: campus intranet, computer help desk, online (class) grades, online (class) registration, online (class) schedules. Campuswide network is available. 100% of college-owned or -operated housing units are wired for high-speed Internet access. Wireless service is available via entire campus.
Library: John Moritz Library. *Books:* 1,374 (physical), 15 (digital/electronic); *Serial titles:* 55 (physical), 13,033 (digital/electronic); *Databases:* 23. Weekly public service hours: 65.

STUDENT LIFE
Housing options: coed. Campus housing is university owned.

Activities and organizations: Student Nurses Association, Methodist Allied Health Student Association, Student Government, Student Ambassadors, Residence Hall Council.

Campus security: 24-hour emergency response devices and patrols, late-night transport/escort service, controlled dormitory access.

Student services: health clinic, personal/psychological counseling, veterans affairs office.

COSTS & FINANCIAL AID
Costs (2019–20) ***Comprehensive fee:*** $25,894 includes full-time tuition ($15,660), mandatory fees ($648), and room and board ($9586). Part-time tuition: $580 per credit hour.

Financial Aid Of all full-time matriculated undergraduates who enrolled in 2017, 415 applied for aid, 368 were judged to have need, 15 had their need fully met. In 2017, 52 non-need-based awards were made. ***Average percent of need met:*** 35. ***Average financial aid package:*** $9709. ***Average need-based loan:*** $4787. ***Average need-based gift aid:*** $6173. ***Average non-need-based aid:*** $4546. ***Average indebtedness upon graduation:*** $33,768.

APPLYING
Standardized Tests *Required:* SAT or ACT (for admission).

Options: electronic application, deferred entrance.

Application fee: $25.

Required: essay or personal statement, high school transcript, minimum 2.5 GPA.

Application deadlines: rolling (freshmen), rolling (transfers).

CONTACT

Ms. Megan Maryott, Director of Enrollment Services, Nebraska Methodist College, 720 North 87th Street, Omaha, NE 68114. *Phone:* 402-354-7111. *Toll-free phone:* 800-335-5510. *Fax:* 402-354-7020. *E-mail:* megan.maryott@methodistcollege.edu.

Nebraska Wesleyan University

Lincoln, Nebraska

http://www.nebrwesleyan.edu/

CONTACT

Mr. Gordie Coffin, Director of Admissions, Nebraska Wesleyan University, 5000 Saint Paul Avenue, Lincoln, NE 68504. *Phone:* 402-465-2218. *Toll-free phone:* 800-541-3818. *Fax:* 402-465-2177. *E-mail:* admissions@nebrwesleyan.edu.

Peru State College

Peru, Nebraska

http://www.peru.edu/

CONTACT

Ms. Micki Willis, Vice President for Enrollment Management and Student Affairs, Peru State College, PO Box 10, Peru, NE 68421. *Phone:* 402-872-2221. *Toll-free phone:* 800-742-4412 (in-state); 800-741-4412 (out-of-state). *Fax:* 402-872-2296. *E-mail:* mwillis@peru.edu.

Purdue University Global

Lincoln, Nebraska

http://www.purdueglobal.edu/

CONTACT

Purdue University Global, 1821 K Street, Lincoln, NE 68508. *Phone:* 402-474-5315. *Toll-free phone:* 844-PURDUE-G.

Purdue University Global

Omaha, Nebraska

http://www.purdueglobal.edu/

CONTACT

Purdue University Global, 5425 North 103rd Street, Omaha, NE 68134. *Phone:* 402-572-8500. *Toll-free phone:* 844-PURDUE-G.

St. Gregory the Great Seminary

Seward, Nebraska

http://www.sggs.edu/

CONTACT

Rev. Peter M. Mitchell, Dean of Men, St. Gregory the Great Seminary, 800 Fletcher Road, Seward, NE 68434. *Phone:* 402-643-4052. *Fax:* 402-643-6964. *E-mail:* sggs@stgregoryseminary.edu.

Union College

Lincoln, Nebraska

http://www.ucollege.edu/

- **Independent Seventh-day Adventist** comprehensive, founded 1891
- **Suburban** 26-acre campus with easy access to Omaha
- **Coed**
- **Moderately difficult** entrance level

FACULTY

Student/faculty ratio: 9:1.

ACADEMICS

Calendar: semesters. *Degrees:* associate, bachelor's, and master's.
Library: Ella Johnson Crandall Library. *Books:* 143,808 (physical), 187,159 (digital/electronic); *Serial titles:* 136 (physical), 136 (digital/electronic); *Databases:* 61. Students can reserve study rooms.

STUDENT LIFE

Housing options: on-campus residence required through junior year; men-only, women-only, special housing for students with disabilities. Campus housing is university owned. Freshman campus housing is guaranteed.

Activities and organizations: drama/theater group, student-run newspaper, choral group, Business and Computer Science Club, Math and Science Club, Nursing Club, Amnesty International, International Club.

Campus security: 24-hour emergency response devices, student patrols, late-night transport/escort service.

Student services: health clinic, personal/psychological counseling.

COSTS & FINANCIAL AID

Costs (2018–19) ***Comprehensive fee:*** $30,850 includes full-time tuition ($22,680), mandatory fees ($1100), and room and board ($7070). Full-time tuition and fees vary according to course load, degree level, and program. Part-time tuition: $945 per credit hour. Part-time tuition and fees vary according to program. ***Required fees:*** $550 per term part-time. ***College room only:*** $4020. Room and board charges vary according to board plan and housing facility.

Financial Aid Of all full-time matriculated undergraduates who enrolled in 2016, 552 applied for aid, 499 were judged to have need, 76 had their need fully met. In 2016, 197 non-need-based awards were made. ***Average percent of need met:*** 65. ***Average financial aid package:*** $17,707. ***Average need-based loan:*** $5000. ***Average need-based gift aid:*** $13,017. ***Average non-need-based aid:*** $8063. ***Average indebtedness upon graduation:*** $35,893.

APPLYING

Standardized Tests *Required:* SAT or ACT (for admission).

Options: electronic application.

Required: high school transcript, minimum 2.5 GPA, 3 letters of recommendation. ***Required for some:*** essay or personal statement, interview.

CONTACT

Kristina Hammer, Assistant Director of Admissions, Union College, 3800 South 48th Street, Lincoln, NE 68506. *Phone:* 402-486-2969 Ext. 2052. *Toll-free phone:* 800-228-4600. *Fax:* 402-486-2895. *E-mail:* enroll@ucollege.edu.

University of Nebraska at Kearney

Kearney, Nebraska

http://www.unk.edu/

- **State-supported** comprehensive, founded 1903, part of University of Nebraska System
- **Small-town** 235-acre campus
- **Coed**
- **Moderately difficult** entrance level

FACULTY

Student/faculty ratio: 14:1.

ACADEMICS

Calendar: semesters. *Degrees:* certificates, bachelor's, master's, and post-master's certificates.
Library: Calvin T. Ryan Library.

STUDENT LIFE

Housing options: on-campus residence required for freshman year; coed. Campus housing is university owned. Freshman campus housing is guaranteed.

Activities and organizations: drama/theater group, student-run newspaper, radio and television station, marching band, national fraternities, national sororities.

Athletics Member NCAA. All Division II.

Campus security: 24-hour emergency response devices and patrols, late-night transport/escort service.

Student services: health clinic, personal/psychological counseling.

COSTS & FINANCIAL AID

Costs (2018–19) ***Tuition:*** state resident $5940 full-time, $198 per credit hour part-time; nonresident $12,930 full-time, $431 per credit hour part-time. Full-time tuition and fees vary according to course level, course load, degree level, location, and program. Part-time tuition and fees vary according to course level, course load, degree level, location, and program. ***Required fees:*** $1573 full-time. ***Room and board:*** $9878; room only: $5058. Room and board charges vary according to board plan and housing facility.

Financial Aid Of all full-time matriculated undergraduates who enrolled in 2017, 3,138 applied for aid, 2,689 were judged to have need, 574 had their need fully met. In 2017, 638 non-need-based awards were made. ***Average percent of need met:*** 66. ***Average financial aid package:*** $11,242. ***Average need-based loan:*** $4051. ***Average need-based gift aid:*** $8412. ***Average non-need-based aid:*** $5367. ***Average indebtedness upon graduation:*** $19,200.

APPLYING

Standardized Tests *Required:* SAT or ACT (for admission).

Options: electronic application.

Application fee: $45.

Required: high school transcript, rank in upper 50% of high school class.

CONTACT

Mr. Dusty Newton, Director of Admissions, University of Nebraska at Kearney, 905 West 25th Street, Kearney, NE 68849-0001. *Phone:* 308-865-8702. *Toll-free phone:* 800-532-7639. *Fax:* 308-865-8987. *E-mail:* admissionsug@unk.edu.

University of Nebraska at Omaha

Omaha, Nebraska

http://www.unomaha.edu/

CONTACT

University of Nebraska at Omaha, 6001 Dodge Street, Omaha, NE 68182. *Phone:* 402-554-3520. *Toll-free phone:* 800-858-8648.

University of Nebraska–Lincoln

Lincoln, Nebraska

http://www.unl.edu/

- **State-supported** university, founded 1869, part of University of Nebraska System
- **Urban** 856-acre campus with easy access to Omaha
- **Endowment** $1.7 billion
- **Coed** 20,830 undergraduate students, 93% full-time, 47% women, 53% men
- **Moderately difficult** entrance level, 80% of applicants were admitted

UNDERGRAD STUDENTS

19,466 full-time, 1,364 part-time. Students come from 51 states and territories; 107 other countries; 24% are from out of state; 3% Black or African American, non-Hispanic/Latino; 7% Hispanic/Latino; 3% Asian, non-Hispanic/Latino; 0.1% Native Hawaiian or other Pacific Islander, non-Hispanic/Latino; 0.2% American Indian or Alaska Native, non-Hispanic/Latino; 3% Two or more races, non-Hispanic/Latino; 1% Race/ethnicity unknown; 9% international; 4% transferred in; 34% live on campus.

Freshmen:

Admission: 14,956 applied, 11,906 admitted, 4,816 enrolled. ***Average high school GPA:*** 3.6. ***Test scores:*** SAT evidence-based reading and writing scores over 500: 93%; SAT math scores over 500: 94%; ACT scores over 18: 97%; SAT evidence-based reading and writing scores over 600: 65%; SAT math scores over 600: 60%; ACT scores over 24: 63%; SAT evidence-based reading and writing scores over 700: 17%; SAT math scores over 700: 21%; ACT scores over 30: 21%.

Retention: 83% of full-time freshmen returned.

FACULTY

Total: 1,397, 93% full-time, 77% with terminal degrees.

Student/faculty ratio: 21:1.

ACADEMICS

Calendar: semesters. *Degrees:* bachelor's, master's, doctoral, post-master's, and postbachelor's certificates.

Special study options: accelerated degree program, adult/continuing education programs, advanced placement credit, cooperative education, distance learning, double majors, English as a second language, honors programs, independent study, internships, off-campus study, part-time degree program, services for LD students, student-designed majors, study abroad, summer session for credit. ***ROTC:*** Army (b), Navy (b), Air Force (b).

Unusual degree programs: 3-2 design/architecture with University of Nebraska-Lincoln, animal science/veterinary science with Iowa State University.

Computers: 455 computers/terminals are available on campus for general student use. Students can access the following: campus intranet, computer help desk, free student e-mail accounts, online (class) grades, online (class) registration, online (class) schedules. Campuswide network is available. 100% of college-owned or -operated housing units are wired for high-speed Internet access. Wireless service is available via entire campus.

Library: Love Memorial Library plus 7 others. *Books:* 1.8 million (physical), 727,811 (digital/electronic); *Serial titles:* 101,076 (physical), 74,949 (digital/electronic); *Databases:* 462. Weekly public service hours: 130; students can reserve study rooms.

STUDENT LIFE

Housing options: on-campus residence required for freshman year; coed, women-only, cooperative, special housing for students with disabilities. Campus housing is university owned. Freshman campus housing is guaranteed.

Activities and organizations: drama/theater group, student-run newspaper, radio station, choral group, marching band, Student Alumni Association, Mexican American Student Association, University Program Council Nebraska, eSAB (Engineering Student Advisory Board), ASUN (Association of Students of the University of Nebraska, student body government), national fraternities, national sororities.

Athletics Member NCAA. All Division I except football (Division I-A). ***Intercollegiate sports:*** badminton M(c)/W(c), baseball M(s), basketball M(s)/W(s), bowling W(s), cross-country running M(s)/W(s), golf M(s)/W(s), gymnastics M(s)/W(s), ice hockey M/W, riflery W(s), sand volleyball W(s), soccer W(s), softball W(s), swimming and diving W(s), table tennis M/W, tennis M(s)/W(s), track and field M(s)/W(s), ultimate Frisbee M/W, volleyball W(s), wrestling M(s). ***Intramural sports:*** badminton M/W, baseball M(c)/W(c), basketball M/W, bowling M/W, crew M(c)/W(c), cross-country running M(c)/W(c), equestrian sports M(c)/W(c), golf M/W, ice hockey M(c)/W(c), lacrosse M(c)/W(c), racquetball M/W, riflery M(c)/W(c), rock climbing M/W, rowing M(c)/W(c), rugby M(c)/W(c), sand volleyball M/W, soccer M(c)/W(c), softball M/W, swimming and diving M(c)/W(c), table tennis M(c)/W(c), tennis M(c)/W(c), track and field M/W, ultimate Frisbee M(c)/W(c), volleyball M/W, water polo M(c)/W(c), weight lifting M(c)/W(c), wrestling M/W.

Campus security: 24-hour emergency response devices and patrols, late-night transport/escort service, controlled dormitory access.

Student services: health clinic, personal/psychological counseling, women's center, legal services, veterans affairs office.

COSTS & FINANCIAL AID

Costs (2018–19) ***Tuition:*** state resident $7350 full-time, $245 per credit hour part-time; nonresident $23,145 full-time, $772 per credit hour part-time. Full-time tuition and fees vary according to course load, location, program, and reciprocity agreements. Part-time tuition and fees vary according to course load, location, program, and reciprocity agreements. ***Required fees:*** $1804 full-time, $17 per credit hour part-time, $395 per term part-time. ***Room and board:*** $11,430. Room and board charges vary according to board plan and housing facility. ***Payment plan:*** installment. ***Waivers:*** employees or children of employees.

Financial Aid Of all full-time matriculated undergraduates who enrolled in 2017, 11,716 applied for aid, 9,140 were judged to have need, 1,407 had their need fully met. 1,240 Federal Work-Study jobs (averaging $2759). In 2017, 1350 non-need-based awards were made. ***Average percent of need met:*** 72. ***Average financial aid package:*** $14,746. ***Average need-based loan:*** $4438. ***Average need-based gift aid:*** $7943. ***Average non-need-based aid:*** $7707. ***Average indebtedness upon graduation:*** $22,676.

APPLYING

Standardized Tests *Required:* SAT or ACT (for admission). *Recommended:* ACT (for admission).

Options: electronic application.

Application fee: $45.

Required: high school transcript, minimum ACT score of 20 or combined total of 1030 or higher on the SAT Evidence-Based Reading and Writing and SAT Math sections or rank in upper 50% of high school class.

Application deadlines: 5/1 (freshmen), 5/1 (out-of-state freshmen), 5/1 (transfers).

Notification: continuous (freshmen), continuous (out-of-state freshmen), continuous (transfers).

CONTACT
Ms. Abby Freeman, Director of Admissions, University of Nebraska–Lincoln, 1410 Q Street, Lincoln, NE 68588-0417. *Phone:* 402-472-2023. *Toll-free phone:* 800-742-8800. *Fax:* 402-472-0670. *E-mail:* admissions@unl.edu.

University of Nebraska Medical Center

Omaha, Nebraska

http://www.unmc.edu/

CONTACT
University of Nebraska Medical Center, Nebraska Medical Center, Omaha, NE 68198. *Toll-free phone:* 800-626-8431 Ext. 6468.

Wayne State College

Wayne, Nebraska

http://www.wsc.edu/

- **State-supported** comprehensive, founded 1910, part of Nebraska State College System
- **Small-town** 128-acre campus
- **Endowment** $22.0 million
- **Coed**
- **Noncompetitive** entrance level

FACULTY
Student/faculty ratio: 19:1.

ACADEMICS
Calendar: semesters. *Degrees:* bachelor's, master's, and post-master's certificates.
Library: U. S. Conn Library. *Books:* 145,315 (physical), 290,865 (digital/electronic); *Serial titles:* 1,045 (physical), 66 (digital/electronic); *Databases:* 49.

STUDENT LIFE
Housing options: on-campus residence required for freshman year; coed. Campus housing is university owned. Freshman campus housing is guaranteed.

Activities and organizations: drama/theater group, student-run newspaper, radio and television station, choral group, marching band, national fraternities, national sororities.

Athletics Member NCAA. All Division II.

Campus security: 24-hour emergency response devices and patrols, student patrols, late-night transport/escort service, controlled dormitory access.

Student services: health clinic, personal/psychological counseling.

COSTS & FINANCIAL AID
Costs (2018–19) ***Tuition:*** state resident $5310 full-time, $177 per credit hour part-time; nonresident $10,620 full-time, $354 per credit hour part-time. Full-time tuition and fees vary according to course level, course load, and location. Part-time tuition and fees vary according to course level, course load, and location. ***Required fees:*** $1679 full-time, $65 per credit hour part-time. ***Room and board:*** $7668; room only: $3870. Room and board charges vary according to board plan and housing facility.

Financial Aid Of all full-time matriculated undergraduates who enrolled in 2017, 2,180 applied for aid, 1,705 were judged to have need, 738 had their need fully met. In 2017, 92 non-need-based awards were made. ***Average percent of need met:*** 61. ***Average financial aid package:*** $9494. ***Average need-based loan:*** $3893. ***Average need-based gift aid:*** $5464. ***Average non-need-based aid:*** $2470.

APPLYING
Options: electronic application, deferred entrance.

Required: high school transcript.

CONTACT
Mr. Kevin Halle, Director of Admissions, Wayne State College, 1111 Main Street, Wayne, NE 68787. *Phone:* 402-375-7234. *Toll-free phone:* 866-WSC-CATS. *Fax:* 402-375-7204. *E-mail:* admit1@wsc.edu.

York College

York, Nebraska

http://www.york.edu/

CONTACT
Ms. Janae Parsons, York College, 1125 East 8th Street, York, NE 68467-2699. *Phone:* 402-363-5627. *Toll-free phone:* 800-950-9675. *Fax:* 402-363-5623. *E-mail:* enroll@york.edu.

NEVADA

Arizona College–Las Vegas

Las Vegas, Nevada

http://www.arizonacollege.edu/

CONTACT
Arizona College–Las Vegas, 2320 South Rancho Drive, Las Vegas, NV 89102.

The Art Institute of Las Vegas

Henderson, Nevada

http://www.artinstitutes.edu/lasvegas/

CONTACT
The Art Institute of Las Vegas, 2350 Corporate Circle Drive, Henderson, NV 89074. *Phone:* 702-369-9944. *Toll-free phone:* 800-833-2678.

Chamberlain College of Nursing

Las Vegas, Nevada

http://www.chamberlain.edu/

CONTACT
Chamberlain College of Nursing, 9901 Covington Cross Drive, Las Vegas, NV 89144. *Toll-free phone:* 877-751-5783.

College of Southern Nevada

Las Vegas, Nevada

http://www.csn.edu/

CONTACT
Admissions and Records, College of Southern Nevada, 6375 West Charleston Boulevard, Las Vegas, NV 89146. *Phone:* 702-651-4060.

DeVry University–Henderson Campus

Henderson, Nevada

http://www.devry.edu/

CONTACT
Admissions Office, DeVry University–Henderson Campus, 2490 Paseo Verde Parkway, Suite 150, Henderson, NV 89074-7120. *Phone:* 702-933-9700. *Toll-free phone:* 866-338-7934.

Great Basin College

Elko, Nevada

http://www.gbcnv.edu/

CONTACT

Ms. Jan King, Director of Admissions and Registrar, Great Basin College, 1500 College Parkway, Elko, NV 89801. *Phone:* 775-753-2102. *E-mail:* jan.king@gbcnv.edu.

Nevada State College

Henderson, Nevada

http://www.nsc.edu/

CONTACT

Adelfa Sullivan, Registrar, Nevada State College, Office of Admissions and Records, 1300 Nevada State Drive, Henderson, NV 89002. *Phone:* 702-992-2115. *Fax:* 702-992-2111. *E-mail:* admissions@nsc.edu.

Pima Medical Institute

Las Vegas, Nevada

http://www.pmi.edu/

CONTACT

Admissions Office, Pima Medical Institute, 3333 East Flamingo Road, Las Vegas, NV 89121. *Phone:* 702-458-9650 Ext. 202. *Toll-free phone:* 800-477-PIMA.

Sierra Nevada College

Incline Village, Nevada

http://www.sierranevada.edu/

- **Independent** comprehensive, founded 1969
- **Small-town** 20-acre campus with easy access to Reno
- **Endowment** $4.3 million
- **Coed**
- **Moderately difficult** entrance level

FACULTY

Student/faculty ratio: 10:1.

ACADEMICS

Calendar: semesters. *Degrees:* certificates, diplomas, bachelor's, and master's.

Library: Prim Library. *Books:* 27,716 (physical), 7,520 (digital/electronic); *Serial titles:* 1,106 (physical); *Databases:* 35. Weekly public service hours: 40.

STUDENT LIFE

Housing options: on-campus residence required through sophomore year; coed, special housing for students with disabilities. Campus housing is university owned. Freshman campus housing is guaranteed.

Activities and organizations: student-run newspaper, choral group, Film Club, International Club, Sustainability Club, Rock Climbing Club, First Generation Club.

Athletics Member NAIA.

Campus security: 24-hour emergency response devices and patrols, student patrols, controlled dormitory access.

Student services: personal/psychological counseling.

COSTS

Costs (2018–19) ***Comprehensive fee:*** $47,598 includes full-time tuition ($33,158), mandatory fees ($1083), and room and board ($13,357). Full-time tuition and fees vary according to course load, degree level, location, program, and reciprocity agreements. Part-time tuition: $1410 per credit hour. Part-time tuition and fees vary according to course load, degree level, location, program, and reciprocity agreements. ***College room only:*** $6711. Room and board charges vary according to board plan.

APPLYING

Standardized Tests *Required:* SAT or ACT (for admission).

Options: electronic application, deferred entrance.

Required: minimum 2.6 GPA. ***Required for some:*** high school transcript, 1 letter of recommendation. ***Recommended:*** essay or personal statement, interview.

CONTACT

Ms. Julie Hernandez, Sierra Nevada College, 999 Tahoe Boulevard, Incline Village, NV 89451. *Phone:* 866-412-4636. *Fax:* 775-831-6223. *E-mail:* admissions@sierranevada.edu.

Truckee Meadows Community College

Reno, Nevada

http://www.tmcc.edu/

- **State-supported** primarily 2-year, founded 1971, part of Nevada System of Higher Education
- **Suburban** 63-acre campus
- **Endowment** $11.1 million
- **Coed** 10,861 undergraduate students, 27% full-time, 53% women, 47% men
- **Noncompetitive** entrance level, 100% of applicants were admitted

UNDERGRAD STUDENTS

2,927 full-time, 7,934 part-time. Students come from 23 states and territories; 20 other countries; 6% are from out of state; 3% Black or African American, non-Hispanic/Latino; 30% Hispanic/Latino; 6% Asian, non-Hispanic/Latino; 1% American Indian or Alaska Native, non-Hispanic/Latino; 4% Two or more races, non-Hispanic/Latino; 2% Race/ethnicity unknown; 0.5% international; 6% transferred in.

Freshmen:

Admission: 3,290 applied, 3,290 admitted, 1,562 enrolled.

Retention: 63% of full-time freshmen returned.

FACULTY

Total: 716, 22% full-time.

Student/faculty ratio: 21:1.

ACADEMICS

Calendar: semesters. *Degrees:* certificates, associate, and bachelor's.

Special study options: academic remediation for entering students, accelerated degree program, adult/continuing education programs, advanced placement credit, cooperative education, distance learning, double majors, English as a second language, independent study, internships, part-time degree program, services for LD students, summer session for credit. ***ROTC:*** Army (c).

Computers: Students can access the following: computer help desk, free student e-mail accounts, online (class) grades, online (class) registration, online (class) schedules. Campuswide network is available. Wireless service is available via entire campus.

Library: Elizabeth Sturm Library plus 2 others. *Books:* 48,770 (physical); *Serial titles:* 36 (physical), 4 (digital/electronic); *Databases:* 93.

STUDENT LIFE

Housing options: college housing not available.

Activities and organizations: drama/theater group, student-run newspaper, Entrepreneurship Club, International Club, Phi Theta Kappa, Student Government Association, Student Media and Broadcasting Club.

Campus security: 24-hour emergency response devices and patrols, late-night transport/escort service.

Student services: personal/psychological counseling, veterans affairs office.

COSTS & FINANCIAL AID

Costs (2019–20) ***Tuition:*** state resident $2370 full-time, $99 per credit part-time; nonresident $9283 full-time, $208 per credit part-time. ***Required fees:*** $300 full-time, $13 per credit part-time.

Financial Aid Of all full-time matriculated undergraduates who enrolled in 2017, 126 Federal Work-Study jobs (averaging $5000). 368 state and other part-time jobs (averaging $5000).

APPLYING

Options: electronic application, early admission.

Application fee: $10.

Application deadlines: rolling (freshmen), rolling (transfers).

Notification: continuous (freshmen), continuous (transfers).

CONTACT

Mr. Andrew Hughes, Director of Admissions and Records, Truckee Meadows Community College, 7000 Dandini Boulevard, Reno, NV 89512-3901. *Phone:* 775-673-7240. *Fax:* 775-673-7028. *E-mail:* ahughes@tmcc.edu.

University of Nevada, Las Vegas

Las Vegas, Nevada

http://www.unlv.edu/

- **State-supported** university, founded 1957, part of Nevada System of Higher Education
- **Urban** 332-acre campus with easy access to Las Vegas
- **Endowment** $55.4 million
- **Coed** 25,282 undergraduate students, 74% full-time, 56% women, 44% men
- **Moderately difficult** entrance level, 82% of applicants were admitted

UNDERGRAD STUDENTS

18,764 full-time, 6,518 part-time. 12% are from out of state; 8% Black or African American, non-Hispanic/Latino; 30% Hispanic/Latino; 16% Asian, non-Hispanic/Latino; 0.9% Native Hawaiian or other Pacific Islander, non-Hispanic/Latino; 0.3% American Indian or Alaska Native, non-Hispanic/Latino; 11% Two or more races, non-Hispanic/Latino; 0.9% Race/ethnicity unknown; 3% international; 10% transferred in.

Freshmen:

Admission: 11,613 applied, 9,527 admitted, 3,964 enrolled. ***Average high school GPA:*** 3.4. ***Test scores:*** SAT evidence-based reading and writing scores over 500: 83%; SAT math scores over 500: 83%; ACT scores over 18: 83%; SAT evidence-based reading and writing scores over 600: 39%; SAT math scores over 600: 34%; ACT scores over 24: 30%; SAT evidence-based reading and writing scores over 700: 4%; SAT math scores over 700: 8%; ACT scores over 30: 4%.

Retention: 76% of full-time freshmen returned.

FACULTY

Total: 1,820, 55% full-time.

Student/faculty ratio: 21:1.

ACADEMICS

Calendar: semesters. *Degrees:* certificates, bachelor's, master's, doctoral, post-master's, and postbachelor's certificates.

Special study options: academic remediation for entering students, adult/continuing education programs, advanced placement credit, cooperative education, distance learning, double majors, English as a second language, honors programs, independent study, internships, part-time degree program, services for LD students, study abroad, summer session for credit. ***ROTC:*** Army (b), Air Force (b).

Computers: 2,100 computers/terminals and 25,000 ports are available on campus for general student use. Students can access the following: campus intranet, computer help desk, free student e-mail accounts, online (class) grades, online (class) registration, online (class) schedules. Campuswide network is available. 100% of college-owned or -operated housing units are wired for high-speed Internet access. Wireless service is available via entire campus.

Library: Lied Library plus 4 others. *Books:* 1.2 million (physical), 1.4 million (digital/electronic); *Serial titles:* 16,265 (physical), 95,398 (digital/electronic); *Databases:* 430. Weekly public service hours: 101; students can reserve study rooms.

STUDENT LIFE

Housing options: coed, special housing for students with disabilities. Campus housing is university owned. Freshman applicants given priority for college housing.

Activities and organizations: drama/theater group, student-run newspaper, radio and television station, choral group, marching band, Social Fraternities and Sororities, Psychology Club, Honors Student Council, Association of Pre-Health Professionals, UNLV Student Nurses Association, national fraternities, national sororities.

Athletics Member NCAA. All Division I except football (Division I-A). ***Intercollegiate sports:*** baseball M(s), basketball M(s)/W(s), cheerleading M(s)/W(s), cross-country running W(s), golf M(s)/W(s), soccer M(s)/W(s), softball W(s), swimming and diving M(s)/W(s), tennis M(s)/W(s), track and field W(s), volleyball W(s). ***Intramural sports:*** badminton M/W, basketball M/W, bowling M/W, football M/W, golf M/W, ice hockey M(c), lacrosse M(c)/W(c), racquetball M/W, soccer M/W, softball M/W, swimming and diving M/W, tennis M/W, volleyball M/W, wrestling M(c).

Campus security: 24-hour emergency response devices and patrols, late-night transport/escort service, controlled dormitory access.

Student services: health clinic, personal/psychological counseling, women's center, legal services, veterans affairs office.

COSTS & FINANCIAL AID

Costs (2018–19) ***One-time required fee:*** $120. ***Tuition:*** state resident $7169 full-time, $224 per credit hour part-time; nonresident $22,316 full-time, $471 per credit hour part-time. Full-time tuition and fees vary according to course level, program, and reciprocity agreements. Part-time tuition and fees vary according to course level, program, and reciprocity agreements. ***Required fees:*** $696 full-time, $15 per credit hour part-time, $348 per term part-time. ***Room and board:*** $10,780; room only: $5880. Room and board charges vary according to board plan and housing facility. ***Payment plans:*** installment, deferred payment. ***Waivers:*** employees or children of employees.

Financial Aid Of all full-time matriculated undergraduates who enrolled in 2017, 14,430 applied for aid, 11,747 were judged to have need, 1,867 had their need fully met. In 2017, 1481 non-need-based awards were made. ***Average percent of need met:*** 67. ***Average financial aid package:*** $8852. ***Average need-based loan:*** $4189. ***Average need-based gift aid:*** $6697. ***Average non-need-based aid:*** $4158. ***Average indebtedness upon graduation:*** $21,333.

APPLYING

Standardized Tests *Required:* SAT or ACT (for admission).

Options: electronic application, early admission, deferred entrance.

Application fee: $60.

Required: high school transcript, minimum 3.0 GPA.

Notification: continuous (freshmen), continuous (transfers).

CONTACT

Kristine Shay, Executive Director of Undergraduate Admissions, University of Nevada, Las Vegas, 4505 S. Maryland Parkway, Box 451021, Las Vegas, NV 89154-1021. *Phone:* 702-774-2922. *E-mail:* kristine.shay@unlv.edu.

University of Nevada, Reno

Reno, Nevada

http://www.unr.edu/

- **State-supported** university, founded 1874, part of Nevada System of Higher Education
- **Urban** 200-acre campus
- **Coed** 17,930 undergraduate students, 85% full-time, 52% women, 48% men
- **Moderately difficult** entrance level, 88% of applicants were admitted

UNDERGRAD STUDENTS

15,200 full-time, 2,730 part-time. Students come from 43 states and territories; 52 other countries; 27% are from out of state; 3% Black or African American, non-Hispanic/Latino; 21% Hispanic/Latino; 8% Asian, non-Hispanic/Latino; 0.6% Native Hawaiian or other Pacific Islander, non-Hispanic/Latino; 0.7% American Indian or Alaska Native, non-Hispanic/Latino; 7% Two or more races, non-Hispanic/Latino; 2% Race/ethnicity unknown; 1% international; 6% transferred in; 16% live on campus.

Freshmen:

Admission: 9,531 applied, 8,402 admitted, 3,365 enrolled. ***Average high school GPA:*** 3.4. ***Test scores:*** SAT evidence-based reading and writing scores over 500: 90%; SAT math scores over 500: 89%; ACT scores over 18: 92%; SAT evidence-based reading and writing scores over 600: 45%; SAT math scores over 600: 44%; ACT scores over 24: 47%; SAT evidence-based reading and writing scores over 700: 7%; SAT math scores over 700: 10%; ACT scores over 30: 10%.

Retention: 81% of full-time freshmen returned.

FACULTY
Total: 1,274, 56% full-time, 64% with terminal degrees.

Student/faculty ratio: 20:1.

ACADEMICS
Calendar: semesters. *Degrees:* certificates, bachelor's, master's, doctoral, post-master's, and postbachelor's certificates.

Special study options: academic remediation for entering students, adult/continuing education programs, advanced placement credit, distance learning, double majors, English as a second language, honors programs, independent study, internships, off-campus study, part-time degree program, services for LD students, study abroad, summer session for credit. ***ROTC:*** Army (b).

Unusual degree programs: 3-2 biotechnology.

Computers: Students can access the following: computer help desk, free student e-mail accounts, online (class) grades, online (class) registration, online (class) schedules. Campuswide network is available. 100% of college-owned or -operated housing units are wired for high-speed Internet access. Wireless service is available via entire campus.
Library: Mathewson-IGT Knowledge Center plus 2 others. *Books:* 1.4 million (physical), 588,940 (digital/electronic). Students can reserve study rooms.

STUDENT LIFE
Housing options: coed, men-only, women-only, special housing for students with disabilities. Campus housing is university owned. Freshman applicants given priority for college housing.

Activities and organizations: drama/theater group, student-run newspaper, radio station, choral group, marching band, Intervarsity Christian Fellowship, Student Ambassadors, Young Democrats, Asian American Association, Blue Crew, national fraternities, national sororities.

Athletics Member NCAA. All Division I except football (Division I-A). ***Intercollegiate sports:*** baseball M(s), basketball M(s)/W(s), cheerleading M(c)/W(c), cross-country running W(s), golf M(s)/W(s)(c), riflery M(s)/W(s), soccer W(s), softball W(s), swimming and diving W(s), tennis M(s)/W(s), track and field W(s), volleyball W(s). ***Intramural sports:*** basketball M/W, bowling M/W, cross-country running M/W, equestrian sports M/W, football M, golf M/W, racquetball M/W, rock climbing M/W, rugby M/W, skiing (cross-country) M/W, skiing (downhill) M/W, soccer M/W, softball M/W, swimming and diving M/W, table tennis M/W, tennis M/W, track and field M/W, ultimate Frisbee M/W, volleyball M/W, water polo M/W.

Campus security: 24-hour emergency response devices and patrols, late-night transport/escort service, controlled dormitory access.

Student services: health clinic, personal/psychological counseling, women's center, legal services, veterans affairs office.

COSTS & FINANCIAL AID
Costs (2018–19) ***Tuition:*** state resident $6990 full-time, $224 per credit part-time; nonresident $21,462 full-time, $470 per credit part-time. Full-time tuition and fees vary according to course level, course load, degree level, and program. Part-time tuition and fees vary according to course level, course load, degree level, and program. ***Required fees:*** $774 full-time, $282 per term part-time. ***Room and board:*** $10,868; room only: $6100. Room and board charges vary according to board plan and housing facility. ***Payment plan:*** installment. ***Waivers:*** senior citizens and employees or children of employees.

Financial Aid Of all full-time matriculated undergraduates who enrolled in 2017, 10,283 applied for aid, 8,014 were judged to have need, 760 had their need fully met. In 2017, 1540 non-need-based awards were made. ***Average percent of need met:*** 60. ***Average financial aid package:*** $9020. ***Average need-based loan:*** $4240. ***Average need-based gift aid:*** $6970. ***Average non-need-based aid:*** $3070. ***Average indebtedness upon graduation:*** $22,600.

APPLYING
Standardized Tests *Required:* SAT or ACT (for admission).

Options: electronic application, early admission, early action, deferred entrance.

Application fee: $60.

Required: high school transcript, minimum 3.0 GPA.

Notification: continuous (freshmen), continuous (out-of-state freshmen), continuous (transfers), rolling (early action).

CONTACT
Dr. Steve Maples, Director of Undergraduate Admissions, University of Nevada, Reno, Mail Stop 120, Reno, NV 89557. *Phone:* 775-784-4700. *Toll-free phone:* 866-263-8232. *Fax:* 775-784-4283. *E-mail:* asknevada@unr.edu.

University of Phoenix–Las Vegas Campus

Las Vegas, Nevada

http://www.phoenix.edu/

CONTACT
Marc Booker, Senior Director, Office of Admissions and Evaluation, University of Phoenix–Las Vegas Campus, 4305 South Riverpoint Parkway, Mail Stop CF-L101, Phoenix, AZ 85040. *Phone:* 602-557-4609. *Toll-free phone:* 866-766-0766. *Fax:* 480-643-1156.

Western Nevada College

Carson City, Nevada

http://www.wnc.edu/

CONTACT
Admissions and Records, Western Nevada College, 2201 West College Parkway, Carson City, NV 89703. *Phone:* 775-445-2377. *Fax:* 775-445-3147. *E-mail:* wncc_aro@wncc.edu.

NEW HAMPSHIRE

Colby-Sawyer College

New London, New Hampshire

http://www.colby-sawyer.edu/

CONTACT
Ms. Jaimee Hofstetter, Director of Enrollment Operations, Colby-Sawyer College, 541 Main Street, New London, NH 03257-4648. *Phone:* 603-526-3887. *Toll-free phone:* 800-272-1015. *Fax:* 603-526-3452. *E-mail:* admissions@colby-sawyer.edu.

Dartmouth College

Hanover, New Hampshire

http://www.dartmouth.edu/

- **Independent** university, founded 1769
- **Small-town** 269-acre campus
- **Endowment** $5.5 billion
- **Coed** 4,417 undergraduate students, 99% full-time, 49% women, 51% men
- **Most difficult** entrance level, 9% of applicants were admitted

UNDERGRAD STUDENTS
4,357 full-time, 60 part-time. Students come from 53 states and territories; 95 other countries; 97% are from out of state; 6% Black or African American, non-Hispanic/Latino; 10% Hispanic/Latino; 15% Asian, non-Hispanic/Latino; 0.3% Native Hawaiian or other Pacific Islander, non-Hispanic/Latino; 2% American Indian or Alaska Native, non-Hispanic/Latino; 5% Two or more races, non-Hispanic/Latino; 1% Race/ethnicity unknown; 9% international; 0.2% transferred in; 87% live on campus.

Freshmen:
Admission: 22,033 applied, 1,925 admitted, 1,167 enrolled. ***Test scores:*** SAT evidence-based reading and writing scores over 500: 100%; SAT math scores over 500: 100%; ACT scores over 18: 100%; SAT evidence-based reading and writing scores over 600: 98%; SAT math scores over 600: 98%; ACT scores over 24: 99%; SAT evidence-based reading and writing scores over 700: 77%; SAT math scores over 700: 83%; ACT scores over 30: 83%.

Retention: 97% of full-time freshmen returned.

FACULTY
Total: 784, 77% full-time, 92% with terminal degrees.

Student/faculty ratio: 7:1.

ACADEMICS
Calendar: quarters. *Degrees:* bachelor's, master's, and doctoral.

Special study options: advanced placement credit, double majors, honors programs, independent study, internships, off-campus study, services for LD students, student-designed majors, study abroad, summer session for credit. ***ROTC:*** Army (c).

Unusual degree programs: 3-2 engineering.

Computers: 200 computers/terminals are available on campus for general student use. Students can access the following: campus intranet, computer help desk, free student e-mail accounts, online (class) grades, online (class) registration, online (class) schedules. Campuswide network is available. 100% of college-owned or -operated housing units are wired for high-speed Internet access. Wireless service is available via entire campus.

Library: Baker-Berry Library plus 8 others. *Books:* 2.5 million (physical), 991,009 (digital/electronic); *Serial titles:* 15,595 (physical). Study areas open 24 hours, 5–7 days a week; students can reserve study rooms.

STUDENT LIFE
Housing options: on-campus residence required for freshman year; coed, cooperative. Campus housing is university owned. Freshman campus housing is guaranteed.

Activities and organizations: drama/theater group, student-run newspaper, radio and television station, choral group, marching band, Dartmouth Student Assembly, Dartmouth Outing Club, Collis After Dark, Green Key Society, GLOS - Greek Letter Organizations and Societies, national fraternities, national sororities.

Athletics Member NCAA. All Division I except football (Division I-AA). ***Intercollegiate sports:*** badminton M(c)/W(c), baseball M, basketball M/W, cheerleading M(c)/W(c), crew M/W, cross-country running M/W, equestrian sports M/W, fencing M(c)/W(c), field hockey W, golf M/W, gymnastics M(c)/W(c), ice hockey M/W, lacrosse M/W, rowing M/W, rugby M(c)/W, sailing M/W, skiing (cross-country) M/W, skiing (downhill) M(c)/W, soccer M/W, softball W, squash M/W, swimming and diving M/W, table tennis M(c)/W(c), tennis M/W, track and field M/W, ultimate Frisbee M(c)/W(c), volleyball M(c)/W, water polo M(c)/W(c), wrestling M(c). ***Intramural sports:*** baseball M, basketball M/W, cross-country running M/W, football M/W, golf M/W, ice hockey M/W, lacrosse M/W, rugby M/W, skiing (cross-country) M/W, skiing (downhill) M/W, soccer M/W, softball M/W, squash M/W, swimming and diving M/W, table tennis M/W, tennis M/W, track and field M/W, volleyball M/W, water polo M/W, weight lifting M/W, wrestling M.

Campus security: 24-hour emergency response devices and patrols, late-night transport/escort service, controlled dormitory access.

Student services: health clinic, personal/psychological counseling, women's center.

COSTS & FINANCIAL AID
Costs (2019–20) ***One-time required fee:*** $418. ***Comprehensive fee:*** $73,578 includes full-time tuition ($55,605), mandatory fees ($1599), and room and board ($16,374). ***College room only:*** $9879. ***Payment plan:*** tuition prepayment.

Financial Aid Of all full-time matriculated undergraduates who enrolled in 2018, 2,503 applied for aid, 2,215 were judged to have need, 2,215 had their need fully met. 1,381 Federal Work-Study jobs (averaging $2234). 598 state and other part-time jobs (averaging $2477). ***Average percent of need met:*** 100. ***Average financial aid package:*** $52,357. ***Average need-based loan:*** $4036. ***Average need-based gift aid:*** $51,118. ***Average indebtedness upon graduation:*** $18,903. ***Financial aid deadline:*** 2/1.

APPLYING
Standardized Tests *Required:* SAT or ACT (for admission), SAT and SAT Subject Tests or ACT (for admission).

Options: electronic application, early admission, early decision, deferred entrance.

Application fee: $80.

Required: essay or personal statement, high school transcript, 3 letters of recommendation, peer evaluation. ***Recommended:*** interview.

Application deadlines: 1/1 (freshmen), 3/1 (transfers).

Early decision deadline: 11/1.

Notification: 4/10 (freshmen), 5/15 (transfers), 12/15 (early decision).

CONTACT
Paul Sunde, Director of Admissions, Dartmouth College, 6016 McNutt Hall, Hanover, NH 03755. *Phone:* 603-646-2875. *E-mail:* admissions.reply@dartmouth.edu.

Franklin Pierce University

Rindge, New Hampshire

http://www.franklinpierce.edu/

- **Independent** comprehensive, founded 1962
- **Rural** 1200-acre campus
- **Endowment** $13.2 million
- **Coed** 1,629 undergraduate students, 87% full-time, 55% women, 45% men
- **Minimally difficult** entrance level, 79% of applicants were admitted

UNDERGRAD STUDENTS
1,413 full-time, 216 part-time. Students come from 27 states and territories; 15 other countries; 81% are from out of state; 7% Black or African American, non-Hispanic/Latino; 7% Hispanic/Latino; 1% Asian, non-Hispanic/Latino; 0.1% Native Hawaiian or other Pacific Islander, non-Hispanic/Latino; 0.4% American Indian or Alaska Native, non-Hispanic/Latino; 1% Two or more races, non-Hispanic/Latino; 7% Race/ethnicity unknown; 3% international; 2% transferred in; 89% live on campus.

Freshmen:

Admission: 5,240 applied, 4,118 admitted, 462 enrolled. ***Average high school GPA:*** 2.9. ***Test scores:*** SAT evidence-based reading and writing scores over 500: 72%; SAT math scores over 500: 72%; ACT scores over 18: 63%; SAT evidence-based reading and writing scores over 600: 18%; SAT math scores over 600: 15%; ACT scores over 24: 33%; SAT evidence-based reading and writing scores over 700: 2%; SAT math scores over 700: 2%; ACT scores over 30: 3%.

Retention: 59% of full-time freshmen returned.

FACULTY
Total: 340, 27% full-time, 53% with terminal degrees.

Student/faculty ratio: 13:1.

ACADEMICS
Calendar: differs by branch and program. *Degrees:* certificates, associate, bachelor's, master's, doctoral, and postbachelor's certificates (profile does not reflect significant enrollment at 6 continuing education sites; master's degree is only offered at these sites).

Special study options: academic remediation for entering students, accelerated degree program, adult/continuing education programs, advanced placement credit, distance learning, double majors, English as a second language, external degree program, freshman honors college, honors programs, independent study, internships, off-campus study, part-time degree program, services for LD students, student-designed majors, study abroad, summer session for credit. ***ROTC:*** Army (c).

Computers: 100 computers/terminals are available on campus for general student use. Students can access the following: campus intranet, computer help desk, free student e-mail accounts, online (class) grades, online (class) registration, online (class) schedules. Campuswide network is available. 100% of college-owned or -operated housing units are wired for high-speed Internet access. Wireless service is available via entire campus.

Library: Frank S. DiPietro Library plus 1 other. *Books:* 105,736 (physical), 246,080 (digital/electronic); *Serial titles:* 72 (physical), 70,000 (digital/electronic); *Databases:* 70. Weekly public service hours: 95.

STUDENT LIFE
Housing options: on-campus residence required for freshman year; coed. Campus housing is university owned. Freshman campus housing is guaranteed.

Activities and organizations: drama/theater group, student-run newspaper, radio and television station, choral group, Peer Leadership,

Health Sciences Club, Student Government, Honors Program, Hope Happens Here.

Athletics Member NCAA. All Division II. ***Intercollegiate sports:*** baseball M(s), basketball M(s)/W(s), cross-country running M(s)/W(s), field hockey W(s), football M(s), golf M(s)/W(s), ice hockey M(s)/W(s), lacrosse M(s)/W(s), rowing W(s), soccer M(s)/W(s), softball W(s), tennis M(s)/W(s), track and field M(s)/W(s), volleyball W(s). ***Intramural sports:*** badminton M/W, baseball M(c), basketball M/W, cheerleading M(c)/W(c), fencing M(c)/W(c), football M/W, rock climbing M/W, rugby M(c)/W(c), sand volleyball M/W, skiing (cross-country) M/W, skiing (downhill) M/W, soccer M/W, softball M/W, table tennis M/W, tennis M/W, ultimate Frisbee M(c)/W(c), volleyball M/W.

Campus security: 24-hour emergency response devices and patrols, student patrols, late-night transport/escort service, controlled dormitory access.

Student services: health clinic, personal/psychological counseling, veterans affairs office.

COSTS & FINANCIAL AID

Costs (2019–20) ***Comprehensive fee:*** $52,100 includes full-time tuition ($34,900), mandatory fees ($3300), and room and board ($13,900). Part-time tuition: $1197 per credit hour. ***College room only:*** $8100.

Financial Aid Of all full-time matriculated undergraduates who enrolled in 2018, 1,196 applied for aid, 1,076 were judged to have need, 261 had their need fully met. In 2018, 298 non-need-based awards were made. ***Average percent of need met:*** 72. ***Average financial aid package:*** $26,363. ***Average need-based loan:*** $4038. ***Average need-based gift aid:*** $23,014. ***Average non-need-based aid:*** $12,148. ***Average indebtedness upon graduation:*** $41,661.

APPLYING

Standardized Tests *Required for some:* SAT or ACT (for admission).

Options: electronic application, early admission, deferred entrance.

Application fee: $40.

Required: essay or personal statement, high school transcript, 1 letter of recommendation. ***Required for some:*** minimum 2.0 GPA. ***Recommended:*** minimum 2.2 GPA, interview.

Application deadlines: rolling (freshmen), rolling (out-of-state freshmen), rolling (transfers).

Notification: continuous (freshmen), continuous (out-of-state freshmen), continuous (transfers).

CONTACT

Ms. Linda Quimby, Vice President for Enrollment, Franklin Pierce University, 40 University Drive, Rindge, NH 03461-0060. *Phone:* 603-899-4050. *Toll-free phone:* 800-437-0048. *E-mail:* admissions@fpc.edu.

Granite State College

Concord, New Hampshire

http://www.granite.edu/

- **State and locally supported** comprehensive, founded 1972, part of University System of New Hampshire
- **Suburban** campus
- **Endowment** $7.5 million
- **Coed** 1,758 undergraduate students, 46% full-time, 73% women, 27% men
- **Noncompetitive** entrance level, 100% of applicants were admitted

UNDERGRAD STUDENTS

807 full-time, 951 part-time. Students come from 42 states and territories; 1 other country; 18% are from out of state; 3% Black or African American, non-Hispanic/Latino; 4% Hispanic/Latino; 1% Asian, non-Hispanic/Latino; 0.4% American Indian or Alaska Native, non-Hispanic/Latino; 2% Two or more races, non-Hispanic/Latino; 6% Race/ethnicity unknown; 0.1% international; 18% transferred in.

Freshmen:

Admission: 263 applied, 263 admitted, 73 enrolled.

Retention: 46% of full-time freshmen returned.

FACULTY

Total: 163, 9% full-time, 32% with terminal degrees.

Student/faculty ratio: 11:1.

ACADEMICS

Calendar: trimesters. *Degrees:* associate, bachelor's, master's, and postbachelor's certificates (offers primarily part-time degree programs; courses offered at 50 locations in New Hampshire).

Special study options: academic remediation for entering students, accelerated degree program, adult/continuing education programs, advanced placement credit, cooperative education, distance learning, double majors, independent study, internships, off-campus study, part-time degree program, services for LD students, student-designed majors, summer session for credit.

Computers: 120 computers/terminals are available on campus for general student use. Students can access the following: campus intranet, computer help desk, free student e-mail accounts, online (class) grades, online (class) registration, online (class) schedules. Campuswide network is available. Wireless service is available via entire campus.

Library: GSC Library and Information Commons. *Books:* 250,000 (digital/electronic); *Databases:* 29. Weekly public service hours: 126.

STUDENT LIFE

Activities and organizations: Alumni Advisory Board, Student Advisory Board.

Student services: personal/psychological counseling.

COSTS

Costs (2019–20) ***Tuition:*** area resident $7536 full-time, $314 per credit part-time; state resident $7536 full-time, $314 per credit part-time; nonresident $8520 full-time, $355 per credit part-time. ***Required fees:*** $225 full-time, $314 per credit part-time, $75 per term part-time.

APPLYING

Options: electronic application.

Required for some: high school transcript, associate degree for some BS programs.

Application deadlines: rolling (freshmen), rolling (transfers).

Notification: continuous (freshmen), continuous (transfers).

CONTACT

Ms. Christine Williams, Assistant Vice President of Enrollment Operations, Granite State College, 25 Hall Street, Concord, NH 03301. *Phone:* 603-228-3000. *Toll-free phone:* 888-228-3000. *Fax:* 603-513-1386. *E-mail:* gsc.admissions@granite.edu.

Hellenic American University

Nashua, New Hampshire

http://www.hauniv.edu/

CONTACT

Hellenic American University, 505 Amherst Street, Nashua, NH 03063.

Keene State College

Keene, New Hampshire

http://www.keene.edu/

- **State-supported** comprehensive, founded 1909, part of University System of New Hampshire
- **Small-town** 150-acre campus
- **Coed**
- **Moderately difficult** entrance level

ACADEMICS

Calendar: semesters. *Degrees:* certificates, bachelor's, master's, post-master's, and postbachelor's certificates.

Library: Mason Library. *Books:* 247,720 (physical), 319,081 (digital/electronic); *Serial titles:* 142 (physical), 73,114 (digital/electronic); *Databases:* 92. Weekly public service hours: 102; students can reserve study rooms.

STUDENT LIFE

Housing options: on-campus residence required through sophomore year; coed, women-only. Campus housing is university owned. Freshman campus housing is guaranteed.

Activities and organizations: drama/theater group, student-run newspaper, radio and television station, choral group, Environmental Outing Club, Social Activities Council, Student Government, Chock Full

O Notes, The Equinox student newspaper, national fraternities, national sororities.

Athletics Member NCAA. All Division III.

Campus security: 24-hour emergency response devices and patrols, late-night transport/escort service, controlled dormitory access, Emergency Notification System.

Student services: health clinic, personal/psychological counseling, women's center, veterans affairs office.

COSTS & FINANCIAL AID

Costs (2018–19) ***Tuition:*** state resident $11,468 full-time, $478 per credit part-time; nonresident $20,432 full-time, $852 per credit part-time. Part-time tuition and fees vary according to course load. ***Required fees:*** $2744 full-time, $111 per credit part-time. ***Room and board:*** $11,026. Room and board charges vary according to board plan and housing facility.

Financial Aid Of all full-time matriculated undergraduates who enrolled in 2017, 3,020 applied for aid, 2,439 were judged to have need, 321 had their need fully met. 947 Federal Work-Study jobs (averaging $2274). 581 state and other part-time jobs (averaging $1227). In 2017, 666 non-need-based awards were made. ***Average percent of need met:*** 65. ***Average financial aid package:*** $13,125. ***Average need-based loan:*** $4257. ***Average need-based gift aid:*** $7143. ***Average non-need-based aid:*** $5334. ***Average indebtedness upon graduation:*** $39,687. ***Financial aid deadline:*** 3/1.

APPLYING

Options: electronic application, deferred entrance.

Application fee: $50.

Required: essay or personal statement, high school transcript. ***Recommended:*** 1 letter of recommendation.

CONTACT

Ms. Peggy Richmond, Director of Admissions, Keene State College, 229 Main Street, Keene, NH 03435-2604. *Phone:* 603-358-2273. *Toll-free phone:* 800-KSC-1909. *Fax:* 603-358-2767. *E-mail:* mrichmon@keene.edu.

New England College

Henniker, New Hampshire

http://www.nec.edu/

- **Independent** comprehensive, founded 1946
- **Small-town** 225-acre campus with easy access to Boston
- **Endowment** $11.9 million
- **Coed** 1,840 undergraduate students, 99% full-time, 58% women, 42% men
- **Minimally difficult** entrance level, 100% of applicants were admitted

UNDERGRAD STUDENTS

1,815 full-time, 25 part-time. Students come from 41 states and territories; 21 other countries; 82% are from out of state; 24% Black or African American, non-Hispanic/Latino; 8% Hispanic/Latino; 2% Asian, non-Hispanic/Latino; 0.2% Native Hawaiian or other Pacific Islander, non-Hispanic/Latino; 0.6% American Indian or Alaska Native, non-Hispanic/Latino; 4% Two or more races, non-Hispanic/Latino; 6% Race/ethnicity unknown; 4% international; 8% transferred in; 41% live on campus.

Freshmen:

Admission: 8,616 applied, 8,608 admitted, 412 enrolled. ***Average high school GPA:*** 2.6.

Retention: 58% of full-time freshmen returned.

FACULTY

Total: 283, 15% full-time, 42% with terminal degrees.

Student/faculty ratio: 16:1.

ACADEMICS

Calendar: semesters for residential undergraduates; 7-week terms for online undergraduate and graduate programs. *Degrees:* associate, bachelor's, master's, and doctoral.

Special study options: academic remediation for entering students, accelerated degree program, adult/continuing education programs, advanced placement credit, distance learning, double majors, English as a second language, external degree program, freshman honors college, honors programs, independent study, internships, off-campus study, part-time degree program, services for LD students, student-designed majors, study abroad, summer session for credit. ***ROTC:*** Army (c), Air Force (c).

Unusual degree programs: business administration; nursing with Massachusetts College of Pharmacy and Health Sciences; education, political science, law with New York Law School.

Computers: 212 computers/terminals and 350 ports are available on campus for general student use. Students can access the following: campus intranet, computer help desk, free student e-mail accounts, online (class) grades, online (class) registration, online (class) schedules, financial aid, billing, advising, degree audit. Campuswide network is available. 100% of college-owned or -operated housing units are wired for high-speed Internet access. Wireless service is available via entire campus.

Library: Danforth Library. *Books:* 98,000 (physical), 152,000 (digital/electronic); *Serial titles:* 101 (physical), 100,000 (digital/electronic); *Databases:* 22. Weekly public service hours: 126; study areas open 24 hours, 5–7 days a week; students can reserve study rooms.

STUDENT LIFE

Housing options: on-campus residence required through junior year; coed. Campus housing is university owned. Freshman campus housing is guaranteed.

Activities and organizations: drama/theater group, student-run newspaper, radio station, Student Senate, Campus Activities Board, Criminal Justice Club, International Student Association, Political Science Club, national fraternities, national sororities.

Athletics Member NCAA. All Division III. ***Intercollegiate sports:*** baseball M, basketball M/W, cross-country running M/W, field hockey W, ice hockey M/W, lacrosse M/W, rugby M(c)/W(c), skiing (downhill) M/W, soccer M/W, softball W, volleyball W, wrestling M. ***Intramural sports:*** basketball M/W, cheerleading W, golf M/W, ice hockey M/W, lacrosse M/W, soccer M/W, softball W, table tennis M/W, tennis M/W, ultimate Frisbee M/W, volleyball M/W.

Campus security: 24-hour emergency response devices and patrols, student patrols, late-night transport/escort service, controlled dormitory access, emergency text system.

Student services: health clinic, personal/psychological counseling, women's center, veterans affairs office.

COSTS & FINANCIAL AID

Costs (2019–20) ***Comprehensive fee:*** $52,840 includes full-time tuition ($37,490), mandatory fees ($1180), and room and board ($14,170). Part-time tuition: $405 per credit hour. ***College room only:*** $7610.

Financial Aid Of all full-time matriculated undergraduates who enrolled in 2018, 1,546 applied for aid, 1,485 were judged to have need, 97 had their need fully met. 397 Federal Work-Study jobs (averaging $1887). 29 state and other part-time jobs (averaging $1096). In 2018, 158 non-need-based awards were made. ***Average percent of need met:*** 52. ***Average financial aid package:*** $20,100. ***Average need-based loan:*** $4030. ***Average need-based gift aid:*** $18,672. ***Average non-need-based aid:*** $20,490. ***Average indebtedness upon graduation:*** $37,747.

APPLYING

Options: electronic application, deferred entrance.

Required: essay or personal statement, high school transcript, 2 letters of recommendation. ***Recommended:*** interview.

Application deadlines: rolling (out-of-state freshmen), 9/5 (transfers).

Notification: continuous (freshmen), continuous (out-of-state freshmen), continuous (transfers).

CONTACT

Emily Lorentsen, Associate Director of Undergraduate Admissions, New England College, 102 Bridge Street, Henniker, NH 03242. *Phone:* 603-428-2392. *Toll-free phone:* 800-521-7642. *Fax:* 603-428-3155. *E-mail:* elorentsen@nec.edu.

New Hampshire Institute of Art

Manchester, New Hampshire

http://www.nhia.edu/

- **Independent** comprehensive, founded 1898
- **Urban** campus with easy access to Boston
- **Endowment** $22.8 million
- **Coed**
- **Moderately difficult** entrance level

FACULTY
Student/faculty ratio: 10:1.

ACADEMICS
Calendar: semesters. *Degrees:* certificates, bachelor's, and master's. **Library:** Teti Library. *Books:* 17,000 (physical), 144,463 (digital/electronic); *Serial titles:* 80 (physical), 7,800 (digital/electronic); *Databases:* 30. Weekly public service hours: 63.

STUDENT LIFE
Housing options: on-campus residence required through sophomore year; coed. Campus housing is university owned and leased by the school. Freshman applicants given priority for college housing.

Activities and organizations: student-run newspaper, radio station, Student Leadership Council, Comic/Arts Club, Neo-Victorian Club, Design Ink, Gay/Straight Alliance.

Campus security: late-night transport/escort service, controlled dormitory access.

Student services: health clinic, personal/psychological counseling.

COSTS
Costs (2018–19) ***Comprehensive fee:*** $40,140 includes full-time tuition ($25,990), mandatory fees ($2690), and room and board ($11,460). Full-time tuition and fees vary according to degree level. Part-time tuition: $3285 per course. Part-time tuition and fees vary according to course load and degree level. ***Required fees:*** $95 per credit hour part-time, $100 per term part-time. ***Room and board:*** Room and board charges vary according to board plan.

APPLYING
Standardized Tests *Required for some:* SAT or ACT (for admission).

Options: electronic application, early action, deferred entrance.

Application fee: $30.

Required: essay or personal statement, high school transcript, portfolio. ***Recommended:*** minimum 2.0 GPA, 2 letters of recommendation.

CONTACT
Mr. Scott Ramon, Director of Student Recruitment, New Hampshire Institute of Art, 148 Concord Street, Manchester, NH 03104-4158. *Phone:* 603-836-2148. *Toll-free phone:* 866-241-4918. *E-mail:* admissions@nhia.edu.

Northeast Catholic College

Warner, New Hampshire

http://www.magdalen.edu/

CONTACT
Admissions Director, Northeast Catholic College, 511 Kearsarge Mountain Road, Warner, NH 03278. *Phone:* 603-456-2656. *Toll-free phone:* 877-498-1723. *Fax:* 603-456-2660. *E-mail:* admissions@magdalen.edu.

Plymouth State University

Plymouth, New Hampshire

http://www.plymouth.edu/

CONTACT
Mr. Tony Trodella, Director of Undergraduate Recruitment, Plymouth State University, Plymouth, NH 03264-1595. *Phone:* 603-535-2237. *Toll-free phone:* 800-842-6900. *Fax:* 603-535-2714. *E-mail:* admissions@plymouth.edu.

Rivier University

Nashua, New Hampshire

http://www.rivier.edu/

- **Independent Roman Catholic** comprehensive, founded 1933
- **Suburban** 68-acre campus with easy access to Boston
- **Coed**
- **Moderately difficult** entrance level

FACULTY
Student/faculty ratio: 13:1.

ACADEMICS
Calendar: semesters. *Degrees:* certificates, associate, bachelor's, master's, doctoral, post-master's, and postbachelor's certificates. **Library:** Regina Library plus 1 other.

STUDENT LIFE
Housing options: coed. Campus housing is university owned. Freshman campus housing is guaranteed.

Activities and organizations: drama/theater group, choral group, Student Government Association, Campus Activities Board, Campus Ministry, Student Nurses Association, Theater Club.

Athletics Member NCAA. All Division III.

Campus security: 24-hour emergency response devices and patrols, late-night transport/escort service, controlled dormitory access.

Student services: health clinic, personal/psychological counseling.

FINANCIAL AID
Financial Aid Of all full-time matriculated undergraduates who enrolled in 2010, 888 applied for aid, 822 were judged to have need, 70 had their need fully met. In 2010, 105 non-need-based awards were made. ***Average percent of need met:*** 59. ***Average financial aid package:*** $14,850. ***Average need-based loan:*** $4378. ***Average need-based gift aid:*** $10,806. ***Average non-need-based aid:*** $5066. ***Average indebtedness upon graduation:*** $43,189.

APPLYING
Standardized Tests *Required for some:* SAT or ACT (for admission), nursing exam. *Recommended:* SAT or ACT (for admission).

Options: electronic application, deferred entrance.

Application fee: $25.

Required: essay or personal statement, high school transcript, 1 letter of recommendation. ***Recommended:*** minimum 2.3 GPA, interview.

CONTACT
Valerie Leclair, Executive Director of Undergraduate and Graduate Admissions, Rivier University, 420 South Main Street, Nashua, NH 03060. *Phone:* 603-897-8515. *Toll-free phone:* 800-44RIVIER. *Fax:* 603-891-1799. *E-mail:* rivadmit@rivier.edu.

See page 493 for display ad and page 1084 for the College Close-Up.

★ Saint Anselm College

Manchester, New Hampshire

http://www.anselm.edu/

- **Independent Roman Catholic** 4-year, founded 1889
- **Suburban** 380-acre campus with easy access to Boston
- **Endowment** $134.6 million
- **Coed** 2,050 undergraduate students, 98% full-time, 61% women, 39% men
- **Moderately difficult** entrance level, 77% of applicants were admitted

UNDERGRAD STUDENTS
2,019 full-time, 31 part-time. Students come from 30 states and territories; 9 other countries; 78% are from out of state; 2% Black or African American, non-Hispanic/Latino; 4% Hispanic/Latino; 1% Asian, non-Hispanic/Latino; 2% Two or more races, non-Hispanic/Latino; 4% Race/ethnicity unknown; 0.8% international; 0.9% transferred in; 91% live on campus.

Freshmen:
Admission: 3,896 applied, 2,986 admitted, 591 enrolled. ***Average high school GPA:*** 3.3. ***Test scores:*** SAT evidence-based reading and writing

scores over 500: 88%; SAT math scores over 500: 98%; ACT scores over 18: 100%; SAT evidence-based reading and writing scores over 600: 62%; SAT math scores over 600: 51%; ACT scores over 24: 86%; SAT evidence-based reading and writing scores over 700: 11%; SAT math scores over 700: 9%; ACT scores over 30: 22%.

Retention: 91% of full-time freshmen returned.

FACULTY

Total: 233, 67% full-time, 74% with terminal degrees.

Student/faculty ratio: 11:1.

ACADEMICS

Calendar: semesters. *Degree:* bachelor's.

Special study options: accelerated degree program, advanced placement credit, double majors, honors programs, independent study, internships, off-campus study, part-time degree program, services for LD students, study abroad, summer session for credit. ***ROTC:*** Army (c).

Unusual degree programs: 3-2 engineering with University of Massachusetts Lowell, The Catholic University of America, University of Notre Dame, Manhattan College; pharmacy, optometry, physical therapy, physician assistant with Massachusetts College of Pharmacy and Health Sciences.

Computers: 400 computers/terminals are available on campus for general student use. Students can access the following: campus intranet, computer help desk, free student e-mail accounts, online (class) registration, online (class) schedules. Campuswide network is available. 100% of college-owned or -operated housing units are wired for high-speed Internet access. Wireless service is available via entire campus.

Library: Geisel Library plus 2 others. Students can reserve study rooms.

STUDENT LIFE

Housing options: coed, men-only, women-only, special housing for students with disabilities. Campus housing is university owned. Freshman campus housing is guaranteed.

Activities and organizations: drama/theater group, student-run newspaper, choral group, Meelia Center for Community Engagement, Anselmian Abbey Players, Club Sports, Service and Solidarity Mission Trips, Saint Anselm College Crier (School Newspaper).

Athletics Member NCAA. All Division II. ***Intercollegiate sports:*** baseball M, basketball M/W, cross-country running M/W, field hockey W, football M, golf M, ice hockey M/W, lacrosse M/W, skiing (downhill) M(c)/W(c), soccer M/W, softball W, tennis M/W, volleyball W. ***Intramural sports:*** basketball M/W, football M/W, ice hockey M/W, racquetball M(c)/W(c), rugby M(c)/W(c), soccer M/W, softball M/W, table tennis M(c)/W(c), tennis M/W, track and field M(c)/W(c), ultimate Frisbee M/W, volleyball M/W.

Campus security: 24-hour emergency response devices and patrols, student patrols, late-night transport/escort service, controlled dormitory access.

Student services: health clinic, personal/psychological counseling.

COSTS & FINANCIAL AID

Costs (2019–20) ***Comprehensive fee:*** $56,850 includes full-time tuition ($40,500), mandatory fees ($1600), and room and board ($14,750). Part-time tuition: $1000 per credit. ***Required fees:*** $600 per term part-time. ***College room only:*** $8850.

Financial Aid Of all full-time matriculated undergraduates who enrolled in 2018, 1,649 applied for aid, 1,374 were judged to have need, 353 had their need fully met. 1,101 Federal Work-Study jobs (averaging $1730). 9 state and other part-time jobs (averaging $2000). In 2018, 560 non-need-based awards were made. ***Average percent of need met:*** 80. ***Average financial aid package:*** $29,735. ***Average need-based loan:*** $3725. ***Average need-based gift aid:*** $25,346. ***Average non-need-based aid:*** $17,512. ***Average indebtedness upon graduation:*** $32,769. ***Financial aid deadline:*** 2/15.

APPLYING

Standardized Tests *Required for some:* SAT or ACT (for admission).

Options: electronic application, early admission, early decision, early action, deferred entrance.

Application fee: $50.

Required: essay or personal statement, high school transcript, 2 letters of recommendation. ***Recommended:*** interview.

Application deadlines: 2/1 (freshmen), rolling (transfers), 11/15 (early action).

Early decision deadline: 12/1.

Notification: 3/15 (freshmen), continuous (transfers), 12/31 (early decision), 1/15 (early action).

CONTACT

Mr. Eric Nichols, Vice President for Enrollment and Dean of Admission, Saint Anselm College, 100 Saint Anselm Drive, Manchester, NH 03102-1310. *Phone:* 603-641-7500. *Toll-free phone:* 888-4ANSELM. *E-mail:* admission@anselm.edu.

See previous page for display ad and page 1090 for the College Close-Up.

★ Southern New Hampshire University

Manchester, New Hampshire

http://www.snhu.edu/

CONTACT

Mr. Tim Whittum, Director of Freshman Admission, Southern New Hampshire University, 2500 North River Road, Manchester, NH 03106-1045. *Phone:* 603-645-9611. *Toll-free phone:* 888-327-7648. *Fax:* 603-645-9693. *E-mail:* t.whittum@snhu.edu.

See below for display ad and page 1116 for the College Close-Up.

Thomas More College of Liberal Arts

Merrimack, New Hampshire

http://www.thomasmorecollege.edu/

- **Independent** 4-year, founded 1978, affiliated with Roman Catholic Church
- **Small-town** 14-acre campus with easy access to Boston
- **Endowment** $551,325
- **Coed**
- **Moderately difficult** entrance level

FACULTY

Student/faculty ratio: 9:1.

ACADEMICS

Calendar: semesters. *Degree:* bachelor's.

Library: Warren Memorial Library plus 1 other. *Books:* 44,075 (physical); *Serial titles:* 43,515 (physical).

STUDENT LIFE

Housing options: on-campus residence required through senior year; men-only, women-only. Campus housing is university owned. Freshman campus housing is guaranteed.

Activities and organizations: drama/theater group, choral group.

Campus security: 24-hour emergency response devices, student patrols, late-night transport/escort service, on-site staff member.

COSTS & FINANCIAL AID

Costs (2018–19) ***Comprehensive fee:*** $31,300 includes full-time tuition ($21,600) and room and board ($9700). Full-time tuition and fees vary according to course load, program, and reciprocity agreements. Part-time tuition: $900 per credit hour. Part-time tuition and fees vary according to course load, program, and reciprocity agreements. ***Room and board:*** Room and board charges vary according to board plan.

Financial Aid Of all full-time matriculated undergraduates who enrolled in 2016, 81 applied for aid, 80 were judged to have need, 17 had their need fully met. In 2016, 33 non-need-based awards were made. ***Average percent of need met:*** 75. ***Average financial aid package:*** $18,718. ***Average need-based loan:*** $4490. ***Average need-based gift aid:*** $16,730. ***Average non-need-based aid:*** $6643. ***Average indebtedness upon graduation:*** $26,828.

APPLYING

Standardized Tests *Recommended:* SAT or ACT (for admission).

Options: electronic application.

Required: essay or personal statement, high school transcript, 2 letters of recommendation. ***Required for some:*** interview.

CONTACT

Mr. Jonathan Rensch, Director of Admissions, Thomas More College of Liberal Arts, 6 Manchester Street, Merrimack, NH 03054-4818. *Phone:* 603-880-8308 Ext. 14. *Toll-free phone:* 800-880-8308. *Fax:* 603-546-0034. *E-mail:* jrensch@thomasmorecollege.edu.

University of New Hampshire

Durham, New Hampshire

http://www.unh.edu/

- **State-supported** university, founded 1866, part of University System of New Hampshire
- **Small-town** 2600-acre campus with easy access to Boston
- **Endowment** $389.5 million
- **Coed** 12,782 undergraduate students, 98% full-time, 55% women, 45% men
- **Moderately difficult** entrance level, 77% of applicants were admitted

UNDERGRAD STUDENTS

12,477 full-time, 305 part-time. Students come from 49 states and territories; 35 other countries; 52% are from out of state; 1% Black or African American, non-Hispanic/Latino; 3% Hispanic/Latino; 3% Asian, non-Hispanic/Latino; 0.1% American Indian or Alaska Native, non-Hispanic/Latino; 2% Two or more races, non-Hispanic/Latino; 4% Race/ethnicity unknown; 4% international; 4% transferred in; 56% live on campus.

Freshmen:

Admission: 20,096 applied, 15,430 admitted, 3,031 enrolled. ***Average high school GPA:*** 3.5. ***Test scores:*** SAT evidence-based reading and writing scores over 500: 93%; SAT math scores over 500: 93%; ACT scores over 18: 98%; SAT evidence-based reading and writing scores over 600: 49%; SAT math scores over 600: 43%; ACT scores over 24: 67%; SAT evidence-based reading and writing scores over 700: 7%; SAT math scores over 700: 8%; ACT scores over 30: 17%.

Retention: 85% of full-time freshmen returned.

FACULTY

Total: 1,008, 63% full-time, 68% with terminal degrees.

Student/faculty ratio: 18:1.

ACADEMICS

Calendar: semesters. *Degrees:* associate, bachelor's, master's, doctoral, and postbachelor's certificates.

Special study options: accelerated degree program, advanced placement credit, distance learning, double majors, English as a second language, honors programs, independent study, internships, off-campus study, part-time degree program, services for LD students, student-designed majors, study abroad, summer session for credit. ***ROTC:*** Army (b), Air Force (b).

Unusual degree programs: 3-2 business administration; social work; occupational therapy.

Computers: 320 computers/terminals are available on campus for general student use. Students can access the following: campus intranet, computer help desk, free student e-mail accounts, online (class) grades, online (class) registration, online (class) schedules. Campuswide network is available. 100% of college-owned or -operated housing units are wired for high-speed Internet access. Wireless service is available via entire campus.

Library: Dimond Library plus 4 others. *Books:* 1.6 million (physical), 889,664 (digital/electronic); *Serial titles:* 749 (physical), 84,556 (digital/electronic); *Databases:* 430. Weekly public service hours: 117; students can reserve study rooms.

STUDENT LIFE

Housing options: coed, special housing for students with disabilities. Campus housing is university owned. Freshman campus housing is guaranteed.

Activities and organizations: drama/theater group, student-run newspaper, radio station, choral group, marching band, Campus Activity Board, The Outing Club, Resident Hall Association, Alpha Phi Omega, Memorial Union Student Organization, national fraternities, national sororities.

Athletics Member NCAA. All Division I except football (Division I-AA). ***Intercollegiate sports:*** archery M(c)/W(c), baseball M(c), basketball M(s)/W(s), crew M(c)/W(c), cross-country running M(s)/W(s), fencing M(c)/W(c), field hockey W(s), golf M(c)/W(c), gymnastics W(s), ice hockey M(s)/W(s), lacrosse M(c)/W(s), riflery M(c)/W(c), rock climbing M(c)/W(c), rugby M(c)/W(c), sailing M(c)/W(c), skiing (cross-country) M(s)/W(s), skiing (downhill) M(s)/W(s), soccer M(s)/W(s), softball W(c), swimming and diving W(s), tennis M(c)/W(c), track and field M(s)/W(s), ultimate Frisbee M(c)/W(c), volleyball M(c)/W(s), wrestling M(c)/W(c).

Intramural sports: basketball M/W, football M/W, ice hockey M/W, sand volleyball M/W, soccer M/W, softball M/W, table tennis M/W, tennis M/W, ultimate Frisbee M/W, volleyball M/W.

Campus security: 24-hour emergency response devices, late-night transport/escort service, controlled dormitory access, lighted sidewalks, emergency phones located across campus, campus-wide 24-hour emergency alert system, 24-hour police coverage.

Student services: health clinic, personal/psychological counseling, women's center, veterans affairs office.

COSTS & FINANCIAL AID

Costs (2018–19) ***Tuition:*** state resident $15,140 full-time, $630 per credit hour part-time; nonresident $30,520 full-time, $1270 per credit hour part-time. Full-time tuition and fees vary according to program. Part-time tuition and fees vary according to course load and program. ***Required fees:*** $3359 full-time, $1680 per year part-time. ***Room and board:*** $11,588; room only: $7220. Room and board charges vary according to board plan and housing facility. ***Payment plan:*** installment. ***Waivers:*** employees or children of employees.

Financial Aid Of all full-time matriculated undergraduates who enrolled in 2017, 9,895 applied for aid, 8,422 were judged to have need, 1,329 had their need fully met. 6,135 Federal Work-Study jobs (averaging $2486). 3,051 state and other part-time jobs (averaging $3644). In 2017, 1867 non-need-based awards were made. ***Average percent of need met:*** 75. ***Average financial aid package:*** $24,654. ***Average need-based loan:*** $3252. ***Average need-based gift aid:*** $6139. ***Average non-need-based aid:*** $6686. ***Average indebtedness upon graduation:*** $40,293.

APPLYING

Standardized Tests *Required:* SAT or ACT (for admission).

Options: electronic application, early action, deferred entrance.

Application fee: $50.

Required: high school transcript, 1 letter of recommendation, Common Application, audition for some majors in music and theater, portfolio for art studio majors. ***Recommended:*** minimum 3.0 GPA.

Application deadlines: 2/1 (freshmen), 2/1 (out-of-state freshmen), 4/1 (transfers), 11/15 (early action).

Notification: continuous until 12/1 (freshmen), continuous (out-of-state freshmen), continuous until 4/15 (transfers), rolling (early action).

CONTACT

Ms. Tara E. Scholder, Interim Director of Admissions, University of New Hampshire, Durham, NH 03824. *Phone:* 603-862-5292. *Fax:* 603-862-0077. *E-mail:* tara.scholder@unh.edu.

University of New Hampshire at Manchester

Manchester, New Hampshire

http://manchester.unh.edu/

CONTACT

Erika Couture, Senior Associate Director of Admission, University of New Hampshire at Manchester, 88 Commerical Street, Manchester, NH 03101. *Phone:* 603-641-4150. *E-mail:* erika.couture@unh.edu.

NEW JERSEY

Bais Medrash Mayan Hatorah

Lakewood, New Jersey

http://www.baismedrashmayanhatorah.com/

CONTACT

Bais Medrash Mayan Hatorah, 101 Milton Street, Lakewood, NJ 08701.

Bais Medrash Toras Chesed

Lakewood, New Jersey

http://www.bmtc.edu/

CONTACT

Bais Medrash Toras Chesed, 910 Monmouth Avenue, Lakewood, NJ 08701.

Berkeley College–Woodland Park Campus

Woodland Park, New Jersey

http://www.berkeleycollege.edu/

- **Proprietary** comprehensive, founded 1931
- **Suburban** 25-acre campus with easy access to New York City
- **Coed** 3,324 undergraduate students, 73% full-time, 72% women, 28% men
- **Minimally difficult** entrance level, 99% of applicants were admitted

UNDERGRAD STUDENTS

2,431 full-time, 893 part-time. Students come from 19 states and territories; 9 other countries; 3% are from out of state; 18% Black or African American, non-Hispanic/Latino; 41% Hispanic/Latino; 1% Asian, non-Hispanic/Latino; 0.1% Native Hawaiian or other Pacific Islander, non-Hispanic/Latino; 0.2% American Indian or Alaska Native, non-Hispanic/Latino; 0.2% Two or more races, non-Hispanic/Latino; 27% Race/ethnicity unknown; 0.5% international; 14% transferred in.

Freshmen:

Admission: 1,105 applied, 1,092 admitted, 461 enrolled.

Retention: 61% of full-time freshmen returned.

FACULTY

Total: 312, 40% full-time, 42% with terminal degrees.

Student/faculty ratio: 14:1.

ACADEMICS

Calendar: semesters. *Degrees:* certificates, associate, bachelor's, and master's.

Special study options: academic remediation for entering students, accelerated degree program, adult/continuing education programs, advanced placement credit, cooperative education, distance learning, honors programs, independent study, internships, off-campus study, part-time degree program. ***ROTC:*** Army (c).

Computers: 955 computers/terminals are available on campus for general student use. Students can access the following: campus intranet, computer help desk, free student e-mail accounts, online (class) grades, online (class) registration, online (class) schedules. Campuswide network is available. Wireless service is available via entire campus.

Library: Walter A. Brower Library. *Books:* 52,322 (physical), 168,797 (digital/electronic); *Serial titles:* 152 (physical), 72,544 (digital/electronic); *Databases:* 84. Students can reserve study rooms.

STUDENT LIFE

Activities and organizations: student-run newspaper, Student Veterans of America, Latino/Hispanic Club, Sister-2-Sister Group, Multicultural Club, Law and Justice Studies Club.

Athletics Member USCAA. ***Intercollegiate sports:*** cross-country running M/W, soccer M.

Campus security: 24-hour emergency response devices and patrols.

Student services: personal/psychological counseling, veterans affairs office.

APPLYING

Options: electronic application, deferred entrance.

Application fee: $50.

Required: essay or personal statement, high school transcript. ***Recommended:*** interview.

Application deadlines: rolling (freshmen), rolling (out-of-state freshmen), rolling (transfers).

Notification: continuous (freshmen), continuous (out-of-state freshmen), continuous (transfers).

CONTACT
Carol J. Covino, Associate Vice President, High School Admissions, Berkeley College–Woodland Park Campus, 44 Rifle Camp Road, Woodland Park, NJ 07424. *Phone:* 973-278-5400. *Toll-free phone:* 800-446-5400. *E-mail:* info@berkeleycollege.edu.

Beth Medrash Govoha
Lakewood, New Jersey

CONTACT
Beth Medrash Govoha, 617 Sixth Street, Lakewood, NJ 08701-2797. *Phone:* 732-367-1060 Ext. 4224.

Bloomfield College
Bloomfield, New Jersey
http://www.bloomfield.edu/

CONTACT
Ms. Nicole Cibelli, Director of Admissions, Bloomfield College, Office of Enrollment Management and Admission, Bloomfield, NJ 07003-9981. *Phone:* 973-748-9000 Ext. 1390. *Toll-free phone:* 800-848-4555 Ext. 230. *Fax:* 973-748-0916. *E-mail:* nicole_cibelli@bloomfield.edu.

Caldwell University
Caldwell, New Jersey
http://www.caldwell.edu/

- **Independent Roman Catholic** comprehensive, founded 1939
- **Suburban** 70-acre campus with easy access to New York City
- **Endowment** $4.3 million
- **Coed** 1,646 undergraduate students, 92% full-time, 67% women, 33% men
- **Moderately difficult** entrance level, 67% of applicants were admitted

UNDERGRAD STUDENTS
1,515 full-time, 131 part-time. Students come from 25 states and territories; 40 other countries; 6% are from out of state; 14% Black or African American, non-Hispanic/Latino; 27% Hispanic/Latino; 3% Asian, non-Hispanic/Latino; 0.2% Native Hawaiian or other Pacific Islander, non-Hispanic/Latino; 0.1% American Indian or Alaska Native, non-Hispanic/Latino; 2% Two or more races, non-Hispanic/Latino; 9% Race/ethnicity unknown; 12% international; 3% transferred in; 36% live on campus.

Freshmen:
Admission: 4,433 applied, 2,954 admitted, 494 enrolled. ***Average high school GPA:*** 3.3. ***Test scores:*** SAT evidence-based reading and writing scores over 500: 70%; SAT math scores over 500: 69%; ACT scores over 18: 65%; SAT evidence-based reading and writing scores over 600: 15%; SAT math scores over 600: 20%; ACT scores over 24: 16%; SAT evidence-based reading and writing scores over 700: 1%; SAT math scores over 700: 7%; ACT scores over 30: 4%.

Retention: 79% of full-time freshmen returned.

FACULTY
Total: 294, 27% full-time.

Student/faculty ratio: 12:1.

ACADEMICS
Calendar: semesters. *Degrees:* bachelor's, master's, doctoral, post-master's, and postbachelor's certificates.

Special study options: academic remediation for entering students, accelerated degree program, adult/continuing education programs, advanced placement credit, distance learning, double majors, honors programs, independent study, internships, part-time degree program, services for LD students, student-designed majors, study abroad, summer session for credit. ***ROTC:*** Army (c).

Unusual degree programs: 3-2 business administration; social work with Rutgers University; biology or psychology/occupational therapy with Columbia University, biology/athletic training with Seton Hall University, psychology/counseling psychology, psychology/applied behavior analysis, education/curriculum and instruction.

Computers: 52 computers/terminals and 796 ports are available on campus for general student use. Students can access the following: campus intranet, computer help desk, free student e-mail accounts, online (class) grades, online (class) registration, online (class) schedules. Campuswide network is available. 100% of college-owned or -operated housing units are wired for high-speed Internet access. Wireless service is available via entire campus.

Library: Jennings Library plus 1 other. *Books:* 142,662 (physical), 166,014 (digital/electronic); *Serial titles:* 88 (physical), 66,812 (digital/electronic); *Databases:* 66. Students can reserve study rooms.

STUDENT LIFE
Housing options: coed. Campus housing is university owned. Freshman applicants given priority for college housing.

Activities and organizations: drama/theater group, student-run newspaper, television station, choral group, marching band, International Student Organization (ISO), Latino American Student Organization (LASO), Filipino Organization Rooted in Caldwell's Excellence (FORCE), Health Professions Club (HPC), Dance Team, national fraternities, national sororities.

Athletics Member NCAA. All Division II. ***Intercollegiate sports:*** baseball M(s), basketball M(s)/W(s), bowling W(s), cross-country running M(s)/W(s), football M(c), lacrosse W(s), soccer M(s)/W(s), softball W(s), tennis W(s), track and field M(s)/W(s), volleyball W(s).

Campus security: 24-hour emergency response devices and patrols, late-night transport/escort service, controlled dormitory access.

Student services: health clinic, personal/psychological counseling, veterans affairs office.

COSTS & FINANCIAL AID
Costs (2019–20) ***Comprehensive fee:*** $48,355 includes full-time tuition ($33,990), mandatory fees ($1950), and room and board ($12,415). Part-time tuition: $950 per credit hour. ***Required fees:*** $235 per term part-time.

Financial Aid Of all full-time matriculated undergraduates who enrolled in 2018, 1,243 applied for aid, 1,192 were judged to have need, 142 had their need fully met. In 2018, 276 non-need-based awards were made. ***Average percent of need met:*** 77. ***Average financial aid package:*** $30,301. ***Average need-based loan:*** $4005. ***Average need-based gift aid:*** $26,901. ***Average non-need-based aid:*** $21,745. ***Average indebtedness upon graduation:*** $31,762.

APPLYING
Standardized Tests *Required:* SAT or ACT (for admission).

Options: electronic application, early admission, early decision, deferred entrance.

Application fee: $50.

Required: essay or personal statement, high school transcript, 2 letters of recommendation. ***Recommended:*** minimum 3.0 GPA, interview, 16 units of college preparatory coursework.

Application deadlines: 4/1 (freshmen), 4/1 (out-of-state freshmen), rolling (transfers), 12/1 (early action).

Notification: 4/15 (freshmen), continuous (transfers), 12/31 (early action).

CONTACT
Mr. Jan Marco Jiras, Director of Admissions, Caldwell University, 120 Bloomfield Avenue, Caldwell, NJ 07006. *Phone:* 973-618-3620. *Fax:* 973-618-3600. *E-mail:* JJiras@caldwell.edu.

Centenary University
Hackettstown, New Jersey
http://www.centenaryuniversity.edu/

CONTACT
Jenna Yount, Director of Admissions, Centenary University, 400 Jefferson Street, Hackettstown, NJ 07840. *Phone:* 908-852-1400 Ext. 2082. *Toll-free phone:* 800-236-8679. *E-mail:* yountj@centenaryuniversity.edu.

Chamberlain College of Nursing

North Brunswick, New Jersey

http://www.chamberlain.edu/

CONTACT

Chamberlain College of Nursing, 630 U.S. Highway 1, North Brunswick, NJ 08902. *Toll-free phone:* 877-751-5783.

★ The College of New Jersey

Ewing, New Jersey

http://www.tcnj.edu/

- **State-supported** comprehensive, founded 1855
- **Suburban** 255-acre campus with easy access to Philadelphia
- **Coed**
- **Very difficult** entrance level

FACULTY

Student/faculty ratio: 13:1.

ACADEMICS

Calendar: semesters. *Degrees:* certificates, bachelor's, master's, post-master's, and postbachelor's certificates.

Library: The College of New Jersey Library. *Books:* 694,461 (physical), 6,455 (digital/electronic); *Serial titles:* 44,898 (physical), 8,859 (digital/electronic); *Databases:* 114. Weekly public service hours: 98; students can reserve study rooms.

STUDENT LIFE

Housing options: on-campus residence required for freshman year; coed, special housing for students with disabilities. Campus housing is university owned. Freshman campus housing is guaranteed.

Activities and organizations: drama/theater group, student-run newspaper, radio and television station, choral group, Student Government Association, College Union Board, Inter-Greek Council, The Signal, national fraternities, national sororities.

Athletics Member NCAA. All Division III.

Campus security: 24-hour emergency response devices and patrols, student patrols, late-night transport/escort service, controlled dormitory access.

Student services: health clinic, personal/psychological counseling, women's center, legal services, veterans affairs office.

COSTS & FINANCIAL AID

Costs (2018–19) ***Tuition:*** state resident $12,947 full-time, $459 per credit hour part-time; nonresident $24,662 full-time, $873 per credit hour part-time. Full-time tuition and fees vary according to course load. Part-time tuition and fees vary according to course load. ***Required fees:*** $3604 full-time, $150 per credit hour part-time. ***Room and board:*** $13,648; room only: $4408. Room and board charges vary according to board plan.

Financial Aid Of all full-time matriculated undergraduates who enrolled in 2018, 4,866 applied for aid, 3,523 were judged to have need, 373 had their need fully met. In 2018, 549 non-need-based awards were made. ***Average percent of need met:*** 43. ***Average financial aid package:*** $11,321. ***Average need-based loan:*** $4264. ***Average need-based gift aid:*** $11,609. ***Average non-need-based aid:*** $4983. ***Average indebtedness upon graduation:*** $38,937. ***Financial aid deadline:*** 10/1.

APPLYING

Standardized Tests *Required:* SAT or ACT (for admission).

Options: electronic application, early decision, deferred entrance.

Application fee: $75.

Required: essay or personal statement, high school transcript. ***Required for some:*** interview, art portfolio or music audition. ***Recommended:*** minimum 2.5 GPA, 3 letters of recommendation.

CONTACT

The College of New Jersey, 2000 Pennington Road, PO Box 7718, Ewing, NJ 08628.

See below for display ad and page 990 for the College Close-Up.

★ College of Saint Elizabeth

Morristown, New Jersey

http://www.cse.edu/

- **Independent Roman Catholic** comprehensive, founded 1899
- **Suburban** 200-acre campus with easy access to New York City
- **Endowment** $19.3 million
- **Coed**
- 65% of applicants were admitted

FACULTY

Student/faculty ratio: 10:1.

ACADEMICS

Calendar: semesters. *Degrees:* certificates, bachelor's, master's, doctoral, and postbachelor's certificates (also offers coed adult undergraduate degree program and coed graduate programs).
Library: Mahoney Library plus 1 other. *Books:* 113,292 (physical), 1.1 million (digital/electronic); *Serial titles:* 240 (physical), 26,767 (digital/electronic); *Databases:* 122. Weekly public service hours: 75.

STUDENT LIFE

Housing options: coed. Campus housing is university owned. Freshman campus housing is guaranteed.

Activities and organizations: drama/theater group, choral group, Student Government Association (SGA), Students Take Action Committee (STAC) Volunteer Organization, International/Intercultural Clubs, College Activities Board (CAB), Campus Ministry.

Athletics Member NCAA. All Division III.

Campus security: 24-hour emergency response devices and patrols, late-night transport/escort service, controlled dormitory access.

Student services: health clinic, personal/psychological counseling.

COSTS

Costs (2018–19) ***Comprehensive fee:*** $45,875 includes full-time tuition ($31,000), mandatory fees ($2131), and room and board ($12,744). Full-time tuition and fees vary according to course load and program. Part-time tuition: $800 per credit hour. Part-time tuition and fees vary according to course load, location, and program. ***Room and board:*** Room and board charges vary according to board plan.

APPLYING

Options: electronic application, deferred entrance.

Application fee: $35.

Required: essay or personal statement, high school transcript, minimum 2.0 GPA, 2 letters of recommendation. ***Recommended:*** interview.

CONTACT

Ms. Adrianna Arroyo, Director of Undergraduate Admissions, College of Saint Elizabeth, 2 Convent Road, Morristown, NJ 07960-6989. *Phone:* 973-290-4700. *Toll-free phone:* 800-210-7900. *Fax:* 973-290-4710. *E-mail:* apply@cse.edu.

DeVry University–North Brunswick Campus

North Brunswick, New Jersey

http://www.devry.edu/

CONTACT

DeVry University–North Brunswick Campus, 630 US Highway 1, North Brunswick, NJ 08902. *Phone:* 732-729-3532. *Toll-free phone:* 866-338-7934.

Drew University

Madison, New Jersey

http://www.drew.edu/

- **Independent** university, founded 1867, affiliated with United Methodist Church
- **Suburban** 186-acre campus with easy access to New York City
- **Coed** 1,668 undergraduate students, 98% full-time, 58% women, 42% men
- **Moderately difficult** entrance level, 69% of applicants were admitted

UNDERGRAD STUDENTS

1,634 full-time, 34 part-time. Students come from 37 states and territories; 47 other countries; 36% are from out of state; 7% Black or African American, non-Hispanic/Latino; 15% Hispanic/Latino; 5% Asian, non-Hispanic/Latino; 0.3% American Indian or Alaska Native, non-Hispanic/Latino; 3% Two or more races, non-Hispanic/Latino; 6% Race/ethnicity unknown; 11% international; 6% transferred in; 80% live on campus.

Freshmen:
Admission: 3,788 applied, 2,622 admitted, 420 enrolled. ***Average high school GPA:*** 3.5. ***Test scores:*** SAT evidence-based reading and writing scores over 500: 97%; SAT math scores over 500: 95%; ACT scores over 18: 99%; SAT evidence-based reading and writing scores over 600: 60%; SAT math scores over 600: 50%; ACT scores over 24: 80%; SAT evidence-based reading and writing scores over 700: 14%; SAT math scores over 700: 11%; ACT scores over 30: 29%.
Retention: 84% of full-time freshmen returned.

FACULTY

Total: 272, 55% full-time.
Student/faculty ratio: 10:1.

ACADEMICS

Calendar: semesters. *Degrees:* bachelor's, master's, doctoral, post-master's, and postbachelor's certificates.

Special study options: accelerated degree program, adult/continuing education programs, advanced placement credit, double majors, English as a second language, freshman honors college, honors programs, independent study, internships, off-campus study, part-time degree program, services for LD students, student-designed majors, study abroad, summer session for credit. ***ROTC:*** Army (c).

Unusual degree programs: 3-2 engineering with Columbia University, Stevens Institute of Technology, Washington University (St Louis); forestry with Duke University; nursing with Drexel University; Business Management with Wake Forest University, Environment Management with Duke University, Forestry with Duke University, Law School with NYU or Seton Hall, MD with Rutgers New Jersey Medical School.

Computers: 95 computers/terminals are available on campus for general student use. Students can access the following: campus intranet, computer help desk, free student e-mail accounts, online (class) grades, online (class) registration, online (class) schedules. Campuswide network is available. 100% of college-owned or -operated housing units are wired for high-speed Internet access. Wireless service is available via entire campus.
Library: Rose Memorial Library plus 1 other. *Books:* 446,142 (physical), 224,692 (digital/electronic); *Serial titles:* 7,192 (physical), 164,691 (digital/electronic); *Databases:* 196. Weekly public service hours: 108; students can reserve study rooms.

STUDENT LIFE

Housing options: coed, special housing for students with disabilities. Campus housing is university owned. Freshman campus housing is guaranteed.

Activities and organizations: drama/theater group, student-run newspaper, radio station, choral group, Drew Organization of Gaming, International Student Association, ARIEL Latin Culture Society, Drew Unversity Chemistry Society, Drew African Students Association.

Athletics Member NCAA. All Division III except golf (Division II). ***Intercollegiate sports:*** baseball M, basketball M/W, cross-country running M/W, equestrian sports W, fencing M/W, field hockey W, golf M/W, lacrosse M/W, rugby M(c)/W(c), soccer M/W, softball W, swimming and diving M/W, tennis M/W, track and field M/W. ***Intramural sports:*** badminton M/W, basketball M/W, football M, racquetball M/W, soccer M/W, squash M/W, table tennis M/W, volleyball M/W.

Campus security: 24-hour emergency response devices and patrols, late-night transport/escort service, controlled dormitory access.

Student services: health clinic, personal/psychological counseling.

COSTS & FINANCIAL AID

Costs (2018–19) ***Comprehensive fee:*** $53,608 includes full-time tuition ($38,668), mandatory fees ($832), and room and board ($14,108). Part-time tuition: $1612 per credit. Part-time tuition and fees vary according to course load. ***College room only:*** $8908. Room and board charges vary according to board plan and housing facility. ***Payment plans:*** tuition prepayment, installment, deferred payment. ***Waivers:*** employees or children of employees.

Financial Aid Of all full-time matriculated undergraduates who enrolled in 2018, 1,173 applied for aid, 1,058 were judged to have need, 159 had their need fully met. 758 Federal Work-Study jobs (averaging $2000). In 2018, 380 non-need-based awards were made. ***Average percent of need met:*** 82. ***Average financial aid package:*** $36,295. ***Average need-based loan:*** $4416. ***Average need-based gift aid:*** $30,806. ***Average non-need-based aid:*** $14,791. ***Average indebtedness upon graduation:*** $23,619.

APPLYING
Options: electronic application, early admission, early decision, early action, deferred entrance.

Application fee: $40.

Required: essay or personal statement, high school transcript, 2 letters of recommendation. ***Recommended:*** interview.

Application deadlines: 2/1 (freshmen), 12/15 (transfers).

Early decision deadline: 11/15.

Notification: 3/18 (freshmen), continuous (transfers), 12/15 (early decision).

CONTACT
Mr. James Skiff, Executive Director, College Admissions, Drew University, 36 Madison Avenue, Madison, NJ 07940-1493. *Phone:* 973-408-DREW. *Fax:* 973-408-3068. *E-mail:* cadm@drew.edu.

Eastern International College

Belleville, New Jersey

http://www.eicollege.edu/

- **Proprietary** primarily 2-year
- **Urban** campus with easy access to Manhattan, New York
- **Coed**

ACADEMICS
Degrees: associate and bachelor's.

CONTACT
Eastern International College, 251 Washington Avenue, Belleville, NJ 07109.

Eastern International College

Jersey City, New Jersey

http://www.eicollege.edu/

CONTACT
Eastern International College, 684 Newark Avenue, Jersey City, NJ 07306.

Eastwick College

Ramsey, New Jersey

http://www.eastwickcollege.edu/

CONTACT
Eastwick College, 10 South Franklin Turnpike, Ramsey, NJ 07446.

Fairleigh Dickinson University, Florham Campus

Madison, New Jersey

http://www.fdu.edu/

- **Independent** comprehensive, founded 1942
- **Suburban** 178-acre campus with easy access to New York City
- **Coed**
- **Moderately difficult** entrance level

FACULTY
Student/faculty ratio: 13:1.

ACADEMICS
Calendar: semesters. *Degrees:* bachelor's, master's, doctoral, post-master's, and postbachelor's certificates.

Library: Monninger Center for Learning and Research. *Books:* 131,212 (physical), 158,628 (digital/electronic); *Serial titles:* 1,423 (physical), 126,248 (digital/electronic); *Databases:* 144. Weekly public service hours: 83.

STUDENT LIFE
Housing options: coed, special housing for students with disabilities. Campus housing is university owned. Freshman applicants given priority for college housing.

Activities and organizations: drama/theater group, student-run newspaper, choral group, national fraternities, national sororities.

Athletics Member NCAA. All Division III.

Campus security: 24-hour emergency response devices and patrols, late-night transport/escort service, controlled dormitory access, trained law enforcement personnel on staff.

Student services: health clinic, personal/psychological counseling, veterans affairs office.

COSTS & FINANCIAL AID
Costs (2018–19) ***One-time required fee:*** $815. ***Comprehensive fee:*** $56,558 includes full-time tuition ($42,096), mandatory fees ($1046), and room and board ($13,416). Full-time tuition and fees vary according to location and program. Part-time tuition: $997 per credit hour. Part-time tuition and fees vary according to location and program. ***Required fees:*** $422 per year part-time. ***College room only:*** $8810. Room and board charges vary according to board plan, housing facility, and location. ***Payment plans:*** installment, deferred payment.

Financial Aid Of all full-time matriculated undergraduates who enrolled in 2017, 2,307 applied for aid, 2,151 were judged to have need, 283 had their need fully met. In 2017, 432 non-need-based awards were made. ***Average percent of need met:*** 73. ***Average financial aid package:*** $40,034. ***Average need-based loan:*** $4420. ***Average need-based gift aid:*** $29,076. ***Average non-need-based aid:*** $17,451. ***Average indebtedness upon graduation:*** $42,122. ***Financial aid deadline:*** 2/15.

APPLYING
Standardized Tests *Required:* SAT or ACT (for admission).

Options: electronic application.

Application fee: $40.

Required: high school transcript, 2 letters of recommendation.

CONTACT
Fairleigh Dickinson University, Florham Campus, 285 Madison Avenue, Madison, NJ 07940-1099. *Toll-free phone:* 800-338-8803.

Fairleigh Dickinson University, Metropolitan Campus

Teaneck, New Jersey

http://www.fdu.edu/

- **Independent** university, founded 1942
- **Suburban** 88-acre campus with easy access to New York City
- **Coed**
- **Moderately difficult** entrance level

FACULTY
Student/faculty ratio: 14:1.

ACADEMICS
Calendar: semesters. *Degrees:* certificates, associate, bachelor's, master's, doctoral, post-master's, and postbachelor's certificates.
Library: Giovatto Library. *Books:* 157,566 (physical); *Serial titles:* 1,217 (physical), 126,248 (digital/electronic); *Databases:* 144. Weekly public service hours: 87.

STUDENT LIFE
Housing options: coed, special housing for students with disabilities. Campus housing is university owned.

Activities and organizations: drama/theater group, student-run newspaper, radio station, choral group, national fraternities, national sororities.

Athletics Member NCAA. All Division I.

Campus security: 24-hour emergency response devices and patrols, late-night transport/escort service, controlled dormitory access, trained law enforcement personnel on staff.

Student services: health clinic, personal/psychological counseling, women's center, veterans affairs office.

COSTS & FINANCIAL AID
Costs (2018–19) ***One-time required fee:*** $815. ***Comprehensive fee:*** $54,102 includes full-time tuition ($39,686), mandatory fees ($1046), and room and board ($13,370). Full-time tuition and fees vary according to location and program. Part-time tuition: $997 per credit hour. Part-time tuition and fees vary according to location and program. ***Required fees:*** $422 per year part-time. ***College room only:*** $8764. Room and board charges vary according to board plan and housing facility. ***Payment plans:*** installment, deferred payment.

Financial Aid Of all full-time matriculated undergraduates who enrolled in 2017, 2,019 applied for aid, 1,964 were judged to have need, 170 had their need fully met. In 2017, 258 non-need-based awards were made. ***Average percent of need met:*** 65. ***Average financial aid package:*** $36,702. ***Average need-based loan:*** $4152. ***Average need-based gift aid:*** $26,806. ***Average non-need-based aid:*** $15,540. ***Average indebtedness upon graduation:*** $40,151. ***Financial aid deadline:*** 2/15.

APPLYING
Standardized Tests *Required:* SAT or ACT (for admission).

Options: electronic application, early admission.

Application fee: $40.

Required: high school transcript, 2 letters of recommendation. ***Required for some:*** interview.

CONTACT
Fairleigh Dickinson University, Metropolitan Campus, 1000 River Road, Teaneck, NJ 07666-1914. *Toll-free phone:* 800-338-8803.

Felician University

Lodi, New Jersey

http://www.felician.edu/

- **Independent Roman Catholic** comprehensive, founded 1942
- **Small-town** 37-acre campus with easy access to New York City
- **Endowment** $6.5 million
- **Coed**
- **Moderately difficult** entrance level

FACULTY
Student/faculty ratio: 14:1.

ACADEMICS
Calendar: semesters. *Degrees:* certificates, associate, bachelor's, master's, doctoral, post-master's, and postbachelor's certificates.
Library: Felician University Library plus 1 other. *Books:* 68,565 (physical), 158,952 (digital/electronic); *Serial titles:* 178 (physical), 51,874 (digital/electronic); *Databases:* 56. Weekly public service hours: 137; students can reserve study rooms.

STUDENT LIFE
Housing options: coed, men-only, women-only, special housing for students with disabilities. Campus housing is university owned. Freshman applicants given priority for college housing.

Activities and organizations: drama/theater group, student-run radio station, choral group, Student Nurses Association, Zeta Alpha Zeta teaching sorority, Campus Activity Board, Students in Free Enterprise (SIFE), Student Government Association.

Athletics Member NCAA, NAIA. All NCAA Division II.

Campus security: 24-hour patrols, student patrols, late-night transport/escort service.

Student services: health clinic, personal/psychological counseling, veterans affairs office.

COSTS & FINANCIAL AID
Costs (2018–19) ***Comprehensive fee:*** $47,200 includes full-time tuition ($31,915), mandatory fees ($2400), and room and board ($12,885). Full-time tuition and fees vary according to program. Part-time tuition: $1055 per credit hour. Part-time tuition and fees vary according to course load and program. ***Required fees:*** $475 per term part-time. ***Room and board:*** Room and board charges vary according to housing facility.

Financial Aid Of all full-time matriculated undergraduates who enrolled in 2016, 1,345 applied for aid, 1,297 were judged to have need, 96 had their need fully met. 49 Federal Work-Study jobs (averaging $2236). In 2016, 78 non-need-based awards were made. ***Average percent of need met:*** 65. ***Average financial aid package:*** $26,743. ***Average need-based loan:*** $4279. ***Average need-based gift aid:*** $13,799. ***Average non-need-based aid:*** $13,431.

APPLYING
Standardized Tests *Required:* SAT or ACT (for admission). *Required for some:* SAT (for admission), ACT (for admission), SAT Subject Tests (for admission). *Recommended:* SAT and SAT Subject Tests or ACT (for admission).

Options: deferred entrance.

Application fee: $30.

Required: essay or personal statement, high school transcript, minimum 2.0 GPA, letters of recommendation. ***Required for some:*** interview.

CONTACT
Colleen Fuller, Director of Undergraduate Admissions, Felician University, 262 South Main Street, Lodi, NJ 07644-2117. *Phone:* 201-355-1444. *E-mail:* fullerc@felician.edu.

Georgian Court University

Lakewood, New Jersey

http://www.georgian.edu/

- **Independent Roman Catholic** comprehensive, founded 1908
- **Suburban** 156-acre campus with easy access to New York City, Philadelphia
- **Endowment** $56.0 million
- **Coed**
- **Moderately difficult** entrance level

FACULTY
Student/faculty ratio: 12:1.

ACADEMICS
Calendar: semesters. *Degrees:* certificates, bachelor's, master's, post-master's, and postbachelor's certificates.
Library: The Sister Mary Joseph Cunningham Library. *Books:* 129,447 (physical), 117,590 (digital/electronic); *Serial titles:* 2,898 (physical), 33,651 (digital/electronic); *Databases:* 115. Weekly public service hours: 85; students can reserve study rooms.

STUDENT LIFE
Housing options: coed. Campus housing is university owned. Freshman campus housing is guaranteed.

Activities and organizations: student-run newspaper, Basketball Club, Black Student Union, Math Club, Dance Theatre Club, History Club.

Athletics Member NCAA. All Division II.

Campus security: 24-hour emergency response devices and patrols, late-night transport/escort service, controlled dormitory access.

Student services: health clinic, personal/psychological counseling, veterans affairs office.

COSTS & FINANCIAL AID
Costs (2018–19) ***Comprehensive fee:*** $43,784 includes full-time tuition ($31,416), mandatory fees ($1560), and room and board ($10,808). Full-time tuition and fees vary according to location, program, and reciprocity agreements. Part-time tuition: $718 per credit hour. Part-time tuition and fees vary according to location, program, and reciprocity agreements. ***Required fees:*** $365 per term part-time.

Financial Aid Of all full-time matriculated undergraduates who enrolled in 2018, 1,275 applied for aid, 1,192 were judged to have need, 245 had their need fully met. 130 Federal Work-Study jobs (averaging $2127). 23 state and other part-time jobs (averaging $1522). In 2018, 173 non-need-based awards were made. ***Average percent of need met:*** 75. ***Average financial aid package:*** $28,852. ***Average need-based loan:*** $6777. ***Average need-based gift aid:*** $19,524. ***Average non-need-based aid:*** $14,866. ***Average indebtedness upon graduation:*** $37,502. ***Financial aid deadline:*** 7/1.

APPLYING
Standardized Tests *Required:* SAT or ACT (for admission).

Options: electronic application, early action, deferred entrance.

Application fee: $40.

Required: high school transcript, minimum 2.5 GPA. ***Required for some:*** essay or personal statement, 2 letters of recommendation, interview.

CONTACT
Director of Undergraduate Admissions, Georgian Court University, 900 Lakewood Avenue, Lakewood, NJ 08701-2697. *Phone:* 732-987-2745. *Toll-free phone:* 800-458-8422. *Fax:* 732-987-2000. *E-mail:* admissions@georgian.edu.

Kean University
Union, New Jersey
http://www.kean.edu/

- **State-supported** university, founded 1855, part of New Jersey State College System
- **Suburban** 240-acre campus with easy access to New York City
- **Coed** 11,824 undergraduate students, 81% full-time, 60% women, 40% men
- **Moderately difficult** entrance level, 86% of applicants were admitted

UNDERGRAD STUDENTS
9,609 full-time, 2,215 part-time. Students come from 22 states and territories; 39 other countries; 2% are from out of state; 21% Black or African American, non-Hispanic/Latino; 30% Hispanic/Latino; 5% Asian, non-Hispanic/Latino; 0.3% Native Hawaiian or other Pacific Islander, non-Hispanic/Latino; 0.2% American Indian or Alaska Native, non-Hispanic/Latino; 2% Two or more races, non-Hispanic/Latino; 8% Race/ethnicity unknown; 2% international; 12% transferred in; 16% live on campus.

Freshmen:
Admission: 9,082 applied, 7,809 admitted, 1,815 enrolled. ***Average high school GPA:*** 3.0. ***Test scores:*** SAT math scores over 500: 52%; ACT scores over 18: 68%; SAT math scores over 600: 9%; ACT scores over 24: 17%; SAT math scores over 700: 1%; ACT scores over 30: 3%.

Retention: 72% of full-time freshmen returned.

FACULTY
Total: 1,393, 26% full-time.

Student/faculty ratio: 17:1.

ACADEMICS
Calendar: semesters. *Degrees:* bachelor's, master's, doctoral, and post-master's certificates.

Special study options: academic remediation for entering students, accelerated degree program, adult/continuing education programs, advanced placement credit, cooperative education, distance learning, double majors, English as a second language, external degree program, independent study, internships, off-campus study, part-time degree program, services for LD students, study abroad, summer session for credit. ***ROTC:*** Army (c), Air Force (c).

Computers: 1,700 computers/terminals and 1,800 ports are available on campus for general student use. Students can access the following: free student e-mail accounts, online (class) grades, online (class) registration, online (class) schedules. Campuswide network is available. 100% of college-owned or -operated housing units are wired for high-speed Internet access. Wireless service is available via entire campus.

Library: Nancy Thompson Library. *Books:* 177,961 (physical), 12,121 (digital/electronic); *Serial titles:* 59,728 (digital/electronic); *Databases:* 244. Weekly public service hours: 102.

STUDENT LIFE
Housing options: coed, special housing for students with disabilities. Campus housing is university owned. Freshman applicants given priority for college housing.

Activities and organizations: drama/theater group, student-run newspaper, radio station, choral group, American Sign Language Club, Kean University Council for Exceptional Children, Kean University Rotaract Action Club, EEO Society, Pre-Medical Pre-Dental Association, national fraternities, national sororities.

Athletics Member NCAA. All Division III. ***Intercollegiate sports:*** baseball M, basketball M/W, field hockey W, football M, lacrosse M/W, soccer M/W, softball W, swimming and diving W, tennis W, volleyball M/W. ***Intramural sports:*** basketball M/W, sand volleyball M/W, soccer M/W, softball M/W, tennis M/W, ultimate Frisbee M/W, volleyball M/W, weight lifting M/W.

Campus security: 24-hour emergency response devices and patrols, student patrols, late-night transport/escort service, controlled dormitory access.

Student services: health clinic, personal/psychological counseling, veterans affairs office.

COSTS & FINANCIAL AID
Costs (2018–19) ***Tuition:*** state resident $9740 full-time, $382 per credit part-time; nonresident $16,775 full-time, $601 per credit part-time. Part-time tuition and fees vary according to course load. ***Required fees:*** $2608 full-time, $90 per credit part-time. ***Room and board:*** $14,470. Room and board charges vary according to board plan, housing facility, and location. ***Payment plan:*** installment. ***Waivers:*** senior citizens and employees or children of employees.

Financial Aid Of all full-time matriculated undergraduates who enrolled in 2018, 8,054 applied for aid, 7,140 were judged to have need, 49 had their need fully met. 248 Federal Work-Study jobs (averaging $3673). In 2018, 214 non-need-based awards were made. ***Average percent of need met:*** 83. ***Average financial aid package:*** $11,118. ***Average need-based loan:*** $4370. ***Average need-based gift aid:*** $8848. ***Average non-need-based aid:*** $2976. ***Average indebtedness upon graduation:*** $33,407.

APPLYING
Standardized Tests *Required:* SAT or ACT (for admission).

Options: electronic application, early action, deferred entrance.

Application fee: $75.

Required: high school transcript, SAT or ACT. ***Required for some:*** interview. ***Recommended:*** essay or personal statement, 2 letters of recommendation.

Application deadlines: 8/15 (freshmen), 8/1 (transfers), 12/1 (early action).

Notification: continuous until 11/1 (freshmen), continuous (transfers), 1/1 (early action).

CONTACT
Mr. Carlos Nazario, Director of Admissions, Kean University, 1000 Morris Avenue, Office of Admissions - Kean Hall, Union, NJ 07083. *Phone:* 908-737-7100. *Fax:* 908-737-7105. *E-mail:* admitme@kean.edu.

Monmouth University
West Long Branch, New Jersey
http://www.monmouth.edu/

CONTACT
Ms. Victoria Bobik, Director of Undergraduate Admission, Monmouth University, 400 Cedar Avenue, West Long Branch, NJ 07764-1898. *Phone:* 732-571-3456. *Toll-free phone:* 800-543-9671. *Fax:* 732-263-5166. *E-mail:* admission@monmouth.edu.

See next page for display ad and page 1048 for the College Close-Up.

Montclair State University
Montclair, New Jersey
http://www.montclair.edu/

- **State-supported** university, founded 1908
- **Suburban** 250-acre campus with easy access to New York City
- **Coed** 16,988 undergraduate students, 89% full-time, 61% women, 39% men
- **Moderately difficult** entrance level, 71% of applicants were admitted

UNDERGRAD STUDENTS
15,133 full-time, 1,855 part-time. Students come from 41 states and territories; 69 other countries; 3% are from out of state; 13% Black or African American, non-Hispanic/Latino; 29% Hispanic/Latino; 6% Asian, non-Hispanic/Latino; 0.2% Native Hawaiian or other Pacific Islander, non-Hispanic/Latino; 0.1% American Indian or Alaska Native, non-Hispanic/Latino; 3% Two or more races, non-Hispanic/Latino; 6%

Race/ethnicity unknown; 2% international; 10% transferred in; 30% live on campus.

Freshmen:

Admission: 14,324 applied, 10,157 admitted, 3,180 enrolled. ***Average high school GPA:*** 3.3. ***Test scores:*** SAT evidence-based reading and writing scores over 500: 77%; SAT math scores over 500: 74%; SAT evidence-based reading and writing scores over 600: 24%; SAT math scores over 600: 18%; SAT evidence-based reading and writing scores over 700: 2%; SAT math scores over 700: 2%.

Retention: 80% of full-time freshmen returned.

FACULTY

Total: 1,855, 34% full-time, 34% with terminal degrees.

Student/faculty ratio: 17:1.

ACADEMICS

Calendar: semesters. *Degrees:* certificates, bachelor's, master's, doctoral, and postbachelor's certificates.

Special study options: academic remediation for entering students, accelerated degree program, adult/continuing education programs, advanced placement credit, cooperative education, double majors, English as a second language, freshman honors college, honors programs, independent study, internships, off-campus study, part-time degree program, services for LD students, study abroad, summer session for credit.

Computers: 800 computers/terminals and 27,000 ports are available on campus for general student use. Students can access the following: campus intranet, computer help desk, free student e-mail accounts, online (class) grades, online (class) registration, online (class) schedules, online storage, online course delivery, online computing lab, student online portal. Campuswide network is available. 100% of college-owned or -operated housing units are wired for high-speed Internet access. Wireless service is available via entire campus.

Library: Sprague Library. *Books:* 432,414 (physical), 157,098 (digital/electronic); *Serial titles:* 9,510 (physical), 62,084 (digital/electronic); *Databases:* 238. Weekly public service hours: 93; students can reserve study rooms.

STUDENT LIFE

Housing options: coed. Campus housing is university owned and is provided by a third party. Freshman campus housing is guaranteed.

Activities and organizations: drama/theater group, student-run newspaper, radio and television station, choral group, Latin American Student Organization, Campus Recreation, MSU Players, Unified Asian American Student Organization, SLAM (Student Life At Montclair), national fraternities, national sororities.

Athletics Member NCAA. All Division III. ***Intercollegiate sports:*** baseball M, basketball M/W, field hockey W, football M, lacrosse M/W, soccer M/W, softball W, swimming and diving M/W, track and field M/W, volleyball W. ***Intramural sports:*** baseball M(c), basketball M/W, cheerleading W(c), fencing W(c), field hockey M(c), ice hockey M(c)/W(c), lacrosse M(c), racquetball M/W, rugby M(c)/W(c), soccer M/W, softball M/W, table tennis M/W, tennis M/W, track and field M(c)/W(c), volleyball M/W, water polo M/W, wrestling M(c)/W(c).

Campus security: 24-hour emergency response devices and patrols, late-night transport/escort service, controlled dormitory access, video surveillance, student escorts.

Student services: health clinic, personal/psychological counseling, women's center, veterans affairs office.

COSTS & FINANCIAL AID

Costs (2018–19) ***Tuition:*** state resident $11,132 full-time, $371 per credit part-time; nonresident $18,920 full-time, $631 per credit part-time. ***Required fees:*** $1658 full-time, $55 per credit part-time. ***Room and board:*** $15,564. Room and board charges vary according to board plan and housing facility. ***Payment plan:*** installment. ***Waivers:*** senior citizens and employees or children of employees.

Financial Aid Of all full-time matriculated undergraduates who enrolled in 2017, 12,427 applied for aid, 10,858 were judged to have need, 56 had their need fully met. 568 Federal Work-Study jobs (averaging $1376). In 2017, 348 non-need-based awards were made. ***Average percent of need met:*** 46. ***Average financial aid package:*** $10,296. ***Average need-based loan:*** $4239. ***Average need-based gift aid:*** $9371. ***Average non-need-based aid:*** $4719. ***Average indebtedness upon graduation:*** $25,597.

APPLYING
Options: electronic application, deferred entrance.

Application fee: $65.

Required: essay or personal statement, high school transcript. ***Required for some:*** interview.

Notification: continuous (freshmen), continuous (transfers).

CONTACT
Jeff Indiveri-Gant, Director of Admissions, Montclair State University, One Normal Avenue, Montclair, NJ 07043-1624. *Phone:* 973-655-3316. *Fax:* 973-655-7700. *E-mail:* undergraduate.admissions@montclair.edu.

New Jersey City University

Jersey City, New Jersey

http://www.njcu.edu/

- **State-supported** comprehensive, founded 1927
- **Urban** 51-acre campus with easy access to New York City
- **Coed** 6,237 undergraduate students, 82% full-time, 59% women, 41% men
- **Moderately difficult** entrance level, 96% of applicants were admitted

UNDERGRAD STUDENTS
5,091 full-time, 1,146 part-time. 1% are from out of state; 23% Black or African American, non-Hispanic/Latino; 40% Hispanic/Latino; 8% Asian, non-Hispanic/Latino; 0.5% Native Hawaiian or other Pacific Islander, non-Hispanic/Latino; 0.4% American Indian or Alaska Native, non-Hispanic/Latino; 2% Two or more races, non-Hispanic/Latino; 4% Race/ethnicity unknown; 1% international; 12% transferred in; 9% live on campus.

Freshmen:
Admission: 4,315 applied, 4,136 admitted, 968 enrolled. ***Average high school GPA:*** 2.9. ***Test scores:*** SAT evidence-based reading and writing scores over 500: 39%; SAT math scores over 500: 43%; SAT evidence-based reading and writing scores over 600: 7%; SAT math scores over 600: 8%; SAT evidence-based reading and writing scores over 700: 1%; SAT math scores over 700: 1%.

Retention: 73% of full-time freshmen returned.

FACULTY
Total: 808, 31% full-time.

Student/faculty ratio: 15:1.

ACADEMICS
Calendar: semesters. *Degrees:* bachelor's, master's, doctoral, and post-master's certificates.

Special study options: academic remediation for entering students, accelerated degree program, adult/continuing education programs, advanced placement credit, cooperative education, distance learning, double majors, English as a second language, honors programs, independent study, internships, off-campus study, part-time degree program, services for LD students, study abroad, summer session for credit. ***ROTC:*** Army (c), Navy (c).

Computers: Students can access the following: free student e-mail accounts, online (class) grades, online (class) registration, online (class) schedules. Campuswide network is available. 100% of college-owned or -operated housing units are wired for high-speed Internet access. Wireless service is available via classrooms, computer centers, computer labs, dorm rooms, learning centers, libraries, student centers.

Library: Congressman Frank J. Guarini Library. *Books:* 300,000 (physical), 150,000 (digital/electronic); *Serial titles:* 150 (physical), 32,000 (digital/electronic); *Databases:* 152. Weekly public service hours: 82.

STUDENT LIFE
Housing options: coed. Campus housing is university owned.

Activities and organizations: drama/theater group, student-run newspaper, radio station, choral group, national fraternities, national sororities.

Athletics Member NCAA. All Division III. ***Intercollegiate sports:*** baseball M, basketball M/W, bowling W, cross-country running M/W, golf M, soccer M/W, softball W, volleyball M/W. ***Intramural sports:*** basketball M/W, bowling M/W, cheerleading M/W, cross-country running M/W, football M/W, golf M, racquetball M/W, soccer M/W, softball M/W, swimming and diving M/W, table tennis M/W, tennis W, track and field M/W, volleyball M/W.

Campus security: 24-hour emergency response devices and patrols, late-night transport/escort service.

Student services: health clinic, personal/psychological counseling, women's center, legal services.

COSTS & FINANCIAL AID
Costs (2018–19) ***Tuition:*** state resident $8518 full-time, $284 per credit hour part-time; nonresident $17,932 full-time, $600 per credit hour part-time. Part-time tuition and fees vary according to course load. ***Required fees:*** $3482 full-time, $115 per credit hour part-time. ***Room and board:*** $12,072. Room and board charges vary according to board plan and housing facility. ***Payment plans:*** installment, deferred payment. ***Waivers:*** senior citizens and employees or children of employees.

Financial Aid Of all full-time matriculated undergraduates who enrolled in 2017, 4,766 applied for aid, 4,508 were judged to have need, 119 had their need fully met. In 2017, 122 non-need-based awards were made. ***Average percent of need met:*** 49. ***Average financial aid package:*** $11,241. ***Average need-based loan:*** $4003. ***Average need-based gift aid:*** $9167. ***Average non-need-based aid:*** $7685. ***Average indebtedness upon graduation:*** $28,538.

APPLYING
Standardized Tests *Recommended:* SAT (for admission).

Options: electronic application, deferred entrance.

Application fee: $50.

Required: essay or personal statement, high school transcript, minimum 2.8 GPA. ***Required for some:*** interview. ***Recommended:*** 1 letter of recommendation.

Notification: continuous (freshmen).

CONTACT
Mr. Jose Balda, Director of Admissions, New Jersey City University, 2039 Kennedy Boulevard, Jersey City, NJ 07305. *Phone:* 201-200-3234. *Toll-free phone:* 888-441-NJCU. *E-mail:* admissions@nicu.edu.

New Jersey Institute of Technology

Newark, New Jersey

http://www.njit.edu/

- **State-supported** university, founded 1881, part of State of New Jersey Department of Education
- **Urban** 48-acre campus with easy access to New York City
- **Endowment** $113.6 million
- **Coed** 8,532 undergraduate students, 80% full-time, 25% women, 75% men
- **Moderately difficult** entrance level, 64% of applicants were admitted

UNDERGRAD STUDENTS
6,827 full-time, 1,705 part-time. Students come from 23 states and territories; 64 other countries; 3% are from out of state; 8% Black or African American, non-Hispanic/Latino; 22% Hispanic/Latino; 22% Asian, non-Hispanic/Latino; 0.1% American Indian or Alaska Native, non-Hispanic/Latino; 3% Two or more races, non-Hispanic/Latino; 8% Race/ethnicity unknown; 5% international; 10% transferred in; 24% live on campus.

Freshmen:
Admission: 8,123 applied, 5,171 admitted, 1,286 enrolled. ***Average high school GPA:*** 3.6. ***Test scores:*** SAT evidence-based reading and writing scores over 500: 99%; SAT math scores over 500: 99%; ACT scores over 18: 100%; SAT evidence-based reading and writing scores over 600: 68%; SAT math scores over 600: 82%; ACT scores over 24: 85%; SAT evidence-based reading and writing scores over 700: 13%; SAT math scores over 700: 30%; ACT scores over 30: 32%.

Retention: 88% of full-time freshmen returned.

FACULTY
Total: 785, 56% full-time.

Student/faculty ratio: 17:1.

ACADEMICS
Calendar: semesters. *Degrees:* bachelor's, master's, doctoral, and postbachelor's certificates.

Special study options: academic remediation for entering students, accelerated degree program, adult/continuing education programs, advanced placement credit, cooperative education, distance learning, double majors, English as a second language, freshman honors college, honors programs, independent study, internships, off-campus study, part-time degree program, services for LD students, study abroad, summer session for credit. ***ROTC:*** Army (c), Air Force (b).

Unusual degree programs: 3-2 business administration; engineering.

Computers: 1,938 computers/terminals are available on campus for general student use. Students can access the following: campus intranet, computer help desk, free student e-mail accounts, online (class) grades, online (class) registration, online (class) schedules. Campuswide network is available. 100% of college-owned or -operated housing units are wired for high-speed Internet access. Wireless service is available via entire campus.

Library: Van Houten Library plus 1 other. *Books:* 138,456 (physical), 185,262 (digital/electronic); *Serial titles:* 50 (physical), 185,301 (digital/electronic); *Databases:* 35. Weekly public service hours: 111; students can reserve study rooms.

STUDENT LIFE

Housing options: coed. Campus housing is university owned.

Activities and organizations: drama/theater group, student-run newspaper, radio station, Student Senate, Student Activities Council, Vector, Institute of Industrial Engineers, WJTB Geek Radio, national fraternities, national sororities.

Athletics Member NCAA. All Division I. ***Intercollegiate sports:*** baseball M(s), basketball M(s)/W(s), bowling M(c), cross-country running M(s)/W(s), fencing M(s)/W(s), ice hockey M(c), lacrosse M(s), soccer M(s)/W(s), swimming and diving M(s), tennis M(s)/W(s), track and field M(s)/W(s), volleyball M(s)/W(s). ***Intramural sports:*** cheerleading M(c)/W(c), racquetball M/W, soccer M/W.

Campus security: 24-hour emergency response devices and patrols, student patrols, late-night transport/escort service, controlled dormitory access.

Student services: health clinic, personal/psychological counseling, women's center.

COSTS & FINANCIAL AID

Costs (2019–20) ***Tuition:*** state resident $14,174 full-time, $539 per credit part-time; nonresident $29,586 full-time, $1265 per credit part-time. ***Required fees:*** $3164 full-time, $186 per credit part-time. ***Room and board:*** $13,600.

Financial Aid Of all full-time matriculated undergraduates who enrolled in 2018, 5,037 applied for aid, 4,451 were judged to have need, 391 had their need fully met. In 2018, 823 non-need-based awards were made. ***Average percent of need met:*** 53. ***Average financial aid package:*** $13,930. ***Average need-based loan:*** $3133. ***Average need-based gift aid:*** $7794. ***Average non-need-based aid:*** $16,643. ***Average indebtedness upon graduation:*** $42,099.

APPLYING

Standardized Tests *Required:* SAT or ACT (for admission).

Options: electronic application, early admission, deferred entrance.

Application fee: $75.

Required: high school transcript, 1 letter of recommendation. ***Required for some:*** essay or personal statement, interview.

Notification: continuous (freshmen), continuous (transfers).

CONTACT

Mr. Stephen M. Eck, Executive Director of University Admissions, New Jersey Institute of Technology, University Heights, Newark, NJ 07102. *Phone:* 973-596-3306. *Toll-free phone:* 800-925-NJIT. *Fax:* 973-596-3461. *E-mail:* admissions@njit.edu.

Pillar College

Newark, New Jersey

http://www.pillar.edu/

CONTACT

Ms. Linda Aarni, Senior Admissions Counselor, Pillar College, 60 Park Place, Suite 701, Newark, NJ 07102. *Phone:* 973-803-5000. *Toll-free phone:* 800-234-9305. *Fax:* 732-356-4846. *E-mail:* info@pillar.edu.

★ Princeton University

Princeton, New Jersey

http://www.princeton.edu/

- **Independent** university, founded 1746
- **Suburban** 600-acre campus with easy access to New York City, Philadelphia
- **Coed** 5,428 undergraduate students, 98% full-time, 49% women, 51% men
- **Most difficult** entrance level, 5% of applicants were admitted

UNDERGRAD STUDENTS

5,321 full-time, 107 part-time. Students come from 53 states and territories; 97 other countries; 82% are from out of state; 8% Black or African American, non-Hispanic/Latino; 10% Hispanic/Latino; 21% Asian, non-Hispanic/Latino; 0.1% Native Hawaiian or other Pacific Islander, non-Hispanic/Latino; 0.2% American Indian or Alaska Native, non-Hispanic/Latino; 5% Two or more races, non-Hispanic/Latino; 1% Race/ethnicity unknown; 12% international; 0.2% transferred in; 96% live on campus.

Freshmen:

Admission: 35,370 applied, 1,940 admitted, 1,338 enrolled. ***Average high school GPA:*** 3.9. ***Test scores:*** SAT evidence-based reading and writing scores over 500: 100%; SAT math scores over 500: 100%; ACT scores over 18: 100%; SAT evidence-based reading and writing scores over 600: 99%; SAT math scores over 600: 99%; ACT scores over 24: 100%; SAT evidence-based reading and writing scores over 700: 80%; SAT math scores over 700: 87%; ACT scores over 30: 90%.

Retention: 98% of full-time freshmen returned.

FACULTY

Total: 1,166, 84% full-time, 87% with terminal degrees.

Student/faculty ratio: 5:1.

ACADEMICS

Calendar: semesters. *Degrees:* bachelor's, master's, and doctoral.

Special study options: advanced placement credit, independent study, off-campus study, services for LD students, student-designed majors, study abroad. ***ROTC:*** Army (b), Navy (c), Air Force (c).

Computers: 500 computers/terminals and 17,000 ports are available on campus for general student use. Students can access the following: campus intranet, computer help desk, free student e-mail accounts, online (class) grades, online (class) registration, online (class) schedules, academic applications and courseware, printing, network file space, website hosting, media lab, broadcast center. Campuswide network is available. 100% of college-owned or -operated housing units are wired for high-speed Internet access. Wireless service is available via entire campus.

Library: Harvey S. Firestone Memorial Library plus 9 others. *Books:* 7.3 million (physical), 2.1 million (digital/electronic); *Serial titles:* 159,820 (physical), 291,025 (digital/electronic); *Databases:* 1,899. Weekly public service hours: 105.

STUDENT LIFE

Housing options: on-campus residence required through sophomore year; coed, men-only, women-only, special housing for students with disabilities. Campus housing is university owned. Freshman campus housing is guaranteed.

Activities and organizations: drama/theater group, student-run newspaper, radio and television station, choral group, marching band.

Athletics Member NCAA. All Division I except football (Division I-AA). ***Intercollegiate sports:*** baseball M, basketball M/W, crew M/W, cross-country running M/W, fencing M/W, field hockey W, golf M/W(c), ice hockey M/W, lacrosse M/W, soccer M/W, softball W, squash M/W, swimming and diving M/W, tennis M/W, track and field M/W, volleyball M/W, water polo M/W, wrestling M. ***Intramural sports:*** badminton M(c)/W(c), baseball M(c), basketball M(c)/W(c), cheerleading M(c)/W(c), cross-country running M(c)/W(c), equestrian sports M(c)/W(c), fencing M(c)/W(c), field hockey W(c), ice hockey M(c)/W(c), lacrosse M(c)/W(c), rugby M(c)/W(c), sailing M(c)/W(c), skiing (downhill) M(c)/W(c), soccer M(c)/W(c), softball W(c), squash M(c)/W(c), swimming and diving M(c)/W(c), table tennis M(c)/W(c), tennis M(c)/W(c), ultimate Frisbee M(c)/W(c), volleyball M(c)/W(c).

Campus security: 24-hour emergency response devices and patrols, student patrols, late-night transport/escort service, controlled dormitory access.

Student services: health clinic, personal/psychological counseling, women's center, legal services.

COSTS & FINANCIAL AID

Costs (2019–20) ***Comprehensive fee:*** $66,700 includes full-time tuition ($49,450), mandatory fees ($890), and room and board ($16,360). Part-time tuition: $6166 per year. ***Required fees:*** $25 per term part-time. ***College room only:*** $9520.

Financial Aid Of all full-time matriculated undergraduates who enrolled in 2018, 3,506 applied for aid, 3,261 were judged to have need, 3,264 had their need fully met. ***Average percent of need met:*** 100. ***Average financial aid package:*** $55,602. ***Average need-based gift aid:*** $53,572. ***Average indebtedness upon graduation:*** $9059.

APPLYING

Standardized Tests *Required:* SAT or ACT (for admission). *Recommended:* SAT Subject Tests (for admission).

Options: electronic application, early action, deferred entrance.

Application fee: $75.

Required: high school transcript, 3 letters of recommendation, graded written paper. ***Recommended:*** interview.

Notification: 4/1 (freshmen), 4/1 (out-of-state freshmen).

CONTACT

Ms. Jill Dolan, Acting Dean of Admissions, Princeton University, Princeton, NJ 08544-1019. *Phone:* 609-258-3040.

Rabbi Jacob Joseph School

Edison, New Jersey

CONTACT

Rabbi Jacob Joseph School, One Plainfield Ave, Edison, NJ 08817.

Rabbinical College of America

Morristown, New Jersey

http://www.rca.edu/

CONTACT

Shoshana Solomon, Registrar, Rabbinical College of America, 226 Sussex Avenue, PO Box 1996, Morristown, NJ 07962-1996. *Phone:* 973-267-9404. *E-mail:* rca079@aol.com.

Ramapo College of New Jersey

Mahwah, New Jersey

http://www.ramapo.edu/

- **State-supported** comprehensive, founded 1969, part of New Jersey State College System
- **Suburban** 300-acre campus with easy access to New York City
- **Coed**
- **Moderately difficult** entrance level

FACULTY

Student/faculty ratio: 18:1.

ACADEMICS

Calendar: semesters. *Degrees:* certificates, bachelor's, master's, post-master's, and postbachelor's certificates.

Library: George T. Potter Library.

STUDENT LIFE

Housing options: coed. Campus housing is university owned. Freshman campus housing is guaranteed.

Activities and organizations: drama/theater group, student-run newspaper, radio and television station, choral group, NORML, 1 Step, Biology & Biochemistry Club, Campus Crusade for Christ, Culture Club, national fraternities, national sororities.

Athletics Member NCAA. All Division III.

Campus security: 24-hour emergency response devices and patrols, late-night transport/escort service, controlled dormitory access, surveillance cameras, patrols by trained security personnel.

Student services: health clinic, personal/psychological counseling, women's center.

COSTS & FINANCIAL AID

Costs (2018–19) ***Tuition:*** state resident $11,902 full-time, $372 per credit part-time; nonresident $21,243 full-time, $664 per credit part-time. Full-time tuition and fees vary according to reciprocity agreements. Part-time tuition and fees vary according to reciprocity agreements. ***Required fees:*** $2472 full-time, $77 per credit part-time. ***Room and board:*** $12,450; room only: $8650. Room and board charges vary according to board plan and housing facility.

Financial Aid Of all full-time matriculated undergraduates who enrolled in 2017, 3,450 applied for aid, 2,709 were judged to have need, 101 had their need fully met. In 2017, 523 non-need-based awards were made. ***Average percent of need met:*** 54. ***Average financial aid package:*** $11,106. ***Average need-based loan:*** $4337. ***Average need-based gift aid:*** $9977. ***Average non-need-based aid:*** $10,895. ***Average indebtedness upon graduation:*** $35,272.

APPLYING

Standardized Tests *Required:* SAT or ACT (for admission).

Options: electronic application, early admission, early decision, deferred entrance.

Application fee: $65.

Required: essay or personal statement, high school transcript. ***Recommended:*** minimum 3.0 GPA.

CONTACT

Associate Director for Freshmen Admissions, Ramapo College of New Jersey, Office of Admissions, 505 Ramapo Valley Road, Mahwah, NJ 07430-1680. *Phone:* 201-684-7300. *Toll-free phone:* 800-9RAMAPO. *Fax:* 201-684-7964. *E-mail:* admissions@ramapo.edu.

★ Rider University

Lawrenceville, New Jersey

http://www.rider.edu/

- **Independent** comprehensive, founded 1865
- **Suburban** 280-acre campus with easy access to New York City, Philadelphia
- **Endowment** $64.3 million
- **Coed** 3,898 undergraduate students, 91% full-time, 58% women, 42% men
- **Moderately difficult** entrance level, 70% of applicants were admitted

UNDERGRAD STUDENTS

3,534 full-time, 364 part-time. Students come from 42 states and territories; 64 other countries; 25% are from out of state; 13% Black or African American, non-Hispanic/Latino; 16% Hispanic/Latino; 5% Asian, non-Hispanic/Latino; 0.2% American Indian or Alaska Native, non-Hispanic/Latino; 4% Two or more races, non-Hispanic/Latino; 2% Race/ethnicity unknown; 3% international; 5% transferred in; 53% live on campus.

Freshmen:

Admission: 9,429 applied, 6,569 admitted, 921 enrolled. ***Average high school GPA:*** 3.4.

Retention: 78% of full-time freshmen returned.

FACULTY

Total: 595, 39% full-time, 69% with terminal degrees.

Student/faculty ratio: 11:1.

ACADEMICS

Calendar: semesters. *Degrees:* certificates, associate, bachelor's, master's, doctoral, post-master's, and postbachelor's certificates.

Special study options: academic remediation for entering students, adult/continuing education programs, advanced placement credit, cooperative education, distance learning, double majors, English as a second language, honors programs, independent study, internships, part-time degree program, services for LD students, study abroad, summer session for credit. ***ROTC:*** Army (c).

Computers: 300 computers/terminals are available on campus for general student use. Students can access the following: computer help desk, free student e-mail accounts, online (class) grades, online (class) registration,

online (class) schedules. Campuswide network is available. 100% of college-owned or -operated housing units are wired for high-speed Internet access. Wireless service is available via entire campus.
Library: Franklin F. Moore Library plus 1 other. *Books:* 311,713 (physical), 174,115 (digital/electronic); *Serial titles:* 723 (physical), 54,382 (digital/electronic); *Databases:* 171. Study areas open 24 hours, 5–7 days a week; students can reserve study rooms.

STUDENT LIFE
Housing options: coed, women-only, special housing for students with disabilities. Campus housing is university owned. Freshman applicants given priority for college housing.

Activities and organizations: drama/theater group, student-run newspaper, radio and television station, choral group, Student Government Association, Greek Council, Association of Commuter Students, Black Student Union, Residence Hall Association, national fraternities, national sororities.

Athletics Member NCAA. All Division I. ***Intercollegiate sports:*** baseball M(s), basketball M(s)/W(s), cheerleading M/W, cross-country running M(s)/W(s), field hockey W(s), golf M(s), soccer M(s)/W(s), softball W(s), swimming and diving M(s)/W(s), tennis M(s)/W(s), track and field M(s)/W(s), volleyball M/W(s), wrestling M(s). ***Intramural sports:*** baseball M, basketball M/W, cheerleading M/W, cross-country running W, equestrian sports M/W(c), golf M, ice hockey M(c), lacrosse M(c)/W, soccer M/W, softball W, tennis M/W, track and field M/W, volleyball M/W, water polo M/W.

Campus security: 24-hour emergency response devices and patrols, student patrols, late-night transport/escort service, controlled dormitory access.

Student services: health clinic, personal/psychological counseling.

COSTS & FINANCIAL AID
Costs (2019–20) ***Comprehensive fee:*** $58,140 includes full-time tuition ($42,120), mandatory fees ($740), and room and board ($15,280). ***College room only:*** $10,020.

Financial Aid Of all full-time matriculated undergraduates who enrolled in 2018, 3,007 applied for aid, 2,750 were judged to have need, 437 had their need fully met. In 2018, 657 non-need-based awards were made. ***Average percent of need met:*** 76. ***Average financial aid package:*** $32,185. ***Average need-based loan:*** $3284. ***Average need-based gift aid:*** $28,285. ***Average non-need-based aid:*** $19,937. ***Average indebtedness upon graduation:*** $36,499.

APPLYING
Options: electronic application, early admission, early action, deferred entrance.

Application fee: $50.

Required: essay or personal statement, high school transcript, 1 letter of recommendation. ***Required for some:*** interview.

Application deadlines: rolling (freshmen), rolling (transfers), 11/15 (early action).

Notification: continuous (freshmen), continuous (transfers), 12/15 (early action).

CONTACT
Mr. William Larrousse, Director of Admissions, Rider University, 2083 Lawrenceville Road, Lawrenceville, NJ 08648. *Phone:* 609-896-5177. *Toll-free phone:* 800-257-9026. *Fax:* 609-895-6645.

See below for display ad and page 1080 for the College Close-Up.

Rowan University
Glassboro, New Jersey
http://www.rowan.edu/

- **State-supported** comprehensive, founded 1923, part of New Jersey State College System
- **Suburban** 921-acre campus with easy access to Philadelphia
- **Endowment** $173.2 million
- **Coed**
- **Moderately difficult** entrance level

FACULTY
Student/faculty ratio: 17:1.

ACADEMICS
Calendar: semesters. *Degrees:* certificates, bachelor's, master's, doctoral, post-master's, and postbachelor's certificates.

Library: Keith and Shirley Campbell Library plus 4 others. *Books:* 328,891 (physical), 494,739 (digital/electronic); *Serial titles:* 129,972 (digital/electronic); *Databases:* 846. Students can reserve study rooms.

STUDENT LIFE
Housing options: on-campus residence required through sophomore year; coed, special housing for students with disabilities. Campus housing is university owned and leased by the school. Freshman campus housing is guaranteed.

Activities and organizations: drama/theater group, student-run newspaper, radio and television station, choral group, Kappa Delta Pi, Public Relations Student Society of America, Student University Programmes, Rowan Television Network, Elementary Education Club, national fraternities, national sororities.

Athletics Member NCAA. All Division III.

Campus security: 24-hour emergency response devices and patrols, student patrols, late-night transport/escort service, controlled dormitory access, EMS service including 2 ambulances, security and campus police trained as police officers in NJ.

Student services: health clinic, personal/psychological counseling, legal services, veterans affairs office.

COSTS & FINANCIAL AID
Costs (2018–19) ***Tuition:*** state resident $9858 full-time, $379 per credit hour part-time; nonresident $18,500 full-time, $712 per credit hour part-time. Full-time tuition and fees vary according to course load, degree level, location, and program. Part-time tuition and fees vary according to course load, degree level, location, and program. ***Required fees:*** $3839 full-time, $164 per credit hour part-time. ***Room and board:*** $12,552; room only: $8072. Room and board charges vary according to board plan and housing facility. ***Payment plans:*** installment, deferred payment.

Financial Aid Of all full-time matriculated undergraduates who enrolled in 2017, 11,131 applied for aid, 9,255 were judged to have need, 1,098 had their need fully met. In 2017, 1094 non-need-based awards were made. ***Average percent of need met:*** 63. ***Average financial aid package:*** $10,296. ***Average need-based loan:*** $4298. ***Average need-based gift aid:*** $8759. ***Average non-need-based aid:*** $7737. ***Average indebtedness upon graduation:*** $35,542.

APPLYING
Standardized Tests *Required:* SAT or ACT (for admission).

Options: electronic application, early admission, deferred entrance.

Application fee: $65.

Required: high school transcript, minimum 2.0 GPA. ***Required for some:*** interview.

CONTACT
Rowan University, 201 Mullica Hill Road, Glassboro, NJ 08028-1701. *Toll-free phone:* 800-447-1165 (in-state); 800-447-1165N (out-of-state).

Rutgers University–Camden

Camden, New Jersey

http://www.camden.rutgers.edu/

- **State-supported** university, founded 1926
- **Urban** 29-acre campus with easy access to Philadelphia
- **Endowment** $1.2 million
- **Coed**
- **Moderately difficult** entrance level

FACULTY
Student/faculty ratio: 11:1.

ACADEMICS
Calendar: semesters. *Degrees:* bachelor's, master's, doctoral, post-master's, and postbachelor's certificates.
Library: Paul Robeson Library plus 1 other. Weekly public service hours: 90; students can reserve study rooms.

STUDENT LIFE
Housing options: coed, special housing for students with disabilities. Campus housing is university owned.

Activities and organizations: drama/theater group, student-run newspaper, radio station, choral group, national fraternities, national sororities.

Athletics Member NCAA. All Division III.

Campus security: 24-hour emergency response devices and patrols, student patrols, late-night transport/escort service, controlled dormitory access.

Student services: health clinic, personal/psychological counseling, women's center, legal services, veterans affairs office.

COSTS & FINANCIAL AID
Costs (2018–19) ***Tuition:*** state resident $11,886 full-time, $383 per credit hour part-time; nonresident $27,664 full-time, $898 per credit hour part-time. Full-time tuition and fees vary according to program. Part-time tuition and fees vary according to course load and program. ***Required fees:*** $2949 full-time, $595 per term part-time. ***Room and board:*** $12,336; room only: $8582. Room and board charges vary according to board plan and housing facility.

Financial Aid Of all full-time matriculated undergraduates who enrolled in 2017, 4,202 applied for aid, 3,917 were judged to have need, 119 had their need fully met. 315 Federal Work-Study jobs (averaging $2539). 617 state and other part-time jobs (averaging $3174). In 2017, 91 non-need-based awards were made. ***Average percent of need met:*** 54. ***Average financial aid package:*** $13,937. ***Average need-based loan:*** $4464. ***Average need-based gift aid:*** $10,656. ***Average non-need-based aid:*** $4688. ***Average indebtedness upon graduation:*** $31,307.

APPLYING
Standardized Tests *Required:* SAT or ACT (for admission).

Options: electronic application, early action, deferred entrance.

Application fee: $70.

Required: essay or personal statement. ***Required for some:*** high school transcript, interview.

CONTACT
Office of Graduate and Undergraduate Admissions, Rutgers University–Camden, 330 Cooper Street, Camden, NJ 08102. *Phone:* 856-225-6104. *E-mail:* admissions@camden.rutgers.edu.

Rutgers University–Newark

Newark, New Jersey

http://www.newark.rutgers.edu/

- **State-supported** university, founded 1908
- **Urban** 40-acre campus with easy access to New York City
- **Endowment** $1.2 million
- **Coed**
- **Moderately difficult** entrance level

FACULTY
Student/faculty ratio: 10:1.

ACADEMICS
Calendar: semesters. *Degrees:* bachelor's, master's, doctoral, post-master's, and postbachelor's certificates.
Library: John Cotton Dana Library plus 4 others. Weekly public service hours: 91; students can reserve study rooms.

STUDENT LIFE
Housing options: coed. Campus housing is university owned.

Activities and organizations: drama/theater group, student-run newspaper, radio station, choral group, marching band, national fraternities, national sororities.

Athletics Member NCAA. All Division III.

Campus security: 24-hour emergency response devices and patrols, student patrols, late-night transport/escort service, controlled dormitory access.

Student services: health clinic, personal/psychological counseling, women's center, legal services, veterans affairs office.

COSTS & FINANCIAL AID
Costs (2018–19) ***Tuition:*** state resident $11,886 full-time, $383 per credit hour part-time; nonresident $28,194 full-time, $915 per credit hour part-time. Full-time tuition and fees vary according to program. Part-time tuition and fees vary according to course load and program. ***Required fees:*** $2523 full-time, $487 per term part-time. ***Room and board:*** $13,536; room only: $8372. Room and board charges vary according to board plan and housing facility.

Financial Aid Of all full-time matriculated undergraduates who enrolled in 2017, 6,421 applied for aid, 6,137 were judged to have need, 94 had their need fully met. 648 Federal Work-Study jobs (averaging $2189). 1,098 state and other part-time jobs (averaging $2872). In 2017, 55 non-need-based awards were made. ***Average percent of need met:*** 56. ***Average financial aid package:*** $14,826. ***Average need-based loan:*** $4645. ***Average need-based gift aid:*** $12,218. ***Average non-need-based aid:*** $5161. ***Average indebtedness upon graduation:*** $29,125.

APPLYING

Standardized Tests *Required:* SAT or ACT (for admission).

Options: electronic application, early action, deferred entrance.

Application fee: $70.

Required: essay or personal statement. ***Required for some:*** high school transcript.

CONTACT

Office of Undergraduate and Graduate Admissions, Rutgers University–Newark, 190 University Avenue, Room 101, Newark, NJ 07102. *Phone:* 973-353-5205. *E-mail:* newarkadmissions@ugadm.rutgers.edu.

Rutgers University–New Brunswick

Piscataway, New Jersey

http://newbrunswick.rutgers.edu/

- **State-supported** university, founded 1766
- **Urban** 2685-acre campus with easy access to New York City
- **Endowment** $1.2 million
- **Coed**
- **Moderately difficult** entrance level

FACULTY

Student/faculty ratio: 13:1.

ACADEMICS

Calendar: semesters. *Degrees:* certificates, diplomas, associate, bachelor's, master's, doctoral, post-master's, and postbachelor's certificates.

Library: Archibald S. Alexander Library plus 15 others. Study areas open 24 hours, 5–7 days a week; students can reserve study rooms.

STUDENT LIFE

Housing options: coed, men-only, women-only, cooperative. Campus housing is university owned.

Activities and organizations: drama/theater group, student-run newspaper, radio and television station, choral group, marching band, national fraternities, national sororities.

Athletics Member NCAA. All Division I except football (Division I-A).

Campus security: 24-hour emergency response devices and patrols, student patrols, late-night transport/escort service, controlled dormitory access.

Student services: health clinic, personal/psychological counseling, women's center, legal services, veterans affairs office.

COSTS & FINANCIAL AID

Costs (2018–19) ***Tuition:*** state resident $11,886 full-time, $383 per credit hour part-time; nonresident $28,194 full-time, $915 per credit hour part-time. Full-time tuition and fees vary according to program. Part-time tuition and fees vary according to course load and program. ***Required fees:*** $3088 full-time, $445 per term part-time. ***Room and board:*** $12,706; room only: $7746. Room and board charges vary according to board plan and housing facility.

Financial Aid Of all full-time matriculated undergraduates who enrolled in 2017, 21,443 applied for aid, 18,264 were judged to have need, 687 had their need fully met. 2,763 Federal Work-Study jobs (averaging $2074). 7,594 state and other part-time jobs (averaging $2333). In 2017, 966 non-need-based awards were made. ***Average percent of need met:*** 52. ***Average financial aid package:*** $14,197. ***Average need-based loan:*** $4890. ***Average need-based gift aid:*** $11,517. ***Average non-need-based aid:*** $9256. ***Average indebtedness upon graduation:*** $34,113.

APPLYING

Standardized Tests *Required:* SAT or ACT (for admission).

Options: electronic application, early action, deferred entrance.

Application fee: $70.

Required: essay or personal statement. ***Required for some:*** high school transcript, interview.

CONTACT

Undergraduate Admissions Office, Rutgers University–New Brunswick, 65 Davidson Road, Room 202, Piscataway, NJ 08854. *Phone:* 732-445-1000. *E-mail:* admissions@ugadm.rutgers.edu.

Saint Peter's University

Jersey City, New Jersey

http://www.saintpeters.edu/

- **Independent Roman Catholic (Jesuit)** comprehensive, founded 1872
- **Urban** 15-acre campus with easy access to New York City
- **Coed**
- **Moderately difficult** entrance level

FACULTY

Student/faculty ratio: 13:1.

ACADEMICS

Calendar: semesters. *Degrees:* certificates, associate, bachelor's, master's, doctoral, post-master's, and postbachelor's certificates.

Library: Theresa and Edward O'Toole Library plus 2 others.

STUDENT LIFE

Housing options: coed, special housing for students with disabilities. Campus housing is university owned. Freshman campus housing is guaranteed.

Activities and organizations: drama/theater group, student-run newspaper, radio station, choral group.

Athletics Member NCAA. All Division I.

Campus security: 24-hour emergency response devices and patrols, late-night transport/escort service, controlled dormitory access, ID checks at residence halls and library.

Student services: health clinic, personal/psychological counseling, veterans affairs office.

FINANCIAL AID

Financial Aid Of all full-time matriculated undergraduates who enrolled in 2017, 2,257 applied for aid, 2,075 were judged to have need, 132 had their need fully met. In 2017, 178 non-need-based awards were made. ***Average percent of need met:*** 79. ***Average financial aid package:*** $32,097. ***Average need-based loan:*** $4048. ***Average need-based gift aid:*** $29,853. ***Average non-need-based aid:*** $21,252. ***Average indebtedness upon graduation:*** $22,317.

APPLYING

Standardized Tests *Required for some:* SAT or ACT (for admission).

Options: early action, deferred entrance.

Required: essay or personal statement, high school transcript, minimum 2.0 GPA, 2 letters of recommendation. ***Required for some:*** interview. ***Recommended:*** interview.

CONTACT

Miss Kacey Tillotson, Director of Undergraduate Admissions, Saint Peter's University, Office of Admission, Lee House, Jersey City 07306. *Phone:* 201-761-7100. *Toll-free phone:* 888-SPC-9933. *E-mail:* ktillotson@saintpeters.edu.

★ Seton Hall University

South Orange, New Jersey

http://www.shu.edu/

CONTACT

Mary Clare Cullum, Director of Undergraduate Admissions, Seton Hall University, Enrollment Management Office, 400 South Orange Avenue, South Orange, NJ 07079-2697. *Phone:* 973-275-2589. *Toll-free phone:* 800-THE HALL. *Fax:* 973-275-2321. *E-mail:* maryclare.cullum@shu.edu.

See next page for display ad and page 1108 for the College Close-Up.

A ★ indicates that the school has detailed information with a Premium Profile on Petersons.com.

Stevens Institute of Technology

Hoboken, New Jersey

http://www.stevens.edu/

- **Independent** university, founded 1870
- **Urban** 55-acre campus with easy access to New York City
- **Coed** 3,431 undergraduate students, 100% full-time, 29% women, 71% men
- **Very difficult** entrance level, 41% of applicants were admitted

UNDERGRAD STUDENTS

3,420 full-time, 11 part-time. Students come from 40 states and territories; 47 other countries; 39% are from out of state; 2% Black or African American, non-Hispanic/Latino; 11% Hispanic/Latino; 15% Asian, non-Hispanic/Latino; 0.1% American Indian or Alaska Native, non-Hispanic/Latino; 4% Race/ethnicity unknown; 4% international; 0.6% transferred in; 64% live on campus.

Freshmen:

Admission: 9,265 applied, 3,838 admitted, 1,009 enrolled. ***Average high school GPA:*** 3.9. ***Test scores:*** SAT evidence-based reading and writing scores over 500: 100%; SAT math scores over 500: 100%; ACT scores over 18: 100%; SAT evidence-based reading and writing scores over 600: 92%; SAT math scores over 600: 98%; ACT scores over 24: 99%; SAT evidence-based reading and writing scores over 700: 37%; SAT math scores over 700: 71%; ACT scores over 30: 85%.

Retention: 95% of full-time freshmen returned.

FACULTY

Total: 392, 67% full-time, 94% with terminal degrees.

Student/faculty ratio: 10:1.

ACADEMICS

Calendar: semesters. *Degrees:* bachelor's, master's, doctoral, and postbachelor's certificates.

Special study options: accelerated degree program, advanced placement credit, cooperative education, distance learning, double majors, honors programs, independent study, internships, off-campus study, services for LD students, study abroad, summer session for credit. ***ROTC:*** Army (c), Air Force (c).

Computers: 11 computers/terminals and 9,600 ports are available on campus for general student use. Students can access the following: campus intranet, computer help desk, free student e-mail accounts, online (class) grades, online (class) registration, online (class) schedules, online account information, debit dining program, laundry status. Campuswide network is available. 100% of college-owned or -operated housing units are wired for high-speed Internet access. Wireless service is available via entire campus.

Library: Samuel C. Williams Library. *Books:* 66,492 (physical), 210,243 (digital/electronic); *Serial titles:* 898 (physical), 35,353 (digital/electronic); *Databases:* 71. Students can reserve study rooms.

STUDENT LIFE

Housing options: coed, women-only. Campus housing is university owned and leased by the school. Freshman campus housing is guaranteed.

Activities and organizations: drama/theater group, student-run newspaper, radio and television station, choral group, Alpha Phi Omega, Computer & Gaming Society (C2GS), Society of Women Engineers, American Society of Mechanical Engineers (ASME), Ethnic Student Council, national fraternities, national sororities.

Athletics Member NCAA. All Division III. ***Intercollegiate sports:*** baseball M, basketball M/W, cross-country running M/W, equestrian sports W, fencing M/W, field hockey W, golf M, lacrosse M/W, soccer M/W, softball W, swimming and diving M/W, tennis M/W, track and field M/W, volleyball M/W, wrestling M. ***Intramural sports:*** archery M(c)/W(c), baseball M(c), basketball M, bowling M(c)/W(c), crew M(c)/W(c), field hockey M, football M/W(c), ice hockey M(c), lacrosse M(c), sailing M(c)/W(c), skiing (cross-country) M(c)/W(c), skiing (downhill) M(c)/W(c), soccer M(c)/W(c), softball W, squash M, ultimate Frisbee M(c), volleyball M(c)/W(c).

Campus security: 24-hour emergency response devices and patrols, late-night transport/escort service, controlled dormitory access.

Student services: health clinic, personal/psychological counseling, women's center, veterans affairs office.

COSTS & FINANCIAL AID

Costs (2019–20) ***Comprehensive fee:*** $69,784 includes full-time tuition ($52,134), mandatory fees ($1880), and room and board ($15,770). Part-time tuition: $1738 per credit. ***College room only:*** $8910.

Financial Aid Of all full-time matriculated undergraduates who enrolled in 2017, 2,361 applied for aid, 2,000 were judged to have need, 325 had their need fully met. In 2017, 912 non-need-based awards were made. ***Average percent of need met:*** 69. ***Average financial aid package:*** $30,331. ***Average need-based loan:*** $4380. ***Average need-based gift aid:*** $13,203. ***Average non-need-based aid:*** $18,498. ***Average indebtedness upon graduation:*** $40,588.

APPLYING

Standardized Tests *Required for some:* SAT or ACT (for admission), SAT and SAT Subject Tests or ACT (for admission), Applicants to Music and Technology or Visual Arts and Technology may submit a digital portfolio in place of standardized test scores. International applicants may submit 2 SAT II scores, 2 AP scores, or 2 IB scores in place of standardized test scores.

Options: electronic application, early admission, early decision, deferred entrance.

Application fee: $70.

Required: essay or personal statement, high school transcript, 2 letters of recommendation. ***Required for some:*** digital portfolio for music and technology or visual arts and technology programs. ***Recommended:*** interview.

Application deadlines: 1/15 (freshmen), 6/1 (transfers).

Early decision deadline: 11/15 (for plan 1), 1/15 (for plan 2).

Notification: 4/1 (freshmen), continuous until 6/30 (transfers), 12/15 (early decision plan 1), 2/15 (early decision plan 2).

CONTACT

Jackie Williams, Dean of Undergraduate Admissions, Stevens Institute of Technology, Castle Point on Hudson, Hoboken, NJ 07030. *Phone:* 201-216-5207. *Toll-free phone:* 800-458-5323. *E-mail:* jackie.williams@stevens.edu.

★ Stockton University

Galloway, New Jersey

http://www.stockton.edu/

- **State-supported** comprehensive, founded 1969, part of New Jersey State College System
- **Suburban** 2000-acre campus with easy access to Philadelphia
- **Endowment** $30.8 million
- **Coed** 8,603 undergraduate students, 95% full-time, 58% women, 42% men
- **Very difficult** entrance level, 84% of applicants were admitted

UNDERGRAD STUDENTS

8,135 full-time, 468 part-time. 2% are from out of state; 8% Black or African American, non-Hispanic/Latino; 14% Hispanic/Latino; 6% Asian, non-Hispanic/Latino; 0.2% Native Hawaiian or other Pacific Islander, non-Hispanic/Latino; 0.2% American Indian or Alaska Native, non-Hispanic/Latino; 2% Two or more races, non-Hispanic/Latino; 2% Race/ethnicity unknown; 0.5% international; 12% transferred in; 37% live on campus.

Freshmen:

Admission: 6,084 applied, 5,133 admitted, 1,595 enrolled. ***Test scores:*** SAT evidence-based reading and writing scores over 500: 75%; SAT math scores over 500: 76%; ACT scores over 18: 81%; SAT evidence-based reading and writing scores over 600: 26%; SAT math scores over 600: 24%; ACT scores over 24: 32%; SAT evidence-based reading and writing scores over 700: 3%; SAT math scores over 700: 4%; ACT scores over 30: 4%.

Retention: 85% of full-time freshmen returned.

FACULTY

Total: 771, 45% full-time, 59% with terminal degrees.

Student/faculty ratio: 17:1.

ACADEMICS

Calendar: semesters. *Degrees:* bachelor's, master's, doctoral, and postbachelor's certificates.

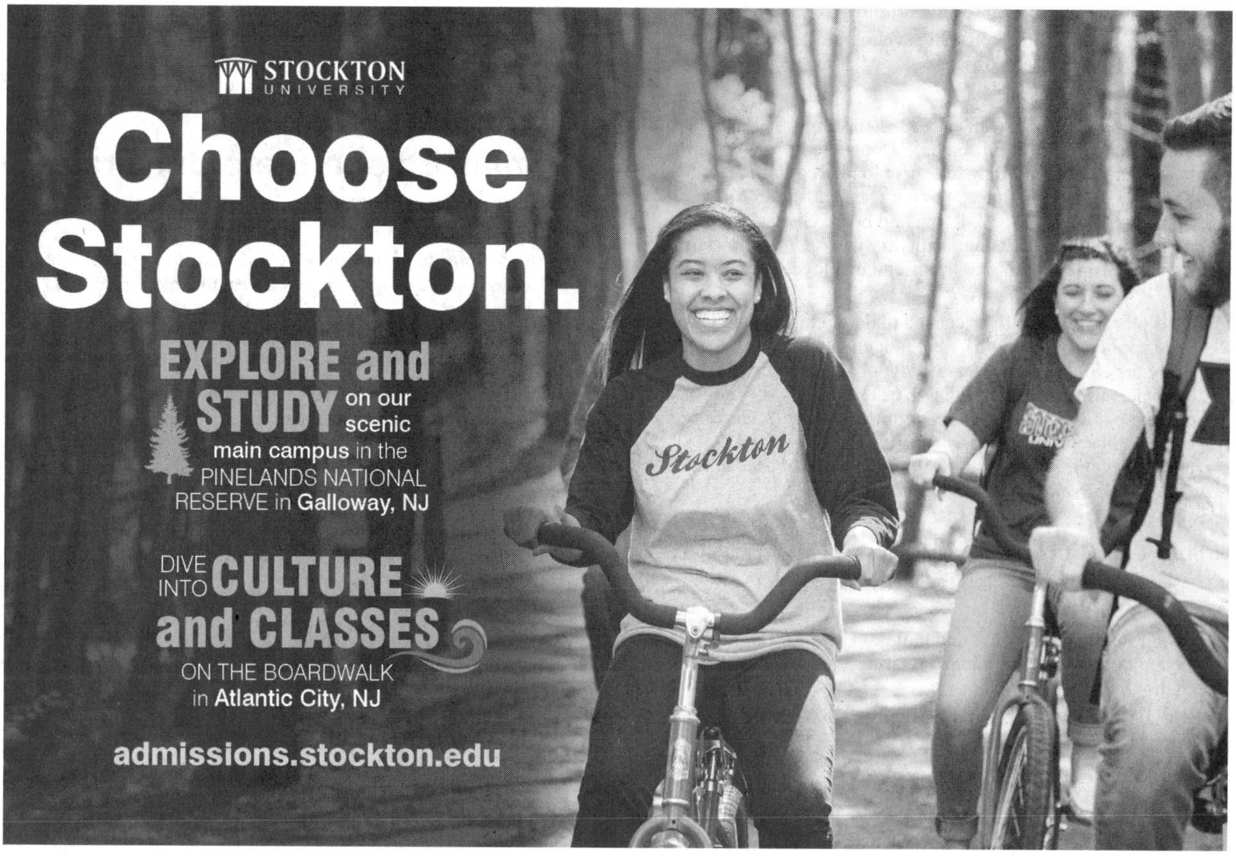

Special study options: academic remediation for entering students, accelerated degree program, adult/continuing education programs, advanced placement credit, distance learning, double majors, English as a second language, honors programs, independent study, internships, off-campus study, part-time degree program, services for LD students, student-designed majors, study abroad, summer session for credit.

Unusual degree programs: 3-2 business administration; engineering with New Jersey Institute of Technology; Rutgers, The State University of New Jersey; Rowan University; public health with Rutgers University, medical technology with University of Delaware.

Computers: 1,224 computers/terminals are available on campus for general student use. Students can access the following: campus intranet, computer help desk, free student e-mail accounts, online (class) grades, online (class) registration, online (class) schedules. Campuswide network is available. 100% of college-owned or -operated housing units are wired for high-speed Internet access. Wireless service is available via entire campus.

Library: Richard E. Bjork Library. *Books:* 215,712 (physical), 165,452 (digital/electronic); *Serial titles:* 85 (physical), 133,008 (digital/electronic); *Databases:* 184. Weekly public service hours: 91.

STUDENT LIFE

Housing options: coed, special housing for students with disabilities. Campus housing is university owned. Freshman campus housing is guaranteed.

Activities and organizations: drama/theater group, student-run newspaper, radio and television station, choral group, Occupational Therapy Club, Sign Language Club, Animal Friendly Organization, Commuters on the Go, Archery Recreational Club of Stockton, national fraternities, national sororities.

Athletics Member NCAA. All Division III. ***Intercollegiate sports:*** baseball M, basketball M/W, crew W, cross-country running M/W, field hockey W, lacrosse M/W, soccer M/W, softball W, tennis W, track and field M/W, volleyball W. ***Intramural sports:*** basketball M/W, bowling M(c)/W(c), crew M(c), fencing M(c), field hockey W(c), golf M(c)/W(c), ice hockey M(c)/W(c), soccer M/W, softball M/W, table tennis M(c)/W(c), tennis M(c)/W(c), ultimate Frisbee M(c)/W(c), volleyball M(c).

Campus security: 24-hour emergency response devices and patrols, late-night transport/escort service, controlled dormitory access.

Student services: health clinic, personal/psychological counseling, women's center, veterans affairs office.

COSTS & FINANCIAL AID

Costs (2018–19) ***Tuition:*** state resident $8862 full-time, $341 per credit part-time; nonresident $15,989 full-time, $615 per credit part-time. Part-time tuition and fees vary according to course load. ***Required fees:*** $4877 full-time, $188 per credit part-time, $120 per term part-time. ***Room and board:*** $12,282; room only: $8232. Room and board charges vary according to board plan and housing facility. ***Payment plans:*** installment, deferred payment. ***Waivers:*** senior citizens and employees or children of employees.

Financial Aid Of all full-time matriculated undergraduates who enrolled in 2018, 7,090 applied for aid, 5,951 were judged to have need, 1,000 had their need fully met. 309 Federal Work-Study jobs (averaging $1806). 895 state and other part-time jobs (averaging $1621). In 2018, 493 non-need-based awards were made. ***Average percent of need met:*** 68. ***Average financial aid package:*** $17,064. ***Average need-based loan:*** $4398. ***Average need-based gift aid:*** $9776. ***Average non-need-based aid:*** $6217. ***Average indebtedness upon graduation:*** $34,735.

APPLYING

Standardized Tests *Required for some:* SAT or ACT (for admission).

Options: electronic application, early admission.

Application fee: $50.

Required: high school transcript, minimum 2.0 GPA. ***Recommended:*** essay or personal statement, minimum 3.0 GPA, 3 letters of recommendation.

Notification: 5/15 (freshmen), continuous until 6/15 (transfers).

CONTACT

Mr. Robert Heinrich, Chief Enrollment Management Officer, Stockton University, 101 Vera King Farris Drive, Galloway, NJ 08205-9441. *Phone:* 609-652-4261. *E-mail:* admissions@stockton.edu.

See previous page for display ad and page 1120 for the College Close-Up.

Strayer University–Cherry Hill Campus

Cherry Hill, New Jersey

http://www.strayer.edu/new-jersey/cherry-hill/

CONTACT

Strayer University–Cherry Hill Campus, 2370 State Route 70 West, Suite 335, Cherry Hill, NJ 08002. *Toll-free phone:* 888-311-0355.

Strayer University–Piscataway Campus

Piscataway, New Jersey

http://www.strayer.edu/new-jersey/piscataway/

CONTACT

Strayer University–Piscataway Campus, 242 Old New Brunswick Road, Suite 220, Piscataway, NJ 08854. *Toll-free phone:* 888-311-0355.

Strayer University–Willingboro Campus

Willingboro, New Jersey

http://www.strayer.edu/new-jersey/willingboro/

CONTACT

Strayer University–Willingboro Campus, 300 Willingboro Parkway, Willingboro Town Center, Suite 125, Willingboro, NJ 08046. *Toll-free phone:* 888-311-0355.

Talmudical Academy of New Jersey

Adelphia, New Jersey

CONTACT

Director of Admissions, Talmudical Academy of New Jersey, 868 Route 524, Adelphia, NJ 07710. *Phone:* 201-431-1600.

Thomas Edison State University

Trenton, New Jersey

http://www.tesu.edu/

- **State-supported** comprehensive, founded 1972
- **Urban** 2-acre campus with easy access to Philadelphia
- **Coed**
- **Noncompetitive** entrance level

ACADEMICS

Calendar: continuous. *Degrees:* certificates, associate, bachelor's, master's, doctoral, and postbachelor's certificates (offers only distance learning degree programs).

STUDENT LIFE

Housing options: college housing not available.

Campus security: 24-hour emergency response devices and patrols, late-night transport/escort service, security officer from 7 am to 11 pm, local police patrol.

COSTS

Costs (2018–19) ***Tuition:*** state resident $7519 full-time, $396 per credit hour part-time; nonresident $9967 full-time, $499 per credit hour part-time.

APPLYING

Options: electronic application.

Application fee: $75.

Required: must be 21 or older and a high school graduate.

CONTACT
Ms. Juliette Punchello, Senior Director, Admissions and Enrollment Services, Thomas Edison State University, 111 West State Street, Trenton, NJ 08608. *Phone:* 888-442-8372. *Toll-free phone:* 888-442-8372. *Fax:* 609-984-8447. *E-mail:* admissions@tesu.edu.

William Paterson University of New Jersey
Wayne, New Jersey
http://www.wpunj.edu/

- **State-supported** comprehensive, founded 1855
- **Suburban** 370-acre campus with easy access to New York City
- **Coed**
- **Moderately difficult** entrance level

FACULTY
Student/faculty ratio: 14:1.

ACADEMICS
Calendar: semesters. *Degrees:* bachelor's, master's, doctoral, post-master's, and postbachelor's certificates.
Library: David and Lorraine Cheng Library. *Books:* 369,216 (physical), 116,597 (digital/electronic); *Serial titles:* 3,772 (physical), 164,249 (digital/electronic); *Databases:* 126. Weekly public service hours: 102; students can reserve study rooms.

STUDENT LIFE
Housing options: coed, special housing for students with disabilities. Campus housing is university owned. Freshman campus housing is guaranteed.

Activities and organizations: drama/theater group, student-run newspaper, radio and television station, choral group, Student Activities Programming Board (SAPB), Students for Awareness Black Leadership and Equality (SABLE), Student Government Association (SGA), The B.A.B.Y. Dolls (Community Service org.), Pioneer Players (drama), national fraternities, national sororities.

Athletics Member NCAA. All Division III.

Campus security: 24-hour emergency response devices and patrols, student patrols, late-night transport/escort service, controlled dormitory access.

Student services: health clinic, personal/psychological counseling, women's center, legal services, veterans affairs office.

COSTS & FINANCIAL AID
Costs (2018–19) ***Tuition:*** state resident $12,936 full-time, $414 per credit part-time; nonresident $21,136 full-time, $685 per credit part-time. Full-time tuition and fees vary according to course load and location. Part-time tuition and fees vary according to course load and location. ***Required fees:*** $124 full-time, $4 per credit part-time. ***Room and board:*** $11,445; room only: $7135. Room and board charges vary according to board plan and housing facility.

Financial Aid Of all full-time matriculated undergraduates who enrolled in 2018, 6,619 applied for aid, 5,574 were judged to have need, 1,422 had their need fully met. 180 Federal Work-Study jobs (averaging $1800). In 2018, 518 non-need-based awards were made. ***Average financial aid package:*** $11,517. ***Average need-based loan:*** $4246. ***Average need-based gift aid:*** $9280. ***Average non-need-based aid:*** $6191. ***Average indebtedness upon graduation:*** $31,105.

APPLYING
Standardized Tests *Required:* SAT or ACT (for admission).

Options: electronic application.

Application fee: $50.

Required: high school transcript, minimum 2.0 GPA. ***Required for some:*** essay or personal statement, 1 letter of recommendation, interview, portfolio for art, audition for music.

CONTACT
Mr. Anthony Leckey, Senior Associate Director of Admissions, William Paterson University of New Jersey, Undergraduate Admissions, 300 Pompton Road, Wayne, NJ 07470. *Phone:* 973-720-2900. *Toll-free phone:* 877-WPU-EXCEL. *Fax:* 973-720-2910. *E-mail:* leckeya@wpunj.edu.

Yeshiva Bais Aharon
Lakewood, New Jersey

CONTACT
Yeshiva Bais Aharon, 905 Park Avenue, Lakewood, NJ 08701.

Yeshiva Gedolah Shaarei Shmuel
Lakewood, New Jersey
http://www.yeshivagedolahshaareishmuel.com/

CONTACT
Yeshiva Gedolah Shaarei Shmuel, 511 Ocean Avenue, Lakewood, NJ 08701.

Yeshiva Gedolah Zichron Leyma
Linden, New Jersey

CONTACT
Yeshiva Gedolah Zichron Leyma, 1000 Orchard Terrace, Linden, NJ 07036.

Yeshivas Be'er Yitzchok
Elizabeth, New Jersey
http://www.elizabethkollel.org/

CONTACT
Yeshivas Be'er Yitzchok, 1391 North Avenue, Elizabeth, NJ 07208.

Yeshiva Toras Chaim
Lakewood, New Jersey

CONTACT
Yeshiva Toras Chaim, 999 Ridge Avenue, Lakewood, NJ 08701.

Yeshiva Yesodei HaTorah
Lakewood, New Jersey

CONTACT
Yeshiva Yesodei HaTorah, 2 Yesodei Court, Lakewood, NJ 08701.

NEW MEXICO

Brookline College
Albuquerque, New Mexico
http://brooklinecollege.edu/

CONTACT
Mr. Andrew Webb, Campus Director, Brookline College, 4201 Central Avenue NW, Suite J, Albuquerque, NM 87105. *Phone:* 505-880-2877. *Toll-free phone:* 888-660-2428. *Fax:* 505-352-0199. *E-mail:* awebb@brooklinecollege.edu.

Eastern New Mexico University
Portales, New Mexico
http://www.enmu.edu/

- **State-supported** comprehensive, founded 1934
- **Rural** 344-acre campus
- **Endowment** $9.8 million
- **Coed**
- **Noncompetitive** entrance level

FACULTY
Student/faculty ratio: 19:1.

ACADEMICS
Calendar: semesters. *Degrees:* certificates, associate, bachelor's, master's, and postbachelor's certificates.

Library: Golden Library plus 2 others.

STUDENT LIFE
Housing options: on-campus residence required for freshman year; coed, women-only, special housing for students with disabilities. Campus housing is university owned. Freshman campus housing is guaranteed.

Activities and organizations: drama/theater group, student-run newspaper, radio and television station, choral group, marching band, Student Government, Student Activities Board, Residence Hall Association, IFC (Inter-Fraternity Council)Panhellenic Council, national fraternities, national sororities.

Athletics Member NCAA. All Division II.

Campus security: 24-hour emergency response devices and patrols, late-night transport/escort service, controlled dormitory access, University Emergency Notification System, security cameras, security lights.

Student services: health clinic, personal/psychological counseling.

COSTS & FINANCIAL AID
Costs (2018–19) ***One-time required fee:*** $95. ***Tuition:*** state resident $3842 full-time, $259 per credit hour part-time; nonresident $5764 full-time, $339 per credit hour part-time. ***Required fees:*** $2364 full-time, $99 per credit hour part-time. ***Room and board:*** $7162; room only: $3496.

Financial Aid Of all full-time matriculated undergraduates who enrolled in 2018, 2,187 applied for aid, 1,739 were judged to have need, 159 had their need fully met. In 2018, 154 non-need-based awards were made. ***Average percent of need met:*** 78. ***Average financial aid package:*** $12,215. ***Average need-based loan:*** $3555. ***Average need-based gift aid:*** $6351. ***Average non-need-based aid:*** $2093. ***Average indebtedness upon graduation:*** $22,439.

APPLYING
Standardized Tests *Required for some:* SAT (for admission), ACT (for admission).

Options: electronic application.

Required: official transcripts from any post-secondary institution attended, good standing with all previous institutions. ***Required for some:*** high school transcript, minimum 2.5 GPA.

CONTACT
Eastern New Mexico University, 1500 South Avenue K, Portales, NM 88130. *Toll-free phone:* 800-367-3668.

EC-Council University

Albuquerque, New Mexico

http://www.eccu.edu/

- **Proprietary** upper-level, founded 2003
- **Coed**

FACULTY
Student/faculty ratio: 5:1.

ACADEMICS
Degrees: bachelor's and master's.

STUDENT LIFE
Housing options: college housing not available.

Student services: veterans affairs office.

APPLYING
Options: electronic application, early admission, deferred entrance.

CONTACT
EC-Council University, 101 C Sun Avenue NE, Albuquerque, NM 87109.

Institute of American Indian Arts

Santa Fe, New Mexico

http://www.iaia.edu/

- **Federally supported** comprehensive, founded 1962
- **Suburban** 140-acre campus with easy access to Albuquerque
- **Coed**

FACULTY
Student/faculty ratio: 7:1.

ACADEMICS
Calendar: semesters. *Degrees:* certificates, associate, bachelor's, and master's.
Library: IAIA Library plus 1 other. Students can reserve study rooms.

STUDENT LIFE
Housing options: on-campus residence required for freshman year; coed, special housing for students with disabilities. Campus housing is university owned. Freshman campus housing is guaranteed.

Activities and organizations: drama/theater group, student-run newspaper, television station.

Campus security: 24-hour patrols, late-night transport/escort service, controlled dormitory access.

Student services: personal/psychological counseling.

COSTS & FINANCIAL AID
Costs (2018–19) ***Tuition:*** state resident $4700 full-time, $196 per semester hour part-time; nonresident $4700 full-time, $196 per semester hour part-time. ***Required fees:*** $280 full-time, $140 per term part-time. ***Room and board:*** $9604; room only: $4144. Room and board charges vary according to board plan and housing facility.

Financial Aid Of all full-time matriculated undergraduates who enrolled in 2011, 263 applied for aid, 261 were judged to have need, 201 had their need fully met. 2 Federal Work-Study jobs (averaging $2300). 3 state and other part-time jobs (averaging $2300). In 2011, 58 non-need-based awards were made. ***Average percent of need met:*** 71. ***Average financial aid package:*** $5005. ***Average need-based gift aid:*** $2500. ***Average non-need-based aid:*** $2500.

APPLYING
Options: electronic application, deferred entrance.

Required: high school transcript. ***Required for some:*** essay or personal statement, interview. ***Recommended:*** interview.

CONTACT
Ms. Mary Silentwalker, Director, Admissions and Recruitment, Institute of American Indian Arts, 83 Avan Nu Po Road, Santa Fe, NM 87508. *Phone:* 505-424-2307. *Fax:* 505-424-0909. *E-mail:* mary.silentwalker@iaia.edu.

National American University

Albuquerque, New Mexico

http://www.national.edu/

CONTACT
Admissions Office, National American University, 10131 Coors Boulevard NW, Suite I-01, Albuquerque, NM 87114. *Toll-free phone:* 800-895-9904.

National American University

Albuquerque, New Mexico

http://www.national.edu/

CONTACT
National American University, 4775 Indian School Road NE, Suite 200, Albuquerque, NM 87110. *Phone:* 505-265-7517. *Toll-free phone:* 800-895-9904.

National College of Midwifery

Taos, New Mexico

http://www.midwiferycollege.org/

CONTACT
Ms. Beth Enson, Dean of Students, National College of Midwifery, 1041 Reed Street, Suite C, Taos, NM 87571. *Phone:* 505-758-8914. *E-mail:* info@midwiferycollege.org.

Navajo Technical University
Crownpoint, New Mexico
http://www.navajotech.edu/

CONTACT
Director of Admission, Navajo Technical University, PO Box 849, Crownpoint, NM 87313. *Phone:* 505-786-4100.

New Mexico Highlands University
Las Vegas, New Mexico
http://www.nmhu.edu/

- **State-supported** comprehensive, founded 1893
- **Small-town** campus
- **Coed**
- **Minimally difficult** entrance level

FACULTY
Student/faculty ratio: 15:1.

ACADEMICS
Calendar: semesters. *Degrees:* bachelor's, master's, post-master's, and postbachelor's certificates.
Library: Thomas C. Donnelly Library.

STUDENT LIFE
Housing options: coed, special housing for students with disabilities. Campus housing is university owned.

Activities and organizations: drama/theater group, student-run radio station, choral group, marching band, Vatos Rugby, Fire Escape Club, MeChA, NMHU Cheerleaders, NMHU Student Ambassadors, national fraternities, national sororities.

Athletics Member NCAA. All Division II.

Campus security: 24-hour emergency response devices and patrols, late-night transport/escort service, controlled dormitory access.

Student services: health clinic, personal/psychological counseling, women's center.

COSTS & FINANCIAL AID
Costs (2018–19) ***One-time required fee:*** $25. ***Tuition:*** state resident $4320 full-time, $180 per credit hour part-time; nonresident $8472 full-time, $353 per credit hour part-time. ***Required fees:*** $1830 full-time, $70 per term part-time. ***Room and board:*** $7872; room only: $3852. Room and board charges vary according to board plan and housing facility.

Financial Aid Of all full-time matriculated undergraduates who enrolled in 2017, 1,063 applied for aid, 974 were judged to have need, 23 had their need fully met. In 2017, 129 non-need-based awards were made. ***Average percent of need met:*** 53. ***Average financial aid package:*** $9683. ***Average need-based loan:*** $4127. ***Average need-based gift aid:*** $7868. ***Average non-need-based aid:*** $2520. ***Average indebtedness upon graduation:*** $18,767. ***Financial aid deadline:*** 6/30.

APPLYING
Options: electronic application, early admission, deferred entrance.

Required: high school transcript, minimum 2.0 GPA. ***Required for some:*** 2 letters of recommendation, interview.

CONTACT
Ms. Jessica Jaramillo, Director of Recruitment and Admissions, New Mexico Highlands University, Box 9000, Las Vegas, NM 87701. *Phone:* 505-454-3394. *Toll-free phone:* 800-338-6648. *E-mail:* admissions@nmhu.edu.

New Mexico Institute of Mining and Technology
Socorro, New Mexico
http://www.nmt.edu/

- **State-supported** university, founded 1889
- **Small-town** 320-acre campus with easy access to Albuquerque
- **Endowment** $45.0 million
- **Coed**
- **Moderately difficult** entrance level

FACULTY
Student/faculty ratio: 11:1.

ACADEMICS
Calendar: semesters. *Degrees:* associate, bachelor's, master's, and doctoral.
Library: The Skeen Library. Students can reserve study rooms.

STUDENT LIFE
Housing options: coed, men-only, women-only. Campus housing is university owned.

Activities and organizations: drama/theater group, student-run newspaper, radio station, choral group.

Campus security: 24-hour emergency response devices and patrols, late-night transport/escort service.

Student services: health clinic, personal/psychological counseling, veterans affairs office.

COSTS & FINANCIAL AID
Costs (2018–19) ***Tuition:*** state resident $6440 full-time, $268 per credit hour part-time; nonresident $20,938 full-time, $872 per credit hour part-time. Full-time tuition and fees vary according to reciprocity agreements. Part-time tuition and fees vary according to course load. ***Required fees:*** $1494 full-time, $18 per credit hour part-time, $444 per term part-time. ***Room and board:*** $8202. Room and board charges vary according to board plan and housing facility.

Financial Aid Of all full-time matriculated undergraduates who enrolled in 2017, 1,159 applied for aid, 691 were judged to have need, 141 had their need fully met. In 2017, 418 non-need-based awards were made. ***Average percent of need met:*** 78. ***Average financial aid package:*** $12,524. ***Average need-based loan:*** $4408. ***Average need-based gift aid:*** $6059. ***Average non-need-based aid:*** $5656. ***Average indebtedness upon graduation:*** $26,817.

APPLYING
Standardized Tests *Required:* SAT or ACT (for admission). *Recommended:* ACT (for admission).

Options: electronic application, deferred entrance.

Application fee: $15.

Required: high school transcript, minimum 2.5 GPA. ***Required for some:*** 2 letters of recommendation. ***Recommended:*** interview.

CONTACT
Mr. Anthony Ortiz, Director of Admissions, New Mexico Institute of Mining and Technology, 801 Leroy Place, Socorro, NM 87801. *Phone:* 575-835-5424. *Toll-free phone:* 800-428-TECH. *Fax:* 575-835-5989. *E-mail:* admission@nmt.edu.

New Mexico State University
Las Cruces, New Mexico
http://www.nmsu.edu/

- **State-supported** university, founded 1888, part of New Mexico State University System
- **Suburban** 900-acre campus with easy access to El Paso, TX
- **Endowment** $167.5 million
- **Coed**
- **Moderately difficult** entrance level

FACULTY
Student/faculty ratio: 16:1.

ACADEMICS
Calendar: semesters. *Degrees:* certificates, associate, bachelor's, master's, doctoral, post-master's, and postbachelor's certificates.
Library: New Mexico State University Library - Zuhl plus 1 other. *Books:* 1.2 million (physical), 160,068 (digital/electronic); *Serial titles:* 23,730 (physical), 135,113 (digital/electronic); *Databases:* 410. Weekly public service hours: 112; students can reserve study rooms.

STUDENT LIFE
Housing options: on-campus residence required for freshman year; coed. Campus housing is university owned. Freshman campus housing is guaranteed.

Activities and organizations: drama/theater group, student-run newspaper, radio and television station, choral group, marching band, national fraternities, national sororities.

Athletics Member NCAA. All Division I except football (Division I-A).

Campus security: 24-hour emergency response devices and patrols, late-night transport/escort service, controlled dormitory access.

Student services: health clinic, personal/psychological counseling, legal services, veterans affairs office.

COSTS & FINANCIAL AID

Costs (2018–19) ***One-time required fee:*** $165. ***Tuition:*** state resident $5515 full-time, $230 per credit hour part-time; nonresident $20,599 full-time, $858 per credit hour part-time. Full-time tuition and fees vary according to course load and reciprocity agreements. Part-time tuition and fees vary according to course load and reciprocity agreements. ***Required fees:*** $1171 full-time, $49 per credit hour part-time. ***Room and board:*** $9252; room only: $5350. Room and board charges vary according to board plan and housing facility.

Financial Aid Of all full-time matriculated undergraduates who enrolled in 2017, 7,296 applied for aid, 6,408 were judged to have need, 845 had their need fully met. 276 Federal Work-Study jobs (averaging $3037). 184 state and other part-time jobs (averaging $6064). In 2017, 1325 non-need-based awards were made. ***Average percent of need met:*** 70. ***Average financial aid package:*** $13,894. ***Average need-based loan:*** $3497. ***Average need-based gift aid:*** $9874. ***Average non-need-based aid:*** $3585. ***Average indebtedness upon graduation:*** $20,354. ***Financial aid deadline:*** 6/30.

APPLYING

Standardized Tests *Required:* SAT or ACT (for admission).

Options: electronic application.

Application fee: $20.

Required: high school transcript, high school course requirements: 4 units of English, 4 of math, 2 of science beyond general science, and 1 foreign language/fine art; must have 2.75 HS GPA, rank in the top 20% of graduating class, or ACT composite score of 21 (SAT of 1060 new format). ***Required for some:*** 3 letters of recommendation.

CONTACT

Danielle Staley, Interim Director of Admissions, New Mexico State University, Box 30001, MSC 3A, Las Cruces, NM 88003-8001. *Phone:* 575-646-3121. *Toll-free phone:* 800-662-6678. *Fax:* 575-646-6330. *E-mail:* admssions@nmsu.edu.

Northern New Mexico College

Española, New Mexico

http://www.nnmc.edu/

CONTACT

Mr. Mike L. Costello, Registrar, Northern New Mexico College, 921 Paseo de Oñate, Española, NM 87532. *Phone:* 505-747-2193. *Fax:* 505-747-2191. *E-mail:* dms@nnmc.edu.

Pima Medical Institute

Albuquerque, New Mexico

http://www.pmi.edu/

CONTACT

Admissions Office, Pima Medical Institute, 4400 Cutler Avenue NE, Albuquerque, NM 87110. *Phone:* 505-881-1234. *Toll-free phone:* 800-477-PIMA. *Fax:* 505-881-5329.

★ St. John's College

Santa Fe, New Mexico

http://www.sjc.edu/

- **Independent** comprehensive, founded 1964
- **Small-town** 250-acre campus with easy access to Albuquerque, NM
- **Endowment** $63.0 million
- **Coed** 320 undergraduate students, 96% full-time, 44% women, 56% men
- **Very difficult** entrance level, 67% of applicants were admitted

UNDERGRAD STUDENTS

306 full-time, 14 part-time. Students come from 42 states and territories; 27 other countries; 87% are from out of state; 0.3% Black or African

American, non-Hispanic/Latino; 13% Hispanic/Latino; 3% Asian, non-Hispanic/Latino; 6% Two or more races, non-Hispanic/Latino; 2% Race/ethnicity unknown; 23% international; 3% transferred in; 87% live on campus.

Freshmen:
Admission: 358 applied, 240 admitted, 71 enrolled. ***Average high school GPA:*** 3.4. ***Test scores:*** SAT evidence-based reading and writing scores over 500: 100%; SAT math scores over 500: 100%; ACT scores over 18: 95%; SAT evidence-based reading and writing scores over 600: 80%; SAT math scores over 600: 60%; ACT scores over 24: 81%; SAT evidence-based reading and writing scores over 700: 50%; SAT math scores over 700: 27%; ACT scores over 30: 45%.

Retention: 76% of full-time freshmen returned.

FACULTY
Total: 48, 83% full-time, 92% with terminal degrees.

Student/faculty ratio: 8:1.

ACADEMICS
Calendar: semesters. *Degrees:* bachelor's and master's.

Special study options: English as a second language, internships, off-campus study, services for LD students, study abroad, summer session for credit.

Computers: 16 computers/terminals and 425 ports are available on campus for general student use. Students can access the following: campus intranet, computer help desk, free student e-mail accounts, free wi-fi access throughout the campus; support for "bring your own"; mobile devices. Campuswide network is available. 100% of college-owned or -operated housing units are wired for high-speed Internet access. Wireless service is available via entire campus.

Library: Meem Library. *Books:* 69,127 (physical); *Serial titles:* 68 (physical); *Databases:* 9. Weekly public service hours: 82; study areas open 24 hours, 5–7 days a week.

STUDENT LIFE
Housing options: on-campus residence required through senior year; coed, men-only, women-only, special housing for students with disabilities. Campus housing is university owned. Freshman campus housing is guaranteed.

Activities and organizations: drama/theater group, student-run newspaper, choral group, Student Government (Polity), Iron Bookworm Workout, Intramural sports, PiYo , International Student Association.

Athletics ***Intramural sports:*** archery M(c)/W(c), basketball M(c)/W(c), fencing M(c)/W, field hockey M/W(c), ice hockey M(c)/W(c), rock climbing M/W, skiing (cross-country) M/W, skiing (downhill) M/W, soccer M(c)/W(c), softball M(c)/W, squash M/W, swimming and diving M/W, table tennis M(c)/W(c), tennis M/W, ultimate Frisbee M/W, volleyball M/W, weight lifting M(c)/W(c).

Campus security: 24-hour emergency response devices and patrols, late-night transport/escort service, controlled dormitory access.

Student services: health clinic, personal/psychological counseling.

COSTS & FINANCIAL AID
Costs (2019–20) ***One-time required fee:*** $100. ***Comprehensive fee:*** $49,270 includes full-time tuition ($35,000), mandatory fees ($1410), and room and board ($12,860). Full-time tuition and fees vary according to location. ***College room only:*** $7152. Room and board charges vary according to board plan, housing facility, and location. ***Payment plan:*** installment. ***Waivers:*** employees or children of employees.

Financial Aid Of all full-time matriculated undergraduates who enrolled in 2018, 307 applied for aid, 303 were judged to have need, 190 had their need fully met. 78 Federal Work-Study jobs (averaging $2717). 104 state and other part-time jobs (averaging $2812). In 2018, 14 non-need-based awards were made. ***Average percent of need met:*** 94. ***Average financial aid package:*** $46,357. ***Average need-based loan:*** $4721. ***Average need-based gift aid:*** $20,780. ***Average non-need-based aid:*** $19,751. ***Average indebtedness upon graduation:*** $44,989.

APPLYING
Standardized Tests *Required for some:* SAT or ACT (for admission), SAT/ACT, TOEFL/IELTS or interview for international applicants; SAT/ACT/CLT for homeschooled students and applicants who have not and will not graduate high school.

Options: electronic application, early admission, early action, deferred entrance.

Required: essay or personal statement, high school transcript, 2 letters of recommendation. ***Required for some:*** outline of curriculum for home-schooled applicants. ***Recommended:*** interview.

Application deadlines: rolling (freshmen), rolling (transfers), 11/15 (early action).

Notification: continuous (freshmen), continuous (transfers), 12/15 (early action).

CONTACT
Ms. Yvette Sobky Shaffer, Director of Admissions, St. John's College, 1160 Camino Cruz Blanca, Santa Fe, NM 87505. *Phone:* 505-984-6060. *Toll-free phone:* 800-331-5232. *E-mail:* santafe.admissions@sjc.edu.

See previous page for display ad and page 1096 for the College Close-Up.

University of New Mexico
Albuquerque, New Mexico
http://www.unm.edu/

- **State-supported** university, founded 1889
- **Urban** 769-acre campus
- **Endowment** $400.8 million
- **Coed** 17,859 undergraduate students, 76% full-time, 56% women, 44% men
- **Moderately difficult** entrance level, 52% of applicants were admitted

UNDERGRAD STUDENTS
13,591 full-time, 4,268 part-time. 10% are from out of state; 2% Black or African American, non-Hispanic/Latino; 49% Hispanic/Latino; 4% Asian, non-Hispanic/Latino; 0.2% Native Hawaiian or other Pacific Islander, non-Hispanic/Latino; 6% American Indian or Alaska Native, non-Hispanic/Latino; 3% Two or more races, non-Hispanic/Latino; 1% Race/ethnicity unknown; 2% international; 9% transferred in; 9% live on campus.

Freshmen:
Admission: 10,912 applied, 5,629 admitted, 2,661 enrolled. ***Average high school GPA:*** 3.4. ***Test scores:*** SAT evidence-based reading and writing scores over 500: 83%; SAT math scores over 500: 81%; ACT scores over 18: 87%; SAT evidence-based reading and writing scores over 600: 42%; SAT math scores over 600: 37%; ACT scores over 24: 39%; SAT evidence-based reading and writing scores over 700: 9%; SAT math scores over 700: 11%; ACT scores over 30: 7%.

Retention: 74% of full-time freshmen returned.

FACULTY
Total: 1,389, 77% full-time, 65% with terminal degrees.

Student/faculty ratio: 16:1.

ACADEMICS
Calendar: semesters. *Degrees:* certificates, bachelor's, master's, doctoral, and post-master's certificates.

Special study options: academic remediation for entering students, accelerated degree program, adult/continuing education programs, advanced placement credit, cooperative education, distance learning, double majors, English as a second language, freshman honors college, honors programs, independent study, internships, off-campus study, part-time degree program, services for LD students, student-designed majors, study abroad, summer session for credit. ***ROTC:*** Army (b), Navy (b), Air Force (b).

Unusual degree programs: 3-2 business administration; engineering; Latin American studies, business.

Computers: 990 computers/terminals and 56,000 ports are available on campus for general student use. Students can access the following: campus intranet, computer help desk, free student e-mail accounts, online (class) grades, online (class) registration, online (class) schedules. Campuswide network is available. 100% of college-owned or -operated housing units are wired for high-speed Internet access. Wireless service is available via entire campus.

Library: College of University Libraries and Learning Sciences plus 7 others. Students can reserve study rooms.

STUDENT LIFE
Housing options: coed, special housing for students with disabilities. Campus housing is university owned and is provided by a third party. Freshman campus housing is guaranteed.

Activities and organizations: drama/theater group, student-run newspaper, radio and television station, choral group, marching band, Associated Students of UNM, Graduate and Professional Students Association, Golden Key National Honor Society, national fraternities, national sororities.

Athletics Member NCAA. All Division I except football (Division I-A). ***Intercollegiate sports:*** baseball M(s), basketball M(s)/W(s), cross-country running M(s)/W(s), golf M(s)/W(s)(c), skiing (cross-country) M(s)/W(s), skiing (downhill) M(s)(c)/W(s), soccer M(s)/W(s), softball W(s), swimming and diving M/W(s), tennis M(s)/W(s), track and field M(s)/W(s), volleyball W(s). ***Intramural sports:*** archery M/W, badminton M/W, basketball M/W, bowling M(c)/W(c), cheerleading M(c)/W(c), fencing M, field hockey W, football M, golf M/W, ice hockey M(c)/W(c), lacrosse M(c)/W(c), racquetball M/W, rugby M(c)/W(c), skiing (cross-country) M/W, skiing (downhill) M/W, soccer M/W, softball M/W, swimming and diving W, table tennis M/W, tennis M/W, ultimate Frisbee M(c)/W(c), volleyball M/W, water polo M/W, wrestling M(c).

Campus security: 24-hour emergency response devices and patrols, student patrols, late-night transport/escort service, controlled dormitory access.

Student services: health clinic, personal/psychological counseling, women's center.

COSTS & FINANCIAL AID
Costs (2018–19) ***Tuition:*** state resident $5418 full-time, $255 per credit hour part-time; nonresident $21,062 full-time, $878 per credit hour part-time. Full-time tuition and fees vary according to course level and program. Part-time tuition and fees vary according to course level, course load, and program. ***Required fees:*** $1904 full-time, $63 per credit hour part-time. ***Room and board:*** $9864. Room and board charges vary according to board plan and housing facility. ***Payment plan:*** installment. ***Waivers:*** senior citizens and employees or children of employees.

Financial Aid Of all full-time matriculated undergraduates who enrolled in 2017, 11,222 applied for aid, 11,105 were judged to have need, 2,681 had their need fully met. ***Average need-based gift aid:*** $6846. ***Average indebtedness upon graduation:*** $21,635. ***Financial aid deadline:*** 5/15.

APPLYING
Standardized Tests *Required:* SAT or ACT (for admission).

Options: electronic application, early admission, deferred entrance.

Application fee: $25.

Required: high school transcript, minimum 2.5 GPA. ***Required for some:*** essay or personal statement, interview.

Application deadlines: rolling (freshmen), rolling (transfers).

Notification: continuous (freshmen), continuous (transfers).

CONTACT
Mr. Matthew Hulett, Director of Admissions and Recruitment Services, University of New Mexico, Office of Admissions, PO Box 4895, Albuquerque, NM 87196-4895. *Phone:* 505-277-8900. *Toll-free phone:* 800-CALL-UNM. *Fax:* 505-277-6686. *E-mail:* apply@unm.edu.

University of the Southwest
Hobbs, New Mexico
http://www.usw.edu/

CONTACT
Lissete Terrazas, Director of Admissions, University of the Southwest, 6610 North Lovington Highway, Hobbs, NM 88240. *Phone:* 575-492-2122. *Toll-free phone:* 800-530-4400. *Fax:* 575-392-6006. *E-mail:* lterrazas@usw.edu.

Western New Mexico University
Silver City, New Mexico
http://www.wnmu.edu/

CONTACT
Mr. Matthew Lara, Director of Admissions, Western New Mexico University, PO Box 680, Silver City, NM 88062-0680. *Phone:* 505-538-6106. *Toll-free phone:* 800-872-WNMU. *Fax:* 505-538-6127. *E-mail:* tresslerd@wnmu.edu.

NEW YORK

Adelphi University
Garden City, New York
http://www.adelphi.edu/

- **Independent** university, founded 1896
- **Suburban** 75-acre campus with easy access to New York City
- **Endowment** $188.6 million
- **Coed** 5,391 undergraduate students, 94% full-time, 68% women, 32% men
- **Moderately difficult** entrance level, 74% of applicants were admitted

UNDERGRAD STUDENTS
5,056 full-time, 335 part-time. Students come from 38 states and territories; 48 other countries; 7% are from out of state; 9% Black or African American, non-Hispanic/Latino; 17% Hispanic/Latino; 11% Asian, non-Hispanic/Latino; 0.2% American Indian or Alaska Native, non-Hispanic/Latino; 2% Two or more races, non-Hispanic/Latino; 7% Race/ethnicity unknown; 4% international; 9% transferred in; 22% live on campus.

Freshmen:
Admission: 13,006 applied, 9,649 admitted, 1,245 enrolled. ***Average high school GPA:*** 3.5. ***Test scores:*** SAT evidence-based reading and writing scores over 500: 93%; SAT math scores over 500: 94%; ACT scores over 18: 98%; SAT evidence-based reading and writing scores over 600: 42%; SAT math scores over 600: 41%; ACT scores over 24: 57%; SAT evidence-based reading and writing scores over 700: 4%; SAT math scores over 700: 8%; ACT scores over 30: 13%.

Retention: 81% of full-time freshmen returned.

FACULTY
Total: 1,060, 32% full-time, 43% with terminal degrees.

Student/faculty ratio: 12:1.

ACADEMICS
Calendar: semesters. *Degrees:* certificates, associate, bachelor's, master's, doctoral, post-master's, and postbachelor's certificates.

ROTC: Army (c), Air Force (c).

Computers: 667 computers/terminals are available on campus for general student use. Students can access the following: campus intranet, computer help desk, free student e-mail accounts, online (class) grades, online (class) registration, online (class) schedules, payment, drop/add classes, check application status. Campuswide network is available. 100% of college-owned or -operated housing units are wired for high-speed Internet access. Wireless service is available via entire campus.
Library: Swirbul Library. *Books:* 537,868 (physical), 240,988 (digital/electronic); *Serial titles:* 430 (physical), 87,949 (digital/electronic); *Databases:* 249. Students can reserve study rooms.

STUDENT LIFE
Housing options: coed, special housing for students with disabilities. Campus housing is university owned. Freshman applicants given priority for college housing.

Activities and organizations: drama/theater group, student-run newspaper, radio station, choral group, Student Activities Board, C. A. L. I. B. E. R. (Cause to Achieve Leadership, Intelligence, Brotherhood, Excellence, and Respect), Commuter Student Organization, Christian Fellowship, Circle K International, national fraternities, national sororities.

Athletics Member NCAA. All Division II. ***Intercollegiate sports:*** baseball M(s), basketball M(s)/W(s), bowling W(s), cross-country running M(s)/W(s), field hockey W(s), golf M(s)/W(s), lacrosse M(s)/W(s), soccer M(s)/W(s), softball W(s), swimming and diving M(s)/W(s), tennis M(s)/W(s), track and field M(s)/W(s), volleyball W(s). ***Intramural sports:*** badminton M(c)/W(c), baseball M(c)/W(c), basketball M/W, cheerleading W, equestrian sports M(c)/W(c), fencing M(c), field hockey W(c), soccer M/W, ultimate Frisbee M(c)/W(c), volleyball M/W.

Campus security: 24-hour emergency response devices and patrols, late-night transport/escort service, controlled dormitory access.

Student services: health clinic, personal/psychological counseling.

COSTS & FINANCIAL AID

Costs (2018–19) ***Comprehensive fee:*** $54,690 includes full-time tuition ($36,920), mandatory fees ($1740), and room and board ($16,030). Full-time tuition and fees vary according to course level, course load, location, program, and student level. Part-time tuition: $1125 per credit hour. Part-time tuition and fees vary according to course level, course load, location, program, and student level. ***Required fees:*** $448 per term part-time. ***Room and board:*** Room and board charges vary according to board plan and housing facility. ***Payment plans:*** tuition prepayment, installment, deferred payment. ***Waivers:*** senior citizens and employees or children of employees.

Financial Aid Of all full-time matriculated undergraduates who enrolled in 2018, 4,077 applied for aid, 3,440 were judged to have need, 656 had their need fully met. 317 Federal Work-Study jobs (averaging $1873). 1,165 state and other part-time jobs (averaging $2181). In 2018, 988 non-need-based awards were made. ***Average percent of need met:*** 48. ***Average financial aid package:*** $22,900. ***Average need-based loan:*** $3859. ***Average need-based gift aid:*** $16,410. ***Average non-need-based aid:*** $16,235. ***Average indebtedness upon graduation:*** $34,980.

APPLYING

Standardized Tests *Required for some:* SAT or ACT (for admission).

Options: electronic application, early action, deferred entrance.

Application fee: $40.

Required: essay or personal statement, high school transcript. ***Required for some:*** interview, auditions/portfolios for performing and fine arts.

Application deadlines: rolling (freshmen), rolling (transfers).

Notification: continuous (freshmen), continuous (transfers).

CONTACT

Ms. Stephanie Espina, Director of Freshman Admissions, Adelphi University, Nexus Building, Room 110, 1 South Avenue, PO Box 701, Garden City, NY 11530-0701. *Phone:* 516-877-3056. *Toll-free phone:* 800-ADELPHI. *Fax:* 516-877-3039. *E-mail:* admissions@adelphi.edu.

Albany College of Pharmacy and Health Sciences

Albany, New York

http://www.acphs.edu/

CONTACT

Mr. Matthew Stever, Director of Admissions, Albany College of Pharmacy and Health Sciences, 106 New Scotland Avenue, Albany, NY 12208. *Phone:* 518-694-7221. *Toll-free phone:* 888-203-8010. *Fax:* 518-694-7322. *E-mail:* admissions@acphs.edu.

Alfred University

Alfred, New York

http://www.alfred.edu/

- **Independent** university, founded 1836
- **Rural** 232-acre campus with easy access to Rochester
- **Endowment** $129.3 million
- **Coed** 1,671 undergraduate students, 94% full-time, 50% women, 50% men
- **Moderately difficult** entrance level, 63% of applicants were admitted

UNDERGRAD STUDENTS

1,572 full-time, 99 part-time. Students come from 43 states and territories; 16 other countries; 18% are from out of state; 11% Black or African American, non-Hispanic/Latino; 10% Hispanic/Latino; 1% Asian, non-Hispanic/Latino; 0.4% American Indian or Alaska Native, non-Hispanic/Latino; 3% Two or more races, non-Hispanic/Latino; 10% Race/ethnicity unknown; 3% international; 6% transferred in; 69% live on campus.

Freshmen:

Admission: 4,296 applied, 2,693 admitted, 437 enrolled. ***Average high school GPA:*** 3.1. ***Test scores:*** SAT evidence-based reading and writing scores over 500: 69%; SAT math scores over 500: 71%; ACT scores over 18: 89%; SAT evidence-based reading and writing scores over 600: 24%; SAT math scores over 600: 27%; ACT scores over 24: 43%; SAT evidence-based reading and writing scores over 700: 4%; SAT math scores over 700: 4%; ACT scores over 30: 14%.

Retention: 73% of full-time freshmen returned.

FACULTY

Total: 194, 80% full-time, 87% with terminal degrees.

Student/faculty ratio: 11:1.

ACADEMICS

Calendar: semesters. *Degrees:* bachelor's, master's, doctoral, and post-master's certificates.

Special study options: advanced placement credit, cooperative education, double majors, honors programs, independent study, internships, off-campus study, part-time degree program, services for LD students, student-designed majors, study abroad, summer session for credit. ***ROTC:*** Army (c).

Computers: 1,231 computers/terminals and 1,231 ports are available on campus for general student use. Students can access the following: campus intranet, computer help desk, free student e-mail accounts, online (class) grades, online (class) registration, online (class) schedules, online bill pay. Campuswide network is available. 100% of college-owned or -operated housing units are wired for high-speed Internet access. Wireless service is available via entire campus.

Library: Herrick Memorial Library plus 1 other. *Books:* 177,734 (physical), 865,873 (digital/electronic); *Serial titles:* 249 (physical), 108,773 (digital/electronic); *Databases:* 330. Study areas open 24 hours, 5–7 days a week; students can reserve study rooms.

STUDENT LIFE

Housing options: on-campus residence required through junior year; coed, men-only, women-only, cooperative, special housing for students with disabilities. Campus housing is university owned. Freshman campus housing is guaranteed.

Activities and organizations: drama/theater group, student-run newspaper, radio station, choral group, Carribean Student Association, Student Activities Board, Art Force 5, Student Senate.

Athletics Member NCAA. All Division III. ***Intercollegiate sports:*** basketball M/W, cross-country running M/W, equestrian sports M/W, football M, lacrosse M/W, skiing (downhill) M/W, soccer M/W, softball W, swimming and diving M/W, tennis M/W, track and field M/W, volleyball W. ***Intramural sports:*** baseball M(c), basketball M/W, bowling M(c)/W(c), cheerleading W(c), football M/W, ice hockey M(c), racquetball M/W, rugby M(c)/W(c), skiing (cross-country) M(c)/W(c), soccer M/W, squash M/W, ultimate Frisbee M(c)/W(c), volleyball M/W.

Campus security: 24-hour emergency response devices, student patrols, late-night transport/escort service, controlled dormitory access.

Student services: health clinic, personal/psychological counseling, women's center.

COSTS & FINANCIAL AID

Costs (2019–20) ***Comprehensive fee:*** $47,488 includes full-time tuition ($33,760), mandatory fees ($1010), and room and board ($12,718). Part-time tuition: $1036 per credit hour. ***Required fees:*** $85 part-time. ***College room only:*** $6418.

Financial Aid Of all full-time matriculated undergraduates who enrolled in 2018, 1,431 applied for aid, 1,301 were judged to have need, 228 had their need fully met. In 2018, 85 non-need-based awards were made. ***Average percent of need met:*** 83. ***Average financial aid package:*** $29,512. ***Average need-based loan:*** $5527. ***Average need-based gift aid:*** $23,230. ***Average non-need-based aid:*** $12,572. ***Average indebtedness upon graduation:*** $34,224. ***Financial aid deadline:*** 3/15.

APPLYING
Standardized Tests *Required:* SAT or ACT (for admission). *Recommended:* SAT (for admission).

Options: electronic application, early admission, early decision, deferred entrance.

Application fee: $50.

Required: essay or personal statement, high school transcript, 1 letter of recommendation. ***Required for some:*** portfolio for applicants to the School of Art and Design. ***Recommended:*** interview.

Application deadlines: rolling (out-of-state freshmen), 8/1 (transfers).

Early decision deadline: 12/1.

Notification: continuous (freshmen), continuous (out-of-state freshmen), continuous (transfers).

CONTACT
Mr. Jake Yale, Director of Admissions, Alfred University, Alumni Hall, Alfred, NY 14802-1205. *Phone:* 607-871-2115. *Toll-free phone:* 800-541-9229. *Fax:* 607-871-2198. *E-mail:* admissions@alfred.edu.

Bard College

Annandale-on-Hudson, New York

http://www.bard.edu/

- **Independent** comprehensive, founded 1860
- **Rural** 1000-acre campus
- **Coed**
- **Moderately difficult** entrance level

FACULTY
Student/faculty ratio: 9:1.

ACADEMICS
Calendar: semesters. *Degrees:* bachelor's, master's, and doctoral.
Library: Stevenson Library plus 3 others. Weekly public service hours: 75; students can reserve study rooms.

STUDENT LIFE
Housing options: on-campus residence required through sophomore year; coed, women-only, cooperative, special housing for students with disabilities. Campus housing is university owned. Freshman campus housing is guaranteed.

Activities and organizations: drama/theater group, student-run newspaper, radio station, choral group.

Athletics Member NCAA, NAIA. All NCAA Division III.

Campus security: 24-hour emergency response devices and patrols, student patrols, late-night transport/escort service, controlled dormitory access.

Student services: health clinic, personal/psychological counseling, legal services.

FINANCIAL AID
Financial Aid Of all full-time matriculated undergraduates who enrolled in 2018, 1,328 applied for aid, 1,272 were judged to have need, 279 had their need fully met. 825 Federal Work-Study jobs (averaging $1694). In 2018, 34 non-need-based awards were made. ***Average percent of need met:*** 79. ***Average financial aid package:*** $48,432. ***Average need-based loan:*** $5519. ***Average need-based gift aid:*** $44,444. ***Average non-need-based aid:*** $23,252. ***Average indebtedness upon graduation:*** $27,726. ***Financial aid deadline:*** 2/15.

APPLYING
Options: electronic application, early admission, early decision, early action, deferred entrance.

Application fee: $50.

Required: essay or personal statement, high school transcript, minimum 3.0 GPA, 3 letters of recommendation.

CONTACT
Ms. Mackie Siebens, Director of Admissions, Bard College, PO Box 5000, 30 Campus Road, Annandale-on-Hudson, NY 12504-5000. *Phone:* 845-758-7472. *Fax:* 845-758-5208. *E-mail:* admission@bard.edu.

★ Barnard College

New York, New York

http://www.barnard.edu/

- **Independent** 4-year, founded 1889
- **Urban** 4-acre campus
- **Endowment** $327.2 million
- **Women only**
- **Most difficult** entrance level

FACULTY
Student/faculty ratio: 10:1.

ACADEMICS
Calendar: semesters. *Degree:* bachelor's.
Library: Lefrak Center plus 20 others. Study areas open 24 hours, 5–7 days a week.

STUDENT LIFE
Housing options: women-only, special housing for students with disabilities. Campus housing is university owned and leased by the school. Freshman campus housing is guaranteed.

Activities and organizations: drama/theater group, student-run newspaper, radio and television station, choral group, marching band, Community Impact (community service), Student Government Association, Take Back the Night, Student Activities Council, Musical Theater Society, national sororities.

Athletics Member NCAA. All Division I.

Campus security: 24-hour emergency response devices and patrols, late-night transport/escort service, controlled dormitory access, gated campus with permanent security posts.

Student services: health clinic, personal/psychological counseling, women's center.

COSTS & FINANCIAL AID
Costs (2018–19) ***Comprehensive fee:*** $72,257 includes full-time tuition ($53,252), mandatory fees ($1780), and room and board ($17,225). Part-time tuition: $1775 per credit hour. ***College room only:*** $10,435. Room and board charges vary according to board plan and housing facility. ***Payment plans:*** tuition prepayment, installment, deferred payment.

Financial Aid Of all full-time matriculated undergraduates who enrolled in 2018, 1,039 applied for aid, 1,006 were judged to have need, 974 had their need fully met. ***Average percent of need met:*** 100. ***Average financial aid package:*** $53,297. ***Average need-based loan:*** $4592. ***Average need-based gift aid:*** $47,970. ***Average indebtedness upon graduation:*** $20,829.

APPLYING
Standardized Tests *Required:* SAT or ACT (for admission).

Options: electronic application, early admission, early decision, deferred entrance.

Application fee: $75.

Required: essay or personal statement, high school transcript, 3 letters of recommendation, Common Application with Barnard Supplement. ***Recommended:*** interview.

CONTACT
Ms. Jennifer Gill Fondiller, Vice President for Enrollment, Barnard College, Barnard College, 3009 Broadway, New York, NY 10027. *Phone:* 212-854-2014. *Fax:* 212-854-6220. *E-mail:* admissions@barnard.edu.

See below for display ad and page 976 for the College Close-Up.

Baruch College of the City University of New York

New York, New York

http://www.baruch.cuny.edu/

- **State and locally supported** comprehensive, founded 1919, part of City University of New York System
- **Urban** 4-acre campus
- **Coed** 15,024 undergraduate students, 77% full-time, 47% women, 53% men
- **Very difficult** entrance level, 39% of applicants were admitted

UNDERGRAD STUDENTS

11,495 full-time, 3,529 part-time. Students come from 26 states and territories; 3% are from out of state; 9% Black or African American, non-Hispanic/Latino; 26% Hispanic/Latino; 32% Asian, non-Hispanic/Latino; 0.1% Native Hawaiian or other Pacific Islander, non-Hispanic/Latino; 0.1% American Indian or Alaska Native, non-Hispanic/Latino; 1% Two or more races, non-Hispanic/Latino; 11% international; 10% transferred in; 2% live on campus.

Freshmen:

Admission: 21,469 applied, 8,436 admitted, 1,692 enrolled. ***Average high school GPA:*** 3.3. ***Test scores:*** SAT evidence-based reading and writing scores over 500: 98%; SAT math scores over 500: 100%; SAT evidence-based reading and writing scores over 600: 75%; SAT math scores over 600: 87%; SAT evidence-based reading and writing scores over 700: 12%; SAT math scores over 700: 37%.

Retention: 89% of full-time freshmen returned.

FACULTY

Total: 1,100, 45% full-time, 62% with terminal degrees.

Student/faculty ratio: 18:1.

ACADEMICS

Calendar: semesters. *Degrees:* bachelor's, master's, and post-master's certificates.

Special study options: accelerated degree program, adult/continuing education programs, advanced placement credit, distance learning, double majors, English as a second language, freshman honors college, honors programs, independent study, internships, part-time degree program, services for LD students, student-designed majors, study abroad, summer session for credit. ***ROTC:*** Army (c).

Computers: 1,300 computers/terminals are available on campus for general student use. Students can access the following: campus intranet, computer help desk, free student e-mail accounts, online (class) grades, online (class) registration, online (class) schedules. Campuswide network is available. 100% of college-owned or -operated housing units are wired for high-speed Internet access. Wireless service is available via classrooms, computer centers, computer labs, learning centers, libraries, student centers.

Library: The William and Anita Newman Library. *Books:* 330,647 (physical), 515,356 (digital/electronic); *Serial titles:* 117,795 (physical), 117,795 (digital/electronic). Students can reserve study rooms.

STUDENT LIFE

Housing options: coed. Campus housing is provided by a third party.

Activities and organizations: drama/theater group, student-run newspaper, radio station, choral group, Accounting Society, Caribbean Students Association, Association of Latino Professionals in Finance and Accounting, Golden Key International Honor Society, Helpline, national fraternities, national sororities.

Athletics Member NCAA. All Division III. ***Intercollegiate sports:*** baseball M, basketball M/W, cheerleading M/W, cross-country running M/W, soccer M, softball W, swimming and diving M/W, tennis M/W, volleyball M/W. ***Intramural sports:*** archery M(c)/W(c), badminton M/W, basketball M/W, cross-country running M/W, racquetball M/W, swimming and diving M/W, table tennis M/W, volleyball M/W.

Campus security: 24-hour emergency response devices and patrols, late-night transport/escort service.

Student services: health clinic, personal/psychological counseling, legal services.

COSTS & FINANCIAL AID

Costs (2018–19) ***Tuition:*** state resident $6530 full-time, $285 per credit hour part-time; nonresident $17,400 full-time, $580 per credit hour part-time. Full-time tuition and fees vary according to course load. Part-time tuition and fees vary according to course load. ***Required fees:*** $585 full-time, $163 per term part-time. ***Room and board:*** Room and board charges vary according to housing facility. ***Payment plans:*** installment, deferred payment. ***Waivers:*** senior citizens and employees or children of employees.

Financial Aid Of all full-time matriculated undergraduates who enrolled in 2018, 8,767 applied for aid, 7,755 were judged to have need, 242 had their need fully met. 1,242 Federal Work-Study jobs (averaging $1006). 50 state and other part-time jobs (averaging $2497). In 2018, 325 non-need-based awards were made. ***Average percent of need met:*** 45. ***Average financial aid package:*** $5365. ***Average need-based loan:*** $6035. ***Average***

need-based gift aid: $8246. ***Average non-need-based aid:*** $2537. ***Average indebtedness upon graduation:*** $9182.

APPLYING
Standardized Tests *Required:* SAT or ACT (for admission).

Options: electronic application, early admission, early decision, deferred entrance.

Application fee: $65.

Required: high school transcript, minimum 2.5 GPA, 16 academic units. ***Required for some:*** interview.

Application deadlines: 2/1 (freshmen), 2/1 (transfers).

Notification: 5/15 (freshmen), continuous until 5/1 (transfers).

CONTACT
Ms. Marisa DeLaCruz, Director of Undergraduate Admissions, Baruch College of the City University of New York, 1 Bernard Baruch Way, New York, NY 10010-5585. *Phone:* 646-312-1383. *Fax:* 646-312-1279. *E-mail:* marisa.delacruz@baruch.cuny.edu.

Be'er Yaakov Talmudic Seminary
Spring Valley, New York

CONTACT
Be'er Yaakov Talmudic Seminary, 12 Jefferson Avenue, Spring Valley, NY 10977.

Beis Medrash Heichal Dovid
Far Rockaway, New York

CONTACT
Beis Medrash Heichal Dovid, 257 Beach 17th Street, Far Rockaway, NY 11691.

Berkeley College–New York City Campus
New York, New York
http://www.berkeleycollege.edu/

- **Proprietary** 4-year, founded 1936
- **Urban** campus with easy access to New York City
- **Coed** 3,293 undergraduate students, 75% full-time, 64% women, 36% men
- **Minimally difficult** entrance level, 100% of applicants were admitted

UNDERGRAD STUDENTS
2,475 full-time, 818 part-time. Students come from 29 states and territories; 52 other countries; 11% are from out of state; 23% Black or African American, non-Hispanic/Latino; 22% Hispanic/Latino; 3% Asian, non-Hispanic/Latino; 0.3% American Indian or Alaska Native, non-Hispanic/Latino; 0.3% Two or more races, non-Hispanic/Latino; 38% Race/ethnicity unknown; 9% international; 12% transferred in.

Freshmen:
Admission: 1,074 applied, 1,074 admitted, 364 enrolled.
Retention: 66% of full-time freshmen returned.

FACULTY
Student/faculty ratio: 23:1.

ACADEMICS
Calendar: semesters. *Degrees:* associate and bachelor's.

Special study options: academic remediation for entering students, accelerated degree program, adult/continuing education programs, advanced placement credit, cooperative education, distance learning, English as a second language, honors programs, independent study, internships, off-campus study, part-time degree program, study abroad.

Computers: 500 computers/terminals are available on campus for general student use. Students can access the following: campus intranet, computer help desk, free student e-mail accounts, online (class) grades, online (class) registration, online (class) schedules. Campuswide network is available. Wireless service is available via entire campus.

Library:***Books:*** 31,426 (physical), 168,797 (digital/electronic); *Serial titles:* 134 (physical), 72,544 (digital/electronic); *Databases:* 84.

STUDENT LIFE
Housing options: college housing not available.

Activities and organizations: student-run newspaper, International Student, Latino/Hispanic Club, Student Veterans of America, Sista Circle, Business Club.

Athletics Member USCAA. ***Intercollegiate sports:*** basketball M/W, cross-country running M/W, soccer M/W, tennis M/W.

Campus security: 24-hour emergency response devices.

Student services: personal/psychological counseling, veterans affairs office.

APPLYING
Options: electronic application, deferred entrance.

Application fee: $50.

Required: essay or personal statement, high school transcript. ***Recommended:*** interview.

Application deadlines: rolling (freshmen), rolling (out-of-state freshmen), rolling (transfers).

Notification: continuous (freshmen), continuous (out-of-state freshmen), continuous (transfers).

CONTACT
Michelle Gomez, Senior Director, High School Admissions, Berkeley College–New York City Campus, 3 East 43 Street, New York, NY 1007. *Phone:* 212-986-4343. *Toll-free phone:* 800-446-5400. *E-mail:* info@berkeleycollege.edu.

Berkeley College–White Plains Campus
White Plains, New York
http://www.berkeleycollege.edu/

- **Proprietary** 4-year, founded 1945
- **Suburban** campus with easy access to New York City
- **Coed** 403 undergraduate students, 89% full-time, 63% women, 37% men
- **Minimally difficult** entrance level, 98% of applicants were admitted

UNDERGRAD STUDENTS
359 full-time, 44 part-time. Students come from 17 states and territories; 8 other countries; 24% are from out of state; 21% Black or African American, non-Hispanic/Latino; 26% Hispanic/Latino; 3% Asian, non-Hispanic/Latino; 0.3% Two or more races, non-Hispanic/Latino; 34% Race/ethnicity unknown; 9% international; 7% transferred in; 20% live on campus.

Freshmen:
Admission: 258 applied, 254 admitted, 97 enrolled.
Retention: 62% of full-time freshmen returned.

FACULTY
Student/faculty ratio: 23:1.

ACADEMICS
Calendar: semesters. *Degrees:* associate and bachelor's.

Special study options: academic remediation for entering students, accelerated degree program, adult/continuing education programs, advanced placement credit, cooperative education, distance learning, honors programs, independent study, internships, off-campus study, part-time degree program, study abroad, summer session for credit.

Computers: 158 computers/terminals are available on campus for general student use. Students can access the following: campus intranet, computer help desk, free student e-mail accounts, online (class) grades, online (class) registration, online (class) schedules. Campuswide network is available. 100% of college-owned or -operated housing units are wired for high-speed Internet access. Wireless service is available via entire campus.

Library:***Books:*** 168,797 (digital/electronic); *Serial titles:* 72,544 (digital/electronic); *Databases:* 84.

STUDENT LIFE
Housing options: coed. Campus housing is university owned.

Activities and organizations: student-run newspaper.

Athletics Member USCAA. ***Intercollegiate sports:*** basketball M/W, cross-country running M/W, soccer M/W, tennis M/W.

Campus security: 24-hour emergency response devices, controlled dormitory access.

Student services: personal/psychological counseling, veterans affairs office.

APPLYING

Options: electronic application, deferred entrance.

Application fee: $50.

Required: essay or personal statement, high school transcript. ***Recommended:*** interview.

Application deadlines: rolling (freshmen), rolling (out-of-state freshmen), rolling (transfers).

Notification: continuous (freshmen), continuous (out-of-state freshmen), continuous (transfers).

CONTACT

Daniel Lapan, Director of Admissions, Berkeley College–White Plains Campus, 99 Church Street, White Plains, NY 10601. *Phone:* 914-694-1122. *Toll-free phone:* 800-446-5400. *E-mail:* info@berkeleycollege.edu.

Beth HaMedrash Shaarei Yosher Institute

Brooklyn, New York

http://www.bethhamedrashshaareiyosher.com/

CONTACT

Director of Admissions, Beth HaMedrash Shaarei Yosher Institute, 4102-10 Sixteenth Avenue, Brooklyn, NY 11204. *Phone:* 718-854-2290.

Beth Hatalmud Rabbinical College

Brooklyn, New York

CONTACT

Rabbi Osina, Director of Admissions, Beth Hatalmud Rabbinical College, 2127 Eighty-second Street, Brooklyn, NY 11214. *Phone:* 718-259-2525.

Beth Medrash Meor Yitzchok

Monsey, New York

http://www.bethmedrashmeoryitzchok.com/

CONTACT

Beth Medrash Meor Yitzchok, 85 Dykstras Way East, Monsey, NY 10952.

Bet Medrash Gadol Ateret Torah

Brooklyn, New York

http://www.betmedrashgadolaterettorah.com/

CONTACT

Bet Medrash Gadol Ateret Torah, 1750 East Fourth Street, Brooklyn, NY 11223.

Binghamton University, State University of New York

Binghamton, New York

http://www.binghamton.edu/

- **State-supported** university, founded 1946, part of State University of New York System
- **Suburban** 930-acre campus
- **Endowment** $109.3 million
- **Coed**
- **Very difficult** entrance level

FACULTY

Student/faculty ratio: 19:1.

ACADEMICS

Calendar: semesters. *Degrees:* bachelor's, master's, doctoral, and post-master's certificates.

Library: Glenn G. Bartle Library plus 4 others. *Books:* 2.3 million (physical), 1.1 million (digital/electronic); *Serial titles:* 683 (physical), 125,064 (digital/electronic); *Databases:* 358. Weekly public service hours: 136; study areas open 24 hours, 5–7 days a week; students can reserve study rooms.

STUDENT LIFE

Housing options: on-campus residence required for freshman year; coed, special housing for students with disabilities. Campus housing is university owned. Freshman campus housing is guaranteed.

Activities and organizations: drama/theater group, student-run newspaper, radio and television station, choral group, Finance Society, Student Volunteer Center, Habitat for Humanity, Pre-Medical Association, Sno-Cats Ski and Snowboard Club, national fraternities, national sororities.

Athletics Member NCAA. All Division I.

Campus security: 24-hour emergency response devices and patrols, student patrols, late-night transport/escort service, controlled dormitory access, only main gate open to traffic 12-5 am, emergency text system, self-defense workshops.

Student services: health clinic, personal/psychological counseling, women's center, legal services, veterans affairs office.

COSTS & FINANCIAL AID

Costs (2018–19) ***Tuition:*** state resident $6870 full-time, $286 per credit hour part-time; nonresident $23,710 full-time, $988 per credit hour part-time. Full-time tuition and fees vary according to program. Part-time tuition and fees vary according to course load and program. ***Required fees:*** $2938 full-time, $118 per credit hour part-time, $24 per term part-time. ***Room and board:*** $15,058; room only: $9882. Room and board charges vary according to board plan and housing facility.

Financial Aid Of all full-time matriculated undergraduates who enrolled in 2018, 9,850 applied for aid, 7,053 were judged to have need, 1,313 had their need fully met. 349 Federal Work-Study jobs (averaging $1942). In 2018, 452 non-need-based awards were made. ***Average percent of need met:*** 70. ***Average financial aid package:*** $14,129. ***Average need-based loan:*** $4736. ***Average need-based gift aid:*** $9655. ***Average non-need-based aid:*** $7644. ***Average indebtedness upon graduation:*** $27,022. ***Financial aid deadline:*** 5/1.

APPLYING

Standardized Tests *Required:* SAT or ACT (for admission).

Options: electronic application, early admission, early action, deferred entrance.

Application fee: $50.

Required: essay or personal statement, high school transcript, 1 letter of recommendation. ***Required for some:*** portfolio, audition.

CONTACT

Krista Medionte-Phillips, Director of Undergraduate Admissions, Binghamton University, State University of New York, PO Box 6001, Binghamton, NY 13902-6001. *Phone:* 607-777-2171. *Fax:* 607-777-4445. *E-mail:* admit@binghamton.edu.

Boricua College

New York, New York

http://www.boricuacollege.edu/

CONTACT

Mrs. Miriam Pfeffer, Director of Student Services, Boricua College, 186 North 6th Street, Brooklyn, NY 11211. *Phone:* 718-782-2200. *Fax:* 718-782-2025. *E-mail:* mpfeffer@boricuacollege.edu.

★ Brooklyn College of the City University of New York

Brooklyn, New York

http://www.brooklyn.cuny.edu/

CONTACT

Office of Admissions, Brooklyn College of the City University of New York, 2900 Bedford Avenue, West Quad Building, Room 222, Brooklyn, NY 11210-2889. *Phone:* 718-951-5001. *Fax:* 718-951-4506. *E-mail:* adminqry@brooklyn.cuny.edu.

A ★ indicates that the school has detailed information with a Premium Profile on Petersons.com.

Bryant & Stratton College–Amherst Campus

Clarence, New York

http://www.bryantstratton.edu/

CONTACT
Mr. Brian K. Dioguardi, Director of Admissions, Bryant & Stratton College–Amherst Campus, Audubon Business Center, 40 Hazelwood Drive, Amherst, NY 14228. *Phone:* 716-691-0012. *Fax:* 716-691-0012. *E-mail:* bkdioguardi@bryantstratton.edu.

Bryant & Stratton College–Buffalo Campus

Buffalo, New York

http://www.bryantstratton.edu/

CONTACT
Mr. Philip J. Struebel, Director of Admissions, Bryant & Stratton College–Buffalo Campus, 465 Main Street, Suite 400, Buffalo, NY 14203. *Phone:* 716-884-9120. *Fax:* 716-884-0091. *E-mail:* pjstruebel@bryantstratton.edu.

Bryant & Stratton College–Orchard Park Campus

Orchard Park, New York

http://www.bryantstratton.edu/

CONTACT
Bryant & Stratton College–Orchard Park Campus, 200 Redtail Road, Orchard Park, NY 14127. *Phone:* 716-677-9500.

Buffalo State College, State University of New York

Buffalo, New York

http://www.buffalostate.edu/

- **State-supported** comprehensive, founded 1867, part of State University of New York System
- **Urban** 115-acre campus
- **Endowment** $42.9 million
- **Coed**
- **Moderately difficult** entrance level

FACULTY
Student/faculty ratio: 16:1.

ACADEMICS
Calendar: semesters. *Degrees:* bachelor's, master's, and post-master's certificates.
Library: E. H. Butler Library plus 1 other.

STUDENT LIFE
Housing options: on-campus residence required through sophomore year; coed. Campus housing is university owned. Freshman campus housing is guaranteed.
Activities and organizations: drama/theater group, student-run newspaper, radio station, choral group, United Student Government, African-American Student Organization, Caribbean Student Organization, The Record, WBNY radio, national fraternities, national sororities.

Athletics Member NCAA. All Division III.

Campus security: 24-hour emergency response devices and patrols, student patrols, late-night transport/escort service, controlled dormitory access.

Student services: health clinic, personal/psychological counseling, women's center, legal services, veterans affairs office.

COSTS & FINANCIAL AID
Costs (2018–19) ***Tuition:*** state resident $6870 full-time, $286 per semester hour part-time; nonresident $16,650 full-time, $694 per semester hour part-time. Part-time tuition and fees vary according to course load. ***Required fees:*** $1340 full-time, $56 per semester hour part-time. ***Room and board:*** $14,050; room only: $8176. Room and board charges vary according to board plan, housing facility, and student level.

Financial Aid ***Average indebtedness upon graduation:*** $26,495. ***Financial aid deadline:*** 5/1.

APPLYING
Standardized Tests *Required:* SAT and SAT Subject Tests or ACT (for admission). *Recommended:* SAT (for admission).

Options: electronic application, early admission, deferred entrance.

Application fee: $50.

Required: high school transcript, minimum 3.0 GPA. ***Required for some:*** essay or personal statement, interview.

CONTACT
Ms. Carmella Thompson, Director of Admissions, Buffalo State College, State University of New York, 110 Moot Hall, Buffalo, NY 14222. *Phone:* 716-878-4017. *Fax:* 716-878-6100. *E-mail:* admissions@buffalostate.edu.

Canisius College

Buffalo, New York

http://www.canisius.edu/

- **Independent Roman Catholic (Jesuit)** comprehensive, founded 1870
- **Urban** 72-acre campus with easy access to Buffalo-Niagara Falls
- **Endowment** $133.9 million
- **Coed** 2,256 undergraduate students, 96% full-time, 48% women, 52% men
- **Moderately difficult** entrance level, 79% of applicants were admitted

UNDERGRAD STUDENTS
2,166 full-time, 90 part-time. Students come from 36 states and territories; 18 other countries; 11% are from out of state; 9% Black or African American, non-Hispanic/Latino; 6% Hispanic/Latino; 3% Asian, non-Hispanic/Latino; 0.2% Native Hawaiian or other Pacific Islander, non-Hispanic/Latino; 0.3% American Indian or Alaska Native, non-Hispanic/Latino; 2% Two or more races, non-Hispanic/Latino; 4% Race/ethnicity unknown; 4% international; 4% transferred in; 42% live on campus.

Freshmen:
Admission: 3,549 applied, 2,793 admitted, 485 enrolled. ***Average high school GPA:*** ####. ***Test scores:*** SAT evidence-based reading and writing scores over 500: 87%; SAT math scores over 500: 84%; ACT scores over 18: 92%; SAT evidence-based reading and writing scores over 600: 40%; SAT math scores over 600: 40%; ACT scores over 24: 55%; SAT evidence-based reading and writing scores over 700: 5%; SAT math scores over 700: 7%; ACT scores over 30: 9%.

Retention: 85% of full-time freshmen returned.

FACULTY
Total: 368, 40% full-time, 57% with terminal degrees.

Student/faculty ratio: 11:1.

ACADEMICS
Calendar: semesters. *Degrees:* associate, bachelor's, master's, post-master's, and postbachelor's certificates.

Special study options: academic remediation for entering students, adult/continuing education programs, advanced placement credit, cooperative education, distance learning, double majors, English as a second language, honors programs, independent study, internships, off-campus study, part-time degree program, services for LD students, study abroad, summer session for credit. ***ROTC:*** Army (b).

Unusual degree programs: 3-2 business administration; engineering with University at Buffalo, the State University of New York.

Computers: 700 computers/terminals are available on campus for general student use. Students can access the following: computer help desk, free student e-mail accounts, online (class) grades, online (class) registration, online (class) schedules, online accounts. Campuswide network is available. 100% of college-owned or -operated housing units are wired for high-speed Internet access. Wireless service is available via entire campus.

Library: Andrew L. Bouwhuis Library plus 1 other. *Books:* 222,252 (physical), 1.7 million (digital/electronic); *Serial titles:* 1,143 (physical),

303,210 (digital/electronic); *Databases:* 108. Weekly public service hours: 110; students can reserve study rooms.

STUDENT LIFE
Housing options: on-campus residence required through sophomore year; coed, special housing for students with disabilities. Campus housing is university owned. Freshman applicants given priority for college housing.

Activities and organizations: drama/theater group, student-run newspaper, radio and television station, choral group, Residence Hall Association, UNITY, Afro-American Society, Project Conservation, FUSION Gaming Society, national fraternities, national sororities.

Athletics Member NCAA. All Division I. ***Intercollegiate sports:*** baseball M(s), basketball M(s)/W(s), cross-country running M(s)/W(s), equestrian sports W(c), golf M(s), ice hockey M(s), lacrosse M(s)/W(s), rugby M(c)/W(c), soccer M(s)/W(s), softball W(s), swimming and diving M(s)/W(s), track and field M(s)/W(s), volleyball M(c)/W(s). ***Intramural sports:*** basketball M/W, bowling M(c)/W(c), cheerleading M(c)/W(c), crew M(c)/W(c), fencing M(c)/W(c), field hockey W(c), golf M(c)/W(c), ice hockey M(c)/W(c), lacrosse M(c), racquetball M/W, riflery M(c)/W(c), skiing (downhill) M(c)/W(c), soccer M/W, softball M/W, tennis M/W, track and field M(c)/W(c), ultimate Frisbee M(c)/W(c), volleyball M/W, wrestling M(c).

Campus security: 24-hour emergency response devices and patrols, late-night transport/escort service, controlled dormitory access.

Student services: health clinic, personal/psychological counseling, veterans affairs office.

COSTS & FINANCIAL AID
Costs (2019–20) ***Comprehensive fee:*** $40,844 includes full-time tuition ($27,940), mandatory fees ($1488), and room and board ($11,416). Part-time tuition: $900 per credit hour. ***Required fees:*** $25 per credit hour part-time, $85 per term part-time. ***College room only:*** $5880.

Financial Aid Of all full-time matriculated undergraduates who enrolled in 2018, 1,764 applied for aid, 1,550 were judged to have need, 362 had their need fully met. 310 Federal Work-Study jobs (averaging $1905). In 2018, 499 non-need-based awards were made. ***Average percent of need met:*** 75. ***Average financial aid package:*** $22,679. ***Average need-based loan:*** $4388. ***Average need-based gift aid:*** $17,184. ***Average non-need-based aid:*** $11,200. ***Average indebtedness upon graduation:*** $34,561. ***Financial aid deadline:*** 5/1.

APPLYING
Standardized Tests *Required:* SAT or ACT (for admission).

Options: electronic application, early admission, early action, deferred entrance.

Required: high school transcript, minimum 2.0 GPA. ***Recommended:*** essay or personal statement, 1 letter of recommendation, interview.

Notification: continuous (freshmen), continuous (transfers).

CONTACT
Mr. Justin P. Rogers, Director of Undergraduate Admissions, Canisius College, 2001 Main Street, Buffalo, NY 14208-1098. *Phone:* 716-888-2200. *Toll-free phone:* 800-843-1517. *Fax:* 716-888-3230. *E-mail:* admissions@canisius.edu.

Cazenovia College

Cazenovia, New York

http://www.cazenovia.edu/

- **Independent** 4-year, founded 1824
- **Small-town** 40-acre campus with easy access to Syracuse
- **Coed**
- **Minimally difficult** entrance level

FACULTY
Student/faculty ratio: 10:1.

ACADEMICS
Calendar: semesters. *Degrees:* certificates, associate, and bachelor's.
Library: Witheral Library. Students can reserve study rooms.

STUDENT LIFE
Housing options: on-campus residence required through junior year; coed, men-only, women-only, special housing for students with disabilities. Campus housing is university owned and leased by the school. Freshman campus housing is guaranteed.

Activities and organizations: drama/theater group, student-run newspaper, radio station, choral group, Activities Board, Multicultural Student Group, performing arts, student radio station, yearbook.

Athletics Member NCAA. All Division III.

Campus security: 24-hour emergency response devices and patrols, late-night transport/escort service, controlled dormitory access.

Student services: health clinic, personal/psychological counseling.

COSTS & FINANCIAL AID
Costs (2018–19) ***Comprehensive fee:*** $48,594 includes full-time tuition ($34,024), mandatory fees ($606), and room and board ($13,964). Full-time tuition and fees vary according to class time, course load, and program. Part-time tuition: $720 per credit hour. Part-time tuition and fees vary according to class time and course load. ***College room only:*** $7810. Room and board charges vary according to board plan and housing facility.

Financial Aid Of all full-time matriculated undergraduates who enrolled in 2017, 725 applied for aid, 725 were judged to have need, 137 had their need fully met. In 2017, 62 non-need-based awards were made. ***Average percent of need met:*** 85. ***Average financial aid package:*** $31,548. ***Average need-based loan:*** $9015. ***Average need-based gift aid:*** $38,809. ***Average non-need-based aid:*** $16,797. ***Average indebtedness upon graduation:*** $35,863.

APPLYING
Standardized Tests *Recommended:* SAT or ACT (for admission).

Options: electronic application, deferred entrance.

Required: high school transcript, 1 letter of recommendation. ***Recommended:*** essay or personal statement, minimum 2.0 GPA, interview, portfolio for art and design students.

CONTACT
Office of Admission and Enrollment Services, Cazenovia College, 3 Sullivan Street, Cazenovia, NY 13035. *Phone:* 315-655-7208. *Toll-free phone:* 800-654-3210. *Fax:* 315-655-4860. *E-mail:* admission@cazenovia.edu.

Central Yeshiva Beth Joseph

Brooklyn, New York

http://www.centralyeshivabethjoseph.com

CONTACT
Central Yeshiva Beth Joseph, 1502 Avenue N, Brooklyn, NY 11230.

Central Yeshiva Tomchei Tmimim-Lubavitch

Brooklyn, New York

CONTACT
Director of Admissions, Central Yeshiva Tomchei Tmimim-Lubavitch, 841-853 Ocean Parkway, Brooklyn, NY 11230. *Phone:* 718-859-7600.

City College of the City University of New York

New York, New York

http://www.ccny.cuny.edu/

- **State and locally supported** comprehensive, founded 1847, part of City University of New York System
- **Urban** 35-acre campus with easy access to New York City
- **Coed**
- **Moderately difficult** entrance level

FACULTY
Student/faculty ratio: 15:1.

ACADEMICS
Calendar: semesters. *Degrees:* bachelor's, master's, doctoral, and post-master's certificates.
Library: Morris Raphael Cohen Library plus 8 others. *Books:* 950,000 (physical), 980,000 (digital/electronic); *Serial titles:* 118,000

(digital/electronic); *Databases:* 308. Weekly public service hours: 99; students can reserve study rooms.

STUDENT LIFE

Housing options: coed. Campus housing is provided by a third party.

Activities and organizations: drama/theater group, student-run newspaper, radio station, choral group, Latin American Engineering Student Assoc./Society of Hispanic Professional Engineers, National Society of Black Engineers, Bangladesh Student Association, Salsa-Mambo, InterVarsity Christian Fellowship, national fraternities.

Athletics Member NCAA. All Division III.

Campus security: 24-hour patrols, late-night transport/escort service, controlled dormitory access.

Student services: health clinic, personal/psychological counseling, veterans affairs office.

COSTS

Costs (2018–19) ***Tuition:*** state resident $6730 full-time, $295 per credit part-time; nonresident $18,000 full-time, $600 per credit part-time. ***Required fees:*** $127 full-time, $40 per term part-time.

APPLYING

Standardized Tests *Required:* SAT or ACT (for admission).

Options: early admission, deferred entrance.

Application fee: $65.

Required: high school transcript. ***Required for some:*** essay or personal statement, letters of recommendation, creative challenge for architecture, supplemental application for engineering.

CONTACT

City College of the City University of New York, 160 Convent Avenue, New York, NY 10031-9198. *Phone:* 212-650-6977.

Clarkson University

Potsdam, New York

http://www.clarkson.edu/

- **Independent** university, founded 1896
- **Small-town** 640-acre campus
- **Endowment** $198.3 million
- **Coed** 3,091 undergraduate students, 98% full-time, 31% women, 69% men
- **Very difficult** entrance level, 71% of applicants were admitted

UNDERGRAD STUDENTS

3,016 full-time, 75 part-time. Students come from 41 states and territories; 35 other countries; 29% are from out of state; 2% Black or African American, non-Hispanic/Latino; 5% Hispanic/Latino; 4% Asian, non-Hispanic/Latino; 0.3% American Indian or Alaska Native, non-Hispanic/Latino; 4% Two or more races, non-Hispanic/Latino; 2% Race/ethnicity unknown; 2% international; 3% transferred in; 80% live on campus.

Freshmen:

Admission: 6,885 applied, 4,894 admitted, 797 enrolled. ***Average high school GPA:*** 3.7. ***Test scores:*** SAT evidence-based reading and writing scores over 500: 96%; SAT math scores over 500: 98%; ACT scores over 18: 100%; SAT evidence-based reading and writing scores over 600: 62%; SAT math scores over 600: 72%; ACT scores over 24: 80%; SAT evidence-based reading and writing scores over 700: 12%; SAT math scores over 700: 22%; ACT scores over 30: 27%.

Retention: 89% of full-time freshmen returned.

FACULTY

Total: 357, 71% full-time, 76% with terminal degrees.

Student/faculty ratio: 13:1.

ACADEMICS

Calendar: semesters. *Degrees:* bachelor's, master's, doctoral, and postbachelor's certificates.

Special study options: accelerated degree program, advanced placement credit, cooperative education, distance learning, double majors, English as a second language, honors programs, independent study, internships, off-campus study, part-time degree program, services for LD students, student-designed majors, study abroad, summer session for credit. ***ROTC:*** Army (b), Air Force (b).

Unusual degree programs: 3-2 engineering.

Computers: 350 computers/terminals and 6,000 ports are available on campus for general student use. Students can access the following: campus intranet, computer help desk, free student e-mail accounts, online (class) grades, online (class) registration, online (class) schedules. Campuswide network is available. 100% of college-owned or -operated housing units are wired for high-speed Internet access. Wireless service is available via entire campus.

Library: Harriet Call Burnap Memorial Library plus 1 other. *Books:* 116,048 (physical), 208,608 (digital/electronic); *Serial titles:* 9,525 (physical), 50,689 (digital/electronic); *Databases:* 134. Weekly public service hours: 97; students can reserve study rooms.

STUDENT LIFE

Housing options: on-campus residence required through senior year; coed, men-only, women-only, special housing for students with disabilities. Campus housing is university owned. Freshman campus housing is guaranteed.

Activities and organizations: drama/theater group, student-run newspaper, radio and television station, choral group, Ski & Snowboard Club, Outing Club, Student Association for Engineering Management, Institute for Electrical and Electronics Engineers, Pep Band, national fraternities, national sororities.

Athletics Member NCAA. All Division III except men's and women's ice hockey (Division I). ***Intercollegiate sports:*** baseball M, basketball M/W, cross-country running M/W, golf M, ice hockey M(s)/W(s), lacrosse M/W, skiing (cross-country) M/W, skiing (downhill) M/W, soccer M/W, softball W, swimming and diving M/W, volleyball W. ***Intramural sports:*** baseball M(c)/W(c), basketball M/W, bowling M(c)/W(c), crew M(c)/W(c), equestrian sports M(c)/W(c), football M/W, golf M(c)/W(c), ice hockey M/W, lacrosse M(c)/W(c), racquetball M(c)/W(c), rowing M(c)/W(c), rugby M(c)/W(c), skiing (cross-country) M(c)/W(c), skiing (downhill) M(c)/W(c), soccer M/W, softball M/W, table tennis M(c)/W(c), tennis M(c)/W(c), ultimate Frisbee M(c)/W(c), volleyball M/W, wrestling M(c).

Campus security: 24-hour emergency response devices and patrols, controlled dormitory access.

Student services: health clinic, personal/psychological counseling, legal services, veterans affairs office.

COSTS & FINANCIAL AID

Costs (2019–20) ***Comprehensive fee:*** $66,468 includes full-time tuition ($49,858), mandatory fees ($1270), and room and board ($15,340). Part-time tuition: $1662 per credit hour. ***College room only:*** $8240.

Financial Aid Of all full-time matriculated undergraduates who enrolled in 2018, 2,640 applied for aid, 2,443 were judged to have need, 573 had their need fully met. 1,543 Federal Work-Study jobs (averaging $1800). 61 state and other part-time jobs (averaging $11,772). In 2018, 458 non-need-based awards were made. ***Average percent of need met:*** 90. ***Average financial aid package:*** $45,326. ***Average need-based loan:*** $4720. ***Average need-based gift aid:*** $33,485. ***Average non-need-based aid:*** $24,913. ***Average indebtedness upon graduation:*** $31,000. ***Financial aid deadline:*** 3/1.

APPLYING

Standardized Tests *Required:* SAT or ACT (for admission). *Recommended:* SAT Subject Tests (for admission).

Options: electronic application, early admission, early decision, deferred entrance.

Application fee: $50.

Required: essay or personal statement, high school transcript, 2 letters of recommendation. ***Recommended:*** interview.

Application deadlines: 1/15 (freshmen), rolling (transfers).

Early decision deadline: 12/1.

Notification: 2/1 (freshmen), continuous (transfers), 1/1 (early decision).

CONTACT

Trish Dobbs, Director of Admissions, Clarkson University, 8 Clarkson Ave, Box 5605, Potsdam, NY 13699. *Phone:* 315-268-6480. *Toll-free phone:* 800-527-6577. *Fax:* 315-268-7647. *E-mail:* admissions@clarkson.edu.

Colgate University

Hamilton, New York

http://www.colgate.edu/

- **Independent** comprehensive, founded 1819
- **Small-town** 575-acre campus with easy access to Syracuse, Utica
- **Coed** 2,958 undergraduate students, 99% full-time, 55% women, 45% men
- **Most difficult** entrance level, 25% of applicants were admitted

UNDERGRAD STUDENTS
2,936 full-time, 22 part-time. Students come from 50 states and territories; 51 other countries; 76% are from out of state; 5% Black or African American, non-Hispanic/Latino; 9% Hispanic/Latino; 5% Asian, non-Hispanic/Latino; 0.1% Native Hawaiian or other Pacific Islander, non-Hispanic/Latino; 0.1% American Indian or Alaska Native, non-Hispanic/Latino; 4% Two or more races, non-Hispanic/Latino; 3% Race/ethnicity unknown; 9% international; 0.7% transferred in; 92% live on campus.

Freshmen:
Admission: 9,716 applied, 2,422 admitted, 815 enrolled. ***Average high school GPA:*** 3.7. ***Test scores:*** SAT evidence-based reading and writing scores over 500: 100%; SAT math scores over 500: 100%; ACT scores over 18: 100%; SAT evidence-based reading and writing scores over 600: 94%; SAT math scores over 600: 94%; ACT scores over 24: 99%; SAT evidence-based reading and writing scores over 700: 50%; SAT math scores over 700: 62%; ACT scores over 30: 84%.

Retention: 94% of full-time freshmen returned.

FACULTY
Total: 355, 94% full-time, 94% with terminal degrees.

Student/faculty ratio: 9:1.

ACADEMICS
Calendar: semesters. *Degrees:* bachelor's and master's.

Special study options: advanced placement credit, double majors, independent study, internships, off-campus study, services for LD students, student-designed majors, study abroad. ***ROTC:*** Army (c).

Unusual degree programs: 3-2 engineering with Columbia University, Rensselaer Polytechnic Institute, Washington University in St. Louis.

Computers: 150 computers/terminals and 12,000 ports are available on campus for general student use. Students can access the following: campus intranet, computer help desk, free student e-mail accounts, online (class) grades, online (class) registration, online (class) schedules, software applications. Campuswide network is available. 100% of college-owned or -operated housing units are wired for high-speed Internet access. Wireless service is available via entire campus.
Library: Case Library and Geyer Center for Information Technology plus 1 other. *Books:* 749,143 (physical), 444,977 (digital/electronic); *Serial titles:* 4,085 (physical), 145,811 (digital/electronic); *Databases:* 305. Study areas open 24 hours, 5–7 days a week; students can reserve study rooms.

STUDENT LIFE
Housing options: on-campus residence required through junior year; coed, cooperative, special housing for students with disabilities. Campus housing is university owned. Freshman campus housing is guaranteed.

Activities and organizations: drama/theater group, student-run newspaper, radio and television station, choral group, COVE (35+ community service groups), Student Government Association, Cultural/ethnic interest groups, Student communications/publications (including WCRU radio station), Club sports/Outdoor Education, national fraternities, national sororities.

Athletics Member NCAA. All Division I. ***Intercollegiate sports:*** badminton M(c)/W(c), baseball M(c), basketball M(s)/W(s), bowling M(c)/W(c), cheerleading M(c)/W(c), cross-country running M/W, equestrian sports M(c)/W(c), fencing M(c)/W(c), field hockey W(s), football M(s), golf M, ice hockey M(s)/W(s), lacrosse M(s)/W(s), rowing M/W, rugby M(c)/W(c), sailing M(c)/W(c), skiing (cross-country) M(c)/W(c), skiing (downhill) M(c)/W(c), soccer M(s)/W(s), softball W(s), squash M(c)/W(c), swimming and diving M/W(s), table tennis M(c)/W(c), tennis M/W, track and field M/W, triathlon M(c)/W(c), ultimate Frisbee M(c)/W(c), volleyball W(s), water polo M(c)/W(c). ***Intramural sports:*** basketball M/W, football M, lacrosse M(c)/W(c), racquetball M/W, rock climbing M(c)/W(c), soccer M(c)/W(c), softball M/W, swimming and diving M(c)/W(c), table tennis M/W, tennis M(c)/W(c), volleyball M(c)/W(c).

Campus security: 24-hour emergency response devices and patrols, student patrols, late-night transport/escort service, controlled dormitory access.

Student services: health clinic, personal/psychological counseling, women's center, legal services.

COSTS & FINANCIAL AID
Costs (2019–20) ***One-time required fee:*** $50. ***Comprehensive fee:*** $72,585 includes full-time tuition ($57,695), mandatory fees ($350), and room and board ($14,540). ***College room only:*** $7020. ***Payment plan:*** tuition prepayment.

Financial Aid Of all full-time matriculated undergraduates who enrolled in 2018, 1,154 applied for aid, 1,016 were judged to have need, 1,014 had their need fully met. 512 Federal Work-Study jobs (averaging $2356). 293 state and other part-time jobs (averaging $2408). ***Average percent of need met:*** 100. ***Average financial aid package:*** $55,110. ***Average need-based loan:*** $3481. ***Average need-based gift aid:*** $50,922. ***Average indebtedness upon graduation:*** $24,243. ***Financial aid deadline:*** 1/15.

APPLYING
Standardized Tests *Required:* SAT or ACT (for admission).

Options: electronic application, early decision, deferred entrance.

Application fee: $60.

Required: essay or personal statement, high school transcript, 3 letters of recommendation, Colgate supplement.

Application deadlines: 1/15 (freshmen), 3/15 (transfers).

Early decision deadline: 11/15.

Notification: 4/1 (freshmen), 5/1 (transfers), 12/15 (early decision plan 1), rolling (early decision plan 2).

CONTACT
Ms. Tara E.W. Bubble, Dean of Admission, Colgate University, Colgate Office of Admission, 13 Oak Drive, Hamilton, NY 13346-1383. *Phone:* 315-228-7401. *Fax:* 315-228-7544. *E-mail:* admission@colgate.edu.

The College at Brockport, State University of New York

Brockport, New York

http://www.brockport.edu/

- **State-supported** comprehensive, founded 1867, part of State University of New York System
- **Small-town** 464-acre campus with easy access to Rochester
- **Endowment** $13.8 million
- **Coed** 7,057 undergraduate students, 90% full-time, 57% women, 43% men
- **Moderately difficult** entrance level, 53% of applicants were admitted

UNDERGRAD STUDENTS
6,343 full-time, 714 part-time. Students come from 25 states and territories; 20 other countries; 2% are from out of state; 11% Black or African American, non-Hispanic/Latino; 8% Hispanic/Latino; 2% Asian, non-Hispanic/Latino; 0.3% American Indian or Alaska Native, non-Hispanic/Latino; 3% Two or more races, non-Hispanic/Latino; 5% Race/ethnicity unknown; 1% international; 13% transferred in; 37% live on campus.

Freshmen:
Admission: 10,535 applied, 5,617 admitted, 1,270 enrolled. ***Average high school GPA:*** 2.9. ***Test scores:*** SAT evidence-based reading and writing scores over 500: 82%; SAT math scores over 500: 84%; ACT scores over 18: 92%; SAT evidence-based reading and writing scores over 600: 24%; SAT math scores over 600: 23%; ACT scores over 24: 35%; SAT evidence-based reading and writing scores over 700: 1%; SAT math scores over 700: 2%; ACT scores over 30: 3%.

Retention: 88% of full-time freshmen returned.

FACULTY
Total: 626, 52% full-time, 55% with terminal degrees.

Student/faculty ratio: 17:1.

ACADEMICS
Calendar: semesters. *Degrees:* certificates, bachelor's, master's, post-master's, and postbachelor's certificates.

Special study options: accelerated degree program, advanced placement credit, cooperative education, distance learning, double majors, English as a second language, freshman honors college, honors programs, independent study, internships, off-campus study, part-time degree program, services for LD students, student-designed majors, study abroad, summer session for credit. ***ROTC:*** Army (b), Navy (c), Air Force (c).

Unusual degree programs: 3-2 business administration; nursing; social work; Biology and Pharm-D with University of Buffalo, accelerated MBA with Rochester Institute of Technology, Doctor of Physical Therapy with SUNY Upstate Medical..

Computers: 1,000 computers/terminals are available on campus for general student use. Students can access the following: campus intranet, computer help desk, free student e-mail accounts, online (class) grades, online (class) registration, online (class) schedules. Campuswide network is available. 100% of college-owned or -operated housing units are wired for high-speed Internet access. Wireless service is available via entire campus.

Library: Drake Memorial Library plus 1 other. *Books:* 500,461 (physical), 185,000 (digital/electronic); *Serial titles:* 4,747 (physical), 113,396 (digital/electronic); *Databases:* 270. Weekly public service hours: 93; students can reserve study rooms.

STUDENT LIFE
Housing options: on-campus residence required through sophomore year; coed, special housing for students with disabilities. Campus housing is university owned. Freshman campus housing is guaranteed.

Activities and organizations: drama/theater group, student-run newspaper, radio and television station, choral group, Habitat for Humanity, Brockport Pre-Professional Health Club, Brockport Psychology Club, Student Nursing Organization, Caribbean Student Association, national fraternities, national sororities.

Athletics Member NCAA, NAIA, USCAA. All NCAA Division III. ***Intercollegiate sports:*** baseball M, basketball M/W, cross-country running M/W, field hockey W, football M, gymnastics W, ice hockey M, lacrosse M/W, soccer M/W, softball W, swimming and diving M/W, tennis W, track and field M/W, ultimate Frisbee W, volleyball W, wrestling M. ***Intramural sports:*** baseball M(c), basketball M/W, cheerleading M(c)/W(c), cross-country running M(c)/W(c), equestrian sports M(c)/W(c), gymnastics M(c)/W(c), ice hockey M(c)/W(c), lacrosse M(c), rugby M(c)/W(c), soccer M/W, softball W(c), swimming and diving M(c)/W(c), table tennis M/W, tennis M(c)/W(c), track and field M(c), ultimate Frisbee M(c)/W(c), volleyball M/W, weight lifting M(c)/W(c).

Campus security: 24-hour emergency response devices and patrols, student patrols, late-night transport/escort service, controlled dormitory access.

Student services: health clinic, personal/psychological counseling, women's center, legal services, veterans affairs office.

COSTS & FINANCIAL AID
Costs (2018–19) ***Tuition:*** state resident $6670 full-time, $278 per credit hour part-time; nonresident $16,320 full-time, $680 per credit hour part-time. Part-time tuition and fees vary according to course load. ***Required fees:*** $1484 full-time, $61 per credit hour part-time, $1484 per year part-time. ***Room and board:*** $12,904; room only: $7974. Room and board charges vary according to board plan and housing facility. ***Payment plans:*** installment, deferred payment. ***Waivers:*** employees or children of employees.

Financial Aid Of all full-time matriculated undergraduates who enrolled in 2017, 4,760 applied for aid, 4,036 were judged to have need, 550 had their need fully met. 459 Federal Work-Study jobs (averaging $2721). 870 state and other part-time jobs (averaging $2036). In 2017, 128 non-need-based awards were made. ***Average percent of need met:*** 70. ***Average financial aid package:*** $11,646. ***Average need-based loan:*** $5037. ***Average need-based gift aid:*** $6930. ***Average non-need-based aid:*** $5151. ***Average indebtedness upon graduation:*** $30,472.

APPLYING
Standardized Tests *Required:* SAT or ACT (for admission). *Recommended:* SAT (for admission), ACT (for admission).

Options: electronic application, deferred entrance.

Application fee: $50.

Required: high school transcript, minimum 2.5 GPA, 1 letter of recommendation. ***Required for some:*** essay or personal statement, interview. ***Recommended:*** essay or personal statement, minimum 3.0 GPA.

Application deadlines: 8/1 (freshmen), 8/1 (out-of-state freshmen), 8/1 (transfers).

Notification: continuous (freshmen), continuous (out-of-state freshmen), continuous (transfers).

CONTACT
Mr. Robert J. Wyant, Director of UG Admissions, The College at Brockport, State University of New York, 350 New Campus Drive, Brockport, NY 14420-2997. *Phone:* 585-395-2751. *Fax:* 585-395-2401. *E-mail:* rwyant@brockport.edu.

College of Mount Saint Vincent
Riverdale, New York
http://www.mountsaintvincent.edu/

- **Independent** comprehensive, founded 1911
- **Suburban** 70-acre campus with easy access to New York City
- **Coed**
- **Moderately difficult** entrance level

FACULTY
Student/faculty ratio: 13:1.

ACADEMICS
Calendar: semesters. *Degrees:* bachelor's, master's, and post-master's certificates.
Library: Elizabeth Seton Library.

STUDENT LIFE
Housing options: coed, special housing for students with disabilities. Campus housing is university owned. Freshman campus housing is guaranteed.

Activities and organizations: drama/theater group, student-run newspaper, radio and television station, choral group.

Athletics Member NCAA. All Division III.

Campus security: 24-hour emergency response devices and patrols, late-night transport/escort service, controlled dormitory access, emergency call boxes.

Student services: health clinic, personal/psychological counseling.

COSTS & FINANCIAL AID
Costs (2018–19) ***Comprehensive fee:*** $48,680 includes full-time tuition ($36,700), mandatory fees ($1480), and room and board ($10,500). Full-time tuition and fees vary according to student level. Part-time tuition: $1060 per credit hour. ***Required fees:*** $45 per credit hour part-time.

Financial Aid Of all full-time matriculated undergraduates who enrolled in 2013, 1,362 applied for aid, 1,250 were judged to have need, 169 had their need fully met. In 2013, 112 non-need-based awards were made. ***Average percent of need met:*** 68. ***Average financial aid package:*** $19,829. ***Average need-based loan:*** $4333. ***Average need-based gift aid:*** $10,243. ***Average non-need-based aid:*** $12,904.

APPLYING
Standardized Tests *Required:* SAT or ACT (for admission).

Options: electronic application, early admission, early action, deferred entrance.

Required: essay or personal statement, high school transcript, minimum 2.0 GPA. ***Required for some:*** interview. ***Recommended:*** 2 letters of recommendation, interview.

CONTACT
College of Mount Saint Vincent, 6301 Riverdale Avenue, Riverdale, NY 10471-1093. *Phone:* 718-405-3268. *Toll-free phone:* 800-665-CMSV.

The College of New Rochelle

New Rochelle, New York

http://www.cnr.edu/

- **Independent** comprehensive, founded 1904
- **Suburban** 20-acre campus with easy access to New York City
- **Endowment** $2.3 million
- **Coed**
- **Moderately difficult** entrance level

FACULTY

Student/faculty ratio: 10:1.

ACADEMICS

Calendar: semesters. *Degrees:* bachelor's, master's, post-master's, and postbachelor's certificates (also offers a non-traditional adult program with significant enrollment not reflected in profile).
Library: Gill Library plus 1 other. *Books:* 93,999 (physical), 153,914 (digital/electronic); *Serial titles:* 886 (physical), 94,336 (digital/electronic); *Databases:* 133. Weekly public service hours: 86; students can reserve study rooms.

STUDENT LIFE

Housing options: coed, special housing for students with disabilities. Campus housing is university owned. Freshman campus housing is guaranteed.

Activities and organizations: choral group, Music Ensembles, CNR Model United Nations, Student Nurses Association, Campus Ministry, Student Government.

Athletics Member NCAA. All Division III except soccer (Division II).

Campus security: 24-hour emergency response devices and patrols, late-night transport/escort service, controlled dormitory access, 24-hour monitored security cameras at residence hall entrances.

Student services: health clinic, personal/psychological counseling.

COSTS

Costs (2018–19) ***Comprehensive fee:*** $52,322 includes full-time tuition ($36,180), mandatory fees ($1580), and room and board ($14,562). Full-time tuition and fees vary according to course load, degree level, and program. Part-time tuition: $1206 per credit. Part-time tuition and fees vary according to course load, degree level, and program. ***Room and board:*** Room and board charges vary according to housing facility.

APPLYING

Standardized Tests *Required:* SAT or ACT (for admission).

Options: electronic application, deferred entrance.

Application fee: $35.

Required: high school transcript. ***Recommended:*** essay or personal statement, 1 letter of recommendation, interview.

CONTACT

Mr. Brian Sondey, Admissions Director, The College of New Rochelle, 29 Castle Place, New Rochelle, NY 10805-2339. *Phone:* 914-654-5921. *Toll-free phone:* 800-933-5923. *Fax:* 914-654-5464. *E-mail:* bsondey@cnr.edu.

The College of Saint Rose

Albany, New York

http://www.strose.edu/

- **Independent** comprehensive, founded 1920
- **Urban** 49-acre campus
- **Endowment** $44.7 million
- **Coed** 2,489 undergraduate students, 97% full-time, 67% women, 33% men
- **Moderately difficult** entrance level, 87% of applicants were admitted

UNDERGRAD STUDENTS

2,402 full-time, 87 part-time. Students come from 34 states and territories; 47 other countries; 12% are from out of state; 17% Black or African American, non-Hispanic/Latino; 7% Hispanic/Latino; 3% Asian, non-Hispanic/Latino; 0.2% Native Hawaiian or other Pacific Islander, non-Hispanic/Latino; 0.5% American Indian or Alaska Native, non-Hispanic/Latino; 12% Two or more races, non-Hispanic/Latino; 4% Race/ethnicity unknown; 3% international; 7% transferred in; 49% live on campus.

Freshmen:
Admission: 6,408 applied, 5,597 admitted, 616 enrolled. ***Average high school GPA:*** 3.3. ***Test scores:*** SAT evidence-based reading and writing scores over 500: 82%; SAT math scores over 500: 77%; ACT scores over 18: 95%; SAT evidence-based reading and writing scores over 600: 28%; SAT math scores over 600: 24%; ACT scores over 24: 39%; SAT evidence-based reading and writing scores over 700: 2%; SAT math scores over 700: 3%; ACT scores over 30: 6%.

Retention: 75% of full-time freshmen returned.

FACULTY

Total: 325, 53% full-time, 66% with terminal degrees.

Student/faculty ratio: 14:1.

ACADEMICS

Calendar: semesters. *Degrees:* certificates, bachelor's, master's, post-master's, and postbachelor's certificates.

Special study options: academic remediation for entering students, accelerated degree program, advanced placement credit, double majors, English as a second language, independent study, internships, off-campus study, part-time degree program, services for LD students, student-designed majors, study abroad, summer session for credit. ***ROTC:*** Army (c), Air Force (c).

Unusual degree programs: 3-2 engineering with Rensselaer Polytechnic Institute; clinical laboratory science, biology/cytotechnology with Albany College of Pharmacy.

Computers: 801 computers/terminals and 4,661 ports are available on campus for general student use. Students can access the following: computer help desk, free student e-mail accounts, online (class) grades, online (class) registration, online (class) schedules. Campuswide network is available. 100% of college-owned or -operated housing units are wired for high-speed Internet access. Wireless service is available via entire campus.
Library: Neil Hellman Library plus 2 others. *Books:* 241,000 (physical), 116,500 (digital/electronic); *Serial titles:* 1,201 (physical), 10 (digital/electronic); *Databases:* 104. Weekly public service hours: 73; students can reserve study rooms.

STUDENT LIFE

Housing options: on-campus residence required for freshman year; coed, men-only, women-only, special housing for students with disabilities. Campus housing is university owned and leased by the school. Freshman campus housing is guaranteed.

Activities and organizations: drama/theater group, student-run newspaper, radio and television station, choral group, Student Association, Student Events Board, Spectrum-ALANA Student Union, Colleges Against Cancer, Music and Entertainment Industry Student Association.

Athletics Member NCAA. All Division II. ***Intercollegiate sports:*** baseball M(s), basketball M(s)/W(s), cross-country running M(s)/W(s), golf M(s)/W(s), lacrosse M(s)/W(s), soccer M(s)/W(s), softball W(s), swimming and diving M(s)/W(s), track and field M(s)/W(s), volleyball W(s). ***Intramural sports:*** baseball M(c), basketball M/W, cheerleading M(c)/W(c), soccer M/W, ultimate Frisbee M(c)/W(c), volleyball M/W.

Campus security: 24-hour emergency response devices and patrols, late-night transport/escort service, controlled dormitory access.

Student services: health clinic, personal/psychological counseling, veterans affairs office.

COSTS & FINANCIAL AID

Costs (2019–20) ***One-time required fee:*** $455. ***Comprehensive fee:*** $46,354 includes full-time tuition ($32,218), mandatory fees ($1168), and room and board ($12,968). Part-time tuition: $1072 per credit hour. ***Required fees:*** $45 per credit hour part-time, $143 per term part-time. ***College room only:*** $6522.

Financial Aid Of all full-time matriculated undergraduates who enrolled in 2017, 2,193 applied for aid, 2,040 were judged to have need, 324 had their need fully met. In 2017, 232 non-need-based awards were made. ***Average percent of need met:*** 79. ***Average financial aid package:*** $23,717. ***Average need-based loan:*** $4303. ***Average need-based gift aid:*** $8183. ***Average non-need-based aid:*** $14,461. ***Average indebtedness upon graduation:*** $37,506. ***Financial aid deadline:*** 5/1.

APPLYING
Standardized Tests *Required for some:* SAT or ACT (for admission).

Options: electronic application, early admission, early action, deferred entrance.

Required: high school transcript, 1 letter of recommendation. ***Required for some:*** interview. ***Recommended:*** essay or personal statement, minimum 2.5 GPA.

Application deadlines: 5/1 (freshmen), 8/1 (transfers), 12/1 (early action).

Notification: continuous (freshmen), continuous (transfers), 12/15 (early action).

CONTACT
Ms. Kathleen Lesko, Assistant Vice President of Undergraduate Admissions, The College of Saint Rose, 1001 Madison Avenue, Albany, NY 12203. *Phone:* 518-454-5154. *Toll-free phone:* 800-637-8556. *Fax:* 518-454-2013. *E-mail:* admit@strose.edu.

★ College of Staten Island of the City University of New York

Staten Island, New York

http://www.csi.cuny.edu/

- **State and locally supported** comprehensive, founded 1955, part of City University of New York
- **Urban** 204-acre campus with easy access to New York City
- **Endowment** $8.8 million
- **Coed** 12,211 undergraduate students, 78% full-time, 54% women, 46% men
- **Noncompetitive** entrance level, 100% of applicants were admitted

UNDERGRAD STUDENTS
9,567 full-time, 2,644 part-time. Students come from 13 states and territories; 102 other countries; 1% are from out of state; 15% Black or African American, non-Hispanic/Latino; 27% Hispanic/Latino; 11% Asian, non-Hispanic/Latino; 0.2% Native Hawaiian or other Pacific Islander, non-Hispanic/Latino; 0.2% American Indian or Alaska Native, non-Hispanic/Latino; 2% Two or more races, non-Hispanic/Latino; 3% international; 5% transferred in; 4% live on campus.

Freshmen:
Admission: 14,443 applied, 14,443 admitted, 2,663 enrolled. ***Average high school GPA:*** 3.0. ***Test scores:*** SAT evidence-based reading and writing scores over 500: 73%; SAT math scores over 500: 76%; SAT evidence-based reading and writing scores over 600: 19%; SAT math scores over 600: 21%; SAT evidence-based reading and writing scores over 700: 2%; SAT math scores over 700: 3%.

Retention: 77% of full-time freshmen returned.

FACULTY
Total: 1,152, 30% full-time, 47% with terminal degrees.

Student/faculty ratio: 18:1.

ACADEMICS
Calendar: semesters. *Degrees:* certificates, associate, bachelor's, master's, doctoral, post-master's, and postbachelor's certificates.

Special study options: academic remediation for entering students, adult/continuing education programs, cooperative education, double majors, English as a second language, honors programs, independent study, internships, services for LD students, student-designed majors, study abroad, summer session for credit.

Computers: 1,700 computers/terminals and 1,400 ports are available on campus for general student use. Students can access the following: computer help desk, free student e-mail accounts, online (class) grades, online (class) registration, online (class) schedules, MyInfo app. Campuswide network is available. 100% of college-owned or -operated housing units are wired for high-speed Internet access. Wireless service is available via entire campus.

Library: College of Staten Island Library. *Books:* 205,415 (physical), 538,477 (digital/electronic); *Serial titles:* 1,842 (physical), 110,942 (digital/electronic); *Databases:* 161. Weekly public service hours: 98; students can reserve study rooms.

STUDENT LIFE
Housing options: coed, special housing for students with disabilities. Campus housing is university owned.

Activities and organizations: drama/theater group, student-run newspaper, radio station, choral group, Pre-Med/Pre-PA Society, International Student Club, United African Students in the USA, The CSI Gamers Club.

Athletics Member NCAA. All Division III. ***Intercollegiate sports:*** baseball M, basketball M/W, cheerleading M(c)/W(c), cross-country running M/W, soccer M/W, softball W, swimming and diving M/W, tennis M/W, track and field M(c)/W(c), volleyball M/W. ***Intramural sports:*** badminton M/W, basketball M/W, cheerleading M/W, football M/W, golf M/W, soccer M/W, swimming and diving M/W, table tennis M/W, tennis M/W, track and field M/W, ultimate Frisbee M/W, volleyball M/W.

Campus security: 24-hour emergency response devices and patrols, student patrols, late-night transport/escort service, controlled dormitory access.

Student services: health clinic, personal/psychological counseling, women's center, veterans affairs office.

COSTS & FINANCIAL AID
Costs (2018–19) ***Tuition:*** state resident $6730 full-time, $295 per credit hour part-time; nonresident $18,000 full-time, $600 per credit hour part-time. ***Required fees:*** $559 full-time, $181 per term part-time. ***Room only:*** $14,315. Room and board charges vary according to housing facility. ***Payment plan:*** installment. ***Waivers:*** senior citizens and employees or children of employees.

Financial Aid Of all full-time matriculated undergraduates who enrolled in 2017, 7,989 applied for aid, 7,229 were judged to have need, 397 had their need fully met. In 2017, 248 non-need-based awards were made. ***Average percent of need met:*** 42. ***Average financial aid package:*** $8359. ***Average need-based loan:*** $9205. ***Average need-based gift aid:*** $7882. ***Average non-need-based aid:*** $4118.

APPLYING
Standardized Tests *Required:* SAT or ACT (for admission).

Options: electronic application, deferred entrance.

Application fee: $65.

Required: high school transcript. ***Required for some:*** essay or personal statement, 2 letters of recommendation, interview.

Application deadlines: rolling (freshmen), rolling (out-of-state freshmen).

Notification: continuous until 2/1 (freshmen), continuous until 2/1 (out-of-state freshmen).

CONTACT
Mr. Emmanuel Esperance Jr., Director of Recruitment and Admissions, College of Staten Island of the City University of New York, 2800 Victory Boulevard, Staten Island, NY 10314-6600. *Phone:* 718-982-2190. *Fax:* 718-982-2500. *E-mail:* emmanuel.esperance@csi.cuny.edu.

See page 531 for display ad and page 992 for the College Close-Up.

The College of Westchester

White Plains, New York

http://www.cw.edu/

- **Proprietary** primarily 2-year, founded 1915
- **Suburban** campus with easy access to New York City
- **Coed**
- **Minimally difficult** entrance level

FACULTY
Student/faculty ratio: 20:1.

ACADEMICS
Calendar: semesters. *Degrees:* certificates, associate, and bachelor's.
Library: Dr. William R. Papallo Library.

STUDENT LIFE
Housing options: college housing not available.

Activities and organizations: student-run newspaper.

Student services: personal/psychological counseling, veterans affairs office.

COSTS
Costs (2018–19) ***Tuition:*** $20,115 full-time, $745 per credit part-time. ***Required fees:*** $900 full-time, $100 per course part-time.

APPLYING
Standardized Tests *Recommended:* SAT (for admission).

Options: electronic application, deferred entrance.

Application fee: $40.

Required: high school transcript, interview. ***Required for some:*** essay or personal statement.

CONTACT
Mr. Matt Curtis, Vice President, Enrollment Management, The College of Westchester, 325 Central Avenue, PO Box 710, White Plains, NY 10602. *Phone:* 914-948-4442 Ext. 313. *Toll-free phone:* 855-403-7722. *Fax:* 914-948-5441. *E-mail:* admissions@cw.edu.

Columbia University

New York, New York

http://www.columbia.edu/

- **Independent** university, founded 1754
- **Urban** 36-acre campus with easy access to New York City
- **Endowment** $10.9 billion
- **Coed** 6,270 undergraduate students, 100% full-time, 49% women, 51% men
- **Most difficult** entrance level, 6% of applicants were admitted

UNDERGRAD STUDENTS
6,270 full-time. Students come from 52 states and territories; 104 other countries; 78% are from out of state; 10% Black or African American, non-Hispanic/Latino; 13% Hispanic/Latino; 22% Asian, non-Hispanic/Latino; 2% American Indian or Alaska Native, non-Hispanic/Latino; 2% Two or more races, non-Hispanic/Latino; 2% Race/ethnicity unknown; 16% international; 2% transferred in; 92% live on campus.

Freshmen:
Admission: 40,203 applied, 2,260 admitted, 1,423 enrolled. ***Test scores:*** SAT evidence-based reading and writing scores over 500: 100%; SAT math scores over 500: 100%; ACT scores over 18: 100%; SAT evidence-based reading and writing scores over 600: 99%; SAT math scores over 600: 99%; ACT scores over 24: 100%; SAT evidence-based reading and writing scores over 700: 81%; SAT math scores over 700: 89%; ACT scores over 30: 97%.

Retention: 99% of full-time freshmen returned.

FACULTY
Student/faculty ratio: 6:1.

ACADEMICS
Calendar: semesters. *Degrees:* bachelor's, master's, and doctoral.

Special study options: accelerated degree program, advanced placement credit, double majors, English as a second language, independent study, internships, off-campus study, services for LD students, student-designed majors, study abroad, summer session for credit. ***ROTC:*** Army (c), Navy (b), Air Force (c).

Unusual degree programs: 3-2 engineering.

Computers: 460 computers/terminals are available on campus for general student use. Students can access the following: campus intranet, computer help desk, free student e-mail accounts, online (class) grades, online (class) registration, online (class) schedules. Campuswide network is available. Wireless service is available via entire campus.
Library: Butler plus 18 others. *Books:* 10.7 million (physical), 2.6 million (digital/electronic); *Databases:* 1,587. Weekly public service hours: 86; study areas open 24 hours, 5–7 days a week; students can reserve study rooms.

STUDENT LIFE
Housing options: on-campus residence required for freshman year; coed, cooperative, special housing for students with disabilities. Campus housing is university owned. Freshman campus housing is guaranteed.

Activities and organizations: drama/theater group, student-run newspaper, radio and television station, choral group, marching band, community service, cultural organizations, performing arts, athletics, publications, national fraternities, national sororities.

Athletics Member NCAA. All Division I except football (Division I-AA). ***Intercollegiate sports:*** archery W, baseball M, basketball M/W, crew M/W, cross-country running M/W, fencing M/W, field hockey W, golf M/W, ice hockey M(c)/W(c), lacrosse M(c)/W, rowing M/W, rugby M(c)/W(c), soccer M/W, softball W, squash M/W, swimming and diving M/W, tennis M/W, track and field M/W, ultimate Frisbee M(c)/W(c), volleyball W, water polo M(c)/W(c), wrestling M. ***Intramural sports:*** archery M(c)/W(c), badminton M(c)/W(c), basketball M/W, equestrian sports M(c)/W(c), football M/W, racquetball M/W, rock climbing M(c)/W(c), sailing M(c)/W(c), skiing (downhill) M(c)/W(c), soccer M/W, squash M/W, table tennis M(c)/W(c), tennis M(c)/W(c), triathlon M(c)/W(c), volleyball M/W.

Campus security: 24-hour emergency response devices and patrols, late-night transport/escort service, controlled dormitory access.

Student services: health clinic, personal/psychological counseling, women's center.

FINANCIAL AID

Financial Aid Of all full-time matriculated undergraduates who enrolled in 2018, 3,323 applied for aid, 3,158 were judged to have need, 2,953 had their need fully met. ***Average percent of need met:*** 100. ***Average financial aid package:*** $60,289. ***Average need-based loan:*** $3684. ***Average need-based gift aid:*** $55,691.

APPLYING

Standardized Tests *Required:* SAT or ACT (for admission).

Options: electronic application, early admission, early decision, deferred entrance.

Application fee: $85.

Required: essay or personal statement, high school transcript, 3 letters of recommendation.

Application deadlines: 1/1 (freshmen), 3/1 (transfers).

Early decision deadline: 11/1.

Notification: 4/1 (freshmen), 5/15 (transfers), 12/15 (early decision).

CONTACT

Ms. Jessica Marinaccio, Dean of Undergraduate Admissions and Financial Aid, Columbia University, 116th Street and Broadway, New York, NY 10027. *Phone:* 212-854-1222.

See previous page for display ad and page 994 for the College Close-Up.

★ Columbia University School of General Studies

New York, New York

http://www.gs.columbia.edu/

CONTACT

Mr. Curtis M. Rodgers, Vice Dean, Columbia University School of General Studies, 2970 Broadway, 408 Lewisohn Hall, MC 4101, New York, NY 10027. *Phone:* 212-854-2772. *Toll-free phone:* 800-895-1169. *Fax:* 212-854-6316. *E-mail:* gsdegree@columbia.edu.

See below for display ad and page 996 for the College Close-Up.

Concordia College–New York

Bronxville, New York

http://www.concordia-ny.edu/

- **Independent Lutheran** comprehensive, founded 1881, part of Concordia University System
- **Suburban** 33-acre campus with easy access to New York City
- **Endowment** $6.4 million
- **Coed**
- **Moderately difficult** entrance level

FACULTY

Student/faculty ratio: 11:1.

ACADEMICS

Calendar: semesters. *Degrees:* certificates, diplomas, associate, bachelor's, and master's.

Library: Scheele Memorial Library plus 1 other.

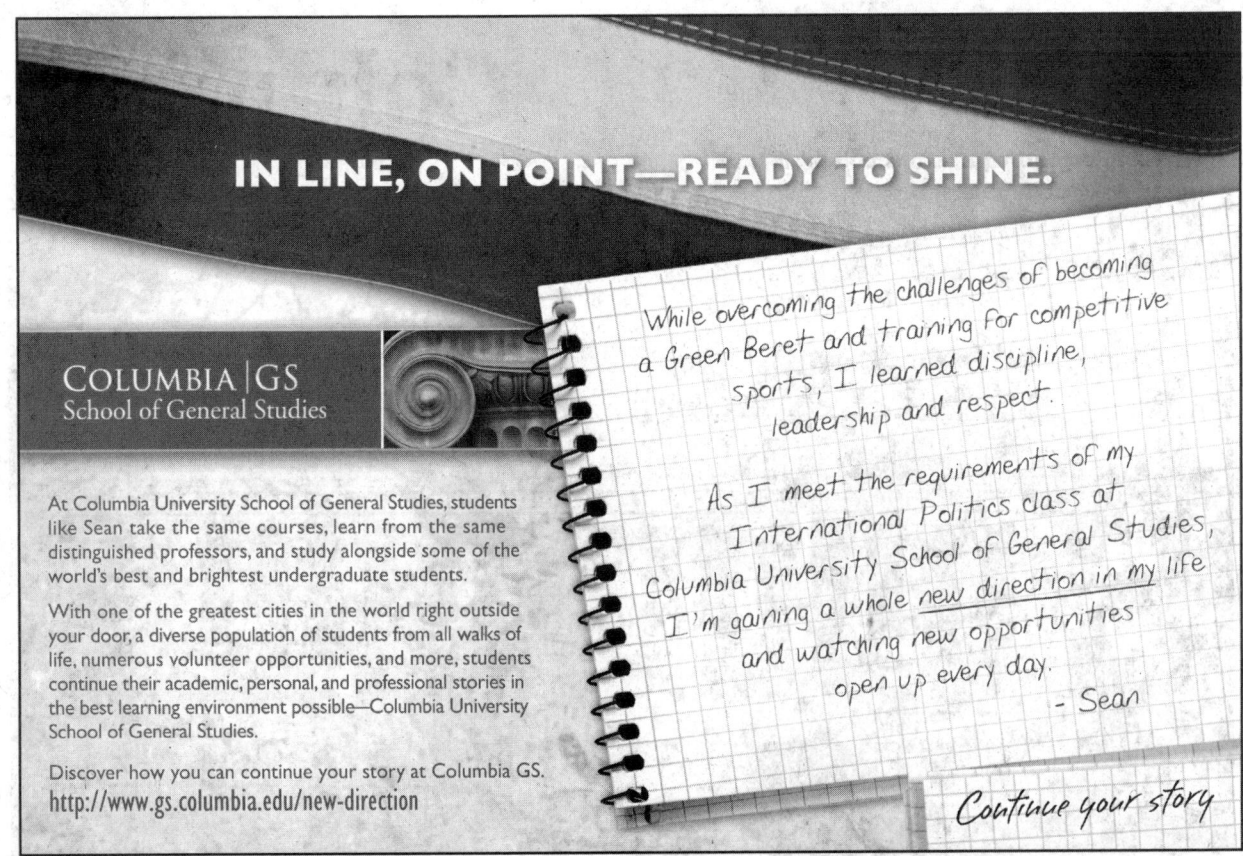

STUDENT LIFE

Housing options: men-only, women-only, special housing for students with disabilities. Campus housing is university owned.

Activities and organizations: drama/theater group, student-run newspaper, choral group, Student Government Association, Choral Groups, Campus Christian Ministries, International and Afro/Latin American Club, Yearbook and newspaper.

Athletics Member NCAA. All Division II.

Campus security: 24-hour emergency response devices and patrols, controlled dormitory access.

Student services: health clinic, personal/psychological counseling.

COSTS & FINANCIAL AID

Costs (2018–19) ***Comprehensive fee:*** $45,590 includes full-time tuition ($31,500), mandatory fees ($1400), and room and board ($12,690). Full-time tuition and fees vary according to class time, course load, location, and program. Part-time tuition: $880 per credit. Part-time tuition and fees vary according to class time, course load, location, and program. ***Room and board:*** Room and board charges vary according to board plan.

Financial Aid Of all full-time matriculated undergraduates who enrolled in 2008, 533 applied for aid, 448 were judged to have need, 89 had their need fully met. In 2008, 100 non-need-based awards were made. ***Average percent of need met:*** 71. ***Average financial aid package:*** $22,309. ***Average need-based loan:*** $4133. ***Average need-based gift aid:*** $11,129. ***Average non-need-based aid:*** $6170. ***Average indebtedness upon graduation:*** $24,153.

APPLYING

Standardized Tests *Required for some:* SAT or ACT (for admission), TOEFL or IELTS for students for whom English is not their first language.

Options: electronic application, early admission, early action, deferred entrance.

Application fee: $60.

Required: essay or personal statement, high school transcript, 2 letters of recommendation. ***Required for some:*** interview. ***Recommended:*** minimum 2.5 GPA.

CONTACT

Ms. Toral Bhatt, Director of Recruitment, Concordia College–New York, 171 White Plains Road, Bronxville, NY 10708. *Phone:* 914-337-9300 Ext. 2124. *Toll-free phone:* 800-YES-COLLEGE. *Fax:* 914-395-4636. *E-mail:* toral.bhatt@concordia-ny.edu.

Cooper Union for the Advancement of Science and Art

New York, New York

http://www.cooper.edu/

- **Independent** comprehensive, founded 1859
- **Urban** campus with easy access to New York City
- **Endowment** $798.9 million
- **Coed**
- **Most difficult** entrance level

FACULTY

Student/faculty ratio: 8:1.

ACADEMICS

Calendar: semesters. *Degrees:* certificates, bachelor's, and master's (also offers master's program primarily made up of currently-enrolled students).

Library: Cooper Union Library. *Books:* 98,400 (physical), 213,578 (digital/electronic); *Serial titles:* 71 (physical), 40,306 (digital/electronic); *Databases:* 48. Weekly public service hours: 69.

STUDENT LIFE

Housing options: coed. Campus housing is university owned. Freshman applicants given priority for college housing.

Activities and organizations: drama/theater group, student-run newspaper, choral group, South Asian Society, Pro Musica, Chinese Student Association, Drama Society, Outdoors Club; Intervarsity Christian Fellowship, national fraternities, national sororities.

Campus security: 24-hour emergency response devices and patrols, controlled dormitory access, security guards.

Student services: personal/psychological counseling, veterans affairs office.

COSTS & FINANCIAL AID

Costs (2018–19) ***Tuition:*** $44,550 full-time, $1310 per credit hour part-time. Full-time tuition and fees vary according to degree level and reciprocity agreements. Part-time tuition and fees vary according to degree level and reciprocity agreements. ***Required fees:*** $1800 full-time, $1075 per term part-time. ***Room only:*** $12,638. Room and board charges vary according to housing facility.

Financial Aid Of all full-time matriculated undergraduates who enrolled in 2017, 497 applied for aid, 413 were judged to have need, 162 had their need fully met. 37 Federal Work-Study jobs (averaging $902). In 2017, 438 non-need-based awards were made. ***Average percent of need met:*** 76. ***Average financial aid package:*** $47,735. ***Average need-based loan:*** $4529. ***Average need-based gift aid:*** $25,221. ***Average non-need-based aid:*** $24,338. ***Average indebtedness upon graduation:*** $18,272.

APPLYING

Standardized Tests *Required:* SAT or ACT (for admission), studio test for architecture, home test for art (for admission). *Required for some:* SAT Subject Tests (for admission).

Options: electronic application, early admission, early decision, deferred entrance.

Application fee: $75.

Required: essay or personal statement, high school transcript. ***Required for some:*** minimum 3.5 GPA, 3 letters of recommendation, interview, portfolio for art, studio test for architecture. ***Recommended:*** minimum 3.0 GPA, 2 letters of recommendation.

CONTACT

Ms. Adrianne Greth, Associate Dean of Admissions, Cooper Union for the Advancement of Science and Art, 30 Cooper Square, New York, NY 10003. *Phone:* 212-353-4121. *Fax:* 212-353-4342. *E-mail:* admissions@cooper.edu.

Cornell University

Ithaca, New York

http://www.cornell.edu/

- **Independent** university, founded 1865, part of State University of New York System
- **Small-town** 745-acre campus with easy access to Syracuse
- **Endowment** $681.5 million
- **Coed** 15,182 undergraduate students, 100% full-time, 53% women, 47% men
- **Most difficult** entrance level, 11% of applicants were admitted

UNDERGRAD STUDENTS

15,182 full-time. Students come from 85 other countries; 59% are from out of state; 7% Black or African American, non-Hispanic/Latino; 13% Hispanic/Latino; 19% Asian, non-Hispanic/Latino; 0.1% Native Hawaiian or other Pacific Islander, non-Hispanic/Latino; 0.4% American Indian or Alaska Native, non-Hispanic/Latino; 5% Two or more races, non-Hispanic/Latino; 8% Race/ethnicity unknown; 11% international; 4% transferred in; 52% live on campus.

Freshmen:

Admission: 51,324 applied, 5,448 admitted, 3,295 enrolled. ***Test scores:*** SAT evidence-based reading and writing scores over 500: 100%; SAT math scores over 500: 100%; ACT scores over 18: 100%; SAT evidence-based reading and writing scores over 600: 98%; SAT math scores over 600: 98%; ACT scores over 24: 100%; SAT evidence-based reading and writing scores over 700: 68%; SAT math scores over 700: 81%; ACT scores over 30: 90%.

Retention: 97% of full-time freshmen returned.

FACULTY

Total: 2,193, 83% full-time, 89% with terminal degrees.

Student/faculty ratio: 9:1.

ACADEMICS

Calendar: semesters. *Degrees:* bachelor's, master's, and doctoral.

Special study options: academic remediation for entering students, accelerated degree program, advanced placement credit, cooperative education, distance learning, double majors, English as a second language, honors programs, independent study, internships, off-campus study, services for LD students, student-designed majors, study abroad, summer session for credit. ***ROTC:*** Army (b), Navy (b), Air Force (b).

Computers: 1,500 computers/terminals are available on campus for general student use. Students can access the following: campus intranet, computer help desk, free student e-mail accounts, online (class) grades, online (class) registration. Campuswide network is available. 100% of college-owned or -operated housing units are wired for high-speed Internet access. Wireless service is available via entire campus.

Library: Main Library plus 16 others. *Books:* 5.1 million (physical), 1.7 million (digital/electronic); *Serial titles:* 240,579 (physical), 148,820 (digital/electronic); *Databases:* 4,207. Weekly public service hours: 146; study areas open 24 hours, 5–7 days a week; students can reserve study rooms.

STUDENT LIFE

Housing options: coed, women-only, cooperative, special housing for students with disabilities. Campus housing is university owned. Freshman campus housing is guaranteed.

Activities and organizations: drama/theater group, student-run newspaper, radio and television station, choral group, marching band, Class Councils, Cornell Hillel, Interfraternity Council/Panhellenic Association, Outing Club, Student Assembly, national fraternities, national sororities.

Athletics Member NCAA. All Division I. ***Intercollegiate sports:*** baseball M, basketball M/W, crew M/W, cross-country running M/W, equestrian sports W, fencing W, field hockey W, football M, golf M, gymnastics W, ice hockey M/W, lacrosse M/W, sailing W, soccer M/W, softball W, squash M/W, swimming and diving M/W, tennis M/W, track and field M/W, ultimate Frisbee M(c)/W(c), volleyball M(c)/W, water polo M(c)/W(c), wrestling M. ***Intramural sports:*** archery M(c)/W(c), badminton M/W, baseball M(c), basketball M/W, bowling M/W, cheerleading W(c), cross-country running M(c)/W(c), equestrian sports M(c)/W(c), fencing M(c)/W(c), field hockey W(c), football M(c)/W(c), golf M/W, gymnastics M(c)/W(c), ice hockey M(c)/W(c), lacrosse W(c), rugby M(c)/W(c), sailing M(c)/W(c), sand volleyball M(c)/W(c), skiing (cross-country) M(c)/W(c), skiing (downhill) M(c)/W(c), soccer M/W, softball M/W, squash M/W, table tennis M/W, tennis M/W, ultimate Frisbee M/W, volleyball M/W, water polo M/W, wrestling M(c)/W(c).

Campus security: 24-hour emergency response devices and patrols, late-night transport/escort service, controlled dormitory access.

Student services: health clinic, personal/psychological counseling, women's center.

COSTS & FINANCIAL AID

Costs (2018–19) ***Comprehensive fee:*** $69,634 includes full-time tuition ($54,584), mandatory fees ($234), and room and board ($14,816). ***College room only:*** $8842. Room and board charges vary according to board plan and housing facility. ***Payment plan:*** installment. ***Waivers:*** employees or children of employees.

Financial Aid Of all full-time matriculated undergraduates who enrolled in 2018, 7,735 applied for aid, 7,163 were judged to have need, 7,163 had their need fully met. 5,417 Federal Work-Study jobs (averaging $2246). 776 state and other part-time jobs (averaging $2332). ***Average percent of need met:*** 100. ***Average financial aid package:*** $48,835. ***Average need-based loan:*** $5255. ***Average need-based gift aid:*** $42,228. ***Average indebtedness upon graduation:*** $29,762. ***Financial aid deadline:*** 2/15.

APPLYING

Standardized Tests *Required:* SAT or ACT (for admission). *Required for some:* SAT Subject Tests (for admission).

Options: electronic application, early decision, deferred entrance.

Application fee: $80.

Required: essay or personal statement, high school transcript, 2 letters of recommendation. ***Required for some:*** interview.

Application deadlines: 1/2 (freshmen), 3/15 (transfers).

Early decision deadline: 11/1.

Notification: 3/31 (freshmen), 6/15 (transfers), 12/15 (early decision).

CONTACT
Mr. Shawn Felton, Director of Undergraduate Admissions, Cornell University, 144 East Avenue, Ithaca, NY 14853. *Phone:* 607-255-5241. *Fax:* 607-255-0659. *E-mail:* admissions@cornell.edu.

The Culinary Institute of America
Hyde Park, New York
http://www.ciachef.edu/

- **Independent** 4-year, founded 1946
- **Suburban** 170-acre campus
- **Endowment** $128.6 million
- **Coed**
- **Moderately difficult** entrance level

FACULTY
Student/faculty ratio: 20:1.

ACADEMICS
Calendar: semesters plus 18 or 21 week externship program. *Degrees:* certificates, associate, bachelor's, and postbachelor's certificates.
Library: Conrad N. Hilton Library. *Books:* 57,977 (physical), 1,149 (digital/electronic); *Serial titles:* 449 (physical), 22,228 (digital/electronic); *Databases:* 75. Weekly public service hours: 92; students can reserve study rooms.

STUDENT LIFE
Housing options: coed. Campus housing is university owned and is provided by a third party. Freshman campus housing is guaranteed.

Activities and organizations: student-run newspaper, Bacchus Wine Society, Tea Club, KACIA, Culinary Christian Fellowship, Black Culinarian Society.

Campus security: 24-hour emergency response devices and patrols, late-night transport/escort service, controlled dormitory access, CCTV & Nightly Visitor Screening.

Student services: health clinic, personal/psychological counseling.

COSTS & FINANCIAL AID
Costs (2018–19) ***Comprehensive fee:*** $44,280 includes full-time tuition ($30,200), mandatory fees ($2520), and room and board ($11,560). Full-time tuition and fees vary according to location. ***College room only:*** $7860. Room and board charges vary according to board plan, housing facility, and location.

Financial Aid Of all full-time matriculated undergraduates who enrolled in 2018, 2,010 applied for aid, 1,788 were judged to have need, 128 had their need fully met. 1,090 Federal Work-Study jobs (averaging $2410). In 2018, 138 non-need-based awards were made. ***Average percent of need met:*** 65. ***Average financial aid package:*** $16,505. ***Average need-based loan:*** $3738. ***Average need-based gift aid:*** $12,799. ***Average non-need-based aid:*** $7454. ***Average indebtedness upon graduation:*** $51,200.

APPLYING
Options: electronic application, early action, deferred entrance.

Application fee: $50.

Required: essay or personal statement, high school transcript, 1 letter of recommendation. ***Required for some:*** Affidavit of Support. ***Recommended:*** minimum 2.0 GPA.

CONTACT
Ms. Rachel Birchwood, Senior Director of Admissions, The Culinary Institute of America, 1946 Campus Drive, Hyde Park, NY 12538. *Phone:* 845-451-1459. *Toll-free phone:* 800-CULINARY. *Fax:* 845-451-1068. *E-mail:* admissions@culinary.edu.

★ Daemen College
Amherst, New York
http://www.daemen.edu/

- **Independent** comprehensive, founded 1947
- **Suburban** 35-acre campus with easy access to Buffalo
- **Endowment** $14.4 million
- **Coed**
- **Moderately difficult** entrance level

FACULTY
Student/faculty ratio: 12:1.

ACADEMICS
Calendar: semesters. *Degrees:* certificates, bachelor's, master's, doctoral, post-master's, and postbachelor's certificates.
Library: Research and Information Commons. *Books:* 85,205 (physical), 138,085 (digital/electronic); *Serial titles:* 488 (physical); *Databases:* 38. Weekly public service hours: 117; students can reserve study rooms.

STUDENT LIFE
Housing options: on-campus residence required for freshman year; coed, special housing for students with disabilities. Campus housing is university owned and leased by the school. Freshman campus housing is guaranteed.

Activities and organizations: drama/theater group, student-run newspaper, choral group, Game Club, Anime Club, Best Buddies, CRU, Pride Club.

Athletics Member NCAA. All Division II.

Campus security: 24-hour emergency response devices and patrols, late-night transport/escort service, controlled dormitory access, 24-hour security cameras.

Student services: personal/psychological counseling, veterans affairs office.

COSTS & FINANCIAL AID
Costs (2018–19) ***Comprehensive fee:*** $41,495 includes full-time tuition ($27,990), mandatory fees ($590), and room and board ($12,915). Full-time tuition and fees vary according to location and reciprocity agreements. Part-time tuition: $933 per credit hour. Part-time tuition and fees vary according to course load, location, and reciprocity agreements. ***Required fees:*** $9 per credit hour part-time, $80 per term part-time. ***Room and board:*** Room and board charges vary according to board plan and housing facility. ***Payment plans:*** installment, deferred payment.

Financial Aid Of all full-time matriculated undergraduates who enrolled in 2017, 1,425 applied for aid, 951 were judged to have need, 117 had their need fully met. 612 Federal Work-Study jobs (averaging $2918). 50 state and other part-time jobs (averaging $2040). In 2017, 441 non-need-based awards were made. ***Average percent of need met:*** 82. ***Average financial aid package:*** $28,324. ***Average need-based loan:*** $4630. ***Average need-based gift aid:*** $11,058. ***Average non-need-based aid:*** $11,119. ***Average indebtedness upon graduation:*** $35,530.

APPLYING
Standardized Tests *Required for some:* SAT or ACT (for admission), SAT/ACT or high school course grades, show rigor of courses and teacher recommendations. *Recommended:* SAT or ACT (for admission).

Options: electronic application, early admission, deferred entrance.

Application fee: $25.

Required: essay or personal statement, high school transcript, 1 letter of recommendation. ***Recommended:*** interview.

CONTACT
Ms. Caroline Marciszewski, Associate Director of Undergraduate Admissions, Daemen College, 4380 Main Street, Amherst, NY 14226-3592. *Phone:* 716-566-7856. *Toll-free phone:* 800-462-7652. *Fax:* 716-839-8229. *E-mail:* admissions@daemen.edu.

Davis College
Johnson City, New York
http://www.davisny.edu/

CONTACT
Ms. Hannah Hempstead, Assistant Director of Admissions for Communication, Davis College, 400 Riverside Drive, Johnson City, NY 13790. *Phone:* 607-729-1581 Ext. 341. *Toll-free phone:* 877-949-3248. *Fax:* 607-770-6886. *E-mail:* hhempstead@davisny.edu.

A ★ indicates that the school has detailed information with a Premium Profile on Petersons.com.

DeVry College of New York–Midtown Manhattan Campus

New York, New York

http://www.devry.edu/

CONTACT

DeVry College of New York–Midtown Manhattan Campus, 180 Madison Avenue, Suite 900, New York, NY 10016. *Phone:* 212-312-4300. *Toll-free phone:* 866-338-7934.

Dominican College

Orangeburg, New York

http://www.dc.edu/

- **Independent** comprehensive, founded 1952
- **Suburban** 70-acre campus with easy access to New York City
- **Endowment** $4.5 million
- **Coed**
- **Noncompetitive** entrance level

FACULTY

Student/faculty ratio: 15:1.

ACADEMICS

Calendar: semesters. *Degrees:* certificates, diplomas, associate, bachelor's, master's, doctoral, and postbachelor's certificates.
Library: Sullivan Library plus 1 other. *Books:* 74,226 (physical), 117,187 (digital/electronic); *Serial titles:* 610 (physical), 75,067 (digital/electronic); *Databases:* 85. Weekly public service hours: 89; students can reserve study rooms.

STUDENT LIFE

Housing options: coed. Campus housing is university owned. Freshman campus housing is guaranteed.

Activities and organizations: drama/theater group, student-run radio station, choral group, Student Government Association, Business Club, Aquin Players Drama Society, Anime Magna and Videogame Club, Student Nursing Association.

Athletics Member NCAA. All Division II.

Campus security: 24-hour emergency response devices and patrols, student patrols, late-night transport/escort service, controlled dormitory access.

Student services: health clinic, personal/psychological counseling.

COSTS & FINANCIAL AID

Costs (2018–19) ***Comprehensive fee:*** $42,150 includes full-time tuition ($28,140), mandatory fees ($860), and room and board ($13,150). Full-time tuition and fees vary according to course load and degree level. Part-time tuition: $851 per credit hour. Part-time tuition and fees vary according to course load, degree level, and program. ***Required fees:*** $200 per term part-time. ***Room and board:*** Room and board charges vary according to board plan and housing facility. ***Payment plans:*** installment, deferred payment.

Financial Aid Of all full-time matriculated undergraduates who enrolled in 2018, 1,133 applied for aid, 1,035 were judged to have need, 124 had their need fully met. In 2018, 160 non-need-based awards were made. ***Average percent of need met:*** 68. ***Average financial aid package:*** $22,960. ***Average need-based loan:*** $5107. ***Average need-based gift aid:*** $19,043. ***Average non-need-based aid:*** $10,531. ***Average indebtedness upon graduation:*** $32,527.

APPLYING

Options: electronic application, deferred entrance.

Application fee: $35.

Required: high school transcript. ***Required for some:*** essay or personal statement, interview. ***Recommended:*** interview.

CONTACT

Mr. Robert Tyrrell, Assistant Director of Freshman Admissions, Dominican College, 470 Western Highway, Orangeburg, NY 10962-1210. *Phone:* 845-359-7906. *Toll-free phone:* 866-432-4636. *Fax:* 845-365-3150. *E-mail:* rob.tyrrell@dc.edu.

D'Youville College

Buffalo, New York

http://www.dyc.edu/

- **Independent** comprehensive, founded 1908
- **Urban** 11-acre campus
- **Endowment** $43.3 million
- **Coed**
- **Moderately difficult** entrance level

FACULTY

Student/faculty ratio: 9:1.

ACADEMICS

Calendar: semesters plus summer session. *Degrees:* bachelor's, master's, doctoral, post-master's, and postbachelor's certificates.
Library: Montante Family Library. *Books:* 69,415 (physical), 75,525 (digital/electronic); *Serial titles:* 572 (physical), 41,529 (digital/electronic); *Databases:* 84. Weekly public service hours: 87; study areas open 24 hours, 5–7 days a week; students can reserve study rooms.

STUDENT LIFE

Housing options: coed, men-only, women-only, special housing for students with disabilities. Campus housing is university owned. Freshman campus housing is guaranteed.

Activities and organizations: drama/theater group, student-run newspaper, choral group, Student Association, Occupational Therapy Student Association, Physical Therapy Student Association, Student Nurses Association, Black Student Union.

Athletics Member NCAA. All Division III.

Campus security: 24-hour emergency response devices and patrols, late-night transport/escort service, controlled dormitory access.

Student services: health clinic, personal/psychological counseling.

COSTS & FINANCIAL AID

Costs (2018–19) ***Comprehensive fee:*** $38,974 includes full-time tuition ($26,120), mandatory fees ($630), and room and board ($12,224). Full-time tuition and fees vary according to course load, degree level, and program. Part-time tuition: $816 per credit hour. Part-time tuition and fees vary according to course load, degree level, and program. No tuition increase for student's term of enrollment. ***Required fees:*** $3 per credit hour part-time, $55 per term part-time. ***Room and board:*** Room and board charges vary according to board plan and housing facility. ***Payment plans:*** installment, deferred payment.

Financial Aid Of all full-time matriculated undergraduates who enrolled in 2015, 810 applied for aid, 720 were judged to have need, 158 had their need fully met. In 2015, 123 non-need-based awards were made. ***Average percent of need met:*** 73. ***Average financial aid package:*** $19,004. ***Average need-based loan:*** $4353. ***Average need-based gift aid:*** $15,177. ***Average non-need-based aid:*** $8739. ***Average indebtedness upon graduation:*** $34,593.

APPLYING

Standardized Tests *Required:* SAT or ACT (for admission).

Options: electronic application, deferred entrance.

Required: high school transcript, minimum 2.0 GPA. ***Required for some:*** essay or personal statement, minimum 3.0 GPA, interview.

CONTACT

Meghan Harmon, Interim Director of Undergraduate Admissions, D'Youville College, 320 Porter Avenue, Buffalo, NY 14201. *Phone:* 716-829-7600. *Toll-free phone:* 800-777-3921. *Fax:* 716-829-7900. *E-mail:* harmonm@dyc.edu.

Elmira College

Elmira, New York

http://www.elmira.edu/

CONTACT

Mr. Christopher R. Coons, Vice President of Enrollment Management, Elmira College, 855 College Avenue, Elmira, NY 14901. *Phone:* 607-735-1724. *Toll-free phone:* 800-935-6472. *Fax:* 607-735-1718. *E-mail:* admissions@elmira.edu.

Eugene Lang College of Liberal Arts

New York, New York

http://www.newschool.edu/lang

- **Independent** 4-year, founded 1975, part of The New School
- **Urban** campus with easy access to New York City
- **Endowment** $322.3 million
- **Coed**
- **Minimally difficult** entrance level

FACULTY
Student/faculty ratio: 17:1.

ACADEMICS
Calendar: semesters. *Degree:* bachelor's.
Library: New School Libraries & Archives plus 3 others. *Books:* 215,937 (physical), 840,933 (digital/electronic); *Serial titles:* 2,265 (physical), 113,452 (digital/electronic); *Databases:* 376. Weekly public service hours: 155; study areas open 24 hours, 5–7 days a week; students can reserve study rooms.

STUDENT LIFE
Housing options: coed, special housing for students with disabilities. Campus housing is university owned and leased by the school. Freshman applicants given priority for college housing.

Activities and organizations: drama/theater group, student-run newspaper, choral group.

Campus security: 24-hour emergency response devices, controlled dormitory access, 24-hour desk attendants in residence halls.

Student services: health clinic, personal/psychological counseling, veterans affairs office.

FINANCIAL AID
Financial Aid Of all full-time matriculated undergraduates who enrolled in 2017, 1,093 applied for aid, 964 were judged to have need, 66 had their need fully met. 130 Federal Work-Study jobs (averaging $3443). In 2017, 475 non-need-based awards were made. ***Average percent of need met:*** 59. ***Average financial aid package:*** $29,671. ***Average need-based loan:*** $4332. ***Average need-based gift aid:*** $15,999. ***Average non-need-based aid:*** $12,921. ***Average indebtedness upon graduation:*** $27,825. ***Financial aid deadline:*** 2/1.

APPLYING
Standardized Tests *Required for some:* TOEFL, IELTS and PTE for some applicants whose first language is not English.

Options: electronic application, early action, deferred entrance.

Application fee: $50.

Required: essay or personal statement, high school transcript, 2 letters of recommendation, online application, 2 supplemental essays, counselor evaluation or teacher evaluation, academic paper (grade preferred). ***Recommended:*** minimum 3.0 GPA.

CONTACT
Ms. Candice MacLusky, Director of Admissions for Lang, Eugene Lang College of Liberal Arts, 65 West 11th Street, New York, NY 10011-8601. *Phone:* 212-229-5155 Ext. 4024. *Toll-free phone:* 800-292-3040. *E-mail:* macluskc@newschool.edu.

Excelsior College

Albany, New York

http://www.excelsior.edu/

- **Independent** comprehensive, founded 1970
- **Suburban** campus with easy access to Albany, NY
- **Coed** 25,423 undergraduate students, 48% women, 52% men

UNDERGRAD STUDENTS
25,423 part-time. Students come from 55 states and territories; 38 other countries; 87% are from out of state; 18% Black or African American, non-Hispanic/Latino; 11% Hispanic/Latino; 3% Asian, non-Hispanic/Latino; 0.6% Native Hawaiian or other Pacific Islander, non-Hispanic/Latino; 0.6% American Indian or Alaska Native, non-Hispanic/Latino; 4% Two or more races, non-Hispanic/Latino; 2% Race/ethnicity unknown; 7% transferred in.

FACULTY
Total: 1,483, 34% with terminal degrees.

Student/faculty ratio: 10:1.

ACADEMICS
Calendar: continuous. *Degrees:* certificates, associate, bachelor's, master's, post-master's, and postbachelor's certificates (offers only external degree programs).

Special study options: adult/continuing education programs, distance learning, external degree program, independent study, part-time degree program, services for LD students, student-designed majors.

Unusual degree programs: 3-2 business administration; nursing; nuclear engineering technology, health care management, business, information technology/business administration; nursing; information technology/cybersecurity.

Computers: Students can access the following: computer help desk, online (class) grades, online (class) registration, online (class) schedules. Campuswide network is available.
Library: Excelsior College Library.

STUDENT LIFE
Housing options: college housing not available.

Student services: veterans affairs office.

COSTS
Costs (2018–19) ***Tuition:*** $510 per credit part-time. Part-time tuition and fees vary according to reciprocity agreements. ***Payment plan:*** installment. ***Waivers:*** employees or children of employees.

APPLYING
Options: electronic application.

Application fee: $50.

Required for some: college transcripts.

Application deadlines: rolling (freshmen), rolling (transfers).

Notification: continuous (freshmen), continuous (transfers).

CONTACT
Excelsior College, 7 Columbia Circle, Albany, NY 12203-5159. *Toll-free phone:* 888-647-2388.

Farmingdale State College

Farmingdale, New York

http://www.farmingdale.edu/

- **State-supported** comprehensive, founded 1912, part of State University of New York System
- **Suburban** 380-acre campus with easy access to New York City
- **Endowment** $5.9 million
- **Coed** 9,916 undergraduate students, 78% full-time, 43% women, 57% men
- **Moderately difficult** entrance level, 46% of applicants were admitted

UNDERGRAD STUDENTS
7,689 full-time, 2,227 part-time. Students come from 14 states and territories; 77 other countries; 0.3% are from out of state; 10% Black or African American, non-Hispanic/Latino; 22% Hispanic/Latino; 9% Asian, non-Hispanic/Latino; 0.2% Native Hawaiian or other Pacific Islander, non-Hispanic/Latino; 0.2% American Indian or Alaska Native, non-Hispanic/Latino; 3% Two or more races, non-Hispanic/Latino; 0.4% Race/ethnicity unknown; 2% international; 12% transferred in; 6% live on campus.

Freshmen:
Admission: 7,500 applied, 3,455 admitted, 1,345 enrolled. ***Average high school GPA:*** 3.2. ***Test scores:*** SAT evidence-based reading and writing scores over 500: 75%; SAT math scores over 500: 83%; ACT scores over 18: 90%; SAT evidence-based reading and writing scores over 600: 16%; SAT math scores over 600: 19%; ACT scores over 24: 31%; SAT math scores over 700: 2%; ACT scores over 30: 1%.

Retention: 84% of full-time freshmen returned.

FACULTY
Total: 748, 33% full-time, 26% with terminal degrees.

Student/faculty ratio: 20:1.

ACADEMICS
Calendar: semesters. *Degrees:* certificates, associate, bachelor's, and master's.

Special study options: academic remediation for entering students, advanced placement credit, cooperative education, distance learning, double majors, independent study, internships, part-time degree program, services for LD students, study abroad, summer session for credit. ***ROTC:*** Army (c), Air Force (c).

Computers: 367 computers/terminals are available on campus for general student use. Students can access the following: computer help desk, free student e-mail accounts, online (class) grades, online (class) registration, online (class) schedules. Campuswide network is available. 100% of college-owned or -operated housing units are wired for high-speed Internet access. Wireless service is available via entire campus.
Library: Greenley Library. *Books:* 120,000 (physical), 165,000 (digital/electronic); *Databases:* 102. Weekly public service hours: 86.

STUDENT LIFE
Housing options: coed. Campus housing is university owned.

Activities and organizations: drama/theater group, student-run radio station, Student Government Association, Ram Nation Radio, Greek Life, E-Sports, Backstage Theater Company, national fraternities, national sororities.

Athletics Member NCAA. All Division III. ***Intercollegiate sports:*** baseball M, basketball M/W, cheerleading W(c), cross-country running M/W, golf M, ice hockey M(c), lacrosse M/W, skiing (downhill) M(c)/W(c), soccer M/W, softball W, tennis M/W, track and field M/W, volleyball W, wrestling M(c). ***Intramural sports:*** basketball M/W, football M/W, sand volleyball M/W, soccer M/W, softball M/W, ultimate Frisbee M/W, volleyball M/W.

Campus security: 24-hour emergency response devices and patrols, controlled dormitory access.

Student services: health clinic, personal/psychological counseling, veterans affairs office.

COSTS & FINANCIAL AID
Costs (2018–19) ***Tuition:*** state resident $6870 full-time, $286 per credit part-time; nonresident $16,650 full-time, $694 per credit part-time. Full-time tuition and fees vary according to program. Part-time tuition and fees vary according to course load and program. ***Required fees:*** $1436 full-time, $59 per credit part-time, $10 per term part-time. ***Room and board:*** $13,238; room only: $8088. Room and board charges vary according to board plan and housing facility. ***Payment plan:*** installment. ***Waivers:*** employees or children of employees.

Financial Aid Of all full-time matriculated undergraduates who enrolled in 2017, 5,473 applied for aid, 4,233 were judged to have need, 149 had their need fully met. In 2017, 81 non-need-based awards were made. ***Average percent of need met:*** 59. ***Average financial aid package:*** $8154. ***Average need-based loan:*** $3732. ***Average need-based gift aid:*** $7250. ***Average non-need-based aid:*** $1705. ***Average indebtedness upon graduation:*** $22,047.

APPLYING
Standardized Tests *Required:* SAT or ACT (for admission).

Options: electronic application, early admission, deferred entrance.

Application fee: $50.

Required: high school transcript, minimum 3.0 GPA. ***Required for some:*** interview.

Application deadlines: rolling (freshmen), rolling (out-of-state freshmen), rolling (transfers).

Notification: continuous (freshmen), continuous (out-of-state freshmen), continuous (transfers).

CONTACT
Jeanne Soto, Interim Director of Admissions, Farmingdale State College, 2350 Broadhollow Road, Farmingdale, NY 11735. *Phone:* 631-420-2200. *Fax:* 631-420-2633. *E-mail:* admissions@farmingdale.edu.

Fashion Institute of Technology
New York, New York
http://www.fitnyc.edu/

- **State and locally supported** comprehensive, founded 1944, part of State University of New York System
- **Urban** 5-acre campus with easy access to New York City
- **Coed, primarily women** 8,555 undergraduate students, 85% full-time, 83% women, 17% men
- **Moderately difficult** entrance level, 53% of applicants were admitted

UNDERGRAD STUDENTS
7,246 full-time, 1,309 part-time. 31% are from out of state; 9% Black or African American, non-Hispanic/Latino; 20% Hispanic/Latino; 12% Asian, non-Hispanic/Latino; 0.2% Native Hawaiian or other Pacific Islander, non-Hispanic/Latino; 0.1% American Indian or Alaska Native, non-Hispanic/Latino; 4% Two or more races, non-Hispanic/Latino; 0.4% Race/ethnicity unknown; 11% international; 9% transferred in; 21% live on campus.

Freshmen:
Admission: 4,507 applied, 2,374 admitted, 1,342 enrolled. ***Average high school GPA:*** 3.6.

Retention: 89% of full-time freshmen returned.

FACULTY
Total: 1,116, 21% full-time.

Student/faculty ratio: 15:1.

ACADEMICS
Calendar: semesters. *Degrees:* certificates, associate, bachelor's, and master's.

Special study options: academic remediation for entering students, advanced placement credit, distance learning, English as a second language, honors programs, independent study, internships, part-time degree program, services for LD students, study abroad, summer session for credit.

Computers: Campuswide network is available.
Library: Gladys Marcus Library.

STUDENT LIFE
Housing options: coed, women-only, special housing for students with disabilities. Campus housing is university owned. Freshman applicants given priority for college housing.

Activities and organizations: drama/theater group, student-run newspaper, radio and television station, choral group.

Athletics Member NJCAA. ***Intercollegiate sports:*** cross-country running M/W, soccer W, swimming and diving M/W, table tennis M/W, tennis M/W, track and field M/W, volleyball W.

Campus security: 24-hour emergency response devices and patrols, late-night transport/escort service, controlled dormitory access.

Student services: health clinic, personal/psychological counseling.

COSTS & FINANCIAL AID
Costs (2018–19) ***Tuition:*** state resident $6870 full-time, $286 per credit hour part-time; nonresident $20,792 full-time, $866 per credit hour part-time. Full-time tuition and fees vary according to degree level. Part-time tuition and fees vary according to degree level. ***Required fees:*** $850 full-time, $24 per credit hour part-time, $65 per term part-time. ***Room and board:*** $18,468. Room and board charges vary according to board plan and housing facility. ***Waivers:*** employees or children of employees.

Financial Aid Of all full-time matriculated undergraduates who enrolled in 2017, 4,604 applied for aid, 3,688 were judged to have need, 1,817 had their need fully met. In 2017, 321 non-need-based awards were made. ***Average percent of need met:*** 68. ***Average financial aid package:*** $12,023. ***Average need-based loan:*** $3149. ***Average need-based gift aid:*** $6591. ***Average non-need-based aid:*** $853. ***Average indebtedness upon graduation:*** $23,968.

APPLYING
Options: electronic application.

Application fee: $50.

Required: essay or personal statement, high school transcript. ***Required for some:*** portfolio for art and design programs.

Application deadlines: 1/1 (freshmen), 1/1 (transfers).

Notification: 4/1 (freshmen), 4/1 (transfers).

CONTACT
Ms. Magda Francois, Director of Admissions and Strategic Recruitment, Fashion Institute of Technology, Seventh Avenue at 27th Street, New York, NY 10001-5992. *E-mail:* fitinfo@fitnyc.edu.

Five Towns College
Dix Hills, New York
http://www.ftc.edu/

CONTACT
Ms. Cynthia Catalano, Admissions, Five Towns College, 305 North Service Road, Dix Hills, NY 11746-6055. *Phone:* 631-424-7000 Ext. 2107. *Fax:* 631-656-2107. *E-mail:* cynthia.catalano@ftc.edu.

★ Fordham University
New York, New York
http://www.fordham.edu/

- **Independent Roman Catholic (Jesuit)** university, founded 1841
- **Urban** 93-acre campus with easy access to New York City
- **Endowment** $729.2 million
- **Coed** 12,366 undergraduate students, 95% full-time, 57% women, 43% men
- **Very difficult** entrance level, 46% of applicants were admitted

UNDERGRAD STUDENTS
11,779 full-time, 587 part-time. Students come from 47 states and territories; 77 other countries; 58% are from out of state; 4% Black or African American, non-Hispanic/Latino; 15% Hispanic/Latino; 11% Asian, non-Hispanic/Latino; 0.1% Native Hawaiian or other Pacific Islander, non-Hispanic/Latino; 0.1% American Indian or Alaska Native, non-Hispanic/Latino; 4% Two or more races, non-Hispanic/Latino; 2% Race/ethnicity unknown; 9% international; 3% transferred in; 50% live on campus.

Freshmen:
Admission: 46,308 applied, 21,313 admitted, 2,299 enrolled. ***Average high school GPA:*** 3.6. ***Test scores:*** SAT evidence-based reading and writing scores over 500: 99%; SAT math scores over 500: 99%; ACT scores over 18: 100%; SAT evidence-based reading and writing scores over 600: 86%; SAT math scores over 600: 85%; ACT scores over 24: 95%; SAT evidence-based reading and writing scores over 700: 30%; SAT math scores over 700: 42%; ACT scores over 30: 58%.
Retention: 90% of full-time freshmen returned.

FACULTY
Total: 1,800, 41% full-time, 66% with terminal degrees.
Student/faculty ratio: 15:1.

ACADEMICS
Calendar: semesters. *Degrees:* bachelor's, master's, doctoral, post-master's, and postbachelor's certificates (branch locations at Rose Hill and Lincoln Center).
Special study options: accelerated degree program, adult/continuing education programs, advanced placement credit, double majors, English as a second language, honors programs, independent study, internships, off-campus study, part-time degree program, services for LD students, student-designed majors, study abroad, summer session for credit. ***ROTC:*** Army (b), Navy (c), Air Force (c).
Unusual degree programs: 3-2 engineering with Columbia University, Case Western Reserve University.
Computers: 2,600 computers/terminals and 2,400 ports are available on campus for general student use. Students can access the following: campus intranet, computer help desk, free student e-mail accounts, online (class) grades, online (class) registration, online (class) schedules, Video Streaming; IP TV Channels; Mobile Apps for University Services; Maker Spaces; University Supplied Software, WebEX Video Conferencing. Campuswide network is available. 100% of college-owned or -operated housing units are wired for high-speed Internet access. Wireless service is available via entire campus.
Library: Walsh Library plus 3 others. *Books:* 1.5 million (physical), 992,000 (digital/electronic); *Serial titles:* 16,353 (physical), 94,307 (digital/electronic); *Databases:* 444. Weekly public service hours: 105; study areas open 24 hours, 5–7 days a week.

STUDENT LIFE
Housing options: coed, special housing for students with disabilities. Campus housing is university owned and leased by the school.
Activities and organizations: drama/theater group, student-run newspaper, radio and television station, choral group, marching band, United Student Government, Commuting Student Association, Residence Hall Association, Ambassador Program (Admission Department Student Tour Guides), Campus Activities Board.
Athletics Member NCAA. All Division I except football (Division I-AA). ***Intercollegiate sports:*** baseball M(s), basketball M(s)/W(s), cheerleading W, crew M(c)/W(s), cross-country running M(s)/W(s), golf M(s), ice hockey M(c), rowing W(s), sailing M(c)/W(c), soccer M(s)/W(s), softball W(s), squash M(s), swimming and diving M(s)/W(s), tennis M(s)/W(s), track and field M(s)/W(s), volleyball W(s), water polo M(s). ***Intramural sports:*** baseball M(c), basketball M/W, lacrosse M(c)/W(c), rowing M(c), rugby M(c)/W(c), soccer M(c)/W(c), softball W(c), squash W(c), tennis W(c), ultimate Frisbee M(c)/W(c), volleyball M/W.
Campus security: 24-hour emergency response devices and patrols, student patrols, late-night transport/escort service, controlled dormitory access.
Student services: health clinic, personal/psychological counseling, veterans affairs office.

COSTS & FINANCIAL AID
Costs (2018–19) ***Comprehensive fee:*** $70,656 includes full-time tuition ($51,285), mandatory fees ($1402), and room and board ($17,969). Part-time tuition: $1710 per credit. Part-time tuition and fees vary according to class time and course load. ***Room and board:*** Room and board charges vary according to board plan, housing facility, and location. ***Payment plan:*** installment. ***Waivers:*** employees or children of employees.
Financial Aid Of all full-time matriculated undergraduates who enrolled in 2018, 7,397 applied for aid, 5,346 were judged to have need, 1,482 had their need fully met. In 2018, 1883 non-need-based awards were made. ***Average percent of need met:*** 77. ***Average financial aid package:*** $38,093. ***Average need-based loan:*** $6072. ***Average need-based gift aid:*** $29,292. ***Average non-need-based aid:*** $19,409. ***Average indebtedness upon graduation:*** $37,429. ***Financial aid deadline:*** 2/1.

APPLYING
Standardized Tests *Required:* SAT or ACT (for admission).
Options: electronic application, early admission, early decision, early action, deferred entrance.
Application fee: $70.
Required: essay or personal statement, high school transcript, 1 letter of recommendation, Common Application. ***Recommended:*** 1 letter of recommendation.
Application deadlines: 11/1 (freshmen), 6/1 (transfers), 11/1 (early action).
Early decision deadline: 11/1.
Notification: 4/1 (freshmen), continuous (transfers), 12/20 (early decision), 12/20 (early action).

CONTACT
Dr. Patricia Peek, Dean of Undergraduate Admission, Fordham University, Office of Undergraduate Admission, Duane Library, 441 East Fordham Road, Bronx, NY 10458. *Phone:* 718-817-3706. *Toll-free phone:* 800-FORDHAM. *Fax:* 718-367-9404. *E-mail:* peek@fordham.edu.

Hamilton College
Clinton, New York
http://www.hamilton.edu/

- **Independent** 4-year, founded 1812
- **Small-town** 1300-acre campus
- **Endowment** $964.2 million
- **Coed** 1,915 undergraduate students, 100% full-time, 53% women, 47% men
- **Very difficult** entrance level, 21% of applicants were admitted

UNDERGRAD STUDENTS
1,907 full-time, 8 part-time. Students come from 45 states and territories; 46 other countries; 71% are from out of state; 4% Black or African American, non-Hispanic/Latino; 10% Hispanic/Latino; 7% Asian, non-Hispanic/Latino; 0.1% American Indian or Alaska Native, non-Hispanic/Latino; 5% Two or more races, non-Hispanic/Latino; 5% Race/ethnicity unknown; 7% international; 0.8% transferred in; 100% live on campus.

Freshmen:
Admission: 6,240 applied, 1,328 admitted, 481 enrolled. ***Test scores:*** SAT evidence-based reading and writing scores over 500: 100%; SAT math scores over 500: 100%; ACT scores over 18: 100%; SAT evidence-based reading and writing scores over 600: 95%; SAT math scores over 600: 96%; ACT scores over 24: 99%; SAT evidence-based reading and writing scores over 700: 62%; SAT math scores over 700: 70%; ACT scores over 30: 84%.

Retention: 94% of full-time freshmen returned.

FACULTY
Total: 229, 83% full-time, 87% with terminal degrees.

Student/faculty ratio: 9:1.

ACADEMICS
Calendar: semesters. *Degree:* bachelor's.

Special study options: accelerated degree program, adult/continuing education programs, advanced placement credit, double majors, English as a second language, independent study, internships, off-campus study, part-time degree program, services for LD students, student-designed majors, study abroad. ***ROTC:*** Army (c), Air Force (c).

Unusual degree programs: 3-2 engineering with Columbia University, Dartmouth College, Rensselaer Polytechnic Institute, Washington University in St. Louis.

Computers: 849 computers/terminals and 10,519 ports are available on campus for general student use. Students can access the following: campus intranet, computer help desk, free student e-mail accounts, online (class) grades, online (class) registration, online (class) schedules. Campuswide network is available. 100% of college-owned or -operated housing units are wired for high-speed Internet access. Wireless service is available via entire campus.

Library: Burke Library plus 1 other. *Books:* 491,977 (physical), 630,432 (digital/electronic); *Serial titles:* 5,000 (physical), 150,000 (digital/electronic); *Databases:* 245. Weekly public service hours: 114; study areas open 24 hours, 5–7 days a week; students can reserve study rooms.

STUDENT LIFE
Housing options: on-campus residence required through senior year; coed, cooperative, special housing for students with disabilities. Campus housing is university owned. Freshman campus housing is guaranteed.

Activities and organizations: drama/theater group, student-run newspaper, radio and television station, choral group, WHCL (Hamilton College Radio), Slow Food, Powder Club, Black & Latin Student Union (BLSU), Hamilton College Climbing Club, national fraternities.

Athletics Member NCAA. All Division III except golf (Division II). ***Intercollegiate sports:*** baseball M, basketball M/W, crew M/W, cross-country running M/W, equestrian sports M(c)/W(c), fencing M(c)/W(c), field hockey W, football M, golf M/W, ice hockey M/W, lacrosse M/W, rugby M(c)/W(c), sailing M(c)/W(c), skiing (cross-country) M(c)/W(c), skiing (downhill) W(c), soccer M/W, softball W, squash M/W, swimming and diving M/W, tennis M/W, track and field M/W, ultimate Frisbee M(c)/W(c), volleyball M(c)/W, water polo M(c). ***Intramural sports:*** badminton M/W, basketball M/W, football M/W, golf M/W, ice hockey M/W, racquetball M/W, skiing (cross-country) M/W, soccer M/W, softball M/W, squash M/W, tennis M/W, volleyball M/W, water polo M/W.

Campus security: 24-hour emergency response devices and patrols, late-night transport/escort service, controlled dormitory access, student safety program.

Student services: health clinic, personal/psychological counseling.

COSTS & FINANCIAL AID
Costs (2019–20) ***Comprehensive fee:*** $70,890 includes full-time tuition ($55,970), mandatory fees ($560), and room and board ($14,360). Part-time tuition: $6996 per course. ***College room only:*** $7850.

Financial Aid Of all full-time matriculated undergraduates who enrolled in 2018, 1,032 applied for aid, 995 were judged to have need, 995 had their need fully met. 625 Federal Work-Study jobs (averaging $1831). 45 state and other part-time jobs (averaging $1944). ***Average percent of need met:*** 100. ***Average financial aid package:*** $49,164. ***Average need-based loan:*** $4346. ***Average need-based gift aid:*** $43,434. ***Average indebtedness upon graduation:*** $20,582. ***Financial aid deadline:*** 1/15.

APPLYING
Standardized Tests *Required:* (for admission).

Options: electronic application, early decision, deferred entrance.

Application fee: $60.

Required: essay or personal statement, high school transcript, 1 letter of recommendation. ***Recommended:*** interview.

Application deadlines: 1/1 (freshmen), 4/1 (transfers).

Early decision deadline: 11/15 (for plan 1), 1/1 (for plan 2).

Notification: 4/1 (freshmen), 5/15 (transfers), 12/15 (early decision plan 1), 2/15 (early decision plan 2).

CONTACT
Ms. T. Peaches Valdes, Dean of Admission, Hamilton College, 198 College Hill Road, Clinton, NY 13323. *Phone:* 800-843-2655. *Toll-free phone:* 800-843-2655. *Fax:* 315-859-4457. *E-mail:* admission@hamilton.edu.

Hartwick College

Oneonta, New York

http://www.hartwick.edu/

- **Independent** 4-year, founded 1797
- **Small-town** 425-acre campus with easy access to Capital District, NY
- **Endowment** $74.3 million
- **Coed** 1,176 undergraduate students, 98% full-time, 59% women, 41% men
- **Moderately difficult** entrance level, 89% of applicants were admitted

UNDERGRAD STUDENTS
1,156 full-time, 20 part-time. Students come from 28 states and territories; 20 other countries; 21% are from out of state; 10% Black or African American, non-Hispanic/Latino; 5% Hispanic/Latino; 3% Asian, non-Hispanic/Latino; 0.2% Native Hawaiian or other Pacific Islander, non-Hispanic/Latino; 2% American Indian or Alaska Native, non-Hispanic/Latino; 14% Race/ethnicity unknown; 2% international; 3% transferred in; 87% live on campus.

Freshmen:
Admission: 3,019 applied, 2,674 admitted, 407 enrolled. ***Average high school GPA:*** ####. ***Test scores:*** SAT evidence-based reading and writing scores over 500: 55%; SAT math scores over 500: 58%; ACT scores over 18: 96%; SAT evidence-based reading and writing scores over 600: 8%; SAT math scores over 600: 13%; ACT scores over 24: 46%; SAT evidence-based reading and writing scores over 700: 1%; SAT math scores over 700: 1%; ACT scores over 30: 7%.

Retention: 69% of full-time freshmen returned.

FACULTY
Total: 161, 61% full-time, 65% with terminal degrees.

Student/faculty ratio: 11:1.

ACADEMICS
Calendar: 4-1-4. *Degree:* bachelor's.

Special study options: accelerated degree program, advanced placement credit, distance learning, double majors, honors programs, independent study, internships, off-campus study, part-time degree program, services for LD students, student-designed majors, study abroad, summer session for credit.

Unusual degree programs: 3-2 business administration with Clarkson University; engineering with Clarkson University, Columbia University; nursing; Occupational or Physical Therapy at Sage Colleges.

Computers: 80 computers/terminals are available on campus for general student use. Students can access the following: computer help desk, free student e-mail accounts, online (class) grades, online (class) registration, online (class) schedules. Campuswide network is available. 100% of college-owned or -operated housing units are wired for high-speed Internet access. Wireless service is available via entire campus. **Library:** Stevens-German Library. *Books:* 209,006 (physical), 4,560 (digital/electronic); *Serial titles:* 1,392 (physical), 38,934 (digital/electronic); *Databases:* 59. Weekly public service hours: 96; students can reserve study rooms.

STUDENT LIFE
Housing options: on-campus residence required through senior year; coed. Campus housing is university owned. Freshman campus housing is guaranteed.

Activities and organizations: drama/theater group, student-run newspaper, radio station, choral group, Student Union, student radio station, Student Senate, Wine to Water, Cardboard Alley Players (theater), national fraternities, national sororities.

Athletics Member NCAA. All Division III. ***Intercollegiate sports:*** basketball M/W, cheerleading W(c), cross-country running M/W, equestrian sports W, field hockey W, football M, lacrosse M/W, soccer M/W, swimming and diving M/W, tennis W, volleyball W. ***Intramural sports:*** basketball M/W, football M, riflery M(c)/W(c), rugby M(c), skiing (downhill) M(c)/W(c), soccer M/W, softball W(c), volleyball M/W.

Campus security: 24-hour emergency response devices and patrols, late-night transport/escort service, controlled dormitory access.

Student services: health clinic, personal/psychological counseling.

COSTS & FINANCIAL AID
Costs (2019–20) ***One-time required fee:*** $400. ***Comprehensive fee:*** $59,756 includes full-time tuition ($45,990), mandatory fees ($936), and room and board ($12,830). Part-time tuition: $1478 per credit hour. ***College room only:*** $6650.

Financial Aid Of all full-time matriculated undergraduates who enrolled in 2018, 1,019 applied for aid, 952 were judged to have need, 143 had their need fully met. 746 Federal Work-Study jobs (averaging $1869). In 2018, 190 non-need-based awards were made. ***Average percent of need met:*** 80. ***Average financial aid package:*** $38,054. ***Average need-based loan:*** $4415. ***Average need-based gift aid:*** $33,033. ***Average non-need-based aid:*** $28,915. ***Average indebtedness upon graduation:*** $27,653.

APPLYING
Standardized Tests *Required for some:* SAT or ACT (for admission).

Options: electronic application, early admission, early decision, deferred entrance.

Required: high school transcript. ***Required for some:*** audition for music program, portfolio for art majors. ***Recommended:*** minimum 2.5 GPA.

Application deadlines: rolling (freshmen), 8/1 (transfers).

Early decision deadline: 11/1.

Notification: continuous (freshmen), continuous until 8/15 (transfers), 12/1 (early decision plan 1), rolling (early decision plan 2).

CONTACT
Ms. Lisa Starkey-Wood, Director of Admissions, Hartwick College, PO Box 4022, Oneonta, NY 13820-4022. *Phone:* 607-431-4150. *Toll-free phone:* 888-HARTWICK. *Fax:* 607-431-4102. *E-mail:* admissions@hartwick.edu.

Helene Fuld College of Nursing
New York, New York
http://www.helenefuld.edu/

CONTACT
Helene Fuld College of Nursing, 24 East 120th Street, New York, NY 10035. *Phone:* 212-616-7271.

Hilbert College
Hamburg, New York
http://www.hilbert.edu/

- **Independent Roman Catholic** comprehensive, founded 1957
- **Suburban** 40-acre campus with easy access to Buffalo
- **Endowment** $7.0 million
- **Coed**
- **Minimally difficult** entrance level

FACULTY
Student/faculty ratio: 12:1.

ACADEMICS
Calendar: semesters. *Degrees:* associate, bachelor's, and master's. **Library:** McGrath Library. *Books:* 36,902 (physical), 9,442 (digital/electronic); *Serial titles:* 172 (physical), 100,109 (digital/electronic); *Databases:* 49. Weekly public service hours: 77; students can reserve study rooms.

STUDENT LIFE
Housing options: coed. Campus housing is university owned and leased by the school. Freshman applicants given priority for college housing.

Activities and organizations: drama/theater group, student-run newspaper, radio station, Student Government Association, Student Business and Accounting Association, SADD, Students in Free Enterprise (SIFE), Criminal Justice Association.

Athletics Member NCAA. All Division III.

Campus security: 24-hour emergency response devices and patrols, student patrols, late-night transport/escort service, controlled dormitory access.

Student services: health clinic, personal/psychological counseling, veterans affairs office.

COSTS & FINANCIAL AID
Costs (2018–19) ***One-time required fee:*** $50. ***Comprehensive fee:*** $31,700 includes full-time tuition ($21,750), mandatory fees ($600), and room and board ($9350). Part-time tuition: $560 per credit hour. ***Required fees:*** $13 per credit hour part-time, $55 per term part-time. ***Room and board:*** Room and board charges vary according to board plan and housing facility.

Financial Aid Of all full-time matriculated undergraduates who enrolled in 2017, 658 applied for aid, 599 were judged to have need, 121 had their need fully met. In 2017, 65 non-need-based awards were made. ***Average percent of need met:*** 74. ***Average financial aid package:*** $15,839. ***Average need-based loan:*** $4996. ***Average need-based gift aid:*** $11,962. ***Average non-need-based aid:*** $6024. ***Average indebtedness upon graduation:*** $19,613.

APPLYING
Standardized Tests *Recommended:* SAT or ACT (for admission).

Options: electronic application, deferred entrance.

Application fee: $25.

Required: high school transcript. ***Required for some:*** interview. ***Recommended:*** essay or personal statement, interview.

CONTACT
Mr. Brian Filjones, Director, Admissions, Hilbert College, 5200 South Park Avenue, Hamburg, NY 14075-1597. *Phone:* 716-649-7900 Ext. 210. *Toll-free phone:* 800-649-8003. *Fax:* 716-649-1152. *E-mail:* bfiljones@hilbert.edu.

Hobart and William Smith Colleges
Geneva, New York
http://www.hws.edu/

- **Independent** comprehensive, founded 1822
- **Small-town** 200-acre campus with easy access to Rochester, Syracuse
- **Endowment** $202.0 million
- **Coed**
- **Very difficult** entrance level

FACULTY
Student/faculty ratio: 10:1.

ACADEMICS
Calendar: semesters. *Degrees:* bachelor's, master's, and postbachelor's certificates.
Library: Warren Hunting Smith Library plus 1 other. *Books:* 389,139 (physical), 285,340 (digital/electronic); *Serial titles:* 1,485 (physical), 57,835 (digital/electronic); *Databases:* 134. Weekly public service hours: 114; study areas open 24 hours, 5–7 days a week; students can reserve study rooms.

STUDENT LIFE

Housing options: on-campus residence required through junior year; coed, men-only, women-only, cooperative. Campus housing is university owned. Freshman campus housing is guaranteed.

Activities and organizations: drama/theater group, student-run newspaper, radio station, choral group, Student Life and Leadership, student government, campus publications, Service Network, sports clubs, national fraternities, national sororities.

Athletics Member NCAA. All Division III except golf (Division II), lacrosse (Division I).

Campus security: 24-hour emergency response devices and patrols, late-night transport/escort service, controlled dormitory access.

Student services: health clinic, personal/psychological counseling, women's center.

COSTS & FINANCIAL AID

Costs (2018–19) ***Comprehensive fee:*** $69,290 includes full-time tuition ($54,060), mandatory fees ($1195), and room and board ($14,035). ***Room and board:*** Room and board charges vary according to board plan. ***Payment plans:*** tuition prepayment, installment.

Financial Aid Of all full-time matriculated undergraduates who enrolled in 2017, 1,560 applied for aid, 1,350 were judged to have need, 473 had their need fully met. 949 Federal Work-Study jobs (averaging $2039). 537 state and other part-time jobs (averaging $1921). In 2017, 669 non-need-based awards were made. ***Average percent of need met:*** 79. ***Average financial aid package:*** $39,749. ***Average need-based loan:*** $3966. ***Average need-based gift aid:*** $35,269. ***Average non-need-based aid:*** $17,584. ***Average indebtedness upon graduation:*** $33,205. ***Financial aid deadline:*** 2/1.

APPLYING

Standardized Tests *Required for some:* SAT or ACT (for admission).

Options: electronic application, early admission, early decision, deferred entrance.

Required: essay or personal statement, high school transcript, 1 letter of recommendation. ***Recommended:*** interview.

CONTACT

Hobart and William Smith Colleges, 300 Pulteney Street, Geneva, NY 14456. *Phone:* 315-781-3622. *Toll-free phone:* 800-852-2256.

★ Hofstra University

Hempstead, New York

http://www.hofstra.edu/

- **Independent** university, founded 1935
- **Suburban** 244-acre campus with easy access to New York City
- **Endowment** $575.8 million
- **Coed** 6,701 undergraduate students, 94% full-time, 55% women, 45% men
- **Moderately difficult** entrance level, 63% of applicants were admitted

UNDERGRAD STUDENTS

6,329 full-time, 372 part-time. Students come from 47 states and territories; 81 other countries; 38% are from out of state; 9% Black or African American, non-Hispanic/Latino; 12% Hispanic/Latino; 11% Asian, non-Hispanic/Latino; 0.2% Native Hawaiian or other Pacific Islander, non-Hispanic/Latino; 0.4% American Indian or Alaska Native, non-Hispanic/Latino; 3% Two or more races, non-Hispanic/Latino; 2% Race/ethnicity unknown; 6% international; 4% transferred in; 45% live on campus.

Freshmen:

Admission: 27,620 applied, 17,456 admitted, 1,555 enrolled. ***Average high school GPA:*** 3.6. ***Test scores:*** SAT evidence-based reading and writing scores over 500: 98%; SAT math scores over 500: 98%; ACT scores over 18: 100%; SAT evidence-based reading and writing scores over 600: 63%; SAT math scores over 600: 61%; ACT scores over 24: 82%; SAT evidence-based reading and writing scores over 700: 11%; SAT math scores over 700: 15%; ACT scores over 30: 30%.

Retention: 82% of full-time freshmen returned.

FACULTY

Total: 1,236, 39% full-time, 64% with terminal degrees.

Student/faculty ratio: 13:1.

ACADEMICS

Calendar: semesters. *Degrees:* certificates, bachelor's, master's, doctoral, post-master's, and postbachelor's certificates.

Special study options: accelerated degree program, advanced placement credit, cooperative education, distance learning, double majors, English as a second language, external degree program, freshman honors college, honors programs, independent study, internships, off-campus study, part-time degree program, services for LD students, student-designed majors, study abroad, summer session for credit. ***ROTC:*** Army (b).

Unusual degree programs: 3-2 business administration; physician assistant studies, computer science, law.

Computers: 1,536 computers/terminals and 1,900 ports are available on campus for general student use. Students can access the following: campus intranet, computer help desk, free student e-mail accounts, online (class) grades, online (class) registration, online (class) schedules, Emergency alert system, online course management system, online card services balance update, online e-portfolio, software tutoring, support for specific tech-enhanced assignments, repair and rebuilding-after-virus services, and printing services. Campuswide network is available. 100% of college-owned or -operated housing units are wired for high-speed Internet access. Wireless service is available via entire campus.

Library: Axinn Library plus 3 others. *Books:* 859,300 (physical), 214,032 (digital/electronic); *Serial titles:* 1,761 (physical), 17,415 (digital/electronic); *Databases:* 241. Weekly public service hours: 110; study areas open 24 hours, 5–7 days a week; students can reserve study rooms.

STUDENT LIFE

Housing options: coed, special housing for students with disabilities. Campus housing is university owned. Freshman applicants given priority for college housing.

Activities and organizations: drama/theater group, student-run newspaper, radio and television station, choral group, Hofstra Rock Climbing, transcenDANCE, DanceWorks, E-Sports, Student Government Association, national fraternities, national sororities.

Athletics Member NCAA. All Division I. ***Intercollegiate sports:*** baseball M(s), basketball M(s)/W(s), cross-country running M(s)/W(s), field hockey W(s), golf M(s)/W(s), lacrosse M(s)/W(s), soccer M(s)/W(s), softball W(s), tennis M(s)/W(s), track and field M(s)/W(s), volleyball W(s), wrestling M(s). ***Intramural sports:*** badminton M(c)/W(c), baseball M(c), basketball M/W, bowling M(c)/W(c), cheerleading M(c)/W(c), crew M(c)/W(c), cross-country running M(c)/W(c), equestrian sports M(c)/W(c), ice hockey M(c)/W(c), lacrosse M(c)/W(c), rock climbing M(c)/W(c), rowing M(c)/W(c), rugby M(c)/W(c), soccer M(c)/W(c), softball M/W, table tennis M(c)/W(c), tennis M(c)/W(c), track and field M(c)/W(c), ultimate Frisbee M(c)/W(c), volleyball M(c)/W(c), weight lifting M(c)/W(c).

Campus security: 24-hour emergency response devices and patrols, student patrols, late-night transport/escort service, controlled dormitory access.

Student services: health clinic, personal/psychological counseling.

COSTS & FINANCIAL AID

Costs (2018–19) ***Comprehensive fee:*** $61,408 includes full-time tuition ($44,640), mandatory fees ($1060), and room and board ($15,708). Full-time tuition and fees vary according to course load. Part-time tuition: $1500 per credit hour. Part-time tuition and fees vary according to course load. No tuition increase for student's term of enrollment. ***Required fees:*** $155 per term part-time. ***College room only:*** $10,640. Room and board charges vary according to board plan and housing facility. ***Payment plan:*** installment. ***Waivers:*** employees or children of employees.

Financial Aid Of all full-time matriculated undergraduates who enrolled in 2018, 4,813 applied for aid, 4,050 were judged to have need, 1,026 had their need fully met. 1,514 Federal Work-Study jobs (averaging $3000). 1,489 state and other part-time jobs (averaging $3200). In 2018, 1589 non-need-based awards were made. ***Average percent of need met:*** 68. ***Average financial aid package:*** $32,000. ***Average need-based loan:*** $4000. ***Average need-based gift aid:*** $22,000. ***Average non-need-based aid:*** $20,000.

APPLYING

Standardized Tests *Required for some:* TOEFL for international students.

Options: electronic application, early admission, early action, deferred entrance.

Application fee: $70.

Required: essay or personal statement, high school transcript, 2 letters of recommendation, Proof of degree required for all; TOEFL required for international students.. ***Required for some:*** interview.

Application deadlines: rolling (freshmen), rolling (transfers), 12/15 (early action).

Notification: continuous (transfers), 1/15 (early action).

CONTACT

Sunil A. Samuel, Assistant Vice President of Admissions, Hofstra University, 100 Hofstra University, Hempstead, NY 11549. *Phone:* 516-463-6700. *Toll-free phone:* 800-HOFSTRA. *Fax:* 516-463-5100. *E-mail:* admission@hofstra.edu.

See this page for display ad and page 1022 for the College Close-Up.

Holy Trinity Orthodox Seminary

Jordanville, New York

http://www.hts.edu/

- **Independent Russian Orthodox** 4-year, founded 1948
- **Rural** 900-acre campus
- **Men only**
- **Noncompetitive** entrance level

FACULTY

Student/faculty ratio: 2:1.

ACADEMICS

Calendar: semesters. *Degree:* certificates and bachelor's.

Library: Holy Trinity Orthodox Seminary Library. *Books:* 40,000 (physical). Weekly public service hours: 40.

STUDENT LIFE

Housing options: men-only. Campus housing is university owned. Freshman campus housing is guaranteed.

Activities and organizations: student-run newspaper, choral group, Student Union.

Campus security: 24-hour emergency response devices.

Student services: health clinic, personal/psychological counseling.

APPLYING

Options: electronic application, deferred entrance.

Application fee: $40.

Required: essay or personal statement, high school transcript, minimum 2.0 GPA, 1 letter of recommendation, Orthodoxy/Orthodox baptism, entrance exam, recommendation from spiritual father or parish priest.

CONTACT

Rev. Fr. Ephraim Willmarth, Assistant Dean and Director of Admissions, Holy Trinity Orthodox Seminary, PO Box 36, Jordanville, NY 13361. *Phone:* 315-858-0945. *Fax:* 315-858-0945. *E-mail:* ejwillmarth@hts.edu.

Houghton College

Houghton, New York

http://www.houghton.edu/

CONTACT

Mr. Ryan Spear, Associate Director of Admission Operations, Houghton College, PO Box 128, Houghton, NY 14744. *Phone:* 585-567-9353. *Toll-free phone:* 800-777-2556. *Fax:* 585-567-9522. *E-mail:* admission@houghton.edu.

Hunter College of the City University of New York

New York, New York

http://www.hunter.cuny.edu/

- **State and locally supported** comprehensive, founded 1870, part of City University of New York System
- **Urban** campus
- **Endowment** $120.0 million
- **Coed** 17,212 undergraduate students, 76% full-time, 65% women, 35% men
- **Moderately difficult** entrance level, 36% of applicants were admitted

UNDERGRAD STUDENTS

13,111 full-time, 4,101 part-time. Students come from 41 states and territories; 162 other countries; 3% are from out of state; 12% Black or African American, non-Hispanic/Latino; 22% Hispanic/Latino; 31% Asian, non-Hispanic/Latino; 0.1% American Indian or Alaska Native, non-Hispanic/Latino; 5% international; 11% transferred in; 1% live on campus.

Freshmen:

Admission: 31,030 applied, 11,300 admitted, 2,598 enrolled. ***Average high school GPA:*** 3.5. ***Test scores:*** SAT evidence-based reading and writing scores over 500: 92%; SAT math scores over 500: 94%; SAT evidence-based reading and writing scores over 600: 33%; SAT math scores over 600: 53%; SAT evidence-based reading and writing scores over 700: 8%; SAT math scores over 700: 12%.

Retention: 85% of full-time freshmen returned.

FACULTY

Total: 2,110, 32% full-time, 54% with terminal degrees.

Student/faculty ratio: 14:1.

ACADEMICS

Calendar: semesters. *Degrees:* bachelor's, master's, doctoral, post-master's, and postbachelor's certificates.

Special study options: advanced placement credit, distance learning, double majors, English as a second language, freshman honors college, honors programs, independent study, internships, off-campus study, part-time degree program, services for LD students, student-designed majors, study abroad, summer session for credit.

Unusual degree programs: 3-2 nursing; social work; anthropology, economics, English, history, mathematics, music, physics, sociology.

Computers: 600 computers/terminals are available on campus for general student use. Students can access the following: computer help desk, free student e-mail accounts, online (class) registration, online (class) schedules. Campuswide network is available. 100% of college-owned or -operated housing units are wired for high-speed Internet access. Wireless service is available via entire campus.

Library: Hunter College Library plus 1 other. *Books:* 438,832 (physical), 602,800 (digital/electronic); *Serial titles:* 3,893 (physical), 105,674 (digital/electronic); *Databases:* 280.

STUDENT LIFE

Housing options: coed.

Activities and organizations: drama/theater group, student-run newspaper, radio and television station, choral group.

Athletics Member NCAA. All Division III. ***Intercollegiate sports:*** basketball M/W, cross-country running M/W, fencing M/W, gymnastics W, soccer M, swimming and diving W, tennis M/W, track and field M/W, volleyball M/W, wrestling M. ***Intramural sports:*** basketball M/W, cross-country running M/W, gymnastics M/W, racquetball M/W, rugby M, soccer M/W, swimming and diving M/W, tennis M/W, volleyball M/W.

Campus security: 24-hour emergency response devices and patrols.

Student services: personal/psychological counseling, women's center.

COSTS & FINANCIAL AID

Costs (2018–19) ***Tuition:*** state resident $6730 full-time, $295 per credit hour part-time; nonresident $18,000 full-time, $600 per credit hour part-time. Full-time tuition and fees vary according to course load, degree level, and program. Part-time tuition and fees vary according to course load, degree level, and program. ***Required fees:*** $450 full-time, $133 per term part-time. ***Room only:*** $4857. Room and board charges vary according to housing facility and location. ***Payment plan:*** installment.

Financial Aid Of all full-time matriculated undergraduates who enrolled in 2018, 10,929 applied for aid, 9,892 were judged to have need, 5,751 had their need fully met. 254 Federal Work-Study jobs (averaging $2303). In 2018, 417 non-need-based awards were made. ***Average percent of need met:*** 82. ***Average financial aid package:*** $8126. ***Average need-based loan:*** $4123. ***Average need-based gift aid:*** $7950. ***Average non-need-based aid:*** $3450. ***Average indebtedness upon graduation:*** $15,096.

APPLYING

Standardized Tests *Required:* SAT or ACT (for admission).

Options: early admission.

Application fee: $65.

Required: high school transcript.

Notification: continuous (freshmen), continuous (transfers).

CONTACT

Ms. Lori Janowski, Associate Director of Undergraduate Admissions, Hunter College of the City University of New York, 695 Park Avenue, New York, NY 10065-5085. *Phone:* 212-772-4490. *Fax:* 212-650-3472. *E-mail:* lori.janowski@hunter.cuny.edu.

Iona College

New Rochelle, New York

http://www.iona.edu/

- **Independent** comprehensive, founded 1940, affiliated with Roman Catholic Church
- **Suburban** 35-acre campus with easy access to New York City
- **Endowment** $130.8 million
- **Coed** 3,287 undergraduate students, 90% full-time, 51% women, 49% men
- **Moderately difficult** entrance level, 88% of applicants were admitted

UNDERGRAD STUDENTS

2,961 full-time, 326 part-time. Students come from 35 states and territories; 38 other countries; 23% are from out of state; 10% Black or African American, non-Hispanic/Latino; 23% Hispanic/Latino; 3% Asian, non-Hispanic/Latino; 0.1% Native Hawaiian or other Pacific Islander, non-Hispanic/Latino; 0.5% American Indian or Alaska Native, non-Hispanic/Latino; 1% Two or more races, non-Hispanic/Latino; 9% Race/ethnicity unknown; 2% international; 3% transferred in; 45% live on campus.

Freshmen:

Admission: 10,062 applied, 8,871 admitted, 853 enrolled. ***Average high school GPA:*** 3.0. ***Test scores:*** SAT evidence-based reading and writing scores over 500: 80%; SAT math scores over 500: 74%; ACT scores over 18: 93%; SAT evidence-based reading and writing scores over 600: 23%; SAT math scores over 600: 18%; ACT scores over 24: 42%; SAT evidence-based reading and writing scores over 700: 1%; SAT math scores over 700: 2%; ACT scores over 30: 8%.

Retention: 75% of full-time freshmen returned.

FACULTY

Total: 329, 53% full-time, 49% with terminal degrees.

Student/faculty ratio: 15:1.

ACADEMICS

Calendar: semesters. *Degrees:* certificates, bachelor's, master's, post-master's, and postbachelor's certificates.

Special study options: accelerated degree program, adult/continuing education programs, advanced placement credit, distance learning, double majors, English as a second language, honors programs, independent study, internships, part-time degree program, services for LD students, study abroad, summer session for credit. ***ROTC:*** Army (c), Air Force (c).

Unusual degree programs: 3-2 business administration.

Computers: 10,000 ports are available on campus for general student use. Students can access the following: campus intranet, computer help desk, free student e-mail accounts, online (class) grades, online (class) registration, online (class) schedules, bill payment. Campuswide network is available. 100% of college-owned or -operated housing units are wired

for high-speed Internet access. Wireless service is available via entire campus.
Library: Ryan Library plus 1 other. *Books:* 268,290 (physical), 330,337 (digital/electronic); *Serial titles:* 112 (physical), 369 (digital/electronic); *Databases:* 160. Weekly public service hours: 101; students can reserve study rooms.

STUDENT LIFE
Housing options: coed, special housing for students with disabilities. Campus housing is university owned and leased by the school. Freshman campus housing is guaranteed.

Activities and organizations: drama/theater group, student-run newspaper, radio and television station, choral group, Student Government Association, Gaels Activities Board, Council for Greek Governance, Student Leader Alliance for Multiculturalism, The Ionian - Student Newspaper, national fraternities, national sororities.

Athletics Member NCAA. All Division I. ***Intercollegiate sports:*** baseball M(s), basketball M(s)/W(s), cross-country running M(s)/W(s), golf M(s), lacrosse W(s), rowing M/W, soccer M(s)/W(s), softball W(s), swimming and diving M(s)/W(s), track and field M(s)/W(s), volleyball W(s), water polo M/W(s). ***Intramural sports:*** basketball M/W, cheerleading M(c)/W(c), football M/W, rugby M(c), soccer M/W, table tennis M/W, volleyball M/W.

Campus security: 24-hour emergency response devices and patrols, controlled dormitory access.

Student services: health clinic, personal/psychological counseling.

COSTS & FINANCIAL AID
Costs (2019–20) ***Tuition:*** $37,972 full-time. ***Required fees:*** $540 per term part-time.

Financial Aid Of all full-time matriculated undergraduates who enrolled in 2018, 2,919 applied for aid, 2,547 were judged to have need, 504 had their need fully met. 453 Federal Work-Study jobs (averaging $2039). In 2018, 356 non-need-based awards were made. ***Average percent of need met:*** 16. ***Average financial aid package:*** $26,735. ***Average need-based loan:*** $2933. ***Average need-based gift aid:*** $6123. ***Average non-need-based aid:*** $21,250. ***Average indebtedness upon graduation:*** $32,396. ***Financial aid deadline:*** 4/15.

APPLYING
Standardized Tests *Required:* SAT or ACT (for admission).

Options: electronic application, early action, deferred entrance.

Required: high school transcript. ***Required for some:*** interview. ***Recommended:*** essay or personal statement, 2 letters of recommendation.

Application deadlines: 2/15 (freshmen), 8/15 (transfers).

Notification: continuous (freshmen), continuous (transfers).

CONTACT
Mr. Bryan Rothstein, Director of Undergraduate Admissions, Iona College, Admissions, 715 North Avenue, New Rochelle, NY 10801. *Phone:* 914-633-2502. *Toll-free phone:* 800-231-IONA. *Fax:* 914-633-2778. *E-mail:* admissions@iona.edu.

Ithaca College
Ithaca, New York
http://www.ithaca.edu/

- **Independent** comprehensive, founded 1892
- **Small-town** 669-acre campus with easy access to Syracuse
- **Endowment** $300.7 million
- **Coed** 6,101 undergraduate students, 98% full-time, 57% women, 43% men
- **Moderately difficult** entrance level, 69% of applicants were admitted

UNDERGRAD STUDENTS
5,991 full-time, 110 part-time. Students come from 45 states and territories; 42 other countries; 55% are from out of state; 6% Black or African American, non-Hispanic/Latino; 9% Hispanic/Latino; 4% Asian, non-Hispanic/Latino; 0.0% Native Hawaiian or other Pacific Islander, non-Hispanic/Latino; 0.1% American Indian or Alaska Native, non-Hispanic/Latino; 3% Two or more races, non-Hispanic/Latino; 3% Race/ethnicity unknown; 2% international; 1% transferred in; 71% live on campus.

Freshmen:
Admission: 15,278 applied, 10,472 admitted, 1,666 enrolled. ***Test scores:*** SAT evidence-based reading and writing scores over 500: 99%; SAT math scores over 500: 98%; ACT scores over 18: 100%; SAT evidence-based reading and writing scores over 600: 74%; SAT math scores over 600: 59%; ACT scores over 24: 85%; SAT evidence-based reading and writing scores over 700: 16%; SAT math scores over 700: 13%; ACT scores over 30: 31%.

Retention: 85% of full-time freshmen returned.

FACULTY
Total: 765, 68% full-time, 66% with terminal degrees.

Student/faculty ratio: 10:1.

ACADEMICS
Calendar: semesters. *Degrees:* certificates, bachelor's, master's, and doctoral.

Special study options: accelerated degree program, adult/continuing education programs, advanced placement credit, distance learning, double majors, freshman honors college, honors programs, independent study, internships, off-campus study, part-time degree program, services for LD students, student-designed majors, study abroad, summer session for credit. ***ROTC:*** Army (c), Air Force (c).

Unusual degree programs: 3-2 engineering with Cornell University, Rensselaer Polytechnic Institute, Clarkson University, Watson School of Engineering at Binghamton University.

Computers: 640 computers/terminals and 20 ports are available on campus for general student use. Students can access the following: campus intranet, computer help desk, free student e-mail accounts, online (class) grades, online (class) registration, online (class) schedules. Campuswide network is available. 100% of college-owned or -operated housing units are wired for high-speed Internet access. Wireless service is available via entire campus.
Library: Ithaca College Library. *Books:* 315,000 (physical), 165,000 (digital/electronic); *Serial titles:* 640 (physical), 68,858 (digital/electronic); *Databases:* 155. Weekly public service hours: 148; study areas open 24 hours, 5–7 days a week.

STUDENT LIFE
Housing options: on-campus residence required through junior year; coed, special housing for students with disabilities. Campus housing is university owned. Freshman campus housing is guaranteed.

Activities and organizations: drama/theater group, student-run newspaper, radio and television station, choral group, Student Governance Council, Colleges Against Cancer, Brothers 4 Brothers, International Club, Asian American Alliance, national fraternities.

Athletics Member NCAA. All Division III. ***Intercollegiate sports:*** baseball M, basketball M/W, crew M/W, cross-country running M/W, field hockey W, football M, gymnastics W, lacrosse M/W, soccer M/W, softball W, swimming and diving M/W, tennis M/W, track and field M/W, volleyball W, wrestling M. ***Intramural sports:*** basketball M/W, equestrian sports M(c)/W(c), fencing M(c), field hockey W(c), football M, golf M/W, ice hockey M(c), lacrosse M(c)/W(c), rugby M(c)/W(c), skiing (downhill) M(c)/W(c), soccer M/W, softball M/W, squash M(c)/W(c), table tennis M(c)/W(c), tennis M/W, ultimate Frisbee M(c)/W(c), volleyball M/W.

Campus security: 24-hour emergency response devices and patrols, student patrols, late-night transport/escort service, controlled dormitory access.

Student services: health clinic, personal/psychological counseling, veterans affairs office.

COSTS & FINANCIAL AID
Costs (2019–20) ***Comprehensive fee:*** $61,130 includes full-time tuition ($45,274) and room and board ($15,856). Part-time tuition: $1509 per credit hour. ***College room only:*** $8768.

Financial Aid Of all full-time matriculated undergraduates who enrolled in 2018, 4,714 applied for aid, 5,522 were judged to have need, 1,736 had their need fully met. 2,949 Federal Work-Study jobs (averaging $2902). 1,742 state and other part-time jobs (averaging $2402). In 2018, 1518 non-need-based awards were made. ***Average percent of need met:*** 87. ***Average financial aid package:*** $38,845. ***Average need-based loan:*** $6006. ***Average need-based gift aid:*** $28,856. ***Average non-need-based aid:*** $16,525. ***Average indebtedness upon graduation:*** $39,913.

APPLYING
Options: electronic application, early admission, early decision, early action, deferred entrance.
Application fee: $60.
Required: essay or personal statement, high school transcript, 1 letter of recommendation. ***Required for some:*** audition for some programs. ***Recommended:*** minimum 3.0 GPA.
Application deadlines: 2/1 (freshmen), 3/1 (transfers), 12/1 (early action).
Early decision deadline: 11/1.
Notification: 4/15 (freshmen), continuous (transfers), 12/15 (early decision), 2/1 (early action).

CONTACT
Ithaca College, 953 Danby Road, Ithaca, NY 14850. *Toll-free phone:* 800-429-4274.

Jamestown Business College
Jamestown, New York
http://www.jbc.edu/

CONTACT
Mrs. Brenda Salemme, Director of Admissions, Jamestown Business College, 7 Fairmount Avenue, Box 429, Jamestown, NY 14702-0429. *Phone:* 716-664-5100. *Fax:* 716-664-3144. *E-mail:* brendasalemme@jbc.edu.

The Jewish Theological Seminary
New York, New York
http://www.jtsa.edu/

CONTACT
Mr. Sergio Lineberge, List College Admissions Coordinator, The Jewish Theological Seminary, 3080 Broadway, New York, NY 10027. *Phone:* 212-678-8820. *E-mail:* lcadmissions@jtsa.edu.

John Jay College of Criminal Justice of the City University of New York
New York, New York
http://www.jjay.cuny.edu/

- **State and locally supported** comprehensive, founded 1964, part of City University of New York
- **Urban** campus with easy access to New York City
- **Coed**
- **Moderately difficult** entrance level

ACADEMICS
Calendar: semesters. *Degrees:* certificates, bachelor's, and master's.
Library: Lloyd George Sealy Library. *Books:* 182,059 (physical), 631,447 (digital/electronic); *Serial titles:* 7,124 (physical), 101,219 (digital/electronic); *Databases:* 178. Weekly public service hours: 77; study areas open 24 hours, 5–7 days a week; students can reserve study rooms.

STUDENT LIFE
Housing options: coed. Campus housing is leased by the school.
Activities and organizations: drama/theater group, student-run newspaper, radio station, choral group, Auxiliary University Program, Student Athlete Advisory Community Club, Environmental Club, Law Society, Artists United.
Athletics Member NCAA. All Division III.
Campus security: 24-hour emergency response devices and patrols, controlled dormitory access.
Student services: health clinic, personal/psychological counseling, women's center, legal services.

COSTS & FINANCIAL AID
Costs (2018–19) ***Tuition:*** state resident $6730 full-time, $295 per credit hour part-time; nonresident $14,400 full-time, $600 per credit hour part-time. ***Required fees:*** $540 full-time, $183 per term part-time.
Financial Aid Of all full-time matriculated undergraduates who enrolled in 2017, 10,370 applied for aid, 9,986 were judged to have need. ***Average percent of need met:*** 85. ***Average financial aid package:*** $8697. ***Average need-based loan:*** $3943. ***Average need-based gift aid:*** $2720.

APPLYING
Standardized Tests *Required:* SAT or ACT (for admission).
Options: deferred entrance.
Application fee: $65.
Required: high school transcript, minimum 2.0 GPA, minimum SAT score of 1100.

CONTACT
Mr. Vincent Papandrea, Director, John Jay College of Criminal Justice of the City University of New York, 524 West 59th Street, L.64.14NB, New York, NY 10019. *Phone:* 212-237-8864. *Toll-free phone:* 877-JOHNJAY. *E-mail:* vpapandrea@jjay.cuny.edu.

The Juilliard School
New York, New York
http://www.juilliard.edu/

- **Independent** comprehensive, founded 1905
- **Urban** campus with easy access to New York City
- **Coed** 585 undergraduate students, 83% full-time, 46% women, 54% men
- **Most difficult** entrance level, 5% of applicants were admitted

UNDERGRAD STUDENTS
487 full-time, 98 part-time. 85% are from out of state; 7% Black or African American, non-Hispanic/Latino; 7% Hispanic/Latino; 12% Asian, non-Hispanic/Latino; 0.2% Native Hawaiian or other Pacific Islander, non-Hispanic/Latino; 6% Two or more races, non-Hispanic/Latino; 12% Race/ethnicity unknown; 23% international; 2% transferred in.

Freshmen:
Admission: 4,045 applied, 199 admitted, 120 enrolled.

FACULTY
Total: 352, 36% full-time.
Student/faculty ratio: 4:1.

ACADEMICS
Calendar: semesters. *Degrees:* diplomas, bachelor's, master's, doctoral, post-master's, and postbachelor's certificates.
Special study options: adult/continuing education programs.
Computers: Campuswide network is available. Wireless service is available via entire campus.
Library: Lila Acheson Wallace Library.

STUDENT LIFE
Housing options: on-campus residence required for freshman year; coed. Campus housing is university owned. Freshman campus housing is guaranteed.
Activities and organizations: drama/theater group, student-run newspaper.
Campus security: 24-hour emergency response devices and patrols, controlled dormitory access, electronically operated main building entrances.
Student services: health clinic, personal/psychological counseling.

COSTS & FINANCIAL AID
Costs (2019–20) ***Comprehensive fee:*** $65,440 includes full-time tuition ($47,370), mandatory fees ($100), and room and board ($17,970).
Financial Aid Of all full-time matriculated undergraduates who enrolled in 2018, 429 applied for aid, 362 were judged to have need, 83 had their need fully met. In 2018, 54 non-need-based awards were made. ***Average percent of need met:*** 74. ***Average financial aid package:*** $36,562. ***Average need-based loan:*** $4604. ***Average need-based gift aid:*** $33,274. ***Average non-need-based aid:*** $21,856. ***Average indebtedness upon graduation:*** $24,702. ***Financial aid deadline:*** 3/1.

APPLYING
Standardized Tests *Required for some:* SAT or ACT (for admission).
Options: electronic application.
Application fee: $110.

Required: essay or personal statement, high school transcript, audition.

Application deadlines: 12/1 (freshmen), 12/1 (out-of-state freshmen), 12/1 (transfers).

Notification: 4/1 (freshmen), 4/1 (out-of-state freshmen), 4/1 (transfers).

CONTACT
Ms. Kathy Tesar, Associate Dean for Enrollment Management, The Juilliard School, 60 Lincoln Center Plaza, New York, NY 10023. *Phone:* 212-799-5000 Ext. 223. *Fax:* 212-724-0263. *E-mail:* admissions@juilliard.edu.

Kehilath Yakov Rabbinical Seminary
Ossining, New York
http://kehilathyakov.com/

CONTACT
Admissions Officer, Kehilath Yakov Rabbinical Seminary, 340 Illington Road, Ossining, NY 10562. *Phone:* 718-963-1212.

Keuka College
Keuka Park, New York
http://www.keuka.edu/

CONTACT
Mrs. Megan Perkins (Ryan), Keuka College, 141 Central Avenue, Keuka Park, NY 14478. *Phone:* 315-279-5254. *Toll-free phone:* 800-33-KEUKA. *Fax:* 315-279-5386. *E-mail:* admissions@keuka.edu.

The King's College
New York, New York
http://www.tkc.edu/

- **Independent nondenominational** 4-year, founded 1939
- **Urban** campus with easy access to New York City
- **Endowment** $488,024
- **Coed**
- **Moderately difficult** entrance level

FACULTY
Student/faculty ratio: 14:1.

ACADEMICS
Calendar: semesters. *Degree:* bachelor's.
Library: Battles Library.

STUDENT LIFE
Housing options: men-only, women-only. Campus housing is university owned and leased by the school. Freshman campus housing is guaranteed.

Activities and organizations: drama/theater group, student-run newspaper, choral group, The King's Players, King's Debate Society, Refuge, Empire State Tribune, The Kings of Swing.

Athletics Member NCCAA, USCAA.

Campus security: 24-hour emergency response devices, 24-hour security/doormen, fire sprinklers, fire/evacuation emergency plan.

Student services: personal/psychological counseling.

COSTS & FINANCIAL AID
Costs (2018–19) ***Tuition:*** $36,000 full-time, $1460 per credit hour part-time. Part-time tuition and fees vary according to course load. ***Required fees:*** $450 full-time, $225 per term part-time. ***Room only:*** $16,840. Room and board charges vary according to location. ***Payment plans:*** installment, deferred payment.

Financial Aid Of all full-time matriculated undergraduates who enrolled in 2017, 415 applied for aid, 365 were judged to have need, 60 had their need fully met. In 2017, 155 non-need-based awards were made. ***Average percent of need met:*** 68. ***Average financial aid package:*** $27,324. ***Average need-based loan:*** $4088. ***Average need-based gift aid:*** $22,539. ***Average non-need-based aid:*** $17,689. ***Average indebtedness upon graduation:*** $35,141.

APPLYING
Standardized Tests *Required:* SAT, ACT or CLT (for admission).

Options: electronic application, early action, deferred entrance.

Application fee: $30.

Required: high school transcript. ***Recommended:*** minimum 3.0 GPA, interview.

CONTACT
Mr. Noah Hunter, Director of Admissions, The King's College, 56 Broadway, New York, NY 10004. *Phone:* 212-659-3615. *Toll-free phone:* 888-969-7200 Ext. 3610. *Fax:* 212-659-3611. *E-mail:* nhunter@tkc.edu.

Lehman College of the City University of New York
Bronx, New York
http://www.lehman.cuny.edu/

- **State and locally supported** comprehensive, founded 1931, part of City University of New York System
- **Urban** 37-acre campus with easy access to New York City
- **Endowment** $7.1 million
- **Coed**
- **Moderately difficult** entrance level

FACULTY
Student/faculty ratio: 17:1.

ACADEMICS
Calendar: semesters. *Degrees:* certificates, bachelor's, master's, and post-master's certificates.
Library: Leonard Lief Library plus 1 other. *Books:* 362,674 (physical); *Serial titles:* 299,414 (physical). Weekly public service hours: 40; students can reserve study rooms.

STUDENT LIFE
Housing options: Campus housing is university owned.

Activities and organizations: drama/theater group, student-run newspaper, radio and television station, choral group, Club Mac, African Students Association, Dominican Student Association, The Sociology Club, Club Live.

Athletics Member NCAA. All Division III.

Campus security: 24-hour emergency response devices and patrols, student patrols, late-night transport/escort service.

Student services: health clinic, personal/psychological counseling, women's center.

COSTS & FINANCIAL AID
Costs (2018–19) ***Tuition:*** state resident $6730 full-time, $295 per credit hour part-time; nonresident $14,400 full-time, $600 per credit hour part-time. Full-time tuition and fees vary according to course load. Part-time tuition and fees vary according to course load. ***Required fees:*** $480 full-time, $130 per term part-time.

Financial Aid Of all full-time matriculated undergraduates who enrolled in 2016, 6,606 applied for aid, 6,407 were judged to have need, 87 had their need fully met. 448 Federal Work-Study jobs (averaging $1846). In 2016, 104 non-need-based awards were made. ***Average percent of need met:*** 54. ***Average financial aid package:*** $9448. ***Average need-based loan:*** $4063. ***Average need-based gift aid:*** $8116. ***Average non-need-based aid:*** $3450. ***Average indebtedness upon graduation:*** $4410.

APPLYING
Standardized Tests *Required:* SAT or ACT (for admission).

Options: deferred entrance.

Application fee: $65.

Required: high school transcript, minimum 3.0 GPA. ***Required for some:*** essay or personal statement, interview.

CONTACT
Ms. Laurie Austin, Director of Admissions, Lehman College of the City University of New York, 250 Bedford Park Boulevard West, Bronx, NY 10468. *Phone:* 718-960-8706. *Toll-free phone:* 877-LEHMAN1. *Fax:* 718-960-8712. *E-mail:* enroll@lehman.cuny.edu.

Le Moyne College
Syracuse, New York
http://www.lemoyne.edu/

- **Independent Roman Catholic (Jesuit)** comprehensive, founded 1946
- **Suburban** 161-acre campus
- **Endowment** $179.1 million
- **Coed**
- **Moderately difficult** entrance level

FACULTY
Student/faculty ratio: 13:1.

ACADEMICS
Calendar: semesters. *Degrees:* bachelor's, master's, post-master's, and postbachelor's certificates.
Library: Noreen Reale Falcone Library. *Books:* 261,183 (physical), 206,330 (digital/electronic); *Serial titles:* 1,391 (physical), 508 (digital/electronic); *Databases:* 270. Weekly public service hours: 109; study areas open 24 hours, 5–7 days a week; students can reserve study rooms.

STUDENT LIFE
Housing options: on-campus residence required through senior year; coed, special housing for students with disabilities. Campus housing is university owned. Freshman campus housing is guaranteed.

Activities and organizations: drama/theater group, student-run newspaper, radio and television station, choral group, Student Programming Board, Outing Club, Performing Arts Groups, Cultural Groups, New Student Orientation Committee.

Athletics Member NCAA. All Division II.

Campus security: 24-hour emergency response devices and patrols, late-night transport/escort service, controlled dormitory access, lighted pathways, closed-circuit security cameras, and emergency code blue phones.

Student services: health clinic, personal/psychological counseling, veterans affairs office.

COSTS & FINANCIAL AID
Costs (2018–19) ***Comprehensive fee:*** $48,405 includes full-time tuition ($33,560), mandatory fees ($1065), and room and board ($13,780). Part-time tuition: $704 per credit hour. Part-time tuition and fees vary according to class time and course load. ***College room only:*** $8590. Room and board charges vary according to board plan and housing facility. ***Payment plans:*** installment, deferred payment.

Financial Aid Of all full-time matriculated undergraduates who enrolled in 2017, 2,159 applied for aid, 1,985 were judged to have need, 491 had their need fully met. 383 Federal Work-Study jobs (averaging $1450). 399 state and other part-time jobs (averaging $1650). In 2017, 302 non-need-based awards were made. ***Average percent of need met:*** 78. ***Average financial aid package:*** $27,162. ***Average need-based loan:*** $4679. ***Average need-based gift aid:*** $22,231. ***Average non-need-based aid:*** $14,922. ***Average indebtedness upon graduation:*** $35,686.

APPLYING
Standardized Tests *Required for some:* SAT or ACT (for admission).

Options: electronic application, early admission, early action, deferred entrance.

Required: essay or personal statement, high school transcript, 3 letters of recommendation. ***Recommended:*** interview.

CONTACT
Le Moyne College, 1419 Salt Springs Road, Syracuse, NY 13214. *Toll-free phone:* 800-333-4733.

★ LIM College
New York, New York
http://www.limcollege.edu/

- **Proprietary** comprehensive, founded 1939
- **Urban** campus with easy access to New York City
- **Coed, primarily women** 1,503 undergraduate students, 93% full-time, 89% women, 11% men
- 83% of applicants were admitted

UNDERGRAD STUDENTS
1,391 full-time, 112 part-time. Students come from 42 states and territories; 28 other countries; 61% are from out of state; 19% Black or African American, non-Hispanic/Latino; 12% Hispanic/Latino; 11% Asian, non-Hispanic/Latino; 0.7% Native Hawaiian or other Pacific Islander, non-Hispanic/Latino; 1% American Indian or Alaska Native, non-Hispanic/Latino; 0.3% Two or more races, non-Hispanic/Latino; 8% Race/ethnicity unknown; 1% international; 13% transferred in; 24% live on campus.

Freshmen:
Admission: 1,348 applied, 1,125 admitted, 298 enrolled. ***Average high school GPA:*** 3.0. ***Test scores:*** SAT evidence-based reading and writing scores over 500: 74%; SAT math scores over 500: 69%; ACT scores over 18: 84%; SAT evidence-based reading and writing scores over 600: 19%; SAT math scores over 600: 11%; ACT scores over 24: 19%; SAT math scores over 700: 1%; ACT scores over 30: 2%.

Retention: 75% of full-time freshmen returned.

FACULTY
Total: 230, 13% full-time.

Student/faculty ratio: 8:1.

ACADEMICS
Calendar: semesters. *Degrees:* certificates, bachelor's, master's, and postbachelor's certificates.

Special study options: academic remediation for entering students, accelerated degree program, advanced placement credit, cooperative education, distance learning, honors programs, internships, off-campus study, part-time degree program, services for LD students, study abroad, summer session for credit.

Computers: 352 computers/terminals are available on campus for general student use. Students can access the following: campus intranet, computer help desk, free student e-mail accounts, online (class) grades, online (class) registration, online (class) schedules. Campuswide network is available. 100% of college-owned or -operated housing units are wired for high-speed Internet access. Wireless service is available via entire campus.
Library: Adrian G. Marcuse Library. *Books:* 15,000 (physical), 700 (digital/electronic); *Serial titles:* 172 (physical); *Databases:* 55. Students can reserve study rooms.

STUDENT LIFE
Housing options: coed. Campus housing is leased by the school.

Activities and organizations: student-run newspaper, Fashion Show Production Club, Lexington Line Magazine, Student Life Activities Board, Dance Team, Black Retail Action Group.

Campus security: 24-hour patrols, controlled dormitory access.

Student services: personal/psychological counseling.

COSTS & FINANCIAL AID
Costs (2019–20) ***Comprehensive fee:*** $48,650 includes full-time tuition ($26,990), mandatory fees ($820), and room and board ($20,840). Part-time tuition: $896 per credit hour. ***College room only:*** $16,840.

Financial Aid ***Average indebtedness upon graduation:*** $40,085.

APPLYING
Options: electronic application, early action.

Application fee: $40.

Required: essay or personal statement, high school transcript, 1 letter of recommendation. ***Required for some:*** interview. ***Recommended:*** minimum 2.0 GPA.

Application deadlines: rolling (freshmen), rolling (out-of-state freshmen), rolling (transfers), 11/15 (early action).

CONTACT
Laura Healy, Associate Director of Admissions Recruitment, LIM College, 12 East 53rd Street, New York, NY 10022. *Phone:* 212-310-0672 Ext. 418. *Toll-free phone:* 800-677-1323. *E-mail:* admissions@limcollege.edu.

Long Island University–LIU Brooklyn

Brooklyn, New York

http://www.liu.edu/

- **Independent** university, founded 1926
- **Urban** 11-acre campus with easy access to New York City
- **Endowment** $92.4 million
- **Coed**
- 84% of applicants were admitted

FACULTY
Student/faculty ratio: 13:1.

ACADEMICS
Calendar: semesters. *Degrees:* associate, bachelor's, master's, doctoral, post-master's, and postbachelor's certificates.
Library: Salena Library. *Books:* 257,706 (physical), 406,939 (digital/electronic); *Serial titles:* 27 (physical), 466,233 (digital/electronic); *Databases:* 495.

STUDENT LIFE
Housing options: coed, special housing for students with disabilities. Campus housing is university owned and leased by the school. Freshman campus housing is guaranteed.

Activities and organizations: drama/theater group, student-run newspaper, radio and television station, choral group, The Student Government Association, The American Pharmacists Association, Hillel Jewish Students Organization, Student Activities Board, Indo American Pharmaceutical Association, national fraternities, national sororities.

Athletics Member NCAA. All Division I.

Campus security: 24-hour emergency response devices and patrols, late-night transport/escort service, controlled dormitory access, lighted pathways/sidewalks.

Student services: health clinic, personal/psychological counseling, veterans affairs office.

COSTS & FINANCIAL AID
Costs (2018–19) ***Comprehensive fee:*** $51,783 includes full-time tuition ($35,737), mandatory fees ($2026), and room and board ($14,020). Part-time tuition: $1115 per credit. ***Required fees:*** $469 per term part-time. ***Room and board:*** Room and board charges vary according to board plan and housing facility.

Financial Aid Of all full-time matriculated undergraduates who enrolled in 2017, 3,128 applied for aid, 2,913 were judged to have need, 51 had their need fully met. 449 Federal Work-Study jobs (averaging $2602). In 2017, 120 non-need-based awards were made. ***Average percent of need met:*** 48. ***Average financial aid package:*** $20,824. ***Average need-based loan:*** $3447. ***Average need-based gift aid:*** $9976. ***Average non-need-based aid:*** $15,289. ***Average indebtedness upon graduation:*** $46,578.

APPLYING
Standardized Tests *Required:* SAT or ACT (for admission).

Options: electronic application, early action, deferred entrance.

Application fee: $50.

Required: essay or personal statement, high school transcript, letters of recommendation. ***Required for some:*** interview.

CONTACT
Mr. Luis Santiago, Dean of Enrollment, Long Island University–LIU Brooklyn, 1 University Plaza, Brooklyn, NY 11201. *Phone:* 718-488-1011. *Toll-free phone:* 800-LIU-PLAN. *Fax:* 718-780-6110. *E-mail:* bkln-admissions@liu.edu.

Long Island University–LIU Post

Brookville, New York

http://www.liu.edu/

- **Independent** university, founded 1954
- **Suburban** 322-acre campus with easy access to New York City
- **Endowment** $100.1 million
- **Coed**
- 83% of applicants were admitted

FACULTY
Student/faculty ratio: 14:1.

ACADEMICS
Calendar: semesters. *Degrees:* associate, bachelor's, master's, doctoral, post-master's, and postbachelor's certificates.
Library: B. Davis Schwartz Memorial Library. *Books:* 459,336 (physical), 203,430 (digital/electronic); *Serial titles:* 482 (physical), 466,233 (digital/electronic); *Databases:* 478.

STUDENT LIFE
Housing options: coed, special housing for students with disabilities. Campus housing is university owned. Freshman campus housing is guaranteed.

Activities and organizations: drama/theater group, student-run newspaper, radio and television station, choral group, marching band, Student Government Association, Student Activities Board, Resident Student Association, Commuter Student Association, Greek Programming Board, national fraternities, national sororities.

Athletics Member NCAA. All Division II.

Campus security: 24-hour emergency response devices and patrols, student patrols, late-night transport/escort service, controlled dormitory access, lighted pathways/sidewalks.

Student services: health clinic, personal/psychological counseling, veterans affairs office.

COSTS & FINANCIAL AID
Costs (2018–19) ***Comprehensive fee:*** $51,783 includes full-time tuition ($35,737), mandatory fees ($2026), and room and board ($14,020). Part-time tuition: $1115 per credit. ***Required fees:*** $469 per term part-time. ***Room and board:*** Room and board charges vary according to board plan and housing facility.

Financial Aid Of all full-time matriculated undergraduates who enrolled in 2017, 2,391 applied for aid, 2,063 were judged to have need, 84 had their need fully met. 535 Federal Work-Study jobs (averaging $2255). In 2017, 268 non-need-based awards were made. ***Average percent of need met:*** 62. ***Average financial aid package:*** $24,166. ***Average need-based loan:*** $3097. ***Average need-based gift aid:*** $6177. ***Average non-need-based aid:*** $15,714. ***Average indebtedness upon graduation:*** $36,533.

APPLYING
Standardized Tests *Required:* SAT or ACT (for admission).

Options: electronic application, early action, deferred entrance.

Application fee: $50.

Required: essay or personal statement, high school transcript, 1 letter of recommendation. ***Required for some:*** interview.

CONTACT
Ms. Anne Marie Caradonna, Director of Admissions Operations, Long Island University–LIU Post, 720 Northern Boulevard, Brookville, NY 11548-1300. *Phone:* 516-299-2900. *Toll-free phone:* 800-LIU-PLAN. *Fax:* 516-299-2137. *E-mail:* post-enroll@liu.edu.

Machzikei Hadath Rabbinical College

Brooklyn, New York

CONTACT
Rabbi Abraham M. Lezerowitz, Director of Admissions, Machzikei Hadath Rabbinical College, 5407 Sixteenth Avenue, Brooklyn, NY 11204-1805. *Phone:* 718-854-8777.

★ Manhattan College

Riverdale, New York

http://www.manhattan.edu/

- **Independent** comprehensive, founded 1853, affiliated with Roman Catholic Church
- **Urban** 31-acre campus with easy access to New York City
- **Endowment** $100.6 million
- **Coed** 3,654 undergraduate students, 95% full-time, 45% women, 55% men
- **Moderately difficult** entrance level, 75% of applicants were admitted

UNDERGRAD STUDENTS
3,455 full-time, 199 part-time. 6% Black or African American, non-Hispanic/Latino; 23% Hispanic/Latino; 5% Asian, non-Hispanic/Latino; 0.2% American Indian or Alaska Native, non-Hispanic/Latino; 2% Two or

more races, non-Hispanic/Latino; 6% Race/ethnicity unknown; 3% international; 5% transferred in; 67% live on campus.

Freshmen:

Admission: 7,882 applied, 5,876 admitted, 815 enrolled. ***Average high school GPA:*** 3.4. ***Test scores:*** SAT evidence-based reading and writing scores over 500: 89%; SAT math scores over 500: 89%; ACT scores over 18: 99%; SAT evidence-based reading and writing scores over 600: 45%; SAT math scores over 600: 41%; ACT scores over 24: 64%; SAT evidence-based reading and writing scores over 700: 4%; SAT math scores over 700: 7%; ACT scores over 30: 14%.

Retention: 82% of full-time freshmen returned.

FACULTY

Total: 466, 52% full-time, 73% with terminal degrees.

Student/faculty ratio: 13:1.

ACADEMICS

Calendar: semesters. *Degrees:* bachelor's, master's, and post-master's certificates.

Special study options: accelerated degree program, adult/continuing education programs, advanced placement credit, cooperative education, distance learning, double majors, English as a second language, honors programs, independent study, internships, off-campus study, part-time degree program, services for LD students, student-designed majors, study abroad, summer session for credit. ***ROTC:*** Army (c), Air Force (b).

Unusual degree programs: 3-2 business administration; engineering; education.

Computers: 450 computers/terminals and 3,000 ports are available on campus for general student use. Students can access the following: campus intranet, computer help desk, free student e-mail accounts, online (class) grades, online (class) registration, online (class) schedules, course management system, degree audit/planning tool, campus card access. Campuswide network is available. 100% of college-owned or -operated housing units are wired for high-speed Internet access. Wireless service is available via entire campus.

Library: Mary Alice and Tom OMalley Library. *Books:* 259,987 (physical), 191,706 (digital/electronic); *Serial titles:* 379 (physical), 186,500 (digital/electronic). Weekly public service hours: 168; study areas open 24 hours, 5–7 days a week.

STUDENT LIFE

Housing options: men-only, women-only, special housing for students with disabilities. Campus housing is university owned. Freshman campus housing is guaranteed.

Activities and organizations: drama/theater group, student-run newspaper, choral group, Society of Hispanic Professional Engineers, Singers, Student Government, Social Life Commission, Manhattan College Players (Theater/Drama group), national fraternities, national sororities.

Athletics Member NCAA. All Division I. ***Intercollegiate sports:*** baseball M(s), basketball M(s)/W(s), cheerleading W, crew M(c)/W, cross-country running M(s)/W(s), golf M(s), lacrosse M(s)/W(s), rugby M(c), soccer M(s)/W(s), softball W(s), swimming and diving M(s)/W(s), track and field M(s)/W(s), volleyball W(s). ***Intramural sports:*** baseball M, basketball M/W, cheerleading M/W, cross-country running M/W, football M/W, soccer M/W, softball M/W, swimming and diving W, track and field M/W, volleyball M/W.

Campus security: 24-hour emergency response devices and patrols, late-night transport/escort service, controlled dormitory access.

Student services: health clinic, personal/psychological counseling, veterans affairs office.

FINANCIAL AID

Financial Aid Of all full-time matriculated undergraduates who enrolled in 2017, 2,865 applied for aid, 3,219 were judged to have need, 465 had their need fully met. In 2017, 933 non-need-based awards were made. ***Average percent of need met:*** 70. ***Average need-based gift aid:*** $14,027. ***Average non-need-based aid:*** $6402. ***Average indebtedness upon graduation:*** $35,000.

APPLYING

Standardized Tests *Required:* SAT or ACT (for admission).

Options: electronic application, early admission, early decision, deferred entrance.

Application fee: $75.

Required: essay or personal statement, high school transcript, minimum 2.5 GPA, 1 letter of recommendation. ***Recommended:*** minimum 3.0 GPA, interview.

Early decision deadline: 11/15.

Notification: continuous until 4/15 (freshmen), continuous until 8/15 (transfers), 12/1 (early decision).

CONTACT

Ms. Tara Fay-Reilly, Director of Undergraduate Admissions, Manhattan College, 4513 Manhattan College Parkway, Riverdale, NY 10471. *Phone:* 718-862-7200. *Toll-free phone:* 800-622-9235. *Fax:* 718-862-8019. *E-mail:* admit@manhattan.edu.

See previous page for display ad and page 1038 for the College Close-Up.

Manhattan School of Music

New York, New York

http://www.msmnyc.edu/

CONTACT

Ms. Amy Anderson, Dean of Enrollment Management, Manhattan School of Music, 120 Claremont Avenue, New York, NY 10027-4698. *Phone:* 917-493-4501. *Fax:* 212-749-3025. *E-mail:* aanderson@msmnyc.edu.

Manhattanville College

Purchase, New York

http://www.mville.edu/

- **Independent** comprehensive, founded 1841
- **Suburban** 100-acre campus with easy access to New York City
- **Endowment** $30.8 million
- **Coed** 1,588 undergraduate students, 95% full-time, 60% women, 40% men
- **Minimally difficult** entrance level, 90% of applicants were admitted

UNDERGRAD STUDENTS

1,513 full-time, 75 part-time. Students come from 32 states and territories; 44 other countries; 27% are from out of state; 10% Black or African American, non-Hispanic/Latino; 27% Hispanic/Latino; 2% Asian, non-Hispanic/Latino; 0.3% Native Hawaiian or other Pacific Islander, non-Hispanic/Latino; 0.2% American Indian or Alaska Native, non-Hispanic/Latino; 3% Two or more races, non-Hispanic/Latino; 4% Race/ethnicity unknown; 7% international; 3% transferred in; 60% live on campus.

Freshmen:

Admission: 3,577 applied, 3,217 admitted, 394 enrolled. ***Average high school GPA:*** 3.2. ***Test scores:*** SAT evidence-based reading and writing scores over 500: 83%; SAT math scores over 500: 78%; ACT scores over 18: 95%; SAT evidence-based reading and writing scores over 600: 30%; SAT math scores over 600: 21%; ACT scores over 24: 45%; SAT evidence-based reading and writing scores over 700: 3%; SAT math scores over 700: 4%; ACT scores over 30: 6%.

Retention: 70% of full-time freshmen returned.

FACULTY

Total: 375, 30% full-time, 51% with terminal degrees.

Student/faculty ratio: 11:1.

ACADEMICS

Calendar: semesters. *Degrees:* bachelor's, master's, doctoral, and post-master's certificates.

Special study options: accelerated degree program, adult/continuing education programs, advanced placement credit, double majors, honors programs, independent study, internships, off-campus study, part-time degree program, services for LD students, student-designed majors, study abroad, summer session for credit.

Unusual degree programs: business administration.

Computers: 125 computers/terminals are available on campus for general student use. Students can access the following: campus intranet, computer help desk, free student e-mail accounts, online (class) grades, online (class) registration, online (class) schedules, Mobile Apps. Campuswide network is available. 100% of college-owned or -operated housing units are wired for high-speed Internet access. Wireless service is available via entire campus.

Library: Manhattanville College Library. *Books:* 189,313 (physical), 177,686 (digital/electronic); *Serial titles:* 926 (physical), 60,205 (digital/electronic); *Databases:* 122. Weekly public service hours: 109; study areas open 24 hours, 5–7 days a week.

STUDENT LIFE

Housing options: coed, special housing for students with disabilities. Campus housing is university owned. Freshman campus housing is guaranteed.

Activities and organizations: drama/theater group, student-run newspaper, radio station, choral group, Students of Caribbean Affiliation (SOCA), Student Government Association (SGA), National Society for Leaderhsip and Success (NSLC), Asian American Student Association (AASA), Active Minds.

Athletics Member NCAA. All Division III. ***Intercollegiate sports:*** baseball M, basketball M/W, cross-country running M/W, field hockey W, golf M/W, ice hockey M/W, lacrosse M/W, soccer M/W, softball W, tennis M/W, track and field M/W, volleyball W.

Campus security: 24-hour emergency response devices and patrols, late-night transport/escort service, controlled dormitory access, officer at the main campus gate 24/7, emergency notification system, seminars on campus safety and security practices.

Student services: health clinic, personal/psychological counseling.

COSTS & FINANCIAL AID

Costs (2019–20) ***Comprehensive fee:*** $54,090 includes full-time tuition ($38,120), mandatory fees ($1450), and room and board ($14,520). Part-time tuition: $865 per credit. ***Required fees:*** $60 per term part-time. ***College room only:*** $8680.

Financial Aid Of all full-time matriculated undergraduates who enrolled in 2018, 1,124 applied for aid, 1,017 were judged to have need, 150 had their need fully met. 725 Federal Work-Study jobs (averaging $1643). In 2018, 409 non-need-based awards were made. ***Average percent of need met:*** 67. ***Average financial aid package:*** $28,115. ***Average need-based loan:*** $4437. ***Average need-based gift aid:*** $5176. ***Average non-need-based aid:*** $21,144. ***Average indebtedness upon graduation:*** $31,237.

APPLYING

Standardized Tests *Required for some:* SAT (for admission), ACT (for admission), SAT or ACT (for admission).

Options: electronic application, early action, deferred entrance.

Application fee: $50.

Required: essay or personal statement, high school transcript, minimum 2.5 GPA, 2 letters of recommendation. ***Required for some:*** interview, If a student is applying for dance, theatre, musical theatre or studio art, please visit https://www.mville.edu/admissions/undergraduate-admissions/find-out-more/art-music-dance-theatre-applicants.

Application deadlines: rolling (freshmen), rolling (transfers).

Notification: continuous (freshmen), continuous (transfers).

CONTACT

Ms. Jessica Holt, Interim Director - Admissions, Manhattanville College, 2900 Purchase Street, Purchase, NY 10577. *Phone:* 914-323-5363. *Toll-free phone:* 800-328-4553. *Fax:* 914-694-1732. *E-mail:* Jessica.Holt@mville.edu.

Maria College

Albany, New York

http://www.mariacollege.edu/

- **Independent** 4-year, founded 1958
- **Urban** 9-acre campus
- **Coed** 912 undergraduate students, 27% full-time, 88% women, 12% men
- **Minimally difficult** entrance level, 25% of applicants were admitted

UNDERGRAD STUDENTS

243 full-time, 669 part-time. Students come from 9 states and territories; 1 other country; 5% are from out of state; 12% Black or African American, non-Hispanic/Latino; 6% Hispanic/Latino; 6% Asian, non-Hispanic/Latino; 0.2% Native Hawaiian or other Pacific Islander, non-Hispanic/Latino; 0.2% American Indian or Alaska Native, non-Hispanic/Latino; 2% Two or more races, non-Hispanic/Latino; 16% Race/ethnicity unknown; 7% transferred in.

Freshmen:
Admission: 293 applied, 73 admitted, 95 enrolled. ***Average high school GPA:*** 2.5. ***Test scores:*** ACT scores over 18: 83%; ACT scores over 24: 33%.

Retention: 83% of full-time freshmen returned.

FACULTY
Total: 88, 36% full-time, 28% with terminal degrees.

Student/faculty ratio: 10:1.

ACADEMICS
Calendar: semesters. *Degrees:* certificates, associate, and bachelor's.

Special study options: adult/continuing education programs, advanced placement credit, cooperative education, distance learning, English as a second language, honors programs, independent study, internships, off-campus study, part-time degree program, services for LD students, summer session for credit.

Computers: 70 computers/terminals are available on campus for general student use. Students can access the following: campus intranet, computer help desk, free student e-mail accounts, online (class) grades, online (class) registration, online (class) schedules. Campuswide network is available. Wireless service is available via entire campus.
Library: Maria College Library. *Books:* 19,779 (physical), 160,512 (digital/electronic); *Serial titles:* 55 (physical), 230,969 (digital/electronic); *Databases:* 27. Weekly public service hours: 131.

STUDENT LIFE
Housing options: college housing not available.

Campus security: late-night transport/escort service, 8:30 am-10 pm security guard coverage in specified campus buildings.

Student services: personal/psychological counseling.

COSTS & FINANCIAL AID
Costs (2018–19) ***Tuition:*** $14,700 full-time, $630 per credit hour part-time. Full-time tuition and fees vary according to course load, program, and reciprocity agreements. Part-time tuition and fees vary according to course load, program, and reciprocity agreements. ***Required fees:*** $440 full-time, $110 per term part-time. ***Payment plan:*** installment. ***Waivers:*** employees or children of employees.

Financial Aid Of all full-time matriculated undergraduates who enrolled in 2018, 282 applied for aid, 251 were judged to have need, 4 had their need fully met. In 2018, 3 non-need-based awards were made. ***Average percent of need met:*** 33. ***Average financial aid package:*** $8758. ***Average need-based loan:*** $3440. ***Average need-based gift aid:*** $6940. ***Average non-need-based aid:*** $6016. ***Average indebtedness upon graduation:*** $18,950.

APPLYING
Standardized Tests *Required for some:* TEAS for AAS in nursing and practical nursing certificate programs. *Recommended:* SAT or ACT (for admission).

Options: electronic application, early admission, deferred entrance.

Application fee: $35.

Required: high school transcript. ***Recommended:*** essay or personal statement, minimum 2.5 GPA, 1 letter of recommendation, interview.

Notification: continuous (freshmen), continuous (transfers).

CONTACT
Mr. John Ramoska, Director of Admissions, Maria College, 700 New Scotland Avenue, Albany, NY 12065. *Phone:* 518-861-2519. *Fax:* 518-453-1366. *E-mail:* admissions@mariacollege.edu.

Marist College
Poughkeepsie, New York
http://www.marist.edu/

- **Independent** comprehensive, founded 1929
- **Suburban** 210-acre campus with easy access to Albany, New York City
- **Endowment** $71.2 million
- **Coed** 5,670 undergraduate students, 91% full-time, 58% women, 42% men
- **Very difficult** entrance level, 46% of applicants were admitted

UNDERGRAD STUDENTS
5,139 full-time, 531 part-time. Students come from 49 states and territories; 64 other countries; 53% are from out of state; 4% Black or African American, non-Hispanic/Latino; 10% Hispanic/Latino; 3% Asian, non-Hispanic/Latino; 0.1% Native Hawaiian or other Pacific Islander, non-Hispanic/Latino; 0.1% American Indian or Alaska Native, non-Hispanic/Latino; 3% Two or more races, non-Hispanic/Latino; 0.7% Race/ethnicity unknown; 2% international; 4% transferred in; 61% live on campus.

Freshmen:
Admission: 11,207 applied, 5,181 admitted, 1,299 enrolled. ***Average high school GPA:*** 3.3. ***Test scores:*** SAT evidence-based reading and writing scores over 500: 97%; SAT math scores over 500: 97%; ACT scores over 18: 99%; SAT evidence-based reading and writing scores over 600: 67%; SAT math scores over 600: 58%; ACT scores over 24: 80%; SAT evidence-based reading and writing scores over 700: 9%; SAT math scores over 700: 10%; ACT scores over 30: 20%.

Retention: 87% of full-time freshmen returned.

FACULTY
Total: 595, 42% full-time, 46% with terminal degrees.

Student/faculty ratio: 16:1.

ACADEMICS
Calendar: semesters. *Degrees:* certificates, bachelor's, master's, and postbachelor's certificates.

Special study options: academic remediation for entering students, accelerated degree program, adult/continuing education programs, advanced placement credit, cooperative education, distance learning, double majors, English as a second language, honors programs, independent study, internships, off-campus study, part-time degree program, services for LD students, study abroad, summer session for credit. ***ROTC:*** Army (b).

Computers: 997 computers/terminals are available on campus for general student use. Students can access the following: campus intranet, computer help desk, free student e-mail accounts, online (class) grades, online (class) registration, online (class) schedules, billing/payments, transcripts, degree audit, financial aid application and award review, student account summary, campus OneCard account, parking registration, cap and gown orders. 100% of college-owned or -operated housing units are wired for high-speed Internet access. Wireless service is available via entire campus.
Library: James A. Cannavino Library. *Books:* 108,161 (physical), 251,090 (digital/electronic); *Serial titles:* 1,085 (physical), 65,765 (digital/electronic); *Databases:* 119. Weekly public service hours: 113; students can reserve study rooms.

STUDENT LIFE
Housing options: coed, special housing for students with disabilities. Campus housing is university owned and is provided by a third party. Freshman campus housing is guaranteed.

Activities and organizations: drama/theater group, student-run newspaper, radio and television station, choral group, marching band, Marist Singers, Dance Club, Student Government, Theater Club, Community Service and Campus Ministry, national fraternities, national sororities.

Athletics Member NCAA. All Division I except football (Division I-AA). ***Intercollegiate sports:*** baseball M(s), basketball M(s)/W(s), bowling M(c)/W(c), cheerleading M(c)/W(c), crew M/W(s), cross-country running M(s)/W(s), equestrian sports M(c)/W(c), fencing M(c)/W(c), ice hockey M(c), lacrosse M(s)/W(s), rugby M(c)/W(c), skiing (downhill) W(c), soccer M(s)/W(s), softball W(s), swimming and diving M(s)/W(s), tennis M(s)/W(s), track and field M(s)/W(s), volleyball M(c)/W(s), water polo W(s). ***Intramural sports:*** basketball M/W, fencing W, football M(c)/W(c), golf M(c)/W(c), soccer M/W, softball M/W, ultimate Frisbee M(c)/W(c), volleyball M/W.

Campus security: 24-hour emergency response devices and patrols, student patrols, late-night transport/escort service, controlled dormitory access, night residence hall monitors.

Student services: health clinic, personal/psychological counseling.

COSTS & FINANCIAL AID

Costs (2019–20) ***Comprehensive fee:*** $58,495 includes full-time tuition ($39,925), mandatory fees ($600), and room and board ($17,970). ***College room only:*** $12,050.

Financial Aid Of all full-time matriculated undergraduates who enrolled in 2018, 3,586 applied for aid, 2,870 were judged to have need, 557 had their need fully met. 1,446 Federal Work-Study jobs (averaging $2672). 571 state and other part-time jobs (averaging $2025). In 2018, 1559 non-need-based awards were made. ***Average percent of need met:*** 67. ***Average financial aid package:*** $25,864. ***Average need-based loan:*** $3953. ***Average need-based gift aid:*** $17,746. ***Average non-need-based aid:*** $10,684. ***Average indebtedness upon graduation:*** $39,035. ***Financial aid deadline:*** 5/1.

APPLYING

Options: electronic application, early admission, early decision, early action, deferred entrance.

Application fee: $50.

Required: essay or personal statement, high school transcript, 2 letters of recommendation.

Application deadlines: 2/1 (freshmen), 6/1 (transfers), 11/15 (early action).

Early decision deadline: 11/15 (for plan 1), 2/1 (for plan 2).

Notification: continuous until 4/1 (freshmen), continuous (transfers), 12/15 (early decision plan 1), 2/15 (early decision plan 2), 1/15 (early action).

CONTACT

Mr. Kent Rinehart, Dean of Undergraduate Admissions, Marist College, 3399 North Road, Poughkeepsie, NY 12601. *Phone:* 845-575-3226. *Toll-free phone:* 800-436-5483. *Fax:* 845-575-3215. *E-mail:* admission@marist.edu.

Marymount Manhattan College

New York, New York

http://www.mmm.edu/

- **Independent** 4-year, founded 1936
- **Urban** campus
- **Endowment** $20.9 million
- **Coed** 2,063 undergraduate students, 90% full-time, 78% women, 22% men
- **Moderately difficult** entrance level, 78% of applicants were admitted

UNDERGRAD STUDENTS

1,861 full-time, 202 part-time. Students come from 50 states and territories; 70 other countries; 63% are from out of state; 9% Black or African American, non-Hispanic/Latino; 16% Hispanic/Latino; 3% Asian, non-Hispanic/Latino; 0.1% Native Hawaiian or other Pacific Islander, non-Hispanic/Latino; 0.2% American Indian or Alaska Native, non-Hispanic/Latino; 4% Two or more races, non-Hispanic/Latino; 6% Race/ethnicity unknown; 4% international; 6% transferred in; 38% live on campus.

Freshmen:

Admission: 5,705 applied, 4,450 admitted, 483 enrolled. ***Average high school GPA:*** 3.5. ***Test scores:*** SAT evidence-based reading and writing scores over 500: 89%; SAT math scores over 500: 76%; ACT scores over 18: 97%; SAT evidence-based reading and writing scores over 600: 43%; SAT math scores over 600: 19%; ACT scores over 24: 59%; SAT evidence-based reading and writing scores over 700: 5%; SAT math scores over 700: 4%; ACT scores over 30: 16%.

Retention: 68% of full-time freshmen returned.

FACULTY

Total: 373, 25% full-time.

Student/faculty ratio: 11:1.

ACADEMICS

Calendar: semesters plus summer and January mini-semesters. *Degree:* bachelor's.

Special study options: academic remediation for entering students, accelerated degree program, adult/continuing education programs, advanced placement credit, distance learning, double majors, honors programs, independent study, internships, off-campus study, part-time degree program, services for LD students, student-designed majors, study abroad, summer session for credit.

Computers: 120 computers/terminals are available on campus for general student use. Students can access the following: campus intranet, computer help desk, free student e-mail accounts, online (class) grades, online (class) registration, online (class) schedules, online payments, direct deposits. Campuswide network is available. 100% of college-owned or -operated housing units are wired for high-speed Internet access. Wireless service is available via entire campus.

Library: Thomas J. Shanahan Library. *Books:* 39,888 (physical), 232,680 (digital/electronic); *Serial titles:* 98 (physical), 54,077 (digital/electronic); *Databases:* 70. Weekly public service hours: 80.

STUDENT LIFE

Housing options: coed, men-only, women-only. Campus housing is university owned and leased by the school. Freshman applicants given priority for college housing.

Activities and organizations: drama/theater group, student-run newspaper, radio station, choral group, Student Government Association (SGA), Black and Latino Student Association (BLSA), The Monitor-Student Newspaper, Musical Theater Association (MTA), Christian Fellowship.

Campus security: 24-hour emergency response devices and patrols, student patrols, 24-hour security in residence halls.

Student services: health clinic, personal/psychological counseling.

COSTS & FINANCIAL AID

Costs (2019–20) ***Comprehensive fee:*** $53,827 includes full-time tuition ($33,980), mandatory fees ($1648), and room and board ($18,199). Part-time tuition: $1132 per credit hour. ***Required fees:*** $603 per term part-time. ***College room only:*** $16,199.

Financial Aid Of all full-time matriculated undergraduates who enrolled in 2017, 1,465 applied for aid, 1,296 were judged to have need, 88 had their need fully met. 107 Federal Work-Study jobs (averaging $3372). In 2017, 143 non-need-based awards were made. ***Average percent of need met:*** 54. ***Average financial aid package:*** $18,930. ***Average need-based loan:*** $4190. ***Average need-based gift aid:*** $15,488. ***Average non-need-based aid:*** $9724. ***Average indebtedness upon graduation:*** $36,417.

APPLYING

Standardized Tests *Required:* SAT or ACT (for admission).

Options: electronic application, deferred entrance.

Application fee: $60.

Required: essay or personal statement, high school transcript, 2 letters of recommendation. ***Required for some:*** interview.

Application deadlines: rolling (freshmen), rolling (transfers).

Notification: continuous (freshmen), continuous (transfers).

CONTACT

Greg Turner, Assistant Director of First-year Admission, Marymount Manhattan College, 221 East 71st Street, New York, NY 10021. *Phone:* 212-517-0444. *Toll-free phone:* 800-627-9668. *E-mail:* gturner@mmm.edu.

Mechon L'Hoyroa

Monsey, New York

http://www.mechonlhoyroa.com/

CONTACT

Mechon L'Hoyroa, 168 Maple Avenue, Monsey, NY 10952.

Medaille College

Buffalo, New York

http://www.medaille.edu/

CONTACT

Christopher LaRusso, Vice President for Enrollment Management and Undergraduate Admissions, Medaille College, Office of Admissions, Buffalo, NY 14214. *Phone:* 716-880-2200. *Toll-free phone:* 800-292-1582. *Fax:* 716-880-2007. *E-mail:* admissionsug@medaille.edu.

Medgar Evers College of the City University of New York

Brooklyn, New York

http://www.mec.cuny.edu/

- **State and locally supported** 4-year, founded 1969, part of City University of New York System
- **Urban** 8-acre campus
- **Endowment** $515,142
- **Coed**
- **Noncompetitive** entrance level

FACULTY
Student/faculty ratio: 18:1.

ACADEMICS
Calendar: semesters. *Degrees:* certificates, associate, and bachelor's.
Library: Charles Evans Inniss Memorial Library plus 1 other.

STUDENT LIFE
Housing options: college housing not available.

Activities and organizations: drama/theater group, student-run newspaper, radio and television station, choral group, American Marketing Association, Drama Students Association, Rising Stars, Medgar Evers College Society of Public Administrators, National Society of Black Accountants.

Athletics Member NCAA. All Division III.

Campus security: 24-hour patrols.

Student services: women's center, legal services.

COSTS & FINANCIAL AID
Costs (2018–19) ***Tuition:*** state resident $6330 full-time, $275 per credit part-time; nonresident $16,800 full-time, $560 per credit part-time. Full-time tuition and fees vary according to course load. Part-time tuition and fees vary according to course load. ***Required fees:*** $320 full-time, $101 per term part-time. ***Payment plans:*** installment, deferred payment.

Financial Aid Of all full-time matriculated undergraduates who enrolled in 2018, 4,281 applied for aid, 4,208 were judged to have need, 62 had their need fully met. ***Average percent of need met:*** 48. ***Average financial aid package:*** $7548. ***Average need-based loan:*** $3593. ***Average need-based gift aid:*** $7921.

APPLYING
Standardized Tests *Recommended:* SAT and SAT Subject Tests or ACT (for admission).

Options: electronic application, deferred entrance.

Application fee: $65.

Required: high school transcript.

CONTACT
Dr. Shannon Clarke-Anderson, Director of Admissions, Medgar Evers College of the City University of New York, 1650 Bedford Avenue, Brooklyn, NY 11225. *Phone:* 718-270-5143. *Fax:* 718-270-6411. *E-mail:* shannon@mec.cuny.edu.

Mercy College

Dobbs Ferry, New York

http://www.mercy.edu/

- **Independent** comprehensive, founded 1951, affiliated with Roman Catholic Church
- **Suburban** 66-acre campus with easy access to New York City
- **Endowment** $245.5 million
- **Coed** 6,611 undergraduate students, 76% full-time, 66% women, 34% men
- **Moderately difficult** entrance level, 79% of applicants were admitted

UNDERGRAD STUDENTS
5,001 full-time, 1,610 part-time. Students come from 36 states and territories; 33 other countries; 8% are from out of state; 22% Black or African American, non-Hispanic/Latino; 41% Hispanic/Latino; 4% Asian, non-Hispanic/Latino; 0.2% Native Hawaiian or other Pacific Islander, non-Hispanic/Latino; 0.4% American Indian or Alaska Native, non-Hispanic/Latino; 1% Two or more races, non-Hispanic/Latino; 8% Race/ethnicity unknown; 1% international; 10% transferred in; 12% live on campus.

Freshmen:
Admission: 6,851 applied, 5,443 admitted, 933 enrolled. ***Average high school GPA:*** 3.0.

Retention: 74% of full-time freshmen returned.

FACULTY
Total: 839, 25% full-time, 21% with terminal degrees.

Student/faculty ratio: 16:1.

ACADEMICS
Calendar: semesters. *Degrees:* certificates, associate, bachelor's, master's, doctoral, post-master's, and postbachelor's certificates.

Special study options: accelerated degree program, adult/continuing education programs, advanced placement credit, cooperative education, distance learning, double majors, freshman honors college, honors programs, independent study, internships, off-campus study, part-time degree program, services for LD students, study abroad, summer session for credit. ***ROTC:*** Army (c), Air Force (c).

Unusual degree programs: 3-2 business administration; education, cybersecurity.

Computers: 1,000 computers/terminals and 600 ports are available on campus for general student use. Students can access the following: campus intranet, computer help desk, free student e-mail accounts, online (class) grades, online (class) registration, online (class) schedules. Campuswide network is available. 100% of college-owned or -operated housing units are wired for high-speed Internet access. Wireless service is available via entire campus.
Library: Mercy College Library plus 3 others. *Books:* 78,894 (physical), 72,328 (digital/electronic); *Serial titles:* 26 (physical), 61,974 (digital/electronic); *Databases:* 43. Students can reserve study rooms.

STUDENT LIFE
Housing options: coed. Campus housing is university owned and leased by the school. Freshman applicants given priority for college housing.

Activities and organizations: student-run newspaper, choral group, Model United Nations, Honors Club and 17 National Honor Societies, Mercy Gives Back, Maverick Society, ROTARACT Club for Community Volunteer Service.

Athletics Member NCAA. All Division II. ***Intercollegiate sports:*** baseball M(s), basketball M(s)/W(s), field hockey W(s), lacrosse M(s)/W(s), soccer M(s)/W(s), softball W(s), volleyball W(s). ***Intramural sports:*** baseball M, basketball M/W, softball W.

Campus security: 24-hour emergency response devices and patrols, late-night transport/escort service, controlled dormitory access.

Student services: health clinic, personal/psychological counseling.

COSTS & FINANCIAL AID
Costs (2018–19) ***Comprehensive fee:*** $33,442 includes full-time tuition ($18,400), mandatory fees ($642), and room and board ($14,400). Full-time tuition and fees vary according to course load. Part-time tuition: $774 per credit. Part-time tuition and fees vary according to course load. ***Required fees:*** $161 per term part-time. ***College room only:*** $9750. Room and board charges vary according to board plan. ***Payment plans:*** installment, deferred payment. ***Waivers:*** senior citizens and employees or children of employees.

Financial Aid Of all full-time matriculated undergraduates who enrolled in 2017, 4,687 applied for aid, 4,421 were judged to have need, 103 had their need fully met. 279 Federal Work-Study jobs. In 2017, 132 non-need-based awards were made. ***Average percent of need met:*** 52. ***Average financial aid package:*** $14,084. ***Average need-based loan:*** $4118. ***Average need-based gift aid:*** $10,674. ***Average non-need-based aid:*** $5224. ***Average indebtedness upon graduation:*** $26,317.

APPLYING
Options: electronic application, deferred entrance.

Application fee: $40.

Required: high school transcript, minimum 2.0 GPA. ***Required for some:*** essay or personal statement, Portfolio required for art program; audition required for music program; R.N. required for nursing program; additional interview with program director required of nursing, occupational therapy, physical therapy, social work, veterinary technology, and computer arts program applicants.. ***Recommended:*** 1 letter of recommendation, interview.

Application deadlines: rolling (freshmen), rolling (transfers).

Notification: continuous (freshmen), continuous (transfers).

CONTACT
Mrs. Allison Gurdineer, Executive Director of Admissions, Mercy College, 555 Broadway, Dobbs Ferry, NY 10522-1189. *Phone:* 877-MERCY-GO. *Toll-free phone:* 877-637-2946 (in-state); 877-MERCY-GO (out-of-state). *Fax:* 914-674-7382. *E-mail:* admissions@mercy.edu.

Mesivta of Eastern Parkway–Yeshiva Zichron Meilech
Brooklyn, New York

CONTACT
Mesivta of Eastern Parkway–Yeshiva Zichron Meilech, 510 Dahill Road, Brooklyn, NY 11218-5559. *Phone:* 718-438-1002.

Mesivta Torah Vodaath Rabbinical Seminary
Brooklyn, New York
http://www.torahvodaath.org/

CONTACT
Rabbi Issac Braun, Administrator, Mesivta Torah Vodaath Rabbinical Seminary, 425 East Ninth Street, Brooklyn, NY 11218-5299. *Phone:* 718-941-8000.

Mesivtha Tifereth Jerusalem of America
New York, New York

CONTACT
Rabbi Fishellis, Director of Admissions, Mesivtha Tifereth Jerusalem of America, 145 East Broadway, New York, NY 10002-6301. *Phone:* 212-964-2830.

Metropolitan College of New York
New York, New York
http://www.mcny.edu/

- **Independent** comprehensive, founded 1964
- **Urban** campus
- **Coed**
- **Moderately difficult** entrance level

FACULTY
Student/faculty ratio: 11:1.

ACADEMICS
Calendar: 3 15-week semesters. *Degrees:* certificates, associate, bachelor's, and master's.
Library: Main Library plus 1 other. *Books:* 26,191 (physical), 156,497 (digital/electronic); *Serial titles:* 29,206 (digital/electronic); *Databases:* 91. Weekly public service hours: 72.

STUDENT LIFE
Housing options: college housing not available.

Activities and organizations: student-run newspaper, Student Government, Student Newsletter, Networking Club, Yearbook Committee.

Campus security: 24-hour patrols.

Student services: personal/psychological counseling.

FINANCIAL AID
Financial Aid Of all full-time matriculated undergraduates who enrolled in 2017, 638 applied for aid, 635 were judged to have need, 4 had their need fully met. In 2017, 16 non-need-based awards were made. ***Average percent of need met:*** 46. ***Average financial aid package:*** $17,286. ***Average need-based loan:*** $4917. ***Average need-based gift aid:*** $12,710. ***Average non-need-based aid:*** $2931.

APPLYING
Standardized Tests *Required for some:* ACCUPLACER. *Recommended:* SAT or ACT (for admission).

Options: electronic application, deferred entrance.

Application fee: $30.

Required: high school transcript, 2 letters of recommendation, interview. ***Recommended:*** essay or personal statement, minimum 3.0 GPA.

CONTACT
Metropolitan College of New York, 60 West Street, New York, NY 10006. *Phone:* 212-343-1234 Ext. 2700. *Toll-free phone:* 800-33-THINK Ext. 5001. *Fax:* 212-343-8470.

Mirrer Yeshiva Central Institute
Brooklyn, New York

CONTACT
Director of Admissions, Mirrer Yeshiva Central Institute, 1791 Ocean Parkway, Brooklyn, NY 11223-2010. *Phone:* 718-645-0536.

★ Molloy College
Rockville Centre, New York
http://www.molloy.edu/

- **Independent** comprehensive, founded 1955
- **Suburban** 30-acre campus with easy access to New York City
- **Endowment** $38.2 million
- **Coed** 3,439 undergraduate students, 80% full-time, 73% women, 27% men
- **Moderately difficult** entrance level, 81% of applicants were admitted

UNDERGRAD STUDENTS
2,762 full-time, 677 part-time. Students come from 33 states and territories; 12 other countries; 4% are from out of state; 10% Black or African American, non-Hispanic/Latino; 17% Hispanic/Latino; 8% Asian, non-Hispanic/Latino; 0.2% Native Hawaiian or other Pacific Islander, non-Hispanic/Latino; 0.3% American Indian or Alaska Native, non-Hispanic/Latino; 2% Two or more races, non-Hispanic/Latino; 2% Race/ethnicity unknown; 0.4% international; 9% transferred in; 8% live on campus.

Freshmen:
Admission: 4,427 applied, 3,587 admitted, 598 enrolled. ***Average high school GPA:*** 3.0. ***Test scores:*** SAT evidence-based reading and writing scores over 500: 90%; SAT math scores over 500: 92%; ACT scores over 18: 97%; SAT evidence-based reading and writing scores over 600: 37%; SAT math scores over 600: 33%; ACT scores over 24: 48%; SAT evidence-based reading and writing scores over 700: 2%; SAT math scores over 700: 3%; ACT scores over 30: 5%.
Retention: 89% of full-time freshmen returned.

FACULTY
Total: 721, 26% full-time, 36% with terminal degrees.

Student/faculty ratio: 10:1.

ACADEMICS
Calendar: 4-1-4. *Degrees:* associate, bachelor's, master's, doctoral, post-master's, and postbachelor's certificates.

Special study options: academic remediation for entering students, accelerated degree program, adult/continuing education programs, advanced placement credit, distance learning, double majors, English as a second language, honors programs, independent study, internships, part-time degree program, services for LD students, student-designed majors, study abroad, summer session for credit. ***ROTC:*** Army (c), Navy (c).

Computers: 750 computers/terminals are available on campus for general student use. Students can access the following: computer help desk, free student e-mail accounts, online (class) grades, online (class) registration, online (class) schedules. Campuswide network is available. 100% of college-owned or -operated housing units are wired for high-speed Internet access. Wireless service is available via entire campus.

A ★ indicates that the school has detailed information with a Premium Profile on Petersons.com.

Library: James Edward Tobin Library plus 1 other. *Books:* 33,809 (physical), 295,138 (digital/electronic); *Serial titles:* 48 (physical), 62,642 (digital/electronic); *Databases:* 198.

STUDENT LIFE

Housing options: coed. Campus housing is university owned. Freshman applicants given priority for college housing.

Activities and organizations: drama/theater group, student-run newspaper, choral group, Molloy Student Government, Molloy Nursing Student Association, Molloy Performing Arts Club, Men's Rugby, MolloyLife Media.

Athletics Member NCAA. All Division II. ***Intercollegiate sports:*** baseball M(s), basketball M(s)/W(s), bowling W(s), cross-country running M(s)/W(s), field hockey W(s), lacrosse M(s)/W(s), rugby W(s), soccer M(s)/W(s), softball W(s), tennis W(s), track and field M(s)/W(s), volleyball W(s). ***Intramural sports:*** cheerleading M(c)/W(c), equestrian sports W(c), rugby M(c), ultimate Frisbee M(c)/W(c).

Campus security: 24-hour emergency response devices and patrols, late-night transport/escort service, controlled dormitory access.

Student services: health clinic, personal/psychological counseling, women's center.

COSTS & FINANCIAL AID

Costs (2018–19) ***Comprehensive fee:*** $46,522 includes full-time tuition ($30,270), mandatory fees ($1220), and room and board ($15,032). Full-time tuition and fees vary according to degree level. Part-time tuition: $1005 per credit hour. Part-time tuition and fees vary according to degree level. ***Room and board:*** Room and board charges vary according to board plan. ***Payment plans:*** installment, deferred payment. ***Waivers:*** senior citizens and employees or children of employees.

Financial Aid Of all full-time matriculated undergraduates who enrolled in 2017, 2,523 applied for aid, 2,260 were judged to have need, 230 had their need fully met. 196 Federal Work-Study jobs (averaging $1636). In 2017, 228 non-need-based awards were made. ***Average percent of need met:*** 48. ***Average financial aid package:*** $16,690. ***Average need-based loan:*** $4119. ***Average need-based gift aid:*** $12,843. ***Average non-need-based aid:*** $9816. ***Average indebtedness upon graduation:*** $34,160. ***Financial aid deadline:*** 5/1.

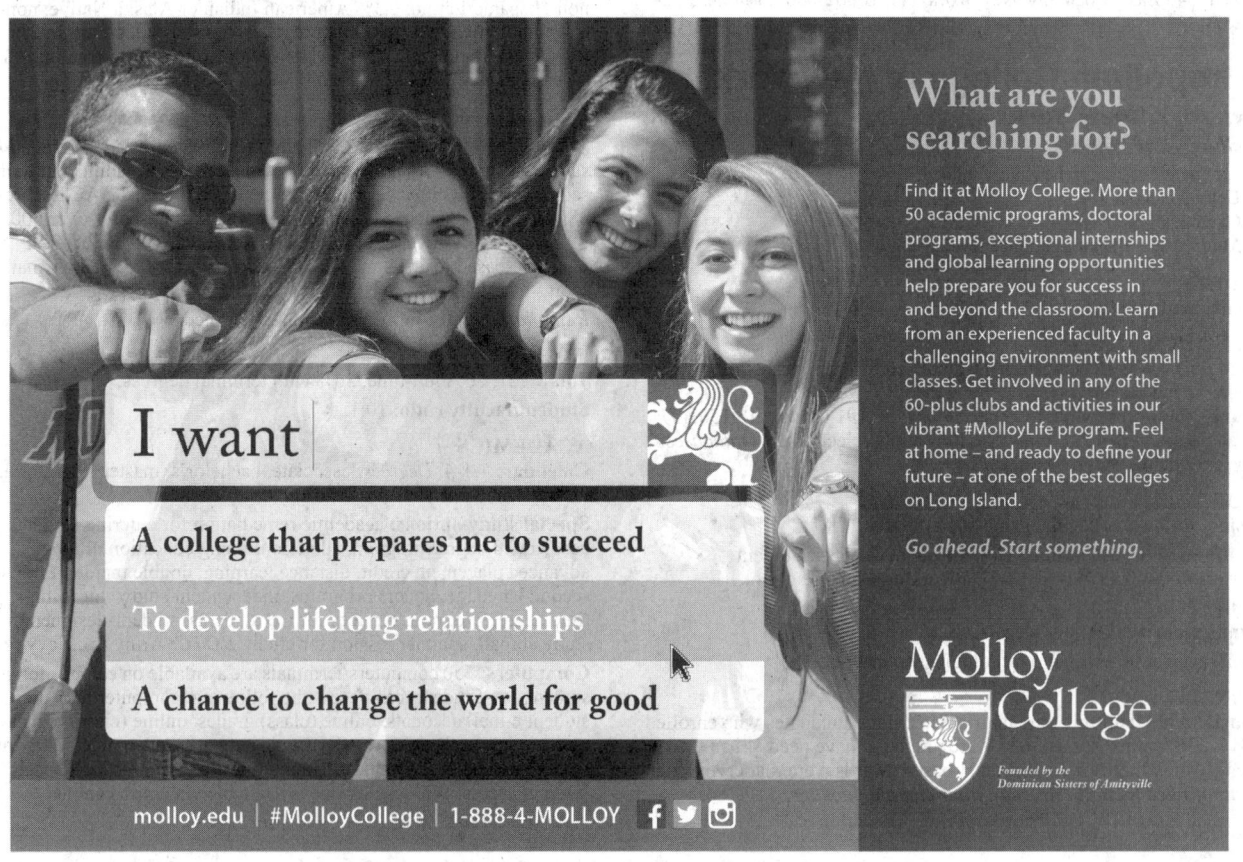

APPLYING

Standardized Tests *Required:* SAT or ACT (for admission).

Options: electronic application, early action, deferred entrance.

Application fee: $40.

Required for some: essay or personal statement, high school transcript, 1 letter of recommendation. ***Recommended:*** interview.

Application deadlines: rolling (freshmen), rolling (transfers).

Notification: continuous (freshmen), continuous (transfers).

CONTACT

Mr. Marc Soevyn, Admissions Counselor, Molloy College, 1000 Hempstead Avenue, PO Box 5002, Rockville Centre, NY 11571-5002. *Phone:* 516-323-4000. *Toll-free phone:* 888-4MOLLOY. *E-mail:* admissions@molloy.edu.

See below for display ad and page 1046 for the College Close-Up.

Monroe College

Bronx, New York

http://www.monroecollege.edu/

CONTACT

Monroe College, 2501 Jerome Avenue, Bronx, NY 10468. *Phone:* 718-933-6700. *Toll-free phone:* 800-55MONROE.

Mount Saint Mary College

Newburgh, New York

http://www.msmc.edu/

- **Independent** comprehensive, founded 1960
- **Suburban** 86-acre campus with easy access to New York City
- **Endowment** $80.3 million
- **Coed** 2,005 undergraduate students, 84% full-time, 71% women, 29% men
- **Moderately difficult** entrance level, 94% of applicants were admitted

UNDERGRAD STUDENTS
1,675 full-time, 330 part-time. Students come from 17 states and territories; 13% are from out of state; 7% Black or African American, non-Hispanic/Latino; 17% Hispanic/Latino; 2% Asian, non-Hispanic/Latino; 0.2% Native Hawaiian or other Pacific Islander, non-Hispanic/Latino; 0.7% American Indian or Alaska Native, non-Hispanic/Latino; 0.9% Two or more races, non-Hispanic/Latino; 15% Race/ethnicity unknown; 0.7% international; 8% transferred in; 48% live on campus.

Freshmen:
Admission: 3,588 applied, 3,365 admitted, 388 enrolled. ***Average high school GPA:*** 3.2. ***Test scores:*** SAT evidence-based reading and writing scores over 500: 85%; SAT math scores over 500: 77%; ACT scores over 18: 90%; SAT evidence-based reading and writing scores over 600: 23%; SAT math scores over 600: 16%; ACT scores over 24: 27%; SAT evidence-based reading and writing scores over 700: 1%; SAT math scores over 700: 1%.

Retention: 85% of full-time freshmen returned.

FACULTY
Total: 249, 32% full-time, 43% with terminal degrees.

Student/faculty ratio: 13:1.

ACADEMICS
Calendar: semesters. *Degrees:* certificates, bachelor's, master's, and post-master's certificates.

Special study options: academic remediation for entering students, accelerated degree program, adult/continuing education programs, advanced placement credit, cooperative education, distance learning, double majors, freshman honors college, honors programs, independent study, internships, off-campus study, part-time degree program, services for LD students, student-designed majors, study abroad, summer session for credit. ***ROTC:*** Army (c).

Unusual degree programs: 3-2 business administration; nursing; social work with Fordham University; publishing, counseling with Pace University.

Computers: 470 computers/terminals are available on campus for general student use. Students can access the following: campus intranet, computer help desk, free student e-mail accounts, online (class) grades, online (class) registration, online (class) schedules. Campuswide network is available. 100% of college-owned or -operated housing units are wired for high-speed Internet access. Wireless service is available via entire campus.

Library: Kaplan Family Library and Learning Center. *Books:* 84,909 (physical), 11,569 (digital/electronic); *Serial titles:* 195 (physical), 59,481 (digital/electronic); *Databases:* 93. Students can reserve study rooms.

STUDENT LIFE
Housing options: on-campus residence required through junior year; coed, men-only, women-only, special housing for students with disabilities. Campus housing is university owned. Freshman campus housing is guaranteed.

Activities and organizations: drama/theater group, student-run newspaper, radio station, choral group, Nursing Student Union, Alpha Knights Step Team, Dance Team, Improvology, Habitat for Humanity.

Athletics Member NCAA. All Division III. ***Intercollegiate sports:*** baseball M, basketball M/W, cheerleading W, cross-country running M/W, golf M, lacrosse M/W, soccer M/W, softball W, swimming and diving M/W, tennis M/W, track and field M/W, volleyball W. ***Intramural sports:*** basketball M/W, bowling M/W, football M, soccer M/W, softball M/W, swimming and diving M/W, table tennis M/W, volleyball M/W.

Campus security: 24-hour emergency response devices and patrols, student patrols, late-night transport/escort service, controlled dormitory access, monitored surveillance cameras in all residence halls.

Student services: health clinic, personal/psychological counseling.

COSTS & FINANCIAL AID
Costs (2018–19) ***Comprehensive fee:*** $46,226 includes full-time tuition ($30,046), mandatory fees ($1072), and room and board ($15,108). Full-time tuition and fees vary according to class time, course load, location, and program. Part-time tuition: $1002 per credit. Part-time tuition and fees vary according to class time, course load, location, and program. ***Required fees:*** $86 per year part-time. ***College room only:*** $8752. Room and board charges vary according to board plan and housing facility. ***Payment plan:*** installment. ***Waivers:*** employees or children of employees.

Financial Aid Of all full-time matriculated undergraduates who enrolled in 2018, 1,524 applied for aid, 1,342 were judged to have need, 214 had their need fully met. 253 Federal Work-Study jobs (averaging $1436). In 2018, 266 non-need-based awards were made. ***Average percent of need met:*** 68. ***Average financial aid package:*** $22,048. ***Average need-based loan:*** $4351. ***Average need-based gift aid:*** $17,339. ***Average non-need-based aid:*** $12,739. ***Average indebtedness upon graduation:*** $29,500. ***Financial aid deadline:*** 3/1.

APPLYING
Standardized Tests *Required:* SAT or ACT (for admission).

Options: electronic application, early admission, deferred entrance.

Application fee: $45.

Required: essay or personal statement, high school transcript. ***Required for some:*** 2 letters of recommendation, interview. ***Recommended:*** minimum 3.0 GPA, 2 letters of recommendation.

Notification: continuous (freshmen).

CONTACT
Ms. Eileen Bardney, Director of Admissions, Mount Saint Mary College, 330 Powell Avenue, Newburgh, NY 12550. *Phone:* 845-569-3254. *Toll-free phone:* 888-937-6762. *Fax:* 845-569-3438. *E-mail:* eileen.bardney@msmc.edu.

Nazareth College of Rochester
Rochester, New York
http://www.naz.edu/

- **Independent** comprehensive, founded 1924
- **Suburban** 150-acre campus
- **Coed** 2,269 undergraduate students, 96% full-time, 74% women, 26% men
- 64% of applicants were admitted

UNDERGRAD STUDENTS
2,176 full-time, 93 part-time. 11% are from out of state; 5% Black or African American, non-Hispanic/Latino; 6% Hispanic/Latino; 3% Asian, non-Hispanic/Latino; 0.2% American Indian or Alaska Native, non-Hispanic/Latino; 2% Two or more races, non-Hispanic/Latino; 4% Race/ethnicity unknown; 1% international.

Freshmen:
Admission: 4,273 applied, 2,719 admitted, 544 enrolled. ***Average high school GPA:*** ####. ***Test scores:*** ACT scores over 18: 98%; ACT scores over 24: 65%; ACT scores over 30: 10%.

FACULTY
Total: 483, 38% full-time, 46% with terminal degrees.

Student/faculty ratio: 9:1.

ACADEMICS
Calendar: semesters. *Degrees:* bachelor's, master's, doctoral, post-master's, and postbachelor's certificates.

Special study options: academic remediation for entering students, adult/continuing education programs, advanced placement credit, cooperative education, double majors, English as a second language, honors programs, independent study, internships, off-campus study, part-time degree program, services for LD students, study abroad, summer session for credit. ***ROTC:*** Army (c), Air Force (c).

Computers: Students can access the following: computer help desk, free student e-mail accounts, online (class) grades, online (class) registration, online (class) schedules. Campuswide network is available. Wireless service is available via entire campus.

Library: Lorette Wilmot Library. Students can reserve study rooms.

STUDENT LIFE
Housing options: on-campus residence required through sophomore year; coed, special housing for students with disabilities. Campus housing is university owned. Freshman campus housing is guaranteed.

Activities and organizations: drama/theater group, student-run newspaper, radio station, choral group, Campus Activities Board, Center for Spirituality, Physical Therapy Club, Diversity Council, Intramurals.

Athletics Member NCAA. All Division III except golf (Division II). ***Intercollegiate sports:*** basketball M/W, crew M/W, cross-country running M/W, equestrian sports M/W, field hockey W, golf M/W, ice hockey M, lacrosse M/W, rugby M, soccer M/W, softball W, swimming and diving M/W, tennis M/W, track and field M/W, volleyball M/W. ***Intramural sports:*** basketball M/W, ice hockey M/W, racquetball M/W, rowing M/W, skiing (downhill) M/W, soccer M/W, ultimate Frisbee M/W, volleyball M/W.

Campus security: 24-hour emergency response devices and patrols, late-night transport/escort service, controlled dormitory access, security beeper, lighted pathways, alert system.

Student services: health clinic, personal/psychological counseling, women's center, veterans affairs office.

COSTS & FINANCIAL AID

Costs (2019–20) ***Comprehensive fee:*** $48,010 includes full-time tuition ($32,850), mandatory fees ($1430), and room and board ($13,730).

Financial Aid Of all full-time matriculated undergraduates who enrolled in 2018, 1,998 applied for aid, 1,797 were judged to have need, 604 had their need fully met. 1,086 Federal Work-Study jobs (averaging $2075). In 2018, 369 non-need-based awards were made. ***Average percent of need met:*** 82. ***Average financial aid package:*** $28,092. ***Average need-based loan:*** $4332. ***Average need-based gift aid:*** $18,131. ***Average non-need-based aid:*** $18,879. ***Average indebtedness upon graduation:*** $42,412.

APPLYING

Standardized Tests *Required for some:* SAT (for admission), SAT or ACT (for admission), Student can submit they ACT or SAT..

Options: electronic application, early admission, early decision, deferred entrance.

Application fee: $45.

Required: essay or personal statement, high school transcript, 1 letter of recommendation. ***Required for some:*** audition/portfolio review. ***Recommended:*** interview.

Application deadlines: 2/1 (freshmen), rolling (transfers).

Early decision deadline: 11/15 (for plan 1), 1/10 (for plan 2).

Notification: continuous until 3/1 (freshmen), continuous (transfers), 12/15 (early decision plan 1), 2/1 (early decision plan 2).

CONTACT

Ms. Meghan Arena, Vice President for Enrollment Management and Student Experience, Nazareth College of Rochester, 4245 East Avenue, Rochester, NY 14618. *Phone:* 585-389-2830. *Toll-free phone:* 800-462-3944. *Fax:* 585-389-2826. *E-mail:* imortim4@naz.edu.

The New School College of Performing Arts

New York, New York

http://www.newschool.edu/performing-arts/

- **Independent** comprehensive, part of The New School
- **Urban** campus with easy access to New York City
- **Endowment** $322.3 million
- **Coed**
- **Moderately difficult** entrance level

FACULTY

Student/faculty ratio: 5:1.

ACADEMICS

Calendar: semesters. *Degrees:* diplomas, bachelor's, and master's.
Library: New School Libraries & Archives plus 3 others. *Books:* 215,937 (physical), 840,933 (digital/electronic); *Serial titles:* 2,265 (physical), 113,452 (digital/electronic); *Databases:* 376. Weekly public service hours: 155; study areas open 24 hours, 5–7 days a week; students can reserve study rooms.

STUDENT LIFE

Housing options: coed, special housing for students with disabilities. Campus housing is university owned and leased by the school. Freshman applicants given priority for college housing.

Activities and organizations: drama/theater group, student-run newspaper, choral group.

Campus security: 24-hour emergency response devices, controlled dormitory access, 24-hour desk attendants in residence halls.

Student services: health clinic, personal/psychological counseling, veterans affairs office.

FINANCIAL AID

Financial Aid Of all full-time matriculated undergraduates who enrolled in 2017, 303 applied for aid, 267 were judged to have need, 21 had their need fully met. 29 Federal Work-Study jobs (averaging $3394). In 2017, 262 non-need-based awards were made. ***Average percent of need met:*** 47. ***Average financial aid package:*** $21,605. ***Average need-based loan:*** $4306. ***Average need-based gift aid:*** $7780. ***Average non-need-based aid:*** $17,827. ***Average indebtedness upon graduation:*** $281,459. ***Financial aid deadline:*** 2/1.

APPLYING

Options: electronic application, early action, deferred entrance.

Application fee: $50.

Required: essay or personal statement, high school transcript, 1 letter of recommendation. ***Required for some:*** interview, prescreening, live audition/interview. ***Recommended:*** minimum 3.0 GPA.

CONTACT

Ms. Amanda Hosking, Director of Admission, The New School College of Performing Arts, 79 Fifth Avenue, New York, NY 10003. *Phone:* 212-229-5150 Ext. 4805. *Toll-free phone:* 800-292-3040. *E-mail:* hoskinga@newschool.edu.

The New School for Public Engagement

New York, New York

http://www.newschool.edu/public-engagement/

- **Independent** comprehensive, founded 1919, part of The New School
- **Urban** campus with easy access to New York City
- **Endowment** $322.3 million
- **Coed**
- **Noncompetitive** entrance level

FACULTY

Student/faculty ratio: 5:1.

ACADEMICS

Calendar: semesters. *Degrees:* certificates, bachelor's, master's, doctoral, post-master's, and postbachelor's certificates.
Library: New School Libraries & Archives plus 3 others. *Books:* 215,937 (physical), 840,933 (digital/electronic); *Serial titles:* 2,265 (physical), 113,452 (digital/electronic); *Databases:* 376. Weekly public service hours: 155; study areas open 24 hours, 5–7 days a week; students can reserve study rooms.

STUDENT LIFE

Housing options: coed, special housing for students with disabilities. Campus housing is university owned and leased by the school. Freshman applicants given priority for college housing.

Activities and organizations: drama/theater group, student-run newspaper, choral group.

Campus security: 24-hour emergency response devices, controlled dormitory access, trained security personnel in central buildings and 24-hour desk attendants in residence halls.

Student services: health clinic, personal/psychological counseling.

FINANCIAL AID

Financial Aid Of all full-time matriculated undergraduates who enrolled in 2017, 140 applied for aid, 128 were judged to have need, 3 had their need fully met. 7 Federal Work-Study jobs (averaging $3707). In 2017, 67 non-need-based awards were made. ***Average percent of need met:*** 48. ***Average financial aid package:*** $20,467. ***Average need-based loan:*** $4743. ***Average need-based gift aid:*** $16,980. ***Average non-need-based aid:*** $3719. ***Average indebtedness upon graduation:*** $54,566. ***Financial aid deadline:*** 2/1.

APPLYING

Options: electronic application, early action, deferred entrance.

Application fee: $50.

Required: essay or personal statement, high school transcript. ***Recommended:*** 1 letter of recommendation.

CONTACT
Ms. Elizabeth Puleio, Associate Director of Admission, The New School for Public Engagement, 72 Fifth Avenue, New York, NY 10011. *Phone:* 212-229-5150 Ext. 3789. *Toll-free phone:* 800-292-3040. *E-mail:* puleioe@newschool.edu.

New York City College of Technology of the City University of New York

Brooklyn, New York

http://www.citytech.cuny.edu/

CONTACT
Alexis Chaconis, Director of Admissions, New York City College of Technology of the City University of New York, 300 Jay Street, Brooklyn, NY 11201-2983. *Phone:* 718-260-5500. *E-mail:* achaconis@citytech.cuny.edu.

New York College of Health Professions

Syosset, New York

http://www.nycollege.edu/

CONTACT
Ms. Mary Rodas, Associate Director of Admissions, New York College of Health Professions, 6801 Jericho Turnpike, Syosset, NY 11791-4413. *Toll-free phone:* 800-922-7337 Ext. 351. *E-mail:* rdodas@nycollege.edu.

New York Institute of Technology

Old Westbury, New York

http://www.nyit.edu/

- **Independent** comprehensive, founded 1955
- **Suburban** 215-acre campus with easy access to New York City
- **Endowment** $110.5 million
- **Coed**
- **Moderately difficult** entrance level

FACULTY
Student/faculty ratio: 13:1.

ACADEMICS
Calendar: semesters. *Degrees:* certificates, diplomas, associate, bachelor's, master's, doctoral, post-master's, and postbachelor's certificates.
Library: George and Gertrude Wisser Memorial Library plus 3 others. *Books:* 89,426 (physical), 70,248 (digital/electronic); *Serial titles:* 2,279 (physical), 23,926 (digital/electronic). Weekly public service hours: 78; students can reserve study rooms.

STUDENT LIFE
Housing options: coed. Campus housing is university owned and leased by the school. Freshman campus housing is guaranteed.

Activities and organizations: student-run newspaper, television station, national fraternities, national sororities.

Athletics Member NCAA. All Division II.

Campus security: 24-hour emergency response devices and patrols, late-night transport/escort service, controlled dormitory access.

Student services: health clinic, personal/psychological counseling, veterans affairs office.

COSTS & FINANCIAL AID
Costs (2018–19) ***Comprehensive fee:*** $51,180 includes full-time tuition ($35,585), mandatory fees ($1305), and room and board ($14,290). Full-time tuition and fees vary according to program. Part-time tuition: $1205 per credit. Part-time tuition and fees vary according to course load and program. ***Required fees:*** $540 per term part-time. ***College room only:*** $9320. Room and board charges vary according to housing facility and location.

Financial Aid Of all full-time matriculated undergraduates who enrolled in 2018, 2,599 applied for aid, 2,362 were judged to have need. In 2018, 484 non-need-based awards were made. ***Average financial aid package:*** $27,482. ***Average need-based loan:*** $4147. ***Average need-based gift aid:*** $9575. ***Average non-need-based aid:*** $16,545.

APPLYING
Standardized Tests *Required:* SAT or ACT (for admission).

Options: electronic application, deferred entrance.

Application fee: $50.

Required: essay or personal statement, high school transcript, 2 letters of recommendation. ***Required for some:*** interview. ***Recommended:*** minimum 2.7 GPA.

CONTACT
Ms. Marcelle Hicks, Senior Director, Undergraduate Admissions, New York Institute of Technology, Old Westbury, NY 11568. *Phone:* 516-686-1020. *Toll-free phone:* 800-345-NYIT. *E-mail:* admissions@nyit.edu.

New York School of Interior Design

New York, New York

http://www.nysid.edu/

CONTACT
Jaspreet Bains, Admissions Associate, New York School of Interior Design, 170 East 70th Street, New York, NY 10021-5110. *Phone:* 212-472-1500 Ext. 212. *Toll-free phone:* 800-336-9743 Ext. 205. *Fax:* 212-472-1867. *E-mail:* admissions@nysid.edu.

New York University

New York, New York

http://www.nyu.edu/

- **Independent** university, founded 1831
- **Urban** 230-acre campus with easy access to New York City
- **Endowment** $4.2 billion
- **Coed** 26,733 undergraduate students, 96% full-time, 58% women, 42% men
- **Very difficult** entrance level, 20% of applicants were admitted

UNDERGRAD STUDENTS
25,725 full-time, 1,008 part-time. Students come from 52 states and territories; 157 other countries; 66% are from out of state; 6% Black or African American, non-Hispanic/Latino; 14% Hispanic/Latino; 19% Asian, non-Hispanic/Latino; 0.2% Native Hawaiian or other Pacific Islander, non-Hispanic/Latino; 0.2% American Indian or Alaska Native, non-Hispanic/Latino; 5% Two or more races, non-Hispanic/Latino; 6% Race/ethnicity unknown; 20% international; 3% transferred in; 42% live on campus.

Freshmen:
Admission: 71,834 applied, 14,359 admitted, 6,174 enrolled. ***Average high school GPA:*** 3.6. ***Test scores:*** SAT evidence-based reading and writing scores over 500: 100%; SAT math scores over 500: 100%; ACT scores over 18: 100%; SAT evidence-based reading and writing scores over 600: 94%; SAT math scores over 600: 90%; ACT scores over 24: 98%; SAT evidence-based reading and writing scores over 700: 43%; SAT math scores over 700: 63%; ACT scores over 30: 73%.
Retention: 94% of full-time freshmen returned.

FACULTY
Total: 6,542, 45% full-time, 73% with terminal degrees.
Student/faculty ratio: 10:1.

ACADEMICS
Calendar: semesters. *Degrees:* certificates, diplomas, associate, bachelor's, master's, doctoral, post-master's, and postbachelor's certificates.

Special study options: accelerated degree program, adult/continuing education programs, advanced placement credit, cooperative education, distance learning, double majors, English as a second language, honors programs, independent study, internships, off-campus study, part-time degree program, services for LD students, student-designed majors, study abroad, summer session for credit. ***ROTC:*** Army (c), Air Force (c).

Unusual degree programs: 3-2 engineering with School of Engineering and College of Arts and Science; nursing; College of Arts and Science,

Gallatin School of Individualized Study, Wagner Graduate School of Public Service.

Computers: Students can access the following: computer help desk, free student e-mail accounts, online (class) grades, online (class) registration, online (class) schedules. Campuswide network is available. 100% of college-owned or -operated housing units are wired for high-speed Internet access. Wireless service is available via entire campus.

Library: Elmer H. Bobst Library plus 10 others. *Books:* 3.4 million (physical), 1.6 million (digital/electronic); *Serial titles:* 51,377 (physical), 197,567 (digital/electronic); *Databases:* 1,152. Study areas open 24 hours, 5–7 days a week; students can reserve study rooms.

STUDENT LIFE

Housing options: coed, special housing for students with disabilities. Campus housing is university owned and leased by the school. Freshman campus housing is guaranteed.

Activities and organizations: drama/theater group, student-run newspaper, radio and television station, choral group, national fraternities, national sororities.

Athletics Member NCAA. All Division III. ***Intercollegiate sports:*** baseball M, basketball M/W, cross-country running M/W, fencing M/W, golf M/W, soccer M/W, softball W, swimming and diving M/W, tennis M/W, track and field M/W, volleyball M/W, wrestling M. ***Intramural sports:*** badminton M(c)/W(c), basketball M/W, bowling M/W, cheerleading M(c)/W(c), equestrian sports M(c)/W(c), football M/W, ice hockey M(c), lacrosse M(c)/W(c), racquetball M(c)/W(c), rowing M(c)/W(c), soccer M/W, softball M/W, squash M(c)/W(c), table tennis M(c)/W(c), triathlon M(c)/W(c), ultimate Frisbee M(c)/W(c), volleyball M/W, water polo M(c)/W(c).

Campus security: 24-hour emergency response devices and patrols, student patrols, late-night transport/escort service, controlled dormitory access.

Student services: health clinic, personal/psychological counseling, women's center, veterans affairs office.

COSTS & FINANCIAL AID

Costs (2018–19) ***Comprehensive fee:*** $69,984 includes full-time tuition ($49,256), mandatory fees ($2572), and room and board ($18,156). Full-time tuition and fees vary according to course load, program, and reciprocity agreements. Part-time tuition: $1451 per credit hour. Part-time tuition and fees vary according to program. ***Required fees:*** $489 per term part-time. ***College room only:*** $13,166. Room and board charges vary according to board plan and housing facility. ***Payment plans:*** tuition prepayment, installment, deferred payment. ***Waivers:*** employees or children of employees.

Financial Aid Of all full-time matriculated undergraduates who enrolled in 2017, 15,956 applied for aid, 12,580 were judged to have need, 1,471 had their need fully met. In 2017, 1071 non-need-based awards were made. ***Average percent of need met:*** 64. ***Average financial aid package:*** $36,209. ***Average need-based loan:*** $5310. ***Average need-based gift aid:*** $31,739. ***Average non-need-based aid:*** $5596. ***Average indebtedness upon graduation:*** $29,923. ***Financial aid deadline:*** 2/15.

APPLYING

Standardized Tests *Required:* (for admission). *Required for some:* SAT and SAT Subject Tests or ACT (for admission).

Options: electronic application, early admission, early decision, deferred entrance.

Application fee: $80.

Required: essay or personal statement, high school transcript, 1 letter of recommendation. ***Required for some:*** audition or a portfolio for some specific programs.

Application deadlines: 1/1 (freshmen), 4/1 (transfers).

Early decision deadline: 11/1 (for plan 1), 1/1 (for plan 2).

Notification: 4/1 (freshmen), 5/15 (transfers), 12/15 (early decision plan 1), 2/15 (early decision plan 2).

CONTACT

Kristy Materasso, Undergraduate Admissions Processing Center, New York University, 383 Lafayette Street, New York, NY 10003. *Phone:* 212-998-4500. *Fax:* 212-995-4902. *E-mail:* admissions@nyu.edu.

★ Niagara University

Niagara Falls, New York

http://www.niagara.edu/

- **Independent** comprehensive, founded 1856, affiliated with Roman Catholic Church
- **Suburban** 160-acre campus with easy access to Buffalo, NY and Toronto, Ontario (Canada)
- **Endowment** $98.0 million
- **Coed**
- **Moderately difficult** entrance level

FACULTY

Student/faculty ratio: 11:1.

ACADEMICS

Calendar: semesters. *Degrees:* certificates, associate, bachelor's, master's, doctoral, post-master's, and postbachelor's certificates.

Library: Our Lady of Angels Library. *Books:* 122,720 (physical), 348,406 (digital/electronic); *Serial titles:* 32,000 (digital/electronic); *Databases:* 111. Weekly public service hours: 107; study areas open 24 hours, 5–7 days a week; students can reserve study rooms.

STUDENT LIFE

Housing options: on-campus residence required through sophomore year; coed. Campus housing is university owned. Freshman campus housing is guaranteed.

Activities and organizations: drama/theater group, student-run newspaper, radio station, choral group, Student Nursing Association, Future Teachers Association, NY Players (theatre), Beta Alpha Psi, Hospitality & Tourism Association, national fraternities, national sororities.

Athletics Member NCAA. All Division I.

Campus security: 24-hour emergency response devices and patrols, late-night transport/escort service, controlled dormitory access, 24-hour escort service, Emergency Notification System.

Student services: health clinic, personal/psychological counseling, veterans affairs office.

COSTS & FINANCIAL AID

Costs (2018–19) ***One-time required fee:*** $200. ***Comprehensive fee:*** $46,380 includes full-time tuition ($31,700), mandatory fees ($1480), and room and board ($13,200). Full-time tuition and fees vary according to program. Part-time tuition: $1060 per credit hour. Part-time tuition and fees vary according to program. ***Room and board:*** Room and board charges vary according to housing facility. ***Payment plans:*** installment, deferred payment.

Financial Aid Of all full-time matriculated undergraduates who enrolled in 2018, 1,999 applied for aid, 1,823 were judged to have need, 887 had their need fully met. 357 Federal Work-Study jobs (averaging $4002). 37 state and other part-time jobs (averaging $6011). In 2018, 425 non-need-based awards were made. ***Average percent of need met:*** 81. ***Average financial aid package:*** $27,511. ***Average need-based loan:*** $4644. ***Average need-based gift aid:*** $23,466. ***Average non-need-based aid:*** $16,072. ***Average indebtedness upon graduation:*** $34,484.

APPLYING

Options: electronic application, early admission, early action, deferred entrance.

Required: high school transcript. ***Recommended:*** minimum 3.0 GPA, 3 letters of recommendation, interview.

CONTACT

Mr. Mark Wojnowski, Director of Undergraduate Admissions, Niagara University, 5795 Lewiston Road, Gacioch Center, Niagara University, NY 14109. *Phone:* 716-286-8700. *Toll-free phone:* 800-462-2111. *Fax:* 716-286-8733. *E-mail:* admissions@niagara.edu.

See next page for display ad and page 1058 for the College Close-Up.

Nyack College

Nyack, New York

http://www.nyack.edu/

- **Independent** comprehensive, founded 1882, affiliated with The Christian and Missionary Alliance
- **Suburban** 125-acre campus with easy access to New York City
- **Coed**
- **Minimally difficult** entrance level

FACULTY

Student/faculty ratio: 12:1.

ACADEMICS

Calendar: semesters. *Degrees:* associate, bachelor's, master's, and doctoral.

Library: Bailey Library plus 3 others.

STUDENT LIFE

Housing options: on-campus residence required through sophomore year; men-only, women-only. Campus housing is university owned. Freshman campus housing is guaranteed.

Activities and organizations: drama/theater group, student-run newspaper, radio station, choral group, Student leadership, Choral groups, Lost & Found, Small group ministries, Intramurals.

Athletics Member NCAA. All Division II.

Campus security: 24-hour emergency response devices and patrols.

Student services: health clinic, personal/psychological counseling.

COSTS & FINANCIAL AID

Costs (2018–19) ***Comprehensive fee:*** $34,800 includes full-time tuition ($25,000), mandatory fees ($350), and room and board ($9450). Part-time tuition: $1040 per credit hour. Part-time tuition and fees vary according to course load. ***Room and board:*** Room and board charges vary according to board plan and housing facility.

Financial Aid Of all full-time matriculated undergraduates who enrolled in 2017, 176 Federal Work-Study jobs (averaging $1028). 239 state and other part-time jobs (averaging $4233). ***Average indebtedness upon graduation:*** $28,926.

APPLYING

Standardized Tests *Required for some:* SAT and SAT Subject Tests or ACT (for admission).

Options: electronic application, early action, deferred entrance.

Application fee: $25.

Required: essay or personal statement, high school transcript, minimum 2.0 GPA, 1 letter of recommendation, signed statement of faith and community life form. ***Required for some:*** interview.

CONTACT

Mr. Dan Bailey, Director of Admissions, Nyack College, 1 South Boulevard, Nyack, NY 10960-3698. *Phone:* 845-675-4401. *Toll-free phone:* 800-33-NYACK. *Fax:* 845-358-3047. *E-mail:* admissions@nyack.edu.

Ohr Hameir Theological Seminary

Cortlandt Manor, New York

http://www.ohrhameir.com/

CONTACT

Director of Admissions, Ohr Hameir Theological Seminary, 141 Furnace Woods Road, Cortlandt Manor, NY 10567. *Phone:* 914-736-1500.

Ohr Somayach/Joseph Tanenbaum Educational Center

Monsey, New York

http://ohr.edu/

- **Independent Jewish** comprehensive, founded 1979
- **Small-town** 7-acre campus with easy access to New York City
- **Men only**
- **Moderately difficult** entrance level

ACADEMICS
Calendar: semesters. *Degree:* master's and doctoral.
Library: Finer Library.

STUDENT LIFE
Housing options: on-campus residence required through senior year; men-only. Campus housing is university owned.

Campus security: 24-hour emergency response devices and patrols, controlled dormitory access.

Student services: personal/psychological counseling.

APPLYING
Options: early admission.

Required: interview. ***Required for some:*** essay or personal statement. ***Recommended:*** high school transcript.

CONTACT
Ohr Somayach/Joseph Tanenbaum Educational Center, PO Box 334, 244 Route 306, Monsey, NY 10952-0334. *Phone:* 845-425-1370 Ext. 22.

★ Pace University
New York, New York
http://www.pace.edu/nyc

- **Independent** university, founded 1906
- **Urban** campus with easy access to New York City
- **Endowment** $169.9 million
- **Coed** 8,960 undergraduate students, 89% full-time, 62% women, 38% men
- **Moderately difficult** entrance level, 76% of applicants were admitted

UNDERGRAD STUDENTS
7,943 full-time, 1,017 part-time. 46% are from out of state; 11% Black or African American, non-Hispanic/Latino; 12% Hispanic/Latino; 8% Asian, non-Hispanic/Latino; 0.1% Native Hawaiian or other Pacific Islander, non-Hispanic/Latino; 0.3% American Indian or Alaska Native, non-Hispanic/Latino; 5% Two or more races, non-Hispanic/Latino; 3% Race/ethnicity unknown; 10% international; 6% transferred in; 42% live on campus.

Freshmen:
Admission: 21,520 applied, 16,327 admitted, 2,013 enrolled. ***Average high school GPA:*** 3.4. ***Test scores:*** SAT evidence-based reading and writing scores over 500: 92%; SAT math scores over 500: 88%; ACT scores over 18: 97%; SAT evidence-based reading and writing scores over 600: 40%; SAT math scores over 600: 29%; ACT scores over 24: 58%; SAT evidence-based reading and writing scores over 700: 4%; SAT math scores over 700: 5%; ACT scores over 30: 9%.

Retention: 79% of full-time freshmen returned.

FACULTY
Total: 1,369, 38% full-time, 55% with terminal degrees.

Student/faculty ratio: 16:1.

ACADEMICS
Calendar: semesters. *Degrees:* certificates, associate, bachelor's, master's, doctoral, post-master's, and postbachelor's certificates.

Special study options: accelerated degree program, adult/continuing education programs, advanced placement credit, cooperative education, distance learning, double majors, English as a second language, freshman honors college, honors programs, independent study, internships, part-time degree program, services for LD students, study abroad, summer session for credit. ***ROTC:*** Army (c).

Unusual degree programs: 3-2 business administration; engineering with Manhattan College, Rensselaer Polytechnic Institute; occupational Therapy with Columbia University, optometry with SUNY College of Optometry, physical therapy with New York Medical College, podiatry with the New York College of Podiatric Medicine.

Computers: 209 computers/terminals are available on campus for general student use. Students can access the following: computer help desk, free student e-mail accounts, online (class) grades, online (class) registration, online (class) schedules, administrative functions (tuition, student records, financial aid, health insurance waiver). Campuswide network is available. 100% of college-owned or -operated housing units are wired for high-speed Internet access. Wireless service is available via entire campus.
Library: Henry Birnbaum Library. *Books:* 382,858 (physical), 224,418 (digital/electronic); *Serial titles:* 73 (physical), 576,860

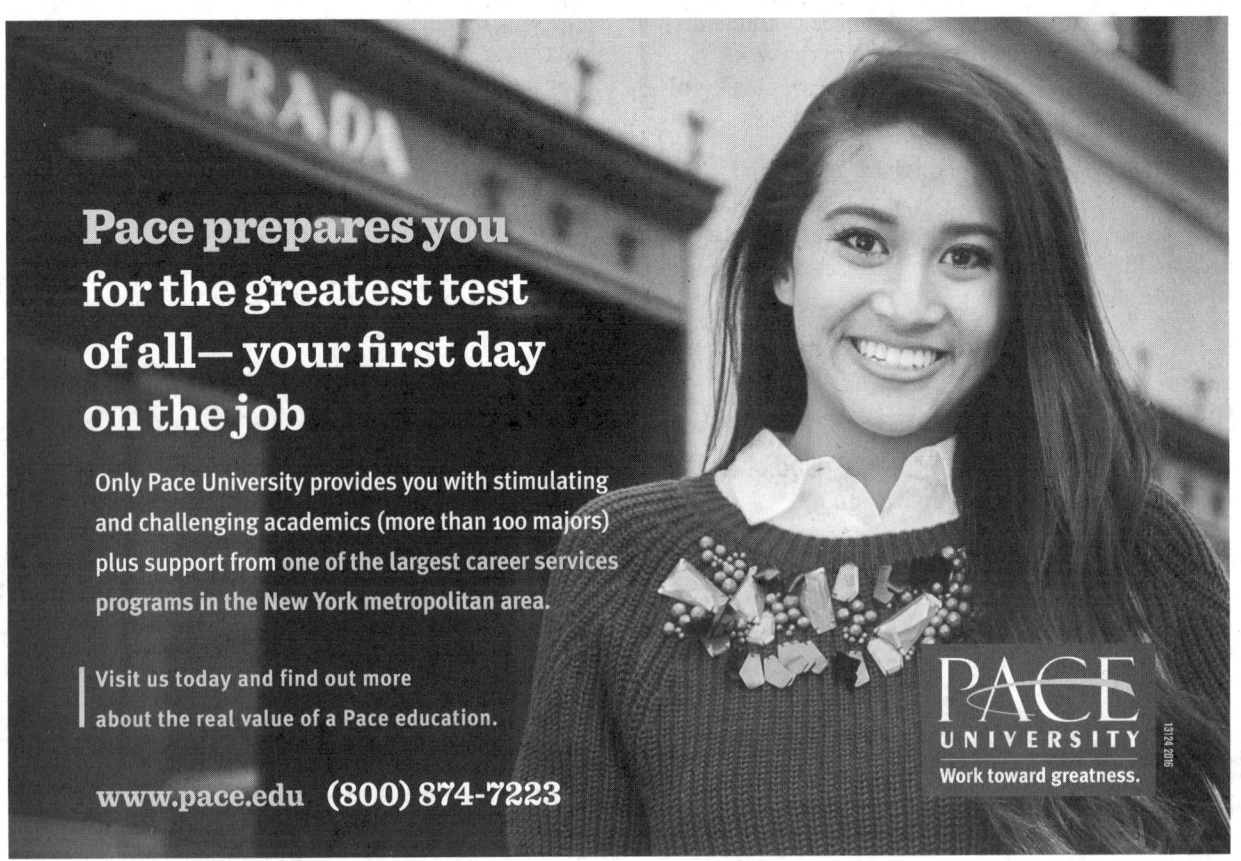

(digital/electronic); *Databases:* 172. Weekly public service hours: 93; students can reserve study rooms.

STUDENT LIFE
Housing options: coed, special housing for students with disabilities. Campus housing is university owned and leased by the school. Freshman campus housing is guaranteed.

Activities and organizations: drama/theater group, student-run newspaper, radio and television station, choral group, Kappa Delta, Sigma Delta Tau, Beta Alpha Psi, Profashionals, Programming and Campus Entertainment Board, national fraternities, national sororities.

Athletics Member NCAA. All Division II. ***Intercollegiate sports:*** baseball M(s), basketball M(s)/W(s), cross-country running M(s)/W(s), field hockey W(s), football M(s), lacrosse M(s)/W(s), soccer W(s), softball W(s), swimming and diving M(s)/W(s), volleyball W(s). ***Intramural sports:*** badminton M/W, basketball M/W, soccer M/W, ultimate Frisbee M/W, volleyball M/W.

Campus security: 24-hour emergency response devices and patrols, late-night transport/escort service, controlled dormitory access.

Student services: health clinic, personal/psychological counseling, veterans affairs office.

COSTS & FINANCIAL AID
Costs (2019–20) ***Comprehensive fee:*** $63,809 includes full-time tuition ($43,624), mandatory fees ($1656), and room and board ($18,529). Part-time tuition: $1251 per credit hour.

Financial Aid Of all full-time matriculated undergraduates who enrolled in 2018, 3,838 applied for aid, 3,442 were judged to have need, 462 had their need fully met. In 2018, 1533 non-need-based awards were made. ***Average percent of need met:*** 68. ***Average financial aid package:*** $31,957. ***Average need-based loan:*** $4247. ***Average need-based gift aid:*** $27,919. ***Average non-need-based aid:*** $20,951. ***Average indebtedness upon graduation:*** $36,113.

APPLYING
Standardized Tests *Required for some:* SAT or ACT (for admission).

Options: electronic application, early decision, early action, deferred entrance.

Application fee: $50.

Required: essay or personal statement, high school transcript, 2 letters of recommendation. ***Recommended:*** interview.

Application deadlines: 2/15 (freshmen), rolling (transfers).

Notification: continuous (freshmen), continuous (transfers).

CONTACT
Mr. Andre Cordon, Dean of Admissions, Pace University, One Pace Plaza, 163 William Street, New York, NY 10038. *Phone:* 212-346-1794. *Toll-free phone:* 800-874-7223. *Fax:* 212-346-1821. *E-mail:* acordon@pace.edu.

See previous page for display ad and page 1070 for the College Close-Up.

Pace University, Pleasantville Campus

Pleasantville, New York

http://www.pace.edu/westchester

- **Independent** university, founded 1906
- **Suburban** campus with easy access to New York City
- **Endowment** $169.9 million
- **Coed** 2,630 undergraduate students, 92% full-time, 60% women, 40% men
- **Moderately difficult** entrance level, 76% of applicants were admitted

UNDERGRAD STUDENTS
2,424 full-time, 206 part-time. 27% are from out of state; 13% Black or African American, non-Hispanic/Latino; 15% Hispanic/Latino; 5% Asian, non-Hispanic/Latino; 0.3% American Indian or Alaska Native, non-Hispanic/Latino; 3% Two or more races, non-Hispanic/Latino; 4% Race/ethnicity unknown; 2% international; 6% transferred in; 56% live on campus.

Freshmen:
Admission: 4,758 applied, 3,602 admitted, 605 enrolled. ***Average high school GPA:*** 3.3. ***Test scores:*** SAT evidence-based reading and writing scores over 500: 89%; SAT math scores over 500: 85%; ACT scores over 18: 95%; SAT evidence-based reading and writing scores over 600: 30%; SAT math scores over 600: 25%; ACT scores over 24: 48%; SAT evidence-based reading and writing scores over 700: 2%; SAT math scores over 700: 3%; ACT scores over 30: 5%.

Retention: 85% of full-time freshmen returned.

FACULTY
Total: 467, 33% full-time, 46% with terminal degrees.

Student/faculty ratio: 11:1.

ACADEMICS
Calendar: semesters. *Degrees:* certificates, diplomas, associate, bachelor's, master's, doctoral, post-master's, and postbachelor's certificates.

Special study options: accelerated degree program, adult/continuing education programs, advanced placement credit, cooperative education, distance learning, double majors, English as a second language, freshman honors college, honors programs, independent study, internships, part-time degree program, services for LD students, study abroad, summer session for credit. ***ROTC:*** Army (c), Air Force (c).

Unusual degree programs: 3-2 business administration; engineering with Manhattan College, Rensselaer Polytechnic Institute; occupational therapy with Columbia University, optometry with SUNY College of Optometry, physical therapy with New York Medical College, podiatry with the New York College of Podiatric Medicine.

Computers: 132 computers/terminals are available on campus for general student use. Students can access the following: computer help desk, free student e-mail accounts, online (class) grades, online (class) registration, online (class) schedules, administrative functions (tuition, student records, financial aid, health insurance waiver). Campuswide network is available. 100% of college-owned or -operated housing units are wired for high-speed Internet access. Wireless service is available via entire campus. **Library:** Edward and Doris Mortola Library. *Books:* 167,456 (physical), 224,418 (digital/electronic); *Serial titles:* 34 (physical), 576,860 (digital/electronic); *Databases:* 172. Weekly public service hours: 113; students can reserve study rooms.

STUDENT LIFE
Housing options: coed. Campus housing is university owned. Freshman campus housing is guaranteed.

Activities and organizations: drama/theater group, student-run newspaper, radio and television station, choral group, Lubin Business Association, National Student Nurses Association, Future Leaders in Healthcare, Black Student Union, Accounting Society, national fraternities, national sororities.

Athletics Member NCAA. All Division II. ***Intercollegiate sports:*** baseball M(s), basketball M(s)/W(s), cross-country running M(s)/W(s), field hockey W(s), football M(s), lacrosse M(s)/W(s), soccer W(s), softball W(s), swimming and diving M(s)/W(s), volleyball W(s). ***Intramural sports:*** badminton M/W, basketball M/W, soccer M/W, softball M/W, tennis M/W, ultimate Frisbee M/W, volleyball M/W.

Campus security: 24-hour emergency response devices and patrols, late-night transport/escort service, controlled dormitory access.

Student services: health clinic, personal/psychological counseling, veterans affairs office.

COSTS & FINANCIAL AID
Costs (2018–19) ***Comprehensive fee:*** $61,880 includes full-time tuition ($43,624), mandatory fees ($1656), and room and board ($16,600). Full-time tuition and fees vary according to location. Part-time tuition: $1251 per credit hour. Part-time tuition and fees vary according to course load and location. ***Room and board:*** Room and board charges vary according to board plan, housing facility, location, and student level. ***Payment plan:*** installment. ***Waivers:*** senior citizens and employees or children of employees.

Financial Aid Of all full-time matriculated undergraduates who enrolled in 2018, 2,102 applied for aid, 1,938 were judged to have need, 361 had their need fully met. In 2018, 400 non-need-based awards were made. ***Average percent of need met:*** 78. ***Average financial aid package:*** $36,894. ***Average need-based loan:*** $4296. ***Average need-based gift aid:*** $32,352. ***Average non-need-based aid:*** $23,976. ***Average indebtedness upon graduation:*** $36,302.

APPLYING
Standardized Tests *Required for some:* SAT or ACT (for admission).

Options: electronic application, early decision, early action, deferred entrance.

Application fee: $50.

Required: essay or personal statement, high school transcript, 2 letters of recommendation. ***Recommended:*** interview.

Application deadlines: 2/15 (freshmen), rolling (transfers).

Notification: continuous (freshmen), continuous (transfers).

CONTACT
Mr. Andre Cordon, Dean of Admission, Pace University, Pleasantville Campus, 861 Bedford Road, Pleasantville, NY 10570. *Phone:* 212-346-1794. *Toll-free phone:* 800-874-PACE. *Fax:* 212-346-1821. *E-mail:* acordon@pace.edu.

Parsons School of Design

New York, New York

http://www.newschool.edu/parsons/

- **Independent** comprehensive, founded 1896, part of The New School
- **Urban** campus with easy access to New York City
- **Endowment** $322.3 million
- **Coed**
- **Moderately difficult** entrance level

FACULTY
Student/faculty ratio: 11:1.

ACADEMICS
Calendar: semesters. *Degrees:* associate, bachelor's, master's, and postbachelor's certificates.
Library: New School Libraries & Archives plus 3 others. *Books:* 215,937 (physical), 840,933 (digital/electronic); *Serial titles:* 2,265 (physical), 113,452 (digital/electronic); *Databases:* 376. Weekly public service hours: 155; study areas open 24 hours, 5–7 days a week; students can reserve study rooms.

STUDENT LIFE
Housing options: coed, special housing for students with disabilities. Campus housing is university owned and leased by the school. Freshman applicants given priority for college housing.

Activities and organizations: drama/theater group, student-run newspaper, choral group.

Campus security: 24-hour emergency response devices, controlled dormitory access, 24-hour security desk personnel.

Student services: health clinic, personal/psychological counseling, veterans affairs office.

FINANCIAL AID
Financial Aid Of all full-time matriculated undergraduates who enrolled in 2017, 1,531 applied for aid, 1,370 were judged to have need, 68 had their need fully met. 145 Federal Work-Study jobs (averaging $3434). In 2017, 1946 non-need-based awards were made. ***Average percent of need met:*** 56. ***Average financial aid package:*** $28,427. ***Average need-based loan:*** $4394. ***Average need-based gift aid:*** $17,295. ***Average non-need-based aid:*** $8274. ***Average indebtedness upon graduation:*** $34,108. ***Financial aid deadline:*** 2/1.

APPLYING
Standardized Tests *Required for some:* TOEFL/IELTS /PTE for students whose native language is not English.

Options: electronic application, early action, deferred entrance.

Application fee: $50.

Required: essay or personal statement, high school transcript, 2 letters of recommendation, online application, Parsons Challenge portfolio, artist statement. ***Recommended:*** minimum 3.0 GPA.

CONTACT
Ms. Erin Stine, Director of Undergraduate Admissions for Parsons School of Design, Parsons School of Design, 72 Fifth Avenue at 13th Street, New York, NY 10011. *Phone:* 212-229-8989. *Toll-free phone:* 800-292-3040. *E-mail:* stinee@newschool.edu.

★ Paul Smith's College

Paul Smiths, New York

http://www.paulsmiths.edu/

CONTACT
Admissions Office, Paul Smith's College, Routes 86 and 30, PO Box 265, Paul Smiths, NY 12970. *Phone:* 518-327-6227. *Toll-free phone:* 800-421-2605. *Fax:* 518-327-6016. *E-mail:* admissions@paulsmiths.edu.

Phillips Beth Israel School of Nursing

New York, New York

http://www.mountsinai.org/locations/beth-israel/pson

CONTACT
Mrs. Bernice Pass-Stern, Assistant Dean, Phillips Beth Israel School of Nursing, 776 Sixth Avenue, 4th Floor, New York, NY 10010-6354. *Phone:* 212-614-6176. *Fax:* 212-614-6109. *E-mail:* bstern@chpnet.org.

Plaza College

Forest Hills, New York

http://www.plazacollege.edu/

CONTACT
Dean Vanessa Lopez, Dean of Admissions, Plaza College, 118-33 Queens Boulevard, Forest Hills, NY 11375. *Phone:* 718-779-1430. *E-mail:* info@plazacollege.edu.

★ Pratt Institute

Brooklyn, New York

http://www.pratt.edu/

- **Independent** comprehensive, founded 1887
- **Urban** 25-acre campus
- **Coed**
- **Very difficult** entrance level

FACULTY
Student/faculty ratio: 10:1.

ACADEMICS
Calendar: semesters plus optional May term and summer session. *Degrees:* associate, bachelor's, master's, and post-master's certificates.
Library: Pratt Institute Library.

STUDENT LIFE
Housing options: coed, special housing for students with disabilities. Campus housing is university owned. Freshman campus housing is guaranteed.

Athletics Member NCAA. All Division III.

Campus security: 24-hour emergency response devices and patrols, late-night transport/escort service.

COSTS & FINANCIAL AID
Costs (2018–19) ***Comprehensive fee:*** $64,492 includes full-time tuition ($49,810), mandatory fees ($2060), and room and board ($12,622). Part-time tuition: $1607 per credit hour. ***College room only:*** $8862. Room and board charges vary according to board plan and housing facility.

Financial Aid Of all full-time matriculated undergraduates who enrolled in 2018, 1,653 applied for aid, 1,449 were judged to have need, 161 had their need fully met. In 2018, 1166 non-need-based awards were made. ***Average percent of need met:*** 55. ***Average financial aid package:*** $30,615. ***Average need-based loan:*** $9724. ***Average need-based gift aid:*** $5729. ***Average non-need-based aid:*** $18,751. ***Average indebtedness upon graduation:*** $39,237. ***Financial aid deadline:*** 3/1.

APPLYING
Standardized Tests *Required:* SAT or ACT (for admission). *Required for some:* SAT Subject Tests (for admission).

Options: electronic application, early action, deferred entrance.

Application fee: $50.

Required: essay or personal statement, high school transcript, 1 letter of recommendation. ***Required for some:*** portfolio. ***Recommended:*** minimum 3.0 GPA.

CONTACT

Mr. Adam Ward, Visit Coordinator, Pratt Institute, 200 Willoughby Avenue, DeKalb Hall, Brooklyn, NY 11205. *Phone:* 718-636-3779. *Toll-free phone:* 800-331-0834. *Fax:* 718-636-3670. *E-mail:* visit@pratt.edu.

See this page for display ad and page 1076 for the College Close-Up.

Purchase College, State University of New York

Purchase, New York

http://www.purchase.edu/

- **State-supported** comprehensive, founded 1967, part of State University of New York System
- **Small-town** 500-acre campus with easy access to New York City
- **Coed** 4,163 undergraduate students, 92% full-time, 58% women, 42% men
- **Moderately difficult** entrance level, 42% of applicants were admitted

UNDERGRAD STUDENTS

3,833 full-time, 330 part-time. Students come from 42 states and territories; 30 other countries; 13% are from out of state; 11% Black or African American, non-Hispanic/Latino; 19% Hispanic/Latino; 4% Asian, non-Hispanic/Latino; 0.2% Native Hawaiian or other Pacific Islander, non-Hispanic/Latino; 0.3% American Indian or Alaska Native, non-Hispanic/Latino; 5% Two or more races, non-Hispanic/Latino; 6% Race/ethnicity unknown; 2% international; 9% transferred in; 68% live on campus.

Freshmen:

Admission: 3,421 applied, 1,453 admitted, 897 enrolled. ***Average high school GPA:*** 3.3. ***Test scores:*** ACT scores over 18: 94%; ACT scores over 24: 54%; ACT scores over 30: 12%.

Retention: 81% of full-time freshmen returned.

FACULTY

Total: 466, 39% full-time.

Student/faculty ratio: 14:1.

ACADEMICS

Calendar: semesters. *Degrees:* certificates, bachelor's, master's, post-master's, and postbachelor's certificates.

Special study options: academic remediation for entering students, adult/continuing education programs, advanced placement credit, double majors, English as a second language, independent study, internships, off-campus study, part-time degree program, services for LD students, student-designed majors, study abroad, summer session for credit.

Computers: 600 computers/terminals and 3,500 ports are available on campus for general student use. Students can access the following: campus intranet, computer help desk, free student e-mail accounts, online (class) grades, online (class) registration, online (class) schedules, CNC-routers; 3D printers; Laser cutters; Vinyl Printers; a Virtual Reality Lab; a fabrication lab; Non-liner edit labs for film; Music Digital Audio Workstations, 24 and 48" plotters for high-quality photographic output; a digital embroidery machine. Campuswide network is available. 100% of college-owned or -operated housing units are wired for high-speed Internet access. Wireless service is available via classrooms, computer centers, computer labs, learning centers, libraries, student centers.

Library: Purchase College Library plus 1 other. *Books:* 237,710 (physical), 11,422 (digital/electronic); *Serial titles:* 107 (physical), 65,714 (digital/electronic); *Databases:* 176.

STUDENT LIFE

Housing options: coed, special housing for students with disabilities. Campus housing is university owned. Freshman applicants given priority for college housing.

Activities and organizations: drama/theater group, student-run newspaper, radio and television station, choral group, Student Union, WPUR radio station, Latinos Unidos, Gay/Lesbian/Bisexual/Transgender Union, Organization of African People in America.

Athletics Member NCAA. All Division III. ***Intercollegiate sports:*** baseball M, basketball M/W, cross-country running M/W, golf M, lacrosse M/W, soccer M/W, softball W, swimming and diving M/W, tennis M/W, volleyball M/W. ***Intramural sports:*** badminton M/W, basketball M/W, bowling M/W, cheerleading M(c)/W(c), cross-country running M/W, fencing M, field hockey W, football M/W, golf M/W, racquetball M/W, skiing (cross-country) M/W, skiing (downhill) M/W, soccer M/W, softball M/W, squash M/W, swimming and diving M/W, table tennis M/W, tennis M/W, volleyball M/W, water polo M/W, weight lifting M/W.

Campus security: 24-hour emergency response devices and patrols, late-night transport/escort service, controlled dormitory access, 24-hour patrols by police officers.

Student services: health clinic, personal/psychological counseling, women's center.

COSTS & FINANCIAL AID

Costs (2018–19) ***One-time required fee:*** $210. ***Tuition:*** state resident $6870 full-time, $286 per credit hour part-time; nonresident $16,650 full-time, $694 per credit hour part-time. Part-time tuition and fees vary according to course load. ***Required fees:*** $1828 full-time, $75 per credit hour part-time. ***Room and board:*** $13,764; room only: $8924. Room and board charges vary according to board plan and housing facility. ***Payment plan:*** installment. ***Waivers:*** employees or children of employees.

Financial Aid Of all full-time matriculated undergraduates who enrolled in 2018, 3,005 applied for aid, 2,423 were judged to have need, 46 had their need fully met. In 2018, 459 non-need-based awards were made. ***Average percent of need met:*** 45. ***Average financial aid package:*** $11,075. ***Average need-based loan:*** $4364. ***Average need-based gift aid:*** $9963. ***Average non-need-based aid:*** $2636.

APPLYING

Options: electronic application, early admission, early action, deferred entrance.

Application fee: $50.

Required: high school transcript, minimum 3.0 GPA. ***Required for some:*** essay or personal statement, 1 letter of recommendation, interview, audition, portfolio.

Application deadlines: 5/15 (freshmen), 5/15 (out-of-state freshmen), rolling (transfers), 11/15 (early action).

Notification: continuous until 5/1 (freshmen), continuous (out-of-state freshmen), continuous (transfers), rolling (early action).

CONTACT

Caitlin Read, Dean of Enrollment Management, Purchase College, State University of New York, 735 Anderson Hill Road, Purchase, NY 10577-1400. *Phone:* 914-251-6300. *Fax:* 914-251-6314. *E-mail:* admission@purchase.edu.

Queens College of the City University of New York

Queens, New York

http://www.qc.cuny.edu/

- **State and locally supported** comprehensive, founded 1937, part of City University of New York
- **Urban** 80-acre campus with easy access to New York City
- **Endowment** $55.5 million
- **Coed** 16,620 undergraduate students, 73% full-time, 54% women, 46% men
- **Very difficult** entrance level, 48% of applicants were admitted

UNDERGRAD STUDENTS

12,201 full-time, 4,419 part-time. Students come from 23 states and territories; 145 other countries; 1% are from out of state; 8% Black or African American, non-Hispanic/Latino; 29% Hispanic/Latino; 29% Asian, non-Hispanic/Latino; 0.4% Native Hawaiian or other Pacific Islander, non-Hispanic/Latino; 0.4% American Indian or Alaska Native, non-Hispanic/Latino; 1% Two or more races, non-Hispanic/Latino; 6% international; 13% transferred in; 2% live on campus.

Freshmen:

Admission: 18,862 applied, 8,987 admitted, 1,953 enrolled. ***Test scores:*** SAT evidence-based reading and writing scores over 500: 88%; SAT math scores over 500: 97%; SAT evidence-based reading and writing scores over 600: 29%; SAT math scores over 600: 37%; SAT evidence-based reading and writing scores over 700: 3%; SAT math scores over 700: 8%.

Retention: 84% of full-time freshmen returned.

FACULTY

Total: 1,629, 36% full-time, 47% with terminal degrees.

Student/faculty ratio: 15:1.

ACADEMICS

Calendar: semesters. *Degrees:* bachelor's, master's, post-master's, and postbachelor's certificates.

Special study options: accelerated degree program, adult/continuing education programs, advanced placement credit, cooperative education, double majors, English as a second language, honors programs, independent study, internships, off-campus study, part-time degree program, services for LD students, study abroad, summer session for credit. ***ROTC:*** Army (c).

Computers: 2,477 computers/terminals are available on campus for general student use. Students can access the following: campus intranet, computer help desk, free student e-mail accounts, online (class) grades, online (class) registration, online (class) schedules. Campuswide network is available. 100% of college-owned or -operated housing units are wired for high-speed Internet access. Wireless service is available via entire campus.

Library: The Benjamin S. Rosenthal Library plus 1 other. *Books:* 842,531 (physical), 405,360 (digital/electronic); *Serial titles:* 198 (physical), 226,727 (digital/electronic); *Databases:* 291. Weekly public service hours: 94; students can reserve study rooms.

STUDENT LIFE

Housing options: coed. Campus housing is university owned.

Activities and organizations: drama/theater group, student-run newspaper, radio station, choral group, Science Fiction and Animation, Chabad of QC, La Tertulia, PRISM: The Sexuality and Gender Alliance of QC, Muslim Students Association, national fraternities, national sororities.

Athletics Member NCAA. All Division II. ***Intercollegiate sports:*** baseball M(s), basketball M(s)/W(s), cross-country running M(s)/W(s), lacrosse W(s), soccer M(s)/W(s), softball W(s), swimming and diving W, tennis M(s)/W(s), track and field M(s)/W(s), volleyball W(s). ***Intramural sports:*** badminton M(c)/W(c), basketball M/W, cross-country running M(c)/W(c), football M/W, soccer M/W, swimming and diving M(c)/W(c), tennis M(c)/W(c), track and field M/W, ultimate Frisbee M(c)/W(c), volleyball M/W.

Campus security: 24-hour emergency response devices and patrols, controlled dormitory access.

Student services: health clinic, personal/psychological counseling, veterans affairs office.

COSTS & FINANCIAL AID

Costs (2018–19) ***Tuition:*** state resident $6730 full-time, $295 per credit part-time; nonresident $18,000 full-time, $600 per credit part-time. Full-time tuition and fees vary according to course load. Part-time tuition and fees vary according to course load. ***Required fees:*** $608 full-time, $209 per term part-time. ***Room and board:*** Room and board charges vary according to board plan and housing facility. ***Payment plan:*** installment. ***Waivers:*** senior citizens and employees or children of employees.

Financial Aid Of all full-time matriculated undergraduates who enrolled in 2018, 9,379 applied for aid, 8,597 were judged to have need, 280 had their need fully met. 243 Federal Work-Study jobs (averaging $3700). In 2018, 106 non-need-based awards were made. ***Average percent of need met:*** 49. ***Average financial aid package:*** $6590. ***Average need-based loan:*** $4124. ***Average need-based gift aid:*** $7716. ***Average non-need-based aid:*** $4664. ***Average indebtedness upon graduation:*** $14,738.

APPLYING

Standardized Tests *Required:* SAT or ACT (for admission). *Required for some:* SAT Subject Tests (for admission).

Options: electronic application, deferred entrance.

Application fee: $65.

Required: high school transcript, minimum 3.0 GPA. ***Required for some:*** essay or personal statement.

Application deadlines: 2/1 (freshmen), 2/1 (transfers).

Notification: 2/1 (freshmen), continuous (transfers).

CONTACT
Ms. Chelsea Lavington, Director of Undergraduate Admissions, Queens College of the City University of New York, 65-30 Kissena Boulevard, Queens, NY 11367. *Phone:* 718-997-5600. *Fax:* 718-997-5617.

Rabbinical Academy Mesivta Rabbi Chaim Berlin

Brooklyn, New York

CONTACT
Executive Administrator, Rabbinical Academy Mesivta Rabbi Chaim Berlin, 1605 Coney Island Avenue, Brooklyn, NY 11230-4715. *Phone:* 718-377-0777. *Fax:* 718-338-5578.

Rabbinical College Beth Shraga

Monsey, New York

CONTACT
Rabbi Sydney Schiff, Director of Admissions, Rabbinical College Beth Shraga, 28 Saddle River Road, Monsey, NY 10952-3035.

Rabbinical College Bobover Yeshiva B'nei Zion

Brooklyn, New York

CONTACT
Director of Admissions, Rabbinical College Bobover Yeshiva B'nei Zion, 1577 Forty-eighth Street, Brooklyn, NY 11219. *Phone:* 718-438-2018.

Rabbinical College of Long Island

Long Beach, New York

CONTACT
Director of Admissions, Rabbinical College of Long Island, 205 West Beech Street, Long Beach, NY 11561-3305. *Phone:* 516-431-7414.

Rabbinical College of Ohr Shimon Yisroel

Brooklyn, New York

CONTACT
Rabbinical College of Ohr Shimon Yisroel, 215-217 Hewes Street, Brooklyn, NY 11211.

Rabbinical College Ohr Yisroel

Brooklyn, New York

http://www.rabbinicalcollegeohryisroel.com/

CONTACT
Rabbinical College Ohr Yisroel, 8800 Seaview Avenue, Brooklyn, NY 11236.

Rabbinical Seminary of America

Flushing, New York

CONTACT
Rabbi Abraham Semmel, Director of Admissions, Rabbinical Seminary of America, 76-01 147th Street, Flushing, NY 11367. *Phone:* 718-268-4700.

Rensselaer Polytechnic Institute

Troy, New York

http://www.rpi.edu/

- **Independent** university, founded 1824
- **Suburban** 284-acre campus with easy access to Albany, NY
- **Endowment** $673.7 million
- **Coed**
- **Very difficult** entrance level

FACULTY
Student/faculty ratio: 13:1.

ACADEMICS
Calendar: semesters. *Degrees:* bachelor's, master's, and doctoral.
Library: Folsom Library plus 2 others. Students can reserve study rooms.

STUDENT LIFE
Housing options: on-campus residence required through sophomore year; coed, special housing for students with disabilities. Campus housing is university owned. Freshman campus housing is guaranteed.

Activities and organizations: drama/theater group, student-run newspaper, radio and television station, choral group, Red Army Spirit Club, Outing Club, Indian Student Association, Chinese American Student Association, pep band, national fraternities, national sororities.

Athletics Member NCAA. All Division III except men's and women's ice hockey (Division I).

Campus security: 24-hour emergency response devices and patrols, late-night transport/escort service, controlled dormitory access, campus foot patrols at night.

Student services: health clinic, personal/psychological counseling, women's center, legal services.

COSTS & FINANCIAL AID
Costs (2018–19) ***Comprehensive fee:*** $69,140 includes full-time tuition ($52,550), mandatory fees ($1330), and room and board ($15,260). Part-time tuition: $1640 per credit hour. ***College room only:*** $8650. Room and board charges vary according to board plan and location.

Financial Aid Of all full-time matriculated undergraduates who enrolled in 2018, 4,331 applied for aid, 3,787 were judged to have need, 607 had their need fully met. 880 Federal Work-Study jobs (averaging $1989). In 2018, 1751 non-need-based awards were made. ***Average percent of need met:*** 78. ***Average financial aid package:*** $41,327. ***Average need-based loan:*** $3904. ***Average need-based gift aid:*** $37,236. ***Average non-need-based aid:*** $20,389. ***Average indebtedness upon graduation:*** $34,595.

APPLYING
Standardized Tests *Required:* SAT or ACT (for admission). *Required for some:* SAT and SAT Subject Tests or ACT (for admission).

Options: electronic application, early admission, early decision, deferred entrance.

Application fee: $70.

Required for some: essay or personal statement, high school transcript, interview, portfolio for electronic arts. ***Recommended:*** minimum 3.0 GPA, 1 letter of recommendation.

CONTACT
Ms. Karen Long, Director, Undergrad Admissions, Rensselaer Polytechnic Institute, 110 8th Street, Troy, NY 12180. *Phone:* 518-276-6216. *Fax:* 518-276-4072. *E-mail:* admissions@rpi.edu.

Roberts Wesleyan College

Rochester, New York

http://www.roberts.edu/

- **Independent** comprehensive, founded 1866, affiliated with Free Methodist Church of North America
- **Suburban** 188-acre campus with easy access to Rochester
- **Endowment** $24.2 million
- **Coed**
- **Moderately difficult** entrance level

FACULTY
Student/faculty ratio: 12:1.

ACADEMICS
Calendar: semesters. *Degrees:* bachelor's, master's, and doctoral.
Library: B. Thomas Golisano Library. *Books:* 128,708 (physical), 6,200 (digital/electronic); *Databases:* 105. Study areas open 24 hours, 5–7 days a week; students can reserve study rooms.

STUDENT LIFE
Housing options: on-campus residence required through senior year; men-only, women-only, special housing for students with disabilities. Campus housing is university owned. Freshman campus housing is guaranteed.

Activities and organizations: drama/theater group, student-run newspaper, choral group, Intramurals, Foot of the Cross, Fellowship of Christian Athletes, Nursing Club, Drama Club.

Athletics Member NCAA, NCCAA. All NCAA Division II.

Campus security: 24-hour emergency response devices and patrols, student patrols, late-night transport/escort service, controlled dormitory access, 24-hour Resident Life staff on-call.

Student services: health clinic, personal/psychological counseling, veterans affairs office.

COSTS & FINANCIAL AID

Costs (2018–19) ***One-time required fee:*** $250. ***Comprehensive fee:*** $42,188 includes full-time tuition ($30,458), mandatory fees ($1110), and room and board ($10,620). Part-time tuition and fees vary according to course load. ***College room only:*** $6630. Room and board charges vary according to board plan and housing facility.

Financial Aid Of all full-time matriculated undergraduates who enrolled in 2018, 1,020 applied for aid, 959 were judged to have need, 130 had their need fully met. 554 Federal Work-Study jobs (averaging $1975). 62 state and other part-time jobs (averaging $1903). In 2018, 201 non-need-based awards were made. ***Average percent of need met:*** 71. ***Average financial aid package:*** $22,429. ***Average need-based loan:*** $5231. ***Average need-based gift aid:*** $17,644. ***Average non-need-based aid:*** $11,459. ***Average indebtedness upon graduation:*** $34,679.

APPLYING

Standardized Tests *Required:* SAT or ACT (for admission).

Options: electronic application, early admission, early action, deferred entrance.

Required: essay or personal statement, high school transcript. ***Recommended:*** minimum 2.7 GPA, interview.

CONTACT

Mr. J. P. Anderson, Associate Vice President of Undergraduate Admissions, Roberts Wesleyan College, 2301 Westside Drive, Rochester, NY 14624-1997. *Phone:* 585-594-6400. *Toll-free phone:* 800-777-4RWC. *Fax:* 585-594-6371. *E-mail:* admissions@roberts.edu.

Rochester Institute of Technology

Rochester, New York

http://www.rit.edu/

- **Independent** university, founded 1829
- **Suburban** 1300-acre campus with easy access to Rochester
- **Endowment** $938.2 million
- **Coed** 13,513 undergraduate students, 92% full-time, 32% women, 68% men
- **Moderately difficult** entrance level, 66% of applicants were admitted

UNDERGRAD STUDENTS

12,486 full-time, 1,027 part-time. Students come from 52 states and territories; 67 other countries; 46% are from out of state; 4% Black or African American, non-Hispanic/Latino; 7% Hispanic/Latino; 9% Asian, non-Hispanic/Latino; 0.1% American Indian or Alaska Native, non-Hispanic/Latino; 4% Two or more races, non-Hispanic/Latino; 6% Race/ethnicity unknown; 6% international; 4% transferred in; 52% live on campus.

Freshmen:

Admission: 19,335 applied, 12,765 admitted, 2,847 enrolled. ***Average high school GPA:*** 3.7. ***Test scores:*** SAT evidence-based reading and writing scores over 500: 98%; SAT math scores over 500: 99%; ACT scores over 18: 100%; SAT evidence-based reading and writing scores over 600: 74%; SAT math scores over 600: 80%; ACT scores over 24: 94%; SAT evidence-based reading and writing scores over 700: 19%; SAT math scores over 700: 36%; ACT scores over 30: 52%.

Retention: 89% of full-time freshmen returned.

FACULTY

Total: 1,425, 73% full-time, 54% with terminal degrees.

Student/faculty ratio: 13:1.

ACADEMICS

Calendar: semesters. *Degrees:* certificates, associate, bachelor's, master's, doctoral, and postbachelor's certificates.

Special study options: accelerated degree program, adult/continuing education programs, advanced placement credit, cooperative education, distance learning, double majors, English as a second language, honors programs, independent study, internships, off-campus study, part-time degree program, services for LD students, student-designed majors, study abroad, summer session for credit. ***ROTC:*** Army (b), Navy (c), Air Force (b).

Computers: 3,500 computers/terminals and 20,000 ports are available on campus for general student use. Students can access the following: campus intranet, computer help desk, free student e-mail accounts, online (class) grades, online (class) registration, online (class) schedules, student account information. Campuswide network is available. 100% of college-owned or -operated housing units are wired for high-speed Internet access. Wireless service is available via entire campus.

Library: Wallace Memorial Library. *Books:* 429,176 (physical), 240,712 (digital/electronic); *Serial titles:* 58,293 (digital/electronic); *Databases:* 113. Weekly public service hours: 147; study areas open 24 hours, 5–7 days a week; students can reserve study rooms.

STUDENT LIFE

Housing options: on-campus residence required for freshman year; coed, men-only, women-only, special housing for students with disabilities. Campus housing is university owned. Freshman campus housing is guaranteed.

Activities and organizations: drama/theater group, student-run newspaper, radio station, choral group, national fraternities, national sororities.

Athletics Member NCAA. All Division III except men's and women's ice hockey (Division I). ***Intercollegiate sports:*** baseball M, basketball M/W, bowling M(c)/W(c), cheerleading M(c)/W(c), crew M/W, cross-country running M/W, equestrian sports M(c)/W(c), fencing M(c)/W(c), field hockey W(c), ice hockey M/W, lacrosse M/W, skiing (downhill) W(c), soccer M/W, softball W, swimming and diving M/W, tennis M/W, track and field M/W, ultimate Frisbee M(c)/W(c), volleyball M(c)/W, water polo M(c)/W(c), wrestling M. ***Intramural sports:*** badminton M/W, basketball M/W, bowling M/W, football M, golf M/W, ice hockey M/W, lacrosse M(c), racquetball M/W, rock climbing M(c)/W(c), soccer M/W, softball M/W, table tennis M/W, tennis M/W, volleyball M/W.

Campus security: 24-hour emergency response devices and patrols, student patrols, late-night transport/escort service, controlled dormitory access.

Student services: health clinic, personal/psychological counseling, women's center, legal services, veterans affairs office.

COSTS & FINANCIAL AID

Costs (2018–19) ***Comprehensive fee:*** $57,176 includes full-time tuition ($43,546), mandatory fees ($584), and room and board ($13,046). Full-time tuition and fees vary according to course load and student level. Part-time tuition and fees vary according to class time and course load. ***Required fees:*** $72 per term part-time. ***College room only:*** $7598. Room and board charges vary according to board plan and housing facility. ***Payment plans:*** tuition prepayment, installment, deferred payment. ***Waivers:*** employees or children of employees.

Financial Aid Of all full-time matriculated undergraduates who enrolled in 2018, 10,239 applied for aid, 9,177 were judged to have need, 7,326 had their need fully met. In 2018, 1560 non-need-based awards were made. ***Average percent of need met:*** 85. ***Average financial aid package:*** $35,000. ***Average need-based loan:*** $5500. ***Average need-based gift aid:*** $30,405. ***Average non-need-based aid:*** $10,700. ***Average indebtedness upon graduation:*** $41,202.

APPLYING

Standardized Tests *Required:* SAT or ACT (for admission).

Options: electronic application, early admission, early decision, deferred entrance.

Application fee: $65.

Required: essay or personal statement, high school transcript. ***Required for some:*** portfolio of original artwork for School of Art, Design and Crafts; interview for BS/MS physician assistant program. ***Recommended:*** minimum 3.4 GPA, 1 letter of recommendation, interview.

Early decision deadline: 11/15 (for plan 1), 1/1 (for plan 2).

Notification: continuous until 2/15 (freshmen), continuous (transfers), 12/15 (early decision).

CONTACT

Ms. Marian Nicoletti, Director of Admission, Rochester Institute of Technology, 60 Lomb Memorial Drive, Rochester, NY 14623-5604. *Phone:* 585-475-6631. *Fax:* 585-475-7424. *E-mail:* admissions@rit.edu.

See previous page for display ad and page 1088 for the College Close-Up.

The Sage Colleges

Troy, New York

http://www.sage.edu/

- **Independent** comprehensive, founded 1916
- **Urban** 23-acre campus
- **Endowment** $36.6 million
- **Coed** 1,477 undergraduate students, 92% full-time, 79% women, 21% men
- **Moderately difficult** entrance level, 93% of applicants were admitted

UNDERGRAD STUDENTS

1,360 full-time, 117 part-time. 9% are from out of state; 11% Black or African American, non-Hispanic/Latino; 10% Hispanic/Latino; 4% Asian, non-Hispanic/Latino; 0.3% Native Hawaiian or other Pacific Islander, non-Hispanic/Latino; 0.3% American Indian or Alaska Native, non-Hispanic/Latino; 4% Two or more races, non-Hispanic/Latino; 9% Race/ethnicity unknown; 1% international; 15% transferred in; 48% live on campus.

Freshmen:

Admission: 2,389 applied, 2,229 admitted, 370 enrolled. ***Test scores:*** SAT evidence-based reading and writing scores over 500: 64%; SAT math scores over 500: 62%; ACT scores over 18: 71%; SAT evidence-based reading and writing scores over 600: 18%; SAT math scores over 600: 13%; ACT scores over 24: 14%; ACT scores over 30: 7%.

Retention: 78% of full-time freshmen returned.

FACULTY

Total: 320, 38% full-time, 53% with terminal degrees.

Student/faculty ratio: 13:1.

ACADEMICS

Calendar: semesters. *Degrees:* bachelor's, master's, doctoral, post-master's, and postbachelor's certificates.

Special study options: accelerated degree program, adult/continuing education programs, advanced placement credit, cooperative education, distance learning, double majors, honors programs, independent study, internships, off-campus study, part-time degree program, services for LD students, student-designed majors, study abroad, summer session for credit. ***ROTC:*** Army (c), Air Force (c).

Unusual degree programs: 3-2 business administration with Sage Graduate School; engineering with Rensselaer Polytechnic Institute; nursing with Sage Graduate School; occupational therapy, physical therapy with Sage Graduate School.

Computers: 416 computers/terminals are available on campus for general student use. Students can access the following: campus intranet, computer help desk, free student e-mail accounts, online (class) grades, online (class) registration, online (class) schedules. Campuswide network is available. 100% of college-owned or -operated housing units are wired for high-speed Internet access. Wireless service is available via classrooms, computer labs, learning centers, libraries, student centers.

Library: James Wheelock Clark Library plus 1 other. *Serial titles:* 217 (physical), 68,930 (digital/electronic); *Databases:* 99. Weekly public service hours: 45; students can reserve study rooms.

STUDENT LIFE

Housing options: coed, women-only. Campus housing is university owned and leased by the school. Freshman campus housing is guaranteed.

Activities and organizations: drama/theater group, student-run newspaper, choral group, Dance Ensamble, SALANA (African American, Latino, Asian, Native American), BLSA (Black Latino), ASIC (Interior Design), AIGA (Graphic Design).

Athletics Member NCAA. All Division III. ***Intercollegiate sports:*** basketball M/W, cross-country running M/W, field hockey W, golf M, lacrosse M/W, soccer M/W, softball W, tennis M/W, track and field M/W, volleyball M/W. ***Intramural sports:*** football M/W, lacrosse W(c), skiing (downhill) M(c)/W(c).

Campus security: 24-hour emergency response devices and patrols, late-night transport/escort service, controlled dormitory access.

Student services: health clinic, personal/psychological counseling, women's center.

COSTS & FINANCIAL AID

Costs (2019–20) ***Tuition:*** $30,383 full-time, $1013 per credit hour part-time. ***Required fees:*** $1500 full-time.

Financial Aid Of all full-time matriculated undergraduates who enrolled in 2018, 1,296 applied for aid, 1,224 were judged to have need. 342 Federal Work-Study jobs (averaging $1930). 31 state and other part-time jobs (averaging $5328). In 2018, 96 non-need-based awards were made. ***Average need-based loan:*** $4202. ***Average need-based gift aid:*** $18,231. ***Average non-need-based aid:*** $14,050. ***Average indebtedness upon graduation:*** $32,497.

APPLYING

Standardized Tests *Required for some:* SAT or ACT (for admission).

Options: electronic application, early admission, early action, deferred entrance.

Application fee: $30.

Required: essay or personal statement, high school transcript, minimum 2.5 GPA, 2 letters of recommendation. ***Required for some:*** portfolio for art and design programs. ***Recommended:*** interview.

Application deadlines: rolling (freshmen), rolling (transfers).

Notification: continuous (freshmen), continuous (transfers).

CONTACT

Ms. Sarah Barrett, Director of Undergraduate Enrollment Management, The Sage Colleges, 65 First Street, Troy, NY 12180. *Phone:* 518-244-2441. *Fax:* 518-292-1912. *E-mail:* barres2@sage.edu.

St. Bonaventure University

St. Bonaventure, New York

http://www.sbu.edu/

- **Independent** comprehensive, founded 1858, affiliated with Roman Catholic Church
- **Small-town** 500-acre campus
- **Endowment** $65.2 million
- **Coed**
- **Moderately difficult** entrance level

FACULTY

Student/faculty ratio: 11:1.

ACADEMICS

Calendar: semesters. *Degrees:* associate, bachelor's, master's, post-master's, and postbachelor's certificates.

Library: Friedsam Memorial Library. *Books:* 371,691 (physical), 1.6 million (digital/electronic); *Serial titles:* 253 (physical), 269,989 (digital/electronic); *Databases:* 64. Weekly public service hours: 109; students can reserve study rooms.

STUDENT LIFE

Housing options: on-campus residence required through junior year; coed, special housing for students with disabilities. Campus housing is university owned. Freshman campus housing is guaranteed.

Activities and organizations: drama/theater group, student-run newspaper, radio and television station, choral group, Student Government Association, Bona Responds, BV newspaper, Students for the Mountain, Student Ambassadors.

Athletics Member NCAA. All Division I.

Campus security: 24-hour emergency response devices and patrols, late-night transport/escort service, controlled dormitory access.

Student services: health clinic, personal/psychological counseling, veterans affairs office.

COSTS & FINANCIAL AID

Costs (2018–19) ***Comprehensive fee:*** $47,351 includes full-time tuition ($33,336), mandatory fees ($965), and room and board ($13,050). Part-time tuition: $991 per credit hour. Part-time tuition and fees vary according to course load. ***College room only:*** $6852. Room and board charges vary according to board plan and housing facility.

Financial Aid Of all full-time matriculated undergraduates who enrolled in 2017, 1,314 applied for aid, 1,171 were judged to have need, 185 had their need fully met. 258 Federal Work-Study jobs (averaging $1150). 367 state and other part-time jobs (averaging $980). In 2017, 371 non-need-based awards were made. ***Average percent of need met:*** 69. ***Average financial aid package:*** $24,420. ***Average need-based loan:*** $4732. ***Average need-based gift aid:*** $22,192. ***Average non-need-based aid:*** $15,721. ***Average indebtedness upon graduation:*** $36,146.

APPLYING

Standardized Tests *Required:* SAT or ACT (for admission). *Required for some:* SAT and SAT Subject Tests or ACT (for admission).

Options: electronic application, deferred entrance.

Required: high school transcript, 1 letter of recommendation. ***Required for some:*** essay or personal statement. ***Recommended:*** essay or personal statement, minimum 3.0 GPA, 3 letters of recommendation, interview.

CONTACT

Mr. Doug Brady, Director of Recruitment, St. Bonaventure University, PO Box D, 3261 West State Road, St. Bonaventure, NY 14778. *Phone:* 716-375-2455. *Toll-free phone:* 800-462-5050. *Fax:* 716-375-4005. *E-mail:* dbrady@sbu.edu.

★ St. Francis College

Brooklyn Heights, New York

http://www.sfc.edu/

CONTACT

Mrs. Lisa Randazzo, Associate Director of Admissions, St. Francis College, 180 Remsen Street, Brooklyn Heights, NY 11201-4398. *Phone:* 718-489-5336. *Fax:* 718-802-0453. *E-mail:* lrandazzo@sfc.edu.

St. John Fisher College

Rochester, New York

http://www.sjfc.edu/

- **Independent** comprehensive, founded 1948, affiliated with Roman Catholic Church
- **Suburban** 154-acre campus
- **Endowment** $93.8 million
- **Coed** 2,752 undergraduate students, 95% full-time, 59% women, 41% men
- **Moderately difficult** entrance level, 64% of applicants were admitted

UNDERGRAD STUDENTS

2,623 full-time, 129 part-time. Students come from 19 states and territories; 3 other countries; 4% are from out of state; 4% Black or African American, non-Hispanic/Latino; 5% Hispanic/Latino; 3% Asian, non-Hispanic/Latino; 0.3% American Indian or Alaska Native, non-Hispanic/Latino; 2% Two or more races, non-Hispanic/Latino; 2% Race/ethnicity unknown; 0.1% international; 6% transferred in; 52% live on campus.

Freshmen:

Admission: 4,594 applied, 2,961 admitted, 601 enrolled. ***Average high school GPA:*** 3.5. ***Test scores:*** SAT evidence-based reading and writing scores over 500: 90%; SAT math scores over 500: 91%; ACT scores over 18: 95%; SAT evidence-based reading and writing scores over 600: 39%; SAT math scores over 600: 42%; ACT scores over 24: 55%; SAT evidence-based reading and writing scores over 700: 2%; SAT math scores over 700: 4%; ACT scores over 30: 7%.

Retention: 87% of full-time freshmen returned.

FACULTY

Total: 449, 51% full-time, 57% with terminal degrees.

Student/faculty ratio: 12:1.

ACADEMICS

Calendar: semesters. *Degrees:* certificates, bachelor's, master's, doctoral, post-master's, and postbachelor's certificates.

Special study options: accelerated degree program, adult/continuing education programs, advanced placement credit, distance learning, double majors, honors programs, independent study, internships, off-campus study, part-time degree program, services for LD students, student-designed majors, study abroad, summer session for credit. ***ROTC:*** Army (c), Navy (c), Air Force (c).

Unusual degree programs: 3-2 engineering with Columbia University, Rensselaer Polytechnic Institute, University of Rochester.

Computers: 550 computers/terminals and 1,875 ports are available on campus for general student use. Students can access the following: campus intranet, computer help desk, free student e-mail accounts, online (class) grades, online (class) registration, online (class) schedules. Campuswide network is available. 100% of college-owned or -operated housing units are wired for high-speed Internet access. Wireless service is available via entire campus.

Library: Charles J. Lavery Library plus 1 other. *Books:* 138,569 (physical), 297,511 (digital/electronic); *Databases:* 156. Students can reserve study rooms.

STUDENT LIFE

Housing options: coed, women-only, special housing for students with disabilities. Campus housing is university owned. Freshman campus housing is guaranteed.

Activities and organizations: drama/theater group, student-run newspaper, television station, choral group, Student Government, Student Activities Board, Commuter Council, Resident Student Association, Teddi Dance for Love.

Athletics Member NCAA. All Division III except golf (Division II). ***Intercollegiate sports:*** baseball M, basketball M/W, crew W, cross-country running M/W, field hockey W, football M, golf M/W, lacrosse M/W, soccer M/W, softball W, tennis M/W, track and field M/W, volleyball M/W. ***Intramural sports:*** basketball M/W, cheerleading W(c), crew M(c), equestrian sports M(c)/W(c), ice hockey M(c)/W(c), rugby M(c)/W(c), soccer M/W, volleyball M.

Campus security: 24-hour emergency response devices and patrols, late-night transport/escort service, controlled dormitory access.

Student services: health clinic, personal/psychological counseling, veterans affairs office.

COSTS & FINANCIAL AID

Costs (2019–20) ***Tuition:*** $34,340 full-time, $936 part-time. ***Required fees:*** $810 full-time.

Financial Aid Of all full-time matriculated undergraduates who enrolled in 2018, 2,341 applied for aid, 2,111 were judged to have need, 636 had their need fully met. 1,220 Federal Work-Study jobs (averaging $1500). In 2018, 507 non-need-based awards were made. ***Average percent of need met:*** 69. ***Average financial aid package:*** $23,459. ***Average need-based loan:*** $4386. ***Average need-based gift aid:*** $18,834. ***Average non-need-based aid:*** $13,292. ***Average indebtedness upon graduation:*** $37,210.

APPLYING

Standardized Tests *Required:* SAT or ACT (for admission).

Options: electronic application, early decision, deferred entrance.

Required: essay or personal statement, high school transcript, minimum 3.0 GPA, 1 letter of recommendation. ***Recommended:*** interview.

Application deadlines: rolling (freshmen), rolling (transfers).

Early decision deadline: 12/1.

Notification: continuous until 12/1 (freshmen), continuous until 9/1 (transfers), 12/15 (early decision).

CONTACT

Mrs. Stacy A. Ledermann, Director of Freshmen Admissions, St. John Fisher College, 3690 East Avenue, Rochester, NY 14618. *Phone:* 585-385-8064. *Toll-free phone:* 800-444-4640. *Fax:* 585-385-8386. *E-mail:* admissions@sjfc.edu.

St. John's University

Queens, New York

http://www.stjohns.edu/

- **Independent** university, founded 1870, affiliated with Roman Catholic Church
- **Urban** 102-acre campus with easy access to New York City
- **Endowment** $716.5 million
- **Coed**
- **Moderately difficult** entrance level

FACULTY

Student/faculty ratio: 17:1.

ACADEMICS

Calendar: semesters. *Degrees:* certificates, bachelor's, master's, doctoral, post-master's, and postbachelor's certificates.

Library: St. John's University Library plus 3 others. *Books:* 534,824 (physical), 608,270 (digital/electronic); *Serial titles:* 68,549 (physical), 88,058 (digital/electronic); *Databases:* 226. Weekly public service hours: 92; students can reserve study rooms.

STUDENT LIFE

Housing options: coed, special housing for students with disabilities. Campus housing is university owned and leased by the school.

Activities and organizations: drama/theater group, student-run newspaper, radio and television station, choral group, Student Government, Incorporated, Haraya (Pan-African Students Coalition), American Pharmaceutical Association, Muslim Students, Pare-Philippine- Americans Reaching Everyone, national fraternities, national sororities.

Athletics Member NCAA. All Division I.

Campus security: 24-hour emergency response devices and patrols, late-night transport/escort service, controlled dormitory access, Emergency Notification System, CNS Boards, Public Address System.

Student services: health clinic, personal/psychological counseling, veterans affairs office.

COSTS & FINANCIAL AID

Costs (2018–19) ***One-time required fee:*** $250. ***Comprehensive fee:*** $58,790 includes full-time tuition ($40,680), mandatory fees ($830), and room and board ($17,280). Full-time tuition and fees vary according to course load, location, program, reciprocity agreements, and student level. Part-time tuition: $1356 per credit. Part-time tuition and fees vary according to course load, location, program, and student level. ***Required fees:*** $313 per term part-time. ***College room only:*** $10,830. Room and board charges vary according to board plan, housing facility, and location.

Financial Aid Of all full-time matriculated undergraduates who enrolled in 2018, 9,522 applied for aid, 8,791 were judged to have need, 1,051 had their need fully met. 753 Federal Work-Study jobs (averaging $2546). In 2018, 705 non-need-based awards were made. ***Average percent of need met:*** 68. ***Average financial aid package:*** $29,457. ***Average need-based loan:*** $4713. ***Average need-based gift aid:*** $8873. ***Average non-need-based aid:*** $19,787. ***Average indebtedness upon graduation:*** $28,264.

APPLYING

Standardized Tests *Required for some:* SAT or ACT (for admission).

Options: electronic application, early admission, early decision, early action, deferred entrance.

Required: high school transcript, minimum 3.0 GPA. ***Required for some:*** essay or personal statement, 2 letters of recommendation, interview. ***Recommended:*** essay or personal statement, 2 letters of recommendation.

CONTACT

St. John's University, 8000 Utopia Parkway, Queens, NY 11439. *Toll-free phone:* 888-9STJOHNS.

St. Joseph's College, Long Island Campus

Patchogue, New York

http://www.sjcny.edu/

- **Independent** comprehensive, founded 1916
- **Suburban** 32-acre campus with easy access to New York City
- **Endowment** $28.5 million
- **Coed** 3,148 undergraduate students, 85% full-time, 68% women, 32% men
- **Moderately difficult** entrance level, 77% of applicants were admitted

UNDERGRAD STUDENTS

2,661 full-time, 487 part-time. Students come from 13 states and territories; 2 other countries; 1% are from out of state; 5% Black or African American, non-Hispanic/Latino; 15% Hispanic/Latino; 2% Asian, non-Hispanic/Latino; 0.1% Native Hawaiian or other Pacific Islander, non-Hispanic/Latino; 0.2% American Indian or Alaska Native, non-

Hispanic/Latino; 2% Two or more races, non-Hispanic/Latino; 11% Race/ethnicity unknown; 15% transferred in.

Freshmen:

Admission: 1,693 applied, 1,298 admitted, 464 enrolled. ***Average high school GPA:*** 3.5. ***Test scores:*** SAT evidence-based reading and writing scores over 500: 84%; SAT math scores over 500: 85%; ACT scores over 18: 91%; SAT evidence-based reading and writing scores over 600: 27%; SAT math scores over 600: 27%; ACT scores over 24: 43%; SAT evidence-based reading and writing scores over 700: 3%; SAT math scores over 700: 3%; ACT scores over 30: 3%.

Retention: 80% of full-time freshmen returned.

FACULTY
Total: 456, 23% full-time, 32% with terminal degrees.

Student/faculty ratio: 14:1.

ACADEMICS
Calendar: 4-1-4. *Degrees:* certificates, bachelor's, master's, and postbachelor's certificates.

Special study options: accelerated degree program, adult/continuing education programs, advanced placement credit, distance learning, double majors, honors programs, independent study, internships, off-campus study, part-time degree program, services for LD students, study abroad, summer session for credit. ***ROTC:*** Army (c), Air Force (c).

Computers: 267 computers/terminals are available on campus for general student use. Students can access the following: campus intranet, computer help desk, free student e-mail accounts, online (class) grades, online (class) registration, online (class) schedules, library databases, learning management system, course evaluations, print management, virtual application labs, office 365, student suggestion box. Campuswide network is available. Wireless service is available via entire campus.
Library: Callahan Library plus 1 other. *Books:* 113,712 (physical), 161,062 (digital/electronic); *Serial titles:* 224 (physical), 59,853 (digital/electronic); *Databases:* 129. Weekly public service hours: 80; students can reserve study rooms.

STUDENT LIFE
Housing options: college housing not available.

Activities and organizations: drama/theater group, student-run newspaper, radio station, choral group, STARS (Students Taking an Active Role in Society), All Greek Life (Alpha Phi Delta and Delta Kappa Epsilon Fraternities), Drama Society, Project Sunshine, SJC Sharps, national fraternities, national sororities.

Athletics Member NCAA. All Division III. ***Intercollegiate sports:*** baseball M, basketball M/W, cross-country running M/W, equestrian sports W(c), golf M, lacrosse M/W, soccer M/W, softball W, swimming and diving W, tennis M/W, track and field M/W, volleyball M/W.

Campus security: 24-hour emergency response devices and patrols, late-night transport/escort service.

Student services: personal/psychological counseling, veterans affairs office.

COSTS & FINANCIAL AID
Costs (2018–19) ***Tuition:*** $27,230 full-time, $882 per credit hour part-time. Full-time tuition and fees vary according to course load, location, and program. Part-time tuition and fees vary according to course load, location, and program. ***Required fees:*** $614 full-time. ***Payment plan:*** installment. ***Waivers:*** employees or children of employees.

Financial Aid Of all full-time matriculated undergraduates who enrolled in 2017, 2,484 applied for aid, 2,058 were judged to have need, 530 had their need fully met. 86 Federal Work-Study jobs (averaging $3464). 82 state and other part-time jobs (averaging $4220). In 2017, 357 non-need-based awards were made. ***Average percent of need met:*** 62. ***Average financial aid package:*** $15,007. ***Average need-based loan:*** $4334. ***Average need-based gift aid:*** $12,296. ***Average non-need-based aid:*** $9639. ***Average indebtedness upon graduation:*** $30,030.

APPLYING
Standardized Tests *Required:* SAT or ACT (for admission).

Options: electronic application, deferred entrance.

Application fee: $25.

Required: essay or personal statement, high school transcript, minimum 3.0 GPA, 2 letters of recommendation. ***Required for some:*** RN for RN-BSN program. ***Recommended:*** interview.

Application deadlines: rolling (freshmen), rolling (transfers).

Notification: continuous until 11/1 (freshmen), continuous (transfers).

CONTACT
Ms. Gigi Lamens, Vice President for Enrollment Management, St. Joseph's College, Long Island Campus, 155 West Roe Boulevard, Patchogue, NY 11772. *Phone:* 631-687-4500. *E-mail:* glamens@sjcny.edu.

St. Joseph's College, New York

Brooklyn, New York

http://www.sjcny.edu/

- **Independent** comprehensive, founded 1916
- **Urban** 5-acre campus with easy access to Manhattan
- **Endowment** $8.5 million
- **Coed** 943 undergraduate students, 87% full-time, 69% women, 31% men
- **Moderately difficult** entrance level, 70% of applicants were admitted

UNDERGRAD STUDENTS
824 full-time, 119 part-time. Students come from 27 states and territories; 26 other countries; 7% are from out of state; 23% Black or African American, non-Hispanic/Latino; 24% Hispanic/Latino; 6% Asian, non-Hispanic/Latino; 0.4% Native Hawaiian or other Pacific Islander, non-Hispanic/Latino; 0.4% American Indian or Alaska Native, non-Hispanic/Latino; 2% Two or more races, non-Hispanic/Latino; 8% Race/ethnicity unknown; 9% transferred in; 9% live on campus.

Freshmen:

Admission: 2,140 applied, 1,493 admitted, 202 enrolled. ***Average high school GPA:*** 3.2. ***Test scores:*** SAT evidence-based reading and writing scores over 500: 82%; SAT math scores over 500: 78%; ACT scores over 18: 92%; SAT evidence-based reading and writing scores over 600: 29%; SAT math scores over 600: 23%; ACT scores over 24: 44%; SAT evidence-based reading and writing scores over 700: 4%; SAT math scores over 700: 2%; ACT scores over 30: 20%.

Retention: 79% of full-time freshmen returned.

FACULTY
Total: 186, 31% full-time, 37% with terminal degrees.

Student/faculty ratio: 11:1.

ACADEMICS
Calendar: semesters. *Degrees:* certificates, bachelor's, master's, and postbachelor's certificates.

Special study options: accelerated degree program, adult/continuing education programs, advanced placement credit, distance learning, double majors, English as a second language, honors programs, independent study, internships, off-campus study, part-time degree program, services for LD students, study abroad, summer session for credit. ***ROTC:*** Army (c), Air Force (c).

Computers: 207 computers/terminals are available on campus for general student use. Students can access the following: campus intranet, computer help desk, free student e-mail accounts, online (class) grades, online (class) registration, online (class) schedules, library databases, learning management system, course evaluations, print management, virtual application labs, office software, student suggestion box. Campuswide network is available. 100% of college-owned or -operated housing units are wired for high-speed Internet access. Wireless service is available via entire campus.
Library: McEntegart Hall Library plus 1 other. *Books:* 91,695 (physical), 161,062 (digital/electronic); *Serial titles:* 36 (physical), 59,853 (digital/electronic); *Databases:* 129. Weekly public service hours: 83; students can reserve study rooms.

STUDENT LIFE
Housing options: coed. Campus housing is leased by the school.

Activities and organizations: drama/theater group, Campus Activities Board (C.A.B.), Student Senate, Chapel Players Dramatic Club, Council of Multicultural Organizations, Dance Club, national fraternities.

Athletics Member NCAA. All Division III. ***Intercollegiate sports:*** baseball M, basketball M/W, cross-country running M/W, soccer M/W, softball W, swimming and diving W, tennis M/W, volleyball M/W.

Campus security: 24-hour emergency response devices and patrols, late-night transport/escort service, controlled dormitory access.

Student services: health clinic, personal/psychological counseling, veterans affairs office.

COSTS & FINANCIAL AID

Costs (2018–19) ***Tuition:*** $27,230 full-time, $882 per credit hour part-time. Full-time tuition and fees vary according to course load and program. Part-time tuition and fees vary according to course load and program. ***Required fees:*** $614 full-time. ***Payment plan:*** installment. ***Waivers:*** employees or children of employees.

Financial Aid Of all full-time matriculated undergraduates who enrolled in 2017, 766 applied for aid, 641 were judged to have need, 101 had their need fully met. 92 Federal Work-Study jobs (averaging $2936). 21 state and other part-time jobs (averaging $1881). In 2017, 107 non-need-based awards were made. ***Average percent of need met:*** 63. ***Average financial aid package:*** $18,393. ***Average need-based loan:*** $3722. ***Average need-based gift aid:*** $15,676. ***Average non-need-based aid:*** $13,709. ***Average indebtedness upon graduation:*** $25,873.

APPLYING

Standardized Tests *Required:* SAT or ACT (for admission).

Options: electronic application, early admission, deferred entrance.

Application fee: $25.

Required: essay or personal statement, high school transcript, minimum 2.5 GPA, 1 letter of recommendation. ***Required for some:*** RN license for the RN to BSN Program. ***Recommended:*** interview.

Application deadlines: rolling (freshmen), rolling (out-of-state freshmen), rolling (transfers).

Notification: continuous until 11/1 (freshmen), continuous (out-of-state freshmen), continuous (transfers).

CONTACT

Ms. Christine Murphy, Vice President for Enrollment Management, St. Joseph's College, New York, 245 Clinton Avenue, Brooklyn, NY 11205. *Phone:* 718-940-5820. *E-mail:* cmurphy@sjcny.edu.

★ St. Lawrence University

Canton, New York

http://www.stlawu.edu/

- **Independent** 4-year, founded 1856
- **Small-town** 1100-acre campus
- **Endowment** $282.1 million
- **Coed**
- **Moderately difficult** entrance level

FACULTY

Student/faculty ratio: 11:1.

ACADEMICS

Calendar: semesters. *Degrees:* bachelor's, master's, and post-master's certificates.

Library: Owen D. Young Library plus 2 others. *Books:* 602,154 (physical), 303,918 (digital/electronic); *Serial titles:* 98,010 (physical), 123,193 (digital/electronic); *Databases:* 170. Students can reserve study rooms.

STUDENT LIFE

Housing options: on-campus residence required through senior year; coed, women-only, cooperative. Campus housing is university owned. Freshman campus housing is guaranteed.

Activities and organizations: drama/theater group, student-run newspaper, radio station, choral group, The Thelomathesian Society (student government), Outing Club, Environmental Action Organization, Association for Campus Entertainment, La Sociedad Hispana, national fraternities, national sororities.

Athletics Member NCAA. All Division III except men's and women's ice hockey (Division I), men's and women's skiing (downhill) (Division I).

Campus security: 24-hour emergency response devices and patrols, student patrols, late-night transport/escort service, controlled dormitory access.

Student services: health clinic, personal/psychological counseling.

COSTS & FINANCIAL AID

Costs (2018–19) ***Comprehensive fee:*** $68,980 includes full-time tuition ($54,454), mandatory fees ($392), and room and board ($14,134). Part-time tuition: $1891 per unit. ***College room only:*** $7614. Room and board charges vary according to board plan. ***Payment plans:*** tuition prepayment, installment.

Financial Aid Of all full-time matriculated undergraduates who enrolled in 2018, 1,803 applied for aid, 1,492 were judged to have need, 381 had their need fully met. 898 Federal Work-Study jobs (averaging $1641). 334 state and other part-time jobs (averaging $1659). In 2018, 782 non-need-based awards were made. ***Average percent of need met:*** 85. ***Average financial aid package:*** $46,622. ***Average need-based loan:*** $4354. ***Average need-based gift aid:*** $40,019. ***Average non-need-based aid:*** $18,770. ***Average indebtedness upon graduation:*** $36,067. ***Financial aid deadline:*** 2/1.

APPLYING

Options: electronic application, early admission, early decision, deferred entrance.

Application fee: $60.

Required: essay or personal statement, high school transcript, 2 letters of recommendation. ***Recommended:*** interview.

CONTACT

Jeremy Freeman, Director of Admissions, St. Lawrence University, 23 Romoda Drive, Canton, NY 13617-1455. *Phone:* 315-229-5261. *Toll-free phone:* 800-285-1856. *Fax:* 315-229-5818. *E-mail:* jfreeman@stlawu.edu.

See previous page for display ad and page 1098 for the College Close-Up.

St. Thomas Aquinas College

Sparkill, New York

http://www.stac.edu/

- **Independent** comprehensive, founded 1952
- **Suburban** 46-acre campus with easy access to New York City
- **Endowment** $30.6 million
- **Coed**
- **Moderately difficult** entrance level

FACULTY

Student/faculty ratio: 12:1.

ACADEMICS

Calendar: semesters. *Degrees:* associate, bachelor's, master's, post-master's, and postbachelor's certificates.

Library: Lougheed Library plus 1 other. *Books:* 50,000 (physical); *Serial titles:* 110 (physical), 75,000 (digital/electronic); *Databases:* 68. Weekly public service hours: 83; students can reserve study rooms.

STUDENT LIFE

Housing options: men-only, women-only, special housing for students with disabilities. Campus housing is university owned. Freshman campus housing is guaranteed.

Activities and organizations: drama/theater group, student-run newspaper, radio station, choral group, Spartan Volunteers, Campus Activities Board, WSTK campus radio, Bowling Club, Laetare Players, national fraternities.

Athletics Member NCAA, NAIA. All NCAA Division II.

Campus security: 24-hour emergency response devices and patrols, student patrols, late-night transport/escort service, controlled dormitory access.

Student services: health clinic, personal/psychological counseling.

COSTS & FINANCIAL AID

Costs (2018–19) ***Comprehensive fee:*** $45,200 includes full-time tuition ($31,150), mandatory fees ($800), and room and board ($13,250). Part-time tuition: $990 per credit hour. ***Required fees:*** $200 per term part-time.

College room only: $7150. Room and board charges vary according to board plan and housing facility.

Financial Aid Of all full-time matriculated undergraduates who enrolled in 2018, 1,045 applied for aid, 800 were judged to have need, 181 had their need fully met. 112 Federal Work-Study jobs (averaging $1345). In 2018, 233 non-need-based awards were made. ***Average percent of need met:*** 40. ***Average financial aid package:*** $18,500. ***Average need-based loan:*** $4800. ***Average need-based gift aid:*** $11,500. ***Average non-need-based aid:*** $15,000. ***Average indebtedness upon graduation:*** $31,000. ***Financial aid deadline:*** 6/30.

APPLYING

Standardized Tests *Required:* SAT or ACT (for admission).

Options: electronic application, deferred entrance.

Application fee: $30.

Required: high school transcript, minimum 2.0 GPA. ***Required for some:*** 3 letters of recommendation. ***Recommended:*** essay or personal statement, 2 letters of recommendation, interview.

CONTACT

Mr. Samantha Bazile, Director of Admissions, St. Thomas Aquinas College, 125 Route 340, Sparkill, NY 10976. *Phone:* 845-398-4104. *Fax:* 845-398-4114. *E-mail:* sbazile@stac.edu.

See previous page for display ad and page 1104 for the College Close-Up.

Sarah Lawrence College

Bronxville, New York

http://www.sarahlawrence.edu/

- **Independent** comprehensive, founded 1926
- **Suburban** 44-acre campus with easy access to New York City
- **Endowment** $113.8 million
- **Coed** 1,410 undergraduate students, 99% full-time, 73% women, 27% men
- **Very difficult** entrance level, 56% of applicants were admitted

UNDERGRAD STUDENTS

1,396 full-time, 14 part-time. Students come from 49 states and territories; 38 other countries; 81% are from out of state; 4% Black or African American, non-Hispanic/Latino; 9% Hispanic/Latino; 5% Asian, non-Hispanic/Latino; 0.1% American Indian or Alaska Native, non-Hispanic/Latino; 6% Two or more races, non-Hispanic/Latino; 10% Race/ethnicity unknown; 12% international; 2% transferred in; 87% live on campus.

Freshmen:

Admission: 3,325 applied, 1,857 admitted, 425 enrolled. ***Average high school GPA:*** 3.7. ***Test scores:*** SAT evidence-based reading and writing scores over 500: 99%; SAT math scores over 500: 99%; ACT scores over 18: 100%; SAT evidence-based reading and writing scores over 600: 91%; SAT math scores over 600: 77%; ACT scores over 24: 94%; SAT evidence-based reading and writing scores over 700: 47%; SAT math scores over 700: 25%; ACT scores over 30: 56%.

Retention: 80% of full-time freshmen returned.

FACULTY

Total: 311, 38% full-time, 70% with terminal degrees.

Student/faculty ratio: 9:1.

ACADEMICS

Calendar: semesters. *Degrees:* bachelor's and master's.

Special study options: accelerated degree program, advanced placement credit, double majors, independent study, internships, off-campus study, services for LD students, student-designed majors, study abroad, summer session for credit. ***ROTC:*** Air Force (c).

Unusual degree programs: 3-2 engineering with Columbia University.

Computers: 143 computers/terminals are available on campus for general student use. Students can access the following: campus intranet, computer help desk, free student e-mail accounts, online (class) grades, online (class) schedules. Campuswide network is available. 100% of college-owned or -operated housing units are wired for high-speed Internet access. Wireless service is available via entire campus.

Library: Esther Rauschenbush Library plus 2 others. *Books:* 235,763 (physical), 407,165 (digital/electronic); *Serial titles:* 4,884 (physical), 43,582 (digital/electronic); *Databases:* 143. Weekly public service hours: 109; study areas open 24 hours, 5–7 days a week; students can reserve study rooms.

STUDENT LIFE

Housing options: on-campus residence required for freshman year; coed, men-only, women-only, cooperative, special housing for students with disabilities. Campus housing is university owned. Freshman campus housing is guaranteed.

Activities and organizations: drama/theater group, student-run newspaper, radio station, choral group, VOX: Voices of Planned Parenthood, SLC Food & Justice Coalition, Rock Climbing Club, Musical Theatre Collective, Interfaith Union.

Athletics Member NCAA. All Division III. ***Intercollegiate sports:*** basketball M/W, crew W, cross-country running M/W, equestrian sports M/W, soccer M/W, softball W, swimming and diving M/W, tennis M/W, volleyball M/W. ***Intramural sports:*** basketball M/W, soccer M/W, squash M/W, table tennis M/W, ultimate Frisbee M/W, volleyball M/W.

Campus security: 24-hour emergency response devices and patrols, late-night transport/escort service, controlled dormitory access.

Student services: health clinic, personal/psychological counseling.

COSTS & FINANCIAL AID

Costs (2018–19) ***Comprehensive fee:*** $71,270 includes full-time tuition ($54,440), mandatory fees ($1460), and room and board ($15,370). Full-time tuition and fees vary according to course load. Part-time tuition: $1815 per credit hour. Part-time tuition and fees vary according to course load. ***Required fees:*** $586 per term part-time. ***College room only:*** $10,130. Room and board charges vary according to board plan. ***Payment plan:*** installment. ***Waivers:*** employees or children of employees.

Financial Aid Of all full-time matriculated undergraduates who enrolled in 2017, 961 applied for aid, 842 were judged to have need, 111 had their need fully met. 571 Federal Work-Study jobs (averaging $2313). 83 state and other part-time jobs (averaging $2627). In 2017, 257 non-need-based awards were made. ***Average percent of need met:*** 76. ***Average financial aid package:*** $34,955. ***Average need-based loan:*** $2976. ***Average need-based gift aid:*** $34,955. ***Average non-need-based aid:*** $16,523. ***Average indebtedness upon graduation:*** $19,610. ***Financial aid deadline:*** 2/1.

APPLYING

Options: electronic application, early admission, early decision, early action, deferred entrance.

Application fee: $60.

Required: essay or personal statement, high school transcript, 2 letters of recommendation, counselor recommendation, school report. ***Recommended:*** minimum 3.0 GPA, interview.

Application deadlines: 1/15 (freshmen), 3/1 (transfers), 11/1 (early action).

Early decision deadline: 11/1 (for plan 1), 1/2 (for plan 2).

Notification: 3/15 (freshmen), 6/1 (transfers), 12/15 (early decision plan 1), 2/15 (early decision plan 2), 12/15 (early action).

CONTACT

Ms. Jennifer Gayles, Director of Admission and Multicultural Recruitment, Sarah Lawrence College, 1 Mead Way, Bronxville, NY 10708-5999. *Phone:* 914-395-2510. *Toll-free phone:* 800-888-2858. *Fax:* 914-395-2515. *E-mail:* slcadmit@sarahlawrence.edu.

★ School of Visual Arts

New York, New York

http://www.sva.edu/

- **Proprietary** comprehensive, founded 1947
- **Urban** 1-acre campus
- **Coed**
- **Moderately difficult** entrance level

FACULTY

Student/faculty ratio: 9:1.

ACADEMICS

Calendar: semesters. *Degrees:* bachelor's and master's.

Library: School of Visual Arts Library.

STUDENT LIFE
Housing options: coed, women-only. Campus housing is university owned, leased by the school and is provided by a third party. Freshman applicants given priority for college housing.

Activities and organizations: student-run newspaper, radio station.

Campus security: 24-hour patrols.

Student services: health clinic, personal/psychological counseling.

COSTS & FINANCIAL AID
Costs (2018–19) ***Comprehensive fee:*** $60,300 includes full-time tuition ($39,900) and room and board ($20,400). Part-time tuition: $1335 per credit hour. ***College room only:*** $17,500. Room and board charges vary according to housing facility.

Financial Aid Of all full-time matriculated undergraduates who enrolled in 2018, 1,445 applied for aid, 1,323 were judged to have need, 36 had their need fully met. In 2018, 452 non-need-based awards were made. ***Average percent of need met:*** 32. ***Average financial aid package:*** $20,517. ***Average need-based loan:*** $4312. ***Average need-based gift aid:*** $15,728. ***Average non-need-based aid:*** $12,106. ***Average indebtedness upon graduation:*** $47,989. ***Financial aid deadline:*** 3/1.

APPLYING
Standardized Tests *Required:* SAT or ACT (for admission).

Options: electronic application, deferred entrance.

Application fee: $50.

Required: essay or personal statement, high school transcript, minimum 2.5 GPA, portfolio. ***Recommended:*** interview.

CONTACT
Admissions Office, School of Visual Arts, 209 East 23rd Street, New York, NY 10010. *Phone:* 212-592-2100. *Toll-free phone:* 800-436-4204. *Fax:* 212-592-2116. *E-mail:* admissions@sva.edu.

Sh'or Yoshuv Rabbinical College
Lawrence, New York

CONTACT
Rabbi Moshe Rubin, Registrar, Sh'or Yoshuv Rabbinical College, 1 Cedarlawn Avenue, Lawrence, NY 11559-1714. *Phone:* 516-239-9002 Ext. 124. *Fax:* 516-977-1282. *E-mail:* mrubin@shoryoshuv.org.

Siena College
Loudonville, New York
http://www.siena.edu/

- **Independent Roman Catholic** comprehensive, founded 1937
- **Suburban** 175-acre campus with easy access to Albany, NY
- **Endowment** $129.3 million
- **Coed**
- **Moderately difficult** entrance level

FACULTY
Student/faculty ratio: 12:1.

ACADEMICS
Calendar: semesters. *Degrees:* certificates, bachelor's, and master's.
Library: J. Spencer and Patricia Standish Library. *Books:* 281,429 (physical), 301,497 (digital/electronic); *Serial titles:* 29,000 (digital/electronic); *Databases:* 172. Weekly public service hours: 102; students can reserve study rooms.

STUDENT LIFE
Housing options: on-campus residence required through senior year; coed, special housing for students with disabilities. Campus housing is university owned. Freshman applicants given priority for college housing.

Activities and organizations: drama/theater group, student-run newspaper, radio and television station, choral group, Outing Club, Best Buddies, Make-a-Wish Wishmakers on Campus, Fitness Club, Psychology Club.

Athletics Member NCAA. All Division I.

Campus security: 24-hour emergency response devices and patrols, late-night transport/escort service, controlled dormitory access.

Student services: health clinic, personal/psychological counseling, women's center, veterans affairs office.

COSTS & FINANCIAL AID
Costs (2018–19) ***One-time required fee:*** $625. ***Comprehensive fee:*** $51,975 includes full-time tuition ($36,675), mandatory fees ($300), and room and board ($15,000). Full-time tuition and fees vary according to course load. Part-time tuition: $675 per credit hour. Part-time tuition and fees vary according to course load. ***Required fees:*** $80 per term part-time. ***College room only:*** $8895. Room and board charges vary according to board plan and housing facility.

Financial Aid Of all full-time matriculated undergraduates who enrolled in 2017, 2,521 applied for aid, 2,274 were judged to have need, 608 had their need fully met. In 2017, 555 non-need-based awards were made. ***Average percent of need met:*** 79. ***Average financial aid package:*** $30,860. ***Average need-based loan:*** $4483. ***Average need-based gift aid:*** $23,536. ***Average non-need-based aid:*** $13,005. ***Average indebtedness upon graduation:*** $35,509. ***Financial aid deadline:*** 2/15.

APPLYING
Standardized Tests *Required for some:* SAT or ACT (for admission).

Options: electronic application, early admission, early decision, early action, deferred entrance.

Application fee: $50.

Required: essay or personal statement, high school transcript, 1 letter of recommendation. ***Required for some:*** interview. ***Recommended:*** interview.

CONTACT
Ms. Katie Szalda, Director of Admissions, Siena College, 515 Loudon Road, Loudonville, NY 12211-1462. *Phone:* 518-782-6767. *Toll-free phone:* 888-AT-SIENA. *Fax:* 518-783-2436. *E-mail:* admissions@siena.edu.

Skidmore College
Saratoga Springs, New York
http://www.skidmore.edu/

- **Independent** 4-year, founded 1903
- **Small-town** 890-acre campus with easy access to Albany, NY
- **Endowment** $376.0 million
- **Coed** 2,612 undergraduate students, 99% full-time, 61% women, 39% men
- **Very difficult** entrance level, 27% of applicants were admitted

UNDERGRAD STUDENTS
2,585 full-time, 27 part-time. Students come from 42 states and territories; 62 other countries; 65% are from out of state; 5% Black or African American, non-Hispanic/Latino; 9% Hispanic/Latino; 5% Asian, non-Hispanic/Latino; 5% Two or more races, non-Hispanic/Latino; 2% Race/ethnicity unknown; 12% international; 1% transferred in; 90% live on campus.

Freshmen:
Admission: 10,796 applied, 2,907 admitted, 678 enrolled. ***Test scores:*** SAT evidence-based reading and writing scores over 500: 97%; SAT math scores over 500: 97%; ACT scores over 18: 99%; SAT evidence-based reading and writing scores over 600: 82%; SAT math scores over 600: 79%; ACT scores over 24: 94%; SAT evidence-based reading and writing scores over 700: 27%; SAT math scores over 700: 27%; ACT scores over 30: 43%.

Retention: 91% of full-time freshmen returned.

FACULTY
Total: 389, 74% full-time, 72% with terminal degrees.

Student/faculty ratio: 8:1.

ACADEMICS
Calendar: semesters plus optional 6-week internship period. *Degree:* bachelor's.

Special study options: accelerated degree program, advanced placement credit, distance learning, double majors, honors programs, independent study, internships, off-campus study, services for LD students, student-designed majors, study abroad, summer session for credit. ***ROTC:*** Army (c), Air Force (c).

Unusual degree programs: 3-2 business administration with Clarkson University, Rochester Institute of Technology, Syracuse University; engineering with Dartmouth College, Clarkson University, Rensselaer

Polytechnic Institute; nursing with New York University; finance or accounting with Syracuse University, physical or occupational therapy with Sage Graduate School, accounting with Wake Forest.

Computers: Students can access the following: campus intranet, computer help desk, free student e-mail accounts, online (class) grades, online (class) registration, online (class) schedules. Campuswide network is available. 100% of college-owned or -operated housing units are wired for high-speed Internet access. Wireless service is available via classrooms, computer centers, computer labs, dorm rooms, learning centers, libraries, student centers.

Library: Scribner Library. *Books:* 415,117 (physical), 85,791 (digital/electronic); *Serial titles:* 2,129 (physical); *Databases:* 404. Weekly public service hours: 109; students can reserve study rooms.

STUDENT LIFE

Housing options: on-campus residence required through sophomore year; coed, women-only, special housing for students with disabilities. Campus housing is university owned. Freshman campus housing is guaranteed.

Activities and organizations: drama/theater group, student-run newspaper, radio and television station, choral group, Student Government Association, Student radio station (WSPN), Benefaction (Student Volunteer), Outing Club, UJIMA.

Athletics Member NCAA. All Division III. ***Intercollegiate sports:*** baseball M, basketball M/W, crew M/W, equestrian sports W, field hockey W, golf M, ice hockey M, lacrosse M/W, soccer M/W, softball W, swimming and diving M/W, tennis M/W, volleyball W. ***Intramural sports:*** basketball M/W, cross-country running M(c)/W(c), ice hockey M(c)/W(c), racquetball M/W, sailing M(c)/W(c), skiing (cross-country) M(c)/W(c), skiing (downhill) M(c)/W(c), soccer M/W, tennis M/W, ultimate Frisbee M(c)/W(c), volleyball M/W.

Campus security: 24-hour emergency response devices and patrols, late-night transport/escort service, controlled dormitory access.

Student services: health clinic, personal/psychological counseling.

COSTS & FINANCIAL AID

Costs (2018–19) ***One-time required fee:*** $150. ***Comprehensive fee:*** $68,764 includes full-time tuition ($53,258), mandatory fees ($1012), and room and board ($14,494). Full-time tuition and fees vary according to course load. Part-time tuition: $1775 per credit hour. Part-time tuition and fees vary according to course load. ***Required fees:*** $25 per term part-time. ***College room only:*** $8568. Room and board charges vary according to board plan and housing facility. ***Payment plans:*** tuition prepayment, installment. ***Waivers:*** senior citizens and employees or children of employees.

Financial Aid Of all full-time matriculated undergraduates who enrolled in 2018, 1,268 applied for aid, 1,086 were judged to have need, 1,025 had their need fully met. In 2018, 10 non-need-based awards were made. ***Average percent of need met:*** 94. ***Average financial aid package:*** $49,600. ***Average need-based loan:*** $4200. ***Average need-based gift aid:*** $46,550. ***Average non-need-based aid:*** $15,300. ***Average indebtedness upon graduation:*** $24,987. ***Financial aid deadline:*** 1/15.

APPLYING

Standardized Tests *Required for some:* SAT or ACT (for admission).

Options: electronic application, early admission, early decision, deferred entrance.

Application fee: $65.

Required: essay or personal statement, high school transcript, 2 letters of recommendation. ***Recommended:*** interview.

Application deadlines: 1/15 (freshmen), 4/1 (transfers).

Early decision deadline: 11/15 (for plan 1), 1/15 (for plan 2).

Notification: 4/1 (freshmen), 4/22 (transfers), 12/15 (early decision plan 1), 2/15 (early decision plan 2).

CONTACT

Ms. Mary Lou Bates, Vice President and Dean of Admissions and Financial Aid, Skidmore College, 815 North Broadway, Saratoga Springs, NY 12866-1632. *Phone:* 518-580-5570. *Toll-free phone:* 800-867-6007. *Fax:* 518-580-5584. *E-mail:* admissions@skidmore.edu.

See below for display ad and page 1112 for the College Close-Up.

State University of New York at Fredonia

Fredonia, New York

http://www.fredonia.edu/

- **State-supported** comprehensive, founded 1826, part of State University of New York System
- **Small-town** 249-acre campus with easy access to Buffalo
- **Endowment** $39.6 million
- **Coed** 4,432 undergraduate students, 97% full-time, 57% women, 43% men
- **Moderately difficult** entrance level, 76% of applicants were admitted

UNDERGRAD STUDENTS

4,313 full-time, 119 part-time. Students come from 29 states and territories; 13 other countries; 4% are from out of state; 9% Black or African American, non-Hispanic/Latino; 10% Hispanic/Latino; 2% Asian, non-Hispanic/Latino; 0.5% American Indian or Alaska Native, non-Hispanic/Latino; 3% Two or more races, non-Hispanic/Latino; 2% Race/ethnicity unknown; 2% international; 8% transferred in; 55% live on campus.

Freshmen:

Admission: 6,183 applied, 4,711 admitted, 1,180 enrolled. ***Average high school GPA:*** 3.2. ***Test scores:*** SAT evidence-based reading and writing scores over 500: 73%; SAT math scores over 500: 72%; ACT scores over 18: 87%; SAT evidence-based reading and writing scores over 600: 25%; SAT math scores over 600: 19%; ACT scores over 24: 49%; SAT evidence-based reading and writing scores over 700: 2%; SAT math scores over 700: 3%; ACT scores over 30: 6%.

Retention: 73% of full-time freshmen returned.

FACULTY

Total: 425, 59% full-time, 57% with terminal degrees.

Student/faculty ratio: 14:1.

ACADEMICS

Calendar: semesters. *Degrees:* bachelor's, master's, and post-master's certificates.

Special study options: accelerated degree program, adult/continuing education programs, advanced placement credit, distance learning, double majors, English as a second language, honors programs, independent study, internships, off-campus study, part-time degree program, services for LD students, student-designed majors, study abroad, summer session for credit.

Unusual degree programs: 3-2 engineering with Clarkson University, State University of New York at Buffalo, Case Western Reserve, Columbia University, Louisiana Technical University, New York State College of Ceramics at Alfred, Ohio State University.

Computers: 500 computers/terminals are available on campus for general student use. Students can access the following: campus intranet, computer help desk, free student e-mail accounts, online (class) grades, online (class) registration, online (class) schedules. Campuswide network is available. 100% of college-owned or -operated housing units are wired for high-speed Internet access. Wireless service is available via entire campus.

Library: Daniel A. Reed Library. *Books:* 18.0 million (physical); *Serial titles:* 48,000 (physical). Weekly public service hours: 68; students can reserve study rooms.

STUDENT LIFE

Housing options: on-campus residence required through sophomore year; coed, men-only, women-only, special housing for students with disabilities. Campus housing is university owned. Freshman campus housing is guaranteed.

Activities and organizations: drama/theater group, student-run newspaper, radio and television station, choral group, Student Association, Fredonia Radio Systems, Colleges Against Cancer, Applied Communication Association, Spectrum Entertainment Board, national fraternities, national sororities.

Athletics Member NCAA. All Division III. ***Intercollegiate sports:*** baseball M, basketball M/W, cheerleading M/W, cross-country running M/W, field hockey M(c)/W(c), ice hockey M, lacrosse M(c)/W, rugby M(c)/W(c), soccer M/W, softball W, swimming and diving M/W, tennis W, track and field M/W, volleyball W. ***Intramural sports:*** basketball M/W, fencing M(c), field hockey W(c), ice hockey M(c), racquetball M/W, rock climbing M/W, sand volleyball M/W, skiing (downhill) M/W, soccer M/W, softball M/W, squash M/W, tennis M/W, ultimate Frisbee M/W, volleyball M/W, water polo M/W.

Campus security: 24-hour emergency response devices and patrols, late-night transport/escort service, controlled dormitory access.

Student services: health clinic, personal/psychological counseling, legal services, veterans affairs office.

COSTS & FINANCIAL AID

Costs (2018–19) ***Tuition:*** state resident $6870 full-time, $286 per credit hour part-time; nonresident $16,650 full-time, $694 per credit hour part-time. ***Required fees:*** $1618 full-time, $67 per credit hour part-time. ***Room and board:*** $12,350; room only: $7500. Room and board charges vary according to board plan and housing facility. ***Payment plan:*** installment.

Financial Aid Of all full-time matriculated undergraduates who enrolled in 2018, 3,847 applied for aid, 3,176 were judged to have need, 581 had their need fully met. 170 Federal Work-Study jobs (averaging $1840). In 2018, 435 non-need-based awards were made. ***Average percent of need met:*** 65. ***Average financial aid package:*** $12,199. ***Average need-based loan:*** $4181. ***Average need-based gift aid:*** $7205. ***Average non-need-based aid:*** $3406. ***Average indebtedness upon graduation:*** $27,058.

APPLYING

Standardized Tests *Required:* SAT or ACT (for admission).

Options: electronic application, early admission, deferred entrance.

Application fee: $50.

Required: essay or personal statement, high school transcript, 1 letter of recommendation. ***Required for some:*** interview, audition for music, dance and theater programs: portfolio for visual arts and technical theatre programs.

Application deadlines: rolling (freshmen), rolling (transfers).

Notification: continuous (freshmen), continuous (transfers).

CONTACT

Mr. Cory M. Bezek, Office of Admissions, State University of New York at Fredonia, 280 Central Avenue, 6th Floor Maytum Hall, Fredonia, NY 14063. *Phone:* 716-673-3251. *Toll-free phone:* 800-252-1212. *Fax:* 716-673-3249. *E-mail:* admissions@fredonia.edu.

State University of New York at New Paltz

New Paltz, New York

http://www.newpaltz.edu/

- **State-supported** comprehensive, founded 1828, part of State University of New York System
- **Small-town** 216-acre campus
- **Endowment** $20.4 million
- **Coed**
- **Very difficult** entrance level

FACULTY

Student/faculty ratio: 16:1.

ACADEMICS

Calendar: semesters. *Degrees:* bachelor's, master's, post-master's, and postbachelor's certificates.

Library: Sojourner Truth Library. *Books:* 455,728 (physical), 149,851 (digital/electronic); *Serial titles:* 234 (physical), 85,306 (digital/electronic); *Databases:* 98. Weekly public service hours: 103; students can reserve study rooms.

STUDENT LIFE

Housing options: on-campus residence required for freshman year; coed, special housing for students with disabilities. Campus housing is university owned. Freshman campus housing is guaranteed.

Activities and organizations: drama/theater group, student-run newspaper, radio and television station, choral group, Student Association, Residence Hall Student Association, Outing Club, The Oracle Newspaper, United Greek Association, national fraternities, national sororities.

Athletics Member NCAA. All Division III.

Campus security: 24-hour emergency response devices and patrols, late-night transport/escort service, controlled dormitory access, safety seminars, RAD Women's Self Defense.

Student services: health clinic, personal/psychological counseling, legal services, veterans affairs office.

COSTS & FINANCIAL AID

Costs (2018–19) ***Tuition:*** state resident $6870 full-time, $286 per credit hour part-time; nonresident $16,650 full-time, $694 per credit hour part-time. ***Required fees:*** $1384 full-time, $40 per credit hour part-time, $210 per term part-time. ***Room and board:*** $13,462; room only: $8862. Room and board charges vary according to board plan.

Financial Aid Of all full-time matriculated undergraduates who enrolled in 2018, 4,983 applied for aid, 3,881 were judged to have need, 334 had their need fully met. In 2018, 56 non-need-based awards were made. ***Average percent of need met:*** 57. ***Average financial aid package:*** $11,606. ***Average need-based loan:*** $4306. ***Average need-based gift aid:*** $5212. ***Average non-need-based aid:*** $3166. ***Average indebtedness upon graduation:*** $25,800.

APPLYING

Standardized Tests *Required:* SAT or ACT (for admission).

Options: electronic application, early admission, early action.

Application fee: $50.

Required: essay or personal statement, high school transcript, 1 letter of recommendation. ***Required for some:*** portfolio for art program, audition for music and theater programs.

CONTACT

Ms. Kimberly A. Strano, Director of Freshman Admissions, State University of New York at New Paltz, 1 Hawk Drive, New Paltz, NY 12561-2499. *Phone:* 845-257-3200. *Toll-free phone:* 877-MY-NP-411. *Fax:* 845-257-3209. *E-mail:* admissions@newpaltz.edu.

★ State University of New York at Oswego

Oswego, New York

http://www.oswego.edu/

- **State-supported** comprehensive, founded 1861, part of State University of New York System
- **Small-town** 696-acre campus with easy access to Syracuse
- **Endowment** $28.8 million
- **Coed**
- **Moderately difficult** entrance level

FACULTY

Student/faculty ratio: 17:1.

ACADEMICS

Calendar: semesters. *Degrees:* bachelor's, master's, post-master's, and postbachelor's certificates.

Library: Penfield Library. *Books:* 331,049 (physical), 154,207 (digital/electronic); *Serial titles:* 1,932 (physical), 55,500 (digital/electronic); *Databases:* 139. Weekly public service hours: 96; study areas open 24 hours, 5–7 days a week; students can reserve study rooms.

STUDENT LIFE

Housing options: on-campus residence required through sophomore year; coed, special housing for students with disabilities. Campus housing is university owned. Freshman campus housing is guaranteed.

Activities and organizations: drama/theater group, student-run newspaper, radio and television station, choral group, club/intramural sports, student radio/television stations (WNYO and WTOP), Outdoor Club, Dance Organization (Del Sarte), Accounting Society, national fraternities, national sororities.

Athletics Member NCAA. All Division III.

Campus security: 24-hour emergency response devices and patrols, controlled dormitory access, Oswego Guardian.

Student services: health clinic, personal/psychological counseling, women's center, legal services, veterans affairs office.

A ★ *indicates that the school has detailed information with a Premium Profile on Petersons.com.*

COSTS & FINANCIAL AID
Costs (2018–19) ***Tuition:*** state resident $6870 full-time, $286 per credit hour part-time; nonresident $16,650 full-time, $694 per credit hour part-time. Part-time tuition and fees vary according to course load. ***Required fees:*** $1570 full-time, $49 per credit hour part-time. ***Room and board:*** $14,140; room only: $8790. Room and board charges vary according to board plan and housing facility.

Financial Aid Of all full-time matriculated undergraduates who enrolled in 2018, 3,708 applied for aid, 4,716 were judged to have need, 539 had their need fully met. 645 Federal Work-Study jobs (averaging $1319). In 2018, 723 non-need-based awards were made. ***Average percent of need met:*** 77. ***Average financial aid package:*** $11,359. ***Average need-based loan:*** $4301. ***Average need-based gift aid:*** $7895. ***Average non-need-based aid:*** $2556. ***Average indebtedness upon graduation:*** $28,006. ***Financial aid deadline:*** 1/1.

APPLYING
Standardized Tests *Required:* SAT or ACT (for admission).

Options: electronic application, early admission, early action, deferred entrance.

Application fee: $50.

Required: essay or personal statement, high school transcript, 1 letter of recommendation. ***Recommended:*** minimum 2.7 GPA, interview.

CONTACT
Mr. Daniel Griffin, Director of Admissions, State University of New York at Oswego, 7060 State Route 104, Oswego, NY 13126. *Phone:* 315-312-2250. *Fax:* 315-312-3260. *E-mail:* admiss@oswego.edu.

See previous page for display ad and page 1118 for the College Close-Up.

State University of New York at Plattsburgh

Plattsburgh, New York

http://www.plattsburgh.edu/

- **State-supported** comprehensive, founded 1889, part of State University of New York System
- **Small-town** 265-acre campus with easy access to Montreal
- **Endowment** $21.1 million
- **Coed** 5,297 undergraduate students, 92% full-time, 57% women, 43% men
- **Moderately difficult** entrance level, 54% of applicants were admitted

UNDERGRAD STUDENTS
4,853 full-time, 444 part-time. Students come from 30 states and territories; 66 other countries; 3% are from out of state; 8% Black or African American, non-Hispanic/Latino; 10% Hispanic/Latino; 2% Asian, non-Hispanic/Latino; 0.1% Native Hawaiian or other Pacific Islander, non-Hispanic/Latino; 0.5% American Indian or Alaska Native, non-Hispanic/Latino; 2% Two or more races, non-Hispanic/Latino; 3% Race/ethnicity unknown; 6% international; 9% transferred in; 55% live on campus.

Freshmen:
Admission: 9,201 applied, 4,992 admitted, 1,144 enrolled. ***Average high school GPA:*** 3.3. ***Test scores:*** SAT evidence-based reading and writing scores over 500: 82%; SAT math scores over 500: 73%; ACT scores over 18: 99%; SAT evidence-based reading and writing scores over 600: 23%; SAT math scores over 600: 20%; ACT scores over 24: 37%; SAT evidence-based reading and writing scores over 700: 2%; SAT math scores over 700: 2%; ACT scores over 30: 3%.

Retention: 78% of full-time freshmen returned.

FACULTY
Total: 436, 62% full-time, 59% with terminal degrees.

Student/faculty ratio: 16:1.

ACADEMICS
Calendar: semesters plus 2 5-week summer sessions and 1 winter session. *Degrees:* certificates, bachelor's, master's, and post-master's certificates.

Special study options: academic remediation for entering students, advanced placement credit, cooperative education, distance learning, double majors, English as a second language, honors programs, independent study, internships, off-campus study, part-time degree program, services for LD students, student-designed majors, study abroad, summer session for credit.

Computers: 450 computers/terminals are available on campus for general student use. Students can access the following: campus intranet, computer help desk, free student e-mail accounts, online (class) grades, online (class) registration, online (class) schedules. Campuswide network is available. 100% of college-owned or -operated housing units are wired for high-speed Internet access. Wireless service is available via entire campus.

Library: Feinberg Library. *Books:* 249,820 (physical), 54,170 (digital/electronic); *Serial titles:* 95 (physical), 463 (digital/electronic); *Databases:* 119. Weekly public service hours: 100; students can reserve study rooms.

STUDENT LIFE
Housing options: on-campus residence required through sophomore year; coed, special housing for students with disabilities. Campus housing is university owned. Freshman campus housing is guaranteed.

Activities and organizations: drama/theater group, student-run newspaper, radio and television station, choral group, Student Association, Honor Societies, Student Media Organizations, service/leadership organizations, intramural and recreational sports, national fraternities, national sororities.

Athletics Member NCAA. All Division III. ***Intercollegiate sports:*** baseball M, basketball M/W, cross-country running M/W, ice hockey M/W, lacrosse M, soccer M/W, softball W, tennis W, track and field M/W, volleyball W. ***Intramural sports:*** basketball M/W, cheerleading M(c)/W(c), fencing W, field hockey M, football M, ice hockey M(c)/W(c), racquetball M/W, rock climbing M(c)/W(c), rugby M(c)/W(c), sand volleyball M/W, soccer M/W, softball M/W, tennis M/W, ultimate Frisbee M/W, volleyball M/W.

Campus security: 24-hour emergency response devices and patrols, late-night transport/escort service, controlled dormitory access.

Student services: health clinic, personal/psychological counseling, women's center, legal services, veterans affairs office.

COSTS & FINANCIAL AID
Costs (2019–20) ***Tuition:*** state resident $6870 full-time, $286 per credit hour part-time; nonresident $16,650 full-time, $694 per credit hour part-time. ***Required fees:*** $1609 full-time, $66 per credit hour part-time. ***Room and board:*** $13,080; room only: $8340.

Financial Aid Of all full-time matriculated undergraduates who enrolled in 2017, 3,964 applied for aid, 3,267 were judged to have need, 574 had their need fully met. 444 Federal Work-Study jobs (averaging $2776). In 2017, 715 non-need-based awards were made. ***Average percent of need met:*** 76. ***Average financial aid package:*** $14,256. ***Average need-based loan:*** $7871. ***Average need-based gift aid:*** $8682. ***Average non-need-based aid:*** $6003. ***Average indebtedness upon graduation:*** $29,510.

APPLYING
Standardized Tests *Required:* SAT or ACT (for admission).

Options: electronic application, early admission, deferred entrance.

Application fee: $50.

Required: essay or personal statement, high school transcript, minimum 2.5 GPA, 1 letter of recommendation. ***Required for some:*** minimum 3.4 GPA. ***Recommended:*** minimum 3.0 GPA, interview.

Application deadlines: rolling (freshmen), rolling (transfers).

Notification: continuous (freshmen), continuous (transfers).

CONTACT
Mrs. Erin Peters, Assistant Director of Admissions, State University of New York at Plattsburgh, 101 Broad Street, Plattsburgh, NY 12901. *Phone:* 888-673-0012. *Toll-free phone:* 888-673-0012. *Fax:* 518-564-2045. *E-mail:* hamm1417@plattsburgh.edu.

State University of New York College at Cortland

Cortland, New York

http://www.cortland.edu/

- **State-supported** comprehensive, founded 1868, part of State University of New York System
- **Small-town** 191-acre campus with easy access to Syracuse
- **Coed**
- **Moderately difficult** entrance level

FACULTY
Student/faculty ratio: 16:1.

ACADEMICS
Calendar: semesters. *Degrees:* bachelor's, master's, post-master's, and postbachelor's certificates.
Library: Memorial Library.

STUDENT LIFE
Housing options: coed, cooperative, special housing for students with disabilities. Campus housing is university owned.

Activities and organizations: drama/theater group, student-run newspaper, radio and television station, choral group.

Athletics Member NCAA. All Division III except golf (Division II).

Campus security: 24-hour emergency response devices and patrols, late-night transport/escort service.

COSTS & FINANCIAL AID
Costs (2018–19) ***Tuition:*** state resident $6870 full-time, $286 per credit hour part-time; nonresident $16,650 full-time, $694 per credit hour part-time. Full-time tuition and fees vary according to course load and degree level. Part-time tuition and fees vary according to course load and degree level. ***Required fees:*** $1666 full-time. ***Room and board:*** $12,486; room only: $7976. Room and board charges vary according to board plan and housing facility.

Financial Aid Of all full-time matriculated undergraduates who enrolled in 2017, 5,080 applied for aid, 3,924 were judged to have need, 454 had their need fully met. In 2017, 237 non-need-based awards were made. ***Average percent of need met:*** 68. ***Average financial aid package:*** $13,591. ***Average need-based loan:*** $4068. ***Average need-based gift aid:*** $4992. ***Average non-need-based aid:*** $2457. ***Average indebtedness upon graduation:*** $29,906.

APPLYING
Standardized Tests *Required for some:* SAT or ACT (for admission).

Options: electronic application, early admission, early action, deferred entrance.

Application fee: $50.

Required: essay or personal statement, high school transcript, minimum 2.3 GPA, 1 letter of recommendation. ***Recommended:*** minimum 3.0 GPA, 3 letters of recommendation, interview.

CONTACT
Director of Admission, State University of New York College at Cortland, PO Box 2000, Cortland, NY 13045. *Phone:* 607-753-4711. *Fax:* 607-753-5998. *E-mail:* admissions@cortland.edu.

State University of New York College at Geneseo

Geneseo, New York

http://www.geneseo.edu/

- **State-supported** comprehensive, founded 1871, part of State University of New York
- **Small-town** 220-acre campus with easy access to Rochester
- **Endowment** $36.5 million
- **Coed** 5,447 undergraduate students, 97% full-time, 61% women, 39% men
- **Moderately difficult** entrance level, 65% of applicants were admitted

UNDERGRAD STUDENTS
5,304 full-time, 143 part-time. Students come from 27 states and territories; 26 other countries; 2% are from out of state; 3% Black or African American, non-Hispanic/Latino; 9% Hispanic/Latino; 6% Asian, non-Hispanic/Latino; 0.1% Native Hawaiian or other Pacific Islander, non-Hispanic/Latino; 0.1% American Indian or Alaska Native, non-Hispanic/Latino; 3% Two or more races, non-Hispanic/Latino; 3% Race/ethnicity unknown; 1% international; 5% transferred in; 55% live on campus.

Freshmen:
Admission: 10,548 applied, 6,836 admitted, 1,343 enrolled. ***Average high school GPA:*** 3.6. ***Test scores:*** SAT evidence-based reading and writing scores over 500: 96%; SAT math scores over 500: 96%; ACT scores over 18: 100%; SAT evidence-based reading and writing scores over 600: 57%; SAT math scores over 600: 56%; ACT scores over 24: 78%; SAT evidence-based reading and writing scores over 700: 9%; SAT math scores over 700: 11%; ACT scores over 30: 14%.

Retention: 85% of full-time freshmen returned.

FACULTY
Total: 379, 68% full-time, 69% with terminal degrees.

Student/faculty ratio: 19:1.

ACADEMICS
Calendar: semesters. *Degrees:* bachelor's and master's.

Special study options: advanced placement credit, distance learning, double majors, English as a second language, honors programs, independent study, internships, off-campus study, part-time degree program, services for LD students, study abroad, summer session for credit. ***ROTC:*** Army (c), Air Force (c).

Unusual degree programs: 3-2 business administration with Alfred University; Binghamton University, State University of New York; Clarkson University; Rochester Institute of Technology; Union College; engineering with Case Western Reserve; Clarkson University; Columbia University; University at Buffalo, State University of New York; Optometry with SUNY College of Optometry, dentistry with SUNY at Buffalo, physical therapy with SUNY Upstate Medical University, osteopathy with New York Institute of Technology College of Osteopathic Medicine.

Computers: 338 computers/terminals and 3,000 ports are available on campus for general student use. Students can access the following: campus intranet, computer help desk, free student e-mail accounts, online (class) grades, online (class) registration, online (class) schedules. Campuswide network is available. 100% of college-owned or -operated housing units are wired for high-speed Internet access. Wireless service is available via entire campus.
Library: Milne Library plus 1 other. *Books:* 330,177 (physical), 64,961 (digital/electronic); *Serial titles:* 20 (physical), 2,226 (digital/electronic); *Databases:* 167. Students can reserve study rooms.

STUDENT LIFE
Housing options: on-campus residence required through sophomore year; coed, special housing for students with disabilities. Campus housing is university owned. Freshman campus housing is guaranteed.

Activities and organizations: drama/theater group, student-run newspaper, radio station, choral group, Phi Alpha Delta, Orchesis, Newman Catholic Community, Golden Key, Alpha Phi Omega, national fraternities, national sororities.

Athletics Member NCAA. All Division III. ***Intercollegiate sports:*** baseball M(c), basketball M/W, cheerleading M(c)/W(c), crew M(c)/W(c), cross-country running M/W, equestrian sports W, fencing M(c)/W(c), field hockey W, ice hockey M/W(c), lacrosse M/W, rugby M(c)/W(c), skiing (downhill) M(c)/W(c), soccer M/W, softball W, swimming and diving M/W, tennis M(c)/W, track and field M/W, ultimate Frisbee M(c)/W(c), volleyball M(c)/W, water polo M(c). ***Intramural sports:*** badminton M/W, basketball M/W, racquetball M/W, soccer M/W, softball M/W, table tennis M/W, tennis M/W, volleyball M/W.

Campus security: 24-hour emergency response devices and patrols, student patrols, late-night transport/escort service, controlled dormitory access.

Student services: health clinic, personal/psychological counseling, legal services, veterans affairs office.

COSTS & FINANCIAL AID
Costs (2018–19) ***Tuition:*** state resident $6870 full-time, $286 per credit hour part-time; nonresident $16,650 full-time, $694 per credit hour part-time. Part-time tuition and fees vary according to course load. ***Required***

fees: $1781 full-time, $74 per credit hour part-time. ***Room and board:*** $13,610; room only: $8126. Room and board charges vary according to board plan and housing facility. ***Payment plans:*** installment, deferred payment.

Financial Aid Of all full-time matriculated undergraduates who enrolled in 2018, 4,126 applied for aid, 2,844 were judged to have need, 352 had their need fully met. 438 Federal Work-Study jobs (averaging $1611). In 2018, 372 non-need-based awards were made. ***Average percent of need met:*** 42. ***Average financial aid package:*** $10,010. ***Average need-based loan:*** $4089. ***Average need-based gift aid:*** $6419. ***Average non-need-based aid:*** $4627. ***Average indebtedness upon graduation:*** $22,854.

APPLYING
Standardized Tests *Required:* SAT or ACT (for admission).

Options: electronic application, early admission, early decision, deferred entrance.

Application fee: $50.

Required: high school transcript. ***Recommended:*** essay or personal statement, 1 letter of recommendation.

Application deadlines: 1/1 (freshmen), rolling (transfers).

Early decision deadline: 11/15.

Notification: 3/1 (freshmen), 12/15 (early decision).

CONTACT
Mr. Kevin J. Reed, Assistant Director of Admissions, State University of New York College at Geneseo, Doty Hall 200, Geneseo, NY 14454-1401. *Phone:* 585-245-5571. *Toll-free phone:* 866-245-5211. *Fax:* 585-245-5550. *E-mail:* admissions@geneseo.edu.

State University of New York College at Old Westbury

Old Westbury, New York

http://www.oldwestbury.edu/

- **State-supported** comprehensive, founded 1965, part of State University of New York System
- **Suburban** 604-acre campus with easy access to New York City
- **Coed**
- **Moderately difficult** entrance level

FACULTY
Student/faculty ratio: 16:1.

ACADEMICS
Calendar: semesters. *Degrees:* certificates, bachelor's, master's, and post-master's certificates.
Library: SUNY College at Old Westbury Library plus 1 other. *Books:* 156,872 (physical), 144,263 (digital/electronic); *Databases:* 138. Weekly public service hours: 99.

STUDENT LIFE
Housing options: coed. Campus housing is university owned. Freshman campus housing is guaranteed.

Activities and organizations: drama/theater group, student-run newspaper, radio station, choral group, Student Government Association, Alianza Latina, PRIDE, Step Tunes, Anime Magna Games Club, national fraternities, national sororities.

Athletics Member NCAA. All Division III.

Campus security: 24-hour emergency response devices and patrols, student patrols, late-night transport/escort service, controlled dormitory access.

Student services: health clinic, personal/psychological counseling, women's center.

COSTS & FINANCIAL AID
Costs (2018–19) ***Tuition:*** state resident $6670 full-time, $278 per credit hour part-time; nonresident $16,320 full-time, $680 per credit hour part-time. Part-time tuition and fees vary according to course load. ***Required fees:*** $1213 full-time, $24 per credit hour part-time, $163 per term part-time. ***Room and board:*** $11,020; room only: $7300. Room and board charges vary according to housing facility.

Financial Aid Of all full-time matriculated undergraduates who enrolled in 2015, 2,853 applied for aid, 2,509 were judged to have need, 182 had their need fully met. 245 Federal Work-Study jobs (averaging $975). In 2015, 26 non-need-based awards were made. ***Average percent of need met:*** 60. ***Average financial aid package:*** $10,395. ***Average need-based loan:*** $3960. ***Average need-based gift aid:*** $6876. ***Average non-need-based aid:*** $5636.

APPLYING
Standardized Tests *Required:* SAT or ACT (for admission).

Options: electronic application, early admission, early decision, deferred entrance.

Application fee: $50.

Required: essay or personal statement, high school transcript, 2 letters of recommendation. ***Required for some:*** interview.

CONTACT
State University of New York College at Old Westbury, PO Box 307, Old Westbury, NY 11568. *Phone:* 516-876-3073. *Fax:* 516-876-3307. *E-mail:* enroll@oldwestbury.edu.

State University of New York College at Oneonta

Oneonta, New York

http://www.oneonta.edu/

- **State-supported** comprehensive, founded 1889, part of State University of New York System
- **Small-town** 250-acre campus
- **Endowment** $49.1 million
- **Coed**
- **Very difficult** entrance level

FACULTY
Student/faculty ratio: 17:1.

ACADEMICS
Calendar: semesters. *Degrees:* bachelor's, master's, post-master's, and postbachelor's certificates.
Library: Milne Library. *Books:* 394,015 (physical), 417,737 (digital/electronic); *Serial titles:* 60 (physical), 119,484 (digital/electronic); *Databases:* 251. Students can reserve study rooms.

STUDENT LIFE
Housing options: on-campus residence required through sophomore year; coed. Campus housing is university owned. Freshman campus housing is guaranteed.

Activities and organizations: drama/theater group, student-run newspaper, radio and television station, choral group, Center for Social Responsibility and Community, Music Industry Club, Terpsichorean Dance Company, Student Government, Zombie Defense Corps, national fraternities, national sororities.

Athletics Member NCAA. All Division III.

Campus security: 24-hour emergency response devices and patrols, late-night transport/escort service, controlled dormitory access, Oneonta Emergency Squad: an organization of student volunteers with first responder credential.

Student services: health clinic, personal/psychological counseling, women's center.

COSTS & FINANCIAL AID
Costs (2018–19) ***Tuition:*** state resident $6670 full-time, $278 per credit hour part-time; nonresident $16,320 full-time, $680 per credit hour part-time. Part-time tuition and fees vary according to course load. ***Required fees:*** $1466 full-time, $42 per credit hour part-time. ***Room and board:*** $12,658; room only: $8350. Room and board charges vary according to housing facility.

Financial Aid Of all full-time matriculated undergraduates who enrolled in 2017, 4,756 applied for aid, 3,580 were judged to have need, 1,353 had their need fully met. In 2017, 392 non-need-based awards were made. ***Average financial aid package:*** $15,505. ***Average need-based loan:*** $4704. ***Average need-based gift aid:*** $8008. ***Average non-need-based aid:*** $4935. ***Average indebtedness upon graduation:*** $26,408.

APPLYING
Standardized Tests *Required:* SAT or ACT (for admission).

Options: electronic application, early admission, early action, deferred entrance.

Application fee: $50.

Required: essay or personal statement, high school transcript. ***Recommended:*** minimum 3.0 GPA, 3 letters of recommendation.

CONTACT

Ms. Karen Brown, Director of Admissions, State University of New York College at Oneonta, Alumni Hall 116, Oneonta, NY 13820-4015. *Phone:* 607-436-2524. *Toll-free phone:* 800-SUNY-123. *Fax:* 607-436-3074. *E-mail:* admissions@oneonta.edu.

State University of New York College at Potsdam

Potsdam, New York

http://www.potsdam.edu/

- **State-supported** comprehensive, founded 1816, part of State University of New York System
- **Small-town** 240-acre campus
- **Endowment** $32.9 million
- **Coed** 3,298 undergraduate students, 98% full-time, 60% women, 40% men
- **Moderately difficult** entrance level, 64% of applicants were admitted

UNDERGRAD STUDENTS

3,221 full-time, 77 part-time. Students come from 28 states and territories; 7 other countries; 4% are from out of state; 13% Black or African American, non-Hispanic/Latino; 15% Hispanic/Latino; 2% Asian, non-Hispanic/Latino; 0.1% Native Hawaiian or other Pacific Islander, non-Hispanic/Latino; 2% American Indian or Alaska Native, non-Hispanic/Latino; 3% Two or more races, non-Hispanic/Latino; 3% Race/ethnicity unknown; 0.2% international; 7% transferred in; 59% live on campus.

Freshmen:

Admission: 6,423 applied, 4,130 admitted, 873 enrolled. ***Average high school GPA:*** ####. ***Test scores:*** SAT evidence-based reading and writing scores over 500: 84%; SAT math scores over 500: 82%; ACT scores over 18: 90%; SAT evidence-based reading and writing scores over 600: 38%; SAT math scores over 600: 26%; ACT scores over 24: 55%; SAT evidence-based reading and writing scores over 700: 3%; SAT math scores over 700: 4%; ACT scores over 30: 14%.

Retention: 75% of full-time freshmen returned.

FACULTY

Total: 346, 73% full-time, 73% with terminal degrees.

Student/faculty ratio: 11:1.

ACADEMICS

Calendar: semesters. *Degrees:* bachelor's, master's, and post-master's certificates.

Special study options: advanced placement credit, distance learning, double majors, honors programs, independent study, internships, off-campus study, part-time degree program, services for LD students, student-designed majors, study abroad, summer session for credit. ***ROTC:*** Army (c), Air Force (c).

Unusual degree programs: 3-2 engineering with Clarkson University; Binghamton University, State University of New York; physics, computer science, chemistry, engineering; mathematics with Clarkson University.

Computers: 608 computers/terminals are available on campus for general student use. Students can access the following: campus intranet, computer help desk, free student e-mail accounts, online (class) grades, online (class) registration, online (class) schedules, online access to financial aid status, unofficial transcripts, billing, meal plan and housing sign-up. Campuswide network is available. 100% of college-owned or -operated housing units are wired for high-speed Internet access. Wireless service is available via classrooms, computer centers, computer labs, dorm rooms, learning centers, libraries, student centers.

Library: F. W. Crumb Memorial Library plus 1 other. *Books:* 249,807 (physical), 43,861 (digital/electronic); *Serial titles:* 3,227 (physical), 107,915 (digital/electronic); *Databases:* 151. Weekly public service hours: 119; study areas open 24 hours, 5–7 days a week; students can reserve study rooms.

STUDENT LIFE

Housing options: on-campus residence required through sophomore year; coed, special housing for students with disabilities. Campus housing is university owned. Freshman campus housing is guaranteed.

Activities and organizations: drama/theater group, student-run newspaper, radio station, choral group, Student Government Association, Crane Student Association, Black Student Alliance, SOCO LOCO, Musical Theatre Organization, national fraternities, national sororities.

Athletics Member NCAA. All Division III. ***Intercollegiate sports:*** basketball M/W, cross-country running M/W, golf M, ice hockey M/W, lacrosse M/W, soccer M/W, swimming and diving M/W, track and field M/W, volleyball W. ***Intramural sports:*** basketball M/W, bowling M(c)/W(c), cheerleading M(c)/W(c), ice hockey M(c)/W(c), racquetball M/W, rugby M(c)/W(c), skiing (downhill) M(c)/W(c), soccer M/W, softball M/W, track and field M(c)/W(c), ultimate Frisbee M(c)/W(c), volleyball M/W.

Campus security: 24-hour emergency response devices and patrols, late-night transport/escort service, controlled dormitory access, RAVE Guardian, Video Surveillance System, security escort service, self-defense education.

Student services: health clinic, personal/psychological counseling, women's center, legal services.

COSTS & FINANCIAL AID

Costs (2018–19) ***Tuition:*** state resident $6870 full-time, $286 per credit hour part-time; nonresident $16,650 full-time, $694 per credit hour part-time. Full-time tuition and fees vary according to course load. Part-time tuition and fees vary according to course load. ***Required fees:*** $1592 full-time, $85 per credit hour part-time. ***Room and board:*** $13,390; room only: $7760. Room and board charges vary according to board plan and housing facility. ***Payment plan:*** installment. ***Waivers:*** employees or children of employees.

Financial Aid Of all full-time matriculated undergraduates who enrolled in 2018, 3,083 applied for aid, 2,547 were judged to have need, 246 had their need fully met. 127 Federal Work-Study jobs (averaging $1709). In 2018, 317 non-need-based awards were made. ***Average percent of need met:*** 83. ***Average financial aid package:*** $15,257. ***Average need-based loan:*** $4229. ***Average need-based gift aid:*** $8301. ***Average non-need-based aid:*** $3879. ***Average indebtedness upon graduation:*** $30,275.

APPLYING

Options: electronic application, early admission, deferred entrance.

Application fee: $50.

Required: high school transcript, minimum 2.5 GPA, 1 letter of recommendation. ***Required for some:*** essay or personal statement, minimum 2.0 GPA, DVD audition for music.

Application deadlines: rolling (freshmen), rolling (transfers).

Notification: continuous (freshmen), continuous (transfers).

CONTACT

Mr. Thomas Nesbitt, Director of Admissions, State University of New York College at Potsdam, 44 Pierrepont Avenue, Potsdam, NY 13676. *Phone:* 315-267-2180. *Toll-free phone:* 877-POTSDAM. *Fax:* 315-267-2163. *E-mail:* admissions@potsdam.edu.

State University of New York College of Agriculture and Technology at Cobleskill

Cobleskill, New York

http://www.cobleskill.edu/

- **State-supported** 4-year, founded 1916, part of State University of New York System
- **Small-town** 950-acre campus with easy access to Albany, NY
- **Endowment** $2.5 million
- **Coed**
- **Minimally difficult** entrance level

FACULTY

Student/faculty ratio: 16:1.

ACADEMICS

Calendar: semesters. *Degrees:* certificates, associate, and bachelor's.

Library: Jared van Wagenen Library. *Books:* 53,260 (physical), 54,322 (digital/electronic); *Serial titles:* 200 (physical), 91,655 (digital/electronic); *Databases:* 60. Weekly public service hours: 76; study areas open 24 hours, 5–7 days a week; students can reserve study rooms.

STUDENT LIFE

Housing options: on-campus residence required through sophomore year; coed, men-only, women-only, special housing for students with disabilities. Campus housing is university owned.

Activities and organizations: drama/theater group, choral group, Dairy Cattle Club, Wildlife Society, Cobleskill Christian Fellowship, Woodsmen's Club, American Fisheries Society.

Athletics Member NCAA. All Division III.

Campus security: 24-hour emergency response devices and patrols, student patrols, late-night transport/escort service, controlled dormitory access, bicycle patrols, horse-mounted patrols.

Student services: health clinic, personal/psychological counseling, veterans affairs office.

COSTS & FINANCIAL AID

Costs (2018–19) ***Tuition:*** state resident $6870 full-time, $286 per credit hour part-time; nonresident $16,650 full-time, $694 per credit hour part-time. Full-time tuition and fees vary according to course level and degree level. Part-time tuition and fees vary according to course level and degree level. ***Required fees:*** $1784 full-time, $71 per credit hour part-time. ***Room and board:*** $13,350; room only: $7960. Room and board charges vary according to board plan and housing facility. ***Payment plans:*** installment, deferred payment.

Financial Aid Of all full-time matriculated undergraduates who enrolled in 2016, 2,058 applied for aid, 1,861 were judged to have need, 13 had their need fully met. 97 Federal Work-Study jobs (averaging $1166). 353 state and other part-time jobs (averaging $1506). In 2016, 61 non-need-based awards were made. ***Average percent of need met:*** 60. ***Average financial aid package:*** $7614. ***Average need-based loan:*** $2279. ***Average need-based gift aid:*** $4333. ***Average non-need-based aid:*** $2623. ***Average indebtedness upon graduation:*** $29,645.

APPLYING

Standardized Tests *Required for some:* SAT or ACT (for admission).

Options: electronic application, early admission.

Application fee: $50.

Required: high school transcript. ***Required for some:*** essay or personal statement, 3 letters of recommendation, interview.

CONTACT

Samara Davis, Office Assistant 1, State University of New York College of Agriculture and Technology at Cobleskill, 213 Knapp Hall, Cobleskill, NY 12043. *Phone:* 518-255-5525. *Toll-free phone:* 800-295-8988. *Fax:* 518-255-6769. *E-mail:* admissions@cobleskill.edu.

State University of New York College of Agriculture & Technology at Morrisville

Morrisville, New York

http://www.morrisville.edu/

CONTACT

Ms. Melissa Ward, Assistant Director of Enrollment Marketing, State University of New York College of Agriculture & Technology at Morrisville, PO Box 901, Morrisville, NY 13408. *Phone:* 315-684-6046. *Toll-free phone:* 800-258-0111. *Fax:* 315-684-6427.

State University of New York College of Environmental Science and Forestry

Syracuse, New York

http://www.esf.edu/

- **State-supported** university, founded 1911, part of State University of New York System
- **Urban** 17-acre campus with easy access to Syracuse
- **Endowment** $37.6 million
- **Coed** 1,861 undergraduate students, 95% full-time, 47% women, 53% men
- **Very difficult** entrance level, 61% of applicants were admitted

UNDERGRAD STUDENTS

1,777 full-time, 84 part-time. 19% are from out of state; 1% Black or African American, non-Hispanic/Latino; 6% Hispanic/Latino; 4% Asian, non-Hispanic/Latino; 0.2% American Indian or Alaska Native, non-Hispanic/Latino; 3% Two or more races, non-Hispanic/Latino; 4% Race/ethnicity unknown; 3% international; 13% transferred in; 35% live on campus.

Freshmen:

Admission: 2,018 applied, 1,239 admitted, 383 enrolled. ***Average high school GPA:*** 3.8. ***Test scores:*** SAT evidence-based reading and writing scores over 500: 96%; SAT math scores over 500: 95%; ACT scores over 18: 99%; SAT evidence-based reading and writing scores over 600: 64%; SAT math scores over 600: 61%; ACT scores over 24: 78%; SAT evidence-based reading and writing scores over 700: 15%; SAT math scores over 700: 12%; ACT scores over 30: 26%.

Retention: 84% of full-time freshmen returned.

FACULTY

Total: 172, 69% full-time, 46% with terminal degrees.

Student/faculty ratio: 13:1.

ACADEMICS

Calendar: semesters. *Degrees:* associate, bachelor's, master's, doctoral, and postbachelor's certificates.

Special study options: accelerated degree program, advanced placement credit, cooperative education, distance learning, double majors, English as a second language, freshman honors college, honors programs, independent study, internships, off-campus study, part-time degree program, services for LD students, study abroad, summer session for credit. ***ROTC:*** Army (c), Air Force (c).

Computers: 350 computers/terminals and 2,250 ports are available on campus for general student use. Students can access the following: campus intranet, computer help desk, free student e-mail accounts, online (class) grades, online (class) registration, online (class) schedules. Campuswide network is available. 100% of college-owned or -operated housing units are wired for high-speed Internet access. Wireless service is available via classrooms, computer centers, computer labs, dorm rooms, libraries, student centers.

Library: F. Franklin Moon Library plus 1 other. *Books:* 57,565 (physical), 444,963 (digital/electronic); *Serial titles:* 1,568 (physical), 163,166 (digital/electronic); *Databases:* 181. Weekly public service hours: 97.

STUDENT LIFE

Housing options: on-campus residence required for freshman year; coed, special housing for students with disabilities. Campus housing is university owned and is provided by a third party. Freshman campus housing is guaranteed.

Activities and organizations: drama/theater group, student-run newspaper, choral group, marching band, Bob Marshall/Outing Club, Forestry Club, Student Environmental Action Coalition, Student Green Campus Initiative, Alpha Phi Omega (Service).

Athletics Member USCAA. ***Intercollegiate sports:*** basketball M, cross-country running M/W, golf M, soccer M/W, track and field M/W. ***Intramural sports:*** archery M/W, badminton M/W, baseball M, basketball M/W, bowling M/W, cheerleading M/W, crew M/W, cross-country running M/W, equestrian sports M/W, fencing M/W, field hockey W, football M, gymnastics M/W, ice hockey M/W, lacrosse M/W, racquetball M/W, riflery M, rugby M/W, sailing M/W, skiing (downhill) M/W, soccer

M/W, softball M/W, squash M/W, swimming and diving M/W, table tennis M/W, tennis M/W, track and field M/W, ultimate Frisbee M/W, volleyball M/W.

Campus security: 24-hour emergency response devices and patrols, late-night transport/escort service, controlled dormitory access.

Student services: health clinic, personal/psychological counseling, women's center, legal services.

COSTS & FINANCIAL AID

Costs (2018–19) ***Tuition:*** state resident $6870 full-time, $286 per credit hour part-time; nonresident $16,650 full-time, $694 per credit hour part-time. Full-time tuition and fees vary according to location. Part-time tuition and fees vary according to course load and location. ***Required fees:*** $1934 full-time, $87 per credit hour part-time. ***Room and board:*** $16,440; room only: $8600. Room and board charges vary according to board plan, housing facility, and location. ***Payment plan:*** installment.

Financial Aid Of all full-time matriculated undergraduates who enrolled in 2017, 1,467 applied for aid, 1,069 were judged to have need, 512 had their need fully met. 180 Federal Work-Study jobs (averaging $1790). 217 state and other part-time jobs (averaging $886). In 2017, 369 non-need-based awards were made. ***Average percent of need met:*** 66. ***Average financial aid package:*** $10,160. ***Average need-based loan:*** $4675. ***Average need-based gift aid:*** $6648. ***Average non-need-based aid:*** $3246. ***Average indebtedness upon graduation:*** $26,679.

APPLYING

Standardized Tests *Required:* SAT or ACT (for admission).

Options: electronic application, early admission, early decision, deferred entrance.

Application fee: $50.

Required: essay or personal statement, high school transcript, minimum 2.5 GPA. ***Recommended:*** 1 letter of recommendation, interview.

Application deadlines: 2/1 (freshmen), rolling (out-of-state freshmen), 3/1 (transfers).

Early decision deadline: 12/1.

Notification: continuous until 2/1 (freshmen), continuous (out-of-state freshmen), continuous (transfers).

CONTACT

Ms. Susan Sanford, Director of Admissions, State University of New York College of Environmental Science and Forestry, Office of Undergraduate Admissions, Gateway Center 1 Forestry Drive, Syracuse, NY 13210-2779. *Phone:* 315-470-6600. *Fax:* 315-470-6933. *E-mail:* esfinfo@esf.edu.

State University of New York College of Technology at Alfred

Alfred, New York

http://www.alfredstate.edu/

- **State-supported** primarily 2-year, founded 1908, part of State University of New York System
- **Rural** 1084-acre campus with easy access to Rochester
- **Endowment** $5.6 million
- **Coed** 3,737 undergraduate students, 92% full-time, 38% women, 62% men
- **Moderately difficult** entrance level, 63% of applicants were admitted

UNDERGRAD STUDENTS

3,456 full-time, 281 part-time. Students come from 32 states and territories; 15 other countries; 4% are from out of state; 12% Black or African American, non-Hispanic/Latino; 9% Hispanic/Latino; 1% Asian, non-Hispanic/Latino; 0.1% Native Hawaiian or other Pacific Islander, non-Hispanic/Latino; 0.3% American Indian or Alaska Native, non-Hispanic/Latino; 3% Two or more races, non-Hispanic/Latino; 2% Race/ethnicity unknown; 0.7% international; 8% transferred in; 63% live on campus.

Freshmen:

Admission: 7,065 applied, 4,449 admitted, 1,222 enrolled. ***Average high school GPA:*** ####. ***Test scores:*** SAT evidence-based reading and writing scores over 500: 66%; SAT math scores over 500: 71%; ACT scores over 18: 85%; SAT evidence-based reading and writing scores over 600: 21%; SAT math scores over 600: 22%; ACT scores over 24: 37%; SAT evidence-based reading and writing scores over 700: 2%; SAT math scores over 700: 3%; ACT scores over 30: 6%.

Retention: 69% of full-time freshmen returned.

FACULTY

Total: 262, 65% full-time, 30% with terminal degrees.

Student/faculty ratio: 18:1.

ACADEMICS

Calendar: semesters. *Degrees:* certificates, associate, and bachelor's.

Special study options: academic remediation for entering students, accelerated degree program, adult/continuing education programs, advanced placement credit, cooperative education, distance learning, double majors, English as a second language, honors programs, independent study, internships, off-campus study, part-time degree program, services for LD students, student-designed majors, study abroad, summer session for credit. ***ROTC:*** Army (c).

Computers: 108 computers/terminals are available on campus for general student use. Students can access the following: campus intranet, computer help desk, free student e-mail accounts, online (class) grades, online (class) registration, online (class) schedules. Campuswide network is available. 100% of college-owned or -operated housing units are wired for high-speed Internet access. Wireless service is available via entire campus.

Library: Walter C. Hinkle Memorial Library plus 1 other. *Books:* 33,901 (physical), 1,901 (digital/electronic); *Serial titles:* 175 (physical); *Databases:* 214. Weekly public service hours: 88.

STUDENT LIFE

Housing options: coed, men-only, women-only, special housing for students with disabilities. Campus housing is university owned. Freshman campus housing is guaranteed.

Activities and organizations: drama/theater group, student-run newspaper, radio station, choral group, Outdoor Recreation Club, Caribbean Student Association, Alfred Programming Board, Pioneer Woodsmen, Disaster Relief Team.

Athletics Member NCAA, USCAA. All Division III. ***Intercollegiate sports:*** baseball M, basketball M/W, cross-country running M/W, equestrian sports M/W, football M, lacrosse M, soccer M/W, softball W, swimming and diving M/W, track and field M/W, volleyball W, wrestling M. ***Intramural sports:*** archery M(c)/W(c), basketball M/W, cheerleading M(c)/W(c), equestrian sports M(c)/W(c), football M, golf M/W, ice hockey M(c), rock climbing M/W, soccer M/W, softball M/W, swimming and diving M/W, tennis M/W, ultimate Frisbee M/W, volleyball M/W.

Campus security: 24-hour emergency response devices and patrols, late-night transport/escort service, controlled dormitory access, residence hall entrance guards.

Student services: health clinic, personal/psychological counseling, veterans affairs office.

COSTS & FINANCIAL AID

Costs (2019–20) ***One-time required fee:*** $110. ***Tuition:*** area resident $6870 full-time, $286 per credit hour part-time; state resident $6870 full-time, $286 per credit hour part-time; nonresident $10,740 full-time, $448 per credit hour part-time. ***Required fees:*** $1700 full-time, $66 per credit hour part-time, $10 per credit hour part-time. ***Room and board:*** $12,570; room only: $7650.

Financial Aid Of all full-time matriculated undergraduates who enrolled in 2017, 3,165 applied for aid, 2,829 were judged to have need, 257 had their need fully met. In 2017, 126 non-need-based awards were made. ***Average percent of need met:*** 58. ***Average financial aid package:*** $11,337. ***Average need-based loan:*** $3842. ***Average need-based gift aid:*** $6801. ***Average non-need-based aid:*** $5855. ***Average indebtedness upon graduation:*** $32,052.

APPLYING

Standardized Tests *Recommended:* SAT or ACT (for admission).

Options: electronic application.

Application fee: $50.

Required: high school transcript, minimum 2.0 GPA, Common Application with essay on supplemental application. ***Recommended:*** essay or personal statement, interview.

Application deadlines: rolling (freshmen), rolling (transfers).

Notification: continuous (freshmen), continuous (transfers).

CONTACT
Ms. Betsy Penrose, Vice President for Enrollment Management, State University of New York College of Technology at Alfred, Huntington Administration Building, 10 Upper College Drive, Alfred, NY 14802. *Phone:* 607-587-3945. *Toll-free phone:* 800-4-ALFRED. *Fax:* 607-587-4299. *E-mail:* admissions@alfredstate.edu.

State University of New York College of Technology at Canton

Canton, New York

http://www.canton.edu/

- **State-supported** 4-year, founded 1906, part of State University of New York System
- **Small-town** 555-acre campus
- **Endowment** $11.9 million
- **Coed**
- **Minimally difficult** entrance level

FACULTY
Student/faculty ratio: 17:1.

ACADEMICS
Calendar: semesters. *Degrees:* certificates, associate, and bachelor's.
Library: Southworth Library. *Books:* 23,958 (physical), 168,143 (digital/electronic); *Serial titles:* 14 (physical), 5,928 (digital/electronic); *Databases:* 84. Weekly public service hours: 125.

STUDENT LIFE
Housing options: on-campus residence required through sophomore year; coed, special housing for students with disabilities. Campus housing is university owned. Freshman applicants given priority for college housing.

Activities and organizations: drama/theater group, choral group, Student Government Alliance, College Activities Board, Greek Council, Brother to Brother, Sister to Sister.

Athletics Member NCAA, USCAA. All Division III.

Campus security: 24-hour emergency response devices and patrols, late-night transport/escort service, controlled dormitory access, student EMS group.

Student services: health clinic, personal/psychological counseling, veterans affairs office.

COSTS & FINANCIAL AID
Costs (2018–19) ***One-time required fee:*** $120. ***Tuition:*** state resident $6870 full-time, $286 per credit hour part-time; nonresident $16,650 full-time, $694 per credit hour part-time. Full-time tuition and fees vary according to degree level. Part-time tuition and fees vary according to degree level. ***Required fees:*** $1519 full-time, $61 per credit hour part-time, $5 per term part-time. ***Room and board:*** $12,900; room only: $7700. Room and board charges vary according to board plan and housing facility. ***Payment plans:*** installment, deferred payment.

Financial Aid Of all full-time matriculated undergraduates who enrolled in 2017, 2,488 applied for aid, 2,279 were judged to have need, 278 had their need fully met. 172 Federal Work-Study jobs (averaging $1381). In 2017, 65 non-need-based awards were made. ***Average percent of need met:*** 12. ***Average financial aid package:*** $11,133. ***Average need-based loan:*** $4073. ***Average need-based gift aid:*** $8332. ***Average non-need-based aid:*** $1941. ***Average indebtedness upon graduation:*** $31,703.

APPLYING
Standardized Tests *Required for some:* SAT or ACT (for admission).

Options: electronic application, deferred entrance.

Application fee: $50.

Required: high school transcript. ***Required for some:*** essay or personal statement, interview. ***Recommended:*** minimum 2.0 GPA.

CONTACT
Melissa Evans, Director of Admissions, State University of New York College of Technology at Canton, 34 Cornell Drive, Canton, NY 13617. *Phone:* 315-386-7123. *Toll-free phone:* 800-388-7123. *Fax:* 315-386-7929. *E-mail:* admissions@canton.edu.

State University of New York College of Technology at Delhi

Delhi, New York

http://www.delhi.edu/

- **State-supported** comprehensive, founded 1913, part of State University of New York System
- **Rural** 625-acre campus
- **Endowment** $7.4 million
- **Coed** 3,178 undergraduate students, 79% full-time, 54% women, 46% men
- **Moderately difficult** entrance level, 64% of applicants were admitted

UNDERGRAD STUDENTS
2,514 full-time, 664 part-time. Students come from 19 states and territories; 4 other countries; 4% are from out of state; 15% Black or African American, non-Hispanic/Latino; 14% Hispanic/Latino; 1% Asian, non-Hispanic/Latino; 0.1% Native Hawaiian or other Pacific Islander, non-Hispanic/Latino; 0.5% American Indian or Alaska Native, non-Hispanic/Latino; 3% Two or more races, non-Hispanic/Latino; 3% Race/ethnicity unknown; 3% international; 11% transferred in; 52% live on campus.

Freshmen:
Admission: 5,935 applied, 3,775 admitted, 788 enrolled. ***Average high school GPA:*** 2.7.

Retention: 79% of full-time freshmen returned.

FACULTY
Total: 240, 63% full-time, 28% with terminal degrees.

Student/faculty ratio: 16:1.

ACADEMICS
Calendar: semesters. *Degrees:* certificates, associate, bachelor's, and master's.

Special study options: academic remediation for entering students, accelerated degree program, adult/continuing education programs, advanced placement credit, distance learning, double majors, English as a second language, honors programs, independent study, internships, off-campus study, part-time degree program, services for LD students, study abroad, summer session for credit.

Computers: 102 computers/terminals are available on campus for general student use. Students can access the following: computer help desk, free student e-mail accounts, online (class) grades, online (class) registration, online (class) schedules. Campuswide network is available. 100% of college-owned or -operated housing units are wired for high-speed Internet access. Wireless service is available via entire campus.
Library: Resnick Library. *Books:* 37,908 (physical), 152,584 (digital/electronic); *Serial titles:* 350,364 (physical), 350,364 (digital/electronic); *Databases:* 68. Weekly public service hours: 93; students can reserve study rooms.

STUDENT LIFE
Housing options: on-campus residence required through sophomore year; coed. Campus housing is university owned. Freshman applicants given priority for college housing.

Activities and organizations: drama/theater group, student-run newspaper, radio and television station, choral group, New York State Association for Veterinary Technicians, National Student Nursing Association, Black Student Union, Bronco's Finest, Equine Club, national fraternities, national sororities.

Athletics Member NCAA. All Division III except golf (Division II). ***Intercollegiate sports:*** basketball M/W, cross-country running M/W, golf M/W, lacrosse M, soccer M/W, softball W, swimming and diving M/W, tennis M/W, track and field M/W, volleyball W. ***Intramural sports:*** badminton M/W, basketball M, bowling M/W, ultimate Frisbee M/W, volleyball M/W.

Campus security: 24-hour emergency response devices and patrols, late-night transport/escort service, controlled dormitory access.

Student services: health clinic, personal/psychological counseling, veterans affairs office.

FINANCIAL AID

Financial Aid Of all full-time matriculated undergraduates who enrolled in 2017, 2,425 applied for aid, 2,141 were judged to have need, 144 had their need fully met. 66 Federal Work-Study jobs (averaging $966). In 2017, 35 non-need-based awards were made. ***Average percent of need met:*** 62. ***Average financial aid package:*** $10,936. ***Average need-based loan:*** $3752. ***Average need-based gift aid:*** $8015. ***Average non-need-based aid:*** $3167. ***Average indebtedness upon graduation:*** $30,159.

APPLYING

Options: electronic application, deferred entrance.

Application fee: $50.

Required: high school transcript. ***Required for some:*** minimum 2.0 GPA, 2 letters of recommendation, associate degree for some bachelor programs, RN license for BSN program. Letters of recommendation required at the graduate level. ***Recommended:*** interview.

Application deadlines: rolling (freshmen), rolling (transfers), 12/1 (early action).

Notification: continuous (freshmen), continuous (transfers), 12/15 (early action).

CONTACT

Robert Piurowski, Director of Admissions and Enrollment Services, State University of New York College of Technology at Delhi, 454 Delhi Drive, Delhi, NY 13753. *Phone:* 607-746-4559. *Toll-free phone:* 800-96-DELHI. *E-mail:* piurowrc@delhi.edu.

State University of New York Downstate Medical Center

Brooklyn, New York

http://www.downstate.edu/

CONTACT

Admissions Office, State University of New York Downstate Medical Center, 450 Clarkson Avenue, Brooklyn, NY 11203-2446. *Phone:* 718-270-2446. *Fax:* 718-270-7592. *E-mail:* admissions@downstate.edu.

State University of New York Empire State College

Saratoga Springs, New York

http://www.esc.edu/

- **State-supported** comprehensive, founded 1971, part of State University of New York System
- **Small-town** campus
- **Endowment** $19.8 million
- **Coed**
- **Noncompetitive** entrance level

FACULTY

Student/faculty ratio: 15:1.

ACADEMICS

Calendar: 5 terms. *Degrees:* certificates, associate, bachelor's, master's, and postbachelor's certificates (branch locations at 7 regional centers with 35 auxiliary units).

Library: ***Books:*** 229,000 (digital/electronic); *Databases:* 94.

STUDENT LIFE

Housing options: college housing not available.

Student services: veterans affairs office.

COSTS

Costs (2018–19) ***Tuition:*** state resident $6670 full-time, $278 per credit part-time; nonresident $16,134 full-time, $680 per credit part-time. Full-time tuition and fees vary according to program. Part-time tuition and fees vary according to program. ***Required fees:*** $535 full-time.

APPLYING

Options: electronic application, deferred entrance.

Application fee: $50.

Required: essay or personal statement, high school transcript.

CONTACT

Ms. Jennifer D'Agostino, Senior Director of Admissions, State University of New York Empire State College, Two Union Avenue, Saratoga Springs, NY 12866. *Phone:* 518-587-2100. *Toll-free phone:* 800-847-3000. *E-mail:* admissions@esc.edu.

State University of New York Maritime College

Throggs Neck, New York

http://www.sunymaritime.edu/

- **State-supported** comprehensive, founded 1874, part of State University of New York System
- **Urban** 55-acre campus with easy access to New York City
- **Endowment** $7.7 million
- **Coed** 1,586 undergraduate students, 97% full-time, 12% women, 88% men
- **Very difficult** entrance level, 72% of applicants were admitted

UNDERGRAD STUDENTS

1,542 full-time, 44 part-time. Students come from 33 states and territories; 15 other countries; 23% are from out of state; 5% Black or African American, non-Hispanic/Latino; 14% Hispanic/Latino; 4% Asian, non-Hispanic/Latino; 0.1% American Indian or Alaska Native, non-Hispanic/Latino; 3% Two or more races, non-Hispanic/Latino; 3% Race/ethnicity unknown; 2% international; 6% transferred in; 89% live on campus.

Freshmen:

Admission: 1,355 applied, 971 admitted, 351 enrolled. ***Average high school GPA:*** 3.3. ***Test scores:*** SAT evidence-based reading and writing scores over 500: 91%; SAT math scores over 500: 93%; ACT scores over 18: 99%; SAT evidence-based reading and writing scores over 600: 41%; SAT math scores over 600: 45%; ACT scores over 24: 61%; SAT evidence-based reading and writing scores over 700: 4%; SAT math scores over 700: 5%; ACT scores over 30: 8%.

Retention: 86% of full-time freshmen returned.

FACULTY

Total: 146, 63% full-time, 35% with terminal degrees.

Student/faculty ratio: 15:1.

ACADEMICS

Calendar: semesters plus 2-month summer sea term. *Degrees:* certificates, associate, bachelor's, master's, and postbachelor's certificates.

Special study options: academic remediation for entering students, advanced placement credit, distance learning, double majors, independent study, internships, off-campus study, part-time degree program, services for LD students, study abroad, summer session for credit. ***ROTC:*** Army (c), Navy (b).

Computers: 160 computers/terminals and 650 ports are available on campus for general student use. Students can access the following: computer help desk, free student e-mail accounts, online (class) grades, online (class) registration, online (class) schedules. Campuswide network is available. 100% of college-owned or -operated housing units are wired for high-speed Internet access. Wireless service is available via classrooms, computer centers, computer labs, dorm rooms, learning centers, libraries, student centers.

Library: Stephen B. Luce Library. *Books:* 41,000 (physical), 60,567 (digital/electronic); *Serial titles:* 125 (physical), 323,000 (digital/electronic); *Databases:* 68. Weekly public service hours: 111; students can reserve study rooms.

STUDENT LIFE

Housing options: on-campus residence required through senior year; coed. Campus housing is university owned.

Activities and organizations: choral group, marching band, Student Government, Maritime Activities and Programs, The Cultural Club, Campus Crusade for Christ, The Maritime Divers Association.

Athletics Member NCAA. All Division III. ***Intercollegiate sports:*** baseball M, basketball M, crew M/W, cross-country running M/W, football M, ice hockey M(c), lacrosse M/W, riflery M(c)/W(c), sailing M/W, soccer M/W, swimming and diving M/W, volleyball W. ***Intramural***

sports: basketball M/W, football M/W, soccer M/W, softball M/W, volleyball M/W, water polo M/W.

Campus security: 24-hour emergency response devices and patrols, student patrols, late-night transport/escort service, controlled dormitory access.

Student services: health clinic, personal/psychological counseling, veterans affairs office.

COSTS & FINANCIAL AID
Costs (2018–19) ***Tuition:*** state resident $6870 full-time, $286 per credit hour part-time; nonresident $16,650 full-time, $694 per credit hour part-time. Full-time tuition and fees vary according to course load. Part-time tuition and fees vary according to course load. ***Required fees:*** $1413 full-time, $59 per term part-time. ***Room and board:*** $12,522; room only: $7792. Room and board charges vary according to board plan and housing facility. ***Payment plan:*** installment.

Financial Aid Of all full-time matriculated undergraduates who enrolled in 2018, 1,216 applied for aid, 822 were judged to have need, 69 had their need fully met. In 2018, 112 non-need-based awards were made. ***Average percent of need met:*** 50. ***Average financial aid package:*** $8523. ***Average need-based loan:*** $3678. ***Average need-based gift aid:*** $6723. ***Average non-need-based aid:*** $2829. ***Average indebtedness upon graduation:*** $34,716.

APPLYING
Standardized Tests *Required:* SAT or ACT (for admission).

Options: electronic application, early decision, deferred entrance.

Application fee: $50.

Required: essay or personal statement. ***Recommended:*** high school transcript, interview.

Application deadlines: 1/31 (freshmen), rolling (transfers).

Early decision deadline: 11/1.

Notification: 3/1 (freshmen), continuous (transfers), 12/15 (early decision).

CONTACT
Mr. Rohan Howell, Dean of Admissions, State University of New York Maritime College, 6 Pennyfield Avenue, Throggs Neck, NY 10465. *Phone:* 718-409-2220. *Fax:* 718-409-7465. *E-mail:* rhowell@sunymaritime.edu.

State University of New York Polytechnic Institute

Utica, New York

http://www.sunypoly.edu/

- **State-supported** comprehensive, founded 1966, part of State University of New York System
- **Suburban** 850-acre campus
- **Endowment** $5.5 million
- **Coed**
- **Moderately difficult** entrance level

FACULTY
Student/faculty ratio: 13:1.

ACADEMICS
Calendar: semesters. *Degrees:* bachelor's, master's, doctoral, post-master's, and postbachelor's certificates.
Library: Peter J. Cayan Library. *Books:* 139,500 (physical), 108,500 (digital/electronic); *Serial titles:* 2,175 (physical), 49,045 (digital/electronic); *Databases:* 50. Weekly public service hours: 87; students can reserve study rooms.

STUDENT LIFE
Housing options: on-campus residence required through sophomore year; coed, special housing for students with disabilities. Campus housing is university owned and leased by the school. Freshman campus housing is guaranteed.

Activities and organizations: student-run newspaper, radio and television station, International Student Association, SUNY Tech Gamers Club, Black and Latino American Student Union, Colleges Against Cancer, BAJA SAE (Society of Automotive Engineers).

Athletics Member NCAA. All Division III.

Campus security: 24-hour emergency response devices and patrols, student patrols, late-night transport/escort service, controlled dormitory access, closed-circuit TV monitors, 24-hour police department.

Student services: health clinic, personal/psychological counseling, legal services.

COSTS & FINANCIAL AID
Costs (2018–19) ***Tuition:*** state resident $6870 full-time, $286 per credit hour part-time; nonresident $16,650 full-time, $694 per credit hour part-time. Full-time tuition and fees vary according to course load, degree level, and location. Part-time tuition and fees vary according to course load, degree level, and location. ***Required fees:*** $1578 full-time, $66 per credit hour part-time. ***Room and board:*** $12,722. Room and board charges vary according to board plan and location.

Financial Aid Of all full-time matriculated undergraduates who enrolled in 2017, 1,563 applied for aid, 1,307 were judged to have need, 1,290 had their need fully met. 152 Federal Work-Study jobs (averaging $1500). In 2017, 263 non-need-based awards were made. ***Average percent of need met:*** 98. ***Average financial aid package:*** $11,381. ***Average need-based loan:*** $4358. ***Average need-based gift aid:*** $8321. ***Average non-need-based aid:*** $4413.

APPLYING
Standardized Tests *Required:* SAT or ACT (for admission).

Options: electronic application, early admission, early action, deferred entrance.

Application fee: $50.

Required: essay or personal statement, high school transcript, minimum 3.0 GPA, 2 letters of recommendation. ***Recommended:*** interview.

CONTACT
Ms. Gina Liscio, Director of Admissions, State University of New York Polytechnic Institute, 100 Seymour Road, Utica, NY 13502. *Phone:* 315-792-7500. *Toll-free phone:* 866-278-6948. *Fax:* 315-792-7837. *E-mail:* admissions@sunyit.edu.

State University of New York Upstate Medical University

Syracuse, New York

http://www.upstate.edu/

CONTACT
Mrs. Donna L. Vavonese, Associate Director of Admissions, State University of New York Upstate Medical University, Weiskotten Hall, 766 Irving Avenue, Syracuse, NY 13210. *Phone:* 315-464-4570. *Toll-free phone:* 800-736-2171. *Fax:* 315-464-8867. *E-mail:* admiss@upstate.edu.

Stony Brook University, State University of New York

Stony Brook, New York

http://www.stonybrook.edu/

- **State-supported** university, founded 1957, part of State University of New York System
- **Suburban** 1450-acre campus with easy access to New York City
- **Endowment** $234.0 million
- **Coed**
- **Very difficult** entrance level

FACULTY
Student/faculty ratio: 18:1.

ACADEMICS
Calendar: semesters. *Degrees:* bachelor's, master's, doctoral, post-master's, and postbachelor's certificates.
Library: Frank Melville, Jr. Memorial Library plus 7 others. *Books:* 1.9 million (physical), 348,868 (digital/electronic); *Serial titles:* 1,225 (physical), 190,674 (digital/electronic); *Databases:* 679. Weekly public service hours: 131; study areas open 24 hours, 5–7 days a week; students can reserve study rooms.

STUDENT LIFE
Housing options: coed. Campus housing is university owned. Freshman campus housing is guaranteed.

Activities and organizations: drama/theater group, student-run newspaper, radio and television station, choral group, marching band, Community Service Organization, Residence Hall Association, Commuter Student Association, Asian Students Alliance, Chinese Association at Stony Brook, national fraternities, national sororities.

Athletics Member NCAA. All Division I.

Campus security: 24-hour emergency response devices and patrols, late-night transport/escort service, controlled dormitory access.

Student services: health clinic, personal/psychological counseling, women's center, legal services, veterans affairs office.

COSTS & FINANCIAL AID

Costs (2018–19) ***Tuition:*** state resident $6870 full-time, $286 per credit hour part-time; nonresident $24,540 full-time, $1023 per credit hour part-time. Full-time tuition and fees vary according to course load and program. Part-time tuition and fees vary according to course load and program. ***Required fees:*** $2755 full-time, $137 per credit hour part-time. ***Room and board:*** $13,698; room only: $8654. Room and board charges vary according to board plan, housing facility, and location.

Financial Aid Of all full-time matriculated undergraduates who enrolled in 2017, 10,935 applied for aid, 9,201 were judged to have need, 1,621 had their need fully met. 499 Federal Work-Study jobs (averaging $2441). 2,514 state and other part-time jobs (averaging $4306). In 2017, 1549 non-need-based awards were made. ***Average percent of need met:*** 66. ***Average financial aid package:*** $13,736. ***Average need-based loan:*** $4636. ***Average need-based gift aid:*** $9188. ***Average non-need-based aid:*** $5559. ***Average indebtedness upon graduation:*** $28,780.

APPLYING

Standardized Tests *Required:* SAT or ACT (for admission).

Options: electronic application, deferred entrance.

Application fee: $50.

Required: essay or personal statement, high school transcript, 1 letter of recommendation. ***Required for some:*** interview, audition. ***Recommended:*** minimum 3.5 GPA.

CONTACT

Ms. Judith Burke-Berhanan, Dean of Undergraduate Admissions, Stony Brook University, State University of New York, Admissions Office, 118 Administration Building, Stony Brook, NY 11794-1901. *Phone:* 631-632-6868. *Fax:* 631-632-9898. *E-mail:* enroll@stonybrook.edu.

Swedish Institute, College of Health Sciences

New York, New York

http://www.swedishinstitute.edu/

CONTACT

Admissions Advisor, Swedish Institute, College of Health Sciences, 226 West 26th Street, New York, NY 10001. *Phone:* 212-914-5900 Ext. 125. *E-mail:* admissions@swedishinstitute.edu.

Syracuse University

Syracuse, New York

http://www.syracuse.edu/

- **Independent** university, founded 1870
- **Urban** 721-acre campus with easy access to Syracuse, NY
- **Endowment** $1.3 billion
- **Coed** 15,226 undergraduate students, 96% full-time, 54% women, 46% men
- **Very difficult** entrance level, 50% of applicants were admitted

UNDERGRAD STUDENTS

14,655 full-time, 571 part-time. Students come from 50 states and territories; 92 other countries; 61% are from out of state; 7% Black or African American, non-Hispanic/Latino; 9% Hispanic/Latino; 7% Asian, non-Hispanic/Latino; 0.1% Native Hawaiian or other Pacific Islander, non-Hispanic/Latino; 0.5% American Indian or Alaska Native, non-Hispanic/Latino; 3% Two or more races, non-Hispanic/Latino; 3% Race/ethnicity unknown; 14% international; 2% transferred in; 53% live on campus.

Freshmen:

Admission: 34,981 applied, 17,643 admitted, 3,599 enrolled. ***Average high school GPA:*** 3.7. ***Test scores:*** SAT evidence-based reading and writing scores over 500: 98%; SAT math scores over 500: 98%; ACT scores over 18: 100%; SAT evidence-based reading and writing scores over 600: 71%; SAT math scores over 600: 72%; ACT scores over 24: 89%; SAT evidence-based reading and writing scores over 700: 13%; SAT math scores over 700: 27%; ACT scores over 30: 32%.

Retention: 90% of full-time freshmen returned.

FACULTY

Total: 1,724, 65% full-time, 65% with terminal degrees.

Student/faculty ratio: 15:1.

ACADEMICS

Calendar: semesters. *Degrees:* certificates, bachelor's, master's, doctoral, post-master's, and postbachelor's certificates.

Special study options: accelerated degree program, adult/continuing education programs, advanced placement credit, cooperative education, distance learning, double majors, English as a second language, freshman honors college, honors programs, independent study, internships, off-campus study, part-time degree program, services for LD students, student-designed majors, study abroad, summer session for credit. ***ROTC:*** Army (b), Air Force (b).

Unusual degree programs: 3-2 engineering with engineering/business administration; arts & sciences/education.

Computers: 3,500 computers/terminals and 678 ports are available on campus for general student use. Students can access the following: campus intranet, computer help desk, free student e-mail accounts, online (class) grades, online (class) registration, online (class) schedules, Library; web conferencing; learning management system (Blackboard); blogging service; personal websites; "View My Advising Report," digital asset management system (Collage);Microsoft Office 365;Lynda.com online video training. Campuswide network is available. 100% of college-owned or -operated housing units are wired for high-speed Internet access. Wireless service is available via classrooms, computer centers, computer labs, dorm rooms, learning centers, libraries, student centers.

Library: E. S. Bird Library plus 4 others. *Books:* 2.6 million (physical), 545,994 (digital/electronic); *Serial titles:* 33,881 (physical), 125,294 (digital/electronic); *Databases:* 586. Weekly public service hours: 146; study areas open 24 hours, 5–7 days a week; students can reserve study rooms.

STUDENT LIFE

Housing options: on-campus residence required through sophomore year; coed, special housing for students with disabilities. Campus housing is university owned. Freshman campus housing is guaranteed.

Activities and organizations: drama/theater group, student-run newspaper, radio and television station, choral group, marching band, Student Association, University Union, Otto, national fraternities, national sororities.

Athletics Member NCAA. All Division I except football (Division I-A). ***Intercollegiate sports:*** badminton M(c)/W(c), baseball M(c), basketball M(s)/W(s), bowling M(c)/W(c), cheerleading M/W, crew M(s)/W(s), cross-country running M(s)/W(s), equestrian sports M(c)/W(c), fencing M(c)/W(c), field hockey W(s), gymnastics M(c)/W(c), ice hockey M(c)/W(s), lacrosse M(s)/W(s), rugby M(c)/W(c), sailing M(c)/W(c), skiing (downhill) W(c), soccer M(s)/W(s), softball W(s), tennis M(c)/W(s), track and field M(s)/W(s), volleyball M(c)/W(s), water polo M(c)/W(c), wrestling M(c). ***Intramural sports:*** basketball M/W, fencing W(c), golf M(c)/W(c), ice hockey M/W, lacrosse M(c)/W(c), racquetball M/W, soccer M/W, softball M/W, swimming and diving M(c)/W(c), table tennis M(c)/W(c), tennis M/W, ultimate Frisbee M(c)/W(c), volleyball M/W.

Campus security: 24-hour emergency response devices and patrols, student patrols, late-night transport/escort service, controlled dormitory access.

Student services: health clinic, personal/psychological counseling, women's center, legal services, veterans affairs office.

COSTS & FINANCIAL AID

Costs (2018–19) ***Comprehensive fee:*** $67,403 includes full-time tuition ($50,230), mandatory fees ($1623), and room and board ($15,550). Full-time tuition and fees vary according to course load. Part-time tuition:

$2043 per credit hour. Part-time tuition and fees vary according to course load. ***College room only:*** $8260. Room and board charges vary according to board plan and housing facility. ***Payment plans:*** tuition prepayment, installment. ***Waivers:*** employees or children of employees.

Financial Aid Of all full-time matriculated undergraduates who enrolled in 2018, 8,564 applied for aid, 6,185 were judged to have need, 2,779 had their need fully met. 5,429 Federal Work-Study jobs (averaging $2951). In 2018, 3521 non-need-based awards were made. ***Average percent of need met:*** 94. ***Average financial aid package:*** $40,030. ***Average need-based loan:*** $4500. ***Average need-based gift aid:*** $32,676. ***Average non-need-based aid:*** $12,070. ***Average indebtedness upon graduation:*** $37,707. ***Financial aid deadline:*** 1/1.

APPLYING

Standardized Tests *Required:* SAT or ACT (for admission).

Options: electronic application, early admission, early decision, deferred entrance.

Application fee: $75.

Required: essay or personal statement, high school transcript, 2 letters of recommendation, Please visit the Apply to Syracuse web page at http://admissions.syr.edu for information on requirements for First-Year, Transfer, and International applicants.. ***Recommended:*** interview.

Application deadlines: 1/1 (freshmen), 7/1 (transfers).

Early decision deadline: 11/15.

Notification: 3/15 (freshmen), continuous (transfers), 12/15 (early decision).

CONTACT

Mr. Maurice Harris, Dean of Admissions, Syracuse University, 900 South Crouse Avenue, Syracuse, NY 13244. *Phone:* 315-443-3611. *E-mail:* orange@syr.edu.

Talmudical Institute of Upstate New York

Rochester, New York

http://www.tiuny.org/

CONTACT

Rabbi Menachem Davidowitz, Director of Admissions, Talmudical Institute of Upstate New York, 769 Park Avenue, Rochester, NY 14607-3046. *Phone:* 716-473-2810. *E-mail:* yeshiva@tiuny.org.

Talmudical Seminary of Bobov

Brooklyn, New York

CONTACT

Talmudical Seminary of Bobov, 5120 New Utrecht Avenue, Brooklyn, NY 11219.

Talmudical Seminary Oholei Torah

Brooklyn, New York

CONTACT

Rabbi Yisroel Friedman, Director of Academic Affairs, Talmudical Seminary Oholei Torah, 667 Eastern Parkway, Brooklyn, NY 11213-3310. *Phone:* 718-363-2034. *E-mail:* info@oholeitorah.com.

Torah Temimah Talmudical Seminary

Brooklyn, New York

CONTACT

Principal, Torah Temimah Talmudical Seminary, 507 Ocean Parkway, Brooklyn, NY 11218-5913. *Phone:* 718-853-8500.

Touro College

New York, New York

http://www.touro.edu/

CONTACT

Mr. David Luk, Associate Director of Admissions, Touro College, 27-33 West 23rd Street, New York, NY 10010. *Phone:* 212-463-0400 Ext. 5644. *Fax:* 212-627-9542. *E-mail:* david.luk@touro.edu.

Trocaire College

Buffalo, New York

http://www.trocaire.edu/

CONTACT

Trocaire College, 360 Choate Avenue, Buffalo, NY 14220-2094. *Phone:* 716-826-2558.

Union College

Schenectady, New York

http://www.union.edu/

- **Independent** 4-year, founded 1795
- **Urban** 100-acre campus
- **Endowment** $427.6 million
- **Coed** 2,206 undergraduate students, 100% full-time, 46% women, 54% men
- **Very difficult** entrance level, 39% of applicants were admitted

UNDERGRAD STUDENTS

2,195 full-time, 11 part-time. 60% are from out of state; 4% Black or African American, non-Hispanic/Latino; 8% Hispanic/Latino; 5% Asian, non-Hispanic/Latino; 0.1% American Indian or Alaska Native, non-Hispanic/Latino; 3% Two or more races, non-Hispanic/Latino; 0.3% Race/ethnicity unknown; 9% international; 88% live on campus.

Freshmen:

Admission: 6,716 applied, 2,598 admitted, 571 enrolled. ***Average high school GPA:*** 3.4. ***Test scores:*** SAT evidence-based reading and writing scores over 500: 94%; SAT math scores over 500: 101%; ACT scores over 18: 100%; SAT evidence-based reading and writing scores over 600: 86%; SAT math scores over 600: 92%; ACT scores over 24: 99%; SAT evidence-based reading and writing scores over 700: 27%; SAT math scores over 700: 46%; ACT scores over 30: 55%.

Retention: 95% of full-time freshmen returned.

FACULTY

Total: 241, 88% full-time, 95% with terminal degrees.

Student/faculty ratio: 10:1.

ACADEMICS

Calendar: trimesters. *Degree:* bachelor's.

Special study options: accelerated degree program, advanced placement credit, double majors, honors programs, independent study, internships, off-campus study, student-designed majors, study abroad, summer session for credit. ***ROTC:*** Army (c), Navy (c), Air Force (c).

Computers: 554 computers/terminals and 3,032 ports are available on campus for general student use. Students can access the following: campus intranet, computer help desk, free student e-mail accounts, online (class) grades, online (class) registration, online (class) schedules, Digital Studio and Learning Commons. Campuswide network is available. 100% of college-owned or -operated housing units are wired for high-speed Internet access. Wireless service is available via entire campus.

Library: Schaffer Library. Study areas open 24 hours, 5–7 days a week; students can reserve study rooms.

STUDENT LIFE

Housing options: on-campus residence required through junior year; coed. Campus housing is university owned. Freshman campus housing is guaranteed.

Activities and organizations: drama/theater group, student-run newspaper, radio and television station, choral group, U-Program (Programming Board), speaker's forum, student newspaper, Concert Committee, ski club, national fraternities, national sororities.

Athletics Member NCAA. All Division III except golf (Division II), men's and women's ice hockey (Division I). ***Intercollegiate sports:*** baseball M, basketball M/W, cheerleading M(c)/W(c), crew M/W, cross-country running M/W, equestrian sports W, field hockey W, football M, golf W, ice hockey M/W, lacrosse M/W, rugby M(c)/W(c), soccer M/W, softball W, swimming and diving M/W, tennis M/W, track and field M/W, ultimate Frisbee M(c)/W(c), volleyball W. ***Intramural sports:*** badminton M(c)/W(c), basketball M/W, bowling M(c)/W(c), equestrian sports M(c)/W(c), fencing M(c), field hockey W(c), football M/W, golf M(c)/W(c), ice hockey M(c)/W(c), lacrosse M(c)/W, racquetball M/W, rock climbing M(c)/W(c), skiing (downhill) M(c)/W(c), soccer M/W, softball M/W, squash M/W, tennis M/W, volleyball M/W, water polo M/W.

Campus security: 24-hour emergency response devices and patrols, late-night transport/escort service, controlled dormitory access, awareness programs, bicycle patrol, shuttle service.

Student services: health clinic, personal/psychological counseling, women's center.

COSTS & FINANCIAL AID
Costs (2018–19) ***Comprehensive fee:*** $68,853 includes full-time tuition ($54,819), mandatory fees ($471), and room and board ($13,563). ***College room only:*** $7437. ***Payment plan:*** installment. ***Waivers:*** senior citizens and employees or children of employees.

Financial Aid Of all full-time matriculated undergraduates who enrolled in 2018, 1,203 applied for aid, 1,091 were judged to have need, 1,087 had their need fully met. In 2018, 678 non-need-based awards were made. ***Average percent of need met:*** 100. ***Average financial aid package:*** $46,068. ***Average need-based loan:*** $5332. ***Average need-based gift aid:*** $39,596. ***Average non-need-based aid:*** $12,950. ***Average indebtedness upon graduation:*** $35,388. ***Financial aid deadline:*** 1/15.

APPLYING
Standardized Tests *Required for some:* SAT (for admission), SAT and SAT Subject Tests or ACT (for admission), SAT I and two SAT II tests or ACT for leadership in medicine program, SAT or ACT for law and public policy program.

Options: electronic application, early admission, early decision, deferred entrance.

Required: essay or personal statement, high school transcript, 2 letters of recommendation. ***Recommended:*** interview.

Application deadlines: 1/15 (freshmen), 4/15 (transfers).

Early decision deadline: 11/15.

Notification: 4/1 (freshmen), continuous (transfers), 12/15 (early decision).

CONTACT
Matthew J. Malatesta, Vice President for Admissions, Financial Aid and Enrollment, Union College, 807 Union Street, Schenectady, NY 12308-2311. *Phone:* 518-388-6112. *Toll-free phone:* 888-843-6688. *Fax:* 518-388-6986. *E-mail:* admissions@union.edu.

★ United States Merchant Marine Academy
Kings Point, New York
http://www.usmma.edu/

- **Federally supported** comprehensive, founded 1943
- **Suburban** 82-acre campus with easy access to New York City
- **Coed**
- **Very difficult** entrance level

FACULTY
Student/faculty ratio: 8:1.

ACADEMICS
Calendar: trimesters. *Degrees:* bachelor's and master's.
Library: Schuyler Otis Bland Memorial Library. *Books:* 176,485 (physical), 2,791 (digital/electronic); *Serial titles:* 1,511 (physical), 505 (digital/electronic); *Databases:* 17. Weekly public service hours: 84.

STUDENT LIFE
Housing options: on-campus residence required through senior year; coed. Campus housing is university owned. Freshman campus housing is guaranteed.

Activities and organizations: drama/theater group, student-run newspaper, choral group, marching band, Regimental Band, CFC, Neuman Club, Honor Guard.

Athletics Member NCAA. All Division III.

Campus security: 24-hour emergency response devices and patrols, controlled dormitory access.

Student services: health clinic, personal/psychological counseling.

COSTS
Costs (2018–19) ***Comprehensive fee:*** includes mandatory fees ($1080). Midshipmen at the United States Merchant Marine Academy receive from the Federal Government their education, room and board, uniforms, and books. However, midshipmen are responsible for the payment of fees for mandatory educational supplies not provided by the government.

APPLYING
Standardized Tests *Required:* SAT or ACT (for admission).

Options: electronic application.

Required: essay or personal statement, high school transcript, 3 letters of recommendation. ***Recommended:*** interview.

CONTACT
Lt. Cdr. Keith L. Watson, Assistant Director of Admissions and Financial Aid, United States Merchant Marine Academy, 300 Steamboat Road, Kings Point, NY 11024-1699. *Phone:* 516-726-5642. *Toll-free phone:* 866-546-4778. *Fax:* 516-773-5390. *E-mail:* admissions@usmma.edu.

See page 1128 for the College Close-Up.

United States Military Academy
West Point, New York
http://www.usma.edu/

- **Federally supported** 4-year, founded 1802
- **Small-town** 16,080-acre campus with easy access to New York City
- **Endowment** $348.2 million
- **Coed**
- 10% of applicants were admitted

FACULTY
Student/faculty ratio: 7:1.

ACADEMICS
Calendar: semesters. *Degree:* bachelor's.
Library: United States Military Academy Library at West Point. *Books:* 422,671 (physical), 931,618 (digital/electronic); *Serial titles:* 110 (physical), 113,741 (digital/electronic); *Databases:* 270. Weekly public service hours: 100.

STUDENT LIFE
Housing options: on-campus residence required through senior year; coed. Campus housing is university owned. Freshman campus housing is guaranteed.

Activities and organizations: drama/theater group, student-run radio station, choral group, Spirit Clubs, Big Brother/Big Sister, Cadet Fine Arts Forum, Film Forum, Philosophy Forum.

Athletics Member NCAA. All Division I except football (Division I-A).

Campus security: 24-hour emergency response devices and patrols, late-night transport/escort service, controlled dormitory access.

Student services: health clinic, personal/psychological counseling, legal services.

COSTS
Costs (2018–19) ***Comprehensive fee:*** Cadets receive a full scholarship and an annual salary. There is no tuition charge, but there is a requirement for an initial deposit. Room, board, and medical and dental care are provided by the US Government. A portion of the cadet pay is deposited to a "Cadet Account" to help pay for uniforms, books, a laptop computer, and incidentals. The only cost is a one-time deposit upon admission to defray the initial issue of uniforms, books, supplies, and equipment. If needed, loans of $100 to $2,000 are available for the deposit. Upon

graduation, cadets incur a 5-year Active Duty service obligation and 3 years of reserve duty in the US Army.

APPLYING
Standardized Tests *Required:* SAT or ACT (for admission).

Options: electronic application.

Required: essay or personal statement, high school transcript, 4 letters of recommendation, Candidates will be notified if they can compete for admission into West Point after the Service Academies Pre-candidate Questionnaire is submitted to West Pointâ??s Admission office. ***Recommended:*** interview.

CONTACT
United States Military Academy, 600 Thayer Road, West Point, NY 10996. *Phone:* 845-938-4041. *E-mail:* admissions@usma.edu.

United Talmudical Seminary

Brooklyn, New York

CONTACT
Director of Admissions, United Talmudical Seminary, 191 Rodney Street, Brooklyn, NY 11211. *Phone:* 718-963-9770.

University at Albany, State University of New York

Albany, New York

http://www.albany.edu/

- **State-supported** university, founded 1844, part of State University of New York System
- **Suburban** 560-acre campus
- **Endowment** $59.8 million
- **Coed**
- **Very difficult** entrance level

FACULTY
Student/faculty ratio: 19:1.

ACADEMICS
Calendar: semesters. *Degrees:* bachelor's, master's, doctoral, post-master's, and postbachelor's certificates.
Library: University Library plus 2 others. *Books:* 2.3 million (physical), 342,263 (digital/electronic); *Serial titles:* 97,614 (digital/electronic). Weekly public service hours: 113; students can reserve study rooms.

STUDENT LIFE
Housing options: on-campus residence required through sophomore year; coed. Campus housing is university owned. Freshman campus housing is guaranteed.

Activities and organizations: drama/theater group, student-run newspaper, radio and television station, choral group, intramural athletics, cultural organizations, political organizations, community service, honor societies, national fraternities, national sororities.

Athletics Member NCAA. All Division I.

Campus security: 24-hour emergency response devices and patrols, late-night transport/escort service, controlled dormitory access, Five Quad Ambulance Service, on-campus car battery assistance.

Student services: health clinic, personal/psychological counseling, legal services.

COSTS & FINANCIAL AID
Costs (2018–19) ***Tuition:*** state resident $6870 full-time, $278 per credit hour part-time; nonresident $23,710 full-time, $898 per credit hour part-time. Part-time tuition and fees vary according to course load. ***Required fees:*** $2946 full-time, $76 per credit hour part-time. ***Room and board:*** $12,942; room only: $8782. Room and board charges vary according to board plan and housing facility.

Financial Aid Of all full-time matriculated undergraduates who enrolled in 2017, 9,827 applied for aid, 8,118 were judged to have need, 489 had their need fully met. In 2017, 646 non-need-based awards were made. ***Average percent of need met:*** 59. ***Average financial aid package:*** $11,046. ***Average need-based loan:*** $4702. ***Average need-based gift aid:*** $7760. ***Average non-need-based aid:*** $4114. ***Average indebtedness upon graduation:*** $21,217.

APPLYING
Standardized Tests *Required:* SAT or ACT (for admission).

Options: electronic application, early admission, early action, deferred entrance.

Application fee: $50.

Required: essay or personal statement, high school transcript, 1 letter of recommendation. ***Required for some:*** portfolio, audition.

CONTACT
University at Albany, State University of New York, Office of Undergraduate Admissions, 1400 Washington Avenue, Albany, NY 12222. *Phone:* 518-442-5435. *Fax:* 518-442-5383. *E-mail:* ugadmissions@albany.edu.

University at Buffalo, the State University of New York

Buffalo, New York

http://www.buffalo.edu/

- **State-supported** university, founded 1846, part of State University of New York System
- **Suburban** 1350-acre campus
- **Endowment** $659.2 million
- **Coed** 21,607 undergraduate students, 92% full-time, 44% women, 56% men
- **Moderately difficult** entrance level, 56% of applicants were admitted

UNDERGRAD STUDENTS
19,941 full-time, 1,666 part-time. 2% are from out of state; 8% Black or African American, non-Hispanic/Latino; 7% Hispanic/Latino; 15% Asian, non-Hispanic/Latino; 0.1% Native Hawaiian or other Pacific Islander, non-Hispanic/Latino; 0.3% American Indian or Alaska Native, non-Hispanic/Latino; 2% Two or more races, non-Hispanic/Latino; 5% Race/ethnicity unknown; 15% international; 9% transferred in; 35% live on campus.

Freshmen:
Admission: 31,196 applied, 17,423 admitted, 4,263 enrolled. ***Average high school GPA:*** ####. ***Test scores:*** SAT evidence-based reading and writing scores over 500: 98%; SAT math scores over 500: 100%; ACT scores over 18: 100%; SAT evidence-based reading and writing scores over 600: 59%; SAT math scores over 600: 69%; ACT scores over 24: 83%; SAT evidence-based reading and writing scores over 700: 9%; SAT math scores over 700: 20%; ACT scores over 30: 21%.

Retention: 87% of full-time freshmen returned.

FACULTY
Total: 1,813, 72% full-time, 92% with terminal degrees.

Student/faculty ratio: 13:1.

ACADEMICS
Calendar: semesters. *Degrees:* certificates, bachelor's, master's, doctoral, and post-master's certificates.

Special study options: academic remediation for entering students, accelerated degree program, advanced placement credit, cooperative education, distance learning, double majors, English as a second language, freshman honors college, honors programs, independent study, internships, off-campus study, part-time degree program, services for LD students, student-designed majors, study abroad, summer session for credit. ***ROTC:*** Army (c).

Unusual degree programs: 3-2 business administration; engineering; nursing; social work; law.

Computers: 3,061 computers/terminals are available on campus for general student use. Students can access the following: campus intranet, computer help desk, free student e-mail accounts, online (class) grades, online (class) registration, online (class) schedules. Campuswide network is available. 100% of college-owned or -operated housing units are wired for high-speed Internet access. Wireless service is available via entire campus.
Library: Lockwood Memorial Library plus 11 others. *Books:* 3.4 million (physical), 826,650 (digital/electronic); *Serial titles:* 2,352 (physical), 175,278 (digital/electronic); *Databases:* 383. Weekly public service hours: 168; study areas open 24 hours, 5–7 days a week; students can reserve study rooms.

STUDENT LIFE
Housing options: coed, special housing for students with disabilities. Campus housing is university owned. Freshman campus housing is guaranteed.

Activities and organizations: drama/theater group, student-run newspaper, radio and television station, choral group, marching band, national fraternities, national sororities.

Athletics Member NCAA. All Division I. ***Intercollegiate sports:*** basketball M(s)/W(s), cross-country running M(s)/W(s), football M(s), soccer M, softball W(s), swimming and diving M, tennis M(s)/W(s), track and field M(s)/W(s), volleyball W(s), wrestling M(s). ***Intramural sports:*** baseball M(c), basketball M/W(c), crew M(c)/W(c), cross-country running M(c)/W(c), equestrian sports M(c)/W(c), fencing M(c)/W(c), field hockey M(c)/W(c), golf M(c)/W(c), gymnastics M(c)/W(c), ice hockey M(c)/W(c), lacrosse M(c)/W(c), rugby M(c)/W(c), sailing M(c)/W(c), skiing (downhill) M(c)/W(c), soccer M(c)/W(c), swimming and diving M(c)/W(c), table tennis M(c)/W(c), tennis M(c)/W(c), track and field M(c)/W(c), ultimate Frisbee M(c)/W(c), volleyball M(c)/W(c), water polo M(c)/W(c), wrestling M(c).

Campus security: 24-hour emergency response devices and patrols, student patrols, late-night transport/escort service, controlled dormitory access.

Student services: health clinic, personal/psychological counseling, women's center, legal services, veterans affairs office.

COSTS & FINANCIAL AID
Costs (2018–19) ***Tuition:*** state resident $6870 full-time, $286 per credit hour part-time; nonresident $24,540 full-time, $1023 per credit hour part-time. Part-time tuition and fees vary according to course load. ***Required fees:*** $3229 full-time, $139 per credit hour part-time. ***Room and board:*** $14,213; room only: $8273. Room and board charges vary according to board plan and housing facility. ***Payment plan:*** installment. ***Waivers:*** minority students.

Financial Aid Of all full-time matriculated undergraduates who enrolled in 2017, 13,809 applied for aid, 10,690 were judged to have need, 742 had their need fully met. 1,026 Federal Work-Study jobs (averaging $1223). 2,972 state and other part-time jobs (averaging $2499). In 2017, 723 non-need-based awards were made. ***Average percent of need met:*** 47. ***Average financial aid package:*** $10,735. ***Average need-based loan:*** $4215. ***Average need-based gift aid:*** $7427. ***Average non-need-based aid:*** $3841. ***Average indebtedness upon graduation:*** $26,062.

APPLYING
Standardized Tests *Required:* SAT or ACT (for admission).

Options: electronic application, early admission, early action.

Application fee: $50.

Required: essay or personal statement, high school transcript, letters of recommendation. ***Required for some:*** portfolio for architecture; audition for dance, music theatre, theatre and music.

Notification: continuous (freshmen), continuous (out-of-state freshmen), continuous (transfers), 1/15 (early action).

CONTACT
Mr. Lee Melvin, Vice Provost for Enrollment Management, University at Buffalo, the State University of New York, 1 Capen Hall, North Campus, Buffalo, NY 14260-1660. *Phone:* 716-645-6900. *Toll-free phone:* 888-UB-ADMIT. *E-mail:* ub-admissions@buffalo.edu.

University of Rochester

Rochester, New York

http://www.rochester.edu/

- **Independent** university, founded 1850
- **Suburban** 655-acre campus
- **Endowment** $2.1 billion
- **Coed**
- **Very difficult** entrance level

FACULTY
Student/faculty ratio: 10:1.

ACADEMICS
Calendar: semesters plus optional summer term. *Degrees:* bachelor's, master's, doctoral, post-master's, and postbachelor's certificates.

Library: Rush Rhees Library plus 7 others. Study areas open 24 hours, 5–7 days a week; students can reserve study rooms.

STUDENT LIFE
Housing options: on-campus residence required through sophomore year; coed. Campus housing is university owned and leased by the school. Freshman campus housing is guaranteed.

Activities and organizations: drama/theater group, student-run newspaper, radio and television station, choral group, marching band, Campus Activities Board, Black Students'; Union, Grassroots (environmental group), Women's Caucus, American Sign Language Club, national fraternities, national sororities.

Athletics Member NCAA. All Division III except squash (Division I).

Campus security: 24-hour emergency response devices and patrols, student patrols, late-night transport/escort service, controlled dormitory access.

Student services: health clinic, personal/psychological counseling, women's center, legal services, veterans affairs office.

COSTS & FINANCIAL AID
Costs (2018–19) ***Comprehensive fee:*** $69,685 includes full-time tuition ($52,867), mandatory fees ($958), and room and board ($15,860). Part-time tuition: $1652 per credit hour. Part-time tuition and fees vary according to course load. ***Room and board:*** Room and board charges vary according to board plan and housing facility.

Financial Aid Of all full-time matriculated undergraduates who enrolled in 2018, 3,875 applied for aid, 3,311 were judged to have need, 2,975 had their need fully met. 2,108 Federal Work-Study jobs (averaging $3114). 478 state and other part-time jobs (averaging $1361). In 2018, 1702 non-need-based awards were made. ***Average percent of need met:*** 95. ***Average financial aid package:*** $49,022. ***Average need-based loan:*** $3655. ***Average need-based gift aid:*** $44,662. ***Average non-need-based aid:*** $13,927. ***Average indebtedness upon graduation:*** $29,553.

APPLYING
Standardized Tests *Required for some:* SAT and SAT Subject Tests or ACT (for admission). *Recommended:* SAT or ACT (for admission), SAT Subject Tests (for admission).

Options: electronic application, early decision, deferred entrance.

Application fee: $50.

Required: essay or personal statement, high school transcript. ***Required for some:*** audition for Eastman School of Music. ***Recommended:*** 2 letters of recommendation, interview.

CONTACT
Office of Admissions, University of Rochester, PO Box 270251, 300 Wilson Boulevard, Rochester, NY 14627-0251. *Phone:* 585-275-3221. *Toll-free phone:* 888-822-2256. *Fax:* 585-461-4595. *E-mail:* admit@admissions.rochester.edu.

U.T.A. Mesivta of Kiryas Joel

Monroe, New York

CONTACT
U.T.A. Mesivta of Kiryas Joel, 48 Bakertown Road, Suite 501, Monroe, NY 10950.

Utica College

Utica, New York

http://www.utica.edu/

- **Independent** comprehensive, founded 1946
- **Suburban** 128-acre campus
- **Endowment** $25.9 million
- **Coed** 3,722 undergraduate students, 78% full-time, 60% women, 40% men
- **Moderately difficult** entrance level, 84% of applicants were admitted

UNDERGRAD STUDENTS
2,909 full-time, 813 part-time. Students come from 48 states and territories; 28 other countries; 12% are from out of state; 10% Black or African American, non-Hispanic/Latino; 9% Hispanic/Latino; 4% Asian, non-Hispanic/Latino; 0.1% Native Hawaiian or other Pacific Islander, non-Hispanic/Latino; 0.5% American Indian or Alaska Native, non-

Hispanic/Latino; 2% Two or more races, non-Hispanic/Latino; 5% Race/ethnicity unknown; 0.8% international; 4% transferred in; 34% live on campus.

Freshmen:

Admission: 4,224 applied, 3,566 admitted, 588 enrolled. ***Average high school GPA:*** 3.2. ***Test scores:*** SAT evidence-based reading and writing scores over 500: 85%; SAT math scores over 500: 85%; ACT scores over 18: 92%; SAT evidence-based reading and writing scores over 600: 30%; SAT math scores over 600: 31%; ACT scores over 24: 45%; SAT evidence-based reading and writing scores over 700: 1%; SAT math scores over 700: 2%; ACT scores over 30: 7%.

Retention: 70% of full-time freshmen returned.

FACULTY

Total: 469, 32% full-time, 40% with terminal degrees.

Student/faculty ratio: 13:1.

ACADEMICS

Calendar: semesters. *Degrees:* certificates, bachelor's, master's, doctoral, and postbachelor's certificates.

Special study options: academic remediation for entering students, accelerated degree program, adult/continuing education programs, advanced placement credit, cooperative education, distance learning, double majors, English as a second language, honors programs, independent study, internships, off-campus study, part-time degree program, services for LD students, study abroad, summer session for credit. ***ROTC:*** Army (b), Air Force (c).

Unusual degree programs: 3-2 engineering with Syracuse University.

Computers: 430 computers/terminals are available on campus for general student use. Students can access the following: computer help desk, free student e-mail accounts, online (class) grades, online (class) registration, online (class) schedules. Campuswide network is available. 100% of college-owned or -operated housing units are wired for high-speed Internet access. Wireless service is available via entire campus.

Library: Frank E. Gannett Memorial Library. *Books:* 307,523 (physical); *Serial titles:* 267,023 (physical). Students can reserve study rooms.

STUDENT LIFE

Housing options: on-campus residence required through sophomore year; coed, special housing for students with disabilities. Campus housing is university owned. Freshman campus housing is guaranteed.

Activities and organizations: drama/theater group, student-run newspaper, radio station, choral group, Physical Therapy Society, Student Nurses Association, Kappa Delta Pi, Student Senate, Utica College Honor Association, national fraternities, national sororities.

Athletics Member NCAA. All Division III except golf (Division II). ***Intercollegiate sports:*** baseball M, basketball M/W, cross-country running M/W, field hockey W, football M, golf M/W, ice hockey M/W, lacrosse M/W, soccer M/W, softball W, swimming and diving M/W, tennis M/W, track and field M/W, volleyball W, water polo W. ***Intramural sports:*** basketball M/W, bowling M/W, cheerleading M(c)/W(c), fencing M(c), field hockey W(c), racquetball M/W, soccer M/W, softball M/W, tennis M/W, volleyball M/W, water polo M/W.

Campus security: 24-hour emergency response devices and patrols, late-night transport/escort service, controlled dormitory access.

Student services: health clinic, personal/psychological counseling, women's center.

COSTS & FINANCIAL AID

Costs (2018–19) ***Comprehensive fee:*** $32,630 includes full-time tuition ($20,832), mandatory fees ($550), and room and board ($11,248). Full-time tuition and fees vary according to course load, degree level, and location. Part-time tuition: $694 per credit hour. Part-time tuition and fees vary according to course load, degree level, and location. ***Required fees:*** $50 per term part-time. ***Room and board:*** Room and board charges vary according to board plan. ***Waivers:*** employees or children of employees.

Financial Aid Of all full-time matriculated undergraduates who enrolled in 2018, 2,685 applied for aid, 2,410 were judged to have need, 225 had their need fully met. In 2018, 255 non-need-based awards were made. ***Average percent of need met:*** 52. ***Average financial aid package:*** $14,592. ***Average need-based loan:*** $4421. ***Average need-based gift aid:*** $4926. ***Average non-need-based aid:*** $4530. ***Average indebtedness upon graduation:*** $29,054.

APPLYING
Standardized Tests *Required for some:* SAT or ACT (for admission).

Options: electronic application, early decision, early action, deferred entrance.

Application fee: $40.

Required: essay or personal statement, high school transcript, minimum 2.0 GPA, 1 letter of recommendation. ***Required for some:*** minimum 3.0 GPA. ***Recommended:*** interview.

Application deadlines: rolling (freshmen), rolling (transfers).

Notification: 9/1 (freshmen), continuous (transfers).

CONTACT
Mr. Jeffrey Gates, Vice President for Enrollment Management, Utica College, 1600 Burrstone Road, Utica, NY 13502-4892. *Phone:* 315-792-3006. *Toll-free phone:* 800-782-8884. *E-mail:* jtgates@utica.edu.

See previous page for display ad and page 1150 for the College Close-Up.

Vassar College

Poughkeepsie, New York

http://www.vassar.edu/

- **Independent** 4-year, founded 1861
- **Suburban** 1000-acre campus with easy access to New York City
- **Endowment** $1.1 billion
- **Coed** 2,463 undergraduate students, 99% full-time, 59% women, 41% men
- **Very difficult** entrance level, 25% of applicants were admitted

UNDERGRAD STUDENTS
2,449 full-time, 14 part-time. Students come from 52 states and territories; 40 other countries; 72% are from out of state; 4% Black or African American, non-Hispanic/Latino; 11% Hispanic/Latino; 12% Asian, non-Hispanic/Latino; 8% Two or more races, non-Hispanic/Latino; 0.8% Race/ethnicity unknown; 9% international; 0.3% transferred in; 97% live on campus.

Freshmen:
Admission: 8,312 applied, 2,043 admitted, 685 enrolled. ***Test scores:*** SAT evidence-based reading and writing scores over 500: 100%; SAT math scores over 500: 100%; ACT scores over 18: 100%; SAT evidence-based reading and writing scores over 600: 99%; SAT math scores over 600: 98%; ACT scores over 24: 99%; SAT evidence-based reading and writing scores over 700: 66%; SAT math scores over 700: 71%; ACT scores over 30: 90%.

FACULTY
Total: 342, 83% full-time, 85% with terminal degrees.

Student/faculty ratio: 8:1.

ACADEMICS
Calendar: semesters. *Degrees:* bachelor's and master's.

Special study options: advanced placement credit, cooperative education, double majors, independent study, internships, off-campus study, part-time degree program, services for LD students, student-designed majors, study abroad.

Unusual degree programs: 3-2 engineering with Dartmouth College.

Computers: 135 computers/terminals are available on campus for general student use. Students can access the following: campus intranet, computer help desk, free student e-mail accounts, online (class) grades, online (class) registration, online (class) schedules, Ethernet. Campuswide network is available. 100% of college-owned or -operated housing units are wired for high-speed Internet access. Wireless service is available via entire campus.

Library: Vassar College Library plus 2 others. *Books:* 1.2 million (physical), 543,272 (digital/electronic); *Serial titles:* 15,914 (physical), 98,004 (digital/electronic); *Databases:* 847. Weekly public service hours: 145; study areas open 24 hours, 5–7 days a week; students can reserve study rooms.

STUDENT LIFE
Housing options: on-campus residence required through senior year; coed, women-only, cooperative, special housing for students with disabilities. Campus housing is university owned. Freshman campus housing is guaranteed.

Activities and organizations: drama/theater group, student-run newspaper, radio station, choral group, Student Association, WVKR radio station, VICE (programming social events), Vassar Greens, Ultimate Frisbee.

Athletics Member NCAA. All Division III except golf (Division II). ***Intercollegiate sports:*** baseball M, basketball M/W, crew M(c)/W(c), cross-country running M/W, fencing M/W, field hockey W, golf W, lacrosse M/W, rugby M(c)/W(c), soccer M/W, squash M/W, swimming and diving M/W, tennis M/W, track and field M/W, volleyball M/W. ***Intramural sports:*** badminton M(c)/W(c), basketball M(c)/W(c), soccer M(c)/W(c), table tennis M(c)/W(c), tennis M(c)/W(c), ultimate Frisbee M(c)/W(c), volleyball M(c)/W(c).

Campus security: 24-hour emergency response devices and patrols, student patrols, late-night transport/escort service, controlled dormitory access.

Student services: health clinic, personal/psychological counseling, women's center, veterans affairs office.

COSTS & FINANCIAL AID
Costs (2018–19) ***One-time required fee:*** $80. ***Comprehensive fee:*** $70,510 includes full-time tuition ($56,130), mandatory fees ($830), and room and board ($13,550). Part-time tuition: $6690 per unit. ***Room and board:*** Room and board charges vary according to housing facility. ***Payment plan:*** installment. ***Waivers:*** employees or children of employees.

Financial Aid Of all full-time matriculated undergraduates who enrolled in 2018, 1,732 applied for aid, 1,526 were judged to have need, 1,526 had their need fully met. 1,133 Federal Work-Study jobs (averaging $2510). 313 state and other part-time jobs (averaging $2451). ***Average percent of need met:*** 100. ***Average financial aid package:*** $54,947. ***Average need-based loan:*** $3315. ***Average need-based gift aid:*** $49,190. ***Average indebtedness upon graduation:*** $21,473. ***Financial aid deadline:*** 2/1.

APPLYING
Standardized Tests *Required:* SAT or ACT (for admission).

Options: electronic application, early decision, deferred entrance.

Application fee: $65.

Required: essay or personal statement, high school transcript, 2 letters of recommendation.

Application deadlines: 1/1 (freshmen), 3/15 (transfers).

Early decision deadline: 11/15 (for plan 1), 1/1 (for plan 2).

Notification: 4/1 (freshmen), 5/10 (transfers), 12/15 (early decision).

CONTACT
Dean Art D. Rodriguez, Dean of Admission and Financial Aid, Vassar College, 124 Raymond Avenue, Poughkeepsie, NY 12604. *Phone:* 845-437-7300. *Toll-free phone:* 800-827-7270. *Fax:* 845-437-7063. *E-mail:* admissions@vassar.edu.

Vaughn College of Aeronautics and Technology

Flushing, New York

http://www.vaughn.edu/

- **Independent** comprehensive, founded 1932
- **Urban** 6-acre campus with easy access to New York City
- **Endowment** $24.4 million
- **Coed, primarily men** 1,538 undergraduate students, 84% full-time, 13% women, 88% men
- **Moderately difficult** entrance level, 82% of applicants were admitted

UNDERGRAD STUDENTS
1,294 full-time, 268 part-time. Students come from 17 states and territories; 22 other countries; 12% are from out of state; 18% Black or African American, non-Hispanic/Latino; 34% Hispanic/Latino; 11% Asian, non-Hispanic/Latino; 1% Native Hawaiian or other Pacific Islander, non-Hispanic/Latino; 0.3% American Indian or Alaska Native, non-Hispanic/Latino; 2% Two or more races, non-Hispanic/Latino; 15% Race/ethnicity unknown; 6% international; 12% transferred in; 12% live on campus.

Freshmen:
Admission: 674 applied, 550 admitted, 313 enrolled. ***Average high school GPA:*** ####. ***Test scores:*** SAT evidence-based reading and writing scores

over 500: 80%; SAT math scores over 500: 83%; ACT scores over 18: 100%; SAT evidence-based reading and writing scores over 600: 18%; SAT math scores over 600: 20%; ACT scores over 24: 64%; SAT evidence-based reading and writing scores over 700: 4%; SAT math scores over 700: 4%; ACT scores over 30: 9%.

Retention: 78% of full-time freshmen returned.

FACULTY
Total: 184, 22% full-time, 20% with terminal degrees.

Student/faculty ratio: 15:1.

ACADEMICS
Calendar: semesters. *Degrees:* certificates, diplomas, associate, bachelor's, and master's.

Special study options: academic remediation for entering students, advanced placement credit, distance learning, double majors, English as a second language, internships, part-time degree program, services for LD students, summer session for credit. ***ROTC:*** Army (c), Air Force (c).

Computers: 220 computers/terminals are available on campus for general student use. Students can access the following: campus intranet, computer help desk, free student e-mail accounts, online (class) grades, online (class) registration, online (class) schedules, Vaughn Student Portal. Campuswide network is available. 100% of college-owned or -operated housing units are wired for high-speed Internet access. Wireless service is available via entire campus.
Library: Library and Learning Commons. Weekly public service hours: 60.

STUDENT LIFE
Housing options: coed, special housing for students with disabilities. Campus housing is university owned. Freshman applicants given priority for college housing.

Activities and organizations: Robotics Club (2106 Vex World Champions), Society of Women Engineers, Engineers Without Borders, The Unmanned Aerial Vehicle (UAV) Club, SHPE (Society of Hispanic Professional Engineers).

Athletics Member USCAA. ***Intercollegiate sports:*** basketball M/W, cross-country running M/W, soccer M, tennis M/W. ***Intramural sports:*** basketball M/W, cross-country running M/W, soccer M, tennis M/W.

Campus security: 24-hour emergency response devices and patrols, controlled dormitory access.

Student services: personal/psychological counseling, veterans affairs office.

COSTS & FINANCIAL AID
Costs (2019–20) ***One-time required fee:*** $160. ***Comprehensive fee:*** $41,364 includes full-time tuition ($25,680), mandatory fees ($960), and room and board ($14,724). Part-time tuition: $855 per credit. ***Required fees:*** $400 part-time. ***College room only:*** $11,425.

Financial Aid Of all full-time matriculated undergraduates who enrolled in 2018, 1,071 applied for aid, 839 were judged to have need, 247 had their need fully met. In 2018, 70 non-need-based awards were made. ***Average percent of need met:*** 82. ***Average financial aid package:*** $9062. ***Average need-based loan:*** $2063. ***Average need-based gift aid:*** $10,990. ***Average non-need-based aid:*** $2387. ***Average indebtedness upon graduation:*** $37,709.

APPLYING
Standardized Tests *Required:* SAT or ACT (for admission). *Recommended:* SAT and SAT Subject Tests or ACT (for admission).

Options: electronic application.

Application fee: $40.

Required: high school transcript. ***Recommended:*** essay or personal statement, 2 letters of recommendation, interview.

Application deadlines: rolling (freshmen), rolling (transfers).

Notification: continuous (freshmen), continuous (transfers).

CONTACT
Mr. Celso Alvarez, Associate Vice President of Enrollment for Admissions, Vaughn College of Aeronautics and Technology, 8601 23rd Avenue, Flushing, NY 11369. *Phone:* 718-429-6600 Ext. 117. *Toll-free phone:* 866-6VAUGHN. *Fax:* 718-779-2231. *E-mail:* celso.alvarez@vaughn.edu.

Villa Maria College
Buffalo, New York
http://www.villa.edu/

- **Independent** 4-year, founded 1960, affiliated with Roman Catholic Church
- **Suburban** 9-acre campus with easy access to Buffalo-Niagara
- **Endowment** $1.9 million
- **Coed**
- **Moderately difficult** entrance level

FACULTY
Student/faculty ratio: 9:1.

ACADEMICS
Calendar: semesters. *Degrees:* certificates, associate, and bachelor's.
Library: Villa Maria College Library. *Books:* 17,213 (physical), 153,087 (digital/electronic); *Serial titles:* 82 (physical); *Databases:* 45.

STUDENT LIFE
Housing options: college housing not available.

Activities and organizations: choral group.

Athletics Member USCAA.

Campus security: 24-hour emergency response devices, late-night transport/escort service, security guard during hours of operation.

Student services: health clinic, personal/psychological counseling, veterans affairs office.

COSTS & FINANCIAL AID
Costs (2018–19) ***Tuition:*** $21,860 full-time, $730 per credit hour part-time. Full-time tuition and fees vary according to degree level, program, and reciprocity agreements. Part-time tuition and fees vary according to course load, degree level, program, and reciprocity agreements. ***Required fees:*** $1150 full-time.

Financial Aid ***Average indebtedness upon graduation:*** $22,658.

APPLYING
Options: electronic application.

Required: high school transcript, application, financial aid forms if applying for assistance, health forms, essay, portfolio and interview for Art programs, audition for music programs. ***Required for some:*** interview. ***Recommended:*** essay or personal statement.

CONTACT
Mr. Brian Emerson, Vice President for Enrollment and Student Services, Villa Maria College, 240 Pine Ridge Road, Buffalo, NY 14225. *Phone:* 716-896-0700 Ext. 1838. *Fax:* 716-896-0705. *E-mail:* admissions@villa.edu.

Wagner College
Staten Island, New York
http://www.wagner.edu/

- **Independent** comprehensive, founded 1883
- **Urban** 105-acre campus with easy access to New York City
- **Endowment** $88.5 million
- **Coed**
- 70% of applicants were admitted

FACULTY
Student/faculty ratio: 13:1.

ACADEMICS
Calendar: semesters. *Degrees:* bachelor's, master's, doctoral, and post-master's certificates.
Library: August Horrmann Library. *Books:* 70,465 (physical), 180,000 (digital/electronic); *Serial titles:* 79,532 (physical); *Databases:* 61. Weekly public service hours: 120; students can reserve study rooms.

STUDENT LIFE
Housing options: coed. Campus housing is university owned and leased by the school. Freshman campus housing is guaranteed.

Activities and organizations: drama/theater group, student-run newspaper, radio station, choral group, marching band, Student Government Association, Student Activities Board, Wagner College

Theatre, Wagner College Choir, student newspaper, national fraternities, national sororities.

Athletics Member NCAA. All Division I except football (Division I-AA).

Campus security: 24-hour emergency response devices and patrols, late-night transport/escort service, controlled dormitory access.

Student services: health clinic, personal/psychological counseling.

FINANCIAL AID

Financial Aid Of all full-time matriculated undergraduates who enrolled in 2016, 1,324 applied for aid, 1,149 were judged to have need, 255 had their need fully met. In 2016, 422 non-need-based awards were made. ***Average percent of need met:*** 70. ***Average financial aid package:*** $29,515. ***Average need-based loan:*** $4937. ***Average need-based gift aid:*** $22,748. ***Average non-need-based aid:*** $17,988.

APPLYING

Standardized Tests *Required for some:* SAT or ACT (for admission).

Options: electronic application, deferred entrance.

Application fee: $60.

Required: essay or personal statement, high school transcript, minimum 2.5 GPA, 2 letters of recommendation. ***Required for some:*** interview. ***Recommended:*** minimum 3.0 GPA, interview.

CONTACT

Mr. James Gibbons, Director of Admissions, Wagner College, One Campus Road, Pape Admissions Building, Staten Island, NY 10301. *Phone:* 718-390-3180. *Toll-free phone:* 800-221-1010. *Fax:* 718-390-3105. *E-mail:* jgibbons@wagner.edu.

Webb Institute

Glen Cove, New York

http://www.webb.edu/

- **Independent** 4-year, founded 1889
- **Suburban** 26-acre campus with easy access to New York City
- **Endowment** $66.3 million
- **Coed**
- **Most difficult** entrance level

FACULTY

Student/faculty ratio: 9:1.

ACADEMICS

Calendar: semesters. *Degree:* bachelor's.

Library: Livingston Library. *Books:* 44,800 (physical), 4,190 (digital/electronic); *Serial titles:* 817 (physical), 43,658 (digital/electronic); *Databases:* 62. Weekly public service hours: 35; study areas open 24 hours, 5–7 days a week.

STUDENT LIFE

Housing options: on-campus residence required through senior year; coed, men-only, women-only. Campus housing is university owned. Freshman campus housing is guaranteed.

Activities and organizations: choral group, Student Organization, Society of Naval Architects and Marine Engineers, American Society of Naval Engineers, Society of Women Engineers, Marine Technology Society.

Campus security: 24-hour emergency response devices and patrols, controlled dormitory access.

Student services: personal/psychological counseling.

COSTS & FINANCIAL AID

Costs (2018–19) ***One-time required fee:*** $3000. ***Comprehensive fee:*** $65,225 includes full-time tuition ($49,750), mandatory fees ($425), and room and board ($15,050). Webb provides scholarships that will fully cover the tuition expenses of U.S. citizens and permanent residents. One-time required fee is for a laptop charged in the first year only.

Financial Aid Of all full-time matriculated undergraduates who enrolled in 2016, 29 applied for aid, 29 were judged to have need. In 2016, 62 non-need-based awards were made. ***Average percent of need met:*** 95. ***Average financial aid package:*** $52,750. ***Average need-based loan:*** $4710. ***Average need-based gift aid:*** $1950. ***Average non-need-based aid:*** $47,000. ***Average indebtedness upon graduation:*** $17,870. ***Financial aid deadline:*** 5/1.

APPLYING

Standardized Tests *Required:* SAT or ACT (for admission), SAT Subject Tests (for admission).

Options: electronic application, early decision, deferred entrance.

Application fee: $60.

Required: essay or personal statement, high school transcript, minimum 3.5 GPA, 2 letters of recommendation, interview, proof of U.S. citizenship or permanent residency status.

CONTACT

Lauren Carballo, Director of Admissions and Student Services, Webb Institute, 298 Crescent Beach Road, Glen Cove, NY 11542. *Phone:* 516-671-8355. *Fax:* 516-674-9838. *E-mail:* admissions@webb.edu.

Wells College

Aurora, New York

http://www.wells.edu/

- **Independent** 4-year, founded 1868
- **Rural** 365-acre campus with easy access to Syracuse
- **Endowment** $23.5 million
- **Coed**
- **Moderately difficult** entrance level

FACULTY

Student/faculty ratio: 10:1.

ACADEMICS

Calendar: semesters. *Degree:* bachelor's.

Library: Louis Jefferson Long Library. Students can reserve study rooms.

STUDENT LIFE

Housing options: on-campus residence required through junior year; coed, women-only, special housing for students with disabilities. Campus housing is university owned. Freshman campus housing is guaranteed.

Activities and organizations: drama/theater group, choral group, Umoja, Prodigy, Red Cross Club, Campus Greens, Programming Board.

Athletics Member NCAA. All Division III.

Campus security: 24-hour emergency response devices and patrols, late-night transport/escort service, controlled dormitory access.

Student services: health clinic, personal/psychological counseling, women's center.

COSTS & FINANCIAL AID

Costs (2018–19) ***Comprehensive fee:*** $54,800 includes full-time tuition ($39,200), mandatory fees ($1500), and room and board ($14,100). Part-time tuition: $800 per credit hour. Part-time tuition and fees vary according to course load. ***Required fees:*** $200 per term part-time. ***College room only:*** $7050. Room and board charges vary according to housing facility.

Financial Aid Of all full-time matriculated undergraduates who enrolled in 2017, 472 applied for aid, 457 were judged to have need, 43 had their need fully met. 64 Federal Work-Study jobs (averaging $1850). 170 state and other part-time jobs (averaging $1850). In 2017, 27 non-need-based awards were made. ***Average percent of need met:*** 77. ***Average financial aid package:*** $35,193. ***Average need-based loan:*** $4071. ***Average need-based gift aid:*** $30,771. ***Average non-need-based aid:*** $21,854. ***Average indebtedness upon graduation:*** $36,804.

APPLYING

Options: electronic application, early admission, early decision, early action, deferred entrance.

Required: essay or personal statement, high school transcript, 2 letters of recommendation. ***Recommended:*** minimum 3.0 GPA, interview.

CONTACT

Wells College, 170 Main Street, Aurora, NY 13026. *Toll-free phone:* 800-952-9355.

Yeshiva and Kolel Bais Medrash Elyon
Monsey, New York

CONTACT
Yeshiva and Kolel Bais Medrash Elyon, 73 Main Street, Monsey, NY 10952.

Yeshiva and Kollel Harbotzas Torah
Brooklyn, New York

CONTACT
Yeshiva and Kollel Harbotzas Torah, 1049 East 15th Street, Brooklyn, NY 11230.

Yeshiva Derech Chaim
Brooklyn, New York

CONTACT
Yeshiva Derech Chaim, 1573 39th Street, Brooklyn, NY 11218.

Yeshiva D'Monsey Rabbinical College
Monsey, New York

CONTACT
Yeshiva D'Monsey Rabbinical College, 2 Roman Boulevard, Monsey, NY 10952.

Yeshiva Gedolah Imrei Yosef D'Spinka
Brooklyn, New York

CONTACT
Yeshiva Gedolah Imrei Yosef D'Spinka, 1466 56th Street, Brooklyn, NY 11219.

Yeshiva Gedolah Kesser Torah
Monsey, New York

CONTACT
Yeshiva Gedolah Kesser Torah, 28 Cedar Lane, Monsey, NY 10952.

Yeshiva Gedola Ohr Yisrael
Brooklyn, New York
http://www.ohryisroel.org/

CONTACT
Yeshiva Gedola Ohr Yisrael, 2899 Nostrand Avenue, Brooklyn, NY 11229.

Yeshiva Karlin Stolin
Brooklyn, New York

CONTACT
Director of Admissions, Yeshiva Karlin Stolin, 1818 54th Street, Brooklyn, NY 11204. *Phone:* 718-232-7800 Ext. 26.

Yeshiva Kollel Tifereth Elizer
Brooklyn, New York

CONTACT
Yeshiva Kollel Tifereth Elizer, 1227 47th Street, Brooklyn, NY 11219.

Yeshiva of Far Rockaway Derech Ayson Rabbinical Seminary
Far Rockaway, New York
http://www.yofr.org/

CONTACT
Yeshiva of Far Rockaway Derech Ayson Rabbinical Seminary, 802 Hicksville Road, Far Rockaway, NY 11691.

Yeshiva of Machzikai Hadas
Brooklyn, New York

CONTACT
Yeshiva of Machzikai Hadas, 1321 43rd Street, Brooklyn, NY 11219.

Yeshiva of Nitra Rabbinical College
Mount Kisco, New York

CONTACT
Administrator, Yeshiva of Nitra Rabbinical College, Croton Lake Road, Mount Kisco, NY 10549. *Phone:* 718-384-5460. *Fax:* 718-387-9400.

Yeshiva of the Telshe Alumni
Riverdale, New York

CONTACT
Yeshiva of the Telshe Alumni, 4904 Independence Avenue, Riverdale, NY 10471.

Yeshiva Ohr Naftoli
New Windsor, New York
http://www.yeshivaohrnaftoli.com/

CONTACT
Yeshiva Ohr Naftoli, 701 Blooming Grove Turnpike, New Windsor, NY 12553.

Yeshiva Shaarei Torah of Rockland
Suffern, New York

CONTACT
Yeshiva Shaarei Torah of Rockland, 91 West Carlton Road, Suffern, NY 10901.

Yeshiva Shaar Ephraim
Monsey, New York

CONTACT
Yeshiva Shaar Ephraim, 178 Maple Avenue, Monsey, NY 10952.

Yeshiva Shaar Hatorah Talmudic Research Institute
Kew Gardens, New York

CONTACT
Assistant Dean, Yeshiva Shaar Hatorah Talmudic Research Institute, 117-06 84th Avenue, Kew Gardens, NY 11418-1469. *Phone:* 718-846-1940.

Yeshivas Maharit D'Satmar
Monroe, New York
http://www.yeshivasmaharit.com/

CONTACT
Yeshivas Maharit D'Satmar, 475 County Route 105, Monroe, NY 10950.

Yeshivas Novominsk
Brooklyn, New York

CONTACT
Yeshivas Novominsk, 1569 47th Street, Brooklyn, NY 11219.

Yeshivath Viznitz
Monsey, New York

CONTACT
Registrar, Yeshivath Viznitz, 15 Elyon Road, Monsey, NY 10952. *Phone:* 914-356-1010.

Yeshivath Zichron Moshe
South Fallsburg, New York

CONTACT
Rabbi Abba Gorelick, Dean, Yeshivath Zichron Moshe, Laurel Park Road, South Fallsburg, NY 12779. *Phone:* 914-434-5240.

Yeshivat Mikdash Melech
Brooklyn, New York

CONTACT
Rabbi S. Beyda, Director of Admissions, Yeshivat Mikdash Melech, 1326 Ocean Parkway, Brooklyn, NY 11230-5601. *Phone:* 718-339-1090. *E-mail:* mikdashmelech@verizon.net.

Yeshiva University
New York, New York
http://www.yu.edu/

CONTACT
Yeshiva University, 500 West 185th Street, New York, NY 10033-3201. *Phone:* 212-960-5277.

Yeshiva Zichron Aryeh
Far Rockaway, New York
http://www.yeshivazichronaryeh.com/

CONTACT
Yeshiva Zichron Aryeh, 1213 Bay 25th Street, Far Rockaway, NY 11691.

York College of the City University of New York
Jamaica, New York
http://www.york.cuny.edu/

CONTACT
Dr. La Toro Yates, Director of Admissions, York College of the City University of New York, 94-20 Guy R. Brewer Boulevard, Jamaica, NY 11451. *Phone:* 718-262-2165. *Fax:* 718-262-2601. *E-mail:* lyates@york.cuny.edu.

NORTH CAROLINA

Apex School of Theology
Durham, North Carolina
http://www.apexsot.edu/

CONTACT
Dr. Henry D. Wells Jr., Registrar, Apex School of Theology, 1701 T.W. Alexander Drive, Durham, NC 27703. *Phone:* 919-572-1625. *Fax:* 919-572-1762. *E-mail:* registrar@apexsot.edu.

Appalachian State University
Boone, North Carolina
http://www.appstate.edu/

- **State-supported** comprehensive, founded 1899, part of University of North Carolina System
- **Small-town** 489-acre campus
- **Endowment** $122.4 million
- **Coed** 17,381 undergraduate students, 94% full-time, 56% women, 44% men
- **Moderately difficult** entrance level, 69% of applicants were admitted

UNDERGRAD STUDENTS
16,421 full-time, 960 part-time. Students come from 46 states and territories; 61 other countries; 8% are from out of state; 3% Black or African American, non-Hispanic/Latino; 6% Hispanic/Latino; 2% Asian, non-Hispanic/Latino; 0.1% Native Hawaiian or other Pacific Islander, non-Hispanic/Latino; 0.3% American Indian or Alaska Native, non-Hispanic/Latino; 4% Two or more races, non-Hispanic/Latino; 1% Race/ethnicity unknown; 0.8% international; 9% transferred in; 33% live on campus.

Freshmen:
Admission: 16,154 applied, 11,221 admitted, 3,445 enrolled. ***Average high school GPA:*** 4.3. ***Test scores:*** SAT evidence-based reading and writing scores over 500: 97%; SAT math scores over 500: 96%; ACT scores over 18: 100%; SAT evidence-based reading and writing scores over 600: 52%; SAT math scores over 600: 44%; ACT scores over 24: 71%; SAT evidence-based reading and writing scores over 700: 5%; SAT math scores over 700: 5%; ACT scores over 30: 13%.

Retention: 87% of full-time freshmen returned.

FACULTY
Total: 1,392, 72% full-time, 92% with terminal degrees.
Student/faculty ratio: 16:1.

ACADEMICS
Calendar: semesters. *Degrees:* bachelor's, master's, doctoral, post-master's, and postbachelor's certificates.

Special study options: academic remediation for entering students, adult/continuing education programs, advanced placement credit, distance learning, double majors, English as a second language, honors programs, independent study, internships, off-campus study, part-time degree program, services for LD students, student-designed majors, study abroad, summer session for credit. ***ROTC:*** Army (b).

Unusual degree programs: 3-2 engineering with Auburn University, Clemson University, North Carolina State University.

Computers: 2,280 computers/terminals are available on campus for general student use. Students can access the following: campus intranet, computer help desk, free student e-mail accounts, online (class) grades, online (class) registration, online (class) schedules. Campuswide network is available. 100% of college-owned or -operated housing units are wired for high-speed Internet access. Wireless service is available via entire campus.
Library: Carol Grotnes Belk Library plus 1 other. *Books:* 666,451 (physical), 831,648 (digital/electronic); *Serial titles:* 12,785 (physical), 161,860 (digital/electronic); *Databases:* 447. Weekly public service hours: 137; students can reserve study rooms.

STUDENT LIFE
Housing options: on-campus residence required for freshman year; coed, women-only, special housing for students with disabilities. Campus housing is university owned. Freshman campus housing is guaranteed.

Activities and organizations: drama/theater group, student-run newspaper, radio and television station, choral group, marching band, Appalachian Educators, Exercise Science Club, App Sits Meditation Club, The Hiking Club, Gaming Club, national fraternities, national sororities.

Athletics Member NCAA, NAIA. All NCAA Division I except football (Division I-A). ***Intercollegiate sports:*** archery M(c)/W(c), baseball M(s), basketball M(s)/W(s), cross-country running M(s)/W(s), equestrian sports W(c), fencing M(c)/W(c), field hockey W(s), golf M(s)/W(s)(c), ice hockey M(c)/W(c), lacrosse M(c)/W(c), rock climbing M(c)/W(c), rugby M(c)/W(c), skiing (downhill) W(c), soccer M(s)/W(s), softball W(s), swimming and diving M(c)/W(c), tennis M(s)/W(s), track and field

M(s)/W(s), triathlon M(c)/W(c), ultimate Frisbee M(c)/W(c), volleyball M(c)/W(s), wrestling M(s). ***Intramural sports:*** badminton M/W, basketball M/W, bowling M/W, cross-country running M/W, golf M/W, racquetball M/W, soccer M/W, softball M/W, swimming and diving M/W, table tennis M/W, tennis M/W, ultimate Frisbee M/W, volleyball M/W, weight lifting M/W.

Campus security: 24-hour emergency response devices and patrols, late-night transport/escort service, controlled dormitory access.

Student services: health clinic, personal/psychological counseling, women's center, legal services, veterans affairs office.

COSTS & FINANCIAL AID

Costs (2018–19) ***Tuition:*** state resident $4242 full-time, $143 per credit hour part-time; nonresident $19,049 full-time, $644 per credit hour part-time. Part-time tuition and fees vary according to course load. No tuition increase for student's term of enrollment. ***Required fees:*** $3122 full-time, $104 per credit hour part-time. ***Room and board:*** $8304; room only: $4470. Room and board charges vary according to board plan and housing facility. ***Payment plan:*** installment. ***Waivers:*** employees or children of employees.

Financial Aid Of all full-time matriculated undergraduates who enrolled in 2018, 11,742 applied for aid, 8,837 were judged to have need, 1,129 had their need fully met. In 2018, 568 non-need-based awards were made. ***Average percent of need met:*** 61. ***Average financial aid package:*** $9717. ***Average need-based loan:*** $4144. ***Average need-based gift aid:*** $8335. ***Average non-need-based aid:*** $3656. ***Average indebtedness upon graduation:*** $23,230.

APPLYING

Standardized Tests *Required:* SAT or ACT (for admission).

Options: electronic application, early action, deferred entrance.

Application fee: $65.

Required: high school transcript. ***Recommended:*** essay or personal statement.

Application deadlines: 3/1 (freshmen), 3/1 (out-of-state freshmen), rolling (transfers), 11/1 (early action).

Notification: continuous until 1/25 (freshmen), continuous until 1/25 (out-of-state freshmen), continuous (transfers), 1/25 (early action).

CONTACT

Mr. Alexis Pope, Director of Admissions, Appalachian State University, ASU Box 32004, Boone, NC 28608. *Phone:* 828-262-2120. *Fax:* 828-262-3296. *E-mail:* admissions@appstate.edu.

Barton College

Wilson, North Carolina

http://www.barton.edu/

- **Independent** comprehensive, founded 1902, affiliated with Christian Church (Disciples of Christ)
- **Small-town** 76-acre campus with easy access to Raleigh-Durham
- **Endowment** $29.1 million
- **Coed** 976 undergraduate students, 95% full-time, 63% women, 37% men
- **Minimally difficult** entrance level, 40% of applicants were admitted

UNDERGRAD STUDENTS

932 full-time, 44 part-time. Students come from 34 states and territories; 25 other countries; 24% are from out of state; 20% Black or African American, non-Hispanic/Latino; 9% Hispanic/Latino; 1% Asian, non-Hispanic/Latino; 0.8% American Indian or Alaska Native, non-Hispanic/Latino; 3% Two or more races, non-Hispanic/Latino; 4% Race/ethnicity unknown; 5% international; 6% transferred in; 51% live on campus.

Freshmen:

Admission: 3,486 applied, 1,381 admitted, 277 enrolled. ***Average high school GPA:*** 3.2. ***Test scores:*** SAT evidence-based reading and writing scores over 500: 62%; SAT math scores over 500: 56%; ACT scores over 18: 75%; SAT evidence-based reading and writing scores over 600: 17%; SAT math scores over 600: 13%; ACT scores over 24: 21%; SAT math scores over 700: 1%; ACT scores over 30: 1%.

Retention: 72% of full-time freshmen returned.

FACULTY

Total: 128, 56% full-time, 55% with terminal degrees.

Student/faculty ratio: 10:1.

ACADEMICS

Calendar: semesters. *Degrees:* bachelor's and master's.

Special study options: academic remediation for entering students, accelerated degree program, adult/continuing education programs, advanced placement credit, distance learning, double majors, honors programs, independent study, internships, part-time degree program, services for LD students, student-designed majors, study abroad, summer session for credit.

Unusual degree programs: 3-2 business administration.

Computers: Students can access the following: campus intranet, computer help desk, free student e-mail accounts, online (class) grades, online (class) registration, online (class) schedules. Campuswide network is available. 100% of college-owned or -operated housing units are wired for high-speed Internet access. Wireless service is available via classrooms, computer centers, computer labs, learning centers, libraries, student centers.

Library: Willis N. Hackney Library. *Books:* 121,046 (physical), 421,508 (digital/electronic); *Serial titles:* 88,792 (digital/electronic); *Databases:* 160. Weekly public service hours: 96; students can reserve study rooms.

STUDENT LIFE

Housing options: on-campus residence required through sophomore year; coed. Campus housing is university owned and leased by the school. Freshman campus housing is guaranteed.

Activities and organizations: drama/theater group, student-run newspaper, radio and television station, choral group, Student Ambassador Program, Barton College Association of Nursing, Barton College Orientation Team, Barton College Catholic Campus Ministries, Minority Student Association, national fraternities, national sororities.

Athletics Member NCAA. All Division II. ***Intercollegiate sports:*** baseball M(s), basketball M(s)/W(s), cheerleading W(s)(c), cross-country running M(s)/W(s), golf M(s)/W(s), lacrosse M(s)/W(s), soccer M(s)/W(s), softball W(s), swimming and diving M(s)/W(s), tennis M(s)/W(s), track and field M(s)/W(s), volleyball M(s)/W(s). ***Intramural sports:*** basketball M/W, football M/W, soccer M/W, softball M/W, volleyball M/W.

Campus security: 24-hour emergency response devices and patrols, late-night transport/escort service, controlled dormitory access.

Student services: health clinic, personal/psychological counseling, women's center, veterans affairs office.

COSTS & FINANCIAL AID

Costs (2019–20) ***Comprehensive fee:*** $42,150 includes full-time tuition ($31,730) and room and board ($10,420). ***College room only:*** $4500.

Financial Aid Of all full-time matriculated undergraduates who enrolled in 2018, 835 applied for aid, 789 were judged to have need, 93 had their need fully met. 186 Federal Work-Study jobs (averaging $800). In 2018, 117 non-need-based awards were made. ***Average percent of need met:*** 65. ***Average financial aid package:*** $23,908. ***Average need-based loan:*** $3752. ***Average need-based gift aid:*** $20,020. ***Average non-need-based aid:*** $11,940. ***Average indebtedness upon graduation:*** $25,529.

APPLYING

Standardized Tests *Required:* SAT or ACT (for admission).

Options: electronic application.

Required for some: high school transcript.

Application deadlines: rolling (freshmen), rolling (transfers).

Notification: continuous (freshmen), continuous (transfers).

CONTACT

Mrs. Amanda Metts, Assistant Vice President for Enrollment Management, Barton College, PO Box 5000, Wilson, NC 27893-7000. *Phone:* 800-345-4973. *Toll-free phone:* 800-345-4973. *Fax:* 252-399-6572. *E-mail:* ahmetts@barton.edu.

Belmont Abbey College

Belmont, North Carolina

http://www.belmontabbeycollege.edu/

CONTACT

Ms. Nicole Focareto, Executive Director of Admissions, Belmont Abbey College, 100 Belmont-Mt. Holly Road, Belmont, NC 28012. *Phone:* 704-461-6214. *Toll-free phone:* 888-BAC-0110. *Fax:* 704-461-6220. *E-mail:* nicolefocareto@bac.edu.

Bennett College

Greensboro, North Carolina

http://www.bennett.edu/

- **Independent United Methodist** 4-year, founded 1873
- **Urban** 60-acre campus
- **Endowment** $12.6 million
- **Women only** 534 undergraduate students, 87% full-time
- **Minimally difficult** entrance level, 96% of applicants were admitted

UNDERGRAD STUDENTS

463 full-time, 71 part-time. Students come from 28 states and territories; 5 other countries; 50% are from out of state; 85% Black or African American, non-Hispanic/Latino; 2% Hispanic/Latino; 0.2% Asian, non-Hispanic/Latino; 4% Two or more races, non-Hispanic/Latino; 7% Race/ethnicity unknown; 0.9% international; 1% transferred in; 69% live on campus.

Freshmen:

Admission: 3,938 applied, 3,794 admitted, 237 enrolled. ***Test scores:*** SAT evidence-based reading and writing scores over 500: 33%; SAT math scores over 500: 20%; ACT scores over 18: 39%; SAT evidence-based reading and writing scores over 600: 3%; SAT math scores over 600: 2%; ACT scores over 24: 8%.

Retention: 53% of full-time freshmen returned.

FACULTY

Total: 61, 59% full-time, 62% with terminal degrees.

Student/faculty ratio: 10:1.

ACADEMICS

Calendar: semesters. *Degree:* bachelor's.

Special study options: academic remediation for entering students, advanced placement credit, cooperative education, distance learning, double majors, English as a second language, honors programs, independent study, internships, off-campus study, part-time degree program, services for LD students, student-designed majors, study abroad, summer session for credit. ***ROTC:*** Army (c), Air Force (c).

Unusual degree programs: 3-2 engineering with North Carolina Agricultural and Technical State University.

Computers: 225 computers/terminals are available on campus for general student use. Students can access the following: campus intranet, computer help desk, free student e-mail accounts, online (class) grades, online (class) registration, online (class) schedules, wireless capability is in all buildings except Steele and Shell halls. Campuswide network is available. 100% of college-owned or -operated housing units are wired for high-speed Internet access. Wireless service is available via entire campus.

Library: Holgate Library. *Books:* 79,536 (physical), 203,358 (digital/electronic); *Serial titles:* 22 (physical), 22,014 (digital/electronic); *Databases:* 143. Weekly public service hours: 83.

STUDENT LIFE

Housing options: on-campus residence required through sophomore year; women-only. Campus housing is university owned. Freshman campus housing is guaranteed.

Activities and organizations: drama/theater group, choral group, national sororities.

Campus security: 24-hour emergency response devices and patrols, late-night transport/escort service, controlled dormitory access, alerts and educational programs are offered.

Student services: health clinic, personal/psychological counseling.

COSTS & FINANCIAL AID

Costs (2018–19) ***One-time required fee:*** $225. ***Comprehensive fee:*** $26,627 includes full-time tuition ($15,964), mandatory fees ($2549), and room and board ($8114). Full-time tuition and fees vary according to course load. Part-time tuition: $665 per credit hour. Part-time tuition and fees vary according to course load. ***Required fees:*** $1067 per term part-time. ***College room only:*** $4040. Room and board charges vary according to board plan. ***Payment plan:*** installment. ***Waivers:*** employees or children of employees.

Financial Aid Of all full-time matriculated undergraduates who enrolled in 2011, 664 applied for aid, 643 were judged to have need, 22 had their need fully met. In 2011, 7 non-need-based awards were made. ***Average percent of need met:*** 47. ***Average financial aid package:*** $13,092. ***Average need-based loan:*** $4170. ***Average need-based gift aid:*** $9402. ***Average non-need-based aid:*** $4714. ***Financial aid deadline:*** 3/15.

APPLYING

Standardized Tests *Required:* SAT or ACT (for admission).

Options: electronic application, deferred entrance.

Application fee: $35.

Required: high school transcript, minimum 2.5 GPA, 2 letters of recommendation. ***Recommended:*** essay or personal statement.

Application deadlines: rolling (freshmen), rolling (transfers).

CONTACT

Mr. James Crawford, Director, Admissions, Bennett College, 900 East Washington Street, Enrollment Management Center, Greensboro, NC 27401. *Phone:* 336-517-1818. *Toll-free phone:* 800-413-5323. *E-mail:* jcrawford@bennett.edu.

Brevard College

Brevard, North Carolina

http://www.brevard.edu/

CONTACT

Mr. David Volrath, Admissions, Brevard College, One Brevard College Drive, Brevard, NC 28712. *Phone:* 828-884-8367. *Toll-free phone:* 800-527-9090. *Fax:* 828-884-3790. *E-mail:* admissions@brevard.edu.

Cabarrus College of Health Sciences

Concord, North Carolina

http://www.cabarruscollege.edu/

CONTACT

McKenzie Allen, Admissions Representative, Cabarrus College of Health Sciences, 401 Medical Park Drive, Concord, NC 28025-2077. *Phone:* 704-403-2589. *Fax:* 704-403-2077. *E-mail:* mckenzie.allen@cabarruscollege.edu.

Campbell University

Buies Creek, North Carolina

http://www.campbell.edu/

CONTACT

Ms. Peggy Mason, Director of Admissions, Campbell University, PO Box 546, 450 Leslie Campbell Avenue, Buies Creek, NC 27506. *Phone:* 910-893-1290. *Toll-free phone:* 800-334-4111. *Fax:* 910-893-1288. *E-mail:* adm@mailcenter.campbell.edu.

Carolina Christian College

Winston-Salem, North Carolina

http://www.carolina.edu/

- **Independent nondenominational** comprehensive, founded 1945
- **Small-town** 2-acre campus
- **Endowment** $250,000
- **Coed**
- **Noncompetitive** entrance level

FACULTY

Student/faculty ratio: 11:1.

ACADEMICS
Calendar: semesters. *Degrees:* associate, bachelor's, and master's.
Library: Aubrey Payne. *Books:* 14,200 (physical), 3,900 (digital/electronic); *Serial titles:* 1,006 (digital/electronic); *Databases:* 4. Weekly public service hours: 2.

STUDENT LIFE
Housing options: college housing not available.

Athletics Member NCCAA. except basketball (Division I-AA)

Campus security: 24-hour emergency response devices.

Student services: personal/psychological counseling.

COSTS & FINANCIAL AID
Costs (2018–19) ***One-time required fee:*** $75. ***Tuition:*** $12,500 full-time, $2750 per term part-time. ***Required fees:*** $1450 full-time, $600 per term part-time.

Financial Aid Of all full-time matriculated undergraduates who enrolled in 2018, 62 applied for aid, 62 were judged to have need, 56 had their need fully met. ***Average percent of need met:*** 95. ***Average financial aid package:*** $10,590. ***Average need-based gift aid:*** $2500.

APPLYING
Options: electronic application.

Application fee: $50.

Required: essay or personal statement, high school transcript, 2 letters of recommendation, interview.

CONTACT
Garriell Lucas, Admission Officer, Carolina Christian College, 4209 Indiana Avenue, Winston-Salem, NC 27105. *Phone:* 336-744-0900.

Carolina College of Biblical Studies

Fayetteville, North Carolina

http://carolinabiblecollege.org/

CONTACT
Carolina College of Biblical Studies, 817 South McPherson Church Road, Fayetteville, NC 28303.

Catawba College

Salisbury, North Carolina

http://www.catawba.edu/

- **Independent** comprehensive, founded 1851, affiliated with United Church of Christ
- **Small-town** 276-acre campus with easy access to Charlotte, NC
- **Endowment** $61.9 million
- **Coed**
- **Moderately difficult** entrance level

FACULTY
Student/faculty ratio: 12:1.

ACADEMICS
Calendar: semesters. *Degrees:* bachelor's and master's.
Library: Corriher-Linn-Black Memorial Library plus 1 other. *Books:* 149,877 (physical), 228,252 (digital/electronic); *Serial titles:* 12,505 (physical), 112,726 (digital/electronic); *Databases:* 100. Weekly public service hours: 83; students can reserve study rooms.

STUDENT LIFE
Housing options: on-campus residence required for freshman year; coed, men-only, women-only. Campus housing is university owned. Freshman campus housing is guaranteed.

Activities and organizations: drama/theater group, student-run newspaper, radio station, choral group, marching band, Volunteer Catawba, Catawba Ambassadors (admissions guides), Blue Masque (drama), Fellowship of Christian Athletes, Wigwam Productions (student activities board).

Athletics Member NCAA. All Division II.

Campus security: 24-hour emergency response devices and patrols, late-night transport/escort service, controlled dormitory access.

Student services: health clinic, personal/psychological counseling.

COSTS & FINANCIAL AID
Costs (2018–19) ***Comprehensive fee:*** $41,008 includes full-time tuition ($30,520) and room and board ($10,488). Full-time tuition and fees vary according to class time, course load, and degree level. Part-time tuition: $816 per credit hour. Part-time tuition and fees vary according to class time, course load, and degree level. ***College room only:*** $6188.

Financial Aid Of all full-time matriculated undergraduates who enrolled in 2017, 1,118 applied for aid, 1,034 were judged to have need, 278 had their need fully met. 105 Federal Work-Study jobs (averaging $1464). 118 state and other part-time jobs (averaging $1314). In 2017, 186 non-need-based awards were made. ***Average percent of need met:*** 78. ***Average financial aid package:*** $25,663. ***Average need-based loan:*** $4134. ***Average need-based gift aid:*** $7357. ***Average non-need-based aid:*** $16,065. ***Average indebtedness upon graduation:*** $29,836.

APPLYING
Options: electronic application, early admission, deferred entrance.

Required: essay or personal statement, high school transcript, minimum 2.0 GPA, 2 letters of recommendation. ***Recommended:*** interview.

CONTACT
Catawba College, 2300 West Innes Street, Salisbury, NC 28144-2488. *Phone:* 704-645-4584. *Toll-free phone:* 800-CATAWBA.

Chamberlain College of Nursing

Charlotte, North Carolina

http://www.chamberlain.edu/

CONTACT
Chamberlain College of Nursing, 2015 Ayrsley Town Boulevard, Charlotte, NC 28273.

Charlotte Christian College and Theological Seminary

Charlotte, North Carolina

http://www.charlottechristian.edu/

- **Independent Christian** comprehensive, founded 1996
- **Urban** 3-acre campus with easy access to Charlotte, NC
- **Coed**

FACULTY
Student/faculty ratio: 5:1.

ACADEMICS
Calendar: quarters. *Degrees:* associate, bachelor's, master's, and doctoral.
Library: CCCTS Library. *Books:* 26,489 (physical), 1,100 (digital/electronic); *Serial titles:* 30 (physical). Weekly public service hours: 50.

STUDENT LIFE
Housing options: college housing not available.

Campus security: 24-hour emergency response devices.

Student services: veterans affairs office.

COSTS & FINANCIAL AID
Costs (2018–19) ***Tuition:*** $10,048 full-time, $454 per credit hour part-time. Full-time tuition and fees vary according to course load and program. Part-time tuition and fees vary according to course load and program. No tuition increase for student's term of enrollment. ***Required fees:*** $420 full-time, $420 per year part-time.

Financial Aid Of all full-time matriculated undergraduates who enrolled in 2017, 16 applied for aid, 16 were judged to have need, 16 had their need fully met. 2 Federal Work-Study jobs (averaging $2364). ***Average percent of need met:*** 100. ***Average financial aid package:*** $7652. ***Average need-based loan:*** $3500. ***Average need-based gift aid:*** $5920. ***Average indebtedness upon graduation:*** $33,034.

APPLYING
Options: electronic application.

Application fee: $50.

Required: essay or personal statement, high school transcript, letters of recommendation, certification of Church membership and involvement.

CONTACT
Mr. George Shears, Director of Admissions, Charlotte Christian College and Theological Seminary, P.O. Box 790106, Charlotte, NC 28206. *Phone:* 704-334-6882 Ext. 115. *Fax:* 704-334-6885. *E-mail:* gshears@charlottechristian.edu.

Chowan University
Murfreesboro, North Carolina
http://www.chowan.edu/

- **Independent Baptist** comprehensive, founded 1848
- **Small-town** 300-acre campus with easy access to Norfolk
- **Endowment** $26.1 million
- **Coed**
- **Minimally difficult** entrance level

FACULTY
Student/faculty ratio: 16:1.

ACADEMICS
Calendar: semesters. *Degrees:* associate, bachelor's, and master's.
Library: Whitaker Library plus 1 other. *Books:* 163,497 (physical), 405,678 (digital/electronic); *Serial titles:* 1,310 (physical), 69,556 (digital/electronic); *Databases:* 135. Weekly public service hours: 84; students can reserve study rooms.

STUDENT LIFE
Housing options: on-campus residence required through sophomore year; men-only, women-only. Campus housing is university owned. Freshman campus housing is guaranteed.

Activities and organizations: drama/theater group, student-run newspaper, choral group, Honors Societies, Rotaract, Campus Ministry, Psychology Club, Science Club, national fraternities, national sororities.

Athletics Member NCAA, NCCAA. All NCAA Division II.

Campus security: 24-hour emergency response devices and patrols, late-night transport/escort service, controlled dormitory access.

Student services: health clinic, personal/psychological counseling, veterans affairs office.

COSTS & FINANCIAL AID
Costs (2018–19) ***Comprehensive fee:*** $34,380 includes full-time tuition ($24,980) and room and board ($9400). Full-time tuition and fees vary according to degree level. Part-time tuition: $400 per credit hour. Part-time tuition and fees vary according to degree level. ***Room and board:*** Room and board charges vary according to board plan.

Financial Aid Of all full-time matriculated undergraduates who enrolled in 2018, 1,305 applied for aid, 1,269 were judged to have need, 152 had their need fully met. 285 Federal Work-Study jobs (averaging $1430). 356 state and other part-time jobs (averaging $3169). In 2018, 88 non-need-based awards were made. ***Average percent of need met:*** 70. ***Average financial aid package:*** $22,274. ***Average need-based loan:*** $3999. ***Average need-based gift aid:*** $20,359. ***Average non-need-based aid:*** $7940. ***Average indebtedness upon graduation:*** $35,882.

APPLYING
Standardized Tests *Required:* SAT or ACT (for admission).

Options: electronic application.

Application fee: $20.

Required: high school transcript. ***Required for some:*** essay or personal statement, interview. ***Recommended:*** minimum 2.0 GPA, 2 letters of recommendation.

CONTACT
Mr. Scott Parker, Director of Admissions Information, Chowan University, One University Place, Murfreesboro, NC 27855. *Phone:* 252-398-6314. *Toll-free phone:* 888-4-CHOWAN. *Fax:* 252-398-1190. *E-mail:* parkes@chowan.edu.

Davidson College
Davidson, North Carolina
http://www.davidson.edu/

- **Independent Presbyterian** 4-year, founded 1837
- **Small-town** 665-acre campus with easy access to Charlotte
- **Endowment** $821.8 million
- **Coed** 1,843 undergraduate students, 100% full-time, 48% women, 52% men
- **Very difficult** entrance level, 20% of applicants were admitted

UNDERGRAD STUDENTS
1,843 full-time. Students come from 48 states and territories; 47 other countries; 78% are from out of state; 7% Black or African American, non-Hispanic/Latino; 8% Hispanic/Latino; 5% Asian, non-Hispanic/Latino; 0.2% Native Hawaiian or other Pacific Islander, non-Hispanic/Latino; 0.5% American Indian or Alaska Native, non-Hispanic/Latino; 4% Two or more races, non-Hispanic/Latino; 1% Race/ethnicity unknown; 7% international; 0.8% transferred in; 95% live on campus.

Freshmen:
Admission: 5,618 applied, 1,130 admitted, 515 enrolled. ***Average high school GPA:*** 3.9. ***Test scores:*** SAT evidence-based reading and writing scores over 500: 99%; SAT math scores over 500: 100%; ACT scores over 18: 100%; SAT evidence-based reading and writing scores over 600: 94%; SAT math scores over 600: 93%; ACT scores over 24: 99%; SAT evidence-based reading and writing scores over 700: 45%; SAT math scores over 700: 44%; ACT scores over 30: 68%.

Retention: 95% of full-time freshmen returned.

FACULTY
Total: 211, 95% full-time, 96% with terminal degrees.

Student/faculty ratio: 10:1.

ACADEMICS
Calendar: semesters. *Degree:* bachelor's.

Special study options: advanced placement credit, double majors, independent study, internships, off-campus study, services for LD students, student-designed majors, study abroad. ***ROTC:*** Army (b).

Unusual degree programs: 3-2 engineering with Columbia University, Washington University in St. Louis.

Computers: Students can access the following: campus intranet, computer help desk, free student e-mail accounts, online (class) grades, online (class) registration, online (class) schedules. Campuswide network is available. 100% of college-owned or -operated housing units are wired for high-speed Internet access. Wireless service is available via entire campus.

Library: E. H. Little Library plus 1 other. *Books:* 484,947 (physical), 1.2 million (digital/electronic); *Serial titles:* 8,359 (physical), 150,122 (digital/electronic); *Databases:* 763. Study areas open 24 hours, 5–7 days a week; students can reserve study rooms.

STUDENT LIFE
Housing options: on-campus residence required through senior year; coed, cooperative. Campus housing is university owned. Freshman campus housing is guaranteed.

Activities and organizations: drama/theater group, student-run newspaper, radio station, choral group, national fraternities, national sororities.

Athletics Member NCAA. All Division I except football (Division I-AA). ***Intercollegiate sports:*** baseball M(s), basketball M(s)/W(s), crew M(c)/W(c), cross-country running M(s)/W(s), fencing M(c)/W(c), field hockey W(s), golf M(s), lacrosse W(s), rugby M(c), sailing M(c)/W(c), soccer M(s)/W(s), squash M(c), swimming and diving M(s)/W(s), tennis M(s)/W(s), track and field M(s)/W(s), ultimate Frisbee M(c)/W(c), volleyball W(s), wrestling M(s). ***Intramural sports:*** baseball M(c), basketball M(c)/W, field hockey W(c), football M/W, golf M(c), lacrosse M(c)/W(c), soccer M(c)/W(c), softball M/W, tennis M(c)/W(c), volleyball M/W(c).

Campus security: 24-hour emergency response devices and patrols, late-night transport/escort service, controlled dormitory access.

Student services: health clinic, personal/psychological counseling, women's center.

COSTS & FINANCIAL AID
Costs (2019–20) ***Comprehensive fee:*** $67,852 includes full-time tuition ($52,524), mandatory fees ($525), and room and board ($14,803). ***College room only:*** $7534.

Financial Aid Of all full-time matriculated undergraduates who enrolled in 2018, 1,085 applied for aid, 918 were judged to have need, 916 had their need fully met. In 2018, 141 non-need-based awards were made. ***Average percent of need met:*** 100. ***Average financial aid package:*** $49,192. ***Average need-based loan:*** $3534. ***Average need-based gift aid:*** $45,442. ***Average non-need-based aid:*** $23,064. ***Average indebtedness upon graduation:*** $22,599. ***Financial aid deadline:*** 2/15.

APPLYING
Standardized Tests *Required:* SAT or ACT (for admission). *Recommended:* SAT and SAT Subject Tests or ACT (for admission).

Options: electronic application, early admission, early decision, deferred entrance.

Application fee: $50.

Required: essay or personal statement, high school transcript, 3 letters of recommendation. ***Recommended:*** interview.

Application deadlines: 1/2 (freshmen), 3/15 (transfers).

Early decision deadline: 11/15 (for plan 1), 1/2 (for plan 2).

Notification: 4/1 (freshmen), 5/15 (transfers), 12/15 (early decision plan 1), 2/1 (early decision plan 2).

CONTACT
Mr. Christopher J. Gruber, Vice President and Dean of Admission and Financial Aid, Davidson College, Box 7156, Davidson, NC 28035-7156. *Phone:* 704-894-2230. *Toll-free phone:* 800-768-0380. *Fax:* 704-894-2016. *E-mail:* admission@davidson.edu.

DeVry University–Charlotte Campus

Charlotte, North Carolina

http://www.devry.edu/

CONTACT
Admissions Office, DeVry University–Charlotte Campus, 2015 Ayrsley Town Boulevard, Suite 109, Charlotte, NC 28273-4068. *Phone:* 704-362-2345. *Toll-free phone:* 866-338-7934.

Duke University

Durham, North Carolina

http://www.duke.edu/

- **Independent** university, founded 1838, affiliated with United Methodist Church
- **Suburban** 8500-acre campus
- **Coed**
- **Most difficult** entrance level

FACULTY
Student/faculty ratio: 6:1.

ACADEMICS
Calendar: semesters. *Degrees:* bachelor's, master's, doctoral, post-master's, and postbachelor's certificates.
Library: Perkins Library.

STUDENT LIFE
Housing options: on-campus residence required through junior year; coed, men-only, women-only. Campus housing is university owned. Freshman campus housing is guaranteed.

Activities and organizations: drama/theater group, student-run newspaper, radio and television station, choral group, marching band, national fraternities, national sororities.

Athletics Member NCAA. All Division I except football (Division I-A).

Campus security: 24-hour emergency response devices and patrols, late-night transport/escort service, controlled dormitory access.

Student services: health clinic, personal/psychological counseling, women's center, legal services.

FINANCIAL AID
Financial Aid Of all full-time matriculated undergraduates who enrolled in 2018, 3,622 applied for aid, 3,024 were judged to have need, 3,024 had their need fully met. 1,889 Federal Work-Study jobs (averaging $2052). 622 state and other part-time jobs (averaging $1989). In 2018, 212 non-need-based awards were made. ***Average percent of need met:*** 100. ***Average financial aid package:*** $54,273. ***Average need-based loan:*** $4126. ***Average need-based gift aid:*** $52,700. ***Average non-need-based aid:*** $71,711. ***Average indebtedness upon graduation:*** $21,525.

APPLYING
Standardized Tests *Required:* SAT and SAT Subject Tests or ACT (for admission).

Options: electronic application, early decision.

Application fee: $85.

Required: essay or personal statement, high school transcript. ***Required for some:*** audition tape for dance, drama, or music; slides of work for art. ***Recommended:*** interview.

CONTACT
Mr. Christoph Guttentag, Director of Admissions, Duke University, Durham, NC 27708. *Phone:* 919-684-3214. *E-mail:* askduke@admiss.duke.edu.

East Carolina University

Greenville, North Carolina

http://www.ecu.edu/

- **State-supported** university, founded 1907, part of University of North Carolina System
- **Urban** 1600-acre campus
- **Endowment** $219.4 million
- **Coed** 23,071 undergraduate students, 85% full-time, 57% women, 43% men
- **Moderately difficult** entrance level, 82% of applicants were admitted

UNDERGRAD STUDENTS
19,562 full-time, 3,509 part-time. Students come from 43 states and territories; 58 other countries; 10% are from out of state; 16% Black or African American, non-Hispanic/Latino; 7% Hispanic/Latino; 2% Asian, non-Hispanic/Latino; 0.1% Native Hawaiian or other Pacific Islander, non-Hispanic/Latino; 0.6% American Indian or Alaska Native, non-Hispanic/Latino; 4% Two or more races, non-Hispanic/Latino; 3% Race/ethnicity unknown; 0.6% international; 8% transferred in; 24% live on campus.

Freshmen:
Admission: 17,551 applied, 14,401 admitted, 4,175 enrolled. ***Average high school GPA:*** 3.8. ***Test scores:*** SAT evidence-based reading and writing scores over 500: 88%; SAT math scores over 500: 97%; ACT scores over 18: 94%; SAT evidence-based reading and writing scores over 600: 25%; SAT math scores over 600: 30%; ACT scores over 24: 28%; SAT evidence-based reading and writing scores over 700: 2%; SAT math scores over 700: 2%; ACT scores over 30: 3%.
Retention: 81% of full-time freshmen returned.

FACULTY
Total: 1,510, 80% full-time, 75% with terminal degrees.
Student/faculty ratio: 19:1.

ACADEMICS
Calendar: semesters. *Degrees:* bachelor's, master's, doctoral, post-master's, and postbachelor's certificates.

Special study options: academic remediation for entering students, accelerated degree program, adult/continuing education programs, advanced placement credit, cooperative education, distance learning, double majors, English as a second language, freshman honors college, honors programs, independent study, internships, off-campus study, part-time degree program, services for LD students, student-designed majors, study abroad, summer session for credit. ***ROTC:*** Army (b), Air Force (b).

Unusual degree programs: 3-2 business administration.

Computers: 2,760 computers/terminals and 2,760 ports are available on campus for general student use. Students can access the following: campus intranet, computer help desk, free student e-mail accounts, online (class) grades, online (class) registration, online (class) schedules. Campuswide network is available. 100% of college-owned or -operated housing units are wired for high-speed Internet access. Wireless service is available via entire campus.

Library: Joyner Library plus 2 others. *Books:* 1.0 million (physical), 873,203 (digital/electronic); *Serial titles:* 8,238 (physical), 109,576 (digital/electronic); *Databases:* 456. Weekly public service hours: 142; study areas open 24 hours, 5–7 days a week; students can reserve study rooms.

STUDENT LIFE

Housing options: on-campus residence required for freshman year; coed, women-only, special housing for students with disabilities. Campus housing is university owned. Freshman campus housing is guaranteed.

Activities and organizations: drama/theater group, student-run newspaper, radio and television station, choral group, marching band, Student Government Association, Student Activities Board, Residence Hall Association, Student Pirate Club, Black Student Union, national fraternities, national sororities.

Athletics Member NCAA. All Division I. ***Intercollegiate sports:*** baseball M(s), basketball M(s)/W(s), cross-country running M(s)/W(s), football M(s), golf M(s)/W(s)(c), lacrosse W(s), soccer W(s), softball W(s), swimming and diving M(s)/W(s), tennis M(s)/W(s), track and field M(s)/W(s), volleyball W(s). ***Intramural sports:*** badminton M(c)/W(c), baseball M(c), basketball M/W, bowling M/W, cheerleading W(c), cross-country running M(c)/W(c), equestrian sports M(c)/W(c), fencing M(c)/W(c), field hockey M(c)/W(c), football M/W, golf M(c)/W(c), ice hockey M(c), lacrosse M(c)/W(c), racquetball M/W, rock climbing M(c)/W(c), rugby M(c)/W(c), skiing (downhill) M(c)/W(c), soccer M/W, softball M/W, swimming and diving M(c)/W(c), table tennis M/W, tennis M/W, ultimate Frisbee M(c)/W(c), volleyball M/W, weight lifting M(c)/W(c), wrestling M(c)/W(c).

Campus security: 24-hour emergency response devices and patrols, student patrols, late-night transport/escort service, controlled dormitory access.

Student services: health clinic, personal/psychological counseling, women's center, legal services, veterans affairs office.

COSTS & FINANCIAL AID

Costs (2018–19) ***Tuition:*** state resident $4452 full-time, $247 per credit hour part-time; nonresident $20,729 full-time, $1151 per credit hour part-time. Full-time tuition and fees vary according to location and program. Part-time tuition and fees vary according to course load, location, and program. No tuition increase for student's term of enrollment. ***Required fees:*** $2736 full-time. ***Room and board:*** $10,354; room only: $5722. Room and board charges vary according to board plan and housing facility. ***Payment plans:*** installment, deferred payment. ***Waivers:*** employees or children of employees.

Financial Aid Of all full-time matriculated undergraduates who enrolled in 2018, 14,741 applied for aid, 11,798 were judged to have need, 1,122 had their need fully met. In 2018, 296 non-need-based awards were made. ***Average percent of need met:*** 63. ***Average financial aid package:*** $10,817. ***Average need-based loan:*** $6843. ***Average need-based gift aid:*** $7907. ***Average non-need-based aid:*** $3949. ***Average indebtedness upon graduation:*** $29,646.

APPLYING

Standardized Tests *Required:* SAT or ACT (for admission).

Options: electronic application, deferred entrance.

Application fee: $75.

Required: high school transcript, minimum 2.5 GPA.

Notification: continuous (freshmen), continuous (transfers).

CONTACT

Dr. Heidi Puckett, Interim Director of Admissions, East Carolina University, East 5th Street, Greenville, NC 27858-4353. *Phone:* 252-328-6444. *E-mail:* puckettth14@ecu.edu.

Elizabeth City State University

Elizabeth City, North Carolina

http://www.ecsu.edu/

- **State-supported** comprehensive, founded 1891, part of University of North Carolina System
- **Small-town** 200-acre campus with easy access to Norfolk
- **Endowment** $6.0 million
- **Coed** 1,636 undergraduate students, 87% full-time, 57% women, 43% men
- **Moderately difficult** entrance level, 59% of applicants were admitted

UNDERGRAD STUDENTS

1,425 full-time, 211 part-time. Students come from 25 states and territories; 5 other countries; 15% are from out of state; 70% Black or African American, non-Hispanic/Latino; 4% Hispanic/Latino; 0.6% Asian, non-Hispanic/Latino; 0.1% Native Hawaiian or other Pacific Islander, non-Hispanic/Latino; 0.5% American Indian or Alaska Native, non-Hispanic/Latino; 4% Two or more races, non-Hispanic/Latino; 3% Race/ethnicity unknown; 0.3% international; 7% transferred in; 51% live on campus.

Freshmen:

Admission: 2,461 applied, 1,462 admitted, 418 enrolled. ***Average high school GPA:*** 3.2. ***Test scores:*** ACT scores over 18: 49%; ACT scores over 24: 5%.

Retention: 72% of full-time freshmen returned.

FACULTY

Total: 135, 86% full-time, 100% with terminal degrees.

Student/faculty ratio: 14:1.

ACADEMICS

Calendar: semesters. *Degrees:* bachelor's and master's.

Special study options: academic remediation for entering students, adult/continuing education programs, advanced placement credit, cooperative education, distance learning, double majors, honors programs, independent study, internships, off-campus study, part-time degree program, services for LD students, study abroad, summer session for credit. ***ROTC:*** Army (b).

Computers: Students can access the following: campus intranet, computer help desk, free student e-mail accounts, online (class) registration, online (class) schedules. Campuswide network is available. Wireless service is available via entire campus.

Library: G. R. Little Library plus 1 other. *Books:* 231,406 (physical), 184,579 (digital/electronic); *Serial titles:* 1,923 (physical), 22,828 (digital/electronic); *Databases:* 101. Weekly public service hours: 82.

STUDENT LIFE

Housing options: coed, men-only, women-only. Campus housing is university owned and leased by the school. Freshman campus housing is guaranteed.

Activities and organizations: drama/theater group, student-run newspaper, choral group, marching band, Vans (Vikings Assisting New Students), Student Activities Committee, Vike Nu' Fashion Troupe, Pep Squad, Essence of Praise, national fraternities, national sororities.

Athletics Member NCAA. All Division II. ***Intercollegiate sports:*** basketball M(s)/W(s), bowling W(s), cheerleading W, cross-country running M/W, football M(s), golf M(s), softball W(s), tennis W(s), volleyball W(s).

Campus security: 24-hour emergency response devices and patrols, controlled dormitory access.

Student services: health clinic, personal/psychological counseling.

COSTS & FINANCIAL AID

Costs (2019–20) ***Tuition:*** area resident $500 full-time; state resident $500 full-time; nonresident $2500 full-time. No tuition increase for student's term of enrollment. ***Required fees:*** $3110 full-time. ***Room and board:*** $9991.

Financial Aid Of all full-time matriculated undergraduates who enrolled in 2017, 1,105 applied for aid, 1,105 were judged to have need. ***Average percent of need met:*** 62. ***Average financial aid package:*** $7742. ***Average need-based gift aid:*** $3884. ***Average indebtedness upon graduation:*** $19,631. ***Financial aid deadline:*** 6/1.

APPLYING
Standardized Tests *Required:* SAT or ACT (for admission).
Options: electronic application, deferred entrance.
Application fee: $30.
Required: high school transcript, minimum 2.3 GPA.

CONTACT
Mr. Darius Eure, Assistant Director, Admissions and Recruitment, Elizabeth City State University, 131 Marion D. Thorpe Administration Building Box 901, 1704 Weeksville Road, Elizabeth City, NC 27909. *Phone:* 252-335-8530. *Toll-free phone:* 800-347-3278. *Fax:* 252-335-3537. *E-mail:* ddeure@ecsu.edu.

Elon University

Elon, North Carolina

http://www.elon.edu/

- **Independent** comprehensive, founded 1889, affiliated with United Church of Christ
- **Suburban** 656-acre campus with easy access to Raleigh
- **Endowment** $230.4 million
- **Coed**
- **Moderately difficult** entrance level

FACULTY
Student/faculty ratio: 12:1.

ACADEMICS
Calendar: semesters 3-week winter term. *Degrees:* bachelor's, master's, and doctoral.
Library: Carol Grotnes Belk. *Books:* 401,760 (physical), 1.3 million (digital/electronic); *Serial titles:* 217 (physical), 64,848 (digital/electronic); *Databases:* 179. Weekly public service hours: 143; study areas open 24 hours, 5–7 days a week; students can reserve study rooms.

STUDENT LIFE
Housing options: on-campus residence required through sophomore year; coed, men-only, women-only. Campus housing is university owned and leased by the school. Freshman campus housing is guaranteed.
Activities and organizations: drama/theater group, student-run newspaper, radio and television station, choral group, marching band, Elon Volunteers, Student Media, Intramural Athletics, Religious Life, Habitat for Humanity, national fraternities, national sororities.
Athletics Member NCAA. All Division I except football (Division I-AA).
Campus security: 24-hour emergency response devices and patrols, late-night transport/escort service, controlled dormitory access, Student Transport Service (Safe Rides).
Student services: health clinic, personal/psychological counseling, women's center.

COSTS & FINANCIAL AID
Costs (2018–19) ***Comprehensive fee:*** $47,549 includes full-time tuition ($34,850), mandatory fees ($469), and room and board ($12,230). Part-time tuition: $1110 per credit hour. Part-time tuition and fees vary according to course load. ***Required fees:*** $167 per term part-time. ***College room only:*** $6020. Room and board charges vary according to board plan and housing facility.
Financial Aid Of all full-time matriculated undergraduates who enrolled in 2018, 2,841 applied for aid, 2,020 were judged to have need, 347 had their need fully met. 1,415 Federal Work-Study jobs (averaging $2374). In 2018, 1442 non-need-based awards were made. ***Average percent of need met:*** 61. ***Average financial aid package:*** $20,456. ***Average need-based loan:*** $4366. ***Average need-based gift aid:*** $15,920. ***Average non-need-based aid:*** $8020. ***Average indebtedness upon graduation:*** $30,625.

APPLYING
Standardized Tests *Required:* SAT or ACT (for admission).
Options: electronic application, early admission, early decision, early action, deferred entrance.
Application fee: $50.
Required: essay or personal statement, high school transcript, counselor evaluation form. ***Required for some:*** interview.

CONTACT
Ms. Melinda Wood, Senior Associate Dean of Admissions, Elon University, 2700 Campus Box, Elon, NC 27244. *Phone:* 336-278-3566. *Toll-free phone:* 800-334-8448. *Fax:* 336-278-7699. *E-mail:* admissions@elon.edu.

Fayetteville State University

Fayetteville, North Carolina

http://www.uncfsu.edu/

- **State-supported** comprehensive, founded 1867, part of University of North Carolina System
- **Urban** 156-acre campus with easy access to Raleigh
- **Coed** 5,473 undergraduate students, 74% full-time, 68% women, 32% men
- **Minimally difficult** entrance level, 68% of applicants were admitted

UNDERGRAD STUDENTS
4,058 full-time, 1,415 part-time. Students come from 40 states and territories; 20 other countries; 7% are from out of state; 63% Black or African American, non-Hispanic/Latino; 8% Hispanic/Latino; 2% Asian, non-Hispanic/Latino; 0.3% Native Hawaiian or other Pacific Islander, non-Hispanic/Latino; 2% American Indian or Alaska Native, non-Hispanic/Latino; 3% Two or more races, non-Hispanic/Latino; 4% Race/ethnicity unknown; 0.6% international; 17% transferred in; 22% live on campus.

Freshmen:
Admission: 4,130 applied, 2,803 admitted, 618 enrolled. ***Average high school GPA:*** 3.4.
Retention: 78% of full-time freshmen returned.

FACULTY
Total: 333, 80% full-time, 71% with terminal degrees.
Student/faculty ratio: 15:1.

ACADEMICS
Calendar: semesters. *Degrees:* bachelor's, master's, and doctoral.
Special study options: academic remediation for entering students, accelerated degree program, adult/continuing education programs, advanced placement credit, cooperative education, distance learning, double majors, honors programs, independent study, internships, part-time degree program, services for LD students, study abroad, summer session for credit. ***ROTC:*** Army (c), Air Force (b).
Unusual degree programs: 3-2 engineering with North Carolina State University.
Computers: 600 computers/terminals and 2,400 ports are available on campus for general student use. Students can access the following: campus intranet, computer help desk, free student e-mail accounts, online (class) grades, online (class) registration, online (class) schedules. Campuswide network is available. 100% of college-owned or -operated housing units are wired for high-speed Internet access. Wireless service is available via classrooms, computer centers, computer labs, learning centers, libraries, student centers.
Library: Charles W. Chestnut Library. *Books:* 223,687 (physical), 224,581 (digital/electronic); *Serial titles:* 314 (physical), 30,747 (digital/electronic); *Databases:* 442. Weekly public service hours: 97; students can reserve study rooms.

STUDENT LIFE
Housing options: coed, men-only, women-only, special housing for students with disabilities. Campus housing is university owned. Freshman applicants given priority for college housing.
Activities and organizations: drama/theater group, student-run newspaper, radio station, choral group, marching band, Student Government Association, Student Activities Council, Pan-Hellenic Council, Residence Hall Association, Illusions and Black Millennium Modeling Clubs, national fraternities, national sororities.
Athletics Member NCAA. All Division II except golf (Division I). ***Intercollegiate sports:*** basketball M(s)/W(s), bowling W, cross-country running M(s)/W(s), football M(s), golf M(s)/W, softball W(s), tennis M/W(s), track and field M/W(s), volleyball W(s). ***Intramural sports:*** baseball M, basketball M/W, bowling M/W, football M, golf M/W, gymnastics M/W, swimming and diving M/W, tennis M, volleyball M/W.

Campus security: 24-hour emergency response devices and patrols, late-night transport/escort service, controlled dormitory access.

Student services: health clinic, personal/psychological counseling, veterans affairs office.

COSTS & FINANCIAL AID
Costs (2018–19) ***Tuition:*** state resident $2982 full-time; nonresident $14,590 full-time. Full-time tuition and fees vary according to course level, course load, degree level, location, and program. Part-time tuition and fees vary according to course level, course load, degree level, location, and program. ***Required fees:*** $1933 full-time. ***Room and board:*** $8236; room only: $4298. Room and board charges vary according to board plan and housing facility. ***Payment plan:*** installment. ***Waivers:*** senior citizens and employees or children of employees.

Financial Aid Of all full-time matriculated undergraduates who enrolled in 2014, 3,562 applied for aid, 3,380 were judged to have need, 373 had their need fully met. In 2014, 2 non-need-based awards were made. ***Average percent of need met:*** 70. ***Average financial aid package:*** $10,632. ***Average need-based loan:*** $4232. ***Average need-based gift aid:*** $7083. ***Average non-need-based aid:*** $750. ***Average indebtedness upon graduation:*** $25,215. ***Financial aid deadline:*** 3/1.

APPLYING
Standardized Tests *Required:* SAT or ACT (for admission).

Options: electronic application, early admission, early decision, early action, deferred entrance.

Application fee: $40.

Required: high school transcript, minimum 2.5 GPA. ***Recommended:*** essay or personal statement.

Notification: continuous (freshmen), continuous (transfers).

CONTACT
Ulisa E. Bowles, Director of Admissions, Fayetteville State University, 1200 Murchison Road, Fayetteville, NC 28301-4298. *Phone:* 910-672-1371. *Toll-free phone:* 800-222-2594. *Fax:* 910-672-1414. *E-mail:* admissions@uncfsu.edu.

Gardner-Webb University
Boiling Springs, North Carolina
http://www.gardner-webb.edu/

CONTACT
Associate Vice President of Undergraduate Admissions, Gardner-Webb University, PO Box 817, 110 South Main Street, Boiling Springs, NC 28017. *Phone:* 704-406-4491. *Toll-free phone:* 800-253-6472. *Fax:* 704-406-4488. *E-mail:* admissions@gardner-webb.edu.

Grace College of Divinity
Fayetteville, North Carolina
http://www.gcd.edu/

CONTACT
Grace College of Divinity, 5117 Cliffdale Road, Fayetteville, NC 28314.

Greensboro College
Greensboro, North Carolina
http://www.greensboro.edu/

- **Independent United Methodist** comprehensive, founded 1838
- **Urban** 75-acre campus with easy access to Charlotte
- **Endowment** $20.5 million
- **Coed**
- **Minimally difficult** entrance level

FACULTY
Student/faculty ratio: 12:1.

ACADEMICS
Calendar: semesters. *Degrees:* certificates, bachelor's, master's, and postbachelor's certificates.
Library: James Addison Jones Library. *Books:* 77,657 (physical), 194,596 (digital/electronic). Weekly public service hours: 60; students can reserve study rooms.

STUDENT LIFE
Housing options: on-campus residence required through sophomore year; coed, men-only, women-only. Campus housing is university owned. Freshman campus housing is guaranteed.

Activities and organizations: drama/theater group, student-run newspaper, choral group, marching band, Pheta VI, Alpha Z Delta, Student Athletic Advisor Counsel, Pride Productions, United African American Society, national fraternities, national sororities.

Athletics Member NCAA. All Division III.

Campus security: 24-hour patrols, late-night transport/escort service, controlled dormitory access.

Student services: health clinic, personal/psychological counseling, veterans affairs office.

COSTS & FINANCIAL AID
Costs (2018–19) ***Comprehensive fee:*** $39,940 includes full-time tuition ($28,440), mandatory fees ($700), and room and board ($10,800). Full-time tuition and fees vary according to degree level and program. Part-time tuition: $750 per credit hour. Part-time tuition and fees vary according to course load, degree level, and program. ***Required fees:*** $700 per year part-time. ***Room and board:*** Room and board charges vary according to housing facility.

Financial Aid Of all full-time matriculated undergraduates who enrolled in 2015, 692 applied for aid, 673 were judged to have need, 54 had their need fully met. 131 Federal Work-Study jobs (averaging $717). In 2015, 24 non-need-based awards were made. ***Average percent of need met:*** 82. ***Average financial aid package:*** $20,493. ***Average need-based loan:*** $7623. ***Average need-based gift aid:*** $8148. ***Average non-need-based aid:*** $10,703. ***Average indebtedness upon graduation:*** $43,509.

APPLYING
Standardized Tests *Required:* SAT or ACT (for admission).

Options: electronic application, early admission, deferred entrance.

Required: high school transcript. ***Required for some:*** interview. ***Recommended:*** essay or personal statement.

CONTACT
Greensboro College, 815 West Market Street, Greensboro, NC 27401-1875. *Toll-free phone:* 800-346-8226.

Guilford College
Greensboro, North Carolina
http://www.guilford.edu/

- **Independent** comprehensive, founded 1837, affiliated with Society of Friends
- **Suburban** 351-acre campus
- **Endowment** $74.5 million
- **Coed**
- **Moderately difficult** entrance level

FACULTY
Student/faculty ratio: 12:1.

ACADEMICS
Calendar: 4-1-4. *Degrees:* bachelor's, master's, and postbachelor's certificates.
Library: Hege Library. *Books:* 164,946 (physical), 326,808 (digital/electronic); *Serial titles:* 4,301 (physical), 45,891 (digital/electronic); *Databases:* 169. Weekly public service hours: 93; students can reserve study rooms.

STUDENT LIFE
Housing options: on-campus residence required through junior year; coed, women-only, cooperative, special housing for students with disabilities. Campus housing is university owned. Freshman campus housing is guaranteed.

Activities and organizations: drama/theater group, student-run newspaper, radio station, choral group, Student Government, Student Radio Station, Student Newspaper.

Athletics Member NCAA. All Division III.

Campus security: 24-hour emergency response devices and patrols, student patrols, late-night transport/escort service, controlled dormitory access.

Student services: health clinic, personal/psychological counseling.

FINANCIAL AID

Financial Aid Of all full-time matriculated undergraduates who enrolled in 2016, 1,206 applied for aid, 1,073 were judged to have need, 597 had their need fully met. In 2016, 131 non-need-based awards were made. ***Average percent of need met:*** 74. ***Average financial aid package:*** $25,481. ***Average need-based loan:*** $3773. ***Average need-based gift aid:*** $4418. ***Average non-need-based aid:*** $9961. ***Average indebtedness upon graduation:*** $35,392.

APPLYING

Standardized Tests *Recommended:* SAT or ACT (for admission).

Options: electronic application, early admission, early decision, early action, deferred entrance.

Required: essay or personal statement, minimum 2.0 GPA. ***Required for some:*** high school transcript, 1 letter of recommendation. ***Recommended:*** minimum 3.0 GPA, interview.

CONTACT

Mr. Kyle Wooden, Interim Director of Admission, Guilford College, 5800 West Friendly Avenue, Greensboro, NC 27410. *Phone:* 336-316-2000. *Toll-free phone:* 800-992-7759. *Fax:* 336-316-2954. *E-mail:* admission@guilford.edu.

Heritage Bible College

Dunn, North Carolina

http://www.heritagebiblecollege.edu/

CONTACT

Ms. Iris Prince, Admissions Director, Heritage Bible College, PO Box 1628, Dunn, NC 28335-1628. *Phone:* 910-892-3178 Ext. 239. *Toll-free phone:* 800-297-6351. *Fax:* 910-891-1660. *E-mail:* iprince@heritagebiblecollege.edu.

High Point University

High Point, North Carolina

http://www.highpoint.edu/

- **Independent United Methodist** university, founded 1924
- **Suburban** 380-acre campus with easy access to Charlotte
- **Endowment** $60.8 million
- **Coed** 4,545 undergraduate students, 99% full-time, 57% women, 43% men
- **Moderately difficult** entrance level, 77% of applicants were admitted

UNDERGRAD STUDENTS

4,504 full-time, 41 part-time. Students come from 46 states and territories; 39 other countries; 76% are from out of state; 5% Black or African American, non-Hispanic/Latino; 5% Hispanic/Latino; 2% Asian, non-Hispanic/Latino; 0.4% American Indian or Alaska Native, non-Hispanic/Latino; 6% Two or more races, non-Hispanic/Latino; 2% Race/ethnicity unknown; 3% international; 1% transferred in; 94% live on campus.

Freshmen:

Admission: 10,098 applied, 7,770 admitted, 1,423 enrolled. ***Average high school GPA:*** 3.3. ***Test scores:*** SAT evidence-based reading and writing scores over 500: 97%; SAT math scores over 500: 97%; ACT scores over 18: 99%; SAT evidence-based reading and writing scores over 600: 50%; SAT math scores over 600: 43%; ACT scores over 24: 65%; SAT evidence-based reading and writing scores over 700: 4%; SAT math scores over 700: 7%; ACT scores over 30: 15%.

Retention: 81% of full-time freshmen returned.

FACULTY

Total: 478, 66% full-time, 65% with terminal degrees.

Student/faculty ratio: 14:1.

ACADEMICS

Calendar: semesters. *Degrees:* bachelor's, master's, doctoral, and postbachelor's certificates.

Special study options: accelerated degree program, advanced placement credit, cooperative education, double majors, English as a second language, honors programs, independent study, internships, services for LD students, student-designed majors, study abroad, summer session for credit. ***ROTC:*** Army (c), Air Force (c).

Unusual degree programs: 3-2 elementary education, strategic communication, athletic training.

Computers: 749 computers/terminals are available on campus for general student use. Students can access the following: campus intranet, computer help desk, free student e-mail accounts, online (class) grades, online (class) registration, online (class) schedules. Campuswide network is available. 100% of college-owned or -operated housing units are wired for high-speed Internet access. Wireless service is available via entire campus.

Library: Smith Library plus 1 other. *Books:* 181,000 (physical), 447,000 (digital/electronic); *Serial titles:* 41,000 (physical), 32,000 (digital/electronic); *Databases:* 185. Weekly public service hours: 168; study areas open 24 hours, 5–7 days a week; students can reserve study rooms.

STUDENT LIFE

Housing options: on-campus residence required through junior year; coed, men-only, women-only, cooperative, special housing for students with disabilities. Campus housing is university owned. Freshman campus housing is guaranteed.

Activities and organizations: drama/theater group, student-run newspaper, radio and television station, choral group, Big Brothers Big Sisters, Campus Activities Team, Purple Reign, Entrepreneurship Club, Volunteer Center, national fraternities, national sororities.

Athletics Member NCAA. All Division I. ***Intercollegiate sports:*** baseball M(s), basketball M(s)/W(s), cheerleading W, cross-country running M(s)/W(s), golf M(s)/W(s)(c), lacrosse M(s)/W(s), soccer M(s)/W(s), track and field M(s)/W(s), volleyball W(s). ***Intramural sports:*** badminton M/W, baseball M(c), basketball M(c)/W(c), bowling M/W, crew M(c)/W(c), cross-country running M(c)/W(c), equestrian sports M(c)/W(c), fencing W(c), football M/W, golf M(c)/W(c), gymnastics M(c)/W(c), ice hockey M(c), lacrosse M(c)/W(c), racquetball M/W, rowing M(c)/W(c), soccer M(c)/W(c), softball W(c), swimming and diving M(c)/W(c), tennis M(c)/W(c), ultimate Frisbee M(c), volleyball M(c)/W(c), water polo M/W, weight lifting M(c)/W(c).

Campus security: 24-hour emergency response devices and patrols, student patrols, late-night transport/escort service, controlled dormitory access.

Student services: health clinic, personal/psychological counseling.

COSTS & FINANCIAL AID

Costs (2018–19) ***Comprehensive fee:*** $49,248 includes full-time tuition ($30,748), mandatory fees ($4370), and room and board ($14,130). Full-time tuition and fees vary according to course load and reciprocity agreements. Part-time tuition: $993 per credit hour. Part-time tuition and fees vary according to course load and reciprocity agreements. ***Required fees:*** $2185 per term part-time. ***Room and board:*** Room and board charges vary according to board plan and housing facility. ***Payment plan:*** installment. ***Waivers:*** employees or children of employees.

Financial Aid Of all full-time matriculated undergraduates who enrolled in 2017, 2,419 applied for aid, 1,899 were judged to have need, 201 had their need fully met. 246 Federal Work-Study jobs (averaging $1052). In 2017, 1409 non-need-based awards were made. ***Average percent of need met:*** 52. ***Average financial aid package:*** $16,266. ***Average need-based loan:*** $4300. ***Average need-based gift aid:*** $12,038. ***Average non-need-based aid:*** $7780. ***Average indebtedness upon graduation:*** $39,597.

APPLYING

Options: electronic application, early decision, early action, deferred entrance.

Application fee: $50.

Required: essay or personal statement, high school transcript, 1 letter of recommendation. ***Recommended:*** interview.

Application deadlines: 3/1 (freshmen), 7/1 (transfers), 11/15 (early action).

Early decision deadline: 11/1 (for plan 1), 2/1 (for plan 2).

Notification: continuous until 2/1 (freshmen), continuous (transfers), 11/27 (early decision plan 1), 2/1 (early decision plan 2), 12/15 (early action).

CONTACT
Dr. Kerr Ramsay, Associate Vice President of Admissions, High Point University, Office of Undergraduate Admissions, One University Parkway, High Point, NC 27268. *Phone:* 336-841-9176. *Toll-free phone:* 800-345-6993. *Fax:* 336-888-6382. *E-mail:* kramsay@highpoint.edu.

Johnson & Wales University
Charlotte, North Carolina
http://www.jwu.edu/charlotte/

CONTACT
Joseph Campos, Director of Admissions, Johnson & Wales University, 801 West Trade Street, Charlotte, NC 28202. *Phone:* 980-598-1100. *Toll-free phone:* 866-598-2427. *Fax:* 980-598-1111. *E-mail:* clt@admissions.jwu.edu.

Johnson C. Smith University
Charlotte, North Carolina
http://www.jcsu.edu/

- **Independent** comprehensive, founded 1867
- **Urban** 100-acre campus with easy access to Atlanta
- **Endowment** $68.2 million
- **Coed** 1,480 undergraduate students, 96% full-time, 61% women, 39% men
- **Moderately difficult** entrance level, 46% of applicants were admitted

UNDERGRAD STUDENTS
1,428 full-time, 52 part-time. Students come from 32 states and territories; 8 other countries; 40% are from out of state; 85% Black or African American, non-Hispanic/Latino; 3% Hispanic/Latino; 0.2% Asian, non-Hispanic/Latino; 0.2% Native Hawaiian or other Pacific Islander, non-Hispanic/Latino; 0.4% American Indian or Alaska Native, non-Hispanic/Latino; 0.8% Two or more races, non-Hispanic/Latino; 8% Race/ethnicity unknown; 1% international; 4% transferred in; 50% live on campus.

Freshmen:
Admission: 6,369 applied, 2,919 admitted, 350 enrolled. ***Average high school GPA:*** 2.8. ***Test scores:*** SAT evidence-based reading and writing scores over 500: 24%; SAT math scores over 500: 23%; ACT scores over 18: 31%; SAT evidence-based reading and writing scores over 600: 4%; SAT math scores over 600: 2%; ACT scores over 24: 2%.

Retention: 69% of full-time freshmen returned.

FACULTY
Total: 164, 53% full-time, 55% with terminal degrees.

Student/faculty ratio: 12:1.

ACADEMICS
Calendar: semesters. *Degrees:* bachelor's and master's.

Special study options: accelerated degree program, adult/continuing education programs, advanced placement credit, cooperative education, distance learning, double majors, English as a second language, independent study, internships, part-time degree program, services for LD students, student-designed majors, study abroad, summer session for credit.

Computers: 125 computers/terminals are available on campus for general student use. Students can access the following: campus intranet, computer help desk, free student e-mail accounts, online (class) grades, online (class) registration, online (class) schedules. Campuswide network is available. 100% of college-owned or -operated housing units are wired for high-speed Internet access. Wireless service is available via entire campus.

Library: James B. Duke Library. *Books:* 105,422 (physical), 203,337 (digital/electronic); *Serial titles:* 107 (physical), 23,465 (digital/electronic); *Databases:* 99. Weekly public service hours: 79; study areas open 24 hours, 5–7 days a week; students can reserve study rooms.

STUDENT LIFE
Housing options: coed, men-only, women-only. Campus housing is university owned and leased by the school. Freshman campus housing is guaranteed.

Activities and organizations: drama/theater group, choral group, marching band, national fraternities, national sororities.

Athletics Member NCAA. All Division II. ***Intercollegiate sports:*** basketball M(s)/W(s), bowling W(s), cheerleading M/W, cross-country running M(s)/W(s), football M(s), golf M(s), softball W(s), tennis M(s)/W(s), track and field M(s)/W(s), volleyball W(s).

Campus security: 24-hour emergency response devices and patrols, late-night transport/escort service, controlled dormitory access.

Student services: health clinic, personal/psychological counseling.

COSTS & FINANCIAL AID
Costs (2018–19) ***Comprehensive fee:*** $25,336 includes full-time tuition ($18,236) and room and board ($7100). Full-time tuition and fees vary according to course load. Part-time tuition: $418 per credit hour. Part-time tuition and fees vary according to course load. ***Room and board:*** Room and board charges vary according to board plan and housing facility. ***Payment plan:*** installment. ***Waivers:*** employees or children of employees.

Financial Aid Of all full-time matriculated undergraduates who enrolled in 2018, 1,362 applied for aid, 1,322 were judged to have need, 97 had their need fully met. 192 Federal Work-Study jobs (averaging $3000). In 2018, 46 non-need-based awards were made. ***Average percent of need met:*** 57. ***Average financial aid package:*** $15,432. ***Average need-based loan:*** $3841. ***Average need-based gift aid:*** $11,869. ***Average non-need-based aid:*** $12,845. ***Financial aid deadline:*** 4/1.

APPLYING
Standardized Tests *Required:* SAT or ACT (for admission).

Options: electronic application, deferred entrance.

Application fee: $25.

Required: high school transcript. ***Recommended:*** essay or personal statement, 1 letter of recommendation.

Notification: continuous (freshmen), continuous (transfers).

CONTACT
Mr. Vory Billups, Director of Admissions, Johnson C. Smith University, 100 Beatties Ford Road, Charlotte, NC 28216. *Phone:* 704-378-1081. *Toll-free phone:* 800-782-7303. *Fax:* 704-378-1242. *E-mail:* vbillups@jcsu.edu.

Lees-McRae College
Banner Elk, North Carolina
http://www.lmc.edu/

- **Independent** 4-year, founded 1900, affiliated with Presbyterian Church (U.S.A.)
- **Rural** 460-acre campus
- **Endowment** $16.4 million
- **Coed** 966 undergraduate students, 95% full-time, 66% women, 34% men
- **Minimally difficult** entrance level, 57% of applicants were admitted

UNDERGRAD STUDENTS
915 full-time, 51 part-time. Students come from 31 states and territories; 16 other countries; 28% are from out of state; 8% Black or African American, non-Hispanic/Latino; 7% Hispanic/Latino; 0.6% Asian, non-Hispanic/Latino; 0.1% Native Hawaiian or other Pacific Islander, non-Hispanic/Latino; 1% American Indian or Alaska Native, non-Hispanic/Latino; 0.6% Two or more races, non-Hispanic/Latino; 7% Race/ethnicity unknown; 3% international; 18% transferred in; 62% live on campus.

Freshmen:
Admission: 1,462 applied, 836 admitted, 212 enrolled. ***Average high school GPA:*** 3.5. ***Test scores:*** ACT scores over 18: 75%; ACT scores over 24: 23%; ACT scores over 30: 2%.

Retention: 66% of full-time freshmen returned.

FACULTY
Total: 121, 50% full-time, 37% with terminal degrees.

Student/faculty ratio: 13:1.

ACADEMICS
Calendar: semesters. *Degree:* bachelor's.

Special study options: academic remediation for entering students, accelerated degree program, adult/continuing education programs, advanced placement credit, cooperative education, double majors, honors programs, independent study, internships, off-campus study, part-time degree program, services for LD students, study abroad, summer session for credit.

Computers: Students can access the following: computer help desk, free student e-mail accounts, online (class) grades, online (class) registration, online (class) schedules. Campuswide network is available. 100% of college-owned or -operated housing units are wired for high-speed Internet access. Wireless service is available via entire campus.

Library: Dotti M. Shelton Learning Commons. *Books:* 70,132 (physical), 200,746 (digital/electronic); *Serial titles:* 225 (physical), 146,361 (digital/electronic); *Databases:* 144. Students can reserve study rooms.

STUDENT LIFE

Housing options: coed, men-only, women-only, special housing for students with disabilities. Campus housing is university owned. Freshman campus housing is guaranteed.

Activities and organizations: drama/theater group, choral group.

Athletics Member NCAA. All Division II. ***Intercollegiate sports:*** basketball M(s)/W(s), cross-country running M(s)/W(s), lacrosse M(s)/W(s), soccer M(s)/W(s), softball W(s), tennis M(s)/W(s), track and field M(s)/W(s), volleyball M(s)/W(s).

Campus security: 24-hour emergency response devices and patrols, controlled dormitory access.

Student services: health clinic, personal/psychological counseling.

COSTS & FINANCIAL AID

Costs (2019–20) ***Comprehensive fee:*** $38,391 includes full-time tuition ($25,625), mandatory fees ($1896), and room and board ($10,870). Part-time tuition: $710 per credit hour. No tuition increase for student's term of enrollment. ***College room only:*** $5320.

Financial Aid Of all full-time matriculated undergraduates who enrolled in 2018, 760 applied for aid, 711 were judged to have need, 7 had their need fully met. In 2018, 60 non-need-based awards were made. ***Average percent of need met:*** 72. ***Average financial aid package:*** $23,399. ***Average need-based loan:*** $3694. ***Average need-based gift aid:*** $6473. ***Average non-need-based aid:*** $9688.

APPLYING

Standardized Tests *Required for some:* SAT or ACT (for admission), SAT or ACT scores for prospective intercollegiate athletes and honors program students.

Options: electronic application, early action.

Application fee: $35.

Required: high school transcript, minimum 2.0 GPA. ***Required for some:*** essay or personal statement, interview.

Application deadlines: rolling (freshmen), rolling (transfers).

Notification: continuous (freshmen), continuous (transfers).

CONTACT

Beverly Hague, Director of Undergraduate and Graduate Admissions, Lees-McRae College, PO Box 128, Banner Elk, NC 28604. *Phone:* 828-898-2417. *Toll-free phone:* 800-280-4562. *Fax:* 828-898-8707. *E-mail:* admissions@lmc.edu.

Lenoir-Rhyne University

Hickory, North Carolina

http://www.lr.edu/

- **Independent Lutheran** comprehensive, founded 1891
- **Small-town** 100-acre campus with easy access to Charlotte
- **Endowment** $106.3 million
- **Coed**
- **Moderately difficult** entrance level

FACULTY

Student/faculty ratio: 13:1.

ACADEMICS

Calendar: semesters. *Degrees:* bachelor's, master's, and doctoral.

Library: Carl Rudisill Library. *Books:* 121,005 (physical), 537,443 (digital/electronic); *Serial titles:* 49 (physical), 28,271 (digital/electronic); *Databases:* 135. Weekly public service hours: 89.

STUDENT LIFE

Housing options: on-campus residence required through junior year; coed. Campus housing is university owned. Freshman campus housing is guaranteed.

Activities and organizations: drama/theater group, student-run newspaper, radio station, choral group, marching band, Circle K, CAB, Nu Generation, Greek Organizations, Sign Troupe, national sororities.

Athletics Member NCAA. All Division II.

Campus security: 24-hour emergency response devices and patrols, late-night transport/escort service, controlled dormitory access.

Student services: health clinic, personal/psychological counseling, veterans affairs office.

COSTS & FINANCIAL AID

Costs (2018–19) ***Comprehensive fee:*** $48,910 includes full-time tuition ($36,400) and room and board ($12,510). Part-time tuition: $1500 per credit. ***Room and board:*** Room and board charges vary according to board plan.

Financial Aid Of all full-time matriculated undergraduates who enrolled in 2017, 1,297 applied for aid, 1,219 were judged to have need, 182 had their need fully met. In 2017, 196 non-need-based awards were made. ***Average percent of need met:*** 73. ***Average financial aid package:*** $30,327. ***Average need-based loan:*** $4265. ***Average need-based gift aid:*** $25,837. ***Average non-need-based aid:*** $19,448. ***Average indebtedness upon graduation:*** $30,156.

APPLYING

Standardized Tests *Required:* SAT or ACT (for admission).

Options: electronic application, early admission, early action, deferred entrance.

Application fee: $35.

Required: high school transcript, minimum 2.5 GPA. ***Recommended:*** essay or personal statement, letters of recommendation.

CONTACT

Lenoir-Rhyne University, 625 7th Avenue NE, Hickory, NC 28601. *Phone:* 828-328-7392. *Toll-free phone:* 800-277-5721.

Living Arts College

Raleigh, North Carolina

http://www.living-arts-college.edu/

CONTACT

Julie Wenta, Director of Admissions, Living Arts College, 3000 Wakefield Crossing Drive, Raleigh, NC 27614. *Phone:* 919-488-5902. *Toll-free phone:* 800-288-7442. *Fax:* 919-488-8490. *E-mail:* jwenta@living-arts-college.edu.

Livingstone College

Salisbury, North Carolina

http://www.livingstone.edu/

CONTACT

Mr. Tony Baldwin, Livingstone College, 701 West Monroe Street, Salisbury, NC 28144. *Phone:* 704-216-6001. *Toll-free phone:* 800-835-3435. *Fax:* 704-216-6215. *E-mail:* admissions@livingstone.edu.

Mars Hill University

Mars Hill, North Carolina

http://www.mhu.edu/

CONTACT

Kristie Vance, Director of Admissions, Mars Hill University, PO Box 370, Mars Hill, NC 28754. *Phone:* 828-689-1201. *Toll-free phone:* 866-648-4968. *Fax:* 828-689-1473. *E-mail:* admissions@mhu.edu.

★ Meredith College

Raleigh, North Carolina

http://www.meredith.edu/

- **Independent** comprehensive, founded 1891
- **Urban** 225-acre campus
- **Undergraduate: women only; graduate: coed**
- **Moderately difficult** entrance level

FACULTY
Student/faculty ratio: 12:1.

ACADEMICS
Calendar: semesters. *Degrees:* bachelor's, master's, and postbachelor's certificates.
Library: Carlyle Campbell Library.

STUDENT LIFE
Housing options: on-campus residence required through sophomore year; women-only. Campus housing is university owned. Freshman campus housing is guaranteed.

Activities and organizations: drama/theater group, student-run newspaper, choral group, Student Government Association, Entertainment Association, Recreation Association, Class Organizations, choral groups.

Athletics Member NCAA. All Division III.

Campus security: 24-hour emergency response devices and patrols, late-night transport/escort service, controlled dormitory access.

Student services: health clinic, personal/psychological counseling.

COSTS & FINANCIAL AID
Costs (2018–19) ***Comprehensive fee:*** $48,106 includes full-time tuition ($37,076), mandatory fees ($100), and room and board ($10,930). Full-time tuition and fees vary according to course load. Part-time tuition: $920 per credit hour. Part-time tuition and fees vary according to course load. ***Required fees:*** $50 per term part-time. ***Room and board:*** Room and board charges vary according to board plan and housing facility.

Financial Aid Of all full-time matriculated undergraduates who enrolled in 2017, 1,274 applied for aid, 1,136 were judged to have need, 201 had their need fully met. In 2017, 124 non-need-based awards were made. ***Average percent of need met:*** 75. ***Average financial aid package:*** $27,707. ***Average need-based loan:*** $4083. ***Average need-based gift aid:*** $23,453. ***Average non-need-based aid:*** $16,687. ***Average indebtedness upon graduation:*** $34,959.

APPLYING
Standardized Tests *Required:* SAT or ACT (for admission).

Options: electronic application, early admission, early decision, deferred entrance.

Application fee: $40.

Required: high school transcript, minimum 2.0 GPA, 2 letters of recommendation. ***Required for some:*** essay or personal statement, interview. ***Recommended:*** essay or personal statement.

CONTACT
Shery Boyles, Director of Admissions, Meredith College, 3800 Hillsborough Street, Raleigh, NC 27807-5298. *Phone:* 919-760-8026. *Toll-free phone:* 800-MEREDITH. *Fax:* 919-760-2298. *E-mail:* admissions@meredith.edu.

Methodist University

Fayetteville, North Carolina

http://www.methodist.edu/

CONTACT
Mr. Jamie Legg, Director of Admissions, Methodist University, 5400 Ramset Street, Fayetteville, NC 28311-1496. *Phone:* 910-630-7027. *Toll-free phone:* 800-488-7110 Ext. 7027. *Fax:* 910-630-7285. *E-mail:* admissions@methodist.edu.

Mid-Atlantic Christian University

Elizabeth City, North Carolina

http://www.macuniversity.edu/

- **Independent Christian** 4-year, founded 1948
- **Small-town** 19-acre campus with easy access to Norfolk
- **Endowment** $3.1 million
- **Coed**
- **Minimally difficult** entrance level

FACULTY
Student/faculty ratio: 11:1.

ACADEMICS
Calendar: semesters. *Degrees:* certificates, associate, bachelor's, and postbachelor's certificates.
Library: Watson-Griffith Library. *Books:* 33,941 (physical), 1,572 (digital/electronic). Students can reserve study rooms.

STUDENT LIFE
Housing options: on-campus residence required through senior year; men-only, women-only. Campus housing is university owned. Freshman campus housing is guaranteed.

Activities and organizations: national sororities.

Athletics Member USCAA.

Campus security: 24-hour emergency response devices, controlled dormitory access.

Student services: personal/psychological counseling.

COSTS & FINANCIAL AID
Costs (2018–19) ***Comprehensive fee:*** $23,450 includes full-time tuition ($14,400), mandatory fees ($450), and room and board ($8600). Full-time tuition and fees vary according to program. Part-time tuition: $450 per credit hour. Part-time tuition and fees vary according to program. ***Required fees:*** $55 per credit hour part-time. ***Room and board:*** Room and board charges vary according to housing facility.

Financial Aid Of all full-time matriculated undergraduates who enrolled in 2015, 170 applied for aid, 156 were judged to have need, 10 had their need fully met. In 2015, 17 non-need-based awards were made. ***Average percent of need met:*** 55. ***Average financial aid package:*** $11,333. ***Average need-based loan:*** $3758. ***Average need-based gift aid:*** $6671. ***Average non-need-based aid:*** $3478. ***Average indebtedness upon graduation:*** $26,414. ***Financial aid deadline:*** 3/1.

APPLYING
Standardized Tests *Required for some:* SAT or ACT (for admission).

Options: electronic application, early admission, deferred entrance.

Application fee: $50.

Required: essay or personal statement, high school transcript, minimum 2.0 GPA, 1 letter of recommendation, reference from church or character reference. ***Required for some:*** interview.

CONTACT
Mid-Atlantic Christian University, 715 North Poindexter Street, Elizabeth City, NC 27909-4054. *Toll-free phone:* 866-996-MACU.

Montreat College

Montreat, North Carolina

http://www.montreat.edu/

CONTACT
Miss Mandi Pike, Senior Admissions Specialist, Montreat College, PO Box 1267, Montreat, NC 28757. *Phone:* 828-669-8012 Ext. 3789. *Toll-free phone:* 800-622-6968. *Fax:* 828-669-0120. *E-mail:* admissions@montreat.edu.

A ★ indicates that the school has detailed information with a Premium Profile on Petersons.com.

North Carolina Agricultural and Technical State University

Greensboro, North Carolina

http://www.ncat.edu/

- **State-supported** university, founded 1891, part of University of North Carolina System
- **Suburban** 200-acre campus with easy access to Charlotte
- **Coed**
- **Moderately difficult** entrance level

FACULTY

Student/faculty ratio: 18:1.

ACADEMICS

Calendar: semesters. *Degrees:* bachelor's, master's, doctoral, post-master's, and postbachelor's certificates.

Library: F. D. Bluford Library.

STUDENT LIFE

Housing options: coed, men-only, women-only. Campus housing is university owned and is provided by a third party. Freshman applicants given priority for college housing.

Activities and organizations: drama/theater group, student-run newspaper, radio and television station, choral group, marching band, Student Government, national fraternities, national sororities.

Athletics Member NCAA. All Division I.

Campus security: 24-hour emergency response devices and patrols, late-night transport/escort service, controlled dormitory access.

Student services: health clinic, personal/psychological counseling.

COSTS & FINANCIAL AID

Costs (2018–19) ***Tuition:*** state resident $3540 full-time; nonresident $16,750 full-time. Full-time tuition and fees vary according to course load, degree level, and program. Part-time tuition and fees vary according to course load, degree level, and program. ***Required fees:*** $3072 full-time. ***Room and board:*** $7644; room only: $4009. Room and board charges vary according to board plan and housing facility.

Financial Aid Of all full-time matriculated undergraduates who enrolled in 2016, 8,221 applied for aid, 7,493 were judged to have need, 489 had their need fully met. In 2016, 179 non-need-based awards were made. ***Average percent of need met:*** 59. ***Average financial aid package:*** $11,092. ***Average need-based loan:*** $4004. ***Average need-based gift aid:*** $8240. ***Average non-need-based aid:*** $5372. ***Average indebtedness upon graduation:*** $34,379.

APPLYING

Standardized Tests *Required:* SAT or ACT (for admission).

Options: early admission, deferred entrance.

Application fee: $55.

Required: high school transcript, minimum 2.0 GPA.

CONTACT

Ms. Cheryl Pollard-Burns, Director of Admissions, North Carolina Agricultural and Technical State University, Webb Hall, 1601 East Market Street, Greensboro, NC 27411. *Phone:* 336-334-7946. *Toll-free phone:* 800-443-8964. *Fax:* 336-334-7478. *E-mail:* uadmit@ncat.edu.

North Carolina Central University

Durham, North Carolina

http://www.nccu.edu/

- **State-supported** comprehensive, founded 1910, part of University of North Carolina System
- **Urban** 115-acre campus with easy access to Raleigh
- **Endowment** $22.9 million
- **Coed**
- **Minimally difficult** entrance level

FACULTY

Student/faculty ratio: 16:1.

ACADEMICS

Calendar: semesters. *Degrees:* bachelor's, master's, and doctoral.

Library: Shepherd Library plus 2 others. Study areas open 24 hours, 5–7 days a week; students can reserve study rooms.

STUDENT LIFE

Housing options: coed. Campus housing is university owned and leased by the school. Freshman applicants given priority for college housing.

Activities and organizations: drama/theater group, student-run newspaper, choral group, marching band, national fraternities, national sororities.

Athletics Member NCAA, NAIA. All NCAA Division I.

Campus security: 24-hour emergency response devices and patrols, student patrols, late-night transport/escort service, controlled dormitory access.

Student services: health clinic, personal/psychological counseling, women's center.

COSTS & FINANCIAL AID

Costs (2018–19) ***Tuition:*** state resident $3728 full-time, $466 per credit hour part-time; nonresident $16,435 full-time, $2054 per credit hour part-time. Part-time tuition and fees vary according to course load. No tuition increase for student's term of enrollment. ***Required fees:*** $2838 full-time, $600 per credit hour part-time. ***Room and board:*** $8446. Room and board charges vary according to board plan, housing facility, and location.

Financial Aid Of all full-time matriculated undergraduates who enrolled in 2017, 5,105 applied for aid, 4,891 were judged to have need, 206 had their need fully met. In 2017, 62 non-need-based awards were made. ***Average percent of need met:*** 57. ***Average financial aid package:*** $14,577. ***Average need-based loan:*** $6701. ***Average need-based gift aid:*** $8826. ***Average non-need-based aid:*** $6217. ***Average indebtedness upon graduation:*** $44,228.

APPLYING

Standardized Tests *Required:* SAT or ACT (for admission).

Options: electronic application, deferred entrance.

Application fee: $40.

Required: high school transcript, minimum 2.5 GPA, University of North Carolina System minimum course requirements.

CONTACT

North Carolina Central University, 1801 Fayetteville Street, Durham, NC 27707-3129. *Toll-free phone:* 877-667-7533.

North Carolina State University

Raleigh, North Carolina

http://www.ncsu.edu/

- **State-supported** university, founded 1887, part of University of North Carolina System
- **Urban** 2137-acre campus with easy access to Raleigh-Durham
- **Endowment** $1.3 billion
- **Coed** 25,199 undergraduate students, 89% full-time, 47% women, 53% men
- **Very difficult** entrance level, 47% of applicants were admitted

UNDERGRAD STUDENTS

22,317 full-time, 2,882 part-time. Students come from 53 states and territories; 105 other countries; 9% are from out of state; 6% Black or African American, non-Hispanic/Latino; 6% Hispanic/Latino; 7% Asian, non-Hispanic/Latino; 0.1% Native Hawaiian or other Pacific Islander, non-Hispanic/Latino; 0.4% American Indian or Alaska Native, non-Hispanic/Latino; 4% Two or more races, non-Hispanic/Latino; 4% Race/ethnicity unknown; 4% international; 5% transferred in; 38% live on campus.

Freshmen:

Admission: 30,193 applied, 14,059 admitted, 4,952 enrolled. ***Average high school GPA:*** 3.8. ***Test scores:*** SAT evidence-based reading and writing scores over 500: 99%; SAT math scores over 500: 99%; ACT scores over 18: 100%; SAT evidence-based reading and writing scores over 600: 87%; SAT math scores over 600: 87%; ACT scores over 24: 97%; SAT evidence-based reading and writing scores over 700: 19%; SAT math scores over 700: 34%; ACT scores over 30: 47%.

Retention: 94% of full-time freshmen returned.

FACULTY
Total: 2,616, 86% full-time, 89% with terminal degrees.
Student/faculty ratio: 13:1.

ACADEMICS
Calendar: semesters. *Degrees:* associate, bachelor's, master's, doctoral, and postbachelor's certificates.

Special study options: academic remediation for entering students, accelerated degree program, adult/continuing education programs, advanced placement credit, cooperative education, distance learning, double majors, English as a second language, honors programs, independent study, internships, off-campus study, part-time degree program, services for LD students, student-designed majors, study abroad, summer session for credit. ***ROTC:*** Army (b), Navy (b), Air Force (b).

Unusual degree programs: 3-2 business administration; engineering; agriculture, life sciences, physical sciences, communication, computer science, economics, foreign languages, history, mathematics, education, statistics, textiles.

Computers: 3,050 computers/terminals are available on campus for general student use. Students can access the following: campus intranet, computer help desk, free student e-mail accounts, online (class) grades, online (class) registration, online (class) schedules, online course materials, homework submission, testing/quizzes, financial aid/cashier's office account balances, blogging service, Web space, unlimited cloud storage, on site hardware and virus removal support. Campuswide network is available. 100% of college-owned or -operated housing units are wired for high-speed Internet access. Wireless service is available via entire campus.
Library: D. H. Hill Jr. Library plus 5 others. *Books:* 2.6 million (physical), 1.2 million (digital/electronic); *Serial titles:* 47,189 (physical), 55,481 (digital/electronic); *Databases:* 635. Weekly public service hours: 146; study areas open 24 hours, 5–7 days a week; students can reserve study rooms.

STUDENT LIFE
Housing options: on-campus residence required for freshman year; coed, men-only, women-only, special housing for students with disabilities. Campus housing is university owned. Freshman campus housing is guaranteed.

Activities and organizations: drama/theater group, student-run newspaper, radio and television station, choral group, marching band, Inter-Residence Council, Student Alumni Association, Student Wolfpack Club, College of Education Graduate Advisory Board, American Society of Mechanical Engineers Student Section, national fraternities, national sororities.

Athletics Member NCAA. All Division I. ***Intercollegiate sports:*** baseball M(s), basketball M(s)/W(s), bowling M(c)/W(c), cheerleading M(s)/W(s), crew M(c)/W(c), cross-country running M(s)/W(s), equestrian sports M(c)/W(c), fencing M(c)/W(c), field hockey M(c)/W(c), football M(s), golf M(s)/W(s)(c), gymnastics M(c)/W(s), ice hockey M(c), lacrosse M(c)/W(c), racquetball M(c)/W(c), riflery M(s)/W(s), rugby M(c)/W(c), sailing M(c)/W(c), skiing (downhill) W(c), soccer M(s)/W(s), softball W(s), swimming and diving M(s)/W(s), table tennis M(c)/W(c), tennis M(s)/W(s), track and field M(s)/W(s), ultimate Frisbee M(c)/W(c), volleyball M(c)/W(s), water polo M(c)/W(c), wrestling M(s). ***Intramural sports:*** badminton M/W, basketball M/W, bowling M/W, football M/W, golf M/W, racquetball M/W, soccer M/W, softball M/W, swimming and diving M/W, table tennis M/W, tennis M/W, track and field M/W, ultimate Frisbee M/W, volleyball M/W.

Campus security: 24-hour emergency response devices and patrols, late-night transport/escort service, controlled dormitory access.

Student services: health clinic, personal/psychological counseling, women's center, legal services, veterans affairs office.

COSTS & FINANCIAL AID
Costs (2019–20) ***Tuition:*** state resident $6535 full-time; nonresident $25,878 full-time. No tuition increase for student's term of enrollment. ***Required fees:*** $2566 full-time. ***Room and board:*** $11,078; room only: $6714.

Financial Aid Of all full-time matriculated undergraduates who enrolled in 2018, 15,503 applied for aid, 10,907 were judged to have need, 2,299 had their need fully met. 1,203 Federal Work-Study jobs (averaging $1725). In 2018, 1007 non-need-based awards were made. ***Average percent of need met:*** 74. ***Average financial aid package:*** $12,946. ***Average need-based loan:*** $3857. ***Average need-based gift aid:*** $9944. ***Average non-need-based aid:*** $5703. ***Average indebtedness upon graduation:*** $24,053.

APPLYING
Standardized Tests *Required:* SAT (for admission), ACT (for admission), SAT or ACT (for admission).

Options: electronic application, early action, deferred entrance.

Application fee: $85.

Required for some: high school transcript, interview, Students applying for studio-based majors must provide a portfolio. Students applying for Professional Golf Management Students must provide a copy of their GHIN/Handicap scores from their local golf facility and a letter of recommendation from their golf coach or a PGA Professional. ***Recommended:*** essay or personal statement.

Application deadlines: 1/15 (freshmen), 2/15 (transfers), 11/1 (early action).

Notification: 3/30 (freshmen), 4/15 (transfers), 1/30 (early action).

CONTACT
Mr. Jon Westover, Associate Vice Provost and Director of Undergraduate Admissions, North Carolina State University, Box 7103, Raleigh, NC 27695. *Phone:* 919-515-2434. *Fax:* 919-515-5039. *E-mail:* undergrad-admissions@ncsu.edu.

North Carolina Wesleyan College
Rocky Mount, North Carolina
http://www.ncwc.edu/

- **Independent** 4-year, founded 1956, affiliated with United Methodist Church
- **Suburban** 200-acre campus
- **Endowment** $10.6 million
- **Coed**
- **Moderately difficult** entrance level

FACULTY
Student/faculty ratio: 16:1.

ACADEMICS
Calendar: semesters. *Degrees:* bachelor's (also offers adult part-time degree program with significant enrollment not reflected in profile).
Library: Elizabeth Braswell Pearsall Library. *Books:* 78,800 (physical), 44,751 (digital/electronic); *Serial titles:* 4,326 (physical), 4,329 (digital/electronic); *Databases:* 86. Students can reserve study rooms.

STUDENT LIFE
Housing options: on-campus residence required through sophomore year; coed, men-only, women-only, special housing for students with disabilities. Campus housing is university owned. Freshman campus housing is guaranteed.

Activities and organizations: drama/theater group, student-run newspaper, choral group, marching band, Refuge Campus Ministry, NCWC Cheerleaders, Voices of Triumph, Campus Crusade for Christ, Visions of Beauty, national fraternities, national sororities.

Athletics Member NCAA. All Division III.

Campus security: 24-hour emergency response devices and patrols, late-night transport/escort service, controlled dormitory access.

Student services: health clinic, personal/psychological counseling.

COSTS & FINANCIAL AID
Costs (2018–19) ***Comprehensive fee:*** $40,200 includes full-time tuition ($29,750), mandatory fees ($400), and room and board ($10,050). Full-time tuition and fees vary according to location. Part-time tuition: $500 per semester hour. Part-time tuition and fees vary according to course load and location. ***College room only:*** $4650. Room and board charges vary according to housing facility.

Financial Aid Of all full-time matriculated undergraduates who enrolled in 2008, 956 applied for aid, 788 were judged to have need, 360 had their need fully met. 323 Federal Work-Study jobs (averaging $1438). 67 state and other part-time jobs (averaging $565). In 2008, 46 non-need-based awards were made. ***Average percent of need met:*** 70. ***Average financial aid package:*** $12,524. ***Average need-based loan:*** $3898. ***Average need-based gift aid:*** $6696. ***Average non-need-based aid:*** $7876. ***Average indebtedness upon graduation:*** $7269.

APPLYING
Standardized Tests *Required:* SAT or ACT (for admission).
Options: electronic application.
Required: high school transcript. ***Required for some:*** essay or personal statement, interview. ***Recommended:*** minimum 2.0 GPA, 2 letters of recommendation, interview.

CONTACT
Mr. Ben Lilley, Assistant Director of Admissions, North Carolina Wesleyan College, 3400 North Wesleyan Boulevard, Rocky Mount, NC 27804. *Phone:* 252-985-5113. *Toll-free phone:* 800-488-6292. *Fax:* 252-985-5295. *E-mail:* blilley@ncwc.edu.

Pfeiffer University
Misenheimer, North Carolina
http://www.pfeiffer.edu/

- **Independent United Methodist** comprehensive, founded 1885
- **Rural** 300-acre campus with easy access to Charlotte
- **Endowment** $15.3 million
- **Coed** 813 undergraduate students, 90% full-time, 52% women, 48% men
- **Moderately difficult** entrance level, 66% of applicants were admitted

UNDERGRAD STUDENTS
732 full-time, 81 part-time. 19% are from out of state; 23% Black or African American, non-Hispanic/Latino; 7% Hispanic/Latino; 1% Asian, non-Hispanic/Latino; 0.2% Native Hawaiian or other Pacific Islander, non-Hispanic/Latino; 0.5% American Indian or Alaska Native, non-Hispanic/Latino; 3% Two or more races, non-Hispanic/Latino; 0.4% Race/ethnicity unknown; 2% international; 7% transferred in; 59% live on campus.

Freshmen:
Admission: 1,860 applied, 1,228 admitted, 277 enrolled. ***Average high school GPA:*** 3.2. ***Test scores:*** SAT evidence-based reading and writing scores over 500: 56%; SAT math scores over 500: 53%; ACT scores over 18: 66%; SAT evidence-based reading and writing scores over 600: 12%; SAT math scores over 600: 12%; ACT scores over 24: 15%; SAT evidence-based reading and writing scores over 700: 1%; SAT math scores over 700: 1%; ACT scores over 30: 3%.
Retention: 61% of full-time freshmen returned.

FACULTY
Total: 126, 64% full-time, 69% with terminal degrees.
Student/faculty ratio: 12:1.

ACADEMICS
Calendar: semesters. *Degrees:* bachelor's, master's, post-master's, and postbachelor's certificates.
Special study options: academic remediation for entering students, accelerated degree program, advanced placement credit, cooperative education, double majors, English as a second language, honors programs, independent study, internships, part-time degree program, services for LD students, study abroad, summer session for credit. ***ROTC:*** Army (c).
Unusual degree programs: 3-2 business administration.
Computers: Students can access the following: campus intranet, computer help desk, free student e-mail accounts, online (class) grades, online (class) registration, online (class) schedules. Campuswide network is available. 100% of college-owned or -operated housing units are wired for high-speed Internet access. Wireless service is available via classrooms, computer centers, student centers.
Library: Gustavus A. Pfeiffer Library. *Books:* 125,000 (physical).

STUDENT LIFE
Housing options: on-campus residence required through senior year; coed, women-only. Campus housing is university owned. Freshman campus housing is guaranteed.
Activities and organizations: drama/theater group, student-run newspaper, choral group, Student Government Association, Religious Life Council, Commuter Student Association, Programming Activities Council, Residence Hall Association.
Athletics Member NCAA. All Division III. ***Intercollegiate sports:*** baseball M, basketball M/W, cheerleading M/W, cross-country running M/W, golf M/W, lacrosse M/W, soccer M/W, softball W, swimming and diving W, tennis M/W, track and field M/W, volleyball W. ***Intramural sports:*** badminton M/W, basketball M/W, football M/W, soccer M/W, softball M/W, tennis M/W, ultimate Frisbee M/W, volleyball M/W, water polo M/W.
Campus security: 24-hour emergency response devices and patrols, late-night transport/escort service, controlled dormitory access.
Student services: health clinic, personal/psychological counseling, women's center.

COSTS & FINANCIAL AID
Costs (2018–19) ***Comprehensive fee:*** $41,460 includes full-time tuition ($29,200), mandatory fees ($1034), and room and board ($11,226). Full-time tuition and fees vary according to course load. Part-time tuition: $460 per semester hour. Part-time tuition and fees vary according to course load. ***Required fees:*** $215 per term part-time. ***College room only:*** $5924. Room and board charges vary according to board plan and housing facility. ***Payment plan:*** installment. ***Waivers:*** employees or children of employees.
Financial Aid Of all full-time matriculated undergraduates who enrolled in 2017, 623 applied for aid, 589 were judged to have need, 96 had their need fully met. In 2017, 75 non-need-based awards were made. ***Average percent of need met:*** 75. ***Average financial aid package:*** $24,502. ***Average need-based loan:*** $3516. ***Average need-based gift aid:*** $21,400. ***Average non-need-based aid:*** $14,609. ***Financial aid deadline:*** 7/1.

APPLYING
Options: electronic application, early admission, deferred entrance.
Required: high school transcript. ***Required for some:*** 2 letters of recommendation. ***Recommended:*** minimum 2.0 GPA, interview.
Application deadlines: rolling (freshmen), rolling (transfers).
Notification: continuous (freshmen), continuous (transfers).

CONTACT
Emily Carella, Director of Undergraduate Admissions, Pfeiffer University, PO Box 960, Misenheimer, NC 28109. *Phone:* 704-463-3047. *Toll-free phone:* 800-338-2060. *Fax:* 704-463-1363. *E-mail:* emily.carella@pfeiffer.edu.

Piedmont International University
Winston-Salem, North Carolina
http://www.piedmontu.edu/

CONTACT
Mr. Joe Edgerton, Undergraduate Admissions Counselor, Piedmont International University, 420 South Broad Street, Winston-Salem, NC 27101. *Phone:* 336-714-7933. *Toll-free phone:* 800-937-5097. *Fax:* 336-725-5522. *E-mail:* stevensons@piedmontu.edu.

Queens University of Charlotte
Charlotte, North Carolina
http://www.queens.edu/

- **Independent Presbyterian** comprehensive, founded 1857
- **Urban** 95-acre campus with easy access to Charlotte, NC
- **Endowment** $91.2 million
- **Coed** 1,766 undergraduate students, 88% full-time, 67% women, 33% men
- **Moderately difficult** entrance level, 79% of applicants were admitted

UNDERGRAD STUDENTS
1,552 full-time, 214 part-time. 43% are from out of state; 16% Black or African American, non-Hispanic/Latino; 10% Hispanic/Latino; 2% Asian, non-Hispanic/Latino; 0.2% Native Hawaiian or other Pacific Islander, non-Hispanic/Latino; 0.7% American Indian or Alaska Native, non-Hispanic/Latino; 0.6% Two or more races, non-Hispanic/Latino; 4% Race/ethnicity unknown; 9% international; 12% transferred in; 68% live on campus.

Freshmen:
Admission: 2,419 applied, 1,900 admitted, 369 enrolled. ***Test scores:*** SAT evidence-based reading and writing scores over 500: 84%; SAT math scores over 500: 84%; ACT scores over 18: 94%; SAT evidence-based reading and writing scores over 600: 37%; SAT math scores over 600: 26%; ACT scores over 24: 47%; SAT evidence-based reading and writing scores over 700: 5%; SAT math scores over 700: 4%; ACT scores over 30: 9%.

Retention: 82% of full-time freshmen returned.

FACULTY
Total: 300, 44% full-time, 58% with terminal degrees.

Student/faculty ratio: 9:1.

ACADEMICS
Calendar: semesters. *Degrees:* bachelor's, master's, and postbachelor's certificates.

Special study options: adult/continuing education programs, advanced placement credit, distance learning, double majors, honors programs, independent study, internships, off-campus study, part-time degree program, study abroad, summer session for credit.

Computers: 220 computers/terminals and 100 ports are available on campus for general student use. Students can access the following: campus intranet, computer help desk, free student e-mail accounts, online (class) grades, online (class) registration, online (class) schedules. Campuswide network is available. 100% of college-owned or -operated housing units are wired for high-speed Internet access. Wireless service is available via entire campus.
Library: Everett Library. *Books:* 41,620 (physical), 228,153 (digital/electronic); *Serial titles:* 106 (physical), 19,724 (digital/electronic); *Databases:* 81. Weekly public service hours: 93; students can reserve study rooms.

STUDENT LIFE
Housing options: on-campus residence required through junior year; coed, special housing for students with disabilities. Campus housing is university owned. Freshman campus housing is guaranteed.

Activities and organizations: drama/theater group, student-run newspaper, radio station, choral group, Senate, College Union Board, Royal Ambassadors, Students for Black Awareness, International Club, national fraternities, national sororities.

Athletics Member NCAA. All Division II except golf (Division I). ***Intercollegiate sports:*** basketball M(s)/W(s), cross-country running M(s)/W(s), golf M(s)/W(s), lacrosse M(s)/W(s), soccer M(s)/W(s), softball W(s), swimming and diving M(s)/W(s), tennis M(s)/W(s), track and field M(s)/W(s), volleyball W(s). ***Intramural sports:*** basketball M/W, cheerleading M/W, fencing W(c), soccer M/W, softball M/W, tennis M/W, triathlon M(c)/W(c), volleyball M/W.

Campus security: 24-hour emergency response devices and patrols, late-night transport/escort service, controlled dormitory access, Emergency Alert System.

Student services: health clinic, personal/psychological counseling.

COSTS & FINANCIAL AID
Costs (2018–19) ***Tuition:*** $33,434 full-time. Full-time tuition and fees vary according to course load, program, and student level. Part-time tuition and fees vary according to course load and program. ***Room only:*** Room and board charges vary according to board plan and housing facility. ***Payment plan:*** installment. ***Waivers:*** employees or children of employees.

Financial Aid Of all full-time matriculated undergraduates who enrolled in 2018, 1,149 applied for aid, 1,012 were judged to have need, 208 had their need fully met. In 2018, 443 non-need-based awards were made. ***Average percent of need met:*** 72. ***Average financial aid package:*** $26,996. ***Average need-based loan:*** $4214. ***Average need-based gift aid:*** $21,269. ***Average non-need-based aid:*** $14,223. ***Average indebtedness upon graduation:*** $22,613.

APPLYING
Standardized Tests *Required:* SAT or ACT (for admission).

Options: electronic application, early action, deferred entrance.

Required: essay or personal statement, high school transcript, 1 letter of recommendation. ***Required for some:*** interview.

Application deadlines: rolling (freshmen), rolling (transfers).

Notification: continuous (freshmen), continuous (transfers).

CONTACT
Evan Sprinkle, Director Traditional Undergraduate Admissions, Queens University of Charlotte, 1900 Selwyn Avenue, Harris Welcome Center, MSC 1428, Charlotte, NC 28274. *Phone:* 704-337-2212. *Toll-free phone:* 800-849-0202. *E-mail:* admissions@queens.edu.

St. Andrews University
Laurinburg, North Carolina
http://www.sa.edu/

- **Independent Presbyterian** comprehensive, founded 1958
- **Small-town** 600-acre campus
- **Coed**
- **Moderately difficult** entrance level

FACULTY
Student/faculty ratio: 14:1.

ACADEMICS
Calendar: semesters. *Degrees:* diplomas, bachelor's, and master's.
Library: DeTamble Library. *Books:* 83,851 (physical), 345,661 (digital/electronic); *Serial titles:* 1,165 (physical), 31,450 (digital/electronic); *Databases:* 90.

STUDENT LIFE
Housing options: on-campus residence required through senior year; coed, men-only, women-only. Campus housing is university owned.

Activities and organizations: drama/theater group, choral group.

Athletics Member NCAA, NAIA. All NCAA Division II.

Campus security: 24-hour emergency response devices and patrols, late-night transport/escort service.

Student services: veterans affairs office.

COSTS & FINANCIAL AID
Costs (2018–19) ***Tuition:*** $25,618 full-time, $288 per credit part-time. Full-time tuition and fees vary according to course load and location. Part-time tuition and fees vary according to location. ***Room only:*** Room and board charges vary according to housing facility.

Financial Aid Of all full-time matriculated undergraduates who enrolled in 2016, 483 applied for aid, 455 were judged to have need, 47 had their need fully met. In 2016, 84 non-need-based awards were made. ***Average percent of need met:*** 70. ***Average financial aid package:*** $21,123. ***Average need-based loan:*** $4538. ***Average need-based gift aid:*** $17,187. ***Average non-need-based aid:*** $10,894. ***Average indebtedness upon graduation:*** $26,209.

APPLYING
Standardized Tests *Recommended:* SAT and SAT Subject Tests or ACT (for admission).

Options: electronic application, deferred entrance.

Application fee: $35.

Required: high school transcript. ***Required for some:*** essay or personal statement, interview. ***Recommended:*** minimum 2.0 GPA.

CONTACT
Erin Balduf, Director of Admissions, St. Andrews University, 1700 Dogwood Mile, Laurinburg, NC 28352. *Phone:* 910-277-5555. *Toll-free phone:* 800-763-0198. *Fax:* 910-277-5087. *E-mail:* admission@sapc.edu.

Saint Augustine's University
Raleigh, North Carolina
http://www.st-aug.edu/

- **Independent Episcopal** 4-year, founded 1867
- **Urban** 122-acre campus
- **Coed**
- **Moderately difficult** entrance level

FACULTY
Student/faculty ratio: 13:1.

ACADEMICS
Calendar: semesters. *Degree:* bachelor's.
Library: Prezell R. Robinson Library. Students can reserve study rooms.

STUDENT LIFE
Housing options: on-campus residence required through sophomore year; men-only, women-only. Campus housing is university owned and leased by the school. Freshman campus housing is guaranteed.

Activities and organizations: drama/theater group, student-run newspaper, radio and television station, choral group, marching band, Campus Activity Board, Christian Fellowship Organization, Collegiate

100 Black Men of America, Student Government Association/Student Leaders, Falcon Fanatic Pep Squad, national fraternities, national sororities.

Athletics Member NCAA. All Division II.

Campus security: 24-hour emergency response devices and patrols, RAVE: Emergency Notification System.

Student services: health clinic, personal/psychological counseling, women's center.

COSTS & FINANCIAL AID
Costs (2018–19) ***Comprehensive fee:*** $25,582 includes full-time tuition ($12,890), mandatory fees ($5000), and room and board ($7692). Full-time tuition and fees vary according to course load. Part-time tuition: $537 per credit hour. Part-time tuition and fees vary according to course load. ***Required fees:*** $208 per credit hour part-time. ***College room only:*** $3182. Room and board charges vary according to housing facility.

Financial Aid Of all full-time matriculated undergraduates who enrolled in 2016, 950 applied for aid, 950 were judged to have need. 462 Federal Work-Study jobs (averaging $1887). In 2016, 39 non-need-based awards were made. ***Average percent of need met:*** 46. ***Average financial aid package:*** $10,315. ***Average need-based gift aid:*** $4670. ***Average non-need-based aid:*** $3750. ***Average indebtedness upon graduation:*** $19,500.

APPLYING
Standardized Tests *Required:* SAT or ACT (for admission).

Options: electronic application, deferred entrance.

Application fee: $50.

Required: high school transcript, minimum 2.0 GPA, 2 letters of recommendation, medical history, background check. ***Required for some:*** essay or personal statement, interview. ***Recommended:*** minimum 2.5 GPA.

CONTACT
Mr. Chris J. Withers, Director of Admissions, Saint Augustine's University, 1315 Oakwood Avenue, Raleigh, NC 27610-2298. *Phone:* 919-516-4012. *Toll-free phone:* 800-948-1126. *Fax:* 919-516-5804. *E-mail:* jesousa@st-aug.edu.

Salem College
Winston-Salem, North Carolina
http://www.salem.edu/

CONTACT
Dean Katherine Knapp Watts, Dean of Admissions and Financial Aid, Salem College, Single Sisters House, 601 South Church Street, Winston-Salem, NC 27101. *Phone:* 336-721-2621. *Toll-free phone:* 800-327-2536. *Fax:* 336-917-5572. *E-mail:* admissions@salem.edu.

Shaw University
Raleigh, North Carolina
http://www.shawu.edu/

- **Independent Baptist** comprehensive, founded 1865
- **Urban** 30-acre campus
- **Coed**
- **Minimally difficult** entrance level

FACULTY
Student/faculty ratio: 17:1.

ACADEMICS
Calendar: semesters. *Degrees:* certificates, bachelor's, and master's.
Library: James E. Cheek Learning Resources Center.

STUDENT LIFE
Housing options: on-campus residence required for freshman year; men-only, women-only. Campus housing is university owned. Freshman applicants given priority for college housing.

Activities and organizations: drama/theater group, student-run newspaper, radio station, choral group, marching band, Student Government Association, choir, University band, academic clubs, International Student Organization, national fraternities, national sororities.

Athletics Member NCAA. All Division II.

Campus security: 24-hour emergency response devices and patrols, late-night transport/escort service, 24-hour electronic surveillance cameras.

Student services: health clinic, personal/psychological counseling.

COSTS & FINANCIAL AID
Costs (2018–19) ***Comprehensive fee:*** $24,638 includes full-time tuition ($11,808), mandatory fees ($4672), and room and board ($8158). Part-time tuition: $492 per credit hour. ***Required fees:*** $93 per credit hour part-time, $290 per term part-time. ***College room only:*** $3842. ***Payment plans:*** installment, deferred payment.

Financial Aid Of all full-time matriculated undergraduates who enrolled in 2005, 2,197 applied for aid, 2,068 were judged to have need, 201 had their need fully met. 347 Federal Work-Study jobs (averaging $1120). In 2005, 117 non-need-based awards were made. ***Average percent of need met:*** 63. ***Average financial aid package:*** $8992. ***Average need-based loan:*** $3394. ***Average need-based gift aid:*** $5898. ***Average non-need-based aid:*** $9333. ***Average indebtedness upon graduation:*** $15,982. ***Financial aid deadline:*** 6/1.

APPLYING
Standardized Tests *Required:* SAT or ACT (for admission).

Options: electronic application, early admission, deferred entrance.

Application fee: $25.

Required: high school transcript, minimum 2.0 GPA.

CONTACT
Shaw University, 118 East South Street, Raleigh, NC 27601-2399. *Toll-free phone:* 800-214-6683.

Southeastern Baptist Theological Seminary
Wake Forest, North Carolina
http://www.sebts.edu/

- **Independent Southern Baptist** comprehensive, founded 1950
- **Suburban** 300-acre campus with easy access to Raleigh
- **Coed** 516 undergraduate students, 60% full-time, 28% women, 72% men
- **Noncompetitive** entrance level, 86% of applicants were admitted

UNDERGRAD STUDENTS
308 full-time, 208 part-time. Students come from 52 states and territories; 30 other countries; 66% are from out of state; 11% Black or African American, non-Hispanic/Latino; 7% Hispanic/Latino; 3% Asian, non-Hispanic/Latino; 1% American Indian or Alaska Native, non-Hispanic/Latino; 1% Race/ethnicity unknown; 0.6% international; 8% transferred in.

Freshmen:
Admission: 109 applied, 94 admitted, 136 enrolled.
Retention: 69% of full-time freshmen returned.

FACULTY
Total: 124, 44% full-time, 68% with terminal degrees.

Student/faculty ratio: 15:1.

ACADEMICS
Calendar: semesters. *Degrees:* certificates, associate, bachelor's, master's, and doctoral.

Special study options: academic remediation for entering students, adult/continuing education programs, distance learning, double majors, independent study, internships, off-campus study, part-time degree program, summer session for credit.

Computers: 55 computers/terminals and 1,100 ports are available on campus for general student use. Students can access the following: campus intranet, free student e-mail accounts, online (class) grades, online (class) registration, online (class) schedules. Campuswide network is available. Wireless service is available via classrooms, libraries, student centers.

Library: The Library at Southeastern plus 1 other. *Books:* 195,926 (physical), 420,952 (digital/electronic); *Serial titles:* 2,286 (physical), 31,776 (digital/electronic); *Databases:* 29. Weekly public service hours: 71; students can reserve study rooms.

STUDENT LIFE

Housing options: on-campus residence required for freshman year; men-only, women-only. Campus housing is university owned and leased by the school. Freshman applicants given priority for college housing.

Activities and organizations: drama/theater group, choral group.

Athletics ***Intramural sports:*** basketball M/W, football M/W, golf M/W, racquetball M/W, table tennis M/W, ultimate Frisbee M/W, volleyball M/W.

Campus security: 24-hour emergency response devices and patrols, late-night transport/escort service.

Student services: health clinic, personal/psychological counseling, women's center.

APPLYING

Standardized Tests *Required:* SAT or ACT (for admission).

Options: electronic application.

Application fee: $40.

Required: essay or personal statement, high school transcript, minimum 2.0 GPA, 3 letters of recommendation.

Notification: continuous until 8/20 (freshmen), continuous until 8/20 (transfers).

CONTACT

Mrs. Samantha Couick, Admissions Counselor, Southeastern Baptist Theological Seminary, 120 South Wingate Street, Wake Forest, NC 27587. *Phone:* 919-761-2283. *Toll-free phone:* 800-284-6317.

Strayer University–Greensboro Campus

Greensboro, North Carolina

http://www.strayer.edu/north-carolina/greensboro/

CONTACT

Strayer University–Greensboro Campus, 4900 Koger Boulevard, Suite 400, Greensboro, NC 27407. *Toll-free phone:* 888-311-0355.

Strayer University–Huntersville Campus

Huntersville, North Carolina

http://www.strayer.edu/north-carolina/huntersville/

CONTACT

Strayer University–Huntersville Campus, 13620 Reese Boulevard, Suite 130, Huntersville, NC 28078. *Toll-free phone:* 888-311-0355.

Strayer University–North Charlotte Campus

Concord, North Carolina

http://www.strayer.edu/north-carolina/north-charlotte/

CONTACT

Strayer University–North Charlotte Campus, 7870 Commons Park Circle NW, Concord, NC 28027. *Toll-free phone:* 888-311-0355.

Strayer University–North Raleigh Campus

Raleigh, North Carolina

http://www.strayer.edu/north-carolina/north-raleigh/

CONTACT

Strayer University–North Raleigh Campus, 8701 Wadford Drive, Raleigh, NC 27616. *Toll-free phone:* 888-311-0355.

Strayer University–Research Triangle Park Campus

Morrisville, North Carolina

http://www.strayer.edu/north-carolina/morrisville

CONTACT

Strayer University–Research Triangle Park Campus, 4 Copley Parkway, Morrisville, NC 27560. *Toll-free phone:* 888-311-0355.

Strayer University–South Charlotte Campus

Charlotte, North Carolina

http://www.strayer.edu/north-carolina/south-charlotte/

CONTACT

Strayer University–South Charlotte Campus, 9101 Kings Parade Boulevard, Suite 200, Charlotte, NC 28273. *Toll-free phone:* 888-311-0355.

Strayer University–South Raleigh Campus

Raleigh, North Carolina

http://www.strayer.edu/north-carolina/south-raleigh/

CONTACT

Strayer University–South Raleigh Campus, 3421 Olympia Drive, Raleigh, NC 27603. *Toll-free phone:* 888-311-0355.

University of Mount Olive

Mount Olive, North Carolina

http://www.umo.edu/

CONTACT

University of Mount Olive, 634 Henderson Street, Mount Olive, NC 28365. *Phone:* 919-658-2502 Ext. 3009. *Toll-free phone:* 800-653-0854.

University of North Carolina at Asheville

Asheville, North Carolina

http://www.unca.edu/

- **State-supported** comprehensive, founded 1927, part of University of North Carolina System
- **Urban** 365-acre campus
- **Endowment** $44.2 million
- **Coed** 3,743 undergraduate students, 86% full-time, 57% women, 43% men
- **Moderately difficult** entrance level, 82% of applicants were admitted

UNDERGRAD STUDENTS

3,232 full-time, 511 part-time. Students come from 44 states and territories; 26 other countries; 12% are from out of state; 5% Black or African American, non-Hispanic/Latino; 6% Hispanic/Latino; 2% Asian, non-Hispanic/Latino; 0.1% Native Hawaiian or other Pacific Islander, non-Hispanic/Latino; 0.6% American Indian or Alaska Native, non-Hispanic/Latino; 4% Two or more races, non-Hispanic/Latino; 3% Race/ethnicity unknown; 1% international; 9% transferred in; 38% live on campus.

Freshmen:

Admission: 3,163 applied, 2,601 admitted, 788 enrolled. ***Average high school GPA:*** 3.4. ***Test scores:*** SAT evidence-based reading and writing scores over 500: 91%; SAT math scores over 500: 84%; ACT scores over 18: 97%; SAT evidence-based reading and writing scores over 600: 49%; SAT math scores over 600: 34%; ACT scores over 24: 58%; SAT evidence-based reading and writing scores over 700: 9%; SAT math scores over 700: 4%; ACT scores over 30: 13%.

Retention: 73% of full-time freshmen returned.

FACULTY
Total: 320, 69% full-time, 72% with terminal degrees.

Student/faculty ratio: 13:1.

ACADEMICS
Calendar: semesters. *Degrees:* bachelor's, master's, and postbachelor's certificates.

Special study options: adult/continuing education programs, advanced placement credit, cooperative education, distance learning, double majors, honors programs, independent study, internships, off-campus study, part-time degree program, services for LD students, student-designed majors, study abroad, summer session for credit.

Computers: 500 computers/terminals and 1,900 ports are available on campus for general student use. Students can access the following: campus intranet, computer help desk, free student e-mail accounts, online (class) grades, online (class) registration, online (class) schedules. Campuswide network is available. 100% of college-owned or -operated housing units are wired for high-speed Internet access. Wireless service is available via classrooms, computer centers, computer labs, dorm rooms, learning centers, libraries, student centers.
Library: Ramsey Library. *Books:* 306,273 (physical), 487,660 (digital/electronic); *Serial titles:* 113 (physical), 82,954 (digital/electronic); *Databases:* 138. Weekly public service hours: 99; students can reserve study rooms.

STUDENT LIFE
Housing options: on-campus residence required for freshman year; coed, special housing for students with disabilities. Campus housing is university owned. Freshman campus housing is guaranteed.

Activities and organizations: drama/theater group, student-run newspaper, radio station, choral group, Student Government Association, Alliance, Black Student Association, Gaming Club, Underdog Productions, national fraternities, national sororities.

Athletics Member NCAA. All Division I. ***Intercollegiate sports:*** archery M(c)/W(c), baseball M(s), basketball M(s)/W(s), cheerleading W(c), cross-country running M(s)/W(s), equestrian sports M(c)/W(c), fencing M(c)/W(c), golf W(s)(c), rugby M(c)/W(c), soccer M(s)/W(s), swimming and diving W(s), tennis M(s)/W(s), track and field M(s)/W(s), volleyball W(s). ***Intramural sports:*** badminton M/W, basketball M/W, football M(c)/W(c), racquetball M/W, soccer M/W, ultimate Frisbee M(c)/W(c), volleyball M/W, water polo M/W.

Campus security: 24-hour emergency response devices and patrols, late-night transport/escort service, controlled dormitory access.

Student services: health clinic, personal/psychological counseling, veterans affairs office.

COSTS & FINANCIAL AID
Costs (2018–19) ***One-time required fee:*** $150. ***Tuition:*** state resident $4914 full-time, $139 per credit hour part-time; nonresident $21,236 full-time, $704 per credit hour part-time. Full-time tuition and fees vary according to course load and degree level. Part-time tuition and fees vary according to course load and degree level. ***Required fees:*** $3023 full-time, $17 per credit hour part-time. ***Room and board:*** $9380; room only: $5288. Room and board charges vary according to board plan and housing facility. ***Payment plan:*** installment. ***Waivers:*** employees or children of employees.

Financial Aid Of all full-time matriculated undergraduates who enrolled in 2017, 2,574 applied for aid, 1,873 were judged to have need, 455 had their need fully met. 55 Federal Work-Study jobs (averaging $2184). 1,900 state and other part-time jobs (averaging $1109). In 2017, 243 non-need-based awards were made. ***Average percent of need met:*** 75. ***Average financial aid package:*** $12,781. ***Average need-based loan:*** $4690. ***Average need-based gift aid:*** $7372. ***Average non-need-based aid:*** $2310. ***Average indebtedness upon graduation:*** $22,545.

APPLYING
Standardized Tests *Required:* SAT or ACT (for admission).

Options: electronic application, deferred entrance.

Application fee: $75.

Required: essay or personal statement, high school transcript, 1 letter of recommendation, minimum course requirement.

Application deadlines: 8/1 (freshmen), 4/15 (transfers).

Notification: continuous until 9/18 (freshmen), continuous (transfers).

CONTACT
Steve McKellips, Senior Director of Admissions and Financial Aid, University of North Carolina at Asheville, Brown Hall, CPO # 1320, Asheville, NC 28804-8510. *Phone:* 828-250-3829. *Toll-free phone:* 800-531-9842. *Fax:* 828-251-6482. *E-mail:* admissions@unca.edu.

The University of North Carolina at Chapel Hill

Chapel Hill, North Carolina

http://www.unc.edu/

- **State-supported** university, founded 1789, part of University of North Carolina System
- **Suburban** 729-acre campus with easy access to Raleigh-Durham
- **Endowment** $3.3 billion
- **Coed** 19,117 undergraduate students, 97% full-time, 59% women, 41% men
- **Very difficult** entrance level, 22% of applicants were admitted

UNDERGRAD STUDENTS
18,526 full-time, 591 part-time. Students come from 52 states and territories; 101 other countries; 15% are from out of state; 8% Black or African American, non-Hispanic/Latino; 8% Hispanic/Latino; 11% Asian, non-Hispanic/Latino; 0.1% Native Hawaiian or other Pacific Islander, non-Hispanic/Latino; 0.5% American Indian or Alaska Native, non-Hispanic/Latino; 5% Two or more races, non-Hispanic/Latino; 4% Race/ethnicity unknown; 3% international; 4% transferred in; 51% live on campus.

Freshmen:
Admission: 43,473 applied, 9,524 admitted, 4,326 enrolled. ***Average high school GPA:*** 4.7. ***Test scores:*** SAT evidence-based reading and writing scores over 500: 99%; SAT math scores over 500: 99%; ACT scores over 18: 100%; SAT evidence-based reading and writing scores over 600: 89%; SAT math scores over 600: 85%; ACT scores over 24: 92%; SAT evidence-based reading and writing scores over 700: 40%; SAT math scores over 700: 46%; ACT scores over 30: 57%.

Retention: 97% of full-time freshmen returned.

FACULTY
Total: 2,310, 72% full-time, 76% with terminal degrees.

Student/faculty ratio: 13:1.

ACADEMICS
Calendar: semesters. *Degrees:* certificates, bachelor's, master's, doctoral, post-master's, and postbachelor's certificates.

Special study options: advanced placement credit, distance learning, double majors, honors programs, independent study, internships, off-campus study, part-time degree program, services for LD students, student-designed majors, study abroad, summer session for credit. ***ROTC:*** Army (b), Navy (b), Air Force (b).

Computers: 867 computers/terminals and 10,000 ports are available on campus for general student use. Students can access the following: computer help desk, free student e-mail accounts, online (class) grades, online (class) registration, online (class) schedules. Campuswide network is available. 100% of college-owned or -operated housing units are wired for high-speed Internet access. Wireless service is available via entire campus.
Library: Davis Library plus 12 others. *Books:* 7.5 million (physical), 1.3 million (digital/electronic); *Serial titles:* 191,333 (digital/electronic); *Databases:* 1,249. Weekly public service hours: 140; study areas open 24 hours, 5–7 days a week; students can reserve study rooms.

STUDENT LIFE
Housing options: on-campus residence required for freshman year; coed, men-only, women-only, special housing for students with disabilities. Campus housing is university owned. Freshman campus housing is guaranteed.

Activities and organizations: drama/theater group, student-run newspaper, radio and television station, choral group, marching band, Residence Hall Association, Carolina Fever, Campus Y, UNC-CH Habitat for Humanity, Carolina for the Kids Foundation (Dance Marathon), national fraternities, national sororities.

Athletics Member NCAA. All Division I except football (Division I-A). ***Intercollegiate sports:*** badminton M(c)/W(c), baseball M(s), basketball M(s)/W(s), cheerleading W(c), crew M(c)/W(s), cross-country running M(s)/W(s), equestrian sports M(c)/W(c), fencing M(s)/W(s), field hockey M(c)/W(s), golf M(s)/W(s), gymnastics M(c)/W(s), ice hockey M(c), lacrosse M(s)/W(s), racquetball M(c)/W(c), rugby M(c)/W(c), sailing M(c)/W(c), skiing (downhill) W(c), soccer M(s)/W(s), softball W(s), swimming and diving M(s)/W(s), tennis M(s)/W(s), track and field M(s)/W(s), triathlon M(c)/W(c), ultimate Frisbee M(c)/W(c), volleyball M(c)/W(s), water polo M(c)/W(c), wrestling M(s). ***Intramural sports:*** badminton M/W, baseball M(c), basketball M(c)/W(c), crew W(c), cross-country running M(c)/W(c), fencing W(c), golf M(c)/W(c), gymnastics W(c), racquetball M/W, sand volleyball M(c)/W(c), soccer M(c)/W(c), softball M/W(c), squash M(c)/W(c), swimming and diving M(c)/W(c), table tennis M/W, tennis M(c)/W(c), track and field M(c)/W(c), ultimate Frisbee M/W, volleyball M/W(c), water polo M/W.

Campus security: 24-hour emergency response devices and patrols, late-night transport/escort service, controlled dormitory access, crime prevention initiatives, campus-wide emergency alert system, cell phone/GPS security options.

Student services: health clinic, personal/psychological counseling, women's center, legal services, veterans affairs office.

COSTS & FINANCIAL AID

Costs (2019–20) ***Tuition:*** state resident $7019 full-time; nonresident $34,198 full-time. ***Required fees:*** $2027 full-time. ***Room and board:*** $11,526; room only: $6810.

Financial Aid Of all full-time matriculated undergraduates who enrolled in 2017, 11,390 applied for aid, 8,477 were judged to have need, 6,419 had their need fully met. 2,381 Federal Work-Study jobs (averaging $1767). In 2017, 751 non-need-based awards were made. ***Average percent of need met:*** 100. ***Average financial aid package:*** $20,312. ***Average need-based loan:*** $4864. ***Average need-based gift aid:*** $18,410. ***Average non-need-based aid:*** $7814. ***Average indebtedness upon graduation:*** $22,466.

APPLYING

Standardized Tests *Required:* SAT or ACT (for admission).

Options: electronic application, early action, deferred entrance.

Application fee: $85.

Required: essay or personal statement, high school transcript, 1 letter of recommendation, counselor's statement.

Application deadlines: 1/15 (freshmen), 2/15 (transfers), 10/15 (early action).

Notification: 3/31 (freshmen), 4/15 (transfers), 1/31 (early action).

CONTACT

Mr. Stephen M. Farmer, Vice Provost for Enrollment and Undergraduate Admissions, The University of North Carolina at Chapel Hill, Chapel Hill, NC 27599. *Phone:* 919-966-3932. *Fax:* 919-962-3045. *E-mail:* unchelp@admissions.unc.edu.

The University of North Carolina at Charlotte

Charlotte, North Carolina

http://www.uncc.edu/

- **State-supported** university, founded 1946, part of University of North Carolina System
- **Suburban** 1000-acre campus with easy access to Charlotte
- **Endowment** $83.2 million
- **Coed** 24,387 undergraduate students, 86% full-time, 47% women, 53% men
- **Moderately difficult** entrance level, 67% of applicants were admitted

UNDERGRAD STUDENTS

21,025 full-time, 3,362 part-time. Students come from 45 states and territories; 92 other countries; 5% are from out of state; 16% Black or African American, non-Hispanic/Latino; 10% Hispanic/Latino; 7% Asian, non-Hispanic/Latino; 0.1% Native Hawaiian or other Pacific Islander, non-Hispanic/Latino; 0.3% American Indian or Alaska Native, non-Hispanic/Latino; 5% Two or more races, non-Hispanic/Latino; 2% Race/ethnicity unknown; 3% international; 12% transferred in; 20% live on campus.

Freshmen:

Admission: 17,119 applied, 11,500 admitted, 3,708 enrolled. ***Average high school GPA:*** 4.1. ***Test scores:*** SAT evidence-based reading and writing scores over 500: 98%; SAT math scores over 500: 98%; ACT scores over 18: 98%; SAT evidence-based reading and writing scores over 600: 51%; SAT math scores over 600: 49%; ACT scores over 24: 50%; SAT evidence-based reading and writing scores over 700: 4%; SAT math scores over 700: 8%; ACT scores over 30: 7%.

Retention: 82% of full-time freshmen returned.

FACULTY

Total: 1,692, 69% full-time, 70% with terminal degrees.

Student/faculty ratio: 19:1.

ACADEMICS

Calendar: semesters. *Degrees:* bachelor's, master's, doctoral, post-master's, and postbachelor's certificates.

Special study options: accelerated degree program, adult/continuing education programs, advanced placement credit, cooperative education, distance learning, double majors, English as a second language, freshman honors college, honors programs, independent study, internships, off-campus study, part-time degree program, services for LD students, study abroad, summer session for credit. ***ROTC:*** Army (b), Air Force (b).

Computers: 1,600 computers/terminals are available on campus for general student use. Students can access the following: computer help desk, free student e-mail accounts, online (class) grades, online (class) registration, online (class) schedules. Campuswide network is available. 100% of college-owned or -operated housing units are wired for high-speed Internet access. Wireless service is available via entire campus.

Library: J. Murrey Atkins Library plus 1 other. *Books:* 812,959 (physical), 980,416 (digital/electronic); *Serial titles:* 4,578 (physical), 92,904 (digital/electronic); *Databases:* 675. Study areas open 24 hours, 5–7 days a week; students can reserve study rooms.

STUDENT LIFE

Housing options: coed, special housing for students with disabilities. Campus housing is university owned.

Activities and organizations: drama/theater group, student-run newspaper, radio station, choral group, marching band, Triveni (Indian Students Association), National Society of Leadership and Success, Kinesiology Student Organization, Habitat for Humanity, 49th Security Division, national fraternities, national sororities.

Athletics Member NCAA. All Division I. ***Intercollegiate sports:*** baseball M(s), basketball M(s)/W(s), cross-country running M(s)/W(s), football M(s), golf M(s)/W(s), soccer M(s)/W(s), softball W(s), tennis M(s)/W(s), track and field M(s)/W(s), volleyball W(s). ***Intramural sports:*** archery M(c)/W(c), badminton M/W, baseball M(c), basketball M/W, bowling M/W, equestrian sports M(c)/W(c), fencing M(c), field hockey M(c)/W(c), football M/W, golf M(c), ice hockey M(c), lacrosse M(c)/W(c), rock climbing M/W, rugby M(c)/W(c), sailing M(c)/W(c), soccer M/W, softball M/W, table tennis M/W, ultimate Frisbee M(c)/W(c), volleyball M/W, water polo M/W, weight lifting M(c)/W(c), wrestling M(c)/W(c).

Campus security: 24-hour emergency response devices and patrols, late-night transport/escort service, controlled dormitory access.

Student services: health clinic, personal/psychological counseling, veterans affairs office.

COSTS & FINANCIAL AID

Costs (2018–19) ***Tuition:*** state resident $3812 full-time; nonresident $17,246 full-time. Full-time tuition and fees vary according to course load and program. Part-time tuition and fees vary according to course load and program. ***Required fees:*** $3232 full-time. ***Room and board:*** $11,100; room only: $6370. Room and board charges vary according to board plan and housing facility. ***Payment plan:*** installment. ***Waivers:*** employees or children of employees.

Financial Aid Of all full-time matriculated undergraduates who enrolled in 2018, 17,116 applied for aid, 13,809 were judged to have need, 1,418 had their need fully met. 1,164 Federal Work-Study jobs (averaging $1737). In 2018, 290 non-need-based awards were made. ***Average percent of need met:*** 56. ***Average financial aid package:*** $9418. ***Average need-based loan:*** $4131. ***Average need-based gift aid:*** $6730. ***Average non-need-based aid:*** $7613. ***Average indebtedness upon graduation:*** $28,050.

APPLYING
Standardized Tests *Required:* SAT or ACT (for admission).

Options: electronic application, early action.

Application fee: $60.

Required: high school transcript, minimum 2.0 GPA.

Application deadlines: 6/1 (freshmen), 6/1 (out-of-state freshmen), 6/1 (transfers), 11/1 (early action).

Notification: continuous until 11/1 (freshmen), continuous until 11/1 (out-of-state freshmen), continuous (transfers), 1/30 (early action).

CONTACT
Ms. Claire Kirby, Director of Admissions, The University of North Carolina at Charlotte, 9201 University City Boulevard, 1st Floor, Cato Hall, Charlotte, NC 28223-0001. *Phone:* 704-687-5507. *Fax:* 704-687-6483. *E-mail:* admissions@uncc.edu.

The University of North Carolina at Greensboro

Greensboro, North Carolina

http://www.uncg.edu/

- **State-supported** university, founded 1891, part of University of North Carolina System
- **Urban** 250-acre campus
- **Endowment** $292.0 million
- **Coed** 16,641 undergraduate students, 86% full-time, 66% women, 34% men
- **Moderately difficult** entrance level, 84% of applicants were admitted

UNDERGRAD STUDENTS
14,265 full-time, 2,376 part-time. Students come from 46 states and territories; 55 other countries; 5% are from out of state; 29% Black or African American, non-Hispanic/Latino; 10% Hispanic/Latino; 5% Asian, non-Hispanic/Latino; 0.1% Native Hawaiian or other Pacific Islander, non-Hispanic/Latino; 0.4% American Indian or Alaska Native, non-Hispanic/Latino; 5% Two or more races, non-Hispanic/Latino; 1% Race/ethnicity unknown; 2% international; 18% transferred in; 34% live on campus.

Freshmen:
Admission: 8,170 applied, 6,846 admitted, 2,979 enrolled. ***Average high school GPA:*** 3.7. ***Test scores:*** SAT evidence-based reading and writing scores over 500: 79%; SAT math scores over 500: 74%; ACT scores over 18: 97%; SAT evidence-based reading and writing scores over 600: 24%; SAT math scores over 600: 14%; ACT scores over 24: 36%; SAT evidence-based reading and writing scores over 700: 2%; SAT math scores over 700: 2%; ACT scores over 30: 4%.

Retention: 76% of full-time freshmen returned.

FACULTY
Total: 1,126, 75% full-time, 71% with terminal degrees.

Student/faculty ratio: 18:1.

ACADEMICS
Calendar: semesters. *Degrees:* bachelor's, master's, doctoral, post-master's, and postbachelor's certificates.

Special study options: academic remediation for entering students, accelerated degree program, adult/continuing education programs, advanced placement credit, distance learning, double majors, English as a second language, freshman honors college, honors programs, independent study, internships, off-campus study, part-time degree program, services for LD students, student-designed majors, study abroad, summer session for credit. ***ROTC:*** Army (c), Air Force (c).

Unusual degree programs: 3-2 nursing; Applied Economics, English, Communication Studies, Mathematics, Applied Geography, Accounting, Economics, Consumer Apparel and Retail Studies, Information Technology and Management, Computer Science, Recreation and Parks Management, Information Syste.

Computers: 474 computers/terminals are available on campus for general student use. Students can access the following: computer help desk, free student e-mail accounts, online (class) grades, online (class) registration, online (class) schedules, wireless printing services, cloud storage services. Campuswide network is available. 100% of college-owned or -operated housing units are wired for high-speed Internet access. Wireless service is available via entire campus.

Library: Walter Clinton Jackson Library plus 4 others. *Books:* 1.2 million (physical), 1.2 million (digital/electronic); *Serial titles:* 18,527 (physical), 109,122 (digital/electronic); *Databases:* 765. Weekly public service hours: 138; study areas open 24 hours, 5–7 days a week; students can reserve study rooms.

STUDENT LIFE
Housing options: coed, special housing for students with disabilities. Campus housing is university owned.

Activities and organizations: drama/theater group, student-run newspaper, radio station, choral group, Alpha Lamda Delta, Beta Gamma Sigma, Sigma Theta Tau, Gamma Zeta, Golden Key, UNCG Leadership Challenge - Bronze, national fraternities, national sororities.

Athletics Member NCAA. All Division I. ***Intercollegiate sports:*** baseball M(s), basketball M(s)/W(s), cross-country running M(s)/W(s), golf M(s)/W(s)(c), soccer M(s)/W(s), softball W(s), tennis M(s)/W(s), track and field M(s)/W(s), volleyball W(s). ***Intramural sports:*** badminton M/W, basketball M/W, cross-country running M(c)/W(c), equestrian sports M(c)/W(c), fencing M(c)/W, field hockey M/W(c), football M(c)/W(c), lacrosse M(c)/W(c), racquetball M/W, rock climbing M/W, rugby M(c)/W(c), sand volleyball M/W, soccer M/W, softball M(c)/W(c), swimming and diving M(c)/W(c), table tennis M/W, tennis M(c)/W(c), ultimate Frisbee M/W, volleyball M(c)/W(c), water polo M/W.

Campus security: 24-hour emergency response devices and patrols, student patrols, late-night transport/escort service, controlled dormitory access.

Student services: health clinic, personal/psychological counseling, women's center, veterans affairs office.

COSTS & FINANCIAL AID
Costs (2018–19) ***Tuition:*** state resident $4422 full-time, $553 per credit hour part-time; nonresident $19,581 full-time, $2448 per credit hour part-time. Part-time tuition and fees vary according to course load. ***Required fees:*** $2897 full-time, $108 per credit hour part-time. ***Room and board:*** $9038; room only: $5382. Room and board charges vary according to board plan and housing facility. ***Payment plan:*** installment. ***Waivers:*** senior citizens and employees or children of employees.

Financial Aid Of all full-time matriculated undergraduates who enrolled in 2018, 12,181 applied for aid, 12,026 were judged to have need, 1,512 had their need fully met. 729 Federal Work-Study jobs (averaging $2275). In 2018, 198 non-need-based awards were made. ***Average percent of need met:*** 73. ***Average financial aid package:*** $11,741. ***Average need-based loan:*** $4199. ***Average need-based gift aid:*** $6310. ***Average non-need-based aid:*** $4005. ***Average indebtedness upon graduation:*** $27,088. ***Financial aid deadline:*** 8/10.

APPLYING
Standardized Tests *Required:* SAT or ACT (for admission).

Options: electronic application.

Application fee: $65.

Required: high school transcript, minimum 2.3 GPA.

Application deadlines: 8/1 (freshmen), 7/15 (transfers).

Notification: continuous until 8/15 (freshmen), continuous (transfers).

CONTACT
Mr. Chris Keller, Director of Admissions, The University of North Carolina at Greensboro, 1400 Spring Garden Street, Greensboro, NC 27412-5001. *Phone:* 336-334-5243. *Fax:* 336-334-5051. *E-mail:* admissions@uncg.edu.

The University of North Carolina at Pembroke

Pembroke, North Carolina

http://www.uncp.edu/

- **State-supported** comprehensive, founded 1887, part of University of North Carolina System
- **Rural** 264-acre campus
- **Endowment** $20.4 million
- **Coed** 6,069 undergraduate students, 81% full-time, 61% women, 39% men
- **Moderately difficult** entrance level, 81% of applicants were admitted

UNDERGRAD STUDENTS

4,945 full-time, 1,124 part-time. Students come from 33 states and territories; 12 other countries; 4% are from out of state; 33% Black or African American, non-Hispanic/Latino; 6% Hispanic/Latino; 2% Asian, non-Hispanic/Latino; 0.1% Native Hawaiian or other Pacific Islander, non-Hispanic/Latino; 15% American Indian or Alaska Native, non-Hispanic/Latino; 4% Two or more races, non-Hispanic/Latino; 1% Race/ethnicity unknown; 0.9% international; 14% transferred in; 34% live on campus.

Freshmen:

Admission: 4,316 applied, 3,506 admitted, 1,233 enrolled. ***Average high school GPA:*** 3.6. ***Test scores:*** SAT evidence-based reading and writing scores over 500: 55%; SAT math scores over 500: 48%; ACT scores over 18: 73%; SAT evidence-based reading and writing scores over 600: 10%; SAT math scores over 600: 6%; ACT scores over 24: 11%; SAT evidence-based reading and writing scores over 700: 1%; ACT scores over 30: 1%.

Retention: 74% of full-time freshmen returned.

FACULTY

Total: 402, 75% full-time, 68% with terminal degrees.

Student/faculty ratio: 16:1.

ACADEMICS

Calendar: semesters. *Degrees:* bachelor's, master's, and post-master's certificates.

Special study options: academic remediation for entering students, accelerated degree program, adult/continuing education programs, advanced placement credit, cooperative education, distance learning, double majors, English as a second language, honors programs, internships, off-campus study, part-time degree program, services for LD students, study abroad, summer session for credit. ***ROTC:*** Army (b), Air Force (b).

Computers: 501 computers/terminals are available on campus for general student use. Students can access the following: campus intranet, computer help desk, free student e-mail accounts, online (class) grades, online (class) registration, online (class) schedules, commuter/off campus connection to network, discounted computer software/hardware. Campuswide network is available. 100% of college-owned or -operated housing units are wired for high-speed Internet access. Wireless service is available via classrooms, computer centers, computer labs, dorm rooms, learning centers, libraries, student centers.

Library: Livermore Library. *Books:* 398,000 (physical), 165,000 (digital/electronic); *Serial titles:* 406 (physical), 54,000 (digital/electronic); *Databases:* 185. Weekly public service hours: 92; students can reserve study rooms.

STUDENT LIFE

Housing options: on-campus residence required for freshman year; coed, men-only, women-only. Campus housing is university owned and is provided by a third party. Freshman applicants given priority for college housing.

Activities and organizations: drama/theater group, student-run newspaper, radio and television station, choral group, marching band, Health Careers Club, Spectrum, Graduate Student Organization, Phi Alpha, National Association for the Advancement of Colored People, national fraternities, national sororities.

Athletics Member NCAA. All Division II except golf (Division I). ***Intercollegiate sports:*** baseball M(s), basketball M(s)/W(s), cheerleading M/W, cross-country running M(s)/W(s), football M(s), golf W(s), soccer M(s)/W(s), softball W(s), swimming and diving W, track and field M(s)/W(s), volleyball W(s), wrestling M(s). ***Intramural sports:*** basketball M/W, bowling M/W, cheerleading M/W, football M, golf M, racquetball M/W, rugby M, sand volleyball M/W, soccer M, softball M/W, swimming and diving M/W, tennis M/W, ultimate Frisbee M/W, volleyball M/W, weight lifting M/W, wrestling M.

Campus security: 24-hour emergency response devices and patrols, late-night transport/escort service, controlled dormitory access.

Student services: health clinic, personal/psychological counseling.

COSTS & FINANCIAL AID

Costs (2019–20) ***Tuition:*** state resident $1000 full-time; nonresident $5000 full-time. ***Required fees:*** $241 full-time. ***Payment plan:*** tuition prepayment.

Financial Aid Of all full-time matriculated undergraduates who enrolled in 2018, 4,406 applied for aid, 3,903 were judged to have need, 298 had their need fully met. 152 Federal Work-Study jobs (averaging $1895). In 2018, 33 non-need-based awards were made. ***Average percent of need met:*** 67. ***Average financial aid package:*** $9295. ***Average need-based loan:*** $4141. ***Average need-based gift aid:*** $6131. ***Average non-need-based aid:*** $2113. ***Average indebtedness upon graduation:*** $26,048.

APPLYING

Standardized Tests *Required:* SAT or ACT (for admission). *Required for some:* TOEFL.

Options: electronic application, deferred entrance.

Application fee: $45.

Required: high school transcript. ***Required for some:*** 1 letter of recommendation, interview. ***Recommended:*** essay or personal statement, minimum 2.0 GPA.

Application deadlines: 6/30 (freshmen), 6/30 (transfers).

Notification: continuous (freshmen), continuous (transfers).

CONTACT

Elizabeth Hunter, Director of Admissions, The University of North Carolina at Pembroke, One University Drive, PO Box 1510, Pembroke, NC 28372-1510. *Phone:* 910-522-6464. *Toll-free phone:* 800-949-UNCP. *Fax:* 910-521-6497. *E-mail:* admissions@uncp.edu.

University of North Carolina School of the Arts

Winston-Salem, North Carolina

http://www.uncsa.edu/

- **State-supported** comprehensive, founded 1963, part of University of North Carolina system
- **Urban** 74-acre campus
- **Endowment** $67.7 million
- **Coed** 890 undergraduate students, 99% full-time, 53% women, 47% men
- 38% of applicants were admitted

UNDERGRAD STUDENTS

884 full-time, 6 part-time. Students come from 46 states and territories; 14 other countries; 49% are from out of state; 9% Black or African American, non-Hispanic/Latino; 8% Hispanic/Latino; 2% Asian, non-Hispanic/Latino; 1% American Indian or Alaska Native, non-Hispanic/Latino; 5% Two or more races, non-Hispanic/Latino; 1% Race/ethnicity unknown; 3% international; 4% transferred in; 59% live on campus.

Freshmen:

Admission: 1,185 applied, 453 admitted, 243 enrolled. ***Average high school GPA:*** 3.8. ***Test scores:*** SAT evidence-based reading and writing scores over 500: 94%; SAT math scores over 500: 91%; ACT scores over 18: 96%; SAT evidence-based reading and writing scores over 600: 56%; SAT math scores over 600: 36%; ACT scores over 24: 62%; SAT evidence-based reading and writing scores over 700: 12%; SAT math scores over 700: 6%; ACT scores over 30: 18%.

Retention: 88% of full-time freshmen returned.

FACULTY

Total: 189, 76% full-time, 43% with terminal degrees.

Student/faculty ratio: 6:1.

ACADEMICS
Calendar: semesters. *Degrees:* certificates, bachelor's, master's, and post-master's certificates.

Special study options: advanced placement credit, English as a second language, independent study, internships, services for LD students, summer session for credit.

Computers: 117 computers/terminals and 1,000 ports are available on campus for general student use. Students can access the following: computer help desk, free student e-mail accounts, online (class) grades, online (class) registration, online (class) schedules. Campuswide network is available. 100% of college-owned or -operated housing units are wired for high-speed Internet access. Wireless service is available via entire campus.
Library: UNCSA Library. *Books:* 101,097 (physical), 37,147 (digital/electronic); *Serial titles:* 1,171 (physical), 73,113 (digital/electronic); *Databases:* 121. Weekly public service hours: 90; students can reserve study rooms.

STUDENT LIFE
Housing options: on-campus residence required through sophomore year; coed. Campus housing is university owned. Freshman campus housing is guaranteed.

Activities and organizations: drama/theater group, student-run newspaper, choral group, A.R.T.S. Club (awareness on social issues through artistic expression), The Artist Underground, Art & Soul, UNCSA Artists of Color.

Campus security: 24-hour emergency response devices and patrols, late-night transport/escort service, controlled dormitory access.

Student services: health clinic, personal/psychological counseling.

COSTS & FINANCIAL AID
Costs (2019–20) ***Tuition:*** state resident $6497 full-time, $266 per credit hour part-time; nonresident $23,040 full-time, $944 per credit hour part-time. No tuition increase for student's term of enrollment. ***Required fees:*** $2861 full-time, $115 per credit hour part-time. ***Room and board:*** $9156; room only: $4654.

Financial Aid Of all full-time matriculated undergraduates who enrolled in 2017, 624 applied for aid, 473 were judged to have need, 61 had their need fully met. 177 Federal Work-Study jobs (averaging $800). In 2017, 49 non-need-based awards were made. ***Average percent of need met:*** 67. ***Average financial aid package:*** $14,145. ***Average need-based loan:*** $4590. ***Average need-based gift aid:*** $9222. ***Average non-need-based aid:*** $3313. ***Average indebtedness upon graduation:*** $28,551.

APPLYING
Standardized Tests *Required:* SAT or ACT (for admission).

Options: deferred entrance.

Application fee: $95.

Required: essay or personal statement, high school transcript, minimum 2.5 GPA, 2 letters of recommendation, interview, audition.

Notification: continuous until 4/1 (freshmen).

CONTACT
Mr. Paul Razza, Director of Admissions, University of North Carolina School of the Arts, 1533 South Main Street, PO Box 12189, Winston-Salem, NC 27127-2738. *Phone:* 336-770-3290. *Fax:* 336-770-3370. *E-mail:* razzap@uncsa.edu.

The University of North Carolina Wilmington

Wilmington, North Carolina

http://www.uncw.edu/

- **State-supported** comprehensive, founded 1947, part of University of North Carolina System
- **Urban** 661-acre campus
- **Endowment** $83.4 million
- **Coed**
- **Moderately difficult** entrance level

FACULTY
Student/faculty ratio: 18:1.

ACADEMICS
Calendar: semesters. *Degrees:* bachelor's, master's, doctoral, post-master's, and postbachelor's certificates.
Library: William Madison Randall Library. *Books:* 573,457 (physical), 272,920 (digital/electronic); *Serial titles:* 4,761 (physical), 71,907 (digital/electronic); *Databases:* 305. Weekly public service hours: 110; study areas open 24 hours, 5–7 days a week; students can reserve study rooms.

STUDENT LIFE
Housing options: on-campus residence required for freshman year; coed, special housing for students with disabilities. Campus housing is university owned and is provided by a third party. Freshman applicants given priority for college housing.

Activities and organizations: drama/theater group, student-run newspaper, radio station, choral group, Student Government Association, Association of Campus Entertainment, Residence Hall Association, Sports Club Council, Graduate Student Association, national fraternities, national sororities.

Athletics Member NCAA. All Division I.

Campus security: 24-hour emergency response devices and patrols, late-night transport/escort service, controlled dormitory access.

Student services: health clinic, personal/psychological counseling, women's center, veterans affairs office.

COSTS & FINANCIAL AID
Costs (2018–19) ***Tuition:*** state resident $4443 full-time, $163 per credit hour part-time; nonresident $18,508 full-time, $680 per credit hour part-time. Full-time tuition and fees vary according to course load and location. Part-time tuition and fees vary according to course load and location. ***Required fees:*** $2557 full-time, $78 per credit hour part-time. ***Room and board:*** $10,686; room only: $6660. Room and board charges vary according to board plan and housing facility.

Financial Aid Of all full-time matriculated undergraduates who enrolled in 2017, 8,824 applied for aid, 7,086 were judged to have need, 656 had their need fully met. In 2017, 281 non-need-based awards were made. ***Average percent of need met:*** 45. ***Average financial aid package:*** $9155. ***Average need-based loan:*** $4181. ***Average need-based gift aid:*** $6834. ***Average non-need-based aid:*** $1758. ***Average indebtedness upon graduation:*** $26,315.

APPLYING
Standardized Tests *Required:* SAT or ACT (for admission).

Options: electronic application, early admission, early action, deferred entrance.

Application fee: $80.

Required: essay or personal statement, high school transcript, 1 letter of recommendation.

CONTACT
UNCW Office of Admissions, The University of North Carolina Wilmington, 601 South College Road, Wilmington, NC 28403-3297. *Phone:* 910-962-3243. *Fax:* 910-962-3038. *E-mail:* admissions@uncw.edu.

Wake Forest University

Winston-Salem, North Carolina

http://www.wfu.edu/

- **Independent** university, founded 1834
- **Suburban** 340-acre campus
- **Coed**
- **Very difficult** entrance level

FACULTY
Student/faculty ratio: 11:1.

ACADEMICS
Calendar: semesters. *Degrees:* bachelor's, master's, doctoral, and postbachelor's certificates.
Library: Z. Smith Reynolds Library.

STUDENT LIFE
Housing options: on-campus residence required through sophomore year; coed. Campus housing is university owned. Freshman campus housing is guaranteed.

Activities and organizations: drama/theater group, student-run newspaper, radio and television station, choral group, marching band, national fraternities, national sororities.

Athletics Member NCAA. All Division I except football (Division I-A).

Campus security: 24-hour emergency response devices and patrols, late-night transport/escort service, controlled dormitory access.

Student services: health clinic, personal/psychological counseling.

COSTS & FINANCIAL AID

Costs (2018–19) ***Comprehensive fee:*** $69,354 includes full-time tuition ($52,348), mandatory fees ($974), and room and board ($16,032). Part-time tuition: $2170 per credit hour. ***College room only:*** $9282.

Financial Aid Of all full-time matriculated undergraduates who enrolled in 2018, 1,927 applied for aid, 1,539 were judged to have need, 1,530 had their need fully met. In 2018, 444 non-need-based awards were made. ***Average percent of need met:*** 100. ***Average financial aid package:*** $50,514. ***Average need-based loan:*** $8306. ***Average need-based gift aid:*** $47,407. ***Average non-need-based aid:*** $13,253. ***Average indebtedness upon graduation:*** $36,863. ***Financial aid deadline:*** 1/1.

APPLYING

Options: electronic application, early admission, early decision.

Application fee: $65.

Required: essay or personal statement, high school transcript, 1 letter of recommendation. ***Recommended:*** interview.

CONTACT

Wake Forest University, 1834 Wake Forest Road, PO Box 7373 Reynolda Station, Winston-Salem, NC 27109. *Phone:* 336-758-5201.

Warren Wilson College

Swannanoa, North Carolina

http://www.warren-wilson.edu/

CONTACT

Monique Cote, Campus Visit Coordinator, Warren Wilson College, PO Box 9000, Asheville, NC 28815-9000. *Phone:* 828-771-2073. *Toll-free phone:* 800-934-3536. *Fax:* 828-298-1440. *E-mail:* admit@warren-wilson.edu.

Western Carolina University

Cullowhee, North Carolina

http://www.wcu.edu/

CONTACT

Office of Undergraduate Admission, Western Carolina University, 102 Camp Building, Cullowhee, NC 28723. *Phone:* 828-227-7317. *Toll-free phone:* 877-WCU4YOU. *E-mail:* admiss@email.wcu.edu.

William Peace University

Raleigh, North Carolina

http://www.peace.edu/

- **Independent** 4-year, founded 1857, affiliated with Presbyterian Church (U.S.A.)
- **Urban** 21-acre campus with easy access to Raleigh-Cary
- **Endowment** $35.6 million
- **Coed**
- **Moderately difficult** entrance level

FACULTY

Student/faculty ratio: 14:1.

ACADEMICS

Calendar: semesters. *Degree:* bachelor's.

Library: Lucy Cooper Finch Library. *Books:* 48,196 (physical), 250,000 (digital/electronic); *Serial titles:* 13 (physical), 25,000 (digital/electronic); *Databases:* 94. Weekly public service hours: 90; students can reserve study rooms.

STUDENT LIFE

Housing options: on-campus residence required through junior year; coed, women-only. Campus housing is university owned, leased by the school and is provided by a third party. Freshman applicants given priority for college housing.

Activities and organizations: drama/theater group, student-run newspaper, choral group, Campus Activities Board, Phi Beta Lambda, Gamma Sigma Sigma, Ambassadors for Christ, Class Councils.

Athletics Member NCAA. All Division III.

Campus security: 24-hour emergency response devices and patrols, late-night transport/escort service, controlled dormitory access.

Student services: health clinic, personal/psychological counseling.

COSTS & FINANCIAL AID

Costs (2018–19) ***Comprehensive fee:*** $41,600 includes full-time tuition ($30,000), mandatory fees ($500), and room and board ($11,100). Full-time tuition and fees vary according to class time and course load. Part-time tuition: $1000 per credit hour. Part-time tuition and fees vary according to class time and course load. ***Room and board:*** Room and board charges vary according to board plan.

Financial Aid Of all full-time matriculated undergraduates who enrolled in 2018, 760 applied for aid, 709 were judged to have need, 22 had their need fully met. In 2018, 95 non-need-based awards were made. ***Average financial aid package:*** $23,876. ***Average need-based loan:*** $4139. ***Average need-based gift aid:*** $13,521. ***Average non-need-based aid:*** $10,727. ***Average indebtedness upon graduation:*** $7386.

APPLYING

Standardized Tests *Required:* SAT or ACT (for admission).

Options: electronic application, early admission, deferred entrance.

Application fee: $35.

Required: high school transcript, minimum 2.5 GPA. ***Required for some:*** essay or personal statement. ***Recommended:*** essay or personal statement, letters of recommendation, interview.

CONTACT

Josh Bistromowitz, Director of Admissions, William Peace University, 15 East Peace Street, Raleigh, NC 27604. *Phone:* 919-508-2000. *E-mail:* admission@peace.edu.

Wingate University

Wingate, North Carolina

http://www.wingate.edu/

CONTACT

Mr. Gabe Hollingsworth, Director of Admissions, Wingate University, PO Box 159, Wingate, NC 28174. *Phone:* 704-233-8000. *Toll-free phone:* 800-755-5550. *Fax:* 704-233-8110. *E-mail:* admit@wingate.edu.

Winston-Salem State University

Winston-Salem, North Carolina

http://www.wssu.edu/

CONTACT

Ms. Tomikia LeGrande, Assistant Vice Chancellor for Enrollment Services, Winston-Salem State University, 601 Martin Luther King, Jr. Drive, Thompson Center, Winston-Salem, NC 27110. *Phone:* 336-750-2070. *Toll-free phone:* 800-257-4052. *Fax:* 336-750-2079. *E-mail:* legrandet@wssu.edu.

NORTH DAKOTA

Bismarck State College

Bismarck, North Dakota

http://www.bismarckstate.edu/

CONTACT

Karen Erickson, Director of Admissions and Enrollment Services, Bismarck State College, PO Box 5587, Bismarck, ND 58506. *Phone:* 701-224-5424. *Toll-free phone:* 800-445-5073. *Fax:* 701-224-5643. *E-mail:* karen.erickson@bismarckstate.edu.

Dickinson State University
Dickinson, North Dakota
http://www.dickinsonstate.edu/

- **State-supported** comprehensive, founded 1918, part of North Dakota University System
- **Small-town** 132-acre campus
- **Coed**
- **Minimally difficult** entrance level

FACULTY
Student/faculty ratio: 9:1.

ACADEMICS
Calendar: semesters. *Degrees:* certificates, associate, bachelor's, and master's.
Library: Stoxen Library plus 1 other. *Books:* 73,571 (physical), 23,355 (digital/electronic); *Serial titles:* 119 (physical), 107,800 (digital/electronic); *Databases:* 71. Weekly public service hours: 56.

STUDENT LIFE
Housing options: on-campus residence required through sophomore year; coed. Campus housing is university owned. Freshman campus housing is guaranteed.

Activities and organizations: drama/theater group, choral group, Rodeo Club, Blue Hawk Brigade, chorale, Business Club, Navigators, national fraternities.

Athletics Member NAIA.

Campus security: 24-hour emergency response devices and patrols, late-night transport/escort service, controlled dormitory access, Crisis Manager App. for Phones, Automated Mass Notification System.

Student services: health clinic, personal/psychological counseling, veterans affairs office.

COSTS & FINANCIAL AID
Costs (2018–19) ***One-time required fee:*** $100. ***Tuition:*** state resident $5558 full-time, $232 per credit hour part-time; nonresident $8336 full-time, $347 per credit hour part-time. Full-time tuition and fees vary according to course load, location, and reciprocity agreements. Part-time tuition and fees vary according to course load, location, and reciprocity agreements. ***Required fees:*** $1210 full-time, $50 per credit hour part-time, $302 per term part-time. ***Room and board:*** $6898; room only: $2900. Room and board charges vary according to board plan, housing facility, and location.

Financial Aid Of all full-time matriculated undergraduates who enrolled in 2017, 686 applied for aid, 483 were judged to have need, 176 had their need fully met. In 2017, 66 non-need-based awards were made. ***Average percent of need met:*** 61. ***Average financial aid package:*** $11,224. ***Average need-based loan:*** $6132. ***Average need-based gift aid:*** $5475. ***Average non-need-based aid:*** $1985. ***Average indebtedness upon graduation:*** $21,356.

APPLYING
Standardized Tests *Required:* SAT or ACT (for admission).

Options: electronic application, early admission, early action, deferred entrance.

Application fee: $35.

Required: high school transcript, minimum 2.0 GPA. ***Required for some:*** essay or personal statement, medical history, proof of measles-rubella shot.

CONTACT
Ms. Heidi Kippenhan, Assistant Dean, Enrollment Management, Dickinson State University, Dickinson, ND 58601. *Phone:* 701-483-2566. *Toll-free phone:* 800-279-4295. *E-mail:* heidi.kippenhan@dickinsonstate.edu.

Mayville State University
Mayville, North Dakota
http://www.mayvillestate.edu/

CONTACT
Jim Morowski, Director of Freshmen Enrollment Services, Mayville State University, 330 3rd Street, NE, Mayville, ND 58257-1299. *Phone:* 701-788-4842. *Toll-free phone:* 800-437-4104. *Fax:* 701-788-4748. *E-mail:* james.morowski@mayvillestate.edu.

Minot State University
Minot, North Dakota
http://www.minotstateu.edu/

- **State-supported** comprehensive, founded 1913, part of North Dakota University System
- **Small-town** 103-acre campus
- **Coed**
- **Moderately difficult** entrance level

FACULTY
Student/faculty ratio: 12:1.

ACADEMICS
Calendar: semesters. *Degrees:* certificates, associate, bachelor's, master's, and postbachelor's certificates.
Library: Gordon B. Olson Library.

STUDENT LIFE
Housing options: on-campus residence required for freshman year; coed, men-only, women-only, special housing for students with disabilities. Campus housing is university owned. Freshman campus housing is guaranteed.
Activities and organizations: drama/theater group, student-run newspaper, radio and television station, choral group, marching band, Residence Hall Association, Student Government Association, Beavers on Business, Student Social Work Organization, National Student Speech and Hearing Association.

Athletics Member NCAA, NAIA, NCCAA. All NCAA Division II.

Campus security: controlled dormitory access, patrols by trained security personnel.

Student services: health clinic, personal/psychological counseling, women's center.

COSTS & FINANCIAL AID
Costs (2018–19) ***Tuition:*** state resident $5616 full-time, $234 per credit hour part-time; nonresident $5616 full-time, $234 per credit hour part-time. Full-time tuition and fees vary according to class time, course load, degree level, location, program, and reciprocity agreements. Part-time tuition and fees vary according to class time, course load, degree level, location, program, and reciprocity agreements. ***Required fees:*** $1448 full-time, $60 per credit hour part-time. ***Room and board:*** $6663; room only: $2663. Room and board charges vary according to board plan and housing facility.

Financial Aid Of all full-time matriculated undergraduates who enrolled in 2017, 1,347 applied for aid, 924 were judged to have need, 329 had their need fully met. 89 Federal Work-Study jobs (averaging $1561). In 2017, 313 non-need-based awards were made. ***Average percent of need met:*** 70. ***Average financial aid package:*** $10,459. ***Average need-based loan:*** $6081. ***Average need-based gift aid:*** $5588. ***Average non-need-based aid:*** $1438. ***Average indebtedness upon graduation:*** $23,282.

APPLYING
Standardized Tests *Required:* SAT or ACT (for admission).

Options: electronic application, deferred entrance.

Application fee: $35.

Required: high school transcript. ***Required for some:*** minimum 2.5 GPA.

CONTACT
Mr. Kevin Harmon, Vice President of Enrollment Management, Minot State University, 500 University Avenue West, Minot, ND 58707-0002. *Phone:* 701-858-3126. *Toll-free phone:* 800-777-0750 Ext. 3350. *Fax:* 701-858-3825. *E-mail:* askmsu@minotstateu.edu.

North Dakota State University

Fargo, North Dakota

http://www.ndsu.edu/

- **State-supported** university, founded 1890, part of North Dakota University System
- **Urban** 2100-acre campus
- **Endowment** $512,215
- **Coed**
- **Moderately difficult** entrance level

FACULTY
Student/faculty ratio: 18:1.

ACADEMICS
Calendar: semesters. *Degrees:* certificates, bachelor's, master's, doctoral, post-master's, and postbachelor's certificates.
Library: North Dakota State University Library plus 6 others. *Books:* 662,884 (physical), 162,977 (digital/electronic); *Serial titles:* 171,924 (physical), 99,565 (digital/electronic); *Databases:* 232. Weekly public service hours: 93; students can reserve study rooms.

STUDENT LIFE
Housing options: on-campus residence required for freshman year; coed, men-only, women-only, special housing for students with disabilities. Campus housing is university owned. Freshman campus housing is guaranteed.

Activities and organizations: drama/theater group, student-run newspaper, radio and television station, choral group, marching band, Saddle and Sirloin, Students Today, Leaders Forever, Chi Alpha Christian Organization, fraternities/sororities, CRU, national fraternities, national sororities.

Athletics Member NCAA. All Division I.

Campus security: 24-hour emergency response devices and patrols, late-night transport/escort service, controlled dormitory access, Pathlight app.

Student services: health clinic, personal/psychological counseling, veterans affairs office.

COSTS & FINANCIAL AID
Costs (2018–19) ***One-time required fee:*** $120. ***Tuition:*** state resident $7957 full-time, $324 per credit hour part-time; nonresident $11,936 full-time, $491 per credit hour part-time. Full-time tuition and fees vary according to course load, program, and reciprocity agreements. Part-time tuition and fees vary according to course load, program, and reciprocity agreements. ***Required fees:*** $1337 full-time, $56 per credit hour part-time. ***Room and board:*** $8565; room only: $3926. Room and board charges vary according to board plan and housing facility.

Financial Aid Of all full-time matriculated undergraduates who enrolled in 2007, 7,109 applied for aid, 4,917 were judged to have need, 980 had their need fully met. In 2007, 1763 non-need-based awards were made. ***Average percent of need met:*** 3. ***Average financial aid package:*** $7030. ***Average need-based loan:*** $4378. ***Average need-based gift aid:*** $3419. ***Average non-need-based aid:*** $1533.

APPLYING
Standardized Tests *Required:* SAT or ACT (for admission).

Options: electronic application.

Application fee: $35.

Required: high school transcript, minimum 2.8 GPA.

CONTACT
Ms. Merideth Sherlin, Director of Admission, North Dakota State University, NDSU Department 2832, PO Box 6050, Fargo, ND 58108-6050. *Phone:* 701-231-8643. *Toll-free phone:* 800-488-6378. *Fax:* 701-231-8802. *E-mail:* ndsu.admission@ndsu.edu.

Rasmussen College Fargo

Fargo, North Dakota

http://www.rasmussen.edu/

- **Proprietary** 4-year, founded 1902, part of Rasmussen College System
- **Suburban** campus
- **Coed**
- **Minimally difficult** entrance level

FACULTY
Student/faculty ratio: 22:1.

ACADEMICS
Calendar: quarters. *Degrees:* certificates, diplomas, associate, and bachelor's.
Library: Rasmussen College Library - Fargo.

STUDENT LIFE
Housing options: college housing not available.

APPLYING
Standardized Tests *Required:* institutional exam (for admission).

Options: electronic application, early admission, deferred entrance.

Required: high school transcript, minimum 2.0 GPA. ***Required for some:*** interview.

CONTACT
Dwayne Bertotto, Vice President of Admissions and Student Experience, Rasmussen College Fargo, 8300 Norman Center Drive, Suite 300, Bloomington, MN 55437. *Phone:* 952-806-3958. *Toll-free phone:* 888-549-6755. *E-mail:* dwayne.bertotto@rasmussen.edu.

Sitting Bull College

Fort Yates, North Dakota

http://www.sittingbull.edu/

CONTACT
Ms. Melody Silk, Director of Registration and Admissions, Sitting Bull College, 1341 92nd Street, Fort Yates, ND 58538-9701. *Phone:* 701-854-3864. *Fax:* 701-854-3403. *E-mail:* melodys@sbcl.edu.

Trinity Bible College and Graduate School

Ellendale, North Dakota

http://www.trinitybiblecollege.edu/

CONTACT
Trinity Bible College and Graduate School, 50 Sixth Avenue South, Ellendale, ND 58436. *Phone:* 701-349-5399. *Toll-free phone:* 800-523-1603. *E-mail:* admissions@trinitybiblecollege.edu.

University of Jamestown

Jamestown, North Dakota

http://www.uj.edu/

- **Independent Presbyterian** comprehensive, founded 1883
- **Small-town** 110-acre campus
- **Endowment** $35.6 million
- **Coed**
- **Minimally difficult** entrance level

FACULTY
Student/faculty ratio: 12:1.

ACADEMICS
Calendar: semesters. *Degrees:* bachelor's, master's, and doctoral.
Library: Raugust Library. *Books:* 94,318 (physical), 15,565 (digital/electronic); *Serial titles:* 822 (physical), 343 (digital/electronic); *Databases:* 87. Weekly public service hours: 89; students can reserve study rooms.

STUDENT LIFE
Housing options: on-campus residence required through junior year; coed, special housing for students with disabilities. Campus housing is university owned and leased by the school. Freshman campus housing is guaranteed.

Activities and organizations: drama/theater group, student-run newspaper, choral group, Cru-Ignite, Student Senate, Relay for Life, Habitat for Humanity, Fellowship of Athletes in Christ.

Athletics Member NAIA.

Campus security: 24-hour emergency response devices, late-night transport/escort service, controlled dormitory access, campus security cameras.

Student services: personal/psychological counseling.

COSTS & FINANCIAL AID

Costs (2018–19) ***Comprehensive fee:*** $29,546 includes full-time tuition ($21,196), mandatory fees ($780), and room and board ($7570). Full-time tuition and fees vary according to course load, degree level, and program. Part-time tuition: $435 per credit hour. Part-time tuition and fees vary according to course load, degree level, and program. ***College room only:*** $3570. Room and board charges vary according to housing facility.

Financial Aid Of all full-time matriculated undergraduates who enrolled in 2017, 661 applied for aid, 554 were judged to have need, 106 had their need fully met. 276 Federal Work-Study jobs (averaging $615). 66 state and other part-time jobs (averaging $617). In 2017, 300 non-need-based awards were made. ***Average percent of need met:*** 71. ***Average financial aid package:*** $16,562. ***Average need-based loan:*** $3870. ***Average need-based gift aid:*** $13,308. ***Average non-need-based aid:*** $8597. ***Average indebtedness upon graduation:*** $28,338.

APPLYING

Standardized Tests *Required:* SAT or ACT (for admission).

Options: electronic application, deferred entrance.

Required: high school transcript, minimum 2.5 GPA. ***Required for some:*** interview.

CONTACT

Mr. Mike Heitkamp, Vice President of Enrollment Management, University of Jamestown, 6081 College Lane, Jamestown, ND 58401. *Phone:* 701-252-3467 Ext. 5512. *Toll-free phone:* 800-336-2554. *Fax:* 701-253-4318. *E-mail:* admissions@uj.edu.

University of Mary

Bismarck, North Dakota

http://www.umary.edu/

CONTACT

Mr. Curtis Ray DeGraw, University of Mary, 7500 University Drive, Bismarck, ND 58504-9652. *Phone:* 701-355-8191. *Toll-free phone:* 800-288-6279. *Fax:* 701-255-7687. *E-mail:* mcheitkamp@umary.edu.

University of North Dakota

Grand Forks, North Dakota

http://www.und.edu/

- **State-supported** university, founded 1883, part of North Dakota University System
- **Urban** 521-acre campus
- **Endowment** $10.7 million
- **Coed** 10,518 undergraduate students, 78% full-time, 44% women, 56% men
- **Minimally difficult** entrance level, 82% of applicants were admitted

UNDERGRAD STUDENTS

8,184 full-time, 2,334 part-time. Students come from 63 states and territories; 78 other countries; 61% are from out of state; 2% Black or African American, non-Hispanic/Latino; 4% Hispanic/Latino; 2% Asian, non-Hispanic/Latino; 0.1% Native Hawaiian or other Pacific Islander, non-Hispanic/Latino; 1% American Indian or Alaska Native, non-Hispanic/Latino; 4% Two or more races, non-Hispanic/Latino; 1% Race/ethnicity unknown; 5% international; 9% transferred in; 27% live on campus.

Freshmen:

Admission: 5,021 applied, 4,128 admitted, 1,835 enrolled. ***Average high school GPA:*** 3.5. ***Test scores:*** SAT evidence-based reading and writing scores over 500: 76%; SAT math scores over 500: 81%; ACT scores over 18: 97%; SAT evidence-based reading and writing scores over 600: 32%; SAT math scores over 600: 34%; ACT scores over 24: 51%; SAT evidence-based reading and writing scores over 700: 6%; SAT math scores over 700: 5%; ACT scores over 30: 10%.

Retention: 80% of full-time freshmen returned.

FACULTY

Total: 760, 94% full-time, 69% with terminal degrees.

Student/faculty ratio: 21:1.

ACADEMICS

Calendar: semesters. *Degrees:* certificates, bachelor's, master's, doctoral, post-master's, and postbachelor's certificates.

Special study options: accelerated degree program, adult/continuing education programs, advanced placement credit, cooperative education, distance learning, double majors, English as a second language, external degree program, honors programs, independent study, internships, off-campus study, part-time degree program, services for LD students, student-designed majors, study abroad, summer session for credit. ***ROTC:*** Army (b), Air Force (b).

Unusual degree programs: 3-2 engineering; applied economics, counseling, chemistry, public administration.

Computers: 500 computers/terminals and 400 ports are available on campus for general student use. Students can access the following: campus intranet, computer help desk, free student e-mail accounts, online (class) grades, online (class) registration, online (class) schedules. Campuswide network is available. 100% of college-owned or -operated housing units are wired for high-speed Internet access. Wireless service is available via classrooms, computer centers, computer labs, dorm rooms, learning centers, libraries, student centers.

Library: Chester Fritz Library plus 2 others. *Books:* 712,457 (physical), 194,647 (digital/electronic); *Serial titles:* 542,772 (physical), 59,846 (digital/electronic); *Databases:* 252. Weekly public service hours: 99.

STUDENT LIFE

Housing options: coed, men-only, women-only, special housing for students with disabilities. Campus housing is university owned.

Activities and organizations: drama/theater group, student-run newspaper, radio and television station, choral group, marching band, Mortar Board, Cru, Greek Liffe, Alpha Kappa Psi, African Student Union, national fraternities, national sororities.

Athletics Member NCAA. All Division I. ***Intercollegiate sports:*** basketball M(s)/W(s), cross-country running M(s)/W(s), football M(s), golf M(s)/W(s), ice hockey M(s), soccer W(s), softball W(s), tennis M(s)/W(s), track and field M(s)/W(s), volleyball W(s). ***Intramural sports:*** basketball M/W, ice hockey M/W, soccer M/W, softball M/W, ultimate Frisbee M/W, volleyball M/W.

Campus security: 24-hour emergency response devices and patrols, late-night transport/escort service, controlled dormitory access.

Student services: health clinic, personal/psychological counseling, women's center, legal services, veterans affairs office.

COSTS & FINANCIAL AID

Costs (2018–19) ***Tuition:*** state resident $7224 full-time, $301 per credit hour part-time; nonresident $19,288 full-time, $803 per credit hour part-time. Full-time tuition and fees vary according to degree level, program, and reciprocity agreements. Part-time tuition and fees vary according to course load, degree level, program, and reciprocity agreements. ***Required fees:*** $1471 full-time. ***Room and board:*** $8974. Room and board charges vary according to board plan and housing facility. ***Payment plan:*** deferred payment. ***Waivers:*** minority students and employees or children of employees.

Financial Aid Of all full-time matriculated undergraduates who enrolled in 2018, 5,958 applied for aid, 4,007 were judged to have need, 1,564 had their need fully met. 1,728 Federal Work-Study jobs (averaging $3000). In 2018, 850 non-need-based awards were made. ***Average percent of need met:*** 56. ***Average financial aid package:*** $14,097. ***Average need-based loan:*** $7614. ***Average need-based gift aid:*** $5795. ***Average non-need-based aid:*** $2179.

APPLYING

Standardized Tests *Required for some:* SAT and SAT Subject Tests or ACT (for admission).

Options: electronic application, deferred entrance.

Application fee: $35.

Required: high school transcript. ***Recommended:*** minimum 2.5 GPA.

Notification: continuous (transfers).

CONTACT

Jennifer Aamodt, University Admissions Director, University of North Dakota, Gorecki Alumni Center, 3501 University Avenue, Stop 8357, Grand Forks, ND 58202. *Phone:* 701-777-3000. *Toll-free phone:* 800-CALL-UND. *Fax:* 701-777-2721. *E-mail:* und.admissions@und.edu.

Valley City State University

Valley City, North Dakota

http://www.vcsu.edu/

- **State-supported** comprehensive, founded 1890, part of North Dakota University System
- **Small-town** 55-acre campus
- **Endowment** $6.8 million
- **Coed** 1,404 undergraduate students, 61% full-time, 58% women, 42% men
- **Noncompetitive** entrance level, 74% of applicants were admitted

UNDERGRAD STUDENTS
862 full-time, 542 part-time. 35% are from out of state; 2% Black or African American, non-Hispanic/Latino; 6% Hispanic/Latino; 0.4% Asian, non-Hispanic/Latino; 0.3% Native Hawaiian or other Pacific Islander, non-Hispanic/Latino; 1% American Indian or Alaska Native, non-Hispanic/Latino; 4% Two or more races, non-Hispanic/Latino; 1% Race/ethnicity unknown; 2% international; 12% transferred in; 29% live on campus.

Freshmen:
Admission: 460 applied, 339 admitted, 166 enrolled. ***Average high school GPA:*** 3.3.

Retention: 68% of full-time freshmen returned.

FACULTY
Total: 110, 61% full-time, 47% with terminal degrees.

Student/faculty ratio: 11:1.

ACADEMICS
Calendar: semesters. *Degrees:* bachelor's and master's.

Special study options: academic remediation for entering students, cooperative education, distance learning, double majors, internships, off-campus study, part-time degree program, services for LD students, student-designed majors, study abroad, summer session for credit.

Computers: 1,200 computers/terminals are available on campus for general student use. Students can access the following: campus intranet, computer help desk, free student e-mail accounts, online (class) grades, online (class) registration, online (class) schedules. Campuswide network is available. 100% of college-owned or -operated housing units are wired for high-speed Internet access. Wireless service is available via entire campus.

Library: Allen Memorial Library. *Books:* 77,906 (physical), 140,050 (digital/electronic); *Serial titles:* 1,301 (physical), 29,378 (digital/electronic); *Databases:* 86. Weekly public service hours: 61; students can reserve study rooms.

STUDENT LIFE
Housing options: on-campus residence required for freshman year; coed, men-only, women-only. Campus housing is university owned. Freshman campus housing is guaranteed.

Activities and organizations: choral group, departmental clubs, Fellowship of Christian Athletes, VCAB, Viking Ambassadors, local fraternities/soroties.

Athletics Member NAIA. ***Intercollegiate sports:*** baseball M(s), basketball M(s)/W(s), cross-country running M(s)/W(s), football M(s), golf M(s), softball W(s), tennis M(c)/W(c), track and field M(s)/W(s), volleyball W(s). ***Intramural sports:*** basketball M/W, bowling M/W, cross-country running M/W, football M/W, golf M/W, ice hockey M/W, racquetball M/W, skiing (cross-country) M/W, soccer M/W, softball M/W, tennis M/W, track and field M/W, volleyball M/W.

Campus security: controlled dormitory access.

Student services: health clinic, personal/psychological counseling.

COSTS & FINANCIAL AID
Costs (2018–19) ***Tuition:*** state resident $5713 full-time, $190 per semester hour part-time; nonresident $15,253 full-time, $508 per semester hour part-time. Full-time tuition and fees vary according to course load, degree level, location, program, and reciprocity agreements. Part-time tuition and fees vary according to course load, degree level, location, program, and reciprocity agreements. ***Required fees:*** $1913 full-time, $80 per semester hour part-time. ***Room and board:*** $6446; room only: $2378. Room and board charges vary according to board plan and housing facility. ***Payment plan:*** installment. ***Waivers:*** employees or children of employees.

Financial Aid Of all full-time matriculated undergraduates who enrolled in 2018, 617 applied for aid, 460 were judged to have need, 201 had their need fully met. In 2018, 94 non-need-based awards were made. ***Average percent of need met:*** 69. ***Average financial aid package:*** $11,869. ***Average need-based loan:*** $5481. ***Average need-based gift aid:*** $5869. ***Average non-need-based aid:*** $2590. ***Average indebtedness upon graduation:*** $27,460.

APPLYING
Standardized Tests *Required:* SAT or ACT (for admission).

Options: electronic application.

Application fee: $35.

Required: high school transcript.

Application deadlines: rolling (freshmen), rolling (out-of-state freshmen), rolling (transfers).

Notification: continuous (freshmen), continuous (out-of-state freshmen), continuous (transfers).

CONTACT
Ms. Charlene Stenson, Director of Enrollment Services, Valley City State University, 101 College Street Southwest, Valley City, ND 58072. *Phone:* 701-845-71. *Toll-free phone:* 800-532-8641 Ext. 7101. *Fax:* 701-845-7299. *E-mail:* c.stenson@vcsu.edu.

OHIO

AIC College of Design

Cincinnati, Ohio

http://www.aic-arts.edu/

- **Independent** primarily 2-year, founded 1976
- **Urban** 3-acre campus with easy access to Cincinnati
- **Coed**
- **Noncompetitive** entrance level

FACULTY
Student/faculty ratio: 5:1.

ACADEMICS
Degrees: associate and bachelor's.
Library: AIC College of Design Library plus 1 other.

STUDENT LIFE
Housing options: college housing not available.

Activities and organizations: AIGA Student Chapter.

Campus security: 24-hour emergency response devices, SMS.

Student services: personal/psychological counseling.

APPLYING
Standardized Tests *Recommended:* SAT or ACT (for admission).

Options: early admission, early decision, deferred entrance.

Application fee: $100.

Required: essay or personal statement, high school transcript, interview. ***Recommended:*** minimum 2.0 GPA, letters of recommendation.

CONTACT
Megan Orsburn, Admissions Assistant, AIC College of Design, 1171 E. Kemper Road, Cincinnati, OH 45246. *Phone:* 513-751-1206.

Allegheny Wesleyan College

Salem, Ohio

http://www.awc.edu/

CONTACT
Admissions Office, Allegheny Wesleyan College, 2161 Woodsdale Road, Salem, OH 44460. *Phone:* 330-337-6403. *Toll-free phone:* 800-292-3153. *E-mail:* college@awc.edu.

Antioch College
Yellow Springs, Ohio
http://www.antiochcollege.edu/

- **Independent** 4-year, founded 2011
- **Rural** 1100-acre campus with easy access to Columbus
- **Endowment** $9.2 million
- **Coed** 102 undergraduate students, 100% full-time, 62% women, 38% men
- **Moderately difficult** entrance level, 84% of applicants were admitted

UNDERGRAD STUDENTS
102 full-time. Students come from 25 states and territories; 3 other countries; 28% are from out of state; 17% Black or African American, non-Hispanic/Latino; 16% Hispanic/Latino; 2% Asian, non-Hispanic/Latino; 1% American Indian or Alaska Native, non-Hispanic/Latino; 6% Two or more races, non-Hispanic/Latino; 5% Race/ethnicity unknown; 12% transferred in; 66% live on campus.

Freshmen:
Admission: 134 applied, 112 admitted, 34 enrolled. ***Average high school GPA:*** 3.1. ***Test scores:*** SAT evidence-based reading and writing scores over 500: 88%; SAT math scores over 500: 75%; ACT scores over 18: 100%; SAT evidence-based reading and writing scores over 600: 63%; SAT math scores over 600: 38%; ACT scores over 24: 75%; SAT evidence-based reading and writing scores over 700: 25%; SAT math scores over 700: 13%; ACT scores over 30: 50%.
Retention: 47% of full-time freshmen returned.

FACULTY
Total: 27, 89% full-time, 70% with terminal degrees.
Student/faculty ratio: 4:1.

ACADEMICS
Calendar: quarters. *Degree:* bachelor's.
Special study options: academic remediation for entering students, advanced placement credit, cooperative education, independent study, off-campus study, services for LD students, student-designed majors, study abroad, summer session for credit.
Computers: 69 computers/terminals are available on campus for general student use. Students can access the following: campus intranet, computer help desk, free student e-mail accounts, online (class) grades, online (class) registration, online (class) schedules. Campuswide network is available. 100% of college-owned or -operated housing units are wired for high-speed Internet access. Wireless service is available via entire campus.
Library: Olive Kettering Library. *Books:* 158,578 (physical), 125,344 (digital/electronic); *Serial titles:* 1,402 (physical), 33,099 (digital/electronic); *Databases:* 199. Weekly public service hours: 72.

STUDENT LIFE
Housing options: on-campus residence required through senior year; coed. Campus housing is university owned.
Activities and organizations: drama/theater group, student-run newspaper, radio station, People of Color Group, Queer Center, Outdoors Club, Antioch Creative Collective, ei@A (Entrepreneurs & Innovation @ Antioch).
Athletics ***Intramural sports:*** basketball M/W, volleyball M/W.
Campus security: 24-hour emergency response devices and patrols, late-night transport/escort service, controlled dormitory access.
Student services: health clinic, personal/psychological counseling.

COSTS
Costs (2019–20) ***One-time required fee:*** $150. ***Comprehensive fee:*** $44,633 includes full-time tuition ($35,949), mandatory fees ($1044), and room and board ($7640). Part-time tuition: $500 per credit hour. No tuition increase for student's term of enrollment. ***College room only:*** $4622.

APPLYING
Options: electronic application, early admission, early decision, deferred entrance.
Required: essay or personal statement, high school transcript, 2 letters of recommendation. ***Required for some:*** interview.
Early decision deadline: 11/15 (for plan 1), 1/2 (for plan 2).
Notification: continuous (freshmen), continuous (out-of-state freshmen), 12/15 (early decision plan 1), 2/1 (early decision plan 2).

CONTACT
Mr. Shane Creepingbear, Associate Director of Admission, Antioch College, South Hall, Yellow Springs, OH 45387. *Phone:* 937-284-0830. *E-mail:* screepingbear@antiochcollege.edu.

Antioch University Midwest
Yellow Springs, Ohio
http://www.antioch.edu/midwest/

- **Independent** upper-level, founded 1988, part of Antioch University
- **Small-town** 100-acre campus with easy access to Dayton
- **Coed**
- **Noncompetitive** entrance level

ACADEMICS
Calendar: semesters. *Degrees:* certificates, bachelor's, master's, post-master's, and postbachelor's certificates.
Library: Midwest Library.

STUDENT LIFE
Housing options: college housing not available.
Campus security: 24-hour emergency response devices.
Student services: personal/psychological counseling.

COSTS
Costs (2018–19) ***Tuition:*** $18,972 full-time, $527 per credit hour part-time. ***Required fees:*** $400 full-time.

APPLYING
Options: electronic application, deferred entrance.
Application fee: $45.

CONTACT
Antioch University Midwest, 900 Dayton Street, Yellow Springs, OH 45387-1609. *Phone:* 937-769-1823.

Art Academy of Cincinnati
Cincinnati, Ohio
http://www.artacademy.edu/

CONTACT
Mr. John J. Wadell, Director of Admissions, Art Academy of Cincinnati, 1212 Jackson Street, Cincinnati, OH 45202-7106. *Phone:* 513-562-8744. *Toll-free phone:* 800-323-5692. *Fax:* 513-562-8778. *E-mail:* admissions@artacademy.edu.

Ashland University
Ashland, Ohio
http://www.ashland.edu/

- **Independent** comprehensive, founded 1878, affiliated with Brethren Church
- **Small-town** 135-acre campus with easy access to Cleveland, Akron
- **Endowment** $36.8 million
- **Coed**
- **Moderately difficult** entrance level

FACULTY
Student/faculty ratio: 12:1.

ACADEMICS
Calendar: semesters. *Degrees:* certificates, diplomas, associate, bachelor's, master's, doctoral, post-master's, and postbachelor's certificates.
Library: Ashland University Library plus 2 others. *Books:* 223,607 (physical), 255,789 (digital/electronic); *Serial titles:* 1,070 (physical), 114,001 (digital/electronic); *Databases:* 200. Weekly public service hours: 102; students can reserve study rooms.

STUDENT LIFE
Housing options: on-campus residence required through junior year; coed, women-only. Campus housing is university owned. Freshman campus housing is guaranteed.

Activities and organizations: drama/theater group, student-run newspaper, radio and television station, choral group, marching band, Campus Activity Board, Fellowship of Christian Athletes, The Well Campus Ministry, intramurals, Sororities, national fraternities, national sororities.

Athletics Member NCAA. All Division II.

Campus security: 24-hour emergency response devices and patrols, student patrols, late-night transport/escort service, controlled dormitory access.

Student services: health clinic, personal/psychological counseling, veterans affairs office.

COSTS & FINANCIAL AID

Costs (2018–19) ***Comprehensive fee:*** $31,284 includes full-time tuition ($20,332), mandatory fees ($1010), and room and board ($9942). Full-time tuition and fees vary according to class time, course level, course load, degree level, location, program, reciprocity agreements, and student level. Part-time tuition: $940 per credit hour. Part-time tuition and fees vary according to class time, course level, course load, degree level, location, program, reciprocity agreements, and student level. ***Required fees:*** $24 per credit hour part-time. ***College room only:*** $5356. Room and board charges vary according to board plan, housing facility, and location.

Financial Aid Of all full-time matriculated undergraduates who enrolled in 2014, 2,191 applied for aid, 1,924 were judged to have need. 1,380 Federal Work-Study jobs (averaging $2589). In 2014, 264 non-need-based awards were made. ***Average financial aid package:*** $17,689. ***Average need-based loan:*** $4836. ***Average need-based gift aid:*** $10,445. ***Average non-need-based aid:*** $5248. ***Average indebtedness upon graduation:*** $36,779.

APPLYING

Standardized Tests *Required:* SAT or ACT (for admission).

Options: electronic application, deferred entrance.

Required: high school transcript, minimum 2.5 GPA, minimum 18 ACT or 860 SAT.

CONTACT

Mr. W. C. Vance, Director of Admissions, Ashland University, 401 College Avenue, Ashland, OH 44805. *Phone:* 419-289-5052. *Toll-free phone:* 800-882-1548. *Fax:* 419-289-5999. *E-mail:* enrollme@ashland.edu.

Aultman College of Nursing and Health Sciences

Canton, Ohio

http://www.aultmancollege.edu/

- **Independent** 4-year, founded 2004
- **Urban** 5-acre campus with easy access to Cleveland
- **Endowment** $1.4 million
- **Coed**
- **Moderately difficult** entrance level

FACULTY

Student/faculty ratio: 7:1.

ACADEMICS

Calendar: semesters. *Degrees:* associate and bachelor's.

Library: Aultman Health Sciences Library plus 1 other. *Books:* 2,448 (physical), 81,000 (digital/electronic); *Serial titles:* 129 (physical), 10,007 (digital/electronic); *Databases:* 145. Study areas open 24 hours, 5–7 days a week.

STUDENT LIFE

Housing options: college housing not available.

Activities and organizations: Aultman College Student Nurse Association, Radiography Club, Aultman College Campus Ministry, Aultman College Veterans Association, Men in Nursing Association.

Campus security: 24-hour emergency response devices and patrols, late-night transport/escort service.

Student services: health clinic.

COSTS

Costs (2018–19) ***One-time required fee:*** $200. ***Tuition:*** $17,510 full-time, $725 per credit hour part-time. Full-time tuition and fees vary according to course load, degree level, and program. Part-time tuition and fees vary according to course load, degree level, and program. ***Required fees:*** $1000 full-time, $500 per term part-time.

APPLYING

Standardized Tests *Required for some:* SAT or ACT (for admission). *Recommended:* SAT or ACT (for admission).

Options: electronic application.

Application fee: $45.

Required: high school transcript. ***Required for some:*** minimum 3.0 GPA, interview.

CONTACT

Mrs. Kelsey Binsley, Enrollment Specialist, Aultman College of Nursing and Health Sciences, 2600 6th Street SW, Canton, OH 44710. *Phone:* 330-363-6773. *Fax:* 330-580-6654. *E-mail:* admissions@aultmancollege.edu.

Baldwin Wallace University

Berea, Ohio

http://www.bw.edu/

- **Independent Methodist** comprehensive, founded 1845
- **Suburban** 100-acre campus with easy access to Cleveland
- **Endowment** $174.8 million
- **Coed** 3,136 undergraduate students, 93% full-time, 54% women, 46% men
- **Moderately difficult** entrance level, 74% of applicants were admitted

UNDERGRAD STUDENTS

2,923 full-time, 213 part-time. Students come from 42 states and territories; 20 other countries; 24% are from out of state; 9% Black or African American, non-Hispanic/Latino; 6% Hispanic/Latino; 1% Asian, non-Hispanic/Latino; 0.1% American Indian or Alaska Native, non-Hispanic/Latino; 5% Two or more races, non-Hispanic/Latino; 0.4% Race/ethnicity unknown; 0.7% international; 5% transferred in; 57% live on campus.

Freshmen:

Admission: 3,926 applied, 2,915 admitted, 677 enrolled. ***Average high school GPA:*** 3.5. ***Test scores:*** SAT evidence-based reading and writing scores over 500: 85%; SAT math scores over 500: 82%; ACT scores over 18: 91%; SAT evidence-based reading and writing scores over 600: 45%; SAT math scores over 600: 31%; ACT scores over 24: 52%; SAT evidence-based reading and writing scores over 700: 6%; SAT math scores over 700: 7%; ACT scores over 30: 11%.

Retention: 82% of full-time freshmen returned.

FACULTY

Total: 460, 48% full-time, 40% with terminal degrees.

Student/faculty ratio: 11:1.

ACADEMICS

Calendar: semesters. *Degrees:* certificates, bachelor's, master's, and post-master's certificates.

Special study options: academic remediation for entering students, accelerated degree program, adult/continuing education programs, advanced placement credit, distance learning, double majors, English as a second language, honors programs, independent study, internships, off-campus study, part-time degree program, services for LD students, student-designed majors, study abroad, summer session for credit. ***ROTC:*** Army (c), Air Force (c).

Unusual degree programs: 3-2 engineering with Case Western Reserve University; social work with Case Western Reserve University; computer information systems, computer science, or human resources/business administration; 4+1 accountancy MAcc.

Computers: 457 computers/terminals and 100 ports are available on campus for general student use. Students can access the following: campus intranet, computer help desk, free student e-mail accounts, online (class) grades, online (class) registration, online (class) schedules. Campuswide network is available. 100% of college-owned or -operated housing units are wired for high-speed Internet access. Wireless service is available via entire campus.

Library: Ritter Library plus 2 others. *Books:* 106,091 (physical), 451,472 (digital/electronic); *Serial titles:* 148 (physical), 86,238 (digital/electronic); *Databases:* 265. Weekly public service hours: 90; study areas open 24 hours, 5–7 days a week; students can reserve study rooms.

STUDENT LIFE

Housing options: on-campus residence required through sophomore year; coed, special housing for students with disabilities. Campus housing is university owned. Freshman applicants given priority for college housing.

Activities and organizations: drama/theater group, student-run newspaper, radio and television station, choral group, marching band, Arts Management Association (AMA), Ohio Collegiate Music Educators Association (OCMEA), Rotaract, Sport Management Club (SMC), Voices of Praise Gospel Choir (VOP), national fraternities, national sororities.

Athletics Member NCAA. All Division III except golf (Division II). ***Intercollegiate sports:*** baseball M, basketball M/W, cross-country running M/W, football M, golf M/W, lacrosse M/W, soccer M/W, softball W, swimming and diving M/W, tennis M/W, track and field M/W, volleyball W, wrestling M. ***Intramural sports:*** archery M(c)/W(c), badminton M/W, basketball M/W, cheerleading W(c), crew M(c)/W(c), football M, golf M/W, racquetball M/W, riflery M(c)/W(c), rowing M(c)/W(c), rugby M(c)/W(c), sailing M(c)/W(c), skiing (cross-country) M(c)/W(c), skiing (downhill) M(c)/W(c), soccer M/W, softball M/W, table tennis M/W, tennis M/W, ultimate Frisbee M/W, volleyball M/W, wrestling M.

Campus security: 24-hour emergency response devices and patrols, student patrols, late-night transport/escort service, controlled dormitory access.

Student services: health clinic, personal/psychological counseling, veterans affairs office.

COSTS & FINANCIAL AID

Costs (2019–20) ***Comprehensive fee:*** $43,640 includes full-time tuition ($33,530) and room and board ($10,110). Part-time tuition: $1042 per credit hour. ***College room only:*** $5678.

Financial Aid Of all full-time matriculated undergraduates who enrolled in 2018, 2,529 applied for aid, 2,209 were judged to have need, 818 had their need fully met. 921 Federal Work-Study jobs (averaging $1361). 500 state and other part-time jobs (averaging $1350). In 2018, 654 non-need-based awards were made. ***Average percent of need met:*** 86. ***Average financial aid package:*** $25,129. ***Average need-based loan:*** $4585. ***Average need-based gift aid:*** $22,405. ***Average non-need-based aid:*** $14,948. ***Average indebtedness upon graduation:*** $33,838.

APPLYING

Standardized Tests *Required for some:* SAT or ACT (for admission).

Options: electronic application, deferred entrance.

Application fee: $25.

Required: essay or personal statement, high school transcript. ***Required for some:*** minimum 3.0 cum GPA and recently graded paper in lieu of ACT or SAT scores for Test Optional applicants. ***Recommended:*** minimum 3.0 GPA, 1 letter of recommendation, interview.

Application deadlines: 5/1 (freshmen), 8/1 (transfers).

Notification: continuous (freshmen), continuous (transfers).

CONTACT

Joyce J. Cendroski, Director of First Year RCMT and Admission, Baldwin Wallace University, Durst Welcome Center, 115 Tressel Street, Berea, OH 44017. *Phone:* 440-826-2222. *Toll-free phone:* 877-BW-APPLY. *Fax:* 440-826-3830. *E-mail:* admission@bw.edu.

Bluffton University

Bluffton, Ohio

http://www.bluffton.edu/

- **Independent Mennonite** comprehensive, founded 1899
- **Small-town** 65-acre campus with easy access to Dayton
- **Endowment** $24.2 million
- **Coed**
- **Moderately difficult** entrance level

FACULTY

Student/faculty ratio: 11:1.

ACADEMICS

Calendar: semesters. *Degrees:* bachelor's, master's, and postbachelor's certificates.

Library: Musselman Library plus 1 other. *Books:* 73,648 (physical), 283,031 (digital/electronic); *Serial titles:* 1,001 (physical), 46,672 (digital/electronic); *Databases:* 258. Weekly public service hours: 74; students can reserve study rooms.

STUDENT LIFE

Housing options: on-campus residence required through senior year; coed, men-only, women-only. Campus housing is university owned. Freshman campus housing is guaranteed.

Activities and organizations: drama/theater group, student-run newspaper, radio station, choral group, Marbeck Center Board, Multicultural Student Organization, Bluffton Education Association, Fellowship of Christian Athletes, Bluffton University Business Leaders.

Athletics Member NCAA. All Division III.

Campus security: 24-hour emergency response devices, controlled dormitory access, night security guards.

Student services: health clinic, personal/psychological counseling.

COSTS & FINANCIAL AID

Costs (2018–19) ***Comprehensive fee:*** $43,566 includes full-time tuition ($32,316), mandatory fees ($450), and room and board ($10,800). Full-time tuition and fees vary according to course load, degree level, and program. Part-time tuition: $1347 per credit hour. Part-time tuition and fees vary according to course load, degree level, and program. ***Required fees:*** $113 per term part-time. ***College room only:*** $5316. Room and board charges vary according to board plan and housing facility.

Financial Aid Of all full-time matriculated undergraduates who enrolled in 2017, 614 applied for aid, 575 were judged to have need, 80 had their need fully met. 442 Federal Work-Study jobs (averaging $2306). 188 state and other part-time jobs (averaging $2907). In 2017, 86 non-need-based awards were made. ***Average percent of need met:*** 75. ***Average financial aid package:*** $27,173. ***Average need-based loan:*** $4551. ***Average need-based gift aid:*** $21,925. ***Average non-need-based aid:*** $16,395. ***Average indebtedness upon graduation:*** $36,796. ***Financial aid deadline:*** 10/1.

APPLYING

Standardized Tests *Required:* SAT or ACT (for admission).

Options: electronic application, deferred entrance.

Required: high school transcript, minimum 2.3 GPA, 1 letter of recommendation, rank in upper 50% of high school class or minimum ACT score of 19. ***Required for some:*** essay or personal statement. ***Recommended:*** interview.

CONTACT

Ms. Emily Warner, Admissions Operation Manager, Bluffton University, 1 University Drive, Bluffton, OH 45817. *Phone:* 419-358-3255. *Toll-free phone:* 800-488-3257. *Fax:* 419-358-3081. *E-mail:* admissions@bluffton.edu.

Bowling Green State University

Bowling Green, Ohio

http://www.bgsu.edu/

- **State-supported** university, founded 1910
- **Small-town** 1338-acre campus with easy access to Toledo
- **Endowment** $162.3 million
- **Coed** 14,858 undergraduate students, 87% full-time, 55% women, 45% men
- **Moderately difficult** entrance level, 72% of applicants were admitted

UNDERGRAD STUDENTS

12,987 full-time, 1,871 part-time. Students come from 51 states and territories; 57 other countries; 12% are from out of state; 8% Black or African American, non-Hispanic/Latino; 4% Hispanic/Latino; 1% Asian, non-Hispanic/Latino; 0.2% American Indian or Alaska Native, non-Hispanic/Latino; 3% Two or more races, non-Hispanic/Latino; 2% Race/ethnicity unknown; 3% international; 4% transferred in; 42% live on campus.

Freshmen:

Admission: 17,028 applied, 12,303 admitted, 3,273 enrolled. ***Average high school GPA:*** 3.4. ***Test scores:*** SAT evidence-based reading and writing scores over 500: 80%; SAT math scores over 500: 76%; ACT scores over 18: 94%; SAT evidence-based reading and writing scores over 600: 30%; SAT math scores over 600: 24%; ACT scores over 24: 39%;

SAT evidence-based reading and writing scores over 700: 3%; SAT math scores over 700: 3%; ACT scores over 30: 6%.

Retention: 77% of full-time freshmen returned.

FACULTY

Total: 1,144, 65% full-time, 59% with terminal degrees.

Student/faculty ratio: 18:1.

ACADEMICS

Calendar: semesters. *Degrees:* certificates, bachelor's, master's, doctoral, post-master's, and postbachelor's certificates.

Special study options: academic remediation for entering students, accelerated degree program, adult/continuing education programs, advanced placement credit, cooperative education, distance learning, double majors, English as a second language, freshman honors college, honors programs, independent study, internships, off-campus study, part-time degree program, services for LD students, student-designed majors, study abroad, summer session for credit. ***ROTC:*** Army (b), Air Force (b).

Computers: 1,500 computers/terminals and 500 ports are available on campus for general student use. Students can access the following: campus intranet, computer help desk, free student e-mail accounts, online (class) grades, online (class) registration, online (class) schedules, wireless networking, OneDrive, Bursar billing information and payment, online mid-term grade reporting, view and change personal information, order official and unofficial transcripts, check meal plan balance, apply for graduation, etc. Campuswide network is available. 100% of college-owned or -operated housing units are wired for high-speed Internet access. Wireless service is available via entire campus.

Library: William T. Jerome Library. *Books:* 1.6 million (physical), 230,668 (digital/electronic); *Serial titles:* 651 (physical), 12,290 (digital/electronic); *Databases:* 303. Weekly public service hours: 110; students can reserve study rooms.

STUDENT LIFE

Housing options: on-campus residence required through sophomore year; coed, men-only, women-only, special housing for students with disabilities. Campus housing is university owned and leased by the school. Freshman campus housing is guaranteed.

Activities and organizations: drama/theater group, student-run newspaper, radio and television station, choral group, marching band, Dance Marathon, Undergraduate Student Government, University Activities Organization, Alpha Phi Omega, Athletic Training Student Organization, national fraternities, national sororities.

Athletics Member NCAA. All Division I. ***Intercollegiate sports:*** baseball M(s), basketball M(s)/W(s), cross-country running M(s)/W(s), football M(s), golf M(s)/W(s), gymnastics W(s), ice hockey M(s), soccer M(s)/W(s), softball W(s), swimming and diving W(s), tennis W(s), track and field W(s), volleyball W(s). ***Intramural sports:*** badminton M/W, baseball M(c), basketball M/W, bowling M(c)/W(c), cross-country running M(c)/W(c), equestrian sports W(c), football M, gymnastics W(c), ice hockey M(c), lacrosse M(c)/W(c), rugby M(c)/W(c), soccer M/W, softball W(c), swimming and diving M(c)/W(c), tennis M(c)/W(c), track and field M(c)/W(c), ultimate Frisbee M/W, volleyball M/W, water polo M(c)/W(c).

Campus security: 24-hour emergency response devices and patrols, student patrols, late-night transport/escort service, controlled dormitory access.

Student services: health clinic, personal/psychological counseling, women's center, legal services, veterans affairs office.

COSTS & FINANCIAL AID

Costs (2018–19) ***Tuition:*** state resident $9096 full-time, $379 per credit hour part-time; nonresident $17,084 full-time, $712 per credit hour part-time. Full-time tuition and fees vary according to course load and location. Part-time tuition and fees vary according to course load and location. ***Required fees:*** $2009 full-time, $83 per credit hour part-time. ***Room and board:*** $9168. Room and board charges vary according to board plan and housing facility. ***Payment plan:*** installment. ***Waivers:*** senior citizens and employees or children of employees.

Financial Aid Of all full-time matriculated undergraduates who enrolled in 2018, 10,726 applied for aid, 8,443 were judged to have need, 1,182 had their need fully met. 391 Federal Work-Study jobs (averaging $1091). In 2018, 2634 non-need-based awards were made. ***Average percent of need met:*** 79. ***Average financial aid package:*** $14,344. ***Average need-based loan:*** $4141. ***Average need-based gift aid:*** $7598. ***Average non-need-based aid:*** $5160. ***Average indebtedness upon graduation:*** $29,958.

APPLYING

Standardized Tests *Required:* SAT or ACT (for admission).

Options: electronic application, deferred entrance.

Application fee: $45.

Required: high school transcript. ***Required for some:*** interview.

Application deadlines: 7/15 (freshmen), 7/15 (out-of-state freshmen), 8/1 (transfers).

Notification: continuous until 8/1 (freshmen), continuous until 8/1 (out-of-state freshmen), continuous (transfers).

CONTACT

Ms. Cecilia Castellano, Vice President for Enrollment, Bowling Green State University, Bowling Green, OH 43403. *Phone:* 419-372-1528. *E-mail:* ccast@bgsu.edu.

Bowling Green State University–Firelands College

Huron, Ohio

http://www.firelands.bgsu.edu/

- **State-supported** primarily 2-year, founded 1968, part of Bowling Green State University System
- **Rural** 216-acre campus with easy access to Cleveland, Toledo
- **Coed**
- **Noncompetitive** entrance level

FACULTY

Student/faculty ratio: 20:1.

ACADEMICS

Calendar: semesters. *Degrees:* certificates, associate, and bachelor's (also offers some upper-level and graduate courses).

Library: BGSU Firelands College Library.

STUDENT LIFE

Housing options: college housing not available.

Activities and organizations: drama/theater group, choral group, Society of Fandom and Gaming, Student Government, Student Theater Guild, Safe Space, Society of Leadership and Success.

Campus security: 24-hour emergency response devices, late-night transport/escort service, patrols by trained security personnel.

COSTS

Costs (2018–19) ***Tuition:*** state resident $4706 full-time, $196 per credit hour part-time; nonresident $12,014 full-time, $510 per credit hour part-time. Full-time tuition and fees vary according to location and reciprocity agreements. Part-time tuition and fees vary according to location and reciprocity agreements. ***Required fees:*** $240 full-time, $9 per credit hour part-time, $120 per term part-time.

APPLYING

Options: electronic application, early admission, deferred entrance.

Application fee: $45.

Required: high school transcript.

CONTACT

Dr. Megan Zahler, Assistant Dean for Strategic Enrollment Planning, Bowling Green State University–Firelands College, One University Drive, Huron, OH 44839-9791. *Phone:* 419-433-5560. *Toll-free phone:* 800-322-4787. *Fax:* 419-372-0604. *E-mail:* mzahler@bgsu.edu.

Bryant & Stratton College–Akron Campus

Akron, Ohio

http://www.bryantstratton.edu/

CONTACT

Bryant & Stratton College–Akron Campus, 190 Montrose West Avenue, Akron, OH 44321.

Bryant & Stratton College–Cleveland Campus

Cleveland, Ohio

http://www.bryantstratton.edu/

CONTACT
Bryant & Stratton College–Cleveland Campus, Cleveland, OH 44114-3203. *Phone:* 216-771-1700. *Fax:* 216-771-7787.

Bryant & Stratton College–Eastlake Campus

Eastlake, Ohio

http://www.bryantstratton.edu/

CONTACT
Ms. Melanie Pettit, Director of Admissions, Bryant & Stratton College–Eastlake Campus, 35350 Curtis Boulevard, Eastlake, OH 44095. *Phone:* 440-510-1112.

Bryant & Stratton College–Parma Campus

Parma, Ohio

http://www.bryantstratton.edu/

CONTACT
Bryant & Stratton College–Parma Campus, 12955 Snow Road, Parma, OH 44130-1005. *Phone:* 216-265-3151. *Toll-free phone:* 866-948-0571.

Capital University

Columbus, Ohio

http://www.capital.edu/

- **Independent** comprehensive, founded 1830, affiliated with Evangelical Lutheran Church in America
- **Suburban** 48-acre campus with easy access to Columbus
- **Endowment** $78.0 million
- **Coed**
- **Moderately difficult** entrance level

FACULTY
Student/faculty ratio: 11:1.

ACADEMICS
Calendar: semesters. *Degrees:* bachelor's, master's, doctoral, and postbachelor's certificates.
Library: Blackmore Library.

STUDENT LIFE
Housing options: on-campus residence required through sophomore year; coed, special housing for students with disabilities. Campus housing is university owned. Freshman campus housing is guaranteed.

Activities and organizations: drama/theater group, student-run newspaper, radio and television station, choral group, Campus Crusade for Christ, student government, University Programming, College Republicans, American Marketing Association, national fraternities, national sororities.

Athletics Member NCAA. All Division III.

Campus security: 24-hour emergency response devices and patrols, late-night transport/escort service, controlled dormitory access.

Student services: health clinic, personal/psychological counseling, veterans affairs office.

COSTS & FINANCIAL AID
Costs (2018–19) ***Comprehensive fee:*** $46,050 includes full-time tuition ($35,146), mandatory fees ($320), and room and board ($10,584). Full-time tuition and fees vary according to course load. Part-time tuition: $1172 per credit hour. Part-time tuition and fees vary according to course load. ***Room and board:*** Room and board charges vary according to board plan and housing facility.

Financial Aid Of all full-time matriculated undergraduates who enrolled in 2017, 2,156 applied for aid, 1,964 were judged to have need, 446 had their need fully met. In 2017, 466 non-need-based awards were made. ***Average percent of need met:*** 78. ***Average financial aid package:*** $28,630. ***Average need-based loan:*** $4642. ***Average need-based gift aid:*** $23,535. ***Average non-need-based aid:*** $20,185. ***Average indebtedness upon graduation:*** $33,496.

APPLYING
Standardized Tests *Required:* SAT or ACT (for admission).

Options: electronic application, deferred entrance.

Application fee: $25.

Required: high school transcript, minimum 2.6 GPA. ***Required for some:*** 1 letter of recommendation, audition for Conservatory of Music. ***Recommended:*** interview.

CONTACT
Mr. Garien Hudson, Director of Admission, Capital University, 1 College and Main, Columbus, OH 43209. *Phone:* 614-236-6232. *Toll-free phone:* 866-544-6175. *Fax:* 614-236-6926. *E-mail:* ghudson@capital.edu.

Case Western Reserve University

Cleveland, Ohio

http://www.case.edu/

- **Independent** university, founded 1826
- **Urban** 267-acre campus
- **Endowment** $1.8 billion
- **Coed**
- **Very difficult** entrance level

FACULTY
Student/faculty ratio: 11:1.

ACADEMICS
Calendar: semesters. *Degrees:* bachelor's, master's, doctoral, post-master's, and postbachelor's certificates.
Library: Kelvin Smith Library plus 6 others. *Books:* 3.4 million (physical); *Serial titles:* 196,361 (physical); *Databases:* 470. Students can reserve study rooms.

STUDENT LIFE
Housing options: on-campus residence required through sophomore year; coed. Campus housing is university owned. Freshman campus housing is guaranteed.

Activities and organizations: drama/theater group, student-run newspaper, radio station, choral group, marching band, SpartaTHON, Quidditch Team, Spartans for Special Olympics, Undergraduate Indian Student Association, Footlighters, national fraternities, national sororities.

Athletics Member NCAA. All Division III.

Campus security: 24-hour emergency response devices and patrols, student patrols, late-night transport/escort service, controlled dormitory access, crime prevention programs.

Student services: health clinic, personal/psychological counseling, women's center, legal services.

COSTS & FINANCIAL AID
Costs (2018–19) ***One-time required fee:*** $555. ***Comprehensive fee:*** $64,232 includes full-time tuition ($48,604), mandatory fees ($438), and room and board ($15,190). Part-time tuition: $2026 per credit hour. Part-time tuition and fees vary according to course load. ***College room only:*** $8830. Room and board charges vary according to board plan, housing facility, and student level.

Financial Aid Of all full-time matriculated undergraduates who enrolled in 2018, 2,963 applied for aid, 2,430 were judged to have need, 1,714 had their need fully met. 1,452 Federal Work-Study jobs (averaging $2662). 161 state and other part-time jobs (averaging $2403). In 2018, 1751 non-need-based awards were made. ***Average percent of need met:*** 90. ***Average financial aid package:*** $44,441. ***Average need-based loan:*** $6216. ***Average need-based gift aid:*** $31,693. ***Average non-need-based aid:*** $24,203. ***Average indebtedness upon graduation:*** $31,820. ***Financial aid deadline:*** 2/1.

APPLYING
Standardized Tests *Required:* SAT or ACT (for admission).

Options: electronic application, early admission, early decision, early action, deferred entrance.

Application fee: $70.

Required: essay or personal statement, high school transcript, 2 letters of recommendation, school report, including a counselor recommendation. ***Recommended:*** interview.

CONTACT

Robert McCullough, Director of Undergraduate Admission, Case Western Reserve University, 10900 Euclid Avenue, Cleveland, OH 44106. *Phone:* 216-368-4450. *Fax:* 216-368-5111. *E-mail:* admission@case.edu.

Cedarville University

Cedarville, Ohio

http://www.cedarville.edu/

- **Independent Baptist** comprehensive, founded 1887
- **Small-town** 441-acre campus with easy access to Columbus, Dayton
- **Endowment** $30.8 million
- **Coed** 3,759 undergraduate students, 87% full-time, 53% women, 47% men
- **Moderately difficult** entrance level, 79% of applicants were admitted

UNDERGRAD STUDENTS

3,278 full-time, 481 part-time. Students come from 48 states and territories; 38 other countries; 57% are from out of state; 1% Black or African American, non-Hispanic/Latino; 2% Hispanic/Latino; 2% Asian, non-Hispanic/Latino; 0.1% Native Hawaiian or other Pacific Islander, non-Hispanic/Latino; 0.3% American Indian or Alaska Native, non-Hispanic/Latino; 3% Two or more races, non-Hispanic/Latino; 3% Race/ethnicity unknown; 2% international; 4% transferred in; 73% live on campus.

Freshmen:

Admission: 3,741 applied, 2,969 admitted, 911 enrolled. ***Average high school GPA:*** 3.8. ***Test scores:*** SAT evidence-based reading and writing scores over 500: 97%; SAT math scores over 500: 95%; ACT scores over 18: 99%; SAT evidence-based reading and writing scores over 600: 70%; SAT math scores over 600: 55%; ACT scores over 24: 74%; SAT evidence-based reading and writing scores over 700: 19%; SAT math scores over 700: 16%; ACT scores over 30: 22%.

Retention: 87% of full-time freshmen returned.

FACULTY

Total: 346, 53% full-time, 58% with terminal degrees.

Student/faculty ratio: 14:1.

ACADEMICS

Calendar: semesters. *Degrees:* certificates, bachelor's, master's, doctoral, post-master's, and postbachelor's certificates.

Special study options: academic remediation for entering students, adult/continuing education programs, advanced placement credit, cooperative education, distance learning, double majors, honors programs, independent study, internships, off-campus study, part-time degree program, services for LD students, student-designed majors, study abroad, summer session for credit. ***ROTC:*** Army (c), Air Force (c).

Computers: 1,500 computers/terminals and 4,000 ports are available on campus for general student use. Students can access the following: campus intranet, computer help desk, free student e-mail accounts, online (class) grades, online (class) registration, online (class) schedules, over 70 software packages. Campuswide network is available. 100% of college-owned or -operated housing units are wired for high-speed Internet access. Wireless service is available via entire campus.

Library: Centennial Library. *Books:* 182,596 (physical), 132,747 (digital/electronic); *Serial titles:* 737 (physical), 27,560 (digital/electronic); *Databases:* 200. Weekly public service hours: 91; students can reserve study rooms.

STUDENT LIFE

Housing options: on-campus residence required through senior year; men-only, women-only, special housing for students with disabilities. Campus housing is university owned. Freshman campus housing is guaranteed.

Activities and organizations: drama/theater group, student-run newspaper, radio station, choral group, Student Nurses Association, Tau Delta Kappa, Mu Kappa, AYO, MISO (Multicultural International Student Org).

Athletics Member NCAA, NCCAA. All NCAA Division II. ***Intercollegiate sports:*** baseball M(s), basketball M(s)/W(s), cheerleading M/W, cross-country running M(s)/W(s), golf M(s), soccer M(s)/W(s), softball W(s), tennis M(s)/W(s), track and field M(s)/W(s), volleyball W(s). ***Intramural sports:*** badminton M/W, basketball M/W, football M/W, golf M/W, racquetball M/W, riflery M(c)/W(c), rock climbing M/W, rugby M(c)/W(c), soccer M/W, swimming and diving M(c)/W(c), table tennis M/W, tennis M/W, ultimate Frisbee M(c)/W(c), volleyball M/W.

Campus security: 24-hour emergency response devices and patrols, late-night transport/escort service, controlled dormitory access.

Student services: health clinic, personal/psychological counseling.

COSTS & FINANCIAL AID

Costs (2019–20) ***Comprehensive fee:*** $38,940 includes full-time tuition ($31,122), mandatory fees ($200), and room and board ($7618). Part-time tuition: $1178 per credit. ***Required fees:*** $50 per term part-time. ***College room only:*** $4318.

Financial Aid Of all full-time matriculated undergraduates who enrolled in 2018, 2,717 applied for aid, 2,295 were judged to have need, 864 had their need fully met. 343 Federal Work-Study jobs (averaging $2227). 1,586 state and other part-time jobs (averaging $1419). In 2018, 831 non-need-based awards were made. ***Average percent of need met:*** 29. ***Average financial aid package:*** $22,873. ***Average need-based loan:*** $5687. ***Average need-based gift aid:*** $6063. ***Average non-need-based aid:*** $19,974. ***Average indebtedness upon graduation:*** $23,822.

APPLYING

Standardized Tests *Required:* SAT or ACT (for admission), SAT or ACT or CLT (for admission).

Options: electronic application, early admission, deferred entrance.

Application fee: $30.

Required: essay or personal statement, high school transcript, minimum 3.0 GPA, 1 letter of recommendation, clear testimony of faith in Jesus Christ and evidence of a consistent Christian lifestyle, minimum ACT score of 22 or SAT score of 1020, minimum 3.0 unweighted, cumulative GPA in college prep course work. ***Required for some:*** interview.

Application deadlines: rolling (freshmen), rolling (out-of-state freshmen), rolling (transfers).

Notification: continuous (freshmen), continuous (out-of-state freshmen), continuous (transfers).

CONTACT

Ms. Becky Hayes, Director of Enrollment Services, Cedarville University, 251 North Main Street, Cedarville, OH 45314-0601. *Phone:* 937-766-7700. *Toll-free phone:* 800-233-2784. *E-mail:* admissions@cedarville.edu.

Central State University

Wilberforce, Ohio

http://www.centralstate.edu/

- **State-supported** 4-year, founded 1887, part of Ohio Board of Regents
- **Rural** 60-acre campus with easy access to Dayton
- **Endowment** $3.9 million
- **Coed** 2,099 undergraduate students, 97% full-time, 60% women, 40% men
- **Minimally difficult** entrance level, 57% of applicants were admitted

UNDERGRAD STUDENTS

2,029 full-time, 70 part-time. Students come from 29 states and territories; 11 other countries; 49% are from out of state; 88% Black or African American, non-Hispanic/Latino; 0.5% Hispanic/Latino; 0.1% Asian, non-Hispanic/Latino; 0.1% American Indian or Alaska Native, non-Hispanic/Latino; 2% Two or more races, non-Hispanic/Latino; 4% Race/ethnicity unknown; 4% international; 5% transferred in; 75% live on campus.

Freshmen:

Admission: 12,353 applied, 7,051 admitted, 792 enrolled. ***Average high school GPA:*** 2.7.

Retention: 54% of full-time freshmen returned.

FACULTY

Total: 201, 51% full-time, 54% with terminal degrees.

Student/faculty ratio: 13:1.

ACADEMICS
Calendar: semesters. *Degree:* bachelor's.

Special study options: adult/continuing education programs, cooperative education, double majors, honors programs, independent study, internships, off-campus study, part-time degree program, services for LD students, study abroad, summer session for credit. ***ROTC:*** Army (b).

Computers: 880 computers/terminals and 2,600 ports are available on campus for general student use. Students can access the following: campus intranet, computer help desk, free student e-mail accounts, online (class) grades, online (class) registration, online (class) schedules. Campuswide network is available. 100% of college-owned or -operated housing units are wired for high-speed Internet access. Wireless service is available via entire campus.

Library: Hallie Q. Brown Memorial Library plus 1 other. *Books:* 362,854 (physical), 187,392 (digital/electronic); *Serial titles:* 69 (physical); *Databases:* 277. Weekly public service hours: 77.

STUDENT LIFE
Housing options: on-campus residence required through sophomore year; coed, men-only, women-only. Campus housing is university owned. Freshman campus housing is guaranteed.

Activities and organizations: drama/theater group, student-run newspaper, radio and television station, choral group, marching band, Student Ambassadors, student government, Campus Tour Guides, Brotherhood of Strong Success, Family Community and Leadership in Action, national fraternities, national sororities.

Athletics Member NCAA. All Division II. ***Intercollegiate sports:*** basketball M(s)/W(s), cheerleading M(s)/W(s), cross-country running M(s)/W(s), football M(s), golf M(s), tennis M(s)/W(s), track and field M(s)/W(s), volleyball W(s). ***Intramural sports:*** basketball M/W, softball M/W, tennis M/W.

Campus security: 24-hour emergency response devices and patrols, controlled dormitory access.

Student services: health clinic, personal/psychological counseling.

COSTS & FINANCIAL AID
Costs (2018–19) ***Tuition:*** state resident $3926 full-time, $275 per credit hour part-time; nonresident $5926 full-time, $625 per credit hour part-time. Full-time tuition and fees vary according to course load and reciprocity agreements. Part-time tuition and fees vary according to course load and reciprocity agreements. ***Required fees:*** $2420 full-time. ***Room and board:*** $10,232; room only: $5500. Room and board charges vary according to board plan and housing facility. ***Payment plan:*** installment. ***Waivers:*** senior citizens and employees or children of employees.

Financial Aid Of all full-time matriculated undergraduates who enrolled in 2017, 1,671 applied for aid, 1,668 were judged to have need, 153 had their need fully met. ***Average percent of need met:*** 9. ***Average financial aid package:*** $9695. ***Average need-based loan:*** $3803. ***Average need-based gift aid:*** $7455.

APPLYING
Options: electronic application.

Application fee: $35.

Required: essay or personal statement, high school transcript. ***Required for some:*** minimum 2.2 GPA, 2 letters of recommendation.

Notification: continuous (freshmen), continuous (transfers).

CONTACT
Mr. James Burrell, Director, Admissions, Central State University, PO Box 1004, 1400 Blush Row Road, Wilberforce, OH 45384. *Phone:* 937-376-6218. *Toll-free phone:* 800-388-CSU1 (in-state); 800-388-2781 (out-of-state). *Fax:* 937-376-6648. *E-mail:* admissions@centralstate.edu.

Chamberlain College of Nursing
Cleveland, Ohio
http://www.chamberlain.edu/

CONTACT
Chamberlain College of Nursing, 6700 Euclid Avenue, Cleveland, OH 44103. *Toll-free phone:* 877-751-5783.

Chamberlain College of Nursing
Columbus, Ohio
http://www.chamberlain.edu/

CONTACT
Admissions, Chamberlain College of Nursing, 1350 Alum Creek Drive, Columbus, OH 43209. *Phone:* 614-252-8890. *Toll-free phone:* 877-751-5783.

Cincinnati Christian University
Cincinnati, Ohio
http://www.ccuniversity.edu/

CONTACT
Cincinnati Christian University, 2700 Glenway Avenue, PO Box 04320, Cincinnati, OH 45204-3200. *Phone:* 513-244-8110. *Toll-free phone:* 800-949-4228 (in-state); 800-949-4CCU (out-of-state).

Cincinnati College of Mortuary Science
Cincinnati, Ohio
http://www.ccms.edu/

CONTACT
Cincinnati College of Mortuary Science, 645 West North Bend Road, Cincinnati, OH 45224-1462. *Phone:* 513-761-2020. *Toll-free phone:* 888-377-8433. *Fax:* 513-761-3333.

Cleveland Institute of Art
Cleveland, Ohio
http://www.cia.edu/

- **Independent** 4-year, founded 1882
- **Urban** 2-acre campus with easy access to Cleveland
- **Endowment** $27.5 million
- **Coed** 670 undergraduate students, 97% full-time, 67% women, 33% men
- **Moderately difficult** entrance level, 73% of applicants were admitted

UNDERGRAD STUDENTS
649 full-time, 21 part-time. Students come from 31 states and territories; 7 other countries; 32% are from out of state; 11% Black or African American, non-Hispanic/Latino; 8% Hispanic/Latino; 3% Asian, non-Hispanic/Latino; 0.2% Native Hawaiian or other Pacific Islander, non-Hispanic/Latino; 0.2% American Indian or Alaska Native, non-Hispanic/Latino; 5% Two or more races, non-Hispanic/Latino; 6% international; 5% transferred in; 48% live on campus.

Freshmen:
Admission: 1,025 applied, 753 admitted, 175 enrolled. ***Average high school GPA:*** 3.3. ***Test scores:*** SAT evidence-based reading and writing scores over 500: 90%; SAT math scores over 500: 81%; ACT scores over 18: 82%; SAT evidence-based reading and writing scores over 600: 45%; SAT math scores over 600: 24%; ACT scores over 24: 35%; SAT evidence-based reading and writing scores over 700: 6%; SAT math scores over 700: 4%; ACT scores over 30: 6%.

Retention: 86% of full-time freshmen returned.

FACULTY
Total: 123, 43% full-time, 63% with terminal degrees.

Student/faculty ratio: 7:1.

ACADEMICS
Calendar: semesters. *Degree:* bachelor's.

Special study options: advanced placement credit, distance learning, double majors, independent study, internships, off-campus study, part-time degree program, services for LD students, study abroad. ***ROTC:*** Army (c), Air Force (c).

Computers: 250 computers/terminals are available on campus for general student use. Students can access the following: campus intranet, computer help desk, free student e-mail accounts, online (class) grades, online (class) registration, online (class) schedules, wireless Internet access available throughout campus. Campuswide network is available. 100% of

college-owned or -operated housing units are wired for high-speed Internet access. Wireless service is available via entire campus.
Library: Jessica R Gund Library. *Books:* 48,478 (physical), 288,857 (digital/electronic); *Serial titles:* 420 (physical), 11 (digital/electronic); *Databases:* 200. Weekly public service hours: 74; students can reserve study rooms.

STUDENT LIFE
Housing options: on-campus residence required through sophomore year; coed. Campus housing is leased by the school. Freshman applicants given priority for college housing.

Activities and organizations: drama/theater group, choral group, marching band, Campus Activities Board, Student Independent Exhibition, International Interior Design Association, Student Leadership Council, Community Outreach Team, national fraternities, national sororities.

Athletics ***Intramural sports:*** basketball M/W, cross-country running M/W, football M/W, golf M/W, racquetball M/W, soccer M/W, softball M/W, swimming and diving M/W, tennis M/W, track and field M/W, ultimate Frisbee M/W, volleyball M/W.

Campus security: 24-hour emergency response devices and patrols, controlled dormitory access.

Student services: health clinic, personal/psychological counseling, women's center.

COSTS & FINANCIAL AID
Costs (2019–20) ***Comprehensive fee:*** $54,640 includes full-time tuition ($40,480), mandatory fees ($2830), and room and board ($11,330). Part-time tuition: $1690 per credit hour. ***Required fees:*** $75 per credit hour part-time. ***College room only:*** $8680.

Financial Aid Of all full-time matriculated undergraduates who enrolled in 2017, 583 applied for aid, 510 were judged to have need, 52 had their need fully met. 137 Federal Work-Study jobs (averaging $1158). In 2017, 82 non-need-based awards were made. ***Average percent of need met:*** 60. ***Average financial aid package:*** $27,398. ***Average need-based loan:*** $4697. ***Average need-based gift aid:*** $23,073. ***Average non-need-based aid:*** $14,168. ***Average indebtedness upon graduation:*** $41,326.

APPLYING
Options: electronic application, early admission, early action, deferred entrance.

Application fee: $40.

Required: essay or personal statement, high school transcript, minimum 2.0 GPA, 1 letter of recommendation, portfolio. ***Recommended:*** interview.

Notification: continuous (freshmen), continuous (transfers).

CONTACT
Mr. Johnathan D Wehner, Vice President for Enrollment Management and Dean of Admissions + Financial Aid, Cleveland Institute of Art, 11610 Euclid Avenue, Cleveland, OH 44106. *Phone:* 216-421-7418. *Toll-free phone:* 800-223-4700. *Fax:* 216-754-3634. *E-mail:* jdwehner@cia.edu.

Cleveland Institute of Music

Cleveland, Ohio

http://www.cim.edu/

CONTACT
Mr. William Fay, Director of Admission, Cleveland Institute of Music, 11021 East Boulevard, Cleveland, OH 44106-1776. *Phone:* 216-795-3107. *Fax:* 216-791-1530. *E-mail:* william.fay@case.edu.

Cleveland State University

Cleveland, Ohio

http://www.csuohio.edu/

- **State-supported** university, founded 1964, part of University System of Ohio
- **Urban** 85-acre campus with easy access to Cleveland, OH
- **Endowment** $66.2 million
- **Coed**
- **Moderately difficult** entrance level

FACULTY
Student/faculty ratio: 17:1.

ACADEMICS
Calendar: semesters. *Degrees:* bachelor's, master's, doctoral, post-master's, and postbachelor's certificates.
Library: Michael Schwartz Library plus 1 other. *Books:* 524,556 (physical), 228,146 (digital/electronic); *Serial titles:* 6,155 (physical), 194 (digital/electronic); *Databases:* 733. Students can reserve study rooms.

STUDENT LIFE
Housing options: coed, special housing for students with disabilities. Campus housing is university owned. Freshman campus housing is guaranteed.

Activities and organizations: drama/theater group, student-run newspaper, radio station, choral group, Black Student Union, Chinese Students and Scholars Association, Through the Cross Campus Ministries, Student Nurses Association, Joint Engineering Council, national fraternities, national sororities.

Athletics Member NCAA. All Division I.

Campus security: 24-hour emergency response devices and patrols, late-night transport/escort service, controlled dormitory access, Campus Watch, CSU Alert Notification System, Community Emergency and Response Team (CERT).

Student services: health clinic, personal/psychological counseling, women's center, veterans affairs office.

FINANCIAL AID
Financial Aid Of all full-time matriculated undergraduates who enrolled in 2018, 7,505 applied for aid, 6,574 were judged to have need, 658 had their need fully met. 311 Federal Work-Study jobs (averaging $3686). In 2018, 767 non-need-based awards were made. ***Average percent of need met:*** 47. ***Average financial aid package:*** $9163. ***Average need-based loan:*** $4031. ***Average need-based gift aid:*** $7171. ***Average non-need-based aid:*** $5161. ***Average indebtedness upon graduation:*** $28,938.

APPLYING
Standardized Tests *Required:* SAT or ACT (for admission).

Options: electronic application, early action, deferred entrance.

Application fee: $30.

Required: high school transcript, minimum 2.3 GPA.

CONTACT
Undergraduate Admissions Office, Cleveland State University, 2121 Euclid Avenue, EC 100, Cleveland, OH 44115. *Phone:* 216-523-7416. *Toll-free phone:* 888-CSU-OHIO. *E-mail:* admissions@csuohio.edu.

The College of Wooster

Wooster, Ohio

http://www.wooster.edu/

- **Independent** 4-year, founded 1866, affiliated with Presbyterian Church (U.S.A.)
- **Small-town** 240-acre campus with easy access to Cleveland
- **Endowment** $280.5 million
- **Coed**
- **Moderately difficult** entrance level

FACULTY
Student/faculty ratio: 11:1.

ACADEMICS
Calendar: semesters. *Degree:* bachelor's.
Library: The College of Wooster Libraries plus 3 others. *Books:* 453,145 (physical), 719,794 (digital/electronic); *Serial titles:* 2,693 (physical), 102,227 (digital/electronic); *Databases:* 568. Weekly public service hours: 112; students can reserve study rooms.

STUDENT LIFE
Housing options: on-campus residence required through senior year; coed, women-only. Campus housing is university owned. Freshman campus housing is guaranteed.

Activities and organizations: drama/theater group, student-run newspaper, radio station, choral group, marching band, Volunteer Network, International Student Association, Inter-Greek Council, Wooster Activities Crew, Women's Athletic and Recreation Association.

Athletics Member NCAA. All Division III.

Campus security: 24-hour emergency response devices and patrols, student patrols, late-night transport/escort service, controlled dormitory access.

Student services: health clinic, personal/psychological counseling, women's center.

COSTS & FINANCIAL AID
Costs (2018–19) ***Comprehensive fee:*** $62,100 includes full-time tuition ($49,810), mandatory fees ($440), and room and board ($11,850). Full-time tuition and fees vary according to course load. Part-time tuition: $1545 per credit hour. Part-time tuition and fees vary according to course load. ***College room only:*** $5750. Room and board charges vary according to board plan and housing facility.

Financial Aid Of all full-time matriculated undergraduates who enrolled in 2018, 1,499 applied for aid, 1,324 were judged to have need, 516 had their need fully met. 524 Federal Work-Study jobs (averaging $1488). 203 state and other part-time jobs (averaging $3672). In 2018, 645 non-need-based awards were made. ***Average percent of need met:*** 93. ***Average financial aid package:*** $43,674. ***Average need-based loan:*** $6658. ***Average need-based gift aid:*** $34,445. ***Average non-need-based aid:*** $25,588. ***Average indebtedness upon graduation:*** $28,021.

APPLYING
Standardized Tests *Required:* SAT or ACT (for admission).

Options: electronic application, early admission, early decision, early action, deferred entrance.

Required: essay or personal statement, high school transcript. ***Recommended:*** letters of recommendation, interview.

CONTACT
Ms. Jennifer Winge, Dean of Admissions, The College of Wooster, 1189 Beall Avenue, Wooster, OH 44691-2363. *Phone:* 330-263-2270. *Toll-free phone:* 800-877-9905. *Fax:* 330-263-2621. *E-mail:* admissions@wooster.edu.

Columbus College of Art & Design

Columbus, Ohio

http://www.ccad.edu/

CONTACT
Columbus College of Art & Design, 60 Cleveland Avenue, Columbus, OH 43215-1758. *Phone:* 614-224-9101. *Toll-free phone:* 877-997-2223. *Fax:* 614-232-8344. *E-mail:* admissions@ccad.edu.

Defiance College

Defiance, Ohio

http://www.defiance.edu/

- **Independent** comprehensive, founded 1850, affiliated with United Church of Christ
- **Small-town** 150-acre campus with easy access to Toledo
- **Endowment** $15.2 million
- **Coed**
- **Moderately difficult** entrance level

FACULTY
Student/faculty ratio: 11:1.

ACADEMICS
Calendar: semesters. *Degrees:* associate, bachelor's, and master's.
Library: Pilgrim Library plus 1 other. *Books:* 62,576 (physical), 271,510 (digital/electronic); *Serial titles:* 308 (physical), 79,914 (digital/electronic); *Databases:* 162. Weekly public service hours: 90; students can reserve study rooms.

STUDENT LIFE
Housing options: on-campus residence required through junior year; coed. Campus housing is university owned. Freshman campus housing is guaranteed.

Activities and organizations: drama/theater group, student-run newspaper, choral group, marching band, Campus Activities Board, Criminal Justice Society, Student Senate, Black Action Student Association, Tau Kappa Epsilon, national fraternities, national sororities.

Athletics Member NCAA. All Division III.

Campus security: late-night transport/escort service, controlled dormitory access.

Student services: personal/psychological counseling, veterans affairs office.

COSTS & FINANCIAL AID
Costs (2018–19) ***Comprehensive fee:*** $42,950 includes full-time tuition ($31,990), mandatory fees ($740), and room and board ($10,220). Full-time tuition and fees vary according to course load. Part-time tuition: $495 per credit hour. Part-time tuition and fees vary according to course load. ***Required fees:*** $100 per term part-time. ***College room only:*** $5500. Room and board charges vary according to board plan and housing facility.

Financial Aid Of all full-time matriculated undergraduates who enrolled in 2018, 457 applied for aid, 438 were judged to have need, 38 had their need fully met. In 2018, 36 non-need-based awards were made. ***Average percent of need met:*** 68. ***Average financial aid package:*** $24,462. ***Average need-based loan:*** $3973. ***Average need-based gift aid:*** $19,662. ***Average non-need-based aid:*** $14,864.

APPLYING
Standardized Tests *Required:* SAT or ACT (for admission).

Options: electronic application, deferred entrance.

Application fee: $25.

Required: high school transcript, minimum 2.3 GPA. ***Required for some:*** essay or personal statement, 1 letter of recommendation, interview.

CONTACT
Mrs. Brenda Averesch, Assistant Dean of Admissions and Financial Aid, Defiance College, 701 North Clinton Street, Defiance, OH 43512. *Phone:* 419-783-2352. *Toll-free phone:* 800-520-4632. *Fax:* 419-783-2468. *E-mail:* baveresch@defiance.edu.

Denison University

Granville, Ohio

http://www.denison.edu/

- **Independent** 4-year, founded 1831
- **Suburban** 931-acre campus with easy access to Columbus
- **Coed**
- **Very difficult** entrance level

FACULTY
Student/faculty ratio: 9:1.

ACADEMICS
Calendar: semesters plus optional May term. *Degree:* bachelor's.
Library: William Howard Doane Library. *Books:* 1.4 million (physical), 912,952 (digital/electronic); *Serial titles:* 540 (physical), 653 (digital/electronic); *Databases:* 464. Weekly public service hours: 104; students can reserve study rooms.

STUDENT LIFE
Housing options: on-campus residence required through senior year; coed, men-only, women-only, cooperative. Campus housing is university owned. Freshman campus housing is guaranteed.

Activities and organizations: drama/theater group, student-run newspaper, radio and television station, choral group, national fraternities, national sororities.

Athletics Member NCAA. All Division III.

Campus security: 24-hour emergency response devices and patrols, student patrols, late-night transport/escort service, controlled dormitory access, security lighting, escort.

Student services: health clinic, personal/psychological counseling, women's center.

COSTS & FINANCIAL AID
Costs (2018–19) ***Comprehensive fee:*** $64,670 includes full-time tuition ($50,790), mandatory fees ($1170), and room and board ($12,710). Part-time tuition: $1590 per credit hour. Part-time tuition and fees vary according to course load. ***College room only:*** $7000. Room and board charges vary according to board plan and housing facility. ***Payment plans:*** installment, deferred payment.

Financial Aid Of all full-time matriculated undergraduates who enrolled in 2018, 1,637 applied for aid, 1,206 were judged to have need, 688 had their need fully met. In 2018, 1159 non-need-based awards were made. ***Average percent of need met:*** 98. ***Average financial aid package:*** $48,177. ***Average need-based loan:*** $4894. ***Average need-based gift aid:***

$46,695. ***Average non-need-based aid:*** $19,769. ***Average indebtedness upon graduation:*** $31,551. ***Financial aid deadline:*** 1/15.

APPLYING

Options: early admission, early decision, deferred entrance.

Required: essay or personal statement, high school transcript, 2 letters of recommendation. ***Recommended:*** interview.

CONTACT

Mr. Michael S. Hills, Director of Admissions, Denison University, 100 West College Street, Granville, OH 43023. *Phone:* 740-587-6627. *Toll-free phone:* 800-DENISON. *E-mail:* hills@denison.edu.

DeVry University–Columbus Campus

Columbus, Ohio

http://www.devry.edu/

CONTACT

Admissions Office, DeVry University–Columbus Campus, 1350 Alum Creek Drive, Columbus, OH 43209. *Phone:* 614-253-7291. *Toll-free phone:* 866-338-7934.

DeVry University–Seven Hills Campus

Seven Hills, Ohio

http://www.devry.edu/

CONTACT

Admissions Office, DeVry University–Seven Hills Campus, 4141 Rockside Road, Suite 110, Seven Hills, OH 44131. *Phone:* 216-328-8754. *Toll-free phone:* 866-338-7934.

Franciscan University of Steubenville

Steubenville, Ohio

http://www.franciscan.edu/

CONTACT

Miss Victoria Kubicz, Assistant Director of Admissions, Franciscan University of Steubenville, 1235 University Boulevard, Steubenville, OH 43952-1763. *Phone:* 740-284-5863. *Toll-free phone:* 800-783-6220. *Fax:* 740-284-5456. *E-mail:* admissions@franciscan.edu.

Franklin University

Columbus, Ohio

http://www.franklin.edu/

CONTACT

Mrs. Lynne Hull, Director of New Student Enrollment, Franklin University, 201 South Grant Avenue, Columbus, OH 43215. *Phone:* 614-947-6046. *Toll-free phone:* 877-341-6300. *E-mail:* hulll@franklin.edu.

Galen College of Nursing

Cincinnati, Ohio

http://www.galencollege.edu/

CONTACT

Galen College of Nursing, 100 East Business Way, Suite 200, Cincinnati, OH 45241. *Toll-free phone:* 877-223-7040.

God's Bible School and College

Cincinnati, Ohio

http://www.gbs.edu/

CONTACT

Heather Couch, Director of Financial Aid and Admissions, God's Bible School and College, 1810 Young Street, Cincinnati, OH 45202-6838. *Phone:* 513-721-7944 Ext. 1161. *Toll-free phone:* 800-486-4637. *Fax:* 513-763-6649. *E-mail:* hcouch@gbs.edu.

Good Samaritan College of Nursing and Health Science

Cincinnati, Ohio

http://www.gscollege.edu/

CONTACT

Admissions Office, Good Samaritan College of Nursing and Health Science, 375 Dixmyth Avenue, Cincinnati, OH 45220. *Phone:* 513-862-2743. *Fax:* 513-862-3572.

Heidelberg University

Tiffin, Ohio

http://www.heidelberg.edu/

- **Independent** comprehensive, founded 1850, affiliated with United Church of Christ
- **Small-town** 115-acre campus with easy access to Toledo, Cleveland, Columbus
- **Endowment** $48.9 million
- **Coed**
- **Moderately difficult** entrance level

FACULTY

Student/faculty ratio: 13:1.

ACADEMICS

Calendar: semesters. *Degrees:* bachelor's and master's.

Library: Beeghly Library plus 1 other. *Books:* 86,891 (physical), 279,499 (digital/electronic); *Serial titles:* 1,293 (physical), 61,058 (digital/electronic); *Databases:* 198. Weekly public service hours: 83.

STUDENT LIFE

Housing options: on-campus residence required through junior year; coed, women-only, cooperative. Campus housing is university owned and leased by the school. Freshman campus housing is guaranteed.

Activities and organizations: drama/theater group, student-run newspaper, radio and television station, choral group, Alpha Phi Omega, BERG Events Council, Student Senate, Campus Fellowship, Black Student Union/World Student Union.

Athletics Member NCAA. All Division III.

Campus security: 24-hour emergency response devices and patrols, student patrols, late-night transport/escort service, controlled dormitory access.

Student services: health clinic, personal/psychological counseling.

COSTS & FINANCIAL AID

Costs (2018–19) ***Comprehensive fee:*** $41,400 includes full-time tuition ($30,400), mandatory fees ($600), and room and board ($10,400). Part-time tuition: $900 per contact hour. ***College room only:*** $5300. Room and board charges vary according to board plan and housing facility.

Financial Aid Of all full-time matriculated undergraduates who enrolled in 2018, 980 applied for aid, 900 were judged to have need, 148 had their need fully met. 672 Federal Work-Study jobs (averaging $2000). 100 state and other part-time jobs (averaging $1000). In 2018, 114 non-need-based awards were made. ***Average percent of need met:*** 81. ***Average financial aid package:*** $27,083. ***Average need-based loan:*** $3921. ***Average need-based gift aid:*** $21,600. ***Average non-need-based aid:*** $15,552. ***Average indebtedness upon graduation:*** $35,872.

APPLYING

Standardized Tests *Required:* SAT or ACT (for admission).

Options: electronic application, deferred entrance.

Required: high school transcript. ***Required for some:*** essay or personal statement, 2 letters of recommendation. ***Recommended:*** essay or personal statement, minimum 2.5 GPA, 1 letter of recommendation.

CONTACT

Mr. Mike Brown, Director of Admission, Heidelberg University, 310 East Market Street, Tiffin, OH 44883. *Phone:* 419-448-2507. *Toll-free phone:* 800-434-3352. *Fax:* 419-448-2334. *E-mail:* mbrown@heidelberg.edu.

Herzing University
Akron, Ohio
http://www.herzing.edu/akron

CONTACT
Herzing University, 1600 South Arlington Street, Suite 100, Akron, OH 44306. *Toll-free phone:* 800-596-0724.

Herzing University
Toledo, Ohio
http://www.herzing.edu/toledo

CONTACT
Herzing University, 5212 Hill Avenue, Toledo, OH 43615. *Toll-free phone:* 800-596-0724.

Hiram College
Hiram, Ohio
http://www.hiram.edu/

- **Independent** comprehensive, founded 1850, affiliated with Christian Church (Disciples of Christ)
- **Rural** 110-acre campus with easy access to Cleveland
- **Endowment** $73.4 million
- **Coed** 1,244 undergraduate students, 66% full-time, 57% women, 43% men
- **Moderately difficult** entrance level, 58% of applicants were admitted

UNDERGRAD STUDENTS
824 full-time, 420 part-time. Students come from 31 states and territories; 8 other countries; 20% are from out of state; 17% Black or African American, non-Hispanic/Latino; 6% Hispanic/Latino; 2% Asian, non-Hispanic/Latino; 0.2% Native Hawaiian or other Pacific Islander, non-Hispanic/Latino; 0.2% American Indian or Alaska Native, non-Hispanic/Latino; 4% Two or more races, non-Hispanic/Latino; 9% Race/ethnicity unknown; 1% international; 3% transferred in; 82% live on campus.

Freshmen:
Admission: 2,687 applied, 1,548 admitted, 233 enrolled. ***Average high school GPA:*** 3.4. ***Test scores:*** SAT evidence-based reading and writing scores over 500: 66%; SAT math scores over 500: 58%; ACT scores over 18: 82%; SAT evidence-based reading and writing scores over 600: 28%; SAT math scores over 600: 25%; ACT scores over 24: 35%; SAT evidence-based reading and writing scores over 700: 7%; ACT scores over 30: 5%.
Retention: 76% of full-time freshmen returned.

FACULTY
Total: 111, 53% full-time, 68% with terminal degrees.
Student/faculty ratio: 10:1.

ACADEMICS
Calendar: semesters. *Degrees:* bachelor's and master's.
Special study options: accelerated degree program, adult/continuing education programs, advanced placement credit, cooperative education, distance learning, double majors, English as a second language, honors programs, independent study, internships, off-campus study, part-time degree program, services for LD students, student-designed majors, study abroad, summer session for credit. ***ROTC:*** Army (c), Air Force (c).
Unusual degree programs: 3-2 engineering with Case Western Reserve University, Washington University in St. Louis; social work with Case Western Reserve University.
Computers: 72 computers/terminals and 3,500 ports are available on campus for general student use. Students can access the following: campus intranet, computer help desk, free student e-mail accounts, online (class) grades, online (class) registration, online (class) schedules. Campuswide network is available. 100% of college-owned or -operated housing units are wired for high-speed Internet access. Wireless service is available via entire campus.
Library: Hiram College Library. *Books:* 177,742 (physical), 168,829 (digital/electronic); *Serial titles:* 85 (physical), 7,340 (digital/electronic); *Databases:* 279. Weekly public service hours: 90.

STUDENT LIFE
Housing options: on-campus residence required through senior year; coed, men-only, women-only, cooperative, special housing for students with disabilities. Campus housing is university owned. Freshman campus housing is guaranteed.
Activities and organizations: drama/theater group, choral group, Black Students United, Intercultural Forum, Terrier Activities Board, Student-Athlete Advisory Committee, Theater Guild.
Athletics Member NCAA. All Division III. ***Intercollegiate sports:*** baseball M, basketball M/W, cheerleading W, football M, golf M/W, lacrosse M/W, soccer M/W, softball W, swimming and diving M/W, volleyball M/W. ***Intramural sports:*** basketball M/W, cross-country running M(c)/W(c), football M/W, rock climbing M(c)/W(c), rugby W(c), skiing (downhill) M(c)/W(c), soccer M/W, swimming and diving M/W, volleyball M/W.
Campus security: 24-hour emergency response devices and patrols, student patrols, late-night transport/escort service, controlled dormitory access.
Student services: health clinic, personal/psychological counseling.

COSTS & FINANCIAL AID
Costs (2019–20) ***Comprehensive fee:*** $46,648 includes full-time tuition ($34,008), mandatory fees ($2350), and room and board ($10,290). Part-time tuition: $1134 per credit hour. No tuition increase for student's term of enrollment. ***College room only:*** $5150.
Financial Aid Of all full-time matriculated undergraduates who enrolled in 2018, 764 applied for aid, 727 were judged to have need, 37 had their need fully met. 557 Federal Work-Study jobs (averaging $2024). In 2018, 75 non-need-based awards were made. ***Average percent of need met:*** 69. ***Average financial aid package:*** $28,530. ***Average need-based loan:*** $3795. ***Average need-based gift aid:*** $23,872. ***Average non-need-based aid:*** $12,748. ***Average indebtedness upon graduation:*** $37,771.

APPLYING
Standardized Tests *Required for some:* SAT or ACT (for admission), SAT or ACT for applicants with cumulative GPA below 2.8, nursing or education applicants, or Trustee and/or President's Scholarships applicants.
Options: electronic application, deferred entrance.
Application fee: $25.
Required: essay or personal statement, high school transcript. ***Recommended:*** minimum 2.8 GPA, interview.
Application deadlines: rolling (freshmen), rolling (transfers).
Notification: continuous (freshmen), continuous (transfers).

CONTACT
Sherman C. Dean II, Director of Admission, Hiram College, PO Box 96, Hiram, OH 44234. *Phone:* 330-569-5169. *Toll-free phone:* 800-362-5280. *Fax:* 330-569-5944. *E-mail:* admission@hiram.edu.

John Carroll University
University Heights, Ohio
http://www.jcu.edu/

- **Independent Roman Catholic (Jesuit)** comprehensive, founded 1886
- **Suburban** 60-acre campus with easy access to Cleveland
- **Endowment** $211.0 million
- **Coed**
- **Moderately difficult** entrance level

FACULTY
Student/faculty ratio: 12:1.

ACADEMICS
Calendar: semesters. *Degrees:* bachelor's, master's, post-master's, and postbachelor's certificates.
Library: Grasselli Library. *Books:* 456,260 (physical), 91,554 (digital/electronic); *Serial titles:* 459,633 (physical), 115,548 (digital/electronic); *Databases:* 279. Weekly public service hours: 111; students can reserve study rooms.

STUDENT LIFE
Housing options: on-campus residence required through sophomore year; coed, women-only, special housing for students with disabilities. Campus housing is university owned. Freshman campus housing is guaranteed.

Activities and organizations: drama/theater group, student-run newspaper, radio and television station, choral group, Community Outreach/Volunteer Service Organization, Student Union, Club Sports, Fraternities and Sororities, Carroll News, national fraternities, national sororities.

Athletics Member NCAA. All Division III.

Campus security: 24-hour emergency response devices and patrols, late-night transport/escort service, controlled dormitory access, student-led EMS program.

Student services: health clinic, personal/psychological counseling, women's center, veterans affairs office.

COSTS & FINANCIAL AID

Costs (2018–19) ***One-time required fee:*** $325. ***Comprehensive fee:*** $53,214 includes full-time tuition ($39,840), mandatory fees ($1500), and room and board ($11,874). Full-time tuition and fees vary according to degree level. Part-time tuition: $1320 per credit hour. Part-time tuition and fees vary according to course load and degree level. ***Room and board:*** Room and board charges vary according to board plan and housing facility.

Financial Aid Of all full-time matriculated undergraduates who enrolled in 2017, 2,507 applied for aid, 2,111 were judged to have need, 488 had their need fully met. In 2017, 777 non-need-based awards were made. ***Average percent of need met:*** 78. ***Average financial aid package:*** $31,429. ***Average need-based loan:*** $4361. ***Average need-based gift aid:*** $25,018. ***Average non-need-based aid:*** $20,256. ***Average indebtedness upon graduation:*** $33,508.

APPLYING

Standardized Tests *Required:* SAT or ACT (for admission).

Options: electronic application, early admission, early action, deferred entrance.

Required: essay or personal statement, high school transcript, 1 letter of recommendation. ***Required for some:*** 2 letters of recommendation, interview.

CONTACT

Mr. Steven P. Vitatoe, Assistant Vice President of Undergraduate Admission, John Carroll University, 1 John Carroll Boulevard, University Heights, OH 44118. *Phone:* 216-397-4277. *Toll-free phone:* 888-335-6800. *E-mail:* svitatoe@jcu.edu.

Kent State University

Kent, Ohio

http://www.kent.edu/

- **State-supported** university, founded 1910, part of Kent State University System
- **Suburban** 866-acre campus with easy access to Cleveland, Akron, Canton
- **Endowment** $129.1 million
- **Coed**
- **Moderately difficult** entrance level

FACULTY

Student/faculty ratio: 20:1.

ACADEMICS

Calendar: semesters. *Degrees:* certificates, bachelor's, master's, doctoral, post-master's, and postbachelor's certificates.

Library: Kent State University Main Library plus 4 others. *Books:* 3.0 million (physical), 1.2 million (digital/electronic); *Serial titles:* 35,857 (physical), 14,996 (digital/electronic); *Databases:* 355. Weekly public service hours: 146; study areas open 24 hours, 5–7 days a week; students can reserve study rooms.

STUDENT LIFE

Housing options: on-campus residence required through sophomore year; coed, men-only, women-only, cooperative, special housing for students with disabilities. Freshman applicants given priority for college housing.

Activities and organizations: drama/theater group, student-run newspaper, radio and television station, choral group, marching band, Black United Students, Running Club, National Society of Leadership and Success, Kent Inter-hall Council, Kent Indian Association, national fraternities, national sororities.

Athletics Member NCAA. All Division I.

Campus security: 24-hour emergency response devices and patrols, student patrols, late-night transport/escort service, controlled dormitory access, campus police and fire department, electronic locks on computer labs, studios and laboratory research areas.

Student services: health clinic, personal/psychological counseling, women's center, legal services, veterans affairs office.

COSTS & FINANCIAL AID

Costs (2018–19) ***One-time required fee:*** $150. ***Tuition:*** state resident $10,012 full-time, $456 per credit hour part-time; nonresident $18,714 full-time, $825 per credit hour part-time. Full-time tuition and fees vary according to course load. Part-time tuition and fees vary according to course load. No tuition increase for student's term of enrollment. ***Room and board:*** $11,362; room only: $7080. Room and board charges vary according to board plan and housing facility.

Financial Aid Of all full-time matriculated undergraduates who enrolled in 2018, 14,923 applied for aid, 12,027 were judged to have need, 1,518 had their need fully met. 243 Federal Work-Study jobs (averaging $3123). In 2018, 2187 non-need-based awards were made. ***Average percent of need met:*** 56. ***Average financial aid package:*** $10,909. ***Average need-based loan:*** $4199. ***Average need-based gift aid:*** $6542. ***Average non-need-based aid:*** $5467. ***Average indebtedness upon graduation:*** $32,800.

APPLYING

Standardized Tests *Required:* SAT or ACT (for admission).

Options: electronic application, deferred entrance.

Application fee: $50.

Required: high school transcript.

CONTACT

Mr. Christopher Buttenschon, Senior Assistant Director of Admissions, Kent State University, 161 Michael Schwartz Center, Admissions Office, Kent, OH 44242-0001. *Phone:* 330-672-2444. *Toll-free phone:* 800-988-KENT. *Fax:* 330-672-2499. *E-mail:* cbuttens@kent.edu.

Kent State University at Ashtabula

Ashtabula, Ohio

http://www.ashtabula.kent.edu/

- **State-supported** primarily 2-year, founded 1958, part of Kent State University System
- **Small-town** 83-acre campus with easy access to Cleveland
- **Coed**
- **Noncompetitive** entrance level

FACULTY

Student/faculty ratio: 20:1.

ACADEMICS

Calendar: semesters. *Degrees:* certificates, associate, and bachelor's (also offers some upper-level and graduate courses).

Library: Kent State at Ashtabula Library. Weekly public service hours: 56.

STUDENT LIFE

Housing options: college housing not available.

Activities and organizations: Student Government, Student Veterans Association, Student Nurses Association, Student Occupational Therapy Association, Media Club.

Campus security: 24-hour emergency response devices.

Student services: veterans affairs office.

COSTS & FINANCIAL AID

Costs (2018–19) ***One-time required fee:*** $150. ***Tuition:*** state resident $5664 full-time, $258 per credit hour part-time; nonresident $14,196 full-time, $627 per credit hour part-time. Full-time tuition and fees vary according to course level and course load. Part-time tuition and fees vary according to course level and course load. No tuition increase for student's term of enrollment.

Financial Aid Of all full-time matriculated undergraduates who enrolled in 2018, 449 applied for aid, 403 were judged to have need, 24 had their need fully met. 6 Federal Work-Study jobs (averaging $3384). In 2018, 8 non-need-based awards were made. ***Average percent of need met:*** 52.

Average financial aid package: $7634. ***Average need-based loan:*** $3631. ***Average need-based gift aid:*** $5194. ***Average non-need-based aid:*** $1705.

APPLYING
Standardized Tests *Required for some:* SAT or ACT (for admission). *Recommended:* SAT or ACT (for admission).

Options: electronic application, deferred entrance.

Application fee: $40.

Required: high school transcript.

CONTACT
Megan Krippel, Admissions Coordinator, Kent State University at Ashtabula, 3300 Lake Road West, Ashtabula, OH 44004. *Phone:* 440-964-4277. *Fax:* 440-964-4269. *E-mail:* ashtabula_admissions@kent.edu.

Kent State University at East Liverpool

East Liverpool, Ohio

http://www.eliv.kent.edu/

- **State-supported** primarily 2-year, founded 1967, part of Kent State University System
- **Small-town** 3-acre campus with easy access to Pittsburgh, Youngstown
- **Coed**
- **Noncompetitive** entrance level

FACULTY
Student/faculty ratio: 25:1.

ACADEMICS
Calendar: semesters. *Degrees:* certificates, associate, and bachelor's.
Library: Paul Blair Memorial Library. Weekly public service hours: 46.

STUDENT LIFE
Housing options: college housing not available.

Activities and organizations: Undergraduate Student Government, Student Nurses Association, Environmental Club, Student Occupational Therapist Assistants, Physical Therapist Assistant Club.

Campus security: 24-hour emergency response devices, student patrols, late-night transport/escort service.

Student services: personal/psychological counseling, veterans affairs office.

COSTS & FINANCIAL AID
Costs (2018–19) ***One-time required fee:*** $150. ***Tuition:*** state resident $5664 full-time, $258 per credit hour part-time; nonresident $14,196 full-time, $627 per credit hour part-time. Full-time tuition and fees vary according to course level and course load. Part-time tuition and fees vary according to course level and course load. No tuition increase for student's term of enrollment.

Financial Aid Of all full-time matriculated undergraduates who enrolled in 2018, 133 applied for aid, 109 were judged to have need, 7 had their need fully met. In 2018, 11 non-need-based awards were made. ***Average percent of need met:*** 57. ***Average financial aid package:*** $8279. ***Average need-based loan:*** $3929. ***Average need-based gift aid:*** $5196. ***Average non-need-based aid:*** $1587.

APPLYING
Standardized Tests *Required for some:* SAT or ACT (for admission). *Recommended:* SAT or ACT (for admission).

Options: electronic application, deferred entrance.

Application fee: $40.

Required: high school transcript.

CONTACT
Office of Admissions, Kent State University at East Liverpool, 400 East 4th Street, East Liverpool, OH 43920-3497. *Phone:* 330-385-3805.

Kent State University at Geauga

Burton, Ohio

http://www.geauga.kent.edu/

- **State-supported** comprehensive, founded 1964, part of Kent State University System
- **Rural** 87-acre campus with easy access to Cleveland, Akron, Youngstown
- **Coed**
- **Noncompetitive** entrance level

FACULTY
Student/faculty ratio: 23:1.

ACADEMICS
Calendar: semesters. *Degrees:* certificates, associate, bachelor's, and master's.
Library: Kent State University at Geauga Library. *Books:* 12,083 (physical); *Serial titles:* 43 (physical). Weekly public service hours: 53.

STUDENT LIFE
Housing options: college housing not available.

Activities and organizations: National Student Nurse Association Twinsburg, Geauga Student Nurses Association, Alpha Delta Nu-Gamma Sigma Chapter, Kent State University Geauga College Republicans, Undergraduate Student Government.

Campus security: 24-hour emergency response devices.

Student services: veterans affairs office.

COSTS & FINANCIAL AID
Costs (2018–19) ***Tuition:*** state resident $258 per credit hour part-time; nonresident $627 per credit hour part-time. Full-time tuition and fees vary according to course level and course load. Part-time tuition and fees vary according to course level and course load. No tuition increase for student's term of enrollment.

Financial Aid Of all full-time matriculated undergraduates who enrolled in 2018, 435 applied for aid, 360 were judged to have need, 43 had their need fully met. 7 Federal Work-Study jobs (averaging $3683). In 2018, 22 non-need-based awards were made. ***Average percent of need met:*** 55. ***Average financial aid package:*** $7094. ***Average need-based loan:*** $3591. ***Average need-based gift aid:*** $5153. ***Average non-need-based aid:*** $1406.

APPLYING
Standardized Tests *Recommended:* SAT or ACT (for admission).

Options: electronic application, deferred entrance.

Application fee: $40.

Required: high school transcript.

CONTACT
Kent State University at Geauga, 14111 Claridon-Troy Road, Burton, OH 44021. *Phone:* 440-834-4187. *Fax:* 440-834-3786. *E-mail:* geaugaadmissions@kent.edu.

Kent State University at Salem

Salem, Ohio

http://www.salem.kent.edu/

- **State-supported** primarily 2-year, founded 1966, part of Kent State University System
- **Rural** 100-acre campus with easy access to Youngstown
- **Coed**
- **Noncompetitive** entrance level

FACULTY
Student/faculty ratio: 19:1.

ACADEMICS
Calendar: semesters. *Degrees:* certificates, associate, and bachelor's (also offers some upper-level and graduate courses).
Library: Kent State Salem Library. *Books:* 23,500 (physical); *Serial titles:* 4,500 (physical).

STUDENT LIFE
Housing options: college housing not available.

Campus security: 24-hour emergency response devices, late-night transport/escort service.

Student services: personal/psychological counseling.

COSTS & FINANCIAL AID

Costs (2018–19) ***One-time required fee:*** $150. ***Tuition:*** state resident $5664 full-time, $258 per credit hour part-time; nonresident $14,366 full-time, $627 per credit hour part-time. Full-time tuition and fees vary according to course level and course load. Part-time tuition and fees vary according to course level and course load. No tuition increase for student's term of enrollment.

Financial Aid Of all full-time matriculated undergraduates who enrolled in 2018, 521 applied for aid, 434 were judged to have need, 37 had their need fully met. 22 Federal Work-Study jobs (averaging $1583). In 2018, 59 non-need-based awards were made. ***Average percent of need met:*** 54. ***Average financial aid package:*** $7474. ***Average need-based loan:*** $3825. ***Average need-based gift aid:*** $5242. ***Average non-need-based aid:*** $1154.

APPLYING

Standardized Tests *Required for some:* SAT or ACT (for admission). *Recommended:* SAT or ACT (for admission).

Options: electronic application, deferred entrance.

Application fee: $40.

Required: high school transcript. ***Required for some:*** essay or personal statement.

CONTACT

Office of Admissions, Kent State University at Salem, 2491 State Route 45 South, Salem, OH 44460-9412. *Phone:* 330-332-0361.

Kent State University at Stark

Canton, Ohio

http://www.stark.kent.edu/

- **State-supported** comprehensive, founded 1946, part of Kent State University System
- **Suburban** 200-acre campus with easy access to Cleveland, Akron, Canton
- **Coed**
- **Noncompetitive** entrance level

FACULTY

Student/faculty ratio: 23:1.

ACADEMICS

Calendar: semesters. *Degrees:* associate, bachelor's, and master's.
Library: Kent State Stark Library. *Serial titles:* 600 (physical). Weekly public service hours: 72; students can reserve study rooms.

STUDENT LIFE

Housing options: college housing not available.

Activities and organizations: drama/theater group, choral group, Music Technology Club, Biology Club, SCRUBS (Nursing Organization), HDFS (Human Development Family Studies), Revive (Faith Based).

Campus security: 24-hour emergency response devices, student patrols, late-night transport/escort service.

Student services: personal/psychological counseling, veterans affairs office.

COSTS & FINANCIAL AID

Costs (2018–19) ***Tuition:*** state resident $258 per credit hour part-time; nonresident $627 per credit hour part-time. Full-time tuition and fees vary according to course level and course load. Part-time tuition and fees vary according to course level and course load. No tuition increase for student's term of enrollment.

Financial Aid Of all full-time matriculated undergraduates who enrolled in 2018, 1,581 applied for aid, 1,293 were judged to have need, 162 had their need fully met. 44 Federal Work-Study jobs (averaging $2045). In 2018, 147 non-need-based awards were made. ***Average percent of need met:*** 57. ***Average financial aid package:*** $7245. ***Average need-based loan:*** $3855. ***Average need-based gift aid:*** $4919. ***Average non-need-based aid:*** $2456.

APPLYING

Standardized Tests *Recommended:* SAT or ACT (for admission).

Options: electronic application, deferred entrance.

Application fee: $40.

Required: high school transcript.

CONTACT

Office of Admissions, Kent State University at Stark, 6000 Frank Avenue NW, North Canton, OH 44720. *Phone:* 330-244-3251. *Fax:* 330-499-0301. *E-mail:* starkadmissions@kent.edu.

Kent State University at Trumbull

Warren, Ohio

http://www.trumbull.kent.edu/

- **State-supported** primarily 2-year, founded 1954, part of Kent State University System
- **Suburban** 438-acre campus with easy access to Akron, Youngstown
- **Coed**
- **Noncompetitive** entrance level

FACULTY

Student/faculty ratio: 25:1.

ACADEMICS

Calendar: semesters. *Degrees:* associate and bachelor's (also offers some upper-level and graduate courses).
Library: Gelbke Library at Kent State Trumbull. *Books:* 40,000 (physical), 100,000 (digital/electronic); *Serial titles:* 40 (physical); *Databases:* 459. Weekly public service hours: 56.

STUDENT LIFE

Housing options: college housing not available.

Activities and organizations: drama/theater group, The National Society for Leadership and Success, Sigma Alpha Pi, Jurisprudence Organization, Student Nurses Association, Pride Alliance, S.E.E.D.S.

Campus security: 24-hour emergency response devices, late-night transport/escort service, patrols by trained security personnel during hours of operation.

Student services: personal/psychological counseling.

COSTS & FINANCIAL AID

Costs (2018–19) ***One-time required fee:*** $150. ***Tuition:*** state resident $5664 full-time, $258 per credit hour part-time; nonresident $14,366 full-time, $627 per credit hour part-time. Full-time tuition and fees vary according to course level and course load. Part-time tuition and fees vary according to course level and course load. No tuition increase for student's term of enrollment.

Financial Aid Of all full-time matriculated undergraduates who enrolled in 2018, 654 applied for aid, 568 were judged to have need, 46 had their need fully met. 12 Federal Work-Study jobs (averaging $1755). In 2018, 42 non-need-based awards were made. ***Average percent of need met:*** 55. ***Average financial aid package:*** $7669. ***Average need-based loan:*** $3756. ***Average need-based gift aid:*** $5144. ***Average non-need-based aid:*** $3150.

APPLYING

Standardized Tests *Recommended:* SAT or ACT (for admission).

Options: electronic application, deferred entrance.

Application fee: $40.

Required: high school transcript.

CONTACT

Office of Enrollment Management, Kent State University at Trumbull, 4314 Mahoning Avenue, NW, Warren, OH 44483-1998. *Phone:* 330-675-8860. *E-mail:* trumbullinfo@kent.edu.

Kent State University at Tuscarawas

New Philadelphia, Ohio

http://www.tusc.kent.edu/

- **State-supported** primarily 2-year, founded 1962, part of Kent State University System
- **Small-town** 180-acre campus with easy access to Akron, Canton
- **Coed**
- **Noncompetitive** entrance level

FACULTY
Student/faculty ratio: 22:1.

ACADEMICS
Calendar: semesters. *Degrees:* certificates, diplomas, associate, and bachelor's (also offers some upper-level and graduate courses).
Library: Kent State Tuscarawas Library. *Books:* 52,500 (physical), 12 (digital/electronic); *Serial titles:* 540 (physical).

STUDENT LIFE
Housing options: college housing not available.

Activities and organizations: choral group, Student Nurses Association, Technology Club, Vet Tech Student Chapter, Realms of Roleplay, Vision.

Athletics Member USCAA.

Campus security: 24-hour emergency response devices.

COSTS & FINANCIAL AID
Costs (2018–19) ***One-time required fee:*** $150. ***Tuition:*** state resident $5664 full-time, $258 per credit hour part-time; nonresident $14,366 full-time, $627 per credit hour part-time. Full-time tuition and fees vary according to course level and course load. Part-time tuition and fees vary according to course level and course load. No tuition increase for student's term of enrollment.

Financial Aid Of all full-time matriculated undergraduates who enrolled in 2018, 700 applied for aid, 576 were judged to have need, 56 had their need fully met. 8 Federal Work-Study jobs (averaging $2325). In 2018, 75 non-need-based awards were made. ***Average percent of need met:*** 58. ***Average financial aid package:*** $7531. ***Average need-based loan:*** $3805. ***Average need-based gift aid:*** $4608. ***Average non-need-based aid:*** $2653.

APPLYING
Standardized Tests *Recommended:* SAT or ACT (for admission).

Options: electronic application, deferred entrance.

Application fee: $40.

Required: high school transcript.

CONTACT
Office of Admissions, Kent State University at Tuscarawas, 330 University Drive NE, New Philadelphia, OH 44663-9403. *Phone:* 330-339-3391. *E-mail:* infotusc@kent.edu.

Kenyon College

Gambier, Ohio

http://www.kenyon.edu/

- **Independent** 4-year, founded 1824
- **Rural** 1000-acre campus with easy access to Columbus
- **Endowment** $208.9 million
- **Coed**
- **Most difficult** entrance level

FACULTY
Student/faculty ratio: 9:1.

ACADEMICS
Calendar: semesters. *Degree:* bachelor's.
Library: Olin Library plus 1 other. *Books:* 495,501 (physical), 42,965 (digital/electronic); *Serial titles:* 1,670 (physical), 43,534 (digital/electronic); *Databases:* 332. Weekly public service hours: 131; students can reserve study rooms.

STUDENT LIFE
Housing options: on-campus residence required through senior year; coed, women-only, special housing for students with disabilities. Campus housing is university owned. Freshman campus housing is guaranteed.

Activities and organizations: drama/theater group, student-run newspaper, radio station, choral group, student advisory groups, student radio station, musical groups, intramural sports and clubs, outdoors club, national fraternities, national sororities.

Athletics Member NCAA. All Division III.

Campus security: 24-hour emergency response devices and patrols, student patrols, late-night transport/escort service, controlled dormitory access.

Student services: health clinic, personal/psychological counseling, women's center.

COSTS & FINANCIAL AID
Costs (2018–19) ***Comprehensive fee:*** $68,440 includes full-time tuition ($53,830), mandatory fees ($2100), and room and board ($12,510). Full-time tuition and fees vary according to reciprocity agreements. Part-time tuition and fees vary according to reciprocity agreements. ***College room only:*** $5470. Room and board charges vary according to housing facility and student level.

Financial Aid Of all full-time matriculated undergraduates who enrolled in 2018, 886 applied for aid, 781 were judged to have need, 781 had their need fully met. In 2018, 312 non-need-based awards were made. ***Average percent of need met:*** 100. ***Average financial aid package:*** $46,004. ***Average need-based loan:*** $3953. ***Average need-based gift aid:*** $42,078. ***Average non-need-based aid:*** $15,754. ***Average indebtedness upon graduation:*** $26,271. ***Financial aid deadline:*** 1/15.

APPLYING
Standardized Tests *Required:* SAT or ACT (for admission).

Options: electronic application, early admission, early decision, deferred entrance.

Required: essay or personal statement, high school transcript, counselor recommendation. ***Recommended:*** 2 letters of recommendation, interview.

CONTACT
Ms. Diane Anci, Vice President of Enrollment Management and Dean of Admissions and Financial Aid, Kenyon College, Ransom Hall, Gambier, OH 43022. *Phone:* 740-427-5776. *Toll-free phone:* 800-848-2468. *Fax:* 740-427-5770. *E-mail:* admissions@kenyon.edu.

Kettering College

Kettering, Ohio

http://www.kc.edu/

CONTACT
Mrs. Becky McDonald, Director of Enrollment Services, Kettering College, 3737 Southern Boulevard, Kettering, OH 45429-1299. *Phone:* 937-395-8628. *Toll-free phone:* 800-433-5262. *Fax:* 937-296-4238.

Lake Erie College

Painesville, Ohio

http://www.lec.edu/

CONTACT
Mrs. Liz Sellers, Director of Admissions, Lake Erie College, 391 West Washington Street, Painesville, OH 44077-3389. *Phone:* 440-375-7251. *Toll-free phone:* 800-916-0904. *Fax:* 440-375-7058. *E-mail:* admissions@lec.edu.

Lourdes University

Sylvania, Ohio

http://www.lourdes.edu/

CONTACT
Amy Houston, Associate Director of Admissions, Lourdes University, 6832 Convent Boulevard, Sylvania, OH 43560. *Phone:* 419-885-5291. *Toll-free phone:* 800-878-3210.

Malone University

Canton, Ohio

http://www.malone.edu/

- **Independent** comprehensive, founded 1892, affiliated with Evangelical Friends Church–Eastern Region
- **Suburban** 96-acre campus with easy access to Cleveland
- **Endowment** $19.4 million
- **Coed**
- **Moderately difficult** entrance level

FACULTY
Student/faculty ratio: 12:1.

ACADEMICS
Calendar: semesters. *Degrees:* bachelor's and master's.
Library: Everett L. Cattell Library plus 1 other. *Books:* 169,479 (physical), 312,753 (digital/electronic); *Serial titles:* 2,035 (physical), 39,854 (digital/electronic); *Databases:* 176. Weekly public service hours: 88.

STUDENT LIFE
Housing options: on-campus residence required through junior year; men-only, women-only, special housing for students with disabilities. Campus housing is university owned. Freshman applicants given priority for college housing.

Activities and organizations: drama/theater group, student-run newspaper, choral group, marching band, Celebration Worship Services (and other Spiritual Formation activities), Student Activities Council, Student Senate, FCA (Fellowship of Christian Athletes), intramural athletics.

Athletics Member NCAA. All Division II.

Campus security: 24-hour emergency response devices and patrols, late-night transport/escort service, controlled dormitory access.

Student services: health clinic, personal/psychological counseling.

COSTS & FINANCIAL AID
Costs (2018–19) ***Comprehensive fee:*** $40,360 includes full-time tuition ($29,900), mandatory fees ($960), and room and board ($9500). Part-time tuition: $500 per credit hour. Part-time tuition and fees vary according to course load. ***Required fees:*** $240 per term part-time. ***College room only:*** $4700. Room and board charges vary according to board plan.

Financial Aid Of all full-time matriculated undergraduates who enrolled in 2017, 939 applied for aid, 879 were judged to have need, 145 had their need fully met. 361 Federal Work-Study jobs (averaging $1866). 109 state and other part-time jobs (averaging $1797). In 2017, 144 non-need-based awards were made. ***Average percent of need met:*** 79. ***Average financial aid package:*** $26,785. ***Average need-based loan:*** $4217. ***Average need-based gift aid:*** $23,026. ***Average non-need-based aid:*** $12,874. ***Average indebtedness upon graduation:*** $32,495. ***Financial aid deadline:*** 7/31.

APPLYING
Standardized Tests *Required:* SAT or ACT (for admission).

Options: electronic application, early admission, deferred entrance.

Application fee: $20.

Required: high school transcript, minimum 2.0 GPA. ***Required for some:*** essay or personal statement. ***Recommended:*** interview.

CONTACT
Mrs. Anissa D. Scott, Assistant Director, Admissions, Malone University, 2600 Cleveland Avenue NW, Canton, OH 44709-3308. *Phone:* 330-471-8153. *Toll-free phone:* 800-521-1146. *Fax:* 330-471-8149. *E-mail:* admissions@malone.edu.

Marietta College

Marietta, Ohio

http://www.marietta.edu/

- **Independent** comprehensive, founded 1835
- **Small-town** 90-acre campus
- **Endowment** $70.3 million
- **Coed**
- **Moderately difficult** entrance level

FACULTY
Student/faculty ratio: 9:1.

ACADEMICS
Calendar: semesters. *Degrees:* certificates, associate, bachelor's, and master's.
Library: Legacy Library. *Books:* 183,103 (physical), 137,587 (digital/electronic); *Serial titles:* 230 (physical), 15,786 (digital/electronic); *Databases:* 186. Weekly public service hours: 95; students can reserve study rooms.

STUDENT LIFE
Housing options: on-campus residence required through senior year; coed, men-only, women-only, special housing for students with disabilities. Campus housing is university owned, leased by the school and is provided by a third party. Freshman campus housing is guaranteed.

Activities and organizations: drama/theater group, student-run newspaper, radio and television station, choral group, Pioneer Activities Council, student government, Panhellenic Council, Inter-Varsity Christian Fellowship, Inter Fraternity Council, national fraternities, national sororities.

Athletics Member NCAA. All Division III.

Campus security: 24-hour emergency response devices and patrols, student patrols, late-night transport/escort service, controlled dormitory access.

Student services: health clinic, personal/psychological counseling.

COSTS & FINANCIAL AID
Costs (2018–19) ***Comprehensive fee:*** $47,370 includes full-time tuition ($35,030), mandatory fees ($1010), and room and board ($11,330). Full-time tuition and fees vary according to course load. Part-time tuition: $1170 per credit hour. Part-time tuition and fees vary according to course load. ***Room and board:*** Room and board charges vary according to board plan and housing facility.

Financial Aid Of all full-time matriculated undergraduates who enrolled in 2018, 790 applied for aid, 712 were judged to have need, 283 had their need fully met. 585 Federal Work-Study jobs (averaging $1990). ***Average percent of need met:*** 92. ***Average financial aid package:*** $36,541. ***Average need-based gift aid:*** $28,541. ***Average indebtedness upon graduation:*** $40,196.

APPLYING
Standardized Tests *Required:* SAT or ACT (for admission). *Recommended:* SAT Subject Tests (for admission).

Options: electronic application, early admission, deferred entrance.

Required: essay or personal statement, high school transcript, minimum 2.5 GPA. ***Recommended:*** minimum 3.4 GPA, letters of recommendation, interview.

CONTACT
Mr. Stephen Lazowski, Vice President for Enrollment Management, Marietta College, 215 Fifth Street, Marietta, OH 45750. *Phone:* 740-376-4503. *Toll-free phone:* 800-331-7896. *Fax:* 740-376-8888. *E-mail:* admit@marietta.edu.

Mercy College of Ohio

Toledo, Ohio

http://www.mercycollege.edu/

- **Independent** comprehensive, founded 1993, affiliated with Roman Catholic Church
- **Urban** campus with easy access to Toledo, OH
- **Coed, primarily women** 1,463 undergraduate students, 30% full-time, 86% women, 14% men
- **Moderately difficult** entrance level, 56% of applicants were admitted

UNDERGRAD STUDENTS
434 full-time, 1,029 part-time. Students come from 30 states and territories; 31% are from out of state; 11% Black or African American, non-Hispanic/Latino; 4% Hispanic/Latino; 2% Asian, non-Hispanic/Latino; 0.5% American Indian or Alaska Native, non-Hispanic/Latino; 4% Two or more races, non-Hispanic/Latino; 0.2% Race/ethnicity unknown; 28% transferred in.

Freshmen:
Admission: 232 applied, 129 admitted, 66 enrolled. ***Test scores:*** SAT math scores over 500: 64%; ACT scores over 18: 75%; SAT math scores over 600: 8%; ACT scores over 24: 15%.

Retention: 81% of full-time freshmen returned.

FACULTY
Total: 219, 23% full-time, 17% with terminal degrees.

Student/faculty ratio: 7:1.

ACADEMICS
Calendar: semesters. *Degrees:* certificates, associate, bachelor's, and master's.

Special study options: academic remediation for entering students, accelerated degree program, advanced placement credit, distance learning, double majors, independent study, internships, part-time degree program, services for LD students, summer session for credit.

Computers: 121 computers/terminals and 121 ports are available on campus for general student use. Students can access the following: computer help desk, free student e-mail accounts, online (class) grades, online (class) registration, online (class) schedules. Campuswide network is available. Wireless service is available via classrooms, computer centers, computer labs, learning centers, libraries, student centers.
Library: Mercy College of Ohio Library. *Books:* 7,081 (physical), 98,167 (digital/electronic); *Serial titles:* 334 (physical), 82,313 (digital/electronic); *Databases:* 15. Weekly public service hours: 57; students can reserve study rooms.

STUDENT LIFE
Activities and organizations: American Assembly of Men in Nursing, National Student Nurses Association, Student Government Association.

Campus security: 24-hour emergency response devices and patrols, late-night transport/escort service.

Student services: personal/psychological counseling.

COSTS & FINANCIAL AID
Costs (2018–19) ***One-time required fee:*** $250. ***Tuition:*** $12,840 full-time, $472 per credit hour part-time. Full-time tuition and fees vary according to course load and program. Part-time tuition and fees vary according to course load and program. ***Required fees:*** $2400 full-time, $60 per credit hour part-time, $300 per term part-time. ***Payment plan:*** installment. ***Waivers:*** employees or children of employees.

Financial Aid Of all full-time matriculated undergraduates who enrolled in 2015, 24 Federal Work-Study jobs (averaging $1744).

APPLYING
Standardized Tests *Required for some:* SAT or ACT (for admission).

Options: electronic application, deferred entrance.

Required: high school transcript, minimum 2.0 GPA.

Application deadlines: rolling (freshmen), rolling (transfers).

Notification: continuous (freshmen), continuous (transfers).

CONTACT
Ms. Kristen Porter, Admissions Officer, Mercy College of Ohio, 2221 Madison Avenue, Toledo, OH 43604. *Phone:* 419-251-1313. *Toll-free phone:* 888-80-MERCY. *Fax:* 419-251-1462. *E-mail:* kristen.porter@mercycollege.edu.

Miami University
Oxford, Ohio
http://miamioh.edu/

- **State-related** university, founded 1809, part of Miami University System
- **Small-town** 2100-acre campus with easy access to Cincinnati
- **Endowment** $534.7 million
- **Coed** 17,327 undergraduate students, 96% full-time, 50% women, 50% men
- **Moderately difficult** entrance level, 75% of applicants were admitted

UNDERGRAD STUDENTS
16,714 full-time, 613 part-time. Students come from 52 states and territories; 102 other countries; 35% are from out of state; 3% Black or African American, non-Hispanic/Latino; 5% Hispanic/Latino; 2% Asian, non-Hispanic/Latino; 0.1% Native Hawaiian or other Pacific Islander, non-Hispanic/Latino; 0.2% American Indian or Alaska Native, non-Hispanic/Latino; 4% Two or more races, non-Hispanic/Latino; 0.4% Race/ethnicity unknown; 15% international; 1% transferred in; 45% live on campus.

Freshmen:
Admission: 30,126 applied, 22,459 admitted, 3,936 enrolled. ***Average high school GPA:*** 3.8. ***Test scores:*** SAT evidence-based reading and writing scores over 500: 97%; SAT math scores over 500: 99%; ACT scores over 18: 100%; SAT evidence-based reading and writing scores over 600: 73%; SAT math scores over 600: 81%; ACT scores over 24: 88%; SAT evidence-based reading and writing scores over 700: 15%; SAT math scores over 700: 33%; ACT scores over 30: 32%.

Retention: 92% of full-time freshmen returned.

FACULTY
Total: 1,312, 76% full-time, 73% with terminal degrees.

Student/faculty ratio: 17:1.

ACADEMICS
Calendar: semesters. *Degrees:* certificates, associate, bachelor's, master's, doctoral, and post-master's certificates.

Special study options: advanced placement credit, cooperative education, distance learning, double majors, English as a second language, honors programs, independent study, internships, off-campus study, services for LD students, student-designed majors, study abroad, summer session for credit. ***ROTC:*** Army (c), Navy (b), Air Force (b).

Unusual degree programs: 3-2 engineering with Case Western Reserve University, Columbia University.

Computers: 652 computers/terminals are available on campus for general student use. Students can access the following: campus intranet, computer help desk, free student e-mail accounts, online (class) grades, online (class) registration, online (class) schedules. Campuswide network is available. 100% of college-owned or -operated housing units are wired for high-speed Internet access. Wireless service is available via entire campus.
Library: King Library plus 3 others. *Books:* 1.3 million (physical), 773,916 (digital/electronic); *Serial titles:* 41,080 (physical), 287,002 (digital/electronic); *Databases:* 778. Weekly public service hours: 168; study areas open 24 hours, 5–7 days a week; students can reserve study rooms.

STUDENT LIFE
Housing options: on-campus residence required through sophomore year; coed, men-only, women-only, special housing for students with disabilities. Campus housing is university owned. Freshman campus housing is guaranteed.

Activities and organizations: drama/theater group, student-run newspaper, radio and television station, choral group, marching band, CRU (formerly Campus Crusade for Christ), Alpha Phi Omega, College Republicans, 4 Paws for Ability, Best Buddies, national fraternities, national sororities.

Athletics Member NCAA. All Division I except football (Division I-A). ***Intercollegiate sports:*** baseball M(s)/W(c), basketball M(s)/W(s), cross-country running M(s)/W(s), equestrian sports M(c)/W(c), fencing M(c)/W(c), field hockey M(c)/W(s), golf M(s), gymnastics M(c)/W(c), ice hockey M(s)/W(c), lacrosse M(c)/W(c), rugby M(c)/W(c), sailing M(c)/W(c), soccer M(c)/W(s), softball M(c)/W(s), swimming and diving M(s)/W(s), tennis M(c)/W(s), track and field M(s)/W(s), ultimate Frisbee M(c)/W(c), volleyball M(c)/W(s), water polo M(c)/W(c), weight lifting M(c)/W(c), wrestling M(c)/W(c). ***Intramural sports:*** badminton M(c)/W(c), baseball M/W, basketball M/W, golf M(c)/W(c), ice hockey M/W, racquetball M/W, soccer M/W, softball M/W, ultimate Frisbee M/W, volleyball M/W.

Campus security: 24-hour emergency response devices and patrols, student patrols, late-night transport/escort service, controlled dormitory access.

Student services: health clinic, personal/psychological counseling, women's center.

COSTS & FINANCIAL AID
Costs (2018–19) ***Tuition:*** state resident $13,966 full-time; nonresident $32,718 full-time. Full-time tuition and fees vary according to location, program, and student level. Part-time tuition and fees vary according to course load, location, program, and student level. No tuition increase for student's term of enrollment. ***Required fees:*** $859 full-time. ***Room and board:*** $13,031; room only: $8063. Room and board charges vary according to board plan, housing facility, and student level. ***Payment plan:*** installment. ***Waivers:*** employees or children of employees.

Financial Aid Of all full-time matriculated undergraduates who enrolled in 2018, 8,601 applied for aid, 5,634 were judged to have need, 1,190 had their need fully met. 3,436 Federal Work-Study jobs (averaging $1063). In 2018, 5275 non-need-based awards were made. ***Average percent of need met:*** 61. ***Average financial aid package:*** $15,185. ***Average need-based loan:*** $4478. ***Average need-based gift aid:*** $11,811. ***Average non-need-based aid:*** $9699. ***Average indebtedness upon graduation:*** $28,648.

APPLYING
Standardized Tests *Required:* SAT or ACT (for admission).

Options: electronic application, early decision, early action, deferred entrance.

Application fee: $50.

Required: essay or personal statement, high school transcript, 1 letter of recommendation.

Application deadlines: 2/1 (freshmen), 11/1 (early action).

Early decision deadline: 11/1.

Notification: 3/15 (freshmen), continuous (transfers), 12/1 (early decision), 12/15 (early action).

CONTACT

Susan K Schaurer, Associate Vice President for Strategic Enrollment Management & Marketing, Miami University, Oxford, OH 45056. *Phone:* 513-529-2531. *E-mail:* admission@miamioh.edu.

Miami University Hamilton

Hamilton, Ohio

http://regionals.miamioh.edu/

- **State-supported** comprehensive, founded 1968, part of Miami University System
- **Suburban** 78-acre campus with easy access to Cincinnati
- **Coed** 4,182 undergraduate students, 78% full-time, 55% women, 45% men
- **Noncompetitive** entrance level

UNDERGRAD STUDENTS

3,280 full-time, 902 part-time. 5% transferred in.

Freshmen:

Admission: 871 enrolled.

FACULTY

Total: 224, 38% full-time.

Student/faculty ratio: 21:1.

ACADEMICS

Calendar: semesters plus summer sessions. *Degrees:* certificates, associate, bachelor's, and master's (degrees awarded by Miami University main campus).

Special study options: academic remediation for entering students, adult/continuing education programs, advanced placement credit, cooperative education, distance learning, double majors, English as a second language, honors programs, internships, part-time degree program, services for LD students, student-designed majors, study abroad, summer session for credit. ***ROTC:*** Navy (c), Air Force (c).

Computers: 300 computers/terminals are available on campus for general student use. Students can access the following: campus intranet, computer help desk, free student e-mail accounts, online (class) grades, online (class) registration, online (class) schedules. Campuswide network is available.
Library: Rentschler Library.

STUDENT LIFE

Housing options: Campus housing is university owned.

Activities and organizations: drama/theater group, Student Government, Campus Activities Committee, Ski Club, Student Nursing Association, OWLS (organization for wiser and world-wide learners).

Athletics *Intercollegiate sports:* baseball M(c), basketball M(c)/W(c), cheerleading W, golf M(c), softball W(c), tennis M(c)/W(c), volleyball W(c). ***Intramural sports:*** basketball M/W, bowling M/W, skiing (cross-country) M/W, soccer M/W, softball M/W, tennis M/W, volleyball M/W, weight lifting M/W.

Campus security: 24-hour emergency response devices and patrols, late-night transport/escort service.

Student services: personal/psychological counseling.

APPLYING

Options: electronic application.

Application fee: $35.

Required: high school transcript.

Application deadlines: rolling (freshmen), rolling (transfers).

Notification: continuous (freshmen), continuous (transfers).

CONTACT

Mr. Archie Nelson, Director of Admission and Financial Aid, Miami University Hamilton, 1601 Peck Boulevard, Hamilton, OH 45011-3399. *Phone:* 513-785-3111. *Fax:* 513-785-1807. *E-mail:* nelsona3@muohio.edu.

Miami University Middletown

Middletown, Ohio

http://regionals.miamioh.edu/

CONTACT

Diane Cantonwine, Assistant Director of Admission and Financial Aid, Miami University Middletown, 4200 East University Boulevard, Middletown, OH 45042-3497. *Phone:* 513-727-3346. *Toll-free phone:* 866-426-4643. *Fax:* 513-727-3223. *E-mail:* cantondm@muohio.edu.

Mount Carmel College of Nursing

Columbus, Ohio

http://www.mccn.edu/

- **Independent** comprehensive, founded 1903
- **Urban** campus with easy access to Columbus
- **Endowment** $1.9 million
- **Coed, primarily women** 873 undergraduate students, 69% full-time, 90% women, 10% men
- **Moderately difficult** entrance level, 63% of applicants were admitted

UNDERGRAD STUDENTS

606 full-time, 267 part-time. 7% are from out of state; 11% Black or African American, non-Hispanic/Latino; 2% Hispanic/Latino; 2% Asian, non-Hispanic/Latino; 0.1% Native Hawaiian or other Pacific Islander, non-Hispanic/Latino; 0.3% American Indian or Alaska Native, non-Hispanic/Latino; 3% Two or more races, non-Hispanic/Latino; 1% Race/ethnicity unknown; 15% transferred in; 1% live on campus.

Freshmen:

Admission: 208 applied, 132 admitted, 68 enrolled. ***Average high school GPA:*** 3.6. ***Test scores:*** ACT scores over 18: 82%; ACT scores over 24: 21%.

Retention: 64% of full-time freshmen returned.

FACULTY

Total: 120, 48% full-time, 24% with terminal degrees.

Student/faculty ratio: 11:1.

ACADEMICS

Calendar: semesters. *Degrees:* bachelor's, master's, doctoral, and post-master's certificates.

Special study options: accelerated degree program, adult/continuing education programs, advanced placement credit, distance learning, honors programs, off-campus study, summer session for credit. ***ROTC:*** Army (c), Air Force (c).

Computers: 25 computers/terminals are available on campus for general student use. Students can access the following: campus intranet, computer help desk, free student e-mail accounts, online (class) grades, online (class) registration, online (class) schedules. Campuswide network is available. 100% of college-owned or -operated housing units are wired for high-speed Internet access. Wireless service is available via entire campus.
Library: The Mount Carmel Health Sciences Library plus 1 other. *Books:* 8,163 (physical), 297,441 (digital/electronic); *Serial titles:* 683 (physical), 48,768 (digital/electronic); *Databases:* 178. Weekly public service hours: 61; study areas open 24 hours, 5–7 days a week; students can reserve study rooms.

STUDENT LIFE

Housing options: on-campus residence required through sophomore year; coed. Campus housing is leased by the school. Freshman applicants given priority for college housing.

Activities and organizations: Campus Ministry, Student Nurses Association of Mount Carmel (SNAM), Mount Carmel Rho Omicron Chapter of Sigma Theta Tau International Honor Society, Student Government Association (SGA), Student Ambassador Program.

Athletics *Intramural sports:* basketball W(c), softball W(c), volleyball M(c)/W(c).

Campus security: 24-hour emergency response devices and patrols, late-night transport/escort service, controlled dormitory access.

Student services: health clinic, personal/psychological counseling.

COSTS & FINANCIAL AID
Costs (2019–20) ***Tuition:*** $20,461 full-time. ***Required fees:*** $884 full-time. ***Room only:*** $5000.

Financial Aid Of all full-time matriculated undergraduates who enrolled in 2018, 487 applied for aid, 434 were judged to have need, 23 had their need fully met. In 2018, 25 non-need-based awards were made. ***Average percent of need met:*** 35. ***Average financial aid package:*** $10,080. ***Average need-based loan:*** $4472. ***Average need-based gift aid:*** $8981. ***Average non-need-based aid:*** $3008. ***Average indebtedness upon graduation:*** $34,996.

APPLYING
Standardized Tests *Required for some:* ACT (for admission).

Options: electronic application.

Application fee: $30.

Required: essay or personal statement, high school transcript, activities/interests resumé. ***Required for some:*** interview. ***Recommended:*** minimum 3.0 GPA.

Notification: continuous (freshmen), continuous (transfers).

CONTACT
Dr. Kim Campbell, Director, Admissions and Recruitment, Mount Carmel College of Nursing, 127 South Davis Avenue, Columbus, OH 43222-1504. *Phone:* 614-234-5144. *Toll-free phone:* 800-556-6942. *Fax:* 614-234-5427. *E-mail:* kcampbell@mccn.edu.

Mount St. Joseph University

Cincinnati, Ohio

http://www.msj.edu/

- **Independent Roman Catholic** comprehensive, founded 1920
- **Suburban** 92-acre campus with easy access to Cincinnati, Ohio
- **Endowment** $39.7 million
- **Coed** 1,448 undergraduate students, 69% full-time, 59% women, 41% men
- **Minimally difficult** entrance level, 60% of applicants were admitted

UNDERGRAD STUDENTS
1,006 full-time, 442 part-time. Students come from 16 states and territories; 18% are from out of state; 10% Black or African American, non-Hispanic/Latino; 2% Hispanic/Latino; 0.4% Asian, non-Hispanic/Latino; 0.1% Native Hawaiian or other Pacific Islander, non-Hispanic/Latino; 0.2% American Indian or Alaska Native, non-Hispanic/Latino; 3% Two or more races, non-Hispanic/Latino; 17% Race/ethnicity unknown; 0.2% international; 3% transferred in; 27% live on campus.

Freshmen:
Admission: 1,832 applied, 1,105 admitted, 318 enrolled. ***Average high school GPA:*** 3.5. ***Test scores:*** ACT scores over 18: 93%; ACT scores over 24: 34%; ACT scores over 30: 4%.

Retention: 73% of full-time freshmen returned.

FACULTY
Total: 220, 45% full-time, 33% with terminal degrees.

Student/faculty ratio: 11:1.

ACADEMICS
Calendar: semesters. *Degrees:* certificates, associate, bachelor's, master's, doctoral, and postbachelor's certificates.

Special study options: academic remediation for entering students, accelerated degree program, advanced placement credit, cooperative education, distance learning, double majors, honors programs, independent study, internships, off-campus study, part-time degree program, services for LD students, study abroad, summer session for credit. ***ROTC:*** Army (c), Air Force (c).

Computers: 172 computers/terminals are available on campus for general student use. Students can access the following: computer help desk, free student e-mail accounts, online (class) grades, online (class) registration, online (class) schedules, wireless printing, storage space. Campuswide network is available. Wireless service is available via entire campus.
Library: Archbishop Alter Library. *Books:* 49,354 (physical), 132,008 (digital/electronic); *Serial titles:* 76 (physical), 30,812 (digital/electronic); *Databases:* 143. Weekly public service hours: 82.

STUDENT LIFE
Housing options: on-campus residence required through sophomore year; coed, special housing for students with disabilities. Campus housing is university owned. Freshman applicants given priority for college housing.

Activities and organizations: drama/theater group, student-run newspaper, choral group, marching band, Black Student Union, Campus Activities Board, Student Government Association, Group Fitness, Residence Hall Council, national fraternities.

Athletics Member NCAA. All Division III except golf (Division II). ***Intercollegiate sports:*** baseball M, basketball M/W, cheerleading W, cross-country running M/W, football M, golf M/W, lacrosse M/W, soccer M/W, softball W, tennis M/W, track and field M/W, volleyball M/W, wrestling M. ***Intramural sports:*** basketball M/W, racquetball M/W, soccer M/W, volleyball M/W.

Campus security: 24-hour emergency response devices and patrols, late-night transport/escort service.

Student services: health clinic, personal/psychological counseling.

COSTS & FINANCIAL AID
Costs (2018–19) ***Comprehensive fee:*** $39,542 includes full-time tuition ($29,100), mandatory fees ($1000), and room and board ($9442). Full-time tuition and fees vary according to course load, location, and reciprocity agreements. Part-time tuition: $540 per credit hour. Part-time tuition and fees vary according to course load, location, and reciprocity agreements. ***Room and board:*** Room and board charges vary according to board plan, housing facility, and location. ***Payment plans:*** installment, deferred payment. ***Waivers:*** senior citizens and employees or children of employees.

Financial Aid Of all full-time matriculated undergraduates who enrolled in 2017, 914 applied for aid, 826 were judged to have need, 133 had their need fully met. 235 Federal Work-Study jobs (averaging $1488). 138 state and other part-time jobs (averaging $1468). In 2017, 151 non-need-based awards were made. ***Average percent of need met:*** 77. ***Average financial aid package:*** $22,394. ***Average need-based loan:*** $4125. ***Average need-based gift aid:*** $17,776. ***Average non-need-based aid:*** $11,293.

APPLYING
Standardized Tests *Required:* SAT or ACT (for admission).

Options: electronic application, deferred entrance.

Application fee: $25.

Required: high school transcript. ***Recommended:*** minimum 3.0 GPA.

Notification: continuous (freshmen), continuous (transfers).

CONTACT
Peggy Minnich, Director of Admission, Mount St. Joseph University, 5701 Delhi Road, Cincinnati, OH 45233-1670. *Phone:* 513-244-4531. *Toll-free phone:* 800-654-9314. *Fax:* 513-244-4629. *E-mail:* admissions@msj.edu.

Mount Vernon Nazarene University

Mount Vernon, Ohio

http://www.mvnu.edu/

- **Independent Nazarene** comprehensive, founded 1968
- **Small-town** 332-acre campus with easy access to Columbus
- **Endowment** $19.7 million
- **Coed**
- **Moderately difficult** entrance level

FACULTY
Student/faculty ratio: 14:1.

ACADEMICS
Calendar: semesters. *Degrees:* associate, bachelor's, and master's.
Library: Thorne Library/Learning Resource Center. *Books:* 100,952 (physical), 790 (digital/electronic); *Serial titles:* 900 (physical), 29,195 (digital/electronic); *Databases:* 242. Weekly public service hours: 93; study areas open 24 hours, 5–7 days a week; students can reserve study rooms.

STUDENT LIFE
Housing options: coed, men-only, women-only, special housing for students with disabilities. Campus housing is university owned. Freshman campus housing is guaranteed.

Activities and organizations: drama/theater group, student-run newspaper, radio station, choral group, Campus Ministry Groups, Student Government Association, Student Education Association, Drama Club, Music Department Ensembles.

Athletics Member NAIA.

Campus security: 24-hour emergency response devices and patrols, late-night transport/escort service, controlled dormitory access.

Student services: health clinic, personal/psychological counseling.

COSTS & FINANCIAL AID

Costs (2018–19) ***Comprehensive fee:*** $37,364 includes full-time tuition ($28,944), mandatory fees ($250), and room and board ($8170). Full-time tuition and fees vary according to program. Part-time tuition: $803 per credit hour. Part-time tuition and fees vary according to course load and program. ***College room only:*** $4564.

Financial Aid Of all full-time matriculated undergraduates who enrolled in 2018, 1,450 applied for aid, 1,378 were judged to have need, 879 had their need fully met. In 2018, 210 non-need-based awards were made. ***Average percent of need met:*** 58. ***Average financial aid package:*** $22,793. ***Average need-based loan:*** $3965. ***Average need-based gift aid:*** $21,647. ***Average non-need-based aid:*** $14,496. ***Average indebtedness upon graduation:*** $22,778.

APPLYING

Standardized Tests *Required:* SAT or ACT (for admission).

Options: electronic application, deferred entrance.

Application fee: $25.

Required: essay or personal statement, high school transcript, minimum 2.5 GPA, 2 letters of recommendation.

CONTACT

Mr. Tracy Waal, Director of Admissions and Student Recruitment, Mount Vernon Nazarene University, 800 Martinsburg Road, Mount Vernon, OH 43050. *Phone:* 740-392-6868 Ext. 4514. *Toll-free phone:* 866-462-6868. *Fax:* 740-393-0511. *E-mail:* admissions@mvnu.edu.

Muskingum University

New Concord, Ohio

http://www.muskingum.edu/

- **Independent** comprehensive, founded 1837, affiliated with Presbyterian Church (U.S.A.)
- **Small-town** 245-acre campus with easy access to Columbus
- **Endowment** $74.3 million
- **Coed** 1,616 undergraduate students, 84% full-time, 56% women, 44% men
- **Moderately difficult** entrance level, 72% of applicants were admitted

UNDERGRAD STUDENTS

1,353 full-time, 263 part-time. Students come from 22 states and territories; 4 other countries; 9% are from out of state; 5% Black or African American, non-Hispanic/Latino; 2% Hispanic/Latino; 0.7% Asian, non-Hispanic/Latino; 0.2% American Indian or Alaska Native, non-Hispanic/Latino; 3% Two or more races, non-Hispanic/Latino; 8% Race/ethnicity unknown; 4% international; 4% transferred in; 64% live on campus.

Freshmen:

Admission: 2,175 applied, 1,570 admitted, 369 enrolled. ***Average high school GPA:*** 3.3. ***Test scores:*** SAT evidence-based reading and writing scores over 500: 74%; SAT math scores over 500: 70%; ACT scores over 18: 86%; SAT evidence-based reading and writing scores over 600: 20%; SAT math scores over 600: 24%; ACT scores over 24: 30%; SAT math scores over 700: 2%; ACT scores over 30: 4%.

Retention: 76% of full-time freshmen returned.

FACULTY

Total: 148, 66% full-time, 69% with terminal degrees.

Student/faculty ratio: 12:1.

ACADEMICS

Calendar: semesters. *Degrees:* bachelor's and master's.

Special study options: accelerated degree program, adult/continuing education programs, advanced placement credit, distance learning, double majors, English as a second language, external degree program, independent study, internships, off-campus study, part-time degree program, services for LD students, student-designed majors, study abroad, summer session for credit.

Computers: 266 computers/terminals are available on campus for general student use. Students can access the following: campus intranet, computer help desk, free student e-mail accounts, online (class) grades, online (class) registration, online (class) schedules. Campuswide network is available. 100% of college-owned or -operated housing units are wired for high-speed Internet access. Wireless service is available via entire campus.

Library: Roberta A. Smith Library. *Books:* 100,648 (physical), 368,006 (digital/electronic); *Serial titles:* 1,085 (physical), 77,990 (digital/electronic); *Databases:* 282. Weekly public service hours: 89; students can reserve study rooms.

STUDENT LIFE

Housing options: on-campus residence required through junior year; coed, men-only, women-only. Campus housing is university owned. Freshman campus housing is guaranteed.

Activities and organizations: drama/theater group, student-run newspaper, radio and television station, choral group, marching band, Campus Crusade for Christ (CRU), Greek Life, Muskingum Programming Board, Game Club, Multicultural Association:Black Student Union, national fraternities, national sororities.

Athletics Member NCAA. All Division III except golf (Division II). ***Intercollegiate sports:*** baseball M, basketball M/W, bowling M/W, cheerleading M(c)/W(c), cross-country running M/W, football M, golf M/W, lacrosse M/W, soccer M/W, softball W, tennis M/W, track and field M/W, ultimate Frisbee M(c)/W(c), volleyball W, wrestling M. ***Intramural sports:*** badminton M/W, basketball M/W, cross-country running M/W, football M/W, golf M/W, racquetball M/W, sand volleyball M/W, soccer M/W, softball M/W, swimming and diving M/W, table tennis M/W, tennis M/W, track and field M/W, volleyball M/W, water polo M/W, weight lifting M/W, wrestling M.

Campus security: 24-hour emergency response devices and patrols, late-night transport/escort service, controlled dormitory access.

Student services: health clinic, personal/psychological counseling, women's center.

COSTS & FINANCIAL AID

Costs (2019–20) ***One-time required fee:*** $250. ***Comprehensive fee:*** $40,640 includes full-time tuition ($28,100), mandatory fees ($778), and room and board ($11,762). Part-time tuition: $625 per credit hour. ***College room only:*** $5860.

Financial Aid Of all full-time matriculated undergraduates who enrolled in 2017, 1,162 applied for aid, 1,107 were judged to have need, 105 had their need fully met. 398 Federal Work-Study jobs (averaging $976). In 2017, 169 non-need-based awards were made. ***Average percent of need met:*** 77. ***Average financial aid package:*** $26,039. ***Average need-based loan:*** $3770. ***Average need-based gift aid:*** $21,380. ***Average non-need-based aid:*** $14,727. ***Average indebtedness upon graduation:*** $38,012.

APPLYING

Standardized Tests *Required:* SAT or ACT (for admission).

Options: electronic application, early admission, deferred entrance.

Required: high school transcript, minimum 2.0 GPA. ***Recommended:*** essay or personal statement, minimum 3.0 GPA, 1 letter of recommendation, interview.

Notification: continuous (freshmen), continuous (transfers).

CONTACT

Mrs. Marcy Ritzert, Director of Admission, Muskingum University, 163 Stormont Street, New Concord, OH 43762. *Phone:* 740-826-8137. *Toll-free phone:* 800-752-6082. *Fax:* 740-826-8100. *E-mail:* adminfo@muskingum.edu.

The North Coast College

Lakewood, Ohio

http://www.thencc.edu/

CONTACT

Regina Reihard, Admissions Representative, The North Coast College, 11724 Detroit Avenue, Lakewood, OH 44107. *Phone:* 216-221-8584 Ext. 113. *E-mail:* rreihard@vmcad.edu.

Notre Dame College
South Euclid, Ohio
http://www.notredamecollege.edu/

CONTACT
Mr. David Armstrong, Dean of Admissions, Notre Dame College, 4545 College Road, South Euclid, OH 44121-4293. *Phone:* 216-373-5214. *Toll-free phone:* 877-NDC-OHIO. *Fax:* 216-381-3802. *E-mail:* admissinos@ndc.edu.

Oberlin College
Oberlin, Ohio
http://www.oberlin.edu/

- **Independent** comprehensive, founded 1833
- **Small-town** 440-acre campus with easy access to Cleveland
- **Endowment** $820.3 million
- **Coed**
- **Very difficult** entrance level

FACULTY
Student/faculty ratio: 10:1.

ACADEMICS
Calendar: 4-1-4. *Degrees:* diplomas, bachelor's, master's, and postbachelor's certificates.
Library: Mudd Center Library plus 3 others. *Books:* 1.4 million (physical), 676,883 (digital/electronic); *Serial titles:* 188,472 (physical). Students can reserve study rooms.

STUDENT LIFE
Housing options: on-campus residence required through senior year; coed, women-only, cooperative, special housing for students with disabilities. Campus housing is university owned. Freshman campus housing is guaranteed.

Activities and organizations: drama/theater group, student-run newspaper, radio station, choral group, Experimental College, Community Outreach, Student Government, Student Cooperative Association, student radio station.

Athletics Member NCAA. All Division III.

Campus security: 24-hour emergency response devices and patrols, student patrols, late-night transport/escort service, controlled dormitory access, crime prevention programs.

Student services: health clinic, personal/psychological counseling, women's center.

COSTS & FINANCIAL AID
Costs (2018–19) ***Comprehensive fee:*** $71,390 includes full-time tuition ($54,346), mandatory fees ($706), and room and board ($16,338). Part-time tuition: $2266 per credit. Part-time tuition and fees vary according to course load. ***College room only:*** $8108. Room and board charges vary according to board plan and housing facility.

Financial Aid Of all full-time matriculated undergraduates who enrolled in 2018, 1,648 applied for aid, 1,412 were judged to have need, 1,412 had their need fully met. In 2018, 1346 non-need-based awards were made. ***Average percent of need met:*** 100. ***Average financial aid package:*** $45,020. ***Average need-based loan:*** $4233. ***Average need-based gift aid:*** $40,459. ***Average non-need-based aid:*** $16,998. ***Average indebtedness upon graduation:*** $27,523. ***Financial aid deadline:*** 2/1.

APPLYING
Standardized Tests *Required:* SAT or ACT (for admission). *Required for some:* SAT and SAT Subject Tests or ACT (for admission).

Options: electronic application, early admission, early decision, deferred entrance.

Required: essay or personal statement, high school transcript, 2 letters of recommendation. ***Required for some:*** interview, audition for the Conservatory of Music, detailed portfolio for homeschooled students. ***Recommended:*** interview.

CONTACT
Manuel Carballo, Vice President and Dean of Admissions and Financial Aid, Oberlin College, College of Arts and Sciences Admissions, 38 East College Street, Oberlin, OH 44074. *Phone:* 440-775-8411. *Toll-free phone:* 800-622-OBIE. *Fax:* 440-775-6905. *E-mail:* college.admissions@oberlin.edu.

Ohio Christian University
Circleville, Ohio
http://www.ohiochristian.edu/

- **Independent** comprehensive, founded 1948, affiliated with Churches of Christ in Christian Union
- **Small-town** 40-acre campus with easy access to Columbus
- **Endowment** $4.1 million
- **Coed**
- **Minimally difficult** entrance level

FACULTY
Student/faculty ratio: 12:1.

ACADEMICS
Calendar: semesters. *Degrees:* associate, bachelor's, and master's.
Library: Melvin Maxwell Memorial Library. *Books:* 59,755 (physical), 96,276 (digital/electronic); *Serial titles:* 143 (physical), 6,473 (digital/electronic). Weekly public service hours: 88; students can reserve study rooms.

STUDENT LIFE
Housing options: men-only, women-only. Campus housing is university owned.

Activities and organizations: drama/theater group, choral group.

Athletics Member NAIA.

Campus security: controlled dormitory access, security checks after midnight.

Student services: personal/psychological counseling, legal services.

COSTS & FINANCIAL AID
Costs (2018–19) ***Comprehensive fee:*** $28,782 includes full-time tuition ($19,456), mandatory fees ($1250), and room and board ($8076). Full-time tuition and fees vary according to class time, course load, degree level, location, and program. Part-time tuition: $886 per credit hour. Part-time tuition and fees vary according to class time, location, and program. ***Required fees:*** $400 per term part-time. ***Room and board:*** Room and board charges vary according to board plan.

Financial Aid Of all full-time matriculated undergraduates who enrolled in 2007, 480 applied for aid, 415 were judged to have need, 100 had their need fully met. 50 Federal Work-Study jobs (averaging $1700). In 2007, 80 non-need-based awards were made. ***Average percent of need met:*** 50. ***Average financial aid package:*** $9500. ***Average need-based loan:*** $4500. ***Average need-based gift aid:*** $4000. ***Average non-need-based aid:*** $1500. ***Average indebtedness upon graduation:*** $30,000.

APPLYING
Standardized Tests *Required for some:* ACT (for admission). *Recommended:* SAT (for admission).

Options: electronic application, early admission.

Application fee: $25.

Required: essay or personal statement, high school transcript, 4 letters of recommendation, medical form. ***Required for some:*** interview.

CONTACT
Ohio Christian University, 1476 Lancaster Pike, Circleville, OH 43113. *Phone:* 740-477-7741. *Toll-free phone:* 877-762-8669.

★ Ohio Dominican University
Columbus, Ohio
http://www.ohiodominican.edu/

- **Independent Roman Catholic** comprehensive, founded 1911
- **Urban** 92-acre campus with easy access to Columbus, OH
- **Endowment** $22.6 million
- **Coed** 1,188 undergraduate students, 80% full-time, 54% women, 46% men
- **Moderately difficult** entrance level, 75% of applicants were admitted

UNDERGRAD STUDENTS
952 full-time, 236 part-time. Students come from 18 states and territories; 11 other countries; 6% are from out of state; 26% Black or African American, non-Hispanic/Latino; 4% Hispanic/Latino; 1% Asian, non-Hispanic/Latino; 0.1% Native Hawaiian or other Pacific Islander, non-Hispanic/Latino; 0.7% American Indian or Alaska Native, non-

Hispanic/Latino; 6% Two or more races, non-Hispanic/Latino; 8% Race/ethnicity unknown; 2% international; 7% transferred in; 43% live on campus.

Freshmen:
Admission: 1,550 applied, 1,168 admitted, 260 enrolled. ***Average high school GPA:*** 3.3. ***Test scores:*** SAT evidence-based reading and writing scores over 500: 55%; ACT scores over 18: 87%; SAT evidence-based reading and writing scores over 600: 14%; ACT scores over 24: 27%; SAT evidence-based reading and writing scores over 700: 5%; ACT scores over 30: 4%.

Retention: 65% of full-time freshmen returned.

FACULTY
Total: 163, 37% full-time, 54% with terminal degrees.

Student/faculty ratio: 14:1.

ACADEMICS
Calendar: semesters. *Degrees:* certificates, associate, bachelor's, master's, and postbachelor's certificates.

Special study options: academic remediation for entering students, accelerated degree program, adult/continuing education programs, advanced placement credit, distance learning, double majors, honors programs, independent study, internships, off-campus study, part-time degree program, services for LD students, student-designed majors, study abroad, summer session for credit. ***ROTC:*** Army (c), Air Force (c).

Unusual degree programs: 3-2 business administration; engineering with software engineering; sport management.

Computers: 350 computers/terminals and 2,300 ports are available on campus for general student use. Students can access the following: campus intranet, computer help desk, free student e-mail accounts, online (class) grades, online (class) registration, online (class) schedules. Campuswide network is available. 100% of college-owned or -operated housing units are wired for high-speed Internet access. Wireless service is available via classrooms, computer centers, computer labs, dorm rooms, learning centers, libraries, student centers.
Library: Ohio Dominican Library. *Books:* 76,976 (physical), 149,521 (digital/electronic); *Serial titles:* 5,327 (physical), 29,439 (digital/electronic); *Databases:* 216. Students can reserve study rooms.

STUDENT LIFE
Housing options: on-campus residence required through sophomore year; coed. Campus housing is university owned. Freshman campus housing is guaranteed.

Activities and organizations: drama/theater group, student-run radio station, choral group, marching band, Panther Activities Council, Student Athletic Advisory Committee, Black Student Union, World Student Club, Panther Players.

Athletics Member NCAA. All Division II. ***Intercollegiate sports:*** baseball M(s), basketball M(s)/W(s), cross-country running M(s)/W(s), football M(s), golf M(s)/W(s), soccer M(s)/W(s), softball W(s), track and field M(s)/W(s), volleyball W(s). ***Intramural sports:*** basketball M/W, cheerleading W(c), sand volleyball M/W, table tennis M/W, ultimate Frisbee M/W.

Campus security: 24-hour emergency response devices and patrols, late-night transport/escort service, controlled dormitory access.

Student services: health clinic, personal/psychological counseling.

COSTS & FINANCIAL AID
Costs (2019–20) ***Comprehensive fee:*** $42,900 includes full-time tuition ($31,100), mandatory fees ($580), and room and board ($11,220). Part-time tuition: $735 per credit hour. ***Required fees:*** $175 per term part-time.

Financial Aid Of all full-time matriculated undergraduates who enrolled in 2017, 200 Federal Work-Study jobs (averaging $2000). ***Average percent of need met:*** 92. ***Average financial aid package:*** $12,467. ***Average indebtedness upon graduation:*** $13,500.

APPLYING
Standardized Tests *Required for some:* SAT or ACT (for admission).

Options: electronic application, deferred entrance.

Required: high school transcript, minimum 2.3 GPA. ***Required for some:*** essay or personal statement. ***Recommended:*** interview.

Application deadlines: rolling (freshmen), rolling (transfers).
Notification: continuous (freshmen), continuous (transfers).

CONTACT
Mr. Michael Halligan, Assoc VP for Undergraduate Admissions, Ohio Dominican University, 1216 Sunbury Road, Columbus, OH 43219. *Phone:* 614-251-4500. *Toll-free phone:* 800-955-6446. *Fax:* 614-251-0156. *E-mail:* admissions@ohiodominican.edu.

Ohio Northern University
Ada, Ohio
http://www.onu.edu/

- **Independent** comprehensive, founded 1871, affiliated with United Methodist Church
- **Small-town** 342-acre campus
- **Endowment** $162.0 million
- **Coed**
- **Moderately difficult** entrance level

FACULTY
Student/faculty ratio: 11:1.

ACADEMICS
Calendar: semesters. *Degrees:* certificates, bachelor's, master's, doctoral, and postbachelor's certificates.
Library: Heterick Memorial Library plus 1 other. Students can reserve study rooms.

STUDENT LIFE
Housing options: on-campus residence required through junior year; coed, men-only, women-only, special housing for students with disabilities. Campus housing is university owned. Freshman campus housing is guaranteed.

Activities and organizations: drama/theater group, student-run newspaper, radio and television station, choral group, marching band, Habitat for Humanity, Student Planning Committee, Student Senate, Northern Christian Fellowship, Marching Band, national fraternities, national sororities.

Athletics Member NCAA. All Division III.

Campus security: 24-hour emergency response devices and patrols, controlled dormitory access.

Student services: health clinic, personal/psychological counseling, legal services.

COSTS & FINANCIAL AID
Costs (2018–19) ***Comprehensive fee:*** $43,910 includes full-time tuition ($31,350), mandatory fees ($910), and room and board ($11,650). Full-time tuition and fees vary according to course load, degree level, and program. Part-time tuition: $1310 per credit hour. Part-time tuition and fees vary according to course load, degree level, and program. ***Room and board:*** Room and board charges vary according to board plan, housing facility, and student level.

Financial Aid Of all full-time matriculated undergraduates who enrolled in 2018, 1,928 applied for aid, 1,738 were judged to have need, 412 had their need fully met. In 2018, 329 non-need-based awards were made. ***Average percent of need met:*** 24. ***Average financial aid package:*** $27,794. ***Average need-based loan:*** $4530. ***Average need-based gift aid:*** $24,130. ***Average non-need-based aid:*** $15,686. ***Average indebtedness upon graduation:*** $39,221.

APPLYING
Standardized Tests *Required:* SAT or ACT (for admission).

Options: electronic application, deferred entrance.

Required: high school transcript. ***Required for some:*** essay or personal statement, 1 letter of recommendation, interview. ***Recommended:*** essay or personal statement.

CONTACT
Ms. Deborah Miller, Director of Admissions, Ohio Northern University, 525 South Main Street, Ada, OH 45810-1599. *Phone:* 419-772-2260 Ext. 2464. *Toll-free phone:* 888-408-4ONU. *Fax:* 419-772-2821. *E-mail:* admissions-ug@onu.edu.

See next page for display ad and page 1068 for the College Close-Up.

The Ohio State University

Columbus, Ohio

http://www.osu.edu/

- **State-supported** university, founded 1870, part of The Ohio State University
- **Urban** 1665-acre campus with easy access to Columbus
- **Endowment** $4.2 billion
- **Coed** 46,820 undergraduate students, 91% full-time, 49% women, 51% men
- **Very difficult** entrance level, 48% of applicants were admitted

UNDERGRAD STUDENTS

42,831 full-time, 3,989 part-time. Students come from 54 states and territories; 71 other countries; 19% are from out of state; 6% Black or African American, non-Hispanic/Latino; 4% Hispanic/Latino; 7% Asian, non-Hispanic/Latino; 0.1% Native Hawaiian or other Pacific Islander, non-Hispanic/Latino; 0.1% American Indian or Alaska Native, non-Hispanic/Latino; 4% Two or more races, non-Hispanic/Latino; 3% Race/ethnicity unknown; 9% international; 5% transferred in; 32% live on campus.

Freshmen:

Admission: 47,782 applied, 22,964 admitted, 7,944 enrolled. ***Test scores:*** SAT evidence-based reading and writing scores over 500: 99%; SAT math scores over 500: 99%; ACT scores over 18: 99%; SAT evidence-based reading and writing scores over 600: 75%; SAT math scores over 600: 88%; ACT scores over 24: 93%; SAT evidence-based reading and writing scores over 700: 23%; SAT math scores over 700: 59%; ACT scores over 30: 52%.

Retention: 95% of full-time freshmen returned.

FACULTY

Total: 5,682, 72% full-time, 88% with terminal degrees.

Student/faculty ratio: 19:1.

ACADEMICS

Calendar: semesters. *Degrees:* certificates, diplomas, associate, bachelor's, master's, doctoral, post-master's, and postbachelor's certificates.

Special study options: academic remediation for entering students, accelerated degree program, adult/continuing education programs, advanced placement credit, cooperative education, distance learning, double majors, English as a second language, freshman honors college, honors programs, independent study, internships, off-campus study, part-time degree program, services for LD students, student-designed majors, study abroad, summer session for credit. ***ROTC:*** Army (b), Navy (b), Air Force (b).

Unusual degree programs: 3-2 business administration.

Computers: Students can access the following: campus intranet, computer help desk, free student e-mail accounts, online (class) grades, online (class) registration, online (class) schedules, admission applications, fee payment. Campuswide network is available. 100% of college-owned or -operated housing units are wired for high-speed Internet access. Wireless service is available via entire campus.

Library: William Oxley Thompson Library plus 10 others. *Books:* 5.0 million (physical), 1.3 million (digital/electronic); *Serial titles:* 664,616 (physical), 55,339 (digital/electronic); *Databases:* 2,046. Study areas open 24 hours, 5–7 days a week; students can reserve study rooms.

STUDENT LIFE

Housing options: on-campus residence required through sophomore year; coed, women-only, cooperative, special housing for students with disabilities. Campus housing is university owned. Freshman campus housing is guaranteed.

Activities and organizations: drama/theater group, student-run newspaper, radio and television station, choral group, marching band, Burritos Club, Vinyl Club, Guitar Club, Artificial Intelligence Club, H20 Students, national fraternities, national sororities.

Athletics Member NCAA. All Division I. ***Intercollegiate sports:*** baseball M(s), basketball M(s)/W(s), cheerleading M(s)/W(s), cross-country running M(s)/W(s), fencing M(s)/W(s), field hockey W(s), football M(s), golf M(s)/W(s), gymnastics M(s)/W(s), ice hockey M(s)/W(s), lacrosse M(s)/W(s), riflery M(s)/W(s), rowing W(s), soccer M(s)/W(s), softball

W(s), swimming and diving M(s)/W(s), tennis M(s)/W(s), track and field M(s)/W(s), volleyball M(s)/W(s), wrestling M(s). ***Intramural sports:*** archery M(c)/W(c), badminton M(c)/W(c), baseball M(c), basketball M(c)/W(c), bowling M(c)/W(c), cheerleading W(c), crew M(c)/W(c), equestrian sports M(c)/W(c), fencing M(c)/W(c), field hockey M(c)/W(c), football M(c), golf M(c)/W(c), gymnastics M(c)/W(c), ice hockey M(c)/W(c), lacrosse M(c)/W(c), racquetball M(c)/W(c), riflery M(c)/W(c), rowing M(c)/W(c), rugby M(c)/W(c), sailing M(c)/W(c), sand volleyball M/W, skiing (downhill) M(c)/W(c), soccer M(c)/W(c), softball M/W(c), squash M(c)/W(c), swimming and diving M(c)/W(c), table tennis M/W, tennis M/W, triathlon M(c)/W(c), ultimate Frisbee M(c)/W(c), volleyball M(c)/W(c), water polo M/W(c), weight lifting M/W(c).

Campus security: 24-hour emergency response devices and patrols, student patrols, late-night transport/escort service, controlled dormitory access.

Student services: health clinic, personal/psychological counseling, legal services, veterans affairs office.

COSTS & FINANCIAL AID

Costs (2018–19) ***Tuition:*** state resident $10,726 full-time, $486 per credit hour part-time; nonresident $30,742 full-time, $1320 per credit hour part-time. Full-time tuition and fees vary according to course load, degree level, location, program, reciprocity agreements, and student level. Part-time tuition and fees vary according to course load, degree level, location, program, reciprocity agreements, and student level. No tuition increase for student's term of enrollment. ***Room and board:*** $12,434. Room and board charges vary according to board plan, housing facility, and location. ***Payment plan:*** installment. ***Waivers:*** senior citizens and employees or children of employees.

Financial Aid Of all full-time matriculated undergraduates who enrolled in 2018, 28,221 applied for aid, 19,909 were judged to have need, 3,990 had their need fully met. 3,037 Federal Work-Study jobs (averaging $2923). In 2018, 8964 non-need-based awards were made. ***Average percent of need met:*** 71. ***Average financial aid package:*** $14,537. ***Average need-based loan:*** $4383. ***Average need-based gift aid:*** $11,252. ***Average non-need-based aid:*** $7211. ***Average indebtedness upon graduation:*** $27,453.

APPLYING

Standardized Tests *Required:* SAT or ACT (for admission).

Options: electronic application, early action, deferred entrance.

Application fee: $60.

Required: essay or personal statement, high school transcript.

Application deadlines: 2/1 (freshmen), 2/1 (out-of-state freshmen), 5/1 (transfers), 11/1 (early action).

Notification: 3/31 (freshmen), 3/31 (out-of-state freshmen), continuous (transfers), 1/31 (early action).

CONTACT

Gail Stephenoff, Interim Executive Director Undergraduate Admissions, The Ohio State University, 281 W. Lane Ave., Student Academic Services Building, Columbus, OH 43210. *Phone:* 614-292-3980. *E-mail:* stephenoff.1@osu.edu.

The Ohio State University at Lima

Lima, Ohio

http://lima.osu.edu/

- **State-supported** comprehensive, founded 1960, part of The Ohio State University
- **Suburban** 562-acre campus
- **Endowment** $5.3 million
- **Coed** 1,010 undergraduate students, 84% full-time, 54% women, 46% men
- **Noncompetitive** entrance level, 99% of applicants were admitted

UNDERGRAD STUDENTS

851 full-time, 159 part-time. Students come from 4 states and territories; 1 other country; 0.3% are from out of state; 4% Black or African American, non-Hispanic/Latino; 5% Hispanic/Latino; 2% Asian, non-Hispanic/Latino; 0.3% American Indian or Alaska Native, non-Hispanic/Latino; 4% Two or more races, non-Hispanic/Latino; 3% Race/ethnicity unknown; 0.2% international; 5% transferred in.

Freshmen:

Admission: 1,704 applied, 1,691 admitted, 370 enrolled. ***Test scores:*** SAT evidence-based reading and writing scores over 500: 65%; SAT math scores over 500: 77%; ACT scores over 18: 85%; SAT evidence-based reading and writing scores over 600: 41%; SAT math scores over 600: 48%; ACT scores over 24: 38%; SAT evidence-based reading and writing scores over 700: 12%; SAT math scores over 700: 13%; ACT scores over 30: 5%.

Retention: 69% of full-time freshmen returned.

FACULTY

Total: 79, 39% full-time, 65% with terminal degrees.

Student/faculty ratio: 19:1.

ACADEMICS

Calendar: semesters. *Degrees:* associate, bachelor's, and master's.

Special study options: academic remediation for entering students, accelerated degree program, adult/continuing education programs, advanced placement credit, cooperative education, distance learning, double majors, English as a second language, freshman honors college, honors programs, independent study, internships, off-campus study, part-time degree program, services for LD students, student-designed majors, study abroad, summer session for credit.

Computers: Students can access the following: campus intranet, computer help desk, free student e-mail accounts, online (class) grades, online (class) registration, online (class) schedules. Campuswide network is available. Wireless service is available via entire campus.

Library: Lima Campus Library. *Books:* 74,972 (physical), 1.4 million (digital/electronic); *Serial titles:* 34 (physical), 54,576 (digital/electronic); *Databases:* 2,056. Weekly public service hours: 57; students can reserve study rooms.

STUDENT LIFE

Housing options: college housing not available.

Activities and organizations: drama/theater group, choral group, United Way Club, Campus Activities Board, Nert Club, Student Senate, Psych Club.

Athletics ***Intercollegiate sports:*** baseball M, basketball M/W, golf M, volleyball W. ***Intramural sports:*** basketball M/W, football M/W, soccer M/W, softball W, ultimate Frisbee M/W, volleyball M/W.

Campus security: 24-hour emergency response devices and patrols, late-night transport/escort service.

Student services: personal/psychological counseling.

COSTS

Costs (2018–19) ***Tuition:*** state resident $7644 full-time, $319 per credit hour part-time; nonresident $27,660 full-time, $1153 per credit hour part-time. Full-time tuition and fees vary according to course load, location, program, reciprocity agreements, and student level. Part-time tuition and fees vary according to course load, location, program, reciprocity agreements, and student level. No tuition increase for student's term of enrollment. ***Payment plan:*** installment. ***Waivers:*** senior citizens and employees or children of employees.

APPLYING

Standardized Tests *Required for some:* SAT or ACT (for admission).

Options: electronic application.

Application fee: $60.

Required: high school transcript.

Application deadlines: 6/1 (freshmen), 6/1 (out-of-state freshmen), 6/1 (transfers).

Notification: continuous (freshmen), continuous (out-of-state freshmen), continuous (transfers).

CONTACT

Kristina Healy, The Ohio State University at Lima, 4240 Campus Drive, Lima, OH 45804. *Phone:* 567-242-7172. *E-mail:* healy.83@osu.edu.

The Ohio State University at Mansfield

Mansfield, Ohio

http://www.mansfield.osu.edu/

- **State-supported** comprehensive, founded 1958, part of The Ohio State University
- **Small-town** 620-acre campus with easy access to Columbus, Cleveland
- **Endowment** $2.3 million
- **Coed** 1,096 undergraduate students, 81% full-time, 52% women, 48% men
- **Noncompetitive** entrance level, 100% of applicants were admitted

UNDERGRAD STUDENTS
883 full-time, 213 part-time. Students come from 6 states and territories; 2 other countries; 0.5% are from out of state; 10% Black or African American, non-Hispanic/Latino; 3% Hispanic/Latino; 3% Asian, non-Hispanic/Latino; 0.2% American Indian or Alaska Native, non-Hispanic/Latino; 4% Two or more races, non-Hispanic/Latino; 3% Race/ethnicity unknown; 5% transferred in; 20% live on campus.

Freshmen:
Admission: 2,695 applied, 2,686 admitted, 438 enrolled. ***Test scores:*** SAT evidence-based reading and writing scores over 500: 80%; SAT math scores over 500: 80%; ACT scores over 18: 86%; SAT evidence-based reading and writing scores over 600: 55%; SAT math scores over 600: 45%; ACT scores over 24: 40%; SAT evidence-based reading and writing scores over 700: 4%; SAT math scores over 700: 6%; ACT scores over 30: 6%.

Retention: 70% of full-time freshmen returned.

FACULTY
Total: 84, 39% full-time, 58% with terminal degrees.

Student/faculty ratio: 19:1.

ACADEMICS
Calendar: semesters. *Degrees:* associate and bachelor's.

Special study options: academic remediation for entering students, adult/continuing education programs, advanced placement credit, cooperative education, distance learning, double majors, English as a second language, freshman honors college, honors programs, independent study, internships, off-campus study, part-time degree program, services for LD students, student-designed majors, study abroad, summer session for credit.

Computers: Students can access the following: campus intranet, computer help desk, free student e-mail accounts, online (class) grades, online (class) registration, online (class) schedules. Campuswide network is available. 100% of college-owned or -operated housing units are wired for high-speed Internet access. Wireless service is available via entire campus.

Library: Bromfield Library & Information Commons. *Books:* 43,903 (physical), 1.4 million (digital/electronic); *Serial titles:* 126 (physical), 54,781 (digital/electronic); *Databases:* 2,075. Weekly public service hours: 63; students can reserve study rooms.

STUDENT LIFE
Housing options: coed, special housing for students with disabilities. Campus housing is university owned. Freshman applicants given priority for college housing.

Activities and organizations: drama/theater group, choral group, Campus Activities Board, Best Buddies, Awakening, College Democrats, College Republicans.

Athletics ***Intercollegiate sports:*** baseball M(c), basketball M(c)/W(c), volleyball W(c). ***Intramural sports:*** baseball M, basketball M/W, cheerleading M(c)/W(c), football M/W, sand volleyball M/W, soccer M/W, tennis M/W, ultimate Frisbee M/W, volleyball M/W.

Campus security: 24-hour emergency response devices and patrols.

Student services: personal/psychological counseling.

COSTS
Costs (2018–19) ***Tuition:*** state resident $7644 full-time, $319 per credit hour part-time; nonresident $27,660 full-time, $1153 per credit hour part-time. Full-time tuition and fees vary according to course load, location, program, reciprocity agreements, and student level. Part-time tuition and fees vary according to course load, location, program, reciprocity agreements, and student level. No tuition increase for student's term of enrollment. ***Room and board:*** $8094; room only: $6422. Room and board charges vary according to board plan, housing facility, and location. ***Payment plan:*** installment. ***Waivers:*** senior citizens and employees or children of employees.

APPLYING
Standardized Tests *Required for some:* SAT or ACT (for admission).

Options: electronic application.

Application fee: $60.

Required: high school transcript.

Application deadlines: 6/1 (freshmen), 6/1 (out-of-state freshmen), 6/1 (transfers).

Notification: continuous (freshmen), continuous (out-of-state freshmen), continuous (transfers).

CONTACT
Jennifer Fry, Director of Enrollment Services, The Ohio State University at Mansfield, 1680 University Drive, Mansfield, OH 44906-1599. *Phone:* 419-755-4300. *E-mail:* mansfield-askabuckeye@osu.edu.

The Ohio State University at Marion

Marion, Ohio

http://osumarion.osu.edu/

- **State-supported** comprehensive, founded 1958, part of The Ohio State University
- **Small-town** 188-acre campus with easy access to Columbus
- **Endowment** $5.6 million
- **Coed** 1,251 undergraduate students, 82% full-time, 49% women, 51% men
- **Noncompetitive** entrance level, 99% of applicants were admitted

UNDERGRAD STUDENTS
1,029 full-time, 222 part-time. Students come from 8 states and territories; 1 other country; 0.6% are from out of state; 4% Black or African American, non-Hispanic/Latino; 4% Hispanic/Latino; 6% Asian, non-Hispanic/Latino; 0.3% American Indian or Alaska Native, non-Hispanic/Latino; 2% Two or more races, non-Hispanic/Latino; 3% Race/ethnicity unknown; 0.1% international; 3% transferred in.

Freshmen:
Admission: 1,329 applied, 1,321 admitted, 488 enrolled. ***Test scores:*** SAT evidence-based reading and writing scores over 500: 84%; SAT math scores over 500: 90%; ACT scores over 18: 89%; SAT evidence-based reading and writing scores over 600: 52%; SAT math scores over 600: 64%; ACT scores over 24: 41%; SAT math scores over 700: 19%; ACT scores over 30: 3%.

Retention: 74% of full-time freshmen returned.

FACULTY
Total: 103, 37% full-time, 63% with terminal degrees.

Student/faculty ratio: 19:1.

ACADEMICS
Calendar: semesters. *Degrees:* associate and bachelor's.

Special study options: academic remediation for entering students, adult/continuing education programs, advanced placement credit, cooperative education, distance learning, double majors, English as a second language, freshman honors college, honors programs, independent study, internships, off-campus study, part-time degree program, services for LD students, student-designed majors, study abroad, summer session for credit.

Computers: Students can access the following: campus intranet, computer help desk, free student e-mail accounts, online (class) grades, online (class) registration, online (class) schedules. Campuswide network is available. Wireless service is available via entire campus.

Library: Marion Campus Library. *Books:* 46,290 (physical), 1.4 million (digital/electronic); *Serial titles:* 54,781 (digital/electronic); *Databases:* 2,056. Weekly public service hours: 57; students can reserve study rooms.

STUDENT LIFE
Housing options: college housing not available.

Activities and organizations: drama/theater group, choral group.

Athletics Member USCAA.

Campus security: 24-hour emergency response devices.

Student services: personal/psychological counseling.

COSTS

Costs (2018–19) ***Tuition:*** state resident $7644 full-time, $319 per credit hour part-time; nonresident $27,660 full-time, $1153 per credit hour part-time. Full-time tuition and fees vary according to course load, location, program, reciprocity agreements, and student level. Part-time tuition and fees vary according to course load, location, program, reciprocity agreements, and student level. No tuition increase for student's term of enrollment. ***Payment plan:*** installment. ***Waivers:*** senior citizens and employees or children of employees.

APPLYING

Standardized Tests *Required for some:* SAT or ACT (for admission).

Options: electronic application.

Application fee: $60.

Required: high school transcript.

Application deadlines: 6/1 (freshmen), 6/1 (out-of-state freshmen), 6/1 (transfers).

Notification: continuous (freshmen), continuous (out-of-state freshmen), continuous (transfers).

CONTACT

The Ohio State University at Marion, 1465 Mount Vernon Avenue, Marion, OH 43302-5695.

The Ohio State University at Newark

Newark, Ohio

http://www.newark.osu.edu/

- **State-supported** comprehensive, founded 1957, part of The Ohio State University
- **Small-town** 111-acre campus with easy access to Columbus
- **Endowment** $4.0 million
- **Coed** 2,870 undergraduate students, 86% full-time, 50% women, 50% men
- **Noncompetitive** entrance level, 100% of applicants were admitted

UNDERGRAD STUDENTS

2,461 full-time, 409 part-time. Students come from 10 states and territories; 1 other country; 0.4% are from out of state; 15% Black or African American, non-Hispanic/Latino; 4% Hispanic/Latino; 5% Asian, non-Hispanic/Latino; 0.1% American Indian or Alaska Native, non-Hispanic/Latino; 6% Two or more races, non-Hispanic/Latino; 3% Race/ethnicity unknown; 5% transferred in; 11% live on campus.

Freshmen:

Admission: 5,381 applied, 5,355 admitted, 1,563 enrolled. ***Test scores:*** SAT evidence-based reading and writing scores over 500: 88%; SAT math scores over 500: 83%; ACT scores over 18: 84%; SAT evidence-based reading and writing scores over 600: 40%; SAT math scores over 600: 39%; ACT scores over 24: 35%; SAT evidence-based reading and writing scores over 700: 6%; SAT math scores over 700: 11%; ACT scores over 30: 3%.

Retention: 70% of full-time freshmen returned.

FACULTY

Total: 161, 29% full-time, 57% with terminal degrees.

Student/faculty ratio: 28:1.

ACADEMICS

Calendar: semesters. *Degrees:* associate, bachelor's, and master's.

Special study options: academic remediation for entering students, adult/continuing education programs, advanced placement credit, cooperative education, distance learning, double majors, English as a second language, freshman honors college, honors programs, independent study, internships, off-campus study, part-time degree program, services for LD students, student-designed majors, study abroad, summer session for credit. ***ROTC:*** Army (b).

Computers: Students can access the following: campus intranet, computer help desk, free student e-mail accounts, online (class) grades, online (class) registration, online (class) schedules. Campuswide network is available. 100% of college-owned or -operated housing units are wired for high-speed Internet access. Wireless service is available via entire campus.

Library: John L. and Christine Warner Library. *Books:* 52,380 (physical), 1.4 million (digital/electronic); *Serial titles:* 491 (physical), 54,576 (digital/electronic); *Databases:* 2,056. Weekly public service hours: 69; students can reserve study rooms.

STUDENT LIFE

Housing options: coed, special housing for students with disabilities. Campus housing is university owned. Freshman applicants given priority for college housing.

Activities and organizations: drama/theater group, choral group, Campus Activities Board, Ebonye Horizons, Journay Campus Ministry, Collegiate 4 - H, American Sign Language.

Athletics ***Intramural sports:*** badminton M/W, basketball M/W, golf M/W, sand volleyball M/W, soccer M/W, softball M/W, table tennis M/W, ultimate Frisbee M/W, volleyball M/W, weight lifting M/W.

Campus security: 24-hour emergency response devices and patrols, late-night transport/escort service.

Student services: personal/psychological counseling, legal services.

COSTS

Costs (2018–19) ***Tuition:*** state resident $7644 full-time, $319 per credit hour part-time; nonresident $27,660 full-time, $1153 per credit hour part-time. Full-time tuition and fees vary according to course load, location, program, reciprocity agreements, and student level. Part-time tuition and fees vary according to course load, location, program, reciprocity agreements, and student level. No tuition increase for student's term of enrollment. ***Room and board:*** $9268; room only: $7596. Room and board charges vary according to board plan, housing facility, and location. ***Payment plan:*** installment. ***Waivers:*** senior citizens and employees or children of employees.

APPLYING

Standardized Tests *Required for some:* SAT or ACT (for admission).

Options: electronic application.

Application fee: $60.

Required: high school transcript.

Application deadlines: 6/1 (freshmen), 6/1 (out-of-state freshmen), 6/1 (transfers).

Notification: continuous (freshmen), continuous (out-of-state freshmen), continuous (transfers).

CONTACT

Ms. Diane Kanney, Director of Enrollment, The Ohio State University at Newark, 1179 University Drive, Newark, OH 43055. *Phone:* 740-366-9333. *E-mail:* kanney.24@osu.edu.

Ohio University

Athens, Ohio

http://www.ohio.edu/

- **State-supported** university, founded 1804, part of Ohio Board of Regents
- **Small-town** 1800-acre campus
- **Endowment** $568.9 million
- **Coed** 22,275 undergraduate students, 77% full-time, 60% women, 40% men
- **Moderately difficult** entrance level, 78% of applicants were admitted

UNDERGRAD STUDENTS

17,041 full-time, 5,234 part-time. Students come from 47 states and territories; 62 other countries; 12% are from out of state; 6% Black or African American, non-Hispanic/Latino; 3% Hispanic/Latino; 1% Asian, non-Hispanic/Latino; 0.1% Native Hawaiian or other Pacific Islander, non-Hispanic/Latino; 0.2% American Indian or Alaska Native, non-Hispanic/Latino; 4% Two or more races, non-Hispanic/Latino; 2% Race/ethnicity unknown; 2% international; 2% transferred in; 43% live on campus.

Freshmen:

Admission: 23,385 applied, 18,311 admitted, 3,993 enrolled. ***Average high school GPA:*** 3.5. ***Test scores:*** SAT evidence-based reading and writing scores over 500: 90%; SAT math scores over 500: 88%; ACT scores over 18: 98%; SAT evidence-based reading and writing scores over 600: 50%; SAT math scores over 600: 40%; ACT scores over 24: 53%;

SAT evidence-based reading and writing scores over 700: 7%; SAT math scores over 700: 7%; ACT scores over 30: 9%.

Retention: 82% of full-time freshmen returned.

FACULTY
Total: 1,251, 79% full-time, 67% with terminal degrees.

Student/faculty ratio: 17:1.

ACADEMICS
Calendar: semesters. *Degrees:* certificates, associate, bachelor's, master's, doctoral, and postbachelor's certificates.

Special study options: academic remediation for entering students, accelerated degree program, adult/continuing education programs, advanced placement credit, cooperative education, distance learning, double majors, English as a second language, external degree program, freshman honors college, honors programs, independent study, internships, off-campus study, part-time degree program, services for LD students, student-designed majors, study abroad, summer session for credit. ***ROTC:*** Army (b), Air Force (b).

Unusual degree programs: 3-2 We have 4+1 program in Biomedical Engineering. "The 4+1 option, which is open only to Ohio University Russ College undergraduates, allows students the opportunity to complete an engineering bachelor's degree and the biomedical engineering master's d.

Computers: 1,000 computers/terminals and 22,000 ports are available on campus for general student use. Students can access the following: campus intranet, computer help desk, free student e-mail accounts, online (class) grades, online (class) registration, online (class) schedules. Campuswide network is available. 100% of college-owned or -operated housing units are wired for high-speed Internet access. Wireless service is available via entire campus.

Library: Alden Library plus 3 others. *Books:* 3.2 million (physical), 1.1 million (digital/electronic); *Serial titles:* 155,515 (physical), 88,338 (digital/electronic); *Databases:* 558. Weekly public service hours: 146; study areas open 24 hours, 5–7 days a week; students can reserve study rooms.

STUDENT LIFE
Housing options: on-campus residence required through sophomore year; coed, women-only, special housing for students with disabilities. Campus housing is university owned. Freshman campus housing is guaranteed.

Activities and organizations: drama/theater group, student-run newspaper, radio and television station, choral group, marching band, Student Senate, Student Alumni Board, International Student Union, University Program Council, Black Student Cultural Programming Board, national fraternities, national sororities.

Athletics Member NCAA. All Division I except football (Division I-A). ***Intercollegiate sports:*** baseball M(s), basketball M(s)/W(s), cheerleading M/W, cross-country running M(s)/W(s), field hockey W(s), golf M(s)/W(s), ice hockey M(c), soccer W(s), softball W(s), swimming and diving W(s), track and field W(s), volleyball W(s), wrestling M(s). ***Intramural sports:*** archery M(c)/W(c), badminton M/W, basketball M/W, bowling M/W, crew M(c)/W(c), equestrian sports M(c)/W(c), fencing M(c)/W(c), golf M(c)/W(c), gymnastics M(c)/W(c), lacrosse M(c)/W(c), racquetball M/W, rugby M(c)/W(c), soccer M(c)/W(c), softball M(c)/W(c), swimming and diving M(c)/W(c), tennis M/W, ultimate Frisbee M(c)/W(c), volleyball M/W, water polo W(c).

Campus security: 24-hour emergency response devices and patrols, student patrols, late-night transport/escort service, controlled dormitory access.

Student services: health clinic, personal/psychological counseling, women's center, legal services, veterans affairs office.

COSTS & FINANCIAL AID
Costs (2018–19) ***Tuition:*** state resident $12,192 full-time, $576 per semester hour part-time; nonresident $21,656 full-time, $1042 per semester hour part-time. Full-time tuition and fees vary according to degree level, location, program, and reciprocity agreements. Part-time tuition and fees vary according to course load, degree level, location, program, and reciprocity agreements. No tuition increase for student's term of enrollment. ***Room and board:*** $11,830; room only: $7060. Room and board charges vary according to board plan. ***Payment plan:*** installment. ***Waivers:*** senior citizens and employees or children of employees.

Financial Aid Of all full-time matriculated undergraduates who enrolled in 2018, 12,027 applied for aid, 9,728 were judged to have need, 720 had their need fully met. 710 Federal Work-Study jobs (averaging $1869). In 2018, 1556 non-need-based awards were made. ***Average percent of need met:*** 49. ***Average financial aid package:*** $8977. ***Average need-based loan:*** $3701. ***Average need-based gift aid:*** $6520. ***Average non-need-based aid:*** $4612. ***Average indebtedness upon graduation:*** $27,993.

APPLYING
Standardized Tests *Required:* SAT or ACT (for admission).

Options: electronic application, early admission, early action, deferred entrance.

Application fee: $50.

Required for some: essay or personal statement, high school transcript, 2 letters of recommendation, Audition required for dance and music programs. Interview required of selected Honors Tutorial College candidates. Portfolio required of visual communication applicants. ***Recommended:*** 2 letters of recommendation.

Application deadlines: 2/1 (freshmen), 6/15 (transfers), 12/1 (early action).

Notification: continuous (freshmen), continuous (transfers), rolling (early action).

CONTACT
Ms. Candace Boeninger, Assistant Vice President and Director, Ohio University, Athens, OH 45701-2979. *Phone:* 740-593-4100. *Fax:* 740-593-0560. *E-mail:* admissions@ohio.edu.

Ohio University–Chillicothe

Chillicothe, Ohio

http://www.chillicothe.ohiou.edu/

CONTACT
Neeley Allen, Coordinator, Recruitment, Ohio University–Chillicothe, 101 University Drive, Chillicothe, OH 45601. *Phone:* 740-774-7241. *Toll-free phone:* 877-462-6824. *Fax:* 740-774-7214. *E-mail:* evelandt@ohio.edu.

Ohio University–Eastern

St. Clairsville, Ohio

http://www.eastern.ohiou.edu/

CONTACT
Ms. Lisa Jeffries, Recruitment Coordinator, Ohio University–Eastern, 45425 National Road, St. Clairsville, OH 43950-9724. *Phone:* 740-699-2504. *Toll-free phone:* 800-648-3331. *E-mail:* jeffriee@ohio.edu.

Ohio University–Lancaster

Lancaster, Ohio

http://www.ohiou.edu/lancaster/

CONTACT
Pat Fox, Enrollment Manager, Ohio University–Lancaster, 1570 Granville Pike, Lancaster, OH 43130-1097. *Phone:* 740-654-6711 Ext. 215. *Toll-free phone:* 888-446-4468. *E-mail:* fox@ohio.edu.

Ohio University–Southern Campus

Ironton, Ohio

http://www.ohiou.edu/

CONTACT
Linda Harlow, Admission, Registration and Records Coordinator, Ohio University–Southern Campus, 1804 Liberty Avenue, Ironton, OH 45638-2214. *Phone:* 740-533-4584. *Toll-free phone:* 800-626-0513. *E-mail:* harlow@ohio.edu.

Ohio University–Zanesville

Zanesville, Ohio

http://www.ohio.edu/zanesville/

- **State-supported** 4-year, founded 1946
- **Rural** 179-acre campus with easy access to Columbus
- **Coed**
- **Noncompetitive** entrance level

FACULTY
Student/faculty ratio: 18:1.

ACADEMICS
Calendar: semesters. *Degrees:* associate and bachelor's (offers first 2 years of most bachelor's degree programs available at the main campus in Athens; also offers several bachelor's degree programs that can be completed at this campus; also offers some graduate courses).
Library: Zanesville Campus Library plus 1 other. Students can reserve study rooms.

STUDENT LIFE
Housing options: college housing not available.

Activities and organizations: student-run radio station, Student Senate, Student Nurses Association, Good Intentions Group, Green Bobcats, Habitat for Humanity Club.

Campus security: student patrols, late-night transport/escort service, night security.

Student services: personal/psychological counseling, legal services, veterans affairs office.

COSTS & FINANCIAL AID
Costs (2018–19) ***Tuition:*** state resident $5280 full-time, $238 per semester hour part-time; nonresident $8272 full-time, $374 per semester hour part-time. No tuition increase for student's term of enrollment. ***Required fees:*** $210 full-time, $9 per semester hour part-time.

Financial Aid Of all full-time matriculated undergraduates who enrolled in 2018, 619 applied for aid, 513 were judged to have need, 21 had their need fully met. 4 Federal Work-Study jobs (averaging $1441). In 2018, 7 non-need-based awards were made. ***Average percent of need met:*** 43. ***Average financial aid package:*** $5620. ***Average need-based loan:*** $2758. ***Average need-based gift aid:*** $4346. ***Average non-need-based aid:*** $1421. ***Average indebtedness upon graduation:*** $27,993.

APPLYING
Standardized Tests *Required for some:* SAT or ACT (for admission).

Options: electronic application.

Application fee: $20.

Required: high school transcript.

CONTACT
Ohio University–Zanesville, Office of Student Services, 1425 Newark Road, Zanesville, OH 43701. *Phone:* 740-588-1440. *Fax:* 740-588-1444. *E-mail:* ouzservices@ohio.edu.

Ohio Wesleyan University

Delaware, Ohio

http://www.owu.edu/

- **Independent United Methodist** 4-year, founded 1842
- **Small-town** 200-acre campus with easy access to Columbus
- **Coed** 1,565 undergraduate students, 99% full-time, 53% women, 47% men
- **Very difficult** entrance level, 71% of applicants were admitted

UNDERGRAD STUDENTS
1,550 full-time, 15 part-time. 54% are from out of state; 10% Black or African American, non-Hispanic/Latino; 6% Hispanic/Latino; 3% Asian, non-Hispanic/Latino; 0.1% Native Hawaiian or other Pacific Islander, non-Hispanic/Latino; 0.1% American Indian or Alaska Native, non-Hispanic/Latino; 5% Two or more races, non-Hispanic/Latino; 2% Race/ethnicity unknown; 5% international; 2% transferred in; 86% live on campus.

Freshmen:
Admission: 4,160 applied, 2,970 admitted, 453 enrolled. ***Average high school GPA:*** 3.4. ***Test scores:*** SAT evidence-based reading and writing scores over 500: 87%; SAT math scores over 500: 88%; ACT scores over 18: 98%; SAT evidence-based reading and writing scores over 600: 49%; SAT math scores over 600: 39%; ACT scores over 24: 70%; SAT evidence-based reading and writing scores over 700: 7%; SAT math scores over 700: 7%; ACT scores over 30: 17%.
Retention: 78% of full-time freshmen returned.

FACULTY
Total: 208, 66% full-time.
Student/faculty ratio: 9:1.

ACADEMICS
Calendar: semesters. *Degree:* bachelor's.

Special study options: double majors, honors programs, internships, off-campus study, services for LD students, student-designed majors, study abroad, summer session for credit. ***ROTC:*** Army (c), Air Force (c).

Unusual degree programs: 3-2 engineering with Alfred University, California Institute of Technology, Case Western Reserve University, Polytechnic University, Rensselaer Polytechnic Institute, Washington University in St. Louis.

Computers: Students can access the following: campus intranet, computer help desk, free student e-mail accounts, online (class) grades, online (class) registration, online (class) schedules. Campuswide network is available. 100% of college-owned or -operated housing units are wired for high-speed Internet access. Wireless service is available via entire campus.
Library: L. A. Beeghly Library.

STUDENT LIFE
Housing options: on-campus residence required through senior year; coed, women-only. Campus housing is university owned. Freshman campus housing is guaranteed.

Activities and organizations: drama/theater group, student-run newspaper, radio station, choral group, national fraternities, national sororities.

Athletics Member NCAA. All Division III. ***Intercollegiate sports:*** baseball M, basketball M/W, cheerleading W(c), crew W, cross-country running M/W, equestrian sports M(c)/W(c), field hockey W, football M, golf M/W, ice hockey M(c)/W(c), lacrosse M/W, rowing W, rugby M(c)/W(c), sailing M(c)/W(c), soccer M/W, softball W, swimming and diving M/W, tennis M/W, track and field M/W, ultimate Frisbee M(c)/W(c), volleyball M(c)/W, wrestling M. ***Intramural sports:*** badminton M/W, basketball M/W, football M/W, golf M/W, lacrosse M/W, racquetball M/W, skiing (cross-country) M/W, skiing (downhill) M/W, soccer M/W, softball M/W, squash M/W, swimming and diving M/W, tennis M/W, track and field M/W, volleyball M/W, water polo M/W.

Campus security: 24-hour emergency response devices and patrols, late-night transport/escort service, controlled dormitory access.

Student services: health clinic, personal/psychological counseling, women's center.

COSTS & FINANCIAL AID
Costs (2018–19) ***Comprehensive fee:*** $58,190 includes full-time tuition ($45,500), mandatory fees ($260), and room and board ($12,430). Full-time tuition and fees vary according to course load. Part-time tuition: $4940 per course. Part-time tuition and fees vary according to course load. ***College room only:*** $6800. Room and board charges vary according to board plan and housing facility. ***Payment plan:*** installment. ***Waivers:*** employees or children of employees.

Financial Aid Of all full-time matriculated undergraduates who enrolled in 2017, 1,239 applied for aid, 1,129 were judged to have need, 200 had their need fully met. In 2017, 397 non-need-based awards were made. ***Average percent of need met:*** 80. ***Average financial aid package:*** $37,783. ***Average need-based loan:*** $4604. ***Average need-based gift aid:*** $32,503. ***Average non-need-based aid:*** $22,751. ***Average indebtedness upon graduation:*** $33,814.

APPLYING
Standardized Tests *Required for some:* SAT or ACT (for admission).

Options: electronic application, early admission, early decision, early action, deferred entrance.

Required: essay or personal statement, high school transcript, minimum 2.5 GPA, 1 letter of recommendation. ***Recommended:*** 2 letters of recommendation, interview.

Early decision deadline: 11/15.

Notification: continuous (freshmen), continuous (out-of-state freshmen), continuous (transfers), 12/1 (early decision), 1/15 (early action).

CONTACT
Ms. Alisha Couch, Director of Admission, Ohio Wesleyan University, 61 South Sandusky Street, Delaware, OH 43015. *Phone:* 740-368-3099. *Toll-free phone:* 800-922-8953. *Fax:* 740-368-3314. *E-mail:* amcouch@owu.edu.

Otterbein University
Westerville, Ohio
http://www.otterbein.edu/

- **Independent United Methodist** comprehensive, founded 1847
- **Suburban** 142-acre campus with easy access to Columbus
- **Endowment** $91.5 million
- **Coed**
- **Moderately difficult** entrance level

FACULTY
Student/faculty ratio: 12:1.

ACADEMICS
Calendar: semesters. *Degrees:* bachelor's, master's, doctoral, and post-master's certificates.
Library: Courtright Memorial Library. *Books:* 281,721 (physical), 243,407 (digital/electronic); *Serial titles:* 15,441 (physical), 7,204 (digital/electronic). Weekly public service hours: 102; students can reserve study rooms.

STUDENT LIFE
Housing options: on-campus residence required through junior year; coed, men-only, women-only. Campus housing is university owned. Freshman campus housing is guaranteed.

Activities and organizations: drama/theater group, student-run newspaper, radio and television station, choral group, marching band, Musical groups, Honoraries, Academic interest clubs, Governance, national fraternities.

Athletics Member NCAA. All Division III.

Campus security: 24-hour emergency response devices and patrols, student patrols, late-night transport/escort service, controlled dormitory access, 24-hour locked residence hall entrances.

Student services: health clinic, personal/psychological counseling.

COSTS & FINANCIAL AID
Costs (2018–19) ***Tuition:*** $31,424 full-time, $564 per credit hour part-time. ***Required fees:*** $450 full-time, $250 per year part-time. ***Room only:*** Room and board charges vary according to board plan and housing facility.

Financial Aid Of all full-time matriculated undergraduates who enrolled in 2018, 2,118 applied for aid, 1,842 were judged to have need, 273 had their need fully met. In 2018, 473 non-need-based awards were made. ***Average percent of need met:*** 69. ***Average financial aid package:*** $22,280. ***Average need-based loan:*** $3850. ***Average need-based gift aid:*** $17,931. ***Average non-need-based aid:*** $14,664. ***Financial aid deadline:*** 6/1.

APPLYING
Standardized Tests *Required:* SAT or ACT (for admission).

Options: electronic application, deferred entrance.

Application fee: $35.

Required: high school transcript. ***Required for some:*** essay or personal statement, 1 letter of recommendation. ***Recommended:*** minimum 2.5 GPA, interview.

CONTACT
Mr. Mark Moffit, Director of Admissions, Otterbein University, 1 South Grove Street, Office of Admission, Westerville, OH 43081-9924. *Phone:* 614-823-1500. *Toll-free phone:* 800-488-8144. *Fax:* 614-823-1200. *E-mail:* uotterb@otterbein.edu.

Pontifical College Josephinum
Columbus, Ohio
http://www.pcj.edu/

CONTACT
Mrs. Arminda Crawford, Secretary for Admissions, Pontifical College Josephinum, 7825 North High Street, Columbus, OH 43235. *Phone:* 614-985-2241. *Toll-free phone:* 888-252-5812. *Fax:* 614-885-2307. *E-mail:* acrawford@pcj.edu.

Rabbinical College of Telshe
Wickliffe, Ohio

CONTACT
Admissions Office, Rabbinical College of Telshe, 28400 Euclid Avenue, Wickliffe, OH 44092-2523. *Phone:* 440-943-5300.

Ross College
Canton, Ohio
http://www.rosseducation.edu/

CONTACT
Ross College, 4300 Munson Street NW, Canton, OH 44718. *Phone:* 330-494-1214. *Toll-free phone:* 866-815-5578.

Shawnee State University
Portsmouth, Ohio
http://www.shawnee.edu/

- **State-supported** comprehensive, founded 1986, part of Ohio Higher Educational System
- **Small-town** 62-acre campus with easy access to Charleston-Huntington-Ashland Area
- **Endowment** $19.3 million
- **Coed**
- **Noncompetitive** entrance level

FACULTY
Student/faculty ratio: 13:1.

ACADEMICS
Calendar: semesters. *Degrees:* certificates, associate, bachelor's, and master's.
Library: Clark Memorial Library. *Books:* 122,670 (physical), 103,584 (digital/electronic); *Serial titles:* 140 (physical), 672 (digital/electronic); *Databases:* 543. Weekly public service hours: 91; study areas open 24 hours, 5–7 days a week; students can reserve study rooms.

STUDENT LIFE
Housing options: on-campus residence required for freshman year; coed. Campus housing is university owned, leased by the school and is provided by a third party. Freshman applicants given priority for college housing.

Activities and organizations: drama/theater group, student-run newspaper, choral group, campus ministry, Health Executives and Administrators Learning Society, Student Programming Board, Student Government Association, national fraternities, national sororities.

Athletics Member NAIA.

Campus security: 24-hour emergency response devices and patrols.

Student services: health clinic, personal/psychological counseling, women's center, veterans affairs office.

COSTS & FINANCIAL AID
Costs (2018–19) ***Tuition:*** state resident $8556 full-time, $348 per credit hour part-time; nonresident $14,714 full-time, $605 per credit hour part-time. Full-time tuition and fees vary according to course load, program, and reciprocity agreements. Part-time tuition and fees vary according to course load, program, and reciprocity agreements. No tuition increase for student's term of enrollment. ***Room and board:*** $10,864; room only: $6896. Room and board charges vary according to board plan and housing facility.

Financial Aid Of all full-time matriculated undergraduates who enrolled in 2016, 2,874 applied for aid, 1,900 were judged to have need, 99 had their need fully met. 60 Federal Work-Study jobs (averaging $1854). In

2016, 404 non-need-based awards were made. ***Average percent of need met:*** 45. ***Average financial aid package:*** $8972. ***Average need-based loan:*** $3964. ***Average need-based gift aid:*** $5855. ***Average non-need-based aid:*** $3875. ***Average indebtedness upon graduation:*** $30,554.

APPLYING
Options: electronic application.

Required: high school transcript. ***Required for some:*** essay or personal statement, minimum 2.7 GPA, interview, ACT/SAT scores if student is under 21.

CONTACT
Amanda Means, Director of Admissions, Shawnee State University, 940 Second Street, Portsmouth, OH 45662. *Phone:* 740-351-3229. *Toll-free phone:* 800-959-2778. *Fax:* 740-351-3111. *E-mail:* ameans@shawnee.edu.

Tiffin University
Tiffin, Ohio
http://www.tiffin.edu/

- **Independent** comprehensive, founded 1888
- **Small-town** 135-acre campus with easy access to Toledo
- **Endowment** $10.9 million
- **Coed** 2,303 undergraduate students, 75% full-time, 50% women, 50% men
- **Moderately difficult** entrance level, 69% of applicants were admitted

UNDERGRAD STUDENTS
1,724 full-time, 579 part-time. Students come from 26 states and territories; 18 other countries; 22% are from out of state; 9% Black or African American, non-Hispanic/Latino; 3% Hispanic/Latino; 0.2% Asian, non-Hispanic/Latino; 0.0% Native Hawaiian or other Pacific Islander, non-Hispanic/Latino; 0.2% American Indian or Alaska Native, non-Hispanic/Latino; 2% Two or more races, non-Hispanic/Latino; 41% Race/ethnicity unknown; 11% international; 6% transferred in; 50% live on campus.

Freshmen:
Admission: 3,977 applied, 2,753 admitted, 481 enrolled. ***Average high school GPA:*** 3.0. ***Test scores:*** SAT evidence-based reading and writing scores over 500: 55%; SAT math scores over 500: 57%; ACT scores over 18: 75%; SAT evidence-based reading and writing scores over 600: 15%; SAT math scores over 600: 8%; ACT scores over 24: 17%; SAT evidence-based reading and writing scores over 700: 1%; ACT scores over 30: 1%.

Retention: 67% of full-time freshmen returned.

FACULTY
Total: 306, 25% full-time, 45% with terminal degrees.

Student/faculty ratio: 14:1.

ACADEMICS
Calendar: semesters. *Degrees:* certificates, associate, bachelor's, master's, post-master's, and postbachelor's certificates.

Special study options: academic remediation for entering students, accelerated degree program, adult/continuing education programs, advanced placement credit, distance learning, double majors, English as a second language, freshman honors college, independent study, internships, off-campus study, services for LD students, study abroad, summer session for credit. ***ROTC:*** Army (c), Air Force (c).

Computers: 280 computers/terminals are available on campus for general student use. Students can access the following: campus intranet, computer help desk, free student e-mail accounts, online (class) grades, online (class) registration, online (class) schedules. Campuswide network is available. 100% of college-owned or -operated housing units are wired for high-speed Internet access. Wireless service is available via entire campus.

Library: Pfeiffer Library plus 1 other. *Books:* 43,505 (physical), 317,775 (digital/electronic); *Serial titles:* 331 (physical), 97,873 (digital/electronic); *Databases:* 216. Weekly public service hours: 73.

STUDENT LIFE
Housing options: on-campus residence required through sophomore year; coed, men-only, women-only. Campus housing is university owned and leased by the school. Freshman campus housing is guaranteed.

Activities and organizations: drama/theater group, student-run newspaper, choral group, marching band, Student Government Association, H2O, International Student Association, Global Affairs Organization, Circle K, national fraternities, national sororities.

Athletics Member NCAA. All Division II. ***Intercollegiate sports:*** baseball M(s), basketball M(s)/W(s), cross-country running M(s)/W(s), football M(s), golf M(s)/W(s), lacrosse W(s), soccer M(s)/W(s), softball W(s), swimming and diving M(s)/W(s), tennis M(s)/W(s), track and field M(s)/W(s), volleyball W(s), wrestling M(s)/W(s). ***Intramural sports:*** basketball M/W, bowling M/W, cheerleading W(c), equestrian sports M(c)/W(c), football M, rugby M(c), soccer M(c)/W(c), softball W, tennis M/W, volleyball M/W.

Campus security: 24-hour emergency response devices, student patrols, late-night transport/escort service, controlled dormitory access.

Student services: health clinic, personal/psychological counseling, women's center.

COSTS & FINANCIAL AID
Costs (2019–20) ***Comprehensive fee:*** $37,650 includes full-time tuition ($25,710), mandatory fees ($400), and room and board ($11,540). Part-time tuition: $857. ***College room only:*** $6180.

Financial Aid Of all full-time matriculated undergraduates who enrolled in 2018, 1,452 applied for aid, 1,320 were judged to have need, 190 had their need fully met. ***Average percent of need met:*** 67. ***Average financial aid package:*** $19,664. ***Average need-based loan:*** $4226. ***Average need-based gift aid:*** $16,031. ***Average indebtedness upon graduation:*** $38,036.

APPLYING
Standardized Tests *Required for some:* SAT or ACT (for admission).

Options: electronic application.

Application fee: $20.

Required: high school transcript. ***Required for some:*** essay or personal statement, interview. ***Recommended:*** minimum 3.0 GPA.

Application deadlines: rolling (freshmen), rolling (transfers).

Notification: continuous (freshmen), continuous (transfers).

CONTACT
Mrs. Sarah Johnson, Director of Undergraduate Admissions, Tiffin University, 155 Miami Street, Tiffin, OH 44883. *Phone:* 419-448-3014. *Toll-free phone:* 800-968-6446. *Fax:* 419-443-5006. *E-mail:* depughst@tiffin.edu.

Tri-State Bible College
South Point, Ohio
http://www.tsbc.edu/

CONTACT
Tri-State Bible College, 506 Margaret Street, PO Box 445, South Point, OH 45680-8402. *Phone:* 740-377-2520.

Union Institute & University
Cincinnati, Ohio
http://www.myunion.edu/

CONTACT
Union Institute & University, 440 East McMillan Street, Cincinnati, OH 45206-1925. *Phone:* 513-487-1173. *Toll-free phone:* 800-486-3116.

The University of Akron
Akron, Ohio
http://www.uakron.edu/

- **State-supported** university, founded 1870
- **Urban** 223-acre campus with easy access to Cleveland
- **Endowment** $191.4 million
- **Coed**
- **Moderately difficult** entrance level

FACULTY
Student/faculty ratio: 18:1.

ACADEMICS
Calendar: semesters. *Degrees:* certificates, associate, bachelor's, master's, doctoral, post-master's, and postbachelor's certificates.
Library: Bierce Library plus 2 others. *Books:* 1.1 million (physical); *Serial titles:* 25,089 (physical). Study areas open 24 hours, 5–7 days a week; students can reserve study rooms.

STUDENT LIFE
Housing options: on-campus residence required for freshman year; coed, special housing for students with disabilities. Campus housing is university owned. Freshman applicants given priority for college housing.
Activities and organizations: drama/theater group, student-run newspaper, radio and television station, choral group, marching band, AK-Rowdies, Akron Animation Association, National Society of Leadership and Success, Golden Key International Honor Society, Alpha Phi Omega, national fraternities, national sororities.
Athletics Member NCAA. All Division I except football (Division I-A).
Campus security: 24-hour emergency response devices and patrols, student patrols, late-night transport/escort service, controlled dormitory access.
Student services: health clinic, personal/psychological counseling, women's center, legal services.

COSTS & FINANCIAL AID
Costs (2018–19) ***Tuition:*** state resident $8618 full-time, $359 per credit hour part-time; nonresident $17,149 full-time, $715 per credit hour part-time. Full-time tuition and fees vary according to course load, degree level, location, and program. Part-time tuition and fees vary according to course load, degree level, location, and program. ***Required fees:*** $1652 full-time. ***Room and board:*** $12,296; room only: $8026. Room and board charges vary according to board plan and housing facility.
Financial Aid Of all full-time matriculated undergraduates who enrolled in 2017, 11,799 applied for aid, 9,312 were judged to have need, 986 had their need fully met. 302 Federal Work-Study jobs (averaging $3307). In 2017, 1777 non-need-based awards were made. ***Average percent of need met:*** 52. ***Average financial aid package:*** $7811. ***Average need-based loan:*** $3927. ***Average need-based gift aid:*** $5276. ***Average non-need-based aid:*** $5150. ***Average indebtedness upon graduation:*** $32,033.

APPLYING
Standardized Tests *Required:* SAT or ACT (for admission).
Options: electronic application, early action, deferred entrance.
Application fee: $45.
Required: high school transcript. ***Required for some:*** essay or personal statement, 3 letters of recommendation, interview.

CONTACT
Ms. Kimberley Gentile, Senior Associate Director of Admissions Outreach, The University of Akron, Office of Admissions, Simmons Hall 109N. *Phone:* 330-972-6345. *Toll-free phone:* 800-655-4884. *E-mail:* gentile@uakron.edu.

The University of Akron Wayne College

Orrville, Ohio

http://www.wayne.uakron.edu/

CONTACT
Ms. Alicia Broadus, Student Services Counselor, The University of Akron Wayne College, Orrville, OH 44667. *Phone:* 800-221-8308 Ext. 8901. *Toll-free phone:* 800-221-8308. *Fax:* 330-684-8989. *E-mail:* wayneadmissions@uakron.edu.

University of Cincinnati

Cincinnati, Ohio

http://www.uc.edu/

- **State-supported** university, founded 1819
- **Urban** 137-acre campus with easy access to Cincinnati
- **Endowment** $1.3 billion
- **Coed**
- **Moderately difficult** entrance level

FACULTY
Student/faculty ratio: 17:1.

ACADEMICS
Calendar: semesters. *Degrees:* certificates, associate, bachelor's, master's, doctoral, post-master's, and postbachelor's certificates.
Library: Walter C. Langsam Library plus 13 others. *Books:* 2.7 million (physical), 1.6 million (digital/electronic); *Serial titles:* 98,491 (physical), 2.1 million (digital/electronic); *Databases:* 1,270. Study areas open 24 hours, 5–7 days a week; students can reserve study rooms.

STUDENT LIFE
Housing options: on-campus residence required for freshman year; coed, men-only, women-only. Campus housing is university owned, leased by the school and is provided by a third party. Freshman campus housing is guaranteed.
Activities and organizations: drama/theater group, student-run newspaper, radio station, choral group, marching band, Serve Beyond Cincinnati, University of Cincinnati Mountaineering Club, Rally Cats, Engineers Without Borders, UC League of Legends, national fraternities, national sororities.
Athletics Member NCAA. All Division I except football (Division I-A).
Campus security: 24-hour emergency response devices and patrols, student patrols, late-night transport/escort service, controlled dormitory access.
Student services: health clinic, personal/psychological counseling, women's center, veterans affairs office.

COSTS & FINANCIAL AID
Costs (2018–19) ***Tuition:*** state resident $9322 full-time, $389 per credit hour part-time; nonresident $24,656 full-time, $1028 per credit hour part-time. Full-time tuition and fees vary according to course load, location, program, and reciprocity agreements. Part-time tuition and fees vary according to course load, location, program, and reciprocity agreements. ***Required fees:*** $1678 full-time, $70 per credit hour part-time. ***Room and board:*** $11,340; room only: $6756. Room and board charges vary according to board plan and housing facility.
Financial Aid Of all full-time matriculated undergraduates who enrolled in 2016, 14,728 applied for aid, 11,674 were judged to have need, 520 had their need fully met. In 2016, 4018 non-need-based awards were made. ***Average percent of need met:*** 39. ***Average financial aid package:*** $8514. ***Average need-based loan:*** $4472. ***Average need-based gift aid:*** $6116. ***Average non-need-based aid:*** $4549. ***Average indebtedness upon graduation:*** $25,877.

APPLYING
Standardized Tests *Required:* SAT or ACT (for admission).
Options: electronic application, early action, deferred entrance.
Application fee: $50.
Required: essay or personal statement, high school transcript. ***Required for some:*** 1 letter of recommendation, audition for performing arts majors.

CONTACT
Dr. Caroline Miller, Vice Provost for Enrollment Management, University of Cincinnati, Office of Admissions, PO Box210091, Cincinnati, OH 45221-0091. *Phone:* 513-556-1100. *Fax:* 513-556-1105. *E-mail:* admissions@uc.edu.

University of Cincinnati Blue Ash College

Cincinnati, Ohio

http://www.ucblueash.edu/

CONTACT
University of Cincinnati Blue Ash College, 9555 Plainfield Road, Cincinnati, OH 45236-1007. *Phone:* 513-745-5700.

University of Cincinnati Clermont College

Batavia, Ohio

http://www.ucclermont.edu/

CONTACT

Mrs. Jamie Adkins, University Services Associate, University of Cincinnati Clermont College, 4200 Clermont College Drive, Batavia, OH 45103. *Phone:* 513-732-5294. *Toll-free phone:* 866-446-2822. *Fax:* 513-732-5303. *E-mail:* jamie.adkins@uc.edu.

University of Dayton

Dayton, Ohio

http://www.udayton.edu/

- **Independent Roman Catholic** university, founded 1850
- **Suburban** 388-acre campus with easy access to Cincinnati
- **Coed** 8,638 undergraduate students, 94% full-time, 48% women, 52% men
- **Moderately difficult** entrance level, 72% of applicants were admitted

UNDERGRAD STUDENTS

8,162 full-time, 476 part-time. Students come from 50 states and territories; 39 other countries; 51% are from out of state; 3% Black or African American, non-Hispanic/Latino; 6% Hispanic/Latino; 1% Asian, non-Hispanic/Latino; 0.1% American Indian or Alaska Native, non-Hispanic/Latino; 5% Two or more races, non-Hispanic/Latino; 1% Race/ethnicity unknown; 5% international; 2% transferred in; 75% live on campus.

Freshmen:

Admission: 16,693 applied, 12,016 admitted, 2,198 enrolled. ***Average high school GPA:*** 3.8. ***Test scores:*** SAT evidence-based reading and writing scores over 500: 96%; SAT math scores over 500: 95%; ACT scores over 18: 100%; SAT evidence-based reading and writing scores over 600: 58%; SAT math scores over 600: 56%; ACT scores over 24: 81%; SAT evidence-based reading and writing scores over 700: 8%; SAT math scores over 700: 15%; ACT scores over 30: 25%.

Retention: 90% of full-time freshmen returned.

FACULTY

Total: 959, 64% full-time, 56% with terminal degrees.

Student/faculty ratio: 15:1.

ACADEMICS

Calendar: semesters plus 2 6-week summer terms. *Degrees:* bachelor's, master's, doctoral, post-master's, and postbachelor's certificates.

Special study options: academic remediation for entering students, accelerated degree program, adult/continuing education programs, advanced placement credit, cooperative education, distance learning, double majors, English as a second language, honors programs, independent study, internships, off-campus study, part-time degree program, services for LD students, student-designed majors, study abroad, summer session for credit. ***ROTC:*** Army (b), Air Force (c).

Unusual degree programs: 3-2 business administration; engineering.

Computers: 7,675 computers/terminals and 19,337 ports are available on campus for general student use. Students can access the following: campus intranet, computer help desk, free student e-mail accounts, online (class) grades, online (class) registration, online (class) schedules, applications, admission/enrollment status, virtual orientation, online digital resources, online courses, assistive technology, learning management system, multimedia labs, payment, cyber cafes, centrally-licensed, downloadable software and training. Campuswide network is available. 100% of college-owned or -operated housing units are wired for high-speed Internet access. Wireless service is available via entire campus.

Library: Roesch Library plus 3 others. *Books:* 881,689 (physical), 972,137 (digital/electronic); *Serial titles:* 2,325 (physical), 96,661 (digital/electronic); *Databases:* 316. Weekly public service hours: 134; students can reserve study rooms.

STUDENT LIFE

Housing options: on-campus residence required through sophomore year; coed, men-only, women-only, special housing for students with disabilities. Campus housing is university owned. Freshman campus housing is guaranteed.

Activities and organizations: drama/theater group, student-run newspaper, radio and television station, choral group, marching band, Student Government Association, Marching Band, Red Scare (basketball student cheering section), Campus Connection, Habitat for Humanity, national fraternities, national sororities.

Athletics Member NCAA. All Division I except football (Division I-AA). ***Intercollegiate sports:*** baseball M(s), basketball M(s)/W(s), cheerleading M/W, crew W, cross-country running M(s)/W(s), golf M(s)/W(c), soccer M(s)/W(s), softball W(s), tennis M(s)/W(s), track and field W(s), volleyball W(s). ***Intramural sports:*** baseball M(c), basketball M(c)/W(c), bowling M/W, crew M(c), cross-country running M(c)/W(c), fencing W(c), field hockey M(c), football M/W, golf M(c)/W(c), gymnastics M(c)/W(c), ice hockey M(c), lacrosse M(c)/W(c), racquetball M(c)/W(c), rugby M(c)/W(c), soccer M(c)/W(c), softball M/W(c), swimming and diving M(c)/W(c), tennis M(c)/W(c), ultimate Frisbee M(c)/W(c), volleyball M(c)/W(c), water polo M(c)/W(c), weight lifting M(c)/W(c), wrestling M(c)/W(c).

Campus security: 24-hour emergency response devices and patrols, student patrols, late-night transport/escort service, controlled dormitory access, approximately 1000 recording video cameras, automated external defibrillators in high density residential facilities and other areas.

Student services: health clinic, personal/psychological counseling, women's center, veterans affairs office.

COSTS & FINANCIAL AID

Costs (2019–20) ***Comprehensive fee:*** $58,150 includes full-time tuition ($44,100) and room and board ($14,050). No tuition increase for student's term of enrollment. ***College room only:*** $8420.

Financial Aid Of all full-time matriculated undergraduates who enrolled in 2018, 6,381 applied for aid, 4,792 were judged to have need, 4,496 had their need fully met. In 2018, 3535 non-need-based awards were made. ***Average percent of need met:*** 82. ***Average financial aid package:*** $31,910. ***Average need-based loan:*** $3162. ***Average need-based gift aid:*** $29,447. ***Average non-need-based aid:*** $19,485. ***Average indebtedness upon graduation:*** $37,533. ***Financial aid deadline:*** 5/1.

APPLYING

Standardized Tests *Required:* SAT or ACT (for admission).

Options: electronic application, early action, deferred entrance.

Required: essay or personal statement, high school transcript, 1 letter of recommendation. ***Required for some:*** audition for music, music therapy, music education programs.

Application deadlines: 6/15 (transfers), 11/1 (early action).

Notification: continuous (transfers), 12/1 (early action).

CONTACT

Mr. Robert Durkle, Dean of Admission and Financial Aid, University of Dayton, 300 College Park, Dayton, OH 45469-1310. *Phone:* 937-229-4411. *Toll-free phone:* 800-837-7433. *Fax:* 937-229-4729. *E-mail:* admission@udayton.edu.

The University of Findlay

Findlay, Ohio

http://www.findlay.edu/

- **Independent** comprehensive, founded 1882, affiliated with Church of God
- **Small-town** 390-acre campus
- **Endowment** $35.3 million
- **Coed** 3,614 undergraduate students, 67% full-time, 67% women, 33% men
- **Moderately difficult** entrance level, 74% of applicants were admitted

UNDERGRAD STUDENTS

2,434 full-time, 1,180 part-time. Students come from 45 states and territories; 28 other countries; 19% are from out of state; 3% Black or African American, non-Hispanic/Latino; 3% Hispanic/Latino; 2% Asian, non-Hispanic/Latino; 0.1% Native Hawaiian or other Pacific Islander, non-Hispanic/Latino; 0.2% American Indian or Alaska Native, non-Hispanic/Latino; 1% Two or more races, non-Hispanic/Latino; 15% Race/ethnicity unknown; 5% international; 2% transferred in; 45% live on campus.

Freshmen:
Admission: 3,462 applied, 2,572 admitted, 560 enrolled. *Test scores:* SAT evidence-based reading and writing scores over 500: 88%; SAT math scores over 500: 87%; ACT scores over 18: 96%; SAT evidence-based reading and writing scores over 600: 43%; SAT math scores over 600: 34%; ACT scores over 24: 50%; SAT evidence-based reading and writing scores over 700: 6%; SAT math scores over 700: 7%; ACT scores over 30: 9%.
Retention: 80% of full-time freshmen returned.

FACULTY
Total: 335, 72% full-time, 45% with terminal degrees.
Student/faculty ratio: 16:1.

ACADEMICS
Calendar: semesters. *Degrees:* certificates, associate, bachelor's, master's, and doctoral.
Special study options: academic remediation for entering students, accelerated degree program, adult/continuing education programs, advanced placement credit, cooperative education, distance learning, double majors, English as a second language, honors programs, independent study, internships, off-campus study, part-time degree program, services for LD students, student-designed majors, study abroad, summer session for credit. *ROTC:* Army (c), Air Force (c).
Unusual degree programs: 3-2 athletic training.
Computers: 151 computers/terminals are available on campus for general student use. Students can access the following: campus intranet, computer help desk, free student e-mail accounts, online (class) grades, online (class) registration, online (class) schedules. Campuswide network is available. 100% of college-owned or -operated housing units are wired for high-speed Internet access. Wireless service is available via entire campus.
Library: Shafer Library plus 4 others. *Books:* 98,272 (physical), 325,566 (digital/electronic); *Serial titles:* 361 (physical), 78,798 (digital/electronic); *Databases:* 173. Weekly public service hours: 94; study areas open 24 hours, 5–7 days a week.

STUDENT LIFE
Housing options: on-campus residence required through sophomore year; coed, women-only. Campus housing is university owned. Freshman campus housing is guaranteed.
Activities and organizations: drama/theater group, student-run newspaper, radio and television station, choral group, marching band, Habitat for Humanity, Pre-Vet Club, Horse Club, Stride, Black Student Union, national fraternities, national sororities.
Athletics Member NCAA. All Division II. *Intercollegiate sports:* baseball M(s), basketball M(s)/W(s), cross-country running M(s)/W(s), football M(s), golf M(s)/W(s), lacrosse W(s), soccer M(s)/W(s), softball W(s), swimming and diving M(s)/W(s), tennis M(s)/W(s), track and field M(s)/W(s), volleyball W(s), wrestling M(s). *Intramural sports:* basketball M/W, bowling M/W, soccer M/W, volleyball M/W.
Campus security: 24-hour emergency response devices and patrols, student patrols, late-night transport/escort service, controlled dormitory access, parking lot and building cameras (over 500), campus police.
Student services: health clinic, personal/psychological counseling, women's center.

COSTS & FINANCIAL AID
Costs (2019–20) ***Comprehensive fee:*** $45,610 includes full-time tuition ($34,200), mandatory fees ($1210), and room and board ($10,200). Part-time tuition: $755 per semester hour. ***Required fees:*** $45 per semester hour part-time, $75 part-time. ***College room only:*** $5090.
Financial Aid Of all full-time matriculated undergraduates who enrolled in 2018, 2,026 applied for aid, 1,748 were judged to have need, 481 had their need fully met. In 2018, 912 non-need-based awards were made. ***Average percent of need met:*** 79. ***Average financial aid package:*** $29,297. ***Average need-based loan:*** $4161. ***Average need-based gift aid:*** $25,689. ***Average non-need-based aid:*** $21,677. ***Average indebtedness upon graduation:*** $37,424. ***Financial aid deadline:*** 9/1.

APPLYING
Standardized Tests *Required:* SAT or ACT (for admission).
Options: electronic application, deferred entrance.
Required: high school transcript, minimum 2.5 GPA. ***Required for some:*** essay or personal statement, 1 letter of recommendation. ***Recommended:*** interview.
Application deadlines: rolling (freshmen), rolling (transfers).
Notification: continuous (freshmen), continuous (transfers).

CONTACT
Ms. Shawn Jordan, Assistant Director of Undergraduate Admissions, The University of Findlay, 1000 North Main Street, Findlay, OH 45840-3653. *Phone:* 419-434-4890. *Toll-free phone:* 800-548-0932. *Fax:* 419-434-4898. *E-mail:* jordan@findlay.edu.

University of Mount Union

Alliance, Ohio

http://www.mountunion.edu/

- **Independent United Methodist** comprehensive, founded 1846
- **Suburban** 123-acre campus with easy access to Cleveland
- **Endowment** $141.9 million
- **Coed** 2,116 undergraduate students, 98% full-time, 47% women, 53% men
- **Moderately difficult** entrance level, 96% of applicants were admitted

UNDERGRAD STUDENTS
2,074 full-time, 42 part-time. Students come from 27 states and territories; 9 other countries; 19% are from out of state; 8% Black or African American, non-Hispanic/Latino; 4% Hispanic/Latino; 0.7% Asian, non-Hispanic/Latino; 0.5% American Indian or Alaska Native, non-Hispanic/Latino; 4% Two or more races, non-Hispanic/Latino; 3% Race/ethnicity unknown; 2% international; 2% transferred in.

Freshmen:
Admission: 2,396 applied, 2,310 admitted, 617 enrolled. *Average high school GPA:* 3.4.
Retention: 77% of full-time freshmen returned.

FACULTY
Total: 253, 57% full-time, 61% with terminal degrees.
Student/faculty ratio: 13:1.

ACADEMICS
Calendar: semesters. *Degrees:* bachelor's, master's, and doctoral.
Special study options: accelerated degree program, adult/continuing education programs, advanced placement credit, cooperative education, distance learning, double majors, English as a second language, honors programs, independent study, internships, off-campus study, part-time degree program, services for LD students, student-designed majors, study abroad, summer session for credit. *ROTC:* Army (c).
Computers: Students can access the following: campus intranet, computer help desk, free student e-mail accounts, online (class) grades, online (class) registration, online (class) schedules. Campuswide network is available. 100% of college-owned or -operated housing units are wired for high-speed Internet access. Wireless service is available via entire campus.
Library: University of Mount Union Library plus 1 other. *Books:* 224,248 (physical), 458,288 (digital/electronic); *Serial titles:* 2,492 (physical), 67,046 (digital/electronic); *Databases:* 230. Study areas open 24 hours, 5–7 days a week; students can reserve study rooms.

STUDENT LIFE
Housing options: on-campus residence required through sophomore year; coed, men-only, women-only, special housing for students with disabilities. Campus housing is university owned. Freshman campus housing is guaranteed.
Activities and organizations: drama/theater group, student-run newspaper, radio and television station, choral group, marching band, Alpha Phi Omega, Student Senate, FCA Fellowship of Christian Athletes, Black Student Union, Raider Programming Board, national fraternities, national sororities.
Athletics Member NCAA. All Division III. *Intercollegiate sports:* baseball M, basketball M/W, cheerleading W, cross-country running M/W, football M, golf M/W, lacrosse M/W, soccer M/W, softball W, swimming and diving M/W, tennis M/W, track and field M/W, volleyball M/W, wrestling M. *Intramural sports:* basketball M/W, bowling M(c)/W(c), ultimate Frisbee M(c)/W(c).

Campus security: 24-hour emergency response devices and patrols, late-night transport/escort service, controlled dormitory access.

Student services: health clinic, personal/psychological counseling.

COSTS & FINANCIAL AID

Costs (2019–20) ***Comprehensive fee:*** $42,200 includes full-time tuition ($31,300), mandatory fees ($400), and room and board ($10,500). Part-time tuition: $1330 per credit hour. ***Required fees:*** $100 part-time. ***College room only:*** $5200. ***Payment plan:*** tuition prepayment.

Financial Aid Of all full-time matriculated undergraduates who enrolled in 2015, 1,778 applied for aid, 1,602 were judged to have need, 224 had their need fully met. 1,257 Federal Work-Study jobs (averaging $1074). 328 state and other part-time jobs (averaging $1487). In 2015, 367 non-need-based awards were made. ***Average percent of need met:*** 78. ***Average financial aid package:*** $22,577. ***Average need-based loan:*** $5877. ***Average need-based gift aid:*** $16,946. ***Average non-need-based aid:*** $12,016. ***Average indebtedness upon graduation:*** $32,680.

APPLYING

Standardized Tests *Required:* SAT or ACT (for admission).

Options: electronic application, early admission, deferred entrance.

Required: essay or personal statement, high school transcript, minimum 2.0 GPA, 1 letter of recommendation. ***Recommended:*** interview.

Application deadlines: rolling (freshmen), rolling (transfers).

Notification: continuous (freshmen), continuous (transfers).

CONTACT

Mr. Eric Young, Director of Admission, University of Mount Union, 1972 Clark Avenue, Alliance, OH 44601. *Phone:* 330-829-8238. *Toll-free phone:* 800-334-6682. *Fax:* 330-823-5097. *E-mail:* admission@mountunion.edu.

University of Northwestern Ohio

Lima, Ohio

http://www.unoh.edu/

CONTACT

Mr. Don Lowden, Director of Admissions, University of Northwestern Ohio, 1441 North Cable Road, Lima, OH 45805-1498. *Phone:* 419-998-3120. *E-mail:* dmlowden@unoh.edu.

University of Rio Grande

Rio Grande, Ohio

http://www.rio.edu/

CONTACT

Kristie Russell, Assistant Director of Admissions, University of Rio Grande, PO Box 500, Rio Grande, OH 45674. *Phone:* 740-245-7208. *Toll-free phone:* 800-282-7201. *Fax:* 740-245-7260. *E-mail:* admissions@rio.edu.

The University of Toledo

Toledo, Ohio

http://www.utoledo.edu/

- **State-supported** university, founded 1872
- **Urban** 858-acre campus with easy access to Detroit
- **Endowment** $306.9 million
- **Coed** 16,065 undergraduate students, 81% full-time, 49% women, 51% men
- **Noncompetitive** entrance level, 94% of applicants were admitted

UNDERGRAD STUDENTS

12,941 full-time, 3,124 part-time. Students come from 49 states and territories; 66 other countries; 21% are from out of state; 11% Black or African American, non-Hispanic/Latino; 5% Hispanic/Latino; 2% Asian, non-Hispanic/Latino; 0.1% Native Hawaiian or other Pacific Islander, non-Hispanic/Latino; 0.2% American Indian or Alaska Native, non-Hispanic/Latino; 4% Two or more races, non-Hispanic/Latino; 4% Race/ethnicity unknown; 6% international; 7% transferred in; 23% live on campus.

Freshmen:

Admission: 10,792 applied, 10,107 admitted, 3,270 enrolled. ***Average high school GPA:*** 3.5. ***Test scores:*** SAT evidence-based reading and writing scores over 500: 79%; SAT math scores over 500: 80%; ACT scores over 18: 88%; SAT evidence-based reading and writing scores over 600: 31%; SAT math scores over 600: 34%; ACT scores over 24: 44%; SAT evidence-based reading and writing scores over 700: 4%; SAT math scores over 700: 8%; ACT scores over 30: 10%.

Retention: 76% of full-time freshmen returned.

FACULTY

Total: 1,119, 69% full-time, 59% with terminal degrees.

Student/faculty ratio: 21:1.

ACADEMICS

Calendar: semesters. *Degrees:* certificates, diplomas, bachelor's, master's, doctoral, post-master's, and postbachelor's certificates.

Special study options: academic remediation for entering students, accelerated degree program, adult/continuing education programs, advanced placement credit, cooperative education, distance learning, double majors, English as a second language, freshman honors college, honors programs, independent study, internships, off-campus study, part-time degree program, services for LD students, student-designed majors, study abroad, summer session for credit. ***ROTC:*** Army (b), Air Force (c).

Unusual degree programs: 3-2 business administration; engineering; nursing; social work; environmental sciences/public health.

Computers: 5,000 computers/terminals and 10,000 ports are available on campus for general student use. Students can access the following: campus intranet, computer help desk, free student e-mail accounts, online (class) grades, online (class) registration, online (class) schedules, online transcripts, student account. Campuswide network is available. 100% of college-owned or -operated housing units are wired for high-speed Internet access. Wireless service is available via entire campus.

Library: Carlson Library plus 3 others. *Books:* 563,687 (physical), 339,697 (digital/electronic); *Serial titles:* 5,602 (physical), 74,382 (digital/electronic); *Databases:* 340. Weekly public service hours: 107; students can reserve study rooms.

STUDENT LIFE

Housing options: on-campus residence required through sophomore year; coed, special housing for students with disabilities. Campus housing is university owned and is provided by a third party. Freshman campus housing is guaranteed.

Activities and organizations: drama/theater group, student-run newspaper, radio and television station, choral group, marching band, Student Government, University YMCA, Newman Club, International Student Association, Campus Activities and Programming, national fraternities, national sororities.

Athletics Member NCAA. All Division I except football (Division I-A). ***Intercollegiate sports:*** baseball M(s), basketball M(s)/W(s), cross-country running M(s)/W(s), golf M(s)/W(s)(c), soccer W(s), softball W(s), swimming and diving W(s), tennis M(s)/W(s), track and field W(s), volleyball W(s). ***Intramural sports:*** badminton M/W, basketball M/W, bowling M/W, cheerleading W, crew M(c)/W(c), fencing M(c), field hockey W(c), football M/W, golf M/W, lacrosse M/W, racquetball M/W, sailing M(c)/W(c), skiing (cross-country) M(c)/W(c), skiing (downhill) M(c)/W(c), soccer M(c)/W(c), softball M/W, swimming and diving M/W, table tennis M/W, tennis M/W, track and field M/W, volleyball M/W, water polo M/W, weight lifting M/W, wrestling M.

Campus security: 24-hour emergency response devices and patrols, student patrols, late-night transport/escort service, controlled dormitory access, bicycle patrols by security staff, crime prevention officer.

Student services: health clinic, personal/psychological counseling, women's center, legal services, veterans affairs office.

COSTS & FINANCIAL AID

Costs (2018–19) ***Tuition:*** state resident $8534 full-time, $356 per credit hour part-time; nonresident $17,894 full-time, $746 per credit hour part-time. Full-time tuition and fees vary according to course load, program, reciprocity agreements, and student level. Part-time tuition and fees vary according to course load, program, reciprocity agreements, and student level. ***Required fees:*** $1261 full-time, $54 per credit hour part-time. ***Room and board:*** $11,434. Room and board charges vary according to board plan and housing facility. ***Payment plan:*** installment. ***Waivers:*** employees or children of employees.

Financial Aid Of all full-time matriculated undergraduates who enrolled in 2018, 10,290 applied for aid, 8,106 were judged to have need, 853 had their need fully met. In 2018, 3192 non-need-based awards were made. ***Average percent of need met:*** 59. ***Average financial aid package:*** $11,469. ***Average need-based loan:*** $3371. ***Average need-based gift aid:*** $9401. ***Average non-need-based aid:*** $6127. ***Average indebtedness upon graduation:*** $25,708.

APPLYING
Standardized Tests *Required:* SAT or ACT (for admission).

Options: electronic application, deferred entrance.

Application fee: $40.

Required: high school transcript. ***Required for some:*** minimum 2.0 GPA, core high school curriculum.

Application deadlines: rolling (freshmen), rolling (transfers).

Notification: continuous (freshmen), continuous (transfers).

CONTACT
William Pierce, Director of Undergraduate Admissions, The University of Toledo, OH. *Phone:* 419-530-5445. *Toll-free phone:* 800-5TOLEDO. *Fax:* 419-530-5713. *E-mail:* william.pierce@utoledo.edu.

Urbana University–A Branch Campus of Franklin University

Urbana, Ohio

http://www.urbana.edu/

CONTACT
Mr. Donnel W. Wiggins, Director of Admissions, Urbana University–A Branch Campus of Franklin University, 579 College Way, Urbana, OH 43078. *Toll-free phone:* 800-7-URBANA. *E-mail:* admiss@urbana.edu.

Ursuline College

Pepper Pike, Ohio

http://www.ursuline.edu/

- **Independent Roman Catholic** comprehensive, founded 1871
- **Suburban** 62-acre campus with easy access to Cleveland
- **Endowment** $43.5 million
- **Coed, primarily women**
- **Minimally difficult** entrance level

FACULTY
Student/faculty ratio: 8:1.

ACADEMICS
Calendar: semesters. *Degrees:* certificates, bachelor's, master's, doctoral, post-master's, and postbachelor's certificates (applications from men are also accepted).
Library: Ralph M. Besse Library. *Books:* 132,089 (physical), 137,533 (digital/electronic); *Serial titles:* 902 (physical), 14,413 (digital/electronic); *Databases:* 162. Weekly public service hours: 91; students can reserve study rooms.

STUDENT LIFE
Housing options: coed, women-only, special housing for students with disabilities. Campus housing is university owned. Freshman campus housing is guaranteed.

Activities and organizations: drama/theater group, Programming Board, Student Nurses of Ursuline College, U-Earth, Women's Circle, Anime Club.

Athletics Member NCAA. All Division II.

Campus security: 24-hour emergency response devices and patrols, late-night transport/escort service, controlled dormitory access.

Student services: personal/psychological counseling.

COSTS & FINANCIAL AID
Costs (2018–19) ***Comprehensive fee:*** $43,166 includes full-time tuition ($32,070), mandatory fees ($320), and room and board ($10,776). Full-time tuition and fees vary according to class time, course load, degree level, location, and program. Part-time tuition: $1069 per credit hour. Part-time tuition and fees vary according to class time, course load, degree level, location, and program. ***Required fees:*** $120 per term part-time. ***Room and board:*** Room and board charges vary according to housing facility.

Financial Aid Of all full-time matriculated undergraduates who enrolled in 2018, 433 applied for aid, 411 were judged to have need, 49 had their need fully met. In 2018, 44 non-need-based awards were made. ***Average percent of need met:*** 69. ***Average financial aid package:*** $24,154. ***Average need-based loan:*** $5249. ***Average need-based gift aid:*** $22,378. ***Average non-need-based aid:*** $9079. ***Average indebtedness upon graduation:*** $29,365.

APPLYING
Standardized Tests *Required:* SAT or ACT (for admission).

Options: electronic application, deferred entrance.

Required: essay or personal statement, high school transcript, 1 letter of recommendation. ***Recommended:*** minimum 2.5 GPA, interview.

CONTACT
Ms. Emily Haggerty, Associate Director, Admission and Recruitment, Ursuline College, 2550 Lander Road, Pepper Pike, OH 44124. *Phone:* 440-684-6107. *Toll-free phone:* 888-URSULINE. *E-mail:* esmith2@ursuline.edu.

Walsh University

North Canton, Ohio

http://www.walsh.edu/

- **Independent Roman Catholic** comprehensive, founded 1958
- **Small-town** 134-acre campus with easy access to Cleveland
- **Endowment** $22.6 million
- **Coed**
- **Moderately difficult** entrance level

FACULTY
Student/faculty ratio: 14:1.

ACADEMICS
Calendar: semesters. *Degrees:* certificates, associate, bachelor's, master's, and doctoral.
Library: Brother Edmond Drouin Library. *Books:* 97,575 (physical), 254,114 (digital/electronic); *Serial titles:* 995 (physical), 82,413 (digital/electronic); *Databases:* 167. Weekly public service hours: 79.

STUDENT LIFE
Housing options: on-campus residence required through senior year; coed, cooperative, special housing for students with disabilities. Campus housing is university owned. Freshman campus housing is guaranteed.

Activities and organizations: drama/theater group, student-run newspaper, radio station, choral group, marching band, Student Government, University Programming Board, Business and Communication Club, Behavioral Science Club, Education Club.

Athletics Member NCAA. All Division II.

Campus security: 24-hour emergency response devices and patrols, late-night transport/escort service, controlled dormitory access.

Student services: health clinic, personal/psychological counseling.

COSTS & FINANCIAL AID
Costs (2018–19) ***Comprehensive fee:*** $40,660 includes full-time tuition ($28,480), mandatory fees ($1500), and room and board ($10,680). Full-time tuition and fees vary according to location. Part-time tuition: $950 per credit hour. Part-time tuition and fees vary according to location. ***Required fees:*** $65 per credit hour part-time. ***College room only:*** $5570. Room and board charges vary according to board plan and housing facility.

Financial Aid Of all full-time matriculated undergraduates who enrolled in 2010, 1,726 applied for aid, 1,661 were judged to have need, 798 had their need fully met. In 2010, 180 non-need-based awards were made. ***Average percent of need met:*** 71. ***Average financial aid package:*** $18,133. ***Average need-based loan:*** $4850. ***Average need-based gift aid:*** $6844. ***Average non-need-based aid:*** $9372. ***Average indebtedness upon graduation:*** $24,753.

APPLYING
Standardized Tests *Required for some:* SAT or ACT (for admission).

Options: electronic application, early admission, deferred entrance.

Application fee: $25.

Required: high school transcript, minimum 2.4 GPA. ***Required for some:*** essay or personal statement, minimum 3.0 GPA, 2 letters of recommendation. ***Recommended:*** interview.

CONTACT
Ms. Melissa Schoeppner, Campus Visit Coordinator, Walsh University, 2020 East Maple, North Canton, OH 44720. *Phone:* 330-490-7172. *Toll-free phone:* 800-362-9846 (in-state); 800-362-8846 (out-of-state). *Fax:* 330-490-7165. *E-mail:* admissions@walsh.edu.

Wilberforce University
Wilberforce, Ohio
http://www.wilberforce.edu/

CONTACT
Ms. Dadra Driscoll, Director, Office of Admissions, Wilberforce University, 1055 N. Bickett Road, PO Box 1001, Wolfe Administration, Wilberforce, OH 45384. *Phone:* 937-708-5556. *Toll-free phone:* 800-367-8568. *E-mail:* ddriscoll@wilberforce.edu.

Wilmington College
Wilmington, Ohio
http://www.wilmington.edu/

CONTACT
Ms. Tina Garland, Director of Admission and Financial Aid, Wilmington College, 1870 Quaker Way, Wilmington, OH 45177. *Phone:* 937-382-6661 Ext. 426. *Toll-free phone:* 800-341-9318. *Fax:* 937-383-8542. *E-mail:* admissions@wilmington.edu.

Wittenberg University
Springfield, Ohio
http://www.wittenberg.edu/

- **Independent** comprehensive, founded 1845, affiliated with Evangelical Lutheran Church
- **Suburban** 114-acre campus with easy access to Columbus, Dayton
- **Coed**
- **Moderately difficult** entrance level

FACULTY
Student/faculty ratio: 13:1.

ACADEMICS
Calendar: semesters. *Degrees:* bachelor's and master's.
Library: Thomas Library plus 1 other. *Books:* 135,595 (digital/electronic); *Serial titles:* 163,369 (digital/electronic); *Databases:* 209. Weekly public service hours: 93.

STUDENT LIFE
Housing options: on-campus residence required through sophomore year; coed, women-only. Campus housing is university owned, leased by the school and is provided by a third party. Freshman campus housing is guaranteed.

Activities and organizations: drama/theater group, student-run newspaper, radio station, choral group, Student Senate, Union Board, Choirs, Weaver Chapel Association, national fraternities, national sororities.

Athletics Member NCAA. All Division III except golf (Division II).

Campus security: 24-hour emergency response devices and patrols, student patrols, late-night transport/escort service, controlled dormitory access, crime prevention programs.

Student services: health clinic, personal/psychological counseling, women's center.

COSTS & FINANCIAL AID
Costs (2018–19) ***Comprehensive fee:*** $49,856 includes full-time tuition ($38,680), mandatory fees ($820), and room and board ($10,356). Part-time tuition: $1289 per credit hour. Part-time tuition and fees vary according to course load. ***College room only:*** $5288. Room and board charges vary according to board plan and housing facility.

Financial Aid Of all full-time matriculated undergraduates who enrolled in 2018, 1,530 applied for aid, 1,355 were judged to have need, 357 had their need fully met. In 2018, 313 non-need-based awards were made. ***Average percent of need met:*** 81. ***Average financial aid package:*** $32,183. ***Average need-based loan:*** $4350. ***Average need-based gift aid:*** $27,774. ***Average non-need-based aid:*** $20,904. ***Average indebtedness upon graduation:*** $37,154.

APPLYING
Standardized Tests *Recommended:* Test score optional.

Options: electronic application, early admission, early decision, early action, deferred entrance.

Application fee: $40.

Required: high school transcript, interview. ***Recommended:*** essay or personal statement.

CONTACT
Ms. Karen Hunt, Director of Admission, Wittenberg University, PO Box 720, Springfield, OH 45501-0720. *Phone:* 877-206-0332 Ext. 6377. *Toll-free phone:* 800-677-7558 Ext. 6314. *Fax:* 937-327-6379. *E-mail:* admission@wittenberg.edu.

Wright State University
Dayton, Ohio
http://www.wright.edu/

- **State-supported** university, founded 1964, part of University System of Ohio
- **Suburban** 557-acre campus with easy access to Dayton, Columbus, Cincinnati
- **Coed**
- **Minimally difficult** entrance level

ACADEMICS
Calendar: semesters. *Degrees:* certificates, bachelor's, master's, doctoral, post-master's, and postbachelor's certificates.
Library: Paul Laurence Dunbar Library plus 1 other. Students can reserve study rooms.

STUDENT LIFE
Housing options: coed, special housing for students with disabilities. Campus housing is university owned and leased by the school.

Activities and organizations: drama/theater group, student-run newspaper, radio and television station, choral group, national fraternities, national sororities.

Athletics Member NCAA. All Division I.

Campus security: 24-hour emergency response devices and patrols, student patrols, late-night transport/escort service, controlled dormitory access.

Student services: health clinic, personal/psychological counseling, women's center, legal services, veterans affairs office.

COSTS & FINANCIAL AID
Costs (2018–19) ***Tuition:*** state resident $9254 full-time, $417 per credit hour part-time; nonresident $18,398 full-time, $838 per credit hour part-time. Full-time tuition and fees vary according to course load, location, reciprocity agreements, and student level. Part-time tuition and fees vary according to course load, location, reciprocity agreements, and student level. No tuition increase for student's term of enrollment. ***Room and board:*** $11,518; room only: $6522. Room and board charges vary according to board plan, housing facility, location, and student level.

Financial Aid Of all full-time matriculated undergraduates who enrolled in 2018, 6,483 applied for aid, 5,288 were judged to have need, 878 had their need fully met. In 2018, 1344 non-need-based awards were made. ***Average percent of need met:*** 62. ***Average financial aid package:*** $10,997. ***Average need-based loan:*** $4093. ***Average need-based gift aid:*** $6866. ***Average non-need-based aid:*** $5067. ***Average indebtedness upon graduation:*** $28,374.

APPLYING
Standardized Tests *Required:* SAT or ACT (for admission).

Options: electronic application, early admission, deferred entrance.

Application fee: $30.

Required: high school transcript. ***Recommended:*** minimum 2.0 GPA.

CONTACT
Wright State University, 3640 Colonel Glenn Highway, E147 Student Union, Dayton, OH 45435. *Phone:* 937-775-5700. *Toll-free phone:* 800-247-1770. *Fax:* 937-775-5795. *E-mail:* admissions@wright.edu.

Wright State University–Lake Campus

Celina, Ohio

http://www.wright.edu/lake/

- **State-supported** comprehensive, founded 1969
- **Small-town** 211-acre campus
- **Coed** 1,063 undergraduate students, 67% full-time, 57% women, 43% men
- **Minimally difficult** entrance level, 99% of applicants were admitted

UNDERGRAD STUDENTS
715 full-time, 348 part-time. 2% Black or African American, non-Hispanic/Latino; 3% Hispanic/Latino; 0.5% Asian, non-Hispanic/Latino; 1% Two or more races, non-Hispanic/Latino; 1% Race/ethnicity unknown; 0.1% international; 3% transferred in; 8% live on campus.

Freshmen:
Admission: 357 applied, 355 admitted, 219 enrolled. ***Average high school GPA:*** 3.1. ***Test scores:*** SAT evidence-based reading and writing scores over 500: 55%; SAT math scores over 500: 78%; ACT scores over 18: 78%; SAT evidence-based reading and writing scores over 600: 11%; ACT scores over 24: 19%; ACT scores over 30: 1%.
Retention: 63% of full-time freshmen returned.

ACADEMICS
Calendar: semesters. *Degrees:* certificates, associate, bachelor's, and master's.
Special study options: academic remediation for entering students, accelerated degree program, adult/continuing education programs, advanced placement credit, cooperative education, distance learning, double majors, honors programs, independent study, internships, off-campus study, part-time degree program, services for LD students, student-designed majors, study abroad, summer session for credit. ***ROTC:*** Army (c), Air Force (c).
Computers: Students can access the following: campus intranet, computer help desk, free student e-mail accounts, online (class) grades, online (class) registration, online (class) schedules. Campuswide network is available. 100% of college-owned or -operated housing units are wired for high-speed Internet access. Wireless service is available via entire campus.
Library: Lake Campus Library & Technology Center plus 1 other.

STUDENT LIFE
Housing options: Campus housing is leased by the school.
Athletics Member USCAA. ***Intercollegiate sports:*** baseball M, basketball M/W, softball W, volleyball W.
Campus security: 24-hour emergency response devices, WSU-Police Department presence, 40 hours per week.
Student services: health clinic, personal/psychological counseling, veterans affairs office.

COSTS & FINANCIAL AID
Costs (2018–19) ***Tuition:*** state resident $6194 full-time, $281 per credit hour part-time; nonresident $15,338 full-time, $702 per credit hour part-time. Full-time tuition and fees vary according to course load, location, reciprocity agreements, and student level. Part-time tuition and fees vary according to course load, location, reciprocity agreements, and student level. No tuition increase for student's term of enrollment. ***Room and board:*** $10,842; room only: $5846. Room and board charges vary according to board plan, housing facility, location, and student level. ***Payment plan:*** installment. ***Waivers:*** senior citizens and employees or children of employees.
Financial Aid Of all full-time matriculated undergraduates who enrolled in 2018, 548 applied for aid, 405 were judged to have need, 96 had their need fully met. In 2018, 112 non-need-based awards were made. ***Average percent of need met:*** 70. ***Average financial aid package:*** $8344. ***Average need-based loan:*** $3758. ***Average need-based gift aid:*** $4994. ***Average non-need-based aid:*** $3107. ***Average indebtedness upon graduation:*** $20,808.

APPLYING
Standardized Tests *Required:* SAT or ACT (for admission).
Options: electronic application, deferred entrance.
Application fee: $30.
Required: high school transcript. ***Recommended:*** minimum 2.0 GPA.
Application deadlines: rolling (freshmen), rolling (transfers).
Notification: continuous (freshmen), continuous (transfers).

CONTACT
Ms. Jill Puthoff, Admissions/Communications Coordinator, Wright State University–Lake Campus, 174 Dwyer Hall, Celina, OH 45822. *Phone:* 419-586-0363. *Toll-free phone:* 800-237-1477. *E-mail:* jill.puthoff@wright.edu.

Xavier University

Cincinnati, Ohio

http://www.xavier.edu/

CONTACT
Xavier University, 3800 Victory Parkway, Cincinnati, OH 45207-5311. *Phone:* 513-745-3301. *Toll-free phone:* 877-XUADMIT. *E-mail:* xuadmit@xavier.edu.

Youngstown State University

Youngstown, Ohio

http://www.ysu.edu/

- **State-supported** comprehensive, founded 1908
- **Urban** 160-acre campus with easy access to Cleveland, Pittsburgh
- **Endowment** $259.3 million
- **Coed** 11,524 undergraduate students, 79% full-time, 53% women, 47% men
- **Minimally difficult** entrance level, 68% of applicants were admitted

UNDERGRAD STUDENTS
9,070 full-time, 2,454 part-time. Students come from 39 states and territories; 77 other countries; 13% are from out of state; 9% Black or African American, non-Hispanic/Latino; 4% Hispanic/Latino; 1% Asian, non-Hispanic/Latino; 0.0% American Indian or Alaska Native, non-Hispanic/Latino; 3% Two or more races, non-Hispanic/Latino; 4% Race/ethnicity unknown; 3% international; 4% transferred in; 21% live on campus.

Freshmen:
Admission: 10,541 applied, 7,148 admitted, 2,322 enrolled. ***Average high school GPA:*** 3.4. ***Test scores:*** SAT evidence-based reading and writing scores over 500: 71%; SAT math scores over 500: 70%; ACT scores over 18: 83%; SAT evidence-based reading and writing scores over 600: 24%; SAT math scores over 600: 26%; ACT scores over 24: 32%; SAT evidence-based reading and writing scores over 700: 3%; SAT math scores over 700: 7%; ACT scores over 30: 4%.
Retention: 75% of full-time freshmen returned.

FACULTY
Total: 1,049, 39% full-time.
Student/faculty ratio: 17:1.

ACADEMICS
Calendar: semesters. *Degrees:* certificates, diplomas, associate, bachelor's, master's, doctoral, post-master's, and postbachelor's certificates.
Special study options: academic remediation for entering students, accelerated degree program, adult/continuing education programs, advanced placement credit, cooperative education, distance learning, double majors, English as a second language, freshman honors college, honors programs, independent study, internships, off-campus study, part-time degree program, services for LD students, student-designed majors, study abroad, summer session for credit. ***ROTC:*** Army (b), Air Force (c).
Unusual degree programs: chemistry, medicine.
Computers: 500 computers/terminals are available on campus for general student use. Students can access the following: campus intranet, computer help desk, free student e-mail accounts, online (class) grades, online (class) registration, online (class) schedules. Campuswide network is

available. 100% of college-owned or -operated housing units are wired for high-speed Internet access. Wireless service is available via entire campus.

Library: William F. Maag, Jr. Library plus 1 other. *Books:* 608,667 (physical), 103,922 (digital/electronic); *Serial titles:* 7,126 (physical), 46,162 (digital/electronic); *Databases:* 262. Weekly public service hours: 84; students can reserve study rooms.

STUDENT LIFE

Housing options: coed, women-only. Campus housing is university owned and is provided by a third party. Freshman applicants given priority for college housing.

Activities and organizations: drama/theater group, student-run newspaper, radio station, choral group, marching band, National Society of Collegiate Scholars, Fraternities/Sororities (IFC, NPHC, Panhellenic), American Society of Mechanical Engineers, MCAT Club, American Medical Student Association, national fraternities, national sororities.

Athletics Member NCAA. All Division I except football (Division I-AA). ***Intercollegiate sports:*** baseball M(s), basketball M(s)/W(s), bowling W, cross-country running M(s)/W(s), golf M(s)/W(s)(c), soccer W(s), softball W(s), swimming and diving W(s), tennis M(s)/W(s), track and field M(s)/W(s), volleyball W(s). ***Intramural sports:*** archery M(c)/W(c), badminton M/W, basketball M/W, bowling M(c)/W(c), cross-country running M/W, equestrian sports M(c)/W(c), fencing M(c)/W(c), field hockey W(c), football M, ice hockey M(c), lacrosse M(c)/W(c), racquetball M(c)/W(c), riflery M(c), rock climbing M/W, rugby W(c), sand volleyball M/W, soccer M/W, table tennis M/W, track and field M(c)/W(c), ultimate Frisbee M(c)/W(c), volleyball M/W, weight lifting M/W, wrestling M(c)/W(c).

Campus security: 24-hour emergency response devices and patrols, student patrols, late-night transport/escort service, controlled dormitory access.

Student services: health clinic, personal/psychological counseling, veterans affairs office.

COSTS & FINANCIAL AID

Costs (2018–19) ***Tuition:*** state resident $8899 full-time, $371 per credit hour part-time; nonresident $14,899 full-time, $621 per credit hour part-time. Full-time tuition and fees vary according to course load. Part-time tuition and fees vary according to course load. No tuition increase for student's term of enrollment. ***Required fees:*** $240 full-time, $34 per term part-time. ***Room and board:*** $9400. Room and board charges vary according to board plan and housing facility. ***Payment plans:*** installment, deferred payment. ***Waivers:*** senior citizens and employees or children of employees.

Financial Aid Of all full-time matriculated undergraduates who enrolled in 2017, 7,256 applied for aid, 6,078 were judged to have need, 471 had their need fully met. In 2017, 1309 non-need-based awards were made. ***Average percent of need met:*** 34. ***Average financial aid package:*** $9695. ***Average need-based loan:*** $3822. ***Average need-based gift aid:*** $5596. ***Average non-need-based aid:*** $4130. ***Average indebtedness upon graduation:*** $30,137.

APPLYING

Standardized Tests *Required:* SAT or ACT (for admission).

Options: electronic application, early admission, deferred entrance.

Application fee: $45.

Required: high school transcript, minimum 2.0 GPA, minimum ACT composite score of 17 or combined SAT score of 910 from evidence-based writing and reading test and math test.

Application deadlines: 8/1 (freshmen), 8/1 (out-of-state freshmen), 8/1 (transfers).

Notification: continuous (freshmen), continuous (out-of-state freshmen), continuous (transfers).

CONTACT

Ms. Sue Davis, Director of Admissions, Youngstown State University, One University Plaza, Youngstown, OH 44555-0001. *Phone:* 330-941-2000. *Toll-free phone:* 877-468-6978. *Fax:* 330-941-3674. *E-mail:* enroll@ysu.edu.

OKLAHOMA

Bacone College

Muskogee, Oklahoma

http://www.bacone.edu/

CONTACT

Bacone College, 2299 Old Bacone Road, Muskogee, OK 74403-1597. *Phone:* 918-781-7342. *Toll-free phone:* 888-682-5514 Ext. 7340.

Cameron University

Lawton, Oklahoma

http://www.cameron.edu/

- **State-supported** comprehensive, founded 1908, part of Oklahoma State Regents for Higher Education
- **Small-town** 360-acre campus
- **Endowment** $18.7 million
- **Coed** 3,944 undergraduate students, 69% full-time, 62% women, 38% men
- **Noncompetitive** entrance level, 100% of applicants were admitted

UNDERGRAD STUDENTS

2,713 full-time, 1,231 part-time. Students come from 32 states and territories; 32 other countries; 12% are from out of state; 12% Black or African American, non-Hispanic/Latino; 15% Hispanic/Latino; 2% Asian, non-Hispanic/Latino; 0.5% Native Hawaiian or other Pacific Islander, non-Hispanic/Latino; 6% American Indian or Alaska Native, non-Hispanic/Latino; 9% Two or more races, non-Hispanic/Latino; 3% Race/ethnicity unknown; 3% international; 8% transferred in; 9% live on campus.

Freshmen:

Admission: 1,120 applied, 1,120 admitted, 664 enrolled. ***Average high school GPA:*** 3.2. ***Test scores:*** ACT scores over 18: 66%; ACT scores over 24: 16%; ACT scores over 30: 1%.

Retention: 60% of full-time freshmen returned.

FACULTY

Total: 252, 54% full-time, 49% with terminal degrees.

Student/faculty ratio: 20:1.

ACADEMICS

Calendar: semesters. *Degrees:* associate, bachelor's, and master's.

Special study options: academic remediation for entering students, accelerated degree program, adult/continuing education programs, advanced placement credit, distance learning, double majors, honors programs, independent study, internships, off-campus study, part-time degree program, services for LD students, student-designed majors, summer session for credit. ***ROTC:*** Army (b).

Computers: 493 computers/terminals are available on campus for general student use. Students can access the following: computer help desk, free student e-mail accounts, online (class) grades, online (class) registration, online (class) schedules, online courses. Campuswide network is available. 100% of college-owned or -operated housing units are wired for high-speed Internet access. Wireless service is available via classrooms, computer centers, computer labs, dorm rooms, learning centers, libraries, student centers.

Library: Cameron University Library. *Books:* 82,620 (physical), 167,401 (digital/electronic); *Serial titles:* 2,000 (physical), 46,664 (digital/electronic); *Databases:* 70. Weekly public service hours: 34; students can reserve study rooms.

STUDENT LIFE

Housing options: men-only, women-only, special housing for students with disabilities. Campus housing is university owned.

Activities and organizations: drama/theater group, student-run newspaper, television station, choral group, Student Government Association, Pre-Nursing Club, Phi Kappa Phi, Health Professions Society, Sigma Tau Delta, national fraternities, national sororities.

Athletics Member NCAA. All Division II. ***Intercollegiate sports:*** baseball M(s), basketball M(s)/W(s), cross-country running M(s)/W(s), golf M(s)/W(s), softball W(s), tennis M(s)/W(s), volleyball W(s).

Intramural sports: badminton M/W, basketball M/W, bowling M/W, racquetball M/W, soccer M/W, softball M/W, table tennis M/W, tennis M/W, volleyball M/W, weight lifting M/W.

Campus security: 24-hour emergency response devices and patrols, late-night transport/escort service, controlled dormitory access.

Student services: health clinic, personal/psychological counseling, veterans affairs office.

COSTS & FINANCIAL AID
Costs (2018–19) ***Tuition:*** state resident $4740 full-time, $158 per credit hour part-time; nonresident $14,160 full-time, $472 per credit hour part-time. Full-time tuition and fees vary according to course level, course load, location, program, and student level. Part-time tuition and fees vary according to course level, course load, location, program, and student level. ***Required fees:*** $1710 full-time, $57 per credit hour part-time. ***Room and board:*** $5452; room only: $2222. Room and board charges vary according to board plan and housing facility. ***Payment plan:*** installment. ***Waivers:*** senior citizens and employees or children of employees.

Financial Aid Of all full-time matriculated undergraduates who enrolled in 2017, 2,150 applied for aid, 1,854 were judged to have need, 116 had their need fully met. 55 Federal Work-Study jobs (averaging $2828). 270 state and other part-time jobs (averaging $2740). In 2017, 287 non-need-based awards were made. ***Average percent of need met:*** 55. ***Average financial aid package:*** $9230. ***Average need-based loan:*** $3816. ***Average need-based gift aid:*** $6727. ***Average non-need-based aid:*** $3473. ***Average indebtedness upon graduation:*** $24,633.

APPLYING
Standardized Tests *Required for some:* SAT or ACT (for admission).

Options: electronic application, deferred entrance.

Application fee: $20.

Required for some: high school transcript.

Application deadlines: rolling (freshmen), rolling (out-of-state freshmen), rolling (transfers).

Notification: continuous (freshmen), continuous (out-of-state freshmen), continuous (transfers).

CONTACT
Ms. Brenda Dally, Director of Admissions, Cameron University, Admissions, 2800 West Gore Boulevard, Lawton, OK 73505-6377. *Phone:* 580-581-2289. *Toll-free phone:* 888-454-7600. *Fax:* 580-581-5514. *E-mail:* brendad@cameron.edu.

East Central University

Ada, Oklahoma

http://www.ecok.edu/

- **State-supported** comprehensive, founded 1909, part of Oklahoma State Regents for Higher Education
- **Small-town** 144-acre campus with easy access to Oklahoma City
- **Endowment** $31.3 million
- **Coed**
- **Minimally difficult** entrance level

FACULTY
Student/faculty ratio: 18:1.

ACADEMICS
Calendar: semesters. *Degrees:* bachelor's, master's, post-master's, and postbachelor's certificates.
Library: Linscheid Library. *Books:* 159,582 (physical), 25,548 (digital/electronic); *Serial titles:* 24,879 (physical), 825 (digital/electronic); *Databases:* 73. Weekly public service hours: 71; students can reserve study rooms.

STUDENT LIFE
Housing options: on-campus residence required for freshman year; coed. Campus housing is university owned.

Activities and organizations: drama/theater group, choral group, marching band, Campus Connection, F.A.T.E, GSA, ECU Wesley, Tigers for Tigers, national fraternities, national sororities.

Athletics Member NCAA. All Division II.

Campus security: 24-hour emergency response devices and patrols, student patrols, late-night transport/escort service, controlled dormitory access, agreements with all local, state, federal, and tribal police departments for added crime and violation prevention.

Student services: health clinic, personal/psychological counseling, veterans affairs office.

COSTS & FINANCIAL AID
Costs (2018–19) ***Tuition:*** state resident $5406 full-time, $180 per semester hour part-time; nonresident $14,616 full-time, $487 per semester hour part-time. No tuition increase for student's term of enrollment. ***Required fees:*** $1404 full-time, $47 per semester hour part-time. ***Room and board:*** $6848; room only: $3538. Room and board charges vary according to board plan and housing facility.

Financial Aid Of all full-time matriculated undergraduates who enrolled in 2017, 2,041 applied for aid, 1,721 were judged to have need, 674 had their need fully met. In 2017, 130 non-need-based awards were made. ***Average percent of need met:*** 86. ***Average financial aid package:*** $6423. ***Average need-based loan:*** $7047. ***Average need-based gift aid:*** $5054. ***Average non-need-based aid:*** $2442. ***Average indebtedness upon graduation:*** $18,140.

APPLYING
Standardized Tests *Required:* ACT (for admission). *Recommended:* SAT or ACT (for admission).

Options: electronic application, early admission.

Application fee: $20.

Required: high school transcript. ***Required for some:*** minimum 2.7 GPA, rank in upper 50% of high school class.

CONTACT
Ms. Kylie Stephens, Admissions Counselor, East Central University, 1100 East 14th Street, PMB R-8, Ada, OK 74820-6999. *Phone:* 580-559-5209. *E-mail:* kstephens@ecok.edu.

Family of Faith Christian University

Shawnee, Oklahoma

http://www.familyoffaith.edu/

CONTACT
Family of Faith Christian University, 30 Kinville, Shawnee, OK 74802.

Langston University

Langston, Oklahoma

http://www.langston.edu/

- **State-supported** comprehensive, founded 1897, part of Oklahoma A&M System
- **Rural** 40-acre campus with easy access to Oklahoma City
- **Endowment** $1.6 million
- **Coed**
- **Moderately difficult** entrance level

FACULTY
Student/faculty ratio: 22:1.

ACADEMICS
Calendar: semesters. *Degrees:* associate, bachelor's, master's, and doctoral.
Library: G. Lamar Harrison Library plus 2 others. *Books:* 44,337 (physical), 189,180 (digital/electronic); *Serial titles:* 111 (physical), 20,763 (digital/electronic); *Databases:* 61. Students can reserve study rooms.

STUDENT LIFE
Housing options: coed, special housing for students with disabilities. Campus housing is university owned and is provided by a third party. Freshman campus housing is guaranteed.

Activities and organizations: drama/theater group, student-run newspaper, radio station, choral group, marching band, Student Government Association, Student Senate, Sorority and Fraternity (Greek Letter), NAACP, Pre- Alumni Council, national fraternities, national sororities.

Athletics Member NAIA.

Campus security: 24-hour emergency response devices and patrols, student patrols, late-night transport/escort service, controlled dormitory access.

Student services: health clinic, personal/psychological counseling, women's center.

FINANCIAL AID

Financial Aid Of all full-time matriculated undergraduates who enrolled in 2015, 1,939 applied for aid, 1,814 were judged to have need, 334 had their need fully met. In 2015, 197 non-need-based awards were made. ***Average percent of need met:*** 54. ***Average financial aid package:*** $10,893. ***Average need-based gift aid:*** $5109. ***Average non-need-based aid:*** $6138. ***Average indebtedness upon graduation:*** $39,681.

APPLYING

Standardized Tests *Required:* SAT or ACT (for admission).

Options: electronic application, deferred entrance.

Required: high school transcript, minimum 2.7 GPA.

CONTACT

Mr. Jeremy Lane, Director of Admissions, Langston University, Box 1550, Langston, OK 73052. *Phone:* 405-466-3428. *Fax:* 405-466-2915. *E-mail:* jlane@langston.edu.

Mid-America Christian University

Oklahoma City, Oklahoma

http://www.macu.edu/

- **Independent** comprehensive, founded 1953, affiliated with Church of God
- **Suburban** 145-acre campus with easy access to Oklahoma City, Oklahoma
- **Endowment** $2.6 million
- **Coed**
- **Noncompetitive** entrance level

FACULTY

Student/faculty ratio: 11:1.

ACADEMICS

Calendar: semesters. *Degrees:* certificates, associate, bachelor's, master's, and post-master's certificates.
Library: Charles Ewing Brown Library. Weekly public service hours: 70; study areas open 24 hours, 5–7 days a week; students can reserve study rooms.

STUDENT LIFE

Housing options: on-campus residence required through sophomore year; men-only, women-only, special housing for students with disabilities. Campus housing is university owned. Freshman campus housing is guaranteed.

Activities and organizations: student-run newspaper, choral group.

Athletics Member NAIA.

Campus security: 24-hour patrols, student patrols.

Student services: personal/psychological counseling, veterans affairs office.

FINANCIAL AID

Financial Aid Of all full-time matriculated undergraduates who enrolled in 2001, 589 applied for aid, 581 were judged to have need, 68 had their need fully met. In 2001, 41 non-need-based awards were made. ***Average percent of need met:*** 75. ***Average financial aid package:*** $6682. ***Average need-based loan:*** $3617. ***Average need-based gift aid:*** $2734. ***Average non-need-based aid:*** $5214.

APPLYING

Standardized Tests *Recommended:* SAT or ACT (for admission).

Options: early admission.

Application fee: $25.

Required: high school transcript. ***Required for some:*** 2 letters of recommendation, interview.

CONTACT

Mid-America Christian University, 3500 Southwest 119th Street, Oklahoma City, OK 73170-4504. *Phone:* 405-692-3281. *Toll-free phone:* 888-436-3035.

National American University

Tulsa, Oklahoma

http://www.national.edu/

CONTACT

National American University, 8040 South Sheridan Road, Tulsa, OK 74133. *Toll-free phone:* 800-209-0338.

Northeastern State University

Tahlequah, Oklahoma

http://www.nsuok.edu/

- **State-supported** comprehensive, founded 1846, part of Regional University System of Oklahoma
- **Small-town** 200-acre campus with easy access to Tulsa
- **Endowment** $5.4 million
- **Coed** 6,741 undergraduate students, 70% full-time, 62% women, 38% men
- **Moderately difficult** entrance level, 97% of applicants were admitted

UNDERGRAD STUDENTS

4,687 full-time, 2,054 part-time. Students come from 26 states and territories; 54 other countries; 5% are from out of state; 4% Black or African American, non-Hispanic/Latino; 6% Hispanic/Latino; 2% Asian, non-Hispanic/Latino; 18% American Indian or Alaska Native, non-Hispanic/Latino; 21% Two or more races, non-Hispanic/Latino; 0.6% Race/ethnicity unknown; 2% international; 13% transferred in; 17% live on campus.

Freshmen:

Admission: 1,474 applied, 1,431 admitted, 854 enrolled. ***Average high school GPA:*** 3.5. ***Test scores:*** ACT scores over 18: 83%; ACT scores over 24: 24%; ACT scores over 30: 3%.

Retention: 64% of full-time freshmen returned.

FACULTY

Total: 427, 66% full-time, 63% with terminal degrees.

Student/faculty ratio: 18:1.

ACADEMICS

Calendar: semesters. *Degrees:* bachelor's, master's, doctoral, post-master's, and postbachelor's certificates.

Special study options: academic remediation for entering students, adult/continuing education programs, advanced placement credit, cooperative education, distance learning, double majors, honors programs, independent study, internships, part-time degree program, services for LD students, student-designed majors, summer session for credit. ***ROTC:*** Army (b).

Computers: 1,160 computers/terminals and 1,200 ports are available on campus for general student use. Students can access the following: campus intranet, computer help desk, free student e-mail accounts, online (class) grades, online (class) registration, online (class) schedules. Campuswide network is available. 100% of college-owned or -operated housing units are wired for high-speed Internet access. Wireless service is available via entire campus.
Library: John Vaughn Library. *Books:* 415,253 (physical), 64,575 (digital/electronic); *Serial titles:* 30,893 (physical), 92,125 (digital/electronic); *Databases:* 143. Weekly public service hours: 114.

STUDENT LIFE

Housing options: on-campus residence required for freshman year; coed, women-only, special housing for students with disabilities. Campus housing is university owned. Freshman applicants given priority for college housing.

Activities and organizations: drama/theater group, student-run newspaper, television station, choral group, marching band, national fraternities, national sororities.

Athletics Member NCAA. All Division II except golf (Division I). ***Intercollegiate sports:*** baseball M(s), basketball M(s)/W(s), football M(s), golf M(s)/W(s), soccer M(s)/W(s), softball W(s), tennis W(s). ***Intramural sports:*** basketball M/W, football M/W, golf M/W, racquetball M/W, soccer M/W, softball M/W, tennis M/W, volleyball M/W.

Campus security: 24-hour emergency response devices and patrols, late-night transport/escort service, controlled dormitory access.

Student services: health clinic, personal/psychological counseling, veterans affairs office.

COSTS & FINANCIAL AID

Costs (2018–19) ***Tuition:*** state resident $5528 full-time, $184 per credit hour part-time; nonresident $13,598 full-time, $453 per credit hour part-time. Full-time tuition and fees vary according to course load and program. Part-time tuition and fees vary according to course load and program. No tuition increase for student's term of enrollment. ***Required fees:*** $1122 full-time, $37 per credit hour part-time. ***Room and board:*** $7638; room only: $3952. Room and board charges vary according to board plan and housing facility. ***Payment plan:*** installment. ***Waivers:*** employees or children of employees.

Financial Aid Of all full-time matriculated undergraduates who enrolled in 2018, 3,972 applied for aid, 3,120 were judged to have need, 1,899 had their need fully met. 200 Federal Work-Study jobs (averaging $1654). 199 state and other part-time jobs (averaging $2271). In 2018, 204 non-need-based awards were made. ***Average percent of need met:*** 92. ***Average financial aid package:*** $13,552. ***Average need-based loan:*** $7501. ***Average need-based gift aid:*** $7270. ***Average non-need-based aid:*** $2764. ***Average indebtedness upon graduation:*** $19,652.

APPLYING

Standardized Tests *Required:* ACT (for admission).

Options: electronic application, deferred entrance.

Application fee: $25.

Required: high school transcript, minimum 2.7 GPA, upper 50% of class or minimum ACT composite of 20. ***Required for some:*** essay or personal statement, letters of recommendation, interview.

Notification: continuous (freshmen), continuous (transfers).

CONTACT

Ms. Damita Cunningham, Assistant Director, Admissions and Recruitment, Northeastern State University, Case Building Room 220, 701 N. Grand Avenue, Tahlequah, OK 74464. *Phone:* 918-444-2207. *Toll-free phone:* 800-722-9614. *E-mail:* cunningham@nsuok.edu.

Northwestern Oklahoma State University

Alva, Oklahoma

http://www.nwosu.edu/

- **State-supported** comprehensive, founded 1897, part of Oklahoma State Regents for Higher Education
- **Rural** 70-acre campus
- **Endowment** $35.7 million
- **Coed** 1,773 undergraduate students, 81% full-time, 59% women, 41% men
- **Moderately difficult** entrance level, 62% of applicants were admitted

UNDERGRAD STUDENTS

1,430 full-time, 343 part-time. Students come from 47 states and territories; 18 other countries; 24% are from out of state; 8% Black or African American, non-Hispanic/Latino; 10% Hispanic/Latino; 0.5% Asian, non-Hispanic/Latino; 0.1% Native Hawaiian or other Pacific Islander, non-Hispanic/Latino; 8% American Indian or Alaska Native, non-Hispanic/Latino; 2% Two or more races, non-Hispanic/Latino; 6% Race/ethnicity unknown; 2% international; 11% transferred in; 30% live on campus.

Freshmen:

Admission: 1,170 applied, 730 admitted, 373 enrolled. ***Average high school GPA:*** 3.3. ***Test scores:*** SAT evidence-based reading and writing scores over 500: 5%; SAT math scores over 500: 6%; ACT scores over 18: 63%; SAT evidence-based reading and writing scores over 600: 2%; SAT math scores over 600: 2%; ACT scores over 24: 17%; SAT math scores over 700: 1%; ACT scores over 30: 1%.

Retention: 60% of full-time freshmen returned.

FACULTY

Total: 159, 57% full-time, 48% with terminal degrees.

Student/faculty ratio: 15:1.

ACADEMICS

Calendar: semesters. *Degrees:* certificates, bachelor's, master's, and doctoral.

Special study options: academic remediation for entering students, adult/continuing education programs, advanced placement credit, cooperative education, distance learning, honors programs, independent study, internships, off-campus study, part-time degree program, services for LD students, study abroad, summer session for credit.

Computers: 260 computers/terminals are available on campus for general student use. Students can access the following: campus intranet, free student e-mail accounts, online (class) grades, online (class) registration, online (class) schedules. Campuswide network is available. 100% of college-owned or -operated housing units are wired for high-speed Internet access. Wireless service is available via classrooms, computer centers, computer labs, learning centers, libraries, student centers.

Library: J. W. Martin Library. *Books:* 91,123 (physical), 213,917 (digital/electronic); *Serial titles:* 23,390 (physical), 6 (digital/electronic); *Databases:* 45. Weekly public service hours: 84; students can reserve study rooms.

STUDENT LIFE

Housing options: on-campus residence required for freshman year; men-only, women-only. Campus housing is university owned. Freshman campus housing is guaranteed.

Activities and organizations: drama/theater group, student-run newspaper, radio and television station, choral group, marching band, Student Government Association, Aggie Club, Delta Mu Delta, Baptist Student Union, SOEA.

Athletics Member NCAA. All Division II. ***Intercollegiate sports:*** baseball M(s), basketball M(s)/W(s), cheerleading M(s)/W(s), cross-country running M(s)/W(s), football M(s), golf M(s)/W(s), soccer W(s), softball W(s), track and field W(s), volleyball W(s). ***Intramural sports:*** basketball M/W, football M/W, sand volleyball M/W, softball M/W, volleyball M/W.

Campus security: 24-hour emergency response devices and patrols, late-night transport/escort service.

Student services: personal/psychological counseling, veterans affairs office.

COSTS & FINANCIAL AID

Costs (2018–19) ***Tuition:*** state resident $6382 full-time; nonresident $13,823 full-time. Full-time tuition and fees vary according to course load, degree level, location, and program. Part-time tuition and fees vary according to course load, degree level, location, and program. No tuition increase for student's term of enrollment. ***Required fees:*** $653 full-time. ***Room and board:*** $4480; room only: $1780. Room and board charges vary according to board plan. ***Payment plan:*** installment. ***Waivers:*** senior citizens and employees or children of employees.

Financial Aid Of all full-time matriculated undergraduates who enrolled in 2018, 1,170 applied for aid, 856 were judged to have need.

APPLYING

Standardized Tests *Required:* SAT or ACT (for admission).

Options: electronic application, early admission.

Application fee: $15.

Required: high school transcript. ***Required for some:*** essay or personal statement, minimum 2.7 GPA, 3 letters of recommendation.

Application deadlines: rolling (freshmen), rolling (out-of-state freshmen), rolling (transfers).

Notification: continuous (freshmen), continuous (out-of-state freshmen), continuous (transfers).

CONTACT

Ms. Paige Fischer, Director of Recruitment, Northwestern Oklahoma State University, 709 Oklahoma Boulevard, Alva, OK 73717-2799. *Phone:* 580-327-8546. *Fax:* 580-327-8699. *E-mail:* recruit@nwosu.edu.

Oklahoma Baptist University
Shawnee, Oklahoma
http://www.okbu.edu/

- **Independent Southern Baptist** comprehensive, founded 1910
- **Small-town** 125-acre campus with easy access to Oklahoma City
- **Endowment** $116.2 million
- **Coed** 1,870 undergraduate students, 95% full-time, 60% women, 40% men
- **Moderately difficult** entrance level, 64% of applicants were admitted

UNDERGRAD STUDENTS
1,785 full-time, 85 part-time. Students come from 45 states and territories; 41 other countries; 36% are from out of state; 5% Black or African American, non-Hispanic/Latino; 2% Hispanic/Latino; 1% Asian, non-Hispanic/Latino; 0.3% Native Hawaiian or other Pacific Islander, non-Hispanic/Latino; 5% American Indian or Alaska Native, non-Hispanic/Latino; 13% Two or more races, non-Hispanic/Latino; 3% Race/ethnicity unknown; 4% international; 4% transferred in; 67% live on campus.

Freshmen:
Admission: 4,434 applied, 2,817 admitted, 527 enrolled. ***Average high school GPA:*** 3.7. ***Test scores:*** ACT scores over 18: 411%; ACT scores over 24: 185%; ACT scores over 30: 55%.

Retention: 78% of full-time freshmen returned.

FACULTY
Total: 187, 58% full-time, 49% with terminal degrees.

Student/faculty ratio: 11:1.

ACADEMICS
Calendar: 4-1-4. *Degrees:* associate, bachelor's, and master's.

Special study options: academic remediation for entering students, advanced placement credit, cooperative education, double majors, honors programs, independent study, internships, off-campus study, part-time degree program, services for LD students, student-designed majors, study abroad, summer session for credit. ***ROTC:*** Air Force (c).

Computers: 175 computers/terminals are available on campus for general student use. Students can access the following: computer help desk, free student e-mail accounts, online (class) grades, online (class) registration, online (class) schedules, campus portal, online course work. Campuswide network is available. 100% of college-owned or -operated housing units are wired for high-speed Internet access. Wireless service is available via entire campus.

Library: Mabee Learning Center. *Books:* 162,334 (physical), 188,606 (digital/electronic); *Serial titles:* 1,140 (physical); *Databases:* 60. Weekly public service hours: 91; students can reserve study rooms.

STUDENT LIFE
Housing options: on-campus residence required through junior year; men-only, women-only. Campus housing is university owned. Freshman campus housing is guaranteed.

Activities and organizations: drama/theater group, student-run newspaper, television station, choral group, marching band, Campus Activities Board, University Concert Series, Student Foundation, Blitz Week Activities, Canterbury.

Athletics Member NCAA, NCCAA. All NCAA Division II except cross-country running (Division I), golf (Division I), men's and women's swimming and diving (Division I). ***Intercollegiate sports:*** baseball M(s), basketball M(s)/W(s), cross-country running M(s)/W(s), football M(s), golf M(s)/W(s), lacrosse W(s), soccer M(s)/W(s), softball W(s), swimming and diving M(s)/W(s), tennis M(s)/W(s), track and field M(s)/W(s), volleyball W(s). ***Intramural sports:*** archery M/W, basketball M/W, bowling M/W, cheerleading W, football M/W, racquetball M/W, riflery M/W, rock climbing M/W, sand volleyball M/W, soccer M/W, softball M/W, table tennis M/W, tennis M/W, ultimate Frisbee M/W, volleyball M/W.

Campus security: 24-hour emergency response devices and patrols, late-night transport/escort service, controlled dormitory access.

Student services: health clinic, personal/psychological counseling.

COSTS & FINANCIAL AID
Costs (2019–20) ***Comprehensive fee:*** $37,354 includes full-time tuition ($26,584), mandatory fees ($3280), and room and board ($7490). Part-time tuition: $864 per credit hour. ***Required fees:*** $3280 per term part-time. ***College room only:*** $3390.

Financial Aid Of all full-time matriculated undergraduates who enrolled in 2018, 1,465 applied for aid, 1,366 were judged to have need, 323 had their need fully met. 120 Federal Work-Study jobs (averaging $911). In 2018, 422 non-need-based awards were made. ***Average percent of need met:*** 84. ***Average financial aid package:*** $24,192. ***Average need-based loan:*** $4028. ***Average need-based gift aid:*** $9460. ***Average non-need-based aid:*** $9972. ***Average indebtedness upon graduation:*** $24,451.

APPLYING
Standardized Tests *Required:* SAT or ACT (for admission).

Options: electronic application, early admission, deferred entrance.

Required: high school transcript, minimum 3.0 GPA. ***Required for some:*** essay or personal statement, interview.

Application deadlines: rolling (freshmen), 8/1 (transfers).

Notification: continuous (freshmen), continuous until 9/1 (transfers).

CONTACT
Mr. Bruce Perkins, Vice President of Enrollment Management, Oklahoma Baptist University, 500 West University, Shawnee, OK 74804. *Phone:* 405-585-5120. *Toll-free phone:* 800-654-3285. *Fax:* 405-585-5017. *E-mail:* bruce.perkins@okbu.edu.

Oklahoma Christian University
Oklahoma City, Oklahoma
http://www.oc.edu/

- **Independent** comprehensive, founded 1950, affiliated with Church of Christ
- **Suburban** 200-acre campus with easy access to Oklahoma City
- **Coed** 1,905 undergraduate students, 93% full-time, 50% women, 50% men
- **Moderately difficult** entrance level, 65% of applicants were admitted

UNDERGRAD STUDENTS
1,767 full-time, 138 part-time. Students come from 42 states and territories; 36 other countries; 54% are from out of state; 5% Black or African American, non-Hispanic/Latino; 7% Hispanic/Latino; 0.8% Asian, non-Hispanic/Latino; 0.1% Native Hawaiian or other Pacific Islander, non-Hispanic/Latino; 2% American Indian or Alaska Native, non-Hispanic/Latino; 7% Two or more races, non-Hispanic/Latino; 0.3% Race/ethnicity unknown; 5% international; 4% transferred in; 77% live on campus.

Freshmen:
Admission: 2,452 applied, 1,588 admitted, 454 enrolled. ***Average high school GPA:*** 3.6. ***Test scores:*** SAT evidence-based reading and writing scores over 500: 78%; SAT math scores over 500: 81%; ACT scores over 18: 91%; SAT evidence-based reading and writing scores over 600: 38%; SAT math scores over 600: 34%; ACT scores over 24: 47%; SAT evidence-based reading and writing scores over 700: 10%; SAT math scores over 700: 9%; ACT scores over 30: 15%.

Retention: 75% of full-time freshmen returned.

FACULTY
Total: 219, 46% full-time, 45% with terminal degrees.

Student/faculty ratio: 14:1.

ACADEMICS
Calendar: semesters. *Degrees:* certificates, bachelor's, master's, and postbachelor's certificates.

Special study options: academic remediation for entering students, accelerated degree program, advanced placement credit, cooperative education, distance learning, double majors, English as a second language, honors programs, independent study, internships, off-campus study, services for LD students, student-designed majors, study abroad, summer session for credit. ***ROTC:*** Army (c), Air Force (c).

Computers: 101 computers/terminals and 450 ports are available on campus for general student use. Students can access the following: campus intranet, computer help desk, free student e-mail accounts, online (class) grades, online (class) registration, online (class) schedules. Campuswide network is available. 100% of college-owned or -operated housing units are wired for high-speed Internet access. Wireless service is available via entire campus.

Library: Tom and Ada Beam Library. *Books:* 108,575 (physical), 66,843 (digital/electronic); *Serial titles:* 1,241 (physical), 42,377 (digital/electronic); *Databases:* 76. Weekly public service hours: 82; students can reserve study rooms.

STUDENT LIFE

Housing options: on-campus residence required through senior year; men-only, women-only, special housing for students with disabilities. Campus housing is university owned. Freshman campus housing is guaranteed.

Activities and organizations: drama/theater group, student-run newspaper, radio and television station, choral group, Ethos, Social Service Clubs, Student Government Association, Freshman Class club, Outreach mission organization.

Athletics Member NCAA. All Division II. ***Intercollegiate sports:*** baseball M(s), basketball M(s)/W(s), bowling M(c)/W(c), cheerleading M(c)/W(c), cross-country running M(s)/W(s), golf M(s), soccer M(s)/W(s), softball W(s), swimming and diving M(s)/W(s), track and field M(s)/W(s), ultimate Frisbee M(s)(c)/W(s)(c). ***Intramural sports:*** basketball M/W, bowling M/W, cross-country running M/W, football M/W, golf M/W, soccer M/W, softball M/W, swimming and diving M/W, table tennis M/W, tennis M/W, track and field M/W, volleyball M/W.

Campus security: 24-hour emergency response devices and patrols, late-night transport/escort service, controlled dormitory access.

Student services: health clinic, personal/psychological counseling, veterans affairs office.

COSTS & FINANCIAL AID

Costs (2019–20) ***Comprehensive fee:*** $32,300 includes full-time tuition ($23,450), mandatory fees ($300), and room and board ($8550). ***College room only:*** $4550.

Financial Aid Of all full-time matriculated undergraduates who enrolled in 2017, 1,455 applied for aid, 1,256 were judged to have need, 493 had their need fully met. In 2017, 505 non-need-based awards were made. ***Average percent of need met:*** 62. ***Average financial aid package:*** $24,125. ***Average need-based loan:*** $2166. ***Average need-based gift aid:*** $3387. ***Average non-need-based aid:*** $7396. ***Average indebtedness upon graduation:*** $30,395.

APPLYING

Standardized Tests *Required:* SAT or ACT (for admission).

Options: electronic application, early admission, deferred entrance.

Application fee: $25.

Required: high school transcript. ***Required for some:*** interview.

Application deadlines: rolling (freshmen), rolling (transfers).

Notification: continuous (freshmen), continuous (transfers).

CONTACT

Ms. Bonnie Howard, Director of Admissions and International Records, Oklahoma Christian University, Box 11000, Oklahoma City, OK 73136-1100. *Phone:* 405-425-5000. *Toll-free phone:* 800-877-5010. *Fax:* 405-425-5208. *E-mail:* admissions@oc.edu.

Oklahoma City University

Oklahoma City, Oklahoma

http://www.okcu.edu/

- **Independent United Methodist** comprehensive, founded 1904
- **Urban** 104-acre campus with easy access to Oklahoma City
- **Endowment** $104.5 million
- **Coed**
- 72% of applicants were admitted

FACULTY

Student/faculty ratio: 11:1.

ACADEMICS

Calendar: semesters. *Degrees:* bachelor's, master's, and doctoral.

Library: Dulaney Browne Library plus 1 other. *Books:* 279,046 (physical), 372,318 (digital/electronic); *Serial titles:* 5,543 (physical), 621,360 (digital/electronic); *Databases:* 114. Weekly public service hours: 99; students can reserve study rooms.

STUDENT LIFE

Housing options: coed, special housing for students with disabilities. Campus housing is university owned and is provided by a third party. Freshman applicants given priority for college housing.

Activities and organizations: drama/theater group, student-run newspaper, television station, choral group, Tri-Beta, Multicultural Student Association, Student Nursing Associate, Fellowship of Christian Athletes, national fraternities, national sororities.

Athletics Member NAIA.

Campus security: 24-hour emergency response devices and patrols, late-night transport/escort service, controlled dormitory access.

Student services: health clinic, personal/psychological counseling.

COSTS & FINANCIAL AID

Costs (2018–19) ***One-time required fee:*** $360. ***Comprehensive fee:*** $39,922 includes full-time tuition ($27,276), mandatory fees ($3750), and room and board ($8896). Full-time tuition and fees vary according to course load. Part-time tuition: $925 per credit hour. ***Required fees:*** $125 per credit hour part-time. ***College room only:*** $4100. Room and board charges vary according to board plan, housing facility, and student level. ***Payment plans:*** installment, deferred payment.

Financial Aid Of all full-time matriculated undergraduates who enrolled in 2018, 1,138 applied for aid, 964 were judged to have need, 807 had their need fully met. 240 Federal Work-Study jobs (averaging $1485). 253 state and other part-time jobs (averaging $1521). In 2018, 168 non-need-based awards were made. ***Average percent of need met:*** 62. ***Average financial aid package:*** $21,913. ***Average need-based loan:*** $3738. ***Average need-based gift aid:*** $18,439. ***Average non-need-based aid:*** $15,420. ***Average indebtedness upon graduation:*** $25,760.

APPLYING

Standardized Tests *Required:* SAT or ACT (for admission).

Options: electronic application, deferred entrance.

Application fee: $55.

Required: essay or personal statement, high school transcript. ***Required for some:*** interview.

CONTACT

Ms. Michelle Cook, Senior Director of Admissions, Oklahoma City University, 2501 North Blackwelder, Oklahoma City, OK 73106. *Phone:* 405-208-5055. *Toll-free phone:* 800-633-7242. *Fax:* 405-208-5916. *E-mail:* michelle.cook@okcu.edu.

Oklahoma Panhandle State University

Goodwell, Oklahoma

http://www.opsu.edu/

CONTACT

Mr. Bobby Jenkins, Registrar and Director of Admissions, Oklahoma Panhandle State University, PO Box 430, 323 Eagle Boulevard, Goodwell, OK 73939-0430. *Phone:* 580-349-1376. *Toll-free phone:* 800-664-6778. *Fax:* 580-349-1371. *E-mail:* opsu@opsu.edu.

Oklahoma State University

Stillwater, Oklahoma

http://www.okstate.edu/

- **State-supported** university, founded 1890, part of Oklahoma State University
- **Small-town** 840-acre campus with easy access to Oklahoma City, Tulsa
- **Endowment** $875.5 million
- **Coed** 20,574 undergraduate students, 86% full-time, 49% women, 51% men
- **Moderately difficult** entrance level, 74% of applicants were admitted

UNDERGRAD STUDENTS

17,684 full-time, 2,890 part-time. Students come from 57 states and territories; 66 other countries; 27% are from out of state; 4% Black or African American, non-Hispanic/Latino; 8% Hispanic/Latino; 2% Asian, non-Hispanic/Latino; 0.1% Native Hawaiian or other Pacific Islander, non-Hispanic/Latino; 4% American Indian or Alaska Native, non-Hispanic/Latino; 10% Two or more races, non-Hispanic/Latino; 0.1% Race/ethnicity unknown; 4% international; 7% transferred in; 43% live on campus.

Freshmen:
Admission: 14,405 applied, 10,629 admitted, 4,166 enrolled. *Average high school GPA:* 3.6. *Test scores:* SAT evidence-based reading and writing scores over 500: 91%; SAT math scores over 500: 87%; ACT scores over 18: 96%; SAT evidence-based reading and writing scores over 600: 48%; SAT math scores over 600: 41%; ACT scores over 24: 60%; SAT evidence-based reading and writing scores over 700: 8%; SAT math scores over 700: 9%; ACT scores over 30: 16%.
Retention: 82% of full-time freshmen returned.

FACULTY
Total: 1,320, 80% full-time, 80% with terminal degrees.
Student/faculty ratio: 20:1.

ACADEMICS
Calendar: semesters. *Degrees:* bachelor's, master's, doctoral, post-master's, and postbachelor's certificates.
Special study options: accelerated degree program, advanced placement credit, distance learning, double majors, English as a second language, freshman honors college, honors programs, independent study, internships, off-campus study, part-time degree program, services for LD students, student-designed majors, study abroad, summer session for credit. *ROTC:* Army (b), Air Force (b).
Unusual degree programs: 3-2 business administration; accounting, special education, biochemistry, early childhood education.
Computers: Students can access the following: campus intranet, computer help desk, free student e-mail accounts, online (class) grades, online (class) registration, online (class) schedules, Computer labs. Campuswide network is available. 99% of college-owned or -operated housing units are wired for high-speed Internet access. Wireless service is available via entire campus.
Library: Edmon Low Library plus 3 others. Weekly public service hours: 146; study areas open 24 hours, 5–7 days a week; students can reserve study rooms.

STUDENT LIFE
Housing options: on-campus residence required for freshman year; coed, men-only, women-only, special housing for students with disabilities. Campus housing is university owned. Freshman applicants given priority for college housing.
Activities and organizations: drama/theater group, student-run newspaper, radio and television station, choral group, marching band, national fraternities, national sororities.
Athletics Member NCAA. All Division I. *Intercollegiate sports:* baseball M(s), basketball M(s)/W(s), cheerleading M(s)/W(s), cross-country running M(s)/W(s), equestrian sports W(s), football M(s), golf M(s)/W(s)(c), soccer M(c)/W(s), softball W(s), tennis M(s)/W(s), track and field M(s)/W(s), wrestling M(s). *Intramural sports:* archery M(c)/W(c), badminton M/W, baseball M(c), basketball M/W, bowling M/W, crew M(c)/W(c), cross-country running M(c)/W(c), football M/W, golf M/W, lacrosse M(c)/W(c), racquetball M/W, riflery M(c)/W(c), rock climbing M/W, rowing M(c)/W(c), rugby M(c)/W(c), sailing M(c)/W(c), soccer M/W, softball M/W, swimming and diving M/W, table tennis M/W, tennis M/W, triathlon M(c)/W(c), ultimate Frisbee M/W, volleyball M/W, water polo M/W, weight lifting M/W, wrestling M/W.
Campus security: 24-hour emergency response devices and patrols, student patrols, late-night transport/escort service, controlled dormitory access.
Student services: health clinic, personal/psychological counseling, legal services, veterans affairs office.

COSTS & FINANCIAL AID
Costs (2018–19) *One-time required fee:* $95. *Tuition:* state resident $5357 full-time, $179 per credit hour part-time; nonresident $20,877 full-time, $696 per credit hour part-time. Full-time tuition and fees vary according to program. Part-time tuition and fees vary according to course load and program. No tuition increase for student's term of enrollment. *Required fees:* $3662 full-time, $122 per credit hour part-time. *Room and board:* $8996; room only: $5096. Room and board charges vary according to board plan and housing facility. *Payment plan:* installment. *Waivers:* children of alumni, senior citizens, and employees or children of employees.
Financial Aid Of all full-time matriculated undergraduates who enrolled in 2017, 12,479 applied for aid, 9,712 were judged to have need, 1,145 had their need fully met. 348 Federal Work-Study jobs (averaging $2506). 4,486 state and other part-time jobs (averaging $3160). In 2017, 4844 non-need-based awards were made. *Average percent of need met:* 74. *Average financial aid package:* $15,272. *Average need-based loan:* $4160. *Average need-based gift aid:* $7822. *Average non-need-based aid:* $6448. *Average indebtedness upon graduation:* $24,701.

APPLYING
Standardized Tests *Required:* SAT or ACT (for admission).
Options: electronic application, deferred entrance.
Application fee: $40.
Required for some: essay or personal statement.
Application deadlines: rolling (freshmen), rolling (out-of-state freshmen), rolling (transfers).
Notification: continuous (freshmen), continuous (out-of-state freshmen), continuous (transfers).

CONTACT
Jeff Hartman, Director of Undergraduate Admissions, Oklahoma State University, Stillwater, OK 74078. *Phone:* 405-744-5358. *Toll-free phone:* 800-233-5019. *Fax:* 405-744-5285. *E-mail:* jeffrey.hartman@okstate.edu.

Oklahoma State University Institute of Technology

Okmulgee, Oklahoma

http://www.osuit.edu/

- **State-supported** primarily 2-year, founded 1946, part of Oklahoma State University
- **Small-town** 160-acre campus with easy access to Tulsa
- **Endowment** $7.6 million
- **Coed**
- **Noncompetitive** entrance level

FACULTY
Student/faculty ratio: 15:1.

ACADEMICS
Calendar: trimesters. *Degrees:* associate and bachelor's.
Library: Oklahoma State University Institute of Technology Library. *Books:* 9,520 (physical), 147,054 (digital/electronic); *Serial titles:* 149 (physical), 70,987 (digital/electronic); *Databases:* 106. Weekly public service hours: 73; students can reserve study rooms.

STUDENT LIFE
Housing options: on-campus residence required for freshman year; coed, men-only. Campus housing is university owned. Freshman applicants given priority for college housing.
Activities and organizations: Phi Theta Kappa, Visual Communications Collective, Air Conditioning and Refrigeration Club, Future Chefs Association, Association of Information Technology Professionals.
Campus security: 24-hour emergency response devices and patrols, late-night transport/escort service, controlled dormitory access.
Student services: health clinic, personal/psychological counseling, veterans affairs office.

COSTS & FINANCIAL AID
Costs (2018–19) *Tuition:* state resident $4350 full-time, $145 per credit hour part-time; nonresident $9960 full-time, $332 per credit hour part-time. Full-time tuition and fees vary according to course level, course load, degree level, location, program, and student level. Part-time tuition and fees vary according to course level, course load, degree level, location, program, and student level. *Required fees:* $1200 full-time, $40 per credit hour part-time. *Room and board:* $6988. Room and board charges vary according to board plan and housing facility.
Financial Aid Of all full-time matriculated undergraduates who enrolled in 2018, 1,419 applied for aid, 1,267 were judged to have need, 8 had their need fully met. In 2018, 29 non-need-based awards were made. *Average percent of need met:* 53. *Average financial aid package:* $10,027. *Average need-based loan:* $3659. *Average need-based gift aid:* $7229. *Average non-need-based aid:* $1956. *Financial aid deadline:* 6/30.

APPLYING
Standardized Tests *Required for some:* SAT or ACT (for admission). *Recommended:* ACT (for admission).

Options: deferred entrance.

Required: high school transcript.

CONTACT
Kyle Gregorio, Assistant Registrar, Oklahoma State University Institute of Technology, 1801 E. 4th Street, Okmulgee, OK 74447. *Phone:* 918-293-5274. *Toll-free phone:* 800-722-4471. *Fax:* 918-293-4643. *E-mail:* kyleg@okstate.edu.

Oklahoma State University–Oklahoma City

Oklahoma City, Oklahoma

http://www.osuokc.edu/

- **State-supported** primarily 2-year, founded 1961, part of Oklahoma State University
- **Urban** 110-acre campus with easy access to Oklahoma City
- **Coed**
- **Noncompetitive** entrance level

FACULTY
Student/faculty ratio: 16:1.

ACADEMICS
Calendar: semesters. *Degrees:* certificates, associate, and bachelor's.
Library: Oklahoma State University, Oklahoma City Library. *Books:* 34,772 (physical), 198,662 (digital/electronic); *Serial titles:* 229 (physical); *Databases:* 72. Weekly public service hours: 75.

STUDENT LIFE
Housing options: college housing not available.

Activities and organizations: OSU-OKC Chapter of the OK Student Nurse Association, Veterinary Technician Association, Hispanic Student Association, Phi Theta Kappa, Student Government Association.

Campus security: 24-hour patrols, late-night transport/escort service.

Student services: veterans affairs office.

COSTS & FINANCIAL AID
Costs (2018–19) ***Tuition:*** state resident $3697 full-time, $147 per credit hour part-time; nonresident $10,778 full-time, $383 per credit hour part-time. Full-time tuition and fees vary according to program. Part-time tuition and fees vary according to program. ***Required fees:*** $781 full-time.

Financial Aid Of all full-time matriculated undergraduates who enrolled in 2017, 1,116 applied for aid, 1,116 were judged to have need, 856 had their need fully met. 192 Federal Work-Study jobs (averaging $275). In 2017, 611 non-need-based awards were made. ***Average percent of need met:*** 81. ***Average financial aid package:*** $1757. ***Average need-based gift aid:*** $2293. ***Average non-need-based aid:*** $1025. ***Average indebtedness upon graduation:*** $3119.

APPLYING
Options: electronic application.

Required for some: high school transcript.

CONTACT
Mr. Kyle Williams, Senior Director of Enrollment Management, Oklahoma State University–Oklahoma City, 900 North Portland Avenue, AD202, Oklahoma City, OK 73107. *Phone:* 405-945-9152. *Toll-free phone:* 800-560-4099. *E-mail:* wilkylw@osuokc.edu.

Oklahoma Wesleyan University

Bartlesville, Oklahoma

http://www.okwu.edu/

CONTACT
Samantha Peterson, Assistant Vice President of Enrollment, Oklahoma Wesleyan University, 2201 Silver Lake Road, Bartlesville, OK 74006. *Phone:* 866-222-8226. *Toll-free phone:* 866-222-8226. *Fax:* 918-335-6229. *E-mail:* admissions@okwu.edu.

Oral Roberts University

Tulsa, Oklahoma

http://www.oru.edu/

- **Independent interdenominational** comprehensive, founded 1963
- **Urban** 263-acre campus
- **Coed**
- **Moderately difficult** entrance level

FACULTY
Student/faculty ratio: 14:1.

ACADEMICS
Calendar: semesters. *Degrees:* certificates, diplomas, bachelor's, master's, and doctoral.
Library: John D. Messick Resources Center.

STUDENT LIFE
Housing options: on-campus residence required through senior year; men-only, women-only, special housing for students with disabilities.

Athletics Member NCAA. All Division I.

Campus security: 24-hour emergency response devices and patrols, late-night transport/escort service.

COSTS & FINANCIAL AID
Costs (2018–19) ***Comprehensive fee:*** $37,178 includes full-time tuition ($26,700), mandatory fees ($1028), and room and board ($9450). Full-time tuition and fees vary according to course load, degree level, and location. Part-time tuition: $1115 per contact hour. Part-time tuition and fees vary according to course load, degree level, and location. ***College room only:*** $4390. Room and board charges vary according to board plan and housing facility.

Financial Aid Of all full-time matriculated undergraduates who enrolled in 2017, 2,264 applied for aid, 2,057 were judged to have need, 882 had their need fully met. In 2017, 667 non-need-based awards were made. ***Average percent of need met:*** 90. ***Average financial aid package:*** $25,595. ***Average need-based loan:*** $7891. ***Average need-based gift aid:*** $17,721. ***Average non-need-based aid:*** $13,540. ***Average indebtedness upon graduation:*** $32,745.

APPLYING
Standardized Tests *Required:* SAT or ACT (for admission).

Options: deferred entrance.

Application fee: $35.

Required: essay or personal statement, high school transcript, minimum 2.0 GPA, 1 letter of recommendation, proof of immunization. ***Required for some:*** interview. ***Recommended:*** interview.

CONTACT
Director of Enrollment, Oral Roberts University, 7777 South Lewis Avenue, Tulsa, OK 74171. *Phone:* 918-495-6529. *Toll-free phone:* 800-678-8876. *Fax:* 918-495-6222. *E-mail:* admissions@oru.edu.

Randall University

Moore, Oklahoma

http://www.ru.edu/

CONTACT
Randall University, PO Box 7208, Moore, OK 73160. *Phone:* 405-912-9007. *Fax:* 405-912-9050. *E-mail:* recruitment@hc.edu.

Rogers State University

Claremore, Oklahoma

http://www.rsu.edu/

- **State-supported** comprehensive, founded 1909, part of Oklahoma State Regents for Higher Education
- **Small-town** 40-acre campus with easy access to Tulsa
- **Endowment** $13.1 million
- **Coed**
- **Noncompetitive** entrance level

FACULTY
Student/faculty ratio: 11:1.

ACADEMICS
Calendar: semesters. *Degrees:* associate, bachelor's, and master's. **Library:** Stratton Taylor Library. *Books:* 80,238 (physical), 298,063 (digital/electronic); *Serial titles:* 491 (physical), 67,126 (digital/electronic); *Databases:* 81. Weekly public service hours: 86; students can reserve study rooms.

STUDENT LIFE
Housing options: coed. Campus housing is university owned.

Activities and organizations: drama/theater group, student-run radio station, choral group, Student Government Association, Student Nurses Association, President's Leadership Class, Pre-Professional Health Club (Pre-SOMA), Student Athlete Advisory Committee, national fraternities, national sororities.

Athletics Member NCAA. All Division II.

Campus security: 24-hour patrols, student patrols, late-night transport/escort service, controlled dormitory access, state-certified law enforcement officers, comprehensive camera surveillance system.

Student services: health clinic, personal/psychological counseling, veterans affairs office.

COSTS & FINANCIAL AID
Costs (2018–19) ***Tuition:*** state resident $4380 full-time; nonresident $12,720 full-time. Full-time tuition and fees vary according to course level, course load, location, program, and student level. Part-time tuition and fees vary according to course level, course load, location, program, and student level. ***Required fees:*** $2820 full-time. ***Room and board:*** $8050; room only: $4600. Room and board charges vary according to housing facility.

Financial Aid Of all full-time matriculated undergraduates who enrolled in 2017, 1,831 applied for aid, 1,584 were judged to have need, 149 had their need fully met. 54 Federal Work-Study jobs (averaging $2900). In 2017, 152 non-need-based awards were made. ***Average percent of need met:*** 50. ***Average financial aid package:*** $9608. ***Average need-based loan:*** $3406. ***Average need-based gift aid:*** $7367. ***Average non-need-based aid:*** $5770. ***Average indebtedness upon graduation:*** $13,052.

APPLYING
Standardized Tests *Required:* SAT or ACT (for admission). *Recommended:* ACT (for admission).

Options: electronic application.

Application fee: $20.

Required: high school transcript. ***Required for some:*** minimum 2.7 GPA, minimum ACT composite of 20 or 2.70, GPA and top 50% rank for baccalaureate programs.

CONTACT
Ms. Joy Lin Hall, Director of Admissions, Rogers State University, 1701 West Will Rogers Boulevard, Claremore, OK 74017. *Phone:* 918-343-7546. *Toll-free phone:* 800-256-7511. *Fax:* 918-343-7595. *E-mail:* admissions@rsu.edu.

Southeastern Oklahoma State University

Durant, Oklahoma

http://www.se.edu/

- **State-supported** comprehensive, founded 1909, part of Oklahoma State Regents for Higher Education
- **Small-town** 276-acre campus
- **Endowment** $23.2 million
- **Coed**
- **Moderately difficult** entrance level

FACULTY
Student/faculty ratio: 18:1.

ACADEMICS
Calendar: semesters. *Degrees:* bachelor's, master's, and post-master's certificates.

Library: Henry G. Bennett Memorial Library plus 1 other. *Books:* 192,351 (physical), 17,845 (digital/electronic); *Serial titles:* 83 (physical), 2,534 (digital/electronic); *Databases:* 108. Weekly public service hours: 79; students can reserve study rooms.

STUDENT LIFE
Housing options: on-campus residence required for freshman year; coed, men-only, women-only, special housing for students with disabilities. Campus housing is university owned. Freshman campus housing is guaranteed.

Activities and organizations: drama/theater group, student-run newspaper, radio station, choral group, marching band, Baptist Collegiate Ministries, Greek Community, Student Government Association, Kappa Kappa Psi, Psychology Club, national fraternities, national sororities.

Athletics Member NCAA. All Division II.

Campus security: 24-hour emergency response devices and patrols, late-night transport/escort service, controlled dormitory access.

Student services: health clinic, personal/psychological counseling.

FINANCIAL AID
Financial Aid Of all full-time matriculated undergraduates who enrolled in 2017, 1,746 applied for aid, 1,577 were judged to have need, 52 had their need fully met. In 2017, 28 non-need-based awards were made. ***Average percent of need met:*** 64. ***Average financial aid package:*** $8802. ***Average need-based loan:*** $2035. ***Average need-based gift aid:*** $2092. ***Average non-need-based aid:*** $835. ***Average indebtedness upon graduation:*** $17,432.

APPLYING
Standardized Tests *Required:* SAT or ACT (for admission).

Options: electronic application.

Application fee: $20.

Required: high school transcript. ***Required for some:*** interview.

CONTACT
Southeastern Oklahoma State University, 1405 North 4th Avenue, Durant, OK 74701-0609. *Toll-free phone:* 800-435-1327.

Southern Nazarene University

Bethany, Oklahoma

http://www.snu.edu/

CONTACT
Dr. Linda Cantwell, Director of Recruitment, Southern Nazarene University, 6729 Northwest 39th Expressway, Bethany, OK 73008. *Phone:* 405-491-6324. *Toll-free phone:* 800-648-9899. *Fax:* 405-491-6320. *E-mail:* admiss@snu.edu.

Southwestern Christian University

Bethany, Oklahoma

http://www.swcu.edu/

CONTACT
Ms. Jessie Burpo, Admissions Counselor, Southwestern Christian University, PO Box 340, Bethany, OK 73008-0340. *Phone:* 405-789-7661 Ext. 3432. *Fax:* 405-495-0078. *E-mail:* admissions@swcu.edu.

Southwestern Oklahoma State University

Weatherford, Oklahoma

http://www.swosu.edu/

CONTACT
Ms. Cassie Jones, Admissions Coordinator, Southwestern Oklahoma State University, John Hays Administration Building, Room 108-C, Weatherford, OK 73096. *Phone:* 580-774-3009. *Fax:* 580-774-3795. *E-mail:* cassie.jones@swosu.edu.

Spartan College of Aeronautics and Technology
Tulsa, Oklahoma
http://www.spartan.edu/

CONTACT
Mr. Mark Fowler, Vice President of Student Records and Finance, Spartan College of Aeronautics and Technology, 8820 East Pine Street, Tulsa, OK 74115. *Phone:* 918-836-6886. *Toll-free phone:* 800-331-1204.

University of Central Oklahoma
Edmond, Oklahoma
http://www.uco.edu/

- **State-supported** comprehensive, founded 1890, part of Oklahoma State Regents for Higher Education
- **Suburban** 210-acre campus with easy access to Oklahoma City
- **Endowment** $25.7 million
- **Coed**
- **Minimally difficult** entrance level

FACULTY
Student/faculty ratio: 18:1.

ACADEMICS
Calendar: semesters. *Degrees:* certificates, associate, bachelor's, and master's.
Library: Max Chambers Library plus 1 other. *Books:* 555,825 (physical), 296,818 (digital/electronic); *Serial titles:* 23,218 (physical), 124,803 (digital/electronic); *Databases:* 239. Weekly public service hours: 107; students can reserve study rooms.

STUDENT LIFE
Housing options: coed, men-only, women-only. Campus housing is university owned and leased by the school.

Activities and organizations: drama/theater group, student-run newspaper, radio and television station, choral group, marching band, Student Government Association, Student Programming Board, International Student Council, Panhellenic Council, Interfraternity Council, national fraternities, national sororities.

Athletics Member NCAA. All Division II.

Campus security: 24-hour emergency response devices and patrols, late-night transport/escort service.

Student services: health clinic, personal/psychological counseling, women's center, veterans affairs office.

COSTS & FINANCIAL AID
Costs (2018–19) ***Tuition:*** state resident $6482 full-time, $216 per credit hour part-time; nonresident $17,369 full-time, $579 per credit hour part-time. Full-time tuition and fees vary according to course level, course load, degree level, location, and program. Part-time tuition and fees vary according to course level, course load, degree level, location, and program. No tuition increase for student's term of enrollment. ***Required fees:*** $1005 full-time, $34 per credit hour part-time. ***Room and board:*** $8050; room only: $3900. Room and board charges vary according to board plan and housing facility.

Financial Aid Of all full-time matriculated undergraduates who enrolled in 2016, 7,448 applied for aid, 6,334 were judged to have need, 621 had their need fully met. 3,125 Federal Work-Study jobs (averaging $4739). In 2016, 396 non-need-based awards were made. ***Average percent of need met:*** 52. ***Average financial aid package:*** $9809. ***Average need-based loan:*** $3959. ***Average need-based gift aid:*** $6245. ***Average non-need-based aid:*** $1541. ***Average indebtedness upon graduation:*** $26,939.

APPLYING
Standardized Tests *Required:* SAT or ACT (for admission). *Required for some:* SAT and SAT Subject Tests or ACT (for admission). *Recommended:* SAT (for admission), ACT (for admission).

Options: electronic application, deferred entrance.

Application fee: $50.

Required: high school transcript, minimum 2.7 GPA, rank in upper 50% of high school class; composite ACT score of 20; 2.7 GPA in core curriculum classes.

CONTACT
Mr. John Stephens, Director of Undergraduate Admissions, University of Central Oklahoma, Office of Undergraduate Admissions, 100 North University Drive, Box 151, Edmond, OK 73034-5209. *Phone:* 405-974-2727. *Fax:* 405-974-3841. *E-mail:* onestop@uco.edu.

University of Oklahoma
Norman, Oklahoma
http://www.ou.edu/

- **State-supported** university, founded 1890
- **Suburban** 3955-acre campus with easy access to Oklahoma City
- **Endowment** $1.1 billion
- **Coed**
- **Moderately difficult** entrance level

FACULTY
Student/faculty ratio: 18:1.

ACADEMICS
Calendar: semesters. *Degrees:* certificates, bachelor's, master's, doctoral, and postbachelor's certificates.
Library: Bizzell Memorial Library plus 5 others. *Books:* 4.4 million (physical), 1.4 million (digital/electronic); *Serial titles:* 71,289 (physical), 128,934 (digital/electronic); *Databases:* 311. Weekly public service hours: 114; students can reserve study rooms.

STUDENT LIFE
Housing options: on-campus residence required for freshman year; coed, men-only, women-only, special housing for students with disabilities. Campus housing is university owned. Freshman campus housing is guaranteed.

Activities and organizations: drama/theater group, student-run newspaper, radio and television station, choral group, marching band, Campus Activities Council Soonerthon, Campus Activities Council Homecoming, Engineers Club, Relay For Life, The Big Event, national fraternities, national sororities.

Athletics Member NCAA. All Division I except football (Division I-A).

Campus security: 24-hour emergency response devices and patrols, late-night transport/escort service, controlled dormitory access, crime prevention programs, police bicycle patrols, self-defense classes, emergency notification system, lighted pathways/sidewalks.

Student services: health clinic, personal/psychological counseling, women's center, legal services, veterans affairs office.

COSTS & FINANCIAL AID
Costs (2018–19) ***Tuition:*** state resident $4788 full-time, $160 per credit hour part-time; nonresident $20,169 full-time, $672 per credit hour part-time. Full-time tuition and fees vary according to course load, degree level, location, and program. Part-time tuition and fees vary according to course load, degree level, location, and program. No tuition increase for student's term of enrollment. ***Required fees:*** $4275 full-time, $134 per credit hour part-time, $127 per term part-time. ***Room and board:*** $10,994; room only: $6378. Room and board charges vary according to board plan and housing facility.

Financial Aid Of all full-time matriculated undergraduates who enrolled in 2017, 11,601 applied for aid, 8,927 were judged to have need, 7,401 had their need fully met. 533 Federal Work-Study jobs (averaging $3191). 105 state and other part-time jobs (averaging $9887). In 2017, 2106 non-need-based awards were made. ***Average percent of need met:*** 85. ***Average financial aid package:*** $14,017. ***Average need-based loan:*** $4464. ***Average need-based gift aid:*** $6261. ***Average non-need-based aid:*** $2452. ***Average indebtedness upon graduation:*** $30,641.

APPLYING
Standardized Tests *Required:* SAT or ACT (for admission).

Options: electronic application.

Application fee: $40.

Required: essay or personal statement, high school transcript, 15 specified curricular units.

CONTACT
Mr. Jeff Blahnik, Director of Admissions, University of Oklahoma, 1000 Asp Avenue, Room 127, Norman, OK 73019-3032. *Phone:* 405-325-2151. *Toll-free phone:* 800-234-6868. *Fax:* 405-325-7478. *E-mail:* admissions@ou.edu.

University of Oklahoma Health Sciences Center

Oklahoma City, Oklahoma

http://www.ouhsc.edu/

- **State-supported** upper-level, founded 1890, part of University of Oklahoma
- **Urban** 300-acre campus with easy access to Oklahoma City
- **Endowment** $312.6 million
- **Coed**

FACULTY
Student/faculty ratio: 10:1.

ACADEMICS
Calendar: semesters. *Degrees:* bachelor's, master's, doctoral, post-master's, and postbachelor's certificates.
Library: Robert M. Bird Health Sciences Library plus 1 other. *Books:* 286,469 (physical), 19,136 (digital/electronic); *Serial titles:* 158 (physical), 26,678 (digital/electronic); *Databases:* 157. Weekly public service hours: 111.

STUDENT LIFE
Housing options: coed. Campus housing is university owned.
Activities and organizations: student-run radio station, OU Health Sciences Center Student Association, OU College of Nursing Student Association, OU College of Medicine Student Association, OU College of Pharmacy Student Counsel, OU College of Allied Health Student Association.
Campus security: 24-hour emergency response devices and patrols, late-night transport/escort service.
Student services: health clinic, personal/psychological counseling, women's center, veterans affairs office.

COSTS
Costs (2018–19) ***Tuition:*** state resident $4788 full-time, $160 per credit hour part-time; nonresident $20,169 full-time, $672 per credit hour part-time. Full-time tuition and fees vary according to course level, course load, degree level, location, program, and student level. Part-time tuition and fees vary according to course level, course load, degree level, location, program, and student level. ***Required fees:*** $2365 full-time, $62 per credit hour part-time, $250 per term part-time. ***Room and board:*** Room and board charges vary according to location.

APPLYING
Options: electronic application, deferred entrance.

CONTACT
University of Oklahoma Health Sciences Center, PO Box 26901, Oklahoma City, OK 73190. *Phone:* 405-271-2347 Ext. 48916.

University of Science and Arts of Oklahoma

Chickasha, Oklahoma

http://www.usao.edu/

- **State-supported** 4-year, founded 1908, part of Oklahoma State Regents for Higher Education
- **Small-town** 75-acre campus with easy access to Oklahoma City
- **Endowment** $13.1 million
- **Coed**
- **Moderately difficult** entrance level

FACULTY
Student/faculty ratio: 12:1.

ACADEMICS
Calendar: trimesters. *Degree:* bachelor's.
Library: Nash Library plus 1 other. *Books:* 87,603 (physical), 4,798 (digital/electronic); *Serial titles:* 22 (physical), 10,500 (digital/electronic); *Databases:* 60. Weekly public service hours: 81.

STUDENT LIFE
Housing options: on-campus residence required for freshman year; coed. Campus housing is university owned. Freshman campus housing is guaranteed.
Activities and organizations: drama/theater group, student-run newspaper, television station, choral group, Student Activities Board, Volunteer Action Council, Psychology Club, Young Democrats, Young Conservatives, national fraternities.
Athletics Member NAIA.
Campus security: 24-hour emergency response devices and patrols, controlled dormitory access.
Student services: health clinic, personal/psychological counseling.

COSTS & FINANCIAL AID
Costs (2018–19) ***Tuition:*** state resident $6030 full-time, $201 per credit hour part-time; nonresident $16,380 full-time, $546 per credit hour part-time. No tuition increase for student's term of enrollment. ***Required fees:*** $1650 full-time, $50 per credit hour part-time. ***Room and board:*** $6100; room only: $3050. Room and board charges vary according to board plan and housing facility.
Financial Aid Of all full-time matriculated undergraduates who enrolled in 2018, 607 applied for aid, 545 were judged to have need, 65 had their need fully met. 158 Federal Work-Study jobs (averaging $1410). In 2018, 115 non-need-based awards were made. ***Average percent of need met:*** 66. ***Average financial aid package:*** $12,801. ***Average need-based loan:*** $3288. ***Average need-based gift aid:*** $10,513. ***Average non-need-based aid:*** $3969. ***Average indebtedness upon graduation:*** $21,276.

APPLYING
Standardized Tests *Required:* SAT or ACT (for admission).
Options: electronic application, deferred entrance.
Application fee: $40.
Required for some: high school transcript, minimum 3.0 GPA, minimum ACT score of 24 and 3.0 GPA/top 50% high school class, 3.0 GPA and top 25% high school class, or minimum ACT score of 22 and 3.0 GPA in 15-unit high school core. ***Recommended:*** minimum ACT score of 24 and 3.0 GPA/top 50% high school class, 3.0 GPA and top 25% high school class, or minimum ACT score of 22 and 3.0 GPA in 15-unit high school core.

CONTACT
Mrs. Laura Coponiti, Dean of Admissions and Financial Aid, University of Science and Arts of Oklahoma, 1727 West Alabama, Chickasha, OK 73018-5322. *Phone:* 405-574-1350. *Toll-free phone:* 800-933-8726. *Fax:* 405-574-1220. *E-mail:* usao-admissions@usao.edu.

The University of Tulsa

Tulsa, Oklahoma

http://www.utulsa.edu/

- **Independent** university, founded 1894, affiliated with Presbyterian Church (U.S.A.)
- **Urban** 209-acre campus with easy access to Tulsa
- **Coed** 3,295 undergraduate students, 96% full-time, 45% women, 55% men
- **Very difficult** entrance level, 41% of applicants were admitted

UNDERGRAD STUDENTS
3,162 full-time, 133 part-time. Students come from 44 states and territories; 55 other countries; 42% are from out of state; 6% Black or African American, non-Hispanic/Latino; 8% Hispanic/Latino; 5% Asian, non-Hispanic/Latino; 3% American Indian or Alaska Native, non-Hispanic/Latino; 5% Two or more races, non-Hispanic/Latino; 2% Race/ethnicity unknown; 15% international; 4% transferred in; 40% live on campus.

Freshmen:
Admission: 8,526 applied, 3,476 admitted, 806 enrolled. ***Test scores:*** SAT evidence-based reading and writing scores over 500: 94%; SAT math scores over 500: 95%; ACT scores over 18: 99%; SAT evidence-based reading and writing scores over 600: 70%; SAT math scores over 600: 65%; ACT scores over 24: 84%; SAT evidence-based reading and writing scores over 700: 26%; SAT math scores over 700: 30%; ACT scores over 30: 48%.
Retention: 88% of full-time freshmen returned.

FACULTY
Total: 465, 77% full-time.
Student/faculty ratio: 11:1.

ACADEMICS

Calendar: semesters. *Degrees:* bachelor's, master's, doctoral, and postbachelor's certificates.

Special study options: accelerated degree program, adult/continuing education programs, advanced placement credit, double majors, English as a second language, honors programs, independent study, internships, part-time degree program, services for LD students, student-designed majors, study abroad, summer session for credit. ***ROTC:*** Air Force (c).

Unusual degree programs: 3-2 business administration; engineering; accountancy, mathematics, athletic training, biochemistry, biology, chemistry, computer science, cyber security, geosciences, geophysics, history, physics, women's and gender studies.

Computers: 710 computers/terminals and 250 ports are available on campus for general student use. Students can access the following: campus intranet, computer help desk, free student e-mail accounts, online (class) grades, online (class) registration, online (class) schedules. Campuswide network is available. 100% of college-owned or -operated housing units are wired for high-speed Internet access. Wireless service is available via entire campus.

Library: McFarlin Library plus 1 other. *Books:* 1.2 million (physical), 460,240 (digital/electronic); *Serial titles:* 59,171 (digital/electronic); *Databases:* 289. Weekly public service hours: 94; study areas open 24 hours, 5–7 days a week; students can reserve study rooms.

STUDENT LIFE

Housing options: on-campus residence required through sophomore year; coed, men-only, women-only, special housing for students with disabilities. Campus housing is university owned. Freshman campus housing is guaranteed.

Activities and organizations: drama/theater group, student-run newspaper, radio and television station, choral group, marching band, Student Association, Residence Hall Association, Pre-Professional organizations, intramural sports, Greek life, national fraternities, national sororities.

Athletics Member NCAA. All Division I except football (Division I-A). ***Intercollegiate sports:*** basketball M(s)/W(s), cheerleading M/W, crew W(s), cross-country running M(s)/W(s), golf W(s)(c), soccer M(s)/W(s), softball W(s), tennis M(s)/W(s), track and field M(s)/W(s), volleyball W(s). ***Intramural sports:*** badminton M/W, basketball M/W, bowling M/W, crew M(c), cross-country running M/W, football M/W, golf W, lacrosse M(c), racquetball M/W, rugby M(c), soccer M/W, softball M/W, squash M/W, table tennis M/W, tennis M/W, track and field M/W, volleyball M/W, weight lifting M/W.

Campus security: 24-hour emergency response devices and patrols, late-night transport/escort service, controlled dormitory access.

Student services: health clinic, personal/psychological counseling, legal services, veterans affairs office.

COSTS & FINANCIAL AID

Costs (2019–20) ***One-time required fee:*** $485. ***Comprehensive fee:*** $53,688 includes full-time tuition ($41,698), mandatory fees ($540), and room and board ($11,450). Part-time tuition: $1497 per credit hour.

Financial Aid Of all full-time matriculated undergraduates who enrolled in 2018, 1,848 applied for aid, 1,596 were judged to have need, 566 had their need fully met. 500 Federal Work-Study jobs (averaging $2523). In 2018, 939 non-need-based awards were made. ***Average percent of need met:*** 69. ***Average financial aid package:*** $30,423. ***Average need-based loan:*** $4217. ***Average need-based gift aid:*** $28,067. ***Average non-need-based aid:*** $10,689. ***Average indebtedness upon graduation:*** $35,985.

APPLYING

Standardized Tests *Required:* SAT or ACT (for admission).

Options: electronic application, early admission, early action, deferred entrance.

Application fee: $50.

Required: essay or personal statement, high school transcript. ***Recommended:*** interview.

Application deadlines: rolling (freshmen), rolling (transfers).

Notification: continuous (freshmen), continuous (transfers).

CONTACT

Ms. Casey Reed, Dean of Admission, The University of Tulsa, 800 South Tucker Drive, Tulsa, OK 74104. *Phone:* 918-631-2307. *Toll-free phone:* 800-331-3050. *Fax:* 918-631-5003. *E-mail:* admission@utulsa.edu.

See below for display ad and page 1148 for the College Close-Up.

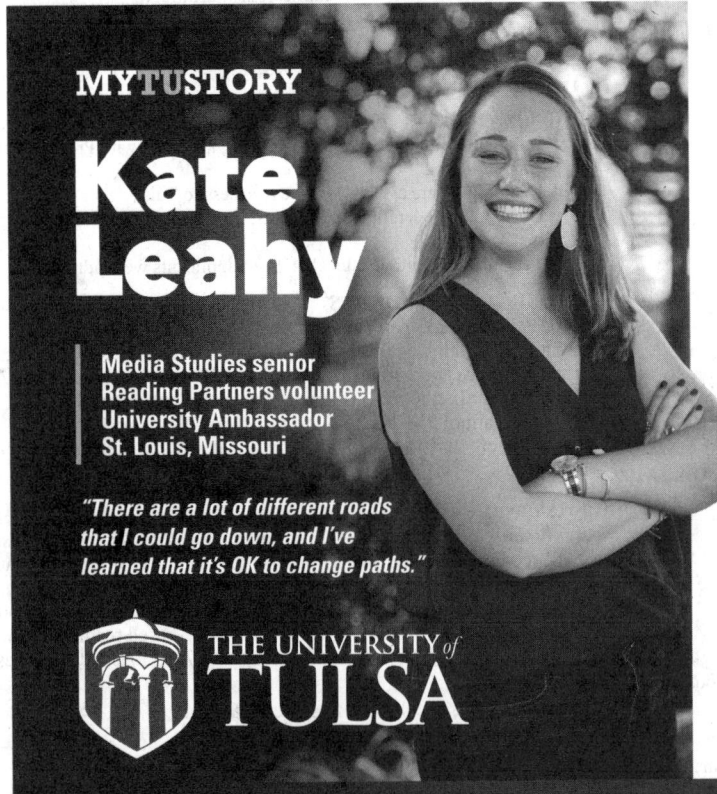

OREGON

American College of Healthcare Sciences

Portland, Oregon

http://www.achs.edu/

- **Independent** comprehensive
- **Coed**
- 50% of applicants were admitted

ACADEMICS

Degrees: certificates, diplomas, associate, bachelor's, master's, and postbachelor's certificates.

Library: ACHS Virtual Library. *Books:* 2,971 (digital/electronic); *Serial titles:* 17,514 (digital/electronic); *Databases:* 70.

APPLYING

Options: electronic application.

Required: essay or personal statement, high school transcript, recommendation from Admissions Committee. ***Required for some:*** letters of recommendation, interview.

CONTACT

American College of Healthcare Sciences, 5005 SW Macadam Avenue, Portland, OR 97239-3719. *Toll-free phone:* 800-487-8839.

Birthingway College of Midwifery

Portland, Oregon

http://www.birthingway.edu/

CONTACT

Director of Admission, Birthingway College of Midwifery, 12113 SE Foster Road, Portland, OR 97299. *Phone:* 503-760-3131. *E-mail:* info@birthingway.edu.

Concordia University

Portland, Oregon

http://www.cu-portland.edu/

CONTACT

Ms. Bobi Swan, Dean of Admission, Concordia University, 2811 Northeast Holman, Portland, OR 97211-6099. *Phone:* 503-493-6526. *Toll-free phone:* 800-321-9371. *Fax:* 503-280-8531. *E-mail:* admissions@cu-portland.edu.

Corban University

Salem, Oregon

http://www.corban.edu/

- **Independent Christian** comprehensive, founded 1935
- **Suburban** 145-acre campus with easy access to Portland
- **Coed**
- **Moderately difficult** entrance level

FACULTY

Student/faculty ratio: 14:1.

ACADEMICS

Calendar: semesters. *Degrees:* associate, bachelor's, master's, and doctoral.

Library: Corban University Library. *Books:* 81,025 (physical), 126,255 (digital/electronic); *Databases:* 14. Students can reserve study rooms.

STUDENT LIFE

Housing options: on-campus residence required through junior year; men-only, women-only. Campus housing is university owned. Freshman campus housing is guaranteed.

Activities and organizations: drama/theater group, student-run newspaper, choral group, Corban Recreation, Corban Community Garden, Stories of Glory, Dens and Leviathans, Corban Students for LIfe.

Athletics Member NAIA, NCCAA.

Campus security: 24-hour emergency response devices and patrols, student patrols, late-night transport/escort service, controlled dormitory access.

Student services: health clinic, personal/psychological counseling, veterans affairs office.

COSTS & FINANCIAL AID

Costs (2018–19) ***One-time required fee:*** $150. ***Comprehensive fee:*** $43,271 includes full-time tuition ($32,380), mandatory fees ($660), and room and board ($10,231). Full-time tuition and fees vary according to course load, degree level, program, and reciprocity agreements. Part-time tuition: $1350 per credit hour. Part-time tuition and fees vary according to course load, degree level, program, and reciprocity agreements. ***Required fees:*** $330 per term part-time. ***College room only:*** $5852. Room and board charges vary according to board plan.

Financial Aid Of all full-time matriculated undergraduates who enrolled in 2017, 789 applied for aid, 730 were judged to have need, 109 had their need fully met. 163 Federal Work-Study jobs (averaging $1820). In 2017, 95 non-need-based awards were made. ***Average percent of need met:*** 71. ***Average financial aid package:*** $23,452. ***Average need-based loan:*** $3738. ***Average need-based gift aid:*** $21,022. ***Average non-need-based aid:*** $4879. ***Average indebtedness upon graduation:*** $40,239.

APPLYING

Standardized Tests *Required:* SAT or ACT (for admission).

Options: electronic application.

Application fee: $40.

Required: essay or personal statement, high school transcript, minimum 2.7 GPA, 2 letters of recommendation.

CONTACT

Jordan Lindsey, Associate Director of Admissions, Corban University, 5000 Deer Park Drive, SE, Salem, OR 97301-9392. *Phone:* 503-375-7156. *Toll-free phone:* 800-845-3005. *Fax:* 503-585-4316. *E-mail:* admissions@corban.edu.

Eastern Oregon University

La Grande, Oregon

http://www.eou.edu/

- **State-supported** comprehensive, founded 1929
- **Rural** 121-acre campus
- **Endowment** $11.3 million
- **Coed** 2,744 undergraduate students, 62% full-time, 60% women, 40% men
- **Minimally difficult** entrance level, 98% of applicants were admitted

UNDERGRAD STUDENTS

1,689 full-time, 1,055 part-time. 32% are from out of state; 2% Black or African American, non-Hispanic/Latino; 11% Hispanic/Latino; 2% Asian, non-Hispanic/Latino; 3% Native Hawaiian or other Pacific Islander, non-Hispanic/Latino; 2% American Indian or Alaska Native, non-Hispanic/Latino; 5% Two or more races, non-Hispanic/Latino; 3% Race/ethnicity unknown; 1% international; 15% transferred in; 15% live on campus.

Freshmen:

Admission: 1,010 applied, 994 admitted, 320 enrolled. ***Average high school GPA:*** 3.4. ***Test scores:*** SAT evidence-based reading and writing scores over 500: 61%; SAT math scores over 500: 59%; ACT scores over 18: 78%; SAT evidence-based reading and writing scores over 600: 21%; SAT math scores over 600: 13%; ACT scores over 24: 18%; SAT evidence-based reading and writing scores over 700: 1%; SAT math scores over 700: 1%; ACT scores over 30: 1%.

Retention: 68% of full-time freshmen returned.

FACULTY

Total: 172, 65% full-time, 55% with terminal degrees.

Student/faculty ratio: 17:1.

ACADEMICS

Calendar: quarters. *Degrees:* certificates, associate, bachelor's, master's, and postbachelor's certificates.

Special study options: academic remediation for entering students, adult/continuing education programs, advanced placement credit, cooperative education, distance learning, double majors, external degree program, honors programs, independent study, internships, off-campus study, part-time degree program, services for LD students, student-designed majors, study abroad, summer session for credit. ***ROTC:*** Army (b).

Computers: Students can access the following: free student e-mail accounts, online (class) grades, online (class) registration, online (class) schedules. Campuswide network is available. 100% of college-owned or -operated housing units are wired for high-speed Internet access. Wireless service is available via entire campus.

Library: Pierce Library. *Books:* 356,951 (physical), 66,379 (digital/electronic); *Serial titles:* 392 (physical), 145 (digital/electronic); *Databases:* 139. Weekly public service hours: 90; students can reserve study rooms.

STUDENT LIFE

Housing options: on-campus residence required for freshman year; coed, special housing for students with disabilities. Campus housing is university owned. Freshman applicants given priority for college housing.

Activities and organizations: drama/theater group, student-run newspaper, radio station, choral group, Outdoor Program, Pre-Professional Health Club, Student Government, International Student Association, Chemistry Club.

Athletics Member NAIA. ***Intercollegiate sports:*** basketball M(s)/W(s), cross-country running M(s)/W(s), football M(s), soccer M(s)/W(s), softball W(s), track and field M(s)/W(s), volleyball W(s), wrestling M(s)/W(s). ***Intramural sports:*** basketball M/W, football M, rock climbing M(c)/W(c), soccer M/W, softball M/W, volleyball M/W.

Campus security: 24-hour emergency response devices, late-night transport/escort service, controlled dormitory access.

Student services: health clinic, personal/psychological counseling, women's center.

FINANCIAL AID

Financial Aid Of all full-time matriculated undergraduates who enrolled in 2017, 1,533 applied for aid, 1,313 were judged to have need, 152 had their need fully met. 148 Federal Work-Study jobs (averaging $1995). In 2017, 172 non-need-based awards were made. ***Average percent of need met:*** 56. ***Average financial aid package:*** $10,016. ***Average need-based loan:*** $4153. ***Average need-based gift aid:*** $8135. ***Average non-need-based aid:*** $1996. ***Average indebtedness upon graduation:*** $27,975.

APPLYING

Standardized Tests *Required:* SAT or ACT (for admission). *Required for some:* SAT and SAT Subject Tests or ACT (for admission).

Options: electronic application, early admission, early action, deferred entrance.

Application fee: $50.

Required: high school transcript, minimum 2.8 GPA. ***Required for some:*** essay or personal statement, 2 letters of recommendation.

Application deadlines: 9/1 (freshmen), 9/1 (transfers), 2/1 (early action).

Notification: continuous (freshmen), continuous (transfers), rolling (early action).

CONTACT

Gina Galaviz, Director, Admissions, Eastern Oregon University, 1 University Boulevard, La Grande, OR 97850-2899. *Phone:* 541-962-3496. *Toll-free phone:* 800-452-8639. *Fax:* 541-962-3418. *E-mail:* admissions@eou.edu.

George Fox University

Newberg, Oregon

http://www.georgefox.edu/

CONTACT

Ms. Lindsay Knox, Director of Undergraduate Admissions, George Fox University, 414 North Meridian Street, Newberg, OR 97132. *Phone:* 503-554-2240. *Toll-free phone:* 800-765-4369. *Fax:* 503-554-3110. *E-mail:* admissions@georgefox.edu.

Gutenberg College

Eugene, Oregon

http://www.gutenberg.edu/

- **Independent Christian** 4-year
- **Urban** campus
- **Coed**
- **Moderately difficult** entrance level

FACULTY

Student/faculty ratio: 2:1.

ACADEMICS

Degree: bachelor's.

STUDENT LIFE

Housing options: cooperative. Campus housing is university owned and leased by the school. Freshman applicants given priority for college housing.

Student services: personal/psychological counseling, legal services.

COSTS

Costs (2018–19) ***Comprehensive fee:*** $18,500 includes full-time tuition ($13,000), mandatory fees ($500), and room and board ($5000). ***Room and board:*** Room and board charges vary according to housing facility.

APPLYING

Standardized Tests *Required:* SAT or ACT (for admission), CLT (for admission).

Options: electronic application, early decision.

Application fee: $40.

Required: essay or personal statement, high school transcript, 2 letters of recommendation, interview.

CONTACT

Dr. Eliot Grasso, Director of Admissions and Development, Gutenberg College, 1883 University Street, Eugene, OR 97403. *Phone:* 541-683-5141. *Fax:* 541-683-6997. *E-mail:* egrasso@gutenberg.edu.

Lewis & Clark College

Portland, Oregon

http://www.lclark.edu/

- **Independent** comprehensive, founded 1867
- **Urban** 137-acre campus with easy access to Portland
- **Endowment** $236.6 million
- **Coed** 2,087 undergraduate students, 99% full-time, 61% women, 39% men
- **Very difficult** entrance level, 74% of applicants were admitted

UNDERGRAD STUDENTS

2,058 full-time, 29 part-time. Students come from 50 states and territories; 55 other countries; 80% are from out of state; 3% Black or African American, non-Hispanic/Latino; 12% Hispanic/Latino; 5% Asian, non-Hispanic/Latino; 0.5% Native Hawaiian or other Pacific Islander, non-Hispanic/Latino; 0.5% American Indian or Alaska Native, non-Hispanic/Latino; 6% Two or more races, non-Hispanic/Latino; 4% Race/ethnicity unknown; 8% international; 2% transferred in; 69% live on campus.

Freshmen:

Admission: 6,139 applied, 4,528 admitted, 562 enrolled. ***Average high school GPA:*** 3.9. ***Test scores:*** SAT evidence-based reading and writing scores over 500: 100%; SAT math scores over 500: 99%; ACT scores over 18: 101%; SAT evidence-based reading and writing scores over 600: 91%; SAT math scores over 600: 67%; ACT scores over 24: 97%; SAT evidence-based reading and writing scores over 700: 35%; SAT math scores over 700: 18%; ACT scores over 30: 47%.

Retention: 82% of full-time freshmen returned.

FACULTY

Total: 480, 44% full-time, 53% with terminal degrees.

Student/faculty ratio: 11:1.

ACADEMICS

Calendar: semesters. *Degrees:* bachelor's, master's, doctoral, and post-master's certificates.

Special study options: advanced placement credit, double majors, English as a second language, honors programs, independent study, internships, off-campus study, services for LD students, student-designed majors, study abroad, summer session for credit. ***ROTC:*** Army (c).

Unusual degree programs: 3-2 engineering with Columbia University (New York), Washington University in St. Louis, University of Southern California.

Computers: 440 computers/terminals are available on campus for general student use. Students can access the following: campus intranet, computer help desk, free student e-mail accounts, online (class) grades, online (class) registration, online (class) schedules. Campuswide network is available. 100% of college-owned or -operated housing units are wired for high-speed Internet access. Wireless service is available via entire campus.

Library: Aubrey Watzek Library plus 1 other. *Books:* 336,148 (physical), 313,729 (digital/electronic); *Serial titles:* 4,973 (physical), 56,436 (digital/electronic); *Databases:* 304. Weekly public service hours: 141; study areas open 24 hours, 5–7 days a week; students can reserve study rooms.

STUDENT LIFE

Housing options: on-campus residence required through sophomore year; coed, women-only. Campus housing is university owned. Freshman campus housing is guaranteed.

Activities and organizations: drama/theater group, student-run newspaper, radio station, choral group, Bacchus Menâ??s Ultimate Frisbee, Artemis Womenâ??s Ultimate Frisbee, International Affairs Symposium, Hillel, Black Student Union.

Athletics Member NCAA. All Division III except golf (Division II). ***Intercollegiate sports:*** baseball M, basketball M/W, crew M/W, cross-country running M/W, football M, golf M/W, lacrosse W(c), rugby M(c)/W(c), soccer M(c)/W, softball W, swimming and diving M/W, tennis M/W, track and field M/W, ultimate Frisbee M(c)/W(c), volleyball W. ***Intramural sports:*** football M/W, soccer M/W, water polo M/W.

Campus security: 24-hour emergency response devices and patrols, late-night transport/escort service, controlled dormitory access.

Student services: health clinic, personal/psychological counseling, veterans affairs office.

COSTS & FINANCIAL AID

Costs (2018–19) ***Comprehensive fee:*** $63,528 includes full-time tuition ($50,574), mandatory fees ($360), and room and board ($12,594). Part-time tuition: $2529 per credit hour. Part-time tuition and fees vary according to course load. ***Required fees:*** $18 per credit hour part-time. ***College room only:*** $7064. Room and board charges vary according to board plan and housing facility. ***Payment plan:*** installment. ***Waivers:*** employees or children of employees.

Financial Aid Of all full-time matriculated undergraduates who enrolled in 2018, 1,417 applied for aid, 1,161 were judged to have need, 443 had their need fully met. 903 Federal Work-Study jobs (averaging $2484). 222 state and other part-time jobs (averaging $4599). In 2018, 689 non-need-based awards were made. ***Average percent of need met:*** 85. ***Average financial aid package:*** $42,683. ***Average need-based loan:*** $4328. ***Average need-based gift aid:*** $35,666. ***Average non-need-based aid:*** $18,688. ***Average indebtedness upon graduation:*** $32,379.

APPLYING

Standardized Tests *Required:* SAT or ACT scores or Test-Optional Portfolio Path materials (for admission).

Options: electronic application, early decision, early action, deferred entrance.

Required: essay or personal statement, high school transcript, 1 letter of recommendation. ***Required for some:*** 2 letters of recommendation, graded writing sample, math or science sample, 2 letters of recommendation for Test Optional Portfolio Path. ***Recommended:*** interview.

Application deadlines: 1/15 (freshmen), 4/1 (transfers), 12/15 (early action).

Early decision deadline: 11/1.

Notification: 4/1 (freshmen), continuous (transfers), 12/15 (early decision), 1/1 (early action).

CONTACT

Lisa Meyer, Vice President and Dean for Enrollment Management, Lewis & Clark College, 0615 Southwest Palatine Hill Road, Portland, OR 97219-7899. *Phone:* 503-768-7040. *Toll-free phone:* 800-444-4111. *Fax:* 503-768-7055. *E-mail:* admissions@lclark.edu.

★ Linfield College

McMinnville, Oregon

http://www.linfield.edu/

- **Independent American Baptist Churches in the USA** 4-year, founded 1858, part of Linfield College
- **Small-town** 189-acre campus with easy access to Portland
- **Endowment** $124.5 million
- **Coed** 1,376 undergraduate students, 97% full-time, 61% women, 39% men
- **Moderately difficult** entrance level, 81% of applicants were admitted

UNDERGRAD STUDENTS

1,334 full-time, 42 part-time. Students come from 18 states and territories; 23 other countries; 42% are from out of state; 2% Black or African American, non-Hispanic/Latino; 17% Hispanic/Latino; 4% Asian, non-Hispanic/Latino; 1% Native Hawaiian or other Pacific Islander, non-Hispanic/Latino; 0.9% American Indian or Alaska Native, non-Hispanic/Latino; 8% Two or more races, non-Hispanic/Latino; 3% Race/ethnicity unknown; 4% international; 4% transferred in; 73% live on campus.

Freshmen:

Admission: 2,199 applied, 1,782 admitted, 326 enrolled. ***Average high school GPA:*** 3.7. ***Test scores:*** SAT evidence-based reading and writing scores over 500: 79%; SAT math scores over 500: 85%; ACT scores over 18: 93%; SAT evidence-based reading and writing scores over 600: 32%; SAT math scores over 600: 28%; ACT scores over 24: 35%; SAT evidence-based reading and writing scores over 700: 4%; SAT math scores over 700: 5%; ACT scores over 30: 12%.

Retention: 79% of full-time freshmen returned.

FACULTY

Total: 203, 61% full-time, 71% with terminal degrees.

Student/faculty ratio: 10:1.

ACADEMICS

Calendar: 4-1-4. *Degrees:* bachelor's and postbachelor's certificates (Linfield College includes the Linfield College McMinnville Campus in McMinnville, Oregon; the Linfield-Good Samaritan School of Nursing in Portland, Oregon(Portland Campus) and the Linfield College Adult Degree Program online).

Special study options: accelerated degree program, adult/continuing education programs, advanced placement credit, distance learning, double majors, English as a second language, external degree program, independent study, internships, off-campus study, part-time degree program, services for LD students, student-designed majors, study abroad, summer session for credit. ***ROTC:*** Air Force (c).

Unusual degree programs: 3-2 engineering with Washington State University, Oregon State University, University of Southern California.

Computers: 250 computers/terminals are available on campus for general student use. Students can access the following: computer help desk, free student e-mail accounts, online (class) grades, online (class) registration, online (class) schedules. Campuswide network is available. 100% of college-owned or -operated housing units are wired for high-speed Internet access. Wireless service is available via entire campus.

Library: Jereld R. Nicholson Library. *Books:* 192,329 (physical), 6,637 (digital/electronic); *Serial titles:* 1,785 (physical), 56,310 (digital/electronic); *Databases:* 192. Weekly public service hours: 95.

STUDENT LIFE

Housing options: on-campus residence required through junior year; coed, men-only, women-only, special housing for students with disabilities. Campus housing is university owned. Freshman campus housing is guaranteed.

Activities and organizations: drama/theater group, student-run newspaper, radio station, choral group, marching band, Hawaiian Club, Linfield Ultimate Players Association, Residence Hall Associations, International Club, Outdoor Club, national fraternities, national sororities.

Athletics Member NCAA. All Division III except golf (Division II). ***Intercollegiate sports:*** baseball M, basketball M/W, cross-country running M/W, football M, golf M/W, lacrosse W, soccer M/W, softball W, swimming and diving M/W, tennis M/W, track and field M/W, volleyball W. ***Intramural sports:*** archery M/W, basketball M/W, bowling M/W, football M/W, sand volleyball M/W, soccer M/W, softball M/W, ultimate Frisbee M/W, volleyball M/W.

Campus security: 24-hour emergency response devices and patrols, late-night transport/escort service, controlled dormitory access.

Student services: health clinic, personal/psychological counseling.

COSTS & FINANCIAL AID

Costs (2019–20) ***Comprehensive fee:*** $56,732 includes full-time tuition ($43,560), mandatory fees ($502), and room and board ($12,670). Part-time tuition: $1360 per semester hour. ***Required fees:*** $280 per year part-time. ***College room only:*** $6970.

Financial Aid Of all full-time matriculated undergraduates who enrolled in 2018, 1,144 applied for aid, 1,015 were judged to have need, 281 had their need fully met. 542 Federal Work-Study jobs (averaging $1455). 525 state and other part-time jobs (averaging $1269). In 2018, 126 non-need-based awards were made. ***Average percent of need met:*** 82. ***Average financial aid package:*** $36,593. ***Average need-based loan:*** $4371. ***Average need-based gift aid:*** $33,269. ***Average non-need-based aid:*** $20,340. ***Average indebtedness upon graduation:*** $34,792.

APPLYING

Standardized Tests *Required for some:* SAT or ACT (for admission).

Options: electronic application, early action, deferred entrance.

Required: essay or personal statement, high school transcript, 1 letter of recommendation. ***Recommended:*** interview.

Application deadlines: 2/1 (freshmen), 4/15 (transfers), 11/1 (early action).

Notification: continuous until 4/1 (freshmen), 5/15 (transfers), 1/15 (early action).

CONTACT

Ms. Lisa Knodle-Bragiel, Director of Admission, Linfield College, 900 SE Baker Street, McMinnville, OR 97128. *Phone:* 503-883-2213. *Toll-free phone:* 800-640-2287. *Fax:* 503-883-2472. *E-mail:* admission@linfield.edu.

See below for display ad and page 1030 for the College Close-Up.

Mount Angel Seminary

Saint Benedict, Oregon

http://www.mountangelabbey.org/seminary/

CONTACT

Registrar/Admissions Officer, Mount Angel Seminary, Saint Benedict, OR 97373. *Phone:* 503-845-3951 Ext. 14. *E-mail:* admissions@mtangel.edu.

Multnomah University

Portland, Oregon

http://www.multnomah.edu/

- **Independent interdenominational** comprehensive, founded 1936
- **Urban** 22-acre campus with easy access to Portland, OR
- **Endowment** $6.9 million
- **Coed**
- **Moderately difficult** entrance level

FACULTY

Student/faculty ratio: 12:1.

ACADEMICS

Calendar: semesters. *Degrees:* bachelor's, master's, doctoral, and postbachelor's certificates.

Library: John Mitchell Library. *Books:* 120,106 (physical), 152,698 (digital/electronic); *Serial titles:* 548 (physical), 20,000 (digital/electronic); *Databases:* 45. Weekly public service hours: 82; students can reserve study rooms.

STUDENT LIFE

Housing options: on-campus residence required through sophomore year; men-only, women-only, special housing for students with disabilities. Campus housing is university owned. Freshman campus housing is guaranteed.

Activities and organizations: choral group, Student Government, Commuter Life, Poetry Club, Brunch Chats, Res Life.

Athletics Member NAIA.

Campus security: 24-hour emergency response devices and patrols, controlled dormitory access.

Student services: personal/psychological counseling, veterans affairs office.

COSTS & FINANCIAL AID

Costs (2018–19) ***Comprehensive fee:*** $34,770 includes full-time tuition ($25,300), mandatory fees ($600), and room and board ($8870). Full-time tuition and fees vary according to course load, degree level, location, and program. Part-time tuition: $800 per quarter hour. Part-time tuition and fees vary according to course load, degree level, location, and program. ***Required fees:*** $155 per term part-time. ***Room and board:*** Room and board charges vary according to board plan and housing facility.

Financial Aid Of all full-time matriculated undergraduates who enrolled in 2009, 503 applied for aid, 441 were judged to have need, 11 had their need fully met. 75 Federal Work-Study jobs (averaging $1500). In 2009, 36 non-need-based awards were made. ***Average percent of need met:*** 50. ***Average financial aid package:*** $9211. ***Average need-based loan:*** $4094. ***Average need-based gift aid:*** $5846. ***Average non-need-based aid:*** $1848. ***Average indebtedness upon graduation:*** $21,020.

APPLYING

Standardized Tests *Recommended:* SAT or ACT (for admission).

Options: electronic application, deferred entrance.

Application fee: $40.

Required: essay or personal statement, high school transcript, minimum 2.5 GPA, 2 letters of recommendation.

CONTACT

Ms. Jenae Johnson, Admissions Counselor, Multnomah University, 8435 Northeast Glisan Street, Portland, OR 97220-5898. *Phone:* 503-251-6467. *Toll-free phone:* 877-251-6560. *Fax:* 503-254-1268. *E-mail:* admiss@multnomah.edu.

New Hope Christian College

Eugene, Oregon

http://www.newhope.edu/

CONTACT

Sarah Slater, Director of Admissions, New Hope Christian College, 2155 Bailey Hill Road, Eugene, OR 97405. *Phone:* 541-485-1780 Ext. 3115. *Toll-free phone:* 800-322-2638. *Fax:* 541-343-5801. *E-mail:* sarahslater@newhope.edu.

Northwest Christian University

Eugene, Oregon

http://www.nwcu.edu/

- **Independent Christian** comprehensive, founded 1895
- **Urban** 8-acre campus with easy access to Portland
- **Endowment** $14.3 million
- **Coed** 593 undergraduate students, 70% full-time, 61% women, 39% men
- **Minimally difficult** entrance level, 62% of applicants were admitted

UNDERGRAD STUDENTS

418 full-time, 175 part-time. Students come from 17 states and territories; 7 other countries; 21% are from out of state; 5% Black or African American, non-Hispanic/Latino; 6% Hispanic/Latino; 2% Asian, non-Hispanic/Latino; 1% Native Hawaiian or other Pacific Islander, non-Hispanic/Latino; 2% American Indian or Alaska Native, non-Hispanic/Latino; 10% Two or more races, non-Hispanic/Latino; 0.9% Race/ethnicity unknown; 1% international; 6% transferred in; 78% live on campus.

Freshmen:

Admission: 479 applied, 299 admitted, 100 enrolled. ***Average high school GPA:*** 3.5. ***Test scores:*** SAT evidence-based reading and writing scores over 500: 60%; SAT math scores over 500: 72%; ACT scores over 18: 76%; SAT evidence-based reading and writing scores over 600: 22%; SAT math scores over 600: 19%; ACT scores over 24: 19%; SAT math scores over 700: 3%; ACT scores over 30: 2%.

Retention: 71% of full-time freshmen returned.

FACULTY

Total: 76, 34% full-time, 22% with terminal degrees.

Student/faculty ratio: 15:1.

ACADEMICS

Calendar: quarters. *Degrees:* associate, bachelor's, master's, and postbachelor's certificates.

Special study options: academic remediation for entering students, accelerated degree program, adult/continuing education programs, advanced placement credit, cooperative education, distance learning, double majors, English as a second language, independent study, internships, part-time degree program, services for LD students, study abroad, summer session for credit. ***ROTC:*** Army (c).

Computers: 16 computers/terminals are available on campus for general student use. Students can access the following: campus intranet, computer help desk, free student e-mail accounts, online (class) grades, online (class) registration, online (class) schedules. Campuswide network is available. Wireless service is available via entire campus.

Library: Edward P. Kellenberger Library. *Books:* 53,806 (physical), 222,316 (digital/electronic); *Serial titles:* 285,351 (digital/electronic); *Databases:* 108. Weekly public service hours: 70.

STUDENT LIFE

Housing options: on-campus residence required through senior year; men-only, women-only. Campus housing is university owned. Freshman campus housing is guaranteed.

Activities and organizations: student-run newspaper, choral group, Embrace the City (community service), FeMystique (Social justice club), Beacon Boards (game board club), History Club, Psychology Club.

Athletics Member NAIA. ***Intercollegiate sports:*** basketball M(s)/W(s), cross-country running M(s)/W(s), golf M(s)/W(s), soccer M(s)/W(s), softball W(s), track and field M(s)/W(s), volleyball W(s). ***Intramural sports:*** basketball M/W, volleyball M/W.

Campus security: 24-hour emergency response devices and patrols, late-night transport/escort service, controlled dormitory access.

Student services: personal/psychological counseling.

COSTS & FINANCIAL AID

Costs (2019–20) ***Comprehensive fee:*** $41,110 includes full-time tuition ($31,200), mandatory fees ($210), and room and board ($9700).

Financial Aid Of all full-time matriculated undergraduates who enrolled in 2018, 323 applied for aid, 287 were judged to have need, 70 had their need fully met. 80 Federal Work-Study jobs (averaging $3250). 2 state and other part-time jobs (averaging $3250). In 2018, 65 non-need-based awards were made. ***Average percent of need met:*** 78. ***Average financial aid package:*** $24,320. ***Average need-based loan:*** $4716. ***Average need-based gift aid:*** $19,989. ***Average non-need-based aid:*** $10,045. ***Average indebtedness upon graduation:*** $28,617.

APPLYING

Standardized Tests *Required:* SAT or ACT (for admission).

Options: electronic application, deferred entrance.

Required: essay or personal statement, minimum 2.5 GPA. ***Required for some:*** high school transcript. ***Recommended:*** interview.

Application deadlines: rolling (freshmen), rolling (transfers).

Notification: continuous (freshmen), continuous (transfers).

CONTACT

Kacie Gerdrum, Dean of Admissions, Northwest Christian University, 828 E. 11th Ave., Eugene, OR 97401-3745. *Phone:* 541-684-7288. *Toll-free phone:* 877-463-6622. *Fax:* 541-684-7317. *E-mail:* kgerdrum@nwcu.edu.

Oregon Health & Science University

Portland, Oregon

http://www.ohsu.edu/

CONTACT

Oregon Health & Science University, 3181 Southwest Sam Jackson Park Road, Portland, OR 97239-3098. *Phone:* 503-494-0954.

Oregon Institute of Technology

Klamath Falls, Oregon

http://www.oit.edu/

- **State-supported** comprehensive, founded 1947
- **Small-town** 190-acre campus
- **Endowment** $7.9 million
- **Coed**
- **Moderately difficult** entrance level

FACULTY
Student/faculty ratio: 16:1.

ACADEMICS
Calendar: quarters. *Degrees:* certificates, associate, bachelor's, master's, and postbachelor's certificates.
Library:*Books:* 140,000 (physical); *Databases:* 70. Students can reserve study rooms.

STUDENT LIFE
Housing options: coed. Campus housing is university owned.

Activities and organizations: student-run newspaper, radio and television station, choral group, Phi Delta Theta, Christian Fellowship, International Club, Society of Women Engineers, Association of Student Mechanical Engineers, national fraternities.

Athletics Member NAIA.

Campus security: 24-hour emergency response devices and patrols, late-night transport/escort service.

Student services: health clinic, personal/psychological counseling, women's center, veterans affairs office.

COSTS & FINANCIAL AID
Costs (2018–19) ***Tuition:*** state resident $8277 full-time, $184 per credit hour part-time; nonresident $26,345 full-time, $585 per credit hour part-time. Full-time tuition and fees vary according to course load, location, program, and reciprocity agreements. Part-time tuition and fees vary according to course load, location, program, and reciprocity agreements. ***Required fees:*** $1710 full-time, $208 per credit hour part-time, $558 per term part-time. ***Room and board:*** $9640; room only: $5860. Room and board charges vary according to board plan and housing facility.

Financial Aid Of all full-time matriculated undergraduates who enrolled in 2016, 1,377 applied for aid, 1,341 were judged to have need, 86 had their need fully met. ***Average percent of need met:*** 39. ***Average financial aid package:*** $11,146. ***Average indebtedness upon graduation:*** $29,685.

APPLYING
Standardized Tests *Required:* SAT or ACT (for admission).

Options: electronic application, deferred entrance.

Application fee: $50.

Required: high school transcript, minimum 3.0 GPA.

CONTACT
Oregon Institute of Technology, 3201 Campus Drive, Klamath Falls, OR 97601-8801. *Toll-free phone:* 800-422-2017.

Oregon State University

Corvallis, Oregon

http://www.oregonstate.edu/

- **State-supported** university, founded 1868
- **Small-town** 422-acre campus
- **Endowment** $624.5 million
- **Coed**
- **Moderately difficult** entrance level

FACULTY
Student/faculty ratio: 18:1.

ACADEMICS
Calendar: quarters. *Degrees:* certificates, bachelor's, master's, doctoral, post-master's, and postbachelor's certificates.
Library: Valley Library plus 2 others. *Books:* 1.7 million (physical), 481,665 (digital/electronic); *Serial titles:* 2,376 (physical), 74,203 (digital/electronic); *Databases:* 150. Weekly public service hours: 138; study areas open 24 hours, 5–7 days a week; students can reserve study rooms.

STUDENT LIFE
Housing options: on-campus residence required for freshman year; coed, special housing for students with disabilities. Campus housing is university owned. Freshman applicants given priority for college housing.

Activities and organizations: drama/theater group, student-run newspaper, radio and television station, choral group, marching band, Ballroom Dance Club, Gaming Club, Organic Growers Club, Blood Drive Association, Residence Hall Association, national fraternities, national sororities.

Athletics Member NCAA. All Division I except football (Division I-A).

Campus security: 24-hour emergency response devices and patrols, student patrols, late-night transport/escort service, controlled dormitory access, crime prevention office.

Student services: health clinic, personal/psychological counseling, women's center, legal services.

COSTS & FINANCIAL AID
Costs (2018–19) ***One-time required fee:*** $350. ***Tuition:*** state resident $9390 full-time, $202 per credit hour part-time; nonresident $28,365 full-time, $608 per credit hour part-time. Full-time tuition and fees vary according to course load, location, and program. Part-time tuition and fees vary according to course load, location, and program. ***Required fees:*** $1776 full-time, $515 per term part-time. ***Room and board:*** $12,855; room only: $8895. Room and board charges vary according to board plan and housing facility.

Financial Aid Of all full-time matriculated undergraduates who enrolled in 2017, 12,517 applied for aid, 9,573 were judged to have need, 1,048 had their need fully met. 1,063 Federal Work-Study jobs (averaging $2832). In 2017, 3180 non-need-based awards were made. ***Average percent of need met:*** 68. ***Average financial aid package:*** $13,346. ***Average need-based loan:*** $5033. ***Average need-based gift aid:*** $7682. ***Average non-need-based aid:*** $5252. ***Average indebtedness upon graduation:*** $28,482.

APPLYING
Standardized Tests *Required:* SAT or ACT (for admission). *Required for some:* SAT Subject Tests (for admission).

Options: electronic application, early action, deferred entrance.

Application fee: $60.

Required: essay or personal statement, high school transcript, minimum 3.0 GPA.

CONTACT
Oregon State University, Corvallis, OR 97331. *Phone:* 541-737-4411. *Toll-free phone:* 800-291-4192.

Oregon State University–Cascades

Bend, Oregon

http://www.osucascades.edu/

CONTACT
Admissions Department, Oregon State University–Cascades, 2600 Northwest College Way, Bend, OR 97701. *Phone:* 541-322-3150. *E-mail:* cascadeadmit@osucascades.edu.

Pacific Northwest College of Art

Portland, Oregon

http://www.pnca.edu/

- **Independent** comprehensive, founded 1909
- **Urban** 2-acre campus with easy access to Portland
- **Endowment** $12.9 million
- **Coed**
- **Noncompetitive** entrance level

FACULTY
Student/faculty ratio: 9:1.

ACADEMICS
Calendar: semesters. *Degrees:* bachelor's and master's.
Library: Albert Solheim Library. *Books:* 34,806 (physical); *Serial titles:* 270 (physical); *Databases:* 52. Weekly public service hours: 87; students can reserve study rooms.

STUDENT LIFE
Housing options: on-campus residence required for freshman year; coed, men-only, women-only, special housing for students with disabilities. Campus housing is provided by a third party. Freshman campus housing is guaranteed.

Campus security: 24-hour emergency response devices, late-night transport/escort service, controlled dormitory access, entrance security guards and patrols during hours of operation.

Student services: personal/psychological counseling.

COSTS & FINANCIAL AID
Costs (2018–19) ***Tuition:*** $37,500 full-time, $1563 per credit hour part-time. Full-time tuition and fees vary according to degree level. Part-time tuition and fees vary according to course load and degree level. ***Required fees:*** $750 full-time, $75 per term part-time. ***Room only:*** $9486.

Financial Aid Of all full-time matriculated undergraduates who enrolled in 2006, 264 applied for aid, 238 were judged to have need, 13 had their need fully met. 33 Federal Work-Study jobs (averaging $1200). 33 state and other part-time jobs (averaging $1200). In 2006, 10 non-need-based awards were made. ***Average percent of need met:*** 54. ***Average financial aid package:*** $11,845. ***Average need-based loan:*** $4040. ***Average need-based gift aid:*** $4699. ***Average non-need-based aid:*** $2442. ***Average indebtedness upon graduation:*** $22,155.

APPLYING
Options: electronic application, early admission, deferred entrance.

Application fee: $45.

Required: essay or personal statement, portfolio of artwork. ***Required for some:*** high school transcript. ***Recommended:*** minimum 2.3 GPA.

CONTACT
Pacific Northwest College of Art, 511 NW Broadway, Portland, OR 97209.

★ Pacific University
Forest Grove, Oregon
http://www.pacificu.edu/

CONTACT
Ms. Karen Dunston, Executive Director, Pacific University, 2043 College Way, Forest Grove, OR 97116-1797. *Phone:* 503-352-2218. *Toll-free phone:* 877-722-8648. *Fax:* 503-352-2975. *E-mail:* admissions@pacificu.edu.

See below for display ad and page 1072 for the College Close-Up.

★ Pioneer Pacific College
Wilsonville, Oregon
http://www.pioneerpacific.edu/

CONTACT
Ms. Juli Lau, Vice President of Admissions, Pioneer Pacific College, 27375 Southwest Parkway Avenue, Wilsonville, OR 97070. *Phone:* 503-682-1862. *Toll-free phone:* 866-PPC-INFO. *Fax:* 503-682-1514. *E-mail:* info@pioneerpacific.edu.

Portland State University
Portland, Oregon
http://www.pdx.edu/

- **State-supported** university, founded 1946
- **Urban** 49-acre campus with easy access to Portland
- **Endowment** $75.2 million
- **Coed** 20,967 undergraduate students, 68% full-time, 54% women, 46% men
- **Moderately difficult** entrance level, 90% of applicants were admitted

UNDERGRAD STUDENTS
14,292 full-time, 6,675 part-time. Students come from 50 states and territories; 70 other countries; 16% are from out of state; 4% Black or African American, non-Hispanic/Latino; 15% Hispanic/Latino; 9% Asian, non-Hispanic/Latino; 0.7% Native Hawaiian or other Pacific Islander,

A ★ indicates that the school has detailed information with a Premium Profile on Petersons.com.

non-Hispanic/Latino; 1% American Indian or Alaska Native, non-Hispanic/Latino; 7% Two or more races, non-Hispanic/Latino; 5% Race/ethnicity unknown; 6% international; 13% transferred in; 9% live on campus.

Freshmen:
Admission: 6,743 applied, 6,082 admitted, 1,743 enrolled. ***Average high school GPA:*** 3.5. ***Test scores:*** SAT evidence-based reading and writing scores over 500: 79%; SAT math scores over 500: 77%; ACT scores over 18: 81%; SAT evidence-based reading and writing scores over 600: 41%; SAT math scores over 600: 27%; ACT scores over 24: 36%; SAT evidence-based reading and writing scores over 700: 6%; SAT math scores over 700: 3%; ACT scores over 30: 6%.

Retention: 74% of full-time freshmen returned.

FACULTY
Total: 1,528, 51% full-time, 52% with terminal degrees.

Student/faculty ratio: 18:1.

ACADEMICS
Calendar: quarters. *Degrees:* certificates, bachelor's, master's, doctoral, and postbachelor's certificates.

Special study options: academic remediation for entering students, accelerated degree program, adult/continuing education programs, advanced placement credit, cooperative education, distance learning, double majors, English as a second language, freshman honors college, honors programs, independent study, internships, off-campus study, part-time degree program, services for LD students, study abroad, summer session for credit. ***ROTC:*** Army (c), Navy (c), Air Force (c).

Computers: Students can access the following: campus intranet, computer help desk, free student e-mail accounts, online (class) grades, online (class) registration, online (class) schedules. Campuswide network is available. Wireless service is available via entire campus.
Library: Branford P. Millar Library plus 1 other. Students can reserve study rooms.

STUDENT LIFE
Housing options: coed, cooperative, special housing for students with disabilities. Campus housing is university owned. Freshman campus housing is guaranteed.

Activities and organizations: drama/theater group, student-run newspaper, radio station, choral group, national fraternities, national sororities.

Athletics Member NCAA. All Division I except football (Division I-AA). ***Intercollegiate sports:*** badminton M(c)/W(c), baseball M(c)/W(c), basketball M/W, crew M(c)/W(c), cross-country running M/W, fencing M(c)/W(c), golf W(c), ice hockey M(c), lacrosse M(c)/W(c), sailing M(c)/W(c), soccer M(c)/W, softball W, tennis M/W, track and field M/W, volleyball W, wrestling M(c)/W(c).

Campus security: 24-hour emergency response devices and patrols, late-night transport/escort service, controlled dormitory access.

Student services: health clinic, personal/psychological counseling, women's center, legal services, veterans affairs office.

COSTS & FINANCIAL AID
Costs (2019–20) ***Tuition:*** state resident $7695 full-time, $171 per credit hour part-time; nonresident $25,650 full-time, $570 per credit hour part-time. ***Required fees:*** $1410 full-time. ***Room and board:*** $13,482; room only: $9204.

Financial Aid Of all full-time matriculated undergraduates who enrolled in 2017, 10,347 applied for aid, 9,264 were judged to have need, 410 had their need fully met. In 2017, 72 non-need-based awards were made. ***Average percent of need met:*** 51. ***Average financial aid package:*** $10,562. ***Average need-based loan:*** $4513. ***Average need-based gift aid:*** $7066. ***Average non-need-based aid:*** $3337. ***Average indebtedness upon graduation:*** $26,867.

APPLYING
Standardized Tests *Required for some:* SAT or ACT (for admission).

Options: electronic application, early admission, deferred entrance.

Application fee: $50.

Required: high school transcript, minimum 3.0 GPA.

Application deadlines: rolling (freshmen), rolling (transfers).
Notification: continuous (freshmen), continuous (transfers).

CONTACT
Yohlunda Mosley, Assistant Vice President for Enrollment, Portland State University, PO Box 751, Portland, OR 97207-0751. *Toll-free phone:* 800-547-8887. *E-mail:* askadm@pdx.edu.

★ Reed College
Portland, Oregon
http://www.reed.edu/

- **Independent** comprehensive, founded 1908
- **Urban** 116-acre campus with easy access to Portland
- **Coed**
- **Very difficult** entrance level

FACULTY
Student/faculty ratio: 10:1.

ACADEMICS
Calendar: semesters. *Degrees:* bachelor's and master's.
Library: Eric V. Hauser Memorial Library plus 1 other. Study areas open 24 hours, 5–7 days a week.

STUDENT LIFE
Housing options: coed, women-only, cooperative, special housing for students with disabilities. Campus housing is university owned. Freshman campus housing is guaranteed.

Activities and organizations: drama/theater group, student-run newspaper, radio station, choral group.

Campus security: 24-hour emergency response devices and patrols, student patrols, late-night transport/escort service, controlled dormitory access.

Student services: health clinic, personal/psychological counseling, women's center, legal services.

COSTS & FINANCIAL AID
Costs (2018–19) ***Comprehensive fee:*** $70,550 includes full-time tuition ($56,030), mandatory fees ($310), and room and board ($14,210). Full-time tuition and fees vary according to degree level. Part-time tuition: $9440 per course. Part-time tuition and fees vary according to course load and degree level. ***College room only:*** $7440. Room and board charges vary according to board plan and housing facility.

Financial Aid Of all full-time matriculated undergraduates who enrolled in 2018, 833 applied for aid, 770 were judged to have need, 751 had their need fully met. ***Average percent of need met:*** 100. ***Average financial aid package:*** $44,317. ***Average need-based loan:*** $2727. ***Average need-based gift aid:*** $39,913. ***Average indebtedness upon graduation:*** $21,697. ***Financial aid deadline:*** 2/1.

APPLYING
Standardized Tests *Required:* SAT or ACT (for admission).

Options: electronic application, early admission, early decision, early action, deferred entrance.

Required: essay or personal statement, high school transcript, 2 letters of recommendation. ***Recommended:*** interview.

CONTACT
Office of Admission, Reed College, 3203 Southeast Woodstock Boulevard, Portland, OR 97202-8199. *Phone:* 800-547-4750. *Toll-free phone:* 800-547-4750. *Fax:* 503-777-7553. *E-mail:* admission@reed.edu.

See next page for display ad and page 1078 for the College Close-Up.

Southern Oregon University
Ashland, Oregon
http://www.sou.edu/

CONTACT
Mr. Kelly Moutsatson, Director of Admissions, Southern Oregon University, 1250 Siskiyou Boulevard, Ashland, OR 97520. *Phone:* 541-552-6411. *Toll-free phone:* 855-470-3377. *Fax:* 541-552-6614. *E-mail:* admissions@sou.edu.

University of Oregon

Eugene, Oregon

http://www.uoregon.edu/

- **State-supported** university, founded 1876
- **Suburban** 295-acre campus with easy access to Portland, Oregon
- **Endowment** $912.5 million
- **Coed** 19,101 undergraduate students, 92% full-time, 54% women, 46% men
- **Moderately difficult** entrance level, 83% of applicants were admitted

UNDERGRAD STUDENTS
17,550 full-time, 1,551 part-time. Students come from 53 states and territories; 83 other countries; 42% are from out of state; 2% Black or African American, non-Hispanic/Latino; 13% Hispanic/Latino; 6% Asian, non-Hispanic/Latino; 0.4% Native Hawaiian or other Pacific Islander, non-Hispanic/Latino; 0.6% American Indian or Alaska Native, non-Hispanic/Latino; 8% Two or more races, non-Hispanic/Latino; 2% Race/ethnicity unknown; 10% international; 6% transferred in; 22% live on campus.

Freshmen:
Admission: 24,474 applied, 20,404 admitted, 4,168 enrolled. ***Average high school GPA:*** 3.6. ***Test scores:*** SAT evidence-based reading and writing scores over 500: 91%; SAT math scores over 500: 90%; ACT scores over 18: 95%; SAT evidence-based reading and writing scores over 600: 53%; SAT math scores over 600: 44%; ACT scores over 24: 63%; SAT evidence-based reading and writing scores over 700: 9%; SAT math scores over 700: 9%; ACT scores over 30: 12%.

Retention: 85% of full-time freshmen returned.

FACULTY
Total: 1,670, 70% full-time, 90% with terminal degrees.

Student/faculty ratio: 17:1.

ACADEMICS
Calendar: quarters. *Degrees:* bachelor's, master's, doctoral, post-master's, and postbachelor's certificates.

Special study options: advanced placement credit, cooperative education, distance learning, double majors, English as a second language, honors programs, independent study, internships, off-campus study, part-time degree program, services for LD students, student-designed majors, study abroad, summer session for credit. ***ROTC:*** Army (b), Air Force (c).

Unusual degree programs: 3-2 engineering with Oregon State University.

Computers: 497 computers/terminals are available on campus for general student use. Students can access the following: campus intranet, computer help desk, free student e-mail accounts, online (class) grades, online (class) registration, online (class) schedules. Campuswide network is available. 100% of college-owned or -operated housing units are wired for high-speed Internet access. Wireless service is available via entire campus.

Library: Knight Library plus 6 others. *Books:* 1.7 million (physical), 927,771 (digital/electronic); *Serial titles:* 74,186 (physical), 157,063 (digital/electronic); *Databases:* 514. Weekly public service hours: 124; students can reserve study rooms.

STUDENT LIFE
Housing options: on-campus residence required for freshman year; coed, cooperative. Campus housing is university owned. Freshman applicants given priority for college housing.

Activities and organizations: drama/theater group, student-run newspaper, radio and television station, choral group, marching band, political and environmental action, cultural organizations, major-specific organizations, community service organizations, club sports, national fraternities, national sororities.

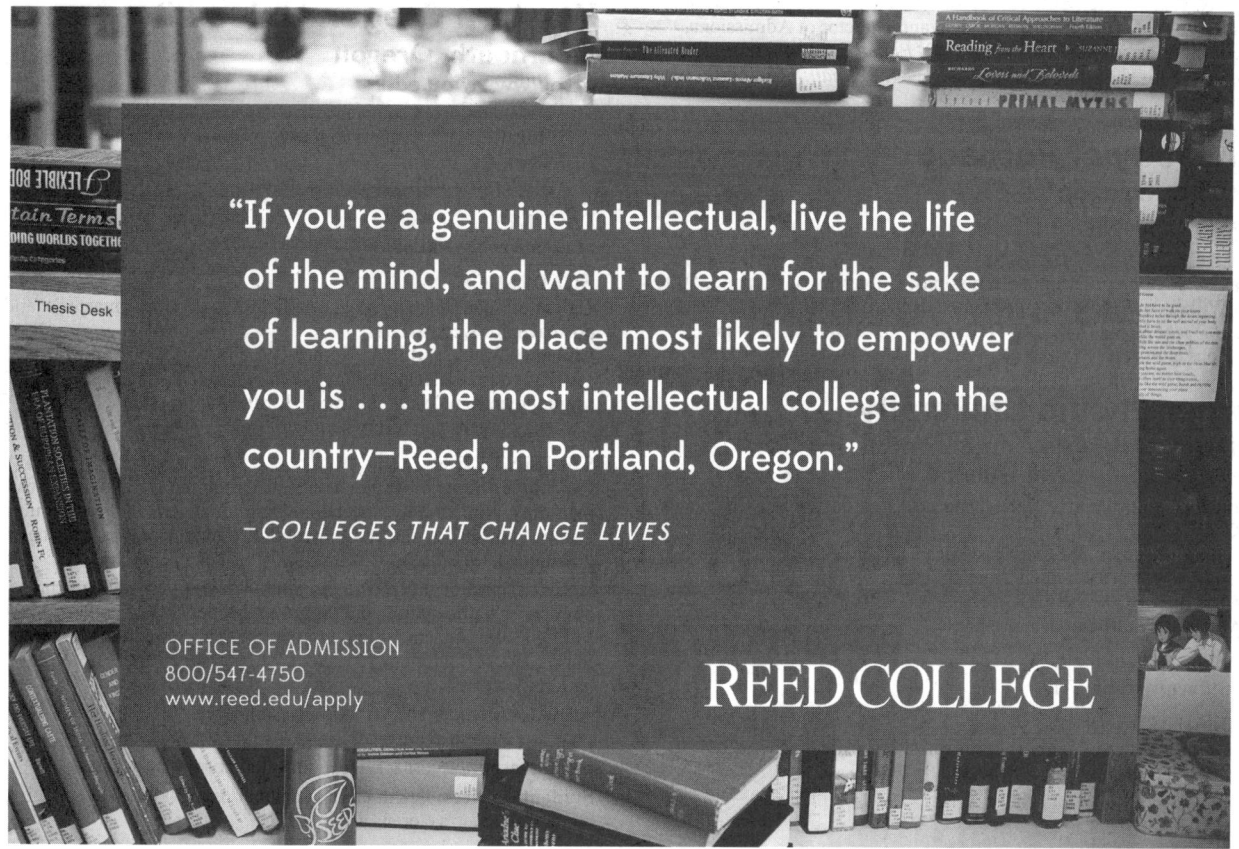

Athletics Member NCAA. All Division I except football (Division I-A). ***Intercollegiate sports:*** baseball M(s), basketball M(s)/W(s), cross-country running M(s)/W(s), golf M(s), lacrosse W(s), sand volleyball W(s), soccer W(s), softball W(s), tennis M(s)/W(s), track and field M(s)/W(s), volleyball W(s). ***Intramural sports:*** badminton M(c)/W(c), baseball M(c), basketball M/W, cross-country running M(c)/W(c), equestrian sports M(c)/W(c), fencing M(c), field hockey M/W, football M/W, golf M(c)/W(c), ice hockey M(c)/W(c), lacrosse M(c)/W(c), rock climbing M(c)/W(c), rowing M(c)/W(c), rugby M(c)/W(c), sailing M(c)/W(c), skiing (downhill) M(c)/W(c), soccer M(c)/W(c), softball M(c)/W(c), squash M(c)/W(c), swimming and diving M(c)/W(c), table tennis M(c)/W(c), tennis M(c)/W(c), track and field M/W, triathlon M(c)/W(c), ultimate Frisbee M(c)/W(c), volleyball M(c)/W(c), water polo M(c)/W(c), weight lifting M(c)/W(c).

Campus security: 24-hour emergency response devices and patrols, late-night transport/escort service, controlled dormitory access, Lighted pathways, emergency phones, self-defense classes.

Student services: health clinic, personal/psychological counseling, women's center, legal services, veterans affairs office.

COSTS & FINANCIAL AID

Costs (2018–19) ***One-time required fee:*** $430. ***Tuition:*** state resident $9765 full-time, $211 per credit hour part-time; nonresident $33,345 full-time, $741 per credit hour part-time. Full-time tuition and fees vary according to course load. Part-time tuition and fees vary according to course load. ***Required fees:*** $2133 full-time. ***Room and board:*** $12,963. Room and board charges vary according to board plan and housing facility. ***Payment plan:*** installment. ***Waivers:*** employees or children of employees.

Financial Aid Of all full-time matriculated undergraduates who enrolled in 2017, 10,529 applied for aid, 7,983 were judged to have need, 419 had their need fully met. 1,271 Federal Work-Study jobs (averaging $1726). 54 state and other part-time jobs (averaging $3277). In 2017, 2803 non-need-based awards were made. ***Average percent of need met:*** 55. ***Average financial aid package:*** $11,002. ***Average need-based loan:*** $4533. ***Average need-based gift aid:*** $9102. ***Average non-need-based aid:*** $5583. ***Average indebtedness upon graduation:*** $25,729.

APPLYING

Standardized Tests *Required:* SAT or ACT (for admission). *Required for some:* SAT and SAT Subject Tests or ACT (for admission).

Options: electronic application, early action, deferred entrance.

Application fee: $65.

Required: essay or personal statement, high school transcript, C+ or better in 15 college preparatory units.

Application deadlines: 1/15 (freshmen), 6/30 (transfers), 11/1 (early action).

Notification: 4/1 (freshmen), 12/15 (early action).

CONTACT

James Rawlins, Assistant Vice President and Director of Admissions, University of Oregon, Eugene, OR 97403. *Phone:* 541-346-3201. *Toll-free phone:* 800-232-3825. *Fax:* 541-346-5815. *E-mail:* uoadmit@uoregon.edu.

University of Portland

Portland, Oregon

http://www.up.edu/

CONTACT

Mr. Jason McDonald, Dean of Admissions, University of Portland, 5000 North Willamette Boulevard, Portland, OR 97203-5798. *Phone:* 503-943-7147. *Toll-free phone:* 888-627-5601. *Fax:* 503-943-7315. *E-mail:* admissions@up.edu.

Warner Pacific University

Portland, Oregon

http://www.warnerpacific.edu/

- **Independent** comprehensive, founded 1937, affiliated with Church of God
- **Urban** 15-acre campus with easy access to Portland
- **Endowment** $10.2 million
- **Coed**
- **Moderately difficult** entrance level

FACULTY

Student/faculty ratio: 7:1.

ACADEMICS

Calendar: semesters. *Degrees:* certificates, associate, bachelor's, master's, and post-master's certificates.

Library: Otto F. Linn Library. *Books:* 65,397 (physical), 164,990 (digital/electronic); *Serial titles:* 257 (physical), 139,309 (digital/electronic); *Databases:* 478. Weekly public service hours: 7.

STUDENT LIFE

Housing options: on-campus residence required through junior year; men-only, women-only, special housing for students with disabilities. Campus housing is university owned. Freshman applicants given priority for college housing.

Activities and organizations: drama/theater group, student-run newspaper, choral group.

Athletics Member NAIA, NCCAA.

Campus security: 24-hour emergency response devices and patrols, student patrols, late-night transport/escort service, controlled dormitory access.

Student services: personal/psychological counseling.

FINANCIAL AID

Financial Aid Of all full-time matriculated undergraduates who enrolled in 2018, 317 applied for aid, 297 were judged to have need, 41 had their need fully met. 247 Federal Work-Study jobs (averaging $2433). In 2018, 17 non-need-based awards were made. ***Average percent of need met:*** 63. ***Average financial aid package:*** $17,382. ***Average need-based loan:*** $4480. ***Average need-based gift aid:*** $10,281. ***Average non-need-based aid:*** $4702. ***Average indebtedness upon graduation:*** $26,540.

APPLYING

Standardized Tests *Required:* SAT or ACT (for admission).

Options: electronic application.

Application fee: $25.

Required: essay or personal statement, high school transcript, minimum 2.5 GPA. ***Required for some:*** 1 letter of recommendation, interview. ***Recommended:*** minimum 3.0 GPA, interview.

CONTACT

Dale Seipp, Vice President for Enrollment Management, Warner Pacific University, 2219 Southeast 68th Avenue, Portland, OR 97215. *Phone:* 503-517-1020. *Toll-free phone:* 800-804-1510. *Fax:* 503-517-1540. *E-mail:* admiss@warnerpacific.edu.

Western Oregon University

Monmouth, Oregon

http://www.wou.edu/

- **State-supported** comprehensive, founded 1856
- **Rural** 157-acre campus with easy access to Portland
- **Coed**
- **Moderately difficult** entrance level

FACULTY

Student/faculty ratio: 15:1.

ACADEMICS

Calendar: quarters. *Degrees:* certificates, bachelor's, master's, and postbachelor's certificates.

Library: Wayne and Lynn Hamersly Library. *Books:* 164,610 (physical), 193,700 (digital/electronic); *Serial titles:* 33,400 (physical), 223,223 (digital/electronic); *Databases:* 291. Study areas open 24 hours, 5–7 days a week; students can reserve study rooms.

STUDENT LIFE

Housing options: on-campus residence required for freshman year; coed, men-only, women-only, special housing for students with disabilities. Campus housing is university owned. Freshman campus housing is guaranteed.

Activities and organizations: drama/theater group, student-run newspaper, radio station, choral group, Model United Nations, Multicultural Student Union, Oregon Student Association, Alternative Spring Break (community service), M.E.Ch.A, national fraternities, national sororities.

Athletics Member NCAA. All Division II.

Campus security: 24-hour emergency response devices and patrols, late-night transport/escort service, controlled dormitory access.

Student services: health clinic, personal/psychological counseling, women's center, veterans affairs office.

COSTS & FINANCIAL AID
Costs (2018–19) ***Tuition:*** state resident $7740 full-time, $172 per credit hour part-time; nonresident $24,615 full-time, $547 per credit hour part-time. Full-time tuition and fees vary according to course load. Part-time tuition and fees vary according to course load. No tuition increase for student's term of enrollment. ***Required fees:*** $1800 full-time. ***Room and board:*** $10,415; room only: $8360. Room and board charges vary according to board plan and housing facility.

Financial Aid Of all full-time matriculated undergraduates who enrolled in 2017, 3,077 applied for aid, 2,571 were judged to have need, 312 had their need fully met. 266 Federal Work-Study jobs (averaging $1305). In 2017, 232 non-need-based awards were made. ***Average percent of need met:*** 63. ***Average financial aid package:*** $10,164. ***Average need-based loan:*** $3811. ***Average need-based gift aid:*** $7577. ***Average non-need-based aid:*** $2509. ***Average indebtedness upon graduation:*** $19,246.

APPLYING
Options: electronic application.

Application fee: $60.

Required: high school transcript, minimum 2.8 GPA, general college preparatory program completion.

CONTACT
Mr. David Compton, Assistant Director of Admissions for Recruitment, Western Oregon University, 345 North Monmouth Avenue, Monmouth, OR 97361. *Phone:* 503-838-8211. *Toll-free phone:* 877-877-1593. *Fax:* 503-838-8067. *E-mail:* wolfgram@wou.edu.

Willamette University
Salem, Oregon
http://www.willamette.edu/

- **Independent United Methodist** comprehensive, founded 1842
- **Urban** 72-acre campus with easy access to Portland
- **Endowment** $225.3 million
- **Coed** 1,810 undergraduate students, 97% full-time, 58% women, 42% men
- **Very difficult** entrance level, 84% of applicants were admitted

UNDERGRAD STUDENTS
1,759 full-time, 51 part-time. 74% are from out of state; 2% Black or African American, non-Hispanic/Latino; 14% Hispanic/Latino; 7% Asian, non-Hispanic/Latino; 0.3% Native Hawaiian or other Pacific Islander, non-Hispanic/Latino; 0.7% American Indian or Alaska Native, non-Hispanic/Latino; 8% Two or more races, non-Hispanic/Latino; 3% Race/ethnicity unknown; 0.8% international; 2% transferred in; 60% live on campus.

Freshmen:
Admission: 4,206 applied, 3,518 admitted, 390 enrolled. ***Average high school GPA:*** 3.8. ***Test scores:*** SAT evidence-based reading and writing scores over 500: 100%; SAT math scores over 500: 96%; ACT scores over 18: 98%; SAT evidence-based reading and writing scores over 600: 76%; SAT math scores over 600: 59%; ACT scores over 24: 85%; SAT evidence-based reading and writing scores over 700: 23%; SAT math scores over 700: 14%; ACT scores over 30: 29%.

Retention: 83% of full-time freshmen returned.

FACULTY
Total: 263, 72% full-time, 81% with terminal degrees.

Student/faculty ratio: 11:1.

ACADEMICS
Calendar: semesters. *Degrees:* bachelor's, master's, and doctoral.

Special study options: accelerated degree program, advanced placement credit, double majors, independent study, internships, off-campus study, part-time degree program, services for LD students, student-designed majors, study abroad. ***ROTC:*** Army (c), Air Force (c).

Unusual degree programs: 3-2 engineering with University of Southern California, Washington University in St. Louis, Columbia University; forestry with Duke University.

Computers: Students can access the following: computer help desk, free student e-mail accounts, online (class) grades, online (class) registration, online (class) schedules. Campuswide network is available. 100% of college-owned or -operated housing units are wired for high-speed Internet access. Wireless service is available via entire campus.

Library: Mark O. Hatfield Library plus 1 other. Study areas open 24 hours, 5–7 days a week; students can reserve study rooms.

STUDENT LIFE
Housing options: on-campus residence required through sophomore year; coed. Campus housing is university owned. Freshman campus housing is guaranteed.

Activities and organizations: drama/theater group, student-run newspaper, radio station, choral group, national fraternities, national sororities.

Athletics Member NCAA. All Division III except golf (Division II). ***Intercollegiate sports:*** baseball M, basketball M/W, crew M/W, cross-country running M/W, football M, golf M/W, lacrosse M(c), soccer M/W, softball W, swimming and diving M/W, tennis M/W, track and field M/W, volleyball W. ***Intramural sports:*** badminton M/W, basketball M/W, bowling M/W, cross-country running M/W, football M/W, golf M/W, racquetball M/W, skiing (cross-country) M(c)/W(c), skiing (downhill) M(c)/W(c), soccer M/W, softball M/W, table tennis M/W, tennis M/W, ultimate Frisbee M/W, volleyball M/W, water polo M/W, weight lifting M/W.

Campus security: 24-hour emergency response devices and patrols, student patrols, late-night transport/escort service, controlled dormitory access.

Student services: health clinic, personal/psychological counseling, women's center.

COSTS & FINANCIAL AID
Costs (2019–20) ***Comprehensive fee:*** $65,014 includes full-time tuition ($51,750), mandatory fees ($324), and room and board ($12,940). Part-time tuition: $1617 per credit hour. ***Payment plan:*** tuition prepayment.

Financial Aid Of all full-time matriculated undergraduates who enrolled in 2018, 1,188 applied for aid, 1,021 were judged to have need, 160 had their need fully met. In 2018, 553 non-need-based awards were made. ***Average percent of need met:*** 78. ***Average financial aid package:*** $37,658. ***Average need-based loan:*** $4395. ***Average need-based gift aid:*** $32,136. ***Average non-need-based aid:*** $22,311. ***Average indebtedness upon graduation:*** $30,740.

APPLYING
Standardized Tests *Recommended:* SAT and SAT Subject Tests or ACT (for admission).

Options: electronic application, early action, deferred entrance.

Required: essay or personal statement, high school transcript, minimum 2.0 GPA, 1 letter of recommendation. ***Recommended:*** interview.

Application deadlines: 1/15 (freshmen), 2/1 (transfers), 11/15 (early action).

Notification: continuous until 5/1 (freshmen), 3/15 (transfers).

CONTACT
Sue Corner, Senior Associate Director of Admission, Willamette University, 900 State Street, Salem, OR 97301. *Phone:* 503-375-5337. *Toll-free phone:* 877-542-2787. *E-mail:* bearcat@willamette.edu.

PENNSYLVANIA

Albright College
Reading, Pennsylvania
http://www.albright.edu/

- **Independent** comprehensive, founded 1856, affiliated with United Methodist Church
- **Suburban** 118-acre campus with easy access to Philadelphia
- **Endowment** $67.7 million
- **Coed** 1,912 undergraduate students, 99% full-time, 60% women, 40% men
- **Moderately difficult** entrance level, 62% of applicants were admitted

UNDERGRAD STUDENTS
1,887 full-time, 25 part-time. Students come from 28 states and territories; 16 other countries; 42% are from out of state; 23% Black or African

American, non-Hispanic/Latino; 15% Hispanic/Latino; 2% Asian, non-Hispanic/Latino; 1% American Indian or Alaska Native, non-Hispanic/Latino; 2% Two or more races, non-Hispanic/Latino; 4% Race/ethnicity unknown; 2% international; 2% transferred in; 80% live on campus.

Freshmen:
Admission: 6,755 applied, 4,188 admitted, 575 enrolled. ***Average high school GPA:*** 3.1.

Retention: 69% of full-time freshmen returned.

FACULTY
Total: 148, 66% full-time, 64% with terminal degrees.

Student/faculty ratio: 14:1.

ACADEMICS
Calendar: 4-1-4. *Degrees:* certificates, bachelor's, and master's.

Special study options: accelerated degree program, adult/continuing education programs, advanced placement credit, distance learning, double majors, honors programs, independent study, internships, off-campus study, services for LD students, student-designed majors, study abroad, summer session for credit.

Computers: Students can access the following: campus intranet, computer help desk, free student e-mail accounts, online (class) grades, online (class) registration, online (class) schedules, online financial statements, housing choices, course management systems. Campuswide network is available. 100% of college-owned or -operated housing units are wired for high-speed Internet access. Wireless service is available via entire campus.
Library: F. W. Gingrich Library plus 1 other. *Databases:* 60. Students can reserve study rooms.

STUDENT LIFE
Housing options: on-campus residence required through senior year; coed, special housing for students with disabilities. Campus housing is university owned and leased by the school. Freshman campus housing is guaranteed.

Activities and organizations: drama/theater group, student-run newspaper, radio and television station, choral group, Greek Organizations (combined), Alpha Phi Omega (service organization), Student Government Association, Albright College Activities Council, Albrightian (newspaper), national fraternities, national sororities.

Athletics Member NCAA. All Division III. ***Intercollegiate sports:*** baseball M, basketball M/W, cheerleading M/W, cross-country running M/W, field hockey W, football M, golf M/W, lacrosse M/W, rugby M(c)/W(c), soccer M/W, softball W, swimming and diving M/W, tennis M/W, track and field M/W, volleyball W. ***Intramural sports:*** basketball M/W, soccer M/W, softball M/W, volleyball M/W.

Campus security: 24-hour emergency response devices and patrols, student patrols, late-night transport/escort service, controlled dormitory access.

Student services: health clinic, personal/psychological counseling, women's center, veterans affairs office.

COSTS & FINANCIAL AID
Costs (2019–20) ***Comprehensive fee:*** $38,122 includes full-time tuition ($24,500), mandatory fees ($1142), and room and board ($12,480). ***College room only:*** $6864.

Financial Aid Of all full-time matriculated undergraduates who enrolled in 2018, 1,552 applied for aid, 1,488 were judged to have need, 166 had their need fully met. In 2018, 132 non-need-based awards were made. ***Average percent of need met:*** 81. ***Average financial aid package:*** $39,431. ***Average need-based loan:*** $3964. ***Average need-based gift aid:*** $35,077. ***Average non-need-based aid:*** $24,449. ***Average indebtedness upon graduation:*** $36,422.

APPLYING
Options: electronic application, deferred entrance.

Application fee: $35.

Required: high school transcript, minimum 2.5 GPA. ***Required for some:*** essay or personal statement, 1 letter of recommendation, interview, secondary school report (guidance department), interview for students applying test-optional.

Application deadlines: rolling (freshmen), rolling (transfers).

Notification: continuous (freshmen), continuous (transfers).

CONTACT
Ms. Jennifer H. Williamson, Director of Admission, Albright College, PO Box 15234, 13th and Bern Streets, Reading, PA 19612-5234. *Phone:* 610-921-7260. *Toll-free phone:* 800-252-1856. *Fax:* 610-921-7294. *E-mail:* admission@albright.edu.

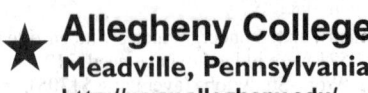

★ Allegheny College

Meadville, Pennsylvania

http://www.allegheny.edu/

- **Independent** 4-year, founded 1815
- **Suburban** 566-acre campus
- **Endowment** $220.8 million
- **Coed** 1,771 undergraduate students, 97% full-time, 56% women, 44% men
- **Very difficult** entrance level, 64% of applicants were admitted

UNDERGRAD STUDENTS
1,724 full-time, 47 part-time. Students come from 46 states and territories; 60 other countries; 48% are from out of state; 9% Black or African American, non-Hispanic/Latino; 9% Hispanic/Latino; 4% Asian, non-Hispanic/Latino; 0.1% Native Hawaiian or other Pacific Islander, non-Hispanic/Latino; 0.3% American Indian or Alaska Native, non-Hispanic/Latino; 5% Two or more races, non-Hispanic/Latino; 2% Race/ethnicity unknown; 4% international; 1% transferred in; 95% live on campus.

Freshmen:
Admission: 5,479 applied, 3,485 admitted, 474 enrolled. ***Average high school GPA:*** 3.5. ***Test scores:*** SAT evidence-based reading and writing scores over 500: 95%; SAT math scores over 500: 93%; ACT scores over 18: 99%; SAT evidence-based reading and writing scores over 600: 65%; SAT math scores over 600: 56%; ACT scores over 24: 75%; SAT evidence-based reading and writing scores over 700: 18%; SAT math scores over 700: 12%; ACT scores over 30: 30%.

Retention: 82% of full-time freshmen returned.

FACULTY
Student/faculty ratio: 10:1.

ACADEMICS
Calendar: semesters. *Degree:* bachelor's.

Special study options: advanced placement credit, double majors, English as a second language, honors programs, independent study, internships, off-campus study, services for LD students, student-designed majors, study abroad. ***ROTC:*** Army (c).

Unusual degree programs: 3-2 engineering with Case Western Reserve University, Washington University, University of Pittsburgh; arts management, public policy and management, health care policy and management, information systems management with Carnegie Mellon University; physician assistant, occupational therapy and psychology with Chatham University.

Computers: 207 computers/terminals and 200 ports are available on campus for general student use. Students can access the following: campus intranet, computer help desk, free student e-mail accounts, online (class) grades, online (class) registration, online (class) schedules, placement testing, course catalog, class lists, transcript review and ordering, billing, payroll time cards, internet kiosks, dataports for laptops, campus organizations, financial aid, room draw, registration, class schedules, grade reports. Campuswide network is available. 100% of college-owned or -operated housing units are wired for high-speed Internet access. Wireless service is available via entire campus.
Library: Lawrence Lee Pelletier Library. *Books:* 468,036 (physical), 456,202 (digital/electronic); *Serial titles:* 72 (physical), 52,931 (digital/electronic). Weekly public service hours: 115; students can reserve study rooms.

STUDENT LIFE
Housing options: on-campus residence required through senior year; coed, men-only, women-only, special housing for students with disabilities. Campus housing is university owned and leased by the school. Freshman campus housing is guaranteed.

Activities and organizations: drama/theater group, student-run newspaper, radio and television station, choral group, Student

Government, Gators Activity Programming, Alpha Phi Omega (service fraternity), Outing Club, Greek life, national fraternities, national sororities.

Athletics Member NCAA. All Division III except golf (Division II). ***Intercollegiate sports:*** baseball M, basketball M/W, cheerleading M(c)/W(c), cross-country running M/W, equestrian sports M(c)/W(c), fencing M(c)/W(c), field hockey W, football M, golf M/W, ice hockey M(c), lacrosse M/W, rugby M(c)/W(c), soccer M/W, softball W, swimming and diving M/W, tennis M/W, track and field M/W, ultimate Frisbee M(c)/W(c), volleyball W. ***Intramural sports:*** basketball M.

Campus security: 24-hour emergency response devices and patrols, student patrols, late-night transport/escort service, controlled dormitory access.

Student services: health clinic, personal/psychological counseling.

COSTS & FINANCIAL AID

Costs (2019–20) ***Comprehensive fee:*** $61,900 includes full-time tuition ($48,760), mandatory fees ($500), and room and board ($12,640). Part-time tuition: $2032 per credit hour. ***Required fees:*** $250 per term part-time. ***College room only:*** $6670.

Financial Aid Of all full-time matriculated undergraduates who enrolled in 2018, 1,469 applied for aid, 1,350 were judged to have need, 367 had their need fully met. 879 Federal Work-Study jobs (averaging $2480). 123 state and other part-time jobs (averaging $4840). In 2018, 341 non-need-based awards were made. ***Average percent of need met:*** 89. ***Average financial aid package:*** $43,273. ***Average need-based loan:*** $4505. ***Average need-based gift aid:*** $36,272. ***Average non-need-based aid:*** $24,286.

APPLYING

Options: electronic application, early admission, early decision, early action, deferred entrance.

Required: essay or personal statement, high school transcript, 2 letters of recommendation, college preparatory program. ***Recommended:*** interview.

Application deadlines: 2/15 (freshmen), 7/1 (transfers), 12/1 (early action).

Early decision deadline: 11/15 (for plan 1), 2/1 (for plan 2).

Notification: 3/15 (freshmen), 8/1 (transfers), 11/30 (early decision plan 1), 2/15 (early decision plan 2), 1/1 (early action).

CONTACT

Ms. Linda Clune, Senior Associate Director of Admissions, Allegheny College, 520 North Main Street, Box 5, Meadville, PA 16335. *Phone:* 814-332-4351. *Toll-free phone:* 800-521-5293. *Fax:* 814-337-0431. *E-mail:* admissions@allegheny.edu.

See below for display ad and page 966 for the College Close-Up.

Alvernia University

Reading, Pennsylvania

http://www.alvernia.edu/

CONTACT

Mr. Dan Hartzman, Director of Undergraduate Admissions, Alvernia University, 400 Saint Bernardine Street, Reading, PA 19607-1799. *Phone:* 610-568-1530. *Toll-free phone:* 888-ALVERNIA. *Fax:* 610-796-2873. *E-mail:* admissions@alvernia.edu.

Arcadia University

Glenside, Pennsylvania

http://www.arcadia.edu/

- **Independent** comprehensive, founded 1853, affiliated with Presbyterian Church (U.S.A.)
- **Suburban** 76-acre campus with easy access to Philadelphia
- **Coed**
- **Moderately difficult** entrance level

FACULTY

Student/faculty ratio: 11:1.

ACADEMICS

Calendar: semesters. *Degrees:* certificates, bachelor's, master's, doctoral, post-master's, and postbachelor's certificates.

Library: Bette E. Landman Library. Students can reserve study rooms.

STUDENT LIFE
Housing options: coed, women-only. Campus housing is university owned and leased by the school. Freshman applicants given priority for college housing.

Activities and organizations: drama/theater group, student-run newspaper, radio station, choral group, Student Program Board, Residence Hall Council, Student Government, Arcadia Christian Fellowship, Student Alumni Association.

Athletics Member NCAA. All Division III.

Campus security: 24-hour emergency response devices and patrols, student patrols, late-night transport/escort service, controlled dormitory access.

Student services: health clinic, personal/psychological counseling.

COSTS & FINANCIAL AID
Costs (2018–19) ***Comprehensive fee:*** $57,380 includes full-time tuition ($42,880), mandatory fees ($700), and room and board ($13,800). Part-time tuition: $715 per credit hour. ***College room only:*** $9000. Room and board charges vary according to board plan and housing facility.

Financial Aid Of all full-time matriculated undergraduates who enrolled in 2016, 2,054 applied for aid, 1,863 were judged to have need, 558 had their need fully met. 140 state and other part-time jobs (averaging $1671). In 2016, 354 non-need-based awards were made. ***Average percent of need met:*** 83. ***Average financial aid package:*** $30,072. ***Average need-based loan:*** $3894. ***Average need-based gift aid:*** $26,516. ***Average non-need-based aid:*** $17,060.

APPLYING
Standardized Tests *Required:* SAT or ACT (for admission).

Options: electronic application, deferred entrance.

Application fee: $30.

Required: essay or personal statement, high school transcript, 2 letters of recommendation. ***Required for some:*** portfolio, audition. ***Recommended:*** minimum 3.0 GPA.

CONTACT
Colleen Pernicello, Director of Undergraduate Admissions, Arcadia University, 450 South Easton Road, Glenside, PA 19038. *Phone:* 215-572-2910. *Toll-free phone:* 877-ARCADIA. *Fax:* 215-572-4049. *E-mail:* admiss@arcadia.edu.

The Art Institute of Pittsburgh
Pittsburgh, Pennsylvania
http://www.artinstitutes.edu/pittsburgh/

CONTACT
The Art Institute of Pittsburgh, 420 Boulevard of the Allies, Pittsburgh, PA 15219. *Phone:* 412-263-6600. *Toll-free phone:* 800-275-2470.

Bloomsburg University of Pennsylvania
Bloomsburg, Pennsylvania
http://www.bloomu.edu/

- **State-supported** comprehensive, founded 1839, part of Pennsylvania State System of Higher Education
- **Small-town** 366-acre campus
- **Endowment** $45.0 million
- **Coed**
- **Minimally difficult** entrance level

FACULTY
Student/faculty ratio: 19:1.

ACADEMICS
Calendar: semesters. *Degrees:* certificates, bachelor's, master's, doctoral, and postbachelor's certificates.
Library: Andruss Library. *Books:* 374,393 (physical), 269,435 (digital/electronic); *Serial titles:* 5,838 (physical), 84,065 (digital/electronic); *Databases:* 165. Weekly public service hours: 98; students can reserve study rooms.

STUDENT LIFE
Housing options: on-campus residence required for freshman year; coed. Campus housing is university owned and leased by the school. Freshman campus housing is guaranteed.

Activities and organizations: drama/theater group, student-run newspaper, radio and television station, choral group, marching band, Living and Learning Communities, Band and Music Groups, Greek Organizations, Residence Hall Councils, Club Sports, national fraternities, national sororities.

Athletics Member NCAA. All Division II except wrestling (Division I).

Campus security: 24-hour emergency response devices and patrols, late-night transport/escort service, controlled dormitory access, monitored surveillance cameras.

Student services: health clinic, personal/psychological counseling, women's center, legal services, veterans affairs office.

COSTS & FINANCIAL AID
Costs (2018–19) ***Tuition:*** state resident $7716 full-time, $322 per credit part-time; nonresident $19,290 full-time, $805 per credit part-time. Full-time tuition and fees vary according to course load and location. Part-time tuition and fees vary according to course load and location. ***Required fees:*** $3242 full-time, $119 per credit part-time, $75 per term part-time. ***Room and board:*** $9686; room only: $6308. Room and board charges vary according to board plan and housing facility.

Financial Aid Of all full-time matriculated undergraduates who enrolled in 2018, 6,750 applied for aid, 4,927 were judged to have need, 562 had their need fully met. 796 Federal Work-Study jobs (averaging $2983). 1,404 state and other part-time jobs (averaging $3249). In 2018, 320 non-need-based awards were made. ***Average percent of need met:*** 54. ***Average financial aid package:*** $9347. ***Average need-based loan:*** $4123. ***Average need-based gift aid:*** $5827. ***Average non-need-based aid:*** $2710. ***Average indebtedness upon graduation:*** $36,908.

APPLYING
Standardized Tests *Required:* SAT or ACT (for admission).

Options: electronic application, early admission, early action, deferred entrance.

Application fee: $35.

Required: high school transcript.

CONTACT
Bloomsburg University of Pennsylvania, 400 East Second Street, Bloomsburg, PA 17815-1301.

Bryn Athyn College of the New Church
Bryn Athyn, Pennsylvania
http://www.brynathyn.edu/

- **Independent Christian** comprehensive, founded 1877, affiliated with Church of the New Jerusalem, part of The Academy of the New Church
- **Suburban** 130-acre campus with easy access to Philadelphia
- **Endowment** $58.8 million
- **Coed** 309 undergraduate students, 91% full-time, 53% women, 47% men
- **Minimally difficult** entrance level, 89% of applicants were admitted

UNDERGRAD STUDENTS
282 full-time, 27 part-time. 22% are from out of state; 16% Black or African American, non-Hispanic/Latino; 8% Hispanic/Latino; 2% Asian, non-Hispanic/Latino; 0.3% Native Hawaiian or other Pacific Islander, non-Hispanic/Latino; 1% American Indian or Alaska Native, non-Hispanic/Latino; 1% Two or more races, non-Hispanic/Latino; 2% Race/ethnicity unknown; 5% international; 7% transferred in; 44% live on campus.

Freshmen:
Admission: 250 applied, 222 admitted, 64 enrolled. ***Average high school GPA:*** 3.4. ***Test scores:*** SAT evidence-based reading and writing scores over 500: 79%; SAT math scores over 500: 79%; ACT scores over 18: 93%; SAT evidence-based reading and writing scores over 600: 31%; SAT math scores over 600: 25%; ACT scores over 24: 33%; SAT evidence-based reading and writing scores over 700: 6%; SAT math scores over 700: 4%.
Retention: 65% of full-time freshmen returned.

FACULTY
Total: 51, 82% full-time, 96% with terminal degrees.

Student/faculty ratio: 6:1.

ACADEMICS
Calendar: trimesters. *Degrees:* associate, bachelor's, and master's.

Special study options: academic remediation for entering students, accelerated degree program, advanced placement credit, cooperative education, English as a second language, independent study, internships, part-time degree program, services for LD students, student-designed majors, study abroad. ***ROTC:*** Army (c), Air Force (c).

Computers: 18 computers/terminals are available on campus for general student use. Students can access the following: campus intranet, computer help desk, free student e-mail accounts, online (class) grades, online (class) registration, online (class) schedules. Campuswide network is available. 100% of college-owned or -operated housing units are wired for high-speed Internet access. Wireless service is available via entire campus.

Library: Swedenborg Library plus 1 other. *Books:* 70,742 (physical), 252 (digital/electronic); *Serial titles:* 834 (physical), 74 (digital/electronic); *Databases:* 13.

STUDENT LIFE
Housing options: men-only, women-only. Campus housing is university owned. Freshman applicants given priority for college housing.

Activities and organizations: drama/theater group, choral group, C.A.R.E. (Community Service), Social council, International Student Organization, Peer Advisory Council, Student Government.

Athletics Member NCAA. All Division III. ***Intercollegiate sports:*** basketball M/W, cross-country running M/W, field hockey W, golf M, ice hockey M, lacrosse M/W, soccer M/W, tennis M/W, volleyball W.

Campus security: 24-hour emergency response devices, controlled dormitory access, 18-hour patrols by trained personnel.

Student services: health clinic, personal/psychological counseling.

COSTS & FINANCIAL AID
Costs (2018–19) ***Comprehensive fee:*** $34,746 includes full-time tuition ($21,360), mandatory fees ($1500), and room and board ($11,886). Part-time tuition: $880 per credit hour. ***Required fees:*** $58 per credit hour part-time. ***College room only:*** $5943. ***Payment plan:*** installment. ***Waivers:*** senior citizens.

Financial Aid Of all full-time matriculated undergraduates who enrolled in 2017, 298 applied for aid, 268 were judged to have need. In 2017, 26 non-need-based awards were made. ***Average percent of need met:*** 78. ***Average financial aid package:*** $9409. ***Average need-based loan:*** $3842. ***Average need-based gift aid:*** $180,342. ***Average non-need-based aid:*** $135,644.

APPLYING
Standardized Tests *Required:* SAT or ACT (for admission).

Options: electronic application, deferred entrance.

Required: essay or personal statement, high school transcript, minimum 2.0 GPA, 1 letter of recommendation. ***Required for some:*** interview.

Application deadlines: rolling (freshmen), rolling (transfers).

Notification: continuous (freshmen), continuous (transfers).

CONTACT
Ms. Nicole D'Amico, Admissions Office, Bryn Athyn College of the New Church, 2945 College Drive, Box 717, Bryn Athyn, PA 19009. *Phone:* 267-502-6000. *Toll-free phone:* 800-767-9552. *Fax:* 267-502-2593. *E-mail:* admissions@brynathyn.edu.

Bryn Mawr College

Bryn Mawr, Pennsylvania

http://www.brynmawr.edu/

- **Independent** comprehensive, founded 1885
- **Suburban** 135-acre campus with easy access to Philadelphia
- **Endowment** $852.7 million
- **Undergraduate: women only; graduate: coed**
- **Most difficult** entrance level

FACULTY
Student/faculty ratio: 8:1.

ACADEMICS
Calendar: semesters. *Degrees:* bachelor's, master's, doctoral, and postbachelor's certificates.
Library: Canaday Library plus 2 others. *Books:* 740,887 (physical), 754,968 (digital/electronic); *Serial titles:* 9,146 (physical), 123,010 (digital/electronic); *Databases:* 170. Weekly public service hours: 105; study areas open 24 hours, 5–7 days a week.

STUDENT LIFE
Housing options: on-campus residence required for freshman year; coed, women-only, cooperative. Campus housing is university owned. Freshman campus housing is guaranteed.

Activities and organizations: drama/theater group, student-run newspaper, radio station, choral group, Student Government Association.

Athletics Member NCAA. All Division III.

Campus security: 24-hour emergency response devices and patrols, late-night transport/escort service, controlled dormitory access, shuttle bus service, awareness programs, bicycle registration, security Web site.

Student services: health clinic, personal/psychological counseling, women's center.

COSTS & FINANCIAL AID
Costs (2018–19) ***Comprehensive fee:*** $68,860 includes full-time tuition ($51,130), mandatory fees ($1230), and room and board ($16,500). Part-time tuition: $6390 per course. ***College room only:*** $9420.

Financial Aid Of all full-time matriculated undergraduates who enrolled in 2018, 801 applied for aid, 713 were judged to have need, 713 had their need fully met. In 2018, 242 non-need-based awards were made. ***Average percent of need met:*** 100. ***Average financial aid package:*** $51,553. ***Average need-based loan:*** $5452. ***Average need-based gift aid:*** $44,589. ***Average non-need-based aid:*** $17,761. ***Average indebtedness upon graduation:*** $25,682. ***Financial aid deadline:*** 1/15.

APPLYING
Standardized Tests *Required for some:* SAT and SAT Subject Tests or ACT (for admission).

Options: electronic application, early admission, early decision, deferred entrance.

Application fee: $50.

Required: essay or personal statement, high school transcript, 3 letters of recommendation. ***Recommended:*** interview.

CONTACT
Dr. Cheryl Lynn Horsey, Chief Enrollment Officer, Bryn Mawr College, 101 North Merion Avenue, Bryn Mawr, PA 19010. *Phone:* 610-526-6522. *Toll-free phone:* 800-BMC-1885. *Fax:* 610-526-7471. *E-mail:* chorsey@brynmawr.edu.

See previous page for display ad and page 984 for the College Close-Up.

Bucknell University

Lewisburg, Pennsylvania

http://www.bucknell.edu/

- **Independent** comprehensive, founded 1846
- **Small-town** 446-acre campus
- **Endowment** $851.3 million
- **Coed** 3,597 undergraduate students, 100% full-time, 51% women, 49% men
- **Most difficult** entrance level, 33% of applicants were admitted

UNDERGRAD STUDENTS
3,581 full-time, 16 part-time. Students come from 42 states and territories; 50 other countries; 79% are from out of state; 4% Black or African American, non-Hispanic/Latino; 7% Hispanic/Latino; 6% Asian, non-Hispanic/Latino; 0.1% American Indian or Alaska Native, non-Hispanic/Latino; 4% Two or more races, non-Hispanic/Latino; 0.2% Race/ethnicity unknown; 7% international; 0.7% transferred in; 92% live on campus.

Freshmen:
Admission: 10,144 applied, 3,352 admitted, 974 enrolled. ***Average high school GPA:*** 3.6. ***Test scores:*** SAT evidence-based reading and writing scores over 500: 100%; SAT math scores over 500: 99%; ACT scores over 18: 100%; SAT evidence-based reading and writing scores over 600: 88%; SAT math scores over 600: 85%; ACT scores over 24: 97%; SAT evidence-based reading and writing scores over 700: 24%; SAT math scores over 700: 44%; ACT scores over 30: 61%.

Retention: 92% of full-time freshmen returned.

FACULTY
Total: 422, 91% full-time, 94% with terminal degrees.

Student/faculty ratio: 9:1.

ACADEMICS
Calendar: semesters. *Degrees:* bachelor's and master's.

Special study options: advanced placement credit, double majors, honors programs, independent study, internships, off-campus study, part-time degree program, services for LD students, student-designed majors, study abroad, summer session for credit. ***ROTC:*** Army (b).

Unusual degree programs: 3-2 engineering; biology, chemistry.

Computers: 1,038 computers/terminals and 190 ports are available on campus for general student use. Students can access the following: campus intranet, computer help desk, free student e-mail accounts, online (class) grades, online (class) registration, online (class) schedules. Campuswide network is available. 100% of college-owned or -operated housing units are wired for high-speed Internet access. Wireless service is available via entire campus.
Library: Ellen Clarke Bertrand Library. *Books:* 673,158 (physical), 849,294 (digital/electronic); *Serial titles:* 264 (physical), 49,759 (digital/electronic); *Databases:* 237. Weekly public service hours: 125.

STUDENT LIFE
Housing options: on-campus residence required through senior year; coed, women-only, cooperative, special housing for students with disabilities. Campus housing is university owned. Freshman campus housing is guaranteed.

Activities and organizations: drama/theater group, student-run newspaper, radio station, choral group, Black Student Union, Outing Club, Activities and Campus Events, French Club, Catholic Campus Ministries, national fraternities, national sororities.

Athletics Member NCAA. All Division I except football (Division I-AA). ***Intercollegiate sports:*** baseball M, basketball M(s)/W(s), cheerleading M(c)/W(c), crew M(c)/W, cross-country running M/W(s), equestrian sports M(c)/W(c), field hockey W(s), golf M/W(c), ice hockey M(c), lacrosse M(s)/W(s), rock climbing M(c)/W(c), rugby M(c)/W(c), sailing M(c)/W(c), skiing (downhill) W(c), soccer M(s)/W, softball W(s), squash M(c)/W(c), swimming and diving M(s)/W, tennis M/W, track and field M/W(s), ultimate Frisbee M(c)/W(c), volleyball M(c)/W(s), water polo M/W, weight lifting M(c)/W(c), wrestling M(s). ***Intramural sports:*** basketball M/W, cross-country running M/W, golf M/W, racquetball M/W, soccer M/W, softball M/W, squash M/W, table tennis M/W, tennis M/W, ultimate Frisbee M/W, volleyball M/W, weight lifting M, wrestling M.

Campus security: 24-hour emergency response devices and patrols, student patrols, late-night transport/escort service, controlled dormitory access.

Student services: health clinic, personal/psychological counseling, women's center.

COSTS & FINANCIAL AID
Costs (2019–20) ***Comprehensive fee:*** $72,370 includes full-time tuition ($57,882), mandatory fees ($314), and room and board ($14,174). Part-time tuition: $6352 per course. ***College room only:*** $8644. ***Payment plan:*** tuition prepayment.

Financial Aid Of all full-time matriculated undergraduates who enrolled in 2018, 1,554 applied for aid, 1,343 were judged to have need. 600 Federal Work-Study jobs (averaging $1500). 50 state and other part-time jobs (averaging $1500). In 2018, 345 non-need-based awards were made. ***Average percent of need met:*** 92. ***Average financial aid package:*** $34,500. ***Average need-based loan:*** $5500. ***Average need-based gift aid:*** $31,600. ***Average non-need-based aid:*** $14,442. ***Average indebtedness upon graduation:*** $31,087. ***Financial aid deadline:*** 1/15.

APPLYING
Options: electronic application, early decision, deferred entrance.

Application fee: $40.

Required: essay or personal statement, high school transcript, 1 letter of recommendation.

Application deadlines: 1/15 (freshmen), 3/15 (transfers).

Early decision deadline: 11/15.

Notification: 4/1 (freshmen), 5/1 (transfers), 12/15 (early decision).

CONTACT
Dean Kevin Mathes, Dean of Admissions, Bucknell University, 1 Dent Drive, Lewisburg, PA 17837. *Phone:* 570-577-3000. *Fax:* 570-577-3538. *E-mail:* admissions@bucknell.edu.

Cabrini University

Radnor, Pennsylvania

http://www.cabrini.edu/

CONTACT
Ms. Shannon Zottola, Assistant Vice President for Enrollment Management, Cabrini University, 610 King of Prussia Road, Radnor, PA 19087-3698. *Phone:* 610-902-1027. *Toll-free phone:* 800-848-1003. *Fax:* 610-902-8508. *E-mail:* admit@cabrini.edu.

Cairn University

Langhorne, Pennsylvania

http://cairn.edu/

- **Independent nondenominational** comprehensive, founded 1913
- **Suburban** 115-acre campus with easy access to Philadelphia
- **Endowment** $11.0 million
- **Coed**
- **Moderately difficult** entrance level

FACULTY
Student/faculty ratio: 12:1.

ACADEMICS
Calendar: semesters. *Degrees:* bachelor's, master's, and postbachelor's certificates.
Library: Masland Learning Resource Center. *Books:* 104,860 (physical), 421,604 (digital/electronic); *Serial titles:* 945 (physical), 53,295 (digital/electronic); *Databases:* 177. Weekly public service hours: 86; students can reserve study rooms.

STUDENT LIFE
Housing options: on-campus residence required through senior year; men-only, women-only, special housing for students with disabilities. Campus housing is university owned. Freshman campus housing is guaranteed.

Activities and organizations: drama/theater group, student-run newspaper, choral group, Ascend (outdoor adventure club), Chi Beta Sigma (Social Work Club), Enactus (Business), Mu Kappa (Missionary Kids Association), Student Visual Arts Society.

Athletics Member NCAA, NCCAA. All NCAA Division III.

Campus security: 24-hour emergency response devices and patrols, student patrols, late-night transport/escort service, controlled dormitory access.

Student services: health clinic, personal/psychological counseling.

COSTS & FINANCIAL AID
Costs (2018–19) ***Comprehensive fee:*** $37,573 includes full-time tuition ($26,979), mandatory fees ($300), and room and board ($10,294). Full-time tuition and fees vary according to course load. Part-time tuition: $800 per credit. Part-time tuition and fees vary according to course load. ***College room only:*** $5389. Room and board charges vary according to board plan and location.

Financial Aid Of all full-time matriculated undergraduates who enrolled in 2017, 640 applied for aid, 585 were judged to have need, 71 had their need fully met. In 2017, 117 non-need-based awards were made. ***Average percent of need met:*** 75. ***Average financial aid package:*** $21,885. ***Average need-based loan:*** $5057. ***Average need-based gift aid:*** $16,755. ***Average non-need-based aid:*** $12,008. ***Average indebtedness upon graduation:*** $35,717.

APPLYING
Standardized Tests *Required:* SAT or ACT (for admission).

Options: electronic application, early admission, deferred entrance.

Application fee: $25.

Required: essay or personal statement, high school transcript, minimum 2.0 GPA, interview.

CONTACT
Mr. Thomas Sherf, Director of Undergraduate Admissions, Cairn University, 200 Manor Avenue, Langhorne, PA 19047. *Phone:* 215-702-4248. *Toll-free phone:* 800-366-0049. *Fax:* 215-702-4248. *E-mail:* admissions@cairn.edu.

California University of Pennsylvania

California, Pennsylvania

http://www.calu.edu/

- **State-supported** comprehensive, founded 1852, part of Pennsylvania State System of Higher Education
- **Rural** 188-acre campus with easy access to Pittsburgh
- **Endowment** $24.1 million
- **Coed** 5,174 undergraduate students, 81% full-time, 54% women, 46% men
- **Moderately difficult** entrance level, 97% of applicants were admitted

UNDERGRAD STUDENTS
4,212 full-time, 962 part-time. Students come from 49 states and territories; 36 other countries; 7% are from out of state; 14% Black or African American, non-Hispanic/Latino; 3% Hispanic/Latino; 0.9% Asian, non-Hispanic/Latino; 0.1% Native Hawaiian or other Pacific Islander, non-Hispanic/Latino; 0.2% American Indian or Alaska Native, non-Hispanic/Latino; 4% Two or more races, non-Hispanic/Latino; 2% Race/ethnicity unknown; 0.9% international; 14% transferred in; 48% live on campus.

Freshmen:
Admission: 2,909 applied, 2,820 admitted, 1,017 enrolled. ***Average high school GPA:*** 3.2. ***Test scores:*** SAT evidence-based reading and writing scores over 500: 57%; SAT math scores over 500: 53%; ACT scores over 18: 71%; SAT evidence-based reading and writing scores over 600: 13%; SAT math scores over 600: 9%; ACT scores over 24: 22%; SAT evidence-based reading and writing scores over 700: 1%; SAT math scores over 700: 1%; ACT scores over 30: 2%.

Retention: 71% of full-time freshmen returned.

FACULTY
Total: 416, 66% full-time, 65% with terminal degrees.

Student/faculty ratio: 20:1.

ACADEMICS
Calendar: semesters. *Degrees:* certificates, associate, bachelor's, master's, doctoral, post-master's, and postbachelor's certificates.

Special study options: academic remediation for entering students, accelerated degree program, adult/continuing education programs, advanced placement credit, cooperative education, distance learning, double majors, English as a second language, honors programs, independent study, internships, off-campus study, part-time degree program, services for LD students, study abroad, summer session for credit. ***ROTC:*** Army (b).

Computers: 1,300 computers/terminals and 18,000 ports are available on campus for general student use. Students can access the following: campus intranet, computer help desk, free student e-mail accounts, online (class) grades, online (class) registration, online (class) schedules. 100% of college-owned or -operated housing units are wired for high-speed Internet access. Wireless service is available via entire campus.
Library: Manderino Library. *Books:* 220,974 (physical), 339,919 (digital/electronic); *Serial titles:* 22,122 (physical), 61,720 (digital/electronic); *Databases:* 96. Students can reserve study rooms.

STUDENT LIFE
Housing options: on-campus residence required for freshman year; coed, special housing for students with disabilities. Campus housing is university owned, leased by the school and is provided by a third party. Freshman campus housing is guaranteed.

Activities and organizations: drama/theater group, student-run newspaper, radio and television station, choral group, marching band, Commuter Council, STAND, Student Activities Board, University Band, Colleges Against Cancer, national fraternities, national sororities.

Athletics Member NCAA. All Division II. ***Intercollegiate sports:*** baseball M(s), basketball M(s)/W(s), cross-country running M(s)/W(s), football M(s), golf M(s)/W(s), soccer M(s)/W(s), softball W(s), swimming and diving W(s), tennis W(s), track and field M(s)/W(s), volleyball W(s). ***Intramural sports:*** archery M(c)/W(c), baseball M(c)/W(c), basketball M/W, cheerleading M(c)/W(c), equestrian sports M(c)/W(c), fencing M(c)/W(c), golf M(c)/W(c), ice hockey M(c)/W(c), lacrosse M(c), rugby M(c)/W(c), soccer M(c)/W(c), ultimate Frisbee M(c), volleyball M(c)/W(c).

Campus security: 24-hour emergency response devices and patrols, student patrols, late-night transport/escort service, controlled dormitory access.

Student services: health clinic, personal/psychological counseling, women's center, legal services, veterans affairs office.

COSTS & FINANCIAL AID
Costs (2019–20) ***Room and board:*** $10,186; room only: $6592.

Financial Aid Of all full-time matriculated undergraduates who enrolled in 2017, 4,171 applied for aid, 3,462 were judged to have need, 242 had their need fully met. In 2017, 103 non-need-based awards were made. ***Average percent of need met:*** 51. ***Average financial aid package:*** $9364. ***Average need-based loan:*** $4244. ***Average need-based gift aid:*** $5982. ***Average non-need-based aid:*** $4150. ***Average indebtedness upon graduation:*** $27,381.

APPLYING
Standardized Tests *Required:* SAT or ACT (for admission).

Options: electronic application, deferred entrance.

Application fee: $35.

Required: high school transcript.

Application deadlines: rolling (freshmen), rolling (transfers).

Notification: continuous (freshmen), continuous (transfers).

CONTACT
Dr. Tracey Sheetz, Dean of Undergraduate Admissions, California University of Pennsylvania, 250 University Avenue, California, PA 15419. *Phone:* 724-938-4404. *Toll-free phone:* 888-412-0479. *Fax:* 724-938-4564. *E-mail:* sheetz@calu.edu.

Carlow University
Pittsburgh, Pennsylvania
http://www.carlow.edu/

- **Independent Roman Catholic** comprehensive, founded 1929
- **Urban** 13-acre campus with easy access to Pittsburgh
- **Coed, primarily women**
- **Minimally difficult** entrance level

FACULTY
Student/faculty ratio: 12:1.

ACADEMICS
Calendar: semesters. *Degrees:* certificates, bachelor's, master's, doctoral, post-master's, and postbachelor's certificates.
Library: Grace Library.

STUDENT LIFE
Housing options: coed, men-only, women-only, special housing for students with disabilities. Campus housing is university owned. Freshman applicants given priority for college housing.

Activities and organizations: drama/theater group, student-run newspaper, choral group, Student Government Association, Campus Activities Board, SPiRiT (Student Ambassadors), SNAP (Student Nursing Association), PSEA (School Education Association), national fraternities.

Athletics Member NAIA, USCAA.

Campus security: 24-hour emergency response devices and patrols, late-night transport/escort service, controlled dormitory access.

Student services: health clinic, personal/psychological counseling.

FINANCIAL AID
Financial Aid Of all full-time matriculated undergraduates who enrolled in 2017, 1,036 applied for aid, 974 were judged to have need, 219 had their need fully met. In 2017, 98 non-need-based awards were made. ***Average percent of need met:*** 63. ***Average financial aid package:*** $19,782. ***Average need-based loan:*** $3469. ***Average need-based gift aid:*** $4364. ***Average non-need-based aid:*** $8541. ***Financial aid deadline:*** 5/1.

APPLYING
Standardized Tests *Required:* SAT or ACT (for admission). *Recommended:* SAT and SAT Subject Tests or ACT (for admission).

Options: electronic application, deferred entrance.

Required: high school transcript. ***Recommended:*** essay or personal statement, minimum 2.5 GPA, interview.

CONTACT
Ms. Wivina Chmura, Director of Undergraduate Admissions, Carlow University, 3333 Fifth Avenue, Pittsburgh, PA 15213. *Phone:* 412-578-8762. *Toll-free phone:* 800-333-CARLOW. *Fax:* 412-578-6668. *E-mail:* admissions@carlow.edu.

Carnegie Mellon University
Pittsburgh, Pennsylvania
http://www.cmu.edu/

- **Independent** university, founded 1900
- **Urban** 153-acre campus with easy access to Pittsburgh
- **Endowment** $1.9 billion
- **Coed** 6,947 undergraduate students, 96% full-time, 50% women, 50% men
- **Most difficult** entrance level, 17% of applicants were admitted

UNDERGRAD STUDENTS
6,680 full-time, 267 part-time. Students come from 50 states and territories; 54 other countries; 86% are from out of state; 4% Black or African American, non-Hispanic/Latino; 9% Hispanic/Latino; 30% Asian, non-Hispanic/Latino; 4% Two or more races, non-Hispanic/Latino; 6% Race/ethnicity unknown; 22% international; 0.4% transferred in; 58% live on campus.

Freshmen:
Admission: 24,351 applied, 4,170 admitted, 1,572 enrolled. ***Average high school GPA:*** 3.8. ***Test scores:*** SAT evidence-based reading and writing scores over 500: 99%; SAT math scores over 500: 100%; ACT scores over 18: 100%; SAT evidence-based reading and writing scores over 600: 98%; SAT math scores over 600: 98%; ACT scores over 24: 99%; SAT evidence-based reading and writing scores over 700: 77%; SAT math scores over 700: 89%; ACT scores over 30: 92%.

Retention: 97% of full-time freshmen returned.

FACULTY
Total: 1,098, 96% full-time, 91% with terminal degrees.

Student/faculty ratio: 13:1.

ACADEMICS
Calendar: semesters. *Degrees:* bachelor's, master's, doctoral, post-master's, and postbachelor's certificates.

Special study options: accelerated degree program, advanced placement credit, cooperative education, distance learning, double majors, independent study, internships, off-campus study, part-time degree program, services for LD students, student-designed majors, study abroad, summer session for credit. ***ROTC:*** Army (c), Navy (b), Air Force (c).

Unusual degree programs: 3-2 business administration; engineering; public management and policy.

Computers: 462 computers/terminals are available on campus for general student use. Students can access the following: campus intranet, computer help desk, free student e-mail accounts, online (class) grades, online (class) registration, online (class) schedules. Campuswide network is available. 100% of college-owned or -operated housing units are wired for high-speed Internet access. Wireless service is available via entire campus.
Library: Hunt Library plus 2 others. Weekly public service hours: 168; study areas open 24 hours, 5–7 days a week; students can reserve study rooms.

STUDENT LIFE
Housing options: on-campus residence required for freshman year; coed, men-only, women-only, special housing for students with disabilities. Campus housing is university owned. Freshman campus housing is guaranteed.

Activities and organizations: drama/theater group, student-run newspaper, radio station, choral group, marching band, national fraternities, national sororities.

Athletics Member NCAA. All Division III except golf (Division II). ***Intercollegiate sports:*** badminton M(c)/W(c), baseball M(c)/W(c), basketball M/W, cross-country running M/W, fencing M(c)/W(c), football M, golf M/W, lacrosse M(c)/W(c), rowing M(c)/W(c), rugby M(c)/W(c), skiing (downhill) M(c)/W(c), soccer M/W, swimming and diving M/W, tennis M/W, track and field M/W, ultimate Frisbee M(c)/W(c), volleyball M(c)/W, water polo M(c)/W(c). ***Intramural sports:*** badminton M/W, basketball M/W, racquetball M/W, soccer M/W, softball M/W, squash M/W, table tennis M/W, tennis M/W, ultimate Frisbee M/W, volleyball M/W, water polo M/W.

Campus security: 24-hour emergency response devices and patrols, late-night transport/escort service, controlled dormitory access.

Student services: health clinic, personal/psychological counseling, legal services, veterans affairs office.

COSTS & FINANCIAL AID

Costs (2019–20) ***Comprehensive fee:*** $72,091 includes full-time tuition ($55,816), mandatory fees ($1303), and room and board ($14,972). Part-time tuition: $776 per unit. ***College room only:*** $8822.

Financial Aid Of all full-time matriculated undergraduates who enrolled in 2018, 3,140 applied for aid, 2,643 were judged to have need, 1,818 had their need fully met. In 2018, 238 non-need-based awards were made. ***Average percent of need met:*** 97. ***Average financial aid package:*** $46,595. ***Average need-based loan:*** $4890. ***Average need-based gift aid:*** $41,432. ***Average non-need-based aid:*** $14,458. ***Average indebtedness upon graduation:*** $27,818. ***Financial aid deadline:*** 2/15.

APPLYING

Standardized Tests *Required:* SAT or ACT (for admission). *Recommended:* SAT Subject Tests (for admission).

Options: electronic application, early admission, early decision, deferred entrance.

Application fee: $75.

Required: essay or personal statement, high school transcript. ***Required for some:*** audition/portfolio for fine arts.

Application deadlines: 1/1 (freshmen), 2/15 (transfers).

Early decision deadline: 11/1.

Notification: 4/1 (freshmen), 5/15 (transfers), 12/15 (early decision).

CONTACT

Mr. Greg Edleman, Director of Admission, Carnegie Mellon University, 5000 Forbes Avenue, Pittsburgh, PA 15213. *Phone:* 412-268-2082. *Fax:* 412-268-7838. *E-mail:* admission@andrew.cmu.edu.

Cedar Crest College

Allentown, Pennsylvania

http://www.cedarcrest.edu/

- **Independent** comprehensive, founded 1867, affiliated with United Church of Christ
- **Suburban** 84-acre campus with easy access to Philadelphia
- **Coed, primarily women**
- **Moderately difficult** entrance level

FACULTY

Student/faculty ratio: 10:1.

ACADEMICS

Calendar: semesters. *Degrees:* certificates, bachelor's, master's, post-master's, and postbachelor's certificates.
Library: Frank M. Cressman Library.

STUDENT LIFE

Housing options: women-only. Campus housing is university owned. Freshman campus housing is guaranteed.

Activities and organizations: drama/theater group, student-run newspaper, radio station, choral group, Student Activities Board, Student Government Association, Commuter Awareness Board, Student Nurse Association, Forensic Student Science organization.

Athletics Member NCAA. All Division III.

Campus security: 24-hour emergency response devices and patrols, late-night transport/escort service, controlled dormitory access, crime prevention programs.

Student services: health clinic, personal/psychological counseling.

COSTS & FINANCIAL AID

Costs (2018–19) ***Comprehensive fee:*** $50,760 includes full-time tuition ($38,616), mandatory fees ($600), and room and board ($11,544). Full-time tuition and fees vary according to class time, course load, and program. Part-time tuition: $1287 per credit. Part-time tuition and fees vary according to class time, course load, and program. ***Required fees:*** $150 per term part-time. ***College room only:*** $5420. Room and board charges vary according to board plan and housing facility. ***Payment plans:*** installment, deferred payment.

Financial Aid Of all full-time matriculated undergraduates who enrolled in 2018, 712 applied for aid, 673 were judged to have need, 107 had their need fully met. In 2018, 51 non-need-based awards were made. ***Average percent of need met:*** 76. ***Average financial aid package:*** $30,400. ***Average need-based loan:*** $4425. ***Average need-based gift aid:*** $26,473. ***Average non-need-based aid:*** $18,424. ***Average indebtedness upon graduation:*** $39,389.

APPLYING

Standardized Tests *Required:* SAT or ACT (for admission).

Options: electronic application, early admission, deferred entrance.

Required: essay or personal statement, high school transcript. ***Required for some:*** 2 letters of recommendation. ***Recommended:*** minimum 2.0 GPA, interview.

CONTACT

Mary Alice Ozechoski, Vice President of Student Affairs and Traditional Enrollment, Cedar Crest College, 100 College Drive, Allentown, PA 18104. *Phone:* 610-606-4666. *Toll-free phone:* 800-360-1222. *E-mail:* admissions@cedarcrest.edu.

Central Penn College

Summerdale, Pennsylvania

http://www.centralpenn.edu/

- **Proprietary** comprehensive, founded 1881
- **Small-town** 35-acre campus with easy access to Harrisburg
- **Coed**
- **Minimally difficult** entrance level

FACULTY

Student/faculty ratio: 10:1.

ACADEMICS

Calendar: quarters. *Degrees:* associate, bachelor's, and master's.
Library: Charles T Jones Leadership Library plus 1 other. *Books:* 24,566 (physical), 140,336 (digital/electronic); *Serial titles:* 67 (physical), 2 (digital/electronic); *Databases:* 34. Weekly public service hours: 74.

STUDENT LIFE

Housing options: coed, men-only, women-only, special housing for students with disabilities. Campus housing is university owned. Freshman applicants given priority for college housing.

Activities and organizations: drama/theater group, student-run newspaper, PTA Club, Student Government Association, Central Penn Players, Student Ambassadors, Colleges Against Cancer.

Athletics Member USCAA.

Campus security: 24-hour emergency response devices and patrols, student patrols, late-night transport/escort service, controlled dormitory access.

Student services: personal/psychological counseling, veterans affairs office.

COSTS & FINANCIAL AID

Costs (2018–19) ***One-time required fee:*** $100. ***Comprehensive fee:*** $26,130 includes full-time tuition ($17,784), mandatory fees ($930), and room and board ($7416). Part-time tuition: $494 per credit hour. ***Required fees:*** $310 per term part-time. ***College room only:*** $5346. Room and board charges vary according to board plan and housing facility.

Financial Aid ***Financial aid deadline:*** 5/1.

APPLYING

Standardized Tests *Required for some:* SAT or ACT (for admission).

Options: electronic application.

Required: high school transcript, minimum 2.0 GPA. ***Required for some:*** 1 letter of recommendation, interview. ***Recommended:*** essay or personal statement, 1 letter of recommendation.

CONTACT

Central Penn College, College Hill & Valley Roads, Summerdale, PA 17093-0309. *Toll-free phone:* 800-759-2727.

Chatham University

Pittsburgh, Pennsylvania

http://www.chatham.edu/

- **Independent** university, founded 1869
- **Urban** 427-acre campus
- **Endowment** $77.7 million
- **Coed, primarily women**
- **Moderately difficult** entrance level

FACULTY

Student/faculty ratio: 10:1.

ACADEMICS

Calendar: 4-4-1. *Degrees:* bachelor's, master's, doctoral, post-master's, and postbachelor's certificates.
Library: Jennie King Mellon Library. *Books:* 88,368 (physical), 1,200 (digital/electronic); *Serial titles:* 92 (physical), 32,874 (digital/electronic); *Databases:* 65. Weekly public service hours: 99; study areas open 24 hours, 5–7 days a week; students can reserve study rooms.

STUDENT LIFE

Housing options: on-campus residence required through sophomore year; coed, women-only. Campus housing is university owned. Freshman campus housing is guaranteed.

Activities and organizations: drama/theater group, student-run newspaper, choral group, Chatham Student Government, Residence Hall Council, Student Athletic Advisory Council (SAAC), Creative Writing Club and MFA Writing Council, Graduate Student Assembly.

Athletics Member NCAA. All Division III.

Campus security: 24-hour emergency response devices and patrols, late-night transport/escort service, controlled dormitory access, self-defense education, well-lighted pathways and sidewalks.

Student services: health clinic, personal/psychological counseling, women's center, veterans affairs office.

COSTS & FINANCIAL AID

Costs (2018–19) ***Comprehensive fee:*** $49,701 includes full-time tuition ($36,276), mandatory fees ($1335), and room and board ($12,090). Part-time tuition: $880 per credit hour. Part-time tuition and fees vary according to course load. ***College room only:*** $6240. Room and board charges vary according to board plan and housing facility.

Financial Aid Of all full-time matriculated undergraduates who enrolled in 2018, 942 applied for aid, 736 were judged to have need, 120 had their need fully met. In 2018, 60 non-need-based awards were made. ***Average percent of need met:*** 64. ***Average financial aid package:*** $36,742. ***Average need-based loan:*** $3981. ***Average need-based gift aid:*** $9292. ***Average non-need-based aid:*** $19,098. ***Average indebtedness upon graduation:*** $35,817.

APPLYING

Options: electronic application, early admission, deferred entrance.

Application fee: $35.

Required: essay or personal statement, high school transcript, minimum 2.0 GPA, 1 letter of recommendation. ***Recommended:*** interview.

CONTACT

Ms. Amy M. Becher, Vice President for Enrollment Management, Chatham University, Woodland, Berry Hall, Pittsburgh, PA 15232. *Phone:* 800-837-1290. *Toll-free phone:* 800-837-1290. *Fax:* 412-365-1609. *E-mail:* admission@chatham.edu.

Chestnut Hill College

Philadelphia, Pennsylvania

http://www.chc.edu/

- **Independent Roman Catholic** comprehensive, founded 1924
- **Suburban** 75-acre campus with easy access to Philadelphia
- **Endowment** $9.4 million
- **Coed**
- **Moderately difficult** entrance level

FACULTY

Student/faculty ratio: 10:1.

ACADEMICS

Calendar: semesters. *Degrees:* certificates, associate, bachelor's, master's, doctoral, post-master's, and postbachelor's certificates (profile includes figures from both traditional and accelerated (part-time) programs).
Library: Logue Library. *Books:* 120,908 (physical), 226,691 (digital/electronic); *Serial titles:* 670 (physical), 271,184 (digital/electronic); *Databases:* 433. Weekly public service hours: 99; students can reserve study rooms.

STUDENT LIFE

Housing options: coed. Campus housing is university owned and leased by the school.

Activities and organizations: drama/theater group, student-run newspaper, radio and television station, choral group, Student Government, Mask and Foil Drama Club, Association for Musical Performance, Campus Ministry Community Service Group, Business Club.

Athletics Member NCAA. All Division II.

Campus security: 24-hour emergency response devices and patrols, late-night transport/escort service, controlled dormitory access.

Student services: health clinic, personal/psychological counseling.

COSTS & FINANCIAL AID

Costs (2018–19) ***One-time required fee:*** $475. ***Comprehensive fee:*** $47,180 includes full-time tuition ($35,950), mandatory fees ($230), and room and board ($11,000). Part-time tuition: $745 per credit hour. Part-time tuition and fees vary according to class time. ***Required fees:*** $230 per year part-time. ***Room and board:*** Room and board charges vary according to housing facility. ***Payment plans:*** installment, deferred payment.

Financial Aid Of all full-time matriculated undergraduates who enrolled in 2018, 988 applied for aid, 933 were judged to have need, 62 had their need fully met. In 2018, 117 non-need-based awards were made. ***Average percent of need met:*** 60. ***Average financial aid package:*** $23,816. ***Average need-based loan:*** $4215. ***Average need-based gift aid:*** $12,835. ***Average non-need-based aid:*** $15,214. ***Average indebtedness upon graduation:*** $32,278. ***Financial aid deadline:*** 6/30.

APPLYING

Standardized Tests *Required:* SAT or ACT (for admission).

Options: electronic application, deferred entrance.

Application fee: $35.

Required: high school transcript. ***Required for some:*** interview. ***Recommended:*** essay or personal statement, .

CONTACT

Ms. Stephanie Williams, Chestnut Hill College, 9601 Germantown Avenue, Philadelphia, PA 19118-2693. *Phone:* 215-248-7001. *Toll-free phone:* 800-248-0052. *Fax:* 215-248-7082. *E-mail:* williamss@chc.edu.

Cheyney University of Pennsylvania

Cheyney, Pennsylvania

http://www.cheyney.edu/

CONTACT

Shon Jeffery, Associate Director of Enrollment Management, Cheyney University of Pennsylvania, 1837 University Circle, PO Box 200, Cheyney, PA 19319. *Phone:* 610-399-2255. *Toll-free phone:* 800-CHEYNEY. *E-mail:* spjeffery@cheyney.edu.

Clarion University of Pennsylvania

Clarion, Pennsylvania

http://www.clarion.edu/

- **State-supported** comprehensive, founded 1867, part of Pennsylvania State System of Higher Education
- **Rural** 201-acre campus
- **Endowment** $37.0 million
- **Coed** 3,942 undergraduate students, 79% full-time, 67% women, 33% men
- **Minimally difficult** entrance level, 94% of applicants were admitted

UNDERGRAD STUDENTS
3,132 full-time, 810 part-time. Students come from 38 states and territories; 8 other countries; 7% are from out of state; 7% Black or African American, non-Hispanic/Latino; 3% Hispanic/Latino; 0.9% Asian, non-Hispanic/Latino; 0.1% Native Hawaiian or other Pacific Islander, non-Hispanic/Latino; 0.2% American Indian or Alaska Native, non-Hispanic/Latino; 2% Two or more races, non-Hispanic/Latino; 3% Race/ethnicity unknown; 0.3% international; 8% transferred in; 35% live on campus.

Freshmen:
Admission: 2,373 applied, 2,233 admitted, 726 enrolled. ***Average high school GPA:*** 3.4. ***Test scores:*** SAT evidence-based reading and writing scores over 500: 68%; SAT math scores over 500: 63%; ACT scores over 18: 84%; SAT evidence-based reading and writing scores over 600: 16%; SAT math scores over 600: 11%; ACT scores over 24: 13%; SAT evidence-based reading and writing scores over 700: 1%; SAT math scores over 700: 1%; ACT scores over 30: 3%.

Retention: 74% of full-time freshmen returned.

FACULTY
Total: 278, 74% full-time, 74% with terminal degrees.

Student/faculty ratio: 18:1.

ACADEMICS
Calendar: semesters. *Degrees:* certificates, associate, bachelor's, master's, doctoral, post-master's, and postbachelor's certificates.

Special study options: academic remediation for entering students, accelerated degree program, adult/continuing education programs, advanced placement credit, cooperative education, distance learning, double majors, English as a second language, honors programs, independent study, internships, off-campus study, part-time degree program, services for LD students, study abroad, summer session for credit. ***ROTC:*** Army (b).

Unusual degree programs: 3-2 engineering with University of Pittsburgh, Case Western Reserve University.

Computers: 950 computers/terminals and 24 ports are available on campus for general student use. Students can access the following: campus intranet, computer help desk, free student e-mail accounts, online (class) grades, online (class) registration, online (class) schedules, Online Learning Management System, web-based personal disk space, other online student services (financial aid, billing etc.). Campuswide network is available. 100% of college-owned or -operated housing units are wired for high-speed Internet access. Wireless service is available via entire campus.

Library: Carlson Library plus 1 other. *Books:* 444,818 (physical), 348,037 (digital/electronic); *Serial titles:* 179 (physical), 57,405 (digital/electronic); *Databases:* 102. Weekly public service hours: 94; students can reserve study rooms.

STUDENT LIFE
Housing options: on-campus residence required through sophomore year; coed, special housing for students with disabilities. Campus housing is university owned. Freshman campus housing is guaranteed.

Activities and organizations: drama/theater group, student-run newspaper, radio and television station, choral group, marching band, The National Student Speech-Language Hearing Association, Phi Eta Sigma freshman honor society, Allies, Black Student Union, Cru, national fraternities, national sororities.

Athletics Member NCAA. All Division II except golf (Division I), wrestling (Division I). ***Intercollegiate sports:*** baseball M(s), basketball M(s)/W(s), cross-country running W(s), football M(s), golf M(s)/W(s), soccer W(s), softball W(s), swimming and diving M(s)/W(s), tennis W(s), track and field W(s), volleyball W(s), wrestling M(s). ***Intramural sports:*** badminton M/W, basketball M/W, equestrian sports M(c)/W(c), golf M/W, racquetball M/W, rock climbing M(c)/W(c), rugby M(c)/W(c), sand volleyball M/W, soccer M/W, softball M/W, table tennis M/W, tennis M/W, track and field M(c)/W(c), ultimate Frisbee M(c)/W(c), volleyball M/W, weight lifting M/W, wrestling M/W.

Campus security: 24-hour emergency response devices and patrols, student patrols, late-night transport/escort service, controlled dormitory access.

Student services: health clinic, personal/psychological counseling, women's center.

COSTS & FINANCIAL AID
Costs (2018–19) ***One-time required fee:*** $50. ***Tuition:*** state resident $7716 full-time, $322 per credit hour part-time; nonresident $11,574 full-time, $482 per credit hour part-time. Full-time tuition and fees vary according to course load and location. Part-time tuition and fees vary according to course load and location. ***Required fees:*** $3459 full-time. ***Room and board:*** $12,670. Room and board charges vary according to board plan and housing facility. ***Payment plans:*** installment, deferred payment. ***Waivers:*** senior citizens and employees or children of employees.

Financial Aid Of all full-time matriculated undergraduates who enrolled in 2018, 2,874 applied for aid, 2,551 were judged to have need, 167 had their need fully met. 314 Federal Work-Study jobs (averaging $1190). 463 state and other part-time jobs (averaging $1851). In 2018, 213 non-need-based awards were made. ***Average percent of need met:*** 50. ***Average financial aid package:*** $10,864. ***Average need-based loan:*** $3893. ***Average need-based gift aid:*** $5834. ***Average non-need-based aid:*** $2291. ***Average indebtedness upon graduation:*** $36,800.

APPLYING
Standardized Tests *Required:* SAT or ACT (for admission). *Required for some:* TOEFL, TSE or IELTS for international students.

Options: electronic application, early admission, deferred entrance.

Application fee: $40.

Required: high school transcript, minimum 2.0 GPA. ***Required for some:*** essay or personal statement, interview, NLN Test for ASN program. ***Recommended:*** essay or personal statement, 2 letters of recommendation, interview.

Application deadlines: rolling (freshmen), rolling (out-of-state freshmen), rolling (transfers).

Notification: continuous (freshmen), continuous (out-of-state freshmen), continuous (transfers).

CONTACT
Ms. Merrilyn Dunlap, Senior Associate Director, Clarion University of Pennsylvania, 314 Becht Hall, 840 Wood Street, Clarion, PA 16214. *Phone:* 814-393-2306. *Toll-free phone:* 800-672-7171. *Fax:* 814-393-2030. *E-mail:* mdunlap@clarion.edu.

Clarks Summit University

South Abington Township, Pennsylvania

http://www.clarkssummitu.edu/

CONTACT
Ms. Patience Schwamb, Director of Student Accounts, Clarks Summit University, 538 Venard Road, Clarks Summit, PA 18411-1297. *Phone:* 570-585-9205. *Toll-free phone:* 800-451-7664. *Fax:* 570-585-9271. *E-mail:* pschwamb@clarkssummitu.edu.

Curtis Institute of Music

Philadelphia, Pennsylvania

http://www.curtis.edu/

CONTACT
Mr. Christopher Hodges, Admissions Officer, Curtis Institute of Music, 1726 Locust Street, Philadelphia, PA 19103-6107. *Phone:* 215-893-5262. *E-mail:* chris.hodges@curtis.edu.

Delaware Valley University

Doylestown, Pennsylvania

http://www.delval.edu/

- **Independent** comprehensive, founded 1896
- **Suburban** 571-acre campus with easy access to Philadelphia
- **Endowment** $33.6 million
- **Coed** 1,982 undergraduate students, 88% full-time, 59% women, 41% men
- **Minimally difficult** entrance level, 66% of applicants were admitted

UNDERGRAD STUDENTS

1,744 full-time, 238 part-time. Students come from 25 states and territories; 8 other countries; 34% are from out of state; 9% Black or African American, non-Hispanic/Latino; 7% Hispanic/Latino; 1% Asian, non-Hispanic/Latino; 0.1% Native Hawaiian or other Pacific Islander, non-Hispanic/Latino; 0.5% American Indian or Alaska Native, non-Hispanic/Latino; 2% Two or more races, non-Hispanic/Latino; 11% Race/ethnicity unknown; 0.6% international; 7% transferred in; 49% live on campus.

Freshmen:

Admission: 2,423 applied, 1,591 admitted, 443 enrolled. ***Average high school GPA:*** 3.3. ***Test scores:*** SAT evidence-based reading and writing scores over 500: 69%; SAT math scores over 500: 67%; ACT scores over 18: 84%; SAT evidence-based reading and writing scores over 600: 23%; SAT math scores over 600: 17%; ACT scores over 24: 51%; SAT evidence-based reading and writing scores over 700: 3%; SAT math scores over 700: 2%; ACT scores over 30: 13%.

Retention: 72% of full-time freshmen returned.

FACULTY

Total: 274, 34% full-time, 24% with terminal degrees.

Student/faculty ratio: 14:1.

ACADEMICS

Calendar: semesters. *Degrees:* certificates, bachelor's, master's, doctoral, and postbachelor's certificates.

Special study options: academic remediation for entering students, accelerated degree program, adult/continuing education programs, advanced placement credit, cooperative education, distance learning, double majors, honors programs, independent study, internships, part-time degree program, services for LD students, study abroad, summer session for credit.

Computers: 160 computers/terminals are available on campus for general student use. Students can access the following: campus intranet, computer help desk, free student e-mail accounts, online (class) grades, online (class) registration, online (class) schedules. Campuswide network is available. 100% of college-owned or -operated housing units are wired for high-speed Internet access. Wireless service is available via entire campus.

Library: Joseph Krauskopf Memorial Library. *Books:* 45,500 (physical), 7,830 (digital/electronic); *Serial titles:* 74 (physical), 113,400 (digital/electronic); *Databases:* 44. Weekly public service hours: 92.

STUDENT LIFE

Housing options: on-campus residence required for freshman year; coed, special housing for students with disabilities. Campus housing is university owned. Freshman campus housing is guaranteed.

Activities and organizations: drama/theater group, choral group, Animal Lifeline Club, Pre-Vet Club, Dairy Society, Sigma Alpha, A-Day, national fraternities, national sororities.

Athletics Member NCAA. All Division III. ***Intercollegiate sports:*** baseball M, basketball M/W, cheerleading W, cross-country running M/W, equestrian sports M/W, fencing M/W, field hockey W, football M, golf M/W, lacrosse M/W, soccer M/W, softball W, tennis M/W, track and field M/W, volleyball W, wrestling M/W. ***Intramural sports:*** basketball M/W, football W, soccer M/W, softball M/W, volleyball M/W.

Campus security: 24-hour emergency response devices and patrols, late-night transport/escort service, controlled dormitory access.

Student services: health clinic, personal/psychological counseling, veterans affairs office.

COSTS & FINANCIAL AID

Costs (2019–20) ***Comprehensive fee:*** $55,240 includes full-time tuition ($38,070), mandatory fees ($2550), and room and board ($14,620). Part-time tuition: $1049 per credit hour. ***Required fees:*** $14 per course part-time. ***College room only:*** $6950.

Financial Aid Of all full-time matriculated undergraduates who enrolled in 2018, 1,537 applied for aid, 1,415 were judged to have need, 230 had their need fully met. 199 Federal Work-Study jobs (averaging $1702). In 2018, 300 non-need-based awards were made. ***Average percent of need met:*** 67. ***Average financial aid package:*** $28,570. ***Average need-based loan:*** $4260. ***Average need-based gift aid:*** $24,864. ***Average non-need-based aid:*** $18,805. ***Average indebtedness upon graduation:*** $42,245.

APPLYING

Standardized Tests *Required:* SAT or ACT (for admission). *Required for some:* TOEFL.

Options: electronic application, deferred entrance.

Application fee: $50.

Required: essay or personal statement, high school transcript, 1 letter of recommendation, Test scores (SAT/ACT), additional short-answer questions for Zoo Science applicants. ***Required for some:*** interview.

Application deadlines: rolling (freshmen), rolling (out-of-state freshmen), rolling (transfers).

Notification: continuous (freshmen), continuous (out-of-state freshmen), continuous (transfers).

CONTACT

Mr. Dwayne Walker, Vice President for Enrollment Management and Director of Admissions, Delaware Valley University, 700 E. Butler Avenue, Doylestown, PA 18901. *Phone:* 215-489-2372. *Toll-free phone:* 800-2DELVAL. *Fax:* 215-230-2968. *E-mail:* dwayne.walker@delval.edu.

DeSales University

Center Valley, Pennsylvania

http://www.desales.edu/

- **Independent Roman Catholic** comprehensive, founded 1964
- **Suburban** 480-acre campus with easy access to Philadelphia, PA
- **Endowment** $80.1 million
- **Coed**
- **Moderately difficult** entrance level

FACULTY

Student/faculty ratio: 12:1.

ACADEMICS

Calendar: semesters. *Degrees:* certificates, bachelor's, master's, doctoral, post-master's, and postbachelor's certificates.

Library: Trexler Library. *Books:* 155,243 (physical), 135,000 (digital/electronic); *Serial titles:* 260 (physical), 19,000 (digital/electronic); *Databases:* 87. Weekly public service hours: 102; students can reserve study rooms.

STUDENT LIFE

Housing options: coed, men-only, women-only, special housing for students with disabilities. Campus housing is university owned. Freshman campus housing is guaranteed.

Activities and organizations: drama/theater group, student-run newspaper, radio and television station, choral group, marching band, College Against Cancer, Outdoor Adventure Club, Student Nursing Association, Criminal Justice Association, Natural Science Club.

Athletics Member NCAA. All Division III.

Campus security: 24-hour emergency response devices and patrols, late-night transport/escort service, controlled dormitory access.

Student services: health clinic, personal/psychological counseling.

COSTS & FINANCIAL AID

Costs (2018–19) ***One-time required fee:*** $200. ***Comprehensive fee:*** $50,200 includes full-time tuition ($36,000), mandatory fees ($1400), and room and board ($12,800). Full-time tuition and fees vary according to class time and course load. Part-time tuition: $1500 per credit hour. Part-time tuition and fees vary according to class time and course load. ***Room and board:*** Room and board charges vary according to board plan and housing facility. ***Payment plans:*** installment, deferred payment.

Financial Aid Of all full-time matriculated undergraduates who enrolled in 2018, 1,713 applied for aid, 1,531 were judged to have need, 321 had their need fully met. 352 Federal Work-Study jobs (averaging $2000). 280 state and other part-time jobs (averaging $1999). In 2018, 354 non-need-based awards were made. ***Average percent of need met:*** 68. ***Average financial aid package:*** $26,116. ***Average need-based loan:*** $4502. ***Average need-based gift aid:*** $20,893. ***Average non-need-based aid:*** $17,677. ***Average indebtedness upon graduation:*** $45,320.

APPLYING

Standardized Tests *Required:* SAT or ACT (for admission).

Options: electronic application, early admission, deferred entrance.

Required: essay or personal statement, high school transcript, letters of recommendation. ***Recommended:*** interview.

CONTACT

Mr. Derrick Wetzel, Director of Admissions, DeSales University, 2755 Station Avenue, Center Valley, PA 18034-9568. *Phone:* 610-282-4443. *Fax:* 610-282-0131. *E-mail:* derrick.wetzell@desales.edu.

DeVry University–Ft. Washington Campus

Fort Washington, Pennsylvania

http://www.devry.edu/

CONTACT

DeVry University–Ft. Washington Campus, 1140 Virginia Drive, Fort Washington, PA 19034. *Phone:* 215-591-5700. *Toll-free phone:* 866-338-7934.

Dickinson College

Carlisle, Pennsylvania

http://www.dickinson.edu/

- **Independent** 4-year, founded 1773
- **Suburban** 144-acre campus with easy access to Harrisburg
- **Endowment** $437.5 million
- **Coed** 2,399 undergraduate students, 98% full-time, 58% women, 42% men
- **Very difficult** entrance level, 49% of applicants were admitted

UNDERGRAD STUDENTS

2,361 full-time, 38 part-time. Students come from 39 states and territories; 49 other countries; 77% are from out of state; 5% Black or African American, non-Hispanic/Latino; 9% Hispanic/Latino; 4% Asian, non-Hispanic/Latino; 0.2% American Indian or Alaska Native, non-Hispanic/Latino; 3% Two or more races, non-Hispanic/Latino; 0.7% Race/ethnicity unknown; 14% international; 0.4% transferred in; 100% live on campus.

Freshmen:

Admission: 6,248 applied, 3,070 admitted, 635 enrolled. ***Test scores:*** SAT evidence-based reading and writing scores over 500: 99%; SAT math scores over 500: 99%; ACT scores over 18: 101%; SAT evidence-based reading and writing scores over 600: 81%; SAT math scores over 600: 72%; ACT scores over 24: 95%; SAT evidence-based reading and writing scores over 700: 21%; SAT math scores over 700: 27%; ACT scores over 30: 49%.

Retention: 91% of full-time freshmen returned.

FACULTY

Total: 285, 78% full-time, 89% with terminal degrees.

Student/faculty ratio: 9:1.

ACADEMICS

Calendar: semesters. *Degree:* bachelor's.

Special study options: accelerated degree program, adult/continuing education programs, advanced placement credit, double majors, English as a second language, independent study, internships, off-campus study, part-time degree program, services for LD students, student-designed majors, study abroad. ***ROTC:*** Army (b).

Unusual degree programs: 3-2 engineering with Case Western Reserve University, Rensselaer Polytechnic Institute, Columbia University; international studies with Johns Hopkins University, Columbia University Mailman School of Public Health.

Computers: 1,720 computers/terminals and 5,400 ports are available on campus for general student use. Students can access the following: campus intranet, computer help desk, free student e-mail accounts, online (class) grades, online (class) registration, online (class) schedules. Campuswide network is available. 100% of college-owned or -operated housing units are wired for high-speed Internet access. Wireless service is available via classrooms, computer centers, computer labs, dorm rooms, libraries, student centers.

Library: Waidner-Spahr Library. *Books:* 516,871 (physical), 653,715 (digital/electronic); *Serial titles:* 3,559 (physical), 99,470 (digital/electronic); *Databases:* 506. Weekly public service hours: 114; students can reserve study rooms.

STUDENT LIFE

Housing options: on-campus residence required through senior year; coed, special housing for students with disabilities. Campus housing is university owned. Freshman campus housing is guaranteed.

Activities and organizations: drama/theater group, student-run newspaper, radio station, choral group, Multi-Organization Board, Outing Club, Student Senate, Admissions Volunteers, WDCV Radio Station, national fraternities, national sororities.

Athletics Member NCAA. All Division III. ***Intercollegiate sports:*** badminton M(c)/W(c), baseball M, basketball M/W, cheerleading M(c)/W(c), cross-country running M/W, equestrian sports M(c)/W(c), fencing M(c)/W(c), field hockey W, football M, golf M/W, ice hockey M(c)/W(c), lacrosse M/W, rock climbing M(c)/W(c), skiing (downhill) M(c)/W(c), soccer M/W, softball W, squash M/W, swimming and diving M/W, tennis M/W, track and field M/W, ultimate Frisbee W(c), volleyball W. ***Intramural sports:*** basketball M(c)/W(c), lacrosse M(c), soccer W(c), squash W(c), tennis W(c), volleyball W(c).

Campus security: 24-hour emergency response devices and patrols, student patrols, late-night transport/escort service, controlled dormitory access.

Student services: health clinic, personal/psychological counseling, women's center.

COSTS & FINANCIAL AID

Costs (2019–20) ***One-time required fee:*** $25. ***Comprehensive fee:*** $70,674 includes full-time tuition ($55,948), mandatory fees ($550), and room and board ($14,176). Part-time tuition: $6995 per course. ***Required fees:*** $70 per course part-time. ***College room only:*** $7310.

Financial Aid Of all full-time matriculated undergraduates who enrolled in 2018, 1,518 applied for aid, 1,430 were judged to have need, 1,107 had their need fully met. 1,032 Federal Work-Study jobs (averaging $2243). 268 state and other part-time jobs (averaging $3525). In 2018, 346 non-need-based awards were made. ***Average percent of need met:*** 98. ***Average financial aid package:*** $48,116. ***Average need-based loan:*** $4840. ***Average need-based gift aid:*** $41,771. ***Average non-need-based aid:*** $11,345. ***Average indebtedness upon graduation:*** $26,977. ***Financial aid deadline:*** 1/15.

APPLYING

Standardized Tests *Recommended:* SAT or ACT (for admission).

Options: electronic application, early decision, early action, deferred entrance.

Application fee: $65.

Required: essay or personal statement, high school transcript, 2 letters of recommendation. ***Recommended:*** minimum 3.0 GPA, interview.

Application deadlines: 1/15 (freshmen), 1/15 (out-of-state freshmen), 4/1 (transfers), 12/1 (early action).

Early decision deadline: 11/15 (for plan 1), 1/15 (for plan 2).

Notification: 3/23 (freshmen), 3/23 (out-of-state freshmen), 5/15 (transfers), 12/15 (early decision plan 1), 2/15 (early decision plan 2), 2/15 (early action).

CONTACT

Catherine Davenport, VP Enrollment Management & Dean of Admissions, Dickinson College, PO Box 1773, Admissions Office, Carlisle, PA 17013-2896. *Phone:* 717-245-1231. *Toll-free phone:* 800-644-1773. *Fax:* 717-245-1442. *E-mail:* admissions@dickinson.edu.

★ Drexel University
Philadelphia, Pennsylvania
http://www.drexel.edu/

- **Independent** university, founded 1891
- **Urban** 96-acre campus with easy access to Philadelphia
- **Endowment** $650.3 million
- **Coed**
- **Moderately difficult** entrance level

FACULTY
Student/faculty ratio: 11:1.

ACADEMICS
Calendar: quarters. *Degrees:* certificates, bachelor's, master's, doctoral, post-master's, and postbachelor's certificates.
Library: W. W. Hagerty Library plus 3 others. *Books:* 286,613 (physical), 215,379 (digital/electronic); *Serial titles:* 126 (physical), 51,775 (digital/electronic); *Databases:* 465. Weekly public service hours: 87; study areas open 24 hours, 5–7 days a week; students can reserve study rooms.

STUDENT LIFE
Housing options: on-campus residence required for freshman year; coed, special housing for students with disabilities. Campus housing is university owned. Freshman campus housing is guaranteed.

Activities and organizations: drama/theater group, student-run newspaper, radio and television station, choral group, Student Government, Black Student Union, Society of Hispanic Professional Engineers, Society of Minority Engineers and Scientists, Campus Activities Board, national fraternities, national sororities.

Athletics Member NCAA. All Division I.

Campus security: 24-hour emergency response devices and patrols, late-night transport/escort service, controlled dormitory access.

Student services: health clinic, personal/psychological counseling, women's center, veterans affairs office.

COSTS & FINANCIAL AID
Costs (2018–19) ***Comprehensive fee:*** $65,892 includes full-time tuition ($49,632), mandatory fees ($2370), and room and board ($13,890). Full-time tuition and fees vary according to course load, location, program, and student level. Part-time tuition: $1116 per credit hour. Part-time tuition and fees vary according to course load and program. ***Required fees:*** $150 per term part-time. ***College room only:*** $8205. Room and board charges vary according to board plan and housing facility.

Financial Aid Of all full-time matriculated undergraduates who enrolled in 2018, 10,231 applied for aid, 9,081 were judged to have need, 2,075 had their need fully met. In 2018, 4267 non-need-based awards were made. ***Average percent of need met:*** 74. ***Average financial aid package:*** $38,636. ***Average need-based loan:*** $10,072. ***Average need-based gift aid:*** $29,091. ***Average non-need-based aid:*** $16,199. ***Financial aid deadline:*** 2/15.

APPLYING
Standardized Tests *Required:* SAT or ACT (for admission).

Options: electronic application, early admission, early decision, early action, deferred entrance.

Application fee: $50.

Required: essay or personal statement, high school transcript, minimum 2.0 GPA. ***Recommended:*** 2 letters of recommendation, interview.

CONTACT
Evelyn Thimba, Vice President, Dean of Admissions, Drexel University, 3141 Chestnut Street, Philadelphia, PA 19104-2875. *Phone:* 215-895-6712. *Toll-free phone:* 800-2-DREXEL. *E-mail:* evelyn.k.thimba@drexel.edu.

See below for display ad and page 1000 for the College Close-Up.

Duquesne University

Pittsburgh, Pennsylvania

http://www.duq.edu/

- **Independent Roman Catholic** university, founded 1878
- **Urban** 50-acre campus with easy access to Pittsburgh
- **Endowment** $308.2 million
- **Coed** 6,013 undergraduate students, 98% full-time, 64% women, 36% men
- **Moderately difficult** entrance level, 72% of applicants were admitted

UNDERGRAD STUDENTS

5,896 full-time, 117 part-time. Students come from 44 states and territories; 44 other countries; 28% are from out of state; 5% Black or African American, non-Hispanic/Latino; 4% Hispanic/Latino; 3% Asian, non-Hispanic/Latino; 0.1% Native Hawaiian or other Pacific Islander, non-Hispanic/Latino; 0.1% American Indian or Alaska Native, non-Hispanic/Latino; 3% Two or more races, non-Hispanic/Latino; 1% Race/ethnicity unknown; 3% international; 3% transferred in; 60% live on campus.

Freshmen:

Admission: 7,505 applied, 5,392 admitted, 1,512 enrolled. ***Average high school GPA:*** 3.8. ***Test scores:*** SAT evidence-based reading and writing scores over 500: 99%; SAT math scores over 500: 99%; ACT scores over 18: 100%; SAT evidence-based reading and writing scores over 600: 63%; SAT math scores over 600: 47%; ACT scores over 24: 83%; SAT evidence-based reading and writing scores over 700: 6%; SAT math scores over 700: 9%; ACT scores over 30: 22%.

Retention: 84% of full-time freshmen returned.

FACULTY

Total: 990, 51% full-time.

Student/faculty ratio: 14:1.

ACADEMICS

Calendar: semesters. *Degrees:* bachelor's, master's, doctoral, post-master's, and postbachelor's certificates.

Special study options: academic remediation for entering students, accelerated degree program, adult/continuing education programs, advanced placement credit, distance learning, double majors, English as a second language, external degree program, freshman honors college, honors programs, independent study, internships, off-campus study, part-time degree program, services for LD students, student-designed majors, study abroad, summer session for credit. ***ROTC:*** Army (b), Navy (c), Air Force (c).

Unusual degree programs: 3-2 engineering with Case Western Reserve University, University of Pittsburgh.

Computers: 1,000 computers/terminals are available on campus for general student use. Students can access the following: campus intranet, computer help desk, free student e-mail accounts, online (class) grades, online (class) registration, online (class) schedules. Campuswide network is available. 100% of college-owned or -operated housing units are wired for high-speed Internet access. Wireless service is available via entire campus.

Library: Gumberg Library plus 1 other. *Books:* 562,314 (physical), 342,710 (digital/electronic); *Serial titles:* 123 (physical), 99,402 (digital/electronic); *Databases:* 227. Weekly public service hours: 112; students can reserve study rooms.

STUDENT LIFE

Housing options: on-campus residence required through sophomore year; coed, men-only, women-only, special housing for students with disabilities. Campus housing is university owned. Freshman campus housing is guaranteed.

Activities and organizations: drama/theater group, student-run newspaper, radio and television station, choral group, marching band, International Student's Org (ISO), Red and Blue Crew, Duquesne University Volunteers (DUV), Duquesne Program Council, Residence Hall Association, national fraternities, national sororities.

Athletics Member NCAA. All Division I except football (Division I-AA). ***Intercollegiate sports:*** basketball M(s)/W(s), bowling W(s), crew W(s), cross-country running M(s)/W(s), lacrosse W(s), soccer M(s)/W(s), swimming and diving W(s), tennis M(s)/W(s), track and field M(s)/W(s), volleyball W(s). ***Intramural sports:*** baseball M(c)/W(c), basketball M/W, crew M(c)/W(c), equestrian sports M(c)/W(c), golf M(c)/W(c), ice hockey M(c)/W(c), lacrosse M(c)/W(c), racquetball M/W, rugby M(c)/W(c), soccer M/W, tennis M(c)/W(c), ultimate Frisbee M/W, volleyball M/W.

Campus security: 24-hour emergency response devices and patrols, late-night transport/escort service, controlled dormitory access, cameras monitor exterior 24-hours/day, card access for buildings, outside warning siren system.

Student services: health clinic, personal/psychological counseling, veterans affairs office.

COSTS & FINANCIAL AID

Costs (2019–20) ***Comprehensive fee:*** $53,080 includes full-time tuition ($39,992) and room and board ($13,088). Part-time tuition: $1325. ***College room only:*** $7194.

Financial Aid Of all full-time matriculated undergraduates who enrolled in 2017, 4,593 applied for aid, 3,956 were judged to have need, 761 had their need fully met. 1,772 Federal Work-Study jobs (averaging $2400). In 2017, 1616 non-need-based awards were made. ***Average percent of need met:*** 72. ***Average financial aid package:*** $25,997. ***Average need-based loan:*** $4437. ***Average need-based gift aid:*** $22,760. ***Average non-need-based aid:*** $14,531. ***Average indebtedness upon graduation:*** $44,228. ***Financial aid deadline:*** 5/1.

APPLYING

Standardized Tests *Required for some:* SAT or ACT (for admission).

Options: electronic application, early admission, early decision, early action, deferred entrance.

Application fee: $50.

Required: high school transcript. ***Required for some:*** essay or personal statement, 1 letter of recommendation, audition for School of Music; 40 hours of volunteer, paid, or shadowing experience for physical therapy. ***Recommended:*** minimum 3.0 GPA, interview.

Application deadlines: 7/1 (transfers), 12/1 (early action).

Early decision deadline: 11/1.

Notification: continuous until 10/1 (freshmen), continuous (out-of-state freshmen), continuous (transfers), 12/15 (early decision), 1/15 (early action).

CONTACT

Ms. Debra Zugates, Director of Admissions, Duquesne University, Administration Building, 600 Forbes Avenue, Pittsburgh, PA 15282-0201. *Phone:* 412-396-5211. *Toll-free phone:* 800-456-0590. *Fax:* 412-396-5644. *E-mail:* admissions@duq.edu.

Eastern University

St. Davids, Pennsylvania

http://www.eastern.edu/

- **Independent Christian** university, founded 1952
- **Suburban** 114-acre campus with easy access to Philadelphia
- **Endowment** $30.7 million
- **Coed** 1,885 undergraduate students, 78% full-time, 68% women, 32% men
- **Moderately difficult** entrance level, 69% of applicants were admitted

UNDERGRAD STUDENTS

1,463 full-time, 422 part-time. Students come from 35 states and territories; 17 other countries; 41% are from out of state; 20% Black or African American, non-Hispanic/Latino; 19% Hispanic/Latino; 2% Asian, non-Hispanic/Latino; 0.1% Native Hawaiian or other Pacific Islander, non-Hispanic/Latino; 0.2% American Indian or Alaska Native, non-Hispanic/Latino; 2% Two or more races, non-Hispanic/Latino; 5% Race/ethnicity unknown; 2% international; 8% transferred in; 79% live on campus.

Freshmen:

Admission: 1,757 applied, 1,204 admitted, 423 enrolled. ***Average high school GPA:*** 3.5. ***Test scores:*** SAT evidence-based reading and writing scores over 500: 77%; SAT math scores over 500: 69%; ACT scores over 18: 73%; SAT evidence-based reading and writing scores over 600: 30%; SAT math scores over 600: 24%; ACT scores over 24: 43%; SAT evidence-based reading and writing scores over 700: 4%; SAT math scores over 700: 3%; ACT scores over 30: 17%.

Retention: 75% of full-time freshmen returned.

FACULTY
Total: 440, 26% full-time, 40% with terminal degrees.

Student/faculty ratio: 10:1.

ACADEMICS
Calendar: semesters. *Degrees:* certificates, diplomas, associate, bachelor's, master's, doctoral, and post-master's certificates.

Special study options: academic remediation for entering students, accelerated degree program, adult/continuing education programs, advanced placement credit, distance learning, double majors, English as a second language, external degree program, honors programs, independent study, internships, off-campus study, part-time degree program, services for LD students, student-designed majors, study abroad, summer session for credit. ***ROTC:*** Army (c), Air Force (c).

Computers: Students can access the following: campus intranet, computer help desk, free student e-mail accounts, online (class) grades, online (class) registration, online (class) schedules, BRIGHTSPACE. Campuswide network is available. 100% of college-owned or -operated housing units are wired for high-speed Internet access. Wireless service is available via entire campus.
Library: Warner Memorial Library plus 1 other. *Books:* 170,630 (physical), 1.6 million (digital/electronic); *Serial titles:* 70 (physical), 61,842 (digital/electronic); *Databases:* 189. Weekly public service hours: 83; students can reserve study rooms.

STUDENT LIFE
Housing options: on-campus residence required through senior year; men-only, women-only, special housing for students with disabilities. Campus housing is university owned and leased by the school. Freshman campus housing is guaranteed.

Activities and organizations: drama/theater group, student-run newspaper, choral group, Wednesday Night Worship, Ultimate Frisbee, Student Activities Board, MAAC, Student Chaplain Program.

Athletics Member NCAA. All Division III. ***Intercollegiate sports:*** baseball M, basketball M/W, cross-country running M/W, field hockey W, golf M/W, lacrosse M/W, soccer M/W, softball W, tennis M/W, track and field M/W, volleyball M/W. ***Intramural sports:*** basketball M/W, soccer M/W, volleyball M/W.

Campus security: 24-hour emergency response devices and patrols, late-night transport/escort service, controlled dormitory access.

Student services: health clinic, personal/psychological counseling, veterans affairs office.

COSTS & FINANCIAL AID
Costs (2019–20) ***One-time required fee:*** $70. ***Comprehensive fee:*** $45,390 includes full-time tuition ($33,304), mandatory fees ($550), and room and board ($11,536). Part-time tuition: $730 per contact hour. ***Required fees:*** $275 per term part-time. ***College room only:*** $6136.

Financial Aid Of all full-time matriculated undergraduates who enrolled in 2017, 1,740 applied for aid, 1,610 were judged to have need, 415 had their need fully met. 337 Federal Work-Study jobs (averaging $1108). In 2017, 101 non-need-based awards were made. ***Average percent of need met:*** 81. ***Average financial aid package:*** $20,817. ***Average need-based loan:*** $4134. ***Average need-based gift aid:*** $7123. ***Average non-need-based aid:*** $13,445. ***Average indebtedness upon graduation:*** $40,488.

APPLYING
Options: electronic application, early admission, deferred entrance.

Application fee: $35.

Required: essay or personal statement, high school transcript, minimum 2.0 GPA, 1 letter of recommendation. ***Recommended:*** 2 letters of recommendation, interview.

Application deadlines: rolling (freshmen), rolling (out-of-state freshmen), rolling (transfers).

Notification: continuous (freshmen), continuous (out-of-state freshmen), continuous (transfers).

CONTACT
Mr. Michael Dziedziak, Executive Director of Enrollment, Eastern University, 1300 Eagle Road, St Davids, PA 19087-3696. *Phone:* 800-452-0996. *Toll-free phone:* 800-452-0996. *Fax:* 610-225-5601. *E-mail:* ugadm@eastern.edu.

East Stroudsburg University of Pennsylvania
East Stroudsburg, Pennsylvania
http://www.esu.edu/

- **State-supported** comprehensive, founded 1893, part of Pennsylvania State System of Higher Education
- **Suburban** 258-acre campus
- **Endowment** $22.2 million
- **Coed** 5,713 undergraduate students, 92% full-time, 56% women, 44% men
- **Moderately difficult** entrance level, 72% of applicants were admitted

UNDERGRAD STUDENTS
5,243 full-time, 470 part-time. Students come from 26 states and territories; 19 other countries; 21% are from out of state; 20% Black or African American, non-Hispanic/Latino; 12% Hispanic/Latino; 2% Asian, non-Hispanic/Latino; 0.2% Native Hawaiian or other Pacific Islander, non-Hispanic/Latino; 0.3% American Indian or Alaska Native, non-Hispanic/Latino; 4% Two or more races, non-Hispanic/Latino; 3% Race/ethnicity unknown; 0.9% international; 8% transferred in; 43% live on campus.

Freshmen:
Admission: 9,713 applied, 6,990 admitted, 1,135 enrolled. ***Average high school GPA:*** 3.2. ***Test scores:*** SAT evidence-based reading and writing scores over 500: 58%; SAT math scores over 500: 53%; ACT scores over 18: 87%; SAT evidence-based reading and writing scores over 600: 15%; SAT math scores over 600: 10%; ACT scores over 24: 31%; SAT evidence-based reading and writing scores over 700: 1%; SAT math scores over 700: 1%; ACT scores over 30: 7%.

Retention: 69% of full-time freshmen returned.

FACULTY
Total: 352, 74% full-time, 52% with terminal degrees.

Student/faculty ratio: 19:1.

ACADEMICS
Calendar: semesters. *Degrees:* certificates, bachelor's, master's, doctoral, post-master's, and postbachelor's certificates.

Special study options: academic remediation for entering students, accelerated degree program, adult/continuing education programs, advanced placement credit, distance learning, double majors, honors programs, independent study, internships, off-campus study, part-time degree program, services for LD students, student-designed majors, study abroad, summer session for credit. ***ROTC:*** Army (b), Air Force (c).

Unusual degree programs: 3-2 engineering with Penn State University Park.

Computers: 500 computers/terminals and 1,500 ports are available on campus for general student use. Students can access the following: campus intranet, computer help desk, free student e-mail accounts, online (class) grades, online (class) registration, online (class) schedules, online classes. Campuswide network is available. 100% of college-owned or -operated housing units are wired for high-speed Internet access. Wireless service is available via classrooms, computer labs, dorm rooms, libraries, student centers.
Library: Kemp Library. *Books:* 227,237 (physical), 411,580 (digital/electronic); *Serial titles:* 3,143 (physical), 76,680 (digital/electronic); *Databases:* 107. Weekly public service hours: 99.

STUDENT LIFE
Housing options: on-campus residence required for freshman year; coed, special housing for students with disabilities. Campus housing is university owned and is provided by a third party. Freshman campus housing is guaranteed.

Activities and organizations: drama/theater group, student-run newspaper, radio station, choral group, marching band, Black Student Union, Council for Exceptional Children, National Student Speech Hearing Language Association, Student Governmnet, Stage II, national fraternities, national sororities.

Athletics Member NCAA. All Division II except golf (Division I). ***Intercollegiate sports:*** baseball M(s), basketball M(s)/W(s), cheerleading M/W, cross-country running M(s)/W(s), equestrian sports M(c)/W(c), field hockey W(s), football M(s), golf M(c)/W, ice hockey M(c)/W(c), lacrosse M(c)/W(s), rugby M(c)/W(c), soccer M(s)/W(s), softball W(s), swimming and diving W(s), tennis M(c)/W(s), track and field M(s)/W(s), ultimate Frisbee M(c)/W(c), volleyball M(c)/W(s), wrestling M(s)/W. ***Intramural sports:*** basketball M/W, gymnastics M(c)/W(c), racquetball M(c)/W(c), sand volleyball M(c)/W(c), soccer M(c)/W(c), softball M/W.

Campus security: 24-hour emergency response devices and patrols, late-night transport/escort service, controlled dormitory access, self-defense education, shuttle buses, lighted pathways/sidewalks, controlled building access.

Student services: health clinic, personal/psychological counseling, women's center, legal services, veterans affairs office.

COSTS & FINANCIAL AID

Costs (2018–19) ***Tuition:*** state resident $7716 full-time, $322 per credit hour part-time; nonresident $19,290 full-time, $805 per credit hour part-time. Full-time tuition and fees vary according to course load, location, and program. Part-time tuition and fees vary according to location and program. No tuition increase for student's term of enrollment. ***Required fees:*** $3002 full-time, $151 per credit hour part-time, $716 per term part-time. ***Room and board:*** $8700; room only: $6120. Room and board charges vary according to board plan and housing facility. ***Payment plan:*** installment. ***Waivers:*** senior citizens and employees or children of employees.

Financial Aid Of all full-time matriculated undergraduates who enrolled in 2017, 5,517 applied for aid, 4,451 were judged to have need, 637 had their need fully met. 118 Federal Work-Study jobs (averaging $1060). 958 state and other part-time jobs (averaging $1160). In 2017, 825 non-need-based awards were made. ***Average percent of need met:*** 68. ***Average financial aid package:*** $10,209. ***Average need-based loan:*** $4470. ***Average need-based gift aid:*** $6062. ***Average non-need-based aid:*** $4413. ***Average indebtedness upon graduation:*** $33,213.

APPLYING

Standardized Tests *Required for some:* SAT or ACT (for admission).

Options: electronic application, deferred entrance.

Application fee: $25.

Required: high school transcript.

Application deadlines: 4/1 (freshmen), 4/1 (out-of-state freshmen), 6/1 (transfers), 11/15 (early action).

Notification: 5/1 (freshmen), continuous (out-of-state freshmen), continuous (transfers), rolling (early action).

CONTACT

Mr. David Bousquet, Vice President of Enrollment Management, East Stroudsburg University of Pennsylvania, 200 Prospect Street, East Stroudsburg, PA 18301. *Phone:* 570-422-3542. *Toll-free phone:* 877-230-5547. *Fax:* 570-422-3933. *E-mail:* admission@esu.edu.

Edinboro University of Pennsylvania

Edinboro, Pennsylvania

http://www.edinboro.edu/

CONTACT

Ms. Melissa Manning, Associate Director of Undergraduate Admissions, Edinboro University of Pennsylvania, Academy Hall, Edinboro, PA 16444. *Phone:* 814-732-2761. *Toll-free phone:* 888-846-2676. *Fax:* 814-732-2420. *E-mail:* eup_admissions@edinboro.edu.

Elizabethtown College

Elizabethtown, Pennsylvania

http://www.etown.edu/

- **Independent** comprehensive, founded 1899, affiliated with Church of the Brethren
- **Small-town** 203-acre campus with easy access to Philadelphia, Baltimore, Harrisburg, Lancaster
- **Endowment** $79.1 million
- **Coed**
- **Moderately difficult** entrance level

FACULTY
Student/faculty ratio: 11:1.

ACADEMICS
Calendar: semesters. *Degrees:* bachelor's and master's.
Library: High Library plus 1 other. *Books:* 253,054 (physical), 5,306 (digital/electronic); *Serial titles:* 1,628 (physical), 7,972 (digital/electronic); *Databases:* 73. Weekly public service hours: 102; students can reserve study rooms.

STUDENT LIFE
Housing options: on-campus residence required through senior year; coed, women-only, special housing for students with disabilities. Campus housing is university owned and leased by the school. Freshman campus housing is guaranteed.

Activities and organizations: drama/theater group, student-run newspaper, radio and television station, choral group, Professional Organizations, Emotion Dance Club, Student Senate, A cappella groups, Religious groups.

Athletics Member NCAA. All Division III.

Campus security: 24-hour emergency response devices and patrols, student patrols, late-night transport/escort service, controlled dormitory access, self-defense workshops, crime prevention program.

Student services: health clinic, personal/psychological counseling.

COSTS & FINANCIAL AID
Costs (2018–19) ***Comprehensive fee:*** $58,310 includes full-time tuition ($46,940) and room and board ($11,370). Full-time tuition and fees vary according to course load. Part-time tuition: $1140 per credit hour. Part-time tuition and fees vary according to course load. ***College room only:*** $5630. Room and board charges vary according to board plan and housing facility.

Financial Aid Of all full-time matriculated undergraduates who enrolled in 2018, 1,356 applied for aid, 1,228 were judged to have need, 282 had their need fully met. 598 Federal Work-Study jobs (averaging $1218). In 2018, 330 non-need-based awards were made. ***Average percent of need met:*** 81. ***Average financial aid package:*** $34,766. ***Average need-based loan:*** $4276. ***Average need-based gift aid:*** $30,526. ***Average non-need-based aid:*** $23,820. ***Average indebtedness upon graduation:*** $40,839.

APPLYING
Standardized Tests *Required:* SAT or ACT (for admission).

Options: electronic application, deferred entrance.

Application fee: $30.

Required: essay or personal statement, high school transcript, minimum 2.0 GPA, 2 letters of recommendation. ***Required for some:*** interview. ***Recommended:*** minimum 3.0 GPA, interview.

CONTACT
Ms. Lauren Deibler, Director of Admissions and Coordinator of International Recruitment, Elizabethtown College, One Alpha Drive, Elizabethtown, PA 17022. *Phone:* 717-361-1400. *Fax:* 717-361-1365. *E-mail:* admissions@etown.edu.

See previous page for display ad and page 1004 for the College Close-Up.

Elizabethtown College School of Continuing and Professional Studies

Elizabethtown, Pennsylvania

http://www.etowndegrees.com/

CONTACT
Ms. Barbara A. Randazzo, Assistant Dean of Enrollment Management, Elizabethtown College School of Continuing and Professional Studies, One Alpha Drive, Elizabethtown College, PA 17022. *Phone:* 717-361-3750. *Toll-free phone:* 800-877-2694. *Fax:* 717-361-1466. *E-mail:* randazzob@etown.edu.

Franklin & Marshall College

Lancaster, Pennsylvania

http://www.fandm.edu/

- **Independent** 4-year, founded 1787
- **Suburban** 209-acre campus with easy access to Philadelphia
- **Coed**
- **Very difficult** entrance level

FACULTY
Student/faculty ratio: 9:1.

ACADEMICS
Calendar: semesters. *Degree:* bachelor's.
Library: Shadek-Fackenthal Library plus 1 other. *Books:* 468,748 (physical), 135,071 (digital/electronic); *Serial titles:* 2,680 (physical), 167,874 (digital/electronic). Weekly public service hours: 110; students can reserve study rooms.

STUDENT LIFE
Housing options: on-campus residence required through senior year; coed, men-only, women-only, cooperative, special housing for students with disabilities. Campus housing is university owned and is provided by a third party. Freshman campus housing is guaranteed.

Activities and organizations: drama/theater group, student-run newspaper, radio station, choral group, Intervarsity, Hillel, Mi Gente Latina, Cia Bella, F&M Players, national fraternities, national sororities.

Athletics Member NCAA. All Division III except wrestling (Division I).

Campus security: 24-hour emergency response devices and patrols, late-night transport/escort service, controlled dormitory access, residence hall security, campus security connected to city police and fire company.

Student services: health clinic, personal/psychological counseling, women's center.

COSTS & FINANCIAL AID
Costs (2018–19) ***One-time required fee:*** $200. ***Comprehensive fee:*** $70,600 includes full-time tuition ($56,450), mandatory fees ($100), and room and board ($14,050). Part-time tuition: $7056 per course. Part-time tuition and fees vary according to course load. ***College room only:*** $8310. Room and board charges vary according to board plan and housing facility. ***Payment plans:*** installment, deferred payment.

Financial Aid Of all full-time matriculated undergraduates who enrolled in 2018, 1,424 applied for aid, 1,239 were judged to have need, 1,239 had their need fully met. In 2018, 34 non-need-based awards were made. ***Average percent of need met:*** 100. ***Average financial aid package:*** $52,703. ***Average need-based loan:*** $4167. ***Average need-based gift aid:*** $47,484. ***Average non-need-based aid:*** $20,673. ***Average indebtedness upon graduation:*** $27,149. ***Financial aid deadline:*** 2/1.

APPLYING
Options: electronic application, early admission, early decision, deferred entrance.

Application fee: $60.

Required: essay or personal statement, high school transcript, 2 letters of recommendation, Common Application Supplement. ***Required for some:*** interview.

CONTACT
Julie Kerich, Director of Admissions, Franklin & Marshall College, PO Box 3003, Lancaster, PA 17604-3003. *Phone:* 717-358-4743. *Toll-free phone:* 877-678-9111. *Fax:* 717-358-4389. *E-mail:* julie.kerich@fandm.edu.

★ Gannon University

Erie, Pennsylvania

http://www.gannon.edu/

- **Independent Roman Catholic** university, founded 1925
- **Urban** 38-acre campus with easy access to Cleveland, Buffalo, Pittsburgh
- **Coed**
- **Moderately difficult** entrance level

FACULTY
Student/faculty ratio: 12:1.

ACADEMICS
Calendar: semesters plus 2 summer sessions. *Degrees:* certificates, associate, bachelor's, master's, doctoral, post-master's, and postbachelor's certificates.
Library: Nash Library. *Books:* 213,041 (physical), 252,244 (digital/electronic); *Serial titles:* 37 (physical), 52,805 (digital/electronic); *Databases:* 45. Weekly public service hours: 97; students can reserve study rooms.

STUDENT LIFE
Housing options: on-campus residence required through sophomore year; coed, special housing for students with disabilities. Campus housing is university owned and leased by the school. Freshman campus housing is guaranteed.
Activities and organizations: drama/theater group, student-run newspaper, radio station, choral group, GU Society of Physician Assistant, GU Habitat for Humanity, Activities Programming Board, Student Occupational Therapy Association, Organization of Women Leaders, national fraternities, national sororities.
Athletics Member NCAA. All Division II.
Campus security: 24-hour emergency response devices and patrols, late-night transport/escort service, controlled dormitory access, security cameras in and outside of campus facilities, including streets and sidewalks.
Student services: health clinic, personal/psychological counseling, veterans affairs office.

FINANCIAL AID
Financial Aid Of all full-time matriculated undergraduates who enrolled in 2018, 2,240 applied for aid, 2,052 were judged to have need, 445 had their need fully met. In 2018, 417 non-need-based awards were made. ***Average percent of need met:*** 73. ***Average financial aid package:*** $26,463. ***Average need-based loan:*** $4408. ***Average need-based gift aid:*** $22,482. ***Average non-need-based aid:*** $16,134.

APPLYING
Standardized Tests *Required:* SAT or ACT (for admission).
Options: electronic application, deferred entrance.
Application fee: $25.
Required: high school transcript, minimum 2.0 GPA, counselor's recommendation. ***Required for some:*** minimum 3.0 GPA, 2 letters of recommendation, interview. ***Recommended:*** essay or personal statement.

CONTACT
Office of Admissions, Gannon University, 109 University Square, Erie, PA 16541. *Phone:* 814-871-7240. *Toll-free phone:* 800-GANNONU. *Fax:* 814-871-5803. *E-mail:* admissions@gannon.edu.

See this page for display ad and page 1014 for the College Close-Up.

Geneva College

Beaver Falls, Pennsylvania

http://www.geneva.edu/

- **Independent** comprehensive, founded 1848, affiliated with Reformed Presbyterian Church of North America
- **Small-town** 55-acre campus with easy access to Pittsburgh
- **Endowment** $42.1 million
- **Coed** 1,376 undergraduate students, 86% full-time, 47% women, 53% men
- **Moderately difficult** entrance level, 63% of applicants were admitted

UNDERGRAD STUDENTS
1,180 full-time, 196 part-time. Students come from 33 states and territories; 8 other countries; 26% are from out of state; 7% Black or African American, non-Hispanic/Latino; 2% Hispanic/Latino; 1% Asian, non-Hispanic/Latino; 0.2% American Indian or Alaska Native, non-Hispanic/Latino; 3% Two or more races, non-Hispanic/Latino; 4% Race/ethnicity unknown; 2% international; 3% transferred in; 65% live on campus.

Freshmen:
Admission: 1,941 applied, 1,229 admitted, 306 enrolled. ***Average high school GPA:*** 3.4. ***Test scores:*** SAT evidence-based reading and writing scores over 500: 186%; SAT math scores over 500: 185%; ACT scores over 18: 78%; SAT evidence-based reading and writing scores over 600: 94%; SAT math scores over 600: 70%; ACT scores over 24: 42%; SAT evidence-based reading and writing scores over 700: 16%; SAT math scores over 700: 15%; ACT scores over 30: 11%.

Retention: 76% of full-time freshmen returned.

FACULTY
Total: 207, 33% full-time, 49% with terminal degrees.

Student/faculty ratio: 12:1.

ACADEMICS
Calendar: semesters. *Degrees:* associate, bachelor's, and master's (also offers non-traditional programs in Philadelphia and western Pennsylvania with significant enrollment not reflected in profile).

Special study options: academic remediation for entering students, accelerated degree program, adult/continuing education programs, advanced placement credit, cooperative education, distance learning, double majors, English as a second language, honors programs, independent study, internships, off-campus study, part-time degree program, services for LD students, student-designed majors, study abroad, summer session for credit. ***ROTC:*** Army (c).

Unusual degree programs: 3-2 divinity with Reformed Presbyterian Theological Seminary.

Computers: 150 computers/terminals and 400 ports are available on campus for general student use. Students can access the following: campus intranet, computer help desk, free student e-mail accounts, online (class) grades, online (class) registration, online (class) schedules. Campuswide network is available. 100% of college-owned or -operated housing units are wired for high-speed Internet access. Wireless service is available via entire campus.
Library: McCartney Library plus 3 others. *Books:* 140,157 (physical), 12,739 (digital/electronic); *Serial titles:* 30,449 (physical); *Databases:* 54. Weekly public service hours: 84.

STUDENT LIFE
Housing options: men-only, women-only. Campus housing is university owned. Freshman campus housing is guaranteed.

Activities and organizations: drama/theater group, student-run newspaper, choral group, marching band, marching band, Genevans Choir, Intramural sports, ministry groups, discipleship groups.

Athletics Member NCAA, NCCAA. All NCAA Division III. ***Intercollegiate sports:*** baseball M, basketball M/W, cross-country running M/W, football M, soccer M/W, softball W, tennis M/W, track and field M/W, volleyball M(c)/W. ***Intramural sports:*** basketball M/W, cheerleading W(c), football M/W, ice hockey M(c), racquetball M/W, rugby M(c)/W(c), skiing (downhill) M(c)/W(c), soccer M/W, softball M/W, table tennis M/W, ultimate Frisbee M/W, volleyball M/W.

Campus security: 24-hour emergency response devices and patrols, late-night transport/escort service, controlled dormitory access.

Student services: health clinic, personal/psychological counseling.

COSTS & FINANCIAL AID
Costs (2019–20) ***Comprehensive fee:*** $38,720 includes full-time tuition ($27,670), mandatory fees ($520), and room and board ($10,530). Part-time tuition: $930 per credit hour. ***Required fees:*** $260 per term part-time. ***College room only:*** $5500.

Financial Aid Of all full-time matriculated undergraduates who enrolled in 2017, 1,023 applied for aid, 927 were judged to have need, 196 had their need fully met. 217 Federal Work-Study jobs (averaging $698). In 2017, 179 non-need-based awards were made. ***Average percent of need met:*** 77. ***Average financial aid package:*** $21,364. ***Average need-based loan:*** $4252. ***Average need-based gift aid:*** $16,975. ***Average non-need-based aid:*** $11,500. ***Average indebtedness upon graduation:*** $36,605.

APPLYING
Standardized Tests *Required:* SAT or ACT (for admission).

Options: electronic application, early admission, deferred entrance.

Application fee: $40.

Required: essay or personal statement, high school transcript, minimum 2.0 GPA. ***Required for some:*** 1 unit of chemistry and physics and 4 units of college-prep mathematics (including trigonometry and pre-calculus) for engineering. ***Recommended:*** minimum 3.0 GPA, 2 letters of recommendation, interview.

Application deadlines: rolling (freshmen), rolling (transfers).

Notification: continuous (freshmen), continuous (transfers).

CONTACT
Mr. David Layton, Associate Vice President for Enrollment, Geneva College, 3200 College Avenue, Beaver Falls, PA 15010-3599. *Phone:* 724-847-6500. *Toll-free phone:* 800-847-8255. *E-mail:* admissions@geneva.edu.

Gettysburg College

Gettysburg, Pennsylvania

http://www.gettysburg.edu/

- **Independent** 4-year, founded 1832, affiliated with Evangelical Lutheran Church in America
- **Suburban** 200-acre campus with easy access to Baltimore and Washington, D.C.
- **Endowment** $313.8 million
- **Coed**
- **Most difficult** entrance level

FACULTY
Student/faculty ratio: 9:1.

ACADEMICS
Calendar: semesters. *Degree:* bachelor's.
Library: Musselman Library. *Books:* 370,500 (physical), 350,000 (digital/electronic); *Databases:* 299. Study areas open 24 hours, 5–7 days a week.

STUDENT LIFE
Housing options: on-campus residence required through senior year; coed, men-only, women-only. Campus housing is university owned. Freshman campus housing is guaranteed.

Activities and organizations: drama/theater group, student-run newspaper, radio and television station, choral group, marching band, community service, music, athletics, student government, national fraternities, national sororities.

Athletics Member NCAA. All Division III.

Campus security: 24-hour emergency response devices and patrols, student patrols, late-night transport/escort service, controlled dormitory access.

Student services: health clinic, personal/psychological counseling, women's center.

COSTS & FINANCIAL AID
Costs (2018–19) ***Comprehensive fee:*** $67,490 includes full-time tuition ($54,480) and room and board ($13,010). ***College room only:*** $6980. Room and board charges vary according to board plan and housing facility.

Financial Aid Of all full-time matriculated undergraduates who enrolled in 2018, 1,788 applied for aid, 1,581 were judged to have need, 1,404 had their need fully met. 318 Federal Work-Study jobs (averaging $865). 1,183 state and other part-time jobs (averaging $812). In 2018, 545 non-need-based awards were made. ***Average percent of need met:*** 90. ***Average financial aid package:*** $42,219. ***Average need-based loan:*** $4468. ***Average need-based gift aid:*** $37,831. ***Average non-need-based aid:*** $15,269. ***Average indebtedness upon graduation:*** $31,670. ***Financial aid deadline:*** 1/15.

APPLYING
Standardized Tests *Required for some:* SAT or ACT (for admission).

Options: electronic application, early admission, early decision, deferred entrance.

Application fee: $60.

Required: essay or personal statement, high school transcript, 2 letters of recommendation. ***Recommended:*** minimum 3.0 GPA, interview, extracurricular activities.

CONTACT
Ms. Gail Sweezey, Director of Admissions, Gettysburg College, 300 North Washington Street, Gettysburg, PA 17325. *Phone:* 717-337-6100. *Toll-free phone:* 800-431-0803. *Fax:* 717-337-6145. *E-mail:* admiss@gettysburg.edu.

Grove City College

Grove City, Pennsylvania

http://www.gcc.edu/

- **Independent Presbyterian** 4-year, founded 1876
- **Small-town** 180-acre campus with easy access to Pittsburgh
- **Endowment** $128.2 million
- **Coed** 2,338 undergraduate students, 98% full-time, 48% women, 52% men
- **Moderately difficult** entrance level, 93% of applicants were admitted

UNDERGRAD STUDENTS

2,280 full-time, 58 part-time. Students come from 42 states and territories; 13 other countries; 45% are from out of state; 0.7% Black or African American, non-Hispanic/Latino; 1% Hispanic/Latino; 2% Asian, non-Hispanic/Latino; 0.1% American Indian or Alaska Native, non-Hispanic/Latino; 3% Two or more races, non-Hispanic/Latino; 0.4% Race/ethnicity unknown; 0.9% international; 2% transferred in; 96% live on campus.

Freshmen:

Admission: 1,544 applied, 1,434 admitted, 608 enrolled. ***Average high school GPA:*** 3.7. ***Test scores:*** SAT evidence-based reading and writing scores over 500: 97%; SAT math scores over 500: 96%; ACT scores over 18: 100%; SAT evidence-based reading and writing scores over 600: 69%; SAT math scores over 600: 57%; ACT scores over 24: 77%; SAT evidence-based reading and writing scores over 700: 19%; SAT math scores over 700: 17%; ACT scores over 30: 27%.

Retention: 87% of full-time freshmen returned.

FACULTY

Total: 221, 72% full-time, 72% with terminal degrees.

Student/faculty ratio: 13:1.

ACADEMICS

Calendar: semesters. *Degree:* bachelor's.

Special study options: accelerated degree program, advanced placement credit, distance learning, double majors, independent study, internships, off-campus study, services for LD students, study abroad, summer session for credit.

Computers: 50 computers/terminals and 8,000 ports are available on campus for general student use. Students can access the following: campus intranet, computer help desk, free student e-mail accounts, online (class) grades, online (class) registration, online (class) schedules. Campuswide network is available. 100% of college-owned or -operated housing units are wired for high-speed Internet access. Wireless service is available via entire campus.

Library: Henry Buhl Library plus 1 other. *Books:* 168,520 (physical), 264,550 (digital/electronic); *Serial titles:* 25 (physical), 45,123 (digital/electronic); *Databases:* 107. Weekly public service hours: 103.

STUDENT LIFE

Housing options: on-campus residence required through senior year; men-only, women-only. Campus housing is university owned. Freshman campus housing is guaranteed.

Activities and organizations: drama/theater group, student-run newspaper, radio and television station, choral group, marching band, Warriors for Christ, Orchesis, Orientation Board, Association for Women Students (AWS), Young Life.

Athletics Member NCAA. All Division III except golf (Division II). ***Intercollegiate sports:*** baseball M, basketball M/W, cross-country running M/W, equestrian sports M(c)/W(c), fencing M(c)/W(c), football M, golf M/W, lacrosse M, rugby M(c)/W(c), soccer M/W, softball W, swimming and diving M/W, tennis M/W, track and field M/W, volleyball M(c)/W, water polo M(c)/W. ***Intramural sports:*** badminton M/W, basketball M/W, bowling M/W, football M/W, racquetball M/W, soccer M/W, softball M, tennis M/W, ultimate Frisbee M/W, volleyball M/W.

Campus security: 24-hour emergency response devices and patrols, student patrols, late-night transport/escort service, controlled dormitory access.

Student services: health clinic, personal/psychological counseling.

COSTS & FINANCIAL AID

Costs (2019–20) ***Comprehensive fee:*** $28,530 includes full-time tuition ($18,470) and room and board ($10,060). Part-time tuition: $595 per credit hour. ***College room only:*** $6160.

Financial Aid Of all full-time matriculated undergraduates who enrolled in 2018, 1,313 applied for aid, 1,078 were judged to have need, 81 had their need fully met. In 2018, 407 non-need-based awards were made. ***Average percent of need met:*** 49. ***Average financial aid package:*** $7999. ***Average need-based loan:*** $18. ***Average need-based gift aid:*** $7999. ***Average non-need-based aid:*** $3420. ***Average indebtedness upon graduation:*** $41,690. ***Financial aid deadline:*** 4/15.

APPLYING

Standardized Tests *Required:* SAT or ACT (for admission), SAT, ACT, and/or CLT test scores (for admission).

Options: electronic application, early admission, early decision, deferred entrance.

Application fee: $50.

Required: essay or personal statement, high school transcript, 2 letters of recommendation. ***Recommended:*** interview.

Application deadlines: 1/20 (freshmen), 8/15 (transfers).

Early decision deadline: 11/1.

Notification: 2/20 (freshmen), continuous (transfers), 12/15 (early decision).

CONTACT

Lee S Wishing, VP Student Recruitment, Grove City College, 100 Campus Drive, Grove City, PA 16127-2104. *Phone:* 724-458-3332. *E-mail:* admissions@gcc.edu.

★ Gwynedd Mercy University

Gwynedd Valley, Pennsylvania

http://www.gmercyu.edu/

- **Independent Roman Catholic** comprehensive, founded 1948
- **Suburban** 170-acre campus with easy access to Philadelphia
- **Endowment** $38.4 million
- **Coed** 2,033 undergraduate students, 93% full-time, 76% women, 24% men
- **Moderately difficult** entrance level, 92% of applicants were admitted

UNDERGRAD STUDENTS

1,898 full-time, 135 part-time. Students come from 22 states and territories; 35 other countries; 14% are from out of state; 22% Black or African American, non-Hispanic/Latino; 5% Hispanic/Latino; 6% Asian, non-Hispanic/Latino; 0.1% Native Hawaiian or other Pacific Islander, non-Hispanic/Latino; 0.5% American Indian or Alaska Native, non-Hispanic/Latino; 0.9% Two or more races, non-Hispanic/Latino; 6% Race/ethnicity unknown; 11% transferred in; 19% live on campus.

Freshmen:

Admission: 1,213 applied, 1,116 admitted, 276 enrolled. ***Average high school GPA:*** 3.2. ***Test scores:*** SAT evidence-based reading and writing scores over 500: 76%; SAT math scores over 500: 61%; ACT scores over 18: 83%; SAT evidence-based reading and writing scores over 600: 23%; SAT math scores over 600: 11%; ACT scores over 24: 27%; SAT evidence-based reading and writing scores over 700: 12%; SAT math scores over 700: 1%; ACT scores over 30: 6%.

Retention: 82% of full-time freshmen returned.

FACULTY

Total: 332, 27% full-time, 25% with terminal degrees.

Student/faculty ratio: 11:1.

ACADEMICS

Calendar: semesters. *Degrees:* bachelor's, master's, doctoral, and post-master's certificates.

Special study options: academic remediation for entering students, accelerated degree program, adult/continuing education programs, advanced placement credit, cooperative education, distance learning, double majors, external degree program, honors programs, independent study, internships, part-time degree program, services for LD students, study abroad, summer session for credit.

Computers: 200 computers/terminals and 1,000 ports are available on campus for general student use. Students can access the following: campus intranet, computer help desk, free student e-mail accounts, online (class) grades, online (class) registration, online (class) schedules. Campuswide network is available. 100% of college-owned or -operated housing units are wired for high-speed Internet access. Wireless service is available via entire campus.
Library: Keiss Library plus 1 other. *Books:* 85,778 (physical), 180,000 (digital/electronic); *Serial titles:* 21 (physical), 111,480 (digital/electronic); *Databases:* 46. Weekly public service hours: 76; students can reserve study rooms.

STUDENT LIFE
Housing options: coed, special housing for students with disabilities. Campus housing is university owned. Freshman applicants given priority for college housing.

Activities and organizations: student-run newspaper, choral group, Voices of Gwynedd, Athletic Association, Student Government, Program Board, Peer Mentors.

Athletics Member NCAA. All Division III. ***Intercollegiate sports:*** baseball M, basketball M/W, cheerleading W, cross-country running M/W, field hockey W, lacrosse M/W, soccer M/W, softball W, tennis M/W, track and field M/W, volleyball W. ***Intramural sports:*** football M.

Campus security: 24-hour emergency response devices and patrols, late-night transport/escort service, controlled dormitory access.

Student services: health clinic, personal/psychological counseling.

COSTS & FINANCIAL AID
Costs (2019–20) ***One-time required fee:*** $780. ***Comprehensive fee:*** $47,050 includes full-time tuition ($33,800), mandatory fees ($780), and room and board ($12,470). Part-time tuition: $632 per credit hour. ***Required fees:*** $17 per credit hour part-time. ***College room only:*** $5520.

Financial Aid Of all full-time matriculated undergraduates who enrolled in 2018, 1,560 applied for aid, 1,438 were judged to have need, 188 had their need fully met. In 2018, 157 non-need-based awards were made. ***Average percent of need met:*** 62. ***Average financial aid package:*** $22,739. ***Average need-based loan:*** $4118. ***Average need-based gift aid:*** $20,411. ***Average non-need-based aid:*** $15,172. ***Average indebtedness upon graduation:*** $44,763. ***Financial aid deadline:*** 5/1.

APPLYING
Standardized Tests *Required:* SAT or ACT (for admission).

Options: electronic application, deferred entrance.

Required for some: essay or personal statement.

Application deadlines: rolling (freshmen), 8/20 (transfers).

Notification: continuous (freshmen), continuous (transfers).

CONTACT
Ms. Michelle Diehl, Director of Admissions, Gwynedd Mercy University, 1325 Sumneytown Pike, Gwynedd Valley, PA 19437-0901. *Phone:* 215-646-7300. *Toll-free phone:* 800-342-5462. *Fax:* 215-641-5556. *E-mail:* admissions@gmercyu.edu.

See below for display ad and page 1016 for the College Close-Up.

Harrisburg University of Science and Technology

Harrisburg, Pennsylvania

http://www.HarrisburgU.edu/

- **Independent** comprehensive, founded 2005
- **Urban** campus
- **Coed**
- **Minimally difficult** entrance level

FACULTY
Student/faculty ratio: 34:1.

ACADEMICS
Calendar: semesters. *Degrees:* bachelor's, master's, and doctoral.
Library: Information Commons. *Books:* 4,130 (physical), 26 (digital/electronic); *Serial titles:* 103 (physical), 126 (digital/electronic); *Databases:* 24. Study areas open 24 hours, 5–7 days a week.

STUDENT LIFE
Housing options: Campus housing is provided by a third party. Freshman applicants given priority for college housing.

Campus security: 24-hour emergency response devices and patrols, trained security personnel during hours of operation.

Student services: personal/psychological counseling.

COSTS & FINANCIAL AID
Costs (2018–19) ***Tuition:*** $23,900 full-time, $1000 per semester hour part-time. Full-time tuition and fees vary according to class time, course level, course load, degree level, location, program, reciprocity agreements, and student level. Part-time tuition and fees vary according to class time, course level, course load, degree level, location, program, reciprocity agreements, and student level. ***Room only:*** $6800. Room and board charges vary according to housing facility. ***Payment plans:*** installment, deferred payment.

Financial Aid Of all full-time matriculated undergraduates who enrolled in 2018, 488 applied for aid, 467 were judged to have need, 81 had their need fully met. In 2018, 43 non-need-based awards were made. ***Average percent of need met:*** 71. ***Average financial aid package:*** $22,885. ***Average need-based loan:*** $3935. ***Average need-based gift aid:*** $20,019. ***Average non-need-based aid:*** $19,305. ***Average indebtedness upon graduation:*** $34,547.

APPLYING
Options: electronic application.

Required: high school transcript. ***Recommended:*** essay or personal statement, interview.

CONTACT
Harrisburg University of Science and Technology, 326 Market Street, Harrisburg, PA 17101. *Phone:* 717-901-5150. *Toll-free phone:* 866-HBG-UNIV.

Haverford College

Haverford, Pennsylvania

http://www.haverford.edu/

- **Independent** 4-year, founded 1833
- **Suburban** 216-acre campus with easy access to Philadelphia
- **Endowment** $518.9 million
- **Coed** 1,310 undergraduate students, 100% full-time, 51% women, 49% men
- **Most difficult** entrance level, 19% of applicants were admitted

UNDERGRAD STUDENTS
1,308 full-time, 2 part-time. Students come from 44 states and territories; 49 other countries; 86% are from out of state; 7% Black or African American, non-Hispanic/Latino; 10% Hispanic/Latino; 13% Asian, non-Hispanic/Latino; 0.2% American Indian or Alaska Native, non-Hispanic/Latino; 3% Two or more races, non-Hispanic/Latino; 3% Race/ethnicity unknown; 11% international; 0.8% transferred in; 98% live on campus.

Freshmen:
Admission: 4,672 applied, 878 admitted, 357 enrolled. ***Test scores:*** SAT evidence-based reading and writing scores over 500: 100%; SAT math scores over 500: 100%; ACT scores over 18: 100%; SAT evidence-based reading and writing scores over 600: 98%; SAT math scores over 600: 97%; ACT scores over 24: 100%; SAT evidence-based reading and writing scores over 700: 65%; SAT math scores over 700: 70%; ACT scores over 30: 97%.

Retention: 97% of full-time freshmen returned.

FACULTY
Total: 159, 85% full-time, 97% with terminal degrees.

Student/faculty ratio: 9:1.

ACADEMICS
Calendar: semesters. *Degree:* bachelor's.

Special study options: advanced placement credit, double majors, independent study, internships, off-campus study, services for LD students, student-designed majors, study abroad. ***ROTC:*** Air Force (c).

Unusual degree programs: 3-2 engineering with California Institute of Technology; city planning with University of Pennsylvania.

Computers: 300 computers/terminals and 1,600 ports are available on campus for general student use. Students can access the following: campus intranet, computer help desk, free student e-mail accounts, online (class) grades, online (class) registration, online (class) schedules. Campuswide network is available. 100% of college-owned or -operated housing units are wired for high-speed Internet access. Wireless service is available via entire campus.

Library: James P. Magill Library plus 3 others. *Books:* 475,604 (physical), 702,593 (digital/electronic); *Serial titles:* 18,525 (physical), 135,312 (digital/electronic); *Databases:* 91. Study areas open 24 hours, 5–7 days a week; students can reserve study rooms.

STUDENT LIFE
Housing options: on-campus residence required for freshman year; coed, men-only, women-only, special housing for students with disabilities. Campus housing is university owned. Freshman campus housing is guaranteed.

Activities and organizations: drama/theater group, student-run newspaper, radio station, choral group, Volunteer Programs, Student government, Choral groups, Multicultural Groups, Orientation Team/Residential Life Leaders.

Athletics Member NCAA. All Division III. ***Intercollegiate sports:*** badminton W(c), baseball M, basketball M/W, crew M(c)/W(c), cross-country running M/W, fencing M/W, field hockey W, golf M(c), lacrosse M/W, rugby M(c), soccer M/W, softball W, squash M/W, tennis M/W, track and field M/W, ultimate Frisbee M(c)/W(c), volleyball M(c)/W, wrestling M(c). ***Intramural sports:*** basketball M/W, ice hockey M(c)/W(c), sailing M(c)/W(c), soccer M/W, softball M/W, tennis M/W, volleyball W.

Campus security: 24-hour emergency response devices and patrols, late-night transport/escort service, controlled dormitory access.

Student services: health clinic, personal/psychological counseling, women's center.

COSTS & FINANCIAL AID
Costs (2018–19) ***One-time required fee:*** $246. ***Comprehensive fee:*** $70,994 includes full-time tuition ($54,100), mandatory fees ($492), and room and board ($16,402). ***College room only:*** $9428. ***Payment plan:*** installment. ***Waivers:*** employees or children of employees.

Financial Aid Of all full-time matriculated undergraduates who enrolled in 2018, 669 applied for aid, 603 were judged to have need, 603 had their need fully met. ***Average percent of need met:*** 100. ***Average financial aid package:*** $54,861. ***Average need-based loan:*** $3517. ***Average need-based gift aid:*** $51,198. ***Average indebtedness upon graduation:*** $11,000.

APPLYING
Standardized Tests *Required:* SAT or ACT (for admission).

Options: electronic application, early admission, early decision, deferred entrance.

Application fee: $65.

Required: essay or personal statement. ***Required for some:*** high school transcript. ***Recommended:*** interview.

Application deadlines: 1/15 (freshmen), 3/31 (transfers).

Early decision deadline: 11/15 (for plan 1), 1/1 (for plan 2).

Notification: 4/1 (freshmen), 5/15 (transfers), 12/15 (early decision plan 1), 2/15 (early decision plan 2).

CONTACT
Mr. Jess Lord, Dean of Admissions and Financial Aid, Haverford College, 370 Lancaster Avenue, Haverford, PA 19041-1392. *Phone:* 610-896-1350. *Fax:* 610-896-1338. *E-mail:* admission@haverford.edu.

Holy Family University

Philadelphia, Pennsylvania

http://www.holyfamily.edu/

- **Independent Roman Catholic** comprehensive, founded 1954
- **Suburban** 47-acre campus with easy access to Philadelphia
- **Endowment** $18.5 million
- **Coed**
- **Minimally difficult** entrance level

FACULTY
Student/faculty ratio: 15:1.

ACADEMICS
Calendar: semesters. *Degrees:* certificates, associate, bachelor's, master's, doctoral, post-master's, and postbachelor's certificates.
Library: Holy Family University Library plus 1 other. *Books:* 75,943 (physical), 27,681 (digital/electronic); *Serial titles:* 1,106 (physical), 22,214 (digital/electronic); *Databases:* 42. Weekly public service hours: 116; students can reserve study rooms.

STUDENT LIFE
Housing options: coed, special housing for students with disabilities. Campus housing is university owned. Freshman campus housing is guaranteed.

Activities and organizations: drama/theater group, student-run newspaper, choral group, Students at Your Service (S.A.Y.S.), Green Team, Campus Ministry Team, Habitat for Humanity, Student Nurses Association of Holy Family.

Athletics Member NCAA. All Division II.

Campus security: 24-hour emergency response devices and patrols, late-night transport/escort service, controlled dormitory access, video surveillance.

Student services: health clinic, personal/psychological counseling.

COSTS & FINANCIAL AID
Costs (2018–19) ***One-time required fee:*** $504. ***Comprehensive fee:*** $43,922 includes full-time tuition ($29,338), mandatory fees ($1008), and room and board ($13,576). Full-time tuition and fees vary according to class time, course level, course load, degree level, program, and reciprocity agreements. Part-time tuition: $627 per credit hour. Part-time tuition and fees vary according to class time, course level, course load, degree level, program, and reciprocity agreements. ***Required fees:*** $112 per term part-time. ***College room only:*** $7140. Room and board charges vary according to board plan and housing facility. ***Payment plans:*** installment, deferred payment.

Financial Aid Of all full-time matriculated undergraduates who enrolled in 2017, 1,371 applied for aid, 1,265 were judged to have need, 159 had their need fully met. 293 Federal Work-Study jobs (averaging $1069). In 2017, 171 non-need-based awards were made. ***Average percent of need met:*** 72. ***Average financial aid package:*** $21,883. ***Average need-based loan:*** $3756. ***Average need-based gift aid:*** $17,716. ***Average non-need-based aid:*** $12,972. ***Average indebtedness upon graduation:*** $36,609.

APPLYING
Standardized Tests *Required:* SAT or ACT (for admission).

Options: electronic application, deferred entrance.

Application fee: $25.

Required: essay or personal statement, high school transcript, minimum 2.0 GPA, 2 letters of recommendation. ***Recommended:*** interview.

CONTACT
Ms. Lauren Campbell, Director of Admissions, Holy Family University, 9801 Frankford Avenue, Philadelphia, PA 19114-2009. *Phone:* 215-637-3050. *Fax:* 215-281-1022. *E-mail:* admissions@holyfamily.edu.

Hussian College, School of Art

Philadelphia, Pennsylvania

http://www.hussiancollege.edu/

CONTACT
Mr. Mark Cernero, Director of Admissions, Hussian College, School of Art, The Bourse, Suite 300, 111 South Independence Mall East, Philadelphia, PA 19106. *Phone:* 215-574-9600. *Fax:* 215-574-9800. *E-mail:* mcernero@hussianart.edu.

Immaculata University

Immaculata, Pennsylvania

http://www.immaculata.edu/

- **Independent Roman Catholic** university, founded 1920
- **Suburban** 373-acre campus with easy access to Philadelphia
- **Endowment** $19.7 million
- **Coed** 1,504 undergraduate students, 55% full-time, 73% women, 27% men
- **Moderately difficult** entrance level, 81% of applicants were admitted

UNDERGRAD STUDENTS
823 full-time, 681 part-time. 25% are from out of state; 16% Black or African American, non-Hispanic/Latino; 7% Hispanic/Latino; 2% Asian, non-Hispanic/Latino; 0.1% Native Hawaiian or other Pacific Islander, non-Hispanic/Latino; 0.1% American Indian or Alaska Native, non-Hispanic/Latino; 2% Two or more races, non-Hispanic/Latino; 1% Race/ethnicity unknown; 2% international; 3% transferred in; 29% live on campus.

Freshmen:
Admission: 1,639 applied, 1,330 admitted, 194 enrolled. ***Average high school GPA:*** 3.4. ***Test scores:*** SAT evidence-based reading and writing scores over 500: 86%; SAT math scores over 500: 78%; ACT scores over 18: 82%; SAT evidence-based reading and writing scores over 600: 43%; SAT math scores over 600: 26%; ACT scores over 24: 55%; SAT evidence-based reading and writing scores over 700: 3%; SAT math scores over 700: 3%; ACT scores over 30: 9%.

Retention: 75% of full-time freshmen returned.

FACULTY
Total: 318, 26% full-time, 50% with terminal degrees.

Student/faculty ratio: 9:1.

ACADEMICS
Calendar: semesters. *Degrees:* certificates, associate, bachelor's, master's, doctoral, and post-master's certificates.

Special study options: academic remediation for entering students, accelerated degree program, adult/continuing education programs, advanced placement credit, distance learning, double majors, honors programs, independent study, internships, off-campus study, part-time degree program, services for LD students, study abroad, summer session for credit. ***ROTC:*** Army (c).

Unusual degree programs: 3-2 business administration with DeSales University; Occupational Therapy with Thomas Jefferson University.

Computers: 600 computers/terminals are available on campus for general student use. Students can access the following: campus intranet, computer help desk, free student e-mail accounts, online (class) grades, online (class) registration, online (class) schedules. Campuswide network is available. Wireless service is available via entire campus.
Library: Gabriele Library. *Books:* 117,336 (physical), 10,448 (digital/electronic); *Databases:* 53. Students can reserve study rooms.

STUDENT LIFE
Housing options: coed, men-only, women-only, special housing for students with disabilities. Campus housing is university owned. Freshman campus housing is guaranteed.

Activities and organizations: drama/theater group, student-run newspaper, choral group, National Society of Leadership and Success, Student Dietetic Association, Immaculata University Chorale, College of Undergraduate Studies Honor Society, Immaculata University Pre-Med.

Athletics Member NCAA. All Division III. ***Intercollegiate sports:*** baseball M, basketball M/W, cross-country running M/W, field hockey W, golf M/W, lacrosse M/W, soccer M/W, softball W, swimming and diving M/W, tennis M/W, track and field M/W, volleyball M/W. ***Intramural sports:*** basketball M/W, cheerleading W(c), soccer M/W, softball M/W, volleyball M/W.

Campus security: 24-hour emergency response devices and patrols, late-night transport/escort service, controlled dormitory access.

Student services: health clinic, personal/psychological counseling.

COSTS & FINANCIAL AID
Costs (2019–20) ***Comprehensive fee:*** $39,970 includes full-time tuition ($26,500), mandatory fees ($850), and room and board ($12,620). Part-time tuition: $540 per credit hour. ***College room only:*** $6390.

Financial Aid Of all full-time matriculated undergraduates who enrolled in 2017, 786 applied for aid, 681 were judged to have need, 85 had their need fully met. In 2017, 151 non-need-based awards were made. ***Average percent of need met:*** 60. ***Average financial aid package:*** $17,211. ***Average need-based loan:*** $4474. ***Average need-based gift aid:*** $7887. ***Average non-need-based aid:*** $8500. ***Average indebtedness upon graduation:*** $48,174.

APPLYING
Options: electronic application, deferred entrance.

Application fee: $35.

Required: essay or personal statement, high school transcript, minimum 2.0 GPA, 1 letter of recommendation. ***Required for some:*** minimum 3.0 GPA, 2 letters of recommendation, audition for music students. ***Recommended:*** minimum 3.0 GPA, interview.

Application deadlines: rolling (freshmen), rolling (transfers).

Notification: continuous (freshmen), continuous (transfers).

CONTACT

Ms. Christine Esbensen, Director of Admissions, Immaculata University, 1145 King Road, Immaculata, PA 19345-0702. *Phone:* 610-647-4400 Ext. 3044. *Toll-free phone:* 877-428-6329. *Fax:* 610-640-0836. *E-mail:* cesbensen@immaculata.edu.

Indiana University of Pennsylvania

Indiana, Pennsylvania

http://www.iup.edu/

- **State-supported** university, founded 1875, part of Pennsylvania State System of Higher Education
- **Small-town** 374-acre campus with easy access to Pittsburgh
- **Endowment** $67.5 million
- **Coed** 9,215 undergraduate students, 91% full-time, 58% women, 42% men
- **Minimally difficult** entrance level, 93% of applicants were admitted

UNDERGRAD STUDENTS

8,359 full-time, 856 part-time. Students come from 29 states and territories; 35 other countries; 5% are from out of state; 12% Black or African American, non-Hispanic/Latino; 5% Hispanic/Latino; 1% Asian, non-Hispanic/Latino; 0.1% American Indian or Alaska Native, non-Hispanic/Latino; 5% Two or more races, non-Hispanic/Latino; 1% Race/ethnicity unknown; 4% international; 4% transferred in; 30% live on campus.

Freshmen:

Admission: 9,522 applied, 8,878 admitted, 1,992 enrolled. ***Test scores:*** SAT evidence-based reading and writing scores over 500: 59%; SAT math scores over 500: 54%; SAT evidence-based reading and writing scores over 600: 16%; SAT math scores over 600: 10%; SAT evidence-based reading and writing scores over 700: 1%; SAT math scores over 700: 1%.

Retention: 71% of full-time freshmen returned.

FACULTY

Total: 654, 83% full-time.

Student/faculty ratio: 16:1.

ACADEMICS

Calendar: semesters. *Degrees:* certificates, associate, bachelor's, master's, doctoral, post-master's, and postbachelor's certificates.

Special study options: academic remediation for entering students, accelerated degree program, adult/continuing education programs, advanced placement credit, cooperative education, distance learning, double majors, English as a second language, external degree program, freshman honors college, honors programs, independent study, internships, off-campus study, part-time degree program, services for LD students, student-designed majors, study abroad, summer session for credit. ***ROTC:*** Army (b).

Unusual degree programs: 3-2 engineering with Drexel University, University of Pittsburgh; Accelerated Pre-Professional Programs: Pre-chiropractic with Logan College of Chiropractic, New York Chiropractic College, Parker College, Sherman Chiropractic College: Pre-Dentistry with Temple University School of Dentistry; Pre-Optometry with Sal.

Computers: 2,363 computers/terminals and 5,000 ports are available on campus for general student use. Students can access the following: computer help desk, free student e-mail accounts, online (class) grades, online (class) registration, online (class) schedules. Campuswide network is available. 100% of college-owned or -operated housing units are wired for high-speed Internet access. Wireless service is available via entire campus.

Library: Stapleton Library plus 1 other. *Books:* 514,631 (physical), 100,229 (digital/electronic); *Serial titles:* 4,858 (physical). Weekly public service hours: 101; study areas open 24 hours, 5–7 days a week; students can reserve study rooms.

STUDENT LIFE

Housing options: on-campus residence required for freshman year; coed, women-only, special housing for students with disabilities. Campus housing is university owned and is provided by a third party. Freshman campus housing is guaranteed.

Activities and organizations: drama/theater group, student-run newspaper, radio and television station, choral group, marching band, Student Government Association, Panhellenic Association, Interfraternity Council, Student Association of Nutrition and Dietetics, Saudi Student Association, national fraternities, national sororities.

Athletics Member NCAA. All Division II. ***Intercollegiate sports:*** baseball M(s), basketball M(s)/W(s), cross-country running M(s)/W(s), field hockey W(s), football M(s), golf M(s), lacrosse W(s), soccer W(s), softball W(s), swimming and diving M(s)/W(s), tennis W(s), track and field M(s)/W(s), volleyball W(s). ***Intramural sports:*** baseball M(c), basketball M/W, cheerleading M(c)/W(c), equestrian sports M(c)/W(c), fencing M(c)/W(c), field hockey W(c), ice hockey M(c)/W(c), lacrosse M(c)/W(c), riflery M(c)/W(c), rugby M(c)/W(c), sailing M(c)/W(c), soccer M/W, swimming and diving M(c)/W(c), tennis M(c)/W(c), ultimate Frisbee M(c)/W(c), volleyball M/W.

Campus security: 24-hour emergency response devices and patrols, late-night transport/escort service, controlled dormitory access.

Student services: health clinic, personal/psychological counseling, legal services, veterans affairs office.

COSTS & FINANCIAL AID

Costs (2018–19) ***Tuition:*** state resident $9570 full-time, $319 per credit hour part-time; nonresident $13,890 full-time, $463 per credit hour part-time. Full-time tuition and fees vary according to course load. Part-time tuition and fees vary according to course load. ***Required fees:*** $3409 full-time, $121 per credit hour part-time, $50 per term part-time. ***Room and board:*** $12,592; room only: $8950. Room and board charges vary according to board plan, housing facility, and location. ***Payment plans:*** installment, deferred payment. ***Waivers:*** senior citizens and employees or children of employees.

Financial Aid Of all full-time matriculated undergraduates who enrolled in 2017, 8,159 applied for aid, 6,827 were judged to have need, 621 had their need fully met. 968 Federal Work-Study jobs (averaging $1919). 886 state and other part-time jobs (averaging $1720). In 2017, 358 non-need-based awards were made. ***Average percent of need met:*** 56. ***Average financial aid package:*** $10,252. ***Average need-based loan:*** $4232. ***Average need-based gift aid:*** $6227. ***Average non-need-based aid:*** $1863. ***Average indebtedness upon graduation:*** $39,284.

APPLYING

Standardized Tests *Required:* SAT or ACT (for admission).

Options: electronic application, early admission, deferred entrance.

Required: high school transcript. ***Recommended:*** essay or personal statement, 2 letters of recommendation.

Application deadlines: rolling (freshmen), rolling (out-of-state freshmen), rolling (transfers).

Notification: continuous (freshmen), continuous (out-of-state freshmen), continuous (transfers).

CONTACT

Patricia McCarthy, Vice President for Enrollment Management, Indiana University of Pennsylvania, 1011 South Drive, Indiana, PA 15705. *Phone:* 724-357-7544. *Toll-free phone:* 800-442-6830. *E-mail:* mccarthy@iup.edu.

Juniata College

Huntingdon, Pennsylvania

http://www.juniata.edu/

- **Independent** comprehensive, founded 1876, affiliated with Church of the Brethren
- **Small-town** 110-acre campus
- **Endowment** $122.3 million
- **Coed** 1,423 undergraduate students, 94% full-time, 57% women, 43% men
- **Moderately difficult** entrance level, 70% of applicants were admitted

UNDERGRAD STUDENTS
1,339 full-time, 84 part-time. Students come from 32 states and territories; 31 other countries; 30% are from out of state; 3% Black or African American, non-Hispanic/Latino; 5% Hispanic/Latino; 3% Asian, non-Hispanic/Latino; 0.2% American Indian or Alaska Native, non-Hispanic/Latino; 3% Two or more races, non-Hispanic/Latino; 2% Race/ethnicity unknown; 7% international; 1% transferred in; 87% live on campus.

Freshmen:
Admission: 2,437 applied, 1,710 admitted, 350 enrolled. ***Average high school GPA:*** 3.8. ***Test scores:*** SAT evidence-based reading and writing scores over 500: 96%; SAT math scores over 500: 94%; ACT scores over 18: 97%; SAT evidence-based reading and writing scores over 600: 61%; SAT math scores over 600: 50%; ACT scores over 24: 74%; SAT evidence-based reading and writing scores over 700: 14%; SAT math scores over 700: 12%; ACT scores over 30: 35%.

Retention: 84% of full-time freshmen returned.

FACULTY
Total: 168, 74% full-time, 68% with terminal degrees.

Student/faculty ratio: 11:1.

ACADEMICS
Calendar: semesters. *Degrees:* certificates, bachelor's, master's, and postbachelor's certificates.

Special study options: advanced placement credit, double majors, English as a second language, honors programs, independent study, internships, off-campus study, part-time degree program, services for LD students, student-designed majors, study abroad, summer session for credit.

Unusual degree programs: 3-2 engineering with Columbia University, Penn State University, Washington University in St. Louis, Clarkson University; nursing with Case Western University, Johns Hopkins University.

Computers: 150 computers/terminals and 257 ports are available on campus for general student use. Students can access the following: campus intranet, computer help desk, free student e-mail accounts, online (class) grades, online (class) registration, online (class) schedules, access to bills. Campuswide network is available. 100% of college-owned or -operated housing units are wired for high-speed Internet access. Wireless service is available via classrooms, computer centers, computer labs, dorm rooms, learning centers, libraries, student centers.
Library: Beeghly Library. *Books:* 139,415 (physical), 467,938 (digital/electronic); *Serial titles:* 379 (physical), 38,606 (digital/electronic); *Databases:* 53. Weekly public service hours: 107.

STUDENT LIFE
Housing options: on-campus residence required through senior year; coed, women-only. Campus housing is university owned. Freshman campus housing is guaranteed.

Activities and organizations: drama/theater group, student-run radio station, choral group, Ministry of Games, Student Government Association, Health Professions Organization, Mud Junkies Ceramics Club, National Society of Leadership and Success.

Athletics Member NCAA. All Division III. ***Intercollegiate sports:*** baseball M, basketball M/W, cross-country running M/W, field hockey W, football M, golf M/W, lacrosse W, rugby M(c)/W(c), soccer M/W, softball W, swimming and diving M/W, tennis M/W, track and field M/W, ultimate Frisbee M(c)/W(c), volleyball M/W. ***Intramural sports:*** basketball M/W, cheerleading W(c), equestrian sports M(c)/W(c), fencing W(c), field hockey M(c), racquetball M/W, skiing (downhill) M(c)/W(c), soccer M/W, swimming and diving M/W, table tennis M(c)/W(c), tennis M(c)/W(c), volleyball M(c)/W(c).

Campus security: 24-hour emergency response devices and patrols, student patrols, late-night transport/escort service, controlled dormitory access.

Student services: health clinic, personal/psychological counseling, women's center.

COSTS & FINANCIAL AID
Costs (2019–20) ***Comprehensive fee:*** $59,875 includes full-time tuition ($46,250), mandatory fees ($825), and room and board ($12,800). Part-time tuition: $1765 per credit hour. ***College room only:*** $6814.

Financial Aid Of all full-time matriculated undergraduates who enrolled in 2018, 1,096 applied for aid, 991 were judged to have need, 191 had their need fully met. In 2018, 313 non-need-based awards were made. ***Average percent of need met:*** 84. ***Average financial aid package:*** $38,359. ***Average need-based loan:*** $5781. ***Average need-based gift aid:*** $32,148. ***Average non-need-based aid:*** $24,404. ***Average indebtedness upon graduation:*** $31,156.

APPLYING
Standardized Tests *Recommended:* SAT (for admission), ACT (for admission), SAT or ACT (for admission).

Options: electronic application, early admission, early decision, early action, deferred entrance.

Required: essay or personal statement, high school transcript, minimum 3.0 GPA, 1 letter of recommendation. ***Recommended:*** interview.

Application deadlines: 3/15 (freshmen), 6/15 (transfers), 1/5 (early action).

Early decision deadline: 11/15.

Notification: 2/1 (freshmen), continuous (transfers), 12/23 (early decision plan 1), rolling (early decision plan 2), 2/15 (early action).

CONTACT
Ms. Terri Bollman-Dalansky, Senior Associate Dean of Admission, Juniata College, 1700 Moore St, Huntingdon, PA 16652. *Phone:* 814-641-3424. *Toll-free phone:* 877-JUNIATA. *Fax:* 814-641-3100. *E-mail:* bollmat@juniata.edu.

Keystone College

La Plume, Pennsylvania

http://www.keystone.edu/

- **Independent** comprehensive, founded 1868
- **Rural** campus
- **Coed** 1,340 undergraduate students, 80% full-time, 62% women, 38% men

UNDERGRAD STUDENTS
1,078 full-time, 262 part-time. 16% are from out of state; 9% Black or African American, non-Hispanic/Latino; 7% Hispanic/Latino; 1% Asian, non-Hispanic/Latino; 0.1% Native Hawaiian or other Pacific Islander, non-Hispanic/Latino; 0.3% American Indian or Alaska Native, non-Hispanic/Latino; 2% Two or more races, non-Hispanic/Latino; 14% Race/ethnicity unknown; 0.1% international; 7% transferred in; 35% live on campus.

Freshmen:
Admission: 329 enrolled. ***Average high school GPA:*** 2.9.

Retention: 62% of full-time freshmen returned.

FACULTY
Total: 188, 28% full-time.

Student/faculty ratio: 11:1.

ACADEMICS
Calendar: semesters. *Degrees:* associate, bachelor's, master's, and postbachelor's certificates.

Special study options: academic remediation for entering students, adult/continuing education programs, advanced placement credit, cooperative education, distance learning, double majors, English as a second language, honors programs, independent study, internships, part-time degree program, services for LD students, study abroad, summer session for credit.

Computers: 100 computers/terminals are available on campus for general student use. Students can access the following: campus intranet, computer help desk, free student e-mail accounts, online (class) grades, online (class) registration, online (class) schedules. Campuswide network is available. 100% of college-owned or -operated housing units are wired for high-speed Internet access. Wireless service is available via entire campus.
Library: Miller Library.

STUDENT LIFE
Housing options: on-campus residence required for freshman year; coed. Campus housing is university owned and leased by the school. Freshman campus housing is guaranteed.

Activities and organizations: drama/theater group, student-run newspaper, radio station, choral group.

Athletics Member NCAA. All Division III.

Student services: health clinic, personal/psychological counseling.

COSTS & FINANCIAL AID
Costs (2019–20) ***Comprehensive fee:*** $38,620 includes full-time tuition ($24,920), mandatory fees ($1800), and room and board ($11,900). Part-time tuition: $550 per credit hour. ***College room only:*** $6000.

Financial Aid Of all full-time matriculated undergraduates who enrolled in 2014, 1,182 applied for aid, 1,100 were judged to have need, 123 had their need fully met. In 2014, 10 non-need-based awards were made. ***Average percent of need met:*** 66. ***Average financial aid package:*** $17,679. ***Average need-based loan:*** $3671. ***Average need-based gift aid:*** $13,989. ***Average non-need-based aid:*** $1467. ***Financial aid deadline:*** 5/1.

APPLYING
Options: electronic application, early admission, deferred entrance.

Required: essay or personal statement, high school transcript. ***Required for some:*** art portfolio for visual arts and art education. ***Recommended:*** interview.

Notification: continuous (freshmen), continuous (transfers).

CONTACT
Jennifer Sekol, Director of Admissions, Keystone College, One College Green, La Plume, PA 18440. *Phone:* 570-945-8111. *Toll-free phone:* 877-4-COLLEGE. *E-mail:* admissions@keystone.edu.

King's College

Wilkes-Barre, Pennsylvania

http://www.kings.edu/

- **Independent Roman Catholic** comprehensive, founded 1946
- **Urban** 48-acre campus
- **Endowment** $82.4 million
- **Coed** 2,269 undergraduate students, 91% full-time, 48% women, 52% men
- **Moderately difficult** entrance level, 78% of applicants were admitted

UNDERGRAD STUDENTS
2,066 full-time, 203 part-time. Students come from 25 states and territories; 10 other countries; 28% are from out of state; 4% Black or African American, non-Hispanic/Latino; 8% Hispanic/Latino; 3% Asian, non-Hispanic/Latino; 0.1% American Indian or Alaska Native, non-Hispanic/Latino; 2% Two or more races, non-Hispanic/Latino; 3% Race/ethnicity unknown; 9% international; 4% transferred in; 48% live on campus.

Freshmen:
Admission: 4,292 applied, 3,330 admitted, 555 enrolled. ***Average high school GPA:*** 3.4. ***Test scores:*** SAT evidence-based reading and writing scores over 500: 82%; SAT math scores over 500: 76%; ACT scores over 18: 92%; SAT evidence-based reading and writing scores over 600: 29%; SAT math scores over 600: 23%; ACT scores over 24: 44%; SAT evidence-based reading and writing scores over 700: 1%; SAT math scores over 700: 3%; ACT scores over 30: 5%.

Retention: 74% of full-time freshmen returned.

FACULTY
Total: 225, 60% full-time, 59% with terminal degrees.

Student/faculty ratio: 13:1.

ACADEMICS
Calendar: semesters. *Degrees:* bachelor's, master's, and postbachelor's certificates.

Special study options: accelerated degree program, adult/continuing education programs, advanced placement credit, distance learning, double majors, English as a second language, honors programs, independent study, internships, off-campus study, part-time degree program, services for LD students, student-designed majors, study abroad, summer session for credit. ***ROTC:*** Army (b), Air Force (c).

Unusual degree programs: 3-2 engineering with University of Notre Dame, Washington University.

Computers: 470 computers/terminals are available on campus for general student use. Students can access the following: computer help desk, free student e-mail accounts, online (class) grades, online (class) registration, online (class) schedules. Campuswide network is available. 100% of college-owned or -operated housing units are wired for high-speed Internet access. Wireless service is available via classrooms, computer labs, dorm rooms, libraries, student centers.

Library: D. Leonard Corgan Library. *Books:* 176,086 (physical); *Databases:* 58. Weekly public service hours: 89; study areas open 24 hours, 5–7 days a week.

STUDENT LIFE
Housing options: on-campus residence required through sophomore year; coed, men-only, women-only, cooperative, special housing for students with disabilities. Campus housing is university owned. Freshman campus housing is guaranteed.

Activities and organizations: drama/theater group, student-run newspaper, radio station, choral group, Association of Campus Events, Student Government Association, Accounting Association, International/Multicultural Club, Biology Club.

Athletics Member NCAA. All Division III. ***Intercollegiate sports:*** baseball M, basketball M/W, cross-country running M/W, field hockey W, football M, golf M/W, ice hockey M/W, lacrosse M/W, soccer M/W, softball W, swimming and diving M/W, tennis M/W, track and field M/W, volleyball W, wrestling M. ***Intramural sports:*** basketball M/W, rugby M, soccer M/W.

Campus security: 24-hour emergency response devices and patrols, late-night transport/escort service, controlled dormitory access.

Student services: health clinic, personal/psychological counseling.

COSTS & FINANCIAL AID
Costs (2019–20) ***Comprehensive fee:*** $52,188 includes full-time tuition ($36,774), mandatory fees ($1950), and room and board ($13,464). Part-time tuition: $600 per credit hour. ***Required fees:*** $90 part-time. ***College room only:*** $7014.

Financial Aid Of all full-time matriculated undergraduates who enrolled in 2018, 1,743 applied for aid, 1,585 were judged to have need, 267 had their need fully met. 167 Federal Work-Study jobs (averaging $1851). 212 state and other part-time jobs (averaging $952). In 2018, 297 non-need-based awards were made. ***Average percent of need met:*** 73. ***Average financial aid package:*** $27,254. ***Average need-based loan:*** $4375. ***Average need-based gift aid:*** $22,356. ***Average non-need-based aid:*** $17,806. ***Average indebtedness upon graduation:*** $39,623.

APPLYING
Standardized Tests *Recommended:* SAT or ACT (for admission).

Options: electronic application, early decision, early action, deferred entrance.

Application fee: $30.

Required: essay or personal statement, high school transcript. ***Recommended:*** interview.

Application deadlines: rolling (freshmen), rolling (out-of-state freshmen), rolling (transfers), 12/1 (early action).

Notification: continuous (freshmen), continuous (out-of-state freshmen), continuous (transfers).

CONTACT
Mr. Robert Reese, Vice President for Enrollment Management, King's College, 133 North River Street, Wilkes-Barre, PA 18711-0801. *Phone:* 570-208-5858. *Toll-free phone:* 888-KINGSPA. *Fax:* 570-208-5971. *E-mail:* admissions@kings.edu.

Kutztown University of Pennsylvania

Kutztown, Pennsylvania

http://www.kutztown.edu/

- **State-supported** comprehensive, founded 1866, part of Pennsylvania State System of Higher Education
- **Rural** 289-acre campus with easy access to Philadelphia
- **Endowment** $22.2 million
- **Coed**
- **Moderately difficult** entrance level

FACULTY
Student/faculty ratio: 18:1.

ACADEMICS
Calendar: semesters. *Degrees:* bachelor's, master's, doctoral, post-master's, and postbachelor's certificates.
Library: Rohrbach Library. *Books:* 317,044 (physical), 299,170 (digital/electronic); *Serial titles:* 88,613 (digital/electronic); *Databases:* 134. Weekly public service hours: 92; students can reserve study rooms.

STUDENT LIFE
Housing options: coed, women-only, cooperative. Campus housing is university owned and leased by the school. Freshman campus housing is guaranteed.

Activities and organizations: drama/theater group, student-run newspaper, radio and television station, choral group, marching band, Marching Unit, Honors Club, American Marketing Association Kutztown Chapter, Humans versus Zombies: Kutztown Chapter, Paws for Love, national fraternities, national sororities.

Athletics Member NCAA. All Division II.

Campus security: 24-hour emergency response devices and patrols, student patrols, late-night transport/escort service, controlled dormitory access, secondary door electronic alarm system in residence halls, 24-hour student desk personnel at main entrance of residence halls.

Student services: health clinic, personal/psychological counseling, women's center.

COSTS & FINANCIAL AID
Costs (2018–19) ***One-time required fee:*** $108. ***Tuition:*** state resident $7716 full-time, $322 per credit part-time; nonresident $11,574 full-time, $805 per credit part-time. Full-time tuition and fees vary according to course load. Part-time tuition and fees vary according to course load. ***Required fees:*** $3086 full-time. ***Room and board:*** $10,334; room only: $6484. Room and board charges vary according to board plan and housing facility. ***Payment plans:*** installment, deferred payment.

Financial Aid Of all full-time matriculated undergraduates who enrolled in 2017, 6,109 applied for aid, 5,140 were judged to have need, 377 had their need fully met. 507 Federal Work-Study jobs (averaging $2900). In 2017, 265 non-need-based awards were made. ***Average percent of need met:*** 44. ***Average financial aid package:*** $9158. ***Average need-based loan:*** $4216. ***Average need-based gift aid:*** $5916. ***Average non-need-based aid:*** $1399. ***Average indebtedness upon graduation:*** $40,864.

APPLYING
Standardized Tests *Required:* SAT or ACT (for admission). *Required for some:* SAT Subject Tests (for admission).

Options: electronic application, early admission, deferred entrance.

Application fee: $35.

Required: high school transcript, minimum 2.0 GPA. ***Required for some:*** audition for music, portfolio and/or art test for arts.

CONTACT
Kutztown University of Pennsylvania, 15200 Kutztown Road, Kutztown, PA 19530-0730. *Phone:* 484-646-4144. *Toll-free phone:* 877-628-1915.

Lackawanna College

Scranton, Pennsylvania

http://www.lackawanna.edu/

- **Independent** primarily 2-year, founded 1894
- **Urban** 4-acre campus
- **Endowment** $5.7 million
- **Coed**
- **Noncompetitive** entrance level

FACULTY
Student/faculty ratio: 16:1.

ACADEMICS
Calendar: semesters. *Degrees:* certificates, diplomas, associate, and bachelor's.
Library: Albright Memorial Library plus 1 other. Students can reserve study rooms.

STUDENT LIFE
Housing options: on-campus residence required through sophomore year; coed, men-only. Campus housing is university owned.

Activities and organizations: Student Government Association, V.O.L.C. (Volunteers of Lackawanna College), Falcon Ambassador Board (FAB), COMMunity Club, Pineapple Club (Hospitality & Culinary Club).

Athletics Member NJCAA.

Campus security: 24-hour emergency response devices and patrols, late-night transport/escort service, controlled dormitory access, patrols by college liaison staff.

Student services: personal/psychological counseling, veterans affairs office.

COSTS & FINANCIAL AID
Costs (2018–19) ***Comprehensive fee:*** $25,960 includes full-time tuition ($14,850), mandatory fees ($810), and room and board ($10,300). Full-time tuition and fees vary according to course load, location, and program. Part-time tuition: $520 per credit. Part-time tuition and fees vary according to course load, location, and program. ***Required fees:*** $405 per term part-time. ***College room only:*** $6500. Room and board charges vary according to board plan. ***Payment plans:*** installment, deferred payment.

Financial Aid Of all full-time matriculated undergraduates who enrolled in 2016, 1,049 applied for aid, 953 were judged to have need, 38 had their need fully met. 80 Federal Work-Study jobs (averaging $779). 21 state and other part-time jobs (averaging $619). In 2016, 18 non-need-based awards were made. ***Average percent of need met:*** 47. ***Average financial aid package:*** $9537. ***Average need-based loan:*** $3247. ***Average need-based gift aid:*** $7272. ***Average non-need-based aid:*** $4882. ***Average indebtedness upon graduation:*** $7347.

APPLYING
Standardized Tests *Recommended:* SAT or ACT (for admission).

Options: electronic application, early admission, deferred entrance.

Application fee: $35.

Required: high school transcript, interview.

CONTACT
Mr. Eddie Perry, Admissions Advisor, Lackawanna College, 501 Vine Street, Scranton, PA 18509. *Phone:* 570-961-7889. *Toll-free phone:* 877-346-3552. *E-mail:* perrye@lackawanna.edu.

Lafayette College

Easton, Pennsylvania

http://www.lafayette.edu/

- **Independent** 4-year, founded 1826, affiliated with Presbyterian Church (U.S.A.)
- **Suburban** 340-acre campus with easy access to New York City, Philadelphia
- **Endowment** $995.3 million
- **Coed** 2,642 undergraduate students, 99% full-time, 52% women, 48% men
- **Very difficult** entrance level, 29% of applicants were admitted

UNDERGRAD STUDENTS
2,603 full-time, 39 part-time. Students come from 46 states and territories; 53 other countries; 81% are from out of state; 5% Black or African American, non-Hispanic/Latino; 7% Hispanic/Latino; 4% Asian, non-Hispanic/Latino; 3% Two or more races, non-Hispanic/Latino; 6% Race/ethnicity unknown; 9% international; 0.4% transferred in; 92% live on campus.

Freshmen:
Admission: 9,237 applied, 2,715 admitted, 733 enrolled. ***Average high school GPA:*** 3.5. ***Test scores:*** SAT evidence-based reading and writing scores over 500: 100%; SAT math scores over 500: 100%; ACT scores over 18: 100%; SAT evidence-based reading and writing scores over 600: 88%; SAT math scores over 600: 86%; ACT scores over 24: 96%; SAT evidence-based reading and writing scores over 700: 29%; SAT math scores over 700: 41%; ACT scores over 30: 53%.

Retention: 93% of full-time freshmen returned.

FACULTY
Total: 297, 80% full-time, 91% with terminal degrees.

Student/faculty ratio: 10:1.

ACADEMICS
Calendar: semesters plus interim January program. *Degree:* bachelor's.

Special study options: academic remediation for entering students, accelerated degree program, advanced placement credit, double majors, honors programs, independent study, internships, off-campus study, part-time degree program, services for LD students, student-designed majors, study abroad, summer session for credit. ***ROTC:*** Army (c).

Computers: 690 computers/terminals and 690 ports are available on campus for general student use. Students can access the following: campus intranet, computer help desk, free student e-mail accounts, online (class) grades, online (class) registration, online (class) schedules. Campuswide network is available. 100% of college-owned or -operated housing units are wired for high-speed Internet access. Wireless service is available via entire campus.
Library: Skillman Library plus 2 others. *Books:* 603,599 (physical), 344,469 (digital/electronic); *Serial titles:* 306 (physical), 68,298 (digital/electronic); *Databases:* 132. Weekly public service hours: 106.

STUDENT LIFE
Housing options: on-campus residence required through senior year; coed, men-only, women-only, special housing for students with disabilities. Campus housing is university owned. Freshman campus housing is guaranteed.

Activities and organizations: drama/theater group, student-run newspaper, radio station, choral group, LAF (Lafayette Activities Forum), Student Government, Crew, International Students Association, Leopards Lair, national fraternities, national sororities.

Athletics Member NCAA. All Division I except football (Division I-AA). ***Intercollegiate sports:*** baseball M, basketball M/W, crew M(c)/W(c), cross-country running M/W, equestrian sports M(c)/W(c), fencing M/W, field hockey W, golf M, ice hockey M(c), lacrosse M/W, rugby M(c)/W(c), skiing (downhill) W(c), soccer M/W, softball W, squash M(c), swimming and diving M/W, tennis M/W, track and field M/W, volleyball W, weight lifting M(c)/W(c), wrestling M(c). ***Intramural sports:*** badminton M/W, baseball M, basketball M/W, bowling M/W, cross-country running M/W, fencing M/W, field hockey W, football M, golf M/W, lacrosse M/W, racquetball M/W, sailing M(c)/W(c), skiing (cross-country) M(c)/W(c), soccer M/W, softball M/W, squash M/W, swimming and diving M/W, table tennis M/W, tennis M/W, track and field M/W, volleyball M/W, weight lifting M/W, wrestling M.

Campus security: 24-hour emergency response devices and patrols, student patrols, late-night transport/escort service, controlled dormitory access.

Student services: health clinic, personal/psychological counseling, women's center.

COSTS & FINANCIAL AID
Costs (2019–20) ***One-time required fee:*** $750. ***Comprehensive fee:*** $71,256 includes full-time tuition ($54,512), mandatory fees ($490), and room and board ($16,254). Part-time tuition: $613 per credit hour. ***College room only:*** $10,057.

Financial Aid Of all full-time matriculated undergraduates who enrolled in 2018, 1,403 applied for aid, 849 were judged to have need, 849 had their need fully met. 588 Federal Work-Study jobs (averaging $1172). In 2018, 181 non-need-based awards were made. ***Average percent of need met:*** 100. ***Average financial aid package:*** $50,594. ***Average need-based loan:*** $3801. ***Average need-based gift aid:*** $45,231. ***Average non-need-based aid:*** $30,781. ***Average indebtedness upon graduation:*** $26,341. ***Financial aid deadline:*** 1/15.

APPLYING
Standardized Tests *Required:* SAT or ACT (for admission). *Recommended:* SAT Subject Tests (for admission).

Options: electronic application, early admission, early decision, deferred entrance.

Application fee: $65.

Required: essay or personal statement, high school transcript, 1 letter of recommendation. ***Recommended:*** interview.

Application deadlines: 1/15 (freshmen), 5/1 (transfers).

Early decision deadline: 11/15.

Notification: 4/1 (freshmen), continuous (transfers).

CONTACT
Mr. Matthew Hyde, Director of Admissions, Lafayette College, 118 Markle Hall, 730 High Street, Easton, PA 18042-1798. *Phone:* 610-330-5100. *Fax:* 610-330-5355. *E-mail:* hydem@lafayette.edu.

Lancaster Bible College

Lancaster, Pennsylvania

http://www.lbc.edu/

- **Independent nondenominational** comprehensive, founded 1933
- **Suburban** 100-acre campus with easy access to Philadelphia
- **Endowment** $14.3 million
- **Coed** 1,688 undergraduate students, 58% full-time, 52% women, 48% men
- **Minimally difficult** entrance level, 57% of applicants were admitted

UNDERGRAD STUDENTS
986 full-time, 702 part-time. Students come from 17 states and territories; 3 other countries; 30% are from out of state; 25% Black or African American, non-Hispanic/Latino; 5% Hispanic/Latino; 1% Asian, non-Hispanic/Latino; 0.1% Native Hawaiian or other Pacific Islander, non-Hispanic/Latino; 0.1% American Indian or Alaska Native, non-Hispanic/Latino; 9% Two or more races, non-Hispanic/Latino; 14% Race/ethnicity unknown; 0.1% international; 22% transferred in; 54% live on campus.

Freshmen:
Admission: 192 applied, 109 admitted, 190 enrolled. ***Average high school GPA:*** 3.1. ***Test scores:*** ACT scores over 18: 71%; ACT scores over 24: 19%.

Retention: 81% of full-time freshmen returned.

FACULTY
Total: 86, 51% full-time, 37% with terminal degrees.

Student/faculty ratio: 15:1.

ACADEMICS
Calendar: semesters. *Degrees:* certificates, associate, bachelor's, master's, doctoral, and postbachelor's certificates.

Special study options: academic remediation for entering students, adult/continuing education programs, advanced placement credit, double majors, independent study, internships, part-time degree program, services for LD students, study abroad, summer session for credit.

Computers: 50 computers/terminals are available on campus for general student use. Campuswide network is available.
Library: Lancaster Bible College Library.

STUDENT LIFE
Housing options: on-campus residence required through senior year; men-only, women-only. Campus housing is university owned. Freshman campus housing is guaranteed.

Activities and organizations: drama/theater group, student-run newspaper, choral group, Student Government Association, Student Missionary Fellowship, International Student Fellowship, Resident Affairs Council, Student Intramural Association.

Athletics Member NCCAA. ***Intercollegiate sports:*** baseball M, basketball M/W, lacrosse W, soccer M/W, volleyball M/W. ***Intramural sports:*** basketball M/W, cheerleading M/W, football M/W, soccer M/W, softball M/W, table tennis M/W, tennis M/W, volleyball M/W.

Campus security: student patrols, late-night transport/escort service, controlled dormitory access.

Student services: health clinic, personal/psychological counseling.

COSTS & FINANCIAL AID
Costs (2018–19) ***One-time required fee:*** $300. ***Comprehensive fee:*** $33,720 includes full-time tuition ($24,290), mandatory fees ($680), and room and board ($8750). Full-time tuition and fees vary according to degree level and student level. Part-time tuition: $810 per credit hour. Part-time tuition and fees vary according to course load and degree level. ***Required fees:*** $35 per credit hour part-time. ***Room and board:*** Room and board charges vary according to board plan. ***Payment plan:*** installment. ***Waivers:*** children of alumni, senior citizens, and employees or children of employees.

Financial Aid Of all full-time matriculated undergraduates who enrolled in 2018, 766 applied for aid, 676 were judged to have need, 234 had their need fully met. 115 Federal Work-Study jobs (averaging $2000). In 2018, 177 non-need-based awards were made. ***Average percent of need met:*** 81. ***Average financial aid package:*** $20,271. ***Average need-based loan:*** $4159. ***Average need-based gift aid:*** $16,847. ***Average non-need-based aid:*** $8942. ***Average indebtedness upon graduation:*** $33,465.

APPLYING

Standardized Tests *Required:* SAT or ACT (for admission).

Options: early admission, deferred entrance.

Application fee: $25.

Required: essay or personal statement, high school transcript, minimum 2.0 GPA, 3 letters of recommendation. ***Required for some:*** interview.

Application deadlines: rolling (freshmen), rolling (transfers).

Notification: continuous (freshmen), continuous (transfers).

CONTACT

Mr. Jared Yoder, Director of Admissions, Lancaster Bible College, PO Box 83403, Lancaster, PA 17608. *Phone:* 717-569-7071. *Toll-free phone:* 800-544-7335. *Fax:* 717-560-8213. *E-mail:* admissions@lbc.edu.

La Roche College

Pittsburgh, Pennsylvania

http://www.laroche.edu/

- **Independent** comprehensive, founded 1963, affiliated with Roman Catholic Church
- **Suburban** 43-acre campus
- **Endowment** $5.7 million
- **Coed**
- **Minimally difficult** entrance level

FACULTY

Student/faculty ratio: 12:1.

ACADEMICS

Calendar: semesters plus summer term. *Degrees:* certificates, associate, bachelor's, master's, doctoral, and postbachelor's certificates.
Library: John J. Wright Library plus 1 other. *Books:* 75,803 (physical), 221,000 (digital/electronic); *Databases:* 1,248.

STUDENT LIFE

Housing options: coed. Campus housing is university owned. Freshman campus housing is guaranteed.

Activities and organizations: student-run newspaper, radio station, American Society of Interior Design, student government, Visions (environmental club).

Athletics Member NCAA. All Division III.

Campus security: 24-hour emergency response devices and patrols, student patrols, late-night transport/escort service, controlled dormitory access.

Student services: health clinic, personal/psychological counseling, veterans affairs office.

COSTS & FINANCIAL AID

Costs (2018–19) ***Comprehensive fee:*** $40,120 includes full-time tuition ($27,714), mandatory fees ($850), and room and board ($11,556). Part-time tuition: $700 per credit hour. ***Required fees:*** $40 per term part-time. ***College room only:*** $7316. Room and board charges vary according to board plan and housing facility.

Financial Aid Of all full-time matriculated undergraduates who enrolled in 2018, 817 applied for aid, 768 were judged to have need, 212 had their need fully met. 149 Federal Work-Study jobs (averaging $1465). In 2018, 49 non-need-based awards were made. ***Average percent of need met:*** 93. ***Average financial aid package:*** $31,921. ***Average need-based loan:*** $4308. ***Average need-based gift aid:*** $8332. ***Average non-need-based aid:*** $19,616. ***Average indebtedness upon graduation:*** $35,357.

APPLYING

Standardized Tests *Required:* SAT or ACT (for admission).

Options: electronic application, early admission, deferred entrance.

Application fee: $50.

Required: high school transcript, minimum 2.0 GPA, 2 letters of recommendation. ***Recommended:*** essay or personal statement, minimum 3.0 GPA, interview.

CONTACT

La Roche College, 9000 Babcock Boulevard, Pittsburgh, PA 15237. *Phone:* 412-536-1272. *Toll-free phone:* 800-838-4LRC. *Fax:* 412-536-1048. *E-mail:* admissions@laroche.edu.

La Salle University

Philadelphia, Pennsylvania

http://www.lasalle.edu/

- **Independent Roman Catholic** comprehensive, founded 1863
- **Urban** 133-acre campus with easy access to Philadelphia
- **Endowment** $84.3 million
- **Coed** 3,904 undergraduate students, 86% full-time, 62% women, 38% men
- **Moderately difficult** entrance level, 81% of applicants were admitted

UNDERGRAD STUDENTS

3,363 full-time, 541 part-time. Students come from 45 other countries; 31% are from out of state; 20% Black or African American, non-Hispanic/Latino; 19% Hispanic/Latino; 5% Asian, non-Hispanic/Latino; 0.2% Native Hawaiian or other Pacific Islander, non-Hispanic/Latino; 0.1% American Indian or Alaska Native, non-Hispanic/Latino; 3% Two or more races, non-Hispanic/Latino; 2% Race/ethnicity unknown; 2% international; 4% transferred in; 48% live on campus.

Freshmen:

Admission: 6,642 applied, 5,392 admitted, 1,049 enrolled. ***Average high school GPA:*** 3.4. ***Test scores:*** SAT evidence-based reading and writing scores over 500: 74%; SAT math scores over 500: 69%; ACT scores over 18: 80%; SAT evidence-based reading and writing scores over 600: 23%; SAT math scores over 600: 14%; ACT scores over 24: 39%; SAT evidence-based reading and writing scores over 700: 2%; SAT math scores over 700: 2%; ACT scores over 30: 9%.

Retention: 74% of full-time freshmen returned.

FACULTY

Total: 512, 43% full-time.

Student/faculty ratio: 11:1.

ACADEMICS

Calendar: semesters. *Degrees:* associate, bachelor's, master's, doctoral, post-master's, and postbachelor's certificates.

Special study options: academic remediation for entering students, accelerated degree program, adult/continuing education programs, advanced placement credit, cooperative education, distance learning, double majors, English as a second language, freshman honors college, honors programs, independent study, internships, off-campus study, part-time degree program, services for LD students, student-designed majors, study abroad, summer session for credit. ***ROTC:*** Army (c), Air Force (c).

Unusual degree programs: 3-2 business administration; communication sciences and disorders/speech language pathology, communication/professional business communication, computer information science, history, elementary/special education, occupational therapy program with Thomas Jefferson University.

Computers: 1,100 computers/terminals are available on campus for general student use. Students can access the following: campus intranet, computer help desk, free student e-mail accounts, online (class) grades, online (class) registration, online (class) schedules, course management system. Campuswide network is available. 100% of college-owned or -operated housing units are wired for high-speed Internet access. Wireless service is available via classrooms, computer centers, computer labs, dorm rooms, learning centers, libraries, student centers.
Library: Connelly Library. *Books:* 314,203 (physical), 819,865 (digital/electronic); *Serial titles:* 2,982 (physical), 139,962 (digital/electronic); *Databases:* 88. Weekly public service hours: 96; students can reserve study rooms.

STUDENT LIFE

Housing options: on-campus residence required through sophomore year; coed, men-only, women-only, special housing for students with disabilities. Campus housing is university owned. Freshman campus housing is guaranteed.

Activities and organizations: drama/theater group, student-run newspaper, radio and television station, choral group, Student Government Association, community service organization, La Salle

Entertainment Organization, The Explorer (yearbook), The Masque (theater group), national fraternities, national sororities.

Athletics Member NCAA. All Division I. ***Intercollegiate sports:*** baseball M(s), basketball M(s)/W(s), cheerleading M/W, crew M(s)/W(s), cross-country running M(s)/W(s), field hockey W(s), golf M(s)/W(s)(c), lacrosse W(s), soccer M(s)/W(s), softball W(s), swimming and diving M(s)/W(s), tennis M(s)/W(s), track and field M(s)/W(s), volleyball W(s), water polo M(s)/W(s). ***Intramural sports:*** basketball M/W, football M/W, ice hockey M(c), lacrosse M(c), rugby M(c)/W(c), softball M/W, ultimate Frisbee M(c)/W(c), volleyball M/W.

Campus security: 24-hour emergency response devices and patrols, student patrols, late-night transport/escort service, controlled dormitory access.

Student services: health clinic, personal/psychological counseling, women's center, veterans affairs office.

COSTS & FINANCIAL AID

Costs (2018–19) ***One-time required fee:*** $300. ***Comprehensive fee:*** $45,790 includes full-time tuition ($29,810), mandatory fees ($900), and room and board ($15,080). Full-time tuition and fees vary according to course load and program. Part-time tuition: $585 per credit hour. Part-time tuition and fees vary according to course load and program. ***Required fees:*** $250 per term part-time. ***College room only:*** $7990. Room and board charges vary according to board plan and housing facility. ***Payment plans:*** installment, deferred payment. ***Waivers:*** employees or children of employees.

Financial Aid Of all full-time matriculated undergraduates who enrolled in 2016, 2,765 applied for aid, 2,605 were judged to have need, 366 had their need fully met. 364 Federal Work-Study jobs (averaging $1837). In 2016, 471 non-need-based awards were made. ***Average percent of need met:*** 75. ***Average financial aid package:*** $32,236. ***Average need-based loan:*** $4822. ***Average need-based gift aid:*** $25,432. ***Average non-need-based aid:*** $19,520. ***Average indebtedness upon graduation:*** $37,002.

APPLYING

Standardized Tests *Required for some:* SAT or ACT (for admission).

Options: electronic application, early admission, early action, deferred entrance.

Required: essay or personal statement, high school transcript, 1 letter of recommendation. ***Recommended:*** interview.

Application deadlines: 8/15 (transfers), 11/15 (early action).

Notification: continuous (freshmen), continuous (transfers).

CONTACT

Mr. James Plunkett, Executive Director of Undergraduate Admission, La Salle University, 1900 West Olney Avenue, Philadelphia, PA 19141-1199. *Phone:* 215-951-1500. *Toll-free phone:* 800-328-1910. *Fax:* 215-951-1656. *E-mail:* admiss@lasalle.edu.

Lebanon Valley College

Annville, Pennsylvania

http://www.lvc.edu/

- **Independent United Methodist** comprehensive, founded 1866
- **Small-town** 357-acre campus
- **Endowment** $67.5 million
- **Coed** 1,744 undergraduate students, 95% full-time, 54% women, 46% men
- **Moderately difficult** entrance level, 78% of applicants were admitted

UNDERGRAD STUDENTS

1,651 full-time, 93 part-time. 20% are from out of state; 3% Black or African American, non-Hispanic/Latino; 5% Hispanic/Latino; 2% Asian, non-Hispanic/Latino; 0.1% Native Hawaiian or other Pacific Islander, non-Hispanic/Latino; 0.1% American Indian or Alaska Native, non-Hispanic/Latino; 3% Two or more races, non-Hispanic/Latino; 1% Race/ethnicity unknown; 1% international; 3% transferred in; 77% live on campus.

Freshmen:

Admission: 2,731 applied, 2,136 admitted, 473 enrolled. ***Average high school GPA:*** 3.6. ***Test scores:*** SAT evidence-based reading and writing scores over 500: 87%; SAT math scores over 500: 87%; ACT scores over 18: 100%; SAT evidence-based reading and writing scores over 600: 47%; SAT math scores over 600: 43%; ACT scores over 24: 66%; SAT evidence-based reading and writing scores over 700: 6%; SAT math scores over 700: 9%; ACT scores over 30: 15%.

Retention: 82% of full-time freshmen returned.

FACULTY

Total: 255, 48% full-time, 54% with terminal degrees.

Student/faculty ratio: 10:1.

ACADEMICS

Calendar: semesters. *Degrees:* bachelor's, master's, doctoral, and postbachelor's certificates.

Special study options: academic remediation for entering students, accelerated degree program, adult/continuing education programs, advanced placement credit, distance learning, double majors, English as a second language, independent study, internships, off-campus study, part-time degree program, services for LD students, student-designed majors, study abroad, summer session for credit.

Unusual degree programs: 3-2 business administration; engineering with Case Western Reserve University, The Penn State University; athletic training, speech language pathology, medical technology.

Computers: 202 computers/terminals are available on campus for general student use. Students can access the following: campus intranet, computer help desk, free student e-mail accounts, online (class) grades, online (class) registration, online (class) schedules. Campuswide network is available. 100% of college-owned or -operated housing units are wired for high-speed Internet access. Wireless service is available via entire campus.

Library: Vernon and Doris Bishop Library. *Books:* 152,349 (physical), 204,880 (digital/electronic); *Serial titles:* 3,047 (physical), 59,331 (digital/electronic); *Databases:* 256. Weekly public service hours: 101; students can reserve study rooms.

STUDENT LIFE

Housing options: on-campus residence required through senior year; coed, special housing for students with disabilities. Campus housing is university owned. Freshman campus housing is guaranteed.

Activities and organizations: drama/theater group, student-run newspaper, choral group, marching band, Mini-THON, Student Government, Colleges Against Cancer, Wig and Buckle Theater Group, Valleyfest, national fraternities, national sororities.

Athletics Member NCAA. All Division III except golf (Division II). ***Intercollegiate sports:*** baseball M, basketball M/W, cross-country running M/W, field hockey W, football M, golf M/W, ice hockey M/W, lacrosse M/W, soccer M/W, softball W, swimming and diving M/W, tennis M/W, track and field M/W, volleyball W. ***Intramural sports:*** archery M(c)/W(c), basketball M/W, cheerleading W(c), equestrian sports M(c)/W(c), football M/W, soccer M(c)/W(c), ultimate Frisbee M(c)/W(c), volleyball M/W, weight lifting W(c).

Campus security: 24-hour emergency response devices and patrols, late-night transport/escort service, controlled dormitory access.

Student services: health clinic, personal/psychological counseling, women's center.

COSTS & FINANCIAL AID

Costs (2019–20) ***Comprehensive fee:*** $57,110 includes full-time tuition ($43,650), mandatory fees ($1260), and room and board ($12,200). ***College room only:*** $5890.

Financial Aid Of all full-time matriculated undergraduates who enrolled in 2018, 1,574 applied for aid, 1,430 were judged to have need, 325 had their need fully met. In 2018, 84 non-need-based awards were made. ***Average percent of need met:*** 81. ***Average financial aid package:*** $34,567. ***Average need-based loan:*** $4049. ***Average need-based gift aid:*** $28,353. ***Average non-need-based aid:*** $21,316. ***Average indebtedness upon graduation:*** $43,880.

APPLYING

Options: electronic application, early decision.

Required: high school transcript. ***Required for some:*** audition for music majors, specific requirements for physical therapy and athletic training programs. ***Recommended:*** 2 letters of recommendation, interview.

Application deadlines: rolling (freshmen), rolling (transfers).

Early decision deadline: 11/1.

Notification: continuous until 11/15 (freshmen), continuous (transfers).

CONTACT
Mr. Edwin Wright, Vice President of Enrollment Management, Lebanon Valley College, 101 North College Avenue, Annville, PA 17003. *Phone:* 717-867-6181. *Toll-free phone:* 866-LVC-4ADM. *Fax:* 717-867-6026. *E-mail:* admission@lvc.edu.

Lehigh University
Bethlehem, Pennsylvania
http://www.lehigh.edu/

- **Independent** university, founded 1865
- **Suburban** 2355-acre campus with easy access to Philadelphia
- **Endowment** $1.3 billion
- **Coed**
- **Most difficult** entrance level

FACULTY
Student/faculty ratio: 9:1.

ACADEMICS
Calendar: semesters. *Degrees:* bachelor's, master's, doctoral, post-master's, and postbachelor's certificates.
Library: E. W. Fairchild-Martindale Library plus 1 other. *Books:* 798,207 (physical), 402,504 (digital/electronic); *Serial titles:* 2,050 (physical), 61,205 (digital/electronic); *Databases:* 191. Weekly public service hours: 83; students can reserve study rooms.

STUDENT LIFE
Housing options: on-campus residence required through sophomore year; coed, special housing for students with disabilities. Campus housing is university owned. Freshman campus housing is guaranteed.

Activities and organizations: drama/theater group, student-run newspaper, radio station, choral group, marching band, Marching 97, Indian Student Association, Accounting Club, Student Senate, Phi Sigma Pi, national fraternities, national sororities.

Athletics Member NCAA. All Division I.

Campus security: 24-hour emergency response devices and patrols, student patrols, late-night transport/escort service, controlled dormitory access, self defense training.

Student services: health clinic, personal/psychological counseling, women's center.

COSTS & FINANCIAL AID
Costs (2018–19) ***Comprehensive fee:*** $66,530 includes full-time tuition ($52,480), mandatory fees ($450), and room and board ($13,600). Part-time tuition: $2190 per credit hour. ***College room only:*** $7930. Room and board charges vary according to board plan and housing facility. ***Payment plans:*** tuition prepayment, installment.

Financial Aid Of all full-time matriculated undergraduates who enrolled in 2018, 2,716 applied for aid, 2,085 were judged to have need, 1,654 had their need fully met. 1,284 Federal Work-Study jobs (averaging $1950). 77 state and other part-time jobs (averaging $1795). In 2018, 248 non-need-based awards were made. ***Average percent of need met:*** 98. ***Average financial aid package:*** $50,425. ***Average need-based loan:*** $4032. ***Average need-based gift aid:*** $44,210. ***Average non-need-based aid:*** $10,574. ***Average indebtedness upon graduation:*** $35,109. ***Financial aid deadline:*** 2/1.

APPLYING
Standardized Tests *Required:* SAT or ACT (for admission). *Recommended:* SAT (for admission), ACT (for admission).

Options: electronic application, early admission, early decision, deferred entrance.

Application fee: $70.

Required: essay or personal statement, high school transcript, 2 letters of recommendation.

CONTACT
Krista Evans, Interim Director of Admissions, Lehigh University, 27 Memorial Drive West, Bethlehem, PA 18015. *Phone:* 610-758-3100. *Fax:* 610-758-4361. *E-mail:* admissions@lehigh.edu.

Lincoln University
Lincoln University, Pennsylvania
http://www.lincoln.edu/

- **State-related** comprehensive, founded 1854
- **Rural** 422-acre campus with easy access to Philadelphia
- **Endowment** $38.6 million
- **Coed**
- **Minimally difficult** entrance level

FACULTY
Student/faculty ratio: 15:1.

ACADEMICS
Calendar: semesters. *Degrees:* certificates, bachelor's, and master's.
Library: Langston Hughes Memorial Library. Weekly public service hours: 80; study areas open 24 hours, 5–7 days a week; students can reserve study rooms.

STUDENT LIFE
Housing options: on-campus residence required for freshman year; coed, men-only, women-only, special housing for students with disabilities. Campus housing is university owned. Freshman applicants given priority for college housing.

Activities and organizations: drama/theater group, student-run newspaper, radio and television station, choral group, marching band, Student Government: Class sections, We R "1" Family, Residence Hall Association, International Students Association, Onyx Dance Troupe, national fraternities, national sororities.

Athletics Member NCAA. All Division II.

Campus security: 24-hour emergency response devices and patrols, late-night transport/escort service, controlled dormitory access, 24-hour command center, gated entrance/exit, medical transports.

Student services: health clinic, personal/psychological counseling, women's center, veterans affairs office.

COSTS & FINANCIAL AID
Costs (2018–19) ***Tuition:*** state resident $7868 full-time, $328 per credit hour part-time; nonresident $13,004 full-time, $545 per credit hour part-time. Full-time tuition and fees vary according to course load, degree level, location, program, and student level. Part-time tuition and fees vary according to course load, degree level, program, and student level. No tuition increase for student's term of enrollment. ***Required fees:*** $3798 full-time, $141 per credit hour part-time. ***Room and board:*** $9588; room only: $5114. Room and board charges vary according to board plan and housing facility. ***Payment plans:*** installment, deferred payment.

Financial Aid Of all full-time matriculated undergraduates who enrolled in 2017, 1,761 applied for aid, 1,660 were judged to have need, 134 had their need fully met. 135 Federal Work-Study jobs (averaging $1551). In 2017, 57 non-need-based awards were made. ***Average percent of need met:*** 39. ***Average financial aid package:*** $13,823. ***Average need-based loan:*** $4111. ***Average need-based gift aid:*** $7158. ***Average non-need-based aid:*** $9385. ***Average indebtedness upon graduation:*** $40,605.

APPLYING
Standardized Tests *Required:* SAT or ACT (for admission).

Options: electronic application, deferred entrance.

Required: high school transcript, minimum 2.0 GPA. ***Recommended:*** essay or personal statement, 2 letters of recommendation, interview.

CONTACT
Ms. Nikoia Forde, Associate Director, Undergraduate Admissions, Lincoln University, 1570 Baltimore Pike, Lincoln University, PA 19352. *Phone:* 484-365-7275. *Toll-free phone:* 800-790-0191. *Fax:* 484-365-8109. *E-mail:* nfredericksen@lincoln.edu.

Lock Haven University of Pennsylvania

Lock Haven, Pennsylvania

http://www.lockhaven.edu/

- **State-supported** comprehensive, founded 1870, part of Pennsylvania State System of Higher Education
- **Rural** 165-acre campus
- **Endowment** $11.0 million
- **Coed** 3,067 undergraduate students, 91% full-time, 58% women, 42% men
- **Moderately difficult** entrance level, 94% of applicants were admitted

UNDERGRAD STUDENTS
2,798 full-time, 269 part-time. Students come from 17 states and territories; 17 other countries; 4% are from out of state; 8% Black or African American, non-Hispanic/Latino; 4% Hispanic/Latino; 1% Asian, non-Hispanic/Latino; 0.6% American Indian or Alaska Native, non-Hispanic/Latino; 0.6% Two or more races, non-Hispanic/Latino; 1% Race/ethnicity unknown; 0.8% international; 5% transferred in; 31% live on campus.

Freshmen:
Admission: 2,560 applied, 2,415 admitted, 692 enrolled. ***Average high school GPA:*** 3.3. ***Test scores:*** SAT evidence-based reading and writing scores over 500: 57%; SAT math scores over 500: 53%; ACT scores over 18: 85%; SAT evidence-based reading and writing scores over 600: 14%; SAT math scores over 600: 10%; ACT scores over 24: 32%; SAT evidence-based reading and writing scores over 700: 1%; SAT math scores over 700: 1%.

Retention: 65% of full-time freshmen returned.

FACULTY
Total: 220, 89% full-time, 84% with terminal degrees.

Student/faculty ratio: 17:1.

ACADEMICS
Calendar: semesters. *Degrees:* associate, bachelor's, and master's.

Special study options: academic remediation for entering students, adult/continuing education programs, advanced placement credit, cooperative education, distance learning, double majors, English as a second language, freshman honors college, honors programs, independent study, internships, off-campus study, part-time degree program, services for LD students, student-designed majors, study abroad, summer session for credit. ***ROTC:*** Army (b).

Unusual degree programs: 3-2 engineering with Penn State University Park.

Computers: 290 computers/terminals are available on campus for general student use. Students can access the following: online (class) registration. Campuswide network is available.

Library: Stevenson Library plus 1 other. *Books:* 239,240 (physical), 216,376 (digital/electronic); *Serial titles:* 37,613 (physical), 61,655 (digital/electronic); *Databases:* 97. Weekly public service hours: 87; students can reserve study rooms.

STUDENT LIFE
Housing options: on-campus residence required through sophomore year; coed. Campus housing is university owned and is provided by a third party. Freshman applicants given priority for college housing.

Activities and organizations: drama/theater group, student-run newspaper, radio and television station, choral group, marching band, Student Government, Residence Hall Association, national fraternities, national sororities.

Athletics Member NCAA. All Division II except field hockey (Division I), wrestling (Division I). ***Intercollegiate sports:*** baseball M(s), basketball M(s)/W(s), cross-country running M(s)/W(s), field hockey W(s), football M(s), lacrosse W(s), soccer M(s)/W(s), softball W(s), swimming and diving W(s), track and field M(s)/W(s), volleyball W(s), wrestling M(s). ***Intramural sports:*** badminton M/W, basketball M/W, cross-country running M/W, fencing M/W, field hockey W, football M, golf M/W, ice hockey M, lacrosse M/W, racquetball M/W, rugby M/W, skiing (cross-country) M/W, skiing (downhill) M/W, soccer M/W, softball M/W, swimming and diving M/W, tennis M/W, track and field M/W, ultimate Frisbee M/W, volleyball M/W, water polo M, weight lifting M/W, wrestling M.

Campus security: 24-hour emergency response devices and patrols, late-night transport/escort service, controlled dormitory access.

Student services: health clinic, personal/psychological counseling, women's center.

COSTS & FINANCIAL AID
Costs (2018–19) ***Tuition:*** state resident $7716 full-time, $322 per credit hour part-time; nonresident $17,290 full-time, $720 per credit hour part-time. Full-time tuition and fees vary according to course load, location, and program. Part-time tuition and fees vary according to course load, location, and program. ***Required fees:*** $3162 full-time, $168 per credit hour part-time. ***Room and board:*** $10,368; room only: $6540. Room and board charges vary according to board plan and housing facility. ***Payment plan:*** installment. ***Waivers:*** minority students, senior citizens, and employees or children of employees.

Financial Aid Of all full-time matriculated undergraduates who enrolled in 2018, 2,438 applied for aid, 2,078 were judged to have need, 1,881 had their need fully met. In 2018, 25 non-need-based awards were made. ***Average percent of need met:*** 87. ***Average financial aid package:*** $9869. ***Average need-based loan:*** $4529. ***Average need-based gift aid:*** $5953. ***Average non-need-based aid:*** $2351. ***Average indebtedness upon graduation:*** $36,662.

APPLYING
Standardized Tests *Required:* SAT or ACT (for admission).

Options: electronic application, deferred entrance.

Application fee: $25.

Required: high school transcript. ***Required for some:*** essay or personal statement. ***Recommended:*** interview.

Application deadlines: rolling (freshmen), rolling (transfers).

Notification: continuous (freshmen), continuous (transfers).

CONTACT
Angelic Hardy, Director of Admissions, Lock Haven University of Pennsylvania, 401 North Fairview Street, Lock Haven, PA 17745-2390. *Phone:* 570-484-2109. *Toll-free phone:* 800-332-8900 (in-state); 800-233-8978 (out-of-state). *Fax:* 570-484-2201. *E-mail:* anh1227@lockhaven.edu.

Lycoming College

Williamsport, Pennsylvania

http://www.lycoming.edu/

- **Independent United Methodist** 4-year, founded 1812
- **Small-town** 35-acre campus
- **Endowment** $207.6 million
- **Coed** 1,142 undergraduate students, 99% full-time, 53% women, 47% men
- **Moderately difficult** entrance level, 66% of applicants were admitted

UNDERGRAD STUDENTS
1,135 full-time, 7 part-time. Students come from 28 states and territories; 18 other countries; 41% are from out of state; 13% Black or African American, non-Hispanic/Latino; 12% Hispanic/Latino; 1% Asian, non-Hispanic/Latino; 0.1% Native Hawaiian or other Pacific Islander, non-Hispanic/Latino; 0.1% American Indian or Alaska Native, non-Hispanic/Latino; 3% Two or more races, non-Hispanic/Latino; 5% Race/ethnicity unknown; 6% international; 2% transferred in; 87% live on campus.

Freshmen:
Admission: 2,430 applied, 1,594 admitted, 323 enrolled. ***Average high school GPA:*** 3.5. ***Test scores:*** SAT evidence-based reading and writing scores over 500: 80%; SAT math scores over 500: 78%; ACT scores over 18: 81%; SAT evidence-based reading and writing scores over 600: 30%; SAT math scores over 600: 26%; ACT scores over 24: 35%; SAT evidence-based reading and writing scores over 700: 3%; SAT math scores over 700: 4%; ACT scores over 30: 6%.

Retention: 75% of full-time freshmen returned.

FACULTY
Total: 116, 76% full-time, 88% with terminal degrees.

Student/faculty ratio: 12:1.

ACADEMICS
Calendar: semesters. *Degree:* bachelor's.

Special study options: adult/continuing education programs, advanced placement credit, cooperative education, double majors, honors programs, independent study, internships, off-campus study, part-time degree program, services for LD students, student-designed majors, study abroad, summer session for credit. ***ROTC:*** Army (c).

Unusual degree programs: 3-2 engineering with Binghamton University, State University of New York; forestry with Duke University; environmental management with Duke University, clinical laboratory science with Susquehanna Health, Robert Packer, Lancaster, and Abington Hospitals.

Computers: 188 computers/terminals and 3,408 ports are available on campus for general student use. Students can access the following: campus intranet, computer help desk, free student e-mail accounts, online (class) grades, online (class) registration, online (class) schedules, online financial aid, free printing up to a limit, password management, free access to Office 365, streaming TV services, mobile phone plans for International students. Campuswide network is available. 100% of college-owned or -operated housing units are wired for high-speed Internet access. Wireless service is available via entire campus.
Library: Snowden Library. *Books:* 135,456 (physical), 134,657 (digital/electronic); *Serial titles:* 1,045 (physical), 18,343 (digital/electronic); *Databases:* 89. Weekly public service hours: 107.

STUDENT LIFE
Housing options: on-campus residence required through senior year; coed, women-only. Campus housing is university owned. Freshman campus housing is guaranteed.

Activities and organizations: drama/theater group, student-run newspaper, radio station, choral group, Campus Activities Board, Lycoming Pom and Dance Club, Society of Physics Students, Black Student Union, Creative Arts Society, national fraternities, national sororities.

Athletics Member NCAA. All Division III except golf (Division II). ***Intercollegiate sports:*** badminton M(c)/W(c), basketball M/W, cheerleading M(c)/W(c), crew M(c)/W(c), cross-country running M/W, equestrian sports M(c)/W(c), fencing M(c)/W(c), football M, golf M/W, lacrosse M/W, rugby M(c), soccer M/W, softball W, swimming and diving M/W, tennis M/W, ultimate Frisbee M(c)/W(c), volleyball W, water polo M(c)/W(c), wrestling M. ***Intramural sports:*** basketball M/W, football M/W, soccer M/W, softball M/W, table tennis M/W, volleyball M/W.

Campus security: 24-hour emergency response devices and patrols, student patrols, late-night transport/escort service, controlled dormitory access.

Student services: health clinic, personal/psychological counseling.

COSTS & FINANCIAL AID
Costs (2019–20) ***One-time required fee:*** $225. ***Comprehensive fee:*** $54,634 includes full-time tuition ($40,896), mandatory fees ($730), and room and board ($13,008).

Financial Aid Of all full-time matriculated undergraduates who enrolled in 2018, 1,021 applied for aid, 977 were judged to have need, 250 had their need fully met. In 2018, 148 non-need-based awards were made. ***Average percent of need met:*** 85. ***Average financial aid package:*** $40,139. ***Average need-based loan:*** $4527. ***Average need-based gift aid:*** $33,028. ***Average non-need-based aid:*** $26,664.

APPLYING
Standardized Tests *Recommended:* SAT or ACT (for admission).

Options: electronic application, early decision, early action, deferred entrance.

Required: essay or personal statement, high school transcript, 2 letters of recommendation. ***Recommended:*** minimum 2.3 GPA, interview.

Early decision deadline: 11/15.

Notification: continuous until 12/15 (freshmen), continuous until 12/15 (transfers), 12/1 (early decision).

CONTACT
Jessica Hess, Director of Admissions, Lycoming College, 700 College Place, Williamsport, PA 17701. *Phone:* 570-321-4318. *Toll-free phone:* 800-345-3920 Ext. 4026. *Fax:* 570-321-4317. *E-mail:* admissions@lycoming.edu.

Manor College

Jenkintown, Pennsylvania

http://www.manor.edu/

- **Independent Byzantine Catholic** primarily 2-year, founded 1947
- **Suburban** 35-acre campus with easy access to Philadelphia
- **Endowment** $2.8 million
- **Coed** 740 undergraduate students, 65% full-time, 67% women, 33% men
- **Minimally difficult** entrance level, 94% of applicants were admitted

UNDERGRAD STUDENTS
480 full-time, 260 part-time. Students come from 6 states and territories; 2 other countries; 3% are from out of state; 34% Black or African American, non-Hispanic/Latino; 14% Hispanic/Latino; 3% Asian, non-Hispanic/Latino; 0.3% Native Hawaiian or other Pacific Islander, non-Hispanic/Latino; 1% American Indian or Alaska Native, non-Hispanic/Latino; 2% Two or more races, non-Hispanic/Latino; 5% Race/ethnicity unknown; 0.3% international; 10% transferred in; 11% live on campus.

Freshmen:
Admission: 857 applied, 804 admitted, 215 enrolled. ***Average high school GPA:*** 2.7. ***Test scores:*** SAT math scores over 500: 21%; ACT scores over 18: 20%; SAT math scores over 600: 7%; ACT scores over 24: 10%; SAT math scores over 700: 5%.
Retention: 58% of full-time freshmen returned.

FACULTY
Total: 68, 54% full-time, 34% with terminal degrees.
Student/faculty ratio: 10:1.

ACADEMICS
Calendar: semesters. *Degrees:* certificates, associate, bachelor's, and postbachelor's certificates.

Special study options: academic remediation for entering students, accelerated degree program, advanced placement credit, distance learning, double majors, honors programs, independent study, internships, part-time degree program, services for LD students, summer session for credit.

Computers: 140 computers/terminals are available on campus for general student use. Students can access the following: computer help desk, free student e-mail accounts, online (class) grades, online (class) registration, online (class) schedules. Campuswide network is available. 100% of college-owned or -operated housing units are wired for high-speed Internet access. Wireless service is available via entire campus.
Library: Basileiad Library. *Books:* 27,188 (physical), 5,037 (digital/electronic); *Serial titles:* 3 (physical); *Databases:* 14. Weekly public service hours: 65.

STUDENT LIFE
Housing options: coed. Campus housing is university owned.

Activities and organizations: choral group, Rotoract (student service organization), Vet Tech Club, Campus Activities Board, Macrinian Yearbook, Phi Theta Kappa (honor society).

Athletics Member NJCAA. ***Intercollegiate sports:*** baseball M, basketball M/W, cross-country running M/W, soccer M/W, track and field M/W, volleyball W.

Campus security: 24-hour emergency response devices and patrols, late-night transport/escort service.

Student services: personal/psychological counseling, veterans affairs office.

COSTS & FINANCIAL AID
Costs (2019–20) ***Comprehensive fee:*** $24,754 includes full-time tuition ($16,428), mandatory fees ($600), and room and board ($7726). Part-time tuition: $669 per credit. ***Required fees:*** $100 per term part-time.

Financial Aid Of all full-time matriculated undergraduates who enrolled in 2009, 35 Federal Work-Study jobs (averaging $3000). 10 state and other part-time jobs (averaging $3600).

APPLYING
Standardized Tests *Recommended:* SAT or ACT (for admission).

Options: electronic application, deferred entrance.

Required: high school transcript, minimum 2.0 GPA. ***Required for some:*** essay or personal statement, interview.

Application deadlines: rolling (freshmen), rolling (transfers).

Notification: continuous (freshmen), continuous (transfers).

CONTACT

Angelica Crespo, Admissions Office Manager, Manor College, 700 Fox Chase Road, Jenkintown, PA 19046. *Phone:* 215-885-2216 Ext. 212. *Fax:* 215-576-6564. *E-mail:* swalker@manor.edu.

Mansfield University of Pennsylvania

Mansfield, Pennsylvania

http://www.mansfield.edu/

- **State-supported** comprehensive, founded 1857, part of Pennsylvania State System of Higher Education
- **Small-town** 174-acre campus
- **Coed** 1,599 undergraduate students, 91% full-time, 61% women, 39% men
- **Moderately difficult** entrance level, 92% of applicants were admitted

UNDERGRAD STUDENTS

1,453 full-time, 146 part-time. 17% are from out of state; 10% Black or African American, non-Hispanic/Latino; 3% Hispanic/Latino; 0.7% Asian, non-Hispanic/Latino; 0.1% Native Hawaiian or other Pacific Islander, non-Hispanic/Latino; 0.1% American Indian or Alaska Native, non-Hispanic/Latino; 3% Two or more races, non-Hispanic/Latino; 2% Race/ethnicity unknown; 0.6% international; 8% transferred in; 53% live on campus.

Freshmen:

Admission: 1,595 applied, 1,464 admitted, 327 enrolled. ***Average high school GPA:*** 3.4. ***Test scores:*** SAT evidence-based reading and writing scores over 500: 67%; SAT math scores over 500: 66%; SAT evidence-based reading and writing scores over 600: 20%; SAT math scores over 600: 11%; SAT evidence-based reading and writing scores over 700: 1%; SAT math scores over 700: 1%.

Retention: 71% of full-time freshmen returned.

FACULTY

Total: 137, 67% full-time, 69% with terminal degrees.

Student/faculty ratio: 15:1.

ACADEMICS

Calendar: semesters. *Degrees:* associate, bachelor's, master's, and postbachelor's certificates.

Special study options: adult/continuing education programs, part-time degree program. ***ROTC:*** Army (c).

Computers: Students can access the following: campus intranet, computer help desk, free student e-mail accounts, online (class) grades, online (class) registration, online (class) schedules. Campuswide network is available. 100% of college-owned or -operated housing units are wired for high-speed Internet access. Wireless service is available via classrooms, computer centers, computer labs, dorm rooms, learning centers, libraries, student centers.

Library: North Hall Library.

STUDENT LIFE

Housing options: on-campus residence required through sophomore year; coed. Campus housing is university owned. Freshman campus housing is guaranteed.

Activities and organizations: drama/theater group, student-run newspaper, radio and television station, choral group, marching band, national fraternities, national sororities.

Athletics Member NCAA. All Division II. ***Intercollegiate sports:*** baseball M(s), basketball M(s)/W(s), cross-country running M(s)/W(s), field hockey W(s), football M(c), soccer W(s), softball W(s), swimming and diving W, track and field M(s)/W(s). ***Intramural sports:*** badminton M/W, basketball M/W, bowling M/W, cheerleading W, cross-country running M/W, equestrian sports M/W, football M/W, golf M/W, racquetball M/W, skiing (cross-country) M/W, skiing (downhill) M/W, soccer M/W, softball M/W, swimming and diving M/W, tennis M/W, track and field M/W, volleyball M/W, water polo M/W, weight lifting M/W.

Campus security: 24-hour emergency response devices and patrols, student patrols, late-night transport/escort service, controlled dormitory access.

Student services: health clinic, personal/psychological counseling, women's center.

COSTS & FINANCIAL AID

Costs (2018–19) ***Tuition:*** state resident $9450 full-time, $315 per credit hour part-time; nonresident $18,900 full-time, $630 per credit hour part-time. ***Required fees:*** $2880 full-time. ***Room and board:*** $11,998; room only: $8468. Room and board charges vary according to board plan. ***Payment plans:*** installment, deferred payment. ***Waivers:*** senior citizens and employees or children of employees.

Financial Aid Of all full-time matriculated undergraduates who enrolled in 2017, 1,295 applied for aid, 1,106 were judged to have need, 695 had their need fully met. In 2017, 149 non-need-based awards were made. ***Average percent of need met:*** 63. ***Average financial aid package:*** $1733. ***Average need-based loan:*** $2008. ***Average need-based gift aid:*** $1418. ***Average non-need-based aid:*** $1405. ***Average indebtedness upon graduation:*** $52,243.

APPLYING

Standardized Tests *Required for some:* SAT or ACT (for admission).

Options: electronic application, early admission, deferred entrance.

Application fee: $25.

Required: high school transcript. ***Required for some:*** interview. ***Recommended:*** essay or personal statement, minimum 2.5 GPA.

CONTACT

Ms. Rachel Green, Director of Admissions, Mansfield University of Pennsylvania, Academy Street, Mansfield, PA 16933. *Phone:* 570-662-4813. *Toll-free phone:* 800-577-6826. *E-mail:* admissions@mnsfld.edu.

Marywood University

Scranton, Pennsylvania

http://www.marywood.edu/

- **Independent Roman Catholic** comprehensive, founded 1915
- **Suburban** 123-acre campus
- **Endowment** $38.0 million
- **Coed** 1,950 undergraduate students, 90% full-time, 68% women, 32% men
- **Moderately difficult** entrance level, 75% of applicants were admitted

UNDERGRAD STUDENTS

1,756 full-time, 194 part-time. Students come from 20 states and territories; 11 other countries; 28% are from out of state; 3% Black or African American, non-Hispanic/Latino; 8% Hispanic/Latino; 2% Asian, non-Hispanic/Latino; 0.1% Native Hawaiian or other Pacific Islander, non-Hispanic/Latino; 0.1% American Indian or Alaska Native, non-Hispanic/Latino; 2% Two or more races, non-Hispanic/Latino; 12% Race/ethnicity unknown; 2% international; 5% transferred in; 35% live on campus.

Freshmen:

Admission: 2,137 applied, 1,607 admitted, 397 enrolled. ***Average high school GPA:*** 3.5. ***Test scores:*** SAT evidence-based reading and writing scores over 500: 83%; SAT math scores over 500: 79%; ACT scores over 18: 95%; SAT evidence-based reading and writing scores over 600: 29%; SAT math scores over 600: 20%; ACT scores over 24: 45%; SAT evidence-based reading and writing scores over 700: 2%; SAT math scores over 700: 1%; ACT scores over 30: 3%.

Retention: 86% of full-time freshmen returned.

FACULTY

Total: 402, 36% full-time.

Student/faculty ratio: 12:1.

ACADEMICS

Calendar: semesters. *Degrees:* certificates, bachelor's, master's, doctoral, post-master's, and postbachelor's certificates.

Special study options: adult/continuing education programs, advanced placement credit, double majors, English as a second language, honors programs, independent study, internships, off-campus study, part-time degree program, services for LD students, student-designed majors, study abroad, summer session for credit. ***ROTC:*** Army (c), Air Force (c).

Unusual degree programs: 3-2 physician assistant, communication sciences disorders, criminal justice, biotechnology, health services administration.

Computers: 359 computers/terminals are available on campus for general student use. Students can access the following: computer help desk, free student e-mail accounts, online (class) grades, online (class) registration, online (class) schedules, degree audit, student account management, financial aid self-service, student planning. Campuswide network is available. 100% of college-owned or -operated housing units are wired for high-speed Internet access. Wireless service is available via entire campus.

Library: Learning Commons plus 2 others. *Books:* 185,509 (physical), 225,884 (digital/electronic); *Serial titles:* 62 (physical), 44,458 (digital/electronic); *Databases:* 62. Weekly public service hours: 99; students can reserve study rooms.

STUDENT LIFE

Housing options: on-campus residence required through sophomore year; coed, women-only, special housing for students with disabilities. Campus housing is university owned. Freshman campus housing is guaranteed.

Activities and organizations: drama/theater group, student-run newspaper, radio and television station, choral group, Phi Beta Lambda (Business Club), Marywood Media Group, Volunteers in Action (VIA), Zeta Phi Delta, American Institute of Architects.

Athletics Member NCAA. All Division III. ***Intercollegiate sports:*** baseball M, basketball M/W, cross-country running M/W, field hockey W, golf M/W, lacrosse M/W, rugby M/W, soccer M/W, softball W, swimming and diving M/W, tennis M/W, track and field M/W, volleyball W. ***Intramural sports:*** basketball M/W, skiing (downhill) M(c)/W(c), soccer M/W, volleyball M/W.

Campus security: 24-hour emergency response devices and patrols, late-night transport/escort service, controlled dormitory access, apartments with deadbolts, self-defense education, lighted pathways, seminars on safety.

Student services: health clinic, personal/psychological counseling, veterans affairs office.

COSTS & FINANCIAL AID

Costs (2019–20) ***Comprehensive fee:*** $49,863 includes full-time tuition ($34,156), mandatory fees ($1750), and room and board ($13,957). Part-time tuition: $650 per credit. ***College room only:*** $7879.

Financial Aid Of all full-time matriculated undergraduates who enrolled in 2018, 1,548 applied for aid, 1,420 were judged to have need, 249 had their need fully met. 918 Federal Work-Study jobs (averaging $1942). In 2018, 271 non-need-based awards were made. ***Average percent of need met:*** 73. ***Average financial aid package:*** $26,557. ***Average need-based loan:*** $4218. ***Average need-based gift aid:*** $21,361. ***Average non-need-based aid:*** $16,668. ***Average indebtedness upon graduation:*** $41,210.

APPLYING

Standardized Tests *Required:* SAT or ACT (for admission).

Options: electronic application, early admission, deferred entrance.

Application fee: $35.

Required: essay or personal statement, high school transcript, minimum 2.5 GPA, 1 letter of recommendation. ***Required for some:*** portfolio for art majors, audition for music majors. ***Recommended:*** interview.

Application deadlines: rolling (freshmen), rolling (transfers).

Notification: continuous (freshmen), continuous (transfers).

CONTACT

Mr. Matthew Herr, Director of University Admissions, Marywood University, 2300 Adams Avenue, Scranton, PA 18509. *Phone:* 570-348-6234. *Toll-free phone:* 866-279-9663. *Fax:* 570-961-4763. *E-mail:* yourfuture@marywood.edu.

See below for display ad and page 1040 for the College Close-Up.

Mercyhurst North East

North East, Pennsylvania

http://northeast.mercyhurst.edu/

CONTACT

Travis Lindahl, Director of Admissions, Mercyhurst North East, 16 West Division Street, North East, PA 16428. *Phone:* 814-725-6217. *Toll-free phone:* 866-846-6042. *Fax:* 814-725-6251. *E-mail:* neadmiss@mercyhurst.edu.

Mercyhurst University

Erie, Pennsylvania

http://www.mercyhurst.edu/

- **Independent Roman Catholic** comprehensive, founded 1926
- **Suburban** 88-acre campus with easy access to Buffalo
- **Endowment** $31.6 million
- **Coed**
- **Moderately difficult** entrance level

FACULTY

Student/faculty ratio: 15:1.

ACADEMICS

Calendar: semesters. *Degrees:* bachelor's, master's, and postbachelor's certificates.

Library: Hammermill Library. *Books:* 108,088 (physical), 134,244 (digital/electronic); *Serial titles:* 500 (physical), 122,471 (digital/electronic); *Databases:* 66. Study areas open 24 hours, 5–7 days a week; students can reserve study rooms.

STUDENT LIFE

Housing options: on-campus residence required through sophomore year; coed, men-only, women-only, special housing for students with disabilities. Campus housing is university owned and leased by the school. Freshman campus housing is guaranteed.

Activities and organizations: drama/theater group, student-run newspaper, choral group, marching band, Student Government, chorus, Admission Ambassadors, Amnesty International, The Merciad (student newspaper).

Athletics Member NCAA. All Division II except men's and women's ice hockey (Division I).

Campus security: 24-hour emergency response devices and patrols, campus-wide camera system.

Student services: health clinic, personal/psychological counseling, veterans affairs office.

COSTS & FINANCIAL AID

Costs (2018–19) ***Comprehensive fee:*** $50,950 includes full-time tuition ($35,400), mandatory fees ($2670), and room and board ($12,880). Full-time tuition and fees vary according to class time, course load, degree level, location, and program. Part-time tuition: $1180 per credit. Part-time tuition and fees vary according to class time, course load, degree level, location, and program. ***Required fees:*** $26 per credit part-time, $710 per term part-time. ***Room and board:*** Room and board charges vary according to board plan, housing facility, and location.

Financial Aid Of all full-time matriculated undergraduates who enrolled in 2015, 1,866 applied for aid, 1,686 were judged to have need, 104 had their need fully met. In 2015, 411 non-need-based awards were made. ***Average percent of need met:*** 50. ***Average financial aid package:*** $26,019. ***Average need-based loan:*** $4360. ***Average need-based gift aid:*** $16,089. ***Average non-need-based aid:*** $15,583. ***Average indebtedness upon graduation:*** $24,739. ***Financial aid deadline:*** 5/1.

APPLYING

Options: electronic application, deferred entrance.

Required: essay or personal statement, high school transcript. ***Required for some:*** 1 letter of recommendation. ***Recommended:*** interview.

CONTACT

Mercyhurst University, 501 East 38th Street, Erie, PA 16546. *Toll-free phone:* 800-825-1926.

Messiah College

Mechanicsburg, Pennsylvania

http://www.messiah.edu/

- **Independent interdenominational** comprehensive, founded 1909
- **Small-town** 485-acre campus
- **Endowment** $138.2 million
- **Coed** 2,734 undergraduate students, 95% full-time, 61% women, 39% men
- **Moderately difficult** entrance level, 79% of applicants were admitted

UNDERGRAD STUDENTS

2,598 full-time, 136 part-time. Students come from 38 states and territories; 30 other countries; 36% are from out of state; 2% Black or African American, non-Hispanic/Latino; 5% Hispanic/Latino; 2% Asian, non-Hispanic/Latino; 0.1% American Indian or Alaska Native, non-Hispanic/Latino; 3% Two or more races, non-Hispanic/Latino; 0.8% Race/ethnicity unknown; 5% international; 4% transferred in; 88% live on campus.

Freshmen:

Admission: 2,530 applied, 1,996 admitted, 647 enrolled. ***Average high school GPA:*** 3.8. ***Test scores:*** SAT evidence-based reading and writing scores over 500: 94%; SAT math scores over 500: 89%; ACT scores over 18: 98%; SAT evidence-based reading and writing scores over 600: 53%; SAT math scores over 600: 47%; ACT scores over 24: 71%; SAT evidence-based reading and writing scores over 700: 12%; SAT math scores over 700: 13%; ACT scores over 30: 20%.

Retention: 87% of full-time freshmen returned.

FACULTY

Total: 357, 55% full-time, 57% with terminal degrees.

Student/faculty ratio: 12:1.

ACADEMICS

Calendar: semesters. *Degrees:* bachelor's, master's, doctoral, post-master's, and postbachelor's certificates.

Special study options: academic remediation for entering students, accelerated degree program, adult/continuing education programs, advanced placement credit, cooperative education, distance learning, double majors, English as a second language, freshman honors college, honors programs, independent study, internships, off-campus study, part-time degree program, services for LD students, student-designed majors, study abroad, summer session for credit.

Unusual degree programs: 3-2 applied health science or biopsychology/occupational therapy with Thomas Jefferson University, biochemistry/pharmacy with the University of the Sciences in Philadelphia, politics/public policy and management with Carnegie Mellon University.

Computers: 571 computers/terminals are available on campus for general student use. Students can access the following: campus intranet, computer help desk, free student e-mail accounts, online (class) grades, online (class) registration, online (class) schedules, access to software. Campuswide network is available. 100% of college-owned or -operated housing units are wired for high-speed Internet access. Wireless service is available via entire campus.

Library: Murray Library. *Books:* 241,426 (physical), 576,178 (digital/electronic); *Serial titles:* 157 (physical), 104,750 (digital/electronic); *Databases:* 135. Weekly public service hours: 96; students can reserve study rooms.

STUDENT LIFE

Housing options: on-campus residence required through senior year; coed, men-only, women-only, special housing for students with disabilities. Campus housing is university owned. Freshman campus housing is guaranteed.

Activities and organizations: drama/theater group, student-run newspaper, radio station, choral group, Outreach teams, student government, choral groups and ensembles, Small Group Program, Outdoors Club.

Athletics Member NCAA. All Division III. ***Intercollegiate sports:*** baseball M, basketball M/W, cross-country running M/W, field hockey W, lacrosse M/W, soccer M/W, softball W, swimming and diving M/W, tennis M/W, track and field M/W, volleyball M/W, wrestling M. ***Intramural sports:*** basketball M/W, field hockey W(c), football M/W, soccer M/W, softball M/W, ultimate Frisbee M(c)/W(c), volleyball M/W.

Campus security: 24-hour emergency response devices and patrols, student patrols, late-night transport/escort service, controlled dormitory access.

Student services: health clinic, personal/psychological counseling.

COSTS & FINANCIAL AID

Costs (2019–20) ***Comprehensive fee:*** $46,700 includes full-time tuition ($35,280), mandatory fees ($840), and room and board ($10,580). Part-time tuition: $1470 per credit hour. ***College room only:*** $5630.

Financial Aid Of all full-time matriculated undergraduates who enrolled in 2018, 2,191 applied for aid, 1,919 were judged to have need, 342 had their need fully met. 804 Federal Work-Study jobs (averaging $2091). 1,107 state and other part-time jobs (averaging $1848). In 2018, 691 non-need-based awards were made. ***Average percent of need met:*** 72. ***Average financial aid package:*** $25,358. ***Average need-based loan:*** $4738. ***Average need-based gift aid:*** $19,479. ***Average non-need-based aid:*** $15,130. ***Average indebtedness upon graduation:*** $39,104.

APPLYING

Standardized Tests *Required:* SAT or ACT (for admission).

Options: electronic application.

Application fee: $50.

Required: essay or personal statement, high school transcript. ***Required for some:*** interview.

Application deadlines: rolling (freshmen), rolling (transfers).

Notification: continuous (freshmen), continuous (transfers).

CONTACT

Dr. John Chopka, Vice President for Enrollment Management, Messiah College, One College Avenue, Suite 3005, Mechanicsburg, PA 17055. *Phone:* 717-691-6000. *Toll-free phone:* 800-233-4220. *Fax:* 717-691-2307. *E-mail:* admiss@messiah.edu.

★ Millersville University of Pennsylvania

Millersville, Pennsylvania

http://www.millersville.edu/

- **State-supported** university, founded 1855, part of Pennsylvania State System of Higher Education
- **Small-town** 250-acre campus
- **Endowment** $11.3 million
- **Coed** 6,779 undergraduate students, 82% full-time, 57% women, 43% men
- **Moderately difficult** entrance level, 78% of applicants were admitted

UNDERGRAD STUDENTS

5,557 full-time, 1,222 part-time. Students come from 33 states and territories; 64 other countries; 7% are from out of state; 9% Black or African American, non-Hispanic/Latino; 11% Hispanic/Latino; 3% Asian, non-Hispanic/Latino; 0.1% Native Hawaiian or other Pacific Islander, non-Hispanic/Latino; 0.4% American Indian or Alaska Native, non-Hispanic/Latino; 1% Two or more races, non-Hispanic/Latino; 1% Race/ethnicity unknown; 0.8% international; 8% transferred in; 32% live on campus.

Freshmen:

Admission: 6,585 applied, 5,134 admitted, 1,360 enrolled. ***Average high school GPA:*** 3.3. ***Test scores:*** SAT evidence-based reading and writing scores over 500: 76%; SAT math scores over 500: 75%; ACT scores over 18: 86%; SAT evidence-based reading and writing scores over 600: 27%; SAT math scores over 600: 20%; ACT scores over 24: 41%; SAT evidence-based reading and writing scores over 700: 3%; SAT math scores over 700: 2%; ACT scores over 30: 9%.

Retention: 75% of full-time freshmen returned.

FACULTY

Total: 463, 62% full-time, 72% with terminal degrees.

Student/faculty ratio: 18:1.

ACADEMICS

Calendar: 4-1-4. *Degrees:* certificates, associate, bachelor's, master's, doctoral, post-master's, and postbachelor's certificates.

Special study options: academic remediation for entering students, accelerated degree program, adult/continuing education programs, advanced placement credit, cooperative education, distance learning, double majors, English as a second language, freshman honors college, honors programs, independent study, internships, off-campus study, part-time degree program, services for LD students, student-designed majors, study abroad, summer session for credit. ***ROTC:*** Army (b).

Unusual degree programs: 3-2 engineering with Penn State University, University of Delaware.

Computers: 430 computers/terminals and 2,500 ports are available on campus for general student use. Students can access the following:

campus intranet, computer help desk, free student e-mail accounts, online (class) grades, online (class) registration, online (class) schedules. Campuswide network is available. 100% of college-owned or -operated housing units are wired for high-speed Internet access. Wireless service is available via entire campus.
Library: The Francine G. McNairy Library and Learning Forum at Ganser Hall. *Books:* 316,579 (physical), 54,885 (digital/electronic); *Serial titles:* 4,191 (physical), 399,958 (digital/electronic); *Databases:* 179. Weekly public service hours: 94; students can reserve study rooms.

STUDENT LIFE
Housing options: on-campus residence required through sophomore year; coed, special housing for students with disabilities. Campus housing is university owned and leased by the school. Freshman campus housing is guaranteed.

Activities and organizations: drama/theater group, student-run newspaper, radio and television station, choral group, marching band, University Activities Board, Honors College Student Association, Mini-THON, Graduate Student Organization, Helping Paws, national fraternities, national sororities.

Athletics Member NCAA. All Division II. ***Intercollegiate sports:*** baseball M(s), basketball M(s)/W(s), cross-country running W(s), field hockey W(s), football M(s), golf M(s)/W(s), lacrosse W(s), soccer M(s)/W(s), softball W(s), swimming and diving W(s), tennis M(s)/W(s), track and field W(s), volleyball W(s), wrestling M(s). ***Intramural sports:*** badminton M/W, basketball M/W, bowling M(c)/W(c), cheerleading M(c)/W(c), cross-country running M(c)/W(c), equestrian sports M(c)/W(c), fencing M(c)/W(c), football M/W, ice hockey M(c)/W(c), lacrosse M(c), rugby M(c)/W(c), soccer M/W, softball M/W, table tennis M/W, ultimate Frisbee M/W, volleyball M/W.

Campus security: 24-hour emergency response devices and patrols, student patrols, late-night transport/escort service, controlled dormitory access.

Student services: health clinic, personal/psychological counseling, women's center, veterans affairs office.

COSTS & FINANCIAL AID
Costs (2018–19) ***Tuition:*** state resident $9570 full-time, $319 per credit part-time; nonresident $19,290 full-time, $805 per credit part-time. Full-time tuition and fees vary according to course load and program. Part-time tuition and fees vary according to course load and program. ***Required fees:*** $2656 full-time, $111 per credit part-time. ***Room and board:*** $13,658. Room and board charges vary according to board plan and housing facility. ***Payment plan:*** installment. ***Waivers:*** senior citizens and employees or children of employees.

Financial Aid Of all full-time matriculated undergraduates who enrolled in 2017, 4,669 applied for aid, 3,887 were judged to have need, 190 had their need fully met. 233 Federal Work-Study jobs (averaging $1321). 1,372 state and other part-time jobs (averaging $1376). In 2017, 270 non-need-based awards were made. ***Average percent of need met:*** 58. ***Average financial aid package:*** $8967. ***Average need-based loan:*** $4075. ***Average need-based gift aid:*** $6356. ***Average non-need-based aid:*** $3161. ***Average indebtedness upon graduation:*** $31,098.

APPLYING
Standardized Tests *Required:* SAT or ACT (for admission).

Options: electronic application, early admission, deferred entrance.

Application fee: $50.

Required: essay or personal statement, high school transcript, minimum 2.0 GPA, Health Examination required for all applicants. High school diploma or GED required for all applicants. SAT or ACT scores required for all applicants. Audition required for music applicants. Portfolio required for art applicants. Associate degree in Nursing or Diploma and RN license required for nur. ***Required for some:*** 1 letter of recommendation, interview, Health Examination required for all applicants. High school diploma or GED required for all applicants. SAT or ACT scores required for all applicants. Audition required for music applicants. Portfolio required for art applicants. Associate degree in Nursing or Diploma and RN license required for nur. ***Recommended:*** minimum 3.0 GPA, 2 letters of recommendation.

Application deadlines: rolling (freshmen), rolling (out-of-state freshmen), rolling (transfers).

Notification: continuous (freshmen), continuous (out-of-state freshmen), continuous (transfers).

CONTACT
Ms. Katy A. Charles, Director of Admissions, Millersville University of Pennsylvania, PO Box 1002, Millersville, PA 17551-0302. *Phone:* 717-871-4625. *Toll-free phone:* 800-MU-ADMIT. *Fax:* 717-871-7973. *E-mail:* admissions@millersville.edu.

See previous page for display ad and page 1042 for the College Close-Up.

★ Misericordia University
Dallas, Pennsylvania
http://www.misericordia.edu/

- **Independent Roman Catholic** comprehensive, founded 1924
- **Small-town** 120-acre campus
- **Endowment** $49.2 million
- **Coed**
- **Moderately difficult** entrance level

FACULTY
Student/faculty ratio: 12:1.

ACADEMICS
Calendar: semesters. *Degrees:* certificates, bachelor's, master's, doctoral, post-master's, and postbachelor's certificates.
Library: Mary Kintz Bevevino Library. *Books:* 80,036 (physical), 13,154 (digital/electronic); *Serial titles:* 8,153 (physical), 28,230 (digital/electronic); *Databases:* 111. Students can reserve study rooms.

STUDENT LIFE
Housing options: coed. Campus housing is university owned and is provided by a third party. Freshman applicants given priority for college housing.

Activities and organizations: drama/theater group, student-run newspaper, radio station, choral group, Physical Therapy club, MSOTA, Colleges against Cancer, Dance Ensemble, Medical Imaging club.

Athletics Member NCAA. All Division III except tennis (Division II).

Campus security: 24-hour emergency response devices and patrols, late-night transport/escort service, controlled dormitory access.

Student services: health clinic, personal/psychological counseling, women's center, veterans affairs office.

COSTS & FINANCIAL AID
Costs (2018–19) ***Comprehensive fee:*** $47,200 includes full-time tuition ($31,530), mandatory fees ($1710), and room and board ($13,960). Full-time tuition and fees vary according to degree level. Part-time tuition: $610 per credit. Part-time tuition and fees vary according to class time and location. ***College room only:*** $7600. Room and board charges vary according to board plan and housing facility. ***Payment plans:*** installment, deferred payment.

Financial Aid Of all full-time matriculated undergraduates who enrolled in 2017, 1,534 applied for aid, 1,361 were judged to have need, 347 had their need fully met. In 2017, 172 non-need-based awards were made. ***Average percent of need met:*** 81. ***Average financial aid package:*** $24,313. ***Average need-based loan:*** $8593. ***Average need-based gift aid:*** $17,695. ***Average non-need-based aid:*** $14,098. ***Average indebtedness upon graduation:*** $47,764. ***Financial aid deadline:*** 5/1.

APPLYING
Standardized Tests *Required:* SAT or ACT (for admission).

Options: electronic application, early admission, deferred entrance.

Application fee: $35.

Required: high school transcript. ***Required for some:*** essay or personal statement, minimum 2.5 GPA, 2 letters of recommendation. ***Recommended:*** interview.

CONTACT
Mr. Glenn Bozinski, Director of Admissions, Misericordia University, 301 Lake Street, Dallas, PA 18612-1098. *Phone:* 570-675-6264. *Toll-free phone:* 866-262-6363. *Fax:* 570-674-6232. *E-mail:* admiss@misericordia.edu.

See next page for display ad and page 1044 for the College Close-Up.

Moore College of Art & Design

Philadelphia, Pennsylvania

http://www.moore.edu/

CONTACT
Ms. Jasmine Zateeny, Assistant Director of Admissions, Recruitment Coordinator, Moore College of Art & Design, 20th and The Parkway, Philadelphia, PA 19103. *Phone:* 215-965-4015. *Toll-free phone:* 800-523-2025. *Fax:* 215-965-8544. *E-mail:* enroll@moore.edu.

Moravian College

Bethlehem, Pennsylvania

http://www.moravian.edu/

- **Independent** comprehensive, founded 1742, affiliated with Moravian Church
- **Suburban** 85-acre campus with easy access to Philadelphia
- **Endowment** $111.3 million
- **Coed**
- **Moderately difficult** entrance level

FACULTY
Student/faculty ratio: 11:1.

ACADEMICS
Calendar: semesters. *Degrees:* bachelor's, master's, doctoral, post-master's, and postbachelor's certificates.
Library: Reeves Library. *Books:* 198,012 (physical), 168,981 (digital/electronic); *Serial titles:* 2,490 (physical), 183 (digital/electronic); *Databases:* 67. Weekly public service hours: 86.

STUDENT LIFE
Housing options: on-campus residence required through senior year; coed, men-only, women-only, special housing for students with disabilities. Campus housing is university owned. Freshman campus housing is guaranteed.
Activities and organizations: drama/theater group, student-run newspaper, radio station, choral group, marching band, Moravian Activities Council, Black Student Union, Habitat for Humanity, Commuter Student Union, American Association of University Women, national fraternities, national sororities.
Athletics Member NCAA. All Division III.
Campus security: 24-hour emergency response devices and patrols, late-night transport/escort service, controlled dormitory access.
Student services: health clinic, personal/psychological counseling.

COSTS & FINANCIAL AID
Costs (2018–19) ***One-time required fee:*** $500. ***Comprehensive fee:*** $57,014 includes full-time tuition ($41,905), mandatory fees ($1731), and room and board ($13,378). Full-time tuition and fees vary according to class time and program. Part-time tuition: $1164 per credit. Part-time tuition and fees vary according to class time. ***College room only:*** $7538. Room and board charges vary according to board plan and housing facility.
Financial Aid Of all full-time matriculated undergraduates who enrolled in 2018, 1,710 applied for aid, 1,565 were judged to have need, 161 had their need fully met. In 2018, 322 non-need-based awards were made. ***Average percent of need met:*** 69. ***Average financial aid package:*** $30,917. ***Average need-based loan:*** $4304. ***Average need-based gift aid:*** $26,629. ***Average non-need-based aid:*** $17,593. ***Average indebtedness upon graduation:*** $35,521.

APPLYING
Standardized Tests *Required:* SAT or ACT (for admission).
Options: electronic application, deferred entrance.
Required: essay or personal statement, high school transcript, 1 letter of recommendation. ***Required for some:*** portfolio for art majors; audition for music majors; 3.3 high school GPA, minimum SAT combined score of 1500 (with no section less than 500) or ACT score of 23 for nursing.

CONTACT
Mr. Scott Myers, Director of Undergraduate Admission, Moravian College, 1200 Main Street, Bethlehem, PA 18018. *Phone:* 610-861-1320 Ext. 7115. *Toll-free phone:* 800-441-3191. *Fax:* 610-625-7930. *E-mail:* myersj02@moravian.edu.

★ Mount Aloysius College
Cresson, Pennsylvania
http://www.mtaloy.edu/

- **Independent Roman Catholic** comprehensive, founded 1939
- **Small-town** 193-acre campus
- **Coed**
- **Minimally difficult** entrance level

FACULTY
Student/faculty ratio: 11:1.

ACADEMICS
Calendar: semesters. *Degrees:* certificates, associate, bachelor's, and master's.
Library: Mount Aloysius College Library.

STUDENT LIFE
Housing options: on-campus residence required through sophomore year; coed. Campus housing is university owned. Freshman campus housing is guaranteed.

Activities and organizations: drama/theater group, student-run newspaper, choral group, Student Government, Campus Activity Board, Student Athletic Advisory Committee, Spirit Team, Dance Team.

Athletics Member NCAA. All Division III.

Campus security: 24-hour emergency response devices and patrols, student patrols, late-night transport/escort service, controlled dormitory access.

Student services: health clinic, personal/psychological counseling.

COSTS & FINANCIAL AID
Costs (2018–19) ***Comprehensive fee:*** $33,758 includes full-time tuition ($21,870), mandatory fees ($1240), and room and board ($10,648). Part-time tuition: $825 per credit hour. ***College room only:*** $5356.

Financial Aid Of all full-time matriculated undergraduates who enrolled in 2018, 975 applied for aid, 848 were judged to have need. In 2018, 127 non-need-based awards were made. ***Average percent of need met:*** 35. ***Average financial aid package:*** $13,900. ***Average need-based loan:*** $4400. ***Average need-based gift aid:*** $3000. ***Average non-need-based aid:*** $5600.

APPLYING
Standardized Tests *Required:* SAT or ACT (for admission). *Recommended:* SAT (for admission), ACT (for admission).

Options: electronic application, early admission, deferred entrance.

Application fee: $30.

Required: high school transcript. ***Required for some:*** essay or personal statement, interview. ***Recommended:*** interview.

CONTACT
Mr. Frank C. Crouse Jr., Vice President for Enrollment Management/Dean of Admissions, Mount Aloysius College, 7373 Admiral Peary Highway, Cresson, PA 16630-1999. *Phone:* 814-886-6383. *Toll-free phone:* 888-823-2220. *Fax:* 814-886-6441. *E-mail:* admissions@mtaloy.edu.

See below for display ad and page 1050 for the College Close-Up.

★ Muhlenberg College
Allentown, Pennsylvania
http://www.muhlenberg.edu/

- **Independent** 4-year, founded 1848, affiliated with Lutheran Church
- **Suburban** 75-acre campus with easy access to Philadelphia
- **Endowment** $246.9 million
- **Coed**
- **Very difficult** entrance level

FACULTY
Student/faculty ratio: 10:1.

ACADEMICS
Calendar: semesters. *Degrees:* certificates, associate, and bachelor's.
Library: Trexler Library. *Books:* 228,069 (physical), 515,579 (digital/electronic); *Serial titles:* 1,183 (physical), 40,276 (digital/electronic); *Databases:* 99. Weekly public service hours: 105; students can reserve study rooms.

STUDENT LIFE
Housing options: on-campus residence required through senior year; coed, women-only, special housing for students with disabilities. Campus housing is university owned and leased by the school. Freshman campus housing is guaranteed.
Activities and organizations: drama/theater group, student-run newspaper, radio and television station, choral group, Theater Association, Environmental Action Team, Jefferson School Partnership, Select Choir, Habitat for Humanity, national fraternities, national sororities.
Athletics Member NCAA. All Division III.
Campus security: 24-hour emergency response devices and patrols, late-night transport/escort service, controlled dormitory access.
Student services: health clinic, personal/psychological counseling.

COSTS & FINANCIAL AID
Costs (2018–19) ***One-time required fee:*** $120. ***Comprehensive fee:*** $64,360 includes full-time tuition ($51,860), mandatory fees ($735), and room and board ($11,765). Part-time tuition: $6100 per course. Part-time tuition and fees vary according to program. ***Required fees:*** $368 per term part-time. ***College room only:*** $6395. Room and board charges vary according to board plan, housing facility, and location.
Financial Aid Of all full-time matriculated undergraduates who enrolled in 2018, 1,573 applied for aid, 1,380 were judged to have need, 266 had their need fully met. In 2018, 644 non-need-based awards were made. ***Average percent of need met:*** 81. ***Average financial aid package:*** $37,874. ***Average need-based loan:*** $4384. ***Average need-based gift aid:*** $34,325. ***Average non-need-based aid:*** $14,525. ***Average indebtedness upon graduation:*** $32,963. ***Financial aid deadline:*** 2/1.

APPLYING
Standardized Tests *Required for some:* SAT or ACT (for admission).
Options: electronic application, early admission, early decision, deferred entrance.
Application fee: $50.
Required: essay or personal statement, high school transcript, 2 letters of recommendation. ***Required for some:*** interview, graded paper. ***Recommended:*** interview.

CONTACT
Muhlenberg College, 2400 Chew Street, Allentown, PA 18104-5586.
See below for display ad and page 1052 for the College Close-Up.

Neumann University
Aston, Pennsylvania
http://www.neumann.edu/

- **Independent Roman Catholic** comprehensive, founded 1965
- **Suburban** 68-acre campus with easy access to Philadelphia
- **Endowment** $30.8 million
- **Coed**
- **Minimally difficult** entrance level

FACULTY
Student/faculty ratio: 15:1.

ACADEMICS
Calendar: semesters. *Degrees:* associate, bachelor's, master's, doctoral, post-master's, and postbachelor's certificates.
Library: Neumann University Library plus 1 other. *Books:* 51,000 (physical), 161,000 (digital/electronic); *Serial titles:* 20 (physical), 100,000 (digital/electronic); *Databases:* 45. Weekly public service hours: 80; students can reserve study rooms.

STUDENT LIFE
Housing options: coed, special housing for students with disabilities. Campus housing is university owned and leased by the school. Freshman applicants given priority for college housing.
Activities and organizations: drama/theater group, student-run newspaper, radio and television station, choral group, Student Nurses Association, Student Activities Board, Boogie Nights, Knights for Education, Neumann Media.
Athletics Member NCAA. All Division III.
Campus security: 24-hour emergency response devices and patrols, late-night transport/escort service, controlled dormitory access.
Student services: health clinic, personal/psychological counseling, veterans affairs office.

COSTS & FINANCIAL AID

Costs (2018–19) ***One-time required fee:*** $100. ***Comprehensive fee:*** $44,420 includes full-time tuition ($30,000), mandatory fees ($1400), and room and board ($13,020). Full-time tuition and fees vary according to degree level. Part-time tuition: $680 per credit hour. Part-time tuition and fees vary according to degree level and program. ***Required fees:*** $90 per term part-time. ***College room only:*** $7840. Room and board charges vary according to board plan and housing facility. ***Payment plans:*** installment, deferred payment.

Financial Aid Of all full-time matriculated undergraduates who enrolled in 2018, 1,338 applied for aid, 1,220 were judged to have need, 115 had their need fully met. In 2018, 204 non-need-based awards were made. ***Average percent of need met:*** 68. ***Average financial aid package:*** $22,378. ***Average need-based loan:*** $4229. ***Average need-based gift aid:*** $8262. ***Average non-need-based aid:*** $12,319. ***Average indebtedness upon graduation:*** $45,011.

APPLYING

Standardized Tests *Required:* SAT or ACT (for admission).

Options: electronic application, deferred entrance.

Application fee: $35.

Required: high school transcript, minimum 2.5 GPA. ***Required for some:*** 1 letter of recommendation. ***Recommended:*** essay or personal statement, interview.

CONTACT

Mr. Edward P. Wright, Director of Undergraduate Admissions, Neumann University, One Neumann Drive, Aston, PA 19014-1298. *Phone:* 610-558-5616. *Toll-free phone:* 800-963-8626. *Fax:* 610-361-2548. *E-mail:* wrighte@neumann.edu.

See below for display ad and page 1054 for the College Close-Up.

Peirce College

Philadelphia, Pennsylvania

http://www.peirce.edu/

- **Independent** comprehensive, founded 1865
- **Urban** 1-acre campus
- **Coed, primarily women**
- **Noncompetitive** entrance level

FACULTY

Student/faculty ratio: 14:1.

ACADEMICS

Calendar: semesters. *Degrees:* certificates, associate, bachelor's, and master's.

Library: Peirce College Library.

STUDENT LIFE

Housing options: college housing not available.

Campus security: 24-hour emergency response devices and patrols, late-night transport/escort service, 24-hour security cameras.

APPLYING

Options: electronic application.

Application fee: $50.

Required: high school transcript.

CONTACT

Mr. Paul Ballentine, Manager, Admissions, Peirce College, 1420 Pine Street, Philadelphia, PA 19102. *Phone:* 215-670-9214. *Toll-free phone:* 888-467-3472. *Fax:* 215-670-9366. *E-mail:* info@peirce.edu.

Penn State Abington

Abington, Pennsylvania

http://www.abington.psu.edu/

- **State-related** 4-year, founded 1950, part of Pennsylvania State University
- **Small-town** campus
- **Coed**
- **Very difficult** entrance level

FACULTY
Student/faculty ratio: 17:1.

ACADEMICS
Calendar: semesters. *Degrees:* certificates, associate, bachelor's, and postbachelor's certificates (enrollment figures include students enrolled at The Graduate School at Penn State who are taking courses at this location).
Library: Penn State Abington Library.

STUDENT LIFE
Housing options: coed, special housing for students with disabilities.

Campus security: 24-hour emergency response devices and patrols.

FINANCIAL AID
Financial Aid Of all full-time matriculated undergraduates who enrolled in 2017, 3,252 applied for aid, 2,504 were judged to have need, 248 had their need fully met. In 2017, 208 non-need-based awards were made. ***Average percent of need met:*** 55. ***Average financial aid package:*** $10,459. ***Average need-based loan:*** $4088. ***Average need-based gift aid:*** $5616. ***Average non-need-based aid:*** $3747. ***Average indebtedness upon graduation:*** $33,043.

APPLYING
Standardized Tests *Required:* SAT or ACT (for admission).

Options: electronic application, early admission, deferred entrance.

Application fee: $65.

Required: high school transcript. ***Required for some:*** interview. ***Recommended:*** essay or personal statement.

CONTACT
Admissions Office, Penn State Abington, 1600 Woodland Road, Abington, PA 19001. *Phone:* 215-881-7600. *Fax:* 215-881-7655. *E-mail:* abingtonadmissions@psu.edu.

Penn State Altoona

Altoona, Pennsylvania

http://www.altoona.psu.edu/

- **State-related** 4-year, founded 1939, part of Pennsylvania State University
- **Suburban** campus
- **Coed**
- **Very difficult** entrance level

FACULTY
Student/faculty ratio: 15:1.

ACADEMICS
Calendar: semesters. *Degrees:* certificates, associate, and bachelor's (enrollment figures include students enrolled at The Graduate School at Penn State who are taking courses at this location).
Library: Robert E. Eiche Library.

STUDENT LIFE
Housing options: coed, cooperative, special housing for students with disabilities. Campus housing is university owned.

Athletics Member NCAA. All Division III.

Campus security: 24-hour emergency response devices and patrols, late-night transport/escort service.

FINANCIAL AID
Financial Aid Of all full-time matriculated undergraduates who enrolled in 2017, 3,365 applied for aid, 2,652 were judged to have need, 538 had their need fully met. In 2017, 233 non-need-based awards were made. ***Average percent of need met:*** 63. ***Average financial aid package:*** $10,106. ***Average need-based loan:*** $4018. ***Average need-based gift aid:*** $5630. ***Average non-need-based aid:*** $3567. ***Average indebtedness upon graduation:*** $41,964.

APPLYING
Standardized Tests *Required:* SAT or ACT (for admission).

Options: electronic application, early admission, deferred entrance.

Application fee: $65.

Required: high school transcript. ***Required for some:*** interview. ***Recommended:*** essay or personal statement.

CONTACT
Admissions Office, Penn State Altoona, 3000 Ivyside Park, Altoona, PA 16601. *Phone:* 814-949-5466. *Toll-free phone:* 800-848-9843. *Fax:* 814-949-5564. *E-mail:* aaadmit@psu.edu.

Penn State Beaver

Monaca, Pennsylvania

http://www.br.psu.edu/

- **State-related** 4-year, founded 1964, part of Pennsylvania State University
- **Small-town** campus
- **Coed**
- **Moderately difficult** entrance level

FACULTY
Student/faculty ratio: 14:1.

ACADEMICS
Calendar: semesters. *Degree:* certificates and bachelor's.

STUDENT LIFE
Housing options: coed, special housing for students with disabilities. Campus housing is university owned. Freshman campus housing is guaranteed.

Athletics Member NJCAA.

FINANCIAL AID
Financial Aid Of all full-time matriculated undergraduates who enrolled in 2017, 561 applied for aid, 498 were judged to have need, 100 had their need fully met. In 2017, 71 non-need-based awards were made. ***Average percent of need met:*** 65. ***Average financial aid package:*** $10,681. ***Average need-based loan:*** $4053. ***Average need-based gift aid:*** $5797. ***Average non-need-based aid:*** $3587. ***Average indebtedness upon graduation:*** $35,519.

APPLYING
Standardized Tests *Required:* SAT or ACT (for admission).

Options: electronic application, early admission, deferred entrance.

Application fee: $65.

Required: high school transcript. ***Required for some:*** interview. ***Recommended:*** essay or personal statement.

CONTACT
Admissions Office, Penn State Beaver, 100 University Drive, Monaca, PA 15061. *Phone:* 724-773-3800. *Fax:* 724-773-3658. *E-mail:* br-admissions@psu.edu.

Penn State Berks

Reading, Pennsylvania

http://www.bk.psu.edu/

- **State-related** 4-year, founded 1924, part of Pennsylvania State University
- **Suburban** campus
- **Coed**
- **Very difficult** entrance level

FACULTY
Student/faculty ratio: 15:1.

ACADEMICS
Calendar: semesters. *Degrees:* certificates, associate, bachelor's, and postbachelor's certificates (enrollment figures include students enrolled at The Graduate School at Penn State who are taking courses at this location).
Library: Thun Library.

STUDENT LIFE
Housing options: coed, special housing for students with disabilities. Campus housing is university owned.

Athletics Member NJCAA.

Campus security: 24-hour emergency response devices and patrols, late-night transport/escort service, controlled dormitory access.

FINANCIAL AID
Financial Aid Of all full-time matriculated undergraduates who enrolled in 2017, 2,398 applied for aid, 1,991 were judged to have need, 354 had their need fully met. In 2017, 128 non-need-based awards were made. ***Average percent of need met:*** 60. ***Average financial aid package:*** $9793. ***Average need-based loan:*** $4259. ***Average need-based gift aid:*** $5503. ***Average non-need-based aid:*** $2943. ***Average indebtedness upon graduation:*** $39,502.

APPLYING
Standardized Tests *Required:* SAT or ACT (for admission).

Options: electronic application, early admission, deferred entrance.

Application fee: $65.

Required: high school transcript. ***Required for some:*** interview. ***Recommended:*** essay or personal statement.

CONTACT
Admissions Office, Penn State Berks, Tulpehocken Road, PO Box 7009, Reading, PA 19610. *Phone:* 610-396-6060. *Fax:* 610-396-6077. *E-mail:* admissionsbk@psu.edu.

Penn State Brandywine

Media, Pennsylvania

http://www.brandywine.psu.edu/

- **State-related** 4-year, founded 1966, part of Pennsylvania State University
- **Small-town** campus
- **Coed**
- **Moderately difficult** entrance level

FACULTY
Student/faculty ratio: 15:1.

ACADEMICS
Calendar: semesters. *Degrees:* certificates, associate, and bachelor's.

STUDENT LIFE
Housing options: coed.

Athletics Member NJCAA.

Campus security: late-night transport/escort service, part-time trained security personnel.

FINANCIAL AID
Financial Aid Of all full-time matriculated undergraduates who enrolled in 2017, 1,235 applied for aid, 1,039 were judged to have need, 137 had their need fully met. In 2017, 112 non-need-based awards were made. ***Average percent of need met:*** 58. ***Average financial aid package:*** $10,385. ***Average need-based loan:*** $3925. ***Average need-based gift aid:*** $5574. ***Average non-need-based aid:*** $4124. ***Average indebtedness upon graduation:*** $33,661.

APPLYING
Standardized Tests *Required:* SAT or ACT (for admission).

Options: electronic application, early admission, deferred entrance.

Application fee: $65.

Required: high school transcript.

CONTACT
Admissions Office, Penn State Brandywine, 25 Yearsley Mill Road, Media, PA 19063. *Phone:* 610-892-1200. *Fax:* 610-892-1320. *E-mail:* bwadmissions@psu.edu.

Penn State DuBois

DuBois, Pennsylvania

http://www.ds.psu.edu/

- **State-related** primarily 2-year, founded 1935, part of Pennsylvania State University
- **Small-town** campus
- **Coed**
- **Moderately difficult** entrance level

FACULTY
Student/faculty ratio: 12:1.

ACADEMICS
Calendar: semesters. *Degrees:* certificates, associate, and bachelor's.

STUDENT LIFE
Housing options: college housing not available.

Athletics Member NJCAA.

FINANCIAL AID
Financial Aid Of all full-time matriculated undergraduates who enrolled in 2017, 461 applied for aid, 420 were judged to have need, 67 had their need fully met. In 2017, 22 non-need-based awards were made. ***Average percent of need met:*** 57. ***Average financial aid package:*** $9809. ***Average need-based loan:*** $3955. ***Average need-based gift aid:*** $5074. ***Average non-need-based aid:*** $2528. ***Average indebtedness upon graduation:*** $36,208.

APPLYING
Standardized Tests *Required:* SAT or ACT (for admission).

Options: electronic application, early admission, deferred entrance.

Application fee: $65.

Required: high school transcript. ***Required for some:*** interview. ***Recommended:*** essay or personal statement.

CONTACT
Admissions Office, Penn State DuBois, 1 College Place, DuBois, PA 15801. *Phone:* 814-375-4720. *Toll-free phone:* 800-346-7627. *Fax:* 814-375-4784. *E-mail:* duboisinfo@psi.edu.

Penn State Erie, The Behrend College

Erie, Pennsylvania

http://www.psbehrend.psu.edu/

- **State-related** comprehensive, founded 1948, part of Pennsylvania State University
- **Suburban** 725-acre campus
- **Coed**
- **Very difficult** entrance level

FACULTY
Student/faculty ratio: 15:1.

ACADEMICS
Calendar: semesters. *Degrees:* certificates, associate, bachelor's, and master's.
Library: John M. Lilley Library.

STUDENT LIFE
Housing options: coed, men-only, women-only, special housing for students with disabilities. Campus housing is university owned.

Athletics Member NCAA. All Division III.

Campus security: 24-hour emergency response devices and patrols, student patrols, late-night transport/escort service, controlled dormitory access.

FINANCIAL AID
Financial Aid Of all full-time matriculated undergraduates who enrolled in 2017, 4,111 applied for aid, 3,177 were judged to have need, 697 had their need fully met. In 2017, 234 non-need-based awards were made. ***Average percent of need met:*** 66. ***Average financial aid package:*** $10,668. ***Average need-based loan:*** $4458. ***Average need-based gift aid:*** $5770. ***Average non-need-based aid:*** $3723. ***Average indebtedness upon graduation:*** $43,039.

APPLYING
Standardized Tests *Required:* SAT or ACT (for admission).

Options: electronic application, early admission, deferred entrance.

Application fee: $65.

Required: high school transcript. ***Required for some:*** interview. ***Recommended:*** essay or personal statement.

CONTACT
Admissions Office, Penn State Erie, The Behrend College, 4701 College Drive, Erie, PA 16563. *Phone:* 814-898-6100. *Toll-free phone:* 866-374-3378. *Fax:* 814-898-6044. *E-mail:* behrend.admissions@psu.edu.

Penn State Fayette, The Eberly Campus

Lemont Furnace, Pennsylvania

http://www.fe.psu.edu/

- **State-related** primarily 2-year, founded 1934, part of Pennsylvania State University
- **Small-town** campus
- **Coed**
- **Moderately difficult** entrance level

FACULTY
Student/faculty ratio: 12:1.

ACADEMICS
Calendar: semesters. *Degrees:* certificates, associate, and bachelor's.

STUDENT LIFE
Housing options: college housing not available.

Athletics Member NJCAA.

Campus security: student patrols, 8-hour patrols by trained security personnel.

FINANCIAL AID
Financial Aid Of all full-time matriculated undergraduates who enrolled in 2017, 589 applied for aid, 542 were judged to have need, 78 had their need fully met. In 2017, 44 non-need-based awards were made. ***Average percent of need met:*** 61. ***Average financial aid package:*** $10,679. ***Average need-based loan:*** $4040. ***Average need-based gift aid:*** $5554. ***Average non-need-based aid:*** $2906. ***Average indebtedness upon graduation:*** $32,520.

APPLYING
Standardized Tests *Required:* SAT or ACT (for admission).

Options: electronic application, early admission, deferred entrance.

Application fee: $65.

Required: high school transcript. ***Required for some:*** interview. ***Recommended:*** essay or personal statement.

CONTACT
Admissions Office, Penn State Fayette, The Eberly Campus, 2201 University Drive, Lemont Furnace, PA 15456. *Phone:* 724-430-4130. *Toll-free phone:* 877-568-4130. *Fax:* 724-430-4175. *E-mail:* feadm@psu.edu.

Penn State Greater Allegheny

McKeesport, Pennsylvania

http://www.ga.psu.edu/

- **State-related** comprehensive, founded 1947, part of Pennsylvania State University
- **Small-town** campus
- **Coed**
- **Moderately difficult** entrance level

FACULTY
Student/faculty ratio: 11:1.

ACADEMICS
Calendar: semesters. *Degrees:* certificates, associate, and bachelor's.

STUDENT LIFE
Housing options: coed, special housing for students with disabilities. Campus housing is university owned. Freshman campus housing is guaranteed.

Athletics Member NJCAA.

Campus security: 24-hour patrols, controlled dormitory access.

FINANCIAL AID
Financial Aid Of all full-time matriculated undergraduates who enrolled in 2017, 451 applied for aid, 410 were judged to have need, 54 had their need fully met. In 2017, 36 non-need-based awards were made. ***Average percent of need met:*** 65. ***Average financial aid package:*** $12,305. ***Average need-based loan:*** $4266. ***Average need-based gift aid:*** $6301. ***Average non-need-based aid:*** $3531. ***Average indebtedness upon graduation:*** $33,929.

APPLYING
Standardized Tests *Required:* SAT or ACT (for admission).

Options: electronic application, early admission, deferred entrance.

Application fee: $65.

Required: high school transcript.

CONTACT
Admissions Office, Penn State Greater Allegheny, 4000 University Drive, McKeesport, PA 15132. *Phone:* 412-675-9010. *Fax:* 412-675-9046. *E-mail:* psuga@psu.edu.

Penn State Harrisburg

Middletown, Pennsylvania

http://www.harrisburg.psu.edu/

- **State-related** comprehensive, founded 1966, part of Pennsylvania State University
- **Small-town** campus
- **Coed**
- **Very difficult** entrance level

FACULTY
Student/faculty ratio: 16:1.

ACADEMICS
Calendar: semesters. *Degrees:* certificates, associate, bachelor's, master's, doctoral, and postbachelor's certificates.
Library: Penn State Harrisburg Library.

STUDENT LIFE
Housing options: special housing for students with disabilities. Campus housing is university owned.

Campus security: 24-hour emergency response devices and patrols, student patrols, late-night transport/escort service, controlled dormitory access.

FINANCIAL AID
Financial Aid Of all full-time matriculated undergraduates who enrolled in 2017, 3,934 applied for aid, 2,772 were judged to have need, 474 had their need fully met. In 2017, 334 non-need-based awards were made. ***Average percent of need met:*** 58. ***Average financial aid package:*** $10,240. ***Average need-based loan:*** $4411. ***Average need-based gift aid:*** $5510. ***Average non-need-based aid:*** $2613. ***Average indebtedness upon graduation:*** $39,995.

APPLYING
Standardized Tests *Required:* SAT or ACT (for admission).

Options: electronic application, early admission, deferred entrance.

Application fee: $65.

Required: high school transcript. ***Required for some:*** interview. ***Recommended:*** essay or personal statement.

CONTACT
Admissions Office, Penn State Harrisburg, 777 West Harrisburg Pike, Middletown, PA 17057. *Phone:* 717-948-6250. *Toll-free phone:* 800-222-2056. *Fax:* 717-948-6325. *E-mail:* hbgadmit@psu.edu.

Penn State Hazleton

Hazleton, Pennsylvania

http://www.hn.psu.edu/

- **State-related** 4-year, founded 1934, part of Pennsylvania State University
- **Small-town** campus
- **Coed**
- **Moderately difficult** entrance level

FACULTY
Student/faculty ratio: 14:1.

ACADEMICS
Calendar: semesters. *Degrees:* certificates, associate, bachelor's, and postbachelor's certificates.

STUDENT LIFE
Housing options: coed. Campus housing is university owned. Freshman campus housing is guaranteed.

Athletics Member NJCAA.

Campus security: 24-hour patrols, late-night transport/escort service, controlled dormitory access.

FINANCIAL AID
Financial Aid Of all full-time matriculated undergraduates who enrolled in 2017, 654 applied for aid, 605 were judged to have need, 118 had their need fully met. In 2017, 56 non-need-based awards were made. ***Average percent of need met:*** 66. ***Average financial aid package:*** $10,943. ***Average need-based loan:*** $4064. ***Average need-based gift aid:*** $5847. ***Average non-need-based aid:*** $3684. ***Average indebtedness upon graduation:*** $39,262.

APPLYING
Standardized Tests *Required:* SAT or ACT (for admission).

Options: electronic application, early admission, deferred entrance.

Application fee: $65.

Required: high school transcript. ***Required for some:*** interview. ***Recommended:*** essay or personal statement.

CONTACT
Admissions Office, Penn State Hazleton, 76 University Drive, Hazleton, PA 18202. *Phone:* 570-450-3142. *Toll-free phone:* 800-279-8495. *Fax:* 570-450-3182. *E-mail:* admissions-hn@psu.edu.

Penn State Lehigh Valley

Center Valley, Pennsylvania

http://www.lv.psu.edu/

- **State-related** 4-year, founded 1912, part of Pennsylvania State University
- **Rural** campus
- **Coed**
- **Moderately difficult** entrance level

FACULTY
Student/faculty ratio: 14:1.

ACADEMICS
Calendar: semesters. *Degrees:* certificates, associate, bachelor's, and postbachelor's certificates (enrollment figures include students enrolled at The Graduate School at Penn State who are taking courses at this location).

STUDENT LIFE
Housing options: college housing not available.

FINANCIAL AID
Financial Aid Of all full-time matriculated undergraduates who enrolled in 2017, 728 applied for aid, 602 were judged to have need, 52 had their need fully met. In 2017, 56 non-need-based awards were made. ***Average percent of need met:*** 51. ***Average financial aid package:*** $9866. ***Average need-based loan:*** $3879. ***Average need-based gift aid:*** $5573. ***Average non-need-based aid:*** $3190. ***Average indebtedness upon graduation:*** $35,805.

APPLYING
Standardized Tests *Required:* SAT or ACT (for admission).

Options: electronic application, early admission, deferred entrance.

Application fee: $65.

Required: high school transcript.

CONTACT
Admissions Office, Penn State Lehigh Valley, 2809 Saucon Valley Road, Center Valley, PA 18034. *Phone:* 610-285-5000. *Fax:* 610-285-5220. *E-mail:* admissions-lv@psu.edu.

Penn State Mont Alto

Mont Alto, Pennsylvania

http://www.ma.psu.edu/

- **State-related** primarily 2-year, founded 1929, part of Pennsylvania State University
- **Small-town** campus
- **Coed**
- **Moderately difficult** entrance level

FACULTY
Student/faculty ratio: 11:1.

ACADEMICS
Calendar: semesters. *Degrees:* certificates, associate, and bachelor's.

STUDENT LIFE
Housing options: coed, special housing for students with disabilities. Campus housing is university owned. Freshman campus housing is guaranteed.

Athletics Member NJCAA.

Campus security: 24-hour patrols, controlled dormitory access.

FINANCIAL AID
Financial Aid Of all full-time matriculated undergraduates who enrolled in 2017, 649 applied for aid, 582 were judged to have need, 116 had their need fully met. In 2017, 55 non-need-based awards were made. ***Average percent of need met:*** 64. ***Average financial aid package:*** $10,886. ***Average need-based loan:*** $4220. ***Average need-based gift aid:*** $4814. ***Average non-need-based aid:*** $3442. ***Average indebtedness upon graduation:*** $44,034.

APPLYING
Standardized Tests *Required:* SAT or ACT (for admission).

Options: electronic application, early admission, deferred entrance.

Application fee: $65.

Required: high school transcript. ***Required for some:*** interview. ***Recommended:*** essay or personal statement.

CONTACT
Admissions Office, Penn State Mont Alto, 1 Campus Drive, Mont Alto, PA 17237. *Phone:* 717-749-6130. *Toll-free phone:* 800-392-6173. *Fax:* 717-749-6132. *E-mail:* psuma@psu.edu.

Penn State New Kensington

New Kensington, Pennsylvania

http://www.nk.psu.edu/

- **State-related** 4-year, founded 1958, part of Pennsylvania State University
- **Small-town** campus
- **Coed**
- **Moderately difficult** entrance level

FACULTY
Student/faculty ratio: 11:1.

ACADEMICS
Calendar: semesters. *Degrees:* certificates, associate, and bachelor's.

STUDENT LIFE
Athletics Member NJCAA.
Campus security: part-time trained security personnel.

FINANCIAL AID
Financial Aid Of all full-time matriculated undergraduates who enrolled in 2017, 482 applied for aid, 419 were judged to have need, 75 had their need fully met. In 2017, 39 non-need-based awards were made. ***Average***

percent of need met: 59. ***Average financial aid package:*** $9197. ***Average need-based loan:*** $3899. ***Average need-based gift aid:*** $5516. ***Average non-need-based aid:*** $3300. ***Average indebtedness upon graduation:*** $32,552.

APPLYING
Standardized Tests *Required:* SAT or ACT (for admission).

Options: electronic application, early admission, deferred entrance.

Application fee: $65.

Required: high school transcript. ***Required for some:*** interview. ***Recommended:*** essay or personal statement.

CONTACT
Admissions Office, Penn State New Kensington, 3550 Seventh Street Road, New Kensington, PA 15068. *Phone:* 724-334-5466. *Toll-free phone:* 888-968-7297. *Fax:* 724-334-6111. *E-mail:* nkadmissions@psu.edu.

Penn State Schuylkill
Schuylkill Haven, Pennsylvania
http://www.sl.psu.edu/

- **State-related** 4-year, founded 1934, part of Pennsylvania State University
- **Small-town** campus
- **Coed**
- **Moderately difficult** entrance level

FACULTY
Student/faculty ratio: 15:1.

ACADEMICS
Calendar: semesters. *Degrees:* certificates, associate, and bachelor's (bachelor's degree programs completed at the Harrisburg campus).

STUDENT LIFE
Housing options: special housing for students with disabilities.

Athletics Member NJCAA.

Campus security: 24-hour patrols, controlled dormitory access.

FINANCIAL AID
Financial Aid Of all full-time matriculated undergraduates who enrolled in 2017, 592 applied for aid, 567 were judged to have need, 88 had their need fully met. In 2017, 26 non-need-based awards were made. ***Average percent of need met:*** 64. ***Average financial aid package:*** $11,397. ***Average need-based loan:*** $3976. ***Average need-based gift aid:*** $5740. ***Average non-need-based aid:*** $2345. ***Average indebtedness upon graduation:*** $33,153.

APPLYING
Standardized Tests *Required:* SAT or ACT (for admission).

Options: electronic application, early admission, deferred entrance.

Application fee: $65.

Required: high school transcript.

CONTACT
Admissions Office, Penn State Schuylkill, 200 University Drive, Schuylkill Haven, PA 17972. *Phone:* 570-385-6252. *Fax:* 570-385-6272. *E-mail:* sl-admissions@psu.edu.

Penn State Shenango
Sharon, Pennsylvania
http://www.shenango.psu.edu/

- **State-related** 4-year, founded 1965, part of Pennsylvania State University
- **Small-town** campus
- **Coed**
- **Moderately difficult** entrance level

FACULTY
Student/faculty ratio: 10:1.

ACADEMICS
Calendar: semesters. *Degrees:* certificates, associate, and bachelor's.

STUDENT LIFE
Housing options: college housing not available.

FINANCIAL AID
Financial Aid Of all full-time matriculated undergraduates who enrolled in 2017, 236 applied for aid, 228 were judged to have need, 16 had their need fully met. In 2017, 17 non-need-based awards were made. ***Average percent of need met:*** 56. ***Average financial aid package:*** $12,554. ***Average need-based loan:*** $3933. ***Average need-based gift aid:*** $5722. ***Average non-need-based aid:*** $4123. ***Average indebtedness upon graduation:*** $32,950.

APPLYING
Standardized Tests *Required:* SAT or ACT (for admission).

Options: electronic application, early admission, deferred entrance.

Application fee: $65.

Required: high school transcript.

CONTACT
Admissions Office, Penn State Shenango, 147 Shenango Avenue, Sharon, PA 16146. *Phone:* 724-983-2803. *Fax:* 724-983-2820. *E-mail:* psushenango@psu.edu.

Penn State University Park
State College, Pennsylvania
http://www.psu.edu/

- **State-related** university, founded 1855, part of The Pennsylvania State University
- **Small-town** 7958-acre campus with easy access to Harrisburg
- **Endowment** $2.8 billion
- **Coed**
- **Very difficult** entrance level

FACULTY
Student/faculty ratio: 16:1.

ACADEMICS
Calendar: semesters. *Degrees:* certificates, associate, bachelor's, master's, doctoral, and postbachelor's certificates.
Library: Pattee and Paterno Libraries plus 4 others. *Books:* 5.0 million (physical), 2.1 million (digital/electronic); *Serial titles:* 84,993 (physical), 160,000 (digital/electronic); *Databases:* 828. Weekly public service hours: 148; study areas open 24 hours, 5–7 days a week; students can reserve study rooms.

STUDENT LIFE
Housing options: on-campus residence required for freshman year; coed, women-only, special housing for students with disabilities. Campus housing is university owned. Freshman campus housing is guaranteed.

Activities and organizations: drama/theater group, student-run newspaper, radio and television station, choral group, marching band, national fraternities, national sororities.

Athletics Member NCAA, USCAA. All Division I except football (Division I-A).

Campus security: 24-hour emergency response devices and patrols, student patrols, late-night transport/escort service, controlled dormitory access.

Student services: health clinic, personal/psychological counseling, women's center, legal services, veterans affairs office.

FINANCIAL AID
Financial Aid Of all full-time matriculated undergraduates who enrolled in 2018, 39,683 applied for aid, 24,050 were judged to have need, 5,370 had their need fully met. 410 Federal Work-Study jobs (averaging $1952). In 2018, 3178 non-need-based awards were made. ***Average percent of need met:*** 64. ***Average financial aid package:*** $11,007. ***Average need-based loan:*** $4743. ***Average need-based gift aid:*** $6599. ***Average non-need-based aid:*** $4730. ***Average indebtedness upon graduation:*** $38,695.

APPLYING
Standardized Tests *Required:* SAT or ACT (for admission).

Options: electronic application, early admission, deferred entrance.

Application fee: $65.

Required: high school transcript. ***Recommended:*** essay or personal statement.

CONTACT
Clark V. Brigger, Executive Director for Undergraduate Admissions, Penn State University Park, 201 Shields Building, University Park, PA 16802. *Phone:* 814-865-5471. *Fax:* 814-863-7590. *E-mail:* admissions@psu.edu.

Penn State Wilkes-Barre

Lehman, Pennsylvania

http://www.wb.psu.edu/

- **State-related** 4-year, founded 1916, part of Pennsylvania State University
- **Rural** campus
- **Coed**
- **Moderately difficult** entrance level

FACULTY
Student/faculty ratio: 11:1.

ACADEMICS
Calendar: semesters. *Degrees:* certificates, associate, bachelor's, and postbachelor's certificates (enrollment figures include students enrolled at The Graduate School at Penn State who are taking courses at this location).

STUDENT LIFE
Housing options: college housing not available.

Athletics Member NJCAA.

FINANCIAL AID
Financial Aid Of all full-time matriculated undergraduates who enrolled in 2017, 385 applied for aid, 351 were judged to have need, 58 had their need fully met. In 2017, 30 non-need-based awards were made. ***Average percent of need met:*** 60. ***Average financial aid package:*** $9937. ***Average need-based loan:*** $4160. ***Average need-based gift aid:*** $5712. ***Average non-need-based aid:*** $2945. ***Average indebtedness upon graduation:*** $37,663.

APPLYING
Standardized Tests *Required:* SAT or ACT (for admission).

Options: electronic application, early admission, deferred entrance.

Application fee: $65.

Required: high school transcript.

CONTACT
Admissions Office, Penn State Wilkes-Barre, Old Route 115, PO Box PSU, Lehman, PA 18627. *Phone:* 570-675-9238. *Fax:* 570-675-9113. *E-mail:* wbadmissions@psu.edu.

Penn State Worthington Scranton

Dunmore, Pennsylvania

http://www.sn.psu.edu/

- **State-related** 4-year, founded 1923, part of Pennsylvania State University
- **Small-town** campus
- **Coed**
- **Moderately difficult** entrance level

FACULTY
Student/faculty ratio: 16:1.

ACADEMICS
Calendar: semesters. *Degrees:* certificates, associate, and bachelor's.

STUDENT LIFE
Housing options: college housing not available.

FINANCIAL AID
Financial Aid Of all full-time matriculated undergraduates who enrolled in 2017, 896 applied for aid, 817 were judged to have need, 92 had their need fully met. In 2017, 36 non-need-based awards were made. ***Average percent of need met:*** 58. ***Average financial aid package:*** $10,433. ***Average need-based loan:*** $4099. ***Average need-based gift aid:*** $5519. ***Average non-need-based aid:*** $4308. ***Average indebtedness upon graduation:*** $36,396.

APPLYING
Standardized Tests *Required:* SAT or ACT (for admission).

Options: electronic application, early admission, deferred entrance.

Application fee: $65.

Required: high school transcript. ***Required for some:*** interview. ***Recommended:*** essay or personal statement.

CONTACT
Admissions Office, Penn State Worthington Scranton, 120 Ridge View Drive, Dunmore, PA 18512. *Phone:* 570-963-2500. *Fax:* 570-963-2524. *E-mail:* wsadmissions@psu.edu.

Penn State York

York, Pennsylvania

http://www.york.psu.edu/

- **State-related** comprehensive, founded 1926, part of Pennsylvania State University
- **Suburban** campus
- **Coed**
- **Moderately difficult** entrance level

FACULTY
Student/faculty ratio: 14:1.

ACADEMICS
Calendar: semesters. *Degrees:* certificates, associate, bachelor's, master's, and postbachelor's certificates (also offers up to 2 years of most bachelor's degree programs offered at University Park campus).

STUDENT LIFE
Housing options: college housing not available.

FINANCIAL AID
Financial Aid Of all full-time matriculated undergraduates who enrolled in 2017, 791 applied for aid, 530 were judged to have need, 72 had their need fully met. In 2017, 95 non-need-based awards were made. ***Average percent of need met:*** 56. ***Average financial aid package:*** $9711. ***Average need-based loan:*** $3958. ***Average need-based gift aid:*** $5370. ***Average non-need-based aid:*** $3488. ***Average indebtedness upon graduation:*** $41,140.

APPLYING
Standardized Tests *Required:* SAT or ACT (for admission).

Options: electronic application, early admission, deferred entrance.

Application fee: $65.

Required: high school transcript.

CONTACT
Admissions Office, Penn State York, 1031 Edgecomb Avenue, York, PA 17403. *Phone:* 717-771-4040. *Toll-free phone:* 800-778-6227. *Fax:* 717-771-4005. *E-mail:* ykadmission@psu.edu.

Pennsylvania Academy of the Fine Arts

Philadelphia, Pennsylvania

http://www.pafa.edu/

- **Independent** comprehensive, founded 1805
- **Urban** campus
- **Coed** 200 undergraduate students
- 90% of applicants were admitted

Freshmen:
Admission: 173 applied, 156 admitted.

FACULTY
Total: 63, 29% full-time.

ACADEMICS
Calendar: semesters. *Degrees:* certificates, bachelor's, master's, and postbachelor's certificates.

Computers: 75 computers/terminals are available on campus for general student use. Students can access the following: free student e-mail accounts.
Library: Arcadia Fine Arts Library.

STUDENT LIFE
Housing options: coed.
Campus security: 24-hour patrols.

COSTS & FINANCIAL AID
Costs (2019–20) ***Tuition:*** $38,926 full-time, $1622 per credit part-time. ***Required fees:*** $1450 full-time. ***Room only:*** $12,010.
Financial Aid Of all full-time matriculated undergraduates who enrolled in 2018, 55 Federal Work-Study jobs (averaging $2000).

APPLYING
Standardized Tests *Required for some:* TOEFL (suggested 600 paper based, 250 computer based, 100 iBT) or IELTS (suggested 6.0 paper based) for international students.
Options: electronic application.
Application fee: $60.
Required: essay or personal statement, minimum 3.0 GPA, 2 letters of recommendation, portfolio of work.
Application deadlines: rolling (out-of-state freshmen), rolling (transfers), 12/1 (early action).
Early decision deadline: 12/1.
Notification: continuous (out-of-state freshmen), continuous (transfers).

CONTACT
Peter Tran, Director of Admissions Operations, Pennsylvania Academy of the Fine Arts, 128 North Broad Street, Philadelphia, PA 19102. *Phone:* 215-391-4111. *Fax:* 215-569-0153. *E-mail:* ptran@pafa.edu.

Pennsylvania College of Art & Design

Lancaster, Pennsylvania

http://www.pcad.edu/

- **Independent** 4-year, founded 1982
- **Urban** campus with easy access to Philadelphia, Baltimore
- **Coed** 251 undergraduate students, 97% full-time, 67% women, 33% men
- **Moderately difficult** entrance level, 44% of applicants were admitted

UNDERGRAD STUDENTS
243 full-time, 8 part-time. 23% are from out of state; 6% Black or African American, non-Hispanic/Latino; 4% Hispanic/Latino; 5% Asian, non-Hispanic/Latino; 0.4% Native Hawaiian or other Pacific Islander, non-Hispanic/Latino; 0.8% American Indian or Alaska Native, non-Hispanic/Latino; 6% Two or more races, non-Hispanic/Latino; 5% Race/ethnicity unknown.

Freshmen:
Admission: 301 applied, 131 admitted, 54 enrolled. ***Average high school GPA:*** 3.0.
Retention: 59% of full-time freshmen returned.

FACULTY
Total: 51, 20% full-time, 41% with terminal degrees.
Student/faculty ratio: 13:1.

ACADEMICS
Calendar: semesters. *Degree:* certificates and bachelor's.
Special study options: advanced placement credit, internships.
Computers: 90 computers/terminals are available on campus for general student use. Students can access the following: campus intranet, computer help desk, free student e-mail accounts, online (class) grades, online (class) registration, online (class) schedules. Campuswide network is available. Wireless service is available via entire campus.
Library: Pennsylvania College of Art & Design Library.

STUDENT LIFE
Housing options: college housing not available.
Activities and organizations: Student Council, Anime Club, Student AIGA, Society of Illustrators - Student Group.
Campus security: late-night transport/escort service, trained evening/weekend security personnel.

COSTS
Costs (2019–20) ***Tuition:*** $25,000 full-time, $1042 per credit part-time. ***Required fees:*** $1600 full-time.

APPLYING
Options: electronic application, deferred entrance.
Application fee: $40.
Required: essay or personal statement, high school transcript, minimum 2.5 GPA, portfolio. ***Required for some:*** 2 letters of recommendation. ***Recommended:*** interview.
Application deadlines: rolling (freshmen), rolling (transfers).
Notification: continuous (freshmen), continuous (transfers).

CONTACT
Natalie A Lascek, Director of Admissions Marketing & Recruitment, Pennsylvania College of Art & Design, 204 North Prince Street, PO Box 59, Lancaster, PA 17608-0059. *Phone:* 717-3967833. *Toll-free phone:* 800-689-0379 Ext. 1001. *E-mail:* nlascek@pcad.edu.

Pennsylvania College of Health Sciences

Lancaster, Pennsylvania

http://www.pacollege.edu/

- **Independent** comprehensive, founded 1903
- **Suburban** 25-acre campus with easy access to Harrisburg
- **Endowment** $5.0 million
- **Coed**
- **Moderately difficult** entrance level

FACULTY
Student/faculty ratio: 12:1.

ACADEMICS
Calendar: semesters. *Degrees:* certificates, associate, bachelor's, master's, and doctoral.
Library: Health Sciences Library. *Books:* 1,185 (physical), 598 (digital/electronic); *Serial titles:* 93 (physical), 13,436 (digital/electronic); *Databases:* 43. Students can reserve study rooms.

STUDENT LIFE
Housing options: college housing not available.
Campus security: 24-hour emergency response devices and patrols, late-night transport/escort service.
Student services: health clinic, personal/psychological counseling.

APPLYING
Standardized Tests *Required for some:* SAT or ACT (for admission).
Options: electronic application, deferred entrance.
Application fee: $35.
Required: minimum 3.0 GPA, 2 letters of recommendation, transcripts of all institutions attended. ***Required for some:*** essay or personal statement.

CONTACT
Pennsylvania College of Health Sciences, 850 Greenfield Road, Lancaster, PA 17601. *Toll-free phone:* 800-622-5443.

Pennsylvania College of Technology

Williamsport, Pennsylvania

http://www.pct.edu/

- **State-related** 4-year, founded 1965
- **Suburban** 994-acre campus
- **Coed**
- **Noncompetitive** entrance level

FACULTY
Student/faculty ratio: 14:1.

ACADEMICS
Calendar: semesters. *Degrees:* certificates, associate, and bachelor's.
Library: Penn College Madigan Library plus 1 other. *Books:* 89,117 (physical), 27,388 (digital/electronic); *Serial titles:* 9,342 (physical), 88,304 (digital/electronic); *Databases:* 169. Weekly public service hours: 86; students can reserve study rooms.

STUDENT LIFE
Housing options: coed, special housing for students with disabilities. Campus housing is university owned.

Activities and organizations: Student Government Association, Residence Hall Association, Wildcats Event Board, Association of Computing Machinery, Campus Ministry International, national fraternities.

Athletics Member NCAA, USCAA. All Division III.

Campus security: 24-hour emergency response devices and patrols, late-night transport/escort service, controlled dormitory access.

Student services: health clinic, personal/psychological counseling.

COSTS & FINANCIAL AID
Costs (2018–19) ***Tuition:*** state resident $16,740 full-time, $475 per credit hour part-time; nonresident $23,880 full-time, $713 per credit hour part-time. Full-time tuition and fees vary according to course load and program. Part-time tuition and fees vary according to course load and program. ***Required fees:*** $2490 full-time, $83 per credit hour part-time. ***Room and board:*** $11,544; room only: $6586. Room and board charges vary according to board plan and housing facility.

Financial Aid Of all full-time matriculated undergraduates who enrolled in 2017, 4,371 applied for aid, 4,194 were judged to have need. 118 Federal Work-Study jobs (averaging $1595). ***Average percent of need met:*** 23. ***Average financial aid package:*** $13,120. ***Average need-based loan:*** $3270. ***Average need-based gift aid:*** $8563. ***Average indebtedness upon graduation:*** $7218.

APPLYING
Standardized Tests *Required for some:* SAT (for admission).

Options: electronic application, early admission, deferred entrance.

Required for some: high school transcript, college transcripts for transfers.

CONTACT
Ashley Murphy, Director of Admissions, Pennsylvania College of Technology, One College Avenue, DIF #119, Williamsport, PA 17701. *Phone:* 570-327-4761 Ext. 7337. *Toll-free phone:* 800-367-9222. *Fax:* 570-321-5551. *E-mail:* admissions@pct.edu.

Pittsburgh Technical College

Oakdale, Pennsylvania

http://www.ptcollege.edu/

- **Proprietary** primarily 2-year, founded 1946
- **Suburban** 180-acre campus with easy access to Pittsburgh
- **Coed**
- 87% of applicants were admitted

FACULTY
Student/faculty ratio: 12:1.

ACADEMICS
Calendar: quarters. *Degrees:* certificates, associate, and bachelor's.
Library: Library Resource Center. *Books:* 7,378 (physical), 46,000 (digital/electronic); *Serial titles:* 116 (physical), 6 (digital/electronic); *Databases:* 12. Weekly public service hours: 58.

STUDENT LIFE
Housing options: coed. Campus housing is university owned and leased by the school.

Activities and organizations: drama/theater group, Software Development Club, Drama Club, DECA, Gay-Straight Alliance, Magic Club.

Campus security: 24-hour emergency response devices and patrols, student patrols, late-night transport/escort service, controlled dormitory access.

Student services: personal/psychological counseling.

COSTS
Costs (2018–19) ***Comprehensive fee:*** $26,847 includes full-time tuition ($16,920) and room and board ($9927). Full-time tuition and fees vary according to degree level and program. No tuition increase for student's term of enrollment. ***College room only:*** $7344. Room and board charges vary according to housing facility. ***Payment plans:*** installment, deferred payment.

APPLYING
Standardized Tests *Required:* entrance exams for practical nursing certificate and nursing and surgical technology Associate degrees (for admission). *Required for some:* SAT or ACT (for admission).

Options: electronic application, deferred entrance.

Required: high school transcript. ***Required for some:*** essay or personal statement, criminal background check, minimum rank in top 80% of class. ***Recommended:*** interview.

CONTACT
Ms. Nancy Goodlin, Admissions Office Assistant, Pittsburgh Technical College, 1111 McKee Road, Oakdale, PA 15071. *Phone:* 412-809-5100. *Toll-free phone:* 800-784-9675. *Fax:* 412-809-5351. *E-mail:* goodlin.nancy@ptcollege.edu.

Point Park University

Pittsburgh, Pennsylvania

http://www.pointpark.edu/

- **Independent** university, founded 1960
- **Urban** campus
- **Endowment** $33.5 million
- **Coed**
- **Moderately difficult** entrance level

FACULTY
Student/faculty ratio: 13:1.

ACADEMICS
Calendar: semesters. *Degrees:* certificates, associate, bachelor's, master's, doctoral, and postbachelor's certificates.
Library: Point Park University Library.

STUDENT LIFE
Housing options: coed, women-only, special housing for students with disabilities. Campus housing is university owned and leased by the school. Freshman campus housing is guaranteed.

Activities and organizations: drama/theater group, student-run newspaper, radio and television station, WPPJ student radio station, The Body Christian Fellowship, Dance Club, Campus Activities Board, Action Sports Club.

Athletics Member NAIA.

Campus security: 24-hour emergency response devices and patrols, late-night transport/escort service, controlled dormitory access, campus patrolled by Accredited Law Enforcement Agency, 24-hour security desk, video security.

Student services: health clinic, personal/psychological counseling, veterans affairs office.

COSTS & FINANCIAL AID
Costs (2018–19) ***Comprehensive fee:*** $43,650 includes full-time tuition ($29,980), mandatory fees ($1470), and room and board ($12,200). Full-time tuition and fees vary according to program. Part-time tuition: $844 per credit. Part-time tuition and fees vary according to program. ***Required fees:*** $165 per term part-time. ***College room only:*** $5320. Room and board charges vary according to board plan and housing facility. ***Payment plans:*** installment, deferred payment.

Financial Aid Of all full-time matriculated undergraduates who enrolled in 2017, 2,516 applied for aid, 2,345 were judged to have need, 296 had their need fully met. In 2017, 162 non-need-based awards were made. ***Average percent of need met:*** 71. ***Average financial aid package:*** $25,353. ***Average need-based loan:*** $5380. ***Average need-based gift aid:*** $19,916. ***Average non-need-based aid:*** $13,043. ***Average indebtedness upon graduation:*** $27,924.

APPLYING
Standardized Tests *Required:* SAT or ACT (for admission).

Options: electronic application, deferred entrance.

Application fee: $40.

Required: high school transcript. ***Required for some:*** essay or personal statement, 2 letters of recommendation, interview, audition. ***Recommended:*** minimum 2.5 GPA.

CONTACT
Point Park University, 201 Wood Street, Pittsburgh, PA 15222-1984. *Phone:* 412-392-3430. *Toll-free phone:* 800-321-0129.

The Restaurant School at Walnut Hill College

Philadelphia, Pennsylvania

http://www.walnuthillcollege.edu/

CONTACT
Mr. John English, Director of Admissions, The Restaurant School at Walnut Hill College, 4207 Walnut Street, Philadelphia, PA 19104-3518. *Phone:* 267-295-2353. *Fax:* 215-222-4219. *E-mail:* jenglish@walnuthillcollege.edu.

Robert Morris University

Moon Township, Pennsylvania

http://www.rmu.edu/

- **Independent** university, founded 1921
- **Suburban** 230-acre campus with easy access to Pittsburgh
- **Endowment** $33.6 million
- **Coed**
- **Minimally difficult** entrance level

FACULTY
Student/faculty ratio: 15:1.

ACADEMICS
Calendar: semesters. *Degrees:* bachelor's, master's, doctoral, and postbachelor's certificates.
Library: Robert Morris University Library. *Books:* 97,693 (physical), 172,931 (digital/electronic); *Serial titles:* 244 (physical), 47,791 (digital/electronic); *Databases:* 104. Weekly public service hours: 101; study areas open 24 hours, 5–7 days a week; students can reserve study rooms.

STUDENT LIFE
Housing options: on-campus residence required for freshman year; coed, men-only, women-only, special housing for students with disabilities. Campus housing is university owned. Freshman applicants given priority for college housing.
Activities and organizations: drama/theater group, student-run newspaper, radio and television station, choral group, marching band, Student Government Association, Residence Hall Association, The Saudi Student Club, National Society of Collegiate Scholars, Top Secret Colonials, national fraternities, national sororities.
Athletics Member NCAA. All Division I.
Campus security: 24-hour emergency response devices and patrols, late-night transport/escort service, controlled dormitory access.
Student services: health clinic, personal/psychological counseling, veterans affairs office.

COSTS & FINANCIAL AID
Costs (2018–19) ***Comprehensive fee:*** $41,700 includes full-time tuition ($29,060), mandatory fees ($1240), and room and board ($11,400). Full-time tuition and fees vary according to course load and program. Part-time tuition: $930 per credit hour. Part-time tuition and fees vary according to program. ***Required fees:*** $80 per credit hour part-time. ***College room only:*** $6340. Room and board charges vary according to board plan and housing facility. ***Payment plans:*** installment, deferred payment.
Financial Aid Of all full-time matriculated undergraduates who enrolled in 2017, 2,996 applied for aid, 2,707 were judged to have need, 347 had their need fully met. In 2017, 670 non-need-based awards were made. ***Average percent of need met:*** 71. ***Average financial aid package:*** $22,897. ***Average need-based loan:*** $6650. ***Average need-based gift aid:*** $16,555. ***Average non-need-based aid:*** $12,841. ***Average indebtedness upon graduation:*** $39,856.

APPLYING
Standardized Tests *Required:* SAT or ACT (for admission).
Options: electronic application, deferred entrance.
Application fee: $30.
Required: high school transcript, minimum 2.0 GPA. ***Required for some:*** interview. ***Recommended:*** essay or personal statement, minimum 3.0 GPA, interview.

CONTACT
Enrollment Services Department, Robert Morris University, 6001 University Boulevard, Moon Township, PA 15108-1189. *Phone:* 412-397-5200. *Toll-free phone:* 800-762-0097. *Fax:* 412-397-2425. *E-mail:* admissionsoffice@rmu.edu.

See page 738 for display ad and page 1086 for the College Close-Up.

Rosemont College

Rosemont, Pennsylvania

http://www.rosemont.edu/

- **Independent Roman Catholic** comprehensive, founded 1921
- **Suburban** 56-acre campus with easy access to Philadelphia
- **Coed**
- **Moderately difficult** entrance level

FACULTY
Student/faculty ratio: 11:1.

ACADEMICS
Calendar: semesters. *Degrees:* bachelor's, master's, and postbachelor's certificates.
Library: Gertrude Kistler Memorial Library plus 1 other. *Books:* 143,162 (physical), 11,582 (digital/electronic); *Serial titles:* 20 (physical), 17,350 (digital/electronic); *Databases:* 40. Students can reserve study rooms.

STUDENT LIFE
Housing options: coed. Campus housing is university owned. Freshman campus housing is guaranteed.
Activities and organizations: drama/theater group, student-run newspaper, choral group.
Athletics Member NCAA. All Division III.
Campus security: 24-hour emergency response devices and patrols, late-night transport/escort service, controlled dormitory access.
Student services: health clinic, personal/psychological counseling.

COSTS & FINANCIAL AID
Costs (2018–19) ***One-time required fee:*** $285. ***Comprehensive fee:*** $32,338 includes full-time tuition ($18,900), mandatory fees ($1000), and room and board ($12,438). Full-time tuition and fees vary according to course load and degree level. Part-time tuition: $715 per credit. Part-time tuition and fees vary according to course load and degree level. ***Required fees:*** $535 per year part-time. ***Room and board:*** Room and board charges vary according to board plan and housing facility.
Financial Aid ***Average indebtedness upon graduation:*** $30,437.

APPLYING
Standardized Tests *Required:* SAT or ACT (for admission).
Options: electronic application, deferred entrance.
Required: high school transcript, minimum 2.0 GPA. ***Required for some:*** essay or personal statement. ***Recommended:*** interview.

CONTACT
Ms. Bettsy Thommen, Director of Admissions, Undergraduate College, Rosemont College, 1400 Montgomery Avenue, Rosemont, PA 19010. *Phone:* 610-527-0200 Ext. 2601. *Toll-free phone:* 888-2-ROSEMONT. *Fax:* 610-520-4399. *E-mail:* bettsy.thommen@rosemont.edu.

Saint Charles Borromeo Seminary, Overbrook

Wynnewood, Pennsylvania

http://www.scs.edu/

- **Independent Roman Catholic** comprehensive, founded 1832
- **Suburban** 77-acre campus with easy access to Philadelphia
- **Coed, primarily men**
- **Moderately difficult** entrance level

FACULTY
Student/faculty ratio: 6:1.

ACADEMICS
Calendar: semesters. *Degrees:* certificates, bachelor's, master's, and postbachelor's certificates (also offers coed part-time programs; students do not apply directly to the Seminary, but instead apply through their local Diocese).
Library: Ryan Memorial Library.

STUDENT LIFE
Housing options: on-campus residence required through senior year; men-only. Campus housing is university owned. Freshman campus housing is guaranteed.
Activities and organizations: drama/theater group, student-run newspaper, choral group, Seminarians for Life, Student Council.
Campus security: 24-hour emergency response devices and patrols.
Student services: health clinic, personal/psychological counseling.

COSTS & FINANCIAL AID
Costs (2018–19) ***Comprehensive fee:*** $34,975 includes full-time tuition ($20,000), mandatory fees ($1275), and room and board ($13,700). Full-time tuition and fees vary according to degree level, program, and student level. Part-time tuition: $950 per course. Part-time tuition and fees vary according to course level. ***Required fees:*** $100 per term part-time. ***College room only:*** $4500.
Financial Aid Of all full-time matriculated undergraduates who enrolled in 2012, 22 applied for aid, 10 were judged to have need, 6 had their need fully met. ***Average percent of need met:*** 60. ***Average financial aid package:*** $20,000. ***Average need-based loan:*** $5500. ***Average need-based gift aid:*** $5000. ***Average indebtedness upon graduation:*** $19,000.

APPLYING
Options: deferred entrance.
Required: essay or personal statement, high school transcript, minimum 2.0 GPA, 3 letters of recommendation, interview, sponsorship by diocese or religious community.

CONTACT
Rev. Joseph Shenosky, Vice Rector, Saint Charles Borromeo Seminary, Overbrook, 100 East Wynnewood Road, Wynnewood, PA 19096. *Phone:* 610-785-6520. *E-mail:* jshenosky@scs.edu.

★ Saint Francis University
Loretto, Pennsylvania
http://www.francis.edu/

- **Independent Roman Catholic** comprehensive, founded 1847
- **Rural** 600-acre campus
- **Endowment** $50.3 million
- **Coed** 2,111 undergraduate students, 70% full-time, 65% women, 35% men
- **Moderately difficult** entrance level, 75% of applicants were admitted

UNDERGRAD STUDENTS
1,485 full-time, 626 part-time. Students come from 36 states and territories; 23 other countries; 29% are from out of state; 8% Black or African American, non-Hispanic/Latino; 2% Hispanic/Latino; 2% Asian, non-Hispanic/Latino; 0.2% Native Hawaiian or other Pacific Islander, non-Hispanic/Latino; 0.3% American Indian or Alaska Native, non-Hispanic/Latino; 2% Two or more races, non-Hispanic/Latino; 2% Race/ethnicity unknown; 1% international; 4% transferred in; 83% live on campus.

Freshmen:
Admission: 1,706 applied, 1,286 admitted, 342 enrolled. ***Average high school GPA:*** 3.5. ***Test scores:*** SAT evidence-based reading and writing scores over 500: 84%; SAT math scores over 500: 83%; ACT scores over 18: 89%; SAT evidence-based reading and writing scores over 600: 40%; SAT math scores over 600: 35%; ACT scores over 24: 52%; SAT evidence-based reading and writing scores over 700: 4%; SAT math scores over 700: 4%; ACT scores over 30: 4%.
Retention: 87% of full-time freshmen returned.

FACULTY
Total: 185, 71% full-time, 55% with terminal degrees.
Student/faculty ratio: 14:1.

ACADEMICS
Calendar: semesters. *Degrees:* certificates, associate, bachelor's, master's, and doctoral.

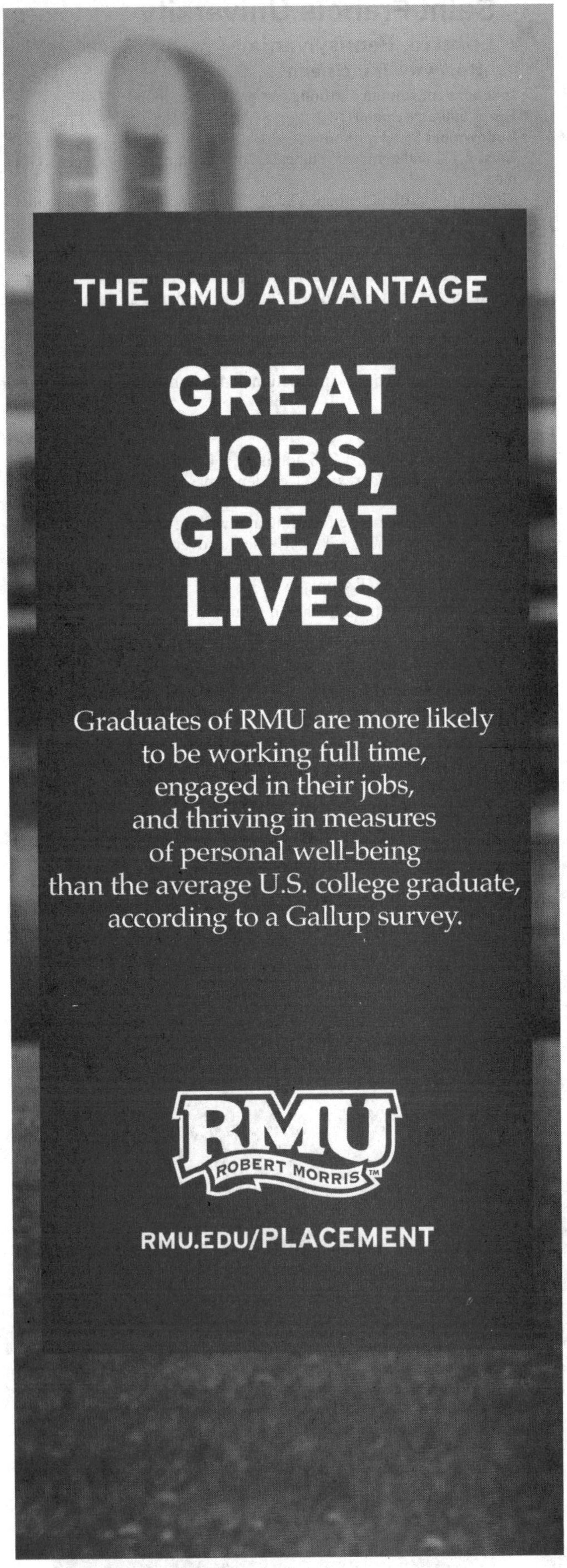

Special study options: academic remediation for entering students, accelerated degree program, adult/continuing education programs, advanced placement credit, cooperative education, distance learning, double majors, English as a second language, external degree program, freshman honors college, honors programs, independent study, internships, off-campus study, part-time degree program, services for LD students, student-designed majors, study abroad, summer session for credit. ***ROTC:*** Army (b).

Unusual degree programs: 3-2 engineering with Penn State University Park, University of Pittsburgh; forestry with Duke University; Optometry with Salus University, osteopathic medicine with Lake Erie College of Osteopathic Medicine, PharmD Duquesne University & Lake Erie College of Osteopathic Medicine, Dental Lake Erie College of Osteopathic Medicine.

Computers: 1,500 computers/terminals are available on campus for general student use. Students can access the following: campus intranet, computer help desk, free student e-mail accounts, online (class) grades, online (class) registration, online (class) schedules. Campuswide network is available. 95% of college-owned or -operated housing units are wired for high-speed Internet access. Wireless service is available via entire campus.

Library: Saint Francis University Library. *Books:* 60,353 (physical), 1.3 million (digital/electronic); *Databases:* 74.

STUDENT LIFE

Housing options: on-campus residence required through junior year; coed, men-only, women-only. Campus housing is university owned and leased by the school. Freshman campus housing is guaranteed.

Activities and organizations: drama/theater group, student-run newspaper, radio station, choral group, marching band, Student Activities Organization, Club Baseball, Student Government Association, Best Buddies, Cru, national fraternities, national sororities.

Athletics Member NCAA. All Division I. ***Intercollegiate sports:*** basketball M(s)/W(s), bowling W, cross-country running M(s)/W(s), field hockey W(s), football M(s), golf M(s)/W(s)(c), lacrosse W(s), soccer M(s)/W(s), softball W(s), swimming and diving W(s), tennis M(s)/W(s), track and field M(s)/W(s), volleyball M(s)/W(s), water polo M. ***Intramural sports:*** baseball M(c)/W(c), basketball M/W, cheerleading M/W, football M, golf M/W, ice hockey M(c)/W(c), lacrosse W, soccer M/W, softball W, swimming and diving W, tennis M/W, track and field M/W, ultimate Frisbee M/W, volleyball M/W.

Campus security: 24-hour emergency response devices and patrols, late-night transport/escort service, controlled dormitory access.

Student services: health clinic, personal/psychological counseling, veterans affairs office.

COSTS & FINANCIAL AID

Costs (2019–20) ***One-time required fee:*** $110. ***Comprehensive fee:*** $50,380 includes full-time tuition ($36,970), mandatory fees ($1300), and room and board ($12,110). Part-time tuition: $1057 per credit. ***College room only:*** $6086.

Financial Aid Of all full-time matriculated undergraduates who enrolled in 2015, 1,497 applied for aid, 1,247 were judged to have need, 347 had their need fully met. 285 Federal Work-Study jobs (averaging $1000). 780 state and other part-time jobs (averaging $1000). In 2015, 289 non-need-based awards were made. ***Average percent of need met:*** 52. ***Average financial aid package:*** $20,018. ***Average need-based loan:*** $4207. ***Average need-based gift aid:*** $16,858. ***Average non-need-based aid:*** $17,963. ***Average indebtedness upon graduation:*** $36,656.

APPLYING

Standardized Tests *Required:* SAT or ACT (for admission).

Options: electronic application, deferred entrance.

Application fee: $30.

Required: essay or personal statement, high school transcript, 1 letter of recommendation. ***Recommended:*** interview.

Application deadlines: rolling (freshmen), rolling (transfers).

Notification: continuous (transfers).

CONTACT

Robert Beener, Dean for Enrollment Management, Saint Francis University, 117 Evergreen Drive, PO Box 600, Loretto, PA 15940-0600.

Phone: 814-472-3100. *Toll-free phone:* 866-DIAL-SFU. *E-mail:* rbeener@francis.edu.

See page 737 for display ad and page 1092 for the College Close-Up.

Saint Joseph's University

Philadelphia, Pennsylvania

http://www.sju.edu/

- **Independent Roman Catholic (Jesuit)** comprehensive, founded 1851
- **Suburban** 114-acre campus with easy access to Philadelphia
- **Endowment** $280.3 million
- **Coed** 4,904 undergraduate students, 89% full-time, 55% women, 45% men
- **Moderately difficult** entrance level, 76% of applicants were admitted

UNDERGRAD STUDENTS

4,350 full-time, 554 part-time. Students come from 36 states and territories; 36 other countries; 53% are from out of state; 6% Black or African American, non-Hispanic/Latino; 7% Hispanic/Latino; 3% Asian, non-Hispanic/Latino; 0.2% Native Hawaiian or other Pacific Islander, non-Hispanic/Latino; 0.1% American Indian or Alaska Native, non-Hispanic/Latino; 3% Two or more races, non-Hispanic/Latino; 2% Race/ethnicity unknown; 2% international; 2% transferred in; 48% live on campus.

Freshmen:

Admission: 8,843 applied, 6,749 admitted, 1,129 enrolled. ***Average high school GPA:*** 3.6. ***Test scores:*** SAT evidence-based reading and writing scores over 500: 97%; SAT math scores over 500: 96%; ACT scores over 18: 99%; SAT evidence-based reading and writing scores over 600: 58%; SAT math scores over 600: 48%; ACT scores over 24: 72%; SAT evidence-based reading and writing scores over 700: 7%; SAT math scores over 700: 8%; ACT scores over 30: 16%.

Retention: 89% of full-time freshmen returned.

FACULTY

Total: 681, 44% full-time.

Student/faculty ratio: 11:1.

ACADEMICS

Calendar: semesters. *Degrees:* associate, bachelor's, master's, doctoral, post-master's, and postbachelor's certificates.

Special study options: accelerated degree program, adult/continuing education programs, advanced placement credit, cooperative education, distance learning, double majors, English as a second language, honors programs, independent study, internships, off-campus study, part-time degree program, services for LD students, student-designed majors, study abroad, summer session for credit. ***ROTC:*** Army (c), Navy (c), Air Force (b).

Computers: 901 computers/terminals are available on campus for general student use. Students can access the following: campus intranet, computer help desk, free student e-mail accounts, online (class) grades, online (class) registration, online (class) schedules. Campuswide network is available. 100% of college-owned or -operated housing units are wired for high-speed Internet access. Wireless service is available via entire campus.

Library: Post Learning Commons and Drexel Library. *Books:* 271,281 (physical), 467,643 (digital/electronic); *Serial titles:* 3,324 (physical), 76,020 (digital/electronic); *Databases:* 219. Weekly public service hours: 109; students can reserve study rooms.

STUDENT LIFE

Housing options: on-campus residence required through sophomore year; coed, men-only, women-only, special housing for students with disabilities. Campus housing is university owned, leased by the school and is provided by a third party. Freshman campus housing is guaranteed.

Activities and organizations: drama/theater group, student-run newspaper, radio station, choral group, Student Union Board, Hand-in-Hand, 54th Airborne / Booster Club, Appalachian Experience, Weekly Service, national fraternities, national sororities.

Athletics Member NCAA. All Division I. ***Intercollegiate sports:*** baseball M(s), basketball M(s)/W(s), cheerleading M(c)/W(c), crew M(s)/W(s), cross-country running M(s)/W(s), field hockey W(s), golf M(s), lacrosse M(s)/W(s), soccer M(s)/W(s), softball W(s), tennis M(s)/W(s), track and field M(s)/W(s). ***Intramural sports:*** baseball M(c), basketball M(c)/W(c), fencing W(c), football M/W, golf M(c)/W(c), ice hockey M(c)/W(c), lacrosse M(c)/W(c), rugby M(c)/W(c), soccer M(c)/W(c), softball W, swimming and diving M(c)/W(c), tennis M(c)/W(c), ultimate Frisbee M(c)/W(c), volleyball M(c)/W(c), water polo M(c)/W(c).

Campus security: 24-hour emergency response devices and patrols, late-night transport/escort service, controlled dormitory access.

Student services: health clinic, personal/psychological counseling, veterans affairs office.

COSTS & FINANCIAL AID

Costs (2019–20) ***Comprehensive fee:*** $61,410 includes full-time tuition ($46,370), mandatory fees ($200), and room and board ($14,840). Part-time tuition: $584 per credit. ***College room only:*** $9424.

Financial Aid Of all full-time matriculated undergraduates who enrolled in 2018, 3,231 applied for aid, 2,714 were judged to have need, 713 had their need fully met. In 2018, 1275 non-need-based awards were made. ***Average percent of need met:*** 79. ***Average financial aid package:*** $31,086. ***Average need-based loan:*** $4378. ***Average need-based gift aid:*** $24,092. ***Average non-need-based aid:*** $14,164.

APPLYING

Options: electronic application, early decision, early action, deferred entrance.

Application fee: $50.

Required: essay or personal statement, high school transcript, 1 letter of recommendation.

Application deadlines: 2/1 (freshmen), 3/1 (transfers), 11/1 (early action).

Early decision deadline: 11/1 (for plan 1), 1/15 (for plan 2).

Notification: 3/15 (freshmen), continuous (transfers), 12/20 (early decision plan 1), 2/15 (early decision plan 2), 12/20 (early action).

CONTACT

Maureen Mathis, Director of Undergraduate Admissions, Saint Joseph's University, 5600 City Avenue, Philadelphia, PA 19131-1395. *Phone:* 610-660-1300. *Toll-free phone:* 888-BE-A-HAWK (in-state); 800-BE-A-HAWK (out-of-state). *E-mail:* admit@sju.edu.

★ Saint Vincent College

Latrobe, Pennsylvania

http://www.stvincent.edu/

- **Independent Roman Catholic** comprehensive, founded 1846
- **Suburban** 200-acre campus with easy access to Pittsburgh
- **Endowment** $109.8 million
- **Coed** 1,676 undergraduate students, 95% full-time, 45% women, 55% men
- **Moderately difficult** entrance level, 68% of applicants were admitted

UNDERGRAD STUDENTS

1,595 full-time, 81 part-time. Students come from 30 states and territories; 8 other countries; 23% are from out of state; 6% Black or African American, non-Hispanic/Latino; 3% Hispanic/Latino; 1% Asian, non-Hispanic/Latino; 0.1% Native Hawaiian or other Pacific Islander, non-Hispanic/Latino; 0.2% American Indian or Alaska Native, non-Hispanic/Latino; 2% Two or more races, non-Hispanic/Latino; 3% Race/ethnicity unknown; 0.7% international; 3% transferred in; 72% live on campus.

Freshmen:

Admission: 2,354 applied, 1,609 admitted, 417 enrolled. ***Average high school GPA:*** 3.5. ***Test scores:*** SAT evidence-based reading and writing scores over 500: 86%; SAT math scores over 500: 85%; ACT scores over 18: 87%; SAT evidence-based reading and writing scores over 600: 41%; SAT math scores over 600: 26%; ACT scores over 24: 46%; SAT evidence-based reading and writing scores over 700: 5%; SAT math scores over 700: 7%; ACT scores over 30: 7%.

Retention: 82% of full-time freshmen returned.

FACULTY

Total: 233, 44% full-time, 61% with terminal degrees.

Student/faculty ratio: 11:1.

ACADEMICS

Calendar: semesters. *Degrees:* certificates, bachelor's, master's, doctoral, and postbachelor's certificates.

Special study options: advanced placement credit, cooperative education, distance learning, double majors, external degree program, honors programs, independent study, internships, part-time degree program, services for LD students, student-designed majors, study abroad, summer session for credit. ***ROTC:*** Army (c), Air Force (c).

Unusual degree programs: 3-2 engineering with University of Pittsburgh, Penn State University, The Catholic University of America; nursing with Carlow University.

Computers: 325 computers/terminals are available on campus for general student use. Students can access the following: campus intranet, computer help desk, free student e-mail accounts, online (class) grades, online (class) registration, online (class) schedules, program requirement evaluation. Campuswide network is available. 100% of college-owned or -operated housing units are wired for high-speed Internet access. Wireless service is available via entire campus.

Library: Latimer Family Library plus 1 other. *Books:* 266,710 (physical); *Serial titles:* 224 (physical). Weekly public service hours: 84.

STUDENT LIFE

Housing options: coed. Campus housing is university owned. Freshman applicants given priority for college housing.

Activities and organizations: drama/theater group, student-run newspaper, choral group, marching band, Activities Programming Board, Orientation Committee, Campus Ministry, Visionaries of Hope.

Athletics Member NCAA. All Division III. ***Intercollegiate sports:*** baseball M, basketball M/W, bowling W, cheerleading W(c), cross-country running M/W, equestrian sports M(c)/W(c), fencing M(c)/W(c), football M, golf M/W, ice hockey M(c), lacrosse M/W, rugby M(c)/W(c), soccer M/W, softball W, swimming and diving M/W, tennis M/W, track and field M/W, volleyball M/W. ***Intramural sports:*** basketball M/W, football M/W, ultimate Frisbee M/W, volleyball M/W.

Campus security: 24-hour emergency response devices and patrols, late-night transport/escort service, controlled dormitory access.

Student services: health clinic, personal/psychological counseling.

COSTS & FINANCIAL AID

Costs (2018–19) ***Comprehensive fee:*** $47,344 includes full-time tuition ($34,520), mandatory fees ($1354), and room and board ($11,470). Full-time tuition and fees vary according to course load and degree level. Part-time tuition: $1080 per credit hour. Part-time tuition and fees vary according to course load and degree level. ***Room and board:*** Room and board charges vary according to board plan and housing facility. ***Payment plan:*** installment. ***Waivers:*** employees or children of employees.

Financial Aid Of all full-time matriculated undergraduates who enrolled in 2018, 1,339 applied for aid, 1,234 were judged to have need, 265 had their need fully met. In 2018, 326 non-need-based awards were made. ***Average percent of need met:*** 79. ***Average financial aid package:*** $31,951. ***Average need-based loan:*** $4362. ***Average need-based gift aid:*** $7209. ***Average non-need-based aid:*** $19,745. ***Average indebtedness upon graduation:*** $37,307.

APPLYING

Standardized Tests *Required:* SAT or ACT (for admission).

Options: early admission, deferred entrance.

Application fee: $25.

Required: essay or personal statement, high school transcript, minimum 2.5 GPA. ***Recommended:*** minimum 3.2 GPA, 3 letters of recommendation, interview.

Application deadlines: 5/1 (freshmen), 7/1 (transfers).

Notification: continuous until 10/1 (freshmen), continuous until 12/1 (transfers).

CONTACT

Ms. Heather Kabala, Dean of Admission, Saint Vincent College, 300 Fraser Purchase Road, Latrobe, PA 15650-2690. *Phone:* 800-782-5549. *Toll-free phone:* 800-782-5549. *Fax:* 724-532-5069. *E-mail:* admission@stvincent.edu.

See below for display ad and page 1106 for the College Close-Up.

The $45 million Sis and Herman Dupré Science Pavilion added the James F. Will Engineering and Biomedical Sciences Hall in 2017.

Seton Hill University
Greensburg, Pennsylvania
http://www.setonhill.edu/

- **Independent Roman Catholic** comprehensive, founded 1883
- **Small-town** 200-acre campus with easy access to Pittsburgh
- **Coed** 1,710 undergraduate students, 93% full-time, 64% women, 36% men
- **Moderately difficult** entrance level, 75% of applicants were admitted

UNDERGRAD STUDENTS
1,592 full-time, 118 part-time. Students come from 31 states and territories; 23 other countries; 23% are from out of state; 9% Black or African American, non-Hispanic/Latino; 4% Hispanic/Latino; 1% Asian, non-Hispanic/Latino; 0.3% Native Hawaiian or other Pacific Islander, non-Hispanic/Latino; 0.3% American Indian or Alaska Native, non-Hispanic/Latino; 3% Two or more races, non-Hispanic/Latino; 0.5% Race/ethnicity unknown; 2% international; 4% transferred in; 47% live on campus.

Freshmen:
Admission: 2,471 applied, 1,853 admitted, 386 enrolled. ***Average high school GPA:*** 3.7. ***Test scores:*** SAT evidence-based reading and writing scores over 500: 82%; SAT math scores over 500: 78%; ACT scores over 18: 96%; SAT evidence-based reading and writing scores over 600: 39%; SAT math scores over 600: 32%; ACT scores over 24: 53%; SAT evidence-based reading and writing scores over 700: 3%; SAT math scores over 700: 4%; ACT scores over 30: 12%.

Retention: 82% of full-time freshmen returned.

FACULTY
Total: 211, 47% full-time, 62% with terminal degrees.

Student/faculty ratio: 14:1.

ACADEMICS
Calendar: semesters. *Degrees:* certificates, bachelor's, master's, and postbachelor's certificates.

Special study options: academic remediation for entering students, adult/continuing education programs, advanced placement credit, distance learning, double majors, English as a second language, honors programs, independent study, internships, off-campus study, part-time degree program, services for LD students, student-designed majors, study abroad, summer session for credit. ***ROTC:*** Army (c).

Unusual degree programs: 3-2 engineering with University of Pittsburgh, Penn State University Park, Georgia Institute of Technology; physician assistant with Seton Hill University, osteopathic medicine or pharmacy with Lake Erie College of Osteopathic Medicine.

Computers: 66 computers/terminals and 66 ports are available on campus for general student use. Students can access the following: campus intranet, computer help desk, free student e-mail accounts, online (class) grades, online (class) registration, online (class) schedules. Campuswide network is available. 100% of college-owned or -operated housing units are wired for high-speed Internet access. Wireless service is available via entire campus.

Library: Reeves Memorial Library. *Books:* 72,274 (physical), 127,160 (digital/electronic); *Serial titles:* 2,919 (physical); *Databases:* 37. Students can reserve study rooms.

STUDENT LIFE
Housing options: on-campus residence required through junior year; coed. Campus housing is university owned. Freshman campus housing is guaranteed.

Activities and organizations: drama/theater group, student-run newspaper, choral group, marching band, Student Body Activities Council, Future Greek leaders, Dietetics Club, Biology Club, intramurals.

Athletics Member NCAA. All Division II except golf (Division I). ***Intercollegiate sports:*** baseball M(s), basketball M(s)/W(s), cross-country running M(s)/W(s), equestrian sports W(s), field hockey W(s), football M(s), golf W(s), lacrosse M(s)/W(s), soccer M(s)/W(s), softball W(s), tennis W(s), track and field M(s)/W(s), volleyball W(s), wrestling M(s).

Campus security: 24-hour emergency response devices and patrols, late-night transport/escort service, controlled dormitory access.

Student services: health clinic, personal/psychological counseling.

COSTS & FINANCIAL AID
Costs (2019–20) ***Comprehensive fee:*** $49,068 includes full-time tuition ($36,306), mandatory fees ($550), and room and board ($12,212). Part-time tuition: $974. ***College room only:*** $6700.

Financial Aid Of all full-time matriculated undergraduates who enrolled in 2017, 1,412 applied for aid, 1,279 were judged to have need, 252 had their need fully met. In 2017, 256 non-need-based awards were made. ***Average percent of need met:*** 74. ***Average financial aid package:*** $26,634. ***Average need-based loan:*** $6502. ***Average need-based gift aid:*** $21,314. ***Average non-need-based aid:*** $16,077. ***Average indebtedness upon graduation:*** $35,356.

APPLYING
Standardized Tests *Recommended:* SAT or ACT (for admission).

Options: electronic application, deferred entrance.

Application fee: $35.

Required: essay or personal statement, high school transcript, 1 letter of recommendation. ***Required for some:*** portfolio for art, audition for music and theatre. ***Recommended:*** interview.

Application deadlines: 8/15 (freshmen), 8/15 (transfers).

Notification: continuous (freshmen), continuous (transfers).

CONTACT
Mrs. Allison Sasso, Director of Admissions, Seton Hill University, 1 Seton Hill Drive, Greensburg, PA 15601. *Phone:* 724-838-4231. *Toll-free phone:* 800-826-6234. *E-mail:* admit@setonhill.edu.

Shippensburg University of Pennsylvania
Shippensburg, Pennsylvania
http://www.ship.edu/

- **State-supported** comprehensive, founded 1871, part of Pennsylvania State System of Higher Education
- **Rural** 200-acre campus
- **Endowment** $38.9 million
- **Coed**
- 84% of applicants were admitted

FACULTY
Student/faculty ratio: 19:1.

ACADEMICS
Calendar: semesters. *Degrees:* certificates, bachelor's, master's, doctoral, post-master's, and postbachelor's certificates.
Library: Ezra Lehman Memorial Library plus 1 other. *Books:* 359,138 (physical), 189,092 (digital/electronic); *Serial titles:* 50 (physical), 255 (digital/electronic); *Databases:* 106. Weekly public service hours: 97.

STUDENT LIFE
Housing options: on-campus residence required for freshman year; coed. Campus housing is provided by a third party. Freshman campus housing is guaranteed.

Activities and organizations: drama/theater group, student-run newspaper, radio and television station, choral group, marching band, national fraternities, national sororities.

Athletics Member NCAA. All Division II.

Campus security: 24-hour emergency response devices and patrols, late-night transport/escort service, controlled dormitory access, surveillance cameras in certain parking lots and buildings; foot, vehicular and bicycle patrols by security officers.

Student services: health clinic, personal/psychological counseling, women's center, veterans affairs office.

COSTS & FINANCIAL AID
Costs (2018–19) ***Tuition:*** state resident $9570 full-time, $319 per credit hour part-time; nonresident $17,362 full-time, $725 per credit hour part-time. Full-time tuition and fees vary according to course load and location. Part-time tuition and fees vary according to course load and location. ***Required fees:*** $3148 full-time, $131 per credit hour part-time. ***Room and board:*** $12,268; room only: $8038. Room and board charges vary according to board plan and housing facility.

Financial Aid Of all full-time matriculated undergraduates who enrolled in 2018, 4,382 applied for aid, 3,566 were judged to have need, 396 had their need fully met. 128 Federal Work-Study jobs (averaging $1336). 608 state and other part-time jobs (averaging $1940). In 2018, 425 non-need-based awards were made. ***Average percent of need met:*** 55. ***Average financial aid package:*** $9929. ***Average need-based loan:*** $4010. ***Average need-based gift aid:*** $7541. ***Average non-need-based aid:*** $5455. ***Average indebtedness upon graduation:*** $34,162.

APPLYING
Standardized Tests *Required:* SAT or ACT (for admission).
Options: electronic application, early admission, early action, deferred entrance.
Application fee: $45.
Required: high school transcript. ***Required for some:*** interview. ***Recommended:*** essay or personal statement, class rank, letters of recommendation.

CONTACT
Mr. William H. Washabaugh, Associate Dean of Admissions, Shippensburg University of Pennsylvania, 1871 Old Main Drive, Shippensburg, PA 17257-2299. *Phone:* 717-477-1231. *Toll-free phone:* 800-822-8028. *Fax:* 717-477-4016. *E-mail:* admiss@ship.edu.

Slippery Rock University of Pennsylvania

Slippery Rock, Pennsylvania

http://www.sru.edu/

- **State-supported** university, founded 1889, part of Pennsylvania State System of Higher Education
- **Small-town** 660-acre campus with easy access to Pittsburgh
- **Endowment** $30.6 million
- **Coed**
- **Moderately difficult** entrance level

FACULTY
Student/faculty ratio: 21:1.

ACADEMICS
Calendar: semesters. *Degrees:* certificates, bachelor's, master's, doctoral, and postbachelor's certificates.
Library: Bailey Library. *Books:* 282,009 (physical), 286,118 (digital/electronic); *Serial titles:* 248 (physical), 49,191 (digital/electronic); *Databases:* 134. Weekly public service hours: 98; students can reserve study rooms.

STUDENT LIFE
Housing options: on-campus residence required for freshman year; coed, special housing for students with disabilities. Campus housing is university owned. Freshman campus housing is guaranteed.
Activities and organizations: drama/theater group, student-run newspaper, radio and television station, choral group, marching band, University Program Board, Interfraternity Council/Panhellenic Council, State Government Association, Black Action Society, Gamer's Guild, national fraternities, national sororities.
Athletics Member NCAA. All Division II.
Campus security: 24-hour emergency response devices and patrols, late-night transport/escort service, controlled dormitory access.
Student services: health clinic, personal/psychological counseling, women's center, legal services, veterans affairs office.

COSTS & FINANCIAL AID
Costs (2018–19) ***Tuition:*** state resident $7716 full-time, $322 per credit hour part-time; nonresident $15,432 full-time, $644 per credit hour part-time. Full-time tuition and fees vary according to course load. Part-time tuition and fees vary according to course load. ***Required fees:*** $2790 full-time, $115 per credit hour part-time. ***Room and board:*** $10,446; room only: $6876. Room and board charges vary according to board plan and housing facility.
Financial Aid Of all full-time matriculated undergraduates who enrolled in 2018, 6,134 applied for aid, 4,911 were judged to have need, 418 had their need fully met. 526 Federal Work-Study jobs (averaging $1540). 946 state and other part-time jobs (averaging $1922). In 2018, 588 non-need-based awards were made. ***Average percent of need met:*** 57. ***Average financial aid package:*** $9246. ***Average need-based loan:*** $4222. ***Average need-based gift aid:*** $5939. ***Average non-need-based aid:*** $2867. ***Average indebtedness upon graduation:*** $35,322.

APPLYING
Standardized Tests *Required:* SAT or ACT (for admission).
Options: electronic application, deferred entrance.
Application fee: $30.
Required: high school transcript. ***Recommended:*** minimum 3.0 GPA.

CONTACT
Slippery Rock University of Pennsylvania, 1 Morrow Way, Slippery Rock, PA 16057-1383. *Phone:* 724-738-2015. *Toll-free phone:* 800-SRU-9111.

Strayer University–Allentown Campus

Allentown, Pennsylvania

http://www.strayer.edu/pennsylvania/allentown/

CONTACT
Strayer University–Allentown Campus, 520 Hamilton Street, Suite 100, Allentown, PA 18101-1502. *Toll-free phone:* 888-311-0355.

Strayer University–Center City Campus

Philadelphia, Pennsylvania

http://www.strayer.edu/pennsylvania/center-city/

CONTACT
Strayer University–Center City Campus, 1601 Cherry Street, Suite 100, Philadelphia, PA 19102. *Toll-free phone:* 888-311-0355.

Strayer University–Delaware County Campus

Springfield, Pennsylvania

http://www.strayer.edu/pennsylvania/delaware-county/

CONTACT
Strayer University–Delaware County Campus, 760 West Sproul Road, Suite 200, Springfield, PA 19064. *Toll-free phone:* 888-311-0355.

Strayer University–Lower Bucks County Campus

Trevose, Pennsylvania

http://www.strayer.edu/pennsylvania/lower-bucks-county/

CONTACT
Strayer University–Lower Bucks County Campus, 3800 Horizon Boulevard, Suite 100, Trevose, PA 19053. *Toll-free phone:* 888-311-0355.

Strayer University–Warrendale Campus

Warrendale, Pennsylvania

http://www.strayer.edu/pennsylvania/warrendale/

CONTACT
Strayer University–Warrendale Campus, 802 Warrendale Village Drive, Warrendale, PA 15086. *Toll-free phone:* 888-311-0355.

Susquehanna University

Selinsgrove, Pennsylvania

http://www.susqu.edu/

- **Independent** 4-year, founded 1858, affiliated with Evangelical Lutheran Church in America
- **Small-town** 325-acre campus
- **Endowment** $143.2 million
- **Coed**
- **Moderately difficult** entrance level

FACULTY
Student/faculty ratio: 12:1.

ACADEMICS
Calendar: semesters. *Degrees:* bachelor's (also offers evening associate degree program limited to local adult students).
Library: Blough-Weis Library. *Books:* 161,900 (physical), 370,171 (digital/electronic); *Serial titles:* 612 (physical), 94,180 (digital/electronic); *Databases:* 137. Weekly public service hours: 106; students can reserve study rooms.

STUDENT LIFE
Housing options: on-campus residence required through senior year; coed. Campus housing is university owned. Freshman campus housing is guaranteed.

Activities and organizations: drama/theater group, student-run newspaper, radio station, choral group, Student Government Association, Alpha Phi Omega, Student Activities Committee, SU Dance Corps, Intramural Sports, national fraternities, national sororities.

Athletics Member NCAA. All Division III.

Campus security: 24-hour emergency response devices and patrols, late-night transport/escort service, controlled dormitory access.

Student services: health clinic, personal/psychological counseling, women's center.

COSTS & FINANCIAL AID
Costs (2018–19) ***Comprehensive fee:*** $59,920 includes full-time tuition ($46,690), mandatory fees ($600), and room and board ($12,630). Part-time tuition: $1485 per credit hour. ***College room only:*** $6630. Room and board charges vary according to board plan. ***Payment plans:*** tuition prepayment, installment.

Financial Aid Of all full-time matriculated undergraduates who enrolled in 2017, 1,961 applied for aid, 1,796 were judged to have need, 324 had their need fully met. 1,265 Federal Work-Study jobs (averaging $2023). In 2017, 456 non-need-based awards were made. ***Average percent of need met:*** 82. ***Average financial aid package:*** $36,552. ***Average need-based loan:*** $4314. ***Average need-based gift aid:*** $31,799. ***Average non-need-based aid:*** $22,119. ***Average indebtedness upon graduation:*** $33,757. ***Financial aid deadline:*** 2/1.

APPLYING
Options: electronic application, early admission, early decision, early action, deferred entrance.

Required: essay or personal statement, high school transcript, minimum 2.5 GPA, 1 letter of recommendation. ***Required for some:*** writing portfolio, audition for music programs. ***Recommended:*** minimum 3.0 GPA, interview.

CONTACT
Mr. Philip Betz, Director of Admissions, Susquehanna University, 514 University Avenue, Selinsgrove, PA 17870. *Phone:* 570-372-4260. *Toll-free phone:* 800-326-9672. *Fax:* 570-372-2722. *E-mail:* suadmiss@susqu.edu.

Swarthmore College
Swarthmore, Pennsylvania
http://www.swarthmore.edu/

- **Independent** 4-year, founded 1864
- **Suburban** 425-acre campus with easy access to Philadelphia
- **Endowment** $1.7 million
- **Coed**
- 11% of applicants were admitted

FACULTY
Student/faculty ratio: 8:1.

ACADEMICS
Calendar: semesters. *Degree:* bachelor's.
Library: McCabe Library plus 6 others.

STUDENT LIFE
Housing options: on-campus residence required for freshman year; coed, men-only, women-only, special housing for students with disabilities. Campus housing is university owned. Freshman campus housing is guaranteed.

Activities and organizations: drama/theater group, student-run newspaper, radio station, choral group, Boy Meets Tractor (sketch comedy troupe), Rhythm N' Motion (performing dance styles of the African Diaspora), Multi (community for people who self-identify as multiracial, multiethnic, multicultural, and/or multireligious), Mixed Company (a cappella group), national fraternities, national sororities.

Athletics Member NCAA. All Division III.

Campus security: 24-hour emergency response devices and patrols, late-night transport/escort service.

Student services: health clinic, personal/psychological counseling, women's center.

COSTS & FINANCIAL AID
Costs (2018–19) ***Comprehensive fee:*** $68,062 includes full-time tuition ($52,190), mandatory fees ($398), and room and board ($15,474). ***Room and board:*** Room and board charges vary according to board plan.

Financial Aid Of all full-time matriculated undergraduates who enrolled in 2018, 998 applied for aid, 906 were judged to have need, 906 had their need fully met. 777 Federal Work-Study jobs (averaging $2026). In 2018, 18 non-need-based awards were made. ***Average percent of need met:*** 100. ***Average financial aid package:*** $52,814. ***Average need-based gift aid:*** $51,079. ***Average non-need-based aid:*** $49,707. ***Average indebtedness upon graduation:*** $22,060. ***Financial aid deadline:*** 1/1.

APPLYING
Standardized Tests *Required:* SAT or ACT (for admission).

Options: early admission, early decision, deferred entrance.

Application fee: $60.

Required: essay or personal statement, high school transcript, 3 letters of recommendation.

CONTACT
Swarthmore College, 500 College Avenue, Swarthmore, PA 19081-1397. *Toll-free phone:* 800-667-3110.

Talmudical Yeshiva of Philadelphia
Philadelphia, Pennsylvania

CONTACT
Rabbi Shmuel Kamenetsky, Co-Dean, Talmudical Yeshiva of Philadelphia, 6063 Drexel Road, Philadelphia, PA 19131-1296. *Phone:* 215-473-1212.

★ Temple University
Philadelphia, Pennsylvania
http://www.temple.edu/

- **State-related** university, founded 1884, part of Commonwealth System of Higher Education
- **Urban** 390-acre campus with easy access to Philadelphia
- **Endowment** $615.4 million
- **Coed** 29,484 undergraduate students, 91% full-time, 53% women, 47% men
- **Moderately difficult** entrance level, 59% of applicants were admitted

UNDERGRAD STUDENTS
26,784 full-time, 2,700 part-time. Students come from 50 states and territories; 125 other countries; 21% are from out of state; 13% Black or African American, non-Hispanic/Latino; 7% Hispanic/Latino; 12% Asian, non-Hispanic/Latino; 0.1% Native Hawaiian or other Pacific Islander, non-Hispanic/Latino; 0.1% American Indian or Alaska Native, non-Hispanic/Latino; 3% Two or more races, non-Hispanic/Latino; 3% Race/ethnicity unknown; 6% international; 8% transferred in; 20% live on campus.

Freshmen:
Admission: 35,501 applied, 20,771 admitted, 5,030 enrolled. ***Average high school GPA:*** 3.6. ***Test scores:*** SAT evidence-based reading and writing scores over 500: 98%; SAT math scores over 500: 97%; ACT scores over 18: 99%; SAT evidence-based reading and writing scores over 600: 66%; SAT math scores over 600: 58%; ACT scores over 24: 81%; SAT evidence-based reading and writing scores over 700: 12%; SAT math scores over 700: 15%; ACT scores over 30: 31%.

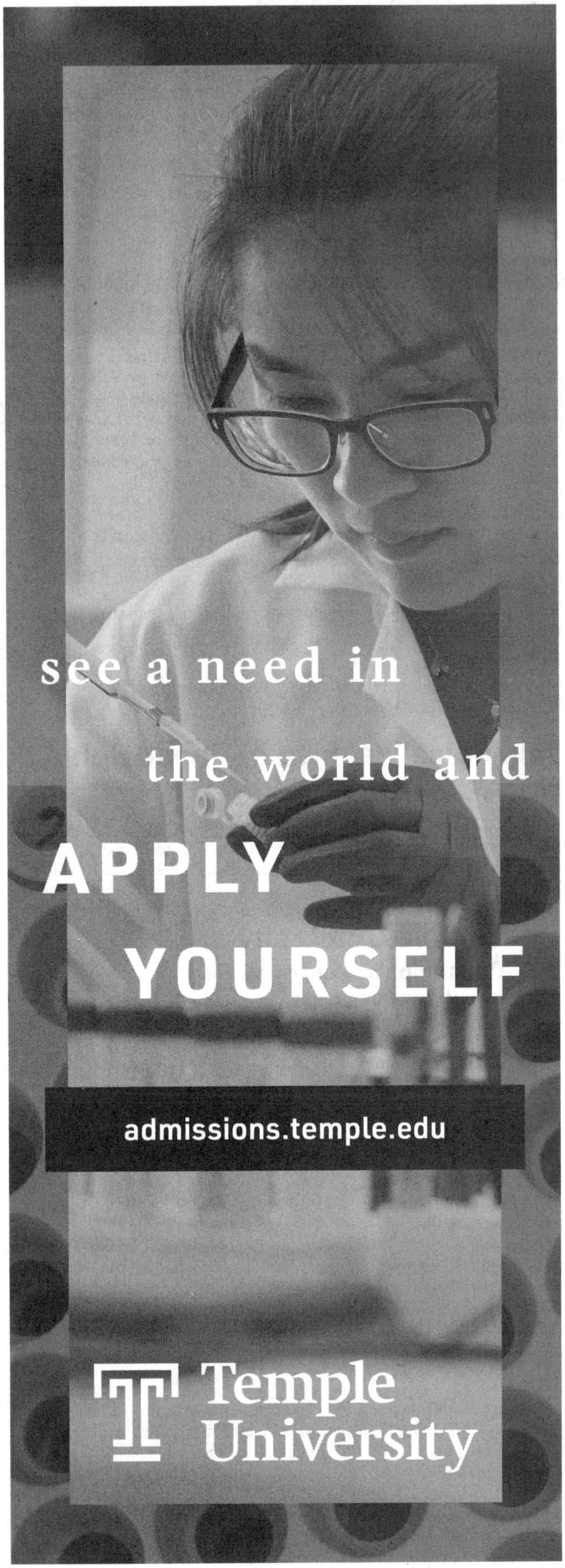
see a need in
the world and
APPLY
YOURSELF
admissions.temple.edu
Temple
University

Retention: 89% of full-time freshmen returned.

FACULTY
Total: 2,874, 55% full-time.

Student/faculty ratio: 14:1.

ACADEMICS
Calendar: semesters. *Degrees:* certificates, diplomas, associate, bachelor's, master's, doctoral, post-master's, and postbachelor's certificates.

Special study options: academic remediation for entering students, accelerated degree program, adult/continuing education programs, advanced placement credit, cooperative education, distance learning, double majors, English as a second language, honors programs, independent study, internships, off-campus study, part-time degree program, services for LD students, study abroad, summer session for credit. ***ROTC:*** Army (b), Navy (c), Air Force (c).

Computers: 15,100 computers/terminals and 49,661 ports are available on campus for general student use. Students can access the following: campus intranet, computer help desk, free student e-mail accounts, online (class) grades, online (class) registration, online (class) schedules, student accounts, Web hosting. Campuswide network is available. 100% of college-owned or -operated housing units are wired for high-speed Internet access. Wireless service is available via entire campus.
Library: Paley Library plus 6 others. *Books:* 3.4 million (physical), 1.6 million (digital/electronic); *Serial titles:* 61,478 (physical), 189,776 (digital/electronic); *Databases:* 773. Students can reserve study rooms.

STUDENT LIFE
Housing options: coed, special housing for students with disabilities. Campus housing is university owned, leased by the school and is provided by a third party.

Activities and organizations: drama/theater group, student-run newspaper, radio and television station, choral group, marching band, Queer Student Union, Habitat for Humanity, Temple University Community Service Association, Gamers Guild, Feminist Alliance, national fraternities, national sororities.

Athletics Member NCAA. All Division I except football (Division I-A). ***Intercollegiate sports:*** basketball M(s)/W(s), crew M(s)/W(s), cross-country running M(s)/W(s), fencing W(s), field hockey W(s), golf M(s), gymnastics W(s), lacrosse W(s), soccer M(s)/W(s), tennis M(s)/W(s), track and field W(s), volleyball W(s). ***Intramural sports:*** badminton M(c)/W(c), baseball M(c), basketball M/W, bowling M(c)/W(c), equestrian sports M(c)/W(c), fencing M(c)/W(c), field hockey W(c), football M/W, gymnastics M(c)/W(c), ice hockey M(c), lacrosse M(c)/W(c), racquetball M(c)/W(c), rugby M(c)/W(c), soccer M/W, softball M/W, swimming and diving M(c)/W(c), tennis M(c)/W(c), track and field M(c)/W(c), ultimate Frisbee M(c)/W(c), volleyball M/W, weight lifting M(c)/W(c), wrestling M(c).

Campus security: 24-hour emergency response devices and patrols, student patrols, late-night transport/escort service, controlled dormitory access.

Student services: health clinic, personal/psychological counseling, women's center, legal services, veterans affairs office.

COSTS & FINANCIAL AID
Costs (2018–19) ***Tuition:*** state resident $16,080 full-time, $670 per credit hour part-time; nonresident $28,176 full-time, $1174 per credit hour part-time. Full-time tuition and fees vary according to course load and program. Part-time tuition and fees vary according to course load and program. ***Required fees:*** $890 full-time, $163 per term part-time. ***Room and board:*** $11,916; room only: $8004. Room and board charges vary according to board plan, housing facility, and location. ***Payment plans:*** installment, deferred payment. ***Waivers:*** employees or children of employees.

Financial Aid Of all full-time matriculated undergraduates who enrolled in 2017, 20,721 applied for aid, 17,962 were judged to have need, 554 had their need fully met. 1,264 Federal Work-Study jobs (averaging $1465). In 2017, 3558 non-need-based awards were made. ***Average percent of need met:*** 62. ***Average financial aid package:*** $12,383. ***Average need-based loan:*** $4539. ***Average need-based gift aid:*** $9352. ***Average non-need-based aid:*** $8194. ***Average indebtedness upon graduation:*** $38,519.

APPLYING
Options: electronic application, early action, deferred entrance.

Application fee: $55.

Required: essay or personal statement, high school transcript. ***Recommended:*** minimum 3.0 GPA, 1 letter of recommendation.

Notification: continuous (freshmen), continuous (transfers).

CONTACT
Ms. Karin Mormando, Director, Undergraduate Admissions, Temple University, 1801 North Broad Street, Philadelphia, PA 19122-6096. *Phone:* 215-204-7200. *Toll-free phone:* 888-340-2222. *E-mail:* tuadm@temple.edu.

See previous page for display ad and page 1122 for the College Close-Up.

Thiel College

Greenville, Pennsylvania

http://www.thiel.edu/

CONTACT
Mr. Stephen Lazowski, Vice President for Enrollment Management, Thiel College, 75 College Avenue, Greenville, PA 16125. *Phone:* 724-589-2182. *Toll-free phone:* 800-248-4435. *Fax:* 724-589-2013. *E-mail:* admissions@thiel.edu.

Thomas Jefferson University

Philadelphia, Pennsylvania

http://www.jefferson.edu/university.html

- **Independent** university, founded 1824
- **Urban** 13-acre campus
- **Coed**
- **Moderately difficult** entrance level

FACULTY
Student/faculty ratio: 15:1.

ACADEMICS
Calendar: semesters. *Degrees:* associate, bachelor's, master's, doctoral, and postbachelor's certificates.

Library: Scott Memorial Library plus 1 other. Study areas open 24 hours, 5–7 days a week; students can reserve study rooms.

STUDENT LIFE
Housing options: coed, men-only, women-only. Campus housing is university owned and is provided by a third party. Freshman campus housing is guaranteed.

Activities and organizations: choral group.

Campus security: 24-hour emergency response devices and patrols, late-night transport/escort service, controlled dormitory access.

Student services: health clinic, personal/psychological counseling.

COSTS & FINANCIAL AID
Costs (2018–19) ***Comprehensive fee:*** $53,966 includes full-time tuition ($39,495), mandatory fees ($1006), and room and board ($13,465). Full-time tuition and fees vary according to degree level and location. Part-time tuition: $605 per credit hour. Part-time tuition and fees vary according to class time and degree level. ***Required fees:*** $30 per credit hour part-time. ***College room only:*** $6295. Room and board charges vary according to board plan, housing facility, and location.

Financial Aid Of all full-time matriculated undergraduates who enrolled in 2017, 2,108 applied for aid, 1,904 were judged to have need, 293 had their need fully met. In 2017, 334 non-need-based awards were made. ***Average percent of need met:*** 72. ***Average financial aid package:*** $29,481. ***Average need-based loan:*** $4370. ***Average need-based gift aid:*** $24,155. ***Average non-need-based aid:*** $12,646. ***Average indebtedness upon graduation:*** $40,100. ***Financial aid deadline:*** 4/15.

APPLYING
Standardized Tests *Required for some:* NET. *Recommended:* SAT or ACT (for admission).

Options: deferred entrance.

Application fee: $50.

Required: essay or personal statement, minimum 3.0 GPA, 2 letters of recommendation, interview. ***Required for some:*** high school transcript.

CONTACT
Ms. Karen Jacobs, Director of Admissions, Thomas Jefferson University, Edison Building, 130 South Ninth Street, Philadelphia, PA 19107. *Phone:* 215-503-8890. *Toll-free phone:* 877-533-3247. *Fax:* 215-503-7241. *E-mail:* chpadmissions@mail.tju.edu.

See next page for display ad and page 1124 for the College Close-Up.

University of Pennsylvania

Philadelphia, Pennsylvania

http://www.upenn.edu/

- **Independent** university, founded 1740
- **Urban** 299-acre campus
- **Endowment** $12.2 billion
- **Coed** 10,183 undergraduate students, 98% full-time, 52% women, 48% men
- **Most difficult** entrance level, 8% of applicants were admitted

UNDERGRAD STUDENTS
9,931 full-time, 252 part-time. 81% are from out of state; 7% Black or African American, non-Hispanic/Latino; 10% Hispanic/Latino; 21% Asian, non-Hispanic/Latino; 0.1% Native Hawaiian or other Pacific Islander, non-Hispanic/Latino; 0.1% American Indian or Alaska Native, non-Hispanic/Latino; 5% Two or more races, non-Hispanic/Latino; 2% Race/ethnicity unknown; 13% international; 1% transferred in; 51% live on campus.

Freshmen:
Admission: 44,491 applied, 3,740 admitted, 2,457 enrolled. ***Average high school GPA:*** 3.9. ***Test scores:*** SAT evidence-based reading and writing scores over 500: 100%; SAT math scores over 500: 100%; ACT scores over 18: 100%; SAT evidence-based reading and writing scores over 600: 99%; SAT math scores over 600: 99%; ACT scores over 24: 100%; SAT evidence-based reading and writing scores over 700: 75%; SAT math scores over 700: 89%; ACT scores over 30: 94%.

Retention: 98% of full-time freshmen returned.

FACULTY
Total: 2,039, 77% full-time, 100% with terminal degrees.

Student/faculty ratio: 6:1.

ACADEMICS
Calendar: semesters plus 2 5-week summer sessions. *Degrees:* certificates, associate, bachelor's, master's, doctoral, post-master's, and postbachelor's certificates (also offers evening program with significant enrollment not reflected in profile).

Special study options: academic remediation for entering students, accelerated degree program, adult/continuing education programs, advanced placement credit, cooperative education, distance learning, double majors, English as a second language, honors programs, independent study, internships, off-campus study, part-time degree program, services for LD students, student-designed majors, study abroad, summer session for credit. ***ROTC:*** Army (c), Navy (b), Air Force (c).

Computers: Students can access the following: campus intranet, computer help desk, free student e-mail accounts, online (class) grades, online (class) registration, online (class) schedules, billing information, financial aid application, status, academic records, student services. Campuswide network is available. 100% of college-owned or -operated housing units are wired for high-speed Internet access. Wireless service is available via entire campus.

Library: Van Pelt Library plus 14 others. *Books:* 6.4 million (physical); *Serial titles:* 188,604 (physical). Study areas open 24 hours, 5–7 days a week; students can reserve study rooms.

STUDENT LIFE
Housing options: coed, special housing for students with disabilities. Campus housing is university owned. Freshman campus housing is guaranteed.

Activities and organizations: drama/theater group, student-run newspaper, radio and television station, choral group, marching band, Kite and Key Society, Social Planning and Events Committee, Hillel at Penn, Sports Club Council, Interfraternity Council, national fraternities, national sororities.

Athletics Member NCAA. All Division I except football (Division I-AA). ***Intercollegiate sports:*** baseball M, basketball M/W, crew M/W, cross-country running M/W, fencing M/W, field hockey W, golf M/W(c), gymnastics W, lacrosse M/W, soccer M/W, softball W, squash M/W, swimming and diving M/W, tennis M/W, track and field M/W, volleyball W, wrestling M. ***Intramural sports:*** badminton M(c)/W(c), baseball M(c)/W(c), basketball M(c)/W(c), cheerleading M/W, equestrian sports M(c)/W(c), fencing W(c), field hockey M(c), golf M(c)/W(c), gymnastics M(c)/W(c), ice hockey M(c)/W(c), lacrosse M/W, rugby M(c)/W(c), sailing M(c)/W(c), skiing (downhill) M(c)/W(c), soccer M/W, softball M/W, squash M/W, swimming and diving M/W, table tennis M/W, tennis M/W, ultimate Frisbee M(c)/W(c), volleyball M/W, water polo M(c)/W(c).

Campus security: 24-hour emergency response devices and patrols, late-night transport/escort service, controlled dormitory access.

Student services: health clinic, personal/psychological counseling, women's center, legal services.

COSTS & FINANCIAL AID

Costs (2019–20) ***Comprehensive fee:*** $73,960 includes full-time tuition ($51,156), mandatory fees ($6614), and room and board ($16,190). ***College room only:*** $10,600. ***Payment plan:*** tuition prepayment.

Financial Aid Of all full-time matriculated undergraduates who enrolled in 2017, 4,882 applied for aid, 4,517 were judged to have need, 4,517 had their need fully met. ***Average percent of need met:*** 100. ***Average financial aid package:*** $51,860. ***Average need-based loan:*** $3783. ***Average need-based gift aid:*** $48,787. ***Average indebtedness upon graduation:*** $22,103.

APPLYING

Standardized Tests *Required:* SAT or ACT (for admission). *Recommended:* SAT Subject Tests (for admission).

Options: electronic application, early admission, early decision, deferred entrance.

Application fee: $75.

Required: essay or personal statement, high school transcript, 2 letters of recommendation.

Application deadlines: 1/5 (freshmen), 3/15 (transfers).

Early decision deadline: 11/1.

Notification: continuous until 4/1 (freshmen), 5/15 (transfers), 12/15 (early decision).

CONTACT

Eric J. Furda, Dean of Admissions, University of Pennsylvania, 3451 Walnut Street, Philadelphia, PA 19104. *Phone:* 215-898-7507. *E-mail:* info@admissions.ugao.upenn.edu.

University of Pittsburgh

Pittsburgh, Pennsylvania

http://www.pitt.edu/

- **State-related** university, founded 1787, part of Commonwealth System of Higher Education
- **Urban** 145-acre campus with easy access to Pittsburgh
- **Endowment** $4.2 billion
- **Coed** 19,330 undergraduate students, 95% full-time, 52% women, 48% men
- **Very difficult** entrance level, 59% of applicants were admitted

UNDERGRAD STUDENTS

18,421 full-time, 909 part-time. Students come from 51 states and territories; 55 other countries; 27% are from out of state; 5% Black or African American, non-Hispanic/Latino; 4% Hispanic/Latino; 10% Asian, non-Hispanic/Latino; 0.1% American Indian or Alaska Native, non-Hispanic/Latino; 4% Two or more races, non-Hispanic/Latino; 1% Race/ethnicity unknown; 5% international; 4% transferred in; 43% live on campus.

Freshmen:

Admission: 29,857 applied, 17,696 admitted, 4,126 enrolled. ***Average high school GPA:*** 4.1. ***Test scores:*** SAT evidence-based reading and writing scores over 500: 99%; SAT math scores over 500: 99%; ACT scores over 18: 99%; SAT evidence-based reading and writing scores over 600: 91%; SAT math scores over 600: 90%; ACT scores over 24: 98%; SAT evidence-based reading and writing scores over 700: 28%; SAT math scores over 700: 42%; ACT scores over 30: 57%.

Retention: 93% of full-time freshmen returned.

FACULTY
Total: 2,339, 77% full-time.

Student/faculty ratio: 14:1.

ACADEMICS
Calendar: semesters plus summer term. *Degrees:* certificates, bachelor's, master's, doctoral, post-master's, and postbachelor's certificates.

Special study options: academic remediation for entering students, accelerated degree program, adult/continuing education programs, advanced placement credit, cooperative education, distance learning, double majors, English as a second language, external degree program, freshman honors college, honors programs, independent study, internships, off-campus study, part-time degree program, services for LD students, student-designed majors, study abroad, summer session for credit. ***ROTC:*** Army (b), Navy (c), Air Force (b).

Unusual degree programs: 3-2 engineering; Computer Science BS/MS, Statistics BA/MA, BA in Legal Studies/Masters of Law.

Computers: 1,156 computers/terminals and 18,250 ports are available on campus for general student use. Students can access the following: campus intranet, computer help desk, free student e-mail accounts, online (class) grades, online (class) registration, online (class) schedules, online class listings, online tuition payment. Campuswide network is available. 100% of college-owned or -operated housing units are wired for high-speed Internet access. Wireless service is available via entire campus.

Library: Hillman Library plus 16 others. *Books:* 4.3 million (physical), 1.7 million (digital/electronic); *Serial titles:* 108,985 (physical), 261,311 (digital/electronic); *Databases:* 571. Weekly public service hours: 145; study areas open 24 hours, 5–7 days a week; students can reserve study rooms.

STUDENT LIFE
Housing options: coed, cooperative, special housing for students with disabilities. Campus housing is university owned. Freshman campus housing is guaranteed.

Activities and organizations: drama/theater group, student-run newspaper, radio and television station, choral group, marching band, Resident Student Association, Black Action Society, Pitt Program Council, Interfraternity Council, Panhellenic Association, national fraternities, national sororities.

Athletics Member NCAA. All Division I except football (Division I-A). ***Intercollegiate sports:*** baseball M(s), basketball M(s)/W(s), cross-country running M(s)/W(s), gymnastics W(s), soccer M(s)/W(s), softball W(s), swimming and diving M(s)/W(s), tennis W(s), track and field M(s)/W(s), volleyball W(s), wrestling M(s). ***Intramural sports:*** archery M(c)/W(c), badminton M/W, baseball M(c), basketball M/W, cross-country running M(c)/W(c), equestrian sports M(c)/W(c), fencing M(c)/W(c), field hockey M(c)/W(c), football M, golf M(c)/W(c), gymnastics M(c)/W(c), ice hockey M(c)/W(c), lacrosse M(c)/W(c), racquetball M(c)/W(c), rowing M(c)/W(c), rugby M(c)/W(c), sailing M(c)/W(c), skiing (downhill) M(c)/W(c), soccer M/W, softball W(c), squash M/W, swimming and diving M(c)/W(c), table tennis M/W, tennis M(c)/W(c), triathlon M(c)/W(c), ultimate Frisbee M/W, volleyball M/W, water polo M(c)/W(c), wrestling M(c)/W(c).

Campus security: 24-hour emergency response devices and patrols, late-night transport/escort service, controlled dormitory access.

Student services: health clinic, personal/psychological counseling, veterans affairs office.

COSTS & FINANCIAL AID
Costs (2018–19) ***Tuition:*** state resident $18,130 full-time, $755 per credit hour part-time; nonresident $31,102 full-time, $1295 per credit hour part-time. Full-time tuition and fees vary according to location and program. Part-time tuition and fees vary according to location and program. ***Required fees:*** $950 full-time, $279 per term part-time. ***Room and board:*** $11,050; room only: $6400. Room and board charges vary according to board plan, housing facility, and location. ***Payment plans:*** installment, deferred payment. ***Waivers:*** employees or children of employees.

Financial Aid Of all full-time matriculated undergraduates who enrolled in 2017, 12,456 applied for aid, 9,552 were judged to have need, 1,163 had their need fully met. In 2017, 608 non-need-based awards were made. ***Average percent of need met:*** 52. ***Average financial aid package:*** $12,078. ***Average need-based loan:*** $4589. ***Average need-based gift aid:*** $9903. ***Average non-need-based aid:*** $9558. ***Average indebtedness upon graduation:*** $39,462.

APPLYING
Standardized Tests *Required:* SAT or ACT (for admission).

Options: electronic application.

Application fee: $45.

Required: high school transcript. ***Recommended:*** essay or personal statement, interview.

Application deadlines: rolling (freshmen), rolling (transfers).

Notification: continuous (freshmen), continuous (transfers).

CONTACT
Marc L. Harding, Chief Enrollment Officer, University of Pittsburgh, 4227 Fifth Avenue, First Floor, Alumni Hall, Pittsburgh, PA 15260. *Phone:* 412-624-7488. *Fax:* 412-648-8815. *E-mail:* oafa@pitt.edu.

University of Pittsburgh at Bradford
Bradford, Pennsylvania
http://www.upb.pitt.edu/

- **State-related** 4-year, founded 1963, part of University of Pittsburgh System
- **Small-town** 317-acre campus with easy access to Buffalo
- **Endowment** $26.7 million
- **Coed** 1,293 undergraduate students, 94% full-time, 56% women, 44% men
- **Minimally difficult** entrance level, 51% of applicants were admitted

UNDERGRAD STUDENTS
1,210 full-time, 83 part-time. Students come from 30 states and territories; 13 other countries; 26% are from out of state; 13% Black or African American, non-Hispanic/Latino; 6% Hispanic/Latino; 3% Asian, non-Hispanic/Latino; 0.1% Native Hawaiian or other Pacific Islander, non-Hispanic/Latino; 0.5% American Indian or Alaska Native, non-Hispanic/Latino; 3% Two or more races, non-Hispanic/Latino; 6% Race/ethnicity unknown; 2% international; 8% transferred in; 72% live on campus.

Freshmen:

Admission: 3,135 applied, 1,602 admitted, 356 enrolled. ***Average high school GPA:*** 3.3. ***Test scores:*** SAT evidence-based reading and writing scores over 500: 73%; SAT math scores over 500: 74%; ACT scores over 18: 83%; SAT evidence-based reading and writing scores over 600: 22%; SAT math scores over 600: 19%; ACT scores over 24: 34%; SAT evidence-based reading and writing scores over 700: 1%; SAT math scores over 700: 3%; ACT scores over 30: 4%.

Retention: 68% of full-time freshmen returned.

FACULTY
Total: 149, 50% full-time, 40% with terminal degrees.

Student/faculty ratio: 16:1.

ACADEMICS
Calendar: semesters. *Degrees:* associate and bachelor's.

Special study options: academic remediation for entering students, accelerated degree program, adult/continuing education programs, advanced placement credit, cooperative education, distance learning, double majors, independent study, internships, off-campus study, part-time degree program, services for LD students, student-designed majors, study abroad, summer session for credit. ***ROTC:*** Army (c).

Computers: 133 computers/terminals and 1,200 ports are available on campus for general student use. Students can access the following: computer help desk, free student e-mail accounts, online (class) grades, online (class) registration, online (class) schedules, online bills. Campuswide network is available. 100% of college-owned or -operated housing units are wired for high-speed Internet access. Wireless service is available via entire campus.

Library: T. Edward and Tullah Hanley Library. *Books:* 107,555 (physical), 1.3 million (digital/electronic); *Serial titles:* 72 (physical), 261,311 (digital/electronic); *Databases:* 581. Weekly public service hours: 86; students can reserve study rooms.

STUDENT LIFE
Housing options: on-campus residence required for freshman year; coed, special housing for students with disabilities. Campus housing is university owned. Freshman campus housing is guaranteed.

Activities and organizations: drama/theater group, student-run radio station, choral group, Student Government Association, Student Activities Board, The Source (student newspaper), Alpha Phi Omega, WDRQ (student radio station), national fraternities, national sororities.

Athletics Member NCAA. All Division III. ***Intercollegiate sports:*** baseball M, basketball M/W, bowling W, golf M, ice hockey M, soccer M/W, softball W, swimming and diving M/W, tennis M/W, volleyball W, wrestling M. ***Intramural sports:*** basketball M/W, cheerleading W(c), football M/W, golf M/W, ice hockey M/W, rock climbing M/W, sand volleyball M/W, skiing (downhill) M/W, soccer M/W, softball M/W, swimming and diving M/W, tennis M/W, ultimate Frisbee M/W, volleyball M/W, water polo M/W.

Campus security: 24-hour emergency response devices and patrols, late-night transport/escort service, controlled dormitory access.

Student services: health clinic, personal/psychological counseling.

COSTS & FINANCIAL AID
Costs (2018–19) ***One-time required fee:*** $90. ***Tuition:*** state resident $12,940 full-time, $539 per credit hour part-time; nonresident $24,184 full-time, $1007 per credit hour part-time. Full-time tuition and fees vary according to course load and program. Part-time tuition and fees vary according to course load and program. ***Required fees:*** $960 full-time, $165 per term part-time. ***Room and board:*** $10,222; room only: $6272. Room and board charges vary according to board plan and housing facility. ***Payment plan:*** installment. ***Waivers:*** employees or children of employees.

Financial Aid Of all full-time matriculated undergraduates who enrolled in 2017, 1,121 applied for aid, 1,021 were judged to have need, 84 had their need fully met. 177 Federal Work-Study jobs (averaging $1980). 95 state and other part-time jobs (averaging $1783). In 2017, 77 non-need-based awards were made. ***Average percent of need met:*** 60. ***Average financial aid package:*** $13,585. ***Average need-based loan:*** $4336. ***Average need-based gift aid:*** $9835. ***Average non-need-based aid:*** $6440. ***Average indebtedness upon graduation:*** $37,735.

APPLYING
Standardized Tests *Required:* SAT or ACT (for admission).

Options: electronic application, deferred entrance.

Required: high school transcript, minimum 2.0 GPA. ***Required for some:*** minimum 3.0 GPA. ***Recommended:*** essay or personal statement, 2 letters of recommendation, interview.

Application deadlines: rolling (freshmen), rolling (out-of-state freshmen), rolling (transfers).

Notification: continuous (freshmen), continuous (out-of-state freshmen), continuous (transfers).

CONTACT
Ms. Vicky Pingie, Associate Director of Admissions, University of Pittsburgh at Bradford, 300 Campus Drive, Bradford, PA 16701. *Phone:* 814-362-7552. *Toll-free phone:* 800-872-1787. *Fax:* 814-362-5150. *E-mail:* monti@pitt.edu.

See below for display ad and page 1144 for the College Close-Up.

University of Pittsburgh at Greensburg

Greensburg, Pennsylvania

http://www.greensburg.pitt.edu/

- **State-related** 4-year, founded 1963, part of University of Pittsburgh System
- **Small-town** 219-acre campus with easy access to Pittsburgh
- **Coed**
- **Moderately difficult** entrance level

ACADEMICS
Calendar: semesters. *Degree:* certificates and bachelor's.
Library: Millstein Library.

STUDENT LIFE
Housing options: coed. Campus housing is university owned.

Activities and organizations: drama/theater group, student-run newspaper, choral group, Habitat for Humanity, Student Government

Association, Student Activities Board, Outdoor Adventure and Community Service, Freshmen Honor Society - Phi Eta Sigma.

Athletics Member NCAA. All Division III.

Campus security: 24-hour emergency response devices and patrols, late-night transport/escort service, controlled dormitory access.

Student services: health clinic, personal/psychological counseling.

COSTS & FINANCIAL AID

Costs (2018–19) ***Tuition:*** state resident $12,940 full-time, $539 per credit hour part-time; nonresident $24,184 full-time, $1007 per credit hour part-time. Full-time tuition and fees vary according to program. Part-time tuition and fees vary according to program. ***Required fees:*** $930 full-time, $174 per term part-time. ***Room and board:*** $10,520; room only: $6450. Room and board charges vary according to board plan and housing facility.

Financial Aid Of all full-time matriculated undergraduates who enrolled in 2017, 1,249 applied for aid, 1,081 were judged to have need, 93 had their need fully met. In 2017, 70 non-need-based awards were made. ***Average percent of need met:*** 57. ***Average financial aid package:*** $11,503. ***Average need-based loan:*** $4181. ***Average need-based gift aid:*** $8725. ***Average non-need-based aid:*** $4345. ***Average indebtedness upon graduation:*** $38,091.

APPLYING

Standardized Tests *Required:* SAT or ACT (for admission).

Options: electronic application, early admission, deferred entrance.

Application fee: $45.

Required: high school transcript, minimum 2.5 GPA. ***Recommended:*** essay or personal statement, interview.

CONTACT

Ms. Heather Kabala, Director of Admissions, University of Pittsburgh at Greensburg, 150 Finoli Drive, Greensburg, PA 15601. *Phone:* 724-836-9880. *Fax:* 724-836-7471. *E-mail:* upgadmit@pitt.edu.

University of Pittsburgh at Johnstown

Johnstown, Pennsylvania

http://www.upj.pitt.edu/

CONTACT

Mr. Ryan Clancy, Office of Admissions, University of Pittsburgh at Johnstown, 157 Blackington Hall, Johnstown, PA 15904. *Phone:* 814-269-7050. *Toll-free phone:* 800-765-4875. *E-mail:* upjadmit@pitt.edu.

The University of Scranton

Scranton, Pennsylvania

http://www.scranton.edu/

- **Independent Roman Catholic (Jesuit)** comprehensive, founded 1888
- **Urban** 50-acre campus
- **Endowment** $187.2 million
- **Coed**
- **Moderately difficult** entrance level

FACULTY

Student/faculty ratio: 12:1.

ACADEMICS

Calendar: semesters. *Degrees:* certificates, bachelor's, master's, doctoral, post-master's, and postbachelor's certificates.

Library: Harry and Jeanette Weinberg Memorial Library. *Books:* 331,804 (physical), 212,028 (digital/electronic); *Serial titles:* 2,677 (physical), 53,194 (digital/electronic); *Databases:* 120. Weekly public service hours: 95; study areas open 24 hours, 5–7 days a week; students can reserve study rooms.

STUDENT LIFE

Housing options: on-campus residence required through sophomore year; coed, men-only, women-only, special housing for students with disabilities. Campus housing is university owned. Freshman campus housing is guaranteed.

Activities and organizations: drama/theater group, student-run newspaper, radio and television station, choral group, Service-oriented student clubs, United Colors, Retreat Programs, Biology/Pre-Medicine clubs, Pre-Law Society.

Athletics Member NCAA. All Division III.

Campus security: 24-hour emergency response devices and patrols, student patrols, late-night transport/escort service, controlled dormitory access, sprinkler systems in all University-owned housing.

Student services: health clinic, personal/psychological counseling, women's center.

COSTS & FINANCIAL AID

Costs (2018–19) ***Comprehensive fee:*** $59,714 includes full-time tuition ($44,132), mandatory fees ($400), and room and board ($15,182). ***College room only:*** $8776. Room and board charges vary according to board plan and housing facility.

Financial Aid Of all full-time matriculated undergraduates who enrolled in 2017, 2,937 applied for aid, 2,564 were judged to have need, 419 had their need fully met. In 2017, 722 non-need-based awards were made. ***Average percent of need met:*** 69. ***Average financial aid package:*** $30,899. ***Average need-based loan:*** $4716. ***Average need-based gift aid:*** $16,323. ***Average non-need-based aid:*** $15,025. ***Average indebtedness upon graduation:*** $41,395.

APPLYING

Standardized Tests *Required:* SAT or ACT (for admission).

Options: electronic application, early admission, early action, deferred entrance.

Required: essay or personal statement, high school transcript, 1 letter of recommendation. ***Required for some:*** interview.

CONTACT

Mr. Joseph Roback, Associate Vice Provost, Admissions and Enrollment, The University of Scranton, The Estate Room 208, Scranton, PA 18510-4501. *Phone:* 570-941-7540. *Toll-free phone:* 888-SCRANTON. *Fax:* 570-941-5928. *E-mail:* admissions@scranton.edu.

The University of the Arts

Philadelphia, Pennsylvania

http://www.uarts.edu/

- **Independent** comprehensive, founded 1876
- **Urban** 21-acre campus with easy access to Philadelphia
- **Coed**
- **Moderately difficult** entrance level

FACULTY

Student/faculty ratio: 8:1.

ACADEMICS

Calendar: semesters. *Degrees:* diplomas, bachelor's, master's, and postbachelor's certificates.

Library: Albert M. Greenfield Library plus 1 other.

STUDENT LIFE

Housing options: coed. Campus housing is university owned and leased by the school. Freshman applicants given priority for college housing.

Activities and organizations: drama/theater group, choral group.

Campus security: 24-hour emergency response devices and patrols, crime prevention workshops and seminars.

Student services: health clinic, personal/psychological counseling.

COSTS & FINANCIAL AID

Costs (2018–19) ***Comprehensive fee:*** $61,102 includes full-time tuition ($44,780) and room and board ($16,322). Part-time tuition: $1866 per credit hour. Part-time tuition and fees vary according to course load. ***College room only:*** $10,540. Room and board charges vary according to board plan and housing facility.

Financial Aid Of all full-time matriculated undergraduates who enrolled in 2017, 1,305 applied for aid, 1,305 were judged to have need, 149 had their need fully met. In 2017, 334 non-need-based awards were made. ***Average percent of need met:*** 62. ***Average financial aid package:*** $29,310. ***Average need-based loan:*** $4103. ***Average need-based gift aid:*** $24,377. ***Average non-need-based aid:*** $16,427. ***Average indebtedness upon graduation:*** $37,575.

APPLYING

Options: electronic application, early admission, deferred entrance.

Application fee: $60.

Required: high school transcript. ***Required for some:*** interview, audition or portfolio required for performing arts programs; portfolio for design, visual arts, film programs. ***Recommended:*** minimum 2.0 GPA.

CONTACT

Ms. Kaitlyn Arillo, Director of Undergraduate Recruitment, The University of the Arts, 320 South Broad Street, Philadelphia, PA 19102-4944. *Phone:* 215-717-6017. *Toll-free phone:* 800-616-ARTS. *Fax:* 215-717-6045. *E-mail:* admissions@uarts.edu.

University of the Sciences

Philadelphia, Pennsylvania

http://www.usciences.edu/

CONTACT

Executive Director of Admission and Enrollment Services, University of the Sciences, 600 South 43rd Street, Philadelphia, PA 19104-4495. *Phone:* 888-996-8747. *Toll-free phone:* 888-996-8747. *Fax:* 215-596-8821. *E-mail:* admit@usciences.edu.

University of Valley Forge

Phoenixville, Pennsylvania

http://www.valleyforge.edu/

- **Independent Assemblies of God** comprehensive, founded 1939
- **Small-town** 150-acre campus with easy access to Philadelphia
- **Endowment** $2.6 million
- **Coed**
- **Minimally difficult** entrance level

FACULTY

Student/faculty ratio: 12:1.

ACADEMICS

Calendar: semesters. *Degrees:* associate, bachelor's, and master's.
Library: Storms Research Center. *Books:* 56,000 (physical), 175,000 (digital/electronic); *Serial titles:* 44 (physical); *Databases:* 48. Weekly public service hours: 81; students can reserve study rooms.

STUDENT LIFE

Housing options: on-campus residence required through senior year; men-only, women-only. Campus housing is university owned. Freshman campus housing is guaranteed.

Activities and organizations: drama/theater group, choral group, Homeless Ministry, The Art Of, Noteworthy, Inspire India, Audience of One.

Athletics Member NCAA, USCAA. All Division III.

Campus security: 24-hour emergency response devices and patrols, student patrols, late-night transport/escort service, controlled dormitory access.

Student services: health clinic, personal/psychological counseling.

COSTS & FINANCIAL AID

Costs (2018–19) ***Comprehensive fee:*** $31,324 includes full-time tuition ($20,266), mandatory fees ($1172), and room and board ($9886). Full-time tuition and fees vary according to course load and location. Part-time tuition: $783 per credit hour. Part-time tuition and fees vary according to course load and location. ***Required fees:*** $256 per term part-time. ***College room only:*** $5386. Room and board charges vary according to board plan, housing facility, and location.

Financial Aid Of all full-time matriculated undergraduates who enrolled in 2016, 640 applied for aid, 583 were judged to have need, 69 had their need fully met. 18 Federal Work-Study jobs (averaging $2671). In 2016, 64 non-need-based awards were made. ***Average percent of need met:*** 56. ***Average financial aid package:*** $13,961. ***Average need-based loan:*** $4059. ***Average need-based gift aid:*** $10,584. ***Average non-need-based aid:*** $8222. ***Average indebtedness upon graduation:*** $34,920.

APPLYING

Standardized Tests *Recommended:* SAT or ACT (for admission).

Options: electronic application, deferred entrance.

Application fee: $25.

Required: essay or personal statement, high school transcript. ***Required for some:*** interview. ***Recommended:*** minimum 2.0 GPA.

CONTACT

Claire M. Eiler, Director of Admissions, University of Valley Forge, 1401 Charlestown Road, Phoenixville, PA 19460. *Phone:* 610-917-1487. *Toll-free phone:* 800-432-8322. *Fax:* 610-917-2069. *E-mail:* admissions@valleyforge.edu.

Ursinus College

Collegeville, Pennsylvania

http://www.ursinus.edu/

- **Independent** 4-year, founded 1869
- **Suburban** 170-acre campus with easy access to Philadelphia
- **Endowment** $144.9 million
- **Coed** 1,435 undergraduate students, 98% full-time, 51% women, 49% men
- **Moderately difficult** entrance level, 71% of applicants were admitted

UNDERGRAD STUDENTS

1,408 full-time, 27 part-time. Students come from 31 states and territories; 20 other countries; 39% are from out of state; 8% Black or African American, non-Hispanic/Latino; 8% Hispanic/Latino; 4% Asian, non-Hispanic/Latino; 0.1% Native Hawaiian or other Pacific Islander, non-Hispanic/Latino; 0.1% American Indian or Alaska Native, non-Hispanic/Latino; 3% Two or more races, non-Hispanic/Latino; 4% Race/ethnicity unknown; 2% international; 1% transferred in; 93% live on campus.

Freshmen:

Admission: 3,361 applied, 2,382 admitted, 378 enrolled. ***Average high school GPA:*** 3.3. ***Test scores:*** SAT evidence-based reading and writing scores over 500: 97%; SAT math scores over 500: 97%; ACT scores over 18: 96%; SAT evidence-based reading and writing scores over 600: 67%; SAT math scores over 600: 58%; ACT scores over 24: 75%; SAT evidence-based reading and writing scores over 700: 8%; SAT math scores over 700: 11%; ACT scores over 30: 14%.

Retention: 89% of full-time freshmen returned.

FACULTY

Total: 171, 71% full-time, 79% with terminal degrees.

Student/faculty ratio: 11:1.

ACADEMICS

Calendar: semesters. *Degree:* bachelor's.

Special study options: advanced placement credit, cooperative education, double majors, English as a second language, honors programs, independent study, internships, off-campus study, services for LD students, student-designed majors, study abroad, summer session for credit.

Unusual degree programs: 3-2 engineering with Columbia University.

Computers: Students can access the following: campus intranet, computer help desk, free student e-mail accounts, online (class) grades, online (class) registration, online (class) schedules. Campuswide network is available. 100% of college-owned or -operated housing units are wired for high-speed Internet access. Wireless service is available via entire campus.
Library: Myrin Library. *Books:* 175,320 (physical), 396,143 (digital/electronic); *Serial titles:* 797 (physical), 52,952 (digital/electronic); *Databases:* 53. Weekly public service hours: 113.

STUDENT LIFE

Housing options: on-campus residence required through senior year; coed, men-only, women-only, special housing for students with disabilities. Campus housing is university owned. Freshman campus housing is guaranteed.

Activities and organizations: drama/theater group, student-run newspaper, radio and television station, choral group, Campus Activities Board, Ursinus College Student Government, Best Buddies, The Grizzly student newspaper, Gender Sexuality Alliance, national fraternities, national sororities.

Athletics Member NCAA. All Division III except golf (Division II). ***Intercollegiate sports:*** baseball M, basketball M/W, cross-country running M/W, field hockey W, football M, golf M/W, gymnastics W, lacrosse

M/W, soccer M/W, softball W, swimming and diving M/W, tennis M/W, track and field M/W, volleyball W, wrestling M. ***Intramural sports:*** badminton M/W, cheerleading M(c)/W(c), cross-country running M(c)/W(c), fencing M(c)/W, field hockey M/W(c), football M/W, rugby M(c)/W(c), sand volleyball M/W, soccer M(c)/W, triathlon M/W, ultimate Frisbee M(c)/W(c), volleyball M(c).

Campus security: 24-hour emergency response devices and patrols, student patrols, late-night transport/escort service, controlled dormitory access.

Student services: health clinic, personal/psychological counseling.

COSTS & FINANCIAL AID

Costs (2019–20) ***Comprehensive fee:*** $66,730 includes full-time tuition ($53,610) and room and board ($13,120). Part-time tuition: $1675 per credit hour.

Financial Aid Of all full-time matriculated undergraduates who enrolled in 2018, 1,201 applied for aid, 1,071 were judged to have need, 259 had their need fully met. 605 Federal Work-Study jobs (averaging $1851). In 2018, 318 non-need-based awards were made. ***Average percent of need met:*** 81. ***Average financial aid package:*** $42,001. ***Average need-based loan:*** $4382. ***Average need-based gift aid:*** $35,652. ***Average non-need-based aid:*** $25,984. ***Average indebtedness upon graduation:*** $42,113. ***Financial aid deadline:*** 2/1.

APPLYING

Standardized Tests *Required for some:* SAT or ACT (for admission).

Options: electronic application, early decision, early action, deferred entrance.

Required: essay or personal statement, high school transcript, 1 letter of recommendation. ***Required for some:*** home schooled students must include detailed information about the depth of their curriculum, including reading lists and standardized tests. ***Recommended:*** interview.

Application deadlines: 2/1 (freshmen), 8/1 (transfers), 11/1 (early action).

Early decision deadline: 12/1.

Notification: continuous (freshmen), continuous (transfers), 12/15 (early decision plan 1), rolling (early decision plan 2), 12/15 (early action).

CONTACT

Ms. Diane Greenwood, Director of Admission, Ursinus College, 601 E. Main Street, Collegeville, PA 19426. *Phone:* 610-409-3200. *Fax:* 610-409-3197. *E-mail:* admission@ursinus.edu.

Villanova University

Villanova, Pennsylvania

http://www.villanova.edu/

- **Independent Roman Catholic** university, founded 1842
- **Suburban** 254-acre campus with easy access to Philadelphia
- **Endowment** $640.0 million
- **Coed**
- **Very difficult** entrance level

FACULTY

Student/faculty ratio: 12:1.

ACADEMICS

Calendar: semesters. *Degrees:* bachelor's, master's, doctoral, post-master's, and postbachelor's certificates.

Library: Falvey Memorial Library plus 1 other. Study areas open 24 hours, 5–7 days a week; students can reserve study rooms.

STUDENT LIFE

Housing options: coed, women-only, special housing for students with disabilities. Campus housing is university owned. Freshman campus housing is guaranteed.

Activities and organizations: drama/theater group, student-run newspaper, radio and television station, choral group, marching band, Blue Key Society, New Student Orientation Counselor Program, Special Olympics, Campus Activities Team, Student Government Association, national fraternities, national sororities.

Athletics Member NCAA. All Division I except football (Division I-AA).

Campus security: 24-hour emergency response devices and patrols, late-night transport/escort service, controlled dormitory access, Nova Alert: email, text messaging for emergency situations.

Student services: health clinic, personal/psychological counseling.

COSTS & FINANCIAL AID

Costs (2018–19) ***One-time required fee:*** $150. ***Comprehensive fee:*** $67,328 includes full-time tuition ($52,578), mandatory fees ($730), and room and board ($14,020). Full-time tuition and fees vary according to degree level and location. Part-time tuition: $2921 per credit hour. Part-time tuition and fees vary according to course load, degree level, location, and program. ***Required fees:*** $365 per term part-time. ***College room only:*** $7470. Room and board charges vary according to board plan and housing facility.

Financial Aid Of all full-time matriculated undergraduates who enrolled in 2018, 3,891 applied for aid, 3,142 were judged to have need, 235 had their need fully met. 2,064 Federal Work-Study jobs (averaging $2828). 52 state and other part-time jobs (averaging $2913). In 2018, 519 non-need-based awards were made. ***Average percent of need met:*** 79. ***Average financial aid package:*** $40,651. ***Average need-based loan:*** $4639. ***Average need-based gift aid:*** $35,229. ***Average non-need-based aid:*** $17,024. ***Average indebtedness upon graduation:*** $35,552. ***Financial aid deadline:*** 1/15.

APPLYING

Standardized Tests *Required:* SAT or ACT (for admission).

Options: electronic application, early admission, early decision, early action, deferred entrance.

Application fee: $80.

Required: essay or personal statement, high school transcript, 1 letter of recommendation.

CONTACT

Villanova University, 800 Lancaster Avenue, Villanova, PA 19085-1699.

Washington & Jefferson College

Washington, Pennsylvania

http://www.washjeff.edu/

- **Independent** comprehensive, founded 1781
- **Suburban** 60-acre campus with easy access to Pittsburgh
- **Endowment** $143.6 million
- **Coed** 1,356 undergraduate students, 100% full-time, 49% women, 51% men
- **Very difficult** entrance level, 82% of applicants were admitted

UNDERGRAD STUDENTS

1,350 full-time, 6 part-time. Students come from 36 states and territories; 37 other countries; 23% are from out of state; 5% Black or African American, non-Hispanic/Latino; 5% Hispanic/Latino; 2% Asian, non-Hispanic/Latino; 0.2% American Indian or Alaska Native, non-Hispanic/Latino; 4% Two or more races, non-Hispanic/Latino; 7% Race/ethnicity unknown; 3% international; 1% transferred in; 93% live on campus.

Freshmen:

Admission: 2,806 applied, 2,311 admitted, 351 enrolled. ***Average high school GPA:*** 3.7. ***Test scores:*** SAT evidence-based reading and writing scores over 500: 95%; SAT math scores over 500: 95%; ACT scores over 18: 99%; SAT evidence-based reading and writing scores over 600: 61%; SAT math scores over 600: 57%; ACT scores over 24: 74%; SAT evidence-based reading and writing scores over 700: 10%; SAT math scores over 700: 12%; ACT scores over 30: 19%.

Retention: 81% of full-time freshmen returned.

FACULTY

Total: 152, 75% full-time, 80% with terminal degrees.

Student/faculty ratio: 11:1.

ACADEMICS

Calendar: 4-1-4. *Degrees:* bachelor's, master's, and postbachelor's certificates.

Special study options: academic remediation for entering students, accelerated degree program, advanced placement credit, double majors, English as a second language, freshman honors college, honors programs, independent study, internships, off-campus study, part-time degree program, services for LD students, student-designed majors, study abroad, summer session for credit. ***ROTC:*** Army (b), Air Force (c).

Unusual degree programs: 3-2 engineering with Columbia University, Case Western Reserve University, Washington University in St. Louis.

Computers: 450 computers/terminals and 2,000 ports are available on campus for general student use. Students can access the following: campus intranet, computer help desk, free student e-mail accounts, online (class) grades, online (class) registration, online (class) schedules. Campuswide network is available. 100% of college-owned or -operated housing units are wired for high-speed Internet access. Wireless service is available via entire campus.
Library: U. Grant Miller Library plus 4 others. *Books:* 91,909 (physical), 6,516 (digital/electronic); *Serial titles:* 654 (physical), 63,356 (digital/electronic); *Databases:* 78. Weekly public service hours: 107.

STUDENT LIFE
Housing options: on-campus residence required through senior year; coed, men-only, women-only, special housing for students with disabilities. Campus housing is university owned. Freshman campus housing is guaranteed.

Activities and organizations: drama/theater group, student-run newspaper, radio station, choral group, Student Government Association, Student Activities Board, Black Student Union, Mock Trial, Latino Culture Association, national fraternities, national sororities.

Athletics Member NCAA. All Division III except golf (Division II). ***Intercollegiate sports:*** baseball M, basketball M/W, cheerleading M(c)/W(c), cross-country running M/W, equestrian sports M(c)/W(c), field hockey W, football M, golf M/W, ice hockey M(c), lacrosse M/W, rugby M(c)/W(c), soccer M/W, softball W, swimming and diving M/W, tennis M/W, track and field M/W, ultimate Frisbee M(c)/W(c), volleyball M(c)/W, water polo M/W, wrestling M. ***Intramural sports:*** basketball M/W, soccer M/W, tennis M/W, triathlon M/W, volleyball M/W.

Campus security: 24-hour emergency response devices and patrols, late-night transport/escort service, controlled dormitory access.

Student services: health clinic, personal/psychological counseling, women's center.

COSTS & FINANCIAL AID
Costs (2018–19) ***Comprehensive fee:*** $60,640 includes full-time tuition ($47,384), mandatory fees ($580), and room and board ($12,676). Part-time tuition: $1188 per credit hour. ***College room only:*** $7438. Room and board charges vary according to board plan and housing facility. ***Payment plans:*** tuition prepayment, installment. ***Waivers:*** employees or children of employees.

Financial Aid Of all full-time matriculated undergraduates who enrolled in 2018, 1,149 applied for aid, 1,066 were judged to have need, 172 had their need fully met. 663 Federal Work-Study jobs (averaging $1782). 210 state and other part-time jobs (averaging $1708). In 2018, 269 non-need-based awards were made. ***Average percent of need met:*** 81. ***Average financial aid package:*** $39,176. ***Average need-based loan:*** $3739. ***Average need-based gift aid:*** $34,328. ***Average non-need-based aid:*** $23,561. ***Average indebtedness upon graduation:*** $45,306.

APPLYING
Options: electronic application, early admission, early decision, early action, deferred entrance.

Application fee: $25.

Required: essay or personal statement, high school transcript, letters of recommendation. ***Recommended:*** interview.

Early decision deadline: 12/1.

Notification: 4/1 (freshmen), 12/15 (early decision).

CONTACT
Mr. Robert Adkins, Dean of Admission, Washington & Jefferson College, 60 South Lincoln Street, Washington, PA 15301. *Phone:* 724-223-6025. *Toll-free phone:* 888-WANDJAY. *Fax:* 724-223-6534. *E-mail:* admission@washjeff.edu.

Waynesburg University

Waynesburg, Pennsylvania

http://www.waynesburg.edu/

- **Independent** comprehensive, founded 1849, affiliated with Presbyterian Church (U.S.A.)
- **Small-town** 30-acre campus with easy access to Pittsburgh
- **Coed** 1,330 undergraduate students, 97% full-time, 57% women, 43% men
- **Moderately difficult** entrance level, 91% of applicants were admitted

UNDERGRAD STUDENTS
1,287 full-time, 43 part-time. Students come from 35 states and territories; 2 other countries; 22% are from out of state; 4% Black or African American, non-Hispanic/Latino; 2% Hispanic/Latino; 0.9% Asian, non-Hispanic/Latino; 0.1% Native Hawaiian or other Pacific Islander, non-Hispanic/Latino; 0.2% American Indian or Alaska Native, non-Hispanic/Latino; 3% Two or more races, non-Hispanic/Latino; 3% Race/ethnicity unknown; 0.2% international; 3% transferred in; 80% live on campus.

Freshmen:
Admission: 1,590 applied, 1,454 admitted, 326 enrolled. ***Average high school GPA:*** 3.6.

Retention: 78% of full-time freshmen returned.

FACULTY
Total: 201, 39% full-time, 41% with terminal degrees.

Student/faculty ratio: 13:1.

ACADEMICS
Calendar: semesters. *Degrees:* bachelor's, master's, and doctoral.

Special study options: accelerated degree program, adult/continuing education programs, advanced placement credit, distance learning, double majors, honors programs, independent study, internships, part-time degree program, services for LD students, study abroad, summer session for credit. ***ROTC:*** Army (c), Air Force (c).

Unusual degree programs: 3-2 engineering with Penn State University.

Computers: 160 computers/terminals are available on campus for general student use. Students can access the following: campus intranet, computer help desk, free student e-mail accounts, online (class) grades, online (class) registration, online (class) schedules. Campuswide network is available. 100% of college-owned or -operated housing units are wired for high-speed Internet access. Wireless service is available via classrooms, computer labs, dorm rooms, learning centers, libraries, student centers.
Library: Eberly Library. *Books:* 71,187 (physical), 162,938 (digital/electronic); *Serial titles:* 159 (physical), 111,249 (digital/electronic); *Databases:* 37.

STUDENT LIFE
Housing options: on-campus residence required through junior year; men-only, women-only, special housing for students with disabilities. Campus housing is university owned. Freshman campus housing is guaranteed.

Activities and organizations: drama/theater group, student-run newspaper, radio and television station, choral group, Student-Pennsylvania State Education Association, Lamplighter Choir, Student Nurses Association, Christian Fellowship.

Athletics Member NCAA. All Division III. ***Intercollegiate sports:*** baseball M, basketball M/W, cross-country running M/W, football M, golf M, lacrosse W, soccer M/W, softball W, tennis M/W, track and field M/W, volleyball W, wrestling M. ***Intramural sports:*** basketball M/W, bowling M/W, racquetball M/W, softball M/W, table tennis M/W, volleyball M/W.

Campus security: 24-hour emergency response devices and patrols, late-night transport/escort service, controlled dormitory access.

Student services: health clinic, personal/psychological counseling.

COSTS & FINANCIAL AID
Costs (2019–20) ***Comprehensive fee:*** $36,090 includes full-time tuition ($24,690), mandatory fees ($880), and room and board ($10,520). Part-time tuition: $1020 per credit hour. ***College room only:*** $5320.

Financial Aid Of all full-time matriculated undergraduates who enrolled in 2018, 1,194 applied for aid, 1,060 were judged to have need, 355 had their need fully met. 700 Federal Work-Study jobs (averaging $1200). In 2018, 227 non-need-based awards were made. ***Average percent of need***

met: 80. ***Average financial aid package:*** $20,659. ***Average need-based loan:*** $5279. ***Average need-based gift aid:*** $15,872. ***Average non-need-based aid:*** $11,886. ***Average indebtedness upon graduation:*** $23,944.

APPLYING

Standardized Tests *Required:* SAT or ACT (for admission).

Options: electronic application, early admission.

Application fee: $20.

Required: high school transcript, minimum 2.8 GPA. ***Required for some:*** essay or personal statement, 2 letters of recommendation. ***Recommended:*** minimum 3.0 GPA, interview.

Application deadlines: rolling (freshmen), rolling (transfers).

Notification: continuous (freshmen), continuous (transfers).

CONTACT

Mrs. Jacqueline Palko, Director of Admissions, Waynesburg University, 51 West College Street, Waynesburg, PA 15370. *Phone:* 724-852-3216. *Toll-free phone:* 800-225-7393. *Fax:* 724-627-8124. *E-mail:* admissions@waynesburg.edu.

West Chester University of Pennsylvania

West Chester, Pennsylvania

http://www.wcupa.edu/

- **State-supported** comprehensive, founded 1871, part of Pennsylvania State System of Higher Education
- **Suburban** 409-acre campus with easy access to Philadelphia
- **Endowment** $25.1 million
- **Coed** 14,567 undergraduate students, 90% full-time, 59% women, 41% men
- **Moderately difficult** entrance level, 74% of applicants were admitted

UNDERGRAD STUDENTS

13,060 full-time, 1,507 part-time. Students come from 28 states and territories; 84 other countries; 13% are from out of state; 11% Black or African American, non-Hispanic/Latino; 6% Hispanic/Latino; 3% Asian, non-Hispanic/Latino; 0.1% Native Hawaiian or other Pacific Islander, non-Hispanic/Latino; 0.1% American Indian or Alaska Native, non-Hispanic/Latino; 4% Two or more races, non-Hispanic/Latino; 1% Race/ethnicity unknown; 0.5% international; 8% transferred in; 36% live on campus.

Freshmen:

Admission: 12,002 applied, 8,934 admitted, 2,777 enrolled. ***Average high school GPA:*** 3.4. ***Test scores:*** SAT evidence-based reading and writing scores over 500: 88%; SAT math scores over 500: 86%; ACT scores over 18: 95%; SAT evidence-based reading and writing scores over 600: 30%; SAT math scores over 600: 23%; ACT scores over 24: 46%; SAT evidence-based reading and writing scores over 700: 2%; SAT math scores over 700: 2%; ACT scores over 30: 6%.

Retention: 85% of full-time freshmen returned.

FACULTY

Total: 981, 70% full-time, 71% with terminal degrees.

Student/faculty ratio: 19:1.

ACADEMICS

Calendar: semesters. *Degrees:* bachelor's, master's, doctoral, post-master's, and postbachelor's certificates.

Special study options: academic remediation for entering students, accelerated degree program, adult/continuing education programs, advanced placement credit, distance learning, double majors, English as a second language, freshman honors college, honors programs, independent study, internships, off-campus study, part-time degree program, services for LD students, student-designed majors, study abroad, summer session for credit. ***ROTC:*** Army (b), Air Force (c).

Unusual degree programs: 3-2 engineering with Pennsylvania State University, Thomas Jefferson University (formerly known as Philadelphia University), Columbia University, and Case Western University.

Computers: 2,204 computers/terminals are available on campus for general student use. Students can access the following: campus intranet, computer help desk, free student e-mail accounts, online (class) grades, online (class) registration, online (class) schedules, virtual software. Campuswide network is available. 100% of college-owned or -operated housing units are wired for high-speed Internet access. Wireless service is available via entire campus.

Library: Francis Harvey Green Library plus 1 other. *Books:* 740,365 (physical), 1.1 million (digital/electronic); *Serial titles:* 1,921 (physical), 127,236 (digital/electronic); *Databases:* 275. Weekly public service hours: 107; study areas open 24 hours, 5–7 days a week.

STUDENT LIFE

Housing options: coed, special housing for students with disabilities. Campus housing is university owned and is provided by a third party. Freshman applicants given priority for college housing.

Activities and organizations: drama/theater group, student-run newspaper, radio and television station, choral group, marching band, Student Government Association, Residence Hall Association, Fraternal Programming Board, Sports Club Council, CRU, national fraternities, national sororities.

Athletics Member NCAA. All Division II except golf (Division I). ***Intercollegiate sports:*** baseball M(s), basketball M(s)/W(s), bowling M(c)/W(c), cheerleading W, equestrian sports M(c)/W(c), fencing M(c)/W(c), field hockey W(s), football M(s), golf M(s)/W(s), gymnastics W(s), ice hockey M(c)/W(c), lacrosse M(c)/W(s), rugby M(c)/W(s), skiing (downhill) M(c)/W(c), soccer M(s)/W(s), softball W(s), swimming and diving M(s)/W(s), tennis M(s)/W(s), track and field M(s)/W(s), ultimate Frisbee M(c)/W(c), volleyball M(c)/W(s), water polo M(c)/W(c), wrestling M(c). ***Intramural sports:*** badminton M/W, basketball M/W, football M/W, racquetball M/W, rock climbing M/W, sand volleyball M/W, soccer M/W, softball M/W, table tennis M/W, tennis M/W, ultimate Frisbee M/W, volleyball M/W.

Campus security: 24-hour emergency response devices and patrols, late-night transport/escort service, controlled dormitory access, camera systems in campus residence halls, recreational and classroom facilities and outdoor areas.

Student services: health clinic, personal/psychological counseling, women's center, legal services, veterans affairs office.

COSTS & FINANCIAL AID

Costs (2018–19) ***Tuition:*** state resident $7716 full-time, $322 per credit part-time; nonresident $19,290 full-time, $805 per credit part-time. Full-time tuition and fees vary according to location. Part-time tuition and fees vary according to location. ***Required fees:*** $2696 full-time, $112 per credit part-time. ***Room and board:*** $9216; room only: $5516. Room and board charges vary according to board plan and housing facility. ***Payment plan:*** installment. ***Waivers:*** senior citizens and employees or children of employees.

Financial Aid Of all full-time matriculated undergraduates who enrolled in 2017, 10,246 applied for aid, 7,663 were judged to have need, 671 had their need fully met. 278 Federal Work-Study jobs (averaging $1799). In 2017, 271 non-need-based awards were made. ***Average percent of need met:*** 51. ***Average financial aid package:*** $8404. ***Average need-based loan:*** $4224. ***Average need-based gift aid:*** $5855. ***Average non-need-based aid:*** $4527. ***Average indebtedness upon graduation:*** $35,464.

APPLYING

Standardized Tests *Required:* SAT or ACT (for admission).

Options: electronic application.

Application fee: $45.

Required: high school transcript. ***Required for some:*** essay or personal statement, interview. ***Recommended:*** minimum 3.0 GPA.

Application deadlines: rolling (freshmen), rolling (transfers).

Notification: continuous (freshmen), continuous (transfers).

CONTACT

Ms. Sarah L. Freed, Assistant Vice President for Admissions, West Chester University of Pennsylvania, University Avenue and High Street, West Chester, PA 19383. *Phone:* 610-436-3411. *Toll-free phone:* 877-315-2165. *Fax:* 610-436-2907. *E-mail:* ugadmiss@wcupa.edu.

Westminster College

New Wilmington, Pennsylvania

http://www.westminster.edu/

- **Independent** comprehensive, founded 1852, affiliated with Presbyterian Church (U.S.A.)
- **Small-town** 350-acre campus with easy access to Pittsburgh
- **Endowment** $110.1 million
- **Coed**
- **Moderately difficult** entrance level

FACULTY
Student/faculty ratio: 11:1.

ACADEMICS
Calendar: semesters. *Degrees:* bachelor's and master's.
Library: McGill Memorial Library plus 1 other. *Books:* 160,296 (physical), 771,138 (digital/electronic); *Serial titles:* 89 (physical), 30,100 (digital/electronic); *Databases:* 70. Weekly public service hours: 104; students can reserve study rooms.

STUDENT LIFE
Housing options: on-campus residence required through junior year; coed, men-only, women-only. Campus housing is university owned. Freshman campus housing is guaranteed.

Activities and organizations: drama/theater group, student-run newspaper, radio and television station, choral group, marching band, Student Government Association, Interfraternity Council/Panhellenic Council, Dance Theatre, Habitat for Humanity, Campus Programming Council, national fraternities, national sororities.

Athletics Member NCAA. All Division III.

Campus security: 24-hour emergency response devices and patrols, late-night transport/escort service, controlled dormitory access.

Student services: health clinic, personal/psychological counseling.

COSTS & FINANCIAL AID
Costs (2018–19) ***Comprehensive fee:*** $47,936 includes full-time tuition ($35,360), mandatory fees ($1446), and room and board ($11,130). Part-time tuition: $1145 per credit hour. ***College room only:*** $5940. Room and board charges vary according to board plan and housing facility.

Financial Aid Of all full-time matriculated undergraduates who enrolled in 2017, 1,077 applied for aid, 1,033 were judged to have need, 198 had their need fully met. 291 Federal Work-Study jobs (averaging $1654). 90 state and other part-time jobs (averaging $1838). In 2017, 151 non-need-based awards were made. ***Average percent of need met:*** 80. ***Average financial aid package:*** $30,623. ***Average need-based loan:*** $4388. ***Average need-based gift aid:*** $26,395. ***Average non-need-based aid:*** $15,019. ***Average indebtedness upon graduation:*** $39,276.

APPLYING
Standardized Tests *Required:* SAT or ACT (for admission).

Options: electronic application, deferred entrance.

Application fee: $35.

Required: essay or personal statement, high school transcript, minimum 2.0 GPA, 2 letters of recommendation. ***Recommended:*** minimum 3.0 GPA, interview.

CONTACT
Dr. Thomas H. Stein, Vice President for Enrollment Management, Westminster College, Remick House, 319 S. Market Street, New Wilmington, PA 16172. *Phone:* 724-946-7105. *Toll-free phone:* 800-942-8033. *Fax:* 724-946-7171. *E-mail:* steinth@westminster.edu.

Widener University

Chester, Pennsylvania

http://www.widener.edu/

- **Independent** comprehensive, founded 1821
- **Suburban** 110-acre campus with easy access to Philadelphia
- **Endowment** $91.8 million
- **Coed** 3,345 undergraduate students, 87% full-time, 57% women, 43% men
- **Moderately difficult** entrance level, 70% of applicants were admitted

UNDERGRAD STUDENTS
2,910 full-time, 435 part-time. 40% are from out of state; 13% Black or African American, non-Hispanic/Latino; 5% Hispanic/Latino; 3% Asian, non-Hispanic/Latino; 0.1% American Indian or Alaska Native, non-Hispanic/Latino; 4% Two or more races, non-Hispanic/Latino; 2% Race/ethnicity unknown; 2% international; 3% transferred in; 47% live on campus.

Freshmen:
Admission: 6,422 applied, 4,474 admitted, 770 enrolled. ***Average high school GPA:*** 3.5. ***Test scores:*** SAT evidence-based reading and writing scores over 500: 85%; SAT math scores over 500: 84%; ACT scores over 18: 91%; SAT evidence-based reading and writing scores over 600: 26%; SAT math scores over 600: 26%; ACT scores over 24: 46%; SAT evidence-based reading and writing scores over 700: 2%; SAT math scores over 700: 4%; ACT scores over 30: 7%.
Retention: 80% of full-time freshmen returned.

FACULTY
Total: 641, 42% full-time, 56% with terminal degrees.

Student/faculty ratio: 14:1.

ACADEMICS
Calendar: semesters. *Degrees:* certificates, associate, bachelor's, master's, doctoral, and post-master's certificates.

Special study options: academic remediation for entering students, accelerated degree program, adult/continuing education programs, advanced placement credit, cooperative education, distance learning, double majors, English as a second language, honors programs, independent study, internships, off-campus study, part-time degree program, services for LD students, student-designed majors, study abroad, summer session for credit. ***ROTC:*** Army (b), Navy (c), Air Force (c).

Unusual degree programs: 3-2 business administration; engineering; social work; physical therapy, education.

Computers: Students can access the following: campus intranet, computer help desk, free student e-mail accounts, online (class) grades, online (class) registration, online (class) schedules. Campuswide network is available. 100% of college-owned or -operated housing units are wired for high-speed Internet access. Wireless service is available via classrooms, computer centers, computer labs, dorm rooms, learning centers, libraries, student centers.
Library: Wolfgram Memorial Library.

STUDENT LIFE
Housing options: on-campus residence required through junior year; coed, men-only, women-only, cooperative. Campus housing is university owned. Freshman campus housing is guaranteed.

Activities and organizations: drama/theater group, student-run television station, choral group, marching band, national fraternities, national sororities.

Athletics Member NCAA. All Division III. ***Intercollegiate sports:*** baseball M, basketball M/W, cheerleading W, cross-country running M/W, field hockey W, football M, golf M/W, lacrosse M/W, soccer M/W, softball W, swimming and diving M/W, track and field M/W, volleyball M/W. ***Intramural sports:*** ice hockey M(c), rugby M(c)/W(c), soccer M(c), volleyball M(c).

Campus security: 24-hour emergency response devices and patrols, late-night transport/escort service, controlled dormitory access.

Student services: health clinic, personal/psychological counseling, veterans affairs office.

COSTS & FINANCIAL AID
Costs (2019–20) ***Comprehensive fee:*** $108,442 includes full-time tuition ($46,378), mandatory fees ($47,328), and room and board ($14,736). Part-time tuition: $1545 per credit hour. ***College room only:*** $7672.

Financial Aid Of all full-time matriculated undergraduates who enrolled in 2018, 2,499 applied for aid, 2,281 were judged to have need, 422 had their need fully met. In 2018, 479 non-need-based awards were made. ***Average percent of need met:*** 72. ***Average financial aid package:*** $34,073. ***Average need-based loan:*** $4413. ***Average need-based gift aid:*** $28,880. ***Average non-need-based aid:*** $24,675.

APPLYING
Standardized Tests *Required:* SAT or ACT (for admission).

Options: electronic application, deferred entrance.

Required: essay or personal statement, high school transcript. ***Required for some:*** minimum 2.9 GPA. ***Recommended:*** interview.

Application deadlines: rolling (freshmen), rolling (transfers).

Notification: continuous (freshmen), continuous (transfers).

CONTACT

Ms. Courtney Kelly, Executive Director of Admissions, Widener University, One University Place, Chester, PA 19013-5792. *Phone:* 610-499-4126. *Toll-free phone:* 888-WIDENER. *Fax:* 610-499-4576. *E-mail:* admissions.office@widener.edu.

Wilkes University

Wilkes-Barre, Pennsylvania

http://www.wilkes.edu/

- **Independent** comprehensive, founded 1933
- **Urban** 25-acre campus
- **Endowment** $51.6 million
- **Coed** 2,455 undergraduate students, 90% full-time, 47% women, 53% men
- **Moderately difficult** entrance level, 75% of applicants were admitted

UNDERGRAD STUDENTS

2,212 full-time, 243 part-time. Students come from 31 states and territories; 13 other countries; 21% are from out of state; 5% Black or African American, non-Hispanic/Latino; 7% Hispanic/Latino; 2% Asian, non-Hispanic/Latino; 0.1% Native Hawaiian or other Pacific Islander, non-Hispanic/Latino; 0.3% American Indian or Alaska Native, non-Hispanic/Latino; 3% Two or more races, non-Hispanic/Latino; 3% Race/ethnicity unknown; 7% international; 6% transferred in; 41% live on campus.

Freshmen:

Admission: 3,932 applied, 2,942 admitted, 650 enrolled. ***Average high school GPA:*** 3.6. ***Test scores:*** SAT evidence-based reading and writing scores over 500: 88%; SAT math scores over 500: 83%; ACT scores over 18: 94%; SAT evidence-based reading and writing scores over 600: 37%; SAT math scores over 600: 35%; ACT scores over 24: 56%; SAT evidence-based reading and writing scores over 700: 3%; SAT math scores over 700: 6%; ACT scores over 30: 6%.

Retention: 76% of full-time freshmen returned.

FACULTY

Total: 416, 43% full-time.

Student/faculty ratio: 14:1.

ACADEMICS

Calendar: semesters. *Degrees:* bachelor's, master's, and doctoral.

Special study options: academic remediation for entering students, accelerated degree program, adult/continuing education programs, advanced placement credit, cooperative education, distance learning, double majors, English as a second language, honors programs, independent study, internships, off-campus study, part-time degree program, services for LD students, student-designed majors, study abroad, summer session for credit. ***ROTC:*** Army (c), Air Force (b).

Computers: 860 computers/terminals are available on campus for general student use. Students can access the following: campus intranet, computer help desk, free student e-mail accounts, online (class) grades, online (class) registration, online (class) schedules. Campuswide network is available. Wireless service is available via classrooms, dorm rooms, libraries, student centers.

Library: Eugene S. Farley Library. *Books:* 184,565 (physical), 8,000 (digital/electronic); *Serial titles:* 60,000 (digital/electronic); *Databases:* 88. Students can reserve study rooms.

STUDENT LIFE

Housing options: on-campus residence required through sophomore year; coed, men-only, women-only. Campus housing is university owned. Freshman campus housing is guaranteed.

Activities and organizations: drama/theater group, student-run newspaper, radio and television station, choral group, marching band.

Athletics Member NCAA. All Division III except golf (Division II). ***Intercollegiate sports:*** baseball M, basketball M/W, cross-country running M/W, field hockey W, football M, golf M/W, ice hockey M/W, lacrosse M/W, soccer M/W, softball W, swimming and diving M/W, tennis M/W, volleyball M/W, wrestling M. ***Intramural sports:*** basketball M/W, cheerleading W(c), cross-country running M(c)/W(c), football M, racquetball M(c)/W(c), rock climbing M(c)/W(c), skiing (downhill) M(c)/W(c), softball M/W, ultimate Frisbee M(c)/W(c), volleyball M/W.

Campus security: 24-hour emergency response devices and patrols, late-night transport/escort service, controlled dormitory access.

Student services: health clinic, personal/psychological counseling, veterans affairs office.

COSTS & FINANCIAL AID

Costs (2018–19) ***Comprehensive fee:*** $50,876 includes full-time tuition ($34,454), mandatory fees ($1740), and room and board ($14,682). ***Room and board:*** Room and board charges vary according to board plan and housing facility. ***Payment plans:*** installment, deferred payment. ***Waivers:*** employees or children of employees.

Financial Aid Of all full-time matriculated undergraduates who enrolled in 2018, 1,901 applied for aid, 1,753 were judged to have need, 217 had their need fully met. In 2018, 139 non-need-based awards were made. ***Average percent of need met:*** 75. ***Average financial aid package:*** $28,186. ***Average need-based loan:*** $4304. ***Average need-based gift aid:*** $23,216. ***Average non-need-based aid:*** $16,921.

APPLYING

Standardized Tests *Required:* SAT or ACT (for admission).

Options: electronic application, early admission, deferred entrance.

Application fee: $40.

Required: high school transcript. ***Recommended:*** interview.

Application deadlines: rolling (freshmen), rolling (out-of-state freshmen), rolling (transfers).

Notification: continuous (freshmen), continuous (out-of-state freshmen), continuous (transfers).

CONTACT

Terese Wignot, Associate Provost Enrollment, Wilkes University, 84 West South Street, Wilkes-Barre, PA 18766. *Phone:* 570-408-4400. *Toll-free phone:* 800-945-5378 Ext. 4400. *Fax:* 570-408-4904. *E-mail:* admissions@wilkes.edu.

See previous page for display ad and page 1162 for the College Close-Up.

Wilson College

Chambersburg, Pennsylvania

http://www.wilson.edu/

CONTACT

Mr. Michael Montana, Director of Admissions, Wilson College, 1015 Philadelphia Avenue, Chambersburg, PA 17201. *Phone:* 717-262-2002 Ext. 3197. *Toll-free phone:* 800-421-8402. *Fax:* 717-262-2546. *E-mail:* admissions@wilson.edu.

Yeshiva Beth Moshe

Scranton, Pennsylvania

CONTACT

Dean, Yeshiva Beth Moshe, 930 Hickory Street, PO Box 1141, Scranton, PA 18505-2124. *Phone:* 717-346-1747.

York College of Pennsylvania

York, Pennsylvania

http://www.ycp.edu/

- **Independent** comprehensive, founded 1787
- **Suburban** 190-acre campus with easy access to Baltimore
- **Coed**
- **Moderately difficult** entrance level

FACULTY

Student/faculty ratio: 15:1.

ACADEMICS

Calendar: semesters. *Degrees:* associate, bachelor's, master's, doctoral, and post-master's certificates.

Library: Schmidt Library.

STUDENT LIFE

Housing options: on-campus residence required through senior year; coed, special housing for students with disabilities. Campus housing is university owned. Freshman campus housing is guaranteed.

Activities and organizations: drama/theater group, student-run newspaper, radio and television station, choral group, Pre-Med Society, Ski and Outdoor Club, Habitat for Humanity, Students in Free Enterprise (SIFE), WVYC Radio Station, national fraternities, national sororities.

Athletics Member NCAA. All Division III.

Campus security: 24-hour emergency response devices and patrols, student patrols, late-night transport/escort service, controlled dormitory access.

Student services: health clinic, personal/psychological counseling.

COSTS & FINANCIAL AID

Costs (2018–19) ***Comprehensive fee:*** $31,300 includes full-time tuition ($18,180), mandatory fees ($1920), and room and board ($11,200). Full-time tuition and fees vary according to program. Part-time tuition: $555 per credit hour. ***Required fees:*** $410 per term part-time. ***College room only:*** $6330. Room and board charges vary according to board plan and housing facility.

Financial Aid Of all full-time matriculated undergraduates who enrolled in 2018, 3,084 applied for aid, 2,517 were judged to have need, 373 had their need fully met. In 2018, 991 non-need-based awards were made. ***Average percent of need met:*** 59. ***Average financial aid package:*** $13,866. ***Average need-based loan:*** $4120. ***Average need-based gift aid:*** $6182. ***Average non-need-based aid:*** $5957. ***Average indebtedness upon graduation:*** $41,848.

APPLYING

Standardized Tests *Required:* SAT or ACT (for admission).

Options: electronic application, deferred entrance.

Required: high school transcript, minimum 2.0 GPA. ***Required for some:*** interview. ***Recommended:*** essay or personal statement, 1 letter of recommendation.

CONTACT

York College of Pennsylvania, 441 Country Club Road, York, PA 17403-3651. *Phone:* 717-815-2257. *Toll-free phone:* 800-455-8018.

RHODE ISLAND

Brown University

Providence, Rhode Island

http://www.brown.edu/

CONTACT

Mr. Logan Powell, Dean of Admission, Brown University, Box 1876, Providence, RI 02912. *Phone:* 401-863-2378. *Fax:* 401-863-9300. *E-mail:* admission_undergraduate@brown.edu.

★ Bryant University

Smithfield, Rhode Island

http://www.bryant.edu/

- **Independent** comprehensive, founded 1863
- **Suburban** 435-acre campus with easy access to Boston, Providence
- **Endowment** $183.8 million
- **Coed** 3,499 undergraduate students, 99% full-time, 38% women, 62% men
- **Moderately difficult** entrance level, 76% of applicants were admitted

UNDERGRAD STUDENTS

3,453 full-time, 46 part-time. Students come from 37 states and territories; 49 other countries; 87% are from out of state; 3% Black or African American, non-Hispanic/Latino; 7% Hispanic/Latino; 4% Asian, non-Hispanic/Latino; 0.1% Native Hawaiian or other Pacific Islander, non-Hispanic/Latino; 0.3% American Indian or Alaska Native, non-Hispanic/Latino; 2% Two or more races, non-Hispanic/Latino; 2% Race/ethnicity unknown; 8% international; 2% transferred in; 81% live on campus.

Freshmen:
Admission: 7,235 applied, 5,475 admitted, 867 enrolled. ***Average high school GPA:*** 3.4. ***Test scores:*** SAT evidence-based reading and writing scores over 500: 96%; SAT math scores over 500: 97%; ACT scores over 18: 100%; SAT evidence-based reading and writing scores over 600: 52%; SAT math scores over 600: 61%; ACT scores over 24: 87%; SAT evidence-based reading and writing scores over 700: 4%; SAT math scores over 700: 13%; ACT scores over 30: 15%.

Retention: 90% of full-time freshmen returned.

FACULTY
Total: 309, 55% full-time, 56% with terminal degrees.

Student/faculty ratio: 13:1.

ACADEMICS
Calendar: semesters. *Degrees:* bachelor's, master's, and postbachelor's certificates.

Special study options: adult/continuing education programs, advanced placement credit, double majors, English as a second language, honors programs, independent study, internships, off-campus study, part-time degree program, services for LD students, study abroad, summer session for credit. ***ROTC:*** Army (c).

Computers: 526 computers/terminals and 4,932 ports are available on campus for general student use. Students can access the following: campus intranet, computer help desk, free student e-mail accounts, online (class) grades, online (class) registration, online (class) schedules, e-mail, online library, student Web hosts. Campuswide network is available. 100% of college-owned or -operated housing units are wired for high-speed Internet access. Wireless service is available via entire campus.
Library: Douglas and Judith Krupp Library plus 1 other. *Books:* 121,623 (physical), 16,854 (digital/electronic); *Serial titles:* 3,183 (physical), 299 (digital/electronic); *Databases:* 80. Weekly public service hours: 110; students can reserve study rooms.

STUDENT LIFE
Housing options: coed, special housing for students with disabilities. Campus housing is university owned. Freshman campus housing is guaranteed.

Activities and organizations: drama/theater group, student-run newspaper, radio and television station, choral group, CALO Community Activism & Leadership Organization, Linked Through Leadership, Technology & Applied Analytics Club, Dawg Pound, Enactus, national fraternities, national sororities.

Athletics Member NCAA. All Division I. ***Intercollegiate sports:*** baseball M(s), basketball M(s)/W(s), bowling M(c)/W(c), cheerleading W(c), crew W(c), cross-country running M(s)/W(s), field hockey W(s), football M(s), golf M(s), ice hockey M(c), lacrosse M(s)/W(s), racquetball M(c)/W(c), rowing W(c), rugby M(c)/W(c), soccer M(s)/W(s), softball W(s), squash M(c)/W(c), swimming and diving M(s)/W(s), tennis M(s)/W(s), track and field M(s)/W(s), ultimate Frisbee M(c)/W(c), volleyball M(c)/W(s). ***Intramural sports:*** badminton M/W, basketball M/W, sand volleyball M/W, soccer M(c)/W, softball M/W, table tennis M/W, tennis M(c)/W(c).

Campus security: 24-hour emergency response devices and patrols, late-night transport/escort service, controlled dormitory access.

Student services: health clinic, personal/psychological counseling, women's center.

COSTS & FINANCIAL AID
Costs (2019–20) ***Comprehensive fee:*** $61,411 includes full-time tuition ($44,498), mandatory fees ($897), and room and board ($16,016). Part-time tuition: $1102 per credit hour. ***College room only:*** $9401.

Financial Aid Of all full-time matriculated undergraduates who enrolled in 2018, 2,429 applied for aid, 2,083 were judged to have need, 623 had their need fully met. In 2018, 312 non-need-based awards were made. ***Average percent of need met:*** 49. ***Average financial aid package:*** $25,821. ***Average need-based loan:*** $4477. ***Average need-based gift aid:*** $10,568. ***Average non-need-based aid:*** $16,640. ***Average indebtedness upon graduation:*** $54,067.

APPLYING
Options: electronic application, early decision, early action, deferred entrance.

Application fee: $50.

Required: essay or personal statement, high school transcript, 1 letter of recommendation, senior year first-quarter grades, three short essay questions in place of test scores. ***Recommended:*** minimum 3.3 GPA, 2 letters of recommendation, interview.

Application deadlines: 2/1 (freshmen), 5/1 (transfers).

Early decision deadline: 11/15.

Notification: 3/15 (freshmen), continuous (transfers), 12/15 (early decision), 1/15 (early action).

CONTACT
Ms. Michelle Cloutier, Vice President for Enrollment Management, Bryant University, 1150 Douglas Pike, Smithfield, RI 02917. *Phone:* 401-232-6100. *Toll-free phone:* 800-622-7001. *Fax:* 401-232-6741. *E-mail:* admission@bryant.edu.

Johnson & Wales University

Providence, Rhode Island

http://www.jwu.edu/providence/

CONTACT
Amy Podbelski, Dean of Undergraduate Admissions, Johnson & Wales University, 8 Abbott Park Place, Providence, RI 02903-3703. *Phone:* 401-598-2310. *Toll-free phone:* 800-342-5598. *Fax:* 401-598-2948. *E-mail:* pvd@admissions.jwu.edu.

New England Institute of Technology

East Greenwich, Rhode Island

http://www.neit.edu/

- **Independent** comprehensive, founded 1940
- **Suburban** 225-acre campus with easy access to Boston
- **Coed** 2,548 undergraduate students, 85% full-time, 33% women, 67% men
- **Minimally difficult** entrance level

UNDERGRAD STUDENTS
2,174 full-time, 374 part-time. Students come from 10 states and territories; 22 other countries; 48% are from out of state; 2% Black or African American, non-Hispanic/Latino; 12% Hispanic/Latino; 0.6% Asian, non-Hispanic/Latino; 3% Two or more races, non-Hispanic/Latino; 61% Race/ethnicity unknown; 2% international; 10% live on campus.

Freshmen:
Admission: 525 enrolled.

FACULTY
Total: 329, 40% full-time, 14% with terminal degrees.

Student/faculty ratio: 16:1.

ACADEMICS
Calendar: quarters. *Degrees:* associate, bachelor's, master's, and doctoral.

Special study options: academic remediation for entering students, accelerated degree program, adult/continuing education programs, advanced placement credit, cooperative education, distance learning, double majors, English as a second language, internships, part-time degree program, services for LD students, student-designed majors, summer session for credit.

Computers: 1,300 computers/terminals are available on campus for general student use. Students can access the following: campus intranet, computer help desk, free student e-mail accounts, online (class) grades, online (class) registration, online (class) schedules. Campuswide network is available. 100% of college-owned or -operated housing units are wired for high-speed Internet access. Wireless service is available via entire campus.
Library: New England Institute of Technology Library. *Books:* 46,006 (physical), 25,801 (digital/electronic); *Serial titles:* 316 (physical), 92,146 (digital/electronic); *Databases:* 64. Weekly public service hours: 66; students can reserve study rooms.

STUDENT LIFE
Housing options: coed. Campus housing is university owned. Freshman applicants given priority for college housing.

Activities and organizations: student-run radio station, Rotaract Club, Student Physical Therapist Assistant Club, Student Nurses Association, Video Club, Criminal Justice Club.

Athletics ***Intramural sports:*** basketball M(c)/W(c), golf M(c)/W(c), soccer M(c)/W(c).

Campus security: 24-hour emergency response devices and patrols, late-night transport/escort service, controlled dormitory access.

Student services: health clinic, personal/psychological counseling.

COSTS & FINANCIAL AID

Costs (2019–20) ***Comprehensive fee:*** $45,180 includes full-time tuition ($29,100), mandatory fees ($1740), and room and board ($14,340). Part-time tuition: $14,550 per year. No tuition increase for student's term of enrollment. ***Required fees:*** $1740 per year part-time. ***Payment plan:*** tuition prepayment.

Financial Aid Of all full-time matriculated undergraduates who enrolled in 2017, 250 Federal Work-Study jobs (averaging $2290).

APPLYING

Options: electronic application, early admission, deferred entrance.

Application fee: $25.

Required: high school transcript, interview. ***Required for some:*** portfolio for advanced standing.

Application deadlines: rolling (freshmen), rolling (out-of-state freshmen), rolling (transfers).

Notification: continuous (freshmen), continuous (out-of-state freshmen), continuous (transfers).

CONTACT

Ms. Lynn M Fawthrop, Vice President of Enrollment Management and Marketing, New England Institute of Technology, One New England Tech Boulevard, East Greenwich, RI 02818. *Phone:* 401-739-5000 Ext. 3315. *Toll-free phone:* 800-736-7744. *Fax:* 401-886-0868. *E-mail:* lmfawthrop@neit.edu.

Providence College

Providence, Rhode Island

http://www.providence.edu/

- **Independent Roman Catholic** comprehensive, founded 1917
- **Suburban** 105-acre campus with easy access to Boston
- **Endowment** $238.5 million
- **Coed** 4,379 undergraduate students, 95% full-time, 55% women, 45% men
- **Moderately difficult** entrance level, 49% of applicants were admitted

UNDERGRAD STUDENTS

4,148 full-time, 231 part-time. Students come from 40 states and territories; 24 other countries; 89% are from out of state; 4% Black or African American, non-Hispanic/Latino; 10% Hispanic/Latino; 1% Asian, non-Hispanic/Latino; 0.3% Native Hawaiian or other Pacific Islander, non-Hispanic/Latino; 0.2% American Indian or Alaska Native, non-Hispanic/Latino; 2% Two or more races, non-Hispanic/Latino; 4% Race/ethnicity unknown; 2% international; 1% transferred in; 81% live on campus.

Freshmen:

Admission: 11,421 applied, 5,593 admitted, 1,122 enrolled. ***Average high school GPA:*** 3.5. ***Test scores:*** SAT evidence-based reading and writing scores over 500: 99%; SAT math scores over 500: 99%; ACT scores over 18: 100%; SAT evidence-based reading and writing scores over 600: 82%; SAT math scores over 600: 77%; ACT scores over 24: 94%; SAT evidence-based reading and writing scores over 700: 15%; SAT math scores over 700: 21%; ACT scores over 30: 37%.

Retention: 93% of full-time freshmen returned.

FACULTY

Total: 488, 62% full-time, 73% with terminal degrees.

Student/faculty ratio: 12:1.

ACADEMICS

Calendar: semesters. *Degrees:* certificates, bachelor's, master's, and postbachelor's certificates.

Special study options: adult/continuing education programs, advanced placement credit, distance learning, double majors, honors programs, independent study, internships, off-campus study, part-time degree program, services for LD students, student-designed majors, study abroad, summer session for credit. ***ROTC:*** Army (b).

Unusual degree programs: 3-2 engineering with Columbia University, Washington University in St. Louis; biology/optometry with New England School of Optometry.

Computers: 460 computers/terminals and 5,000 ports are available on campus for general student use. Students can access the following: campus intranet, computer help desk, free student e-mail accounts, online (class) grades, online (class) registration, online (class) schedules. Campuswide network is available. 100% of college-owned or -operated housing units are wired for high-speed Internet access. Wireless service is available via entire campus.

Library: Phillips Memorial Library. *Books:* 286,704 (physical), 1.0 million (digital/electronic); *Serial titles:* 241 (physical), 58,816 (digital/electronic); *Databases:* 397. Weekly public service hours: 116; students can reserve study rooms.

STUDENT LIFE

Housing options: on-campus residence required through junior year; coed, men-only, women-only, special housing for students with disabilities. Campus housing is university owned. Freshman campus housing is guaranteed.

Activities and organizations: drama/theater group, student-run newspaper, radio and television station, choral group, Student Congress, Board of Multicultural Student Affairs, Campus Ministry, Dance Club, Board of Programmers.

Athletics Member NCAA. All Division I. ***Intercollegiate sports:*** basketball M(s)/W(s), cross-country running M(s)/W(s), field hockey W(s), ice hockey M(s)/W(s), lacrosse M(s), soccer M(s)/W(s), softball W(s), swimming and diving M/W, tennis W, track and field M(s)/W(s), volleyball W(s). ***Intramural sports:*** badminton M/W, basketball M(c)/W(c), cheerleading M(c)/W(c), cross-country running M/W, fencing W, football M/W, golf M(c)/W(c), ice hockey M(c)/W, lacrosse M/W(c), racquetball M(c)/W(c), rugby M(c)/W(c), sailing M(c)/W(c), soccer M/W, softball M/W, table tennis M/W, track and field M/W, ultimate Frisbee M(c)/W(c), volleyball M(c)/W(c), water polo M/W, wrestling M(c)/W(c).

Campus security: 24-hour emergency response devices and patrols, late-night transport/escort service, controlled dormitory access.

Student services: health clinic, personal/psychological counseling, legal services.

COSTS & FINANCIAL AID

Costs (2019–20) ***Comprehensive fee:*** $67,578 includes full-time tuition ($51,490), mandatory fees ($948), and room and board ($15,140). Part-time tuition: $2145 per credit hour. ***College room only:*** $8730.

Financial Aid Of all full-time matriculated undergraduates who enrolled in 2018, 2,645 applied for aid, 1,957 were judged to have need, 437 had their need fully met. In 2018, 604 non-need-based awards were made. ***Average percent of need met:*** 84. ***Average financial aid package:*** $35,421. ***Average need-based loan:*** $4542. ***Average need-based gift aid:*** $30,322. ***Average non-need-based aid:*** $21,040. ***Average indebtedness upon graduation:*** $39,370. ***Financial aid deadline:*** 2/1.

APPLYING

Standardized Tests *Required for some:* TOEFL or IELTS if English is not the applicant's first language.

Options: electronic application, early decision, early action, deferred entrance.

Application fee: $65.

Required: essay or personal statement, high school transcript, 2 letters of recommendation.

Application deadlines: 1/15 (freshmen), 4/1 (transfers), 11/1 (early action).

Early decision deadline: 11/15 (for plan 1), 1/15 (for plan 2).

Notification: 4/1 (freshmen), 4/15 (transfers), 1/1 (early decision plan 1), 2/15 (early decision plan 2), 1/1 (early action).

CONTACT

Mr. Raul Fonts, Associate Vice President/Dean of Admission and Financial Aid, Providence College, 1 Cunningham Square, Providence, RI 02918. *Phone:* 401-865-2535. *Toll-free phone:* 800-721-6444. *Fax:* 401-865-2826. *E-mail:* rfonts@providence.edu.

Rhode Island College

Providence, Rhode Island

http://www.ric.edu/

- **State-supported** comprehensive, founded 1854
- **Suburban** 180-acre campus with easy access to Boston
- **Endowment** $18.2 million
- **Coed** 6,688 undergraduate students, 76% full-time, 69% women, 31% men
- **Moderately difficult** entrance level, 73% of applicants were admitted

UNDERGRAD STUDENTS

5,108 full-time, 1,580 part-time. 15% are from out of state; 10% Black or African American, non-Hispanic/Latino; 21% Hispanic/Latino; 3% Asian, non-Hispanic/Latino; 0.1% Native Hawaiian or other Pacific Islander, non-Hispanic/Latino; 0.4% American Indian or Alaska Native, non-Hispanic/Latino; 2% Two or more races, non-Hispanic/Latino; 6% Race/ethnicity unknown; 0.2% international; 10% transferred in; 14% live on campus.

Freshmen:

Admission: 4,613 applied, 3,360 admitted, 848 enrolled. ***Test scores:*** SAT evidence-based reading and writing scores over 500: 58%; SAT math scores over 500: 52%; ACT scores over 18: 53%; SAT evidence-based reading and writing scores over 600: 13%; SAT math scores over 600: 8%; ACT scores over 24: 9%; SAT evidence-based reading and writing scores over 700: 2%; SAT math scores over 700: 1%.

Retention: 73% of full-time freshmen returned.

FACULTY

Total: 747, 45% full-time, 40% with terminal degrees.

Student/faculty ratio: 14:1.

ACADEMICS

Calendar: semesters. *Degrees:* certificates, bachelor's, master's, doctoral, post-master's, and postbachelor's certificates.

Special study options: academic remediation for entering students, adult/continuing education programs, advanced placement credit, double majors, English as a second language, honors programs, independent study, internships, off-campus study, part-time degree program, services for LD students, student-designed majors, study abroad, summer session for credit. ***ROTC:*** Army (c).

Unusual degree programs: 3-2 public administration with University of Rhode Island.

Computers: 250 computers/terminals are available on campus for general student use. Students can access the following: computer help desk, free student e-mail accounts, online (class) grades, online (class) registration, online (class) schedules. Campuswide network is available. 100% of college-owned or -operated housing units are wired for high-speed Internet access. Wireless service is available via classrooms, computer centers, computer labs, dorm rooms, learning centers, libraries, student centers.

Library: Adams Library. *Books:* 306,080 (physical), 302,387 (digital/electronic); *Serial titles:* 3,081 (physical), 52,652 (digital/electronic); *Databases:* 123. Weekly public service hours: 80.

STUDENT LIFE

Housing options: coed, special housing for students with disabilities. Campus housing is university owned. Freshman applicants given priority for college housing.

Activities and organizations: drama/theater group, student-run newspaper, radio and television station, choral group, Theta Phi Alpha, Delta Phi Epsilon, Alpha Sigma Tau, Sojourn Collegiate Ministries, Student Community Government, national fraternities, national sororities.

Athletics Member NCAA. All Division III except golf (Division II). ***Intercollegiate sports:*** baseball M, basketball M/W, cross-country running M/W, golf M/W, gymnastics W, lacrosse W, soccer M/W, softball W, swimming and diving W, tennis M/W, track and field M/W, volleyball W, wrestling M. ***Intramural sports:*** badminton M/W, basketball M/W, football M, soccer M/W, softball M/W, swimming and diving M/W, tennis M/W, volleyball M/W, water polo M/W.

Campus security: 24-hour emergency response devices and patrols, late-night transport/escort service, controlled dormitory access.

Student services: health clinic, personal/psychological counseling, women's center, legal services, veterans affairs office.

COSTS & FINANCIAL AID

Costs (2018–19) ***Tuition:*** state resident $7790 full-time, $306 per credit part-time; nonresident $20,553 full-time, $755 per credit part-time. Part-time tuition and fees vary according to course load. ***Required fees:*** $1139 full-time, $39 per credit part-time. ***Room and board:*** $12,978. Room and board charges vary according to housing facility. ***Payment plan:*** installment. ***Waivers:*** employees or children of employees.

Financial Aid Of all full-time matriculated undergraduates who enrolled in 2018, 4,333 applied for aid, 3,639 were judged to have need, 538 had their need fully met. In 2018, 129 non-need-based awards were made. ***Average percent of need met:*** 65. ***Average financial aid package:*** $9185. ***Average need-based loan:*** $3790. ***Average need-based gift aid:*** $6848. ***Average non-need-based aid:*** $2143. ***Average indebtedness upon graduation:*** $26,594.

APPLYING

Standardized Tests *Required:* SAT or ACT (for admission).

Options: electronic application, early admission.

Application fee: $50.

Required: essay or personal statement, high school transcript, 1 letter of recommendation, 1 letter from a guidance counselor. ***Required for some:*** interview. ***Recommended:*** minimum 3.0 GPA.

Notification: continuous until 12/15 (freshmen), continuous (out-of-state freshmen), continuous (transfers).

CONTACT

Jason Anthony, Director of Admissions, Rhode Island College, 600 Mount Pleasant Avenue, Providence, RI 02908-1927. *Phone:* 401-456-8234. *Toll-free phone:* 800-669-5760. *Fax:* 401-456-8817. *E-mail:* admissions@ric.edu.

Rhode Island School of Design

Providence, Rhode Island

http://www.risd.edu/

- **Independent** comprehensive, founded 1877
- **Urban** 19-acre campus with easy access to Boston, MA
- **Endowment** $351.4 million
- **Coed** 1,994 undergraduate students, 100% full-time, 68% women, 32% men
- 24% of applicants were admitted

UNDERGRAD STUDENTS

1,994 full-time. Students come from 48 states and territories; 46 other countries; 95% are from out of state; 4% Black or African American, non-Hispanic/Latino; 9% Hispanic/Latino; 18% Asian, non-Hispanic/Latino; 0.2% American Indian or Alaska Native, non-Hispanic/Latino; 5% Two or more races, non-Hispanic/Latino; 4% Race/ethnicity unknown; 30% international; 3% transferred in; 60% live on campus.

Freshmen:

Admission: 3,913 applied, 934 admitted, 473 enrolled. ***Average high school GPA:*** 3.6. ***Test scores:*** SAT evidence-based reading and writing scores over 500: 98%; SAT math scores over 500: 93%; ACT scores over 18: 99%; SAT evidence-based reading and writing scores over 600: 76%; SAT math scores over 600: 68%; ACT scores over 24: 86%; SAT evidence-based reading and writing scores over 700: 20%; SAT math scores over 700: 40%; ACT scores over 30: 46%.

Retention: 94% of full-time freshmen returned.

FACULTY

Total: 440, 37% full-time, 70% with terminal degrees.

Student/faculty ratio: 10:1.

ACADEMICS

Calendar: 4-1-4. *Degrees:* bachelor's and master's.

Special study options: advanced placement credit, double majors, honors programs, independent study, internships, off-campus study, services for LD students, study abroad. ***ROTC:*** Army (c).

Computers: 65 computers/terminals and 400 ports are available on campus for general student use. Students can access the following: campus intranet, computer help desk, free student e-mail accounts, online

(class) grades, online (class) registration, online (class) schedules. Campuswide network is available. 100% of college-owned or -operated housing units are wired for high-speed Internet access. Wireless service is available via entire campus.
Library: Fleet Library. *Books:* 131,412 (physical), 178,450 (digital/electronic); *Serial titles:* 1,662 (physical), 800 (digital/electronic); *Databases:* 48. Weekly public service hours: 89; students can reserve study rooms.

STUDENT LIFE
Housing options: on-campus residence required through sophomore year; coed, special housing for students with disabilities. Campus housing is university owned and leased by the school. Freshman campus housing is guaranteed.

Activities and organizations: drama/theater group, student-run newspaper, radio station, choral group, athletic clubs, Religious clubs, South Asian Student Association, RISD Global Initiative, Community Service Club.

Athletics ***Intramural sports:*** basketball M(c)/W(c), equestrian sports M(c)/W(c), fencing M(c)/W(c), field hockey M(c)/W(c), ice hockey M(c)/W(c), skiing (downhill) M(c)/W(c), soccer M(c)/W(c), swimming and diving M(c)/W(c), tennis M(c)/W(c), ultimate Frisbee M(c)/W(c), volleyball M(c)/W(c).

Campus security: 24-hour emergency response devices and patrols, late-night transport/escort service, controlled dormitory access.

Student services: health clinic, personal/psychological counseling, legal services.

COSTS & FINANCIAL AID
Costs (2019–20) ***Comprehensive fee:*** $66,580 includes full-time tuition ($51,800), mandatory fees ($1060), and room and board ($13,720).

Financial Aid Of all full-time matriculated undergraduates who enrolled in 2018, 887 applied for aid, 794 were judged to have need, 28 had their need fully met. ***Average percent of need met:*** 66. ***Average financial aid package:*** $35,064. ***Average need-based loan:*** $6750. ***Average need-based gift aid:*** $30,418. ***Average indebtedness upon graduation:*** $35,398. ***Financial aid deadline:*** 2/15.

APPLYING
Standardized Tests *Required:* SAT or ACT (for admission).

Options: electronic application, early decision, deferred entrance.

Application fee: $60.

Required: essay or personal statement, high school transcript, portfolio, drawing assignments. ***Recommended:*** 3 letters of recommendation.

Application deadlines: 2/1 (freshmen), 3/15 (transfers).

Early decision deadline: 11/1.

CONTACT
James O'Hara, Vice President for Enrollment, Rhode Island School of Design, 2 College Street, Providence, RI 02903-2784. *Phone:* 401-454-6300. *Toll-free phone:* 800-364-7473. *Fax:* 401-454-6309. *E-mail:* admissions@risd.edu.

Roger Williams University

Bristol, Rhode Island

http://www.rwu.edu/

- **Independent** comprehensive, founded 1956
- **Small-town** 140-acre campus with easy access to Boston
- **Endowment** $67.6 million
- **Coed**
- 82% of applicants were admitted

FACULTY
Student/faculty ratio: 14:1.

ACADEMICS
Calendar: semesters. *Degrees:* certificates, associate, bachelor's, master's, doctoral, and postbachelor's certificates.
Library: Roger Williams University Library plus 1 other. *Books:* 219,429 (physical), 448,637 (digital/electronic); *Serial titles:* 493 (physical), 52,585 (digital/electronic); *Databases:* 189. Weekly public service hours: 111; students can reserve study rooms.

STUDENT LIFE
Housing options: on-campus residence required through sophomore year; coed, special housing for students with disabilities. Campus housing is university owned. Freshman campus housing is guaranteed.

Activities and organizations: drama/theater group, student-run newspaper, radio station, choral group, Campus Entertainment Network, Dance Club, WQRI 88.3 Radio Station, Habitat for Humanity.

Athletics Member NCAA. All Division III.

Campus security: 24-hour emergency response devices and patrols, late-night transport/escort service, controlled dormitory access, Rave Guardian Emergency Communication App.

Student services: health clinic, personal/psychological counseling, women's center, veterans affairs office.

COSTS & FINANCIAL AID
Costs (2018–19) ***Comprehensive fee:*** $48,074 includes full-time tuition ($30,326), mandatory fees ($2184), and room and board ($15,564). Full-time tuition and fees vary according to class time, course load, degree level, and program. Part-time tuition and fees vary according to class time, course load, degree level, and program. No tuition increase for student's term of enrollment. ***College room only:*** $8310. Room and board charges vary according to board plan and housing facility.

Financial Aid Of all full-time matriculated undergraduates who enrolled in 2018, 3,089 applied for aid, 2,578 were judged to have need, 266 had their need fully met. 1,427 Federal Work-Study jobs (averaging $1858). In 2018, 1173 non-need-based awards were made. ***Average percent of need met:*** 81. ***Average financial aid package:*** $22,916. ***Average need-based loan:*** $4294. ***Average need-based gift aid:*** $15,125. ***Average non-need-based aid:*** $12,688. ***Average indebtedness upon graduation:*** $44,886. ***Financial aid deadline:*** 2/1.

APPLYING
Standardized Tests *Required for some:* SAT or ACT (for admission).

Options: electronic application, early action, deferred entrance.

Application fee: $50.

Required: essay or personal statement, 1 letter of recommendation. ***Required for some:*** high school transcript, portfolio review, audition, specific preparatory courses for visual arts studies, graphic design communications, architecture, creative writing, dance and theater.

CONTACT
Roger Williams University, 1 Old Ferry Road, Bristol, RI 02809. *Toll-free phone:* 800-458-7144.

Salve Regina University

Newport, Rhode Island

http://www.salve.edu/

- **Independent Roman Catholic** comprehensive, founded 1934
- **Suburban** 80-acre campus with easy access to Boston, Providence
- **Endowment** $62.7 million
- **Coed** 2,021 undergraduate students, 97% full-time, 67% women, 33% men
- 76% of applicants were admitted

UNDERGRAD STUDENTS
1,957 full-time, 64 part-time. Students come from 35 states and territories; 17 other countries; 82% are from out of state; 2% Black or African American, non-Hispanic/Latino; 7% Hispanic/Latino; 1% Asian, non-Hispanic/Latino; 0.0% Native Hawaiian or other Pacific Islander, non-Hispanic/Latino; 0.2% American Indian or Alaska Native, non-Hispanic/Latino; 3% Two or more races, non-Hispanic/Latino; 5% Race/ethnicity unknown; 2% international; 2% transferred in; 60% live on campus.

Freshmen:
Admission: 4,721 applied, 3,596 admitted, 497 enrolled. ***Average high school GPA:*** 3.4.

Retention: 83% of full-time freshmen returned.

FACULTY
Total: 278, 46% full-time, 49% with terminal degrees.
Student/faculty ratio: 14:1.

ACADEMICS
Calendar: semesters. *Degrees:* certificates, associate, bachelor's, master's, doctoral, post-master's, and postbachelor's certificates.

Special study options: accelerated degree program, adult/continuing education programs, advanced placement credit, double majors, English as a second language, honors programs, independent study, internships, off-campus study, part-time degree program, services for LD students, study abroad, summer session for credit. ***ROTC:*** Army (c).

Unusual degree programs: 3-2 business administration; nursing; administration of justice, holistic counseling, international relations, MBA, management, rehabilitation counseling.

Computers: 215 computers/terminals are available on campus for general student use. Students can access the following: campus intranet, computer help desk, free student e-mail accounts, online (class) grades, online (class) registration, online (class) schedules. Campuswide network is available. 100% of college-owned or -operated housing units are wired for high-speed Internet access. Wireless service is available via entire campus.
Library: McKillop Library. *Books:* 147,721 (physical), 347,549 (digital/electronic); *Serial titles:* 195 (physical), 75,064 (digital/electronic); *Databases:* 82. Weekly public service hours: 58; students can reserve study rooms.

STUDENT LIFE
Housing options: on-campus residence required through sophomore year; coed, men-only, women-only. Campus housing is university owned and leased by the school. Freshman campus housing is guaranteed.

Activities and organizations: drama/theater group, student-run newspaper, radio station, choral group, Orpheus Musical Society, Student Government Association, Student Outdoor Adventures, Student Nurse Organization, Stagefright Theatre Company.

Athletics Member NCAA. All Division III. ***Intercollegiate sports:*** baseball M, basketball M/W, cross-country running M/W, equestrian sports W, field hockey W, football M, ice hockey M/W, lacrosse M/W, rugby M(c)/W(c), sailing M/W, soccer M/W, softball W, tennis M/W, track and field W, volleyball W. ***Intramural sports:*** baseball M, basketball M/W, cheerleading W(c), football M/W, golf M/W, ice hockey M, lacrosse M, rugby M(c)/W(c), soccer M/W, softball M/W, swimming and diving M(c)/W(c), tennis M/W, ultimate Frisbee M/W, volleyball M/W, weight lifting M/W.

Campus security: 24-hour emergency response devices and patrols, late-night transport/escort service, controlled dormitory access.

Student services: health clinic, personal/psychological counseling, veterans affairs office.

COSTS & FINANCIAL AID
Costs (2019–20) ***Comprehensive fee:*** $56,410 includes full-time tuition ($40,750), mandatory fees ($700), and room and board ($14,960). Part-time tuition: $1358 per credit.

Financial Aid Of all full-time matriculated undergraduates who enrolled in 2018, 1,687 applied for aid, 1,497 were judged to have need, 170 had their need fully met. 699 Federal Work-Study jobs (averaging $737). 33 state and other part-time jobs (averaging $585). In 2018, 410 non-need-based awards were made. ***Average percent of need met:*** 67. ***Average financial aid package:*** $28,323. ***Average need-based loan:*** $4429. ***Average need-based gift aid:*** $23,290. ***Average non-need-based aid:*** $15,236. ***Average indebtedness upon graduation:*** $30,692.

APPLYING
Options: electronic application, early action, deferred entrance.

Application fee: $50.

Required: essay or personal statement, high school transcript, 2 letters of recommendation. ***Recommended:*** minimum 2.7 GPA.

Application deadlines: 2/1 (freshmen), rolling (transfers), 11/1 (early action).

Notification: 12/25 (freshmen), continuous (transfers).

CONTACT
Dean Colleen Emerson, Dean of Undergraduate Admissions, Salve Regina University, 100 Ochre Point Avenue, Newport, RI 02840-4192. *Phone:* 401-341-2908. *Toll-free phone:* 888-GO SALVE. *Fax:* 401-848-2823. *E-mail:* emersonc@salve.edu.

★ University of Rhode Island
Kingston, Rhode Island
http://www.uri.edu/

- **State-supported** university, founded 1892
- **Small-town** 1200-acre campus
- **Endowment** $107.8 million
- **Coed**
- **Moderately difficult** entrance level

FACULTY
Student/faculty ratio: 17:1.

ACADEMICS
Calendar: semesters. *Degrees:* bachelor's, master's, doctoral, and postbachelor's certificates.
Library: Robert L. Carothers Library and Learning Commons plus 3 others. Study areas open 24 hours, 5–7 days a week; students can reserve study rooms.

STUDENT LIFE
Housing options: coed, cooperative, special housing for students with disabilities. Campus housing is university owned and leased by the school. Freshman campus housing is guaranteed.

Activities and organizations: drama/theater group, student-run newspaper, radio and television station, choral group, marching band, Student Entertainment Committee, student radio station, Intramural sport clubs, Student Alumni Association, student newspaper, national fraternities, national sororities.

Athletics Member NCAA. All Division I.

Campus security: 24-hour emergency response devices and patrols, student patrols, late-night transport/escort service, controlled dormitory access.

Student services: health clinic, personal/psychological counseling, women's center.

COSTS & FINANCIAL AID
Costs (2018–19) ***Tuition:*** state resident $12,248 full-time, $510 per credit hour part-time; nonresident $28,972 full-time, $1207 per credit hour part-time. Full-time tuition and fees vary according to course load, location, and reciprocity agreements. Part-time tuition and fees vary according to course load, location, and reciprocity agreements. ***Required fees:*** $1890 full-time, $51 per credit hour part-time, $58 per term part-time. ***Room and board:*** $7850; room only: $4500. Room and board charges vary according to board plan and housing facility.

Financial Aid Of all full-time matriculated undergraduates who enrolled in 2018, 12,856 applied for aid, 11,146 were judged to have need, 4,900 had their need fully met. 631 Federal Work-Study jobs (averaging $1807). In 2018, 1039 non-need-based awards were made. ***Average percent of need met:*** 57. ***Average financial aid package:*** $16,753. ***Average need-based loan:*** $6760. ***Average need-based gift aid:*** $10,292. ***Average non-need-based aid:*** $6603. ***Average indebtedness upon graduation:*** $34,050.

APPLYING
Standardized Tests *Required:* SAT or ACT (for admission).

Options: electronic application, early admission, early action, deferred entrance.

Application fee: $65.

Required: essay or personal statement, high school transcript, 1 letter of recommendation, list of senior courses. ***Required for some:*** 2 letters of recommendation.

CONTACT
Ms. Joanne Lynch, Assistant Dean of Admissions, University of Rhode Island, Undergraduate Admission Office, Newman Hall, 14 Upper College Road, Kingston, RI 02881. *Phone:* 401-874-7110. *Fax:* 401-874-5523. *E-mail:* lynch@uri.edu.

SOUTH CAROLINA

Allen University

Columbia, South Carolina

http://www.allenuniversity.edu/

CONTACT

Terri Parker, Director of Admission, Allen University, 1530 Harden Street, Columbia, SC 29204. *Phone:* 803-376-5733. *Toll-free phone:* 877-625-5368. *E-mail:* tparker@allenuniversity.edu.

Anderson University

Anderson, South Carolina

http://www.andersonuniversity.edu/

- **Independent Baptist** comprehensive, founded 1911
- **Urban** 271-acre campus with easy access to Greenville
- **Endowment** $44.7 million
- **Coed**
- **Minimally difficult** entrance level

FACULTY

Student/faculty ratio: 14:1.

ACADEMICS

Calendar: semesters. *Degrees:* bachelor's, master's, and doctoral.
Library: Thrift Library. *Books:* 90,729 (physical), 99,204 (digital/electronic); *Serial titles:* 14,268 (physical), 174,052 (digital/electronic); *Databases:* 200. Weekly public service hours: 88; students can reserve study rooms.

STUDENT LIFE

Housing options: on-campus residence required through sophomore year; men-only, women-only. Campus housing is university owned. Freshman campus housing is guaranteed.

Activities and organizations: drama/theater group, student-run newspaper, choral group, Baptist Collegiate Ministries, Gamma Beta Phi, Anderson University Education Club, Ducks Unlimited, Council of Exceptional Children.

Athletics Member NCAA. All Division II.

Campus security: 24-hour emergency response devices and patrols, late-night transport/escort service, controlled dormitory access.

Student services: health clinic, personal/psychological counseling.

COSTS & FINANCIAL AID

Costs (2018–19) ***Comprehensive fee:*** $37,830 includes full-time tuition ($25,140), mandatory fees ($2860), and room and board ($9830). Full-time tuition and fees vary according to course load and program. Part-time tuition: $625 per credit hour. Part-time tuition and fees vary according to course load and program. ***College room only:*** $5030. Room and board charges vary according to board plan and housing facility.

Financial Aid Of all full-time matriculated undergraduates who enrolled in 2018, 2,308 applied for aid, 1,954 were judged to have need, 556 had their need fully met. 205 Federal Work-Study jobs (averaging $4000). 242 state and other part-time jobs (averaging $1100). In 2018, 492 non-need-based awards were made. ***Average percent of need met:*** 72. ***Average financial aid package:*** $20,554. ***Average need-based loan:*** $4246. ***Average need-based gift aid:*** $17,701. ***Average non-need-based aid:*** $12,380. ***Average indebtedness upon graduation:*** $48,455. ***Financial aid deadline:*** 7/1.

APPLYING

Standardized Tests *Required:* SAT or ACT (for admission).

Options: electronic application, deferred entrance.

Application fee: $25.

Required: high school transcript. ***Required for some:*** essay or personal statement, 2 letters of recommendation, interview. ***Recommended:*** minimum 2.9 GPA.

CONTACT

Mr. Jacob Queen, Director of Admission, Anderson University, 316 Boulevard, Anderson, SC 29621. *Phone:* 864-231-5795. *Toll-free phone:* 800-542-3594. *E-mail:* jqueen@andersonuniversity.edu.

Benedict College

Columbia, South Carolina

http://www.benedict.edu/

CONTACT

Benedict College, 1600 Harden Street, Columbia, SC 29204. *Phone:* 803-705-4491. *Toll-free phone:* 800-868-6598.

Bob Jones University

Greenville, South Carolina

http://www.bju.edu/

- **Independent Christian** university, founded 1927
- **Urban** 225-acre campus
- **Coed**
- **Minimally difficult** entrance level

FACULTY

Student/faculty ratio: 13:1.

ACADEMICS

Calendar: semesters. *Degrees:* associate, bachelor's, master's, doctoral, and post-master's certificates.
Library: Mack Library plus 2 others.

STUDENT LIFE

Housing options: on-campus residence required through senior year; men-only, women-only, special housing for students with disabilities. Campus housing is university owned. Freshman campus housing is guaranteed.

Activities and organizations: drama/theater group, student-run newspaper, radio and television station, choral group, Community Service Council, Missions Advance, Societies, Mission Prayer Band, University Business Association.

Athletics Member NCCAA.

Campus security: 24-hour patrols, student patrols, late-night transport/escort service, controlled dormitory access, 24/7 emergency dispatcher.

Student services: health clinic, personal/psychological counseling.

COSTS & FINANCIAL AID

Costs (2018–19) ***Comprehensive fee:*** $25,126 includes full-time tuition ($17,250), mandatory fees ($900), and room and board ($6976). Full-time tuition and fees vary according to course load and program. Part-time tuition: $860 per credit hour. Part-time tuition and fees vary according to course load and program. ***Required fees:*** $488 per degree program part-time.

Financial Aid Of all full-time matriculated undergraduates who enrolled in 2017, 1,862 applied for aid, 1,653 were judged to have need, 269 had their need fully met. In 2017, 470 non-need-based awards were made. ***Average percent of need met:*** 61. ***Average financial aid package:*** $12,290. ***Average need-based loan:*** $3814. ***Average need-based gift aid:*** $10,486. ***Average non-need-based aid:*** $5069. ***Average indebtedness upon graduation:*** $21,153.

APPLYING

Options: electronic application.

Required: essay or personal statement, high school transcript, 3 letters of recommendation.

CONTACT

Mr. Gary Deedrick, Director of Admission, Bob Jones University, 1700 Wade Hampton Boulevard, Greenville, SC 29614. *Phone:* 864-242-5100. *Toll-free phone:* 800-252-6363. *Fax:* 800-232-9258. *E-mail:* admission@bju.edu.

Charleston Southern University

Charleston, South Carolina

http://www.charlestonsouthern.edu/

- **Independent Baptist** comprehensive, founded 1964
- **Suburban** 500-acre campus
- **Endowment** $18.2 million
- **Coed**
- **Moderately difficult** entrance level

FACULTY
Student/faculty ratio: 15:1.

ACADEMICS
Calendar: 4-4-1. *Degrees:* bachelor's, master's, and post-master's certificates.
Library: L. Mendel Rivers Library plus 1 other. *Books:* 117,095 (physical), 303,641 (digital/electronic); *Serial titles:* 4,761 (physical), 53,688 (digital/electronic); *Databases:* 177. Weekly public service hours: 83; students can reserve study rooms.

STUDENT LIFE
Housing options: on-campus residence required for freshman year; men-only, women-only. Campus housing is university owned. Freshman applicants given priority for college housing.

Activities and organizations: drama/theater group, student-run newspaper, choral group, marching band, Student Government, Baptist Student Union, Fellowship of Christian Athletes, national fraternities, national sororities.

Athletics Member NCAA. All Division I except football (Division I-AA).

Campus security: 24-hour emergency response devices and patrols, late-night transport/escort service, controlled dormitory access.

Student services: personal/psychological counseling.

FINANCIAL AID
Financial Aid Of all full-time matriculated undergraduates who enrolled in 2007, 1,968 applied for aid, 1,749 were judged to have need, 421 had their need fully met. 614 Federal Work-Study jobs (averaging $1406). In 2007, 306 non-need-based awards were made. ***Average percent of need met:*** 73. ***Average financial aid package:*** $15,036. ***Average need-based loan:*** $4804. ***Average need-based gift aid:*** $11,008. ***Average non-need-based aid:*** $10,832. ***Average indebtedness upon graduation:*** $20,252.

APPLYING
Standardized Tests *Required:* SAT or ACT (for admission).

Options: electronic application.

Application fee: $40.

Required: high school transcript, minimum 2.0 GPA. ***Required for some:*** essay or personal statement, 1 letter of recommendation, interview.

CONTACT
Mr. Jim Rhoden, Director of Enrollment Management, Charleston Southern University, Charleston, SC 29423-8087. *Phone:* 843-863-7050. *Toll-free phone:* 800-947-7474. *E-mail:* enroll@csuniv.edu.

The Citadel, The Military College of South Carolina

Charleston, South Carolina

http://www.citadel.edu/

- **State-supported** comprehensive, founded 1842
- **Suburban** 300-acre campus
- **Endowment** $254.3 million
- **Coed, primarily men**
- **Moderately difficult** entrance level

FACULTY
Student/faculty ratio: 12:1.

ACADEMICS
Calendar: semesters. *Degrees:* bachelor's, master's, post-master's, and postbachelor's certificates.
Library: Daniel Library. *Books:* 182,744 (physical), 225,852 (digital/electronic); *Serial titles:* 97 (physical); *Databases:* 250. Students can reserve study rooms.

STUDENT LIFE
Housing options: on-campus residence required through senior year; coed. Campus housing is university owned. Freshman campus housing is guaranteed.

Activities and organizations: student-run newspaper, choral group, marching band, The Republican Society, Semper Fi Society, American Society of Civil Engineers, Campus Outreach, Criminal Justice Society.

Athletics Member NCAA. All Division I except football (Division I-AA).

Campus security: 24-hour patrols.

Student services: health clinic, personal/psychological counseling, veterans affairs office.

COSTS & FINANCIAL AID
Costs (2018–19) ***Tuition:*** state resident $12,516 full-time, $485 per credit hour part-time; nonresident $34,988 full-time, $902 per credit hour part-time. Full-time tuition and fees vary according to class time, degree level, program, and student level. Part-time tuition and fees vary according to class time and program. ***Required fees:*** $2133 full-time. ***Room and board:*** $6904.

Financial Aid Of all full-time matriculated undergraduates who enrolled in 2018, 2,006 applied for aid, 1,558 were judged to have need, 465 had their need fully met. 96 Federal Work-Study jobs (averaging $3542). In 2018, 615 non-need-based awards were made. ***Average percent of need met:*** 65. ***Average financial aid package:*** $18,477. ***Average need-based loan:*** $4286. ***Average need-based gift aid:*** $17,996. ***Average non-need-based aid:*** $15,808. ***Average indebtedness upon graduation:*** $31,029.

APPLYING
Standardized Tests *Required:* SAT or ACT (for admission).

Options: electronic application.

Application fee: $40.

Required: high school transcript. ***Recommended:*** interview.

CONTACT
Lt. Col. John W. Powell Jr., Director of Admissions, The Citadel, The Military College of South Carolina, 171 Moultrie Street, Charleston, SC 29409. *Phone:* 843-953-5230. *Toll-free phone:* 800-868-1842. *Fax:* 843-953-7036. *E-mail:* john.powell@citadel.edu.

Claflin University

Orangeburg, South Carolina

http://www.claflin.edu/

CONTACT
Claflin University, 400 Magnolia Street, Orangeburg, SC 29115. *Phone:* 803-535-5340. *Toll-free phone:* 800-922-1276.

★ Clemson University

Clemson, South Carolina

http://www.clemson.edu/

- **State-supported** university, founded 1889
- **Small-town** 1400-acre campus
- **Endowment** $518.6 million
- **Coed**
- **Very difficult** entrance level

FACULTY
Student/faculty ratio: 16:1.

ACADEMICS
Calendar: semesters. *Degrees:* bachelor's, master's, doctoral, and post-master's certificates.
Library: Robert Muldrow Cooper Library plus 1 other. Study areas open 24 hours, 5–7 days a week; students can reserve study rooms.

STUDENT LIFE
Housing options: on-campus residence required for freshman year; coed, men-only, women-only. Campus housing is university owned. Freshman campus housing is guaranteed.

Activities and organizations: drama/theater group, student-run newspaper, radio and television station, choral group, marching band, Student Government, Fellowship of Christian Athletes, Tiger Band, national fraternities, national sororities.

Athletics Member NCAA. All Division I except football (Division I-A).

Campus security: 24-hour emergency response devices and patrols, late-night transport/escort service, controlled dormitory access.

Student services: health clinic, personal/psychological counseling, legal services.

FINANCIAL AID
Financial Aid Of all full-time matriculated undergraduates who enrolled in 2018, 12,570 applied for aid, 9,047 were judged to have need, 1,259 had their need fully met. 1,168 Federal Work-Study jobs (averaging

$2888). In 2018, 5144 non-need-based awards were made. ***Average percent of need met:*** 52. ***Average financial aid package:*** $11,743. ***Average need-based loan:*** $4320. ***Average need-based gift aid:*** $9629. ***Average non-need-based aid:*** $5447. ***Average indebtedness upon graduation:*** $32,285.

APPLYING

Standardized Tests *Required:* SAT or ACT (for admission).

Options: electronic application.

Application fee: $70.

Required: high school transcript. ***Recommended:*** essay or personal statement.

CONTACT

Clemson University, Clemson, SC 29634.

See below for display ad and page 988 for the College Close-Up.

Coastal Carolina University

Conway, South Carolina

http://www.coastal.edu/

- **State-supported** comprehensive, founded 1954
- **Suburban** 621-acre campus
- **Endowment** $44.7 million
- **Coed** 9,917 undergraduate students, 90% full-time, 54% women, 46% men
- **Moderately difficult** entrance level, 70% of applicants were admitted

UNDERGRAD STUDENTS

8,941 full-time, 976 part-time. Students come from 50 states and territories; 61 other countries; 51% are from out of state; 19% Black or African American, non-Hispanic/Latino; 5% Hispanic/Latino; 0.9% Asian, non-Hispanic/Latino; 0.1% Native Hawaiian or other Pacific Islander, non-Hispanic/Latino; 0.3% American Indian or Alaska Native, non-Hispanic/Latino; 5% Two or more races, non-Hispanic/Latino; 2% Race/ethnicity unknown; 1% international; 7% transferred in; 44% live on campus.

Freshmen:

Admission: 14,057 applied, 9,777 admitted, 2,329 enrolled. ***Average high school GPA:*** 3.6. ***Test scores:*** SAT evidence-based reading and writing scores over 500: 87%; SAT math scores over 500: 83%; ACT scores over 18: 93%; SAT evidence-based reading and writing scores over 600: 23%; SAT math scores over 600: 18%; ACT scores over 24: 28%; SAT evidence-based reading and writing scores over 700: 2%; SAT math scores over 700: 1%; ACT scores over 30: 3%.

Retention: 69% of full-time freshmen returned.

FACULTY

Total: 784, 63% full-time, 57% with terminal degrees.

Student/faculty ratio: 17:1.

ACADEMICS

Calendar: semesters. *Degrees:* certificates, bachelor's, master's, doctoral, post-master's, and postbachelor's certificates.

Special study options: accelerated degree program, adult/continuing education programs, advanced placement credit, cooperative education, distance learning, double majors, honors programs, independent study, internships, part-time degree program, services for LD students, student-designed majors, study abroad, summer session for credit. ***ROTC:*** Army (b).

Computers: 1,400 computers/terminals are available on campus for general student use. Students can access the following: computer help desk, free student e-mail accounts, online (class) grades, online (class) registration, online (class) schedules. Campuswide network is available. Wireless service is available via entire campus.

Library: Kimbel Library. *Books:* 129,696 (physical), 433,254 (digital/electronic); *Serial titles:* 622 (physical), 79,146 (digital/electronic); *Databases:* 213. Weekly public service hours: 168; study areas open 24 hours, 5–7 days a week.

STUDENT LIFE

Housing options: on-campus residence required through sophomore year; coed, special housing for students with disabilities. Campus housing is university owned. Freshman campus housing is guaranteed.

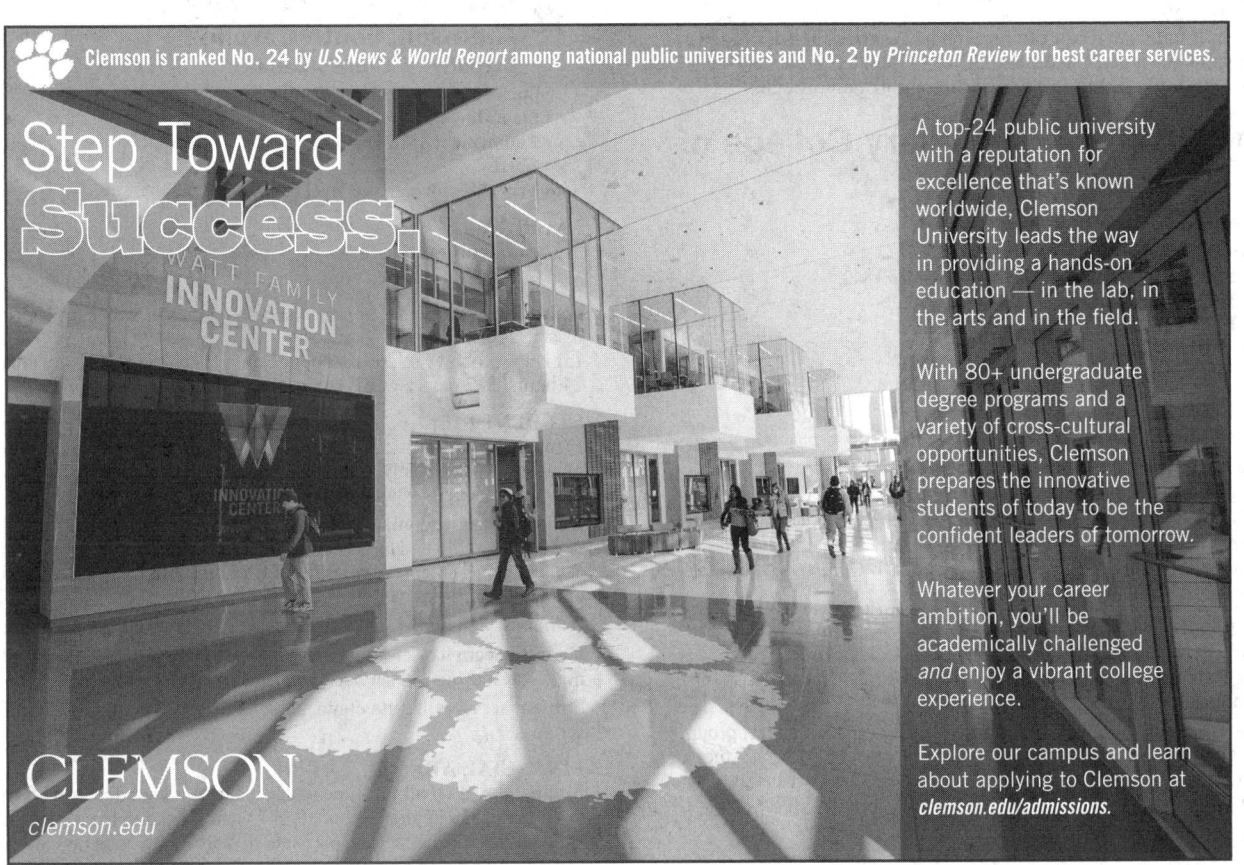

Activities and organizations: drama/theater group, student-run newspaper, radio station, choral group, marching band, Club Rugby,

Outdoor Adventure Club, Alpha Delta Pi, Salt Water Anglers, Aqua League (Scuba Club), national fraternities, national sororities.

Athletics Member NCAA. All Division I. ***Intercollegiate sports:*** baseball M(s), basketball M(s)/W(s), cheerleading M(c)/W(c), cross-country running M(s)/W(s), equestrian sports M(c)/W(c), field hockey M(c)/W(c), football M(s), golf M(s)/W(s), lacrosse M(c)/W(s), rugby M(c)/W(c), sailing M(c)/W(c), sand volleyball W(s), soccer M(s)/W(s), softball W(s), swimming and diving M(c)/W(c), tennis M(s)/W(s), track and field M(s)/W(s), volleyball M(c)/W(s), weight lifting M(c)/W(c), wrestling M(c). ***Intramural sports:*** badminton M/W, basketball M/W, lacrosse M/W, sand volleyball M/W, soccer M/W, softball M/W, table tennis M/W, tennis M/W, volleyball M/W.

Campus security: 24-hour emergency response devices and patrols, late-night transport/escort service.

Student services: health clinic, personal/psychological counseling, women's center, veterans affairs office.

COSTS & FINANCIAL AID

Costs (2018–19) ***Tuition:*** state resident $11,356 full-time, $483 per credit hour part-time; nonresident $26,468 full-time, $1107 per credit hour part-time. Full-time tuition and fees vary according to course load, degree level, and reciprocity agreements. Part-time tuition and fees vary according to course load, degree level, and reciprocity agreements. ***Required fees:*** $180 full-time, $5 per credit hour part-time. ***Room and board:*** $9190; room only: $5440. Room and board charges vary according to board plan and housing facility. ***Payment plan:*** installment. ***Waivers:*** senior citizens and employees or children of employees.

Financial Aid Of all full-time matriculated undergraduates who enrolled in 2017, 7,459 applied for aid, 6,300 were judged to have need, 636 had their need fully met. 221 Federal Work-Study jobs (averaging $1973). 1,485 state and other part-time jobs (averaging $1829). In 2017, 1697 non-need-based awards were made. ***Average percent of need met:*** 46. ***Average financial aid package:*** $10,780. ***Average need-based loan:*** $9360. ***Average need-based gift aid:*** $5286. ***Average non-need-based aid:*** $14,557. ***Average indebtedness upon graduation:*** $37,226.

APPLYING

Standardized Tests *Required:* SAT or ACT (for admission).

Options: electronic application, deferred entrance.

Application fee: $45.

Required: high school transcript, minimum 2.0 GPA. ***Recommended:*** essay or personal statement, 1 letter of recommendation, interview.

Application deadlines: rolling (freshmen), rolling (transfers).

Notification: continuous (freshmen), continuous (transfers).

CONTACT

Ms. Amanda E. Craddock, Assistant Provost for Admissions and Merit Awards, Coastal Carolina University, PO Box 261954, Conway, SC 29528-6054. *Phone:* 843-349-2170. *Toll-free phone:* 800-277-7000. *Fax:* 843-349-6436. *E-mail:* acraddoc@coastal.edu.

Coker College

Hartsville, South Carolina

http://www.coker.edu/

- **Independent** comprehensive, founded 1908
- **Small-town** 37-acre campus with easy access to Charlotte
- **Endowment** $29.2 million
- **Coed**
- **Moderately difficult** entrance level

FACULTY

Student/faculty ratio: 13:1.

ACADEMICS

Calendar: semesters. *Degrees:* bachelor's and master's (also offers evening program with significant enrollment not reflected in profile). **Library:** The Charles W. and Joan S. Coker Library-Information Technology Center plus 1 other. *Books:* 81,626 (physical), 15,760 (digital/electronic). Weekly public service hours: 87; students can reserve study rooms.

STUDENT LIFE

Housing options: coed, special housing for students with disabilities. Campus housing is university owned. Freshman campus housing is guaranteed.

Activities and organizations: drama/theater group, choral group, Student Government Association.

Athletics Member NCAA. All Division II except lacrosse (Division I).

Campus security: 24-hour patrols, late-night transport/escort service, controlled dormitory access.

Student services: health clinic, personal/psychological counseling.

COSTS & FINANCIAL AID

Costs (2018–19) ***Comprehensive fee:*** $38,618 includes full-time tuition ($29,328), mandatory fees ($200), and room and board ($9090). Full-time tuition and fees vary according to course load, degree level, location, and program. Part-time tuition: $1222 per credit hour. Part-time tuition and fees vary according to course load, degree level, location, and program. ***College room only:*** $4190. Room and board charges vary according to board plan and housing facility.

Financial Aid Of all full-time matriculated undergraduates who enrolled in 2017, 934 applied for aid, 824 were judged to have need, 154 had their need fully met. 71 Federal Work-Study jobs (averaging $831). In 2017, 110 non-need-based awards were made. ***Average percent of need met:*** 69. ***Average financial aid package:*** $20,820. ***Average need-based loan:*** $4216. ***Average need-based gift aid:*** $7883. ***Average non-need-based aid:*** $16,116. ***Average indebtedness upon graduation:*** $9601.

APPLYING

Standardized Tests *Required:* SAT or ACT (for admission).

Options: electronic application, early action, deferred entrance.

Required: high school transcript. ***Required for some:*** essay or personal statement, interview, audition or portfolio for certain programs.

CONTACT

Mr. Adam Connolly, Vice President for Enrollment Management, Coker College, 300 E. College Avenue, Hartsville, SC 29550. *Phone:* 843-383-8050. *Toll-free phone:* 800-950-1908. *Fax:* 843-383-8056. *E-mail:* admissions@coker.edu.

College of Charleston

Charleston, South Carolina

http://www.cofc.edu/

- **State-supported** comprehensive, founded 1770
- **Urban** 66-acre campus
- **Endowment** $92.3 million
- **Coed** 9,880 undergraduate students, 92% full-time, 64% women, 36% men
- **Moderately difficult** entrance level, 79% of applicants were admitted

UNDERGRAD STUDENTS

9,103 full-time, 777 part-time. Students come from 48 states and territories; 62 other countries; 34% are from out of state; 8% Black or African American, non-Hispanic/Latino; 6% Hispanic/Latino; 2% Asian, non-Hispanic/Latino; 0.2% Native Hawaiian or other Pacific Islander, non-Hispanic/Latino; 0.4% American Indian or Alaska Native, non-Hispanic/Latino; 4% Two or more races, non-Hispanic/Latino; 1% Race/ethnicity unknown; 1% international; 5% transferred in; 31% live on campus.

Freshmen:

Admission: 11,675 applied, 9,254 admitted, 2,199 enrolled. ***Average high school GPA:*** 3.9. ***Test scores:*** SAT evidence-based reading and writing scores over 500: 95%; SAT math scores over 500: 90%; ACT scores over 18: 98%; SAT evidence-based reading and writing scores over 600: 50%; SAT math scores over 600: 33%; ACT scores over 24: 63%; SAT evidence-based reading and writing scores over 700: 7%; SAT math scores over 700: 6%; ACT scores over 30: 13%.

Retention: 79% of full-time freshmen returned.

FACULTY

Total: 958, 58% full-time, 68% with terminal degrees.

Student/faculty ratio: 15:1.

ACADEMICS

Calendar: semesters. *Degrees:* certificates, bachelor's, master's, post-master's, and postbachelor's certificates (also offers graduate degree programs through University of Charleston, South Carolina).

Special study options: accelerated degree program, adult/continuing education programs, advanced placement credit, cooperative education, distance learning, double majors, English as a second language, honors programs, independent study, internships, off-campus study, part-time degree program, services for LD students, study abroad, summer session for credit. ***ROTC:*** Air Force (c).

Unusual degree programs: 3-2 computer science, mathematics.

Computers: 325 computers/terminals are available on campus for general student use. Students can access the following: campus intranet, computer help desk, free student e-mail accounts, online (class) grades, online (class) registration, online (class) schedules. Campuswide network is available. 80% of college-owned or -operated housing units are wired for high-speed Internet access. Wireless service is available via entire campus.

Library: Marlene and Nathan Addlestone Library plus 3 others. *Books:* 608,954 (physical), 635,379 (digital/electronic); *Serial titles:* 418 (physical), 89,449 (digital/electronic); *Databases:* 339. Weekly public service hours: 112; students can reserve study rooms.

STUDENT LIFE

Housing options: coed, men-only, women-only, special housing for students with disabilities. Campus housing is university owned and leased by the school. Freshman applicants given priority for college housing.

Activities and organizations: drama/theater group, student-run newspaper, radio and television station, choral group, Student Government Association, Cougar Activities Board, Black Student Union, Charleston Miracle, Intramural Basketball, national fraternities, national sororities.

Athletics Member NCAA. All Division I. ***Intercollegiate sports:*** baseball M(s), basketball M(s)/W(s), cheerleading M/W, cross-country running M(s)/W(s), equestrian sports W, golf M(s)/W(s), sailing M/W, sand volleyball W, soccer M(s)/W(s), softball W(s), tennis M(s)/W(s), volleyball W(s). ***Intramural sports:*** badminton M/W, baseball M(c), basketball M/W, crew M(c)/W(c), fencing M(c)/W(c), golf M(c)/W(c), gymnastics M(c)/W(c), ice hockey M(c)/W(c), lacrosse M(c)/W(c), racquetball M/W, rock climbing M/W, rowing M(c)/W(c), rugby M(c)/W(c), soccer M/W, softball M/W, squash M(c)/W(c), swimming and diving M(c)/W(c), table tennis M/W, tennis M(c)/W(c), ultimate Frisbee M(c)/W(c), volleyball M/W, weight lifting M/W.

Campus security: 24-hour emergency response devices and patrols, student patrols, late-night transport/escort service, controlled dormitory access.

Student services: health clinic, personal/psychological counseling, women's center, veterans affairs office.

COSTS & FINANCIAL AID

Costs (2018–19) ***Tuition:*** state resident $12,418 full-time, $517 per credit hour part-time; nonresident $31,600 full-time, $1317 per credit hour part-time. Full-time tuition and fees vary according to student level. Part-time tuition and fees vary according to course load and student level. ***Required fees:*** $460 full-time, $16 per term part-time, $16 per term part-time. ***Room and board:*** $12,166; room only: $7866. Room and board charges vary according to board plan and housing facility. ***Payment plan:*** installment. ***Waivers:*** senior citizens and employees or children of employees.

Financial Aid Of all full-time matriculated undergraduates who enrolled in 2018, 5,974 applied for aid, 4,585 were judged to have need, 680 had their need fully met. In 2018, 1882 non-need-based awards were made. ***Average percent of need met:*** 53. ***Average financial aid package:*** $14,110. ***Average need-based loan:*** $3513. ***Average need-based gift aid:*** $2671. ***Average non-need-based aid:*** $12,252. ***Average indebtedness upon graduation:*** $27,731.

APPLYING

Standardized Tests *Required:* SAT or ACT (for admission). *Required for some:* International applicants not submitting an SAT/ACT score should submit an English language proficiency test score (TOEFL, IELTS, or iTEP).

Options: electronic application, early decision, early action, deferred entrance.

Application fee: $50.

Required: essay or personal statement, high school transcript. ***Required for some:*** letters of recommendation for Honors College.

Application deadlines: 2/15 (freshmen), 6/1 (transfers), 12/1 (early action).

Early decision deadline: 11/1.

Notification: 4/1 (freshmen), continuous (transfers), 12/1 (early decision), 1/1 (early action).

CONTACT

Ms. Suzette Stille, Dean of Admissions, College of Charleston, 66 George Street, Charleston, SC 29424-0001. *Phone:* 843-953-5670. *Fax:* 843-953-6322. *E-mail:* admissions@cofc.edu.

Columbia College

Columbia, South Carolina

http://www.columbiasc.edu/

- **Independent United Methodist** comprehensive, founded 1854
- **Suburban** 59-acre campus
- **Endowment** $25.6 million
- **Coed, primarily women**
- **Moderately difficult** entrance level

FACULTY

Student/faculty ratio: 15:1.

ACADEMICS

Calendar: semesters. *Degrees:* bachelor's and master's.

Library: J. Edens Drake Library. *Books:* 128,000 (physical), 92 (digital/electronic); *Serial titles:* 310 (physical); *Databases:* 84. Weekly public service hours: 70; students can reserve study rooms.

STUDENT LIFE

Housing options: on-campus residence required through sophomore year; women-only. Campus housing is university owned. Freshman campus housing is guaranteed.

Activities and organizations: drama/theater group, student-run newspaper, choral group.

Athletics Member NAIA.

Campus security: 24-hour emergency response devices and patrols, late-night transport/escort service, controlled dormitory access.

Student services: health clinic, personal/psychological counseling, women's center.

COSTS & FINANCIAL AID

Costs (2018–19) ***One-time required fee:*** $150. ***Comprehensive fee:*** $27,400 includes full-time tuition ($19,500) and room and board ($7900). Full-time tuition and fees vary according to class time and location. Part-time tuition: $650 per semester hour. Part-time tuition and fees vary according to class time and location. ***College room only:*** $3900. Room and board charges vary according to board plan and housing facility.

Financial Aid Of all full-time matriculated undergraduates who enrolled in 2005, 794 applied for aid, 698 were judged to have need, 310 had their need fully met. 200 Federal Work-Study jobs (averaging $1000). In 2005, 152 non-need-based awards were made. ***Average percent of need met:*** 70. ***Average financial aid package:*** $20,052. ***Average need-based loan:*** $3810. ***Average need-based gift aid:*** $8495. ***Average non-need-based aid:*** $7775. ***Average indebtedness upon graduation:*** $25,333.

APPLYING

Options: electronic application.

Required: high school transcript. ***Required for some:*** interview. ***Recommended:*** essay or personal statement.

CONTACT

Mr. Ryan Longe, Director of Admissions Operations, Columbia College, 1301 Columbia College Drive, Columbia, SC 29203. *Phone:* 803-786-3871. *Toll-free phone:* 800-277-1301. *E-mail:* rlonge@columbiasc.edu.

Columbia International University
Columbia, South Carolina
http://www.ciu.edu/

CONTACT
Ms. Jen Johnson, Undergraduate Admissions Office, Columbia International University, Columbia, SC 29230-3122. *Phone:* 803-777-2227. *Toll-free phone:* 800-777-2227 Ext. 5024. *Fax:* 803-786-4041. *E-mail:* yesciu@ciu.edu.

Converse College
Spartanburg, South Carolina
http://www.converse.edu/

- **Independent** comprehensive, founded 1889
- **Urban** 70-acre campus
- **Undergraduate: women only; graduate: coed**
- **Moderately difficult** entrance level

FACULTY
Student/faculty ratio: 13:1.

ACADEMICS
Calendar: 4-1-4. *Degrees:* bachelor's, master's, and post-master's certificates.
Library: Mickel Library. *Books:* 165,873 (physical), 252,047 (digital/electronic); *Databases:* 30.

STUDENT LIFE
Housing options: on-campus residence required through senior year; women-only. Campus housing is university owned. Freshman campus housing is guaranteed.

Activities and organizations: drama/theater group, student-run newspaper, choral group, Student Government, student volunteer services, Student Christian Organization, Student Activities Committee, Athletic Association.

Athletics Member NCAA. All Division II.

Campus security: 24-hour emergency response devices and patrols, late-night transport/escort service, controlled dormitory access.

Student services: health clinic, personal/psychological counseling, women's center.

COSTS & FINANCIAL AID
Costs (2018–19) ***Comprehensive fee:*** $29,620 includes full-time tuition ($18,340), mandatory fees ($350), and room and board ($10,930). Part-time tuition: $875 per credit. Part-time tuition and fees vary according to course load. ***Room and board:*** Room and board charges vary according to board plan.

Financial Aid Of all full-time matriculated undergraduates who enrolled in 2017, 801 applied for aid, 699 were judged to have need, 127 had their need fully met. 57 Federal Work-Study jobs (averaging $1385). 95 state and other part-time jobs (averaging $1566). In 2017, 94 non-need-based awards were made. ***Average percent of need met:*** 64. ***Average financial aid package:*** $15,674. ***Average need-based loan:*** $4383. ***Average need-based gift aid:*** $12,363. ***Average non-need-based aid:*** $5054. ***Average indebtedness upon graduation:*** $29,580.

APPLYING
Standardized Tests *Required:* SAT or ACT (for admission).

Options: electronic application, deferred entrance.

Required: high school transcript. ***Recommended:*** essay or personal statement, minimum 3.0 GPA.

CONTACT
Admissions, Converse College, 580 East Main Street, Spartanburg, SC 29302. *Phone:* 864-596-9040. *Toll-free phone:* 800-766-1125. *E-mail:* admissions@converse.edu.

★ Erskine College
Due West, South Carolina
http://www.erskine.edu/

CONTACT
Ms. Tobe Frierson, Senior Admissions Specialist, Erskine College, 2 Washington Street, PO Box 338, Due West, SC 29639. *Phone:* 864-379-8838. *Toll-free phone:* 800-241-8721.

See next page for display ad and page 1010 for the College Close-Up.

Francis Marion University
Florence, South Carolina
http://www.fmarion.edu/

- **State-supported** comprehensive, founded 1970
- **Rural** 400-acre campus
- **Endowment** $25.7 million
- **Coed**
- **Moderately difficult** entrance level

FACULTY
Student/faculty ratio: 16:1.

ACADEMICS
Calendar: semesters. *Degrees:* bachelor's, master's, and post-master's certificates.
Library: James A. Rogers Library plus 1 other. *Books:* 343,000 (digital/electronic).

STUDENT LIFE
Housing options: men-only, women-only, special housing for students with disabilities. Campus housing is university owned and is provided by a third party. Freshman applicants given priority for college housing.

Activities and organizations: drama/theater group, student-run newspaper, choral group, Baptist Collegiate Ministries, University Programming Board, Psychology Club, Student Alumni Association, Young Gifted and Blessed Chorus, national fraternities, national sororities.

Athletics Member NCAA. All Division II except golf (Division I), soccer (Division I).

Campus security: 24-hour emergency response devices and patrols, late-night transport/escort service, controlled dormitory access.

Student services: health clinic, personal/psychological counseling.

COSTS & FINANCIAL AID
Costs (2018–19) ***Tuition:*** state resident $10,384 full-time, $519 per credit hour part-time; nonresident $20,768 full-time, $1038 per credit hour part-time. Full-time tuition and fees vary according to degree level and program. Part-time tuition and fees vary according to course load, degree level, and program. ***Required fees:*** $776 full-time, $16 per credit hour part-time, $126 per term part-time. ***Room and board:*** $7948; room only: $4916. Room and board charges vary according to board plan and housing facility.

Financial Aid Of all full-time matriculated undergraduates who enrolled in 2017, 2,576 applied for aid, 2,327 were judged to have need, 235 had their need fully met. In 2017, 65 non-need-based awards were made. ***Average percent of need met:*** 64. ***Average financial aid package:*** $12,396. ***Average need-based loan:*** $4142. ***Average need-based gift aid:*** $7682. ***Average non-need-based aid:*** $2252. ***Average indebtedness upon graduation:*** $32,346.

APPLYING
Standardized Tests *Required:* SAT or ACT (for admission).

Options: electronic application, early admission, deferred entrance.

Application fee: $41.

Required: minimum 2.0 GPA. ***Required for some:*** essay or personal statement, high school transcript.

CONTACT
Jamie Hunt, Director of Admissions, Francis Marion University, PO Box 100547, Florence, SC 29502-0547. *Phone:* 843-661-1231. *Toll-free phone:* 800-368-7551. *Fax:* 843-661-4635. *E-mail:* admissions@fmarion.edu.

A ★ indicates that the school has detailed information with a Premium Profile on Petersons.com.

Furman University

Greenville, South Carolina

http://www.furman.edu/

- **Independent** comprehensive, founded 1826
- **Suburban** 800-acre campus
- **Coed** 2,768 undergraduate students, 97% full-time, 59% women, 41% men
- **Moderately difficult** entrance level, 61% of applicants were admitted

UNDERGRAD STUDENTS
2,677 full-time, 91 part-time. Students come from 46 states and territories; 34 other countries; 68% are from out of state; 7% Black or African American, non-Hispanic/Latino; 6% Hispanic/Latino; 2% Asian, non-Hispanic/Latino; 0.2% American Indian or Alaska Native, non-Hispanic/Latino; 3% Two or more races, non-Hispanic/Latino; 2% Race/ethnicity unknown; 4% international; 0.7% transferred in; 91% live on campus.

Freshmen:
Admission: 5,469 applied, 3,339 admitted, 711 enrolled. ***Test scores:*** SAT evidence-based reading and writing scores over 500: 99%; SAT math scores over 500: 110%; ACT scores over 18: 100%; SAT evidence-based reading and writing scores over 600: 87%; SAT math scores over 600: 76%; ACT scores over 24: 94%; SAT evidence-based reading and writing scores over 700: 29%; SAT math scores over 700: 27%; ACT scores over 30: 52%.
Retention: 91% of full-time freshmen returned.

FACULTY
Total: 327, 72% full-time, 86% with terminal degrees.
Student/faculty ratio: 10:1.

ACADEMICS
Calendar: semesters. *Degrees:* bachelor's, master's, and postbachelor's certificates.
Special study options: accelerated degree program, adult/continuing education programs, advanced placement credit, double majors, independent study, internships, part-time degree program, services for LD students, student-designed majors, study abroad, summer session for credit. ***ROTC:*** Army (b).
Unusual degree programs: 3-2 engineering with Georgia Institute of Technology, Clemson University, Auburn University, North Carolina State University, Washington University in St. Louis.
Computers: 500 computers/terminals are available on campus for general student use. Students can access the following: campus intranet, computer help desk, free student e-mail accounts, online (class) grades, online (class) registration, online (class) schedules. Campuswide network is available. 100% of college-owned or -operated housing units are wired for high-speed Internet access. Wireless service is available via entire campus.
Library: James Buchanan Duke Library plus 3 others. *Books:* 601,063 (physical), 921,761 (digital/electronic); *Serial titles:* 704,239 (physical). Study areas open 24 hours, 5–7 days a week.

STUDENT LIFE
Housing options: on-campus residence required through senior year; coed, men-only, women-only, special housing for students with disabilities. Campus housing is university owned. Freshman campus housing is guaranteed.
Activities and organizations: drama/theater group, student-run newspaper, radio and television station, choral group, marching band, national fraternities, national sororities.
Athletics Member NCAA. All Division I except football (Division I-AA). ***Intercollegiate sports:*** baseball M(s), basketball M(s)/W(s), cheerleading W(s), cross-country running M(s)/W(s), equestrian sports W(c), golf M(s)/W(s), lacrosse M/W, rugby M(c), soccer M(s)/W(s), softball W(s), swimming and diving M(c)/W(c), tennis M(s)/W(s), track and field M(s)/W(s), ultimate Frisbee M(c)/W(c), volleyball W(s). ***Intramural sports:*** basketball M/W, bowling M/W, racquetball M(c)/W(c), rock climbing M(c)/W(c), soccer M/W, softball M/W, volleyball M/W, weight lifting M(c)/W(c).
Campus security: 24-hour emergency response devices and patrols, student patrols, late-night transport/escort service, controlled dormitory access.

Student services: health clinic, personal/psychological counseling, women's center.

COSTS & FINANCIAL AID

Costs (2018–19) ***Comprehensive fee:*** $62,244 includes full-time tuition ($49,152), mandatory fees ($380), and room and board ($12,712). Part-time tuition: $1536 per credit. Part-time tuition and fees vary according to course load. ***College room only:*** $6954. Room and board charges vary according to board plan and housing facility. ***Payment plan:*** installment. ***Waivers:*** employees or children of employees.

Financial Aid Of all full-time matriculated undergraduates who enrolled in 2018, 1,528 applied for aid, 1,214 were judged to have need, 528 had their need fully met. In 2018, 1212 non-need-based awards were made. ***Average percent of need met:*** 81. ***Average financial aid package:*** $41,883. ***Average need-based loan:*** $4265. ***Average need-based gift aid:*** $30,365. ***Average non-need-based aid:*** $18,905. ***Average indebtedness upon graduation:*** $34,072. ***Financial aid deadline:*** 3/1.

APPLYING

Options: electronic application, early decision, early action.

Application fee: $50.

Required: essay or personal statement, high school transcript.

Application deadlines: 1/15 (freshmen), 1/15 (transfers), 11/1 (early action).

Early decision deadline: 11/1.

Notification: 3/1 (freshmen), 3/1 (transfers), 11/15 (early decision), 12/20 (early action).

CONTACT

Mr. Christine Pochard, Associate VP for Enrollment Management & Dean of Admission, Furman University, 3300 Poinsett Highway, Greenville, SC 29613. *Phone:* 864-6178192. *Fax:* 864-294-2018. *E-mail:* admissions@furman.edu.

Lander University

Greenwood, South Carolina

http://www.lander.edu/

CONTACT

Ms. Jennifer M. Mathis, Director of Admissions, Lander University, 320 Stanley Avenue, Greenwood, SC 29649. *Phone:* 864-388-8307. *Toll-free phone:* 888-452-6337. *Fax:* 864-388-8125. *E-mail:* admissions@lander.edu.

Limestone College

Gaffney, South Carolina

http://www.limestone.edu/

- **Independent** comprehensive, founded 1845
- **Suburban** 123-acre campus with easy access to Charlotte
- **Endowment** $20.5 million
- **Coed** 2,279 undergraduate students, 79% full-time, 56% women, 44% men
- **Minimally difficult** entrance level, 44% of applicants were admitted

UNDERGRAD STUDENTS

1,797 full-time, 482 part-time. Students come from 30 states and territories; 31 other countries; 42% are from out of state; 44% Black or African American, non-Hispanic/Latino; 4% Hispanic/Latino; 0.6% Asian, non-Hispanic/Latino; 0.7% American Indian or Alaska Native, non-Hispanic/Latino; 0.1% Two or more races, non-Hispanic/Latino; 3% Race/ethnicity unknown; 4% international; 2% transferred in; 75% live on campus.

Freshmen:

Admission: 3,057 applied, 1,350 admitted, 387 enrolled. ***Average high school GPA:*** 3.3. ***Test scores:*** SAT evidence-based reading and writing scores over 500: 69%; SAT math scores over 500: 71%; ACT scores over 18: 85%; SAT evidence-based reading and writing scores over 600: 15%; SAT math scores over 600: 11%; ACT scores over 24: 18%; SAT evidence-based reading and writing scores over 700: 2%; SAT math scores over 700: 2%; ACT scores over 30: 1%.

Retention: 52% of full-time freshmen returned.

FACULTY

Total: 285, 33% full-time, 50% with terminal degrees.

Student/faculty ratio: 10:1.

ACADEMICS

Calendar: semesters. *Degrees:* associate, bachelor's, and master's.

Special study options: academic remediation for entering students, accelerated degree program, adult/continuing education programs, advanced placement credit, distance learning, double majors, honors programs, independent study, internships, part-time degree program, services for LD students, student-designed majors, summer session for credit.

Computers: 137 computers/terminals are available on campus for general student use. Students can access the following: campus intranet, computer help desk, free student e-mail accounts, online (class) grades, online (class) registration, online (class) schedules. Campuswide network is available. 100% of college-owned or -operated housing units are wired for high-speed Internet access. Wireless service is available via classrooms, dorm rooms, learning centers, libraries, student centers.

Library: A. J. Eastwood Library plus 1 other. *Books:* 67,000 (physical), 239,537 (digital/electronic); *Serial titles:* 111 (physical), 482,082 (digital/electronic); *Databases:* 156. Weekly public service hours: 70.

STUDENT LIFE

Housing options: on-campus residence required through junior year; men-only, women-only. Campus housing is university owned. Freshman applicants given priority for college housing.

Activities and organizations: drama/theater group, choral group, marching band, Fellowship of Christian Athletes, Student Government Association, Student Alumni Leadership Council, Campus Crusade (CRU), Limestone Activities Board (LAB), national fraternities, national sororities.

Athletics Member NCAA. All Division II except golf (Division I). ***Intercollegiate sports:*** baseball M(s), basketball M(s)/W(s), cheerleading M(s)/W(s), cross-country running M(s)/W(s), field hockey W(s), football M(s), golf M(s)/W(s), gymnastics W(s), lacrosse M(s)/W(s), soccer M(s)/W(s), softball W(s), swimming and diving M(s)/W(s), tennis M(s)/W(s), track and field M(s)/W(s), volleyball M(s)/W(s), wrestling M(s)/W(s). ***Intramural sports:*** badminton M/W, basketball M/W, bowling M/W, racquetball M/W, soccer M/W, table tennis M/W, ultimate Frisbee M/W, volleyball M/W, weight lifting M/W.

Campus security: 24-hour emergency response devices and patrols, late-night transport/escort service, controlled dormitory access.

Student services: health clinic, personal/psychological counseling, veterans affairs office.

COSTS & FINANCIAL AID

Costs (2019–20) ***Comprehensive fee:*** $36,200 includes full-time tuition ($25,200), mandatory fees ($1100), and room and board ($9900). Part-time tuition: $1038 per credit hour. ***Required fees:*** $1038 per credit hour part-time.

Financial Aid Of all full-time matriculated undergraduates who enrolled in 2017, 2,224 applied for aid, 2,137 were judged to have need, 122 had their need fully met. 102 Federal Work-Study jobs (averaging $1253). In 2017, 61 non-need-based awards were made. ***Average percent of need met:*** 44. ***Average financial aid package:*** $12,023. ***Average need-based loan:*** $3738. ***Average need-based gift aid:*** $9908. ***Average non-need-based aid:*** $6180. ***Average indebtedness upon graduation:*** $30,562.

APPLYING

Standardized Tests *Required:* SAT or ACT (for admission). *Required for some:* minimum score of 500 on TOEFL or proof of successfully completed ESL program for students whose native language is not English.

Options: electronic application.

Application fee: $25.

Required: high school transcript, minimum 2.0 GPA. ***Recommended:*** 2 letters of recommendation, interview.

Application deadlines: rolling (freshmen), rolling (transfers).

Notification: continuous (freshmen), continuous (transfers).

CONTACT

Ms. Lisa Hobbs, Admissions Office Manager, Limestone College, 1115 College Drive, Gaffney, SC 29340-3799. *Phone:* 864-488-4554. *Toll-free phone:* 800-795-7151. *Fax:* 864-487-8706. *E-mail:* lhobbs@limestone.edu.

Medical University of South Carolina

Charleston, South Carolina

http://www.musc.edu/

CONTACT
Lyla E. Hudson, Director of Admissions, Medical University of South Carolina, 41 Bee Street MSC203, Charleston, SC 29425-2030. *Phone:* 843-792-7408. *E-mail:* hudsonly@musc.edu.

Morris College

Sumter, South Carolina

http://www.morris.edu/

- **Independent** 4-year, founded 1908, affiliated with Baptist Educational and Missionary Convention of South Carolina
- **Urban** 34-acre campus with easy access to Columbia, SC
- **Endowment** $10.9 million
- **Coed**
- **Noncompetitive** entrance level

FACULTY
Student/faculty ratio: 13:1.

ACADEMICS
Calendar: semesters. *Degree:* bachelor's.
Library: Richardson-Johnson Learning Resources Center plus 1 other. *Books:* 95,133 (physical), 37,342 (digital/electronic); *Serial titles:* 427 (physical), 4 (digital/electronic); *Databases:* 74. Weekly public service hours: 76.

STUDENT LIFE
Housing options: men-only, women-only. Campus housing is university owned. Freshman campus housing is guaranteed.

Activities and organizations: drama/theater group, student-run radio station, choral group, Student Government Association, New Emphasis on Nontraditional Students (NEONS), Block M Club, Pre Alumni Council, Baptist Student Union.

Athletics Member NAIA.

Campus security: 24-hour emergency response devices and patrols.

Student services: health clinic, personal/psychological counseling, veterans affairs office.

COSTS & FINANCIAL AID
Costs (2018–19) ***Comprehensive fee:*** $19,915 includes full-time tuition ($12,521), mandatory fees ($1361), and room and board ($6033). Part-time tuition: $522 per credit hour. ***College room only:*** $2650.

Financial Aid Of all full-time matriculated undergraduates who enrolled in 2017, 887 applied for aid, 859 were judged to have need, 10 had their need fully met. 300 Federal Work-Study jobs (averaging $818). ***Average percent of need met:*** 85. ***Average financial aid package:*** $12,100. ***Average need-based loan:*** $3900. ***Average need-based gift aid:*** $7400. ***Average indebtedness upon graduation:*** $17,125.

APPLYING
Options: electronic application, deferred entrance.

Required: high school transcript. ***Required for some:*** interview.

CONTACT
Ms. Gloria Scriven, Assistant Director of Admissions and Records, Morris College, 100 West College Street, Sumter, SC 29150-3502. *Phone:* 803-934-3239. *Toll-free phone:* 866-853-1345. *Fax:* 803-773-8241. *E-mail:* gscriven@morris.edu.

Newberry College

Newberry, South Carolina

http://www.newberry.edu/

- **Independent Evangelical Lutheran** 4-year, founded 1856
- **Small-town** 90-acre campus with easy access to Columbia and Greenville, SC
- **Endowment** $18.8 million
- **Coed**
- **Moderately difficult** entrance level

FACULTY
Student/faculty ratio: 14:1.

ACADEMICS
Calendar: semesters. *Degree:* bachelor's.
Library: Wessels Library. *Books:* 36,525 (physical), 295,982 (digital/electronic); *Serial titles:* 33 (physical), 10,000 (digital/electronic); *Databases:* 108. Weekly public service hours: 91.

STUDENT LIFE
Housing options: on-campus residence required through senior year; coed, men-only, women-only. Campus housing is university owned and is provided by a third party. Freshman applicants given priority for college housing.

Activities and organizations: drama/theater group, student-run radio station, choral group, marching band, National Society of Leadership and Success, Kappa Delta, Sigma Sigma Sigma, Alpha Xi Delta, Kappa Alpha Order, national fraternities, national sororities.

Athletics Member NCAA. All Division II.

Campus security: 24-hour emergency response devices and patrols, late-night transport/escort service, controlled dormitory access.

Student services: health clinic, personal/psychological counseling, veterans affairs office.

COSTS & FINANCIAL AID
Costs (2018–19) ***Comprehensive fee:*** $37,090 includes full-time tuition ($24,174), mandatory fees ($2250), and room and board ($10,666). Full-time tuition and fees vary according to course load. Part-time tuition: $820 per credit hour. Part-time tuition and fees vary according to course load. ***Required fees:*** $70 per credit hour part-time. ***Room and board:*** Room and board charges vary according to board plan and housing facility.

Financial Aid Of all full-time matriculated undergraduates who enrolled in 2017, 1,089 applied for aid, 996 were judged to have need, 171 had their need fully met. In 2017, 166 non-need-based awards were made. ***Average percent of need met:*** 74. ***Average financial aid package:*** $22,183. ***Average need-based loan:*** $3558. ***Average need-based gift aid:*** $19,296. ***Average non-need-based aid:*** $10,302. ***Average indebtedness upon graduation:*** $22,380.

APPLYING
Standardized Tests *Required:* SAT or ACT (for admission).

Options: electronic application, deferred entrance.

Required: high school transcript, minimum 2.0 GPA. ***Required for some:*** essay or personal statement, interview.

CONTACT
Mr. Joel Vander Horst, Dean of Enrollment Management, Newberry College, 2100 College Street, Newberry, SC 29108. *Phone:* 803-947-2110. *Toll-free phone:* 800-845-4955. *Fax:* 803-321-5138. *E-mail:* admissions@newberry.edu.

North Greenville University

Tigerville, South Carolina

http://www.ngu.edu/

- **Independent Southern Baptist** comprehensive, founded 1892
- **Rural** 380-acre campus with easy access to Greenville
- **Endowment** $258.4 million
- **Coed**
- **Minimally difficult** entrance level

FACULTY
Student/faculty ratio: 14:1.

ACADEMICS
Calendar: semesters. *Degrees:* bachelor's, master's, and doctoral.
Library: Hester Memorial Library. *Books:* 70,000 (physical), 250,000 (digital/electronic); *Serial titles:* 250 (physical), 150 (digital/electronic); *Databases:* 103. Weekly public service hours: 85.

STUDENT LIFE
Housing options: on-campus residence required through sophomore year; men-only, women-only. Campus housing is university owned. Freshman campus housing is guaranteed.

Activities and organizations: drama/theater group, student-run radio station, choral group, marching band, Baptist Student Union, Fellowship of Christians in Service, Fellowship of Christian Athletes, Black Student Fellowship, Education Club.

Athletics Member NCAA, NCCAA. All NCAA Division II.

Campus security: 24-hour emergency response devices and patrols, late-night transport/escort service, controlled dormitory access.

Student services: personal/psychological counseling.

COSTS & FINANCIAL AID

Costs (2018–19) ***Comprehensive fee:*** $29,990 includes full-time tuition ($19,750) and room and board ($10,240). Full-time tuition and fees vary according to course load. Part-time tuition: $480 per credit hour. ***College room only:*** $4900. Room and board charges vary according to housing facility.

Financial Aid Of all full-time matriculated undergraduates who enrolled in 2015, 1,143 applied for aid, 1,143 were judged to have need, 1,143 had their need fully met. In 2015, 1989 non-need-based awards were made. ***Average financial aid package:*** $5783. ***Average need-based gift aid:*** $5783. ***Average non-need-based aid:*** $7081.

APPLYING

Standardized Tests *Required:* SAT or ACT (for admission). *Required for some:* CPT. *Recommended:* CPT.

Options: electronic application, early admission, deferred entrance.

Application fee: $30.

Required: high school transcript. ***Required for some:*** interview. ***Recommended:*** minimum 2.0 GPA.

CONTACT

North Greenville University, PO Box 1892, Tigerville, SC 29688-1892. *Phone:* 864-977-7052. *Toll-free phone:* 800-468-6642 Ext. 7001.

Presbyterian College

Clinton, South Carolina

http://www.presby.edu/

- **Independent** comprehensive, founded 1880, affiliated with Presbyterian Church (U.S.A.)
- **Small-town** 240-acre campus with easy access to Greenville, Spartanburg
- **Endowment** $90.2 million
- **Coed**
- **Very difficult** entrance level

FACULTY

Student/faculty ratio: 13:1.

ACADEMICS

Calendar: semesters. *Degrees:* bachelor's and doctoral.
Library: James H. Thomason Library. *Books:* 108,925 (physical), 227,396 (digital/electronic); *Serial titles:* 702 (physical), 16,342 (digital/electronic); *Databases:* 71. Study areas open 24 hours, 5–7 days a week; students can reserve study rooms.

STUDENT LIFE

Housing options: on-campus residence required through senior year; coed, men-only, women-only. Campus housing is university owned. Freshman campus housing is guaranteed.

Activities and organizations: drama/theater group, student-run newspaper, choral group, Student Volunteer Services, Intramural sports, Student Union Board, Fellowship of Christian Athletes, Student Government Association, national fraternities, national sororities.

Athletics Member NCAA. All Division I.

Campus security: 24-hour emergency response devices and patrols, late-night transport/escort service, controlled dormitory access.

Student services: health clinic, personal/psychological counseling.

COSTS & FINANCIAL AID

Costs (2018–19) ***Comprehensive fee:*** $49,140 includes full-time tuition ($35,800), mandatory fees ($2860), and room and board ($10,480). Full-time tuition and fees vary according to course load and reciprocity agreements. Part-time tuition: $1492 per credit hour. Part-time tuition and fees vary according to course load and program. ***Required fees:*** $26 per credit hour part-time, $25 per term part-time. ***College room only:*** $5100. Room and board charges vary according to board plan and housing facility.

Financial Aid Of all full-time matriculated undergraduates who enrolled in 2018, 836 applied for aid, 734 were judged to have need, 247 had their need fully met. In 2018, 102 non-need-based awards were made. ***Average percent of need met:*** 86. ***Average financial aid package:*** $37,073. ***Average need-based loan:*** $3872. ***Average need-based gift aid:*** $31,185. ***Average non-need-based aid:*** $19,998. ***Average indebtedness upon graduation:*** $31,925. ***Financial aid deadline:*** 6/30.

APPLYING

Standardized Tests *Required for some:* SAT or ACT (for admission).

Options: electronic application, early decision, early action, deferred entrance.

Required: essay or personal statement, high school transcript, minimum 2.0 GPA, 1 letter of recommendation. ***Recommended:*** interview.

CONTACT

Mr. Mark O. Fox, Director of Admissions, Presbyterian College, 503 South Broad Street, Clinton, SC 29325. *Phone:* 864-833-8232. *Toll-free phone:* 800-476-7272. *Fax:* 864-833-8195. *E-mail:* mfox@presby.edu.

South Carolina State University

Orangeburg, South Carolina

http://www.scsu.edu/

CONTACT

Mrs. Gennifer Bookhardt, South Carolina State University, PO Box 7127, 300 College Street NE, Orangeburg, SC 29117. *Phone:* 803-536-7186. *Toll-free phone:* 800-260-5956. *Fax:* 803-536-8990. *E-mail:* admissions@scsu.edu.

Southern Wesleyan University

Central, South Carolina

http://www.swu.edu/

CONTACT

Mrs. Beth Roe, Director of First Year Experience, Southern Wesleyan University, PO Box 1020, 907 Wesleyan Drive, Central, SC 29630-1020. *Phone:* 864-644-5149. *Toll-free phone:* 800-CU-AT-SWU. *Fax:* 864-644-5901. *E-mail:* broe@swu.edu.

South University

Columbia, South Carolina

http://www.southuniversity.edu/columbia/

CONTACT

South University, 9 Science Court, Columbia, SC 29203. *Phone:* 803-799-9082. *Toll-free phone:* 866-629-3031.

Strayer University–Charleston Campus

North Charleston, South Carolina

http://www.strayer.edu/south-carolina/charleston/

CONTACT

Strayer University–Charleston Campus, 5010 Wetland Crossing, North Charleston, SC 29418. *Toll-free phone:* 888-311-0355.

Strayer University–Columbia Campus

Columbia, South Carolina

http://www.strayer.edu/south-carolina/columbia/

CONTACT

Strayer University–Columbia Campus, 200 Center Point Circle, Suite 300, Columbia, SC 29210. *Toll-free phone:* 888-311-0355.

Strayer University–Greenville Campus
Greenville, South Carolina
http://www.strayer.edu/south-carolina/greenville/

CONTACT
Strayer University–Greenville Campus, 777 Lowndes Hill Road, Building 3, Suite 300, Greenville, SC 29607. *Toll-free phone:* 888-311-0355.

University of South Carolina
Columbia, South Carolina
http://www.sc.edu/

- **State-supported** university, founded 1801, part of University of South Carolina System
- **Urban** 444-acre campus
- **Coed** 26,733 undergraduate students, 96% full-time, 53% women, 47% men
- **Moderately difficult** entrance level, 63% of applicants were admitted

UNDERGRAD STUDENTS
25,633 full-time, 1,100 part-time. 38% are from out of state; 9% Black or African American, non-Hispanic/Latino; 5% Hispanic/Latino; 3% Asian, non-Hispanic/Latino; 0.1% Native Hawaiian or other Pacific Islander, non-Hispanic/Latino; 0.2% American Indian or Alaska Native, non-Hispanic/Latino; 4% Two or more races, non-Hispanic/Latino; 0.8% Race/ethnicity unknown; 3% international; 7% transferred in; 27% live on campus.

Freshmen:
Admission: 30,778 applied, 19,438 admitted, 5,854 enrolled. ***Average high school GPA:*** 4.2. ***Test scores:*** SAT evidence-based reading and writing scores over 500: 99%; SAT math scores over 500: 99%; ACT scores over 18: 100%; SAT evidence-based reading and writing scores over 600: 77%; SAT math scores over 600: 71%; ACT scores over 24: 87%; SAT evidence-based reading and writing scores over 700: 16%; SAT math scores over 700: 21%; ACT scores over 30: 33%.

Retention: 88% of full-time freshmen returned.

FACULTY
Total: 2,200, 69% full-time, 73% with terminal degrees.

Student/faculty ratio: 17:1.

ACADEMICS
Calendar: semesters. *Degrees:* certificates, associate, bachelor's, master's, doctoral, post-master's, and postbachelor's certificates.

Special study options: accelerated degree program, adult/continuing education programs, advanced placement credit, cooperative education, distance learning, double majors, English as a second language, freshman honors college, honors programs, independent study, internships, part-time degree program, services for LD students, student-designed majors, study abroad, summer session for credit. ***ROTC:*** Army (b), Navy (b), Air Force (b).

Computers: Students can access the following: computer help desk, free student e-mail accounts, online (class) grades, online (class) registration, online (class) schedules. Campuswide network is available. Wireless service is available via entire campus.
Library: Thomas Cooper Library plus 6 others. *Books:* 1.8 million (physical), 1.1 million (digital/electronic); *Serial titles:* 72,412 (physical), 18,860 (digital/electronic); *Databases:* 574.

STUDENT LIFE
Housing options: on-campus residence required for freshman year; coed, men-only, women-only, special housing for students with disabilities. Campus housing is university owned. Freshman campus housing is guaranteed.

Activities and organizations: drama/theater group, student-run newspaper, radio and television station, choral group, marching band, national fraternities, national sororities.

Athletics Member NCAA. All Division I except football (Division I-A). ***Intercollegiate sports:*** baseball M(s), basketball M(s)/W(s), cross-country running W(s), equestrian sports W(s), golf M(s)/W(s)(c), soccer M(s)/W(s), softball W(s), swimming and diving M(s)/W(s), tennis M(s)/W(s), track and field M(s)/W(s), volleyball W(s). ***Intramural sports:*** badminton M(c)/W(c), baseball M(c), basketball M/W, bowling M/W, equestrian sports M(c)/W(c), fencing M(c)/W(c), field hockey W(c), football M/W, golf M/W, gymnastics W(c), ice hockey M(c), lacrosse M(c)/W(c), racquetball M/W, rock climbing M(c)/W(c), rugby M(c)/W(c), sailing M(c)/W(c), soccer M/W, softball M/W, swimming and diving M/W, table tennis M/W, tennis M/W, ultimate Frisbee M(c)/W(c), volleyball M/W, water polo M(c)/W(c), weight lifting M/W, wrestling M(c).

Campus security: 24-hour emergency response devices and patrols, student patrols, late-night transport/escort service, controlled dormitory access.

Student services: health clinic, personal/psychological counseling, women's center.

COSTS & FINANCIAL AID
Costs (2018–19) ***Tuition:*** state resident $12,216 full-time, $509 per credit hour part-time; nonresident $32,898 full-time, $1371 per credit hour part-time. Full-time tuition and fees vary according to program and reciprocity agreements. Part-time tuition and fees vary according to course load. ***Required fees:*** $400 full-time, $17 per credit hour part-time. ***Room and board:*** $10,388; room only: $6530. Room and board charges vary according to board plan, housing facility, and location. ***Payment plan:*** deferred payment. ***Waivers:*** senior citizens and employees or children of employees.

Financial Aid Of all full-time matriculated undergraduates who enrolled in 2018, 16,678 applied for aid, 12,543 were judged to have need, 3,135 had their need fully met. In 2018, 8394 non-need-based awards were made. ***Average percent of need met:*** 72. ***Average financial aid package:*** $12,025. ***Average need-based loan:*** $4456. ***Average need-based gift aid:*** $5839. ***Average non-need-based aid:*** $6548. ***Average indebtedness upon graduation:*** $28,169.

APPLYING
Standardized Tests *Required:* SAT or ACT (for admission).

Options: electronic application, early action.

Application fee: $65.

Required: high school transcript, minimum 2.0 GPA.

CONTACT
Dr. Mary Wagner, Director, Undergraduate Admissions, University of South Carolina, Columbia, SC 29208. *Phone:* 803-777-7700. *Toll-free phone:* 800-868-5872. *Fax:* 803-777-0101. *E-mail:* wagnermt@mailbox.sc.edu.

University of South Carolina Aiken
Aiken, South Carolina
http://www.usca.edu/

- **State-supported** comprehensive, founded 1961, part of University of South Carolina System
- **Suburban** 453-acre campus with easy access to Columbia
- **Endowment** $26.6 million
- **Coed** 3,344 undergraduate students, 80% full-time, 65% women, 35% men
- **Moderately difficult** entrance level, 51% of applicants were admitted

UNDERGRAD STUDENTS
2,670 full-time, 674 part-time. Students come from 32 states and territories; 33 other countries; 12% are from out of state; 26% Black or African American, non-Hispanic/Latino; 5% Hispanic/Latino; 1% Asian, non-Hispanic/Latino; 0.1% Native Hawaiian or other Pacific Islander, non-Hispanic/Latino; 0.4% American Indian or Alaska Native, non-Hispanic/Latino; 4% Two or more races, non-Hispanic/Latino; 1% Race/ethnicity unknown; 3% international; 12% transferred in; 27% live on campus.

Freshmen:
Admission: 3,115 applied, 1,587 admitted, 550 enrolled. ***Average high school GPA:*** 3.9. ***Test scores:*** SAT evidence-based reading and writing scores over 500: 62%; SAT math scores over 500: 71%; ACT scores over 18: 73%; SAT evidence-based reading and writing scores over 600: 14%; SAT math scores over 600: 20%; ACT scores over 24: 16%; SAT evidence-based reading and writing scores over 700: 1%; SAT math scores over 700: 2%; ACT scores over 30: 1%.

Retention: 64% of full-time freshmen returned.

FACULTY
Total: 296, 52% full-time, 56% with terminal degrees.

Student/faculty ratio: 15:1.

ACADEMICS
Calendar: semesters. *Degrees:* bachelor's and master's.

Special study options: adult/continuing education programs, advanced placement credit, cooperative education, distance learning, double majors, English as a second language, honors programs, independent study, internships, off-campus study, part-time degree program, services for LD students, student-designed majors, study abroad, summer session for credit.

Computers: 550 computers/terminals and 1,400 ports are available on campus for general student use. Students can access the following: computer help desk, free student e-mail accounts, online (class) grades, online (class) registration, online (class) schedules. Campuswide network is available. 100% of college-owned or -operated housing units are wired for high-speed Internet access. Wireless service is available via entire campus.
Library: Gregg-Graniteville Library. *Books:* 133,161 (physical), 407,453 (digital/electronic); *Serial titles:* 16,034 (physical), 125,380 (digital/electronic); *Databases:* 217. Weekly public service hours: 78; students can reserve study rooms.

STUDENT LIFE
Housing options: on-campus residence required for freshman year; coed, special housing for students with disabilities. Campus housing is university owned. Freshman applicants given priority for college housing.

Activities and organizations: drama/theater group, student-run newspaper, choral group, National Society of Leadership and Success, Pacer Fanatics, Alpha Omicron Pi, Zeta Tau Alpha, Phi Mu, national fraternities, national sororities.

Athletics Member NCAA. All Division II. ***Intercollegiate sports:*** baseball M(s), basketball M(s)/W(s), cross-country running W(s), golf M(s), soccer M(s)/W(s), softball W(s), tennis M(s)/W(s), volleyball W(s). ***Intramural sports:*** basketball M/W, cheerleading M(c)/W(c), equestrian sports M(c)/W(c), lacrosse M(c), rugby M(c), soccer M/W, swimming and diving M(c)/W(c), tennis M(c)/W(c), ultimate Frisbee M/W, volleyball M/W.

Campus security: 24-hour emergency response devices and patrols, late-night transport/escort service, controlled dormitory access.

Student services: health clinic, personal/psychological counseling, veterans affairs office.

COSTS & FINANCIAL AID
Costs (2018–19) ***Tuition:*** state resident $10,398 full-time, $433 per credit hour part-time; nonresident $20,856 full-time, $869 per credit hour part-time. Full-time tuition and fees vary according to program and reciprocity agreements. Part-time tuition and fees vary according to course load, program, and reciprocity agreements. ***Required fees:*** $362 full-time, $13 per credit hour part-time, $25 per term part-time. ***Room and board:*** $7766; room only: $5066. Room and board charges vary according to board plan and housing facility. ***Payment plan:*** deferred payment. ***Waivers:*** senior citizens and employees or children of employees.

Financial Aid Of all full-time matriculated undergraduates who enrolled in 2017, 2,711 applied for aid, 1,823 were judged to have need, 344 had their need fully met. 61 Federal Work-Study jobs (averaging $2075). 386 state and other part-time jobs (averaging $1844). In 2017, 171 non-need-based awards were made. ***Average percent of need met:*** 62. ***Average financial aid package:*** $11,898. ***Average need-based loan:*** $4113. ***Average need-based gift aid:*** $7264. ***Average non-need-based aid:*** $1775. ***Average indebtedness upon graduation:*** $28,908.

APPLYING
Standardized Tests *Required:* SAT or ACT (for admission).

Options: electronic application, early admission, deferred entrance.

Application fee: $45.

Required: high school transcript.

Application deadlines: 7/1 (freshmen), 7/1 (out-of-state freshmen), 7/1 (transfers).

Notification: continuous (freshmen), continuous (out-of-state freshmen), continuous (transfers).

CONTACT
Mr. Andrew Hendrix, Director of Admissions, University of South Carolina Aiken, 471 University Parkway, Aiken, SC 29801-6309. *Phone:* 803-641-3366. *Toll-free phone:* 888-WOW-USCA. *Fax:* 803-641-3727. *E-mail:* admit@usca.edu.

University of South Carolina Beaufort

Bluffton, South Carolina

http://www.uscb.edu/

CONTACT
Ms. Monica Williams, University of South Carolina Beaufort, 1 University Boulevard, Bluffton, SC 29909. *Phone:* 843-208-8112. *Fax:* 843-208-8015. *E-mail:* monicaw@sc.edu.

University of South Carolina Union

Union, South Carolina

http://uscunion.sc.edu/

- **State-supported** primarily 2-year, founded 1965, part of University of South Carolina System
- **Small-town** 7-acre campus with easy access to Charlotte, North Carolina
- **Endowment** $1.2 million
- **Coed** 905 undergraduate students, 54% full-time, 53% women, 47% men
- **Minimally difficult** entrance level, 67% of applicants were admitted

UNDERGRAD STUDENTS
487 full-time, 418 part-time. Students come from 3 states and territories; 1 other country; 2% are from out of state; 43% Black or African American, non-Hispanic/Latino; 3% Hispanic/Latino.

Freshmen:
Admission: 1,378 applied, 930 admitted. ***Average high school GPA:*** 3.3. ***Test scores:*** ACT scores over 18: 75%; ACT scores over 24: 5%.

FACULTY
Total: 42, 29% full-time.

Student/faculty ratio: 18:1.

ACADEMICS
Calendar: semesters. *Degrees:* associate and bachelor's.

Special study options: advanced placement credit, cooperative education, distance learning, double majors, independent study, internships, part-time degree program, study abroad, summer session for credit.

Computers: 100 computers/terminals are available on campus for general student use. Students can access the following: campus intranet, computer help desk, free student e-mail accounts, online (class) grades, online (class) registration, online (class) schedules. Campuswide network is available. Wireless service is available via entire campus.
Library: Union Carnegie Library plus 1 other. Study areas open 24 hours, 5–7 days a week.

STUDENT LIFE
Housing options: college housing not available.

Activities and organizations: drama/theater group, choral group.

Athletics Member NJCAA. ***Intramural sports:*** baseball M, soccer M/W, softball W.

Campus security: 24-hour emergency response devices.

Student services: personal/psychological counseling, veterans affairs office.

COSTS & FINANCIAL AID
Costs (2018–19) ***Tuition:*** state resident $285 per credit hour part-time; nonresident $721 per credit hour part-time. Full-time tuition and fees vary according to class time, course load, degree level, location, program, and student level. Part-time tuition and fees vary according to class time, location, program, and student level. ***Payment plan:*** deferred payment. ***Waivers:*** senior citizens.

Financial Aid Of all full-time matriculated undergraduates who enrolled in 2017, 16 Federal Work-Study jobs (averaging $3400).

APPLYING
Standardized Tests *Required:* SAT or ACT (for admission).

Options: electronic application.

Application fee: $40.

Required: high school transcript.

Application deadlines: rolling (freshmen), rolling (transfers).

Notification: continuous (freshmen), continuous (transfers).

CONTACT

Mr. Michael B. Greer, Director of Enrollment Services, University of South Carolina Union, PO Drawer 729, Union, SC 29379-0729. *Phone:* 864-424-8039. *E-mail:* greerm@mailbox.sc.edu.

University of South Carolina Upstate

Spartanburg, South Carolina

http://www.uscupstate.edu/

CONTACT

Ms. Donette Stewart, Associate Vice Chancellor for Enrollment Services, University of South Carolina Upstate, 800 University Way, Spartanburg, SC 29303. *Phone:* 864-503-5280. *Toll-free phone:* 800-277-8727. *Fax:* 864-503-5727. *E-mail:* dstewart@uscupstate.edu.

Voorhees College

Denmark, South Carolina

http://www.voorhees.edu/

CONTACT

Adrain West, Dean of Enrollment Management, Voorhees College, PO Box 678, Denmark, SC 29042. *Phone:* 803-780-1269. *Toll-free phone:* 866-237-4570. *E-mail:* west@voorhees.edu.

Winthrop University

Rock Hill, South Carolina

http://www.winthrop.edu/

- **State-supported** comprehensive, founded 1886, part of South Carolina Commission on Higher Education
- **Suburban** 456-acre campus with easy access to Charlotte
- **Coed** 4,887 undergraduate students, 89% full-time, 70% women, 30% men
- **Moderately difficult** entrance level, 67% of applicants were admitted

UNDERGRAD STUDENTS

4,331 full-time, 556 part-time. Students come from 41 states and territories; 66 other countries; 9% are from out of state; 29% Black or African American, non-Hispanic/Latino; 5% Hispanic/Latino; 1% Asian, non-Hispanic/Latino; 0.1% Native Hawaiian or other Pacific Islander, non-Hispanic/Latino; 0.3% American Indian or Alaska Native, non-Hispanic/Latino; 4% Two or more races, non-Hispanic/Latino; 0.1% Race/ethnicity unknown; 1% international; 6% transferred in; 48% live on campus.

Freshmen:

Admission: 5,175 applied, 3,481 admitted, 991 enrolled. ***Average high school GPA:*** 4.0. ***Test scores:*** SAT evidence-based reading and writing scores over 500: 72%; SAT math scores over 500: 59%; ACT scores over 18: 93%; SAT evidence-based reading and writing scores over 600: 26%; SAT math scores over 600: 15%; ACT scores over 24: 41%; SAT evidence-based reading and writing scores over 700: 3%; SAT math scores over 700: 2%; ACT scores over 30: 7%.

Retention: 75% of full-time freshmen returned.

FACULTY

Total: 546, 52% full-time, 59% with terminal degrees.

Student/faculty ratio: 14:1.

ACADEMICS

Calendar: semesters. *Degrees:* certificates, bachelor's, master's, post-master's, and postbachelor's certificates.

Special study options: adult/continuing education programs, advanced placement credit, cooperative education, distance learning, double majors, honors programs, independent study, internships, off-campus study, part-time degree program, services for LD students, student-designed majors, study abroad, summer session for credit. ***ROTC:*** Army (c), Air Force (c).

Computers: 620 computers/terminals are available on campus for general student use. Students can access the following: campus intranet, computer help desk, free student e-mail accounts, online (class) grades, online (class) registration, online (class) schedules, university services. Campuswide network is available. 100% of college-owned or -operated housing units are wired for high-speed Internet access. Wireless service is available via entire campus.

Library: Dacus Library plus 1 other. *Books:* 356,611 (physical), 281,972 (digital/electronic); *Serial titles:* 540 (physical), 36,003 (digital/electronic); *Databases:* 133. Weekly public service hours: 144; study areas open 24 hours, 5–7 days a week; students can reserve study rooms.

STUDENT LIFE

Housing options: on-campus residence required through sophomore year; coed, women-only, special housing for students with disabilities. Campus housing is university owned. Freshman campus housing is guaranteed.

Activities and organizations: drama/theater group, student-run newspaper, radio station, choral group, Association of Ebonites, WU Crew, Greek Life, DiGiorgio Student Union, Campus Ministries, national fraternities, national sororities.

Athletics Member NCAA. All Division I. ***Intercollegiate sports:*** baseball M(s), basketball M(s)/W(s), cheerleading M(c)/W(c), cross-country running M(s)/W(s), fencing M(c)/W(c), golf M(s)/W(s)(c), lacrosse M(c)/W, rugby M(c), soccer M(s)/W(s), softball W(s), tennis M(s)/W(s), track and field M(s)/W(s), volleyball W(s). ***Intramural sports:*** badminton M/W, basketball M/W, cross-country running M/W, equestrian sports M(c)/W(c), football M/W, golf M/W, racquetball M/W, soccer M/W, softball M/W, swimming and diving M/W, table tennis M/W, tennis M/W, ultimate Frisbee M/W, volleyball M/W, water polo M/W, weight lifting M/W.

Campus security: 24-hour emergency response devices and patrols, late-night transport/escort service, controlled dormitory access.

Student services: health clinic, personal/psychological counseling, veterans affairs office.

COSTS & FINANCIAL AID

Costs (2018–19) ***Tuition:*** state resident $15,230 full-time, $635 per credit hour part-time; nonresident $29,486 full-time, $1229 per credit hour part-time. Full-time tuition and fees vary according to degree level, reciprocity agreements, and student level. Part-time tuition and fees vary according to degree level and student level. ***Required fees:*** $360 full-time. ***Room and board:*** $8948; room only: $5416. Room and board charges vary according to board plan and housing facility. ***Payment plan:*** installment. ***Waivers:*** senior citizens and employees or children of employees.

Financial Aid Of all full-time matriculated undergraduates who enrolled in 2018, 3,758 applied for aid, 3,275 were judged to have need, 434 had their need fully met. 148 Federal Work-Study jobs (averaging $2002). In 2018, 576 non-need-based awards were made. ***Average percent of need met:*** 56. ***Average financial aid package:*** $13,642. ***Average need-based loan:*** $4185. ***Average need-based gift aid:*** $9191. ***Average non-need-based aid:*** $4329. ***Average indebtedness upon graduation:*** $33,499.

APPLYING

Standardized Tests *Required:* SAT or ACT (for admission).

Options: electronic application, deferred entrance.

Application fee: $40.

Required: high school transcript, minimum 3.0 GPA. ***Required for some:*** essay or personal statement.

Notification: continuous (freshmen), continuous (transfers).

CONTACT

David Rollings, Director of Admissions Ops and Systems, Winthrop University, Joynes Hall 226, Rock Hill, SC 29733. *Phone:* 803-323-2191. *Toll-free phone:* 800-763-0230. *E-mail:* rollingsd@winthrop.edu.

Wofford College

Spartanburg, South Carolina

http://www.wofford.edu/

- **Independent** 4-year, founded 1854, affiliated with United Methodist Church
- **Urban** 170-acre campus
- **Endowment** $194.0 million
- **Coed** 1,608 undergraduate students, 99% full-time, 53% women, 47% men
- **Very difficult** entrance level, 64% of applicants were admitted

UNDERGRAD STUDENTS

1,588 full-time, 20 part-time. Students come from 42 states and territories; 24 other countries; 44% are from out of state; 8% Black or African American, non-Hispanic/Latino; 4% Hispanic/Latino; 2% Asian, non-Hispanic/Latino; 0.1% American Indian or Alaska Native, non-Hispanic/Latino; 3% Two or more races, non-Hispanic/Latino; 1% Race/ethnicity unknown; 2% international; 1% transferred in; 97% live on campus.

Freshmen:
Admission: 3,520 applied, 2,238 admitted, 465 enrolled. ***Average high school GPA:*** 3.6. ***Test scores:*** SAT evidence-based reading and writing scores over 500: 99%; SAT math scores over 500: 100%; ACT scores over 18: 100%; SAT evidence-based reading and writing scores over 600: 82%; SAT math scores over 600: 61%; ACT scores over 24: 97%; SAT evidence-based reading and writing scores over 700: 16%; SAT math scores over 700: 18%; ACT scores over 30: 36%.

Retention: 88% of full-time freshmen returned.

FACULTY

Total: 182, 81% full-time, 80% with terminal degrees.

Student/faculty ratio: 10:1.

ACADEMICS

Calendar: 4-1-4. *Degree:* bachelor's.

Special study options: accelerated degree program, advanced placement credit, double majors, independent study, internships, off-campus study, part-time degree program, student-designed majors, study abroad, summer session for credit. ***ROTC:*** Army (b).

Computers: 233 computers/terminals are available on campus for general student use. Students can access the following: campus intranet, computer help desk, free student e-mail accounts, online (class) grades, online (class) registration, online (class) schedules. Campuswide network is available. Wireless service is available via entire campus.
Library: Sandor Teszler Library. *Books:* 114,660 (physical), 498,046 (digital/electronic); *Serial titles:* 372 (physical), 78,078 (digital/electronic); *Databases:* 201.

STUDENT LIFE

Housing options: on-campus residence required through senior year; coed. Campus housing is university owned. Freshman applicants given priority for college housing.

Activities and organizations: drama/theater group, student-run newspaper, radio station, choral group, W.A.R. - Wofford Athletics and Recreation, W.A.C. - Wofford Activities Council, Twin Towers - Service Organization, Math Academy, Arcadia Volunteer Corp, national fraternities, national sororities.

Athletics Member NCAA. All Division I except football (Division I-AA). ***Intercollegiate sports:*** baseball M(s), basketball M(s)/W(s), cheerleading W, cross-country running M(s)/W(s), golf M(s)/W(s)(c), lacrosse W(s), riflery M(s)/W(s), soccer M(s)/W(s), tennis M(s)/W(s), track and field M(s)/W(s), volleyball W(s). ***Intramural sports:*** basketball M/W, football M/W, soccer M/W, softball M/W, table tennis M/W, tennis M/W, ultimate Frisbee M/W.

Campus security: 24-hour emergency response devices and patrols, late-night transport/escort service, controlled dormitory access.

Student services: health clinic, personal/psychological counseling.

COSTS & FINANCIAL AID

Costs (2019–20) ***Comprehensive fee:*** $58,935 includes full-time tuition ($44,135), mandatory fees ($1575), and room and board ($13,225). Part-time tuition: $1825 per credit hour. ***College room only:*** $7315.

Financial Aid Of all full-time matriculated undergraduates who enrolled in 2018, 1,220 applied for aid, 1,001 were judged to have need, 399 had their need fully met. In 2018, 443 non-need-based awards were made. ***Average percent of need met:*** 83. ***Average financial aid package:*** $38,257. ***Average need-based loan:*** $4280. ***Average need-based gift aid:*** $33,590. ***Average non-need-based aid:*** $18,031. ***Average indebtedness upon graduation:*** $31,865. ***Financial aid deadline:*** 3/1.

APPLYING

Options: electronic application, early admission, early decision, early action, deferred entrance.

Application fee: $35.

Required: essay or personal statement, high school transcript. ***Recommended:*** 2 letters of recommendation, interview.

Application deadlines: 1/15 (freshmen), rolling (transfers), 11/15 (early action).

Early decision deadline: 11/1.

Notification: 3/1 (freshmen), continuous (transfers), 12/1 (early decision), 2/1 (early action).

CONTACT

Ms. Britt Shisler, Visit Coordinator, Wofford College, 429 N. Church Street, Spartanburg, SC 29303. *Phone:* 864-597-4132. *Fax:* 864-597-4147. *E-mail:* admission@wofford.edu.

SOUTH DAKOTA

Augustana University

Sioux Falls, South Dakota

http://www.augie.edu/

- **Independent** comprehensive, founded 1860, affiliated with Evangelical Lutheran Church in America
- **Urban** 100-acre campus
- **Endowment** $81.0 million
- **Coed**
- **Moderately difficult** entrance level

FACULTY

Student/faculty ratio: 12:1.

ACADEMICS

Calendar: 4-1-4. *Degrees:* bachelor's and master's.
Library: Mikkelsen Library. Students can reserve study rooms.

STUDENT LIFE

Housing options: on-campus residence required through sophomore year; coed, special housing for students with disabilities. Campus housing is university owned. Freshman campus housing is guaranteed.

Activities and organizations: drama/theater group, student-run newspaper, choral group, Augieholics (student athletics support organization), intramurals, Union Board of Governors (student union), Augie Green, Campus Ministries.

Athletics Member NCAA. All Division II.

Campus security: 24-hour emergency response devices and patrols, late-night transport/escort service, controlled dormitory access, special "day lighting" night lights throughout the campus grounds.

Student services: health clinic, personal/psychological counseling.

COSTS & FINANCIAL AID

Costs (2018–19) ***Comprehensive fee:*** $41,266 includes full-time tuition ($32,488), mandatory fees ($530), and room and board ($8248). Full-time tuition and fees vary according to course load and degree level. Part-time tuition and fees vary according to course load and degree level. ***College room only:*** $3778. Room and board charges vary according to board plan and housing facility.

Financial Aid Of all full-time matriculated undergraduates who enrolled in 2018, 1,242 applied for aid, 1,061 were judged to have need, 153 had their need fully met. 350 Federal Work-Study jobs (averaging $1784). 129 state and other part-time jobs (averaging $850). In 2018, 633 non-need-based awards were made. ***Average percent of need met:*** 84. ***Average financial aid package:*** $27,248. ***Average need-based loan:*** $4658.

Average need-based gift aid: $23,899. ***Average non-need-based aid:*** $16,682. ***Average indebtedness upon graduation:*** $38,588.

APPLYING
Standardized Tests *Required:* SAT or ACT (for admission).

Options: electronic application, deferred entrance.

Required: high school transcript, minimum 2.7 GPA, minimum ACT score of 20. ***Recommended:*** essay or personal statement, 1 letter of recommendation, interview.

CONTACT
Nancy Davidson, Vice President for Enrollment, Augustana University, 2001 South Summit Avenue, Sioux Falls, SD 57197. *Phone:* 605-274-5516. *Toll-free phone:* 800-727-2844. *Fax:* 605-274-5518. *E-mail:* admission@augie.edu.

Black Hills State University

Spearfish, South Dakota

http://www.bhsu.edu/

- **State-supported** comprehensive, founded 1883, part of South Dakota Board of Regents
- **Small-town** 123-acre campus
- **Coed**
- 87% of applicants were admitted

ACADEMICS
Calendar: semesters. *Degrees:* associate, bachelor's, master's, post-master's, and postbachelor's certificates.
Library: E. Y. Berry Library. Students can reserve study rooms.

STUDENT LIFE
Housing options: on-campus residence required through sophomore year; coed, men-only, women-only, special housing for students with disabilities. Campus housing is university owned. Freshman applicants given priority for college housing.

Activities and organizations: drama/theater group, student-run newspaper, radio and television station, choral group, Student Activities Committee, Student Government, national fraternities, national sororities.

Athletics Member NCAA. All Division II.

Campus security: 24-hour patrols, late-night transport/escort service, controlled dormitory access.

Student services: health clinic, personal/psychological counseling, veterans affairs office.

COSTS
Costs (2018–19) ***Tuition:*** state resident $7626 full-time, $291 per credit hour part-time; nonresident $10,671 full-time, $393 per credit hour part-time. Full-time tuition and fees vary according to course load, location, and reciprocity agreements. Part-time tuition and fees vary according to course load, location, and reciprocity agreements. ***Required fees:*** $1107 full-time. ***Room and board:*** $6978; room only: $3530. Room and board charges vary according to board plan, housing facility, and location. ***Payment plans:*** installment, deferred payment.

APPLYING
Standardized Tests *Required:* SAT or ACT (for admission).

Application fee: $20.

Required: high school transcript, minimum 2.0 high school GPA in core curriculum.

CONTACT
Mrs. Beth Oaks, Director of Admissions, Black Hills State University, 1200 University Street, Unit 9502, Spearfish, SD 57799-9502. *Phone:* 605-642-6343. *Toll-free phone:* 800-255-2478. *Fax:* 605-642-6254. *E-mail:* admissions@bhsu.edu.

Dakota State University

Madison, South Dakota

http://www.dsu.edu/

- **State-supported** comprehensive, founded 1881, part of South Dakota Board of Regents
- **Rural** 62-acre campus with easy access to Sioux Falls
- **Endowment** $15.2 million
- **Coed** 2,993 undergraduate students, 48% full-time, 41% women, 59% men
- **Moderately difficult** entrance level, 83% of applicants were admitted

UNDERGRAD STUDENTS
1,448 full-time, 1,545 part-time. Students come from 49 states and territories; 31 other countries; 39% are from out of state; 3% Black or African American, non-Hispanic/Latino; 4% Hispanic/Latino; 2% Asian, non-Hispanic/Latino; 0.1% Native Hawaiian or other Pacific Islander, non-Hispanic/Latino; 0.6% American Indian or Alaska Native, non-Hispanic/Latino; 4% Two or more races, non-Hispanic/Latino; 0.7% Race/ethnicity unknown; 1% international; 8% transferred in; 36% live on campus.

Freshmen:
Admission: 1,056 applied, 879 admitted, 405 enrolled. ***Average high school GPA:*** 3.2. ***Test scores:*** SAT evidence-based reading and writing scores over 500: 66%; SAT math scores over 500: 63%; ACT scores over 18: 90%; SAT evidence-based reading and writing scores over 600: 29%; SAT math scores over 600: 32%; ACT scores over 24: 47%; SAT math scores over 700: 6%; ACT scores over 30: 9%.

Retention: 67% of full-time freshmen returned.

FACULTY
Total: 153, 66% full-time, 57% with terminal degrees.

ACADEMICS
Calendar: semesters. *Degrees:* certificates, associate, bachelor's, master's, doctoral, and postbachelor's certificates.

Special study options: academic remediation for entering students, advanced placement credit, cooperative education, distance learning, double majors, honors programs, independent study, internships, off-campus study, part-time degree program, services for LD students, study abroad, summer session for credit. ***ROTC:*** Army (c), Air Force (c).

Computers: 110 computers/terminals are available on campus for general student use. Students can access the following: campus intranet, computer help desk, free student e-mail accounts, online (class) grades, online (class) registration, online (class) schedules. Campuswide network is available. 100% of college-owned or -operated housing units are wired for high-speed Internet access. Wireless service is available via entire campus.
Library: Karl E. Mundt Library plus 1 other. *Books:* 49,261 (physical), 218,951 (digital/electronic); *Serial titles:* 200 (physical), 120 (digital/electronic); *Databases:* 140. Weekly public service hours: 85.

STUDENT LIFE
Housing options: on-campus residence required through sophomore year; coed, men-only. Campus housing is university owned and leased by the school. Freshman campus housing is guaranteed.

Activities and organizations: drama/theater group, student-run newspaper, radio station, choral group, Gaming Club, Computer Club, Student Senate, Fellowship of Christian Athletes, Campus Crusade for Christ (Cru).

Athletics Member NAIA. ***Intercollegiate sports:*** baseball M(s), basketball M(s)/W(s), cheerleading M/W, cross-country running M(s)/W(s), football M(s), golf M/W, softball W(s), track and field M(s)/W(s), volleyball W(s). ***Intramural sports:*** basketball M/W, softball W, table tennis M/W, tennis M/W, volleyball W.

Campus security: late-night transport/escort service, controlled dormitory access.

Student services: health clinic, personal/psychological counseling, veterans affairs office.

COSTS & FINANCIAL AID
Costs (2018–19) ***Tuition:*** state resident $7299 full-time, $243 per credit hour part-time; nonresident $10,272 full-time, $342 per credit hour part-time. Full-time tuition and fees vary according to location and reciprocity

agreements. Part-time tuition and fees vary according to location and reciprocity agreements. ***Required fees:*** $1977 full-time, $40 per credit hour part-time. ***Room and board:*** $6873; room only: $3723. Room and board charges vary according to board plan and housing facility. ***Payment plan:*** installment. ***Waivers:*** senior citizens and employees or children of employees.

Financial Aid Of all full-time matriculated undergraduates who enrolled in 2017, 1,160 applied for aid, 943 were judged to have need, 85 had their need fully met. 133 Federal Work-Study jobs (averaging $2103). 24 state and other part-time jobs (averaging $7038). In 2017, 126 non-need-based awards were made. ***Average percent of need met:*** 54. ***Average financial aid package:*** $8324. ***Average need-based loan:*** $4222. ***Average need-based gift aid:*** $4575. ***Average non-need-based aid:*** $5327. ***Average indebtedness upon graduation:*** $29,962.

APPLYING

Standardized Tests *Required:* SAT or ACT (for admission).

Options: electronic application, deferred entrance.

Application fee: $20.

Required: high school transcript, minimum 2.6 GPA.

Application deadlines: rolling (freshmen), rolling (out-of-state freshmen), rolling (transfers).

Notification: continuous (freshmen), continuous (out-of-state freshmen), continuous (transfers).

CONTACT

Ms. Tory Bickett, Admissions Senior Secretary, Dakota State University, 820 North Washington, Madison, SD 57042-1799. *Phone:* 605-256-5178. *Toll-free phone:* 888-DSU-9988. *Fax:* 605-256-5020. *E-mail:* admissions@dsu.edu.

Dakota Wesleyan University

Mitchell, South Dakota

http://www.dwu.edu/

CONTACT

Mrs. Melissa Herr-Valburg, Director of Admissions, Dakota Wesleyan University, 1200 West University Avenue, Mitchell, SD 57301-4398. *Phone:* 605-995-2600 Ext. 2652. *Toll-free phone:* 800-333-8506. *Fax:* 605-995-2699. *E-mail:* admissions@dwu.edu.

Mount Marty College

Yankton, South Dakota

http://www.mtmc.edu/

- **Independent Roman Catholic** comprehensive, founded 1936
- **Small-town** 80-acre campus
- **Endowment** $26.6 million
- **Coed** 862 undergraduate students, 58% full-time, 57% women, 43% men
- **Minimally difficult** entrance level, 69% of applicants were admitted

UNDERGRAD STUDENTS

497 full-time, 365 part-time. Students come from 28 states and territories; 11 other countries; 47% are from out of state; 2% Black or African American, non-Hispanic/Latino; 8% Hispanic/Latino; 1% Asian, non-Hispanic/Latino; 0.1% Native Hawaiian or other Pacific Islander, non-Hispanic/Latino; 3% American Indian or Alaska Native, non-Hispanic/Latino; 0.9% Two or more races, non-Hispanic/Latino; 2% Race/ethnicity unknown; 2% international; 8% transferred in; 75% live on campus.

Freshmen:

Admission: 523 applied, 362 admitted, 135 enrolled.

Retention: 71% of full-time freshmen returned.

FACULTY

Total: 49, 88% full-time, 61% with terminal degrees.

Student/faculty ratio: 11:1.

ACADEMICS

Calendar: semesters. *Degrees:* certificates, associate, bachelor's, master's, doctoral, and post-master's certificates.

Special study options: academic remediation for entering students, accelerated degree program, adult/continuing education programs, advanced placement credit, cooperative education, distance learning, double majors, honors programs, independent study, internships, off-campus study, part-time degree program, services for LD students, student-designed majors, summer session for credit. ***ROTC:*** Army (c).

Computers: 8 computers/terminals are available on campus for general student use. Students can access the following: campus intranet, computer help desk, free student e-mail accounts, online (class) grades, online (class) registration, online (class) schedules. Campuswide network is available. 100% of college-owned or -operated housing units are wired for high-speed Internet access. Wireless service is available via entire campus.

Library: Mount Marty College Library. *Books:* 80,395 (physical), 16,584 (digital/electronic); *Serial titles:* 171 (physical); *Databases:* 83. Weekly public service hours: 81; study areas open 24 hours, 5–7 days a week; students can reserve study rooms.

STUDENT LIFE

Housing options: on-campus residence required through senior year; coed, men-only, women-only. Campus housing is university owned. Freshman campus housing is guaranteed.

Activities and organizations: drama/theater group, choral group, Campus Ministry, Student Government Association, Nursing Club, Education Club, Theater Club.

Athletics Member NAIA. ***Intercollegiate sports:*** archery M(s)/W(s), baseball M(s), basketball M(s)/W(s), cross-country running M(s)/W(s), golf M(s), riflery M(c)/W(c), soccer M(s)/W(s), softball W(s), tennis M(s)/W(s), track and field M(s)/W(s), volleyball W(s). ***Intramural sports:*** basketball M/W, soccer M/W, softball W, volleyball M/W.

Campus security: 24-hour emergency response devices and patrols, late-night transport/escort service, controlled dormitory access.

Student services: health clinic, personal/psychological counseling.

COSTS & FINANCIAL AID

Costs (2019–20) ***Comprehensive fee:*** $36,271 includes full-time tuition ($25,975), mandatory fees ($2150), and room and board ($8146). Part-time tuition: $540 per credit hour. ***Required fees:*** $45 per credit hour part-time.

Financial Aid Of all full-time matriculated undergraduates who enrolled in 2018, 437 applied for aid, 389 were judged to have need, 142 had their need fully met. In 2018, 71 non-need-based awards were made. ***Average percent of need met:*** 84. ***Average financial aid package:*** $27,555. ***Average need-based loan:*** $4490. ***Average need-based gift aid:*** $17,708. ***Average non-need-based aid:*** $11,896. ***Average indebtedness upon graduation:*** $38,026.

APPLYING

Standardized Tests *Required:* SAT or ACT (for admission).

Options: electronic application, early admission, deferred entrance.

Application fee: $35.

Required: high school transcript, minimum 2.0 GPA. ***Recommended:*** interview.

Application deadlines: rolling (freshmen), rolling (transfers).

Notification: continuous (freshmen), continuous (transfers).

CONTACT

Stephanie Moser, Dean of Enrollment, Mount Marty College, 1105 W. 8th Street, Yankton, SD 57078. *Phone:* 605-668-1545. *Toll-free phone:* 800-658-4552. *E-mail:* stephanie.moser@mtmc.edu.

National American University

Ellsworth AFB, South Dakota

http://www.national.edu/

CONTACT

Admissions Office, National American University, 1000 Ellsworth Street, Rushmore Center, Suite 2400B, Ellsworth AFB, SD 57706.

National American University
Rapid City, South Dakota
http://www.national.edu/

CONTACT
Ms. Angela Beck, Director of Enrollment Management, National American University, 321 Kansas City Street, Rapid City, SD 57701. *Phone:* 605-394-4902. *Toll-free phone:* 800-209-0490. *Fax:* 605-394-4871. *E-mail:* abeck@national.edu.

National American University
Sioux Falls, South Dakota
http://www.national.edu/

CONTACT
Ms. Lisa Houtsma, Director of Admissions, National American University, 5801 South Corporate Place, Sioux Falls, SD 57108. *Phone:* 605-336-4600. *Toll-free phone:* 800-388-5430. *Fax:* 605-336-4605. *E-mail:* lhoutsma@national.edu.

National American University
Watertown, South Dakota
http://www.national.edu/

CONTACT
National American University, 925 29th Street SE, Watertown, SD 57201.

Northern State University
Aberdeen, South Dakota
http://www.northern.edu/

- **State-supported** comprehensive, founded 1901, part of South Dakota Board of Regents
- **Small-town** 72-acre campus
- **Endowment** $30.8 million
- **Coed** 3,051 undergraduate students, 44% full-time, 58% women, 42% men
- **Minimally difficult** entrance level, 88% of applicants were admitted

UNDERGRAD STUDENTS
1,333 full-time, 1,718 part-time. Students come from 39 states and territories; 35 other countries; 30% are from out of state; 2% Black or African American, non-Hispanic/Latino; 4% Hispanic/Latino; 2% Asian, non-Hispanic/Latino; 0.2% Native Hawaiian or other Pacific Islander, non-Hispanic/Latino; 3% American Indian or Alaska Native, non-Hispanic/Latino; 3% Two or more races, non-Hispanic/Latino; 0.4% Race/ethnicity unknown; 4% international; 3% transferred in; 37% live on campus.

Freshmen:
Admission: 1,066 applied, 942 admitted, 339 enrolled. ***Average high school GPA:*** 3.3. ***Test scores:*** SAT evidence-based reading and writing scores over 500: 55%; SAT math scores over 500: 73%; ACT scores over 18: 82%; SAT evidence-based reading and writing scores over 600: 36%; SAT math scores over 600: 36%; ACT scores over 24: 32%; ACT scores over 30: 2%.
Retention: 75% of full-time freshmen returned.

FACULTY
Total: 102, 89% full-time, 78% with terminal degrees.
Student/faculty ratio: 19:1.

ACADEMICS
Calendar: semesters. *Degrees:* certificates, associate, bachelor's, master's, and postbachelor's certificates.
Special study options: academic remediation for entering students, accelerated degree program, adult/continuing education programs, advanced placement credit, cooperative education, distance learning, double majors, English as a second language, freshman honors college, honors programs, independent study, internships, off-campus study, part-time degree program, services for LD students, student-designed majors, study abroad, summer session for credit.
Computers: 130 computers/terminals and 20 ports are available on campus for general student use. Students can access the following: campus intranet, computer help desk, free student e-mail accounts, online (class) grades, online (class) registration, online (class) schedules. Campuswide network is available. 100% of college-owned or -operated housing units are wired for high-speed Internet access. Wireless service is available via entire campus.
Library: Beulah Williams Library. *Books:* 156,950 (physical), 15,000 (digital/electronic); *Serial titles:* 7,000 (physical), 250 (digital/electronic); *Databases:* 80. Weekly public service hours: 90; students can reserve study rooms.

STUDENT LIFE
Housing options: on-campus residence required through sophomore year; coed. Campus housing is university owned. Freshman campus housing is guaranteed.
Activities and organizations: drama/theater group, student-run newspaper, television station, choral group, marching band.
Athletics Member NCAA. All Division II. ***Intercollegiate sports:*** baseball M(s), basketball M(s)/W(s), cross-country running M(s)/W(s), football M(s), soccer W(s), softball W(s), swimming and diving W(s), track and field M(s)/W(s), volleyball W(s), wrestling M(s). ***Intramural sports:*** badminton M(c)/W(c), basketball M/W, cheerleading W(c), football M/W, racquetball M/W, rugby M(c)/W(c), soccer M/W, softball M/W, table tennis M/W, ultimate Frisbee M/W, volleyball M/W.
Campus security: 24-hour emergency response devices, controlled dormitory access.
Student services: health clinic, personal/psychological counseling, legal services, veterans affairs office.

COSTS & FINANCIAL AID
Costs (2018–19) ***Tuition:*** state resident $7191 full-time, $240 per credit hour part-time; nonresident $10,120 full-time, $337 per credit hour part-time. Full-time tuition and fees vary according to course load, program, and reciprocity agreements. Part-time tuition and fees vary according to course load, program, and reciprocity agreements. ***Required fees:*** $1089 full-time, $36 per credit hour part-time. ***Room and board:*** $7844; room only: $3640. Room and board charges vary according to board plan and housing facility. ***Payment plan:*** installment. ***Waivers:*** senior citizens and employees or children of employees.
Financial Aid Of all full-time matriculated undergraduates who enrolled in 2017, 1,001 applied for aid, 793 were judged to have need, 223 had their need fully met. 302 Federal Work-Study jobs (averaging $2484). 339 state and other part-time jobs (averaging $1078). In 2017, 129 non-need-based awards were made. ***Average percent of need met:*** 74. ***Average financial aid package:*** $10,864. ***Average need-based loan:*** $5593. ***Average need-based gift aid:*** $4862. ***Average non-need-based aid:*** $1623. ***Average indebtedness upon graduation:*** $29,968.

APPLYING
Standardized Tests *Required:* SAT or ACT (for admission).
Options: electronic application, early admission, deferred entrance.
Application fee: $20.
Required: high school transcript, minimum 2.6 GPA.
Application deadlines: rolling (freshmen), rolling (out-of-state freshmen), rolling (transfers).
Notification: continuous (freshmen), continuous (out-of-state freshmen), continuous (transfers).

CONTACT
Dr. Jeremy Reed, Vice President of Enrollment Management and Student Affairs, Northern State University, 1200 South Jay Street, Aberdeen, SD 57401. *Phone:* 605-626-2530. *Toll-free phone:* 800-678-5330. *Fax:* 605-626-2531. *E-mail:* admissions@northern.edu.

Oglala Lakota College
Kyle, South Dakota
http://www.olc.edu/

CONTACT
Director of Admissions, Oglala Lakota College, 490 Piya Wiconi Road, Kyle, SD 57752-0490. *Phone:* 605-455-2321 Ext. 236. *E-mail:* lmeseteth@olc.edu.

Presentation College

Aberdeen, South Dakota

http://www.presentation.edu/

CONTACT

Mr. Robert Schuchardt, Vice President for Student Services, Presentation College, 1500 North Main Street, Aberdeen, SD 57401. *Phone:* 605-229-8406. *Toll-free phone:* 800-437-6060. *Fax:* 605-229-8425. *E-mail:* admit@presentation.edu.

Sinte Gleska University

Mission, South Dakota

http://www.sintegleska.edu/

CONTACT

Mr. Jack Herman, Registrar and Director of Admissions, Sinte Gleska University, 101 Antelope Lake Circle, PO Box 105, Mission, SD 57555. *Phone:* 605-856-8100 Ext. 8479.

South Dakota School of Mines and Technology

Rapid City, South Dakota

http://www.sdsmt.edu/

CONTACT

Genene Sigler, Applications Processor, South Dakota School of Mines and Technology, 501 East Saint Joseph Street, Rapid City, SD 57701-3995. *Phone:* 605-394-2414 Ext. 5209. *Toll-free phone:* 800-544-8162. *Fax:* 605-394-1979. *E-mail:* admissions@sdsmt.edu.

South Dakota State University

Brookings, South Dakota

http://www.sdstate.edu/

CONTACT

Ms. Michelle Kuebler, Assistant Director of Admissions, South Dakota State University, PO Box 2201, Brookings, SD 57007. *Phone:* 605-688-4121. *Toll-free phone:* 800-952-3541. *Fax:* 605-688-6891. *E-mail:* sdsu.admissions@sdstate.edu.

University of Sioux Falls

Sioux Falls, South Dakota

http://www.usiouxfalls.edu/

- **Independent American Baptist Churches in the USA** comprehensive, founded 1883
- **Suburban** 140-acre campus
- **Endowment** $30.4 million
- **Coed** 1,319 undergraduate students, 86% full-time, 62% women, 38% men
- **Moderately difficult** entrance level, 91% of applicants were admitted

UNDERGRAD STUDENTS

1,137 full-time, 182 part-time. Students come from 32 states and territories; 11 other countries; 42% are from out of state; 6% Black or African American, non-Hispanic/Latino; 2% Hispanic/Latino; 1% Asian, non-Hispanic/Latino; 0.2% Native Hawaiian or other Pacific Islander, non-Hispanic/Latino; 0.2% American Indian or Alaska Native, non-Hispanic/Latino; 6% Two or more races, non-Hispanic/Latino; 1% Race/ethnicity unknown; 1% international; 7% transferred in; 55% live on campus.

Freshmen:

Admission: 2,000 applied, 1,825 admitted, 311 enrolled. ***Average high school GPA:*** 3.4. ***Test scores:*** SAT evidence-based reading and writing scores over 500: 83%; SAT math scores over 500: 100%; ACT scores over 18: 90%; SAT evidence-based reading and writing scores over 600: 33%; SAT math scores over 600: 17%; ACT scores over 24: 37%; ACT scores over 30: 5%.

Retention: 73% of full-time freshmen returned.

FACULTY

Total: 122, 49% full-time, 44% with terminal degrees.

Student/faculty ratio: 13:1.

ACADEMICS

Calendar: 4-1-4. *Degrees:* certificates, associate, bachelor's, master's, post-master's, and postbachelor's certificates.

Special study options: academic remediation for entering students, accelerated degree program, adult/continuing education programs, advanced placement credit, distance learning, double majors, honors programs, independent study, internships, off-campus study, part-time degree program, services for LD students, student-designed majors, study abroad, summer session for credit. ***ROTC:*** Air Force (c).

Unusual degree programs: 3-2 business administration.

Computers: 190 computers/terminals are available on campus for general student use. Students can access the following: campus intranet, computer help desk, free student e-mail accounts, online (class) grades, online (class) registration, online (class) schedules. Campuswide network is available. 100% of college-owned or -operated housing units are wired for high-speed Internet access. Wireless service is available via entire campus.

Library: Norman B. Mears Library. *Books:* 55,448 (physical), 158,760 (digital/electronic); *Serial titles:* 361 (physical), 30,000 (digital/electronic); *Databases:* 58. Weekly public service hours: 78.

STUDENT LIFE

Housing options: on-campus residence required through sophomore year; coed, women-only. Campus housing is university owned. Freshman campus housing is guaranteed.

Activities and organizations: drama/theater group, student-run newspaper, radio and television station, choral group, Campus Ministries, Student Senate, Fellowship of Christian Athletes, Association for Supervision and Curriculum Development, Service Core.

Athletics Member NCAA. All Division II except golf (Division I). ***Intercollegiate sports:*** baseball M(s), basketball M(s)/W(s), cheerleading M(s)/W(s), cross-country running M(s)/W(s), football M(s), golf M(s)/W(s), soccer W(s), softball W(s), swimming and diving W(s), tennis W(s), track and field M(s)/W(s), volleyball W(s). ***Intramural sports:*** basketball M/W, football M/W, sand volleyball M/W, soccer M/W, softball M/W, table tennis M/W, ultimate Frisbee M/W, volleyball M/W.

Campus security: 24-hour emergency response devices and patrols, student patrols, late-night transport/escort service, controlled dormitory access.

Student services: personal/psychological counseling.

COSTS & FINANCIAL AID

Costs (2019–20) ***Comprehensive fee:*** $26,460 includes full-time tuition ($18,610), mandatory fees ($300), and room and board ($7550). Part-time tuition: $370 per semester hour. ***College room only:*** $3970.

Financial Aid Of all full-time matriculated undergraduates who enrolled in 2018, 956 applied for aid, 782 were judged to have need, 146 had their need fully met. 107 Federal Work-Study jobs (averaging $1500). In 2018, 271 non-need-based awards were made. ***Average percent of need met:*** 76. ***Average financial aid package:*** $12,765. ***Average need-based loan:*** $4405. ***Average need-based gift aid:*** $8292. ***Average non-need-based aid:*** $5474. ***Average indebtedness upon graduation:*** $33,862.

APPLYING

Standardized Tests *Required:* SAT or ACT (for admission).

Options: electronic application, deferred entrance.

Application fee: $25.

Required: high school transcript. ***Required for some:*** essay or personal statement, 2 letters of recommendation, interview. ***Recommended:*** minimum 2.8 GPA.

Application deadlines: rolling (freshmen), rolling (transfers).

Notification: continuous (freshmen), continuous (transfers).

CONTACT

Mr. Ben Weins, Director of Admissions, University of Sioux Falls, 1101 West 22nd Street, Sioux Falls, SD 57105-1699. *Phone:* 605-331-6700. *Toll-free phone:* 800-888-1047. *Fax:* 605-331-6615. *E-mail:* admissions@usiouxfalls.edu.

University of South Dakota

Vermillion, South Dakota

http://www.usd.edu/

- **State-supported** university, founded 1862, part of South Dakota Board of Regents
- **Small-town** 274-acre campus
- **Endowment** $243.9 million
- **Coed** 7,590 undergraduate students, 65% full-time, 63% women, 37% men
- **Moderately difficult** entrance level, 86% of applicants were admitted

UNDERGRAD STUDENTS
4,969 full-time, 2,621 part-time. Students come from 47 states and territories; 51 other countries; 35% are from out of state; 3% Black or African American, non-Hispanic/Latino; 4% Hispanic/Latino; 1% Asian, non-Hispanic/Latino; 0.1% Native Hawaiian or other Pacific Islander, non-Hispanic/Latino; 2% American Indian or Alaska Native, non-Hispanic/Latino; 4% Two or more races, non-Hispanic/Latino; 0.7% Race/ethnicity unknown; 2% international; 7% transferred in; 34% live on campus.

Freshmen:
Admission: 4,119 applied, 3,534 admitted, 1,370 enrolled. ***Average high school GPA:*** 3.4. ***Test scores:*** SAT evidence-based reading and writing scores over 500: 86%; SAT math scores over 500: 80%; ACT scores over 18: 90%; SAT evidence-based reading and writing scores over 600: 35%; SAT math scores over 600: 42%; ACT scores over 24: 41%; SAT evidence-based reading and writing scores over 700: 5%; SAT math scores over 700: 9%; ACT scores over 30: 6%.

Retention: 77% of full-time freshmen returned.

FACULTY
Total: 682, 57% full-time, 47% with terminal degrees.

Student/faculty ratio: 17:1.

ACADEMICS
Calendar: semesters. *Degrees:* certificates, bachelor's, master's, doctoral, and postbachelor's certificates.

Special study options: academic remediation for entering students, accelerated degree program, adult/continuing education programs, advanced placement credit, distance learning, double majors, English as a second language, honors programs, independent study, internships, off-campus study, part-time degree program, services for LD students, student-designed majors, study abroad, summer session for credit. ***ROTC:*** Army (b).

Unusual degree programs: 3-2 business administration; engineering; BA/BS English with MA, BS/MS Physics,BS/MS Computer Science, BA/BS Psychology with MA, BS/MS Biology.

Computers: 975 computers/terminals are available on campus for general student use. Students can access the following: campus intranet, computer help desk, free student e-mail accounts, online (class) grades, online (class) registration, online (class) schedules. Campuswide network is available. 100% of college-owned or -operated housing units are wired for high-speed Internet access. Wireless service is available via entire campus.
Library: I. D. Weeks Library plus 2 others. *Books:* 528,075 (physical), 152,540 (digital/electronic); *Serial titles:* 4,739 (physical), 154,738 (digital/electronic); *Databases:* 230. Weekly public service hours: 103; students can reserve study rooms.

STUDENT LIFE
Housing options: on-campus residence required through sophomore year; coed, special housing for students with disabilities. Campus housing is university owned. Freshman campus housing is guaranteed.

Activities and organizations: drama/theater group, student-run newspaper, radio and television station, choral group, marching band, Dakotathon, International Club, SERVE, Campus Activities Board, national fraternities, national sororities.

Athletics Member NCAA. All Division I. ***Intercollegiate sports:*** basketball M(s)/W(s), cross-country running M(s)/W(s), football M(s), golf M/W(s)(c), soccer W(s), softball W(s), swimming and diving M(s)/W(s), tennis W(s), track and field M(s)/W(s), triathlon W(s), volleyball W(s). ***Intramural sports:*** archery M(c)/W(c), baseball M(c)/W(c), basketball M/W, fencing M(c)/W(c), field hockey W(c), football M, golf M/W, racquetball M/W, rugby W(c), soccer M(c)/W(c), softball M/W, table tennis M/W, tennis M/W, ultimate Frisbee M(c)/W(c), volleyball M/W, weight lifting M/W.

Campus security: 24-hour emergency response devices and patrols, student patrols, late-night transport/escort service, controlled dormitory access.

Student services: health clinic, personal/psychological counseling, legal services, veterans affairs office.

COSTS & FINANCIAL AID
Costs (2018–19) ***Tuition:*** state resident $7451 full-time, $248 per credit hour part-time; nonresident $10,815 full-time, $361 per credit hour part-time. Full-time tuition and fees vary according to location, program, and reciprocity agreements. Part-time tuition and fees vary according to location, program, and reciprocity agreements. ***Required fees:*** $1610 full-time, $54 per credit hour part-time. ***Room and board:*** $8216; room only: $4188. Room and board charges vary according to board plan and housing facility. ***Payment plan:*** installment. ***Waivers:*** children of alumni, senior citizens, and employees or children of employees.

Financial Aid Of all full-time matriculated undergraduates who enrolled in 2017, 3,872 applied for aid, 2,879 were judged to have need, 448 had their need fully met. In 2017, 918 non-need-based awards were made. ***Average percent of need met:*** 57. ***Average financial aid package:*** $8638. ***Average need-based loan:*** $4411. ***Average need-based gift aid:*** $4720. ***Average non-need-based aid:*** $2307. ***Average indebtedness upon graduation:*** $29,548.

APPLYING
Standardized Tests *Required:* SAT or ACT (for admission), College Preparatory program required for all degree seeking students. (for admission).

Options: electronic application, early admission.

Application fee: $20.

Required: high school transcript.

Application deadlines: rolling (freshmen), rolling (out-of-state freshmen), rolling (transfers).

Notification: continuous (freshmen), continuous (out-of-state freshmen), continuous (transfers).

CONTACT
Mr. Travis Vlasman, Senior Associate Director of Admissions, University of South Dakota, 414 East Clark Street, Vermillion, SD 57069-2390. *Phone:* 605-658-6228. *Toll-free phone:* 877-269-6837. *Fax:* 605-677-6323. *E-mail:* Travis.Vlasman@usd.edu.

TENNESSEE

American Baptist College

Nashville, Tennessee

http://www.abcnash.edu/

- **Independent Baptist** 4-year, founded 1924
- **Urban** 52-acre campus with easy access to Nashville
- **Endowment** $626,121
- **Coed**
- **Noncompetitive** entrance level

FACULTY
Student/faculty ratio: 12:1.

ACADEMICS
Calendar: semesters. *Degrees:* diplomas, associate, and bachelor's.
Library: T. L. Holcolm Library. *Books:* 14,290 (physical); *Serial titles:* 2 (physical); *Databases:* 2. Weekly public service hours: 2; students can reserve study rooms.

STUDENT LIFE
Housing options: coed, men-only, women-only. Campus housing is university owned.

Activities and organizations: choral group, Student Government Association, Vespers Service, Baptist Student Union, Choir, Greek Letter Fraternity and Hoi Adelphoi Fraternity, national fraternities.

Campus security: 24-hour emergency response devices and patrols, controlled dormitory access.

Student services: health clinic.

COSTS & FINANCIAL AID

Costs (2018–19) ***Comprehensive fee:*** $13,737 includes full-time tuition ($8760), mandatory fees ($657), and room and board ($4320). Full-time tuition and fees vary according to course load and program. Part-time tuition: $380 per credit hour. Part-time tuition and fees vary according to course load and program. ***College room only:*** $2120. Room and board charges vary according to board plan and housing facility.

Financial Aid Of all full-time matriculated undergraduates who enrolled in 2014, 128 applied for aid, 128 were judged to have need. 5 Federal Work-Study jobs (averaging $7452). ***Average percent of need met:*** 40. ***Average financial aid package:*** $10,412. ***Average need-based loan:*** $3823. ***Average need-based gift aid:*** $8263. ***Average indebtedness upon graduation:*** $9743. ***Financial aid deadline:*** 7/23.

APPLYING

Standardized Tests *Required:* (for admission).

Options: electronic application, deferred entrance.

Application fee: $30.

Required: essay or personal statement, high school transcript, minimum 2.0 GPA, 2 letters of recommendation, official transcript(s). ***Required for some:*** interview.

CONTACT

American Baptist College, 1800 Baptist World Center Drive, Nashville, TN 37207.

Aquinas College

Nashville, Tennessee

http://www.aquinascollege.edu/

CONTACT

Ms. Connie Hansom, Director of Admissions, Aquinas College, 4210 Harding Pike, Nashville, TN 37205-2005. *Phone:* 615-297-7545 Ext. 411. *Toll-free phone:* 800-649-9956. *Fax:* 615-279-3893. *E-mail:* hansomc@aquinascollege.edu.

Austin Peay State University

Clarksville, Tennessee

http://www.apsu.edu/

- **State-supported** comprehensive, founded 1927
- **Suburban** 169-acre campus with easy access to Nashville
- **Endowment** $9.9 million
- **Coed** 9,871 undergraduate students, 71% full-time, 59% women, 41% men
- **Moderately difficult** entrance level, 94% of applicants were admitted

UNDERGRAD STUDENTS

6,993 full-time, 2,878 part-time. Students come from 48 states and territories; 23 other countries; 11% are from out of state; 22% Black or African American, non-Hispanic/Latino; 8% Hispanic/Latino; 1% Asian, non-Hispanic/Latino; 0.3% Native Hawaiian or other Pacific Islander, non-Hispanic/Latino; 0.3% American Indian or Alaska Native, non-Hispanic/Latino; 7% Two or more races, non-Hispanic/Latino; 2% Race/ethnicity unknown; 0.6% international; 9% transferred in; 16% live on campus.

Freshmen:

Admission: 7,704 applied, 7,230 admitted, 2,009 enrolled. ***Average high school GPA:*** 3.3. ***Test scores:*** SAT evidence-based reading and writing scores over 500: 71%; SAT math scores over 500: 65%; ACT scores over 18: 84%; SAT evidence-based reading and writing scores over 600: 35%; SAT math scores over 600: 18%; ACT scores over 24: 29%; SAT evidence-based reading and writing scores over 700: 6%; SAT math scores over 700: 6%; ACT scores over 30: 4%.

Retention: 66% of full-time freshmen returned.

FACULTY

Total: 694, 53% full-time.

Student/faculty ratio: 18:1.

ACADEMICS

Calendar: semesters. *Degrees:* certificates, associate, bachelor's, master's, doctoral, post-master's, and postbachelor's certificates.

Special study options: academic remediation for entering students, accelerated degree program, adult/continuing education programs, advanced placement credit, cooperative education, distance learning, double majors, English as a second language, honors programs, independent study, internships, part-time degree program, services for LD students, study abroad, summer session for credit. ***ROTC:*** Army (b), Air Force (c).

Computers: 1,400 computers/terminals are available on campus for general student use. Students can access the following: campus intranet, computer help desk, free student e-mail accounts, online (class) grades, online (class) registration, online (class) schedules. Campuswide network is available. Wireless service is available via entire campus.

Library: Felix G. Woodward Library. *Books:* 196,384 (physical), 397,836 (digital/electronic); *Serial titles:* 53,295 (physical), 59,165 (digital/electronic); *Databases:* 299. Weekly public service hours: 109.

STUDENT LIFE

Housing options: on-campus residence required for freshman year; coed, men-only, women-only, special housing for students with disabilities. Campus housing is university owned.

Activities and organizations: drama/theater group, student-run newspaper, radio and television station, choral group, marching band, national fraternities, national sororities.

Athletics Member NCAA. All Division I except football (Division I-AA). ***Intercollegiate sports:*** baseball M(s), basketball M(s)/W(s), cheerleading M(s)/W(s), cross-country running M(s)/W(s), golf M(s)/W(s)(c), soccer W(s), softball W(s), tennis M(s)/W(s), track and field W(s), volleyball W(s). ***Intramural sports:*** badminton M/W, basketball M/W, football M/W, golf M/W, racquetball M/W, soccer M/W, softball M/W, table tennis M/W, ultimate Frisbee M/W, volleyball M/W.

Campus security: 24-hour emergency response devices and patrols, student patrols, late-night transport/escort service, controlled dormitory access.

Student services: health clinic, personal/psychological counseling, veterans affairs office.

COSTS & FINANCIAL AID

Costs (2018–19) ***One-time required fee:*** $75. ***Tuition:*** state resident $6696 full-time, $266 per credit hour part-time; nonresident $22,692 full-time, $901 per credit hour part-time. Full-time tuition and fees vary according to location and program. Part-time tuition and fees vary according to location and program. ***Required fees:*** $1529 full-time. ***Room and board:*** $9170; room only: $5520. Room and board charges vary according to board plan and housing facility. ***Payment plan:*** installment. ***Waivers:*** senior citizens and employees or children of employees.

Financial Aid Of all full-time matriculated undergraduates who enrolled in 2017, 6,549 applied for aid, 5,808 were judged to have need. 117 Federal Work-Study jobs (averaging $2492). 577 state and other part-time jobs (averaging $1580). In 2017, 595 non-need-based awards were made. ***Average financial aid package:*** $11,444. ***Average need-based loan:*** $3831. ***Average need-based gift aid:*** $7917. ***Average non-need-based aid:*** $4817. ***Average indebtedness upon graduation:*** $25,279.

APPLYING

Standardized Tests *Required for some:* SAT or ACT (for admission).

Options: electronic application, deferred entrance.

Application fee: $25.

Required: high school transcript. ***Required for some:*** minimum 2.8 GPA.

Notification: continuous (freshmen), continuous (transfers).

CONTACT

Ms. Amy Corlew, Director of Admissions, Austin Peay State University, 601 College Street, Clarksville, TN 37044. *Phone:* 931-221-7661. *Toll-free phone:* 800-844-2778. *Fax:* 931-221-6168. *E-mail:* admissions@apsu.edu.

Baptist College of Health Sciences

Memphis, Tennessee

http://www.bchs.edu/

- **Independent Southern Baptist** comprehensive, founded 1994
- **Urban** 17-acre campus with easy access to Memphis, TN
- **Endowment** $45.3 million
- **Coed, primarily women** 1,056 undergraduate students, 46% full-time, 89% women, 11% men
- **Moderately difficult** entrance level, 59% of applicants were admitted

UNDERGRAD STUDENTS
489 full-time, 567 part-time. Students come from 13 states and territories; 30% are from out of state; 43% Black or African American, non-Hispanic/Latino; 3% Hispanic/Latino; 2% Asian, non-Hispanic/Latino; 2% Two or more races, non-Hispanic/Latino; 1% Race/ethnicity unknown; 10% live on campus.

Freshmen:
Admission: 462 applied, 273 admitted. ***Average high school GPA:*** 3.2. ***Test scores:*** ACT scores over 18: 100%; ACT scores over 24: 29%; ACT scores over 30: 3%.
Retention: 74% of full-time freshmen returned.

FACULTY
Total: 65.
Student/faculty ratio: 11:1.

ACADEMICS
Calendar: trimesters. *Degree:* bachelor's and doctoral.

Special study options: accelerated degree program, advanced placement credit, distance learning, double majors, honors programs, part-time degree program, services for LD students, summer session for credit.

Computers: 26 computers/terminals are available on campus for general student use. Students can access the following: campus intranet, computer help desk, free student e-mail accounts, online (class) grades, online (class) registration, online (class) schedules. Campuswide network is available. 100% of college-owned or -operated housing units are wired for high-speed Internet access. Wireless service is available via entire campus.
Library: Health Sciences Library. *Books:* 1,869 (physical), 4,542 (digital/electronic); *Serial titles:* 3 (physical), 134,650 (digital/electronic); *Databases:* 46. Students can reserve study rooms.

STUDENT LIFE
Housing options: coed. Campus housing is university owned.

Activities and organizations: Student Government Association, Student Nursing Association, Allied Health Organization.

Campus security: 24-hour emergency response devices, late-night transport/escort service, controlled dormitory access, trained security personnel.

Student services: health clinic, personal/psychological counseling.

COSTS
Costs (2019–20) ***Tuition:*** $10,560 full-time, $440 per credit hour part-time. ***Required fees:*** $1340 full-time. ***Room only:*** $2900.

APPLYING
Standardized Tests *Required:* SAT or ACT (for admission).

Options: electronic application.

Application fee: $25.

Required: high school transcript, minimum 2.8 GPA, immunizations, health physical. ***Required for some:*** interview.

CONTACT
Ms. Lissa Morgan, Manager of Admissions/Retention, Baptist College of Health Sciences, 1003 Monroe Avenue, Memphis, TN 38104. *Phone:* 901-572-2441. *Toll-free phone:* 866-575-2247. *E-mail:* lissa.morgan@bchs.edu.

Belhaven University

Memphis, Tennessee

http://memphis.belhaven.edu/

CONTACT
Don Jones, Director of Admission, Belhaven University, 5100 Poplar Avenue, Suite 200, Memphis, TN 38137. *Phone:* 901-888-3343. *Fax:* 901-888-0771. *E-mail:* memphisadmission@belhaven.edu.

Belmont University

Nashville, Tennessee

http://www.belmont.edu/

- **Independent Christian** university, founded 1951
- **Urban** 77-acre campus
- **Endowment** $107.8 million
- **Coed**
- **Moderately difficult** entrance level

FACULTY
Student/faculty ratio: 14:1.

ACADEMICS
Calendar: semesters. *Degrees:* bachelor's, master's, doctoral, and post-master's certificates.
Library: Lila D. Bunch Library plus 1 other. *Books:* 184,352 (physical), 224,292 (digital/electronic); *Serial titles:* 1,033 (physical), 94,560 (digital/electronic); *Databases:* 288. Weekly public service hours: 127; students can reserve study rooms.

STUDENT LIFE
Housing options: on-campus residence required through sophomore year; men-only, women-only. Campus housing is university owned. Freshman campus housing is guaranteed.

Activities and organizations: drama/theater group, student-run newspaper, radio and television station, choral group, marching band, Service Corp, Alpha Sigma Tau, Phi Mu, Phi Kappa Tau, MOB, national fraternities, national sororities.

Athletics Member NCAA. All Division I.

Campus security: 24-hour emergency response devices and patrols, late-night transport/escort service, controlled dormitory access, bicycle patrol.

Student services: health clinic, personal/psychological counseling, women's center.

COSTS & FINANCIAL AID
Costs (2018–19) ***Comprehensive fee:*** $46,430 includes full-time tuition ($32,720), mandatory fees ($1590), and room and board ($12,120). Full-time tuition and fees vary according to course load and location. Part-time tuition: $1240 per credit hour. Part-time tuition and fees vary according to course load and location. ***College room only:*** $6660. Room and board charges vary according to board plan and housing facility. ***Payment plans:*** installment, deferred payment.
Financial Aid Of all full-time matriculated undergraduates who enrolled in 2018, 4,388 applied for aid, 3,356 were judged to have need, 315 had their need fully met. In 2018, 1701 non-need-based awards were made. ***Average percent of need met:*** 56. ***Average financial aid package:*** $20,334. ***Average need-based loan:*** $4289. ***Average need-based gift aid:*** $16,511. ***Average non-need-based aid:*** $7988. ***Average indebtedness upon graduation:*** $30,465.

APPLYING
Standardized Tests *Required:* SAT or ACT (for admission).

Options: electronic application, early admission, deferred entrance.

Application fee: $50.

Required: essay or personal statement, high school transcript. ***Required for some:*** interview, resumé of activities.

CONTACT
Mr. David Mee, Associate Provost and Dean of Enrollment, Belmont University, 1900 Belmont Boulevard, Nashville, TN 37212-3757. *Phone:* 615-460-5479. *Fax:* 615-460-5434. *E-mail:* david.mee@belmont.edu.

Bethel University

McKenzie, Tennessee

http://www.bethelu.edu/

- **Independent Cumberland Presbyterian** comprehensive, founded 1842
- **Small-town** 100-acre campus
- **Endowment** $2.9 million
- **Coed**
- **Minimally difficult** entrance level

FACULTY
Student/faculty ratio: 14:1.

ACADEMICS
Calendar: semesters. *Degrees:* associate, bachelor's, and master's.
Library: Burroughs Learning Center plus 1 other. *Books:* 24,618 (physical), 175,995 (digital/electronic); *Serial titles:* 26 (physical), 58,233 (digital/electronic); *Databases:* 92. Students can reserve study rooms.

STUDENT LIFE
Housing options: on-campus residence required through junior year; coed, men-only, women-only, special housing for students with disabilities. Campus housing is university owned and leased by the school. Freshman applicants given priority for college housing.

Activities and organizations: drama/theater group, choral group, marching band, Campus Crusade for Christ, STEA (Education), Student Government Association, Students in Free Enterprise (SIFE), Arete.

Athletics Member NAIA.

Campus security: night patrols by trained security personnel.

Student services: personal/psychological counseling.

COSTS
Costs (2018–19) ***Comprehensive fee:*** $25,750 includes full-time tuition ($15,292), mandatory fees ($1260), and room and board ($9198). Full-time tuition and fees vary according to course load and program. Part-time tuition: $462 per credit hour. Part-time tuition and fees vary according to course load and program. ***Required fees:*** $53 per credit hour part-time. ***College room only:*** $5814. Room and board charges vary according to board plan and housing facility.

APPLYING
Standardized Tests *Recommended:* SAT or ACT (for admission).

Options: electronic application, early admission, deferred entrance.

Application fee: $30.

Required: high school transcript, minimum 2.0 GPA. ***Required for some:*** essay or personal statement, interview.

CONTACT
Tina Hodges, Admissions Coordinator, Bethel University, 325 Cherry Avenue, McKenzie, TN 38201. *Phone:* 731-352-4030. *Fax:* 731-352-4069. *E-mail:* hodgest@bethelu.edu.

Bryan College

Dayton, Tennessee

http://www.bryan.edu/

- **Independent interdenominational** comprehensive, founded 1930
- **Small-town** 130-acre campus
- **Coed**
- **Moderately difficult** entrance level

FACULTY
Student/faculty ratio: 15:1.

ACADEMICS
Calendar: semesters. *Degrees:* diplomas, associate, bachelor's, master's, and postbachelor's certificates.
Library: Bryan College Library.

STUDENT LIFE
Housing options: on-campus residence required through senior year; men-only, women-only, special housing for students with disabilities. Campus housing is university owned. Freshman campus housing is guaranteed.

Activities and organizations: drama/theater group, student-run newspaper, choral group, Practical Christian Involvement (PCI), International Students Association, Rugby club, Nutella Club, Navigators.

Athletics Member NAIA.

Campus security: controlled dormitory access, police patrols, night watch.

Student services: health clinic, personal/psychological counseling.

COSTS & FINANCIAL AID
Costs (2018–19) ***Comprehensive fee:*** $34,300 includes full-time tuition ($26,800) and room and board ($7500). Part-time tuition: $1200 per credit hour. ***Room and board:*** Room and board charges vary according to housing facility.

Financial Aid Of all full-time matriculated undergraduates who enrolled in 2018, 558 applied for aid, 514 were judged to have need, 202 had their need fully met. ***Average financial aid package:*** $23,310. ***Average need-based loan:*** $3684. ***Average need-based gift aid:*** $13,777. ***Average indebtedness upon graduation:*** $24,610.

APPLYING
Standardized Tests *Required:* SAT or ACT (for admission).

Options: electronic application, early action, deferred entrance.

Application fee: $35.

Required: essay or personal statement, high school transcript, minimum 2.0 GPA, 3 letters of recommendation, minimum ACT score of 18 or RSAT of 940. ***Required for some:*** interview.

CONTACT
Mr. Andrew Smith, Senior Enrollment Counselor, Bryan College, 721 Bryan Drive, Dayton, TN 37321-7000. *Phone:* 423-775-2041 Ext. 218. *Toll-free phone:* 800-277-9522. *Fax:* 423-775-7199. *E-mail:* admissions@bryan.edu.

Carson-Newman University

Jefferson City, Tennessee

http://www.cn.edu/

- **Independent Southern Baptist** comprehensive, founded 1851
- **Small-town** 90-acre campus with easy access to Knoxville
- **Endowment** $54.6 million
- **Coed** 1,774 undergraduate students, 94% full-time, 59% women, 41% men
- **Moderately difficult** entrance level, 66% of applicants were admitted

UNDERGRAD STUDENTS
1,661 full-time, 113 part-time. 19% are from out of state; 9% Black or African American, non-Hispanic/Latino; 3% Hispanic/Latino; 0.7% Asian, non-Hispanic/Latino; 0.1% Native Hawaiian or other Pacific Islander, non-Hispanic/Latino; 0.7% American Indian or Alaska Native, non-Hispanic/Latino; 3% Two or more races, non-Hispanic/Latino; 0.9% Race/ethnicity unknown; 3% international; 6% transferred in; 49% live on campus.

Freshmen:
Admission: 3,736 applied, 2,467 admitted, 483 enrolled. ***Average high school GPA:*** 3.5. ***Test scores:*** SAT evidence-based reading and writing scores over 500: 71%; SAT math scores over 500: 67%; ACT scores over 18: 87%; SAT evidence-based reading and writing scores over 600: 25%; SAT math scores over 600: 14%; ACT scores over 24: 35%; SAT evidence-based reading and writing scores over 700: 3%; SAT math scores over 700: 3%; ACT scores over 30: 6%.

Retention: 63% of full-time freshmen returned.

FACULTY
Total: 247, 49% full-time, 55% with terminal degrees.

Student/faculty ratio: 13:1.

ACADEMICS
Calendar: semesters. *Degrees:* associate, bachelor's, master's, doctoral, and post-master's certificates.

Special study options: academic remediation for entering students, accelerated degree program, adult/continuing education programs, advanced placement credit, English as a second language, honors programs, internships, off-campus study, part-time degree program, services for LD students, student-designed majors, study abroad, summer session for credit. ***ROTC:*** Army (b).

Unusual degree programs: 3-2 engineering with Georgia Institute of Technology, University of Tennessee, Tennessee Technological University; pharmacy with Campbell University, Mercer University, University of Georgia.

Computers: 200 computers/terminals and 200 ports are available on campus for general student use. Students can access the following: campus intranet, computer help desk, free student e-mail accounts, online (class) grades, online (class) registration, online (class) schedules. Campuswide network is available. 100% of college-owned or -operated housing units are wired for high-speed Internet access. Wireless service is available via entire campus.

Library: Stephens-Burnett Library plus 3 others. Study areas open 24 hours, 5–7 days a week; students can reserve study rooms.

STUDENT LIFE

Housing options: on-campus residence required through junior year; men-only, women-only, special housing for students with disabilities. Campus housing is university owned. Freshman campus housing is guaranteed.

Activities and organizations: drama/theater group, student-run newspaper, choral group, marching band, Baptist Student Union, Fellowship of Christian Athletes, Student Government Association, Student Ambassadors Association, Columbians, national fraternities, national sororities.

Athletics Member NCAA. All Division II except golf (Division I). ***Intercollegiate sports:*** baseball M(s), basketball M(s)/W(s), cross-country running M(s)/W(s), football M(s), golf M(s)/W, soccer M(s)/W(s), softball W(s), swimming and diving M(s)/W(s), tennis M(s)/W(s), track and field M(s)/W(s), volleyball W(s). ***Intramural sports:*** badminton M/W, baseball M/W, basketball M/W, football M/W, golf M/W, racquetball M/W, skiing (downhill) M/W, soccer M/W, softball M/W, swimming and diving M/W, table tennis M/W, tennis M/W, volleyball M/W.

Campus security: 24-hour emergency response devices and patrols, late-night transport/escort service, controlled dormitory access.

Student services: health clinic, personal/psychological counseling.

COSTS & FINANCIAL AID

Costs (2019–20) ***Comprehensive fee:*** $36,710 includes full-time tuition ($26,700), mandatory fees ($1200), and room and board ($8810). Part-time tuition: $1090 per credit hour. ***College room only:*** $3930.

Financial Aid Of all full-time matriculated undergraduates who enrolled in 2018, 1,368 applied for aid, 1,368 were judged to have need, 302 had their need fully met. In 2018, 131 non-need-based awards were made. ***Average percent of need met:*** 80. ***Average financial aid package:*** $22,336. ***Average need-based loan:*** $3586. ***Average need-based gift aid:*** $19,792. ***Average non-need-based aid:*** $10,560. ***Average indebtedness upon graduation:*** $24,557.

APPLYING

Standardized Tests *Required:* SAT or ACT (for admission).

Options: electronic application, deferred entrance.

Required: high school transcript, minimum 2.3 GPA, medical history. ***Required for some:*** essay or personal statement. ***Recommended:*** interview.

Notification: continuous (freshmen), continuous (transfers).

CONTACT

Mr. Aaron Porter, Vice President for Enrollment Management, Carson-Newman University, 1646 Russell Avenue, PO Box 557, Jefferson City, TN 37760. *Phone:* 865-471-3223. *Toll-free phone:* 800-678-9061. *Fax:* 865-471-4817. *E-mail:* cnadmiss@cn.edu.

Christian Brothers University

Memphis, Tennessee

http://www.cbu.edu/

- **Independent Roman Catholic** comprehensive, founded 1871
- **Urban** 75-acre campus with easy access to Memphis
- **Endowment** $38.6 million
- **Coed** 1,674 undergraduate students, 88% full-time, 51% women, 49% men
- **Moderately difficult** entrance level, 56% of applicants were admitted

UNDERGRAD STUDENTS

1,476 full-time, 198 part-time. Students come from 28 states and territories; 30 other countries; 25% are from out of state; 26% Black or African American, non-Hispanic/Latino; 8% Hispanic/Latino; 5% Asian, non-Hispanic/Latino; 0.1% Native Hawaiian or other Pacific Islander, non-Hispanic/Latino; 0.8% American Indian or Alaska Native, non-Hispanic/Latino; 5% Two or more races, non-Hispanic/Latino; 18% Race/ethnicity unknown; 4% international; 4% transferred in; 40% live on campus.

Freshmen:

Admission: 2,810 applied, 1,574 admitted, 395 enrolled. ***Average high school GPA:*** 3.7. ***Test scores:*** ACT scores over 18: 90%; ACT scores over 24: 47%; ACT scores over 30: 11%.

Retention: 79% of full-time freshmen returned.

FACULTY

Total: 194, 54% full-time, 65% with terminal degrees.

Student/faculty ratio: 13:1.

ACADEMICS

Calendar: semesters. *Degrees:* associate, bachelor's, and master's.

Special study options: accelerated degree program, adult/continuing education programs, advanced placement credit, cooperative education, distance learning, double majors, honors programs, independent study, internships, part-time degree program, services for LD students, student-designed majors, study abroad, summer session for credit. ***ROTC:*** Army (c), Navy (c), Air Force (c).

Unusual degree programs: 3-2 engineering with Rhodes College.

Computers: 310 computers/terminals are available on campus for general student use. Students can access the following: campus intranet, computer help desk, free student e-mail accounts, online (class) grades, online (class) registration, online (class) schedules. Campuswide network is available. 100% of college-owned or -operated housing units are wired for high-speed Internet access. Wireless service is available via entire campus.

Library: Plough Memorial Library and Media Center. *Books:* 69,362 (physical), 180,750 (digital/electronic); *Serial titles:* 111 (physical), 39 (digital/electronic); *Databases:* 25. Weekly public service hours: 70; students can reserve study rooms.

STUDENT LIFE

Housing options: on-campus residence required through sophomore year; coed, men-only, women-only. Campus housing is university owned. Freshman campus housing is guaranteed.

Activities and organizations: choral group, Black Student Association, Tri-Beta, Hola CBU, Delta Sigma Pi, national fraternities, national sororities.

Athletics Member NCAA. All Division II except golf (Division I). ***Intercollegiate sports:*** baseball M(s), basketball M(s)/W(s), cross-country running M(s)/W(s), golf M(s)/W(s), rugby M(c)/W(c), soccer M(s)/W(s), softball W(s), tennis M(s)/W(s), track and field M(s)/W(s), volleyball W(s). ***Intramural sports:*** basketball M/W, soccer M/W, softball M/W, ultimate Frisbee M(c)/W(c), volleyball M/W.

Campus security: 24-hour emergency response devices and patrols, late-night transport/escort service, controlled dormitory access.

Student services: health clinic, personal/psychological counseling.

COSTS & FINANCIAL AID

Costs (2018–19) ***Comprehensive fee:*** $40,220 includes full-time tuition ($31,900), mandatory fees ($920), and room and board ($7400). Full-time tuition and fees vary according to class time, course load, and program. Part-time tuition: $1135 per credit hour. Part-time tuition and fees vary according to class time, course load, and program. ***Required fees:*** $215 per term part-time. ***Room and board:*** Room and board charges vary according to housing facility. ***Payment plan:*** installment. ***Waivers:*** employees or children of employees.

Financial Aid Of all full-time matriculated undergraduates who enrolled in 2018, 1,359 applied for aid, 976 were judged to have need, 168 had their need fully met. 128 Federal Work-Study jobs (averaging $1108). 102 state and other part-time jobs (averaging $1069). In 2018, 368 non-need-based awards were made. ***Average percent of need met:*** 71. ***Average financial aid package:*** $25,525. ***Average need-based loan:*** $2771. ***Average need-based gift aid:*** $20,664. ***Average non-need-based aid:*** $18,501. ***Average indebtedness upon graduation:*** $36,886.

APPLYING

Standardized Tests *Required:* SAT or ACT (for admission).

Options: electronic application, deferred entrance.

Application fee: $25.

Required: essay or personal statement, high school transcript, minimum 2.0 GPA. ***Required for some:*** 2 letters of recommendation. ***Recommended:*** interview.

Application deadlines: rolling (out-of-state freshmen), 8/23 (transfers).

Notification: 12/1 (freshmen), continuous (out-of-state freshmen), continuous (transfers).

CONTACT

Ms. Kristi Forman, Director of Admissions, Christian Brothers University, 650 East Parkway South, Memphis, TN 38104. *Phone:* 901-321-3205. *Toll-free phone:* 877-321-4CBU. *Fax:* 901-321-3202. *E-mail:* admissions@cbu.edu.

Cumberland University

Lebanon, Tennessee

http://www.cumberland.edu/

CONTACT

Ms. Beatrice LaChance, Director of Enrollment Services, Cumberland University, One Cumberland Square, Lebanon, TN 37087. *Phone:* 615-547-1244. *Toll-free phone:* 800-467-0562. *Fax:* 615-444-2569. *E-mail:* admissions@cumberland.edu.

Daymar College

Clarksville, Tennessee

http://www.daymarcollege.edu/

CONTACT

Daymar College, 2691 Trenton Road, Clarksville, TN 37040. *Phone:* 931-552-7600 Ext. 204.

Daymar College

Murfreesboro, Tennessee

http://www.daymarcollege.edu/

CONTACT

Daymar College, 415 Golden Bear Court, Murfreesboro, TN 37128.

DeVry University–Nashville Campus

Nashville, Tennessee

http://www.devry.edu/

CONTACT

Admissions Office, DeVry University–Nashville Campus, 3343 Perimeter Hill Drive, Suite 200, Nashville, TN 37211-4147. *Phone:* 615-445-3456. *Toll-free phone:* 866-338-7934.

East Tennessee State University

Johnson City, Tennessee

http://www.etsu.edu/

- **State-supported** university, founded 1911, part of State University and Community College System of Tennessee
- **Small-town** 366-acre campus
- **Endowment** $113.3 million
- **Coed** 11,268 undergraduate students, 85% full-time, 57% women, 43% men
- **Moderately difficult** entrance level, 87% of applicants were admitted

UNDERGRAD STUDENTS

9,533 full-time, 1,735 part-time. Students come from 42 states and territories; 60 other countries; 20% are from out of state; 6% Black or African American, non-Hispanic/Latino; 3% Hispanic/Latino; 1% Asian, non-Hispanic/Latino; 0.1% Native Hawaiian or other Pacific Islander, non-Hispanic/Latino; 0.2% American Indian or Alaska Native, non-Hispanic/Latino; 3% Two or more races, non-Hispanic/Latino; 1% Race/ethnicity unknown; 3% international; 10% transferred in; 25% live on campus.

Freshmen:

Admission: 8,009 applied, 6,978 admitted, 1,976 enrolled. ***Average high school GPA:*** 3.4. ***Test scores:*** ACT scores over 18: 88%; ACT scores over 24: 40%; ACT scores over 30: 7%.

Retention: 73% of full-time freshmen returned.

FACULTY

Total: 1,023, 59% full-time.

Student/faculty ratio: 15:1.

ACADEMICS

Calendar: semesters. *Degrees:* certificates, bachelor's, master's, doctoral, post-master's, and postbachelor's certificates.

Special study options: adult/continuing education programs, advanced placement credit, cooperative education, distance learning, double majors, English as a second language, external degree program, freshman honors college, honors programs, independent study, internships, off-campus study, part-time degree program, services for LD students, student-designed majors, study abroad, summer session for credit. ***ROTC:*** Army (b).

Computers: 1,400 computers/terminals are available on campus for general student use. Students can access the following: computer help desk, free student e-mail accounts, online (class) grades, online (class) registration, online (class) schedules. Campuswide network is available. Wireless service is available via entire campus.

Library: Charles C. Sherrod Library plus 2 others. *Books:* 731,960 (physical), 98,312 (digital/electronic); *Databases:* 210. Study areas open 24 hours, 5–7 days a week; students can reserve study rooms.

STUDENT LIFE

Housing options: coed, men-only, women-only, special housing for students with disabilities. Campus housing is university owned.

Activities and organizations: drama/theater group, student-run newspaper, radio and television station, choral group, marching band, honor societies, Volunteer ETSU, religious groups, residence hall councils, national fraternities, national sororities.

Athletics Member NCAA. All Division I except football (Division I-AA). ***Intercollegiate sports:*** baseball M(s), basketball M(s)/W(s), cross-country running M(s)/W(s), golf M(s)/W(s)(c), soccer M(s)/W(s), softball W(s), tennis M(s)/W(s), track and field M(s)/W(s), volleyball W(s). ***Intramural sports:*** basketball M/W, cross-country running M/W, football M/W, golf M/W, racquetball M/W, softball M/W, tennis M/W, volleyball W, weight lifting M.

Campus security: 24-hour emergency response devices and patrols, student patrols, late-night transport/escort service, controlled dormitory access.

Student services: health clinic, personal/psychological counseling, women's center, veterans affairs office.

FINANCIAL AID

Financial Aid Of all full-time matriculated undergraduates who enrolled in 2015, 8,121 applied for aid, 6,967 were judged to have need, 517 had their need fully met. 359 state and other part-time jobs (averaging $1156).

In 2015, 1145 non-need-based awards were made. ***Average percent of need met:*** 54. ***Average financial aid package:*** $10,182. ***Average need-based loan:*** $4198. ***Average need-based gift aid:*** $6449. ***Average non-need-based aid:*** $9680. ***Average indebtedness upon graduation:*** $27,866.

APPLYING
Standardized Tests *Required:* SAT or ACT (for admission).

Options: electronic application, early admission.

Application fee: $25.

Required: high school transcript, minimum 2.3 GPA, minimum 2.3 high school GPA or ACT score of 19.

Application deadlines: rolling (freshmen), rolling (transfers).

Notification: continuous (freshmen), continuous (transfers).

CONTACT
Mr. Michelle Williams, Director of Admissions, East Tennessee State University, PO Box 70731, Johnson City, TN 37614-0734. *Phone:* 423-439-4213. *Toll-free phone:* 800-462-3878. *Fax:* 423-439-4630. *E-mail:* go2etsu@etsu.edu.

Fisk University

Nashville, Tennessee

http://www.fisk.edu/

CONTACT
Ms. Loretta McDonald, Dean of the Office of Recruitment and Admission, Fisk University, 1000 17th Avenue North, Nashville, TN 37208-3051. *Phone:* 615-329-8503. *Toll-free phone:* 888-702-0022. *Fax:* 615-329-8774. *E-mail:* lmcdonald@fisk.edu.

Freed-Hardeman University

Henderson, Tennessee

http://www.fhu.edu/

CONTACT
Freed-Hardeman University, 158 East Main Street, Henderson, TN 38340-2399. *Phone:* 731-989-6557. *Toll-free phone:* 800-FHU-FHU-1.

Huntington University of Health Sciences

Knoxville, Tennessee

http://www.huhs.edu/

- **Proprietary** comprehensive, founded 1984
- **Suburban** campus
- **Coed** 115 undergraduate students, 21% full-time, 83% women, 17% men
- **Noncompetitive** entrance level, 100% of applicants were admitted

UNDERGRAD STUDENTS
24 full-time, 91 part-time. Students come from 33 states and territories; 72 other countries; 96% are from out of state; 5% Black or African American, non-Hispanic/Latino; 11% Hispanic/Latino; 1% Asian, non-Hispanic/Latino; 1% American Indian or Alaska Native, non-Hispanic/Latino; 2% Race/ethnicity unknown; 2% international; 23% transferred in.

Freshmen:
Admission: 5 applied, 5 admitted, 3 enrolled.
Retention: 50% of full-time freshmen returned.

FACULTY
Total: 19, 16% full-time, 37% with terminal degrees.

Student/faculty ratio: 13:1.

ACADEMICS
Calendar: continuous. *Degrees:* certificates, diplomas, associate, bachelor's, master's, and doctoral (offers only external degree programs conducted through home study).

Special study options: academic remediation for entering students, accelerated degree program, adult/continuing education programs, distance learning, external degree program, independent study, part-time degree program, summer session for credit.

Library: HUHS Online Library. *Books:* 9,130 (digital/electronic); *Serial titles:* 484,490 (digital/electronic); *Databases:* 13.

STUDENT LIFE
Housing options: college housing not available.

COSTS
Costs (2019–20) ***Tuition:*** $6360 full-time, $265 per credit hour part-time. ***Required fees:*** $250 full-time.

APPLYING
Options: deferred entrance.

Application fee: $75.

Required: minimum 2.0 GPA. ***Required for some:*** high school transcript, interview.

Application deadlines: rolling (freshmen), rolling (out-of-state freshmen), rolling (transfers).

Notification: continuous (freshmen), continuous (out-of-state freshmen), continuous (transfers).

CONTACT
Gregory Scott, Director of Admissions, Huntington University of Health Sciences, 118 Legacy View Way, Knoxville, TN 37918. *Phone:* 865-524-8079 Ext. 1. *Toll-free phone:* 800-290-4226. *Fax:* 865-524-8339. *E-mail:* admissions@huhs.edu.

Johnson University

Knoxville, Tennessee

http://www.johnsonu.edu/

- **Independent** comprehensive, founded 1893, affiliated with Christian Churches and Churches of Christ
- **Rural** 175-acre campus with easy access to Knoxville
- **Coed**
- **Moderately difficult** entrance level

FACULTY
Student/faculty ratio: 20:1.

ACADEMICS
Calendar: semesters. *Degrees:* certificates, associate, bachelor's, master's, doctoral, and post-master's certificates.
Library: Glass Memorial Library plus 1 other. Weekly public service hours: 80.

STUDENT LIFE
Housing options: on-campus residence required through senior year; men-only, women-only. Campus housing is university owned.

Activities and organizations: drama/theater group, student-run newspaper, radio station, choral group, Student Government Association, International student Association, Harvesters (Missions), International Justice Mission, Students Promoting Social Unity.

Athletics Member NCCAA.

Campus security: 24-hour emergency response devices and patrols, student patrols, controlled dormitory access.

Student services: health clinic, personal/psychological counseling.

COSTS & FINANCIAL AID
Costs (2018–19) ***Comprehensive fee:*** $22,760 includes full-time tuition ($14,880), mandatory fees ($1180), and room and board ($6700). Full-time tuition and fees vary according to class time, course load, degree level, location, and program. Part-time tuition: $470 per credit hour. Part-time tuition and fees vary according to class time, course load, degree level, location, and program. ***College room only:*** $3000. Room and board charges vary according to board plan, housing facility, and location.

Financial Aid Of all full-time matriculated undergraduates who enrolled in 2017, 655 applied for aid, 555 were judged to have need, 66 had their need fully met. In 2017, 99 non-need-based awards were made. ***Average percent of need met:*** 64. ***Average financial aid package:*** $11,438. ***Average need-based loan:*** $4320. ***Average need-based gift aid:*** $8142. ***Average non-need-based aid:*** $4772. ***Average indebtedness upon graduation:*** $24,353.

APPLYING
Standardized Tests *Required:* SAT or ACT (for admission).

Options: electronic application, early admission, deferred entrance.

Application fee: $35.

Required: essay or personal statement, high school transcript, minimum 2.5 GPA, 3 letters of recommendation. ***Required for some:*** interview.

CONTACT
Ms. Julee Schultz, Director of Admissions, Johnson University, 7900 Johnson Drive, Knoxville, TN 37998. *Phone:* 865-251-2233. *Toll-free phone:* 800-827-2122. *Fax:* 865-251-2336. *E-mail:* jschultz@johnsonu.edu.

King University

Bristol, Tennessee

http://www.king.edu/

- **Independent** comprehensive, founded 1867, affiliated with Presbyterian Church (U.S.A.)
- **Suburban** 135-acre campus
- **Endowment** $33.4 million
- **Coed** 1,579 undergraduate students, 92% full-time, 62% women, 38% men
- **Moderately difficult** entrance level, 59% of applicants were admitted

UNDERGRAD STUDENTS
1,460 full-time, 119 part-time. Students come from 41 states and territories; 24 other countries; 40% are from out of state; 6% Black or African American, non-Hispanic/Latino; 3% Hispanic/Latino; 0.9% Asian, non-Hispanic/Latino; 0.1% Native Hawaiian or other Pacific Islander, non-Hispanic/Latino; 0.3% American Indian or Alaska Native, non-Hispanic/Latino; 1% Two or more races, non-Hispanic/Latino; 14% Race/ethnicity unknown; 3% international; 3% transferred in; 21% live on campus.

Freshmen:
Admission: 1,152 applied, 683 admitted, 188 enrolled. ***Average high school GPA:*** 3.4.

Retention: 69% of full-time freshmen returned.

FACULTY
Total: 255, 34% full-time, 53% with terminal degrees.

Student/faculty ratio: 13:1.

ACADEMICS
Calendar: semesters. *Degrees:* associate, bachelor's, master's, doctoral, and post-master's certificates.

Special study options: adult/continuing education programs, advanced placement credit, distance learning, double majors, honors programs, independent study, internships, off-campus study, part-time degree program, services for LD students, student-designed majors, study abroad, summer session for credit. ***ROTC:*** Army (c).

Unusual degree programs: 3-2 engineering with The University of Tennessee.

Computers: 90 computers/terminals and 500 ports are available on campus for general student use. Students can access the following: campus intranet, computer help desk, free student e-mail accounts, online (class) grades, online (class) registration, online (class) schedules, Student Portal. Campuswide network is available. 100% of college-owned or -operated housing units are wired for high-speed Internet access. Wireless service is available via entire campus.

Library: E. W. King Library plus 3 others. *Books:* 75,745 (physical), 191,050 (digital/electronic); *Serial titles:* 150 (physical); *Databases:* 99. Weekly public service hours: 85.

STUDENT LIFE
Housing options: on-campus residence required through junior year; men-only, women-only, special housing for students with disabilities. Campus housing is university owned. Freshman campus housing is guaranteed.

Activities and organizations: drama/theater group, student-run newspaper, choral group, Student Government Association, Women in STEM, King Security and Intelligence Studies Student Group, Enactus, STEA-KE.

Athletics Member NCAA. All Division II. ***Intercollegiate sports:*** baseball M(s), basketball M(s)/W(s), cheerleading M/W(s), cross-country running M(s)/W(s), golf M(s)/W(s), soccer M(s)/W(s), softball W(s), swimming and diving M(s)/W(s), tennis M(s)/W(s), track and field M(s)/W(s), volleyball M(s)/W(s), wrestling M(s)/W(s). ***Intramural sports:*** basketball M/W, bowling M/W, racquetball M(c)/W(c), sand volleyball M(c)/W(c), soccer M/W, softball M/W, table tennis M(c)/W(c), tennis M(c)/W(c), ultimate Frisbee M/W, volleyball M/W.

Campus security: 24-hour emergency response devices and patrols, late-night transport/escort service, controlled dormitory access.

Student services: personal/psychological counseling.

COSTS & FINANCIAL AID
Costs (2019–20) ***Comprehensive fee:*** $49,640 includes full-time tuition ($38,948), mandatory fees ($1668), and room and board ($9024). ***College room only:*** $4532.

Financial Aid Of all full-time matriculated undergraduates who enrolled in 2018, 1,302 applied for aid, 1,197 were judged to have need, 153 had their need fully met. 126 Federal Work-Study jobs (averaging $1150). 121 state and other part-time jobs (averaging $1185). In 2018, 90 non-need-based awards were made. ***Average percent of need met:*** 68. ***Average financial aid package:*** $16,476. ***Average need-based loan:*** $4538. ***Average need-based gift aid:*** $13,828. ***Average non-need-based aid:*** $10,178. ***Average indebtedness upon graduation:*** $29,023.

APPLYING
Options: electronic application, deferred entrance.

Required: high school transcript. ***Required for some:*** essay or personal statement. ***Recommended:*** minimum 3.0 GPA.

Application deadlines: rolling (freshmen), rolling (transfers).

Notification: continuous (freshmen), continuous (transfers).

CONTACT
Mr. Tom VerDow, Director of Undergraduate Recruitment, King University, 1350 King College Road, Bristol, TN 37620. *Phone:* 423-652-4149. *Toll-free phone:* 800-362-0014. *Fax:* 423-652-4727. *E-mail:* admissions@king.edu.

Lane College

Jackson, Tennessee

http://www.lanecollege.edu/

CONTACT
Dr. Monica C. Scott, Director of Enrollment Management, Lane College, 545 Lane Avenue, Jackson, TN 38301. *Phone:* 731-426-7533. *Toll-free phone:* 800-960-7533. *Fax:* 731-426-7559. *E-mail:* mclayborne@lanecollege.edu.

Lee University

Cleveland, Tennessee

http://www.leeuniversity.edu/

- **Independent** comprehensive, founded 1918, affiliated with Church of God
- **Small-town** 120-acre campus with easy access to Chattanooga, TN
- **Endowment** $21.9 million
- **Coed** 4,883 undergraduate students, 77% full-time, 61% women, 39% men
- **Moderately difficult** entrance level, 83% of applicants were admitted

UNDERGRAD STUDENTS
3,780 full-time, 1,103 part-time. Students come from 50 states and territories; 47 other countries; 54% are from out of state; 5% Black or African American, non-Hispanic/Latino; 2% Hispanic/Latino; 0.7% Asian, non-Hispanic/Latino; 0.2% Native Hawaiian or other Pacific Islander, non-Hispanic/Latino; 0.4% American Indian or Alaska Native, non-Hispanic/Latino; 3% Two or more races, non-Hispanic/Latino; 10% Race/ethnicity unknown; 2% international; 4% transferred in; 47% live on campus.

Freshmen:
Admission: 2,443 applied, 2,029 admitted, 880 enrolled. ***Average high school GPA:*** 3.7. ***Test scores:*** SAT evidence-based reading and writing scores over 500: 85%; SAT math scores over 500: 73%; ACT scores over 18: 93%; SAT evidence-based reading and writing scores over 600: 46%; SAT math scores over 600: 26%; ACT scores over 24: 62%; SAT evidence-based reading and writing scores over 700: 7%; SAT math scores over 700: 5%; ACT scores over 30: 19%.

Retention: 79% of full-time freshmen returned.

FACULTY
Total: 476, 40% full-time, 54% with terminal degrees.

Student/faculty ratio: 16:1.

ACADEMICS
Calendar: semesters. *Degrees:* bachelor's, master's, doctoral, and post-master's certificates.

Special study options: academic remediation for entering students, adult/continuing education programs, advanced placement credit, cooperative education, distance learning, double majors, English as a second language, external degree program, honors programs, independent study, internships, off-campus study, part-time degree program, services for LD students, student-designed majors, study abroad, summer session for credit.

Computers: 460 computers/terminals and 650 ports are available on campus for general student use. Students can access the following: campus intranet, computer help desk, free student e-mail accounts, online (class) grades, online (class) registration, online (class) schedules. Campuswide network is available. 95% of college-owned or -operated housing units are wired for high-speed Internet access. Wireless service is available via entire campus.
Library: William G. Squires Library plus 2 others. *Books:* 158,156 (physical), 303,576 (digital/electronic); *Serial titles:* 244 (physical), 97,212 (digital/electronic); *Databases:* 137. Weekly public service hours: 93; students can reserve study rooms.

STUDENT LIFE
Housing options: on-campus residence required through sophomore year; men-only, women-only. Campus housing is university owned and leased by the school. Freshman campus housing is guaranteed.

Activities and organizations: drama/theater group, student-run newspaper, choral group, Student Leadership Council, CRU, Big Pal Little Pal, Delta Zeta Tau, Crossover.

Athletics Member NCAA, NCCAA. All NCAA Division II.
Intercollegiate sports: baseball M(s), basketball M(s)/W(s), cross-country running M(s)/W(s), golf M(s)/W(s), lacrosse W(s), soccer M(s)/W(s), softball W(s), tennis M(s)/W(s), track and field M(s)/W(s), volleyball W(s). ***Intramural sports:*** basketball M/W, bowling M/W, football M/W, golf M/W, racquetball M/W, rugby M(c)/W(c), sand volleyball M/W, soccer M/W, softball M/W, table tennis M/W, tennis M/W, ultimate Frisbee M(c)/W(c), volleyball M/W.

Campus security: 24-hour emergency response devices and patrols, late-night transport/escort service, controlled dormitory access.

Student services: health clinic, personal/psychological counseling, veterans affairs office.

COSTS & FINANCIAL AID
Costs (2019–20) ***Comprehensive fee:*** $27,095 includes full-time tuition ($18,120), mandatory fees ($650), and room and board ($8325). Part-time tuition: $755 per credit hour. ***Required fees:*** $35 per term part-time. ***College room only:*** $4575.

Financial Aid Of all full-time matriculated undergraduates who enrolled in 2018, 3,320 applied for aid, 2,577 were judged to have need, 486 had their need fully met. 311 Federal Work-Study jobs (averaging $1401). 782 state and other part-time jobs (averaging $1685). In 2018, 726 non-need-based awards were made. ***Average percent of need met:*** 55. ***Average financial aid package:*** $14,010. ***Average need-based loan:*** $4175. ***Average need-based gift aid:*** $11,230. ***Average non-need-based aid:*** $7720. ***Average indebtedness upon graduation:*** $32,039.

APPLYING
Standardized Tests *Required:* SAT or ACT (for admission). *Recommended:* SAT (for admission), ACT (for admission).

Options: electronic application, early admission, deferred entrance.

Application fee: $25.

Required: high school transcript, minimum 2.0 GPA, MMR immunization record. ***Required for some:*** 3 letters of recommendation.

Application deadlines: rolling (freshmen), rolling (out-of-state freshmen), rolling (transfers).

Notification: continuous (freshmen), continuous (out-of-state freshmen), continuous (transfers).

CONTACT
Mr. Phillip Cook, Vice President for Enrollment, Lee University, 1120 N. Ocoee Street, Cleveland, TN 37311. *Phone:* 423-614-8500. *Toll-free phone:* 800-533-9930. *Fax:* 423-614-8533. *E-mail:* admissions@leeuniversity.edu.

LeMoyne-Owen College

Memphis, Tennessee

http://www.loc.edu/

CONTACT
LeMoyne-Owen College, 807 Walker Avenue, Memphis, TN 38126-6595. *Phone:* 901-435-1500. *Toll-free phone:* 800-737-7778.

Lincoln Memorial University

Harrogate, Tennessee

http://www.lmunet.edu/

- **Independent** university, founded 1897
- **Small-town** 1000-acre campus
- **Endowment** $40.8 million
- **Coed**
- **Moderately difficult** entrance level

FACULTY
Student/faculty ratio: 14:1.

ACADEMICS
Calendar: semesters. *Degrees:* associate, bachelor's, master's, doctoral, and post-master's certificates.
Library: Carnegie-Vincent Library. *Books:* 85,346 (physical), 355,314 (digital/electronic); *Serial titles:* 1,548 (physical), 32,592 (digital/electronic); *Databases:* 225. Weekly public service hours: 92; students can reserve study rooms.

STUDENT LIFE
Housing options: coed, men-only, women-only, special housing for students with disabilities. Campus housing is university owned and leased by the school.

Activities and organizations: drama/theater group, student-run radio and television station, choral group, Enactus, Pre-Vet Club, Pre-Med Club, Fishing Club, Earth Club, national fraternities, national sororities.

Athletics Member NCAA. All Division II.

Campus security: 24-hour emergency response devices and patrols, late-night transport/escort service.

Student services: health clinic, personal/psychological counseling, veterans affairs office.

COSTS & FINANCIAL AID
Costs (2018–19) ***Comprehensive fee:*** $29,250 includes full-time tuition ($21,480) and room and board ($7770). Full-time tuition and fees vary according to course load, degree level, location, and program. Part-time tuition: $895 per credit hour. Part-time tuition and fees vary according to course load, degree level, location, and program. ***College room only:*** $3450. Room and board charges vary according to board plan and housing facility.

Financial Aid Of all full-time matriculated undergraduates who enrolled in 2016, 1,058 applied for aid, 946 were judged to have need, 307 had their need fully met. In 2016, 77 non-need-based awards were made. ***Average percent of need met:*** 83. ***Average financial aid package:*** $22,114. ***Average need-based loan:*** $6522. ***Average need-based gift aid:*** $14,876. ***Average non-need-based aid:*** $9788. ***Average indebtedness upon graduation:*** $18,038.

APPLYING
Standardized Tests *Required:* SAT or ACT (for admission).

Options: electronic application.

Required: high school transcript, immunization records, financial aid application. ***Recommended:*** minimum 3.0 GPA.

CONTACT
Lincoln Memorial University, 6965 Cumberland Gap Parkway, Harrogate, TN 37752-1901. *Phone:* 423-869-6280. *Toll-free phone:* 800-325-0900.

Lipscomb University

Nashville, Tennessee

http://www.lipscomb.edu/

- **Independent** university, founded 1891, affiliated with Church of Christ
- **Suburban** 89-acre campus
- **Endowment** $79.1 million
- **Coed** 2,938 undergraduate students, 93% full-time, 61% women, 39% men
- **Moderately difficult** entrance level, 60% of applicants were admitted

UNDERGRAD STUDENTS

2,738 full-time, 200 part-time. Students come from 47 states and territories; 44 other countries; 36% are from out of state; 7% Black or African American, non-Hispanic/Latino; 8% Hispanic/Latino; 3% Asian, non-Hispanic/Latino; 0.1% Native Hawaiian or other Pacific Islander, non-Hispanic/Latino; 0.1% American Indian or Alaska Native, non-Hispanic/Latino; 3% Two or more races, non-Hispanic/Latino; 0.9% Race/ethnicity unknown; 3% international; 6% transferred in; 47% live on campus.

Freshmen:

Admission: 3,638 applied, 2,165 admitted, 666 enrolled. ***Average high school GPA:*** 3.7. ***Test scores:*** SAT evidence-based reading and writing scores over 500: 91%; SAT math scores over 500: 87%; ACT scores over 18: 98%; SAT evidence-based reading and writing scores over 600: 52%; SAT math scores over 600: 42%; ACT scores over 24: 64%; SAT evidence-based reading and writing scores over 700: 12%; SAT math scores over 700: 17%; ACT scores over 30: 21%.

Retention: 81% of full-time freshmen returned.

FACULTY

Total: 587, 39% full-time, 51% with terminal degrees.

Student/faculty ratio: 14:1.

ACADEMICS

Calendar: semesters. *Degrees:* associate, bachelor's, master's, doctoral, and postbachelor's certificates.

Special study options: academic remediation for entering students, accelerated degree program, adult/continuing education programs, advanced placement credit, distance learning, double majors, English as a second language, honors programs, independent study, internships, part-time degree program, services for LD students, student-designed majors, study abroad, summer session for credit. ***ROTC:*** Army (c), Air Force (c).

Computers: 150 computers/terminals are available on campus for general student use. Students can access the following: campus intranet, computer help desk, free student e-mail accounts, online (class) grades, online (class) registration, online (class) schedules. Campuswide network is available. 100% of college-owned or -operated housing units are wired for high-speed Internet access. Wireless service is available via entire campus.

Library: Beaman Library plus 1 other. *Books:* 157,824 (physical), 167,520 (digital/electronic); *Serial titles:* 253 (physical), 489 (digital/electronic); *Databases:* 100. Students can reserve study rooms.

STUDENT LIFE

Housing options: on-campus residence required through junior year; men-only, women-only. Campus housing is university owned. Freshman applicants given priority for college housing.

Activities and organizations: drama/theater group, student-run newspaper, radio and television station, choral group, Sigma Pi Beta, business fraternities, Multicultural Association, Alpha Phi Chi men's service club, Pi Kappa Sigma women's service club.

Athletics Member NCAA. All Division I. ***Intercollegiate sports:*** baseball M(s), basketball M(s)/W(s), cross-country running M(s)/W(s), golf M(s)/W(s)(c), ice hockey M(c), soccer M(s)/W(s), softball W(s), tennis M(s)/W(s), track and field M(s)/W(s), volleyball W(s). ***Intramural sports:*** basketball M/W, football M/W, golf M/W, racquetball M/W, sand volleyball M/W, soccer M/W, softball M/W, table tennis M/W, ultimate Frisbee M/W, volleyball M/W.

Campus security: 24-hour emergency response devices and patrols, late-night transport/escort service, controlled dormitory access.

Student services: health clinic, personal/psychological counseling, veterans affairs office.

COSTS & FINANCIAL AID

Costs (2019–20) ***Comprehensive fee:*** $46,704 includes full-time tuition ($30,860), mandatory fees ($2564), and room and board ($13,280). Part-time tuition: $1286 per credit hour.

Financial Aid Of all full-time matriculated undergraduates who enrolled in 2018, 2,639 applied for aid, 1,701 were judged to have need, 450 had their need fully met. 239 Federal Work-Study jobs. In 2018, 836 non-need-based awards were made. ***Average percent of need met:*** 62. ***Average financial aid package:*** $29,133. ***Average need-based loan:*** $5459. ***Average need-based gift aid:*** $25,903. ***Average non-need-based aid:*** $17,045. ***Average indebtedness upon graduation:*** $32,369.

APPLYING

Standardized Tests *Required:* SAT or ACT (for admission).

Options: electronic application, early admission, deferred entrance.

Application fee: $50.

Required: essay or personal statement, high school transcript, minimum 2.5 GPA, 1 letter of recommendation. ***Recommended:*** interview.

Application deadlines: rolling (freshmen), rolling (transfers).

Notification: continuous (freshmen), continuous (transfers).

CONTACT

Mr. Johnathan Akin, Assistant Vice President of Undergraduate Admissions, Lipscomb University, One University Park Drive, Nashville, TN 37204-3951. *Phone:* 615-966-6150. *Toll-free phone:* 877-582-4766. *Fax:* 615-966-1804. *E-mail:* admissions@lipscomb.edu.

Martin Methodist College

Pulaski, Tennessee

http://www.martinmethodist.edu/

CONTACT

Lisa Smith, Director of Admissions, Martin Methodist College, 433 West Madison Street, Pulaski, TN 38478-2716. *Phone:* 931-363-9868. *Toll-free phone:* 800-467-1273. *Fax:* 931-363-9818. *E-mail:* admit@martinmethodist.edu.

Maryville College

Maryville, Tennessee

http://www.maryvillecollege.edu/

- **Independent Presbyterian** 4-year, founded 1819
- **Suburban** 263-acre campus
- **Endowment** $69.2 million
- **Coed**
- **Moderately difficult** entrance level

FACULTY

Student/faculty ratio: 13:1.

ACADEMICS

Calendar: 4-1-4. *Degree:* bachelor's.

Library: Lamar Memorial Library plus 1 other. *Books:* 123,369 (physical), 272,064 (digital/electronic); *Serial titles:* 181 (physical), 37,204 (digital/electronic); *Databases:* 112. Weekly public service hours: 93; students can reserve study rooms.

STUDENT LIFE

Housing options: on-campus residence required through senior year; coed, men-only, women-only, special housing for students with disabilities. Campus housing is university owned. Freshman campus housing is guaranteed.

Activities and organizations: drama/theater group, student-run newspaper, choral group, Voices of Praise, student government, Student Programming Board, Global Citizenship, Peer Mentors.

Athletics Member NCAA. All Division III.

Campus security: 24-hour emergency response devices and patrols, late-night transport/escort service, controlled dormitory access, campus-wide emergency alert system via cell phones, home phones, and email.

Student services: health clinic, personal/psychological counseling, veterans affairs office.

COSTS & FINANCIAL AID
Costs (2018–19) ***Comprehensive fee:*** $46,304 includes full-time tuition ($34,070), mandatory fees ($810), and room and board ($11,424). Part-time tuition: $876 per credit hour. Part-time tuition and fees vary according to course load. ***Required fees:*** $15 per credit hour part-time, $195 per term part-time. ***College room only:*** $5674. Room and board charges vary according to board plan and housing facility.

Financial Aid Of all full-time matriculated undergraduates who enrolled in 2018, 1,102 applied for aid, 909 were judged to have need, 205 had their need fully met. 616 Federal Work-Study jobs (averaging $1718). In 2018, 188 non-need-based awards were made. ***Average percent of need met:*** 81. ***Average financial aid package:*** $32,852. ***Average need-based loan:*** $4371. ***Average need-based gift aid:*** $26,039. ***Average non-need-based aid:*** $21,769. ***Average indebtedness upon graduation:*** $12,654.

APPLYING
Standardized Tests *Required:* SAT or ACT (for admission).

Options: electronic application, early admission, deferred entrance.

Required: high school transcript, minimum 2.5 GPA, letters of recommendation. ***Required for some:*** essay or personal statement, interview.

CONTACT
Ms. Arielle Kilday, Associate Director of Admissions, Maryville College, 502 East Lamar Alexander Parkway, Maryville, TN 37804-5907. *Phone:* 865-981-8042. *Toll-free phone:* 800-597-2687. *Fax:* 865-981-8005. *E-mail:* admissions@maryvillecollege.edu.

Mid-America Baptist Theological Seminary

Cordova, Tennessee

http://www.mabts.edu/

- **Independent Southern Baptist** comprehensive, founded 1972
- **Suburban** campus with easy access to Memphis
- **Endowment** $3.6 million
- **Men only**
- **Noncompetitive** entrance level

FACULTY
Student/faculty ratio: 11:1.

ACADEMICS
Calendar: semesters. *Degrees:* associate, bachelor's, master's, and doctoral.
Library: Ora Byram Allison Memorial Library. Students can reserve study rooms.

STUDENT LIFE
Housing options: men-only, women-only, special housing for students with disabilities. Campus housing is university owned.

Campus security: 24-hour emergency response devices.

COSTS
Costs (2018–19) ***Tuition:*** $9450 full-time, $315 per credit hour part-time. Full-time tuition and fees vary according to course load, degree level, and location. Part-time tuition and fees vary according to course load and location. ***Required fees:*** $500 full-time, $250 per term part-time. ***Room only:*** Room and board charges vary according to housing facility and location.

APPLYING
Options: electronic application.

Application fee: $25.

Required: essay or personal statement, 2 letters of recommendation. ***Required for some:*** high school transcript.

CONTACT
Mid-America Baptist Theological Seminary, 2095 Appling Road, Cordova, TN 38016. *Toll-free phone:* 800-968-4508.

Middle Tennessee State University

Murfreesboro, Tennessee

http://www.mtsu.edu/

- **State-supported** university, founded 1911
- **Urban** 500-acre campus with easy access to Nashville
- **Coed** 19,518 undergraduate students, 80% full-time, 54% women, 46% men
- **Moderately difficult** entrance level, 94% of applicants were admitted

UNDERGRAD STUDENTS
15,586 full-time, 3,932 part-time. 19% Black or African American, non-Hispanic/Latino; 6% Hispanic/Latino; 3% Asian, non-Hispanic/Latino; 0.1% Native Hawaiian or other Pacific Islander, non-Hispanic/Latino; 0.2% American Indian or Alaska Native, non-Hispanic/Latino; 4% Two or more races, non-Hispanic/Latino; 0.2% Race/ethnicity unknown; 3% international; 10% transferred in; 14% live on campus.

Freshmen:
Admission: 8,055 applied, 7,534 admitted, 2,900 enrolled. ***Average high school GPA:*** 3.5. ***Test scores:*** SAT evidence-based reading and writing scores over 500: 88%; SAT math scores over 500: 83%; ACT scores over 18: 90%; SAT evidence-based reading and writing scores over 600: 50%; SAT math scores over 600: 35%; ACT scores over 24: 42%; SAT evidence-based reading and writing scores over 700: 10%; SAT math scores over 700: 6%; ACT scores over 30: 8%.
Retention: 76% of full-time freshmen returned.

FACULTY
Total: 1,256, 75% full-time, 68% with terminal degrees.
Student/faculty ratio: 18:1.

ACADEMICS
Calendar: semesters. *Degrees:* certificates, bachelor's, master's, doctoral, post-master's, and postbachelor's certificates.

Special study options: adult/continuing education programs, external degree program, part-time degree program. ***ROTC:*** Army (b), Air Force (c).

Computers: Students can access the following: computer help desk, free student e-mail accounts, online (class) grades, online (class) registration, online (class) schedules. Campuswide network is available.
Library: James E. Walker Library.

STUDENT LIFE
Housing options: coed, men-only, women-only, special housing for students with disabilities. Campus housing is university owned.

Activities and organizations: drama/theater group, student-run newspaper, radio and television station, choral group, marching band, national fraternities, national sororities.

Athletics Member NCAA. All Division I except football (Division I-A). ***Intercollegiate sports:*** baseball M(s), basketball M(s)/W(s), cheerleading M(s)/W(s), cross-country running M(s)/W(s), equestrian sports M/W, golf M(s), soccer W(s), softball W(s), tennis M(s)/W(s), track and field M(s)/W(s), volleyball W(s). ***Intramural sports:*** badminton M/W, basketball M/W, bowling M(c)/W(c), fencing M(c)/W(c), field hockey M(c)/W(c), football M, ice hockey M(c)/W(c), lacrosse M(c)/W(c), racquetball M(c)/W(c), riflery M/W(c), rock climbing M(c)/W(c), rugby M(c)/W(c), soccer M(c)/W, softball M/W, swimming and diving M/W, tennis M/W, ultimate Frisbee M(c)/W(c), volleyball M(c)/W(c), wrestling M(c)/W(c).

Campus security: 24-hour emergency response devices and patrols, student patrols, late-night transport/escort service, controlled dormitory access.

Student services: health clinic, personal/psychological counseling, women's center, legal services, veterans affairs office.

COSTS & FINANCIAL AID
Costs (2018–19) ***Tuition:*** state resident $7380 full-time, $293 per credit hour part-time; nonresident $26,538 full-time, $1053 per credit hour part-time. Full-time tuition and fees vary according to course load and program. Part-time tuition and fees vary according to course load and program. ***Required fees:*** $1826 full-time, $76 per credit hour part-time. ***Room and board:*** $9436; room only: $5436. Room and board charges vary according to board plan and housing facility. ***Payment plan:*** installment. ***Waivers:*** employees or children of employees.

Financial Aid Of all full-time matriculated undergraduates who enrolled in 2018, 13,346 applied for aid, 10,474 were judged to have need, 1,228 had their need fully met. 227 Federal Work-Study jobs (averaging $2873). In 2018, 2040 non-need-based awards were made. ***Average percent of need met:*** 64. ***Average financial aid package:*** $10,068. ***Average need-based loan:*** $4011. ***Average need-based gift aid:*** $6040. ***Average non-need-based aid:*** $8275. ***Average indebtedness upon graduation:*** $25,774.

APPLYING
Standardized Tests *Required:* SAT or ACT (for admission).

Application fee: $25.

Required: high school transcript, minimum 3.0 GPA. ***Required for some:*** essay or personal statement.

CONTACT
Middle Tennessee State University, 1301 East Main Street, Murfreesboro, TN 37132. *Toll-free phone:* 800-331-MTSU.

Mid-South Christian College
Memphis, Tennessee
http://www.midsouthchristian.edu/

CONTACT
Mrs. Wendy Lambert, Student Recruiter, Mid-South Christian College, PO Box 181056, Memphis, TN 38181. *Phone:* 901-375-4400 Ext. 103. *Fax:* 901-375-4085. *E-mail:* wendylambert@midsouthcc.org.

Milligan College
Milligan College, Tennessee
http://www.milligan.edu/

- **Independent Christian** comprehensive, founded 1866
- **Suburban** 235-acre campus
- **Endowment** $46.0 million
- **Coed** 829 undergraduate students, 89% full-time, 57% women, 43% men
- **Moderately difficult** entrance level, 83% of applicants were admitted

UNDERGRAD STUDENTS
734 full-time, 95 part-time. Students come from 32 states and territories; 17 other countries; 36% are from out of state; 4% Black or African American, non-Hispanic/Latino; 5% Hispanic/Latino; 2% Asian, non-Hispanic/Latino; 0.4% Native Hawaiian or other Pacific Islander, non-Hispanic/Latino; 2% Two or more races, non-Hispanic/Latino; 0.4% Race/ethnicity unknown; 5% international; 7% transferred in; 75% live on campus.

Freshmen:
Admission: 482 applied, 402 admitted, 155 enrolled. ***Average high school GPA:*** 3.8. ***Test scores:*** SAT evidence-based reading and writing scores over 500: 92%; SAT math scores over 500: 91%; ACT scores over 18: 98%; SAT evidence-based reading and writing scores over 600: 56%; SAT math scores over 600: 35%; ACT scores over 24: 58%; SAT evidence-based reading and writing scores over 700: 9%; SAT math scores over 700: 11%; ACT scores over 30: 16%.

Retention: 71% of full-time freshmen returned.

FACULTY
Total: 178, 54% full-time, 58% with terminal degrees.

Student/faculty ratio: 9:1.

ACADEMICS
Calendar: semesters. *Degrees:* certificates, bachelor's, master's, doctoral, and postbachelor's certificates.

Special study options: academic remediation for entering students, adult/continuing education programs, advanced placement credit, cooperative education, distance learning, double majors, honors programs, independent study, internships, off-campus study, part-time degree program, student-designed majors, study abroad, summer session for credit.

Unusual degree programs: 3-2 pharmacy with East Tennessee State University.

Computers: 102 computers/terminals are available on campus for general student use. Students can access the following: campus intranet, computer help desk, free student e-mail accounts, online (class) grades, online (class) registration, online (class) schedules. Campuswide network is available. 100% of college-owned or -operated housing units are wired for high-speed Internet access. Wireless service is available via classrooms, computer centers, computer labs, dorm rooms, libraries, student centers.

Library: P. H. Welshimer Memorial Library plus 1 other. *Books:* 173,242 (physical), 281,617 (digital/electronic); *Serial titles:* 932 (physical), 44,498 (digital/electronic); *Databases:* 95. Weekly public service hours: 89; students can reserve study rooms.

STUDENT LIFE
Housing options: on-campus residence required through senior year; men-only, women-only. Campus housing is university owned. Freshman campus housing is guaranteed.

Activities and organizations: drama/theater group, student-run newspaper, radio and television station, choral group, Student Government Association, Vespers-worship team, LINC-service organization, Campus Activities Board, Club Ultimate-frisbee.

Athletics Member NAIA. ***Intercollegiate sports:*** baseball M(s), basketball M(s)/W(s), cheerleading W(s)(c), cross-country running M(s)/W(s), golf M(s)/W(s), soccer M(s)/W(s), softball W(s), swimming and diving M(s)/W(s), tennis M(s)/W(s), track and field M(s)/W(s), triathlon M(s)(c)/W(s)(c), volleyball M(s)(c)/W(s). ***Intramural sports:*** basketball M/W, football M/W, softball M/W, table tennis M/W, ultimate Frisbee M(c)/W(c), volleyball M/W.

Campus security: 24-hour emergency response devices and patrols, late-night transport/escort service, controlled dormitory access.

Student services: health clinic, personal/psychological counseling.

COSTS & FINANCIAL AID
Costs (2019–20) ***Comprehensive fee:*** $41,950 includes full-time tuition ($33,450), mandatory fees ($1200), and room and board ($7300). No tuition increase for student's term of enrollment. ***Required fees:*** $930 per semester hour part-time, $375 per term part-time. ***College room only:*** $3650.

Financial Aid Of all full-time matriculated undergraduates who enrolled in 2018, 677 applied for aid, 595 were judged to have need, 206 had their need fully met. 126 Federal Work-Study jobs (averaging $1200). 141 state and other part-time jobs (averaging $1509). In 2018, 122 non-need-based awards were made. ***Average percent of need met:*** 80. ***Average financial aid package:*** $25,278. ***Average need-based loan:*** $4763. ***Average need-based gift aid:*** $21,595. ***Average non-need-based aid:*** $12,642. ***Average indebtedness upon graduation:*** $28,449.

APPLYING
Standardized Tests *Required:* SAT or ACT (for admission).

Options: electronic application, deferred entrance.

Application fee: $30.

Required: essay or personal statement, high school transcript, minimum 2.0 GPA, 2 letters of recommendation. ***Required for some:*** interview. ***Recommended:*** minimum 3.0 GPA.

Notification: continuous (freshmen), continuous (transfers).

CONTACT
Ms. Kristin Wright, Director of Admissions, Milligan College, PO Box 210, Milligan College, TN 37682. *Phone:* 423-461-8730. *Toll-free phone:* 800-262-8337. *Fax:* 423-461-8982. *E-mail:* admissions@milligan.edu.

National College
Bristol, Tennessee
http://www.national-college.edu/

CONTACT
National College, 1328 Highway 11 West, Bristol, TN 37620. *Phone:* 423-878-4440. *Toll-free phone:* 888-9-JOBREADY.

Nossi College of Art
Nashville, Tennessee
http://www.nossi.edu/

- **Proprietary** 4-year, founded 1973
- **Urban** 10-acre campus with easy access to Nashville
- **Coed**

FACULTY
Student/faculty ratio: 8:1.

ACADEMICS
Calendar: semesters. *Degrees:* associate and bachelor's.
Library: Learning Resource Center.

STUDENT LIFE
Housing options: college housing not available.

Activities and organizations: Kappa Pi, CMA.EDU, Fashion Alliance, national fraternities, national sororities.

Campus security: gated entrance, ID badges for building access, doors are locked at all times.

COSTS
Costs (2018–19) ***Tuition:*** $17,700 full-time. No tuition increase for student's term of enrollment. ***Required fees:*** $100 full-time.

APPLYING
Standardized Tests *Required for some:* ACT (for admission).

Options: electronic application, early admission.

Application fee: $100.

Required: essay or personal statement, high school transcript, interview, portfolio of work.

CONTACT
Ms. Mitzi Hatfield, Admissions Director, Nossi College of Art, 590 Cheron Road, Madison, TN 37115. *Phone:* 615-514-2787 (ARTS). *Toll-free phone:* 888-986-ARTS. *Fax:* 615-514-2788. *E-mail:* admissions@nossi.edu.

O'More School of Design at Belmont University

Nashville, Tennessee

http://www.omorecollege.edu/

- **Independent** 4-year, founded 1970
- **Small-town** 7-acre campus with easy access to Nashville
- **Coed**
- **Moderately difficult** entrance level

FACULTY
Student/faculty ratio: 7:1.

ACADEMICS
Calendar: semesters. *Degree:* bachelor's.
Library: McAfee Library. *Books:* 2,242 (physical); *Databases:* 30. Weekly public service hours: 40.

STUDENT LIFE
Housing options: college housing not available.

Activities and organizations: Student Activities Council, Magnolia Social, O'More Fashion Association, LeP (Interior Design Association), Graphic Designers Guild.

Campus security: on-campus security/contracted security until 10pm M-F, 24-hour studio key access.

FINANCIAL AID
Financial Aid Of all full-time matriculated undergraduates who enrolled in 2015, 147 applied for aid, 130 were judged to have need, 18 had their need fully met. 13 Federal Work-Study jobs (averaging $1285). 17 state and other part-time jobs (averaging $2130). In 2015, 34 non-need-based awards were made. ***Average percent of need met:*** 76. ***Average financial aid package:*** $16,617. ***Average need-based loan:*** $4762. ***Average need-based gift aid:*** $13,756. ***Average non-need-based aid:*** $5934. ***Average indebtedness upon graduation:*** $31,773.

APPLYING
Standardized Tests *Required:* SAT or ACT (for admission).

Options: electronic application, early admission, deferred entrance.

Application fee: $50.

Required: high school transcript, interview, minimum 3.0 GPA or ACT score of 20. ***Required for some:*** essay or personal statement.

CONTACT
Tori Bagsby, Admissions Manager, O'More School of Design at Belmont University, 423 South Margin Street, Franklin, TN 37064-2816. *Phone:* 615-794-4254 Ext. 230. *Toll-free phone:* 888-662-1970. *Fax:* 615-790-1662. *E-mail:* tbagsby@omorecollege.edu.

Remington College–Memphis Campus

Memphis, Tennessee

http://www.remingtoncollege.edu/

CONTACT
Randal Hayes, Director of Recruitment, Remington College–Memphis Campus, 2710 Nonconnah Boulevard, Memphis, TN 38132. *Phone:* 901-345-1000. *Toll-free phone:* 800-323-8122. *Fax:* 901-396-8310. *E-mail:* randal.hayes@remingtoncollege.edu.

Rhodes College

Memphis, Tennessee

http://www.rhodes.edu/

- **Independent** comprehensive, founded 1848
- **Urban** 100-acre campus with easy access to Memphis
- **Endowment** $359.3 million
- **Coed** 2,008 undergraduate students, 99% full-time, 56% women, 44% men
- **Very difficult** entrance level, 45% of applicants were admitted

UNDERGRAD STUDENTS
1,992 full-time, 16 part-time. Students come from 46 states and territories; 35 other countries; 71% are from out of state; 9% Black or African American, non-Hispanic/Latino; 6% Hispanic/Latino; 6% Asian, non-Hispanic/Latino; 0.1% Native Hawaiian or other Pacific Islander, non-Hispanic/Latino; 0.2% American Indian or Alaska Native, non-Hispanic/Latino; 5% Two or more races, non-Hispanic/Latino; 2% Race/ethnicity unknown; 5% international; 0.3% transferred in; 69% live on campus.

Freshmen:
Admission: 5,093 applied, 2,269 admitted, 543 enrolled. ***Average high school GPA:*** 3.9. ***Test scores:*** SAT evidence-based reading and writing scores over 500: 100%; SAT math scores over 500: 100%; ACT scores over 18: 100%; SAT evidence-based reading and writing scores over 600: 89%; SAT math scores over 600: 80%; ACT scores over 24: 96%; SAT evidence-based reading and writing scores over 700: 27%; SAT math scores over 700: 31%; ACT scores over 30: 50%.

Retention: 90% of full-time freshmen returned.

FACULTY
Total: 222, 81% full-time, 92% with terminal degrees.

Student/faculty ratio: 10:1.

ACADEMICS
Calendar: semesters. *Degrees:* bachelor's and master's (master's degree in accounting only).

Special study options: advanced placement credit, cooperative education, double majors, honors programs, independent study, internships, off-campus study, part-time degree program, services for LD students, student-designed majors, study abroad, summer session for credit. ***ROTC:*** Army (c), Navy (c), Air Force (c).

Unusual degree programs: 3-2 engineering with Washington University in St. Louis, Christian Brothers University, University of Memphis, The University of Tennessee.

Computers: 1,000 computers/terminals are available on campus for general student use. Students can access the following: campus intranet, computer help desk, free student e-mail accounts, online (class) grades, online (class) registration, online (class) schedules. Campuswide network is available. 100% of college-owned or -operated housing units are wired for high-speed Internet access. Wireless service is available via entire campus.
Library: Paul Barret, Jr. Library. *Books:* 246,054 (physical); *Serial titles:* 94,665 (digital/electronic); *Databases:* 151. Weekly public service hours: 113.

STUDENT LIFE
Housing options: on-campus residence required through sophomore year; coed, men-only, women-only. Campus housing is university owned. Freshman campus housing is guaranteed.

Activities and organizations: drama/theater group, student-run newspaper, radio and television station, choral group, Rhodes Outdoors Club, South Asian Culture and Advocacy, Rhodes College Crew Team, Gender and Sexuality Alliance, Culture of Consent, national fraternities, national sororities.

Athletics Member NCAA. All Division III except golf (Division II). ***Intercollegiate sports:*** badminton M(c)/W(c), baseball M, basketball M/W, crew M(c)/W(c), cross-country running M/W, equestrian sports M(c)/W(c), fencing M(c)/W(c), field hockey W, football M, golf M/W, ice hockey M(c), lacrosse M/W, rugby M(c), soccer M/W, softball W, swimming and diving M/W, tennis M/W, track and field M/W, ultimate Frisbee M(c)/W(c), volleyball W, wrestling M(c). ***Intramural sports:*** basketball M/W, racquetball M/W, soccer M/W, squash M(c), volleyball M/W.

Campus security: 24-hour emergency response devices and patrols, student patrols, late-night transport/escort service.

Student services: health clinic, personal/psychological counseling, women's center.

COSTS & FINANCIAL AID
Costs (2019–20) ***Comprehensive fee:*** $59,293 includes full-time tuition ($47,580), mandatory fees ($310), and room and board ($11,403). Part-time tuition: $1970 per credit hour. ***College room only:*** $5373.

Financial Aid Of all full-time matriculated undergraduates who enrolled in 2018, 1,369 applied for aid, 987 were judged to have need, 420 had their need fully met. In 2018, 873 non-need-based awards were made. ***Average percent of need met:*** 90. ***Average financial aid package:*** $40,793. ***Average need-based loan:*** $5997. ***Average need-based gift aid:*** $33,275. ***Average non-need-based aid:*** $25,679. ***Average indebtedness upon graduation:*** $24,187. ***Financial aid deadline:*** 3/1.

APPLYING
Standardized Tests *Required:* SAT or ACT (for admission).

Options: electronic application, early admission, early decision, early action, deferred entrance.

Required: essay or personal statement, high school transcript. ***Recommended:*** letters of recommendation, interview.

Application deadlines: 1/15 (freshmen), 1/15 (transfers), 11/15 (early action).

Early decision deadline: 11/1 (for plan 1), 11/1 (for plan 2).

Notification: 4/1 (freshmen), 4/1 (transfers), 12/1 (early decision plan 1), 2/1 (early decision plan 2), 1/15 (early action).

CONTACT
Mr. Carey Thompson, Vice President of Enrollment and Communications, Dean of Admissions, Rhodes College, 2000 N. Parkway, Memphis, TN 38112. *Phone:* 901-843-3700. *Toll-free phone:* 800-844-5969. *Fax:* 901-843-3631. *E-mail:* adminfo@rhodes.edu.

South College
Knoxville, Tennessee
http://www.southcollegetn.edu/

CONTACT
Mr. Walter Hosea, Director of Admissions, South College, 720 North Fifth Avenue, Knoxville, TN 37917. *Phone:* 865-524-3043 Ext. 1825. *E-mail:* whosea@southcollegetn.edu.

Southern Adventist University
Collegedale, Tennessee
http://www.southern.edu/

- **Independent Seventh-day Adventist** comprehensive, founded 1892
- **Small-town** 1000-acre campus with easy access to Chattanooga
- **Endowment** $38.1 million
- **Coed**
- **Moderately difficult** entrance level

FACULTY
Student/faculty ratio: 14:1.

ACADEMICS
Calendar: semesters. *Degrees:* certificates, associate, bachelor's, master's, doctoral, and post-master's certificates.
Library: McKee Library plus 7 others. *Books:* 173,284 (physical), 107,663 (digital/electronic); *Serial titles:* 510 (physical), 170 (digital/electronic); *Databases:* 160. Weekly public service hours: 82; students can reserve study rooms.

STUDENT LIFE
Housing options: on-campus residence required through junior year; men-only, women-only. Campus housing is university owned. Freshman campus housing is guaranteed.

Activities and organizations: drama/theater group, student-run newspaper, radio and television station, choral group, Asian Club, Black Christian Union, Business Society, School of Nursing, Student Ministerial Association.

Campus security: 24-hour emergency response devices and patrols, student patrols, late-night transport/escort service, controlled dormitory access.

Student services: health clinic, personal/psychological counseling.

COSTS & FINANCIAL AID
Costs (2018–19) ***Comprehensive fee:*** $28,890 includes full-time tuition ($21,100), mandatory fees ($850), and room and board ($6940). Full-time tuition and fees vary according to course load. Part-time tuition: $890 per credit hour. Part-time tuition and fees vary according to course load. ***Required fees:*** $850 per term part-time. ***College room only:*** $4400. Room and board charges vary according to board plan.

Financial Aid Of all full-time matriculated undergraduates who enrolled in 2017, 1,704 applied for aid, 1,464 were judged to have need, 24 had their need fully met. 801 Federal Work-Study jobs (averaging $2500). In 2017, 575 non-need-based awards were made. ***Average percent of need met:*** 68. ***Average financial aid package:*** $16,298. ***Average need-based loan:*** $4660. ***Average need-based gift aid:*** $10,702. ***Average non-need-based aid:*** $7645. ***Average indebtedness upon graduation:*** $33,445.

APPLYING
Standardized Tests *Required:* SAT or ACT (for admission).

Options: electronic application, deferred entrance.

Application fee: $25.

Required: high school transcript, minimum 2.5 GPA. ***Required for some:*** essay or personal statement, minimum 2.3 GPA.

CONTACT
Jennifer Landivar, Applications Manager, Southern Adventist University, PO Box 370, Collegedale, TN 37315-0370. *Phone:* 423-236-2655. *Toll-free phone:* 800-768-8437. *Fax:* 423-236-1835. *E-mail:* jlandivar@southern.edu.

Strayer University–Knoxville Campus
Knoxville, Tennessee
http://www.strayer.edu/tennessee/knoxville/

CONTACT
Strayer University–Knoxville Campus, 10118 Parkside Drive, Suite 200, Knoxville, TN 37922. *Toll-free phone:* 888-311-0355.

Strayer University–Nashville Campus
Nashville, Tennessee
http://www.strayer.edu/tennessee/nashville/

CONTACT
Strayer University–Nashville Campus, 1809 Dabbs Avenue, Nashville, TN 37210. *Toll-free phone:* 888-311-0355.

Strayer University–Shelby Campus

Memphis, Tennessee

http://www.strayer.edu/tennessee/shelby/

CONTACT
Strayer University–Shelby Campus, 7275 Appling Farms Parkway, Memphis, TN 38133. *Toll-free phone:* 888-311-0355.

Strayer University–Thousand Oaks Campus

Memphis, Tennessee

http://www.strayer.edu/tennessee/thousand-oaks/

CONTACT
Strayer University–Thousand Oaks Campus, 2620 Thousand Oaks Boulevard, Suite 1100, Memphis, TN 38118. *Toll-free phone:* 888-311-0355.

Tennessee State University

Nashville, Tennessee

http://www.tnstate.edu/

CONTACT
Dr. John Cade, Associate Vice President/Interim Vice President, Tennessee State University, 3500 John A. Merritt Boulevard, Nashville, TN 37209. *Phone:* 615-963-5101. *E-mail:* jcade@tnstate.edu.

Tennessee Technological University

Cookeville, Tennessee

http://www.tntech.edu/

- **State-supported** university, founded 1915, part of Tennessee Board of Regents
- **Small-town** campus
- **Endowment** $65.9 million
- **Coed**
- **Moderately difficult** entrance level

FACULTY
Student/faculty ratio: 18:1.

ACADEMICS
Calendar: semesters. *Degrees:* bachelor's, master's, doctoral, post-master's, and postbachelor's certificates.
Library: Angelo and Jennette Volpe Library and Media Center. *Books:* 235,249 (physical), 267,168 (digital/electronic); *Serial titles:* 120,118 (physical); *Databases:* 193.

STUDENT LIFE
Housing options: on-campus residence required for freshman year; coed, men-only, women-only, special housing for students with disabilities. Campus housing is university owned. Freshman campus housing is guaranteed.

Activities and organizations: drama/theater group, student-run newspaper, choral group, marching band, Baptist Collegiate Center, Fellowship of Christian Athletes, University Christian Student Center, Residence Hall Association, national fraternities, national sororities.

Athletics Member NCAA. All Division I except football (Division I-AA).

Campus security: 24-hour emergency response devices and patrols, late-night transport/escort service, controlled dormitory access, student safety organization, lighted pathways.

Student services: health clinic, personal/psychological counseling, women's center, veterans affairs office.

COSTS & FINANCIAL AID
Costs (2018–19) ***Tuition:*** state resident $8731 full-time, $390 per credit hour part-time; nonresident $24,595 full-time, $1051 per credit hour part-time. Full-time tuition and fees vary according to program. Part-time tuition and fees vary according to program. ***Room and board:*** $9736; room only: $5060. Room and board charges vary according to board plan and housing facility.

Financial Aid Of all full-time matriculated undergraduates who enrolled in 2016, 7,301 applied for aid, 5,815 were judged to have need, 538 had their need fully met. 456 Federal Work-Study jobs (averaging $963). In 2016, 1620 non-need-based awards were made. ***Average percent of need met:*** 60. ***Average financial aid package:*** $10,151. ***Average need-based loan:*** $4029. ***Average need-based gift aid:*** $5694. ***Average non-need-based aid:*** $9264. ***Average indebtedness upon graduation:*** $22,018.

APPLYING
Standardized Tests *Required:* SAT or ACT (for admission). *Recommended:* ACT (for admission).

Options: electronic application, early admission, deferred entrance.

Application fee: $25.

Required: high school transcript, minimum 2.5 GPA. ***Recommended:*** interview.

CONTACT
Tennessee Technological University, North Dixie Avenue, Cookeville, TN 38505. *Toll-free phone:* 800-255-8881.

Tennessee Wesleyan University

Athens, Tennessee

http://www.tnwesleyan.edu/

- **Independent United Methodist** comprehensive, founded 1857
- **Small-town** 40-acre campus with easy access to Knoxville, Chattanooga
- **Endowment** $9.4 million
- **Coed**
- **Minimally difficult** entrance level

FACULTY
Student/faculty ratio: 12:1.

ACADEMICS
Calendar: semesters. *Degrees:* bachelor's and master's (profile includes information for both the main and branch campuses).
Library: Merner-Pfeiffer Library plus 1 other. *Books:* 52,465 (physical), 356,697 (digital/electronic); *Serial titles:* 82 (physical); *Databases:* 76. Weekly public service hours: 69.

STUDENT LIFE
Housing options: men-only, women-only. Campus housing is university owned. Freshman campus housing is guaranteed.

Activities and organizations: drama/theater group, student-run newspaper, choral group, Student Government Association, national sororities.

Athletics Member NAIA.

Campus security: 24-hour patrols, late-night transport/escort service, controlled dormitory access, night patrols by trained security personnel.

Student services: health clinic, personal/psychological counseling, veterans affairs office.

COSTS & FINANCIAL AID
Costs (2018–19) ***Comprehensive fee:*** $32,180 includes full-time tuition ($23,300), mandatory fees ($1000), and room and board ($7880). Full-time tuition and fees vary according to program. Part-time tuition: $590 per credit hour. Part-time tuition and fees vary according to program. ***Required fees:*** $10 per credit hour part-time. ***College room only:*** $2230. Room and board charges vary according to board plan and housing facility. ***Payment plans:*** installment, deferred payment.

Financial Aid Of all full-time matriculated undergraduates who enrolled in 2018, 863 applied for aid, 744 were judged to have need, 256 had their need fully met. 76 Federal Work-Study jobs (averaging $1119). 6 state and other part-time jobs (averaging $2301). In 2018, 73 non-need-based awards were made. ***Average percent of need met:*** 70. ***Average financial aid package:*** $17,144. ***Average need-based loan:*** $3968. ***Average need-based gift aid:*** $8416. ***Average non-need-based aid:*** $14,161. ***Average indebtedness upon graduation:*** $24,785.

APPLYING
Standardized Tests *Required:* SAT or ACT (for admission).

Options: electronic application, deferred entrance.

Required: high school transcript, minimum 2.3 GPA, 1 letter of recommendation. ***Required for some:*** essay or personal statement, interview. ***Recommended:*** essay or personal statement.

CONTACT
Ms. Joanne Landers, Vice President for Admissions, Tennessee Wesleyan University, 204 East College Street, Athens, TN 37303. *Phone:* 423-746-7504. *Toll-free phone:* 800-PICK-TWU. *Fax:* 423-745-9335. *E-mail:* admissions@twcnet.edu.

Trevecca Nazarene University
Nashville, Tennessee
http://www.trevecca.edu/

- **Independent Nazarene** comprehensive, founded 1901
- **Urban** 80-acre campus
- **Endowment** $28.9 million
- **Coed** 2,311 undergraduate students, 82% full-time, 62% women, 38% men
- **Moderately difficult** entrance level, 64% of applicants were admitted

UNDERGRAD STUDENTS
1,886 full-time, 425 part-time. 35% are from out of state; 13% Black or African American, non-Hispanic/Latino; 9% Hispanic/Latino; 1% Asian, non-Hispanic/Latino; 0.1% Native Hawaiian or other Pacific Islander, non-Hispanic/Latino; 0.4% American Indian or Alaska Native, non-Hispanic/Latino; 3% Two or more races, non-Hispanic/Latino; 6% Race/ethnicity unknown; 6% international; 4% transferred in; 39% live on campus.

Freshmen:
Admission: 1,671 applied, 1,070 admitted, 380 enrolled. ***Average high school GPA:*** 3.4. ***Test scores:*** SAT evidence-based reading and writing scores over 500: 81%; SAT math scores over 500: 74%; ACT scores over 18: 93%; SAT evidence-based reading and writing scores over 600: 36%; SAT math scores over 600: 30%; ACT scores over 24: 39%; SAT evidence-based reading and writing scores over 700: 3%; SAT math scores over 700: 3%; ACT scores over 30: 11%.

FACULTY
Total: 272, 36% full-time, 63% with terminal degrees.
Student/faculty ratio: 18:1.

ACADEMICS
Calendar: semesters. *Degrees:* certificates, associate, bachelor's, master's, doctoral, and post-master's certificates.
Special study options: academic remediation for entering students, adult/continuing education programs, advanced placement credit, distance learning, double majors, internships, services for LD students, study abroad, summer session for credit. ***ROTC:*** Army (c).
Computers: 200 computers/terminals and 1,460 ports are available on campus for general student use. Students can access the following: campus intranet, computer help desk, free student e-mail accounts, online (class) grades, online (class) registration, online (class) schedules, Non-traditional and graduate students are registered through Academic Records. Campuswide network is available. 100% of college-owned or -operated housing units are wired for high-speed Internet access. Wireless service is available via entire campus.
Library: Waggoner Library. *Books:* 85,560 (physical), 49,113 (digital/electronic); *Serial titles:* 299 (physical), 60,127 (digital/electronic); *Databases:* 44. Weekly public service hours: 91; students can reserve study rooms.

STUDENT LIFE
Housing options: on-campus residence required through senior year; men-only, women-only. Campus housing is university owned.
Activities and organizations: drama/theater group, student-run newspaper, choral group, marching band.
Athletics Member NCAA. All Division II except golf (Division I). ***Intercollegiate sports:*** baseball M(s), basketball M(s)/W(s), cross-country running M(s)/W(s), golf M(s)/W(s), soccer M(s)/W(s), softball W(s), track and field M(s)/W(s), volleyball W(s). ***Intramural sports:*** basketball M/W, football M/W, soccer M/W, softball M/W, tennis M/W, ultimate Frisbee M/W, volleyball M/W.
Campus security: 24-hour patrols, late-night transport/escort service, weather alert warning system (phone, email, siren).
Student services: health clinic, personal/psychological counseling.

COSTS & FINANCIAL AID
Costs (2019–20) ***Comprehensive fee:*** $34,998 includes full-time tuition ($25,198), mandatory fees ($900), and room and board ($8900). ***College room only:*** $4450. ***Payment plan:*** tuition prepayment.
Financial Aid ***Average indebtedness upon graduation:*** $24,249.

APPLYING
Standardized Tests *Required:* SAT or ACT (for admission).
Options: electronic application, early admission, deferred entrance.
Required: high school transcript, minimum 2.5 GPA, minimum ACT composite score of 18, SAT Evidence-Based Reading and Writing and Math score of 940, medical history and immunization records.
Notification: continuous (freshmen), continuous (transfers).

CONTACT
Ms. Melinda Miller, Director of Undergraduate Admissions, Trevecca Nazarene University, 333 Murfreesboro Road, Nashville, TN 37210. *Phone:* 615-248-1320. *Toll-free phone:* 888-210-4TNU. *Fax:* 615-248-7406. *E-mail:* admissions_und@trevecca.edu.

Tusculum University
Greeneville, Tennessee
http://www.tusculum.edu/

- **Independent Presbyterian** comprehensive, founded 1794
- **Small-town** 140-acre campus
- **Endowment** $21.1 million
- **Coed**
- **Moderately difficult** entrance level

FACULTY
Student/faculty ratio: 17:1.

ACADEMICS
Calendar: semesters. *Degrees:* associate, bachelor's, and master's.
Library: Thomas J. Garland Library plus 2 others. Students can reserve study rooms.

STUDENT LIFE
Housing options: coed, men-only, women-only, special housing for students with disabilities. Campus housing is university owned. Freshman campus housing is guaranteed.
Activities and organizations: drama/theater group, student-run newspaper, radio and television station, choral group, marching band.
Athletics Member NCAA. All Division II.
Campus security: 24-hour emergency response devices and patrols, student patrols, late-night transport/escort service, controlled dormitory access, trained security personnel on duty.
Student services: health clinic, personal/psychological counseling, women's center.

COSTS & FINANCIAL AID
Costs (2018–19) ***Comprehensive fee:*** $34,050 includes full-time tuition ($24,860) and room and board ($9190). Part-time tuition: $768 per credit hour. ***College room only:*** $5600.
Financial Aid Of all full-time matriculated undergraduates who enrolled in 2016, 1,286 applied for aid, 1,196 were judged to have need, 103 had their need fully met. 293 Federal Work-Study jobs (averaging $963). In 2016, 72 non-need-based awards were made. ***Average percent of need met:*** 77. ***Average financial aid package:*** $17,079. ***Average need-based loan:*** $4098. ***Average need-based gift aid:*** $9629. ***Average non-need-based aid:*** $8329. ***Average indebtedness upon graduation:*** $33,916.

APPLYING
Standardized Tests *Required:* SAT or ACT (for admission).
Options: electronic application, early admission, early decision, deferred entrance.

CONTACT
Tusculum University, PO Box 50627, Greeneville, TN 37743-9997. *Phone:* 423-636-7300 Ext. 5374. *Toll-free phone:* 800-729-0256. *E-mail:* admissions@tusculum.edu.

Union University

Jackson, Tennessee

http://www.uu.edu/

- **Independent Southern Baptist** comprehensive, founded 1823
- **Suburban** 360-acre campus with easy access to Memphis
- **Endowment** $39.1 million
- **Coed**
- **Moderately difficult** entrance level

FACULTY

Student/faculty ratio: 9:1.

ACADEMICS

Calendar: 4-1-4. *Degrees:* certificates, associate, bachelor's, master's, doctoral, post-master's, and postbachelor's certificates.
Library: The Logos Library plus 1 other. *Books:* 136,991 (physical), 265,352 (digital/electronic); *Serial titles:* 2,362 (physical), 33,609 (digital/electronic); *Databases:* 135. Weekly public service hours: 93; students can reserve study rooms.

STUDENT LIFE

Housing options: on-campus residence required through junior year; men-only, women-only, special housing for students with disabilities. Campus housing is university owned. Freshman applicants given priority for college housing.

Activities and organizations: drama/theater group, student-run newspaper, choral group, Campus Ministries, Student Government Association, Student Activities Council, Students in Free Enterprise (SIFE), national fraternities, national sororities.

Athletics Member NCAA. All Division II.

Campus security: 24-hour emergency response devices and patrols, student patrols, late-night transport/escort service.

Student services: health clinic, personal/psychological counseling.

COSTS & FINANCIAL AID

Costs (2018–19) ***Comprehensive fee:*** $43,090 includes full-time tuition ($31,550), mandatory fees ($1340), and room and board ($10,200). Full-time tuition and fees vary according to class time, course load, degree level, location, and program. Part-time tuition: $1015 per credit hour. Part-time tuition and fees vary according to class time, course load, degree level, location, and program. ***Required fees:*** $45 per credit hour part-time. ***College room only:*** $7900. Room and board charges vary according to board plan and housing facility. ***Payment plans:*** installment, deferred payment.

Financial Aid Of all full-time matriculated undergraduates who enrolled in 2018, 1,532 applied for aid, 1,343 were judged to have need, 161 had their need fully met. In 2018, 305 non-need-based awards were made. ***Average percent of need met:*** 68. ***Average financial aid package:*** $26,846. ***Average need-based loan:*** $4374. ***Average need-based gift aid:*** $6137. ***Average non-need-based aid:*** $13,810. ***Average indebtedness upon graduation:*** $49,824.

APPLYING

Standardized Tests *Required:* SAT or ACT (for admission).

Options: electronic application, early admission, deferred entrance.

Application fee: $35.

Required: high school transcript, minimum 2.5 GPA. ***Required for some:*** 3 letters of recommendation. ***Recommended:*** essay or personal statement, interview.

CONTACT

Mr. Robbie Graves, Director of Enrollment Services, Union University, 1050 Union University Drive, Jackson, TN 38305-3697. *Phone:* 731-661-5590. *Toll-free phone:* 800-33-UNION. *Fax:* 731-661-5589. *E-mail:* rgraves@uu.edu.

University of Memphis

Memphis, Tennessee

http://www.memphis.edu/

- **State-supported** university, founded 1912
- **Urban** 1160-acre campus with easy access to Memphis
- **Endowment** $216.2 million
- **Coed** 17,233 undergraduate students, 70% full-time, 59% women, 41% men
- **Moderately difficult** entrance level, 84% of applicants were admitted

UNDERGRAD STUDENTS

12,064 full-time, 5,169 part-time. Students come from 47 states and territories; 49 other countries; 12% are from out of state; 37% Black or African American, non-Hispanic/Latino; 6% Hispanic/Latino; 4% Asian, non-Hispanic/Latino; 0.1% Native Hawaiian or other Pacific Islander, non-Hispanic/Latino; 0.2% American Indian or Alaska Native, non-Hispanic/Latino; 4% Two or more races, non-Hispanic/Latino; 1% Race/ethnicity unknown; 2% international; 8% transferred in; 14% live on campus.

Freshmen:
Admission: 14,160 applied, 11,923 admitted, 2,480 enrolled. ***Average high school GPA:*** 3.5. ***Test scores:*** SAT evidence-based reading and writing scores over 500: 77%; SAT math scores over 500: 66%; ACT scores over 18: 91%; SAT evidence-based reading and writing scores over 600: 37%; SAT math scores over 600: 25%; ACT scores over 24: 40%; SAT evidence-based reading and writing scores over 700: 7%; SAT math scores over 700: 9%; ACT scores over 30: 8%.

Retention: 76% of full-time freshmen returned.

FACULTY

Total: 1,477, 61% full-time, 59% with terminal degrees.

Student/faculty ratio: 16:1.

ACADEMICS

Calendar: semesters. *Degrees:* bachelor's, master's, doctoral, post-master's, and postbachelor's certificates.

Special study options: accelerated degree program, adult/continuing education programs, advanced placement credit, cooperative education, distance learning, double majors, English as a second language, external degree program, honors programs, independent study, internships, off-campus study, part-time degree program, services for LD students, student-designed majors, study abroad, summer session for credit. ***ROTC:*** Army (b), Navy (b), Air Force (b).

Computers: 1,255 computers/terminals and 35 ports are available on campus for general student use. Students can access the following: campus intranet, computer help desk, free student e-mail accounts, online (class) grades, online (class) registration, online (class) schedules. Campuswide network is available. 100% of college-owned or -operated housing units are wired for high-speed Internet access. Wireless service is available via entire campus.
Library: McWherter Library plus 4 others. *Books:* 1.4 million (physical), 315,573 (digital/electronic); *Serial titles:* 17,630 (physical), 256,700 (digital/electronic); *Databases:* 400. Weekly public service hours: 91; students can reserve study rooms.

STUDENT LIFE

Housing options: coed, men-only, women-only, cooperative, special housing for students with disabilities. Campus housing is university owned.

Activities and organizations: drama/theater group, student-run newspaper, radio station, choral group, marching band, Student Activities Council, Fraternity and Sorority Life, Black Student Association, Student Government Association, Up 'til Dawn- St. Jude Philanthropy, national fraternities, national sororities.

Athletics Member NCAA. All Division I except football (Division I-A). ***Intercollegiate sports:*** baseball M(s), basketball M(s)/W(s), cheerleading M(s)/W(s), cross-country running M(s)/W(s), golf M(s)/W(s), riflery M(s)/W(s), soccer M(s)/W(s), softball W(s), tennis M(s)/W(s), track and field M(s)/W(s), volleyball W(s). ***Intramural sports:*** badminton M/W, basketball M/W, equestrian sports W(c), football M/W, golf M/W, lacrosse M(c), racquetball M/W, rugby M(c), soccer M/W, softball M/W, table tennis M/W, ultimate Frisbee M/W, volleyball M/W, water polo M(c).

Campus security: 24-hour emergency response devices and patrols, student patrols, late-night transport/escort service, controlled dormitory access.

Student services: health clinic, personal/psychological counseling, women's center, veterans affairs office.

COSTS & FINANCIAL AID

Costs (2018–19) ***Tuition:*** state resident $8064 full-time, $320 per credit hour part-time; nonresident $19,776 full-time, $808 per credit hour part-time. Full-time tuition and fees vary according to course load, degree level, program, and reciprocity agreements. Part-time tuition and fees vary according to course load, degree level, and program. ***Required fees:*** $1637 full-time, $114 per credit hour part-time. ***Room and board:*** $9975; room only: $5985. Room and board charges vary according to board plan, housing facility, and location. ***Payment plan:*** installment. ***Waivers:*** senior citizens and employees or children of employees.

Financial Aid Of all full-time matriculated undergraduates who enrolled in 2018, 10,996 applied for aid, 9,182 were judged to have need, 1,153 had their need fully met. 162 Federal Work-Study jobs (averaging $2517). In 2018, 1527 non-need-based awards were made. ***Average percent of need met:*** 70. ***Average financial aid package:*** $7491. ***Average need-based loan:*** $3990. ***Average need-based gift aid:*** $5474. ***Average non-need-based aid:*** $6203. ***Average indebtedness upon graduation:*** $26,961.

APPLYING

Standardized Tests *Required:* SAT or ACT (for admission).

Options: electronic application, early admission.

Application fee: $25.

Required: high school transcript. ***Required for some:*** essay or personal statement, minimum 2.0 GPA, 2 letters of recommendation, interview.

Application deadlines: 7/1 (freshmen), 7/1 (out-of-state freshmen), 7/1 (transfers).

Notification: continuous (freshmen), continuous (out-of-state freshmen), continuous (transfers).

CONTACT

Drusilla Welch, Associate Director of Operations for Admissions, University of Memphis, Admissions Operations, 204A Wilder Tower, Memphis, TN 38152. *Phone:* 901-678-3007. *Toll-free phone:* 800-669-2678. *E-mail:* dwelch@memphis.edu.

The University of Tennessee

Knoxville, Tennessee

http://www.utk.edu/

- **State-supported** university, founded 1794, part of University of Tennessee System
- **Urban** 600-acre campus
- **Endowment** $508.8 million
- **Coed** 22,815 undergraduate students, 94% full-time, 51% women, 49% men
- **Moderately difficult** entrance level, 77% of applicants were admitted

UNDERGRAD STUDENTS

21,489 full-time, 1,326 part-time. Students come from 46 states and territories; 43 other countries; 16% are from out of state; 6% Black or African American, non-Hispanic/Latino; 4% Hispanic/Latino; 4% Asian, non-Hispanic/Latino; 0.2% American Indian or Alaska Native, non-Hispanic/Latino; 3% Two or more races, non-Hispanic/Latino; 2% Race/ethnicity unknown; 1% international; 6% transferred in; 32% live on campus.

Freshmen:

Admission: 18,872 applied, 14,526 admitted, 5,215 enrolled. ***Average high school GPA:*** 4.0. ***Test scores:*** SAT evidence-based reading and writing scores over 500: 98%; SAT math scores over 500: 96%; ACT scores over 18: 100%; SAT evidence-based reading and writing scores over 600: 66%; SAT math scores over 600: 57%; ACT scores over 24: 86%; SAT evidence-based reading and writing scores over 700: 12%; SAT math scores over 700: 17%; ACT scores over 30: 36%.

Retention: 87% of full-time freshmen returned.

FACULTY

Total: 1,799, 89% full-time, 83% with terminal degrees.

Student/faculty ratio: 17:1.

ACADEMICS

Calendar: semesters. *Degrees:* bachelor's, master's, doctoral, and postbachelor's certificates.

Special study options: accelerated degree program, advanced placement credit, cooperative education, distance learning, double majors, English as a second language, external degree program, freshman honors college, honors programs, independent study, internships, off-campus study, part-time degree program, services for LD students, student-designed majors, study abroad, summer session for credit. ***ROTC:*** Army (b), Air Force (b).

Computers: 1,325 computers/terminals are available on campus for general student use. Students can access the following: campus intranet, computer help desk, free student e-mail accounts, online (class) grades, online (class) registration, online (class) schedules, course management system. Campuswide network is available. 100% of college-owned or -operated housing units are wired for high-speed Internet access. Wireless service is available via entire campus.

Library: John C. Hodges Library plus 4 others. *Books:* 1.5 million (physical), 824,325 (digital/electronic); *Serial titles:* 51,489 (physical), 158,361 (digital/electronic); *Databases:* 737. Weekly public service hours: 160; study areas open 24 hours, 5–7 days a week; students can reserve study rooms.

STUDENT LIFE

Housing options: on-campus residence required for freshman year; coed, men-only, women-only, special housing for students with disabilities. Campus housing is university owned. Freshman campus housing is guaranteed.

Activities and organizations: drama/theater group, student-run newspaper, radio and television station, choral group, marching band, Fraternities/Sororities, Religious organizations, Campus Events Board, Black Cultural Programming Committee, Student Government Association, national fraternities, national sororities.

Athletics Member NCAA. All Division I. ***Intercollegiate sports:*** baseball M(s), basketball M(s)/W(s), crew W(s), cross-country running M/W, football M(s), golf M(s)/W(s), soccer W(s), softball W(s), swimming and diving M(s)/W(s), tennis M(s)/W(s), track and field M(s)/W(s), volleyball W(s). ***Intramural sports:*** badminton M/W, baseball M(c), basketball M/W, bowling M/W, crew M(c)/W(c), cross-country running M(c)/W(c), equestrian sports M(c)/W(c), fencing M(c)/W(c), field hockey M/W, golf M(c)/W(c), gymnastics M(c)/W(c), ice hockey M(c)/W(c), lacrosse M(c)/W(c), racquetball M/W, rock climbing M(c)/W(c), rowing M(c)/W(c), rugby M(c)/W(c), sailing M(c)/W(c), sand volleyball M/W, skiing (downhill) M(c)/W(c), soccer M/W, softball M/W, swimming and diving M(c)/W(c), table tennis M/W, tennis M/W, triathlon M(c)/W(c), ultimate Frisbee M/W, volleyball M/W, water polo M/W, weight lifting M/W, wrestling M(c)/W(c).

Campus security: 24-hour emergency response devices and patrols, late-night transport/escort service, controlled dormitory access.

Student services: health clinic, personal/psychological counseling, women's center, veterans affairs office.

COSTS & FINANCIAL AID

Costs (2018–19) ***Tuition:*** state resident $11,110 full-time, $371 per credit hour part-time; nonresident $29,300 full-time, $1130 per credit hour part-time. Full-time tuition and fees vary according to course level, location, program, reciprocity agreements, and student level. Part-time tuition and fees vary according to course level, location, program, reciprocity agreements, and student level. ***Required fees:*** $1896 full-time. ***Room and board:*** $11,240. Room and board charges vary according to board plan and housing facility. ***Payment plan:*** installment. ***Waivers:*** senior citizens and employees or children of employees.

Financial Aid Of all full-time matriculated undergraduates who enrolled in 2018, 18,681 applied for aid, 12,095 were judged to have need, 2,513 had their need fully met. 687 Federal Work-Study jobs (averaging $2904). In 2018, 3445 non-need-based awards were made. ***Average percent of need met:*** 57. ***Average financial aid package:*** $13,685. ***Average need-based loan:*** $6993. ***Average need-based gift aid:*** $10,750. ***Average non-need-based aid:*** $6327. ***Average indebtedness upon graduation:*** $25,372.

APPLYING

Standardized Tests *Required:* SAT or ACT (for admission).

Options: electronic application, early action.

Application fee: $50.

Required: essay or personal statement, high school transcript, minimum 2.0 GPA. ***Recommended:*** 1 letter of recommendation.

Application deadlines: rolling (freshmen), rolling (out-of-state freshmen), 7/1 (transfers), 11/1 (early action).

Notification: continuous until 9/15 (freshmen), continuous until 9/15 (out-of-state freshmen), continuous (transfers), 12/15 (early action).

CONTACT

Mr. Clayton Alexander, Associate Director, The University of Tennessee, 320 Student Services Building, Knoxville, TN 37996-0230. *Phone:* 865-974-2184. *E-mail:* admissions@utk.edu.

The University of Tennessee at Chattanooga

Chattanooga, Tennessee

http://www.utc.edu/

- **State-supported** comprehensive, founded 1886, part of University of Tennessee System
- **Urban** 425-acre campus
- **Coed**
- **Moderately difficult** entrance level

FACULTY

Student/faculty ratio: 19:1.

ACADEMICS

Calendar: semesters. *Degrees:* certificates, bachelor's, master's, doctoral, post-master's, and postbachelor's certificates.

Library: UTC Library plus 1 other. *Books:* 743,490 (physical); *Databases:* 219. Study areas open 24 hours, 5–7 days a week; students can reserve study rooms.

STUDENT LIFE

Housing options: on-campus residence required for freshman year; coed, special housing for students with disabilities. Campus housing is university owned. Freshman applicants given priority for college housing.

Activities and organizations: drama/theater group, student-run newspaper, choral group, marching band, national fraternities, national sororities.

Athletics Member NCAA. All Division I except football (Division I-AA).

Campus security: 24-hour emergency response devices.

Student services: health clinic, personal/psychological counseling, women's center, veterans affairs office.

COSTS & FINANCIAL AID

Costs (2018–19) ***Tuition:*** state resident $6888 full-time, $287 per credit hour part-time; nonresident $23,006 full-time, $959 per credit hour part-time. Full-time tuition and fees vary according to degree level. Part-time tuition and fees vary according to degree level. ***Required fees:*** $1776 full-time, $59 per credit hour part-time, $205 per term part-time. ***Room and board:*** $9050; room only: $5600. Room and board charges vary according to board plan, housing facility, and location.

Financial Aid Of all full-time matriculated undergraduates who enrolled in 2018, 8,083 applied for aid, 5,718 were judged to have need, 702 had their need fully met. 184 Federal Work-Study jobs (averaging $2646). 105 state and other part-time jobs (averaging $1917). In 2018, 1048 non-need-based awards were made. ***Average percent of need met:*** 63. ***Average financial aid package:*** $10,411. ***Average need-based loan:*** $3845. ***Average need-based gift aid:*** $8311. ***Average non-need-based aid:*** $3274. ***Average indebtedness upon graduation:*** $24,274.

APPLYING

Standardized Tests *Required:* SAT or ACT (for admission).

Options: electronic application, early admission, deferred entrance.

Application fee: $30.

Required: high school transcript, 2.5 GPA with minimum ACT score of 21/SAT of 990 or minimum GPA of 2.85 with minimum ACT score of 18/SAT score of 870.

CONTACT

Ms. Lee Pierce, Director of Admissions, The University of Tennessee at Chattanooga, 615 McCallie Avenue, 101 University Center, Department 5105, Chattanooga, TN 37403. *Phone:* 423-425-4662. *Toll-free phone:* 800-882-6627. *Fax:* 423-425-4157. *E-mail:* admissions@utc.edu.

The University of Tennessee at Martin

Martin, Tennessee

http://www.utm.edu/

- **State-supported** comprehensive, founded 1900, part of University of Tennessee System
- **Small-town** 250-acre campus
- **Endowment** $35.0 million
- **Coed** 6,694 undergraduate students, 71% full-time, 60% women, 40% men
- **Moderately difficult** entrance level, 69% of applicants were admitted

UNDERGRAD STUDENTS

4,748 full-time, 1,946 part-time. Students come from 44 states and territories; 20 other countries; 9% are from out of state; 13% Black or African American, non-Hispanic/Latino; 3% Hispanic/Latino; 0.8% Asian, non-Hispanic/Latino; 0.4% American Indian or Alaska Native, non-Hispanic/Latino; 2% Two or more races, non-Hispanic/Latino; 2% international; 7% transferred in; 30% live on campus.

Freshmen:

Admission: 8,047 applied, 5,544 admitted, 1,143 enrolled. ***Average high school GPA:*** 3.5. ***Test scores:*** ACT scores over 18: 99%; ACT scores over 24: 44%; ACT scores over 30: 7%.

Retention: 74% of full-time freshmen returned.

FACULTY

Total: 506, 56% full-time, 50% with terminal degrees.

Student/faculty ratio: 15:1.

ACADEMICS

Calendar: semesters. *Degrees:* bachelor's and master's.

Special study options: accelerated degree program, adult/continuing education programs, advanced placement credit, cooperative education, distance learning, double majors, English as a second language, honors programs, independent study, internships, off-campus study, part-time degree program, services for LD students, student-designed majors, study abroad, summer session for credit. ***ROTC:*** Army (b).

Computers: 1,214 computers/terminals and 6,425 ports are available on campus for general student use. Students can access the following: campus intranet, computer help desk, free student e-mail accounts, online (class) grades, online (class) registration, online (class) schedules, online fee payments, degree progress, financial aid data, housing applications, transcripts. Campuswide network is available. 100% of college-owned or -operated housing units are wired for high-speed Internet access. Wireless service is available via entire campus.

Library: Paul Meek Library. *Books:* 302,341 (physical), 92,351 (digital/electronic); *Serial titles:* 47,314 (physical), 350,984 (digital/electronic); *Databases:* 231. Weekly public service hours: 92; study areas open 24 hours, 5–7 days a week.

STUDENT LIFE

Housing options: on-campus residence required for freshman year; men-only, women-only, special housing for students with disabilities. Campus housing is university owned. Freshman applicants given priority for college housing.

Activities and organizations: drama/theater group, student-run newspaper, radio and television station, choral group, marching band, Student Government Association, Black Student Association, National Society for Leadership and Success, Phi Eta Sigma, League of Striving Artists, national fraternities, national sororities.

Athletics Member NCAA. All Division I except football (Division I-AA). ***Intercollegiate sports:*** baseball M(s), basketball M(s)/W(s), cheerleading W(s), cross-country running M(s)/W(s), equestrian sports W(s), golf M(s), riflery M(s)/W(s), sand volleyball W(s), soccer W(s), softball W(s), tennis W(s), volleyball W(s). ***Intramural sports:*** basketball M/W, football M/W, golf M/W, racquetball M/W, soccer M/W, softball M/W, tennis M/W, ultimate Frisbee M/W, volleyball M/W, water polo M/W.

Campus security: 24-hour emergency response devices and patrols, student patrols, controlled dormitory access.

Student services: health clinic, personal/psychological counseling, women's center, veterans affairs office.

COSTS & FINANCIAL AID

Costs (2018–19) ***Tuition:*** state resident $8052 full-time, $335 per credit hour part-time; nonresident $14,092 full-time, $587 per credit hour part-time. Full-time tuition and fees vary according to student level. Part-time tuition and fees vary according to course level and course load. ***Required fees:*** $1460 full-time, $61 per credit hour part-time. ***Room and board:*** $6164; room only: $2820. Room and board charges vary according to board plan and housing facility. ***Payment plans:*** installment, deferred payment. ***Waivers:*** senior citizens and employees or children of employees.

Financial Aid Of all full-time matriculated undergraduates who enrolled in 2018, 4,421 applied for aid, 3,530 were judged to have need, 883 had their need fully met. 270 Federal Work-Study jobs (averaging $2521). In 2018, 353 non-need-based awards were made. ***Average percent of need met:*** 45. ***Average financial aid package:*** $11,535. ***Average need-based loan:*** $4138. ***Average need-based gift aid:*** $6530. ***Average non-need-based aid:*** $1949. ***Average indebtedness upon graduation:*** $27,866.

APPLYING

Standardized Tests *Required:* SAT or ACT (for admission).

Options: electronic application, early admission, deferred entrance.

Application fee: $30.

Required: high school transcript, minimum 2.7 GPA.

Application deadlines: rolling (freshmen), rolling (transfers).

Notification: continuous until 8/1 (freshmen), continuous until 8/1 (transfers).

CONTACT

Ms. Destin Tucker, Director of Admission, The University of Tennessee at Martin, 200 Hall-Moody Administration Building, Martin, TN 38238. *Phone:* 731-881-7020. *Toll-free phone:* 800-829-8861. *Fax:* 731-881-7029. *E-mail:* dtucker@utm.edu.

The University of the South

Sewanee, Tennessee

http://www.sewanee.edu/

- **Independent Episcopal** comprehensive, founded 1857
- **Small-town** 13,000-acre campus with easy access to Chattanooga
- **Endowment** $411.0 million
- **Coed** 1,698 undergraduate students, 99% full-time, 51% women, 49% men
- **Very difficult** entrance level, 65% of applicants were admitted

UNDERGRAD STUDENTS

1,678 full-time, 20 part-time. Students come from 44 states and territories; 22 other countries; 78% are from out of state; 5% Black or African American, non-Hispanic/Latino; 5% Hispanic/Latino; 2% Asian, non-Hispanic/Latino; 0.1% American Indian or Alaska Native, non-Hispanic/Latino; 3% Two or more races, non-Hispanic/Latino; 3% international; 1% transferred in; 98% live on campus.

Freshmen:

Admission: 3,465 applied, 2,258 admitted, 477 enrolled. ***Test scores:*** SAT evidence-based reading and writing scores over 500: 98%; SAT math scores over 500: 97%; ACT scores over 18: 99%; SAT evidence-based reading and writing scores over 600: 80%; SAT math scores over 600: 69%; ACT scores over 24: 87%; SAT evidence-based reading and writing scores over 700: 27%; SAT math scores over 700: 23%; ACT scores over 30: 40%.

Retention: 89% of full-time freshmen returned.

FACULTY

Total: 237, 71% full-time, 87% with terminal degrees.

Student/faculty ratio: 10:1.

ACADEMICS

Calendar: semesters. *Degrees:* bachelor's, master's, doctoral, post-master's, and postbachelor's certificates.

Special study options: advanced placement credit, double majors, independent study, internships, off-campus study, services for LD students, student-designed majors, study abroad, summer session for credit.

Unusual degree programs: 3-2 engineering with Columbia University, Rensselaer Polytechnic Institute, Vanderbilt University, Washington University in St. Louis.

Computers: 150 computers/terminals and 3,000 ports are available on campus for general student use. Students can access the following: computer help desk, free student e-mail accounts, online (class) grades, online (class) registration, online (class) schedules. Campuswide network is available. 100% of college-owned or -operated housing units are wired for high-speed Internet access. Wireless service is available via entire campus.

Library: Jessie Ball duPont Library. *Books:* 512,993 (physical), 563,193 (digital/electronic); *Serial titles:* 4,034 (physical), 22,304 (digital/electronic); *Databases:* 382. Study areas open 24 hours, 5–7 days a week; students can reserve study rooms.

STUDENT LIFE

Housing options: on-campus residence required through senior year; coed, men-only, women-only. Campus housing is university owned. Freshman campus housing is guaranteed.

Activities and organizations: drama/theater group, student-run newspaper, radio station, choral group, Sewanee Outing Program, Sewanee Outreach, Organization for Cross Cultural Understanding, Alpha Phi Omega (APO) National Service Fraternity, African American Alliance, national fraternities, national sororities.

Athletics Member NCAA. All Division III. ***Intercollegiate sports:*** baseball M, basketball M/W, cheerleading W, crew M(c)/W(c), cross-country running M/W, equestrian sports M/W, fencing M(c)/W(c), field hockey W, football M, golf M/W, ice hockey M(c)/W(c), lacrosse M/W, rugby M(c)/W(c), soccer M/W, softball W, squash M(c)/W(c), swimming and diving M/W, tennis M/W, track and field M/W, volleyball W. ***Intramural sports:*** basketball M/W, football M/W, soccer M/W, table tennis M/W.

Campus security: 24-hour emergency response devices and patrols, late-night transport/escort service, controlled dormitory access.

Student services: health clinic, personal/psychological counseling, women's center.

COSTS & FINANCIAL AID

Costs (2019–20) ***Comprehensive fee:*** $59,740 includes full-time tuition ($46,200), mandatory fees ($272), and room and board ($13,268). Part-time tuition: $1470 per credit hour. ***College room only:*** $6876.

Financial Aid Of all full-time matriculated undergraduates who enrolled in 2018, 1,019 applied for aid, 786 were judged to have need, 252 had their need fully met. 397 Federal Work-Study jobs (averaging $1639). 157 state and other part-time jobs (averaging $3230). In 2018, 730 non-need-based awards were made. ***Average percent of need met:*** 84. ***Average financial aid package:*** $35,337. ***Average need-based loan:*** $4340. ***Average need-based gift aid:*** $29,514. ***Average non-need-based aid:*** $16,348. ***Average indebtedness upon graduation:*** $28,976.

APPLYING

Standardized Tests *Required for some:* TOEFL for international students. *Recommended:* SAT or ACT (for admission).

Options: electronic application, early admission, early decision, early action, deferred entrance.

Required: essay or personal statement, high school transcript, 2 letters of recommendation. ***Recommended:*** interview.

Application deadlines: 2/1 (freshmen), 4/1 (transfers), 12/1 (early action).

Early decision deadline: 11/15 (for plan 1), 1/15 (for plan 2).

Notification: continuous (transfers), 12/15 (early decision plan 1), 2/15 (early decision plan 2).

CONTACT

Ms. Lisa Burns, Associate Dean of Admission, The University of the South, 735 University Avenue, Sewanee, TN 37383. *Phone:* 931-598-1238. *Toll-free phone:* 800-522-2234. *Fax:* 931-598-3248. *E-mail:* admiss@sewanee.edu.

Vanderbilt University

Nashville, Tennessee

http://www.vanderbilt.edu/

- **Independent** university, founded 1873
- **Urban** 330-acre campus with easy access to Nashville, TN
- **Endowment** $3.8 billion
- **Coed**
- **Most difficult** entrance level

FACULTY
Student/faculty ratio: 8:1.

ACADEMICS
Calendar: semesters. *Degrees:* bachelor's, master's, and doctoral.
Library: Jean and Alexander Heard Library plus 7 others. *Books:* 3.1 million (physical), 1.7 million (digital/electronic); *Databases:* 3,700.

STUDENT LIFE
Housing options: on-campus residence required for freshman year; coed, men-only, women-only, special housing for students with disabilities. Campus housing is university owned. Freshman campus housing is guaranteed.

Activities and organizations: drama/theater group, student-run newspaper, radio and television station, choral group, marching band, national fraternities, national sororities.

Athletics Member NCAA. All Division I except football (Division I-A).

Campus security: 24-hour emergency response devices and patrols, student patrols, late-night transport/escort service, controlled dormitory access.

Student services: health clinic, personal/psychological counseling, women's center.

COSTS & FINANCIAL AID
Costs (2018–19) ***Comprehensive fee:*** $66,050 includes full-time tuition ($48,600), mandatory fees ($1216), and room and board ($16,234). Part-time tuition: $2025 per credit hour. ***College room only:*** $10,620. Room and board charges vary according to board plan. ***Payment plans:*** tuition prepayment, installment.

Financial Aid Of all full-time matriculated undergraduates who enrolled in 2018, 3,874 applied for aid, 3,371 were judged to have need, 3,371 had their need fully met. 1,696 Federal Work-Study jobs (averaging $2380). In 2018, 704 non-need-based awards were made. ***Average percent of need met:*** 100. ***Average financial aid package:*** $51,787. ***Average need-based loan:*** $3429. ***Average need-based gift aid:*** $49,076. ***Average non-need-based aid:*** $24,217. ***Average indebtedness upon graduation:*** $22,854.

APPLYING
Standardized Tests *Required:* SAT or ACT (for admission).

Options: electronic application, early admission, early decision, deferred entrance.

Application fee: $50.

Required: essay or personal statement, high school transcript, 3 letters of recommendation, 3 letters of recommendation (2 from teachers in core subject areas and 1 from counselor).

CONTACT
Mr. John O. Gaines, Director of Undergraduate Admissions, Vanderbilt University, 2305 West End Avenue, Nashville, TN 37203. *Phone:* 615-936-2811. *Toll-free phone:* 800-288-0432. *Fax:* 615-343-8326. *E-mail:* admissions@vanderbilt.edu.

See page 1152 for the College Close-Up.

Visible Music College

Memphis, Tennessee

http://visible.edu/

CONTACT
Visible Music College, 200 Madison Avenue, Memphis, TN 38103.

Watkins College of Art, Design, & Film

Nashville, Tennessee

http://www.watkins.edu/

CONTACT
Ms. Jaime Raybin, Recruiter, Watkins College of Art, Design, & Film, 2298 Rosa L. Parks Boulevard, Nashville, TN 37228. *Phone:* 615-383-4848 Ext. 5397. *Fax:* 615-383-4849. *E-mail:* admissions@watkins.edu.

Welch College

Gallatin, Tennessee

http://www.welch.edu/

- **Independent Free Will Baptist** comprehensive, founded 1942
- **Suburban** 120-acre campus with easy access to Nashville
- **Endowment** $2.5 million
- **Coed**
- **Noncompetitive** entrance level

FACULTY
Student/faculty ratio: 8:1.

ACADEMICS
Calendar: semesters. *Degrees:* associate, bachelor's, and master's.
Library: Welch Library. *Books:* 64,478 (physical), 48,741 (digital/electronic); *Databases:* 56.

STUDENT LIFE
Housing options: on-campus residence required through senior year; men-only, women-only. Campus housing is university owned. Freshman campus housing is guaranteed.

Activities and organizations: drama/theater group, choral group, GMF-Global Missions Fellowship, Four Women's Societies, Four Men's Societies.

Athletics Member NCCAA.

Campus security: 24-hour emergency response devices, student patrols, late-night transport/escort service, controlled dormitory access.

Student services: personal/psychological counseling.

COSTS & FINANCIAL AID
Costs (2018–19) ***Comprehensive fee:*** $26,716 includes full-time tuition ($19,012) and room and board ($7704). Full-time tuition and fees vary according to location. Part-time tuition: $648 per credit hour. Part-time tuition and fees vary according to location. ***College room only:*** $2926. Room and board charges vary according to board plan. ***Payment plans:*** installment, deferred payment.

Financial Aid Of all full-time matriculated undergraduates who enrolled in 2011, 178 applied for aid, 172 were judged to have need. 7 Federal Work-Study jobs (averaging $1871). 101 state and other part-time jobs (averaging $1960). ***Average percent of need met:*** 71. ***Average financial aid package:*** $5331. ***Average need-based loan:*** $2195. ***Average need-based gift aid:*** $4214. ***Average indebtedness upon graduation:*** $19,688.

APPLYING
Standardized Tests *Required:* SAT or ACT (for admission).

Options: electronic application, early admission, deferred entrance.

Application fee: $35.

Required: essay or personal statement, high school transcript, 3 letters of recommendation, medical history.

CONTACT
Mr. Daniel Webster, Director of Enrollment Services, Welch College, 1045 Bison Trail, Gallatin, TN 37066. *Phone:* 615-675-5295. *Toll-free phone:* 800-763-9222. *Fax:* 615-296-0400. *E-mail:* daniel.webster@welch.edu.

Williamson College

Franklin, Tennessee

http://www.williamsoncc.edu/

CONTACT
Ms. Laura Flowers, Admissions Coordinator, Williamson College, 274 Mallory Station Road, Franklin, TN 37067. *Phone:* 615-771-7821. *Fax:* 615-771-7810. *E-mail:* laura@williamsoncc.edu.

TEXAS

Abilene Christian University

Abilene, Texas

http://www.acu.edu/

- **Independent** university, founded 1906, affiliated with Church of Christ
- **Urban** 262-acre campus
- **Endowment** $384.6 million
- **Coed**
- **Moderately difficult** entrance level

FACULTY
Student/faculty ratio: 13:1.

ACADEMICS
Calendar: semesters. *Degrees:* certificates, associate, bachelor's, master's, doctoral, post-master's, and postbachelor's certificates.
Library: Brown Library. *Books:* 406,890 (physical), 347,095 (digital/electronic); *Serial titles:* 20,683 (physical), 52,058 (digital/electronic); *Databases:* 109. Weekly public service hours: 97; students can reserve study rooms.

STUDENT LIFE
Housing options: on-campus residence required through sophomore year; men-only, women-only. Campus housing is university owned. Freshman campus housing is guaranteed.

Activities and organizations: drama/theater group, student-run newspaper, radio and television station, choral group, marching band, Student Association, Graduate Students Association, Spring Break Campaigns, International Students Association, LYNAY.

Athletics Member NCAA. All Division I.

Campus security: 24-hour emergency response devices and patrols, student patrols, late-night transport/escort service, controlled dormitory access.

Student services: health clinic, personal/psychological counseling, veterans affairs office.

COSTS & FINANCIAL AID
Costs (2018–19) ***Comprehensive fee:*** $45,200 includes full-time tuition ($34,800), mandatory fees ($50), and room and board ($10,350). Full-time tuition and fees vary according to course load. Part-time tuition: $1442 per credit hour. Part-time tuition and fees vary according to course load. ***College room only:*** $5030. Room and board charges vary according to board plan and housing facility. ***Payment plans:*** tuition prepayment, installment.

Financial Aid Of all full-time matriculated undergraduates who enrolled in 2018, 2,540 applied for aid, 2,248 were judged to have need, 639 had their need fully met. In 2018, 1169 non-need-based awards were made. ***Average percent of need met:*** 68. ***Average financial aid package:*** $24,771. ***Average need-based loan:*** $4189. ***Average need-based gift aid:*** $22,072. ***Average non-need-based aid:*** $17,023.

APPLYING
Standardized Tests *Required:* SAT or ACT (for admission).

Options: electronic application, early admission, early action.

Application fee: $50.

Required: high school transcript. ***Required for some:*** essay or personal statement.

CONTACT
Admissions, Abilene Christian University, ACU Box 29000, Abilene, TX 79699-9000. *Phone:* 325-674-2650. *Toll-free phone:* 800-460-6228. *Fax:* 325-674-2130. *E-mail:* info@admissions.acu.edu.

Amberton University

Garland, Texas

http://www.amberton.edu/

CONTACT
Academic Dean, Amberton University, 1700 Eastgate Drive, Garland, TX 75041-5595. *Phone:* 972-279-6511. *E-mail:* advisor@amberton.edu.

American InterContinental University Houston

Houston, Texas

http://www.aiuniv.edu/

CONTACT
American InterContinental University Houston, 9999 Richmond Avenue, Houston, TX 77042. *Phone:* 877-564-6248. *Toll-free phone:* 888-607-9888.

Angelo State University

San Angelo, Texas

http://www.angelo.edu/

- **State-supported** comprehensive, founded 1928, part of Texas Tech University System
- **Urban** 268-acre campus
- **Endowment** $189.3 million
- **Coed** 8,752 undergraduate students, 63% full-time, 57% women, 43% men
- **Moderately difficult** entrance level, 73% of applicants were admitted

UNDERGRAD STUDENTS
5,499 full-time, 3,253 part-time. Students come from 39 states and territories; 26 other countries; 3% are from out of state; 6% Black or African American, non-Hispanic/Latino; 36% Hispanic/Latino; 1% Asian, non-Hispanic/Latino; 0.2% Native Hawaiian or other Pacific Islander, non-Hispanic/Latino; 0.4% American Indian or Alaska Native, non-Hispanic/Latino; 3% Two or more races, non-Hispanic/Latino; 0.1% Race/ethnicity unknown; 3% international; 5% transferred in; 34% live on campus.

Freshmen:
Admission: 4,152 applied, 3,035 admitted, 1,428 enrolled. ***Test scores:*** SAT evidence-based reading and writing scores over 500: 67%; SAT math scores over 500: 65%; ACT scores over 18: 78%; SAT evidence-based reading and writing scores over 600: 20%; SAT math scores over 600: 13%; ACT scores over 24: 25%; SAT evidence-based reading and writing scores over 700: 2%; SAT math scores over 700: 3%; ACT scores over 30: 6%.

Retention: 67% of full-time freshmen returned.

FACULTY
Total: 435, 71% full-time, 59% with terminal degrees.

Student/faculty ratio: 20:1.

ACADEMICS
Calendar: semesters. *Degrees:* certificates, bachelor's, master's, and doctoral.

Special study options: academic remediation for entering students, advanced placement credit, distance learning, double majors, English as a second language, honors programs, independent study, internships, part-time degree program, study abroad, summer session for credit. ***ROTC:*** Air Force (b).

Unusual degree programs: 3-2 business administration.

Computers: 750 computers/terminals and 3,900 ports are available on campus for general student use. Students can access the following: campus intranet, computer help desk, free student e-mail accounts, online (class) grades, online (class) registration, online (class) schedules, online courses, tuition payments, book purchase, parking permits, university calendar, discounted hardware and software. Campuswide network is available. 100% of college-owned or -operated housing units are wired for high-speed Internet access. Wireless service is available via entire campus.
Library: Porter Henderson Library. *Books:* 309,338 (physical), 100,539 (digital/electronic); *Serial titles:* 105 (physical), 54,329 (digital/electronic); *Databases:* 243. Weekly public service hours: 137; study areas open 24 hours, 5–7 days a week; students can reserve study rooms.

STUDENT LIFE
Housing options: on-campus residence required through sophomore year; coed, special housing for students with disabilities. Campus housing is university owned.

Activities and organizations: drama/theater group, student-run newspaper, radio and television station, choral group, marching band, Association of Mexican-American Students, Block and Bridle Club, Air Force ROTC, University Center Program Council, Baptist Student Union, national fraternities, national sororities.

Athletics Member NCAA. All Division II except golf (Division I). ***Intercollegiate sports:*** baseball M(s), basketball M(s)/W(s), cross-country running M(s)/W(s), football M(s), golf W(s), soccer W(s), softball W(s), tennis W, track and field M(s)/W(s), volleyball W(s). ***Intramural sports:*** badminton M/W, basketball M/W, bowling M/W, football M/W, golf M/W, racquetball M/W, soccer M/W, softball M/W, swimming and diving M/W, table tennis M/W, tennis M/W, ultimate Frisbee M/W, volleyball M/W, weight lifting M/W.

Campus security: 24-hour emergency response devices and patrols, student patrols, late-night transport/escort service, controlled dormitory access.

Student services: health clinic, personal/psychological counseling, veterans affairs office.

COSTS & FINANCIAL AID
Costs (2019–20) ***Tuition:*** state resident $5415 full-time, $181 per credit hour part-time; nonresident $18,075 full-time, $601 per credit hour part-time. No tuition increase for student's term of enrollment. ***Required fees:*** $3306 full-time. ***Room and board:*** $9130.

Financial Aid Of all full-time matriculated undergraduates who enrolled in 2017, 4,246 applied for aid, 3,566 were judged to have need, 418 had their need fully met. In 2017, 979 non-need-based awards were made. ***Average percent of need met:*** 81. ***Average financial aid package:*** $10,925. ***Average need-based loan:*** $3812. ***Average need-based gift aid:*** $3578. ***Average non-need-based aid:*** $3501. ***Average indebtedness upon graduation:*** $24,496.

APPLYING
Standardized Tests *Required:* SAT or ACT (for admission).

Options: electronic application, early admission, deferred entrance.

Application fee: $35.

Required: high school transcript, high school class rank.

Application deadlines: rolling (freshmen), rolling (transfers).

Notification: continuous (freshmen), continuous (transfers).

CONTACT
Ms. Sharla Adam, Director of Admissions, Angelo State University, 2601 West Avenue N., San Angelo, TX 76909. *Phone:* 325-942-2185. *Toll-free phone:* 800-946-8627. *Fax:* 325-942-2078. *E-mail:* admissions@angelo.edu.

Arlington Baptist University

Arlington, Texas

http://www.abu.edu/

- **Independent Baptist** comprehensive, founded 1939
- **Urban** 32-acre campus with easy access to Dallas-Fort Worth
- **Endowment** $17,000
- **Coed**
- **Noncompetitive** entrance level

FACULTY
Student/faculty ratio: 9:1.

ACADEMICS
Calendar: semesters. *Degrees:* bachelor's and master's.
Library: Earl K. Oldham Library. *Databases:* 5. Weekly public service hours: 73.

STUDENT LIFE
Housing options: men-only, women-only. Campus housing is university owned. Freshman campus housing is guaranteed.

Activities and organizations: choral group, Collegians.

Athletics Member NCCAA.

Campus security: controlled dormitory access, night security guards.

Student services: personal/psychological counseling, veterans affairs office.

COSTS & FINANCIAL AID
Costs (2018–19) ***One-time required fee:*** $250. ***Comprehensive fee:*** $20,490 includes full-time tuition ($13,100), mandatory fees ($990), and room and board ($6400). Full-time tuition and fees vary according to course load. Part-time tuition: $405 per credit hour. Part-time tuition and fees vary according to course load. ***Required fees:*** $445 per term part-time. ***Room and board:*** Room and board charges vary according to board plan.

Financial Aid Of all full-time matriculated undergraduates who enrolled in 2006, 164 applied for aid, 118 were judged to have need, 93 had their need fully met. ***Average financial aid package:*** $6847. ***Average indebtedness upon graduation:*** $4838.

APPLYING
Standardized Tests *Required for some:* SAT or ACT (for admission).

Options: electronic application, early admission, deferred entrance.

Application fee: $25.

Required: essay or personal statement, 1 letter of recommendation, pastoral recommendation, medical examination. ***Required for some:*** high school transcript, interview.

CONTACT
Melissa Hayward, Admissions Specialist, Arlington Baptist University, 3001 West Division, Arlington, TX 76012-3425. *Phone:* 817-461-8741. *Fax:* 817-274-1138. *E-mail:* mhayward@abu.edu.

The Art Institute of Austin, a branch of The Art Institute of Houston

Austin, Texas

http://www.artinstitutes.edu/austin

CONTACT
The Art Institute of Austin, a branch of The Art Institute of Houston, 101 W. Louis Henna Boulevard, Suite 100, Austin, TX 78728. *Phone:* 512-691-1707. *Toll-free phone:* 866-583-7952.

The Art Institute of Dallas, a branch of Miami International University of Art & Design

Dallas, Texas

http://www.artinstitutes.edu/dallas/

CONTACT
The Art Institute of Dallas, a branch of Miami International University of Art & Design, 8080 Park Lane, Suite 100, Dallas, TX 75231-5993. *Phone:* 214-692-8080. *Toll-free phone:* 800-275-4243.

The Art Institute of Houston

Houston, Texas

http://www.artinstitutes.edu/houston/

CONTACT
The Art Institute of Houston, 4140 Southwest Freeway, Houston, TX 77027. *Phone:* 713-623-2040. *Toll-free phone:* 800-275-4244.

The Art Institute of San Antonio, a branch of The Art Institute of Houston

San Antonio, Texas

http://www.artinstitutes.edu/san-antonio/

CONTACT
The Art Institute of San Antonio, a branch of The Art Institute of Houston, 1000 IH-10 West, Suite 200, San Antonio, TX 78230. *Phone:* 210-338-7320. *Toll-free phone:* 888-222-0040.

Austin College
Sherman, Texas
http://www.austincollege.edu/

- **Independent Presbyterian** comprehensive, founded 1849
- **Small-town** 60-acre campus with easy access to Dallas-Fort Worth
- **Coed** 1,288 undergraduate students, 100% full-time, 51% women, 49% men
- **Moderately difficult** entrance level, 55% of applicants were admitted

UNDERGRAD STUDENTS
1,284 full-time, 4 part-time. Students come from 30 states and territories; 16 other countries; 7% are from out of state; 10% Black or African American, non-Hispanic/Latino; 21% Hispanic/Latino; 13% Asian, non-Hispanic/Latino; 0.2% Native Hawaiian or other Pacific Islander, non-Hispanic/Latino; 0.5% American Indian or Alaska Native, non-Hispanic/Latino; 5% Two or more races, non-Hispanic/Latino; 0.4% Race/ethnicity unknown; 2% international; 1% transferred in; 86% live on campus.

Freshmen:
Admission: 3,832 applied, 2,120 admitted, 435 enrolled. ***Average high school GPA:*** 3.6. ***Test scores:*** SAT evidence-based reading and writing scores over 500: 97%; SAT math scores over 500: 97%; ACT scores over 18: 99%; SAT evidence-based reading and writing scores over 600: 61%; SAT math scores over 600: 57%; ACT scores over 24: 61%; SAT evidence-based reading and writing scores over 700: 18%; SAT math scores over 700: 14%; ACT scores over 30: 12%.

Retention: 82% of full-time freshmen returned.

FACULTY
Total: 113, 88% full-time, 88% with terminal degrees.

Student/faculty ratio: 11:1.

ACADEMICS
Calendar: 4-1-4. *Degrees:* bachelor's and master's.

Special study options: advanced placement credit, double majors, honors programs, independent study, internships, off-campus study, part-time degree program, services for LD students, student-designed majors, study abroad, summer session for credit.

Unusual degree programs: 3-2 engineering with University of Texas at Dallas, Texas A&M University, Washington University in St. Louis, Columbia University.

Computers: 160 computers/terminals are available on campus for general student use. Students can access the following: campus intranet, computer help desk, free student e-mail accounts, online (class) grades, online (class) registration, online (class) schedules. Campuswide network is available. 100% of college-owned or -operated housing units are wired for high-speed Internet access. Wireless service is available via entire campus.

Library: Abell Library. *Books:* 227,390 (physical). Study areas open 24 hours, 5–7 days a week; students can reserve study rooms.

STUDENT LIFE
Housing options: on-campus residence required through junior year; coed, men-only, women-only, special housing for students with disabilities. Campus housing is university owned. Freshman campus housing is guaranteed.

Activities and organizations: drama/theater group, student-run newspaper, choral group, Inter-Varsity Christian Fellowship (IVCF), Campus Activity Board (CAB), Indian Cultural Association, Students Today Alumni Tomorrow (STAT), ACtivators.

Athletics Member NCAA. All Division III. ***Intercollegiate sports:*** baseball M, basketball M/W, cheerleading M(c)/W(c), cross-country running M/W, football M, soccer M/W, softball W, swimming and diving M/W, tennis M/W, volleyball W, water polo M/W. ***Intramural sports:*** basketball M/W, football M/W, soccer M/W, softball M/W, ultimate Frisbee M/W, volleyball M/W.

Campus security: 24-hour emergency response devices and patrols, late-night transport/escort service, controlled dormitory access.

Student services: health clinic, personal/psychological counseling.

COSTS & FINANCIAL AID
Costs (2019–20) ***One-time required fee:*** $25. ***Comprehensive fee:*** $53,932 includes full-time tuition ($40,970), mandatory fees ($210), and room and board ($12,752). ***College room only:*** $5900.

Financial Aid Of all full-time matriculated undergraduates who enrolled in 2018, 1,012 applied for aid, 889 were judged to have need, 249 had their need fully met. In 2018, 390 non-need-based awards were made. ***Average percent of need met:*** 87. ***Average financial aid package:*** $35,321. ***Average need-based loan:*** $4115. ***Average need-based gift aid:*** $32,056. ***Average non-need-based aid:*** $25,033.

APPLYING
Standardized Tests *Required for some:* SAT or ACT (for admission).

Options: electronic application, early admission, early decision, early action, deferred entrance.

Required: high school transcript. ***Required for some:*** essay or personal statement. ***Recommended:*** minimum 3.0 GPA, 2 letters of recommendation, interview.

Application deadlines: 3/1 (freshmen), 8/1 (transfers), 12/1 (early action).

Early decision deadline: 11/1.

Notification: 4/1 (freshmen), 12/4 (early decision), 1/15 (early action).

CONTACT
Mrs. Baylee Kowert, Executive Director of Institutional Enrollment, Austin College, 900 North Grand Avenue, Suite 6N, Sherman, TX 75090-4400. *Phone:* 903-813-3000. *Toll-free phone:* 800-596-4276 (in-state); 800-526-4276 (out-of-state). *Fax:* 903-813-3198. *E-mail:* admission@austincollege.edu.

Austin Community College District
Austin, Texas
http://www.austincc.edu/

- **State and locally supported** primarily 2-year, founded 1972
- **Urban** campus with easy access to Austin
- **Endowment** $5.9 million
- **Coed** 40,799 undergraduate students, 22% full-time, 56% women, 44% men
- **Noncompetitive** entrance level

UNDERGRAD STUDENTS
8,983 full-time, 31,816 part-time. Students come from 52 states and territories; 94 other countries; 2% are from out of state; 7% Black or African American, non-Hispanic/Latino; 37% Hispanic/Latino; 5% Asian, non-Hispanic/Latino; 0.2% Native Hawaiian or other Pacific Islander, non-Hispanic/Latino; 0.7% American Indian or Alaska Native, non-Hispanic/Latino; 4% Two or more races, non-Hispanic/Latino; 0.8% Race/ethnicity unknown; 1% international.

FACULTY
Total: 1,856, 31% full-time, 23% with terminal degrees.

Student/faculty ratio: 20:1.

ACADEMICS
Calendar: semesters. *Degrees:* certificates, associate, bachelor's, and postbachelor's certificates.

Special study options: academic remediation for entering students, accelerated degree program, adult/continuing education programs, advanced placement credit, cooperative education, distance learning, English as a second language, honors programs, independent study, internships, part-time degree program, services for LD students, summer session for credit. ***ROTC:*** Army (c), Air Force (c).

Computers: 2,090 computers/terminals are available on campus for general student use. Students can access the following: computer help desk, free student e-mail accounts, online (class) grades, online (class) registration, online (class) schedules. Campuswide network is available. Wireless service is available via entire campus.

Library: Main Library plus 11 others. *Books:* 158,142 (physical), 50,957 (digital/electronic); *Serial titles:* 394 (physical), 83,559 (digital/electronic); *Databases:* 110. Weekly public service hours: 83; students can reserve study rooms.

STUDENT LIFE
Housing options: college housing not available.

Activities and organizations: Intramurals, Students for Environmental Outreach, Phi Theta Kappa (PTK), National Society of Collegiate Scholars, Students for Community Involvement.

Athletics ***Intramural sports:*** basketball M/W, soccer M/W, volleyball W.

Campus security: 24-hour emergency response devices, late-night transport/escort service.

Student services: personal/psychological counseling, veterans affairs office.

COSTS & FINANCIAL AID
Costs (2018–19) ***Tuition:*** area resident $2010 full-time, $67 per credit hour part-time; state resident $10,290 full-time, $343 per credit hour part-time; nonresident $12,480 full-time, $416 per credit hour part-time. Full-time tuition and fees vary according to course load. Part-time tuition and fees vary according to course load. ***Required fees:*** $540 full-time, $18 per credit hour part-time. ***Payment plan:*** installment. ***Waivers:*** senior citizens and employees or children of employees.

Financial Aid Of all full-time matriculated undergraduates who enrolled in 2018, 4,879 applied for aid, 4,091 were judged to have need. 270 Federal Work-Study jobs (averaging $2407). 27 state and other part-time jobs (averaging $2479). ***Average need-based loan:*** $3326. ***Average need-based gift aid:*** $4225.

APPLYING
Options: electronic application.

Required: high school transcript.

Application deadlines: rolling (freshmen), rolling (transfers).

CONTACT
Mrs. Linda Terry, Executive Director, Admissions and Records, Austin Community College District, 5930 Middle Fiskville Road, Austin, TX 78752. *Phone:* 512-223-7503. *Fax:* 512-223-7963. *E-mail:* admission@austincc.edu.

Austin Graduate School of Theology

Austin, Texas

http://www.austingrad.edu/

- **Independent** upper-level, founded 1917, affiliated with Church of Christ
- **Urban** 2-acre campus with easy access to Austin
- **Endowment** $4.6 million
- **Coed**
- **Minimally difficult** entrance level

FACULTY
Student/faculty ratio: 4:1.

ACADEMICS
Calendar: semesters. *Degrees:* bachelor's and master's.
Library: David Worley Library.

STUDENT LIFE
Housing options: college housing not available.

Activities and organizations: Student Association (government).

APPLYING
Options: electronic application, early admission, deferred entrance.

CONTACT
Dawn Bond, Director of Admissions, Austin Graduate School of Theology, 7640 Guadalupe Street, Austin, TX 78752. *Phone:* 512-476-2772. *Toll-free phone:* 866-AUS-GRAD. *Fax:* 512-476-3919. *E-mail:* registrar@austingrad.edu.

Baptist Health System School of Health Professions

San Antonio, Texas

http://www.bshp.edu/

CONTACT
Baptist Health System School of Health Professions, 8400 Datapoint Drive, San Antonio, TX 78229.

Baptist Missionary Association Theological Seminary

Jacksonville, Texas

http://www.bmats.edu/

CONTACT
Baptist Missionary Association Theological Seminary, 1530 East Pine Street, Jacksonville, TX 75766-5407. *Phone:* 903-586-2501 Ext. 229. *Toll-free phone:* 800-259-5673.

Baptist University of the Americas

San Antonio, Texas

http://www.bua.edu/

- **Independent Baptist** 4-year, founded 1947
- **Urban** 75-acre campus with easy access to San Antonio
- **Endowment** $2.1 million
- **Coed**

FACULTY
Student/faculty ratio: 8:1.

ACADEMICS
Calendar: semesters May term is a two week intensive course. *Degrees:* certificates, diplomas, associate, and bachelor's (associate degree in Cross-Cultural Studies).
Library: Baptist University of the Americas Learning Resource Center plus 1 other. *Books:* 21,947 (physical), 362 (digital/electronic); *Serial titles:* 252 (physical), 252 (digital/electronic); *Databases:* 8. Weekly public service hours: 72; students can reserve study rooms.

STUDENT LIFE
Housing options: coed, men-only, women-only, special housing for students with disabilities. Campus housing is university owned.

Activities and organizations: choral group, Called Club, Spanish Club, Missions Society, Business Society, BUA Band.

Campus security: 24-hour emergency response devices, student patrols, late-night transport/escort service, Gate code is required to enter the residence area.

Student services: personal/psychological counseling.

FINANCIAL AID
Financial Aid Of all full-time matriculated undergraduates who enrolled in 2018, 2 Federal Work-Study jobs (averaging $2624). 60 state and other part-time jobs (averaging $2400).

APPLYING
Standardized Tests *Required:* SAT and SAT Subject Tests or ACT (for admission), ACCUPLACER, THEA (Texas Higher Education Assessment), CPT (Computer Proficiency Test) and TSI (for admission). *Recommended:* SAT or ACT (for admission).

Required: essay or personal statement, high school transcript, minimum 2.0 GPA, 2 letters of recommendation, meningitis vaccination for students under 22 years. ***Required for some:*** minimum 2.0 GPA, 2 letters of recommendation, interview. ***Recommended:*** minimum 2.0 GPA, 2 letters of recommendation.

CONTACT
Admissions Counselor, Baptist University of the Americas, 8019 Pan Am Expressway, San Antonio, TX 78224. *Phone:* 210-924-4338 Ext. 229. *Toll-free phone:* 800-721-1396. *Fax:* 210-924-2701. *E-mail:* admissions@bua.edu.

Baylor University

Waco, Texas

http://www.baylor.edu/

- **Independent Baptist** university, founded 1845
- **Urban** 1000-acre campus with easy access to Dallas-Fort Worth
- **Endowment** $1.3 billion
- **Coed** 14,188 undergraduate students, 99% full-time, 60% women, 40% men
- **Moderately difficult** entrance level, 52% of applicants were admitted

UNDERGRAD STUDENTS
13,976 full-time, 212 part-time. Students come from 51 states and territories; 72 other countries; 32% are from out of state; 6% Black or African American, non-Hispanic/Latino; 16% Hispanic/Latino; 7% Asian, non-Hispanic/Latino; 0.1% Native Hawaiian or other Pacific Islander, non-Hispanic/Latino; 0.4% American Indian or Alaska Native, non-Hispanic/Latino; 5% Two or more races, non-Hispanic/Latino; 0.5% Race/ethnicity unknown; 3% international; 2% transferred in; 36% live on campus.

Freshmen:
Admission: 34,681 applied, 17,910 admitted, 3,366 enrolled. ***Test scores:*** SAT evidence-based reading and writing scores over 500: 99%; SAT math scores over 500: 99%; ACT scores over 18: 100%; SAT evidence-based reading and writing scores over 600: 76%; SAT math scores over 600: 73%; ACT scores over 24: 92%; SAT evidence-based reading and writing scores over 700: 17%; SAT math scores over 700: 23%; ACT scores over 30: 42%.
Retention: 89% of full-time freshmen returned.

FACULTY
Total: 1,392, 79% full-time, 66% with terminal degrees.
Student/faculty ratio: 14:1.

ACADEMICS
Calendar: semesters. *Degrees:* bachelor's, master's, doctoral, and post-master's certificates.
Special study options: accelerated degree program, advanced placement credit, double majors, honors programs, internships, part-time degree program, services for LD students, student-designed majors, study abroad, summer session for credit. ***ROTC:*** Army (b), Air Force (b).
Unusual degree programs: 3-2 clinical laboratory science.
Computers: Students can access the following: campus intranet, computer help desk, free student e-mail accounts, online (class) grades, online (class) registration, online (class) schedules. Campuswide network is available. 99% of college-owned or -operated housing units are wired for high-speed Internet access. Wireless service is available via entire campus.
Library: Moody Memorial Library plus 8 others.

STUDENT LIFE
Housing options: on-campus residence required for freshman year; coed, men-only, women-only, cooperative, special housing for students with disabilities. Campus housing is university owned. Freshman campus housing is guaranteed.
Activities and organizations: drama/theater group, student-run newspaper, radio and television station, choral group, marching band, national fraternities, national sororities.
Athletics Member NCAA. All Division I except football (Division I-A). ***Intercollegiate sports:*** baseball M(s), basketball M(s)/W(s), cheerleading M(s)/W(s), cross-country running M(s)/W(s), equestrian sports W(s), golf M(s)/W(s)(c), soccer W(s), softball W(s), tennis M(s)/W(s), track and field M(s)/W(s), volleyball W(s). ***Intramural sports:*** baseball M(c), basketball M/W, bowling M/W, crew M(c)/W(c), cross-country running M/W, fencing M(c), field hockey W(c), football M/W, golf M(c), gymnastics M(c)/W(c), lacrosse M(c)/W(c), racquetball M/W, rock climbing M(c)/W(c), rowing M(c)/W(c), rugby M(c)/W(c), sailing M(c)/W(c), skiing (downhill) M(c)/W(c), soccer M(c)/W(c), softball M/W, swimming and diving M(c)/W(c), table tennis M/W, tennis M(c)/W(c), track and field M/W, triathlon M(c)/W(c), ultimate Frisbee M(c)/W(c), volleyball M(c), water polo M(c)/W(c).
Campus security: 24-hour emergency response devices and patrols, late-night transport/escort service, controlled dormitory access.
Student services: health clinic, personal/psychological counseling, legal services.

COSTS & FINANCIAL AID
Costs (2019–20) ***Comprehensive fee:*** $60,356 includes full-time tuition ($42,842), mandatory fees ($4522), and room and board ($12,992). Part-time tuition: $1785 per semester hour. ***Required fees:*** $188 per semester hour part-time. ***College room only:*** $7150.
Financial Aid Of all full-time matriculated undergraduates who enrolled in 2018, 8,994 applied for aid, 7,606 were judged to have need, 1,065 had their need fully met. 5,069 Federal Work-Study jobs (averaging $2876). In 2018, 5165 non-need-based awards were made. ***Average percent of need met:*** 66. ***Average financial aid package:*** $31,333. ***Average need-based loan:*** $3270. ***Average need-based gift aid:*** $25,716. ***Average non-need-based aid:*** $15,993. ***Average indebtedness upon graduation:*** $50,172.

APPLYING
Standardized Tests *Required:* SAT or ACT (for admission).
Options: electronic application, early admission, early action, deferred entrance.
Required: high school transcript. ***Required for some:*** essay or personal statement, minimum 2.5 GPA, 2 letters of recommendation.
Application deadlines: 2/1 (freshmen), rolling (transfers), 11/1 (early action).
Notification: 4/10 (freshmen), continuous (transfers), 1/15 (early action).

CONTACT
Ms. Jessica King Gereghty, Assistant Vice President of Undergraduate Admissions, Baylor University, PO Box 97056, Waco, TX 76798. *Phone:* 254-710-3435. *Toll-free phone:* 800-BAYLORU. *Fax:* 254-710-3436. *E-mail:* admissions@baylor.edu.

Brazosport College
Lake Jackson, Texas
http://www.brazosport.edu/

CONTACT
Brazosport College, 500 College Drive, Lake Jackson, TX 77566-3199. *Phone:* 979-230-3020.

Chamberlain College of Nursing
Houston, Texas
http://www.chamberlain.edu/

CONTACT
Director of Recruitment, Chamberlain College of Nursing, 11025 Equity Drive, Houston, TX 77041. *Phone:* 713-277-9800. *Toll-free phone:* 877-751-5783.

Chamberlain College of Nursing
Irving, Texas
http://www.chamberlain.edu/

CONTACT
Chamberlain College of Nursing, 4800 Regent Boulevard, Irving, TX 75063. *Toll-free phone:* 866-593-8669.

Chamberlain College of Nursing
Pearland, Texas
http://www.chamberlain.edu/

CONTACT
Chamberlain College of Nursing, 12000 Shadow Creek Parkway, Pearland, TX 77584. *Toll-free phone:* 877-751-5783.

College of Biblical Studies–Houston
Houston, Texas
http://www.cbshouston.edu/

- **Independent nondenominational** 4-year, founded 1976
- **Urban** 14-acre campus with easy access to Houston
- **Endowment** $656,713
- **Coed**
- **Noncompetitive** entrance level

FACULTY
Student/faculty ratio: 10:1.

ACADEMICS
Calendar: semesters. *Degrees:* certificates, associate, and bachelor's.
Library: College of Biblical Studies Library. *Books:* 88,005 (physical), 161,601 (digital/electronic); *Serial titles:* 476 (physical), 5,325

(digital/electronic). Weekly public service hours: 53; students can reserve study rooms.

STUDENT LIFE
Housing options: college housing not available.

Activities and organizations: choral group, Student Ministries.

Campus security: 24-hour emergency response devices, late-night transport/escort service, hourly patrols by trained security guards and police.

Student services: personal/psychological counseling.

COSTS & FINANCIAL AID
Costs (2018–19) ***Tuition:*** $6576 full-time, $274 per credit hour part-time. ***Required fees:*** $370 full-time, $185 per term part-time. ***Payment plans:*** installment, deferred payment.

Financial Aid ***Financial aid deadline:*** 8/5.

APPLYING
Options: electronic application.

Application fee: $40.

Required: essay or personal statement, high school transcript. ***Required for some:*** interview.

CONTACT
Admissions Office, College of Biblical Studies–Houston, 7000 Regency Square Boulevard, Houston, TX 77036. *Phone:* 713-772-4253. *Toll-free phone:* 844-227-9673. *E-mail:* admissions@cbshouston.edu.

Concordia University Texas
Austin, Texas
http://www.concordia.edu/

CONTACT
Ms. Kristin Coulter, Director of Admissions, Concordia University Texas, 11400 Concordia University Drive, Austin, TX 78726. *Phone:* 800-865-4282. *Toll-free phone:* 800-865-4282. *Fax:* 512-313-3999. *E-mail:* admissions@concordia.edu.

Criswell College
Dallas, Texas
http://www.criswell.edu/

- **Independent** comprehensive, founded 1970, affiliated with Southern Baptist Convention
- **Urban** campus with easy access to Dallas-Fort Worth
- **Endowment** $15.0 million
- **Coed**
- **Minimally difficult** entrance level

FACULTY
Student/faculty ratio: 8:1.

ACADEMICS
Calendar: semesters. *Degrees:* associate, bachelor's, and master's.
Library: Wallace Library. *Books:* 45,906 (physical), 200,891 (digital/electronic); *Serial titles:* 8 (physical), 19,721 (digital/electronic); *Databases:* 71. Students can reserve study rooms.

STUDENT LIFE
Housing options: college housing not available.

Campus security: 24-hour emergency response devices, late-night transport/escort service, electronically-operated building entrances.

Student services: personal/psychological counseling.

COSTS & FINANCIAL AID
Costs (2018–19) ***Tuition:*** $9960 full-time, $415 per credit hour part-time. Full-time tuition and fees vary according to course load. Part-time tuition and fees vary according to course load. ***Required fees:*** $750 full-time, $750 per year part-time.

Financial Aid Of all full-time matriculated undergraduates who enrolled in 2017, 87 applied for aid, 69 were judged to have need, 6 had their need fully met. In 2017, 11 non-need-based awards were made. ***Average percent of need met:*** 43. ***Average financial aid package:*** $8901. ***Average need-based loan:*** $4278. ***Average need-based gift aid:*** $6453. ***Average non-need-based aid:*** $5745.

APPLYING
Standardized Tests *Required for some:* SAT or ACT (for admission).

Options: electronic application.

Application fee: $35.

Required: essay or personal statement, 1 letter of recommendation. ***Required for some:*** high school transcript.

CONTACT
Sam Hagos, Enrollment Assistant, Criswell College, 4010 Gaston Avenue, Dallas, TX 75246. *Phone:* 214-818-1391. *Toll-free phone:* 800-899-0012. *E-mail:* shagos@criswell.edu.

Dallas Baptist University
Dallas, Texas
http://www.dbu.edu/

- **Independent** comprehensive, founded 1965, affiliated with Baptist General Convention of Texas
- **Suburban** 368-acre campus with easy access to Dallas-Fort Worth
- **Endowment** $51.4 million
- **Coed** 3,014 undergraduate students, 78% full-time, 58% women, 42% men
- **Moderately difficult** entrance level, 88% of applicants were admitted

UNDERGRAD STUDENTS
2,364 full-time, 650 part-time. Students come from 36 states and territories; 47 other countries; 8% are from out of state; 10% Black or African American, non-Hispanic/Latino; 18% Hispanic/Latino; 2% Asian, non-Hispanic/Latino; 0.3% Native Hawaiian or other Pacific Islander, non-Hispanic/Latino; 0.7% American Indian or Alaska Native, non-Hispanic/Latino; 0.9% Two or more races, non-Hispanic/Latino; 8% international; 7% transferred in; 64% live on campus.

Freshmen:
Admission: 2,757 applied, 2,428 admitted, 548 enrolled. ***Average high school GPA:*** 3.5. ***Test scores:*** SAT evidence-based reading and writing scores over 500: 95%; SAT math scores over 500: 95%; ACT scores over 18: 93%; SAT evidence-based reading and writing scores over 600: 53%; SAT math scores over 600: 38%; ACT scores over 24: 32%; SAT evidence-based reading and writing scores over 700: 8%; SAT math scores over 700: 4%; ACT scores over 30: 4%.
Retention: 77% of full-time freshmen returned.

FACULTY
Total: 636, 21% full-time, 53% with terminal degrees.

Student/faculty ratio: 13:1.

ACADEMICS
Calendar: 4-1-4. *Degrees:* certificates, associate, bachelor's, master's, doctoral, post-master's, and postbachelor's certificates.

Special study options: academic remediation for entering students, accelerated degree program, adult/continuing education programs, advanced placement credit, distance learning, double majors, English as a second language, honors programs, independent study, internships, off-campus study, part-time degree program, services for LD students, study abroad, summer session for credit. ***ROTC:*** Army (c), Air Force (c).

Unusual degree programs: 3-2 business administration.

Computers: 214 computers/terminals are available on campus for general student use. Students can access the following: computer help desk, free student e-mail accounts, online (class) grades, online (class) registration, online (class) schedules. Campuswide network is available. 100% of college-owned or -operated housing units are wired for high-speed Internet access. Wireless service is available via entire campus.
Library: Vance Memorial Library plus 3 others. *Books:* 247,606 (physical), 153,056 (digital/electronic); *Serial titles:* 561 (physical), 46,112 (digital/electronic); *Databases:* 203. Weekly public service hours: 108.

STUDENT LIFE
Housing options: men-only, women-only, special housing for students with disabilities. Campus housing is university owned and leased by the school. Freshman applicants given priority for college housing.

Activities and organizations: drama/theater group, choral group, Ministry Fellowship, Baptist Student Ministry, Student Government

Association, Student Education Association, International Student Organization.

Athletics Member NCAA, NCCAA. All NCAA Division II except baseball (Division I). ***Intercollegiate sports:*** baseball M(s), basketball M(s), cheerleading W(c), cross-country running M/W(s), golf M/W(s), ice hockey M(c), lacrosse M(c), soccer M/W(s), tennis M/W(s), track and field M/W(s), volleyball W(s). ***Intramural sports:*** basketball M/W, football M/W, golf M/W, soccer M/W, softball M/W, table tennis M/W, tennis M/W, ultimate Frisbee M/W, volleyball M/W.

Campus security: 24-hour emergency response devices and patrols, late-night transport/escort service, controlled dormitory access.

Student services: health clinic, personal/psychological counseling, veterans affairs office.

COSTS & FINANCIAL AID

Costs (2019–20) ***Comprehensive fee:*** $38,546 includes full-time tuition ($29,220), mandatory fees ($1100), and room and board ($8226). Part-time tuition: $974 per credit hour. ***Required fees:*** $550 part-time. ***College room only:*** $4015.

Financial Aid Of all full-time matriculated undergraduates who enrolled in 2018, 2,001 applied for aid, 1,510 were judged to have need, 489 had their need fully met. 95 Federal Work-Study jobs (averaging $2402). 12 state and other part-time jobs (averaging $688). In 2018, 350 non-need-based awards were made. ***Average percent of need met:*** 57. ***Average financial aid package:*** $16,668. ***Average need-based loan:*** $4166. ***Average need-based gift aid:*** $3988. ***Average non-need-based aid:*** $9533. ***Average indebtedness upon graduation:*** $22,246.

APPLYING

Standardized Tests *Required:* SAT or ACT (for admission).

Options: electronic application, early admission, deferred entrance.

Application fee: $25.

Required: essay or personal statement, high school transcript, minimum 2.5 GPA, rank in upper 50% of high school class. ***Recommended:*** interview.

Application deadlines: rolling (freshmen), rolling (out-of-state freshmen), rolling (transfers).

Notification: continuous (freshmen), continuous (out-of-state freshmen), continuous (transfers).

CONTACT

Mr. Richard Nassar, Director of Admissions, Dallas Baptist University, 3000 Mountain Creek Parkway, Dallas, TX 75211-9299. *Phone:* 214-333-5360. *Toll-free phone:* 800-460-1328. *Fax:* 214-333-5447. *E-mail:* richardn@dbu.edu.

Dallas Christian College

Dallas, Texas

http://www.dallas.edu/

- **Independent** 4-year, founded 1950, affiliated with Christian Churches and Churches of Christ
- **Suburban** 22-acre campus with easy access to Dallas-Fort Worth
- **Endowment** $169,907
- **Coed** 212 undergraduate students, 79% full-time, 40% women, 60% men
- **Moderately difficult** entrance level, 37% of applicants were admitted

UNDERGRAD STUDENTS

167 full-time, 45 part-time. Students come from 11 states and territories; 5 other countries; 16% are from out of state; 24% Black or African American, non-Hispanic/Latino; 15% Hispanic/Latino; 1% Asian, non-Hispanic/Latino; 0.5% Native Hawaiian or other Pacific Islander, non-Hispanic/Latino; 10% Two or more races, non-Hispanic/Latino; 5% Race/ethnicity unknown; 3% international; 13% transferred in; 46% live on campus.

Freshmen:

Admission: 132 applied, 49 admitted, 49 enrolled. ***Average high school GPA:*** 3.1.

Retention: 50% of full-time freshmen returned.

FACULTY

Total: 56, 14% full-time, 29% with terminal degrees.

Student/faculty ratio: 16:1.

ACADEMICS

Calendar: semesters. *Degrees:* associate, bachelor's, and postbachelor's certificates.

Special study options: academic remediation for entering students, accelerated degree program, adult/continuing education programs, advanced placement credit, distance learning, double majors, independent study, internships, part-time degree program, summer session for credit.

Computers: 16 computers/terminals are available on campus for general student use. Students can access the following: free student e-mail accounts, online (class) grades, online (class) registration, online (class) schedules. Campuswide network is available. 100% of college-owned or -operated housing units are wired for high-speed Internet access. Wireless service is available via entire campus.

Library: The Crawford Library. *Books:* 35,000 (physical), 26,000 (digital/electronic); *Serial titles:* 100 (physical); *Databases:* 60.

STUDENT LIFE

Housing options: on-campus residence required through sophomore year; men-only, women-only. Campus housing is university owned.

Activities and organizations: drama/theater group, choral group.

Athletics Member NCCAA. ***Intercollegiate sports:*** baseball M, basketball M/W, cross-country running W, soccer M, track and field W, volleyball W. ***Intramural sports:*** basketball M/W, sand volleyball M/W, soccer M/W, table tennis M/W, volleyball M/W.

Campus security: controlled dormitory access.

Student services: personal/psychological counseling.

COSTS & FINANCIAL AID

Costs (2018–19) ***Comprehensive fee:*** $25,516 includes full-time tuition ($15,596), mandatory fees ($910), and room and board ($9010). Full-time tuition and fees vary according to program. Part-time tuition: $557 per credit hour. Part-time tuition and fees vary according to program. ***Required fees:*** $285 per term part-time. ***Payment plan:*** installment. ***Waivers:*** children of alumni and employees or children of employees.

Financial Aid Of all full-time matriculated undergraduates who enrolled in 2005, 189 applied for aid, 132 were judged to have need. 36 Federal Work-Study jobs (averaging $1404). In 2005, 26 non-need-based awards were made. ***Average percent of need met:*** 43. ***Average financial aid package:*** $3940. ***Average need-based loan:*** $3589. ***Average need-based gift aid:*** $1282. ***Average non-need-based aid:*** $3664. ***Average indebtedness upon graduation:*** $15,000.

APPLYING

Standardized Tests *Required:* SAT or ACT (for admission).

Options: electronic application, deferred entrance.

Application fee: $30.

Required for some: high school transcript.

Application deadlines: rolling (freshmen), rolling (transfers).

CONTACT

Ms. Ashley Hudspeth, Admissions Counselor, Dallas Christian College, 2700 Christian Parkway, Dallas, TX 75234-7299. *Phone:* 972-241-3371 Ext. 195. *Toll-free phone:* 800-688-1029. *Fax:* 972-241-8021. *E-mail:* ahudspeth@dallas.edu.

Dallas International University

Dallas, Texas

http://www.diu.edu/

CONTACT

Dallas International University, 7500 West Camp Wisdom Road, Dallas, TX 75236.

Dallas Nursing Institute

Dallas, Texas

http://www.dni.edu/

CONTACT

Dallas Nursing Institute, 12170 N. Abrams Road, Suite 200, Dallas, TX 75243.

DeVry University–Irving Campus

Irving, Texas

http://www.devry.edu/

CONTACT
DeVry University–Irving Campus, 4800 Regent Boulevard, Suite 200, Irving, TX 75063. *Phone:* 972-929-6777. *Toll-free phone:* 866-338-7934.

East Texas Baptist University

Marshall, Texas

http://www.etbu.edu/

- **Independent Baptist** comprehensive, founded 1912
- **Small-town** 250-acre campus
- **Endowment** $71.5 million
- **Coed** 1,485 undergraduate students, 87% full-time, 55% women, 45% men
- **Moderately difficult** entrance level, 54% of applicants were admitted

UNDERGRAD STUDENTS
1,296 full-time, 189 part-time. Students come from 24 states and territories; 6 other countries; 11% are from out of state; 16% Black or African American, non-Hispanic/Latino; 10% Hispanic/Latino; 0.4% Asian, non-Hispanic/Latino; 0.1% Native Hawaiian or other Pacific Islander, non-Hispanic/Latino; 0.2% American Indian or Alaska Native, non-Hispanic/Latino; 4% Two or more races, non-Hispanic/Latino; 0.4% Race/ethnicity unknown; 0.8% international; 9% transferred in; 81% live on campus.

Freshmen:
Admission: 1,849 applied, 1,007 admitted, 403 enrolled. ***Average high school GPA:*** 3.4. ***Test scores:*** SAT evidence-based reading and writing scores over 500: 67%; SAT math scores over 500: 64%; ACT scores over 18: 82%; SAT evidence-based reading and writing scores over 600: 12%; SAT math scores over 600: 9%; ACT scores over 24: 20%; ACT scores over 30: 1%.

Retention: 63% of full-time freshmen returned.

FACULTY
Total: 149, 48% full-time, 57% with terminal degrees.

Student/faculty ratio: 15:1.

ACADEMICS
Calendar: semesters. *Degrees:* certificates, bachelor's, and master's.

Special study options: accelerated degree program, adult/continuing education programs, advanced placement credit, distance learning, double majors, English as a second language, honors programs, independent study, internships, off-campus study, part-time degree program, services for LD students, student-designed majors, study abroad, summer session for credit.

Computers: 301 computers/terminals and 800 ports are available on campus for general student use. Students can access the following: campus intranet, free student e-mail accounts, online (class) grades, online (class) registration, online (class) schedules. Campuswide network is available. 100% of college-owned or -operated housing units are wired for high-speed Internet access. Wireless service is available via entire campus.

Library: Mamye Jarrett Library. *Books:* 89,001 (physical), 520,411 (digital/electronic); *Serial titles:* 1,119 (physical), 81,485 (digital/electronic); *Databases:* 184. Weekly public service hours: 88.

STUDENT LIFE
Housing options: on-campus residence required through senior year; men-only, women-only. Campus housing is university owned. Freshman applicants given priority for college housing.

Activities and organizations: drama/theater group, choral group, marching band, Fellowship of Christian Athletes (FCA), Student Foundation, Student Government Association (SGA), Enactus, Chem Club.

Athletics Member NCAA. All Division III. ***Intercollegiate sports:*** baseball M, basketball M/W, cross-country running M/W, football M, golf M/W, soccer M/W, softball W, tennis M/W, track and field M/W, volleyball W. ***Intramural sports:*** basketball M/W, football M/W, sand volleyball M/W, soccer M/W, softball M/W, table tennis M/W, ultimate Frisbee M/W, volleyball M/W.

Campus security: 24-hour emergency response devices and patrols, student patrols, late-night transport/escort service, controlled dormitory access.

Student services: personal/psychological counseling.

COSTS & FINANCIAL AID
Costs (2019–20) ***Comprehensive fee:*** $36,538 includes full-time tuition ($26,100), mandatory fees ($1110), and room and board ($9328). Part-time tuition: $870 per credit hour. ***Required fees:*** $46 per credit hour part-time. ***College room only:*** $4576.

Financial Aid Of all full-time matriculated undergraduates who enrolled in 2017, 1,134 applied for aid, 1,035 were judged to have need, 158 had their need fully met. 98 Federal Work-Study jobs (averaging $1006). 279 state and other part-time jobs (averaging $1378). In 2017, 180 non-need-based awards were made. ***Average percent of need met:*** 30. ***Average financial aid package:*** $19,994. ***Average need-based loan:*** $3791. ***Average need-based gift aid:*** $6040. ***Average non-need-based aid:*** $12,339. ***Average indebtedness upon graduation:*** $30,367.

APPLYING
Standardized Tests *Required:* SAT or ACT (for admission).

Options: electronic application.

Application fee: $25.

Required: high school transcript.

Application deadlines: 8/27 (freshmen), 8/27 (out-of-state freshmen), 8/27 (transfers).

Notification: continuous (freshmen), continuous (transfers).

CONTACT
Mr. Jeremy Johnson, Assistant Vice President for Enrollment, East Texas Baptist University, One Tiger Drive, Marshall, TX 75670. *Phone:* 903-923-2010. *Toll-free phone:* 800-804-ETBU. *Fax:* 903-923-2001. *E-mail:* admissions@etbu.edu.

Gemini School of Visual Arts & Communication

Cedar Park, Texas

http://www.geminischool.com/

CONTACT
Gemini School of Visual Arts & Communication, 501 Prize Oaks Drive, Cedar Park, TX 78613.

Grace School of Theology

Conroe, Texas

http://www.gsot.edu/

CONTACT
Grace School of Theology, 3705 College Park Drive Suite 140, Conroe, TX 77384-4894.

Hallmark University

San Antonio, Texas

http://www.hallmarkuniversity.edu/

- **Independent** comprehensive, founded 1969
- **Suburban** 2-acre campus with easy access to San Antonio
- **Coed**
- **Moderately difficult** entrance level

FACULTY
Student/faculty ratio: 20:1.

ACADEMICS
Calendar: continuous. *Degrees:* associate, bachelor's, and master's.
Library: Randall K. Williams Assessment Center/ Virtual Library plus 1 other. *Books:* 172,325 (digital/electronic); *Serial titles:* 26,880 (digital/electronic); *Databases:* 32. Weekly public service hours: 4.

STUDENT LIFE
Housing options: college housing not available.

Activities and organizations: Alpha Beta Kappa Honor Society, Student Veteran's Organization.

Campus security: 24-hour emergency response devices and patrols, security guard on duty during hours when students are on campus.

Student services: veterans affairs office.

COSTS
Costs (2018–19) ***One-time required fee:*** $110. ***Tuition:*** $36,806 full-time. Full-time tuition and fees vary according to degree level, location, and program. ***Required fees:*** $900 full-time. ***Payment plans:*** tuition prepayment, installment.

APPLYING
Standardized Tests *Required:* Wonderlic aptitude test for Main Campus, Aviation Assessment for Satellite Campus, SAT/ACT is used for some degree programs (for admission).

Options: electronic application, early admission.

Required: high school transcript, interview, hybrid readiness test (main campus only). ***Required for some:*** essay or personal statement, letters of recommendation.

CONTACT
Ms. Jennifer Sanchez, Director of Admissions, Hallmark University, 10401 IH-10 West, San Antonio, TX 78230. *Phone:* 210-690-9000 Ext. 7540. *Toll-free phone:* 800-880-6600. *Fax:* 210-697-8225. *E-mail:* jsanchez@hallmarkuniversity.edu.

Hardin-Simmons University
Abilene, Texas
http://www.hsutx.edu/

- **Independent Baptist** comprehensive, founded 1891
- **Urban** 220-acre campus
- **Endowment** $176.2 million
- **Coed** 1,765 undergraduate students, 92% full-time, 53% women, 47% men
- **Moderately difficult** entrance level, 84% of applicants were admitted

UNDERGRAD STUDENTS
1,625 full-time, 140 part-time. Students come from 18 states and territories; 26 other countries; 3% are from out of state; 9% Black or African American, non-Hispanic/Latino; 19% Hispanic/Latino; 2% Asian, non-Hispanic/Latino; 0.3% American Indian or Alaska Native, non-Hispanic/Latino; 4% Two or more races, non-Hispanic/Latino; 1% Race/ethnicity unknown; 3% international; 6% transferred in; 54% live on campus.

Freshmen:
Admission: 1,766 applied, 1,487 admitted, 484 enrolled. ***Average high school GPA:*** 3.5. ***Test scores:*** SAT evidence-based reading and writing scores over 500: 80%; SAT math scores over 500: 77%; ACT scores over 18: 85%; SAT evidence-based reading and writing scores over 600: 23%; SAT math scores over 600: 20%; ACT scores over 24: 31%; SAT evidence-based reading and writing scores over 700: 4%; SAT math scores over 700: 3%; ACT scores over 30: 3%.

FACULTY
Student/faculty ratio: 12:1.

ACADEMICS
Calendar: semesters. *Degrees:* bachelor's, master's, doctoral, post-master's, and postbachelor's certificates.

Special study options: academic remediation for entering students, accelerated degree program, adult/continuing education programs, advanced placement credit, distance learning, double majors, honors programs, independent study, internships, off-campus study, part-time degree program, services for LD students, study abroad, summer session for credit.

Computers: 115 computers/terminals are available on campus for general student use. Students can access the following: campus intranet, computer help desk, free student e-mail accounts, online (class) grades, online (class) registration, online (class) schedules. Campuswide network is available. 100% of college-owned or -operated housing units are wired for high-speed Internet access. Wireless service is available via entire campus.

Library: Richardson Library plus 1 other. *Books:* 201,169 (physical), 41,773 (digital/electronic); *Serial titles:* 183 (physical), 67,899 (digital/electronic); *Databases:* 142. Weekly public service hours: 89.

STUDENT LIFE
Housing options: on-campus residence required through sophomore year; men-only, women-only. Campus housing is university owned. Freshman campus housing is guaranteed.

Activities and organizations: drama/theater group, student-run newspaper, choral group, marching band, Baptist Student Ministries, Student Government, Alpha Phi Omega, Student Activities Board, Fellowship of Christian Athletes.

Athletics Member NCAA. All Division III. ***Intercollegiate sports:*** baseball M, basketball M/W, cheerleading M(c)/W(c), cross-country running M/W, football M, golf M/W, soccer M/W, softball W, tennis M/W, track and field M/W, volleyball W. ***Intramural sports:*** badminton M/W, basketball M/W, bowling M/W, football M/W, golf M/W, gymnastics M(c)/W(c), lacrosse M(c)/W(c), racquetball M/W, soccer M/W, softball W, swimming and diving M(c)/W(c), table tennis M(c)/W(c), tennis M(c)/W(c), ultimate Frisbee M/W, volleyball M/W.

Campus security: 24-hour emergency response devices and patrols, late-night transport/escort service, controlled dormitory access.

Student services: personal/psychological counseling.

COSTS & FINANCIAL AID
Costs (2019–20) ***Comprehensive fee:*** $39,990 includes full-time tuition ($28,390), mandatory fees ($1750), and room and board ($9850). Part-time tuition: $850 per credit hour. ***Required fees:*** $400 per term part-time. ***College room only:*** $4470.

Financial Aid Of all full-time matriculated undergraduates who enrolled in 2018, 1,350 applied for aid, 1,244 were judged to have need, 231 had their need fully met. In 2018, 373 non-need-based awards were made. ***Average percent of need met:*** 74. ***Average financial aid package:*** $24,415. ***Average need-based loan:*** $4107. ***Average need-based gift aid:*** $7088. ***Average non-need-based aid:*** $14,960. ***Average indebtedness upon graduation:*** $36,053.

APPLYING
Standardized Tests *Required:* SAT or ACT (for admission).

Options: electronic application, deferred entrance.

Required: high school transcript, minimum 2.0 GPA.

Application deadlines: rolling (freshmen), rolling (transfers).

Notification: continuous (freshmen), continuous (transfers).

CONTACT
Mr. Grant Greenwood, Director of Undergraduate Admissions and Recruiting, Hardin-Simmons University, Box 16050, Abilene, TX 79698-0001. *Phone:* 325-670-1422. *Toll-free phone:* 877-464-7889. *E-mail:* grant.t.greenwood@hsutx.edu.

Houston Baptist University
Houston, Texas
http://www.hbu.edu/

- **Independent Baptist** comprehensive, founded 1960
- **Suburban** 100-acre campus with easy access to Houston
- **Endowment** $102.8 million
- **Coed**
- **Moderately difficult** entrance level

FACULTY
Student/faculty ratio: 14:1.

ACADEMICS
Calendar: semesters. *Degrees:* bachelor's, master's, and doctoral.
Library: Moody Library. *Books:* 109,715 (physical); *Serial titles:* 252 (physical), 57,209 (digital/electronic); *Databases:* 111. Students can reserve study rooms.

STUDENT LIFE
Housing options: on-campus residence required for freshman year; coed, men-only, women-only, special housing for students with disabilities. Campus housing is university owned. Freshman campus housing is guaranteed.

Activities and organizations: drama/theater group, student-run newspaper, choral group, marching band, Filipino Student Association, Baptist Student Ministry, Nursing Student Association, Phi Mu, Alpha Epsilon Delta, national fraternities, national sororities.

Athletics Member NCAA. All Division I.

Campus security: 24-hour emergency response devices and patrols, late-night transport/escort service, controlled dormitory access.

Student services: health clinic, personal/psychological counseling, veterans affairs office.

COSTS & FINANCIAL AID

Costs (2018–19) ***Comprehensive fee:*** $41,344 includes full-time tuition ($30,480), mandatory fees ($2050), and room and board ($8814). Part-time tuition: $1270 per semester hour. Part-time tuition and fees vary according to course load. ***Required fees:*** $1025 per term part-time. ***College room only:*** $4800. Room and board charges vary according to board plan and housing facility.

Financial Aid Of all full-time matriculated undergraduates who enrolled in 2018, 1,466 applied for aid, 1,382 were judged to have need, 200 had their need fully met. 888 Federal Work-Study jobs (averaging $986). In 2018, 435 non-need-based awards were made. ***Average percent of need met:*** 69. ***Average financial aid package:*** $28,187. ***Average need-based loan:*** $4241. ***Average need-based gift aid:*** $21,688. ***Average non-need-based aid:*** $14,579. ***Average indebtedness upon graduation:*** $33,667.

APPLYING

Standardized Tests *Required:* SAT or ACT (for admission).

Options: electronic application, deferred entrance.

Required: high school transcript. ***Required for some:*** essay or personal statement.

CONTACT

Mr. James Steen, Vice President for Enrollment Management, Houston Baptist University, 7502 Fondren Road, Houston, TX 77074-3298. *Phone:* 281-649-3752. *Toll-free phone:* 800-696-3210. *Fax:* 281-649-3217. *E-mail:* jsteen@hbu.edu.

Howard Payne University

Brownwood, Texas

http://www.hputx.edu/

- **Independent** comprehensive, founded 1889, affiliated with Baptist General Convention of Texas
- **Small-town** 80-acre campus
- **Endowment** $56.5 million
- **Coed**
- **Moderately difficult** entrance level

FACULTY

Student/faculty ratio: 10:1.

ACADEMICS

Calendar: semesters. *Degrees:* certificates, bachelor's, and master's.
Library: Walker Memorial Library. *Books:* 125,784 (physical), 144,053 (digital/electronic); *Serial titles:* 27,347 (physical). Weekly public service hours: 84.

STUDENT LIFE

Housing options: on-campus residence required through sophomore year; men-only, women-only. Campus housing is university owned. Freshman campus housing is guaranteed.

Activities and organizations: drama/theater group, student-run newspaper, choral group, marching band, Baptist Student Ministry, Fellowship of Christian Athletes, Gaming Guild, Spanish Club, Social Work Club, national fraternities, national sororities.

Athletics Member NCAA. All Division III.

Campus security: 24-hour emergency response devices and patrols, late-night transport/escort service, controlled dormitory access.

Student services: health clinic, personal/psychological counseling.

COSTS & FINANCIAL AID

Costs (2018–19) ***Comprehensive fee:*** $36,476 includes full-time tuition ($25,290), mandatory fees ($2800), and room and board ($8386). Full-time tuition and fees vary according to course load, location, and program. Part-time tuition: $845 per credit hour. Part-time tuition and fees vary according to location and program. ***Room and board:*** Room and board charges vary according to board plan and housing facility.

Financial Aid Of all full-time matriculated undergraduates who enrolled in 2018, 745 applied for aid, 697 were judged to have need, 107 had their need fully met. In 2018, 105 non-need-based awards were made. ***Average percent of need met:*** 78. ***Average financial aid package:*** $21,443. ***Average need-based loan:*** $5011. ***Average need-based gift aid:*** $17,120. ***Average non-need-based aid:*** $13,786. ***Average indebtedness upon graduation:*** $34,875.

APPLYING

Standardized Tests *Required:* SAT or ACT (for admission). *Required for some:* ACCUPLACER.

Options: electronic application, early admission.

Required: high school transcript. ***Required for some:*** 3 letters of recommendation, interview. ***Recommended:*** essay or personal statement, minimum 3.0 GPA.

CONTACT

Mrs. P. J. Gramling, Director of Admission, Howard Payne University, 1000 Fisk Street, Brownwood, TX 76801. *Phone:* 325-649-8406. *Toll-free phone:* 800-880-4478. *Fax:* 325-649-8901. *E-mail:* enroll@hputx.edu.

Huston-Tillotson University

Austin, Texas

http://www.htu.edu/

- **Independent interdenominational** comprehensive, founded 1875
- **Urban** 23-acre campus
- **Coed**
- **Moderately difficult** entrance level

ACADEMICS

Calendar: semesters. *Degrees:* associate, bachelor's, and master's.
Library: Downs-Jones Library.

STUDENT LIFE

Housing options: on-campus residence required for freshman yearCampus housing is university owned. Freshman campus housing is guaranteed.

Activities and organizations: drama/theater group, choral group, Campus Ministries, Zeta Phi Beta Sorority, Inc, Alpha Phi Alpha Fraternity, Inc, The Gentlemen's Club, Pre-Alumni Council, national fraternities, national sororities.

Athletics Member NAIA.

Campus security: 24-hour emergency response devices and patrols, late-night transport/escort service, controlled dormitory access.

Student services: health clinic, personal/psychological counseling.

COSTS

Costs (2018–19) ***Comprehensive fee:*** $21,914 includes full-time tuition ($12,262), mandatory fees ($2084), and room and board ($7568). Full-time tuition and fees vary according to course load. Part-time tuition: $410 per credit hour. Part-time tuition and fees vary according to course load. ***College room only:*** $3642. Room and board charges vary according to housing facility. ***Payment plans:*** installment, deferred payment.

APPLYING

Standardized Tests *Required:* SAT or ACT (for admission). *Recommended:* SAT (for admission), ACT (for admission), SAT and SAT Subject Tests or ACT (for admission).

Options: electronic application, deferred entrance.

Application fee: $25.

Required: high school transcript, minimum 2.5 GPA. ***Required for some:*** interview.

CONTACT

Ms. Shakitha Stinson, Director of Admission, Huston-Tillotson University, 900 Chicon Street, Austin, TX 78702. *Phone:* 512-505-3029. *Fax:* 512-505-3192. *E-mail:* slstinson@htu.edu.

Jarvis Christian College
Hawkins, Texas
http://www.jarvis.edu/

CONTACT
Mr. Brandon Byrd, Director of Admissions and Enrollment, Jarvis Christian College, PO Box 1470, Hawkins, TX 75765-9989. *Phone:* 903-730-4890 Ext. 2201. *Fax:* 903-769-4842.

The King's University
Southlake, Texas
http://www.tku.edu/

CONTACT
Tyler Maxey, Director of Admissions, The King's University, 2121 E. Southlake Boulevard, Southlake, TX 76092. *Phone:* 817-552-7570. *Toll-free phone:* 888-779-8040. *E-mail:* tyler.maxey@tku.edu.

Lamar University
Beaumont, Texas
http://www.lamar.edu/

- **State-supported** university, founded 1923, part of Texas State University System
- **Suburban** 292-acre campus with easy access to Houston
- **Endowment** $114.9 million
- **Coed** 8,904 undergraduate students, 64% full-time, 58% women, 42% men
- **Minimally difficult** entrance level, 86% of applicants were admitted

UNDERGRAD STUDENTS
5,735 full-time, 3,169 part-time. Students come from 37 states and territories; 46 other countries; 3% are from out of state; 27% Black or African American, non-Hispanic/Latino; 19% Hispanic/Latino; 5% Asian, non-Hispanic/Latino; 0.1% Native Hawaiian or other Pacific Islander, non-Hispanic/Latino; 0.6% American Indian or Alaska Native, non-Hispanic/Latino; 1% Two or more races, non-Hispanic/Latino; 1% Race/ethnicity unknown; 1% international; 8% transferred in; 26% live on campus.

Freshmen:
Admission: 5,652 applied, 4,842 admitted, 1,464 enrolled. ***Average high school GPA:*** 3.3. ***Test scores:*** SAT evidence-based reading and writing scores over 500: 65%; SAT math scores over 500: 62%; ACT scores over 18: 76%; SAT evidence-based reading and writing scores over 600: 17%; SAT math scores over 600: 12%; ACT scores over 24: 24%; SAT evidence-based reading and writing scores over 700: 2%; SAT math scores over 700: 2%; ACT scores over 30: 4%.

Retention: 64% of full-time freshmen returned.

FACULTY
Total: 614, 79% full-time, 61% with terminal degrees.

Student/faculty ratio: 18:1.

ACADEMICS
Calendar: semesters. *Degrees:* bachelor's, master's, doctoral, post-master's, and postbachelor's certificates.

Special study options: academic remediation for entering students, accelerated degree program, advanced placement credit, cooperative education, distance learning, double majors, English as a second language, freshman honors college, honors programs, independent study, internships, off-campus study, part-time degree program, services for LD students, student-designed majors, study abroad, summer session for credit. ***ROTC:*** Air Force (c).

Computers: 1,104 computers/terminals are available on campus for general student use. Students can access the following: campus intranet, computer help desk, free student e-mail accounts, online (class) grades, online (class) registration, online (class) schedules. Campuswide network is available. 100% of college-owned or -operated housing units are wired for high-speed Internet access. Wireless service is available via entire campus.

Library: Mary and John Gray Library plus 1 other. *Books:* 496,121 (physical), 91,469 (digital/electronic); *Serial titles:* 42,694 (physical), 47,629 (digital/electronic); *Databases:* 142. Weekly public service hours: 87; students can reserve study rooms.

STUDENT LIFE
Housing options: on-campus residence required for freshman year; coed, special housing for students with disabilities. Campus housing is university owned. Freshman campus housing is guaranteed.

Activities and organizations: drama/theater group, student-run newspaper, television station, choral group, marching band, national fraternities, national sororities.

Athletics Member NCAA. All Division I except football (Division I-AA). ***Intercollegiate sports:*** baseball M(s), basketball M(s)/W(s), cheerleading M/W, cross-country running M(s)/W(s), golf M(s)/W(s)(c), soccer W(s), softball W, tennis M(s)/W(s), track and field M(s)/W(s), volleyball W(s). ***Intramural sports:*** badminton M/W, basketball M/W, cross-country running M/W, football M, golf M/W, racquetball M/W, rugby M/W, sailing M/W, soccer M/W, softball M/W, swimming and diving M/W, table tennis M/W, tennis M/W, track and field M/W, volleyball M/W, weight lifting M/W.

Campus security: 24-hour emergency response devices and patrols, student patrols, late-night transport/escort service, controlled dormitory access.

Student services: health clinic, personal/psychological counseling, veterans affairs office.

COSTS & FINANCIAL AID
Costs (2018–19) ***One-time required fee:*** $10. ***Tuition:*** state resident $7391 full-time, $246 per credit hour part-time; nonresident $19,841 full-time, $661 per credit hour part-time. Full-time tuition and fees vary according to course load, location, and program. Part-time tuition and fees vary according to course load, location, and program. No tuition increase for student's term of enrollment. ***Required fees:*** $2801 full-time, $382 per credit hour part-time. ***Room and board:*** $8920; room only: $5670. Room and board charges vary according to board plan. ***Payment plan:*** installment. ***Waivers:*** senior citizens and employees or children of employees.

Financial Aid ***Average indebtedness upon graduation:*** $35,651.

APPLYING
Standardized Tests *Required:* SAT or ACT (for admission).

Options: electronic application, early admission.

Application fee: $25.

Required: high school transcript. ***Required for some:*** essay or personal statement.

CONTACT
Celeste Contreras, Director of Admissions, Lamar University, PO Box 10009, Beaumont, TX 77710. *Phone:* 409-880-8888. *Fax:* 409-880-8463. *E-mail:* admissions@lamar.edu.

LeTourneau University
Longview, Texas
http://www.letu.edu/

- **Independent nondenominational** comprehensive, founded 1946
- **Suburban** 162-acre campus
- **Coed** 2,801 undergraduate students, 47% full-time, 48% women, 52% men
- **Moderately difficult** entrance level, 46% of applicants were admitted

UNDERGRAD STUDENTS
1,317 full-time, 1,484 part-time. 33% are from out of state; 7% Black or African American, non-Hispanic/Latino; 9% Hispanic/Latino; 2% Asian, non-Hispanic/Latino; 0.1% Native Hawaiian or other Pacific Islander, non-Hispanic/Latino; 0.6% American Indian or Alaska Native, non-Hispanic/Latino; 5% Two or more races, non-Hispanic/Latino; 17% Race/ethnicity unknown; 2% international; 6% transferred in; 69% live on campus.

Freshmen:
Admission: 1,922 applied, 875 admitted, 335 enrolled. ***Average high school GPA:*** 3.6. ***Test scores:*** SAT evidence-based reading and writing scores over 500: 93%; SAT math scores over 500: 91%; ACT scores over 18: 97%; SAT evidence-based reading and writing scores over 600: 53%; SAT math scores over 600: 50%; ACT scores over 24: 58%; SAT

evidence-based reading and writing scores over 700: 10%; SAT math scores over 700: 15%; ACT scores over 30: 18%.

Retention: 79% of full-time freshmen returned.

FACULTY

Total: 249, 35% full-time, 53% with terminal degrees.

Student/faculty ratio: 15:1.

ACADEMICS

Calendar: semesters. *Degrees:* associate, bachelor's, and master's.

Special study options: accelerated degree program, advanced placement credit, cooperative education, distance learning, double majors, English as a second language, freshman honors college, honors programs, independent study, internships, part-time degree program, services for LD students, study abroad, summer session for credit.

Computers: Students can access the following: campus intranet, computer help desk, free student e-mail accounts, online (class) grades, online (class) registration, online (class) schedules. Campuswide network is available. 100% of college-owned or -operated housing units are wired for high-speed Internet access. Wireless service is available via entire campus.

Library: Margaret Estes Library plus 1 other. *Books:* 36,096 (physical), 233,126 (digital/electronic); *Serial titles:* 29,406 (digital/electronic); *Databases:* 95. Weekly public service hours: 87.

STUDENT LIFE

Housing options: on-campus residence required through junior year; men-only, women-only, special housing for students with disabilities. Campus housing is university owned. Freshman campus housing is guaranteed.

Activities and organizations: drama/theater group, choral group.

Athletics Member NCAA. All Division III. ***Intercollegiate sports:*** baseball M, basketball M/W, cross-country running M/W, golf M/W, rugby M(c)/W(c), soccer M/W, softball W, tennis M/W, track and field M/W, volleyball W. ***Intramural sports:*** badminton M/W, basketball M/W, sand volleyball M/W, soccer M/W, softball M/W, swimming and diving M(c)/W(c), table tennis M/W, tennis M/W, ultimate Frisbee M/W, volleyball M/W.

Campus security: 24-hour emergency response devices and patrols, student patrols, late-night transport/escort service, controlled dormitory access.

Student services: personal/psychological counseling.

COSTS & FINANCIAL AID

Costs (2019–20) ***Comprehensive fee:*** $41,240 includes full-time tuition ($30,520), mandatory fees ($750), and room and board ($9970).

Financial Aid Of all full-time matriculated undergraduates who enrolled in 2018, 1,021 applied for aid, 909 were judged to have need, 128 had their need fully met. In 2018, 321 non-need-based awards were made. ***Average percent of need met:*** 69. ***Average financial aid package:*** $23,406. ***Average need-based loan:*** $4558. ***Average need-based gift aid:*** $18,518. ***Average non-need-based aid:*** $14,467. ***Average indebtedness upon graduation:*** $36,643. ***Financial aid deadline:*** 8/1.

APPLYING

Standardized Tests *Required for some:* SAT or ACT (for admission).

Options: electronic application, deferred entrance.

Application deadlines: rolling (freshmen), rolling (transfers).

Notification: continuous (freshmen), continuous (transfers).

CONTACT

LeTourneau University, PO Box 7001, Longview, TX 75607-7001. *Toll-free phone:* 800-759-8811.

Lubbock Christian University

Lubbock, Texas

http://www.lcu.edu/

- **Independent** comprehensive, founded 1957, affiliated with Church of Christ
- **Suburban** 120-acre campus
- **Endowment** $19.7 million
- **Coed** 6,439 undergraduate students, 97% full-time, 91% women, 9% men
- **Moderately difficult** entrance level, 90% of applicants were admitted

UNDERGRAD STUDENTS

6,272 full-time, 167 part-time. Students come from 34 states and territories; 19 other countries; 10% are from out of state; 4% Black or African American, non-Hispanic/Latino; 24% Hispanic/Latino; 0.7% Asian, non-Hispanic/Latino; 0.4% Native Hawaiian or other Pacific Islander, non-Hispanic/Latino; 1% American Indian or Alaska Native, non-Hispanic/Latino; 0.1% Race/ethnicity unknown; 2% international; 2% transferred in; 37% live on campus.

Freshmen:

Admission: 696 applied, 624 admitted, 294 enrolled. ***Average high school GPA:*** 3.6. ***Test scores:*** SAT evidence-based reading and writing scores over 500: 66%; SAT math scores over 500: 68%; ACT scores over 18: 88%; SAT evidence-based reading and writing scores over 600: 29%; SAT math scores over 600: 22%; ACT scores over 24: 36%; SAT evidence-based reading and writing scores over 700: 4%; SAT math scores over 700: 4%; ACT scores over 30: 10%.

Retention: 69% of full-time freshmen returned.

FACULTY

Total: 190, 50% full-time, 53% with terminal degrees.

Student/faculty ratio: 13:1.

ACADEMICS

Calendar: semesters. *Degrees:* bachelor's and master's.

Special study options: academic remediation for entering students, adult/continuing education programs, advanced placement credit, cooperative education, distance learning, double majors, honors programs, internships, part-time degree program, services for LD students, study abroad, summer session for credit. ***ROTC:*** Army (c), Air Force (c).

Computers: 169 computers/terminals are available on campus for general student use. Students can access the following: campus intranet, computer help desk, free student e-mail accounts, online (class) grades, online (class) registration, online (class) schedules. Campuswide network is available. 100% of college-owned or -operated housing units are wired for high-speed Internet access. Wireless service is available via entire campus.

Library: University Library. *Books:* 124,676 (physical), 176,165 (digital/electronic); *Serial titles:* 5 (digital/electronic); *Databases:* 92. Weekly public service hours: 93.

STUDENT LIFE

Housing options: on-campus residence required through sophomore year; men-only, women-only. Campus housing is university owned. Freshman campus housing is guaranteed.

Activities and organizations: drama/theater group, student-run newspaper, radio station, choral group, Student Senate, Enactus, Ag Club, Behavioral Science Society, International Student Association.

Athletics Member NCAA. All Division II. ***Intercollegiate sports:*** baseball M(s), basketball M(s)/W(s), cheerleading M/W, cross-country running M(s)/W(s), golf M(s)/W(s), soccer M(s)/W(s), softball W(s), track and field M/W, volleyball W(s). ***Intramural sports:*** basketball M/W, cross-country running M/W, football M/W, golf M/W, rock climbing M/W, soccer M/W, softball M/W, table tennis M/W, track and field M/W, ultimate Frisbee M/W, volleyball M/W.

Campus security: 24-hour patrols, late-night transport/escort service, controlled dormitory access.

Student services: health clinic, personal/psychological counseling.

COSTS & FINANCIAL AID

Costs (2019–20) ***Comprehensive fee:*** $31,270 includes full-time tuition ($23,330) and room and board ($7940). Part-time tuition: $755 per credit hour. ***Required fees:*** $60 per term part-time.

Financial Aid Of all full-time matriculated undergraduates who enrolled in 2018, 1,095 applied for aid, 940 were judged to have need, 105 had their need fully met. 632 Federal Work-Study jobs (averaging $1733). 14 state and other part-time jobs (averaging $735). In 2018, 204 non-need-based awards were made. ***Average percent of need met:*** 64. ***Average financial aid package:*** $16,179. ***Average need-based loan:*** $4221. ***Average need-based gift aid:*** $11,974. ***Average non-need-based aid:*** $6569. ***Average indebtedness upon graduation:*** $39,288.

APPLYING

Standardized Tests *Required:* SAT or ACT (for admission).

Options: electronic application, early decision, early action.

Application fee: $25.

Required: high school transcript.

Application deadlines: 6/1 (freshmen), 6/1 (out-of-state freshmen), rolling (transfers), 6/15 (early action).

Early decision deadline: 10/31 (for plan 1), 1/1 (for plan 2).

Notification: continuous (freshmen), continuous (out-of-state freshmen), continuous (transfers), 12/15 (early decision plan 1), 2/15 (early decision plan 2), 7/15 (early action).

CONTACT

Mr. Chris Hayes, Director of Admissions, Lubbock Christian University, 5601 19th Street, Lubbock, TX 79407. *Phone:* 806-720-7156. *Toll-free phone:* 800-933-7601. *Fax:* 806-720-7162. *E-mail:* admissions@lcu.edu.

McMurry University

Abilene, Texas

http://www.mcm.edu/

- **Independent United Methodist** comprehensive, founded 1923
- **Suburban** 52-acre campus
- **Endowment** $81.5 million
- **Coed**
- **Moderately difficult** entrance level

FACULTY

Student/faculty ratio: 11:1.

ACADEMICS

Calendar: semesters plus May term. *Degrees:* bachelor's and master's.
Library: Jay-Rollins Library. *Books:* 128,329 (physical), 193,689 (digital/electronic); *Serial titles:* 115 (physical), 377 (digital/electronic); *Databases:* 95. Weekly public service hours: 86.

STUDENT LIFE

Housing options: on-campus residence required through junior year; coed, men-only, women-only. Campus housing is university owned and is provided by a third party. Freshman campus housing is guaranteed.

Activities and organizations: drama/theater group, student-run newspaper, choral group, marching band, Alpha Phi Omega, Religious Life Council, McMurry Student Government, Campus Activity Board, Servant Leadership.

Athletics Member NCAA, NCCAA. All NCAA Division III.

Campus security: 24-hour emergency response devices and patrols, late-night transport/escort service, controlled dormitory access.

Student services: health clinic, personal/psychological counseling, veterans affairs office.

COSTS & FINANCIAL AID

Costs (2018–19) ***One-time required fee:*** $175. ***Comprehensive fee:*** $35,846 includes full-time tuition ($27,154), mandatory fees ($90), and room and board ($8602). Full-time tuition and fees vary according to course load. Part-time tuition: $848 per credit hour. Part-time tuition and fees vary according to course load. ***Required fees:*** $3 per credit hour part-time. ***College room only:*** $4186. Room and board charges vary according to board plan and housing facility.

Financial Aid Of all full-time matriculated undergraduates who enrolled in 2017, 823 applied for aid, 777 were judged to have need, 94 had their need fully met. 130 Federal Work-Study jobs (averaging $975). 40 state and other part-time jobs (averaging $1106). In 2017, 103 non-need-based awards were made. ***Average percent of need met:*** 72. ***Average financial aid package:*** $21,941. ***Average need-based loan:*** $4260. ***Average need-based gift aid:*** $16,829. ***Average non-need-based aid:*** $11,582. ***Average indebtedness upon graduation:*** $31,350.

APPLYING

Standardized Tests *Required:* SAT or ACT (for admission).

Options: electronic application, deferred entrance.

Application fee: $25.

Required: essay or personal statement, high school transcript, minimum 2.0 GPA. ***Required for some:*** 3 letters of recommendation, interview.

CONTACT

Ms. Teresa Bridwell, Admission Counselor, McMurry University, 1 McMurry University, #278, Abilene, TX 79697. *Phone:* 325-793-4700. *Toll-free phone:* 800-460-2392. *Fax:* 325-793-4701. *E-mail:* admissions@mcm.edu.

Messenger College

Euless, Texas

http://www.messengercollege.edu/

- **Independent Pentecostal** 4-year, founded 1987
- **Suburban** 3-acre campus with easy access to Dallas-Fort Worth
- **Endowment** $543,454
- **Coed** 45 undergraduate students, 76% full-time, 51% women, 49% men
- **Moderately difficult** entrance level, 27% of applicants were admitted

UNDERGRAD STUDENTS

34 full-time, 11 part-time. Students come from 12 states and territories; 73% are from out of state; 4% Black or African American, non-Hispanic/Latino; 20% Hispanic/Latino; 7% Two or more races, non-Hispanic/Latino; 4% Race/ethnicity unknown; 4% transferred in; 58% live on campus.

Freshmen:

Admission: 44 applied, 12 admitted, 8 enrolled. ***Average high school GPA:*** 3.2.

Retention: 89% of full-time freshmen returned.

FACULTY

Total: 24, 8% full-time, 13% with terminal degrees.

ACADEMICS

Calendar: semesters. *Degrees:* associate and bachelor's.

Special study options: academic remediation for entering students, advanced placement credit, cooperative education, distance learning, double majors, external degree program, honors programs, independent study, internships, part-time degree program.

Computers: 5 computers/terminals are available on campus for general student use. Students can access the following: campus intranet, free student e-mail accounts, online (class) grades, online (class) registration, online (class) schedules. Campuswide network is available. 100% of college-owned or -operated housing units are wired for high-speed Internet access. Wireless service is available via entire campus.
Library: McDole-McDonald Library. *Books:* 12,617 (physical), 10,290 (digital/electronic); *Serial titles:* 12,705 (physical), 14,979 (digital/electronic); *Databases:* 15. Students can reserve study rooms.

STUDENT LIFE

Housing options: men-only, women-only. Campus housing is university owned.

Campus security: 24-hour emergency response devices, student patrols, controlled dormitory access.

COSTS & FINANCIAL AID

Costs (2019–20) ***Comprehensive fee:*** $17,230 includes full-time tuition ($9750), mandatory fees ($1330), and room and board ($6150). Part-time tuition: $325 per credit hour. ***Required fees:*** $660 per term part-time. ***College room only:*** $3350.

Financial Aid Of all full-time matriculated undergraduates who enrolled in 2010, 64 applied for aid, 64 were judged to have need. 16 Federal Work-Study jobs (averaging $460). ***Average percent of need met:*** 44. ***Average financial aid package:*** $8338. ***Average need-based loan:*** $3791. ***Average need-based gift aid:*** $5198. ***Average indebtedness upon graduation:*** $20,805.

APPLYING

Standardized Tests *Required for some:* SAT or ACT (for admission).

Options: electronic application, early admission.

Application fee: $35.

Required: essay or personal statement, high school transcript, minimum 2.0 GPA, 3 letters of recommendation, health form. ***Required for some:*** interview.

Application deadlines: 8/14 (freshmen), 8/14 (out-of-state freshmen), 8/14 (transfers).

Notification: continuous (freshmen), continuous (out-of-state freshmen), continuous (transfers).

CONTACT

Olivia Carter, Teaching & Academic Assistant, Messenger College, 400 South Industrial Boulevard, Suite 300, Euless, TX 76040. *Phone:* 817-554-5950 Ext. 165. *Toll-free phone:* 800-385-8940. *Fax:* 817-391-4003. *E-mail:* enrollment@messengercollege.edu.

Midland College

Midland, Texas

http://www.midland.edu/

- **State and locally supported** 4-year, founded 1969
- **Suburban** 163-acre campus
- **Coed**
- **Noncompetitive** entrance level

FACULTY
Student/faculty ratio: 17:1.

ACADEMICS
Calendar: semesters. *Degrees:* certificates, associate, and bachelor's.
Library: Murray Fasken Learning Resource Center. Weekly public service hours: 84.

STUDENT LIFE
Housing options: coed, men-only, women-only. Campus housing is university owned.

Activities and organizations: drama/theater group, student-run newspaper, choral group, OIKOS, Midland College Latin American Student Society, Student Government Association, Student Nurses Association, Baptist Student Ministries.

Athletics Member NJCAA.

Campus security: 24-hour patrols, controlled dormitory access.

Student services: personal/psychological counseling, veterans affairs office.

FINANCIAL AID
Financial Aid Of all full-time matriculated undergraduates who enrolled in 2017, 5,640 applied for aid, 3,630 were judged to have need, 137 had their need fully met. 30 Federal Work-Study jobs (averaging $49,712). 10 state and other part-time jobs (averaging $24,745). In 2017, 133 non-need-based awards were made. ***Average percent of need met:*** 57. ***Average financial aid package:*** $7934. ***Average need-based loan:*** $2985. ***Average need-based gift aid:*** $4059. ***Average non-need-based aid:*** $1524.

APPLYING
Options: electronic application.

CONTACT
Ms. Amy Webb, Enrollment Services and Navigation Director, Midland College, 3600 North Garfield, Midland, TX 79705-6399. *Phone:* 432-685-4816. *E-mail:* amyw@midland.edu.

Midwestern State University

Wichita Falls, Texas

http://www.mwsu.edu/

CONTACT
Ms. Leah Vineyard, Interim Director of Admissions, Midwestern State University, 3410 Taft Boulevard, Wichita Falls, TX 76308. *Phone:* 940-397-4343. *Toll-free phone:* 800-842-1922. *Fax:* 940-397-4672. *E-mail:* leah.vineyard@mwsu.edu.

National American University

Austin, Texas

http://www.national.edu/

CONTACT
National American University, 13801 Burnet Road, Suite 300, Austin, TX 78727. *Toll-free phone:* 888-628-8392.

National American University

Georgetown, Texas

http://www.national.edu/

CONTACT
National American University, 1015 West University Avenue, Suite 700, Georgetown, TX 78628. *Toll-free phone:* 888-628-8392.

National American University

Houston, Texas

http://www.national.edu/

CONTACT
National American University, 11511 Katy Freeway, Suite 200, Houston, TX 77079. *Toll-free phone:* 855-455-8029.

National American University

Lewisville, Texas

http://www.national.edu/

CONTACT
National American University, 475 State Highway 121 Bypass, Suite 150, Lewisville, TX 75067. *Toll-free phone:* 800-548-0605.

National American University

Mesquite, Texas

http://www.national.edu/

CONTACT
National American University, 18600 LBJ Freeway, Mesquite, TX 75150. *Toll-free phone:* 800-548-0605.

National American University

Richardson, Texas

http://www.national.edu/

CONTACT
National American University, 300 North Coit Road, Suite 225, Richardson, TX 75080. *Toll-free phone:* 800-548-0605.

North American University

Stafford, Texas

http://www.na.edu/

- **Independent** comprehensive, founded 2010
- **Urban** 12-acre campus with easy access to Houston, TX
- **Coed**
- **Minimally difficult** entrance level

FACULTY
Student/faculty ratio: 19:1.

ACADEMICS
Calendar: semesters. *Degrees:* bachelor's and master's.
Library: North American University Library. *Books:* 4,857 (physical), 168,629 (digital/electronic); *Serial titles:* 3 (physical), 2 (digital/electronic); *Databases:* 8. Weekly public service hours: 61; students can reserve study rooms.

STUDENT LIFE
Housing options: men-only, women-only. Campus housing is leased by the school.

Activities and organizations: Computer Science, Women's Computer Science, NAU Care Services, Student Athlete Association, Harmony Stallions Association.

Student services: personal/psychological counseling.

COSTS
Costs (2018–19) ***One-time required fee:*** $110. ***Comprehensive fee:*** $18,800 includes full-time tuition ($9450), mandatory fees ($450), and room and board ($8900). Full-time tuition and fees vary according to course load, degree level, and program. Part-time tuition: $475 per credit hour. Part-time tuition and fees vary according to course load, degree level, and program. No tuition increase for student's term of enrollment. ***Required fees:*** $225 per term part-time. ***College room only:*** $4500. Room and board charges vary according to board plan.

APPLYING
Standardized Tests *Recommended:* SAT or ACT (for admission).

Options: electronic application, early admission, deferred entrance.

Required: high school transcript, interview. ***Required for some:*** essay or personal statement, 1 letter of recommendation. ***Recommended:*** minimum 2.7 GPA.

CONTACT
Mr. Shawn Washington, Associate Director of Admissions, North American University, 11929 West Airport Boulevard, Stafford, TX 77477. *Phone:* 832-230-5555. *E-mail:* admissions@na.edu.

Our Lady of the Lake University

San Antonio, Texas

http://www.ollusa.edu/

- **Independent Roman Catholic** comprehensive, founded 1895
- **Urban** 75-acre campus with easy access to San Antonio, TX
- **Endowment** $27.7 million
- **Coed**
- 91% of applicants were admitted

FACULTY
Student/faculty ratio: 14:1.

ACADEMICS
Calendar: semesters plus summer sessions. *Degrees:* bachelor's, master's, and doctoral.
Library: The Sueltenfuss Library. *Books:* 82,924 (physical), 51,160 (digital/electronic); *Serial titles:* 16,651 (physical), 167,665 (digital/electronic); *Databases:* 96. Weekly public service hours: 95; study areas open 24 hours, 5–7 days a week.

STUDENT LIFE
Housing options: coed, women-only, special housing for students with disabilities. Campus housing is university owned.

Activities and organizations: drama/theater group, student-run newspaper, television station, choral group, First Year Connection, Kappa Delta Chi, Epsilon Sigma Alpha, Social Justice Organization, Higher Achievement Through Leadership Opportunities, national sororities.

Athletics Member NAIA.

Campus security: 24-hour emergency response devices and patrols, late-night transport/escort service, controlled dormitory access.

Student services: health clinic, personal/psychological counseling, women's center, veterans affairs office.

COSTS & FINANCIAL AID
Costs (2018–19) ***Comprehensive fee:*** $38,342 includes full-time tuition ($27,912), mandatory fees ($828), and room and board ($9602). Full-time tuition and fees vary according to course load and location. Part-time tuition: $895 per credit hour. Part-time tuition and fees vary according to course load and location. ***Required fees:*** $414 per term part-time. ***College room only:*** $5814. Room and board charges vary according to board plan and housing facility. ***Payment plans:*** installment, deferred payment.

Financial Aid Of all full-time matriculated undergraduates who enrolled in 2016, 1,084 applied for aid, 1,016 were judged to have need, 418 had their need fully met. In 2016, 108 non-need-based awards were made. ***Average percent of need met:*** 84. ***Average financial aid package:*** $22,549. ***Average need-based loan:*** $4785. ***Average need-based gift aid:*** $15,648. ***Average non-need-based aid:*** $8806. ***Average indebtedness upon graduation:*** $34,224.

APPLYING
Standardized Tests *Required:* SAT or ACT (for admission).

Options: early action.

Application fee: $35.

Required: high school transcript, minimum 2.0 GPA.

CONTACT
Shannon Tijerina, Assistant Director of Traditional Admissions, Our Lady of the Lake University, 411 Southwest 24th Street, San Antonio, TX 78207-4689. *Phone:* 210-434-6711 Ext. 4133. *Toll-free phone:* 800-436-6558. *Fax:* 210-431-4036. *E-mail:* sytijeria@lake.ollusa.edu.

Paul Quinn College

Dallas, Texas

http://www.pqc.edu/

CONTACT
Paul Quinn College, 3837 Simpson-Stuart Road, Dallas, TX 75241-4331. *Phone:* 214-379-5494. *Toll-free phone:* 877-346-1063.

Prairie View A&M University

Prairie View, Texas

http://www.pvamu.edu/

- **State-supported** university, founded 1878, part of Texas A&M University System
- **Small-town** 1502-acre campus with easy access to Houston
- **Endowment** $80.9 million
- **Coed** 8,531 undergraduate students, 93% full-time, 64% women, 36% men
- **Moderately difficult** entrance level, 74% of applicants were admitted

UNDERGRAD STUDENTS
7,953 full-time, 578 part-time. Students come from 40 states and territories; 26 other countries; 8% are from out of state; 84% Black or African American, non-Hispanic/Latino; 9% Hispanic/Latino; 2% Asian, non-Hispanic/Latino; 0.1% Native Hawaiian or other Pacific Islander, non-Hispanic/Latino; 0.2% American Indian or Alaska Native, non-Hispanic/Latino; 2% Two or more races, non-Hispanic/Latino; 0.2% Race/ethnicity unknown; 1% international; 6% transferred in; 45% live on campus.

Freshmen:
Admission: 7,158 applied, 5,321 admitted, 2,177 enrolled. ***Average high school GPA:*** 3.2. ***Test scores:*** SAT evidence-based reading and writing scores over 500: 45%; SAT math scores over 500: 38%; ACT scores over 18: 55%; SAT evidence-based reading and writing scores over 600: 7%; SAT math scores over 600: 5%; ACT scores over 24: 11%.
Retention: 74% of full-time freshmen returned.

FACULTY
Total: 506, 86% full-time, 37% with terminal degrees.
Student/faculty ratio: 18:1.

ACADEMICS
Calendar: semesters. *Degrees:* bachelor's, master's, doctoral, post-master's, and postbachelor's certificates.

Special study options: academic remediation for entering students, accelerated degree program, advanced placement credit, cooperative education, distance learning, double majors, honors programs, independent study, internships, off-campus study, part-time degree program, services for LD students, study abroad, summer session for credit. ***ROTC:*** Army (b), Navy (b), Air Force (c).

Computers: 3,500 computers/terminals are available on campus for general student use. Students can access the following: campus intranet, computer help desk, free student e-mail accounts, online (class) grades, online (class) registration, online (class) schedules. Campuswide network is available. 100% of college-owned or -operated housing units are wired for high-speed Internet access. Wireless service is available via entire campus.
Library: John B. Coleman Library plus 3 others. *Books:* 232,516 (physical), 344,581 (digital/electronic); *Serial titles:* 199 (physical); *Databases:* 23. Weekly public service hours: 97; students can reserve study rooms.

STUDENT LIFE
Housing options: men-only, women-only, special housing for students with disabilities. Campus housing is provided by a third party. Freshman applicants given priority for college housing.

Activities and organizations: drama/theater group, student-run newspaper, radio and television station, choral group, marching band, Student Government Association, Campus Activities Board, National Association for the Advancement of Colored People, National Society of Black Engineers, Peer Advisors to Leadership Students, national fraternities, national sororities.

Athletics Member NCAA, NAIA. All NCAA Division I except football (Division I-AA). ***Intercollegiate sports:*** baseball M(s), basketball M(s)/W(s), bowling W(s), cheerleading M(s)/W(s), cross-country running M(s)/W(s), golf M(s)/W(s)(c), soccer W(s), softball W(s), tennis M(s)/W(s), track and field M(s)/W(s), volleyball W(s). ***Intramural sports:*** basketball M/W, football M/W, rugby M/W, soccer M, swimming and diving M/W, tennis M/W, volleyball W, weight lifting M/W.

Campus security: 24-hour emergency response devices and patrols, late-night transport/escort service, controlled dormitory access.

Student services: health clinic, personal/psychological counseling, women's center, veterans affairs office.

COSTS & FINANCIAL AID

Costs (2019–20) ***One-time required fee:*** $40. ***Tuition:*** state resident $7043 full-time; nonresident $21,912 full-time. No tuition increase for student's term of enrollment. ***Required fees:*** $3743 full-time. ***Room and board:*** $8859; room only: $5890.

Financial Aid Of all full-time matriculated undergraduates who enrolled in 2017, 6,868 applied for aid, 6,347 were judged to have need, 659 had their need fully met. 576 Federal Work-Study jobs (averaging $2693). 37 state and other part-time jobs (averaging $2064). In 2017, 174 non-need-based awards were made. ***Average percent of need met:*** 72. ***Average financial aid package:*** $15,438. ***Average need-based loan:*** $7495. ***Average need-based gift aid:*** $8018. ***Average non-need-based aid:*** $6741. ***Average indebtedness upon graduation:*** $35,858. ***Financial aid deadline:*** 3/15.

APPLYING

Standardized Tests *Required:* SAT or ACT (for admission).

Options: electronic application, early admission, deferred entrance.

Application fee: $40.

Required: high school transcript, minimum 2.8 GPA.

Notification: 8/15 (freshmen), 8/15 (transfers).

CONTACT

Ms. Nicole Woods, Administrative Assistant, Prairie View A&M University, PO Box 519, MS #1009, Prairie View, TX 77446-0188. *Phone:* 936-261-1000. *E-mail:* admissions@pvamu.edu.

Rice University

Houston, Texas

http://www.rice.edu/

- **Independent** university, founded 1912
- **Urban** 300-acre campus with easy access to Houston
- **Endowment** $6.3 billion
- **Coed** 3,992 undergraduate students, 98% full-time, 48% women, 52% men
- **Most difficult** entrance level, 11% of applicants were admitted

UNDERGRAD STUDENTS

3,899 full-time, 93 part-time. Students come from 53 states and territories; 55 other countries; 53% are from out of state; 7% Black or African American, non-Hispanic/Latino; 15% Hispanic/Latino; 26% Asian, non-Hispanic/Latino; 0.2% Native Hawaiian or other Pacific Islander, non-Hispanic/Latino; 0.2% American Indian or Alaska Native, non-Hispanic/Latino; 4% Two or more races, non-Hispanic/Latino; 2% Race/ethnicity unknown; 12% international; 1% transferred in; 71% live on campus.

Freshmen:

Admission: 20,923 applied, 2,328 admitted, 958 enrolled. ***Test scores:*** SAT evidence-based reading and writing scores over 500: 100%; SAT math scores over 500: 100%; ACT scores over 18: 101%; SAT evidence-based reading and writing scores over 600: 96%; SAT math scores over 600: 97%; ACT scores over 24: 99%; SAT evidence-based reading and writing scores over 700: 77%; SAT math scores over 700: 88%; ACT scores over 30: 92%.

Retention: 97% of full-time freshmen returned.

FACULTY

Total: 879, 78% full-time, 90% with terminal degrees.

Student/faculty ratio: 6:1.

ACADEMICS

Calendar: semesters. *Degrees:* bachelor's, master's, and doctoral.

Special study options: accelerated degree program, advanced placement credit, double majors, English as a second language, honors programs, independent study, internships, off-campus study, services for LD students, student-designed majors, study abroad, summer session for credit. ***ROTC:*** Army (c), Navy (b), Air Force (c).

Computers: 245 computers/terminals are available on campus for general student use. Students can access the following: campus intranet, computer help desk, free student e-mail accounts, online (class) grades, online (class) registration, online (class) schedules. Campuswide network is available. 100% of college-owned or -operated housing units are wired for high-speed Internet access. Wireless service is available via entire campus.

Library: Fondren Library. *Books:* 3.0 million (physical), 51,950 (digital/electronic); *Serial titles:* 172,172 (digital/electronic).

STUDENT LIFE

Housing options: coed. Campus housing is university owned. Freshman applicants given priority for college housing.

Activities and organizations: drama/theater group, student-run newspaper, radio and television station, choral group, marching band, Drama Club, Community service/volunteer program, intramural sports, College government, Marching Owl Band.

Athletics Member NCAA. All Division I except football (Division I-A). ***Intercollegiate sports:*** badminton M(c)/W(c), baseball M(s), basketball M(s)/W(s), cheerleading W, crew M(c)/W(c), cross-country running M(s)/W(s), equestrian sports W(c), fencing M(c)/W(c), golf M(s), lacrosse M(c), rugby M(c)/W(c), sailing M(c)/W(c), soccer M(c)/W(s), swimming and diving W(s), tennis M(s)/W(s), track and field M(s)/W(s), ultimate Frisbee M(c)/W(c), volleyball M(c)/W(s), water polo M(c)/W(c). ***Intramural sports:*** badminton M/W, basketball M/W, cross-country running M/W, football M, golf M/W, racquetball M/W, soccer M/W, softball M/W, swimming and diving M/W, table tennis M/W, tennis M/W, track and field M/W, ultimate Frisbee M/W, volleyball M/W, water polo M/W.

Campus security: 24-hour emergency response devices and patrols, late-night transport/escort service, controlled dormitory access.

Student services: health clinic, personal/psychological counseling, women's center.

COSTS & FINANCIAL AID

Costs (2019–20) ***Comprehensive fee:*** $63,252 includes full-time tuition ($48,330), mandatory fees ($782), and room and board ($14,140). Part-time tuition: $2014 per credit hour. ***College room only:*** $9700.

Financial Aid Of all full-time matriculated undergraduates who enrolled in 2017, 2,818 applied for aid, 1,529 were judged to have need, 1,525 had their need fully met. In 2017, 437 non-need-based awards were made. ***Average percent of need met:*** 100. ***Average financial aid package:*** $44,799. ***Average need-based loan:*** $3237. ***Average need-based gift aid:*** $40,285. ***Average non-need-based aid:*** $20,779. ***Average indebtedness upon graduation:*** $26,556. ***Financial aid deadline:*** 4/15.

APPLYING

Standardized Tests *Required:* SAT or ACT (for admission). *Recommended:* SAT Subject Tests (for admission).

Options: electronic application, early decision, deferred entrance.

Application fee: $75.

Required: essay or personal statement, high school transcript, 2 letters of recommendation. ***Required for some:*** portfolio for architecture, audition for music. ***Recommended:*** interview.

Application deadlines: 1/1 (freshmen), 3/15 (transfers).

Early decision deadline: 11/1.

Notification: 4/1 (freshmen), continuous until 5/15 (transfers), 12/15 (early decision).

CONTACT

Yvonne Romero Da Silva, Vice President for Enrollment, Rice University, 6100 Main Street, PO Box 1892, Houston, TX 77251-1892. *Phone:* 713-348-RICE. *E-mail:* admi@rice.edu.

Rio Grande Bible Institute

Edinburg, Texas

http://www.riogrande.edu/

CONTACT

David Loyola, Director of Admissions, Rio Grande Bible Institute, 4300 S US Hwy 281, Edinburg, TX 78539. *Phone:* 956-380-8100. *Fax:* 956-380-8256. *E-mail:* admisiones@riogrande.edu.

St. Edward's University

Austin, Texas

http://www.stedwards.edu/

CONTACT

Ms. Kelsey McClure, Administrative Coordinator, St. Edward's University, 3001 South Congress Avenue, Austin, TX 78704. *Phone:* 512-448-8500. *Toll-free phone:* 800-555-0164. *Fax:* 512-464-8877. *E-mail:* seu.admit@stedwards.edu.

St. Mary's University

San Antonio, Texas

http://www.stmarytx.edu/

- **Independent Roman Catholic** comprehensive, founded 1852
- **Urban** 135-acre campus with easy access to San Antonio
- **Endowment** $183.0 million
- **Coed** 2,373 undergraduate students, 95% full-time, 55% women, 45% men
- **Moderately difficult** entrance level, 75% of applicants were admitted

UNDERGRAD STUDENTS

2,262 full-time, 111 part-time. Students come from 32 states and territories; 34 other countries; 8% are from out of state; 3% Black or African American, non-Hispanic/Latino; 67% Hispanic/Latino; 2% Asian, non-Hispanic/Latino; 0.2% American Indian or Alaska Native, non-Hispanic/Latino; 1% Two or more races, non-Hispanic/Latino; 3% Race/ethnicity unknown; 8% international; 4% transferred in; 56% live on campus.

Freshmen:

Admission: 5,350 applied, 4,011 admitted, 640 enrolled. ***Average high school GPA:*** 3.6. ***Test scores:*** SAT evidence-based reading and writing scores over 500: 92%; SAT math scores over 500: 87%; ACT scores over 18: 98%; SAT evidence-based reading and writing scores over 600: 43%; SAT math scores over 600: 34%; ACT scores over 24: 46%; SAT evidence-based reading and writing scores over 700: 7%; SAT math scores over 700: 7%; ACT scores over 30: 9%.

Retention: 75% of full-time freshmen returned.

FACULTY

Total: 404, 54% full-time, 73% with terminal degrees.

Student/faculty ratio: 11:1.

ACADEMICS

Calendar: semesters. *Degrees:* bachelor's, master's, doctoral, post-master's, and postbachelor's certificates.

Special study options: academic remediation for entering students, adult/continuing education programs, advanced placement credit, cooperative education, distance learning, double majors, English as a second language, honors programs, independent study, internships, off-campus study, part-time degree program, services for LD students, study abroad, summer session for credit. ***ROTC:*** Army (b), Air Force (c).

Computers: 200 computers/terminals and 125 ports are available on campus for general student use. Students can access the following: campus intranet, computer help desk, free student e-mail accounts, online (class) grades, online (class) registration, online (class) schedules. Campuswide network is available. 100% of college-owned or -operated housing units are wired for high-speed Internet access. Wireless service is available via entire campus.

Library: Louis J. Blume Library plus 1 other. *Books:* 207,131 (physical), 479,714 (digital/electronic); *Serial titles:* 429 (physical), 99,503 (digital/electronic); *Databases:* 134. Weekly public service hours: 100.

STUDENT LIFE

Housing options: on-campus residence required for freshman year; coed, special housing for students with disabilities. Campus housing is university owned. Freshman applicants given priority for college housing.

Activities and organizations: drama/theater group, student-run newspaper, choral group, Alpha Phi Omega (Professional Service Fraternity), Beta Beta Beta Biological Honor Society, Delta Sigma Pi (Professional Business Fraternity), Society of Hispanic Engineers, Pre-Medical Society, national fraternities, national sororities.

Athletics Member NCAA. All Division II. ***Intercollegiate sports:*** baseball M(s), basketball M(s)/W(s), cheerleading M/W, golf M(s), soccer M(s)/W(s), softball W, tennis M(s)/W(s), volleyball W(s). ***Intramural sports:*** badminton M/W, basketball M/W, football M/W, racquetball M/W, rock climbing M/W, sand volleyball M/W, soccer M/W, softball M/W, swimming and diving M/W, table tennis M/W, tennis M/W, ultimate Frisbee M(c)/W(c), volleyball M/W.

Campus security: 24-hour emergency response devices and patrols, late-night transport/escort service, controlled dormitory access.

Student services: health clinic, personal/psychological counseling.

COSTS & FINANCIAL AID

Costs (2019–20) ***Comprehensive fee:*** $42,860 includes full-time tuition ($31,170), mandatory fees ($970), and room and board ($10,720). Part-time tuition: $970 per credit hour. ***Required fees:*** $270 per term part-time. ***College room only:*** $6860.

Financial Aid Of all full-time matriculated undergraduates who enrolled in 2018, 1,813 applied for aid, 1,598 were judged to have need, 196 had their need fully met. 447 Federal Work-Study jobs (averaging $2087). 61 state and other part-time jobs (averaging $2430). In 2018, 471 non-need-based awards were made. ***Average percent of need met:*** 77. ***Average financial aid package:*** $28,040. ***Average need-based loan:*** $4235. ***Average need-based gift aid:*** $22,804. ***Average non-need-based aid:*** $18,709. ***Average indebtedness upon graduation:*** $35,111. ***Financial aid deadline:*** 6/1.

APPLYING

Standardized Tests *Required:* SAT or ACT (for admission).

Options: electronic application, deferred entrance.

Required: essay or personal statement, high school transcript, minimum 2.5 GPA, 1 letter of recommendation. ***Required for some:*** interview.

Application deadlines: rolling (freshmen), rolling (transfers).

Notification: continuous (freshmen), continuous (transfers).

CONTACT

Ms. Melissa Romero, Associate Director, Freshman Admission, St. Mary's University, One Camino Santa Maria, Box #3, San Antonio, TX 78228. *Phone:* 210-436-3126. *Toll-free phone:* 800-367-7868. *Fax:* 210-431-6742. *E-mail:* uadm@stmarytx.edu.

Sam Houston State University

Huntsville, Texas

http://www.shsu.edu/

- **State-supported** university, founded 1879, part of Texas State University System
- **Small-town** campus with easy access to Houston
- **Endowment** $96.5 million
- **Coed**
- **Moderately difficult** entrance level

FACULTY

Student/faculty ratio: 23:1.

ACADEMICS

Calendar: semesters. *Degrees:* bachelor's, master's, doctoral, and postbachelor's certificates.

Library: Newton Gresham Library. Students can reserve study rooms.

STUDENT LIFE

Housing options: on-campus residence required for freshman year; coed, women-only, special housing for students with disabilities. Campus housing is university owned and is provided by a third party. Freshman campus housing is guaranteed.

Activities and organizations: drama/theater group, student-run newspaper, radio and television station, choral group, marching band, national fraternities, national sororities.

Athletics Member NCAA. All Division I except football (Division I-AA).

Campus security: 24-hour emergency response devices and patrols, student patrols, late-night transport/escort service, controlled dormitory access.

Student services: health clinic, personal/psychological counseling, legal services, veterans affairs office.

COSTS & FINANCIAL AID
Costs (2018–19) ***Tuition:*** state resident $7020 full-time, $234 per credit hour part-time; nonresident $19,470 full-time, $649 per credit hour part-time. Full-time tuition and fees vary according to course load and location. Part-time tuition and fees vary according to course load and location. No tuition increase for student's term of enrollment. ***Required fees:*** $3163 full-time. ***Room and board:*** $9180; room only: $5240. Room and board charges vary according to board plan and housing facility.

Financial Aid Of all full-time matriculated undergraduates who enrolled in 2016, 11,217 applied for aid, 9,556 were judged to have need, 895 had their need fully met. In 2016, 476 non-need-based awards were made. ***Average percent of need met:*** 77. ***Average financial aid package:*** $11,263. ***Average need-based loan:*** $7582. ***Average need-based gift aid:*** $7560. ***Average non-need-based aid:*** $2624. ***Average indebtedness upon graduation:*** $27,920.

APPLYING
Standardized Tests *Required:* SAT or ACT (for admission).

Options: electronic application, early admission.

Application fee: $45.

Required: high school transcript.

CONTACT
Ms. Angie Taylor, Director of Admissions, Sam Houston State University, Box 2418, Huntsville, TX 77341. *Phone:* 936-294-1845. *Toll-free phone:* 866-232-7528 Ext. 1828. *Fax:* 936-294-3758. *E-mail:* agb003@shsu.edu.

Schreiner University

Kerrville, Texas

http://www.schreiner.edu/

- **Independent Presbyterian** comprehensive, founded 1923
- **Small-town** 211-acre campus with easy access to San Antonio, Austin
- **Endowment** $69.2 million
- **Coed**
- **Moderately difficult** entrance level

FACULTY
Student/faculty ratio: 13:1.

ACADEMICS
Calendar: semesters. *Degrees:* certificates, associate, bachelor's, and master's.
Library: W. M. Logan Library. *Books:* 80,478 (physical); *Serial titles:* 404 (physical). Weekly public service hours: 30; students can reserve study rooms.

STUDENT LIFE
Housing options: on-campus residence required through junior year; coed, special housing for students with disabilities. Campus housing is university owned. Freshman campus housing is guaranteed.

Activities and organizations: drama/theater group, student-run newspaper, choral group, Student Senate, Greek Life, Campus Ministry, honor societies, Hall Councils, national fraternities, national sororities.

Athletics Member NCAA. All Division III.

Campus security: 24-hour emergency response devices and patrols, student patrols, late-night transport/escort service, controlled dormitory access.

Student services: health clinic, personal/psychological counseling.

COSTS & FINANCIAL AID
Costs (2018–19) ***Comprehensive fee:*** $38,468 includes full-time tuition ($25,990), mandatory fees ($1970), and room and board ($10,508). Full-time tuition and fees vary according to course load, location, and program. Part-time tuition: $1111 per credit hour. Part-time tuition and fees vary according to course load and program. ***Required fees:*** $1290 per year part-time, $645 per term part-time. ***College room only:*** $5156. Room and board charges vary according to board plan and housing facility.

Financial Aid Of all full-time matriculated undergraduates who enrolled in 2017, 949 applied for aid, 845 were judged to have need, 116 had their need fully met. In 2017, 97 non-need-based awards were made. ***Average percent of need met:*** 71. ***Average financial aid package:*** $22,685. ***Average need-based loan:*** $4174. ***Average need-based gift aid:*** $7966. ***Average non-need-based aid:*** $13,790. ***Average indebtedness upon graduation:*** $37,071. ***Financial aid deadline:*** 5/15.

APPLYING
Standardized Tests *Required:* SAT or ACT (for admission).

Options: electronic application, deferred entrance.

Application fee: $25.

Required: high school transcript.

CONTACT
Caroline Randall, Director of Admissions, Schreiner University, 2100 Memorial Boulevard, Kerrville, TX 78028. *Phone:* 800-343-4919. *Toll-free phone:* 800-343-4919. *E-mail:* carandall@schreiner.edu.

★ Southern Methodist University

Dallas, Texas

http://www.smu.edu/

- **Independent** university, founded 1911, affiliated with United Methodist Church
- **Urban** 234-acre campus with easy access to Dallas-Fort Worth
- **Endowment** $1.5 billion
- **Coed**
- **Moderately difficult** entrance level

FACULTY
Student/faculty ratio: 11:1.

ACADEMICS
Calendar: semesters. *Degrees:* bachelor's, master's, doctoral, post-master's, and postbachelor's certificates.
Library: Fondren Library plus 7 others. *Books:* 3.0 million (physical), 1.2 million (digital/electronic); *Serial titles:* 16,580 (physical), 139,891 (digital/electronic); *Databases:* 667. Weekly public service hours: 150; study areas open 24 hours, 5–7 days a week; students can reserve study rooms.

STUDENT LIFE
Housing options: on-campus residence required through sophomore year; coed, special housing for students with disabilities. Campus housing is university owned, leased by the school and is provided by a third party. Freshman campus housing is guaranteed.

Activities and organizations: drama/theater group, student-run newspaper, radio and television station, choral group, marching band, Program Council, Student Senate, Student Foundation, Residence Hall Association, SPARC (Students Promoting Awareness, Responsibility, and Citizenship), national fraternities, national sororities.

Athletics Member NCAA. All Division I except football (Division I-A).

Campus security: 24-hour emergency response devices and patrols, late-night transport/escort service, controlled dormitory access.

Student services: health clinic, personal/psychological counseling, women's center, veterans affairs office.

COSTS & FINANCIAL AID
Costs (2018–19) ***Comprehensive fee:*** $71,338 includes full-time tuition ($48,365), mandatory fees ($6128), and room and board ($16,845). Part-time tuition: $2020 per credit hour. Part-time tuition and fees vary according to course load. ***Room and board:*** Room and board charges vary according to board plan and housing facility. ***Payment plans:*** tuition prepayment, installment.

Financial Aid Of all full-time matriculated undergraduates who enrolled in 2018, 2,443 applied for aid, 1,964 were judged to have need, 761 had their need fully met. In 2018, 2493 non-need-based awards were made. ***Average percent of need met:*** 86. ***Average financial aid package:*** $44,493. ***Average need-based loan:*** $4200. ***Average need-based gift aid:*** $21,799. ***Average non-need-based aid:*** $27,283. ***Average indebtedness upon graduation:*** $38,086.

APPLYING
Standardized Tests *Required:* SAT or ACT (for admission). *Required for some:* SAT Subject Tests (for admission).

Options: electronic application, early decision, early action, deferred entrance.

Application fee: $60.

Required: high school transcript, minimum 2.0 GPA, 1 letter of recommendation, statement of good standing from prior institution(s). ***Recommended:*** essay or personal statement, minimum 2.7 GPA.

CONTACT
Ms. Elena Hicks, Dean of Undergraduate Admission, Southern Methodist University, PO Box 750181, Dallas, TX 75275-0181. *Phone:* 214-768-3417. *Toll-free phone:* 800-323-0672. *Fax:* 214-768-1083. *E-mail:* ugadmission@smu.edu.

See below for display ad and page 1114 for the College Close-Up.

South Texas College
McAllen, Texas
http://www.southtexascollege.edu/

CONTACT
Mr. Matthew Hebbard, Director of Enrollment Services and Registrar, South Texas College, 3201 West Pecan, McAllen, TX 78501. *Phone:* 956-872-2147. *Toll-free phone:* 800-742-7822. *E-mail:* mshebbar@southtexascollege.edu.

South University
Round Rock, Texas
http://www.southuniversity.edu/austin.aspx

CONTACT
Director of Admissions, South University, 1220 West Louis Henna Boulevard, Round Rock, TX 78681. *Phone:* 512-516-8800. *Toll-free phone:* 877-659-5706. *Fax:* 512-516-8680.

Southwestern Adventist University
Keene, Texas
http://www.swau.edu/

- **Independent Seventh-day Adventist** comprehensive, founded 1894
- **Small-town** 150-acre campus with easy access to Dallas-Fort Worth
- **Endowment** $11.4 million
- **Coed**
- **Minimally difficult** entrance level

FACULTY
Student/faculty ratio: 12:1.

ACADEMICS
Calendar: semesters. *Degrees:* certificates, associate, bachelor's, and master's.
Library: Chan Shun Centennial Library. *Books:* 90,431 (physical), 29,515 (digital/electronic); *Serial titles:* 5,000 (digital/electronic); *Databases:* 85. Weekly public service hours: 60; students can reserve study rooms.

STUDENT LIFE
Housing options: men-only, women-only, cooperative. Campus housing is university owned. Freshman campus housing is guaranteed.

Activities and organizations: drama/theater group, student-run newspaper, radio and television station, choral group, Student Association, Enactus (to enable progress through entrepreneurial action), Education/Psychology Club, Theology Club, Nursing Club.

Athletics Member USCAA.

Campus security: 24-hour emergency response devices, student patrols, controlled dormitory access.

Student services: health clinic, personal/psychological counseling.

COSTS
Costs (2018–19) ***Comprehensive fee:*** $29,164 includes full-time tuition ($20,904), mandatory fees ($660), and room and board ($7600). Full-time tuition and fees vary according to program. Part-time tuition: $871 per semester hour. Part-time tuition and fees vary according to program.

Required fees: $660 per term part-time. ***College room only:*** $3800. Room and board charges vary according to board plan.

APPLYING
Standardized Tests *Required:* SAT or ACT (for admission).

Options: electronic application, early admission, deferred entrance.

Application fee: $25.

Required: high school transcript, minimum 2.5 GPA. ***Required for some:*** essay or personal statement, 1 letter of recommendation, interview.

CONTACT
Ms. Rahneeka Hazelton, Director of Admissions, Southwestern Adventist University, 100 West Hillcrest, Keene, TX 76059. *Phone:* 817-202-6733. *Toll-free phone:* 800-433-2240. *E-mail:* rahneeka@swau.edu.

Southwestern Assemblies of God University
Waxahachie, Texas
http://www.sagu.edu/

- **Independent** comprehensive, founded 1927, affiliated with Assemblies of God
- **Small-town** 70-acre campus with easy access to Dallas-Fort Worth
- **Endowment** $10.3 million
- **Coed**
- **Noncompetitive** entrance level

FACULTY
Student/faculty ratio: 16:1.

ACADEMICS
Calendar: semesters. *Degrees:* associate, bachelor's, and master's.
Library: P. C. Nelson Memorial Library plus 1 other. *Books:* 100,582 (physical), 256 (digital/electronic); *Serial titles:* 414 (physical), 13,284 (digital/electronic); *Databases:* 70. Weekly public service hours: 90; students can reserve study rooms.

STUDENT LIFE
Housing options: on-campus residence required through senior year; coed, women-only. Campus housing is university owned. Freshman campus housing is guaranteed.

Activities and organizations: drama/theater group, student-run newspaper, choral group, Student Congress, Southwestern Missions Association, Street Hope, Gold Jackets, Women in Ministry.

Athletics Member NAIA, NCCAA.

Campus security: 24-hour patrols, late-night transport/escort service, controlled dormitory access, camera surveillance, 24-hour dispatch monitored fire alarm systems (offsite).

Student services: health clinic, personal/psychological counseling.

COSTS & FINANCIAL AID
Costs (2018–19) ***Comprehensive fee:*** $28,452 includes full-time tuition ($19,992), mandatory fees ($960), and room and board ($7500). Full-time tuition and fees vary according to course load, degree level, and location. Part-time tuition and fees vary according to course load, degree level, and location. ***Room and board:*** Room and board charges vary according to board plan, housing facility, and location.

Financial Aid Of all full-time matriculated undergraduates who enrolled in 2000, 1,116 applied for aid, 1,002 were judged to have need, 110 had their need fully met. 178 Federal Work-Study jobs (averaging $3278). 7 state and other part-time jobs (averaging $890). In 2000, 316 non-need-based awards were made. ***Average percent of need met:*** 64. ***Average financial aid package:*** $6728. ***Average need-based loan:*** $3177. ***Average need-based gift aid:*** $3511. ***Average indebtedness upon graduation:*** $13,938. ***Financial aid deadline:*** 7/1.

APPLYING
Standardized Tests *Required:* SAT or ACT (for admission). *Recommended:* ACT (for admission).

Options: electronic application.

Application fee: $35.

Required: essay or personal statement, high school transcript, minimum 2.0 GPA, 1 letter of recommendation.

CONTACT
Mr. Joshua Martin, Assistant Dean of Admissions, Southwestern Assemblies of God University, 1200 Sycamore Street, Waxahachie, TX 75165. *Phone:* 972-825-4821. *Toll-free phone:* 888-937-7248. *E-mail:* jmartin@sagu.edu.

Southwestern Christian College
Terrell, Texas
http://www.swcc.edu/

CONTACT
Admissions Department, Southwestern Christian College, Box 10, 200 Bowser Street, Terrell, TX 75160. *Phone:* 214-524-3341.

Southwestern University
Georgetown, Texas
http://www.southwestern.edu/

- **Independent Methodist** 4-year, founded 1840
- **Suburban** 700-acre campus with easy access to Austin
- **Endowment** $281.5 million
- **Coed** 1,430 undergraduate students, 99% full-time, 55% women, 45% men
- **Very difficult** entrance level, 45% of applicants were admitted

UNDERGRAD STUDENTS
1,416 full-time, 14 part-time. Students come from 34 states and territories; 12 other countries; 9% are from out of state; 5% Black or African American, non-Hispanic/Latino; 24% Hispanic/Latino; 3% Asian, non-Hispanic/Latino; 0.2% American Indian or Alaska Native, non-Hispanic/Latino; 4% Two or more races, non-Hispanic/Latino; 0.9% Race/ethnicity unknown; 1% international; 3% transferred in; 78% live on campus.

Freshmen:
Admission: 4,551 applied, 2,049 admitted, 442 enrolled. ***Test scores:*** SAT evidence-based reading and writing scores over 500: 97%; SAT math scores over 500: 97%; ACT scores over 18: 99%; SAT evidence-based reading and writing scores over 600: 69%; SAT math scores over 600: 49%; ACT scores over 24: 72%; SAT evidence-based reading and writing scores over 700: 17%; SAT math scores over 700: 12%; ACT scores over 30: 22%.

Retention: 81% of full-time freshmen returned.

FACULTY
Total: 144, 76% full-time, 93% with terminal degrees.

Student/faculty ratio: 11:1.

ACADEMICS
Calendar: semesters. *Degree:* bachelor's.

Special study options: advanced placement credit, double majors, honors programs, independent study, internships, off-campus study, services for LD students, student-designed majors, study abroad, summer session for credit. ***ROTC:*** Air Force (c).

Unusual degree programs: 3-2 engineering with Engineering school accredited by the Accreditation Board for Engineering and Technology (ABET).

Computers: 410 computers/terminals are available on campus for general student use. Students can access the following: campus intranet, computer help desk, free student e-mail accounts, online (class) grades, online (class) registration, online (class) schedules, transcripts. Campuswide network is available. 100% of college-owned or -operated housing units are wired for high-speed Internet access. Wireless service is available via entire campus.
Library: A. Frank Smith, Jr. Library Center. *Books:* 267,609 (physical), 566,353 (digital/electronic); *Serial titles:* 245 (physical), 73,126 (digital/electronic); *Databases:* 156. Weekly public service hours: 90; study areas open 24 hours, 5–7 days a week.

STUDENT LIFE
Housing options: on-campus residence required through sophomore year; coed, men-only, women-only, special housing for students with disabilities. Campus housing is university owned. Freshman campus housing is guaranteed.

Activities and organizations: drama/theater group, student-run newspaper, radio station, choral group, Students for Environmental Activism and Knowledge (SEAK), Alpha Phi Omega, Women's Panhellenic, Men's IFC, Coalition for Diversity and Social Justice, national fraternities, national sororities.

Athletics Member NCAA. All Division III. ***Intercollegiate sports:*** baseball M, basketball M/W, cross-country running M/W, football M, golf M/W, lacrosse M/W, soccer M/W, softball W, swimming and diving M/W, tennis M/W, track and field M/W, volleyball W. ***Intramural sports:*** basketball M/W, cheerleading M(c)/W(c), fencing M(c), field hockey W(c), football M/W, sand volleyball M/W, soccer M/W, table tennis M/W, ultimate Frisbee M(c)/W(c), volleyball M/W.

Campus security: 24-hour emergency response devices and patrols, late-night transport/escort service, controlled dormitory access.

Student services: health clinic, personal/psychological counseling, women's center.

COSTS & FINANCIAL AID

Costs (2019–20) ***Comprehensive fee:*** $55,880 includes full-time tuition ($43,560) and room and board ($12,320). Part-time tuition: $1815 per credit hour. ***College room only:*** $6670.

Financial Aid Of all full-time matriculated undergraduates who enrolled in 2018, 1,059 applied for aid, 903 were judged to have need, 244 had their need fully met. 219 Federal Work-Study jobs (averaging $2199). 433 state and other part-time jobs (averaging $2499). In 2018, 500 non-need-based awards were made. ***Average percent of need met:*** 87. ***Average financial aid package:*** $37,110. ***Average need-based loan:*** $4425. ***Average need-based gift aid:*** $31,848. ***Average non-need-based aid:*** $22,521. ***Average indebtedness upon graduation:*** $34,133.

APPLYING

Standardized Tests *Required:* SAT or ACT (for admission).

Options: electronic application, early admission, early decision, early action, deferred entrance.

Required: essay or personal statement, high school transcript, 1 letter of recommendation, counselor recommendation. ***Recommended:*** interview.

Application deadlines: 2/1 (freshmen), 2/1 (out-of-state freshmen), 4/1 (transfers), 12/1 (early action).

Early decision deadline: 11/1.

Notification: 4/1 (freshmen), 4/1 (out-of-state freshmen), 7/1 (transfers), 12/1 (early decision), 3/1 (early action).

CONTACT

Mrs. Christine Bowman, Dean of Enrollment Services, Southwestern University, 1001 East University Avenue, Georgetown, TX 78626. *Phone:* 512-863-1200. *Toll-free phone:* 800-252-3166. *Fax:* 512-863-9601. *E-mail:* admission@southwestern.edu.

Southwest University at El Paso

El Paso, Texas

http://southwestuniversity.edu/

CONTACT

Southwest University at El Paso, 1414 Geronimo Drive, El Paso, TX 79925.

Stephen F. Austin State University

Nacogdoches, Texas

http://www.sfasu.edu/

- **State-supported** comprehensive, founded 1923
- **Small-town** 419-acre campus
- **Endowment** $81.7 million
- **Coed**
- **Moderately difficult** entrance level

FACULTY

Student/faculty ratio: 19:1.

ACADEMICS

Calendar: semesters. *Degrees:* bachelor's, master's, and doctoral.

Library: Ralph W. Steen Library. *Books:* 685,436 (physical), 341,357 (digital/electronic); *Serial titles:* 5,582 (physical), 119,163 (digital/electronic); *Databases:* 265. Weekly public service hours: 99; students can reserve study rooms.

STUDENT LIFE

Housing options: on-campus residence required through sophomore year; coed, men-only, women-only, special housing for students with disabilities. Campus housing is university owned and is provided by a third party. Freshman campus housing is guaranteed.

Activities and organizations: drama/theater group, student-run newspaper, radio and television station, choral group, marching band, Residence Hall Association, Baptist Student Ministries, Greek Life, Student Activities Association, Student Government Association, national fraternities, national sororities.

Athletics Member NCAA. All Division I except football (Division I-AA).

Campus security: 24-hour emergency response devices and patrols, student patrols, late-night transport/escort service, controlled dormitory access.

Student services: health clinic, personal/psychological counseling, veterans affairs office.

COSTS & FINANCIAL AID

Costs (2018–19) ***Tuition:*** state resident $7260 full-time, $242 per credit hour part-time; nonresident $19,710 full-time, $657 per credit hour part-time. Full-time tuition and fees vary according to course load, degree level, and location. Part-time tuition and fees vary according to course load, degree level, and location. No tuition increase for student's term of enrollment. ***Required fees:*** $183 per credit hour part-time. ***Room and board:*** $8964. Room and board charges vary according to board plan and housing facility.

Financial Aid Of all full-time matriculated undergraduates who enrolled in 2018, 8,177 applied for aid, 6,661 were judged to have need, 938 had their need fully met. In 2018, 830 non-need-based awards were made. ***Average percent of need met:*** 60. ***Average financial aid package:*** $11,829. ***Average need-based loan:*** $4626. ***Average need-based gift aid:*** $7359. ***Average non-need-based aid:*** $2748. ***Average indebtedness upon graduation:*** $30,101.

APPLYING

Standardized Tests *Required:* SAT or ACT (for admission).

Options: electronic application.

Application fee: $45.

Required: high school transcript.

CONTACT

Mr. Kevin Davis, Associate Director of Admissions, Stephen F. Austin State University, PO Box 13051, SFA Station, Nacogdoches, TX 75962. *Phone:* 936-468-2504. *Toll-free phone:* 800-731-2902. *Fax:* 936-468-3849. *E-mail:* admissions@sfasu.edu.

Strayer University–Cedar Hill Campus

Cedar Hill, Texas

http://www.strayer.edu/texas/cedar-hill/

CONTACT

Strayer University–Cedar Hill Campus, 610 Uptown Boulevard, Suite 3500, Cedar Hill, TX 75104. *Toll-free phone:* 888-311-0355.

Strayer University–North Austin Campus

Austin, Texas

http://www.strayer.edu/texas/north-austin/

CONTACT

Strayer University–North Austin Campus, 8501 North Mopac Expressway, Suite 100, Austin, TX 78759. *Toll-free phone:* 888-311-0355.

Strayer University–North Dallas Campus

Farmers Branch, Texas

http://www.strayer.edu/texas/north-dallas

CONTACT

Strayer University–North Dallas Campus, 2711 LBJ Freeway, Suite 450, Farmers Branch, TX 75234-7315.

Strayer University–Northwest Houston Campus

Houston, Texas

http://www.strayer.edu/texas/northwest-houston/

CONTACT

Strayer University–Northwest Houston Campus, 10343 Sam Houston Park Drive, Suite 110, Houston, TX 77064. *Toll-free phone:* 888-311-0355.

Strayer University–San Antonio Campus

San Antonio, Texas

http://www.strayer.edu/texas/san-antonio

CONTACT

Strayer University–San Antonio Campus, 40 NE Loop 410, Suite 500, San Antonio, TX 78216.

Strayer University–Stafford Campus

Stafford, Texas

http://www.strayer.edu/texas/stafford

CONTACT

Strayer University–Stafford Campus, 12603 Southwest Freeway, Suite 400, Stafford, TX 77477.

Sul Ross State University

Alpine, Texas

http://www.sulross.edu/

CONTACT

Sul Ross State University, PO Box C - 114, Alpine, TX 79832. *Phone:* 432-837-8050. *Toll-free phone:* 888-722-7778.

Tarleton State University

Stephenville, Texas

http://www.tarleton.edu/

- **State-supported** comprehensive, founded 1899, part of Texas A&M University System
- **Small-town** 175-acre campus with easy access to Fort Worth
- **Endowment** $29.8 million
- **Coed**
- **Moderately difficult** entrance level

FACULTY

Student/faculty ratio: 17:1.

ACADEMICS

Calendar: semesters. *Degrees:* certificates, associate, bachelor's, master's, and doctoral.

Library: Dick Smith Library plus 1 other. Students can reserve study rooms.

STUDENT LIFE

Housing options: on-campus residence required through sophomore year; coed, men-only, women-only, cooperative. Campus housing is university owned and leased by the school. Freshman campus housing is guaranteed.

Activities and organizations: drama/theater group, student-run newspaper, radio station, choral group, marching band, Student Government Association, Student Programming Association, Kappa Delta Rho, Delta Zeta, Chi Alpha, national fraternities, national sororities.

Athletics Member NCAA. All Division II.

Campus security: 24-hour emergency response devices and patrols, student patrols, late-night transport/escort service, controlled dormitory access.

Student services: health clinic, personal/psychological counseling, legal services, veterans affairs office.

COSTS & FINANCIAL AID

Costs (2018–19) ***Tuition:*** state resident $5025 full-time, $167 per credit hour part-time; nonresident $17,475 full-time, $583 per credit hour part-time. Full-time tuition and fees vary according to course load, degree level, program, and student level. Part-time tuition and fees vary according to course load, degree level, program, and student level. No tuition increase for student's term of enrollment. ***Required fees:*** $4066 full-time. ***Room and board:*** $9872; room only: $6220. Room and board charges vary according to board plan and housing facility.

Financial Aid Of all full-time matriculated undergraduates who enrolled in 2018, 6,605 applied for aid, 5,331 were judged to have need, 116 had their need fully met. ***Average percent of need met:*** 51. ***Average financial aid package:*** $9196. ***Average need-based loan:*** $4219. ***Average need-based gift aid:*** $6917. ***Average indebtedness upon graduation:*** $24,872. ***Financial aid deadline:*** 11/1.

APPLYING

Standardized Tests *Required:* SAT or ACT (for admission).

Options: electronic application, early action.

Application fee: $45.

Required: high school transcript.

CONTACT

Ms. Cindy Hess, Director of Undergraduate Admissions, Tarleton State University, Box T-0030, Tarleton Station, Stephenville, TX 76402. *Phone:* 254-968-9123. *Toll-free phone:* 800-687-8236. *Fax:* 254-968-9951. *E-mail:* uadm@tarleton.edu.

Texas A&M International University

Laredo, Texas

http://www.tamiu.edu/

- **State-supported** comprehensive, founded 1969, part of Texas A&M University System
- **Urban** 300-acre campus
- **Endowment** $52.1 million
- **Coed** 6,992 undergraduate students, 75% full-time, 60% women, 40% men
- **Moderately difficult** entrance level, 52% of applicants were admitted

UNDERGRAD STUDENTS

5,235 full-time, 1,757 part-time. Students come from 26 states and territories; 24 other countries; 1% are from out of state; 0.4% Black or African American, non-Hispanic/Latino; 95% Hispanic/Latino; 0.4% Asian, non-Hispanic/Latino; 0.2% Two or more races, non-Hispanic/Latino; 0.5% Race/ethnicity unknown; 2% international; 7% transferred in; 9% live on campus.

Freshmen:

Admission: 7,211 applied, 3,761 admitted, 1,273 enrolled. ***Average high school GPA:*** 3.6. ***Test scores:*** SAT evidence-based reading and writing scores over 500: 60%; SAT math scores over 500: 55%; ACT scores over 18: 52%; SAT evidence-based reading and writing scores over 600: 13%; SAT math scores over 600: 8%; ACT scores over 24: 10%; SAT evidence-based reading and writing scores over 700: 1%; SAT math scores over 700: 1%; ACT scores over 30: 1%.

Retention: 77% of full-time freshmen returned.

FACULTY

Total: 361, 58% full-time, 53% with terminal degrees.

Student/faculty ratio: 21:1.

ACADEMICS

Calendar: semesters. *Degrees:* bachelor's, master's, and doctoral.

Special study options: academic remediation for entering students, advanced placement credit, distance learning, double majors, English as a second language, honors programs, independent study, internships, part-time degree program, services for LD students, study abroad, summer session for credit. ***ROTC:*** Army (b).

Computers: 970 computers/terminals are available on campus for general student use. Students can access the following: free student e-mail accounts, online (class) grades, online (class) registration, online (class) schedules. Campuswide network is available. 100% of college-owned or -operated housing units are wired for high-speed Internet access. Wireless service is available via entire campus.

Library: Sue and Radcliff Killam Library. *Books:* 256,158 (physical), 620,245 (digital/electronic); *Serial titles:* 6,348 (physical), 80,261 (digital/electronic); *Databases:* 282. Weekly public service hours: 96; students can reserve study rooms.

STUDENT LIFE

Housing options: coed. Campus housing is university owned and is provided by a third party.

Activities and organizations: student-run newspaper, choral group, Student Government Association, Campus Activities Board, Greek Association, Criminal Justice Association, Ballet Folklorico, national fraternities, national sororities.

Athletics ***Intercollegiate sports:*** baseball M(s), basketball M(s)/W(s), cross-country running M(s)/W(s), golf M(s), soccer M(s)/W(s), softball W(s), volleyball W(s). ***Intramural sports:*** badminton M/W, basketball M/W, soccer M/W, softball M/W, table tennis M/W, ultimate Frisbee M/W, volleyball M/W.

Campus security: 24-hour emergency response devices and patrols, late-night transport/escort service, controlled dormitory access, active shooter response training for faculty, staff, and new students; timely on-going threat information dissemination.

Student services: health clinic, personal/psychological counseling, veterans affairs office.

COSTS & FINANCIAL AID

Costs (2019–20) ***Tuition:*** state resident $4773 full-time, $159 per credit hour part-time; nonresident $17,433 full-time, $581 per credit hour part-time. No tuition increase for student's term of enrollment. ***Required fees:*** $4071 full-time, $269 per credit hour part-time, $133 per credit hour part-time. ***Room and board:*** $8618; room only: $5732.

Financial Aid Of all full-time matriculated undergraduates who enrolled in 2017, 5,016 applied for aid, 4,342 were judged to have need, 19 had their need fully met. 104 Federal Work-Study jobs (averaging $1951). 26 state and other part-time jobs (averaging $1757). In 2017, 329 non-need-based awards were made. ***Average percent of need met:*** 67. ***Average financial aid package:*** $9553. ***Average need-based loan:*** $2845. ***Average need-based gift aid:*** $6936. ***Average non-need-based aid:*** $3924. ***Average indebtedness upon graduation:*** $17,394. ***Financial aid deadline:*** 7/30.

APPLYING

Standardized Tests *Required:* SAT or ACT (for admission).

Options: electronic application, deferred entrance.

Required: high school transcript.

Notification: continuous (freshmen), continuous (transfers).

CONTACT

Ms. Rosie A. Dickinson, Admissions Director, Office of Admissions, Texas A&M International University, 5201 University Boulevard, Laredo, TX 78041-1900. *Phone:* 956-326-2202. *Toll-free phone:* 888-489-2648. *E-mail:* adms@tamiu.edu.

Texas A&M University

College Station, Texas

http://www.tamu.edu/

- **State-supported** university, founded 1876, part of Texas A&M University System
- **Suburban** campus with easy access to Houston
- **Endowment** $11.6 billion
- **Coed**
- **Moderately difficult** entrance level

FACULTY

Student/faculty ratio: 20:1.

ACADEMICS

Calendar: semesters. *Degrees:* bachelor's, master's, doctoral, post-master's, and postbachelor's certificates.

Library: Sterling C. Evans Library plus 9 others. *Books:* 4.3 million (physical), 1.9 million (digital/electronic); *Serial titles:* 10,083 (physical), 199,378 (digital/electronic); *Databases:* 1,162. Weekly public service hours: 144; study areas open 24 hours, 5–7 days a week; students can reserve study rooms.

STUDENT LIFE

Housing options: coed, men-only, women-only, special housing for students with disabilities. Campus housing is university owned, leased by the school and is provided by a third party.

Activities and organizations: drama/theater group, student-run newspaper, radio and television station, choral group, marching band, Memorial Student Center, Corps of Cadets, Fish Camp, Student Government, national fraternities, national sororities.

Athletics Member NCAA. All Division I except football (Division I-A).

Campus security: 24-hour emergency response devices and patrols, late-night transport/escort service, controlled dormitory access, student escorts.

Student services: health clinic, personal/psychological counseling, women's center, legal services.

COSTS & FINANCIAL AID

Costs (2018–19) ***Tuition:*** state resident $7406 full-time, $247 per credit hour part-time; nonresident $33,074 full-time, $1102 per credit hour part-time. Full-time tuition and fees vary according to program. Part-time tuition and fees vary according to program. No tuition increase for student's term of enrollment. ***Required fees:*** $3562 full-time. ***Room and board:*** $10,436. Room and board charges vary according to board plan, housing facility, and location.

Financial Aid Of all full-time matriculated undergraduates who enrolled in 2017, 29,196 applied for aid, 21,397 were judged to have need, 4,507 had their need fully met. In 2017, 4832 non-need-based awards were made. ***Average percent of need met:*** 72. ***Average financial aid package:*** $16,695. ***Average need-based loan:*** $8173. ***Average need-based gift aid:*** $10,569. ***Average non-need-based aid:*** $3987. ***Average indebtedness upon graduation:*** $23,505.

APPLYING

Standardized Tests *Required:* SAT or ACT (for admission).

Options: electronic application.

Application fee: $75.

Required: essay or personal statement, high school transcript. ***Required for some:*** Apply Texas application, minimum SAT math score of 550 or ACT math score of 24 for the College of Engineering.

CONTACT

Office of Admissions, Texas A&M University, Freshman Admissions, PO Box 30014, College Station, TX 77842-3014. *Phone:* 979-845-1060. *Fax:* 979-845-1808.

Texas A&M University–Central Texas

Killeen, Texas

http://www.tamuct.edu/

- **State-supported** upper-level, founded 2009, part of Texas A&M University System
- **Rural** 662-acre campus
- **Coed** 1,913 undergraduate students, 36% full-time, 57% women, 43% men

UNDERGRAD STUDENTS

684 full-time, 1,229 part-time. Students come from 33 states and territories; 6 other countries; 5% are from out of state; 27% Black or African American, non-Hispanic/Latino; 24% Hispanic/Latino; 3% Asian, non-Hispanic/Latino; 0.6% Native Hawaiian or other Pacific Islander, non-Hispanic/Latino; 0.5% American Indian or Alaska Native, non-Hispanic/Latino; 2% Two or more races, non-Hispanic/Latino; 1% Race/ethnicity unknown; 0.1% international; 101% transferred in.

FACULTY

Total: 190, 33% full-time, 49% with terminal degrees.

Student/faculty ratio: 20:1.

ACADEMICS
Calendar: semesters. *Degrees:* certificates, bachelor's, master's, and post-master's certificates.

Special study options: accelerated degree program, advanced placement credit, cooperative education, distance learning, double majors, independent study, internships, off-campus study, part-time degree program, services for LD students, study abroad, summer session for credit. ***ROTC:*** Army (b).

Computers: 48 computers/terminals are available on campus for general student use. Students can access the following: computer help desk, free student e-mail accounts, online (class) grades, online (class) registration, online (class) schedules. Campuswide network is available. Wireless service is available via entire campus.
Library: University Library. *Books:* 86,646 (physical), 387,198 (digital/electronic); *Serial titles:* 160 (physical), 173,928 (digital/electronic); *Databases:* 283. Weekly public service hours: 81; students can reserve study rooms.

STUDENT LIFE
Housing options: college housing not available.

Activities and organizations: student-run newspaper.

Athletics ***Intramural sports:*** rugby M(c)/W(c).

Campus security: 24-hour emergency response devices and patrols.

Student services: personal/psychological counseling, veterans affairs office.

COSTS
Costs (2019–20) ***Tuition:*** state resident $20,325 full-time, $185 part-time; nonresident $30,284 full-time, $601 part-time. No tuition increase for student's term of enrollment. ***Required fees:*** $2085 full-time, $211 part-time.

APPLYING
Options: electronic application, deferred entrance.

Notification: continuous (transfers).

CONTACT
Mr. Joshua Smith, Director, Undergraduate Admissions and Recruitment, Texas A&M University–Central Texas, 1001 Leadership Place, Killeen, TX 76549. *Phone:* 254-519-5438. *Fax:* 254-501-5808.

Texas A&M University–Commerce

Commerce, Texas

http://www.tamuc.edu/

- **State-supported** university, founded 1889, part of Texas A&M University System
- **Small-town** 1883-acre campus with easy access to Dallas-Fort Worth
- **Coed**
- **Moderately difficult** entrance level

FACULTY
Student/faculty ratio: 18:1.

ACADEMICS
Calendar: semesters. *Degrees:* bachelor's, master's, doctoral, and postbachelor's certificates.
Library: Gee Library.

STUDENT LIFE
Housing options: on-campus residence required for freshman year; coed, women-only, special housing for students with disabilities. Campus housing is university owned. Freshman campus housing is guaranteed.

Activities and organizations: drama/theater group, student-run newspaper, radio and television station, choral group, marching band, National Society for Leadership and Success, Residence Hall Association, Indian Students Association, The Pride Alliance, National Association of Colored Women's Club, Inc, national fraternities, national sororities.

Athletics Member NCAA. All Division II.

Campus security: 24-hour emergency response devices and patrols, controlled dormitory access.

Student services: health clinic, personal/psychological counseling, legal services, veterans affairs office.

COSTS & FINANCIAL AID
Costs (2018–19) ***Tuition:*** state resident $4790 full-time, $160 per credit hour part-time; nonresident $17,240 full-time, $575 per credit hour part-time. Full-time tuition and fees vary according to course load, degree level, location, program, and reciprocity agreements. Part-time tuition and fees vary according to course load, degree level, location, program, and reciprocity agreements. ***Required fees:*** $3958 full-time. ***Room and board:*** $8326; room only: $4426. Room and board charges vary according to board plan and housing facility.

Financial Aid Of all full-time matriculated undergraduates who enrolled in 2017, 4,418 applied for aid, 3,915 were judged to have need, 953 had their need fully met. 131 Federal Work-Study jobs (averaging $2287). 21 state and other part-time jobs (averaging $2935). In 2017, 178 non-need-based awards were made. ***Average percent of need met:*** 55. ***Average financial aid package:*** $10,028. ***Average need-based loan:*** $3652. ***Average need-based gift aid:*** $8418. ***Average non-need-based aid:*** $2498. ***Average indebtedness upon graduation:*** $27,118.

APPLYING
Standardized Tests *Required:* SAT or ACT (for admission).

Options: electronic application, deferred entrance.

Required: high school transcript. ***Required for some:*** interview for honors college.

CONTACT
Mr. Jody Todhunter, Director of Admissions, Texas A&M University–Commerce, PO Box 3011, Commerce, TX 75429. *Phone:* 903-886-5072. *Toll-free phone:* 888-868-2682. *Fax:* 903-468-8698. *E-mail:* admissions@tamu-commerce.edu.

Texas A&M University–Corpus Christi

Corpus Christi, Texas

http://www.tamucc.edu/

- **State-supported** university, founded 1947, part of Texas A&M University System
- **Suburban** 317-acre campus
- **Endowment** $12.4 million
- **Coed**
- **Moderately difficult** entrance level

FACULTY
Student/faculty ratio: 18:1.

ACADEMICS
Calendar: semesters. *Degrees:* bachelor's, master's, and doctoral.
Library: Mary and Jeff Bell Library. *Books:* 329,340 (physical), 145,756 (digital/electronic); *Serial titles:* 10,348 (physical), 80,843 (digital/electronic); *Databases:* 271. Weekly public service hours: 106; students can reserve study rooms.

STUDENT LIFE
Housing options: coed. Campus housing is provided by a third party.

Activities and organizations: drama/theater group, student-run newspaper, choral group, Student Accounting Society: Alpha Epsilon Delta, Student Art Association: Golden Key, Islander Cultural Alliance: Kinesiology Club, Graduate Student Association: Sea Turtle Club, Student Nurses Association, national fraternities, national sororities.

Athletics Member NCAA. All Division I.

Campus security: 24-hour emergency response devices and patrols, late-night transport/escort service, controlled dormitory access.

Student services: health clinic, personal/psychological counseling, veterans affairs office.

COSTS & FINANCIAL AID
Costs (2018–19) ***Tuition:*** state resident $4719 full-time, $175 per credit hour part-time; nonresident $14,527 full-time, $586 per credit hour part-time. Full-time tuition and fees vary according to course load, degree level, location, program, and student level. Part-time tuition and fees vary according to course load, degree level, location, program, and student level. No tuition increase for student's term of enrollment. ***Required fees:*** $4336 full-time, $429 per credit hour part-time. ***Room and board:*** Room and board charges vary according to board plan and housing facility. ***Payment plans:*** tuition prepayment, installment.

Financial Aid Of all full-time matriculated undergraduates who enrolled in 2018, 6,110 applied for aid, 5,272 were judged to have need, 977 had their need fully met. 207 Federal Work-Study jobs (averaging $3348). 253 state and other part-time jobs (averaging $3516). In 2018, 357 non-need-based awards were made. ***Average percent of need met:*** 52. ***Average financial aid package:*** $11,859. ***Average need-based loan:*** $3949. ***Average need-based gift aid:*** $8647. ***Average non-need-based aid:*** $2664. ***Average indebtedness upon graduation:*** $18,078.

APPLYING
Standardized Tests *Required:* SAT or ACT (for admission).

Options: electronic application.

Application fee: $50.

Required: high school transcript, minimum 2.0 GPA.

CONTACT
Mrs. Monica Martinez, Assistant Director of Admissions, Texas A&M University–Corpus Christi, SSC 107, 6300 Ocean Drive, Unit 5774, Corpus Christi, TX 78412-5774. *Phone:* 361-825-2624. *Toll-free phone:* 800-482-6822. *Fax:* 361-825-5887. *E-mail:* monica.martinez@tamucc.edu.

Texas A&M University–Kingsville
Kingsville, Texas
http://www.tamuk.edu/

- **State-supported** university, founded 1925, part of Texas A&M University System
- **Small-town** 250-acre campus
- **Coed**
- **Moderately difficult** entrance level

ACADEMICS
Calendar: semesters. *Degrees:* bachelor's, master's, doctoral, post-master's, and postbachelor's certificates.
Library: James C. Jernigan Library. Students can reserve study rooms.

STUDENT LIFE
Housing options: on-campus residence required for freshman year; coed, men-only, women-only. Campus housing is university owned. Freshman campus housing is guaranteed.

Activities and organizations: drama/theater group, student-run newspaper, radio and television station, choral group, marching band, national fraternities, national sororities.

Athletics Member NCAA. All Division II.

Campus security: controlled dormitory access.

Student services: health clinic, personal/psychological counseling, veterans affairs office.

COSTS & FINANCIAL AID
Costs (2018–19) ***Tuition:*** state resident $8462 full-time, $120 per credit hour part-time; nonresident $22,034 full-time, $465 per credit hour part-time. Full-time tuition and fees vary according to course load and degree level. Part-time tuition and fees vary according to course load and degree level. No tuition increase for student's term of enrollment. ***Required fees:*** $4131 full-time. ***Room and board:*** $9096. Room and board charges vary according to board plan and housing facility.

Financial Aid Of all full-time matriculated undergraduates who enrolled in 2017, 4,229 applied for aid, 3,866 were judged to have need, 131 had their need fully met. In 2017, 336 non-need-based awards were made. ***Average percent of need met:*** 54. ***Average financial aid package:*** $12,565. ***Average need-based loan:*** $6724. ***Average need-based gift aid:*** $7249. ***Average non-need-based aid:*** $5497. ***Average indebtedness upon graduation:*** $29,454.

APPLYING
Standardized Tests *Required:* SAT or ACT (for admission).

Options: electronic application.

Application fee: $25.

Required for some: essay or personal statement, high school transcript, minimum 2.0 GPA, 2 letters of recommendation, written statement and two letters of recommendation for alternate admissions process.

CONTACT
Laura Knippers, Associate Director of Admissions, Texas A&M University–Kingsville, MSC 128, 700 University Boulevard, Kingsville, TX 78363. *Phone:* 361-593-2311. *Toll-free phone:* 800-687-6000. *E-mail:* laura.knippers@tamuk.edu.

Texas A&M University–San Antonio
San Antonio, Texas
http://www.tamusa.edu/

CONTACT
Ms. Jennifer Zamarripa, Director of Admissions and Registrar, Texas A&M University–San Antonio, One University Way, San Antonio, TX 78224. *Phone:* 210-932-6201. *E-mail:* jennifer.zamarripa@tamusa.tamus.edu.

Texas A&M University–Texarkana
Texarkana, Texas
http://www.tamut.edu/

- **State-supported** comprehensive, founded 1971, part of Texas A&M University System
- **Small-town** 1-acre campus
- **Endowment** $6.8 million
- **Coed**
- **Noncompetitive** entrance level

FACULTY
Student/faculty ratio: 15:1.

ACADEMICS
Calendar: semesters. *Degrees:* bachelor's, master's, and doctoral.
Library: John F. Moss Library plus 1 other. *Books:* 128,838 (physical), 583,387 (digital/electronic); *Serial titles:* 1,184 (physical), 72,678 (digital/electronic); *Databases:* 299. Weekly public service hours: 84; students can reserve study rooms.

STUDENT LIFE
Housing options: coed. Campus housing is university owned.

Activities and organizations: student-run newspaper, Campus Activities Board, Student Government Association, Alpha Sigma Alpha, Omega Delta Chi, Phi Lambda Chi.

Athletics Member NAIA.

Campus security: 24-hour patrols, late-night transport/escort service.

Student services: personal/psychological counseling, veterans affairs office.

COSTS & FINANCIAL AID
Costs (2018–19) ***One-time required fee:*** $30. ***Tuition:*** state resident $5978 full-time, $244 per credit hour part-time; nonresident $21,014 full-time, $745 per credit hour part-time. No tuition increase for student's term of enrollment. ***Required fees:*** $2092 full-time, $111 per credit hour part-time, $150 per term part-time. ***Room and board:*** $8732; room only: $4596. Room and board charges vary according to board plan and housing facility.

Financial Aid Of all full-time matriculated undergraduates who enrolled in 2017, 962 applied for aid, 826 were judged to have need, 67 had their need fully met. 25 Federal Work-Study jobs (averaging $1958). In 2017, 117 non-need-based awards were made. ***Average percent of need met:*** 69. ***Average financial aid package:*** $10,840. ***Average need-based loan:*** $3567. ***Average need-based gift aid:*** $8905. ***Average non-need-based aid:*** $2222. ***Average indebtedness upon graduation:*** $18,843.

APPLYING
Standardized Tests *Required:* SAT or ACT (for admission).

Options: electronic application.

Application fee: $30.

Required: high school transcript.

CONTACT
Ms. Chrissy Gonzalez, Assistant Director of Admissions, Texas A&M University–Texarkana, Texarkana, TX 75505-5518. *Phone:* 903-223-3180. *E-mail:* admissions@tamut.edu.

Texas Christian University

Fort Worth, Texas

http://www.tcu.edu/

- **Independent** university, founded 1873, affiliated with Christian Church (Disciples of Christ)
- **Suburban** 299-acre campus with easy access to Dallas-Fort Worth
- **Endowment** $1.6 billion
- **Coed** 9,445 undergraduate students, 97% full-time, 59% women, 41% men
- **Very difficult** entrance level, 41% of applicants were admitted

UNDERGRAD STUDENTS

9,162 full-time, 283 part-time. Students come from 53 states and territories; 77 other countries; 48% are from out of state; 6% Black or African American, non-Hispanic/Latino; 14% Hispanic/Latino; 3% Asian, non-Hispanic/Latino; 0.2% Native Hawaiian or other Pacific Islander, non-Hispanic/Latino; 0.8% American Indian or Alaska Native, non-Hispanic/Latino; 1% Two or more races, non-Hispanic/Latino; 1% Race/ethnicity unknown; 5% international; 5% transferred in; 51% live on campus.

Freshmen:

Admission: 20,156 applied, 8,210 admitted, 2,194 enrolled. ***Test scores:*** SAT evidence-based reading and writing scores over 500: 96%; SAT math scores over 500: 96%; ACT scores over 18: 100%; SAT evidence-based reading and writing scores over 600: 66%; SAT math scores over 600: 62%; ACT scores over 24: 89%; SAT evidence-based reading and writing scores over 700: 12%; SAT math scores over 700: 20%; ACT scores over 30: 36%.

Retention: 92% of full-time freshmen returned.

FACULTY

Total: 1,041, 67% full-time, 69% with terminal degrees.

Student/faculty ratio: 13:1.

ACADEMICS

Calendar: semesters. *Degrees:* certificates, diplomas, bachelor's, master's, doctoral, post-master's, and postbachelor's certificates.

Special study options: accelerated degree program, advanced placement credit, distance learning, double majors, English as a second language, honors programs, independent study, internships, part-time degree program, services for LD students, student-designed majors, study abroad, summer session for credit. ***ROTC:*** Army (b), Air Force (b).

Computers: 1,400 computers/terminals and 10,000 ports are available on campus for general student use. Students can access the following: campus intranet, computer help desk, free student e-mail accounts, online (class) grades, online (class) registration, online (class) schedules. Campuswide network is available. 100% of college-owned or -operated housing units are wired for high-speed Internet access. Wireless service is available via entire campus.

Library: Mary Couts Burnett Library. *Books:* 1.4 million (physical), 1.2 million (digital/electronic); *Serial titles:* 11,126 (physical), 143,171 (digital/electronic); *Databases:* 554. Weekly public service hours: 139; study areas open 24 hours, 5–7 days a week; students can reserve study rooms.

STUDENT LIFE

Housing options: on-campus residence required through sophomore year; coed, men-only, women-only, special housing for students with disabilities. Campus housing is university owned and leased by the school. Freshman campus housing is guaranteed.

Activities and organizations: drama/theater group, student-run newspaper, radio and television station, choral group, marching band, Entrepreneurship Club, Foodies, National Society of Collegiate Scholars, College Republicans, Best Buddies, national fraternities, national sororities.

Athletics Member NCAA. All Division I. ***Intercollegiate sports:*** baseball M(s), basketball M(s)/W(s), cross-country running M(s)/W(s), equestrian sports W(s), football M(s), golf M(s)/W(s)(c), gymnastics M(c)/W(c), ice hockey M(c), lacrosse M(c)/W(c), riflery W(s), rock climbing M(c)/W(c), rowing M(c)/W(c), rugby M(c)/W(c), sand volleyball W(s), soccer M(c)/W(s), swimming and diving M(s)/W(s), tennis M(s)/W(s), track and field M(s)/W(s), triathlon M(c)/W(c), ultimate Frisbee M(c)/W(c), volleyball M(c)/W(s), water polo M(c)/W(c). ***Intramural sports:*** baseball M(c), basketball M/W, bowling M/W, football M/W, golf M(c)/W(c), racquetball M/W, sand volleyball M/W, soccer M/W(c), table tennis M/W, tennis M(c)/W(c), ultimate Frisbee M/W, volleyball M/W(c).

Campus security: 24-hour emergency response devices and patrols, late-night transport/escort service, controlled dormitory access.

Student services: health clinic, personal/psychological counseling, women's center, veterans affairs office.

COSTS & FINANCIAL AID

Costs (2019–20) ***Comprehensive fee:*** $62,360 includes full-time tuition ($49,160) and room and board ($13,200). ***College room only:*** $8060.

Financial Aid Of all full-time matriculated undergraduates who enrolled in 2018, 4,660 applied for aid, 3,612 were judged to have need, 863 had their need fully met. 1,344 Federal Work-Study jobs (averaging $2100). In 2018, 2693 non-need-based awards were made. ***Average percent of need met:*** 65. ***Average financial aid package:*** $32,632. ***Average need-based loan:*** $4360. ***Average need-based gift aid:*** $29,991. ***Average non-need-based aid:*** $18,839. ***Average indebtedness upon graduation:*** $49,197. ***Financial aid deadline:*** 5/1.

APPLYING

Standardized Tests *Required:* SAT or ACT (for admission).

Options: electronic application, early decision, early action, deferred entrance.

Application fee: $50.

Required: essay or personal statement, high school transcript, 2 letters of recommendation.

Application deadlines: 2/1 (freshmen), 8/1 (transfers), 11/1 (early action).

Early decision deadline: 11/1.

Notification: 4/1 (freshmen), continuous (transfers), 12/1 (early decision), 12/15 (early action).

CONTACT

Mandy Castro, Director of Freshman Admission, Texas Christian University, Office of Admission, Box 297013, Fort Worth, TX 76129. *Phone:* 817-257-7490. *Toll-free phone:* 800-828-3764. *Fax:* 817-257-7268. *E-mail:* frogmail@tcu.edu.

Texas College

Tyler, Texas

http://www.texascollege.edu/

CONTACT

Mr. Ronald MsDowell, Director of Financial Aid, Texas College, 2404 North Grand Avenue, Tyler, TX 75702. *Phone:* 903-593-8311 Ext. 2297. *Toll-free phone:* 800-306-6299. *Fax:* 903-593-6551. *E-mail:* rmcdowell@texascollege.edu.

Texas Lutheran University

Seguin, Texas

http://www.tlu.edu/

- **Independent** comprehensive, founded 1891, affiliated with Evangelical Lutheran Church
- **Suburban** 196-acre campus with easy access to San Antonio, Austin
- **Coed** 1,411 undergraduate students, 95% full-time, 50% women, 50% men
- **Moderately difficult** entrance level, 54% of applicants were admitted

UNDERGRAD STUDENTS

1,338 full-time, 73 part-time. 2% are from out of state; 9% Black or African American, non-Hispanic/Latino; 37% Hispanic/Latino; 0.7% Asian, non-Hispanic/Latino; 0.1% Native Hawaiian or other Pacific Islander, non-Hispanic/Latino; 0.2% American Indian or Alaska Native, non-Hispanic/Latino; 0.4% Two or more races, non-Hispanic/Latino; 2% Race/ethnicity unknown; 0.4% international; 5% transferred in; 55% live on campus.

Freshmen:

Admission: 2,198 applied, 1,193 admitted, 364 enrolled. ***Average high school GPA:*** 3.6. ***Test scores:*** SAT evidence-based reading and writing scores over 500: 74%; SAT math scores over 500: 76%; ACT scores over 18: 85%; SAT evidence-based reading and writing scores over 600: 22%;

SAT math scores over 600: 18%; ACT scores over 24: 44%; SAT evidence-based reading and writing scores over 700: 2%; SAT math scores over 700: 1%; ACT scores over 30: 9%.

Retention: 71% of full-time freshmen returned.

FACULTY
Total: 134, 64% full-time, 65% with terminal degrees.

Student/faculty ratio: 14:1.

ACADEMICS
Calendar: semesters. *Degrees:* bachelor's and master's.

Special study options: advanced placement credit, double majors, external degree program, honors programs, independent study, internships, part-time degree program, services for LD students, study abroad, summer session for credit. ***ROTC:*** Army (c), Navy (c).

Unusual degree programs: engineering with Texas A&M University, Texas Tech University, Texas State University.

Computers: Students can access the following: campus intranet, computer help desk, free student e-mail accounts, online (class) grades, online (class) registration, online (class) schedules, free printing. Campuswide network is available. 100% of college-owned or -operated housing units are wired for high-speed Internet access. Wireless service is available via entire campus.

Library: Blumberg Memorial Library plus 1 other. Weekly public service hours: 86; students can reserve study rooms.

STUDENT LIFE
Housing options: coed, special housing for students with disabilities. Campus housing is university owned. Freshman campus housing is guaranteed.

Activities and organizations: drama/theater group, student-run newspaper, choral group, Alpha Lambda Delta, Pre Health Professions Club, Xi Tau, Sigma Phi Theta, Mexican American Student Association.

Athletics Member NCAA. All Division III except golf (Division II). ***Intercollegiate sports:*** baseball M, basketball M/W, cross-country running M/W, football M, golf M/W, soccer M/W, softball W, tennis M/W, track and field M/W, volleyball W. ***Intramural sports:*** basketball M/W, bowling M/W, football M, racquetball M/W, softball M/W, tennis M/W, volleyball M/W.

Campus security: 24-hour emergency response devices and patrols, late-night transport/escort service, controlled dormitory access.

Student services: health clinic, personal/psychological counseling, women's center.

COSTS & FINANCIAL AID
Costs (2018–19) ***One-time required fee:*** $300. ***Comprehensive fee:*** $40,110 includes full-time tuition ($29,650), mandatory fees ($310), and room and board ($10,150). Full-time tuition and fees vary according to course load. Part-time tuition: $980 per semester hour. ***Required fees:*** $155 per term part-time. ***College room only:*** $5750. Room and board charges vary according to board plan and housing facility. ***Payment plan:*** installment. ***Waivers:*** children of alumni and employees or children of employees.

Financial Aid Of all full-time matriculated undergraduates who enrolled in 2018, 1,213 applied for aid, 1,094 were judged to have need, 286 had their need fully met. In 2018, 248 non-need-based awards were made. ***Average percent of need met:*** 84. ***Average financial aid package:*** $25,663. ***Average need-based loan:*** $4137. ***Average need-based gift aid:*** $22,801. ***Average non-need-based aid:*** $16,787. ***Average indebtedness upon graduation:*** $33,813.

APPLYING
Standardized Tests *Required:* SAT or ACT (for admission).

Options: electronic application, early admission.

Required: high school transcript. ***Required for some:*** letters of recommendation.

CONTACT
Mrs. Alecia McCain, Director for Admissions Recruiting, Texas Lutheran University, 1000 West Court Street, Seguin, TX 78155-5999. *Phone:* 830-372-6078. *Toll-free phone:* 800-771-8521. *Fax:* 830-372-8096. *E-mail:* almccain@tlu.edu.

Texas Southern University
Houston, Texas

http://www.tsu.edu/

CONTACT
Enrollment Services Customer Service Center, Texas Southern University, 3100 Cleburne Street, Houston, TX 77004-4598. *Phone:* 713-313-7071. *Fax:* 713-313-7851. *E-mail:* eservices@em.tsu.edu.

Texas State University
San Marcos, Texas

http://www.txstate.edu/

- **State-supported** university, founded 1899, part of Texas State University System
- **Suburban** 491-acre campus with easy access to San Antonio, Austin
- **Endowment** $186.7 million
- **Coed**
- **Moderately difficult** entrance level

FACULTY
Student/faculty ratio: 21:1.

ACADEMICS
Calendar: semesters. *Degrees:* bachelor's, master's, doctoral, and postbachelor's certificates.

Library: Alkek Library plus 1 other. *Books:* 1.5 million (physical), 664,569 (digital/electronic); *Serial titles:* 32,501 (physical), 129,479 (digital/electronic); *Databases:* 503. Weekly public service hours: 103; students can reserve study rooms.

STUDENT LIFE
Housing options: on-campus residence required for freshman year; coed, men-only, women-only. Campus housing is university owned. Freshman campus housing is guaranteed.

Activities and organizations: drama/theater group, student-run newspaper, radio station, choral group, marching band, Veterans Alliance of Texas State, Texas State Strutters (Dance performance group), Student Foundation, Sport Clubs Alliance, Student Association for Campus Activities, national fraternities, national sororities.

Athletics Member NCAA. All Division I.

Campus security: 24-hour emergency response devices and patrols, late-night transport/escort service, controlled dormitory access, Emergency Notification System (electronic signs) within classrooms and offices.

Student services: health clinic, personal/psychological counseling, legal services, veterans affairs office.

COSTS & FINANCIAL AID
Costs (2018–19) ***Tuition:*** state resident $8335 full-time, $278 per credit hour part-time; nonresident $20,785 full-time, $693 per credit hour part-time. Full-time tuition and fees vary according to course load and degree level. Part-time tuition and fees vary according to course load and degree level. No tuition increase for student's term of enrollment. ***Required fees:*** $2600 full-time, $56 per credit hour part-time, $464 per term part-time. ***Room and board:*** $9374; room only: $6580. Room and board charges vary according to board plan and housing facility. ***Payment plans:*** tuition prepayment, installment.

Financial Aid Of all full-time matriculated undergraduates who enrolled in 2018, 26,222 applied for aid, 16,876 were judged to have need, 2,853 had their need fully met. 763 Federal Work-Study jobs (averaging $2983). 182 state and other part-time jobs (averaging $3220). In 2018, 840 non-need-based awards were made. ***Average percent of need met:*** 62. ***Average financial aid package:*** $10,721. ***Average need-based loan:*** $3994. ***Average need-based gift aid:*** $7732. ***Average non-need-based aid:*** $3953. ***Average indebtedness upon graduation:*** $25,853.

APPLYING
Standardized Tests *Required:* SAT or ACT (for admission). *Required for some:* TOEFL for international students. *Recommended:* SAT (for admission), ACT (for admission).

Options: electronic application, early admission, deferred entrance.

Application fee: $75.

Required: essay or personal statement, high school transcript.

CONTACT
Texas State University, 429 N. Guadalupe Street, San Marcos, TX 78666. *Phone:* 512-245-2364. *Fax:* 512-245-8100. *E-mail:* admissions@txstate.edu.

Texas Tech University

Lubbock, Texas

http://www.ttu.edu/

- **State-supported** university, founded 1923, part of Texas Tech University System
- **Urban** 1839-acre campus
- **Endowment** $764.5 million
- **Coed** 31,957 undergraduate students, 87% full-time, 47% women, 53% men
- **Moderately difficult** entrance level, 71% of applicants were admitted

UNDERGRAD STUDENTS
27,648 full-time, 4,309 part-time. Students come from 52 states and territories; 98 other countries; 6% are from out of state; 7% Black or African American, non-Hispanic/Latino; 30% Hispanic/Latino; 3% Asian, non-Hispanic/Latino; 0.1% Native Hawaiian or other Pacific Islander, non-Hispanic/Latino; 0.4% American Indian or Alaska Native, non-Hispanic/Latino; 3% Two or more races, non-Hispanic/Latino; 0.4% Race/ethnicity unknown; 3% international; 8% transferred in; 26% live on campus.

Freshmen:
Admission: 24,452 applied, 17,280 admitted, 6,171 enrolled. ***Average high school GPA:*** 3.6. ***Test scores:*** SAT evidence-based reading and writing scores over 500: 96%; SAT math scores over 500: 94%; ACT scores over 18: 99%; SAT evidence-based reading and writing scores over 600: 42%; SAT math scores over 600: 37%; ACT scores over 24: 57%; SAT evidence-based reading and writing scores over 700: 4%; SAT math scores over 700: 6%; ACT scores over 30: 10%.

Retention: 85% of full-time freshmen returned.

FACULTY
Total: 1,802, 89% full-time.

Student/faculty ratio: 20:1.

ACADEMICS
Calendar: semesters. *Degrees:* bachelor's, master's, doctoral, and postbachelor's certificates.

Special study options: academic remediation for entering students, accelerated degree program, advanced placement credit, cooperative education, distance learning, double majors, English as a second language, external degree program, freshman honors college, honors programs, independent study, internships, off-campus study, part-time degree program, services for LD students, student-designed majors, study abroad, summer session for credit. ***ROTC:*** Army (b), Air Force (b).

Unusual degree programs: 3-2 business administration; engineering; agribusiness, agricultural & applied economics, architecture, environmental design, hospitality & retail management, interdisciplinary studies, languages & cultures, mathematics, music education, personal financial planning, political science, psycho.

Computers: 2,087 computers/terminals and 3,250 ports are available on campus for general student use. Students can access the following: campus intranet, computer help desk, free student e-mail accounts, online (class) grades, online (class) registration, online (class) schedules, online degree plans, accounts, transcripts, financial aid, course and instructor evaluations, scholarship applications and submissions. Campuswide network is available. 100% of college-owned or -operated housing units are wired for high-speed Internet access. Wireless service is available via classrooms, computer centers, computer labs, dorm rooms, learning centers, libraries, student centers.

Library: Texas Tech Library plus 3 others. *Books:* 2.9 million (physical), 159,373 (digital/electronic); *Serial titles:* 1,464 (physical), 200,332 (digital/electronic); *Databases:* 405. Weekly public service hours: 146; study areas open 24 hours, 5–7 days a week; students can reserve study rooms.

STUDENT LIFE
Housing options: on-campus residence required for freshman year; coed, men-only, women-only, special housing for students with disabilities. Campus housing is university owned. Freshman campus housing is guaranteed.

Activities and organizations: drama/theater group, student-run newspaper, radio station, choral group, marching band, Society of Petroleum Engineers, Hispanic Student Society, Pre-Nursing Association, Alpha Lambda Delta and Phi Eta Sigma, Catholic Student Association, national fraternities, national sororities.

Athletics Member NCAA. All Division I except football (Division I-A). ***Intercollegiate sports:*** baseball M(s), basketball M(s)/W(s), cross-country running M(s)/W(s), golf M(s)/W(s), soccer W(s), softball W(s), tennis M(s)/W(s), track and field M(s)/W(s), volleyball W(s). ***Intramural sports:*** archery M/W, badminton M(c)/W(c), baseball M(c), basketball M/W, bowling M/W, equestrian sports M(c)/W(c), fencing M(c)/W(c), golf M/W, gymnastics M(c)/W(c), ice hockey M(c), lacrosse M(c)/W(c), racquetball M/W, rock climbing M(c)/W(c), rugby M(c)/W(c), sand volleyball M/W, soccer M/W, softball M/W, swimming and diving M(c)/W(c), table tennis M/W, tennis M/W, triathlon M(c)/W(c), ultimate Frisbee M(c)/W(c), volleyball M/W, water polo M(c)/W(c), weight lifting M/W, wrestling M(c)/W(c).

Campus security: 24-hour emergency response devices and patrols, late-night transport/escort service, controlled dormitory access.

Student services: health clinic, personal/psychological counseling, legal services, veterans affairs office.

COSTS & FINANCIAL AID
Costs (2018–19) ***Tuition:*** state resident $8220 full-time, $274 per credit hour part-time; nonresident $20,670 full-time, $689 per credit hour part-time. Full-time tuition and fees vary according to course load, location, program, and reciprocity agreements. Part-time tuition and fees vary according to course load, location, program, and reciprocity agreements. ***Required fees:*** $2825 full-time, $54 per credit hour part-time, $610 per term part-time. ***Room and board:*** $9772; room only: $6236. Room and board charges vary according to board plan and housing facility. ***Payment plan:*** installment. ***Waivers:*** senior citizens and employees or children of employees.

Financial Aid Of all full-time matriculated undergraduates who enrolled in 2016, 16,239 applied for aid, 13,251 were judged to have need, 1,075 had their need fully met. 360 Federal Work-Study jobs (averaging $2520). 6 state and other part-time jobs (averaging $1296). In 2016, 3132 non-need-based awards were made. ***Average percent of need met:*** 67. ***Average financial aid package:*** $15,085. ***Average need-based loan:*** $5307. ***Average need-based gift aid:*** $7786. ***Average non-need-based aid:*** $3564. ***Average indebtedness upon graduation:*** $30,759.

APPLYING
Standardized Tests *Required:* SAT or ACT (for admission).

Options: electronic application.

Application fee: $75.

Required: high school transcript. ***Recommended:*** essay or personal statement.

Application deadlines: 8/1 (freshmen), rolling (transfers).

Notification: 9/1 (freshmen), continuous (transfers).

CONTACT
Jamie Hansard, Executive Director, Office of Undergraduate Admissions, Texas Tech University, 2500 Broadway, Lubbock, TX 79409. *Phone:* 806-742-1480. *Fax:* 806-742-0062. *E-mail:* admissions@ttu.edu.

Texas Wesleyan University

Fort Worth, Texas

http://www.txwes.edu/

CONTACT
Mrs. Djuana Young, Associate Vice President for Enrollment, Admissions, Texas Wesleyan University, 1201 Wesleyan Street, Fort Worth, TX 76105-1536. *Phone:* 817-531-4422. *Toll-free phone:* 800-580-8980. *Fax:* 817-531-7515. *E-mail:* admissions@txwes.edu.

Texas Woman's University

Denton, Texas

http://www.twu.edu/

- **State-supported** university, founded 1901
- **Suburban** 270-acre campus with easy access to Dallas-Fort Worth
- **Endowment** $72.2 million
- **Coed, primarily women** 10,390 undergraduate students, 66% full-time, 88% women, 12% men
- **Moderately difficult** entrance level, 87% of applicants were admitted

UNDERGRAD STUDENTS

6,880 full-time, 3,510 part-time. Students come from 32 states and territories; 23 other countries; 2% are from out of state; 17% Black or African American, non-Hispanic/Latino; 30% Hispanic/Latino; 9% Asian, non-Hispanic/Latino; 0.5% American Indian or Alaska Native, non-Hispanic/Latino; 4% Two or more races, non-Hispanic/Latino; 0.8% Race/ethnicity unknown; 0.9% international; 13% transferred in; 19% live on campus.

Freshmen:

Admission: 5,727 applied, 4,971 admitted, 1,244 enrolled. ***Average high school GPA:*** 3.2. ***Test scores:*** SAT evidence-based reading and writing scores over 500: 72%; SAT math scores over 500: 66%; ACT scores over 18: 73%; SAT evidence-based reading and writing scores over 600: 23%; SAT math scores over 600: 16%; ACT scores over 24: 22%; SAT evidence-based reading and writing scores over 700: 2%; SAT math scores over 700: 2%; ACT scores over 30: 2%.

Retention: 73% of full-time freshmen returned.

FACULTY

Total: 939, 54% full-time, 59% with terminal degrees.

Student/faculty ratio: 18:1.

ACADEMICS

Calendar: semesters. *Degrees:* bachelor's, master's, doctoral, post-master's, and postbachelor's certificates.

Special study options: academic remediation for entering students, accelerated degree program, adult/continuing education programs, advanced placement credit, cooperative education, distance learning, double majors, honors programs, independent study, internships, off-campus study, part-time degree program, services for LD students, study abroad, summer session for credit. ***ROTC:*** Army (c), Navy (c), Air Force (c).

Computers: 296 computers/terminals and 592 ports are available on campus for general student use. Students can access the following: campus intranet, computer help desk, free student e-mail accounts, online (class) grades, online (class) registration, online (class) schedules. Campuswide network is available. 100% of college-owned or -operated housing units are wired for high-speed Internet access. Wireless service is available via entire campus.

Library: Blagg-Huey Library. *Books:* 387,169 (physical), 504,151 (digital/electronic); *Serial titles:* 131,848 (physical), 209,764 (digital/electronic); *Databases:* 306. Weekly public service hours: 116; students can reserve study rooms.

STUDENT LIFE

Housing options: on-campus residence required through sophomore year; coed, men-only, women-only, special housing for students with disabilities. Campus housing is university owned, leased by the school and is provided by a third party. Freshman campus housing is guaranteed.

Activities and organizations: drama/theater group, student-run newspaper, choral group, Residence Hall Association, Helping Hands Service Ambassadors, Athenian Honor Society, Phi Kappa Phi Student Scholars, University Network Intercultural Team and Education, national fraternities, national sororities.

Athletics Member NCAA. All Division II. ***Intercollegiate sports:*** basketball W(s), gymnastics W(s), soccer W(s), softball W(s), volleyball W(s). ***Intramural sports:*** basketball M/W, football M/W, sand volleyball M/W, soccer M/W, tennis M/W, volleyball M/W, weight lifting M/W.

Campus security: 24-hour emergency response devices and patrols, late-night transport/escort service, controlled dormitory access.

Student services: health clinic, personal/psychological counseling, women's center, legal services, veterans affairs office.

COSTS & FINANCIAL AID

Costs (2019–20) ***Tuition:*** area resident $6789 full-time, $226 per credit hour part-time; state resident $6789 full-time, $226 per credit hour part-time; nonresident $19,449 full-time, $648 per credit hour part-time. No tuition increase for student's term of enrollment. ***Required fees:*** $2959 full-time, $98 per credit hour part-time, $298 per term part-time. ***Room and board:*** $8950; room only: $5250.

Financial Aid Of all full-time matriculated undergraduates who enrolled in 2017, 5,490 applied for aid, 4,801 were judged to have need, 1,381 had their need fully met. 353 Federal Work-Study jobs (averaging $3007). 76 state and other part-time jobs (averaging $1325). In 2017, 402 non-need-based awards were made. ***Average percent of need met:*** 84. ***Average financial aid package:*** $14,065. ***Average need-based loan:*** $6858. ***Average need-based gift aid:*** $7675. ***Average non-need-based aid:*** $4595. ***Average indebtedness upon graduation:*** $22,794. ***Financial aid deadline:*** 3/15.

APPLYING

Standardized Tests *Required for some:* SAT or ACT (for admission).

Options: electronic application, early admission, deferred entrance.

Application fee: $50.

Required: minimum 2.0 GPA, Transcripts from prior colleges attended. ***Required for some:*** high school transcript.

Application deadlines: 8/25 (freshmen), 8/25 (transfers).

Notification: continuous (freshmen), continuous (transfers).

CONTACT

Ms. Nikki Young, Interim Director of Admissions, Texas Woman's University, P.O. Box 425589, Denton, TX 76204. *Phone:* 940-898-3188. *Toll-free phone:* 866-809-6130. *Fax:* 940-898-3081. *E-mail:* admissions@twu.edu.

Trinity University

San Antonio, Texas

http://www.trinity.edu/

- **Independent** comprehensive, founded 1869, affiliated with Presbyterian Church
- **Urban** 117-acre campus with easy access to San Antonio
- **Endowment** $1.2 billion
- **Coed**
- **Very difficult** entrance level

FACULTY

Student/faculty ratio: 9:1.

ACADEMICS

Calendar: semesters. *Degrees:* bachelor's and master's.

Library: Elizabeth Huth Coates Library plus 1 other. *Books:* 716,500 (physical); *Serial titles:* 1,907 (physical), 95,000 (digital/electronic); *Databases:* 297. Weekly public service hours: 96; students can reserve study rooms.

STUDENT LIFE

Housing options: on-campus residence required through junior year; coed. Campus housing is university owned. Freshman campus housing is guaranteed.

Activities and organizations: drama/theater group, student-run newspaper, radio and television station, choral group, Tiger Stand Band, Alpha Phi Omega, Association of Student Representatives, Acabellas/Trinitones, Multicultural Network.

Athletics Member NCAA. All Division III except golf (Division II).

Campus security: 24-hour emergency response devices and patrols, late-night transport/escort service, controlled dormitory access.

Student services: health clinic, personal/psychological counseling.

COSTS & FINANCIAL AID

Costs (2018–19) ***Comprehensive fee:*** $56,440 includes full-time tuition ($42,360), mandatory fees ($616), and room and board ($13,464). Full-time tuition and fees vary according to course load. Part-time tuition: $1765 per credit hour. Part-time tuition and fees vary according to course load. ***Required fees:*** $13 per credit hour part-time. ***College room only:*** $8690. Room and board charges vary according to board plan.

Financial Aid Of all full-time matriculated undergraduates who enrolled in 2018, 1,482 applied for aid, 1,134 were judged to have need, 488 had their need fully met. In 2018, 1216 non-need-based awards were made. ***Average percent of need met:*** 92. ***Average financial aid package:*** $39,603. ***Average need-based loan:*** $4727. ***Average need-based gift aid:*** $32,162. ***Average non-need-based aid:*** $21,339. ***Average indebtedness upon graduation:*** $42,036.

APPLYING

Standardized Tests *Required:* SAT or ACT (for admission).

Options: electronic application, early decision, early action, deferred entrance.

Required: essay or personal statement, high school transcript, 2 letters of recommendation. ***Recommended:*** interview.

CONTACT

Office of Admissions, Trinity University, One Trinity Place, Northrup Hall 140, San Antonio, TX 78212-7200. *Phone:* 210-999-7207. *Toll-free phone:* 800-TRINITY. *Fax:* 210-999-8164. *E-mail:* admissions@trinity.edu.

Tyler Junior College

Tyler, Texas

http://www.tjc.edu/

- **State and locally supported** primarily 2-year, founded 1926
- **Suburban** 137-acre campus
- **Endowment** $42.2 million
- **Coed** 10,106 undergraduate students, 60% full-time, 62% women, 38% men
- **Noncompetitive** entrance level, 100% of applicants were admitted

UNDERGRAD STUDENTS

6,026 full-time, 4,080 part-time. Students come from 27 states and territories; 31 other countries; 3% are from out of state; 21% Black or African American, non-Hispanic/Latino; 26% Hispanic/Latino; 2% Asian, non-Hispanic/Latino; 0.1% Native Hawaiian or other Pacific Islander, non-Hispanic/Latino; 0.9% American Indian or Alaska Native, non-Hispanic/Latino; 0.5% Two or more races, non-Hispanic/Latino; 0.7% Race/ethnicity unknown; 0.4% international; 6% transferred in; 11% live on campus.

Freshmen:

Admission: 10,778 applied, 10,778 admitted, 3,296 enrolled.

Retention: 54% of full-time freshmen returned.

FACULTY

Total: 559, 56% full-time, 9% with terminal degrees.

Student/faculty ratio: 20:1.

ACADEMICS

Calendar: semesters. *Degrees:* certificates, diplomas, associate, and bachelor's.

Special study options: academic remediation for entering students, accelerated degree program, adult/continuing education programs, advanced placement credit, distance learning, freshman honors college, honors programs, part-time degree program, services for LD students, study abroad, summer session for credit.

Computers: Students can access the following: campus intranet, computer help desk, free student e-mail accounts, online (class) grades, online (class) registration, online (class) schedules. Campuswide network is available. 100% of college-owned or -operated housing units are wired for high-speed Internet access. Wireless service is available via entire campus.

Library: Vaughn Library and Learning Resource Center. *Books:* 85,418 (physical), 135,816 (digital/electronic); *Databases:* 100. Weekly public service hours: 74.

STUDENT LIFE

Housing options: coed, men-only, women-only. Campus housing is university owned and is provided by a third party.

Activities and organizations: drama/theater group, student-run newspaper, choral group, marching band, Student Government, Religious Affiliation Clubs, Phi Theta Kappa, national sororities.

Athletics Member NJCAA. ***Intercollegiate sports:*** baseball M, basketball M(s)/W(s), cheerleading W(s), football M(s), golf M, soccer M(s)/W(s), softball W(s), tennis M(s)/W(s), volleyball W(s). ***Intramural sports:*** basketball M/W, cheerleading W, racquetball M/W, volleyball M/W, weight lifting M/W.

Campus security: 24-hour emergency response devices and patrols, controlled dormitory access.

Student services: health clinic, personal/psychological counseling, veterans affairs office.

FINANCIAL AID

Financial Aid ***Average indebtedness upon graduation:*** $14,743. ***Financial aid deadline:*** 6/1.

APPLYING

Options: electronic application, early admission.

Required: high school transcript.

Application deadlines: rolling (freshmen), rolling (transfers).

Notification: continuous (freshmen), continuous (transfers).

CONTACT

Tyler Junior College, PO Box 9020, Tyler, TX 75711-9020. *Toll-free phone:* 800-687-5680.

University of Dallas

Irving, Texas

http://www.udallas.edu/

- **Independent Roman Catholic** university, founded 1955
- **Suburban** 215-acre campus with easy access to Dallas-Fort Worth
- **Endowment** $76.0 million
- **Coed** 1,471 undergraduate students, 98% full-time, 53% women, 47% men
- **Moderately difficult** entrance level, 61% of applicants were admitted

UNDERGRAD STUDENTS

1,447 full-time, 24 part-time. Students come from 22 other countries; 47% are from out of state; 2% Black or African American, non-Hispanic/Latino; 24% Hispanic/Latino; 7% Asian, non-Hispanic/Latino; 0.1% Native Hawaiian or other Pacific Islander, non-Hispanic/Latino; 0.4% American Indian or Alaska Native, non-Hispanic/Latino; 3% Two or more races, non-Hispanic/Latino; 2% Race/ethnicity unknown; 3% international; 3% transferred in; 60% live on campus.

Freshmen:

Admission: 4,188 applied, 2,554 admitted, 376 enrolled. ***Average high school GPA:*** 3.9. ***Test scores:*** SAT evidence-based reading and writing scores over 500: 96%; SAT math scores over 500: 92%; ACT scores over 18: 99%; SAT evidence-based reading and writing scores over 600: 66%; SAT math scores over 600: 51%; ACT scores over 24: 68%; SAT evidence-based reading and writing scores over 700: 20%; SAT math scores over 700: 13%; ACT scores over 30: 23%.

Retention: 80% of full-time freshmen returned.

FACULTY

Total: 194, 72% full-time, 79% with terminal degrees.

Student/faculty ratio: 10:1.

ACADEMICS

Calendar: semesters. *Degrees:* bachelor's, master's, doctoral, post-master's, and postbachelor's certificates.

Special study options: advanced placement credit, double majors, independent study, internships, off-campus study, part-time degree program, services for LD students, student-designed majors, study abroad, summer session for credit. ***ROTC:*** Army (c), Air Force (c).

Unusual degree programs: 3-2 engineering with University of Texas at Arlington; nursing with Texas Woman's University.

Computers: 125 computers/terminals are available on campus for general student use. Students can access the following: campus intranet, computer help desk, free student e-mail accounts, online (class) grades, online (class) registration, online (class) schedules. Campuswide network is available. 100% of college-owned or -operated housing units are wired for high-speed Internet access. Wireless service is available via entire campus.

Library: William A. Blakley Library. *Books:* 235,868 (physical), 237,409 (digital/electronic); *Serial titles:* 294 (physical), 179 (digital/electronic); *Databases:* 215. Weekly public service hours: 99.

STUDENT LIFE

Housing options: on-campus residence required through junior year; coed, men-only, women-only. Campus housing is university owned. Freshman campus housing is guaranteed.

Activities and organizations: drama/theater group, student-run newspaper, choral group, CAB (Campus Activities Board), Residence Hall Association, Student Government, Best Buddies, Alexander Hamilton Society.

Athletics Member NCAA. All Division III. ***Intercollegiate sports:*** baseball M, basketball M/W, cross-country running M/W, golf M/W, lacrosse M/W, soccer M/W, softball W, track and field M/W, volleyball W. ***Intramural sports:*** basketball M, equestrian sports M(c)/W(c), football M/W, rugby M(c)/W(c), sailing M(c)/W(c), soccer M/W, softball M/W, swimming and diving M(c)/W(c), tennis M(c)/W(c), ultimate Frisbee M(c)/W(c), volleyball M/W.

Campus security: 24-hour emergency response devices and patrols, late-night transport/escort service, controlled dormitory access.

Student services: health clinic, personal/psychological counseling.

COSTS & FINANCIAL AID

Costs (2019–20) ***Comprehensive fee:*** $56,412 includes full-time tuition ($40,652), mandatory fees ($3000), and room and board ($12,760). Part-time tuition: $1653 per credit hour. ***College room only:*** $6900.

Financial Aid Of all full-time matriculated undergraduates who enrolled in 2017, 1,006 applied for aid, 909 were judged to have need, 177 had their need fully met. 253 Federal Work-Study jobs (averaging $1554). 5 state and other part-time jobs (averaging $1460). In 2017, 394 non-need-based awards were made. ***Average percent of need met:*** 78. ***Average financial aid package:*** $32,282. ***Average need-based loan:*** $4881. ***Average need-based gift aid:*** $27,941. ***Average non-need-based aid:*** $20,241. ***Average indebtedness upon graduation:*** $35,993.

APPLYING

Standardized Tests *Required:* SAT or ACT (for admission).

Options: electronic application, early action, deferred entrance.

Application fee: $50.

Required: essay or personal statement, high school transcript, 2 letters of recommendation. ***Required for some:*** interview.

Application deadlines: 8/1 (freshmen), 8/1 (out-of-state freshmen), 8/1 (transfers), 12/1 (early action).

Notification: continuous (freshmen), continuous (out-of-state freshmen), continuous (transfers), 1/15 (early action).

CONTACT

MIchael Probus, Director of Undergraduate Admission, University of Dallas, 1845 East Northgate Drive, Irving, TX 75062-4736. *Phone:* 800-628-6999. *Toll-free phone:* 800-628-6999. *Fax:* 972-721-5017. *E-mail:* crusader@udallas.edu.

University of Houston

Houston, Texas

http://www.uh.edu/

- **State-supported** university, founded 1927, part of University of Houston System
- **Urban** 594-acre campus with easy access to Houston
- **Endowment** $826.3 million
- **Coed** 38,348 undergraduate students, 73% full-time, 50% women, 50% men
- **Moderately difficult** entrance level, 62% of applicants were admitted

UNDERGRAD STUDENTS

28,029 full-time, 10,319 part-time. Students come from 51 states and territories; 100 other countries; 2% are from out of state; 10% Black or African American, non-Hispanic/Latino; 35% Hispanic/Latino; 22% Asian, non-Hispanic/Latino; 0.1% Native Hawaiian or other Pacific Islander, non-Hispanic/Latino; 0.1% American Indian or Alaska Native, non-Hispanic/Latino; 3% Two or more races, non-Hispanic/Latino; 2% Race/ethnicity unknown; 4% international; 14% transferred in; 17% live on campus.

Freshmen:

Admission: 22,461 applied, 14,002 admitted, 5,198 enrolled. ***Average high school GPA:*** 3.8. ***Test scores:*** SAT evidence-based reading and writing scores over 500: 96%; SAT math scores over 500: 96%; ACT scores over 18: 98%; SAT evidence-based reading and writing scores over 600: 57%; SAT math scores over 600: 56%; ACT scores over 24: 65%; SAT evidence-based reading and writing scores over 700: 8%; SAT math scores over 700: 14%; ACT scores over 30: 13%.

Retention: 85% of full-time freshmen returned.

FACULTY

Total: 2,450, 64% full-time, 77% with terminal degrees.

Student/faculty ratio: 22:1.

ACADEMICS

Calendar: semesters. *Degrees:* bachelor's, master's, and doctoral.

Special study options: academic remediation for entering students, adult/continuing education programs, advanced placement credit, cooperative education, distance learning, double majors, freshman honors college, honors programs, independent study, internships, off-campus study, part-time degree program, services for LD students, study abroad, summer session for credit. ***ROTC:*** Army (b), Navy (c), Air Force (b).

Unusual degree programs: 3-2 business administration.

Computers: 1,010 computers/terminals and 80,482 ports are available on campus for general student use. Students can access the following: campus intranet, computer help desk, free student e-mail accounts, online (class) grades, online (class) registration, online (class) schedules, Bus loop schedule; Academic calendar; Student media; Alerts; Social Media Directory. Campuswide network is available. 100% of college-owned or -operated housing units are wired for high-speed Internet access. Wireless service is available via entire campus.

Library: M. D. Anderson Library plus 4 others. *Books:* 1.5 million (physical), 724,075 (digital/electronic); *Serial titles:* 50,880 (physical), 108,834 (digital/electronic); *Databases:* 419. Weekly public service hours: 122; study areas open 24 hours, 5–7 days a week; students can reserve study rooms.

STUDENT LIFE

Housing options: coed, special housing for students with disabilities. Campus housing is university owned and is provided by a third party.

Activities and organizations: drama/theater group, student-run newspaper, radio and television station, choral group, marching band, Graduate Indian Student Organization, Filipino Student Association, The National Society of Leadership and Success, Houston Panhellenic Council, Society of Women Engineers, national fraternities, national sororities.

Athletics Member NCAA. All Division I except football (Division I-A). ***Intercollegiate sports:*** baseball M(s), basketball M(s)/W(s), cross-country running M(s)/W(s), golf M(s), soccer W(s), softball W(s), swimming and diving W(s), tennis W(s), track and field M(s)/W(s), volleyball W(s). ***Intramural sports:*** badminton M/W, basketball M/W, bowling M(c)/W, fencing M(c), field hockey W(c), golf M/W, racquetball M/W, rock climbing M/W, soccer M/W, softball M/W, swimming and diving M/W, table tennis M/W, tennis M/W, track and field M/W, ultimate Frisbee M(c)/W(c), volleyball M/W(c), water polo M(c)/W(c), weight lifting M/W.

Campus security: 24-hour emergency response devices and patrols, student patrols, late-night transport/escort service, controlled dormitory access.

Student services: health clinic, personal/psychological counseling, women's center, legal services, veterans affairs office.

COSTS & FINANCIAL AID

Costs (2019–20) ***Tuition:*** state resident $10,271 full-time, $342 per credit hour part-time; nonresident $25,934 full-time, $864 per credit hour part-time. No tuition increase for student's term of enrollment. ***Required fees:*** $1002 full-time. ***Room and board:*** $9368.

Financial Aid Of all full-time matriculated undergraduates who enrolled in 2018, 19,880 applied for aid, 16,523 were judged to have need, 2,009 had their need fully met. 900 Federal Work-Study jobs (averaging $3994). 222 state and other part-time jobs (averaging $3919). In 2018, 838 non-need-based awards were made. ***Average percent of need met:*** 58. ***Average financial aid package:*** $12,979. ***Average need-based loan:*** $7154.

Average need-based gift aid: $8551. *Average non-need-based aid:* $4367. *Average indebtedness upon graduation:* $24,018.

APPLYING
Standardized Tests *Required:* SAT or ACT (for admission).

Options: electronic application.

Application fee: $75.

Required: high school transcript.

Application deadlines: 6/7 (freshmen), 6/7 (out-of-state freshmen), 6/28 (transfers).

Notification: continuous (freshmen), continuous (out-of-state freshmen), continuous (transfers).

CONTACT
Mardell Maxwell, Exec Director, Admissions, University of Houston, Welcome Center, 4400 University Boulevard, Houston, TX 77204-2023. *Phone:* 713-743-1010. *Fax:* 713-743-9633. *E-mail:* mrmaxwe2@central.uh.edu.

University of Houston–Clear Lake

Houston, Texas

http://www.uhcl.edu/

- **State-supported** comprehensive, founded 1971, part of University of Houston System
- **Suburban** 524-acre campus with easy access to Houston
- **Coed** 6,212 undergraduate students, 50% full-time, 62% women, 38% men
- **Minimally difficult** entrance level, 45% of applicants were admitted

UNDERGRAD STUDENTS
3,099 full-time, 3,113 part-time. Students come from 19 other countries; 8% Black or African American, non-Hispanic/Latino; 41% Hispanic/Latino; 6% Asian, non-Hispanic/Latino; 0.3% American Indian or Alaska Native, non-Hispanic/Latino; 3% Two or more races, non-Hispanic/Latino; 1% Race/ethnicity unknown; 1% international; 25% transferred in; 3% live on campus.

Freshmen:
Admission: 1,830 applied, 823 admitted, 237 enrolled. *Average high school GPA:* 3.4. *Test scores:* SAT evidence-based reading and writing scores over 500: 85%; SAT math scores over 500: 89%; ACT scores over 18: 96%; SAT evidence-based reading and writing scores over 600: 35%; SAT math scores over 600: 22%; ACT scores over 24: 30%; SAT evidence-based reading and writing scores over 700: 3%; SAT math scores over 700: 3%; ACT scores over 30: 7%.

Retention: 74% of full-time freshmen returned.

FACULTY
Student/faculty ratio: 15:1.

ACADEMICS
Calendar: semesters. *Degrees:* bachelor's, master's, doctoral, post-master's, and postbachelor's certificates.

Special study options: academic remediation for entering students, advanced placement credit, distance learning, double majors, English as a second language, independent study, internships, off-campus study, part-time degree program, services for LD students, study abroad, summer session for credit.

Computers: 723 computers/terminals are available on campus for general student use. Students can access the following: campus intranet, computer help desk, free student e-mail accounts, online (class) grades, online (class) registration, online (class) schedules. Campuswide network is available. Wireless service is available via entire campus.

Library: Alfred R. Neuman Library. *Books:* 441,306 (physical), 503,332 (digital/electronic); *Serial titles:* 5,402 (physical), 93,891 (digital/electronic); *Databases:* 212. Weekly public service hours: 89; students can reserve study rooms.

STUDENT LIFE
Housing options: special housing for students with disabilities. Campus housing is provided by a third party. Freshman applicants given priority for college housing.

Activities and organizations: drama/theater group, student-run newspaper.

Athletics *Intramural sports:* badminton M/W, basketball M/W, bowling M/W, football M/W, table tennis M/W, tennis M/W, volleyball M/W.

Campus security: 24-hour emergency response devices and patrols, student patrols, late-night transport/escort service.

Student services: health clinic, personal/psychological counseling, women's center, veterans affairs office.

COSTS & FINANCIAL AID
Costs (2019–20) *Tuition:* area resident $6790 full-time; state resident $6790 full-time; nonresident $22,980 full-time. *Required fees:* $784 full-time. *Room only:* $4310.

Financial Aid Of all full-time matriculated undergraduates who enrolled in 2016, 1,916 applied for aid, 1,810 were judged to have need, 66 had their need fully met. In 2016, 252 non-need-based awards were made. *Average percent of need met:* 45. *Average financial aid package:* $8767. *Average need-based loan:* $4452. *Average need-based gift aid:* $6891. *Average non-need-based aid:* $2149.

APPLYING
Standardized Tests *Required:* SAT or ACT (for admission).

Options: electronic application, early admission, deferred entrance.

Application fee: $45.

Required: high school transcript, State of Texas Uniform Admission Policy criteria. *Required for some:* essay or personal statement, 2 letters of recommendation.

Application deadlines: 8/1 (freshmen), 8/1 (out-of-state freshmen).

CONTACT
University of Houston–Clear Lake, 2700 Bay Area Boulevard, Houston, TX 77058-1002.

University of Houston–Downtown

Houston, Texas

http://www.uhd.edu/

- **State-supported** comprehensive, founded 1974, part of University of Houston System
- **Urban** 24-acre campus
- **Coed** 12,680 undergraduate students, 49% full-time, 60% women, 40% men
- **Noncompetitive** entrance level, 83% of applicants were admitted

UNDERGRAD STUDENTS
6,201 full-time, 6,479 part-time. 1% are from out of state; 19% Black or African American, non-Hispanic/Latino; 50% Hispanic/Latino; 9% Asian, non-Hispanic/Latino; 0.2% Native Hawaiian or other Pacific Islander, non-Hispanic/Latino; 0.3% American Indian or Alaska Native, non-Hispanic/Latino; 1% Two or more races, non-Hispanic/Latino; 0.8% Race/ethnicity unknown; 6% international; 17% transferred in.

Freshmen:
Admission: 4,416 applied, 3,673 admitted, 1,068 enrolled. *Test scores:* SAT evidence-based reading and writing scores over 500: 56%; SAT math scores over 500: 59%; ACT scores over 18: 62%; SAT evidence-based reading and writing scores over 600: 8%; SAT math scores over 600: 4%; ACT scores over 24: 5%.

Retention: 71% of full-time freshmen returned.

FACULTY
Total: 751, 49% full-time, 63% with terminal degrees.

Student/faculty ratio: 19:1.

ACADEMICS
Calendar: semesters. *Degrees:* bachelor's, master's, and postbachelor's certificates.

Special study options: academic remediation for entering students, advanced placement credit, distance learning, double majors, English as a second language, honors programs, independent study, internships, off-campus study, part-time degree program, services for LD students, study abroad, summer session for credit. *ROTC:* Army (c), Air Force (c).

Computers: Students can access the following: computer help desk, free student e-mail accounts, online (class) grades, online (class) registration, online (class) schedules. Campuswide network is available. Wireless service is available via entire campus.

Library: W. I. Dykes Library. Study areas open 24 hours, 5–7 days a week; students can reserve study rooms.

STUDENT LIFE
Housing options: college housing not available.

Activities and organizations: drama/theater group, student-run newspaper, radio station, Student Government Association, Campus Activities Board, Professional Accounting Society, American Marketing Association, Bilingual Education Student Organization, national fraternities, national sororities.

Athletics ***Intramural sports:*** badminton M/W, baseball M(c), basketball M(c)/W(c), bowling M/W, cheerleading M(c)/W(c), soccer M(c)/W(c), tennis M/W, volleyball M(c)/W(c), weight lifting M(c)/W(c).

Campus security: 24-hour emergency response devices and patrols, late-night transport/escort service.

Student services: health clinic, personal/psychological counseling, legal services, veterans affairs office.

COSTS & FINANCIAL AID
Costs (2019–20) ***Tuition:*** state resident $6990 full-time, $233 per credit hour part-time; nonresident $19,650 full-time, $655 per credit hour part-time. ***Required fees:*** $1196 full-time.

Financial Aid Of all full-time matriculated undergraduates who enrolled in 2018, 7,074 applied for aid, 6,247 were judged to have need, 173 had their need fully met. In 2018, 384 non-need-based awards were made. ***Average percent of need met:*** 43. ***Average financial aid package:*** $10,277. ***Average need-based loan:*** $8151. ***Average need-based gift aid:*** $5574. ***Average non-need-based aid:*** $2137. ***Average indebtedness upon graduation:*** $26,811.

APPLYING
Standardized Tests *Required:* SAT or ACT (for admission).

Options: electronic application.

Application fee: $50.

Required: high school transcript.

CONTACT
Mr. Jordan Green, Assistant Director, Customer Services Undergraduate Admissions, University of Houston–Downtown, One Main Street, Suite GSB308, Houston, TX 77002. *Phone:* 713-221-8021. *Fax:* 713-221-8157. *E-mail:* uhdadmit@uhd.edu.

University of Houston–Victoria

Victoria, Texas

http://www.uhv.edu/

CONTACT
Mrs. Trudy Wortham, Registrar, University of Houston–Victoria, 3007 North Ben Wilson, Victoria, TX 77901. *Phone:* 361-485-4521 Ext. 4184. *Toll-free phone:* 877-970-4848 Ext. 110. *E-mail:* worthamt@uhv.edu.

University of Mary Hardin-Baylor

Belton, Texas

http://www.umhb.edu/

- **Independent Southern Baptist** comprehensive, founded 1845
- **Small-town** 340-acre campus with easy access to Austin
- **Endowment** $88.2 million
- **Coed** 3,397 undergraduate students, 94% full-time, 65% women, 35% men
- **Moderately difficult** entrance level, 87% of applicants were admitted

UNDERGRAD STUDENTS
3,181 full-time, 216 part-time. Students come from 34 states and territories; 25 other countries; 3% are from out of state; 14% Black or African American, non-Hispanic/Latino; 22% Hispanic/Latino; 2% Asian, non-Hispanic/Latino; 0.1% Native Hawaiian or other Pacific Islander, non-Hispanic/Latino; 0.8% American Indian or Alaska Native, non-Hispanic/Latino; 3% Two or more races, non-Hispanic/Latino; 2% Race/ethnicity unknown; 0.9% international; 7% transferred in; 59% live on campus.

Freshmen:
Admission: 11,783 applied, 10,214 admitted, 875 enrolled. ***Average high school GPA:*** 3.6. ***Test scores:*** SAT evidence-based reading and writing scores over 500: 85%; SAT math scores over 500: 80%; ACT scores over 18: 92%; SAT evidence-based reading and writing scores over 600: 32%; SAT math scores over 600: 21%; ACT scores over 24: 38%; SAT evidence-based reading and writing scores over 700: 3%; SAT math scores over 700: 2%; ACT scores over 30: 5%.

Retention: 73% of full-time freshmen returned.

FACULTY
Total: 277, 60% full-time, 63% with terminal degrees.

Student/faculty ratio: 18:1.

ACADEMICS
Calendar: semesters. *Degrees:* bachelor's, master's, doctoral, and post-master's certificates.

Special study options: academic remediation for entering students, adult/continuing education programs, advanced placement credit, distance learning, double majors, English as a second language, honors programs, independent study, internships, off-campus study, part-time degree program, services for LD students, study abroad, summer session for credit. ***ROTC:*** Army (b), Air Force (c).

Unusual degree programs: 3-2 business administration.

Computers: 275 computers/terminals and 1,000 ports are available on campus for general student use. Students can access the following: campus intranet, computer help desk, free student e-mail accounts, online (class) grades, online (class) registration, online (class) schedules. Campuswide network is available. 100% of college-owned or -operated housing units are wired for high-speed Internet access. Wireless service is available via entire campus.
Library: Townsend Memorial Library. *Books:* 183,933 (physical), 28,294 (digital/electronic); *Serial titles:* 340 (physical), 277,950 (digital/electronic); *Databases:* 146. Weekly public service hours: 99; students can reserve study rooms.

STUDENT LIFE
Housing options: men-only, women-only, special housing for students with disabilities. Campus housing is university owned. Freshman applicants given priority for college housing.

Activities and organizations: drama/theater group, student-run newspaper, choral group, Baptist Student Ministry, Student Government Association, Nursing Student Association, Campus Activities Board, Search Cru.

Athletics Member NCAA. All Division III except golf (Division II). ***Intercollegiate sports:*** baseball M, basketball M/W, cross-country running M/W, football M, golf M/W, gymnastics W, soccer M/W, softball W, tennis M/W, volleyball W. ***Intramural sports:*** basketball M/W, football M/W, golf M/W, soccer M/W, softball M/W, table tennis M/W, tennis M/W, ultimate Frisbee M/W, volleyball M/W.

Campus security: 24-hour emergency response devices and patrols, late-night transport/escort service, controlled dormitory access.

Student services: health clinic, personal/psychological counseling, veterans affairs office.

COSTS & FINANCIAL AID
Costs (2018–19) ***Comprehensive fee:*** $35,336 includes full-time tuition ($24,640), mandatory fees ($2250), and room and board ($8446). Full-time tuition and fees vary according to course load and degree level. Part-time tuition: $880 per credit hour. Part-time tuition and fees vary according to course load and degree level. ***Room and board:*** Room and board charges vary according to board plan and housing facility. ***Payment plan:*** installment. ***Waivers:*** employees or children of employees.

Financial Aid Of all full-time matriculated undergraduates who enrolled in 2018, 2,831 applied for aid, 2,563 were judged to have need, 173 had their need fully met. In 2018, 389 non-need-based awards were made. ***Average percent of need met:*** 57. ***Average financial aid package:*** $18,315. ***Average need-based loan:*** $4205. ***Average need-based gift aid:*** $14,331. ***Average non-need-based aid:*** $7709. ***Average indebtedness upon graduation:*** $38,369.

APPLYING
Standardized Tests *Required:* SAT or ACT (for admission).

Options: electronic application, early admission, deferred entrance.

Application fee: $35.

Required: high school transcript. ***Required for some:*** essay or personal statement, interview.

Application deadlines: rolling (freshmen), rolling (transfers).

Notification: continuous (freshmen), continuous (transfers).

CONTACT
Mr. Nick Jones, Associate Director, Admissions and Recruiting, University of Mary Hardin-Baylor, 900 College Street UMHB Box 8004, Belton, TX 76513. *Phone:* 254-295-4249. *Toll-free phone:* 800-727-8642. *E-mail:* njones@umhb.edu.

University of North Texas

Denton, Texas

http://www.unt.edu/

- **State-supported** university, founded 1890, part of University of North Texas System
- **Suburban** 875-acre campus with easy access to Dallas-Fort Worth
- **Endowment** $166.4 million
- **Coed**
- **Moderately difficult** entrance level

FACULTY
Student/faculty ratio: 24:1.

ACADEMICS
Calendar: semesters. *Degrees:* bachelor's, master's, doctoral, and postbachelor's certificates.
Library: Willis Library plus 5 others. *Books:* 2.1 million (physical), 1.0 million (digital/electronic); *Serial titles:* 19,763 (physical), 166,076 (digital/electronic); *Databases:* 391. Weekly public service hours: 168; study areas open 24 hours, 5–7 days a week; students can reserve study rooms.

STUDENT LIFE
Housing options: on-campus residence required for freshman year; coed, special housing for students with disabilities. Campus housing is university owned. Freshman applicants given priority for college housing.

Activities and organizations: drama/theater group, student-run newspaper, radio and television station, choral group, marching band, Student Government Association, Residence Hall Association, Panhellenic Association, Interfraternity Council, Black Student Union, national fraternities, national sororities.

Athletics Member NCAA. All Division I except football (Division I-A).

Campus security: 24-hour emergency response devices and patrols, late-night transport/escort service, controlled dormitory access.

Student services: health clinic, personal/psychological counseling, legal services, veterans affairs office.

COSTS & FINANCIAL AID
Costs (2018–19) ***Tuition:*** state resident $8403 full-time, $280 per semester hour part-time; nonresident $20,853 full-time, $695 per semester hour part-time. Full-time tuition and fees vary according to course load and program. Part-time tuition and fees vary according to course load and program. No tuition increase for student's term of enrollment. ***Required fees:*** $2847 full-time, $95 per semester hour part-time. ***Room and board:*** $9727. Room and board charges vary according to board plan and housing facility.

Financial Aid Of all full-time matriculated undergraduates who enrolled in 2018, 18,708 applied for aid, 15,599 were judged to have need, 1,273 had their need fully met. In 2018, 2833 non-need-based awards were made. ***Average percent of need met:*** 53. ***Average financial aid package:*** $11,415. ***Average need-based loan:*** $4124. ***Average need-based gift aid:*** $8425. ***Average non-need-based aid:*** $5105. ***Average indebtedness upon graduation:*** $25,808.

APPLYING
Standardized Tests *Required:* SAT or ACT (for admission).

Options: electronic application, early admission, deferred entrance.

Application fee: $75.

Required: high school transcript. ***Required for some:*** essay or personal statement.

CONTACT
Mr. Randall Nunn, Associate Director of Admissions, University of North Texas, Denton, TX 76203. *Phone:* 940-565-3920. *Toll-free phone:* 800-868-8211. *E-mail:* randall.nunn@unt.edu.

University of North Texas at Dallas

Dallas, Texas

http://untdallas.edu/

- **State-supported** comprehensive, founded 2001, part of University of North Texas System
- **Urban** 264-acre campus with easy access to Dallas-Fort Worth
- **Endowment** $823,724
- **Coed**
- 74% of applicants were admitted

FACULTY
Student/faculty ratio: 15:1.

ACADEMICS
Degrees: bachelor's, master's, and doctoral.
Library: UNTD Library. *Books:* 3,980 (physical), 44,401 (digital/electronic); *Serial titles:* 330 (physical), 10,899 (digital/electronic); *Databases:* 281.

STUDENT LIFE
Activities and organizations: national fraternities, national sororities.

Campus security: 24-hour emergency response devices, late-night transport/escort service.

Student services: personal/psychological counseling, veterans affairs office.

COSTS & FINANCIAL AID
Costs (2018–19) ***Tuition:*** state resident $7548 full-time, $252 per credit hour part-time; nonresident $19,788 full-time, $660 per credit hour part-time. Full-time tuition and fees vary according to degree level. Part-time tuition and fees vary according to degree level. No tuition increase for student's term of enrollment. ***Required fees:*** $300 full-time, $10 per credit hour part-time. ***Room and board:*** $8948. Room and board charges vary according to board plan and housing facility.

Financial Aid Of all full-time matriculated undergraduates who enrolled in 2017, 1,469 applied for aid, 1,400 were judged to have need, 77 had their need fully met. In 2017, 152 non-need-based awards were made. ***Average percent of need met:*** 46. ***Average financial aid package:*** $9796. ***Average need-based loan:*** $4230. ***Average need-based gift aid:*** $6835. ***Average non-need-based aid:*** $6012. ***Average indebtedness upon graduation:*** $6566.

APPLYING
Standardized Tests *Required:* SAT or ACT (for admission).

Options: electronic application.

Application fee: $50.

Required: high school transcript.

CONTACT
Mr. Jason Faulk, Director of Undergraduate Admission, University of North Texas at Dallas, 7300 University Hill Drive, Admin (B1)105, Dallas 76039. *Phone:* 972-780-3642. *E-mail:* admissions@untdallas.edu.

University of Phoenix–Dallas Campus

Dallas, Texas

http://www.phoenix.edu/

CONTACT
Marc Booker, Senior Director, Office of Admissions and Evaluation, University of Phoenix–Dallas Campus, 4035 South Riverpoint Parkway, Mail Stop CF-L101, Phoenix, AZ 85040. *Phone:* 602-557-4609. *Toll-free phone:* 866-766-0766. *Fax:* 480-643-1156.

University of Phoenix–Houston Campus

Houston, Texas

http://www.phoenix.edu/

CONTACT

Marc Booker, Senior Director, Office of Admissions and Evaluation, University of Phoenix–Houston Campus, 4305 South Riverpoint Parkway, Mail Stop CF-L101, Phoenix, AZ 85040. *Phone:* 602-557-4609. *Toll-free phone:* 866-766-0766. *Fax:* 480-643-1156.

University of Phoenix–San Antonio Campus

San Antonio, Texas

http://www.phoenix.edu/

CONTACT

University of Phoenix–San Antonio Campus, 8200 IH-10 West, San Antonio, TX 78230. *Toll-free phone:* 866-766-0766.

University of St. Thomas

Houston, Texas

http://www.stthom.edu/

- **Independent Roman Catholic** comprehensive, founded 1947
- **Urban** 23-acre campus with easy access to Houston, TX
- **Endowment** $102.4 million
- **Coed** 2,047 undergraduate students, 77% full-time, 63% women, 37% men
- **Moderately difficult** entrance level, 82% of applicants were admitted

UNDERGRAD STUDENTS

1,573 full-time, 474 part-time. Students come from 33 states and territories; 58 other countries; 2% are from out of state; 7% Black or African American, non-Hispanic/Latino; 47% Hispanic/Latino; 12% Asian, non-Hispanic/Latino; 0.2% Native Hawaiian or other Pacific Islander, non-Hispanic/Latino; 0.2% American Indian or Alaska Native, non-Hispanic/Latino; 2% Two or more races, non-Hispanic/Latino; 2% Race/ethnicity unknown; 8% international; 10% transferred in; 20% live on campus.

Freshmen:

Admission: 1,216 applied, 1,000 admitted, 355 enrolled. ***Average high school GPA:*** 3.6. ***Test scores:*** SAT evidence-based reading and writing scores over 500: 94%; SAT math scores over 500: 91%; ACT scores over 18: 100%; SAT evidence-based reading and writing scores over 600: 38%; SAT math scores over 600: 32%; ACT scores over 24: 50%; SAT evidence-based reading and writing scores over 700: 6%; SAT math scores over 700: 7%; ACT scores over 30: 11%.

Retention: 82% of full-time freshmen returned.

FACULTY

Total: 337, 46% full-time, 66% with terminal degrees.

Student/faculty ratio: 10:1.

ACADEMICS

Calendar: semesters. *Degrees:* diplomas, bachelor's, master's, doctoral, and postbachelor's certificates.

Special study options: accelerated degree program, adult/continuing education programs, advanced placement credit, distance learning, double majors, honors programs, independent study, internships, off-campus study, part-time degree program, services for LD students, student-designed majors, study abroad, summer session for credit. ***ROTC:*** Army (c), Air Force (c).

Unusual degree programs: 3-2 business administration; engineering with University of Notre Dame, University of Houston, Texas A&M University, The Catholic University of America.

Computers: 490 computers/terminals and 800 ports are available on campus for general student use. Students can access the following: campus intranet, computer help desk, free student e-mail accounts, online (class) grades, online (class) registration, online (class) schedules. Campuswide network is available. 100% of college-owned or -operated housing units are wired for high-speed Internet access. Wireless service is available via entire campus.

Library: Doherty Library. *Books:* 262,245 (physical), 2,496 (digital/electronic); *Serial titles:* 74,347 (physical), 74,347 (digital/electronic); *Databases:* 274. Weekly public service hours: 100.

STUDENT LIFE

Housing options: coed, men-only, women-only, special housing for students with disabilities. Campus housing is university owned. Freshman applicants given priority for college housing.

Activities and organizations: drama/theater group, choral group, Health Occupations Students of America (HOSA), Filipino Student Association (FSA), Tri-Beta, Psi Chi, Pre-Health Professional Society.

Athletics Member NAIA. ***Intercollegiate sports:*** basketball M(s)/W(s), cross-country running M(s)/W(s), golf M(s)/W(s), soccer M(s)/W(s), volleyball W(s). ***Intramural sports:*** badminton M(c)/W(c), baseball M(c)/W(c), basketball M(c)/W(c), cheerleading M(c)/W(c), fencing M(c)/W(c), sand volleyball M(c)/W(c), soccer M(c)/W(c), table tennis M(c)/W(c), tennis M(c)/W(c).

Campus security: 24-hour emergency response devices and patrols, late-night transport/escort service, controlled dormitory access.

Student services: personal/psychological counseling.

COSTS & FINANCIAL AID

Costs (2019–20) ***Comprehensive fee:*** $40,760 includes full-time tuition ($30,800), mandatory fees ($660), and room and board ($9300). Part-time tuition: $1100 per credit hour. ***College room only:*** $5710.

Financial Aid Of all full-time matriculated undergraduates who enrolled in 2018, 1,131 applied for aid, 1,079 were judged to have need, 81 had their need fully met. 78 Federal Work-Study jobs (averaging $3843). 3 state and other part-time jobs (averaging $3510). In 2018, 373 non-need-based awards were made. ***Average percent of need met:*** 66. ***Average financial aid package:*** $25,607. ***Average need-based loan:*** $4457. ***Average need-based gift aid:*** $23,273. ***Average non-need-based aid:*** $12,181. ***Average indebtedness upon graduation:*** $29,896.

APPLYING

Standardized Tests *Required:* SAT or ACT (for admission).

Options: electronic application, early action, deferred entrance.

Required: minimum 2.8 GPA. ***Recommended:*** 3 letters of recommendation.

Notification: continuous until 11/1 (freshmen), continuous (transfers).

CONTACT

Mr. Marcos Canales, Assistant Director of Freshman Admissions, University of St. Thomas, 3800 Montrose Boulevard, Houston, TX 77006-4696. *Phone:* 713-525-3542. *Toll-free phone:* 800-856-8565. *Fax:* 713-525-3558. *E-mail:* admissions@stthom.edu.

The University of Texas at Arlington

Arlington, Texas

http://www.uta.edu/

CONTACT

Dr. Hans Gatterdam, Executive Director of Admissions, Records and Registration, The University of Texas at Arlington, UTA Box 19088, 701 South Nedderman Drive, Arlington, TX 76019-0088. *Phone:* 817-272-3275. *Fax:* 817-272-5114.

The University of Texas at Austin

Austin, Texas

http://www.utexas.edu/

- **State-supported** university, founded 1883, part of University of Texas System
- **Urban** 431-acre campus with easy access to Austin
- **Endowment** $4.0 billion
- **Coed** 40,804 undergraduate students, 93% full-time, 54% women, 46% men
- **Moderately difficult** entrance level, 39% of applicants were admitted

UNDERGRAD STUDENTS

38,097 full-time, 2,707 part-time. Students come from 52 states and territories; 102 other countries; 6% are from out of state; 4% Black or

African American, non-Hispanic/Latino; 24% Hispanic/Latino; 22% Asian, non-Hispanic/Latino; 0.1% Native Hawaiian or other Pacific Islander, non-Hispanic/Latino; 0.1% American Indian or Alaska Native, non-Hispanic/Latino; 4% Two or more races, non-Hispanic/Latino; 0.9% Race/ethnicity unknown; 5% international; 4% transferred in; 18% live on campus.

Freshmen:
Admission: 50,575 applied, 19,482 admitted, 8,960 enrolled. ***Test scores:*** SAT evidence-based reading and writing scores over 500: 99%; SAT math scores over 500: 98%; ACT scores over 18: 99%; SAT evidence-based reading and writing scores over 600: 84%; SAT math scores over 600: 79%; ACT scores over 24: 89%; SAT evidence-based reading and writing scores over 700: 37%; SAT math scores over 700: 46%; ACT scores over 30: 56%.
Retention: 95% of full-time freshmen returned.

FACULTY
Total: 2,994, 83% full-time, 88% with terminal degrees.
Student/faculty ratio: 18:1.

ACADEMICS
Calendar: semesters. *Degrees:* certificates, bachelor's, master's, doctoral, and postbachelor's certificates.
Special study options: academic remediation for entering students, accelerated degree program, advanced placement credit, cooperative education, distance learning, double majors, English as a second language, honors programs, independent study, internships, off-campus study, part-time degree program, services for LD students, student-designed majors, study abroad, summer session for credit. ***ROTC:*** Army (b), Navy (b), Air Force (b).
Unusual degree programs: 3-2 business administration; engineering; nursing; social work; computer science.
Computers: 3,150 computers/terminals are available on campus for general student use. Students can access the following: campus intranet, computer help desk, free student e-mail accounts, online (class) grades, online (class) registration, online (class) schedules. Campuswide network is available. 100% of college-owned or -operated housing units are wired for high-speed Internet access. Wireless service is available via entire campus.
Library: PCL (Perry Castaneda Library) plus 19 others. *Books:* 11.5 million (physical), 1.5 million (digital/electronic); *Serial titles:* 252,967 (physical), 471,535 (digital/electronic); *Databases:* 941. Weekly public service hours: 94; study areas open 24 hours, 5–7 days a week; students can reserve study rooms.

STUDENT LIFE
Housing options: coed, men-only, women-only, special housing for students with disabilities. Campus housing is university owned. Freshman applicants given priority for college housing.
Activities and organizations: drama/theater group, student-run newspaper, radio and television station, choral group, marching band, Alpha Phi Omega, University Panhellenic Council, Asian Business Students Association, Longhorn Band Student Organization, Campus Events + Entertainment, national fraternities, national sororities.
Athletics Member NCAA. All Division I except football (Division I-A). ***Intercollegiate sports:*** archery M(c)/W(c), badminton M(c)/W(c), baseball M(s)/W(c), basketball M(s)/W(s), crew M(c)/W(s), cross-country running M(s)/W(s), fencing M(c)/W(c), golf M(s)/W(s)(c), gymnastics M(c)/W(c), ice hockey M(c)/W(c), lacrosse M(c)/W(c), racquetball M(c)/W(c), rock climbing M(c)/W(c), rugby M(c)/W(c), sailing M(c)/W(c), soccer M(c)/W(s), softball W(s), swimming and diving M(s)/W(s), table tennis M(c)/W(c), tennis M(s)/W(s), track and field M(s)/W(s), ultimate Frisbee M(c)/W(c), volleyball M(c)/W(s), water polo M(c)/W(c), weight lifting M(c)/W(c), wrestling M(c)/W(c). ***Intramural sports:*** basketball M/W, football M/W, golf M/W, racquetball M/W, rock climbing M/W, soccer M/W, softball M/W, swimming and diving M/W, table tennis M/W, tennis M/W, track and field M/W, ultimate Frisbee M/W, volleyball M/W.
Campus security: 24-hour emergency response devices and patrols, late-night transport/escort service, controlled dormitory access.
Student services: health clinic, personal/psychological counseling, women's center, legal services, veterans affairs office.

COSTS & FINANCIAL AID
Costs (2018–19) ***Tuition:*** state resident $10,606 full-time; nonresident $37,480 full-time. Full-time tuition and fees vary according to course load and program. Part-time tuition and fees vary according to course load and program. No tuition increase for student's term of enrollment. ***Room and board:*** $10,804. Room and board charges vary according to housing facility. ***Payment plan:*** installment. ***Waivers:*** senior citizens and employees or children of employees.
Financial Aid Of all full-time matriculated undergraduates who enrolled in 2017, 22,544 applied for aid, 15,083 were judged to have need, 3,322 had their need fully met. 1,084 Federal Work-Study jobs (averaging $2031). 192 state and other part-time jobs (averaging $1665). In 2017, 292 non-need-based awards were made. ***Average percent of need met:*** 70. ***Average financial aid package:*** $12,215. ***Average need-based loan:*** $4786. ***Average need-based gift aid:*** $9535. ***Average non-need-based aid:*** $2514. ***Average indebtedness upon graduation:*** $24,244.

APPLYING
Standardized Tests *Required:* SAT or ACT (for admission).
Options: electronic application.
Application fee: $75.
Required: essay or personal statement, high school transcript.
Application deadlines: 12/1 (freshmen), 12/1 (out-of-state freshmen), 3/1 (transfers).
Notification: continuous (freshmen), continuous (transfers).

CONTACT
Miguel Wasielewski, Executive Director of Admissions, The University of Texas at Austin, Office of Admissions, PO Box 8058, PO Box 8058, Austin, TX 78713-8058. *Phone:* 512-475-7399. *E-mail:* admissions@austin.utexas.edu.

The University of Texas at Dallas
Richardson, Texas
http://www.utdallas.edu/

- **State-supported** university, founded 1969, part of University of Texas System
- **Suburban** 500-acre campus with easy access to Dallas-Fort Worth
- **Endowment** $482.8 million
- **Coed**
- **Very difficult** entrance level

FACULTY
Student/faculty ratio: 23:1.

ACADEMICS
Calendar: semesters. *Degrees:* bachelor's, master's, doctoral, and postbachelor's certificates.
Library: Eugene McDermott Library plus 1 other. *Books:* 652,018 (physical), 1.5 million (digital/electronic); *Serial titles:* 135,287 (physical), 149,406 (digital/electronic); *Databases:* 530. Weekly public service hours: 152; study areas open 24 hours, 5–7 days a week; students can reserve study rooms.

STUDENT LIFE
Housing options: coed. Campus housing is university owned. Freshman applicants given priority for college housing.
Activities and organizations: drama/theater group, student-run newspaper, radio and television station, choral group, Student Government Association, Golden Key National Honor Society, Muslim Students Association, Indian Student Association, Friendship Association of Chinese Students and Scholars, national fraternities, national sororities.
Athletics Member NCAA. All Division III.
Campus security: 24-hour emergency response devices and patrols, student patrols, late-night transport/escort service, controlled dormitory access.
Student services: health clinic, personal/psychological counseling, women's center, legal services, veterans affairs office.

COSTS & FINANCIAL AID
Costs (2018–19) ***Tuition:*** state resident $13,034 full-time; nonresident $36,876 full-time. Full-time tuition and fees vary according to course load and degree level. Part-time tuition and fees vary according to course load and degree level. No tuition increase for student's term of enrollment.

Room and board: $11,532. Room and board charges vary according to board plan and housing facility.

Financial Aid Of all full-time matriculated undergraduates who enrolled in 2017, 9,660 applied for aid, 8,058 were judged to have need, 1,165 had their need fully met. In 2017, 3181 non-need-based awards were made. ***Average percent of need met:*** 64. ***Average financial aid package:*** $13,396. ***Average need-based loan:*** $4467. ***Average need-based gift aid:*** $9376. ***Average non-need-based aid:*** $11,579. ***Average indebtedness upon graduation:*** $23,884.

APPLYING
Standardized Tests *Required:* SAT or ACT (for admission). *Required for some:* THEA.

Options: electronic application, deferred entrance.

Application fee: $50.

Required: essay or personal statement, high school transcript. ***Required for some:*** interview. ***Recommended:*** 3 letters of recommendation.

CONTACT
Enrollment Services, The University of Texas at Dallas, 800 West Campbell Road, Mail Station ROC12, Richardson, TX 75083-0688. *Phone:* 972-883-2270. *Toll-free phone:* 800-889-2443. *Fax:* 972-883-2599. *E-mail:* interest@utdallas.edu.

The University of Texas at El Paso

El Paso, Texas

http://www.utep.edu/

- **State-supported** university, founded 1913, part of University of Texas System
- **Urban** 360-acre campus
- **Coed** 21,464 undergraduate students, 65% full-time, 53% women, 47% men
- **Minimally difficult** entrance level, 100% of applicants were admitted

UNDERGRAD STUDENTS
14,044 full-time, 7,420 part-time. Students come from 53 states and territories; 80 other countries; 4% are from out of state; 2% Black or African American, non-Hispanic/Latino; 83% Hispanic/Latino; 0.9% Asian, non-Hispanic/Latino; 0.1% Native Hawaiian or other Pacific Islander, non-Hispanic/Latino; 0.1% American Indian or Alaska Native, non-Hispanic/Latino; 0.9% Two or more races, non-Hispanic/Latino; 0.5% Race/ethnicity unknown; 6% international; 9% transferred in.

Freshmen:
Admission: 9,382 applied, 9,382 admitted, 2,835 enrolled. ***Average high school GPA:*** 3.3. ***Test scores:*** SAT evidence-based reading and writing scores over 500: 62%; SAT math scores over 500: 62%; ACT scores over 18: 68%; SAT evidence-based reading and writing scores over 600: 17%; SAT math scores over 600: 13%; ACT scores over 24: 19%; SAT evidence-based reading and writing scores over 700: 2%; SAT math scores over 700: 1%; ACT scores over 30: 2%.

Retention: 73% of full-time freshmen returned.

FACULTY
Total: 1,315, 61% full-time.

Student/faculty ratio: 21:1.

ACADEMICS
Calendar: semesters. *Degrees:* certificates, diplomas, bachelor's, master's, and doctoral.

Special study options: distance learning, double majors, honors programs, independent study, study abroad. ***ROTC:*** Army (b).

Computers: Students can access the following: computer help desk, free student e-mail accounts, online (class) grades, online (class) registration, online (class) schedules. Campuswide network is available. 100% of college-owned or -operated housing units are wired for high-speed Internet access. Wireless service is available via entire campus.
Library: University Library. *Books:* 914,412 (physical), 407,455 (digital/electronic); *Serial titles:* 15,278 (physical), 101,613 (digital/electronic); *Databases:* 395.

STUDENT LIFE
Housing options: coed. Campus housing is university owned.

Activities and organizations: drama/theater group, student-run newspaper, radio station, choral group, marching band, national fraternities, national sororities.

Athletics Member NCAA. All Division I except football (Division I-A). ***Intercollegiate sports:*** basketball M(s)/W(s), cross-country running M(s)/W(s), golf M(s), riflery M/W, softball W(s), tennis W(s), track and field M(s)/W(s), volleyball W(s). ***Intramural sports:*** archery M/W, badminton M/W, basketball M/W, bowling M/W, fencing M, field hockey M/W, golf M/W, gymnastics M/W, ice hockey M(c), racquetball M/W, rock climbing M/W, sand volleyball M/W, skiing (downhill) M, soccer M/W, squash M/W, swimming and diving M/W, tennis M/W, track and field M/W, volleyball M/W, water polo M/W, weight lifting M, wrestling M/W.

Campus security: 24-hour emergency response devices and patrols, late-night transport/escort service.

Student services: health clinic, personal/psychological counseling, women's center, legal services.

FINANCIAL AID
Financial Aid Of all full-time matriculated undergraduates who enrolled in 2017, 12,305 applied for aid, 10,363 were judged to have need, 1,622 had their need fully met. In 2017, 655 non-need-based awards were made. ***Average percent of need met:*** 55. ***Average financial aid package:*** $11,820. ***Average need-based loan:*** $6172. ***Average need-based gift aid:*** $7873. ***Average non-need-based aid:*** $4229. ***Average indebtedness upon graduation:*** $23,632.

APPLYING
Standardized Tests *Required:* SAT or ACT (for admission).

Options: deferred entrance.

Required: high school transcript.

CONTACT
Mr. Michael J. Talamantes, Director of Admissions and Recruitment, The University of Texas at El Paso, Academic Services Building, Room 102, El Paso, TX 779968. *Phone:* 915-747-5890. *Toll-free phone:* 877-74MINER. *Fax:* 915-747-5890. *E-mail:* futureminer@utep.edu.

The University of Texas at San Antonio

San Antonio, Texas

http://www.utsa.edu/

- **State-supported** university, founded 1969, part of University of Texas System
- **Suburban** 725-acre campus with easy access to San Antonio
- **Endowment** $134.5 million
- **Coed**
- **Moderately difficult** entrance level

FACULTY
Student/faculty ratio: 25:1.

ACADEMICS
Calendar: semesters. *Degrees:* certificates, bachelor's, master's, doctoral, and postbachelor's certificates.
Library: John Peace Library plus 3 others. Students can reserve study rooms.

STUDENT LIFE
Housing options: coed. Campus housing is university owned and is provided by a third party.

Activities and organizations: student-run newspaper, radio and television station, choral group, marching band, Student Government, VOICES, Chi Alpha Christian Fellowship, Hispanic Student Association, Panhellenic Council, national fraternities, national sororities.

Athletics Member NCAA. All Division I.

Campus security: 24-hour emergency response devices and patrols, late-night transport/escort service, controlled dormitory access, close to 1000 security cameras, Reverse 911 emergency telephone notification system, warning speaker arrays.

Student services: health clinic, personal/psychological counseling, women's center, veterans affairs office.

FINANCIAL AID
Financial Aid Of all full-time matriculated undergraduates who enrolled in 2017, 16,976 applied for aid, 14,613 were judged to have need, 1,073 had their need fully met. In 2017, 781 non-need-based awards were made. ***Average percent of need met:*** 52. ***Average financial aid package:*** $10,359. ***Average need-based loan:*** $4114. ***Average need-based gift aid:*** $7937. ***Average non-need-based aid:*** $3622. ***Average indebtedness upon graduation:*** $24,585.

APPLYING
Standardized Tests *Required:* SAT or ACT (for admission).
Options: electronic application.
Application fee: $60.
Required: high school transcript. ***Required for some:*** transfer applicants with less than 30 hours must meet freshman requirements and have a 2.25 GPA on a 4.0 scale and submit all college transcripts; transfer applicants with 30 or more completed hours must have a 2.25 GPA on a 4.0 scale and submit all college transcripts. ***Recommended:*** essay or personal statement, 1 letter of recommendation.

CONTACT
Mrs. Beverly Woodson Day, Director of Admissions, The University of Texas at San Antonio, One UTSA Circle, San Antonio, TX 78249. *Phone:* 210-458-4536. *Toll-free phone:* 800-669-0919. *Fax:* 210-458-2001. *E-mail:* prospects@utsa.edu.

The University of Texas at Tyler
Tyler, Texas
http://www.uttyler.edu/

CONTACT
Ms. Sarah Bowdin, Interim Assistant Vice President for Enrollment Management, The University of Texas at Tyler, 3900 University Boulevard, Tyler, TX 75799-0001. *Phone:* 903-566-7057. *Toll-free phone:* 800-UTTYLER. *Fax:* 903-566-7068. *E-mail:* admissions@uttyler.edu.

The University of Texas Health Science Center at Houston
Houston, Texas
http://www.uthouston.edu/

CONTACT
The University of Texas Health Science Center at Houston, PO Box 20036, Houston, TX 77225-0036. *Phone:* 713-500-3388.

The University of Texas Health Science Center at San Antonio
San Antonio, Texas
http://www.uthscsa.edu/

CONTACT
The University of Texas Health Science Center at San Antonio, 7703 Floyd Curl Drive, San Antonio, TX 78229-3900. *Phone:* 210-567-2659.

The University of Texas MD Anderson Cancer Center
Houston, Texas
http://www.mdanderson.org/education-and-research/

CONTACT
The University of Texas MD Anderson Cancer Center, 1515 Holcombe Boulevard, Houston, TX 77030.

The University of Texas Medical Branch
Galveston, Texas
http://www.utmb.edu/

CONTACT
The University of Texas Medical Branch, 301 University Boulevard, Galveston, TX 77555. *Phone:* 409-772-1215.

The University of Texas of the Permian Basin
Odessa, Texas
http://www.utpb.edu/

- **State-supported** comprehensive, founded 1969, part of The University of Texas System
- **Urban** 600-acre campus
- **Endowment** $42.2 million
- **Coed** 6,065 undergraduate students, 36% full-time, 57% women, 43% men
- **Moderately difficult** entrance level, 82% of applicants were admitted

UNDERGRAD STUDENTS
2,192 full-time, 3,873 part-time. Students come from 42 states and territories; 36 other countries; 3% are from out of state; 5% Black or African American, non-Hispanic/Latino; 47% Hispanic/Latino; 3% Asian, non-Hispanic/Latino; 0.2% Native Hawaiian or other Pacific Islander, non-Hispanic/Latino; 0.4% American Indian or Alaska Native, non-Hispanic/Latino; 2% Two or more races, non-Hispanic/Latino; 3% Race/ethnicity unknown; 2% international; 7% transferred in; 19% live on campus.

Freshmen:
Admission: 940 applied, 768 admitted, 396 enrolled. ***Test scores:*** SAT math scores over 500: 65%; ACT scores over 18: 75%; SAT math scores over 600: 19%; ACT scores over 24: 17%; SAT math scores over 700: 1%; ACT scores over 30: 1%.
Retention: 66% of full-time freshmen returned.

FACULTY
Total: 290, 40% full-time, 47% with terminal degrees.
Student/faculty ratio: 27:1.

ACADEMICS
Calendar: semesters. *Degrees:* bachelor's, master's, and postbachelor's certificates.
Special study options: academic remediation for entering students, accelerated degree program, advanced placement credit, cooperative education, distance learning, double majors, English as a second language, honors programs, independent study, internships, part-time degree program, services for LD students, study abroad, summer session for credit.
Unusual degree programs: 3-2 business administration.
Computers: 511 computers/terminals are available on campus for general student use. Students can access the following: campus intranet, computer help desk, free student e-mail accounts, online (class) grades, online (class) registration, online (class) schedules. Campuswide network is available. 100% of college-owned or -operated housing units are wired for high-speed Internet access. Wireless service is available via entire campus.
Library: J. Conrad Dunagan Library. *Books:* 294,556 (physical), 1.0 million (digital/electronic); *Serial titles:* 358 (physical), 86,390 (digital/electronic); *Databases:* 226. Weekly public service hours: 86; students can reserve study rooms.

STUDENT LIFE
Housing options: coed. Campus housing is university owned.
Activities and organizations: drama/theater group, student-run newspaper, choral group, marching band, The American Society for Mechanical Engineers, The Student Veteran Association, Marketing Experiences, The National Society for Leadership and Success, Students in Free Enterprise, national fraternities.

Athletics Member NCAA. All Division II except golf (Division I). ***Intercollegiate sports:*** baseball M(s), basketball M(s)/W(s), cheerleading M(s)/W(s), cross-country running M(s)/W(s), football M(s), golf M(s)/W(s), soccer M(s)/W(s), softball W(s), swimming and diving M(s)/W(s), tennis M(s)/W(s), volleyball W(s). ***Intramural sports:*** basketball M/W, bowling M/W, cross-country running M/W, golf M/W, soccer M/W, softball W, swimming and diving M/W, tennis M/W, volleyball M/W.

Campus security: 24-hour emergency response devices and patrols, late-night transport/escort service, controlled dormitory access.

Student services: health clinic, personal/psychological counseling, veterans affairs office.

COSTS & FINANCIAL AID

Costs (2018–19) ***Tuition:*** state resident $5662 full-time, $189 per credit hour part-time; nonresident $6812 full-time. Full-time tuition and fees vary according to course load, degree level, and location. Part-time tuition and fees vary according to course load, degree level, and location. No tuition increase for student's term of enrollment. ***Required fees:*** $1462 full-time, $70 per credit hour part-time. ***Room and board:*** $10,944; room only: $7200. Room and board charges vary according to board plan and housing facility. ***Payment plan:*** installment.

Financial Aid Of all full-time matriculated undergraduates who enrolled in 2018, 2,371 applied for aid, 2,066 were judged to have need, 306 had their need fully met. In 2018, 985 non-need-based awards were made. ***Average percent of need met:*** 100. ***Average financial aid package:*** $17,965. ***Average need-based loan:*** $4207. ***Average need-based gift aid:*** $17,554. ***Average non-need-based aid:*** $2398. ***Average indebtedness upon graduation:*** $13,445.

APPLYING

Standardized Tests *Required:* SAT or ACT (for admission).

Options: electronic application.

Application fee: $40.

Required: high school transcript.

Notification: continuous (freshmen), continuous (transfers).

CONTACT

Scott Smiley, Director of Admissions, The University of Texas of the Permian Basin, 4901 East University Boulevard, Odessa, TX 79762-0001. *Phone:* 432-552-2605. *Toll-free phone:* 866-552-UTPB. *Fax:* 432-552-3605. *E-mail:* admissions@utpb.edu.

The University of Texas Rio Grande Valley

Edinburg, Texas

http://www.utrgv.edu/

- **State-supported** university, founded 1927, part of University of Texas System
- **Small-town** 414-acre campus with easy access to McAllen, Edinburg, Mission
- **Coed** 24,678 undergraduate students, 78% full-time, 57% women, 43% men
- **Noncompetitive** entrance level, 81% of applicants were admitted

UNDERGRAD STUDENTS

19,128 full-time, 5,550 part-time. Students come from 33 states and territories; 50 other countries; 1% are from out of state; 0.4% Black or African American, non-Hispanic/Latino; 90% Hispanic/Latino; 1% Asian, non-Hispanic/Latino; 0.3% Two or more races, non-Hispanic/Latino; 3% Race/ethnicity unknown; 2% international; 7% transferred in; 4% live on campus.

Freshmen:

Admission: 10,710 applied, 8,636 admitted, 4,565 enrolled. ***Test scores:*** SAT evidence-based reading and writing scores over 500: 68%; SAT math scores over 500: 63%; ACT scores over 18: 70%; SAT evidence-based reading and writing scores over 600: 18%; SAT math scores over 600: 11%; ACT scores over 24: 12%; SAT evidence-based reading and writing scores over 700: 1%; SAT math scores over 700: 1%; ACT scores over 30: 1%.

Retention: 71% of full-time freshmen returned.

ACADEMICS

Calendar: semesters. *Degrees:* bachelor's, master's, doctoral, and post-master's certificates.

Special study options: academic remediation for entering students, accelerated degree program, adult/continuing education programs, advanced placement credit, cooperative education, distance learning, double majors, English as a second language, honors programs, independent study, internships, off-campus study, part-time degree program, services for LD students, study abroad, summer session for credit. ***ROTC:*** Army (b).

Unusual degree programs: 3-2 business administration.

Computers: Students can access the following: campus intranet, computer help desk, free student e-mail accounts, online (class) grades, online (class) registration, online (class) schedules. Campuswide network is available. 66% of college-owned or -operated housing units are wired for high-speed Internet access. Wireless service is available via entire campus.

Library: University Library. Students can reserve study rooms.

STUDENT LIFE

Housing options: men-only, women-only, special housing for students with disabilities. Campus housing is university owned.

Activities and organizations: drama/theater group, student-run newspaper, radio and television station, choral group, Alpha Lambda Delta National Honor Society for First-Year Students, The National Society of Collegiate Scholars, Golden Key International Honor Society, Pre-Medical Bio-Medical Society, Environmental Awareness Club, national fraternities, national sororities.

Athletics Member NCAA. All Division I. ***Intercollegiate sports:*** baseball M, basketball M/W, cross-country running M/W, golf M, soccer M/W, tennis M/W, track and field M/W, volleyball W.

Campus security: 24-hour emergency response devices and patrols, late-night transport/escort service.

Student services: health clinic, personal/psychological counseling, veterans affairs office.

COSTS & FINANCIAL AID

Costs (2018–19) ***Tuition:*** state resident $6345 full-time, $376 per credit hour part-time; nonresident $18,795 full-time, $791 per credit hour part-time. Full-time tuition and fees vary according to degree level and program. Part-time tuition and fees vary according to degree level and program. No tuition increase for student's term of enrollment. ***Required fees:*** $1468 full-time, $185 per credit hour part-time. ***Room and board:*** $8124; room only: $4976. Room and board charges vary according to board plan and housing facility. ***Payment plans:*** installment, deferred payment.

Financial Aid Of all full-time matriculated undergraduates who enrolled in 2017, 14,435 applied for aid, 13,829 were judged to have need, 345 had their need fully met. 764 Federal Work-Study jobs (averaging $2694). 428 state and other part-time jobs (averaging $2056). In 2017, 389 non-need-based awards were made. ***Average percent of need met:*** 78. ***Average financial aid package:*** $10,132. ***Average need-based loan:*** $4417. ***Average need-based gift aid:*** $10,676. ***Average non-need-based aid:*** $3329. ***Average indebtedness upon graduation:*** $16,129.

APPLYING

Standardized Tests *Required:* SAT or ACT (for admission).

Options: electronic application.

Required: high school transcript, minimum 2.0 GPA. ***Required for some:*** interview.

Application deadlines: 7/1 (freshmen), 7/1 (transfers).

Notification: continuous (freshmen).

CONTACT

Dr. Debbie Gilchrist, Interim Registrar, The University of Texas Rio Grande Valley, Office of Enrollment Services, 1201 West University Drive, Edinburg, TX 78539. *Phone:* 956-665-2926. *Toll-free phone:* 888-882-4026. *Fax:* 956-665-2212. *E-mail:* debbie.gilchrist@utrgv.edu.

University of the Incarnate Word

San Antonio, Texas

http://www.uiw.edu/

- **Independent Roman Catholic** comprehensive, founded 1881
- **Urban** 200-acre campus with easy access to San Antonio
- **Endowment** $142.0 million
- **Coed** 5,558 undergraduate students, 74% full-time, 61% women, 39% men
- **Minimally difficult** entrance level, 88% of applicants were admitted

UNDERGRAD STUDENTS
4,103 full-time, 1,455 part-time. Students come from 46 states and territories; 44 other countries; 6% are from out of state; 7% Black or African American, non-Hispanic/Latino; 56% Hispanic/Latino; 2% Asian, non-Hispanic/Latino; 0.3% Native Hawaiian or other Pacific Islander, non-Hispanic/Latino; 0.3% American Indian or Alaska Native, non-Hispanic/Latino; 2% Two or more races, non-Hispanic/Latino; 10% Race/ethnicity unknown; 5% international; 9% transferred in; 18% live on campus.

Freshmen:
Admission: 4,894 applied, 4,304 admitted, 822 enrolled. ***Average high school GPA:*** 3.5. ***Test scores:*** SAT evidence-based reading and writing scores over 500: 68%; SAT math scores over 500: 62%; ACT scores over 18: 68%; SAT evidence-based reading and writing scores over 600: 20%; SAT math scores over 600: 14%; ACT scores over 24: 16%; SAT evidence-based reading and writing scores over 700: 1%; SAT math scores over 700: 1%.

Retention: 74% of full-time freshmen returned.

FACULTY
Total: 766, 45% full-time, 28% with terminal degrees.

Student/faculty ratio: 15:1.

ACADEMICS
Calendar: semesters. *Degrees:* diplomas, associate, bachelor's, master's, and doctoral.

Special study options: academic remediation for entering students, accelerated degree program, adult/continuing education programs, advanced placement credit, cooperative education, distance learning, double majors, English as a second language, freshman honors college, honors programs, independent study, internships, off-campus study, part-time degree program, services for LD students, study abroad, summer session for credit. ***ROTC:*** Army (c).

Unusual degree programs: 3-2 business administration; Accounting.

Computers: 406 computers/terminals are available on campus for general student use. Students can access the following: computer help desk, free student e-mail accounts, online (class) grades, online (class) registration, online (class) schedules. Campuswide network is available. 100% of college-owned or -operated housing units are wired for high-speed Internet access. Wireless service is available via entire campus.
Library: J. E. and M. E. Mabee Library plus 1 other. *Books:* 159,953 (physical), 60,292 (digital/electronic); *Serial titles:* 1,063 (physical), 86,652 (digital/electronic); *Databases:* 206. Weekly public service hours: 105.

STUDENT LIFE
Housing options: coed, men-only, women-only, special housing for students with disabilities. Campus housing is university owned.

Activities and organizations: drama/theater group, student-run newspaper, radio and television station, choral group, marching band, Business Club, Biology Club, Student Government Association, International Students Association, Multicultural Greek Council, national fraternities, national sororities.

Athletics Member NCAA. All Division I except football (Division I-AA), softball (Division II). ***Intercollegiate sports:*** baseball M(s), basketball M(s)/W(s), cross-country running M(s)/W(s), golf M(s)/W(s)(c), soccer M(s)/W(s), softball W(s), swimming and diving M(s)/W(s), tennis M(s)/W(s), track and field M(s)/W(s), volleyball W(s). ***Intramural sports:*** basketball M/W, cheerleading M/W, football M/W, racquetball M/W, soccer M/W, softball M/W, tennis M/W, ultimate Frisbee M/W, volleyball M/W, water polo M/W.

Campus security: 24-hour emergency response devices and patrols, late-night transport/escort service, controlled dormitory access.

Student services: health clinic, personal/psychological counseling, veterans affairs office.

COSTS & FINANCIAL AID
Costs (2019–20) ***Comprehensive fee:*** $45,400 includes full-time tuition ($29,900), mandatory fees ($2676), and room and board ($12,824). Part-time tuition: $950 per credit hour.

Financial Aid Of all full-time matriculated undergraduates who enrolled in 2017, 3,571 applied for aid, 3,374 were judged to have need, 248 had their need fully met. In 2017, 2 non-need-based awards were made. ***Average percent of need met:*** 58. ***Average financial aid package:*** $20,157. ***Average need-based loan:*** $3744. ***Average need-based gift aid:*** $15,472. ***Average non-need-based aid:*** $2356. ***Average indebtedness upon graduation:*** $3909.

APPLYING
Standardized Tests *Required:* SAT or ACT (for admission).

Options: electronic application, deferred entrance.

Application fee: $20.

Required: high school transcript. ***Required for some:*** essay or personal statement. ***Recommended:*** minimum 2.0 GPA, interview.

Application deadlines: rolling (freshmen), rolling (transfers).

Notification: continuous (freshmen), continuous (transfers).

CONTACT
Ms. Jessica Delarosa, Assistant Director of Undergraduate Admissions, University of the Incarnate Word, 4301 Broadway Avenue, San Antonio, TX 78209. *Phone:* 210-829-6005. *Toll-free phone:* 800-749-WORD. *Fax:* 210-829-3921. *E-mail:* jsdelaro@uiwtx.edu.

Wade College

Dallas, Texas

http://www.wadecollege.edu/

- **Proprietary** primarily 2-year, founded 1965
- **Urban** 175-acre campus with easy access to Dallas Fort Worth
- **Coed**
- **Minimally difficult** entrance level

FACULTY
Student/faculty ratio: 12:1.

ACADEMICS
Calendar: trimesters. *Degrees:* associate and bachelor's.
Library: College Library. *Books:* 8,500 (physical), 45,000 (digital/electronic); *Databases:* 10.

STUDENT LIFE
Activities and organizations: student-run newspaper, Wade College Student Association.

Campus security: 24-hour emergency response devices and patrols, late-night transport/escort service, controlled dormitory access.

Student services: veterans affairs office.

COSTS
Costs (2018–19) ***Tuition:*** $24,975 full-time, $1665 per course part-time. Full-time tuition and fees vary according to course load and degree level. Part-time tuition and fees vary according to course load and degree level. No tuition increase for student's term of enrollment. ***Required fees:*** $25 full-time, $25 per degree program part-time.

APPLYING
Options: electronic application.

Required: high school transcript, interview.

CONTACT
Wade College, Infomart, 1950 North Stemmons Freeway, Suite 4080, LB 562, Dallas, TX 75207. *Phone:* 214-637-3530. *Toll-free phone:* 800-624-4850.

Wayland Baptist University

Plainview, Texas

http://www.wbu.edu/

- **Independent Baptist** comprehensive, founded 1908
- **Small-town** 80-acre campus
- **Endowment** $82.8 million
- **Coed**
- **Minimally difficult** entrance level

FACULTY
Student/faculty ratio: 8:1.

ACADEMICS
Calendar: semesters. *Degrees:* associate, bachelor's, master's, and doctoral (branch locations in Anchorage, AK; Amarillo, TX; Luke Air Force Base, AZ; Glorieta, NM; Aiea, HI; Lubbock, TX; San Antonio, TX; Wichita Falls, TX).
Library: J.E. and L.E. Mabee Learning Resource Center. *Books:* 130,903 (physical), 49,479 (digital/electronic); *Serial titles:* 555,663 (digital/electronic); *Databases:* 104.

STUDENT LIFE
Housing options: on-campus residence required through junior year; men-only, women-only. Campus housing is university owned. Freshman campus housing is guaranteed.

Activities and organizations: drama/theater group, student-run newspaper, radio and television station, choral group, marching band, Student Government, Wayland Singers, Baptist Student Ministries, International Choir, President's Ambassadors, national fraternities, national sororities.

Athletics Member NAIA.

Campus security: 24-hour emergency response devices and patrols, security lighting, campus police department.

Student services: health clinic, personal/psychological counseling.

COSTS & FINANCIAL AID
Costs (2018–19) ***Comprehensive fee:*** $27,934 includes full-time tuition ($18,780), mandatory fees ($1290), and room and board ($7864). Full-time tuition and fees vary according to course load and location. Part-time tuition: $626 per credit hour. Part-time tuition and fees vary according to course load and location. ***College room only:*** $3196. Room and board charges vary according to board plan and housing facility.

Financial Aid Of all full-time matriculated undergraduates who enrolled in 2017, 977 applied for aid, 977 were judged to have need, 55 had their need fully met. 123 Federal Work-Study jobs (averaging $1447). 225 state and other part-time jobs (averaging $2171). In 2017, 101 non-need-based awards were made. ***Average percent of need met:*** 44. ***Average financial aid package:*** $11,880. ***Average need-based loan:*** $4154. ***Average need-based gift aid:*** $9079. ***Average non-need-based aid:*** $5321. ***Average indebtedness upon graduation:*** $29,555.

APPLYING
Standardized Tests *Required:* SAT or ACT (for admission).

Options: electronic application.

Application fee: $35.

Required: high school transcript. ***Required for some:*** interview.

CONTACT
Ms. Debbie Stennett, Director of Student Admissions, Wayland Baptist University, 1900 West 7th Street, CMB 1294, Plainview, TX 79072. *Phone:* 806-291-3500. *Toll-free phone:* 800-588-1928. *Fax:* 806-291-1973. *E-mail:* admityou@wbu.edu.

West Coast University

Dallas, Texas

http://www.westcoastuniversity.edu/

CONTACT
West Coast University, 8435 N. Stemmons Freeway, Dallas, TX 75247. *Toll-free phone:* 866-508-2684.

West Texas A&M University

Canyon, Texas

http://www.wtamu.edu/

- **State-supported** comprehensive, founded 1909, part of Texas A&M University System
- **Small-town** 128-acre campus
- **Endowment** $80.4 million
- **Coed**
- **Moderately difficult** entrance level

FACULTY
Student/faculty ratio: 20:1.

ACADEMICS
Calendar: semesters. *Degrees:* bachelor's, master's, and doctoral.
Library: Cornette Library plus 3 others. *Books:* 305,487 (physical), 516,531 (digital/electronic); *Serial titles:* 12,207 (physical), 12,592 (digital/electronic); *Databases:* 181. Weekly public service hours: 91; students can reserve study rooms.

STUDENT LIFE
Housing options: on-campus residence required through sophomore year; coed, men-only, women-only, special housing for students with disabilities. Campus housing is university owned. Freshman campus housing is guaranteed.

Activities and organizations: drama/theater group, student-run newspaper, radio station, choral group, marching band, Residence Hall Association, Wesley, Student Government, SAGE, Baptist Student Ministries, national fraternities, national sororities.

Athletics Member NCAA. All Division II.

Campus security: 24-hour emergency response devices and patrols, late-night transport/escort service, controlled dormitory access.

Student services: health clinic, personal/psychological counseling, veterans affairs office.

FINANCIAL AID
Financial Aid Of all full-time matriculated undergraduates who enrolled in 2017, 4,407 applied for aid, 3,496 were judged to have need, 138 had their need fully met. In 2017, 831 non-need-based awards were made. ***Average percent of need met:*** 57. ***Average financial aid package:*** $9366. ***Average need-based loan:*** $3087. ***Average need-based gift aid:*** $6285. ***Average non-need-based aid:*** $2892. ***Average indebtedness upon graduation:*** $23,670.

APPLYING
Standardized Tests *Required:* SAT or ACT (for admission).

Options: electronic application, deferred entrance.

Application fee: $40.

Required: high school transcript, class rank and Texas high school curriculum or equivalent.

CONTACT
Mrs. Tana Miller, Assistant Vice President for SEES/Registrar, West Texas A&M University, WTAMU Box 60907, Canyon, TX 79016-0001. *Phone:* 806-651-4911. *Toll-free phone:* 800-99-WTAMU. *Fax:* 806-651-5285. *E-mail:* tmiller@wtamu.edu.

Wiley College

Marshall, Texas

http://www.wileyc.edu/

CONTACT
Ms. Alvena Jones, Interim Director of Admissions/Recruitment, Wiley College, 711 Wiley Avenue, Marshall, TX 75670-5199. *Phone:* 903-927-3222. *Toll-free phone:* 800-658-6889. *Fax:* 903-923-8878. *E-mail:* ajones@wileyc.edu.

COLLEGES AT-A-GLANCE

UTAH

Ameritech College of Healthcare

Draper, Utah

http://www.ameritech.edu/

CONTACT
Ameritech College of Healthcare, 12257 South Business Park Drive, Suite 108, Draper, UT 84020-6545.

Brigham Young University

Provo, Utah

http://www.byu.edu/

- **Independent** university, founded 1875, affiliated with The Church of Jesus Christ of Latter-day Saints, part of Church Education System (CES) of The Church of Jesus Christ of Latter-day Saints
- **Suburban** 557-acre campus with easy access to Salt Lake City
- **Coed**
- **Moderately difficult** entrance level

FACULTY
Student/faculty ratio: 20:1.

ACADEMICS
Calendar: semesters. *Degrees:* bachelor's, master's, doctoral, post-master's, and postbachelor's certificates.
Library: Harold B. Lee Library plus 2 others.

STUDENT LIFE
Housing options: men-only, women-only, special housing for students with disabilities. Campus housing is university owned.

Athletics Member NCAA. All Division I except football (Division I-A).

Campus security: 24-hour emergency response devices and patrols, late-night transport/escort service, controlled dormitory access.

COSTS & FINANCIAL AID
Costs (2018–19) ***Comprehensive fee:*** $13,248 includes full-time tuition ($5620) and room and board ($7628). Part-time tuition: $294 per credit hour. Part-time tuition and fees vary according to course load. ***Room and board:*** Room and board charges vary according to board plan, housing facility, and location.

Financial Aid Of all full-time matriculated undergraduates who enrolled in 2017, 17,083 applied for aid, 14,239 were judged to have need, 407 had their need fully met. In 2017, 6980 non-need-based awards were made. ***Average percent of need met:*** 35. ***Average financial aid package:*** $7968. ***Average need-based loan:*** $4061. ***Average need-based gift aid:*** $5613. ***Average non-need-based aid:*** $4364. ***Average indebtedness upon graduation:*** $15,701.

APPLYING
Standardized Tests *Required:* SAT or ACT (for admission).

Options: electronic application, early admission, deferred entrance.

Application fee: $35.

Required: essay or personal statement, high school transcript, 1 letter of recommendation, interview.

CONTACT
Dean of Admissions, Brigham Young University, A-153 Abraham Smoot Building, Provo, UT 84602. *Phone:* 801-422-2507. *Fax:* 801-422-0005. *E-mail:* admissions@byu.edu.

Broadview University–West Jordan

West Jordan, Utah

http://www.broadviewuniversity.edu/

CONTACT
Broadview University–West Jordan, 1902 West 7800 South, West Jordan, UT 84088. *Toll-free phone:* 866-304-4224.

Careers Unlimited

Orem, Utah

http://www.ucdh.edu/

CONTACT
Careers Unlimited, 1176 South 1480 West, Orem, UT 84058.

Dixie State University

St. George, Utah

http://www.dixie.edu/

CONTACT
Dixie State University, 225 South 700 East, St. George, UT 84770-3876. *Phone:* 435-652-7698.

Eagle Gate College

Layton, Utah

http://eaglegatecollege.edu/

CONTACT
Eagle Gate College, 915 North 400 West, Layton, UT 84041. *Phone:* 801-546-7500. *Toll-free phone:* 866-29-EAGLE.

Eagle Gate College

Murray, Utah

http://eaglegatecollege.edu/

CONTACT
Eagle Gate College, 5588 South Green Street, Murray, UT 84123. *Phone:* 801-333-8100. *Toll-free phone:* 866-29-EAGLE.

Independence University

Salt Lake City, Utah

http://www.independence.edu/

CONTACT
Ms. Deborah Hopkins, Enrollment Manager, Independence University, 4021 South 700 East, Suite 400, Salt Lake City, UT 84107. *Toll-free phone:* 800-917-6391.

Midwives College of Utah

Salt Lake City, Utah

http://www.midwifery.edu/

- **Independent** comprehensive, founded 1980
- **Urban** campus with easy access to Salt Lake City
- **Women only**

ACADEMICS
Calendar: semesters. *Degrees:* bachelor's and master's.
Library: MCU Library. *Books:* 644 (physical); *Serial titles:* 5 (digital/electronic). Weekly public service hours: 35.

STUDENT LIFE
Housing options: college housing not available.

Student services: personal/psychological counseling.

COSTS
Costs (2018–19) ***One-time required fee:*** $235. ***Tuition:*** $4400 full-time, $2200 per year part-time. ***Required fees:*** $345 full-time, $345 per year part-time.

APPLYING
Options: electronic application, deferred entrance.

Application fee: $50.

Required: essay or personal statement, 2 letters of recommendation. ***Required for some:*** high school transcript, interview, transcripts from previous college.

CONTACT
Mel Smith-Tourville, Admissions Director, Midwives College of Utah, 1174 East Graystone Way, Suite 2, Suite 2, Salt Lake City, UT 84106. *Phone:* 801-649-5230. *Toll-free phone:* 866-680-2756. *Fax:* 866-207-2024. *E-mail:* admission@midwifery.edu.

Neumont College of Computer Science

Salt Lake City, Utah

http://www.neumont.edu/

- **Proprietary** 4-year, founded 2002
- **Urban** campus with easy access to Salt Lake City
- **Coed**
- **Moderately difficult** entrance level

FACULTY

Student/faculty ratio: 29:1.

ACADEMICS

Calendar: quarters. *Degree:* bachelor's.

STUDENT LIFE

Housing options: on-campus residence required for freshman year; coed, special housing for students with disabilities. Campus housing is university owned and leased by the school. Freshman campus housing is guaranteed.

Activities and organizations: Unified Student Government, Society of Women Engineers, Pathfinder- (RPG group), Game Gurus, Soccer Club.

Campus security: 24-hour emergency response devices and patrols.

Student services: health clinic, personal/psychological counseling.

COSTS & FINANCIAL AID

Costs (2018–19) ***One-time required fee:*** $2500. ***Tuition:*** $22,950 full-time, $6000 per term part-time. Full-time tuition and fees vary according to course load, degree level, program, and student level. Part-time tuition and fees vary according to course load, degree level, program, and student level. ***Required fees:*** $1800 full-time. ***Room only:*** $5970. Room and board charges vary according to housing facility. ***Payment plans:*** installment, deferred payment.

Financial Aid ***Average indebtedness upon graduation:*** $39,623. ***Financial aid deadline:*** 7/30.

APPLYING

Standardized Tests *Required:* SAT or ACT (for admission).

Options: electronic application.

Application fee: $35.

Required: essay or personal statement, high school transcript. ***Recommended:*** 2 letters of recommendation, interview.

CONTACT

Neumont College of Computer Science, 143 South Main Street, Salt Lake City, UT 84111. *Toll-free phone:* 888-NEUMONT.

New Charter University

Salt Lake City, Utah

http://www.new.edu/

CONTACT

Ms. Tammy J. Kassner, Director of Admissions, New Charter University, 2919 John Hawkins Parkway, Birmingham, AL 35244. *Phone:* 205-871-9288 Ext. 107. *Toll-free phone:* 888-639-1388. *Fax:* 800-871-9294. *E-mail:* admissions@aju.edu.

Nightingale College

Ogden, Utah

http://www.nightingale.edu/

CONTACT

Nightingale College, 4155 Harrison Boulevard #100, Ogden, UT 84403.

Southern Utah University

Cedar City, Utah

http://www.suu.edu/

- **State-supported** comprehensive, founded 1897, part of Utah System of Higher Education
- **Small-town** 130-acre campus
- **Endowment** $273.2 million
- **Coed**
- **Moderately difficult** entrance level

FACULTY

Student/faculty ratio: 19:1.

ACADEMICS

Calendar: semesters. *Degrees:* certificates, diplomas, associate, bachelor's, and master's.

Library: Gerald R Sherratt Library. *Books:* 241,434 (physical), 441,219 (digital/electronic); *Serial titles:* 676 (physical), 22,603 (digital/electronic); *Databases:* 218. Students can reserve study rooms.

STUDENT LIFE

Housing options: coed, special housing for students with disabilities. Campus housing is university owned.

Activities and organizations: drama/theater group, student-run newspaper, radio and television station, choral group, national fraternities, national sororities.

Athletics Member NCAA. All Division I.

Campus security: 24-hour emergency response devices, student patrols, late-night transport/escort service, controlled dormitory access.

Student services: health clinic, personal/psychological counseling, women's center.

COSTS & FINANCIAL AID

Costs (2018–19) ***Tuition:*** state resident $6006 full-time; nonresident $19,822 full-time. Full-time tuition and fees vary according to program. Part-time tuition and fees vary according to course load and program. ***Required fees:*** $764 full-time. ***Room and board:*** $7250; room only: $3350. Room and board charges vary according to board plan and housing facility.

Financial Aid Of all full-time matriculated undergraduates who enrolled in 2017, 4,367 applied for aid, 3,750 were judged to have need, 431 had their need fully met. In 2017, 1581 non-need-based awards were made. ***Average percent of need met:*** 61. ***Average financial aid package:*** $9765. ***Average need-based loan:*** $3675. ***Average need-based gift aid:*** $4872. ***Average non-need-based aid:*** $6476. ***Average indebtedness upon graduation:*** $18,185.

APPLYING

Standardized Tests *Required:* SAT or ACT (for admission).

Options: electronic application, deferred entrance.

Application fee: $50.

Required: high school transcript.

CONTACT

Southern Utah University, 351 West University Boulevard, Cedar City, UT 84720-2498. *Phone:* 435-586-7740.

Stevens-Henager College

Logan, Utah

http://www.stevenshenager.edu/

CONTACT

Stevens-Henager College, 755 South Main Street, Logan, UT 84321. *Toll-free phone:* 800-622-2640.

Stevens-Henager College

Orem, Utah

http://www.stevenshenager.edu/

CONTACT

Stevens-Henager College, 1476 South Sandhill Road, Orem, UT 84058. *Toll-free phone:* 800-622-2640.

Stevens-Henager College

St. George, Utah

http://www.stevenshenager.edu/

CONTACT

Stevens-Henager College, 720 South River Road, Suite C-130, St. George, UT 84790. *Toll-free phone:* 800-622-2640.

Stevens-Henager College

Salt Lake City, Utah

http://www.stevenshenager.edu/

CONTACT

Stevens-Henager College, 383 West Vine Street, Salt Lake City, UT 84123. *Toll-free phone:* 800-622-2640.

Stevens-Henager College

West Haven, Utah

http://www.stevenshenager.edu/

CONTACT

Admissions Office, Stevens-Henager College, 1890 South 1350 West, West Haven, UT 84401. *Phone:* 801-394-7791. *Toll-free phone:* 800-622-2640.

University of Utah

Salt Lake City, Utah

http://www.utah.edu/

- **State-supported** university, founded 1850, part of Utah System of Higher Education
- **Urban** 1535-acre campus with easy access to Salt Lake City
- **Endowment** $958.0 million
- **Coed**
- **Moderately difficult** entrance level

FACULTY

Student/faculty ratio: 16:1.

ACADEMICS

Calendar: semesters. *Degrees:* bachelor's, master's, doctoral, post-master's, and postbachelor's certificates.
Library: J. Willard Marriott Library plus 3 others. *Books:* 3.2 million (physical), 460,000 (digital/electronic); *Serial titles:* 500 (physical), 11,500 (digital/electronic); *Databases:* 325. Weekly public service hours: 111; students can reserve study rooms.

STUDENT LIFE

Housing options: coed, men-only, women-only, special housing for students with disabilities. Campus housing is university owned.

Activities and organizations: drama/theater group, student-run newspaper, radio station, choral group, marching band, TEK Club, International Business Club, Golden Key International Honours Society, Tennis Club, Thai Student Association, national fraternities, national sororities.

Athletics Member NCAA. All Division I.

Campus security: 24-hour emergency response devices and patrols, student patrols, late-night transport/escort service, controlled dormitory access.

Student services: health clinic, personal/psychological counseling, women's center, veterans affairs office.

COSTS & FINANCIAL AID

Costs (2018–19) ***Tuition:*** state resident $7997 full-time, $225 per credit hour part-time; nonresident $27,990 full-time, $772 per credit hour part-time. Full-time tuition and fees vary according to course level, course load, degree level, location, program, and student level. Part-time tuition and fees vary according to course level, course load, degree level, location, program, and student level. ***Required fees:*** $1225 full-time. ***Room and board:*** $10,262; room only: $5323. Room and board charges vary according to board plan, housing facility, and location. ***Payment plans:*** installment, deferred payment.

Financial Aid Of all full-time matriculated undergraduates who enrolled in 2018, 10,834 applied for aid, 8,374 were judged to have need, 1,135 had their need fully met. 850 Federal Work-Study jobs (averaging $1897). In 2018, 2674 non-need-based awards were made. ***Average percent of need met:*** 65. ***Average financial aid package:*** $19,812. ***Average need-based loan:*** $4168. ***Average need-based gift aid:*** $7361. ***Average non-need-based aid:*** $6508. ***Average indebtedness upon graduation:*** $21,792.

APPLYING

Standardized Tests *Required:* SAT or ACT (for admission).

Options: electronic application, early admission, early action, deferred entrance.

Application fee: $55.

Required: high school transcript.

CONTACT

Mateo Remsburg, Associate Director, Office of Admissions, University of Utah, 201 S. 1460 E., Room 250 S., Salt Lake City, UT 84112. *Phone:* 801-581-8761. *Toll-free phone:* 800-685-8856. *Fax:* 801-585-3257. *E-mail:* mremsburg@sa.utah.edu.

Utah State University

Logan, Utah

http://www.usu.edu/

- **State-supported** university, founded 1888, part of Utah System of Higher Education
- **Urban** 456-acre campus
- **Endowment** $377.0 million
- **Coed** 24,880 undergraduate students, 70% full-time, 54% women, 46% men
- **Moderately difficult** entrance level, 89% of applicants were admitted

UNDERGRAD STUDENTS

17,394 full-time, 7,486 part-time. Students come from 53 states and territories; 59 other countries; 27% are from out of state; 0.9% Black or African American, non-Hispanic/Latino; 6% Hispanic/Latino; 1% Asian, non-Hispanic/Latino; 0.3% Native Hawaiian or other Pacific Islander, non-Hispanic/Latino; 2% American Indian or Alaska Native, non-Hispanic/Latino; 2% Two or more races, non-Hispanic/Latino; 4% Race/ethnicity unknown; 1% international; 6% transferred in.

Freshmen:

Admission: 15,099 applied, 13,446 admitted, 4,429 enrolled. ***Average high school GPA:*** 3.6. ***Test scores:*** SAT evidence-based reading and writing scores over 500: 90%; SAT math scores over 500: 86%; ACT scores over 18: 91%; SAT evidence-based reading and writing scores over 600: 50%; SAT math scores over 600: 41%; ACT scores over 24: 53%; SAT evidence-based reading and writing scores over 700: 11%; SAT math scores over 700: 10%; ACT scores over 30: 16%.

Retention: 73% of full-time freshmen returned.

FACULTY

Total: 1,289, 78% full-time, 68% with terminal degrees.

Student/faculty ratio: 20:1.

ACADEMICS

Calendar: semesters. *Degrees:* certificates, associate, bachelor's, master's, doctoral, and postbachelor's certificates.

Special study options: academic remediation for entering students, accelerated degree program, adult/continuing education programs, advanced placement credit, cooperative education, distance learning, double majors, English as a second language, freshman honors college, honors programs, independent study, internships, off-campus study, part-time degree program, services for LD students, student-designed majors, study abroad, summer session for credit. ***ROTC:*** Army (b), Air Force (b).

Computers: 1,000 computers/terminals are available on campus for general student use. Students can access the following: computer help desk, free student e-mail accounts, online (class) grades, online (class) registration, online (class) schedules. Campuswide network is available. 100% of college-owned or -operated housing units are wired for high-speed Internet access. Wireless service is available via classrooms, computer centers, computer labs, dorm rooms, learning centers, libraries, student centers.

Library: Merrill-Cazier Library plus 4 others. *Books:* 1.9 million (physical), 768,007 (digital/electronic); *Serial titles:* 44,565 (physical), 74,377 (digital/electronic); *Databases:* 4,418. Weekly public service hours: 101; students can reserve study rooms.

STUDENT LIFE
Housing options: coed, men-only, women-only, special housing for students with disabilities. Campus housing is university owned.

Activities and organizations: drama/theater group, student-run newspaper, radio station, choral group, marching band, Latter-Day Saints Student Association, multicultural clubs, volunteer groups, college councils, national fraternities, national sororities.

Athletics Member NCAA. All Division I except football (Division I-A). ***Intercollegiate sports:*** baseball M(c), basketball M(s)/W(s), cross-country running M(s)/W(s), equestrian sports M(c)/W(c), golf M(s), gymnastics W(s), ice hockey M(c), racquetball M(c)/W(c), rugby M(c)/W(c), soccer M(c)/W(s), softball W(s), tennis M(s)/W(s), track and field M(s)/W(s), ultimate Frisbee M(c)/W(c), volleyball M(c)/W(s). ***Intramural sports:*** basketball M/W, football M/W, lacrosse M(c)/W(c), soccer M/W, softball M/W, swimming and diving M(c)/W(c), table tennis M/W, tennis M/W, ultimate Frisbee M/W, volleyball M/W, wrestling M(c).

Campus security: 24-hour emergency response devices and patrols, student patrols, late-night transport/escort service.

Student services: health clinic, personal/psychological counseling, women's center, legal services, veterans affairs office.

COSTS & FINANCIAL AID
Costs (2018–19) ***Tuition:*** state resident $6342 full-time; nonresident $20,423 full-time. Full-time tuition and fees vary according to course level, course load, program, and reciprocity agreements. Part-time tuition and fees vary according to course level, course load, program, and reciprocity agreements. ***Required fees:*** $1082 full-time. ***Room and board:*** $6400; room only: $2240. Room and board charges vary according to board plan and housing facility. ***Payment plan:*** deferred payment. ***Waivers:*** minority students, children of alumni, adult students, senior citizens, and employees or children of employees.

Financial Aid Of all full-time matriculated undergraduates who enrolled in 2018, 11,270 applied for aid, 9,204 were judged to have need, 796 had their need fully met. In 2018, 2404 non-need-based awards were made. ***Average percent of need met:*** 62. ***Average financial aid package:*** $11,579. ***Average need-based loan:*** $4427. ***Average need-based gift aid:*** $5116. ***Average non-need-based aid:*** $3295. ***Average indebtedness upon graduation:*** $21,080.

APPLYING
Standardized Tests *Required:* SAT or ACT (for admission).

Options: electronic application, deferred entrance.

Application fee: $50.

Required: high school transcript. ***Recommended:*** minimum 2.8 GPA.

Application deadlines: rolling (freshmen), rolling (transfers).

Notification: continuous (freshmen), continuous (transfers).

CONTACT
Mr. Jeff Sorenson, Assistant Director, Admissions Office, Utah State University, 0160 Old Main Hill, Logan, UT 84322-0160. *Phone:* 435-797-1079. *Toll-free phone:* 800-488-8108. *Fax:* 435-797-3708. *E-mail:* admit@usu.edu.

Utah Valley University

Orem, Utah

http://www.uvu.edu/

- **State-supported** comprehensive, founded 1941, affiliated with Advent Christian Church, part of Utah System of Higher Education
- **Suburban** 524-acre campus with easy access to Salt Lake City
- **Coed** 39,397 undergraduate students, 49% full-time, 47% women, 53% men
- 100% of applicants were admitted

UNDERGRAD STUDENTS
19,261 full-time, 20,136 part-time. Students come from 50 states and territories; 71 other countries; 12% are from out of state; 1% Black or African American, non-Hispanic/Latino; 12% Hispanic/Latino; 1% Asian, non-Hispanic/Latino; 0.8% Native Hawaiian or other Pacific Islander, non-Hispanic/Latino; 0.6% American Indian or Alaska Native, non-Hispanic/Latino; 3% Two or more races, non-Hispanic/Latino; 1% Race/ethnicity unknown; 2% international; 7% transferred in.

Freshmen:
Admission: 10,117 applied, 10,117 admitted, 4,803 enrolled. ***Average high school GPA:*** 3.4.

Retention: 64% of full-time freshmen returned.

FACULTY
Total: 2,096, 35% full-time, 28% with terminal degrees.

Student/faculty ratio: 25:1.

ACADEMICS
Calendar: semesters. *Degrees:* certificates, diplomas, associate, bachelor's, master's, and postbachelor's certificates.

Special study options: academic remediation for entering students, advanced placement credit, cooperative education, distance learning, double majors, English as a second language, honors programs, independent study, internships, off-campus study, part-time degree program, services for LD students, student-designed majors, study abroad, summer session for credit. ***ROTC:*** Army (b), Air Force (c).

Computers: Students can access the following: campus intranet, computer help desk, free student e-mail accounts, online (class) grades, online (class) registration, online (class) schedules. Campuswide network is available. Wireless service is available via entire campus.
Library: Utah Valley University Library plus 1 other. Students can reserve study rooms.

STUDENT LIFE
Housing options: college housing not available.

Activities and organizations: drama/theater group, student-run newspaper, television station, choral group, national fraternities, national sororities.

Athletics Member NCAA. All Division I. ***Intercollegiate sports:*** baseball M(s), basketball M(s)/W(s), cross-country running M(s)/W(s), golf M(s)/W(s)(c), soccer W(s), softball W(s), track and field M(s)/W(s), volleyball W(s), wrestling M(s).

Campus security: 24-hour patrols.

Student services: health clinic, personal/psychological counseling, women's center, legal services, veterans affairs office.

COSTS & FINANCIAL AID
Costs (2018–19) ***Tuition:*** state resident $5036 full-time, $207 per credit part-time; nonresident $15,606 full-time, $642 per credit part-time. Full-time tuition and fees vary according to course load and program. Part-time tuition and fees vary according to course load. ***Required fees:*** $690 full-time, $345 per term part-time. ***Payment plan:*** deferred payment. ***Waivers:*** employees or children of employees.

Financial Aid Of all full-time matriculated undergraduates who enrolled in 2018, 12,443 applied for aid, 10,737 were judged to have need, 800 had their need fully met. In 2018, 604 non-need-based awards were made. ***Average percent of need met:*** 61. ***Average financial aid package:*** $7986. ***Average need-based loan:*** $2568. ***Average need-based gift aid:*** $5112. ***Average non-need-based aid:*** $5173. ***Average indebtedness upon graduation:*** $18,880.

APPLYING
Options: electronic application, deferred entrance.

Application fee: $35.

Required: high school transcript.

Notification: continuous (freshmen), continuous (out-of-state freshmen), continuous (transfers).

CONTACT
Mr. Kristopher Coles, Director of Admissions, Utah Valley University, 800 West University Parkway, Orem, UT 84058-5999. *Phone:* 801-863-6368. *Fax:* 801-863-7229. *E-mail:* coleskr@uvu.edu.

Weber State University
Ogden, Utah
http://www.weber.edu/

- **State-supported** comprehensive, founded 1889, part of Utah System of Higher Education
- **Urban** 504-acre campus with easy access to Salt Lake City
- **Endowment** $149.0 million
- **Coed** 27,465 undergraduate students, 42% full-time, 55% women, 45% men
- **Noncompetitive** entrance level, 100% of applicants were admitted

UNDERGRAD STUDENTS
11,444 full-time, 16,021 part-time. Students come from 54 states and territories; 61 other countries; 8% are from out of state; 1% Black or African American, non-Hispanic/Latino; 11% Hispanic/Latino; 2% Asian, non-Hispanic/Latino; 0.5% Native Hawaiian or other Pacific Islander, non-Hispanic/Latino; 0.5% American Indian or Alaska Native, non-Hispanic/Latino; 3% Two or more races, non-Hispanic/Latino; 5% Race/ethnicity unknown; 1% international; 5% transferred in; 4% live on campus.

Freshmen:
Admission: 7,251 applied, 7,251 admitted, 3,317 enrolled. ***Average high school GPA:*** 3.3. ***Test scores:*** ACT scores over 18: 78%; ACT scores over 24: 31%; ACT scores over 30: 5%.

Retention: 65% of full-time freshmen returned.

FACULTY
Total: 1,404, 37% full-time, 33% with terminal degrees.

Student/faculty ratio: 21:1.

ACADEMICS
Calendar: semesters. *Degrees:* certificates, associate, bachelor's, master's, post-master's, and postbachelor's certificates.

Special study options: academic remediation for entering students, accelerated degree program, adult/continuing education programs, advanced placement credit, cooperative education, distance learning, double majors, English as a second language, external degree program, freshman honors college, honors programs, independent study, internships, off-campus study, part-time degree program, services for LD students, student-designed majors, study abroad, summer session for credit. ***ROTC:*** Army (b), Navy (c), Air Force (c).

Computers: 650 computers/terminals are available on campus for general student use. Students can access the following: campus intranet, computer help desk, free student e-mail accounts, online (class) grades, online (class) registration, online (class) schedules. Campuswide network is available. 100% of college-owned or -operated housing units are wired for high-speed Internet access. Wireless service is available via entire campus.

Library: Stewart Library. *Books:* 498,531 (physical); *Serial titles:* 425 (physical); *Databases:* 223,410.

STUDENT LIFE
Housing options: men-only, women-only, cooperative, special housing for students with disabilities. Campus housing is university owned and is provided by a third party.

Activities and organizations: drama/theater group, student-run newspaper, radio and television station, choral group, marching band, LDSSA (Latter-day Saint Student Association), SAA (Student Alumni Association), GSA (Gay-Straight Alliance), Chinese Club, Golden Key Honor Society, national fraternities, national sororities.

Athletics Member NCAA. All Division I. ***Intercollegiate sports:*** archery M(c)/W(c), baseball M(c), basketball M(s)/W(s), bowling M(c)/W(c), cheerleading M(s)/W(s), cross-country running M(s)/W(s), football M(s), golf M(s)/W(s)(c), ice hockey M(c), lacrosse M(c), racquetball M/W, rugby M(c), skiing (downhill) W(c), soccer M(c)/W(s), softball W(s), swimming and diving M(c)/W(c), tennis M(s)(c)/W(s)(c), track and field M(s)/W(s), volleyball M(c)/W(s), weight lifting M(c)/W(c), wrestling M(c). ***Intramural sports:*** racquetball M(c)/W(c), rock climbing M/W, tennis M(c)/W(c), ultimate Frisbee M(c)/W(c), volleyball M(c)/W(c).

Campus security: 24-hour emergency response devices and patrols, student patrols, late-night transport/escort service, controlled dormitory access.

Student services: health clinic, personal/psychological counseling, women's center, legal services, veterans affairs office.

COSTS & FINANCIAL AID
Costs (2018–19) ***Tuition:*** state resident $4892 full-time, $2886 per year part-time; nonresident $14,679 full-time, $8661 per year part-time. Full-time tuition and fees vary according to course level, course load, degree level, program, and reciprocity agreements. Part-time tuition and fees vary according to course level, course load, degree level, program, and reciprocity agreements. ***Required fees:*** $948 full-time, $593 per year part-time. ***Room and board:*** $8400. Room and board charges vary according to board plan and housing facility. ***Payment plan:*** installment. ***Waivers:*** senior citizens and employees or children of employees.

Financial Aid Of all full-time matriculated undergraduates who enrolled in 2017, 7,369 applied for aid, 6,348 were judged to have need, 2,023 had their need fully met. In 2017, 2226 non-need-based awards were made. ***Average financial aid package:*** $6703. ***Average need-based loan:*** $3674. ***Average need-based gift aid:*** $4863. ***Average non-need-based aid:*** $3841. ***Average indebtedness upon graduation:*** $20,312.

APPLYING
Standardized Tests *Required for some:* ACCUPLACER. *Recommended:* SAT or ACT (for admission).

Options: electronic application, early admission, deferred entrance.

Application fee: $30.

Required: high school transcript.

Notification: continuous (freshmen), continuous (out-of-state freshmen), continuous (transfers).

CONTACT
Andrew Young, Associate Director of Admissions, Weber State University, 1137 University Circle, Ogden, UT 84408-1137. *Phone:* 801-626-6050. *Toll-free phone:* 800-848-7700 (in-state); 800-848-7770 (out-of-state). *Fax:* 801-626-6747. *E-mail:* andrewyoung@weber.edu.

Western Governors University
Salt Lake City, Utah
http://www.wgu.edu/

CONTACT
Western Governors University, 4001 South 700 East, Suite 700, Salt Lake City, UT 84107. *Phone:* 801-274-3280 Ext. 336. *Toll-free phone:* 866-225-5948.

Westminster College
Salt Lake City, Utah
http://www.westminstercollege.edu/

- **Independent** comprehensive, founded 1875
- **Suburban** 27-acre campus
- **Endowment** $77.4 million
- **Coed**
- **Moderately difficult** entrance level

FACULTY
Student/faculty ratio: 9:1.

ACADEMICS
Calendar: semesters. *Degrees:* bachelor's, master's, and postbachelor's certificates.

Library: Giovale Library plus 1 other. *Books:* 95,039 (physical), 364,687 (digital/electronic); *Databases:* 56. Students can reserve study rooms.

STUDENT LIFE
Housing options: on-campus residence required through sophomore year; coed, special housing for students with disabilities. Campus housing is university owned and leased by the school. Freshman campus housing is guaranteed.

Activities and organizations: drama/theater group, student-run newspaper, choral group, Westminster Ski and Snowboard Club (WSSC), Residence Hall Association (Residential Government), Feminist Club, Latin X, Theatre Society.

Athletics Member NCAA. All Division II.

Campus security: 24-hour emergency response devices and patrols, student patrols, late-night transport/escort service, controlled dormitory access.

Student services: health clinic, personal/psychological counseling, veterans affairs office.

COSTS & FINANCIAL AID

Costs (2018–19) ***One-time required fee:*** $300. ***Comprehensive fee:*** $43,524 includes full-time tuition ($33,480), mandatory fees ($520), and room and board ($9524). Full-time tuition and fees vary according to course load and program. Part-time tuition: $1395 per credit hour. Part-time tuition and fees vary according to course load and program. ***Required fees:*** $154 per credit hour part-time. ***College room only:*** $5526. Room and board charges vary according to board plan and housing facility. ***Payment plans:*** installment, deferred payment.

Financial Aid Of all full-time matriculated undergraduates who enrolled in 2018, 1,350 applied for aid, 1,171 were judged to have need, 272 had their need fully met. In 2018, 506 non-need-based awards were made. ***Average percent of need met:*** 80. ***Average financial aid package:*** $28,582. ***Average need-based loan:*** $4361. ***Average need-based gift aid:*** $23,545. ***Average non-need-based aid:*** $15,553. ***Average indebtedness upon graduation:*** $29,713.

APPLYING

Standardized Tests *Required:* SAT or ACT (for admission).

Options: electronic application, deferred entrance.

Application fee: $50.

Required: essay or personal statement, high school transcript, minimum 2.5 GPA, 1 letter of recommendation. ***Recommended:*** interview.

CONTACT

Jen Dahl, Director of Admissions, Westminster College, 1840 South 1300 East, Salt Lake City, UT 84105-3697. *Phone:* 801-832-2200. *Toll-free phone:* 800-748-4753. *Fax:* 801-832-3101. *E-mail:* admission@westminstercollege.edu.

VERMONT

Bennington College

Bennington, Vermont

http://www.bennington.edu/

- **Independent** comprehensive, founded 1932
- **Small-town** 440-acre campus with easy access to Albany, NY
- **Endowment** $19.2 million
- **Coed**
- **Very difficult** entrance level

FACULTY

Student/faculty ratio: 10:1.

ACADEMICS

Calendar: semesters plus winter work term in January and February. *Degrees:* bachelor's and master's.

Library: Crossett Library plus 1 other. *Books:* 89,000 (physical), 162,000 (digital/electronic); *Serial titles:* 200 (physical), 48,000 (digital/electronic); *Databases:* 56. Weekly public service hours: 111; students can reserve study rooms.

STUDENT LIFE

Housing options: on-campus residence required through senior year; coed. Campus housing is university owned and leased by the school. Freshman campus housing is guaranteed.

Activities and organizations: drama/theater group, student-run newspaper, radio station, choral group, Program Activity Council, Bennington Free Press, Student Endowment for the Arts, SILO: Student Journal of Arts and Letters, The Purple Carrot Farm.

Campus security: 24-hour emergency response devices and patrols, late-night transport/escort service, controlled dormitory access, prevention/awareness program.

Student services: health clinic, personal/psychological counseling.

COSTS & FINANCIAL AID

Costs (2018–19) ***One-time required fee:*** $650. ***Comprehensive fee:*** $69,470 includes full-time tuition ($53,160), mandatory fees ($700), and room and board ($15,610). Full-time tuition and fees vary according to degree level. Part-time tuition: $2215 per credit hour. ***College room only:*** $8460. Room and board charges vary according to board plan.

Financial Aid Of all full-time matriculated undergraduates who enrolled in 2017, 487 applied for aid, 444 were judged to have need, 73 had their need fully met. 362 Federal Work-Study jobs (averaging $2364). 116 state and other part-time jobs (averaging $2181). In 2017, 225 non-need-based awards were made. ***Average percent of need met:*** 84. ***Average financial aid package:*** $45,496. ***Average need-based loan:*** $3534. ***Average need-based gift aid:*** $40,598. ***Average non-need-based aid:*** $26,899. ***Average indebtedness upon graduation:*** $27,965. ***Financial aid deadline:*** 1/3.

APPLYING

Options: electronic application, early admission, early decision, early action, deferred entrance.

Required: essay or personal statement, high school transcript, 2 letters of recommendation, graded analytic paper. ***Recommended:*** interview.

CONTACT

Mr. Fumio Sugihara, Director of Admissions, Bennington College, One College Drive, Bennington, VT 05201-6003. *Phone:* 802-440-4316. *Toll-free phone:* 800-833-6845. *Fax:* 802-440-4320. *E-mail:* admissions@bennington.edu.

Castleton University

Castleton, Vermont

http://www.castleton.edu/

CONTACT

Mr. Maurice Ouimet Jr., Dean of Enrollment, Castleton University, 62 Alumni Drive, Woodruff Hall, Castleton, VT 05735. *Phone:* 802-468-1213. *Toll-free phone:* 800-639-8521. *Fax:* 802-468-1476. *E-mail:* info@castleton.edu.

See next page for display ad and page 986 for the College Close-Up.

Champlain College

Burlington, Vermont

http://www.champlain.edu/

- **Independent** comprehensive, founded 1878
- **Suburban** 27-acre campus with easy access to Montreal
- **Endowment** $24.3 million
- **Coed** 2,240 undergraduate students, 96% full-time, 41% women, 59% men
- **Moderately difficult** entrance level, 75% of applicants were admitted

UNDERGRAD STUDENTS

2,158 full-time, 82 part-time. Students come from 43 states and territories; 79% are from out of state; 3% Black or African American, non-Hispanic/Latino; 7% Hispanic/Latino; 3% Asian, non-Hispanic/Latino; 0.2% American Indian or Alaska Native, non-Hispanic/Latino; 3% Two or more races, non-Hispanic/Latino; 9% Race/ethnicity unknown; 0.8% international; 2% transferred in; 71% live on campus.

Freshmen:

Admission: 4,977 applied, 3,753 admitted, 538 enrolled. ***Average high school GPA:*** 3.4. ***Test scores:*** SAT evidence-based reading and writing scores over 500: 89%; SAT math scores over 500: 93%; ACT scores over 18: 93%; SAT evidence-based reading and writing scores over 600: 40%; SAT math scores over 600: 56%; ACT scores over 24: 61%; SAT evidence-based reading and writing scores over 700: 7%; SAT math scores over 700: 9%; ACT scores over 30: 16%.

Retention: 78% of full-time freshmen returned.

FACULTY

Total: 274, 42% full-time, 46% with terminal degrees.

Student/faculty ratio: 14:1.

ACADEMICS

Calendar: semesters. *Degrees:* certificates, associate, bachelor's, master's, and postbachelor's certificates.

COLLEGES AT-A-GLANCE

Special study options: adult/continuing education programs, advanced placement credit, cooperative education, distance learning, double majors, independent study, internships, off-campus study, part-time degree program, services for LD students, study abroad, summer session for credit. ***ROTC:*** Army (c).

Computers: 640 computers/terminals are available on campus for general student use. Students can access the following: campus intranet, computer help desk, free student e-mail accounts, online (class) grades, online (class) registration, online (class) schedules. Campuswide network is available. 100% of college-owned or -operated housing units are wired for high-speed Internet access. Wireless service is available via entire campus.

Library: Miller Information Commons. *Books:* 50,200 (physical), 210,502 (digital/electronic); *Serial titles:* 150 (physical), 65,578 (digital/electronic); *Databases:* 151. Weekly public service hours: 105; students can reserve study rooms.

STUDENT LIFE

Housing options: coed, women-only, special housing for students with disabilities. Campus housing is university owned and leased by the school. Freshman campus housing is guaranteed.

Activities and organizations: drama/theater group, student-run newspaper, radio station, choral group, Diversity Champlain, International Club, community service organization, Champlain Players (theater group), Outing Club/Skiing Snowboarding Club.

Athletics ***Intramural sports:*** basketball M/W, cross-country running M(c)/W(c), equestrian sports M(c)/W(c), fencing W, football M/W, ice hockey M, lacrosse M, rock climbing M/W, rugby M(c)/W(c), skiing (cross-country) M/W, skiing (downhill) M(c)/W(c), soccer M/W, table tennis M/W, tennis M/W, ultimate Frisbee M/W, volleyball M/W.

Campus security: 24-hour emergency response devices and patrols, late-night transport/escort service, controlled dormitory access.

Student services: health clinic, personal/psychological counseling, women's center.

COSTS & FINANCIAL AID

Costs (2019–20) ***Comprehensive fee:*** $57,594 includes full-time tuition ($41,728), mandatory fees ($100), and room and board ($15,766). Part-time tuition: $1762 per credit hour. ***Payment plan:*** tuition prepayment.

Financial Aid Of all full-time matriculated undergraduates who enrolled in 2018, 1,614 applied for aid, 1,429 were judged to have need, 207 had their need fully met. In 2018, 165 non-need-based awards were made. ***Average percent of need met:*** 69. ***Average financial aid package:*** $28,783. ***Average need-based loan:*** $3708. ***Average need-based gift aid:*** $23,508. ***Average non-need-based aid:*** $14,219. ***Average indebtedness upon graduation:*** $35,383. ***Financial aid deadline:*** 1/15.

APPLYING

Options: electronic application, early admission, early decision, deferred entrance.

Required: essay or personal statement, high school transcript. ***Required for some:*** portfolio for creative media, filmmaking, game art and animation, game design, and graphic design and digital media majors. ***Recommended:*** 2 letters of recommendation.

Application deadlines: 1/15 (freshmen), rolling (transfers).

Early decision deadline: 11/15.

Notification: 3/15 (freshmen), continuous (transfers), 12/15 (early decision).

CONTACT

Diane Soboski, Director of Undergraduate Admissions, Champlain College, PO Box 670, Burlington, VT 05401. *Phone:* 802-865-5740. *Toll-free phone:* 800-570-5858. *Fax:* 802-860-2767. *E-mail:* admission@champlain.edu.

College of St. Joseph

Rutland, Vermont

http://www.csj.edu/

CONTACT

Mr. Alan Young, Dean of Admissions, College of St. Joseph, 71 Clement Road, Rutland, VT 05701-3899. *Phone:* 802-773-5227. *Toll-free phone:* 877-270-9998. *Fax:* 802-776-5310. *E-mail:* admissions@csj.edu.

Goddard College
Plainfield, Vermont
http://www.goddard.edu/

CONTACT
Admissions Office, Goddard College, 123 Pitkin Road, Plainfield, VT 05667-9432. *Phone:* 800-906-8312. *Toll-free phone:* 800-906-8312. *Fax:* 802-454-1029. *E-mail:* admissions@goddard.edu.

Landmark College
Putney, Vermont
http://www.landmark.edu/

CONTACT
Admissions Main Desk, Landmark College, Admissions Office, River Road South, Putney, VT 05346. *Phone:* 802-387-6718. *Fax:* 802-387-6868. *E-mail:* admissions@landmark.edu.

Marlboro College
Marlboro, Vermont
http://www.marlboro.edu/

- **Independent** comprehensive, founded 1946
- **Rural** 350-acre campus
- **Endowment** $37.3 million
- **Coed**
- **Moderately difficult** entrance level

FACULTY
Student/faculty ratio: 5:1.

ACADEMICS
Calendar: semesters. *Degrees:* bachelor's and master's.
Library: Rice-Aron Library. *Books:* 88,500 (physical), 137,548 (digital/electronic); *Serial titles:* 5,400 (physical), 150 (digital/electronic); *Databases:* 75. Study areas open 24 hours, 5–7 days a week.

STUDENT LIFE
Housing options: on-campus residence required for freshman year; coed, women-only, cooperative, special housing for students with disabilities. Campus housing is university owned. Freshman campus housing is guaranteed.

Activities and organizations: drama/theater group, student-run newspaper, radio station, choral group, outdoor program, theater, farm program, Gay/Lesbian/Bisexual Alliance, madrigal and a cappella groups.

Campus security: 24-hour emergency response devices and patrols.

Student services: health clinic, personal/psychological counseling, women's center, veterans affairs office.

COSTS & FINANCIAL AID
Costs (2018–19) ***Comprehensive fee:*** $53,225 includes full-time tuition ($39,870), mandatory fees ($970), and room and board ($12,385). Full-time tuition and fees vary according to reciprocity agreements. Part-time tuition: $1329 per credit hour. Part-time tuition and fees vary according to course load. ***Required fees:*** $105 per term part-time. ***College room only:*** $7142. Room and board charges vary according to board plan.

Financial Aid Of all full-time matriculated undergraduates who enrolled in 2018, 125 applied for aid, 118 were judged to have need, 17 had their need fully met. In 2018, 24 non-need-based awards were made. ***Average percent of need met:*** 85. ***Average financial aid package:*** $39,397. ***Average need-based loan:*** $4837. ***Average need-based gift aid:*** $33,953. ***Average non-need-based aid:*** $27,383. ***Average indebtedness upon graduation:*** $28,381. ***Financial aid deadline:*** 3/1.

APPLYING
Standardized Tests *Recommended:* SAT or ACT (for admission).

Options: electronic application, early admission, early decision, early action, deferred entrance.

Application fee: $50.

Required: essay or personal statement, high school transcript, 2 letters of recommendation, analytical essay. ***Required for some:*** interview. ***Recommended:*** interview.

CONTACT
Marlboro College, PO Box A, South Road, Marlboro, VT 05344. *Toll-free phone:* 800-343-0049.

Middlebury College
Middlebury, Vermont
http://www.middlebury.edu/

- **Independent** comprehensive, founded 1800
- **Small-town** 350-acre campus
- **Endowment** $1.1 billion
- **Coed** 2,579 undergraduate students, 99% full-time, 53% women, 47% men
- **Most difficult** entrance level, 17% of applicants were admitted

UNDERGRAD STUDENTS
2,551 full-time, 28 part-time. Students come from 52 states and territories; 68 other countries; 94% are from out of state; 4% Black or African American, non-Hispanic/Latino; 10% Hispanic/Latino; 7% Asian, non-Hispanic/Latino; 5% Two or more races, non-Hispanic/Latino; 2% Race/ethnicity unknown; 11% international; 0.3% transferred in; 95% live on campus.

Freshmen:
Admission: 9,227 applied, 1,542 admitted, 628 enrolled. ***Test scores:*** SAT evidence-based reading and writing scores over 500: 100%; SAT math scores over 500: 100%; ACT scores over 18: 100%; SAT evidence-based reading and writing scores over 600: 97%; SAT math scores over 600: 95%; ACT scores over 24: 99%; SAT evidence-based reading and writing scores over 700: 53%; SAT math scores over 700: 64%; ACT scores over 30: 87%.

Retention: 96% of full-time freshmen returned.

FACULTY
Total: 357, 84% full-time, 94% with terminal degrees.

Student/faculty ratio: 8:1.

ACADEMICS
Calendar: 4-1-4. *Degrees:* bachelor's, master's, and doctoral.

Special study options: accelerated degree program, advanced placement credit, double majors, honors programs, independent study, internships, off-campus study, services for LD students, student-designed majors, study abroad, summer session for credit. ***ROTC:*** Army (c).

Unusual degree programs: 3-2 engineering with Columbia University, Dartmouth College.

Computers: Students can access the following: campus intranet, computer help desk, free student e-mail accounts, online (class) grades, online (class) registration, online (class) schedules, personal Web pages, file servers. Campuswide network is available. Wireless service is available via entire campus.
Library: Davis Family Library plus 2 others. *Books:* 764,667 (physical), 644,056 (digital/electronic); *Databases:* 695. Weekly public service hours: 112; students can reserve study rooms.

STUDENT LIFE
Housing options: on-campus residence required through junior year; coed, special housing for students with disabilities. Campus housing is university owned. Freshman campus housing is guaranteed.

Activities and organizations: drama/theater group, student-run newspaper, radio station, choral group, Middlebury College Activities Board, Middlebury Mountain Club, Student Government Association, International Students Organization, WRMC.

Athletics Member NCAA. All Division III except golf (Division II), men's and women's skiing (cross-country) (Division I), skiing (downhill) (Division I). ***Intercollegiate sports:*** baseball M, basketball M/W, cross-country running M/W, field hockey W, football M, golf M/W, ice hockey M/W, lacrosse M/W, skiing (cross-country) M/W, skiing (downhill) M(c)/W, soccer M/W, softball W, squash M/W, swimming and diving M/W, tennis M/W, track and field M/W, volleyball W. ***Intramural sports:*** badminton M(c)/W(c), basketball M/W, crew M(c)/W(c), equestrian sports M(c)/W(c), fencing M(c), field hockey W(c), football M/W, golf M/W, ice hockey M/W, rugby M(c)/W(c), sailing M(c)/W(c), soccer M/W, softball M/W, squash M/W, tennis M/W, ultimate Frisbee M(c)/W(c), volleyball M(c), water polo M(c)/W(c).

Campus security: 24-hour emergency response devices and patrols, student patrols, late-night transport/escort service, controlled dormitory access.

Student services: health clinic, personal/psychological counseling, women's center.

COSTS & FINANCIAL AID

Costs (2019–20) ***Comprehensive fee:*** $72,248 includes full-time tuition ($55,790), mandatory fees ($426), and room and board ($16,032). ***Payment plan:*** tuition prepayment.

Financial Aid Of all full-time matriculated undergraduates who enrolled in 2018, 1,501 applied for aid, 1,178 were judged to have need, 1,178 had their need fully met. In 2018, 5 non-need-based awards were made. ***Average percent of need met:*** 100. ***Average financial aid package:*** $52,352. ***Average need-based loan:*** $3788. ***Average need-based gift aid:*** $49,003. ***Average non-need-based aid:*** $25,000. ***Average indebtedness upon graduation:*** $18,955. ***Financial aid deadline:*** 11/1.

APPLYING

Standardized Tests *Required:* SAT and SAT Subject Tests or ACT (for admission).

Options: electronic application, early admission, early decision, deferred entrance.

Application fee: $65.

Required: essay or personal statement, high school transcript, 2 letters of recommendation. ***Recommended:*** interview.

Application deadlines: 1/1 (freshmen), 3/1 (transfers).

Early decision deadline: 11/1.

Notification: 3/31 (freshmen), 4/10 (transfers), 12/15 (early decision).

CONTACT

Mr. Greg Buckles, Dean of Admissions, Middlebury College, Emma Willard House, Middlebury, VT 05753-6002. *Phone:* 802-443-3000. *Fax:* 802-443-2056. *E-mail:* admissions@middlebury.edu.

New England Culinary Institute

Montpelier, Vermont

http://www.neci.edu/

CONTACT

Adonica Williams, New England Culinary Institute, 7 School Street, Montpelier, VT 05602-3115. *Phone:* 802-225-3210. *Toll-free phone:* 877-223-6324. *Fax:* 802-225-3280. *E-mail:* admissions@neci.edu.

Northern Vermont University–Johnson

Johnson, Vermont

http://www.northernvermont.edu/

CONTACT

Bethany Harrington, Admissions Specialist, Northern Vermont University–Johnson, 337 College Hill, Johnson, VT 05656. *Phone:* 802-635-1219. *Toll-free phone:* 800-635-2356. *Fax:* 802-635-1230. *E-mail:* admissions@jsc.edu.

★ Northern Vermont University–Lyndon

Lyndonville, Vermont

http://www.northernvermont.edu/

- **State-supported** comprehensive, founded 2018, part of Vermont State Colleges System
- **Rural** 175-acre campus
- **Coed**
- **Moderately difficult** entrance level

FACULTY

Student/faculty ratio: 15:1.

ACADEMICS
Calendar: semesters. *Degrees:* certificates, diplomas, associate, bachelor's, master's, and post-master's certificates.
Library: Samuel Read Hall Library (NVU-Lyndon) and Willey Library (NVU-Johnson). Weekly public service hours: 38.

STUDENT LIFE
Housing options: on-campus residence required through sophomore year; coed, women-only, cooperative, special housing for students with disabilities. Campus housing is university owned and leased by the school. Freshman campus housing is guaranteed.

Activities and organizations: drama/theater group, student-run newspaper, radio and television station, choral group, American Meteorological Society, ASSIST and SERVE, Student Government, Campus Activities, Outing Club, Dance Club.

Athletics Member NCAA. All Division III.

Campus security: 24-hour emergency response devices, student patrols, late-night transport/escort service, controlled dormitory access.

Student services: health clinic, personal/psychological counseling, veterans affairs office.

COSTS
Costs (2018–19) ***Tuition:*** state resident $10,944 full-time; nonresident $24,264 full-time. Full-time tuition and fees vary according to course load. Part-time tuition and fees vary according to course load. ***Required fees:*** $1490 full-time. ***Room and board:*** $11,598; room only: $6312. Room and board charges vary according to board plan and housing facility.

APPLYING
Options: electronic application, early admission, deferred entrance.

Application fee: $36.

Required: high school transcript, minimum 2.0 GPA, 1 letter of recommendation. ***Required for some:*** essay or personal statement, minimum 3.0 GPA. ***Recommended:*** minimum 3.0 GPA, interview.

CONTACT
Ms. Cheri Goldrick, Admissions Assistant, Northern Vermont University–Lyndon, 1001 College Road, PO Box 919, Lyndonville, VT 05851. *Phone:* 802-626-6451. *Toll-free phone:* 800-225-1998. *Fax:* 802-626-6335. *E-mail:* admissions@lyndonstate.edu.

See previous page for display ad and page 1066 for the College Close-Up.

Norwich University
Northfield, Vermont
http://www.norwich.edu/

CONTACT
Norwich University, 158 Harmon Drive, Northfield, VT 05663. *Phone:* 802-485-2658. *Toll-free phone:* 800-468-6679.

Saint Michael's College
Colchester, Vermont
http://www.smcvt.edu/

- **Independent Roman Catholic** comprehensive, founded 1904
- **Suburban** 440-acre campus with easy access to Montreal
- **Endowment** $87.5 million
- **Coed**
- **Moderately difficult** entrance level

FACULTY
Student/faculty ratio: 13:1.

ACADEMICS
Calendar: semesters. *Degrees:* bachelor's, master's, post-master's, and postbachelor's certificates.
Library: Durick Library. *Books:* 231,418 (physical), 231,171 (digital/electronic); *Serial titles:* 1,653 (physical), 128,515 (digital/electronic); *Databases:* 142. Weekly public service hours: 102.

STUDENT LIFE
Housing options: on-campus residence required through senior year; coed, men-only, women-only, special housing for students with disabilities. Campus housing is university owned. Freshman campus housing is guaranteed.

Activities and organizations: drama/theater group, student-run newspaper, radio station, choral group, Student Association (governing board), Mobilization of Volunteer Efforts (MOVE), Wilderness Program, Martin Luther King Society, ShredMC.

Athletics Member NCAA. All Division II except skiing (downhill) (Division I).

Campus security: 24-hour emergency response devices and patrols, student patrols, late-night transport/escort service, controlled dormitory access, bicycle patrols, fire and rescue squad with professionals and trained student volunteers.

Student services: health clinic, personal/psychological counseling, women's center, veterans affairs office.

COSTS & FINANCIAL AID
Costs (2018–19) ***Comprehensive fee:*** $57,595 includes full-time tuition ($45,050), mandatory fees ($325), and room and board ($12,220). Full-time tuition and fees vary according to course load. Part-time tuition: $1445 per credit hour. Part-time tuition and fees vary according to course load. ***Room and board:*** Room and board charges vary according to board plan and housing facility.

Financial Aid Of all full-time matriculated undergraduates who enrolled in 2018, 1,210 applied for aid, 1,062 were judged to have need, 250 had their need fully met. In 2018, 547 non-need-based awards were made. ***Average percent of need met:*** 76. ***Average financial aid package:*** $31,371. ***Average need-based loan:*** $4432. ***Average need-based gift aid:*** $27,022. ***Average non-need-based aid:*** $18,771. ***Average indebtedness upon graduation:*** $38,040.

APPLYING
Options: electronic application, early action, deferred entrance.

Application fee: $50.

Required: essay or personal statement, high school transcript, 1 letter of recommendation. ***Recommended:*** minimum 3.0 GPA, 3 letters of recommendation, interview.

CONTACT
Mr. Michael Stefanowicz, Director of Admission, Saint Michael's College, One Winooski Park, Colchester, VT 05439. *Phone:* 802-654-2108. *Toll-free phone:* 800-762-8000. *Fax:* 802-654-2906. *E-mail:* admission@smcvt.edu.

Southern Vermont College
Bennington, Vermont
http://www.svc.edu/

- **Independent** 4-year, founded 1926
- **Small-town** 371-acre campus with easy access to Albany, NY
- **Endowment** $3.5 million
- **Coed**
- **Noncompetitive** entrance level

FACULTY
Student/faculty ratio: 14:1.

ACADEMICS
Calendar: semesters. *Degrees:* certificates, associate, and bachelor's.
Library: Southern Vermont College Library. *Books:* 10,025 (physical), 8,818 (digital/electronic); *Serial titles:* 792 (physical); *Databases:* 70. Students can reserve study rooms.

STUDENT LIFE
Housing options: on-campus residence required through junior year; coed. Campus housing is university owned. Freshman campus housing is guaranteed.

Activities and organizations: drama/theater group, Student Government Association, Mountaineer Event Board, Japanese Culture and Anime Club, Big Brothers Big Sisters, Moosecorps.

Athletics Member NCAA. All Division III.

Campus security: 24-hour patrols, late-night transport/escort service, controlled dormitory access.

Student services: health clinic, personal/psychological counseling.

COSTS & FINANCIAL AID

Costs (2018–19) ***One-time required fee:*** $100. ***Comprehensive fee:*** $36,511 includes full-time tuition ($25,236), mandatory fees ($275), and room and board ($11,000). Part-time tuition: $1052 per credit hour. Part-time tuition and fees vary according to course load. ***Room and board:*** Room and board charges vary according to board plan and housing facility.

Financial Aid Of all full-time matriculated undergraduates who enrolled in 2017, 307 applied for aid, 307 were judged to have need. 99 Federal Work-Study jobs (averaging $1500). 6 state and other part-time jobs (averaging $1500). In 2017, 34 non-need-based awards were made. ***Average percent of need met:*** 42. ***Average financial aid package:*** $16,000. ***Average need-based loan:*** $4500. ***Average need-based gift aid:*** $16,000. ***Average non-need-based aid:*** $12,000. ***Average indebtedness upon graduation:*** $35,728.

APPLYING

Standardized Tests *Required:* SAT or ACT (for admission).

Options: electronic application, early admission, deferred entrance.

Application fee: $30.

Required: high school transcript. ***Required for some:*** college transcripts for transfer students. ***Recommended:*** essay or personal statement, minimum 2.0 GPA.

CONTACT

Southern Vermont College, 897 Monument Avenue, Bennington, VT 05201. *Phone:* 802-447-6300. *Fax:* 802-681-2868. *E-mail:* admissions@svc.edu.

Sterling College

Craftsbury Common, Vermont

http://www.sterlingcollege.edu/

CONTACT

Tim Patterson, Director of Admission and Financial Aid, Sterling College, PO Box 72, Craftsbury Common, VT 05827. *Phone:* 802-586-7711 Ext. 135. *Toll-free phone:* 800-648-3591 Ext. 100. *Fax:* 802-586-2596. *E-mail:* tpatterson@sterlingcollege.edu.

University of Vermont

Burlington, Vermont

http://www.uvm.edu/

- **State-supported** university, founded 1791
- **Suburban** 459-acre campus
- **Endowment** $490.8 million
- **Coed** 11,328 undergraduate students, 92% full-time, 59% women, 41% men
- **Moderately difficult** entrance level, 68% of applicants were admitted

UNDERGRAD STUDENTS

10,434 full-time, 894 part-time. Students come from 50 states and territories; 51 other countries; 71% are from out of state; 1% Black or African American, non-Hispanic/Latino; 4% Hispanic/Latino; 3% Asian, non-Hispanic/Latino; 3% Two or more races, non-Hispanic/Latino; 2% Race/ethnicity unknown; 5% international; 4% transferred in; 51% live on campus.

Freshmen:

Admission: 21,263 applied, 14,365 admitted, 2,531 enrolled. ***Average high school GPA:*** 3.6. ***Test scores:*** SAT evidence-based reading and writing scores over 500: 99%; SAT math scores over 500: 98%; ACT scores over 18: 100%; SAT evidence-based reading and writing scores over 600: 77%; SAT math scores over 600: 66%; ACT scores over 24: 90%; SAT evidence-based reading and writing scores over 700: 17%; SAT math scores over 700: 17%; ACT scores over 30: 36%.

Retention: 87% of full-time freshmen returned.

FACULTY

Total: 814, 76% full-time, 72% with terminal degrees.

Student/faculty ratio: 17:1.

ACADEMICS

Calendar: semesters. *Degrees:* bachelor's, master's, doctoral, post-master's, and postbachelor's certificates.

Special study options: adult/continuing education programs, advanced placement credit, cooperative education, distance learning, double majors, freshman honors college, honors programs, independent study, internships, off-campus study, part-time degree program, services for LD students, student-designed majors, study abroad, summer session for credit. ***ROTC:*** Army (b).

Unusual degree programs: 3-2 law with Vermont Law School.

Computers: 530 computers/terminals and 300 ports are available on campus for general student use. Students can access the following: campus intranet, computer help desk, free student e-mail accounts, online (class) grades, online (class) registration, online (class) schedules, Web pages, online course support, learning management system. Campuswide network is available. 100% of college-owned or -operated housing units are wired for high-speed Internet access. Wireless service is available via entire campus.

Library: David W. Howe Memorial Library plus 3 others. *Books:* 1.2 million (physical), 334,751 (digital/electronic); *Serial titles:* 42,611 (physical), 90,435 (digital/electronic); *Databases:* 395. Weekly public service hours: 102; study areas open 24 hours, 5–7 days a week; students can reserve study rooms.

STUDENT LIFE

Housing options: on-campus residence required through sophomore year; coed. Campus housing is university owned. Freshman campus housing is guaranteed.

Activities and organizations: drama/theater group, student-run newspaper, radio and television station, choral group, Ski and Snowboard Club, Outing Club, Volunteer in Action, Climbing Team, national fraternities, national sororities.

Athletics Member NCAA. All Division I. ***Intercollegiate sports:*** badminton M(c)/W(c), baseball M(c)/W(c), basketball M(s)/W(s), cheerleading M(c)/W(c), crew M(c)/W(c), cross-country running M/W, equestrian sports M(c)/W(c), fencing M(c)/W(c), field hockey W(s), football M(c)/W(c), golf M(c), gymnastics M(c)/W(c), ice hockey M(s)/W(s), lacrosse M(s)/W(s), riflery M(c)/W(c), rock climbing M(c)/W(c), rugby M(c)/W(c), sailing M(c)/W(c), skiing (cross-country) M(s)/W(s), skiing (downhill) M(s)/W(s), soccer M(s)/W(s), squash M(c)/W(c), swimming and diving W, table tennis M(c)/W(c), tennis M(c)/W(c), track and field M/W, triathlon M(c)/W(c), ultimate Frisbee M(c)/W(c), volleyball M(c)/W(c), water polo M(c)/W(c), wrestling M(c)/W(c). ***Intramural sports:*** badminton M/W, basketball M/W, football M/W, ice hockey M/W, soccer M/W, tennis M/W, ultimate Frisbee M/W, volleyball M/W.

Campus security: 24-hour emergency response devices and patrols, late-night transport/escort service, controlled dormitory access.

Student services: health clinic, personal/psychological counseling, women's center, legal services, veterans affairs office.

COSTS & FINANCIAL AID

Costs (2018–19) ***Tuition:*** state resident $15,936 full-time, $664 per credit hour part-time; nonresident $40,176 full-time, $1674 per credit hour part-time. Full-time tuition and fees vary according to reciprocity agreements. Part-time tuition and fees vary according to course load and reciprocity agreements. ***Required fees:*** $2340 full-time, $20 per credit hour part-time. ***Room and board:*** $12,492; room only: $8196. Room and board charges vary according to board plan and housing facility. ***Payment plan:*** installment. ***Waivers:*** employees or children of employees.

Financial Aid Of all full-time matriculated undergraduates who enrolled in 2017, 7,053 applied for aid, 5,654 were judged to have need, 892 had their need fully met. 1,500 Federal Work-Study jobs (averaging $1600). In 2017, 3119 non-need-based awards were made. ***Average percent of need met:*** 68. ***Average financial aid package:*** $26,256. ***Average need-based loan:*** $4604. ***Average need-based gift aid:*** $17,169. ***Average non-need-based aid:*** $13,726. ***Average indebtedness upon graduation:*** $32,950.

APPLYING

Standardized Tests *Required:* SAT or ACT (for admission).

Options: electronic application, early admission, early action, deferred entrance.

Application fee: $55.

Required: essay or personal statement, high school transcript, 1 letter of recommendation. ***Required for some:*** audition for music or music education.

Application deadlines: 1/15 (freshmen), 1/15 (out-of-state freshmen), 4/15 (transfers), 11/1 (early action).

Notification: 3/31 (freshmen), 3/31 (out-of-state freshmen), continuous (transfers), 12/15 (early action).

CONTACT
Mr. Ryan Hargraves, Director of Admissions, University of Vermont, Office of Admissions, 194 South Prospect Street, Burlington, VT 05401. *Phone:* 802-656-3370. *Fax:* 802-656-8611. *E-mail:* admissions@uvm.edu.

Vermont Technical College

Randolph Center, Vermont

http://www.vtc.edu/

- **State-supported** comprehensive, founded 1866, part of Vermont State Colleges System
- **Rural** 544-acre campus
- **Endowment** $5.5 million
- **Coed** 1,610 undergraduate students, 66% full-time, 48% women, 52% men
- **Moderately difficult** entrance level, 69% of applicants were admitted

UNDERGRAD STUDENTS
1,069 full-time, 541 part-time. Students come from 23 states and territories; 6 other countries; 15% are from out of state; 1% Black or African American, non-Hispanic/Latino; 2% Hispanic/Latino; 0.9% Asian, non-Hispanic/Latino; 0.2% American Indian or Alaska Native, non-Hispanic/Latino; 17% Two or more races, non-Hispanic/Latino; 3% Race/ethnicity unknown; 2% international; 21% transferred in; 31% live on campus.

Freshmen:
Admission: 1,039 applied, 718 admitted, 283 enrolled. ***Average high school GPA:*** 3.2. ***Test scores:*** SAT evidence-based reading and writing scores over 500: 100%; SAT math scores over 500: 100%; ACT scores over 18: 90%; SAT evidence-based reading and writing scores over 600: 33%; SAT math scores over 600: 33%; ACT scores over 24: 31%; ACT scores over 30: 10%.

Retention: 71% of full-time freshmen returned.

FACULTY
Total: 165, 48% full-time, 19% with terminal degrees.

Student/faculty ratio: 12:1.

ACADEMICS
Calendar: semesters. *Degrees:* certificates, associate, bachelor's, and master's.

Special study options: academic remediation for entering students, accelerated degree program, advanced placement credit, cooperative education, distance learning, double majors, English as a second language, honors programs, independent study, internships, part-time degree program, services for LD students, summer session for credit. ***ROTC:*** Army (c).

Computers: 480 computers/terminals and 600 ports are available on campus for general student use. Students can access the following: campus intranet, computer help desk, free student e-mail accounts, online (class) grades, online (class) registration, online (class) schedules, online (network) file storage. Campuswide network is available. 98% of college-owned or -operated housing units are wired for high-speed Internet access. Wireless service is available via entire campus.
Library: Hartness Library. *Books:* 59,000 (physical).

STUDENT LIFE
Housing options: on-campus residence required through sophomore year; coed. Campus housing is university owned.

Activities and organizations: student-run radio and television station, choral group, Student Council (student government), Adventurer's Guild (board and video gaming), WVTC (student radio station), Outing Club, Veterinary Technology Club.

Athletics Member USCAA. ***Intercollegiate sports:*** baseball M, basketball M/W, soccer M/W, softball W. ***Intramural sports:*** basketball M/W, bowling M(c)/W(c), cross-country running M/W, fencing M(c), field hockey W(c), football M/W, golf M(c)/W(c), ice hockey M(c)/W(c), racquetball M/W, riflery M(c)/W(c), rock climbing M(c)/W(c), rugby M(c), skiing (cross-country) M(c)/W(c), skiing (downhill) M(c)/W(c), soccer M/W, softball M/W, swimming and diving M/W, table tennis M/W, tennis M/W, volleyball M/W, water polo M/W, weight lifting M(c)/W(c).

Campus security: 24-hour emergency response devices and patrols, late-night transport/escort service, controlled dormitory access.

Student services: health clinic.

COSTS & FINANCIAL AID
Costs (2019–20) ***Tuition:*** state resident $14,304 full-time, $596 per credit hour part-time; nonresident $27,336 full-time, $1139 per credit hour part-time. ***Required fees:*** $1667 full-time, $49 per credit hour part-time. ***Room and board:*** $10,920; room only: $6504.

Financial Aid Of all full-time matriculated undergraduates who enrolled in 2018, 921 applied for aid, 852 were judged to have need, 59 had their need fully met. 154 Federal Work-Study jobs (averaging $1252). In 2018, 68 non-need-based awards were made. ***Average percent of need met:*** 49. ***Average financial aid package:*** $12,000. ***Average need-based loan:*** $3764. ***Average need-based gift aid:*** $8272. ***Average non-need-based aid:*** $5532. ***Average indebtedness upon graduation:*** $24,480.

APPLYING
Standardized Tests *Required for some:* SAT (for admission).

Options: electronic application.

Application fee: $47.

Required: high school transcript. ***Required for some:*** essay or personal statement, 2 letters of recommendation. ***Recommended:*** minimum 3.0 GPA, 2 letters of recommendation, interview.

Application deadlines: rolling (freshmen), rolling (transfers).

Notification: continuous (freshmen), continuous (transfers).

CONTACT
Jessica Van Deren, Assistant Dean of Admissions, Vermont Technical College, PO Box 500, Randolph Center, VT 05061. *Phone:* 802-728-1244. *Toll-free phone:* 800-442-VTC1. *Fax:* 802-728-1390. *E-mail:* admissions@vtc.edu.

VIRGINIA

American National University

Danville, Virginia

http://www.an.edu/

CONTACT
Admissions Office, American National University, 336 Old Riverside Drive, Danville, VA 24541. *Phone:* 434-793-6822. *Toll-free phone:* 888-9-JOBREADY.

American National University

Harrisonburg, Virginia

http://www.an.edu/

CONTACT
Jack Evey, Campus Director, American National University, 1515 Country Club Road, Harrisonburg, VA 22802. *Phone:* 540-432-0943. *Toll-free phone:* 888-9-JOBREADY.

American National University

Lynchburg, Virginia

http://www.an.edu/

CONTACT
Admissions Representative, American National University, 104 Candlewood Court, Lynchburg, VA 24502. *Phone:* 804-239-3500. *Toll-free phone:* 888-9-JOBREADY.

American National University
Salem, Virginia
http://www.an.edu/

CONTACT
Director of Admissions, American National University, 1813 East Main Street, Salem, VA 24153. *Phone:* 540-986-1800. *Toll-free phone:* 888-9-JOBREADY. *Fax:* 540-444-4198.

Argosy University, Northern Virginia
Arlington, Virginia
http://www.argosy.edu/locations/northern-virginia/

CONTACT
Argosy University, Northern Virginia, 1550 Wilson Boulevard, Suite 600, Arlington, VA 22209. *Phone:* 703-526-5800. *Toll-free phone:* 866-703-2777.

The Art Institute of Virginia Beach, a branch of The Art Institute of Atlanta
Virginia Beach, Virginia
http://www.artinstitutes.edu/virginia-beach/

CONTACT
The Art Institute of Virginia Beach, a branch of The Art Institute of Atlanta, Two Columbus Center, 4500 Main Street, Suite 100, Virginia Beach, VA 23462. *Phone:* 757-493-6700. *Toll-free phone:* 877-437-4428.

Averett University
Danville, Virginia
http://www.averett.edu/

- **Independent** comprehensive, founded 1859, affiliated with Baptist General Association of Virginia
- **Small-town** 185-acre campus with easy access to Greensboro, NC
- **Endowment** $29.1 million
- **Coed** 965 undergraduate students, 97% full-time, 43% women, 57% men
- **Moderately difficult** entrance level, 61% of applicants were admitted

UNDERGRAD STUDENTS
934 full-time, 31 part-time. Students come from 24 states and territories; 20 other countries; 44% are from out of state; 29% Black or African American, non-Hispanic/Latino; 4% Hispanic/Latino; 0.6% Asian, non-Hispanic/Latino; 0.4% Native Hawaiian or other Pacific Islander, non-Hispanic/Latino; 0.4% American Indian or Alaska Native, non-Hispanic/Latino; 4% Two or more races, non-Hispanic/Latino; 6% international; 7% transferred in; 58% live on campus.

Freshmen:
Admission: 2,812 applied, 1,711 admitted, 292 enrolled. ***Average high school GPA:*** 3.3. ***Test scores:*** SAT evidence-based reading and writing scores over 500: 48%; SAT math scores over 500: 47%; ACT scores over 18: 60%; SAT evidence-based reading and writing scores over 600: 8%; SAT math scores over 600: 6%; ACT scores over 24: 20%; ACT scores over 30: 3%.

Retention: 63% of full-time freshmen returned.

FACULTY
Total: 123, 42% full-time, 44% with terminal degrees.

Student/faculty ratio: 12:1.

ACADEMICS
Calendar: semesters. *Degree:* bachelor's.

Special study options: academic remediation for entering students, accelerated degree program, adult/continuing education programs, advanced placement credit, cooperative education, distance learning, double majors, external degree program, honors programs, independent study, internships, off-campus study, part-time degree program, services for LD students, student-designed majors, study abroad, summer session for credit.

Computers: 150 computers/terminals and 25 ports are available on campus for general student use. Students can access the following: computer help desk, free student e-mail accounts, online (class) grades, online (class) registration, online (class) schedules. Campuswide network is available. 100% of college-owned or -operated housing units are wired for high-speed Internet access. Wireless service is available via entire campus.

Library: Mary B. Blount Library. *Books:* 86,432 (physical), 313,632 (digital/electronic); *Serial titles:* 98 (physical), 35,069 (digital/electronic); *Databases:* 160. Weekly public service hours: 81; students can reserve study rooms.

STUDENT LIFE
Housing options: on-campus residence required through junior year; coed, men-only, women-only. Campus housing is university owned. Freshman campus housing is guaranteed.

Activities and organizations: drama/theater group, student-run newspaper, choral group, Cougar Activities Board (CAB), Student Athletic Advisory Committee (SAAC), Student Government Association (SGA), FOCUS/Christian Student Fellowship, Rainbow Club, national fraternities.

Athletics Member NCAA. All Division III. ***Intercollegiate sports:*** baseball M, basketball M/W, cheerleading M(c)/W(c), cross-country running M/W, equestrian sports M(c)/W(c), football M, golf M, lacrosse M/W, soccer M/W, softball W, tennis M/W, volleyball W, wrestling M. ***Intramural sports:*** soccer M/W, volleyball M/W.

Campus security: 24-hour emergency response devices and patrols, late-night transport/escort service, controlled dormitory access.

Student services: health clinic, personal/psychological counseling, veterans affairs office.

COSTS & FINANCIAL AID
Costs (2018–19) ***Comprehensive fee:*** $44,496 includes full-time tuition ($34,400), mandatory fees ($120), and room and board ($9976). Full-time tuition and fees vary according to class time, course load, degree level, location, and program. Part-time tuition: $1075 per credit. Part-time tuition and fees vary according to class time, course load, degree level, location, and program. ***Required fees:*** $30 per term part-time. ***College room only:*** $6370. Room and board charges vary according to board plan and housing facility. ***Payment plan:*** installment. ***Waivers:*** senior citizens and employees or children of employees.

Financial Aid Of all full-time matriculated undergraduates who enrolled in 2018, 849 applied for aid, 801 were judged to have need, 110 had their need fully met. 176 Federal Work-Study jobs (averaging $962). In 2018, 132 non-need-based awards were made. ***Average percent of need met:*** 72. ***Average financial aid package:*** $27,059. ***Average need-based loan:*** $3951. ***Average need-based gift aid:*** $23,577. ***Average non-need-based aid:*** $16,030. ***Average indebtedness upon graduation:*** $31,127.

APPLYING
Standardized Tests *Required:* SAT or ACT (for admission), TOEFL for international students (for admission).

Options: electronic application, deferred entrance.

Required: high school transcript, minimum 2.5 GPA. ***Recommended:*** essay or personal statement, 1 letter of recommendation, interview.

Notification: continuous (freshmen), continuous (transfers).

CONTACT
Mr. Joel Nester, Director of Admissions and International Counselor, Averett University, 420 West Main Street, English Hall, Danville, VA 24541. *Phone:* 434-791-5663. *Toll-free phone:* 800-AVERETT. *E-mail:* joel.nester@averett.edu.

Bethel College
Hampton, Virginia
http://www.bcva.edu/

CONTACT
Ms. Nanette Bartholomew, Student Affairs, Bethel College, 1705 Todds Lane, Hampton, VA 23666. *Phone:* 757-826-1883 Ext. 215.

Bluefield College

Bluefield, Virginia

http://www.bluefield.edu/

- **Independent Southern Baptist** comprehensive, founded 1922
- **Small-town** 82-acre campus
- **Endowment** $6.7 million
- **Coed**
- 91% of applicants were admitted

FACULTY
Student/faculty ratio: 14:1.

ACADEMICS
Calendar: semesters. *Degrees:* bachelor's and master's.
Library: Easley Library. *Books:* 44,352 (physical), 165,829 (digital/electronic); *Serial titles:* 7,976 (physical), 334 (digital/electronic); *Databases:* 72. Students can reserve study rooms.

STUDENT LIFE
Housing options: on-campus residence required through junior year; men-only, women-only. Campus housing is university owned. Freshman applicants given priority for college housing.

Activities and organizations: drama/theater group, student-run newspaper, choral group, Baptist Collegiate Ministries, Fellowship of Christian Athletes, Student Union Board, Student Government Association, Arts Club.

Athletics Member NAIA, NCCAA.

Campus security: controlled dormitory access, night security patrols.

Student services: personal/psychological counseling.

COSTS & FINANCIAL AID
Costs (2018–19) ***Comprehensive fee:*** $34,314 includes full-time tuition ($24,520), mandatory fees ($770), and room and board ($9024). Full-time tuition and fees vary according to course load and program. Part-time tuition: $970 per credit hour. Part-time tuition and fees vary according to course load and program. ***Required fees:*** $28 per credit hour part-time. ***College room only:*** $3770. Room and board charges vary according to housing facility.

Financial Aid Of all full-time matriculated undergraduates who enrolled in 2018, 742 applied for aid, 693 were judged to have need, 70 had their need fully met. 82 Federal Work-Study jobs (averaging $1035). 26 state and other part-time jobs (averaging $181). In 2018, 74 non-need-based awards were made. ***Average percent of need met:*** 66. ***Average financial aid package:*** $17,231. ***Average need-based loan:*** $4062. ***Average need-based gift aid:*** $13,602. ***Average non-need-based aid:*** $7593. ***Average indebtedness upon graduation:*** $27,855.

APPLYING
Standardized Tests *Required:* SAT or ACT (for admission).

Options: electronic application.

Required: high school transcript, minimum 2.0 GPA. ***Required for some:*** essay or personal statement.

CONTACT
Mr. Matthew Hamilton, Director of Traditional Admissions, Bluefield College, 3000 College Avenue, Bluefield, VA 24605-1799. *Phone:* 276-326-4602. *Toll-free phone:* 800-872-0175. *Fax:* 276-326-4395. *E-mail:* mrh263676@bluefield.edu.

Bon Secours Memorial College of Nursing

Richmond, Virginia

http://www.bsmcon.edu/

CONTACT
Bon Secours Memorial College of Nursing, 8550 Magellan Parkway, Suite 1100, Richmond, VA 23227-1149. *Toll-free phone:* 866-238-7414.

Bridgewater College

Bridgewater, Virginia

http://www.bridgewater.edu/

- **Independent** comprehensive, founded 1880, affiliated with Church of the Brethren
- **Small-town** 300-acre campus
- **Endowment** $98.1 million
- **Coed** 1,839 undergraduate students, 100% full-time, 56% women, 44% men
- **Moderately difficult** entrance level, 66% of applicants were admitted

UNDERGRAD STUDENTS
1,832 full-time, 7 part-time. Students come from 28 states and territories; 22 other countries; 25% are from out of state; 16% Black or African American, non-Hispanic/Latino; 7% Hispanic/Latino; 1% Asian, non-Hispanic/Latino; 0.2% Native Hawaiian or other Pacific Islander, non-Hispanic/Latino; 0.3% American Indian or Alaska Native, non-Hispanic/Latino; 5% Two or more races, non-Hispanic/Latino; 3% Race/ethnicity unknown; 2% international; 2% transferred in; 82% live on campus.

Freshmen:
Admission: 6,360 applied, 4,203 admitted, 590 enrolled. ***Average high school GPA:*** 3.5. ***Test scores:*** SAT evidence-based reading and writing scores over 500: 75%; SAT math scores over 500: 72%; ACT scores over 18: 82%; SAT evidence-based reading and writing scores over 600: 26%; SAT math scores over 600: 18%; ACT scores over 24: 35%; SAT evidence-based reading and writing scores over 700: 5%; SAT math scores over 700: 3%; ACT scores over 30: 10%.

Retention: 68% of full-time freshmen returned.

FACULTY
Total: 169, 69% full-time, 67% with terminal degrees.

Student/faculty ratio: 14:1.

ACADEMICS
Calendar: semesters. *Degrees:* bachelor's and master's.

Special study options: adult/continuing education programs, advanced placement credit, distance learning, double majors, honors programs, independent study, internships, off-campus study, part-time degree program, services for LD students, study abroad, summer session for credit.

Unusual degree programs: 3-2 engineering with Virginia Polytechnic Institute and State University; 3-2 athletic training (internal); 4-1 digital media strategy (internal); 3-4 Veterinary Science with Virginia Tech.

Computers: 135 computers/terminals and 701 ports are available on campus for general student use. Students can access the following: campus intranet, computer help desk, free student e-mail accounts, online (class) grades, online (class) registration, online (class) schedules, course management system, campus bulletin board system. Campuswide network is available. 100% of college-owned or -operated housing units are wired for high-speed Internet access. Wireless service is available via entire campus.

Library: Alexander Mack Memorial Library. *Books:* 105,776 (physical), 23,752 (digital/electronic); *Serial titles:* 264 (physical), 130 (digital/electronic); *Databases:* 110. Weekly public service hours: 92.

STUDENT LIFE
Housing options: on-campus residence required through junior year; coed, men-only, women-only, special housing for students with disabilities. Campus housing is university owned.

Activities and organizations: drama/theater group, student-run newspaper, radio station, choral group, Eagle Productions (program board), Physics Club, Active Minds, BC Allies.

Athletics Member NCAA. All Division III. ***Intercollegiate sports:*** baseball M, basketball M/W, cheerleading M(c)/W(c), cross-country running M/W, equestrian sports M(c)/W(c), field hockey W, football M, golf M/W, lacrosse M/W, soccer M/W, softball W, swimming and diving M/W, tennis M/W, track and field M/W, volleyball W, wrestling M(c). ***Intramural sports:*** badminton M/W, basketball M/W, bowling M/W, football M/W, golf M/W, racquetball M/W, sand volleyball M/W, soccer M/W, softball M/W, table tennis M/W, tennis M/W, ultimate Frisbee M/W, volleyball M/W.

Campus security: 24-hour emergency response devices and patrols, controlled dormitory access, emergency alert system.

Student services: health clinic, personal/psychological counseling.

COSTS & FINANCIAL AID
Costs (2019–20) ***Comprehensive fee:*** $49,570 includes full-time tuition ($35,700), mandatory fees ($900), and room and board ($12,970). Part-time tuition: $1230 per credit hour. ***Required fees:*** $40 part-time.

Financial Aid Of all full-time matriculated undergraduates who enrolled in 2018, 1,639 applied for aid, 1,518 were judged to have need, 397 had their need fully met. 435 Federal Work-Study jobs (averaging $1438). 139 state and other part-time jobs (averaging $853). In 2018, 309 non-need-based awards were made. ***Average percent of need met:*** 85. ***Average financial aid package:*** $32,671. ***Average need-based loan:*** $4114. ***Average need-based gift aid:*** $29,398. ***Average non-need-based aid:*** $21,457. ***Average indebtedness upon graduation:*** $33,744.

APPLYING
Standardized Tests *Required:* SAT or ACT (for admission).

Options: electronic application, deferred entrance.

Required: high school transcript. ***Recommended:*** minimum 3.0 GPA.

Notification: continuous (freshmen), continuous (transfers).

CONTACT
Mr. Jarret L. Smith, Director of Admissions, Bridgewater College, 402 East College Street, Bridgewater, VA 22812. *Phone:* 540-828-5469. *Toll-free phone:* 800-759-8328. *Fax:* 540-828-5481. *E-mail:* admissions@bridgewater.edu.

Bryant & Stratton College–Hampton Campus

Hampton, Virginia

http://www.bryantstratton.edu/

CONTACT
Bryant & Stratton College–Hampton Campus, 4410 East Claiborne Square, Suite 233, Hampton, VA 23666.

Bryant & Stratton College–Richmond Campus

Richmond, Virginia

http://www.bryantstratton.edu/

CONTACT
Mr. David K. Mayle, Director of Admissions, Bryant & Stratton College–Richmond Campus, 8141 Hull Street Road, Richmond, VA 23235-6411. *Phone:* 804-745-2444. *Fax:* 804-745-6884. *E-mail:* tlawson@bryanstratton.edu.

Bryant & Stratton College–Virginia Beach Campus

Virginia Beach, Virginia

http://www.bryantstratton.edu/

CONTACT
Bryant & Stratton College–Virginia Beach Campus, 301 Centre Pointe Drive, Virginia Beach, VA 23462. *Phone:* 757-499-7900 Ext. 173.

Centura College

Virginia Beach, Virginia

http://www.centuracollege.edu/

CONTACT
Admissions Office, Centura College, 2697 Dean Drive, Suite 100, Virginia Beach, VA 23452. *Phone:* 757-340-2121. *Toll-free phone:* 877-575-5627. *Fax:* 757-340-9704.

Chamberlain College of Nursing

Arlington, Virginia

http://www.chamberlain.edu/

CONTACT
Admissions, Chamberlain College of Nursing, 2450 Crystal Drive, Suite 319, Arlington, VA 22202. *Phone:* 703-416-7300. *Toll-free phone:* 877-751-5783.

Christendom College

Front Royal, Virginia

http://www.christendom.edu/

- **Independent Roman Catholic** comprehensive, founded 1977
- **Rural** 200-acre campus with easy access to Washington, DC
- **Endowment** $15.8 million
- **Coed**
- **Moderately difficult** entrance level

FACULTY
Student/faculty ratio: 15:1.

ACADEMICS
Calendar: semesters. *Degrees:* associate, bachelor's, and master's.
Library: St. John the Evangelist Library. *Books:* 100,000 (physical), 1,000 (digital/electronic); *Serial titles:* 250 (physical), 1,000 (digital/electronic); *Databases:* 45. Weekly public service hours: 97.

STUDENT LIFE
Housing options: on-campus residence required through senior year; men-only, women-only. Campus housing is university owned. Freshman campus housing is guaranteed.

Activities and organizations: drama/theater group, student-run newspaper, choral group, drama, choir, Chester-Belloc Debate Society, Swing Dance Club, Shields of Rose Pro-life group.

Athletics Member USCAA.

Campus security: 24-hour emergency response devices, late-night transport/escort service, night patrols by trained security personnel.

Student services: health clinic, personal/psychological counseling.

COSTS & FINANCIAL AID
Costs (2018–19) ***Comprehensive fee:*** $36,640 includes full-time tuition ($25,460), mandatory fees ($900), and room and board ($10,280).

Financial Aid Of all full-time matriculated undergraduates who enrolled in 2018, 270 applied for aid, 270 were judged to have need. 201 state and other part-time jobs (averaging $2873). In 2018, 170 non-need-based awards were made. ***Average percent of need met:*** 73. ***Average financial aid package:*** $19,348. ***Average need-based loan:*** $7110. ***Average need-based gift aid:*** $11,894. ***Average non-need-based aid:*** $11,114. ***Average indebtedness upon graduation:*** $32,750.

APPLYING
Standardized Tests *Required:* SAT or ACT (for admission).

Options: electronic application, early admission, early action.

Required: essay or personal statement, high school transcript, 1 letter of recommendation. ***Required for some:*** 2 letters of recommendation, two writing samples for those with SAT scores lower than 1000 or ACT scores lower than 21. ***Recommended:*** minimum 2.0 GPA, interview.

CONTACT
Mr. Sam Phillips, Director of Admissions, Christendom College, 134 Christendom Drive, Front Royal, VA 22630. *Phone:* 800-877-5456 Ext. 1290. *Toll-free phone:* 800-877-5456. *E-mail:* sam.phillips@christendom.edu.

Christopher Newport University

Newport News, Virginia

http://www.cnu.edu/

- **State-supported** comprehensive, founded 1960
- **Suburban** 260-acre campus with easy access to Virginia Beach
- **Endowment** $35.4 million
- **Coed** 4,857 undergraduate students, 99% full-time, 56% women, 44% men
- **Moderately difficult** entrance level, 68% of applicants were admitted

UNDERGRAD STUDENTS
4,789 full-time, 68 part-time. Students come from 34 states and territories; 34 other countries; 8% are from out of state; 6% Black or African American, non-Hispanic/Latino; 6% Hispanic/Latino; 3% Asian, non-Hispanic/Latino; 0.1% Native Hawaiian or other Pacific Islander, non-Hispanic/Latino; 0.2% American Indian or Alaska Native, non-Hispanic/Latino; 5% Two or more races, non-Hispanic/Latino; 3% Race/ethnicity unknown; 0.4% international; 3% transferred in; 78% live on campus.

Freshmen:
Admission: 7,430 applied, 5,035 admitted, 1,228 enrolled. ***Average high school GPA:*** 3.8. ***Test scores:*** SAT evidence-based reading and writing scores over 500: 98%; SAT math scores over 500: 95%; ACT scores over 18: 99%; SAT evidence-based reading and writing scores over 600: 60%; SAT math scores over 600: 41%; ACT scores over 24: 72%; SAT evidence-based reading and writing scores over 700: 9%; SAT math scores over 700: 7%; ACT scores over 30: 15%.

Retention: 87% of full-time freshmen returned.

FACULTY
Total: 465, 61% full-time, 67% with terminal degrees.

Student/faculty ratio: 15:1.

ACADEMICS
Calendar: semesters. *Degrees:* bachelor's and master's.

Special study options: advanced placement credit, double majors, honors programs, independent study, internships, off-campus study, student-designed majors, study abroad, summer session for credit. ***ROTC:*** Army (b).

Computers: 540 computers/terminals and 1,000 ports are available on campus for general student use. Students can access the following: campus intranet, computer help desk, free student e-mail accounts, online (class) grades, online (class) registration, online (class) schedules. Campuswide network is available. 100% of college-owned or -operated housing units are wired for high-speed Internet access. Wireless service is available via entire campus.

Library: Paul and Rosemary Trible Library. *Books:* 229,577 (physical), 578,114 (digital/electronic); *Serial titles:* 745 (physical), 65,202 (digital/electronic); *Databases:* 282. Weekly public service hours: 101; study areas open 24 hours, 5–7 days a week; students can reserve study rooms.

STUDENT LIFE
Housing options: on-campus residence required through junior year; coed. Campus housing is university owned. Freshman campus housing is guaranteed.

Activities and organizations: drama/theater group, student-run newspaper, radio and television station, choral group, marching band, Intervarsity Christian Fellowship, Alpha Delta Pi, Delta Gamma, Gamma Phi Beta, Alpha Phi, national fraternities, national sororities.

Athletics Member NCAA. All Division III except golf (Division II). ***Intercollegiate sports:*** baseball M, basketball M/W, cheerleading M(c)/W(c), crew M(c)/W(c), cross-country running M/W, equestrian sports M(c)/W(c), field hockey W, football M, golf M/W, gymnastics M(c)/W(c), ice hockey M(c), lacrosse M/W, rowing M(c)/W(c), rugby M(c), sailing M(c)/W(c), skiing (cross-country) M(c)/W(c), skiing (downhill) W(c), soccer M/W, softball W, swimming and diving M(c)/W(c), table tennis M(c)/W(c), tennis M/W, track and field M/W, ultimate Frisbee M(c)/W(c), volleyball M(c)/W. ***Intramural sports:*** basketball M/W, football M/W, sand volleyball M/W, soccer M/W, softball M/W, ultimate Frisbee M/W, volleyball M/W.

Campus security: 24-hour emergency response devices and patrols, late-night transport/escort service, controlled dormitory access.

Student services: health clinic, personal/psychological counseling, veterans affairs office.

COSTS & FINANCIAL AID
Costs (2018–19) ***Tuition:*** state resident $9032 full-time, $376 per credit hour part-time; nonresident $21,498 full-time, $895 per credit hour part-time. Full-time tuition and fees vary according to course load. Part-time tuition and fees vary according to course load. ***Required fees:*** $5722 full-time, $238 per credit hour part-time. ***Room and board:*** $11,460; room only: $7054. Room and board charges vary according to board plan and housing facility. ***Payment plan:*** installment. ***Waivers:*** senior citizens and employees or children of employees.

Financial Aid Of all full-time matriculated undergraduates who enrolled in 2018, 3,127 applied for aid, 2,156 were judged to have need, 436 had their need fully met. 98 Federal Work-Study jobs (averaging $1490). 1,446 state and other part-time jobs (averaging $2146). In 2018, 770 non-need-based awards were made. ***Average percent of need met:*** 68. ***Average financial aid package:*** $9449. ***Average need-based loan:*** $4386. ***Average need-based gift aid:*** $6334. ***Average non-need-based aid:*** $3329. ***Average indebtedness upon graduation:*** $31,767.

APPLYING
Standardized Tests *Required for some:* SAT or ACT (for admission).

Options: electronic application, early admission, early decision, early action, deferred entrance.

Application fee: $65.

Required: essay or personal statement, high school transcript. ***Required for some:*** interview. ***Recommended:*** minimum 3.5 GPA, 2 letters of recommendation.

Application deadlines: 2/1 (freshmen), 2/1 (out-of-state freshmen), 3/1 (transfers), 12/1 (early action).

Early decision deadline: 11/15.

Notification: 3/15 (freshmen), 3/15 (out-of-state freshmen), 4/15 (transfers), 12/15 (early decision), 1/15 (early action).

CONTACT
Mr. Rob J. Lange III, Dean of Admission, Christopher Newport University, Office of Admission, 1 Avenue of the Arts, Newport News, VA 23606-3072. *Phone:* 757-594-7015. *Toll-free phone:* 800-333-4268. *Fax:* 757-594-7333. *E-mail:* admit@cnu.edu.

The College of William and Mary

Williamsburg, Virginia

http://www.wm.edu/

- **State-supported** university, founded 1693
- **Small-town** 1200-acre campus with easy access to Richmond
- **Endowment** $935.5 million
- **Coed** 6,377 undergraduate students, 99% full-time, 58% women, 42% men
- **Most difficult** entrance level, 37% of applicants were admitted

UNDERGRAD STUDENTS
6,300 full-time, 77 part-time. Students come from 55 states and territories; 84 other countries; 31% are from out of state; 7% Black or African American, non-Hispanic/Latino; 9% Hispanic/Latino; 8% Asian, non-Hispanic/Latino; 0.1% Native Hawaiian or other Pacific Islander, non-Hispanic/Latino; 0.2% American Indian or Alaska Native, non-Hispanic/Latino; 5% Two or more races, non-Hispanic/Latino; 6% Race/ethnicity unknown; 6% international; 3% transferred in; 71% live on campus.

Freshmen:
Admission: 14,644 applied, 5,406 admitted, 1,545 enrolled. ***Average high school GPA:*** 4.2. ***Test scores:*** SAT evidence-based reading and writing scores over 500: 100%; SAT math scores over 500: 100%; ACT scores over 18: 100%; SAT evidence-based reading and writing scores over 600: 94%; SAT math scores over 600: 88%; ACT scores over 24: 97%; SAT evidence-based reading and writing scores over 700: 56%; SAT math scores over 700: 54%; ACT scores over 30: 77%.

Retention: 95% of full-time freshmen returned.

ACADEMICS
Calendar: semesters. *Degrees:* bachelor's, master's, doctoral, post-master's, and postbachelor's certificates.

Special study options: accelerated degree program, advanced placement credit, distance learning, double majors, English as a second language, honors programs, independent study, internships, off-campus study, part-time degree program, services for LD students, student-designed majors, study abroad, summer session for credit. ***ROTC:*** Army (b).

Unusual degree programs: 3-2 elementary education, secondary education, special education, chemistry, public policy.

Computers: 400 computers/terminals and 8,000 ports are available on campus for general student use. Students can access the following:

campus intranet, computer help desk, free student e-mail accounts, online (class) grades, online (class) registration, online (class) schedules. Campuswide network is available. 100% of college-owned or -operated housing units are wired for high-speed Internet access. Wireless service is available via entire campus.

Library: Earl Gregg Swem Library plus 7 others. *Books:* 1.1 million (physical), 2.2 million (digital/electronic); *Serial titles:* 40,428 (physical), 153,205 (digital/electronic); *Databases:* 540. Weekly public service hours: 110; study areas open 24 hours, 5–7 days a week; students can reserve study rooms.

STUDENT LIFE

Housing options: on-campus residence required for freshman year; coed, special housing for students with disabilities. Campus housing is university owned and leased by the school. Freshman campus housing is guaranteed.

Activities and organizations: drama/theater group, student-run newspaper, radio and television station, choral group, Alma Mater Productions, Student Assembly, Residence Hall Association, Alpha Phi Omega, International Relations Club, national fraternities, national sororities.

Athletics Member NCAA. All Division I. ***Intercollegiate sports:*** baseball M(s), basketball M(s)/W(s), cross-country running M(s)/W(s), field hockey W(s), football M(s), golf M(s)/W(s), gymnastics M(s)/W(s), lacrosse W(s), soccer M(s)/W(s), swimming and diving M/W(s), tennis M(s)/W(s), track and field M(s)/W(s), volleyball W(s). ***Intramural sports:*** badminton M(c)/W(c), baseball M(c), basketball M/W, cheerleading M(c)/W(c), crew M(c)/W(c), cross-country running M(c)/W(c), equestrian sports M(c)/W(c), fencing M(c)/W(c), field hockey M(c)/W(c), football M/W, golf M(c)/W(c), gymnastics M(c)/W(c), ice hockey M(c), lacrosse M(c)/W(c), racquetball M(c)/W(c), rock climbing M(c)/W(c), rowing M(c)/W(c), rugby M(c)/W(c), sailing M(c)/W(c), soccer M/W, softball M/W, squash M(c)/W(c), swimming and diving M(c)/W(c), table tennis M(c)/W(c), tennis M(c)/W(c), triathlon M(c)/W(c), ultimate Frisbee M(c)/W(c), volleyball M/W, water polo M(c)/W(c), weight lifting M/W, wrestling M(c).

Campus security: 24-hour emergency response devices and patrols, late-night transport/escort service, controlled dormitory access.

Student services: health clinic, personal/psychological counseling, legal services.

COSTS & FINANCIAL AID

Costs (2018–19) ***Tuition:*** state resident $17,434 full-time, $425 per credit hour part-time; nonresident $38,735 full-time, $1235 per credit hour part-time. ***Required fees:*** $5966 full-time. ***Room and board:*** $12,236; room only: $7436. Room and board charges vary according to board plan and housing facility. ***Payment plan:*** installment. ***Waivers:*** senior citizens and employees or children of employees.

Financial Aid Of all full-time matriculated undergraduates who enrolled in 2017, 3,225 applied for aid, 2,369 were judged to have need, 577 had their need fully met. 559 Federal Work-Study jobs (averaging $972). In 2017, 325 non-need-based awards were made. ***Average percent of need met:*** 81. ***Average financial aid package:*** $23,807. ***Average need-based loan:*** $3620. ***Average need-based gift aid:*** $17,561. ***Average non-need-based aid:*** $7405. ***Average indebtedness upon graduation:*** $24,072.

APPLYING

Standardized Tests *Required:* SAT or ACT (for admission).

Options: electronic application, early admission, early decision, deferred entrance.

Application fee: $75.

Required: essay or personal statement, high school transcript, 1 letter of recommendation. ***Recommended:*** 2 letters of recommendation.

Application deadlines: 1/1 (freshmen), 3/1 (transfers).

Early decision deadline: 11/1.

Notification: 4/1 (freshmen), 5/1 (transfers), 12/1 (early decision).

CONTACT

Mr. David Trott, Associate Dean of Admission, The College of William and Mary, PO Box 8795, Williamsburg, VA 23187-8795. *Phone:* 757-221-3059. *Fax:* 757-221-1242. *E-mail:* admission@wm.edu.

Culinary Institute of Virginia

Norfolk, Virginia

http://www.chefva.com/

CONTACT

Director of Admissions, Culinary Institute of Virginia, 2428 Almeda Avenue, Suite 316, Norfolk, VA 23513. *Phone:* 757-858-2433. *Toll-free phone:* 866-619-CHEF. *E-mail:* hsadmissions@chefva.com.

DeVry University–Arlington Campus

Arlington, Virginia

http://www.devry.edu/

CONTACT

DeVry University–Arlington Campus, 2450 Crystal Drive, Arlington, VA 22202. *Phone:* 703-414-4000. *Toll-free phone:* 866-338-7934.

DeVry University–Chesapeake Campus

Chesapeake, Virginia

http://www.devry.edu/

CONTACT

Admissions Office, DeVry University–Chesapeake Campus, 1317 Executive Boulevard, Suite 100, Chesapeake, VA 23320-3671. *Phone:* 757-382-5680. *Toll-free phone:* 866-338-7934.

Eastern Mennonite University

Harrisonburg, Virginia

http://www.emu.edu/

- **Independent Mennonite** comprehensive, founded 1917
- **Small-town** 93-acre campus
- **Endowment** $27.5 million
- **Coed** 1,041 undergraduate students, 82% full-time, 64% women, 36% men
- **Moderately difficult** entrance level, 59% of applicants were admitted

UNDERGRAD STUDENTS

850 full-time, 191 part-time. Students come from 30 states and territories; 33 other countries; 38% are from out of state; 9% Black or African American, non-Hispanic/Latino; 7% Hispanic/Latino; 3% Asian, non-Hispanic/Latino; 0.2% Native Hawaiian or other Pacific Islander, non-Hispanic/Latino; 0.3% American Indian or Alaska Native, non-Hispanic/Latino; 4% Two or more races, non-Hispanic/Latino; 4% Race/ethnicity unknown; 4% international; 4% transferred in; 44% live on campus.

Freshmen:

Admission: 1,245 applied, 737 admitted, 201 enrolled. ***Average high school GPA:*** 3.6. ***Test scores:*** SAT evidence-based reading and writing scores over 500: 79%; SAT math scores over 500: 76%; ACT scores over 18: 96%; SAT evidence-based reading and writing scores over 600: 37%; SAT math scores over 600: 28%; ACT scores over 24: 65%; SAT evidence-based reading and writing scores over 700: 3%; SAT math scores over 700: 5%; ACT scores over 30: 29%.

Retention: 70% of full-time freshmen returned.

FACULTY

Total: 184, 52% full-time, 48% with terminal degrees.

Student/faculty ratio: 9:1.

ACADEMICS

Calendar: semesters. *Degrees:* certificates, associate, bachelor's, master's, doctoral, and postbachelor's certificates.

Special study options: adult/continuing education programs, advanced placement credit, distance learning, double majors, English as a second language, honors programs, independent study, internships, off-campus study, part-time degree program, services for LD students, study abroad, summer session for credit.

Unusual degree programs: 3-2 engineering with The Catholic University of America.

Computers: 154 computers/terminals are available on campus for general student use. Students can access the following: campus intranet, computer help desk, free student e-mail accounts, online (class) grades, online (class) registration, online (class) schedules. Campuswide network is available. 100% of college-owned or -operated housing units are wired for high-speed Internet access. Wireless service is available via entire campus.
Library: Sadie Hartzler Library. *Books:* 137,998 (physical), 236,023 (digital/electronic); *Serial titles:* 2,083 (physical), 79,742 (digital/electronic); *Databases:* 156. Weekly public service hours: 92.

STUDENT LIFE
Housing options: on-campus residence required through junior year; coed, cooperative, special housing for students with disabilities. Campus housing is university owned. Freshman campus housing is guaranteed.

Activities and organizations: drama/theater group, student-run newspaper, choral group, Young People's Christian Association, Student Government Association, Student Education Association, Creation Care Council, Black Student Union.

Athletics Member NCAA. All Division III except golf (Division II). ***Intercollegiate sports:*** baseball M, basketball M/W, cross-country running M/W, field hockey W, golf M/W, soccer M/W, softball W, track and field M/W, volleyball M/W. ***Intramural sports:*** basketball M/W, football M/W, golf M/W, lacrosse M(c), rock climbing M/W, soccer M/W, softball M/W, table tennis M/W, tennis M/W, volleyball M/W.

Campus security: 24-hour emergency response devices, controlled dormitory access.

Student services: health clinic, personal/psychological counseling.

COSTS & FINANCIAL AID
Costs (2018–19) ***Comprehensive fee:*** $48,260 includes full-time tuition ($36,760), mandatory fees ($340), and room and board ($11,160). Part-time tuition: $1400 per credit hour. Part-time tuition and fees vary according to course load. ***Room and board:*** Room and board charges vary according to board plan and housing facility. ***Payment plan:*** installment. ***Waivers:*** employees or children of employees.

Financial Aid Of all full-time matriculated undergraduates who enrolled in 2016, 840 applied for aid, 772 were judged to have need, 133 had their need fully met. 316 Federal Work-Study jobs (averaging $1266). 49 state and other part-time jobs (averaging $1453). In 2016, 168 non-need-based awards were made. ***Average percent of need met:*** 75. ***Average financial aid package:*** $31,315. ***Average need-based loan:*** $8346. ***Average need-based gift aid:*** $19,417. ***Average non-need-based aid:*** $15,317. ***Average indebtedness upon graduation:*** $39,845.

APPLYING
Standardized Tests *Required:* SAT or ACT (for admission).

Options: electronic application, deferred entrance.

Application fee: $25.

Required: high school transcript, minimum 2.2 GPA, Community Lifestyle Commitment. ***Required for some:*** 2 letters of recommendation. ***Recommended:*** interview.

Application deadlines: rolling (freshmen), rolling (transfers).

Notification: continuous (freshmen), continuous (transfers).

CONTACT
Matthew Ruth, Director of Admissions, Eastern Mennonite University, 1200 Park Road, Harrisonburg, VA 22802. *Phone:* 540-432-4118. *Toll-free phone:* 800-368-2665. *Fax:* 540-432-4444. *E-mail:* admiss@emu.edu.

ECPI University
Virginia Beach, Virginia
http://www.ecpi.edu/

- **Proprietary** comprehensive, founded 1966
- **Suburban** 8-acre campus
- **Coed**
- **Moderately difficult** entrance level

FACULTY
Student/faculty ratio: 16:1.

ACADEMICS
Calendar: continuous. *Degrees:* certificates, diplomas, associate, bachelor's, and master's.
Library: ECPI-Virginia Beach Campus Library plus 14 others. *Books:* 25,945 (physical), 189,050 (digital/electronic); *Serial titles:* 118 (physical); *Databases:* 83. Weekly public service hours: 62; students can reserve study rooms.

STUDENT LIFE
Housing options: college housing not availableCampus housing is provided by a third party.

Activities and organizations: Student Electronic Technicians Association (SETA), Institute of Electrical and Electronic Engineers (IEEE), Phi Theta Kappa Honor Society, Information Technology Exchange (ITE), Medical Student Association, national fraternities, national sororities.

Campus security: building and parking lot security.

Student services: personal/psychological counseling, veterans affairs office.

COSTS
Costs (2018–19) ***One-time required fee:*** $100. ***Tuition:*** $15,984 full-time. Full-time tuition and fees vary according to course load, degree level, location, program, and reciprocity agreements. No tuition increase for student's term of enrollment. ***Payment plans:*** tuition prepayment, installment.

APPLYING
Options: electronic application, deferred entrance.

Application fee: $45.

Required: high school transcript, interview, Entrance Exam. ***Required for some:*** minimum 2.5 GPA.

CONTACT
Mr. Chad Samuelson, University Director of Student Recruitment, ECPI University, 5555 Greenwich Road, Virginia Beach, VA 23462. *Phone:* 757-671-7171 Ext. 55839. *Toll-free phone:* 844-611-0766. *E-mail:* csamuelson@ecpi.edu.

Emory & Henry College
Emory, Virginia
http://www.ehc.edu/

- **Independent United Methodist** comprehensive, founded 1836
- **Rural** 330-acre campus
- **Endowment** $81.8 million
- **Coed**
- 72% of applicants were admitted

FACULTY
Student/faculty ratio: 11:1.

ACADEMICS
Calendar: semesters. *Degrees:* bachelor's, master's, and doctoral.
Library: Kelly Library plus 1 other. *Books:* 225,739 (physical), 126,654 (digital/electronic); *Serial titles:* 728 (physical), 113,345 (digital/electronic); *Databases:* 105. Weekly public service hours: 90; students can reserve study rooms.

STUDENT LIFE
Housing options: on-campus residence required through junior year; coed, men-only, women-only, special housing for students with disabilities. Campus housing is university owned. Freshman campus housing is guaranteed.

Activities and organizations: drama/theater group, student-run newspaper, radio and television station, choral group, marching band, E&H Outdoor Program, Alpha Psi Omega Honors Fraternity, Alpha Phi Omega Honors Fraternity, Blue Key/ Cardinal Key Honors Society, The Emory Activities Board.

Athletics Member NCAA. All Division III.

Campus security: 24-hour emergency response devices and patrols, late-night transport/escort service, controlled dormitory access.

Student services: health clinic, personal/psychological counseling.

COSTS & FINANCIAL AID

Costs (2018–19) ***Comprehensive fee:*** $47,100 includes full-time tuition ($34,500), mandatory fees ($500), and room and board ($12,100). Full-time tuition and fees vary according to degree level, location, and student level. Part-time tuition and fees vary according to course load, degree level, location, and student level. No tuition increase for student's term of enrollment. ***College room only:*** $6300. Room and board charges vary according to board plan and housing facility.

Financial Aid Of all full-time matriculated undergraduates who enrolled in 2018, 903 applied for aid, 849 were judged to have need, 214 had their need fully met. 450 Federal Work-Study jobs (averaging $2000). In 2018, 104 non-need-based awards were made. ***Average percent of need met:*** 73. ***Average financial aid package:*** $32,909. ***Average need-based loan:*** $4380. ***Average need-based gift aid:*** $27,726. ***Average non-need-based aid:*** $19,130. ***Average indebtedness upon graduation:*** $31,283.

APPLYING

Standardized Tests *Required:* SAT or ACT (for admission).

Options: electronic application, early decision.

Required: high school transcript. ***Recommended:*** essay or personal statement, interview.

CONTACT

Mr. Matt Crisman, Director of Admissions, Emory & Henry College, PO Box 947, Emory, VA 24327-0947. *Phone:* 276-944-6491. *Toll-free phone:* 800-848-5493. *E-mail:* mcrisman@ehc.edu.

Ferrum College

Ferrum, Virginia

http://www.ferrum.edu/

CONTACT

Ms. Gilda Q. Woods, Associate Vice President for Enrollment Management and Dean of Admissions, Ferrum College, Spilman-Daniel House, PO Box 1000, Ferrum, VA 24088-9001. *Phone:* 540-365-4290. *Toll-free phone:* 800-868-9797. *Fax:* 540-365-4266. *E-mail:* admissions@ferrum.edu.

George Mason University

Fairfax, Virginia

http://www.gmu.edu/

- **State-supported** university, founded 1972
- **Suburban** 817-acre campus with easy access to Washington, DC
- **Endowment** $84.9 million
- **Coed** 26,192 undergraduate students, 81% full-time, 50% women, 50% men
- **Moderately difficult** entrance level, 81% of applicants were admitted

UNDERGRAD STUDENTS

21,213 full-time, 4,979 part-time. Students come from 49 states and territories; 106 other countries; 10% are from out of state; 11% Black or African American, non-Hispanic/Latino; 15% Hispanic/Latino; 20% Asian, non-Hispanic/Latino; 0.3% Native Hawaiian or other Pacific Islander, non-Hispanic/Latino; 0.1% American Indian or Alaska Native, non-Hispanic/Latino; 5% Two or more races, non-Hispanic/Latino; 3% Race/ethnicity unknown; 5% international; 11% transferred in; 23% live on campus.

Freshmen:

Admission: 19,557 applied, 15,852 admitted, 3,711 enrolled. ***Average high school GPA:*** 3.7. ***Test scores:*** SAT evidence-based reading and writing scores over 500: 97%; SAT math scores over 500: 96%; ACT scores over 18: 99%; SAT evidence-based reading and writing scores over 600: 59%; SAT math scores over 600: 51%; ACT scores over 24: 80%; SAT evidence-based reading and writing scores over 700: 11%; SAT math scores over 700: 14%; ACT scores over 30: 27%.

Retention: 86% of full-time freshmen returned.

FACULTY

Total: 2,765, 48% full-time.

Student/faculty ratio: 17:1.

ACADEMICS

Calendar: semesters. *Degrees:* bachelor's, master's, doctoral, post-master's, and postbachelor's certificates.

Special study options: accelerated degree program, adult/continuing education programs, advanced placement credit, cooperative education, distance learning, double majors, English as a second language, freshman honors college, honors programs, independent study, internships, off-campus study, part-time degree program, services for LD students, student-designed majors, study abroad, summer session for credit. ***ROTC:*** Army (b), Air Force (c).

Computers: 622 computers/terminals and 45,871 ports are available on campus for general student use. Students can access the following: campus intranet, computer help desk, free student e-mail accounts, online (class) grades, online (class) registration, online (class) schedules. Campuswide network is available. 100% of college-owned or -operated housing units are wired for high-speed Internet access. Wireless service is available via entire campus.

Library: Fenwick Library plus 3 others. *Books:* 1.1 million (physical), 1.4 million (digital/electronic); *Serial titles:* 1,049 (physical), 127,898 (digital/electronic); *Databases:* 772. Weekly public service hours: 100; study areas open 24 hours, 5–7 days a week; students can reserve study rooms.

STUDENT LIFE

Housing options: coed, special housing for students with disabilities. Campus housing is university owned and leased by the school. Freshman campus housing is guaranteed.

Activities and organizations: drama/theater group, student-run newspaper, radio and television station, choral group, Catholic Campus Ministry, Indian Student Association, Black Student Alliance, Muslim Student Association, CRU (Campus Crusade for Christ), national fraternities, national sororities.

Athletics Member NCAA. All Division I. ***Intercollegiate sports:*** baseball M(s), basketball M(s)/W(s), crew W(s), cross-country running M(s)/W(s), golf M(s), lacrosse W(s), soccer M(s)/W(s), softball W(s), swimming and diving M(s)/W(s), tennis M(s)/W(s), track and field M(s)/W(s), volleyball M(s)/W(s), wrestling M(s). ***Intramural sports:*** badminton M(c)/W(c), baseball M(c), basketball M/W, bowling M(c)/W(c), crew M(c)/W(c), cross-country running M(c)/W(c), equestrian sports M(c)/W(c), fencing M(c)/W(c), field hockey M(c)/W(c), football M(c), golf M/W, ice hockey M(c), lacrosse M(c)/W(c), rugby M(c)/W(c), soccer M(c)/W(c), softball M/W(c), swimming and diving M/W, tennis M(c)/W(c), track and field M(c)/W(c), ultimate Frisbee M(c)/W(c), volleyball M(c)/W(c), water polo M/W, wrestling M(c).

Campus security: 24-hour emergency response devices and patrols, student patrols, late-night transport/escort service, controlled dormitory access.

Student services: health clinic, personal/psychological counseling, women's center, veterans affairs office.

COSTS & FINANCIAL AID

Costs (2018–19) ***Tuition:*** state resident $9060 full-time, $378 per credit hour part-time; nonresident $32,520 full-time, $1355 per credit hour part-time. Full-time tuition and fees vary according to course load. Part-time tuition and fees vary according to course load. ***Required fees:*** $3402 full-time, $142 per credit hour part-time. ***Room and board:*** $11,460. Room and board charges vary according to board plan and housing facility. ***Payment plans:*** installment, deferred payment. ***Waivers:*** senior citizens and employees or children of employees.

Financial Aid Of all full-time matriculated undergraduates who enrolled in 2017, 13,964 applied for aid, 11,574 were judged to have need, 218 had their need fully met. 626 Federal Work-Study jobs (averaging $2050). In 2017, 1441 non-need-based awards were made. ***Average percent of need met:*** 55. ***Average financial aid package:*** $14,053. ***Average need-based loan:*** $4411. ***Average need-based gift aid:*** $6752. ***Average non-need-based aid:*** $4998. ***Average indebtedness upon graduation:*** $30,790.

APPLYING

Standardized Tests *Required for some:* SAT or ACT (for admission).

Options: electronic application, early admission, early action, deferred entrance.

Application fee: $70.

Required: high school transcript. ***Required for some:*** essay or personal statement, audition for dance and music, portfolio for art and visual technology and computer game design, interview and audition or portfolio for theater. ***Recommended:*** 3 letters of recommendation.

Application deadlines: 1/15 (freshmen), 3/1 (transfers), 11/15 (early action).

Notification: 4/1 (transfers), 12/15 (early action).

CONTACT
Melissa Bevacqua, Director, Undergraduate Admissions, George Mason University, 4400 University Drive, MSN 3A4, Fairfax, VA 22030-4444. *Phone:* 703-993-2291. *Toll-free phone:* 888-627-6612. *Fax:* 703-993-2392. *E-mail:* mbevacqu@gmu.edu.

Hampden-Sydney College
Hampden-Sydney, Virginia
http://www.hsc.edu/

- **Independent** 4-year, founded 1776, affiliated with Presbyterian Church (U.S.A.)
- **Rural** 1343-acre campus with easy access to Richmond, Lynchburg, Charlottesville
- **Endowment** $170.7 million
- **Men only** 1,072 undergraduate students, 100% full-time
- **Moderately difficult** entrance level, 59% of applicants were admitted

UNDERGRAD STUDENTS
1,070 full-time, 2 part-time. Students come from 31 states and territories; 5 other countries; 30% are from out of state; 5% Black or African American, non-Hispanic/Latino; 4% Hispanic/Latino; 0.7% Asian, non-Hispanic/Latino; 0.1% Native Hawaiian or other Pacific Islander, non-Hispanic/Latino; 0.5% American Indian or Alaska Native, non-Hispanic/Latino; 3% Two or more races, non-Hispanic/Latino; 1% Race/ethnicity unknown; 0.4% international; 1% transferred in; 98% live on campus.

Freshmen:
Admission: 3,240 applied, 1,912 admitted, 343 enrolled. ***Average high school GPA:*** 3.5. ***Test scores:*** SAT evidence-based reading and writing scores over 500: 88%; SAT math scores over 500: 87%; SAT evidence-based reading and writing scores over 600: 48%; SAT math scores over 600: 36%; SAT evidence-based reading and writing scores over 700: 5%; SAT math scores over 700: 5%.

Retention: 81% of full-time freshmen returned.

FACULTY
Total: 111, 86% full-time, 86% with terminal degrees.
Student/faculty ratio: 10:1.

ACADEMICS
Calendar: semesters. *Degree:* bachelor's.

Special study options: academic remediation for entering students, advanced placement credit, cooperative education, double majors, honors programs, independent study, internships, off-campus study, study abroad, summer session for credit. ***ROTC:*** Army (c).

Unusual degree programs: 3-2 engineering with University of Virginia, Old Dominion University.

Computers: 200 computers/terminals are available on campus for general student use. Students can access the following: campus intranet, computer help desk, free student e-mail accounts, online (class) grades, online (class) registration, online (class) schedules. Campuswide network is available. 100% of college-owned or -operated housing units are wired for high-speed Internet access. Wireless service is available via entire campus.

Library: Walter M. Bortz III Library. *Books:* 211,996 (physical), 184,419 (digital/electronic); *Serial titles:* 57 (physical), 103,133 (digital/electronic); *Databases:* 95. Weekly public service hours: 99; students can reserve study rooms.

STUDENT LIFE
Housing options: on-campus residence required through senior year; men-only, special housing for students with disabilities. Campus housing is university owned. Freshman campus housing is guaranteed.

Activities and organizations: drama/theater group, student-run newspaper, radio station, choral group, Republican Society, Pre-Health Society, Outdoors Club, Tiger Athletic Club, Pre-Law Society, national fraternities.

Athletics Member NCAA. All Division III. ***Intercollegiate sports:*** baseball M, basketball M, crew M(c), cross-country running M, fencing M(c), football M, golf M, lacrosse M, riflery M(c), rugby M(c), soccer M, swimming and diving M, tennis M, ultimate Frisbee M(c). ***Intramural sports:*** archery M(c), basketball M, fencing M(c), football M, lacrosse M(c), racquetball M(c), riflery M(c), soccer M, softball M, swimming and diving M(c), volleyball M, water polo M(c), wrestling M(c).

Campus security: 24-hour emergency response devices and patrols.

Student services: health clinic, personal/psychological counseling.

COSTS & FINANCIAL AID
Costs (2019–20) ***Comprehensive fee:*** $60,602 includes full-time tuition ($44,532), mandatory fees ($2358), and room and board ($13,712). Part-time tuition: $1394 per credit hour.

Financial Aid Of all full-time matriculated undergraduates who enrolled in 2018, 832 applied for aid, 732 were judged to have need, 192 had their need fully met. 191 Federal Work-Study jobs (averaging $1413). In 2018, 328 non-need-based awards were made. ***Average percent of need met:*** 80. ***Average financial aid package:*** $33,849. ***Average need-based loan:*** $4145. ***Average need-based gift aid:*** $30,385. ***Average non-need-based aid:*** $17,967. ***Average indebtedness upon graduation:*** $33,777.

APPLYING
Standardized Tests *Required:* SAT or ACT (for admission). *Recommended:* SAT and SAT Subject Tests or ACT (for admission).

Options: electronic application, early admission, early decision, early action.

Application fee: $30.

Required: essay or personal statement, high school transcript, 2 letters of recommendation. ***Recommended:*** interview.

Early decision deadline: 11/1.

Notification: 4/15 (freshmen), 7/31 (transfers), 12/1 (early decision), 12/1 (early action).

CONTACT
Dean Anita Garland, Dean of Admissions, Hampden-Sydney College, PO Box 667, Hampden-Sydney, VA 23943-0667. *Phone:* 434-223-6120. *Toll-free phone:* 800-755-0733. *Fax:* 434-223-6346. *E-mail:* hsapp@hsc.edu.

Hampton University
Hampton, Virginia
http://www.hamptonu.edu/

- **Independent** comprehensive, founded 1868
- **Urban** 314-acre campus with easy access to Norfolk
- **Coed**
- **Moderately difficult** entrance level

FACULTY
Student/faculty ratio: 13:1.

ACADEMICS
Calendar: semesters. *Degrees:* certificates, associate, bachelor's, master's, doctoral, and post-master's certificates.
Library: William R. and Norma B. Harvey Library plus 4 others. *Books:* 307,143 (physical), 91,991 (digital/electronic); *Serial titles:* 8,240 (physical); *Databases:* 115. Study areas open 24 hours, 5–7 days a week; students can reserve study rooms.

STUDENT LIFE
Housing options: on-campus residence required for freshman year; coed, men-only, women-only, special housing for students with disabilities. Campus housing is university owned. Freshman applicants given priority for college housing.

Activities and organizations: drama/theater group, student-run newspaper, radio station, choral group, marching band, Student Government, student leaders, Student Union Board, student recruitment team, resident assistants, national fraternities, national sororities.

Athletics Member NCAA. All Division I.

Campus security: 24-hour emergency response devices and patrols.

Student services: health clinic, personal/psychological counseling, women's center, veterans affairs office.

FINANCIAL AID
Financial Aid Of all full-time matriculated undergraduates who enrolled in 2017, 2,380 applied for aid, 1,918 were judged to have need, 847 had their need fully met. 273 Federal Work-Study jobs (averaging $1413). In 2017, 61 non-need-based awards were made. ***Average percent of need met:*** 46. ***Average financial aid package:*** $5794. ***Average need-based loan:*** $5125. ***Average need-based gift aid:*** $5071. ***Average non-need-based aid:*** $6988. ***Average indebtedness upon graduation:*** $33,095. ***Financial aid deadline:*** 4/15.

APPLYING
Standardized Tests *Required for some:* SAT or ACT (for admission).

Options: electronic application, early admission, early action, deferred entrance.

Application fee: $35.

Required: essay or personal statement, high school transcript, minimum 2.5 GPA, 1 letter of recommendation. ***Required for some:*** interview, audition for music.

CONTACT
Ms. Patra Johnson, Director, Freshman Studies, Hampton University, 204 Student Center, Hampton, VA 23668. *Phone:* 757-727-5901. *Toll-free phone:* 800-624-3328. *Fax:* 757-727-5095. *E-mail:* patra.johnson@hamptonu.edu.

Hollins University

Roanoke, Virginia

http://www.hollins.edu/

- **Independent** comprehensive, founded 1842
- **Suburban** 475-acre campus
- **Endowment** $186.3 million
- **Undergraduate: women only; graduate: coed** 676 undergraduate students, 99% full-time, 100% women
- **Moderately difficult** entrance level, 48% of applicants were admitted

UNDERGRAD STUDENTS
666 full-time, 10 part-time. Students come from 44 states and territories; 16 other countries; 50% are from out of state; 10% Black or African American, non-Hispanic/Latino; 8% Hispanic/Latino; 2% Asian, non-Hispanic/Latino; 0.3% Native Hawaiian or other Pacific Islander, non-Hispanic/Latino; 0.6% American Indian or Alaska Native, non-Hispanic/Latino; 7% Two or more races, non-Hispanic/Latino; 2% Race/ethnicity unknown; 7% international; 2% transferred in; 87% live on campus.

Freshmen:
Admission: 2,842 applied, 1,375 admitted, 199 enrolled. ***Average high school GPA:*** 3.7. ***Test scores:*** SAT evidence-based reading and writing scores over 500: 98%; SAT math scores over 500: 92%; ACT scores over 18: 97%; SAT evidence-based reading and writing scores over 600: 70%; SAT math scores over 600: 31%; ACT scores over 24: 66%; SAT evidence-based reading and writing scores over 700: 16%; SAT math scores over 700: 4%; ACT scores over 30: 16%.

Retention: 78% of full-time freshmen returned.

FACULTY
Total: 98, 71% full-time, 86% with terminal degrees.

Student/faculty ratio: 10:1.

ACADEMICS
Calendar: 4-1-4. *Degrees:* bachelor's, master's, and post-master's certificates.

Special study options: accelerated degree program, adult/continuing education programs, advanced placement credit, cooperative education, double majors, honors programs, independent study, internships, off-campus study, part-time degree program, services for LD students, student-designed majors, study abroad.

Computers: 102 computers/terminals and 1,000 ports are available on campus for general student use. Students can access the following: campus intranet, computer help desk, free student e-mail accounts, online (class) grades, online (class) registration, online (class) schedules. Campuswide network is available. 100% of college-owned or -operated housing units are wired for high-speed Internet access. Wireless service is available via entire campus.

Library: Wyndham Robertson Library plus 1 other. *Books:* 246,065 (physical), 122,121 (digital/electronic); *Serial titles:* 1,160 (physical), 51,262 (digital/electronic); *Databases:* 130. Weekly public service hours: 94.

STUDENT LIFE
Housing options: on-campus residence required through senior year; women-only, special housing for students with disabilities. Campus housing is university owned. Freshman campus housing is guaranteed.

Activities and organizations: drama/theater group, choral group, Hollins Activity Board, Black Student Alliance, Hollins Repertory Dance Club, Arts Association, Voices for Unity.

Athletics Member NCAA. All Division III. ***Intercollegiate sports:*** basketball W, cross-country running W, equestrian sports W, lacrosse W, soccer W, swimming and diving W, tennis W, volleyball W.

Campus security: 24-hour emergency response devices and patrols, late-night transport/escort service, controlled dormitory access.

Student services: health clinic, personal/psychological counseling, women's center.

COSTS & FINANCIAL AID
Costs (2019–20) ***Comprehensive fee:*** $53,940 includes full-time tuition ($39,360), mandatory fees ($650), and room and board ($13,930). Part-time tuition: $1233 per credit hour. ***Required fees:*** $325 per year part-time. ***Payment plan:*** tuition prepayment.

Financial Aid Of all full-time matriculated undergraduates who enrolled in 2018, 555 applied for aid, 509 were judged to have need, 123 had their need fully met. 120 Federal Work-Study jobs (averaging $1500). 186 state and other part-time jobs (averaging $1500). In 2018, 149 non-need-based awards were made. ***Average percent of need met:*** 85. ***Average financial aid package:*** $37,488. ***Average need-based loan:*** $4530. ***Average need-based gift aid:*** $33,408. ***Average non-need-based aid:*** $31,221. ***Average indebtedness upon graduation:*** $33,408.

APPLYING
Standardized Tests *Required:* SAT or ACT (for admission).

Options: electronic application, early admission, early decision, early action, deferred entrance.

Required: essay or personal statement, high school transcript, 1 letter of recommendation. ***Recommended:*** interview.

Application deadlines: rolling (freshmen), 11/15 (early action).

Early decision deadline: 11/1.

Notification: continuous (freshmen).

CONTACT
Ms. Madeline Aliff, Director of Recruitment, Hollins University, 7916 Williamson Road, Box 9707, Roanoke, VA 24020. *Phone:* 540-362-6401. *Toll-free phone:* 800-456-9595. *Fax:* 540-362-6218. *E-mail:* huadm@hollins.edu.

IGlobal University

Vienna, Virginia

http://www.igu.edu/

CONTACT
IGlobal University, 8133 Leesburg Pike, #230, Vienna, VA 22182.

James Madison University

Harrisonburg, Virginia

http://www.jmu.edu/

- **State-supported** comprehensive, founded 1908
- **Small-town** 721-acre campus
- **Coed**
- **Very difficult** entrance level

FACULTY
Student/faculty ratio: 16:1.

ACADEMICS
Calendar: semesters. *Degrees:* bachelor's, master's, and doctoral (also offers specialist in education degree).
Library: Carrier Library plus 2 others. Students can reserve study rooms.

STUDENT LIFE
Housing options: on-campus residence required for freshman year; coed, special housing for students with disabilities. Campus housing is university owned and leased by the school. Freshman campus housing is guaranteed.

Activities and organizations: drama/theater group, student-run newspaper, radio station, choral group, marching band, national fraternities, national sororities.

Athletics Member NCAA. All Division I except football (Division I-AA).

Campus security: 24-hour emergency response devices and patrols, student patrols, late-night transport/escort service, controlled dormitory access, lighted pathways.

Student services: health clinic, personal/psychological counseling, women's center.

COSTS & FINANCIAL AID
Costs (2018–19) ***Tuition:*** state resident $6620 full-time, $220 per credit hour part-time; nonresident $23,334 full-time, $777 per credit hour part-time. ***Required fees:*** $4766 full-time. ***Room and board:*** $10,092; room only: $5220. Room and board charges vary according to board plan.

Financial Aid Of all full-time matriculated undergraduates who enrolled in 2018, 11,326 applied for aid, 7,847 were judged to have need, 5,234 had their need fully met. In 2018, 218 non-need-based awards were made. ***Average percent of need met:*** 37. ***Average financial aid package:*** $8755. ***Average need-based loan:*** $4228. ***Average need-based gift aid:*** $6908. ***Average non-need-based aid:*** $5823. ***Average indebtedness upon graduation:*** $29,189.

APPLYING
Options: electronic application, early action, deferred entrance.

Application fee: $70.

Required: high school transcript. ***Recommended:*** minimum 3.0 GPA.

CONTACT
James Madison University, 800 South Main Street, Harrisonburg, VA 22807. *Phone:* 540-568-5681.

Jefferson College of Health Sciences
Roanoke, Virginia
http://www.jchs.edu/

- **Independent** comprehensive, founded 1982
- **Urban** 1-acre campus
- **Endowment** $2.4 million
- **Coed**
- **Moderately difficult** entrance level

ACADEMICS
Calendar: semesters. *Degrees:* certificates, associate, bachelor's, master's, and doctoral.
Library: JCHS Library. *Books:* 4,971 (physical), 41,000 (digital/electronic); *Serial titles:* 99 (physical), 65 (digital/electronic); *Databases:* 29.

STUDENT LIFE
Housing options: coed. Campus housing is university owned.

Activities and organizations: student-run newspaper, choral group, Jefferson Activities Group (JAG), Student Ambassadors, Hands of Healing, American Medical Students Association (AMSA), Student Nurses Association.

Campus security: 24-hour emergency response devices and patrols, late-night transport/escort service, controlled dormitory access.

Student services: personal/psychological counseling.

COSTS & FINANCIAL AID
Costs (2018–19) ***Comprehensive fee:*** $36,380 includes full-time tuition ($26,416), mandatory fees ($450), and room and board ($9514). Full-time tuition and fees vary according to course load. Part-time tuition: $765 per credit hour. Part-time tuition and fees vary according to course load. ***Required fees:*** $150 per year part-time. ***Room and board:*** Room and board charges vary according to location.

Financial Aid Of all full-time matriculated undergraduates who enrolled in 2016, 582 applied for aid, 559 were judged to have need.

APPLYING
Standardized Tests *Required:* SAT or ACT (for admission). *Recommended:* SAT (for admission).

Options: electronic application, early action, deferred entrance.

Application fee: $35.

Required: high school transcript, minimum 2.5 GPA. ***Required for some:*** interview.

CONTACT
Jefferson College of Health Sciences, 101 Elm Avenue SE, Roanoke, VA 24013. *Phone:* 540-985-8309. *Toll-free phone:* 888-985-8483.

★ Liberty University
Lynchburg, Virginia
http://www.liberty.edu/

- **Independent nondenominational** comprehensive, founded 1971
- **Suburban** 6500-acre campus
- **Coed** 13,560 undergraduate students, 95% full-time, 54% women, 46% men
- **Minimally difficult** entrance level, 53% of applicants were admitted

UNDERGRAD STUDENTS
12,849 full-time, 711 part-time. Students come from 52 states and territories; 84 other countries; 61% are from out of state; 4% Black or African American, non-Hispanic/Latino; 5% Hispanic/Latino; 2% Asian, non-Hispanic/Latino; 0.1% Native Hawaiian or other Pacific Islander, non-Hispanic/Latino; 0.4% American Indian or Alaska Native, non-Hispanic/Latino; 3% Two or more races, non-Hispanic/Latino; 12% Race/ethnicity unknown; 4% international; 11% transferred in; 58% live on campus.

Freshmen:
Admission: 12,429 applied, 6,587 admitted, 2,987 enrolled. ***Average high school GPA:*** 3.5. ***Test scores:*** SAT evidence-based reading and writing scores over 500: 75%; SAT math scores over 500: 75%; ACT scores over 18: 95%; SAT evidence-based reading and writing scores over 600: 28%; SAT math scores over 600: 23%; ACT scores over 24: 55%; SAT evidence-based reading and writing scores over 700: 8%; SAT math scores over 700: 8%; ACT scores over 30: 19%.

Retention: 85% of full-time freshmen returned.

ACADEMICS
Calendar: semesters. *Degrees:* certificates, associate, bachelor's, master's, doctoral, post-master's, and postbachelor's certificates (also offers external degree program with significant enrollment not reflected in profile).

Special study options: academic remediation for entering students, accelerated degree program, advanced placement credit, cooperative education, distance learning, double majors, English as a second language, external degree program, honors programs, independent study, internships, off-campus study, part-time degree program, services for LD students, student-designed majors, study abroad, summer session for credit. ***ROTC:*** Army (b), Air Force (c).

Computers: 1,640 computers/terminals are available on campus for general student use. Students can access the following: computer help desk, free student e-mail accounts, online (class) grades, online (class) registration, online (class) schedules. Campuswide network is available. 100% of college-owned or -operated housing units are wired for high-speed Internet access. Wireless service is available via entire campus.
Library: Jerry Falwell Library plus 1 other. *Books:* 313,657 (physical), 377,967 (digital/electronic); *Serial titles:* 4,323 (physical), 118,877 (digital/electronic); *Databases:* 512. Students can reserve study rooms.

STUDENT LIFE
Housing options: on-campus residence required through senior year; men-only, women-only, special housing for students with disabilities. Campus housing is university owned. Freshman campus housing is guaranteed.

Activities and organizations: drama/theater group, student-run newspaper, radio station, choral group, marching band, Campus Serve.

Athletics Member NCAA. All Division I except football (Division I-AA). ***Intercollegiate sports:*** baseball M(s), basketball M(s)/W(s), cheerleading M(s)/W(s), crew M(c)/W(c), cross-country running M(s)/W(s), equestrian sports W(c), field hockey W(s), golf M(s), ice hockey M(c)/W(c), lacrosse W(s), soccer M(s)/W(s), softball W(s), swimming and diving W(s), tennis M(s)/W(s), track and field M(s)/W(s), volleyball M(c)/W(s). ***Intramural sports:*** archery M(c)/W(c), basketball M/W, football M/W, gymnastics M(c)/W(c), lacrosse M(c), racquetball M(c)/W(c), skiing (downhill) M(c)/W(c), soccer M/W, softball M/W, table tennis M/W, tennis M/W, ultimate Frisbee M(c)/W(c), volleyball M/W, wrestling M(c).

Campus security: 24-hour patrols, late-night transport/escort service, 24-hour emergency dispatch.

Student services: health clinic, personal/psychological counseling.

COSTS & FINANCIAL AID

Costs (2019–20) ***Comprehensive fee:*** $35,446 includes full-time tuition ($23,800), mandatory fees ($1106), and room and board ($10,540). Part-time tuition: $815 per credit. ***College room only:*** $6760.

Financial Aid Of all full-time matriculated undergraduates who enrolled in 2018, 11,731 applied for aid, 9,370 were judged to have need, 1,021 had their need fully met. In 2018, 2237 non-need-based awards were made. ***Average percent of need met:*** 55. ***Average financial aid package:*** $14,818. ***Average need-based loan:*** $4277. ***Average need-based gift aid:*** $10,779. ***Average non-need-based aid:*** $7343. ***Average indebtedness upon graduation:*** $22,836. ***Financial aid deadline:*** 3/1.

APPLYING

Standardized Tests *Required:* SAT or ACT (for admission).

Options: electronic application.

Application fee: $50.

Required: essay or personal statement, high school transcript, minimum 2.0 GPA. ***Recommended:*** minimum 2.0 GPA.

Application deadlines: rolling (freshmen), rolling (transfers).

Notification: continuous (freshmen), continuous (transfers).

CONTACT

Dr. Terry Elam, Director of Admissions, Liberty University, 1971 University Boulevard, Lynchburg, VA 24515. *Phone:* 434-592-3966. *Toll-free phone:* 800-543-5317. *Fax:* 800-542-2311. *E-mail:* admissions@liberty.edu.

Longwood University

Farmville, Virginia

http://www.longwood.edu/

- **State-supported** comprehensive, founded 1839
- **Small-town** 60-acre campus with easy access to Richmond
- **Endowment** $59.1 million
- **Coed**
- **Moderately difficult** entrance level

FACULTY

Student/faculty ratio: 14:1.

ACADEMICS

Calendar: semesters. *Degrees:* bachelor's, master's, post-master's, and postbachelor's certificates.

Library: The Janet D. Greenwood Library. *Books:* 216,525 (physical), 333,909 (digital/electronic); *Serial titles:* 2,667 (physical), 403 (digital/electronic); *Databases:* 295. Weekly public service hours: 93.

STUDENT LIFE

Housing options: on-campus residence required through sophomore year; coed, women-only, special housing for students with disabilities. Campus housing is university owned. Freshman campus housing is guaranteed.

Activities and organizations: drama/theater group, student-run newspaper, radio station, choral group, Alpha Lambda Delta, Student Nursing Association, Longwood University, Bare Naked Ladies, Chi Alpha, Sigma Alpha Pi, national fraternities, national sororities.

Athletics Member NCAA. All Division I.

Campus security: 24-hour emergency response devices and patrols, late-night transport/escort service, controlled dormitory access.

Student services: health clinic, personal/psychological counseling.

COSTS & FINANCIAL AID

Costs (2018–19) ***Tuition:*** state resident $7940 full-time, $273 per credit hour part-time; nonresident $23,300 full-time, $785 per credit hour part-time. Full-time tuition and fees vary according to course load and program. Part-time tuition and fees vary according to course load and program. ***Required fees:*** $5400 full-time, $180 per credit hour part-time. ***Room and board:*** $11,026; room only: $7336. Room and board charges vary according to board plan, housing facility, and location.

Financial Aid Of all full-time matriculated undergraduates who enrolled in 2017, 3,007 applied for aid, 2,383 were judged to have need, 237 had their need fully met. 266 Federal Work-Study jobs (averaging $2000). In 2017, 288 non-need-based awards were made. ***Average percent of need met:*** 73. ***Average financial aid package:*** $11,061. ***Average need-based loan:*** $4235. ***Average need-based gift aid:*** $7227. ***Average non-need-based aid:*** $3666. ***Average indebtedness upon graduation:*** $29,904.

APPLYING

Standardized Tests *Required:* SAT or ACT (for admission).

Options: electronic application, early admission, early action, deferred entrance.

Application fee: $50.

Required: essay or personal statement, high school transcript. ***Recommended:*** 3 letters of recommendation.

CONTACT

Mr. Jason Faulk, Dean of Admissions, Longwood University, 201 High Street, Farmville, VA 23909. *Phone:* 434-395-2809. *Toll-free phone:* 800-281-4677. *Fax:* 434-395-2332. *E-mail:* faulkjc@longwood.edu.

Mary Baldwin University

Staunton, Virginia

http://www.marybaldwin.edu/

- **Independent** comprehensive, founded 1842
- **Small-town** 59-acre campus
- **Endowment** $35.1 million
- **Coed, primarily women**
- **Moderately difficult** entrance level

FACULTY

Student/faculty ratio: 9:1.

ACADEMICS

Calendar: 4-1-4. *Degrees:* certificates, bachelor's, master's, doctoral, and postbachelor's certificates.

Library: Grafton Library. *Books:* 104,405 (physical), 367,524 (digital/electronic); *Serial titles:* 348 (physical), 31,879 (digital/electronic); *Databases:* 76. Weekly public service hours: 92; students can reserve study rooms.

STUDENT LIFE

Housing options: on-campus residence required through senior year; coed, women-only. Campus housing is university owned. Freshman campus housing is guaranteed.

Activities and organizations: drama/theater group, choral group, marching band, Minority Clubs United, Greater Things Dance Ministry, MBU Cheer, Ladies of Elegance, Math Club.

Athletics Member NCAA. All Division III.

Campus security: 24-hour emergency response devices and patrols, late-night transport/escort service, controlled dormitory access.

Student services: health clinic, personal/psychological counseling.

COSTS & FINANCIAL AID

Costs (2018–19) ***Comprehensive fee:*** $40,495 includes full-time tuition ($30,690), mandatory fees ($395), and room and board ($9410). Part-time tuition: $460 per semester hour. Part-time tuition and fees vary according to program. ***Required fees:*** $60 per term part-time. ***Room and board:*** Room and board charges vary according to housing facility and student level.

Financial Aid Of all full-time matriculated undergraduates who enrolled in 2018, 924 applied for aid, 855 were judged to have need, 73 had their need fully met. 226 Federal Work-Study jobs (averaging $1300). 84 state and other part-time jobs (averaging $1389). In 2018, 69 non-need-based awards were made. ***Average percent of need met:*** 91. ***Average financial aid package:*** $27,093. ***Average need-based loan:*** $4069. ***Average need-based gift aid:*** $23,495. ***Average non-need-based aid:*** $17,317. ***Average indebtedness upon graduation:*** $37,097.

APPLYING

Standardized Tests *Required:* SAT or ACT (for admission).

Options: electronic application, early admission, deferred entrance.

Required: high school transcript. ***Required for some:*** essay or personal statement, 1 letter of recommendation, interview. ***Recommended:*** 1 letter of recommendation.

CONTACT

Mr. Matthew Munsey, Director of Admissions, Mary Baldwin University, Frederick and New Streets, Staunton, VA 24401. *Phone:* 540-887-7211. *Toll-free phone:* 800-468-2262. *Fax:* 540-887-7292. *E-mail:* mmunsey@marybaldwin.edu.

Marymount University

Arlington, Virginia

http://www.marymount.edu/

- **Independent** comprehensive, founded 1950, affiliated with Roman Catholic Church
- **Suburban** 21-acre campus with easy access to Washington, DC
- **Endowment** $46.3 million
- **Coed** 2,287 undergraduate students, 91% full-time, 64% women, 36% men
- **Moderately difficult** entrance level, 91% of applicants were admitted

UNDERGRAD STUDENTS

2,070 full-time, 217 part-time. Students come from 38 states and territories; 62 other countries; 40% are from out of state; 14% Black or African American, non-Hispanic/Latino; 18% Hispanic/Latino; 8% Asian, non-Hispanic/Latino; 0.3% Native Hawaiian or other Pacific Islander, non-Hispanic/Latino; 0.3% American Indian or Alaska Native, non-Hispanic/Latino; 3% Two or more races, non-Hispanic/Latino; 5% Race/ethnicity unknown; 17% international; 10% transferred in; 30% live on campus.

Freshmen:

Admission: 2,873 applied, 2,611 admitted, 422 enrolled. ***Average high school GPA:*** 3.3. ***Test scores:*** SAT evidence-based reading and writing scores over 500: 71%; SAT math scores over 500: 63%; ACT scores over 18: 68%; SAT evidence-based reading and writing scores over 600: 26%; SAT math scores over 600: 19%; ACT scores over 24: 38%; SAT evidence-based reading and writing scores over 700: 3%; SAT math scores over 700: 3%; ACT scores over 30: 2%.

Retention: 72% of full-time freshmen returned.

FACULTY

Total: 343, 48% full-time, 66% with terminal degrees.

Student/faculty ratio: 13:1.

ACADEMICS

Calendar: semesters plus 2 summer terms. *Degrees:* certificates, bachelor's, master's, doctoral, post-master's, and postbachelor's certificates.

Special study options: academic remediation for entering students, accelerated degree program, advanced placement credit, distance learning, double majors, honors programs, independent study, internships, off-campus study, part-time degree program, services for LD students, student-designed majors, study abroad, summer session for credit. ***ROTC:*** Army (c), Air Force (c).

Unusual degree programs: 3-2 business administration; information technology, health sciences.

Computers: 270 computers/terminals are available on campus for general student use. Students can access the following: campus intranet, computer help desk, free student e-mail accounts, online (class) grades, online (class) registration, online (class) schedules, Online drive space. Campuswide network is available. 100% of college-owned or -operated housing units are wired for high-speed Internet access. Wireless service is available via entire campus.

Library: Emerson C. Reinsch Library plus 1 other. Weekly public service hours: 104; students can reserve study rooms.

STUDENT LIFE

Housing options: on-campus residence required through sophomore year; coed, women-only, special housing for students with disabilities. Campus housing is university owned and leased by the school. Freshman applicants given priority for college housing.

Activities and organizations: drama/theater group, student-run newspaper, choral group, Fashion Club, Student Nurses Association, International Club, Association for Campus Events, Blue Harmony (show choir).

Athletics Member NCAA. All Division III. ***Intercollegiate sports:*** baseball M, basketball M/W, cheerleading W(c), cross-country running M/W, golf M/W, ice hockey M(c), lacrosse M/W, soccer M/W, swimming and diving M/W, tennis M/W, track and field M/W, triathlon M(c)/W(c), volleyball M/W. ***Intramural sports:*** basketball M/W, soccer M/W, ultimate Frisbee M/W, volleyball M, water polo M/W.

Campus security: 24-hour emergency response devices and patrols, student patrols, late-night transport/escort service, controlled dormitory access.

Student services: health clinic, personal/psychological counseling, veterans affairs office.

COSTS & FINANCIAL AID

Costs (2018–19) ***One-time required fee:*** $460. ***Comprehensive fee:*** $44,655 includes full-time tuition ($30,990), mandatory fees ($475), and room and board ($13,190). Part-time tuition: $1010 per credit hour. ***Required fees:*** $11 per credit hour part-time. ***Room and board:*** Room and board charges vary according to board plan and housing facility. ***Payment plan:*** installment. ***Waivers:*** senior citizens and employees or children of employees.

Financial Aid Of all full-time matriculated undergraduates who enrolled in 2018, 1,397 applied for aid, 1,282 were judged to have need, 136 had their need fully met. 912 Federal Work-Study jobs (averaging $1987). In 2018, 431 non-need-based awards were made. ***Average percent of need met:*** 58. ***Average financial aid package:*** $21,642. ***Average need-based loan:*** $4430. ***Average need-based gift aid:*** $7388. ***Average non-need-based aid:*** $14,059. ***Average indebtedness upon graduation:*** $33,856.

APPLYING

Standardized Tests *Required for some:* SAT or ACT (for admission).

Options: electronic application, early action, deferred entrance.

Application fee: $40.

Required: high school transcript, minimum 2.6 GPA, 1 letter of recommendation. ***Required for some:*** essay or personal statement, interview. ***Recommended:*** essay or personal statement.

Application deadlines: rolling (freshmen), rolling (transfers), 11/15 (early action).

Notification: continuous (freshmen), continuous (transfers), 12/14 (early action).

CONTACT

Mr. John Sawyer, Director of Undergraduate Admissions, Marymount University, 2807 North Glebe Road, Arlington, VA 22207. *Phone:* 703-284-1500. *Toll-free phone:* 800-548-7638. *Fax:* 703-522-0349. *E-mail:* admissions@marymount.edu.

Norfolk State University

Norfolk, Virginia

http://www.nsu.edu/

CONTACT

Mr. Kevin M. Holmes, Director of Recruitment and Admissions, Norfolk State University, 700 Park Avenue, Norfolk, VA 23504. *Phone:* 757-823-9222. *Toll-free phone:* 800-274-1821. *Fax:* 757-823-2078. *E-mail:* admissions@nsu.edu.

Old Dominion University

Norfolk, Virginia

http://www.odu.edu/

- **State-supported** university, founded 1930
- **Urban** 251-acre campus with easy access to Virginia Beach
- **Endowment** $249.7 million
- **Coed** 19,372 undergraduate students, 77% full-time, 55% women, 45% men
- **Moderately difficult** entrance level, 87% of applicants were admitted

UNDERGRAD STUDENTS
15,003 full-time, 4,369 part-time. Students come from 50 states and territories; 88 other countries; 8% are from out of state; 31% Black or African American, non-Hispanic/Latino; 9% Hispanic/Latino; 5% Asian, non-Hispanic/Latino; 0.3% Native Hawaiian or other Pacific Islander, non-Hispanic/Latino; 0.3% American Indian or Alaska Native, non-Hispanic/Latino; 7% Two or more races, non-Hispanic/Latino; 3% Race/ethnicity unknown; 1% international; 10% transferred in; 25% live on campus.

Freshmen:
Admission: 13,335 applied, 11,600 admitted, 3,176 enrolled. ***Average high school GPA:*** 3.3. ***Test scores:*** SAT evidence-based reading and writing scores over 500: 80%; SAT math scores over 500: 72%; ACT scores over 18: 81%; SAT evidence-based reading and writing scores over 600: 32%; SAT math scores over 600: 21%; ACT scores over 24: 32%; SAT evidence-based reading and writing scores over 700: 3%; SAT math scores over 700: 3%; ACT scores over 30: 6%.

Retention: 79% of full-time freshmen returned.

FACULTY
Total: 1,559, 55% full-time, 65% with terminal degrees.

Student/faculty ratio: 18:1.

ACADEMICS
Calendar: semesters. *Degrees:* certificates, bachelor's, master's, doctoral, post-master's, and postbachelor's certificates.

ROTC: Army (b), Navy (b).

Unusual degree programs: 3-2 engineering; nursing; International Studies, Dental Hygiene, Communication/Humanities, Interdisciplinary Studies/Humanities, Women's Studies/Humanities, Computer Science, Philosophy/Humanities, Accounting, Math, Art History, Studio Arts, Fine Arts, Geography, Economics, P.

Computers: 2,030 computers/terminals and 12,372 ports are available on campus for general student use. Students can access the following: campus intranet, computer help desk, free student e-mail accounts, online (class) grades, online (class) registration, online (class) schedules, online courses. Campuswide network is available. 100% of college-owned or -operated housing units are wired for high-speed Internet access. Wireless service is available via entire campus.

Library: Patricia W. and Douglas Perry Library plus 3 others. *Books:* 1.0 million (physical), 1.5 million (digital/electronic); *Serial titles:* 19,020 (physical), 110,572 (digital/electronic); *Databases:* 550. Weekly public service hours: 146; study areas open 24 hours, 5–7 days a week; students can reserve study rooms.

STUDENT LIFE
Housing options: coed, women-only, special housing for students with disabilities. Campus housing is university owned and leased by the school. Freshman campus housing is guaranteed.

Activities and organizations: drama/theater group, student-run newspaper, radio station, choral group, marching band, Asian Pacific American Student Union, Student Government Association, Student Veterans Association, Colleges Against Cancer, Student Activities Council, national fraternities, national sororities.

Athletics Member NCAA. All Division I. ***Intercollegiate sports:*** baseball M(s), basketball M(s)/W(s), cheerleading M(s)/W(s), crew M(c)/W(s), equestrian sports M(c)/W(c), field hockey W(s), football M(s), golf M(s)/W(s), ice hockey M(c)/W(c), lacrosse M(c)/W(s), rugby M(c)/W(c), sailing M/W, soccer M(s)/W(s), softball W(c), swimming and diving M(s)/W(s), tennis M(s)/W(s), ultimate Frisbee M(c)/W(c), volleyball M(c)/W(c), wrestling M(s). ***Intramural sports:*** badminton M/W, basketball M/W, golf M/W, racquetball M/W, soccer M/W, softball M/W, table tennis M/W, ultimate Frisbee M/W, volleyball M/W.

Campus security: 24-hour emergency response devices and patrols, student patrols, late-night transport/escort service, controlled dormitory access.

Student services: health clinic, personal/psychological counseling, women's center, veterans affairs office.

COSTS & FINANCIAL AID
Costs (2018–19) ***Tuition:*** state resident $10,872 full-time, $352 per credit hour part-time; nonresident $29,772 full-time, $982 per credit hour part-time. Full-time tuition and fees vary according to location. Part-time tuition and fees vary according to location. ***Required fees:*** $312 full-time, $66 per term part-time. ***Room and board:*** $12,338; room only: $7248. Room and board charges vary according to board plan, housing facility, location, and student level. ***Payment plans:*** installment, deferred payment. ***Waivers:*** senior citizens and employees or children of employees.

Financial Aid Of all full-time matriculated undergraduates who enrolled in 2018, 12,100 applied for aid, 10,292 were judged to have need, 1,285 had their need fully met. 200 Federal Work-Study jobs (averaging $2400). In 2018, 983 non-need-based awards were made. ***Average percent of need met:*** 42. ***Average financial aid package:*** $10,655. ***Average need-based loan:*** $4175. ***Average need-based gift aid:*** $6859. ***Average non-need-based aid:*** $5098. ***Average indebtedness upon graduation:*** $33,545.

APPLYING
Standardized Tests *Required for some:* SAT or ACT (for admission).

Options: electronic application, early admission, early action, deferred entrance.

Application fee: $50.

Required: high school transcript, minimum 2.7 GPA. ***Recommended:*** essay or personal statement, 1 letter of recommendation.

Application deadlines: 2/1 (freshmen), 5/1 (transfers), 12/1 (early action).

Notification: continuous (freshmen), continuous (transfers), 1/15 (early action).

CONTACT
Ms. Shereen Williams, Customer Service Manager, Admissions Office, Old Dominion University, 108 Rollins Hall, 5215 Hampton Boulevard, Norfolk, VA 23529. *Phone:* 757-683-3648. *Toll-free phone:* 800-348-7926. *Fax:* 757-683-3255. *E-mail:* admissions@odu.edu.

Patrick Henry College

Purcellville, Virginia

http://www.phc.edu/

CONTACT
Mr. Stephen C. Allen, Director of Admissions and Communications, Patrick Henry College, 10 Patrick Henry Circle, Purcellville, VA 20132. *Phone:* 540-338-1776. *Toll-free phone:* 888-338-1776. *Fax:* 540-441-8119. *E-mail:* admissions@phc.edu.

Radford University

Radford, Virginia

http://www.radford.edu/

- **State-supported** university, founded 1910
- **Small-town** 204-acre campus
- **Endowment** $50.3 million
- **Coed** 7,926 undergraduate students, 95% full-time, 57% women, 43% men
- **Minimally difficult** entrance level, 75% of applicants were admitted

UNDERGRAD STUDENTS
7,556 full-time, 370 part-time. Students come from 41 states and territories; 62 other countries; 6% are from out of state; 17% Black or African American, non-Hispanic/Latino; 7% Hispanic/Latino; 2% Asian, non-Hispanic/Latino; 0.1% Native Hawaiian or other Pacific Islander, non-Hispanic/Latino; 0.3% American Indian or Alaska Native, non-Hispanic/Latino; 5% Two or more races, non-Hispanic/Latino; 2% Race/ethnicity unknown; 1% international; 7% transferred in; 41% live on campus.

Freshmen:
Admission: 14,161 applied, 10,561 admitted, 1,762 enrolled. ***Average high school GPA:*** 3.3. ***Test scores:*** SAT evidence-based reading and writing scores over 500: 69%; SAT math scores over 500: 59%; ACT scores over 18: 72%; SAT evidence-based reading and writing scores over 600: 18%; SAT math scores over 600: 9%; ACT scores over 24: 20%; SAT evidence-based reading and writing scores over 700: 1%; SAT math scores over 700: 1%; ACT scores over 30: 1%.

Retention: 71% of full-time freshmen returned.

FACULTY
Total: 737, 63% full-time, 63% with terminal degrees.

Student/faculty ratio: 16:1.

ACADEMICS

Calendar: semesters. *Degrees:* certificates, bachelor's, master's, doctoral, post-master's, and postbachelor's certificates.

Special study options: accelerated degree program, advanced placement credit, distance learning, double majors, English as a second language, honors programs, independent study, internships, off-campus study, part-time degree program, services for LD students, student-designed majors, study abroad, summer session for credit. ***ROTC:*** Army (b).

Computers: 900 computers/terminals are available on campus for general student use. Students can access the following: campus intranet, computer help desk, free student e-mail accounts, online (class) grades, online (class) registration, online (class) schedules, online financial aid status and student accounts payable. Campuswide network is available. 100% of college-owned or -operated housing units are wired for high-speed Internet access. Wireless service is available via entire campus.

Library: McConnell Library. *Books:* 271,383 (physical), 332,165 (digital/electronic); *Serial titles:* 558 (physical), 28,298 (digital/electronic); *Databases:* 535. Students can reserve study rooms.

STUDENT LIFE

Housing options: on-campus residence required through sophomore year; coed, special housing for students with disabilities. Campus housing is university owned and leased by the school. Freshman campus housing is guaranteed.

Activities and organizations: drama/theater group, student-run newspaper, radio station, choral group, Radford Crafty, American Sign Language Club, Radford Student Programming and Campus Events (R-SPaCE), National Society for Collegiate Scholars, Scholar-Citizen Initiative Student Organization, national fraternities, national sororities.

Athletics Member NCAA. All Division I. ***Intercollegiate sports:*** baseball M(s), basketball M(s)/W(s), cross-country running M(s)/W(s), golf M(s)/W(s)(c), lacrosse W(s), soccer M(s)/W(s), softball W(s), tennis M(s)/W(s), track and field W(s), volleyball W(s). ***Intramural sports:*** basketball M/W, bowling M(c)/W(c), cheerleading M(c)/W(c), cross-country running M/W, equestrian sports M(c)/W(c), fencing W(c), football M/W, ice hockey M(c)/W(c), lacrosse M(c)/W(c), riflery M(c)/W(c), rugby M(c)/W(c), skiing (downhill) M(c)/W(c), soccer M(c)/W(c), softball M/W, swimming and diving M(c)/W(c), table tennis M/W, tennis M/W, ultimate Frisbee M/W, volleyball M/W, wrestling M(c)/W(c).

Campus security: 24-hour emergency response devices and patrols, late-night transport/escort service, controlled dormitory access.

Student services: health clinic, personal/psychological counseling, veterans affairs office.

COSTS & FINANCIAL AID

Costs (2018–19) ***Tuition:*** state resident $7922 full-time, $329 per credit hour part-time; nonresident $19,557 full-time, $814 per credit hour part-time. Full-time tuition and fees vary according to course load. Part-time tuition and fees vary according to course load. ***Required fees:*** $3288 full-time, $138 per credit hour part-time. ***Room and board:*** $9406; room only: $5177. Room and board charges vary according to board plan and housing facility. ***Payment plan:*** installment. ***Waivers:*** senior citizens and employees or children of employees.

Financial Aid Of all full-time matriculated undergraduates who enrolled in 2018, 6,103 applied for aid, 4,983 were judged to have need, 991 had their need fully met. 442 Federal Work-Study jobs (averaging $2452). 264 state and other part-time jobs (averaging $2208). In 2018, 383 non-need-based awards were made. ***Average percent of need met:*** 78. ***Average financial aid package:*** $10,794. ***Average need-based loan:*** $4113. ***Average need-based gift aid:*** $8102. ***Average non-need-based aid:*** $3748. ***Average indebtedness upon graduation:*** $31,547.

APPLYING

Standardized Tests *Recommended:* SAT or ACT (for admission).

Options: electronic application, early admission, early action, deferred entrance.

Required: high school transcript.

Application deadlines: 2/1 (freshmen), 6/1 (transfers), 12/1 (early action).

Notification: 4/1 (freshmen), continuous (transfers), 1/15 (early action).

CONTACT

Ms. Mildred Johnson, Dean of Admissions, Radford University, PO Box 6903, Radford, VA 24142. *Phone:* 540-831-5371. *Fax:* 540-831-5038. *E-mail:* admissions@radford.edu.

Randolph College

Lynchburg, Virginia

http://www.randolphcollege.edu/

- **Independent Methodist** comprehensive, founded 1891
- **Suburban** 100-acre campus
- **Coed** 600 undergraduate students, 98% full-time, 63% women, 37% men
- **Moderately difficult** entrance level, 87% of applicants were admitted

UNDERGRAD STUDENTS

586 full-time, 14 part-time. 23% are from out of state; 16% Black or African American, non-Hispanic/Latino; 7% Hispanic/Latino; 3% Asian, non-Hispanic/Latino; 0.2% Native Hawaiian or other Pacific Islander, non-Hispanic/Latino; 6% Two or more races, non-Hispanic/Latino; 0.7% Race/ethnicity unknown; 3% international; 6% transferred in; 77% live on campus.

Freshmen:

Admission: 1,576 applied, 1,366 admitted, 166 enrolled. ***Average high school GPA:*** 3.4. ***Test scores:*** SAT evidence-based reading and writing scores over 500: 71%; SAT math scores over 500: 68%; ACT scores over 18: 75%; SAT evidence-based reading and writing scores over 600: 33%; SAT math scores over 600: 16%; ACT scores over 24: 41%; SAT evidence-based reading and writing scores over 700: 2%; ACT scores over 30: 11%.

Retention: 65% of full-time freshmen returned.

FACULTY

Total: 69, 99% full-time, 93% with terminal degrees.

Student/faculty ratio: 9:1.

ACADEMICS

Calendar: semesters. *Degrees:* bachelor's and master's.

Special study options: adult/continuing education programs, part-time degree program.

Computers: Students can access the following: campus intranet, computer help desk, free student e-mail accounts, online (class) grades, online (class) registration, online (class) schedules. Campuswide network is available. Wireless service is available via entire campus.

Library: Lipscomb Library.

STUDENT LIFE

Housing options: on-campus residence required through senior year; coed. Campus housing is university owned. Freshman campus housing is guaranteed.

Athletics Member NCAA. All Division III. ***Intercollegiate sports:*** basketball M/W, cross-country running M/W, equestrian sports M/W, lacrosse M/W, soccer M/W, softball W, tennis M/W, volleyball W.

Campus security: 24-hour emergency response devices and patrols, late-night transport/escort service.

COSTS & FINANCIAL AID

Costs (2019–20) ***Comprehensive fee:*** $54,711 includes full-time tuition ($40,521), mandatory fees ($610), and room and board ($13,580). Part-time tuition: $1625 per credit hour.

Financial Aid Of all full-time matriculated undergraduates who enrolled in 2018, 516 applied for aid, 486 were judged to have need, 88 had their need fully met. In 2018, 94 non-need-based awards were made. ***Average percent of need met:*** 76. ***Average financial aid package:*** $35,000. ***Average need-based loan:*** $4745. ***Average need-based gift aid:*** $30,447. ***Average non-need-based aid:*** $24,779. ***Average indebtedness upon graduation:*** $42,183.

APPLYING

Standardized Tests *Required:* SAT or ACT (for admission).

Options: electronic application, early admission, early action, deferred entrance.

Required: essay or personal statement, high school transcript, 2 letters of recommendation. ***Recommended:*** interview.

CONTACT
Michael Quinn, Randolph College, 2500 Rivermont Avenue, Lynchburg, VA 24503-1555. *Phone:* 434-947-8100. *Toll-free phone:* 800-745-7692. *Fax:* 434-947-8996. *E-mail:* admissions@randolphcollege.edu.

Randolph-Macon College
Ashland, Virginia
http://www.rmc.edu/

- **Independent United Methodist** 4-year, founded 1830
- **Suburban** 124-acre campus with easy access to Richmond
- **Endowment** $166.2 million
- **Coed** 1,488 undergraduate students, 98% full-time, 53% women, 47% men
- **Moderately difficult** entrance level, 67% of applicants were admitted

UNDERGRAD STUDENTS
1,464 full-time, 24 part-time. Students come from 30 states and territories; 28 other countries; 22% are from out of state; 10% Black or African American, non-Hispanic/Latino; 4% Hispanic/Latino; 1% Asian, non-Hispanic/Latino; 0.2% Native Hawaiian or other Pacific Islander, non-Hispanic/Latino; 0.5% American Indian or Alaska Native, non-Hispanic/Latino; 4% Two or more races, non-Hispanic/Latino; 1% Race/ethnicity unknown; 2% international; 3% transferred in; 83% live on campus.

Freshmen:
Admission: 2,907 applied, 1,951 admitted, 420 enrolled. ***Average high school GPA:*** 3.6. ***Test scores:*** SAT evidence-based reading and writing scores over 500: 86%; SAT math scores over 500: 79%; ACT scores over 18: 89%; SAT evidence-based reading and writing scores over 600: 41%; SAT math scores over 600: 29%; ACT scores over 24: 52%; SAT evidence-based reading and writing scores over 700: 5%; SAT math scores over 700: 5%; ACT scores over 30: 10%.

Retention: 86% of full-time freshmen returned.

FACULTY
Total: 172, 65% full-time, 78% with terminal degrees.

Student/faculty ratio: 11:1.

ACADEMICS
Calendar: 4-1-4. *Degree:* bachelor's.

Special study options: academic remediation for entering students, accelerated degree program, advanced placement credit, double majors, honors programs, independent study, internships, off-campus study, part-time degree program, services for LD students, study abroad, summer session for credit. ***ROTC:*** Army (c).

Unusual degree programs: 3-2 business administration; engineering with University of Virginia; forestry with Duke University; Accounting, Virginia Commonwealth University; BS/MD Eastern VA Medical School.

Computers: 345 computers/terminals and 3,400 ports are available on campus for general student use. Students can access the following: campus intranet, computer help desk, free student e-mail accounts, online (class) registration, online (class) schedules. Campuswide network is available. 100% of college-owned or -operated housing units are wired for high-speed Internet access. Wireless service is available via entire campus.

Library: McGraw-Page Library. *Books:* 129,311 (physical), 457,041 (digital/electronic); *Serial titles:* 430 (physical), 144,340 (digital/electronic); *Databases:* 148. Study areas open 24 hours, 5–7 days a week; students can reserve study rooms.

STUDENT LIFE
Housing options: on-campus residence required through junior year; coed, men-only, women-only, special housing for students with disabilities. Campus housing is university owned. Freshman campus housing is guaranteed.

Activities and organizations: drama/theater group, student-run newspaper, radio and television station, choral group, marching band, Habitat for Humanity, Macon Outdoors, Relay for Life, College Panhellenic Council, R-MC Angler's Club, national fraternities, national sororities.

Athletics Member NCAA. All Division III. ***Intercollegiate sports:*** baseball M, basketball M/W, cheerleading M(c)/W(c), equestrian sports M(c)/W(c), field hockey W, football M, golf M/W, lacrosse M/W, soccer M/W, softball W, swimming and diving M/W, tennis M/W, volleyball M/W. ***Intramural sports:*** badminton M/W, basketball M/W, cheerleading M(c)/W(c), cross-country running M(c)/W(c), football M/W, lacrosse M/W, racquetball M/W, rugby M/W, soccer M/W, softball M/W, table tennis M/W, tennis M/W, ultimate Frisbee M/W, volleyball M/W, water polo M/W.

Campus security: 24-hour emergency response devices and patrols, late-night transport/escort service, controlled dormitory access.

Student services: health clinic, personal/psychological counseling, women's center.

COSTS & FINANCIAL AID
Costs (2019–20) ***One-time required fee:*** $100. ***Comprehensive fee:*** $54,770 includes full-time tuition ($41,200), mandatory fees ($1350), and room and board ($12,220). Part-time tuition: $4450 per course. ***Required fees:*** $110 per credit hour part-time. ***College room only:*** $6800.

Financial Aid Of all full-time matriculated undergraduates who enrolled in 2018, 1,258 applied for aid, 1,035 were judged to have need, 313 had their need fully met. In 2018, 414 non-need-based awards were made. ***Average percent of need met:*** 81. ***Average financial aid package:*** $30,349. ***Average need-based loan:*** $4216. ***Average need-based gift aid:*** $26,668. ***Average non-need-based aid:*** $21,305. ***Average indebtedness upon graduation:*** $23,336. ***Financial aid deadline:*** 3/1.

APPLYING
Standardized Tests *Required:* SAT or ACT (for admission). *Recommended:* SAT Subject Tests (for admission).

Options: electronic application, early admission, early action, deferred entrance.

Required: essay or personal statement, high school transcript, minimum 2.0 GPA, 1 letter of recommendation. ***Recommended:*** interview.

Application deadlines: 3/1 (freshmen), 4/1 (transfers), 11/15 (early action).

Notification: 4/1 (freshmen), continuous until 5/1 (transfers).

CONTACT
Erin Slater, Director of Admissions, Randolph-Macon College, PO Box 5005, Ashland, VA 23005-5505. *Phone:* 804-752-7305. *Toll-free phone:* 800-888-1762. *Fax:* 804-752-4707. *E-mail:* admissions@rmc.edu.

Regent University
Virginia Beach, Virginia
http://www.regent.edu/

- **Independent Christian** comprehensive, founded 1977
- **Suburban** 70-acre campus
- **Endowment** $80.2 million
- **Coed** 4,646 undergraduate students, 52% full-time, 62% women, 38% men
- **Minimally difficult** entrance level, 84% of applicants were admitted

UNDERGRAD STUDENTS
2,402 full-time, 2,244 part-time. Students come from 50 states and territories; 19 other countries; 58% are from out of state; 27% Black or African American, non-Hispanic/Latino; 9% Hispanic/Latino; 1% Asian, non-Hispanic/Latino; 0.4% Native Hawaiian or other Pacific Islander, non-Hispanic/Latino; 0.5% American Indian or Alaska Native, non-Hispanic/Latino; 5% Two or more races, non-Hispanic/Latino; 1% Race/ethnicity unknown; 0.6% international; 20% transferred in; 15% live on campus.

Freshmen:
Admission: 2,854 applied, 2,405 admitted, 467 enrolled. ***Average high school GPA:*** 3.5. ***Test scores:*** SAT evidence-based reading and writing scores over 500: 71%; SAT math scores over 500: 57%; ACT scores over 18: 85%; SAT evidence-based reading and writing scores over 600: 31%; SAT math scores over 600: 17%; ACT scores over 24: 39%; SAT evidence-based reading and writing scores over 700: 6%; SAT math scores over 700: 4%; ACT scores over 30: 9%.

Retention: 77% of full-time freshmen returned.

FACULTY
Total: 907, 16% full-time, 69% with terminal degrees.

Student/faculty ratio: 21:1.

ACADEMICS
Calendar: trimesters. *Degrees:* certificates, associate, bachelor's, master's, doctoral, post-master's, and postbachelor's certificates.

Special study options: academic remediation for entering students, adult/continuing education programs, advanced placement credit, distance learning, double majors, external degree program, freshman honors college, honors programs, internships, off-campus study, part-time degree program, services for LD students, study abroad, summer session for credit. ***ROTC:*** Army (c), Navy (c).

Unusual degree programs: 3-2 business administration with Regent University; nursing with Regent University.

Computers: 70 computers/terminals and 75 ports are available on campus for general student use. Students can access the following: campus intranet, computer help desk, free student e-mail accounts, online (class) grades, online (class) registration, online (class) schedules. Campuswide network is available. 100% of college-owned or -operated housing units are wired for high-speed Internet access. Wireless service is available via entire campus.
Library: Regent University Library plus 1 other. *Books:* 314,660 (physical), 531,636 (digital/electronic); *Serial titles:* 97 (physical), 95,377 (digital/electronic); *Databases:* 159. Weekly public service hours: 99; students can reserve study rooms.

STUDENT LIFE
Housing options: on-campus residence required for freshman year; men-only, women-only, special housing for students with disabilities. Campus housing is university owned. Freshman applicants given priority for college housing.

Activities and organizations: drama/theater group, student-run newspaper, choral group, College Student Leadership Board, Student Activities Board, Psychology Club, Student Alumni Ambassadors (SAA), Undergraduate Debate Association, national fraternities, national sororities.

Athletics Member NCCAA. ***Intercollegiate sports:*** basketball M(s)/W(s), cheerleading M(s)/W(s), cross-country running M(s)/W(s), soccer M(s)/W(s), track and field M(s)/W(s), volleyball W(s). ***Intramural sports:*** basketball M/W, soccer M/W, softball M/W, ultimate Frisbee M/W, volleyball M/W.

Campus security: 24-hour emergency response devices and patrols, student patrols, late-night transport/escort service, controlled dormitory access.

Student services: personal/psychological counseling, veterans affairs office.

COSTS & FINANCIAL AID
Costs (2019–20) ***Comprehensive fee:*** $26,360 includes full-time tuition ($17,880), mandatory fees ($1400), and room and board ($7080). Part-time tuition: $596 per credit hour. ***Required fees:*** $700 part-time. ***College room only:*** $4560.

Financial Aid Of all full-time matriculated undergraduates who enrolled in 2017, 2,030 applied for aid, 1,859 were judged to have need, 170 had their need fully met. In 2017, 296 non-need-based awards were made. ***Average percent of need met:*** 60. ***Average financial aid package:*** $10,819. ***Average need-based loan:*** $3703. ***Average need-based gift aid:*** $8566. ***Average non-need-based aid:*** $7253. ***Average indebtedness upon graduation:*** $28,035.

APPLYING
Standardized Tests *Required for some:* SAT or ACT (for admission).

Options: electronic application, deferred entrance.

Application fee: $50.

Required: high school transcript. ***Required for some:*** essay or personal statement, minimum 3.0 GPA.

Application deadlines: rolling (freshmen), rolling (out-of-state freshmen), 8/1 (transfers).

Notification: continuous (freshmen), continuous (out-of-state freshmen), continuous (transfers).

CONTACT
Mrs. Heidi Cece, Associate Vice President, Enrollment Management, Regent University, 1000 Regent University Drive, Virginia Beach, VA 23464. *Phone:* 800-373-5504. *Toll-free phone:* 800-373-5504. *Fax:* 757-352-4839. *E-mail:* admissions@regent.edu.

Roanoke College
Salem, Virginia
http://www.roanoke.edu/

- **Independent** 4-year, founded 1842, affiliated with Evangelical Lutheran Church in America
- **Suburban** 80-acre campus
- **Endowment** $152.6 million
- **Coed** 2,017 undergraduate students, 97% full-time, 58% women, 42% men
- **Moderately difficult** entrance level, 72% of applicants were admitted

UNDERGRAD STUDENTS
1,956 full-time, 61 part-time. Students come from 39 states and territories; 32 other countries; 44% are from out of state; 5% Black or African American, non-Hispanic/Latino; 5% Hispanic/Latino; 1% Asian, non-Hispanic/Latino; 0.1% Native Hawaiian or other Pacific Islander, non-Hispanic/Latino; 0.2% American Indian or Alaska Native, non-Hispanic/Latino; 4% Two or more races, non-Hispanic/Latino; 2% international; 3% transferred in; 77% live on campus.

Freshmen:
Admission: 5,122 applied, 3,713 admitted, 576 enrolled. ***Average high school GPA:*** 3.5. ***Test scores:*** SAT evidence-based reading and writing scores over 500: 91%; SAT math scores over 500: 85%; ACT scores over 18: 98%; SAT evidence-based reading and writing scores over 600: 41%; SAT math scores over 600: 27%; ACT scores over 24: 61%; SAT evidence-based reading and writing scores over 700: 6%; SAT math scores over 700: 4%; ACT scores over 30: 11%.

Retention: 78% of full-time freshmen returned.

FACULTY
Total: 220, 76% full-time, 75% with terminal degrees.

Student/faculty ratio: 11:1.

ACADEMICS
Calendar: semesters. *Degree:* bachelor's.

Special study options: accelerated degree program, adult/continuing education programs, advanced placement credit, distance learning, double majors, English as a second language, honors programs, independent study, internships, off-campus study, part-time degree program, services for LD students, study abroad, summer session for credit.

Unusual degree programs: 3-2 engineering with Virginia Polytechnic Institute and State University.

Computers: 228 computers/terminals and 1,600 ports are available on campus for general student use. Students can access the following: campus intranet, computer help desk, free student e-mail accounts, online (class) grades, online (class) registration, online (class) schedules, discounts on computer hardware and software purchases, free office software, free security software. Campuswide network is available. 100% of college-owned or -operated housing units are wired for high-speed Internet access. Wireless service is available via entire campus.
Library: Fintel Library. *Books:* 188,670 (physical), 227,793 (digital/electronic); *Serial titles:* 249 (physical), 89,398 (digital/electronic); *Databases:* 294. Weekly public service hours: 93; study areas open 24 hours, 5–7 days a week; students can reserve study rooms.

STUDENT LIFE
Housing options: on-campus residence required through senior year; coed, women-only, special housing for students with disabilities. Campus housing is university owned. Freshman campus housing is guaranteed.

Activities and organizations: drama/theater group, student-run newspaper, radio station, choral group, Habitat for Humanity, Nerf Gun Wars, Student Firearms Association, Biology Club, Lambda Alliance, national fraternities, national sororities.

Athletics Member NCAA. All Division III. ***Intercollegiate sports:*** baseball M, basketball M/W, cross-country running M/W, field hockey W, golf M, lacrosse M/W, soccer M/W, softball W, swimming and diving M/W, tennis M/W, track and field M/W, volleyball W. ***Intramural sports:*** badminton M(c)/W(c), baseball M(c), basketball M/W, cheerleading M(c)/W(c), equestrian sports W(c), football M/W, ice hockey M(c), rock climbing M(c)/W(c), rugby M(c)/W(c), soccer M/W(c), softball M/W, tennis M(c)/W(c), ultimate Frisbee M(c)/W(c), volleyball M/W.

Campus security: 24-hour emergency response devices and patrols, late-night transport/escort service, controlled dormitory access.

Student services: health clinic, personal/psychological counseling.

COSTS & FINANCIAL AID

Costs (2019–20) ***One-time required fee:*** $125. ***Comprehensive fee:*** $59,568 includes full-time tuition ($43,818), mandatory fees ($1616), and room and board ($14,134). Part-time tuition: $2096 per course. ***Required fees:*** $60 per term part-time. ***College room only:*** $6562.

Financial Aid Of all full-time matriculated undergraduates who enrolled in 2018, 1,648 applied for aid, 1,472 were judged to have need, 335 had their need fully met. In 2018, 462 non-need-based awards were made. ***Average percent of need met:*** 82. ***Average financial aid package:*** $38,206. ***Average need-based loan:*** $4506. ***Average need-based gift aid:*** $30,413. ***Average non-need-based aid:*** $22,756. ***Average indebtedness upon graduation:*** $41,187.

APPLYING

Standardized Tests *Required:* SAT or ACT (for admission).

Options: electronic application, early admission, early decision, deferred entrance.

Application fee: $30.

Required: high school transcript, SAT or ACT scores or must meet specific criteria to apply test-optional.. ***Recommended:*** essay or personal statement, 1 letter of recommendation, interview.

Application deadlines: 3/15 (freshmen), 3/15 (out-of-state freshmen), 8/1 (transfers).

Early decision deadline: 11/15.

Notification: continuous until 4/1 (freshmen), continuous until 4/1 (out-of-state freshmen), continuous until 8/15 (transfers), 12/15 (early decision).

CONTACT

Dr. Brenda Poggendorf, Vice President for Enrollment, Roanoke College, 221 College Lane, Salem, VA 24153-3794. *Phone:* 540-375-2270. *Toll-free phone:* 800-388-2276. *Fax:* 540-375-2267. *E-mail:* poggendorf@roanoke.edu.

Sentara College of Health Sciences

Chesapeake, Virginia

http://www.sentara.edu/

- **Independent** 4-year, founded 1892
- **Urban** campus with easy access to Virginia Beach
- **Coed**

ACADEMICS

Calendar: semesters. *Degrees:* associate and bachelor's.

Library: Sentara Healthcare Library. *Books:* 1,790 (physical); *Serial titles:* 65 (physical); *Databases:* 29.

STUDENT LIFE

Housing options: college housing not available.

Activities and organizations: Sentara Nursing Student Association (SNSA), Alpha Eta National Honor Society for Allied Health Professionals, Sigma Theta Tau International Nursing Honor Society, Chi Kappa Chapter (STTI), Student Community Outreach Program of Excellence (SCOPE).

Campus security: 24-hour emergency response devices.

Student services: personal/psychological counseling.

COSTS

Costs (2018–19) ***One-time required fee:*** $85. ***Tuition:*** $10,472 full-time, $357 per credit hour part-time. Full-time tuition and fees vary according to course level, course load, degree level, and program. Part-time tuition and fees vary according to course level, course load, degree level, and program. ***Required fees:*** $2447 full-time, $2447 per year part-time.

APPLYING

Standardized Tests *Required:* ATI Teas (BSN, CVT, ST) (for admission).

Options: electronic application.

Application fee: $85.

Required for some: high school transcript, minimum 3.5 GPA, For our BSN, early Admission option: earn courses, cumulative GPA of 3.3 on all college transcripts.

CONTACT

Sentara College of Health Sciences, 1441 Crossways Boulevard, Crossways I, Suite 105, Chesapeake, VA 23320. *Phone:* 757-388-2604.

Shenandoah University

Winchester, Virginia

http://www.su.edu/

- **Independent United Methodist** university, founded 1875
- **Suburban** 359-acre campus with easy access to Washington, D.C.
- **Endowment** $63.4 million
- **Coed**
- 83% of applicants were admitted

FACULTY

Student/faculty ratio: 10:1.

ACADEMICS

Calendar: semesters. *Degrees:* certificates, bachelor's, master's, doctoral, post-master's, and postbachelor's certificates.

Library: Alson H. Smith, Jr. Library plus 1 other. *Books:* 122,422 (physical), 217,000 (digital/electronic); *Serial titles:* 700 (physical), 86,500 (digital/electronic); *Databases:* 135. Weekly public service hours: 96; students can reserve study rooms.

STUDENT LIFE

Housing options: on-campus residence required through sophomore year; coed, special housing for students with disabilities. Campus housing is university owned and leased by the school. Freshman campus housing is guaranteed.

Activities and organizations: drama/theater group, student-run newspaper, radio station, choral group, Student Government Association, Graduate Student Assembly, Campus Activities Network, Athletic Training Club, Variety of Groups for Professional Fraternities.

Athletics Member NCAA. All Division III except golf (Division II).

Campus security: 24-hour emergency response devices and patrols, late-night transport/escort service, controlled dormitory access, LiveSafe mobile app, anonymous reporting, side-door alarms, campus shuttle, Safe in Sixty Seconds Program, Safe Walk/Safe Ride Program.

Student services: health clinic, personal/psychological counseling, women's center, veterans affairs office.

COSTS & FINANCIAL AID

Costs (2018–19) ***Comprehensive fee:*** $42,900 includes full-time tuition ($31,280), mandatory fees ($1250), and room and board ($10,370). Full-time tuition and fees vary according to course load and program. Part-time tuition: $910 per credit hour. Part-time tuition and fees vary according to course load and program. ***Required fees:*** $90 per term part-time. ***Room and board:*** Room and board charges vary according to board plan and housing facility.

Financial Aid Of all full-time matriculated undergraduates who enrolled in 2018, 1,761 applied for aid, 1,522 were judged to have need, 248 had their need fully met. 953 Federal Work-Study jobs (averaging $1923). 517 state and other part-time jobs (averaging $1959). In 2018, 405 non-need-based awards were made. ***Average percent of need met:*** 66. ***Average financial aid package:*** $21,297. ***Average need-based loan:*** $4431. ***Average need-based gift aid:*** $9271. ***Average non-need-based aid:*** $11,029. ***Average indebtedness upon graduation:*** $34,121.

APPLYING

Standardized Tests *Required:* SAT or ACT (for admission).

Options: electronic application.

Application fee: $30.

Required: high school transcript. ***Required for some:*** essay or personal statement, interview, audition for conservatory applicants, interview for some Conservatory programs and for Guaranteed Admission for Health Professions programs.

CONTACT

Mr. Thomas McKenna, Associate Director of Admissions, Shenandoah University, 1460 University Drive, Wilkins Building, Admissions Office, Winchester, VA 22601-5195. *Phone:* 540-545-7327. *Toll-free phone:* 800-432-2266. *Fax:* 540-665-4627. *E-mail:* admit@su.edu.

Southern Virginia University
Buena Vista, Virginia
http://www.svu.edu/

CONTACT
Mr. Tony Caputo, Dean of Admissions, Southern Virginia University, One University Hill Drive, Buena Vista, VA 24416. *Phone:* 540-261-2756. *Toll-free phone:* 800-229-8420. *Fax:* 540-261-8559. *E-mail:* admissions@southernvirginia.edu.

South University
Glen Allen, Virginia
http://www.southuniversity.edu/richmond

CONTACT
South University, 2151 Old Brick Road, Glen Allen, VA 23060. *Phone:* 804-727-6800. *Toll-free phone:* 888-422-5076.

South University
Virginia Beach, Virginia
http://www.southuniversity.edu/virginia-beach

CONTACT
South University, 301 Bendix Road, Suite 100, Virginia Beach, VA 23452. *Phone:* 757-493-6900. *Toll-free phone:* 877-206-1845.

Stratford University
Alexandria, Virginia
http://www.stratford.edu/

CONTACT
Admissions, Stratford University, 2900 Eisenhower Avenue, Alexandria, VA 22314. *Phone:* 571-699-3200. *Toll-free phone:* 800-444-0804. *E-mail:* alexandriaadmissions@stratford.edu.

Stratford University
Falls Church, Virginia
http://www.stratford.edu/

CONTACT
Admissions, Stratford University, 7777 Leesburg Pike, Falls Church, VA 22043. *Phone:* 703-821-8570. *Toll-free phone:* 800-444-0804. *E-mail:* fcadmissions@stratford.edu.

Stratford University
Glen Allen, Virginia
http://www.stratford.edu/

CONTACT
Admissions, Stratford University, 11104 West Broad Street, Glen Allen, VA 23060. *Phone:* 804-290-4231. *Toll-free phone:* 877-373-5173. *E-mail:* gaadmissions@stratford.edu.

Stratford University
Newport News, Virginia
http://www.stratford.edu/

CONTACT
Admissions, Stratford University, 836 J. Clyde Morris Boulevard, Newport News, VA 23601. *Phone:* 757-873-4235. *Toll-free phone:* 855-873-4235. *E-mail:* newportnewsadmissions@stratford.edu.

Stratford University
Virginia Beach, Virginia
http://www.stratford.edu/

CONTACT
Admissions, Stratford University, 555 South Independence Boulevard, Virginia Beach, VA 23452. *Phone:* 757-497-4466. *Toll-free phone:* 866-528-8363. *E-mail:* virginiabeachadmissions@stratford.edu.

Stratford University
Woodbridge, Virginia
http://www.stratford.edu/

CONTACT
Admissions, Stratford University, 14349 Gideon Drive, Woodbridge, VA 22192. *Phone:* 703-897-1982. *Toll-free phone:* 888-546-1250. *E-mail:* woodbridgeadmissions@stratford.edu.

Strayer University–Alexandria Campus
Alexandria, Virginia
http://www.strayer.edu/virginia/alexandria/

CONTACT
Strayer University–Alexandria Campus, 2730 Eisenhower Avenue, Alexandria, VA 22314. *Toll-free phone:* 888-311-0355.

Strayer University–Arlington Campus
Arlington, Virginia
http://www.strayer.edu/virginia/arlington/

CONTACT
Strayer University–Arlington Campus, 2121 15th Street North, Arlington, VA 22201. *Toll-free phone:* 888-311-0355.

Strayer University–Chesapeake Campus
Chesapeake, Virginia
http://www.strayer.edu/virginia/chesapeake/

CONTACT
Strayer University–Chesapeake Campus, 676 Independence Parkway, Suite 300, Chesapeake, VA 23320. *Toll-free phone:* 888-311-0355.

Strayer University–Chesterfield Campus
Midlothian, Virginia
http://www.strayer.edu/virginia/chesterfield/

CONTACT
Strayer University–Chesterfield Campus, 15521 Midlothian Turnpike, Suite 401, Midlothian, VA 23113. *Toll-free phone:* 888-311-0355.

Strayer University–Fredericksburg Campus
Fredericksburg, Virginia
http://www.strayer.edu/virginia/fredericksburg/

CONTACT
Strayer University–Fredericksburg Campus, 150 Riverside Parkway, Suite 100, Fredericksburg, VA 22406. *Toll-free phone:* 888-311-0355.

Strayer University–Henrico Campus

Glen Allen, Virginia

http://www.strayer.edu/virginia/henrico/

CONTACT
Strayer University–Henrico Campus, 11501 Nuckols Road, Glen Allen, VA 23059. *Toll-free phone:* 888-311-0355.

Strayer University–Loudoun Campus

Ashburn, Virginia

http://www.strayer.edu/virginia/loudoun/

CONTACT
Strayer University–Loudoun Campus, 45150 Russell Branch Parkway, Suite 200, Ashburn, VA 20147. *Toll-free phone:* 888-311-0355.

Strayer University–Manassas Campus

Manassas, Virginia

http://www.strayer.edu/virginia/manassas/

CONTACT
Strayer University–Manassas Campus, 9990 Battleview Parkway, Manassas, VA 20109. *Toll-free phone:* 888-311-0355.

Strayer University–Newport News Campus

Newport News, Virginia

http://www.strayer.edu/virginia/newport-news/

CONTACT
Strayer University–Newport News Campus, 99 Old Oyster Point Road, Newport News, VA 23602. *Toll-free phone:* 888-311-0355.

Strayer University–Virginia Beach Campus

Virginia Beach, Virginia

http://www.strayer.edu/virginia/virginia-beach/

CONTACT
Strayer University–Virginia Beach Campus, 249 Central Park Avenue, Suite 350, Virginia Beach, VA 23462. *Toll-free phone:* 888-311-0355.

Strayer University–Woodbridge Campus

Woodbridge, Virginia

http://www.strayer.edu/virginia/woodbridge/

CONTACT
Strayer University–Woodbridge Campus, 13385 Minnieville Road, Woodbridge, VA 22192. *Toll-free phone:* 888-311-0355.

Sweet Briar College

Sweet Briar, Virginia

http://www.sbc.edu/

- **Independent** comprehensive, founded 1901
- **Rural** 3250-acre campus
- **Endowment** $74.8 million
- **Women only** 336 undergraduate students, 99% full-time
- **Minimally difficult** entrance level, 76% of applicants were admitted

UNDERGRAD STUDENTS
331 full-time, 5 part-time. Students come from 33 states and territories; 6 other countries; 48% are from out of state; 9% Black or African American, non-Hispanic/Latino; 8% Hispanic/Latino; 2% Asian, non-Hispanic/Latino; 0.3% Native Hawaiian or other Pacific Islander, non-Hispanic/Latino; 3% Two or more races, non-Hispanic/Latino; 2% Race/ethnicity unknown; 3% international; 4% transferred in; 93% live on campus.

Freshmen:
Admission: 654 applied, 495 admitted, 110 enrolled. ***Average high school GPA:*** 3.5. ***Test scores:*** SAT evidence-based reading and writing scores over 500: 80%; SAT math scores over 500: 66%; ACT scores over 18: 95%; SAT evidence-based reading and writing scores over 600: 41%; SAT math scores over 600: 17%; ACT scores over 24: 41%; SAT evidence-based reading and writing scores over 700: 10%; SAT math scores over 700: 1%; ACT scores over 30: 14%.

Retention: 72% of full-time freshmen returned.

FACULTY
Total: 75, 80% full-time, 76% with terminal degrees.

Student/faculty ratio: 5:1.

ACADEMICS
Calendar: semesters. *Degrees:* bachelor's and master's.

Special study options: adult/continuing education programs, advanced placement credit, double majors, honors programs, independent study, internships, off-campus study, part-time degree program, services for LD students, student-designed majors, study abroad, summer session for credit.

Unusual degree programs: 3-2 engineering with Virginia Polytechnic Institute and State University, University of Virginia, Columbia University, Washington University in St. Louis.

Computers: Students can access the following: campus intranet, computer help desk, free student e-mail accounts, online (class) grades, online (class) registration, online (class) schedules. Campuswide network is available. 100% of college-owned or -operated housing units are wired for high-speed Internet access. Wireless service is available via entire campus.

Library: Mary Helen Cochran Library plus 1 other. *Books:* 245,124 (physical); *Serial titles:* 1,215 (physical), 31,479 (digital/electronic); *Databases:* 214. Study areas open 24 hours, 5–7 days a week.

STUDENT LIFE
Housing options: on-campus residence required through senior year; women-only. Campus housing is university owned. Freshman campus housing is guaranteed.

Activities and organizations: drama/theater group, student-run newspaper, radio station, choral group.

Athletics Member NCAA. All Division III. ***Intercollegiate sports:*** cross-country running W, equestrian sports W, field hockey W, golf W, lacrosse W, soccer W, softball W, swimming and diving W, tennis W.

Campus security: 24-hour emergency response devices and patrols, student patrols, late-night transport/escort service, controlled dormitory access, front gate security.

Student services: health clinic, personal/psychological counseling, women's center, veterans affairs office.

COSTS & FINANCIAL AID
Costs (2019–20) ***Comprehensive fee:*** $35,220 includes full-time tuition ($21,420), mandatory fees ($600), and room and board ($13,200).

Financial Aid Of all full-time matriculated undergraduates who enrolled in 2016, 281 applied for aid, 257 were judged to have need, 61 had their need fully met. In 2016, 20 non-need-based awards were made. ***Average percent of need met:*** 81. ***Average financial aid package:*** $34,064. ***Average need-based loan:*** $7457. ***Average need-based gift aid:*** $28,297. ***Average non-need-based aid:*** $29,940. ***Average indebtedness upon graduation:*** $31,269.

APPLYING
Standardized Tests *Required for some:* SAT or ACT (for admission).

Options: electronic application, deferred entrance.

Required: essay or personal statement, high school transcript. ***Recommended:*** 2 letters of recommendation.

Application deadlines: rolling (out-of-state freshmen), rolling (transfers), 10/1 (early action).

Notification: continuous (freshmen), continuous (out-of-state freshmen), continuous (transfers), rolling (early action).

CONTACT
Elizabeth Clarke, Dir. Admissions Strategy, Sweet Briar College, PO Box 1052, Sweet Briar, VA 24595. *Phone:* 434-381-6720. *Toll-free phone:* 800-381-6142. *E-mail:* admissions@sbc.edu.

University of Lynchburg

Lynchburg, Virginia

http://www.lynchburg.edu/

- **Independent** comprehensive, founded 1903, affiliated with Christian Church (Disciples of Christ)
- **Suburban** 264-acre campus
- **Endowment** $109.7 million
- **Coed** 2,086 undergraduate students, 93% full-time, 61% women, 39% men
- **Moderately difficult** entrance level, 100% of applicants were admitted

UNDERGRAD STUDENTS
1,930 full-time, 156 part-time. Students come from 33 states and territories; 11 other countries; 29% are from out of state; 11% Black or African American, non-Hispanic/Latino; 5% Hispanic/Latino; 1% Asian, non-Hispanic/Latino; 0.5% American Indian or Alaska Native, non-Hispanic/Latino; 3% Two or more races, non-Hispanic/Latino; 4% Race/ethnicity unknown; 1% international; 4% transferred in; 74% live on campus.

Freshmen:
Admission: 3,830 applied, 3,830 admitted, 516 enrolled. ***Average high school GPA:*** 3.4. ***Test scores:*** SAT evidence-based reading and writing scores over 500: 79%; SAT math scores over 500: 70%; ACT scores over 18: 88%; SAT evidence-based reading and writing scores over 600: 31%; SAT math scores over 600: 16%; ACT scores over 24: 43%; SAT evidence-based reading and writing scores over 700: 2%; SAT math scores over 700: 2%; ACT scores over 30: 11%.

Retention: 79% of full-time freshmen returned.

FACULTY
Total: 270, 69% full-time, 76% with terminal degrees.
Student/faculty ratio: 11:1.

ACADEMICS
Calendar: semesters. *Degrees:* bachelor's, master's, doctoral, post-master's, and postbachelor's certificates.

Special study options: accelerated degree program, adult/continuing education programs, advanced placement credit, distance learning, double majors, English as a second language, honors programs, independent study, internships, off-campus study, part-time degree program, services for LD students, student-designed majors, study abroad, summer session for credit.

Unusual degree programs: engineering with Old Dominion University, University of Virginia.

Computers: 300 computers/terminals are available on campus for general student use. Students can access the following: campus intranet, computer help desk, free student e-mail accounts, online (class) grades, online (class) registration, online (class) schedules. Campuswide network is available. 100% of college-owned or -operated housing units are wired for high-speed Internet access. Wireless service is available via entire campus.

Library: Knight-Capron Library. *Books:* 109,236 (physical), 323,591 (digital/electronic); *Serial titles:* 109 (physical), 58,732 (digital/electronic); *Databases:* 98. Study areas open 24 hours, 5–7 days a week; students can reserve study rooms.

STUDENT LIFE
Housing options: on-campus residence required through junior year; coed, special housing for students with disabilities. Campus housing is university owned. Freshman campus housing is guaranteed.

Activities and organizations: drama/theater group, student-run newspaper, choral group, Student Government Association, Student Activities Board, Enrollment Student Ambassadors, Emergency Services, Greek Life, national fraternities, national sororities.

Athletics Member NCAA. All Division III. ***Intercollegiate sports:*** baseball M, basketball M/W, cheerleading M/W, cross-country running M/W, equestrian sports M/W, field hockey W, golf M, lacrosse M/W, soccer M/W, softball W, tennis M/W, track and field M/W, volleyball W. ***Intramural sports:*** basketball M(c)/W(c), golf M(c)/W(c), lacrosse M(c)/W(c), rugby M/W, soccer M(c)/W(c), tennis M(c)/W(c), volleyball M/W, wrestling M(c).

Campus security: 24-hour emergency response devices and patrols, late-night transport/escort service, controlled dormitory access.

Student services: health clinic, personal/psychological counseling, veterans affairs office.

COSTS & FINANCIAL AID

Costs (2018–19) ***Comprehensive fee:*** $50,330 includes full-time tuition ($38,560), mandatory fees ($970), and room and board ($10,800). Part-time tuition: $525 per credit hour. Part-time tuition and fees vary according to course load. ***Required fees:*** $5 per credit hour part-time. ***College room only:*** $5800. Room and board charges vary according to housing facility. ***Payment plans:*** tuition prepayment, installment. ***Waivers:*** adult students, senior citizens, and employees or children of employees.

Financial Aid Of all full-time matriculated undergraduates who enrolled in 2018, 1,687 applied for aid, 1,547 were judged to have need, 323 had their need fully met. In 2018, 463 non-need-based awards were made. ***Average percent of need met:*** 76. ***Average financial aid package:*** $29,919. ***Average need-based loan:*** $3399. ***Average need-based gift aid:*** $26,512. ***Average non-need-based aid:*** $19,944. ***Average indebtedness upon graduation:*** $36,076.

APPLYING

Standardized Tests *Required:* SAT or ACT (for admission).

Options: electronic application, early admission, early decision, deferred entrance.

Application fee: $30.

Required: high school transcript. ***Recommended:*** essay or personal statement, 2 letters of recommendation, interview.

Application deadlines: rolling (freshmen), rolling (transfers).

Early decision deadline: 11/15.

Notification: continuous (freshmen), continuous (transfers), 12/15 (early decision).

CONTACT

Ms. Sharon Walters-Bower, Director of Admissions, University of Lynchburg, 1501 Lakeside Drive, Lynchburg, VA 24501-3199. *Phone:* 434-544-8300. *Toll-free phone:* 800-426-8101. *Fax:* 434-544-8653. *E-mail:* admissions@lynchburg.edu.

See previous page for display ad and page 1138 for the College Close-Up.

University of Management and Technology

Arlington, Virginia

http://www.umtweb.edu/

- **Proprietary** comprehensive, founded 1998
- **Urban** campus with easy access to Washington, DC
- **Coed**

FACULTY

Student/faculty ratio: 25:1.

ACADEMICS

Calendar: continuous. *Degrees:* certificates, associate, bachelor's, master's, doctoral, post-master's, and postbachelor's certificates.
Library: ***Books:*** 9,149 (physical), 35 (digital/electronic).

STUDENT LIFE

Student services: veterans affairs office.

COSTS & FINANCIAL AID

Costs (2018–19) ***Tuition:*** $9360 full-time. ***Required fees:*** $90 full-time.

Financial Aid Of all full-time matriculated undergraduates who enrolled in 2014, 71 applied for aid, 67 were judged to have need, 67 had their need fully met. ***Average percent of need met:*** 100. ***Average financial aid package:*** $16,980. ***Average need-based loan:*** $3414. ***Average need-based gift aid:*** $3989. ***Average indebtedness upon graduation:*** $15,415.

APPLYING

Application fee: $30.

CONTACT

University of Management and Technology, 1901 Fort Myer Drive, Arlington, VA 22209-1609. *Toll-free phone:* 800-924-4883.

University of Mary Washington

Fredericksburg, Virginia

http://www.umw.edu/

- **State-supported** comprehensive, founded 1908
- **Small-town** 234-acre campus with easy access to Richmond; Washington, D.C.
- **Endowment** $50.0 million
- **Coed**
- **Very difficult** entrance level

FACULTY

Student/faculty ratio: 14:1.

ACADEMICS

Calendar: semesters. *Degrees:* certificates, bachelor's, master's, and postbachelor's certificates.
Library: Simpson Library plus 2 others. *Books:* 373,290 (physical), 243,338 (digital/electronic); *Serial titles:* 3,164 (physical), 76,994 (digital/electronic); *Databases:* 210. Weekly public service hours: 90; students can reserve study rooms.

STUDENT LIFE

Housing options: on-campus residence required through sophomore year; coed, women-only, special housing for students with disabilities. Campus housing is university owned. Freshman campus housing is guaranteed.

Activities and organizations: drama/theater group, student-run newspaper, radio station, choral group, Class Council, Campus Programming Board, Community Outreach and Participation, Association of Residence Halls, Student Government Association.

Athletics Member NCAA. All Division III.

Campus security: 24-hour emergency response devices and patrols, student patrols, late-night transport/escort service, controlled dormitory access, self-defense and safety classes. Guardian App.

Student services: health clinic, personal/psychological counseling, veterans affairs office.

COSTS & FINANCIAL AID

Costs (2018–19) ***Tuition:*** state resident $5772 full-time; nonresident $20,362 full-time. Full-time tuition and fees vary according to course load, degree level, and location. Part-time tuition and fees vary according to course load, degree level, and location. ***Required fees:*** $5858 full-time. ***Room and board:*** $11,118; room only: $7326. Room and board charges vary according to board plan and housing facility.

Financial Aid Of all full-time matriculated undergraduates who enrolled in 2017, 2,640 applied for aid, 1,823 were judged to have need, 187 had their need fully met. In 2017, 1072 non-need-based awards were made. ***Average percent of need met:*** 43. ***Average financial aid package:*** $9995. ***Average need-based loan:*** $4109. ***Average need-based gift aid:*** $3368. ***Average non-need-based aid:*** $3374. ***Average indebtedness upon graduation:*** $32,820. ***Financial aid deadline:*** 6/1.

APPLYING

Standardized Tests *Required for some:* SAT or ACT (for admission).

Options: electronic application, early admission, early decision, early action, deferred entrance.

Application fee: $50.

Required: essay or personal statement, high school transcript.

CONTACT

Ms. Melissa Yakabouski, Director of Undergraduate Admissions, University of Mary Washington, 1301 College Avenue, Fredericksburg, VA 22401-5358. *Phone:* 540-654-1669. *Toll-free phone:* 800-468-5614. *Fax:* 540-654-1857. *E-mail:* myak@umw.edu.

University of Richmond

Richmond, Virginia

http://www.richmond.edu/

- **Independent** comprehensive, founded 1830
- **Suburban** 350-acre campus
- **Endowment** $2.5 billion
- **Coed** 3,227 undergraduate students, 94% full-time, 52% women, 48% men
- **Very difficult** entrance level, 30% of applicants were admitted

UNDERGRAD STUDENTS
3,019 full-time, 208 part-time. Students come from 48 states and territories; 63 other countries; 81% are from out of state; 7% Black or African American, non-Hispanic/Latino; 9% Hispanic/Latino; 8% Asian, non-Hispanic/Latino; 0.1% American Indian or Alaska Native, non-Hispanic/Latino; 4% Two or more races, non-Hispanic/Latino; 5% Race/ethnicity unknown; 10% international; 2% transferred in; 91% live on campus.

Freshmen:
Admission: 11,882 applied, 3,585 admitted, 832 enrolled. ***Test scores:*** SAT evidence-based reading and writing scores over 500: 100%; SAT math scores over 500: 99%; ACT scores over 18: 100%; SAT evidence-based reading and writing scores over 600: 89%; SAT math scores over 600: 91%; ACT scores over 24: 96%; SAT evidence-based reading and writing scores over 700: 35%; SAT math scores over 700: 51%; ACT scores over 30: 75%.

Retention: 94% of full-time freshmen returned.

FACULTY
Total: 439, 78% full-time, 85% with terminal degrees.

Student/faculty ratio: 8:1.

ACADEMICS
Calendar: semesters. *Degrees:* certificates, bachelor's, master's, and doctoral.

Special study options: advanced placement credit, double majors, English as a second language, honors programs, independent study, internships, off-campus study, part-time degree program, services for LD students, student-designed majors, study abroad, summer session for credit. ***ROTC:*** Army (b).

Unusual degree programs: 3-2 engineering with Columbia University, University of Virginia; Duke University Environmental Studies, Virginia Commonwealth University Environmental Studies.

Computers: 971 computers/terminals and 4,608 ports are available on campus for general student use. Students can access the following: campus intranet, computer help desk, free student e-mail accounts, online (class) grades, online (class) registration, online (class) schedules. Campuswide network is available. 100% of college-owned or -operated housing units are wired for high-speed Internet access. Wireless service is available via entire campus.

Library: Boatwright Memorial Library plus 2 others. *Books:* 541,127 (physical), 578,842 (digital/electronic); *Serial titles:* 427 (physical), 154,436 (digital/electronic); *Databases:* 460. Weekly public service hours: 100; study areas open 24 hours, 5–7 days a week; students can reserve study rooms.

STUDENT LIFE
Housing options: coed, men-only, women-only, special housing for students with disabilities. Campus housing is university owned. Freshman campus housing is guaranteed.

Activities and organizations: drama/theater group, student-run newspaper, radio station, choral group, Greek Life, Sport Clubs, SpiderBoard Concert, SpiderFest, Block Parties, national fraternities, national sororities.

Athletics Member NCAA. All Division I except football (Division I-AA). ***Intercollegiate sports:*** baseball M(s), basketball M(s)/W(s), cross-country running M/W(s), field hockey W(s), golf M(s)/W(s)(c), lacrosse M(s)/W(s), soccer W(s), swimming and diving W(s), tennis M(s)/W(s), track and field W(s). ***Intramural sports:*** archery M(c)/W(c), badminton M(c)/W(c), baseball M(c), basketball M/W, crew M(c)/W(c), equestrian sports M(c)/W(c), field hockey M(c)/W(c), golf M/W, ice hockey M(c)/W(c), lacrosse M(c)/W(c), racquetball M/W, rugby M(c)/W(c), soccer M/W, softball M/W, squash M/W, swimming and diving M(c)/W(c), table tennis M/W, tennis M/W, track and field M(c)/W(c), ultimate Frisbee M(c)/W(c), volleyball M/W, water polo M(c)/W(c), wrestling M(c).

Campus security: 24-hour emergency response devices and patrols, late-night transport/escort service, controlled dormitory access.

Student services: health clinic, personal/psychological counseling, women's center.

COSTS & FINANCIAL AID
Costs (2019–20) ***Comprehensive fee:*** $67,590 includes full-time tuition ($54,690) and room and board ($12,900). Part-time tuition: $2231 per credit hour. ***College room only:*** $6000. ***Payment plan:*** tuition prepayment.

Financial Aid Of all full-time matriculated undergraduates who enrolled in 2018, 1,621 applied for aid, 1,284 were judged to have need, 1,050 had their need fully met. 697 Federal Work-Study jobs (averaging $1509). In 2018, 610 non-need-based awards were made. ***Average percent of need met:*** 100. ***Average financial aid package:*** $49,423. ***Average need-based loan:*** $3718. ***Average need-based gift aid:*** $43,705. ***Average non-need-based aid:*** $23,157. ***Average indebtedness upon graduation:*** $27,406. ***Financial aid deadline:*** 2/1.

APPLYING
Standardized Tests *Required:* SAT or ACT (for admission).

Options: electronic application, early decision, early action, deferred entrance.

Application fee: $50.

Required: essay or personal statement, high school transcript, 1 letter of recommendation.

Application deadlines: 1/15 (freshmen), 2/15 (transfers), 11/1 (early action).

Early decision deadline: 11/1.

Notification: 4/1 (freshmen), 4/15 (transfers), 12/15 (early decision), 1/20 (early action).

CONTACT
Mr. Gil Villanueva, Dean of Admission, University of Richmond, Queally Center for Admission and Career Services, 30 UR Drive, University of Richmond, VA 23173. *Phone:* 804-289-8640. *Toll-free phone:* 800-700-1662. *Fax:* 804-287-6003. *E-mail:* admissions@richmond.edu.

University of Valley Forge Virginia Campus

Woodbridge, Virginia

http://www.valleyforge.edu/

CONTACT
Admissions Coordinator, University of Valley Forge Virginia Campus, 13909 Smoketown Road, Woodbridge, VA 22192. *Phone:* 703-580-4810 Ext. 210. *Toll-free phone:* 800-432-8322.

University of Virginia

Charlottesville, Virginia

http://www.virginia.edu/

- **State-supported** university, founded 1819
- **Suburban** 1167-acre campus with easy access to Richmond
- **Endowment** $6.3 billion
- **Coed** 16,787 undergraduate students, 95% full-time, 55% women, 45% men
- **Very difficult** entrance level, 26% of applicants were admitted

UNDERGRAD STUDENTS
16,007 full-time, 780 part-time. Students come from 52 states and territories; 125 other countries; 28% are from out of state; 7% Black or African American, non-Hispanic/Latino; 6% Hispanic/Latino; 15% Asian, non-Hispanic/Latino; 0.1% Native Hawaiian or other Pacific Islander, non-Hispanic/Latino; 0.1% American Indian or Alaska Native, non-Hispanic/Latino; 5% Two or more races, non-Hispanic/Latino; 6% Race/ethnicity unknown; 4% international; 4% transferred in; 38% live on campus.

Freshmen:
Admission: 37,182 applied, 9,828 admitted, 3,822 enrolled. ***Average high school GPA:*** 4.3. ***Test scores:*** SAT evidence-based reading and writing scores over 500: 100%; SAT math scores over 500: 100%; ACT scores over 18: 100%; SAT evidence-based reading and writing scores over 600: 95%; SAT math scores over 600: 92%; ACT scores over 24: 97%; SAT evidence-based reading and writing scores over 700: 55%; SAT math scores over 700: 62%; ACT scores over 30: 81%.

Retention: 97% of full-time freshmen returned.

FACULTY
Total: 1,573, 95% full-time, 89% with terminal degrees.

Student/faculty ratio: 15:1.

ACADEMICS
Calendar: semesters. *Degrees:* certificates, bachelor's, master's, doctoral, post-master's, and postbachelor's certificates.

Special study options: accelerated degree program, adult/continuing education programs, advanced placement credit, cooperative education, distance learning, double majors, English as a second language, honors programs, independent study, internships, part-time degree program, services for LD students, student-designed majors, study abroad, summer session for credit. ***ROTC:*** Army (b), Navy (b), Air Force (b).

Unusual degree programs: 3-2 education.

Computers: 250 computers/terminals are available on campus for general student use. Students can access the following: campus intranet, computer help desk, free student e-mail accounts, online (class) grades, online (class) registration, online (class) schedules, online course management tool. Campuswide network is available. 100% of college-owned or -operated housing units are wired for high-speed Internet access. Wireless service is available via classrooms, computer centers, computer labs, dorm rooms, learning centers, libraries, student centers.
Library: Alderman Library plus 14 others. *Books:* 5.1 million (physical), 785,258 (digital/electronic); *Serial titles:* 7,910 (physical), 207,644 (digital/electronic); *Databases:* 1,340. Weekly public service hours: 149; study areas open 24 hours, 5–7 days a week; students can reserve study rooms.

STUDENT LIFE
Housing options: on-campus residence required for freshman year; coed. Campus housing is university owned. Freshman campus housing is guaranteed.

Activities and organizations: drama/theater group, student-run newspaper, radio and television station, choral group, marching band, Madison House, student government, university guides, University Union, The Cavalier Daily, national fraternities, national sororities.

Athletics Member NCAA. All Division I except football (Division I-A). ***Intercollegiate sports:*** baseball M(s), basketball M(s)/W(s), crew W(s), cross-country running M(s)/W(s), field hockey W(s), golf M(s)/W(s)(c), lacrosse M(s)/W(s), soccer M(s)/W(s), softball W(s), squash M(s)/W(s), swimming and diving M(s)/W(s), tennis M(s)/W(s), track and field M(s)/W(s), volleyball W(s), wrestling M(s). ***Intramural sports:*** archery M(c)/W(c), badminton M(c)/W(c), baseball M(c), basketball M(c)/W(c), cheerleading M(c)/W(c), crew M(c)/W, cross-country running M(c)/W(c), equestrian sports M(c)/W(c), fencing M(c)/W(c), field hockey W(c), football M, golf M(c)/W(c), gymnastics M(c)/W(c), ice hockey M(c), lacrosse W(c), racquetball M(c)/W(c), riflery M(c)/W(c), rock climbing M(c)/W(c), rugby M(c)/W(c), sailing M(c)/W(c), skiing (downhill) M(c)/W(c), soccer M(c)/W(c), softball W(c), squash M(c)/W(c), swimming and diving M(c)/W(c), tennis M(c)/W(c), track and field M(c)/W(c), ultimate Frisbee M(c)/W(c), volleyball M(c)/W(c), water polo M(c)/W(c), wrestling M(c)/W(c).

Campus security: 24-hour emergency response devices and patrols, student patrols, late-night transport/escort service, controlled dormitory access.

Student services: health clinic, personal/psychological counseling, women's center, legal services.

FINANCIAL AID
Financial Aid Of all full-time matriculated undergraduates who enrolled in 2018, 9,532 applied for aid, 5,571 were judged to have need, 5,571 had their need fully met. In 2018, 493 non-need-based awards were made. ***Average percent of need met:*** 100. ***Average financial aid package:*** $28,986. ***Average need-based loan:*** $6038. ***Average need-based gift aid:*** $23,439. ***Average non-need-based aid:*** $5042. ***Average indebtedness upon graduation:*** $24,682.

APPLYING
Standardized Tests *Required:* SAT or ACT (for admission).

Options: electronic application, early action, deferred entrance.

Application fee: $70.

Required: essay or personal statement, high school transcript, 2 letters of recommendation.

Application deadlines: 1/1 (freshmen), 3/1 (transfers), 11/1 (early action).

Notification: 4/1 (freshmen), 5/1 (transfers), 1/31 (early action).

CONTACT
Mr. Gregory W. Roberts, Dean of Admission, University of Virginia, PO Box 400160, Charlottesville, VA 22904-4727. *Phone:* 434-982-3200. *Fax:* 434-924-3587. *E-mail:* undergrad-admission@virginia.edu.

The University of Virginia's College at Wise

Wise, Virginia

http://www.uvawise.edu/

- **State-supported** 4-year, founded 1954, part of University of Virginia
- **Small-town** 396-acre campus
- **Endowment** $6.5 billion
- **Coed**
- **Moderately difficult** entrance level

FACULTY
Student/faculty ratio: 12:1.

ACADEMICS
Calendar: semesters. *Degree:* bachelor's.
Library: University of Virginia's College at Wise Library. *Books:* 148,612 (physical), 179,697 (digital/electronic); *Serial titles:* 719 (physical), 3,284 (digital/electronic); *Databases:* 124. Weekly public service hours: 78; study areas open 24 hours, 5–7 days a week; students can reserve study rooms.

STUDENT LIFE
Housing options: on-campus residence required for freshman year; coed, men-only, women-only, special housing for students with disabilities. Campus housing is university owned.

Activities and organizations: drama/theater group, student-run newspaper, radio and television station, choral group, marching band, Student Government, Student Activities Board, Multicultural Association, Residence Hall Association, intramurals, national fraternities, national sororities.

Athletics Member NCAA. All Division II.

Campus security: 24-hour emergency response devices and patrols, student patrols, late-night transport/escort service, self-defense, informal discussions, pamphlets/posters/films, and crime prevention office.

Student services: health clinic, personal/psychological counseling.

FINANCIAL AID
Financial Aid Of all full-time matriculated undergraduates who enrolled in 2018, 1,101 applied for aid, 966 were judged to have need, 268 had their need fully met. In 2018, 93 non-need-based awards were made. ***Average percent of need met:*** 87. ***Average financial aid package:*** $16,027. ***Average need-based loan:*** $3253. ***Average need-based gift aid:*** $8615. ***Average non-need-based aid:*** $7663. ***Average indebtedness upon graduation:*** $30,381. ***Financial aid deadline:*** 2/15.

APPLYING
Standardized Tests *Required:* SAT or ACT (for admission).

Options: early admission, early action.

Application fee: $25.

Required: high school transcript, minimum 2.3 GPA. ***Recommended:*** 2 letters of recommendation.

CONTACT
Mr. Russell D. Necessary, Vice Chancellor for Enrollment Management and Student Life, The University of Virginia's College at Wise, 1 College Avenue, Wise, VA 24293. *Phone:* 276-328-0322. *Toll-free phone:* 888-282-9324. *Fax:* 276-328-0251. *E-mail:* admissions@uvawise.edu.

Virginia Baptist College

Fredericksburg, Virginia

http://www.vbc.edu/

CONTACT
Virginia Baptist College, 4111 Plank Road, Fredericksburg, VA 22407.

Virginia Commonwealth University
Richmond, Virginia
http://www.vcu.edu/

- **State-supported** university, founded 1838
- **Urban** 174-acre campus
- **Endowment** $147.3 million
- **Coed** 24,058 undergraduate students, 85% full-time, 60% women, 40% men
- 77% of applicants were admitted

UNDERGRAD STUDENTS
20,508 full-time, 3,550 part-time. Students come from 44 states and territories; 80 other countries; 7% are from out of state; 19% Black or African American, non-Hispanic/Latino; 10% Hispanic/Latino; 14% Asian, non-Hispanic/Latino; 0.1% Native Hawaiian or other Pacific Islander, non-Hispanic/Latino; 0.2% American Indian or Alaska Native, non-Hispanic/Latino; 7% Two or more races, non-Hispanic/Latino; 3% Race/ethnicity unknown; 3% international; 7% transferred in; 28% live on campus.

Freshmen:
Admission: 16,847 applied, 12,901 admitted, 4,543 enrolled. ***Average high school GPA:*** 3.7. ***Test scores:*** SAT evidence-based reading and writing scores over 500: 93%; SAT math scores over 500: 88%; ACT scores over 18: 94%; SAT evidence-based reading and writing scores over 600: 50%; SAT math scores over 600: 33%; ACT scores over 24: 56%; SAT evidence-based reading and writing scores over 700: 9%; SAT math scores over 700: 7%; ACT scores over 30: 16%.

Retention: 85% of full-time freshmen returned.

FACULTY
Total: 2,158, 59% full-time.

Student/faculty ratio: 18:1.

ACADEMICS
Calendar: semesters. *Degrees:* certificates, bachelor's, master's, doctoral, post-master's, and postbachelor's certificates.

Special study options: academic remediation for entering students, accelerated degree program, adult/continuing education programs, advanced placement credit, cooperative education, distance learning, double majors, English as a second language, freshman honors college, honors programs, independent study, internships, off-campus study, part-time degree program, services for LD students, student-designed majors, study abroad, summer session for credit. ***ROTC:*** Army (c).

Computers: 2,500 computers/terminals and 90,000 ports are available on campus for general student use. Students can access the following: campus intranet, computer help desk, free student e-mail accounts, online (class) grades, online (class) registration, online (class) schedules. Campuswide network is available. 100% of college-owned or -operated housing units are wired for high-speed Internet access. Wireless service is available via entire campus.
Library: Cabell Library and Thompkins McCaw Library plus 3 others. *Databases:* 500. Weekly public service hours: 146; study areas open 24 hours, 5–7 days a week; students can reserve study rooms.

STUDENT LIFE
Housing options: coed. Campus housing is university owned. Freshman applicants given priority for college housing.

Activities and organizations: drama/theater group, student-run newspaper, radio and television station, choral group, national fraternities, national sororities.

Athletics Member NCAA. All Division I. ***Intercollegiate sports:*** baseball M(s), basketball M(s)/W(s), cross-country running M(s)/W(s), field hockey W(s), golf M(s), lacrosse W(s), soccer M(s)/W(s), tennis M(s)/W(s), track and field M(s)/W(s), volleyball W(s). ***Intramural sports:*** badminton M(c)/W(c), baseball M(c), basketball M(c)/W(c), bowling M(c)/W(c), equestrian sports M(c)/W(c), fencing W(c), field hockey M(c), ice hockey M(c), lacrosse M(c)/W(c), rowing M(c)/W(c), rugby M(c)/W(c), soccer M(c)/W(c), softball W(c), swimming and diving M(c)/W(c), table tennis M(c)/W(c), tennis M(c)/W(c), triathlon M(c)/W(c), ultimate Frisbee M(c)/W(c), volleyball M(c)/W(c).

Campus security: 24-hour emergency response devices and patrols, student patrols, late-night transport/escort service, controlled dormitory access, security personnel in res. halls, RAD classes/special event coverage, more than 90 sworn officers and 200 security personnel.

Student services: health clinic, personal/psychological counseling, women's center, veterans affairs office.

COSTS & FINANCIAL AID
Costs (2018–19) ***Tuition:*** state resident $12,094 full-time, $417 per credit hour part-time; nonresident $32,742 full-time, $1129 per credit hour part-time. ***Required fees:*** $2396 full-time, $9 per credit hour part-time. ***Room and board:*** $10,428. Room and board charges vary according to board plan and housing facility. ***Payment plan:*** installment. ***Waivers:*** employees or children of employees.

Financial Aid Of all full-time matriculated undergraduates who enrolled in 2017, 14,326 applied for aid, 12,299 were judged to have need, 414 had their need fully met. 816 Federal Work-Study jobs (averaging $2230). 1 state and other part-time job (averaging $500). In 2017, 1471 non-need-based awards were made. ***Average percent of need met:*** 51. ***Average financial aid package:*** $12,040. ***Average need-based loan:*** $4338. ***Average need-based gift aid:*** $9775. ***Average non-need-based aid:*** $7368. ***Average indebtedness upon graduation:*** $32,617.

APPLYING
Standardized Tests *Required for some:* SAT or ACT (for admission).

Options: electronic application, early admission, deferred entrance.

Application fee: $65.

Required: high school transcript.

Notification: 11/1 (freshmen).

CONTACT
Ms. Sybil C. Halloran, Senior Associate Vice Provost of Strategic Enrollment Management, Virginia Commonwealth University, 901 West Franklin Street, Richmond, VA 23284-9005. *Phone:* 804-828-6125. *Toll-free phone:* 800-841-3638. *E-mail:* schallor@vcu.edu.

Virginia International University
Fairfax, Virginia
http://www.viu.edu/

CONTACT
Admissions Department, Virginia International University, 4401 Village Drive, Fairfax, VA 22030. *Phone:* 703-591-7042 Ext. 313. *Toll-free phone:* 800-514-6848. *Fax:* 703-591-7048. *E-mail:* admissions@viu.edu.

★ Virginia Military Institute
Lexington, Virginia
http://www.vmi.edu/

- **State-supported** 4-year, founded 1839
- **Small-town** 134-acre campus
- **Endowment** $381.9 million
- **Coed**
- **Moderately difficult** entrance level

FACULTY
Student/faculty ratio: 11:1.

ACADEMICS
Calendar: semesters. *Degree:* bachelor's.
Library: Preston Library. *Books:* 280,000 (physical), 240,000 (digital/electronic); *Databases:* 150. Weekly public service hours: 113.

STUDENT LIFE
Housing options: on-campus residence required through senior year; coed. Campus housing is university owned. Freshman campus housing is guaranteed.

Activities and organizations: drama/theater group, student-run newspaper, choral group, marching band, Newman Club, Officers Christian Fellowship, strength and fitness organizations, Promaji, Pre-Law Society.

Athletics Member NCAA. All Division I.

Campus security: 24-hour emergency response devices and patrols, student patrols.

Student services: health clinic, personal/psychological counseling.

COSTS & FINANCIAL AID

Costs (2018–19) ***Tuition:*** state resident $9284 full-time, $340 per credit hour part-time; nonresident $36,128 full-time, $1060 per credit hour part-time. ***Required fees:*** $9578 full-time, $72 per term part-time. ***Room and board:*** $9482.

Financial Aid Of all full-time matriculated undergraduates who enrolled in 2018, 1,155 applied for aid, 921 were judged to have need, 404 had their need fully met. In 2018, 167 non-need-based awards were made. ***Average percent of need met:*** 80. ***Average financial aid package:*** $26,987. ***Average need-based loan:*** $441. ***Average need-based gift aid:*** $12,636. ***Average non-need-based aid:*** $6747. ***Average indebtedness upon graduation:*** $31,893.

APPLYING

Standardized Tests *Required:* SAT or ACT (for admission).

Options: electronic application, early decision.

Application fee: $40.

Required: high school transcript. ***Recommended:*** essay or personal statement, 2 letters of recommendation, interview, statement of good standing from prior institution.

CONTACT

Office of Admissions, Virginia Military Institute, Lexington, VA 24450. *Phone:* 800-767-4207. *Toll-free phone:* 800-767-4207. *Fax:* 540-464-7746. *E-mail:* admissions@vmi.edu.

Virginia Polytechnic Institute and State University

Blacksburg, Virginia

http://www.vt.edu/

- **State-supported** university, founded 1872
- **Small-town** 2600-acre campus
- **Endowment** $1.1 billion
- **Coed** 27,811 undergraduate students, 98% full-time, 43% women, 57% men
- **Moderately difficult** entrance level, 65% of applicants were admitted

UNDERGRAD STUDENTS

27,180 full-time, 631 part-time. Students come from 48 states and territories; 86 other countries; 24% are from out of state; 4% Black or African American, non-Hispanic/Latino; 6% Hispanic/Latino; 10% Asian, non-Hispanic/Latino; 0.1% Native Hawaiian or other Pacific Islander, non-Hispanic/Latino; 0.1% American Indian or Alaska Native, non-Hispanic/Latino; 5% Two or more races, non-Hispanic/Latino; 3% Race/ethnicity unknown; 7% international; 4% transferred in; 33% live on campus.

Freshmen:

Admission: 31,936 applied, 20,709 admitted, 6,285 enrolled. ***Average high school GPA:*** 4.0. ***Test scores:*** SAT evidence-based reading and writing scores over 500: 99%; SAT math scores over 500: 99%; ACT scores over 18: 99%; SAT evidence-based reading and writing scores over 600: 75%; SAT math scores over 600: 73%; ACT scores over 24: 85%; SAT evidence-based reading and writing scores over 700: 17%; SAT math scores over 700: 30%; ACT scores over 30: 34%.

FACULTY

Total: 2,256, 82% full-time, 80% with terminal degrees.

Student/faculty ratio: 14:1.

ACADEMICS

Calendar: semesters. *Degrees:* bachelor's, master's, doctoral, post-master's, and postbachelor's certificates.

Special study options: accelerated degree program, adult/continuing education programs, advanced placement credit, cooperative education, distance learning, double majors, English as a second language, honors programs, independent study, internships, part-time degree program, services for LD students, study abroad, summer session for credit. ***ROTC:*** Army (b), Navy (b), Air Force (b).

Computers: Students can access the following: campus intranet, computer help desk, free student e-mail accounts, online (class) grades, online (class) registration, online (class) schedules. Campuswide network is available. Wireless service is available via entire campus.

Library: Newman Library plus 2 others. Study areas open 24 hours, 5–7 days a week.

STUDENT LIFE

Housing options: on-campus residence required for freshman year; coed, men-only, women-only, special housing for students with disabilities. Campus housing is university owned. Freshman campus housing is guaranteed.

Activities and organizations: drama/theater group, student-run newspaper, radio and television station, choral group, marching band, Virginia Tech Union, Student Government Association, International student organizations, national fraternities, national sororities.

Athletics Member NCAA. All Division I except football (Division I-A). ***Intercollegiate sports:*** baseball M, basketball M, cross-country running M/W, golf M(s), lacrosse W(s), soccer M(s)/W(s), swimming and diving M(s)/W(s), tennis M(s)/W(s), track and field M(s)/W(s), ultimate Frisbee M/W, volleyball W. ***Intramural sports:*** baseball M(c), basketball M, bowling M/W, crew M(c)/W(c), cross-country running M/W, equestrian sports M(c)/W(c), fencing M(c)/W(c), field hockey M(c)/W(c), football M/W, golf M/W, gymnastics M(c)/W(c), ice hockey M/W, lacrosse M(c)/W(c), racquetball M/W, riflery M(c)/W(c), rugby M(c)/W(c), soccer M/W, softball M/W, swimming and diving M/W, table tennis M/W, tennis M/W, volleyball M/W, water polo M/W.

Campus security: 24-hour emergency response devices and patrols, student patrols, late-night transport/escort service, controlled dormitory access.

Student services: health clinic, personal/psychological counseling, women's center, legal services, veterans affairs office.

COSTS & FINANCIAL AID

Costs (2018–19) ***Tuition:*** state resident $11,420 full-time, $476 per hour part-time; nonresident $29,104 full-time, $1213 per hour part-time. Full-time tuition and fees vary according to course load and program. Part-time tuition and fees vary according to course load and program. ***Required fees:*** $2200 full-time, $550 per term part-time. ***Room and board:*** $8934. Room and board charges vary according to board plan and housing facility. ***Payment plan:*** installment. ***Waivers:*** senior citizens.

Financial Aid Of all full-time matriculated undergraduates who enrolled in 2017, 16,636 applied for aid, 11,042 were judged to have need, 1,693 had their need fully met. In 2017, 2269 non-need-based awards were made. ***Average percent of need met:*** 56. ***Average financial aid package:*** $10,980. ***Average need-based loan:*** $4692. ***Average need-based gift aid:*** $7432. ***Average non-need-based aid:*** $3696. ***Average indebtedness upon graduation:*** $31,494. ***Financial aid deadline:*** 1/15.

APPLYING

Standardized Tests *Required:* SAT or ACT (for admission).

Options: electronic application, early admission, early decision, deferred entrance.

Application fee: $60.

Required: high school transcript. ***Recommended:*** essay or personal statement.

Application deadlines: 1/15 (freshmen), 2/15 (transfers), 12/1 (early action).

Early decision deadline: 11/1 (for plan 1), 12/15 (for plan 2).

Notification: 4/1 (freshmen), 5/1 (transfers), 2/22 (early action).

CONTACT

Mr. Juan P. Espinoza, Associated Vice Provost for Enrollment Management and Director of Undergraduate Admissions, Virginia Polytechnic Institute and State University, Blacksburg, VA 24061. *Phone:* 540-231-6267. *Fax:* 540-231-3242. *E-mail:* admissions@vt.edu.

Virginia State University

Petersburg, Virginia

http://www.vsu.edu/

CONTACT

Mr. Rodney Hall, Director of Enrollment Services, Virginia State University, Office of Admissions, Petersburg, VA 23806. *Phone:* 804-524-2954. *Toll-free phone:* 800-871-7611. *Fax:* 804-524-5055. *E-mail:* rhall@vsu.edu.

Virginia Union University

Richmond, Virginia

http://www.vuu.edu/

CONTACT
Ms. Danitra Morrison, Assistant Director of Admissions, Virginia Union University, 1500 North Lombardy Street, Richmond, VA 23220-1170. *Phone:* 804-257-5853. *Toll-free phone:* 800-368-3227. *Fax:* 804-342-3511. *E-mail:* dvmorrison@vuu.edu.

Virginia University of Lynchburg

Lynchburg, Virginia

http://www.vul.edu/

CONTACT
Ms. Cheryl Glass, Director of Admissions, Virginia University of Lynchburg, 2058 Garfield Avenue, Lynchburg, VA 24501. *Phone:* 434-528-5276 Ext. 106. *Fax:* 434-528-4275. *E-mail:* cglass@vul.edu.

Virginia Wesleyan University

Virginia Beach, Virginia

http://www.vwu.edu/

- **Independent United Methodist** comprehensive, founded 1961
- **Urban** 284-acre campus with easy access to Hampton Roads
- **Endowment** $56.6 million
- **Coed**
- **Moderately difficult** entrance level

FACULTY
Student/faculty ratio: 12:1.

ACADEMICS
Calendar: 4-1-4. *Degrees:* certificates, bachelor's, and master's.
Library: H. C. Hofheimer II Library plus 1 other. *Books:* 118,216 (physical), 256,770 (digital/electronic); *Serial titles:* 111 (physical), 71,260 (digital/electronic); *Databases:* 73. Weekly public service hours: 93; study areas open 24 hours, 5–7 days a week; students can reserve study rooms.

STUDENT LIFE
Housing options: on-campus residence required through senior year; coed, women-only, special housing for students with disabilities. Campus housing is university owned. Freshman campus housing is guaranteed.

Activities and organizations: drama/theater group, student-run newspaper, radio station, choral group, Wesleyan Activities Council, community service, Student Government Association, student newspaper, Black Student Union, national fraternities, national sororities.

Athletics Member NCAA. All Division III.

Campus security: 24-hour emergency response devices and patrols, late-night transport/escort service, controlled dormitory access, well-lit pathways.

Student services: health clinic, personal/psychological counseling, women's center, veterans affairs office.

COSTS & FINANCIAL AID
Costs (2018–19) ***One-time required fee:*** $1520. ***Comprehensive fee:*** $45,916 includes full-time tuition ($36,010), mandatory fees ($650), and room and board ($9256). Full-time tuition and fees vary according to course load. Part-time tuition: $1500 per credit hour. Part-time tuition and fees vary according to course load. ***Room and board:*** Room and board charges vary according to board plan and housing facility.

Financial Aid Of all full-time matriculated undergraduates who enrolled in 2017, 1,138 applied for aid, 1,138 were judged to have need, 147 had their need fully met. 192 Federal Work-Study jobs (averaging $1331). In 2017, 184 non-need-based awards were made. ***Average percent of need met:*** 63. ***Average financial aid package:*** $24,610. ***Average need-based loan:*** $6767. ***Average need-based gift aid:*** $22,042. ***Average non-need-based aid:*** $17,331. ***Average indebtedness upon graduation:*** $32,404.

APPLYING
Standardized Tests *Required:* SAT or ACT (for admission).

Options: electronic application.

Required: high school transcript. ***Required for some:*** interview. ***Recommended:*** letters of recommendation.

CONTACT
Ms. Elizabeth Clarke, Assistant Vice President for Enrollment, Virginia Wesleyan University, 5817 Wesleyan Drive, Virginia Beach, VA 23455. *Phone:* 757-455-3208. *Toll-free phone:* 800-737-8684. *Fax:* 757-461-5238. *E-mail:* admissions@vwu.edu.

Washington and Lee University

Lexington, Virginia

http://www.wlu.edu/

- **Independent** comprehensive, founded 1749
- **Small-town** 415-acre campus
- **Endowment** $1.5 billion
- **Coed** 1,827 undergraduate students, 100% full-time, 48% women, 52% men
- **Most difficult** entrance level, 22% of applicants were admitted

UNDERGRAD STUDENTS
1,823 full-time, 4 part-time. Students come from 50 states and territories; 33 other countries; 84% are from out of state; 2% Black or African American, non-Hispanic/Latino; 5% Hispanic/Latino; 3% Asian, non-Hispanic/Latino; 3% Two or more races, non-Hispanic/Latino; 0.7% Race/ethnicity unknown; 4% international; 0.2% transferred in; 75% live on campus.

Freshmen:
Admission: 5,455 applied, 1,200 admitted, 471 enrolled. ***Test scores:*** SAT evidence-based reading and writing scores over 500: 100%; ACT scores over 18: 100%; SAT evidence-based reading and writing scores over 600: 99%; ACT scores over 24: 100%; SAT evidence-based reading and writing scores over 700: 55%; ACT scores over 30: 90%.

Retention: 96% of full-time freshmen returned.

FACULTY
Total: 234, 87% full-time, 87% with terminal degrees.

Student/faculty ratio: 8:1.

ACADEMICS
Calendar: 4-4-2. *Degree:* bachelor's and doctoral.

Special study options: advanced placement credit, double majors, honors programs, independent study, internships, off-campus study, services for LD students, student-designed majors, study abroad. ***ROTC:*** Army (c).

Computers: 176 computers/terminals and 1,200 ports are available on campus for general student use. Students can access the following: campus intranet, computer help desk, free student e-mail accounts, online (class) grades, online (class) registration, online (class) schedules. Campuswide network is available. 100% of college-owned or -operated housing units are wired for high-speed Internet access. Wireless service is available via entire campus.
Library: James G. Leyburn Library plus 2 others. *Books:* 1.0 million (physical), 321,493 (digital/electronic); *Serial titles:* 66,967 (digital/electronic); *Databases:* 441. Study areas open 24 hours, 5–7 days a week; students can reserve study rooms.

STUDENT LIFE
Housing options: on-campus residence required through junior year; coed, men-only, women-only, special housing for students with disabilities. Campus housing is university owned. Freshman campus housing is guaranteed.

Activities and organizations: drama/theater group, student-run newspaper, radio and television station, choral group, Mock Convention, General Activities Board, Nabors Service League, Outing Club, Sports Clubs, national fraternities, national sororities.

Athletics Member NCAA. All Division III except golf (Division II). ***Intercollegiate sports:*** baseball M, basketball M/W, cross-country running M/W, equestrian sports M/W, field hockey W, football M, golf M/W, lacrosse M/W, rugby M(c), soccer M/W, swimming and diving M/W, tennis M/W, track and field M/W, volleyball W, wrestling M. ***Intramural sports:*** badminton M/W, baseball M(c), cheerleading M/W, equestrian sports W(c), golf M/W, ice hockey M(c), rock climbing M(c)/W(c), table tennis M/W, tennis M/W, track and field M/W, ultimate Frisbee M/W, volleyball W.

Campus security: 24-hour emergency response devices and patrols, late-night transport/escort service, controlled dormitory access, Emergency Alert System.

Student services: health clinic, personal/psychological counseling.

COSTS & FINANCIAL AID

Costs (2018–19) ***Comprehensive fee:*** $66,380 includes full-time tuition ($51,420), mandatory fees ($1035), and room and board ($13,925). Full-time tuition and fees vary according to degree level. Part-time tuition: $1714 per credit hour. Part-time tuition and fees vary according to degree level. ***College room only:*** $7300. Room and board charges vary according to board plan. ***Waivers:*** employees or children of employees.

Financial Aid Of all full-time matriculated undergraduates who enrolled in 2018, 887 applied for aid, 835 were judged to have need, 835 had their need fully met. 238 Federal Work-Study jobs (averaging $2000). 409 state and other part-time jobs (averaging $2000). In 2018, 134 non-need-based awards were made. ***Average percent of need met:*** 100. ***Average financial aid package:*** $53,443. ***Average need-based loan:*** $871. ***Average need-based gift aid:*** $46,849. ***Average non-need-based aid:*** $40,050. ***Average indebtedness upon graduation:*** $21,758. ***Financial aid deadline:*** 2/15.

APPLYING

Standardized Tests *Required:* SAT or ACT (for admission).

Options: electronic application, early decision, deferred entrance.

Application fee: $60.

Required: high school transcript, 3 letters of recommendation. ***Recommended:*** essay or personal statement, interview.

Application deadlines: 1/1 (freshmen), 4/1 (transfers).

Early decision deadline: 11/1.

Notification: 4/1 (freshmen), continuous (transfers), 12/22 (early decision).

CONTACT

Sally S. Richmond, Vice President for Admissions and Financial Aid, Washington and Lee University, 204 West Washington Street, Lexington, VA 24450-2116. *Phone:* 540-458-8710. *Fax:* 540-458-8062. *E-mail:* admissions@wlu.edu.

WASHINGTON

Antioch University Seattle

Seattle, Washington

http://www.antioch.edu/seattle/

CONTACT

Admissions Office, Antioch University Seattle, 2400 3rd Avenue, Suite 200, Seattle, WA 98121. *Phone:* 206-268-4202. *Toll-free phone:* 888-268-4477. *E-mail:* admissions@antiochseattle.edu.

Argosy University, Seattle

Seattle, Washington

http://www.argosy.edu/locations/seattle/

CONTACT

Argosy University, Seattle, 2601-A Elliott Avenue, Seattle, WA 98121. *Phone:* 206-283-4500. *Toll-free phone:* 866-283-2777.

The Art Institute of Seattle

Seattle, Washington

http://www.artinstitutes.edu/seattle/

CONTACT

The Art Institute of Seattle, 2323 Elliott Avenue, Seattle, WA 98121-1642. *Phone:* 206-448-6600. *Toll-free phone:* 800-275-2471.

Bastyr University

Kenmore, Washington

http://www.bastyr.edu/

CONTACT

Ms. Lauren Marani, Assistant Director of Admissions, Bastyr University, 14500 Juanita Drive NE, Kenmore, WA 98028-4966. *Phone:* 425-602-1300. *Fax:* 425-602-3090. *E-mail:* admissions@bastyr.edu.

Bellevue College

Bellevue, Washington

http://www.bellevuecollege.edu/

CONTACT

Morenika Jacobs, Associate Dean of Enrollment Services, Bellevue College, 3000 Landerholm Circle, SE, Bellevue, WA 98007-6484. *Phone:* 425-564-2205. *Fax:* 425-564-4065.

Cascadia College

Bothell, Washington

http://www.cascadia.edu/

CONTACT

Ms. Erin Blakeney, Dean for Student Success, Cascadia College, 18345 Campus Way, NE, Bothell, WA 98011. *Phone:* 425-352-8000. *Fax:* 425-352-8137. *E-mail:* admissions@cascadia.edu.

Central Washington University

Ellensburg, Washington

http://www.cwu.edu/

- **State-supported** comprehensive, founded 1891
- **Small-town** 380-acre campus with easy access to Seattle
- **Endowment** $5.7 million
- **Coed** 14,427 undergraduate students, 70% full-time, 53% women, 47% men
- **Moderately difficult** entrance level, 64% of applicants were admitted

UNDERGRAD STUDENTS

10,101 full-time, 4,326 part-time. 8% are from out of state; 4% Black or African American, non-Hispanic/Latino; 16% Hispanic/Latino; 4% Asian, non-Hispanic/Latino; 0.9% Native Hawaiian or other Pacific Islander, non-Hispanic/Latino; 0.5% American Indian or Alaska Native, non-Hispanic/Latino; 8% Two or more races, non-Hispanic/Latino; 13% Race/ethnicity unknown; 3% international; 9% transferred in; 31% live on campus.

Freshmen:

Admission: 12,320 applied, 7,932 admitted, 2,274 enrolled. ***Average high school GPA:*** 3.1. ***Test scores:*** SAT evidence-based reading and writing scores over 500: 62%; SAT math scores over 500: 61%; ACT scores over 18: 57%; SAT evidence-based reading and writing scores over 600: 13%; SAT math scores over 600: 17%; ACT scores over 24: 20%; SAT evidence-based reading and writing scores over 700: 1%; SAT math scores over 700: 1%; ACT scores over 30: 2%.

Retention: 69% of full-time freshmen returned.

FACULTY

Total: 678, 62% full-time, 59% with terminal degrees.

Student/faculty ratio: 18:1.

ACADEMICS

Calendar: quarters. *Degrees:* certificates, bachelor's, master's, post-master's, and postbachelor's certificates.

Special study options: academic remediation for entering students, advanced placement credit, cooperative education, distance learning, double majors, English as a second language, freshman honors college, honors programs, independent study, internships, off-campus study, part-time degree program, services for LD students, student-designed majors, study abroad, summer session for credit. ***ROTC:*** Army (b), Air Force (b).

Computers: 791 computers/terminals and 3,100 ports are available on campus for general student use. Students can access the following: campus intranet, computer help desk, free student e-mail accounts, online

(class) grades, online (class) registration, online (class) schedules, online data storage, office software. Campuswide network is available. 100% of college-owned or -operated housing units are wired for high-speed Internet access. Wireless service is available via entire campus.
Library: James E. Brooks Library plus 2 others. *Books:* 900,981 (physical), 251,073 (digital/electronic); *Serial titles:* 327 (physical), 72,453 (digital/electronic); *Databases:* 112. Weekly public service hours: 101; students can reserve study rooms.

STUDENT LIFE
Housing options: on-campus residence required for freshman year; coed, special housing for students with disabilities. Campus housing is university owned. Freshman campus housing is guaranteed.

Activities and organizations: drama/theater group, student-run newspaper, radio and television station, choral group, marching band, SISTERS, Brother 2 Brother, Cosplay, Alpha Kappa Si, Society of Human Resource Management.

Athletics Member NCAA. All Division II. ***Intercollegiate sports:*** archery M(c)/W(c), baseball M(s), basketball M(s)/W(s), bowling M(c)/W(c), cheerleading M/W, cross-country running M(s)/W(s), equestrian sports M(c)/W(c), fencing M(c)/W(c), football M(s), golf M(c), ice hockey M(c)/W(c), lacrosse M(c)/W(c), rock climbing M(c)/W(c), rugby M(s)/W(s), soccer M(c)/W(s), softball W(s), swimming and diving M(c)/W(c), tennis M(c)/W(c), track and field M(s)/W(s), ultimate Frisbee M(c)/W(c), volleyball W(s), water polo M(c)/W(c), wrestling M(c)/W(c). ***Intramural sports:*** badminton M/W, basketball M/W, rock climbing M/W, skiing (cross-country) M/W, soccer M/W, softball M/W, table tennis M/W, tennis M/W, volleyball M/W.

Campus security: 24-hour emergency response devices and patrols, late-night transport/escort service, controlled dormitory access, alert update system: emergency notification across digital platforms, Rape Aggression Defense System: realistic self-defense for women.

Student services: health clinic, personal/psychological counseling, veterans affairs office.

COSTS & FINANCIAL AID
Costs (2019–20) ***Tuition:*** area resident $6170 full-time; state resident $6170 full-time; nonresident $21,151 full-time. ***Required fees:*** $1191 full-time. ***Room and board:*** $13,066; room only: $5783.

Financial Aid Of all full-time matriculated undergraduates who enrolled in 2017, 7,667 applied for aid, 6,497 were judged to have need, 237 had their need fully met. In 2017, 8 non-need-based awards were made. ***Average percent of need met:*** 57. ***Average financial aid package:*** $10,533. ***Average need-based loan:*** $3714. ***Average need-based gift aid:*** $3640. ***Average non-need-based aid:*** $1156. ***Average indebtedness upon graduation:*** $22,900.

APPLYING
Standardized Tests *Required:* SAT or ACT (for admission).

Options: electronic application.

Application fee: $50.

Required: high school transcript, minimum 2.0 GPA. ***Required for some:*** essay or personal statement, interview.

Application deadlines: rolling (out-of-state freshmen), 3/1 (transfers).

Notification: continuous (freshmen), continuous (out-of-state freshmen), continuous (transfers).

CONTACT
Ms. Sharon O'Hare, Vice President of Strategic Enrollment Management, Central Washington University, 400 East University Way, Ellensburg, WA 98926-7463. *Phone:* 509-963-1211. *Fax:* 509-963-3065. *E-mail:* admissions@cwu.edu.

Charter College

Vancouver, Washington

http://www.chartercollege.edu/

CONTACT
Charter College, 17720 SE Mill Plain Boulevard, Suite 170, Vancouver, WA 98683.

City University of Seattle

Seattle, Washington

http://www.cityu.edu/

CONTACT
Student Services Center, City University of Seattle, 11900 NE First Street, Bellevue, WA 98005. *Phone:* 888-422-4898. *Toll-free phone:* 800-426-5596. *E-mail:* info@cityu.edu.

Clark College

Vancouver, Washington

http://www.clark.edu/

- **State-supported** primarily 2-year, founded 1933, part of Washington State Board for Community and Technical Colleges
- **Urban** 101-acre campus with easy access to Portland
- **Endowment** $61.0 million
- **Coed**
- **Noncompetitive** entrance level

FACULTY
Student/faculty ratio: 24:1.

ACADEMICS
Calendar: quarters. *Degrees:* certificates, diplomas, associate, and bachelor's.
Library: Lewis D. Cannell Library. Students can reserve study rooms.

STUDENT LIFE
Housing options: college housing not available.

Activities and organizations: drama/theater group, student-run newspaper, choral group.

Campus security: 24-hour patrols, late-night transport/escort service, security staff during hours of operation.

Student services: health clinic, personal/psychological counseling, legal services, veterans affairs office.

COSTS
Costs (2018–19) ***Tuition:*** state resident $4287 full-time, $113 per credit hour part-time; nonresident $9718 full-time, $291 per credit hour part-time. Full-time tuition and fees vary according to course level, course load, degree level, program, and reciprocity agreements. Part-time tuition and fees vary according to course level, course load, degree level, program, and reciprocity agreements.

APPLYING
Options: electronic application, early admission, deferred entrance.

Application fee: $25.

CONTACT
Ms. Vanessa Watkins, Associate Director of Entry Services, Clark College, Vancouver, WA 98663. *Phone:* 360-992-2308. *Fax:* 360-992-2867. *E-mail:* admissions@clark.edu.

Cornish College of the Arts

Seattle, Washington

http://www.cornish.edu/

- **Independent** 4-year, founded 1914
- **Urban** 4-acre campus with easy access to Seattle
- **Coed**
- **Moderately difficult** entrance level

FACULTY
Student/faculty ratio: 6:1.

ACADEMICS
Calendar: semesters. *Degrees:* bachelor's and postbachelor's certificates.
Library: Cornish Library. *Books:* 30,000 (physical), 130,000 (digital/electronic).

STUDENT LIFE
Housing options: on-campus residence required for freshman year; coed. Campus housing is university owned. Freshman campus housing is guaranteed.

Activities and organizations: drama/theater group, choral group, Student Leadership Council, Black Student Alliance, Sigma Alpha Phi, AIGA, Cheese Tasting.

Campus security: 24-hour emergency response devices and patrols, late-night transport/escort service, controlled dormitory access.

Student services: personal/psychological counseling.

COSTS & FINANCIAL AID
Costs (2018–19) ***Comprehensive fee:*** $53,142 includes full-time tuition ($40,442), mandatory fees ($1200), and room and board ($11,500). Full-time tuition and fees vary according to course load and program. Part-time tuition: $1686 per credit hour. Part-time tuition and fees vary according to course load. ***Required fees:*** $600 per term part-time. ***College room only:*** $8400. Room and board charges vary according to board plan and housing facility.

Financial Aid Of all full-time matriculated undergraduates who enrolled in 2015, 629 applied for aid, 559 were judged to have need, 45 had their need fully met. In 2015, 142 non-need-based awards were made. ***Average percent of need met:*** 59. ***Average financial aid package:*** $24,566. ***Average need-based loan:*** $4930. ***Average need-based gift aid:*** $18,098. ***Average non-need-based aid:*** $9626. ***Average indebtedness upon graduation:*** $37,686.

APPLYING
Standardized Tests *Recommended:* SAT or ACT (for admission).

Options: electronic application, early action, deferred entrance.

Application fee: $60.

Required: essay or personal statement, high school transcript, minimum 2.5 GPA, portfolio or audition. ***Required for some:*** 2 letters of recommendation. ***Recommended:*** 2 letters of recommendation, interview.

CONTACT
Ms. Sharron Starling, Director of Admissions, Cornish College of the Arts, 1000 Lenora Street, Seattle, WA 98121. *Phone:* 206-726-5017. *Toll-free phone:* 800-726-ARTS. *Fax:* 206-720-1011. *E-mail:* admissions@cornish.edu.

DigiPen Institute of Technology
Redmond, Washington
http://www.digipen.edu/

- **Proprietary** comprehensive, founded 1988
- **Suburban** 3-acre campus with easy access to Seattle
- **Coed** 1,064 undergraduate students, 93% full-time, 23% women, 77% men
- **Minimally difficult** entrance level, 57% of applicants were admitted

UNDERGRAD STUDENTS
991 full-time, 73 part-time. 50% are from out of state; 0.9% Black or African American, non-Hispanic/Latino; 6% Hispanic/Latino; 7% Asian, non-Hispanic/Latino; 0.3% Native Hawaiian or other Pacific Islander, non-Hispanic/Latino; 0.3% American Indian or Alaska Native, non-Hispanic/Latino; 6% Two or more races, non-Hispanic/Latino; 20% Race/ethnicity unknown; 10% international; 9% transferred in.

Freshmen:
Admission: 669 applied, 379 admitted, 218 enrolled.

Retention: 70% of full-time freshmen returned.

FACULTY
Total: 172, 40% full-time, 29% with terminal degrees.

Student/faculty ratio: 11:1.

ACADEMICS
Calendar: semesters. *Degrees:* bachelor's and master's.

Special study options: academic remediation for entering students, accelerated degree program, advanced placement credit, cooperative education, English as a second language, independent study, internships, services for LD students, summer session for credit.

Computers: 1,040 computers/terminals are available on campus for general student use. Students can access the following: campus intranet, computer help desk, free student e-mail accounts, online (class) grades, online (class) registration, online (class) schedules. Campuswide network is available. 100% of college-owned or -operated housing units are wired for high-speed Internet access. Wireless service is available via entire campus.

Library: DigiPen Library. *Books:* 5,946 (physical), 196,396 (digital/electronic); *Serial titles:* 36 (physical), 6,756 (digital/electronic); *Databases:* 11. Weekly public service hours: 84.

STUDENT LIFE
Housing options: coed, men-only, women-only, special housing for students with disabilities. Campus housing is leased by the school and is provided by a third party. Freshman applicants given priority for college housing.

Activities and organizations: choral group, PRISM Club, Cage of the Week Club, Halo Club, Outbreak Club, Wellness Club.

Campus security: 24-hour patrols, late-night transport/escort service, controlled dormitory access, on-site security during campus hours.

Student services: personal/psychological counseling.

COSTS & FINANCIAL AID
Costs (2019–20) ***One-time required fee:*** $150. ***Tuition:*** $32,400 full-time, $1045 per credit part-time. ***Required fees:*** $200 full-time. ***Room only:*** $7500.

Financial Aid Of all full-time matriculated undergraduates who enrolled in 2018, 592 applied for aid, 512 were judged to have need. 22 Federal Work-Study jobs (averaging $2000). In 2018, 10 non-need-based awards were made. ***Average percent of need met:*** 24. ***Average financial aid package:*** $7966. ***Average need-based loan:*** $3695. ***Average need-based gift aid:*** $7860. ***Average non-need-based aid:*** $6028. ***Average indebtedness upon graduation:*** $28,539.

APPLYING
Standardized Tests *Required for some:* SAT or ACT (for admission).

Options: electronic application, deferred entrance.

Application fee: $60.

Required: essay or personal statement, high school transcript, minimum 2.5 GPA. ***Required for some:*** pre-calculus for Bachelor of Science, art portfolio for BFA in Digital Art and Animation, performance portfolio for BA in Music and Sound Design, design portfolio for Bachelor of Art in Game Design. ***Recommended:*** 2 letters of recommendation.

Application deadlines: rolling (freshmen), rolling (transfers).

Notification: continuous (freshmen), continuous (transfers).

CONTACT
Ms. Emily Kirby, Director of Admissions, DigiPen Institute of Technology, 9931 Willows Road NE, Redmond, WA 98052. *Phone:* 425-629-4862. *Toll-free phone:* 866-478-5236. *Fax:* 425-558-0378. *E-mail:* admissions@digipen.edu.

Eastern Washington University
Cheney, Washington
http://www.ewu.edu/

- **State-supported** comprehensive, founded 1882
- **Suburban** 335-acre campus with easy access to Spokane
- **Coed** 11,410 undergraduate students, 87% full-time, 54% women, 46% men
- 63% of applicants were admitted

UNDERGRAD STUDENTS
9,912 full-time, 1,498 part-time. 6% are from out of state; 4% Black or African American, non-Hispanic/Latino; 17% Hispanic/Latino; 3% Asian, non-Hispanic/Latino; 0.3% Native Hawaiian or other Pacific Islander, non-Hispanic/Latino; 1% American Indian or Alaska Native, non-Hispanic/Latino; 7% Two or more races, non-Hispanic/Latino; 3% Race/ethnicity unknown; 4% international; 10% transferred in; 17% live on campus.

Freshmen:
Admission: 8,367 applied, 5,310 admitted, 1,758 enrolled. ***Average high school GPA:*** 3.2. ***Test scores:*** SAT evidence-based reading and writing scores over 500: 51%; SAT math scores over 500: 63%; ACT scores over 18: 68%; SAT evidence-based reading and writing scores over 600: 8%; SAT math scores over 600: 24%; ACT scores over 24: 18%; SAT evidence-based reading and writing scores over 700: 1%; SAT math scores over 700: 1%; ACT scores over 30: 3%.

Retention: 74% of full-time freshmen returned.

FACULTY
Total: 730, 65% full-time, 46% with terminal degrees.

Student/faculty ratio: 21:1.

ACADEMICS
Calendar: quarters. *Degrees:* certificates, bachelor's, master's, doctoral, and postbachelor's certificates.

Special study options: academic remediation for entering students, accelerated degree program, adult/continuing education programs, advanced placement credit, cooperative education, distance learning, double majors, English as a second language, honors programs, independent study, internships, off-campus study, part-time degree program, services for LD students, student-designed majors, study abroad, summer session for credit. ***ROTC:*** Army (b).

Unusual degree programs: 3-2 exercise science/occupational therapy, therapeutic recreation, interdisciplinary studies.

Computers: Students can access the following: campus intranet, computer help desk, free student e-mail accounts, online (class) grades, online (class) registration, online (class) schedules, network disk storage; discounted software; laptops, still and video cameras, projectors for checkout; print credit; black white laser, color laser, and color photo options, large format print service. Campuswide network is available. 100% of college-owned or -operated housing units are wired for high-speed Internet access. Wireless service is available via entire campus.
Library: John F. Kennedy Library. Students can reserve study rooms.

STUDENT LIFE
Housing options: on-campus residence required for freshman year; coed, special housing for students with disabilities. Campus housing is university owned. Freshman campus housing is guaranteed.

Activities and organizations: drama/theater group, student-run newspaper, radio station, choral group, marching band, national fraternities, national sororities.

Athletics Member NCAA. All Division I except football (Division I-AA). ***Intercollegiate sports:*** archery M(c)/W(c), baseball M(c), basketball M(s)/W(s), cheerleading W(c), cross-country running M(s)/W(s), equestrian sports M(c)/W(c), fencing M(c)/W(c), golf W(s)(c), ice hockey M(c)/W(c), rugby M(c)/W(c), soccer M(c)/W(s), softball W(c), tennis M(s)/W(s), track and field M(s)/W(s), volleyball W(s). ***Intramural sports:*** baseball M/W, basketball M/W, bowling M/W, cross-country running M/W, football M/W, golf W, racquetball M/W, soccer M/W, softball M/W, tennis M/W, track and field M/W, ultimate Frisbee M(c)/W(c), volleyball M/W, wrestling M(c)/W(c).

Campus security: 24-hour emergency response devices and patrols, student patrols, late-night transport/escort service, controlled dormitory access.

Student services: health clinic, personal/psychological counseling, women's center.

COSTS & FINANCIAL AID
Costs (2019–20) ***Tuition:*** area resident $6522 full-time; state resident $6522 full-time, $218 per credit hour part-time; nonresident $24,018 full-time, $801 per credit hour part-time. ***Required fees:*** $939 full-time. ***Room and board:*** $12,708; room only: $7260.

Financial Aid Of all full-time matriculated undergraduates who enrolled in 2017, 7,534 applied for aid, 6,410 were judged to have need, 390 had their need fully met. 193 Federal Work-Study jobs (averaging $3072). 149 state and other part-time jobs (averaging $3237). In 2017, 543 non-need-based awards were made. ***Average percent of need met:*** 59. ***Average financial aid package:*** $13,581. ***Average need-based loan:*** $4128. ***Average need-based gift aid:*** $8360. ***Average non-need-based aid:*** $4203. ***Average indebtedness upon graduation:*** $24,877.

APPLYING
Standardized Tests *Required:* SAT or ACT (for admission).

Application fee: $60.

Required: high school transcript, minimum 2.0 GPA. ***Required for some:*** essay or personal statement. ***Recommended:*** minimum 3.0 GPA.

CONTACT
Jana Jaraysi, Director of Recruitment, Eastern Washington University, 304 Sutton Hall, Cheney, WA 99004-2447. *Phone:* 509-359-2450. *Fax:* 509-359-6692. *E-mail:* admissions@ewu.edu.

The Evergreen State College
Olympia, Washington
http://www.evergreen.edu/

- **State-supported** comprehensive, founded 1967, part of Washington State Public Baccalaureate Institution
- **Rural** 1000-acre campus with easy access to Seattle
- **Endowment** $13.4 million
- **Coed** 3,018 undergraduate students, 92% full-time, 58% women, 42% men
- **Moderately difficult** entrance level, 95% of applicants were admitted

UNDERGRAD STUDENTS
2,781 full-time, 237 part-time. Students come from 42 states and territories; 11 other countries; 18% are from out of state; 5% Black or African American, non-Hispanic/Latino; 12% Hispanic/Latino; 3% Asian, non-Hispanic/Latino; 0.5% Native Hawaiian or other Pacific Islander, non-Hispanic/Latino; 3% American Indian or Alaska Native, non-Hispanic/Latino; 7% Two or more races, non-Hispanic/Latino; 5% Race/ethnicity unknown; 0.2% international; 14% transferred in; 23% live on campus.

Freshmen:
Admission: 1,194 applied, 1,137 admitted, 309 enrolled. ***Average high school GPA:*** 3.1. ***Test scores:*** SAT evidence-based reading and writing scores over 500: 85%; SAT math scores over 500: 63%; ACT scores over 18: 87%; SAT evidence-based reading and writing scores over 600: 44%; SAT math scores over 600: 20%; ACT scores over 24: 50%; SAT evidence-based reading and writing scores over 700: 7%; SAT math scores over 700: 2%; ACT scores over 30: 14%.

Retention: 66% of full-time freshmen returned.

FACULTY
Total: 190, 71% full-time, 82% with terminal degrees.

Student/faculty ratio: 21:1.

ACADEMICS
Calendar: quarters. *Degrees:* bachelor's and master's.

Special study options: accelerated degree program, advanced placement credit, double majors, independent study, internships, off-campus study, part-time degree program, services for LD students, student-designed majors, study abroad, summer session for credit.

Computers: 556 computers/terminals are available on campus for general student use. Students can access the following: campus intranet, computer help desk, free student e-mail accounts, online (class) grades, online (class) registration, online (class) schedules, online payment, student accounts history, financial aid records, academic history, housing application, evaluations. Campuswide network is available. 100% of college-owned or -operated housing units are wired for high-speed Internet access. Wireless service is available via entire campus.
Library: Daniel J. Evans Library. *Books:* 377,812 (physical), 216,358 (digital/electronic); *Serial titles:* 69 (physical), 73,705 (digital/electronic); *Databases:* 103. Weekly public service hours: 77; students can reserve study rooms.

STUDENT LIFE
Housing options: coed, special housing for students with disabilities. Campus housing is university owned. Freshman campus housing is guaranteed.

Activities and organizations: drama/theater group, student-run newspaper, radio and television station, choral group, Flaming Eggplant, Geoduck Student Union, Cooper Point Journal, Gaming Guild, Myco-Collective.

Athletics Member NCAA, NAIA. All NCAA Division II. ***Intercollegiate sports:*** basketball M(s)/W(s), soccer M(s)/W(s), track and field M/W, volleyball W(s). ***Intramural sports:*** archery M(c)/W(c), badminton M/W, basketball M/W, crew M(c)/W(c), fencing M(c)/W(c), rock climbing M(c)/W(c), sailing M(c)/W(c), skiing (downhill) M(c)/W(c), soccer M/W, volleyball M/W.

Campus security: 24-hour emergency response devices and patrols, student patrols, late-night transport/escort service, controlled dormitory access, car lockouts, jump-starts.

Student services: health clinic, personal/psychological counseling, women's center, veterans affairs office.

COSTS & FINANCIAL AID

Costs (2018–19) ***Tuition:*** state resident $6825 full-time, $228 per credit hour part-time; nonresident $25,335 full-time, $845 per credit hour part-time. Full-time tuition and fees vary according to course load, location, and program. Part-time tuition and fees vary according to course load, location, and program. ***Required fees:*** $849 full-time, $9 per credit hour part-time, $15 per term part-time. ***Room and board:*** $11,346; room only: $8046. Room and board charges vary according to board plan, housing facility, location, and student level. ***Payment plan:*** installment. ***Waivers:*** senior citizens and employees or children of employees.

Financial Aid Of all full-time matriculated undergraduates who enrolled in 2017, 2,591 applied for aid, 2,277 were judged to have need, 106 had their need fully met. In 2017, 28 non-need-based awards were made. ***Average percent of need met:*** 64. ***Average financial aid package:*** $12,729. ***Average need-based loan:*** $4118. ***Average need-based gift aid:*** $10,009. ***Average non-need-based aid:*** $3182. ***Average indebtedness upon graduation:*** $19,763.

APPLYING

Standardized Tests *Required:* SAT or ACT (for admission).

Options: electronic application, deferred entrance.

Application fee: $50.

Required: high school transcript, minimum 2.0 GPA. ***Required for some:*** essay or personal statement.

Application deadlines: 2/1 (freshmen), 2/1 (transfers).

Notification: continuous until 11/1 (freshmen), continuous until 11/1 (transfers).

CONTACT

Eric Pedersen, Director of Admissions, The Evergreen State College, 2700 Evergreen Parkway, NW, Olympia, WA 98505. *Phone:* 360-867-6170. *Fax:* 360-867-5114. *E-mail:* admissions@evergreen.edu.

Faith International University

Tacoma, Washington

http://www.faithseminary.edu/

CONTACT

Faith International University, 3504 North Pearl Street, Tacoma, WA 98407. *Toll-free phone:* 888-777-7675.

Gonzaga University

Spokane, Washington

http://www.gonzaga.edu/

- **Independent Roman Catholic** university, founded 1887
- **Urban** 152-acre campus
- **Endowment** $276.0 million
- **Coed** 5,317 undergraduate students, 99% full-time, 53% women, 47% men
- **Moderately difficult** entrance level, 66% of applicants were admitted

UNDERGRAD STUDENTS

5,244 full-time, 73 part-time. Students come from 45 states and territories; 26 other countries; 52% are from out of state; 1% Black or African American, non-Hispanic/Latino; 11% Hispanic/Latino; 5% Asian, non-Hispanic/Latino; 0.3% Native Hawaiian or other Pacific Islander, non-Hispanic/Latino; 0.6% American Indian or Alaska Native, non-Hispanic/Latino; 6% Two or more races, non-Hispanic/Latino; 3% Race/ethnicity unknown; 1% international; 3% transferred in; 52% live on campus.

Freshmen:

Admission: 8,400 applied, 5,512 admitted, 1,197 enrolled. ***Average high school GPA:*** 3.8. ***Test scores:*** SAT evidence-based reading and writing scores over 500: 99%; SAT math scores over 500: 99%; ACT scores over 18: 99%; SAT evidence-based reading and writing scores over 600: 76%; SAT math scores over 600: 68%; ACT scores over 24: 87%; SAT evidence-based reading and writing scores over 700: 13%; SAT math scores over 700: 17%; ACT scores over 30: 29%.

Retention: 94% of full-time freshmen returned.

FACULTY

Total: 813, 56% full-time, 50% with terminal degrees.

Student/faculty ratio: 12:1.

ACADEMICS

Calendar: semesters. *Degrees:* bachelor's, master's, and doctoral.

Special study options: accelerated degree program, adult/continuing education programs, advanced placement credit, distance learning, double majors, English as a second language, honors programs, independent study, internships, off-campus study, part-time degree program, services for LD students, study abroad, summer session for credit. ***ROTC:*** Army (b).

Unusual degree programs: 3-2 business administration.

Computers: 500 computers/terminals and 900 ports are available on campus for general student use. Students can access the following: campus intranet, computer help desk, free student e-mail accounts, online (class) grades, online (class) registration, online (class) schedules. Campuswide network is available. 100% of college-owned or -operated housing units are wired for high-speed Internet access. Wireless service is available via entire campus.

Library: Ralph E. and Helen Higgins Foley Center plus 1 other. *Books:* 291,713 (physical), 76,847 (digital/electronic); *Serial titles:* 11,876 (physical), 60,184 (digital/electronic); *Databases:* 254. Weekly public service hours: 112; study areas open 24 hours, 5–7 days a week; students can reserve study rooms.

STUDENT LIFE

Housing options: on-campus residence required through sophomore year; coed, men-only, women-only, special housing for students with disabilities. Campus housing is university owned and leased by the school. Freshman campus housing is guaranteed.

Activities and organizations: drama/theater group, student-run newspaper, radio and television station, choral group, Student Body Association, Kennel Club, Search, Circle K, Encore.

Athletics Member NCAA. All Division I. ***Intercollegiate sports:*** baseball M(s), basketball M(s)/W(s), cross-country running M(s)/W(s), golf M(s)/W(s), rowing M(s)/W(s), soccer M(s)/W(s), tennis M(s)/W(s), track and field M(s)/W(s), volleyball W(s). ***Intramural sports:*** badminton M/W, basketball M/W, cheerleading M(c)/W(c), football M/W, golf M(c)/W(c), ice hockey M(c)/W(c), lacrosse M(c)/W(c), racquetball M/W, rugby M(c)/W(c), skiing (downhill) M(c)/W(c), soccer M(c)/W(c), softball M/W, swimming and diving M(c)/W(c), tennis M/W, track and field M(c)/W(c), triathlon M(c)/W(c), ultimate Frisbee M(c)/W(c), water polo M(c)/W(c), weight lifting M(c)/W(c), wrestling M.

Campus security: 24-hour emergency response devices and patrols, late-night transport/escort service, controlled dormitory access.

Student services: health clinic, personal/psychological counseling, veterans affairs office.

COSTS & FINANCIAL AID

Costs (2019–20) ***Comprehensive fee:*** $57,470 includes full-time tuition ($44,280), mandatory fees ($860), and room and board ($12,330). Part-time tuition: $1210 per credit. ***Required fees:*** $105 per term part-time. ***College room only:*** $6240.

Financial Aid Of all full-time matriculated undergraduates who enrolled in 2017, 3,490 applied for aid, 2,752 were judged to have need, 662 had their need fully met. 441 Federal Work-Study jobs (averaging $1978). 132 state and other part-time jobs (averaging $2274). In 2017, 720 non-need-based awards were made. ***Average percent of need met:*** 79. ***Average financial aid package:*** $30,171. ***Average need-based loan:*** $5929. ***Average need-based gift aid:*** $8490. ***Average non-need-based aid:*** $14,488. ***Average indebtedness upon graduation:*** $30,576.

APPLYING

Standardized Tests *Required:* SAT or ACT (for admission).

Options: electronic application, early action, deferred entrance.

Application fee: $50.

Required: essay or personal statement, high school transcript, 1 letter of recommendation. ***Recommended:*** interview.

Application deadlines: 2/1 (freshmen), 6/1 (transfers), 11/15 (early action).

Notification: 3/15 (freshmen), continuous (transfers), 1/15 (early action).

CONTACT

Ms. Julie McCulloh, Dean of Admission, Gonzaga University, 502 East Boone Avenue, Spokane, WA 99258-0102. *Phone:* 800-322-2584. *Toll-free phone:* 800-322-2584 Ext. 6572. *Fax:* 509-313-6572. *E-mail:* admissions@gonzaga.edu.

Heritage University

Toppenish, Washington

http://www.heritage.edu/

CONTACT
Olivia Gutierrez, Director of Admissions, Heritage University, 3240 Fort Road, Toppenish, WA 98948-9599. *Phone:* 509-865-8697. *Toll-free phone:* 888-272-6190. *Fax:* 509-865-4469. *E-mail:* admissions@heritage.edu.

Northwest College of Art & Design

Tacoma, Washington

http://www.ncad.edu/

- **Proprietary** 4-year, founded 1982
- **Urban** campus with easy access to Seattle
- **Coed** 104 undergraduate students, 100% full-time, 69% women, 31% men

UNDERGRAD STUDENTS
104 full-time. 6% Black or African American, non-Hispanic/Latino; 7% Hispanic/Latino; 11% Asian, non-Hispanic/Latino; 3% American Indian or Alaska Native, non-Hispanic/Latino; 6% Race/ethnicity unknown.

FACULTY
Total: 12.

Student/faculty ratio: 5:1.

ACADEMICS
Calendar: semesters. *Degree:* bachelor's.

Special study options: accelerated degree program, double majors, internships, services for LD students, summer session for credit.

Computers: 86 computers/terminals are available on campus for general student use. Students can access the following: campus intranet, computer help desk, online (class) grades, online (class) schedules. Campuswide network is available. Wireless service is available via entire campus.
Library: Northwest College of Art & Design Library plus 1 other. *Books:* 1,686 (physical); *Serial titles:* 366 (physical). Weekly public service hours: 40.

COSTS & FINANCIAL AID
Costs (2019–20) ***Tuition:*** $18,000 full-time, $765 per credit hour part-time. ***Required fees:*** $100 full-time, $100 per year part-time.

Financial Aid Of all full-time matriculated undergraduates who enrolled in 2016, 91 applied for aid, 91 were judged to have need, 72 had their need fully met. ***Average percent of need met:*** 63. ***Average financial aid package:*** $12,093. ***Average need-based loan:*** $7995. ***Average need-based gift aid:*** $10,549. ***Average non-need-based aid:*** $1413.

APPLYING
Required: essay or personal statement, high school transcript, interview, 5 piece portfolio.

CONTACT
Mrs. Ashley Miller, Admissions Representative, Northwest College of Art & Design, 1126 Pacific Avenue, Suite 101, Tacoma, WA 98402. *Phone:* 253-2721126. *Toll-free phone:* 800-769-ARTS. *Fax:* 253-5729058. *E-mail:* amiller@ncad.edu.

Northwest Indian College

Bellingham, Washington

http://www.nwic.edu/

CONTACT
Office of Admissions, Northwest Indian College, 2522 Kwina Road, Bellingham, WA 98226. *Phone:* 360-676-2772. *Toll-free phone:* 866-676-2772. *Fax:* 360-392-4333. *E-mail:* admissions@nwic.edu.

Northwest University

Kirkland, Washington

http://www.northwestu.edu/

- **Independent** comprehensive, founded 1934, affiliated with Assemblies of God
- **Suburban** 56-acre campus with easy access to Seattle
- **Endowment** $6.8 million
- **Coed**
- **Moderately difficult** entrance level

FACULTY
Student/faculty ratio: 14:1.

ACADEMICS
Calendar: semesters. *Degrees:* certificates, diplomas, associate, bachelor's, master's, and doctoral.
Library: Hurst Library. *Books:* 170,000 (physical); *Serial titles:* 7,000 (physical); *Databases:* 81. Weekly public service hours: 91; study areas open 24 hours, 5–7 days a week; students can reserve study rooms.

STUDENT LIFE
Housing options: on-campus residence required through sophomore year; men-only, women-only. Campus housing is university owned. Freshman campus housing is guaranteed.

Activities and organizations: drama/theater group, student-run newspaper, choral group, Student Ministries, Pursuit (worship service), Northwest University Business Club, Environmental Stewardship Club.

Athletics Member NAIA.

Campus security: 24-hour emergency response devices and patrols, late-night transport/escort service, controlled dormitory access.

Student services: health clinic, personal/psychological counseling.

COSTS & FINANCIAL AID
Costs (2018–19) ***Comprehensive fee:*** $40,170 includes full-time tuition ($31,100), mandatory fees ($440), and room and board ($8630). Full-time tuition and fees vary according to class time, course load, location, program, and reciprocity agreements. Part-time tuition: $1250 per credit hour. Part-time tuition and fees vary according to class time, course load, and location. ***Required fees:*** $120 per term part-time. ***College room only:*** $4315. Room and board charges vary according to housing facility and location.

Financial Aid Of all full-time matriculated undergraduates who enrolled in 2017, 1,116 applied for aid, 984 were judged to have need, 115 had their need fully met. 81 Federal Work-Study jobs (averaging $1821). 2 state and other part-time jobs (averaging $2396). In 2017, 172 non-need-based awards were made. ***Average percent of need met:*** 70. ***Average financial aid package:*** $18,885. ***Average need-based loan:*** $4012. ***Average need-based gift aid:*** $15,573. ***Average non-need-based aid:*** $10,813. ***Average indebtedness upon graduation:*** $24,930.

APPLYING
Standardized Tests *Required:* SAT or ACT (for admission).

Options: electronic application, early action, deferred entrance.

Application fee: $30.

Required: essay or personal statement, high school transcript, minimum 2.3 GPA, 2 letters of recommendation. ***Required for some:*** interview.

CONTACT
Andy Hall, Northwest University, 5520 108th Avenue NE, PO Box 579, Kirkland, WA 98083-0579. *Phone:* 425-889-5212. *Toll-free phone:* 800-669-3781. *Fax:* 425-889-5224. *E-mail:* admissions@northwestu.edu.

Olympic College

Bremerton, Washington

http://www.olympic.edu/

CONTACT
Ms. Nora Downard, Program Manager, Olympic College, 1600 Chester Avenue, Bremerton, WA 98337-1699. *Phone:* 360-475-7445. *Toll-free phone:* 800-259-6718. *Fax:* 360-475-7202. *E-mail:* ndownard@olympic.edu.

Pacific Lutheran University

Tacoma, Washington

http://www.plu.edu/

- **Independent** comprehensive, founded 1890, affiliated with Evangelical Lutheran Church in America
- **Suburban** 156-acre campus with easy access to Seattle
- **Endowment** $99.8 million
- **Coed** 2,769 undergraduate students, 98% full-time, 64% women, 36% men
- **Moderately difficult** entrance level, 80% of applicants were admitted

UNDERGRAD STUDENTS

2,712 full-time, 57 part-time. Students come from 43 states and territories; 26 other countries; 22% are from out of state; 4% Black or African American, non-Hispanic/Latino; 12% Hispanic/Latino; 10% Asian, non-Hispanic/Latino; 1% Native Hawaiian or other Pacific Islander, non-Hispanic/Latino; 0.6% American Indian or Alaska Native, non-Hispanic/Latino; 10% Two or more races, non-Hispanic/Latino; 1% Race/ethnicity unknown; 3% international; 6% transferred in; 44% live on campus.

Freshmen:

Admission: 3,740 applied, 2,984 admitted, 649 enrolled. ***Average high school GPA:*** 3.7. ***Test scores:*** SAT evidence-based reading and writing scores over 500: 91%; SAT math scores over 500: 90%; ACT scores over 18: 96%; SAT evidence-based reading and writing scores over 600: 46%; SAT math scores over 600: 37%; ACT scores over 24: 54%; SAT evidence-based reading and writing scores over 700: 8%; SAT math scores over 700: 6%; ACT scores over 30: 17%.

Retention: 83% of full-time freshmen returned.

FACULTY

Total: 269, 74% full-time, 77% with terminal degrees.

Student/faculty ratio: 15:1.

ACADEMICS

Calendar: 4-1-4. *Degrees:* certificates, bachelor's, master's, doctoral, and post-master's certificates.

Special study options: advanced placement credit, cooperative education, distance learning, double majors, English as a second language, honors programs, independent study, internships, part-time degree program, services for LD students, student-designed majors, study abroad, summer session for credit. ***ROTC:*** Army (b).

Unusual degree programs: 3-2 engineering with Columbia University (New York), Washington University in St. Louis.

Computers: 522 computers/terminals and 3,500 ports are available on campus for general student use. Students can access the following: campus intranet, computer help desk, free student e-mail accounts, online (class) grades, online (class) registration, online (class) schedules. Campuswide network is available. 100% of college-owned or -operated housing units are wired for high-speed Internet access. Wireless service is available via entire campus.

Library: Robert A. L. Mortvedt Library. *Books:* 222,754 (physical), 40,703 (digital/electronic); *Serial titles:* 34,315 (physical); *Databases:* 118. Weekly public service hours: 80; students can reserve study rooms.

STUDENT LIFE

Housing options: on-campus residence required through sophomore year; coed, women-only, special housing for students with disabilities. Campus housing is university owned. Freshman campus housing is guaranteed.

Activities and organizations: drama/theater group, student-run newspaper, radio and television station, choral group, Chemistry Club, Delta Iota Chi, Black Student Union, APISA, Na Hoaloha O Hawaii.

Athletics Member NCAA. All Division III. ***Intercollegiate sports:*** baseball M, basketball M/W, cheerleading W(c), cross-country running M/W, football M, golf M/W, lacrosse M(c)/W(c), rowing M(c)/W, soccer M/W, softball W, swimming and diving M/W, tennis M/W, track and field M/W, ultimate Frisbee M(c)/W(c), volleyball W, wrestling M(c)/W(c). ***Intramural sports:*** basketball M/W, soccer M/W, volleyball M/W, water polo M/W.

Campus security: 24-hour emergency response devices and patrols, student patrols, late-night transport/escort service, controlled dormitory access.

Student services: health clinic, personal/psychological counseling, women's center.

COSTS & FINANCIAL AID

Costs (2019–20) ***Comprehensive fee:*** $54,550 includes full-time tuition ($43,264), mandatory fees ($410), and room and board ($10,876). Part-time tuition: $1352 per credit hour. ***College room only:*** $4940.

Financial Aid Of all full-time matriculated undergraduates who enrolled in 2017, 2,183 applied for aid, 1,976 were judged to have need, 330 had their need fully met. In 2017, 110 non-need-based awards were made. ***Average percent of need met:*** 86. ***Average financial aid package:*** $32,319. ***Average need-based loan:*** $5443. ***Average need-based gift aid:*** $11,539. ***Average non-need-based aid:*** $13,122.

APPLYING

Standardized Tests *Required:* SAT or ACT (for admission).

Options: electronic application, deferred entrance.

Application fee: $40.

Required: essay or personal statement, high school transcript, 1 letter of recommendation. ***Required for some:*** interview. ***Recommended:*** minimum 2.5 GPA.

Application deadlines: rolling (freshmen), rolling (out-of-state freshmen), rolling (transfers).

Notification: continuous (freshmen), continuous (out-of-state freshmen), continuous (transfers).

CONTACT

Melody A. Ferguson, Director of Admission, Pacific Lutheran University, 12180 Park Avenue S., Tacoma, WA 98447. *Phone:* 253-535-7151. *Toll-free phone:* 800-274-6758. *Fax:* 253-536-5136. *E-mail:* admission@plu.edu.

Peninsula College

Port Angeles, Washington

http://www.pencol.edu/

CONTACT

Ms. Pauline Marvin, Peninsula College, 1502 East Lauridsen Boulevard, Port Angeles, WA 98362. *Phone:* 360-417-6596. *Toll-free phone:* 877-452-9277. *Fax:* 360-457-8100. *E-mail:* admissions@pencol.edu.

Pima Medical Institute

Seattle, Washington

http://www.pmi.edu/

CONTACT

Admissions Office, Pima Medical Institute, 9709 Third Avenue NE, Suite 400, Seattle, WA 98115. *Phone:* 206-322-6100. *Toll-free phone:* 800-477-PIMA.

Renton Technical College

Renton, Washington

http://www.rtc.edu/

- **State-supported** primarily 2-year, founded 1942, part of Washington State Board for Community and Technical Colleges
- **Suburban** 30-acre campus with easy access to Seattle
- **Endowment** $837,103
- **Coed** 3,546 undergraduate students, 35% full-time, 33% women, 67% men
- **Noncompetitive** entrance level

UNDERGRAD STUDENTS

1,245 full-time, 2,301 part-time. 16% Black or African American, non-Hispanic/Latino; 13% Hispanic/Latino; 19% Asian, non-Hispanic/Latino; 1% Native Hawaiian or other Pacific Islander, non-Hispanic/Latino; 0.5% American Indian or Alaska Native, non-Hispanic/Latino; 6% Two or more races, non-Hispanic/Latino; 6% Race/ethnicity unknown; 0.9% international.

FACULTY

Total: 242, 29% full-time.

Student/faculty ratio: 16:1.

ACADEMICS
Calendar: quarters. *Degrees:* certificates, diplomas, associate, and bachelor's.

Special study options: academic remediation for entering students, adult/continuing education programs, advanced placement credit, cooperative education, distance learning, English as a second language, internships, off-campus study, part-time degree program, services for LD students, summer session for credit.

Computers: 96 computers/terminals are available on campus for general student use. Students can access the following: computer help desk, free student e-mail accounts, online (class) grades, online (class) registration, online (class) schedules, We provide numerous computer labs and classroom (podium-like setup) for instructional purposes. Campuswide network is available.
Library: Renton Technical College Library. *Books:* 24,464 (physical), 64,437 (digital/electronic); *Serial titles:* 354 (physical), 19,981 (digital/electronic); *Databases:* 22. Weekly public service hours: 62.

STUDENT LIFE
Housing options: college housing not available.

Campus security: patrols by security, security system.

Student services: personal/psychological counseling, veterans affairs office.

COSTS
Costs (2018–19) ***Tuition:*** state resident $4836 full-time, $125 per credit hour part-time; nonresident $139 per credit hour part-time. Full-time tuition and fees vary according to course load, degree level, and program. Part-time tuition and fees vary according to course load, degree level, and program. ***Payment plan:*** installment. ***Waivers:*** employees or children of employees.

APPLYING
Standardized Tests *Required for some:* ACT ASSET, CLEP, ACCUPLACER, DSP.

Options: electronic application, early admission.

Application fee: $30.

Required for some: essay or personal statement, high school transcript, interview.

Application deadlines: rolling (freshmen), rolling (transfers).

Notification: continuous (freshmen), continuous (transfers).

CONTACT
Patrick Brown, Director of Enrollment Services/Registrar, Renton Technical College, 3000 NE Fourth Street, Renton, WA 98056. *Phone:* 425-2352352 Ext. 5537. *E-mail:* pbrown@rtc.edu.

Saint Martin's University

Lacey, Washington

http://www.stmartin.edu/

- **Independent Roman Catholic** comprehensive, founded 1895
- **Suburban** 300-acre campus with easy access to Seattle
- **Endowment** $21.8 million
- **Coed** 1,344 undergraduate students, 87% full-time, 48% women, 52% men
- **Moderately difficult** entrance level, 96% of applicants were admitted

UNDERGRAD STUDENTS
1,172 full-time, 172 part-time. Students come from 34 states and territories; 6 other countries; 28% are from out of state; 6% Black or African American, non-Hispanic/Latino; 13% Hispanic/Latino; 9% Asian, non-Hispanic/Latino; 5% Native Hawaiian or other Pacific Islander, non-Hispanic/Latino; 1% American Indian or Alaska Native, non-Hispanic/Latino; 7% Two or more races, non-Hispanic/Latino; 3% Race/ethnicity unknown; 6% international; 11% transferred in; 39% live on campus.

Freshmen:
Admission: 1,125 applied, 1,075 admitted, 241 enrolled. ***Average high school GPA:*** 3.4. ***Test scores:*** SAT evidence-based reading and writing scores over 500: 81%; SAT math scores over 500: 77%; ACT scores over 18: 80%; SAT evidence-based reading and writing scores over 600: 34%; SAT math scores over 600: 29%; ACT scores over 24: 29%; SAT evidence-based reading and writing scores over 700: 3%; SAT math scores over 700: 3%; ACT scores over 30: 6%.

Retention: 78% of full-time freshmen returned.

FACULTY
Total: 197, 40% full-time, 55% with terminal degrees.

Student/faculty ratio: 11:1.

ACADEMICS
Calendar: semesters. *Degrees:* certificates, bachelor's, master's, post-master's, and postbachelor's certificates.

Special study options: academic remediation for entering students, adult/continuing education programs, advanced placement credit, cooperative education, distance learning, double majors, English as a second language, honors programs, independent study, internships, off-campus study, part-time degree program, services for LD students, study abroad, summer session for credit. ***ROTC:*** Army (c), Air Force (c).

Unusual degree programs: 3-2 business administration; engineering.

Computers: 80 computers/terminals and 130 ports are available on campus for general student use. Students can access the following: campus intranet, computer help desk, free student e-mail accounts, online (class) grades, online (class) registration, online (class) schedules. Campuswide network is available. 100% of college-owned or -operated housing units are wired for high-speed Internet access. Wireless service is available via entire campus.
Library: O'Grady Library. *Books:* 88,291 (physical), 233,172 (digital/electronic); *Serial titles:* 98 (physical), 54,407 (digital/electronic); *Databases:* 114. Weekly public service hours: 88; students can reserve study rooms.

STUDENT LIFE
Housing options: on-campus residence required through sophomore year; coed. Campus housing is university owned. Freshman campus housing is guaranteed.

Activities and organizations: drama/theater group, student-run newspaper, choral group.

Athletics Member NCAA. All Division II except golf (Division I). ***Intercollegiate sports:*** baseball M(s), basketball M(s)/W(s), cross-country running M(s)/W(s), golf M(s)/W(s), soccer M/W(s), softball W(s), track and field M(s)/W(s), volleyball W(s). ***Intramural sports:*** basketball M/W, bowling M/W, golf M/W, soccer M/W, softball M/W, table tennis M/W, tennis M/W, ultimate Frisbee M/W, volleyball M/W.

Campus security: 24-hour emergency response devices and patrols, student patrols, late-night transport/escort service, controlled dormitory access, close-circuit TV cameras throughout campus, emergency text messaging/notification.

Student services: health clinic, personal/psychological counseling.

COSTS & FINANCIAL AID
Costs (2019–20) ***Comprehensive fee:*** $50,560 includes full-time tuition ($38,150), mandatory fees ($410), and room and board ($12,000). Part-time tuition: $1275 per credit. ***College room only:*** $5750.

Financial Aid Of all full-time matriculated undergraduates who enrolled in 2017, 882 applied for aid, 820 were judged to have need, 204 had their need fully met. In 2017, 129 non-need-based awards were made. ***Average percent of need met:*** 79. ***Average financial aid package:*** $29,720. ***Average need-based loan:*** $4028. ***Average need-based gift aid:*** $26,817. ***Average non-need-based aid:*** $15,107. ***Average indebtedness upon graduation:*** $26,761.

APPLYING
Standardized Tests *Required:* SAT or ACT (for admission).

Options: electronic application, deferred entrance.

Required: essay or personal statement, high school transcript, 1 letter of recommendation.

Notification: continuous (freshmen), continuous (out-of-state freshmen), continuous (transfers).

CONTACT
Dr. Pamela Holsinger-Fuchs, Dean of Enrollment, Saint Martin's University, 5000 Abbey Way SE, Lacey, WA 98503. *Phone:* 360-438-4592. *Toll-free phone:* 800-368-8803. *Fax:* 360-412-6189. *E-mail:* admissions@stmartin.edu.

Seattle Pacific University

Seattle, Washington

http://www.spu.edu/

- **Independent Free Methodist** comprehensive, founded 1891
- **Urban** 40-acre campus
- **Coed**
- **Moderately difficult** entrance level

FACULTY

Student/faculty ratio: 13:1.

ACADEMICS

Calendar: quarters. *Degrees:* bachelor's, master's, doctoral, and post-master's certificates.

Library: University Library.

STUDENT LIFE

Housing options: on-campus residence required through sophomore year; coed, special housing for students with disabilities. Campus housing is university owned. Freshman campus housing is guaranteed.

Activities and organizations: drama/theater group, student-run newspaper, radio station, choral group, Centurions, Falconettes, forensics organization, Amnesty International, University Players.

Athletics Member NCAA. All Division II.

Campus security: 24-hour emergency response devices and patrols, student patrols, late-night transport/escort service, closed-circuit TV monitors.

Student services: health clinic, personal/psychological counseling.

COSTS & FINANCIAL AID

Costs (2018–19) ***Comprehensive fee:*** $54,735 includes full-time tuition ($42,480), mandatory fees ($459), and room and board ($11,796). Part-time tuition: $1180 per credit hour. Part-time tuition and fees vary according to course load. ***College room only:*** $6399. Room and board charges vary according to board plan and housing facility. ***Payment plans:*** installment, deferred payment.

Financial Aid Of all full-time matriculated undergraduates who enrolled in 2018, 2,192 applied for aid, 1,899 were judged to have need, 109 had their need fully met. 388 Federal Work-Study jobs (averaging $2668). 96 state and other part-time jobs (averaging $3202). In 2018, 681 non-need-based awards were made. ***Average percent of need met:*** 78. ***Average financial aid package:*** $36,825. ***Average need-based loan:*** $4694. ***Average need-based gift aid:*** $36,415. ***Average non-need-based aid:*** $25,477. ***Average indebtedness upon graduation:*** $28,586.

APPLYING

Standardized Tests *Required:* SAT or ACT (for admission). *Required for some:* SAT and SAT Subject Tests or ACT (for admission).

Options: electronic application, early admission, early action.

Application fee: $50.

Required: essay or personal statement, high school transcript, minimum 2.5 GPA, 2 letters of recommendation. ***Recommended:*** interview.

CONTACT

Ineliz Soto-Fuller, Director of Undergraduate Admissions, Seattle Pacific University, 3307 3rd Avenue, West, Seattle, WA 98119-1997. *Phone:* 206-281-2021. *Toll-free phone:* 800-366-3344. *Fax:* 206-281-2544. *E-mail:* admissions@spu.edu.

Seattle University

Seattle, Washington

http://www.seattleu.edu/

- **Independent Roman Catholic** comprehensive, founded 1891
- **Urban** 50-acre campus with easy access to Seattle
- **Coed** 4,764 undergraduate students, 95% full-time, 61% women, 39% men
- **Moderately difficult** entrance level, 76% of applicants were admitted

UNDERGRAD STUDENTS

4,519 full-time, 245 part-time. Students come from 50 states and territories; 101 other countries; 59% are from out of state; 3% Black or African American, non-Hispanic/Latino; 12% Hispanic/Latino; 16% Asian, non-Hispanic/Latino; 0.8% Native Hawaiian or other Pacific Islander, non-Hispanic/Latino; 0.3% American Indian or Alaska Native, non-Hispanic/Latino; 8% Two or more races, non-Hispanic/Latino; 6% Race/ethnicity unknown; 11% international; 9% transferred in; 50% live on campus.

Freshmen:

Admission: 8,640 applied, 6,536 admitted, 1,083 enrolled. ***Average high school GPA:*** 3.6. ***Test scores:*** SAT evidence-based reading and writing scores over 500: 98%; SAT math scores over 500: 97%; ACT scores over 18: 100%; SAT evidence-based reading and writing scores over 600: 63%; SAT math scores over 600: 55%; ACT scores over 24: 85%; SAT evidence-based reading and writing scores over 700: 11%; SAT math scores over 700: 14%; ACT scores over 30: 30%.

Retention: 85% of full-time freshmen returned.

FACULTY

Total: 729, 70% full-time, 78% with terminal degrees.

Student/faculty ratio: 11:1.

ACADEMICS

Calendar: quarters. *Degrees:* bachelor's, master's, doctoral, post-master's, and postbachelor's certificates.

Special study options: accelerated degree program, adult/continuing education programs, advanced placement credit, double majors, English as a second language, freshman honors college, honors programs, independent study, internships, off-campus study, part-time degree program, services for LD students, student-designed majors, study abroad, summer session for credit. ***ROTC:*** Army (b), Navy (c), Air Force (c).

Computers: 467 computers/terminals are available on campus for general student use. Students can access the following: campus intranet, computer help desk, free student e-mail accounts, online (class) grades, online (class) registration, online (class) schedules. Campuswide network is available. 99% of college-owned or -operated housing units are wired for high-speed Internet access. Wireless service is available via entire campus.

Library: Lemieux Library & McGoldrick Learning Commons plus 1 other. *Books:* 472,572 (physical), 257,641 (digital/electronic); *Serial titles:* 118,353 (physical), 8,597 (digital/electronic); *Databases:* 235. Students can reserve study rooms.

STUDENT LIFE

Housing options: on-campus residence required through sophomore year; coed, special housing for students with disabilities. Campus housing is university owned and leased by the school. Freshman campus housing is guaranteed.

Activities and organizations: drama/theater group, student-run newspaper, radio station, choral group, Student Government of Seattle University (SGSU), Student Events and Activities Council (SEAC), Redzone, Dance Marathon, Hui 'O Nani Hawaii Club.

Athletics Member NCAA. All Division I. ***Intercollegiate sports:*** baseball M, basketball M(s)/W(s), cheerleading M(c)/W(c), crew W(c), cross-country running M(s)/W(s), golf M(s), soccer M(s)/W(s), softball W(s), swimming and diving M(s)/W(s), tennis M/W, track and field M(s)/W(s), volleyball W(s). ***Intramural sports:*** archery M(c)/W(c), basketball M/W, crew M(c)/W(c), fencing W, field hockey M, football M/W, riflery M(c)/W(c), rock climbing M/W, skiing (downhill) M(c)/W(c), soccer M/W, softball M/W, tennis M/W, ultimate Frisbee M/W, volleyball M/W, water polo M/W.

Campus security: 24-hour emergency response devices and patrols, late-night transport/escort service, controlled dormitory access.

Student services: health clinic, personal/psychological counseling, women's center.

COSTS & FINANCIAL AID

Costs (2019–20) ***Comprehensive fee:*** $59,121 includes full-time tuition ($45,765), mandatory fees ($825), and room and board ($12,531). Part-time tuition: $1017 per credit. ***College room only:*** $8481.

Financial Aid Of all full-time matriculated undergraduates who enrolled in 2018, 3,206 applied for aid, 2,622 were judged to have need, 803 had their need fully met. 506 Federal Work-Study jobs (averaging $1.9 million). 531 state and other part-time jobs (averaging $2.5 million). In 2018, 269 non-need-based awards were made. ***Average percent of need met:*** 81. ***Average financial aid package:*** $37,437. ***Average need-based loan:*** $5828. ***Average need-based gift aid:*** $26,825. ***Average non-need-based aid:*** $14,482. ***Average indebtedness upon graduation:*** $28,851.

APPLYING
Standardized Tests *Required:* SAT or ACT (for admission).
Options: electronic application, early action, deferred entrance.
Application fee: $55.
Required: essay or personal statement, high school transcript, minimum 2.5 GPA, 2 letters of recommendation.
Application deadlines: rolling (freshmen), 3/1 (transfers), 11/15 (early action).
Notification: continuous until 3/1 (freshmen), continuous (transfers).

CONTACT
Seattle University, 902 12th Avenue, PO Box 222000, Seattle, WA 98122-1090. *Toll-free phone:* 800-542-0833 (in-state); 800-426-7123 (out-of-state).

University of Puget Sound

Tacoma, Washington

http://www.pugetsound.edu/

- **Independent** comprehensive, founded 1888
- **Urban** 97-acre campus with easy access to Seattle
- **Endowment** $369.0 million
- **Coed** 2,364 undergraduate students, 99% full-time, 60% women, 40% men
- **Moderately difficult** entrance level, 88% of applicants were admitted

UNDERGRAD STUDENTS
2,348 full-time, 16 part-time. Students come from 44 states and territories; 6 other countries; 77% are from out of state; 2% Black or African American, non-Hispanic/Latino; 9% Hispanic/Latino; 6% Asian, non-Hispanic/Latino; 0.6% Native Hawaiian or other Pacific Islander, non-Hispanic/Latino; 0.1% American Indian or Alaska Native, non-Hispanic/Latino; 9% Two or more races, non-Hispanic/Latino; 4% Race/ethnicity unknown; 0.4% international; 2% transferred in; 66% live on campus.

Freshmen:
Admission: 5,730 applied, 5,060 admitted, 653 enrolled. ***Average high school GPA:*** 3.5. ***Test scores:*** SAT evidence-based reading and writing scores over 500: 93%; SAT math scores over 500: 91%; ACT scores over 18: 100%; SAT evidence-based reading and writing scores over 600: 67%; SAT math scores over 600: 55%; ACT scores over 24: 85%; SAT evidence-based reading and writing scores over 700: 19%; SAT math scores over 700: 14%; ACT scores over 30: 37%.
Retention: 81% of full-time freshmen returned.

FACULTY
Total: 288, 80% full-time.
Student/faculty ratio: 11:1.

ACADEMICS
Calendar: semesters. *Degrees:* bachelor's, master's, and doctoral.
Special study options: advanced placement credit, cooperative education, double majors, honors programs, independent study, internships, part-time degree program, services for LD students, student-designed majors, study abroad, summer session for credit. ***ROTC:*** Army (c).
Unusual degree programs: 3-2 engineering with Washington University in St. Louis, Columbia University, University of Southern California.
Computers: 329 computers/terminals are available on campus for general student use. Students can access the following: campus intranet, computer help desk, free student e-mail accounts, online (class) grades, online (class) registration, online (class) schedules, financial aid, admission, student employment. Campuswide network is available. 100% of college-owned or -operated housing units are wired for high-speed Internet access. Wireless service is available via entire campus.
Library: Collins Memorial Library.

STUDENT LIFE
Housing options: on-campus residence required through sophomore year; coed, special housing for students with disabilities. Campus housing is university owned. Freshman campus housing is guaranteed.
Activities and organizations: drama/theater group, student-run newspaper, radio station, choral group, Puget Sound Outdoors, Repertory Dance Group, Ka Ohana me ke Aloha, Student Theatre Productions, Relay for Life, national fraternities, national sororities.
Athletics Member NCAA. All Division III except golf (Division II). ***Intercollegiate sports:*** baseball M, basketball M/W, cheerleading M/W, crew M/W, cross-country running M/W, fencing M(c)/W(c), football M, golf M/W, ice hockey M(c)/W(c), lacrosse M(c)/W, rugby M(c)/W(c), sailing M(c)/W(c), skiing (downhill) W(c), soccer M/W, softball W, swimming and diving M/W, tennis M/W, track and field M/W, ultimate Frisbee M(c)/W(c), volleyball W. ***Intramural sports:*** basketball M/W, football M(c)/W, soccer M/W, softball M/W, volleyball M/W.
Campus security: 24-hour emergency response devices and patrols, student patrols, late-night transport/escort service, controlled dormitory access.
Student services: health clinic, personal/psychological counseling.

COSTS & FINANCIAL AID
Costs (2019–20) ***Comprehensive fee:*** $64,740 includes full-time tuition ($51,470), mandatory fees ($270), and room and board ($13,000). Part-time tuition: $6500 per unit. ***College room only:*** $7020.
Financial Aid Of all full-time matriculated undergraduates who enrolled in 2018, 1,525 applied for aid, 1,264 were judged to have need, 262 had their need fully met. 519 Federal Work-Study jobs (averaging $2965). 870 state and other part-time jobs (averaging $2734). In 2018, 1060 non-need-based awards were made. ***Average percent of need met:*** 77. ***Average financial aid package:*** $35,216. ***Average need-based loan:*** $4390. ***Average need-based gift aid:*** $30,159. ***Average non-need-based aid:*** $17,438. ***Average indebtedness upon graduation:*** $32,999.

APPLYING
Options: electronic application, early admission, early decision, early action, deferred entrance.
Application fee: $60.
Required: essay or personal statement, high school transcript, 2 letters of recommendation. ***Recommended:*** minimum 3.0 GPA, interview.

CONTACT
Laura Martin-Fedich, Vice President for Enrollment, University of Puget Sound, 1500 North Warner Street, CMB 1062, Tacoma, WA 98416. *Phone:* 253-879-3211. *Toll-free phone:* 800-396-7191. *Fax:* 253-879-3993. *E-mail:* admission@pugetsound.edu.

University of Washington

Seattle, Washington

http://www.washington.edu/

- **State-supported** university, founded 1861, part of University of Washington
- **Urban** 634-acre campus with easy access to Seattle, WA
- **Endowment** $3.4 billion
- **Coed** 32,099 undergraduate students, 92% full-time, 53% women, 47% men
- **Very difficult** entrance level, 49% of applicants were admitted

UNDERGRAD STUDENTS
29,496 full-time, 2,603 part-time. Students come from 51 states and territories; 86 other countries; 19% are from out of state; 3% Black or African American, non-Hispanic/Latino; 8% Hispanic/Latino; 25% Asian, non-Hispanic/Latino; 0.4% Native Hawaiian or other Pacific Islander, non-Hispanic/Latino; 0.5% American Indian or Alaska Native, non-Hispanic/Latino; 7% Two or more races, non-Hispanic/Latino; 1% Race/ethnicity unknown; 16% international; 22% transferred in; 29% live on campus.

Freshmen:
Admission: 45,907 applied, 22,350 admitted, 7,161 enrolled. ***Average high school GPA:*** 3.8. ***Test scores:*** SAT evidence-based reading and writing scores over 500: 97%; SAT math scores over 500: 98%; ACT scores over 18: 98%; SAT evidence-based reading and writing scores over 600: 79%; SAT math scores over 600: 83%; ACT scores over 24: 89%; SAT evidence-based reading and writing scores over 700: 26%; SAT math scores over 700: 49%; ACT scores over 30: 54%.
Retention: 94% of full-time freshmen returned.

FACULTY
Total: 2,675, 75% full-time, 64% with terminal degrees.

Student/faculty ratio: 19:1.

ACADEMICS
Calendar: quarters. *Degrees:* bachelor's, master's, doctoral, and post-master's certificates.

Special study options: adult/continuing education programs, advanced placement credit, cooperative education, distance learning, double majors, English as a second language, external degree program, honors programs, independent study, internships, off-campus study, part-time degree program, services for LD students, student-designed majors, study abroad, summer session for credit. ***ROTC:*** Army (b), Navy (b), Air Force (b).

Computers: 919 computers/terminals are available on campus for general student use. Students can access the following: computer help desk, free student e-mail accounts, online (class) grades, online (class) registration, online (class) schedules. Campuswide network is available. 100% of college-owned or -operated housing units are wired for high-speed Internet access. Wireless service is available via entire campus.
Library: Odegaard Undergraduate Library plus 12 others. *Books:* 9.0 million (physical), 1.2 million (digital/electronic); *Serial titles:* 156,594 (physical), 183,555 (digital/electronic); *Databases:* 283. Weekly public service hours: 124; study areas open 24 hours, 5–7 days a week; students can reserve study rooms.

STUDENT LIFE
Housing options: coed, special housing for students with disabilities. Campus housing is university owned, leased by the school and is provided by a third party.

Activities and organizations: drama/theater group, student-run newspaper, radio and television station, choral group, marching band, Interfraternity Council/Pan-Hellenic Council, Taiwanese Student Association, Chinese Student Association, Yacht Club, Asian American Intervarsity Christian Fellowship/Muslim Students Association, national fraternities, national sororities.

Athletics Member NCAA, NAIA. All NCAA Division I except football (Division I-A). ***Intercollegiate sports:*** baseball M(s), basketball M(s)/W(s), cheerleading M(s)/W(s), crew M(s)/W(s), cross-country running M(s)/W(s), golf M(s)/W(s)(c), gymnastics W(s), rowing M(s)/W(s), soccer M(s)/W(s), softball W(s), tennis M(s)/W(s), track and field M(s)/W(s), volleyball W(s). ***Intramural sports:*** archery M(c)/W(c), badminton M/W, baseball M(c)/W(c), basketball M/W, bowling M/W(c), crew M(c)/W(c), equestrian sports M(c)/W(c), football M/W, ice hockey M(c)/W(c), lacrosse M(c)/W(c), racquetball M/W, rock climbing M/W, rowing M/W, rugby M(c)/W(c), sailing M(c)/W(c), skiing (cross-country) M(c)/W(c), skiing (downhill) M(c)/W(c), soccer M/W, softball M/W, squash M(c)/W(c), swimming and diving M/W, table tennis M(c)/W(c), tennis M/W, triathlon M(c)/W(c), ultimate Frisbee M/W, volleyball M/W, water polo M(c)/W(c), wrestling M(c)/W(c).

Campus security: 24-hour emergency response devices and patrols, late-night transport/escort service, controlled dormitory access.

Student services: health clinic, personal/psychological counseling, women's center, legal services, veterans affairs office.

COSTS & FINANCIAL AID
Costs (2018–19) ***Tuition:*** state resident $10,127 full-time, $338 per credit part-time; nonresident $35,508 full-time, $1184 per credit part-time. Full-time tuition and fees vary according to course load and location. Part-time tuition and fees vary according to course load and location. ***Required fees:*** $1080 full-time, $28 per credit part-time, $84 per term part-time. ***Room and board:*** $12,798. Room and board charges vary according to board plan, housing facility, and location. ***Payment plan:*** tuition prepayment. ***Waivers:*** senior citizens and employees or children of employees.

Financial Aid Of all full-time matriculated undergraduates who enrolled in 2018, 16,791 applied for aid, 12,493 were judged to have need, 2,575 had their need fully met. 628 Federal Work-Study jobs (averaging $4665). 52 state and other part-time jobs (averaging $4940). In 2018, 2638 non-need-based awards were made. ***Average percent of need met:*** 75. ***Average financial aid package:*** $16,900. ***Average need-based loan:*** $4047. ***Average need-based gift aid:*** $15,804. ***Average non-need-based aid:*** $4618. ***Average indebtedness upon graduation:*** $20,094.

APPLYING
Options: electronic application, early admission.

Application fee: $80.

Required: essay or personal statement. ***Required for some:*** high school transcript.

Notification: 3/15 (freshmen), 6/30 (transfers).

CONTACT
Philip Ballinger, Associate Vice Provost for Enrollment, University of Washington, Seattle, WA 98195. *Phone:* 206-543-0852. *Fax:* 206-221-2305. *E-mail:* philipba@uw.edu.

University of Washington, Bothell

Bothell, Washington

http://www.uwb.edu/

- **State-supported** comprehensive, founded 1990, part of University of Washington
- **Suburban** 127-acre campus with easy access to Seattle
- **Endowment** $4.1 million
- **Coed** 5,401 undergraduate students, 86% full-time, 48% women, 52% men
- **Moderately difficult** entrance level, 79% of applicants were admitted

UNDERGRAD STUDENTS
4,623 full-time, 778 part-time. Students come from 25 states and territories; 24 other countries; 2% are from out of state; 7% Black or African American, non-Hispanic/Latino; 10% Hispanic/Latino; 29% Asian, non-Hispanic/Latino; 0.5% Native Hawaiian or other Pacific Islander, non-Hispanic/Latino; 0.5% American Indian or Alaska Native, non-Hispanic/Latino; 6% Two or more races, non-Hispanic/Latino; 2% Race/ethnicity unknown; 9% international; 14% transferred in; 6% live on campus.

Freshmen:
Admission: 3,022 applied, 2,398 admitted, 781 enrolled. ***Average high school GPA:*** 3.4. ***Test scores:*** SAT evidence-based reading and writing scores over 500: 79%; SAT math scores over 500: 86%; ACT scores over 18: 85%; SAT evidence-based reading and writing scores over 600: 33%; SAT math scores over 600: 39%; ACT scores over 24: 46%; SAT evidence-based reading and writing scores over 700: 4%; SAT math scores over 700: 8%; ACT scores over 30: 5%.

Retention: 87% of full-time freshmen returned.

FACULTY
Total: 340, 59% full-time, 51% with terminal degrees.

Student/faculty ratio: 20:1.

ACADEMICS
Calendar: quarters. *Degrees:* bachelor's and master's.

Special study options: adult/continuing education programs, advanced placement credit, cooperative education, distance learning, double majors, English as a second language, honors programs, independent study, internships, off-campus study, part-time degree program, services for LD students, student-designed majors, study abroad, summer session for credit. ***ROTC:*** Army (c), Navy (c), Air Force (c).

Computers: 538 computers/terminals are available on campus for general student use. Students can access the following: campus intranet, computer help desk, free student e-mail accounts, online (class) grades, online (class) registration, online (class) schedules. Campuswide network is available. 100% of college-owned or -operated housing units are wired for high-speed Internet access. Wireless service is available via classrooms, computer centers, computer labs, learning centers, libraries, student centers.
Library: Campus Library. *Books:* 119,564 (physical), 1.2 million (digital/electronic); *Serial titles:* 1,100 (physical), 183,555 (digital/electronic); *Databases:* 283. Weekly public service hours: 86; students can reserve study rooms.

STUDENT LIFE
Housing options: coed, special housing for students with disabilities. Campus housing is university owned and leased by the school. Freshman applicants given priority for college housing.

Activities and organizations: student-run newspaper, radio station, Campus Events Board, Social Justice Organizers, Associated Students of University of Washington Bothell (ASUWB), Recreation and Intramurals Program, Club Council.

Athletics ***Intramural sports:*** basketball M/W, football M/W, soccer M/W, softball M/W, tennis M/W, ultimate Frisbee M(c)/W(c), volleyball M/W.

Campus security: 24-hour emergency response devices and patrols, late-night transport/escort service.

Student services: personal/psychological counseling, veterans affairs office.

COSTS & FINANCIAL AID
Costs (2018–19) ***Tuition:*** state resident $10,127 full-time, $339 per credit part-time; nonresident $35,508 full-time, $1184 per credit part-time. Full-time tuition and fees vary according to course load. Part-time tuition and fees vary according to course load. ***Required fees:*** $1011 full-time, $34 per credit part-time. ***Room and board:*** $11,877. Room and board charges vary according to board plan, housing facility, and location. ***Payment plans:*** tuition prepayment, installment. ***Waivers:*** senior citizens and employees or children of employees.

Financial Aid Of all full-time matriculated undergraduates who enrolled in 2018, 3,046 applied for aid, 2,587 were judged to have need, 280 had their need fully met. 52 Federal Work-Study jobs (averaging $5031). 17 state and other part-time jobs (averaging $4149). In 2018, 41 non-need-based awards were made. ***Average percent of need met:*** 70. ***Average financial aid package:*** $14,757. ***Average need-based loan:*** $4248. ***Average need-based gift aid:*** $14,194. ***Average non-need-based aid:*** $6883. ***Average indebtedness upon graduation:*** $18,177.

APPLYING
Standardized Tests *Required:* SAT or ACT (for admission).

Options: electronic application.

Application fee: $60.

Required: essay or personal statement, high school transcript, minimum 2.0 GPA. ***Required for some:*** 1 letter of recommendation.

Application deadlines: 1/15 (freshmen), 1/15 (transfers).

Notification: continuous (freshmen), continuous (transfers).

CONTACT
Steve Syverson, Assistant Vice Chancellor for Enrollment Management, University of Washington, Bothell, 18115 Campus Way NE, Bothell, WA 98011. *Phone:* 425-352-5000. *E-mail:* steves47@uw.edu.

University of Washington, Tacoma

Tacoma, Washington

http://www.tacoma.uw.edu/

- **State-supported** comprehensive, founded 1990, part of University of Washington
- **Urban** 31-acre campus with easy access to Seattle
- **Endowment** $40.5 million
- **Coed** 4,544 undergraduate students, 88% full-time, 51% women, 49% men
- **Moderately difficult** entrance level, 86% of applicants were admitted

UNDERGRAD STUDENTS
3,995 full-time, 549 part-time. Students come from 29 states and territories; 20 other countries; 1% are from out of state; 9% Black or African American, non-Hispanic/Latino; 15% Hispanic/Latino; 20% Asian, non-Hispanic/Latino; 1% Native Hawaiian or other Pacific Islander, non-Hispanic/Latino; 0.8% American Indian or Alaska Native, non-Hispanic/Latino; 9% Two or more races, non-Hispanic/Latino; 2% Race/ethnicity unknown; 4% international; 14% transferred in; 6% live on campus.

Freshmen:
Admission: 2,036 applied, 1,742 admitted, 643 enrolled. ***Average high school GPA:*** 3.3. ***Test scores:*** SAT evidence-based reading and writing scores over 500: 74%; SAT math scores over 500: 73%; ACT scores over 18: 68%; SAT evidence-based reading and writing scores over 600: 28%; SAT math scores over 600: 22%; ACT scores over 24: 24%; SAT evidence-based reading and writing scores over 700: 3%; SAT math scores over 700: 3%; ACT scores over 30: 2%.

Retention: 81% of full-time freshmen returned.

FACULTY
Total: 338, 77% full-time, 57% with terminal degrees.

Student/faculty ratio: 16:1.

ACADEMICS
Calendar: quarters. *Degrees:* bachelor's, master's, doctoral, and postbachelor's certificates.

Special study options: academic remediation for entering students, advanced placement credit, distance learning, double majors, external degree program, honors programs, independent study, internships, off-campus study, part-time degree program, services for LD students, student-designed majors, study abroad, summer session for credit. ***ROTC:*** Army (c), Navy (c), Air Force (c).

Computers: 166 computers/terminals are available on campus for general student use. Students can access the following: campus intranet, computer help desk, free student e-mail accounts, online (class) grades, online (class) registration, online (class) schedules, learning management system, course management system. Campuswide network is available. 100% of college-owned or -operated housing units are wired for high-speed Internet access. Wireless service is available via entire campus.
Library: University of Washington Tacoma Library. *Books:* 133,442 (physical), 1.2 million (digital/electronic); *Serial titles:* 924 (physical), 183,555 (digital/electronic); *Databases:* 283. Weekly public service hours: 84; students can reserve study rooms.

STUDENT LIFE
Housing options: Campus housing is leased by the school. Freshman applicants given priority for college housing.

Activities and organizations: drama/theater group, student-run newspaper, choral group, Accounting Student Association, International Student Association, Partners in Action to Transform Healthcare (PATH), Asian Pacific Islander Student Union (APISU).

Athletics ***Intramural sports:*** badminton M/W, basketball M/W, soccer M(c)/W(c), volleyball M(c)/W(c), wrestling M(c)/W(c).

Campus security: 24-hour emergency response devices and patrols, late-night transport/escort service, key card access to buildings after hours.

Student services: health clinic, personal/psychological counseling, veterans affairs office.

COSTS & FINANCIAL AID
Costs (2018–19) ***Tuition:*** state resident $10,127 full-time, $339 per credit part-time; nonresident $35,508 full-time, $1184 per credit part-time. Full-time tuition and fees vary according to course load. Part-time tuition and fees vary according to course load. ***Required fees:*** $1134 full-time, $38 per credit part-time. ***Room and board:*** $11,028. Room and board charges vary according to housing facility and location. ***Payment plans:*** tuition prepayment, installment. ***Waivers:*** senior citizens and employees or children of employees.

Financial Aid Of all full-time matriculated undergraduates who enrolled in 2018, 3,298 applied for aid, 2,885 were judged to have need, 312 had their need fully met. 63 Federal Work-Study jobs (averaging $4493). 34 state and other part-time jobs (averaging $4933). In 2018, 255 non-need-based awards were made. ***Average percent of need met:*** 69. ***Average financial aid package:*** $14,791. ***Average need-based loan:*** $4276. ***Average need-based gift aid:*** $13,485. ***Average non-need-based aid:*** $2742. ***Average indebtedness upon graduation:*** $15,601.

APPLYING
Standardized Tests *Required:* SAT or ACT (for admission).

Options: electronic application, deferred entrance.

Application fee: $60.

Required: essay or personal statement. ***Required for some:*** high school transcript, 3 letters of recommendation.

Notification: continuous (freshmen), continuous (transfers).

CONTACT
Ms. Megan Cooley, Associate Director of University Recruitment, University of Washington, Tacoma, 1900 Commerce Street, Tacoma, WA 98402-3100. *Phone:* 253-692-4738. *Toll-free phone:* 800-736-7750. *Fax:* 253-692-4414. *E-mail:* uwtinfo@uw.edu.

Walla Walla University

College Place, Washington

http://www.wallawalla.edu/

CONTACT

Mr. Dallas Weis, Director of Admissions, Walla Walla University, Marketing and Enrollment Services, 204 S. College Avenue, College Place, WA 99324. *Phone:* 509-527-2327. *Toll-free phone:* 800-541-8900. *Fax:* 509-527-2397.

Washington State University

Pullman, Washington

http://www.wsu.edu/

- **State-supported** university, founded 1890
- **Small-town** 620-acre campus with easy access to Spokane
- **Endowment** $1.0 billion
- **Coed** 18,632 undergraduate students, 95% full-time, 49% women, 51% men
- **Moderately difficult** entrance level, 79% of applicants were admitted

UNDERGRAD STUDENTS

17,653 full-time, 979 part-time. Students come from 50 states and territories; 75 other countries; 16% are from out of state; 4% Black or African American, non-Hispanic/Latino; 14% Hispanic/Latino; 6% Asian, non-Hispanic/Latino; 0.5% Native Hawaiian or other Pacific Islander, non-Hispanic/Latino; 0.6% American Indian or Alaska Native, non-Hispanic/Latino; 7% Two or more races, non-Hispanic/Latino; 2% Race/ethnicity unknown; 5% international; 7% transferred in; 25% live on campus.

Freshmen:

Admission: 20,762 applied, 16,305 admitted, 4,543 enrolled. ***Average high school GPA:*** 3.4. ***Test scores:*** SAT evidence-based reading and writing scores over 500: 80%; SAT math scores over 500: 81%; ACT scores over 18: 88%; SAT evidence-based reading and writing scores over 600: 32%; SAT math scores over 600: 29%; ACT scores over 24: 44%; SAT evidence-based reading and writing scores over 700: 4%; SAT math scores over 700: 5%; ACT scores over 30: 8%.

Retention: 80% of full-time freshmen returned.

FACULTY

Total: 1,803, 74% full-time, 78% with terminal degrees.

Student/faculty ratio: 15:1.

ACADEMICS

Calendar: semesters. *Degrees:* certificates, bachelor's, master's, doctoral, post-master's, and postbachelor's certificates.

Special study options: academic remediation for entering students, accelerated degree program, adult/continuing education programs, advanced placement credit, cooperative education, distance learning, double majors, English as a second language, external degree program, freshman honors college, honors programs, independent study, internships, off-campus study, part-time degree program, services for LD students, student-designed majors, study abroad, summer session for credit. ***ROTC:*** Army (b), Navy (c), Air Force (b).

Computers: 2,500 computers/terminals and 2,500 ports are available on campus for general student use. Students can access the following: campus intranet, computer help desk, free student e-mail accounts, online (class) grades, online (class) registration, online (class) schedules. Campuswide network is available. 100% of college-owned or -operated housing units are wired for high-speed Internet access. Wireless service is available via classrooms, computer centers, computer labs, dorm rooms, learning centers, libraries, student centers.

Library: Holland and Terrell Libraries plus 3 others. *Books:* 2.4 million (physical), 750,000 (digital/electronic); *Serial titles:* 93,000 (digital/electronic); *Databases:* 216. Weekly public service hours: 140; students can reserve study rooms.

STUDENT LIFE

Housing options: on-campus residence required for freshman year; coed, men-only, women-only, cooperative, special housing for students with disabilities. Campus housing is university owned. Freshman campus housing is guaranteed.

Activities and organizations: drama/theater group, student-run newspaper, radio and television station, choral group, marching band, Panhellenic Association - Sororities, Interfraternity Council - Fraternities, Student Entertainment Board, International Students Council, ChiLaStAl (Chicana/o Latina/o Student Alliance), national fraternities, national sororities.

Athletics Member NCAA. All Division I except football (Division I-A). ***Intercollegiate sports:*** baseball M(s), basketball M(s)/W(s), bowling M(c)/W(c), cheerleading M/W, crew M(c)/W(s), cross-country running M(s)/W(s), equestrian sports W(c), fencing M(c)/W(c), golf M(s)/W(s)(c), ice hockey M(c)/W(c), lacrosse M(c)/W(c), rowing M(c)/W, rugby M(c)/W(c), skiing (cross-country) M(c)/W(c), skiing (downhill) W(c), soccer M(c)/W(s), softball W(c), swimming and diving W(s), tennis M(c)/W(s), track and field M(s)/W(s), triathlon M(c)/W(c), ultimate Frisbee M(c)/W(c), volleyball M(c)/W(s), water polo W(c), weight lifting M(c)/W(c), wrestling M(c). ***Intramural sports:*** badminton M/W, basketball M/W, football M/W, golf M/W, racquetball M/W, rock climbing M/W, sand volleyball M/W, soccer M/W, softball M/W, table tennis M/W, tennis M/W, triathlon M/W, ultimate Frisbee M/W, volleyball M/W.

Campus security: 24-hour emergency response devices and patrols, student patrols, late-night transport/escort service, controlled dormitory access.

Student services: health clinic, personal/psychological counseling, women's center, legal services.

FINANCIAL AID

Financial Aid Of all full-time matriculated undergraduates who enrolled in 2017, 16,761 applied for aid, 13,115 were judged to have need, 1,422 had their need fully met. In 2017, 4217 non-need-based awards were made. ***Average percent of need met:*** 64. ***Average financial aid package:*** $13,059. ***Average need-based loan:*** $4282. ***Average need-based gift aid:*** $11,013. ***Average non-need-based aid:*** $4280. ***Average indebtedness upon graduation:*** $27,094. ***Financial aid deadline:*** 1/31.

APPLYING

Standardized Tests *Required:* SAT or ACT (for admission).

Options: electronic application.

Application fee: $50.

Required: high school transcript, minimum 2.0 GPA. ***Recommended:*** essay or personal statement.

Application deadlines: 1/31 (freshmen), rolling (out-of-state freshmen), 1/31 (transfers).

Notification: continuous until 11/1 (freshmen), continuous (out-of-state freshmen), continuous until 11/1 (transfers).

CONTACT

Ms. Wendy Peterson, Director of Admissions, Washington State University, PO Box 641067, Pullman, WA 99164-1067. *Phone:* 888-468-6978. *Toll-free phone:* 888-468-6978. *Fax:* 509-335-4902. *E-mail:* admissions@wsu.edu.

Washington State University–Global Campus

Pullman, Washington

http://www.globalcampus.wsu.edu/

- **State-supported** comprehensive
- **Coed**
- **Moderately difficult** entrance level

ACADEMICS

Calendar: semesters. *Degrees:* certificates, bachelor's, master's, post-master's, and postbachelor's certificates.

STUDENT LIFE

Student services: veterans affairs office.

APPLYING

Standardized Tests *Required:* SAT or ACT (for admission).

Options: electronic application.

Application fee: $50.

Required: high school transcript, minimum 2.0 GPA. ***Recommended:*** essay or personal statement.

CONTACT
Ms. Wendy Peterson, Director of Admissions, Washington State University–Global Campus, 370 Lighty Student Services Building, PO Box 641067, Pullman, WA 99164-1067. *Phone:* 509-335-5586. *Toll-free phone:* 800-222-4978. *Fax:* 509-335-4902. *E-mail:* admissions@wsu.edu.

Washington State University–Spokane

Spokane, Washington

http://www.spokane.wsu.edu/

- **State-supported** upper-level, founded 1989
- **Urban** 48-acre campus
- **Coed** 576 undergraduate students, 93% full-time, 86% women, 14% men
- **Moderately difficult** entrance level

UNDERGRAD STUDENTS
536 full-time, 40 part-time. Students come from 11 states and territories; 6 other countries; 9% are from out of state; 4% Black or African American, non-Hispanic/Latino; 10% Hispanic/Latino; 6% Asian, non-Hispanic/Latino; 0.2% Native Hawaiian or other Pacific Islander, non-Hispanic/Latino; 0.9% American Indian or Alaska Native, non-Hispanic/Latino; 5% Two or more races, non-Hispanic/Latino; 3% Race/ethnicity unknown; 1% international; 17% transferred in.

Freshmen:
Admission: 2 applied.

ACADEMICS
Calendar: semesters. *Degrees:* bachelor's, master's, and doctoral.

Special study options: accelerated degree program, adult/continuing education programs, advanced placement credit, cooperative education, distance learning, double majors, English as a second language, external degree program, freshman honors college, honors programs, independent study, internships, off-campus study, part-time degree program, services for LD students, student-designed majors, study abroad, summer session for credit.

Computers: Campuswide network is available. Wireless service is available via entire campus.

STUDENT LIFE
Housing options: college housing not available.

Activities and organizations: ASWSU Spokane, Simulation Club, Multicultural Club, IHI Open School (Interprofessional Club), Diversity Club.

Campus security: 24-hour emergency response devices and patrols.

Student services: personal/psychological counseling, veterans affairs office.

APPLYING
Standardized Tests *Required:* SAT or ACT (for admission).

Options: electronic application.

Application fee: $50.

Notification: continuous until 11/1 (transfers).

CONTACT
Ms. Wendy Peterson, Director of Admissions, Washington State University–Spokane, 412 East Spokane Falls Boulevard, PO Box 1495, Spokane, WA 99210-1495. *Phone:* 509-335-5586. *Fax:* 509-335-4902. *E-mail:* admissions@wsu.edu.

Washington State University–Tri-Cities

Richland, Washington

http://www.tricities.wsu.edu/

- **State-supported** comprehensive, founded 1989
- **Urban** 84-acre campus
- **Coed** 1,625 undergraduate students, 78% full-time, 57% women, 43% men
- **Moderately difficult** entrance level, 65% of applicants were admitted

UNDERGRAD STUDENTS
1,262 full-time, 363 part-time. Students come from 18 states and territories; 6 other countries; 3% are from out of state; 1% Black or African American, non-Hispanic/Latino; 35% Hispanic/Latino; 4% Asian, non-Hispanic/Latino; 0.2% Native Hawaiian or other Pacific Islander, non-Hispanic/Latino; 0.4% American Indian or Alaska Native, non-Hispanic/Latino; 3% Two or more races, non-Hispanic/Latino; 4% Race/ethnicity unknown; 0.6% international; 14% transferred in.

Freshmen:
Admission: 663 applied, 432 admitted, 209 enrolled. ***Average high school GPA:*** 3.4. ***Test scores:*** SAT evidence-based reading and writing scores over 500: 64%; SAT math scores over 500: 73%; ACT scores over 18: 81%; SAT evidence-based reading and writing scores over 600: 29%; SAT math scores over 600: 25%; ACT scores over 24: 38%; SAT evidence-based reading and writing scores over 700: 6%; SAT math scores over 700: 5%; ACT scores over 30: 13%.

Retention: 76% of full-time freshmen returned.

ACADEMICS
Calendar: semesters. *Degrees:* certificates, bachelor's, master's, doctoral, and postbachelor's certificates.

Special study options: accelerated degree program, adult/continuing education programs, advanced placement credit, cooperative education, distance learning, double majors, English as a second language, external degree program, independent study, internships, part-time degree program, services for LD students, study abroad, summer session for credit.

Computers: Students can access the following: campus intranet, computer help desk, free student e-mail accounts, online (class) grades, online (class) registration. Campuswide network is available. Wireless service is available via entire campus.
Library: Max E. Benitz Memorial Library plus 2 others.

STUDENT LIFE
Housing options: coed. Campus housing is provided by a third party.

Activities and organizations: American Society of Civil Engineers, Environmental Club, Gaming Club, Pre-Health Club, Robotics Club.

Athletics ***Intercollegiate sports:*** rugby M(c), soccer M(c)/W(c), volleyball W(c). ***Intramural sports:*** basketball M/W, football M/W, tennis M/W, ultimate Frisbee M/W.

Campus security: 24-hour emergency response devices.

Student services: personal/psychological counseling, veterans affairs office.

APPLYING
Standardized Tests *Required:* SAT or ACT (for admission).

Options: electronic application.

Application fee: $50.

Required: high school transcript, minimum 2.0 GPA. ***Recommended:*** essay or personal statement.

Application deadlines: 1/31 (freshmen), 1/31 (transfers).

Notification: continuous until 11/1 (freshmen), continuous (out-of-state freshmen), continuous until 11/1 (transfers).

CONTACT
Ms. Jana Kay Lunstad, Director of Enrollment & Campus Registrar, Washington State University–Tri-Cities, 2710 Crimson Way, Richland, WA 99354. *Phone:* 509-372-7250. *E-mail:* admissions@tricity.wsu.edu.

Washington State University–Vancouver

Vancouver, Washington

http://www.vancouver.wsu.edu/

- **State-supported** comprehensive, founded 1989
- **Suburban** 351-acre campus with easy access to Portland, OR
- **Coed** 3,181 undergraduate students, 79% full-time, 53% women, 47% men
- **Moderately difficult** entrance level, 64% of applicants were admitted

UNDERGRAD STUDENTS
2,517 full-time, 664 part-time. Students come from 23 states and territories; 15 other countries; 5% are from out of state; 2% Black or African American, non-Hispanic/Latino; 13% Hispanic/Latino; 7% Asian, non-Hispanic/Latino; 0.7% Native Hawaiian or other Pacific Islander, non-Hispanic/Latino; 0.4% American Indian or Alaska Native, non-Hispanic/Latino; 6% Two or more races, non-Hispanic/Latino; 4% Race/ethnicity unknown; 1% international; 19% transferred in.

Freshmen:
Admission: 1,225 applied, 781 admitted, 375 enrolled. ***Average high school GPA:*** 3.4. ***Test scores:*** SAT evidence-based reading and writing scores over 500: 79%; SAT math scores over 500: 76%; ACT scores over 18: 83%; SAT evidence-based reading and writing scores over 600: 36%; SAT math scores over 600: 24%; ACT scores over 24: 39%; SAT evidence-based reading and writing scores over 700: 5%; SAT math scores over 700: 2%; ACT scores over 30: 9%.

Retention: 74% of full-time freshmen returned.

ACADEMICS
Calendar: semesters. *Degrees:* certificates, bachelor's, master's, and doctoral.

Special study options: accelerated degree program, adult/continuing education programs, advanced placement credit, cooperative education, distance learning, double majors, English as a second language, external degree program, honors programs, independent study, internships, off-campus study, part-time degree program, services for LD students, student-designed majors, study abroad, summer session for credit. ***ROTC:*** Army (c), Air Force (c).

Computers: Students can access the following: free student e-mail accounts, online (class) grades, online (class) registration, online (class) schedules. Campuswide network is available. Wireless service is available via classrooms, computer centers, computer labs, learning centers, libraries, student centers.
Library: WSU Vancouver Library plus 1 other. Students can reserve study rooms.

STUDENT LIFE
Housing options: college housing not available.

Activities and organizations: student-run newspaper, radio station.

Athletics ***Intramural sports:*** basketball M/W, soccer M/W, volleyball M/W.

Campus security: 24-hour emergency response devices and patrols, student patrols.

Student services: personal/psychological counseling, veterans affairs office.

APPLYING
Standardized Tests *Required:* SAT or ACT (for admission).

Options: electronic application.

Application fee: $50.

Required: high school transcript, minimum 2.0 GPA. ***Recommended:*** essay or personal statement.

Application deadlines: 1/31 (freshmen), 1/31 (transfers).

Notification: continuous until 11/1 (freshmen), continuous (out-of-state freshmen), continuous until 11/1 (transfers).

CONTACT
Ms. Kim Hiatt, Associate Director of Admissions, Washington State University–Vancouver, 14204 NE Salmon Creek Avenue, Vancouver, WA 98686. *Phone:* 360-546-9779. *Fax:* 360-546-9032. *E-mail:* van.admissions@wsu.edu.

Western Washington University

Bellingham, Washington

http://www.wwu.edu/

- **State-supported** comprehensive, founded 1893
- **Small-town** 223-acre campus with easy access to Seattle, WA and Vancouver, BC Canada
- **Endowment** $85.2 million
- **Coed** 15,170 undergraduate students, 92% full-time, 57% women, 43% men
- **Moderately difficult** entrance level, 88% of applicants were admitted

UNDERGRAD STUDENTS
13,893 full-time, 1,277 part-time. Students come from 48 states and territories; 42 other countries; 14% are from out of state; 2% Black or African American, non-Hispanic/Latino; 9% Hispanic/Latino; 6% Asian, non-Hispanic/Latino; 0.2% Native Hawaiian or other Pacific Islander, non-Hispanic/Latino; 0.3% American Indian or Alaska Native, non-Hispanic/Latino; 9% Two or more races, non-Hispanic/Latino; 2% Race/ethnicity unknown; 1% international; 8% transferred in; 26% live on campus.

Freshmen:
Admission: 11,124 applied, 9,751 admitted, 3,147 enrolled. ***Average high school GPA:*** 3.5. ***Test scores:*** SAT evidence-based reading and writing scores over 500: 92%; SAT math scores over 500: 89%; ACT scores over 18: 96%; SAT evidence-based reading and writing scores over 600: 54%; SAT math scores over 600: 40%; ACT scores over 24: 63%; SAT evidence-based reading and writing scores over 700: 10%; SAT math scores over 700: 7%; ACT scores over 30: 20%.

Retention: 81% of full-time freshmen returned.

FACULTY
Total: 949, 67% full-time, 74% with terminal degrees.

Student/faculty ratio: 18:1.

ACADEMICS
Calendar: quarters. *Degrees:* certificates, bachelor's, master's, and post-master's certificates.

Special study options: accelerated degree program, advanced placement credit, cooperative education, distance learning, double majors, English as a second language, external degree program, honors programs, independent study, internships, off-campus study, part-time degree program, services for LD students, student-designed majors, study abroad, summer session for credit.

Computers: 2,268 computers/terminals are available on campus for general student use. Students can access the following: computer help desk, free student e-mail accounts, online (class) grades, online (class) registration, online (class) schedules. Campuswide network is available. 99% of college-owned or -operated housing units are wired for high-speed Internet access. Wireless service is available via entire campus.
Library: Wilson Library plus 2 others. *Books:* 631,958 (physical), 363,547 (digital/electronic); *Serial titles:* 21,547 (physical), 101,542 (digital/electronic); *Databases:* 95. Weekly public service hours: 97; students can reserve study rooms.

STUDENT LIFE
Housing options: coed, special housing for students with disabilities. Campus housing is university owned. Freshman campus housing is guaranteed.

Activities and organizations: drama/theater group, student-run newspaper, radio and television station, choral group, Intramurals, Residence Hall Association, Associated Students, Outdoor Center, Ethnic Student Center.

Athletics Member NCAA. All Division II except golf (Division I). ***Intercollegiate sports:*** basketball M(s)/W(s), crew W(s), cross-country running M(s)/W(s), golf M(s)/W(s), soccer M(s)/W(s), softball M/W(s), track and field M(s)/W(s), volleyball W(s). ***Intramural sports:*** baseball M(c), basketball M/W, crew M(c)/W(c), equestrian sports M(c)/W(c), fencing M(c), field hockey W(c), football M/W, golf M/W, ice hockey M(c), lacrosse M(c)/W(c), racquetball M/W, rock climbing M/W, rugby M(c)/W(c), sailing M(c)/W(c), skiing (downhill) M(c)/W(c), soccer M/W, softball M, swimming and diving M(c)/W(c), table tennis M/W, tennis M/W, ultimate Frisbee M(c)/W(c), volleyball M(c)/W(c), water polo M(c)/W(c), wrestling M(c)/W(c).

Campus security: 24-hour emergency response devices and patrols, student patrols, late-night transport/escort service, controlled dormitory access.

Student services: health clinic, personal/psychological counseling, women's center, legal services, veterans affairs office.

COSTS & FINANCIAL AID
Costs (2018–19) ***Tuition:*** state resident $7038 full-time, $235 per credit hour part-time; nonresident $22,450 full-time, $748 per credit hour part-time. Full-time tuition and fees vary according to course load, location, and reciprocity agreements. Part-time tuition and fees vary according to course load, location, and reciprocity agreements. ***Required fees:*** $1094

full-time. ***Room and board:*** $11,466. Room and board charges vary according to board plan, housing facility, and location. ***Payment plan:*** installment. ***Waivers:*** minority students, senior citizens, and employees or children of employees.

Financial Aid Of all full-time matriculated undergraduates who enrolled in 2018, 9,585 applied for aid, 6,771 were judged to have need, 1,033 had their need fully met. 167 Federal Work-Study jobs (averaging $4388). 400 state and other part-time jobs (averaging $4380). In 2018, 344 non-need-based awards were made. ***Average percent of need met:*** 93. ***Average financial aid package:*** $16,294. ***Average need-based loan:*** $4595. ***Average need-based gift aid:*** $9577. ***Average non-need-based aid:*** $1854. ***Average indebtedness upon graduation:*** $11,907.

APPLYING

Standardized Tests *Required:* SAT or ACT (for admission).

Options: electronic application, early action, deferred entrance.

Application fee: $60.

Required: high school transcript. ***Recommended:*** essay or personal statement.

Application deadlines: 1/31 (freshmen), 3/1 (transfers).

Notification: continuous until 11/1 (freshmen), continuous until 5/1 (transfers).

CONTACT

Cezar Mesquita, Director of Admissions, Western Washington University, 516 High Street, Bellingham, WA 98225-5996. *Phone:* 360-650-3440. *E-mail:* admissions@wwu.edu.

Whitman College

Walla Walla, Washington

http://www.whitman.edu/

- **Independent** 4-year, founded 1859
- **Small-town** 117-acre campus
- **Endowment** $518.3 million
- **Coed**
- **Very difficult** entrance level

FACULTY

Student/faculty ratio: 9:1.

ACADEMICS

Calendar: semesters. *Degree:* bachelor's.

Library: Penrose Library plus 1 other. *Books:* 406,675 (physical), 305,206 (digital/electronic); *Serial titles:* 5,082 (physical), 98,012 (digital/electronic); *Databases:* 206. Weekly public service hours: 84; study areas open 24 hours, 5–7 days a week; students can reserve study rooms.

STUDENT LIFE

Housing options: on-campus residence required through sophomore year; coed, women-only. Campus housing is university owned. Freshman campus housing is guaranteed.

Activities and organizations: drama/theater group, student-run newspaper, radio station, choral group, national fraternities, national sororities.

Athletics Member NCAA. All Division III.

Campus security: 24-hour emergency response devices and patrols, student patrols, late-night transport/escort service, controlled dormitory access.

Student services: health clinic, personal/psychological counseling, women's center.

COSTS & FINANCIAL AID

Costs (2018–19) ***Comprehensive fee:*** $64,882 includes full-time tuition ($51,370), mandatory fees ($394), and room and board ($13,118). Part-time tuition: $2140 per credit. Part-time tuition and fees vary according to course load. ***College room only:*** $5844. Room and board charges vary according to board plan, housing facility, and location.

Financial Aid Of all full-time matriculated undergraduates who enrolled in 2018, 758 applied for aid, 638 were judged to have need, 195 had their need fully met. 470 Federal Work-Study jobs (averaging $2462). 55 state and other part-time jobs (averaging $1706). In 2018, 484 non-need-based awards were made. ***Average percent of need met:*** 94. ***Average financial aid package:*** $43,371. ***Average need-based loan:*** $4279. ***Average need-based gift aid:*** $38,369. ***Average non-need-based aid:*** $12,212. ***Average indebtedness upon graduation:*** $25,356. ***Financial aid deadline:*** 1/15.

APPLYING

Standardized Tests *Required for some:* SAT or ACT (for admission).

Options: electronic application, early decision, deferred entrance.

Application fee: $50.

Required: high school transcript. ***Required for some:*** statement of good standing from prior institutions. ***Recommended:*** essay or personal statement, interview.

CONTACT

Whitman College, Penrose House, 345 Boyer Avenue, Walla Walla, WA 99362. *Phone:* 509-527-5176. *Toll-free phone:* 877-462-9448. *E-mail:* admission@whitman.edu.

Whitworth University

Spokane, Washington

http://www.whitworth.edu/

- **Independent Presbyterian** comprehensive, founded 1890
- **Suburban** 200-acre campus
- **Endowment** $151.2 million
- **Coed** 2,355 undergraduate students, 98% full-time, 60% women, 40% men
- **Moderately difficult** entrance level, 91% of applicants were admitted

UNDERGRAD STUDENTS

2,304 full-time, 51 part-time. Students come from 35 states and territories; 38 other countries; 26% are from out of state; 2% Black or African American, non-Hispanic/Latino; 10% Hispanic/Latino; 5% Asian, non-Hispanic/Latino; 0.8% Native Hawaiian or other Pacific Islander, non-Hispanic/Latino; 0.7% American Indian or Alaska Native, non-Hispanic/Latino; 9% Two or more races, non-Hispanic/Latino; 0.9% Race/ethnicity unknown; 4% international; 4% transferred in; 51% live on campus.

Freshmen:

Admission: 3,731 applied, 3,387 admitted, 696 enrolled. ***Average high school GPA:*** 3.6. ***Test scores:*** SAT evidence-based reading and writing scores over 500: 91%; SAT math scores over 500: 89%; ACT scores over 18: 94%; SAT evidence-based reading and writing scores over 600: 54%; SAT math scores over 600: 45%; ACT scores over 24: 60%; SAT evidence-based reading and writing scores over 700: 12%; SAT math scores over 700: 13%; ACT scores over 30: 17%.

Retention: 82% of full-time freshmen returned.

FACULTY

Total: 314, 61% full-time, 61% with terminal degrees.

Student/faculty ratio: 11:1.

ACADEMICS

Calendar: 4-1-4. *Degrees:* bachelor's, master's, post-master's, and postbachelor's certificates.

Special study options: adult/continuing education programs, advanced placement credit, double majors, honors programs, independent study, internships, off-campus study, part-time degree program, services for LD students, student-designed majors, study abroad, summer session for credit. ***ROTC:*** Army (c).

Unusual degree programs: 3-2 engineering with Seattle Pacific University, University of Southern California, Washington University in St. Louis, Columbia University, Washington State University; nursing with Washington State University; athletic training at Whitworth University.

Computers: 280 computers/terminals and 950 ports are available on campus for general student use. Students can access the following: campus intranet, computer help desk, free student e-mail accounts, online (class) grades, online (class) registration, online (class) schedules, learning management system. Campuswide network is available. 100% of college-owned or -operated housing units are wired for high-speed Internet access. Wireless service is available via entire campus.

Library: Harriet Cheney Cowles Library. *Books:* 217,713 (physical), 447,336 (digital/electronic); *Serial titles:* 1,549 (physical), 41,985

(digital/electronic); *Databases:* 207. Weekly public service hours: 97; students can reserve study rooms.

STUDENT LIFE
Housing options: on-campus residence required through sophomore year; coed, men-only, women-only. Campus housing is university owned. Freshman campus housing is guaranteed.

Activities and organizations: drama/theater group, student-run newspaper, radio station, choral group, International Club, Whitworth Student Investment Group, En Christo, Hawaiian Club, Swing and Ballroom Dance Club.

Athletics Member NCAA. All Division III. ***Intercollegiate sports:*** baseball M, basketball M/W, cross-country running M/W, football M, golf M/W, lacrosse W, soccer M/W, softball W, swimming and diving M/W, tennis M/W, track and field M/W, volleyball W. ***Intramural sports:*** badminton M/W, basketball M(c)/W, cheerleading M(c)/W(c), football M/W, soccer M/W, softball M/W, table tennis M/W, tennis M/W, ultimate Frisbee M(c)/W(c), volleyball M/W.

Campus security: 24-hour emergency response devices and patrols, late-night transport/escort service, controlled dormitory access.

Student services: health clinic, personal/psychological counseling.

COSTS & FINANCIAL AID
Costs (2019–20) ***Comprehensive fee:*** $56,740 includes full-time tuition ($43,800), mandatory fees ($1140), and room and board ($11,800). Part-time tuition: $1825 per credit hour. ***Required fees:*** $508 part-time. ***College room only:*** $6450.

Financial Aid Of all full-time matriculated undergraduates who enrolled in 2018, 1,821 applied for aid, 1,631 were judged to have need, 310 had their need fully met. 848 Federal Work-Study jobs (averaging $2774). 71 state and other part-time jobs (averaging $3646). In 2018, 583 non-need-based awards were made. ***Average percent of need met:*** 81. ***Average financial aid package:*** $38,637. ***Average need-based loan:*** $4492. ***Average need-based gift aid:*** $30,617. ***Average non-need-based aid:*** $20,509. ***Average indebtedness upon graduation:*** $29,442.

APPLYING
Standardized Tests *Required for some:* SAT or ACT (for admission).

Options: electronic application, early admission, early action, deferred entrance.

Required: essay or personal statement, high school transcript, 1 letter of recommendation. ***Required for some:*** minimum 3.0 GPA, 2 letters of recommendation, interview.

Application deadlines: rolling (freshmen), rolling (out-of-state freshmen), rolling (transfers), 1/15 (early action).

Notification: continuous (freshmen), continuous (out-of-state freshmen), continuous (transfers), rolling (early action).

CONTACT
Ms. Lara Ramsay, Director of Admission, Whitworth University, 300 West, Hawthorne Road, Spokane, WA 99251. *Phone:* 509-777-4347. *Toll-free phone:* 800-533-4668. *Fax:* 509-777-3758. *E-mail:* admission@whitworth.edu.

WEST VIRGINIA

Alderson Broaddus University

Philippi, West Virginia

http://www.ab.edu/

CONTACT
Mr. Erika L. Thon, Director of Admissions, Alderson Broaddus University, 101 College Hill Drive, Campus Box 2003, Philippi, WV 26416. *Phone:* 304-457-6256. *Toll-free phone:* 800-263-1549. *Fax:* 304-457-6239. *E-mail:* thonel@ab.edu.

American Public University System

Charles Town, West Virginia

http://www.apus.edu/

- **Proprietary** comprehensive, founded 1991
- **Rural** campus with easy access to Washington, DC
- **Coed** 37,746 undergraduate students, 6% full-time, 36% women, 64% men
- **Noncompetitive** entrance level

UNDERGRAD STUDENTS
2,324 full-time, 35,422 part-time. 16% Black or African American, non-Hispanic/Latino; 13% Hispanic/Latino; 2% Asian, non-Hispanic/Latino; 0.9% Native Hawaiian or other Pacific Islander, non-Hispanic/Latino; 0.6% American Indian or Alaska Native, non-Hispanic/Latino; 4% Two or more races, non-Hispanic/Latino; 7% Race/ethnicity unknown; 0.7% international; 14% transferred in.

Freshmen:
Admission: 1,324 enrolled.
Retention: 98% of full-time freshmen returned.

FACULTY
Student/faculty ratio: 20:1.

ACADEMICS
Calendar: courses start on the first Monday of each month. *Degrees:* certificates, associate, bachelor's, master's, doctoral, and postbachelor's certificates (profile includes American Public University, American Military University and American Community College).

Special study options: advanced placement credit, distance learning, external degree program, independent study, internships, part-time degree program, services for LD students, summer session for credit.

Computers: Students can access the following: free student e-mail accounts, online (class) grades, online (class) registration, online (class) schedules.
Library: APUS Online Library.

STUDENT LIFE
Housing options: college housing not available.

COSTS
Costs (2018–19) ***Tuition:*** $6480 full-time, $270 per credit hour part-time. ***Required fees:*** $400 full-time. ***Payment plan:*** installment. ***Waivers:*** employees or children of employees.

APPLYING
Options: electronic application, deferred entrance.

Required: high school transcript.

CONTACT
Mr. Greg Hill, Assistant Vice President, Prospect Management and Undergraduate Admissions, American Public University System, 111 West Congress Street, Charles Town, WV 25414. *Phone:* 877-468-6268. *Toll-free phone:* 877-755-2787. *Fax:* 304-724-3788. *E-mail:* info@apus.edu.

Appalachian Bible College

Mount Hope, West Virginia

http://www.abc.edu/

- **Independent nondenominational** comprehensive, founded 1950
- **Small-town** 110-acre campus
- **Endowment** $316,677
- **Coed**
- **Noncompetitive** entrance level

FACULTY
Student/faculty ratio: 8:1.

ACADEMICS
Calendar: semesters. *Degrees:* certificates, diplomas, associate, bachelor's, master's, and postbachelor's certificates.
Library: John Van Pufflen Library.

STUDENT LIFE
Housing options: on-campus residence required for freshman year; men-only, women-only. Campus housing is university owned. Freshman campus housing is guaranteed.

Activities and organizations: drama/theater group, choral group.

Athletics Member NCCAA.

Campus security: 24-hour emergency response devices, controlled dormitory access, patrols by trained security personnel.

Student services: health clinic, personal/psychological counseling.

COSTS & FINANCIAL AID
Costs (2018–19) ***Comprehensive fee:*** $21,880 includes full-time tuition ($13,010), mandatory fees ($910), and room and board ($7960). Full-time tuition and fees vary according to course load. Part-time tuition: $395 per credit hour. Part-time tuition and fees vary according to course load. ***Required fees:*** $42 per credit hour part-time, $160 per term part-time. ***Room and board:*** Room and board charges vary according to housing facility. ***Payment plans:*** installment, deferred payment.

Financial Aid Of all full-time matriculated undergraduates who enrolled in 2018, 150 applied for aid, 107 were judged to have need, 1 had their need fully met. 23 Federal Work-Study jobs (averaging $721). In 2018, 8 non-need-based awards were made. ***Average percent of need met:*** 67. ***Average financial aid package:*** $13,038. ***Average need-based loan:*** $4223. ***Average need-based gift aid:*** $12,160. ***Average non-need-based aid:*** $5309. ***Average indebtedness upon graduation:*** $3043.

APPLYING
Standardized Tests *Required:* SAT or ACT (for admission).

Options: electronic application, early admission, deferred entrance.

Application fee: $35.

Required: essay or personal statement, high school transcript, 2 letters of recommendation. ***Required for some:*** interview. ***Recommended:*** minimum 2.3 GPA.

CONTACT
Miss Megan Mullens, Admissions Assistant, Appalachian Bible College, 161 College Drive, Mount Hope, WV 25880. *Phone:* 304-877-6428 Ext. 313. *Toll-free phone:* 800-678-9ABC. *Fax:* 304-877-5082. *E-mail:* admissions@abc.edu.

Bethany College
Bethany, West Virginia
http://www.bethanywv.edu/

CONTACT
Ms. Mollie Cecere, Director of Enrollment, Bethany College, Center for Enrollment and Financial Aid, 31 E. Campus Drive #4, Bethany, WV 26032. *Phone:* 304-829-7611. *Toll-free phone:* 800-922-7611. *Fax:* 304-829-7142. *E-mail:* enrollment@bethanywv.edu.

Bluefield State College
Bluefield, West Virginia
http://www.bluefieldstate.edu/

CONTACT
Bluefield State College, 219 Rock Street, Bluefield, WV 24701-2198. *Phone:* 304-327-4067. *Toll-free phone:* 800-344-8892 Ext. 4065 (in-state); 800-654-7798 Ext. 4065 (out-of-state).

Concord University
Athens, West Virginia
http://www.concord.edu/

- **State-supported** comprehensive, founded 1872, part of State College System of West Virginia
- **Rural** 100-acre campus
- **Endowment** $24.5 million
- **Coed**
- **Minimally difficult** entrance level

FACULTY
Student/faculty ratio: 15:1.

ACADEMICS
Calendar: semesters. *Degrees:* bachelor's, master's, and post-master's certificates.
Library: J. Frank Marsh Library. *Books:* 162,020 (physical), 34,329 (digital/electronic); *Serial titles:* 68 (physical), 110 (digital/electronic); *Databases:* 14. Weekly public service hours: 77; study areas open 24 hours, 5–7 days a week; students can reserve study rooms.

STUDENT LIFE
Housing options: coed, men-only, women-only. Campus housing is university owned. Freshman campus housing is guaranteed.

Activities and organizations: drama/theater group, student-run newspaper, radio and television station, choral group, marching band, Service Groups, student government, student-run publications, intramurals, Student Activities Committee, national fraternities, national sororities.

Athletics Member NCAA. All Division II.

Campus security: 24-hour emergency response devices and patrols, student patrols, late-night transport/escort service, controlled dormitory access.

Student services: health clinic, personal/psychological counseling, veterans affairs office.

COSTS & FINANCIAL AID
Costs (2018–19) ***Tuition:*** state resident $7876 full-time; nonresident $17,320 full-time. Full-time tuition and fees vary according to course load and program. Part-time tuition and fees vary according to course load and program. ***Required fees:*** $150 full-time. ***Room and board:*** $8988; room only: $4502. Room and board charges vary according to board plan.

Financial Aid Of all full-time matriculated undergraduates who enrolled in 2018, 1,420 applied for aid, 1,222 were judged to have need, 458 had their need fully met. 180 Federal Work-Study jobs (averaging $2041). In 2018, 221 non-need-based awards were made. ***Average percent of need met:*** 83. ***Average financial aid package:*** $8491. ***Average need-based loan:*** $3335. ***Average need-based gift aid:*** $5995. ***Average non-need-based aid:*** $4096. ***Average indebtedness upon graduation:*** $21,176. ***Financial aid deadline:*** 4/15.

APPLYING
Standardized Tests *Required:* SAT or ACT (for admission).

Options: electronic application, early admission.

Required: high school transcript, minimum 2.0 GPA. ***Required for some:*** essay or personal statement, interview. ***Recommended:*** interview.

CONTACT
Mr. Jamie Ealy, Vice President of Enrollment Management, Concord University, 1000 Vermillion Street, Athens, WV 24712. *Phone:* 304-384-6305. *Toll-free phone:* 888-384-5249. *Fax:* 304-384-9044. *E-mail:* admissions@concord.edu.

Davis & Elkins College
Elkins, West Virginia
http://www.dewv.edu/

CONTACT
Ms. ReneÃ© Heckel, Director of Enrollment Management, Davis & Elkins College, 100 Campus Drive, Elkins, WV 26241. *Phone:* 304-637-1974. *Toll-free phone:* 800-624-3157. *Fax:* 304-637-1800. *E-mail:* admiss@davisandelkins.edu.

Fairmont State University
Fairmont, West Virginia
http://www.fairmontstate.edu/

CONTACT
Mrs. Amie Fazalare, Director of Recruiting, Fairmont State University, 1201 Locust Avenue, Fairmont, WV 26554. *Phone:* 304-367-4892. *Toll-free phone:* 800-641-5678. *Fax:* 304-367-4789. *E-mail:* admit@fairmontstate.edu.

Glenville State College

Glenville, West Virginia

http://www.glenville.edu/

CONTACT

Ms. Ashley Weir, Admission Counselor, Glenville State College, 200 High Street, Glenville, WV 26351-1200. *Phone:* 304-462-4128 Ext. 6133. *Toll-free phone:* 800-924-2010. *Fax:* 304-462-8619. *E-mail:* ashley.weir@glenville.edu.

Marshall University

Huntington, West Virginia

http://www.marshall.edu/

- **State-supported** university, founded 1837, part of University System of West Virginia
- **Urban** 114-acre campus
- **Coed** 9,593 undergraduate students, 78% full-time, 58% women, 42% men
- **Moderately difficult** entrance level, 91% of applicants were admitted

UNDERGRAD STUDENTS

7,460 full-time, 2,133 part-time. 18% are from out of state; 6% Black or African American, non-Hispanic/Latino; 2% Hispanic/Latino; 0.9% Asian, non-Hispanic/Latino; 0.1% Native Hawaiian or other Pacific Islander, non-Hispanic/Latino; 0.3% American Indian or Alaska Native, non-Hispanic/Latino; 3% Two or more races, non-Hispanic/Latino; 1% Race/ethnicity unknown; 2% international; 5% transferred in.

Freshmen:

Admission: 4,987 applied, 4,519 admitted, 1,681 enrolled. ***Average high school GPA:*** 3.5. ***Test scores:*** SAT evidence-based reading and writing scores over 500: 76%; SAT math scores over 500: 62%; ACT scores over 18: 86%; SAT evidence-based reading and writing scores over 600: 28%; SAT math scores over 600: 17%; ACT scores over 24: 33%; SAT evidence-based reading and writing scores over 700: 3%; SAT math scores over 700: 6%; ACT scores over 30: 5%.

Retention: 72% of full-time freshmen returned.

FACULTY

Total: 712, 68% full-time, 60% with terminal degrees.

Student/faculty ratio: 19:1.

ACADEMICS

Calendar: semesters. *Degrees:* certificates, bachelor's, master's, doctoral, post-master's, and postbachelor's certificates.

Special study options: academic remediation for entering students, accelerated degree program, adult/continuing education programs, advanced placement credit, cooperative education, distance learning, double majors, English as a second language, honors programs, independent study, internships, off-campus study, part-time degree program, services for LD students, study abroad, summer session for credit. *ROTC:* Army (b).

Computers: 1,200 computers/terminals and 500 ports are available on campus for general student use. Students can access the following: campus intranet, computer help desk, free student e-mail accounts, online (class) grades, online (class) registration, online (class) schedules, virtual computer lab: remote and Web conferencing. Campuswide network is available. 100% of college-owned or -operated housing units are wired for high-speed Internet access. Wireless service is available via classrooms, computer centers, computer labs, dorm rooms, learning centers, libraries, student centers.

Library: John Deaver Drinko Library plus 1 other. *Books:* 398,144 (physical), 224,894 (digital/electronic); *Serial titles:* 2,030 (physical), 49,727 (digital/electronic); *Databases:* 256. Weekly public service hours: 133; study areas open 24 hours, 5–7 days a week; students can reserve study rooms.

STUDENT LIFE

Housing options: on-campus residence required through sophomore year; coed, women-only, special housing for students with disabilities. Campus housing is university owned and is provided by a third party. Freshman campus housing is guaranteed.

Activities and organizations: drama/theater group, student-run newspaper, radio and television station, choral group, marching band, Campus Crusade for Christ, Gamma Beta Phi, The International Students'; Organization, Newman Association, Phi Alpha Theta, national fraternities, national sororities.

Athletics Member NCAA. All Division I except football (Division I-A). ***Intercollegiate sports:*** baseball M(s), basketball M(s)/W(s), cross-country running M(s)/W(s), golf M(s)/W(s)(c), lacrosse M(c), rugby M(c)/W(c), soccer M(s)/W(s), softball W(s), swimming and diving W(s), tennis W(s), track and field M(s)/W(s), volleyball W(s). ***Intramural sports:*** basketball M/W, bowling M/W, football M/W, golf M/W, racquetball M/W, soccer M/W, softball M/W, swimming and diving M/W, tennis M/W, track and field M/W, volleyball M/W.

Campus security: 24-hour emergency response devices and patrols, student patrols, late-night transport/escort service, controlled dormitory access.

Student services: health clinic, personal/psychological counseling, women's center, legal services, veterans affairs office.

COSTS & FINANCIAL AID

Costs (2018–19) ***Tuition:*** state resident $7006 full-time, $292 per credit hour part-time; nonresident $17,492 full-time, $729 per credit hour part-time. Full-time tuition and fees vary according to degree level, location, program, and reciprocity agreements. Part-time tuition and fees vary according to course load, degree level, location, program, and reciprocity agreements. ***Required fees:*** $1122 full-time, $47 per credit hour part-time. ***Room and board:*** $10,450; room only: $6454. Room and board charges vary according to board plan and housing facility. ***Payment plan:*** installment. ***Waivers:*** children of alumni, senior citizens, and employees or children of employees.

Financial Aid Of all full-time matriculated undergraduates who enrolled in 2018, 6,543 applied for aid, 5,357 were judged to have need, 1,545 had their need fully met. In 2018, 945 non-need-based awards were made. ***Average percent of need met:*** 47. ***Average financial aid package:*** $11,290. ***Average need-based loan:*** $6791. ***Average need-based gift aid:*** $6568. ***Average non-need-based aid:*** $2771. ***Average indebtedness upon graduation:*** $27,420.

APPLYING

Standardized Tests *Required:* SAT or ACT (for admission).

Options: electronic application, deferred entrance.

Application fee: $40.

Required for some: high school transcript.

Application deadlines: rolling (freshmen), rolling (transfers).

Notification: continuous (freshmen), continuous (transfers).

CONTACT

Dr. Tammy Johnson, Director of Admissions, Marshall University, 1 John Marshall Drive, Huntington, WV 25755. *Phone:* 800-642-3499. *Toll-free phone:* 800-642-3499. *Fax:* 304-696-3135. *E-mail:* admissions@marshall.edu.

Ohio Valley University

Vienna, West Virginia

http://www.ovu.edu/

CONTACT

Mrs. Valerie Wright, Admissions Office Manager, Ohio Valley University, 1 Campus View Drive, Vienna, WV 26105. *Phone:* 304-865-6200. *Toll-free phone:* 877-446-8668. *Fax:* 304-865-6001. *E-mail:* admissions@ovu.edu.

Potomac State College of West Virginia University

Keyser, West Virginia

http://www.potomacstatecollege.edu/

- **State-supported** primarily 2-year, founded 1901, part of West Virginia Higher Education Policy Commission
- **Small-town** 18-acre campus
- **Coed** 1,340 undergraduate students, 76% full-time, 56% women, 44% men
- **Noncompetitive** entrance level, 76% of applicants were admitted

UNDERGRAD STUDENTS
1,018 full-time, 322 part-time. 20% are from out of state; 8% Black or African American, non-Hispanic/Latino; 3% Hispanic/Latino; 1% Asian, non-Hispanic/Latino; 0.1% Native Hawaiian or other Pacific Islander, non-Hispanic/Latino; 0.2% American Indian or Alaska Native, non-Hispanic/Latino; 4% Two or more races, non-Hispanic/Latino; 1% Race/ethnicity unknown; 0.4% international; 4% transferred in; 52% live on campus.

Freshmen:
Admission: 2,284 applied, 1,726 admitted, 537 enrolled. ***Average high school GPA:*** 3.1.

Retention: 39% of full-time freshmen returned.

FACULTY
Total: 80, 61% full-time, 25% with terminal degrees.

Student/faculty ratio: 22:1.

ACADEMICS
Calendar: semesters. *Degrees:* associate and bachelor's.

Special study options: academic remediation for entering students, adult/continuing education programs, advanced placement credit, cooperative education, distance learning, double majors, honors programs, independent study, internships, part-time degree program, services for LD students, study abroad, summer session for credit.

Computers: 69 computers/terminals are available on campus for general student use. Students can access the following: computer help desk, free student e-mail accounts, online (class) grades, online (class) registration, online (class) schedules. 100% of college-owned or -operated housing units are wired for high-speed Internet access. Wireless service is available via classrooms, computer labs, libraries, student centers.
Library: Mary F. Shipper Library. *Books:* 7,011 (physical), 617,383 (digital/electronic); *Serial titles:* 19 (physical), 93,783 (digital/electronic); *Databases:* 687.

STUDENT LIFE
Housing options: on-campus residence required through sophomore year; coed. Campus housing is university owned. Freshman applicants given priority for college housing.

Activities and organizations: drama/theater group, student-run newspaper, choral group, Agriculture and Forestry Club, Black Student Alliance, Gamers and Geeks Club, Campus and Community Ministries.

Athletics Member NJCAA. ***Intercollegiate sports:*** baseball M(s), basketball M(s)/W(s), cross-country running M(s)/W(s), lacrosse M(s)/W(s), soccer M/W, softball W(s), volleyball W(s). ***Intramural sports:*** basketball M/W, football M/W, soccer M/W, softball M/W, table tennis M/W, ultimate Frisbee M/W, volleyball M/W.

Campus security: 24-hour patrols, late-night transport/escort service, controlled dormitory access.

Student services: health clinic, personal/psychological counseling, veterans affairs office.

COSTS & FINANCIAL AID
Costs (2018–19) ***Tuition:*** state resident $4488 full-time, $187 per credit hour part-time; nonresident $11,376 full-time, $474 per credit hour part-time. Full-time tuition and fees vary according to degree level and program. Part-time tuition and fees vary according to degree level. ***Room and board:*** $8524. Room and board charges vary according to board plan and housing facility. ***Payment plan:*** deferred payment. ***Waivers:*** employees or children of employees.

Financial Aid Of all full-time matriculated undergraduates who enrolled in 2017, 1,059 applied for aid, 843 were judged to have need, 73 had their need fully met. In 2017, 57 non-need-based awards were made. ***Average percent of need met:*** 65. ***Average financial aid package:*** $4355. ***Average need-based loan:*** $3039. ***Average need-based gift aid:*** $3418. ***Average non-need-based aid:*** $1907. ***Average indebtedness upon graduation:*** $18,208.

APPLYING
Options: electronic application.

Required: high school transcript.

Application deadlines: rolling (freshmen), rolling (transfers).

CONTACT
Ms. Beth Little, Director of Enrollment Services, Potomac State College of West Virginia University, 75 Arnold Street, Keyser, WV 26726. *Phone:* 304-788-6820. *Toll-free phone:* 800-262-7332 Ext. 6820. *Fax:* 304-788-6939. *E-mail:* go2psc@mail.wvu.edu.

Salem International University

Salem, West Virginia

http://www.salemu.edu/

CONTACT
Mrs. Brenda Davis, Admissions Representative, Salem International University, PO Box 500, Salem, WV 26426-0500. *Phone:* 304-326-1359. *Toll-free phone:* 888-235-5024. *Fax:* 304-326-1592. *E-mail:* admissions@salemiu.edu.

Shepherd University

Shepherdstown, West Virginia

http://www.shepherd.edu/

- **State-supported** comprehensive, founded 1871, part of West Virginia Higher Education Policy Commission
- **Small-town** 325-acre campus with easy access to Washington, D.C.
- **Endowment** $25.9 million
- **Coed**
- **Moderately difficult** entrance level

FACULTY
Student/faculty ratio: 15:1.

ACADEMICS
Calendar: semesters. *Degrees:* bachelor's, master's, and doctoral.
Library: Scarborough Library. *Books:* 143,245 (physical), 6,727 (digital/electronic); *Serial titles:* 373 (physical), 69,441 (digital/electronic); *Databases:* 71. Weekly public service hours: 87; study areas open 24 hours, 5–7 days a week; students can reserve study rooms.

STUDENT LIFE
Housing options: on-campus residence required through senior year; coed, special housing for students with disabilities. Campus housing is university owned. Freshman campus housing is guaranteed.

Activities and organizations: drama/theater group, student-run newspaper, radio station, choral group, marching band, Relay for Life, Student Government Association, Ram Marching Band, Sigma Sigma Sigma, Alpha Phi Omega, national fraternities, national sororities.

Athletics Member NCAA. All Division II.

Campus security: 24-hour emergency response devices and patrols, late-night transport/escort service, controlled dormitory access, student security in academic buildings, RAVE emergency alert system.

Student services: health clinic, personal/psychological counseling, veterans affairs office.

COSTS & FINANCIAL AID
Costs (2018–19) ***Tuition:*** state resident $7548 full-time, $315 per credit hour part-time; nonresident $18,052 full-time, $752 per credit hour part-time. Full-time tuition and fees vary according to program and reciprocity agreements. Part-time tuition and fees vary according to program. ***Room and board:*** $10,500. Room and board charges vary according to board plan and housing facility.

Financial Aid Of all full-time matriculated undergraduates who enrolled in 2018, 2,422 applied for aid, 1,709 were judged to have need, 448 had their need fully met. 105 Federal Work-Study jobs (averaging $1850). 418 state and other part-time jobs (averaging $2021). In 2018, 553 non-need-based awards were made. ***Average percent of need met:*** 73. ***Average financial aid package:*** $12,813. ***Average need-based loan:*** $4059. ***Average need-based gift aid:*** $5743. ***Average non-need-based aid:*** $11,230. ***Average indebtedness upon graduation:*** $28,175.

APPLYING
Standardized Tests *Required:* SAT or ACT (for admission).

Options: electronic application, early admission, early action, deferred entrance.

Application fee: $45.

Required: high school transcript, minimum 2.0 GPA. ***Recommended:*** essay or personal statement, minimum 3.0 GPA, 2 letters of recommendation.

CONTACT
Ms. Kristen Lorenz, Director of Admissions, Shepherd University, PO Box 5000, Shepherdstown, WV 25443-5000. *Phone:* 304-876-5212. *Toll-free phone:* 800-344-5231. *Fax:* 304-876-5165. *E-mail:* admission@shepherd.edu.

Strayer University–Teays Valley Campus

Scott Depot, West Virginia

http://www.strayer.edu/west-virginia/teays-valley/

CONTACT
Strayer University–Teays Valley Campus, 135 Corporate Center Drive, Scott Depot, WV 25560. *Toll-free phone:* 888-311-0355.

University of Charleston

Charleston, West Virginia

http://www.ucwv.edu/

- **Independent** comprehensive, founded 1888
- **Small-town** 40-acre campus
- **Coed**
- **Moderately difficult** entrance level

ACADEMICS
Calendar: semesters. *Degrees:* associate, bachelor's, master's, and doctoral.
Library: Schoenbaum Library plus 1 other. *Books:* 189,000 (physical), 210,000 (digital/electronic); *Databases:* 56. Students can reserve study rooms.

STUDENT LIFE
Housing options: on-campus residence required through sophomore year; coed, special housing for students with disabilities. Campus housing is university owned. Freshman campus housing is guaranteed.

Activities and organizations: student-run newspaper, choral group, marching band, Student Activities Board, American Society of Interior Designers, Student Government Association, Capito Association of Nursing Students, International Student Organization, national fraternities, national sororities.

Athletics Member NCAA. All Division II.

Campus security: 24-hour emergency response devices and patrols, student patrols, late-night transport/escort service, controlled dormitory access, radio connection to city police and ambulance.

Student services: health clinic, personal/psychological counseling, veterans affairs office.

COSTS & FINANCIAL AID
Costs (2018–19) ***Comprehensive fee:*** $40,080 includes full-time tuition ($29,900), mandatory fees ($1000), and room and board ($9180). Full-time tuition and fees vary according to location and program. Part-time tuition: $380 per credit hour. Part-time tuition and fees vary according to course load, location, and program. ***College room only:*** $5000. Room and board charges vary according to board plan, housing facility, and location.

Financial Aid ***Financial aid deadline:*** 8/15.

APPLYING
Options: electronic application, early admission, deferred entrance.

Application fee: $25.

Required: high school transcript, minimum 2.3 GPA. ***Required for some:*** interview. ***Recommended:*** essay or personal statement.

CONTACT
Sandy Dolin, Application Coordinator, University of Charleston, 2300 MacCorkle Avenue, SE, Charleston, WV 25304. *Phone:* 304-357-4752. *Toll-free phone:* 800-995-GOUC. *E-mail:* admissions@ucwv.edu.

West Liberty University

West Liberty, West Virginia

http://www.westliberty.edu/

CONTACT
Ms. Stephanie North, Admissions Counselor, West Liberty University, 208 University Drive, West Liberty, WV 26074. *Phone:* 304-336-8078. *Toll-free phone:* 800-732-6204 (in-state); 866-WESTLIB (out-of-state). *Fax:* 304-336-8403. *E-mail:* wladmsn1@westliberty.edu.

West Virginia State University

Institute, West Virginia

http://www.wvstateu.edu/

- **State-supported** comprehensive, founded 1891, part of West Virginia four-year public higher education system
- **Small-town** 98-acre campus
- **Endowment** $7.1 million
- **Coed** 3,571 undergraduate students, 46% full-time, 59% women, 41% men
- **Minimally difficult** entrance level, 98% of applicants were admitted

UNDERGRAD STUDENTS
1,644 full-time, 1,927 part-time. Students come from 25 states and territories; 13 other countries; 15% are from out of state; 14% Black or African American, non-Hispanic/Latino; 2% Hispanic/Latino; 0.6% Asian, non-Hispanic/Latino; 0.3% Native Hawaiian or other Pacific Islander, non-Hispanic/Latino; 1% American Indian or Alaska Native, non-Hispanic/Latino; 7% Two or more races, non-Hispanic/Latino; 4% Race/ethnicity unknown; 2% international; 6% transferred in; 21% live on campus.

Freshmen:
Admission: 3,182 applied, 3,105 admitted, 324 enrolled. ***Average high school GPA:*** 3.1. ***Test scores:*** SAT evidence-based reading and writing scores over 500: 47%; SAT math scores over 500: 43%; ACT scores over 18: 69%; SAT evidence-based reading and writing scores over 600: 4%; ACT scores over 24: 15%; ACT scores over 30: 1%.

Retention: 59% of full-time freshmen returned.

FACULTY
Total: 193, 55% full-time, 48% with terminal degrees.

Student/faculty ratio: 13:1.

ACADEMICS
Calendar: semesters. *Degrees:* bachelor's, master's, post-master's, and postbachelor's certificates.

Special study options: academic remediation for entering students, accelerated degree program, adult/continuing education programs, advanced placement credit, cooperative education, double majors, external degree program, honors programs, internships, part-time degree program, services for LD students, summer session for credit. ***ROTC:*** Army (b).

Computers: 625 computers/terminals and 5,500 ports are available on campus for general student use. Students can access the following: campus intranet, computer help desk, free student e-mail accounts, online (class) grades, online (class) registration, online (class) schedules. Campuswide network is available. 100% of college-owned or -operated housing units are wired for high-speed Internet access. Wireless service is available via entire campus.
Library: Drain-Jordan Library. *Books:* 135,848 (physical), 25,361 (digital/electronic); *Serial titles:* 1,454 (physical), 33,375 (digital/electronic); *Databases:* 28. Weekly public service hours: 82.

STUDENT LIFE
Housing options: on-campus residence required through sophomore year; coed, special housing for students with disabilities. Campus housing is university owned.

Activities and organizations: student-run newspaper, radio station, choral group, marching band, Student Social Work Organization 20, WVSU College Chapter - NAACP 17, CHOICES Peer Educators 13, WVSU International Student Services 13, C.E. Jones Historical Society 12, national fraternities, national sororities.

Athletics Member NCAA. All Division II. ***Intercollegiate sports:*** baseball M(s), basketball M(s)/W(s), cross-country running W(s), football M(s), golf M(s), softball W(s), tennis M(s)/W(s), volleyball W(s). ***Intramural sports:*** baseball M, basketball M/W, cheerleading W, cross-country running W, football M, golf M, softball W, tennis M/W, volleyball W.

Campus security: 24-hour emergency response devices and patrols, late-night transport/escort service, controlled dormitory access.

Student services: health clinic, personal/psychological counseling, veterans affairs office.

COSTS & FINANCIAL AID

Costs (2019–20) ***Tuition:*** state resident $8050 full-time, $332 per credit hour part-time; nonresident $17,166 full-time, $746 per credit hour part-time. ***Required fees:*** $700 full-time. ***Room and board:*** $12,486; room only: $7852.

Financial Aid ***Financial aid deadline:*** 6/15.

APPLYING

Standardized Tests *Required:* SAT or ACT (for admission).

Options: electronic application.

Application fee: $20.

Required: high school transcript, minimum 2.0 GPA, minimum ACT composite score of 18 (870 SAT).

Notification: continuous (freshmen), continuous (out-of-state freshmen), continuous (transfers).

CONTACT

Jameelah Means, Interim Director of Admissions, West Virginia State University, PO Box 1000, Ferrell Hall, Room 106, Institute, WV 25112-1000. *Phone:* 304-204-4340. *Toll-free phone:* 800-987-2112. *Fax:* 304-766-5182. *E-mail:* jmeans9@wvstateu.edu.

West Virginia University

Morgantown, West Virginia

http://www.wvu.edu/

- **State-supported** university, founded 1867, part of West Virginia Higher Education Policy Commission
- **Small-town** 1892-acre campus with easy access to Pittsburgh
- **Endowment** $574.9 million
- **Coed**
- **Moderately difficult** entrance level

FACULTY

Student/faculty ratio: 20:1.

ACADEMICS

Calendar: semesters. *Degrees:* bachelor's, master's, and doctoral.

Library: Downtown Library Complex plus 5 others. *Books:* 1.1 million (physical), 621,166 (digital/electronic); *Serial titles:* 56,340 (physical), 96,553 (digital/electronic); *Databases:* 975. Study areas open 24 hours, 5–7 days a week; students can reserve study rooms.

STUDENT LIFE

Housing options: on-campus residence required for freshman year; coed, men-only, women-only, cooperative, special housing for students with disabilities. Campus housing is university owned and leased by the school. Freshman campus housing is guaranteed.

Activities and organizations: drama/theater group, student-run newspaper, radio station, choral group, marching band, Residential Hall Association, Alpha Phi Omega, WVU Greek System, Mountaineer Maniacs, Campus Crusade for Christ, national fraternities, national sororities.

Athletics Member NCAA. All Division I except football (Division I-A).

Campus security: 24-hour emergency response devices and patrols, student patrols, late-night transport/escort service, controlled dormitory access, patrol officers just for housing.

Student services: health clinic, personal/psychological counseling, women's center, legal services, veterans affairs office.

COSTS & FINANCIAL AID

Costs (2018–19) ***Tuition:*** state resident $8856 full-time, $369 per credit hour part-time; nonresident $24,950 full-time, $1040 per credit hour part-time. Full-time tuition and fees vary according to location, program, and reciprocity agreements. Part-time tuition and fees vary according to course load, location, program, and reciprocity agreements. ***Room and board:*** $10,918. Room and board charges vary according to board plan, housing facility, and location.

Financial Aid Of all full-time matriculated undergraduates who enrolled in 2017, 16,394 applied for aid, 10,783 were judged to have need, 1,160 had their need fully met. In 2017, 3344 non-need-based awards were made. ***Average financial aid package:*** $7488. ***Average need-based loan:*** $4225. ***Average need-based gift aid:*** $5812. ***Average non-need-based aid:*** $4737. ***Average indebtedness upon graduation:*** $32,541. ***Financial aid deadline:*** 3/1.

APPLYING

Standardized Tests *Required:* SAT or ACT (for admission).

Options: electronic application.

Application fee: $45.

Required: high school transcript, minimum 2.0 GPA. ***Required for some:*** essay or personal statement, minimum 2.3 GPA.

CONTACT

Ms. Marilyn Potts, Director of Admissions, West Virginia University, PO Box 6009, Morgantown, WV 26506-6009. *Phone:* 304-293-2121. *Toll-free phone:* 800-344-9881. *Fax:* 304-293-3080. *E-mail:* marilyn.potts@mail.wvu.edu.

West Virginia University at Parkersburg

Parkersburg, West Virginia

http://www.wvup.edu/

CONTACT

Christine Post, Associate Dean of Enrollment Management, West Virginia University at Parkersburg, 300 Campus Drive, Parkersburg, WV 26104. *Phone:* 304-424-8223 Ext. 223. *Toll-free phone:* 800-WVA-WVUP. *Fax:* 304-424-8332. *E-mail:* christine.post@mail.wvu.edu.

West Virginia University Institute of Technology

Beckley, West Virginia

http://www.wvutech.edu/

- **State-supported** 4-year, founded 1895
- **Small-town** 114-acre campus
- **Endowment** $532.6 million
- **Coed** 1,755 undergraduate students, 67% full-time, 46% women, 54% men
- **Minimally difficult** entrance level, 61% of applicants were admitted

UNDERGRAD STUDENTS

1,175 full-time, 580 part-time. Students come from 31 states and territories; 29 other countries; 11% are from out of state; 6% Black or African American, non-Hispanic/Latino; 3% Hispanic/Latino; 0.8% Asian, non-Hispanic/Latino; 0.3% American Indian or Alaska Native, non-Hispanic/Latino; 6% Two or more races, non-Hispanic/Latino; 2% Race/ethnicity unknown; 5% international; 6% transferred in; 23% live on campus.

Freshmen:

Admission: 1,517 applied, 920 admitted, 367 enrolled. ***Average high school GPA:*** 3.5. ***Test scores:*** SAT math scores over 500: 64%; ACT scores over 18: 80%; SAT math scores over 600: 19%; ACT scores over 24: 25%; SAT math scores over 700: 2%; ACT scores over 30: 3%.

Retention: 56% of full-time freshmen returned.

FACULTY

Total: 124, 77% full-time, 55% with terminal degrees.

Student/faculty ratio: 13:1.

ACADEMICS

Calendar: semesters. *Degrees:* bachelor's and postbachelor's certificates.

Special study options: academic remediation for entering students, advanced placement credit, cooperative education, distance learning, double majors, independent study, internships, part-time degree program, services for LD students, student-designed majors, study abroad, summer session for credit. ***ROTC:*** Army (b).

Unusual degree programs: 3-2 teacher education with West Virginia University.

Computers: 200 computers/terminals are available on campus for general student use. Students can access the following: computer help desk, free student e-mail accounts, online (class) grades, online (class) registration, online (class) schedules, electronic course materials. Campuswide network is available. 100% of college-owned or -operated housing units are wired for high-speed Internet access. Wireless service is available via classrooms, computer centers, computer labs, dorm rooms, learning centers, libraries, student centers.

Library: Vining Library plus 1 other. *Books:* 14,844 (physical), 586,819 (digital/electronic); *Serial titles:* 154 (physical), 95,919 (digital/electronic). Students can reserve study rooms.

STUDENT LIFE

Housing options: on-campus residence required through sophomore year; coed. Campus housing is university owned. Freshman campus housing is guaranteed.

Activities and organizations: drama/theater group, student-run newspaper, Christian Student Union, Student Activities Board, Alpha Phi Omega, Student Government Association, American Society of Mechanical Engineers, national fraternities, national sororities.

Athletics Member NAIA, USCAA. ***Intercollegiate sports:*** baseball M(s), basketball M(s)/W(s), cross-country running M(s)/W(s), golf M(s), soccer M(s)/W(s), softball W(s), swimming and diving M(s)/W(s), volleyball W(s), wrestling M(s). ***Intramural sports:*** badminton M(c)/W(c), basketball M(c)/W(c), cheerleading M(c)/W(c), soccer M(c)/W(c), ultimate Frisbee M(c)/W(c), volleyball M(c)/W(c).

Campus security: 24-hour emergency response devices and patrols.

Student services: health clinic, personal/psychological counseling, veterans affairs office.

COSTS & FINANCIAL AID

Costs (2018–19) ***Tuition:*** state resident $7464 full-time, $311 per credit hour part-time; nonresident $18,648 full-time, $777 per credit hour part-time. Full-time tuition and fees vary according to program. Part-time tuition and fees vary according to course load and program. ***Room and board:*** $11,390. Room and board charges vary according to board plan and housing facility. ***Payment plan:*** installment. ***Waivers:*** senior citizens.

Financial Aid Of all full-time matriculated undergraduates who enrolled in 2017, 940 applied for aid, 736 were judged to have need, 46 had their need fully met. In 2017, 25 non-need-based awards were made. ***Average financial aid package:*** $7441. ***Average need-based loan:*** $3781. ***Average need-based gift aid:*** $3086. ***Average non-need-based aid:*** $2843. ***Average indebtedness upon graduation:*** $28,859.

APPLYING

Standardized Tests *Required:* SAT or ACT (for admission). *Required for some:* TOEFL or IELTS.

Options: electronic application, early admission.

Required: high school transcript, minimum 2.0 GPA, minimum ACT composite score of 18 or 870 SAT math and verbal or minimum 3.0 high school GPA.

Application deadlines: rolling (freshmen), rolling (out-of-state freshmen), rolling (transfers).

Notification: continuous until 8/15 (freshmen), continuous (out-of-state freshmen), continuous until 8/15 (transfers).

CONTACT

William Allen Jr., Dean of Enrollment Services, West Virginia University Institute of Technology, Old Main Box 80, 405 Fayette Pike, Montgomery, WV 25136. *Phone:* 304-442-3146. *Toll-free phone:* 888-554-8324. *Fax:* 304-442-3067. *E-mail:* tech-admissions@mail.wvu.edu.

West Virginia Wesleyan College

Buckhannon, West Virginia

http://www.wvwc.edu/

- **Independent** comprehensive, founded 1890, affiliated with United Methodist Church
- **Small-town** 180-acre campus
- **Endowment** $47.4 million
- **Coed**
- **Moderately difficult** entrance level

FACULTY
Student/faculty ratio: 13:1.

ACADEMICS
Calendar: semesters. *Degrees:* bachelor's, master's, post-master's, and postbachelor's certificates.
Library: Annie Merner Pfeifer Library plus 1 other. *Books:* 122,495 (physical), 271,641 (digital/electronic); *Serial titles:* 11,057 (physical), 112,139 (digital/electronic); *Databases:* 110. Students can reserve study rooms.

STUDENT LIFE
Housing options: on-campus residence required through senior year; coed, men-only, women-only, special housing for students with disabilities. Campus housing is university owned. Freshman campus housing is guaranteed.

Activities and organizations: drama/theater group, student-run newspaper, radio station, choral group, marching band, Campus Activities Board, Green Club, WE LEAD, Wesleyan Ambassadors, Enactus, national fraternities, national sororities.

Athletics Member NCAA. All Division II except baseball (Division III), men's and women's basketball (Division III), men's and women's cross-country running (Division III), field hockey (Division III), men's and women's golf (Division III), men's and women's lacrosse (Division III), men's and women's soccer (Division III), softball (Division III), men's and women's swimming and diving (Division III), men's and women's tennis (Division III), men's and women's track and field (Division III), volleyball (Division III).

Campus security: 24-hour emergency response devices and patrols, student patrols, late-night transport/escort service, controlled dormitory access.

Student services: health clinic, personal/psychological counseling.

COSTS & FINANCIAL AID
Costs (2018–19) ***Comprehensive fee:*** $40,496 includes full-time tuition ($30,462), mandatory fees ($1178), and room and board ($8856). Full-time tuition and fees vary according to course load and student level. Part-time tuition and fees vary according to course load. ***College room only:*** $4326. Room and board charges vary according to housing facility.

Financial Aid Of all full-time matriculated undergraduates who enrolled in 2018, 1,016 applied for aid, 916 were judged to have need, 234 had their need fully met. In 2018, 246 non-need-based awards were made. ***Average percent of need met:*** 81. ***Average financial aid package:*** $29,728. ***Average need-based loan:*** $3231. ***Average need-based gift aid:*** $26,581. ***Average non-need-based aid:*** $18,236. ***Average indebtedness upon graduation:*** $31,412.

APPLYING
Standardized Tests *Required:* SAT or ACT (for admission). *Required for some:* SAT Subject Tests (for admission).

Options: electronic application, deferred entrance.

Application fee: $35.

Required: high school transcript. ***Required for some:*** letters of recommendation. ***Recommended:*** essay or personal statement, interview.

CONTACT
John Waltz, Vice President for Enrollment Management, West Virginia Wesleyan College, 59 College Avenue, Buckhannon, WV 26201. *Phone:* 304-473-8510. *Toll-free phone:* 800-722-9933. *Fax:* 304-473-8108. *E-mail:* admission@wvwc.edu.

See previous page for display ad and page 1156 for the College Close-Up.

Wheeling Jesuit University

Wheeling, West Virginia

http://www.wju.edu/

CONTACT
Mr. Christopher Rouhier, Senior Admissions Representative, Wheeling Jesuit University, 316 Washington Avenue, Wheeling, WV 26003. *Phone:* 304-243-2106. *Toll-free phone:* 800-624-6992 Ext. 2359. *Fax:* 304-243-2397. *E-mail:* crouhier@wju.edu.

WISCONSIN

Alverno College

Milwaukee, Wisconsin

http://www.alverno.edu/

- **Independent Roman Catholic** comprehensive, founded 1887
- **Urban** 46-acre campus
- **Endowment** $30.0 million
- **Undergraduate: women only; graduate: coed** 1,219 undergraduate students, 82% full-time, 99% women, 1% men
- **Moderately difficult** entrance level, 67% of applicants were admitted

UNDERGRAD STUDENTS
995 full-time, 224 part-time. Students come from 14 states and territories; 1 other country; 7% are from out of state; 14% Black or African American, non-Hispanic/Latino; 30% Hispanic/Latino; 5% Asian, non-Hispanic/Latino; 0.7% American Indian or Alaska Native, non-Hispanic/Latino; 5% Two or more races, non-Hispanic/Latino; 0.2% Race/ethnicity unknown; 0.2% international; 9% transferred in; 17% live on campus.

Freshmen:
Admission: 747 applied, 501 admitted, 187 enrolled. ***Average high school GPA:*** 3.1. ***Test scores:*** ACT scores over 18: 71%; ACT scores over 24: 11%.

Retention: 68% of full-time freshmen returned.

FACULTY
Total: 231, 39% full-time, 47% with terminal degrees.

Student/faculty ratio: 10:1.

ACADEMICS
Calendar: semesters. *Degrees:* associate, bachelor's, master's, doctoral, post-master's, and postbachelor's certificates (also offers weekend program with significant enrollment not reflected in profile).

Special study options: academic remediation for entering students, accelerated degree program, adult/continuing education programs, advanced placement credit, double majors, honors programs, independent study, internships, part-time degree program, services for LD students, student-designed majors, study abroad, summer session for credit. ***ROTC:*** Army (c), Air Force (c).

Unusual degree programs: math/computer science with UW-Milwaukee; fresh water sciences with UW-Milwaukee.

Computers: 664 computers/terminals are available on campus for general student use. Students can access the following: campus intranet, computer help desk, free student e-mail accounts, online (class) registration, online (class) schedules. Campuswide network is available. 100% of college-owned or -operated housing units are wired for high-speed Internet access. Wireless service is available via classrooms, computer centers, computer labs, dorm rooms, libraries.
Library: Alverno College Library. *Books:* 65,917 (physical), 157,042 (digital/electronic); *Serial titles:* 478 (physical), 52,613 (digital/electronic); *Databases:* 57. Weekly public service hours: 84.

STUDENT LIFE
Housing options: women-only. Campus housing is university owned. Freshman campus housing is guaranteed.

Activities and organizations: drama/theater group, student-run newspaper, radio station, choral group, Alverno Cru, CHICA, Love Your Melon Crew, Circle K, Gay-Straight Alliance.

Athletics Member NCAA. All Division III. ***Intercollegiate sports:*** basketball W, cross-country running W, soccer W, softball W, tennis W, volleyball W.

Campus security: 24-hour emergency response devices and patrols, late-night transport/escort service, controlled dormitory access, well-lit parking lots and pathways, emergency first-aid and CPR, crisis intervention team and plan in place.

Student services: health clinic, personal/psychological counseling.

COSTS & FINANCIAL AID
Costs (2018–19) ***Comprehensive fee:*** $36,848 includes full-time tuition ($27,552), mandatory fees ($750), and room and board ($8546). Full-time tuition and fees vary according to program. Part-time tuition: $1148 per

credit hour. Part-time tuition and fees vary according to program. ***Room and board:*** Room and board charges vary according to board plan and housing facility. ***Payment plans:*** installment, deferred payment. ***Waivers:*** employees or children of employees.

Financial Aid Of all full-time matriculated undergraduates who enrolled in 2018, 928 applied for aid, 885 were judged to have need. 572 Federal Work-Study jobs (averaging $2088). In 2018, 84 non-need-based awards were made. ***Average financial aid package:*** $24,196. ***Average need-based loan:*** $4635. ***Average need-based gift aid:*** $15,894. ***Average non-need-based aid:*** $10,848. ***Average indebtedness upon graduation:*** $36,994.

APPLYING
Standardized Tests *Required:* SAT or ACT (for admission).

Options: electronic application, deferred entrance.

Required: essay or personal statement, high school transcript, minimum 2.0 college GPA. ***Recommended:*** minimum 2.0 GPA, interview.

Application deadlines: rolling (freshmen), rolling (transfers).

Notification: continuous (freshmen), continuous (transfers).

CONTACT
Ms. Janet Stikel, Director of Admissions, Alverno College, 3400 South 43 Street, PO Box 343922, Milwaukee, WI 53234-3922. *Phone:* 414-382-6110. *Toll-free phone:* 800-933-3401. *Fax:* 414-382-6055. *E-mail:* admissions@alverno.edu.

Bellin College

Green Bay, Wisconsin

http://www.bellincollege.edu/

CONTACT
Kathryn Wall, Director of Enrollment Management, Bellin College, 3201 Eaton Road, Green Bay, WI 54311. *Phone:* 920-433-6651. *Toll-free phone:* 800-236-8707. *E-mail:* admissions@bellincollege.edu.

Beloit College

Beloit, Wisconsin

http://www.beloit.edu/

- **Independent** 4-year, founded 1846
- **Small-town** 84-acre campus with easy access to Chicago, Milwaukee
- **Endowment** $160.9 million
- **Coed** 1,275 undergraduate students, 96% full-time, 55% women, 45% men
- 56% of applicants were admitted

UNDERGRAD STUDENTS
1,228 full-time, 47 part-time. Students come from 44 states and territories; 44 other countries; 84% are from out of state; 7% Black or African American, non-Hispanic/Latino; 11% Hispanic/Latino; 4% Asian, non-Hispanic/Latino; 0.2% Native Hawaiian or other Pacific Islander, non-Hispanic/Latino; 0.2% American Indian or Alaska Native, non-Hispanic/Latino; 4% Two or more races, non-Hispanic/Latino; 4% Race/ethnicity unknown; 18% international; 2% transferred in; 88% live on campus.

Freshmen:
Admission: 4,200 applied, 2,369 admitted, 266 enrolled. ***Average high school GPA:*** 3.3. ***Test scores:*** SAT evidence-based reading and writing scores over 500: 95%; SAT math scores over 500: 93%; ACT scores over 18: 96%; SAT evidence-based reading and writing scores over 600: 61%; SAT math scores over 600: 62%; ACT scores over 24: 63%; SAT evidence-based reading and writing scores over 700: 17%; SAT math scores over 700: 25%; ACT scores over 30: 24%.

Retention: 78% of full-time freshmen returned.

FACULTY
Total: 135, 87% full-time, 90% with terminal degrees.

Student/faculty ratio: 11:1.

ACADEMICS
Calendar: semesters. *Degree:* bachelor's.

Special study options: adult/continuing education programs, advanced placement credit, double majors, English as a second language, independent study, internships, off-campus study, services for LD students, student-designed majors, study abroad, summer session for credit.

Unusual degree programs: 3-2 engineering with Columbia University, Rensselaer Polytechnic Institute, Washington University in St. Louis; forestry with Duke University.

Computers: 300 computers/terminals are available on campus for general student use. Students can access the following: campus intranet, computer help desk, free student e-mail accounts, online (class) grades, online (class) registration, online (class) schedules. Campuswide network is available. 100% of college-owned or -operated housing units are wired for high-speed Internet access. Wireless service is available via entire campus.

Library: Morse Library and Black Information Center. *Books:* 207,000 (physical), 210,000 (digital/electronic); *Serial titles:* 11,700 (physical), 76,000 (digital/electronic); *Databases:* 151. Weekly public service hours: 109; students can reserve study rooms.

STUDENT LIFE
Housing options: on-campus residence required through junior year; coed, women-only, cooperative. Campus housing is university owned. Freshman campus housing is guaranteed.

Activities and organizations: drama/theater group, student-run newspaper, radio and television station, choral group, BSFFA - Beloit Science Fiction and Fantasy Association, Ceramics Club, Anthropology Club, Yoga Club, Outdoor Environmental Club, national fraternities, national sororities.

Athletics Member NCAA. All Division III. ***Intercollegiate sports:*** baseball M, basketball M/W, cross-country running M/W, football M, ice hockey M(c)/W(c), lacrosse M/W, soccer M/W, softball W, swimming and diving M/W, tennis W, track and field M/W, volleyball W. ***Intramural sports:*** archery M(c)/W(c), badminton M/W, basketball M/W, fencing M(c), field hockey W(c), football M, golf M(c)/W(c), racquetball M/W, sailing M(c)/W(c), skiing (downhill) M(c)/W(c), soccer M/W, ultimate Frisbee M/W, volleyball M/W.

Campus security: 24-hour emergency response devices and patrols, late-night transport/escort service, controlled dormitory access.

Student services: health clinic, personal/psychological counseling, women's center.

COSTS & FINANCIAL AID
Costs (2018–19) ***Comprehensive fee:*** $58,870 includes full-time tuition ($49,564), mandatory fees ($476), and room and board ($8830). Part-time tuition: $1549 per unit. ***College room only:*** $5030. Room and board charges vary according to board plan. ***Payment plan:*** installment. ***Waivers:*** employees or children of employees.

Financial Aid Of all full-time matriculated undergraduates who enrolled in 2018, 803 applied for aid, 732 were judged to have need, 214 had their need fully met. In 2018, 456 non-need-based awards were made. ***Average percent of need met:*** 95. ***Average financial aid package:*** $46,286. ***Average need-based loan:*** $7234. ***Average need-based gift aid:*** $35,970. ***Average non-need-based aid:*** $28,647. ***Average indebtedness upon graduation:*** $31,675. ***Financial aid deadline:*** 3/1.

APPLYING
Standardized Tests *Required for some:* SAT or ACT (for admission).

Options: electronic application, early decision, early action.

Required: essay or personal statement, high school transcript, 1 letter of recommendation. ***Recommended:*** interview.

Application deadlines: 1/15 (freshmen), rolling (transfers).

Early decision deadline: 11/1.

Notification: continuous (freshmen), continuous (transfers), 12/1 (early decision).

CONTACT
Ms. Kate Virgo, Interim Director of Enrollment Operations, Beloit College, 700 College Street, Beloit, WI 53511-5596. *Phone:* 608-363-2380. *Toll-free phone:* 800-9-BELOIT. *Fax:* 608-363-2179. *E-mail:* virgok@beloit.edu.

Bryant & Stratton College–Bayshore Campus

Glendale, Wisconsin

http://www.bryantstratton.edu/

CONTACT
Bryant & Stratton College–Bayshore Campus, 500 West Silver Spring Drive, Bayshore Town Center, Suite K340, Glendale, WI 53217.

Bryant & Stratton College–Milwaukee Campus

Milwaukee, Wisconsin

http://www.bryantstratton.edu/

CONTACT
Mr. Dan Basile, Director of Admissions, Bryant & Stratton College–Milwaukee Campus, 310 West Wisconsin Avenue, Suite 500 East, Milwaukee, WI 53203-2214. *Phone:* 414-276-5200.

Bryant & Stratton College–Wauwatosa Campus

Wauwatosa, Wisconsin

http://www.bryantstratton.edu/

CONTACT
Bryant & Stratton College–Wauwatosa Campus, 10950 West Potter Road, Wauwatosa, WI 53226. *Phone:* 414-302-7000 Ext. 502.

Cardinal Stritch University

Milwaukee, Wisconsin

http://www.stritch.edu/

- **Independent Roman Catholic** university, founded 1937
- **Suburban** 40-acre campus with easy access to Milwaukee
- **Endowment** $19.4 million
- **Coed**
- **Moderately difficult** entrance level

FACULTY
Student/faculty ratio: 10:1.

ACADEMICS
Calendar: semesters. *Degrees:* certificates, associate, bachelor's, master's, doctoral, post-master's, and postbachelor's certificates.
Library: Cardinal Stritch University Library. *Books:* 122,184 (physical), 146,127 (digital/electronic); *Serial titles:* 66 (physical), 68 (digital/electronic); *Databases:* 71. Weekly public service hours: 90.

STUDENT LIFE
Housing options: on-campus residence required for freshman year; coed. Campus housing is university owned and leased by the school. Freshman campus housing is guaranteed.

Activities and organizations: drama/theater group, choral group, Student Government, Student Programming Board, Hispanic Club, University Ministry, Circle K International, national fraternities.

Athletics Member NAIA.

Campus security: 24-hour emergency response devices and patrols, controlled dormitory access.

Student services: health clinic, personal/psychological counseling.

COSTS & FINANCIAL AID
Costs (2018–19) ***Comprehensive fee:*** $38,622 includes full-time tuition ($29,998) and room and board ($8624). Full-time tuition and fees vary according to degree level, program, and reciprocity agreements. Part-time tuition: $936 per credit hour. Part-time tuition and fees vary according to course load, degree level, program, and reciprocity agreements. ***Room and board:*** Room and board charges vary according to board plan and housing facility.

Financial Aid Of all full-time matriculated undergraduates who enrolled in 2018, 612 applied for aid, 571 were judged to have need, 54 had their need fully met. 348 Federal Work-Study jobs (averaging $2057). In 2018, 220 non-need-based awards were made. ***Average percent of need met:*** 72. ***Average financial aid package:*** $24,575. ***Average need-based loan:*** $4141. ***Average need-based gift aid:*** $19,843. ***Average non-need-based aid:*** $18,965. ***Average indebtedness upon graduation:*** $28,270.

APPLYING
Standardized Tests *Required for some:* SAT or ACT (for admission), TOEFL for international students.

Options: electronic application, deferred entrance.

Required for some: high school transcript, minimum 2.0 GPA.

CONTACT
Mary-Grace Linse, Associate Director of Undergraduate Admissions, Cardinal Stritch University, 6801 N. Yates Road, Milwaukee, WI 53217. *Phone:* 414-410-4052. *Toll-free phone:* 800-347-8822 Ext. 4040. *Fax:* 414-410-4058. *E-mail:* admissions@stritch.edu.

Carroll University

Waukesha, Wisconsin

http://www.carrollu.edu/

- **Independent Presbyterian** comprehensive, founded 1846
- **Suburban** 136-acre campus with easy access to Milwaukee
- **Endowment** $57.5 million
- **Coed**
- **Moderately difficult** entrance level

FACULTY
Student/faculty ratio: 16:1.

ACADEMICS
Calendar: semesters. *Degrees:* bachelor's, master's, doctoral, and postbachelor's certificates.
Library: Todd Wehr Memorial Library.

STUDENT LIFE
Housing options: on-campus residence required through sophomore year; coed, women-only, special housing for students with disabilities. Campus housing is university owned. Freshman campus housing is guaranteed.

Activities and organizations: drama/theater group, student-run newspaper, radio station, choral group, College Activities Board, Student Senate, Black Student Union, Intervarsity Christian Fellowship, Latin American Student Organization, national sororities.

Athletics Member NCAA. All Division III.

Campus security: 24-hour emergency response devices and patrols, student patrols, late-night transport/escort service, controlled dormitory access.

Student services: health clinic, personal/psychological counseling.

COSTS & FINANCIAL AID
Costs (2018–19) ***One-time required fee:*** $270. ***Comprehensive fee:*** $41,814 includes full-time tuition ($31,162), mandatory fees ($756), and room and board ($9896). Full-time tuition and fees vary according to program. Part-time tuition: $400 per credit hour. Part-time tuition and fees vary according to course load and program. ***College room only:*** $5180. Room and board charges vary according to board plan and housing facility. ***Payment plans:*** installment, deferred payment.

Financial Aid Of all full-time matriculated undergraduates who enrolled in 2018, 2,420 applied for aid, 2,094 were judged to have need, 757 had their need fully met. 639 Federal Work-Study jobs (averaging $2276). 1,492 state and other part-time jobs (averaging $2250). In 2018, 597 non-need-based awards were made. ***Average percent of need met:*** 87. ***Average financial aid package:*** $25,956. ***Average need-based loan:*** $4237. ***Average need-based gift aid:*** $20,071. ***Average non-need-based aid:*** $16,675. ***Average indebtedness upon graduation:*** $35,997.

APPLYING
Standardized Tests *Required:* SAT or ACT (for admission). *Recommended:* ACT (for admission).

Options: electronic application, deferred entrance.

Required: high school transcript, minimum 2.0 GPA, 1 letter of recommendation. ***Required for some:*** essay or personal statement. ***Recommended:*** interview.

CONTACT
Mr. James Wiseman, Vice President of Enrollment, Carroll University, 100 North East Avenue, Waukesha, WI 53186-5593. *Phone:* 262-524-7221. *Toll-free phone:* 800-CARROLL. *Fax:* 262-524-7139. *E-mail:* info@carrollu.edu.

Carthage College

Kenosha, Wisconsin

http://www.carthage.edu/

- **Independent** comprehensive, founded 1847, affiliated with Evangelical Lutheran Church in America
- **Suburban** 72-acre campus with easy access to Chicago, Milwaukee
- **Coed** 2,776 undergraduate students, 95% full-time, 56% women, 44% men
- **Moderately difficult** entrance level, 105% of applicants were admitted

UNDERGRAD STUDENTS
2,649 full-time, 127 part-time. Students come from 37 states and territories; 17 other countries; 64% are from out of state; 6% Black or African American, non-Hispanic/Latino; 14% Hispanic/Latino; 2% Asian, non-Hispanic/Latino; 0.2% Native Hawaiian or other Pacific Islander, non-Hispanic/Latino; 0.5% American Indian or Alaska Native, non-Hispanic/Latino; 3% Two or more races, non-Hispanic/Latino; 5% Race/ethnicity unknown; 1% international; 3% transferred in; 66% live on campus.

Freshmen:
Admission: 5,260 applied, 5,500 admitted, 763 enrolled. ***Average high school GPA:*** 3.3. ***Test scores:*** SAT evidence-based reading and writing scores over 500: 80%; SAT math scores over 500: 83%; ACT scores over 18: 96%; SAT evidence-based reading and writing scores over 600: 35%; SAT math scores over 600: 30%; ACT scores over 24: 49%; SAT evidence-based reading and writing scores over 700: 7%; SAT math scores over 700: 4%; ACT scores over 30: 11%.

Retention: 77% of full-time freshmen returned.

FACULTY
Total: 338, 53% full-time, 51% with terminal degrees.

Student/faculty ratio: 12:1.

ACADEMICS
Calendar: 4-1-4. *Degrees:* bachelor's and master's.

Special study options: accelerated degree program, adult/continuing education programs, advanced placement credit, double majors, honors programs, internships, off-campus study, part-time degree program, services for LD students, student-designed majors, study abroad, summer session for credit. ***ROTC:*** Army (c), Air Force (c).

Unusual degree programs: 3-2 engineering with Case Western Reserve University; occupational therapy with Washington University in St. Louis.

Computers: 130 computers/terminals are available on campus for general student use. Students can access the following: campus intranet, computer help desk, free student e-mail accounts, online (class) grades, online (class) registration, online (class) schedules. Campuswide network is available. 96% of college-owned or -operated housing units are wired for high-speed Internet access. Wireless service is available via entire campus.

Library: Hedberg Library. *Books:* 103,144 (physical), 328,850 (digital/electronic); *Serial titles:* 4,243 (physical), 555,934 (digital/electronic); *Databases:* 334. Students can reserve study rooms.

STUDENT LIFE
Housing options: on-campus residence required through junior year; coed, men-only, women-only. Campus housing is university owned and leased by the school. Freshman campus housing is guaranteed.

Activities and organizations: drama/theater group, student-run newspaper, radio station, choral group, Tau Sigma Chi, Alpha Phi Omega, Intervarsity Christian Fellowship, Alpha Lambda Delta, Beta Beta Beta, national fraternities, national sororities.

Athletics Member NCAA. All Division III except golf (Division II). ***Intercollegiate sports:*** baseball M, basketball M/W, bowling M(c)/W(c), cross-country running M/W, football M, golf M/W, ice hockey M(c)/W(c), lacrosse M/W, soccer M/W, softball W, swimming and diving M/W, tennis M/W, track and field M/W, volleyball M/W, water polo W. ***Intramural sports:*** basketball M/W, football M/W, racquetball M/W, rock climbing M/W, soccer M/W, softball M/W, volleyball M/W.

Campus security: 24-hour emergency response devices and patrols, student patrols, late-night transport/escort service, controlled dormitory access.

Student services: health clinic, personal/psychological counseling.

COSTS & FINANCIAL AID
Costs (2019–20) ***Comprehensive fee:*** $101,800 includes full-time tuition ($45,100), mandatory fees ($45,100), and room and board ($11,600). Part-time tuition: $595 per credit. ***Required fees:*** $595 per credit part-time.

Financial Aid Of all full-time matriculated undergraduates who enrolled in 2018, 2,165 applied for aid, 2,165 were judged to have need, 960 had their need fully met. 849 Federal Work-Study jobs (averaging $1882). In 2018, 496 non-need-based awards were made. ***Average percent of need met:*** 79. ***Average financial aid package:*** $39,017. ***Average need-based loan:*** $10,258. ***Average need-based gift aid:*** $32,872. ***Average non-need-based aid:*** $24,268. ***Average indebtedness upon graduation:*** $54,496.

APPLYING
Standardized Tests *Recommended:* SAT and SAT Subject Tests or ACT (for admission).

Options: electronic application, deferred entrance.

Application fee: $35.

Required: high school transcript. ***Required for some:*** minimum 2.3 GPA, 2 letters of recommendation, statement of good standing from prior institution(s). ***Recommended:*** essay or personal statement, interview.

Application deadlines: rolling (freshmen), rolling (transfers).

Notification: continuous (freshmen), continuous (transfers).

CONTACT
Mr. Nick Mulvey, Vice President for Enrollment, Carthage College, 2001 Alford Park Drive, Kenosha, WI 53140. *Phone:* 262-551-5762. *Toll-free phone:* 800-351-4058. *E-mail:* admissions@carthage.edu.

Columbia College of Nursing

Glendale, Wisconsin

http://www.ccon.edu/

CONTACT
Columbia College of Nursing, 4425 North Port Washington Road, Glendale, WI 53212. *Phone:* 414-326-2336.

Concordia University Wisconsin

Mequon, Wisconsin

http://www.cuw.edu/

- **Independent** comprehensive, founded 1881, affiliated with Lutheran Church–Missouri Synod, part of Concordia University System
- **Suburban** 192-acre campus with easy access to Milwaukee
- **Coed**
- **Moderately difficult** entrance level

FACULTY
Student/faculty ratio: 11:1.

ACADEMICS
Calendar: 4-1-4. *Degrees:* certificates, associate, bachelor's, master's, doctoral, and post-master's certificates.
Library: Rinker Memorial Library.

STUDENT LIFE
Housing options: men-only, women-only. Campus housing is university owned. Freshman applicants given priority for college housing.

Activities and organizations: drama/theater group, student-run newspaper, radio station, choral group.

Athletics Member NCAA. All Division III.

Campus security: 24-hour patrols, student patrols, late-night transport/escort service, controlled dormitory access.

Student services: health clinic, personal/psychological counseling.

COSTS & FINANCIAL AID
Costs (2018–19) ***Comprehensive fee:*** $40,300 includes full-time tuition ($29,180), mandatory fees ($270), and room and board ($10,850). Full-

time tuition and fees vary according to program. Part-time tuition and fees vary according to program. ***Room and board:*** Room and board charges vary according to board plan.

Financial Aid Of all full-time matriculated undergraduates who enrolled in 2018, 2,381 applied for aid, 2,042 were judged to have need. In 2018, 2501 non-need-based awards were made. ***Financial aid deadline:*** 4/15.

APPLYING
Standardized Tests *Required:* SAT or ACT (for admission).

Required: high school transcript, minimum 2.0 GPA. ***Required for some:*** essay or personal statement, minimum 3.0 GPA, 3 letters of recommendation. ***Recommended:*** interview.

CONTACT
Ms. Julie Schroeder, Concordia University Wisconsin, Admissions Office, 12800 North Lake Drive, Mequon, WI 53097. *Phone:* 262-243-4305 Ext. 4305. *Toll-free phone:* 888-628-9472. *E-mail:* admission@cuw.edu.

Edgewood College
Madison, Wisconsin
http://www.edgewood.edu/

- **Independent Roman Catholic** comprehensive, founded 1927
- **Urban** 55-acre campus
- **Endowment** $37.8 million
- **Coed**
- **Moderately difficult** entrance level

FACULTY
Student/faculty ratio: 9:1.

ACADEMICS
Calendar: semesters. *Degrees:* certificates, bachelor's, master's, doctoral, and postbachelor's certificates.
Library: Oscar Rennebohm Library. *Books:* 82,008 (physical), 140,319 (digital/electronic); *Serial titles:* 219 (physical), 38,116 (digital/electronic); *Databases:* 90. Weekly public service hours: 98; students can reserve study rooms.

STUDENT LIFE
Housing options: on-campus residence required through sophomore year; coed, cooperative, special housing for students with disabilities. Campus housing is university owned. Freshman campus housing is guaranteed.

Activities and organizations: drama/theater group, student-run newspaper, choral group, Circle K, Student Education Association, Student Government Association, Rotaract, Ambassadors.

Athletics Member NCAA. All Division III.

Campus security: 24-hour emergency response devices and patrols, student patrols, late-night transport/escort service, controlled dormitory access, lighted pathways/sidewalks, Eagle Alert System, Public Address System, Safe Ride Shuttle, extensive video surveillance system.

Student services: health clinic, personal/psychological counseling, veterans affairs office.

COSTS & FINANCIAL AID
Costs (2018–19) ***Comprehensive fee:*** $40,520 includes full-time tuition ($29,500) and room and board ($11,020). Full-time tuition and fees vary according to degree level. Part-time tuition: $927 per credit. Part-time tuition and fees vary according to course load and degree level. ***Room and board:*** Room and board charges vary according to housing facility.

Financial Aid Of all full-time matriculated undergraduates who enrolled in 2017, 1,143 applied for aid, 1,008 were judged to have need, 150 had their need fully met. 408 Federal Work-Study jobs (averaging $2060). 592 state and other part-time jobs (averaging $1991). In 2017, 240 non-need-based awards were made. ***Average percent of need met:*** 76. ***Average financial aid package:*** $22,093. ***Average need-based loan:*** $5765. ***Average need-based gift aid:*** $15,514. ***Average non-need-based aid:*** $7003. ***Average indebtedness upon graduation:*** $38,769.

APPLYING
Standardized Tests *Required:* SAT or ACT (for admission).

Options: electronic application, deferred entrance.

Application fee: $30.

Required: high school transcript, minimum 2.5 GPA, two of the following: cumulative high school GPA of 2.5 on a 4.0 scale, a rank in the top 50% of their high school graduating class and/or a composite score of 18 on the ACT or an equivalent SAT score. ***Required for some:*** essay or personal statement, 2 letters of recommendation, interview.

CONTACT
Ms. Christine Benedict, Vice President for Enrollment Management, Edgewood College, 1000 Edgewood College Drive, Madison, WI 53711-1997. *Phone:* 608-663-2294. *Toll-free phone:* 800-444-4861 Ext. 2294. *Fax:* 608-663-2214. *E-mail:* admissions@edgewood.edu.

Herzing University
Brookfield, Wisconsin
http://www.herzing.edu/brookfield

CONTACT
Herzing University, 555 South Executive Drive, Brookfield, WI 53005. *Toll-free phone:* 800-596-0724.

Herzing University
Kenosha, Wisconsin
http://www.herzing.edu/kenosha

CONTACT
Herzing University, 4006 Washington Road, Kenosha, WI 53144. *Toll-free phone:* 800-596-0724.

Herzing University
Madison, Wisconsin
http://www.herzing.edu/madison/

CONTACT
Herzing University, 5218 East Terrace Drive, Madison, WI 53718. *Toll-free phone:* 800-596-0724.

Herzing University Online
Menomonee Falls, Wisconsin
http://www.herzingonline.edu/

CONTACT
Herzing University Online, W140N8917 Lilly Road, Menomonee Falls, WI 53051. *Toll-free phone:* 866-508-0748.

Lakeland University
Plymouth, Wisconsin
http://www.lakeland.edu/

CONTACT
Mr. Nick Spaeth, Director of Admissions, Lakeland University, PO Box 359, Nash Visitors Center, Sheboygan, WI 53082-0359. *Phone:* 920-565-1007. *Toll-free phone:* 800-569-2166. *Fax:* 920-565-1215. *E-mail:* admissions@lakeland.edu.

Lawrence University
Appleton, Wisconsin
http://www.lawrence.edu/

- **Independent** 4-year, founded 1847
- **Small-town** 88-acre campus
- **Endowment** $339.8 million
- **Coed** 1,472 undergraduate students, 96% full-time, 53% women, 47% men
- **Very difficult** entrance level, 62% of applicants were admitted

UNDERGRAD STUDENTS
1,420 full-time, 52 part-time. Students come from 47 states and territories; 37 other countries; 73% are from out of state; 5% Black or African American, non-Hispanic/Latino; 10% Hispanic/Latino; 5% Asian, non-Hispanic/Latino; 0.1% Native Hawaiian or other Pacific Islander, non-Hispanic/Latino; 0.3% American Indian or Alaska Native, non-Hispanic/Latino; 4% Two or more races, non-Hispanic/Latino; 1% Race/ethnicity unknown; 13% international; 0.9% transferred in; 94% live on campus.

Freshmen:
Admission: 3,502 applied, 2,188 admitted, 400 enrolled. ***Average high school GPA:*** 3.5. ***Test scores:*** SAT evidence-based reading and writing scores over 500: 98%; SAT math scores over 500: 98%; ACT scores over 18: 100%; SAT evidence-based reading and writing scores over 600: 77%; SAT math scores over 600: 76%; ACT scores over 24: 90%; SAT evidence-based reading and writing scores over 700: 33%; SAT math scores over 700: 37%; ACT scores over 30: 42%.

Retention: 85% of full-time freshmen returned.

FACULTY
Total: 204, 85% full-time, 87% with terminal degrees.

Student/faculty ratio: 8:1.

ACADEMICS
Calendar: trimesters. *Degree:* bachelor's.

Special study options: advanced placement credit, double majors, independent study, internships, off-campus study, part-time degree program, services for LD students, student-designed majors, study abroad.

Unusual degree programs: 3-2 engineering with Columbia University, Rensselaer Polytechnic Institute, Washington University in St. Louis; forestry with Duke University; Occupational therapy with Washington University in St. Louis Law with Marquette University.

Computers: 250 computers/terminals and 400 ports are available on campus for general student use. Students can access the following: campus intranet, computer help desk, free student e-mail accounts, online (class) grades, online (class) registration, online (class) schedules, online transcripts, financial aid, financial account information. Campuswide network is available. 100% of college-owned or -operated housing units are wired for high-speed Internet access. Wireless service is available via entire campus.
Library: Seeley G. Mudd Library. *Books:* 553,969 (physical), 220,704 (digital/electronic); *Serial titles:* 544 (physical), 68,015 (digital/electronic); *Databases:* 160. Weekly public service hours: 110; students can reserve study rooms.

STUDENT LIFE
Housing options: on-campus residence required through senior year; coed, men-only, women-only, cooperative, special housing for students with disabilities. Campus housing is university owned. Freshman campus housing is guaranteed.

Activities and organizations: drama/theater group, student-run newspaper, radio station, choral group, Gaming, Dance, Lawrence International, Outdoor Recreation Club, Sustainable Lawrence University Gardens (SLUG), national fraternities, national sororities.

Athletics Member NCAA. All Division III. ***Intercollegiate sports:*** baseball M, basketball M/W, crew M(c)/W(c), cross-country running M/W, fencing M/W, football M, ice hockey M/W(c), soccer M/W, softball W, swimming and diving M/W, tennis M/W, track and field M/W, ultimate Frisbee M(c)/W(c), volleyball W. ***Intramural sports:*** badminton M/W, basketball M/W, golf M(c)/W(c), rock climbing M(c)/W(c), sailing M(c)/W(c), skiing (downhill) M/W, soccer M/W, table tennis M/W, triathlon M(c)/W(c), volleyball M/W, water polo M/W.

Campus security: 24-hour emergency response devices and patrols, student patrols, late-night transport/escort service, controlled dormitory access, evening patrols by trained security personnel.

Student services: health clinic, personal/psychological counseling.

COSTS & FINANCIAL AID
Costs (2019–20) ***Comprehensive fee:*** $59,841 includes full-time tuition ($48,822), mandatory fees ($300), and room and board ($10,719). ***College room only:*** $5448.

Financial Aid Of all full-time matriculated undergraduates who enrolled in 2018, 1,009 applied for aid, 860 were judged to have need, 369 had their need fully met. In 2018, 511 non-need-based awards were made. ***Average percent of need met:*** 93. ***Average financial aid package:*** $41,150. ***Average need-based loan:*** $4364. ***Average need-based gift aid:*** $36,245. ***Average non-need-based aid:*** $23,806. ***Average indebtedness upon graduation:*** $31,136.

APPLYING
Standardized Tests *Required for some:* English Language Proficiency Exam (SAT/TOEFL/IELTS/ACT).

Options: electronic application, early decision, early action, deferred entrance.

Required: essay or personal statement, high school transcript, 1 letter of recommendation. ***Required for some:*** audition for music majors. ***Recommended:*** minimum 3.0 GPA, interview.

Application deadlines: 1/15 (freshmen), 7/1 (transfers), 12/1 (early action).

Early decision deadline: 10/31 (for plan 1), 11/1 (for plan 2).

Notification: continuous until 4/1 (freshmen), continuous until 7/15 (transfers), 12/1 (early decision plan 1), 12/15 (early decision plan 2), 1/25 (early action).

CONTACT
Ms. Mary Beth Petrie, Admissions Director, Lawrence University, 711 East Boldt Way, Admissions Office, Appleton, WI 54911. *Phone:* 920-832-6502. *Toll-free phone:* 800-227-0982. *Fax:* 920-832-6782. *E-mail:* marybeth.petrie@lawrence.edu.

Maranatha Baptist University
Watertown, Wisconsin
http://www.mbu.edu/

- **Independent Baptist** comprehensive, founded 1968
- **Small-town** 60-acre campus with easy access to Milwaukee
- **Coed**
- **Noncompetitive** entrance level

FACULTY
Student/faculty ratio: 11:1.

ACADEMICS
Calendar: semesters. *Degrees:* certificates, associate, bachelor's, master's, and doctoral.
Library: Cedarholm Library and Resource Center. Students can reserve study rooms.

STUDENT LIFE
Housing options: on-campus residence required through senior year; men-only, women-only. Campus housing is university owned. Freshman campus housing is guaranteed.

Activities and organizations: drama/theater group, choral group.

Athletics Member NCAA, NCCAA. All NCAA Division III.

Campus security: student patrols, late-night transport/escort service, controlled dormitory access.

Student services: health clinic, personal/psychological counseling.

COSTS & FINANCIAL AID
Costs (2018–19) ***Comprehensive fee:*** $22,510 includes full-time tuition ($14,250), mandatory fees ($1160), and room and board ($7100). Full-time tuition and fees vary according to location and program. Part-time tuition: $594 per semester hour. Part-time tuition and fees vary according to course load. ***Required fees:*** $48 per semester hour part-time.

Financial Aid Of all full-time matriculated undergraduates who enrolled in 2016, 591 applied for aid, 530 were judged to have need, 70 had their need fully met. In 2016, 69 non-need-based awards were made. ***Average percent of need met:*** 56. ***Average financial aid package:*** $10,216. ***Average need-based loan:*** $4061. ***Average need-based gift aid:*** $7075. ***Average non-need-based aid:*** $4186. ***Average indebtedness upon graduation:*** $21,432.

APPLYING
Standardized Tests *Required:* SAT or ACT (for admission).

Options: electronic application.

Application fee: $50.

Required: essay or personal statement, high school transcript, 4 letters of recommendation.

CONTACT
Jonathan Sheeley, Director of Admissions, Maranatha Baptist University, 745 West Main Street, Watertown, WI 53094. *Phone:* 920-206-2327. *Toll-free phone:* 800-622-2947. *Fax:* 920-261-9109. *E-mail:* admissions@mbu.edu.

Marian University

Fond du Lac, Wisconsin

http://www.marianuniversity.edu/

- **Independent Roman Catholic** comprehensive, founded 1936
- **Small-town** 78-acre campus with easy access to Milwaukee
- **Endowment** $11.7 million
- **Coed**
- **Moderately difficult** entrance level

FACULTY

Student/faculty ratio: 9:1.

ACADEMICS

Calendar: semesters. *Degrees:* certificates, bachelor's, master's, doctoral, post-master's, and postbachelor's certificates.
Library: Cardinal Meyer Library plus 1 other. *Books:* 210,079 (physical), 147,236 (digital/electronic); *Databases:* 1,805.

STUDENT LIFE

Housing options: on-campus residence required through sophomore year; coed, special housing for students with disabilities. Campus housing is university owned. Freshman campus housing is guaranteed.

Activities and organizations: student-run newspaper, choral group, Student Senate, Student Nurses Association, Student Education Association, Science and Math Association, Business Club, national sororities.

Athletics Member NCAA. All Division III.

Campus security: 24-hour emergency response devices and patrols, student patrols, late-night transport/escort service, controlled dormitory access.

Student services: health clinic, personal/psychological counseling, veterans affairs office.

COSTS & FINANCIAL AID

Costs (2018–19) ***Comprehensive fee:*** $34,622 includes full-time tuition ($26,950), mandatory fees ($450), and room and board ($7222). Full-time tuition and fees vary according to course load and program. Part-time tuition: $450 per credit hour. Part-time tuition and fees vary according to course load and program. ***College room only:*** $4352. Room and board charges vary according to board plan.

Financial Aid Of all full-time matriculated undergraduates who enrolled in 2015, 1,271 applied for aid, 1,176 were judged to have need, 66 had their need fully met. 146 Federal Work-Study jobs (averaging $443). 342 state and other part-time jobs (averaging $1465). In 2015, 87 non-need-based awards were made. ***Average percent of need met:*** 60. ***Average financial aid package:*** $16,769. ***Average need-based loan:*** $3444. ***Average need-based gift aid:*** $12,996. ***Average non-need-based aid:*** $6038. ***Average indebtedness upon graduation:*** $30,565.

APPLYING

Standardized Tests *Required:* SAT or ACT (for admission). *Recommended:* ACT (for admission).

Options: electronic application, deferred entrance.

Application fee: $20.

Required: high school transcript. ***Required for some:*** interview. ***Recommended:*** interview.

CONTACT

Shannon LaLuzerne, Dean of Admission, Marian University, 45 S. National Avenue, Fond du Lac, WI 54935-4699. *Phone:* 920-923-7650. *Toll-free phone:* 800-2-MARIAN. *E-mail:* admission@marianuniversity.edu.

Marquette University

Milwaukee, Wisconsin

http://www.marquette.edu/

- **Independent Roman Catholic (Jesuit)** university, founded 1881
- **Urban** 107-acre campus with easy access to Milwaukee
- **Coed** 8,435 undergraduate students, 96% full-time, 54% women, 46% men
- **Moderately difficult** entrance level, 82% of applicants were admitted

UNDERGRAD STUDENTS

8,121 full-time, 314 part-time. 69% are from out of state; 4% Black or African American, non-Hispanic/Latino; 13% Hispanic/Latino; 7% Asian, non-Hispanic/Latino; 0.1% Native Hawaiian or other Pacific Islander, non-Hispanic/Latino; 0.2% American Indian or Alaska Native, non-Hispanic/Latino; 3% Two or more races, non-Hispanic/Latino; 0.4% Race/ethnicity unknown; 3% international; 2% transferred in; 54% live on campus.

Freshmen:

Admission: 15,574 applied, 12,717 admitted, 2,164 enrolled. ***Test scores:*** SAT evidence-based reading and writing scores over 500: 99%; SAT math scores over 500: 97%; ACT scores over 18: 100%; SAT evidence-based reading and writing scores over 600: 64%; SAT math scores over 600: 59%; ACT scores over 24: 84%; SAT evidence-based reading and writing scores over 700: 9%; SAT math scores over 700: 15%; ACT scores over 30: 26%.

Retention: 87% of full-time freshmen returned.

FACULTY

Total: 1,194, 56% full-time, 73% with terminal degrees.

Student/faculty ratio: 14:1.

ACADEMICS

Calendar: semesters. *Degrees:* bachelor's, master's, doctoral, post-master's, and postbachelor's certificates.

Special study options: accelerated degree program, adult/continuing education programs, advanced placement credit, cooperative education, distance learning, double majors, English as a second language, honors programs, independent study, internships, off-campus study, part-time degree program, services for LD students, student-designed majors, study abroad, summer session for credit. ***ROTC:*** Army (b), Navy (b), Air Force (b).

Unusual degree programs: 3-2 business administration; engineering; exercise science/clinical and translational rehabilitation health sciences, speech and language pathology, international affairs, physical therapy.

Computers: Students can access the following: campus intranet, computer help desk, free student e-mail accounts, online (class) grades, online (class) registration, online (class) schedules, AV Software, MATLAB, Printwise. Campuswide network is available. 100% of college-owned or -operated housing units are wired for high-speed Internet access. Wireless service is available via classrooms, computer centers, computer labs, dorm rooms, learning centers, libraries, student centers.

Library: Raynor Memorial Libraries plus 1 other. Study areas open 24 hours, 5–7 days a week; students can reserve study rooms.

STUDENT LIFE

Housing options: on-campus residence required through sophomore year; coed, men-only, women-only, cooperative, special housing for students with disabilities. Campus housing is university owned. Freshman campus housing is guaranteed.

Activities and organizations: drama/theater group, student-run newspaper, radio and television station, choral group, Student Government, club sports, community service organizations, band/jazz/orchestra, Residence Hall Association, national fraternities, national sororities.

Athletics Member NCAA. All Division I. ***Intercollegiate sports:*** basketball M(s)/W(s), cheerleading M/W, cross-country running M(s)/W(s), golf M(s), lacrosse M(s)/W(s), soccer M(s)/W(s), tennis M(s)/W(s), track and field M(s)/W(s), volleyball W(s). ***Intramural sports:*** badminton M/W, baseball M(c), basketball M(c)/W(c), crew M(c)/W(c), cross-country running M(c)/W(c), equestrian sports M(c)/W(c), fencing M(c), field hockey W(c), football M/W, golf M(c)/W(c), ice hockey M(c), lacrosse M(c)/W(c), rowing M(c)/W(c), rugby M(c)/W(c), sailing M(c)/W(c), sand volleyball M/W, skiing (downhill) M(c)/W(c), soccer M(c)/W(c), softball M/W(c), swimming and diving M(c)/W(c), table tennis M(c)/W(c), tennis M(c)/W(c), ultimate Frisbee M(c)/W(c), volleyball M(c)/W(c), water polo M(c)/W(c), weight lifting M/W.

Campus security: 24-hour emergency response devices and patrols, student patrols, late-night transport/escort service.

Student services: health clinic, personal/psychological counseling.

COSTS & FINANCIAL AID
Costs (2019–20) ***Required fees:*** $586 full-time. ***Room and board:*** $13,200; room only: $8660.

Financial Aid Of all full-time matriculated undergraduates who enrolled in 2018, 5,764 applied for aid, 4,736 were judged to have need, 1,039 had their need fully met. In 2018, 3097 non-need-based awards were made. ***Average percent of need met:*** 77. ***Average financial aid package:*** $30,471. ***Average need-based loan:*** $5799. ***Average need-based gift aid:*** $24,379. ***Average non-need-based aid:*** $14,045. ***Average indebtedness upon graduation:*** $37,175.

APPLYING
Standardized Tests *Required:* SAT or ACT (for admission).

Options: electronic application, deferred entrance.

Required: essay or personal statement, high school transcript, minimum 2.5 GPA. ***Recommended:*** minimum 3.4 GPA.

Notification: 12/23 (freshmen), continuous (transfers).

CONTACT
Mr. Brian Troyer, Dean of Undergraduate Admissions, Marquette University, PO Box 1881, Milwaukee, WI 53201-1881. *Phone:* 414-288-7004. *Toll-free phone:* 800-222-6544. *Fax:* 414-288-3764. *E-mail:* admissions@marquette.edu.

Milwaukee Institute of Art and Design

Milwaukee, Wisconsin

http://www.miad.edu/

CONTACT
David Sigman, Director of Admissions, Milwaukee Institute of Art and Design, 273 East Erie Street, Milwaukee, WI 53202. *Phone:* 414-847-3200. *Toll-free phone:* 888-749-MIAD. *Fax:* 414-291-8077. *E-mail:* admissions@miad.edu.

Milwaukee School of Engineering

Milwaukee, Wisconsin

http://www.msoe.edu/

- **Independent** comprehensive, founded 1903
- **Urban** 22-acre campus
- **Endowment** $65.0 million
- **Coed, primarily men**
- **Moderately difficult** entrance level

FACULTY
Student/faculty ratio: 16:1.

ACADEMICS
Calendar: quarters. *Degrees:* bachelor's and master's.
Library: Walter Schroeder. *Books:* 51,408 (physical), 370,802 (digital/electronic); *Serial titles:* 345 (physical), 114,238 (digital/electronic); *Databases:* 124. Weekly public service hours: 96; students can reserve study rooms.

STUDENT LIFE
Housing options: on-campus residence required through sophomore year; coed, special housing for students with disabilities. Campus housing is university owned. Freshman campus housing is guaranteed.

Activities and organizations: drama/theater group, student-run radio station, choral group, Student Union Board, Greek Council, Student Government Association, Residence Hall Association, Intervarsity Christian Fellowship, national fraternities, national sororities.

Athletics Member NCAA. All Division III.

Campus security: 24-hour emergency response devices and patrols, late-night transport/escort service, controlled dormitory access.

Student services: health clinic, personal/psychological counseling, women's center.

COSTS & FINANCIAL AID
Costs (2018–19) ***Comprehensive fee:*** $50,157 includes full-time tuition ($39,039), mandatory fees ($1710), and room and board ($9408). Full-time tuition and fees vary according to course load. Part-time tuition: $678 per credit hour. Part-time tuition and fees vary according to course load. ***Required fees:*** $13 per credit hour part-time. ***College room only:*** $5889. Room and board charges vary according to board plan and housing facility.

Financial Aid Of all full-time matriculated undergraduates who enrolled in 2017, 2,172 applied for aid, 1,980 were judged to have need, 355 had their need fully met. 267 Federal Work-Study jobs (averaging $1206). In 2017, 402 non-need-based awards were made. ***Average percent of need met:*** 77. ***Average financial aid package:*** $30,233. ***Average need-based loan:*** $4320. ***Average need-based gift aid:*** $26,431. ***Average non-need-based aid:*** $14,091. ***Average indebtedness upon graduation:*** $38,421.

APPLYING
Standardized Tests *Required:* SAT or ACT (for admission).

Options: electronic application, deferred entrance.

Required: high school transcript, minimum 3.0 GPA. ***Required for some:*** essay or personal statement, interview.

CONTACT
Seandra Mitchell, Director, Undergraduate Admission, Milwaukee School of Engineering, 1025 N. Broadway, Milwaukee, WI 53202. *Phone:* 414-277-6762. *Toll-free phone:* 800-332-6763. *E-mail:* mitchell@msoe.edu.

Mount Mary University

Milwaukee, Wisconsin

http://www.mtmary.edu/

- **Independent Roman Catholic** comprehensive, founded 1913
- **Urban** 80-acre campus with easy access to Milwaukee
- **Endowment** $17.0 million
- **Undergraduate: women only; graduate: coed**
- **Moderately difficult** entrance level

FACULTY
Student/faculty ratio: 11:1.

ACADEMICS
Calendar: semesters. *Degrees:* bachelor's, master's, doctoral, post-master's, and postbachelor's certificates.
Library: The Patrick and Beatrice Haggerty Library. *Books:* 77,098 (physical), 142,434 (digital/electronic); *Serial titles:* 5,268 (physical), 155,028 (digital/electronic); *Databases:* 92. Students can reserve study rooms.

STUDENT LIFE
Housing options: on-campus residence required for freshman year; women-only. Campus housing is university owned. Freshman applicants given priority for college housing.

Activities and organizations: student-run newspaper, choral group, Programming and Activities Council, Student Government Association, International Club, Caroline Hall Council, Department Affiliated Clubs.

Athletics Member NCAA. All Division III.

Campus security: 24-hour emergency response devices and patrols, late-night transport/escort service, controlled dormitory access.

Student services: personal/psychological counseling.

COSTS & FINANCIAL AID
Costs (2018–19) ***Comprehensive fee:*** $38,700 includes full-time tuition ($29,510), mandatory fees ($590), and room and board ($8600). Full-time tuition and fees vary according to degree level and program. Part-time tuition: $895 per credit hour. Part-time tuition and fees vary according to course load, degree level, and program. ***Required fees:*** $370 per year part-time. ***Room and board:*** Room and board charges vary according to board plan.

Financial Aid Of all full-time matriculated undergraduates who enrolled in 2018, 619 applied for aid, 594 were judged to have need, 53 had their need fully met. 100 Federal Work-Study jobs (averaging $1620). 76 state and other part-time jobs (averaging $1580). In 2018, 42 non-need-based awards were made. ***Average percent of need met:*** 70. ***Average financial aid package:*** $25,352. ***Average need-based loan:*** $4433. ***Average need-based gift aid:*** $20,616. ***Average non-need-based aid:*** $13,289. ***Average indebtedness upon graduation:*** $27,854.

APPLYING
Standardized Tests *Required:* SAT or ACT (for admission).

Options: electronic application, deferred entrance.

Required: high school transcript. ***Required for some:*** essay or personal statement, 1 letter of recommendation. ***Recommended:*** minimum 2.5 GPA.

CONTACT
Liz Saffold, Admission Counselor Assistant/Receptionist, Mount Mary University, 2900 North Menomonee River Parkway, Milwaukee, WI 53222. *Phone:* 414-930-3000 Ext. 219. *Toll-free phone:* 800-321-6265. *Fax:* 414-256-0180. *E-mail:* mmu-admiss@mtmary.edu.

Northland College

Ashland, Wisconsin

http://www.northland.edu/

- **Independent** 4-year, founded 1892, affiliated with United Church of Christ
- **Small-town** 130-acre campus
- **Endowment** $22.6 million
- **Coed**
- **Moderately difficult** entrance level

FACULTY
Student/faculty ratio: 11:1.

ACADEMICS
Calendar: 4-4-1. *Degree:* bachelor's.
Library: Dexter Library. *Books:* 74,451 (physical); *Serial titles:* 82 (physical), 50 (digital/electronic); *Databases:* 38. Weekly public service hours: 88; students can reserve study rooms.

STUDENT LIFE
Housing options: on-campus residence required through junior year; coed, women-only, special housing for students with disabilities. Campus housing is university owned. Freshman campus housing is guaranteed.

Activities and organizations: drama/theater group, student-run newspaper, choral group, Northland Volunteer Program, Northland College Student Association, Native American Student Association, Environmental Council, SAAC (Student Athlete Organization).

Athletics Member NCAA. All Division III.

Campus security: 24-hour emergency response devices and patrols, late-night transport/escort service, controlled dormitory access.

Student services: health clinic, personal/psychological counseling.

COSTS & FINANCIAL AID
Costs (2018–19) ***Comprehensive fee:*** $45,359 includes full-time tuition ($34,666), mandatory fees ($1517), and room and board ($9176). Full-time tuition and fees vary according to course load. Part-time tuition: $670 per credit. Part-time tuition and fees vary according to course load. ***College room only:*** $4234. Room and board charges vary according to board plan and housing facility.

Financial Aid Of all full-time matriculated undergraduates who enrolled in 2018, 540 applied for aid, 492 were judged to have need, 82 had their need fully met. 285 Federal Work-Study jobs (averaging $1572). 199 state and other part-time jobs (averaging $1733). In 2018, 57 non-need-based awards were made. ***Average percent of need met:*** 78. ***Average financial aid package:*** $30,675. ***Average need-based loan:*** $4218. ***Average need-based gift aid:*** $26,499. ***Average non-need-based aid:*** $20,021. ***Average indebtedness upon graduation:*** $31,106.

APPLYING
Standardized Tests *Required for some:* SAT or ACT (for admission).

Options: electronic application, deferred entrance.

Required: high school transcript.

CONTACT
Teege Mettille, Executive Director of Admissions, Northland College, 1411 Ellis Avenue, Ashland, WI 54806. *Phone:* 715-682-1224. *Toll-free phone:* 800-753-1840 (in-state); 800-753-1040 (out-of-state). *Fax:* 715-682-1258. *E-mail:* admit@northland.edu.

Purdue University Global

Milwaukee, Wisconsin

http://www.purdueglobal.edu/

CONTACT
Purdue University Global, 201 West Wisconsin Avenue, Milwaukee, WI 53203.

Rasmussen College Green Bay

Green Bay, Wisconsin

http://www.rasmussen.edu/

CONTACT
Ms. Susan Hammerstrom, Director of Admissions, Rasmussen College Green Bay, 904 South Taylor Street, Suite 100, Green Bay, WI 54303. *Phone:* 920-593-8400. *Toll-free phone:* 888-549-6755. *E-mail:* susan.hammerstrom@rasmussen.edu.

Rasmussen College Wausau

Wausau, Wisconsin

http://www.rasmussen.edu/

CONTACT
Ms. Susan Hammerstrom, Director of Admissions, Rasmussen College Wausau, 1101 Westwood Drive, Wausau, WI 54401. *Phone:* 715-841-8000. *Toll-free phone:* 888-549-6755. *E-mail:* susan.hammerstrom@rasmussen.edu.

Ripon College

Ripon, Wisconsin

http://www.ripon.edu/

- **Independent** 4-year, founded 1851
- **Small-town** 250-acre campus with easy access to Milwaukee
- **Endowment** $84.5 million
- **Coed**
- **Moderately difficult** entrance level

FACULTY
Student/faculty ratio: 12:1.

ACADEMICS
Calendar: semesters. *Degree:* bachelor's.
Library: Lane Library. *Books:* 160,664 (physical), 142,427 (digital/electronic); *Serial titles:* 86 (physical), 61,132 (digital/electronic); *Databases:* 26. Weekly public service hours: 52; students can reserve study rooms.

STUDENT LIFE
Housing options: on-campus residence required through senior year; coed, men-only, women-only. Campus housing is university owned. Freshman campus housing is guaranteed.

Activities and organizations: drama/theater group, student-run newspaper, radio station, choral group, Environmental Group, Student Senate, Community Service Coalition, SMAC (Student Media and Activities Committee), national fraternities, national sororities.

Athletics Member NCAA. All Division III.

Campus security: 24-hour emergency response devices and patrols, student patrols, late-night transport/escort service, controlled dormitory access.

Student services: health clinic, personal/psychological counseling.

COSTS & FINANCIAL AID
Costs (2018–19) ***Comprehensive fee:*** $52,208 includes full-time tuition ($43,508), mandatory fees ($300), and room and board ($8400). Part-time tuition: $1500 per credit.

Financial Aid Of all full-time matriculated undergraduates who enrolled in 2012, 840 applied for aid, 760 were judged to have need, 135 had their need fully met. 437 Federal Work-Study jobs (averaging $1777). 326 state and other part-time jobs (averaging $1727). In 2012, 124 non-need-based awards were made. ***Average percent of need met:*** 84. ***Average financial aid package:*** $25,418. ***Average need-based loan:*** $5329. ***Average need-***

based gift aid: $19,763. ***Average non-need-based aid:*** $10,803. ***Average indebtedness upon graduation:*** $31,216.

APPLYING
Options: electronic application, deferred entrance.

Application fee: $30.

Required: high school transcript, minimum 2.0 GPA, 1 letter of recommendation. ***Required for some:*** essay or personal statement, interview. ***Recommended:*** essay or personal statement, interview.

CONTACT
Office of Admission, Ripon College, 300 Seward Street, PO Box 248, Ripon, WI 54971. *Phone:* 920-748-8337. *Toll-free phone:* 800-947-4766. *Fax:* 920-748-8335. *E-mail:* adminfo@ripon.edu.

See below for display ad and page 1082 for the College Close-Up.

St. Norbert College

De Pere, Wisconsin

http://www.snc.edu/

- **Independent Roman Catholic** comprehensive, founded 1898
- **Suburban** 113-acre campus
- **Endowment** $145.8 million
- **Coed** 2,132 undergraduate students, 98% full-time, 59% women, 41% men
- **Moderately difficult** entrance level, 78% of applicants were admitted

UNDERGRAD STUDENTS
2,083 full-time, 49 part-time. Students come from 26 states and territories; 18 other countries; 21% are from out of state; 2% Black or African American, non-Hispanic/Latino; 5% Hispanic/Latino; 1% Asian, non-Hispanic/Latino; 0.9% American Indian or Alaska Native, non-Hispanic/Latino; 1% Two or more races, non-Hispanic/Latino; 0.8% Race/ethnicity unknown; 2% international; 1% transferred in; 82% live on campus.

Freshmen:
Admission: 4,118 applied, 3,199 admitted, 620 enrolled. ***Average high school GPA:*** 3.6. ***Test scores:*** ACT scores over 18: 99%; ACT scores over 24: 61%; ACT scores over 30: 10%.

Retention: 83% of full-time freshmen returned.

FACULTY
Total: 203, 68% full-time, 78% with terminal degrees.

Student/faculty ratio: 13:1.

ACADEMICS
Calendar: semesters. *Degrees:* bachelor's and master's.

Special study options: academic remediation for entering students, advanced placement credit, distance learning, double majors, English as a second language, honors programs, independent study, internships, off-campus study, part-time degree program, services for LD students, student-designed majors, study abroad, summer session for credit. ***ROTC:*** Army (b).

Computers: 167 computers/terminals are available on campus for general student use. Students can access the following: campus intranet, computer help desk, free student e-mail accounts, online (class) grades, online (class) registration, online (class) schedules. Campuswide network is available. 100% of college-owned or -operated housing units are wired for high-speed Internet access. Wireless service is available via classrooms, computer centers, computer labs, dorm rooms, learning centers, libraries, student centers.

Library: Miriam B. and James J. Mulva Library plus 1 other. *Books:* 252,444 (physical), 207,312 (digital/electronic); *Serial titles:* 103,421 (physical), 103,236 (digital/electronic). Weekly public service hours: 116; students can reserve study rooms.

STUDENT LIFE
Housing options: on-campus residence required through senior year; coed, women-only, special housing for students with disabilities. Campus housing is university owned. Freshman campus housing is guaranteed.

Activities and organizations: drama/theater group, student-run newspaper, radio and television station, choral group, Pre-Health Science Club, Adventure Club, CC Hams, BUD, American Medical Student Association, national fraternities, national sororities.

Athletics Member NCAA. All Division III except golf (Division II). ***Intercollegiate sports:*** baseball M, basketball M/W, cross-country running M/W, football M, golf M/W, ice hockey M/W, soccer M/W, softball W, swimming and diving M/W, tennis M/W, track and field M/W, volleyball M/W. ***Intramural sports:*** basketball M/W, cheerleading W, football M/W, rowing M(c)/W(c), skiing (downhill) M(c)/W(c), soccer M/W, triathlon M(c)/W(c), ultimate Frisbee M(c)/W(c), volleyball M/W.

Campus security: 24-hour emergency response devices and patrols, student patrols, late-night transport/escort service, controlled dormitory access.

Student services: health clinic, personal/psychological counseling, women's center.

COSTS & FINANCIAL AID

Costs (2019–20) ***Comprehensive fee:*** $49,964 includes full-time tuition ($38,714), mandatory fees ($815), and room and board ($10,435). Part-time tuition: $1209 per credit. ***College room only:*** $5841.

Financial Aid Of all full-time matriculated undergraduates who enrolled in 2017, 1,696 applied for aid, 1,464 were judged to have need, 394 had their need fully met. 387 Federal Work-Study jobs (averaging $1267). In 2017, 518 non-need-based awards were made. ***Average percent of need met:*** 81. ***Average financial aid package:*** $26,919. ***Average need-based loan:*** $4941. ***Average need-based gift aid:*** $20,869. ***Average non-need-based aid:*** $13,542. ***Average indebtedness upon graduation:*** $33,866.

APPLYING

Standardized Tests *Required:* SAT or ACT (for admission).

Options: electronic application, deferred entrance.

Required: high school transcript. ***Recommended:*** essay or personal statement, interview.

Application deadlines: rolling (freshmen), rolling (out-of-state freshmen), rolling (transfers).

Notification: continuous (freshmen), continuous (out-of-state freshmen), continuous (transfers).

CONTACT

Mr. Mark Selin, Executive Director of Enrollment and Marketing, St. Norbert College, 100 Grant Street, De Pere, WI 54115-2099. *Phone:* 920-403-3005. *Toll-free phone:* 800-236-4878. *Fax:* 920-403-4072. *E-mail:* admit@snc.edu.

See below for display ad and page 1102 for the College Close-Up.

Silver Lake College of the Holy Family

Manitowoc, Wisconsin

http://www.sl.edu/

- **Independent Roman Catholic** comprehensive, founded 1869
- **Rural** 30-acre campus with easy access to Milwaukee
- **Endowment** $7.2 million
- **Coed**
- **Minimally difficult** entrance level

FACULTY

Student/faculty ratio: 9:1.

ACADEMICS

Calendar: semesters. *Degrees:* certificates, bachelor's, master's, and postbachelor's certificates.

Library: The Erma M. and Theodore M. Zigmunt Library. *Books:* 53,862 (physical), 93 (digital/electronic); *Serial titles:* 488 (physical); *Databases:* 32. Weekly public service hours: 80; study areas open 24 hours, 5–7 days a week; students can reserve study rooms.

STUDENT LIFE

Housing options: on-campus residence required through junior year; coed, men-only, women-only, special housing for students with disabilities. Campus housing is university owned. Freshman campus housing is guaranteed.

Activities and organizations: choral group, Wellness Club, Card and Game Club, Student For Life, Campus Activity Board, Silver Lake Serves.

Athletics Member NAIA, USCAA.

Campus security: 24-hour emergency response devices and patrols, student patrols, late-night transport/escort service, controlled dormitory access.

Student services: health clinic, personal/psychological counseling.

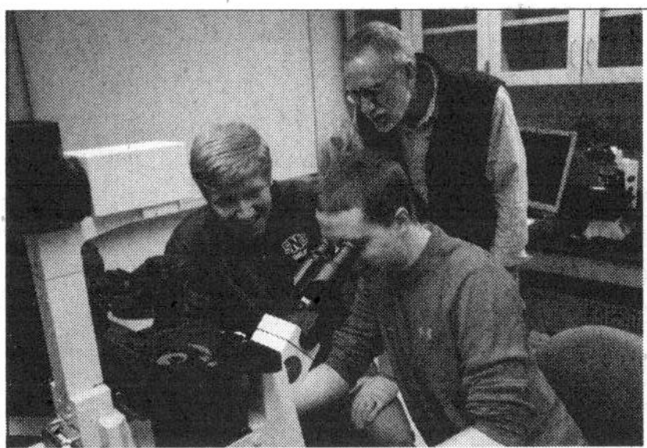

COSTS & FINANCIAL AID
Costs (2018–19) ***One-time required fee:*** $290. ***Comprehensive fee:*** $35,900 includes full-time tuition ($27,800), mandatory fees ($300), and room and board ($7800). Full-time tuition and fees vary according to course load and degree level. Part-time tuition: $560 per credit hour. Part-time tuition and fees vary according to course load and degree level. ***College room only:*** $3600. Room and board charges vary according to board plan and housing facility.

Financial Aid Of all full-time matriculated undergraduates who enrolled in 2011, 157 applied for aid, 149 were judged to have need, 17 had their need fully met. 97 Federal Work-Study jobs (averaging $1429). 3 state and other part-time jobs (averaging $2450). In 2011, 7 non-need-based awards were made. ***Average percent of need met:*** 77. ***Average financial aid package:*** $18,970. ***Average need-based loan:*** $4210. ***Average need-based gift aid:*** $14,197. ***Average non-need-based aid:*** $10,140. ***Average indebtedness upon graduation:*** $35,164.

APPLYING
Standardized Tests *Recommended:* SAT or ACT (for admission).

Options: electronic application, deferred entrance.

Application fee: $50.

Required: high school transcript, minimum 2.0 GPA, 1 letter of recommendation. ***Required for some:*** essay or personal statement, interview.

CONTACT
Daniel Connolly, Director of Enrollment Management, Silver Lake College of the Holy Family, 2406 South Alverno Road, Manitowoc, WI 54220-9319. *Phone:* 920-686-6175. *Toll-free phone:* 800-236-4752 Ext. 175. *Fax:* 920-686-6322. *E-mail:* dan.connolly@sl.edu.

University of Wisconsin–Baraboo/Sauk County

Baraboo, Wisconsin

http://www.baraboo.uwc.edu/

- **State-supported** primarily 2-year, founded 1968, part of University of Wisconsin System
- **Small-town** 68-acre campus with easy access to Madison
- **Coed**

FACULTY
Student/faculty ratio: 16:1.

ACADEMICS
Calendar: semesters. *Degrees:* certificates, associate, and bachelor's.
Library: T. N. Savides Library plus 1 other.

STUDENT LIFE
Housing options: college housing not available.

Activities and organizations: drama/theater group, student-run newspaper, choral group.

Athletics Member NJCAA.

Student services: personal/psychological counseling.

APPLYING
Standardized Tests *Required:* ACT (for admission).

Options: electronic application.

Application fee: $50.

Required: high school transcript.

CONTACT
University of Wisconsin–Baraboo/Sauk County, 1006 Connie Road, Baraboo, WI 53913.

University of Wisconsin–Barron County

Rice Lake, Wisconsin

http://www.barron.uwc.edu/

- **State-supported** primarily 2-year, founded 1968, part of University of Wisconsin System
- **Small-town** 110-acre campus
- **Coed**

FACULTY
Student/faculty ratio: 12:1.

ACADEMICS
Calendar: semesters. *Degrees:* associate and bachelor's.
Library: UW Barron County Library plus 1 other.

STUDENT LIFE
Housing options: college housing not available.

APPLYING
Standardized Tests *Required:* ACT (for admission).

Options: electronic application, deferred entrance.

Application fee: $50.

Required: high school transcript.

CONTACT
University of Wisconsin–Barron County, 1800 College Drive, Rice Lake, WI 54868.

University of Wisconsin–Eau Claire

Eau Claire, Wisconsin

http://www.uwec.edu/

- **State-supported** comprehensive, founded 1916, part of University of Wisconsin System
- **Small-town** 337-acre campus with easy access to Minneapolis-St. Paul
- **Endowment** $73.3 million
- **Coed** 10,113 undergraduate students, 93% full-time, 62% women, 38% men
- **Moderately difficult** entrance level, 86% of applicants were admitted

UNDERGRAD STUDENTS
9,448 full-time, 665 part-time. Students come from 41 states and territories; 24 other countries; 30% are from out of state; 1% Black or African American, non-Hispanic/Latino; 3% Hispanic/Latino; 3% Asian, non-Hispanic/Latino; 0.2% American Indian or Alaska Native, non-Hispanic/Latino; 2% Two or more races, non-Hispanic/Latino; 0.1% Race/ethnicity unknown; 2% international; 5% transferred in; 35% live on campus.

Freshmen:
Admission: 5,855 applied, 5,037 admitted, 2,325 enrolled. ***Test scores:*** SAT evidence-based reading and writing scores over 500: 85%; SAT math scores over 500: 87%; ACT scores over 18: 98%; SAT evidence-based reading and writing scores over 600: 34%; SAT math scores over 600: 35%; ACT scores over 24: 52%; SAT evidence-based reading and writing scores over 700: 7%; SAT math scores over 700: 3%; ACT scores over 30: 6%.

Retention: 82% of full-time freshmen returned.

FACULTY
Total: 559, 68% full-time, 69% with terminal degrees.

Student/faculty ratio: 22:1.

ACADEMICS
Calendar: semesters. *Degrees:* certificates, associate, bachelor's, master's, doctoral, post-master's, and postbachelor's certificates.

Special study options: academic remediation for entering students, accelerated degree program, advanced placement credit, cooperative education, distance learning, double majors, English as a second language, external degree program, honors programs, independent study, internships, off-campus study, part-time degree program, services for LD students, student-designed majors, study abroad, summer session for credit. ***ROTC:*** Army (b).

Computers: 900 computers/terminals are available on campus for general student use. Students can access the following: campus intranet, computer help desk, free student e-mail accounts, online (class) grades, online (class) registration, online (class) schedules, course management system, online library databases and card catalog, other online library services (e.g. Interlibrary loan), library reference staff online chat, check open seats in computer labs, laptop check out, poster printing. Campuswide network is available. 100% of college-owned or -operated housing units are wired for high-speed Internet access. Wireless service is available via entire campus.

Library: William D. McIntyre Library. *Books:* 432,031 (physical), 203,469 (digital/electronic); *Serial titles:* 141 (physical), 216,577 (digital/electronic); *Databases:* 233. Weekly public service hours: 112; study areas open 24 hours, 5–7 days a week; students can reserve study rooms.

STUDENT LIFE

Housing options: on-campus residence required through sophomore year; coed. Campus housing is university owned and leased by the school. Freshman campus housing is guaranteed.

Activities and organizations: drama/theater group, student-run newspaper, radio and television station, choral group, marching band, Student Wisconsin Education Association, Pre- Professional Health Club, Kinesiology Club, RHA (Residence Hall Association), Blugold Beginnings, national fraternities, national sororities.

Athletics Member NCAA. All Division III. ***Intercollegiate sports:*** basketball M/W, cross-country running M/W, football M, golf M/W, gymnastics W, ice hockey M/W, soccer W, softball W, swimming and diving M/W, tennis M/W, track and field M/W, volleyball W, wrestling M. ***Intramural sports:*** baseball M(c)/W(c), basketball M/W, bowling M(c)/W(c), cheerleading M(c)/W(c), equestrian sports M(c)/W(c), football M/W, ice hockey M(c)/W(c), lacrosse M(c)/W(c), rugby M(c)/W(c), sand volleyball M/W, skiing (cross-country) M(c)/W(c), soccer M(c)/W(c), softball M/W, table tennis M(c)/W(c), tennis M/W, triathlon M(c)/W(c), ultimate Frisbee M(c)/W(c), volleyball M(c)/W(c).

Campus security: 24-hour emergency response devices and patrols, student patrols, late-night transport/escort service, controlled dormitory access.

Student services: health clinic, personal/psychological counseling, women's center, legal services, veterans affairs office.

COSTS & FINANCIAL AID

Costs (2018–19) ***Tuition:*** state resident $7361 full-time, $307 per credit part-time; nonresident $15,637 full-time, $652 per credit part-time. Full-time tuition and fees vary according to program and reciprocity agreements. Part-time tuition and fees vary according to program and reciprocity agreements. ***Required fees:*** $1459 full-time, $61 per credit part-time. ***Room and board:*** $7813; room only: $4657. Room and board charges vary according to board plan and housing facility. ***Payment plan:*** installment.

Financial Aid Of all full-time matriculated undergraduates who enrolled in 2017, 6,997 applied for aid, 4,867 were judged to have need, 1,094 had their need fully met. 4,060 Federal Work-Study jobs (averaging $1546). In 2017, 610 non-need-based awards were made. ***Average percent of need met:*** 83. ***Average financial aid package:*** $9551. ***Average need-based loan:*** $4508. ***Average need-based gift aid:*** $6285. ***Average non-need-based aid:*** $2242. ***Average indebtedness upon graduation:*** $26,800.

APPLYING

Standardized Tests *Required:* SAT or ACT (for admission).

Options: electronic application, early admission.

Application fee: $50.

Required: essay or personal statement, high school transcript.

Application deadlines: 8/20 (freshmen), 8/20 (transfers).

Notification: continuous (freshmen), continuous (transfers).

CONTACT

Heather Kretz, Director of Admissions, University of Wisconsin–Eau Claire, PO Box 4004, Eau Claire, WI 54702-4004. *Phone:* 715-836-5188. *Fax:* 715-831-4799. *E-mail:* admissions@uwec.edu.

University of Wisconsin–Green Bay

Green Bay, Wisconsin

http://www.uwgb.edu/

CONTACT

Ms. Jen Jones, Director of Admissions, University of Wisconsin–Green Bay, 2420 Nicolet Drive, Green Bay, WI 54311-7001. *Phone:* 920-465-2111. *Fax:* 920-465-5754. *E-mail:* uwgb@uwgb.edu.

University of Wisconsin–La Crosse

La Crosse, Wisconsin

http://www.uwlax.edu/

- **State-supported** comprehensive, founded 1909, part of University of Wisconsin System
- **Suburban** 128-acre campus
- **Endowment** $25.6 million
- **Coed** 9,676 undergraduate students, 94% full-time, 56% women, 44% men
- **Moderately difficult** entrance level, 78% of applicants were admitted

UNDERGRAD STUDENTS

9,130 full-time, 546 part-time. Students come from 42 states and territories; 30 other countries; 17% are from out of state; 0.8% Black or African American, non-Hispanic/Latino; 3% Hispanic/Latino; 2% Asian, non-Hispanic/Latino; 0.1% American Indian or Alaska Native, non-Hispanic/Latino; 3% Two or more races, non-Hispanic/Latino; 0.1% Race/ethnicity unknown; 1% international; 4% transferred in; 35% live on campus.

Freshmen:

Admission: 6,048 applied, 4,730 admitted, 2,166 enrolled. ***Test scores:*** SAT evidence-based reading and writing scores over 500: 85%; SAT math scores over 500: 96%; ACT scores over 18: 100%; SAT evidence-based reading and writing scores over 600: 48%; SAT math scores over 600: 52%; ACT scores over 24: 63%; SAT evidence-based reading and writing scores over 700: 4%; ACT scores over 30: 7%.

Retention: 86% of full-time freshmen returned.

FACULTY

Total: 625, 74% full-time, 71% with terminal degrees.

Student/faculty ratio: 19:1.

ACADEMICS

Calendar: semesters. *Degrees:* certificates, associate, bachelor's, master's, doctoral, post-master's, and postbachelor's certificates.

Special study options: academic remediation for entering students, advanced placement credit, distance learning, double majors, English as a second language, honors programs, independent study, internships, off-campus study, part-time degree program, services for LD students, study abroad, summer session for credit. ***ROTC:*** Army (b).

Unusual degree programs: 3-2 engineering with University of Wisconsin-Madison; University of Wisconsin-Milwaukee; University of Wisconsin-Platteville; University of Minnesota-Duluth; Winona State University; physical therapy and physics; physical therapy and biology.

Computers: 200 computers/terminals are available on campus for general student use. Students can access the following: campus intranet, computer help desk, free student e-mail accounts, online (class) grades, online (class) registration, online (class) schedules. Campuswide network is available. 100% of college-owned or -operated housing units are wired for high-speed Internet access. Wireless service is available via entire campus.

Library: Murphy Library plus 1 other. *Books:* 422,070 (physical), 670,354 (digital/electronic); *Serial titles:* 7,822 (physical), 135,820 (digital/electronic); *Databases:* 230. Weekly public service hours: 107; students can reserve study rooms.

STUDENT LIFE

Housing options: on-campus residence required for freshman year; coed, special housing for students with disabilities. Campus housing is university owned. Freshman applicants given priority for college housing.

Activities and organizations: drama/theater group, student-run newspaper, radio and television station, choral group, marching band, Sports and Activities Club, Residential Hall Council, Religious/Spiritual Organizations, Human Diversity Organizations, Departmental/Professional, national fraternities, national sororities.

Athletics Member NCAA, NAIA. All NCAA Division III. ***Intercollegiate sports:*** baseball M, basketball M/W, cross-country running M/W, football M, gymnastics W, soccer W, softball W, swimming and diving M/W, tennis M/W, track and field M/W, volleyball W, wrestling M. ***Intramural sports:*** archery M(c)/W(c), badminton M/W, basketball M/W, bowling M(c)/W(c), equestrian sports M(c)/W(c), ice hockey M(c)/W(c), lacrosse M(c)/W(c), racquetball M/W, rugby M(c)/W(c), skiing (cross-country) M(c)/W(c), skiing (downhill) M(c)/W(c), soccer M(c)/W(c), softball

M/W, table tennis M/W, tennis M/W, triathlon M(c)/W(c), ultimate Frisbee M/W, volleyball M(c)/W(c), weight lifting M/W.

Campus security: 24-hour emergency response devices and patrols, late-night transport/escort service, controlled dormitory access.

Student services: health clinic, personal/psychological counseling, legal services, veterans affairs office.

COSTS & FINANCIAL AID
Costs (2018–19) ***Tuition:*** state resident $7885 full-time; nonresident $16,254 full-time. Full-time tuition and fees vary according to reciprocity agreements. Part-time tuition and fees vary according to course load and reciprocity agreements. ***Required fees:*** $1348 full-time. ***Room and board:*** $6331; room only: $3825. Room and board charges vary according to board plan and housing facility. ***Payment plan:*** installment.

Financial Aid Of all full-time matriculated undergraduates who enrolled in 2017, 6,810 applied for aid, 4,282 were judged to have need, 1,113 had their need fully met. 452 Federal Work-Study jobs (averaging $1544). In 2017, 372 non-need-based awards were made. ***Average percent of need met:*** 73. ***Average financial aid package:*** $8315. ***Average need-based loan:*** $4454. ***Average need-based gift aid:*** $5810. ***Average non-need-based aid:*** $1628. ***Average indebtedness upon graduation:*** $26,706.

APPLYING
Standardized Tests *Required:* SAT or ACT (for admission).

Options: electronic application.

Application fee: $50.

Required: essay or personal statement, high school transcript.

Application deadlines: rolling (freshmen), rolling (transfers).

Notification: continuous (freshmen), continuous (transfers).

CONTACT
Mr. Corey Sjoquist, Director of Admissions, University of Wisconsin–La Crosse, 1725 State Street, La Crosse, WI 54601. *Phone:* 608-785-8939. *Fax:* 608-785-8940. *E-mail:* admissions@uwlax.edu.

University of Wisconsin–Madison
Madison, Wisconsin
http://www.wisc.edu/

- **State-supported** university, founded 1848, part of University of Wisconsin System
- **Urban** 936-acre campus with easy access to Milwaukee
- **Endowment** $2.5 billion
- **Coed**
- **Very difficult** entrance level

FACULTY
Student/faculty ratio: 18:1.

ACADEMICS
Calendar: semesters. *Degrees:* bachelor's, master's, doctoral, and postbachelor's certificates.
Library: Memorial Library plus 40 others. Study areas open 24 hours, 5–7 days a week; students can reserve study rooms.

STUDENT LIFE
Housing options: coed, men-only, women-only, cooperative. Campus housing is university owned. Freshman applicants given priority for college housing.

Activities and organizations: drama/theater group, student-run newspaper, radio station, choral group, marching band, national fraternities, national sororities.

Athletics Member NCAA. All Division I except football (Division I-A).

Campus security: 24-hour emergency response devices and patrols, late-night transport/escort service, controlled dormitory access.

Student services: health clinic, personal/psychological counseling, women's center, veterans affairs office.

COSTS & FINANCIAL AID
Costs (2018–19) ***Tuition:*** state resident $9273 full-time, $386 per credit hour part-time; nonresident $35,523 full-time, $1480 per credit hour part-time. Full-time tuition and fees vary according to program and reciprocity agreements. Part-time tuition and fees vary according to course load, program, and reciprocity agreements. ***Required fees:*** $1282 full-time, $101 per credit hour part-time. ***Room and board:*** $11,114. Room and board charges vary according to board plan and housing facility.

Financial Aid Of all full-time matriculated undergraduates who enrolled in 2018, 15,891 applied for aid, 10,635 were judged to have need, 3,584 had their need fully met. In 2018, 2143 non-need-based awards were made. ***Average percent of need met:*** 75. ***Average financial aid package:*** $18,194. ***Average need-based loan:*** $5446. ***Average need-based gift aid:*** $12,751. ***Average non-need-based aid:*** $4108. ***Average indebtedness upon graduation:*** $28,229.

APPLYING
Standardized Tests *Required:* SAT or ACT (for admission).

Options: electronic application, early action, deferred entrance.

Application fee: $60.

Required: essay or personal statement, high school transcript. *Recommended:* 2 letters of recommendation.

CONTACT
Office of Admissions and Recruitment, University of Wisconsin–Madison, 702 West Johnson Street, Suite 101, Madison, WI 53706-1481. *Phone:* 608-262-3961. *Fax:* 608-262-7706. *E-mail:* onwisconsin@admissions.wisc.edu.

University of Wisconsin–Marshfield/Wood County
Marshfield, Wisconsin
http://marshfield.uwc.edu/

- **State-supported** primarily 2-year, founded 1963, part of University of Wisconsin System
- **Small-town** 114-acre campus
- **Coed**

FACULTY
Student/faculty ratio: 15:1.

ACADEMICS
Calendar: semesters. *Degrees:* certificates, associate, and bachelor's.
Library: Hamilton Roddis Memorial Library plus 1 other.

STUDENT LIFE
Activities and organizations: drama/theater group, student-run newspaper, choral group.

Campus security: 24-hour patrols, patrols by city police.

APPLYING
Standardized Tests *Required:* ACT (for admission).

Options: electronic application, early admission, deferred entrance.

Application fee: $50.

Required: high school transcript.

CONTACT
University of Wisconsin–Marshfield/Wood County, 2000 West 5th Street, Marshfield, WI 54449.

University of Wisconsin–Milwaukee
Milwaukee, Wisconsin
http://www.uwm.edu/

- **State-supported** university, founded 1956, part of University of Wisconsin System
- **Urban** 104-acre campus with easy access to Milwaukee
- **Endowment** $167.2 million
- **Coed** 20,256 undergraduate students, 82% full-time, 53% women, 47% men
- **Moderately difficult** entrance level, 72% of applicants were admitted

UNDERGRAD STUDENTS
16,669 full-time, 3,587 part-time. Students come from 52 states and territories; 91 other countries; 11% are from out of state; 7% Black or African American, non-Hispanic/Latino; 11% Hispanic/Latino; 7% Asian, non-Hispanic/Latino; 0.1% Native Hawaiian or other Pacific Islander, non-Hispanic/Latino; 0.4% American Indian or Alaska Native, non-Hispanic/Latino; 4% Two or more races, non-Hispanic/Latino; 0.6%

Race/ethnicity unknown; 4% international; 7% transferred in; 20% live on campus.

Freshmen:
Admission: 10,046 applied, 7,211 admitted, 3,220 enrolled. ***Average high school GPA:*** 3.1. ***Test scores:*** SAT evidence-based reading and writing scores over 500: 91%; SAT math scores over 500: 85%; ACT scores over 18: 92%; SAT evidence-based reading and writing scores over 600: 39%; SAT math scores over 600: 37%; ACT scores over 24: 40%; SAT evidence-based reading and writing scores over 700: 3%; SAT math scores over 700: 4%; ACT scores over 30: 5%.

Retention: 74% of full-time freshmen returned.

FACULTY
Total: 1,546, 64% full-time, 49% with terminal degrees.

Student/faculty ratio: 19:1.

ACADEMICS
Calendar: semesters. *Degrees:* certificates, bachelor's, master's, doctoral, post-master's, and postbachelor's certificates.

Special study options: academic remediation for entering students, accelerated degree program, adult/continuing education programs, advanced placement credit, cooperative education, distance learning, double majors, English as a second language, external degree program, freshman honors college, honors programs, independent study, internships, off-campus study, part-time degree program, services for LD students, student-designed majors, study abroad, summer session for credit. ***ROTC:*** Army (c), Navy (c), Air Force (c).

Computers: 500 computers/terminals are available on campus for general student use. Students can access the following: campus intranet, computer help desk, free student e-mail accounts, online (class) grades, online (class) registration, online (class) schedules. Campuswide network is available. 100% of college-owned or -operated housing units are wired for high-speed Internet access. Wireless service is available via classrooms, computer centers, computer labs, dorm rooms, learning centers, libraries, student centers.

Library: Golda Meir Library. *Books:* 2.5 million (physical), 178,268 (digital/electronic); *Serial titles:* 112,752 (physical). Students can reserve study rooms.

STUDENT LIFE
Housing options: on-campus residence required for freshman year; coed, special housing for students with disabilities. Campus housing is university owned. Freshman applicants given priority for college housing.

Activities and organizations: drama/theater group, student-run newspaper, choral group, national fraternities, national sororities.

Athletics Member NCAA. All Division I. ***Intercollegiate sports:*** baseball M(s), basketball M(s)/W(s), bowling M(c)/W(c), cross-country running M(s)/W(s), equestrian sports M(c)/W(c), football M(c)/W(c), ice hockey M(c)/W(c), lacrosse M(c)/W(c), rugby M(c)/W(c), sailing M(c)/W(c), soccer M(s)/W(s), swimming and diving M(s)/W(s), tennis W(s), track and field M(s)/W(s), ultimate Frisbee M(c)/W(c), volleyball M(c)/W(s). ***Intramural sports:*** badminton M/W, baseball M(c)/W(c), basketball M/W, cross-country running M/W, football M/W, racquetball M/W, skiing (downhill) M(c)/W(c), soccer M/W, swimming and diving M/W, tennis M(c)/W(c), track and field M(c)/W(c), volleyball M/W.

Campus security: 24-hour emergency response devices and patrols, student patrols, late-night transport/escort service, controlled dormitory access.

Student services: health clinic, personal/psychological counseling, women's center, legal services.

COSTS & FINANCIAL AID
Costs (2019–20) ***Tuition:*** area resident $9588 full-time; state resident $9588 full-time; nonresident $20,868 full-time. ***Room and board:*** $10,792.

Financial Aid Of all full-time matriculated undergraduates who enrolled in 2017, 13,434 applied for aid, 11,204 were judged to have need, 753 had their need fully met. In 2017, 422 non-need-based awards were made. ***Average percent of need met:*** 50. ***Average financial aid package:*** $9130. ***Average need-based loan:*** $4340. ***Average need-based gift aid:*** $6396. ***Average non-need-based aid:*** $1875. ***Average indebtedness upon graduation:*** $37,979.

APPLYING
Standardized Tests *Required for some:* SAT or ACT (for admission), TOEFL for students whose native language is not English and who were not educated in an entirely English-speaking country.

Options: electronic application, deferred entrance.

Application fee: $50.

Required: high school transcript. ***Recommended:*** essay or personal statement.

Application deadlines: rolling (freshmen), 8/10 (transfers).

Notification: continuous (freshmen), continuous (transfers).

CONTACT
Mr. Patrick Fay, Interim Director, Undergraduate Admissions, University of Wisconsin–Milwaukee, PO Box 413, Milwaukee, WI 53201-0413. *Phone:* 414-229-4445. *E-mail:* uwmlook@uwm.edu.

University of Wisconsin–Oshkosh
Oshkosh, Wisconsin
http://www.uwosh.edu/

CONTACT
Associate Director of Admissions, University of Wisconsin–Oshkosh, 800 Algoma Boulevard, Oshkosh, WI 54901. *Phone:* 920-424-0202. *E-mail:* oshadmuw@uwosh.edu.

University of Wisconsin–Parkside
Kenosha, Wisconsin
http://www.uwp.edu/

- **State-supported** comprehensive, founded 1968, part of University of Wisconsin System
- **Suburban** 700-acre campus with easy access to Chicago, Milwaukee
- **Coed**
- **Moderately difficult** entrance level

FACULTY
Student/faculty ratio: 19:1.

ACADEMICS
Calendar: semesters. *Degrees:* certificates, associate, bachelor's, and master's.
Library: UWP Library. Students can reserve study rooms.

STUDENT LIFE
Housing options: on-campus residence required through sophomore year; coed, special housing for students with disabilities. Campus housing is university owned.

Activities and organizations: drama/theater group, student-run newspaper, radio station, choral group, Habitat for Humanity, Criminal Justice Association, Next Level Gaming, Parkside Asian Organization, Active Minds, national fraternities, national sororities.

Athletics Member NCAA. All Division II.

Campus security: 24-hour emergency response devices and patrols, late-night transport/escort service, controlled dormitory access.

Student services: health clinic, personal/psychological counseling, women's center, veterans affairs office.

COSTS & FINANCIAL AID
Costs (2018–19) ***One-time required fee:*** $260. ***Tuition:*** state resident $6298 full-time, $262 per credit hour part-time; nonresident $14,287 full-time, $595 per credit hour part-time. Full-time tuition and fees vary according to course load, program, and reciprocity agreements. Part-time tuition and fees vary according to course load, program, and reciprocity agreements. ***Required fees:*** $1351 full-time, $45 per credit hour part-time. ***Room and board:*** $8026; room only: $4494. Room and board charges vary according to board plan and housing facility.

Financial Aid Of all full-time matriculated undergraduates who enrolled in 2016, 2,537 applied for aid, 2,080 were judged to have need, 281 had their need fully met. 117 Federal Work-Study jobs (averaging $1564). In 2016, 87 non-need-based awards were made. ***Average percent of need met:*** 66. ***Average financial aid package:*** $9703. ***Average need-based loan:*** $4494. ***Average need-based gift aid:*** $6311. ***Average non-need-based aid:*** $2149. ***Average indebtedness upon graduation:*** $28,504.

APPLYING
Standardized Tests *Required for some:* SAT or ACT (for admission).
Options: electronic application.
Application fee: $50.
Required: high school transcript, minimum of 17 high school units distribution.

CONTACT
Troy Moldenhauer, Director, Admissions and Recruitment, University of Wisconsin–Parkside, PO Box 2000, 900 Wood Road, Kenosha, WI 53141-2000. *Phone:* 262-595-2355. *Fax:* 262-595-2006. *E-mail:* moldenht@uwp.edu.

University of Wisconsin–Platteville
Platteville, Wisconsin
http://www.uwplatt.edu/

- **State-supported** comprehensive, founded 1866, part of University of Wisconsin System
- **Small-town** 821-acre campus
- **Endowment** $28.6 million
- **Coed**
- 79% of applicants were admitted

FACULTY
Student/faculty ratio: 21:1.

ACADEMICS
Calendar: semesters. *Degrees:* certificates, associate, bachelor's, master's, and postbachelor's certificates.
Library: Karrmann Library plus 1 other. *Books:* 167,304 (physical), 59,292 (digital/electronic); *Serial titles:* 1,151 (physical), 44,687 (digital/electronic); *Databases:* 123. Weekly public service hours: 87.

STUDENT LIFE
Housing options: on-campus residence required through sophomore year; coed, men-only, women-only, cooperative, special housing for students with disabilities. Campus housing is university owned. Freshman campus housing is guaranteed.
Activities and organizations: drama/theater group, student-run newspaper, radio and television station, choral group, marching band, Criminal Justice Association, Platteville Gaming Association, Dodgeball, American Society of Mechanical Engineers, Outdoor Adventure Club, national fraternities, national sororities.
Athletics Member NCAA. All Division III.
Campus security: 24-hour emergency response devices and patrols, student patrols, late-night transport/escort service, controlled dormitory access.
Student services: health clinic, personal/psychological counseling, women's center, veterans affairs office.

FINANCIAL AID
Financial Aid Of all full-time matriculated undergraduates who enrolled in 2002, 3,289 applied for aid, 2,468 were judged to have need. 382 Federal Work-Study jobs (averaging $1392). In 2002, 652 non-need-based awards were made. ***Average financial aid package:*** $6161. ***Average need-based loan:*** $3499. ***Average need-based gift aid:*** $3599. ***Average non-need-based aid:*** $1427. ***Average indebtedness upon graduation:*** $15,785.

APPLYING
Standardized Tests *Required:* SAT or ACT (for admission).
Application fee: $50.
Required: high school transcript. ***Recommended:*** essay or personal statement.

CONTACT
Ms. Heidi Tuescher-Gille, Director of Admission and Enrollment Services, University of Wisconsin–Platteville, 1 University Plaza, 1300 Ullsvik Hall, Platteville, WI 53818-3099. *Phone:* 608-342-1125. *Toll-free phone:* 877-897-5288. *Fax:* 608-342-1122. *E-mail:* tuescheh@uwplatt.edu.

University of Wisconsin–Richland
Richland Center, Wisconsin
http://richland.uwc.edu/

- **State-supported** primarily 2-year, founded 1967, part of University of Wisconsin System
- **Small-town** 135-acre campus
- **Coed**

FACULTY
Student/faculty ratio: 8:1.

ACADEMICS
Calendar: semesters. *Degrees:* certificates, associate, and bachelor's.
Library: Miller Memorial Library plus 1 other.

STUDENT LIFE
Housing options: coed. Campus housing is provided by a third party.
Activities and organizations: drama/theater group, choral group.
Student services: personal/psychological counseling.

APPLYING
Standardized Tests *Required:* ACT (for admission).
Options: electronic application.
Application fee: $50.
Required: high school transcript.

CONTACT
University of Wisconsin–Richland, 1200 Highway 14 West, Richland Center, WI 53581.

University of Wisconsin–River Falls
River Falls, Wisconsin
http://www.uwrf.edu/

- **State-supported** comprehensive, founded 1874, part of University of Wisconsin System
- **Suburban** 303-acre campus with easy access to Minneapolis-St. Paul
- **Endowment** $25.8 million
- **Coed** 5,725 undergraduate students, 91% full-time, 63% women, 37% men
- **Moderately difficult** entrance level, 75% of applicants were admitted

UNDERGRAD STUDENTS
5,206 full-time, 519 part-time. Students come from 33 states and territories; 14 other countries; 50% are from out of state; 1% Black or African American, non-Hispanic/Latino; 4% Hispanic/Latino; 3% Asian, non-Hispanic/Latino; 0.1% Native Hawaiian or other Pacific Islander, non-Hispanic/Latino; 0.1% American Indian or Alaska Native, non-Hispanic/Latino; 3% Two or more races, non-Hispanic/Latino; 0.2% Race/ethnicity unknown; 2% international; 6% transferred in; 47% live on campus.

Freshmen:
Admission: 3,209 applied, 2,409 admitted, 1,264 enrolled. ***Average high school GPA:*** 3.4. ***Test scores:*** SAT evidence-based reading and writing scores over 500: 82%; SAT math scores over 500: 73%; ACT scores over 18: 94%; SAT evidence-based reading and writing scores over 600: 27%; SAT math scores over 600: 27%; ACT scores over 24: 36%; SAT math scores over 700: 5%; ACT scores over 30: 4%.
Retention: 75% of full-time freshmen returned.

FACULTY
Total: 380, 70% full-time, 66% with terminal degrees.
Student/faculty ratio: 18:1.

ACADEMICS
Calendar: semesters. *Degrees:* certificates, associate, bachelor's, master's, post-master's, and postbachelor's certificates.
Special study options: academic remediation for entering students, adult/continuing education programs, advanced placement credit, distance learning, double majors, English as a second language, external degree program, honors programs, independent study, internships, off-campus study, part-time degree program, services for LD students, study abroad, summer session for credit. ***ROTC:*** Army (b).

Unusual degree programs: 3-2 engineering with University of Wisconsin-Madison, University of Wisconsin-Milwaukee, University of Wisconsin-Platteville, University of Minnesota-Twin Cities, University of Minnesota-Duluth.

Computers: 800 computers/terminals are available on campus for general student use. Students can access the following: computer help desk, free student e-mail accounts, online (class) grades, online (class) registration, online (class) schedules. Campuswide network is available. 100% of college-owned or -operated housing units are wired for high-speed Internet access. Wireless service is available via entire campus.
Library: Chalmer Davee Library. *Books:* 268,085 (physical), 433,534 (digital/electronic); *Serial titles:* 35 (physical). Weekly public service hours: 46; study areas open 24 hours, 5–7 days a week; students can reserve study rooms.

STUDENT LIFE
Housing options: on-campus residence required through sophomore year; coed, women-only, special housing for students with disabilities. Campus housing is university owned. Freshman campus housing is guaranteed.

Activities and organizations: drama/theater group, student-run newspaper, radio and television station, choral group, Intervarsity Christian Fellowship, UW Pre-Vet Club, National Association for Music Education, Aspiring Educators, Agricultural Business and Marketing Society, national fraternities, national sororities.

Athletics Member NCAA. All Division III. ***Intercollegiate sports:*** baseball M(c)/W(c), basketball M/W, cheerleading M(c)/W(c), cross-country running M/W, football M, golf W, ice hockey M/W, lacrosse M(c)/W, rock climbing M(c)/W(c), soccer M(c)/W, softball W, tennis M(c)/W, track and field M/W, ultimate Frisbee M(c)/W(c), volleyball M(c)/W. ***Intramural sports:*** badminton M/W, basketball M/W, football M/W, soccer M/W, softball M/W, tennis M/W, ultimate Frisbee M/W, volleyball M/W.

Campus security: 24-hour emergency response devices and patrols, student patrols, late-night transport/escort service, controlled dormitory access.

Student services: health clinic, personal/psychological counseling, veterans affairs office.

FINANCIAL AID
Financial Aid Of all full-time matriculated undergraduates who enrolled in 2017, 3,845 applied for aid, 2,854 were judged to have need, 54 had their need fully met. 396 Federal Work-Study jobs (averaging $1195). In 2017, 489 non-need-based awards were made. ***Average percent of need met:*** 54. ***Average financial aid package:*** $7196. ***Average need-based loan:*** $4204. ***Average need-based gift aid:*** $5188. ***Average non-need-based aid:*** $1896. ***Average indebtedness upon graduation:*** $27,684.

APPLYING
Standardized Tests *Required:* SAT or ACT (for admission). *Recommended:* ACT (for admission).

Options: electronic application, deferred entrance.

Application fee: $50.

Required: essay or personal statement, high school transcript. ***Recommended:*** rank in upper 40% of high school class.

Application deadlines: rolling (freshmen), rolling (out-of-state freshmen), rolling (transfers).

Notification: continuous (freshmen), continuous (out-of-state freshmen), continuous (transfers).

CONTACT
Sarah Nelson, Director of Admissions, University of Wisconsin–River Falls, 410 South Third Street, Admissions Office - 112 South Hall, River Falls, WI 54022. *Phone:* 715-425-3500. *E-mail:* admissions@uwrf.edu.

University of Wisconsin–Rock County

Janesville, Wisconsin

http://rock.uwc.edu/

- **State-supported** primarily 2-year, founded 1966, part of University of Wisconsin System
- **Small-town** 50-acre campus with easy access to Milwaukee
- **Coed**

FACULTY
Student/faculty ratio: 16:1.

ACADEMICS
Calendar: semesters. *Degrees:* certificates, associate, and bachelor's.
Library: Gary J. Lenox Library plus 1 other.

STUDENT LIFE
Housing options: college housing not available.

APPLYING
Standardized Tests *Required:* ACT (for admission).

Options: electronic application, deferred entrance.

Application fee: $50.

Required: high school transcript.

CONTACT
University of Wisconsin–Rock County, 2909 Kellogg Avenue, Janesville, WI 53546. *Toll-free phone:* 888-INFO-UWC.

University of Wisconsin–Stevens Point

Stevens Point, Wisconsin

http://www.uwsp.edu/

- **State-supported** comprehensive, founded 1894, part of University of Wisconsin System
- **Small-town** 400-acre campus
- **Endowment** $28.6 million
- **Coed**
- **Moderately difficult** entrance level

FACULTY
Student/faculty ratio: 17:1.

ACADEMICS
Calendar: semesters. *Degrees:* associate, bachelor's, master's, and doctoral.
Library: Learning Resources Center plus 1 other. *Books:* 420,414 (physical), 247,207 (digital/electronic); *Serial titles:* 7,192 (physical), 133,235 (digital/electronic); *Databases:* 204. Study areas open 24 hours, 5–7 days a week; students can reserve study rooms.

STUDENT LIFE
Housing options: on-campus residence required through sophomore year; coed, men-only, women-only. Campus housing is university owned. Freshman applicants given priority for college housing.

Activities and organizations: drama/theater group, student-run newspaper, radio and television station, choral group, The Wildlife Society, Student Impact, WWSP 90-FM radio station, Gender and Sexuality Alliance, Student Wisconsin Education Association, national fraternities, national sororities.

Athletics Member NCAA. All Division III.

Campus security: 24-hour emergency response devices and patrols, student patrols, late-night transport/escort service, controlled dormitory access.

Student services: health clinic, personal/psychological counseling, women's center, veterans affairs office.

COSTS & FINANCIAL AID
Costs (2018–19) ***Tuition:*** state resident $8308 full-time, $407 per credit part-time; nonresident $16,576 full-time, $752 per credit part-time. Full-time tuition and fees vary according to course load, location, program, reciprocity agreements, and student level. Part-time tuition and fees vary according to course load, location, program, reciprocity agreements, and student level. ***Required fees:*** $1426 full-time. ***Room and board:*** $7290; room only: $4420. Room and board charges vary according to board plan and housing facility. ***Payment plans:*** installment, deferred payment.

Financial Aid Of all full-time matriculated undergraduates who enrolled in 2018, 5,348 applied for aid, 3,983 were judged to have need, 2,561 had their need fully met. 1,241 Federal Work-Study jobs (averaging $2317). In 2018, 729 non-need-based awards were made. ***Average percent of need met:*** 78. ***Average financial aid package:*** $9814. ***Average need-based loan:*** $4648. ***Average need-based gift aid:*** $6398. ***Average non-need-***

based aid: $1534. ***Average indebtedness upon graduation:*** $31,715. ***Financial aid deadline:*** 5/1.

APPLYING
Standardized Tests *Required:* SAT or ACT (for admission).

Options: electronic application, deferred entrance.

Application fee: $50.

Required: high school transcript. ***Recommended:*** essay or personal statement, 3 letters of recommendation.

CONTACT
Mr. William Jordan, Director of Admissions, University of Wisconsin–Stevens Point, 102 Student Services Center, Stevens Point, WI 54481. *Phone:* 715-346-4021. *Fax:* 715-346-3296. *E-mail:* bjordan@uwsp.edu.

University of Wisconsin–Stout

Menomonie, Wisconsin

http://www.uwstout.edu/

- **State-supported** comprehensive, founded 1891, part of University of Wisconsin System
- **Small-town** 120-acre campus with easy access to Minneapolis-St. Paul
- **Coed**
- **Moderately difficult** entrance level

FACULTY
Student/faculty ratio: 20:1.

ACADEMICS
Calendar: 4-1-4. *Degrees:* certificates, bachelor's, master's, doctoral, post-master's, and postbachelor's certificates.
Library: Library Learning Center.

STUDENT LIFE
Housing options: on-campus residence required through sophomore year; coed, special housing for students with disabilities. Campus housing is university owned. Freshman campus housing is guaranteed.

Activities and organizations: drama/theater group, student-run newspaper, radio station, choral group, marching band, national fraternities, national sororities.

Athletics Member NCAA. All Division III.

Campus security: 24-hour emergency response devices and patrols, student patrols, controlled dormitory access.

Student services: health clinic, personal/psychological counseling, legal services.

FINANCIAL AID
Financial Aid Of all full-time matriculated undergraduates who enrolled in 2017, 5,154 applied for aid, 3,714 were judged to have need, 591 had their need fully met. 1,726 Federal Work-Study jobs (averaging $1627). In 2017, 182 non-need-based awards were made. ***Average percent of need met:*** 85. ***Average financial aid package:*** $11,237. ***Average need-based loan:*** $4729. ***Average need-based gift aid:*** $6033. ***Average non-need-based aid:*** $1865. ***Average indebtedness upon graduation:*** $30,409.

APPLYING
Standardized Tests *Required:* SAT or ACT (for admission).

Options: electronic application.

Application fee: $50.

Required: high school transcript. ***Required for some:*** minimum 2.8 GPA. ***Recommended:*** minimum 2.5 GPA.

CONTACT
Dr. Pamela Holsinger-Fuchs, Executive Director of Enrollment Services, University of Wisconsin–Stout, Admissions, Bowman Hall, Menomonie, WI 54751. *Phone:* 715-232-2639. *Toll-free phone:* 800-HI-STOUT. *Fax:* 715-232-1667. *E-mail:* admissions@uwstout.edu.

University of Wisconsin–Superior

Superior, Wisconsin

http://www.uwsuper.edu/

- **State-supported** comprehensive, founded 1893, part of University of Wisconsin System
- **Suburban** 230-acre campus
- **Coed** 2,294 undergraduate students, 78% full-time, 62% women, 38% men
- **Minimally difficult** entrance level, 74% of applicants were admitted

UNDERGRAD STUDENTS
1,793 full-time, 501 part-time. Students come from 49 other countries; 49% are from out of state; 2% Black or African American, non-Hispanic/Latino; 3% Hispanic/Latino; 0.7% Asian, non-Hispanic/Latino; 1% American Indian or Alaska Native, non-Hispanic/Latino; 4% Two or more races, non-Hispanic/Latino; 0.2% Race/ethnicity unknown; 10% international; 11% transferred in; 31% live on campus.

Freshmen:
Admission: 936 applied, 690 admitted, 326 enrolled. ***Average high school GPA:*** 3.2. ***Test scores:*** SAT evidence-based reading and writing scores over 500: 71%; SAT math scores over 500: 86%; ACT scores over 18: 84%; SAT evidence-based reading and writing scores over 600: 29%; SAT math scores over 600: 48%; ACT scores over 24: 29%; SAT evidence-based reading and writing scores over 700: 5%; SAT math scores over 700: 19%; ACT scores over 30: 5%.

Retention: 70% of full-time freshmen returned.

FACULTY
Total: 222, 51% full-time, 44% with terminal degrees.

Student/faculty ratio: 14:1.

ACADEMICS
Calendar: semesters. *Degrees:* certificates, associate, bachelor's, master's, post-master's, and postbachelor's certificates.

Special study options: academic remediation for entering students, accelerated degree program, adult/continuing education programs, advanced placement credit, cooperative education, distance learning, double majors, English as a second language, external degree program, independent study, internships, off-campus study, part-time degree program, services for LD students, student-designed majors, study abroad, summer session for credit. ***ROTC:*** Air Force (c).

Unusual degree programs: 3-2 engineering with Michigan Technological University, University of Wisconsin–Madison; forestry with Michigan Technological University.

Computers: 375 computers/terminals are available on campus for general student use. Students can access the following: campus intranet, computer help desk, free student e-mail accounts, online (class) grades, online (class) registration, online (class) schedules. Campuswide network is available. 100% of college-owned or -operated housing units are wired for high-speed Internet access. Wireless service is available via entire campus.
Library: Jim Dan Hill Library.

STUDENT LIFE
Housing options: on-campus residence required through sophomore year; coed, women-only, special housing for students with disabilities. Campus housing is university owned. Freshman campus housing is guaranteed.

Activities and organizations: drama/theater group, student-run newspaper, radio station, choral group.

Athletics Member NCAA. All Division III. ***Intercollegiate sports:*** baseball M, basketball M/W, cross-country running M/W, ice hockey M/W, soccer M/W, softball W, tennis M/W, track and field M/W, volleyball W. ***Intramural sports:*** badminton M/W, baseball M(c), basketball M/W, bowling M/W, football M/W, ice hockey M(c)/W(c), racquetball M/W, riflery M/W, rock climbing M/W, soccer M/W, softball M/W, swimming and diving M/W, table tennis M/W, tennis M(c)/W(c), ultimate Frisbee M(c)/W(c), volleyball M(c)/W(c).

Campus security: 24-hour emergency response devices and patrols, student patrols, late-night transport/escort service, controlled dormitory access.

Student services: health clinic, personal/psychological counseling, women's center, veterans affairs office.

COSTS & FINANCIAL AID
Costs (2018–19) ***Tuition:*** state resident $6535 full-time; nonresident $14,108 full-time. Full-time tuition and fees vary according to course load and reciprocity agreements. Part-time tuition and fees vary according to course load and reciprocity agreements. ***Required fees:*** $1574 full-time. ***Room and board:*** $6730; room only: $3600. Room and board charges vary according to board plan and housing facility. ***Payment plan:*** installment.

Financial Aid Of all full-time matriculated undergraduates who enrolled in 2018, 1,372 applied for aid, 1,111 were judged to have need, 174 had their need fully met. In 2018, 54 non-need-based awards were made. ***Average percent of need met:*** 82. ***Average financial aid package:*** $11,210. ***Average need-based loan:*** $3741. ***Average need-based gift aid:*** $5484. ***Average non-need-based aid:*** $2444. ***Average indebtedness upon graduation:*** $30,223.

APPLYING
Standardized Tests *Required:* SAT or ACT (for admission).

Options: electronic application, deferred entrance.

Application fee: $44.

Required: high school transcript. ***Required for some:*** interview. ***Recommended:*** essay or personal statement.

Notification: continuous until 9/16 (freshmen), continuous (transfers).

CONTACT
University of Wisconsin–Superior, Belknap and Catlin, PO Box 2000, Superior, WI 54880-4500.

University of Wisconsin–Waukesha

Waukesha, Wisconsin

http://www.waukesha.uwc.edu/

- **State-supported** primarily 2-year, founded 1966, part of University of Wisconsin System
- **Small-town** 86-acre campus with easy access to Milwaukee
- **Coed**

FACULTY
Student/faculty ratio: 17:1.

ACADEMICS
Calendar: semesters. *Degrees:* associate and bachelor's.
Library: University of Wisconsin-Waukesha Library plus 1 other.

STUDENT LIFE
Housing options: college housing not available.

Activities and organizations: drama/theater group, student-run newspaper, choral group.

Athletics Member NJCAA.

Campus security: late-night transport/escort service, part-time patrols by trained security personnel.

Student services: personal/psychological counseling.

APPLYING
Standardized Tests *Required:* ACT (for admission).

Options: electronic application, early admission, deferred entrance.

Application fee: $50.

Required: high school transcript.

CONTACT
University of Wisconsin–Waukesha, 1500 North University Drive, Waukesha, WI 53188.

University of Wisconsin–Whitewater

Whitewater, Wisconsin

http://www.uww.edu/

- **State-supported** comprehensive, founded 1868, part of University of Wisconsin System
- **Small-town** 400-acre campus with easy access to Milwaukee
- **Coed**
- **Moderately difficult** entrance level

FACULTY
Student/faculty ratio: 20:1.

ACADEMICS
Calendar: semesters. *Degrees:* associate, bachelor's, master's, and doctoral.
Library: Andersen Library. Students can reserve study rooms.

STUDENT LIFE
Housing options: on-campus residence required through sophomore year; coed, special housing for students with disabilities. Campus housing is university owned. Freshman campus housing is guaranteed.

Activities and organizations: drama/theater group, student-run newspaper, radio and television station, choral group, marching band, Adult Student Connection, Pan Hellenic Council, Sigma Alpha Lambda (Academic Honors), Cru (Faith-Related Organization), National Society of Leadership and Success, national fraternities, national sororities.

Athletics Member NCAA. All Division III.

Campus security: 24-hour emergency response devices and patrols, student patrols, late-night transport/escort service, controlled dormitory access.

Student services: health clinic, personal/psychological counseling, women's center, legal services, veterans affairs office.

COSTS & FINANCIAL AID
Costs (2018–19) ***Tuition:*** state resident $6519 full-time, $272 per credit hour part-time; nonresident $15,092 full-time, $629 per credit hour part-time. Full-time tuition and fees vary according to course load, degree level, and reciprocity agreements. ***Required fees:*** $1173 full-time. ***Room and board:*** $6786; room only: $4206. Room and board charges vary according to board plan and housing facility. ***Payment plans:*** installment, deferred payment.

Financial Aid Of all full-time matriculated undergraduates who enrolled in 2017, 7,783 applied for aid, 5,649 were judged to have need, 2,264 had their need fully met. 470 Federal Work-Study jobs (averaging $1070). 2,365 state and other part-time jobs (averaging $1903). In 2017, 581 non-need-based awards were made. ***Average percent of need met:*** 63. ***Average financial aid package:*** $8590. ***Average need-based loan:*** $4329. ***Average need-based gift aid:*** $6028. ***Average non-need-based aid:*** $2147. ***Average indebtedness upon graduation:*** $28,050.

APPLYING
Standardized Tests *Required:* SAT or ACT (for admission).

Options: electronic application, deferred entrance.

Application fee: $50.

Required: high school transcript. ***Recommended:*** essay or personal statement.

CONTACT
Mr. Jeremy Reed, Director of Admissions, University of Wisconsin–Whitewater, 800 West Main Street, Whitewater, WI 53190-1790. *Phone:* 262-472-1440. *E-mail:* uwwadmit@uww.edu.

Viterbo University

La Crosse, Wisconsin

http://www.viterbo.edu/

CONTACT
Mr. Eric Schmidt, Freshman Admission Counselor/Associate Director for Admission, Viterbo University, 900 Viterbo Drive, La Crosse, WI 54601. *Phone:* 608-796-3017. *Toll-free phone:* 800-VITERBO. *E-mail:* admission@viterbo.edu.

Wisconsin Lutheran College

Milwaukee, Wisconsin

http://www.wlc.edu/

- **Independent** comprehensive, founded 1973, affiliated with Wisconsin Evangelical Lutheran Synod
- **Suburban** 54-acre campus
- **Endowment** $32.9 million
- **Coed**
- **Moderately difficult** entrance level

FACULTY
Student/faculty ratio: 10:1.

ACADEMICS
Calendar: semesters. *Degrees:* bachelor's and master's.
Library: Marvin M. Schwan Library. *Books:* 64,947 (physical), 3,778 (digital/electronic); *Serial titles:* 19 (physical), 37,529 (digital/electronic); *Databases:* 28.

STUDENT LIFE
Housing options: on-campus residence required through junior year; men-only, women-only. Campus housing is university owned. Freshman campus housing is guaranteed.

Activities and organizations: student-run newspaper, choral group.

Athletics Member NCAA. All Division III except golf (Division II).

Campus security: 24-hour emergency response devices and patrols, late-night transport/escort service, controlled dormitory access, closed-circuit TV monitors.

Student services: health clinic, personal/psychological counseling.

COSTS & FINANCIAL AID
Costs (2018–19) ***Comprehensive fee:*** $39,915 includes full-time tuition ($29,410), mandatory fees ($315), and room and board ($10,190). Part-time tuition: $765 per credit hour. ***Room and board:*** Room and board charges vary according to board plan and housing facility.

Financial Aid Of all full-time matriculated undergraduates who enrolled in 2018, 877 applied for aid, 794 were judged to have need, 158 had their need fully met. 77 Federal Work-Study jobs (averaging $2258). 323 state and other part-time jobs (averaging $2168). In 2018, 148 non-need-based awards were made. ***Average percent of need met:*** 80. ***Average financial aid package:*** $23,597. ***Average need-based loan:*** $3984. ***Average need-based gift aid:*** $19,528. ***Average non-need-based aid:*** $12,920. ***Average indebtedness upon graduation:*** $31,002.

APPLYING
Standardized Tests *Required:* SAT or ACT (for admission).

Options: electronic application, deferred entrance.

Required: high school transcript. ***Required for some:*** interview.

CONTACT
Wisconsin Lutheran College, 8800 West Bluemound Road, Milwaukee, WI 53226-9942.

WYOMING

University of Wyoming

Laramie, Wyoming

http://www.uwyo.edu/

- **State-supported** university, founded 1886
- **Small-town** 835-acre campus
- **Endowment** $517.5 million
- **Coed** 9,998 undergraduate students, 85% full-time, 51% women, 49% men
- **Moderately difficult** entrance level, 96% of applicants were admitted

UNDERGRAD STUDENTS
8,457 full-time, 1,541 part-time. Students come from 51 states and territories; 61 other countries; 34% are from out of state; 1% Black or African American, non-Hispanic/Latino; 7% Hispanic/Latino; 1% Asian, non-Hispanic/Latino; 0.1% Native Hawaiian or other Pacific Islander, non-Hispanic/Latino; 0.6% American Indian or Alaska Native, non-Hispanic/Latino; 4% Two or more races, non-Hispanic/Latino; 11% Race/ethnicity unknown; 4% international; 11% transferred in; 25% live on campus.

Freshmen:
Admission: 5,238 applied, 5,034 admitted, 1,859 enrolled. ***Average high school GPA:*** 3.5. ***Test scores:*** SAT evidence-based reading and writing scores over 500: 85%; SAT math scores over 500: 84%; ACT scores over 18: 96%; SAT evidence-based reading and writing scores over 600: 44%; SAT math scores over 600: 41%; ACT scores over 24: 61%; SAT evidence-based reading and writing scores over 700: 7%; SAT math scores over 700: 7%; ACT scores over 30: 14%.

Retention: 78% of full-time freshmen returned.

FACULTY
Total: 738, 99% full-time, 79% with terminal degrees.

Student/faculty ratio: 15:1.

ACADEMICS
Calendar: semesters. *Degrees:* certificates, bachelor's, master's, doctoral, and postbachelor's certificates.

Special study options: accelerated degree program, advanced placement credit, cooperative education, distance learning, double majors, external degree program, honors programs, independent study, internships, off-campus study, part-time degree program, services for LD students, student-designed majors, study abroad, summer session for credit. ***ROTC:*** Army (b), Air Force (b).

Computers: 1,683 computers/terminals and 10 ports are available on campus for general student use. Students can access the following: campus intranet, computer help desk, free student e-mail accounts, online (class) grades, online (class) registration, online (class) schedules. Campuswide network is available. 100% of college-owned or -operated housing units are wired for high-speed Internet access. Wireless service is available via classrooms, computer centers, computer labs, dorm rooms, learning centers, libraries, student centers.
Library: William Robertson Coe Library plus 4 others. *Books:* 1.8 million (physical), 1.2 million (digital/electronic); *Serial titles:* 14,085 (physical), 96,240 (digital/electronic); *Databases:* 1,043. Study areas open 24 hours, 5–7 days a week; students can reserve study rooms.

STUDENT LIFE
Housing options: on-campus residence required for freshman year; coed, men-only, women-only, special housing for students with disabilities. Campus housing is university owned. Freshman campus housing is guaranteed.

Activities and organizations: drama/theater group, student-run newspaper, radio and television station, choral group, marching band, national fraternities, national sororities.

Athletics Member NCAA. All Division I except football (Division I-A). ***Intercollegiate sports:*** baseball M(c), basketball M(s)/W(s), cross-country running M(s)/W(s), equestrian sports M(c)/W(c), fencing M(c)/W(c), golf M(s)/W(s)(c), ice hockey M(c)/W(c), lacrosse M(c)/W(c), racquetball M(c)/W(c), riflery M(c)/W(c), rugby M(c)/W(c), skiing (cross-country) M(c)/W(c), skiing (downhill) W(c), soccer M(c)/W(s), softball W(c), swimming and diving M(s)/W(s), tennis M(c)/W(s), track and field M(s)/W(s), triathlon M(c)/W(c), volleyball W(s), water polo M(c), wrestling M(s). ***Intramural sports:*** badminton M/W, basketball M/W, bowling M/W, football M/W, golf M/W, racquetball M(c)/W(c), soccer M/W, softball M/W, swimming and diving M/W, table tennis M/W, tennis M/W, track and field M/W, triathlon M/W, ultimate Frisbee M/W, volleyball M/W, water polo M/W, weight lifting M/W, wrestling M/W.

Campus security: 24-hour emergency response devices and patrols, student patrols, late-night transport/escort service, controlled dormitory access.

Student services: health clinic, personal/psychological counseling, women's center, legal services, veterans affairs office.

COSTS & FINANCIAL AID
Costs (2019–20) ***One-time required fee:*** $40. ***Tuition:*** area resident $4020 full-time, $134 part-time; state resident $4020 full-time, $134 per credit hour part-time; nonresident $16,110 full-time, $537 per credit hour part-time. ***Required fees:*** $1380 full-time. ***Room and board:*** $10,320; room only: $4493.

Financial Aid Of all full-time matriculated undergraduates who enrolled in 2017, 5,441 applied for aid, 3,888 were judged to have need, 668 had their need fully met. 271 Federal Work-Study jobs (averaging $2103). In 2017, 1639 non-need-based awards were made. ***Average percent of need met:*** 60. ***Average financial aid package:*** $10,356. ***Average need-based loan:*** $4233. ***Average need-based gift aid:*** $4889. ***Average non-need-based aid:*** $4055. ***Average indebtedness upon graduation:*** $24,474.

APPLYING
Standardized Tests *Required:* SAT or ACT (for admission).

Options: electronic application, deferred entrance.

Application fee: $40.

Required: high school transcript, minimum 3.0 GPA, pre-college curriculum, minimum ACT composite score of 21 or SAT of 980.

Application deadlines: 8/10 (freshmen), 8/10 (out-of-state freshmen), 8/10 (transfers).

Notification: continuous (freshmen), continuous (out-of-state freshmen), continuous (transfers).

CONTACT
Katie Watson, Assistant Director of Admissions, University of Wyoming, 1000 E. University Avenue, Dept 3435, Laramie, WY 82071. *Phone:* 307-766-4261. *Toll-free phone:* 800-342-5996. *Fax:* 307-766-4042. *E-mail:* admissions@uwyo.edu.

AMERICAN SAMOA

American Samoa Community College

Pago Pago, American Samoa

http://www.amsamoa.edu/

- **Territory-supported** primarily 2-year, founded 1969
- **Rural** 20-acre campus
- **Endowment** $3.1 million
- **Coed**
- **Noncompetitive** entrance level

FACULTY
Student/faculty ratio: 20:1.

ACADEMICS
Calendar: semesters. *Degrees:* certificates, associate, and bachelor's.
Library: ASCC Learning Resource Center/Library plus 1 other. *Books:* 33,000 (physical); *Serial titles:* 330 (physical). Weekly public service hours: 43.

STUDENT LIFE
Housing options: college housing not available.

Activities and organizations: student-run newspaper, Student Government Association, Phi Theta Kappa, ASCC Research Foundation Student Club, Fa'aSamoa (Samoan culture) Club, Journalism Club.

Campus security: 24-hour emergency response devices and patrols.

Student services: health clinic, personal/psychological counseling, legal services, veterans affairs office.

COSTS & FINANCIAL AID
Costs (2018–19) ***Tuition:*** territory resident $3300 full-time, $110 per credit part-time; nonresident $3600 full-time, $120 per credit part-time. Full-time tuition and fees vary according to course level, course load, and degree level. Part-time tuition and fees vary according to course level, course load, and degree level. ***Required fees:*** $650 full-time, $550 per term part-time.

Financial Aid Of all full-time matriculated undergraduates who enrolled in 2017, 532 applied for aid, 532 were judged to have need. 110 Federal Work-Study jobs (averaging $60,937). ***Average percent of need met:*** 54. ***Average financial aid package:*** $2726. ***Average need-based gift aid:*** $2726.

APPLYING
Standardized Tests *Recommended:* SAT and SAT Subject Tests or ACT (for admission).

Options: electronic application, early admission, deferred entrance.

CONTACT
Elizabeth Leuma, Admissions Officer, American Samoa Community College, PO Box 2609, Pago Pago 96799, American Samoa. *Phone:* 684-699-9155 Ext. 411. *Fax:* 684-699-1083.

GUAM

Pacific Islands University

Mangilao, Guam

http://www.piu.edu/

CONTACT
Ethel Laco, Admissions Office, Pacific Islands University, 172 Kinney's Road, Mangilao, GU 96913. *Phone:* 671-734-1812. *Fax:* 671-734-1813. *E-mail:* guamcampus@pibc.edu.

University of Guam

Mangilao, Guam

http://www.uog.edu/

- **Territory-supported** comprehensive, founded 1952
- **Suburban** 100-acre campus
- **Coed** 3,421 undergraduate students, 79% full-time, 57% women, 43% men
- **Noncompetitive** entrance level, 79% of applicants were admitted

UNDERGRAD STUDENTS
2,708 full-time, 713 part-time. Students come from 26 states and territories; 19 other countries; 0.7% are from out of state; 0.7% Black or African American, non-Hispanic/Latino; 0.7% Hispanic/Latino; 45% Asian, non-Hispanic/Latino; 47% Native Hawaiian or other Pacific Islander, non-Hispanic/Latino; 0.1% American Indian or Alaska Native, non-Hispanic/Latino; 3% Race/ethnicity unknown; 0.9% international; 4% transferred in.

Freshmen:
Admission: 645 applied, 511 admitted, 541 enrolled. ***Average high school GPA:*** 3.2.

Retention: 73% of full-time freshmen returned.

FACULTY
Total: 294, 46% full-time.

ACADEMICS
Calendar: semesters. *Degrees:* certificates, bachelor's, master's, and postbachelor's certificates.

Special study options: academic remediation for entering students, accelerated degree program, advanced placement credit, cooperative education, distance learning, double majors, English as a second language, honors programs, independent study, internships, off-campus study, part-time degree program, services for LD students, study abroad, summer session for credit. ***ROTC:*** Army (b).

Computers: 262 computers/terminals and 262 ports are available on campus for general student use. Students can access the following: campus intranet, computer help desk, free student e-mail accounts, online (class) grades, online (class) registration, online (class) schedules. Campuswide network is available. 100% of college-owned or -operated housing units are wired for high-speed Internet access.
Library: University of Guam Robert F. Kennedy Memorial Library. *Books:* 213,916 (physical), 153,000 (digital/electronic); *Serial titles:* 1,527 (physical); *Databases:* 60. Weekly public service hours: 60; study areas open 24 hours, 5–7 days a week; students can reserve study rooms.

STUDENT LIFE
Housing options: coed. Campus housing is university owned.

Activities and organizations: drama/theater group, student-run newspaper, choral group, American Marketing Association, Student Nurses Association of Guam, Social Work Student Alliance, Association of Early Childhood Education International, Public Administration and Legal Studies.

Athletics ***Intramural sports:*** basketball M/W, crew M(c)/W(c), football M, soccer M/W, softball M/W, volleyball M/W.

Campus security: 24-hour emergency response devices and patrols, late-night transport/escort service, Sexual Harassment Training Requirement for all Students, Faculty, Staff, and Administrators.

Student services: health clinic, personal/psychological counseling, women's center.

COSTS
Costs (2019–20) ***Tuition:*** territory resident $5040 full-time, $210 per credit hour part-time; nonresident $12,096 full-time, $504 per credit hour part-time. ***Required fees:*** $764 full-time, $382 per term part-time. ***Room and board:*** $3850.

APPLYING
Options: electronic application, deferred entrance.

Application fee: $52.

Required: high school transcript.

Application deadlines: 6/1 (freshmen), 6/1 (out-of-state freshmen), 6/1 (transfers).

Notification: continuous (freshmen), continuous (transfers).

CONTACT
Ms. Betty Jean Bailey, Records Supervisor, University of Guam, Admissions and Records Office, UOG Station, Mangilao, GU 96923. *Phone:* 671-735-2213. *Fax:* 671-735-2203. *E-mail:* admitme@triton.uog.edu.

NORTHERN MARIANA ISLANDS

Northern Marianas College

Saipan, Northern Mariana Islands

http://www.marianas.edu/

CONTACT
Ms. Leilani M. Basa-Alam, Admission Specialist, Northern Marianas College, PO Box 501250, Saipan, MP 96950-1250. *Phone:* 670-234-3690 Ext. 1539. *Fax:* 670-235-4967. *E-mail:* leilanib@nmcnet.edu.

PUERTO RICO

Albizu University

San Juan, Puerto Rico

http://www.albizu.edu/

- **Independent** university, founded 1966
- **Urban** campus
- **Endowment** $732,270
- **Coed**
- **Noncompetitive** entrance level

FACULTY
Student/faculty ratio: 10:1.

ACADEMICS
Calendar: semesters. *Degrees:* bachelor's, master's, and doctoral.
Library: Carlos Albizu Miranda plus 2 others.

STUDENT LIFE
Housing options: college housing not available.

Activities and organizations: student-run newspaper, Student Council, Community Services, Gender and Sexual Diversity Organization, OASIS, Speech/Language Pathology Students Organization.

Campus security: 24-hour emergency response devices, late-night transport/escort service, security cameras.

FINANCIAL AID
Financial Aid Of all full-time matriculated undergraduates who enrolled in 2018, 381 applied for aid, 381 were judged to have need. ***Average percent of need met:*** 100. ***Average financial aid package:*** $4925. ***Average need-based loan:*** $3000. ***Average need-based gift aid:*** $4925.

APPLYING
Standardized Tests *Required:* CEEB or SAT (for admission).

Options: early admission, deferred entrance.

Application fee: $75.

Required: minimum 2.0 GPA, 2 letters of recommendation. ***Required for some:*** health certificate, Good Conduct Crete, official university transcript.

CONTACT
Albizu University, 151 Tanca Street, San Juan, PR 00901.

American University of Puerto Rico

Bayamon, Puerto Rico

http://www.aupr.edu/

CONTACT
Ms. Keren Llanos Figueroa, Director of Admissions, American University of Puerto Rico, PO Box 2037, Bayamon, PR 00960-2037. *Phone:* 787-620-2040 Ext. 2020. *Fax:* 787-785-7377. *E-mail:* kllanos@aupr.edu.

American University of Puerto Rico

Manati, Puerto Rico

http://www.aupr.edu/

CONTACT
American University of Puerto Rico, Carretera Estatal #2 Km. 48.7, PO Box 1082, Manati, PR 00674-1082.

Atenas College

Manati, Puerto Rico

http://www.atenascollege.edu/

CONTACT
Atenas College, Paseo de La Atenas #101 Altos, Manati, PR 00674.

Atlantic University College

Guaynabo, Puerto Rico

http://www.atlanticu.edu/

CONTACT
Ms. Zaida Perez, Admission's Officer, Atlantic University College, PO Box 3918, Guaynabo, PR 00970. *Phone:* 787-720-1022 Ext. 13. *E-mail:* admisiones@atlanticcollege.edu.

Bayamón Central University

Bayamón, Puerto Rico

http://www.ucb.edu.pr/

CONTACT
Bayamón Central University, PO Box 1725, Bayamón, PR 00960-1725. *Phone:* 787-786-3030 Ext. 2102.

Caribbean University

Bayamón, Puerto Rico

http://www.caribbean.edu/

- **Independent** comprehensive, founded 1969
- **Urban** 16-acre campus with easy access to San Juan
- **Coed**
- **Minimally difficult** entrance level

FACULTY
Student/faculty ratio: 14:1.

ACADEMICS
Calendar: semesters. *Degrees:* certificates, associate, bachelor's, master's, and doctoral.
Library: Biblioteca Virgilio Davila, Recinto de Bayamon plus 4 others. *Books:* 76,606 (physical), 139,981 (digital/electronic); *Databases:* 2,346.

STUDENT LIFE
Housing options: college housing not available.

Activities and organizations: drama/theater group, choral group, Engineering Student Association, Nursing, Social Work, Speech Therapy, Criminal Justices.

Campus security: 24-hour patrols.

Student services: health clinic, personal/psychological counseling.

APPLYING
Standardized Tests *Required for some:* College Board math/verbal test for engineering.

Options: deferred entrance.

Application fee: $30.

Required: high school transcript. ***Required for some:*** minimum 2.0 GPA, 1 letter of recommendation, interview.

CONTACT
Caribbean University, Box 493, Bayamón, PR 00960-0493. *Phone:* 787-780-0070 Ext. 1129.

Caribbean University–Carolina
Carolina, Puerto Rico
http://www.caribbean.edu/

CONTACT
Caribbean University–Carolina, Calle Ignacio Arzuaga #208, Carolina, PR 00985.

Caribbean University–Ponce
Ponce, Puerto Rico
http://www.caribbean.edu/

CONTACT
Caribbean University–Ponce, Ave. Ednita Nazario #1015, Ponce, PR 00716-7733.

Caribbean University–Vega Baja
Vega Baja, Puerto Rico
http://www.caribbean.edu/

CONTACT
Caribbean University–Vega Baja, Carr 671 K.M. 5, Sector El Criollo, Bo. Algarrobo, Vega Baja, PR 00964.

Centro de Estudios Multidisciplinarios
Bayamon, Puerto Rico
http://www.cemcollege.edu/

CONTACT
Centro de Estudios Multidisciplinarios, Calle Degetau #25, Bayamon, PR 00961.

Centro de Estudios Multidisciplinarios
Humacao, Puerto Rico
http://www.cemcollege.edu/

CONTACT
Centro de Estudios Multidisciplinarios, Calle Dr. Vidal #8 y #53, Humacao, PR 00791. *Phone:* 787-850-8333.

Centro de Estudios Multidisciplinarios
Mayaguez, Puerto Rico
http://www.cemcollege.edu/

CONTACT
Centro de Estudios Multidisciplinarios, Calle Cristy #56, Mayaguez, PR 00680.

Centro de Estudios Multidisciplinarios
Rio Piedras, Puerto Rico
http://www.cemcollege.edu/

CONTACT
Admissions Department, Centro de Estudios Multidisciplinarios, Calle 13 #1206, Ext. San Agustin, Rio Piedras, PR 00926. *Phone:* 787-765-4210 Ext. 115. *Toll-free phone:* 877-779-CDEM.

Colegio Universitario de San Juan
San Juan, Puerto Rico
http://www.cunisanjuan.edu/

- **City-supported** 4-year, founded 1971
- **Urban** 5-acre campus
- **Coed**
- **Noncompetitive** entrance level

FACULTY
Student/faculty ratio: 22:1.

ACADEMICS
Calendar: semesters. *Degrees:* certificates, diplomas, associate, and bachelor's.
Library: Access to Information Center. *Books:* 17,569 (physical), 228,547 (digital/electronic); *Serial titles:* 82,010 (digital/electronic); *Databases:* 69. Weekly public service hours: 81; students can reserve study rooms.

STUDENT LIFE
Housing options: college housing not available.

Campus security: 24-hour emergency response devices and patrols.

Student services: personal/psychological counseling.

COSTS
Costs (2018–19) ***Tuition:*** commonwealth resident $2040 full-time; nonresident $2040 full-time. ***Required fees:*** $330 full-time.

APPLYING
Options: electronic application.

Application fee: $15.

Required: high school transcript, minimum 2.0 GPA, medical history. ***Required for some:*** interview.

CONTACT
Colegio Universitario de San Juan, Jose R. Oliver Street, Hato Rey, PR 00918. *Phone:* 787-250-7111 Ext. 2227.

Columbia Central University
Caguas, Puerto Rico
http://www.columbiacentral.edu/

- **Proprietary** comprehensive, founded 1966
- **Urban** 6-acre campus with easy access to San Juan
- **Coed** 1,050 undergraduate students, 55% full-time, 58% women, 42% men
- **Noncompetitive** entrance level, 90% of applicants were admitted

UNDERGRAD STUDENTS
581 full-time, 469 part-time. Students come from 1 other state; 14% transferred in.

Freshmen:
Admission: 190 applied, 171 admitted, 172 enrolled. ***Average high school GPA:*** 2.0.

FACULTY
Total: 90, 32% full-time, 51% with terminal degrees.

Student/faculty ratio: 17:1.

ACADEMICS
Calendar: semesters. *Degrees:* certificates, associate, bachelor's, and master's.

Special study options: accelerated degree program, part-time degree program.

A ★ indicates that the school has detailed information with a Premium Profile on Petersons.com.

Computers: 185 computers/terminals are available on campus for general student use. Students can access the following: free student e-mail accounts, online (class) grades, online (class) registration, online (class) schedules, online courses, technical support, Microsoft office 365 products, Microsoft Imagine, Virtual library services, Moodle E-learning platform. Campuswide network is available. Wireless service is available via entire campus.
Library: Efrain Sola Bezares Library plus 1 other. *Books:* 9,494 (physical), 759 (digital/electronic); *Serial titles:* 19 (physical), 13,966 (digital/electronic); *Databases:* 26. Weekly public service hours: 81; students can reserve study rooms.

STUDENT LIFE
Housing options: college housing not available.

Campus security: 24-hour patrols.

Student services: personal/psychological counseling.

COSTS & FINANCIAL AID
Costs (2019–20) ***Comprehensive fee:*** $16,707 includes full-time tuition ($9630), mandatory fees ($180), and room and board ($6897). Part-time tuition: $1665 per semester hour. ***Required fees:*** $230 per semester hour part-time.
Financial Aid Of all full-time matriculated undergraduates who enrolled in 2008, 974 applied for aid, 818 were judged to have need. 61 Federal Work-Study jobs (averaging $982). ***Average percent of need met:*** 11. ***Average financial aid package:*** $4035.

APPLYING
Options: electronic application.

Application fee: $10.

Required: high school transcript, minimum 2.0 GPA. ***Required for some:*** essay or personal statement, 3 letters of recommendation, interview, Immunization Certificate for candidates who are under 21.

Notification: continuous (freshmen).

CONTACT
Mrs. Brendaliz Zayas, Vice President of Student Affairs and Enrollment, Columbia Central University, PO Box 8517, Caguas, PR 00726, Puerto Rico. *Phone:* 787-743-4041 Ext. 224. *Fax:* 787-744-7031. *E-mail:* bzayas@columbiacentral.edu.

Columbia Central University

Yauco, Puerto Rico

http://www.columbiacentral.edu/

- **Proprietary** 4-year, founded 1966
- **Urban** campus with easy access to Ponce, Mayaguez
- **Coed** 283 undergraduate students, 55% full-time, 68% women, 32% men
- **Minimally difficult** entrance level, 94% of applicants were admitted

UNDERGRAD STUDENTS
155 full-time, 128 part-time. Students come from 1 other state; 100% Hispanic/Latino.

Freshmen:
Admission: 114 applied, 107 admitted, 56 enrolled. ***Average high school GPA:*** 3.0.

FACULTY
Total: 28, 25% full-time, 21% with terminal degrees.

Student/faculty ratio: 10:1.

ACADEMICS
Calendar: trimesters. *Degrees:* certificates, associate, and bachelor's.

Special study options: adult/continuing education programs, cooperative education, distance learning, internships, part-time degree program, services for LD students.

Computers: 14 computers/terminals and 20 ports are available on campus for general student use. Students can access the following: campus intranet, computer help desk, free student e-mail accounts, online (class) grades, online (class) registration, online (class) schedules. Campuswide network is available. Wireless service is available via entire campus.
Library: Centro de Informacion y Recursos Integrados (CIRI). *Books:* 2,362 (physical), 759 (digital/electronic); *Serial titles:* 547 (physical), 231,831 (digital/electronic); *Databases:* 26. Weekly public service hours: 64; students can reserve study rooms.

STUDENT LIFE
Housing options: college housing not available.

Activities and organizations: Student Association Pharmacy Technicians, Student Association Graphic Design, Student Council.

Campus security: trained security personnel during hours of operation.

Student services: personal/psychological counseling.

COSTS
Costs (2018–19) ***Tuition:*** $9810 full-time, $1665 per semester hour part-time. ***Required fees:*** $60 full-time, $230 per semester hour part-time. ***Payment plan:*** installment. ***Waivers:*** employees or children of employees.

APPLYING
Options: electronic application, deferred entrance.

Application fee: $10.

Required: high school transcript, minimum 2.0 GPA.

Notification: continuous (freshmen).

CONTACT
Mrs. Carmen Ivette Pabon, Admissions Coordinator, Columbia Central University, PO Box 3062, Yauco, PR 00698. *Phone:* 787-856-0945 Ext. 117. *Fax:* 787-267-0994. *E-mail:* cipabon@columbiacentral.edu.

Conservatorio de Musica de Puerto Rico

San Juan, Puerto Rico

http://www.cmpr.edu/

- **Commonwealth-supported** comprehensive
- **Urban** 4-acre campus with easy access to Old San Juan
- **Endowment** $1.0 million
- **Coed**
- **Moderately difficult** entrance level

FACULTY
Student/faculty ratio: 6:1.

ACADEMICS
Calendar: semesters. *Degrees:* bachelor's, master's, and postbachelor's certificates.
Library: Biblioteca Amaury Veray plus 1 other. *Books:* 29,276 (physical), 80,545 (digital/electronic); *Serial titles:* 197 (physical), 80,942 (digital/electronic); *Databases:* 108.

STUDENT LIFE
Housing options: college housing not available.

Activities and organizations: choral group.

Campus security: 24-hour patrols.

COSTS
Costs (2018–19) ***One-time required fee:*** $225. ***Tuition:*** commonwealth resident $2520 full-time; nonresident $2520 full-time. ***Required fees:*** $425 full-time.

APPLYING
Application fee: $75.

Required: high school transcript, minimum 2.0 GPA, instrument audition, ear training test. ***Required for some:*** essay or personal statement, minimum 3.0 GPA. ***Recommended:*** interview.

CONTACT
Mrs. Ana Marta Arraiza, Admission Coordinator, Conservatorio de Musica de Puerto Rico, 951 Ponce de Leon Avenue, San Juan, PR 00907-3373. *Phone:* 787-751-0160 Ext. 275. *Fax:* 787-758-9511. *E-mail:* aarraiza2@cmpr.gobierno.pr.

Dewey University–Carolina

Carolina, Puerto Rico

http://www.dewey.edu/

CONTACT
Dewey University–Carolina, Carr. #3, Km. 11, Parque Industrial de Carolina, Lote 7, Carolina, PR 00986.

Dewey University–Hato Rey

Hato Rey, Puerto Rico

http://www.dewey.edu/

CONTACT

Dewey University–Hato Rey, 427 Avenida Barbosa, Hato Rey, PR 00923.

Dewey University–Manati

Manati, Puerto Rico

http://www.dewey.edu/

CONTACT

Dewey University–Manati, Carr. 604, Km. 49.1 Barrio Tierras Nuevas, Salientes, Manati, PR 00674. *Toll-free phone:* 866-773-3939.

EDIC College

Caguas, Puerto Rico

http://www.ediccollege.edu/

CONTACT

EDIC College, Ave. Rafael Cordero Calle Génova Urb. Caguas Norte, Caguas, PR 00726.

EDP University of Puerto Rico

Hato Rey, Puerto Rico

http://www.edpuniversity.edu/

- **Independent** comprehensive, founded 1968
- **Urban** 1-acre campus with easy access to San Juan
- **Coed**
- **Noncompetitive** entrance level

FACULTY

Student/faculty ratio: 12:1.

ACADEMICS

Calendar: semesters. *Degrees:* associate, bachelor's, master's, and postbachelor's certificates.

Library: Centro de Recursos para la Informacion plus 2 others. *Books:* 16,163 (physical), 50 (digital/electronic); *Serial titles:* 48 (physical), 13,800 (digital/electronic); *Databases:* 30. Weekly public service hours: 82; students can reserve study rooms.

STUDENT LIFE

Housing options: college housing not available.

Activities and organizations: choral group, Student Council, Graduate Student Association, Dance Group.

Campus security: 24-hour emergency response devices, student patrols, late-night transport/escort service, security and emergency telephones during working hours.

Student services: personal/psychological counseling.

COSTS & FINANCIAL AID

Costs (2018–19) ***Tuition:*** $5280 full-time, $176 per credit hour part-time. Full-time tuition and fees vary according to course load and program. Part-time tuition and fees vary according to course load and program. ***Required fees:*** $920 full-time, $460 per term part-time.

Financial Aid Of all full-time matriculated undergraduates who enrolled in 2011, 1,028 applied for aid, 1,028 were judged to have need. 35 Federal Work-Study jobs (averaging $1972). ***Average percent of need met:*** 90. ***Average financial aid package:*** $5587. ***Average need-based loan:*** $3137. ***Average need-based gift aid:*** $5416. ***Average indebtedness upon graduation:*** $4256.

APPLYING

Standardized Tests *Required:* CEEB, institutional admission exam (for admission).

Options: electronic application, early admission, early decision, deferred entrance.

Application fee: $15.

Required: high school transcript, minimum 1.6 GPA. ***Required for some:*** essay or personal statement, minimum 2.5 GPA, 3 letters of recommendation, interview. ***Recommended:*** minimum 2.0 GPA.

CONTACT

Mr. Oscar Morales, Dean of Student Affairs, EDP University of Puerto Rico, Avenue Ponce de Leon, #560, Hato Rey, PR 00918, Puerto Rico. *Phone:* 787-765-3560 Ext. 2272. *Fax:* 787-777-0024. *E-mail:* oscarmorales@edpuniversity.edu.

EDP University of Puerto Rico–San Sebastian

San Sebastian, Puerto Rico

http://www.edpuniversity.edu/

- **Independent** comprehensive, founded 1976
- **Rural** campus
- **Coed**
- **Minimally difficult** entrance level

FACULTY

Student/faculty ratio: 20:1.

ACADEMICS

Calendar: semesters. *Degrees:* associate, bachelor's, and master's.

Library: Juan S. Robles Library. *Books:* 11,683 (physical), 222,135 (digital/electronic); *Serial titles:* 11 (physical), 25,540 (digital/electronic); *Databases:* 12. Weekly public service hours: 85; students can reserve study rooms.

STUDENT LIFE

Housing options: college housing not available.

Activities and organizations: student-run radio station, Nursing, Physical Therapy, Information Systems (SITA), Pharmacy, Digital Fashion Design.

Campus security: private security.

Student services: personal/psychological counseling.

COSTS & FINANCIAL AID

Costs (2018–19) ***Tuition:*** $5280 full-time, $176 per credit hour part-time. Full-time tuition and fees vary according to course load and program. Part-time tuition and fees vary according to course load and program. ***Required fees:*** $920 full-time, $460 per term part-time.

Financial Aid Of all full-time matriculated undergraduates who enrolled in 2012, 1,098 applied for aid, 1,097 were judged to have need. 32 Federal Work-Study jobs (averaging $1714). ***Average percent of need met:*** 92. ***Average financial aid package:*** $5000. ***Average need-based loan:*** $2601. ***Average need-based gift aid:*** $4545.

APPLYING

Standardized Tests *Required:* College Board exam or institutional entrance test (for admission).

Application fee: $15.

Required: high school transcript, minimum 1.6 GPA. ***Required for some:*** essay or personal statement, minimum 2.5 GPA, interview.

CONTACT

Dra. Pilar Cordero de Vidal, Student Affairs Dean, EDP University of Puerto Rico–San Sebastian, Avenue Betances #49, San Sebastian, PR 00685. *Phone:* 787-896-2252 Ext. 3313. *Fax:* 787-896-5960. *E-mail:* pcordero@edpuniversity.edu.

Escuela de Artes Plasticas y Diseño de Puerto Rico

San Juan, Puerto Rico

http://www.eap.edu/

- **Commonwealth-supported** 4-year, founded 1966
- **Urban** campus
- **Endowment** $2.5 million
- **Coed** 441 undergraduate students, 73% full-time, 71% women, 29% men
- **Moderately difficult** entrance level, 94% of applicants were admitted

UNDERGRAD STUDENTS

322 full-time, 119 part-time. Students come from 2 states and territories; 0.2% Black or African American, non-Hispanic/Latino; 100% Hispanic/Latino; 27% transferred in.

Freshmen:
Admission: 82 applied, 77 admitted, 69 enrolled. ***Average high school GPA:*** 3.5.
Retention: 86% of full-time freshmen returned.

FACULTY
Total: 62, 42% full-time, 65% with terminal degrees.
Student/faculty ratio: 12:1.

ACADEMICS
Calendar: semesters 3 semesters each calendar year; participant in Year Round Pell. *Degree:* bachelor's.
Special study options: academic remediation for entering students, adult/continuing education programs, advanced placement credit, independent study, internships, part-time degree program, services for LD students, study abroad, summer session for credit.
Computers: 98 computers/terminals and 98 ports are available on campus for general student use. Students can access the following: computer help desk, free student e-mail accounts, library online catalog, wireless access. Wireless service is available via entire campus.
Library: Francisco Oller Library. *Books:* 23,366 (physical); *Serial titles:* 449 (digital/electronic); *Databases:* 3. Weekly public service hours: 59.

STUDENT LIFE
Housing options: college housing not available.
Activities and organizations: Student government, CINEAP, Arte-Sanacion.
Campus security: 24-hour emergency response devices and patrols, security cameras.
Student services: personal/psychological counseling.

COSTS & FINANCIAL AID
Costs (2018–19) ***Tuition:*** commonwealth resident $2860 full-time; nonresident $5020 full-time. ***Required fees:*** $602 full-time. ***Payment plan:*** installment. ***Waivers:*** employees or children of employees.
Financial Aid Of all full-time matriculated undergraduates who enrolled in 2007, 276 applied for aid, 276 were judged to have need. 10 Federal Work-Study jobs (averaging $1850). ***Average percent of need met:*** 82. ***Financial aid deadline:*** 5/25.

APPLYING
Standardized Tests *Recommended:* SAT (for admission).
Application fee: $25.
Required: high school transcript, minimum 2.0 GPA, portfolio or seminar.
Notification: 5/18 (freshmen), 5/18 (transfers).

CONTACT
Alicea Denizard, Officer of Admissions, Escuela de Artes Plasticas y Diseño de Puerto Rico, PO Box 902112, San Juan, PR 00902-1112. *Phone:* 787-725-8120 Ext. 373. *E-mail:* admisiones@eap.edu.

Humacao Community College

Humacao, Puerto Rico

http://www.hccpr.edu/

- **Independent** primarily 2-year
- **Urban** campus
- **Endowment** $1.3 million
- **Coed**
- **Noncompetitive** entrance level

FACULTY
Student/faculty ratio: 30:1.

ACADEMICS
Calendar: trimesters. *Degrees:* certificates, diplomas, associate, and bachelor's.
Library: Santiago N. Manuez Educational Resources Center plus 1 other. *Books:* 5,320 (physical); *Serial titles:* 43 (physical), 2 (digital/electronic); *Databases:* 5. Weekly public service hours: 56.

STUDENT LIFE
Housing options: college housing not available.
Activities and organizations: Enactus Humacao Community College, Students Council.
Campus security: 24-hour emergency response devices and patrols.
Student services: personal/psychological counseling.

COSTS & FINANCIAL AID
Costs (2018–19) ***One-time required fee:*** $140. ***Tuition:*** $4932 full-time, $2466 per year part-time. Full-time tuition and fees vary according to course load and degree level. Part-time tuition and fees vary according to course load and degree level. ***Required fees:*** $450 full-time, $450 per year part-time.
Financial Aid Of all full-time matriculated undergraduates who enrolled in 2017, 64 Federal Work-Study jobs (averaging $546).

APPLYING
Application fee: $15.
Required: high school transcript, interview. ***Required for some:*** certificate of Immunization for students under 21 years.

CONTACT
Mrs. Arlene Osorio, Recruitment and Promotion Official, Humacao Community College, PO Box 9139, Humacao, PR 00792, Puerto Rico. *Phone:* 787-852-1430 Ext. 225. *Fax:* 787-850-1577. *E-mail:* arlene.osorio@hccpr.edu.

Inter American University of Puerto Rico, Aguadilla Campus

Aguadilla, Puerto Rico

http://www.aguadilla.inter.edu/

- **Independent** comprehensive, founded 1957, part of Inter American University of Puerto Rico
- **Small-town** 50-acre campus
- **Endowment** $239.0 million
- **Coed** 3,667 undergraduate students, 86% full-time, 58% women, 42% men
- **Moderately difficult** entrance level

UNDERGRAD STUDENTS
3,141 full-time, 526 part-time. Students come from 23 states and territories; 1 other country; 2% are from out of state; 0.1% Black or African American, non-Hispanic/Latino; 100% Hispanic/Latino; 0.1% American Indian or Alaska Native, non-Hispanic/Latino; 5% transferred in.

Freshmen:
Admission: 1,748 applied, 797 enrolled. ***Average high school GPA:*** 3.1.

FACULTY
Total: 228, 35% full-time, 100% with terminal degrees.
Student/faculty ratio: 30:1.

ACADEMICS
Calendar: semesters. *Degrees:* certificates, diplomas, bachelor's, and master's.
Special study options: academic remediation for entering students, accelerated degree program, adult/continuing education programs, advanced placement credit, cooperative education, distance learning, double majors, English as a second language, external degree program, honors programs, independent study, internships, part-time degree program, services for LD students, study abroad, summer session for credit. ***ROTC:*** Army (b), Air Force (b).
Computers: 861 computers/terminals are available on campus for general student use. Students can access the following: campus intranet, free student e-mail accounts, online (class) grades, online (class) registration, online (class) schedules. Campuswide network is available. Wireless service is available via entire campus.
Library: Manuel Mendez Ballester Information Access Center. *Books:* 62,162 (physical), 249,610 (digital/electronic); *Serial titles:* 100 (physical); *Databases:* 75. Weekly public service hours: 80; students can reserve study rooms.

STUDENT LIFE
Housing options: college housing not available.

Activities and organizations: drama/theater group, student-run newspaper, choral group, Criminal Justice Association, Microbiot Science Association, Social Workers Association, Nursing Association, Psychology Association.

Athletics ***Intercollegiate sports:*** baseball M(s), basketball M(s)/W(s), cross-country running M(s)/W(s), soccer M(s)/W(s), softball M(s)/W(s), swimming and diving M(s)/W(s), table tennis M(s)/W(s), tennis M(s)/W(s), track and field M(s)/W(s), volleyball M(s)/W(s), weight lifting M(s)/W(s), wrestling M(s)/W(s). ***Intramural sports:*** basketball M/W, cross-country running M/W, soccer M/W, softball M/W, table tennis M/W, tennis M/W, track and field M/W, volleyball M/W, weight lifting M/W.

Campus security: 24-hour emergency response devices and patrols.

Student services: personal/psychological counseling, veterans affairs office.

COSTS

Costs (2018–19) ***Tuition:*** $4488 full-time, $187 per credit part-time. Full-time tuition and fees vary according to course load. Part-time tuition and fees vary according to course load. ***Required fees:*** $754 full-time, $313 per semester part-time. ***Payment plan:*** deferred payment. ***Waivers:*** employees or children of employees.

APPLYING

Standardized Tests *Required:* SAT or ACT (for admission), PAA (for admission).

Options: electronic application.

Required: high school transcript, minimum 2.0 GPA.

Application deadlines: rolling (freshmen), rolling (transfers).

CONTACT

Mrs. Daisy Irizarry, Administrative Assistant, Inter American University of Puerto Rico, Aguadilla Campus, PO Box 20,000, Road 459 Intersection 463, Aguadilla, PR 00605. *Phone:* 787-891-0925 Ext. 2181. *Fax:* 787-882-3020.

Inter American University of Puerto Rico, Arecibo Campus

Arecibo, Puerto Rico

http://www.arecibo.inter.edu/

CONTACT

Ms. Provi Montalvo, Admission Director, Inter American University of Puerto Rico, Arecibo Campus, PO Box 4050, Arecibo, PR 00614-4050. *Phone:* 787-878-5475. *Fax:* 787-880-1624. *E-mail:* pmontalvo@arecibo.inter.edu.

Inter American University of Puerto Rico, Barranquitas Campus

Barranquitas, Puerto Rico

http://www.br.inter.edu/

- **Independent** comprehensive, founded 1957, part of Inter American University of Puerto Rico
- **Small-town** campus with easy access to 35 miles from San Juan
- **Endowment** $239.0 million
- **Coed** 1,521 undergraduate students, 87% full-time, 62% women, 38% men
- 40% of applicants were admitted

UNDERGRAD STUDENTS

1,324 full-time, 197 part-time. Students come from 4 states and territories; 0.2% are from out of state; 100% Hispanic/Latino; 0.1% American Indian or Alaska Native, non-Hispanic/Latino; 2% transferred in.

Freshmen:

Admission: 946 applied, 380 admitted, 367 enrolled. ***Average high school GPA:*** 3.1.

Retention: 69% of full-time freshmen returned.

FACULTY

Total: 145, 21% full-time, 23% with terminal degrees.

Student/faculty ratio: 21:1.

ACADEMICS

Calendar: semesters. *Degrees:* certificates, associate, bachelor's, and master's.

Special study options: adult/continuing education programs, cooperative education, distance learning, English as a second language, external degree program, honors programs, off-campus study, part-time degree program, services for LD students, summer session for credit. ***ROTC:*** Army (c).

Computers: 378 computers/terminals and 378 ports are available on campus for general student use. Students can access the following: campus intranet, computer help desk, free student e-mail accounts, online (class) grades, online (class) registration, online (class) schedules. Campuswide network is available. Wireless service is available via entire campus.

Library: Centro de Accoso a la InformaciÃ³n (CAI), Recinto de Barranquitas. *Books:* 40,014 (physical), 286,834 (digital/electronic); *Serial titles:* 60 (physical), 58,313 (digital/electronic); *Databases:* 83. Weekly public service hours: 72; students can reserve study rooms.

STUDENT LIFE

Activities and organizations: Nursing Student Organization, Honor Program Student Organization, Culinary Arts Student Organization, Poly-Inter Alumni Association Student Chapter.

Athletics ***Intercollegiate sports:*** baseball M(s), basketball M(s), cross-country running M/W, softball M/W, tennis M/W, volleyball M(s)/W(s), weight lifting M/W. ***Intramural sports:*** basketball M, cross-country running M/W, softball M/W, table tennis M/W, tennis M/W, track and field M/W, volleyball M/W.

Campus security: 24-hour emergency response devices and patrols.

Student services: health clinic, personal/psychological counseling.

COSTS

Costs (2018–19) ***One-time required fee:*** $100. ***Tuition:*** $5610 full-time, $3020 per year part-time. Full-time tuition and fees vary according to course load, degree level, and program. Part-time tuition and fees vary according to course load, degree level, and program. ***Required fees:*** $652 full-time, $524 per year part-time, $262 per term part-time. ***Payment plan:*** deferred payment. ***Waivers:*** minority students and employees or children of employees.

APPLYING

Standardized Tests *Required:* CEEB (for admission). *Required for some:* SAT or ACT (for admission). *Recommended:* SAT (for admission), SAT Subject Tests (for admission).

CONTACT

Mrs. Aramilda Cartagena, Dean of Students, Inter American University of Puerto Rico, Barranquitas Campus, PO Box 517, Barranquitas, PR 00794, Puerto Rico. *Phone:* 787-857-3600 Ext. 2009. *Fax:* 787-857-2125. *E-mail:* aramildacartagena@br.inter.edu.

Inter American University of Puerto Rico, Bayamón Campus

Bayamón, Puerto Rico

http://bayamon.inter.edu/

- **Independent** comprehensive, founded 1912, part of Inter American University of Puerto Rico
- **Suburban** 51-acre campus with easy access to San Juan
- **Endowment** $239.0 million
- **Coed** 4,188 undergraduate students, 88% full-time, 44% women, 56% men
- 31% of applicants were admitted

UNDERGRAD STUDENTS

3,703 full-time, 485 part-time. Students come from 15 states and territories; 2 other countries; 0.6% are from out of state; 0.3% Black or African American, non-Hispanic/Latino; 98% Hispanic/Latino; 0.1% Native Hawaiian or other Pacific Islander, non-Hispanic/Latino; 0.6% American Indian or Alaska Native, non-Hispanic/Latino; 3% transferred in.

Freshmen:

Admission: 2,920 applied, 897 admitted, 874 enrolled. ***Average high school GPA:*** 3.2.

Retention: 71% of full-time freshmen returned.

FACULTY
Total: 251, 36% full-time, 33% with terminal degrees.

Student/faculty ratio: 25:1.

ACADEMICS
Calendar: semesters. *Degrees:* certificates, associate, bachelor's, and master's.

Special study options: accelerated degree program, adult/continuing education programs, advanced placement credit, cooperative education, distance learning, external degree program, honors programs, independent study, internships, part-time degree program, services for LD students, summer session for credit. ***ROTC:*** Army (c).

Computers: 730 computers/terminals are available on campus for general student use. Students can access the following: computer help desk, free student e-mail accounts, online (class) grades, online (class) registration. Campuswide network is available. Wireless service is available via entire campus.
Library: Centro de Acceso a la Informacion plus 1 other. *Books:* 28,998 (physical), 248,232 (digital/electronic); *Serial titles:* 123 (physical); *Databases:* 88. Weekly public service hours: 75; students can reserve study rooms.

STUDENT LIFE
Housing options: men-only, women-only. Campus housing is university owned.

Activities and organizations: drama/theater group, student-run radio station, choral group, Consejo de Estudiantes, Asociacion Estudiantes de Ingenieria, Asociacion Estudiantes de Aviacion, Estudiantes Unidos por la Ciencia, Asociacion de Estudiantes de Administracion de Empresas.

Athletics *Intercollegiate sports:* baseball M(s), basketball M(s)/W(s), cross-country running M(s)/W(s), softball M(s)/W(s), swimming and diving M(s)/W(s), table tennis M(s)/W(s), track and field M(s)/W(s), volleyball M(s)/W(s), weight lifting M(s). ***Intramural sports:*** basketball M/W, cross-country running M/W, softball M/W, swimming and diving M/W, table tennis M/W, tennis M/W, track and field M/W, volleyball M/W, weight lifting M.

Campus security: 24-hour patrols.

Student services: health clinic, personal/psychological counseling, veterans affairs office.

COSTS & FINANCIAL AID
Costs (2019–20) *Comprehensive fee:* $14,063 includes full-time tuition ($4488), mandatory fees ($1452), and room and board ($8123). Part-time tuition: $187 per credit. ***Required fees:*** $345 part-time. ***College room only:*** $5271.

Financial Aid Of all full-time matriculated undergraduates who enrolled in 2018, 2,578 applied for aid, 2,539 were judged to have need. ***Average percent of need met:*** 26. ***Average financial aid package:*** $3917. ***Average need-based loan:*** $2152. ***Average need-based gift aid:*** $3544.

APPLYING
Standardized Tests *Required:* CEEB (for admission). *Required for some:* SAT (for admission).

Options: electronic application.

Required: high school transcript, minimum 2.0 GPA. ***Required for some:*** minimum 2.5 GPA for engineering program.

Notification: continuous (freshmen), continuous (transfers).

CONTACT
Ms. Aurelis Baez, Director of Students Services, Inter American University of Puerto Rico, Bayamón Campus, 500 Dr. John Will Harris Road, Bayamón, PR 00957. *Phone:* 787-279-1912 Ext. 2017. *Fax:* 787-279-2205. *E-mail:* abaez@bayamon.inter.edu.

Inter American University of Puerto Rico, Fajardo Campus

Fajardo, Puerto Rico

http://www.fajardo.inter.edu/

- **Independent** comprehensive, founded 1965, part of Inter American University of Puerto Rico
- **Small-town** 11-acre campus with easy access to San Juan
- **Endowment** $4.3 million
- **Coed** 1,769 undergraduate students, 84% full-time, 60% women, 40% men
- **Moderately difficult** entrance level, 88% of applicants were admitted

UNDERGRAD STUDENTS
1,481 full-time, 288 part-time. Students come from 3 states and territories; 100% Hispanic/Latino.

Freshmen:
Admission: 708 applied, 626 admitted, 446 enrolled. ***Average high school GPA:*** 2.0.

Retention: 74% of full-time freshmen returned.

FACULTY
Total: 116, 35% full-time, 31% with terminal degrees.

Student/faculty ratio: 11:1.

ACADEMICS
Calendar: semesters. *Degrees:* certificates, associate, bachelor's, and master's.

Special study options: academic remediation for entering students, adult/continuing education programs, advanced placement credit, cooperative education, distance learning, English as a second language, external degree program, honors programs, independent study, internships, off-campus study, part-time degree program, services for LD students, summer session for credit. ***ROTC:*** Army (c).

Computers: 280 computers/terminals are available on campus for general student use. Students can access the following: free student e-mail accounts, online (class) grades, online (class) registration, online (class) schedules. Campuswide network is available. Wireless service is available via entire campus.
Library: Antonio S. Belaval Library plus 1 other. *Books:* 47,697 (physical), 262,990 (digital/electronic); *Databases:* 36. Students can reserve study rooms.

STUDENT LIFE
Housing options: college housing not available.

Activities and organizations: choral group, Future Teachers Association, Criminal Justice Student Association, Honor Program Association, Computer Science Association, Social Work Association.

Athletics *Intercollegiate sports:* baseball M, basketball M(s)/W, cheerleading W, softball W, track and field M(s)/W(s), volleyball M/W.

Campus security: 24-hour patrols.

Student services: personal/psychological counseling.

COSTS
Costs (2019–20) *Tuition:* $187 per credit hour part-time.

APPLYING
Standardized Tests *Required:* College Board exam (for admission).

Options: electronic application, early admission, deferred entrance.

Required: high school transcript. ***Required for some:*** interview.

CONTACT
Ms. Ghisita M. Garcia, Administrative Assistant II, Inter American University of Puerto Rico, Fajardo Campus, Call Box 70003, Fajardo, PR 00738-7003. *Phone:* 787-863-2390 Ext. 2210. *Fax:* 787-860-3470. *E-mail:* ghisita.garcia@fajardo.inter.edu.

Inter American University of Puerto Rico, Guayama Campus

Guayama, Puerto Rico

http://www.guayama.inter.edu/

CONTACT

Mrs. Laura E. Ferrer, Director of Admissions, Inter American University of Puerto Rico, Guayama Campus, Call Box 10004, Guayama, PR 00785. *Phone:* 787-864-2222 Ext. 2220. *Fax:* 787-864-8232. *E-mail:* laura.ferrer@guayama.inter.edu.

Inter American University of Puerto Rico, Metropolitan Campus

San Juan, Puerto Rico

http://metro.inter.edu/

- **Independent** comprehensive, founded 1960, part of Inter American University of Puerto Rico
- **Urban** campus with easy access to San Juan
- **Endowment** $224.1 million
- **Coed**
- **Moderately difficult** entrance level

ACADEMICS

Calendar: trimesters. *Degrees:* certificates, associate, bachelor's, master's, doctoral, post-master's, and postbachelor's certificates.
Library: Centro de Acceso a la Informacion plus 1 other. *Books:* 121,223 (physical); *Serial titles:* 311 (physical); *Databases:* 24. Students can reserve study rooms.

STUDENT LIFE

Housing options: college housing not available.

Activities and organizations: drama/theater group, student-run newspaper, choral group, Intercultural Student Association, Club Rotaract, Roots and Shoots Inter Metro, Chemical Students Association, Social Work Students Association.

Campus security: 24-hour emergency response devices and patrols, Video Security System.

Student services: personal/psychological counseling, women's center, veterans affairs office.

FINANCIAL AID

Financial Aid Of all full-time matriculated undergraduates who enrolled in 1999, 4,328 applied for aid, 3,935 were judged to have need, 29 had their need fully met. ***Average percent of need met:*** 11. ***Average financial aid package:*** $2144. ***Average need-based loan:*** $1149. ***Average need-based gift aid:*** $1617. ***Financial aid deadline:*** 4/30.

APPLYING

Standardized Tests *Required:* CEEB (for admission). *Required for some:* SAT or ACT (for admission).

Options: electronic application.

Required: high school transcript, minimum 2.0 GPA.

CONTACT

Inter American University of Puerto Rico, Metropolitan Campus, PO Box 191293, San Juan, PR 00919-1293. *Phone:* 787-250-1912 Ext. 2204.

Inter American University of Puerto Rico, Ponce Campus

Mercedita, Puerto Rico

http://www.ponce.inter.edu/

CONTACT

Mr. Franco Diaz, Admissions Officer, Inter American University of Puerto Rico, Ponce Campus, 104 Turpo Industrial Park, Road #1, Mercedita, PR 00715-1602. *Phone:* 787-284-1912 Ext. 2025. *Fax:* 787-841-0103. *E-mail:* fidiaz@ponce.inter.edu.

Inter American University of Puerto Rico, San Germán Campus

San Germán, Puerto Rico

http://www.sg.inter.edu/

- **Independent** university, founded 1912, part of Inter American University of Puerto Rico
- **Small-town** 283-acre campus with easy access to Ponce, Aguadilla, Mayaguez
- **Endowment** $239.0 million
- **Coed** 3,787 undergraduate students, 89% full-time, 52% women, 48% men
- **Moderately difficult** entrance level, 45% of applicants were admitted

UNDERGRAD STUDENTS

3,379 full-time, 408 part-time. Students come from 7 states and territories; 1 other country; 0.3% are from out of state; 0.2% Black or African American, non-Hispanic/Latino; 99% Hispanic/Latino; 0.2% American Indian or Alaska Native, non-Hispanic/Latino; 3% transferred in; 7% live on campus.

Freshmen:
Admission: 2,054 applied, 925 admitted, 820 enrolled. ***Average high school GPA:*** 3.2.

Retention: 78% of full-time freshmen returned.

FACULTY

Total: 291, 33% full-time, 42% with terminal degrees.

Student/faculty ratio: 13:1.

ACADEMICS

Calendar: semesters. *Degrees:* certificates, associate, bachelor's, master's, doctoral, and postbachelor's certificates.

Special study options: academic remediation for entering students, accelerated degree program, adult/continuing education programs, advanced placement credit, cooperative education, distance learning, double majors, English as a second language, external degree program, honors programs, independent study, internships, off-campus study, part-time degree program, services for LD students, summer session for credit. ***ROTC:*** Army (c), Navy (c), Air Force (c).

Computers: 950 computers/terminals are available on campus for general student use. Students can access the following: campus intranet, computer help desk, free student e-mail accounts, online (class) grades, online (class) registration, online (class) schedules. Campuswide network is available. Wireless service is available via entire campus.
Library: Juan Cancio Ortiz Library. *Books:* 125,059 (physical), 3,850 (digital/electronic); *Serial titles:* 240 (physical), 594,924 (digital/electronic); *Databases:* 96. Weekly public service hours: 69.

STUDENT LIFE

Housing options: men-only, women-only. Campus housing is university owned.

Activities and organizations: choral group, Tomorrows Leaders Association, Business Professionals of America, Sociedad de Honor en Biologia Beta Beta Beta (TriBeta), Asociacion Estudiantes de Enfermería, Asociacion de Estudiantes del Programa de Honor, national fraternities.

Athletics ***Intercollegiate sports:*** baseball M(s), basketball M(s)/W(s), cross-country running M(s)/W(s), sand volleyball M/W, soccer M/W, softball W, swimming and diving M/W, table tennis M(s)/W(s), tennis M(s)/W(s), track and field M(s)/W(s), volleyball M(s)/W(s), weight lifting M(s)/W(s), wrestling M. ***Intramural sports:*** baseball M, basketball M/W, cheerleading M/W, cross-country running M/W, softball M/W, table tennis M/W, tennis M/W, track and field M/W, volleyball M/W, weight lifting M/W.

Campus security: 24-hour patrols.

Student services: health clinic, personal/psychological counseling.

COSTS & FINANCIAL AID

Costs (2018–19) ***Comprehensive fee:*** $10,242 includes full-time tuition ($5610), mandatory fees ($732), and room and board ($3900). Full-time tuition and fees vary according to degree level. Part-time tuition: $187 per credit hour. Part-time tuition and fees vary according to degree level. ***Required fees:*** $187 per credit hour part-time, $732 per year part-time. ***College room only:*** $2400. Room and board charges vary according to board plan and housing facility. ***Payment plan:*** installment. ***Waivers:*** employees or children of employees.

Financial Aid Of all full-time matriculated undergraduates who enrolled in 2009, 2,797 applied for aid, 2,755 were judged to have need, 4 had their need fully met. ***Average percent of need met:*** 12. ***Average financial aid package:*** $2009. ***Average need-based loan:*** $3080. ***Average need-based gift aid:*** $642.

APPLYING

Standardized Tests *Required:* CEEB (for admission). *Required for some:* SAT or ACT (for admission).

Options: electronic application, early admission.

Required: high school transcript, medical history, vaccination. ***Required for some:*** 1 letter of recommendation, interview. ***Recommended:*** essay or personal statement, minimum 2.0 GPA.

Notification: continuous (freshmen), continuous (transfers).

CONTACT

Prof. Mildred Camacho, Director of Admissions, Inter American University of Puerto Rico, San Germán Campus, PO Box 5100, San German, PR 00683-5008. *Phone:* 787-264-1912 Ext. 7283. *Toll-free phone:* 800-981-8075. *Fax:* 787-892-7020. *E-mail:* milcama@intersg.edu.

National University College

Arecibo, Puerto Rico

http://www.nuc.edu/

CONTACT

National University College, Calle Manuel Pérez Avilés, Avenida VÃ-ctor Rojas, Arecibo, PR 00612.

National University College

Bayamón, Puerto Rico

http://www.nuc.edu/

CONTACT

Admissions, National University College, PO Box 2036, National College Plaza Building, Bayamón, PR 00960. *Toll-free phone:* 800-780-5134.

National University College

Caguas, Puerto Rico

http://www.nuc.edu/

CONTACT

National University College, 190 Avenida Gautier Benitez Esquina Avenida Federico Degatau, Caguas, PR 00725. *Toll-free phone:* 800-780-5134.

National University College

Ponce, Puerto Rico

http://www.nuc.edu/

CONTACT

National University College, PO Box 801243, Ponce, PR 00716.

National University College

Rio Grande, Puerto Rico

http://www.nuc.edu/

CONTACT

National University College, Carretera #3 Km. 22.1, Bo. CiÃ©naga Baja, Rio Grande, PR 00745. *Toll-free phone:* 800-981-0812.

Polytechnic University of Puerto Rico

Hato Rey, Puerto Rico

http://www.pupr.edu/

- **Independent** comprehensive, founded 1966
- **Urban** 10-acre campus with easy access to San Juan
- **Endowment** $14.3 million
- **Coed**
- **Minimally difficult** entrance level

FACULTY

Student/faculty ratio: 14:1.

ACADEMICS

Calendar: trimesters. *Degrees:* associate, bachelor's, master's, and doctoral.

Library: Biblioteca de la Unidersidad Politecnica de Puerto Rico. *Books:* 66,518 (physical), 61,939 (digital/electronic); *Serial titles:* 1,794 (physical), 15,595 (digital/electronic); *Databases:* 46. Weekly public service hours: 82; study areas open 24 hours, 5–7 days a week; students can reserve study rooms.

STUDENT LIFE

Housing options: coed. Campus housing is university owned.

Activities and organizations: choral group, ASCE (American Society of Civil Engineering), PRWEA (Puerto Rico Water and Environment Association), ACI (American Concrete Institute), SAE PUPR AERO DESIGN TEAM, SHPE (Society of Hispanic Professional Engineers).

Campus security: 24-hour emergency response devices and patrols, late-night transport/escort service, controlled dormitory access, over 350 security cameras on campus.

Student services: health clinic, personal/psychological counseling, veterans affairs office.

COSTS

Costs (2018–19) ***Comprehensive fee:*** $20,538 includes full-time tuition ($7740), mandatory fees ($870), and room and board ($11,928). Full-time tuition and fees vary according to course level, degree level, and program. Part-time tuition: $215 per credit hour. Part-time tuition and fees vary according to course level, degree level, and program. ***Required fees:*** $290 per term part-time. ***College room only:*** $4950.

APPLYING

Standardized Tests *Recommended:* CEEB or PEAU.

Options: electronic application.

Application fee: $30.

Required: high school transcript, minimum 2.0 GPA.

CONTACT

Ms. Teresa Cardona, Director of Admissions, Polytechnic University of Puerto Rico, PO Box 192017, San Juan, PR 00919-2017. *Phone:* 787-622-8000 Ext. 240. *Fax:* 787-764-8712. *E-mail:* tcardona@pupr.edu.

Pontifical Catholic University of Puerto Rico

Ponce, Puerto Rico

http://www.pucpr.edu/

CONTACT

Sra. Ana O. Bonilla, Director of Admissions, Pontifical Catholic University of Puerto Rico, 2250 Avenida Las Americas Avenue, Suite 584, Ponce, PR 00717-9777. *Phone:* 787-841-2000 Ext. 1004. *Toll-free phone:* 800-961-7696. *Fax:* 787-840-4295. *E-mail:* admissions@email.pucpr.edu.

Pontifical Catholic University of Puerto Rico–Arecibo Campus

Arecibo, Puerto Rico

http://www.pucpr.edu/arecibo/

CONTACT

Pontifical Catholic University of Puerto Rico–Arecibo Campus, Bo. Santana Carr. 662 Km. 2.3, Arecibo, PR 00614-4045.

Pontifical Catholic University of Puerto Rico–Mayaguez Campus

Mayaguez, Puerto Rico

http://www.pucpr.edu/mayaguez/

CONTACT

Pontifical Catholic University of Puerto Rico–Mayaguez Campus, 482 Sur Calle Ramon Emerito Betances, Mayaguez, PR 00680.

Theological University of the Caribbean

Saint Just, Puerto Rico

http://www.utcpr.edu/

- **Independent Pentecostal** comprehensive, founded 1956
- **Suburban** 4-acre campus with easy access to San Juan
- **Endowment** $1.0 million
- **Coed** 265 undergraduate students, 71% full-time, 46% women, 54% men
- 100% of applicants were admitted

UNDERGRAD STUDENTS

187 full-time, 78 part-time. Students come from 1 other state; 100% Hispanic/Latino.

Freshmen:

Admission: 48 applied, 48 admitted, 48 enrolled.

Retention: 36% of full-time freshmen returned.

FACULTY

Total: 53, 38% full-time, 30% with terminal degrees.

Student/faculty ratio: 23:1.

ACADEMICS

Calendar: semesters. *Degrees:* certificates, diplomas, associate, bachelor's, and master's.

Special study options: distance learning, honors programs, independent study, internships, off-campus study, part-time degree program, services for LD students, summer session for credit.

Computers: 3 computers/terminals and 3 ports are available on campus for general student use. Students can access the following: campus intranet, computer help desk, free student e-mail accounts, online (class) grades, online (class) registration, online (class) schedules. Campuswide network is available. 90% of college-owned or -operated housing units are wired for high-speed Internet access. Wireless service is available via entire campus.

Library: Juan L. Lugo Library plus 1 other. *Books:* 17,258 (physical); *Serial titles:* 45 (physical). Weekly public service hours: 61.

STUDENT LIFE

Housing options: coed. Campus housing is university owned.

Activities and organizations: Student Council, Missionary Evangelistic Association, Ministerial Association, FESI, Free Night.

Campus security: patrols by security personnel at night since 6:00 pm to midnight; Security Cameras.

Student services: personal/psychological counseling.

COSTS & FINANCIAL AID

Costs (2019–20) ***Comprehensive fee:*** $7924 includes full-time tuition ($4524), mandatory fees ($1000), and room and board ($2400). Part-time tuition: $21 per credit hour. ***Required fees:*** $154 per credit hour part-time, $3696 per term part-time. ***College room only:*** $1200.

Financial Aid Of all full-time matriculated undergraduates who enrolled in 2017, 251 applied for aid, 251 were judged to have need. ***Average financial aid package:*** $4054. ***Average need-based loan:*** $1899. ***Average need-based gift aid:*** $4054. ***Average indebtedness upon graduation:*** $8906. ***Financial aid deadline:*** 6/30.

APPLYING

Options: early admission.

Application fee: $45.

Required: high school transcript, medical certificate, certificate of immunization, 1 2x2 photo, Bible content exam.

Notification: continuous (freshmen).

CONTACT

Mrs. Avianny Paulino, Recruitment Officer, Theological University of the Caribbean, PO Box 901, Saint Just, PR 00978-901. *Phone:* 787-761-0640 Ext. 1246. *Fax:* 787-748-9220. *E-mail:* promocion@utcpr.edu.

Universidad Adventista de las Antillas

Mayagüez, Puerto Rico

http://www.uaa.edu/esp/

CONTACT

Mrs. Yolanda Ferrer, Director of Admissions, Universidad Adventista de las Antillas, Oficina de Admisiones, PO Box 118, Mayaguez, PR 00681-0118. *Phone:* 787-834-9595 Ext. 2208. *Fax:* 787-834-9597. *E-mail:* admissions@uaa.edu.

Universidad Central del Caribe

Bayamón, Puerto Rico

http://www.uccaribe.edu/

CONTACT

Admissions Department, Universidad Central del Caribe, PO Box 60-327, Bayamón, PR 00960-6032. *Phone:* 787-740-1611.

Universidad del Este

Carolina, Puerto Rico

http://www.suagm.edu/une/

CONTACT

Universidad del Este, PO Box 2010, Carolina, PR 00984. *Phone:* 787-257-7373 Ext. 3401.

Universidad del Turabo

Gurabo, Puerto Rico

http://www.suagm.edu/ut/

CONTACT

Universidad del Turabo, PO Box 3030, Gurabo, PR 00778-3030. *Phone:* 787-743-7979 Ext. 4351.

Universidad Metropolitana

San Juan, Puerto Rico

http://www.suagm.edu/umet/

CONTACT

Mrs. Yadira Rivera Lugo, Director of Admissions, Universidad Metropolitana, Box 21150, San Juan, PR 00928-1150. *Phone:* 787-766-1717 Ext. 6683. *Toll-free phone:* 800-747-8362. *E-mail:* yrivera@suagm.edu.

Universidad Pentecostal Mizpa

San Juan, Puerto Rico

http://www.mizpa.edu/

CONTACT

Omar Alicea, Recruitment, Universidad Pentecostal Mizpa, Bo Caimito Road 199, Apartado 20966, San Juan, PR 00928-0966. *Phone:* 787-720-4476. *Fax:* 787-720-2012.

University of Puerto Rico–Aguadilla

Aguadilla, Puerto Rico

http://www.uprag.edu/

CONTACT

Ms. Melba Serrano Lugo, Admissions Officer, University of Puerto Rico–Aguadilla, PO Box 6150, Aguadilla, PR 00604. *Phone:* 787-890-2681 Ext. 280.

COLLEGES AT-A-GLANCE

University of Puerto Rico–Arecibo

Arecibo, Puerto Rico

http://www.upra.edu/

CONTACT
University of Puerto Rico–Arecibo, Carretera 653 Km. 0.8, Sector Las Dunas, PO Box 4010, Arecibo, PR 00614. *Phone:* 787-878-2830 Ext. 4101.

University of Puerto Rico–Bayamón

Bayamón, Puerto Rico

http://www.uprb.edu/

- **Commonwealth-supported** 4-year, founded 1971, part of University of Puerto Rico System
- **Urban** 78-acre campus with easy access to San Juan
- **Coed** 4,189 undergraduate students, 87% full-time, 51% women, 49% men
- **Very difficult** entrance level, 70% of applicants were admitted

UNDERGRAD STUDENTS
3,643 full-time, 546 part-time. Students come from 3 other countries; 1% are from out of state; 100% Hispanic/Latino; 19% transferred in.

Freshmen:
Admission: 1,564 applied, 1,093 admitted, 978 enrolled. ***Average high school GPA:*** 3.6.

Retention: 81% of full-time freshmen returned.

FACULTY
Total: 227, 82% full-time, 53% with terminal degrees.

Student/faculty ratio: 20:1.

ACADEMICS
Calendar: semesters. *Degrees:* associate and bachelor's.

Special study options: academic remediation for entering students, adult/continuing education programs, advanced placement credit, cooperative education, honors programs, independent study, internships, part-time degree program, services for LD students, summer session for credit.

Computers: 496 computers/terminals and 496 ports are available on campus for general student use. Students can access the following: campus intranet, free student e-mail accounts, online (class) grades, online (class) registration, online (class) schedules. Campuswide network is available. Wireless service is available via entire campus.
Library: Centro Recursos para el Aprendizaje. *Books:* 54,105 (physical), 4,871 (digital/electronic); *Serial titles:* 386 (physical), 2,947 (digital/electronic); *Databases:* 103. Weekly public service hours: 78; students can reserve study rooms.

STUDENT LIFE
Housing options: college housing not available.

Activities and organizations: drama/theater group, choral group, The National Society of Collegiate Scholars at UPRB (NSCS), American Medical Student Association (AMSA), Med Life Capitulo Vaquero, Asociacion de Estudiantes de Computadoras (AECC), Asociacion de Estudiantes de Contabilidad (ASEC).

Athletics Member NCAA. All Division II. ***Intercollegiate sports:*** basketball M(s)/W(s), cross-country running M(s)/W(s), tennis M(s)/W(s), track and field M(s)/W(s), volleyball M(s)/W(s).

Campus security: 24-hour patrols.

Student services: health clinic, personal/psychological counseling.

COSTS & FINANCIAL AID
Costs (2018–19) ***Tuition:*** commonwealth resident $3910 full-time, $115 per credit part-time; nonresident $5865 full-time, $173 per credit part-time. Full-time tuition and fees vary according to class time, course load, and program. Part-time tuition and fees vary according to class time, course load, and program. No tuition increase for student's term of enrollment. ***Required fees:*** $174 full-time. ***Payment plan:*** deferred payment. ***Waivers:*** employees or children of employees.

Financial Aid Of all full-time matriculated undergraduates who enrolled in 2016, 315 Federal Work-Study jobs (averaging $1111).

APPLYING
Standardized Tests *Required:* College Board exam (for admission).

Options: electronic application.

Application fee: $30.

Required: high school transcript.

Application deadlines: 1/6 (freshmen), 2/15 (transfers).

Notification: 5/1 (freshmen), continuous until 7/1 (transfers).

CONTACT
Ms. Carmen I. Montes Burgos, Director, Office of Admissions, University of Puerto Rico–Bayamón, OPEI Office, Street 174 #170 Minillas Industrial Park, Bayamon, PR 00959-1919. *Phone:* 787-993-8952 Ext. 4016. *Fax:* 787-993-8929. *E-mail:* carmen.montes1@upr.edu.

University of Puerto Rico–Carolina

Carolina, Puerto Rico

http://www.uprc.edu/

CONTACT
Ms. Celia Mendez, Admissions Officer, University of Puerto Rico–Carolina, PO Box 4800, Carolina, PR 00984-4800. *Phone:* 787-757-1485.

University of Puerto Rico–Cayey

Cayey, Puerto Rico

http://www.cayey.upr.edu/

CONTACT
University of Puerto Rico–Cayey, 205 Avenue Antonio R. Barcelo, Cayey, PR 00736. *Phone:* 787-738-2161 Ext. 2233.

University of Puerto Rico–Humacao

Humacao, Puerto Rico

http://www.uprh.edu/

- **Commonwealth-supported** 4-year, founded 1962, part of University of Puerto Rico System
- **Suburban** 62-acre campus with easy access to San Juan
- **Coed**
- **Moderately difficult** entrance level

FACULTY
Student/faculty ratio: 17:1.

ACADEMICS
Calendar: semesters. *Degrees:* associate and bachelor's.
Library: Aguedo Mojica Marrero. *Books:* 101,475 (physical), 200 (digital/electronic); *Serial titles:* 15 (physical), 43,942 (digital/electronic); *Databases:* 7. Weekly public service hours: 92; study areas open 24 hours, 5–7 days a week; students can reserve study rooms.

STUDENT LIFE
Housing options: college housing not available.

Activities and organizations: drama/theater group, student-run newspaper, radio and television station, choral group, marching band, Accounting Students Association, Management Students Association, Microbiology Students Association, Human Resources Students Association, Biology Students Association.

Campus security: 24-hour emergency response devices and patrols, late-night transport/escort service, 24-hour gate security.

Student services: personal/psychological counseling, women's center.

FINANCIAL AID
Financial Aid Of all full-time matriculated undergraduates who enrolled in 2001, 3,515 applied for aid, 2,883 were judged to have need, 7 had their need fully met. 278 Federal Work-Study jobs (averaging $1318). ***Average percent of need met:*** 50. ***Average financial aid package:*** $3929. ***Average need-based loan:*** $3295. ***Average need-based gift aid:*** $3664. ***Average indebtedness upon graduation:*** $2749. ***Financial aid deadline:*** 6/30.

APPLYING
Standardized Tests *Required:* Pruebas de Evaluacion y Admision Universitaria (PEAU) (for admission).

Options: electronic application, deferred entrance.

Required: high school transcript. ***Required for some:*** interview.

CONTACT
Mrs. Debbie GarcÃ-a, Admissions Officer, University of Puerto Rico–Humacao, Call Box 860, Humacao, PR 00792. *Phone:* 787-850-9301. *Fax:* 787-850-9428. *E-mail:* debbie.garcia@upr.edu.

University of Puerto Rico–Mayagüez

Mayagüez, Puerto Rico

http://www.uprm.edu/

CONTACT
Ms. Sheila Marty-Rodriquez, Director, Admissions Office, University of Puerto Rico–Mayagüez, PO Box 9000, Mayagüez, PR 00681-9000. *Phone:* 787-265-5465. *Fax:* 787-265-5465. *E-mail:* smarty@uprm.edu.

University of Puerto Rico–Medical Sciences Campus

San Juan, Puerto Rico

http://www.rcm.upr.edu/

CONTACT
University of Puerto Rico–Medical Sciences Campus, PO Box 365067, San Juan, PR 00936-5067. *Phone:* 787-758-2525 Ext. 5214.

University of Puerto Rico–Ponce

Ponce, Puerto Rico

http://www.uprp.edu/

CONTACT
University of Puerto Rico–Ponce, PO Box 7186, Ponce, PR 00732-7186. *Phone:* 787-844-8181 Ext. 2533.

University of Puerto Rico–Río Piedras

San Juan, Puerto Rico

http://www.uprrp.edu/

CONTACT
Mrs. Cruz B. Valentin, Director of Admissions, University of Puerto Rico–Río Piedras, PO Box 23300, San Juan, PR 00931-3300. *Phone:* 787-764-0000 Ext. 85700.

University of Puerto Rico–Utuado

Utuado, Puerto Rico

http://www.uprutuado.edu/

CONTACT
Mrs. Maria Robles Serrano, Admissions Officer, University of Puerto Rico–Utuado, PO Box 2500, Utuado, PR 00641-2500. *Phone:* 787-894-2828 Ext. 2240.

University of the Sacred Heart

San Juan, Puerto Rico

http://www.sagrado.edu/

CONTACT
Mr. Luis Heviquez, Director of Admissions, University of the Sacred Heart, PO Box 12383, San Juan, PR 00914-0383. *Phone:* 787-728-1515 Ext. 3237.

VIRGIN ISLANDS

University of the Virgin Islands

St. Thomas, Virgin Islands

http://www.uvi.edu/

- **Territory-supported** comprehensive, founded 1962
- **Small-town** 518-acre campus
- **Coed**
- **Noncompetitive** entrance level

FACULTY
Student/faculty ratio: 12:1.

ACADEMICS
Calendar: semesters. *Degrees:* associate, bachelor's, master's, doctoral, and post-master's certificates.
Library: Ralph M. Paiewonsky Library. Students can reserve study rooms.

STUDENT LIFE
Housing options: coed, men-only, women-only. Campus housing is university owned.
Activities and organizations: drama/theater group, student-run newspaper, radio station, choral group, Student Government Association, Golden Key Honor Society, Student Nurses Association, National Student Exchange Club, St. Kitts and Nevis, national sororities.
Athletics Member NAIA.
Campus security: 24-hour emergency response devices and patrols.
Student services: health clinic, personal/psychological counseling.

COSTS & FINANCIAL AID
Costs (2018–19) ***Tuition:*** territory resident $4631 full-time, $154 per credit part-time; nonresident $13,892 full-time, $463 per credit part-time. Full-time tuition and fees vary according to reciprocity agreements. Part-time tuition and fees vary according to course load and reciprocity agreements. ***Required fees:*** $604 full-time, $254 per term part-time. ***Room and board:*** $9900; room only: $4120. Room and board charges vary according to board plan and housing facility.
Financial Aid Of all full-time matriculated undergraduates who enrolled in 2007, 1,202 applied for aid, 1,118 were judged to have need, 10 had their need fully met. 39 Federal Work-Study jobs (averaging $2130). 28 state and other part-time jobs (averaging $1900). In 2007, 5 non-need-based awards were made. ***Average financial aid package:*** $4450. ***Average need-based loan:*** $3240. ***Average need-based gift aid:*** $3440. ***Average non-need-based aid:*** $8500. ***Average indebtedness upon graduation:*** $9480.

APPLYING
Options: electronic application, early admission, deferred entrance.
Application fee: $25.
Recommended: high school transcript, minimum 2.0 GPA.

CONTACT
University of the Virgin Islands, 2 John Brewers Bay, St. Thomas, VI 00802. *Toll-free phone:* 877-468-6884.

CANADA

CANADA

Acadia University

Wolfville, Nova Scotia, Canada

http://www.acadiau.ca/

- **Province-supported** comprehensive, founded 1838
- **Small-town** 250-acre campus with easy access to Halifax, Nova Scotia
- **Coed** 3,348 undergraduate students, 95% full-time, 57% women, 43% men
- **Moderately difficult** entrance level, 27% of applicants were admitted

UNDERGRAD STUDENTS
3,195 full-time, 153 part-time. Students come from 12 provinces and territories; 50 other countries; 47% are from out of state; 8% transferred in.

Freshmen:
Admission: 4,573 applied, 1,252 admitted, 830 enrolled.
Retention: 76% of full-time freshmen returned.

FACULTY
Total: 245.
Student/faculty ratio: 15:1.

ACADEMICS
Calendar: Canadian standard year. *Degrees:* certificates, bachelor's, master's, doctoral, and postbachelor's certificates.
Special study options: academic remediation for entering students, advanced placement credit, cooperative education, distance learning, double majors, English as a second language, honors programs, internships, off-campus study, part-time degree program, services for LD students, study abroad, summer session for credit.
Computers: 7,000 ports are available on campus for general student use. Students can access the following: campus intranet, computer help desk, free student e-mail accounts, online (class) grades, online (class) registration, online (class) schedules. Campuswide network is available. 100% of college-owned or -operated housing units are wired for high-speed Internet access. Wireless service is available via classrooms, dorm rooms, learning centers, libraries, student centers.
Library: Vaughan Memorial Library.

STUDENT LIFE
Housing options: coed, women-only. Campus housing is university owned. Freshman campus housing is guaranteed.
Activities and organizations: drama/theater group, student-run newspaper, radio station, choral group, Dance Acadia, Power Cheerleading, Water Watch Canada, LINC, Biology.
Athletics Member CIS. ***Intercollegiate sports:*** basketball M(s)/W(s), cross-country running W, football M(s), ice hockey M(s), rugby W(s), soccer M(s)/W(s), swimming and diving M(s)/W(s), track and field W, volleyball W. ***Intramural sports:*** basketball M/W, cheerleading M/W, equestrian sports M(c)/W(c), fencing M(c)/W(c), field hockey W(c), ice hockey M/W(c), lacrosse M(c)/W(c), rugby M(c), soccer M/W, ultimate Frisbee M/W, volleyball M/W.
Campus security: 24-hour emergency response devices and patrols, student patrols, late-night transport/escort service, controlled dormitory access, video surveillance, emergency response, emergency notification, emergency management planning.
Student services: health clinic, personal/psychological counseling, women's center, legal services.

APPLYING
Options: electronic application, deferred entrance.
Application fee: $40 Canadian dollars.
Required: high school transcript, minimum 2.5 GPA. ***Required for some:*** essay or personal statement, 1 letter of recommendation, interview, Auditions for music programs.
Notification: continuous (freshmen), continuous (out-of-state freshmen), continuous (transfers).

CONTACT
Ms. Leigh-Ann Murphy, Manager of Admissions, Acadia University, 15 University Avenue, Wolfville, NS B4P 2R6, Canada. *Phone:* 902-585-1016. *Toll-free phone:* 877-585-1121. *Fax:* 902-585-1092. *E-mail:* admissions@acadiau.ca.

Alberta Bible College

Calgary, Alberta, Canada

http://www.abccampus.ca/

CONTACT
Craig Reid, Recruitment Officer, Alberta Bible College, 635 Northmount Drive, NW, Calgary, AB T2K 3J6, Canada. *Phone:* 403-282-2994 Ext. 225. *Toll-free phone:* 877-542-9492. *E-mail:* admissions@abccampus.ca.

Alberta College of Art & Design

Calgary, Alberta, Canada

http://www.acad.ca/

- **Province-supported** 4-year, founded 1926
- **Urban** 1-acre campus with easy access to Calgary
- **Endowment** $4.4 million
- **Coed**
- **Moderately difficult** entrance level

FACULTY
Student/faculty ratio: 16:1.

ACADEMICS
Calendar: semesters. *Degree:* bachelor's.
Library: Luke Lindoe Library.

STUDENT LIFE
Housing options: coed, special housing for students with disabilities. Campus housing is provided by a third party.
Activities and organizations: The Rendez-Vous Collective, Conceptual Arts Club, Arts Mob, Anime and Gaming Club, ACAD Glass.
Campus security: 24-hour emergency response devices and patrols, late-night transport/escort service, controlled dormitory access.
Student services: health clinic, personal/psychological counseling.

APPLYING
Options: electronic application, early decision.
Application fee: $85 Canadian dollars.
Required: essay or personal statement, high school transcript, minimum 2.0 GPA, portfolio of artwork.

CONTACT
Alberta College of Art & Design, 1407 14 Avenue NW, Calgary, AB T2N 4R3, Canada. *Toll-free phone:* 800-251-8290.

Ambrose University

Calgary, Alberta, Canada

http://www.ambrose.edu/

- **Independent** comprehensive, founded 1941, affiliated with The Christian and Missionary Alliance
- **Urban** 37-acre campus
- **Endowment** $6.0 million
- **Coed**

FACULTY
Student/faculty ratio: 13:1.

ACADEMICS
Calendar: semesters. *Degrees:* certificates, diplomas, bachelor's, and master's (graduate and professional degrees are offered by Canadian Theological Seminary).

Library: Archibald Foundation Library. *Books:* 127,484 (physical), 150,000 (digital/electronic); *Serial titles:* 152 (physical), 60,338 (digital/electronic); *Databases:* 42. Weekly public service hours: 81; students can reserve study rooms.

STUDENT LIFE
Housing options: on-campus residence required for freshman year; men-only, women-only. Campus housing is university owned. Freshman applicants given priority for college housing.

Activities and organizations: drama/theater group, student-run newspaper, choral group, Coffee Club, Business Society, Hockey Club, Biology Club, Outdoors Club.

Campus security: 24-hour emergency response devices, student patrols, late-night transport/escort service, controlled dormitory access.

Student services: personal/psychological counseling.

COSTS & FINANCIAL AID
Costs (2018–19) ***Comprehensive fee:*** $19,008 Canadian dollars includes full-time tuition ($11,400 Canadian dollars), mandatory fees ($908 Canadian dollars), and room and board ($6700 Canadian dollars). Full-time tuition and fees vary according to course load, degree level, and program. Part-time tuition: $380 Canadian dollars per credit hour. Part-time tuition and fees vary according to course load, degree level, and program. ***Required fees:*** $30 Canadian dollars per credit hour part-time. ***College room only:*** $3600 Canadian dollars. Room and board charges vary according to board plan and housing facility. ***Payment plans:*** installment, deferred payment.

Financial Aid Of all full-time matriculated undergraduates who enrolled in 2016, 236 applied for aid. ***Average financial aid package:*** $1700. ***Financial aid deadline:*** 6/1.

APPLYING
Standardized Tests *Required for some:* SAT or ACT (for admission).

Options: electronic application, early admission, deferred entrance.

Application fee: $70.

Required: high school transcript. ***Required for some:*** essay or personal statement, 3 letters of recommendation, interview, minimum 60% overall average on 5 grade-12 level courses, program-specific requirements.

CONTACT
Kalie Eeles, Enrolment Coordinator, Ambrose University, 150 Ambrose Circle SW, Calgary, AB T3H 0L5, Canada. *Phone:* 403-410-2000 Ext. 2954. *Toll-free phone:* 800-461-1222. *Fax:* 403-571-6556. *E-mail:* enrolment@ambrose.edu.

Athabasca University
Athabasca, Alberta, Canada
http://www.athabascau.ca/

- **Province-supported** comprehensive, founded 1970
- **Small-town** 480-acre campus
- **Endowment** $1.0 million
- **Coed**
- **Noncompetitive** entrance level

ACADEMICS
Calendar: continuous. *Degrees:* certificates, diplomas, bachelor's, master's, doctoral, post-master's, and postbachelor's certificates (offers only external degree programs).
Library: Athabasca University Library.

STUDENT LIFE
Housing options: college housing not available.

Activities and organizations: student-run newspaper.

Campus security: 24-hour emergency response devices.

APPLYING
Options: electronic application.

Application fee: $60 Canadian dollars.

CONTACT
Information Centre, Athabasca University, 1 University Drive, Athabasca, AB T9S 3A3, Canada. *Phone:* 800-788-9041. *Toll-free phone:* 800-788-9041. *Fax:* 780-675-6437.

Bishop's University
Sherbrooke, Quebec, Canada
http://www.ubishops.ca/

CONTACT
Mr. Doug McCooeye, Manager Student Recruitment, Admissions and Student Exchange, Bishop's University, 2600 College Street, Sherbrooke, QC J1M 1Z7, Canada. *Phone:* 819-822-9600 Ext. 2206. *Toll-free phone:* 877-822-8200. *E-mail:* admissions@ubishops.ca.

Booth University College
Winnipeg, Manitoba, Canada
http://www.boothuc.ca/

CONTACT
Chantel Burt, Director of Admission, Booth University College, 447 Webb Place, Winnipeg, MB R3B 2P2, Canada. *Phone:* 204-924-4867. *Toll-free phone:* 877-942-6684. *E-mail:* cburt@boothcollege.ca.

Brandon University
Brandon, Manitoba, Canada
http://www.brandonu.ca/

- **Province-supported** comprehensive, founded 1899
- **Small-town** 30-acre campus
- **Endowment** $24.0 million
- **Coed**
- **Noncompetitive** entrance level

FACULTY
Student/faculty ratio: 11:1.

ACADEMICS
Calendar: Canadian standard year. *Degrees:* certificates, bachelor's, and master's.
Library: John E. Robbins Library.

STUDENT LIFE
Housing options: coed, men-only, women-only. Campus housing is university owned. Freshman campus housing is guaranteed.

Activities and organizations: drama/theater group, student-run newspaper, radio station, choral group, Psychology Club, zoology club, Inter-Varsity Christian Fellowship, International Students Club, Business Administration Club.

Athletics Member CIS.

Campus security: 24-hour emergency response devices, controlled dormitory access, night residence hall security personnel.

Student services: personal/psychological counseling.

COSTS
Costs (2018–19) ***Tuition:*** area resident $3984 Canadian dollars full-time, $133 Canadian dollars per credit hour part-time; nonresident $266 Canadian dollars per credit hour part-time; International tuition $7968 Canadian dollars full-time. Full-time tuition and fees vary according to class time, course level, course load, degree level, location, program, reciprocity agreements, and student level. Part-time tuition and fees vary according to class time, course level, course load, degree level, location, program, reciprocity agreements, and student level. ***Required fees:*** $526 Canadian dollars full-time, $45 Canadian dollars per credit hour part-time, $109 Canadian dollars per term part-time. ***Room and board:*** $9645 Canadian dollars; room only: $5574 Canadian dollars. Room and board charges vary according to board plan, gender, and location.

APPLYING
Options: electronic application, deferred entrance.

Application fee: $68 Canadian dollars.

Required: high school transcript. ***Required for some:*** criminal and child abuse registry checks.

CONTACT
Murray Kerr, Director of Admissions, Brandon University, 270 18th Street, Brandon, MB R7A 6A9, Canada. *Phone:* 204-727-7352. *Toll-free phone:* 800-644-7644. *Fax:* 204-728-3221. *E-mail:* kerr@brandonu.ca.

Briercrest College
Caronport, Saskatchewan, Canada
http://www.briercrest.ca/

CONTACT
Mr. Ralph Troshke, Director of Enrolment, Briercrest College, 510 College Drive, Caronport, SK S0H 0S0, Canada. *Phone:* 306-756-3200. *Toll-free phone:* 800-667-5199. *Fax:* 800-667-5199. *E-mail:* admissions@briercrest.ca.

British Columbia Institute of Technology
Burnaby, British Columbia, Canada
http://www.bcit.ca/

CONTACT
Ms. Anna Dosen, Supervisor of Admissions, British Columbia Institute of Technology, 3700 Willingdon Avenue, Burnaby, BC V5G 3H2, Canada. *Phone:* 604-432-8496. *Toll-free phone:* 866-434-1610. *Fax:* 604-431-6917.

Brock University
St. Catharines, Ontario, Canada
http://www.brocku.ca/

- **Province-supported** university, founded 1964
- **Urban** 540-acre campus with easy access to Toronto, ON and Buffalo, NY
- **Coed**

FACULTY
Student/faculty ratio: 30:1.

ACADEMICS
Calendar: Canadian standard year. *Degrees:* certificates, bachelor's, master's, and doctoral.
Library: James A. Gibson Library plus 1 other. *Books:* 492,672 (physical). Students can reserve study rooms.

STUDENT LIFE
Housing options: coed, special housing for students with disabilities. Campus housing is university owned and leased by the school. Freshman campus housing is guaranteed.

Activities and organizations: drama/theater group, student-run newspaper, radio and television station, choral group, International Students Association, Brock University Student Association, Business Administration Association, Brock Christian Fellowship, Ace Brock.

Athletics Member CIS.

Campus security: 24-hour emergency response devices and patrols, student patrols, late-night transport/escort service, controlled dormitory access.

Student services: health clinic, personal/psychological counseling, women's center.

COSTS
Costs (2018–19) ***Tuition:*** province resident $7149 Canadian dollars full-time; nonresident $7149 Canadian dollars full-time; International tuition $24,386 Canadian dollars full-time. Full-time tuition and fees vary according to course load, degree level, program, and student level. Part-time tuition and fees vary according to course load, program, and student level. ***Room and board:*** $6954 Canadian dollars. Room and board charges vary according to board plan and housing facility.

APPLYING
Standardized Tests *Required:* SAT or ACT (for admission).

Options: electronic application.

Required: high school transcript. ***Required for some:*** essay or personal statement, interview, audition for Dramatic Arts and Music programs, profile questionnaire for Concurrent Education programs. ***Recommended:*** minimum 3.0 GPA.

CONTACT
Mrs. Lynn Thompson-Dovi, Admissions Officer, International Undergraduate, Brock University, 1812 Sir Isaac Brock Way, L2S 3A1, Canada. *Phone:* 905-688-5550 Ext. 3431. *E-mail:* central@brocku.ca.

Cape Breton University
Sydney, Nova Scotia, Canada
http://www.cbu.ca/

CONTACT
Cape Breton University, Box 5300, 1250 Grand Lake Road, Sydney, NS B1P 6L2, Canada. *Phone:* 902-563-1117. *Toll-free phone:* 888-959-9995.

Capilano University
North Vancouver, British Columbia, Canada
http://www.capilanou.ca/

- **Public** 4-year, founded 1967, part of British Columbia's Advanced Education system
- **Suburban** 44-hectare campus with easy access to Vancouver
- **Endowment** $7.6 million
- **Coed** 7,311 undergraduate students, 74% full-time, 61% women, 39% men
- **Noncompetitive** entrance level

UNDERGRAD STUDENTS
5,436 full-time, 1,875 part-time. Students come from 12 provinces and territories; 87 other countries; 5% are from out of state.

Freshmen:
Admission: 2,200 applied, 442 enrolled.

Retention: 64% of full-time freshmen returned.

FACULTY
Total: 633, 27% full-time, 29% with terminal degrees.

Student/faculty ratio: 17:1.

ACADEMICS
Calendar: semesters. *Degrees:* certificates, diplomas, associate, bachelor's, and postbachelor's certificates.

Special study options: academic remediation for entering students, advanced placement credit, cooperative education, distance learning, English as a second language, independent study, internships, off-campus study, part-time degree program, services for LD students, study abroad, summer session for credit.

Computers: 1,083 computers/terminals are available on campus for general student use. Students can access the following: computer help desk, free student e-mail accounts, online (class) grades, online (class) registration, online (class) schedules. 100% of college-owned or -operated housing units are wired for high-speed Internet access. Wireless service is available via entire campus.
Library: Capilano University Library. *Books:* 73,290 (physical), 178,273 (digital/electronic); *Serial titles:* 122 (physical), 34,260 (digital/electronic); *Databases:* 136. Weekly public service hours: 73; students can reserve study rooms.

STUDENT LIFE
Housing options: coed, men-only, women-only, special housing for students with disabilities. Campus housing is leased by the school. Freshman applicants given priority for college housing.

Activities and organizations: student-run newspaper, radio station, choral group.

Campus security: 24-hour emergency response devices and patrols, late-night transport/escort service.

Student services: health clinic, personal/psychological counseling, women's center, legal services.

COSTS
Costs (2019–20) ***Required fees:*** $264 Canadian dollars full-time, $13 Canadian dollars per credit part-time, $29 Canadian dollars per term part-time.

APPLYING
Options: electronic application, early admission.

Required for some: essay or personal statement, minimum 2.0 GPA.

Application deadlines: 3/31 (freshmen), 3/31 (transfers).

CONTACT
Capilano University, 2055 Purcell Way, North Vancouver, BC V7J 3H5, Canada.

Carleton University
Ottawa, Ontario, Canada
http://www.carleton.ca/

CONTACT
Ms. Jean Mullan, Director, Undergraduate Recruitment Office, Carleton University, 1125 Colonel By Drive, Ottawa, ON K1S 5B6, Canada. *Phone:* 613-520-3663. *Toll-free phone:* 888-354-4414. *E-mail:* liaison@admissions.carleton.ca.

Centennial College
Scarborough, Ontario, Canada
http://www.centennialcollege.ca/

- **Province-supported** 4-year, part of Ontario College Application System
- **Urban** campus with easy access to Greater Toronto Area
- **Coed**

ACADEMICS
Calendar: semesters. *Degrees:* certificates, diplomas, bachelor's, and postbachelor's certificates.
Library: Centennial College Libraries. Study areas open 24 hours, 5–7 days a week; students can reserve study rooms.

STUDENT LIFE
Housing options: Campus housing is university owned. Freshman applicants given priority for college housing.

Activities and organizations: choral group.

Athletics Member CIS.

Campus security: 24-hour emergency response devices and patrols, late-night transport/escort service.

Student services: personal/psychological counseling.

APPLYING
Options: electronic application.

Application fee: $95 Canadian dollars.

Required: high school transcript.

CONTACT
Centennial College, PO Box 631, Station 'A', Scarborough, ON M1K 5E9, Canada. *Toll-free phone:* 800-268-4419.

Columbia Bible College
Abbotsford, British Columbia, Canada
http://www.columbiabc.edu/

CONTACT
Nathan Martin, Admissions Coordinator, Columbia Bible College, 2940 Clearbrook Road, Abbotsford, BC V2T 2Z8, Canada. *Phone:* 604-853-3358 Ext. 309. *Toll-free phone:* 800-283-0881. *Fax:* 604-853-3063. *E-mail:* nathan.martin@columbiabc.edu.

Concordia University
Montréal, Quebec, Canada
http://www.concordia.ca/

- **Province-supported** university, founded 1974, part of Quebec University Network
- **Urban** 52-acre campus with easy access to Montreal
- **Coed**
- **Moderately difficult** entrance level

FACULTY
Student/faculty ratio: 25:1.

ACADEMICS
Calendar: semesters. *Degrees:* certificates, diplomas, bachelor's, master's, doctoral, and postbachelor's certificates.
Library: Webster Library plus 1 other. *Books:* 994,394 (physical), 556,907 (digital/electronic); *Serial titles:* 18,752 (physical), 140,024 (digital/electronic); *Databases:* 1,000. Weekly public service hours: 70; study areas open 24 hours, 5–7 days a week; students can reserve study rooms.

STUDENT LIFE
Housing options: coed, special housing for students with disabilities. Campus housing is university owned. Freshman applicants given priority for college housing.

Activities and organizations: drama/theater group, student-run newspaper, radio and television station, choral group, Undergraduate Student Union, departmental clubs, religious clubs, ethnic clubs, social action groups, national fraternities, national sororities.

Athletics Member CIS.

Campus security: 24-hour emergency response devices and patrols, student patrols, late-night transport/escort service, controlled dormitory access.

Student services: health clinic, personal/psychological counseling, women's center.

COSTS & FINANCIAL AID
Costs (2018–19) ***Tuition:*** province resident $2391 Canadian dollars full-time, $80 Canadian dollars per credit part-time; nonresident $7403 Canadian dollars full-time, $247 Canadian dollars per credit part-time; International tuition $18,289 Canadian dollars full-time. Full-time tuition and fees vary according to course load. Part-time tuition and fees vary according to course load. ***Required fees:*** $1424 Canadian dollars full-time, $40 Canadian dollars per credit part-time, $29 Canadian dollars per term part-time. ***Room and board:*** $10,300 Canadian dollars; room only: $6000 Canadian dollars. Room and board charges vary according to housing facility and location.

Financial Aid Of all full-time matriculated undergraduates who enrolled in 2017, 349 state and other part-time jobs (averaging $1286). ***Financial aid deadline:*** 3/31.

APPLYING
Options: electronic application, deferred entrance.

Application fee: $100 Canadian dollars.

Required: high school transcript, minimum 2.5 GPA. ***Required for some:*** essay or personal statement, minimum 3.7 GPA, 2 letters of recommendation, interview, portfolio and/or auditions are for performing and visual arts, interview/essay/portfolio for communications, letter of intent and interview for some education programs.

CONTACT
Dr. Matthew Stiegemeyer, Director, Student Recruitment (Enrolment and Student Services), Concordia University, 1455 de Maisonneuve Boulevard West, Building LB-718, Montreal, QC H3G 1M8, Canada. *Phone:* 514-848-2424 Ext. 4781. *Fax:* 514-848-2837. *E-mail:* matthew.stiegemeyer@concordia.ca.

Concordia University of Edmonton
Edmonton, Alberta, Canada
http://www.concordia.ab.ca/

- **Independent Lutheran** comprehensive, founded 1921
- **Urban** 15-acre campus
- **Coed**
- **Moderately difficult** entrance level

FACULTY
Student/faculty ratio: 18:1.

ACADEMICS
Calendar: semesters. *Degrees:* certificates, diplomas, bachelor's, master's, and postbachelor's certificates.
Library: Arnold Guebert Memorial Library plus 1 other.

STUDENT LIFE
Housing options: men-only, women-only. Campus housing is university owned.

Activities and organizations: drama/theater group, student-run newspaper, choral group, concert choir, Concordia Business Association, Science Club, Education Undergraduate Society, Psychology Students' Association.

Athletics Member CIS.

Campus security: 24-hour patrols, late-night transport/escort service.

Student services: personal/psychological counseling.

FINANCIAL AID
Financial Aid In 2017, 305 non-need-based awards were made. ***Financial aid deadline:*** 10/15.

APPLYING
Options: electronic application, early admission.

Required: high school transcript, minimum 2.0 GPA. ***Required for some:*** essay or personal statement, 2 letters of recommendation, interview.

CONTACT
Student and Enrollment Services, Concordia University of Edmonton, 7128 Ada Boulevard, Edmonton, AB T5B 4E4, Canada. *Phone:* 780-479-9220. *Toll-free phone:* 866-479-5200. *Fax:* 780-378-8460. *E-mail:* admits@concordia.ab.ca.

Crandall University
Moncton, New Brunswick, Canada
http://www.crandallu.ca/

CONTACT
Mrs. Lorrie Weir, Admissions Administrative Assistant, Crandall University, Box 6004, Moncton, NB E1C 9L7, Canada. *Phone:* 506-858-8970 Ext. 434. *Toll-free phone:* 888-968-6228. *Fax:* 506-863-6460. *E-mail:* admissions@crandallu.ca.

Dalhousie University
Halifax, Nova Scotia, Canada
http://www.dal.ca/

CONTACT
Ashley Jordan, Assistant Registrar, Associate Director Admissions, Dalhousie University, Office of the Registrar, Halifax, NS B3H 4H6, Canada. *Phone:* 902-494-1833. *Fax:* 902-494-1630. *E-mail:* admissions@dal.ca.

École Polytechnique de Montréal
Montréal, Quebec, Canada
http://www.polymtl.ca/

CONTACT
École Polytechnique de Montréal, CP 6079, Succursale Centre-Ville, Montréal, QC H3C 3A7, Canada.

Emily Carr University of Art + Design
Vancouver, British Columbia, Canada
http://www.ecuad.ca/

CONTACT
Sara Liao, Admissions, Emily Carr University of Art + Design, 1399 Johnston Street, Vancouver, BC V6H 3R9, Canada. *Phone:* 604-844-3800. *Toll-free phone:* 800-832-7788. *Fax:* 604-844-3801. *E-mail:* admissions@ecuad.ca.

Emmanuel Bible College
Kitchener, Ontario, Canada
http://www.emmanuelbiblecollege.ca/

CONTACT
Emmanuel Bible College, 100 Fergus Avenue, Kitchener, ON N2A 2H2, Canada. *Phone:* 519-894-8900 Ext. 224.

Eston College
Eston, Saskatchewan, Canada
http://www.estoncollege.ca/

CONTACT
Admissions, Eston College, 730 1st Street E., Box 579, Eston, SK S0L 1A0, Canada. *Phone:* 306-962-3621. *Toll-free phone:* 888-440-3424. *Fax:* 306-962-3810. *E-mail:* admissions@estoncollege.ca.

HEC Montreal
Montréal, Quebec, Canada
http://www.hec.ca/

- **Province-supported** comprehensive, founded 1910, part of Universite de Montreal
- **Urban** 9-acre campus with easy access to Montreal, QC
- **Coed**
- **Moderately difficult** entrance level

FACULTY
Student/faculty ratio: 23:1.

ACADEMICS
Calendar: trimesters. *Degrees:* certificates, bachelor's, master's, doctoral, and postbachelor's certificates.
Library: HEC Montreal Library plus 1 other. *Books:* 116,690 (physical), 206,337 (digital/electronic); *Serial titles:* 952 (physical), 111,941 (digital/electronic); *Databases:* 161. Weekly public service hours: 100; students can reserve study rooms.

STUDENT LIFE
Housing options: coed. Campus housing is university owned. Freshman applicants given priority for college housing.

Activities and organizations: student-run newspaper, AEMBA (MBA Students' Association), AEHEC (BBA Students'; Association), AEPC (Certificate Students'; Association), AECS (Graduate Students'; Association).

Campus security: 24-hour emergency response devices and patrols.

Student services: health clinic, personal/psychological counseling.

COSTS & FINANCIAL AID
Costs (2018–19) ***Tuition:*** province resident $2456 Canadian dollars full-time, $82 Canadian dollars per credit part-time; nonresident $7632 Canadian dollars full-time, $254 Canadian dollars per credit part-time; International tuition $25,000 Canadian dollars full-time. Full-time tuition and fees vary according to program. Part-time tuition and fees vary according to program. ***Required fees:*** $1540 Canadian dollars full-time, $48 Canadian dollars per credit part-time, $84 Canadian dollars per credit part-time. ***Room and board:*** $3930 Canadian dollars. Room and board charges vary according to board plan and housing facility.

Financial Aid Of all full-time matriculated undergraduates who enrolled in 2017, 2,500 applied for aid, 2,500 were judged to have need. 7 state and other part-time jobs (averaging $3300). ***Average financial aid package:*** $8200. ***Average need-based loan:*** $3200. ***Average need-based gift aid:*** $6600. ***Average indebtedness upon graduation:*** $3200.

APPLYING
Options: electronic application, deferred entrance.

Application fee: $88 Canadian dollars.

Required: high school transcript. ***Required for some:*** R score, collegial/college performance rating.

CONTACT
Mrs. Virginie Lefebvre, Assistant Registrar, HEC Montreal, 3000 Chemin de la Cote-Sainte-Catherine, Montreal, QC H3T 2A7, Canada. *Phone:* 514-340-6151. *Fax:* 514-340-5640.

Heritage College and Seminary

Cambridge, Ontario, Canada

http://www.heritagecambridge.com/

CONTACT
Mr. Mark Walther, Assistant Dean of Students, Heritage College and Seminary, New York, NY 10023-6588. *Phone:* 519-651-2869 Ext. 251. *Toll-free phone:* 800-465-1961. *Fax:* 519-651-2870. *E-mail:* mwalther@heritagecollege.net.

Horizon College & Seminary

Saskatoon, Saskatchewan, Canada

http://www.horizon.edu/

CONTACT
Mrs. Jenn Lundy, Assistant Registrar, Horizon College & Seminary, 1303 Jackson Avenue, Saskatoon, SK S7H 2M9, Canada. *Phone:* 306-374-6655 Ext. 225. *Toll-free phone:* 877-374-6655. *Fax:* 306-373-6968. *E-mail:* admissions@horizon.edu.

The King's University

Edmonton, Alberta, Canada

http://www.kingsu.ca/

CONTACT
Ms. Hilda Buisman, Director of Admissions, The King's University, 9125-50 Street, Edmonton, AB T6B 2H3, Canada. *Phone:* 780-465-3500 Ext. 8031. *Toll-free phone:* 800-661-8582. *Fax:* 780-465-3534. *E-mail:* admissions@kingsu.ca.

Kingswood University

Sussex, New Brunswick, Canada

http://www.kingswood.edu/

CONTACT
Mrs. Shelley Vail, Associate Director for Admissions and Financial Aid, Kingswood University, PO Box 5125, Sussex, NB E4E 5L2, Canada. *Phone:* 506-432-4422. *Toll-free phone:* 888-432-4422. *Fax:* 506-432-4442. *E-mail:* vails@kingswood.edu.

Lakehead University

Thunder Bay, Ontario, Canada

http://www.lakeheadu.ca/

CONTACT
Mr. Nicholas Chamut, Manager of Undergraduate Admissions, Lakehead University, 955 Oliver Road, Thunder Bay, ON P7B 5E1, Canada. *Phone:* 807-343-8676. *Toll-free phone:* 800-465-3959. *Fax:* 807-766-7209. *E-mail:* admissions@lakeheadu.ca.

Laurentian University

Sudbury, Ontario, Canada

http://www.laurentian.ca/

CONTACT
Laurentian University, 935 Ramsey Lake Road, P3E 2C6, Canada. *Phone:* 800-263-4188. *Toll-free phone:* 800-263-4188. *E-mail:* explore@laurentian.ca.

Master's College and Seminary

Peterborough, Ontario, Canada

http://www.mcs.edu/

- **Independent Pentecostal** 4-year, founded 1939
- **Suburban** campus with easy access to Toronto
- **Endowment** $970,384
- **Coed**
- **Noncompetitive** entrance level

FACULTY
Student/faculty ratio: 16:1.

ACADEMICS
Calendar: semesters. *Degree:* certificates, diplomas, and bachelor's. **Library:** Robert and Shirley Taitinger Learning Commons. *Books:* 35,418 (physical), 5,422 (digital/electronic); *Serial titles:* 542 (physical). Weekly public service hours: 71.

STUDENT LIFE
Housing options: on-campus residence required for freshman year; men-only, women-only. Campus housing is leased by the school. Freshman campus housing is guaranteed.

Campus security: 24-hour emergency response devices, controlled dormitory access.

COSTS
Costs (2018–19) ***One-time required fee:*** $535 Canadian dollars. ***Comprehensive fee:*** $15,682 Canadian dollars includes full-time tuition ($6848 Canadian dollars), mandatory fees ($1414 Canadian dollars), and room and board ($7420 Canadian dollars). Full-time tuition and fees vary according to course load, location, and program. Part-time tuition: $214 Canadian dollars per credit hour. Part-time tuition and fees vary according to course load, location, and program. ***Required fees:*** $29 Canadian dollars per credit hour part-time. ***Room and board:*** Room and board charges vary according to board plan.

APPLYING
Options: electronic application, deferred entrance.

Application fee: $75 Canadian dollars.

Required: essay or personal statement, high school transcript, 3 letters of recommendation, Christian commitment. ***Required for some:*** interview. ***Recommended:*** minimum 2.0 GPA.

CONTACT
Ms. Flora Anthony, Admissions Counsellor, Master's College and Seminary, 780 Argyle Street, Peterborough, ON K9H 5T2, Canada. *Phone:* 800-295-6368 Ext. 237. *Toll-free phone:* 800-295-6368. *Fax:* 705-749-0417. *E-mail:* flora.anthony@mcs.edu.

McGill University

Montréal, Quebec, Canada

http://www.mcgill.ca/

CONTACT
Enrollment Services, McGill University, 845 Sherbrooke Street West, James Administration Building, Room 205, Montreal, QC H3A 2T5, Canada. *Phone:* 514-398-3910. *Fax:* 514-398-4193. *E-mail:* admissions@mcgill.ca.

McMaster University

Hamilton, Ontario, Canada

http://www.mcmaster.ca/

CONTACT
Olivia Demerling, Admissions Officer, McMaster University, 1280 Main Street West, Hamilton, ON L8S 4M2, Canada. *Phone:* 905-525-4600. *Fax:* 905-527-1105. *E-mail:* admitmac@mcmaster.ca.

Memorial University of Newfoundland

St. John's, Newfoundland and Labrador, Canada

http://www.mun.ca/

CONTACT
Ms. Marian Abbott, Admissions Office, Memorial University of Newfoundland, Elizabeth Avenue, St. John's, NL A1C 5S7, Canada. *Phone:* 709-737-3705. *E-mail:* sturecru@morgan.ucs.mun.ca.

Mount Allison University

Sackville, New Brunswick, Canada

http://www.mta.ca/

CONTACT
Mr. Curtis Michaelis, Manager of Admissions, Mount Allison University, 65 York Street, Sackville, NB E4L 1E4, Canada. *Phone:* 506-364-3294. *Fax:* 506-364-2272. *E-mail:* admissions@mta.ca.

Mount Royal University
Calgary, Alberta, Canada
http://www.mtroyal.ca/

CONTACT
Admissions Office, Mount Royal University, 4825 Mount Royal Gate SW, Calgary, AB T3E 6K6, Canada. *Phone:* 403-440-5000. *Toll-free phone:* 877-440-5001.

Mount Saint Vincent University
Halifax, Nova Scotia, Canada
http://www.msvu.ca/

CONTACT
Ms. Heidi Tattrie, Assistant Registrar/Admissions, Mount Saint Vincent University, 166 Bedford Highway, Halifax, NS B3M2J6, Canada. *Phone:* 902-457-6117. *Toll-free phone:* 877-733-6788. *Fax:* 902-457-6498. *E-mail:* admissions@msvu.ca.

Ner Israel Yeshiva College of Toronto
Thornhill, Ontario, Canada
http://www.neryisroel.info/

CONTACT
Rabbi Y. Kravetz, Director of Admissions, Ner Israel Yeshiva College of Toronto, 8950 Bathurst Street, Thornhill, ON L4J 8A7, Canada. *Phone:* 905-731-1224.

Nipissing University
North Bay, Ontario, Canada
http://www.nipissingu.ca/

CONTACT
Ms. Lori-Ann Beckford, Assistant Registrar, Liaison, Nipissing University, 100 College Drive, Box 5002, North Bay, ON P1B 8L7, Canada. *Phone:* 705-474-3461 Ext. 4518. *Fax:* 705-474-1947. *E-mail:* liaison@nipissingu.ca.

NSCAD University
Halifax, Nova Scotia, Canada
http://www.nscad.ca/

CONTACT
Mr. Terry Bailey, Director of Admissions and Enrollment Services, NSCAD University, 5163 Duke Street, Halifax, NS B3J 3J6, Canada. *Phone:* 902-494-8129. *Toll-free phone:* 888-444-5989. *Fax:* 902-425-2987. *E-mail:* admissions@nscad.ca.

Okanagan College
Kelowna, British Columbia, Canada
http://www.okanagan.bc.ca/

CONTACT
Mr. Allan Hickey, Associate Registrar Systems, Okanagan College, 1000 K.L.O. Road, Kelowna, BC V1Y 4X8, Canada. *Phone:* 250-762-5445 Ext. 4332. *Toll-free phone:* 877-755-2266. *E-mail:* ahickey@okanagan.bc.ca.

Prairie Bible Institute
Three Hills, Alberta, Canada
http://www.prairie.edu/

CONTACT
Mr. Kevin Kirk, Vice President, Marketing and Enrollment Management, Prairie Bible Institute, 350 5th Avenue, NE, Box 4000, Three Hills, AB T0M 2N0, Canada. *Phone:* 403-443-5511 Ext. 3007. *Toll-free phone:* 800-661-2425. *E-mail:* admissions@prairie.edu.

Providence University College & Theological Seminary
Otterburne, Manitoba, Canada
http://www.prov.ca/

CONTACT
Mr. Adrian Enns, Director of College Enrollment, Providence University College & Theological Seminary, 10 College Crescent, Otterburne, MB R0A 1G0, Canada. *Phone:* 204-433-7488. *Toll-free phone:* 800-668-7768. *Fax:* 204-433-7158. *E-mail:* info@prov.ca.

Queen's University at Kingston
Kingston, Ontario, Canada
http://www.queensu.ca/

CONTACT
Ms. Iveta Reinikovaite, Admission Coordinator, Queen's University at Kingston, Undergraduate Admissions, Gordon Hall, 74 Union Street, Kingston, ON K7L 3N6, Canada. *Phone:* 613-533-2218. *Fax:* 613-533-6810. *E-mail:* admission@queensu.ca.

Redeemer University College
Ancaster, Ontario, Canada
http://www.redeemer.ca/

- **Independent interdenominational** 4-year, founded 1980
- **Small-town** 86-acre campus with easy access to Toronto
- **Coed** 688 undergraduate students, 94% full-time, 62% women, 38% men
- 94% of applicants were admitted

UNDERGRAD STUDENTS
650 full-time, 38 part-time. Students come from 6 provinces and territories; 16 other countries; 5% are from out of state; 6% transferred in.

Freshmen:
Admission: 247 applied, 231 admitted, 120 enrolled.
Retention: 78% of full-time freshmen returned.

FACULTY
Total: 74, 55% full-time, 65% with terminal degrees.
Student/faculty ratio: 11:1.

ACADEMICS
Calendar: semesters. *Degree:* certificates and bachelor's.
Special study options: academic remediation for entering students, cooperative education, double majors, honors programs, independent study, internships, off-campus study, part-time degree program, services for LD students, study abroad, summer session for credit.
Computers: 81 computers/terminals are available on campus for general student use. Students can access the following: campus intranet, computer help desk, free student e-mail accounts, online (class) grades, online (class) schedules. Campuswide network is available. 100% of college-owned or -operated housing units are wired for high-speed Internet access. Wireless service is available via entire campus.
Library: Peter Turkstra Library. *Books:* 92,733 (physical); *Serial titles:* 93 (physical), 9,387 (digital/electronic); *Databases:* 21. Students can reserve study rooms.

STUDENT LIFE
Housing options: on-campus residence required through sophomore year; men-only, women-only. Campus housing is university owned. Freshman campus housing is guaranteed.
Activities and organizations: drama/theater group, student-run newspaper, choral group, Church in the Box, Service Learning Trips, Deedz, Athletics and Recreation, Concert Choir.
Athletics ***Intercollegiate sports:*** badminton M/W, basketball M(s)/W(s), cross-country running M/W, soccer M/W, volleyball M/W. ***Intramural sports:*** basketball M/W, ice hockey M, rugby M, soccer M/W, squash M/W, tennis M/W, ultimate Frisbee M/W, volleyball M/W.
Campus security: 24-hour emergency response devices, student patrols, late-night transport/escort service, controlled dormitory access.
Student services: personal/psychological counseling.

COSTS & FINANCIAL AID
Costs (2019–20) ***Comprehensive fee:*** $18,969 Canadian dollars includes full-time tuition ($9800 Canadian dollars), mandatory fees ($621 Canadian dollars), and room and board ($8548 Canadian dollars). Part-time tuition: $980 Canadian dollars per course. ***Required fees:*** $43 Canadian dollars part-time. ***College room only:*** $6200 Canadian dollars.
Financial Aid Of all full-time matriculated undergraduates who enrolled in 2010, 640 applied for aid, 607 were judged to have need, 200 had their need fully met. 385 state and other part-time jobs (averaging $1238). In 2010, 99 non-need-based awards were made. ***Average percent of need met:*** 82. ***Average financial aid package:*** $12,582. ***Average need-based loan:*** $7464. ***Average need-based gift aid:*** $4587. ***Average non-need-based aid:*** $3061. ***Average indebtedness upon graduation:*** $23,598. ***Financial aid deadline:*** 3/31.

APPLYING
Standardized Tests *Required for some:* SAT or ACT (for admission).
Options: electronic application, deferred entrance.
Application fee: $40 Canadian dollars.
Required: essay or personal statement, high school transcript, minimum 2.0 GPA, 1 letter of recommendation. ***Required for some:*** interview.
Application deadlines: rolling (freshmen), rolling (transfers).
Notification: continuous (freshmen), continuous (transfers).

CONTACT
Mr. Willem deRuijter, Director, Admissions, Redeemer University College, 777 Garner Road East, Ancaster, ON L9K 1J4, Canada. *Phone:* 905-648-2131 Ext. 4471. *Toll-free phone:* 800-263-6467. *Fax:* 905-648-2134. *E-mail:* recruitment@redeemer.ca.

Rocky Mountain College
Calgary, Alberta, Canada
http://www.rockymountaincollege.ca/

CONTACT
Rocky Mountain College, 4039 Brentwood Road, NW, Calgary, AB T2L 1L1, Canada. *Phone:* 403-284-5100 Ext. 222. *Toll-free phone:* 877-YOUnRMC.

Royal Military College of Canada
Kingston, Ontario, Canada
http://www.rmc.ca/

CONTACT
Royal Military College of Canada, PO Box 17000, Station Forces, Kingston, ON K7K 7B4, Canada. *Phone:* 613-541-6000 Ext. 6579.

Royal Roads University
Victoria, British Columbia, Canada
http://www.royalroads.ca/

CONTACT
Royal Roads University, 2005 Sooke Road, Victoria, BC V9B 5Y2, Canada. *Phone:* 250-391-2511. *Toll-free phone:* 800-788-8028.

Ryerson University
Toronto, Ontario, Canada
http://www.ryerson.ca/

CONTACT
Michelle Beaton, Manager of International Student Recruitment, Ryerson University, 350 Victoria Street, Toronto, ON M5B 2K3, Canada. *Phone:* 416-979-5080. *Fax:* 416-979-5067. *E-mail:* inquire@ryerson.ca.

St. Francis Xavier University
Antigonish, Nova Scotia, Canada
http://www.stfx.ca/

CONTACT
Ms. Sarah Murray, Admissions Officer, St. Francis Xavier University, PO Box 5000, Antigonish, NS B2G 2W5, Canada. *Phone:* 902-867-2219. *Toll-free phone:* 877-867-7839 (in-state); 877-867-STFX (out-of-state). *Fax:* 902-867-2329. *E-mail:* mbarry@stfx.ca.

Saint Mary's University
Halifax, Nova Scotia, Canada
http://www.smu.ca/

CONTACT
Mr. Greg Ferguson, Director of Admissions, Saint Mary's University, Halifax, NS B3H 3C3, Canada. *Phone:* 902-420-5415. *Fax:* 902-496-8100. *E-mail:* greg.ferguson@smu.ca.

Saint Paul University
Ottawa, Ontario, Canada
http://www.ustpaul.ca/

CONTACT
Admission and Recruitment Office, Saint Paul University, 223 Main Street, Ottawa, ON K1S 1C4, Canada. *Phone:* 613-236-1393 Ext. 8990. *Toll-free phone:* 800-637-6859. *Fax:* 613-782-3014. *E-mail:* admission@ustpaul.ca.

St. Thomas University
Fredericton, New Brunswick, Canada
http://www.stu.ca/

- **Independent Roman Catholic** 4-year, founded 1910
- **Small-town** 16-acre campus
- **Endowment** $17.9 million
- **Coed**
- **Moderately difficult** entrance level

FACULTY
Student/faculty ratio: 16:1.

ACADEMICS
Calendar: semesters. *Degrees:* certificates, bachelor's, and postbachelor's certificates.
Library: Harriet Irving Library plus 2 others. *Books:* 976,313 (physical), 532,787 (digital/electronic); *Serial titles:* 2,449 (physical), 44,800 (digital/electronic). Weekly public service hours: 113; students can reserve study rooms.

STUDENT LIFE
Housing options: coed, women-only, special housing for students with disabilities. Campus housing is university owned. Freshman campus housing is guaranteed.
Activities and organizations: drama/theater group, student-run newspaper, radio station, choral group, Theatre St. Thomas, St. Thomas Student Union, Criminology Society, Model UN, International Students' Association.
Athletics Member CIS.
Campus security: 24-hour emergency response devices and patrols, student patrols, late-night transport/escort service, controlled dormitory access.
Student services: health clinic, personal/psychological counseling, women's center.

COSTS & FINANCIAL AID
Costs (2018–19) ***Comprehensive fee:*** $16,682 Canadian dollars includes full-time tuition ($6776 Canadian dollars), mandatory fees ($885 Canadian dollars), and room and board ($9021 Canadian dollars). Full-time tuition and fees vary according to course load, degree level, and program. Part-time tuition: $681 Canadian dollars per course. Part-time tuition and fees vary according to course load. ***Required fees:*** $56 Canadian dollars per course part-time. ***Room and board:*** Room and board charges vary according to board plan, housing facility, and location. ***Payment plans:*** installment, deferred payment.
Financial Aid ***Financial aid deadline:*** 3/1.

APPLYING
Standardized Tests *Recommended:* SAT (for admission).
Options: electronic application, early action.
Application fee: $55 Canadian dollars.

Required: essay or personal statement, high school transcript, minimum 3.0 GPA. ***Required for some:*** interview.

CONTACT
Ms. Kathryn Monti, Director of Admissions, St. Thomas University, Duffie Hall, Fredericton, NB E3B 5G3, Canada. *Phone:* 506-452-0532. *Fax:* 506-452-0617. *E-mail:* admissions@stu.ca.

Simon Fraser University

Burnaby, British Columbia, Canada

http://www.sfu.ca/

- **Province-supported** university, founded 1965
- **Suburban** 174-hectare campus with easy access to Vancouver
- **Coed**
- **Moderately difficult** entrance level

FACULTY
Student/faculty ratio: 22:1.

ACADEMICS
Calendar: trimesters. *Degrees:* certificates, diplomas, bachelor's, master's, doctoral, post-master's, and postbachelor's certificates.
Library: Bennett Library plus 2 others. *Books:* 1.5 million (physical), 1.1 million (digital/electronic); *Serial titles:* 2,500 (physical), 98,000 (digital/electronic). Weekly public service hours: 103; students can reserve study rooms.

STUDENT LIFE
Housing options: coed, special housing for students with disabilities. Campus housing is university owned. Freshman applicants given priority for college housing.

Activities and organizations: student-run newspaper, radio station, The Peak Newspaper, orientation/peer leaders, Crisis line, Women's Centre, Simon Fraser Public Interest Research Group.

Athletics Member NCAA. All Division II.

Campus security: 24-hour emergency response devices and patrols, student patrols, late-night transport/escort service, controlled dormitory access, safe-walk stations, 24-hour safe study area.

Student services: health clinic, personal/psychological counseling, women's center.

APPLYING
Standardized Tests *Required for some:* SAT or ACT (for admission).

Options: electronic application, early admission, early action, deferred entrance.

Application fee: $78 Canadian dollars.

Required: high school transcript, minimum 3.0 GPA. ***Required for some:*** essay or personal statement, interview.

CONTACT
Louise Legris, Director of Admissions, Simon Fraser University, 8888 University Drive, MBC 3200, Burnaby, BC V5A 1S6, Canada. *Phone:* 778-782-3498. *Fax:* 778-782-4969.

Southern Alberta Institute of Technology

Calgary, Alberta, Canada

http://www.sait.ca/

CONTACT
Southern Alberta Institute of Technology, 1301 16th Avenue NW, Calgary, AB T2M 0L4, Canada. *Phone:* 403-284-8857. *Toll-free phone:* 877-284-SAIT.

Steinbach Bible College

Steinbach, Manitoba, Canada

http://www.sbcollege.ca/

CONTACT
Mrs. Kaylene Buhler, Admissions Counselor, Steinbach Bible College, 50 PTH 12 North, Steinbach, MB R5G 1T4, Canada. *Phone:* 204-326-6451 Ext. 232. *Toll-free phone:* 800-230-8478. *Fax:* 204-326-6908. *E-mail:* info@sbcollege.ca.

Summit Pacific College

Abbotsford, British Columbia, Canada

http://www.summitpacific.ca/

CONTACT
Ms. Melody Deeley, Admissions and Registration, Summit Pacific College, Box 1700, Abbotsford, BC V2S 7E7, Canada. *Phone:* 604-851-7225. *Toll-free phone:* 800-976-8388. *E-mail:* registrar@summitpacific.ca.

Télé-université

Québec, Quebec, Canada

http://www.teluq.uquebec.ca/

CONTACT
Ms. Louise Bertrand, Registraire, Télé-université, 455, rue de l'Église, C.P. 4800, succ. Terminus, Québec, QC G1K 9H5, Canada. *Phone:* 418-657-2262 Ext. 5307. *Toll-free phone:* 888-843-4333.

Thompson Rivers University

Kamloops, British Columbia, Canada

http://www.tru.ca/

CONTACT
Mr. Josh Keller, Director, Student Recruitment and Liaison, Thompson Rivers University, 900 McGill Road, Kamloops, BC V2C 0C8, Canada. *Phone:* 250-828-5008. *Fax:* 250-828-5159. *E-mail:* jkeller@tru.ca.

Trent University

Peterborough, Ontario, Canada

http://www.trentu.ca/

- **Province-supported** university, founded 1963
- **Suburban** 1400-acre campus with easy access to Toronto
- **Coed**
- **Moderately difficult** entrance level

ACADEMICS
Calendar: Canadian standard year. *Degrees:* certificates, diplomas, bachelor's, master's, and doctoral.
Library: Thomas J. Bata Library plus 1 other. Students can reserve study rooms.

STUDENT LIFE
Housing options: coed, women-only. Campus housing is university owned. Freshman campus housing is guaranteed.

Activities and organizations: drama/theater group, student-run newspaper, radio station, choral group, Trent Radio, Trent International Program, Trent Central Student Association, Arthur (student newspaper), Excalibur (yearbook).

Athletics Member CIS.

Campus security: 24-hour emergency response devices and patrols, student patrols, late-night transport/escort service, controlled dormitory access.

Student services: health clinic, personal/psychological counseling, women's center.

COSTS
Costs (2018–19) ***Tuition:*** province resident $6798 Canadian dollars full-time, $1360 Canadian dollars per credit part-time; nonresident $4106 Canadian dollars per credit part-time; International tuition $20,367 Canadian dollars full-time. Full-time tuition and fees vary according to course load, degree level, and program. Part-time tuition and fees vary according to course load, degree level, and program. ***Required fees:*** $1660 Canadian dollars full-time, $136 Canadian dollars per credit part-time. ***Room and board:*** $10,095 Canadian dollars. Room and board charges vary according to board plan, housing facility, and location. ***Payment plans:*** installment, deferred payment.

APPLYING
Options: electronic application, deferred entrance.

Application fee: $150 Canadian dollars.

Required: high school transcript, minimum 2.8 GPA. ***Required for some:*** essay or personal statement, interview.

CONTACT
Mr. Kevin Whitmore, Director, Recruitment and Admissions, Trent University, 1600 West Bank Drive, Peterborough, ON K9J 7B8, Canada. *Phone:* 705-748-1011 Ext. 7748. *Fax:* 705-748-1629. *E-mail:* admissions@trentu.ca.

Trinity Western University
Langley, British Columbia, Canada
http://www.twu.ca/

CONTACT
Trinity Western University, 7600 Glover Road, Langley, BC V2Y 1Y1, Canada. *Toll-free phone:* 888-468-6898.

Tyndale University College & Seminary
Toronto, Ontario, Canada
http://www.tyndale.ca/

- **Independent interdenominational** comprehensive, founded 1894
- **Urban** 56-acre campus
- **Endowment** $2.0 million
- **Coed** 479 undergraduate students, 73% full-time, 48% women, 52% men
- **Moderately difficult** entrance level, 53% of applicants were admitted

UNDERGRAD STUDENTS
348 full-time, 131 part-time. Students come from 7 provinces and territories; 12 other countries; 30% live on campus.

Freshmen:
Admission: 368 applied, 196 admitted, 193 enrolled.
Retention: 49% of full-time freshmen returned.

FACULTY
Total: 54.
Student/faculty ratio: 23:1.

ACADEMICS
Calendar: semesters. *Degrees:* certificates, bachelor's, master's, and doctoral.
Special study options: academic remediation for entering students, accelerated degree program, adult/continuing education programs, honors programs, off-campus study, part-time degree program, summer session for credit.
Computers: 30 computers/terminals are available on campus for general student use. Students can access the following: free student e-mail accounts, online (class) grades, online (class) registration, online (class) schedules. Campuswide network is available. Wireless service is available via entire campus.
Library: J. William Horsey Library.

STUDENT LIFE
Housing options: men-only, women-only. Campus housing is university owned. Freshman applicants given priority for college housing.
Activities and organizations: drama/theater group, student-run newspaper, choral group, choir, student government, Urban Ministry Team, Steadfast drama team.
Athletics ***Intercollegiate sports:*** basketball M/W, ice hockey M, ultimate Frisbee M(s)/W(s), volleyball M(s)/W(s). ***Intramural sports:*** badminton M(c)/W(c), basketball M(c), football M, golf M, skiing (cross-country) M(c)/W(c), skiing (downhill) M(c)/W(c), soccer M(c)/W(c), softball M/W, swimming and diving M(c)/W(c), ultimate Frisbee M/W, volleyball M/W, weight lifting M(c)/W(c).
Campus security: 24-hour patrols, student patrols, late-night transport/escort service, controlled dormitory access.
Student services: personal/psychological counseling.

APPLYING
Options: electronic application, deferred entrance.
Application fee: $50 Canadian dollars.
Required: high school transcript, minimum 2.0 GPA, all post-secondary transcripts. ***Required for some:*** 1 letter of recommendation, interview. ***Recommended:*** essay or personal statement.
Application deadlines: rolling (freshmen), rolling (out-of-state freshmen), rolling (transfers).
Notification: continuous (freshmen), continuous (out-of-state freshmen), continuous (transfers).

CONTACT
Justin Hackett, Director, Admissions, Tyndale University College & Seminary, 3377 Bayview Avenue, Toronto, ON M2M 3S4, Canada. *Phone:* 416-218-6757. *Toll-free phone:* 877-896-3253. *E-mail:* admissions@tydale.ca.

Université de Moncton
Moncton, New Brunswick, Canada
http://www.umoncton.ca/

CONTACT
Miss Nicole Savois, Chief Admission Officer, Université de Moncton, Moncton, NB E1A 3E9, Canada. *Phone:* 506-858-4115. *Toll-free phone:* 800-363-8336. *E-mail:* gallanrm@umoncton.ca.

Université de Montréal
Montréal, Quebec, Canada
http://www.umontreal.ca/

CONTACT
Mme. Marie-Claude Binette, Registrar, Université de Montréal, Bureau du registraire, CP 6128, Succursale Centre-Ville, Montreal, QC H3C 3J7, Canada. *Phone:* 514-343-2214. *Toll-free phone:* 866-977-7076 (in-state); 800-977-0761 (out-of-state). *Fax:* 514-343-2097. *E-mail:* marie-claude.binette@umontreal.ca.

Université de Saint-Boniface
Saint-Boniface, Manitoba, Canada
http://www.ustboniface.ca/

CONTACT
Université de Saint-Boniface, 200 avenue de la Cathèdrale, Saint-Boniface, MB R2H 0H7, Canada.

Université de Sherbrooke
Sherbrooke, Quebec, Canada
http://www.usherbrooke.ca/

- **Independent** university, founded 1954
- **Urban** 800-acre campus with easy access to Montreal
- **Coed** 14,971 undergraduate students, 80% full-time, 53% women, 47% men
- **Moderately difficult** entrance level, 58% of applicants were admitted

UNDERGRAD STUDENTS
11,978 full-time, 2,993 part-time. Students come from 7 provinces and territories; 76 other countries; 1% are from out of state.

Freshmen:
Admission: 17,665 applied, 10,228 admitted, 3,234 enrolled.

FACULTY
Total: 3,173, 37% full-time.

ACADEMICS
Calendar: Canadian standard year. *Degrees:* certificates, diplomas, bachelor's, master's, and doctoral.
Special study options: accelerated degree program, adult/continuing education programs, cooperative education, English as a second language, internships, off-campus study, part-time degree program, services for LD students, study abroad, summer session for credit.
Computers: 300 computers/terminals are available on campus for general student use. Students can access the following: campus intranet, computer help desk, free student e-mail accounts, online (class) registration, online (class) schedules. Campuswide network is available. 100% of college-owned or -operated housing units are wired for high-speed Internet access. Wireless service is available via entire campus.
Library: Bibliotheque Roger-Maltais plus 5 others. Weekly public service hours: 73; students can reserve study rooms.

STUDENT LIFE
Housing options: coed, cooperative. Campus housing is university owned and is provided by a third party.
Activities and organizations: drama/theater group, student-run newspaper, radio station, choral group.
Athletics Member CIS. ***Intercollegiate sports:*** badminton M/W, cheerleading M/W, cross-country running M/W, football M(s), golf M, rugby M/W, soccer M/W, swimming and diving M/W. ***Intramural sports:*** badminton M/W, basketball M/W, fencing W, field hockey M, ice hockey M, racquetball M/W, soccer M/W, squash M/W, track and field M/W, ultimate Frisbee M/W, volleyball M/W, water polo M/W.
Campus security: 24-hour emergency response devices and patrols, late-night transport/escort service.
Student services: health clinic, personal/psychological counseling.

COSTS & FINANCIAL AID
Costs (2019–20) ***Required fees:*** $14 Canadian dollars per credit part-time, $66 Canadian dollars per term part-time. ***Room and board:*** $9200 Canadian dollars; room only: $4992 Canadian dollars.
Financial Aid ***Financial aid deadline:*** 3/31.

APPLYING
Options: electronic application.
Application fee: $75 Canadian dollars.
Required: high school transcript. ***Required for some:*** interview, Test of French level, Casper test.
Notification: continuous (freshmen).

CONTACT
Mme. Lisa BEDARD, Admissions Officer, Université de Sherbrooke, 2500 boulevard de l'Universite, Sherbrooke, QC J1K 2R1. *Phone:* 819-821-7687. *Toll-free phone:* 800-267-UDES.

Université du Québec à Chicoutimi
Chicoutimi, Quebec, Canada
http://www.uqac.ca/

CONTACT
Jean Wauthier, Admissions Officer, Université du Québec à Chicoutimi, 555, boulevard de L'Université, Chicoutimi, QC G7H 2B1, Canada. *Phone:* 418-545-5005. *E-mail:* czoccast@uqac.uquebec.ca.

Université du Québec à Montréal
Montréal, Quebec, Canada
http://www.uqam.ca/

CONTACT
Ms. Lucille Boisselle-Roy, Admissions Officer, Université du Québec à Montréal, CP 8888, Succursale Centreville, Montréal, QC H2L 4S8, Canada. *Phone:* 514-987-3132. *E-mail:* admission@uqam.ca.

Université du Québec à Rimouski
Rimouski, Quebec, Canada
http://www.uqar.ca/

CONTACT
Ms. Marie Saint-Laurent, Admissions Officer, Université du Québec à Rimouski, 300 Allee des Ursulines, CP3300, Rimouski QC G5L 3A1, Canada. *Phone:* 418-724-1433. *E-mail:* philippe_horth@uqar.uquebec.ca.

Université du Québec à Trois-Rivières
Trois-Rivières, Quebec, Canada
http://www.uqtr.ca/

CONTACT
Ms. Jean Bois, Admissions Officer, Université du Québec à Trois-Rivières, 3351 blvd des Forges, Case post 500, Trois-Rivières, QC G9A 5H7, Canada. *Phone:* 819-376-5011. *Toll-free phone:* 800-365-0922. *Fax:* 819-376-5232. *E-mail:* registraire@uqtr.ca.

Université du Québec, École de technologie supérieure
Montréal, Quebec, Canada
http://www.etsmtl.ca/

CONTACT
Mme. Francine Gamache, Registraire, Université du Québec, École de technologie supérieure, 1100, rue Notre Dame Ouest, Montréal, QC H3C 1K3, Canada. *Phone:* 514-396-8885. *E-mail:* admission@ets.mtl.ca.

Université du Québec en Abitibi-Témiscamingue
Rouyn-Noranda, Quebec, Canada
http://www.uqat.ca/

CONTACT
Mrs. Monique Fay, Admissions Officer, Université du Québec en Abitibi-Témiscamingue, 445 boulevard de l'Université, Rouyn-Noranda, QC J9X 5E4, Canada. *Phone:* 819-762-0971. *E-mail:* micheline.chevalier@uqat.uquebec.ca.

Université du Québec en Outaouais
Gatineau, Quebec, Canada
http://www.uqo.ca/

CONTACT
Registrar's Office, Université du Québec en Outaouais, CP 1250, Succursale Hull, 101 Saint-Jean-Bosco, 101 rue Saint-Jean-Bosco, Gatineau, QC J8X 3X7, Canada. *Phone:* 819-595-3900 Ext. 1850. *Toll-free phone:* 800-567-1283. *Fax:* 819-773-1835. *E-mail:* registraire@uqo.ca.

Université Laval
Québec, Quebec, Canada
http://www.ulaval.ca/

CONTACT
Promotion and Recruitment Division, Université Laval, Quebec, QC G1K 7P4, Canada. *Phone:* 418-656-2764. *Toll-free phone:* 877-785-2825. *Fax:* 418-656-5216. *E-mail:* info@dap.ulaval.ca.

Université Sainte-Anne
Church Point, Nova Scotia, Canada
http://www.usainteanne.ca/

- **Province-supported** comprehensive, founded 1890
- **Rural** 115-acre campus
- **Endowment** $2.7 million
- **Coed** 319 undergraduate students, 97% full-time, 65% women, 35% men
- **Moderately difficult** entrance level, 87% of applicants were admitted

UNDERGRAD STUDENTS
308 full-time, 11 part-time. Students come from 1 other province; 3 other countries; 18% are from out of state; 100% international; 15% transferred in; 52% live on campus.

Freshmen:
Admission: 209 applied, 181 admitted, 115 enrolled.
Retention: 86% of full-time freshmen returned.

FACULTY
Total: 72, 60% full-time, 33% with terminal degrees.

ACADEMICS
Calendar: semesters. *Degrees:* certificates, diplomas, bachelor's, and master's.
Special study options: academic remediation for entering students, adult/continuing education programs, cooperative education, distance learning, double majors, English as a second language, off-campus study, part-time degree program, services for LD students, study abroad.
Unusual degree programs: 3-2 education.

Computers: 45 computers/terminals are available on campus for general student use. Students can access the following: campus intranet, computer help desk, free student e-mail accounts, online (class) grades, online (class) registration, online (class) schedules. Campuswide network is available. 100% of college-owned or -operated housing units are wired for high-speed Internet access. Wireless service is available via entire campus.
Library: BibliothÃ¨que Louis-R.-Comeau plus 1 other. *Books:* 76,000 (physical); *Serial titles:* 52 (physical); *Databases:* 27. Weekly public service hours: 78.

STUDENT LIFE
Housing options: coed, special housing for students with disabilities. Campus housing is university owned and is provided by a third party.

Activities and organizations: drama/theater group, Student Organization, Enactus, Club de Plein Air, Education Committee, Association des étudiants internationaux de l'Université Sainte-Anne.

Athletics Member CIS. ***Intercollegiate sports:*** badminton M/W, volleyball M(c)/W(c). ***Intramural sports:*** badminton M/W, cross-country running M/W, ice hockey M/W, rugby W, soccer M, swimming and diving M/W, table tennis M/W, tennis M/W, volleyball M/W, weight lifting M/W.

Campus security: 24-hour emergency response devices and patrols, student patrols, late-night transport/escort service, 14-hour patrols by trained security personnel.

Student services: health clinic, personal/psychological counseling.

COSTS & FINANCIAL AID
Costs (2018–19) ***Comprehensive fee:*** $10,139 Canadian dollars includes full-time tuition ($5593 Canadian dollars) and room and board ($4545 Canadian dollars). Full-time tuition and fees vary according to course load, location, and program. Part-time tuition and fees vary according to course load, location, and program. ***Required fees:*** $1448 Canadian dollars per term part-time. ***College room only:*** $2195 Canadian dollars. Room and board charges vary according to board plan, housing facility, and location. ***Payment plan:*** installment. ***Waivers:*** children of alumni, senior citizens, and employees or children of employees.

Financial Aid Of all full-time matriculated undergraduates who enrolled in 2013, 3 were judged to have need. ***Financial aid deadline:*** 11/15.

APPLYING
Options: electronic application, early admission, deferred entrance.

Application fee: $50.

Required: high school transcript. ***Required for some:*** essay or personal statement, 3 letters of recommendation, Criminal record check.

Application deadlines: rolling (freshmen), rolling (out-of-state freshmen).

Early decision deadline: rolling.

Notification: continuous (freshmen), continuous (out-of-state freshmen), rolling (early decision).

CONTACT
Ms. Nora Saulnier, Admissions Officer, Université Sainte-Anne, 1695, Highway 1, Church Point, NS B0W 1M0. *Phone:* 902-769-2114 Ext. 7116. *E-mail:* admission@usainteanne.ca.

University of Alberta
Edmonton, Alberta, Canada
http://www.ualberta.ca/

CONTACT
Melissa Padfield, Deputy Registrar, University of Alberta, Administration Building, Edmonton, AB T6G 2M7, Canada. *Phone:* 780-492-3113. *Toll-free phone:* 855-492-3113. *Fax:* 780-492-7172.

The University of British Columbia
Vancouver, British Columbia, Canada
http://www.ubc.ca/

CONTACT
The University of British Columbia, 2075 Wesbrook Mall, Vancouver, BC V6T 1Z1, Canada. *Phone:* 604-822-3014.

The University of British Columbia–Okanagan Campus
Kelowna, British Columbia, Canada
http://www.ok.ubc.ca/

CONTACT
International Student Recruitment, The University of British Columbia–Okanagan Campus, UC222 University Centre, 3333 University Way, Kelowna, BC V1V 1V7, Canada. *Phone:* 250-807-9447. *Fax:* 250-807-8552.

University of Calgary
Calgary, Alberta, Canada
http://www.ucalgary.ca/

CONTACT
Mr. Kaili Xu, Associate Registrar, Undergraduate Admissions, University of Calgary, 2500 University Drive NW, Calgary, AB T2N 1N4, Canada. *Phone:* 403-210-7625. *E-mail:* future.students@ucalgary.ca.

University of Guelph
Guelph, Ontario, Canada
http://www.uoguelph.ca/

- **Province-supported** university, founded 1964
- **Suburban** 1017-acre campus with easy access to Toronto
- **Endowment** $419.1 million
- **Coed**
- **Moderately difficult** entrance level

FACULTY
Student/faculty ratio: 23:1.

ACADEMICS
Calendar: trimesters. *Degrees:* certificates, diplomas, associate, bachelor's, master's, and doctoral.
Library: University of Guelph Library plus 1 other. *Books:* 1.3 million (physical), 35,000 (digital/electronic); *Serial titles:* 1,617 (physical), 21,287 (digital/electronic); *Databases:* 280. Students can reserve study rooms.

STUDENT LIFE
Housing options: coed, women-only, cooperative, special housing for students with disabilities. Campus housing is university owned and is provided by a third party. Freshman campus housing is guaranteed.

Activities and organizations: drama/theater group, student-run newspaper, radio station, choral group, Guelph Gryphon Athletics, Habitat for Humanity, Curtain Call Productions, West Indian Students Association, OXFAM-Guelph Chapter.

Athletics Member CIS.

Campus security: 24-hour emergency response devices and patrols, student patrols, late-night transport/escort service, controlled dormitory access, video camera surveillance in parking lots, alarms in women's locker room.

Student services: health clinic, personal/psychological counseling, women's center, legal services.

COSTS
Costs (2018–19) ***Tuition:*** province resident $6571 Canadian dollars full-time, $1313 Canadian dollars per credit part-time; nonresident $6571 Canadian dollars full-time; International tuition $20,840 Canadian dollars full-time. Full-time tuition and fees vary according to degree level and program. Part-time tuition and fees vary according to course load, degree level, and program. No tuition increase for student's term of enrollment. ***Required fees:*** $22,501 Canadian dollars full-time, $514 Canadian dollars per credit part-time. ***Room and board:*** $11,132 Canadian dollars; room only: $6082 Canadian dollars. Room and board charges vary according to board plan and housing facility.

APPLYING
Standardized Tests *Required:* SAT or ACT (for admission).

Options: electronic application, early admission, deferred entrance.

Application fee: $150 Canadian dollars.

Required: high school transcript, minimum 3.0 GPA. ***Required for some:*** essay or personal statement.

CONTACT
Ms. Janette Hogan, Assistant Registrar, Admissions, University of Guelph, L-3 University Centre, Guelph, ON N1G 2W1, Canada. *Phone:* 519-824-4120 Ext. 58529. *Fax:* 519-766-9481. *E-mail:* jhogan@uoguelph.ca.

University of King's College

Halifax, Nova Scotia, Canada

http://www.ukings.ca/

- **Province-supported** comprehensive, founded 1789
- **Urban** 4-acre campus
- **Endowment** $38.0 million
- **Coed**
- **Moderately difficult** entrance level

FACULTY
Student/faculty ratio: 21:1.

ACADEMICS
Calendar: Canadian standard year. *Degrees:* bachelor's and master's.
Library: University of King's College Library. Students can reserve study rooms.

STUDENT LIFE
Housing options: coed, women-only. Campus housing is university owned. Freshman applicants given priority for college housing.

Activities and organizations: drama/theater group, student-run newspaper, radio station, choral group, King's Theatrical Society, student newspaper, King's College Dance Collective, St. Andrew's Missionary Society, King's Independent Film-Makers Society.

Campus security: student patrols, late-night transport/escort service, controlled dormitory access.

Student services: health clinic, personal/psychological counseling, women's center, legal services.

APPLYING
Standardized Tests *Required for some:* SAT or ACT (for admission).

Options: electronic application, early admission, early decision, deferred entrance.

Application fee: $65 Canadian dollars.

Required: high school transcript, minimum 3.0 GPA. ***Required for some:*** essay or personal statement, writing sample.

CONTACT
Ms. Tara Wigglesworth-Hines, Assistant Registrar/Admissions, University of King's College, Registrar's Office, Halifax, NS B3H 3A1, Canada. *Phone:* 902-422-1271. *Fax:* 902-425-8183. *E-mail:* admissions@ukings.ns.ca.

University of Lethbridge

Lethbridge, Alberta, Canada

http://www.uleth.ca/

CONTACT
Registrar's Office, University of Lethbridge, 4401 University Drive, Lethbridge, AB T1K 3M4, Canada. *Phone:* 403-320-5700. *Fax:* 403-329-5159. *E-mail:* regoffice@uleth.ca.

University of Manitoba

Winnipeg, Manitoba, Canada

http://www.umanitoba.ca/

CONTACT
Mr. Peter Dueck, Director of Enrollment Services, University of Manitoba, Winnipeg, MB R3T 2N2, Canada. *Phone:* 204-474-6382.

University of New Brunswick Fredericton

Fredericton, New Brunswick, Canada

http://www.unb.ca/

CONTACT
University of New Brunswick Fredericton, PO Box 4400, Fredericton, NB E3B 5A3, Canada. *Phone:* 506-453-4865.

University of New Brunswick Saint John

Saint John, New Brunswick, Canada

http://www.unb.ca/

CONTACT
University of New Brunswick Saint John, PO Box 5050, Saint John, NB E2L 4L5, Canada.

University of Northern British Columbia

Prince George, British Columbia, Canada

http://www.unbc.ca/

CONTACT
Pamela Flagel, Associate Registrar Enrollment, University of Northern British Columbia, Office of the Registrar, 3333 University Way, Prince George, BC V2N 4Z9, Canada. *Phone:* 250-960-6300. *Fax:* 250-960-6330. *E-mail:* registrar-info@unbc.ca.

University of Ottawa

Ottawa, Ontario, Canada

http://www.uottawa.ca/

CONTACT
University of Ottawa, 550 Cumberland Street, Ottawa, ON K1N 6N5, Canada. *Phone:* 613-562-5800 Ext. 1594.

University of Prince Edward Island

Charlottetown, Prince Edward Island, Canada

http://home.upei.ca/

CONTACT
University of Prince Edward Island, 550 University Avenue, Charlottetown, PE C1A 4P3, Canada. *Phone:* 902-566-0634.

University of Regina

Regina, Saskatchewan, Canada

http://www.uregina.ca/

- **Province-supported** university, founded 1974, part of intentionally left blank
- **Urban** 76-hectare campus
- **Endowment** $48.7 million
- **Coed** 13,668 undergraduate students, 84% full-time, 61% women, 39% men
- **Minimally difficult** entrance level, 64% of applicants were admitted

UNDERGRAD STUDENTS
11,431 full-time, 2,237 part-time. Students come from 13 provinces and territories; 119 other countries; 16% are from out of state; 4% transferred in; 10% live on campus.

Freshmen:
Admission: 7,435 applied, 4,770 admitted, 2,163 enrolled. ***Average high school GPA:*** 3.7.

Retention: 83% of full-time freshmen returned.

FACULTY
Total: 562, 75% with terminal degrees.
Student/faculty ratio: 23:1.

ACADEMICS
Calendar: semesters. *Degrees:* certificates, diplomas, bachelor's, master's, doctoral, and postbachelor's certificates.

Special study options: academic remediation for entering students, adult/continuing education programs, advanced placement credit, cooperative education, distance learning, double majors, English as a second language, honors programs, independent study, internships, off-campus study, part-time degree program, services for LD students, student-designed majors, study abroad, summer session for credit.

Computers: 412 computers/terminals are available on campus for general student use. Students can access the following: computer help desk, free student e-mail accounts, online (class) grades, online (class) registration, online (class) schedules. Campuswide network is available. 100% of college-owned or -operated housing units are wired for high-speed Internet access. Wireless service is available via entire campus.
Library: Dr. John Archer Library plus 5 others. *Books:* 806,988 (physical), 802,795 (digital/electronic); *Serial titles:* 163,120 (physical), 131,946 (digital/electronic); *Databases:* 519. Weekly public service hours: 105; students can reserve study rooms.

STUDENT LIFE
Housing options: special housing for students with disabilities. Campus housing is university owned. Freshman campus housing is guaranteed.

Activities and organizations: drama/theater group, student-run newspaper, University of Regina Students' Union, Biology Undergraduate and Graduate Society, Institute of Electrical and Electronics Engineers (IEEE) U of R Students Branch, UR Toastmasters, Inter-Varsity Christian Fellowship.

Athletics Member CIS. ***Intercollegiate sports:*** basketball M(s)/W(s), cross-country running M(s)/W(s), football M(s), ice hockey M(s)/W(s), soccer W(s), swimming and diving M(s)/W(s), track and field M(s)/W(s), volleyball M(s)/W(s). ***Intramural sports:*** badminton M/W, basketball M/W, bowling M/W, cheerleading M(c)/W(c), fencing M(c)/W(c), football M/W, golf M(c)/W(c), rowing M(c)/W(c), rugby M(c)/W(c), soccer M/W, softball M/W(c), tennis M/W, ultimate Frisbee M/W, volleyball M/W.

Campus security: 24-hour emergency response devices and patrols, controlled dormitory access, CCTV, card access and some alarm monitoring.

Student services: health clinic, personal/psychological counseling, women's center.

COSTS
Costs (2019–20) ***Required fees:*** $784 Canadian dollars full-time. ***Room and board:*** $7447 Canadian dollars; room only: $6552 Canadian dollars.

APPLYING
Standardized Tests *Required for some:* SAT or ACT (for admission).

Options: electronic application, early admission, early action, deferred entrance.

Application fee: $100 Canadian dollars.

Required: high school transcript, minimum 2.3 GPA. ***Required for some:*** essay or personal statement, 2 letters of recommendation, interview, portfolio, audition, 2.3 minimum GPA.

Application deadlines: 8/15 (freshmen), 8/15 (transfers), 6/15 (early action).

CONTACT
Ms. Christine McBain, Associate Director, Enrolment Services, University of Regina, 3737 Wascana Parkway, Regina, SK S4S 0A2, Canada. *Phone:* 306-585-5345. *Toll-free phone:* 800-644-4756. *Fax:* 306-337-2525. *E-mail:* enrolment.services@uregina.ca.

University of Saskatchewan
Saskatoon, Saskatchewan, Canada
http://www.usask.ca/

- **Province-supported** university, founded 1907
- **Urban** 1865-acre campus
- **Coed**
- 65% of applicants were admitted

FACULTY
Student/faculty ratio: 20:1.

ACADEMICS
Calendar: Canadian standard year. *Degrees:* certificates, diplomas, bachelor's, master's, doctoral, and postbachelor's certificates.
Library: University of Saskatchewan Main Library plus 7 others.

STUDENT LIFE
Housing options: coed. Campus housing is university owned.

Activities and organizations: drama/theater group, student-run newspaper, choral group.

Athletics Member CIS.

Campus security: 24-hour emergency response devices and patrols, student patrols, late-night transport/escort service, controlled dormitory access.

Student services: health clinic, personal/psychological counseling, women's center, legal services.

FINANCIAL AID
Financial Aid ***Financial aid deadline:*** 3/15.

APPLYING
Options: electronic application, early admission.

Application fee: $90 Canadian dollars.

Required: high school transcript. ***Required for some:*** essay or personal statement, interview.

CONTACT
University of Saskatchewan, 105 Administration Place, Saskatoon, SK S7N 5A2, Canada. *Phone:* 306-966-5788.

University of the Fraser Valley
Abbotsford, British Columbia, Canada
http://www.ufv.ca/

- **Province-supported** comprehensive, founded 1974
- **Urban** 64-hectare campus with easy access to Vancouver
- **Endowment** $11.0 million
- **Coed**

ACADEMICS
Calendar: semesters. *Degrees:* certificates, diplomas, associate, bachelor's, master's, and postbachelor's certificates.
Library: Peter Jones Library plus 3 others. *Books:* 181,000 (physical), 37,000 (digital/electronic). Students can reserve study rooms.

STUDENT LIFE
Housing options: coed. Campus housing is university owned. Freshman applicants given priority for college housing.

Activities and organizations: drama/theater group, student-run newspaper, radio station.

Athletics Member CIS.

Campus security: 24-hour emergency response devices and patrols, late-night transport/escort service, controlled dormitory access.

Student services: personal/psychological counseling.

COSTS
Costs (2018–19) ***Tuition:*** province resident $4873 Canadian dollars full-time, $162 Canadian dollars per credit hour part-time; nonresident $4873 Canadian dollars full-time, $162 Canadian dollars per credit hour part-time; International tuition $17,150 Canadian dollars full-time. Full-time tuition and fees vary according to course load. Part-time tuition and fees vary according to course load. ***Required fees:*** $526 Canadian dollars full-time, $158 Canadian dollars per term part-time. ***Room and board:*** $7941 Canadian dollars; room only: $5941 Canadian dollars. Room and board charges vary according to board plan.

APPLYING
Options: electronic application, early admission, deferred entrance.

Application fee: $45 Canadian dollars.

Required: high school transcript. ***Required for some:*** essay or personal statement, 2 letters of recommendation, interview, minimum GPA of 2.0 to 2.67.

CONTACT
Mr. Daniel Goertz, Recruitment Coordinator, University of the Fraser Valley, 33844 King Road, Abbotsford, BC V2S 7M8, Canada. *Phone:* 604-504-7441 Ext. 4693. *Toll-free phone:* 888-504-7441. *E-mail:* daniel.goertz@ufv.ca.

University of Toronto

Toronto, Ontario, Canada

http://www.utoronto.ca/

- **Province-supported** university, founded 1827
- **Urban** 714-hectare campus with easy access to Greater Toronto Area
- **Endowment** $2.4 billion
- **Coed**
- **Very difficult** entrance level

FACULTY
Student/faculty ratio: 24:1.

ACADEMICS
Calendar: fall/winter terms and a summer session. *Degrees:* certificates, diplomas, bachelor's, master's, and doctoral.
Library: Robarts Library plus 43 others. *Books:* 19.4 million (physical), 6.0 million (digital/electronic). Students can reserve study rooms.

STUDENT LIFE
Housing options: coed, women-only. Campus housing is university owned and leased by the school. Freshman campus housing is guaranteed.

Activities and organizations: drama/theater group, student-run newspaper, radio station, choral group, national fraternities, national sororities.

Athletics Member CIS.

Campus security: 24-hour emergency response devices and patrols, student patrols, late-night transport/escort service.

Student services: health clinic, personal/psychological counseling, women's center, legal services.

FINANCIAL AID
Financial Aid Of all full-time matriculated undergraduates who enrolled in 2017, 3,500 state and other part-time jobs.

APPLYING
Standardized Tests *Required:* SAT and SAT Subject Tests or ACT (for admission).

Options: electronic application, deferred entrance.

Application fee: $255 Canadian dollars.

Required: high school transcript. ***Required for some:*** essay or personal statement, interview.

CONTACT
University of Toronto, 27 King's College Circle, Toronto, ON M5S 1A1, Canada. *Phone:* 416-978-2190. *Fax:* 416-978-7022.

University of Victoria

Victoria, British Columbia, Canada

http://www.uvic.ca/

CONTACT
Mr. Bruno Rocca, Student Recruitment Director, University of Victoria, PO Box 1700, STN CSC, Victoria, BC V8W 2Y2, Canada. *Phone:* 250-721-8121 Ext. 8109. *Fax:* 250-721-6225. *E-mail:* admit@uvic.ca.

University of Waterloo

Waterloo, Ontario, Canada

http://www.uwaterloo.ca/

- **Province-supported** university, founded 1957
- **Suburban** 1112-acre campus with easy access to Toronto
- **Endowment** $294.5 million
- **Coed**
- **Moderately difficult** entrance level

FACULTY
Student/faculty ratio: 26:1.

ACADEMICS
Calendar: trimesters. *Degrees:* bachelor's, master's, and doctoral.
Library: Dana Porter Library plus 11 others. Students can reserve study rooms.

STUDENT LIFE
Housing options: coed. Campus housing is university owned. Freshman campus housing is guaranteed.

Activities and organizations: drama/theater group, student-run newspaper, choral group, marching band, national fraternities, national sororities.

Campus security: 24-hour emergency response devices and patrols, student patrols, late-night transport/escort service, controlled dormitory access.

Student services: health clinic, personal/psychological counseling, women's center, legal services.

COSTS
Costs (2018–19) ***Tuition:*** province resident $9262 Canadian dollars full-time, $737 Canadian dollars per course part-time; International tuition $33,289 Canadian dollars full-time. Full-time tuition and fees vary according to course load, degree level, program, and student level. Part-time tuition and fees vary according to course load, degree level, program, and student level. ***Required fees:*** $800 Canadian dollars full-time, $65 Canadian dollars per term part-time. ***Room and board:*** $10,525 Canadian dollars; room only: $5775 Canadian dollars. Room and board charges vary according to board plan, housing facility, and location.

APPLYING
Options: electronic application, early admission, deferred entrance.

Application fee: $140 Canadian dollars.

Required: high school transcript. ***Required for some:*** essay or personal statement, interview. ***Recommended:*** essay or personal statement.

CONTACT
University of Waterloo, 200 University Avenue West, Waterloo, ON N2L 3G1, Canada. *Phone:* 519-888-4567. *E-mail:* myapplication@uwaterloo.ca.

The University of Western Ontario

London, Ontario, Canada

http://www.uwo.ca/

CONTACT
Undergraduate Recruitment and Admissions, The University of Western Ontario, Western University, London, ON N6A 3K7, Canada. *Phone:* 519-661-2100. *Fax:* 519-661-3710. *E-mail:* reg-admissions@uwo.ca.

University of Windsor

Windsor, Ontario, Canada

http://www.uwindsor.ca/

CONTACT
Ms. Charlene Yates, Associate Registrar, University of Windsor, Office of the Registrar, 401 Sunset Avenue, Windsor, ON N9B 3P4, Canada. *Phone:* 519-253-3000 Ext. 3332. *Toll-free phone:* 800-864-2860. *Fax:* 519-971-3653. *E-mail:* registrar@uwindsor.ca.

The University of Winnipeg

Winnipeg, Manitoba, Canada

http://www.uwinnipeg.ca/

CONTACT
Mr. Colin Russell, Registrar, The University of Winnipeg, 515 Portage Avenue, Winnipeg, MB R3B 2E9, Canada. *Phone:* 204-786-9776. *Fax:* 204-786-8656. *E-mail:* admissions@uwinnipeg.ca.

Vancouver Island University

Nanaimo, British Columbia, Canada

http://www.viu.ca/

CONTACT
Mr. Andrew Amour, Associate Registrar, Admissions and Registration, Vancouver Island University, 900 Fifth Street, Nanaimo, BC V9R 5S5, Canada. *Phone:* 250-740-6355. *Fax:* 250-740-6479.

Vanguard College
Edmonton, Alberta, Canada
http://www.vanguardcollege.com/

CONTACT
Vanguard College, 12140 103rd Street, Edmonton, AB T5G 2J9, Canada. *Phone:* 780-452-0808 Ext. 231. *Toll-free phone:* 866-222-0808. *E-mail:* admissions@vanguardcollege.com.

Wilfrid Laurier University
Waterloo, Ontario, Canada
http://www.wlu.ca/

CONTACT
Wilfrid Laurier University, 75 University Avenue West, Waterloo, ON N2L 3C5, Canada. *Phone:* 519-884-0710 Ext. 6099.

York University
Toronto, Ontario, Canada
http://www.yorku.ca/

CONTACT
International Recruitment, York University, N301 Bennett Centre for Student Services, 4700 Keele Street, Toronto, ON M3J 1P3, Canada. *Phone:* 416-736-5825. *Fax:* 416-736-5741. *E-mail:* intlenq@yorku.ca.

INTERNATIONAL

BULGARIA

★ American University in Bulgaria
Blagoevgrad, Bulgaria
http://www.aubg.edu/

- **Independent** comprehensive, founded 1991
- **Small-town** 12-acre campus with easy access to Sofia, Bulgaria
- **Endowment** $27.4 million
- **Coed** 880 undergraduate students, 100% full-time, 54% women, 46% men
- **Very difficult** entrance level, 80% of applicants were admitted

UNDERGRAD STUDENTS
880 full-time. Students come from 40 other countries; 100% Race/ethnicity unknown; 0.6% transferred in; 77% live on campus.

Freshmen:
Admission: 579 applied, 462 admitted, 251 enrolled. ***Average high school GPA:*** 3.8. ***Test scores:*** SAT evidence-based reading and writing scores over 500: 89%; SAT math scores over 500: 92%; ACT scores over 18: 100%; SAT evidence-based reading and writing scores over 600: 53%; SAT math scores over 600: 78%; ACT scores over 24: 100%; SAT evidence-based reading and writing scores over 700: 3%; SAT math scores over 700: 31%; ACT scores over 30: 67%.

Retention: 94% of full-time freshmen returned.

FACULTY
Total: 83, 58% full-time, 70% with terminal degrees.

Student/faculty ratio: 16:1.

ACADEMICS
Calendar: semesters. *Degrees:* bachelor's and master's.

Special study options: advanced placement credit, double majors, honors programs, independent study, internships, services for LD students, student-designed majors, study abroad.

Computers: 373 computers/terminals and 8 ports are available on campus for general student use. Students can access the following: campus intranet, computer help desk, free student e-mail accounts, online (class) grades, online (class) registration, online (class) schedules. Campuswide network is available. 100% of college-owned or -operated housing units are wired for high-speed Internet access. Wireless service is available via entire campus.

Library: Panitza Library. *Books:* 122,369 (physical), 326,128 (digital/electronic); *Serial titles:* 170 (physical), 62,637 (digital/electronic); *Databases:* 34. Weekly public service hours: 56; study areas open 24 hours, 5–7 days a week; students can reserve study rooms.

STUDENT LIFE
Housing options: on-campus residence required through senior year; coed, special housing for students with disabilities. Campus housing is university owned. Freshman campus housing is guaranteed.

Activities and organizations: drama/theater group, student-run newspaper, radio station, choral group, Computer Science Student Union, AUBG Political Science Club, Better Community Club, AUBG Broadway Performance Club, Business Club.

Athletics *Intramural sports:* basketball M/W, cheerleading W(c), equestrian sports M(c)/W(c), football M(c), gymnastics W, soccer M(c), softball M/W, volleyball M/W.

Campus security: 24-hour emergency response devices and patrols, controlled dormitory access.

Student services: health clinic, personal/psychological counseling.

COSTS
Costs (2019–20) *Comprehensive fee:* $14,650 includes full-time tuition ($12,300), mandatory fees ($610), and room and board ($1740). Part-time tuition: $1025 per credit hour. ***College room only:*** $1440.

APPLYING
Standardized Tests *Required for some:* TOEFL, IELTS, or ESOL for students whose primary language is not English. *Recommended:* SAT or ACT (for admission).

Options: electronic application, early admission, deferred entrance.

Required: essay or personal statement, high school transcript, minimum 3.0 GPA, 2 letters of recommendation.

CONTACT
Ms. Boriana Shalyavska, Director of Admissions, American University in Bulgaria, 1 Izmirliev Square, 1st Floor, Blagoevgrad 2700. *Phone:* 359-73 888 218. *Fax:* 359-73 883 227. *E-mail:* admissions@aubg.edu.

EGYPT

The American University in Cairo
Cairo, Egypt
http://www.aucegypt.edu/

- **Independent** comprehensive, founded 1919
- **Suburban** 260-acre campus with easy access to Cairo
- **Endowment** $519
- **Coed**
- **Very difficult** entrance level

FACULTY
Student/faculty ratio: 11:1.

A ★ indicates that the school has detailed information with a Premium Profile on Petersons.com.

ACADEMICS
Calendar: semesters. *Degrees:* diplomas, bachelor's, master's, and doctoral (majority of students are Egyptians; enrollment open to all nationalities).
Library: American University in Cairo Library plus 1 other. *Books:* 546,020 (physical), 311,887 (digital/electronic); *Databases:* 123. Weekly public service hours: 80; students can reserve study rooms.

STUDENT LIFE
Housing options: men-only, women-only, special housing for students with disabilities. Campus housing is university owned and leased by the school. Freshman applicants given priority for college housing.

Activities and organizations: drama/theater group, student-run newspaper, choral group, AIESEC, Theater and Film Club, VIA, ACT, Mashrou3 Kheir.

Campus security: 24-hour emergency response devices and patrols, controlled dormitory access.

Student services: health clinic, personal/psychological counseling.

FINANCIAL AID
Financial Aid ***Average financial aid package:*** $3711. ***Average need-based gift aid:*** $2991. ***Financial aid deadline:*** 3/14.

APPLYING
Standardized Tests *Required for some:* SAT or ACT (for admission), SAT Subject Tests (for admission).

Options: electronic application, early admission, early action, deferred entrance.

Application fee: $85.

Required: essay or personal statement, high school transcript, minimum 2.0 GPA.

CONTACT
Ms. Randa Kamel, Chief Enrollment Officer, The American University in Cairo, AUC Avenue, PO Box 74 New Cairo 11835, Cairo, Egypt. *Phone:* 202-26154601. *E-mail:* randakamel@aucegypt.edu.

FRANCE

The American University of Paris

Paris, France

http://www.aup.edu/

- **Independent** comprehensive, founded 1962
- **Urban** campus with easy access to Paris, France
- **Endowment** $852,072
- **Coed**
- **Moderately difficult** entrance level

FACULTY
Student/faculty ratio: 9:1.

ACADEMICS
Calendar: semesters. *Degrees:* bachelor's and master's.
Library: AUP Library. *Books:* 41,927 (physical), 545,019 (digital/electronic); *Serial titles:* 28 (physical), 44,960 (digital/electronic); *Databases:* 48. Students can reserve study rooms.

STUDENT LIFE
Housing options: on-campus residence required for freshman yearCampus housing is provided by a third party.

Activities and organizations: drama/theater group, student-run newspaper, television station, choral group, AUP Student Media (ASM) - Print, Video, Audio, Student Government Association (SGA), Sports Association, BVSyria (Refugee Assistance), Environmental and Community Services Committee.

Campus security: 24-hour emergency response devices, valid student ID required for all building entries.

Student services: personal/psychological counseling.

COSTS & FINANCIAL AID
Costs (2018–19) ***Tuition:*** 30,080 euros full-time, 940 euros per credit part-time. Full-time tuition and fees vary according to degree level. Part-time tuition and fees vary according to course load and degree level. ***Required fees:*** 1340 euros full-time. ***Room only:*** Room and board charges vary according to housing facility.

Financial Aid Of all full-time matriculated undergraduates who enrolled in 2018, 291 applied for aid, 278 were judged to have need, 6 had their need fully met. In 2018, 10 non-need-based awards were made. ***Average percent of need met:*** 22. ***Average financial aid package:*** $12,931. ***Average need-based loan:*** $4741. ***Average need-based gift aid:*** $10,750. ***Average non-need-based aid:*** $4382. ***Average indebtedness upon graduation:*** $56,876.

APPLYING
Standardized Tests *Required for some:* TOEFL, TOEIC or IELTS for students whose primary language is not English. *Recommended:* SAT or ACT (for admission).

Options: electronic application, deferred entrance.

Application fee: $70.

Required: essay or personal statement, high school transcript, 2 letters of recommendation. ***Recommended:*** minimum 3.0 GPA, interview.

CONTACT
International Admissions Office Counselors, The American University of Paris, 5 boulevard de la Tour Maubourg, Paris 75007, France. *Phone:* -+33 1 40 62 07 20. *Fax:* +33 1 47 05 34 32. *E-mail:* admissions@aup.edu.

The New School–Parsons Paris

Paris, France

http://www.newschool.edu/parsons-paris/

- **Independent** comprehensive, founded 2013, part of The New School
- **Urban** campus with easy access to Paris
- **Endowment** $322.3 million
- **Coed**
- **Moderately difficult** entrance level

FACULTY
Student/faculty ratio: 8:1.

ACADEMICS
Calendar: semesters. *Degrees:* bachelor's and master's.
Library:***Books:*** 840,933 (digital/electronic); *Serial titles:* 113,452 (digital/electronic); *Databases:* 376.

STUDENT LIFE
Housing options: coed. Campus housing is provided by a third party. Freshman applicants given priority for college housing.

Activities and organizations: drama/theater group, student-run newspaper, choral group.

Campus security: 24-hour emergency response devices.

Student services: health clinic, personal/psychological counseling, legal services, veterans affairs office.

FINANCIAL AID
Financial Aid Of all full-time matriculated undergraduates who enrolled in 2017, 42 applied for aid, 31 were judged to have need, 1 had their need fully met. In 2017, 96 non-need-based awards were made. ***Average percent of need met:*** 54. ***Average financial aid package:*** $26,626. ***Average need-based loan:*** $5303. ***Average need-based gift aid:*** $8509. ***Average non-need-based aid:*** $9071. ***Average indebtedness upon graduation:*** $25,884.

APPLYING
Options: electronic application, early action, deferred entrance.

Application fee: $50.

Required: essay or personal statement, high school transcript, 2 letters of recommendation.

CONTACT
Mr. Mike Fakih, Director of Admissions, The New School–Parsons Paris, 79 Fifth Avenue, 5th floor, New York, NY 10011. *Phone:* 212-229-5150. *Toll-free phone:* 800-292-3040. *E-mail:* fakihm@newschool.edu.

Paris College of Art
Paris, France
http://www.paris.edu/

- **Independent** comprehensive
- **Urban** campus
- **Coed**

ACADEMICS
Calendar: semesters. *Degrees:* certificates, bachelor's, and master's.

STUDENT LIFE
Housing options: college housing not available.

Student services: personal/psychological counseling.

COSTS & FINANCIAL AID
Costs (2018–19) ***Tuition:*** 28,900 euros full-time. Full-time tuition and fees vary according to program. Part-time tuition and fees vary according to course load.

Financial Aid Of all full-time matriculated undergraduates who enrolled in 2010, 46 applied for aid, 41 were judged to have need. 40 state and other part-time jobs (averaging $2300). In 2010, 14 non-need-based awards were made. ***Average percent of need met:*** 75. ***Average financial aid package:*** $11,500. ***Average need-based gift aid:*** $8600. ***Average non-need-based aid:*** $4200. ***Financial aid deadline:*** 8/1.

APPLYING
Standardized Tests *Required for some:* SAT or ACT (for admission).

Required: essay or personal statement, high school transcript, interview. ***Required for some:*** letters of recommendation.

CONTACT
Paris College of Art, 15 rue Fénelon, 75010 Paris, France.

Schiller International University
Paris, France
http://www.schiller.edu/

CONTACT
Schiller International University, 9 rue d'Yvart, F-75015 Paris, France. *Toll-free phone:* 800-261-9571 (in-state); 800-261-9751 (out-of-state).

GERMANY

Schiller International University
Heidelberg, Germany
http://www.schiller.edu/

CONTACT
Ms. Kamala Dontamsetti, Associate Director of Admissions, Schiller International University, 300 East Bay Drive, Largo, FL 33770. *Phone:* 727-736-5082 Ext. 234. *Toll-free phone:* 800-261-9571 (in-state); 800-261-9751 (out-of-state). *Fax:* 727-734-0359. *E-mail:* kamala_dontamsetti@schiller.edu.

GREECE

American College of Thessaloniki
Pylea, Greece
http://www.act.edu/

- **Independent** comprehensive, founded 1886
- **Suburban** 62-acre campus with easy access to Thessaloniki
- **Endowment** $6.0 million
- **Coed** 512 undergraduate students, 89% full-time, 52% women, 48% men
- **Minimally difficult** entrance level, 96% of applicants were admitted

UNDERGRAD STUDENTS
457 full-time, 55 part-time. Students come from 26 other countries; 0.8% transferred in.

Freshmen:
Admission: 114 applied, 109 admitted, 75 enrolled. ***Average high school GPA:*** 3.4.

Retention: 87% of full-time freshmen returned.

FACULTY
Total: 64, 30% full-time, 45% with terminal degrees.

Student/faculty ratio: 18:1.

ACADEMICS
Calendar: semesters. *Degrees:* certificates, bachelor's, and master's.

Special study options: academic remediation for entering students, accelerated degree program, advanced placement credit, double majors, English as a second language, honors programs, independent study, internships, part-time degree program, services for LD students, study abroad, summer session for credit.

Computers: 165 computers/terminals and 30 ports are available on campus for general student use. Students can access the following: campus intranet, computer help desk, free student e-mail accounts, online (class) grades, online (class) schedules. Campuswide network is available. 100% of college-owned or -operated housing units are wired for high-speed Internet access. Wireless service is available via entire campus.
Library: Bissell Library plus 1 other. *Books:* 27,086 (physical), 190,171 (digital/electronic); *Serial titles:* 20 (physical), 42,603 (digital/electronic); *Databases:* 23. Weekly public service hours: 54; students can reserve study rooms.

STUDENT LIFE
Housing options: coed. Campus housing is university owned, leased by the school and is provided by a third party. Freshman applicants given priority for college housing.

Activities and organizations: drama/theater group, student-run newspaper, radio station, Model MUN, Tennis Club, The Geopolitical Circle, Painting Club, Photography Club.

Athletics ***Intercollegiate sports:*** basketball M, soccer M, table tennis M/W, tennis M/W. ***Intramural sports:*** basketball M, lacrosse M/W, sailing M/W, sand volleyball M/W, soccer M, table tennis M/W, tennis M/W, volleyball M/W.

Campus security: 24-hour emergency response devices and patrols, controlled dormitory access.

Student services: health clinic, personal/psychological counseling.

COSTS
Costs (2019–20) ***One-time required fee:*** 70 euros. ***Tuition:*** 8400 euros full-time, 280 euros per credit part-time. ***Required fees:*** 100 euros full-time.

APPLYING
Options: electronic application, deferred entrance.

Application fee: 75 euros.

Required: high school transcript, CV. ***Required for some:*** essay or personal statement, interview. ***Recommended:*** minimum 2.0 GPA.

Application deadlines: rolling (freshmen), rolling (transfers).

Notification: continuous (freshmen), continuous (transfers).

CONTACT
Mrs. Roula Lebetli, Director of Admissions, American College of Thessaloniki, PO Box 21021, Pylea, Thessaloniki 55510. *Phone:* 30-2310-398239. *Fax:* 30-2310-398389. *E-mail:* admissions@act.edu.

DEREE - The American College of Greece
Athens, Greece
http://www.acg.edu/

- **Independent** comprehensive, founded 1875
- **Suburban** 64-acre campus with easy access to Athens
- **Coed** 3,317 undergraduate students, 39% full-time, 53% women, 47% men
- **Moderately difficult** entrance level, 83% of applicants were admitted

UNDERGRAD STUDENTS
1,280 full-time, 2,037 part-time. Students come from 62 other countries; 3% transferred in; 9% live on campus.

Freshmen:
Admission: 599 applied, 499 admitted, 429 enrolled. ***Average high school GPA:*** 3.3.
Retention: 84% of full-time freshmen returned.

FACULTY
Total: 302, 50% full-time.
Student/faculty ratio: 11:1.

ACADEMICS
Calendar: semesters 2 summer sessions. *Degrees:* bachelor's, master's, and postbachelor's certificates.
Special study options: academic remediation for entering students, accelerated degree program, adult/continuing education programs, advanced placement credit, double majors, English as a second language, honors programs, independent study, internships, part-time degree program, services for LD students, student-designed majors, study abroad, summer session for credit.
Computers: 306 computers/terminals are available on campus for general student use. Students can access the following: computer help desk, free student e-mail accounts, online (class) grades, online (class) registration, online (class) schedules, learning management system. Campuswide network is available. 100% of college-owned or -operated housing units are wired for high-speed Internet access. Wireless service is available via computer centers, computer labs, dorm rooms, learning centers, libraries.
Library: John S. Bailey Library plus 1 other. *Books:* 129,000 (physical), 316,000 (digital/electronic); *Serial titles:* 60 (physical), 13,000 (digital/electronic); *Databases:* 45. Weekly public service hours: 72; students can reserve study rooms.

STUDENT LIFE
Housing options: coed, special housing for students with disabilities. Campus housing is university owned. Freshman applicants given priority for college housing.
Activities and organizations: drama/theater group, student-run newspaper, choral group, DEREE Ambassadors, DEREE Orientation Leaders, Debate Club, DEREE SAB (Student Activities Board), Innovation and Entrepreneurship Clib.
Athletics *Intercollegiate sports:* basketball M(s)/W(s), rugby M, soccer M(s)/W, swimming and diving M/W, volleyball M/W(s), water polo M. ***Intramural sports:*** archery M/W, basketball M/W, rock climbing M/W, soccer M/W, swimming and diving M/W, table tennis M/W, tennis M/W, track and field M/W, volleyball M/W.
Campus security: 24-hour emergency response devices and patrols, controlled dormitory access.
Student services: health clinic, personal/psychological counseling.

COSTS & FINANCIAL AID
Costs (2019–20) *Tuition:* $13,120 full-time. No tuition increase for student's term of enrollment. ***Required fees:*** $1240 full-time.
Financial Aid *Financial aid deadline:* 9/1.

APPLYING
Options: electronic application, deferred entrance.
Required: essay or personal statement, high school transcript, minimum 2.1 GPA, 1 letter of recommendation, interview.
Application deadlines: rolling (freshmen), rolling (transfers).
Notification: continuous until 6/15 (freshmen), 6/15 (transfers).

CONTACT
Ms. Loukia Kanatsouli, Dean of Enrollment and International Students, DEREE - The American College of Greece, 6 Gravias Street, Aghia Paraskevi, Athens 15342, Greece. *Phone:* 30-210-600-9800 Ext. 1474. *Fax:* 30-210-608-2344. *E-mail:* lkanatsouli@acg.edu.

IRELAND

American College Dublin
Dublin, Ireland
http://www.amcd.ie/

CONTACT
American College Dublin, 2 Merrion Square, Dublin 2, Ireland.

Institute of Public Administration
Dublin, Ireland
http://www.ipa.ie/

CONTACT
Dr. Denis O'Brien, Registrar, Institute of Public Administration, 57-61 Lansdowne Road, Dublin 4, Ireland. *Phone:* 353-1-240-3600. *Fax:* 353-1-668-9135. *E-mail:* undergrad@ipa.ie.

ITALY

★ The American University of Rome
Rome, Italy
http://www.aur.edu/

CONTACT
Ms. Jessica York, Admissions Counselor, The American University of Rome, Via Pietro Roselli 4, Rome 00153, Italy. *Phone:* -+39 0658330919. *Toll-free phone:* 877-592-1287. *Fax:* +39 0658330992. *E-mail:* admissions@aur.edu.

See next page for display ad and page 970 for the College Close-Up.

John Cabot University
Rome, Italy
http://www.johncabot.edu/

- **Independent** comprehensive, founded 1972
- **Urban** campus with easy access to Rome
- **Coed** 1,497 undergraduate students
- 58% of applicants were admitted

UNDERGRAD STUDENTS
Students come from 40 states and territories; 70 other countries; 46% live on campus.

Freshmen:
Admission: 791 applied, 461 admitted. ***Average high school GPA:*** 3.1.
Retention: 98% of full-time freshmen returned.

FACULTY
Total: 150, 23% full-time, 63% with terminal degrees.
Student/faculty ratio: 9:1.

ACADEMICS
Calendar: semesters. *Degrees:* associate, bachelor's, and master's.
Special study options: adult/continuing education programs, advanced placement credit, double majors, English as a second language, freshman honors college, honors programs, independent study, internships, part-time degree program, services for LD students, study abroad, summer session for credit.
Computers: 153 computers/terminals are available on campus for general student use. Students can access the following: campus intranet, computer help desk, free student e-mail accounts, online (class) grades, online (class) registration, online (class) schedules. Campuswide network is available. 100% of college-owned or -operated housing units are wired for high-speed Internet access. Wireless service is available via entire campus.
Library: Frohring Library. *Books:* 34,218 (physical); *Databases:* 39. Weekly public service hours: 86; students can reserve study rooms.

STUDENT LIFE
Housing options: coed, men-only, women-only, special housing for students with disabilities. Campus housing is leased by the school and is provided by a third party. Freshman campus housing is guaranteed.

Activities and organizations: drama/theater group, student-run newspaper, Student Government, Model United Nations, Student Newspaper, Queer Alliance Club, Grassroots.

Athletics ***Intercollegiate sports:*** basketball M/W, soccer M/W, volleyball M/W. ***Intramural sports:*** basketball M/W, cheerleading M/W, cross-country running M/W, skiing (downhill) M/W, soccer M/W, volleyball M/W, weight lifting M(c)/W(c).

Campus security: 24-hour emergency response devices and patrols, controlled dormitory access.

Student services: health clinic, personal/psychological counseling.

COSTS
Costs (2019–20) ***Comprehensive fee:*** $35,890 includes full-time tuition ($24,900) and room and board ($10,990). No tuition increase for student's term of enrollment. ***College room only:*** $9800.

APPLYING
Standardized Tests *Required for some:* SAT or ACT (for admission), SAT and SAT Subject Tests or ACT (for admission).

Options: early admission, early decision, early action, deferred entrance.

Application fee: $50.

Required: essay or personal statement, high school transcript, 2 letters of recommendation, interview. ***Required for some:*** English Proficiency for non-US applicants. ***Recommended:*** minimum 2.5 GPA.

Application deadlines: 3/31 (freshmen), 3/1 (out-of-state freshmen), 6/1 (transfers), 11/15 (early action).

Early decision deadline: 11/15.

Notification: 8/5 (freshmen), 4/1 (out-of-state freshmen), 6/15 (transfers), 12/15 (early action).

CONTACT
Ms. Stefania Corrado, Associate Coordinator of DS Admissions, John Cabot University, Roma 00165. *Phone:* 855-528-7662. *Toll-free phone:* 855-528-7662. *E-mail:* admissions@johncabot.edu.

See previous page for display ad and page 1026 for the College Close-Up.

KENYA

United States International University–Africa

Nairobi, Kenya

http://www.usiu.ac.ke/

CONTACT
United States International University–Africa, PO Box 14634, Thika Road Kasarani, Nairobi 00800, Kenya. *Phone:* 254-02-3606563.

LEBANON

American University of Beirut

Beirut, Lebanon

http://www.aub.edu.lb/

- **Independent** university, founded 1866
- **Urban** 61-acre campus with easy access to Beirut
- **Endowment** $731.4 million
- **Coed** 7,341 undergraduate students, 95% full-time, 49% women, 51% men
- 70% of applicants were admitted

UNDERGRAD STUDENTS
6,964 full-time, 377 part-time. Students come from 79 other countries; 0.4% transferred in; 15% live on campus.

Freshmen:
Admission: 5,178 applied, 3,600 admitted, 1,848 enrolled. ***Test scores:*** SAT evidence-based reading and writing scores over 500: 18%; SAT math scores over 500: 20%; SAT evidence-based reading and writing scores over 600: 6%; SAT math scores over 600: 15%; SAT evidence-based reading and writing scores over 700: 1%; SAT math scores over 700: 6%.

Retention: 92% of full-time freshmen returned.

FACULTY
Total: 1,200, 76% full-time, 60% with terminal degrees.

Student/faculty ratio: 11:1.

ACADEMICS
Calendar: semesters. *Degrees:* certificates, diplomas, bachelor's, master's, doctoral, and postbachelor's certificates.

Special study options: academic remediation for entering students, advanced placement credit, double majors, English as a second language, honors programs, independent study, internships, services for LD students, study abroad, summer session for credit.

Computers: 1,760 computers/terminals and 1,452 ports are available on campus for general student use. Students can access the following: campus intranet, computer help desk, free student e-mail accounts, online (class) grades, online (class) registration, online (class) schedules. Campuswide network is available. 100% of college-owned or -operated housing units are wired for high-speed Internet access. Wireless service is available via entire campus.

Library: Jafet Library plus 3 others. *Books:* 400,000 (physical), 1.0 million (digital/electronic); *Serial titles:* 500 (physical), 130,000 (digital/electronic); *Databases:* 350. Weekly public service hours: 107; study areas open 24 hours, 5–7 days a week; students can reserve study rooms.

STUDENT LIFE
Housing options: on-campus residence required for freshman year; men-only, women-only. Campus housing is university owned. Freshman campus housing is guaranteed.

Activities and organizations: drama/theater group, student-run newspaper, choral group, Red Cross Club, Biology Society, Business Society, Music Club, Institute of Electrical and Electronics Engineer IEEE.

Athletics ***Intercollegiate sports:*** archery M/W, badminton M/W, basketball M(s)/W(s), cheerleading M/W, cross-country running M(s)/W(s), football M(s)/W(s), rugby M(s)/W(s), soccer M(s)/W(s), squash M/W, swimming and diving M(s)/W(s), table tennis M(s)/W(s), tennis M(s)/W(s), track and field M(s)/W(s), ultimate Frisbee M(s)/W(s), volleyball M(s)/W(s), water polo M(s)/W(s). ***Intramural sports:*** football M/W, rugby M/W, soccer M/W.

Campus security: 24-hour emergency response devices and patrols, late-night transport/escort service, controlled dormitory access.

Student services: health clinic, personal/psychological counseling, legal services.

FINANCIAL AID
Financial Aid Of all full-time matriculated undergraduates who enrolled in 2017, 3,870 applied for aid, 3,033 were judged to have need. 24 state and other part-time jobs (averaging $2256). In 2017, 33 non-need-based awards were made. ***Average need-based loan:*** $6697. ***Average non-need-based aid:*** $24,720. ***Average indebtedness upon graduation:*** $19,214. ***Financial aid deadline:*** 12/20.

APPLYING
Standardized Tests *Required:* SAT (for admission). *Required for some:* SAT Subject Tests (for admission), TOEFL, IELTS.

Options: electronic application, early admission, early decision, early action, deferred entrance.

Application fee: $80.

Required: high school transcript. ***Required for some:*** essay or personal statement, 2 letters of recommendation, interview.

Application deadlines: 12/20 (freshmen), 12/20 (out-of-state freshmen).

Early decision deadline: 10/31.

Notification: 3/30 (freshmen), 3/30 (out-of-state freshmen), continuous (transfers), 1/31 (early decision).

CONTACT
Dr. Salim Kanaan, Director of Admissions Office, American University of Beirut, PO Box 11-0236, Riad El-Solh, 1107 2020. *Phone:* 961-1374374 Ext. 2592. *Fax:* 961-1750775. *E-mail:* admissions@aub.edu.lb.

Lebanese American University

Beirut, Lebanon

http://www.lau.edu.lb/

- **Private** comprehensive, founded 1835
- **Urban** 50-acre campus with easy access to Beirut, Byblos, Tripoli
- **Endowment** $516.7 million
- **Coed** 7,433 undergraduate students, 94% full-time, 50% women, 50% men
- **Moderately difficult** entrance level, 90% of applicants were admitted

UNDERGRAD STUDENTS
7,012 full-time, 421 part-time. Students come from 78 other countries; 19% are from out of state; 0.9% transferred in; 5% live on campus.

Freshmen:
Admission: 4,852 applied, 4,346 admitted, 1,657 enrolled. ***Average high school GPA:*** 2.8. ***Test scores:*** SAT evidence-based reading and writing scores over 500: 60%; SAT math scores over 500: 87%; SAT evidence-based reading and writing scores over 600: 14%; SAT math scores over 600: 47%; SAT evidence-based reading and writing scores over 700: 1%; SAT math scores over 700: 13%.

Retention: 87% of full-time freshmen returned.

FACULTY
Total: 815, 38% full-time, 51% with terminal degrees.

Student/faculty ratio: 16:1.

ACADEMICS
Calendar: semesters. *Degrees:* bachelor's, master's, doctoral, and postbachelor's certificates.

Special study options: academic remediation for entering students, advanced placement credit, double majors, honors programs, internships, part-time degree program, services for LD students, study abroad, summer session for credit.

Computers: 1,948 computers/terminals and 2,200 ports are available on campus for general student use. Students can access the following: campus intranet, computer help desk, free student e-mail accounts, online (class) grades, online (class) registration, online (class) schedules, online forms requests, online and mobile course management system. Campuswide network is available. 100% of college-owned or -operated housing units are wired for high-speed Internet access. Wireless service is available via entire campus.

Library: LAU Libraries plus 3 others. *Books:* 424,537 (physical), 556,586 (digital/electronic); *Serial titles:* 473 (physical), 131,038 (digital/electronic); *Databases:* 154. Weekly public service hours: 88; students can reserve study rooms.

STUDENT LIFE
Housing options: coed, men-only, women-only, special housing for students with disabilities. Campus housing is university owned, leased by the school and is provided by a third party.

Activities and organizations: drama/theater group, student-run newspaper, choral group, Event Organization Club, Astronomy Club, Human Rights Club, International Affairs Club, Red Cross Club.

Athletics ***Intercollegiate sports:*** badminton M/W, basketball M(s)/W(s), cheerleading M/W, cross-country running M/W, rugby M(s)/W, skiing (downhill) W, soccer M(s)/W(s), swimming and diving M(s)/W(s), table tennis M(s)/W(s), tennis M(s)/W(s), track and field M(s)/W(s), triathlon M(s), volleyball M(s)/W(s), water polo M(s). ***Intramural sports:*** archery M/W, basketball M/W, soccer M/W, swimming and diving M/W, table tennis M/W, tennis M/W, volleyball M/W.

Campus security: 24-hour emergency response devices and patrols.

Student services: health clinic, personal/psychological counseling, women's center.

COSTS
Costs (2018–19) ***Tuition:*** $17,940 full-time, $757 per credit part-time. Full-time tuition and fees vary according to course load, degree level, and program. Part-time tuition and fees vary according to course load, degree level, and program. ***Required fees:*** $415 full-time, $235 per year part-time. ***Room only:*** Room and board charges vary according to housing facility and location. ***Payment plans:*** installment, deferred payment. ***Waivers:*** employees or children of employees.

APPLYING
Standardized Tests *Required:* SAT or ACT (for admission). *Required for some:* SAT and SAT Subject Tests or ACT (for admission), SAT Subject Tests (for admission), Institutional English Test (English Entrance Exam EEE) or International TOFEL.

Options: electronic application, deferred entrance.

Application fee: $85.

Required: high school transcript, minimum 2.0 GPA.

Application deadlines: 7/15 (freshmen), 7/15 (out-of-state freshmen), 7/15 (transfers).

Notification: continuous (freshmen), continuous (out-of-state freshmen), continuous (transfers).

CONTACT
Nada Hajj, University Director of Admissions, Lebanese American University, PO Box 13-5053 Chouran Beirut 1102 2801, Lebanon, Beirut. *Phone:* 961-1786456 Ext. 1111. *Fax:* 961-1786456. *E-mail:* nhajj@lau.edu.lb.

MEXICO

Instituto Tecnológico y de Estudios Superiores de Monterrey, Campus Central de Veracruz

Córdoba, Mexico

http://www.itesm.mx/

CONTACT
Ing. Luis Pablo Villareal, Registrar, Instituto Tecnológico y de Estudios Superiores de Monterrey, Campus Central de Veracruz, Avenida Eugenio Garza Sada 1, Apartado Postal 314, 94500 Córdoba, Veracruz, Mexico. *Phone:* -27-13-23-40 Ext. 123.

Instituto Tecnológico y de Estudios Superiores de Monterrey, Campus Chiapas

Tuxtla Gutiérrez, Mexico

http://www.itesm.mx/

CONTACT
Lic. Luis Enrique Cancino, Registrar, Instituto Tecnológico y de Estudios Superiores de Monterrey, Campus Chiapas, Carretera a Tapanatepec Km 149&746, Apartado Postal 312, 29000 Tuxtla Gutiérrez, Chiapas, Mexico. *Phone:* -96-15-1723.

Instituto Tecnológico y de Estudios Superiores de Monterrey, Campus Chihuahua

Chihuahua, Mexico

http://www.itesm.mx/

CONTACT
Ing. Juan Manuel Fernandez, Registrar, Instituto Tecnológico y de Estudios Superiores de Monterrey, Campus Chihuahua, Colegio Militar 4700, Colonia Nombre de Dios, Apartado Postal 728, 31300 Chihuahua, Chihuahua, Mexico. *Phone:* -14-17-48-58 Ext. 117.

Instituto Tecnológico y de Estudios Superiores de Monterrey, Campus Ciudad de México

Ciudad de Mexico, Mexico

http://www.itesm.mx/

CONTACT

Admissions Office, Instituto Tecnológico y de Estudios Superiores de Monterrey, Campus Ciudad de México, Calle del Puente #222 esquina con Periférico, 14380 Colonia Huipulco, Tlalpan, MDF, Mexico. *Phone:* -5-673-6488.

Instituto Tecnológico y de Estudios Superiores de Monterrey, Campus Ciudad Juárez

Ciudad Juárez, Mexico

http://www.itesm.mx/

CONTACT

Lic. Alberto Trejo, Registrar, Instituto Tecnológico y de Estudios Superiores de Monterrey, Campus Ciudad Juárez, Boulevard Tomas Fernandez y Avenida A J Bermudez, Apartado Postal 3105-J, 32320 Ciudad Juárez, Chihuahua, Mexico. *Phone:* -16-17-88-07 Ext. 113.

Instituto Tecnológico y de Estudios Superiores de Monterrey, Campus Ciudad Obregón

Ciudad Obregón, Mexico

http://www.itesm.mx/

CONTACT

Lic. Judith Almeida, Registrar, Instituto Tecnológico y de Estudios Superiores de Monterrey, Campus Ciudad Obregón, Dr Norman E Borlaug Km 14, Apartado Postal 662, 85000 Ciudad Obregón, Sonora, Mexico. *Phone:* -64-15-03-12.

Instituto Tecnológico y de Estudios Superiores de Monterrey, Campus Colima

Colima, Mexico

http://www.itesm.mx/

CONTACT

Lic. Manuel Perez Rivera, Registrar, Instituto Tecnológico y de Estudios Superiores de Monterrey, Campus Colima, Prolongacion Ignacio Sandoval s/n, Fraccionamiento Jardines de Vista Hermosa, Apartado Postal 190, 28010 Colima, Colima, Mexico. *Phone:* -33-12-53-39.

Instituto Tecnológico y de Estudios Superiores de Monterrey, Campus Cuernavaca

Temixco, Mexico

http://www.itesm.mx/

CONTACT

Lic. Miguel Angel Machua, Registrar, Instituto Tecnológico y de Estudios Superiores de Monterrey, Campus Cuernavaca, Paseo de la Reforma 182-A, Colonia Lomas de Cuernavaca, 62000 Temixco, Morelos, Mexico. *Phone:* -73 18-49-57.

Instituto Tecnológico y de Estudios Superiores de Monterrey, Campus Estado de México

Estado de Mexico, Mexico

http://www.itesm.mx/

CONTACT

Prof. Jose de Jesus Molina, Registrar, Instituto Tecnológico y de Estudios Superiores de Monterrey, Campus Estado de México, Carretera Lago de Guadalupe Km. 3.5, Atizapan de Zaragoza, Estado de Mexico 52926, Mexico. *Phone:* -5-873-3600.

Instituto Tecnológico y de Estudios Superiores de Monterrey, Campus Guadalajara

Zapopan, Mexico

http://www.itesm.mx/

CONTACT

Ms. Janet Martell Sotomayor, Registration Director, Instituto Tecnológico y de Estudios Superiores de Monterrey, Campus Guadalajara, Avenida General Ramón Corona 2514, Colonia Nuevo Mexico, 45140 Zapopan, Jalisco, Mexico. *Phone:* -3-669-3006.

Instituto Tecnológico y de Estudios Superiores de Monterrey, Campus Hidalgo

Pachuca, Mexico

http://www.itesm.mx/

CONTACT

Lic. Lizbet Melo, Registrar, Instituto Tecnológico y de Estudios Superiores de Monterrey, Campus Hidalgo, Boulevard Felipe Angeles s/n al lado de la Unidad Deportiva, Apartado Postal 337, 42090 Pachuca, Hidalgo, Mexico. *Phone:* -714-25-00 Ext. 128.

Instituto Tecnológico y de Estudios Superiores de Monterrey, Campus Irapuato

Irapuato, Mexico

http://www.itesm.mx/

CONTACT

Ing. Marcela Beltrán, Registrar, Instituto Tecnológico y de Estudios Superiores de Monterrey, Campus Irapuato, Paseo Mirador del Valle No. 445, Col. Villas de Irapuato, Apartado Postal 568, 36660 Irapuato, Guanajuato, Mexico. *Phone:* -46-230342.

Instituto Tecnológico y de Estudios Superiores de Monterrey, Campus Laguna

Torreón, Mexico

http://www.itesm.mx/

CONTACT

Ing. Aroldo Camargo Soto, Registrar, Instituto Tecnológico y de Estudios Superiores de Monterrey, Campus Laguna, Paseo del Tecnologico s/n Ampliacion La Rosita, Apartado Postal 506, 27250 Torreón, Coahuila, Mexico. *Phone:* -17-20-66-61 Ext. 23.

Instituto Tecnológico y de Estudios Superiores de Monterrey, Campus León

León, Mexico

http://www.itesm.mx/

CONTACT
Lic. Eddie Villegas, Registrar, Instituto Tecnológico y de Estudios Superiores de Monterrey, Campus León, Avenida Eugenio Garza Sada s/n Colonia Cerro Gordo, Apartado Postal 872, 37120 León, Guanajuato, Mexico. *Phone:* -47-17-10-00 Ext. 131.

Instituto Tecnológico y de Estudios Superiores de Monterrey, Campus Monterrey

Monterrey, Mexico

http://www.itesm.mx/

CONTACT
Lic. Carlos Ordoñez, International Student Advisor, Instituto Tecnológico y de Estudios Superiores de Monterrey, Campus Monterrey, Avenida Eugenio Garza Sada 2501 Sur Colonia Tecnnologico, Sucursal de Correos J, 64849 Monterrey, Nuevo León, Mexico. *Phone:* -52 81 8328 4065 Ext. 3942.

Instituto Tecnológico y de Estudios Superiores de Monterrey, Campus Querétaro

Santiago de Querétaro, Mexico

http://www.itesm.mx/

CONTACT
Lic. Marco Vinicio Lopez, Registrar, Instituto Tecnológico y de Estudios Superiores de Monterrey, Campus Querétaro, Avenida Epigmenio González #500, Apartado Postal 37, 76130 Querétaro, Querétaro, Mexico. *Phone:* -42-17-38-25 Ext. 156.

Instituto Tecnológico y de Estudios Superiores de Monterrey, Campus Saltillo

Saltillo, Mexico

http://www.itesm.mx/

CONTACT
Lic. Esteban Ramos, Registrar, Instituto Tecnológico y de Estudios Superiores de Monterrey, Campus Saltillo, Prolongacion Juan de la Barrera 1241 Ote, Apartado Postal 539, 25270 Saltillo, Coahuila, Mexico. *Phone:* -84-15-06-90 Ext. 12.

Instituto Tecnológico y de Estudios Superiores de Monterrey, Campus San Luis Potosí

San Luis Potosí, Mexico

http://www.itesm.mx/

CONTACT
Ing. Consuelo Gonzalez, Registrar, Instituto Tecnológico y de Estudios Superiores de Monterrey, Campus San Luis Potosí, Avenida Robles 600, Colonia Jacarandas, Apartado Postal 1473 Suc E, 78140 San Luis Potosí, SLP, Mexico. *Phone:* -48 13-3441 Ext. 14.

Instituto Tecnológico y de Estudios Superiores de Monterrey, Campus Sinaloa

Culiacán, Mexico

http://www.itesm.mx/

CONTACT
Lic. Hugo Guerrero, Registrar, Instituto Tecnológico y de Estudios Superiores de Monterrey, Campus Sinaloa, Boulevard Culiacán 3773, Apartado Postal 69-F, 80800 Culiacán, Sinaloa, Mexico. *Phone:* -67-14-03-69.

Instituto Tecnológico y de Estudios Superiores de Monterrey, Campus Sonora Norte

Hermosillo, Mexico

http://www.itesm.mx/

CONTACT
Ing. Victor Eduardo Perez Orozco, Library and Admissions/Registration Director, Instituto Tecnológico y de Estudios Superiores de Monterrey, Campus Sonora Norte, Carretera Hermosillo-Nogales Km 9, Apartado Postal 216, 83000 Hermosillo, Sonora, Mexico. *Phone:* -62-15-52-05 Ext. 131.

Instituto Tecnológico y de Estudios Superiores de Monterrey, Campus Tampico

Altimira, Mexico

http://www.itesm.mx/

CONTACT
Ing. Javier Ponce, Registrar, Instituto Tecnológico y de Estudios Superiores de Monterrey, Campus Tampico, Boulevard Petrocel Km 1.3, Corredor Industrial, Carretera Tampico-Mante, 89120 Altimira, Tamaulipas, Mexico. *Phone:* -126-4-19-79.

Instituto Tecnológico y de Estudios Superiores de Monterrey, Campus Toluca

Toluca, Mexico

http://www.itesm.mx/

CONTACT
Ing. Victor M. Martinez Orta, Registrar, Instituto Tecnológico y de Estudios Superiores de Monterrey, Campus Toluca, Ex-hacienda La Pila, 100 metros al norte de San Antonio Buenavista, 50252 Toluca, Estado de Mexico, Mexico. *Phone:* -72-74-11-92.

Instituto Tecnológico y de Estudios Superiores de Monterrey, Campus Zacatecas

Zacatecas, Mexico

http://www.itesm.mx/

CONTACT
Lic. de Lourdes Zorrilla, Business Affairs Director and Registrar, Instituto Tecnológico y de Estudios Superiores de Monterrey, Campus Zacatecas, Calzada Pedro Coronel #16, Frente al Club Bernades, Municipio de Guadalupe, 98000 Zacatecas, Zacatecas, Mexico. *Phone:* -49 23-00-40.

Universidad de las Americas, A.C.
Mexico City, Mexico
http://www.udladf.mx/

CONTACT
Universidad de las Americas, A.C., Calle de Puebla 223, Col. Roma, 06700 Mexico City, Mexico.

Universidad de las Américas Puebla
Puebla, Mexico
http://www.udlap.mx/

CONTACT
Miss Madet Ruisenor-Quintero, Director of Student Enrollment Office, Universidad de las Américas Puebla, Ex-Hacienda Santa Catarina Martir, Cholula, Puebla 72820, Mexico. *Phone:* -52 229-2024.

Universidad de Monterrey
San Pedro Garza Garcia, Mexico
http://www.udem.edu.mx/

CONTACT
Universidad de Monterrey, Av. Ignacio Morones Prieto 4500 Pte, 66238 San Pedro Garza Garcia, NL, Mexico. *Toll-free phone:* 800-801-UDEM.

MONACO

The International University of Monaco
Monte Carlo, Monaco
http://www.monaco.edu/

CONTACT
Dr. Gisele Dudognon, Director of Admissions, The International University of Monaco, 2, Avenue Albert II, MC-98000 Principality of Monaco, Monaco. *Phone:* -377 97986 994. *Fax:* 377 92052 830. *E-mail:* gdudognon@monaco.edu.

SOUTH AFRICA

University of South Africa
Pretoria, South Africa
http://www.unisa.ac.za/

CONTACT
Contact Centre, University of South Africa, PO Box 392, Pretoria 0003, South Africa. *Phone:* 27-11 670-9000. *Fax:* 012 429 4150. *E-mail:* study-info@unisa.ac.za.

SPAIN

Saint Louis University–Madrid Campus
Madrid, Spain
http://www.slu.edu/madrid

- **Independent Roman Catholic (Jesuit)** comprehensive, founded 1967
- **Urban** 1-acre campus with easy access to Madrid, Spain
- **Coed**
- **Moderately difficult** entrance level

FACULTY
Student/faculty ratio: 11:1.

ACADEMICS
Calendar: semesters. *Degrees:* bachelor's and master's.
Library: Main Library plus 1 other. Students can reserve study rooms.

STUDENT LIFE
Housing options: men-only, women-only. Campus housing is provided by a third party. Freshman campus housing is guaranteed.
Activities and organizations: drama/theater group, student-run newspaper, choral group, Student Government, Campus Ambassadors, Student Magazine, Theatre Club, Babel Language Exchange.
Campus security: 24-hour emergency response devices.
Student services: personal/psychological counseling, veterans affairs office.

COSTS
Costs (2018–19) ***One-time required fee:*** 225 euros. ***Comprehensive fee:*** 28,260 euros includes full-time tuition (20,460 euros), mandatory fees (180 euros), and room and board (7620 euros). Part-time tuition and fees vary according to course load and degree level. ***College room only:*** 4600 euros. Room and board charges vary according to housing facility.

APPLYING
Standardized Tests *Required for some:* IB, A-Levels, French Baccalaureate, Selectividad, Maturita, or Abitur.
Options: electronic application, deferred entrance.
Required: essay or personal statement, high school transcript, minimum 2.5 GPA. ***Recommended:*** 2 letters of recommendation.

CONTACT
Ms. Heidi Buffington, Director of Admissions, Saint Louis University–Madrid Campus, Avenida del Valle, 34, Madrid 28003, Spain. *Phone:* -34 91-554-5858 Ext. 206. *Fax:* 34 91-554-6202. *E-mail:* heidi.buffington@slu.edu.

Schiller International University
Madrid, Spain
http://www.schiller.edu/

CONTACT
Ms. Kamala Dontamsetti, Associate Director of Admissions, Schiller International University, 300 East Bay Drive, Largo, FL 33700. *Phone:* 727-736-5082 Ext. 234. *Toll-free phone:* 800-261-9571 (in-state); 800-261-9751 (out-of-state). *Fax:* 727-734-0359. *E-mail:* admissions@schiller.edu.

SWITZERLAND

Ecole Hôtelière de Lausanne
Lausanne, Switzerland
http://www.ehl.edu/

CONTACT
Ecole Hôtelière de Lausanne, Route de Cojonnex 18, Le Chalet-a-Gobet, CH-1000 Lausanne 25, Switzerland. *Phone:* -41 21 785 1111.

Franklin University Switzerland
Sorengo, Switzerland
http://www.fus.edu/

- **Independent** comprehensive, founded 1969
- **Suburban** 7-acre campus with easy access to Milan, Italy
- **Coed**
- **Moderately difficult** entrance level

FACULTY
Student/faculty ratio: 9:1.

ACADEMICS
Calendar: semesters. *Degrees:* bachelor's and master's.
Library: David R. Grace Library plus 2 others.

STUDENT LIFE
Housing options: on-campus residence required through sophomore year; coed. Campus housing is university owned and leased by the school. Freshman campus housing is guaranteed.

Activities and organizations: drama/theater group, student-run newspaper, Student Government Association, Newspaper, Literary Society, Drama Club, Peer Educators Program.

Campus security: 24-hour emergency response devices, student patrols, late-night transport/escort service, controlled dormitory access, late night patrols by professional security service personnel.

Student services: health clinic, personal/psychological counseling.

COSTS & FINANCIAL AID
Costs (2018–19) ***Comprehensive fee:*** $54,310 includes full-time tuition ($39,600), mandatory fees ($1420), and room and board ($13,290). ***College room only:*** $10,900.

Financial Aid Of all full-time matriculated undergraduates who enrolled in 2017, 147 applied for aid, 127 were judged to have need. In 2017, 82 non-need-based awards were made. ***Average financial aid package:*** $25,897. ***Average need-based loan:*** $4312. ***Average need-based gift aid:*** $20,157. ***Average non-need-based aid:*** $12,287.

APPLYING
Options: electronic application, deferred entrance.

Application fee: $90.

Required: essay or personal statement, high school transcript, minimum 2.0 GPA, 3 letters of recommendation. ***Recommended:*** interview.

CONTACT
Franklin University Switzerland, Via Ponte Tresa 29, CH-6924 Sorengo, Switzerland.

Glion Institute of Higher Education
Glion-sur-Montreux, Switzerland
http://www.glion.edu/

CONTACT
Admissions, Glion Institute of Higher Education, Route de Glion 111, CH-1823 Glion-sur-Montreux, Switzerland. *Phone:* 41-0 21 989 26 77. *Fax:* 41-0 21 989 26 78. *E-mail:* info@glion.edu.

International University in Geneva
Geneva, Switzerland
http://www.iun.ch/

CONTACT
Ms. Virginie Morel, Admissions Officer, International University in Geneva, Geneva 1215, Switzerland. *Phone:* -41 22710-7110. *Fax:* 41 22710-7111. *E-mail:* bachelor@iun.ch.

Les Roches International School of Hotel Management
Bluche, Switzerland
http://www.lesroches.edu/

CONTACT
Enrollment Management Department, Les Roches International School of Hotel Management, CH-3975 Bluche, Switzerland. *Phone:* 41-021 989 26 44. *Fax:* 41-021 989 26 45. *E-mail:* info@lesroches.edu.

TAIWAN

Christ's College
Taipei, Taiwan
http://www.cct.edu.tw/

CONTACT
Ms. Lucy Li, Recruiter, Christ's College, No. 51, Ziqiang Road, Tamsui District, New Taipei City 251, Taiwan. *Phone:* -+886-2-2809-7661. *Fax:* +886-2-8809-1084. *E-mail:* lucyli@christs-college.org.

UNITED ARAB EMIRATES

The American University in Dubai
Dubai, United Arab Emirates
http://www.aud.edu/

- **Proprietary** comprehensive, founded 1995
- **Urban** campus
- **Coed**
- 74% of applicants were admitted

FACULTY
Student/faculty ratio: 15:1.

ACADEMICS
Calendar: semesters. *Degrees:* certificates, bachelor's, and master's.
Library: University Library. *Books:* 47,378 (physical), 300,000 (digital/electronic); *Serial titles:* 85 (physical); *Databases:* 48.

STUDENT LIFE
Housing options: men-only, women-only. Campus housing is university owned. Freshman campus housing is guaranteed.

Activities and organizations: drama/theater group, student-run newspaper, Student Government Association, Community Service Club, Drama Club, Music Club, Debate Club.

Campus security: 24-hour patrols.

Student services: health clinic, personal/psychological counseling.

APPLYING
Options: electronic application, early admission.

Application fee: 55 United Arab Emirates dirhams.

Required: high school transcript, minimum 2.0 GPA, 2 letters of recommendation. ***Required for some:*** interview. ***Recommended:*** essay or personal statement.

CONTACT
Mrs. Carol Maalouf, Director of Admissions, The American University in Dubai, PO Box 28282, Dubai, United Arab Emirates. *Phone:* -971 4 399 9000 Ext. 170. *Fax:* 971 4 399 8899. *E-mail:* admissions@aud.edu.

★ American University of Sharjah
Sharjah, United Arab Emirates
http://www.aus.edu/

CONTACT
American University of Sharjah, PO Box 26666, Sharjah, United Arab Emirates. *Phone:* -+971 6 515 1000. *Fax:* + 971 6 515 2200. *E-mail:* inforequest@aus.edu.

United Arab Emirates University
Al-Ain, United Arab Emirates
http://www.uaeu.ac.ae/

CONTACT
United Arab Emirates University, PO Box 15551, Al Ain, Abu Dhabi, United Arab Emirates.

A ★ indicates that the school has detailed information with a Premium Profile on Petersons.com.

UNITED KINGDOM

Hult International Business School

London, United Kingdom

http://www.hult.edu/

- **Independent** comprehensive, founded 1959
- **Urban** campus with easy access to San Francisco, London, Boston
- **Coed** 1,487 undergraduate students, 100% full-time, 36% women, 64% men
- **Moderately difficult** entrance level, 50% of applicants were admitted

UNDERGRAD STUDENTS
1,487 full-time. Students come from 12 states and territories; 136 other countries; 46% are from out of state; 0.5% Black or African American, non-Hispanic/Latino; 0.7% Hispanic/Latino; 0.3% Asian, non-Hispanic/Latino; 0.1% Two or more races, non-Hispanic/Latino; 4% Race/ethnicity unknown; 93% international; 6% transferred in.

Freshmen:
Admission: 4,012 applied, 2,009 admitted, 592 enrolled. ***Average high school GPA:*** 3.0.

Retention: 81% of full-time freshmen returned.

FACULTY
Total: 99, 39% full-time, 41% with terminal degrees.

Student/faculty ratio: 15:1.

ACADEMICS
Calendar: 5-term academic calendar: required fall, winter, spring terms; optional Summer 1, Summer 2 terms. *Degrees:* bachelor's, master's, and doctoral.

Special study options: academic remediation for entering students, accelerated degree program, advanced placement credit, English as a second language, honors programs, independent study, internships, services for LD students, study abroad, summer session for credit.

Computers: Students can access the following: campus intranet, computer help desk, free student e-mail accounts, online (class) grades, online (class) registration, online (class) schedules. Campuswide network is available. 100% of college-owned or -operated housing units are wired for high-speed Internet access. Wireless service is available via entire campus.
Library: Main Library plus 3 others. *Books:* 198,590 (digital/electronic); *Databases:* 23.

STUDENT LIFE
Housing options: on-campus residence required through sophomore year; coed. Campus housing is leased by the school. Freshman applicants given priority for college housing.

Activities and organizations: drama/theater group, student-run newspaper, choral group, Language Cafe, Model United Nations, International Law Society, Hult RISE (charity club), Consultancy Club.

Athletics ***Intercollegiate sports:*** basketball M/W, soccer M/W.
Intramural sports: badminton M/W, baseball M/W, cheerleading W, golf M/W, rugby M, skiing (downhill) M/W, swimming and diving M/W, table tennis M/W.

Campus security: 24-hour emergency response devices and patrols, controlled dormitory access.

Student services: personal/psychological counseling.

COSTS
Costs (2019–20) ***One-time required fee:*** $850. ***Comprehensive fee:*** $59,650 includes full-time tuition ($41,650) and room and board ($18,000). ***College room only:*** $14,000.

APPLYING
Standardized Tests *Required for some:* SAT or ACT (for admission), TOEFL, IELTS, or PTE for non-native English speakers.

Options: electronic application.

Application fee: 75 British pounds.

Required: essay or personal statement, high school transcript, 2 letters of recommendation. ***Required for some:*** interview.

Application deadlines: rolling (freshmen), rolling (transfers).

Notification: continuous (freshmen), continuous (transfers).

CONTACT
Mr. Niccolo Del Monte, Vice President, Undergraduate Enrollment, Hult International Business School, 35 Commercial Road, London E1 1LD, United Kingdom. *Phone:* -44 207 341 8555. *E-mail:* niccolo.delmonte@hult.edu.

London Metropolitan University

London, United Kingdom

http://www.londonmet.ac.uk/

CONTACT
London Metropolitan University, 166-220 Holloway Road, London N7 8DB, United Kingdom.

Open University

Milton Keynes, United Kingdom

http://www.open.ac.uk/

CONTACT
Open University, Walton Hall, Milton Keynes MK7 6AA, United Kingdom.

Regent's University London

London, United Kingdom

http://www.regents.ac.uk/

CONTACT
Admissions Director, Regent's University London, Inner Circle, Regent's Park, London NW1 4NS, United Kingdom. *Phone:* 44-0 207 487 7505. *Fax:* 44-0 207 487 7425. *E-mail:* bacl@regents.ac.uk.

Richmond, The American International University in London

Richmond, United Kingdom

http://www.richmond.ac.uk/

CONTACT
Mr. Nick Atkinson, Director of United States Admissions, Richmond, The American International University in London, 343 Congress Street, Suite 3100, Boston, MA 02210-1214. *Phone:* 617-450-5617. *Fax:* 617-450-5601. *E-mail:* us_admissions@richmond.ac.uk.

College Close-Ups

NOTICE: Certain portions of or information contained in this book have been submitted and paid for by the educational institution identified, and such institutions take full responsibility for the accuracy, timeliness, completeness and functionality of such content. Such portions or information include (i) each display ad in the "Profiles" section from pages 55 through 1272 that comprises a half or full page of information covering a single educational institution, and (ii) each two-page description in the "College Close-Up" section from pages 1274 through 1606.

A ★ indicates that the school has detailed information with a Premium Profile on Petersons.com.

ACADEMY OF ART UNIVERSITY

SAN FRANCISCO, CALIFORNIA

The College

In 1929, Academy of Art University founder Richard S. Stephens, who was the advertising Creative Director of *Sunset* magazine, acted on his belief that "aspiring artists and designers, given proper instruction, hard work, and dedication, can learn the skills needed to become successful professionals." His new School of Advertising Art consisted of 46 students meeting in one room on San Francisco's Kearny Street.

The instructors, who were professional artists, brought real-world problems, situations, solutions, and practical experience to the students. Based on this idea, the school's philosophy was formulated: Hire established professionals to teach the art and design professionals of tomorrow. At that time, advertising consisted primarily of illustrations, photos, and copy. Consequently, it became necessary to teach beginning students the fundamentals of drawing, painting, color, light, and photography as well as layout and typography.

When Richard A. Stephens succeeded his father as President in 1951, the Foundations Department was added, ensuring all students mastered the basic principles of traditional art and design. Illustration soon expanded to include fine arts (drawing, painting, sculpture, and printmaking), and advertising design led to the School of Graphic Design. A Fashion School (design, knitwear, textiles, and merchandising) and an Interior Design School were also added. In 1966, the Academy officially became a college, and a decade later began offering the Master of Fine Arts degree. Later, five more buildings were purchased, and by 1992, the student body comprised more than 2,500 students.

The leadership of the Academy was then turned over to the third generation. Dr. Elisa Stephens, granddaughter of the school's founder, quickly determined that the school's small School of Web Design & New Media had enormous potential to prepare students for multimedia careers with such companies as Pixar, Adobe, and Walt Disney Productions. It is now one of the largest departments at the Academy. In 2004, the name of the school was changed from Academy of Art College to Academy of Art University, in recognition of its depth, scope, and quality.

Today, Academy of Art University is the largest accredited private art and design university in the United States. Nearly one third of the student body is made up of international students. The Academy has over 50 facilities that house classrooms, cafes, studios, galleries, museum, library, chapel, and residence halls. The students, who are admitted through an open-enrollment policy, aspire to earn A.A., B.A., B.F.A., B.S., B.Arch., M.A., M.F.A., or M.Arch. degrees or an Art Teaching Credential. Students can study through the Academy's flexible online programs or in San Francisco.

The Academy maintains a system of courtesy shuttles to connect the different points of the campus, all located within the city limits of San Francisco, one of the world's most vibrant and beautiful cities. The instructors, who are working art and design professionals from around the world, are drawn to the Academy and to the creative and intellectual center that is the Bay Area. Extensive senior-year internship programs allow students to gain valuable experience and develop strong portfolios in their chosen field prior to graduation.

Academy of Art University is an accredited member of the WASC Senior College and University Commission (WSCUC), National Association of Schools of Art and Design (NASAD), Council for Interior Design Accreditation (CIDA) for B.F.A.-IAD and M.F.A.-IAD, National Architectural Accrediting Board (NAAB) for B.Arch. and M.Arch., and California Commission on Teacher Credentialing (CTC).

Location

The city of San Francisco is one of the great cultural centers of the world; a melting pot of diversity, culture, and creativity that has spawned major museums and galleries, world-class opera and theaters, dance companies, film production and recording studios, technological innovation, performing artists ranging from classical to popular music, and numerous other cultural opportunities. The city's status as a tourist mecca located on the Pacific Rim ensures that one encounters people from all corners of the world.

The climate is moderate and offers kaleidoscopic blends of sunshine and fog most of the year. The Northpoint campus is located at the historic Cannery building near world-famous Pier 39, where students can view Alcatraz Island and the world famous Golden Gate Bridge from their classroom windows. In addition, four campus buildings are located two blocks from historic Union Square, in the commercial heart of the city, and three others are located near the Financial District. Shop 657, a store in Union Square, opened in December 2014 to display school designs and provide merchandising students real-world experience. The city offers myriad locations for field trips and studio visits. World-renowned artists display their creations in the Academy's five nonprofit art galleries, which are open to the public. The Academy is an urban institution that both draws upon and contributes to the cultural wealth of the community in which it resides.

Degrees and Areas of Study

Academy of Art University offers A.A., B.A., B.F.A., B.S., B.Arch., M.A., M.F.A., M.Arch. degrees, Art Teaching Credential, and a tuition free pre-college art experience programs. Areas of study are available online and in San Francisco in the following: acting* (speech, improv, physical acting), advertising (creative strategy, art direction, copywriting, television commercials), animation & visual effects (background painting/ layout design, character development, storyboard art, 3-D modeling, VFX/compositing), architecture (structures, materials and methods of construction, design process, structural and environmental systems), art education (learning to teach in museums, developmental psychology, teaching art in the community), art history (Renaissance art, American art history, ancient art history, looking at art, philosophy), art teaching credential (learning to teach both children and adults), automotive restoration*, communications & media technologies (journalism, editing, short-form documentary), costume design (design research, production bible, costume consistency, hair and makeup), fashion (design, knitwear, textiles), fashion journalism (fashion writing, editorials for magazines, newspaper writing, fashion news, social media), fashion marketing (market research, analysis of business trends, digital and social media trends, effective branding, written communication), fashion merchandising (fashion business analysis, product selection, effective business plan), fashion product development (identify materials, manufacturing process, understanding of brand, consumer, and price point, technical drawings, knowledge of computer software), fashion styling (advanced skills for styling fashion products, photography, composition, lighting, hair styling, make-up artistry, art direction, production management), fashion textile design (design research, sketchbook, concept selection, original design production, trial and self-edit designs), fashion visual merchandising (research and concept development, visual presentation, creative merchandising concepts, verbal and written presentation), footwear & accessory design, fine art (painting, printmaking, sculpture), game development (game engines, prototyping, level design, game art, 3-D modeling), game programming (engineering and programming techniques, math and object-oriented programming, complex algorithms, writing code), graphic design (corporate and brand identity, package design, print and collateral), illustration (children's books, editorial, comic books), industrial design (furniture design, product design, toy design, transportation design), interior architecture & design (commercial and residential design, furniture design), jewelry & metal arts (fashion jewelry design, enameling, stone setting, casting, welded and fabricated sculpture), landscape architecture (plant design, elements in landscape, grading and drainage, urban open spaces), motion pictures & television (cinematography, directing, editing, producing, production design, screenwriting), music production & sound design for visual media (harmony, arranging, orchestration, music production techniques, scoring for film), photography (architecture, advertising, digital documentary, editorial, fashion, fine art, landscape, photojournalism, portraiture), studio production for advertising & design, visual development (concept art for animation, film, and games; digital painting; character design; cinematic storytelling; Marquette sculpting; environment creation), web design & new media (user experience design, interactive design, new media, web design), and writing for film, television & digital media.

* Acting and automotive restoration degrees are currently not available online.

Academic Environment and Enrichment

The Bachelor of Fine Arts degree requires foundations courses, major courses, art electives, and liberal arts courses. Fundamental courses are related specifically to students' majors to prepare them to begin intense focus courses in their field by the sophomore year. All major courses of study are structured so the student builds upon skills learned the previous semester and advances to the next level of technical or creative proficiency. Some related major courses may be taken concurrently.

Liberal arts courses teach practical applications for forging a professional career in art and design. International students who come from countries where English is not the primary language may take additional EAP

(English for Art Purposes) classes, as determined by English language proficiency testing. Students are advised to meet with departmental directors at least once during the academic year to have their progress assessed. Portfolios are reviewed before the junior year to determine whether or not a student has progressed sufficiently to continue study at the Academy.

Academic Facilities

Academy of Art University's industry-standard facilities offer students the tools they need to prepare for professional careers in art and design. The Academy invests in top-notch equipment to ensure it remains on the cutting edge of technology. Learning on industry-standard equipment, students gain hands-on experience.

Academy of Art University students have access to an array of digital tools. The School of Game Development and the School of Animation & Visual Effects provide the latest equipment like HTC Vive and Oculus Rifts/Gear, as well as a video and Cintiq lab, green screen studio, and sound booth. The School of Web Design & New Media houses a usability lab with the most current software, while the School of Music Production & Sound Design for Visual Media offers the latest sound design and video editing tools and is proud to have a new flagship mixing console, the Avid S6. The Academy is the first university in California to offer this new console and the second organization in California other than Skywalker Sound to own the console.

The School of Advertising is designed to look, feel, and function like an ad agency. Young & Hungry, a student run ad agency, offers opportunities for students to gain agency experience before graduation. Located in the heart of San Francisco's Financial District, the School of Graphic Design has the latest industry tools that enable students to have a seamless transition into the world of work following graduation. And the School of Illustration is housed in a unique historic building in San Francisco's Union Square District. The original libraries, meeting rooms, theater, and a ballroom are transformed into drawing/painting studios and classrooms.

Undergraduate and graduate students in Architecture, Interior Architecture & Design, and Landscape Architecture share an 800-square-foot materials library and plotting room, as well as a model shop. The School of Industrial Design offers multiple shop facilities and a 3-D computer lab. The School of Landscape Architecture benefits from being located in San Francisco, the hub of urban landscape design.

Fashion students have access to studio facilities for women's, men's and children's wear, as well as textile design, knitwear design, and fashion merchandising and marketing. Surrounded by world-renowned museums and galleries, the School of Fine Art and the School of Art History facilities include thousands of square feet of studio space with everything their students need to bring their individual visions to life.

The School of Motion Pictures & Television and the School of Acting facilities include a postproduction area, green screen studio, screenwriting lab, VR equipment, and several soundstage studios. Students of the School of Communications & Media Technologies have access to a cutting-edge radio studio and television studio, complete with robotic cameras and drones, anchor desks and interview sets, teleprompters, and green screens. School of Photography facilities are equipped with both traditional and digital photographic technology.

The library provides advanced digital tools, making it possible for students to access extensive art and design image resources and information on demand. The Academy Resource Center offers all students free learning support services including study hall tutoring, academic coaching, English as second language support programs, a writing lab, and a multimedia language lab.

Costs

For Fall 2019, undergraduate tuition will be $963 per credit unit. Full-time students must carry at least 12 semester units per term. There is a nonrefundable $50 fee when applying. Lab fees run from $25 to $400 per semester, depending on the class. Tuition and fees are subject to change at any time. Art supplies can run from $250 to $1,500 per semester, depending on the major. The Academy has most of the expensive technical equipment available for students to borrow or use in a lab. Academy of Art University operates many residence halls within the city. Several housing options are offered, and costs vary based on the building and room/unit assigned. For further information, students may contact the Department of Housing and Residence Life directly at 415-618-6335.

Financial Aid

The Academy offers financial aid packages consisting of grants, loans, and work-study to eligible students with a demonstrated need. Low-interest loans are available to all eligible students, regardless of need. As financial aid programs, procedures, and eligibility requirements change frequently, applicants should contact the Financial Aid Office at financialaid@academyart.edu or 800-544-2787 x 6190 (toll-free, U.S. only).

Faculty

The Academy averages 1,138 instructors in fall/spring semester, most of whom are full-time art and design professionals and part-time teachers. The student-teacher ratio for undergraduate classes averages 14:1.

Student Government

Although there is no formal student government, each department has between two and three student representatives who meet with the President as needed throughout the semester to discuss any student issues.

Admission Requirements

Applicants for the A.A., B.A., B.F.A., B.S., and B.Arch. programs must have a high school diploma or equivalent. There is no portfolio requirement. M.A., M.F.A., and M.Arch. Applicants must have a bachelor's degree and submit a portfolio and statement of intent. International students take written and speech tests to determine which EAP (English for Art Purposes) classes may have to be completed. Most EAP classes can be taken in conjunction with art and design classes. All foundations classes offer specialized EAP sections with instructors trained for language assistance. The application fee is $50 for domestic and $150 for international students.

What Sets Academy of Art University Apart

The Academy is one of the few art and design schools that believes in nurturing the whole artist; this includes developing athletic ability along with artistic talent. Students can participate in intercollegiate, intramural, and club sports. With Pacific West honors and national championships, the Academy offers basketball, baseball, softball, cross country, track and field, soccer, golf, volleyball, and tennis for its students to partake in. Furthermore, the Academy is proud to be the only art school in the NCAA Division II. Students have gone on to compete in the Olympics and have been drafted by professional leagues to play their sport professionally.

Application and Information

Students may apply to enter the Academy at the beginning of the spring, fall, or summer semesters. Information in this profile is subject to change. Students should contact Academy of Art University for current information or visit www.academyart.edu to learn about total costs, median student loan debt, potential occupations, and other information.

Academy of Art University
79 New Montgomery Street
San Francisco, California 94105
Phone: 415-274-2222
800-544-2787 (U.S. only)
Fax: 415-618-6287
E-mail: info@academyart.edu
Website: www.academyart.edu
https://www.facebook.com/AcademyofArtUniversity
https://twitter.com/academy_of_art
http://www.pinterest.com/academyofartuni
https://www.linkedin.com/school/academy-of-art-university/
http://instagram.com/academy_of_art
http://www.youtube.com/user/academyofartu

Academy of Art University's downtown campus.

COLLEGE CLOSE-UPS

ALLEGHENY COLLEGE

MEADVILLE, PENNSYLVANIA

ALLEGHENY COLLEGE

The College

One of Loren Pope's 40 "Colleges That Change Lives," Allegheny is cited as the premiere college in the country for students with "unusual combinations" of interests and talents. On its historic campus—where the liberal arts and sciences have been taught for more than 200 years—students develop combinations of majors and minors in areas that may, at first glance, seem unrelated: biology and economics, political science and music, history and psychology. Allegheny students share an abiding passion for learning and life, a spirit of camaraderie, and a respect for shared inquiry that spans all areas of study. Neuroscience majors play in the Civic Symphony and build houses during Alternative Spring Break. Students prepare for law school while playing basketball and interning in Washington, D.C. Computer science majors present work in philosophy at national conferences.

Building on a combination of academic disciplines and passions, every student completes the comprehensive Senior Project under the guidance of a faculty adviser in his or her major field. The project demonstrates the skills most prized by employers and graduate schools: the ability to complete a major assignment, work independently, analyze and synthesize information, and to write and speak persuasively.

Allegheny students are encouraged to explore all of their interests and to look at academic disciplines from multiple perspectives, which leads them to extraordinary outcomes. Biochemistry majors use the skills they learned in communication arts to start marketing careers with the Environmental Protection Agency. English majors collaborate with the College's pre-health advisers and enjoy acceptance rates to medical school between 80 and 100 percent—twice the national average. And over 95 percent of Allegheny's job-seeking graduates find employment within six months.

Leaders in business, government, medicine, education, and community service frequently declare that the future belongs to individuals who are innovators, inventors, and big-picture thinkers, those who think both analytically and creatively. It is this preparation for the global marketplace, and for life, that Allegheny, with its emphasis on "unusual combinations," is nationally known for providing.

Location

Central campus looks like a traditional college with a rich liberal arts heritage and tradition, with its 79 acres of rolling lawns and brick walkways, historic buildings, and century-old oaks and elms. A 203-acre recreational complex and a 283-acre nature reserve complement state-of-the-art classrooms, labs, theaters, studios and other facilities.

The campus overlooks the town of Meadville, a county seat that features a courthouse, hospital, a variety of industries, and more. Allegheny students connect with the community in many ways, from running after-school programs to taking in the latest movies, from creating art installations to checking out live music.

Allegheny students live in a section of the country that most people get to see only on vacation. Northwest Pennsylvania is a nature-lover's paradise of verdant, undisturbed forests and streams and lakes that are gems of biodiversity. It's no wonder that the College has one of the oldest Outing Clubs in the country.

Allegheny is ideally situated within two hours of the social and transportation hubs of Pittsburgh, Cleveland, and Buffalo. Being just close enough to major cities allows for frequent excursions to major sporting events, concerts, and other attractions.

Majors and Degrees

Allegheny students can earn the Bachelor of Arts (B.A.) or the Bachelor of Science (B.S.) degree in the following programs of study; art and technology; art (studio); biochemistry; biology; business; chemistry; communication arts; community and justice studies; computer science; creative writing; economics; English; environmental geology; environmental science & sustainability; French; geology; global health studies; history; integrative informatics; international studies; mathematics; music; neuroscience; philosophy; physics; political science; psychology; religious studies; Spanish; theatre; women's, gender, and sexuality studies; and self-designed majors.

In addition to the above majors, minors are available in: Asian studies, astronomy, black studies, Chinese studies, classical studies, dance and movement studies, education studies, energy & society, environmental writing, French studies, German, Jewish studies, journalism in the public interest, Latin, Latin American and Caribbean studies, Middle East and North African studies, music history, music performance, music theory, and writing.

Dedicated advisers are available for students interested in: pre-dental, pre-law, pre-medicine, pre-nursing, pre-pharmacy, and pre-veterinary.

Students may also take advantage of accelerated master's and doctoral degree programs, teacher certification programs, and engineering cooperative programs with other top institutions.

Academic Programs

Allegheny College believes so strongly in unusual combinations that they are built right into its curriculum; it is one of the few liberal arts colleges nationally that requires students to choose a minor as well as a major. In some ways, this may make school more difficult. But most students at Allegheny are individuals for whom the most difficult thing would be to give up some vital part of themselves. Some Allegheny students have majors and minors that complement each other in predictable ways—an international studies major with a minor in French, for example. But there are other students whose majors and minors represent very different aspects of themselves—an environmental science & sustainability major with a minor in creative writing or a chemistry major with a minor in history. Coupled with experiential learning and the distinctive Senior Project, seeing academic disciplines from multiple perspectives leads to extraordinary outcomes.

During the first two years, every Allegheny student participates in seminars that focus on written and oral communication as well as academic and career advising, and the faculty instructor serves as adviser for both years. This progressive course sequence, in addition to the Junior Seminar and Senior Project, helps students create a four-year experience to match all of their needs and goals.

Under the guidance of a faculty adviser in his or her major field, every student completes the Senior Project, a significant piece of original scholarly work with a creative, analytical, or experimental focus. The project mirrors a master's thesis and requires project management skills, independent work, writing and presentation skills, and the ability to analyze and synthesize information. Allegheny has required a senior capstone experience since the college's first commencement ceremony in 1821. The Council on Undergraduate Research recognized Allegheny as the top baccalaureate college in the nation for providing high-quality research experiences to undergraduates.

In the National Survey of Student Engagement, responses by college freshmen placed Allegheny within the top 10 percent in the United States for both a supportive campus environment and level of academic challenge.

Off-Campus Programs

Allegheny College recognizes the enormous academic, professional, and personal value of studying off-campus, nationally or internationally. Allegheny students can experience multiple off-campus adventures, learning with an eclectic group of students with diverse academic majors and interests. The Gateway facilitates a variety of opportunities through study abroad, career services, community service, and more.

The College sponsors semester and year-long study-away programs, some of which require skills in languages other than English, and others with no language requirements. More than 190 Allegheny students and faculty participate in 40 Allegheny-sponsored study abroad programs in 20 countries.

In addition, faculty members lead students each year on intensive three-week experiential learning seminars. These for-credit, faculty-designed programs occur at the end of each spring semester. Recent excursions took students to Austria, the Czech Republic, England, Germany, India, Japan, Turkey, and South Africa.

The Office of Career Education maintains a database of 2,500 internship and shadowing opportunities, including especially popular ones in Boston, New York City, Los Angeles, and Washington, D.C. Students at Allegheny can choose among several kinds of internships, including academic internships taken for credit that often take place during a spring or fall semester and noncredit internships throughout the summer.

Academic Facilities

Allegheny boasts the nationally acclaimed Steffee Hall of Life Sciences, which incorporates state-of-the-art labs located right next to classrooms and faculty offices. An environmental science & sustainability center features the best in sustainable practices with a living wall, aquaponics equipment, and solar panels. Students also benefit from the GIS learning lab, planetarium, and seismographic network station.

The multimillion-dollar Vukovich Center for Communication Arts, which meets LEED certification standards and has a rooftop garden, features a learning theater, scene and costume shops, and video production facilities. Language students enjoy a multimedia learning lab, and dancers work in bright, functional studio and performance spaces. The Bowman, Penelec, and Megahan art galleries display student and faculty work as well as visiting exhibits.

Allegheny's Learning Commons provides academic support to all students through professional guidance, peer mentors, training, and effective learning tools. The center is housed in Pelletier Library, which offers more than 900,000 volumes, as well as extensive digital resources, research tools, and unique meeting spaces.

Costs

For 2018–19, tuition and fees were $47,040. The standard first-year room and board was $12,140.

Financial Aid

Through the generous support of its alumni, Allegheny is able to provide over $43 million in achievement-based scholarships; need-based grant assistance; and aid awarded to students from federal, state, and private sources. Allegheny's financial assistance allows many students the opportunity to make a college choice based on value and fit, rather than financial constraints.

Allegheny's Trustee Scholarships are awarded without regard to financial need to students who have balanced academic excellence with other distinctive activities while in high school. Awards range up to $140,000, distributed equally over four years of study at Allegheny (up to $35,000 per year), and renew automatically.

Faculty

Whether it's conducting research, teaching a First-Year Seminar, leading a three-week study tour, co-authoring an article or making an authentic French dinner, faculty work and learn alongside students every day. There's no graduate school buffer between undergraduates and faculty. Students don't have to wait behind graduate students for research positions on faculty-led projects or compete against hundreds of other students for the lead roles in plays or an editorship at the literary magazine.

Of the 173 full-time faculty members, 91 percent have earned the highest degree in their fields. The student to faculty ratio is 11:1, and introductory classes have an average of 19 students. Advanced classes have an average of 12 students, and some seminars have fewer than 10. Of all classes, 88 percent have fewer than 30 students.

Every student has a faculty adviser for the first two years and a faculty adviser in his/her major field for the final two years. Culminating with their work guiding students through the Senior Project, faculty members are not only supportive and engaging teachers but true leaders and mentors.

Student Government

The Allegheny Student Government is the official voice and administrative unit of the student body. This extremely active and influential organization concerns itself with the quality of the educational, cultural, and social aspects of the Allegheny community. Its members organize and coordinate programs of a cocurricular and extracurricular nature and sponsor more than 120 student-run clubs and organizations.

Students serve on every major college committee, including faculty searches, sustainability efforts, and strategic planning. Their presence exemplifies the importance placed on student participation and represents the influence students have on the institution.

Admission Requirements

From the time a prospective student first contacts Allegheny, the College's holistic approach is directed to addressing his or her unique character, needs, and aspirations. During the application process, primary attention is focused on those criteria that indicate academic promise, including difficulty of high school classes, GPA, and class rank. Careful consideration is also given to those personal qualities that are important in the total success of the college experience: school and community activities, recommendation letters, and the personal essay. Students are encouraged to share additional information through the College's application supplement and an interview and visit. Allegheny embraces the concept that standardized test scores do not exclusively reflect a student's full range of abilities or potential to succeed in college. As a result, Allegheny is now test optional. ACT and SAT I scores are optional for U.S. citizens and permanent residents.

The result is a highly personalized approach to the selection of students that remains consistent with the aims of the College, respects the individuality of each applicant, and ensures equal consideration of every candidate. The College encourages diversity and actively seeks students from all ethnic, religious, racial, political, geographic, and socioeconomic backgrounds.

Application and Information

Office of Admissions
Allegheny College
520 North Main Street
Meadville, Pennsylvania 16335
Phone: 814-332-4351
800-521-5293 (toll-free)
Fax: 814-337-0431
E-mail: admissions@allegheny.edu
Web site: http://www.allegheny.edu/admissions
http://www.allegheny.edu/distinctions
http://www.allegheny.edu/visit
http://www.allegheny.edu/apply

Recognized among Loren Pope's *40 "Colleges That Change Lives,"* Allegheny College is one of the nation's most historic and innovative institutions of higher education. Allegheny is one of the only colleges in the country that requires students to choose both a major and minor, ensuring they develop the skills needed to be analytical and creative.

COLLEGE CLOSE-UPS

AMDA COLLEGE AND CONSERVATORY OF THE PERFORMING ARTS

LOS ANGELES, CALIFORNIA AND NEW YORK, NEW YORK

AMDA
AMDA College and Conservatory of the Performing Arts — LOS ANGELES CAMPUS
The American Musical and Dramatic Academy — NEW YORK CITY CAMPUS

AMDA

Over the past 55 years, AMDA has remained at the forefront of performing arts higher education, training actors, dancers, and singers for film, stage, and television. With full accreditation from the National Association of Schools of Theatre, it offers four B.F.A. degrees, three A.O.S. degrees, and three certificate paths for acting, dance theatre, and music theatre.

Students can study at AMDA campuses in Los Angeles and New York City, two of the most influential entertainment hubs in the world. AMDA College and Conservatory of the Performing Arts in Los Angeles and the American Musical and Dramatic Academy in New York provide greater understanding of dance, film, popular music, theatre, and television industries throughout the world.

Founded in 1964, AMDA pioneered the concept of training students to become triple threats: actors, dancers, and singers. More than 55 years later, AMDA continues to create innovative performing arts programs that address the entertainment industry's needs. Its innovative learning environment helps students develop the confidence, imagination, skills, and power to contribute to their communities as artists, conscientious citizens, entrepreneurs, lifelong learners, and visionaries.

Alumni consistently perform in Broadway productions, star in television shows and films, and dance on stages throughout the world. Alumni also perform improvisation, one-person shows, and stand-up comedy, and they take part in commercial concerts, music videos, and pop/rock tours. In addition, they have built outstanding careers as casting directors, choreographers, composers, directors, stage managers, talent agents, and writers.

According to Niche.com's rankings, the American Musical and Dramatic Academy is among the 10 Best Colleges for Performing Arts in America. The college also ranked fourth on *Playbill* magazine's list of the 10 most represented colleges on Broadway during the 2018 to 2019 season.

AMDA is a private, nonprofit, 501(c)(3) entity and has been accredited, both institutionally and programmatically, by the National Association of Schools of Theatre (NAST) since 1984. NAST has been designated by the United States Department of Education as the agency responsible for the accreditation throughout the United States of freestanding institutions and units offering theatre and theatre-related programs (both degree and nondegree granting). AMDA is licensed to operate in the state of New York by the Bureau of Proprietary School Supervision (BPSS) under the New York State Department of Education. AMDA is licensed to operate in the state of California by the Bureau for Private Postsecondary Education (BPPE) under the Department of Consumer Affairs.

Location

AMDA's campuses in New York City and Los Angeles, California consist not only of the traditional buildings, theatres, and classrooms but also the cities of New York and Los Angeles themselves.

Both campus locations offer access to countless attractions including amusement parks, art galleries, film studios, movie theatres, playhouses, and shopping venues. ABC Studios, Broadway, Central Park, Columbus Circle, the Lincoln Center, and Times Square are just some of the attractions in New York City. Places of interest in (or near) Los Angeles include the Capitol Records Building, Disneyland, the Getty Center, Runyon Canyon Park, and Universal Studios Hollywood.

Majors and Degrees

The AMDA College and Conservatory of the Performing Arts in Los Angeles offers four-year Bachelor of Fine Arts and two-year Associate of Occupations Studies degrees. The American Musical and Dramatic Academy in New York City offers two-year Conservatory certificate programs with an option to transfer to the Los Angeles campus to complete a B.F.A. program.

Bachelor of Fine Arts Degree Programs

The B.F.A. in Acting develops the physical and vocal foundations necessary for professional acting and expands students' depth of knowledge, instincts, and skills.

The B.F.A. in Music Theatre focuses on individual voice instruction and performance skills within a musical theatre foundation.

The B.F.A. in Dance Theatre focuses on dance techniques that build artistry, stamina, and strength and trains students to blend technical choreography with interpretive storytelling.

The B.F.A. in Performing Arts provides foundational work in all performance areas: acting, dance, improvisation, musical theatre, singing, and stage combat.

Associate of Occupational Studies Degree Programs

The A.O.S. in Acting prepares students for working in theatre, television and film through an immersive program built upon performance-based courses.

The A.O.S. in Musical Theatre offers interdisciplinary arts training for the emerging musical theatre performer through a balanced emphasis on music, acting, and dance.

The A.O.S. in Dance Theatre is designed for ambitious dancers and offers a rigorous course of physical study while providing immersion in theatrical, commercial and concert dance disciplines

Conservatory Certificate Programs

The Studio in Acting for Stage, Film, and Television teaches the theories and techniques of effective character development, movement, and vocal control.

The Integrated Program in Acting, Dance, and Music Theatre focuses on developing a strong foundation in a variety of acting techniques, dance styles, and musical skills.

The Dance Theatre Conservatory expands students' repertoire through a range of disciplines, genres, and styles that span both contemporary and classical dance.

Academic Programs

AMDA's academics emphasize creative maturity, stylistic depth, and professional excellence, and are designed to help students reach their full artistic potential through a deep-rooted foundation in the performing arts. Students complete rigorous curricula and receive intensive, hands-on instruction from some of the best professionals in the industry. They build a strong foundation in the performing arts and create impressive performance resumes. Students can also participate in industry panel nights, which provide exposure to casting directors for Broadway, film, and television; directors and producers; talent agents; record producers; and other industry professionals.

Classes at AMDA average 12 to 18 students to ensure individualized attention. There are more than 30 performing opportunities each term to help students build performance resumes.

Academic Facilities

AMDA Los Angeles' campus is anchored in the Tower Building, an eight-story, historic art-deco building which houses administrative offices, classrooms, studio spaces, a costume shop, a stage combat armory, a computer lab, a library, the AMDA Café, the campus store and a black box theatre. The Vine Building houses classrooms, laboratory theatres, studios, private voice rooms, a general education classroom, student lounge, the film production office and the scene shop, and storage space for costumes, props, and production sets. AMDA Los Angeles features four main theatres featuring full theatrical lighting and sound packages. An outdoor amphitheater hosts everything from theatrical performances to dances. Six nearby buildings serve as residence halls, with a range of student housing options.

AMDA New York's main facility is located at 211 West 61st Street, in the heart of the Upper West Side of Manhattan. The building's four floors house classrooms, rehearsal studios, private voice rooms, student lounges, a performing arts library, a student store and administrative offices. Its secondary location is at 73rd Street and Broadway in the Ansonia, and features a theatre, additional performance space, studios, and private voice rooms. The Ansonia Building features a 100-seat, black box-style theatre that can be arranged in multiple layouts. It is equipped with two dressing rooms, a costume shop, a workshop, backstage space and prop storage, dedicated lighting, and a sound system. Studio apartments are available for students in two buildings within walking distance.

Both AMDA campuses provide plenty of training spaces outside the classroom: studios and private voice rooms, a range of stereo and audiovisual equipment, pianos, ballet barres and sprung floors in the dance studios, and other rehearsal equipment. AMDA is equipped with the latest technological resources devoted to filmmaking and TV show creation, including full shooting setups with lighting instruments, cameras and playback, and editing equipment.

Costs

For the 2019–20 academic year, tuition and fees for the B.F.A., A.O.S., and Conservatory programs totaled $40,444. On-campus housing is $9,750 while off-campus housing is estimated at $12,500. Books are estimated at $1,200 per academic year. Transportation, food, personal, and other miscellaneous costs vary by individual.

Financial Aid

Financial aid is available to help pay for the student's education. Major forms of financial aid include gift aid (merit- and need-based grants and scholarships) and self-help aid (loans and work). AMDA offers payment plans, grants and scholarships, Federal Direct Stafford loans, Federal Parent PLUS loans, and other alternative loan programs. Ninety-five present of AMDA students receive institutional support in the form of scholarships and/or grants.

In order to be considered for financial aid, AMDA requires that all U.S. citizens and permanent residents complete the FAFSA (Free Application for Federal Student Aid). AMDA'S school code for both locations is 016082.

Faculty

AMDA prides itself on utilizing the best and the brightest performing arts professionals in the world in its faculty. The unrivaled access and industry insight these faculty members provide helps students become well-rounded, business-savvy, working professionals.

Students graduate from AMDA prepared to pursue success on the world stage. Their connections with faculty-mentors enable them to start building their professional networks from the moment they begin their programs. These networks along with comprehensive training make it possible for students to excel in their chosen crafts.

Student Life

From full-scale mainstage productions to student-directed films, AMDA gives every student countless opportunities to perform, starting on the very first day of class. As performing artists, maintaining high quality physical and mental health is critical for students who must meet rigorous academic and performance demands, and AMDA provides opportunities for such on both campuses.

International students are vital members of AMDA's community. They come from 51 countries and represent 8 percent of the college's student population. The college provides extensive resources to help them reach their full creative potential. International Student Services including dedicated advisers that help students navigate the United States immigration system and transition to U.S. culture and AMDA campus life.

Application and Information

Applicants must complete the online application, fulfill the audition requirement, provide letters of recommendation, and submit official transcripts from every education institution listed on their application.

AMDA offers numerous audition opportunities in locations throughout the United States and the world. AMDA encourages you to schedule your audition at either the New York City or Los Angeles campus. You must be a junior or senior in high school or a high school graduate to request an audition. Further audition details are available at https://www.amda.edu/admissions/audition/requirements.

Additional information regarding AMDA is available by contacting the following:

AMDA College and Conservatory of the Performing Arts
6305 Yucca Street
Los Angeles, California 90028
Phone: 800-367-7908
E-mail: info@amda.edu

The American Musical and Dramatic Academy
211 West 61st Street
New York, New York 10023
Phone: 212-787-5300
E-mail: info@amda.edu

Website: https://www.amda.edu
AMDA (Facebook)
amdaofficial (Instagram)
AMDA NY & LA (Twitter)

Unparalleled Performing Arts Education in the USA!

COLLEGE CLOSE-UPS

AMERICAN UNIVERSITY OF ROME

ROME, ITALY

The University

Preparing students from around the world to live and work across cultures, The American University of Rome (AUR) offers undergraduate students a one-of-a-kind liberal arts education that combines academia with hands-on practical experience through internships and field experience. Students leave AUR trained in the fundamental skills of language, communication, and critical thinking that allow them to continue to learn and thrive in a complex and interconnected world. Studying at AUR is an exceptional educational experience and, for many students, the time spent in Rome is a life-transforming experience.

Founded in 1969, The American University of Rome is the oldest, private independent American institution of higher education in Rome, offering undergraduate degrees in ten disciplines. Faculty encourage students to think broadly and to combine their knowledge from various areas in order to get the most out of their studies. The interdisciplinary nature of the degree programs at AUR produces talented and creative graduates that can combine knowledge from a variety of fields as they pursue their careers.

The student body at AUR is both academically impressive and diverse. Although the student body is relatively small (500–600 enrolled undergraduates) students hail from 50 countries. They bring their unique perspectives into the classroom to enhance discussions and educate their peers on their particular cultures and backgrounds. Students form lifelong international friendships and often go on to develop multinational collaborative ventures even years after graduation. There is also a strong alumni network, and AUR graduates frequently find themselves connecting with alumni across the globe.

The American University of Rome is fully accredited by the Middle States Commission on Higher Education and is licensed by the State of Delaware Department of Education to award associate, bachelor's, and master's degrees. AUR is incorporated in the District of Columbia as a not-for-profit institution.

Location

AUR's location is truly breathtaking. The campus sits on the Giancarlo hill overlooking Rome, just a few minutes' walk from the historic Trastevere district. With its own gardens of Roman pines, it offers spectacular views. The campus is close to two city parks, Villa Sciarra and Villa Pamphili. The neighborhood hosts diplomatic residences and international academies, and offers a full range of amenities, including restaurants, shops, cafés, and outdoor markets.

Students have easy access to Trastevere and the center of Rome and are encouraged to immerse themselves in the city and Italian culture. They can also explore during classes, with study trips throughout the city, giving students direct exposure to a thriving, historic, and contemporary European capital.

From Rome, students also have easy access to the rest of Europe. In under two hours on the plane they can explore Germany, France, and Spain, among others. AUR students often travel around Europe together in groups during the winter holidays and spring break.

Majors and Degrees

The American University of Rome offers ten bachelor's degree programs in Archaeology and Classics; Art History; Business Administration; Communication; English Writing, Literature, and Publishing; Film and Digital Media; Fine Arts; Interdisciplinary Studies; International Relations and Global Politics; and Travel and Tourism Management. Students often double-major or add one of 23 available minors in a separate field in order to combine their skills and further the interdisciplinary nature of their specific degree programs.

There are also two associate degree programs and three graduate degree programs.

Academic Programs

AUR's general education requirements reflect the key concepts that make an American liberal arts university education unique. In addition to preparing students in the foundational skills of English writing, mathematics, the sciences, and the fundamentals of the Italian language, the general education program offers students the opportunity to develop the critical and creative capacity to explore larger questions of knowledge and meaning. Students will learn an interdisciplinary approach to complex topics and to examine concepts from a variety of angles.

Completion of the General Education program is a requirement for all bachelor's degrees, and makes use of courses throughout the AUR curriculum. Consistent with the mission of the University, the program develops important practical skills, addresses social issues of diversity, multiculturalism and ethics and draws on the rich resources of the city of Rome as a learning tool. Reflecting the mission of the institution, it strives to ensure that all students, regardless of major, will share a common dialogue which will prepare them to live and work across cultures.

AUR's First Year Program is a signature, one-semester course required of all first year students, irrespective of their choice of major. All first-year students encounter the same questions, experiences, and texts and the critical discussions that emerge from small seminars, make this program distinctive and stimulating.

AUR follows a semester calendar (fall and spring) and also offers a shorter winter session and summer session. All classes are taught in English.

Off-Campus Programs

While all degree programs at the American University of Rome have a strong career focus, AUR has developed a number of internship programs to get students involved in their fields outside of the classroom in order to enhance career development. Based on their particular majors and expressed interests, AUR places students in internships in Italy and other locations and positions around the world. Internship programs encourage students to think creatively and critically by applying their academic knowledge to the workplace. In the past, students have taken part in internship programs at the following institutions: Amnesty International; The Italian Banking, Insurance, and Finance Federation; The Rome Chamber Music Festival; the Smithsonian Cultural Rescue Initiative; MediaLab; and the Skeletal Analysis Laboratory.

While AUR is already a study-abroad experience for most students, there are also opportunities in other locations outside of Italy, including China, Denmark, Ecuador, England, Greece, Spain, and the United States. The AUR Study Abroad Offices are available to assist incoming and current students explore the benefits of particular programs.

Academic Facilities

AUR is an urban campus of around 30,000 square feet that provides study space, equipment, and an environment conducive to study and learning. Administrative and academic offices, computer labs, and a student lounge are housed in a four-story villa. Adjacent to the villa, a five-story building offers faculty offices, classrooms, a science lab, a computer classroom, art studios, and tutoring centers. Other campus facilities include an auditorium and a multimedia lab. Another two-story villa, Evans Hall, is AUR's library which houses 15,000 volumes, 1,200 DVDs and videos, and provides access to important online databases and a vast network of Roman libraries.

There is a main general purpose computer lab with 55 PCs and several print stations; PC teaching classroom; Mac-based multimedia laboratory; 14 library workstations; and wireless internet access throughout the campus and its gardens and terraces.

Costs

The estimated cost of attendance for academic year 2019–20 includes the following: full-time tuition, $24,480; new student orientation fee, $230; permit to stay, $200; and health insurance, $225.

Shared University housing is available for those who students who want it, or students are free to find their own accommodation in Rome. Students who choose university-facilitated housing are placed in furnished accommodations in areas surrounding the university campus. The cost of University housing is $9,700 for the academic year. Beyond that, a student's cost of living will vary depending on personal lifestyle and preferences.

Financial Aid

The American University of Rome's dedicated financial aid office guides students as they consider how they will finance their education and related expenses. The University offers different comprehensive financial assistance programs.

AUR has an array of scholarship and grant programs for students in need of financial assistance. Incoming students are automatically considered for merit scholarships upon acceptance. The University also has several specific interest and heritage-based scholarships, such as the Michael D'Angelo Fine Arts Scholarship and the Sons of Italy Scholarship.

Returning resident students who have already completed a minimum of one semester with AUR may receive training in various areas of the University in exchange for partial remission of fees and tuition or tuition reimbursement if tuition has been paid in full.

The American University of Rome participates in U.S. Title IV Direct Lending, to cover the estimated cost of attendance. Veteran's benefits may also be utilized; there are several degree programs that are listed as approved training for eligible U.S. citizens at the Department of Veterans Affairs.

Applicants must complete the Free Application for Federal Student Aid (FAFSA) and submit it to the University. Incoming students are encouraged to reach out the AUR Financial Aid Office upon acceptance for assistance in locating the best possible funding sources.

Faculty

There are 70 full and part-time faculty members with a wide range of professional skills, knowledge, and international expertise. AUR prides itself on a robust academic curriculum that features small classes, average size 18, with a 16:1 student/faculty ratio overall allowing for personal attention.

Student Life

AUR's academic program is complemented by a rich variety of extracurricular activities including clubs, performing groups, local events, and athletics. The activities and facilities are designed to promote students' personal growth, leadership development, social responsibility, multicultural competence, and intellectual inquiry.

Admission Requirements

AUR requires a minimum high school GPA of 3.0. However, each applicant is reviewed individually; leadership, motivation, academic improvement, the level of the high school program's difficulty, involvement in activities, and potential for growth are important considerations in the selection process. SAT and ACT scores are optional requirements for U.S. applicants.

Applicants must submit a completed application form (on the University's website or via the Common Application), a $50 nonrefundable application fee, a personal statement, an essay, official high school and/or university transcripts, an academic recommendation letter, a copy of a valid passport, and official TOEFF or IELTS scores for applicants whose native language is not English.

Application and Information

Applications are reviewed on a rolling basis, with preference given to early applicants. Due to student visa purposes, Non-EU/EAA students are encouraged to complete their applications as soon as possible. Applicants will be contacted for an interview once the completed application and all supporting materials have been submitted.

Once admitted, students will be sent an acceptance package and information regarding enrollment, housing, and registration. The enrollment confirmation form and tuition deposit payment must be received by May 1 for the fall semester and November 1 for the spring semester.

Prospective students are encouraged to visit the campus. Further information may be obtained via the University's website and by contacting the University directly.

The American University of Rome
Via Pietro Roselli, 4
00153 Rome, Italy
Phone: +39-0658330919 (direct dial from U.S.)
877-592-1287 (toll-free to Rome from U.S.)
888-791-8327 (toll-free in the U.S.)
Fax: +39-0658330992 (direct fax from U.S.)
866-287-2025 (toll-free fax in the U.S.)
Skype: auradmissions or 415-992-5213
E-mail: admissions@aur.edu
Website: http://www.aur.edu
http://www.facebook.com/TheAmericanUniversityofRome
https://twitter.com/Life_at_AUR

At The American University of Rome we use the Eternal City as an extension of our classroom.

COLLEGE CLOSE-UPS

AQUINAS COLLEGE

GRAND RAPIDS, MICHIGAN

AQUINAS COLLEGE

The College

Aquinas College is an inclusive four-year institution that provides a liberal arts education with a global perspective, emphasizes career preparation focused on leadership and service to others, and fosters a commitment to lifelong learning dedicated to the pursuit of truth and the common good. Aquinas is recognized nationally for strong academic programs, athletics, success in sustainability and service.

Recently named a #11 Best Value - Regional Universities Midwest, Top 50 Catholic college, Aquinas College offers over 60 undergraduate areas of study and is located on the eastern edge of the city of Grand Rapids. Aquinas enjoys all of the advantages of Michigan's second-largest city and is just a 3-hour drive from Detroit or Chicago.

The campus abounds with natural beauty and has been called the most beautiful small campus in Michigan. Its 90 species of trees, winding woodland paths and inviting creeks and ponds create a peaceful 117-acre environment that students of all ages find welcoming.

Founded by the Dominican Sisters of Grand Rapids in 1886, Aquinas is rooted in Catholic and Dominican tradition. For more than 130 years, Aquinas College has educated and inspired students to transform the world by helping them realize their purpose and empowering them to make a difference through vocations and careers that will enrich them and enhance the broader community.

Aquinas has a 96% placement rate, with graduates finding employment or enrolling in graduate school within six months of graduation. Internship partners include Amway, Disney, Steelcase, Spectrum Health, Grand Rapids Art Museum, Van Andel Research Institute, the Detroit Tigers, and many more.

Arriving from places as near as Grand Rapids, Chicago, and Detroit and as far as China and South America, the approximately 1,900 students include 1,300 full-time, 175 part-time, 150 graduate students, 100 dually enrolled high school students, and almost 200 students in nursing, which is a collaborative program with the University of Detroit Mercy. The Insignis program at Aquinas encourages students of exceptional academic ability to participate in social and intellectual activities such as lectures and receptions for visiting scholars and trips to places of cultural interest. Aquinas offers more than 70 student organizations, ranging from intramural teams and departmental clubs to a wide variety of musical groups, student publications, and service organizations.

In addition to its undergraduate degrees, Aquinas also offers Master in the Art of Teaching, Master of Art in Counseling, Master in Education, and Master of Management graduate degrees.

Location

Aquinas' location in Grand Rapids allows students to reap the benefits of West Michigan's economic, educational, and cultural center. The city was recognized as one of the "Top 52 Places to Go in the World" by The New York Times. With more than one million people in the greater metropolitan area, students have the opportunity to take advantage of the thriving city that was recently ranked the #7 fastest growing economy in the U.S. There are cosmopolitan amenities ranging from four-star hotels and restaurants to top-notch cultural facilities and entertainment venues. Established attractions include ArtPrize, Laughfest, the Gerald R. Ford Presidential Museum, the Van Andel Public Museum, the John Ball Zoo, the 10,000-seat Fifth Third Park for Whitecaps minor-league baseball, the 70-acre Frederik Meijer Gardens, and the 12,000-seat Van Andel Arena, home to the Grand Rapids Griffins AHL hockey team and a venue for nationally known music concerts and performances. Grand Rapids boasts several professional performance groups including Opera Grand Rapids, the Grand Rapids Symphony, and the Grand Rapids Ballet Company.

Majors and Degrees

Aquinas College offers the following undergraduate degree programs: Bachelor of Arts, Bachelor of Fine Arts, Bachelor of Arts in general education, Bachelor of Music, Bachelor of Music Education, Bachelor of Science, Bachelor of Professional Accountancy, Bachelor of Science in Business Administration, Bachelor of Science in Sustainable Business, and Bachelor of Science in International Business. A Bachelor of Science in Nursing degree program is offered in collaboration with the University of Detroit Mercy and Mercy Health St. Mary's. A Bachelor of Science in Engineering degree program is offered in collaboration with the Western Michigan University, in addition to an accelerated bachelor's to master's degree program (4+1).

Majors and programs of study are offered in:

- accounting
- art
- art history
- biochemistry and molecular biology
- biology and health sciences
- business administration
- business administration/accounting
- business administration/chemistry
- business administration/communication
- business administration/computer information systems
- business administration/economics
- business administration/music
- business administration/sport management
- business administration/theatre
- business administration/visual arts
- Catholic studies
- chemistry
- child life
- communication
- community leadership
- computer information systems
- data analytics
- economics
- education
- engineering
- English
- English as a second language
- environmental studies
- exercise science
- French
- geography and environmental studies
- German
- health education
- health science
- history
- international studies
- international business
- Irish studies
- Japanese
- journalism/publications
- learning disabilities
- management information systems
- marketing
- mathematics
- nursing
- music
- philosophy
- physical education
- physics
- political science
- pre-law
- psychology
- sociology
- Spanish
- studio art: ceramics, drawing, painting, photography, print-making, sculpture
- sustainable business
- theatre
- theatre for social change
- theology
- translation and interpretation
- urban studies
- women's studies
- world languages

Associate degrees are also available, including the Associate of Arts and the Associate of Science.

Pre-professional programs include dentistry, law, medicine, occupational therapy, physical therapy, physician's assistant studies, and veterinary science.

Academic Programs

Aquinas students receive a four-year liberal arts education, which prepares them for employment, lifelong learning, and critical thinking. Students make real the vision of the college: Aquinas College is an exceptional Catholic liberal arts college that prepares individuals for careers of leadership and service in developing a sustainable and just global community.

In addition to their major and minor fields of study, students take a First-Year Experience Course and an integrated skills course called Inquiry and Expression. This course spans the first semester of the freshman year and has an emphasis on writing integrated with reading critically, oral communication skills, critical thinking, library/electronic research methods, computer utilization, and basic quantitative reasoning. As juniors, they are required to take three hours in Theological Foundation. Students are also required to be proficient in a second language through the 102 level. There also is a distribution plan in the general education plan covering social science, natural world, humanities, cross-cultural awareness, and mathematics.

The AQ Advantage Center expands learning beyond the classroom by housing co-curricular opportunities for study away, internships, faculty-guided research, and career services.

Aquinas sees a liberal arts education as career preparation. The Aquinas general education plan exposes students to the necessary skills that enable them to become critical thinkers, articulate speakers, strong writers, and effective problem solvers. Aquinas faculty members insist that students carry values as well as skills into the workplace. The College's curriculum, with its more than 60 majors, is designed to provide students with both breadth and depth and to foster a thirst for knowledge and truth and a spirit of intellectual dialogue and inquiry. Coupled with nationally recognized internship programs, it prepares students to both live and work in the rapidly changing world of today and tomorrow.

Aquinas also accepts credit through CLEP, Advanced Placement, and International Baccalaureate.

Off-Campus Programs

Study Away at Aquinas offers strong academic, credit-bearing educational opportunities that develop intercultural competence and globally-relevant leadership skills. Programs are offered in Costa Rica, England, France, Germany, Italy, Japan, or Spain. Students have the option of participating in the Dominican College Campus Interchange Program.

The Aquinas Ireland Study Away Program is a cultural immersion experience in Ireland that includes academics, internships, excursions, housing and community engagement. More than 1,000 students have participated in the program, which is based on the College's closed campus in Tully Cross.

The Dominican Exchange Program offers an experience at another campus through a sister-school relationship with fellow Dominican-rooted institutions around the country: Barry University in Miami Shores, Florida; Dominican University in San Rafael, California; and St. Thomas Aquinas College in Sparkill, New York.

Athletics

- Baseball (M,W)
- Golf (M,W)
- Softball (W)
- Basketball (M,W)
- Ice Hockey (M,W)
- Tennis (M,W)
- Bowling (M,W)
- Indoor Track (M,W)
- Volleyball (M,W)
- Cheerleading (co-ed)
- Irish Dance (W)
- Cross Country (M,W)
- Lacrosse (M,W)
- Dance (W)
- Outdoor Track (M,W)
- Esports (M,W)
- Soccer (M,W)

Academic Facilities

The Albertus Magnus Hall of Science is currently undergoing a $32 million expansion and renovation that will pave the way for new programs, innovative research, and student engagement. The Grace Hauenstein Library is a $6 million facility with resources that include a public access catalog, audiovisual materials, circulation and course reserve materials, reference services, and interlibrary loan services (free access to more than 60 million books and documents from libraries across the country). Other facilities include the Cook Carriage House student center and the Art and Music Center, which features a 200-seat recital hall, an art gallery, and a sculpture studio. The Aquinas Performing Arts Center is a $7 million state-of-the-art theater venue. Five apartment buildings also provide on-campus housing for upperclassmen.

The campus offers high-speed wireless internet connection, and kiosks and computer labs are located across campus in classrooms, residence halls, the Grace Hauenstein Library, and common areas.

Costs

Tuition for 2019-20 is $30,256 (12-18 credits), or $16,628 per semester. Room and board is $9,598 (standard). Required fees are $598 per year. Other expenses, including books, travel, and personal supplies, average $2,000 per year.

Financial Aid

Aquinas College awards both merit-based financial assistance and traditional need-based assistance to qualified students. The Spectrum Scholarship Program recognizes students' achievements in academics, leadership, and service. Nearly 100% of Aquinas students receive some form of financial assistance. The College administers the traditional grant and loan programs, including Federal Direct Loans and Parent PLUS loans. Athletic grants are also available. The College participates in an automatic payment program. This plan assists students in paying costs over a period of time. To apply for financial assistance, students must complete the Free Application for Federal Student Aid (FAFSA).

Faculty

Aquinas faculty members are teachers first. While research plays an important part in the Aquinas faculty's development, teaching remains the number-one priority. In addition to teaching, faculty members serve as academic advisers, mentors, and advisers to various clubs and organizations on campus. With a student-professor ratio of 11:1, faculty members give individual attention and assistance to students. All classes and labs are taught by faculty members, not graduate assistants. More than 80 percent of Aquinas faculty members have doctoral or terminal degrees.

Student Government

The Student Senate is the governing body of Aquinas students. Senators are chosen by securing 25 signatures of students in support of their involvement. These students have both voice and vote on issues facing the College's Academic Assembly. The Senate is responsible for many of the academic, social, recreational, and cultural activities on the campus.

Admission Requirements

Freshman and transfer applications are received on a rolling basis. There is no fee for filing an application for admission. A candidate for admission to Aquinas should present a completed application for admission, an official high-school transcript, the results of the ACT or SAT and a minimum of 15 acceptable academic units from an accredited high school. The admissions office reserves the right to review applications on a case-by-case basis. Curriculum, extracurricular activities, and any extenuating circumstances are considered in the decision. Letters of recommendation are encouraged but not required.

Application and Information

Prospective students may submit a free application for admission at https://www.aquinas.edu/undergraduate. For further information, interested students should contact:

Damon Bouwkamp
Senior Associate Director of Admissions
bouwkdam@aquinas.edu
(616) 632-2863
Aquinas College
1700 Fulton E
Grand Rapids, Michigan 49506-1801
Phone: 616-632-8900
800-678-9593 (toll-free)
E-mail: admissions@aquinas.edu
Website: aquinas.edu

ASSUMPTION COLLEGE

WORCESTER, MASSACHUSETTS

ASSUMPTION COLLEGE

The College

Assumption College, established in 1904 by the Augustinians of the Assumption, is a coeducational institution known for its classic liberal arts curriculum and strong academic programs in business and professional studies. The College's 2,000 undergraduates choose among 30 majors and 47 minors, gaining a depth and breadth of knowledge that serves as a foundation for personal fulfillment and lifelong success. Students' educational experience is grounded in the rich Catholic intellectual tradition, which cultivates both the mind and the personal values students require to meet the demands of a constantly changing world. Undergraduate and graduate students are guided by faculty and staff members in a thriving community that develops individuals known for critical intelligence, thoughtful citizenship, and compassionate service.

The academic journey is characterized by individual attention and the quest for personal excellence. With a student-faculty ratio of just 11:1, Assumption's professors serve as mentors who challenge students to ask questions, find their own answers, and grow—intellectually, socially, and spiritually. Students are encouraged to pursue hands-on experience at internships and to participate in individual research projects. The result? Ninety-five percent of the graduates who responded to a survey six months after graduation are either employed, enrolled in graduate school, or engaged in community service.

At Assumption, 90 percent of the undergraduates live on campus and housing is guaranteed for all four years. The campus is lively seven days a week with academic programming, activities sponsored by student clubs and organizations, community service opportunities, campus ministry programs, and intercollegiate, intramural, and club sports. The College's state-of-the-art recreation center offers a number of opportunities for students to exercise or participate in intramural sports.

Location

The College's 185-acre campus is situated in a beautiful, residential neighborhood just minutes from downtown Worcester, Massachusetts. Worcester, the second-largest city in New England, is a vibrant college town, home to 35,000 students. The city offers extensive opportunities for internships in virtually every field, as well as numerous entertainment and community service options. Great restaurants, cultural venues and programs, and retail shops provide students with an array of off-campus activities. Worcester is also centrally located to exciting urban areas such as Boston; Providence, Rhode Island; and Hartford, Connecticut only an hour's drive away. The mountains of Vermont and New Hampshire provide skiing, hiking, and sightseeing opportunities. There are numerous daily commuter trains to Boston as well as other transportation options.

Majors and Degrees

Assumption offers undergraduate and graduate degrees.

Undergraduates pursue Bachelor of Arts degrees. The most popular majors include English (concentrations in literature or writing and mass communications), history, political science, psychology, the natural sciences (biology, biotechnology and molecular biology, neuroscience, chemistry, and environmental science), education, human services and rehabilitation studies, and business disciplines such as accounting, international business, management, marketing, and organizational communication. Minors are offered in 47 areas. Pre-professional advising programs are available for medicine, law, and dentistry.

The College has also developed partnerships with a number of highly regarded institutions to provide students with additional options, including engineering with the University of Notre Dame and Washington University in St. Louis, environmental science with Duke University, and law (3+3 programs) with Duquesne, Vermont, University of St. Thomas, and Western New England law schools. There are agreements for numerous medical professions as well, and joint seven-year programs are also available for those interested in podiatry or optometry.

Assumption College offers graduate degrees in applied behavior analysis, business, special education, school counseling, clinical counseling psychology, health advocacy, and rehabilitation counseling. An accelerated 6-in-5 combined bachelor's and master's degree is offered in several programs.

Academic Programs

The College's classic liberal arts curriculum promotes lively discussion of the books, ideas, people, and events that have shaped civilization. Faculty members and students explore the rich Catholic intellectual tradition together as they seek truth and the nature of the world.

Assumption also offers academic programs and courses that help students achieve their full potential. The College's Honors Program and the Fortin and Gonthier Core Texts and Enduring Questions Program encourage students to challenge themselves intellectually through intensive study and independent research. The SOPHIA (SOPHomore Initiative at Assumption) program is designed to help students discover a deeper connection between their spiritual, personal, and professional lives. Air Force and Army ROTC are also available at a neighboring institution.

Assumption College follows a traditional two-semester calendar, from late August to mid-May, as well as an optional January intersession. The Graduate Studies programs and the Center for Continuing and Career Education also offer two summer sessions for students.

Undergraduates complete a core curriculum that provides a strong foundation in the liberal arts, in addition to developing the skills and knowledge necessary for their professional career. Students must complete 120 credit hours in all academic programs to earn a degree.

Off-Campus Programs

The College and eleven other institutions of higher learning compose the Colleges of Worcester Consortium, which combines resources to offer the 35,000 college students in the area even greater academic and social opportunities. Assumption students may cross-register for academic credit at any of the participating colleges and enjoy their social and cultural events. Free transportation to and from other participating institutions is available.

Eligible students may choose to spend a semester or a year abroad. Assumption opened a campus in Rome in February 2013. The campus provides the opportunity for a close learning community where students live, study, and travel together in the city that forged the foundations of Western Civilization. The College's students have studied abroad in Australia, Austria, Chile, China, Costa Rica, the Czech Republic, England, France, Germany, Greece, Ireland, Italy, Japan, the Netherlands, Spain, and other locations. There are also numerous one- and two-week international experiences led by Assumption faculty.

Eighty-four percent of Assumption students have undertaken at least one internship, where they explore their professional choices and broaden their workplace skills at local, regional, national, and international sites. In recent years, they have interned at PBS, the U.S. House of Representatives, Ralph Lauren, the Hungarian Embassy, Smith Barney, Fidelity, *The Rachel Ray Show, The Daily Show with Jon Stewart*, ABC News, PricewaterhouseCoopers, AT&T, Sony Japan, and countless other organizations.

Campus Facilities

The recently constructed Tsotsis Family Academic Center is a 62,000-square-foot building that features 13 high-tech, flexible classrooms; seminar rooms; common study spaces; a 400-seat performance hall with a rehearsal room, both of which are equipped with a sophisticated sound system not found in any other higher education institution on the East Coast; and a multi-function space that can accommodate 400 people.

The Testa Science Center houses the Department of Natural Sciences and features multiuse classrooms with state-of-the-art technology, ten teaching laboratories, seven laboratories dedicated to faculty and student research, a greenhouse, and student lounge areas.

The Information Technology Center houses computer labs, technology-rich classrooms, and an experienced support staff. Students can learn Web authoring, graphics and animation, digital video, and multimedia production. The digital audio studio is available to all students and faculty members.

Assumption offers a variety of housing options to accommodate the 90 percent of students who choose to live on campus. There are traditional residence halls, suites, a living and learning residence, and apartments with full kitchens. All resident students have individual hard-wired and wireless Internet access in their rooms. The College's stadium and athletic facilities support Assumption's 24 NCAA Division II intercollegiate teams, recreational programs, and the physical well-being of the campus community.

Costs

For 2018–19, tuition was $40,208, room and board were $12,684, and student fees were $750. The board plan is required for all first-year students.

Financial Aid

The College offers financial aid based on demonstrated need and scholastic achievement. The College requires that students submit the Free Application for Federal Student Aid (FAFSA),which is available on October 1. This form should be filed by February 15, so that the College may consider the information as it makes financial aid awards.

All applicants for admission are considered for merit awards of up to $24,000 per year. Funds awarded through this program reflect the College's commitment to academic excellence and student leadership. The College also awards up to fifty $26,000 Light the Way Scholarships each year to students who are working to positively impact the work in their own meaningful way.

Faculty

More than 94 percent of the Assumption College faculty members hold the highest degree in their field. They are active scholars presenting their ideas and research at professional conferences, writing books and articles, and publishing in journals. With a student-to-faculty ratio of 11:1, professors work closely with students and challenge them to explore new paths of knowledge and make their own discoveries. All of Assumption's academic advisors are full-time faculty members.

Student Organizations and Government

There are more than 60 clubs and organizations on campus, offering students many opportunities in community service, sports, academics, leadership, and special interests. The Student Government Association (SGA), the elected representatives of the student body, coordinates official communication between the student community and the College administration and officially recognizes student clubs and activities.

Admission Requirements

All applicants must graduate from an accredited secondary school with a minimum of 18 academic units. These units should include 4 years of English, 3 years of mathematics, 2 years of a foreign language, 2 years of history, 2 years of science, and 5 additional academic units.

Admission to Assumption is test-score optional. When submitting an application, an essay and recommendations are required. Interviews are recommended, but not required.

The number of solid academic courses, including the number of honors-level or Advanced Placement–level courses, is considered during the application review process.

The Admissions Committee understands that grading standards vary from school to school and from one course to another. Class rank provides some context within which to place the grades of students applying from a given school, but is not the only factor weighed when considering a student for admission. Some schools also provide grade distribution charts. The Committee also considers whether the applicant's grade point average or rank in class is weighted or unweighted.

Application and Information

Campus visits are strongly recommended. Appointments can be scheduled Monday through Friday and most Saturdays in the fall.

Applicants must submit a completed application, a $50 application fee, official transcripts, a recommendation letter, and an essay. Applications for early action admission must be received by November 1. There is a second early action admission deadline of December 15. The deadline for regular admission is February 15. Students may complete the Common Application and Supplement at www.commonapp.org.

For more information, students should contact:

Office of Admissions
Assumption College
500 Salisbury Street
P.O. Box 15005
Worcester, Massachusetts 01609-1296
Phone: 508-767-7285
866-477-7776 (toll-free)
E-mail: admissions@assumption.edu
Website: www.assumption.edu
twitter.com/AssumptionNews
facebook.com/assumptioncollege

Assumption provides an environment that encourages a quest for knowledge, personal growth, and discovery.

BARNARD COLLEGE

NEW YORK, NEW YORK

The College

The founders of Barnard College were among the pioneers in the late nineteenth-century crusade who sought to make access to higher education available to women. Founded in 1889 and formally partnered with Columbia University since 1900, the College serves more than 2,600 students today from almost every state and more than fifty countries. It offers the intimacy of a small college with the added advantages of a large research university. Barnard remains affiliated with Columbia, with students at both schools regularly cross-registering for courses taught at either institution. Barnard students have access to the University's resources and graduates receive their degree from Columbia. At the same time, Barnard College remains a small, independent liberal arts college, devoted solely to the undergraduate education of women. The College maintains its own Board of Trustees, faculty, administrative staff, endowment, admissions process, and sole ownership of its property and physical plant.

The self-contained Barnard campus occupies 4+ acres of urban property along Broadway between 116th and 120th streets and serves as an oasis from the hustle and bustle of New York City. Its location on the upper west side of Manhattan grants students access to thousands of internship opportunities in addition to unparalleled cultural, intellectual, and social resources. Forty-five percent of students identify as students of color, and 13 percent come from non-college backgrounds.

Location

Barnard is located north of Central Park on the upper west side of Manhattan, in the safe and student-friendly Morningside Heights neighborhood. The campus is directly across from Columbia University, and has numerous educational and cultural institutions as neighbors, including the Jewish Theological Seminary, Bank Street School of Education, St. John the Divine church, and Grant's tomb. Abounding with cultural, educational, internship, and professional opportunities and more than 500,000 college students, New York is Barnard's laboratory.

Majors and Degrees

Students can earn a Bachelor of Arts (B.A.) in the following subjects: Africana studies, American studies, ancient studies, anthropology, architecture, art history, Asian and Middle Eastern cultures, astronomy, biochemistry, biological sciences, chemistry, classics (Greek and Latin), comparative literature, computer science, dance, economics, education, English, environmental biology science or studies, European studies, film studies, French, German, history, human rights, Italian, Jewish studies, mathematics and applied mathematics, medieval and Renaissance studies, music, neuroscience, philosophy, physics, political science, psychology, religion, Russian and Slavic studies, sociology, Spanish and Latin American cultures, statistics, theater, urban studies, and women's, gender, and sexuality studies. The College provides an excellent education program, leading to teaching certification with a specific urban studies track, and prepares students for programs in health and medicine, law, and business, as well as further study in a variety of graduate programs.

Barnard College also offers double- and joint-degree programs in cooperation with other schools within the Columbia community as well as several 4+1 programs for a graduate degree. These include a five-year M.P.A./M.I.A. (3-2) program offered in conjunction with the School of International and Public Affairs (SIPA), a double-degree program with List College of the Jewish Theological Seminary, and through the Fu Foundation School of Engineering and Applied Science at Columbia, Barnard students can pursue a five-year (3-2) program in all branches of engineering. The 4+1 programs are in partnership with a number of Columbia's programs: the School of International and Public Affairs (SIPA), the School of Engineering and Applies Sciences (SEAS), the Mailman School of Public Health, the Harriman Institute for Russian, European and Eastern European Studies, the Graduate School of Arts and Sciences Oral History program (OHMA), and the Graduate School of Arts and Sciences Quantitative Methods in the Social Sciences program(QMSS).

Academic Programs

Two required courses, First-Year Seminar and First-Year Writing, set the foundation for a Barnard education with small seminar classes, limited to 16 and 12 students, respectively. In addition to these First Year Experience courses, Barnard's flexible general education requirements are organized around Foundation Requirements in four subject areas and Modes of Thinking that connect to six themes. A generous list of courses allows for students to choose which options interest them most. Barnard students shape their educational experience by choosing courses that enhance the way they view the world.

Advanced placement and I.B. credit are available. Barnard operates on a two-semester calendar, with classes beginning in early September. The fall semester ends in mid-December; classes resume for the spring semester in mid-January and end in mid-May.

Off-Campus Programs

As an independent partner of Columbia University, Barnard offers students open access to courses, libraries, and other facilities of the University. With special permission, students may also register for selected classes in Columbia's graduate and professional schools. In addition, two highly selective lesson exchange programs with the Juilliard School and the nearby Manhattan School of Music allow qualified Barnard students to take music lessons in a conservatory setting.

Barnard has a rich history and tradition of study abroad dating back to the 1930s. Today, qualified students are eligible to study in nearly 100 programs in more than fifty countries worldwide and nearly forty percent of Barnard students spend a semester or year abroad. Students are currently studying in Argentina, Australia, Austria, Bolivia, Brazil, Chile, China, Costa Rica, Czech Republic, Denmark, Ecuador, England, France, Germany, Greece, Hungary, Ireland, Israel, Italy, Japan, Jordan, Kenya, Madagascar, Netherlands, New Zealand, Panama, Peru, Russia, Scotland, Senegal, South Africa, Spain, Switzerland, and other locations. Students may also participate in a domestic exchange with Spelman College in Atlanta or Howard University in Washington, D.C.

Barnard's location offers its students a variety of work experiences and 75 percent of students will complete an internship.

Academic Facilities

Barnard's campus blends classic and modern architecture. The Cheryl and Philip Milstein Teaching and Learning Center, which opened in fall 2018, serves as the academic hub in the heart of the Barnard College campus. The 128,000 square-foot building includes a 40,000 square-foot library and centers for pedagogy, media, data analysis, movement, and design. The Center includes the Vagelos Computational Science Center, homes for the Barnard Center for Research on Women and the Athena Center for Leadership Studies, and social and study spaces for students. Historic Milbank Hall anchors the north end of campus, topped by the 2,500-square-foot Arthur Ross Greenhouse, housing administrative and faculty offices in addition to the Minor Latham Playhouse.

The south end of the campus, referred to as the Quad, contains the Brooks, Reid, Hewitt, and Sulzberger residence halls; first-year students are housed in the Quad. Additional housing (twelve residence halls in total) provides those entering as first-years guaranteed housing for four years of continuous enrollment at

Barnard. The Diana Center, a 70,000 square-foot student center, added a new element of design in 2010. Its seven-story glass structure stretches across campus, linking the historic gates of the entrance at the south end of campus, to one of the original campus buildings, Milbank Hall, on the north.

Costs

Tuition and fees for 2018–19 were $55,032. Room and board costs are an additional $17,225.

Financial Aid

Financial aid at Barnard is awarded based upon demonstrated need. Federal funds and institutional grants are administered as determined by federal and institutional methodology. Barnard provides no merit or athletic scholarships. Once need has been established, Barnard covers 100 percent of demonstrated need with a combination of grants, loans, and work-study or student employment. Approximately 40 percent of the students at Barnard receive some form of financial aid.

Barnard College has a need-blind admission policy in which first-year applicants who are U.S. citizens or permanent residents are judged solely on merit without reference to financial circumstances. International and transfer students are considered for need-based aid from a limited pool of funding.

Faculty

Barnard College employs more than 300 teaching faculty members with a student-faculty ratio of 9:1. Barnard's faculty includes editors of leading scholarly journals, prize-winning novelists and translators, and frequent winners of awards from respected foundations, corporations, and government agencies. They are actively engaged in research and publication in their respective fields, but they regard teaching as their primary commitment. From the start of their time at the College, all students have faculty advisers who assist them in selecting courses and designing individual academic programs, in addition to a vast network of decanal, staff, and peer advising.

Student Life

Barnard women have access to more than eighty clubs and organizations on the College campus alone. Add to this list the hundreds of additional dually recognized clubs with members from both Barnard and Columbia, provided for through Barnard's long-standing partnership with the University, and strong friendships develop among students from both sides of Broadway. Student groups include performance groups, academic and pre-professional, ethnic and cultural, language, community service, and publications. Social interaction and cooperation between Barnard and Columbia groups is virtually seamless, with Barnard women regularly joining and leading a variety of Columbia organizations. Students, faculty members, and administrators also serve on tripartite committees and share responsibility for policy on curriculum, housing, financial aid, orientation, and the library.

On Barnard's campus, every student service is designed to meet the needs of a women-focused community. Primary Health Services, Furman Counseling Center, the academic advising program, and a unique Career Development and graduate school/fellowships advising Center called Beyond Barnard create programs to provide the kind of support young women may need as they navigate their academic experiences and life beyond college. The Athena Center for Leadership studies also provides Barnard students with the unique opportunity to become an Athena scholar and dedicate a portion of their studies to leadership development, history, and skills, culminating in a senior capstone project.

Admission Requirements

The Committee on Admissions selects motivated women of proven academic strength who exhibit intellectual and personal maturity. Careful consideration is given to candidates' high school records, recommendations, writing skills, standardized test scores, special abilities and interests, and personal and educational context.

Admission to Barnard is highly selective and candidates for admission to the first-year class are expected to have taken a highly rigorous college-preparatory program. Students educated in a non-English-speaking setting or who have studied in English for less than four years must also take the TOEFL or IELTS exam. Interview opportunities are available for first-year students, but are not required. Barnard also enrolls a robust transfer class for fall and spring semesters and offers visiting student opportunities.

Application and Information

Applicants for first-year admission should apply in the fall of their senior year of high school. Applications must be received by January 1 and must include the non-refundable application fee. Students are notified in late March. Well-qualified high school seniors who have selected Barnard as their first-choice college are encouraged to apply under the binding early decision plan. Early decision applications must be submitted by November 1. Barnard accepts sophomore and junior transfer students. Transfer and visiting student applications must be submitted by March 15 for consideration for September entrance and by November 1 for consideration for January entrance.

For more information about Barnard College, students should contact:

Dean of Admissions
Barnard College, Office of Admissions
3009 Broadway
New York, New York 10027
Phone: 212-854-2014
Fax: 212-280-8797
E-mail: admissions@barnard.edu
Website: http://www.admissions.barnard.edu

A view of Milbank Hall from the Diana, Barnard's multipurpose student center.

BENTLEY UNIVERSITY

WALTHAM, MASSACHUSETTS

BENTLEY UNIVERSITY

The University

Bentley University provides a modern business education to prepare students for today's complex business world. The Bentley experience has been designed to give students more: Business plus the arts and sciences. Classroom learning plus real-world experience. World-class technology plus global perspective. As a result, Bentley students are highly sought after by today's leading organizations because of their professionalism, exposure to state-of-the-art research tools, and diverse, real-world experience. In its 2016 "Best Undergraduate Business Schools" issue, *Bloomberg Businessweek* ranked Bentley 10th among the country's top undergraduate business programs.

Located on a classic New England campus minutes from Boston, Bentley offers a wide variety of majors and minors, as well as optional liberal studies and business studies majors designed to create a modern intersection of the arts and sciences and business that's unique in higher education. This fusion of business fundamentals and liberal arts enables Bentley students to think outside of the box when faced with critical decisions in the workplace.

Bentley was recently ranked #1 in the country for its career services office and #1 in the country for internship opportunities by the Princeton Review in 2019. The Office of Career Services offers resources including an on-campus recruiting program involving 1,000 national and international companies; an online job and internship database; career fairs; workshops on topics such as interviewing and networking; and a Career Development Seminar (CDI 101) for first-year students.

This approach works: 99 percent of students in the Class of 2018 found employment or enrolled in graduate school within six months of graduation. The median annual salary was $59,000.

Approximately 98 percent of freshmen live on campus. Twenty-three residence halls provide a range of housing options: dorms, suites, and apartments. Housing is provided for all four years; all residence halls are air-conditioned and typically include study lounges, exercise facilities, TV lounges, and game rooms. Bentley has a variety of meal plans for students to choose from as they move into suites and apartments with kitchens. There are eleven places on campus to dine, offering an array of food options from buffet-style cafeterias to Currito and Dunkin's.

Students live and learn in a multicultural environment that prepares them to thrive in today's diverse world. International students representing nearly 100 countries make up 18 percent of the undergraduate student body and bring valuable perspectives to the Bentley community.

Supporting Bentley's commitment to diversity are offices such as the Multicultural Center, Spiritual Life Center, Center for International Students and Scholars, Center for Women in Business, and the Women's Center.

The newly renovated Student Center is the hub of campus activity and is home to the main dining room, the pub, eateries, student services, and more than 100 student organizations. These groups represent academics, the arts and media, religions, fraternity and sorority life, and cultural interests.

Athletic programs are a Bentley hallmark and include intramurals, recreational sports, and more than 20 varsity teams in NCAA Divisions I and II. The Dana Athletic Center houses a weight and fitness complex, food court, locker rooms, a gym, a basketball court, volleyball and racquetball courts, a competition-size pool with a diving tank, and saunas. Outdoor facilities include soccer and baseball fields, a track, and tennis courts. Bentley's brand-new arena is home to the school's Division I hockey team and other campus activities.

Location

Bentley's location in Waltham, Massachusetts—just minutes west of Boston—puts the city within easy reach. As the country's ultimate university town, Boston's options range from theater to art exhibits, dance clubs to concerts, and championship sports to world-class shopping. Bentley's free shuttle makes regular trips to Harvard Square in Cambridge, just a subway ride from Boston. Boston also offers many opportunities for internships and jobs after graduation.

Majors and Degrees

The Bentley curriculum is a ground-breaking integration of business and the arts and sciences that has been featured in the *Wall Street Journal*.

To that end, Bachelor of Science (B.S.) degree programs enable students to gain in-depth knowledge and skills in specific business disciplines: accountancy, actuarial science, computer information systems, corporate finance and accounting, creative industries, data analytics, economics–finance, finance, information design and corporate communication, information systems audit and control, management, managerial economics, marketing, mathematical sciences, and professional sales.

Bentley also offers Bachelor of Arts (B.A.) degree programs with majors in English, health sciences, Hispanic studies, history, international affairs, liberal arts, media and culture, philosophy, public policy, and sustainability science. All B.A. students gain business experience through either the Business Studies Major (BSM) or minor. All students can also choose from one of 35 minors, including entrepreneurial studies, law, and sports management.

The Liberal Studies Major (LSM), an optional double major, can be combined with any business program. It provides students with a competitive edge by building meaningful connections across and within disciplines. To complete the LSM, students do not need to take any extra courses beyond those normally required. It allows students to add another credential to their degree, helping them stand out to employers. LSM concentrations include American studies; diversity and society; earth, environment, and global sustainability; ethics and social responsibility; global perspectives; health and industry; media arts and society; and quantitative perspectives.

Academic Programs

The Honors Program provides our most academically-talented students, selected each year from the top 10 percent of applicants, access to challenging, seminar-style courses each semester, small classes, as well as research funding and fellowships. Honors Program students also enjoy co-curricular activities designed to enhance the academic curriculum.

The Women's Leadership Program is sponsored by Bentley's Center for Women and Business, and gives participants the opportunity to participate in workshops, roundtables, and special events that explore critical gender equity issues on a deeper level, while developing effective leadership and communications skills. The program also includes a $10,000 annual award toward tuition, totaling $40,000 over four years.

The Falcon Fast-Track Program is a streamlined graduate school enrollment option for top-tier Bentley graduates with a GPA of 3.2 or higher. This new program allows qualified Bentley graduates to obtain a master's degree after completing a bachelor's degree (up to five years after graduation) without going through the traditional application process, including waiver of the GMAT or GRE, and no application fee.

Off-Campus Programs

Hands-on experience is emphasized across the curriculum. Internships, study abroad, service-learning, and corporate partnerships allow students to apply classroom theory in the community.

Each year, more than 92 percent of students complete at least one internship and 71 percent complete two or more, building valuable work experience and networking connections. Some of the top internship employers include Fidelity Investments, the TJX Companies, Liberty Mutual, Bain & Company, and all of the Big Four accounting firms.

Bentley students can gain insight into different cultures by studying abroad. Programs take place in more than 26 countries and vary in length from one week to a full academic year.

Through Bentley's Service-Learning Center, students build skills in business, communication, and teamwork while assisting nonprofit and community-based organizations both locally and internationally.

Academic Facilities

Concepts taught in the classroom are put to use in several high-tech learning laboratories.

Bentley's financial Trading Room combines state-of-the-art technology and real-time data to offer first-hand exposure to financial concepts in simulated trading sessions. Resources include Bloomberg, Capital IQ, Datastream, FactSet, Thomson One Analytics, Portfolio Analysis, MATLAB, S&P Compustat, and Worldscope.

The Center for Marketing Technology plays an integral role in marketing programs. Students gain a full grasp of software options, familiarity with research tools and techniques, and knowledge of new digital marketing frameworks.

The Accounting Center for Electronic Learning and Business Management (ACELAB) introduces cutting-edge technologies that are reshaping the accounting profession. Students have access to auditing and tax preparation software as well as other professional applications from industry leaders such as SAP and Oracle.

The Center for Languages and International Collaboration (CLIC) is a key resource for language courses, international studies majors, and students with an interest in global issues. The center promotes collaboration among Bentley students and their counterparts overseas.

The Media and Culture Labs and Studio feature resources for video production and editing as well as digital photography. The lab provides students with industry-standard software programs for screenwriting, sound mixing, graphic design, and DVD authoring.

The User Experience Center (UXC) features labs ideal for usability testing. Students use the applications employed by technical communicators, web developers, user-interface designers, and usability specialists.

The CIS Learning and Technology Sandbox is a collaborative space for learning new technologies. Its resources include Google TVs, Xbox 360 with Kinect, study spaces, large-screen TVs, a smart board, specialized networking equipment, and the latest in Windows, Linux, and Android development software.

The Bentley Library is outfitted with computer workstations, group study rooms, and wireless network access. It also has an exceptional number of online database resources, research guides, and consultation appointments are available to assist students with their projects.

Costs

Tuition for resident and nonresident students during the 2019–20 academic year is $50,060. Room and board (double room, meal plan) costs are $16,960. Additional expenses include books, supplies, technology fee, and personal and travel expenses.

Financial Aid

Bentley's financial aid program includes both scholarships based on academic achievement, which are awarded through the admission process, as well as grants based on financial need. Bentley administered nearly $100 million in aid to undergraduate students last year. More than 80 percent of aid awarded comes from Bentley-funded grants and scholarships. Currently, more than 70 percent of undergraduates receive some type of financial assistance—either grants, scholarships, loans, and/or work study.

Faculty

Bentley faculty members are teacher-scholars known for their classroom skills and cutting-edge research. They bring practical, real-world experience to the classroom, based on years of professional involvement in their fields. Faculty research focuses on issues of prime importance to current business practice. Much of the research is conducted in partnership with leading organizations. A student-faculty ratio of 11:1 and average class size of 26 ensure a personal experience for students. All courses are taught by professors; there are no teaching assistants. Students often note that professors are accessible to them outside of the classroom.

Student Government

Bentley has a number of student governing groups, including the Student Government Association, Residence Hall Association, and the Graduate Student Association.

Admission Requirements

Applicants are encouraged to complete a competitive university preparatory program. Recommendations include four years of English, four years of mathematics (preferably algebra I and II, geometry, and pre-calculus or its equivalent), and three to four years each of history, laboratory science, and a foreign language.

Along with the application, students must submit a secondary school transcript, letters of recommendation from a teacher and a counselor, and official scores of either the SAT or ACT. Bentley has a separate application for transfer students. Applicants who are nonnative speakers of English must also submit official scores of the Test of English as a Foreign Language (TOEFL).

Application and Information

Bentley University accepts the Common Application. Candidates for the fall semester are notified in late March; spring semester candidates and transfers are notified on a rolling basis.

Prospective students can visit bentley.edu/undergraduate/applying for application information and deadlines.

For more information, students should contact:

Office of Undergraduate Admission
Bentley University
175 Forest Street
Waltham, Massachusetts 02452-4705
Phone: 781-891-2244
800-523-2354 (toll-free)
Fax: 781-891-3414
E-mail: ugadmission@bentley.edu
Website: bentley.edu/undergraduate
facebook.com/bentleyadmission
twitter.com/ugabentley

Bentley opened the new arena, home to the Division I hockey team, in February 2018.

COLLEGE CLOSE-UPS

BOSTON COLLEGE

CHESTNUT HILL, MASSACHUSETTS

The University

Boston College (BC) was founded in 1863 by the Jesuits to serve the sons of Boston's Irish immigrants. Today a coeducational university on more than 239 acres in Chestnut Hill, BC may seem a world apart from the small school in the crowded heart of Boston that was its first home. Through more than fifteen decades of growth and change, however, BC has held fast to the Jesuit ideals that inspired its founders. A Jesuit education today, as a century ago, is grounded in the liberal arts and in a commitment to the service of others.

Undergraduates may enroll in the Morrissey College of Arts and Sciences, the Wallace E. Carroll School of Management, the Connell School of Nursing, or the Lynch School of Education.

BC's approximately 9,000 undergraduates come from many backgrounds. The university draws from nearly all fifty states and more than fifty-five countries. Students' religious and cultural backgrounds are similarly diverse. Today, the university's AHANA (African American, Hispanic, Asian, and Native American) and international students make up approximately 30 percent of the undergraduate student body.

In today's complex and increasingly diverse world, the university believes that the best education is one that broadens a student's capacity to reason, think, and make critical judgments in a wide range of areas. Thus, each BC student fulfills a core of liberal arts courses from which he or she can pursue degrees in more than fifty areas of study and choose from more than 1,400 course offerings throughout the university.

According to several recent national publications, BC is in the top tier of the nation's colleges and universities. The foundation for that achievement is the university's scholars and researchers—834 full-time professionals who make up the faculty. The kinship between teachers and students is one of the hallmarks of a BC education; that relationship is nurtured by a student-teacher ratio of 12.2:1. The median class size at the university is 20 students.

At BC, learning continues beyond the classroom in more than 225 student-run organizations. These include student government, honor societies, language and cultural organizations, performance ensembles, political groups, pre-professional clubs, publications, and service organizations. BC also sponsors thirteen varsity teams for men and sixteen for women, all of which compete at the NCAA Division I level. The College also supports over sixty club and intramural sports.

Boston College's public affairs office maintains university profiles on major social networking sites including: Twitter (http://twitter.com/BostonCollege), Facebook (http://www.facebook.com/BostonCollege), YouTube (http://www.youtube.com/bostoncollege), Instagram (http://instagram.com/BostonCollege), and LinkedIn (https://www.linkedin.com/school/boston-college/).

Location

Located in the Chestnut Hill section of Newton, BC sits on the doorstep of one of America's great cities, a center of culture and education for more than three centuries. It is an energetic, cosmopolitan city that draws life and enthusiasm from the more than 200,000 college students in residence during the academic year. Located just 6 miles from downtown Boston and with easy access to the city via the trolley system that stops at the foot of the campus, BC offers the best of both worlds: a scenic suburban setting neighboring an exciting metropolitan center.

Majors and Degrees

The College of Arts and Sciences (A&S) is the oldest and largest of the four undergraduate schools at BC. A&S students must complete thirty-eight 1-semester courses, thirty-two of which are in A&S departments. The normal course load is five courses per semester for the first three years and four courses per semester during the senior year. The undergraduate curriculum includes the university core curriculum and ten to twelve courses in the major field, with the remainder of courses chosen as electives. A&S offers degrees in the following areas: art history, biochemistry, biology, chemistry, classical studies, communication, computer science, economics, English, environmental geosciences, environmental studies, film studies, French, geology, geological studies, geophysics, German studies, Hispanic studies, history, independent major, international studies, Islamic civilizations and societies, Italian, linguistics, mathematics, music, neuroscience, philosophy, physics, political science, psychology, Russian, Slavic studies, sociology, studio art, theater, and theology. Pre-professional advisement is also available in medical, dental, veterinary, and legal programs. Students can also select from twenty-one departmental minors, or seventeen interdisciplinary minors.

The Carroll School of Management educates students to be leaders in business and industry and in public agencies, educational institutions, and service organizations. The Carroll School offers concentrations in accounting, accounting information systems, computer science, corporate reporting and analysis, economics, finance, general management, information systems, management and leadership, marketing, operations management, and new co-concentration options in entrepreneurship, business analytics, and managing for social impact and the public good.

The Lynch School of Education and Human Development prepares students for education and human services professions. Programs provide a general education, professional preparation, and specialized education in the major field. Fieldwork in area schools is closely linked to course work in each specialization. The Lynch School awards degrees upon completion of thirty-eight courses, including the university core curriculum, a major field of study in education, and a second major in a subject field or an interdisciplinary area in A&S that complements the student's program. Areas of specialization include applied psychology and human development, elementary education, and secondary education. The Lynch School also offers interdisciplinary majors in American heritages, general science, mathematics/computer science, and perspectives on Spanish America.

The Connell School of Nursing offers a four-year program of study leading to a Bachelor of Science degree. The three major components to the curriculum are nursing major courses, electives, and the required university core curriculum. In all courses, principles of wellness, illness, rehabilitation, and health maintenance serve as a theoretical basis in preparing students for professional nursing practice. Nursing courses include traditional classes, simulated and audiovisual laboratory activities on campus, and clinical learning activities in health-care settings.

Academic Programs

Every BC education is centered on a core curriculum—a set of required courses. BC offers a core curriculum because it believes in the unity of knowledge. While the core, which is continually reviewed by a committee of faculty members, varies somewhat by school, its common elements include literature, natural science, writing, philosophy, theology, social science, history, mathematics, fine arts, and cultural diversity.

There are a wide variety of extraordinary academic programs available to BC students to enhance their educational experience. They include, among others, honors programs within each of the university's four undergraduate schools, Undergraduate Faculty Research Fellows, the Scholar of the College, PULSE, and Perspectives on Western Culture.

Off-Campus Programs

BC encourages all students to take part in internship programs. Approximately 87 percent of BC undergraduates participate in at least one internship or prepracticum placement during their college years. Internships can be paid or unpaid and may take place during the academic year or the summer; some carry academic credit.

BC students may take on the challenge of international study in more than sixty programs administered by BC at universities in more than forty countries. BC students who study abroad typically do so in their junior year, but there is also a range of full-year and summer-abroad opportunities. The Office of International Programs helps students with program selection and applications and maintains a library of reference books and professional evaluations of international study programs.

Academic Facilities

BC's eight libraries contain more than 3.2 million printed volumes, over 4.3 million items in microform, 844,953 e-books, 271,792 government documents, 42,277 serial subscriptions, and a wide collection of films and archival items. The resources of the library system range from some of Europe's earliest printed books to hundreds of computerized databases. Students with personal computers have dorm-room access to these databases as well as to Quest and other library information sources through Agora, the campus information network. BC also offers a 24/7 "Ask a Librarian" e-mail service and the capability to text questions to a librarian. In addition, all of BC's libraries and classrooms offer a wireless network that provides access to these resources and the Internet.

Research laboratories in the state-of-the-art science facilities have been specially designed to accommodate the advanced instrumentation required for modern science and to provide flexibility for accommodating new equipment. The $85-million expansion to the Higgins Biology and Physics Center was carefully designed to place classrooms, laboratories, computer facilities, and office space in proximity and to facilitate interaction among faculty members, researchers, and students. In addition to the Center's seventeen teaching laboratories, special working labs are designed and outfitted for research and teaching in the fields of biology and physics.

Boston College opened Stokes Hall in January 2013. This $78-million facility was strategically designed to foster interdisciplinary collaboration among BC's humanities departments and enhanced student-faculty interaction, with thirty-six state-of-the-art classrooms and 200 faculty offices for the Classical Studies, English, History, Philosophy, and Theology departments. Stokes Hall also houses the Academic Advising Center, College of Arts and Sciences Honors Department, and Office of First Year Experience, as well as common areas, conference rooms, a coffee shop, and an outdoor garden and plaza that provide multiple meeting spaces to connect students and faculty.

In 2016, BC opened a new residence hall with 490 beds, as well as a new museum of art which hosts modern architecture with larger space for exhibits, functions, and meetings.

In 2018, BC opened the newly constructed Fish Field House which provides 115,700 square feet of indoor practice space for football, as well as re-designed outdoor athletics fields for baseball and soccer. A new, state of the art, recreation complex is finishing the final stages of construction, and should be open in the summer of 2019.

Costs

Tuition for the 2018–19 academic year was $54,600, which included a student activity fee and campus health fee of $864. The total for room and board was $14,478, which included the board plan. Freshman mandatory fees include a one-time required charge of $520 for first-year orientation and student identification.

Financial Aid

BC maintains a financial aid program to assist deserving and qualified students who might otherwise not be able to attend the university. Boston College is committed to providing funds to meet the full demonstrated need of every admitted student who applies for financial aid. Overall, 67 percent of students receive some form of financial aid with the University awarding over $137 million annually in need-based scholarships and grants. Assistance for freshmen alone included more than $40 million in need-based scholarships and grants. The university offers financial aid to students based on need as demonstrated by completion of the College Scholarship Service's Financial Aid PROFILE and the Free Application for Federal Student Aid (FAFSA). All requirements and deadlines and complete instructions are available in BC admission literature. An application for financial aid in no way affects a decision on admission.

Each year, BC chooses 15 incoming freshmen as Presidential Scholars to receive merit-based, full-tuition scholarships. Students are selected from all candidates who apply through the early action program.

Faculty

BC has 834 full-time faculty members. Of these faculty members, 98 percent hold doctoral degrees. Approximately 50 Jesuits live on BC-owned property and make up one of the largest Apostolic Jesuit communities in the world. About a quarter of those members are active in the College's administration and teaching.

Student Government

The Undergraduate Government of Boston College (UGBC), formed in 1968, is led by the president and vice president, who are elected in the spring of each year by the entire student body. UGBC's goal is to serve the students by providing services and opportunities and by representing them in the best manner possible to the university community. To accomplish this goal, UGBC provides many educational, social, and cultural programs, such as concerts, lectures, roundtables, and more.

Admission Requirements

The undergraduate admission staff pays particular attention to students who have done well in a demanding college-preparatory curriculum, including Advanced Placement (AP) and honors courses when available. For the class of 2022, there were 31,084 applications for 2,327 places. The majority of incoming freshmen ranked comfortably in the top 10 percent of their high school class. The SAT scores of the middle half of admitted freshmen were 1320–1490. On the ACT, scores of the middle half were between 31 and 34.

Application and Information

Students applying to Boston College for a place in the freshman class must complete both the Common Application and the Boston College Supplemental Application. All applicants should submit the BC Supplemental Application as soon as they have decided to apply to Boston College. Students are encouraged to review the electronic application instructions on BC's website at http://www.bc.edu/content/bc/admission/undergrad/process.html and then apply at http://www.commonapp.org.

Students applying through the regular admission program must submit the Common Application and all other required forms, along with the $80 application fee, by January 1. Candidates are notified of action taken on their application in early April. Admitted students intending to matriculate are required to forward a confirmation fee to the Admission Office postmarked by May 1.

Students with superior academic credentials who view Boston College as a top choice may apply through the nonbinding early action program. These applicants must submit both application forms, along with the $80 application fee, by November 1. Candidates learn of their admission decision before December 25 but have the standard deadline (May 1) to reserve their places as freshmen. Boston College does permit students to apply under early action if they have applied to an early decision college.

BC accepts approximately 125 transfer students each year. Transfer candidates should request applications for transfer admission from the Office of Undergraduate Admission or via the website at http://www.bc.edu/transfer. In addition to high school records and standardized test results, transfer applicants must furnish transcripts from all postsecondary institutions they have attended.

For more information, students should contact:

Office of Undergraduate Admission
Devlin Hall 208
Boston College
Chestnut Hill, Massachusetts 02467
Phone: 617-552-3100
800-360-2522 (toll-free)
Fax: 617-552-0798
Website: http://www.bc.edu

BOSTON UNIVERSITY

BOSTON, MASSACHUSETTS

The University

Located in the heart of historic Boston, Boston University (BU) is a private teaching and research university ranked #42 in the nation by *U.S. News & World Report*. With ten undergraduate schools and colleges; over 300 programs of study; more than 650+ in-depth, global courses; and more than 100 study-abroad programs, the challenges at BU are vast and varied. BU students come from all fifty states and more than 100 countries; they are bright, driven, and inquisitive. Students study with world-renowned faculty, 90 percent of whom have a Ph.D. or equivalent. Faculty members include Fulbright scholars, Guggenheim scholars, Sloan Research fellows, Pulitzer Prize winners, a MacArthur fellow, and a former Poet Laureate. With an average class size of 27 and a 10:1 student-to-faculty ratio, these amazing professors become more than just a face students see in class. There are hundreds of research projects that allow undergraduates to work directly with faculty as early as freshman year through the Undergraduate Research Opportunities Program (UROP).

Location

Students experience the city as an extension of campus. Boston provides an environment rich in intellectual and cultural stimuli thanks to its remarkable concentration of higher education institutions, world-renowned medical centers, and historic and cultural attractions. The city provides many opportunities for impressive internship and research positions and is home to world-class attractions including the Museum of Fine Arts, Fenway Park, Boston Symphony Orchestra, and a thriving theater district. With four years of guaranteed campus housing, and 75 percent of undergraduates living on campus all four years, the campus feels like a true residential community in the heart of Boston.

Majors and Degrees

Of the University's seventeen schools and colleges, ten offer opportunities for undergraduate study.

As BU's largest academic division, the College of Arts & Sciences (CAS) offers a diverse learning community with world-class research faculty. Students may major in American studies; ancient Greek; ancient Greek and Latin; anthropology; anthropology and religion; archaeology; architectural studies; astronomy; astronomy and physics; biochemistry and molecular biology; biology; biology with a specialization in behavioral biology; biology with a specialization in cell biology, molecular biology, and genetics; biology with a specialization in ecology and conservation biology; biology with a specialization in neurobiology; chemistry; chemistry with specialization in biochemistry; chemistry with specialization in teaching; Chinese language and literature; cinema and media studies (also offered in COM); classical civilization; classics and philosophy; classics and religion; comparative literature; computer science; earth and environmental sciences; economics; economics and mathematics; English; environmental analysis and policy; French and linguistics; French studies; geophysics and planetary sciences; German language and literature; history; history of art and architecture; Italian studies; Japanese and linguistics; Japanese language and literature; Latin; linguistics; linguistics and philosophy; linguistics and speech, language, and hearing sciences (also offered in Sargent); marine science; mathematics (includes statistics); mathematics and computer science; mathematics and mathematics education; mathematics and philosophy; neuroscience; philosophy; philosophy and neuroscience; philosophy and physics; philosophy and political science; philosophy and psychology; philosophy and religion; physics; political science; pre-dentistry; pre-law; pre-medicine; pre-veterinary medicine; psychology; religion; Russian language and literature; sociology; Spanish; and Spanish and linguistics. Special curricula include a seven-year accelerated program in liberal arts and medicine; the Modular Medical/Dental Integrated Curriculum (MMEDIC); the BU dual-degree program; the Wheelock/CAS double-degree program; and various combined B.A./M.A. degree programs.

The College of Fine Arts (CFA) offers programs in the School of Music (composition and theory, music education, performance, and nonperformance), the School of Theatre (acting, design, stage management, production, and theater arts/performing), and the School of Visual Arts (art education, graphic design, painting, printmaking, and sculpture).

The College of General Studies (CGS) offers spring admission to the Boston-London Program. This demanding, two-year program in the liberal arts and sciences stresses an interdisciplinary and global approach to learning. Students begin course work in Boston in January with classes in the humanities, social sciences, and rhetoric, before gaining global perspectives in London during a six-week summer term of intensive study. Students complete the CGS curriculum in their sophomore year, then continue into one of BU's degree-granting schools or colleges to complete their studies. For students who are unable to go abroad, a similar program is offered during the summer in Boston.

Located in one of the largest media markets in the nation, the College of Communication (COM) offers majors in advertising; cinema and media studies (also offered in CAS); film and television (production, writing, management); journalism (with specialization available in broadcast, magazine, news-editorial, online, and photojournalism); media science; and public relations.

Majors in the College of Engineering (ENG) include biomedical engineering (a program consistently ranked among the top in the country by U.S. News & World Report), computer engineering, electrical engineering, mechanical engineering, and mechanical engineering with specialization in aerospace.

The College of Health & Rehabilitation Sciences: Sargent College is one of the oldest and top-ranked health sciences schools in the country. It offers programs in behavior and health; health science; human physiology; a combined major in linguistics and speech, language, and hearing sciences; nutrition; and speech, language, and hearing sciences. Also offered is a six-year B.S./D.P.T. program.

The Frederick S. Pardee School of Global Studies is housed within the College of Arts & Sciences and is dedicated to advancing human progress and educating the next generation of global leaders. The school's education, research, and initiatives aim to produce globally competent citizens and leaders. Consisting of two divisions—international studies and regional studies—the school offers programs in Asian studies, European studies, international relations, Latin American studies, and Middle East and North Africa studies.

Located in one of the hospitality and tourism capitals of the world, the School of Hospitality Administration (SHA) offers a rigorous program in the management of hotels, restaurants, food and beverage service, travel and tourism, and entertainment. SHA offers majors in hospitality and communication and hospitality administration, with concentrations in event management, hospitality marketing, and hospitality real estate development.

With a unique global curriculum, the Questrom School of Business (Questrom) offers concentrations in accounting, entrepreneurship, finance, general management, health and life sciences management, international management, law, management information systems, marketing, operations and technology management, organizational behavior, real estate, retailing, and strategy and innovation.

Areas of concentration in the Wheelock College of Education & Human Development include bilingual education (includes TESOL), deaf studies, early childhood education, elementary education, English education, mathematics education, modern foreign languages education, science education, social studies education, and special education. The Wheelock/CAS double-degree program is also offered.

Academic Programs

A Boston University education combines the elements of a traditional liberal arts education with training for the professions. Highly qualified freshmen may also be invited to participate in the prestigious Arvind & Chandan Nandlal Kilachand Honors College.

Students complete general education requirements through the BU Hub, an innovative new general education program that is integrated with majors and minors and enables students to develop six core capacities. Students take courses of interest while exploring areas ranging from global citizenship to scientific and social inquiry to ethical reasoning or digital communication. The Hub is robust in its options for experiential learning and co-curriculars, and its signature feature, the BU Cross-College Challenge, offers an opportunity to work with a team of students and faculty drawn from across BU's schools and colleges.

Boston University has more than 100 study-abroad opportunities that take students around the world for courses, internships, and fieldwork. Opportunities are offered on six continents, in over twenty-five countries, and in cities such as Auckland, Dresden, London, Los Angeles, Madrid, Paris, Shanghai, Sydney, and Washington, D.C. Programs offered include studies in art/architecture, business/economics, engineering, health and human services, journalism/communications, visual/performing arts, and many more.

Boston University operates on a calendar of two semesters and two summer terms. Students generally take four courses each semester.

Academic Facilities

The Yawkey Center for Student Services is home to BU's Center for Career Development, Educational Resource Center, Pre-Professional Advising Office with pre-med and pre-law advising services, and the two-story Marciano Commons dining hall. The Engineering Product Innovation Center (EPIC) is a 15,000-square-foot facility where undergraduates can experiment with developing new products, from design to manufacturing. The BUild Lab: IDG Capital Student Innovation Center fosters innovation and entrepreneurship across the campus and any area of study. Students can connect with advisers, find funding sources, collaborate with other students on projects, and get help with matters from design and prototyping to legal advice and marketing. West campus features the modern Student Village, including Agganis Arena; the Fitness & Recreation Center, complete with a 35-foot rock-climbing wall; and high-rise, apartment-style dorms. The Questrom School of Business building also offers technologically advanced educational facilities, with a dedicated career center and management library. The new Joan & Edgar Booth Theatre and College of Fine Arts Production Center, studio space for visual arts students, practice rooms for music, and a 575-seat music performance center are indicative of BU's support for the arts. More than 2.8 million library volumes and over 4.7 million microform units are contained in Mugar Memorial Library, where the Twentieth-Century Archives are held, including the papers of Dr. Martin Luther King, Jr., Theodore Roosevelt, Robert Frost, and Bette Davis.

Costs

Tuition for 2019–20 is $54,720, estimated room and board costs are $16,160, and University and college fees are $1,172. These costs are exclusive of books, supplies, transportation, and personal expenses.

Financial Assistance

Boston University helps students realize their dreams with several different kinds of financial aid: BU scholarships, federal and state grants, federal loans, federal work-study awards, and financing and payment plan options. Financial aid is offered on the basis of calculated financial eligibility, and two or more types of aid are often combined in award packages. Students must submit the FAFSA and the CSS Profile by established deadlines to be considered. Thanks to the BU Scholarship Assurance, the Boston University aid offered in a student's first year is guaranteed for each undergraduate year. In addition, the Trustee Scholarship (full tuition) and the Presidential Scholarship ($20,000) are offered based on merit to the highest achieving students who apply for admission.

The University makes every effort to assist students with calculated financial eligibility, however funds are limited. All applicants who anticipate the need for financial aid are encouraged to apply.

Admission Requirements

The Board of Admissions considers each candidate individually. Primary emphasis is placed on the strength of the secondary school record, but required test scores, character, breadth of interest, school recommendations, and other personal qualifications are also carefully evaluated. Students are required to submit the SAT or the ACT, with the exception of those applying to the College of Fine Arts. A full listing of the standardized testing requirements can be found on the BU Admissions website at www.bu.edu/admissions/apply/. Secondary school graduation or an equivalency diploma is required of all candidates; for the College of Fine Arts a prescreening, audition, or a portfolio may be required, depending on the program of interest. For the accelerated medical program, interviews and SAT Subject Test scores are required. Boston University offers programs of early decision (binding agreement), early decision 2 (binding agreement), and deferred admission.

Transfer applicants are considered for September or January admission. Transfer students are not eligible for admission to the accelerated liberal arts/medical program or the six-year Bachelor of Science in Health Studies/Doctor of Physical Therapy program. January admission to the College of Fine Arts School of Theatre is also not available to transfer students.

Boston University admits qualified students to all its programs and activities regardless of their race, color, national origin, religion, sex, age, or disability.

Application and Information

Boston University accepts either the Common Application or the Coalition Application. Information on applying is available online at www.bu.edu/admissions/apply/. The deadline for regular decision applications is January 6. Applicants for early decision must apply by November 1. Accelerated medical program applications are due November 15. The deadline for the Trustee Scholarship (full tuition) and the Presidential Scholarship ($20,000) is December 1. Transfer students applying for September admission should submit their applications, CSS Profile, and FAFSA forms by March 1 or by November 1 for January admission.

Boston University Admissions
233 Bay State Road
Boston, Massachusetts 02215
Phone: 617-353-2300
E-mail: admissions@bu.edu
Website: http://www.bu.edu/admissions
http://www.facebook.com/BUadmissions
https://twitter.com/ApplyToBU
https://www.instagram.com/applytobu

Students at Boston University find that nothing separates them from Boston's world-class museums, vibrant culture, legendary sports teams, rich history, or world-renowned scientific and medical communities.

BRYN MAWR COLLEGE
BRYN MAWR, PENNSYLVANIA

BRYN MAWR COLLEGE

The College

Every year, 1,300 undergraduate students and 400 graduate students from around the world gather on Bryn Mawr College's historic campus to study with leading scholars, conduct advanced research, and expand the boundaries of what's possible. As a women's college, Bryn Mawr strives for academic excellence, opportunity for women, respect for the individual, and purposeful action in the world. Bryn Mawr's prestigious alumnae include the first woman to be president of Harvard University, one of the first women to receive the Nobel Peace Prize, the first woman neurosurgeon, and the first and only woman to receive four Academy Awards.

The undergraduate college is known as one of the most academically rigorous liberal arts colleges in the nation and consistently ranks among the top feeder schools to the world's premier graduate programs and professional schools. Students can pursue independent and interdepartmental majors, as well as minors and concentrations. Joint academic programs and offerings also exist with Haverford, Swarthmore, and the University of Pennsylvania.

Bryn Mawr's Leadership, Innovation, and Liberal Arts Center (LILAC) integrates fieldwork with theoretical study through civic engagement, professional development, and their Praxis program, providing students with extensive opportunities for internships, research, and service in nearby Philadelphia and beyond. Through these extensive offerings, students are involved in the local, national, and global communities.

Bryn Mawr offers a unique interdisciplinary experience, 360° Course Clusters, in which a cohort of students takes several courses together to engage multiple aspects of a topic or theme, giving students an opportunity to investigate thoroughly and thoughtfully a multitude of perspectives. Typical 360°s focus on the history, economic concerns, cultural intersections, and political impact of an era, decision, event, policy, or important scientific innovation. 360° participants hone their arguments and insights through writing and research, develop strategies for teamwork that push the limits of their talents and creativity, and work with professors and scholars to promote big-picture thinking. Each 360° includes an experiential learning component like travel abroad or local community work.

Diversity is central to Bryn Mawr's mission to sustain a community inclusive in nature and democratic in practice. Students of color and international students make up 56 percent of the undergraduate enrollment. Bryn Mawr's students come from 49 U.S. states, districts, and territories and 67 other countries. Above all else, Bryn Mawr students share a tremendous respect for individual differences. The result is a community that resounds with the energy, healthy friction, and range of perspectives that can only come from true cultural and ideological diversity. The diversity that Bryn Mawr students experience, in and out of the classroom, helps prepare them to be confident global citizens and leaders.

Bryn Mawr students share a commitment to a community that is based on inclusion and support, reinforced by the College's Honor Code, a set of principles stressing personal integrity and mutual respect. In the words of one graduating senior, "This is a place where being yourself makes you feel part of something larger than yourself. A strong sense of self is what we all have in common."

Bryn Mawr is a charter member of the Centennial Conference and is home to twelve NCAA varsity athletic teams. Students may compete in badminton, basketball, crew, cross-country, field hockey, lacrosse, soccer, swimming, tennis, indoor track and field, outdoor track and field, and volleyball. The Bern Schwartz Fitness and Athletic Center offers enhanced spaces for training, fitness, and aquatics.

Goodhart Hall serves as a hub for the College's performing arts scene and boasts a theater for 500+, a teaching theater, scene shop, music rooms, and several performance spaces. Other performance spaces include the Pembroke Dance Studio and the Denbigh Dance Studio. Bryn Mawr students participate in more than 100 active student organizations. The tri-college community of Haverford, Swarthmore, and Bryn Mawr also sponsors many student groups and activities. Bryn Mawr's relationship with Haverford College is particularly close. Just a 30-minute walk or a 10-minute ride on the bi-college Blue Bus brings students from one campus to the other.

Location

Students at Bryn Mawr have the best of it all in terms of location. The campus itself is a picture-perfect example of Collegiate Gothic that it has been used as the backdrop for several motion pictures. A quick 5-minute walk into the suburban town of Bryn Mawr finds an eclectic mix of funky independent and favorite franchise coffee shops, eateries, and retailers; an historic movie theater; and a commuter train that can take students to the heart of Philadelphia in about 20 minutes. Philadelphia has a bustling arts scene and nightlife and is home to more than 250,000 college students. Bryn Mawr students enjoy a rich academic and social life on their own campus, on tri-college campuses, and in Philadelphia.

Almost all students live on campus in one of thirteen main residence halls. Two of the buildings are listed on the National Register of Historic Places, and one is also a National Historic Landmark.

Majors and Degrees

Bryn Mawr College grants the Bachelor of Arts (A.B.) degree with majors, minors, and concentrations in more than forty areas: Africana studies; anthropology; Arabic, astronomy; biology; biochemistry and molecular biology; chemistry; child and family studies; Chinese; classical and Near Eastern archaeology; classical culture and society; classical languages; comparative literature; computational methods; computer science; creative writing; dance; East Asian languages and cultures; economics; education; English; environmental studies; film studies; fine arts; French and Francophone studies; gender and sexuality studies; geoarchaeology; geology; German and German studies; Greek; growth and structure of cities; Hebrew and Judaic studies; health studies; history; history of art; international studies; Italian studies; Japanese; Latin; Latin American, Iberian, and Latina/o studies; linguistics; mathematics; Middle Eastern studies; museum studies; music; neurosciences; peace, conflict, and social justice studies; philosophy; physics; political science; psychology; religion; Romance languages; Russian; sociology; Spanish; theater studies; and visual studies. In consultation with faculty and academic advisers, students may apply to partnership programs for combined undergraduate/graduate degrees from the University of Pennsylvania in engineering, education, city planning, and bioethics. Other partnership programs are available in public health from Boston University, and Chinese studies from Zhejiang University. Combined undergraduate programs in engineering are also available through Cal Tech and Columbia University.

There are approximately 3,000 course exchanges between Bryn Mawr and Haverford each year, selected from a jointly published course list. Bryn Mawr students may major in any of Haverford's coordinate departments or in astronomy, classics, fine arts, music, religion, or visual studies while earning a Bachelor of Arts degree from Bryn Mawr. Students may also apply to obtain their master's through the combined A.B./M.A. program in chemistry, classical and Near Eastern archaeology, French, Greek studies, Latin language and Roman studies, classical studies, history of art, mathematics, and physics or the combined A.B./M.S.S. with Bryn Mawr's Graduate School of Social Work and Social Research.

Academic Programs

The Bryn Mawr curriculum is designed to encourage breadth of learning and training in the fundamentals of scholarship. At some point during their first three years at Bryn Mawr, students are required to complete Approaches to Inquiry, a curriculum designed to introduce possibilities and problems in scientific investigation, critical interpretation, cross-cultural analysis, and inquiry into the past. Many options are available to fulfill these requirements and students are encouraged to explore many areas of interest. Innovative curricular options include interdisciplinary programs like the Growth and Structure of Cities and the Museum Studies programs; 360° Course Clusters; and Focus Courses, which are demanding, half-semester courses that may ignite a new intellectual passion. The curriculum encourages independence within a rigorous but flexible framework. Students choose and plan their major in consultation with a dean and faculty adviser. Some students take advantage of this freedom to design an independent major, while others fashion their own intellectual perspectives by enrolling in courses that span academic fields or participating in independent research experiences. With certain restrictions, full-time Bryn Mawr students may also take courses at Swarthmore College, the University of Pennsylvania, and Villanova University during the academic year without paying additional fees.

Off-Campus Programs

Bryn Mawr is only 20 minutes by car or seven short stops by train from Philadelphia, the nation's sixth-largest city. Philadelphia is an incredible resource for Bryn Mawr—a truly accessible city, rich with cultural and professional opportunities, including the Philadelphia Museum of Art, the Philadelphia Orchestra, the Pennsylvania Ballet, numerous theaters, professional sports teams, and some of the nation's most important historic sites. Students may also take advantage of internship opportunities in Center City law firms, art galleries, government agencies, hospitals, TV studios, banks, and schools. When Philadelphia seems too small, Bryn Mawr students can take advantage of one of Bryn Mawr's many study-abroad opportunities.

Academic Facilities

Bryn Mawr ranks highly among U.S. colleges and universities in the percentage of graduates going on to earn a Ph.D. Bryn Mawr students have unlimited access to libraries and laboratories equal to those of many graduate programs, allowing students to pursue independent research at a level unavailable at most undergraduate institutions. These resources include an extensive array of laboratory equipment for the study of science, such as a robotics lab, laser with rangefinder, DNA analyzers, and a geological subsurface profiling system. The first phase of the Park Science Building renovation to update and expand the many laboratory spaces and equipment was recently completed. More than 1 million volumes in a network of open-stack libraries are available to Bryn Mawr students, as well as access to the libraries of both Haverford and Swarthmore Colleges via the Tripod Library System.

In addition, the College has recently enhanced several of its buildings to support student inquiry in all of the liberal arts, including a $19-million renovation of the Marjorie Goodhart Theater which consists of a new state-of-the-art theater, practice rooms, a teaching theater, and scene shop; the upgrade of Dalton Hall, home to Bryn Mawr's social science labs and classrooms; and Bettws-y-Coed, a center for the study of psychology complete with new labs, faculty offices, and meeting rooms. Four former faculty residences have also been renovated to house the student activities village, Cambrian Row.

Costs

In 2019–20, Bryn Mawr tuition, room and board, and fees totaled $71,540.

Financial Aid

To apply for financial aid, students must submit the Free Application for Federal Student Aid (FAFSA), the College Scholarship Service (CSS) Profile form, and if applicable, the CSS Noncustodial Parent Profile. The College also requires a signed copy of the custodial and noncustodial parents' prior-prior year federal income tax returns, including W-2 forms, and all schedules and attachments. The student's federal income tax return is only required if the student is selected for verification. Tax returns must be submitted to The College Board's Institutional Documentation Service (IDOC). Applicants who are not citizens of the U.S. may file the (CSS) Profile. Non–U.S. citizens must also submit letters (in English) from their parents' employers stating gross income and the value of any perquisites, subsidies, and benefits directly to the Office of Financial Aid. Prospective first-year students are notified of admission and financial aid decisions simultaneously. Students must apply for financial aid in their first year to be considered for aid in subsequent years.

Faculty

The Bryn Mawr faculty has 159 full-time members, of whom 59 percent are women and 25 percent are professors of color. The College's student-faculty ratio is 9:1. Few colleges or universities can genuinely claim the intellectual curiosity, intensity, and passion found at Bryn Mawr. Classes are small (many have fewer than 15 students), and faculty members come to know their students as individuals. That means more than just being on a first-name basis. In fact, Bryn Mawr faculty members, world-renowned leaders in their fields, regard their students as junior colleagues, fully capable of working at a high level, developing their own ideas, and making important contributions. It is in this way that, perhaps more than at any other school, Bryn Mawr feels like a graduate school on an undergraduate level.

Student Government

Bryn Mawr's culture of innovative leadership dates back to 1892 and the founding of the Student Self-Government Association (SGA), the oldest undergraduate governing body in the country. SGA gives Bryn Mawr students the responsibility of running many campus organizations and activities and participating in discussions and resolutions of important issues, such as curriculum and faculty appointments.

Admission Requirements

Every year, Bryn Mawr receives many more outstanding applications for admission than can be admitted into the first-year class of about 360 students. As members of the Common Application and Coalition Application, Bryn Mawr practices holistic review, with admission decisions based on a number of factors. Strength of the applicant's high school curriculum within the context of the high school and academic performance are of significant importance. Other factors considered are a student's writing, recommendations from the high school counselor and academic teachers, test scores (optional for U.S. citizens and permanent residents), involvement in school and community, and diverse or unique perspectives and talents a student might bring to the Bryn Mawr community. A school program giving good preparation for study at Bryn Mawr includes four years of English grammar, composition, and literature; at least three years of mathematics (preferably up to statistics, pre-calculus, or calculus); three years of one modern or ancient language, or a good foundation in two languages; work in history; and at least three courses in science, including two lab sciences (preferably biology, chemistry, or physics). Non-U.S. citizens and non-U.S. permanent residents are required to submit standardized test scores (SAT I or ACT) as well as either the TOEFL or IELTS if their primary language is not English and/or their language of instruction over the past four years has not been English. Complete details may be found on the Bryn Mawr website. An interview, either with an admissions representative or with a local alumnae representative, is strongly recommended, but not required. Bryn Mawr accepts the Common Application and Coalition Application and waives the application fees when students apply online. Application forms should be submitted by November 15 for fall early decision applicants, by January 1 for winter early decision applicants, and by January 15 for regular decision applicants. Transfer students must complete a minimum of two years of work at Bryn Mawr to qualify for the A.B. degree.

Application and Information

The Office of Admissions is open from 9 a.m. to 5 p.m. on weekdays and some Saturdays throughout the year. Please visit the College website http://www.brynmawr.edu/admissions to plan a visit. Bryn Mawr accepts both the Common Application (http://www.commonapplication.org) and the Coalition Application (http://www.coalitionforcollegeaccess.org/). For additional information, prospective students should contact:

Bryn Mawr College Office of Admissions
101 North Merion Avenue
Bryn Mawr, Pennsylvania 19010-2899
Phone: 610-526-5152
Fax: 610-526-7471
E-mail: admissions@brynmawr.edu
Websites: http://www.brynmawr.edu
http://www.brynmawr.edu/admissions/
http://www.themawryouknow.blogs.brynmawr.edu
http://www.facebook.com/BMCadmissions
http://www.instagram.com/bmc_admissions
http://twitter.com/BrynMawrCollege

Bryn Mawr means "big hill" in Welsh.

CASTLETON UNIVERSITY
CASTLETON, VERMONT

Castleton
A VERMONT UNIVERSITY

COLLEGE CLOSE-UPS

The University

Castleton University is dedicated to educating future leaders of Vermont and beyond, just as it has been since its founding in 1787. With more than 230 years of service to students, Castleton is the first institution of higher education in Vermont, and the eighteenth-oldest in the United States. Steeped in history, the University cherishes its long-standing traditions, with a focus on innovation through all facets of the student experience.

Sixty-five percent of Castleton's 2,000 students call Vermont home, while the remaining students come from across the United States and more than 40 countries. New England and the Middle Atlantic states are the most predominant areas represented in the University's out-of-state population.

Castleton students are positioned for success the moment they arrive on campus thanks to the First-Year Seminar, an immersive program designed to teach new students how to navigate and excel in their new educational pursuits. First-year students also benefit from an innovative cultural program known as Soundings, which introduces a world of theater, music, dance, film, debate, and lecture brought to Castleton by renowned performers and scholars.

Eleven residence halls on campus provide more than just housing to 1,100 students, they provide learning opportunities where students are challenged to build communities, interact with their peers, learn to respect and appreciate differences and become more involved in community governance. Each residence hall room has both wired and wireless high-speed internet free of charge, and is comfortably furnished. On-campus residence halls include corridor and suite options, and if students are looking for additional independence, the university's newest apartment-style living option in downtown Rutland offers just that. Off-campus housing is available through private landlords in Castleton and neighboring towns. Other amenities include ample free parking for all students, and meal plans that provide three location options for dining; Huden Dining Hall, The Fireside Café, and The Coffee Cottage.

Students further their experience outside of the classroom with more than 50 clubs and organizations including club sports; a nationally-recognized student newspaper; radio station; and clubs related to politics and government, academic majors, and community service. Vermont provides a majestic backdrop for an active student body that takes advantage of free skiing at nearby Pico Mountain, some of the best hiking and biking trails in the state, and countless other outdoor recreational opportunities provided by nearby Lake Bomoseen. At the varsity level, Castleton sponsors 28 NCAA Division III sports including men's and women's alpine skiing, baseball, men's and women's basketball, men's and women's cross-country, field hockey, football, men's golf, men's and women's ice hockey, men's and women's lacrosse, men's and women's Nordic skiing, men's and women's soccer, softball, men's and women's track and field, men's and women's tennis, women's volleyball, and men's wrestling. In addition to the more than 600 student-athletes participating in a varsity sport, there are also countless intramural opportunities throughout the year that serve the entire student population in a fun and supportive atmosphere.

Castleton's facilities are among the finest in New England as virtually every building on campus has either been built or renovated since 2002. The largest project of the last decade was focused solely on the student experience, and resulted in a $25.7 million project that included a new multi-sport stadium, athletic complex, and campus center.

Location

Nestled at the base of the Green Mountains to the east and the Adirondacks to the west, Castleton is located in a quintessential Vermont village. The small-town feelings of safety and authenticity surround the University, but it is also just a short drive from Vermont's cities of Rutland and Burlington. Major cities such as New York, Boston, Hartford, and Montreal are all just a train ride or easy drive away, and students also have access to Rutland Airport with flights in and out of Boston several times each day.

Majors and Degrees

Castleton offers more than 75 programs of study for undergraduate and graduate students. Students may pursue B.A. or B.S. degrees in: accounting, American literature, art, biology, chemistry, children's literature, computer information systems, criminal justice, digital media, ecological studies, economics, elementary education, English, environmental science, exercise science, forensic psychology, geography, geology, global studies, graphic design, health education, health science, history, journalism, kinesiology, management, marketing, mass media, mathematics, music, music education, nursing, philosophy, physical education, political science, psychology, public relations, secondary education, social studies, social work, sociology, Spanish, special education, sport management, theater arts, world literature, and women's and gender studies. A.A. or A.S. degrees may be pursued in: business, media and communication, computer programming, criminal justice, and general studies.

Academic Programs

Castleton University is committed to providing a holistic educational experience, relying on a strong liberal arts foundation to provide its students with the critical thinking, problem-solving, and creative skills needed to succeed in tomorrow's workplace. This foundation is complimented by a focus on career preparation through experiential learning. With more than 400 partnerships in the region, Castleton offers students opportunities through civic engagement, internships, and research.

Castleton students benefit from access to local employers, a state-of-the-art makerspace, and a flourishing entrepreneurial spirit in the region. In 2017 Castleton was the recipient of a five-year grant from the McNair Foundation worth more than $1 million to help its students gain entry into doctoral programs. This new addition complements the growing number of pre-professional offerings such as pre-law, pre-med, and pre-pharmacy as well as the countless research opportunities available through student-faculty partnerships and other off-campus opportunities.

Castleton students typically enroll in five courses each 15-week semester. In addition to the traditional calendar, Castleton also offers summer and January terms to allow students to stay on track for degree completion.

Academic Facilities

The Calvin Coolidge Library is home to a 500,000-volume collection of books, periodicals, microforms, and nonprint media.

Access includes outside scholarly resources through online databases and several inter-library relationships throughout the state of Vermont and beyond.

The Stafford Academic Center is a modern academic building that houses the largest lecture hall on campus, computing and media services, several computer labs, the nursing program's simulation lab, and is connected to the Calvin Coolidge Library. In addition to being a hub for student research and IT support, Stafford is also home to the mathematics, education, and nursing programs.

Leavenworth Hall is home to the social sciences, languages, and media and communication departments. This academic building includes state-of-the-art video editing bays, a television studio, and student lounge among its highlights. The courtyard and outdoor classroom are among students' favorite places to hang out and catch up.

The university's award-winning student newspaper, *The Spartan*, provides communication students with an experiential learning opportunity as soon as their first year.

The Fine Arts Center is the hub of student creativity. Home to Castleton fine and performing arts, music, athletic bands, and graphic design programs, students have every opportunity to showcase talents of their own, or take in a show from a variety of world-renowned guest artists in the 500-seat Casella Theater.

The Jeffords Science Center houses the psychological sciences and natural sciences programs. Offering laboratory and classroom space, as well as a large lecture hall, greenhouse and gardens, Jeffords is well equipped to help students find solutions to the scientific questions of tomorrow.

Home to Glenbrook Gymnasium, two athletic training rooms, team rooms, and strength training facilities for all 600 student-athletes, the Spartan Athletic Complex is the hub for Spartan Pride as well as home to the athletic training, physical education, health education, and sport management programs.

Costs

Costs for 2019–20 are: Vermont resident undergraduate tuition is $11,496 (per year), nonresident undergraduate tuition is $27,984 (per year); room and board is $10,920 (per year); and total fees are $1,396 (per year).

Financial Aid

More than 80 percent of Castleton University's full-time undergraduate students receive financial assistance from federal, state, and University programs or other public and private sources. Grants, loans, and student work programs are available for qualified students. Applicants for financial aid should file the Free Application for Federal Student Aid (FAFSA) form by April 1 of the senior year in high school. All financial aid awards are based on need. Castleton offers an array of need- and merit-based scholarships for first-year, transfer, international, and returning students.

Faculty

Castleton has nearly 100 full-time faculty members, 96 percent of whom hold terminal degrees in their chosen field. Part-time faculty members, many of whom are experienced experts in the professional world, complement the program offerings and bolster the learning experience. Students benefit from 1:1 faculty advising and a 14:1 student-faculty ratio in the classroom.

Student Government

The Student Government Association (SGA) operates with three distinctive branches: Congress, University Court, and Campus Activities Board (CAB). All students participating in any facet of these groups are considered active members of the SGA. The SGA represents the Castleton student body and administers the student activity fee which is assessed to all students to fund activities and the more than 50 clubs and organizations on campus.

Admission Requirements

Applicants are evaluated on the basis of their secondary school records, standardized test scores, and recommendations. Admission is granted to those applicants who have demonstrated their ability and potential to meet the challenges of a postsecondary learning experience.

Application and Information

Students may apply for admission through the Common Application. Under Castleton's rolling admission policy, applications are processed throughout the year, and candidates are notified of the admission decision as soon as their files are complete. Students are admitted in the fall and spring semesters.

For more information about Castleton University or to arrange a campus visit, students should contact:

Office of Admissions
Castleton University
Castleton, Vermont 05735
Phone: 802-468-1213
800-639-8521 (toll-free)
Fax: 802-468-1476
E-mail: info@castleton.edu
Website: www.castleton.edu

The Castleton campus is nestled at the base of the Green Mountains, and has a panoramic view of every season.

CLEMSON UNIVERSITY

CLEMSON, SOUTH CAROLINA

The University

A top-24 public university with a reputation for excellence that's known worldwide, Clemson University leads the way in providing a hands-on education—in the lab, in the arts, and in the field. Clemson was founded in 1889 with a mission to be a "high seminary of learning" dedicated to teaching, research, and service. Today, Clemson is one of the country's most selective public research universities, and these three concepts remain prevalent, providing the framework for an exceptional educational experience.

At Clemson University, professors take the time to get to know students and explore innovative ways of teaching. Exceptional teaching is one reason Clemson's retention and graduation rates rank among the highest in the country for public universities.

Exceptional teaching is also why Clemson continues to attract an increasingly talented student body. In 2018, more than half of the entering freshmen were ranked in the top 10 percent of their high school classes, and the freshman class averaged 29 on the ACT.

Clemson is committed to world-class research and is ranked in the highest research university category by the Carnegie Classification of Institutions of Higher Education. The University is also invested in the success of its students. Student retention at Clemson is consistently more than 90 percent. Much of this is due to the Academic Success Center (ASC). Established in 2001, the ASC has been recognized nationally and internationally by organizations related to tutoring, supplemental instruction, and collegiate learning. The ASC moved into a new, 35,000 square-foot facility in 2012 where it offers free one-on-one tutoring services for more than 80 courses and provides tutoring for additional courses as the need arises. Peer-assisted learning, academic skills workshops, and academic counseling are also available—free to all Clemson students. It is estimated that more than 50 percent of freshmen use ASC services during their first semester.

Clemson has also received national recognition for its innovative Communication Across the Curriculum (CAC) program. At Clemson, CAC is a standard teaching method used in nearly every department. Professors use CAC to focus on providing real-life challenges that require students to think and communicate effectively.

From cheering on the Tigers at a football game to socializing in the Hendrix Student Center, Clemson students can participate in a wide variety of activities outside the classroom. The more than 500 campus clubs and organizations include fraternities and sororities, as well as honorary, international, military, performing arts, political, professional, religious, service, social interest, special interest, sports and fitness, and student media programs and activities.

With 19 intercollegiate sports, Clemson offers exciting spectator sports year-round. Clemson is a charter member of the Atlantic Coast Conference (ACC) and is an NCAA Division I school. Admission to most regular-season home events is included in University fees for full-time students.

Clemson University is accredited by the Commission on Colleges of the Southern Association of Colleges and Schools to award bachelor's, master's, specialist, and doctoral degrees. Questions about the accreditation of Clemson University can be directed to the Commission on Colleges at 1866 Southern Lane, Decatur, Georgia 30033-4097; phone: 404-679-4500.

Location

Approximately midway between Charlotte, North Carolina, and Atlanta, Georgia, Clemson University is located on 1,400 acres in the foothills of the Blue Ridge Mountains and along the shores of Hartwell Lake. Great weather and proximity to natural wonders and large cities offer year-round recreational opportunities.

The University's enrollment of more than 24,000 undergraduate and graduate students makes it a defining presence in Clemson, South Carolina, a town of about 14,000. Students may live on campus in one of the 27 residence halls and five apartment communities, most of which are within a 15-minute walk to class or downtown. More than 99 percent of students live on campus their freshman year.

Majors and Degrees

Clemson offers nearly 80 undergraduate and more than 120 graduate degree programs through seven academic colleges: Agriculture, Forestry, and Life Sciences; Architecture, Arts, and Humanities; Behavioral, Social and Health Sciences; Business; Engineering, Computing and Applied Sciences; Education; and Science. Undergraduate students can earn B.A., B.S., or preprofessional degrees in accounting; agribusiness; agricultural education; agricultural mechanization and business; animal and veterinary sciences; anthropology; architecture; art; biochemistry; bioengineering; biological sciences; biosystems engineering; chemical engineering; chemistry; civil engineering; communication; computer engineering; computer information systems; computer science; construction science and management; criminal justice; early childhood education; economics; electrical engineering; elementary education; English; environmental and natural resources; environmental engineering; financial management; food science and human nutrition; forest resource management; genetics; geology; graphic communications; health science; history; horticulture; industrial engineering; landscape architecture; language and international health; language and international trade; management; marketing; materials science and engineering; mathematical sciences; mathematics teaching; mechanical engineering; microbiology; modern languages (American Sign Language, Chinese, French, German, Italian, Japanese, and Spanish); nursing; packaging science; Pan African studies; parks, recreation, and tourism management; philosophy; physics; plant and environmental sciences; political science; prepharmacy; preprofessional health studies; preveterinary medicine; production studies in performing arts; psychology; religious studies; science teaching; secondary education; sociology; special education; sports communication; turfgrass; wildlife and fisheries biology; women's leadership; and world cinema.

Academic Programs

Clemson's academic year is divided into two semesters. The fall semester begins in mid-August and the spring semester starts in early January. Three summer sessions and four mini-semesters are also available. Students average 16 credit hours per semester, and Clemson requires all students to complete some general education classes specified by the University before graduation. The number of completed credit hours required for graduation varies, depending on the major.

Calhoun Honors College is a University-wide program that combines the strengths of a public, land-grant university with those of a highly selective small college. Calhoun scholars may choose to pursue departmental honors within their specific academic discipline. In addition, EUREKA! (Experiences in Undergraduate Research, Exploration, and Knowledge Advancement) is a unique and exciting program that enables honors students to pursue research and scholarly activities with faculty members across all disciplines. The advantages of membership in the Honors College include priority registration, extended library loan privileges, honors research grants, and a special living-learning community.

The National Scholars Program is a highly selective program for exceptional students who strive to meet their highest intellectual potential. One of its goals is to develop the interests and talents students need to compete for Rhodes, Marshall, and Truman scholarships; Fulbright Grants; National Science Foundation Graduate Fellowships; and other prestigious international fellowships. In 2017–18, six Clemson students received National Science Foundation Graduate Fellowships. Three Clemson graduates received Fulbright grants to conduct research or teach abroad, and two students received honorable mentions for the Goldwater Scholars award.

Clemson's Creative Inquiry (CI) program allows undergraduate students to engage in research about problems that spring from their own curiosity, from a professor's challenge, or from the pressing needs of the world around them. Team-based investigations are led by a faculty mentor and typically span two to four semesters. Students take ownership of their projects and take the risks necessary to solve problems and get answers. This invaluable experience produces exceptional graduates, capable of thinking critically, solving problems as a team, and communicating and presenting their ideas to others. In 2017–18, 4,838 students participated in 414 Creative Inquiry projects.

Clemson's nationally recognized Programs for Educational Enrichment and Retention (PEER) is committed to improving the academic performance of underrepresented students in engineering and science.

Off-Campus Programs

Clemson's students are strongly encouraged to incorporate a study-abroad experience in their overall Clemson journey. Programs are available on six continents for all disciplines and interests. These include faculty-led programs, exchange programs, and programs available through Clemson's partnerships with study-abroad providers and institutions.

Students in a variety of majors also have opportunities at other Clemson campuses around the world, including the Archbold Center in Dominica; the Daniel Center in Genoa, Italy; and the Clemson University Brussels Center in Belgium. There are other campuses around South Carolina, including Greenville, Greenwood, and Charleston.

The Cooperative Education program provides an opportunity for students to alternate periods of academic study with semesters of paid, career-related, engaged-learning experiences to bridge the gap between academic study and its application in professional practice. Clemson's Center for Career and Professional Development helps to pair students with companies seeking interns or co-op students. The Princeton Review ranks Clemson's career services program as the number-two career office in the nation, and with help from the career center, about 2,200 students participate in academic internships and co-ops annually. Because co-op experiences have been proven to enhance academic performance and provide a competitive edge when seeking full-time employment, Clemson students can now add on-campus internship experiences to their resumes. Students can work part- or full-time, with many in full-time positions having the option of earning credit. The University has made an investment to fund a portion of these experiences, so these on-campus jobs are paid positions.

Academic Facilities

The Clemson campus is a blend of historic buildings and advanced research facilities surrounded by stately trees and lush greenery.

Clemson's main library, the Robert M. Cooper Library, is located at the center of campus and provides a variety of services and up-to-date collections. The University's wireless networking capability lets students communicate with professors and classmates, read online course materials, check email, and conduct research—all from their own laptops.

The campus offers an array of facilities and programs designed to enhance a student's entire educational experience. These include the Pearce Center for Professional Communication, Class of 1941 Studio for Student Communication, Rutland Institute for Ethics, and the Academic Success Center.

Clemson real estate holdings also include more than 32,000 acres of forestry and agricultural lands throughout the state, most of which are dedicated to the University's research and service missions.

Costs

For the 2018–19 academic year, undergraduate tuition and fees were $15,374 for South Carolina residents and $37,128 for out-of-state residents. Room and board costs were approximately $10,832, and books and supplies were around $1,392. Estimated personal and transportation expenses were $3,672, and the one-time laptop computer cost was about $1,666.

Financial Aid

Financial aid is usually awarded based on need to supplement the amount students and their parents can contribute to college expenses. The University also awards some scholarships based entirely on academic merit. Clemson offers financial aid in the form of grants, scholarships, loans, and part-time employment, and 87 percent of all students receive financial aid at Clemson.

The Office of Admissions automatically reviews each applicant to Clemson for scholarship eligibility (no additional scholarship application required). Test scores, class rank, GPA and financial need are all considered when awarding scholarships. Incoming freshmen must apply for admission by December 1 to be considered. Test scores need to be received by Clemson by December 31 for scholarship consideration. The high school transcript submitted for admission evaluation will be the same transcript used to determine merit scholarship eligibility. Information regarding scholarship packages will be communicated to students in the spring. To be eligible for federal and state-based aid, students are encouraged to complete the FAFSA located at fafsa.gov by January 2. For more information regarding specific scholarship types and amounts, visit clemson.edu/financial-aid.

Faculty

Clemson has more than 1,000 full-time faculty members, with around 87 percent holding a Ph.D. or terminal degree in their fields. In addition, the University has more than 100 part-time faculty members. Faculty honors include the Fulbright Scholarship, Guggenheim Fellowship, National Science Foundation CAREER Award, National Institutes of Health Senior Scientist Award, and membership in the American Academy of Arts and Sciences. The median undergraduate class size is 19, and the student-to-faculty ratio is 16:1.

Admission Requirements

In 2018, the University received about 28,845 applications for a fall freshman class of 3,792. Transfer applications were received from 3,050 students, 1,528 of whom enrolled. Undergraduate applications are available online at clemson.edu/admissions.

For freshman applicants, the following factors are considered: class standing, standardized test scores (SAT or ACT), high school curriculum, grades, and choice of major. Entering freshmen must have completed 4 credits of English, 3 credits of mathematics, 3 credits of laboratory science, 3 credits of a foreign language (in the same language), 3 credits of social sciences, 1 credit of U.S. history, 1 credit of physical education or ROTC, and 1 credit of fine arts.

To be considered for transfer admission, candidates must have completed a full year of college study (a minimum of 30 semester hours or 45 quarter hours of transferable work completed after secondary school conclusion), earned a minimum cumulative GPA of at least 2.5 on a 4.0 scale (3.0 preferred), and completed freshman-level courses in English, science, and mathematics for their intended major at Clemson. Students may also transfer into Clemson after successful completion of their freshman year through the Bridge to Clemson program, a collaborative first-year academic and residential life partnership between Clemson University and Tri-County Technical College. Bridge is available by invitation only to qualified Clemson freshman applicants who have the potential to be successful at Clemson but, due to its competitive admissions landscape, could not be admitted directly into the University for their freshman year.

Application and Information

Application deadlines for freshman admissions are December 1 (priority date for fall semester), May 1 (fall semester), and December 15 (spring semester). For transfer admissions, the application deadlines are July 1 (fall semester) and December 15 (spring semester).

Office of Admissions
Clemson University
105 Sikes Hall, Box 345124
Clemson, South Carolina 29634-5124
Phone: 864-656-2287
Fax: 864-656-2464
E-mail: cuadmissions@clemson.edu
Website: http://www.clemson.edu/admissions

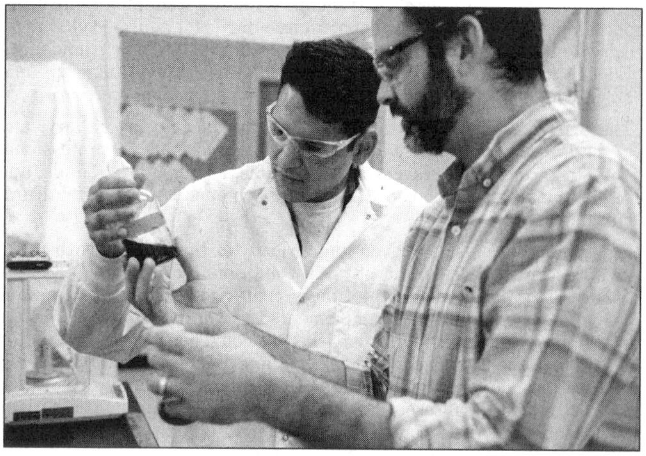

Hands-on problem solving and real-world experiences make Clemson students exceptionally prepared for postgraduate education and future career opportunities.

THE COLLEGE OF NEW JERSEY

EWING TOWNSHIP, NEW JERSEY

TCNJ
THE COLLEGE OF
NEW JERSEY

The College

The College of New Jersey (TCNJ) welcomes students who have the talent and motivation to succeed in a highly rigorous academic environment. Founded in 1855, the College enrolls about 6,500 full-time undergraduates, two thirds of whom reside on campus. Today it is heralded by U.S. News & World Report, Barron's, Money Magazine, and numerous other publications as one of the most competitive and accomplished schools in the nation, public or private. TCNJ serves a diverse student body, preparing graduates to excel as leaders in their chosen fields.

TCNJ has set the standard for public higher education. Students appreciate The College's atmosphere, a school large enough to provide a full range of academic and extracurricular choices, yet small enough to be a genuine residential community of friends and fellow learners. With professors committed to collaboration in and out of the classroom and facilities of enviable quality, TCNJ represents an exceptional value in higher education.

In order to enhance student development and empowerment, TCNJ's curriculum is built around five Signature Experiences which permeate every major across seven academic schools. Small classes prioritizing discussion and inquiry create a Personalized, Rigorous, and Collaborative Learning Environment where students and faculty work side by side in developing skills and applying concepts. Undergraduate Research, Mentored Internships, and Field Experiences give TCNJ students opportunities to get out of the classroom, develop their professional skill sets, and discover exciting career paths and academic endeavors. Passion for civic responsibility and a commitment to Community-Engaged Learning ensures that TCNJ graduates enter the professional world as top-notch scholars and citizens. Opportunities for Global Engagement found on the TCNJ campus and facilitated through internationally recognized study-abroad programs allow students to expand their internal scope and frame their academic goals and achievements in a truly global context. Finally, academic and extracurricular programs designed to foster Leadership Development help students build confidence and decision-making skills that they will need to solve the problems of tomorrow and build a brighter future.

All first- and second-year students at TCNJ are guaranteed on-campus housing, and most juniors and seniors continue to live on campus. Rooming arrangements are quite flexible, from doubles in freshman residence halls to suites and single rooms and on-campus town houses or apartments for upper class students. Over 200 student organizations on campus offer numerous opportunities for leadership development, community engagement, and the cultivation of lifelong friendships. Engaged and motivated within and beyond the classroom, an exceptional 96 percent of first-year students return for their sophomore year.

The arts flourish in two theaters, a recital hall, an art gallery, and numerous other campus venues. Student performances, professional groups on tour, and a large variety of films, lectures, local bands, and solo entertainers fill the academic year with opportunities for cultural enrichment.

Student wellness is also given high priority at the College, with many facilities for recreation and physical conditioning. In fall 2015, TCNJ opened a brand-new student fitness center as part of the Campus Town project. This facility complements the workout spaces, 25-meter swimming and diving pool, and basketball court housed in Packer Hall; the weight room and indoor track in the Student Recreation Center; and the numerous, well-lit athletic fields across campus. In addition to these recreational resources, TCNJ employs dieticians, nutritionists, and other specialists committed to promoting healthy lifestyles and overall wellness in the realms of mind, body, and spirit.

As one of the top-ranked Division III members of the National Collegiate Athletic Association, TCNJ offers twenty sports: ten for men and ten for women. Since 1979, TCNJ student-athletes have amassed an aggregate of more than seventy first- and second-place finishes. TCNJ has produced over 40 individual national champions and more than 50 CoSIDA Academic All-Americans. In the past two decades, TCNJ has finished in the top ten of the Learfield Sports Director's Cup races more than fifteen times.

In addition to its NCAA athletics, TCNJ offers a wide variety of recreation programs for intramural competition and self-governing club sports teams. Each year, more than 3,500 students play with these less demanding, but still spirited and competitive organizations.

Location

Students at The College of New Jersey live and learn on a picturesque, 289-acre campus located in suburban Ewing Township, approximately 15 minutes from downtown Princeton; 10 minutes from Bucks County, Pennsylvania; and 5 miles from the state capital of Trenton. Woodlands and lakes surround academic and residential buildings, which bear a distinctive Neoclassical Georgian Colonial aesthetic. The campus is 30 miles from the theaters and museums of Philadelphia and 60 miles from those in New York City, and public and mass transit services are easily accessible. In 2015, TCNJ completed the first phase of the Campus Town project. Adding an attractive downtown component to an already appealing campus, Campus Town offers students brand new residential opportunities, a pristine Barnes and Noble bookstore and café, and a comprehensive fitness center. Retail and dining establishments have been incorporated as well, with additional businesses scheduled to open throughout 2019.

Majors and Degrees

The College of New Jersey offers rigorous, personalized programs culminating in the Bachelor of Arts, Bachelor of Fine Arts, Bachelor of Music, Bachelor of Science, Bachelor of Science in Engineering, and Bachelor of Science in Nursing degrees.

TCNJ grants degrees in the following majors: accountancy; African American studies; art history; art education; biology*; biomedical engineering; business administration (specializations in finance, interdisciplinary business, management, and marketing); chemistry*; civil engineering; communication studies; computer engineering; computer science; criminology; early childhood education; economics*; education of the deaf and hard of hearing; electrical engineering; elementary education; engineering science (specializations in engineering management or policy and society); English*; health and exercise science; health and physical education; history*; interactive multimedia; international studies; integrative-STEM education (iSTEM education); journalism and professional writing; mathematics*; mechanical engineering; music (options in education and performance); nursing; philosophy; physics*; political science; psychology; public health; self-designed major; sociology; Spanish; special education; speech pathology and audiology; technology education /pre-engineering; urban education; visual arts (options in fine arts, graphic design, and lens-based art); and women, gender, and sexuality studies.

**Programs in which students may prepare for teacher certification*

Specialized Programs: TCNJ offers a number of 5-year combined Master of Arts in Teaching degrees with dual certification in elementary education, and either special education, urban education, or deaf and hard-of-hearing education. Students may also enroll in a 7-year B.S./M.D. degree program with the New Jersey Medical School (Newark) or a 7-year B.S./O.D. degree program with the State University of New York College of Optometry. The College also offers a Medical Careers Advisory Committee for premed students and a Pre-Law Advisement Committee for students planning a career in law. Sixty-four percent of TCNJ undergraduates seeking admission to medical school and 88 percent seeking admission to law school are accepted into their top choice programs. Both of these figures significantly exceed national averages.

Academic Programs

All academic courses contain significant out-of-class requirements, which foster deeper student-faculty collaboration. All baccalaureate degrees require at least thirty-two courses, including a core curriculum in the traditional arts and sciences. The average class size is 23 students for upper-division lectures.

The thirty-week academic year is divided into Fall and Spring semesters; during the summer, courses are offered in two 5-week sessions and one 6-week session. Winter Session also guarantees all of the benefits of full-time TCNJ courses in a more compact time frame, in addition to study-abroad opportunities. For those students who find that they cannot fit study abroad into their standard semester, Winter and Summer Session students travel everywhere from New Orleans to London.

Seminars, independent studies, and capstone courses give students the opportunity for challenging advanced study in close collaboration with faculty mentors. Many TCNJ students publish the results of these endeavors in academic journals or present them at national and regional conferences.

The College of New Jersey Honors Program offers top-tier students highly intensive academic experiences without adding extra obstructions on the path toward degree completion. Honors courses promote an interdisciplinary perspective and curriculum, concentrating on central themes relevant to cultural development. All honors classes are small, personalized, and stimulating.

Off-Campus Programs

TCNJ offers students a variety of full-year and one-semester study abroad programs as well as study opportunities with other colleges and universities within the United States. Exchange programs are available in 80 cities in Australia, Austria, Canada, Denmark, France, Germany, Greece, Israel, Japan, Mexico, the United Kingdom, and numerous other countries. National exchanges are available at more than 130 participating institutions in the United States, the U.S. Virgin Islands, Puerto Rico, and Guam.

Academic Facilities

TCNJ has been nationally recognized as one of the most beautiful campuses in the nation. Within the past several years, the beautiful campus has grown with the addition of a Science Complex, Biology Building, Social Science Building, College Spiritual Center, Art and Interactive Media Building, Education Building, student apartments, and a state-of-the-art library, which serves as the intellectual and social hub of campus. In 2017 alone, TCNJ was proud to reopen the renovated Brower Student Center and cut the ribbon on an all new STEM (science, technology, engineering, and mathematics) complex. Campus wide networking provides full Internet accessibility from all residence hall rooms and more than twenty student computing laboratories.

Costs

For up-to-date information on in-state and out-of-state tuition and fees costs, as well as room and board figures, prospective students should head online and visit studentaccounts.tcnj.edu/tuition-fees/.

Financial Aid

Over 50 percent of full-time undergraduates receive some form of financial aid, such as federal, state, and institutional grants; merit scholarships; student employment; and loan assistance. Students who submit the Free Application for Federal Student Aid (FAFSA) or Renewal FAFSA are given full consideration for need-based aid at the federal and state levels.

Scholarships and grants include The College of New Jersey Merit Scholars Program, Founders Scholars, Provost Scholars, Bonner Scholars, Chairman of the Board Merit Scholars, the New Jersey Tuition Aid Grant, Federal Pell Grants, Educational Opportunity Fund (EOF) Promise Award, and Army and Air Force ROTC Scholarships, as well as other institutional scholarships. Loans include the Federal Subsidized and Unsubsidized Stafford Loans, the Federal Perkins Loan, the Federal Parent Loan for Undergraduate Students (PLUS), the New Jersey CLASS Loan, private/alternative loans, nursing loans, and short-term emergency loan funds. Student employment options include the need-based Federal Work-Study Program (on- and off-campus positions) as well as institutionally supported campus jobs.

Faculty

The approximately 335 full-time members of the College of New Jersey faculty are teachers and scholars possessing terminal degrees in their respective fields. They are also active researchers, authors, artists, performers, and regular contributors in their academic disciplines. A wide majority of classes are led by full-time faculty members; there are no classes taught by graduate assistants. TCNJ boasts a student-faculty ratio of 13:1. From their first day, students work closely with faculty mentors, contributing to a wide array of projects. Members of the faculty have attracted many significant grants, fellowships, and awards, including the Bancroft Prize in History, Fulbright Scholarships, and grants from the National Science Foundation, the National Institute for Advanced Study, the Guggenheim Foundation, and the National Endowment for the Humanities. Faculty members mentor their students, preparing them for careers, graduate and professional schools, and prestigious fellowships such as the Fulbright, Truman, and Marshall Fellowships.

Student Governance and Programming

The Student Government Association at the College is governed by elected representatives and works to support and empower all undergraduate students. Members of the Student Finance Board oversee and administer approximately $500,000 in student funds. The College Union Board sponsors a wide range of special events, including recent visits by Hasan Minhaj, Soledad O'Brien, John Oliver, and Gloria Steinem.

Admission Requirements

The College of New Jersey seeks students who show intellectual curiosity, academic talent, and the potential to contribute to TCNJ's vibrant community. The College is committed to attracting students from diverse economic, racial, social, and geographic backgrounds. A high school record of college-preparatory credits, rigorous Honors and Advanced Placement courses, high school class rank, SAT or ACT scores, special interests, skills, and qualities can be influential in application review. Certain departments, such as Art and Music, waive the SAT/ACT submission requirement and use additional criteria such as portfolio submissions and auditions to evaluate candidates seeking admission. The College of New Jersey reviews candidates holistically and takes into consideration the variations in high schools and communities from which the applicants hail.

Application and Information

The College of New Jersey is a member of the Common Application. The deadline for applications for Spring enrollment is November 1. The Regular Decision application deadline for Fall enrollment is February 1. There is a $75 application fee. Candidates who apply only to The College of New Jersey under the Early Decision agreement can apply up until November 1 to receive the earliest possible admissions notification on or before December 1. Early Decision applicants unable to complete and submit their application prior to the initial deadline may apply up until January 1 and receive notification on or before February 1. Students applying to the seven-year Accelerated Medical program must apply by November 1. For Fall enrollment, the College requires incoming students to pay an enrollment deposit of $600 on or before May 1.

For more information, students should contact:
The College of New Jersey
P.O. Box 7718
Ewing, New Jersey 08628-0718
United States
Phone: 609-771-2131
Website: http://www.tcnj.edu

Breathtaking, Neoclassical Georgian Colonial architecture is just one of many features distinguishing The College of New Jersey as an enticing option for students from across the country and throughout the world.

COLLEGE OF STATEN ISLAND OF THE CITY UNIVERSITY OF NEW YORK

STATEN ISLAND, NEW YORK

THE CITY UNIVERSITY OF NEW YORK College of Staten Island

The College and the University

The College of Staten Island (CSI) is a four-year senior college within the City University of New York (CUNY) and is Staten Island's only public institution of higher learning. CSI is dedicated to access and excellence and currently serves over 13,250 students.

Offering over eighty programs and areas of study, the College ensures that students receive a thorough liberal arts education through core requirements that include classes in the arts and humanities, mathematics, sciences, and social sciences.

In addition to the exciting array of undergraduate degrees and majors available, CSI also awards master's degrees in the following disciplines: Accounting; Biology; Biology: Biotechnology Track; Business Management: Strategic Management Track; Business Management: Large-Scale Data Analysis Track; Cinema and Media Studies; Clinical Mental Health Counseling; Computer Science; Education: Adolescence, Childhood, Special Education 1–6, and Special Education 7–12 tracks; Electrical Engineering; English; Environmental Science; Healthcare Management; History; Liberal Studies; Neuroscience; Nursing: Adult-Gerontological Health; Social Work; and Teaching of English to Speakers of Other Languages. CSI also offers the following post-master's and advanced certificates: Adult-Gerontological Health Nursing, Autism Spectrum Disorders, Bilingual Education, Business Analytics of Large-Scale Data, Leadership in Education, Public History, and Teaching of English to Speakers of Other Languages. CSI proudly confers the Clinical Doctorate in Physical Therapy (D.P.T.) and the Doctorate of Nurse Practice (D.N.P.).

Housing: CSI offers students an opportunity to live on campus in luxury apartment-style housing. Located in two brand-new buildings, Dolphin Cove North and South contain 133 furnished apartments housing 454 residents. The buildings offer both private and semi-private bedroom accommodations with semi-private bathrooms and full kitchens. Other amenities include a study lounge, fitness center, and convenient parking. Housing is filled on a first-come, first-served basis.

Location

Conveniently located in the heart of Staten Island, CSI's park-like 204-acre property is the largest single college campus, public or private, in New York City. Classrooms and academic offices are located in fourteen neo-Georgian buildings that form two quadrangles connected by the campus walk, which extends between the Library and the Campus Center. The Library, Dolphin Cove North and South, the Campus Center, the Biological Sciences/Chemical Sciences building, the Center for the Arts, and the Sports and Recreation Center provide outstanding facilities for scholastic and community activities.

CSI St. George, an extension of the CSI Willowbrook campus, located at 120 Stuyvesant Place, is home to a dynamic 16,000 square-foot facility a few blocks from the Staten Island Ferry, with convenient access for full- and part-time students from Staten Island, as well as commuters from Manhattan, Brooklyn, and the Bronx.

CSI's location offers students the better of two worlds, with Staten Island providing a suburban environment with some of the most interesting landscapes in the metropolitan area, and Manhattan, the center of cultural and social life in the city, being only 25 minutes from the Island by ferry. In addition, the Verrazano-Narrows Bridge provides direct access between Staten Island and Brooklyn.

Majors and Degrees

CSI offers the following associate degrees: Business (A.A.S.): Accounting, Finance, Information Systems, International Business, Management, and Marketing specializations; Computer Technology (A.A.S.): Programming and Information Science sequences; Engineering Science (A.S.); Liberal Arts and Sciences (A.A./A.S.); and Nursing (A.A.S.).

CSI offers the following bachelor's degree programs: Accounting (B.S.); African and African Diaspora Studies (B.A.); American Studies (B.A.); Art (B.A./B.F.A.): Studio Art and Photography concentrations; Biochemistry (B.S.); Biology* (B.S.): Bioinformatics, Ecology, Evolution, and Behavioral Biology, Molecular, Cellular, and Developmental Biology, Neuroscience, and Health Science options; Business (B.S.): Finance, International Business, Management, and Marketing concentrations; Chemistry* (B.S.); Cinema Studies (B.A.): Critical Studies and Production concentrations; Communications (B.S.): Journalism, Media Studies, Design and Digital Media, and Corporate Communications concentrations; Computer Science (B.S.); Computer Science/Mathematics (B.S.); Drama (B.S.); Earth and Environmental Science (B.S.); Earth Science* (B.S.); Economics (B.A./B.S.): Business and Finance specializations; Education: Early Childhood, Childhood, and Adolescence programs; Electrical Engineering (B.S.); Engineering Science (B.S.): Computer and Mechanical specializations; English* (B.A.): Writing, Linguistics, Literature, and Dramatic Literature concentrations; Geography (B.A.); History* (B.A.); Information Systems and Informatics (B.S.); International Studies (B.A.); Italian Studies* (B.A.); Mathematics* (B.S.): Pure and Applied Mathematics emphases; Medical Technology (B.S.); Music (B.A./B.S.): Classical Performance, Literature and Theory, Music Technology, Jazz Studies and Performance concentrations; Nursing (B.S.); Philosophy (B.A.); Philosophy and Political Science (B.A., dual major); Physics* (B.S.); Political Science (B.A.); Pre-Professional Preparation: Dentistry, Law, Medicine, Optometry, Physical Therapy, Chiropractic, and Podiatry programs; Psychology (B.A./B.S.); Science Letters and Society (B.A.): Early Childhood sequence (Birth–2) and Childhood sequence (1–6); Social Work (B.S.S.W.); Sociology–Anthropology (B.A.); Spanish* (B.A.); and Women's, Gender, and Sexuality Studies (B.A.).

**Adolescence Education track (grades 7–12) available.*

Academic Programs

CSI offers two-year programs in career areas and in liberal arts and sciences, and four-year programs with majors in the traditional fields of study. General education requirements have been established for all degrees. Credit may be awarded for internships, research, and experiential learning. Students may graduate with honors in most bachelor's degree majors.

The College offers classes scheduled during both the day and evening, seven days a week, with a variety of course combinations leading to associate and bachelor's degrees, providing opportunities for nontraditional students to pursue a college education at more convenient times. CSI also offers intensive summer and winter sessions.

Honors Programs: The College offers several honors programs. Programs include Macaulay Honors College at CSI (MHC), the College's most selective full scholarship program*; the Verrazano Honors Program, a local honors program that creates learning communities and provides scholarships for study abroad; and Teacher Education Honors Academy at CSI (TEHA), a scholarship program designed to highly train select students to teach mathematics and science in New York City Department of Education middle and high schools.

**Scholarship receipt subject to eligibility requirements.*

Off-Campus Programs

CSI students may use the resources of and receive credit for courses taken at other CUNY colleges to support their education. The College also gives a number of courses for credit at off-campus locations throughout the city through internships at major corporations and other sites. Exceptional study-abroad opportunities are available through CSI's Center for Global Engagement, which offers students the option of earning academic credit for study in Australia, Belgium, China, Costa Rica, Cuba, Denmark, Ecuador, England, France, Greece, Hungary, Ireland, Italy, Japan, Northern Ireland, Spain, Sweden, Taiwan, or Trinidad and Tobago. Students may also pursue study-abroad programs in additional countries through the College Consortium for International Studies (CCIS).

Academic Facilities

The academic buildings are designed to house approximately 300 state-of-the-art laboratories and classrooms; each has its own computer lab, study lounge for students, and faculty offices.

The Campus Center is where students can relax, dine, and be entertained. The two-story rotunda at the heart of the structure contains the main dining facilities, the College's health services, a bookstore, offices for student organizations, study lounges, a small performance/café space, game rooms with the latest game consoles, and the state-of-the-art student-operated studios of WSIA 88.9, the only FM radio station on Staten Island.

The Center for the Arts complex provides facilities for teaching in the instructional wing and performance spaces in the public wing. The complex of public facilities includes a 911-seat auditorium, a 442-seat fully equipped theater, a 156-seat recital hall, a 143-seat lecture hall, an experimental Black Box Theater, art galleries, and a conference center. Classrooms, lecture halls, studios, screening rooms, and offices for faculty members are located in the instructional wing.

The CSI Library is staffed with librarians trained in every discipline offered at the College, who also hold faculty status and rank. The Library's total collection consists of approximately 532,189 books and ebooks, 77,283 electronic journals, 220 electronic resources, 19,800 streaming video titles, and 5,000 sound recordings. The Library's online catalog provides complete access to the collections, including access to holdings of other CUNY libraries. Students also have electronic access to database and research tools 24 hours a day via the Internet. In addition, the Library maintains a collection of current textbooks donated by the CSI Student Government. These and other course materials are available at the Reserve Desk. Wireless laptops are loaned to students for use throughout the Library. The Library building also houses the Office of Academic Support and the Cybercafé, which offers Starbucks® coffee.

The laboratory science building provides facilities for teaching and for two research centers: the Center for Environmental Science and the Center for Developmental Neuroscience and Developmental Disabilities. It consists of a research wing and an instructional wing. State-of-the-art laboratories serve students and faculty members in their teaching and research.

The CSI Astrophysical Observatory is a world-class resource that has been recognized by the International Astronomical Union as an official asteroid-tracking station.

CSI is dedicated to keeping its campus up-to-date during these technology-centric times. Planned updates include the highly innovative Interdisciplinary High-Performance Computational Center and expansions to the Library and Campus Center.

Costs

For 2019–20, undergraduate tuition for New York State (NYS) residents is $295 per credit for resident part-time matriculated students, $3,365 per semester for resident full-time matriculated students, and $430 per credit for resident non-degree students. Nonresident full- and part-time students are charged $600 per credit, and nonresident non-degree students are charged $890 per credit. Graduate NYS resident tuition is $5,385 per semester for students attending the College full-time and $455 per credit for resident part-time students. Nonresidents are charged $830 per credit for full- and part-time attendance.

Financial Aid

Financial aid is available through state and federal programs and includes the New York State Tuition Assistance Program (TAP) awards, Federal Pell Grants, Supplemental Educational Opportunity Grants (SEOG), Search for Elevation and Education through Knowledge (SEEK) awards, the Accelerated Study in Associate Programs (ASAP) awards, Federal Work-Study Program awards, and student loan programs. Information about programs, application procedures, and deadlines is available from the Office of Student Financial Aid.

The CSI Scholarship is awarded annually to incoming freshmen, transfer, and current students with a 90.00 or 3.25 (or higher) GPA. Further information about scholarships is available from the Office of Fellowship and Scholarship Opportunities.

Faculty

The College has a full-time faculty of 404, of whom approximately 90 percent hold a doctoral degree or the highest attainable degree in their field. Numerous faculty members have made significant contributions in many areas of scholarship, creativity, and public service and have received prestigious grants and awards.

Student Government

A single body, the Senate, is composed of 25 elected students and represents the interests of the College's students, serving as liaison to faculty and administrators. The Senate derives funding from the Student Activity Fee and sponsors many academic and nonacademic programs benefiting students.

Admission Requirements

A freshman applicant seeking admission to a bachelor's degree program must pass the CUNY Assessment Tests (CATs) in reading, writing, and mathematics unless he or she qualifies for exemption based on their high SAT, ACT, or Regents Examination scores. Admission to a bachelor's degree program is determined by the applicant's high school courses, academic average, and the combined verbal and mathematics SAT scores. The College accepts applicants whose scores reach or exceed the College's minimum bachelor's degree program requirements. A faculty admissions committee may consider admitting applicants whose scores approach the College's minimum requirements. Entering first-year students may be admitted to associate-level programs if they have graduated from an accredited high school or have earned a high school equivalency diploma. A transfer applicant with 30 or more credits completed at the time of application must have a minimum cumulative GPA of 2.00. Applicants with fewer than 30 credits must have a GPA of at least 2.00 and must meet freshman entrance criteria.

Application and Information

Requests for further information and application materials should be directed to:

College of Staten Island/The City University of New York
Office of Recruitment and Admissions, Building 2A, Room 103
Staten Island, New York 10314
Phone: 718-982-2010
E-mail: admissions@csi.cuny.edu
Website: www.csi.cuny.edu

The CSI Library offers access to over 532,000 books and 77,000 electronic journals. All CSI students may also use the libraries and databases of other CUNY schools, allowing them access to millions of resources.

COLUMBIA UNIVERSITY
Columbia College/The Fu Foundation School of Engineering and Applied Science
NEW YORK, NEW YORK

The University

Columbia College and The Fu Foundation School of Engineering and Applied Science (Columbia Engineering) offer their students the unique advantages proved by both a major research university and a small, selective college. Students benefit from over 250 years of rich history and distinction, easy access to the immense resources of New York City and a dynamic residential community where "Columbia Blue" is worn with pride at events ranging from Lions' basketball games to the World Leaders Forum, from the Varsity Show to the annual tree-lighting ceremony.

The Columbia College student body is composed of approximately 4,500 students; the Columbia Engineering student body has roughly 1,500. Students come from all fifty states and over ninety countries. They represent a dazzling array of ethnic, social, economic, cultural, religious, and geographic backgrounds. The diversity of Columbia's student body reflects the diversity of New York City, the world's most international city.

Columbia guarantees four years of on-campus housing to all entering first-year students. More than 95 percent of undergraduates remain in University residence halls for all four years.

Columbia students take part in extracurricular groups of all kinds: artistic (theater, music, dance, film, and visual arts), athletic (thirty-one Division I varsity sports and dozens of club and intramural sports), communications (the *Columbia Daily Spectator*, the *Columbia Journal of Literary Criticism*, WKCR-FM, and many others), community service (Big Brother/Big Sister programs, after-hours tutoring programs, a volunteer ambulance squad, and partnerships with dozens of hospitals, soup kitchens, and homeless shelters), and pre-professional (the Charles Drew Pre-Medical Society, the Society of Hispanic Professional Engineers, and more). Other groups represent students' ethnic, religious, political, and gender identities. There are twenty-eight fraternities and sororities. Alfred Lerner Hall houses office and meeting space for student organizations, a black box theatre, a cinema, the Berick Center for Student Advising, and many dining options.

Location

Columbia shares its Manhattan neighborhood, Morningside Heights, with a number of other notable institutions: Barnard College, the Cathedral of St. John the Divine, Union Theological Seminary, Jewish Theological Seminary, and the Manhattan School of Music, to name a few. Many faculty members from Columbia and the other surrounding schools make their homes in the neighborhood. Morningside Heights is an area known for bookstores, wonderfully varied restaurants, and merchants that cater to student tastes, student budgets, and student hours. Columbia students enjoy a college town community in addition to the opportunities New York City has to offer.

Students are encouraged to take advantage of New York's breathtaking variety of cultural, recreational, and professional resources. Through the Columbia Arts Initiative, students can receive discounted tickets to Broadway shows, film screenings, art galleries, and cultural events in New York City. Passport to NYC offers students free access to over thirty museums throughout the city. Columbia students can be found any day of the week exploring the Metropolitan Museum of Art, the Museum of Modern Art, the Guggenheim Museum, the Museum of African Art, or the Museo del Barrio. They might be discovering the theatrical offerings on, off, or "off-off" Broadway; attending the opera, ballet, or symphony at Lincoln Center; enjoying jazz in Greenwich Village or amateur night at the Apollo; sampling *pai gwat* in Chinatown; or jogging in Central Park. Columbia's Center for Career Education offers students opportunities to explore career pathways in depth; nowhere else in the world does the concentration of industries allow such a range of possibilities for internships and post-graduate employment. New York's public transportation system puts the entire city within easy reach of Columbia students; the campus is directly served by a subway line and five bus routes.

Majors and Degrees

Columbia College grants the B.A. degree in more than eighty programs of study in the humanities, social sciences, and pure sciences, including many interdisciplinary majors. Columbia Engineering grants the B.S. degree in sixteen engineering fields. A five-year program that begins in either school allows students to receive both a B.A. from Columbia College and a B.S. from Columbia Engineering.

Joint degree programs offer selected students the opportunity to combine their undergraduate work with study in Columbia University's schools of law and international affairs and with the Juilliard School.

Academic Programs

Columbia College is known for its Core Curriculum, a set of common courses required of all undergraduates and considered the necessary general education for students, regardless of their choice in major. The communal learning—with all students encountering the same texts and issues at the same time—and the critical dialogue experienced in small seminars are the distinctive features of the Core. Begun in 1919, the Core Curriculum is one of the founding experiments in liberal higher education in the United States, and it remains vibrant a century later. One of the signature courses in the Core is Contemporary Civilization, a year-long historical survey of Western civilization's religious, political, and moral philosophies; another is Literature Humanities, a year-long introduction to Western culture's most seminal and meaningful literary works. A second year of humanities offers a semester each of music and art appreciation, encouraging students to experience the cultural treasures of New York City. The Global Core requirement enlarges the scope of inquiry beyond the Western focus in order to promote learning and thought about the variety of cultures and the diversity of traditions that interact in the United States and the world today. Frontiers of Science outlines the approaches that scientists take to answer compelling problems in the natural world and introduces students to scientific research methods. University Writing equips students with the ability and thoughtfulness to read and write essays in order to participate in the academic conversations that form Columbia's intellectual community. The Core is the critical examination of challenging ideas. It's a shared connection with classmates, professors, and other Columbians since 1919. Core classrooms are places where the pursuit of better questions is just as important as the pursuit of better answers.

The strength of Columbia Engineering's education is in its unique vision—Engineering for Humanity—preparing students not only to be world-class engineers but also to be global leaders across industries who are equipped and motivated to address the most pressing global challenges in the areas of sustainability, health, security, connectivity, and creativity. In addition to taking rigorous math and science courses typically offered at top undergraduate programs, Columbia Engineering students benefit from programming that fosters innovation and entrepreneurship, and are also required to take courses in the liberal arts alongside their College counterparts, providing them with interdisciplinary tools for real-world problem solving. This type of broad academic exposure is what alumni often cite as the foundation of their later academic and professional success. Another hallmark of the Columbia Engineering education is the Art of Engineering, where first-year students are introduced to the field through interactive lectures, hands-on group projects, and guest speakers. Past examples of projects include mathematically modeling the U.S. elections, designing vital signs monitors, and modifying a laser pointer to transmit digital data over long distances. In addition to the technical issues discussed in the course, other key issues of importance in professional engineering such as ethics, project management, and societal impact are addressed.

Off-Campus Programs

Columbia maintains a network of global centers, developing opportunities for research, scholarship, teaching, and service across borders. With eight international locations ranging from Turkey to Chile and from Kenya to China, undergraduate options include summer Arabic language programs in Amman, Jordan, or a semester-long French literature program in Paris. Columbia also has direct enrollment agreements with many partner institutions abroad, as well as a growing number of exchange programs with universities abroad.

Altogether, Columbia students, with the help of advisers from Global Programs, may choose from over 150 study-abroad programs on nearly every continent.

Academic Facilities

Columbia has the fifth-largest research library system in the world, consisting of 12 million volumes and 26 million manuscripts within 3,000 collections. The LEED Gold–certified Northwest Corner Building houses cutting-edge labs that bring together researchers in biology, chemistry, physics, and engineering, as well as a science library, lecture hall, and café. Students may also make use of an electronic music lab, a cyclotron, an oral history collection, the facilities and programs of the Lamont-Doherty Earth Observatory, and oceanographic research ships.

Costs

Tuition for the 2018–19 academic year was $59,985. Room and board for all first-year students was $13,864. With typical fees, books, and supplies, the total cost of a year at Columbia was approximately $77,259.

Financial Aid

Columbia awards more than $168 million annually in scholarships and grants, and the average amount awarded is $53,830. Additionally, 50 percent of Columbia students receive grants from the university. All first-year candidates who are U.S. citizens, have U.S. permanent resident or political refugee status, or are undocumented students who reside in the U.S. are considered for admission without regard to their financial need. International students who do not fit into the above categories should be aware that their admissions process is not need-blind; their financial need is taken into account at the time of admission. Regardless of citizenship, Columbia meets the full demonstrated need of every student admitted as a first-year or transfer student. All financial aid at Columbia is based on need, in the form of grants and student work only, not loans. Prospective students should go to http://cc-seas.financialaid.columbia.edu/ for information on specific requirements and deadlines.

Faculty

The student-to-faculty ratio is 6:1. Core Curriculum classes are capped at 22 students, and 80 percent of classes have 20 students or fewer. The Columbia faculty is committed to both teaching and research, and all faculty members, including the president of the University, teach undergraduates.

Admission Requirements

The Columbia first-year class of 1,400 students is selected from a much larger pool of applicants through a holistic, committee-based review process. There are no specific course requirements for admission, but applicants must present evidence that they are prepared for college work in a variety of disciplines as required for the Columbia degree. Accordingly, the following preparation is strongly recommended: 4 years of English, including meaningful work in literature and writing; 3 (preferably 4) years of mathematics, including pre-calculus and calculus where offered; 3 (preferably 4) years of history and social studies; 3 or more years of the same foreign language; and 3 (preferably 4) years of laboratory science (including chemistry and physics where available). Modifying the preparatory program just outlined—by taking more work in some subjects and less in others—is not only acceptable but may be desirable in individual cases.

Standardized tests are required for admission, according to the following guidelines. Students must take *either* the SAT *or* the ACT, and they may self-report their scores. Students who take the SAT more than once are evaluated on the highest score they receive in any individual section. Applicants taking the ACT more than once are evaluated on the highest score received in any individual section. The writing component of both exams is not required. Only admitted students who choose to enroll at Columbia must have their official scores sent by the testing agency.

While Columbia does not require SAT or ACT writing tests or SAT Subject Tests, students who have taken these exams may submit their results if they wish them to be considered.

Transfer students may enter Columbia in the fall term only.

Columbia College and Columbia Engineering each have a Visiting Students Program, which allow students to attend for one or both semesters of their sophomore, junior, or senior year.

Application and Information

Students may apply via the Common Application or the Coalition Application. Students for whom Columbia is their definite first choice are encouraged to apply early decision. The early decision deadline is November 1, and candidates are notified by mid-December. Students admitted to Columbia under early decision are required to matriculate at Columbia and withdraw their applications to other colleges. The regular decision deadline is January 1, and candidates are notified by April 1. Admitted students must respond to Columbia's offer of admission by May 1.

For further information, interested students should contact:

Undergraduate Admissions
Columbia University
1130 Amsterdam Avenue, MC 2807
New York, New York 10027
Phone: 212-854-2522
Fax: 212-854-1209
E-mail: ugrad-ask@columbia.edu
Website: http://undergrad.admissions.columbia.edu/
http://www.youtube.com/columbiaadmissions
http://www.instagram.com/columbiaadmissions

COLUMBIA UNIVERSITY SCHOOL OF GENERAL STUDIES

NEW YORK, NEW YORK

COLUMBIA | GS
School of General Studies

The University and the School

The Columbia University School of General Studies (GS), founded in 1947, is the finest liberal arts college in the United States dedicated specifically to returning and nontraditional students seeking a rigorous, traditional, Ivy League undergraduate education full or part time. Students come from a variety of backgrounds and, for personal or professional reasons, most have interrupted their educations, never attended college, or are only able to attend part time. GS is unique among colleges of its type, because its students are fully integrated into the Columbia undergraduate curriculum: they take the same courses, with the same faculty members, and earn the same degree as all other undergraduates at the University.

In the classroom, the diversity and varied personal experiences of the student body promote discussion and debate that is unparalleled in the Ivy League, fostering an environment of academic rigor and intellectual development. GS enrolls world-class dancers, athletes, and musicians; bankers and small business owners; and military veterans. There are more than 2,100 undergraduate degree candidates and more than 400 Postbac Premed students. The average age of the GS student body is 27, and more than 70 percent of GS students attend classes full time.

In addition to its core undergraduate program, GS is home to the Columbia University Postbaccalaureate Premedical Program, as well as dual- and joint-degree programs with Sciences Po, Trinity College Dublin, City University of Hong Kong, and List College of the Jewish Theological Seminary. GS also offers combined undergraduate/graduate degree programs with Columbia's Schools of Engineering and Applied Science, Social Work, International and Public Affairs, Law, Business, Dental Medicine, and Public Health, as well as Teachers College and the College of Physicians and Surgeons. More than 70 percent of GS students go on to earn advanced degrees after graduation.

Location

Columbia University is located in Morningside Heights, on the Upper West Side of Manhattan. The University's neighbors include the Union Theological Seminary, the Jewish Theological Seminary, the Manhattan School of Music, Mount Sinai St. Luke's Hospital, Riverside Church, and the historic Cathedral of St. John the Divine, the largest cathedral in the world. The diversity of intellectual and social activities offered by these institutions is one of Columbia's great assets; another is New York City itself, which offers Columbia students a rich and almost boundless variety of social and cultural opportunities.

Majors and Degrees

GS offers an Ivy League liberal arts education leading to a Bachelor of Arts degree, and students may choose from more than eighty majors and concentrations, including African American studies; American studies; ancient studies; anthropology; applied mathematics; archaeology; architecture; art history; astronomy; astrophysics; biochemistry; biology; biophysics; business management; chemical physics; chemistry; classics; comparative literature and society; computer science; creative writing; dance; data science; drama and theater arts; earth and environmental science; East Asian studies; economics; education; English; environmental biology; environmental chemistry; environmental science; ethnicity and race studies; evolutionary biology of the human species; film and media studies; financial economics; French; German literature and cultural history; Hispanic studies; history; human rights; information science, Italian cultural studies; Italian language and literature; jazz studies; Jewish studies; Latin American and Caribbean studies; Latin American and Iberian cultures; linguistics; mathematics; medieval and renaissance studies; Middle Eastern, South Asian, and African studies; modern Greek studies; music; neuroscience and behavior; philosophy; physics; political science; Portuguese studies; psychology; regional studies; religion; Russian language and culture; Russian literature and culture; Slavic studies; sociology; statistics; sustainable development; urban studies; visual arts; women's and gender studies; and Yiddish studies.

GS is also home to the Columbia University Postbaccalaureate Premedical Program, the oldest and largest of its kind in the United States, which aims to meet the needs of college graduates who wish to pursue a medical education, but who have taken few or none of the core science courses required for admission to medical school, dental school, veterinary medical school, or other allied health graduate programs. Additionally, the program provides students with opportunities for practical clinical and research experience, guidance throughout the medical school application process, and institutional support through a letter of recommendation.

Academic Programs

The School of General Studies offers a traditional liberal arts education designed to provide students with the broad knowledge and intellectual skills that foster continued education and growth in the years after college as well as providing a sound foundation for positions of responsibility in the professional world.

Requirements for the bachelor's degree comprise three elements: (1) core requirements, intended to develop critical skills in writing and quantitative reasoning while providing exposure to a range of knowledge and disciplines; (2) major requirements, designed to provide students sustained and coherent exposure to a particular discipline in an area of strong intellectual interest; and (3) elective courses. Students are required to complete a minimum of 124 points for the bachelor's degree; 60 of these may be in transfer credit, but at least 64 points (including the last 30 points) must be completed at Columbia.

Off-Campus Programs

Columbia students are encouraged to enhance their academic experiences through the more than 150 study-abroad programs offered in more than 100 cities around the world. Options include studying in Paris at the Columbia University Global Center, in Kyoto at the Consortium for Japanese Studies, in Kenya completing the Tropical Biology and Sustainability Program, or in Cuba taking courses at the University of Havana, to name a few.

Academic Facilities

The Columbia University Libraries constitute the nation's fifth-largest academic library system, with a collection of more than 13 million volumes, more than 160,000 journals and serials, and an extensive array of additional resources. Of the twenty-two libraries in the system, five are designated Distinctive Collections because of their unusual depth and nationally recognized excellence. The Fairchild Life Sciences Building houses research facilities, laboratories, electron microscopes, and a vast amount of biochemical equipment used for teaching and research. The University's physics building has been the scene of many important developments in the recent history of physics, including the invention of the laser and the first U.S. demonstration of nuclear fission.

Costs

For the 2018–19 academic year, tuition was $1,822 per point (credit), and annual living (room and board) and personal expenses (books, local commuting costs, and other expenses) were $24,170.

Financial Aid

The School of General Studies awards financial aid based upon need and academic ability. Approximately 70 percent of GS degree candidates receive some form of financial aid, including federal Pell grants, New York State grants, federal unsubsidized and subsidized loans, institutional scholarships, and Federal Work-Study Program awards. The average scholarship award ranges from $8,000 to $10,000 for first-year students.

Faculty

All undergraduate liberal arts courses at Columbia University are taught by members of the Columbia University Faculty of Arts and Sciences. These distinguished scholars in virtually every discipline also teach students in Columbia College, the Graduate School of Arts and Sciences, the School of the Arts, and the School of Professional Studies. The student-faculty ratio is 6:1, and GS students have many opportunities to work closely with faculty members, both in small classes and research projects. Faculty members also serve as departmental advisors to students majoring in their area of study and maintain regular office hours.

Student Government

One student represents GS in the University Senate, a decision-making body comprising students, faculty members, and administrative staff members from each division of the University. In addition, two GS students sit as voting members on the Committee on Instruction, which oversees the curriculum of the School. The General Studies Student Council elects officers each year and sponsors activities for students and the Premedical Association sponsors events related to the medical school admissions process.

Admission Requirements

The GS admission policy is geared to the maturity and varied backgrounds of its students. Aptitude and motivation are considered along with past academic performance, standardized test scores, and employment history. The School's admission decisions are based on a careful review of each application and reflect the Admissions Committee's considered judgment of the applicant's maturity, academic potential, and present ability to undertake course work at Columbia.

Admission requirements include a completed application form; an autobiographical statement; two letters of recommendation from academic or professional evaluators; official transcripts from all high schools, colleges, and universities attended; official SAT or ACT scores (some applicants may also take the General Studies Admissions Examination); and a nonrefundable application fee of $80.

Students from outside the United States may apply to the School of General Studies to start or complete a baccalaureate degree. In addition to the materials previously described, international applicants must submit official scores from the Duolingo English Test, TOEFL, or IELTS.

Application and Information

Fall early action applications completed by January 15 will receive a March 1 decision; applications completed by March 1 will receive a decision by May 1. Spring early action applications completed by September 1 will receive an October 1 decision; applications completed by October 1 will receive a decision by November 15.

For more information, students should contact:

Curtis M. Rodgers, Vice Dean
Office of Admissions and Educational Financing
School of General Studies
408 Lewisohn Hall
2970 Broadway
Columbia University, Mail Code 4101
New York, New York 10027
Phone: 212-854-2772
E-mail: gsdegree@columbia.edu
Website: http://gs.columbia.edu
http://facebook.com/ColumbiaGS
http://instagram.com/columbiageneralstudies
http://twitter.com/ColumbiaGS
http://youtube.com/GSColumbia

Morningside Campus, Columbia University.

DEAN COLLEGE
FRANKLIN, MASSACHUSETTS

The College

Founded in 1865, Dean is a unique New England college awarding both four-year baccalaureate and two-year associate degrees. Students may choose from over two-dozen academic programs supported by state-of-the-art facilities, a dedicated teaching faculty, and professional advising known for exceptional personalized academic support.

Located 45 minutes outside Boston in the town of Franklin, Massachusetts, Dean's attractive 100-acre campus is home to WGAO-FM, the Joan Phelps Palladino School of Dance, and several buildings listed on the National Register of Historic Places. There are two fitness centers, a gymnasium, and athletic fields, as well as a library learning commons, an advising center, a 214-seat theater, and numerous dance studios.

Nearly all of Dean's 1,200 full-time students live on campus, and housing is available for all four years. The student body is impressively diverse with more than 30 states and 25 countries represented (and an additional 500 part-time students). The College sponsors 16 NCAA Division III athletic teams, an Honors Program, internship and study abroad opportunities, an executive lecture series, and dozens of clubs, performance groups, and student organizations.

Dean College graduates are very successful. Of those receiving a bachelor's degree last year, 95 percent were employed or attending graduate school within a year. Among associate degree graduates, 98 percent were accepted as transfers to highly selective universities across the United States or had plans to continue their bachelor's degree at Dean.

Location

Dean's home town, Franklin, is a charming, historic Massachusetts community. The suburban setting is safe and convenient to downtown Boston with many local stores and restaurants to support an active college campus. The Commuter Rail—just three blocks from Dean—provides frequent train service to Boston, and students can reach popular destinations such as baseball's Fenway Park, the TD Garden, Museum of Fine Arts, and Harvard Square in less than an hour. Providence, Rhode Island, is even closer (40 minutes) where students can shop at Providence Place or see events at the Dunkin' Donuts Center and Rhode Island Center for the Performing Arts.

The area's biggest attractions are only minutes from Dean: Patriot Place and Gillette Stadium (home of the New England Patriots), the fashionable Wrentham Outlets, and Xfinity Center outdoor amphitheater. For day trips, students can easily get to the beaches on Cape Cod, see Newport's mansions, or reach the mountains in nearby New Hampshire and Vermont.

Areas of Study

Dean College offers a wide range of Bachelor's and Associate Degree Programs across four academic schools: the School of the Arts, School of Business, Palladino School of Dance, and School of Liberal Arts.

Areas of study include: arts and entertainment management, athletic coaching and recreation management, pre-athletic training, biology, business management, communications, criminal justice and homeland security, dance (B.A. and B.F.A. degrees), early childhood education, English, entertainment industry management, exercise science, family and childhood studies, global studies, health and the human experience, health sciences, history, human services, individually designed programs, liberal arts and studies, marketing, pre-law, pre-nursing, psychology, sociology, sport management, sports broadcasting, and theatre (acting, musical theatre, and technical theatre).

Academic Programs

Dean is accredited by the New England Association of Schools and Colleges. Bachelor's degree candidates must complete a required internship or other experiential learning opportunity related to their major.

The Honors Program at Dean offers academically talented students an opportunity to engage in stimulating and challenging courses, seminars, and colloquia. Students who meet the honors entrance criteria enroll in special course sections reserved for honors students or may enhance non-honors courses with additional intensive readings and analysis approved by the instructors. The Honors Program also offers exciting academic and cultural activities outside the traditional classroom environment.

Study-abroad and study-away opportunities are increasingly popular at Dean. Students may choose programs across the globe through cooperative arrangements facilitated by the College, such as programs in London and Buenos Aires, or take advantage of Dean's relationship with the Washington Center Program for study and internships in Washington, D.C.

The Dean Leadership Institute sponsors an Executive Lecture Series that brings leaders in business, media, and the arts to campus. Featured speakers share their insights into post-graduate opportunities and help build each student's career network. Recent guests include Bert Jacobs (Life is Good), Anne Finucane (Bank of America), and Michael Spillane (Nike).

The Arch Learning Community provides comprehensive support for students with diagnosed learning differences. Arch students receive dedicated academic advising and coaching as well as a cohort educational model specially designed to help students maximize their academic and personal potential. The program works with students to find success within the rigors of a traditional college curriculum.

Academic Facilities

Students have access to a wide range of facilities, including the Green Family Library-Learning Commons and E. Ross Anderson Library, Berenson Writing Center, and Morton Family Learning Center—all housed under one roof. Together, these form the hub of Dean's academic support efforts. There are print and online resources for class projects, academic coaches to provide professional one-on-one mentoring, peer and professional tutoring services, the Technology Service Center, and space for weekly faculty drop-in sessions where students can participate in group or individual advising.

Other academic facilities include the A.W. Pierce Technology and Science Center, which houses science and computer labs as well as the Alden Center high-tech master classroom; the Dean College Children's Center, an on-campus pre-school, which doubles as a learning laboratory for student teachers; and Campus Center, where students can find the Advising Center, Main Stage Theater, Guidrey Center, student activities office, and newly renovated classrooms featuring cutting-edge technology.

Costs

The basic costs related to attending Dean College for 2019–20 are $40,414 for tuition and fees and $17,258 for room and board.

Financial Aid

Dean College awards more than $25 million in scholarships and grants annually to assist their students in funding their educations. Ninety-five percent of Dean students receive some form of merit-based aid with an average award amount of $20,000 per year. These awards are based solely on the information students provide in their application for admission—not financial need—and help to reduce the average cost of attendance by over 30 percent. In addition, most students apply for—and receive—federal and state financial aid, which is separate from (and can be added to) Dean's scholarship awards.

Student financial aid packages are generally a combination of grants, loans, and work-study, contingent upon demonstrated need and the availability of funds. The College participates in all Federal Title IV and Federal Family Education Loan Programs. Students must submit the Free Application for Federal Student Aid (FAFSA) in order to be considered for need-based aid. Upon receipt of a valid FAFSA, full-time students are considered for all of the financial aid programs that Dean administers. Residents of Massachusetts and other reciprocal states may also be eligible for state scholarships, grants, or loans.

Faculty

Dean's dedicated faculty members, advisers, and educational specialists—some of the best in their respective fields—offer direct, personal involvement to help students obtain the full value of their college experience. The average class size is 18 students.

Student Government

The Student Government Association serves as a liaison between the student body and Dean College administration. It disseminates information about College policies, seeks out student opinion, allocates funds collected from the activities fee to clubs and organizations through a budget request process, and coordinates the activities of various clubs, groups, and organizations campus wide.

Admission Requirements

Every application to Dean is carefully reviewed by the Admission Committee. In addition to the application form, students must submit an official high school transcript. A letter of recommendation from a guidance counselor or teacher, a personal statement or essay, and SAT or ACT scores are all optional. Interviews are not required but are offered as students visit campus. Students applying for the dance and theatre programs must audition.

Application and Information

Students who identify Dean as a top choice may choose to apply under the early action plan, with an application deadline of November 1 or December 1. The College accepts applications on a rolling basis thereafter, though it is recommended that applications be submitted by March 15 to ensure access to the highest level of financial aid and priority in housing and class registration. Once an application is complete, an admissions decision is typically made within four weeks.

For more information, contact:

Office of Admissions
Dean College
99 Main Street
Franklin, Massachusetts 02038
Phone: 508-541-1508
877-TRY-DEAN (toll-free)
E-mail: admissions@dean.edu
Website: http://www.dean.edu

Dean Hall, built in 1865 when Dean College was established.

DREXEL UNIVERSITY
PHILADELPHIA, PENNSYLVANIA

The University

Drexel University is a comprehensive global research university that has maintained a reputation for academic excellence since its founding in 1891. The University's use-inspired approach to learning prepares undergraduates for a variety of careers and graduate school. Cooperative education is a vital part of a Drexel education. Students gain professional experience in jobs related to their career interests by alternating classroom study with periods of meaningful employment. The 2018 undergraduate enrollment numbered 13,938 full-time students representing 46 states and 126 other countries. International students compose about 15 percent of the undergraduate population. Drexel University grants bachelor's, master's, and doctoral degrees—as well as certificates—in a variety of programs.

Drexel offers 18 Division I varsity athletic programs and competes in the Colonial Athletic Association Conference. The University also sponsors intramural and club sports.

There is always something to do on campus, including events such as dances, lectures, excursions, community service projects, free movie screenings from the Campus Activities Board (CAB), and other activities related to Drexel's more than 30 active fraternities and sororities. Students can also take part in performing arts groups in dance, theater, and music. In all, there are over 350 student organizations.

Location

Drexel is located in the heart of Philadelphia, the nation's sixth-largest city, and shares its University City neighborhood with five other universities. With thousands of college student residents, University City is a great place for students to spend their college years—in an urban campus setting, surrounded by the amenities of the city and the diversity of their peers. Philadelphia is home to some of the nation's best historical and cultural attractions and offers a vibrant social and cultural scene, dynamic arts, and highly competitive professional athletic teams. Drexel's location offers easy access to public transportation and the Drexel shuttle provides convenient, free transportation between campuses for Drexel students. Adjacent to Drexel's University City Campus, Amtrak's 30th Street Station is a hub for trains and buses to the Philadelphia suburbs, New York City, Washington, DC, and the Philadelphia International Airport.

Academic Disciplines

Whatever their interests, students at Drexel are at the forefront of their fields. Drexel offers more than 80 undergraduate majors and over 20 accelerated degree programs. Academic majors include fields such as business, computing and informatics, culinary arts and science, education, engineering, entrepreneurship, exploratory studies, health professions, hospitality, humanities and social sciences, media arts and design, nursing, public health, sciences, and undeclared.

Accelerated and joint degree programs allow students to earn both a bachelor's and an advanced degree in a shortened period of time. Drexel's accelerated and joint degree options include the BA/BS/JD in law; BA/BS+MD in medicine; BS/DPT in physical therapy; BS/MHS in physician assistant studies; BS/MPH in public health; BS/MBA programs in business, computing and security technology, culinary arts and science, design and merchandising, entertainment and arts management, hospitality management, information systems, and music industry; BS/MS programs in accounting, biomedical engineering, communication, computing and informatics, education, engineering, and psychology; BS/MA in creative arts in therapy and dance/movement therapy; BA/BS/MS in science, technology, and security; and BA/BS in history/MS in library and information sciences.

Academic Enhancement Programs

Qualified students can apply to the Honors Program, one of many exciting opportunities offered by the Pennoni Honors College. The Honors Program offers enhanced academic and extracurricular options to talented students through course work, speakers, social activities, and travel. Honors students receive benefits such as small Honors classes, Honors housing, free tickets to cultural events in Philadelphia, Honors-specific advising and mentoring, and priority registration for classes. Students in the Honors Program who satisfy the requirements are eligible for Graduation with Honors or, for the most accomplished students, Graduation with Distinction.

Drexel is an R1-level comprehensive research institution committed to use-inspired research with real-world applications. Research at Drexel is driven by faculty from all disciplines and students are encouraged to seek opportunities to partner with world-renowned faculty or develop independent research projects. The STAR (Students Tackling Advanced Research) Scholars program invites qualified students to participate in faculty-mentored research projects in their chosen fields as early as their first year. Students who take part in research may be eligible for stipends or academic credit.

Opportunities for Enrichment

Drexel's experiential learning model recognizes the importance of both academic and professional preparation. Drexel's cooperative education program (Drexel Co-op) provides professional employment experiences for students, giving them the opportunity to test-drive a career before they enter the workforce. The benefits are obvious—during their time at Drexel, students experience up to three different co-ops (up to 18 months). Drexel Co-op connects them with industry leaders and brings their cooperative education experiences back into the classroom. Because of this, Drexel students graduate having already built a professional network, and they typically receive higher starting salaries than their counterparts from other schools.

Drexel brings an international dimension to University life through its academic programs, study and cooperative education abroad, major research projects, global classrooms, conferences, and cultural events. Last year, more than 900 Drexel students had an international experience studying, doing research, and participating in service learning abroad. These students represented every major and took advantage of more than 150 program opportunities. With programs in Africa, Asia, Europe, Latin America, and the Pacific, locations are as varied as the interests of Drexel students.

Students can also become civically engaged and fulfill public service and leadership roles at Drexel's Lindy Center for Civic Engagement.

Academic Facilities

Drexel has three campus locations: University City Campus, Center City Campus, and Queen Lane Campus. The University's library system comprises the W. W. Hagerty Library, the Library Learning Terrace, the Legal Research Center, and three health sciences libraries. The W. W. Hagerty Library, the University's central library located on the University City campus, maintains subscriptions to nearly 12,000 electronic journals, which are accessed via the library website, along with academic journals and 200 databases. Students may borrow laptops for use in the library. The Library Learning Terrace, a 3,000-square-foot flexible learning space located in a residence hall and staffed by librarians, enables students to learn and research collaboratively through a variety of technologies. The Legal Research Center on the third floor of the Kline School of Law shares University databases while continuing to acquire new material. The additional libraries on the health sciences campuses provide study space, 75,000 books, and network access to the same set of online journals and databases.

The University is comprised of many state-of-the-art spaces for students. One popular student location is the 12-story, 177,500-square-foot Gerri C. LeBow Hall, which houses the LeBow College of Business, along with the Chestnut Square complex, which features mixed-use housing and retail, including a Shake Shack. The URBN Center houses the Westphal College of Media Arts & Design, providing space for exhibitions, labs, studios, and a black box theater. The five-story, 130,000-square-foot Papadakis Integrated Sciences Building features classrooms and North America's largest biowall. In addition, The Summit at University City provides more student housing and mixed-use commercial space.

Costs

For the 2019–20 academic year, Drexel's estimated cost of attendance for a full-time undergraduate student starting as a first-year student includes $52,146 in tuition, $2,405 in fees, and $14,241 in room and board. Students also incur additional costs for books (which vary by program), a computer for personal use, transportation, and miscellaneous personal costs.

Financial Aid

First-year students eligible for merit and/or need-based funds were awarded financial aid in the 2018–19 academic year. The average financial aid awards for full-time degree-seeking undergraduates in the 2018–19 academic year, including all grant and scholarship sources, was $30,732. All incoming students are encouraged to submit both the CSS Profile and the Free Application for Federal Student Aid (FAFSA) by specific deadlines. Financial aid notifications to students begin mid-December for students accepted during Early Action and Early Decision. The Drexel Liberty Scholars Program also provides 50 full-tuition and fees scholarships to low-income students who live in Philadelphia. The Drexel Global Scholar program grants full-tuition scholarships to exceptional international students who are also committed to global leadership.

Faculty

The University requires faculty members engaged in research and graduate-level teaching to also teach at the undergraduate level, allowing all students to benefit from the research activities of the faculty. Specially selected faculty members serve as advisors for first-year students. The student–faculty ratio is 11:1.

Admission Requirements

All colleges within the University require completion of a college-preparatory program in high school that includes at least 3 years of mathematics and 1 year of laboratory science. Students applying to a major in the sciences or business and engineering are required to take 4 years of mathematics (through trigonometry) and 2 years of laboratory science. Engineering requires 4 years of mathematics (through trigonometry and precalculus), chemistry, and physics. Biomedical engineering requires 1 year of calculus and 1 year of physics. Computer science and software engineering require 4 years of math (including trigonometry and calculus) and 2 years of lab science. The quality of academic performance is more important than merely meeting minimum requirements. The strength of preparation is judged primarily by rigor of course work or relative grade point average (GPA), by the degree of improvement in the quality of the academic record, and by the comments and recommendations from principals, school counselors, or teachers. First-year applicants are required to submit standardized test scores—including the SAT, ACT, SAT Subject, AP, or IB—and can also utilize Drexel's flexible testing policy. Students who were admitted and enrolled in the fall of 2018 had an average SAT math score (25th–75th percentiles) of 590–710 and an average SAT critical reading score (25th–75th percentiles) of 580–670. The essay from the Common Application or personal statement is required of all full-time applicants (except nursing ACE). Applicants to the Westphal College of Media Arts & Design or those seeking a custom-designed major may also be required to submit a writing supplement or portfolio. Transfer applicants should complete a minimum of 24 college credits from a regionally accredited institution. Transfer applicants who have fewer than 24 college credits prior to their application will also need to submit their high school transcript and SAT or ACT scores.

Application and Information

There are a few different ways for full-time undergraduate students to apply for admission. First-year students may submit the Common Application. There is a $50 application fee and all Common Application waivers are honored. First-year students may apply under Early Action, Early Decision, or Regular Decision options. Early Decision is binding and, if admitted, students must withdraw all other applications and commit to enrolling at Drexel. Early Action and Early Decision deadlines are November 1, with admission decisions rendered in mid-December. Applications for Regular Decision have a deadline of January 15, with admission decisions rendered no later than April 1. Applications for the BS+MD Early Assurance degree program are due on November 1. Drexel subscribes to the College Board candidate's reply date of May 1. More information can be found at https://drexel.edu/undergrad/apply/freshman. Full-time undergraduate transfer students may apply using the Common Application or the Drexel University Application. For transfer application deadlines, please visit https://drexel.edu/undergrad/apply/deadlines.

Undergraduate Admissions
Drexel University
3141 Chestnut Street
Philadelphia, Pennsylvania 19104-2876
Phone: 215-895-2400; 800-2-DREXEL (toll-free)
Fax: 215-895-1285
E-mail: enroll@drexel.edu
Website: drexel.edu/admissions (admissions)
drexel.edu/undergrad/apply (application)
facebook.com/DrexelAdmission (Facebook)
twitter.com/DrexelAdmission (Twitter)
drexeladmission (Snapchat)

Drexel students on Chestnut St. in University City, Philadephia, Pennsylvania.

COLLEGE CLOSE-UPS

EARLHAM COLLEGE

RICHMOND, INDIANA

The College

Established in 1847, Earlham College is a selective, private liberal arts college. With its emphasis on experiential learning and profound inquiry, an Earlham education is excellent preparation not just for a first job, but a career and a lifetime of rewarding involvement.

Earlham has shaped its curriculum through an initiative called EPIC (Earlham Program for an Integrated Curriculum) in order to help its students connect their academic and personal passions with career preparation and opportunities to make a positive difference in the world. EPIC offers students multidisciplinary experiences that combine guided research opportunities, international education, and internships as well as academic centers devoted to entrepreneurship, global health, and social justice.

Among its distinctions, Earlham is committed to funding an internship, research experience or community-based project for every student. Called the EPIC Advantage, the program offers these funded experiences to help students connect high-impact experiences with their traditional course work and even extracurricular activities.

Earlham is a residential college of about 1,100 students. A global perspective comes naturally to the campus community. Earlham is ranked fifth by *U.S. News & World Report* among liberal arts colleges in the U.S. for the percentage of international students enrolled. With such a variety of students, campus life at Earlham is both lively and welcoming.

Besides traditional residence halls, Earlham has friendship and theme housing for those who share like interests. Yet one kind of housing isn't found at Earlham—sororities and fraternities. Earlham's inclusive community has never had them.

Founded by Quakers, Earlham College has prepared students to contribute to the social good since its inception. Earlham embraces cultural and individual differences alike and offers unparalleled opportunities for leadership, friendship, and community.

Earlham sponsors 19 NCAA Division III sports teams; most compete in the Heartland Collegiate Athletic Conference. The College also sponsors a hunt seat equestrian team, an Ultimate (Frisbee) team that competes on the club level, and numerous recreational sports.

Earlham is accredited by the Higher Learning Commission of the North Central Association of Colleges and Schools.

Location

The Earlham campus is located on 800 acres in the city of Richmond, Indiana. It is situated along the Indiana-Ohio border, about an hour's drive from Indianapolis, Cincinnati, or Dayton. Richmond, named the No. 1 small city in Indiana by *Cities Journal*, has a population of 36,000 and a rich heritage of music, culture, and architecture.

Majors and Degrees

Earlham offers a diverse range of degree programs including: African and African American Studies; ancient and classical studies; art; biochemistry; biology; chemistry; Chinese studies*; comparative languages and linguistics; computer science; economics; English; environmental sustainability; film studies*; French and Francophone studies; geology; German language and literature; global management (with tracks in finance, international business, leadership and change, marketing, social entrepreneurship and social change, and supply chain and operations/management information technology); history; human development and social relations; international studies; Japanese language and linguistics*; Japanese studies; Jewish studies*; mathematics; museum studies*; music; neuroscience; peace and global studies; philosophy; physics and astronomy; politics; pre-engineering; pre-health; pre-law; psychology; public health*; public policy; religion; sociology/anthropology; Spanish and Hispanic studies; TESOL*; theatre arts; and women's, gender, sexuality studies. (*Indicates programs that are available as minors only.)

In addition to more than 30 undergraduate majors, Earlham offers two dual-degree programs: a 3+2 degree for engineering and a 3+1 degree program that allows students to earn both a B.A. and a M.A.T. in just four years.

Academic Programs

Earlham is one of the only colleges in the United States to offer a funded summer internship, research experience, or community-based project to every student. Eligible experiences take place in the summer anytime between a student's first year and fourth year of enrollment. Earlham helps students create an opportunity to put their education into practice without having to worry about finances. Even if the opportunity is on another continent, EPIC Advantage will cover the travel expenses. Earlham's collaborative advising model, which includes a team of academic and career advisers, helps each student to consider the available opportunities and integrate their experiences into academic plans and career aspirations. There is also funding to support other high-impact learning experiences, including student-faculty research, so many Earlham students benefit from multiple opportunities.

Earlham's unique approach to academic life, high-impact experiences, teaching, and mentoring has been uncommonly effective:

Graduates from the past five years have earned such prestigious awards as the Rhodes Scholarship, Fulbright Scholarship, the Watson Fellowship, the National Science Foundation Pre-Doctoral Fellowship, the Samuel Huntington Public Service Award, and a Fellowship at the Carnegie Endowment for International Peace.

Of all colleges and universities in the U.S., Earlham also ranks in the top 2 percent for its percentage of graduates who go on to earn research doctorates.

A team of recent Earlham graduates won the 2016 Hult Prize, beating out 25,000 entrants in the world's largest student competition for the social good. They are using $1 million in prize money to launch a business that is already revolutionizing public transportation in several cities in Kenya.

Off-Campus Programs

Earlham's off-campus study programs send students all over the globe to explore new places and experience new cultures. In addition, Earlham's EPIC Advantage program provides another way to take part in off-campus experiences, including an internship, research opportunity, or a community-based project.

Semester-long programs include: Border Studies (Tucson), Ecuador, England, France/Senegal, Germany/Austria, Greece, Japan, Middle East/Jordan, New Zealand, Spain, or Tibetan Studies (India).

May Term programs include: Bahamas, Benin, Berlin, Borneo, Canada, China, Costa Rica, Curaçao, England, Galápagos Islands, Greece, Hawaii, Iceland, Italy, Martinique, Spain, or Turkey.

Internship, research, and project locations funded by Earlham's EPIC Advantage include local, regional, U.S., and international sites.

Academic Facilities

Earlham's academic facilities are state-of-the-art and designed to foster collaboration. In recent years the College has invested more than $70 million in its campus, including new and renovated student center, science facilities, and a center for visual and performing arts.

Costs

Earlham College tuition and fees for the 2019–20 academic year are $58,265.

Financial Aid

Earlham believes that paying for college should not be a barrier to going to college and is committed to creating financial access to qualified students from all backgrounds. The College offers scholarships to high academic achievers (up to full tuition), to those who demonstrate a financial need and a commitment to volunteer service, to Quakers, and to highly qualified members of underrepresented racial and ethnic groups. Financial aid can also include loans and student employment.

Faculty

Recognized for their commitment to undergraduate teaching, Earlham's faculty members combine their love of scholarship with their teaching. It's a potent combination and it is the College's student body that benefits. In Princeton Review's Best 384 Colleges - 2019 Edition, Earlham is ranked 7th nationally for "Best Classroom Experience." U.S. News and World Report regularly adds Earlham to its list of schools with a strong commitment to undergraduate teaching.

All Earlham professors also actively engage students as true partners in learning, and an unusually high number participate in scholarly or creative projects with their students. A large percentage of Earlham professors include students in their research on some of the important challenges facing the world today, often leading to coauthored publications.

Students learn to be colleagues as part of their education. That's part of why everyone in the Earlham community is on a first-name basis, from students to staff, professors to the College president.

Most classes are small. Seventy percent have fewer than 15 students.

Student Life

With a long and varied list of active, student-led organizations to choose from, Earlham students have every chance to get involved outside of the classroom. Some of the more popular organizations include dance teams, Frisbee golf, Ultimate, cultural clubs, and political clubs. In addition, there are numerous co-ops on campus, including the Barn Co-op, home to Earlham's Equestrian Team horses and other horses boarded by students.

Besides the 19 varsity sports the College sponsors, there are numerous club teams and opportunities to participate in intramural sports. For those desiring a workout, Earlham has extensive wellness facilities, including a field house, swimming pool, weight room, climbing wall, exercise classes, and a walking track.

The activity calendar at Earlham is packed with speakers, theatre productions, art exhibits and much more. The campus also kicks off each school year with Sunsplash, an annual festival that includes live music from major bands, and wraps up each year with SpringFest, an outdoor event with inflatable games and other excuses to let loose.

Admission Requirements

Earlham is selective, with six applicants for every seat in the first-year class. The College seeks students who are academically prepared, intellectually curious, and who possess a variety of special talents and interests. Earlham also looks for students who are comfortable in their own skin and embrace differences.

Earlham takes a holistic approach in its review of students' applications for admission, giving consideration to academic achievement, writing ability (the essay is very important), and letters of recommendation from teachers and guidance counselors. In determining academic ability and college readiness, the College gives particular weight to a student's performance in high school courses and the quality of their chosen college preparatory academic program. Earlham also recognizes applicants' commitments, accomplishments and contributions beyond the classroom

Earlham uses the Common Application, which includes a guidance counselor recommendation and a teacher recommendation. Earlham expects high school applicants to have completed at least 15 academic high school units or the equivalent: 4 in English, 3 in mathematics, and 2 or more in a second language, science, and history or social studies. Experience in the area of studio or performing arts is very desirable. Earlham has a test-optional policy which means applicants are not required to submit any standardized test scores (Home-schooled and international students are required to submit standardized testing.)

Application and Information

Earlham College offers application plans for early decision (application materials due Nov. 15), early action (application materials due Dec. 1), and regular decision (application materials due Feb. 15). More information about these plans is available online at Earlham.edu/apply.

Contact Information

Office of Admissions
801 National Road West
Richmond, Indiana 47374
Phone: 765-983-1600
800-EARLHAM (toll-free)
E-mail: admissions@earlham.edu
Website: earlham.edu/admissions
facebook.com/earlhamcollege

ELIZABETHTOWN COLLEGE

ELIZABETHTOWN, PENNSYLVANIA

Elizabethtown College

The College

Founded in 1899, and located in historic Lancaster County, Pennsylvania, Elizabethtown College offers students 59 majors, over 100 minors and concentrations in liberal arts, sciences, and professional studies. A selective, private institution, the College is driven by its motto, "Educate for Service," and links classroom instruction with experiential learning through Signature Learning Experiences (SLEs), which supplement classroom learning and include choices in supervised research, cross-cultural experiences, community-based learning, internships, and capstone courses. SLEs prepare students for lives of purpose and are the hallmarks of the Elizabethtown experience.

Home to 1,595 full time undergraduate students in our traditional program, hailing from 28 states and 23 countries, approximately 84 percent live on the 204-acre campus in residence halls, townhouses and apartments, and college-owned houses called student-directed learning communities, where students commit to community-focused service work.

In addition to an active intramural and club sports program, Blue Jay Athletics fields 24 NCAA Division III teams for Men (Baseball, Basketball, Cross Country, Golf, Lacrosse, Soccer, Swimming, Tennis, indoor and outdoor Track & Field, Volleyball, Wrestling) and Women (Basketball, Cross Country, Field Hockey, Golf, Lacrosse, Soccer, Softball, Swimming, Tennis, indoor and outdoor Track & Field, Volleyball).

The Center for Student Success offers academic advising, individual academic coaching, tutoring, and writing support for all students. Student Wellness provides individual and group counseling in a diversity affirming environment, delivers health services in partnership with Penn State Health, and offers robust health promotion programs through The Well. Career Services assists with career exploration, job shadow, and internship options, and prepares students for the job search process. The Center for Student Involvement promotes strengths-based initiatives for cultivating lives of purpose and meaning including the Called to Lead program, civic and community engagement and interfaith programs.

The Office of Diversity is committed to valuing and fostering the diversity reflected in our life together and in the world beyond the campus. The Mosaic House serves as a gathering place for students of diverse backgrounds and interests.

The campus offers five dining venues: The Marketplace (traditional dining); The Jay's Nest (deli/quick-serve/convenience store); The Blue Bean (which proudly serves Starbucks); The Jay Truck (food truck); and a smoothie bar and cafe in the new Bowers Center. Recreational spaces and offerings include Thompson Gymnasium, an outdoor mondo-surface track, a swimming pool and lots of walking/running paths and green space. The newly opened Bowers Center for Sports, Fitness and Well-being, with more than 78,000 square feet, will house wellness programming, intramural and club sports, intercollegiate athletics, fitness studios, cardio, strength and conditioning areas, a 180-meter indoor track, wellness classrooms and areas for meditation and yoga, meeting and gathering spaces for students, a smoothie bar, spin studio, training and athletic treatment areas, and office space for health educators and campus recreation. The KAV is a multipurpose entertainment and educational space. Leffler Chapel and Performance Center features an 840-seat auditorium. The campus events calendar boasts more than 125 arts and cultural happenings each academic year, not including student-run programming from OSA and the 80+ campus clubs.

Elizabethtown holds accreditations from the Middle States Commission for Higher Education (MSCHE), American Chemical Society for Clinical Lab Services (ACS), National Association of Schools of Music (NASM), National Council on Social Work Education (CSWE), Accreditation Council for Occupational Therapy Education (ACOTE), Association of Collegiate Business Schools and Programs (ACBSP), and the Accreditation Board for Engineering and Technology Inc. for Computer Engineering and Engineering (ABET).

Location

Elizabethtown borough is a community of close to 12,000 people located in historic Lancaster County in south-central Pennsylvania, 20 minutes from Harrisburg (state capital), Hershey, and Lancaster; 90 minutes from Philadelphia and Baltimore; and a few hours from New York and Washington, D.C. The Amtrak station in Elizabethtown offers train service to and from New York, Philadelphia, and Pittsburgh. The Harrisburg International Airport is 15 minutes away.

Majors and Degrees

Bachelor of Arts degrees awarded: Communications, Criminal Justice, Economics, English, English Education (7-12), Fine Arts, Fine Arts Education (K-12), French, German, Graphic Design, History, Individualized, Interfaith Leadership Studies, Japanese, Legal Studies, Music, Philosophy, Political Science, Psychology, Religious Studies, Sociology-Anthropology, Spanish, Spanish Education (K-12), and Theatre.

Bachelor of Science degrees awarded: Accounting, Actuarial Science, Biochemistry (Pre-Medicine), Biology (Allied Health, Biological Science, Pre-medicine), Biology Education (7-12), Biotechnology, Business Administration (Accounting, Economics, Entrepreneurship and Family Business, Finance, Management, Marketing), Business Data Science, Chemistry (ACS Professional, Chemical Physics, Chemistry Management, Forensic Science, Premedical) , Chemistry Education (7-12), Chemistry Laboratory Sciences, Computer Engineering, Computer Science, Data Science, Early Childhood Education (Pre-K through 4, Dual Special Education Certification, English as a Second Language), Elementary & Middle-level Education (English as a Second Language) (4-8), Engineering (Biomedical, Civil, Electrical, Environmental, Industrial and Systems, Mechanical), Environmental Science,, Finance, Financial Economics, Health Science, Information Systems, Individualized, International Business (Accounting, Economics, Entrepreneurship & Family Business, Finance, Management, Marketing, Self-Designed), Marketing, Mathematical Business, Mathematics (Applied Mathematics, Pure Mathematics), Mathematics Education (7-12), Neuroscience, Physics, Physics Education (7-12). Also awarded: Bachelor of Music degree in Music Education (K-12) and Music Therapy and the Bachelor of Social Work.

Masters degrees awarded are a Master of Occupational Therapy; a Master of Public Policy(4+1); a Master of Special Education (4+1); a Master of Education in Curriculum and Instruction in Peace Education; a Master of Music Education; and beginning in 2020, a Master of Physician Assistant Studies. The School of Continuing and Professional Studies offers a Master of Business Administration and a Master of Science in Strategic Leadership, Master of Education in Special Education, and graduate certificates in Health Care Administration and Strategic Leadership.. More than 100 minors, concentrations, endorsements, and certifications are offered.

A Doctorate degree is awarded in Occupational Therapy.

The College offers a variety of cooperative programs that allow qualified students to combine undergraduate studies with direct admission into graduate school. These include a special partnership with Northumbria University in the UK; the Law Early Admissions Program with Drexel University Thomas R. Kline School of Law, Duquesne University School of Law, and Widener University Schools of Law; the 4+1 Masters in Molecular Medicine with Drexel University College of Medicine; a Masters of Public Health with Penn State College of Medicine; the Physician Assistant Program with Penn State College of Medicine; the Primary Care Program with Penn State College of Medicine; the Cardiovascular Invasive Specialty Program with Pennsylvania College of Health Sciences; the 3+4 or 4+4 Doctor of Dental Medicine with Lake Erie College of Osteopathic Medicine; 4+4 Doctor of Dental Surgery with West Virginia University School of Dentistry; and the 3+4 or 4+4 Doctor of Pharmaceutical with Lake Erie College of Osteopathic Medicine and the 3+3

Doctor of Physical Therapy with Thomas Jefferson University and Widener University.

Academic Programs

An interdisciplinary first-year seminar and a strong core curriculum create a solid foundation for a student's chosen area of study. The core develops critical analysis and communication skills that ensure adaptability in the ever-changing global marketplace. Independent and directed studies, undergraduate research, and internships are available.

The Elizabethtown College Honors Program offers top students a highly selective program of study with the opportunity for a stipend to fund professional development, research, or travel-related study.

Called to Lead is a leadership-building program that helps students aspire to lead purposeful lives. Scholarship and Creative Arts Days, held each spring, give students of all majors and class years the opportunity to showcase their research or creative works. The Center for Global Understanding and Peacemaking, Bowers Writers House, and The Young Center for Anabaptist and Pietist Studies all offer a variety of academic programming that further reinforce classroom experiences. The Social Enterprise Institute offers students the opportunity to collaborate with faculty and industry fellows to create sustainable social and economic value both domestically and internationally. The Momentum program, a pre-orientation program, helps first-generation college students prepare for the academic expectations of Elizabethtown.

Off-Campus Programs

During their time at Elizabethtown, each student is guaranteed to experience at least two of the following Signature Learning Experiences: undergraduate research, study abroad, community-based learning, internships/fieldwork, and capstone course work.

Students may study abroad for a semester in 45 different locations on six continents through the College's affiliate programs. Short-term academic study tours or service-learning trips are offered. The Center for Community and Civic Engagement offers numerous community-based learning experiences locally, regionally, and nationally.

Academic Facilities

The High Library contains more than 241,000 volumes and an extensive collection of journals and other research materials; computers and printers; conference rooms; and private, individual, and group study areas. Librarians help students with research projects and using library resources effectively.

The campus features numerous academic buildings, including the James B. Hoover Center for Business and The Masters Center for Science, Mathematics, and Engineering. The Baugher Student center is home to the Tempest Theatre and a dance studio, and Zug Memorial Hall houses a recital hall and private and group practice rooms. Steinman Center for Communications and Arts features a television studio, radio station, and office space for the College newspaper. The College houses three art galleries and the Masters Mineral Gallery.

Elizabethtown is home to The Young Center for Anabaptist and Pietist Studies, a world-renowned research center focusing on the Amish and other similar religions. The High Center, a local research and resource center for family-owned businesses, partners with academic departments for events and programs. The Social Enterprise Institute brings together faculty members, industry fellows of the Institute and students, to collaborate on social enterprise development initiatives.

Costs

For 2019–20, tuition was reduced by 32% to $32,000 and room and meals are $11,710, for a total comprehensive fee of $43,710. Students should also plan for an additional $2,150 for books, transportation, and personal expenses, for a total cost of $45,860. Financial aid is based on this figure.

Financial Aid

Elizabethtown College works with students and their families to make education affordable. About 97 percent of students receive some form of aid; packages typically combine scholarships, grants, loans, and student employment. About 86 percent of Elizabethtown's first-year students receive renewable merit-based scholarships, which are awarded on a competitive basis and without regard to need.

To apply for aid, students must file the Free Application for Federal Student Aid (FAFSA). Students are assigned a personal financial aid counselor to help them throughout their years at the College. Elizabethtown's deadline for financial consideration is March 15.

Faculty

Elizabethtown has a teaching faculty of 124 full-time professors. The student-faculty ratio is 11:1. Of the full-time faculty members, 94 percent hold a Ph.D. or the highest earned degree in their field. In addition to being assigned a faculty adviser for the First-Year Seminar program, when students declare a major, they are also assigned a new faculty adviser within the academic department of their declared major.

Student Government

Students play an active role in campus governance through Student Senate. Representative members of Student Senate are elected from each class. They advocate for students, coordinate special events, and allocate funds for student activities and the more than eighty student-directed clubs and organizations.

Admission Requirements

Elizabethtown believes the right fit is more than just SAT scores and GPA; other admission factors considered at the College are academic, cocurricular, and social fit. Admissions decisions are made without regard to sex, sexual orientation, race, religion, physical handicap, or place of residence. On average, 71 percent of all applicants are accepted. The middle 50 percent of enrolled students scored between 1070 and 1290 on the evidence-based reading and writing section and mathematics section of the SAT, and 63 percent were in the top 25 percent of their high school class.

The College is a diverse and exciting community, one that is composed of students who display leadership abilities and special talents. Campus interviews are highly recommended but not required for most students, although the College reserves the right to require interviews in special cases. Applicants to the Honors Program and occupational therapy program are required to interview. Auditions are required for music students.

Early admission is available for highly qualified high school juniors.

Application and Information

The College operates on a rolling admission basis—applications are processed as they are received—and the application deadline is April 1. Students can apply using the Common Application or online at the College's website. Applicants must submit a high school transcript, SAT or ACT scores, and a personal statement, essay, or graded paper. Early application is strongly recommended. Accepted students should notify the College of their decision to attend by May 1. Students who are interested in the Elizabethtown College Honors Program must submit a completed application by January 15.

For more information, students should contact:
Lauren Deibler, Director of Admissions
Elizabethtown College
One Alpha Drive
Elizabethtown, Pennsylvania 17022-2298
Phone: 717-361-1400; Fax: 717-361-1365
E-mail: admissions@etown.edu; Website: http://www.etown.edu

Elizabethtown College, home to about 1,598 full-time students, offers more than fifty-nine majors, forty-seven minors, and forty-eight concentrations.

ELMHURST COLLEGE

ELMHURST, ILLINOIS

COLLEGE CLOSE-UPS

The College

A private college in the heart of the Chicago metropolitan area, Elmhurst College is committed to helping students navigate and succeed in their college journey—and in the world beyond. An Elmhurst education is about more than courses and credits; it's about experiential learning, exploring the globe, challenging oneself and successfully launching into the real world.

Elmhurst is one of the top regional colleges in the Midwest, according to U.S. News & World Report, and it also ranks among the best values in the region. With more than 60 undergraduate majors and 15 graduate programs, Elmhurst boasts a student-to-faculty ratio of just 14 to 1. In small classes, professors get to know their students as individuals.

Beyond the classroom, students get plenty of opportunities to put their passions and talents into action in more than 100 campus activities. Elmhurst's 20 athletic teams compete in NCAA Division III athletics in the CCIW conference, one of the strongest in the Midwest.

More than 80 percent of Elmhurst undergraduates gain on-the-job experience through internships or service work, and nearly 94 percent of Elmhurst graduates find full-time employment or enter graduate school within a year of graduation. The College's robust career programs include more than 2,000 options for internships and other professional experiences.

Students come to Elmhurst from many states and countries, and from nearly every religious, racial and ethnic background. The student body comprises about 2,800 full-time undergraduate students, 250 adults pursuing an undergraduate degree and 600 graduate students.

Elmhurst College is accredited by the Department of Education of the State of Illinois, and by the Higher Learning Commission, a member of the North Central Association of Colleges and Schools. The baccalaureate degree in nursing and master's degree in nursing at Elmhurst College are accredited by the Commission on Collegiate Nursing Education (http://www.aacn.nche.edu/ccne-accreditation).

Location

Elmhurst's 48-acre grounds are an arboretum, with more than 800 varieties of trees, shrubs and other woody plants. The gorgeous campus is a green oasis in the heart of a quiet, safe suburb—but it's also just a few blocks from the Elmhurst Metra station, where students can catch the train for a 30-minute ride to downtown Chicago, providing easy access to world-class cultural, entertainment, and professional opportunities.

Academics

With more than 60 undergraduate majors and 16 pre-professional programs, Elmhurst boasts a student-to-faculty ratio of just 14 to 1. In small classes, students work closely with faculty members who are experts in their fields—and whose primary mission is teaching.

Many students collaborate with faculty on high-level research projects, studying subjects ranging from metastatic breast cancer to the effect of acting lessons on aging brains. An Honors Program offers special opportunities for students who are especially motivated by academic challenges and allows students to study abroad within their first year.

Beyond the classroom, Elmhurst offers study-abroad opportunities in more than 60 countries. A special January Term offers undergraduate students the chance to undertake courses and field projects off campus.

Career Development

Elmhurst students gain real-world experience starting their first year. Internships, professional mentors, and shadowing experiences help them define their future and provide them the skills to succeed. Nearly 94 percent of Elmhurst College graduates are employed or in graduate school within a year of graduating.

Facilities

The Elmhurst campus combines the high-tech necessities of a modern education with the charm of a classic college campus. Its classic red-brick buildings boast wireless Internet access, smart classrooms, and more. In addition, the College has a long tradition of responsible stewardship of the environment. From low-impact lighting and permeable paving to a LEED-certified residence hall, Elmhurst incorporates green principles throughout campus life.

Costs

Full-time undergraduate tuition for 2018–19 was $37,454; basic room and board was $10,510.

Financial Aid

Elmhurst College is committed to making college affordable; 100 percent of new students receive financial aid in the form of grants, scholarships, loans, and work-study. Scholarship competitions are available for first-generation first-year students and for first-year students with significant service and a 3.0 GPA or higher to earn up to full-tuition.

Campus Life

Students at Elmhurst find plenty of opportunities to put their passions and talents into action. The College offers more than 100 student organizations, including everything from Habitat for Humanity to the Black Student Union to religious groups and Greek life.

Many Elmhurst students live on campus, where they find all the amenities of home—free laundry plus the convenience of close proximity to classes, the library, the gym and all your favorite student activities. The College's six residence halls host offer gender neutral housing options and are equipped with full kitchens, cozy gathering spots, Internet access, and free cable TV. Each hall sponsors a variety of events—like movies, workshops, and barbecues.

Elmhurst also offers an array of services and resources designed to help students navigate the pressures of college life. Services in the Division of Student Affairs include individual counseling, support with housing issues, comprehensive health care services, transition assistance, and diversity education.

Admission Requirements

Elmhurst gives preference to students who have completed a strong college preparatory curriculum and have demonstrated the ability to succeed through test scores and supplemental materials.

Application and Information

To apply, prospective students should submit the following:

- **The application for admission.** Students may apply online at https://connect.elmhurst.edu/apply.
- **High school transcript** or GED test results.
- **Scores from the ACT or SAT,** sent directly from the testing corporation to Elmhurst. (Elmhurst's SAT code is 1204 and ACT code is 1020).
- **A personal statement or essay** (encouraged, but not required).

Elmhurst has an Early Action deadline (nonbinding) of November 1 with a December 1 notification. Rolling admission notifications begin mid-December.

Prospective students are encouraged to visit the campus, either individually or as part of a scheduled event. Admission events range from campus tours and open houses to information sessions and overnight visits.

The Office of Admission at Elmhurst College welcomes students' questions and comments.

For more information, please contact:

Office of Admission
Elmhurst College
190 Prospect Avenue
Elmhurst, Illinois 60126-3296
United States
Phone: 630-617-3400
800-697-1871 (toll-free)
E-mail: admit@elmhurst.edu
Website: http://www.elmhurst.edu/admission

The Elmhurst College campus is within easy access of the limitless opportunities of downtown Chicago.

EMERSON COLLEGE
BOSTON, MASSACHUSETTS

Emerson
COLLEGE

The College

Founded in 1880 and located in the heart of Boston, Massachusetts, Emerson College is the nation's premier institution for the study of communication and the arts. Students may choose from nearly 30 undergraduate programs supported by state-of-the-art facilities and a nationally renowned faculty. Emerson's campus is home to WERS-FM, the oldest noncommercial radio station in Boston; the historic 1,200-seat Cutler Majestic Theatre; and *Ploughshares*, the award-winning literary journal for new writing.

Emerson College offers educational programs that prepare undergraduate and graduate men and women to assume positions of responsibility and leadership in communication and the arts and to pursue scholarship and work that brings innovation to these disciplines.

Originally a small, regional school of oratory, Emerson has evolved into a diverse, coeducational, and multifaceted degree-granting institution with a liberal arts rather than conservatory orientation. But its mission and focus remains largely the same: to explore and push the boundaries of communication, art, and culture and, thereby, to contribute to the advancement of society.

Many of the College's 37,000+ alumni remain active participants in the life of Emerson. Although concentrated in Massachusetts, California, and New York, Emersonians can be found working in virtually every major media, entertainment, or arts enterprise across the country.

The College's 3,813 undergraduate and 653 graduate students come from across the United States and forty-nine countries. Many undergraduate students live on campus, some in special learning communities, such as the Writers' Block, Film Immersion, and Performing Cultures. There is a fitness center, athletic field, and several residence halls, including a fourteen-story campus center and residence hall that houses a gymnasium and student-services offices. Emerson opened a new 18-story residence hall and a new 18,000 square-foot Dining Center in fall 2017, and will add a new student center in 2019.

Emerson is fully accredited by the New England Association of Schools and Colleges as authorized by the Commission on Institutions of Higher Education. Emerson is also accredited by the Council on Academic Accreditation of the American Speech-Language-Hearing Association and the Massachusetts Department of Education.

Location

Emerson College is located in Boston, Massachusetts, the most popular college city in the U.S. Emerson's campus is in the heart of downtown Boston and the city's Theatre District, just steps from the Massachusetts State House, Boston Common, the historic Freedom Trail, Boston Public Garden, Chinatown, and countless restaurants and museums.

Emerson College's Boston campus is located at the gateway to the city's bustling Theatre District, in close proximity to cultural resources, media outlets, and public transportation. It comprises a cluster of eleven buildings near the intersection of Boylston and Tremont Streets (adjacent to historic Boston Common) plus the magnificent Paramount Center, a performing arts and residence center on nearby Washington Street. The College also has facilities in Los Angeles and the Netherlands.

The Boston campus has been assembled during the past 30 years as the College moved to the Theatre District from the Back Bay. Since 1993, Emerson has invested more than $500 million in preserving and restoring historic spaces and also creating new facilities. Emerson's decision to create the "Campus on the Common" is widely credited with reviving and revitalizing this section of Boston, attracting the development of private residences, hotels, restaurants, and other retail spaces. Emerson is continuing its legacy of preservation and restoration through its recently completed renovation of the Colonial Theatre and the Little Building residence hall slated to re-open in Fall 2019. When these projects are completed, the College will be able to house nearly 70 percent of its students and will have preserved several additional historic spaces for future generations.

Majors and Degrees

Boston's Emerson College offers Bachelor of Arts, Bachelor of Fine Arts, and Bachelor of Science degrees. Undergraduates can major in acting; business of creative enterprises; comedic arts; communication disorders; communication studies; creative writing; film art; journalism; marketing communication; media arts production; media studies; musical theatre; political communication; production; public relations; sports communication; stage and production management; stage and screen design/technology; theatre; theatre design/technology; theatre education; theatre education and performance; theatre and performance; or writing, literature, and publishing. The individually-designed interdisciplinary program also allows students to create their own major from the multitude of programs offered in communication, arts, and the liberal arts with faculty approval.

Academic Programs

The Institute for Liberal Arts and Interdisciplinary Studies is also home to Emerson's highly competitive Honors Program. Emerson offers a wide range of student support services including the Academic Advising Center, Career Services, disability services, and the Lacerte Family Writing and Academic Resource Center.

Emerson College is committed to creating a campus environment that supports and promotes superior research, premier creative activities, and innovative scholarly pursuits. The mission of the Office of Research and Creative Scholarship (ORCS) is to serve the Emerson community by providing information, personal assistance, services, and programs to those who seek financial support for scholarly endeavors. The Office will also provide college-wide leadership in the development of research and sponsored program activities, and work closely with faculty, staff and senior administrators in shaping the effort to build a more robust program of grants and sponsored research.

Off-Campus Programs

Hundreds of internship placements exist throughout Boston and in major cities across the country, including Emerson College's Los Angeles center—a state-of-the-art facility home to a residential study and internship program in the hub of the global entertainment industry. Emerson also offers a semester-long program in Washington, DC. Students also have the option to register for courses with six other arts colleges in Boston through the ProArts Consortium.

The Office of Internationalization and Global Engagement (IGE) seeks to enhance global engagement by utilizing Emerson's collective talent, energy, human and financial resources to support compelling transformation and change in international education across disciplines and around the world. Students can study abroad at the college's castle in the Netherlands; 20+ additional study abroad opportunities in China, the Czech Republic, Greece, Spain, and more.

Emerson, in partnership with Paris College of Art, has developed a new Global B.F.A. in Film Art. Students in this joint B.F.A. degree program will study for three academic years in Paris and complete three summers in Boston and one summer in Emerson's Kasteel Well program in the Netherlands.

Academic Facilities

More than half of Emerson's facilities are new or renovated since 2002. Students have access to the highest quality equipment, clinical facilities devoted to communication disorders research and treatment, and an integrated digital newsroom for aspiring journalists.

The College also owns more performance space than any other institution in Boston. The eleven-story Tufte Performance and Production Center has rehearsal space, a theatre design/technology center, makeup lab, and costume shop. Emerson's Paramount Center performance facility houses a sound stage, black box theater, scene shop, film screening room, and residence hall. Other performance facilities include the Cutler Majestic Theatre, a 1,200-seat Broadway-style theatre, renovated in 2002, and the Bill Bordy Auditorium and Theater.

Emerson has one of the largest installations of film, video, and audio post-production facilities of any college in the country. Digital production labs contain workstations with multimedia production and digital video/audio applications. Emerson has been designated a New Media Center since 1995. Emerson also has numerous radio, television, and film outlets and facilities.

Clinical facilities include the Robbins Speech, Language and Hearing Center in the Department of Communication Sciences and Disorders. Graduate students work with patients and participate in a variety of Emerson-run clinics that are widely recognized in the field.

In addition, the Iwasaki Library houses more than 180,000 volumes and serial subscriptions, 10,000 microforms, 11,000 audiovisual materials, and 8,000 e-books. Students can access the resources of a dozen cooperating libraries through Emerson College's membership in the Fenway Library Consortium.

Costs

In the 2019–20 academic year, full-time undergraduate student tuition is $48,560, room and board (for a double room) is $18,400, and the student services fee is $872.

Financial Aid

Emerson offers a variety of financial assistance programs. Approximately 75 percent of Emerson's student body receives financial assistance to help pay for their education. Sources of support may include institutional gift aid, academic scholarships, need-based grants, loan programs, work-study, and payment plans. There are also merit scholarships available through the Office of Undergraduate Admission. All applicants are automatically reviewed for eligibility for these merit scholarships once they have submitted their application.

Faculty

With a student-faculty ratio of 13:1, students at Emerson College develop close relationships with remarkably talented and active instructors who are experts in their fields. Emerson's 479 full- and part-time faculty members are nationally recognized and award-winning authors, directors, researchers, producers, journalists, playwrights, actors, and more. The majority of the faculty has earned doctorates or the highest degree obtainable in their field.

Student Life

Emerson students are doers and learners, creating and collaborating even after class is over for the day. The college offers more than 90 student organizations and performance groups, student publications, and honor societies. Emerson also supports 14 NCAA Division III men's and women's athletic teams.

The College has five residence halls, four of which are newly renovated or brand new within the last 10 years. Students use the nearby Boston Common for relaxation and recreational activities such as tennis, softball, running, Quidditch, and ice-skating. The Field at Rotch Playground, located a mile from campus, serves as a practice and playing field while the Bobbi Brown and Steven Plofker Gym is the site for men's and women's basketball and volleyball games and other events.

Admission Requirements

Admission is competitive; each year, more than 15,000 applications are received for a class of approximately 900 new first-year students. Selection is based on academic promise as indicated by secondary school performance, recommendations, and writing competency. Emerson has a Test Optional admission policy. Students are welcome to submit SAT or ACT scores or may submit a test optional essay or major-related creative sample in their place. TOEFL, IELTS or other exams are required if English is not the first language. Emerson also considers personal qualities as seen in extracurricular activities, community involvement, and demonstrated leadership.

Application and Information

Emerson College accepts the Common Application and the Emerson Application. Students are required to complete all parts of their chosen application, including the Emerson-specific questions and writing supplement. There are additional requirements for students applying to Performing Arts programs, Comedic Arts, Film Art or Media Arts Production.

The deadline for fall admission for first-year students is January 15 (Early Action is November 1), and for transfer students, the priority deadline is March 15. The spring admission priority deadline is November 1 for first-year students and transfer students.

Emerson College Admissions
120 Boylston Street
Boston, Massachusetts 02116
United States
Phone: 617-824-8600
E-mail: admission@emerson.edu
Website: www.emerson.edu

ERSKINE COLLEGE
DUE WEST, SOUTH CAROLINA

ERSKINE

The College

Erskine College has been preparing students to flourish in lives of learning, service, and leadership for more than 175 years. With its heritage of thoughtful scholarship, Christian commitment, and intentional community, Erskine offers a rich undergraduate experience. Founded by the Associate Reformed Presbyterian Church in 1839, it is the oldest four-year private Christian college in South Carolina and is accredited by the Southern Association of Colleges and Schools Commission on Colleges. Erskine provides an environment in which students can be challenged and inspired. Students work hard, think creatively and critically, and explore options across a variety of disciplines.

Erskine fields 22 intercollegiate teams in NCAA Division II as part of Conference Carolinas and offers intramural and recreational programs as well. Athletic facilities include a full court basketball gymnasium with an attached auxiliary gym and aerobics facility, racquetball courts, a rock climbing wall, a weight-training facility, baseball fields, softball fields, and two football-sized intramural activity fields. The Galloway gymnasium on campus houses a basketball arena along with volleyball and classroom facilities. Students have several dining options, including Moffatt Dining Hall, Snapper's Restaurant in the Watkins Student Center, and Erskine's own campus coffee shop, Java City.

Erskine is a residential campus offering numerous student organizations to complement the academic experience. Living on campus affords opportunities for fellowship and leadership through residence life, student government, and various student organizations, including Christian ministries, literary and honor societies, service clubs, and interest groups. Each residence hall provides fellowship opportunities, such as cookouts and movie nights. Erskine's small size means students can get to know just about everyone on campus, including their professors, who can become mentors and friends.

Location

Erskine College is located in Due West, a town of 1,200 residents located in historic Abbeville County, South Carolina, an area rich in colonial, Revolutionary War, and Civil War history. Erskine's 90-acre campus, with its tree-lined green spaces, gardens, and stately architecture, has been recognized as one of the 50 Most Beautiful Christian Colleges and Universities in the nation by Christian Universities Online.

The town and the college, with a number of antebellum buildings, are listed on the National Register of Historic Places. Erskine is located near lakes and recreational areas and within easy access to Interstate Routes 26 and 85 and the cities of Atlanta, Charlotte, Columbia, and Greenville. Due West is located about 30 minutes from the cities of Greenwood and Anderson, giving the town a calm and unplugged feeling. Greenville, an hour from Due West, is among the fastest growing cities in the country and features a thriving downtown environment, award-winning restaurants, and exciting weekend activities. Abbeville, with its quaint town square and historic playhouse, is only about 15 minutes from Due West.

Majors and Degrees

The College offers Bachelor of Arts (B.A.) and Bachelor of Science (B.S.) degrees. A B.A. candidate can choose from the following majors: American studies, Bible and religion, biology, chemistry, English, health science, history, mathematics, music, philosophy, political science, psychology, and social studies. A B.S. candidate can choose from the following majors: biology, business administration, chemistry, early childhood education, elementary education, health science, music education, physical education and coaching, psychology, special education, and sport management.

Students may choose from the following minors: Bible and religion, biology, business administration, chemistry, Christian education, Christian leadership, English, family studies, global studies, graphic design, health, healthcare management, history, information technology, mathematics, music, music studies, philosophy, physical education, physics, political science, psychology, secondary education, social entrepreneurship and innovation, theater, and visual art.

Erskine College maintains an engineering dual-degree program with Clemson University. Students in this program typically complete three years at Erskine and two to three years at Clemson, earning a B.S. degree in engineering from Clemson and a B.A. degree in biology, chemistry, or mathematics from Erskine.

Academic Programs

At Erskine, students are taught by professors, not graduate students, and the curriculum is based on the liberal arts tradition. Erskine also offers a number of pre-professional programs. More than 96 percent of Erskine's faculty members hold terminal degrees in their subject areas. Small class sizes, along with professors' efforts to promote mentoring relationships with students, help to spur students to academic growth and prepare them for leadership. Students can work with faculty members to craft a course of study that suits their individual strengths and career interests.

Off-Campus Programs

Erskine offers opportunities for study abroad with the University of St. Andrews at St. Andrews in Scotland; with the OSAP program at Oxford University in England; with the University of Aix in Aix-en-Provence, France; with Tandem Escuela Internacional in Madrid, Spain; with the Universidad de Alicante in Alicante, Spain; and with the Universidad Veracruzana in Jalapa, Mexico. A student may choose to study abroad for either fall or spring semester or a full year.

Pre-professional externships at Erskine College are offered in several areas, including health-related fields (medicine, dentistry, medical technology, pharmacy, etc.), business, engineering, journalism, law and government, library science, ministry, social services, and veterinary medicine.

The college offers two summer semester terms in which students have the opportunity to travel with professors for course credit. In the past, students have traveled to Brazil, China, England, Germany, Lithuania, Scotland, and Spain. In the Department of Political Science, students are offered the chance to travel to the state capital of Columbia or to the nation's capital in Washington, D.C., where they meet with congressional and state representatives and form relationships for future experiences in government, nonprofits, and lobbying organizations.

Academic Facilities

All academic buildings on campus are wireless, and Erskine has developed innovative uses of technology to increase person-to-person communication and maximize student learning. Along with the successful use of technology, personal interaction that leads to lasting friendships and discovery within a community of learners continues as a primary focus on the Erskine campus.

Notable among Erskine's 11 academic buildings are the Bowie Arts Center, a 14,000-square-foot museum and gallery featuring an exhibit hall as well as a state-of-the-art classroom; the Daniel-Moultrie Science Center, a 46,000-square-foot facility featuring an auditorium, classrooms, state-of-the-art labs, a live animal room, and a greenhouse; the Moss Mathematics and Music Educational Facility, a 24,000-square-foot two-story building equipped with classrooms, computer labs, and state-of-the-art sound studios for vocal and instrumental performances; and Memorial Hall, which houses Erskine's musical performance theater and is directly connected to the Moss facility.

The climate-controlled McCain Library Department of Archives and Special Collections, located across from the McCain Library in Reid Hall and maintained by an archivist from the library staff, is used by both students and area historians. Reid Hall also houses the business department and contains a multimedia classroom.

Costs

For the 2019–20 academic year, Erskine's tuition is $36,150. Room and board charges are $11,350. Additional fees amount to approximately $1,000 annually.

Financial Aid

Financial aid is offered to a large percentage of Erskine's students through multiple endowed scholarships, grants, state aid, loans, and work-study assignments. Erskine offers merit scholarships to students that range from $7,500 to $14,000 based on high school academic performance. The school also accepts all applicable state aid programs from the state of South Carolina. Federal funds are available to students through the Federal Pell Grant, Federal work-study programs, and Federal Supplemental Educational Opportunity Grants. Additionally, applicants can participate in Erskine's Presidential Scholarship, an invitational academic competition that grants full scholarships (tuition, room, board, and fees) to two students per year. Students who participate in the Presidential Scholarship are also considered for the Solomon Award, which covers tuition for a four-year period.

Faculty

The Erskine full-time faculty numbers 40 men and women; 96 percent have earned the highest degree in their field. With an average class size of 20, a student-faculty ratio of 13:1, and private offices for all full-time faculty members, Erskine promotes a personal as well as an academic relationship between students and faculty members. All classroom instruction is done by faculty members and they are happy to assist and encourage students who wish to pursue undergraduate research through tutorials or summer research projects. These projects are carried out in an atmosphere free of competition from graduate students for books, laboratories, or professors' time. Erskine emphasizes advising and academic counseling for students throughout their four years.

Student Government

Erskine encourages students to get involved on campus. Positions of leadership are open to students of all class years in a variety of organizations. All students are represented by elected delegates to the Student Government Association's Student Senate and have formal representation at most college-wide committees involved in decision-making and policy formation.

Admission Requirements

Erskine College seeks students who are committed to serious academic study and critical thinking. Applicants are expected to have completed at least 15 secondary school college preparatory units, 4 of which must be in English, 3 in mathematics, 3 in science, 3 in social studies, and 2 in a foreign language. Electives are also highly encouraged. Students applying to Erskine are required to submit scores from the SAT, ACT, or CLT for admission consideration. Students interested in the college's academic competition are encouraged to plan ahead and submit these scores as soon as possible. Campus visits are strongly recommended; the admissions process is a personal one. Transfer students are evaluated after submitting an application for admission and submitting a transcript from an accredited higher education institution showing at least 24 hours of course work completed at a 2.0 GPA.

Application and Information

Erskine's application can be found online at http://know.erskine.edu. Students fill out a brief online inquiry form providing contact information and program interests. After this form is submitted, students will be directed to a personalized web page giving them more information about the college. On this page, students will find a link to the official application. Admission applications are reviewed and admissions decisions are made on a rolling basis. The priority deadline for applications is May 1; all students who wish to be considered for academic merit scholarships should have a completed application on file in the Office of Undergraduate Admissions before this date. All students are encouraged to include Erskine (003432) on their FAFSA submission.

Dr. Timothy E. Rees

Dean of Enrollment

Erskine College
P.O. Box 338
2 Washington Street
Due West, South Carolina 29639
Phone: 864-379-8838
E-mail: admissions@erskine.edu
Website: http://visit.erskine edu

FRANKLIN COLLEGE

FRANKLIN, INDIANA

The College

At Franklin, we believe your potential is unlimited. That's why we have designed a liberal arts curriculum, the Franklin College Pursuit, that is designed to expand your interests and passions across disciplinary lines all while preparing you for an impactful career. You will have endless opportunities to reach your goals. You'll learn just as much outside the classroom as you will inside it—critically seeking out all perspectives and examining issues from a multitude of angles. A holistic education isn't just about checking off distribution requirements. Instead its about understanding how subjects relate and using those skills to solve real-world problems. It is about activities and involvement that hone your leadership skills. And it is about practical experiences through internships and research that set you apart. Employers tell us that's what they want—and its why our graduates are admitted to graduate school and employed in their field at such high rates.

Franklin believes liberal arts means small classes and dedicated faculty who challenge you to discover your deepest abilities and then empower you to achieve that potential. faculty-student relationships are guided by mutual respect, strong mentorship, and a partnership towards excellence. With just over 1000 students, a faculty-student ratio of 11 to 1, and no large classrooms on campus—you will experience a personal education with you and your passions at the core.

Location

Located twenty minutes south of Indianapolis, Franklin College offers students the best of both a small community and vibrant city. Indianapolis, the state's capital city and the twelfth largest city in the U.S, has 48,000 businesses offering students a wide variety of internship opportunities. Rated as one of US News and World Reports best places to live and work, Indianapolis has a wide variety of athletic, cultural, and entertainment events that appeal to all students.

Majors and Degrees

Franklin College offers more than sixty academic majors and minors in the following areas: accounting, actuarial science, art (ceramics, painting, photography: digital fine arts), art history, biochemistry, biology, business (finance, general, international business, management, and marketing), chemistry, computer science, creative writing, criminal justice, ecology/conservation, economics, elementary education, English, environmental science, exercise science, French, graphic design, history, mathematical science (applied, pure, and quantitative analysis), multimedia journalism (broadcasting and news-editorial), music (instrumental and vocal), philosophy, political science, psychology, public relations, quantitative analysis, religious studies, sociology, software engineering, Spanish, and theater. Additional minors include American studies, biomedical physics, Canadian studies, coaching, education, English as a New Language (elementary education), fitness, international relations, leadership, neuroscience, nonprofit leadership, rhetoric, visual communications.

Preparation for graduate school is exceptional, with 90 percent of students gaining admission to medical school and 100 percent of recent applicants accepted to law school.

Students considering a career in dentistry, medical technology, medicine, occupational therapy, optometry, pharmacy, physical therapy, or veterinary medicine arrange their program with the advice of the preprofessional adviser of the science division.

Business students repeatedly score in the top 5 percent on the National College Business Examination.

The Pulliam School of Journalism is one of a few comprehensive journalism schools housed at a small liberal arts institution. In addition to media opportunities including a student newspaper, Franklin College students participate in the Statehouse Files—a student run newswire providing articles on Indiana's political scene to media outlets around the region.

Engineering is offered as a 3+2 program. Students earn a Bachelor of Arts degree from Franklin College and a Bachelor of Science degree in one of the engineering disciplines from the Purdue School of Engineering and Technology (IUPUI).

Academic Programs

The relevant and responsive liberal arts curriculum is the heart of a Franklin College education, an education that nurtures personal and professional development. The Pursuit is designed to provide a breadth of experience in the liberal arts while preparing students to think critically; communicate effectively; apply knowledge and skills; solve problems; and reflect on events, actions, and behaviors in a rapidly changing world. The curriculum scaffolds foundational skills yet permits each student to design a learning experience that best suits individual needs, strengths, and interests.

Design and key features:

The Pursuit at Franklin College can aptly be summed up as a carefully crafted, intentional intersection of liberal arts education and experience-based preparation for the world of work. We not only think this is a winning intersection; we know it is.

"A robust first-year experience"—Students take a small, topic-based seminar in the fall and throughout the year benefit from a series of workshops, peer interactions, and skill-building opportunities as well as from individualized guidance by trained staff and advisors.

"A continued liberal arts and sciences experience that is relevant and responsive"—Specially designed courses ensure students learn to value different ways of knowing, that they learn to see the world through a variety of lenses, and that they understand how values are formulated from different perspectives.

"Immersive, applied experiences"— Internship opportunities are being expanded so that all students undertake at least one, but also: every course that students take in January will now be experience-based, situating their primary means of student learning somewhere other than in the traditional classroom.

"Overt opportunities to use technology"—Wherever possible, both in- and out-of-classroom experiences will involve technology, whether that means learning to write code during a January immersive term, conducting research on equipment in a community research lab, or honing digital presentation skills.

"Undergraduate research opportunities"—Year by year, every student will learn how to conduct research of an increasingly professional caliber, gaining confidence as well as the ability to pursue and answer a meaningful research question, skills that are highly valued by employers and graduate programs alike.

"Cohesive professional development opportunities"—Every single major will integrate uniquely designed opportunities for its students to develop as professionals in that field, offering students a clear vision of the path between their college education and the post-college world of work.

Franklin College operates on a 4-1-4 academic calendar, which allows tremendous opportunities for students throughout the academic year. The fall semester begins toward the end of August and ends mid-December; the spring semester begins in February and ends in the middle of May. The two semesters are broken up by a special four-week Immersive Term program during the month of January. Immersive Term is designed to allow students to study in areas of particular interest to them, either within or outside their major field of study. Some January classes offer students the opportunity to travel to locations such as Uganda, England, France, Italy, Guatemala and Mexico.

Students can also take advantage of internship opportunities during Immersive Term, offering practical experience under the supervision of a professional. Internships are available during Immersive Term, summer, fall semester, and spring semester. Franklin students can count up to sixteen hours of internship credit towards their graduation requirements and still graduate within four years. On time, prepared completion is the goal. The location of the college in proximity to downtown Indianapolis allows students to complete internships with nationally known Fortune 500 companies. One-hundred percent of Franklin College students complete an internship or significant undergraduate research prior to graduation.

Franklin gives credit in seventeen academic areas for successful scores on CLEP subject examinations; credit is also granted for successful scores on the Advanced Placement tests of the College Board. The Running Start Program enables talented high school students to get an early start on their college education.

Academic Facilities

Franklin College has two campus buildings listed on the National Historic Register. Old Main, the original home of the college, and Shirk Hall, home of the Pulliam School of Journalism, are footholds of the rich past and recent renovation of the Franklin College campus. Classrooms and administrative, business, and professorial offices, along with computer laboratories, occupy Old Main; Shirk Hall also houses classrooms and the radio station.

The new Franklin College Science Center houses all natural sciences and psychology with state of the art labs, greenhouse and classroom space as well as outdoor classrooms and wetlands used by the ecology and biology programs. The Spurlock Center gymnasium and fitness center provide workout and weight equipment to students in order to maintain a healthy lifestyle.

The Lilly Center for exploration houses the Professional Development, Career Services, Global Studies and Service Learning programs.. State-of-the-art conference rooms and computer facilities enhance Franklin's career programming commitment to its students.

In addition to more than 117,000 volumes and collections of microfilm, slides, art reproductions, recordings, and periodicals, The B.F. Hamilton library houses Governor George Branigin's personal archives and HamiltonONE—a hub for student success which includes the Academic Resource Center and Academic Resource Center which provides a variety of tutoring, academic and disability services.

The Johnson Center for Fine Arts provides classrooms and practice and performance accommodations for music, studio arts, theater and general student use.

Costs

The direct cost for the 2018-19 academic year was $41,956. This amount was derived from tuition, which was $31,810; residence hall, which was $5,682; activity fees of $200; and Immersive term meal fees of $427 plus the meal plan, which was $3,837.

Financial Aid

The Franklin College financial aid program assists students who might not otherwise be able to attend college and rewards applicants for excellent academic achievement in high school. Awards are based on scholarship, curricular and extracurricular activities, and financial need. Aid involving financial need includes Franklin College grants, loans, and employment. Franklin participates in the Federal Direct Loan and Federal Work-Study programs. Merit-based scholarships ranging from $2,000 to full-tuition are awarded to students based on academic performance, activities, and standardized test scores. Scholarships are renewable for each of the recipient's four academic years at Franklin, provided students maintain specific GPA requirements and advance in class status each year. Franklin College encourages all students and families to file the Free Application for Federal Student Aid (FAFSA) in order to receive additional financial aid.

Student Organizations

Franklin College offers more than sixty clubs and organizations such as Student Congress, Black Student Union, Greek Life, and Student Entertainment Board. These organizations allow students to plan on-campus concerts/events, represent the student body to change campus policies, and volunteer their time with the college's Habitat for Humanity programs from the first year. In addition to the existing organizations, the college allows students to set up new groups of their interests.

Admission Requirements

Applications for admission to Franklin College are evaluated on an individual basis. A student's potential academic and personal contributions to the college, recommendations, school and community activities, academic record, and standardized test scores are taken into consideration by the Admissions Committee. A student should complete a strong college-preparatory program. Candidates for admission are urged to visit the campus in order to experience the college community. Franklin offers a variety of visit opportunities, from personal visits to open houses, all providing opportunities to meet current students, professors, and coaches, and to take a campus tour.

Application and Information

To be considered for admission, an applicant must submit a completed Franklin College or Common Application), a transcript of all secondary school and college work attempted, and either SAT or ACT scores. Self-reported scores are acceptable. Recommendations and an optional essay are recommended. Decisions are made on a rolling basis.

Office of Admissions
Franklin College
101 Branigin Boulevard
Franklin, Indiana 46131
Phone: 317-738-8075
888-852-6471 (toll-free)
Fax: 317-738-8274
E-mail: admissions@FranklinCollege.edu
Website: http://www.franklincollege.edu/admissions/

Old Main is the oldest academic building on the Franklin College campus.

COLLEGE CLOSE-UPS

GANNON UNIVERSITY
ERIE, PENNSYLVANIA

Believe in the possibilities.

The University

Gannon University is a place where lives are transformed, lifelong friendships made, and futures forged, a place where possibilities are discovered and become reality.

A Catholic, diocesan university founded in 1925, Gannon is more than a brick-and-mortar institution. It is a close-knit family of dedicated faculty, staff, and students inspired to solve problems, meet challenges, and make a difference in the process. It is a family that values faith, leadership, inclusiveness, and social responsibility—and puts those values into action locally and across the world.

Gannon's expert faculty and staff prepare students to be global citizens and leaders through innovative programs that are grounded in the liberal arts, sciences, and professional specializations and complemented by unique research, internship, and travel-abroad opportunities. Students don't have to imagine themselves interning at a Fortune 500 company, building an instrument for a NASA-funded project, or being immersed in the culture and history of Italy or Thailand or Spain. It happens at Gannon every day.

School pride doesn't end with academics. The entire Gannon community rallies around the Golden Knights and Lady Knights who excel in NCAA Division II athletics. Student-athletes can take their pick of 21 scholarship-granting varsity sports and year-round intramural and club sports. The campus includes the Recreation and Wellness Center, which recently underwent an expansion project that included a complete interior renovation, new cardio equipment, new locker rooms, and the addition of a 51,300 square-foot, indoor fieldhouse that features an 80-yard practice facility open to all students.

Students looking for a different kind of team can participate in service learning projects, or join any of more than 130 student clubs and organizations that offer a chance to bond with new friends over shared interests—two of the many ways Gannon students make memories that last a lifetime.

Location

Located in downtown Erie, Pennsylvania, Gannon is within walking distance of shops, restaurants, theaters, and professional sports venues and just minutes from Erie's bayfront and the beaches of Presque Isle State Park. Cleveland, Buffalo, and Pittsburgh all are within a two-hour drive.

Gannon's residence halls, apartments, academic buildings, administrative offices, and chapel are centered around the Waldron Campus Center—the heart of Gannon's campus—where members of the University's community meet, dine, study, and socialize. All campus housing is within three blocks of the cafeteria, Recreation and Wellness Center, library, and classrooms, creating a special, close-knit atmosphere in an urban setting. Students live and work near many of the businesses, organizations, and government agencies that are active partners in providing hands-on learning opportunities, including internships and service-learning experiences.

Majors and Degrees

The challenge at Gannon is not a lack of career paths—it's which one to choose. Students have their pick of more than 100 undergraduate, graduate, and online academic programs, all taught by faculty members who are experts in their field.

The College of Humanities, Education and Social Sciences offers programs in advertising communication, criminal justice, digital media communication, English, foreign language and international studies, foreign language and literature, history, interdisciplinary studies, journalism communications, legal studies, mortuary science, performance for media and stage, philosophy, political science, prelaw, a 3+3 prelaw program that includes early admission to Duquesne University, psychology, public relations, public service and global affairs, social work, theatre and communication arts, theatre technologies and design, or theology.

Future educators can choose from several programs in the School of Education including early childhood education PreK–4, early childhood education PreK–4/special education PreK–8, middle level education 4–8 and middle level education 4–8/special education PreK–8, and secondary education (in biology, English, mathematics and social studies).

The Morosky College of Health Professions and Sciences offers the following degrees: athletic training (master's), medical laboratory science, nursing, nutrition and human performance, occupational therapy (five-year direct-entry master's and a doctorate offered at the Ruskin, Florida campus), physical therapy (direct-entry doctorate), physician assistant (five-year direct-entry master's), public health, radiologic sciences, respiratory care, sport and exercise science, and undecided health science.

Degrees are also offered in biochemistry, biology, chemical engineering (cooperative program), chemistry, freshwater and marine biology, mathematics and science. Students who wish to enter chiropractic, dental, medical, optometry, pharmacy, podiatry, or veterinary school can choose from among 11 preprofessional programs.

The College of Engineering and Business offers degrees in biomedical engineering, computer science, electrical engineering (including a five-year co-op program), environmental engineering, industrial engineering, information systems, mechanical engineering (including a five-year co-op program), software engineering, and a dual-degree program in partnership with Esslingen University of Applied Sciences in which students earn bachelor's degrees in software engineering or computer science as well as software technology.

The most recent additions include programs in cyber engineering and cybersecurity with an Institute for Cyber Health and Knowledge that will serve as the global headquarters for academic, industry, and business owners to design, integrate and protect cybernetic intelligence and data systems worldwide.

Programs in the Dahlkemper School of Business include accounting, economics, entrepreneurship, finance, healthcare management, international management, management, management information systems, marketing, risk management and insurance, sport management and marketing, and supply chain management.

Academic Programs

Gannon's academic calendar consists of two full semesters running from August to December and from January to May, with optional summer classes. Basic graduation requirements for bachelor's degree candidates are 128 credit hours, including completion of requirements for the major and the liberal studies program. Associate degree students must complete 60 to 68 credit hours, depending on the program.

Academic Facilities

Nash Library, the hub of academic life at Gannon, reopened in 2017, following a complete exterior and interior renovation of the 82,000 square-foot building. The transformed library features new student study spaces, group collaboration spaces, the University's Writing and Research and S.T.E.M. centers, a full-service information technology help desk, new spaces for the university's archives and special collections, a reading room and a coffeehouse. The renovation follows the recent reopening of Beyer Hall after a 40,000 square-foot expansion project that created a collaborative space where students from around the world come together to learn, participate in campus life and organizations, and discover ways to engage the world.

Also new this year is the Donald M. and Judith C. Alstadt Environmental Center, waterfront property on 3.57 acres at the edge of the Allegheny National Forest that will be used by Gannon students and faculty to live, learn, and conduct research in a setting that offers unparalleled direct access to diverse ecosystems.

Gannon's academic facilities do more than house programs. They are the spaces where students learn by doing.

The Center for Business Ingenuity brings together the Dahlkemper School of business, Gannon's Small Business Development Center, and the Erie Technology Incubator under one roof, creating unprecedented collaboration between business students, entrepreneurs, business faculty, and consultants in a facility that looks and feels like a major corporate headquarters.

Gannon's mechanical, biomedical, and industrial and robotics engineering programs are located in another exceptional learning environment, the Center for Advanced Engineering, also home to the industrial engineering laboratory and the only biomedical engineering lab of its kind in the region.

Budding biologists, doctors, physicists, chemists, and engineers will spend much of their time in the Zurn Science Center, which houses laboratory space, an open-engineering computer lab, and 3-D printers for student use. Criminal justice students can investigate simulated crime scenes, conduct research in a state-of-the-art forensics lab, and train in interrogation rooms and a virtual reality firearms simulator in the forensic investigation center.

The Morosky College of Health Professions and Sciences is located in the Robert H. Morosky Academic Center, a 99,000 square-foot facility that includes classrooms, labs, and a state-of-the-art patient simulation center, the largest and most comprehensive one in the region. Nursing, respiratory care, radiologic science, physician assistant, and occupational therapy students come together at the center to take part in collaborative, hands-on learning.

Gannon's advertising, digital media communication, journalism, and theater programs, along with Gannon's award-winning radio station and student newspaper, are housed in the new Center for Communication Arts. Other academic buildings include the A. J. Palumbo Center, home to the College of Humanities, Education and Social Sciences, and Scottino Hall, home to the acclaimed Schuster Theatre.

Costs

Full-time tuition for 2018–19 was $15,590 per semester ($16,530 for engineering and health sciences), or $31,180 per academic year ($33,060 for engineering and health sciences). Tuition for part-time students was $755 to $810 per credit hour. Room and board range from $5,725 to $7,530 per semester. The total cost for the academic year at Gannon was $32,136 for commuting students and between $43,586 and $47,884 for resident students, depending on the program of study.

Financial Aid

Gannon is dedicated to ensuring a high-quality education is within everyone's reach: More than $27 million in student scholarship and financial aid is provided to 94 percent of undergraduate students. Students seeking financial aid can file the admissions and financial aid applications as early as October 1 and should file by the preferred deadline of March 15. Numerous employment and scholarship opportunities are available to qualified students. Each year the University offers its top incoming freshmen the ability to compete for full-tuition scholarships. The application deadline for this competition is December 15 with an on-campus competition in late January or early February.

Faculty

Gannon's faculty numbers more than 400 and 69 percent of the full-time faculty members have either doctoral or terminal degrees. The student-to-faculty ratio is 13:1, and average class size is approximately 25 students.

Admission Requirements

Gannon University actively recruits students of all races, faith traditions, and ages from all geographic regions of North America and abroad. Applicants must submit scores (including senior-year scores) on either the SAT or ACT; an up-to-date official transcript of the high school record (plus official college transcripts for transfer applicants); and a completed application form. Applications can be completed online at www.gannon.edu/apply or via the Common Application.

Admission decisions are based upon numerous factors, most importantly the high school record as demonstrated through grades and SAT and/or ACT scores and other test scores that may be available. Recommendations and personal statements also affect admission decisions. Transfer and international students should check with the admissions office for special application procedures.

Application and Information

Gannon operates on a rolling admissions basis; there is no deadline for filing applications with the exception of the physician assistant program, which has a deadline of December 1 for the fall semester. Due to the competitiveness of some programs, students interested in the nursing or occupational therapy programs are strongly encouraged to file applications in September. Early applications are recommended, as are enrollment deposits.

To find out more, contact:
Office of Admissions
Gannon University
109 University Square
Erie, Pennsylvania 16541
Phone: 814-871-7240
800-GANNON-U (426-6668, toll-free)
Fax: 814-871-5803
E-mail: admissions@gannon.edu
Website: http://www.gannon.edu

GWYNEDD MERCY UNIVERSITY
GWYNEDD VALLEY, PENNSYLVANIA

Gwynedd Mercy University

The University

Gwynedd Mercy University (GMercyU) is a Catholic university with a strong foundation in the liberal arts and a deep commitment to the Mercy tradition of service to society. GMercyU believes that each person has the power to make a difference — to another individual, to a community, to the world.

The University supports students in their quest to become their best selves with the help of a dedicated team of professors who take an interest in who they are, and who they aspire to be. Students are encouraged to join a growing team of *Distinctive Mercy Graduates* who are doing more than launching successful careers; they're living productive and meaningful lives. With excellent programs in nursing, health professions, arts and sciences, education, and business, GMercyU supports students in making a difference in their own lives and in the lives of others.

GMercyU is set on 314 beautiful acres in southeastern Pennsylvania and is home to nearly 2,000 undergraduate students, 19 NCAA Division III athletic teams, and dozens of clubs and organizations. The University is large enough to offer a vibrant campus life but small enough that students get the personal attention they need to achieve their goals.

In addition to taking classes, students can join the University's nationally-renowned choir, join the Griffin Student Leadership Institute, improve the lives of others through Alternative Spring Break, be part of a winning athletic team, or choose from many other options. Students also can enjoy several on-campus dining choices or take a free shuttle to nearby restaurants when they're looking for a change of scene.

With more than 21,000 alumni, Gwynedd Mercy University has a strong reputation for preparing *Distinctive Mercy Graduates* who make a difference in the world. In 2017, PayScale also ranked GMercyU in the Top 25 percent of schools nationwide for 20-year net return on investment, and 100% of first-time, full-time students received financial aid in 2017-18. Gwynedd Mercy University is also considered a military-friendly college.

Location

Gwynedd Mercy University's idyllic 314-acre campus is located in Gwynedd Valley, Pennsylvania, a suburb 30 miles from downtown Philadelphia. While on campus, students can enjoy beautiful outdoor spaces perfect for a long run, a friendly game of Frisbee, or a quiet lunch with friends on a colorful hammock. Philadelphia's South Street, sports arenas, and some of the best restaurants and concert venues around are just a 30-minute car or train ride from campus. In addition to the vibrant city life of Philadelphia, New Jersey beaches, the Pocono Mountains, Washington D.C., and New York City are just about two hours from campus. Students can take advantage of free shuttle service to the local train station or to the many shops, restaurants, and entertainment areas nearby.

In Fall 2018, GMercyU announced the purchase of its new East Campus, which nearly doubles the size of campus to 314 acres. The property is adjacent to its Gwynedd Valley campus and is a part of a broader plan to enhance existing programs and support the introduction of new programs.

Majors and Degrees

Gwynedd Mercy University offers baccalaureate degrees in accounting, behavioral/social gerontology, biology, digital communication, computer information science, criminal justice, education/special education, finance, history, human resource management, human services, management, marketing, mathematics, medical laboratory science, nursing, occupational science/pre-OT, philosophy, psychology, radiologic technology, radiation therapy, respiratory care, social work, and sports management.

Associate degrees are awarded in liberal studies, natural science, and respiratory care. GMercyU also offers a number of master's degrees in business, education, and nursing, including a 4+1 MBA program on campus. Students who want to earn their doctorate degrees can choose from programs in education and nursing. Many graduate programs are offered in accelerated and/or online formats.

Academic Programs

The academic year is divided into two semesters, and most baccalaureate degree programs require the completion of a minimum of 120 credit hours. All of Gwynedd Mercy University's undergraduate programs include a strong focus on the liberal arts to ensure students develop some of today's most in-demand skills, including communication, critical thinking, and problem-solving. Liberal arts courses include language; literature and the fine arts; humanities; and behavioral, social, and natural sciences. Students have access to the Academic Resource Center for tutoring and writing assistance at no additional charge.

Individualized credit-bearing internships and work experience programs are available and recommended in all majors to give students firsthand experience in their chosen field before they graduate. Nearby Fortune 500 companies offer a variety of experiences to students in business and accounting, for example. TAP, GMercyU's Teacher Apprentice Program, places every education major in the classroom one day a week beginning in their first year, and education students also complete pre-student teaching and student teaching experiences. All health professions and nursing programs require clinical experience. Students also have the opportunity to conduct research and present at academic and industry conferences, depending on their major. Students are encouraged to develop a global perspective through various study abroad and Alternative Spring Break service opportunities.

Off-Campus Programs

The excellent, on-campus simulation and laboratory facilities are extended by affiliations with more than 200 hospitals and health care agencies in Pennsylvania, New Jersey, and Delaware, where nursing and health professions students may complete their clinical experiences. Gwynedd Mercy University also maintains a close relationship with nearby school districts and companies, including the Philadelphia School District, Johnson & Johnson, Merck, McNeil, Sun Company, just to name a few.

Academic Facilities

Gwynedd Mercy University has expanded its physical facilities as its student enrollment has increased. Frances M. Maguire Hall is home to the Frances M. Maguire School of Nursing and Health Professions as well as the Division of Natural Sciences. This 50,000 square-foot state-of-the-art facility offers laboratories for areas such as nursing skills, respiratory care, radiation therapy, organic chemistry, and microbiology. The University's SIM® family includes newborn, infant, child, and adult simulation mannequins that allow students to practice techniques before performing them on real patients in clinical settings. An advanced video system also gives students real-time feedback on care techniques.

Gwynedd Mercy University's newest academic building on its main campus, University Hall, opened in the spring of 2014. The building is the home of the School of Business and Education. University Hall features state-of-the-art technology to further enhance educational opportunities, including a Financial Trading Room, equipped with a real-time stock ticker.

The Griffin Complex houses the University's recreation facilities, including a full gymnasium and track, racquetball court, cardio room, and weight room.

The University's Julia Ball Auditorium is a 400-seat space for theatrical productions, musical events, and other cultural and academic programs. The Valie Genuardi Hobbit House is a fully licensed academic lab school located right on campus. It is home to nursery and pre-kindergarten students, and also provides a place for students in the School of Business and Education to gain valuable, hands-on experience.

The Keiss Library and Learning Commons links academic support services, library services, and career development services, providing a one-stop academic center that facilitates student success.

Costs

The published 2019–20 academic year tuition for full-time students (12 to 18 credits per semester) is $33,800. The published tuition for health professions and nursing students is $35,800. Room and board costs average $12,750. Professional liability fees for students enrolled in clinical components and lab fees are extra. The University offers generous scholarships ranging from $10,000 to full tuition, and other financial aid to qualified students.

Financial Aid

Gwynedd Mercy University strives to make a quality education accessible to all. GMercyU's tuition and aid amounts makes them a competitive value in the Pennsylvania region, and they work closely with you to find the best options to pay for your education. Financial aid, which includes federal, state, and other available funds, is awarded on the basis of demonstrated financial need, academic proficiency, and responsible campus citizenship. In 2017–18, 100 percent of the University's first-time full-time students received some form of financial aid.

Faculty

The University's student-faculty ratio is 11:1, allowing for personal attention, advising, and after-class instruction. For nursing students in the clinical setting, there are never more than 8 students to 1 clinical adviser; in the health professions programs, there often is one-to-one instruction. The quality of teaching is enhanced by the diversified interests of the faculty. Faculty members teach both day and evening classes, allowing students the greatest flexibility in scheduling. Tutoring is available in all disciplines at no additional charge.

Student Government

All students are encouraged to take part in the responsibilities of student government. Student participation and shared responsibility for the welfare of the University are promoted through a framework of committees.

Admission Requirements

Admission to Gwynedd Mercy University is based on a student's high school record, rank in class, SAT or ACT scores, counselor's recommendation, and choice of major. Entrance requirements vary with the program. The rolling admission policy generally allows students to be informed of an admission decision within two to three weeks of submitting their completed application.

Gwynedd Mercy University awards credit for satisfactory completion of Advanced Placement courses, provided students receive an AP exam score of 3 or higher.

A minimum 2.0 grade point average (on a 4.0 scale) is generally required to transfer from another institution. Gwynedd Mercy University does, however, retain the right to require a higher GPA for admission to some programs.

Gwynedd Mercy University is committed to maintaining a positive learning, working, and living environment that is free from unlawful discrimination and harassment. Gwynedd Mercy University does not discriminate against any applicant for admission to or employment at the University because of race, religion, age, gender, sexual orientation, gender identity, national origin, disability, color, marital status, veteran status, genetic characteristics, or any other characteristic protected by federal, state or local law ("Protected Classes"). This includes, but is not limited to, admissions, financial aid, educational services, and student programs and activities, as well as to all terms and conditions of employment including, but not limited to, recruitment, selection, hiring, placement, transfer, promotion, training, compensation, benefits, discipline, and termination. The University will not tolerate unlawful acts of discrimination or harassment based upon Protected Classes, or related retaliation against or by any employee or student.

Application and Information

All prospective applicants are encouraged to visit the campus to meet with an admission counselor, dean, or professor. To apply for admission, applicants should complete the online application available at gmercyu.edu/apply. First-time freshmen must also submit an official high school transcript or equivalency certificate; results of the SAT or ACT (for recent high school graduates); and a letter of recommendation (optional but recommended). All applicants should verify that they meet the specific requirements and have the necessary high school prerequisites for admission.

Students who wish to transfer to Gwynedd Mercy University should submit the same online application, high school and college transcripts, and a letter of recommendation.

For additional information or to schedule campus tours and visits, students are encouraged to register with the Office of Admissions at admissions@gmercyu.edu or contact the office at 215-641-5510.

For more information, contact:

Office of Admissions
Gwynedd Mercy University
1325 Sumneytown Pike
P.O. Box 901
Gwynedd Valley, Pennsylvania 19437-9923
Phone: 800-342-5462 (toll-free)
215-641-5510
E-mail: admissions@gmercycu.edu
Website: gmercyu.edu/admissions-aid/undergraduate-admissions
twitter.com/GMercyU
facebook.com/GMercyU
instagram.com/gmercyu

Students walk to and from classes in University Hall, the newest academic building on campus.

HARDING UNIVERSITY

SEARCY, ARKANSAS

HARDING UNIVERSITY

The University

Harding University was founded on Christian principles and a liberal arts tradition. Since 1924, Harding has challenged its students to pursue scholarship, service, teamwork, excellence, and commitment. The largest private university in Arkansas, it is ranked by *U.S. News and World Report* and Princeton Review as one of the top liberal arts universities in the South and attracts exceptional high school students representing every U.S. state and more than 54 nations and territories.

Harding University is accredited by the Higher Learning Commission and maintains specialized accreditation for its programs as appropriate to its educational purpose. Students have opportunities for hands-on learning whether it be engineering majors developing concept, design, and construction of an off-road vehicle; journalism majors managing, writing and editing for the student newspaper; or nursing majors conducting exam simulations on high-fidelity mannequins. With a student-teacher ratio of 14 to 1, strong relationships are built in and out of the classroom.

Students can cultivate friendships and interests with 120 academic and professional organizations and 31 social clubs. Ranging from the arts, music, politics, business, diversity, children, missions, service, and the environment, the clubs on campus offer a variety of interests to explore.

Provided with a Christian perspective through which to appreciate various disciplines, students excel as scholars and develop leadership skills. As a result, Harding alumni display character, conviction, and a competitive edge and are prepared for success at prestigious graduate schools and companies throughout the nation.

Location

Harding is located in Searcy, Arkansas, and offers students a hometown feeling with easy access to major cities. The University is about an hour away from Little Rock, Arkansas, and the Bill and Hillary Clinton National Airport and is about 2 hours away from Memphis, Tennessee. Located in The Natural State, University students have several nearby options such as the Little Red River, Pinnacle Mountain, and Petit Jean State Parks for fishing, camping, hiking, and other outdoor activities. Arkansas is home to 52 state parks.

Majors and Degrees

Housed within nine colleges, the University offers more than 100 academic majors, including 14 preprofessional programs, taught by top instructors.

Within the College of Allied Health, students may earn a Bachelor of Arts degree in communication sciences and disorders, a Bachelor of Science in exercise and sport sciences, a Master of Science degree in speech-language pathology, a Master of Science degree in physician assistant studies, and a Doctor of Physical Therapy degree.

The College of Arts and Humanities offers a wide range of degrees in the humanities, arts, communication, English language and literature, foreign language and international studies, history and political science, interior design, medical humanities, music, and theater.

In the College of Bible and Ministry, there are degrees in Bible and ministry, family ministry, leadership and ministry, missions, and preaching.

Students in the Paul R. Carter College of Business Administration may earn the Bachelor of Business Administration in accounting, finance, international business, information systems, management, marketing and professional sales, and a Master of Business Administration.

Those interested in teaching may earn degrees in birth–kindergarten early childhood/special education integrated, elementary education, middle level education English/language arts/math 4–8, middle level education English/language arts/science 4–8, middle level education English/language arts/social science 4–8, middle level math/science 4–8, middle level science/social sciences 4–8, middle level social sciences/math 4–8, secondary education, and special education in the Cannon-Clary College of Education. Students can also earn a Master of Arts, Master of Arts in Teaching, Master of Education, Master of Science, Master of Science in Education, Master of Science in Marriage and Family Therapy, educational specialist, and educational doctorate. Students can also earn several additional endorsements.

The Carr College of Nursing offers a Bachelor of Science in Nursing, enabling students to take the NCLEX-RN exam after graduation. There also is a Master of Science in Nursing degree program, preparing students to be family nurse practitioners.

Students can earn a Doctor of Pharmacy degree through the University's four-year program in the College of Pharmacy.

The College of Sciences allows students to study health sciences, behavioral sciences, biology, chemistry, computer science, engineering (civil, computer, electrical, and mechanical) and physics, exercise and sport sciences, family and consumer sciences, kinesiology, mathematics, medical humanities, medical laboratory science, psychology, and social work.

The Honors College offers a Bachelor of Arts in interdisciplinary studies for its students.

In addition, teaching licensure may be obtained in the following areas: art, biology, chemistry, drama/speech, English, family and consumer sciences, French, kinesiology, mathematics, music, social science, Spanish, and theater 7–12.

Academic Programs

For the basic requirements necessary for each degree, prospective students should visit the Harding University online catalog at www.harding.edu/catalog. Specific inquires may be addressed to catalog@harding.edu.

Students may apply and participate in the Honors College with acceptance based on acceptance to the University and an ACT score of 27 or higher or an SAT evidence-based reading and writing, plus math score of 1280 or higher. These students may take honors-level courses and graduate with honors.

Off-Campus Programs

Harding offers multiple study abroad programs in locations such as Australia, Chile, England, France, Greece, Italy, and Zambia that will help expand cultural awareness and understanding. Nearly 50 percent of each graduating class takes advantage of one of Harding's international experiences. At each location, students are accompanied and taught by University faculty. Costs are based on 16 tuition hours and include housing and meals.

Academic Facilities

Harding's campus consists of 13 academic buildings, cafeteria, two auditoriums, a world-class recreation center, a library, a performing arts center, a student center, student health services, 14 residence halls, and six apartment complexes.

Costs

The basic undergraduate, on-campus cost for 2018-19 for 15 hours of enrollment per semester was $10,005 for a semester and $20,010 for the year. Tuition was $638 per course hour. Students paid $520 a year for a required technology fee, a one-time $205 first-year experience fee, $3,764 for a standard dorm room, and $3,406 for a standard meal plan of 190 meals. The overall total came to $27,905.

Financial Aid

On average, 92 percent of Harding University freshman students receive financial assistance. The University awards more than $22 million in institutional scholarships and grants and nearly $9 million in federal and state scholarships and grants.

Admission Requirements

Students wishing to apply to Harding must have a 19 ACT or 900 SAT and 3.0 high school GPA (on a 4.0 scale). In addition, high school graduates should have completed at least 15 units in academic subjects. Specifically, an applicant should have completed 4 units of English, 3 units of mathematics (taken from general math, geometry, algebra, trigonometry, precalculus, or calculus), 3 units of social studies (taken from civics, American history, world history, or geography), and 2 units of natural science (taken from physical science, biology, physics, or chemistry). Students planning to major in any area of health care are strongly encouraged to take one or more chemistry courses while in high school. Although not required for admission, two years of foreign language is recommended. The additional units may come from any academic area.

Application and Information

Prospective students may apply online at www.harding.edu/apply/.

Because Harding receives so many applications, it recommends that students apply before fall of their senior year of high school—even if they haven't taken the ACT or SAT. Admissions advisers are glad to help students through this process.

For more information, prospective students should contact:

Harding University
Box 12255
Searcy, Arkansas 72149-5615
Phone: 501-279-4407
Website: http://www.harding.edu
http://www.facebook.com/HardingU
http://www.twitter.com/HardingU

Harding University's student population represents all 50 states and 54 nations and territories. With more than 5,900 students, Harding is the largest private college or university in Arkansas.

HILLSDALE COLLEGE
HILLSDALE, MICHIGAN

HILLSDALE COLLEGE
PURSUING TRUTH · DEFENDING LIBERTY SINCE 1844

The College

Hillsdale College is a private, independent, nonsectarian, Christian institution of higher learning founded in 1844 by men and women who described themselves as "grateful to God for the inestimable blessings" resulting from civil and religious liberty and as "believing that the diffusion of sound learning is essential to the perpetuity of those blessings." The College has maintained institutional independence since its founding by refusing to accept aid from or control by federal authorities. Private support from a national constituency has enabled Hillsdale to continue its trusteeship of the intellectual and spiritual inheritance tracing to Athens and Jerusalem, a heritage finding its clearest expression in the American experiment of self-government under law.

The undergraduate enrollment for fall 2018 was 1,468—52 percent men and 48 percent women—from fifty states and twelve foreign countries. Approximately 33 percent of students are from Michigan. The entering freshman class in 2018 had the following mid-range scores: high school grade-point average of 3.86–4.0, ACT of 29–32, and SAT of 1300–1450. All Hillsdale students sign an Honor Code challenging self-government and committing them to honesty, duty, and respect.

Location

Hillsdale College is located in the south-central town of Hillsdale, Michigan (population 10,000) near the Indiana and Ohio borders. Stores, churches, restaurants, and coffee shops are within walking distance of the campus.

Majors and Degrees

Hillsdale awards Bachelor of Arts and Bachelor of Science degrees in accounting, applied mathematics, art, biochemistry, biology, chemistry, classics, economics, English, exercise science, financial management, French, German, Greek, history, Latin, marketing/management, mathematics, music, philosophy, physical education, physics, politics, psychology, religion, rhetoric and public address, Spanish, sport management, sport psychology, and theater. Interdisciplinary majors are available in American studies, Christian studies, comparative literature, European studies, international studies in business and foreign language, political economy, and sociology and social thought. Preprofessional programs are offered in allied health sciences (including optometry, pharmacy, and physical therapy), dentistry, education, engineering, environmental sciences, journalism, law, medicine and osteopathy, theology, and veterinary medicine. The Van Andel Graduate School of Statesmanship offers a Doctor of Philosophy in politics and a Master of Arts in politics.

The Academic Program

Hillsdale operates on a two-semester schedule. Two 3-week summer sessions are also offered.

The College offers a traditional liberal arts curriculum. Every Hillsdale College student is required to complete a structured core of courses in the humanities, natural sciences, and social sciences. Required courses include Western and American Heritage, U.S. Constitution, Great Books in the Western and British/American Traditions, Classical Logic and Rhetoric, Western Philosophical Tradition, and Western Theological Tradition. To graduate, students must complete a minimum 124 hours of course work and fulfill the requirements of at least one major field. The B.A. program includes a foreign language proficiency requirement. The B.S. program requires additional studies in mathematics and the natural sciences.

The Center for Constructive Alternatives conducts four week-long symposia during the academic year and is one of the largest college lecture series in America. These programs, with themes ranging from historical to political, business, science, and the arts, bring distinguished scholars and public figures to the campus. All students are required to enroll in at least one seminar for credit during their time at Hillsdale.

The Collegiate Scholars Program enriches the academic experience of high-performing students by providing opportunities to become deeply versed in the contents and methods of inquiry of the liberal arts. A combination of seminars, campus lectures and discussions, retreats, subsidized foreign travel, and the completion of an interdisciplinary senior thesis help to meet this goal.

Off-Campus Programs

For forty years, the Washington-Hillsdale Internship Program (WHIP) has provided students the opportunity to participate in full-time, academically intensive internships in Washington, D.C. Past interns and fellows have been placed in locations such as the U.S. Senate, the White House, news and media outlets, and national security agencies. Students complement their internships with classes at Hillsdale's Allan P. Kirby, Jr. Center for Constitutional Studies and Citizenship.

Hillsdale students are able to study abroad for a summer or a semester at one of the more than thirty colleges of Oxford University. Hillsdale also offers a summer business program in cooperation with Regent's College in London, England, and the opportunity to study at the University of St. Andrews in St. Andrews, Scotland. Science students benefit from Hillsdale's 685-acre field research laboratory in northern Michigan, a marine biology program in the Florida Keys, and internship opportunities with the Omaha Zoo. Foreign language students frequently study abroad in Argentina, France, Germany, and Spain.

Academic Facilities

The Hillsdale College Mossey Library features a collection of more than 2,900,000 volumes (print and electronic), including rare and special holdings such as the Ludwig von Mises and Russell Kirk collections.

Lane and Kendall Halls contain classroom space and faculty offices for the humanities and social sciences, as well as a special laboratory for experimental psychology. Strosacker Science Center and the Herbert Henry Dow Science Building provide classrooms and laboratories for the natural sciences. The Joseph H. Moss Family Laboratory Wing includes state-of-the-art laboratories and a greenhouse. Slayton Arboretum is a 48-acre campus garden and bird sanctuary used by students to conduct research. At the Mary Randall Preschool, nursery school children are taught by students specializing in early childhood education and psychology. Hillsdale Academy, a K–12 private school, provides additional opportunities for classroom observation.

The Roche Sports Complex houses the Dawn Tibbetts Potter Arena, with a student fitness center and basketball/volleyball courts, the John "Jack" McAvoy Natatorium for swimming and diving, an exercise physiology and sports medicine facility, four racquetball courts, and a weight/fitness room. Adjacent is the Frank "Muddy" Waters Stadium, which features an artificial surface football field; all-weather, Olympic-quality eight-lane running track; and fields for soccer, baseball, and women's softball. The Margot V. Biermann Athletic Center houses four acrylic tennis courts and a six-lane, 200-meter NCAA regulation Mondo surface track.

The Fine Arts Building is home to the departments of art and theater. It features Daughtrey Gallery, a prop- and scene-construction shop, a sound studio, graphics lab, black box theatre, and the Markel Auditorium, a 353-seat performance hall (with orchestra pit). Howard Music Hall houses the McNamara Rehearsal Hall, Conrad Recital Hall, studio space for percussion and jazz studies, offices, and practice rooms.

The Grewcock Student Union houses the cafeteria, bookstore, student mail center, offices for student activities and publications, a lounge and game area, and AJ's Café. In addition to serving as a course for Hillsdale's cross-country teams, Hayden Park, located northeast of campus, provides a place for club and intramural sports, mountain biking, cross-country skiing, and general outdoor recreation. The 27,000-square-foot Christ Chapel will open in 2019, serving as a center for campus spiritual life and as a symbol of Hillsdale's Christian roots and identity.

Faculty

The faculty consists of 143 full-time members with a 9:1 student-teacher ratio and average class sizes of 13. The size and closeness of the College community enable personal attention and faculty mentorship inside the classroom and during office visits after class. Each student has a faculty advisor for core and major coursework.

Athletics

Hillsdale's Charger athletes compete in 14 intercollegiate NCAA Division II varsity sports as part of the Great Midwest Athletic Conference. Hillsdale College sponsors varsity basketball, cross-country, swimming, softball, tennis, indoor and outdoor track and field, and volleyball for women, and varsity baseball, basketball, cross-country, golf, football, tennis, and indoor and outdoor track and field for men.

Student Life

Four national fraternities, three national sororities, a newspaper and radio station, and more than 100 other social, academic, spiritual, and service organizations provide Hillsdale students with a diverse array of cocurricular opportunities. A resident drama troupe and dance company, a concert choir and chamber chorale, a jazz program, instrumental chamber ensembles, and a symphony orchestra and band constitute the College's performing arts organizations. The Student Activities Board hosts campus-wide social functions throughout the year, including events like Garden Party, Homecoming, President's Ball, and Centralhallapalooza.

Hillsdale students are housed in single-sex dormitories, fraternity and sorority houses, and off-campus houses. Each College-owned residence hall is supervised by a resident director and resident advisers. All freshmen (except commuters) are required to live on campus; upperclass students seeking to live off campus must apply to the deans.

Special student services provided by the College include career planning and placement counseling; academic advising and tutoring; and a health service staffed by a physician, a resident nurse, and counselors.

Costs

Annual tuition for the 2018–19 academic year was $26,300, room was $5,440, board was $5,560, and mandatory fees were $1,278. Books, supplies, and personal expenses (including travel, recreation, and clothing) are estimated at $3,200 per year.

Financial Aid

Academic scholarships are awarded on a competitive basis, regardless of financial need. The application for admission also serves as the application for merit-based aid. Athletic scholarships are awarded on a competitive basis in men's baseball, football, and golf; men's and women's basketball, tennis, track, and cross-country; and women's swimming, softball, and volleyball. The departments of art and music also award a select number of scholarships based on strength of portfolio/audition. To apply for aid on the basis of financial need, students are required to file Hillsdale's Confidential Family Financial Statement (CFFS). Because Hillsdale does not accept government funds, either directly for its operations or indirectly in the form of student aid, the FAFSA is not applicable; government funds are replaced with private dollars. Grants and loans are available from the College.

Admission Requirements

A formal application to Hillsdale College includes: (1) a completed application form; (2) the scores from either the Scholastic Aptitude Test (SAT), the American College Test (ACT), or the Classic Learning Test (CLT); (3) an official transcript of high school grades (and post-secondary grades, if available); (4) thoughtful essay and short answer responses; (5) two academic letters of recommendation; and (6) a résumé of extracurricular activities, volunteerism, leadership, and work experience. An interview is recommended, but not required. Transfer students must include a Dean of Students Transfer Form and official college transcript(s). International students must submit all required documents in English; the ACT, SAT, or CLT is required, the TOEFL is optional.

Application and Information

Students may apply to Hillsdale College any time after the completion of the junior year of high school. A formal application includes a completed application form accompanied by a nonrefundable fee of $35 (free if submitted online) and all required credentials. Application plans include early decision (November 1), spring admission (December 1), priority scholarship (January 1), and regular decision (April 1). Hillsdale College has been distinguished since its founding in 1844 by voluntarily adhering to a nondiscriminatory policy regarding race, religion, sex, and national or ethnic origin. All records and forms should be mailed to:

Admissions Office
Hillsdale College
33 East College Street
Hillsdale, Michigan 49242-1298
Phone: 517-607-2327
Fax: 517-607-2223
E-mail: admissions@hillsdale.edu
Website: http://www.hillsdale.edu

Central Hall, on the campus of Hillsdale College, stands as an enduring symbol of the school's independence.

HOFSTRA UNIVERSITY

HEMPSTEAD, NEW YORK

HOFSTRA UNIVERSITY. pride and purpose

The University

Since its founding in 1935, Hofstra has evolved into an internationally renowned university that continues to achieve recognition as an institution of academic excellence. Hofstra has 28 academic accreditations and 32 total accreditations, and consistently earns recognition on the best college lists of *U.S. News & World Report*, The Princeton Review, *Fiske Guide to Colleges*, PayScale College ROI and Salary Reports, and *Forbes* magazine. Additionally, Hofstra has consistently been named to the President's Higher Education Community Service Honor Roll and is the only university to host three consecutive U.S. presidential debates (2008, 2012, and 2016).

Hofstra offers more than 160 undergraduate and more than 165 graduate program options. More than 100 dual-degree program options are also offered, giving students the opportunity to earn both a graduate and undergraduate degree in less time than if each degree was pursued separately. Students can choose from internationally recognized programs within Hofstra's various schools and colleges:

- Academic Health Sciences Center, including the Donald and Barbara Zucker School of Medicine at Hofstra/Northwell; the Hofstra Northwell School of Graduate Nursing and Physician Assistant Studies at Hofstra University; and the School of Health Professions and Human Services.
- Frank G. Zarb School of Business
- Fred DeMatteis School of Engineering and Applied Science
- Hofstra College of Liberal Arts and Sciences, including the Peter S. Kalikow School of Government, Public Policy, and International Affairs; the School of Education; the School of Humanities, Fine and Performing Arts; and the School of Natural Sciences and Mathematics
- Honors College
- Lawrence Herbert School of Communication
- Maurice A. Deane School of Law
- Hofstra University Continuing Education

Students live and learn in one of the university's 35 residence halls, each with a community and life of its own. Hofstra hosts hundreds of social, academic, and cultural events each year, drawing together scholars, business leaders, authors, celebrities, health care professionals, politicians, and journalists from across the nation and around the world.

The David S. Mack Sports and Exhibition Complex, a 5,025-seat arena, is home to various Hofstra Pride athletic teams. It is also the site for events such as commencements, exhibitions, trade shows, televised political events—including U.S. presidential debates—and concerts. Other recreational and athletic facilities include an indoor, Olympic-size swimming pool; a state-of-the-art fitness center; and various athletic fields. In addition, Hofstra offers 21 varsity sports that compete at the NCAA Division I level; 29 local/national fraternities and sororities; and more than 220 academic, media, multicultural, performance, preprofessional, religious, social/political, and sports clubs and organizations.

Location

Hofstra's 244-acre suburban campus is a short train ride from all the cultural, recreational, internship, and career opportunities New York City has to offer—and only minutes from beautiful beaches, shopping malls, restaurants, and two major airports.

Majors and Degrees

The Bachelor of Arts (B.A.) is awarded in African studies; American studies; anthropology; art history; Asian studies; biology; chemistry; Chinese; Chinese studies; classics; comparative literature and languages; computer science; criminology; dance; drama; early childhood education and childhood education (with dual major in another discipline); economics; elementary education; engineering science; English; English education; film studies and production; fine arts; foreign language education (French, German, Italian, Russian, Spanish); French; geography; geology; German; global studies; Hebrew; history; individually designed B.A. major in humanities, natural sciences, or social sciences; Italian; Japanese and Japanese studies; Jewish studies; journalism; labor studies; Latin; Latin American and Caribbean studies; liberal arts; linguistics; mass media studies; math education (with a dual major in another discipline); mathematical economics; mathematics; music; philosophy; physics; political science; pre-health with a concentration in humanities and social sciences; psychology; public relations; public policy and public service; radio production and studies; religion; rhetorical studies; Russian; science education (biology, chemistry, earth science, physics); science technology, engineering and mathematics (STEM); social studies education (with a dual major in another discipline); sociology; Spanish; speech-language-hearing sciences; sustainability studies; television production and studies; urban ecology; and women's studies.

The Bachelor of Business Administration (B.B.A.) is awarded in accounting, business analytics, entrepreneurship, finance, information systems, international business, legal studies in business, management, marketing, and supply chain management.

The Bachelor of Science (B.S.) is offered in applied physics, athletic training, biochemistry, biology, business economics, chemistry, civil engineering, community health, computer engineering, computer science, computer science and mathematics (dual major), early childhood education/childhood education, electrical engineering, environmental resources, exercise science, fine arts, forensic science, geographic information systems, geology, health education, health science, industrial engineering, mathematical business economics, mathematical finance, mathematics, mechanical engineering, music, neuroscience, philosophy, physics, pre-medical, psychology, sustainability studies, urban ecology, video/television, video/television and business, video/television and film, and video/television.

The Bachelor of Science in Education (B.S.Ed.) is offered with specializations in dance, fine arts, music, and physical education.

The Bachelor of Engineering (B.E.) is offered in engineering science with specializations in biomedical engineering and civil engineering.

The Bachelor of Fine Arts (B.F.A.) is awarded in theater arts and dance.

Combined (dual) degrees offered include Bachelor of Arts/Juris Doctor (B.A./J.D.), in collaboration with the Maurice A. Deane School of Law; Juris Doctor/Master of Business Administration (J.D./MBA) in collaboration with the Maurice A. Deane School of Law and the Frank G. Zarb School of Business; Juris Doctor/Master of Public Health (J.D./M.P.H.) in collaboration with the Maurice A. Dean School of Law and the School of Health Professions and Human Services; Medical Doctorate/Master of Public Health in collaboration with the Donald and Barbara Zucker School of Medicine at Hofstra/Northwell and the School of Health Professions and Human Services; B.S./M.S. in physician assistant studies; B.S./M.D. and B.A./M.D., through the Donald and Barbara Zucker School of Medicine at Hofstra/Northwell; and various majors and concentrations leading to the B.A./MBA, B.S./MBA, B.A./M.S.Ed., B.A./M.A., B.A./M.S., B.S./M.S., B.B.A./M.S.Ed., B.B.A./M.S., B.B.A./MBA, B.S./M.S.Ed., B.S./M.A., B.A./M.F.A., M.A./MBA, and M.D./Ph.D.

Academic Programs

Requirements for graduation vary among schools and majors. A liberal arts core curriculum is an integral part of all areas of concentration. The University calendar is organized on a traditional fall and spring semester system, and offers an optional January session and three optional Summer sessions (between May and August).

Hofstra offers innovative programs designed to meet the needs of its diverse student body. These include Honors College, Legal Education Accelerated Program (LEAP), Hofstra 4+4 Program, First-Year Connections, and living/learning communities.

Honors College students can elect to study in any of the University's undergraduate programs and are involved in all fields of advanced study.

The Legal Education Accelerated Program allows students to earn both a B.A. and a J.D. in just six years.

The Hofstra 4+4 Program allows students to earn both a bachelor's degree (B.A. or B.S.) and M.D. in eight years in collaboration with the Donald and Barbara Zucker School of Medicine at Hofstra/Northwell.

First-Year Connections, an optional integrated academic and social program, helps first-year students connect with one another as well as with all the resources and opportunities offered at the University. The program offers seminars and course clusters, that satisfy general education requirements for all majors, and features small classes taught by distinguished faculty.

Through Hofstra's living/learning communities, students are exposed to environments that are intellectually stimulating, supportive, and conducive to building lasting friendships and a memorable first-year experience. These communities are associated with several first-year clusters and seminars, giving students the opportunity to live with students who are in their classes and who share their interests.

Off-Campus Programs

Hofstra extends learning beyond the classroom through varied internship programs and study-abroad opportunities. The internship programs take advantage of Hofstra's proximity to New York City, allowing students to gain real-life experience in areas such as finance, business, media, advertising, and entertainment. Through study-abroad programs in Europe, Asia, South America, and other locations, students can explore the world while earning college credits. More information is available at hofstra.edu/studyabroad.

Academic Facilities

Hofstra students connect with the real world through experiential learning and build leadership skills by participating in service projects that give back to the community. Students have the opportunity to work in cutting-edge facilities, including the Martin B. Greenberg Trading Room; a big data lab; a robotics and advanced manufacturing lab; a cell and tissue engineering lab; and WRHU-88.7FM Radio Hofstra University, recipient of two prestigious Marconi Awards from the National Association of Broadcasters and among the top college radio stations in the country.

Costs

The 2018–19 annual tuition and fees for a full-time undergraduate student are $44,640. The cost of a housing and dining plan is approximately $16,768. The full tuition and fees schedule is available at hofstra.edu/tuition.

Financial Aid

Hofstra University works hard to make a private college education affordable for students and families, and offers several financial aid options for new undergraduates, including interest-free payment plans and a four-year locked-in rate for tuition and fees (hofstra.edu/lockedintuitionrate) that can help students manage costs from admission through graduation. Detailed information can be found at hofstra.edu/FinancialAid.

Faculty

All classes at Hofstra are taught by distinguished faculty members who are committed to excellence in teaching, scholarly research, and service. With an average undergraduate class size of 21 and a student-faculty ratio of 13:1, students are encouraged to debate, question, conduct research, discuss, and think critically in an open, collaborative learning environment.

Student Government

The Student Government Association (SGA) is Hofstra University's student-run governing body and is comprised of full-time undergraduate students; the SGA acts as a liaison between Hofstra students and the University's faculty, administration, and Board of Trustees. In addition, SGA plans and executes multiple programs and initiatives throughout the academic year, and oversees and finances of more than 200 clubs and organizations.

Admission Requirements

Hofstra is a competitive institution that seeks to enroll students who demonstrate academic ability, intellectual curiosity, and the motivation to succeed and contribute to the campus community. Careful consideration is given to a student's high school record, types of courses taken, SAT or ACT scores (if applicable), letters of recommendation, extracurricular involvement, and the personal essay. Submitting standardized test scores to Hofstra is optional. Prospective students should visit hofstra.edu/testing policy for more information. The most competitive applicants will have followed a rigorous college preparatory curriculum and will have taken advantage of honors and advanced placement–level courses where appropriate. The Office of Admission prefers a high school curriculum that includes 4 years of English, 3 to 4 years of social studies, 2 to 3 years of foreign language, 3 years of mathematics (4 years for engineering applicants), and 3 years of science (4 years for engineering applicants). Campus visits are strongly recommended. Hofstra accepts applications from first-year, transfer, and international students.

Application and Information

For students whose first choice is Hofstra, there are two early action periods: (1) When an application is submitted by November 15, notification is made to the student by December 15; and (2) When an application is submitted by December 15, notification is made to the student by January 15. Students applying for regular decision are considered on a rolling basis.

First-year applicants must submit an application, $70 application fee, high school transcript, SAT or ACT scores (if applicable), essay, and letter of recommendation. Hofstra accepts applications via mail or online and participates in the Common Application.

For more information, contact:
Hofstra University
Office of Undergraduate Admission
100 Hofstra University
Hempstead, New York 11549-1000
Phone: 516-463-6700
Fax: 516-463-5100
E-mail: admission@hofstra.edu
Website: http://www.hofstra.edu/admission

Hofstra students live and learn in the best of both worlds. Professors teach in traditional classroom settings, but lectures expand into the world beyond. With NYC only a 45-minute train ride away, students can immerse themselves in diverse cultural and entertainment activities, while applying what they learn in the classroom at internships and co-op programs.

HOLY NAMES UNIVERSITY

OAKLAND, CALIFORNIA

HOLY NAMES UNIVERSITY
Since 1868

COLLEGE CLOSE-UPS

The University

Founded in 1868, Holy Names University (HNU) empowers a diverse student body for leadership and service through liberal arts and professional education. It consistently ranks as one of the most diverse universities in the nation, and it receives the highest accreditation from the Western Association of Schools and Colleges.

Roughly 1,000 students have access to 15 bachelor's degrees, seven master's degrees, and four degree-completion programs. Small class sizes, dedicated teachers, personal attention, and a social-justice focus prepare students for leadership roles in service to their communities.

Location

Holy Names University is situated on 60 wooded acres in the hills of Oakland, California. Its location offers a spectacular view of Oakland, San Francisco, and the Bay. The area's coastal climate provides temperate winters; clear, sunny fall and spring days; and sunny, breezy summers. The University's location amongst the hills provides a safe, beautiful, tranquil place to learn. Parks that surround the campus provide outdoor recreation like bicycling, hiking, and horseback riding.

HNU's close proximity to Oakland, Berkeley, and San Francisco provides easy access to urban amenities like museums, performing arts, and professional sporting events. Attractions like Carmel, Lake Tahoe, Monterey Bay, and Yosemite National Park are within driving distance.

Majors and Degrees

Holy Names University is comprised of four schools, each of which offers the following programs of study:

The School of Arts and Sciences: biology, community health sciences (B.S.), kinesiology (B.A. and B.S.), communication studies, and a self-designed major (may be across schools) with concentrations in diversity studies, English literature, Latin American and Latinx studies, digital arts, music, philosophy, religious studies, and writing for professionals.

The School of Nursing and Health Professions: nursing (post-licensure, RN to B.S.N.), and nursing (pre-licensure, generic B.S.N.).

The School of Education: liberal studies (B.A.).

The School of Business and Applied Social Sciences: accounting (B.S.); business (B.A.) with the following emphases: finance, international business, management, marketing, or sports management; criminology; international relations; politics and history; psychobiology; and sociology.

Academic Programs

The Connections Project First-Year Experience program is designed to help first-year students connect with the HNU community in meaningful ways that will support their social and academic transition into college life, including learning how to learn; learning how to serve; and learning how to lead.

Providing students with comprehensive support, the staff and departments in the Advising and Learning Resources area assist with academic planning, tutoring and other learning supports, and disability services. The University strives to provide a wide range of resources for academic success and to work with students to identify and achieve their academic goals.

HNU's Center for Social Justice and Civic Engagement has the goal of aligning educational actions with institutional mission. The work of the Center has been recognized as enriching the understanding of social issues through personal exploration and socially responsible leadership at the University and within the local and global community.

Off-Campus Programs

HNU's Center for Social Justice and Civic Engagement organizes the following student trips each year:

- HNU students and staff participate in the annual School of the Americas Watch Vigil and Protest, representing the HNU community in Nogales, Arizona. The delegation participates in activities to promote justice and peace, and to bring awareness to immigration policies.
- HNU students travel with faculty and staff to Tutwiler, Mississippi, to work with Habitat for Humanity to build a home for a community resident. Students also visit several civil rights landmarks throughout the South, including the National Civil Rights Museum at the Lorraine Motel in Memphis, Tennessee, where Dr. Martin Luther King Jr. was assassinated.

Costs

For the 2019–20 academic year, full-time undergraduate tuition totals $39,576 with a campus fee of $526 per year. Residence hall room rates range from $6,638 to $10,204 per year and meal plans cost up to $6,570 per year, depending on the options selected.

Financial Aid

Holy Names University is one of the most affordable private universities in the San Francisco Bay Area. In fact, nearly all incoming freshman and day transfer students receive University grants and/or scholarships such as the following: Holy Names University Grants, athletic scholarships, Catholic High Schools scholarship, merit scholarships, and the Sister Marie Rose Durocher Scholarship.

Many undergraduate students also qualify for one or more of these financial aid resources: Cal Grant A & B (California state grants), Federal Pell Grant, Federal Direct Subsidized Stafford Loans, Federal Direct Unsubsidized Stafford Loans, Federal Parent Plus Loans, Federal Perkins Loans, private loans, and student employment.

Faculty

Holy Names University's faculty is highly qualified; 90 percent of full-time faculty members have the highest possible degree in their field. A low 13:1 student-faculty ratio facilitates interaction and involvement with students.

Faculty members bring unique experiences and perspectives to their classrooms. For example, students learn about Central America's history from a professor who grew up in El Salvador. They learn accounting and marketing strategies from a professor who's also a Certified Public Accountant and former entrepreneur.

Student Life

Holy Names is a close-knit community where students build meaningful partnerships with faculty members. On-campus housing gives them the opportunity to create friendships and build strong ties with fellow students from diverse backgrounds and origins.

One of HNU's assets is its diversity. The student population is 67 percent female and 33 percent male; 34 percent are first-generation college students. The student body is 43.3 percent Hispanic, 18.4 percent black, 18.1 percent white, 8.6 percent Asian, 3.4 percent international, 1.9 percent Native Hawaiian/Pacific islander, and .2 percent American Indian or Alaskan.

Residential living also provides easy access to opportunities that enable students to express their creativity, have fun, help others, and take on leadership roles. Students can enjoy a wide range of activities—these are just a few options:

- Attend events like carnivals, dances, and intercollegiate athletic games (Holy Names is NCAA Division II)
- Become peer mentors
- Engage in spiritual growth through the Campus Ministry
- Join or start a student club and organizations, such as the HNU Black Student Union, Dance Force, Freaks and Geeks, and Latinos Unidos
- Participate in student government
- Pursue social justice work through the Center for Social Justice and Civic Engagement

Admission Requirements

First-year applicants are considered for admission based on the overall strength of their high school preparation, SAT or ACT scores (SAT code is 4059 and ACT code is 0230), extracurricular activities, and individual talents and achievements from either a state-accredited high school of the completion of the equivalent of a high school education and other documentation as required.

Application and Information

Applications are accepted for both fall and spring semesters on a rolling basis. Eligible incoming freshman students who complete the Application for Admission by the March 2 priority deadline will be automatically awarded scholarships based on academic merit.

All applicants are strongly encouraged to complete the Free Application for Federal Student Aid (FAFSA) by the March 2 priority deadline. In addition, California residents should submit a GPA Verification Form to the California Student Aid Commission by March 2, the deadline for Cal Grant eligibility.

There is no fee to apply online or with a paper application. Undergraduate applicants can also apply through The Common Application.

For additional information, prospective students should contact:
Holy Names University
Office of Undergraduate Admission
3500 Mountain Boulevard
Oakland, California 94619
Phone: 510-436-1351
Fax: 510-436-1325
E-mail: admissions@hnu.edu
Website: https://www.hnu.edu

Holy Names University's location in the Oakland Hills provides wonderful views of the San Francisco Bay and infinite opportunities for personal and career development.

JOHN CABOT UNIVERSITY

ROME, ITALY

The University

John Cabot University (JCU) was founded in 1972 and is the first overseas American university in Italy with regional accreditation by the Middle States Commission on Higher Education. JCU is a liberal arts university following the American system of education but with a distinctive European and international character. Located in the historic center of Rome, the University has unparalleled access to history, culture, and the active international communities associated with the United Nations organizations and embassies present in the city. With a commitment to a serious liberal arts education and a unique relationship with leading multinational corporations, media, and other cultural and international organizations, JCU provides students with the academic training and opportunities to participate in exclusive internships that will allow them to enter directly into challenging careers after graduation, or to continue their studies at prestigious graduate programs.

The University has a diverse and unique student body, comprised of American, Italian, and international students from more than seventy countries. This group is complemented by visiting American students from universities across the United States. The visiting students bring their own regional diversity, which enhances the international environment at JCU, resulting in a dynamic and engaging student body. JCU's commitment to creating a student community of both degree-seeking and visiting students results in the friendly, close community of a small campus, with the wide-ranging networks that come from studying with a large pool of students from across the United States.

The average class size is 15 students, and there are approximately 100 full- and part-time faculty members with advanced degrees from prestigious universities all over the world. Students work closely with professors and receive the individual attention needed to develop their academic abilities. JCU graduates are accepted into acclaimed graduate programs in the United States, the United Kingdom, and Europe, such as Columbia University, Johns Hopkins University, London School of Economics, and the University of Oxford.

The University is licensed by the Delaware Department of Education to award its degrees and is authorized by the Italian Ministry of Research and Instruction to operate as an institution of American higher education in Rome. John Cabot University was accredited in 2003 by the Middle States Commission on Higher Education (http://www.msche.org).

Location

John Cabot University is located in Rome, Italy, in the picturesque Trastevere neighborhood, just down the river from the Vatican; across the river from Piazza Navona, the Pantheon, and the Spanish Steps; and a short walk from the Colosseum and Roman Forum. The University has three campuses within a 15-minute walk of each other and student residences with 24/7 security close to campus. The Guarini Campus consists of a main building with three floors and an adjacent wing connected by terraces and courtyards. The property offers students a quiet atmosphere in which to study and interact, while historic, bustling Rome is just a few steps away. Surrounded by the gardens of the Accademia dei Lincei (the National Academy of Sciences, of which Galileo was an early member) and the Villa Farnesina of Raphael's famous frescoes, the Guarini Campus is buttressed by the Aurelian Wall of the Roman Empire. The Guarini Campus is approached through the Porta Settimiana, which was built in the third century and later rebuilt by Pope Alexander VI Borgia in 1498. JCU also has spacious classrooms, a cafeteria, and the Student Services office in the Tiber Campus, which is located along the banks of the Tiber River. JCU's Critelli Campus, also along the Tiber River, was opened in 2018 and houses administrative offices as well as classrooms. All three campuses are equipped with WiFi, and classrooms are furnished with multimedia equipment. JCU's fine arts and art history classes often meet at famous monuments such as the Colosseum and the Forum. In essence, all of Rome is John Cabot University's campus, and students take advantage of JCU's urban setting, meeting with friends and faculty at local cafés as well as in many of the piazzas that are tucked away within the streets of Rome's historic center.

Majors and Degrees

John Cabot University offers the Bachelor of Arts degree in thirteen majors: art history, business administration, classical studies, communications, economics and finance, English literature, history, humanistic studies, international affairs, international business, Italian studies, marketing, and political science. JCU also offers a joint degree in communications with the University of Milan, as well as a dual degree in marketing with Pace University in New York City. Students may select minors in all of the major areas except international business, as well as in creative writing, entrepreneurship, philosophy, and psychology. John Cabot offers the Associate of Arts degree in all major fields of study. JCU also introduced a Master's degree in Art History in 2017, the first U.S.-accredited graduate degree program in art history based entirely in Rome.

Each of these programs is designed to offer a unique learning and living experience in a setting rich in history, culture, and geopolitical interaction. All majors are complemented by internship opportunities at the United Nations, museums, and international firms in Rome. JCU's Career Services Center offers support for students' preparation and transition into post-graduate activities, with 580 internship and job opportunities each year. JCU's 10,000-member alumni network spans 110 countries and includes business leaders, politicians, diplomats, artists, scholars, and entrepreneurs, providing additional opportunities for graduates to continue their career development through international connections.

Academic Programs

The American higher education system encourages experimentation and breadth, particularly during the first two years of the university experience. The curricula of the University's programs are divided into two basic categories: the general distribution requirements of the first two years of study, which give the student a broad exposure to the basic disciplines of the liberal arts educational experience, and the specific requirements of each degree awarded by the University.

The general distribution requirements and other introductory courses equip the student to select an area of specialization as a degree candidate. The degree requirements include ten to twelve core courses deemed by faculty members to be essential to the discipline of the degree. Other requisites include electives that support the core program and allow the student to take courses in other discipline areas of particular interest.

The academic year is divided into two semesters of fifteen weeks each, beginning in late August and mid-January. In one semester, a student normally takes five courses, earning 15 credits in the semester and 30 credits in the year. Two 5-week summer sessions allow students to take one or two additional courses per summer session. To earn the Bachelor of Arts degree, a student must complete 120 credits (forty courses); to earn the Associate of Arts degree, a student must complete 60 credits (twenty courses).

JCU accepts up to 60 transfer credits, including the IB diploma, AP exams, UK A-Levels, and other college-level courses.

Special programs include English language preparation for university study (ENLUS) for non-native English speakers, after which students who successfully complete the program may transfer directly into one of JCU's degree programs.

Off-Campus Programs

The Going Global program at JCU offers degree-seeking students the opportunity to study at partner universities in the United States, Mexico, Europe, Africa, Asia, and the Middle East. This opportunity contributes to educational growth and cultural awareness, and helps prepare students for careers in international fields.

Academic Facilities

The Frohring Library provides the latest in online access to academic journals and indexes, and is the University center for research in support of the academic programs as well as a quiet place for study and pleasure reading. The University's four computer laboratories contain desktop computers (Macs and PCs) equipped with the latest software as well as printers and a full-color scanner. The University is equipped with high-speed WiFi across campus, a studio art facility, a fitness center, a cafeteria, and a digital media lab.

Costs

Tuition for 2019–20 is $24,900 and housing costs begin at $4,900 per semester.

Financial Aid

U.S. citizens and eligible non-citizens attending John Cabot University may apply for Title IV Federal Student Aid, including Federal Direct Subsidized, Unsubsidized, and Parent Loans for Undergraduate Students(PLUS). Academic scholarships are awarded by the University each year, based on merit and need; they include the Presidential Scholarship, the Italian Merit Scholarship, the Expansion Scholarship for Latin American students, the Dean's List Scholarship, and the assistance grant. JCU certifies enrollment for U.S. veterans and their dependents studying on the Post-9/11 GI Bill.

Faculty

The University has a distinguished faculty of professors from around the world who are actively engaged in research. In addition to teaching, faculty members take part in academic advising and co-curricular activities, such as field trips, lectures, and seminars.

Student Government

Student Government at JCU contributes significantly to the quality of student life. A Student Senate is elected each year to represent students' interests, acting as a link between students, faculty, and staff. The Student Government works with a faculty adviser in planning social, cultural, intellectual, and sports activities to respond to students' interests and needs.

Admission Requirements

Successful applicants must have a scholastic record demonstrating a commitment to their studies and the ability to succeed at college-level work.

The previous school's documentation of the applicant's academic ability, motivation, character, and contribution to school life is very important. The University does not prescribe a fixed secondary school course of study but considers both the quality and breadth of the student's record. Results of the SAT or the ACT are required for high school students graduating from an American secondary school.

The University is open to all applicants without regard to race, national origin, religion, or gender.

For applicants coming from the U.S. secondary school system, a standard college-preparatory program is expected. For applicants from other national systems, an essential requirement is successful completion of a secondary school program permitting university admission in the respective system. Students holding the Italian Diploma di Maturità, the International Baccalaureate, or other equivalent academic credentials may be granted advanced standing.

Applicants who did not attend an English-language secondary school or university for at least two years must demonstrate sufficient preparation in the English language. Standardized test scores, such as the Test of English as a Foreign Language (TOEFL) or the International English Language Testing System (IELTS), are required.

Application and Information

Admissions decisions are based on the review of official transcripts, results of standardized tests, the student's GPA, final examination results, a personal statement, an interview, and letters of recommendation from teachers or school counselors. A completed application must be accompanied by a nonrefundable application fee of $50. Students may complete the application online or apply through the Common Application. The University has four application deadlines for fall: November 15 (Early Action), March 1 (Regular Decision), June 1 (Late Decision), and July 31 (Late Decision II, only available to students who do not require a study visa). The spring application deadlines are October 15 (Regular Decision), November 15 (Late Decision), and December 15 (Late Decision II, only available to students who do not require a study visa). Candidates are urged to submit their application and supporting documents as early as possible, as greater scholarship funds may be available.

Students may apply online at https://netcommunity.johncabot.edu/application#.

For additional information, prospective students should contact:

Admissions Office
John Cabot University
Caroline Critelli Guarini Campus
P.zza Giuseppe Gioachino Belli, 11
00153 Rome
Italy
Phone: 855-JCU ROMA (toll free)
E-mail: admissions@johncabot.edu
Website: http://www.johncabot.edu
https://www.facebook.com/JohnCabotUniversity
http://twitter.com/JohnCabotRome
http://instagram.com/johncabotuniversity

John Cabot University is located in the picturesque Trastevere neighborhood, just down the river from the Vatican, and a short walk from the Colosseum and Roman Forum.

JOHNS HOPKINS UNIVERSITY
Krieger School of Arts and Sciences and Whiting School of Engineering
BALTIMORE, MARYLAND

JOHNS HOPKINS UNIVERSITY

COLLEGE CLOSE-UPS

The University

As America's first research institution, Johns Hopkins University is well known for innovative advances in everything from technology to history and sociology. The university emphasizes the importance of exploration and discovery in the undergraduate experience. Learning occurs through hands-on experiences across all academic disciplines and within every subject imaginable. The academic experience is built around freedom, which allows students to create their own unique interdisciplinary paths. They choose classes they are genuinely interested in, not just required to take, so there's a real sense of curiosity around learning that extends beyond the classroom setting.

Collaborative learning is fundamental to the academic culture and cross-disciplinary partnerships occur between students of all academic areas. Hopkins professors, another invaluable resource, are enthusiastic about teaching and often include undergraduates in their own groundbreaking research. Students get to know their professors and classmates the way they would at a small liberal arts college but have all of the opportunities of a major research institution with a global reach. As a part of this community, undergraduates not only work alongside experts who share their interests but they also run with projects of their own design. In fact, the university remains a national leader of research funding and students in all programs within the Krieger School of Arts & Sciences and Whiting School of Engineering gain practical experiences through research conducted both on and off campus. Every day, faculty and students together create meaningful contributions to academic discourse and make important discoveries. Almost 75 percent of students across all disciplines participate in research, which takes place in labs, museums, and unconventional places throughout campus and the city of Baltimore.

The Homewood campus brings together students with varied interests. Diversity of thought, culture, and experiences cultivates a dynamic, open-minded environment. With over 300 student-run organizations, students find leadership opportunities and the chance to get involved on campus and in their local and global communities.

Location

Located in Baltimore, Maryland, the undergraduate Homewood campus is a traditional college campus with all the advantages of a major city just beyond its front gates. The 140-acre campus, featuring grassy quads and brick buildings, is surrounded by residential areas and neighborhoods that boast one-of-a-kind boutiques, restaurants, historic theaters, and a thriving arts and entertainment district. Baltimore's cultural and networking resources make it an extension of the classroom and an integral part of a Hopkins education. The experiences Hopkins students find in Baltimore create lasting memories and offer preparation for future success in a wide variety of industries. An entrepreneurial hub, Baltimore is the ideal environment to build professional networks, access coveted internships and careers, and get startups off the ground. Undergrads intern at major corporations, government agencies, and nonprofits and make lasting connections with help from the broader Hopkins network. Hopkins students also embrace the University's long-standing commitment to Baltimore and use their skills to make an impact on the city that becomes their second home.

Majors and Degrees

Academics at Hopkins are interdisciplinary and collaboration is encouraged—between students and faculty and across disciplines. The majority of programs combine different areas of study to enable students to make connections across academic boundaries and discover new interests. This establishes a dynamic, engaging learning environment where students from various backgrounds bring an array of perspectives to class discussions. More than 60 percent of Hopkins students pursue a double major or minor, often creating unique combinations like electrical engineering and romance languages or biomedical engineering and business. The full list of majors and minors can be found online at apply.jhu.edu/majors.

Academic Programs

Undergraduates in all programs in the Krieger School of Arts & Sciences and Whiting School of Engineering gain practical experience through innovative research. Several funded programs, such as the Provost's Undergraduate Research Award and the Woodrow Wilson Undergraduate Research Fellowship, are available to give participants the chance to complete projects of their own design. Students also encounter real-world experiences—like implementing marketing plans for local companies and heading startup businesses on campus through the Center for Leadership Education—as well as classes in business, marketing, and communications, accounting and financial management, and entrepreneurship and management. Students can pursue their creative interests through the Center for Visual Arts, which offers nearly 40 studio courses and state-of-the-art equipment for student use.

Students interested in pursuing law or medicine choose any major/minor combination but follow a pre-law or pre-med advising track offered through the Office of Pre-Professional Advising. The biomedical engineering (BME) program at Johns Hopkins, widely regarded as one of the best in the world, is the only undergraduate limited-enrollment major.

Several combined programs are available for undergraduates who want to broaden their educational experience. The Peabody Double Degree Program allows qualified students to simultaneously earn a bachelor of music from the Johns Hopkins Peabody Institute and a B.A or B.S. from Johns Hopkins University. The Direct Matriculation Programs: Master's in International Studies and Master's in Global Health Studies, allow qualified students displaying a strong interest in either area to pursue a combined bachelor's/master's degree with the Johns Hopkins School of Advanced International Studies (SAIS) or the Johns Hopkins Bloomberg School of Public Health. The University also offers the Army ROTC program on campus and the Air Force ROTC program in cooperation with the University of Maryland, College Park.

Off-Campus Programs

Off campus, the city of Baltimore provides unique academic, cultural, and pre-professional experiences. Some classes partner with local organizations to give students practical experiences that complement classroom lectures—like engineering a "fish ladder" at Maryland's Bloede Dam or replicating ancient Greek pottery work at Baltimore Clayworks. Due to the vast network of Hopkins schools and facilities that extends throughout Baltimore (and abroad), undergraduates have the chance to take courses and participate in research at the other renowned divisions of Johns Hopkins University, including the Peabody Conservatory, the School of Nursing, the Bloomberg School of Public Health, the Nitze School of Advanced International Studies, the School of Education, the Carey Business School, and the School of Medicine. In addition to local programs and opportunities, each year more than 500 students study abroad in nearly 30 countries all over the globe. The University also participates in a cooperative program with other colleges in the Baltimore area, such as the Maryland Institute College of Art (MICA), which Hopkins partnered with to open the Johns Hopkins–MICA Film Centre.

Academic Facilities

Collaborative learning is fundamental to the academic environment and many of the newest buildings were designed to foster collaboration across disciplines. Brody Learning Commons (BLC) is one of the most popular places for students to gather, study, and work together. Designed with student input, the building is directly connected to the library and contains the latest learning technology—like interactive projectors that allow students to write on walls and video teleconferencing capabilities—in an eco-friendly, energy-efficient space. The Undergraduate Teaching Labs (UTL), a 105,000-square-foot facility equipped with the latest lab technology, enables synergistic, cross-disciplinary partnerships and research opportunities. Malone Hall was built in 2014 and is a hub for the computer science department, where faculty and students work on innovative projects. The Milton S. Eisenhower Library on the Homewood campus is part of the University's Sheridan Libraries, which comprise the Milton S. Eisenhower Library (including the rare books collection), the John Work Garrett Library, the Albert D. Hutzler Undergraduate Reading Room, and the George Peabody Library. Together, these libraries provide one of the most comprehensive learning resources in the world. Two on-campus creative centers provide resources for students in the arts: the Mattin Student Arts Center contains theaters, a dance studio, music practice rooms, film and digital labs, darkrooms, and art studios; the Brown Foundation Digital Media Center offers digital tools like high-end computers and cameras that enable digital and audio composition and editing, animation, virtual painting, 3-D modeling, and workshops for programs like Adobe After Effects. Off campus, just a short shuttle ride away, the JHU Technology Ventures office allows student entrepreneurs to collaborate, strategize, and get their ideas off the ground.

Costs

Costs for 2018–19 were $53,740 for tuition and $15,836 for room and meals, plus personal expenses like books and travel. (Expenses such as travel and room and meals vary based on choices.)

Financial Aid

A landmark gift by Michael R. Bloomberg '64 reflects the university's mission by supporting need-blind admissions and meeting 100% of demonstrated need with no-loan financial aid packages. Students who are primed to thrive on a campus where diversity of thought drives our academic culture shouldn't be limited by their family's ability to pay. With the potential to graduate debt-free, equipped with an education that opens doors, our students have the freedom to boldly explore ways to apply their knowledge and talents. More details, including financial aid application requirements and deadlines and net price calculator tools, are available online at finaid.jhu.edu.

Faculty

As a global research university, Johns Hopkins attracts esteemed faculty. Hopkins professors are world-class scholars and experts in their fields who are constantly making important contributions to their industries and academia at large. They've accomplished impressive feats such as placing 100 percent of their class in finance jobs, winning Nobel Prizes, making scientific breakthroughs, leading global initiatives, and being granted awards for decades-long research studies. They're enthusiastic about teaching, often including undergraduates in their own groundbreaking research, and are always accessible to advise and assist students. Faculty are readily available to students and it's not unusual to brainstorm research ideas over coffee or debate philosophical theories during office hours.

Admission Requirements

Johns Hopkins seeks students who are eager to take advantage of the resources and opportunities at the University and who will contribute to the campus community. The student's academic character, intellectual curiosity, impact and initiative, and extracurricular involvement play a significant role in application review. A student's intellectual interests and accomplishments are of primary importance, and the admissions committee considers each applicant's scholastic record, standardized test results, essays, and recommendations from secondary school officials. In addition to the application and the Hopkins supplement, including a school-specific essay, other required documents include: two teacher recommendations, the secondary school report, and scores on the SAT or the ACT. The University enrolls a first-year class of approximately 1,300 men and women from across the globe. In addition, transfer students from other colleges and universities are admitted to the sophomore and junior classes. Prospective students should refer to apply.jhu.edu/apply for more information about the application process.

Application and Information

Johns Hopkins accepts the Coalition Application, the Common Application, and the Universal College Application, all with a Johns Hopkins supplement. Students who are certain Johns Hopkins is the place for them should consider applying under the Early Decision plan. This requires that the application be submitted by November 1. The deadline for the Regular Decision application is usually January 1. (Note: Deadlines can vary slightly from year to year; see apply.jhu.edu/apply for specific dates.) Notification is given by April 1 for Regular Decision students and by December 15 for those applying under the Early Decision plan. Students wishing to enroll in the biomedical engineering (BME) program must indicate BME as their first choice major on their application. Students applying to the Direct Matriculation Program: Master's in International Studies or Direct Matriculation Program: Master's in Global Health Studies (DMP) must submit an additional application and essay to be considered. First-year students who apply to the BME major or Direct Matriculation Program receive notification at the time of their admission to Johns Hopkins University. Students interested in pursuing a research project of their own design can also apply to the Woodrow Wilson Undergraduate Research Fellowship, which awards up to $10,000 to arts and sciences undergraduates. The Wilson Fellowship application deadline is in January and the date varies slightly from year to year.

Office of Undergraduate Admissions
Johns Hopkins University
Mason Hall
3400 N. Charles Street
Baltimore, Maryland 21218-2683
Phone: 410-516-8171
Fax: 410-516-6025
E-mail: gotojhu@jhu.edu
Website: http://apply.jhu.edu

Johns Hopkins undergrads walking to class on the Homewood campus.

LINFIELD COLLEGE

McMINNVILLE, OREGON

Linfield College

The College

Linfield College (1858) is an independent, coeducational, residential, comprehensive liberal arts and sciences college dedicated to providing an educational environment conducive to learning and participation. There are 1,500 full-time students on the McMinnville campus. These students come primarily from the thirteen Western states (twenty-one states overall) but also from twenty-four other countries. Students of color make up 35 percent of the student body, and 4 percent of students are international. Most students are between 18 and 22. Linfield is primarily residential, with seventeen residence halls, each accommodating between 10 and 100 residents. Each hall establishes its own calendar of social, educational, and recreational events throughout the year. Students who reside on campus eat their meals in the College dining hall. Houses and apartments are available for upper-division students. Social clubs, professional organizations, four sororities and four fraternities, service clubs, and almost forty other organizations, including a new marching band, play an important role in the daily life of a Linfield student. Linfield's winning athletics tradition fosters participation at all levels of competition. Women compete in intercollegiate basketball, cross-country, golf, lacrosse, soccer, softball, swimming, tennis, track and field, and volleyball. Men compete in intercollegiate baseball, basketball, cross-country, football, golf, soccer, swimming, tennis, and track and field. Linfield also has an extensive and active year-round intramural program.

Linfield hosts the Oregon Nobel Laureate Symposium, one of five such symposiums worldwide. At each symposium, several Nobel laureates come to share their backgrounds and expertise within the context of a basic theme.

The Linfield–Good Samaritan School of Nursing, an academic unit of the College at its Portland campus, prepares students for careers in nursing. This campus, at the Good Samaritan Hospital and Medical Center, has residence facilities, food service options, and a residence life program. In 2006, the Portland campus programs became open only to transfer admission.

Location

Located in McMinnville, 40 miles southwest of Portland, Linfield College is a leader in the cultural, educational, and recreational events of the fast-growing community of 35,000. Linfield is situated on 189 acres with most classrooms no more than a 10-minute walk from any of the twenty-four on-campus apartment buildings and residence halls. With most students living on campus, Linfield offers a welcoming and lively community.

Coffeehouses, cinemas, boutiques, a community theater, the Evergreen Air and Space Museum (including an IMAX theater and water park), bowling alleys, and a wide variety of restaurants are within walking distance for Linfield students. The central Oregon coast is an hour to the west, and the outdoor activity areas of the Oregon Cascade Range, including year-round skiing at Mount Hood, are two hours to the east. Salem, the state capital of Oregon, is 25 miles to the southeast, and Eugene is 80 miles south. Rainfall in western Oregon averages 42 inches annually and the winter temperature averages 41°F.

Majors and Degrees

Linfield offers the Bachelor of Arts degree in communication arts, creative writing, Francophone African Studies, French studies, German, German studies, global cultural studies, history, intercultural communication, international relations, Japanese, Japanese studies, journalism and media studies, Latin American/Latino studies, literature, music, philosophy, political science, religious studies, Spanish, studio art, and theater arts. The Bachelor of Arts or Bachelor of Science degree is offered in accounting, anthropology, applied physics, biochemistry and molecular biology, biology, chemistry, computing science, digital arts, economics, elementary education, environmental studies, exercise science, finance, health education, international business, management, marketing, mathematics, physical activity and fitness studies, physical education, physics, psychology, sociology, sport management and wine studies. A Bachelor of Science in Nursing (B.S.N.) is also available. The College has programs to prepare students for advanced study in any health profession, including medicine, as well as law. The education department offers a strong program of teacher certification at the secondary and elementary levels.

Academic Programs

The academic year is divided into two 15-week semesters (fall and spring) and a four-week winter term in January. The January Term offers regular departmental courses and off-campus and international study. Academic courses are assigned 1–5 semester credit hours each; 125 credits are required for a B.A. or a B.S. degree. Students divide their time equally among required general education courses, a major area of study, and elective subjects. The Linfield Curriculum courses, selected to provide a solid foundation in the liberal arts, require students to take 3 semester hours in each of the six Modes of Inquiry as well as one upper-division course in one of these areas. These Modes of Inquiry are as follows: Vital Past; Ultimate Questions; Individuals, Systems, and Societies; Natural World; Creative Studies; and Quantitative Reasoning. In addition, students are required to take a writing-intensive course, a course addressing global pluralisms, and a course dealing with United States pluralism. Individually designed majors are available with faculty approval. Students majoring in a foreign language spend an academic year in a country in which the language being studied is the native tongue.

Through the college's English Language and Culture Program, Linfield offers courses designed to help international students whose native language is not English to achieve competence in academic and social English skills, so that they may work effectively in their undergraduate classes at Linfield.

Off-Campus Programs

Off-campus educational experiences include the Semester Abroad program, involving four months of study in Australia, Austria, Chile, China, Ecuador, England, France, Germany, Hong Kong, Ireland, Japan, Korea, New Zealand, Norway, and Spain. Transportation for the first round-trip is included in the cost of tuition, and most of these study programs cost the same as a semester on campus. January Term study-abroad programs for four weeks are also offered. Recent offerings included Health Care in Kenya; China's Solutions to Energy Issues in the Twenty-first Century; Art and Visual Culture of Catalonia, Spain; and Australia: From Colony to Asian Power.

Academic Facilities

In recent years, the College has opened two residence halls, six apartment buildings, the James F. Miller Fine Arts Center, the Marshall Theatre and communication arts facility, the Vivian A. Bull Center for Music, and the Nicholson Library. The library covers 56,000 square feet and combines traditional collections of books and journals with the new and changing digital and electronic technology to provide access to the web and web-based designs. The studio theater has an audience seating capacity of up to 140 and includes space for set construction and design.

In 2011, Linfield reopened the former library to provide new classroom and office space for the departments of business, economics, English, and philosophy. This state-of-the-art facility, T. J. Day Hall, includes the College's writing center and the Program for Liberal Arts and Civic Engagement (PLACE). PLACE connects the Linfield student experience with civic discourse and real-world application. T. J. Day Hall is Linfield's first LEED-certified Gold building, underscoring the College's commitment to sustainability and conservation.

Murdock and Graf Halls house the biology, chemistry, and physics departments and up-to-date laboratories and equipment. Other facilities include art galleries and studios, a 250-watt FM radio station, an experimental psychology lab, dance and music studios, a preschool, and a 425-seat auditorium that houses a three-manual, 48-rank Casavant pipe organ.

Linfield students benefit from a communications and technology network that includes phone service, voice mail, e-mail, and wireless Internet connections in each residence hall room. In addition, there is wireless access in the library and all other areas of the campus.

The Health and Physical Education/Recreation Complex houses three gymnasiums; weight rooms; fitness laboratories with a hydrostatic weighing tank, a metabolic and pulmonary measuring system, and an electrocardiovascular exercise ECG system; an eight-lane, 25-yard indoor pool; handball and racquetball courts; classrooms; offices; and a 28,000-square-foot field house.

Costs

For 2018–19, tuition and fees were $42,700 per two-semester year, board was $5,590, and a double room was $6,830. There was a $255 per-credit fee for on-campus January Term classes.

Financial Aid

Eligibility for most of Linfield's assistance programs is based on need as determined by a federally approved needs analysis processor. The only form required for need-based programs is the Free Application for Federal Student Aid (FAFSA). Linfield participates in the federal grant, loan, and work programs, and other forms of financial assistance on the basis of demonstrated need.

The College awards scholarships to full-time students based on scholastic achievement, independent of financial need. These academic scholarships vary from 30 to 60 percent of tuition. A number of criteria are used when determining scholarships, including grade point average, strength of curriculum, and standardized test scores. Linfield sponsors special scholarships for National Merit finalists. The College also sponsors an annual Scholarship and Visit Weekend program in February. Participation is limited to high school seniors who meet particular academic requirements and apply by December 1. Each academic department offers prizes ranging from $12,000 to $20,000, divided over the student's four years at Linfield. Scholarships are also available to students from the departments of music, theater, and communication who demonstrate outstanding leadership and community service. Financial assistance for non–U.S. citizens is limited to partial-tuition scholarships and the opportunity to work part-time on campus.

Faculty

There are 129 faculty members, each of whom is committed to undergraduate teaching and scholarship. Ninety-five percent have doctoral or other terminal degrees within their field. The student-faculty ratio is 10:1, and faculty members serve as academic advisers. There are no teaching assistants.

Student Government

Students have a significant voice in establishing and changing College policies and regulations. The Student Senate, chosen through campus elections, is the focus of student opinion and debate. Students are represented on most College governing councils and committees with faculty members and trustees, and they are encouraged to express and implement their ideas on academic or extracurricular matters.

Admission Requirements

Admission to Linfield College is selective. Admission is granted to students who are likely to grow and succeed in a personal and challenging liberal arts environment. Each applicant is judged on individual merit, based on high school performance, a writing sample, recommendations from teachers and counselors, precollege standardized test results (ACT or SAT), and the depth and quality of an applicant's involvement in community and school activities. Linfield is a member of the Common Application Association. Students may opt to pursue Linfield's test optional admission process, as well.

International students whose education has been in a language other than English must submit certified English translations of their academic work. Proficiency in English is required, as demonstrated by an official TOEFL score report or other English proficiency exam.

Application and Information

The early action deadline is November 1 (with notification by January 15) and the regular decision priority deadline is February 1 (with notification by April 1).

Interviews are not required, but students are encouraged to visit. Appointments should be made in advance and can be requested online at http://www.linfield.edu/stopby. The Linfield website provides students with information on academic programs, student life, and athletics.

Interested students are encouraged to contact:

Office of Admission
Linfield College
900 SE Baker Street
McMinnville, Oregon 97128
Phone: 503-883-2213
800-640-2287 (toll-free)
Fax: 503-883-2472
E-mail: admission@linfield.edu
Website: http://www.linfield.edu/admission
https://www.facebook.com/LinfieldCollege/
https://twitter.com/linfieldcollege
https://www.instagram.com/linfieldcollege/

Linfield College is located 1 hour southwest of Portland, Oregon's largest city, on nearly 200 acres. Nearly sixty buildings, many built in Georgian colonial style, house forty academic departments among a grove of oak trees.

COLLEGE CLOSE-UPS

LOS ANGELES FILM SCHOOL
LOS ANGELES, CALIFORNIA

THE LOS ANGELES® FILM SCHOOL

The University

The mission of The Los Angeles Film School is to inspire students with an inventive method of education that concentrates on preparation for career opportunities in the entertainment industry. The school's curriculum integrates technical knowledge with artistic exploration and creativity, taught by a staff of passionate professionals. Education is delivered through reflective teaching methods and hands-on learning in the heart of Hollywood, the world's entertainment capital. Its programs are designed to immerse aspiring talent in industry practices and current technologies, enabling students to discover their individual voices through collaboration and realize their career goals in the entertainment industry.

In the spring of 1999, a group of Hollywood professionals with a love for all things film founded the School, with an official groundbreaking ceremony just a few months later. Acclaimed director, Oliver Stone, spoke at the School's dedication, followed by a professional stunt team free-falling off the school's roof.

The School offers career-focused, accredited Bachelor of Science and Associate of Science degrees both on campus and online. Students learn industry-current techniques from professionals whose credentials include Grammy awards, Oscar awards and work on films such as "The Kids Are Alright," "The Fighter," "The Lion King," and "Ice Age," as well as games like "Medal of Honor" and "Age of Empires." Students also learn while working with the industry-standard technology, including a fully-digital high-definition Dolby surround, RealD 3-D theater.

Los Angeles Film School graduates are making their marks in the entertainment industry. Recoding alumnus Ari Levine has been nominated for a total of nine Grammys, including Song of the Year, Record of the Year, Album of the Year, and Producer of the Year. Film grad Hannah Lux Davis is an award-winning music video director with directing credits Ariana Grande's hit singles including "Thank U, Next," "7 Rings," "Breathin," "Into You," and many more. In 2018, the Recording Academy honored Hannah Lux Davis as "Women Architects of Sound in Music." Other notable Film grads include Brandon Trost and Kyle Newachek who have credits for movies like "Can You Ever Forgive Me?", "The Disaster Artist," and "This is the End," and the TV shows "Workaholics" and "Community." Computer animation grads are experiencing career success with the creation of video games like "Jack Powers: Bane of the Shadow King," and for work on sci-fi movies including "Return of the Killer Shrews." A sampling of the School's computer animation graduate work can be found on the school's YouTube channel (https://www.youtube.com/user/losangelesfilmschool).

The Los Angeles Film School is a private educational institution granted approval to operate by the Bureau for Private Postsecondary Education under the California Private Postsecondary Education Act of 2009. It is accredited by the Accrediting Commission of Career Schools and Colleges (ACCSC, listed by the U.S. Department of Education a recognized accrediting agency).

The School is approved for Army, Air Force, Coast Guard, Marine Corps, and Navy and U.S. Government tuition assistance and is part of the Service members Opportunity College Consortium (SOCC).

Location

The campus of the Los Angeles Film School is in Hollywood, California, a city often recognized as "The Entertainment Capital of the World." The campus is built on sites rich with Hollywood entertainment history and spans several buildings that include animation labs, sound stages, recording studios, and more.

Los Angeles is the cultural, financial and commercial center of Southern California. L.A. is also billed as the "creative capital of the world," boasting the highest percentage of creative workers in the country—with more artists, writers, filmmakers, actors, dancers, and musicians living and working in metro L.A. than any other city.

Majors and Degrees

The Los Angeles Film School offers both on-campus and online programs.

Bachelor of Science degree programs offered on-campus include: film (with concentrations in production, cinematography, directing, or producing), animation (with concentrations in visual effects or game art), music production, audio production, and entertainment business.

Bachelor of Science degree programs available online include: animation (with concentrations in environment and character design or visual effects), digital filmmaking, entertainment business (with concentrations in music business or entertainment business), graphic design, and music production.

The School also offers Associate of Science degree programs in film, audio production, and music production.

Academic Programs

The keys to unlocking and managing a successful career in the entertainment industry are research, networking, preparation, professionalism, and the ability to stay current with industry practices and trends. The School's Career Development Department works in conjunction with students' education curricula to prepare them with interpersonal and professional skills, support their vocational goals, and help to bridge the gap between academia and the workplace.

The Los Angeles Film School has full-time, dedicated staff members available to facilitate local and long-distance transitions for enrolled and active students. A housing coordinator assists students in finding accommodations that fit a wide range of budgetary and lifestyle preferences, in addition to student roommate selection.

The School's International Student Center assists global students with admissions, enrollment, and securing a visa, and also provides tutoring, information about housing and the local area, and career assistance.

Online students have access to the School's Media Center, tech support, and career development.

Academic Facilities

Several buildings make up the School's Hollywood campus, most in close proximity to each other along the famous Sunset Boulevard. At 6363 Sunset is the historic RCA Building, which was once used as a recording studio by several legendary artists such as Elvis Presley,

The Rolling Stones and The Grateful Dead. It now houses everything from sound stages to a Dolby Digital movie theatre, which seats over 300 people.

At 6353 Sunset is the School's editing and animation labs and a fully-functional sound stage complete with green screen set among other exciting spaces. It's just steps away from iconic Hollywood landmarks such as the Walk of Fame, Capitol Records, and The Pantages Theatre.

The Los Angeles Recording School, a division of The Los Angeles Film School, was founded in 1985 as The Los Angeles Recording Workshop and is located at 6690 Sunset. This is where the School's audio and music students practice, learning a wide variety of recording skills in labs such as an SSL Duality Studio and Foley Suite.

The Ivar Theatre, a live venue hall, has been a Hollywood landmark since the 1950s and now hosts classes in live sound as well as concerts, film productions and student-produced performances.

Costs

Costs at the Los Angeles Film School vary based on the program of study and the academic year. For the 2018–19 academic year, costs for tuition, tech kit, textbooks, and technology fees for the Bachelor of Science programs ranged from $13,900 to $21,450. Living expenses (housing, utilities, food, transportation, travel, parking, and miscellaneous) are estimated at $24,000 per academic year.

Financial Aid

The Los Angeles Film School offers several student financial aid opportunities: Pell grants, Federal Supplement al Educational Opportunity Grants (FSEOG), the Direct Loan Program, the Federal Work-Study program, a variety of GI Bill programs, and a small number of institutional scholarships and grants.

All students who wish to receive federal or state funds must complete the Free Application for Federal Student Aid (FASFA). Students may be asked to submit documentation such as tax returns, birth certificates and Social Security cards, along with other items necessary to verify financial or dependency status. Students who do not wish to submit requested documentation will not receive a financial aid award. Students who are eligible for VA benefits may contact the School's military department (military@lafilm.edu) for a list of required documents or additional information. Students progressing to their second academic year of study (and every year thereafter) are notified two months before the new academic year that it is time to reapply for financial aid.

Faculty

The Los Angeles Film School's prime location provides access to many of the industry's top professionals. The faculty is a team of award-winning, experienced entertainment business veterans and highly qualified academic educators. Some members of the faculty teach between projects; others make the School their home base, creating a group of committed educators who are well-versed in current entertainment media development and production.

Student Activities

In addition to classes and hands-on learning, students at The Los Angeles Film School can take part in many fun, entertaining, and networking events throughout the year. The 340-seat, RealD 3-D theater attracts moviemakers from all over the world to screen their films. The School hosts exclusive screenings followed by Q&As with directors, screenwriters, producers, actors, and others. The Brain Lobby serves as an excellent gallery for student work during the annual Animation Smash for Animation students. In addition to screenings and film festivals, The Los Angeles Film School hosts on- and off-campus networking events.

Admission Requirements

The Los Angeles Film School seeks students who are serious about pursuing careers in the world of entertainment media. They must show dedication and commitment to the art. Prospective students are encouraged to visit the school and discuss their personal, educational, and occupational goals with the Office of Admissions.

The School has an open enrollment policy, with new start dates every four weeks. Enrollment is open to high school graduates, or equivalent, who are seriously interested in the field of professional filmmaking, animation and VFX, music production, audio production, graphic design, and entertainment business. Previous experience in these fields is not required for admission.

Application and information

The School's student success teams in the Admissions Department will guide students through the enrollment process. They are the main point of contact and are available to answer any questions that prospective students may have. They are also there to assist with the application process including getting students in touch with a financial aid adviser to help finance their education. After notification of acceptance, students should complete and submit the Free Application for Federal Student Aid (FAFSA) at fafsa.ed.gov.

Prospective students must submit an application for admission and pay the $75.00 application fee. To be eligible for admission, applicants must be a high school graduate or possess a recognized high school equivalency (GED or HiSET exam scores). An applicant to a bachelor's degree completion program must have an associate degree from a recognized accredited institution.

To meet admissions requirements, an applicant must provide documentation supporting one of the following: an official high school transcript or diploma or recognized equivalent, an official college transcript documenting completion of an associate degree from an accredited institution (for bachelor's degree completion program only), and must have the ability to read and write English at the level of a graduate of an American high school as demonstrated by the possession of a high school diploma, GED, or passage of the California high school proficiency exam.

The Los Angeles Film School
6363 Sunset Boulevard
Hollywood, California 90028
Phone: 888-688-5277 (toll-free)
877-952-3456 (toll-free, admissions)
323-860-0789
Website: https://go.lafilm.edu
https://www.youtube.com/user/losangelesfilmschool

LOYOLA UNIVERSITY MARYLAND

BALTIMORE, MARYLAND

LOYOLA
UNIVERSITY MARYLAND

The University

With just over 4,000 undergraduates from 39 states, more than 30 countries, and six continents, Loyola University Maryland is big enough to inspire and challenge students, and small enough for opportunities to be accessible to them. Loyola makes it easy for students to embrace new challenges, feel comfortable taking risks, and connect to the experiences and resources they need to develop as learners, leaders, and professionals. Our students feel called and confident in trying new activities, pursuing their talents, sharing their research, and asking bold questions. Surrounded by people from different backgrounds and with diverse interests, students are members of a student body that is sure to enrich their college experience.

At Loyola University Maryland, higher education is as much social, physical, and spiritual as it is intellectual. With more than 200 student-led clubs and organizations, collegiate and intramural athletics, service opportunities, lectures, concerts, and on-campus events, Greyhounds have a world of opportunity to get involved and pursue their passions—and even discover new ones. Loyola's offices of student engagement, student activities, and student life offer further opportunities throughout the year for students to get off campus and explore and experience Baltimore and beyond.

As a Jesuit, Catholic university, Loyola fosters a community rooted in spirituality that is integrated into daily life through experience, discernment, service, and the promotion of social justice. Our students serve on campus, in the local community, and around the globe with myriad programs and partnerships through the Center for Community Service and Justice. Regardless of religious beliefs and faith traditions, we invite all members of our community to grow in spirituality through daily Mass and prayer, faith-based student organizations, retreats, reflection, and interfaith dialogue.

Location

Loyola's beautiful Evergreen campus is in a residential area of North Baltimore, five miles from the city's Inner Harbor area. This location offers students the best of both worlds: the advantage of quiet residential living on 80 wooded acres that offer grassy quadrangles, Gothic-style buildings, nationally-ranked residence halls, and state-of-the-art classrooms and facilities—all within a few minutes of the attractions and amenities of city life. Make no mistake; with 120,000 students at 13 universities, Baltimore is very much a college town. The fourth-largest metropolitan area in the United States, Baltimore/Washington D.C. offers a wide variety of theaters, museums, professional and intercollegiate sports events, and historical points of interest.

Loyola attracts the types of students who are also attracted to Baltimore, people eager to shape their lives—and their city—according to their ideals. Whether you dream of forming your own tech startup, opening a craft brewery, or becoming a social activist in a region that's ripe for change, Baltimore is the ideal place to begin.

Majors and Degrees

Loyola offers more than 30 majors and more than 45 minors. The Bachelor of Arts degree is awarded in art history, classical civilization, classics, communication, comparative cultures and literary studies, computer science, economics, elementary education, English, fine arts, French, German, global studies, history, philosophy, political science, psychology, sociology, Spanish, speech-language-hearing sciences, theology, and writing. The Bachelor of Business Administration degree is awarded in accounting, business economics, finance, information systems, international business, management, and marketing. The Bachelor of Science degree is awarded in biology, chemistry, computer science, data science, engineering (with concentrations in mechanical, computer, electrical, and materials), forensic studies, mathematics, statistics, and physics.

Academic Programs

The curriculum at Loyola is divided into three parts: the core, the major, and electives. The core contains those courses that Loyola considers essential to the liberal arts curriculum. These courses, which are required of all students regardless of major, are completed throughout the four years. The core consists of a classical or modern language, English literature, writing, mathematics and natural science, social science, fine arts, history, philosophy, ethics, and theology. Majors enable students to pursue their specialized area of study in depth. Electives give students the opportunity to broaden their intellectual and cultural background in areas of special interest. To prepare for graduate study, students may enroll in one of three pre-professional programs: pre-health, pre-medical, or pre-law.

Messina, Loyola's first-year experience, is designed to help students adjust quickly to college life and to forge a clear path to success at Loyola and in the life and career that will follow. Messina offers a similarly distinctive and powerful beginning, an opportunity to explore a wide range of academic disciplines, appreciate their interconnectedness, and take to heart the importance of learning in a student's personal and intellectual growth.

Off-Campus Programs

Loyola University Maryland participates in a cooperative program with Notre Dame of Maryland University, Johns Hopkins University, Goucher College, Morgan State University, Towson University, the Peabody Conservatory of Music, Stevenson University, University of Maryland (Baltimore County), and the Maryland Institute College of Art. Loyola students may cross-register at any of these area colleges and universities.

Nearly two-thirds of students participate in Loyola's extensive study abroad program, which includes programs and exchanges taught in English, total immersion programs taught in the host country's native language, and combinations of the two. Students in good academic standing may pursue studies abroad through Loyola's programs in Accra, Ghana; Alcalá, Spain; Amsterdam, Netherlands; Athens, Greece; Auckland, New Zealand; Bangkok, Thailand; Beijing, China; Berlin, Germany; Budapest, Hungary; Cape Town, South Africa; Copenhagen, Denmark; Cork, Ireland; Dubai, United Arab Emirates; Glasgow, Scotland; Leuven, Belgium; Lyon, France; Madrid, Spain; Melbourne, Australia; Montpellier, France; Newcastle, England; Osaka, Japan; Paris, France; Rome, Italy; Santiago, Italy; and Singapore. Loyola also offers summer and winter study tours and assists students in applying to a variety of non-Loyola affiliated international study programs each year.

Academic Facilities

The Donnelly Science Center houses class laboratory spaces, research laboratories, offices, a conference room for the natural sciences, storage, a vivarium, a microscopy center, and a robotics laboratory. Spacious hallways connecting the building's wings on all levels include spaces for science displays and gathering areas for students and faculty in biology, chemistry, physics, computer science, and engineering.

The Sellinger School of Business and Management is Loyola's AACSB-accredited business school. Highlights of this school include experiential learning requirements, the Sellinger Scholars honors program, many student associations, and the Student Experiential Learning Lab, a state-of-the-art trading room that allows students access to the three most widely used databases in the finance industry—Reuters, Morningstar, and Bloomberg—and features a six-screen video display for breaking news and real-time market updates and a scrolling price ticker.

The DeChiaro College Center is home to the fine arts and communication departments. Loyola's music department is located on the ground floor, with soundproof private practice rooms, voice and piano lesson rooms, an electronic music studio, and instrument storage. Studio Arts and Photography are on the upper floors, with black-and-white and alternative-process darkrooms, a clay green room, and studio space for students. The Julio Art Gallery features rotating exhibits and regular talks by guest artists. McManus Theatre and Loyola's Black Box Theatre host student productions throughout the year. Other on-campus spaces include both painting and printmaking studios, digital laboratories, electronic music and podcasting studios, and Loyola's student-run radio and television station studios.

Costs

For 2019–20, tuition for all undergraduate students is $48,700 per year. Housing costs are $10,470 or $11,800, depending upon the specific residence hall in which the student lives. The base meal plan for first-year residential students is $4,240 per year and student fees are estimated at $1,400.

Financial Aid

Loyola maintains a strong commitment to helping make our high-quality Jesuit education affordable for all qualified students and their families. That's why more than 85 percent of undergraduate students receive some form of financial assistance from institutional, federal, state, and private sources. Students are required to submit the Free Application for Federal Student Aid (FAFSA) and the CSS Profile Application to be considered for need-based financial aid.

All applicants (first-year, transfer, and international) are eligible to receive merit-based scholarships, and every student who completes an application for admission is automatically considered for merit scholarships. You will be notified of your merit scholarship award at the time of admission.

Faculty

With a faculty-student ratio of approximately 12:1 and an average class size of 20, students are individually taught—and taught as individuals. Our 359 full-time faculty are committed teachers and advisors, scholars, and experts and in their fields; 70 percent are tenured or on the tenure track. Loyola professors push students to the limits of their intellect and imagination. Beyond academic rigor, the cornerstone of intellectual life at Loyola is relationships between faculty and students: relationships that help students discover strengths, that instill confidence—and that celebrate and champion achievement. Ask any Loyola graduate what made the difference in their academic journey, and they'll not only say it was their professors, but they'll likely name a name and share a story, a specific example, of a meaningful relationship with a faculty member who became a mentor.

Student Government

The Student Government serves three chief functions, which make its existence not only valuable but also necessary. These functions are to represent the student body outside the University, to provide leadership within the student body, and to perform services—both social and academic—for the students. Responsibility for budgeting activities also rests with the Student Government. The president of the Student Government is a member of the College Academic Council.

Admission Requirements

The admission evaluation at Loyola combines an analysis of academic information submitted along with a review of recommendations, the record of extracurricular involvement, and evidence of special talent, leadership, and service. The admission committee does not use a formula or have strict cutoffs. Instead, the admission office's goal is to conduct a balanced and holistic review, taking several factors into account. Submission of SAT and ACT scores is optional for all first-year applicants, excluding home-school students. Students who choose not to submit standardized test scores must submit an additional teacher letter of recommendation or personal essay. Students may apply early action (nonbinding) or regular decision (nonbinding).

Application and Information

Interested students seeking to enroll at Loyola may apply online using the Common Application. Each applicant must submit a school counselor letter of recommendation, a teacher letter of recommendation, and a personal statement. Applicants for financial aid must file the Free Application for Federal Student Aid (FAFSA) to be considered for federal student aid in addition to the CSS Profile application to be considered for all forms of institutionally funded need-based aid. A $60 application fee must accompany the application for admission.

For additional information, students are encouraged to contact:

Undergraduate Admission Office
Loyola University Maryland
4501 North Charles Street
Baltimore, Maryland 21210-2699
Phone: 410-617-5012
800-221-9107 (toll-free)
Website: http://www.loyola.edu/undergraduate
http://www.facebook.com/LoyolaMarylandAdmission
https://twitter.com/LOYOLAdmission
https://instagram.com/LOYOLAdmission

Loyola University Maryland has a vibrant and active student community. Whether you're looking for adventure, leadership, professional experiences, friendship, or the latest foodie trends, we're confident that Loyola has a place for you.

LUTHER COLLEGE
DECORAH, IOWA

The College

Luther College, founded in 1861 by Norwegian immigrants, is a four-year residential liberal arts college of the Lutheran church (ELCA). The College is an academic community of faith and learning where students of promise from all beliefs and backgrounds have the freedom to learn, to express themselves, to perform, to compete, and to grow. Located in Decorah, Iowa, the College is home to more than 2,005 students from 40 states and 74 countries. Twenty-seven percent of the students are from Iowa; 82 percent come from the four-state area of Iowa, Minnesota, Wisconsin, and Illinois. In 2018-19, 169 international students chose to study at Luther.

In keeping with its liberal arts tradition, the College requires students to develop a depth of knowledge in their chosen major and a breadth of knowledge through exposure to a wide range of subjects and intellectual approaches (general requirements). Learning at Luther is about engagement: faculty members who are passionate in their teaching and scholarship; students who are bright, active, and involved; and a College community characterized by personal attention, hands-on experiences, academic challenge, and community support. At Luther, all students become immersed in the liberal arts through the College's Paideia program. This program, which is uncommon in its approach, helps train students' minds and develop their research and writing skills as they explore human cultures and history. In addition, Luther offers a Phi Beta Kappa chapter and departmental honor societies, evidence of the quality of teaching and learning on campus.

At Luther, students are encouraged to seek out connections between their lives in the classroom and their lives outside the classroom. The College provides a stimulating cultural and educational atmosphere by bringing distinguished public figures, theatre groups, musicians, and educators to the campus. Cocurricular activities are an important part of college life. The College sponsors five choirs, three orchestras, three bands, two jazz bands, and a full visual and performing arts program. Numerous student organizations and societies provide ample opportunities for student involvement in meaningful activities. As a community of faith, students can participate in chapel, weekly Sunday worship, and outreach teams.

Nineteen intercollegiate sports are offered. Men compete in ten intercollegiate sports: baseball, basketball, cross-country, football, golf, soccer, swimming, tennis, track and field, and wrestling. Women compete in nine intercollegiate sports: basketball, cross-country, golf, soccer, softball, swimming, tennis, track and field, and volleyball. Club sports include Ultimate Frisbee and rugby. Seventy percent of the student body is involved in an extensive intramural and recreational sports program. Available for recreational use are twelve newly renovated tennis courts, an eight-lane polyurethane 400-meter track, numerous cross-country running and ski trails, and 15 acres of intramural fields. The well-equipped Regents Center houses four hardwood basketball courts, a wrestling complex, three racquetball courts, and a 3,000-seat gymnasium. A sports forum accommodates a six-lane, 200-meter indoor track; six indoor tennis courts; locker rooms; and athletic training facilities. The Legends Fitness for Life Center provides the latest fitness equipment and a 30-foot-high rock-climbing wall. Luther offers an aquatic center, which opened in 2013 and features an eight-lane stainless steel pool complete with diving well. Legacy Field, a brand new football field installed in 2017, features distinctive blue turf.

Location

The College is located in Decorah, a city of 8,000 people in the scenic bluff country of northeast Iowa. The Upper Iowa River, which runs through the campus, is designated as a National Scenic and Recreational River. Rich in Scandinavian heritage, Decorah is a popular recreation area, providing opportunities for canoeing, kayaking, fishing, hunting, cross-country skiing, camping, hiking, biking, and spelunking. Three airports are located within a 75-mile radius of Decorah: in Rochester, Minnesota; Waterloo, Iowa; and La Crosse, Wisconsin.

Majors and Degrees

Luther College grants the Bachelor of Arts (B.A.) degree and offers majors in accounting, Africana studies, allied health sciences, anthropology, art, Biblical languages, biology, chemistry, classics, communication studies, computer science, data science, economics, elementary education, English, environmental studies, exercise science, French, German, health promotion, history, international studies, management, mathematics, mathematics/statistics, music, neuroscience, Nordic studies, nursing, philosophy, physics, political science, psychology, religion, social work, sociology, Spanish, theatre, visual communication, and women and gender studies. Preprofessional preparation is offered in dentistry, engineering, law, medicine, optometry, pharmacy, physical therapy, seminary, and veterinary medicine.

Academic Programs

Luther operates on a 4-1-4 academic calendar. The first semester runs from September to December, followed by a three-week January Term, and the second semester, which runs from February to May. Two four-week summer sessions are offered in June and July. All students must complete at least 128 semester hours of credit, including two January-term courses in order to graduate from Luther. Other requirements for graduation include four common foundational courses: Paideia (111 and 112); foreign language (typically one or two courses); religion (two courses, one of which must be in Biblical studies); and wellness (two 1-credit courses). In addition to a focused area of study (the major, which usually requires eight to ten courses), Luther requires all students to take courses in three general fields of inquiry: the natural world (two courses); human behavior (two courses); and human expression (two courses). Before graduating, students are required to bring together all they have learned in two culminating experiences: senior project (one course); and Paideia 450. Luther students also develop the perspectives and skills they will utilize in their lives as citizens and professionals equipped for distinguished service. Qualified students may develop interdisciplinary majors with faculty advisers.

Off-Campus Programs

Luther operates under the belief that the best education connects students with global issues and helps them engage with the larger world. Luther is consistently ranked among the top baccalaureate colleges in the nation for the number of students studying abroad prior to graduation.

Luther's off-campus programs not only span the globe, but also offer in-depth and immersive study in a wide variety of subjects. Students may participate in programs during fall and spring semesters, the January Term, and summer sessions.

The College's signature off-campus programs include an academic-year program in Nottingham, England; a semester program in Sliema, Malta; a semester program in Münster, Germany; and a semester program in Coldigioco, Italy. In addition, Luther is part of a thirteen-college consortium which runs a successful Washington Semester in Washington, D.C. Students also have options for urban study at several centers in Chicago.

Each January Term, 300–400 Luther students study on eighteen to twenty-five faculty-led domestic and international programs.

Finally, Luther students have a wide variety of off-campus options through Luther-affiliated programs, such as those sponsored by the Institute for Study Abroad–Butler University, the Institute for the International Education of Students (IES), and International Studies Abroad (ISA), among others.

Academic Facilities

The 1,000-acre campus includes Preus Library, housing 340,812 volumes, over 800 print periodicals, 200,000 electronic books, and the College art collection. The library's circulation desk, research help desk, technology help desk, and Digital Media Center connect students with the resources they need. Two science teaching facilities, Sampson Hoffland Laboratories and Valders Hall of Science, feature modern, well-equipped labs as well as a planetarium, a greenhouse, an herbarium, a live-animal center, a human anatomy laboratory, a natural history museum, and a psychology sleep laboratory. Within easy walking distance of the campus, the field study area offers an ideal setting for studies in aquatic biology, ecology, and field biology. Five ponds, two reestablished prairies, marshes, wooded areas, and agricultural lands are available for classwork and independent study. The College has wired and wireless networking support throughout the campus. Residence halls, classrooms, and labs are outfitted with computers, printers, and academic software. Multiple connections to the Internet provide high bandwidth and reliable connectivity.

Luther College maintains radio station KWLC-AM, and the College's affiliate station, KLSE-FM, is part of the Minnesota Public Radio network. Luther is also home to one of the largest archaeological research centers in Iowa.

The Language Learning Center houses computer facilities and video screening rooms, as well as a foreign language media library with over 800 foreign language films, audio books, and print books for language learners.

The economics and business, mathematics, and computer science departments are located in Luther's high-tech, fully networked

F. W. Olin Building.

The award-winning Jenson-Noble Hall of Music contains 32,000 square feet of classrooms, studios, practice rooms, and rehearsal rooms for keyboard, vocal, and instrumental music. The Center for Faith and Life (CFL) houses a 42-stop/62-rank organ in the 1,600-seat auditorium for the performing arts. A 200-seat recital hall, a 24-hour meditation chapel, and one of four campus art galleries are located in the CFL as well. The Center for the Arts serves as the home for theatre, dance, and the visual arts.

Costs

For 2019-20, the comprehensive fee is $53,830, which includes tuition, room, board, a technology fee, subscription to student publications, and admission to Luther-supported concerts, lectures, and other events. A room telephone, cable TV, computer access from residence hall rooms, and a health-service program are also included. Private music lessons are $510 per semester. It is estimated that an additional $3,015 is adequate for books, clothing, entertainment, and other personal expenses.

Financial Aid

More than 98 percent of all Luther students receive financial aid in the form of grants, scholarships, low-interest loans, and work-study jobs on campus. Luther awards Founders, President's, and Dean's Scholarships to students demonstrating superior academic achievement. The amount of aid given is determined by an analysis of the Free Application for Federal Student Aid (FAFSA).

Faculty

There are 175 full-time faculty members; 95 percent hold a Ph.D., first professional, or other terminal degree. The student-faculty ratio is 11:1.

Student Government

Students share in the governance of the College and participate in social and cultural programming. They have full membership on most College committees, majority representation in the Community Assembly, and nonvoting representation on the Board of Regents.

Admission Requirements

Admission is selective. An applicant must be a graduate of an accredited high school and have completed at least 4 units of English, 3 units of mathematics, 3 units of social science, and 2 units of natural science. It is strongly recommended that the applicant have at least two years of a foreign language. Transfer students may enroll at the beginning of the fall or spring semester or the January term.

Application and Information

An application, SAT or ACT scores, an educator's reference, a personal statement/essay, and a transcript of previous academic work are required for admission. On-campus interviews are recommended but not required. For more information about Luther, students should contact:

Admissions Office
Luther College
700 College Drive
Decorah, Iowa 52101-1042
Phone: 563-387-1287
800-458-8437 (toll-free)
Fax: 563-387-2159
E-mail: admissions@luther.edu (admissions)
finaid@luther.edu (financial aid)
global@luther.edu (international)
Website: http://admissions.luther.edu
http://www.facebook.com/luthercollege1861
http://twitter.com/luthercollege

Luther College students learn in a community that emphasizes challenging academics, a world-class music program, competitive athletics, and opportunities to put their classroom learning to the test through internships, independent research, and study abroad. Typically, 97 percent of Luther graduates are employed, attending graduate school, or engaged in an internship or volunteer work within eight months of graduation.

MANHATTAN COLLEGE

RIVERDALE, NEW YORK

The College

Manhattan College has more than sixty programs that build upon a strong liberal arts foundation and offer professional preparation in business, education and health, liberal arts, science, and engineering. Learning extends beyond the classroom through internships in New York City and beyond.

The College is one of only a few U.S. colleges to have chapters of all five of these distinguished national honor societies: Phi Beta Kappa, Beta Gamma Sigma, Kappa Delta Pi, Sigma Xi, and Beta Pi.

Manhattan College ranks among the top 15 Catholic colleges in the United States on Forbes' list of *Best Value Colleges 2017: The 300 Schools Worth the Investment.*

Following in the Lasallian Catholic tradition, many Manhattan College students actively define their commitment to social justice by balancing their traditional lifestyles with immersion and service experiences around the city, country, and world.

Each year, Campus Ministry and Social Action (CMSA) organizes several L.O.V.E. programs (Lasallian Outreach Volunteer Experience), which give students the opportunity to travel to some of the world's poorest areas in New Orleans, West Virginia, Kenya, Ecuador, and the Dominican Republic to volunteer with people of very different socioeconomic backgrounds.

Closer to home, the Lasallian Collegians volunteer on campus and in New York City by arranging school blood drives, toy drives, soup kitchen trips, and food runs. In addition, the Arches offers freshman students the opportunity to live in a community in Lee Hall and take one class together each semester of their freshman year that incorporates cultural excursions and service projects in New York City. Many former Arches students say the friendships they made through the program last well beyond graduation.

The tight-knit College community is comprised of 3,927 students. With a 12:1 student-to-faculty ratio, professors know students personally and care about their success. The majority of students live on the traditional collegiate campus, just a subway ride from midtown Manhattan.

Location

Manhattan College's 23-acre campus is located 10 miles north of midtown Manhattan in the suburban Riverdale section of the Bronx, about a mile from Westchester County. The College is located in the world's greatest cultural hub, where renowned museums and landmarks serve as off-campus classrooms. Students have access to internship and job opportunities at some of the country's most prestigious companies. From Fortune 500 companies to independent start-ups, students can find an organization in New York City to support their career goals.

Majors and Degrees

Business: The O'Malley School of Business, accredited by AACSB International, has programs leading to a Bachelor of Science in Business Administration degree with majors in accounting, business analytics, computer information systems, economics, finance, global business studies, management, and marketing.

In addition, Manhattan College also offers the following graduate programs: the Bachelor of Science in Professional Accounting/Master of Business Administration and the Bachelor of Science in Business/Master of Business Administration, which offer students the opportunity to complete a five-year multiple award program.

Education and Health: The School of Education and Health offers a curriculum leading to a Bachelor of Arts degree in childhood education, childhood/special education (dual program), and adolescent education. The kinesiology curriculum leads to a Bachelor of Science degree in physical education and exercise science. The health curriculum leads to a Bachelor of Science degree in allied health, with a concentration in health care administration or general sciences. Curricula in radiological and health sciences lead to a Bachelor of Science in radiation therapy or nuclear medicine technology. In addition, the School of Education and Health offers the five-year childhood/special education program, which allows the student to receive a bachelor's and master's degree with eligibility to pursue certification for grades 1–6 in regular and special education. The School of Education and Health also offers master's degrees and professional diplomas in school counseling, mental health counseling, special education, and school building leadership. All programs are approved by the New York State Education Department and accredited by the Teacher Education Accreditation Council (TEAC).

Engineering: The School of Engineering has a well-deserved reputation as one of the best college engineering schools in the nation and offers programs leading to a Bachelor of Science degree in chemical, civil, computer, electrical, and mechanical engineering. The program is fully accredited by the Educational Accreditation Commission of ABET. Graduate programs are also available in chemical, civil, computer, electrical, environmental, and mechanical engineering.

Liberal Arts: The curriculum of the School of Liberal Arts provides programs that lead to a Bachelor of Arts or Bachelor of Science degree with majors in the humanities and the social sciences, including art history, communication, economics, English, French, government, history, labor studies, philosophy, psychology, religious studies, sociology, and Spanish. Interdisciplinary majors include international studies, peace studies, and urban studies.

Science: In the School of Science, programs lead to a Bachelor of Science or Bachelor of Arts degree with majors in biochemistry, biology, chemistry, computer science, environmental science, mathematics, and physics. Pre-medical, pre-dental, and pre–veterinary studies programs are also available. In addition, Manhattan College also offers the following graduate programs: Applied Mathematics–Data Analytics and Computer Science.

Academic Programs

The core curriculum shared by the Schools of Liberal Arts and Science studies some of the vital works of humankind, explores new ideas, examines the meaning of scientific experimentation, and encourages a student to develop his or her thinking and leadership abilities. The major programs offer advanced work in specific humanistic and scientific disciplines and opportunities to work on research projects in collaboration with faculty scholars.

In the School of Engineering, all engineering students follow a common core curriculum during the first two years and choose a major at the beginning of the junior year. Each curriculum includes a generous selection of courses in basic sciences, the engineering sciences, humanistic studies, and mathematics.

The O'Malley School of Business prepares students for positions of executive responsibility in business, government, and nonprofit organizations. The business curriculum is based on a strong commitment to liberal education and is well balanced between professional business courses, humanities, sciences, and social sciences. This is a reflection of the school's belief that executives should be broadly educated and should involve themselves, as well as their organizations, in efforts to solve social problems.

The School of Education and Health prepares students for teaching, counseling, and health professions. Students complete the College's core curriculum in liberal arts and sciences and then complete a major in various programs in the school's three departments: education, kinesiology, and radiological and health professions. All programs include internships/practicums in schools, hospitals, or other institutions. Graduates of the school's teacher-preparation programs receive New York State provisional teaching certification. The school also offers a five-year B.A./M.S. program in childhood/special education and special education.

Off-Campus Programs

Manhattan College also offers study-abroad programs in many countries; arrangements can be made to study in a country of choice. Students in the O'Malley School of Business may participate in the International Field Studies Seminar. As participants, they spend time in another country studying the effect of that environment on international firms. Career services and co-op education integrate classroom theory with the practical experience of a job in industry, business, the social services, the arts, or government. Portions of the education courses are conducted in New York City schools, so that student teachers may gain experience in urban education at an early stage.

Academic Facilities

There are more than forty scientific and engineering laboratories at Manhattan, including the Research and Learning Center, as well as a modern language laboratory and a computer information systems laboratory. Manhattan's O'Malley Library is a state-of-the-art facility featuring modern accommodations for study and research.

The Raymond W. Kelly ('63) Student Commons, which opened in the fall of 2014, is a 70,000-square-foot building, which has quickly become a focal point on campus. It enhances the College's ability to integrate academics and student life, and provides space for fitness and wellness programming, cultural and community events, dining, student activities, and student collaboration.

The Higgins Engineering and Science Center is slated to open in the Fall of 2020. It will provide the necessary resources for a 21st-century education in engineering and the sciences. Fourteen ultramodern laboratories will support and expand teaching and research in each of the College's engineering and science disciplines. There also will be space for collaborative learning and interdisciplinary partnerships among students and faculty.

Costs

For 2019–20, the tuition for Manhattan College new students will be $40,400 per year plus program fee. Room and board for the year will be $16,870.

Financial Aid

Manhattan grants or administers financial assistance in the form of tuition awards to students on the basis of need and/or ability. Need is evaluated by submitting the FAFSA. In addition to a merit scholarship fund, Manhattan offers endowed scholarships, special category scholarships and student athletic grants, Federal Pell Grants, Federal Supplemental Educational Opportunity Grants, student loans, Federal Work-Study Program awards, and New York State financial assistance are also available to students who qualify. Forty-eight percent of all students receive merit aid with 94 percent of the students receiving aid.

Faculty

Manhattan's faculty has 219 full-time faculty members. Ninety-three percent of the faculty members hold doctorates. They are available to students for informal guidance and counseling and serve as official moderators of many campus organizations.

Admission Requirements and Application Information

An application for admission to Manhattan College may be submitted using the Common Application or a Manhattan College Application. An application fee of $75 is required.

In reviewing applications for admission, the most emphasis is placed upon student course selection and the rigor of the course curriculum as well as on cumulative grade point average. All applicants must have completed a minimum of 16 units in academic subjects to be qualified for admission.

Applicants for freshman admission need to submit SAT or ACT scores. Only a student's highest scores are considered for admission and scholarship eligibility.

Grades and examination scores alone do not adequately evaluate a student's ability to be successful in college. Therefore, appropriate character references are considered important when reviewing candidates for admission. One letter of recommendation from a teacher or guidance counselor is required. Applicants must also submit a brief personal statement or college essay.

Interviews are recommended but not required as part of the admissions process.

Applications are reviewed on a rolling admission basis. Manhattan will consider for admission any qualified student upon completion of the junior year. Students must continue to demonstrate progress at the same academic level in their senior year and that all secondary school graduation requirements must be met, and a diploma issued, in order to enroll. Junior college or other transfer students are welcome. Manhattan College requires applicants whose native language is not English to take the Test of English as a Foreign Language (TOEFL), IELTS, the SAT, or ACT exam. The average SAT score is 1100–1240.

The high school report, recommendation letters, and transcript must be submitted by the high school guidance counselor. There is a rolling admissions policy and a March 1 priority deadline for financial aid applications.

For more information, contact:

Tara Fay-Reilly
Director of Undergraduate Admissions
Manhattan College
Riverdale, New York 10471
United States
Phone: 718-862-7200
800-MC2-XCEL (toll-free)
E-mail: admit@manhattan.edu
Website: http://www.manhattan.edu

Manhattan College centers a great deal of its campus activity around the main quadrangle.

COLLEGE CLOSE-UPS

MARYWOOD UNIVERSITY
SCRANTON, PENNSYLVANIA

Marywood
UNIVERSITY

The University

Marywood University enrolls more than 2,600 students in its undergraduate, graduate, and doctoral programs. Founded in 1915 by the Sisters, Servants of the Immaculate Heart of Mary, the University provides a framework for educational excellence that enables students to develop fully as persons and to master professional and leadership skills necessary for meeting human needs.

Students at Marywood have the opportunity to build on their academic interests and proactively shape their educational experience. Marywood believes in the power of the individual and in the premise that education is the most empowering tool.

Marywood is fully accredited by the Commission on Higher Education of the Middle States Association of Colleges and Schools. Program-specific accreditations are available to review online at www.marywood.edu/academics.

Marywood's athletic programs provide students with opportunities to play on competitive intercollegiate, club, and intramural teams. Students compete on an intercollegiate basis in baseball, basketball, cross-country, field hockey, golf, lacrosse, rugby, soccer, softball, swimming/diving, tennis, track and field, and volleyball. Marywood is a member of NCAA Division III, the Atlantic East Conference, and the Eastern College Athletic Conference.

Prospective students can connect with Marywood through social networks including Facebook (facebook.com/marywoodu), Twitter (twitter.com/marywoodu), and YouTube (youtube.com/marywoodu).

Location

Marywood's campus is part of an attractive residential area of Scranton, in northeastern Pennsylvania. With a population of 78,000, Scranton is the fifth-largest city in Pennsylvania. Marywood is close to many major cities of the Northeast; traveling by car, it is 2½ hours to New York and Philadelphia, 4 hours to Washington, D.C., and 5½ hours to Boston. Several airlines serve the Wilkes-Barre/Scranton International Airport, which is 20 minutes from the campus. The Pocono Mountains, offering spectacular scenery and an abundance of outdoor recreational opportunities, including downhill skiing, are a short distance from campus.

Academic Programs

All students are required to complete a core curriculum in the liberal arts in addition to the courses in their major. Opportunities for undergraduates abound through double majors, honors and independent-study programs, practicums, internships, and study abroad. Army and Air Force ROTC programs are available.

Majors and Degrees

At the undergraduate level, Marywood awards the Bachelor of Arts (B.A.), Bachelor of Architecture (B.Arch.), Bachelor of Business Administration (B.B.A.), Bachelor of Environmental Design in Architecture (B.E.D.A.), Bachelor of Fine Arts (B.F.A.), Bachelor of Interior Architecture (B.I.A.), Bachelor of Music (B.M.), Bachelor of Science (B.S.), Bachelor of Science in Nursing (B.S.N.), and Bachelor of Social Work (B.S.W.).

Marywood offers majors in the following areas of study: accounting, ad hoc (self-designed), advertising and public relations, architecture and interior architecture/design, art (studio: ceramics, painting, sculpture, illustration; design: graphic design, photography), art therapy, arts administration (art, music, theater), athletic training, aviation management, biology, biology secondary education, biotechnology, communication sciences and disorders (speech-language pathology), computer science, criminal justice, cyber security (information security), digital media and broadcast production (broadcast, corporate), early childhood and elementary education, early childhood and elementary education/special education, English (literature and writing), English secondary education, environmental science, exercise science, financial planning, health services administration, history, history/pre-law, history secondary education, hospitality management, international business, journalism, management, marketing, mathematics, mathematics secondary education, medical laboratory science, music education, music performance, music therapy, nursing, nutrition and dietetics, philosophy, pre-physician assistant studies, psychology, psychology/clinical practice, religious studies, respiratory therapy, retail business management, sociology, social work, Spanish, Spanish secondary education, and theater.

Off-Campus Programs

Study-abroad opportunities are available in countries such as Australia, Canada, England, France, Mexico, and Spain. Through Studio Art Centers International (SACI), art students may study in Florence, Italy.

Academic Facilities

In recent years, the University has made major improvements to campus, including new athletic, residence, and dining facilities, and one of the finest studio arts facilities in the northeast. The Learning Commons is a 21st century–style library featuring four levels of open, accessible, and technologically advanced facilities. The Insalaco Center for Studio Arts features 60,000 square feet of fully equipped studios, labs, and classroom spaces for a broad variety of artistic disciplines. The Center for Architectural Studies offers students two levels of studio space in a spacious, adaptive re-use of Marywood's former gymnasium and pool space. A Center for Communication Arts offers a wide range of media tools, including a soundstage for television production and audio recording, a radio station, video and editing rooms, an animation studio, and print journalism facilities.

Costs

Tuition for full-time students (12–18 credits per semester) for the 2019-20 academic year is a flat fee of $34,154. There is also a general fee of $1,500 for full-time students. Costs for room and board for a full academic year are approximately $14,100, depending on which meal plan is selected and the desired room occupancy.

Financial Aid

Marywood offers a comprehensive program of financial aid to assist students in meeting educational costs. Eligibility for federal and state programs is based on demonstrated financial need, as determined by a federal eligibility formula that analyzes family income and assets. In addition, approximately $29 million in institutional aid is awarded annually to Marywood students. Applicants to Marywood are considered for all financial assistance programs for which they qualify. Candidates are required to submit the Free Application for Federal Student Aid (FAFSA) and the Marywood application form.

Faculty

Among faculty members at Marywood, 156 are full-time, and 98 of these hold a Ph.D. or the highest degree in their field. The student-faculty ratio is 12:1. Faculty members are evaluated on their teaching and on their scholarly and artistic activities.

Student Government

All matriculated students in the undergraduate school are members of the Student Government Association (SGA). The SGA operates with a number of committees, including the Student Council, the Resident Committee, and the Commuter Committee. The association plays a key role in establishing a positive campus environment.

Admission Requirements

Candidates for admission should demonstrate reasonable progress toward graduation in an accredited secondary school, have graduated from a secondary school, or offer evidence of an equivalent secondary education. Each candidate should show satisfactory academic preparation in 16 units of subject matter, including 4 units of English, 3 units of social studies, 2 units of mathematics, 1 unit of science with laboratory, and 6 additional units. Prospective students should check with the Office of University Admissions regarding current standardized test requirements.

In addition to fulfilling general admission requirements, candidates for admission to a degree program in architecture, art, education, music, nursing, pre–physician assistant studies, and speech language pathology must meet special standards established by the department. Prior to enrollment, music, theater, and art candidates are required to audition or to present an art portfolio.

For certain programs, candidates without the recommended distribution of units may be eligible for admission if their course work as a whole and the results of their tests offer evidence of a strong foundation for college work. Candidates who are deficient in required course work may complete the appropriate work during the summer or first year in college.

A student who demonstrates satisfactory academic performance at another college may apply for admission as a transfer student. Academic courses presented for transfer should be equivalents of courses required by the programs of study at Marywood. Students should have earned a grade of C or higher in their course work; C– will not transfer. A student should expect to earn a minimum of 42 credits at Marywood; ordinarily, at least one half of the credits required for a major must also be earned at Marywood.

International candidates are required to meet the academic standards for admission, demonstrate proficiency in the use of the English language, and submit documentation of having sufficient funds to cover educational and living expenses for the duration of study. To certify proficiency in the use of English, international applicants whose primary language is not English must submit scores from the Test of English as a Foreign Language (TOEFL) or the IELTS.

Application and Information

Applications for admission are considered on a rolling basis; however, candidates are strongly encouraged to submit applications by March 1. Applications received after March 1 are considered on the basis of available space in particular programs. To be considered for admission, freshman applicants must submit to the Office of University Admissions a completed application, a nonrefundable $35 application fee (waived if applying online), an official high school transcript, an official report of scores from the SAT or ACT, and at least one letter of recommendation. Students can apply online at www.marywood.edu/admissions/applying.

Transfer students must submit a completed application, a nonrefundable $35 application fee (waived if applying online), an official high school transcript, official academic transcript(s) reflecting all college course work for which the candidate has enrolled, and at least one letter of recommendation.

All submitted credentials become the property of Marywood and are not returnable to the applicant. Admission standards and policies are free of discrimination on grounds of race, color, national origin, sex, age, or disability.

For further information, interested students should contact:

Matthew Herr, Senior Director
Office of University Admissions
Marywood University
2300 Adams Avenue
Scranton, Pennsylvania 18509
Phone: 866-279-9663
Fax: 570-961-4763
E-mail: yourfuture@marywood.edu
Website: http://www.marywood.edu/admissions
www.facebook.com/marywoodu
www.twitter.com/marywoodu
www.youtube.com/marywoodu

The majestic Rotunda located in the Liberal Arts Center on Marywood's campus.

MILLERSVILLE UNIVERSITY OF PENNSYLVANIA

MILLERSVILLE, PENNSYLVANIA

Millersville University

The University

Millersville University of Pennsylvania, nestled in the hills of Amish country, offers a wide range of programs and a commitment to high-quality undergraduate and graduate instruction. Millersville's student body of approximately 8,100, including 7,200 undergraduates, is large enough for the University to offer over 100 academic programs, plus master's and doctoral degree programs. The University is also small enough to provide friendly service and individual attention. Students report that the relaxed, friendly campus atmosphere is one component of their superior collegiate experience at Millersville. The campus features a beautiful green and flowered landscape, a pond with resident swans, and clean, well-maintained facilities.

Millersville University was established more than 150 years ago, in 1855, as a normal school, the first one in Pennsylvania. It remained a teachers college until 1962 when it was authorized to offer liberal arts degrees. It has been Millersville University of Pennsylvania since 1983.

Students most frequently cite Millersville's excellent academic reputation and affordable tuition as the top two reasons why they chose the University. Education, business administration, psychology, biology, English, speech communications, and sociology are among the most popular majors offered. Millersville's undergraduates are diverse; one in nine students attends part-time, 23 percent are members of a racial/ethnic minority group, and 10 percent are more than 25 years old. Thirty-three percent of Millersville undergraduates are from Lancaster County, 63 percent from elsewhere in Pennsylvania, 5 percent from out of state, and 2 percent from other countries.

The University offers 19 intercollegiate varsity sports in NCAA Division II as well as intramural and club sports. There are a wide range of special interest clubs, fraternities and sororities, musical organizations, publications, and broad cultural programs available.

Thirty-one percent of undergraduates live on campus in residence halls, with the rest commuting from home or living nearby. Coed dormitories and apartments are available for students. Freshmen and sophomores not commuting from home are required to live on campus. The possession, use, or sale of alcoholic beverages and illegal drugs is prohibited on the University campus. Smoking is prohibited in all academic and residential buildings on campus. Freshmen are permitted to have cars on campus.

Special services provided for students include free tutoring, academic advisement, career planning and placement, personal counseling, health services, wellness activities, and special facilities for commuters.

Location

Millersville is three miles from Lancaster City, a growing metropolitan area. Lancaster County is an exceptionally friendly and beautiful area with a large number of art galleries, stores, restaurants, theaters, parks, and tourist attractions. The campus is served by the area bus system, and Lancaster has Amtrak service for easy access to nearby cities like Philadelphia, which is an hour and a half away; Washington, D.C., which is two and a half hours away; and New York City, which is three hours away. Baltimore is also an easy hour and a half drive from campus. There is also air service nearby.

Lancaster County is one of the fastest-growing counties in Pennsylvania and has one of the lowest unemployment rates in the state. The local economy is sound and diverse. Sixty percent of Millersville graduates choose to settle within the county.

Majors and Degrees

Millersville offers the Bachelor of Arts degree in anthropology, art, biology, chemistry, earth sciences, economics, English, environmental geology, French, geography, German, government and political affairs, history, international studies, mathematics, music, philosophy, physics, psychology, social work, sociology, and Spanish.

The Bachelor of Science degree is offered in allied health technology; applied engineering, safety and technology; biology; business administration; chemistry; communications and theatre; computer science; geology; mathematics; meteorology; occupational safety and environmental health; ocean sciences and coastal sciences; and physics.

The Bachelor of Science in Education degree with teaching certification is offered in art education, biology, chemistry, earth sciences, Pre-K–4 education, English, French, German, mathematics, middle level education, music education, physics, social studies, Spanish, special education, and technology education. Millersville now offers degree programs in inclusive education, allowing students to specialize in an age group and subject area while also learning how to teach students with special needs.

The University also offers the Bachelor of Fine Arts degree in art; the Bachelor of Science in nursing degree for RNs only (fully online and on-campus options are available); and the Associate of Technology degree in applied engineering, safety and technology.

Other new academic programs have been added to Millersville's offerings to better serve the student body with specialized degrees. The multidisciplinary studies major allows students to work with a faculty advisor to combine their unique areas of interest and create a custom degree focus. The Paul H. Slaugh Jr. entrepreneurship minor allows students to combine entrepreneurship with a major of their choosing. Millersville now also offers degree programs in entertainment technology, sports journalism, and environmental hazards and emergency management. Students should refer to the website for a complete listing. More than 65 minors are offered along with engineering programs for chemistry majors. Special advisement is available for students interested in pre-medicine and pre-law.

Academic Programs

Millersville University places a strong emphasis on the liberal arts. Nearly half of the courses required for all its undergraduate degrees, including those with technical or professional majors, are in the liberal arts. This prepares students for a lifetime of learning and gives them a background in writing, speaking, analysis, and critical thinking across a broad range of subjects.

Millersville's baccalaureate degree programs have four common curricular elements: proficiency requirements in English composition and speech; the general education program, which constitutes about half the curriculum; the major field of study; and elective courses, if needed, to meet the minimum of 120 credits required for graduation. Within this framework, students have many choices in developing programs of study.

The general education program has requirements in writing, speaking, humanities, natural sciences and mathematics, social sciences, and interdisciplinary and/or multicultural study. There is also a health and physical education requirement.

Millersville offers a University Honors College, departmental honors programs, independent study, a pass/fail option, and asuccessful Exploratory Program for undeclared students who are deciding about a major.

The University operates on a 4-1-4 academic calendar with summer sessions.

Off-Campus Programs

An exchange agreement with Franklin & Marshall College allows Millersville students to take select Franklin & Marshall courses not offered at Millersville. Cooperative education internships are available to students in most majors, and some majors offer or require specialized internships. Millersville has study-abroad programs in Australia, Chile, China, England, France, Germany, Ireland, Japan, Peru, Scotland, South Africa, Spain, and other countries. Qualified students who wish to study abroad elsewhere may do so through the University's cooperative arrangements with other colleges and universities. Students may also choose to student teach or participate in an internship abroad.

Academic Facilities

With numerous study areas, classrooms, and even a café, the new Dr. Francine G. McNairy Library and Learning Forum is a relaxing and visually pleasing place where students can study and work. Materials from other libraries are available through interlibrary loan.

The University's computing facilities support both PC and Apple platforms. There are more than 400 terminals and computer stations available in multiple computer labs across campus. On-campus access to the Internet is available for all faculty members and students. Wireless access is available in all buildings, residence halls, classrooms, and offices.

Other University facilities include an extensive scientific instrumentation inventory, industry and technology laboratories, a variety of art studios and galleries, two visual and performing arts centers, a state-of-the-art sound studio, three gymnasiums, two swimming pools, radio and television production facilities, soundproof music practice modules, and a language laboratory.

Costs

Annual tuition and fees in 2018-19 were $12,226 (based on 30 credits per semester) for Pennsylvania residents and $22,196 for out-of-state students. Annual room and board charges for 2018-19 were $13,806.

Financial Aid

Approximately 82 percent of Millersville undergraduates receive financial aid through grants, scholarships, employment, and loans. Scholarships are available on the basis of academic performance. Federal Pell, Federal Supplemental Educational Opportunity grants, and Pennsylvania Higher Education Assistance Agency (PHEAA) grants are awarded on the basis of need. Students may also qualify for Federal Perkins Loans and Federal Stafford Student Loans. On-campus and off-campus job opportunities are plentiful, with nearly one-third of students holding an on-campus job.

Students applying for a federal or state grant, Federal Work-Study, or a Federal Perkins Loan must complete the Free Application for Federal Student Aid. The forms are available from high school guidance offices, from the Financial Aid Office, or online at http://www.fafsa.ed.gov. Deadlines are given in the forms' instructions.

Faculty

Millersville University faculty members are dedicated to teaching and to offering individual attention. In 2016–17 the University employed 475 full and part-time faculty. Ninety-eight percent of the full-time faculty members have earned the highest degree in their field. The University keeps a relatively low student-faculty ratio of 22:1 and an average class size of approximately 25. No classes are taught by graduate or teaching assistants.

Student Government

Millersville University students participate in University governance through the Student Senate, faculty-student committees, and representation on the Faculty Senate, the Council of Trustees, and the Millersville Borough Council. The Student Senate works with faculty members and the administration on major University policies.

Admission Requirements

Millersville University admits approximately 60 percent of its applicants. More than 80 percent of its full-time freshmen rank in the top 40 percent of their high school class. Academic records are the most important factor in admission decisions. Applicants must have successfully completed at least 4 years of high school English, 3 years of social studies, 3 years of mathematics, and 3 years of science (1 unit must be a lab). In addition, 2 years of foreign language is strongly recommended.

Since meeting people with different backgrounds and interests is an important part of the college experience, Millersville University is committed to recruiting a diversified student body. SAT or ACT scores are required. Letters of recommendations are encouraged. Out-of-state, international, nontraditional, and transfer applicants are welcome. Exceptional high school students may apply for early admission at the end of their junior year. Admitted applicants may request to defer their admission for up to two semesters. Advanced standing is offered through CLEP and AP examinations.

Application and Information

To apply, students should submit an online application with a $40 processing fee and official copies of the high school record and SAT or ACT scores (freshman applicants only, transfer students must submit official transcripts from all previous institutions). A 3–5 minute video essay can be submitted instead of a written application essay. The paper application fee is $50. The University has a rolling admission policy, and students are encouraged to apply early (by mid-November) in their senior year for fall admission. Applicants are usually notified of a decision within a month after a completed application and required materials are received. Students can apply to Millersville via the Pennsylvania State System of Higher Education App or the Common App.

For application forms and additional information, students should contact:

Office of Admissions
Millersville University of Pennsylvania
P.O. Box 1002
Millersville, Pennsylvania 17551-0302
Phone: 717-871-4625
800-MU-ADMIT (toll-free)
E-mail: admissions@millersville.edu
Website: www.millersville.edu
YouTube: www.youtube.com/millersvilleu
Facebook: www.facebook.com/villeadmissions
Twitter: https://twitter.com/VilleAdmissions
Virtual tour: www.youvisit.com/millersville

Millersville University has more than 100 undergraduate programs available and state-of-the-art facilities. Students can find their path at a top-ranked public university that is committed to their future.

MISERICORDIA UNIVERSITY

DALLAS, PENNSYLVANIA

The University

Misericordia University is a high-quality liberal arts and professional studies institution rooted in service to others and committed to challenging academics and the personal attention students deserve. Founded by the Religious Sisters of Mercy in 1924, Misericordia offers undergraduate and graduate programs to resident and commuter students, as well as adult students. Current enrollment is more than 2,600 men and women.

The University cultivates a spirit of community service and a lifelong love of learning in its students through extracurricular activities, experiential learning, and challenging academic programs. In the National Survey of Student Engagement, Misericordia students say they are more involved in learning and have better relationships with faculty members and peers than students at other similar institutions. Misericordia is also ranked in the top tier of U.S. News & World Report's America's Best Regional Universities–North Category 2019.

Misericordia operates twelve residential facilities, including five residence halls, a town house complex, and off-campus housing, with a total capacity of more than 1,100 students. This includes three nearby homes are reserved for upper-level students. Residents have a number of options, including single rooms and wellness housing. Each residence hall offers study rooms, laundry facilities, and recreational lounges. The Metz Dining Hall is located in the Banks Student Life Center, which also houses a "We Proudly Brew Starbucks" coffee shop, a Chick-fil-A Express, and the Chopping Block restaurant, and the renovated Student Union that features flat-screen televisions as well as pool and foosball tables.

There are numerous campus activities. Besides Student Government, there are over 40 chartered student clubs and organizations. Cultural events, Campus Ministry, intramural and intercollegiate athletic programs including esports, performing arts shows, art exhibits, and many other social activities complement the academic experience. The Metz Field House provides enhanced facilities for student athletes. In keeping with the University's tradition of Mercy, Service, Justice, and Hospitality, students have opportunities to develop leadership potential through service projects. Misericordia earned a spot on the President's National Community Service Honor Roll for the past several years.

On spring break, students have served the needy in rural Appalachia, the Gulf Coast, Texas, California, Philadelphia, and the South Bronx. Students have volunteered abroad in Jamaica, Guyana, and Romania.

Personalized attention is the key to the support available in the Student Success Center. A psychologist, counselors, therapists, and peer counselors conduct workshops each semester on a variety of topics, including test anxiety, stress management, time management, and goal setting. Many services are free of charge to students and contacts are confidential..

First-year students may join the Guaranteed Placement Program (GPP) through the Insalaco Center for Career Development. The GPP program includes academic standards, cocurricular activities (such as leadership and service projects), internships, resume development, etiquette development, and interviewing skills. If a student fulfills the program's requirements and is not employed in his or her field or enrolled in graduate or professional school within six months of graduation, a paid internship is assured. The center also co-presents the Choice Program, which offers special guidance for students who have not declared a major. Opportunities for career exploration, cooperative education, and internships help students develop the skills they need to be successful when they enter the working world.

Student Health Services staff members provide first aid, assessment and treatment of common illnesses, and referrals for more serious health conditions. Health center activities are directed by a nurse practitioner. A self-care room offers reference materials and up-to-date information on personal health concerns. All services are confidential.

A rapidly evolving world has increased the number of adults who seek higher education. Misericordia offers bachelor's, master's, and doctoral programs for adult learners in several formats. The Ruth Matthews Bourger Women with Children program provides housing and support services for single women with children who are working toward their undergraduate degree. Convenient evening, online, and weekend formats also are available for people with families and full-time jobs.

Master's degrees are available in education, nurse practitioner studies, occupational therapy, physician assistant, speech/language pathology, business administration, and organizational management. A doctoral program in physical therapy is available to students entering in a full-time format, and doctoral programs in occupational therapy and nursing practice are available for graduate students via part-time study, including online and in-class components.

The University is fully accredited by the Middle States Association of Colleges and Schools. The medical imaging, nursing, occupational therapy, physical therapy, social work, and speech-language pathology programs are accredited by the National League for Nursing Accrediting Commission, the Council on Social Work Education, the Joint Review Committee on Education in Radiologic Technology, the American Occupational Therapy Association, the American Physical Therapy Association, and the American Speech-Language and Hearing Association. The ARC-PA has granted Accreditation - Provisional status to the Misericordia University Physician Assistant Program.

Location

Located in northeastern Pennsylvania, Misericordia University is the oldest four-year institution of higher education in Luzerne County. Expansive lawns and thick stands of trees dominate the 115-acre upper and expanding lower campuses. It is 9 miles from the city of Wilkes-Barre. The area offers shopping centers, malls, cinemas, skiing, professional sporting events, and a variety of cultural activities. Pennsylvania's largest natural lake and two state parks are nearby, as are Pocono ski resorts. Metropolitan New York and Philadelphia are each within a 3-hour drive. Public and university-sponsored transportation serves the campus.

Majors and Degrees

Misericordia University awards the Bachelor of Arts (B.A.) degree in English, history, government, law and national security, medical and health humanities, and philosophy. The Bachelor of Science (B.S.) degree is awarded in accounting, biochemistry, biology, business administration, chemistry, clinical laboratory science, computer science, diagnostic medical sonography, early childhood and special education, health care management, health science, information technology, mass communications and design, mathematics, medical imaging, middle level education, professional studies, psychology, secondary education, sport management, and statistics. The Bachelor of Science in Nursing (B.S.N.) is awarded to nursing majors, and a Bachelor of Social Work (B.S.W.) is awarded to social work majors. Specializations in exercise science, IT security, marketing, medical science, patient navigation, pre-law, respiratory therapy, sport communications, surgical technology, and preprofessional occupations are also available. Certificate programs include addictions counseling, diagnostic medical sonography, patient navigation, post-professional pediatrics certificate for occupational therapists and physical therapists, and secondary education. These may be taken in support of several degrees offered by Misericordia or as stand-alone programs.

The University also offers five-year entry-level graduate majors in occupational therapy and speech-language pathology. Students graduate with a master's degree in speech-language pathology or occupational therapy and a bachelor's degree in health sciences. The physical therapy program is a 6½-year doctoral program. Students graduate with a bachelor's degree in one of several areas and a Doctor of Physical Therapy (D.P.T.) degree.

Academic Programs

Candidates for any bachelor's degree must fulfill a 49-credit liberal arts core curriculum and must complete the requirements of at least one major (credits vary, but no less than 30 credits in a major). The typical requirement for a baccalaureate degree is a total of 121 credits. Other options include minors, specializations, and free electives. Interested students should consult the academic catalog for the most current information.

Courses are offered on a semester basis, beginning in August and January and ending in December and May. Summer, weekend, online, and accelerated courses are also available.

Academic Facilities

The chemistry, physics, and biology departments all have fully equipped research laboratories available to students in these fields. State-of-the-art equipment includes high-performance liquid chromatography (HPLC), a rotary evaporator, and a new gas chromatograph mass spectrometer. The science building contains a gross anatomy laboratory, a rare asset for a university of this size. The University also houses an energized radiation laboratory for the medical imaging program. The Passan Hall–College of Health Sciences provides classrooms and high-tech laboratories for the occupational therapy, physical therapy, speech-language pathology, and nursing programs in a facility devoted to these majors.

In addition to the four main computer labs, most other campus buildings and common areas offer wireless Internet access. The University operates MyMU, a secure online portal where students can access e-mail, course schedules, class registration tools, and student account and registration information from a single sign-on.

Mercy Hall, the original administrative building, offers multi-purpose academic classrooms and facilities. Many key student service departments, including the registrar, student accounts, and financial aid are centralized in one area in Mercy Hall. Sandy and Marlene Insalaco Hall houses the Pauly Friedman Art Gallery, Intermetzo Café, computer labs, an ensemble room, fine arts classroom, music teaching and practice areas, and the Assistive Technology Research Institute.

The new Michael and Tina MacDowell Residence Hall hosts three ultramodern classrooms on the first floor.

The three-story Mark Kintz Bevevino Library covers 37,500 square feet and houses stacks for 90,000 volumes. Materials include information and communication technology and a reference section that offers books, serials, and a variety of periodicals as well as reference search tools.

Costs

Full-time undergraduate tuition for 2017–18 was $31,530 per year. The general fee was $1,710. Housing options include traditional rooms, suites, town houses, and lower-campus housing. The median room cost was $8,326. The median board cost is $4,630.

Financial Aid

All students applying for financial aid must complete the Free Application for Federal Student Aid (FAFSA) by May 1, but it can be completed as early as October 1 of senior year. This is used for Federal Pell Grants, Federal Supplemental Educational Opportunity Grants (FSEOG), subsidized and unsubsidized Federal Direct Student Loans, Federal Perkins Loans, nursing loans, and the Federal Work-Study Program. This application is also the basis upon which state and institutional aid is awarded. The University also offers a no-interest monthly payment plan. Many scholarships are available including $20 million in presidential scholarships based on academic ability and $4.6 million in McAuley Awards for students who have experience in leadership roles and volunteer service.

Faculty

There are 138 full-time faculty members. A student-faculty ratio of 11.3:1 results in students receiving a great deal of individual attention from a highly qualified faculty; 78 percent of the faculty members hold doctorates. Besides student academic advising, the faculty members also serve as advisers to clubs.

Student Government

An active student government organization serves as a liaison between the students and the faculty and staff members. The administration enables students to become involved by serving as student representatives on various University committees.

Admission Requirements

Misericordia University admits applicants based on their secondary school record, high school recommendation, extracurricular activities, and personal promise. The University requires SAT or ACT scores.

Transfer students with a cumulative average of at least 2.0 (4.0 scale) may be considered for admission and may receive advanced standing. Some majors require a 2.5 or higher cumulative average. Transfer students must submit official high school transcripts and transcripts of work completed at other colleges and universities.

Application and Information

Applicants must submit the free online application, available at misericordia.edu/apply, transcripts, and SAT or ACT scores.

The University considers applications on a rolling basis. Usually, candidates are notified of the admission decision within three weeks of receipt of all required materials.

For more information, students should contact:

Office of Admissions
Misericordia University
301 Lake Street
Dallas, Pennsylvania 18612-1090
Phone: 570-674-6461
866-262-6363 (toll free)
Fax: 570-675-2441
E-mail: admiss@misericordia.edu
Website: http://admissions.misericordia.edu
www.twitter.com/misericordiaUAD
www.facebook.com/misericordiauniversity
www.facebook.com/misericoridau

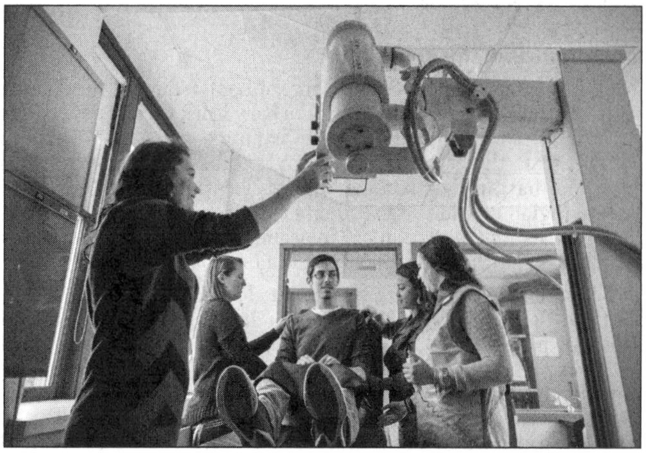

Misericordia University offers multiple medical and health science degree options on the undergraduate and graduate levels.

COLLEGE CLOSE-UPS

MOLLOY COLLEGE
ROCKVILLE CENTRE, NEW YORK

Molloy College

The College

What college offers a great education with small classes, wonderful internships, community service projects, and international trips, plus an amazing campus life program to round out the college experience? Welcome to Molloy College, where you can truly "live your story."

Molloy, an independent, private Catholic college based in Rockville Centre, New York was founded in 1955 by the Sisters of Saint Dominic of Amityville, New York. The College serves a student population of more than 4,900 undergraduate and graduate students. Molloy students can earn degrees in a variety of outstanding academic programs, including nursing, business, education, social work, music therapy, and many more.

Prospective students are always looking for an academic environment that offers the best fit for the student and the best value for their tuition dollar. Molloy was recently named by *The Wall Street Journal* as the #18 ranked "value-added" college in the nation, a testament to our tremendous academic programs. Molloy also earned important recognition from another source, when *Newsday* produced an enrollment overview of the many private colleges in the Long Island region. While most of Molloy's competitors struggled in the 2012-2017 period, Molloy "saw the largest increase, rising more than 11 percent."

Molloy continues to earn recognition in many areas. College Factual recently named Molloy the #1 college for health professions, as well as naming Molloy's undergraduate nursing program the best in the nation. Molloy's accounting students have the highest pass rate on Long Island for the CPA exam, and the College's music therapy program is ranked 16th in the nation by TheBestSchools.org. In addition, the College's residence halls were voted Best in New York by Niche.com, and these rankings also referenced Molloy's freshmen retention rate, which is among the highest in the country (89 percent). Also of note, Molloy graduates' starting salaries have ranked among the highest in the U.S. in surveys conducted by Georgetown University and PayScale.com.

Location and Environment

Molloy is located on the South Shore of Long Island in the Village of Rockville Centre. Its proximity to New York City—just a short train ride away from the 30-acre campus—allows students to benefit from the cultural, social, and professional opportunities that Manhattan has to offer. Molloy's location in the New York metro region provides its students with numerous opportunities for internships and clinical placements, critical for helping students land their first job upon graduation.

Molloy College also offers off-campus locations for study at the Suffolk Center in East Farmingdale and at area hospitals and schools, all designed to provide convenience for graduate and continuing education students. Most recently, Molloy opened a new facility at 50 Broadway in Manhattan's downtown Oculus District. The new building houses the Molloy/CAP21 B.F.A. musical conservatory program, in addition to hosting a variety of lectures and other academic programs.

Majors and Degrees

Molloy offers the A.A. degree in liberal arts; the A.A.S. degree in cardiovascular technology and respiratory care; and the B.A. or B.S. degree in accounting, art, biology, business management, communications, computer science, computer information systems, criminal justice, education, English, earth and environmental studies, finance, history, interdisciplinary studies, marketing, mathematics, modern languages, music, music therapy, new media, nuclear medicine technology, nursing, philosophy, political science, psychology, respiratory care, sociology, speech language pathology/audiology, and theology; the B.S.W. degree in Social Work; and the B.F.A. in art, music, and theatre arts. Teacher certification programs are available in childhood (1–6), adolescence (7–12), special education, and birth–grade 2 childhood special education.

On the graduate level, Molloy offers a Master of Science degree as well as post-master's certification in nursing and education. M.B.A. programs are available in business, accounting, healthcare, marketing, and personal financial planning; a master's program in clinical mental health counseling was recently launched as well. A master's in social work is offered through Molloy's partnership with Fordham University. Molloy also offers graduate degrees in criminal justice, music therapy, and speech-language pathology. The College offers three doctoral programs: a Ph.D. in nursing and a Doctor of Nursing Practice (D.N.P.), as well as an Ed.D. in Education.

Students interested in pre-dental, pre-law, pre-medical, or pre-veterinary programs are offered special advisement.

Articulation agreements with community colleges and established transfer credit policies ensure ease of transferability. Experienced admissions counselors will evaluate transfer applicants' credits and help plan toward a path toward degree completion.

Academic Programs

At Molloy, small class size, engaging and experienced faculty, and renowned academic programs help ensure student success, both in the classroom and beyond.

Molloy strives to make the college experience convenient for all students. The College offers evening and weekend classes, many in online and hybrid formats, with accelerated schedules designed to accommodate students' busy schedules.

A minimum of 128 credit hours is required for a baccalaureate degree; these courses include a strong liberal arts general education curriculum for every major field of study. Students may choose a double major, and many minors are available. Molloy has a 4-1-4 academic calendar.

Students may earn CLEP and CPE credit, and advanced placement credit is granted for a score of 3 or better on the AP exam. Qualified full-time students may participate in the Army ROTC program at Hofstra University or St. John's University on a cross-enrolled basis. Molloy students may also elect Air Force ROTC on a cross-enrolled basis with New York Institute of Technology.

Off-Campus Programs

The vast majority of students at Molloy enjoy an internship at some point in their academic careers. These real-world experiences are a crucial part of the learning process and ensure that students enter their chosen field ready to make strong contributions. Molloy's location in the New York metro region provides its students with numerous opportunities for all-important internships and clinical placements that can lead to a full-time job.

Molloy students are also instilled with the belief that they can make a difference beyond the classroom. As part of Molloy's tradition of service, students become involved in projects that help underserved populations in New York City, New Orleans, Puerto Rico and Haiti, to name but a few locations. Through the College's international education program, students seek enrichment and greater understanding of the world by participating in trips to Europe, Japan, South America, and other locales around the globe.

Facilities

In recent years, Molloy has added a number of new facilities, including two residence halls, a student center, and a performing arts theatre, all of which enhance the student experience. Additionally, Molloy recently opened the Barbara H. Hagan School of Nursing to support its nationally ranked nursing program. The College is slated to open its newest residence hall in fall 2019.

Molloy is a wireless campus and its computer labs house more than 325 PCs. Many departments have their own computer labs with state-of-the-art equipment.

The James E. Tobin (JET) Library is the center of academic research on the Molloy College campus. Beyond the library's physical collection of books, media, and periodicals, it also provides 24/7 access to over 250,000 ebooks as well as full text to over 170 million articles contained within its 80+ subscription databases. The facility itself contains reference computers, three classrooms, a media center, and designated areas for both group and private study. The Information Commons, located in the Public Square, offers an additional 40 computers as well as four study rooms that can be reserved in advance. Reference services are available to both on-campus and remote researchers in a variety of ways, including a chat service that is available all of the hours the library is open. Additionally, the Public Square provides numerous music studios, for both individual and group study.

The Wilbur Arts Center features art studios, a cable television studio, and the Lucille B. Hays Theatre. The school also has six science labs, a language lab, the education resource center, new state-of-the-art nursing labs, and a behavioral sciences research facility.

Costs

For 2018–19, tuition was $30,270 and required fees were $1,190. Students can expect to spend about $1,400 on books.

Financial Aid

Financial aid, which is based on academic achievement and financial need, is awarded to more than 85 percent of the student body. Aid is awarded in the form of scholarships, grants, loans, and Federal Work-Study Program employment. Merit-based scholarships and grants are also available.

Students are required to complete the FAFSA application every year. Full- and partial-tuition scholarships are available through the following: Molloy Scholars, Presidential Dominican Scholarships, Presidential Business Scholarships, Dean Scholarships, Academic Achievement, Fine Arts Scholarships, Community Service Awards, and other funded scholarships. The Transfer Scholarship Program awards partial-tuition scholarships to students transferring into Molloy College with at least a 3.0 cumulative GPA. Nursing transfers are required to have a 3.3 GPA to be eligible for a transfer scholarship. Athletic grants (Division II only) are awarded to full-time students who show superior athletic ability in baseball, basketball, bowling, cross-country, equestrian, field hockey, indoor and outdoor track, lacrosse, soccer, softball, tennis, or volleyball. Most recently, Molloy announced that it would be offering scholarships for students participating in e-sports.

Faculty

Molloy's 10:1 undergraduate student-faculty ratio reflects the College's commitment to its students. In addition, the College has increased the number of faculty members by more than 10 percent in recent years. Of those faculty members, more than 77 percent have doctoral degrees.

Student Organizations and Activities

Molloy offers plenty of opportunities for its 4,900+ undergraduate and graduate students.

There are more than 50 academic programs, approximately 60 clubs and honor societies, various service opportunities, and NCAA Division II athletics, providing abundant opportunities for each student to not only strive for academic excellence, but also explore new interests, pursue athletics, and enrich the community.

Admission Requirements

While Molloy is a selective college, admissions counselors respect each individual applicant and consider the whole student—not just test scores—when making admissions decision. Prospective freshmen must submit their high school credentials, SAT or ACT scores, the Molloy application, and a $40 nonrefundable application fee. While not required, a personal interview is strongly suggested.

Entrance requirements include graduation from high school or equivalent with 20.5 units, including the following: 4 units of English, 3 units of a foreign language, 3 units of mathematics, 4 units of social studies, and 3 units of science. Those who plan to major in mathematics must have 4 units of high school mathematics and 2 units of science, including either chemistry or physics. Biology majors must have biology, chemistry, physics, and 4 units of mathematics. Nursing majors must have biology and chemistry. Cardio-respiratory science majors must have biology, chemistry, and mathematics. Nuclear medicine majors must have high school algebra and biology. Applicants lacking above requirements are reviewed on an individual basis.

Application Information

Molloy College offers rolling admissions at the undergraduate level. Early action on admission will be made promptly on applications received by December 1 of the senior year from well-qualified students who have filed all their credentials with the admissions office.

Prospective students are invited to visit the campus. Questions or requests for more information can be directed to:

Undergraduate Admissions
Molloy College
1000 Hempstead Avenue
Rockville Centre, New York 11571
Phone: 516-323-4000
888-4-MOLLOY (toll-free)
E-mail: admissions@molloy.edu
Website: http://www.molloy.edu
http://www.facebook.com/GoMolloy
http://www.twitter.com/MolloyCollege

MONMOUTH UNIVERSITY
WEST LONG BRANCH, NEW JERSEY

MONMOUTH
UNIVERSITY

The College

Monmouth University is a first-tier, private university located along New Jersey's northern coastline that offers a welcoming and dynamic setting for student development. Innovative academic programs, individual faculty attention, and nationally ranked Division I athletics make this private university a great place for students to prepare for their futures.

Monmouth's beautiful coastal campus sits at the heart of a vibrant culture rich in history, the arts, technology, and entrepreneurship. Just an hour from New York and Philadelphia, the University provides a welcoming and dynamic setting that prepares students to succeed in life after graduation. Renowned faculty are actively involved in advancing academic research nationwide while encouraging meaningful community involvement and critical thinking for self-fulfillment.

A comprehensive selection of in-demand degree programs are led by innovative faculty in a small class setting, where students are active participants in their education.

Monmouth has a diverse student body comprising approximately 6,400 undergraduate and graduate students. While many are from the Northeast, students come from all across the United States, as well as nations around the world. Monmouth offers traditional residence halls and garden-style apartments. Some University-sponsored beachfront campus housing is also offered to students who meet certain requirements.

Students at Monmouth have an assortment of extracurricular activities to choose from, including more than 120 student-run clubs and organizations, such as the Student Government Association, the campus newspaper (The Outlook), the FM radio station (WMCX), the television station (Hawk TV), the online news portal (The Verge), the yearbook (Shadows), the literary magazine (Monmouth Review), and various sororities and fraternities. Special events are held throughout the year, including art exhibits, concerts, lectures, and sightseeing trips. Monmouth's Alternative Spring Break provides students with the opportunity to travel globally to take part in service projects and community building.

Students can also cheer on Monmouth's 23 NCAA Division I men's and women's athletic programs. The teams compete primarily in the Metro Atlantic Athletic Conference (MAAC), with the exception of football, which competes in the full-scholarship Big South Conference, and bowling, a member of the Southland Bowling League. The University's basketball and track and field teams compete in the 153,200-square-foot OceanFirst Bank Center, a 4,200-seat venue that opened in 2009. All Monmouth students have access to the arena, which also houses a 200-meter, six-lane indoor track; fitness center; conference space; the University Store; and luxury suites. The University's football, lacrosse, and outdoor track and field programs open their new home in fall 2017, with the debut of Monmouth Stadium. The new stadium will accommodate 4,200 fans and feature state-of-the-art media facilities and end zone to end zone seating.

Monmouth offers something for everyone, and it strives to ensure that students have the resources and support to pursue their goals. The Center for Student Success (CSS) assists students through a variety of academic and career counseling services and programs. Graduates benefit from continued relationships with the Monmouth family. Many return to campus to visit friends, discuss projects with faculty members, and even recruit the next generation of alumni.

Location

Monmouth's coastal campus provides a safe, suburban setting in one of the world's largest metropolitan regions, ideally positioned to help students develop and pursue their career interests while enjoying rich cultural opportunities. Approximately one hour from both New York City and Philadelphia, and one mile from the coastal beaches of the Atlantic Ocean, the University is also at the heart of the coast's vibrant tri-city region.

Economic and political centers of the country and the world are made real and accessible through fascinating internships, a robust study-abroad program, and multiple field experience opportunities. Corporate global headquarters, world-class museums, Madison Square Garden, the Barclays Center, and other sports hubs, shops, restaurants, and theaters are all within reach of the campus.

Majors and Degrees

Monmouth University offers 32 baccalaureate degree programs in six academic schools that share the University's commitment to providing a rigorous academic experience grounded in the liberal arts. The Leon Hess Business School awards bachelor's degrees in business administration with concentrations in accounting; economics; finance; economics and finance; international business; management and decision sciences; marketing; marketing, management, and decision sciences; and real estate. The School of Education awards bachelor's degrees that allow students to earn certification as elementary and secondary school teachers; the school also offers various endorsements, such as English as a second language and teacher of students with disabilities. The Wayne D. McMurray School of Humanities and Social Sciences awards bachelor's degrees in anthropology, art, communication, criminal justice, English, fine arts, foreign language, history, homeland security, music, political science, psychology, and sociology. A Spanish and international business B.A. degree is awarded jointly through the Leon Hess Business School and the School of Humanities and Social Sciences. The School of Science awards bachelor's degrees in biology, chemistry, clinical laboratory sciences, computer science, marine and environmental biology and policy, mathematics, medical laboratory science, and software engineering. The School of Social Work awards the Bachelor of Social Work degree. The Marjorie K. Unterberg School of Nursing and Health Studies awards bachelor's degrees in health studies and health and physical education, as well as the Bachelor of Science in Nursing. A pre-professional advising program is available for students who intend to pursue careers in medicine, dentistry, or other healthcare fields. Monmouth also offers a number of Five-Year Baccalaureate/Master's programs, which enable qualified students to earn a bachelor's and a master's degree in five years in business, computer science, criminal justice, education (select programs), English, history, social work, or software engineering.

Academic Programs

The curriculum at Monmouth University is focused on learning experiences that are both high impact and immersive, extending beyond the classroom, and designed to prepare students for life after college.

Monmouth challenges students in a demanding college environment built on a regimen of reading, deliberating, writing, experimenting, and discussion that ignites curiosity, helps uncover latent passions, and discover a greater sense of purpose.

Transformative learning extends beyond the lecture hall, through a campus-wide culture of teaching excellence that includes linked-learning communities, first-year and senior seminars, study abroad, common readings, experiential education opportunities, community-based participatory research and service-learning courses. Students study abroad in Australia, England, Italy, Spain, and more. Additionally, Monmouth's alternative break allows students to take part in service projects and community building activities in locales around the globe including Guatemala, Haiti, and Nicaragua.

Monmouth students have access to internships, practicums, and even employment opportunities during their course of study. Many students have internships in New York City and Philadelphia, with industry leaders including JPMorgan Chase, NBCUniversal, L'Oreal, and others. The University also partners with the Washington Center, allowing students to earn credit for experiential learning gained through internships and symposia in the nation's capital.

Monmouth's location and network provide tremendous academic opportunities to students. For example, students in Monmouth's music industry program interface with industry professionals in and beyond the classroom, managing their own record label, Blue Hawk Records. There is a real spirit of entrepreneurship on campus that comes to life through student activities like the student-managed investment fund Hawk Capital. Marine and environmental biology and policy students benefit from the University's proximity to coastal waterways.

Qualified students accepted to the University's Honors School participate in an educational environment that encourages and supports intellectual and personal excellence. First-year courses are clustered to enhance interactive learning, with professors who develop common themes and assignments. Honors classes are distinguished by in-depth coverage of material through discussion and writing, smaller class sizes, and a heightened student-faculty rapport. In their final year, each Honors School student researches, writes, and publicly presents an honors thesis, guided by a faculty member who serves as their academic mentor.

Academic Facilities

Monmouth's 55 buildings provide a synthesis of historical architecture and modern aesthetics. The campus' signature building is Woodrow Wilson Hall, a National Historic Landmark, which served as Daddy Warbucks' mansion in the 1982 film *Annie*. The library, the former mansion of Murry and Leonie Guggenheim, is listed on the National Register of History Places and holds 290,000 print and online monographs, 180 databases (abstracts and full-text, e-books, motion picture, image, tools), over 74,000 electronic and print journal subscriptions, and over 1,200 media items. The Lauren K. Woods Theatre, once the Guggenheim carriage house, is a showcase for professional and student performances and that offer students direct experience with all phases of the theater arts.

The Jules L. Plangere Jr. Center for Communication, which is home to the Department of Communication, provides state-of-the-art studios and editing facilities. Joan and Robert Rechnitz Hall houses the Department of Art and Design and features an art gallery, Mac labs, a reception area, and an animation and editing studio. The newest facility is Pozycki Hall, a two-story addition to the Samuel E. and Mollie Bey Hall and home to the Kislak Real Estate Institute. It includes a 150-seat lecture hall, student lounge, general and computer classrooms, and spacious meeting rooms.

Costs

For 2018–19, tuition and fees were approximately $39,600 per year. Annual room and board costs were approximately $14,500; actual costs are determined by the room and meal plan selected.

Financial Aid

At Monmouth, 99 percent of first-year students receive some form of financial aid. About 96 percent receive a scholarship or grant (federal, state, or University); the average scholarship/grant package is $22,521; and the average financial aid package, including student loans and work study, is approximately $26,944. All this, combined with the fact that Monmouth awards more than $59 million in institutional aid to students each year, makes Monmouth an affordable option for many families.

A wide range of University scholarships and grants are offered to all prospective full-time, first-year, and transfer students on the basis of academic performance.

The University participates in all federal and state grant and loan programs. To establish eligibility and to capitalize on available assistance, students should complete the Free Application for Federal Student Aid (FAFSA), which is available after October 1. Students and their families may call 732-571-3463, e-mail finaid@monmouth.edu, or visit the Financial Aid Office for assistance.

Students interested in attending Monmouth can get an estimate of their eligibility for federal, state, and institutional aid, even before submitting their application. To complete the University's Net Price Calculator, visit www.monmouth.edu/netpricecalculator.

Faculty

The University's professors are leaders in their fields and contribute through research, publishing, and consulting services to their respective academic areas. There are 302 full-time and 385 part-time faculty members. Approximately 75 percent of full-time faculty members have doctorates or terminal degrees in their fields. The average class size is 21, and the student-faculty ratio is 13:1.

Student Government

The Student Government Association (SGA) is an important and necessary voice in the University community; its views are recognized and respected. Monmouth students who wish to get involved with SGA can also do so as general members. This flexible form of involvement does not require a student to run for a position or participate in any one of the elections that are sponsored by SGA. More information is available at www.monmouth.edu/sga.

Admission Requirements

Many factors are considered in an admission application. For first-year applicants, a committee evaluates the high school transcripts and SAT or ACT scores, one letter of recommendation, and a personal essay. A resume of activities including leadership positions held and other information supporting the application are also welcome. Campus tours and information sessions with admission counselors are available. Transfer students must submit official transcripts from all colleges attended. If transfer students have earned fewer than 24 transferable credits, they must fulfill first-year admission requirements as well. Nursing applicants must apply by December 1 and submit a nursing-specific essay.

Application and Information

Early action is a nonbinding option for students who wish to receive an early response from Monmouth. December 1 is the deadline for early action and nursing applicants, and admission decisions are mailed by January 15. The application deadline for regular decision is March 1, with an admission decision notification date prior to April 1. Applications received after March 1 are considered on a space-available basis. First-year housing is guaranteed for students who submit the required enrollment deposit, housing deposit, and housing contract by May 1. Students who submit their deposits and housing contract after May 1 may be placed on a wait list for admission and/or housing.

For further information, students should contact:

Office of Undergraduate Admissions
Monmouth University
400 Cedar Avenue
West Long Branch, New Jersey 0774-1898
Phone: 732-571-3456
800-543-9671 (toll-free)
Fax: 732-263-5166
E-mail: admission@monmouth.edu
Website: http://www.monmouth.edu
http://www.facebook.com/monmouthuniversity
http://www.twitter.com/monmouthu
http://www.youtube.com/monmouthuniversity

Monmouth University's Woodrow Wilson Hall is designated as a National Historic Landmark.

COLLEGE CLOSE-UPS

MOUNT ALOYSIUS COLLEGE

CRESSON, PENNSYLVANIA

Mount Aloysius College

The College

Mount Aloysius College is a private, comprehensive, Catholic liberal arts college sponsored by the Sisters of Mercy. The College welcomes people of all faith traditions. Established in 1853, Mount Aloysius College offers both undergraduate and graduate education. Since the founding of the College, nearly 17,000 students have become proud Mount Aloysius alumni. The College is committed to providing small class sizes, and students benefit from accessible faculty and staff. Mount Aloysius students come mostly from throughout Pennsylvania and the mid-Atlantic Region. There are approximately 2,500 students enrolled (unduplicated headcount).

Mount Aloysius College is one of 17 Mercy Colleges nationwide. Students are encouraged to synthesize faith with learning, to develop competence with compassion, to apply their talents and gifts to the service of others, and to assume leadership in their community.

Student activities play a distinctive role in personal growth. At Mount Aloysius College, there are approximately 100 organized clubs, groups, honor societies, and an intramural sports program. Activities include a student newspaper, residence hall associations, student government, cheerleading, dance team, scholarship-funded theater and choir programs, and a student activities planning board. Mount Aloysius fun includes social events, intramural sports, athletic events, comedians, live music, theater, educational events, campus forums, and awesome guest lectures.

Mount Aloysius College is a member of NCAA Division III. Athletic programs involve both women and men and include basketball, cross-country, golf, soccer, and tennis. Men's baseball and women's bowling, softball, lacrosse, and volleyball are offered. Athletes benefit from the Ray S. and Louise S. Walker Athletic Field Complex, which includes a softball, turfed baseball field and soccer field. The Calandra-Smith baseball complex houses the Mountie Stables which offer players and fans lockers, showers, a press box, and concession facilities. The College's soccer field was recently updated to include a turf field, bleachers, a press box and stadium lighting.

The Athletic Convocation and Wellness Center is a spectacular 87,400 square-foot multipurpose facility on the western edge of the beautiful 193-acre campus. This facility takes Mount Aloysius athletics to a new level and adds a welcomed special events venue to the southern Allegheny Mountains. This Center houses a main gymnasium and events venue with seating for over 2,500, home and visitor locker rooms, training facilities, high-tech classrooms, a conference center, and office space. On the ground floor, a new state-of-the-art wellness center offers both cardio and resistance training in a spacious, modern environment.

The Bertschi Center and Technology Commons—with open architecture, vivid colors, and glass walls offering great views of the campus and surrounding mountains—is an additional social, technology, and special events venue that serves both commuter and resident students.

The main campus building is a picturesque structure dating to 1897. It houses the admissions, financial aid, security, health, and academic offices, along with the Office of the President, classrooms, and the Wolf-Kuhn Art Gallery. Cosgrave Center is the hub of campus life. The building contains the Dining Hall, Snack Bar, Bookstore, Child Care Center (part of the elementary education/early childhood program at the College), lounges, recreational rooms, student affairs offices, and meeting rooms. Residence halls include Ihmsen Hall; the Misciagna Residence—a state-of-the-art residence hall, providing 25 suites and private bathrooms; McAuley Hall featuring double and single rooms, a large multipurpose room, and study lounge; and Saint Gert's and Saint Joseph's residence halls. Alumni Hall is a historic, multipurpose facility used for College drama, musicals, lectures, and performing arts events. The College operates 12 months per year and opens its facilities to the Southern Allegheny community.

The College is 100 percent wireless, and smart classrooms are located throughout the campus.

Mount Aloysius is fully accredited by the Middle States Association of Colleges and Schools and approved by the Pennsylvania Department of Education.

In addition to its undergraduate programs—both associate and bachelor's degrees—Mount Aloysius offers master's degree programs in business administration and counseling.

Location

Mount Aloysius College is located in the scenic Southern Allegheny Mountains of west-central Pennsylvania, in the town of Cresson. Convenient and accessible from U.S. Route 22, the College's setting is rural but mere minutes from State College, Altoona, Johnstown, and Pittsburgh, Pennsylvania. Outdoor lovers are at home here. The area has warm, beautiful summers; brisk, breathtaking autumns; invigorating winters; and cool, blooming springs. Facilities are available for biking, golfing, swimming, horseback riding, waterskiing, boating, hiking, spelunking, cross-country and downhill skiing, picnicking, and amusement parks. A well-kept system of State Parks is convenient to the College as are shopping malls, golf courses, and numerous historical sites.

Majors and Degrees

Mount Aloysius College awards bachelor's and associate degrees in the arts, sciences, and health studies fields in both career-oriented and traditional liberal arts programs. Baccalaureate degrees are available in accounting (includes a fifth-year MBA option), American Sign Language/English interpreter education, behavioral and social science, biology and general science, business administration (includes a fifth-year MBA option), computer science, criminology, dentistry (4-4), elementary/early childhood education and secondary education (with certifications), English, natural science, history/political science, humanities, information technology, math/science, medical imaging, natural resource management, nursing (RN-BSN program), nursing (2+2), occupational therapy (3-2), osteopathic medicine (3-4), pharmacy (3-3), physical therapy (4-3), physician assistant studies (3-2), prelaw, psychology, ultrasonography,and undeclared. The College now also offers degrees in Communication Studies and Cybersecurity and Digital Forensics. Associate degrees are offered in applied technology, business administration, criminology, early childhood studies, general studies, legal studies, liberal arts, nursing, physical therapist assistant studies, radiography/medical imaging, sign language/deaf studies, and surgical technology. The College also confers the MBA and a master's degree in counseling.

Academic Programs

Whether preparing students for careers upon graduation or for graduate school, Mount Aloysius recognizes the importance of a liberal arts education. In addition to receiving solid preparation for a chosen career, every student at the College receives a foundation in the arts, sciences, and humanities through an outstanding core curriculum. Strong emphasis is placed on the specialized courses within each program of study, and many academic programs combine classroom experience with internships and related training at area clinical sites, agencies, and institutions. In addition to its regular academic programs, Mount Aloysius offers independent and directed study with a commitment to service, a central component of a Mercy education. The College has an excellent honors program and academic services area. The academic calendar has two traditional semesters and optional summer sessions.

Off-Campus Programs

An important feature of many academic programs is off-campus training. The majority of the College's programs of study require credit-yielding practicums at partnering hospitals, public and private schools, or health or human service agencies. Students in all health programs benefit from required clinical training during their time at the College.

Academic Facilities

The Mount Aloysius College Library is a state-of-the-art learning and study facility offering unprecedented access to a world of information. With a cybersecurity lab and more than 80,000 print and nonprint titles, the Library is an impressive, 31,000 square-foot facility with ample seating, four group-study rooms, reading lounge, and an unparalleled 18,000-volume Ecumenical Collection donated by Pastor Gerald Myers. This facility is completely automated, with an online catalog and access to remote libraries and the Internet through more than 30 workstations. The Library also houses the Information Technology Center, home to 15 multimedia workstations and the latest educational software.

Pierce Hall serves as the campus science center and has over 45,000 square feet of newly renovated and added lab and classroom space. The facility will be officially renamed the Learning Center for Health Science & Technology.

Academic Hall is home to the College Honors Program. It houses classrooms, labs, seminar rooms, faculty offices, and electronic classrooms. The College is proud of its bridge to the past and its progress in providing 21st-century learning facilities.

Costs

Annual tuition and fees for the 2018–19 academic year for full-time students were $21,870; room and board were $10,176. Up-to-date cost information is available online at http://www.mtaloy.edu/tuition-fees/tuition-and-fees.

Financial Aid

Mount Aloysius prides itself on affordability. Many MAC students hail from proud families of modest means and many are first-generation students. The College understands the expense involved in acquiring a quality education and encourages students to apply for all available aid. Through the Office of Financial Aid, the College assists students in applying for state and federal grants, loans, work-study awards, merit scholarships, need-based aid and more. The College awards academic monies based on GPA and SAT or ACT scores. These awards are renewable over a four-year period and range from $1,500 to $14,000 per year. Mount Aloysius College participates in all federal and state programs; fully

94 percent of Mount Aloysius College students receive some form of financial aid. U.S. News & World Report has ranked Mount Aloysius College as one of the best-priced private liberal arts colleges in the United States.

Faculty

The Mount Aloysius faculty consists of approximately 175 members, whose primary responsibility is teaching and advising students. Many faculty members hold advanced or terminal degrees and are expected to maintain close instructional ties with students. Many professors hold national, professional certificates in such disciplines as criminology, education, law, and nursing. The Mount Aloysius student-faculty ratio of 11:1 allows close contact between students and faculty members, providing personal attention in a highly structured environment—a key ingredient in the College's academic philosophy.

Student Government

The Student Government Association (SGA) represents students on all issues that concern the College. The SGA appoints student representatives to all student-oriented College committees. The College encourages student participation in the general governance structure and other matters concerning the development and implementation of policies on residential student life.

Recognitions

Mount Aloysius was recently named one of 100 Best Value Colleges in the U.S. It is a College of Distinction, a Catholic College of Distinction and a Pennsylvania College of Distinction; three separate academic areas—business, education, and nursing—have also earned College of Distinction status. It has also received the Homeschooling Parent's Seal of Approval. Mount Aloysius was one of four colleges deemed "an engine of opportunity" in a White House Report. In the past year, the College's Theatre productions have earned several awards from the prestigious Kennedy Center. The Nursing Division boasts NCLEX pass rates that beat both state and national averages. The American Sign Language/English Interpreter program is an accredited bachelor's program. Mount Aloysius College has also been designated as a Military Friendly College.

Admission Requirements

The College enrolls a freshman class of approximately 350 students. The total class of 550 includes transfer students. Admission is selective, based on academic promise, as indicated by a student's secondary school performance and activities, standardized test scores, and special experience and talents. Applicants are required to have or expected to earn a diploma from an approved secondary school or a GED diploma. Submission of official transcripts and SAT or ACT scores is no longer required but will be reviewed. In addition to the general admission requirements, specific admission requirements exist for the health programs.

For further information, students should visit the College's website at http://www.mtaloy.edu. Prospective students are encouraged to visit the scenic 193-acre campus. The College is open Monday to Friday from 8:30 a.m. to 5 p.m. and on select weekends.

Application and Information

To apply for admission to Mount Aloysius College, candidates are encouraged to submit their application and $30 application fee to the Office of Undergraduate and Graduate Admissions. In addition, students may apply online.

For further information, students should contact:

Office of Undergraduate and Graduate Admissions
Mount Aloysius College
7373 Admiral Peary Highway
Cresson, Pennsylvania 16630
Phone: 814-886-6383
888-823-2220 (toll-free)
Fax: 814-886-6441
E-mail: admissions@mtaloy.edu
Website: http://www.mtaloy.edu

Mount Aloysius College, located on a beautiful 193-acre campus in Cresson, Pennsylvania provides a safe, vibrant learning community. Nestled in the southern Allegheny Mountains, Mount Aloysius is one of 17 U.S. Mercy colleges and universities. Mount Aloysius offers year-round recreational and cultural opportunities. Students enjoy both the security of the campus and the proximity to State College to the east and Pittsburgh to the west. Mount Aloysius College is minutes away from all the amenities of Altoona and Johnstown, Pennsylvania. Interstate highways, the Pennsylvania Turnpike, AMTRAK train service, bus service, and several regional airports—including Pittsburgh International Airport—make Mount Aloysius College convenient from anywhere.

MUHLENBERG COLLEGE

ALLENTOWN, PENNSYLVANIA

The College

Founded in 1848, Muhlenberg College is a top-tier liberal arts college that offers an extensive array of pre-professional programs than most institutions of its size. Its mission is to develop independent critical thinkers who are intellectually agile, characterized by a zeal for reasoned and civil debate, knowledgeable about the achievements and traditions of diverse civilizations and cultures, able to express ideas with clarity and grace, committed to lifelong learning, equipped with ethical values, and prepared for lives of leadership and service.

Muhlenberg students achieve the College's goals by assuming strong individual responsibility for intense involvement in academic work and for personal involvement within the College community. The more than 115 student organizations and 22 NCAA Division III varsity sports provide outlets for the diverse cultural, athletic, religious, social, leadership, and service interests of students. The campus is primarily residential; more than 90 percent of the 2,200 students live on campus. Muhlenberg students are smart, open-minded individuals of all backgrounds who care deeply about the world and each other. They love to learn, are good citizens and friends, and are motivated for professional success. But they don't take themselves too seriously.

Muhlenberg students are guided by an active Career Center and more than 2,100 alumni who are part of The Muhlenberg Network, in advising, mentoring, and opening doors to professional opportunities. More than 90 percent are employed and/or attending graduate school within one year of graduation. About one third of a typical graduating class proceeds immediately to graduate or professional school, while two thirds pursue a career immediately upon graduation.

Location

Located less than 90 miles west of New York City and 60 miles north of Philadelphia, Muhlenberg's campus in Allentown, Pennsylvania is beautiful and convenient. Allentown is Pennsylvania's third-largest and fastest-growing city. It is home to one of the best park systems in the United States—and thanks to more than $1 billion in recent investments, was recently honored as a finalist for a global award for excellence. It is a magnet for entrepreneurs and new businesses ranging from tech and design to logistics, finance, medicine, and biotechnology. These businesses offer internships and full-time employment to Muhlenberg students and alumni.

Majors and Degrees

Muhlenberg offers the Bachelor of Arts (B.A.) degree in the following fields: accounting, American studies, anthropology, art history, business administration, dance, economics, English, film studies, finance, French, history, international studies, Jewish studies, media and communication, music, philosophy, philosophy/political thought, political economy and public policy, political science, psychology, public health, religious studies, Russian studies, sociology, Spanish, studio art, and theatre. The Bachelor of Science (B.S.) degree is offered in the following fields: biochemistry, biology, chemistry, computer science, environmental science, mathematics, neuroscience, physical science, physics and sustainability studies. Students may also design their own major. Minors are offered in most of the major fields, as well as in Africana studies, analytics, Asian studies, creative writing, documentary storymaking, German studies, innovation and entrepreneurship, Italian studies, Latin American and Caribbean studies, statistics, and women's and gender studies. Muhlenberg also offers students cooperative programs with Boston University in medicine, public health and management; a 3-4 dental program with the University of Pennsylvania; a 3-3 B.S. program in physical therapy with Thomas Jefferson University; a 3-2 B.S./M.S. program in occupational therapy with Thomas Jefferson University; a 3-3 program with Villanova University Charles Widger School of Law; a 3-2/4-2 combined program in engineering, offered in cooperation with Columbia University; a 3-4 dual-admission program with SUNY College of Optometry; an Early Assurance Program with Temple University School of Medicine; graduate programs at American University in finance; at Penn State College of Medicine in public health; and at Lehigh University in management. In addition, students may receive certification to teach at the elementary and secondary levels.

Academic Programs

Muhlenberg's academic programs emphasize breadth of study in the liberal arts as well as in-depth study of a particular academic major. All students must fulfill requirements in the arts, foreign culture, the humanities, social sciences, and natural sciences. Strong achievement on Advanced Placement examinations may enable a student to receive advanced placement, possibly with credit. Scores of 4 or 5 earn automatic credit.

Students work closely with academic advisers to formulate programs well suited to their individual interests, abilities, needs, and goals. Generally, students are expected to declare their major at the end of the sophomore year; however, many students later change their academic major without difficulty. A double major is possible, and about a third of Muhlenberg students graduate with a double major. The College also enriches the freshman-year experience through more than 35 special-focus First-Year Seminars. Seniors have the opportunity to synthesize and integrate their academic experience through a Culminating Undergraduate Experience (CUE).

Off-Campus Programs

Study abroad is available through Muhlenberg's Semester-in-London Program, Netherlands semester, Dublin semester, or more than 160 affiliate agreements with international universities all over the world. More than half of Muhlenberg students choose to study abroad.

Students may participate in a variety of internships in local, national, and international businesses; health-care facilities; schools; public agencies; theaters; broadcasting stations; and magazines. Government internships in Harrisburg, Pennsylvania, and Washington, D.C., and an Ethics and Public Affairs semester in Washington, D.C., and a studio semester in New York City through the Theatre Program as well as a New York City semester at Jewish Theological Seminary also are available.

Students may enroll in courses offered at any of the five other member institutions of the Lehigh Valley Association of Independent Colleges: Lafayette College, Lehigh University, Cedar Crest College, DeSales University, and Moravian College.

Academic Facilities

Muhlenberg's library collection, housed in the Harry C. Trexler Library, contains more than 310,000 volumes as well as numerous government documents, periodicals, and electronic and online resources. Students may also use library materials owned by the other institutions participating in the Lehigh Valley Association of Independent Colleges.

The Baker Center for the Arts was designed for Muhlenberg by the well-known architect Philip Johnson. It houses a modern theater complex, a recital hall, classrooms, art studios, and a fine arts gallery. The Trexler Pavilion for Theater and Dance provides dance performance and studio space, a proscenium theater, a Black Box theater, a costume shop, and additional rehearsal spaces.

Life science facilities include numerous laboratories, classrooms, two electron microscopes, a DNA sequencer, an isolation room used for growing and studying viruses, and a museum of natural history. Facilities supporting students in the physical sciences include equipment for optics, electronics, and atomic, nuclear, and solid-state physics. The College supports both Microsoft and Apple applications throughout campus.

Costs

The comprehensive tuition and fees for the 2018–19 academic year were $52,595. The room and board fee averaged $11,640. The total cost for a resident student was approximately $64,235.

Financial Aid

Muhlenberg College endeavors to make its educational opportunities available to all qualified students, regardless of their financial circumstances. While most financial aid at Muhlenberg is based on financial need as demonstrated by the College Scholarship Service Financial Aid PROFILE and FAFSA, there is also significant merit aid available. Typically, about 94 percent of Muhlenberg's students qualify for and receive grant and/or scholarship aid. The average gift aid for first-year students is $34,266. Merit scholarships range from $1,000 to $40,000.

Faculty

The Muhlenberg faculty consists of 185 full-time and 123 part-time members. While many faculty members are distinguished for their scholarly research, teaching is the main emphasis of their work. Professors, at all levels, work closely with students both inside and outside of the classroom. Many department heads teach introductory courses, and no courses are taught by graduate students or teaching assistants.

Student Government

Muhlenberg students are expected to demonstrate a high level of responsibility with regard to their own governance and to participate extensively in internal decision-making and communication processes throughout the campus. These responsibilities are coordinated by the Student Government, which transacts all business pertaining to the student body. In addition, two students serve as representatives to the Board of Trustees, and students hold membership on many faculty committees.

Admission Requirements

The College's admissions process is holistic, selecting students who give evidence of ability and scholastic achievement, seriousness of purpose, and the capacity to make constructive contributions to the College community and the world. In terms of academic quality, the middle range for the SAT reading and writing is 590–680; and 580–680 for math. The ACT middle range is 26–30. Average GPA is 3.3 on a 4.0 unweighted scale.

Muhlenberg also has a long-standing test optional policy. An on-campus interview is strongly recommended for all applicants and required for students who choose not to submit standardized test scores.

Application and Information

Prospective first-year students may apply for admission under either the Early Decision or Regular Decision plan. About half of the first-year class is admitted through Early Decision. In addition, transfer admission is offered for both fall and spring semesters. Application requirements and deadlines for first-year and transfer admission are as follows:

First-Year:
Early Decision I - November 15
Early Decision II and Regular Decision - February 1

Transfer:
December 10 (for spring)
June 15 (for fall)

For further information, interested students should contact:
Melissa W. Falk
Dean of Admissions and Financial Aid
Muhlenberg College
Allentown, Pennsylvania 18104-5586
Phone: 484-664-3200
E-mail: admissions@muhlenberg.edu
Website: www.muhlenberg.edu

Located 90 miles west of New York City and 60 miles north of Philadelphia, Muhlenberg's campus in Allentown, Pennsylvania, is beautiful and convenient.

NEUMANN UNIVERSITY
ASTON, PENNSYLVANIA

NEUMANN UNIVERSITY® CATHOLIC EDUCATION IN THE FRANCISCAN TRADITION

COLLEGE CLOSE-UPS

The University

Neumann University (http://www.neumann.edu), a Catholic co-educational institution in the Franciscan tradition, recognizes the value of developing intellectual excellence, professional competence, and strong community life. As a university that balances the liberal arts with the professions, Neumann was founded to meet and expand the educational and professional horizons of men and women through instruction that is based on values, ethical behavior, and service to others. With its Living and Learning Center residence halls, Neumann University is able to serve a diverse geographic and demographic population.

Founded and sponsored by the Sisters of St. Francis of Philadelphia, the University is committed to a varied student body and welcomes students of all denominations. Enrollment is around 2,700.

The Life Center houses the Meagher Theatre, the Bruder Athletic Center, and the Crossroads Cafe dining facility. Intercollegiate sports include women's basketball, cross-country, field hockey, golf, ice hockey, indoor track, lacrosse, soccer, softball, swimming, tennis, track, and volleyball; and men's baseball, basketball, cross-country, golf, ice hockey, indoor track, lacrosse, soccer, tennis, track, and volleyball. Neumann University competes as a member of the National Collegiate Athletic Association (NCAA) Division III, the Atlantic East Conference, and the Eastern Collegiate Athletic Conference (ECAC). Intramural sports and club teams are available to all members of the campus community.

The residence halls are designed to provide a state-of-the-art residential experience, with a focus on education within a real-world living environment. Technologically smart, the halls connect students to both faculty members and friends via wireless Internet, which is available in every suite and apartment. The center also houses a separate computer lab, a fitness center, a reflection room, various study rooms with warming kitchens for group study or meetings, and a laundry.

The University provides a full range of services to students, including career placement, career and personal counseling, a tutoring program, and health services.

Neumann students are involved in a wide variety of campus and community activities. Major and special interest clubs are available for student participation. Clubs bring together students who share common interests and help foster new friendships.

At Neumann, the spiritual dimension of one's life is recognized as integral to total human development. The Ministry Team provides a pastoral presence on campus and promotes a sense of community. The entire University community is invited to serve the needs of the poor and neglected in society through various outreach programs, with special attention to the need for peace and justice in the world today.

Neumann is well positioned to respond to the academic and extracurricular needs of students who are of traditional or nontraditional age, commuters or residents, and full-time or part-time.

In addition to undergraduate programs, Neumann confers master's degrees in accounting, athletic training, education, nursing, organizational and strategic leadership, pastoral counseling, and sport business as well as doctoral degrees in education (Ed.D.), counselor education and supervision (Ph.D.), and physical therapy (D.P.T.).

Location

Neumann, with a beautiful 68-acre suburban campus in Aston, Delaware County, Pennsylvania, is a short distance from Philadelphia; Wilmington, Delaware; southern New Jersey; and Maryland. It is easily accessible from major arteries such as I-95, Route 476, Route 1, and the Pennsylvania Turnpike.

Majors and Degrees

Neumann offers strong academic majors leading to a Bachelor of Arts degree or a Bachelor of Science degree in accounting, arts production and performance, biology, business administration, communication and digital media, computer information systems, criminal justice, cybersecurity, data science and analytics, education, English, health sciences, liberal arts, marketing, nursing, political science, psychology, public safety administration, social work, and sport management. The education programs lead to teacher certification in early elementary (PK–4), special education (PK–8) or secondary education. Pre-professional programs in engineering, law, medicine, pharmacy, and physical therapy are also available. An accelerated evening program for adults leads to an Associate of Arts, Bachelor of Arts, or Bachelor of Science degree in liberal studies or professional studies.

Academic Programs

The academic program at Neumann University is composed of a core curriculum (required of all students), a major area of study (chosen by each student), and a wide range of elective offerings. Students may also choose a minor area of study. The University's broad base of liberal arts offerings prepares students for the intellectual and social challenges they will face in the employment marketplace and throughout their lives. The core is intended to provide basic knowledge of the liberal arts and sciences; develop verbal, written, and symbolic communication skills; and stimulate interest in a broad range of topics for the purpose of enhancing the individual's contributions to society, thereby enabling the individual to realize full human potential.

Classroom instruction is supplemented by field experience and internships, through which students can earn credit and gain experience by working in a job related to their career interest. Fieldwork and student teaching are required of all education majors. Clinical practice for the nursing major occurs in a variety of health-care facilities in the tri-state area.

The honors program is an opportunity for academically talented students to explore imaginative and innovative perspectives on learning. It is also an opportunity to stimulate and motivate students to expand their knowledge and interest and to strive for greater excellence. Moreover, it is a reward for prior perseverance and dedication as well as an obligation to use skills and abilities in service to others. Admission to the honors program is by invitation.

Neumann University has transfer articulation agreements with numerous schools throughout the area.

Academic Facilities

The Child Development Center is a state-of-the-art, octagonal-shaped building, specifically designed to house an educational program for preschoolers. As a state-licensed day-care facility, it enrolls children of Neumann students, the faculty, and the community. The Child Development Center is part of the Division of Education and Human Services. Students enrolled in education courses use the center for observation, practical experience, and student teaching.

The Academic Computing Center is located on the ground floor of the University. The computers are viewed as tools to support all fields of study and all students and faculty members. Neumann University provides wireless access across campus. Computers are available to all students, as is software related to various academic disciplines.

The University library contains a balanced collection of more than 55,000 physical volumes and films, 20,000 e-books, and nearly

100,000 electronic journals. E-books and journals can be accessed from anywhere with an Internet connection. Collaboration with faculty and membership in local consortia (TCLC, SEPCHE) ensures access to the most relevant resources for academic success. Professional librarians provide in-person research support seven days a week and also create online Research Guides and video tutorials for around-the-clock assistance. Librarians also provide cutting-edge instruction to help develop essential 21st-century skills like critical thinking, technological literacy, and information management. Quiet study rooms, collaborative group spaces, and an open computer lab and Wi-Fi collectively support student study needs.

Costs

Annual tuition and fees for full-time students (12 to 19 credits per semester) in 2018–19 was $31,400. Room and board is $13,020.

Financial Aid

Typically, about 98 percent of Neumann undergraduate students receive some form of financial aid (scholarships, grants, and student loans).

Neumann offers a variety of renewable scholarships each year to entering full-time freshmen and transfer students. Interested applicants should contact the Office of Admissions and Financial Aid as soon as possible to determine eligibility.

In addition to Neumann scholarships, funds are available through the Federal Pell Grant, Federal Supplemental Educational Opportunity Grant, and Federal Work-Study Programs. Many states provide grant money to attend Neumann (non-Pennsylvania residents should check with their state's higher education agency for details). Veterans Administration benefits can be received by qualified veterans or their dependents. Federal Stafford Student Loans and Federal PLUS Program loans are available and can be applied for through Neumann's preferred lender or any participating bank. Neumann also offers institutional need-based grants. All students requesting financial aid must complete the Free Application for Federal Student Aid (FAFSA) each year to determine eligibility. In order to expedite processing, the FAFSA should be submitted by March 15 for the following school year. Financial aid funds are renewable annually based on need, as determined by the FAFSA results.

Faculty

Neumann students describe faculty members as sincere, hard-working, determined, and energetic. Faculty members view themselves, first, as teachers and are proud partners in their students' journeys toward professional careers. Each student has a faculty adviser, who assists in arranging a program designed to meet the student's educational goals. Many faculty members serve as moderators of student clubs. The student-faculty ratio is 14:1.

Student Government

The Student Government Association (SGA) is the representative body for all students. Its function is to implement the aims and purposes of the University, foster cooperation in student relationships, assist the University in being responsive to the needs of the student body, and encourage personal responsibility for an intelligent system of student self-government. Through the Student Activities Board, social functions are planned throughout the year. Students serve on various University committees, including the Student Affairs Committee of the Board, Academic Advising Committee, Honors Program Committee, Registration/Orientation Task Force, and Student Judicial Board. For full-time students, a Student Government Association fee of $85 per semester is required.

Admission Requirements

Neumann has a rolling admission policy and accepts applications throughout the year. Applicants are considered on the basis of high school record, SAT or ACT scores, recommendations, class rank, and other indicators of potential to succeed in university-level studies. Applications for admission are reviewed without regard to sex, race, creed, color, national origin, age, sexual orientation, pregnancy, military status, religion, or disability. Applicants should be graduates of an accredited high school (or present equivalent credentials) and have a recommended curriculum of 16 units of high school course work, distributed as follows: 4 in English, 2 to 3 in science, 2 in mathematics, 2 in social studies, 2 in foreign language, and 4 in electives. Students intending to pursue a major in biology or clinical laboratory science must have at least 1 year of high school biology and chemistry, and high school physics is highly recommended.

Neumann participates in the Advanced Placement (AP) Program and the College-Level Examination Program (CLEP).

An interview and tour of the campus are highly recommended for all prospective students and parents. Visits can be arranged by contacting the Office of Undergraduate Admission at 610-558-5616 or www.neumann.edu/visit.

Application and Information

Applicants for freshman admission are requested to have SAT or ACT scores and high school transcripts sent to the Office of Undergraduate Admission. Our application is available online at http://www.neumann.edu/apply, and it is free.

Neumann University welcomes applications from students who have attended or are currently attending either two-year or four-year regionally accredited institutions of higher learning.

For further information, students should contact:

Office of Admissions
Neumann University
One Neumann Drive
Aston, Pennsylvania 19014-1298
United States
Phone: 610-558-5616
800-9NEUMANN (toll-free)
E-mail: neumann@neumann.edu
Website: http://www.neumann.edu

Students love the newest building on campus, the Mirenda Center for Sport, Spirituality, and Character Development.

NEW COLLEGE OF FLORIDA

SARASOTA, FLORIDA

The College

New College of Florida offers serious students the opportunity to pursue rigorous academic study in an environment designed to promote depth in thinking, free exchange of ideas, and highly individualized interaction with faculty members. The College was founded as a private institution in 1960 with a devotion to the values implicit in a liberal arts and sciences education, and a dedication to creating an innovative academic program where talented students and outstanding faculty members could come together to pursue learning through small classes, seminars, and independent study, and to pursue advanced undergraduate research.

In 2001, New College was designated as the official Honors College in the liberal arts and sciences for the State University System of Florida. New College is regularly featured in guidebooks as being among the nation's leading educational values and as one of the country's top small, public colleges. New College is also known as one of the nation's top producers of Fulbright scholarship recipients, with 46 in the last decade alone, a better per-capita performance than almost all U.S. colleges and universities.

About 80 percent of New College graduates go on to pursue graduate or professional study at leading institutions, in recent years including Harvard, Yale, MIT, Georgetown, Berkeley, and Oxford.

New College's student population is 838, of whom approximately 62 percent are women. Approximately 20 percent of students are out-of-state or overseas residents. The College has begun a growth initiative and plans to gradually increase enrollment to 1,200 by 2023.

The College's 110-acre bayfront location near the Gulf of Mexico includes basketball, racquetball, tennis, and volleyball courts; a multipurpose soccer, softball, and athletic field; a running trail; a 25-meter swimming pool; and a comprehensive fitness center. The New College sailing team is part of the Inter-Collegiate Sailing Association of North America (ICSA). Students also compete in recreational and intramural sports including soccer, tennis, fencing, flag football, softball, and swimming. Sailboats, kayaks, and canoes are also available free of charge.

Location

On the coastline in southwest Florida, New College serves as the northern gateway to Sarasota, a bustling city 50 miles south of Tampa. Sarasota is noted for its recreational and cultural attractions, including beautiful white-sand beaches, professional theater, orchestra, opera, and ballet companies, and an abundance of art and music venues. Notably, New College sits adjacent to the world-famous John and Mable Ringling Museum of Art, which offers students free entry to view its Baroque and Renaissance art collections.

Many major airlines serve Sarasota-Bradenton International Airport, which is near the College. Buses link the campus to downtown, shopping malls, parks, and beaches, though bicycling is the favored means of transportation among students.

Majors and Degrees

New College awards the Bachelor of Arts degree in liberal arts and sciences. Each of the College's nearly forty different areas of concentration (majors) is an individualized program that students design in consultation with faculty members. These include anthropology; applied mathematics; art; art history; biochemistry; biology; biopsychology; chemistry; Chinese language and culture; classics; computer science; economics; English; environmental studies; European studies; French language/French studies; gender studies; general studies; German studies/German language and literature; history; humanities; international and area studies; literature; marine biology; mathematics; medieval and Renaissance studies; music; natural sciences; philosophy; physics; political science; psychology; public policy; religion; Russian language and literature; social sciences; sociology; Spanish language and literature; theater; and urban studies. Students may also pursue special program areas of concentration with faculty approval. Pre-medical, pre-law, pre-M.B.A., pre-veterinary, and other advanced-degree program advising and guidelines are provided by faculty members and by the Center for Career Engagement and Opportunity. New College also offers a master's degree program in data science.

Academic Programs

New College's distinctive curriculum enables students, in close consultation with faculty members, to develop programs of seminars, tutorials, independent research, internships, and off-campus experiences that meet each student's personal academic interests and goals.

At the end of each semester, students receive detailed narrative evaluations that are far more comprehensive than grades, as well as satisfactory/unsatisfactory assessments of their work from individual faculty members. Graduation requirements include satisfactory completion of seven academic contracts (a set of academic courses and other goals for the semester, planned by the student and faculty adviser), three independent-study projects, a senior thesis or project, and an oral baccalaureate examination. In addition to the requirements for individual majors, students must complete eight courses within the liberal arts curriculum, with at least one course each in the humanities, social sciences, natural sciences, and diverse perspectives. Students must also meet basic proficiency in mathematics and English language and advanced proficiency in written and oral English language.

The College operates on a 4-1-4 calendar year, including a January interterm when students undertake independent study projects, such as library, laboratory, or field research; internships; and performing arts projects, all of which they design and complete under faculty sponsorship.

Off-Campus Programs

New College believes that internships, fieldwork, and independent research can make a significant contribution to an undergraduate education, and facilitates such study through its flexible, individualized curriculum and special support services. New College is a member of the National Student Exchange, which provides access to nearly 200 universities with programs in the U.S. and abroad (many with comparable tuition costs) and the Consortium for Innovative Environments in Learning. New College is also a member of the Cross-College Alliance with four other higher education institutions in the Sarasota area that allow students to cross-register for courses at each other's campuses.

Academic Facilities

New College's Jane Bancroft Cook Library is befitting of one of the country's leading colleges and has an open stack arrangement that allows free access to most materials. With a resident collection of more than 285,000 items, and unmediated access to more than 11 million items from the State University System of Florida Libraries, Cook Library provides research-level collections to students and faculty. The library also boasts access to the University of South Florida electronic collections. In total, the library has access to more than 10,000 electronic serial titles, including scholarly journals, newspapers, digital images and videos, and datasets. A comprehensive online interlibrary loan system gives students convenient access to holdings of libraries worldwide. In addition, the library offers research instruction, digital services, data management and grant compliance services, and numerous workshops, lectures, seminars, and other offerings. Robust wireless network access is available to all users.

The Harry Sudakoff Conference Center hosts visiting lecturers, meetings of campus and community organizations, and special events. The Caples Fine Arts Complex includes the 264-seat Mildred Sainer Music and Arts Pavilion, which features student, local, and national performances; the Lota Mundy Music Building, which houses eight music practice rooms and the Benjamin and Barbara Slavin Electronic Music Studio; the Christianne Felsmann Fine Arts Building; the Betty Isermann Fine Arts Gallery and Studio; and a sculpture studio.

The R. V. Heiser Natural Sciences Complex houses laboratories, classrooms, offices, a state-of-the-art optical spectroscopy and nanomaterials laboratory, a research greenhouse, herbarium, a computer lab, two electron microscopes, and an auditorium. An $8 million addition that opened in fall 2017 expanded Heiser by 50 percent. The Rhoda and Jack Pritzker Marine Biology Research Center, one of the leading marine research centers in southwest Florida, features culture rooms, laboratories, and aquariums with water drawn from Sarasota Bay.

The College's 35,000 square-foot Academic Center, which opened in 2011, was awarded LEED Gold certification by the U.S. Green Building Council. It includes a state-of-the-art computer lab, classrooms, faculty offices, and a student lounge.

Costs

For the 2019–20 academic year, the estimated in-state tuition and fees at New College of Florida are $6,916 and out-of-state tuition and fees are $29,944. Room and board costs are $9,529.

Financial Aid

Most students receive scholarship funding from either New College of Florida or the New College Foundation. Approximately 96 percent of New College students receive some form of financial assistance, including academic scholarships and need-based financial aid. To apply for federal and need-based financial aid, students should file the Free Application for Federal Student Aid (FAFSA). November 1 is the priority date for need-based financial aid. No additional forms are required for most of the College's scholarship programs. New College of Florida guarantees an offer of scholarship funding to all admitted applicants with admission files completed by April 15, so long as they are US citizens or eligible non-citizens, and have not yet earned a bachelor's or advanced degree. The same deadline applies to freshmen, transfers, and internationals.

Faculty

Of New College's full-time faculty members, 97 percent hold the highest degree awarded in their field of study, usually the doctorate. They come to New College from the finest universities nationally and abroad, drawn to an environment that emphasizes excellence in teaching and fosters a close-knit community of scholars. Faculty members sponsor individual students in the formulation of their academic programs, gradually moving toward a form of mentorship through which joint research is sometimes pursued. A 10:1 student-faculty ratio is a key factor in the College's individualized approach to education. At New College, all classes are taught by faculty, not by teaching assistants.

Student Government

Student input is a decisive factor in campus governance. Elected student representatives serve on the Board of Trustees and most major policymaking committees, and are voting participants in divisional and campus-wide faculty meetings. The New College Student Alliance, the College's student government, has authority over funding for recreational events, social events, student clubs and organizations on campus, and allocation of the Green Fee for environmentally friendly projects.

Admission Requirements

New College of Florida seeks highly capable students eager to take responsibility for their own education. The admissions staff reviews each candidate individually, assessing his or her potential for success within, and contribution to, the College's unique environment. Course selection, academic record, and writing ability are focal points of the committee's review. The majority (60 percent) of the first-year students entering in fall 2018 ranked in the top 20 percent of their high school class.

The middle 50 percent of SAT takers had a combined score of 1230–1400 on the evidence-based reading/writing and math sections. The middle 50 percent of ACT takers had a composite score of 25–31.

All prospective students may apply for entrance to the fall term. Only prospective transfer students may apply the spring term. Candidates must submit an admission application, fee or fee waiver, Self-reported Student Academic Record (SSAR), SAT or ACT scores, and a letter of recommendation. A campus visit and demonstrated interest are also recommended for all those with serious interest in applying.

Application and Information

Admissions application materials and descriptive literature are available through the New College Office of Admissions and Financial Aid. The deadline for priority admission is November 1. All students who meet this deadline will receive a decision by April 1, however some students will receive their decisions sooner. Applications will continue to be accepted on a rolling basis November 2 through April 15. Those students who apply during that time will receive their decisions on a rolling basis. A completed application and all supporting documents must be submitted to the Office of Admissions and Financial Aid before a candidate is considered for admission.

Inquiries and application requests should be directed to:

Joy Hamm
Dean of Admissions and Financial Aid
New College of Florida
5800 Bay Shore Road
Sarasota, Florida 34243-2109
United States
Phone: 941-487-5000
Fax: 941-487-5001
E-mail: admissions@ncf.edu
Website: http://www.ncf.edu
http://www.facebook.com/newcollegeofflorida
http://twitter.com/NewCollegeofFL
http://www.youtube.com/user/NewCollegeofFL

New College of Florida's historic waterfront campus features spectacular sunsets, wetlands, an intertidal lagoon, and boat access.

COLLEGE CLOSE-UPS

NIAGARA UNIVERSITY

NIAGARA UNIVERSITY, NEW YORK

NIAGARA UNIVERSITY

The University

Niagara University (NU), founded in 1856, is a private, comprehensive university rooted in a Catholic and Vincentian tradition. The suburban campus combines the old and new; both ivy-covered buildings and modern architectural structures line its picturesque landscape. The University is easily accessible via the New York State Thruway, both the Buffalo and Niagara Falls international airports, and rail and bus service.

There are approximately 3,100 undergraduate and 850 graduate students enrolled at Niagara. A large percentage of these students take advantage of the more than 100 extracurricular and cocurricular activities offered. Volunteer work in the community is popular among the students and enhances learning and community relations.

University sports teams compete on the Division I level and are members of the NCAA, the Metro Atlantic Athletic Conference and the Atlantic Hockey Association. Intercollegiate sports for men include baseball, basketball, cross-country, golf, ice hockey, soccer, swimming and diving, and tennis. Intercollegiate sports for women include basketball, cross-country, golf, lacrosse, outdoor track and field, soccer, softball, swimming and diving, tennis, and volleyball. Club sports include cheerleading, danceline, hockey, rugby, skiing, wrestling, and many others. The Kiernan Recreation Center offers a variety of sports and recreational facilities, including a multipurpose gymnasium, a swimming and diving pool, an indoor track, racquetball courts, free weight and Nautilus rooms, and aerobics rooms. There are several outdoor athletic fields as well as basketball and tennis courts.

Additional student services include the Student Health Center; the Office of Academic Support, which provides free tutoring services; and the Office of Career Services, which offers professional and career counseling. Other services include counseling, new student orientation, academic support, and veterans' affairs.

Niagara University's housing accommodations include five residence halls, a grouping of five small cottages, and a student apartment complex.

The University offers graduate studies in business, counseling, criminal justice, education, finance, interdisciplinary studies, information security and digital forensics, sport management and a Ph.D. in leadership and policy.

Location

Niagara University's picturesque 160-acre campus is located in the town of Lewiston, New York, two minutes off the I-190 on Route 104. The campus is situated on Monteagle Ridge overlooking the lower Niagara River, which connects the two Great Lakes of Erie and Ontario. The University's suburban campus setting is just a few miles from the world-famous Niagara Falls, 20 minutes from Buffalo, which offers a variety of cultural events, sports, and entertainment opportunities, and just 90 minutes from Rochester and Toronto, Canada's largest metropolitan area. In addition, the University is minutes away from the quaint village of Lewiston, New York, and the city of Niagara Falls, New York.

Majors and Degrees

The **College of Arts and Sciences** offers the Bachelor of Arts degree in art history with museum studies, chemistry, communication studies, English, environmental science, French, gerontology, history, international studies, liberal arts, life sciences, mathematics, philosophy, political science, psychology, religious studies, social sciences, sociology, and Spanish. The Bachelor of Science degree is awarded in actuarial science, biochemistry, biology (with a concentration in biotechnology), chemistry, computer and information sciences, criminal justice, environmental science, mathematics, nursing, psychology, and social work. This division also offers the Bachelor of Fine Arts degree in theatre studies (with concentrations in performance, design and production, and theatre specializations). Preprofessional programs are offered in dentistry, law, medicine, pharmacy, veterinary medicine, and Army ROTC. An Associate of Arts degree is available in general studies. Enrichment courses in fine arts and languages are also available. A combination five-year B.S./M.S. program is available to students in the criminal justice program; psychology majors can engage in a six-year B.A./M.S. program in clinical mental health counseling; and an accelerated nursing program and an R.N.-to-B.S.N. program is offered for students who already have their R.N.

Preprofessional Partnerships: NU offers a number of preprofessional partnerships. These include a 3+4 partnership in pharmacy with the State University of New York at Buffalo (SUNY), a 2+3 partnership in pharmacy with Lake Erie College of Osteopathic Medicine (LECOM), a 3+4 partnership in medicine with LECOM, and a 3+4 partnership in dentistry with SUNY at Buffalo. Qualified premedical Niagara students are eligible to apply for the early assurance program sponsored by the SUNY at Buffalo.

Niagara University's **College of Business Administration** is accredited by AACSB International—The Association to Advance Collegiate Schools of Business and offers a B.B.A. and a combination B.B.A./M.B.A. degree (five-year program) in accounting. This division offers B.S. degrees in economics, finance, management (with concentrations in human resources, international business, and supply chain management), and marketing (with a concentration in food marketing), as well as a B.A. in economics. In addition, an A.A.S. degree can be earned in business. Students gain real-world experiences through internships, study abroad, and via cooperative education programs as well as research being conducted in several business-focused campus centers.

Holding the highest accreditations possible in both the United States and Canada—the United States Council for the Accreditation of Educator Preparation (CAEP) and Canada's Ontario College of Teachers—Niagara University's **College of Education** provides students with an option of earning dual certification to teach in both countries. The College of Education offers bachelor's degree programs leading to New York state initial certification in early childhood and childhood (birth–grade 6), childhood (grades 1–6), childhood and middle childhood (grades 1–9), middle childhood and adolescence (grades 5–12), special education and childhood (grades 1–6), special education and adolescence (grades 7–12), and in Teaching English to Speakers of Other Languages (TESOL). All education majors pursue an academic concentration to establish expertise in one of the following subject areas: business, English language arts, French, liberal arts, mathematics, social studies, and Spanish. Business education is offered only for grades 5–12. The academic concentrations in biology, chemistry, or liberal arts can only be pursued in the early childhood and childhood (birth–grade 6), and special education and childhood (grades 1–6). Most other states, and Puerto Rico, have reciprocity agreements with New York, so an NU education would qualify education majors to teach in those states as well.

The **College of Hospitality and Tourism Management** provides a career-oriented curriculum leading to a B.S. degree in three specific areas: hotel and restaurant management (with concentrations in food and beverage management; luxury hospitality operations; and hotel planning, development, and operations), sport management (with concentrations in sport operations and revenue management), and tourism and recreation management (with concentrations in event and meeting management and tourism destination management). The College of Hospitality and Tourism Management offered the world's first bachelor's degree in tourism. NU's hotel and restaurant program, the second oldest in New York state, was the seventh program nationally to be accredited by the Accreditation Commission for Programs in Hospitality Administration by the Council of Hotel, Restaurant, and Institutional Education. The College introduces students to a comprehensive body of knowledge about the hotel, restaurant, tourism, and recreational areas and applies this knowledge to current industry challenges. The College requires that its students accumulate 800 hours of industry-related experience. These and other practical experiences offer NU students the knowledge necessary to advance in the field. Students work with industry leaders in classroom projects, join academic clubs and professional organizations, and participate in special trips to trade shows and conventions and specially designed study-abroad experiences, making NU a national leader in the area.

For students who are undecided about which major to choose, Niagara University offers its award-winning **Academic Exploration Program (AEP).** AEP provides a structured opportunity for students to participate in a thorough, organized process of selecting a major that meets their academic talents and career goals while fulfilling requirements to graduate with classmates on time.

Academic Programs

Niagara University's curricula enable students to pursue their academic preferences and to complete courses that lead to proficiency in other academic areas. The Honors program provides special academic opportunities that stimulate, encourage, and challenge participants. In addition, an accelerated three-year degree program is offered to qualified students.

Niagara grants credit for successful scores on the Advanced Placement, College-Level Examination Program, and the International Baccalaureate tests.

Internships, research, and independent study are available in many academic programs. An Army ROTC program is also offered.

NU is fully accredited by the Middle States Association of Colleges and Schools. The University's programs in the respective areas are accredited by the Council for the Accreditation of Educator Preparation, AACSB International–The Association to Advance Collegiate Schools of Business, and the Council on Social Work Education. The chemistry department has the approval of the American Chemical Society. The travel, hotel, and restaurant administration program is accredited by the Commission for Programs in Hospitality Administration.

Off-Campus Programs

For those students who wish to study abroad, the University offers programs in Argentina, Australia, Chile, China, England, France, Ireland, Italy, Japan, Spain, Thailand, and many other countries. Students may choose from more than 200 programs in more than 30 countries available through the University's membership in the American Institute for Foreign Studies, Center for Cross-Cultural Study, College Consortium for International Studies, Global Learning Semesters, and Semester at Sea.

Academic Facilities

In recent years, Niagara University has experienced a process of transformation that has significantly developed the physical character of the University's campus and its 21st-century approach to teaching and learning.

The $33 million B. Thomas Golisano Center for Integrated Sciences offers 50,000 square-feet of learning space and cutting-edge equipment that encourages collaboration among scientific disciplines. The Academic Complex, the home to the College of Education and the College of Business Administration (Bisgrove Hall), is a state-of-the-art learning facility, with a simulated trading floor. The newly renovated and expanded Russell J. Salvatore Dining Commons features presentation-style cooking, a variety of comfortable seating options, and bold colors and design elements that create an inviting environment for NU students to gather and enjoy meals.

Costs

Tuition for 2018–19 was $31,700. Room and board (with a choice of meal plans) cost an additional $13,200 per year. Fees were estimated at $1,450 per year. Niagara estimates that an additional $2,500 to $3,050 per year is adequate for books, laundry, and other essentials, such as travel to and from home.

Financial Aid

Ninety-nine percent of the entering freshmen and transfer students received a financial aid package which may include merit-based scholarships, loans, grants, or campus employment. Students seeking financial aid should file the Free Application for Federal Student Aid (FAFSA). New York state residents should also file a Tuition Assistance Program (TAP) application.

Faculty

Niagara University has a dedicated, accessible faculty that genuinely cares about the academic and personal growth of their students. Their commitment to teaching is their primary concern. A student-to-faculty ratio of 12:1 and an average class size of approximately 20 allow personal attention and classroom interaction.

Admission Requirements

Niagara University welcomes students who have demonstrated aptitude and academic achievement at the high school level. The university has adopted a test-optional admissions policy for most first-year undergraduate applicants, beginning with the fall 2018 entry year. Niagara has joined a growing number of the nation's most competitive and well-respected institutions by giving students the option to submit or withhold standardized test scores (SAT/ACT) as part of their admissions application. The Office of Undergraduate Admissions will continue to accept standardized test scores from students who believe their results are reflective of their academic abilities to succeed at the university. If they feel that it doesn't reflect their ability and academic skills, they have the option of not submitting.

The few exceptions to this test-optional policy include students who are seeking entrance into a nursing or biology major, those who wish to be considered for Trustees or Presidential Scholarships, students looking to apply for science-related scholarships such as NUSURF (Niagara University Science Undergraduate Research Fellowship), and home-schooled students.

International students are required to submit the results of their TOEFL examination and a translation of their academic documentation. Interviews are recommended. Transfer students are accepted in any semester. (Transfer credit is evaluated individually by the dean of each division.) Students who complete high school in less than four years are eligible for early admission. Students may also apply under an early action program. Economically and educationally disadvantaged students from New York State are eligible to apply for admission through the Higher Educational Opportunity Program (HEOP).

Application and Information

Niagara operates on a rolling admission basis and adheres to the College Board Candidates Reply Date. Nursing and theatre applicants are encouraged to apply by mid-December of their senior year. A visit to the campus is recommended, and overnight accommodations in a residence hall are available through the Niagara Nights program.

Information on all aspects of the University can be obtained by contacting the Office of Admissions or by visiting www.niagara.edu.

Mark Wojnowski
Director of Admissions
Niagara University
Niagara University, New York 14109-2011
Phone: 716-286-8700
800-462-2111 (toll-free)
Fax: 716-286-8710
E-mail: admissions@niagara.edu
Website: http://www.niagara.edu
http://www.facebook.com/niagarau
http://twitter.com/niagarauniv
http://instagram.com/NiagaraUniversity

Adjacent to the international border between the United States and Canada, Niagara University's 160-acre campus runs along the top of picturesque Monteagle Ridge, overlooking the Niagara River gorge just 4 miles north of the world-famous waterfalls.

COLLEGE CLOSE-UPS

NORTHEASTERN UNIVERSITY

BOSTON, MASSACHUSETTS

Northeastern

The University

Founded in 1898, Northeastern is a global research university and the recognized leader in experience-driven lifelong learning. Northeastern's world-renowned experiential approach empowers their students, faculty, alumni, and partners to create impact far beyond the confines of discipline, degree, and campus. The academic curriculum is enhanced by experiential learning through research, professional, global, regional, and service experiences. Anchored by the world's largest, most innovative cooperative education program, Northeastern prepares students for a lifetime of achievement and allows them to make an impact on the world before they graduate.

The current undergraduate enrollment of 18,299 is comprised of students of all backgrounds and interests, giving Northeastern its diverse culture and community. Students can participate in more than 400 student clubs and organizations, engage in cutting-edge research with faculty from various disciplines, and perform with an award-winning a cappella group. They can join Northeastern's student-run venture accelerator, IDEA, play varsity or club basketball, tutor local children, and more. Students have countless opportunities to make lifelong friendships, to try something brand new—a class, a sport, or a career path—to hone their leadership skills, and find a place where they belong. Quiet corners of the campus feel far from city streets and give students a secluded haven to read, write, or relax. The 73-acre campus is dynamic and welcoming, a beautiful stretch of leafy green in the heart of Boston.

Location

Northeastern's Boston campus is located in the heart of the city, where the distinctive neighborhoods of Back Bay, South End, Fenway, and Roxbury meet. Over half of the student body lives on campus and many of the residence halls have amazing views of the Boston skyline.

The Back Bay area, known for its many cultural and educational institutions, is just steps away from Symphony Hall, the New England Conservatory of Music, the Museum of Fine Arts, and the Isabella Stewart Gardner Museum. The South End is home to elegant Victorian row houses, a vibrant arts scene, hidden gardens, and some of the finest dining in Boston. The Fenway area, with its beautiful rose garden, bicycle and jogging paths, and Fenway Park (home of the Boston Red Sox), is just a few blocks away.

Majors and Degrees

Northeastern offers over 175 majors and 120 combined majors across eight colleges. Combined majors pair together two areas of study into one interdisciplinary program. Half of Northeastern students have more than just a major—either a double major, a major and a minor, or another combination.

The College of Arts, Media and Design awards undergraduate degrees in architecture, art, communication studies, design, game art and animation, games, journalism, landscape architecture, media and screen studies, media arts, music, music industry, music technology, studio art, and theatre.

The D'Amore-McKim School of Business offers two degree options: the Bachelor of Science in Business Administration (B.S.B.A.) and the Bachelor of Science in International Business (B.S.I.B.). The college offers concentrations in accounting, entrepreneurship and innovation, finance, management, management information systems, marketing, and supply chain management.

The Khoury College of Computer Sciences awards degrees in computer science, cybersecurity, and data science. Khoury also offers combined majors that pair computer science with over 20 different academic fields.

The College of Engineering offers degrees in bioengineering, chemical, civil, computer, electrical, environmental, industrial, and mechanical engineering.

The Bouvé College of Health Sciences awards degrees in health science, nursing, pharmaceutical sciences, and pharmacy.

The College of Science offers degrees in applied physics, behavioral neuroscience, biochemistry, biology, biomedical physics, cell and molecular biology, chemistry, ecology and evolutionary biology, environmental science, environmental studies, linguistics, marine biology, mathematics, physics, and psychology.

The College of Social Sciences and Humanities awards undergraduate degrees in African American studies, American Sign Language, anthropology, Asian studies, criminal justice, economics, English, history, human services, international affairs, philosophy, political science, religious studies, sociology, and Spanish.

The Explore Program for undeclared students offers a wide array of academic opportunities designed to help students who feel strongly about exploring their options before making a commitment to a major. The program provides the support and guidance students need to explore and eventually choose one of Northeastern's undergraduate programs.

Combined majors are unique, hybrid degree programs that combine multiple academic fields—allowing students to pursue more than one interest area—all while staying on track for graduation. Northeastern offers over 120 defined combined majors with curriculum specific to each individual academic program.

Academic Programs

At the heart of a Northeastern education are award-winning faculty mentors, a rigorous and innovative curriculum, undergraduate research, and global experiences that challenge and transform. Northeastern's innovative programs encompass over 175 majors and 120 combined majors, along with a variety of concentrations and honors, pre-professional, and study-abroad programs.

Northeastern's approach to education integrates a challenging academic curriculum with immersive experiences including research, service-learning, opportunities across all seven continents, and the university's signature cooperative education program (co-op), enabling students to make deep connections between their field of study and the world around them. Personalized, guided, and supported flexibility enables students to choose a four- or five-year path with up to 18 months of real-world experience, creating a strong professional network and giving students confidence—as well as a significant edge in the job market. Students learn which careers are a good fit for them—and which are not—all before graduating. Over half of students are offered full-time jobs from previous co-op employers. Northeastern partners with over 2,943 co-op employers around the globe, including some of the world's largest and most reputable companies: Apple, Bank of America, The Boston Globe, Child Family Health International, Google, Hill Holiday, P&G, Pixar, Samsung, and Vogue, just to name a few. Experiential learning opportunities—including global co-ops, service-learning, research, programs at their regional campuses, and study abroad—are available in 136 countries around the world.

NORTHERN ARIZONA UNIVERSITY
FLAGSTAFF, ARIZONA

NAU NORTHERN ARIZONA UNIVERSITY

The University

Founded in 1899, Northern Arizona University (NAU) is a fully accredited four-year public university centered on students. For those interested in a collaborative community with a breadth of stellar programs and a dedicated research agenda, NAU offers an environment ideal for academic achievement, personal growth, professional outcomes, and adventure.

The university's Flagstaff campus offers the amenities of a big-campus with a small-campus feel—all in a beautiful mountain location that ranks among the best college towns in the nation. NAU also has innovative partnerships with numerous Arizona community colleges, which gives students affordable and convenient options for transferring into an NAU bachelor's degree program.

NAU offers a comprehensive range of nearly 100 majors to choose from and many nationally ranked programs taught by professors who work alongside you as mentors and teammates. Students have an abundance of opportunities to participate in important research and creative and scholarly projects alongside faculty who bring their focus to their labs and their passion to the classrooms. Nearly 3,000 students participate in research and professional internships each year. Through the "Accelerated Program," high-achieving students can even work simultaneously on select master's degrees and graduate in as few as five years with both a bachelor's and a master's degree. And students can find everything they need to accomplish their goals, including programs and support services that are second to none—from enrollment through graduation and beyond.

NAU also delivers a predictable price tag through its fixed tuition rate, known as The Pledge. Students who attend the Flagstaff campus will pay the same fixed tuition rate for up to four years with a no-increases guarantee. Those who live in one of 14 Western states can save nearly 40 percent on the out-of-state tuition rate through the Western Undergraduate Exchange (WUE). Every major at NAU is eligible for the WUE rate.

Location

With a population of about 70,000, Flagstaff is a vibrant high-elevation mountain town that breaks Arizona's desert stereotype. Temperatures rarely exceed 90 degrees in the summer, fall brings a brilliant change of color, winter snowfall averages more than 100 inches, and spring bursts with blossoms. The region's unparalleled natural scenery is enhanced by hundreds of great restaurants and a robust arts and entertainment scene. The four-season climate provides recreational opportunities that range from scenic hiking and biking to skiing and snowboarding. The campus sits just 75 miles south of the Grand Canyon—close enough that studies might bring students there to collect water samples from the Colorado River, discuss issues related to Native populations, participate in interactive painting workshops, or explore the art and culture of the region.

Flagstaff's charm, location, and recreational opportunities consistently earn top honors and distinctions from national publications. Time.com named it one of the nation's happiest cities, and the American Institute for Economic Research's 2017 College Destinations Index named Flagstaff the No. 1 Best College Town in Arizona and No. 3 in the nation. Outside Magazine also has named Flagstaff among the best places to live in the United States. Prospective students can explore some of the most popular local sights through NAU's fully immersive online regional tour: nau.edu/explore.

In addition to Northern Arizona University's Flagstaff campus, NAU has locations throughout the state that provide a convenient way for students to complete an NAU degree at an Arizona community college. Online options also allow students to take classes that work with their schedule.

Academics

NAU offers nearly 100 bachelor's degrees, about 64 master's degrees, 14 doctoral degrees, and a wide range of minors, certificates, and emphases, so students are sure to find a program that's right for them. Majors and programs are organized by academic discipline under nine colleges: the College of Arts and Letters; the College of Education; the College of Engineering, Informatics and Applied Sciences; The College of the Environment, Forestry and Natural Sciences; the College of Health and Human Services; the College of Social and Behavioral Sciences; The W. A. Franke College of Business; the Honors College; and the Graduate College. Some of the most popular majors include biomedical science, criminology and criminal justice, nursing, mechanical engineering, elementary education, and hotel and restaurant management.

Through the Honors College, students can pursue a rewarding and enriching academic path that emphasizes small, interactive classes where students gain critical-thinking skills that appeal to employers and graduate schools. The new 200,000-square foot Honors College facility, which opened fall 2018, provides meaningful engagement living and working with other motivated students who share a passion for learning.

To complete a bachelor's degree at NAU, students must complete 120 units of credit, including all liberal studies and capstone requirements, and all requirements for a student's specific academic plan. Other requirements, such as a minimum GPA, also apply. Detailed information can be found at nau.edu/academics.

Beyond the Classroom

A degree from NAU represents a quality educational experience—one that incorporates a practical learning approach beyond any textbook. Nearly 600 NAU students each year travel to partner institutions in one of more than 60 foreign countries as part of our international-award-winning study-abroad experiences. Those wishing to stay closer to home can study at one of 200 U.S. institutions through the National Student Exchange program. An internationalization strategy at NAU incorporates global cultures into every discipline. And the Interdisciplinary Global Programs in a STEM field, business, or hospitality infuse language, culture, and a year abroad into students' studies—participants graduate with two degrees: one in their field of study and one in their chosen foreign language.

A signature of the NAU undergraduate experience is a focus on engaged and active learning. Nearly 3,000 students each year engage in practical research opportunities alongside skilled faculty and mentors. More than 1,000 students convene each spring for the Undergraduate Symposium, a large-scale event where students share their research and discoveries and present scholarly and creative work to their peers, professors, and the Flagstaff community.

NAU also takes advantage of its prime location with world-class outdoor education opportunities. An interdisciplinary Grand Canyon semester offers students immersion in the science, culture, and politics of one of the truly unique regions of the U.S. Flagstaff is the world's first International Dark Sky City and offers unparalleled night skies and stargazing facilities for astronomical research, including the Discovery Channel Telescope, the world's fifth-largest. And the 50,000-acre Centennial Forest offers forestry majors and students in other environmental studies programs the chance to conduct research and practice maintenance of a variety of ecosystems.

Facilities

With nearly 90 percent of freshmen choosing to live on campus, students begin to build their community the moment they arrive at NAU. Freshman housing options are based upon each student's academic interests, so they select a room in the Residential College that aligns with their major and career interests and live alongside others who are on a similar journey. Multiple Academic Success Centers on campus provide distinct types of tutoring, most at no cost. And the 225,000-square-foot Cline Library offers an array of services, research materials, and study spaces, and students can reserve rooms, check out laptops, and get help with technology or writing.

NAU is ranked as one of the top 100 research universities without a medical school by the National Science Foundation. The visually striking, five-story Science and Health Building serves as a symbol of the university's rise to scientific and research prominence. This is where students interested in medicine, dentistry, research, or science education will take some of their first steps toward a professional career. The university's one-of-a-kind Native American Cultural Center was built with input from 22 tribes and reflects NAU's commitment to Indigenous students and to helping others learn more about these cultures.

NAU's Aquatic and Tennis Complex attracts international athletes and Olympic teams for high-altitude training, and a world-class recreation facility at the Health and Learning Center offers a 38-foot climbing wall, an indoor jogging track, a fully equipped weight room, cardio studio, and much more.

A visit to campus is the best way to learn more about the university's impressive facilities; for those who can't make it to Flagstaff in person, NAU's online virtual tour is the next best thing: nau.edu/virtualtour.

Costs

NAU tuition and fees for 2019–20 are $11,896 per academic year for Arizona residents and $26,516 for nonresidents. Under the Western Undergraduate Exchange (WUE) program, students from 14 qualifying states pay a tuition rate nearly 40 percent lower than the out-of-state rate. The 2019–20 WUE tuition and fee rate is $17,221 per academic year. Tuition rates are set each spring by the Arizona Board of Regents. Room, board, books, transportation, and personal expenses vary by student and are not included in the tuition costs.

NAU makes financial planning for college easier with The Pledge, a four-year fixed-tuition guarantee. Students who attend on the Flagstaff campus will pay the same fixed-tuition rate for up to four years. In addition, students with a meal plan will have the same rates for up to two years. More details of The Pledge can be found at nau.edu/pledge.

Financial Aid

Students are automatically considered for merit scholarships when they apply and have submitted their test scores. Arizona residents might be eligible for the Lumberjack Scholars Award, which covers up to 100 percent of the cost of in-state tuition. Nonresidents might be eligible for a number of awards including the President's Excellence Scholarship, valued at $36,000 over four years. NAU's friendly financial aid staff is available to help students explore other opportunities such as private scholarships, grants, and loans in order to make their education as affordable as possible. More details regarding financial aid can be found at nau.edu/finaid.

Faculty

Northern Arizona University is designed for discovery. The faculty and staff care about student success and encourage students to push past their limits and develop new strengths. From biology to social sciences, professors weave interactive learning into NAU's curriculum, providing students with the hands-on experience they need to succeed and opportunities to make original contributions to a field of study.

NAU professors from a variety of disciplines are among the leading experts in their fields, such as astronomy professor David Trilling, who is one of the world's foremost asteroid researchers and works on several NASA-funded projects investigating hundreds of asteroids, including those that could strike Earth. Biology professor Kiisa Nishikawa's muscle function theory is improving prosthetic devices and neuromuscular disease treatment. And entomology professor Rich Hofstetter studies how loud rock music might slow the infestation of bark beetles, which destroy pine trees and increase wildfire danger in Southwestern forests.

Student Clubs and Organizations

Getting involved in campus life is one of the best ways students can gain leadership skills and define their own NAU experience. Northern Arizona University offers more than 400 clubs and organizations ranging from sport clubs and intramurals to sororities and fraternities. There is also a wide range of leadership, academic, and service organizations related to almost every hobby, passion, or academic interest students might have.

Studies have shown that students who are involved in campus activities are more likely to be successful; it's also a great way to meet new friends. NAU students can join organizations such as First Jacks, which empowers first-generation college students toward personal and academic success; or find a sense of of 'ohana, or family, with the HAPA Hawaiian Club. The university's thriving intramural sports program ranges from favorites such as basketball and soccer to unique sports such as Canoe Battleship and even Quidditch. NAU's ultra-competitive ice hockey team, the IceJacks, is one of nearly 40 club sports and ranks among the top teams in the American Collegiate Hockey Association's Western region. Whatever a student's interest, pursuits, or background, there is a club or organization offering a sense of community and a chance to get involved.

Admission Requirements and Application Information

NAU applicants will be offered admission if they demonstrate a 3.0 high school core GPA and have no deficiencies in the 16 required college preparatory courses. Students will be considered for admission if they have a 2.5 high school core GPA and no more than one deficiency in any two areas of the college preparatory courses. Additionally, applicants with mathematics and science combination deficiencies are not admissible.

Students can apply online. They are required to access their high school transcripts and self-report them on the online application. NAU also requests that students send ACT and/or SAT scores in order to be considered for scholarships. A $25 application fee is required. Deadlines and additional details are available online at nau.edu/admissions.

Northern Arizona University
University Admissions
P.O. Box 4084
Student and Academic Services Building (#60)
Flagstaff, Arizona 86011-4084
Phone: 888-628-2968 (toll-free)
Fax: 928-523-6023
Email: admissions@nau.edu
Website: nau.edu

NORTHERN KENTUCKY UNIVERSITY
HIGHLAND HEIGHTS, KENTUCKY

The University

Northern Kentucky University (NKU) was founded in 1968 and is the newest of Kentucky's eight state universities. Nestled in a quiet suburb, NKU is just minutes from the entertainment and career opportunities of downtown Cincinnati. NKU has an enrollment of more than 14,000 students from forty-five states and sixty-one countries and is accredited by the Southern Association of Colleges and Schools. The Salmon P. Chase College of Law is accredited by both the American Bar Association and the Association of American Law Schools.

There are more than 220 student organizations and NKU's athletic teams compete in the NCAA Division I Horizon League Conference. Intercollegiate sports are offered for men and women in basketball, cross-country, track, golf, soccer, and tennis; for men in baseball; and for women in fast-pitch softball and volleyball. Intramural activities vary by semester, but include basketball, dodgeball, field hockey, flag football, ice hockey, racquetball, soccer, softball, taekwando, volleyball, and many others. A complete list can be found online at http://campusrec.nku.edu.

Majors and Degrees

NKU offers 72 bachelor's degrees, 2 associate degrees, 23 graduate programs, 10 doctoral and post master's programs, the Juris Doctor, as well as 16 graduate certificates.

Academic Programs

NKU operates on a semester calendar. To receive a bachelor's degree, students must complete a minimum of 120 credit hours. At least 60 credit hours are required for the associate degree.

The University offers a variety of career planning and placement, internship, independent study, work-study, and cooperative-education programs. There is also an advising, counseling, and testing Center available. Other programs include an honors college, a program that allows for the dual enrollment of high school students, a program where students can combine their career interests in the liberal arts and engineering fields, and University 101, an orientation program for freshmen students.

NKU recognizes credit earned through the Advanced Placement (AP) Program and the general, subject, and institutional tests of specific College-Level Examination Program (CLEP). A maximum of 45 credit hours may be applied toward the bachelor's degree from the AP and CLEP examinations. The International Baccalaureate program allows students to earn credit in science, mathematics, psychology, and languages.

Off-Campus Programs

More than 330 students participated in study-abroad programs in twenty-six countries worldwide.

Academic Facilities

Among the academic facilities at NKU are an anthropology museum, a biology museum, and an art gallery with rotating exhibits. NKU also has a laser projection planetarium; laboratories for nursing, respiratory care, and radiologic technology; the 9,000-seat BB&T Arena; and the James C. and Rachel M. Votruba Student Union, a student-centered facility, and focal point for campus programs and student organizations.

NKU's Griffin Hall, the home of the College of Informatics, is designed to help students interested in communication and media, computer science, information technology, or management information systems become the new generation of professionals who will build the region's information economy. The Health Innovation Center supports an integrated portfolio of programs to prepare a new generation of health care professionals for the future and to provide solutions to the population health and wellness challenges of the region and Commonwealth. It is an advanced facility designed to transdisciplinary research and collaboration between campus and the community. The W. Frank Steely Library contains 311,155 book titles and maintains 1,729 paper periodical subscriptions (additional periodicals are available in electronic format). Computer laboratories offer students opportunities to learn and utilize a variety of software programs. The Computer Science Department and Criminal Justice Department have collaborated to offer students a computer forensics minor to teach students how to handle digital evidence and how to present such evidence in court.

Costs

Tuition and fees for 2018-2019 were $9,360 for Kentucky students and $18,720 for nonresidents. Other costs included $7,700–$9,800 for room and meals, about $850 for books and supplies, and $3,000 for miscellaneous expenses.

Financial Aid

Northern Kentucky University awards more than $6 million in academic scholarships each year to the incoming freshman class. The University awards scholarships to highly motivated students who demonstrate strong academic performance. Kentucky residents who achieve a 2.5 GPA and a 21 ACT or 1060 SAT are considered for academic awards. Nonresident students should review scholarships.nku.edu for information on scholarship opportunities. The University offers numerous scholarship levels. Each scholarship level has merit guidelines that students must meet to qualify. To be considered for academic scholarships, interested students need to apply for admission by February 15 (based on availability of funds). For fall 2019, there is no separate scholarship application for general Northern Kentucky University academic scholarships. Students who qualify for a scholarship receive an award letter upon acceptance to NKU. Prospective students can visit scholarships.nku.edu for information on additional scholarship opportunities that require an application, letters of recommendation, or an essay. There is no deadline for the University's financial aid application; however, students who wish to receive institutional aid must apply by February 1 for priority consideration. Applicants are notified of acceptance on a rolling basis.

Faculty

More than 82 percent of the faculty members at NKU hold a doctoral degree or the terminal degree in their field. Classes are small, with an average class size of 24 and a student-faculty ratio of 18:1. All classes are taught by faculty members; no classes are taught by graduate assistants.

Student Government

Student Government (SG) is the elected student assembly at Northern Kentucky University. It is the official student voice on campus and represents the student viewpoint on University committees. All SG meetings are open, and students are encouraged to attend.

Admission Requirements

Incoming freshmen must submit an application for admission; arrange for the official ACT, SAT, or COMPASS score report to be sent; and request that the high school send an official transcript.

Based on the review of official test results, students are admitted into one of two categories: regular admission or admission with conditions. Students who have two or more deficiencies are encouraged to retake the ACT or SAT so an additional review can be completed. Students with two or more deficiencies may be asked to submit an essay, letters of recommendation, and an activities portfolio before an admission decision can be rendered. Students with two or more deficiencies who are offered admission will be required to participate in the Pathfinders Program, which is designed to enhance student engagement and provide tools needed for future academic achievement. The program includes: mandatory advising, completion of University 101 (Introduction to College) course, participation in study tables, tutoring, and college success workshops. Some degree programs require that students meet additional criteria; more information is available in the current catalog (http://www.nku.edu).

Application and Information

The $40 paper application fee may be waived for applicants with demonstrated need. The fall semester early action and scholarship deadline is February 15, assured consideration deadline is February 15, enrollment confirmation deadline is May 1, and the final deadline is July 1. The priority application deadline for the nursing program is January 31. The priority application deadline for the respiratory care program is February 15.

For more information, students should contact:
Office of Admissions
Northern Kentucky University
Highland Heights, Kentucky 41099
Phone: 859-572-5220
800-637-9948 (toll-free)
E-mail: beanorse@nku.edu
Website: http://admissions.nku.edu
http://www.facebook.com/nkuedu
http://twitter.com.nkuedu

NORTHERN VERMONT UNIVERSITY

JOHNSON, VERMONT AND LYNDONVILLE, VERMONT

Northern Vermont UNIVERSITY

The University

Set in the heart of Vermont's mountains, Northern Vermont University (NVU), with two campuses, at Johnson and Lyndon, and an online division, guides curious, motivated, engaged students on their path to success and their place in the world. The university boasts a 95 percent job placement rate for its graduates. NVU's 2,500 plus students hail from Vermont, New England, and around the world.

On July 1, 2018, Johnson State College and Lyndon State College joined to become Northern Vermont University. By combining more than 200 years of history in liberal arts and professional learning, NVU and its two campuses offer expanded access to a faculty with a broad range of expertise and experience.

Students collaborate with, and learn from, a network of peers and staff. Members of the strong alumni network live all over the world. On these close-knit campuses, relationships last a lifetime. Alumni help graduates get a foot in the door to launch their professions.

NVU offers in-demand degrees in biology, business, computer information systems, criminal justice, education, psychology and human services, and specialized degrees in animation and illustration, atmospheric sciences, climate change science, electronic journalism arts, fine woodworking and furniture design, music business and industry, mountain recreation management, studio arts, and theater.

NVU students enroll at either campus. Students can take classes at both, on campus and via online and telepresence classrooms.

NVU–Lyndon: The Lyndon campus, located in Vermont's Northeast Kingdom, offers distinct professional programs based in a liberal arts core, where every degree is infused with career-ready skills. Programs such as atmospheric sciences, mountain recreation management, electronic journalism arts, music business and industry, and exercise science prepare students for career success through real-world experiences such as internships and practicums.

Music business and industry interns can be found working on concert tours for world-famous musicians. Atmospheric sciences students regularly take first place in national competitions. Electronic journalism arts students routinely win national awards for their daily live news broadcasts—including a coveted Emmy award.

NVU–Johnson: The Johnson campus, designated by COPLAC as Vermont's premier public liberal arts institution, offers an immersive, high-impact, liberal arts experience that prepares students for meaningful careers and lifelong growth. Students are prepared to thrive in an ever-changing world.

Faculty members are active scholars and researchers committed to student success. Cross-disciplinary learning—through research, internships, student teaching, and other forms of experiential learning—enhances the student experience. Environmental and social awareness is a fundamental component of an NVU–Johnson education.

Location

NVU and its two campuses are located in the northern tier of Vermont. The 350-acre Johnson campus sits on a breathtaking hilltop amidst the Green Mountain range. Situated near Stowe, the campus is 1 hour from Burlington (Vermont's largest city), 3.5 hours from Boston, 1.5 hours from Montreal, and has access to six major ski resorts.

The modern 174-acre Lyndon campus is in Lyndonville, high on a beautiful hillside overlooking Burke Mountain in the heart of Vermont's scenic Northeast Kingdom. Nearby are two major ski areas and the Kingdom Trails mountain biking network. Lyndon is easily accessible from all points by Interstate 91, 3 hours from Boston and Springfield, Massachusetts, and 2.5 hours from Montreal.

Majors and Degrees

NVU offers bachelor's degrees in accounting, animation and illustration, anthropology and sociology, art, atmospheric sciences, biology, biology (field naturalist), business administration, childhood education, cinema production, climate change science, computer information systems, creative writing, criminal justice (restorative justice), early childhood education, electronic journalism arts, elementary education, English, environmental science, exercise science, explorations/undecided, fine woodworking and furniture design, global studies, graphic design, health science, history, interdisciplinary studies, journalism, liberal studies, mathematics, media arts, mountain recreation management, music, music business and industry, music education, musical theater, natural sciences, outdoor education, political science, psychology, psychology and human services, secondary education, studio arts, sustainability studies, and wellness and alternative medicine. NVU offers online bachelor's degrees in accounting, business, criminal justice (restorative justice), early childhood education, interdisciplinary studies, professional studies, psychology, and wellness and alternative medicine.

Associate's degrees are offered in applied science, business administration, cinema production, computing, criminal justice, electronic journalism arts, fine woodworking and furniture design, general studies, human services, mathematics, mountain recreation management, music business and industry, photography, special education, technical theater, and visual arts.

There are graduate programs in clinical mental health counseling, education, liberal studies, and studio arts.

Academics

Established in 1828, NVU–Johnson is designated by COPLAC as Vermont's premier public liberal arts institution with curriculum in professional programs and liberal arts and sciences.

Lyndon was established in 1911. Today, NVU–Lyndon is best known for innovative professional programs that combine real-world experience and career-ready skills, with a traditional education in the liberal arts.

NVU operates on a two-semester calendar plus a summer session and a two-week winter term. To graduate with a bachelor's degree, students must complete 120 credit hours and meet university and program requirements. Sixty credit hours are required for associate's degrees. Incoming students are tested for competence in writing and mathematics; deficiencies must be made up in noncredit classes during the first two semesters.

NVU's Academic Support Centers, Career Services, Financial Aid Offices, Student Life, and Health Services are just some of the entities that serve the needs and promote the well-being of students. Complete information can be found at NorthernVermont.edu.

Off-Campus Programs

Out-of-classroom and off-campus study is an integral part of the curriculum in the form of paid and unpaid internships, site visits, hands-on projects, research, independent study, field trips, and domestic and international study-away programs.

Academic Facilities

The NVU–Johnson campus has well-equipped facilities for arts, sciences, computing, and traditional classroom-based learning. The campus has one large lecture hall, a telepresence classroom, a geology lab, a chemistry lab, and an exercise physiology lab. There are seven computing labs for student use, including two all-Mac labs for media arts students. The recently renovated Visual Arts Center hosts facilities for traditional photography and ceramics, as well as two painting studios and a sculpture studio. Performing arts and theater tech students make their home in Dibden Center for the arts, which houses a 500-seat theater, practice rooms, and a MIDI lab and recording studio. The campus student center offers a game room, fireplace lounge, and a performance space for smaller events. The library holdings consist of more than 111,000 volumes, 6,500 e-books, 384 print journals, and 36,000 e-journals.

The NVU–Lyndon campus is modern and well-equipped. There are smart classrooms, two lecture halls, six computer classrooms, six science labs, and two general computer labs. There is a digital media, graphic design, video editing, and photo lab; a GIS-mapping lab; comprehensive weather center, atmospheric science lab, and observation deck; two exercise science labs; a recording studio/music business and industry lab; an instructional materials center for education majors; a psychology lab and reading lab; and the News7 broadcast production studio. The Alexander Twilight Theatre and Moore Community Room provide flexible space for gatherings, activities, and performances of all kinds. The library holdings include more than 60,000 print volumes and 100,000 managed electronic and print resources, including periodicals, e-books, and e-reference sources; and 10,000 audio visual materials including music, films, and documentaries.

Costs

The 2019–20 tuition for Vermont residents is $11,256 per year; for nonresidents, it is $24,960. The NEBHE regional program allows for a $6,500 discount for New England students in eligible programs (program eligibility by state can be found at NorthernVermont.edu/FinancialAid); there are also regionally based discounts ranging from $4,500–$6,500 for non-NEBHE students. Room and board (21-meal plan) for one academic year is $10,920. Required fees, not including health and accident insurance or the orientation/matriculation fee, total $1,166. Total expenses for a Vermont resident living on campus are $23,542; for a nonresident, $37,246. Complete information on costs can be found at NorthernVermont.edu/Tuition.

Financial Aid

Financial aid is available in the form of loans, grants, and campus employment under the Federal Work-Study program. Approximately 89 percent of the student population receives some type of financial aid from institutional and outside sources. Applicants for aid are required to complete the Free Application for Federal Student Aid (FAFSA). NVU offers merit-based scholarships as well.

Faculty

Northern Vermont University's faculty consists of 94 full-time and 168 part-time across the two campuses. The majority of NVU faculty hold the highest degree in their field. Some are successful entrepreneurs, offering real-world expertise to back up their classroom teaching. Faculty across both campuses are involved in research and offer research opportunities to NVU students.

Faculty members serve as academic advisors and mentors to students and student organizations. Student evaluation of teaching is a formal process and is used in personnel decisions.

Student Life

A full slate of cultural activities such as movies, lectures, theater, dance, and music keep students entertained. Campus events range from the intellectual to the physical, with abundant opportunities for learning and fun. A rich mix of off-campus travel, adventure programming, and community service is offered to enrich life outside the classroom.

There are more than thirty student organizations on each campus, including the campus radio stations; theater and dance groups; and numerous sports, social, service, and academic clubs.

Outdoor activities are around every corner. Students enjoy the three nearby ski areas, on Burke Mountain, Smugglers' Notch, and Jay Peak; run white water rivers; and bike Kingdom Trails, one of the best mountain biking networks in the U.S. The Long Trail System and other walking, hiking, and cross-country ski trails are nearby. On campus, there are indoor climbing centers, disc golf, ropes courses, terrain parks, biking and hiking trails, and skate parks.

On the Johnson campus, there are four residence halls and college apartments for both graduate and undergraduate students. Students who live on campus eat at the Stearns Dining Hall and the Common Grounds Cafe. All students are allowed to have vehicles on campus.

At Lyndon, there are eight residence halls, including a 132-unit, apartment-style hall for juniors and seniors. Students who live on campus eat at the Stevens Dining Hall and the Hornet's Nest Snack Bar. All students are allowed to have vehicles on campus.

Athletics

NVU boasts two athletic departments, one for each campus. Athletes compete in Division III at the varsity level, for either the Johnson Badgers or the Lyndon Hornets. Johnson Badgers: basketball (men, women), cross-country (men, women), golf (men), lacrosse (men), soccer (men, women), softball (women), tennis (men, women), track and field (men, women), triathlon (women), and volleyball (men, women). Lyndon Hornets: baseball (men), basketball (men, women), cross-country (men, women), lacrosse (men, women), soccer (men, women), softball (women), tennis (men, women), track and field (men, women), and volleyball (women). As Hornets or Badgers, the teams will even play each other!

Admission Requirements

NVU emphasizes academic success as reflected on high school or college transcripts, and social and academic potential as reflected in a letter of recommendation. NVU seeks applicants whose academic record reveals maturity and motivation as well as a sense of responsibility and leadership. International students can find detailed information on the university's website. The SAT is optional. Complete information about admissions requirements is available at NorthernVermont.edu/Apply.

Admission requirements for transfer students are the same as those for first-year applicants; an official transcript must also be obtained from each college-level institution that the applicant has attended.

Application and Information

Interested students can apply online at NorthernVermont.edu/Apply. A nonrefundable $50 fee must accompany each application. Northern Vermont University also accepts the Common Application.

For further information, students should contact:

Northern Vermont University
E-mail: Admissions@NorthernVermont.edu
Website: NorthernVermont.edu

Northern Vermont University–Johnson
Office of Admissions
337 College Hill
Johnson, Vermont 05056
Phone: 800-635-2356

Northern Vermont University–Lyndon
Office of Admissions
P.O. Box 919
1001 College Rd.
Lyndonville, Vermont 05851
Phone: 800-225-1998

Climate Change Science is just one of the cutting-edge degrees offered at Northern Vermont University.

OHIO NORTHERN UNIVERSITY

ADA, OHIO

OHIO NORTHERN UNIVERSITY

The University

Ohio Northern University (ONU) has a 94 percent job and graduate school placement rate. Its long-standing success is partly because of excellent professors, partly because of ambitious students, and partly because the University has always been rooted in the future. At ONU, students move toward a career long before they graduate—and ONU's alumni successes prove it. With top-ranked programs and opportunities outside the classroom, any path a student chooses at ONU will be grounded in concrete applications for the future. Established in 1871 and comprised of five colleges (Arts & Sciences, Business Administration, Engineering, Pharmacy, and Law), ONU's beautiful residential campus is made up of more than sixty modern residences and academic buildings and provides a vibrant campus experience.

Students can choose from a variety of campus activities including more than 200 student organizations; four national sororities and six national fraternities; fine arts, music, and theatrical events; and intramural and club sports. Residence hall living is an integral part of the educational program, contributing to a student's personal development. There are nine residence halls on campus as well as eight campus apartment complexes and an Affinity Housing complex.

The ONU Polar Bears compete successfully at the NCAA Division III level in twenty-three varsity sports as part of the highly respected Ohio Athletic Conference. ONU has twelve men's teams (baseball, basketball, cross-country, football, golf, lacrosse, soccer, swimming and diving, tennis, indoor and outdoor track, and wrestling) and eleven women's teams (basketball, cross-country, fast-pitch softball, golf, lacrosse, soccer, swimming and diving, tennis, indoor and outdoor track, and volleyball). In fall 2019, ONU will begin competing in esports.

Location

Ohio Northern University's campus is situated on 342 beautiful acres in the village of Ada (population 5,500). Located in northwestern Ohio, ONU is easily accessible by major highways and conveniently located near major cities such as Columbus, Dayton, Toledo, and Fort Wayne, Indiana.

Majors and Degrees

Ohio Northern University offers the undergraduate degrees: Bachelor of Arts, Bachelor of Fine Arts, Bachelor of Music, Bachelor of Science, Bachelor of Science in Business Administration, Bachelor of Science in Civil Engineering, Bachelor of Science in Medical Laboratory Science, Bachelor of Science in Computer Engineering, Bachelor of Science in Electrical Engineering, Bachelor of Science in Mechanical Engineering, and Bachelor of Science in Nursing. In addition to the undergraduate programs, ONU offers a Master of Science in Accounting; Juris Doctor; Doctor of Pharmacy (Pharm.D.), which is a 0-6, direct entry program; and the Master of Laws (LL.M.) in Democratic Governance and Rule of Law. The 3+3 Law Admissions Program leads to an approved bachelor's degree plus a juris doctorate degree. Majors considered for the 3+3 Admissions Program include business administration; chemistry; English; history; philosophy; philosophy, politics, and economics (PPE); political science; religion; and sociology.

Majors are offered in accounting; advertising design; applied mathematics; art education; biochemistry; biology; chemistry; civil engineering; communication studies; computer engineering; computer science; construction management; creative writing; criminal justice; early childhood education; electrical engineering; engineering education; engineering exploratory; environmental and field biology; exercise physiology; forensic biology; French; German; graphic design; history; international theatre production; language arts education; literature; management; manufacturing technology; marketing; mathematical statistics; mathematics; mechanical engineering; medical laboratory science; middle childhood education; molecular biology; multimedia journalism; music; music education; musical theatre; music performance; nursing; pharmaceutical and healthcare business; pharmacy; philosophy; philosophy, politics, and economics; physics; political science; professional writing; psychology; public health; public relations; religion; risk management and insurance; social studies; sociology; Spanish; sport management; studio arts; technology education; theatre; youth ministry; undecided business; undecided general studies; and undecided sciences.

Special preprofessional programs are available in dentistry, law, medicine, occupational therapy, physical therapy, physician assistant, seminary, and veterinary medicine. Teacher licensure programs are offered at the early childhood, middle childhood, adolescent/young adult, and multiage levels within 16 programs and two endorsement areas.

Changes in programs of study are updated at www.onu.edu.

Academic Programs

The Getty College of Arts & Sciences creatively combines a traditional liberal arts education with cutting-edge preprofessional studies. The college offers more than 50 majors in 17 academic departments, and students can earn a Bachelor of Arts, Bachelor of Fine Arts, Bachelor of Music, Bachelor of Science, Bachelor of Science in Medical Laboratory Science, or Bachelor of Science in Nursing.

Thirteen students in the sciences have been honored by the Barry M. Goldwater Scholarship and Excellence in Education Foundation in the past eleven years. The college has also been recognized as one of the top 200 programs in the nation for creative students in *Creative Colleges: A Guide for Student Actors, Artists, Dancers, Musicians and Writers.*

Working closely with dedicated faculty members, students complete the general education requirements, delve deeply into advanced courses, and engage in high-impact learning through research, internships, practicum experiences, study abroad, and more.

The Dicke College of Business Administration focuses on creating ethical, entrepreneurial, and professional business and civic leaders. The college offers a rigorous academic curriculum with signature programs in pharmaceutical and healthcare business, and risk management and insurance. Internships are required by the college and are available year-round. There are international programs, including study abroad, work abroad, and study tours. An office of experiential learning supports students looking for these opportunities. The course of study for the Bachelor of Science in Business Administration includes a four-year business core experience themed around strategic business planning. Personal attention and mentoring from faculty members, small intimate classes, and active student organizations combine with an emphasis on experiential learning, global awareness, and the entrepreneurial spirit. The college is accredited by the AACSB International—The Association to Advance Collegiate Schools of Business. The Dicke College of Business Administration is ranked by *Bloomberg Businessweek* among the top 50 undergraduate business programs in the United States and No. 1 in Ohio for teaching quality.

The T. J. Smull College of Engineering is noted for its hands-on learning; small, intimate classes; dedicated, accessible professors; and world-class, top-ranked instruction. Ranked thirtieth in the nation for undergraduate engineering programs by *U.S. News & World Report*, ONU's engineering and computer science programs prepare graduates who think critically, lead confidently, and have solid technical foundations upon which to build successful long-term careers. From strong lab components to a host of experiential learning opportunities, ONU's faculty is committed to helping its students achieve their educational goals and realize their dreams. The college features six accredited, disciplinary majors in civil, computer, electrical, and mechanical engineering; computer science; and engineering education, a degree option supporting the demand for high school math teachers with engineering degrees. A new, state-of-the-art engineering building will open in fall 2019.

The courses for the first academic year are essentially the same for each degree program, offering students an easy track to move from one program to another if initially uncertain which disciplines they prefer to study.

An optional five-year co-op program is available for students in each program, provided they maintain a minimum 2.5 GPA. The college focuses on high-impact learning as an essential part of an engineering education; thus, in addition to a co-op program, students apply their classroom learning in freshman design projects, senior capstone projects, national design competitions, and numerous engineering projects in community service (EPICS). Further, many opportunities are available for valuable work experience through the co-op and internship programs, with a historically high job-placement rate for graduates.

For more than 130 years, the Raabe College of Pharmacy has offered distinctive, challenging, and comprehensive training for some of the nation's most talented pharmacists. This University signature program features a six-year Doctor of Pharmacy (Pharm.D.) degree accredited by the American Council on Pharmaceutical Education. This program is direct-entry, admitting students immediately from high school into the college's professional program. This approach enables students to take pharmacy courses from the very first day. A rigorous curriculum utilizes an innovative modular format to organize learning around the human body systems and patient care implementation.

Cutting-edge clinical facilities include the Pharmacy Skills Center, where students access state-of-the-art compounding/counseling pods with portable OTC simulation stations. Students gain considerable experience through a strong undergraduate research program and through the college's on-campus pharmacy facility. Faculty members are teaching-focused but remain current in their research disciplines. Upon graduation, students are well schooled in every aspect of pharmacy and have a high placement rate.

Off-Campus Programs

Many majors may take part in study-abroad programs developed in consultation with faculty members. Field experiences and internships are available to most majors. Externships are required of all pharmacy majors and place students in retail and clinical experiences. Teacher licensure requires one semester of primary or secondary classroom teaching experience under the supervision of practicing teachers. Additional opportunities include computer science and mathematics co-op programs (professional practice), engineering co-op programs (professional practice, domestic and international), and an honors program. All off-campus learning experiences carry credit.

Academic Facilities

Among the nineteen modern academic buildings on campus, the newest is the Mathile Center for the Natural Sciences, which expands the science-learning environment. This 95,145-square-foot student-centered academic research and learning facility blends hands-on teaching excellence with advanced technology in a functional modern environment.

The College of Business Administration's Dicke Hall offers students a modern setting for high-tech classrooms, meeting rooms and a 150-seat lecture forum.

ONU's Heterick Memorial Library and the Taggart Law Library provide information resources and services to support course offerings and foster independent study.

The Freed Center for the Performing Arts houses Communications and Theatre Arts classrooms and features a 550-seat theater/concert hall, a 120-seat studio theater, and television and radio production facilities. WONB-FM is the commercial-free voice of ONU.

Costs

Tuition and fees charges for the 2019–20 year are $33,440 for the Colleges of Arts & Sciences and Business Administration; $38,140 for the College of Engineering; and $39,360 for the College of Pharmacy. These totals do not include room and board.

Financial Aid

Even with one of the highest returns on investment in the nation, ONU invests more than $48 million toward merit-based scholarships and need-based resources. To be considered, the student should submit the FAFSA to the University along with the admission application.

Faculty

More than 210 full-time faculty members bring extensive academic, work, travel, and life experience to their classrooms. Ohio Northern values excellence, innovation, technology, diversity, and its people. With an 11:1 student-faculty ratio, students get lots of personal attention from professors who are passionate about teaching and mentoring.

Student Government

The Student Senate provides self-government in many areas of student life and seeks to further ideals of character and service to the University. The Student Senate serves as the official representative group of the student body to the University administration and agencies in matters pertaining to the student body.

Admission Requirements

High school students applying for admission to the University should present an official transcript indicating at least 16 total units of study, including work in specific academic areas as indicated by each college. Applicants are also required to submit scores on the ACT and/or SAT. For scholarship purposes, the traditional sections of the ACT and the SAT are considered. An on-campus interview is also recommended.

Application and Information

In the colleges of Arts & Sciences, Business Administration, and Engineering, a student's file is considered complete when it contains the application, official high school transcript, and ACT and/or SAT scores. The College of Pharmacy requires a personal statement and a recommendation in addition to the previous items.

The College of Pharmacy's priority application deadline is December 1 for entering freshmen. A campus visit is strongly encouraged for consideration for admittance into this college.

Requests for catalogs or additional information should be directed to:

Office of Admissions
Ohio Northern University
525 South Main Street
Ada, Ohio 45810
Phone: 888-408-4668 (toll-free)
Fax: 419-772-2821
E-mail: admissions-ug@onu.edu
Website: www.onu.edu
www.facebook.com/ohionorthern
www.twitter.com/ohionorthern

Pharmacy students (from left) Ruth Aminu, Emily Somerfield, Alicia Sawmiller, and Caleb VonStein work in the Pharmacy Skills Center of the Ohio Northern University College of Pharmacy. An Ohio Northern University education is based on experiential, hands-on learning, and students are guided by professors who know them personally and care about their lifelong success.

PACE UNIVERSITY

NEW YORK CITY AND WESTCHESTER, NEW YORK

PACE UNIVERSITY

The University

Founded in 1906, Pace University is a leading private metropolitan university that offers an exceptional liberal arts education combined with superior professional preparation, two strategic undergraduate New York locations, and robust scholarships and financial aid. The diverse student population of 8,914 undergraduates (6,284 in New York City and 2,630 in Westchester) is enrolled in more than 3,000 courses across 100-plus majors and combined, accelerated bachelor's and graduate degree programs. These are offered through five undergraduate schools and colleges: the Lubin School of Business, the Dyson College of Arts and Sciences, the Seidenberg School of Computer Science and Information Systems, the School of Education, and the College of Health Professions. Pace facilitates more than 5,000 internships, co-op experiences, practicums, field experiences, and clinical assignments every year.

Many student-led clubs and organizations are active on the campus, including the Pace Advertising Club, African Students Association, the Pace Association for Collegiate Entrepreneurs, the Student Government Association, and the Collegiate Psychology Club. Pace also offers many campus activities, including student government associations, fraternities, sororities, two campus newspapers, two literary magazines, two yearbooks, and two campus broadcasting systems. Athletic facilities are available for students, and intercollegiate sports include baseball, basketball, cross-country, cheerleading, dance, women's field hockey, football, lacrosse, women's soccer, women's softball, swimming and diving, and women's volleyball.

The student body is diverse, representing forty-nine states, five U.S. territories, and more than 100 countries.

Location

Pace University is a multicampus institution with campuses in both New York City and Westchester, New York. Both locations are within reach of cultural, business, and social resources and opportunities. The New York City campus is located in the heart of the Financial District in lower Manhattan, and within a short walking distance of Wall Street and the South Street Seaport. Lincoln Center, Broadway theaters, museums, and many world-famous attractions are minutes away by public transportation. Located 35 miles north of New York City, the newly renovated Westchester campus offers a traditional college experience: state-of-the-art science and video production labs, competitive athletics, fraternities and sororities, and access to internship opportunities at many Fortune 500 companies.

Students can take courses at either campus, and housing is available in both New York City and Westchester residence halls.

Majors and Degrees

The following programs are offered at both the New York City and Westchester campuses. The Bachelor of Business Administration (B.B.A.) is offered with majors in accounting (with concentrations in forensic accounting and internal auditing), accounting—public, finance, general business, information systems, international management, management (with concentrations in business, entrepreneurship, health care, hospitality and tourism, and human resources), and marketing (with concentrations in advertising and integrated marketing communications, global marketing management, and sports marketing). In addition, a five-year combined B.B.A./M.B.A in public accounting is available for qualified students. The Bachelor of Arts (B.A.) degree is granted in adolescent education (with concentrations in biology, chemistry, earth science, English, history/social studies, mathematics, and Spanish), applied psychology and human relations, biology, childhood education, computer science, early childhood education, economics, environmental studies, film and screen studies, health science, history, information systems, liberal studies, mathematics, philosophy and religious studies, political science, and psychology. The Bachelor of Science (B.S.) degree is offered in biochemistry, biology, business economics, chemistry, computer science, criminal justice, economics, environmental science, health science, information systems, information systems, information technology, mathematics, professional computer studies, and professional studies.

Certain programs are available only on one campus. The B.S. programs in biology–pre-professional (occupational therapy, optometry, and podiatry) and forensic science; the B.B.A. programs in arts and entertainment management, and business analytics; the B.F.A. programs in acting, art, commercial dance, musical theater, and production and design for stage and screen; and the B.A. programs in acting; acting for film, television, voice-overs, and commercials; American studies; art; art history; communication science and disorders; communication studies; directing; English language and literature; language, culture, and world trade; global Asia studies; global professional studies; Latin American studies; modern languages and culture; peace and justice studies; sociology-anthropology; Spanish; stage management; teaching students with speech and language disabilities; theater arts (acting and design/technical); and women's and gender studies are offered only at the New York City campus. The B.A. programs in biological psychology, communication arts and journalism, communications, digital journalism, digital cinema and filmmaking, English, English and communications, education, global professional studies, and personality and social psychology, and the B.S. programs in nursing are available at the Westchester campus only.

Pace University offers a five-year engineering programs in cooperation with Manhattan College and Rensselaer Polytechnic Institute. Students attend Pace for three years and either Manhattan College or Rensselaer for two years. Upon successful completion, students receive a B.S. degree in chemistry from Pace and either a Bachelor of Chemical Engineering (B.C.E.) in chemical engineering from Manhattan or a B.S. degree in engineering from Rensselaer.

Academic Programs

The Pace Path is an innovative program unique to Pace University that helps each student become successful in college, career, and life. Each student develops strengths in managing oneself, interpersonal relations, and organizational awareness through co-curricular activities with an academic program. This is accomplished through collaboration with Pace faulty, advisers, staff, coaches, and mentors. The Pace Path is framed by Pace's historic mission of *Opportunitas* and prepares innovative thinkers through a powerful combination of knowledge in the professions, real-world experience, and rigorous liberal arts curriculum.

The Pforzheimer Honors College is a highly esteemed opportunity at Pace—a community of talented undergraduate scholars studying under the distinguished faculty of the University's five undergraduate schools and colleges. It is a place to excel and realize potential.

Pace University's internship program is nationally recognized and offers qualified students the opportunity to gain experience in their field of study while earning a four-year degree. Students can choose full-time, part-time, or summer positions working in an area directly related to their major course of study. Over 4,000 Pace students participate each year in internships, faculty-sponsored research, consulting projects, fieldwork, and practicums—Pace's Career Services team is one of the largest in the New York Metropolitan area.

Academic Facilities

Pace University opened its second new high-rise (34 stories) residence hall on its New York City campus in fall 2015. It is the tallest university residence hall in the world. In addition, there are brand new science labs, art studios, an honors student lounge, and School of Performing Arts studios. The Westchester campus had the most visible and dramatic changes with new modern residence halls, enlarged student centers, digital video/filmmaking facilities, new environmental center with indoor and outdoor classrooms, expanded athletic fields, and new field house.

Costs

For the 2018–19 academic year, undergraduate tuition was $43,624 per year for full-time study. The cost for an on-campus double-occupancy room and board was $16,600–$19,200, with different housing options available.

Financial Aid

Pace University strives to provide opportunities to students of diverse backgrounds and varied circumstances and is committed to offering financial aid to students to the fullest extent of its resources. University-sponsored scholarships are awarded to students on the basis of academic merit, service to the community, and financial need. The goal is to offer every student as much financial assistance as possible, based upon availability and need. Last year, ninety-two percent of first-year students received financial aid. Pace's comprehensive student financial aid assistance program includes scholarships, grants, on-campus employment, student loans (federal and alternative plans), and tuition payment plans. Pace participates in all federal financial aid programs and the New York State Tuition Assistance Program (TAP) and honors awards from other states' incentive grant programs.

Students should submit the Free Application for Federal Student Aid (FAFSA) by November 15 for priority consideration for the fall semester. Pace University's new Net Price Calculator (www.pace.edu/calculator) is an online tool designed to help students and their families estimate their financial aid package. Many find that Pace is actually more affordable than similar public and private colleges due to the scholarship and financial aid awards offered to families.

Faculty

First and foremost, Pace University professors are dedicated teachers. All Pace classes are taught by professors. Students will never take a course taught by a teaching assistant. Faculty members also bring real-world experience and scholarship into the classroom through their work with outside companies and organizations and by leading cutting-edge research projects. Faculty members come from the best graduate and doctoral programs in the country. Professors—90 percent of whom hold Ph.D.'s—have earned degrees from the University of Pennsylvania, Harvard, Brown, Columbia, and Yale. Pace professors work closely with students to not only broaden their academic horizons, but to show how their work in the classroom is applicable to their future careers.

Admission Requirements

A minimum of 16 academic units from an accredited secondary school, or equivalent, are required. Academic subjects in high school should be distributed as follows: 4 years of English, 3–4 years of college-preparatory mathematics, 2 years of foreign language, 3–4 years of history/social science, 2 years of laboratory science, and 2–3 units of academic electives. All domestic applicants are required to take either the SAT or ACT examination and have results forwarded to the University. International students are required to take the TOEFL, IELTS, or PTE.

Application and Information

Students can apply online at www.pace.edu/apply.

For more information contact:

Pace University
861 Bedford Road
Pleasantville, New York 10570-2799
Phone: 800-874-7223 (toll-free)
E-mail: infoctr@pace.edu
Website: http://www.pace.edu

PACIFIC UNIVERSITY

FOREST GROVE, OREGON

Pacific University Oregon

The University

Pacific University is a private, fully accredited university in Oregon offering more than sixty undergraduate fields of study and more than 20 graduate and professional degree programs in the arts & sciences, business, education, health professions, and optometry.

Pacific is rare in that its 3,900-plus students are evenly split between undergraduate and graduate programs. The unique mix of undergraduate, graduate and degree programs provides students with direct pathways to advanced degrees, as well as opportunities to engage in research and scholarship that aren't often available in bachelor's programs. Pacific is the No. 1 private research university in the Pacific Northwest and No. 10 on the west coast, falling just behind institutions including Stanford, USC and Caltech. Students regularly conduct research alongside their professors and have the opportunity to publish and present nationally.

Pacific's focus is on teaching and learning in a close nurturing environment. Classes are taught by faculty members, not teaching assistants, and classes are small, allowing professors to get to know their students as individuals. About one in four students — from freshmen to doctoral candidates — are the first in their families to attend college, and Pacific students experience greater socioeconomic growth as a result of their educations than their peers at other colleges in the Northwest.

At Pacific, students are encouraged to pursue their passions, melding rigorous academics with community engagement, study abroad, and cocurricular activities. There are more than sixty student interest groups at Pacific, including student media, academic societies, religious and political organizations, and service clubs. One of the largest student organizations, Na Haumana O Hawai'i, unites Pacific's large population of students from Hawai'i and presents an authentic lu'au each year.

Pacific also is a member of the NCAA Division III Northwest Conference. Almost a third of undergraduate students participate in varsity and junior varsity athletics, including baseball, basketball, cross-country, football, golf, lacrosse, rowing, soccer, swimming, tennis, track & field, volleyball and wrestling. The campus athletic center houses gymnasiums, a fitness center, a state-of-the-art indoor field house, handball/racquetball courts, a wrestling room, and a sports medicine training facility. The Lincoln Park Athletic Complex, a partnership with the City of Forest Grove, features a 1,100-seat stadium with a nine-lane, 400-meter track, a FieldTurf soccer/football/lacrosse field, a Bond baseball field with turf infield, and a varsity softball field.

Outside of formal sports, Pacific students also enjoy informal sports and the outdoor opportunities unique to the Northwest. An outdoor recreation program offers training, equipment and organized trips for snowboarding and skiing, rock climbing, camping, kayaking and more, and Forest Grove is optimally placed just an hour from the Oregon Coast, Columbia River Gorge and Cascade Mountains.

Pacific consistently holds a place in U.S. News & World Report's Best Regional Universities in the West, Forbes' list of America's Top Colleges, and Washington Monthly's Best Bang for the Buck schools. It also was named the best undergraduate accounting program in Oregon and the National Optometric Association School of the Year in 2018.

Locations

Pacific University was founded in Forest Grove, Oregon, in 1849, and was the first chartered university west of the Mississippi. The historic college town on the west end of the Portland Metro Area is home to the 55-acre oak-covered campus that serves most undergraduates, as well as the College of Optometry, College of Education, College of Business and Master of Fine Arts in Writing Program.

Pacific also offers health professions and an MBA program on its growing campus in Hillsboro, Oregon, the fifth-largest city in the state. Located on the regional light-rail line in the Hillsboro Health and Education District, the Hillsboro Campus connects students with world-class learning opportunities and real-world experience as they connect with local businesses, hospitals, and non-profit organizations.

A small campus in Eugene, Oregon, offers undergraduate and graduate teaching programs, as well as Pacific's Master of Social Work Program.

And Pacific's newest campus in Woodburn — one of the most diverse and fastest-growing communities in Oregon — offers undergraduate and graduate teaching programs embedded in the local school district and community.

Majors and Degrees

Pacific University is known for its excellent liberal arts foundation, as well as the superior preparation its students receive to go on to careers and advanced study. In particular, the University is heralded for its graduate programs in health professions, as well as its undergraduate preparation for healthcare fields and medical school. Pacific offers several advanced pathways into graduate programs, including three-year tracks to pharmacy and athletic training programs.

Pacific emphasizes the education benefits of research projects, internships, study-abroad experiences, and service learning. Most freshmen participate in a semester-long first-year seminar program designed to introduce students to college-level writing and research expectations. The core curriculum emphasizes writing, reasoning, and communication skills, as well as global perspectives and service. Pacific University also requires most students to complete a senior capstone, a year-long research project designed and implemented by students and culminating in a presentation to the University community.

Most undergraduate programs operate on a two-semester calendar with an optional short term and limited summer courses. Many graduate and professional programs have year-round calendars.

The Pacific University College of Arts & Sciences offers most undergraduate majors, including programs in anthropology/sociology, applied science, art, bioinformatics, biology, chemistry, computer science, criminal justice, dance, economics, English, environmental science, exercise science, history, international studies, mathematics, media arts, modern languages, music, music therapy, philosophy, physics, politics and government, psychology, public health, social work, and theatre. The College of Arts & Sciences also offers a nationally recognized, low-residency Master of Fine Arts in Writing program, and a Master of Social Work program.

The College of Business offers undergraduate tracks in accounting, finance, international business, marketing, and business administration, as well as a one-year MBA program.

The College of Health Professions provides an undergraduate program in dental hygiene studies and an online bachelor of health science program, as well as graduate programs in athletic training, audiology, healthcare administration, occupational therapy, pharmacy, physical therapy, physician assistant studies, and professional psychology as well as a graduate-level certificate program in gerontology.

The College of Education offers an undergraduate major in education and learning, as well as a Bachelor of Education in elementary education and English language learning. Graduate programs in the College of Education include a fifth-year Master of Arts in Teaching, a Master of Arts in teaching special education, a Master of Education, and several endorsement options. Also available is a master's degree in speech-language pathology, as well as an undergraduate minor in communication sciences and disorders that prepares students for the speech-language pathology program.

The College of Optometry offers a Doctor of Optometry program, as well as master's and Ph.D. programs in vision science.

Costs

Tuition and fees for the 2018–19 school year were $44,298 for undergraduates in the College of Arts & Sciences. Room and board were $12,528 for a double room and a University meal plan.

Financial Aid

Financial assistance at Pacific is awarded on the basis of demonstrated need, academic merit, and talent. The Free Application for Federal Student Aid (FAFSA) is used in evaluating need. Prospective students are encouraged to apply for financial assistance by submitting the FAFSA to the federal processor as soon after October 1 as possible. Pacific provides financial assistance through grants, scholarships, loans, and part-time employment. For more information prospective students can e-mail financialaid@pacificu.edu.

Faculty

Pacific's outstanding faculty members provide the foundation for the University's academic program. A student-faculty ratio of 10:1 and an average class size of 19 students in undergraduate courses allows for personal attention from the professors. Pacific University does not use graduate or teaching assistants; all faculty members teach their own courses.

Admission Requirements

Pacific University is selective in considering new students. Primary consideration is given to a candidate's academic preparation and potential for successful study at the college level, as assessed by evaluating the student's transcripts of college-preparatory work, counselor and teacher recommendations, personal essay, SAT and/or ACT scores, and other student-submitted information. Transfer students must submit high school records and test scores if they have completed less than 30 semester hours, plus official transcripts from any institution previously attended.

Application and Information

Students may apply early and may be notified early through the modified rolling admissions plan. Pacific University is an exclusive member of the Common Application. For additional information, interested students should contact:

Office of Admissions
Pacific University
2043 College Way
Forest Grove, Oregon 97116
Phone: 503-352-2218
800-677-6712 (toll-free)
E-mail: admissions@pacificu.edu
Website: http://www.pacificu.edu
http://www.facebook.com/pacificu
http://www.twitter.com/pacificu

PEPPERDINE UNIVERSITY
Seaver College
MALIBU, CALIFORNIA

PEPPERDINE

The University and The College

Pepperdine University is a private, faith-based university committed to the highest standards of academic excellence and Christian values, where students are strengthened for lives of purpose, service, and leadership.

Seaver College, Pepperdine's undergraduate liberal arts college, is comprised of approximately 3,300 students, 52 percent of which come from California. Thirty-six percent hail from the other forty-nine states, and 12 percent are international. The 2018–19 freshmen class had an average high school GPA of 3.75. It's this diversity of backgrounds and worldviews that helps contribute to Pepperdine's unique educational experience.

Nestled between the Santa Monica Mountains and the Pacific Ocean, Pepperdine's Malibu campus provides fantastic on-campus housing options for all students. Students are required to live on campus during their first and second years, and also have premium residence halls available as upperclassmen.

Students have a wide range of extracurricular activities and organizations to choose from, including social, honor, service, spiritual, professional, divisional, and special interest clubs. Pepperdine provides students with interests in communications and media the chance to be involved with the campus radio station, weekly student newspaper and television broadcast.

Pepperdine has 17 Division One men's and women's athletic programs that have won an impressive 13 national team championships and 12 individual national championships. As a member of the West Coast Conference, the University houses a 3,500-seat gymnasium, an Olympic-size swimming pool, a tennis pavilion and sixteen additional tennis courts, an intramural field, and a 2,000-seat baseball stadium.

Pepperdine's graduate schools include the School of Law, School of Public Policy, School of Education and Psychology, and the George L. Graziado School of Business and Management. These distinguished programs offer master's degrees in law, dispute resolution, public policy, business, and more.

Location

Overlooking the Pacific Ocean in scenic Malibu, California, and less than an hour from downtown Los Angeles, Seaver's Malibu campus offers both the benefits of a small coastal community and the advantages of proximity to a major metropolitan area.

Malibu is a pristine beach community with excellent restaurants, a movie theater, and shopping centers complete with banking facilities and industry-leading brands. The winding seashore and rugged beauty of Malibu connects students to a litany of nightlife options in Santa Monica, Hollywood, and Los Angeles. Malibu's clean air provides an environment conducive to study, while the moderate climate permits year-round outdoor recreation. In addition to making use of the physical education facilities on campus, students can enjoy swimming, surfing, horseback riding, fishing, hiking, boating, kayaking, and other activities in the vicinity. As an international epicenter of culture, industry, and trade, Los Angeles provides students with a one-of-a-kind living experience.

Majors and Degrees

Students can choose from forty-five majors and thirty-seven minors. Seaver College awards the Bachelor of Arts in advertising, art, art history, biology, chemistry, communication, creative writing, economics, English, film studies, French, German, Hispanic studies (Spanish), history, integrated marketing communication, international studies, Italian, journalism, liberal arts, math education, media production, music, natural science, philosophy, political science, psychology, public relations, religion, sociology, sport administration, sports medicine, theater and music, theater and media production, and theater arts.

The Bachelor of Science is awarded in accounting, biology, business administration, chemistry, computer science and mathematics, international business, mathematics, nutritional science, physics, and sports medicine. A teacher education program offers credentials in single or multiple subjects.

Academic Programs

The academic programs at Seaver College provide students with a liberal arts education in a Christian atmosphere that sharpens critical thinking, improves information literacy, and builds a learning community. Students must complete 128 units for the B.A. or B.S. degree, including 64 units in general education requirements and 40 or more in upper-division studies.

Major requirements may be fulfilled through three basic arrangements. Students who specialize in a discipline must complete at least 24 units of upper-division work in their chosen discipline. Students may choose an interdisciplinary major, entailing at least 40 units of upper-division work, with courses ranging broadly across disciplinary lines within a division and on occasion crossing divisional lines, in one of the following fields of study: communication, English, humanities, international studies, liberal arts, or religion. Alternatively, students may initiate a contract major by presenting an application for specific upper-division courses to the Dean of Seaver College.

Seaver College functions on a semester plan; the regular academic year consists of two semesters from late August to April. In addition to the regular academic year, summer sessions run from early May to August.

At Seaver, instruction and study are adapted both to students' abilities and to the nature of the course content, instead of utilizing only the traditional lecture method. Programs involve several types of learning experiences: seminars, integrated lectures, individual study, fieldwork, and laboratories. Students are never taught by a teacher's assistant at Pepperdine; the average class size is 17 students and a student-to-faculty ratio of 13:1 fosters an environment where professors are invested in the growth and success of their students.

The Dean's List of undergraduate students is published each semester, comprised of the top 10 percent of the class with a grade point index no lower than 3.5. Other honors include cum laude for students graduating with a scholastic level of at least 3.5, magna cum laude for 3.7, and summa cum laude for 3.9.

Off-Campus Programs

At Seaver, students have the opportunity to study abroad in Buenos Aires, Argentina; Florence, Italy; Heidelberg, Germany; Lausanne, Switzerland; London, England; and Shanghai, China. The academic programs emphasize European, Latin American, or Asian history and culture. Seaver also offers an internship-based program in Washington, D.C. and summer special interest programs in Spain, Thailand, East Africa, and the Middle East. Classes are taught by Seaver faculty members. Serious study and the daily experiences of living in another country give students a special depth of understanding of other cultures and a broader world perspective.

The Buenos Aires program accommodates approximately 60 students who live in the homes of carefully selected host families. The Florence program houses approximately 55 students who live in a Florentine villa and residential complex with classrooms, a library, a computer facility, and recreational facilities. The Heidelberg program has space for approximately 50 students at the Moore Haus, located near the city's famous castle. Classes are held in modern facilities in downtown Heidelberg. The Lausanne program accommodates about 70 students. The Pepperdine facility is located in La Croisée near the center of Lausanne, which has a picturesque view of Lake Geneva and the French Alps. The London program has space for approximately 40 students in the Knightsbridge area. In addition to living quarters, the facility includes classrooms, a library, a computer room, offices, and a student center. The Shanghai program accommodates approximately 40 students who live in the Pepperdine-owned jia, meaning "house," which is located in the French Concession area near the American Consulate. The majority of the international program facilities are University-owned.

Academic Facilities

The Malibu campus is home to academic complexes containing seminar and lecture rooms, art studios, communication facilities, science and computer laboratories, mini-theaters, a recital hall, and administrative offices. The newly renovated Payson Library is the global gateway to knowledge and provides students access to thousands of online journals, articles, and periodicals through various databases. Payson Library serves as a sanctuary for study, learning, and research by encouraging discovery, contemplation, social discourse, and creative expression.

The 300-seat George Elkins Auditorium is used for public presentations and lectures. The Center for the Arts facility includes the renowned Frederick R. Weisman Museum of Art and the Smothers Theatre, which seats 450 people and is used for dance, music, and theater performances. The Center for Communication and Business building houses a state-of-the-art radio and television production center where students have the opportunity to work on Pepperdine's cable television and radio stations.

Costs

Costs for the 2018–19* academic year were $53,680 for tuition, $15,320 for room and board, and $252 for additional fees.

Financial Aid

Approximately 85 percent of Seaver's students receive some form of financial assistance through scholarships, loans, grants, work-study programs, or jobs within the University. To be eligible for financial assistance from institutional resources, an undergraduate student must be enrolled in at least 12 units. To ensure full consideration, the Free Application for Federal Student Aid (FAFSA) should be submitted by the priority deadlines of November 1 for early action and February 15 for regular decision for the fall semester and October 15 for the spring semester. Students who qualify should also apply for the Cal Grant (California residents only). Prospective students will receive their estimated financial assistance award after admission to the University but prior to the enrollment deadline.

Faculty

Seaver College's faculty includes men and women of high academic distinction whose primary focus is instruction with a secondary focus on research. Fifty-four percent of faculty members are full-time, and 85 percent of full-time faculty members hold a doctorate or terminal degree in their field. Upon enrollment, each student is assigned an academic adviser from among the faculty members. A qualified counseling staff is also available to assist with personal, professional, and academic needs.

Student Government

The Student Government Association (SGA) is composed of student leaders dedicated to providing Pepperdine's students with quality representation through innovative advocacy programs. SGA serves as the voice of the students to the Seaver administration and works in coordination with the Student Activities Office in establishing activities and maintaining school policies. Seaver has more than 1,000 programmed on-campus events each year including movies, sightseeing trips, guest performances, dances, speakers, and more. Pepperdine has eight nationally recognized sororities and five fraternities and there are over 110 different student clubs and organizations on campus that focus on a range of interests, including academic, language, art, music, dance, drama, sports, and politics.

Admission Requirements

Applicants are admitted on the basis of their academic record, SAT or ACT scores, and personal information and references. Transfer applicants are high school graduates who have taken any transferable college units after graduating high school. Students who took colleges courses prior to graduating high school are not considered transfer students and should apply as a first-year student. To ensure full consideration for the fall semester, students should apply by the early action deadline of November 1 or regular application deadline of January 15. October 1 is the regular deadline for the spring semester. Decision letter dates are announced in the current application form.

Seaver College seeks to enroll a diverse student body. As such, Pepperdine University does not unlawfully discriminate on the basis of any status or condition protected by applicable federal or state law in the administration of its educational policies, admission, financial assistance, employment, educational programs, or activities.

Application and Information

To request information, students should contact:

Office of Admission
Seaver College
Pepperdine University
Malibu, California 90263-4392
Phone: 310-506-4392
E-mail: admission-seaver@pepperdine.edu
Website: http://seaver.pepperdine.edu/admission
https://seaver.pepperdine.edu/admission/risingtide (Docuseries)
http://on.fb.me/Seaver_Admission (Facebook)
http://twitter.com/#!/SeaverAdmission (Twitter)
http://instagram.com/seaveradmission# (Instagram)
http://bit.ly/YouTube_Pepperdine (YouTube)
http://pinterest.com/seaveradmission/ (Pinterest)

The 830-acre Malibu campus of Pepperdine University, Seaver College, overlooks the Pacific Ocean, 30 miles west of Los Angeles, California.

COLLEGE CLOSE-UPS

PRATT INSTITUTE
BROOKLYN, NEW YORK

Pratt

The Institute

Industrialist and philanthropist Charles Pratt founded Pratt Institute in 1887 to educate students for various professions on a non-degree level. As the educational preparation necessary for various professions expanded, Pratt Institute moved to offer baccalaureate degrees with its first granted in 1938 and its first graduate degree granted in 1950. Now, with twenty-five undergraduate majors and concentrations, Pratt offers students a wide variety of programs in which to major or take elective courses.

With its undergraduate ranked programs in art, design, and architecture ranked among the top five or ten in the country, Pratt has been ranked among the top design schools in the United States by Business Week. Pratt was also ranked number one in the country for its fine arts and studio programs by USA Today.

In addition to the four-year programs on its Brooklyn campus, Pratt offers students several additional locations to pursue their education: a two-year program in Utica, New York, at PrattMWP; and an associate degree program in fine art, graphic design, illustration, and gaming as well as a two- and four-year degree in construction management in Manhattan.

Although the characteristics and educational requirements of the professions for which Pratt prepares students have changed over the course of a century, the Institute has succeeded in pursuing its abiding purpose—to blend theoretical learning with professional and humanistic development—and has kept its curricula current by hiring practicing professionals to teach. Standards are high, modeled after the professional world. Faculty members connect students with internships and eventually jobs after graduation. Industry projects and internships provide students with real-world experience. Ninety-five percent of Pratt's graduates are working within the first year after graduation.

Pratt Institute offers four-year bachelor's, two-year associate's, and master's degrees. Pratt's national and international reputation attracts undergraduate and graduate students from forty-eight U.S. states and over eighty-five countries. Students who choose Pratt are committed to the study of art, design, architecture, or creative writing and to their career objectives.

A short subway or bus ride from the museums, galleries, and design centers of both Manhattan and Brooklyn, Pratt Institute's main campus in Brooklyn, New York features twenty-five buildings of differing architectural styles spread throughout a beautifully landscaped 25-acre campus. The campus was ranked by Architectural Digest as one of the top ten campuses nationwide with the best architecture. It includes a contemporary sculpture garden (ranked among the top ten campus art collections by Public Art Review), an athletic center, residence halls, dining halls, outstanding studio facilities, and historic buildings. Nineteen of the buildings house studios, classrooms, laboratories, administrative offices, auditoria, sports facilities, food services, and student centers. A new green LEED gold-certified building houses student administrative services including admissions, undergraduate and graduate digital arts programs, and various administrative offices, including student financial services and the registrar's offices. Six buildings are student residences, including the Stabile Hall freshman residence, which provides studio space on each floor; a new freshman residence hall is under construction. There is adequate parking for residents and commuters. Student services include career planning and placement, health and counseling, a disabilities office, a HEOP program, and student development. More than sixty student organizations are available including fraternities and sororities, honorary societies, professional societies, and clubs.

Location

Pratt Institute, the country's premier college of art, design, writing, and architecture, has its main campus in the Clinton Hill neighborhood of Brooklyn, just minutes from downtown Manhattan. Almost ninety percent of Pratt's freshmen and over half of its undergraduates live on the tree-lined Brooklyn campus. Close to the Brooklyn Museum and the Brooklyn Academy of Music, Pratt is ideally located, providing students with a green oasis just minutes from the art capital of the world, Manhattan. The Manhattan campus is located in Chelsea. The Utica campus, home to the first two years of Pratt's programs in fine art, communications design, photography, and art and design education (teacher certification) with automatic relocation to the Brooklyn campus for the junior year, is located in upstate New York.

Majors and Degrees

Pratt Institute offers the Bachelor of Architecture, Bachelor of Fine Arts, Bachelor of Art, Bachelor of Industrial Design, Bachelor of Professional Studies, Bachelor of Science, Associate of Occupational Studies, and Associate of Applied Science degrees.

The Bachelor of Architecture degree program is a five-year, accredited program. For the Bachelor of Fine Arts degree, a candidate may choose to major in art and design education (art teacher certification), history of art and design, communications design (advertising art direction, graphic design, and illustration), digital arts (3-D animation, 2-D animation, and interactive arts), fashion design, film, fine arts (ceramics, drawing, jewelry, painting, printmaking, sculpture, and integrated practices), interior design, photography, or writing. The Bachelor of Arts is offered in critical and visual studies. The Bachelor of Industrial Design is offered for students interested in product and furniture design. In the Bachelor of Professional Studies degree program, the major is in construction management. Students seeking the Bachelor of Science degree can major in construction management or professional services management.

The two-year Associate of Occupational Studies degree is offered in game design and interactive media, graphic design, and illustration. The Associate of Applied Science is offered in painting/drawing and graphic design/illustration. The two-year Associate of Applied Science degree is transferable to a four-year program.

Students may also earn combined bachelor's/master's degrees. B.F.A./M.A. in art and design education.

Academic Programs

Educating artists and creative professionals to be responsible contributors to society has been the mission of Pratt Institute since it assembled its first group of students in 1887. Within the structure of that professional education, Pratt students are encouraged to acquire the diverse knowledge that is necessary for them to succeed in their chosen fields including sustainability. In addition to the professional studies, the curriculum in each of Pratt's schools includes a broad range of liberal arts courses. Students from all schools take these courses together and have the opportunity to examine the interrelationships of art, science, technology, and human need.

At the time of graduation, students in the associate degree programs have completed 66 credit hours of course work. In the bachelor's programs, credit-hour requirements are 126 credits with opportunities to take electives in other disciplines or minors, depending on the particular program. For the Bachelor of Architecture degree, 170 credits are required.

Pratt's academic calendar consists of two semesters plus optional summer terms that allow students to choose alternative courses or various options usually not offered during the fall or spring semester.

Off-Campus Programs

Pratt Institute offers credit for a wide variety of off-campus study programs. The internship program offers qualified students challenging on-the-job experience related to their major fields of interest; this extension of the classroom and laboratory into the professional world adds a practical dimension to periods of on-campus study.

International programs, available during all academic sessions, have included semester programs in the cities of Copenhagen, Rome and Berlin. Summer programs are offered in Copenhagen, Havana, Rome, Tokyo and Venice . New programs are developed regularly in these and other countries.

Academic Facilities

Founded as the first free library in Brooklyn, the Pratt Institute Library has more than 176,674 bound volumes, 84,604 art books, 237 print and online art and art history journals, a rare book collection, and subscriptions to journals online through JSTOR, EBSCO, and others. The library also has serial backfiles and other material, including government documents; 251,603 audiovisual materials; and 3,996 microforms and subscribes to 925 periodicals—the largest collection of any independent art school. With their ID cards, Pratt students also have access to numerous college libraries in the metropolitan area.

Extensive studio and state-of-the-art computer lab facilities are provided for all Pratt students. In the School of Art and Design, these include studio, shop, and technical facilities for work in all media, from the traditional to the most experimental. Gallery space, both on campus and at Pratt Manhattan, is extensive, showing the work of students, alumni, faculty members, staff members, and other well-known artists, architects, and designers.

Costs

Tuition for the 2019-20 academic year is $51,754. Room charges are $9,422. per academic year. A meal plan is available, and costs about $3,872 for the year. The fees are approximately $2,060. The estimated cost of books and supplies is $1,750 per academic year. Students should allow an additional $3,000 for transportation and personal expenses. For an updated list of tuition and fees, prospective students should visit www.pratt.edu/admissions/financing-your-education/financing-undergraduate/cost-of-attendance.

Financial Aid

Pratt Institute offers an extensive program of merit-based scholarships, need-based grants, loans, and awards based on academic achievement, talent, financial need, or all three. More than 75 percent of Pratt students receive financial assistance through one or more of these kinds of aid.

Faculty

The faculty at Pratt Institute is exceptional in that a large number of practicing professionals augment the regular full-time faculty. There are 163 full-time and 992 part-time faculty members. In small classes and studios, students have easy access to professors whose natural environment is the design studio, the architectural office, or the industrial research department. Faculty members often connect students with internships and eventually jobs.

Student Government

The Student Government Association (SGA) maintains primary responsibility for all student interests and involvement at Pratt. All undergraduate students are encouraged to become involved in the SGA, whose main functions are allocating and administering funds collected through the student activities fee, scheduling student activities, and representing the student viewpoint to the rest of the Pratt community.

Admission Requirements

Pratt Institute attracts and enrolls highly motivated and talented students from diverse backgrounds. Applications are welcome from all qualified students, regardless of sex, gender, race, color, religion or creed, marital status, age, sexual orientation, status as a veteran, political beliefs, disability, citizenship, genetic information, or national or ethnic origin Admission standards at Pratt are high. One of the major components for admission consideration in art, design, or architecture is the evaluation of a student's art or writing portfolio, which must be submitted along with the other required documents.

All applicants to four-year programs must submit official transcripts, test scores, and a visual or writing portfolio with the exception of construction management applicants who are not required to submit a portfolio. Instructions may be found at www.pratt.edu/apply.

The admission committee bases its decisions on careful reviews of all credentials submitted by applicants in relation to the requirements of the program to which students seek admission. International students must submit TOEFL or IELTS scores or SAT scores, but not both. In certain cases, extraordinary talent may offset a low grade or a test score.

Application and Information

Pratt has two admissions deadlines: November 1 for early action and January 5 for regular admissions. To receive full consideration, students must submit their applications by January 5 for anticipated entrance in the fall semester and by October 1 for anticipated entrance in the spring semester. Additional details regarding application deadlines can be found on Pratt's website: https://www.pratt.edu/admissions/applying/applying-undergraduate/ug-application-requirements.

For more information about Pratt Institute, students should contact:

Office of Admissions
Pratt Institute
200 Willoughby Avenue
Brooklyn, New York 11205
Phone: 718-636-3514
800-331-0834 (toll-free)
E-mail: admissions@pratt.edu
Website: www.pratt.edu
www.pratt.edu/request (Catalog request)
www.pratt.edu/visit (Visit information and online campus tour registration)
http://on.fb.me/pratt_admissions (Facebook)

Pratt's campus in the spring. *© 2014 Bob Handelman*

REED COLLEGE

PORTLAND, OREGON

The College

Referred to as one of the most intellectual colleges in the country, Reed is known for its high standards of scholarly practice, creative thinking, and engaged citizenship. A genuine enthusiasm for academic work and intellectual exchange is valued, and the Honor Principle, Reed's ethos that guides both academic and campus life, ensures personal responsibility and mutual respect within its small community of 1,483 students and 153 faculty members. More than four-fifths of Reed's students come from outside the Northwest, with one-fifth from the Northeast and one-tenth from outside of the United States. Over 30 percent of Reed's students identify with historically underrepresented racial and ethnic backgrounds. Reed's twenty-four residence halls enable approximately 80 percent of students to live on campus.

At its founding, Reed rejected fraternal societies and varsity sports. The goal was to foster a climate of inclusivity and collaboration focused on academics. This atmosphere persists, with student groups—social, religious, and cultural—open to all and wellness and the development of athletic skills taking precedence over competition.

Location

Reed's 116-acre wooded campus is located in a residential section of southeast Portland. The city, a welcoming metropolis, offers a thriving local music scene, diverse restaurants and food carts, tranquil Japanese and Chinese gardens, noisy downtown clubs, a plethora of bridges and bike paths, and the largest independent bookstore in the world. Just 90 minutes west of Portland are the wild beaches of the Pacific Ocean; 90 minutes east are the ski slopes of Mount Hood where Reed owns a ski cabin for use by the college community.

Majors and Degrees

Reed College awards the Bachelor of Arts degree in a variety of traditional fields as well as in interdisciplinary combinations. Students may select from the following majors: American studies, anthropology, art, biochemistry and molecular biology, biology, chemistry, chemistry-physics, Chinese literature, classics, classics-religion, comparative literature, comparative race and ethnicity studies, computer science, dance, dance-theater, economics, English literature, environmental studies, French literature, German literature, history, history-literature, international and comparative policy studies, linguistics, literature-theater, mathematics, mathematics-computer science, mathematics-economics, mathematics-physics, music, neuroscience, philosophy, physics, political science, psychology, religion, Russian literature, sociology, Spanish literature, and theatre.

Students may also design their own interdisciplinary majors. The approval of such special programs, which link two or more disciplines, is reviewed by the student's adviser and the departments concerned.

Reed offers several combined 3-2 programs, which allow students to graduate with degrees from Reed and an affiliated institution. Science programs and institutions include engineering, computer science (California Institute of Technology, Columbia University, and Rensselaer Polytechnic Institute) and forestry-environmental sciences (Duke University). The college also has a combined program in visual arts (Pacific Northwest College of Art).

Academic Programs

Hallmarks of academic life at Reed include the small-group conference method of teaching and its reliance on active student participation; a de-emphasizing of grades coupled with comprehensive narrative feedback; a yearlong interdisciplinary humanities program; and distribution requirements that balance breadth of learning with the depth of designing an in-depth senior thesis. In addition to fulfilling the requirements for the major, taking the humanities course, and writing the senior thesis, students must satisfy a distributional requirement, consisting of core classes from each of the following academic groups: arts, literature, and languages; history and social sciences; laboratory sciences and mathematics.

Off-Campus Programs

Reed participates in domestic exchange programs with Howard University in Washington, D.C.; Sarah Lawrence College in New York; and Sea Education Association in Massachusetts. In addition, Reed provides study-abroad opportunities for students in Australia, Argentina, Botswana, China, Costa Rica, Cuba, the Czech Republic, Ecuador, Egypt, France, Germany, Greece, Hungary, Ireland, Israel, Italy, Kenya, Lebanon, Morocco, Palestine, Russia, South Africa, Spain, Taiwan, Tanzania, Turkey, Turks and Caicos, and the United Kingdom. Students may also arrange independent study plans in consultation with appropriate faculty members, the director for off-campus studies, and the registrar.

Academic Facilities

Students have access to Reed's substantial library collection by searching the online catalog in the library or from any computer on the campus network. Through its participation in Summit, a union catalog of Oregon and Washington academic libraries, Reed provides online access to other library catalogs and databases. Students may borrow materials directly from academic libraries in the Portland area, as well as from collections worldwide through interlibrary loan. In addition, the Reed library houses a first-rate art gallery, a language lab, and a multimedia resource facility. The Reed library is open 18 hours most days and 24 hours a day during examinations.

The science laboratories at Reed are among the best equipped of any undergraduate college in the United States. These include the A.A. Knowlton Laboratory of Physics, the Arthur F. Scott Laboratory of Chemistry, and the L.E. Griffin Memorial Biology Building. Reed's nuclear research reactor (the only such reactor in the country that is staffed primarily by undergraduates) and radiochemistry lab are actively used for student research, instruction, and training. For those interested in the arts, the campus houses studio art facilities, performing arts facilities, twenty instrumental practice rooms, a computer music laboratory, a recording system, and an 800-seat auditorium. In fall 2013, Reed opened a new $28-million Performing Arts Building, representing a major step forward in the college's commitment to the important role the arts play at Reed. Other popular facilities include a radio station and Reed's newly expanded sports center, which offers a climbing wall and a nationally recognized outdoor program.

Costs

Tuition for 2019–20 is $58,130, and room and board is $14,620. The student body fee is $310, bringing the yearly total cost to approximately $73,060. The cost of books and incidental expenses averages approximately $2,000.

Financial Aid

Over half of the Reed student body receives financial assistance from the college. A full need-based financial aid program makes Reed accessible to students from a wide range of economic backgrounds. The college guarantees to meet the full demonstrated need of all continuing students in good academic standing who complete their financial aid applications on time. Reed's own funds are the primary source of grants to students, making up 83 percent of the average financial aid package in 2017–18. Reed also administers federal and state grants as well as federally subsidized loan programs. Campus employment and work-study programs are available. The size of a financial aid award is based solely upon analysis of the student's need. The average amount awarded to students receiving financial aid in 2018–19 was $45,550, which includes grants, loans, and work opportunities. Reed students' average graduating loan debt for all four years is $17,336, well below the national average.

Faculty

All classes at Reed are taught by professors rather than by teaching assistants. Classes are small, averaging about 15 students. The opportunity to work closely with faculty members is noted by students as one of the great benefits of a Reed education. Reed faculty members point to the opportunity to work with students who are serious scholars as one of the great benefits of teaching at Reed. Faculty members commit themselves primarily to teaching, with scholarly and scientific research furthering this primary goal; they view students as partners in learning, often serving as coauthors and co-investigators on professional papers and research projects. This close association is due, in large part, to a 10:1 student-faculty ratio and the one-on-one relationship between thesis adviser (a professor) and student during the senior year.

Student Government

The Student Senate is the central body in student governance. The Senate consists of the student body president, vice president, and 8 student representatives, all elected by the students. Its two primary functions are to allocate student body funds and to represent student interests and concerns to the faculty, administration, and Reed College Board of Trustees. The Senate distributes approximately $40,000 each semester to the many student organizations on campus. As agreed under the community constitution, students participate fully in discussions and decisions on a wide variety of issues. The Student Committee on Academic Policy and Planning participates in debate about the curriculum at Reed; many other committees, from the Library Board to the Reactor Committee, have substantial student input. The Senate and student body president make all student appointments to such committees.

Admission Requirements

Reed welcomes applications from first-year and transfer candidates who are genuinely committed to the pursuit of a liberal arts education and a rigorous academic program. Those applicants are admitted who, in the view of the Admission Committee, are most likely to become successful members of and contribute significantly and honorably to the Reed community. The college is committed to maintaining a student body distinguished by its intellectual passion and its diverse range of backgrounds, interests, and talents.

Admission decisions are based on many factors, but academic accomplishments and talents are given the greatest weight in the selection process. A strong secondary school preparation, including honors and advanced courses where available, improves a student's chances for admission. Such a program usually includes 4 years of English and 3 to 4 years of mathematics (through pre-calculus), science, foreign language, and history or social studies. Given the wide variation in high school programs and quality, however, there are no fixed requirements for secondary school courses. Applicants are expected to have obtained a secondary school diploma prior to enrollment, although exceptions are occasionally made. There are no cutoff points for high school or college grades or for test scores.

Reed recognizes qualities of character—in particular, motivation, intellectual curiosity, individual responsibility, and community and social consciousness—as important considerations in the selection process, beyond a demonstrated commitment to academic excellence. Thus, the Admission Committee looks for students whose accomplishments and interests in various fields of endeavor will contribute to the overall liveliness of the Reed community. Personal interviews, either on or off campus, are not a requirement in the admission process but are recommended whenever possible. Applications for early decision should be submitted by November 15 (Option I) or December 20 (Option II), early action applications should be submitted by November 15, regular freshman admission by January 15, and transfer candidates by March 1.

Application and Information

The Office of Admission is open Monday through Friday from 8:30 a.m. until 5 p.m. (Pacific time) all year, except for major holidays. The Admission Office is also open on select Saturdays in the spring and fall. Reed College uses both the Coalition Application and the Common Application; students can find a complete list of application requirements online at reed.edu/apply/guide-to-applying.

For further information or to arrange a campus tour, overnight stay, information session, or interview, students should contact:

Office of Admission
Reed College
3203 Southeast Woodstock Boulevard
Portland, Oregon 97202-8199
Phone: 503-777-7511
800-547-4750 (toll-free)
Fax: 503-777-7553
E-mail: admission@reed.edu
Website: reed.edu

Students at Reed College have a great appreciation for intellectual inquiry and passionate discussion, wherever it can be found.

RIDER UNIVERSITY

LAWRENCEVILLE, NEW JERSEY

1865

The University

When students join Rider University's vibrant living-and-learning community, life—and learning—is never the same. Guided by Rider's gifted faculty and supported by its staff, Rider students discover powerful new ways to connect learning to the world around them.

The University is located in central New Jersey, easily accessible to New York City and Philadelphia, offering students great opportunities for exploration, culture, leadership development, internships, and jobs.

Students are at the heart of everything that happens at Rider. The University's student-centered commitment begins with professors who are focused on teaching and mentoring students. That commitment is shared by the entire University community, where every staff member is available to support students and their goals. It's a unique environment dedicated to giving students the self-confidence, skills and strong foundation essential for professional and personal success.

Students come to Rider from 38 states, three U.S. territories, and 68 countries. Each year, Rider enrolls 3,800 undergraduate and 1,000 graduate students.

The greatest legacy of a Rider education is measured by the success of its alumni. Rider alumni have gone on to great success at many of the country's top-ranked graduate and professional schools. They have competed for and won prestigious internships, research grants, scholarships, and fellowships—including numerous Fulbright Scholars.

The outcomes of a Rider education are clear: over 93 percent of Rider graduates are employed full- or part-time, pursuing graduate study, or involved in a volunteer or fellowship position within six months of graduating. And, 273 Rider alumni are presidents, CEOs, and leaders of national or international corporations or organizations.

Location

Rider's central location between two vibrant metropolitan centers—New York and Philadelphia—offers great opportunities for adventure, exploration, culture and shopping, plus internships and jobs. Rider is just minutes away from historic downtown Princeton, incredible nature trails, shopping malls, and more. Students can head an hour in any direction to laze at the beach, downhill ski, or enjoy the sights and sounds of the big city. Whether it's for sightseeing or shows, auditions or internships, Rider is only 90 minutes by train to the heart of Manhattan or an hour to downtown Philadelphia.

Majors and Degrees

At Rider, students can choose from nearly 70 undergraduate and 35 graduate programs through five colleges/schools: College of Business Administration; College of Liberal Arts and Sciences; College of Education and Human Services; School of Fine and Performing Arts; and College of Continuing Studies. Interdisciplinary majors are plentiful, and dual majors are encouraged.

Academic Programs

Lessons learned in the classroom at Rider are complemented and reinforced with rich hands-on experiences. Students have the opportunity to participate in impressive professional internships, student-faculty research, honors and study-abroad programs, and volunteer experiences.

Rider students do lab work, perform on stage, hold leadership roles on campus, and work at the TV station as early as freshman year. Education majors are guaranteed 700 hours of classroom experience through field placements that begin in the sophomore year. Each year, Rider students complete more than 1,000 internships, co-ops, and field placements as part of their degree studies. Rider's award-winning Model UN program, innovative Global Village class, and a wealth of study-abroad and international partnership programs provide opportunities for students to experience the world in a new way.

Learning is enhanced by course work that reflects the latest best practices and technology, and guest lectures by leading experts. With plenty of real-world opportunities in nearby New York and Philadelphia, these great cities are true learning laboratories for students.

By building on these experiences, achievements, credentials, and contacts, Rider students discover what they love to do most—and stand out from the competition when they graduate.

Each of Rider's colleges has a career adviser who specializes in providing the support and preparation needed to move students from their majors to relevant careers. Students begin planning for the future in their first semester, using the expert resources of the Career Development and Success Center to create a compelling professional portfolio and a targeted resume. More information is available online at www.rider.edu/careers.

Students also have opportunities to develop polished interview skills through interactive workshops and alumni videos, launch their job search through the Rider career "handshake" site, and shadow and network with Rider alumni. Rider also hosts career fairs attended each year by hundreds of employers who come to campus to recruit candidates.

Costs

Rider is proud to be private and affordable. Students benefit from the many advantages of Rider's private university experience, and generous scholarship and financial aid programs that focus on making its bottom-line costs extremely competitive with most public colleges and universities.

For the 2018–19 academic year, tuition was $42,120 for full-time students. There is a student activities fee of $145 per semester and a technology fee of $225 per semester. There may be additional fees associated with certain academic programs.

Housing options ranged from $5,210 to $6,540 per semester, depending on the type of residence selected. Meal plans ranged from $2,630 to $2,710 per semester. Additional details can be found online at http://www.rider.edu/offices-services/financial-aid-scholarships/tuition-fees/housing-and-dining-rates.

Financial Aid

Financial aid is personal and tailored to each student's needs and circumstances, starting with the assigning of a personal financial aid advisor to each student. Ninety-nine percent of Rider students receive various forms of financial aid and 98 percent receive Rider-funded scholarships and gift aid. The average annual student assistance package at Rider is more than $34,000. More information on financial aid and scholarship availability can be found at http://www.rider.edu/offices-services/financial-aid-scholarships.

Faculty

Rider's professors are passionate about their disciplines, but teaching is their top priority. They are distinguished authors, educators, scholars, scientists, performing artists, and researchers; an impressive 99 percent hold a doctorate or the highest degree in their field. With an average class size of 22 and a 11:1 student/faculty ratio, classes at Rider are small and collegial.

Student Life

Rider's focus on engaged learning helps students grow, professionally and personally, through abundant global and cultural experiences, honors and leadership development programs, service-learning opportunities, and exposure to the arts.

Rider's vibrant and active campus community includes student government, more than 150 student organizations, fraternities and sororities, plus 20 NCAA Division I men's and women's teams, and 28 club and intramural sports. Getting involved offers students the chance to inspire and lead others, manage budgets, plan successful events, and engage in big-picture thinking.

Admission Requirements

Rider University welcomes students with a variety of academic backgrounds. When reviewing an application for admission, the Undergraduate Admission Office takes a holistic approach by assessing academic performance, letters of recommendation, and admission essay. Once the committee has reviewed the entirety of the student's academic experience, an admission decision will be made.

Potential students must submit official transcripts from their high school or for any college work they may have completed while in high school, a letter of recommendation and a $50 nonrefundable application fee. Rider is Test Optional so students may apply to the University without submitting the results of their standardized testing. For those students submitting scores from the SAT or ACT test, the writing section is not required.

Application and Information

The application deadlines for the fall semester are the following: Early Action (nonbinding), November 15; musical theatre, December 1; and scholarship deadline, January 15. For spring admission, the scholarship deadline is December 15.

Campus tours are offered Monday through Friday at 10 a.m. and 1 p.m. and select Saturdays at 10 a.m. or 1 p.m. To register for a tour online, visit http://rider.edu/visit.

For details on application dates and more, visit http://www.rider.edu/applynow.
Office of Admission
Rider University
2083 Lawrenceville Road
Lawrenceville, New Jersey 08648
Phone: 609-896-5000 (Main)
800-257-9026 (Admission)
E-mail: admissions@rider.edu
Website: http://www.rider.edu

Rider University's vibrant and engaged learning community brings together people from diverse backgrounds, talents, and perspectives to explore subjects, tackle problems, share ideas, embark on adventures, and create solutions.

RIPON COLLEGE
RIPON, WISCONSIN

The College

Established in 1851, Ripon College is Wisconsin's best-value private college and a national leader in liberal arts education, devoted to ensuring every student realizes their unique potential. Ripon's five-course, 20-credit Catalyst curriculum rigorously develops the 21st-century skills employers seek while streamlining the path to graduation. Catalyst ensures students are able to complete multiple majors and minors, study abroad and hold internships in four years. Students enjoy extensive freedom to pursue their passions and craft their own academic program of study. Graduates who complete the Catalyst curriculum earn a Concentration in Applied Innovation, which documents on the transcript that a graduate has mastered the skills of oral communication, writing, critical thinking, collaboration, quantitative reasoning, information literacy, integration and intercultural competence.

Students are overwhelmingly satisfied with the amount of personalized attention they receive from devoted faculty and staff. Within six months of graduation, 98 percent of alumni are employed, in graduate school or student-teaching. An analysis of Department of Education College Scorecard data of alumni 10 years post-graduation shows Ripon graduates are the highest earners of all Wisconsin college graduates.

Ripon is a member of the prestigious Associated Colleges of the Midwest (ACM). The College competes athletically as part of the Midwest Conference and offers 21 NCAA Division III varsity teams. Ripon has a student-to-faculty ratio of 12:1, and the average class size is fewer than 20 students. The new $23.5 million Willmore Center provides students with state-of-the-art facilities to train, work out, study, and learn, and boasts the best NCAA indoor track in Wisconsin. More information is available at ripon.edu/willmore-center.

Location

The College is in the historic city of Ripon, Wisconsin—a friendly, safe community of just under 8,000 people, 80 miles northwest of Milwaukee, 70 miles southwest of Green Bay, 73 miles northeast of Madison, 180 miles northwest of Chicago, and 255 miles southeast of the Twin Cities in Minnesota. The nearest airport is 40 minutes away in Appleton, Wisconsin.

The campus comprises 250 tree-lined acres and 27 buildings, 10 of which are listed on the National Register of Historic Places. A sustainable campus, Ripon is home to the Ceresco Prairie Conservancy with 130 acres of native prairie, oak savanna, and wetland habitat in the making.

Majors and Degrees

Ripon College offers a four-year graduation guarantee with over 80 areas of study, including a variety of fast-track pre-professional programs. Every student graduates with a concentration in Applied Innovation upon completing the five-course, 20-credit Catalyst curriculum.

Majors include anthropology, art history, biology, business management, chemistry, chemistry–biology, communication, computer science-chemistry, computer science-interdisciplinary, computer science-mathematics, computer science-physics, economics, educational studies, English, environmental studies, exercise science-athletic training, exercise science-human performance, exercise science-physical education, exercise science-sports management, finance, foreign languages, global studies, history, mathematics, music, music education, philosophy, physical science, physics, politics and government, psychobiology, psychology, religion, sociology, Spanish, studio art, and theatre.

Minors include adapted physical education, American studies, ARMS (Ancient, Renaissance, and Medieval Studies), anthropology, art history, biology, business management, chemistry, classical studies, coaching, communication, computer and data sciences, criminal justice, economics, educational studies, English, entrepreneurship, environmental biology, Francophone studies, French, health, history, Latin American and Caribbean studies, law and society, mathematics, military leadership, music, national security studies, nonprofit management, philosophy, physics, politics and government, psychology, religion, sociology, Spanish, strength and conditioning, studio art, theatre, and women's and gender studies.

Ripon College offers fast-track programs that allow students to get professional degrees sooner in certain fields. There are currently fast-track programs in engineering with Washington University; law with Marquette University, American University, Mitchell Hamline University, and St. Thomas University; and osteopathic medicine with Lake Erie College of Osteopathic Medicine. Other pre-professional programs available include: government service, journalism, library and information science, military leadership, ministry, pre-med and health sciences (medicine, dentistry, veterinary medicine, optometry, podiatry, physical therapy, pharmacy, nursing, chiropractic medicine and sports medicine), and social work.

Teacher certification is offered in early childhood, elementary, middle/junior high, secondary, and bilingual/ESL. In addition, Ripon offers licensure in 26 subject areas. Teacher certification programs approved by the Wisconsin Department of Public Instruction prepare students for licensure at the early childhood/middle childhood level (grades PK through 5), the middle childhood/early adolescence level (grades 1 through 8), and the early adolescence/adolescence level (grades 6 through 12). The educational studies department also offers PK–12 certification programs in art, foreign languages (French and Spanish), music, physical education, physical education and health, and theatre (pending program approval).

Academic Programs

Ripon's innovative new curriculum, Catalyst, began with the first-year class in fall 2016. The five-course, 20-credit curriculum rigorously develops the 21st-century skills that employers seek while streamlining the path to graduation. Catalyst ensures students have extensive freedom and are able to complete multiple majors and minors, study abroad, and hold internships in four years.

Ripon's liberal arts curriculum introduces students to a wide variety of disciplines. About 40 percent of students complete double or triple majors, while some create special self-designed majors. Hallmarks of a Ripon education are excellent written and oral communication skills; critical-thinking and problem-solving skills; quantitative analysis; intercultural competence; collaboration; and informational literacy. Students enjoy limitless opportunities to explore serious research pursuits alongside faculty as an undergraduate, no matter what the student's major.

A Ripon education can take students anywhere, as demonstrated by the College's talented and well-known alumni. One student studied psychology and played basketball at Ripon, then become a seven-time Grammy winner: jazz singer Al Jarreau (1962). Another, Oliver Williamson (1954) earned a Nobel Prize in economics. Jeff Bantle (1980), a chief flight director with NASA, helped guide the space shuttle into orbit, and Gail Dobish (1976) is an international opera star. Neonatologist Dr. Jonathan Muraskas (1978) is credited with saving the world's smallest premature baby, and Richard Threlkeld (1959) covered the world as former Moscow correspondent for CBS News. Other entertainment notables include Harrison Ford (1964), Spencer Tracy (1924), and Justin Neibank (1978). Recent alumni Zach Morris (2002) studied at Oxford University as a Rhodes Scholar and also found time to play touch football with former President Bill Clinton and spend an evening at Buckingham Palace with Queen Elizabeth.

Off-Campus Programs

United States or abroad? Three weeks, one semester, two semesters? Students can choose from more than 40 programs, each officially sanctioned by and affiliated with Ripon. Although most programs are connected with a major or minor program, all are open to every Ripon student, regardless of major. Scholarships are available to pursue off-campus study.

Programs are offered throughout the United States, including Chicago; Knoxville, Tennessee; Nashville, Tennessee; a southwest Indian reservation; Washington, D.C.; Woods Hole, Massachusetts; and experiences at sea. International programs are offered in Europe, Africa, South America, Central America, India, and Asia.

Ripon College offers three-week Liberal Arts In Focus courses in January, May, and August. Taught in short, intensive blocks, In Focus courses are designed as immersion experiences to provide a bridge between the theory and content of disciplines. Recent courses have included history lessons in Italy; intensive biology field studies in Costa Rica and the Wilderness Field Station near Ely, Minnesota; and a unique English course in Great Britain covering children's fantasy literature from Beatrix Potter to Harry Potter.

Academic Facilities

The 27 buildings on the Ripon campus include historic limestone structures and more modern facilities. Recent updates include a $23.5 million athletics, health, and wellness center; a new Center for Career and Professional Development; a completely renovated recital hall; an apartment-style residence hall; and enhancements to the student union, dining facilities, and student activity spaces.

The athletics, health, and wellness center features new high-tech classrooms, a state-of-the-art fitness center, an NCAA indoor track and field, performance courts, fitness studios, athletic training center, an open-air atrium, new conference and meeting spaces, competition swimming and diving facilities, and other enhancements.

C. J. Rodman Center for the Arts is home to a theatre with a state-of-the-art computerized lighting system, a recital hall with one of only 50 existing Bedient organs, an art gallery, a high-tech lab, and a sculpture garden.

Bovay's Study Bar & Mercantile opened in March 2017 in a historic building in downtown Ripon. This unique venue features a high-tech collaborative study space, a study bar with barista coffee service, a mercantile with official Ripon College apparel and gifts, and flexible meeting space. Student interns working in the space will benefit from hands-on experiential training in marketing, merchandising, and small-business management.

Ripon College provides a secure, high-speed Wi-Fi network across campus and in every building. In addition, a state-of-the-art fiber optic network (10 Gb/s) connects all academic buildings, administrative buildings, and residence halls.

Students, faculty, and staff are issued a G Suite account that offers a variety of productivity tools (Gmail, Calendar, Drive, Docs, Forms, Hangouts) to enhance campus collaboration and communication. Multi-functional devices (MFDs) are located in every academic and administrative building to service the campus printing, copying and scanning needs. The College also has 3-D printers that several faculty have incorporated into their course curricula.

Open-use computer labs are located across campus, offering both Windows and Mac OS devices, projectors, and MFDs.

Ripon College partners with Apogee to provide a cutting-edge cable TV/video solution. With the IPTV service, Stream2, students can view HD content live, on-demand, or recorded (20 hours of DVR storage per user) on their laptops, tablets, and smartphones.

Library staff provide friendly and efficient circulation, reference, instruction, and interlibrary loan services that aid in research. The library also houses the College archives, a computer lab, digital media stations, and more than 25 online databases. Library holdings include access to more than 300,000 physical and electronic books and 55,000 periodicals.

Costs

Tuition for the 2019-20 academic year was $44,813, room and board is $8,653, and fees are $300, for a total cost of $53,766.

Financial Aid

Pursuing a college degree is an important investment, so financial circumstances will never affect Ripon's admission decision. The College provides 100 percent of students with the financial assistance necessary to graduate and works to ensure a great economic value per every dollar spent.

Ripon offers its students competitive packages with funding from many sources: merit-based scholarships, need-based grants, educational loans, work-study, and scholarships from outside organizations. Academic scholarships range from $22,000 to $35,000 per year.

Student Organizations and Activities

From Love Your Melon to fencing, Ripon College hosts more than 60 student-run clubs and organizations. Students are encouraged to lead the programs, supported by the Student Senate's activity fee. This allows students to collaborate on conceiving, organizing, marketing, and developing unique activities.

Ripon's NCAA Division III Intercollegiate Teams compete in the Midwest Conference. Men's varsity sports include: baseball, basketball, cross-country, cycling, football, soccer, swimming and diving, tennis, and indoor and outdoor track and field. Women's varsity sports include: basketball, cross-country, cycling, dance, soccer, softball, swimming and diving, tennis, indoor and outdoor track and field, and volleyball.

In addition, Ripon offers a variety of intramural sports throughout the year, including kickball, dodgeball, flag football, indoor soccer, inner-tube water polo, basketball, bowling, badminton, whiffle ball, video games, volleyball, Ultimate Frisbee, and aerobics.

Admission Requirements

Ripon encourages applications from those students who are best prepared to benefit from and contribute to the academic and extracurricular programs that it offers. In evaluating applications, attention is paid to evidence of academic achievement, as indicated both by the distribution of courses taken in secondary school and by performance in those courses.

Ripon is test optional; test scores will be considered if the applicant chooses to submit them.

For further information, students should contact:

Leigh D. Mlodzik
Dean of Admission
Ripon College
300 Seward Street
P.O. Box 248
Ripon, Wisconsin 54971-0248
Phone: 800-947-4766 (toll-free)
E-mail: adminfo@ripon.edu
Website: http://www.ripon.edu

Ripon College's new $23.5 million Willmore Center was host to the 2018 Midwest Conference Indoor Track and Field and 2019 Women's Basketball Championships.

RIVIER UNIVERSITY

NASHUA, NEW HAMPSHIRE

The University

Rivier University, a private Catholic university founded in 1933 by the Sisters of the Presentation of Mary, has earned a reputation for excellence with distinguished academic programs. Rivier offers many of the region's leading programs at the undergraduate, graduate, postgraduate, and doctoral levels.

Rivier's School of Undergraduate Studies enrolls approximately 1,400 students, including more than 940 full-time day students. With a 12:1 student-faculty ratio, day students have plenty of opportunities to connect with faculty and become active members of the academic community.

The majority of undergraduate students enroll from the six New England states. Rivier also attracts students from all over the United States as well as international students representing countries in Africa, Asia, Europe, and the Middle East. Students who live on campus reside in four modern residence halls, some with suite-style options. Rivier also provides substance-free housing and honors housing. The Dion Center features the University's student center and the newly renovated Dining Center which offers a healthy, upscale dining experience. The commuter lounge, a campus store, student development offices, and meeting rooms are also available in the Dion Center.

The Office of Student Affairs, the Student Government Association, and more than 13 student clubs and organizations provide a calendar of social, cultural, and recreational activities, including concerts, live entertainment, films, and sporting events. The University and student organizations frequently organize outings, including trips to locations such as Boston and New York. Students also enjoy performances by the University Dance Team and Rivier Theater Company.

Rivier's orientation for new students introduces them to the University's wide array of services, such as academic advisers, the Academic Support Center, and peer tutors. The Health Services Center and the Wellness and Counseling Center ensure students' physical and emotional well-being. Campus Ministry staff coordinate spiritual activities and service opportunities.

Be Remarkable

University programs feature a strong liberal arts foundation and proactive professional preparation. Students are encouraged to "Be Remarkable" through Rivier's unique combination of classroom learning, real-world experiences, and career preparation. Vocational exploration begins in the first year, and a personal, four-year academic and professional action plan is offered to each student, charting a path to achieving their goals. Close collaboration between academics, Student Advising, faculty, and the Career Development Center facilitates students' achievement and tracks progress on their plans.

Employment Promise Program

Rivier University has instituted an innovative Employment Promise Program to enhance career preparation and employability of students in all academic disciplines. The program demonstrates the University's confidence in its educational experience marked by distinctive academic programs, committed faculty, and active learning. Through this initiative, the University promises invested students that they will secure a job within nine months of graduation. If they do not, they will receive additional support in the form of payment of monthly federal subsidized student loans for up to one year or enrollment in up to six Rivier master's degree courses tuition-free. Rivier is the only institution in New Hampshire to offer this program.

Athletics

Rivier is a Division III member of the NCAA and sponsors 13 intercollegiate sports. Rivier Raiders compete in men's and women's soccer, volleyball, cross-country, basketball, and lacrosse; men's baseball; and women's field hockey and softball. The men's volleyball team has been nationally ranked every year since 2001 and recently captured heir 9th NCAA championship. The Muldoon Health and Fitness Center is home to Rivier's varsity athletics, fitness activities, and recreation programs including volleyball, floor hockey, basketball, weight training, indoor soccer, and more. The campus also has a turf rectangular field and a natural grass softball field, as well as a beach volleyball court and cross-country trail. Student athletes can take advantage of an on-campus athletic training clinic for injury assessment and rehabilitation. Rivier is constructing a new Athletics Pavilion, elevating the game-day experience for athletes and fans. Features will include spectator seating, team rooms and conference space, a training room, locker rooms, and a press box.

Location

Nashua (population approximately 87,000) is located in southern New Hampshire. The city of Boston lies within easy access 40 miles to the south. Local access to public transportation provides for easy travel to and from the campus. Recreational activities abound year-round at nearby lakes and ski areas, in the White Mountains to the north, and at the seacoast, just an hour's drive to the east. The Manchester airport is a 15-minute drive from campus, convenient for students who must access air travel.

Majors and Degrees

Rivier University awards Bachelor of Arts and Bachelor of Science degrees in the following areas: biology, biology education, biotechnology, business, criminal justice, cybersecurity management, early childhood education, education and community leadership, elementary education, English, English education, finance, global studies, history, homeland and international security, human development, human services, liberal studies, marketing, mathematics, mathematics education, nursing, political science, psychology (with optional track in substance use disorders), public health, secondary education, social studies education, sociology, special education, and sport management. The University offers preprofessional programs in law, dentistry, medicine, and veterinary medicine.

Academic Programs

Professional studies and liberal arts programs prepare students for a rapidly changing, highly technological, and global society. The broad-based curriculum focuses on preparing students for rewarding careers and furthering their personal growth. The University launched a new core curriculum, offering opportunities for service learning, servant leadership, civic engagement, and community service to support the intellectual growth of students and enhance student leadership. Students choose from courses in three areas: humanities and social sciences, mathematics and natural sciences, and languages in the core complement. The new core is aligned with the Association of American Colleges and Universities' (AAC&U) essential learning outcomes, which provide Rivier graduates with the strong intellectual and practical skills that are in demand in the workplace. A bachelor's degree requires a minimum of 120 credits with a grade point average of at least 2.0. For an associate degree, the student must complete a minimum of 60 credits with a grade point average of at least 2.0.

All departments encourage qualified students to pursue internships in their field of study. Students in Rivier's public health major will work alongside public health professionals at local agencies, and a study-abroad component offers first-hand global perspective and experience. Education majors student teach in local schools. Nursing majors complete clinical rotations in healthcare facilities throughout southern New Hampshire and northern Massachusetts. History, law, and political science majors may work in a law office, business, legal-assistance agency, or government agency. Sociology and psychology majors work with local social service agencies. English and marketing majors work in public relations, broadcasting, or corporate communications positions. Business majors work in advertising, management, and technology.

Honors and awards for students include placement on the dean's list, membership in Kappa Gamma Pi or Psi Chi, listing in *Who's Who Among Students in American Universities and Colleges*, listing in *The National Dean's List*, and degrees with honors. Academically talented students may also apply to the four-year Global Scholars Honors Program.

The academic year is divided into two 14-week semesters. Students usually take five courses each semester. Additional courses are offered during the summer. Academic credit may be granted to incoming freshmen on the basis of Advanced Placement test and CLEP examination scores. Students may also "challenge" courses and receive credit by special examination.

Off-Campus Programs

Through Rivier University's membership in the New Hampshire College and University Council, a sixteen-member consortium of senior and two-year colleges, Rivier students may register for courses at any of the member colleges and receive transfer credits.

Academic Facilities

Academic facilities include Memorial Hall, which houses 14 classrooms, the Office of Global Engagement, faculty offices, a lecture hall, a behavioral science lab, and Rivier's art gallery. The Academic Computer Center features up to 68 workstations with a full range of cutting-edge software and Internet/email access. Regina Library provides access to more than 90,000 print volumes, 45,000 e-books and over 90 research databases, as well as more than 3 million volumes in 12 area libraries on virtually every academic subject. The Writing and Resource Center offers assistance from professional writing consultants as well as peer tutors. Other academic facilities include nursing and science laboratories; a physical assessment lab and nursing skills simulation lab, which provide nursing students with practical experience using blood pressure cuffs, ophthalmoscopes, IV pumps, high-fidelity patient simulators, and more; the McLean Center for Finance and Economics; the BAE Student Research Lab; a clinical psychology lab; electronic classrooms offering multimedia learning tools; and the Benoit Education Center, which houses the eight-classroom Landry Early Childhood Center, observation rooms, and an educational resource center. A new 35,000 square foot Science Center is scheduled for Fall 2020.

Costs

Tuition and fees for the academic year 2019–20 are $32,440; room and board, $13,790; and books and supplies, approximately $1,400.

Financial Aid

Financial aid is awarded on the basis of the financial need of the student and family. Approximately 98 percent of Rivier's full-time undergraduate students receive financial aid from the University or from government or private sources. Federal aid includes Federal Pell Grants, Federal Supplemental Educational Opportunity Grants, Federal Perkins Loans, Federal Direct Stafford Student Loans, the Federal Direct PLUS loan program, and the Federal Work-Study Program. To be considered for financial aid, a student must file the Free Application for Federal Student Aid (FAFSA) with the federal government as soon as possible after October 1 for the coming year. FAFSA results should be on file with the University Financial Aid Office prior to March 1 for the following academic year. Each applicant is assessed individually to determine the best combination of grant, work, scholarship, and loan amounts to meet the need of the student. The University awards more than $13 million in institutional need-based and merit-based scholarships and grants annually. For more information, students should contact the Office of Financial Aid.

Faculty

The University employs 64 full-time faculty members. Part-time instructors in specialized areas are working professionals who bring current knowledge and expertise in their field to their classes. All classes are taught by faculty members, and department chairs serve as academic advisers to students in their major programs.

Student Government

Every full-time day student automatically becomes a member of the Student Government Association (SGA) upon registration and payment of the student activity fee. The SGA's main goals are to stimulate active participation in all University functions; to establish and maintain effective channels of communication among members of the University community and the community at large; to foster a mutual trust; to encourage a spirit of cooperation; and to initiate new endeavors. The SGA also supervises student clubs and organizations and oversees their finances. The SGA Executive Board serves as the channel of communication through which the views of the students on institutional policies reach the University administration.

Admission Requirements

Applicants for admission should ordinarily have completed, in an accredited high school, a minimum of 16 academic units, including 4 of English, 2 of a modern foreign language (optional), 3 of mathematics, 2 of social science, 1 of laboratory science, and 3 of electives. The most successful candidates are in the upper half of their class, with at least a B average. The University does not require SAT or ACT scores as part of a student's overall admissions file, except for nursing students. While nursing students are required to provide SAT or ACT scores, all other students have the option to submit their scores. A personal interview is strongly recommended but not required.

Rivier welcomes applications from qualified transfer candidates from accredited institutions, as well as applications from international students. Transfer students must forward transcripts of all previous college work and a high school transcript. International students must fulfill the requirements for general admission; they may also be required to submit Test of English as a Foreign Language (TOEFL) scores. Deferred admission may be granted to students who wish to postpone entrance for up to one year, provided they have not been enrolled full-time at another postsecondary institution.

Application and Information

Applications must be accompanied by an essay, one letter of recommendation, and a high school transcript. The School of Undergraduate Studies employs a system of rolling admission that allows qualified students to be admitted approximately one month after their application is completed. Transfers should apply by June 1 for fall admission and by December 1 for spring admission. Those applying for financial aid should observe the March 1 deadline. Interviews are arranged through the Admissions Office. Students may apply online using the Common Application or the application on the University's website.

For an application or additional information, please contact:

Office of Undergraduate Admissions
Rivier University
420 South Main Street
Nashua, New Hampshire 03060
Phone: 603-897-8507
Fax: 603-891-1799
E-mail: admissions@rivier.edu
Website: http://www.rivier.edu

Students enjoy Rivier's great location in the heart of New England—approximately an hour's drive from Boston, the mountains, and the seacoast.

ROBERT MORRIS UNIVERSITY

MOON TOWNSHIP, PENNSYLVANIA

The University

A private university in Pittsburgh's suburban hills, Robert Morris University is set on a 230-acre former estate that is a short drive from the cultural and commercial opportunities of a major city. Founded in 1921, RMU is a nationally ranked, doctoral degree-granting university and one of Pennsylvania's most affordable private universities. RMU enrolls approximately 5,000 students in more than 90 undergraduate and graduate programs of study.

The university built its reputation in the business fields of accounting, finance, marketing, and management. It has grown to include programs in engineering, mathematics, science, informatics, humanities, social sciences, nursing, education, and psychology. RMU is a teaching-centered institution with small classes taught by professors. Internships, service-learning activities, study abroad, leadership roles, and other learning outside the classroom is documented in the Student Engagement Transcript.

Since 2011 the growing campus has added three major academic buildings, two residence halls, a student recreation and fitness center, and the new UPMC Events center, which combines regional conference and meeting space with a 4,000-seat arena for the Colonials' NCAA Division I basketball and volleyball teams as well as concerts and speakers.

RMU is a residential university, with more than 80 percent of freshmen living in campus housing. Students can participate in any of nearly 100 clubs and organizations. The Student Life features a full calendar of events, while business organizations, professional clubs, and honor societies provide students with career preparation opportunities. Visiting international scholars and a variety of study abroad options enrich students' global perspectives.

The university's competitive athletics program fields 16 NCAA Division I teams, including the Pittsburgh area's only Division I men's and women's ice hockey teams. The Colonials will host the NCAA Frozen Four in 2021. Students can also participate in a number of club teams and intramural sports on campus.

Location

The 230-acre main campus is located in Moon Township, Pennsylvania, just 15 minutes from Pittsburgh International Airport and 17 miles from downtown Pittsburgh. The RMU Island Sports Center is 15 minutes from campus on Neville Island.

Majors and Degrees

Robert Morris University offers 58 undergraduate programs of study: accounting, actuarial science, advertising, biology, biology education, biomedical engineering, business, business education, communication studies, clinical psychology, clinical-sport psychology, computer information systems, corporate communication, criminal justice, cyber forensics and information security, data analytics, digital cinema and television, economics, education (early childhood, special education, middle level, and secondary), engineering, English studies, English education, environmental science, finance, financial mathematics, graphic design, health services administration, history, hospitality and tourism management, industrial engineering, industrial-organizational psychology, information sciences, interaction design, journalism, management, manufacturing engineering, marketing, mathematics, mathematics education, mechanical engineering, nuclear medicine technology, nursing, organizational leadership, photography, political science, pre-medicines, psychology, public relations, social science, social studies education, sociology, software engineering, special education, sport management, sport psychology, statistics and predictive analysis, and writing.

Fully online bachelor's degree programs are available in business, criminal justice, cyber forensics and information security, English, health services administration, hospitality and tourism management, organizational leadership, psychology, and R.N.–M.S.N.

The University offers five-year integrated bachelor's/master's degree programs, medical school affiliation, cooperative education programs, an integrated 3+3 J.D. program with three law school partners, and an honors program.

Academic Programs

Robert Morris operates on a two-semester schedule with various summer sessions. A total of 120 credits are required for most bachelor's degrees. Internship or co-op credits of 3 to 12 hours may be used toward degree requirements. The

University participates in a cross-registration program with nine local colleges through the Pittsburgh Council on Higher Education consortium.

Academic Facilities

All facilities are equipped with learning technology, including state-of-the-art laboratories and studios, simulation equipment, and videoconferencing. Learning resources include a traditional library with more than 137,000 bound volumes, 80 reference databases, and 600 periodical subscriptions.

Costs

Annual tuition for the 2019–20 year is a $29,930 flat rate, based on a 24- to 36-credit, two-semester schedule. Annual room and board is $11,780 based on double occupancy and the Patriot meal plan.

Financial Aid

Ninety percent of RMU undergraduates who request it receive some sort of financial aid, including scholarships, grants, loans, and work-study programs. Both need-based and achievement-based awards are available. All applicants must complete the admissions application, the Free Application for Federal Student Aid, and the grant forms from their own state.

Faculty

The University has more than 480 full- and part-time faculty members; 87 percent of full-time faculty members hold terminal degrees. The student-faculty ratio is 15:1 and the average class size is 22. Students may take advantage of the expertise offered by the faculty in academic advisement and counseling, as well as counseling from the staff at the Center for Student Success.

Student Government

The Student Government Association represents all student organizations, including fraternities and sororities. Members participate in the planning of all social and cultural events on campus.

Admission Requirements

First-time freshmen must submit an application for admission with a $30 application fee (waived for online applicants), official high school transcripts or GED credential, and official SAT or ACT scores. Preference is given to applicants with a minimum 3.0 high school GPA and a combined SAT score of 1000 (Reading + Math) or a composite ACT score of 22.

Transfer students who have earned credits from another regionally accredited institution must submit transcripts from all postsecondary institutions attended and must have a minimum 2.0 GPA. Students with less than 30 college credits must also submit high school transcripts or GED credential.

Certain select academic programs have higher admissions criteria. Students are encouraged to arrange for a campus visit with an admissions counselor.

Application and Information

Students are encouraged to submit applications in the fall of their senior year of high school. Official transcripts and counselor recommendations should accompany the application; there is a $30 application processing fee that is waived for online applicants.

Robert Morris uses a rolling admission system; students are considered for acceptance as soon as all application materials have been received and evaluated.

For additional information and application materials, students should contact:

Kellie Laurenzi
Dean of Admissions
Robert Morris University
6001 University Boulevard
Moon Township, Pennsylvania 15108
Phone: 800-762-0097 (toll-free)
Website: http://www.rmu.edu
http://www.facebook.com/RMUpgh
http://twitter.com/rmu
http://www.youtube.com/RMUNewsTube

RMU students engage in a campus tradition: taking selfies with "Bronze Bob," a statue of university namesake Robert Morris.

ROCHESTER INSTITUTE OF TECHNOLOGY

ROCHESTER, NEW YORK

RIT

COLLEGE CLOSE-UPS

The University

Rochester Institute of Technology (RIT) is among the world's leading career-oriented, technological universities. RIT offers more than ninety undergraduate programs in areas such as engineering, computing and information sciences, engineering technology, business, hospitality, science, art, design, photography, film and animation, biomedical sciences, game design and development, and the liberal arts including communications, economics, international and global studies, psychology, advertising and public relations, and public policy. Students may choose from more than eighty different minors to develop personal and professional interests that complement their academic program. RIT is a world leader in experiential education, which includes cooperative education, internships, study abroad, and undergraduate research. As home to the National Technical Institute for the Deaf (NTID), RIT is a world leader in providing access services for deaf and hard-of-hearing students and has nearly 1,100 deaf and hard-of-hearing students from around the United States and the world. RIT enrolls students from every state and more than 100 countries.

Close to 70 percent of RIT's approximately 12,500 full-time undergraduate students live on the campus in residence halls or campus apartments.

Each year, RIT's more than 300 student organizations sponsor over 1,300 on-campus activities. RIT offers 23 varsity sports, including Division I men's and women's hockey. Recreational facilities are exceptional and include two ice rinks, an aquatics center, a field house with an indoor track, and fitness facilities.

Location

The greater Rochester area has a population of about 800,000. Per-capita income is among the highest in the nation for metropolitan centers. The area's many internationally known industries employ a high proportion of scientists, technologists, and skilled workers. Rochester's industries have always been closely associated with RIT's programs and progress. Rochester is also a hub for higher education with twelve colleges and universities in the area.

Majors and Degrees

The College of Engineering Technology offers the Bachelor of Science (B.S.) degree in applied technical leadership (upper-division, online only), civil engineering technology, computer engineering technology, electrical engineering technology, electrical/mechanical engineering technology, robotics and manufacturing engineering technology, and mechanical engineering technology. It also grants the Bachelor of Science in environmental sustainability, health and safety, packaging science, and media arts and technology. An undeclared option allowing freshmen to delay selecting a major for up to a year is available in the School of Engineering Technology.

The E. Philip Saunders College of Business offers the B.S. in accounting, finance, new media marketing, international business, hospitality and tourism management, management information systems, marketing, and supply chain management. A 4+1 M.B.A. option is available, as are several minors, including entrepreneurship, digital business, and supply chain management. An undeclared option allowing freshmen to delay the selection of their major for up to one year is available.

The B. Thomas Golisano College of Computing and Information Sciences offers the B.S. in computer science, computing security, computing and information technologies, game design and development, human-centered computing, new media interactive development, software engineering, and web and mobile computing. The college also offers a computing exploration option for undeclared freshman students.

The Kate Gleason College of Engineering grants the B.S. in biomedical engineering, chemical engineering, computer engineering, electrical engineering, industrial and systems engineering, mechanical engineering, and microelectronic engineering. Degree options in aerospace, automotive, bioengineering, biomedical, energy and environment, ergonomics, information systems, manufacturing, and software engineering are also offered within the college. Accelerated B.S./M.S. options are available. The Engineering Exploration Program, which allows freshmen to delay the selection of their major for up to one year, is available.

The College of Health Sciences and Technology offers B.S. programs in biomedical sciences, diagnostic medical sonography, exercise science, nutrition management, nutritional sciences, and a five-year physician assistant B.S./M.S. program.

The College of Art and Design offers the Bachelor of Fine Arts in 3-D digital graphics, advertising photography, film and animation, fine art photography, studio arts (with options in ceramics, expanded forms, furniture design, glass, metal and jewelry design, non-toxic printmaking, painting and sculpture), graphic design, illustration, industrial design, interior design, medical illustration, new media design and imaging, photojournalism, and visual media. The college also offers B.S. programs in biomedical photographic communications, imaging and photographic technology, and motion picture science. An undeclared option allowing freshmen to delay the selection of their major for up to one year is available in the School of Art, the School of Design, and the School of Photographic Arts and Sciences.

The College of Liberal Arts offers B.S. programs in advertising and public relations, applied modern language and culture (with options in Chinese, Japanese, and Spanish), communication, criminal justice, digital humanities and social sciences, economics, journalism, international and global studies, museum studies, philosophy, psychology, public policy, and sociology and anthropology. The Liberal Arts Exploration Program is designed to help undecided students formulate education and career plans.

The College of Science offers B.S. programs in applied mathematics, applied statistics and actuarial sciences, biology, biochemistry, bioinformatics, biotechnology and molecular bioscience, chemistry, computational mathematics, environmental science, imaging science, and physics. Special options are available in premedical studies (medicine, dentistry, veterinary medicine). Minors are available in astronomy, exercise science, imaging science, mathematics, physics, and statistics. Accelerated B.S./M.S. and B.S./M.B.A. programs are available. General Science Exploration allows freshmen to delay the selection of their major for up to one year.

Home of the National Technical Institute for the Deaf, RIT is a world leader in providing educational opportunities and access services for deaf and hard-of-hearing students. Qualified deaf and hard-or-hearing students can enroll in any RIT bachelor's degree program. NTID awards associate degree programs and offers pre-baccalaureate studies for deaf and hard-of-hearing students. The associate degree programs prepare students for immediate employment after graduation or transfer into one of RIT's bachelor's degree programs. The pre-baccalaureate studies program prepares students for entry into RIT's bachelor's degree programs. Nearly 600 of the 1,100 deaf and hard-of-hearing students at RIT are enrolled in bachelor's degree programs in the other eight colleges.

Academic Programs

Most students entering as freshmen enroll directly in the academic program of their choice. Options for undeclared students are offered by most colleges as described above. A University Exploration program is available for entering freshmen who wish to explore programs in two or more colleges. Students interested in pre-law, pre-medical, and other pre-health professions may enroll in any major at RIT and take advantage of pre-professional advising programs that provide the guidance necessary to complete the admission requirements for graduate programs in law, medicine, and other health professions. Undergraduates may choose from more than eighty different minors. Double-majors and accelerated dual-degree (combined bachelor's/masters) options are available. The RIT honors program admits approximately 150 freshmen annually. Air Force and Army ROTC programs are available on the campus. A Naval ROTC program is offered jointly with the University of Rochester.

Every academic program at RIT offers some form of experiential education opportunity, including cooperative education, internships, study abroad, undergraduate research, and industry-sponsored projects. Co-op students alternate periods of full-time study with periods of full-time paid work experience directly related to their field of study and career interests. Last year, more than 4,400 students completed approximately 6,000 co-op assignments with nearly 2,300 employers, earning collectively in excess of $45 million.

Off-Campus Programs

RIT has four international locations. RIT Croatia is located in Dubrovnik and Zagreb, Croatia and offers undergraduate degree programs in hospitality and service management, information technology, and international business. RIT Kosovo in Pristina provides career-oriented programs that foster links between the university, industry, and government in support of workforce development. RIT Dubai offers graduate and undergraduate programs in business, engineering, service leadership, and information sciences.

Academic Facilities

Excellent facilities add to the quality of academic life. Students have access to some of the most up-to-date microelectronic, telecommunications, and computer engineering facilities in the U.S. RIT's Wallace Center is a true multimedia learning center. Its collections are exceptionally extensive in the areas of art and design, education for the deaf, photography, and printing.

Students use state-of-the-art computer equipment regardless of their major. Central computer systems can be accessed via a high-speed data network connecting the library, academic facilities, residence hall rooms, and on-campus apartments. There are more than sixty locations campuswide, with wireless networking connectivity utilizing 802.11b technology. The RIT campus network is served by two OC3 connections, each operating at a data rate of 155 Mbps, and one T3 connection operating at 45 Mbps. RIT is among a select group of institutions with access to the Internet2 research network, a collaborative research and development effort led by more than 170 U.S. universities working in partnership with industry and government.

Costs

For 2018–19, undergraduate tuition for the academic year (two semesters) was $43,546. Fees, including the activities and health fees, are $584. Room and board (twenty meals per week) cost $13,046.

Financial Aid

Approximately 77 percent of RIT's full-time undergraduates receive some form of financial aid that includes RIT scholarships, alumni or industry-supported scholarships, and state and federal government grants. A variety of loans and part-time work positions are available. The FAFSA must be submitted by March 1. Giving full recognition to scholarship apart from financial need, RIT awards a number of academic scholarships based on grades, test scores, and activities. Freshmen applying by January 15 and transfers applying by March 1 are considered for these scholarships.

Faculty

There are 1,045 full-time faculty members, 380 part-time faculty members, and an administrative and supporting staff of more than 2,200. Approximately 73 percent of the faculty members have earned a Ph.D. or the terminal degree in their field.

Student Government

The Student Government is the representative body for students. It works with RIT administration, faculty, and staff members to communicate the needs and desires of the student body and to communicate decisions of the administration to students. Fraternity and sorority members, off-campus and hearing-impaired students, and students from minority groups elect special representative bodies. All full-time and part-time undergraduate and graduate students are represented in Student Government.

Admission Requirements

Admission to RIT is competitive and varies from selective to highly selective depending on the desired program of study. The major factors determining freshman admission are strength of academic program, high school performance, and ACT or SAT test results (which may be self-reported for admission review purposes). College performance is the main factor for transfer candidates. Students applying for programs in art, design, and film and animation must submit a portfolio as part of the application process.

RIT promotes and values diversity and admits qualified men and women of any race, color, national or ethnic origin, religion, sexual orientation, gender identity, gender expression, or marital status. RIT does not discriminate on the basis of handicap in the recruitment or admission of students or in the operation of any of its programs or activities, as specified by federal laws and regulations.

Application and Information

An application, a nonrefundable processing fee of $65, official transcripts of all secondary school or college records, and SAT or ACT scores (for prospective freshmen) should be forwarded to RIT. Two Early Decision (ED) plans are available: For ED I, freshman applicants should provide all required materials for fall entry by November 1. For ED II, freshman applicants should provide all required materials for fall entry by January 1. Early Decision applicants who are admitted and submit the $300 acceptance deposit on or before the ED deposit deadlines, are expected to withdraw applications to all other colleges/universities. For Regular Decision, freshman applicants who provide all required materials for fall entry by January 15 receive admission notification by March 15. Prospective freshmen who apply after January 15 are considered on a space-available basis. It is strongly recommended that transfer applicants file their materials on or before March 1 for fall or summer admission and November 1 for spring admission. Fall applicants to the physician assistant program must have all application materials in by December 1.

For application forms, students should contact:

Director of Undergraduate Admissions
Rochester Institute of Technology
60 Lomb Memorial Drive
Rochester, New York 14623-5604
Phone: 585-475-6631
Fax: 585-475-7424
E-mail: admissions@rit.edu
Website: http://www.rit.edu
http://www.facebook.com/RITfb
http://twitter.com/RITAdmissions

A view of the campus.

COLLEGE CLOSE-UPS

SAINT ANSELM COLLEGE
MANCHESTER, NEW HAMPSHIRE

SAINT ANSELM COLLEGE 1889

The College

Saint Anselm College is a nationally-ranked private, Catholic, undergraduate institution with approximately 2,000 students. Founded in 1889 by the world's oldest religious order, the Benedictines—a Catholic order that has endured and thrived for more than 1,500 years—Saint Anselm is accredited by the New England Association of Schools and Colleges and holds membership in the Association of American Colleges, The American Council on Education, the National Catholic Educational Association, and the National Association of Independent Colleges and Universities. It is the third-oldest Catholic college in New England.

Saint Anselm College prepares students for life. With a liberal arts education, graduates are ready for real career experience, and for the challenges that lie ahead. They take their Saint Anselm experience with them to think critically, communicate effectively, and solve problems creatively.

Saint Anselm graduates are CEOs, doctors, lawyers, nurses, engineers, teachers, marketers, and researchers. They are humanitarians, healers, and philanthropists. They graduate Saint Anselm with the drive to achieve, empowered to make the world a better place. In fact, 99 percent of the class of 2017 was employed, in graduate school, or engaged in service within six months of graduation.

There's much to see and do on campus from open skate nights at Sullivan Arena to spring concerts on the quad. Academic buildings, such as the Goulet Science Center and Gadbois Hall, house innovative labs where remarkable research happens every day. There are cell culture labs, climate-controlled environmental chambers, a greenhouse, a sleep lab, SimMan labs, and more. In the library, students have access to the latest technological advances and a range of workspaces for individuals and groups.

The Roger & Francine Jean Student Center, opened in 2018, is a one-stop shop for student life. Home to offices such as Student Engagement and Leadership, Campus Ministry, the Intercultural Center, the Career Development Center, the Academic Resource Center, and the Meelia Center for Community Engagement, it is a hub of activity, community, and opportunity. Students can also get the latest Saint Anselm gear in the bookstore or pick up a coffee from Starbucks in the Gallo Café. Recreational facilities include the Carr Center with basketball courts and the 9,000 square-foot, three-level fitness center. Saint Anselm College boasts some of the top athletic facilities in the Northeast-10 Conference. The College's eighteen intercollegiate athletic teams play all of their home contests on campus (with the exception of the golf team) at Grappone Stadium, Sullivan Arena, or Melucci Field.

Ninety-one percent of Saint Anselm students live on campus in traditional residence halls, suites, townhouses, or apartments. Whether students live on campus or commute, everyone has access to Saint Anselm College's amazing food, ranked eighth in the nation by the Princeton Review.

New Hampshire Institute of Politics: Saint Anselm is home to the New Hampshire Institute of Politics & Political Library (NHIOP), which offers unparalleled opportunities for students to be in the front row of the democratic process. Its auditorium, West Wing, TV studio, and classrooms are where students meet today's prominent political policy thinkers and researchers, journalists and authors, scientists, industry executives, global leaders, and presidential candidates. The Institute, nationally known to political scholars and strategists, is an essential campaign stop for presidential candidates. All of the U.S. presidents in the last fifty years have visited Saint Anselm.

Location

Saint Anselm College is located on 380 acres in Manchester, New Hampshire and is an hour drive from Boston, the Atlantic Ocean and New Hampshire seacoast, and the White Mountains. Just minutes from downtown Manchester, students can find all the venues a small city has to offer: great restaurants and coffee shops, a theater, museum, minor league baseball and hockey teams, and a concert and sports arena to name a few. The Manchester-Boston Regional Airport is also just minutes from the College.

Majors and Degrees

At Saint Anselm College, students may earn a Bachelor of Arts degree in the following academic programs and majors: accounting, American studies, behavioral neuroscience, biochemistry, biology, business, chemistry, classical archaeology, classics, communication, computer science (including concentrations with business or mathematics), criminal justice, economics, education (secondary and elementary), engineering (3-2 program), English, environmental science, environmental studies, finance, fine arts, forensic science, French, German studies, great books, history, international business, international relations, mathematics, mathematics with economics, marketing, natural science, peace and justice studies, philosophy, physics, politics, psychology, social work, sociology, Spanish, and theology. The college also offers a Bachelor of Science in Nursing (BSN).

Saint Anselm students may pursue pre-professional programs in dentistry, law, medicine, theology, veterinary medicine, and other allied health fields, such as pharmacy, physical therapy, and physician assistant.

The engineering physics (3-2) program partners with the University of Notre Dame, University of Massachusetts-Lowell, Catholic University of America, and Manhattan College.

Off-Campus Programs

At Saint Anselm College, a liberal arts education gives students a solid foundation for any career, but opportunities outside the classroom give students a competitive edge and real job experience.

Students find all kinds of experiential learning opportunities at Saint Anselm including internships, research, study abroad, and volunteering. Students of all majors and interests can find opportunities for internships through the Career Development Center, which also brings employers to campus and advises students throughout their job search.

Internships are offered in Boston, New York City, Washington, D.C., Manchester, and beyond. Some recent internships opportunities have included: the Boston Bruins, United States Secret Service, Fidelity Investments, the White House, Fox News, and the American Cancer Society.

Many students work closely on research projects with faculty members on campus to gain valuable lab skills, but there are also opportunities at local hospitals and businesses.

Students interested in study abroad can travel the world visiting such places as Thailand, Morocco, and South Africa. In recent years, students have studied marine biology on Australia's Great Barrier Reef, art history in the museums of Florence, finance in London, language in Spain and France, the culture of peace in Peru, and political history in Ireland. Saint Anselm College offers a semester abroad in Orvieto, Italy, with classes taught by Saint Anselm College faculty. If studying abroad for an entire semester seems too long, Saint Anselm students have traveled with faculty members on week-long trips to places such as China, Panama, and Vietnam.

Saint Anselm students have gained essential leadership and organizational skills through volunteering, doing everything from teaching English to new Americans to working the crisis hotline at the YWCA. In addition, every winter and spring break, Saint Anselm students travel to organizations around the country to volunteer at service sites through Service & Solidarity Mission trips. These service trips challenge students, giving them valuable perspectives and changing their views on the world.

Costs

For the 2019–20 academic year, tuition is $40,500, room and board is $14,750, and fees are $1,300.

Financial Aid

Saint Anselm provides students with financial aid opportunities through both private and federal aid programs. The College provides financial aid to offset the reasonable monetary investment that the student and family are expected to contribute. Ninety-nine percent of the College's undergraduates receive some degree of financial aid. Saint Anselm's financial aid opportunities include grants, loans, scholarships, and employment positions.

Merit scholarships are awarded to outstanding students. Two forms are required in applying for aid; the student must submit the CSS/Financial Aid PROFILE and the Free Application for Federal Student Aid (FAFSA).

Faculty

With an average class size of 18 and a student-faculty ratio of 11 to 1, students receive individual attention in small classes. With 220 professors and no teaching assistants, Saint Anselm faculty members are committed to the success of their students.

Student Life

With more than sixty clubs and organizations, twenty varsity athletic teams, a performing arts center, and an art gallery, Saint Anselm students have plenty of activities to explore. From the soccer club to the mock trial team to the Muslim Student Association, there is a club for every interest, cultural to academic.

Students interested in service will be right at home volunteering through the Meelia Center for Community Engagement or through Campus Ministry. Saint Anselm students volunteered more than 51,000 hours last year. Service & Solidarity Mission trips, held during each winter and spring break, allow Saint Anselm students to volunteer at locations around the country.

Saint Anselm College is part of the Division II Northeast-10 and ECAC Conferences and offers men's intercollegiate baseball, basketball, cross-country, football, golf, ice hockey, lacrosse, soccer, and tennis; and women's basketball, cross-country, field hockey, ice hockey, lacrosse, skiing, soccer, softball, tennis, and volleyball. Saint Anselm also has a variety of club, recreational, and intramural sports teams.

Admission Requirements

In reviewing applicants for the first-year class, admission considers each prospective student carefully. Counselors assess each applicant's secondary school performance, SAT or ACT scores (optional for non-nursing majors, nursing majors must submit scores), recommendation letters, and the written essay. Of highest priority is the applicant's secondary school transcript, with a specific focus on both the rigor of course study and the marks received. Saint Anselm invites transfer and international students to apply.

Saint Anselm College has the following admission deadlines:

- Early action—November 15
- Early decision—December 1
- Nursing majors—must apply by one of the early deadlines
- Regular decision—February 1

Saint Anselm College invites students and families to visit campus for a tour, information session, and/or interview.

For more information, prospective students should contact:

Office of Admission
Saint Anselm College
100 Saint Anselm Drive
Manchester, New Hampshire 03102
Phone: 603-641-7500
888-426-7356 (toll-free)
E-mail: admission@anselm.edu
Website: http://www.anselm.edu

Saint Anselm's campus is home to students, instructors, researchers, and administrators, all striving to create a community where learning shapes living and where the search for knowledge takes place in an environment that values critical thinking, multicultural exchange, and service to humanity.

SAINT FRANCIS UNIVERSITY

LORETTO, PENNSYLVANIA

The University

As the first Franciscan university in the nation, Saint Francis University has been educating competent, caring professionals for 170 years. The private, Catholic, coeducational institution founded by the Franciscan Friars of the Third Order Regular, welcomes students of all faiths and currently enrolls more than 2,600 students from more than 20 countries.

The University offers highly targeted, career-focused programs grounded in the liberal arts tradition of inquiry and self-discovery. The values of respect, drive, generosity, and joy run deep in the University culture and help to prepare ethical, knowledgeable professionals with a passion to shape the world. This holistic approach to career preparation is supported by respected faculty who work closely with students in small settings to meet individual goals.

Saint Francis students are encouraged to make a difference through research and service projects, and many start as early as their freshman year. Undergraduate students work alongside Ph.D. faculty members conducting research and service projects as part of classes and through specialized learning centers such as the Center for Watershed Research and Service, The Keirn Family World War II Museum, the Center for the Study of Occupational Regulation, and the Center for Rural Cancer Survivorship.

Every student is encouraged to look beyond the classroom for career and personal growth through service leadership, undergraduate research, internships, and global opportunities. Saint Francis students graduate with a custom transcript in addition to their academic transcript known as their L.I.S.T. (Leadership, Involvement, Service Transcript) that quantifies these co-curricular accomplishments for employers.

The University is home to a vibrant campus life experience which capitalizes on its natural, rural setting as well as activities organized through student leaders. There are more than 50 official clubs and organizations including Campus Ministry, club sports, Greek Life, the Literary Guild, and marching band. Athletics also plays a major role in the student life with over twenty NCAA Division I sports for men and women ranging from football to water polo.

Location

Saint Francis University's picturesque campus is situated on 600 acres in the heart of the Allegheny Mountains. The campus is located in the borough of Loretto, which has a population of approximately 1,400. The campus is 6 miles from the county seat of Ebensburg, which has a population of 4,000. The cities of Johnstown and Altoona are within 25 miles of Loretto and have populations of 35,000 and 55,000, respectively. The University is a 90-minute drive east of Pittsburgh.

Majors and Degrees

Saint Francis University offers more than 60 academic majors and a wide variety of minors and concentrations through three distinct academic schools. Each school couples classroom curriculum with embedded research and outreach centers for in-depth experiences.

School of Science, Technology, Engineering, Arts & Mathematics: arts and letters, aviation concentration, aquarium and zoo sciences, biology, biochemistry, chemistry, computer science, cybersecurity administration, engineering, English, environmental engineering, environmental studies, fermentation, history, international studies, mathematics, petroleum and natural gas engineering, philosophy, political sciences, pre-law, pre-professional (dentistry, optometry, pharmacy, veterinary), public administration/government services, religious studies, Spanish, and women's studies.

School of Business: accounting, business analytics, communications, criminal justice, digital media, economics, entrepreneurship concentration, finance, healthcare management, management, management information systems (M.I.S.), marketing, MBA (5-year, undergraduate entry), and sociology.

School of Health Sciences and Education: early childhood education, exercise physiology, healthcare studies (pre–allied health, pre-occupational therapy, pre-physician assistant), middle childhood education, nursing, occupational therapy (5-year master's degree), physical therapy (6-year doctorate program), and physician assistant sciences (5-year master's degree), psychology, public health and social work.

The University is accredited by the Middle States Association of Colleges and Schools. Many departmental programs also hold program-level accreditations. A complete list of accreditations may be found in the University catalog or online at www.francis.edu.

Academic Programs

The program of study leading to a bachelor's degree is usually completed in eight semesters. To qualify for graduation, a student must follow a program of study approved by the University that totals at least 128 credits distributed among liberal arts courses, major requirements, collateral requirements, and general electives. All students, regardless of major, are required to complete the University's general education program of 58 credits. A majority of academic programs integrate hands-on learning opportunities using undergraduate research, clinical fieldwork experiences, study abroad, or independent study.

Off-Campus Programs

Students at Saint Francis University may, with permission of the University's administration, spend their junior year of study abroad or may earn credit for participation in summer programs conducted in Canada, France, Germany, Spain, and other countries by accredited American colleges and universities.

Students are encouraged to take advantage of the University's study abroad facility in Ambialet, France, anytime throughout their academic career. The Semester in France program offers study for students within any major for the same tuition costs as studying on campus.

A number of departments offer students the opportunity for off-campus study. For some majors, such as nursing, occupational therapy, physical therapy, physician assistant science, education, medical technology, and social work, internships and/or clinical rotations are required. Saint Francis University strongly encourages students in all other academic majors to complement their field of study with an internship, study abroad, a community service experience, or academic research with a faculty member.

Academic Facilities

The Campus Mall is flanked by academic buildings dedicated to each of the three academic schools. The newest construction projects include a re-imagined space for The Shields School of Business and a state-of-the art 70,000 square-foot science center. Currently underway is a 10,000 square-foot addition to the Sullivan Hall, which will provide health science majors a new space to practice real-world healthcare scenarios. These projects complement the DiSepio Institute for Rural Health and Wellness Center which provides a clinical training area for health sciences. Students in the School of STEAM conduct archival research in the newly opened Keirn Family World War II Museum.

Costs

For 2018–19, tuition was $35,210. In addition, there were fees for expenses associated with lodging, food, insurance, facilities, technology, orientation, and travel. The estimated total per student ranged from $47,500 to $49,182. Detailed cost breakdowns are available on the University website, www.francis.edu.

Financial Aid

Approximately 98 percent of the Saint Francis University student body receives financial aid. In addition to participating in federal and state need-based student aid programs, Saint Francis University offers its own substantial grant program and a generous scholarship program that is based on SAT or ACT scores, high school average, and class rank. Academic awards range from $1,000 to $18,000 annually.

Faculty

Faculty members are chosen for their knowledge of subject matter, as well as for their ability to communicate. Of the teaching faculty at Saint Francis University, 82 percent hold a doctorate or the highest degree attainable in their specific field of expertise. No teaching assistants or graduate students teach classes at Saint Francis University.

Student Clubs and Organizations

Saint Francis University offers an extensive list of co-curricular organizations for students. Over 60 clubs and organizations allow students to choose to become involved in areas of interest. A Greek life community, Student Government Association, and Student Activities Organization provide students additional leadership and involvement opportunities. Several club sport teams are available for students.

Admission Requirements

The admission committee considers applicants and renders decisions on the basis of the secondary school record, the recommendation of the secondary school principal or counselor, and the results of the SAT or ACT. Applicants to the School of Health Science should be aware of specified application requirements and deadlines. Applicants should have a minimum of 16 academic units and are strongly encouraged to visit the University campus for an admission interview and tour. Interviews and campus tours are available Monday through Friday throughout the year and select Saturday mornings while classes are in session.

Transfer students must submit a formal transfer application and a college clearance form in addition to official transcripts from each high school and college previously attended. Transfer students receive an advanced standing evaluation after an offer of admission has been made.

Saint Francis University, an equal opportunity/affirmative action employer, complies with applicable federal and state laws regarding nondiscrimination and affirmative action, including Title IX of the Educational Amendments of 1972, Titles VI and VII of the Civil Rights Act of 1964, and Section 504 of the Rehabilitation Act of 1973. Saint Francis University is committed to a policy of non-discrimination and equal opportunity in employment, education programs and activities, and admissions that includes all persons regardless of race, gender, color, religion, national origin or ancestry, age, marital status, disability, or Vietnam-era veteran status. Inquiries or complaints may be addressed to the University's Director of Human Resources/Affirmative Action/Title IX Coordinator, Saint Francis University, Loretto, Pennsylvania 15940; telephone: 814-472-3264. For other University information, students should call 814-472-3000 or visit the website at www.francis.edu.

Application and Information

The University operates under a rolling admission policy. The occupational therapy and physical therapy programs have a January 15 priority application deadline. The Physician Assistant Sciences program has a November 15 priority application deadline. For more information about Saint Francis University, students should contact:

Vice President for Enrollment Management
Saint Francis University
P.O. Box 600
Loretto, Pennsylvania 15940
Phone: 814-472-3100
866-342-5738 (toll-free)
E-mail: admissions@francis.edu
Website: http://www.francis.edu
http://www.facebook.com/SaintFrancisUniversity
http://twitter.com/SaintFrancisPA
https://www.instagram.com/saintfrancispa

In the fall of 2016, following a year-long $7 million renovation and expansion project, Schwab Hall welcomed students once more, this time re-imagined as home to The Shields School of Business. The project was funded entirely by donations from alumni and friends of the University.

COLLEGE CLOSE-UPS

ST. JOHN'S COLLEGE
ANNAPOLIS, MARYLAND

The College

Founded in 1696, St. John's College in Annapolis, Maryland is among the oldest colleges in the country and offers students a unique education in the liberal arts. Its sole undergraduate program, the Bachelor of Arts (B.A.) in liberal arts, is based on the great books of Western civilization.

The College, which has no religious affiliation, has 450 students from all 50 states and 20 countries. Every class is small (12 to 21 students) with seminar-style discussions led by one or two faculty members. The vibrant community is complemented by the College's campus in Santa Fe, New Mexico, where students may transfer for a year or more.

St. John's College is one of forty colleges profiled in Loren Pope's book, Colleges that Change Lives, in which he described the college as "intellectual" and "indispensable." Discussion in the classroom tends to spill into student life as well. "Johnnies"—as students at the school are known—are original and unconventional, love big questions and discussion, and debate the ideas of thinkers, authors, scientists, philosophers, musicians, mathematicians, politicians, and more who changed the world.

The Liberal Arts

St. John's has one academic program: reading and discussing the great books of Western civilization. Alongside names such as Plato, Shakespeare, Euclid, Nietzsche, Einstein, and Austen, Johnnies wrestle with ideas in interdisciplinary classes with fewer than 20 students. All students follow the same curriculum and graduate with a B.A. in Liberal Arts, having taken seminars, laboratories, math tutorials, music tutorials, and language tutorials.

Seminars at St. John's include:

- classics
- economics
- literature
- history
- philosophy
- political science
- psychology
- theology

Math tutorial classes include:

- algebra
- astronomy
- calculus
- geometry
- number theory
- relativity

Science laboratories cover the following subjects:

- astronomy/astrophysics
- biology
- chemistry
- genetics
- physics

The music tutorial classes include chorus and music theory. Students also take language tutorials, which cover ancient Greek, French, and English-language poetry.

During junior and senior year, students also take elective classes called preceptorials. Past preceptorial subjects have included:

- Gabriel García Márquez, *One Hundred Years of Solitude*
- Immanuel Kant, *Critique of Practical Reason*
- *The Neuroscience of Vision*
- Laozi and Zhuangzi
- Bertrand Russell, *An Introduction to Mathematical Philosophy*
- Readings from Muslim Philosophers who Introduced Ancient Greek Thought into Western Europe
- Early Buddhist Discourses
- *What is a (Modernist) Painting?*
- Herman Melville, *Moby Dick*
- Flannery O'Connor, *Wise Blood* and selected short stories
- Maimonides, *Guide to the Perplexed*
- Cosmology
- The Poetry of John Donne and Emily Dickinson

Graduate Programs in the Liberal Arts

St. John's College has a Master of Arts (M.A.) in Liberal Arts program that allows students—including executives, professionals, teachers, and writers—to expand their understanding of themselves and the world. They achieve this goal by reading, contemplating, and discussing great texts like Euripides's Electra, Shakespeare's King Lear, de Tocqueville's Democracy in America, and Kierkegaard's Philosophical Fragments.

The University Honors Program allows students to participate in enriched educational experiences and offers opportunities that include honors sections of required academic courses, honors seminars, independent research, and specialized study abroad.

Academic Facilities

Northeastern is home to more than 40 research centers and undergraduates have ample opportunities to work alongside their professors to aid and conduct research on a variety of topics. The 220,000 square-foot Interdisciplinary Science and Engineering Complex has further evolved Northeastern's research enterprise by providing state-of-the-art infrastructure and fostering collaboration across disciplines.

The university library system is comprised of Snell Library, a 240,000-square-foot central library on the Boston campus, the School of Law Library, and a supplemental collection at the Nahant Marine Science Center. Snell also houses the Digital Media Commons, a dedicated media lab and digital creativity space that offers flexible work areas, professional-grade technology, high-power computer workstations, printers, scanners, a 3D printing studio, and a recording studio.

Costs

For the 2018–19 academic year, the estimated tuition is $50,450 and room and board fees are estimated at $16,270. Regardless of time to degree, tuition is charged only while students are earning academic credit. All tuition and fees are subject to approval and revision by the Board of Trustees. For the most up to date information, please visit studentfinance.northeastern.edu.

Financial Aid

The university operates a substantial aid program designed to make attendance feasible for all qualified students. Northeastern is dedicated to meeting full demonstrated need for incoming domestic financial aid applicants. By coordinating the resources of the university and various public and private scholarship programs, the Office of Student Financial Services was able to provide $281 million in grant and scholarship assistance. More than 75 percent of students receive some form of financial aid. Northeastern participates in all federal aid programs. Financial aid is based on need and academic merit and may consist of scholarships, grants, loans, work-study employment, or any combination of these funds. To apply, students must file the Free Application for Federal Student Aid (FAFSA) and a CSS Profile form, available through the College Board, by the priority filing deadline that corresponds with their application type.

Faculty

The university has more than 1,380 full-time faculty members with a variety of research and teaching interests. Academic counselors in each college work closely with students to assist them in developing programs suited to their interests and abilities. Co-op advisors assist students in resume-building and honing interview skills, while helping students develop contacts with businesses to support networking and professional opportunities.

Admission Requirements

Students may enter the university with advanced credit on the basis of test scores on Advanced Placement (AP) examinations, the International Baccalaureate (IB) examinations, or with successful completion of accredited college-level courses. In addition to the application for admission, prospective freshmen must submit official high school transcript(s) (or official GED score reports); official transcripts for any college-level coursework taken while a secondary-school student; written recommendations from their secondary school counselor and a teacher; and scores from the SAT (Northeastern's College Board code is 3667) or ACT, including the writing section. Please visit the university's website for additional admission details for specific student populations and transfer admissions requirements (northeastern.edu/admissions).

Application and Information

Admission to Northeastern is selective and competitive. For the freshman class entering in Fall 2018, the university received more than 62,000 applications for 2,800 seats in the freshman class. Students are reviewed in the context of their environment, with attention paid to their academic course selections and rigor, academic achievement, extracurricular involvement and impact, and their potential fit with Northeastern, including the demonstration of personal traits like leadership, adaptability, a global perspective, or an entrepreneurial spirit.

Northeastern offers four decision plans for first year students: Early Decision I, Early Action, Early Decision II, and Regular Decision. The deadline for Early Decision I is November 1, and the deadline for Early Decision II is January 1; both of these programs are binding admission programs. Students who have carefully explored their college options and have decided that Northeastern is where they want to enroll may choose to apply under the Early Decision program. November 1 is the deadline for Early Action, and January 1 is the deadline for Regular Decision; both of these programs are non-binding. For transfer students, the admissions deadlines are April 1 for fall and October 1 for spring admission. Fall transfer and spring admission decisions are made on a space-available, rolling basis.

Please visit the university's website for application requirements, additional admission details for specific student populations, and information about transfer admissions requirements (northeastern.edu/admissions).

Northeastern offers a variety of visit options including information sessions and campus tours. For more information, or to register, visit northeastern.edu/admissions/connect/visit.

For more information, students should contact:

The Office of Undergraduate Admissions
240 West Village F
Northeastern University
360 Huntington Avenue
Boston, Massachusetts 02115
Phone: 617-373-2200
E-mail: admissions@northeastern.edu
Website: northeastern.edu/admissions

Northeastern's Centennial Common—a typical quad where students relax, study, and hang out with friends.

The College also offers the M.A. in Liberal Arts as well as an M.A. in Eastern Classics program at its Santa Fe campus.

Student Life in Annapolis

St. John's College is located at the center of historic Annapolis, just 30 miles outside of Washington, D.C. Students live and study along cobblestone streets by the Chesapeake Bay. Annapolis is a bustling college town filled with restaurants, college students, and the Maryland state capital.

The heart of student life is on campus. All freshmen are guaranteed housing on campus; over 80 percent of Johnnies live on campus and eat in the dining hall. There are over 50 clubs and study groups devised and sustained entirely by students. These include the campus newspaper, known as the Gadfly; the theater group, known as King William Players; choirs; orchestra; student government; LGBT groups; the film society; and more. Over 50% of Johnnies play intramural sports, including soccer, basketball, tennis, and dodgeball. There are four intercollegiate sports: crew, croquet, fencing, and sailing. Croquet is particularly popular for the annual Annapolis Cup against the United States Naval Academy.

Costs

For academic year 2019-20 the undergraduate tuition is $35,000 ($17,500 per semester); room and board is $13,635 ($6,817.50 per semester); and the activity fees and other fees total $635 ($317.50 per semester). A typical student budget would include about $630 for books, $400 for personal expenses, and transportation costs depending on the distance of the student's home from campus.

Financial Aid

St. John's College is committed to making college affordable for all students. In service of this goal, St. John's has reduced its tuition by $17,000 dollars for the 2019-20 academic year and going forward. In addition, St. John's provides generous need-based and merit-based financial aid, and the vast majority of St. John's students receive financial aid. All applicants, including international applicants, are eligible to be considered for need based aid. All applicants are also eligible for merit scholarships up to the full cost of tuition for 2019-2020.

Career Opportunities

Nearly 70 percent of graduates pursue advanced degrees. St. John's College is in the top 2 percent of all colleges and universities in the nation for percent of alumni who go on to earn Ph.D.'s; in the top 1 percent for degrees in the humanities; and in the top 4 percent for those in science and engineering.

More than half of Johnnies pursue internships during their time at St. John's, many of which are funded by the college. The Career Services Office gives students personalized assistance with internships, graduate school, and job applications. A recent survey revealed the following career paths of some alumni: business (20 percent), education (19 percent), communication and the arts (15 percent), law (10 percent), health and medicine (9 percent), computers/science and mathematics (8 percent), and social sciences (2 percent).

Application Information

The St. John's application process is different. While the Admissions Committee (both admissions officers and faculty) considers traditional factors, such as the applicant's academic record, letters of recommendation, and test scores (which are optional for most students), the most important factor the committee considers is the writing supplement each applicant submits. The committee reads the essays of every single applicant to St. John's before making an admissions decision.

Because St. John's welcomes all serious applicants, there is no application fee.

Applicants may apply Early Action, Regular Fall, Rolling, or Regular Spring (Santa Fe campus only). Early Action acceptances are nonbinding. Except for Regular Spring applicants for the Santa Fe campus, all accepted students have until May 1 to make enrollment decisions and deposits. The deadline for Early Action is November 15, with the admissions decision returned December 15. The deadline for Regular Fall is January 15, with the admissions decision returned February 15. The deadline for Rolling Fall is after February 15, with admissions decisions returned within two to three weeks.

Visiting is the best way to learn about St. John's. Students can explore campus, take a tour with a current student, attend a class, talk with a faculty member, meet with an admissions officer, eat in the dining hall, and even stay overnight. If visiting St. John's poses a financial hardship, there is funding available to assist interested students with travel expenses. More information is available online at http://www.sjc.edu/admissions-and-aid/undergraduate-admissions/visit/

For more information, prospective students should contact:
St. John's College
60 College Avenue
Annapolis, Maryland 21401
Phone: 410-626-2522
800-727-9238 (toll-free)
E-mail: Annapolis.Admissions@sjc.edu
Website: http://www.sjc.edu/

St. John's College, founded in 1696 in Annapolis, Maryland, is one of the oldest colleges in the country.

COLLEGE CLOSE-UPS

ST. JOHN'S COLLEGE
SANTA FE, NEW MEXICO

sjc | St. John's College

The College

Nestled in the foothills of the Rocky Mountains, St. John's College in Santa Fe, New Mexico offers students a unique education in the liberal arts. Its sole undergraduate program, the Bachelor of Arts (B.A.) in liberal arts, is based on the great books of Western civilization.

The College, which has no religious affiliation, has 450 students from all 50 states and 20 countries. Every class is small (12 to 21 students) with seminar-style discussions led by one or two faculty members. The vibrant community is complemented by the College's campus in Santa Fe, New Mexico, where students may transfer for a year or more.

St. John's College is one of forty colleges profiled in Loren Pope's book, Colleges that Change Lives, in which he described the college as "intellectual" and "indispensable." Discussion in the classroom tends to spill into student life as well. "Johnnies"—as students at the school are known—are original and unconventional, love big questions and discussion, and debate the ideas of thinkers, authors, scientists, philosophers, musicians, mathematicians, politicians, and more who changed the world.

The Liberal Arts

St. John's has one academic program: reading and discussing the great books of Western civilization. Alongside names such as Plato, Shakespeare, Euclid, Nietzsche, Einstein, and Austen, Johnnies wrestle with ideas in interdisciplinary classes with fewer than 20 students. All students follow the same curriculum and graduate with a B.A. in Liberal Arts, having taken seminars, laboratories, math tutorials, music tutorials, and language tutorials. Seminars at St. John's include:

- classics
- economics
- English/literature
- history
- philosophy
- political science
- psychology
- religion/theology

Math tutorial classes include:

- algebra
- astronomy
- calculus
- geometry
- number theory
- relativity

Science laboratories cover the following subjects:

- astronomy/astrophysics
- biology
- chemistry
- genetics
- physics

The music tutorial classes include chorus and music theory. Students also take language tutorials, which cover ancient Greek, French, and poetry.

During junior and senior year, students also take elective classes called preceptorials. Past preceptorial subjects have included:

- Gabriel García Márquez, One Hundred Years of Solitude
- Immanuel Kant, Critique of Practical Reason
- The Neuroscience of Vision
- Laozi and Zhuangzi
- Bertrand Russell, An Introduction to Mathematical Philosophy
- Readings from Muslim Philosophers who Introduced Ancient Greek Thought into Western Europe
- Early Buddhist Discourses
- What is a (Modernist) Painting?
- Melville, Moby Dick
- Flannery O'Connor, Wise Blood and selected short stories
- Maimonides, Guide to the Perplexed
- Cosmology
- The Poetry of John Donne and Emily Dickinson

Graduate Programs in the Liberal Arts

St. John's College also offers M.A. (Master of Arts) programs in Liberal Arts and Eastern Classics. These programs allow students—including executives, professionals, teachers, and writers—to expand their understanding of themselves and the world. They achieve this goal by reading, contemplating, and discussing great texts like The Mahabharata, Shakespeare's King Lear, de Tocqueville's Democracy in America, and Laozi's Tao Te Ching.

The College also offers the M.A. in Liberal Arts at its Annapolis campus.

Student Life in Sante Fe

St. John's College's 260-acre campus, located between downtown Santa Fe and the Santa Fe National Forest, gives students easy access to the tranquility of nature and the culture of a world-renowned artistic and cultural hub known for its world-class museums, hundreds of art galleries, live music venues, and amazing restaurants.

Student life is centered on campus; all freshmen are guaranteed housing on campus, and over 80 percent of students live on campus and eat in the dining hall. Johnnies are members of a vibrant community, with more than fifty clubs founded and maintained entirely by the students. These include The Moon, a student-run newspaper; Chrysostomos, a theater group, Student Polity, the student government organization; choirs, instrumental groups, LGBT groups, painting, pottery and other art groups, and more. In addition, they engage in community service through Project Politae (and volunteer at community organizations throughout Santa Fe).

Students also enjoy a variety of campus events like concerts, parties, picnics, open mic nights, movies, and game nights, and have easy access to outdoor activities like backpacking, rock climbing, rafting, and skiing, as well as intramural sports and world class gym facilities.

Costs

For academic year 2019-20 the undergraduate tuition is $35,000 ($17,500 per semester); room and board is $12,860 ($6,430 per semester); and the activity fee and other fees total $1,410 ($705 per semester). A typical student budget would include about $630 for books, $400 for personal expenses, and transportation costs depending on the distance of the student's home from campus.

Financial Aid

St. John's College is committed to making college affordable for all students. In service of this goal, St. John's has reduced its tuition by $17,000 dollars for the 2019-20 academic year and going forward. In addition, St. John's provides generous need-based and merit-based financial aid, and the vast majority of St. John's students receive financial aid. All applicants, including international applicants, are eligible to be considered for need based aid. All applicants are also eligible for merit scholarships up to the full cost of tuition for 2019-2020, and all New Mexico residents admitted to the Santa Fe campus of St. John's College will receive a $10,000 dollar grant in addition to any other financial aid and scholarships.

Career Opportunities

Nearly 70 percent of graduates pursue advanced degrees. St. John's College is in the top 2 percent of all colleges and universities in the nation for percent of alumni who go on to earn Ph.D.'s; in the top 1 percent for degrees in the humanities; and in the top 4 percent for those in science and engineering.

More than half of Johnnies pursue internships during their time at St. John's, many of which are funded by the college. The Office of Personal and Professional Development gives students personalized assistance with internships, graduate school, and job applications. A recent survey revealed the following career paths of some alumni: business (20 percent), education (19 percent), communication and the arts (15 percent), law (10 percent), health and medicine (9 percent), computers/science and mathematics (8 percent), and social sciences (2 percent).

Application Information

The St. John's application process is different. While the Admissions Committee (both admissions officers and faculty) considers traditional factors, such as the applicant's academic record, letters of recommendation, and test scores (which are optional for most students), the most important factor the committee considers is the writing supplement each applicant submits. The committee reads the essays of every single applicant to St. John's before making an admissions decision. Because St. John's welcomes all serious applicants, there is no application fee.

Applicants may apply Early Action, Regular Fall, Rolling, or Regular Spring (Santa Fe campus only). Early Action acceptances are nonbinding. Except for Regular Spring applicants for the Santa Fe campus, all accepted students have until May 1 to make enrollment decisions and deposits. The deadline for Early Action is November 15, with the admissions decision returned December 15. The deadline for Regular Fall is January 15, with the admissions decision returned February 15. The deadline for Rolling Fall is after February 15, with admissions decisions returned within two to three weeks.

Visiting is the best way to learn about St. John's. Students can explore campus, take a tour with a current student, attend a class, talk with a faculty member, meet with an admissions officer, eat in the dining hall, and even stay overnight. If visiting St. John's poses a financial hardship, there is funding available to assist interested students with travel expenses. More information is available online at http://www.sjc.edu/admissions-and-aid/undergraduate-admissions/visit/.

For more information, prospective students should contact:
St. John's College
1160 Camino Cruz Blanca
Santa Fe, New Mexico 87505
United States
Phone: 505-984-6060
Fax: 505-984-6162
E-mail: SantaFe.Admissions@sjc.edu
Website: http://www.sjc.edu

St. John's College's New Mexico campus boasts 260 stunning acres and is located in Santa Fe, which was just named as one of the top 20 college towns in the country.

ST. LAWRENCE UNIVERSITY
CANTON, NEW YORK

ST. LAWRENCE UNIVERSITY

The University

From deep exploration in classrooms and labs to bold adventures across the globe, St. Lawrence University students seek insight and knowledge through experience. Every academic, extracurricular, and personal journey they pursue is a chance to ask better questions, magnify understanding, and put their boldest ideas to the test. As the world around us searches for answers to the most pressing complex issues facing local and global communities today, St. Lawrence graduates are in demand because they are equipped with the tools, knowledge, inspiration and passion needed to tackle them. That's why 97 percent of the most recent graduating class were employed or enrolled in graduate school less than a year after graduation.

Founded in 1856, St. Lawrence is the oldest continuously coeducational degree-granting institution of higher learning in New York State. Initially established as a theology school for the Universalist Church, it quickly evolved into the liberal arts college that it is today. St. Lawrence is a private, nonsectarian university of approximately 2,400 undergraduate students, with a small graduate program in education. St. Lawrence is known for its residential/academic First-Year Program, its international study opportunities and area studies programs, its students' strong interest in the environment and the outdoors, and its empowering and supportive community.

St. Lawrence students enthusiastically engage in extracurricular opportunities. There are more than 150 student clubs and organizations, with new ones created each year based on student interest. The University routinely hosts well-known speakers, as well as alumni who return to campus to mentor students, while lectures, concerts, plays, and films are regulars on the weekly events calendar.

St. Lawrence students have historically placed high value on athletic activity, and a large number participate in varsity, intramural, or club sports. Most of the 34 varsity men's and women's teams compete at the NCAA Division III level, with the exception of men's and women's ice hockey, which compete in Division I, and riding, Alpine skiing, Nordic skiing, squash, and men's crew. Recreational facilities include cross-country ski and running trails; indoor and outdoor tennis courts; an athletic complex with a gymnasium, two field houses, a 133-station fitness center, a three-story climbing wall, and a pool; an ice rink; an equestrian center; a boathouse; a golf course; a nine-lane all-weather track; an artificial-turf field for lacrosse and field hockey; ten squash courts; and performance fields for soccer, football, baseball, and softball.

Residential life is an important aspect of the St. Lawrence experience. The University's innovative and highly regarded First-Year Program creates communities in which groups of approximately 30–35 first-year students live and learn together. In the upperclass years, students can choose from traditional residence halls, Greek chapter houses, suites, and theme cottages that focus on student interests, such as low-impact living and community service. Seniors may also choose townhouses. St. Lawrence sponsors a full range of student services from counseling to career planning.

Location

St. Lawrence is situated on a 1,000-acre campus in the village of Canton, New York (population 6,400), the seat of St. Lawrence County. Canton, with its Victorian homes, tree-lined streets, village green, farmer's market, restaurants, and small shops, is typical of college towns throughout the Northeast. Students and residents often mix in stores, at athletic events, and in community projects. Ottawa, Canada's capital, is 75 minutes to the north, while Lake Placid, one of America's hiking and skiing meccas, is 90 minutes to the southeast.

Majors and Degrees

St. Lawrence offers the Bachelor of Arts and Bachelor of Science degrees; students can choose from 69 majors and have the option of picking from 41 minors. Combined five-year programs with other institutions are in place in engineering, management and data science, and specialized advising is offered in preparation for postgraduate work in dentistry, law, medicine, nursing, physical therapy, and veterinary medicine.

Academic Programs

St. Lawrence's foremost mission is to provide its students with a liberal arts education. Students complete requirements in eight areas and concentrated work in a major field as well as demonstrating competence in writing. Close faculty-student interaction is a hallmark of a St. Lawrence education as professors are well known for unlocking the brilliant potential found within every student. Every semester, many students engage in independent or honors projects, often working with professors on joint research projects that lead to publication in leading scholarly journals. A senior project is required in most majors.

Off-Campus Programs

St. Lawrence University supports a variety of off-campus programs on six continents that allow students to enrich their majors, expand their world, gain cross-cultural skills, and prepare them to be unequaled agents of change. Nearly 70 percent of St. Lawrence students study off campus during their collegiate careers. St. Lawrence operates or has partnered with other carefully selected programs in Australia, Austria, Canada, China, Costa Rica, the Czech Republic, Denmark, England, France, India, Italy, Japan, Jordan, Kenya, New Zealand, Spain, Thailand, and Trinidad and Tobago. The Kenya program is based at the University-owned and operated campus in the suburbs of Nairobi. The program strives to provide students with a unique study-abroad experience. In addition, the University's membership in the International Student Exchange Program (ISEP) permits students to directly enroll in universities in more than 50 additional countries. St. Lawrence also operates a program at Fisk University in Nashville, Tennessee, and administers its own Adirondack Semester Program, Sustainability Program, and the Liberal Arts in New York City Semester Program. The University also enrolls students in The Washington Center internship program, located in Washington, D.C.

Academic Facilities

Owen D. Young Library and Launders Science Library contain more than a million volumes as well as electronic resources and ample space for reading and research. Griffiths Arts Center is the home of the University's Art and Art History program, as well as the Performance and Communication Arts department. The building features two theaters, an art gallery in which selections from St. Lawrence's 7,000-piece permanent collection are frequently shown, and the Peterson-Kermani Performance Hall, a 19,000-square-foot space for the performing arts. A unified science complex houses the departments of Biology, Chemistry, Physics, Psychology, Geology, Mathematics, Computer Science, and Statistics, and is connected via a covered hallway to the science library and new Center for Student Achievement. The 130,000-square-foot Johnson Hall of Science was the first LEED-certified gold science building in New York State. Richardson Hall, St. Lawrence's oldest building and on the National Register of Historic Places, is home to the English and Religious Studies departments. Other departments can be found in academic buildings clustered on one part of the campus, so classrooms are not far apart.

Costs

The comprehensive fee for 2019–20 is $71,395, including tuition, fees, room, and board.

Financial Aid

St. Lawrence awards both merit scholarships and need-based financial aid. More than a third of accepted students receive a merit scholarship, and nearly 55 percent receive need-based aid. St. Lawrence is committed to assisting as many students as possible and recognizes academic and personal achievement in making financial aid decisions. To apply for need-based financial aid, students must file the Free Application for Federal Student Aid (FAFSA) between October 1 and February 1 and request that the results be sent directly to St. Lawrence.

Faculty

The 216 members of St. Lawrence's faculty are teachers and scholars who pride themselves on not just knowing student names, but knowing students. While teaching and advising are their primary responsibilities, they are also active researchers, artists, performers, and regular contributors in their academic disciplines. Faculty members teach all courses at St. Lawrence; no undergraduate courses are taught by graduate students. Active teaching assistants and tutoring programs, involving qualified upperclass students, are closely supervised by faculty members. The student-faculty ratio is 11:1. Faculty members hold regular office hours, serve as academic advisers to students, and frequently take part in extracurricular activities on campus.

Student Government

The Thelomathesian Society, comprised of all students on campus, is governed by a senate of elected representatives. The senate distributes funds in support of student activities and provides two student delegates to the University's Board of Trustees.

Admission Requirements

St. Lawrence seeks students who can be successful in a demanding academic program and who can contribute to the quality of life of the community. The University is committed to enrolling students who represent the widest possible diversity of economic, social, ethnic, and geographic backgrounds. Academic preparation and ability are the most important criteria, but demonstrated ability in the creative arts, athletics, and/or social service is also a measure of a student's potential to benefit the St. Lawrence community. Submitting standardized test scores (SAT or ACT) is optional for domestic candidates. International applicants are required to submit SAT scores. A campus visit is strongly encouraged, and interviews may be scheduled on-campus or off-campus in certain areas.

Although there is no set distribution of required high school courses, successful applicants typically show strong preparation in the humanities, social sciences, mathematics, and natural sciences. Honors, Advanced Placement, and International Baccalaureate courses are opportunities for applicants to demonstrate intellectual maturity and curiosity, qualities highly valued in the admission process.

Application and Contact Information

St. Lawrence uses the Common Application as its sole application form. The application processing fee is $60, which is waived if candidates have made an official visit to campus. Regular Decision applications must be submitted by February 1, with notification by mail in mid-March. Students who decide that St. Lawrence is their first choice may apply Early Decision. The priority window for Early Decision begins November 1; students may commit to Early Decision at any point until February 1. Early Decision candidates are usually notified by mail within two weeks of receipt of a completed application.

Transfer candidates should submit applications no later than November 1 for the spring semester or March 1 for the fall semester.

For additional information, students should contact:

Office of Admissions and Financial Aid
St. Lawrence University
23 Romoda Drive
Canton, New York 13617
Phone: 315-229-5261 (Admissions)
800-285-1856 (Admissions, toll-free)
315-229-5265 (Financial aid)
800-355-0863 (Financial aid, toll-free)
E-mail: admissions@stlawu.edu or finaid@stlawu.edu
Website: http://www.stlawu.edu
http://www.facebook.com/StLawrenceU
http://twitter.com/StLawrenceU
http://instagram.com/StLawrenceU
http://www.youtube.com/StLawrenceU

Located in the center of campus, the Sullivan Student Center is home to the Northstar Café, Career Services, the Campus Mailroom, Student Activities, Volunteer Services, Residence Life, and plenty of comfortable student study and meeting spaces.

SAINT MARY'S COLLEGE

NOTRE DAME, INDIANA

Saint Mary's College
NOTRE DAME, IN

The College

Saint Mary's College is a Catholic undergraduate women's college located in Notre Dame, Indiana, offering graduate programs for women and men. The Sisters of the Holy Cross founded the College in 1844.

Saint Mary's College has an undergraduate community of 1,600 academically motivated women from 46 states and 10 countries determined to make the world a better place. As a women's College, our students are more likely to speak up, ask for instruction, and become leaders when integrated into co-ed classes and work settings. At Saint Mary's accomplished, passionate, confident, women express themselves, share their dreams, push each other, support each other, encourage each other, are inspired, and strive to inspire. Ninety-three percent of the school's graduates complete their degrees in four years, and whether they choose new careers, graduate school, or postgraduate service, Saint Mary's alumnae are prepared for life.

Saint Mary's unique relationship with the University of Notre Dame provides access to the exciting atmosphere of a large university—just across the street. Students at both schools can take courses at either institution. Saint Mary's students can audition for Notre Dame's legendary marching band or work for The Observer, the student newspaper for Saint Mary's and Notre Dame. In addition, students participate in dances, concerts, lectures, and social organizations on both campuses. Holy Cross College is also just next door to Saint Mary's College. Holy Cross congregations founded all three campuses.

Saint Mary's residential campus becomes the students' second home. Saint Mary's five residence halls include Opus Hall, which offers apartment-style living for seniors on campus. Residence halls host events and compete with each other in intramural athletics. Each hall also sponsors a local nonprofit organization that provides students with service opportunities. All residence halls have chapels, and the Church of Our Lady of Loretto, the main worship space, offers daily Mass on campus.

As an NCAA Division III school and a member of the Michigan Intercollegiate Athletic Association (MIAA), Saint Mary's sponsors varsity teams in basketball, cross-country, golf, lacrosse, soccer, softball, tennis, and volleyball. Club sports, co-sponsored with Notre Dame, include gymnastics and figure skating. In addition, Saint Mary's offers many intramural sports. The new Angela Athletic & Wellness Complex opened in spring of 2018, complete with a training and fitness center with weight and cardio machines, an indoor track, fitness classes for every level, a cafe, and study spaces.

Location

Saint Mary's beautiful 100-acre campus, set alongside the Saint Joseph River, is across the street from the University of Notre Dame, next door to Holy Cross College, minutes north of the city of South Bend (population 101,000), 90 miles from Chicago and 140 miles from Indianapolis. The South Bend community provides opportunities for internships, field practicums, and volunteer service. Eighty percent of Saint Mary's students engage in service by the time they graduate (the national average is approximately 55 percent).

Majors and Degrees

Saint Mary's College offers seven undergraduate degree programs: Bachelor of Arts, Bachelor of Science, Bachelor of Science in Nursing, Bachelor of Social Work, Bachelor of Business Administration, Bachelor of Fine Arts, and Bachelor of Music, and more than 40 academic programs. The College offers more than 40 minors, including American history, anthropology, computer science, environmental studies, justice studies, Latin American studies, and women's studies.

Saint Mary's also offers four coeducational graduate degrees: a Master of Science in Data Science, a Master of Science in Speech Language Pathology, a Doctor of Nursing Practice, and a Master in Autism Studies.

In addition, the Five-Year Dual Degree in Engineering Program with the University of Notre Dame leads to a bachelor's degree from Saint Mary's College and a Bachelor of Science in Engineering degree from Notre Dame in aerospace, chemical, civil, computer, electrical, environmental, or mechanical engineering.

Saint Mary's education department, accredited by the National Council for Accreditation of Teacher Education, offers an elementary education major (grades K–6) and a secondary education minor (grades 5–12). With an elementary education major, students can also receive mild intervention licensure (K–6) and an Indiana reading licensure (P–12). Saint Mary's also offers minors in English as a second language and early childhood education. In addition, the department offers programs for those interested in teaching the visual arts or music. Secondary education requires a major in one of the following: English, Spanish, mathematics, science (science majors must complete licensing requirements in chemistry or life science), history (history majors must complete additional course work in political science and one of the following: sociology, psychology, economics), and political science (political science majors must complete additional course work in history and one of the following: sociology, psychology, economics).

Academic Programs

In addition to completing the required credit hours in her chosen field, every undergraduate student completes a senior comprehensive in her major (a thesis, a research or creative project, or a written or oral examination). All undergraduate students must also complete a writing-intensive "W" course, usually in the first year, and an advanced portfolio of writing in the major discipline, usually in the senior year.

Off-Campus Programs

Intercultural competence is a cornerstone of the liberal arts education. Saint Mary's combines that with travel and adventure through study-abroad experiences in more 15 locations. Saint Mary's students may also study through a cooperative program with the University of Notre Dame. Domestic programs include a semester at American University in Washington, D.C. for political science majors, opportunities for student teachers in Native American communities, and the Catalyst Trip, a journey to sites significant to the history of social justice.

Academic Facilities

Librarians at the Cushwa-Leighton Library help students navigate research assignments, using a collection of over 228,000 books, dozens of online databases, and thousands of online journals. The library also houses a 24/7 computing center, faculty instructional design support, and a collection of rare and historic books. Research help is available in person or by phone, email, or live online chat.

Laboratory facilities are available for biology, chemistry, and physics in the newly renovated Science Hall, and for psychology and language students. Art studios, music practice rooms, O'Laughlin Auditorium, and Little Theatre provide space for fine arts creation, practice, and performance. Spes Unica Hall, an academic building, provides students with technology-equipped classrooms, group and individual study spaces, and presentation spaces.

The Early Childhood Development Center provides education and psychology majors with a unique opportunity to work with young children on campus.

Costs

Expenses for the 2018–19 academic year include tuition and fees, $42,220; room and board, $12,580 (average).

Financial Aid

The College strives to make a Saint Mary's education available for every admitted student by offering financial aid packages that might include institutional need-based assistance, merit scholarships, and work-study opportunities in addition to state and federal grants and loans. One-hundred percent of admitted students receive merit-based scholarships.

The priority deadline for applicants to complete the Free Application for Federal Student Aid (FAFSA) is March 1.

Faculty

Saint Mary's professors are experts in their fields of study and mentors to their students inside and outside the classroom. Our small class sizes allow students to connect with their professors. Students are encouraged to ask questions, work together, and get involved in various projects. Our faculty typically know each student by name so there is no getting lost in the shuffle. Most importantly, they become mentors and advisors, leading our students towards academic and professional success.

Student Government

The Student Government Association (SGA) is a dynamic student-led organization that sponsors extracurricular and co-curricular activities including service projects, social events, and learning experiences. It provides student participants with leadership opportunities that often include leadership training. SGA has voting representatives on the president's two highest advisory boards, the Student Affairs Council and the Academic Affairs Council. A student is also a voting member of the College's Board of Trustees.

Admission Requirements

Applicants for undergraduate admission to Saint Mary's College should be impending graduates of an accredited high school. Home-schooled students are also encouraged to apply. All applicants must complete a four-year, college-preparatory curriculum that consists of a minimum of 16 academic (Carnegie) units where one unit represents one full year of study. The minimum requirements are: 4 units of English, 2 units of the same foreign language, 3 units of college-preparatory mathematics (beginning with algebra I), 2 units of laboratory science, and 2 units of history or social science. The remaining required units should consist of three additional units in the above listed subjects.

Applications must include an academic transcript showing current rank and senior-year courses (if available), a secondary school report, and SAT or ACT scores. Saint Mary's offers students the ability to apply without their test scores. In order for students to qualify for this, they must have a minimum 3.2 GPA out of 4.0. In lieu of test scores, they are asked to submit an academic writing sample and an academic teacher recommendation from grades 10-12 and an essay. There is no application fee, and Saint Mary's is a member of the Common Application.

Saint Mary's encourages students to visit the campus for a tour and informational meeting with an admission counselor. Arrangements to attend classes, meet with coaches, stay overnight, or have an admission meeting via phone or Skype can be made by contacting the Office of Admission.

Application and Information

Saint Mary's has two application and notification programs: early decision and modified rolling regular admission. Students who have selected Saint Mary's as their first choice for admission may apply under the early decision program. The application deadline is November 15, and the notification date is January 15. Students who apply for modified rolling admission, and those whose application files are complete on or before the end of November are notified of the admission decision prior to the Christmas holiday. After that, applications are reviewed in the order in which they become complete. The priority application deadline for regular admission is February 15. Applications are accepted, however, as long as space is available.

Interested students are encouraged to contact:

Office of Admission
Saint Mary's College
Notre Dame, Indiana 46556-5001
Call (574) 284-4587
Text (574) 213-0281
Email admission@saintmarys.edu
Visit saintmarys.edu;
@saintmaryscollege on Facebook and Instagram

We promise you discovery. Discovery of yourselves, discovery of the universe, and your place in it.
—Sister Madeleva Wolfe, CSC,
President of Saint Mary's College from 1934–1961

COLLEGE CLOSE-UPS

ST. NORBERT COLLEGE

DE PERE, WISCONSIN

The College

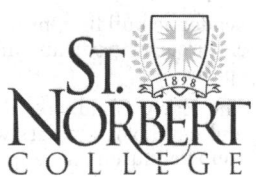

St. Norbert College is a private institution that was founded in 1898. It has a total undergraduate enrollment of 2,047 students on a scenic, riverfront campus that spans 112 acres in the metropolitan Green Bay area. At St. Norbert, the undergraduate curriculum is guided by a liberal arts core and the opportunity for students to pursue any of more than 30 majors, including pre-professional programs, or design their own.

St. Norbert College (SNC) is the only institution of higher education in the world sponsored by the Norbertines, a Catholic order devoted to living in community and serving others. The college welcomes students of all faiths who aspire to develop their full potential in understanding and serving the world. St. Norbert has grown to become an influential part of business, educational, service, theological and cultural experiences throughout northeastern Wisconsin. It is conveniently located within three hours of Chicago, Milwaukee, and Madison, Wisconsin.

St. Norbert's academic and student experience highlights include:

- 97 percent of SNC students receive financial aid
- SNC provides a four-year graduation guarantee
- Roughly 30 percent of SNC students study abroad via programs that span 29 countries
- Students can choose from more than 30 majors or design their own
- The student-to-faculty ratio is 13:1
- First-year students are eligible for collaborative research fellowships and internships
- International students from 20+ countries call SNC their home away from home
- SNC has 90 student organizations and clubs
- SNC has 23 varsity athletic teams and a distinguished history of Division III championships
- Students contribute 28,000+ hours of service annually
- Within one year of graduation, 96 percent of SNC students are employed or attending graduate school
- SNC's chef-prepared meals are nationally ranked and recognized

The college's motto is *docere et exemplo*, to teach by word and example.

Students at St. Norbert exhibit a strong sense of community, school pride, and an appreciation for the diverse perspectives and global opportunities available to them. They often highlight the relationships they have developed with peers and faculty, as well as the rewards of volunteering in the local community.

Location

The 112-acre St. Norbert campus is located on the Fox River in De Pere, Wisconsin, just minutes south of Green Bay, a metropolitan area of about 300,000 people. Rich in industry, culture, arts, and entertainment, De Pere and the greater Green Bay area are recognized among the 100 best communities for young people by America's Promise Alliance. The campus is part of a vibrant 18-county region of 1.2 million people, home to Fortune 500 companies, hospitals, schools, and service organizations, many of which offer internships for students.

Majors and Degrees

St. Norbert offers programs leading to the Bachelor of Arts, Bachelor of Science, Bachelor of Music, and Bachelor of Business Administration degrees.

Programs of study at St. Norbert include: accounting, American studies, art–fine arts, art–graphic design, biology–biomedical, biology–organismal, business administration, chemistry, chemistry–biochemistry, classical studies, communication and media studies, computer science, computer science–business information systems, computer science–graphic design and implementation, economics, education, English, English–creative writing, environmental science, French, geography, geology, German, history, human services (social work), integrative studies, international business and language area studies, international studies, Japanese, leadership studies, mathematics, military science/ROTC, music, natural sciences, nursing, peace and justice, philosophy, physics, political science, pre-dental, pre-engineering, pre-law, pre-medical, pre-pharmacy, pre-veterinary, psychology, religious studies, religious studies–youth ministry, sociology, Spanish, teacher education, theatre studies, and women's and gender studies.

Graduate Programs: Through its Donald J. Schneider School of Business & Economics, the college offers a Master of Business Administration degree. St. Norbert also offers Master of Arts in Liberal Studies and Master of Theological Studies degrees.

Academic Programs

As a liberal arts institution, St. Norbert equips students with exceptional communication, critical-thinking, problem-solving, and leadership skills. An honors program offers additional challenge for students who demonstrate exceptional academic ability.

The academic centers at St. Norbert enrich students' academic experience and serve as valuable resources for the community. The centers include the Center for Exceptional Leadership, the Center for Norbertine Studies, the Norman Miller Center for Peace, Justice & Public Understanding, the Sturzl Center for Service & Learning, the Center for Global Engagement, the Center for Business & Economic Analysis, and the Strategic Research Institute.

Off-Campus Programs

St. Norbert students, regardless of major, can spend a summer, a semester, or a year abroad. In fact, 30 percent of St. Norbert students spend at least one semester abroad compared to less than 4 percent nationally. The college has more than 75 study-abroad program sites in 29 countries on six continents. An international-study component is a part of majors in French, Spanish, and German, as well as both the international business program and the international studies major.

St. Norbert considers international experience vital to today's graduates and it is a key component of the college's educational mission. St. Norbert's international curriculum prepares students to live in a global society. A Washington semester is also available through American University in Washington, D.C.

First-year students still undecided about their life path can participate in the Gap Experience, which takes them from the Canadian north shore of Lake Superior to the natural wonders of Guatemala, all while earning college credit toward their degree.

Additional service-learning opportunities are available throughout the year, including the TRIPS (Turning Responsibility Into Powerful Service) program in local, national, and international locations.

Academic Facilities

The facilities that define St. Norbert's campus include buildings of rich historical significance as well as state-of-the art new construction.

The Mulva Library features 250,000 volumes, enhanced technology, flexible study and classroom spaces, and a 24-hour computer study area. A high-tech multimedia studio on the lower level of the library opened in 2013 and has become a favorite place for students to collaborate on group projects.

The F. K. Bemis International Center provides students with opportunities to prepare for careers with greater international emphasis. The center also serves as a resource for K–12 schools and Wisconsin businesses for language instruction, translation, and interpretation.

The stunning Gehl-Mulva Science Center, completed in 2015, is home to St. Norbert's science programs as well as the Medical College of Wisconsin's northeast Wisconsin campus. The 160,000-square-foot facility features classrooms and labs equipped with the latest technology.

A signature addition to the campus, the new Mulva Family Fitness & Sports Center is home to the college's indoor sports, health, and wellness facilities, and aquatics center. Schneider Stadium is an outdoor athletics complex that provides a modern venue for football, soccer, and track and field.

Michels Commons is a hub for student life with chef-prepared meals at Ruth's Marketplace and a popular gathering place in Dale's Sports Lounge. St. Norbert ranks in the top 3 percent of all colleges in the nation for its food.

The Cassandra Voss Center offers innovative, holistic programming about gender, identity, and diversity, attracting leading figures in the field as speakers.

Fifteen residence halls provide the link between living and learning for roughly 85 percent of St. Norbert students. Some residence halls focus on community service or feature campus programs, such as the honors program. An apartment-style residence hall offers upperclassmen a transitional experience to living on their own. Many halls have chapels for students.

Costs

For 2018–19, tuition and required fees for full-time students totaled $38,129 for the year. Room and board costs averaged $10,556 per year.

Financial Aid

Students share in more than $60 million of financial aid each year, including scholarships and grants, campus jobs, and educational loans. Roughly 97 percent of St. Norbert students receive financial aid, with an average aid amount of more than $24,000 per year. There are both need-based and merit-based awards as well as full Army ROTC scholarships each year. A multitude of work-study positions exist on campus, as well as paid community internships.

Need-based awards are made on the basis of the Free Application for Federal Student Aid (FAFSA; St. Norbert College's code is 003892) and the St. Norbert College institutional application for financial aid. First-year applicants should submit their FAFSA by Jan. 1 of their senior year of high school.

Faculty

Ninety-two percent of the 200 full-time faculty members at St. Norbert hold a doctoral or other terminal degree in their field. The student-to-faculty ratio is 13:1, and student success is the top priority of the faculty. They work closely with students in their major area of study, help students prepare for graduate school, write letters of recommendation, and work with those who seek independent study and research opportunities. Research fellowships and collaborations with faculty members are available to all students—as early as their first year—who may ultimately have the opportunity to present their research findings collaboratively with faculty members at national conferences.

Student Government

The Student Government Association is active on campus, with representation extending as far as the college's board of trustees. The president of the college and his cabinet respect the voice of the student body, and openly discuss issues that impact students and the college community. There are more than 90 organizations in which students can get involved.

Admission Requirements

St. Norbert College welcomes enrollment from a diverse group of students who are prepared academically and who will make a contribution to the college's living and learning community. Students who are likely to succeed are accepted based on their holistic achievements, not just grades and test scores. The average GPA of admitted students is 3.5, and the average ACT composite score is 25. Students with superior test scores and grades are invited to enroll in the honors program. The college encourages and welcomes applications from international, transfer, and diverse students.

Application and Information

Because St. Norbert gives preference to qualified students according to the date of admission and enrollment deposit, it benefits students to apply as early as possible in their senior year. Students are notified about admission decisions on a rolling basis beginning in late September. A $350 nonrefundable deposit is required to confirm enrollment.

For more information about St. Norbert College, students should contact:

Ed Lamm
Vice President for Enrollment Management and Communications
St. Norbert College
100 Grant Street
De Pere, Wisconsin 54115
Phone: 920-403-3005
800-236-4878 (toll-free)
E-mail: admit@snc.edu
Website: http://www.snc.edu
http://www.snc.edu/go/socialmedia

A welcoming, supportive community greets first-year students at Convocation.

COLLEGE CLOSE-UPS

ST. THOMAS AQUINAS COLLEGE

SPARKILL, NEW YORK

ST. THOMAS AQUINAS COLLEGE

The College

St. Thomas Aquinas College (STAC) is a four-year liberal arts college that offers over 100 different majors, minors, specializations, and dual degree programs with a total student body of approximately 2,800 in all programs, on and off campus. Much growth and development have taken place over the College's history. The College offers a Master of Science in Education (M.S.Ed.), with concentrations in autism, literacy, and special education, and postgraduate certificate programs in autism, literacy, and special education. The College also offers a Master of Business Administration (M.B.A.) program with concentrations in finance, management, marketing, sports administration, and general M.B.A. St. Thomas Aquinas College has a Master of Science in Teaching (M.S.T.) program available for individuals without a background in teacher education who are seeking a career change. The College is home to New York University's Master in Social Work program. Then there's the School of Arts and Sciences - Master of Public Administration in Criminal Justice.

The suburban, metropolitan campus includes two residential complexes, with a third residential complex underway in 2019: Aquinas Village, comprises self-contained townhouse units that house 300 students, and the McNelis Commons, which comprises townhouse residential units that house 375 students and a common dining hall and laundry building. Approximately 40 percent of the College's full-time student population lives on campus.

The College provides extracurricular activities through 40+ different organizations, including the Spartan Volunteers, a community service program; a student-run radio station (WSTK); the Laetare Players dramatic and musical club; and the student-edited campus newspaper and yearbook. The College has NCAA Division II teams in men's and women's cross-country, indoor and outdoor track and field, basketball, soccer, lacrosse, and tennis; women's field hockey and softball; and men's baseball and golf. Also, on the varsity sport roster are sprint football, women's triathlon, women's bowling, and e-sports. There are several club sports including ice hockey, cheerleading and dance, bowling, and ski and snowboarding, and intramural athletics.

The College has a campus ministry office, a health office, and residence life, career development, and counseling services.

Location

The College is located in Rockland County, just 15 miles north of New York City, giving students quick access to learning, cultural, internship, and career opportunities in one of the world's most exciting cities.

Majors and Degrees

St. Thomas Aquinas College's School of Arts & Sciences offers degrees in the humanities, mathematics, natural sciences, and social sciences. Programs are available in art therapy, art and visual communications in graphic design or media art, communication arts, creative writing, English, journalism, philosophy and religious studies, Romance languages, Spanish, mathematics, computer sciences, biochemistry, biology, exercise science, forensic science, medical technology, natural sciences, criminal justice, psychology, therapeutic recreation, social science, and history. There are specializations in biology, chemistry, and physics. Minors include art therapy, biology, chemistry, communication arts, computer information science, criminal justice, English, fine arts, history, journalism, mathematics, performing arts, physics, public relations, religious studies, social media, sociology, Spanish, therapeutic recreation, and creative writing. A full listing of all programs can be found online at www.stac.edu.

The School of Business offers accounting (and accounting as a dual degree with an M.B.A. degree), finance, hospitality management, management, marketing, and sport management. Minors are offered in business management, marketing, economics, human resource management, international business, sport management, and management information systems. Specializations are in management relations/industrial and organizational psychology.

The School of Education offers programs in grades 1–6 childhood education, the same plus special education, birth–6 early childhood and childhood education, and grades 7–12 adolescence education. An art education program with certifications in grades K–12 is offered as well as a middle school extension that adds to either the elementary or secondary degree, enabling the student to certify for all middle school grades. The School of Education also offers several dual-degree programs: B.S./B.A. and M.S.Ed. in childhood (B.S.) and special education (M.S.Ed.), grades 1–6; mathematics (B.S.) and special education (M.S.Ed.), grades 7–12; social sciences (B.S.) and special education (M.S.Ed.), grades 7–12; and Spanish (B.A.) and special education (M.S.Ed.), grades 7–12.

The College offers a five-year dual degree program in mathematics with The George Washington University (GWU) or Manhattan College. Students study at St. Thomas Aquinas College for three years. After completion of their final two years at either GWU or Manhattan, they earn a B.S. in mathematics from STAC and a B.S. in engineering from one of the other two institutions. The College also offers several dual-degree options in biology: a dual degree in biology (B.S. from STAC), a dual degree in biology (B.S. from STAC) and physical therapy (D.P.T. from New York Medical College), a dual degree in biology (B.S. from STAC) and chiropractic (D.C. from New York Chiropractic College), and a dual degree in biology (B.S. from STAC) and podiatry (D.P.M. from New York College of Podiatric Medicine). There are several other strategic alliances, such as preferred admission to St. John's University School of Law in New York and a similar program with Barry University School of Law in Florida that includes scholarship funds. St. Thomas Aquinas College also has strategic agreements with St. John's University for an M.P.S. in sport management and a Master of Public Health.

Academic Programs

The College strives to develop students who are not only generally educated but also possess advanced knowledge in specialized areas, who are prepared for further study, and have the drive to undertake fulfilling careers. To earn a bachelor's degree, students must complete a total of 120 semester hours, including a minimum of 51 credits in a core curriculum; complete all requirements for the specific major; and complete the final 30 hours at the college. St. Thomas Aquinas College awards up to 30 credits for life experience and up to 30 credits for achievement on the College-Level Examination Program (CLEP). The College operates on a semester calendar (quarterly on the M.B.A. level). Students may enroll in classes in the fall, winter (a one-month session), spring, and summer (three separate sessions). Undergraduate students can apply for the fall and spring semesters. Graduate education students can apply for the fall, spring, and summer semesters. Classes are scheduled during the day and evening, and students are permitted considerable academic flexibility in planning their programs.

Students can pursue independent study and internships, and many majors require a field practicum. The College maintains an active Center for Academic Excellence as a resource for enhancing academic performance, and students are encouraged to meet regularly with faculty advisers for academic guidance and career direction.

The College has a widely recognized program for college-age learning-disabled students, called the Pathways Program (at an additional cost). The College also participates in the New York State Higher Education Opportunity Program and provides an honors program (freshman applicants only) for exceptionally qualified students with 70 percent tuition scholarships. The honors program includes summer study at Oxford University. The Aquinas Leaders Work Scholarship program is for qualified students (freshmen applicants only) with strong academic abilities and a desire to gain work experience each semester that can be related to academic pursuits.

Aquinas Leaders receive financial awards that cover approximately 60 percent of tuition costs over four years.

Off-Campus Programs

The College offers a variety of degree programs to active-duty military personnel, spouses, and dependents at the United States Military Academy at West Point. Associate and bachelor degrees are offered in a variety of areas at a discounted tuition rate.

Through articulation agreements with high schools, students can take college-level courses for credit at their own high schools at a substantially discounted tuition rate. This program provides high school students an opportunity to get a jump-start on their college careers by immersing them in college-level coursework and providing them with transferrable college credits for it.

The study-abroad program provides opportunities at colleges and universities in such places as Brazil, Canada, England, France, Hungary, Ireland, Italy, Morocco, and Spain. Several other locations are also available.

Academic Facilities

Borelli Hall, a green-designed, LEED-certified Silver building, features new classrooms with interactive board technologies. Costello Hall houses the science laboratories, technology theaters, and Azarian-McCullough Art Gallery. Spellman Hall houses a multiroom technology corridor, with a state-of-the-art communication studio where students produce their own news show, and technology and language labs. Lougheed Library provides a variety of online research opportunities for students. The Bloomberg Professional Laboratory provides students with the same platform for news, data, analytics, and research used by the world's leading banks, corporations, government agencies and public policy makers, law firms, libraries, energy companies, and media outlets. Aquinas Hall houses athletic facilities and a fitness center. Maguire Hall is home to classrooms, art studios, and the Sullivan Theater. Additional meeting areas are provided in the Romano Student-Alumni Center and in the two residence complexes, McNelis Commons and Aquinas Village. There is an after-hours club in the McNelis Commons dining hall for student activities.

Costs

For 2019–20, the tuition for full-time study (12 to 16 credits per semester) is $32,250; annual fees are $800. Room and board at the College Commons are $13,650. Certain studio, laboratory, and computer courses carry fees.

Financial Aid

St. Thomas Aquinas College is committed to making and keeping education affordable and has elected to participate in the New York State Enhanced Tuition Award Program for the 2018-2019 academic year. The College is committed to providing students with the resources necessary to continue their education. Students must submit the Free Application for Federal Student Aid (FAFSA) each year. The College awards academic and merit scholarships from $5,000 up to 70 percent and provides need-based aid from the College as well as athletic grants and all federal and New York State aid programs.

St. Thomas Aquinas College strives to partner with the student to make college education affordable. The College has one of the lowest private college tuition rates in New York State, and scholarships make it even more affordable. The College is also a member of the Yellow Ribbon program for veterans enabling a qualified veteran to study with a full tuition scholarship.

STAC has partnered with RaiseMe to offer high school students the opportunity to earn "micro-scholarships" as early as 9th grade for their accomplishments in high school, making access to higher education more affordable.

Faculty

The faculty has 70 full-time and 55 part-time members; 80 percent have terminal degrees. The student-faculty ratio is 12:1. All faculty members take part in the academic advising of students and serve on College committees. Many serve as advisers to extracurricular activities.

Student Government

The Student Government comprises elected members who officially represent the student body, are responsible for planning and implementing student-originated programs, and coordinate and oversee all extracurricular organizations. Through its various offices, students play a vital part in offering consultation on new policies, planning social and cultural events, managing student funds, and operating the judicial system. In addition, the College Forum, consisting of elected students, faculty members, alumni, administrators, and trustees, meets regularly to discuss policies, procedures, long-range plans, and any problems affecting the College.

Admission Requirements

All applicants must have successfully completed an approved secondary school program or the equivalent, including 4 years in English, 3 years in mathematics, 3 years in science, 2 years of a foreign language, and 4 years of social studies. The College considers applicants whose high school background varies from the recommended pattern. Freshman applicants must submit the application for admission, including an essay, high school transcripts, SAT and/or ACT scores, and a letter of recommendation. Transfer students must submit the application and official transcripts of all previous college work. An academic evaluation is prepared for every matriculant. The College is a member of the Common Application and students are strongly encouraged to apply online through that service.

Application and Information

Candidates should submit completed application forms to the Admissions and Financial Aid Office and must request that their official transcripts be sent to the Admissions Office from their school. Students are notified of the admission decision on a rolling basis upon receipt of all the credentials. The College is a member of the Common Application and students can find the link to apply on its website, http://www.stac.edu/apply.

St. Thomas Aquinas College does not discriminate in its educational programs, activities or employment practices based on race, color, national origin, sex, sexual orientation or expression, disability, age, religion, ancestry, genetic information, marital status, veteran status or any other legally protected category. Announcement of this policy is in accordance with State and with Federal law, including Title VI and Title VII of the Civil Rights Act of 1964, Title IX of the Education Amendments of 1972, Section 504 of the Rehabilitation Act of 1973, the Age Discrimination in Employment Act of 1967 and the Americans with Disabilities Act of 1990. For more information, please contact EEO, Section 504/ADA and Title IX Compliance Officer, 125 Route 340, Sparkill, New York 10976; phone: 845-398-4044.

For more information or an application, students should contact:
Admissions and Financial Aid Office
St. Thomas Aquinas College
125 Route 340
Sparkill, New York 10976-1050
Phone: 845-398-4100
E-mail: admissions@stac.edu
Website: http://www.stac.edu

Entrance to St. Thomas Aquinas College Campus

SAINT VINCENT COLLEGE

LATROBE, PENNSYLVANIA

The College

Founded in 1846, Saint Vincent College is the first Benedictine college in the United States. It is an educational community rooted in the tradition of the Catholic faith, the heritage of Benedictine monasticism, and the love of values inherent in the liberal approach to life and learning. There are 1,595 full-time undergraduate students and 81 part-time students, of whom 70 percent reside on campus. The College welcomes students from twenty-nine states and six other countries. In addition to more than fifty programs in the liberal arts and sciences, the College offers the Master of Science degrees in education: in counselor education, curriculum and instruction, instructional design and technology, special education, and school administration and supervision. The College also offers postbaccalaureate and certification programs in special education, instructional technology specialist, principal, early childhood director, English as a second language, and online teaching. Other graduate and professional programs include a Master of Science in management: operational excellence, a Master of Science in criminology, and a Doctor of Nurse Anesthesia Practice.

Student services include advising, athletics, career placement and planning, computer assistance, and a wellness center. Students choose from more than fifty social, political, cultural, service, recreational, and religious student organizations. Saint Vincent College is accredited by the Department of Education of the Commonwealth of Pennsylvania, the Middle States Association of Colleges and Schools, and the Association of Collegiate Business Schools and Programs.

Location

Saint Vincent College is located on 200 acres in the Laurel Highlands of southwestern Pennsylvania. Noted for its beautiful countryside, the region offers abundant opportunities for outdoor recreation and adventure. Excellent sites for hiking, mountain biking, skiing, camping, and white-water rafting are less than half an hour from the campus in ten state forests. Pittsburgh, a regional center of culture and the arts, is only 35 miles to the west. The city offers music, museums, theater, shopping, nightlife, and sports.

Majors and Degrees

The College offers more than fifty degree programs; the most popular majors are biology, criminology, law and society, management, psychology, and accounting. The College is organized into three schools: the Alex G. McKenna School of Business, Economics, and Government; the Herbert W. Boyer School of Natural Sciences, Mathematics, and Computing; the School of Arts, Humanities, and Social Sciences.

The McKenna School includes majors in the areas of accounting, business economics, business education information technology, criminology, law and society, economics, finance, international business, joint economics and mathematics, joint finance and mathematics, management, marketing, politics, political science, and public policy. The Herbert W. Boyer School of Natural Sciences, Mathematics, and Computing offers degrees in biochemistry, bioinformatics, biology, chemistry, computer science, cybersecurity, engineering science, environmental chemistry, environmental science, information technology, integrated science, mathematics, mathematics/actuarial science, mathematics/engineering, physics, and physics education. The School of Arts, Humanities and Social Sciences offers majors in anthropology, arts administration, art education, communication, digital art and media, education (pre-K-4 or middle grade), English, history, liberal arts, music, music performance, philosophy, philosophy/politics, philosophy/theology, pre-law, psychology, public history, sociology, Spanish, studio arts, and theology. Middle grade certification is offered in language arts, mathematics, science, and social studies, while minors in K–12 and secondary education include art, biology, business computing and information technology, chemistry, Chinese, English, French, mathematics, physics, social studies, and Spanish.

The College offers both a four-year degree in engineering science, with a five-year cooperative liberal arts and engineering program.

Saint Vincent offers pre–health training in accelerated osteopathic medicine, accelerated podiatric medicine, allopathic medicine, chiropractic medicine, dental medicine, optometry, osteopathic medicine, pharmacy, podiatric medicine and veterinary medicine in cooperation with various professional schools.

Students may select minor areas of study in accounting, anthropology, art history, biochemistry, biology, biological psychology, biotechnology, chemistry, children's literature, children's studies, Chinese, Chinese language and culture, communication, computer science, creative writing, criminology, law and society, cybersecurity, disability studies, disability studies with certification, economics, entrepreneurship, education K-12, English, environmental science, environmental studies, finance, forensic science (computer security, financial investigations, or natural science), French, German, global security, history, international business, international studies, Italian, Latin, literary translation, management, marketing, mathematics, medieval studies, music, music history, operational excellence, peace and justice studies, philosophy, physics, politics, psychology, public administration, public health, public history, sacred music, secondary education, sociology, Spanish, studio arts, and theology. Certificates are offered in addiction specialist, biotechnology and global engagement.

Academic Programs

An academic year consists of two semesters, fall and spring, with the opportunity to earn credits in the summer. Saint Vincent College requires each student to complete a minimum of 124 credits, satisfy the requirements for the major(s) as specified by the department(s) or school(s), achieve an overall grade point average of at least 2.0 as well as a grade point average of at least 2.0 in the major, and satisfy the capstone requirement as specified by the major department(s) or school(s). Each student must complete a core curriculum. The core curriculum provides all students with a broadly based education that provides a general body of knowledge in the humanities, social sciences, natural sciences, and mathematics; an interdisciplinary view of that knowledge base; and the skills to increase that general body of knowledge throughout their lives. Special programs include national and international academic honor societies, an internship program, an interdisciplinary writing program, and an honors program. An annual Academic Conference allows students to showcase their work across a variety of disciplines.

Off-Campus Programs

Saint Vincent students may choose to learn in surrounding communities, those across the country, or around the world.

Service plays a prominent role in the life of the campus—nearly two-thirds of seniors take part in a service project, and every student organization completes at least one service project each year. There are numerous local service opportunities, as well as service trips to Alaska, Appalachia, New Jersey, and abroad in Brazil, China, Guatemala, Haiti, Jamaica and Taiwan, and an annual pilgrimage to Rome.

Saint Vincent College encourages students of all majors and backgrounds to study abroad for a semester, academic, year, summer or spring in diverse locations worldwide. Students may take classes abroad in their major, earn credit toward the College core, complete an internship or study a foreign language. Popular programs include short-term Global Perspectives courses in Iceland, New Zealand, South Africa, Taiwan, Mexico, Peru and the United Kingdom. Affordable, high-quality semester exchange and direct enrollment placements, too, are available in 49 countries.

From the breadth of the liberal arts curriculum to the excitement of hands-on learning, Saint Vincent's goal is to encourage a love for learning that endures.

Academic Facilities

Saint Vincent College has invested more than $100 million in campus facilities during the past ten years, including the $45-million Dupré Science Pavilion, where every student takes at least two laboratory classes. Its James F. Will Engineering and Biomedical Sciences Hall, opened in 2017, is specifically designed for collaborative, interdisciplinary learning.

The result is a modern, student-friendly campus that features accessible computer laboratories and workstations; fiber-optic

cabling between buildings; Wi-Fi across campus and specialized laboratories for the study of astronomy, ecology, genetics, geology, human anatomy, life sciences, microbiology, optics, organic chemistry, physiology, and other subjects. From the multimedia computer lab to the nature reserve (created by the late golfing legend and College supporter Arnold Palmer) to the $14-million Fred Rogers Center for Early Learning and Children's Media, Saint Vincent offers many resources to help students intensify their learning.

Traditionally, Benedictine institutions have granted a place of honor to the library. Open 89 hours a week, the Dale P. Latimer Library is currently undergoing a renovation that will transform the building, which serves every Saint Vincent College student, into an information and technology hub that also features galleries, storage and display space for the College's stunning art and rare book collections.

The Robert S. Carey Student Center, covering more than 2 acres, contains the Frank and Elizabeth Resnik Swimming Pool, a gymnasium, performing arts center, wellness center, bookstore, fitness center, locker rooms and training rooms, snack bar, student lounge, chapel, billiards room, art gallery, art studios, and music practice rooms.

Costs

Tuition and fees at Saint Vincent for 2019-20 are $18,064 per semester, and room and board costs average $5,902 per semester, depending on accommodations and meal plan. Books and supplies average $1,350 per year. Costs are subject to change.

Financial Aid

Saint Vincent College offers a comprehensive program of financial aid in the form of scholarships, grants, loans, part-time employment, and deferred-payment schedules and coordinates programs from the federal and state financial aid program. In 2018-19, 100 percent of first-year students who applied for financial aid were offered assistance. The College annually awards qualified freshmen academic scholarships of up to $21,000 per year, renewable for up to four years, for excellence in academic achievement. In addition, the College offers first-generation grants, out-of-state grants, and grants to graduates of Catholic high schools and Benedictine parishes, among others. Other financial aid opportunities include Federal Direct Student Loans and Federal PLUS loans. Residents of Pennsylvania may be eligible for the Pennsylvania Higher Education Assistance Agency Grant program. In order to be considered for financial aid, students must complete the Free Application for Federal Student Aid (FAFSA).

Faculty

The faculty numbers 105 members, of whom 90 percent hold terminal degrees. Members of the faculty have earned doctorates or terminal degrees at such schools as Catholic University of America, Cornell, Duke, Fordham, Northwestern, Notre Dame, NYU, Stanford, Yale, and the Universities of California, Chicago, and Pennsylvania. Faculty members are engaged as principal investigators in research and other projects funded through government agencies such as the National Science Foundation and the U.S. Department of Education and private foundations. The student-faculty ratio is 11:1, and no classes are taught by teaching assistants. Faculty members have chosen to teach at Saint Vincent in part because they value the quality of student-teacher interaction, specifically the emphasis on high standards, personalized learning, fieldwork, hands-on experience, and the high level of classroom participation.

Student Government and Student Activities

The Student Government Association (SGA) acts as a liaison between the administration and the student body by representing and being attentive to student concerns and interests. SGA strives to enhance the quality of student life while seeking to preserve the College's commitment to traditional, Benedictine values and a strong liberal arts education. All class officers, senators, and representatives can vote in the senate that makes up the student government.

The sense of community that Saint Vincent is known for is fostered from the day students arrive on campus. Orientation lasts through the first five weeks of the fall semester and involves more than 150 upperclassmen. Their mission is to make each incoming student's transition to SVC a smooth one. Every freshman is matched with an older student who serves as a big brother or big sister throughout the first year.

In the residence halls (where more than 70 percent of students live), trained student prefects foster a safe living environment and provide guidance and advice, along with activities and educational programs. The Residence Life staff strive to create an engaging and comforta-ble residential atmosphere which is supportive to the academic mission of the College.

The College community is proud of the Catholic, Benedictine tradition that has shaped life on the campus for more than 170 years. Campus Ministry, in keeping with the tradition of hospitality, engages the college community, especially the students, of all faith traditions, by providing opportunities to explore, celebrate, act on and live their faith through prayer, education, service and Christian living.

Admission Requirements

Saint Vincent College has a rolling admission policy. Adequate preparation for college is an important determinant for a successful college education. Fifteen secondary school academic units are required for admission to Saint Vincent College. These 15 units must include 4 units of English, 3 or more units of college-preparatory mathematics, 1 unit of laboratory science, and 3 units of social science; 2 units of a foreign language are preferred among 5 elective units. Engineering students must have 1 unit in plane geometry, 1 unit in intermediate algebra, 1 unit in physics, and ½ unit in trigonometry in addition to those listed above. Art education, graphic design and studio arts majors must submit a portfolio for acceptance to the Fine Arts Department, and students seeking a major in music or music performance must audition for acceptance.

Transfer students are invited to apply to Saint Vincent College, which awards generous scholarships to academically capable transfer students. The applicant's academic achievement and personal history at the postsecondary schools previously attended are of primary importance in the decision for admission.

Application and Information

To be considered for admission, a freshman applicant must submit a completed application form with the nonrefundable $25 application fee, an official high school transcript, and an official copy of the test results from the SAT or ACT.

An application and additional information may be obtained by contacting:

Office of Admission and Financial Aid
Saint Vincent College
300 Fraser Purchase Road
Latrobe, Pennsylvania 15650-2690
Phone: 800-782-5549 (toll-free)
E-mail: admission@stvincent.edu
Website: http://www.stvincent.edu
Instagram: @SaintVincentCollege
Snapchat: mysaintvincent
YouTube: SaintVincentCollege
Twitter: @MySaintVincent
Facebook: SaintVincentCollege

Saint Vincent College offers a warm and welcoming atmosphere combined with technologically advanced facilities including the $45-million Sis and Herman Dupré Science Pavilion, dedicated in 2013 and expanded in 2017.

SETON HALL UNIVERSITY

SOUTH ORANGE, NEW JERSEY

SETON HALL UNIVERSITY 1856

COLLEGE CLOSE-UPS

The University

As one of the nation's leading Catholic universities, Seton Hall provides great minds with rigorous and challenging academic opportunities in over ninety academic programs that are highly ranked by the Princeton Review, *U.S. News & World Report,* and *Bloomberg Businessweek.* Seton Hall offers all the advantages of a large research university—national reputation; challenging academic programs; notable alumni; state-of-the-art facilities; renowned faculty; and extensive opportunities for internships, research, and scholarship— with all the benefits of a small, supportive, and nurturing environment. The 14:1 student-to-faculty ratio and average class size of 21 students means faculty members know more about each student than just their name.

The University's accomplished faculty members include Fulbright Scholars, prominent researchers, authors, artists, filmmakers, former school superintendents and principals, leaders in nursing, former ambassadors, analysts, and lawmakers—all of whom are dedicated to their fields and their students. They have graduated from some of the nation's leading institutions, including Seton Hall, Harvard, Columbia, Yale, Princeton, and Dartmouth. While faculty members shine in the lecture halls and on the national stage every day, they also meet regularly with students outside the classroom and help them learn to think critically.

Seton Hall offers more than 17,000 internship opportunities, and over 81 percent of students have an internship—or two—on their resume before graduation. This is just one of the reasons Seton Hall graduates have an employment rate of over 90 percent and mid-career earnings 50 percent higher than the national average. Seton Hall was recently ranked in the top 5 in the nation for providing internship opportunities. This national reputation coupled with the University's stellar academic programs draws over 550 employers to campus each year to recruit graduates.

Seton Hall is a Catholic university with a 160-year tradition of educational excellence. A welcoming community, Seton Hall embraces students of all faiths and inspires them to become servant-leaders who make a difference in the world. The University community performs over 40,000 hours of community service annually.

Location

Nestled in the suburban village of South Orange, New Jersey, Seton Hall provides small-town charm combined with big-city opportunities. The University's 58-acre, suburban, park-like campus sits proudly in this picturesque town with tree-lined streets; historic, gracious homes; and quaint shops just 14 miles from New York City—close to all the action, but not engulfed by it.

The bustling town center—with diners, pizzerias, banks, pharmacies, Starbucks, Cold Stone Creamery, a gourmet marketplace, South Orange Performing Arts Center, a movie theater, and more—is just a 5-minute walk from campus. The train station, right in the center of town, provides a direct link to NYC's Penn Station, just 30 minutes away.

The University takes full advantage of all the Big Apple has to offer; after all, it's where the worlds of entertainment, art, publishing, global finance, international diplomacy, and fashion collide. NYC is also one of the world's largest job markets, brimming with internship and job placement opportunities in a variety of companies. Seton Hall students have interned at leading companies like Goldman Sachs, American Express, CNN, the U.S. Secret Service, the United Nations, The *New York Times*, Prudential, The Museum of Natural History, Lockheed Martin, NBC, Sony Music, JPMorgan Chase, Lincoln Center and more.

One of the wealthiest states in the nation, New Jersey is brimming with opportunity. Seton Hall's backyard boasts a powerhouse corporate corridor of more than fifty Fortune 500 companies, pharmaceutical giants, and major corporations. For students, this means networking, internships, and career opportunities.

Academic Programs

Seton Hall is a place where great minds are exposed to even greater opportunities. This is evident in the dozens of student and alumni national scholars and fellows, including nearly 20 prestigious Fulbright Scholars since 2009, as well as Rhodes, Udall, Pickering, Marshall, Critical Language, and Truman Scholars and more than 100,000 alumni who are now successful as CEOs, judges, doctors, principals, CFOs, journalists, nurses, diplomats, and more. About 1,000 Seton Hall graduates have served in executive positions at firms like Oppenheimer, Visiting Nurse Service of New York, American Express, and Merrill Lynch. They have served as elected officials in Washington, D.C., and in hundreds of state capitals and town halls throughout the country. In New Jersey alone, almost 20 percent of the state legislators holds a Seton Hall degree.

Seton Hall's commitment to academic excellence is evident in the more than ninety academic programs offered through six undergraduate schools and colleges. In addition, the University has recently opened a medical school in partnership with Hackensack Meridian Health and is also offering a joint bachelor's/MD program to incoming freshman.

Majors and Degrees

Accounting•
Accounting (5-year B.S./M.S. dual-degree∞)
Africana Studies•
American Humanics√
Ancient Greek†
Anthropology•
Applied Scientific Mathematics†
Arabic†
Archaeology†
Art (Art History•, Fine Arts•, Graphic Interactive and Advertising Design•)
Asian Studies•
Athletic Training (5-year B.S./M.S. or B.A./M.S. dual-degree)∞
Biochemistry
Biology (B.A. or B.S.)
Broadcasting, Visual and Interactive Media•
Business Administration•‡
Catholic Studies•‡
Catholic Theology•
Chemistry•
Classical Culture†
Classical Languages†
Classical Studies•
Communication•
Computer Graphics√
Computer Science•
Creative Writing
Criminal Justice•
Data Visualization and Analysis√
Digital Media and Video√
Digital Media Production for the Web√
Diplomacy and International Relations•
Early Childhood (integrated with elementary and special education)
Elementary Education (integrated with early childhood and special education)
Education with Speech Language Pathology (6-year B.S.E./M.S. dual- degree)∞
Economics (B.A. or B.S.)
Engineering (Biomedical, Chemical, Civil, Computer, Electrical, Industrial, Mechanical)§
English•
Entrepreneurial Studies√
Environmental Sciences†
Environmental Studies•
Ethics and Applied Ethics†
Finance
French•
Gerontology√
Graphic, Interactive, and Advertising Design
History•
Information Technologies√
Information Technology Management‡
International Business
International Relations
Italian•
Italian Studies†
Journalism•
Latin†
Latin America and Latino/ Latina Studies•
Law (3+3 program)∞
Legal Studies in Business†
Liberal Studies
Management
Marketing
Mathematical Finance
Mathematics•
M.B.A. (5-year B.S./M.B.A. or B.A./ M.B.A. dual-degree)∞
Medicine (Joint bachelors/MD)
Modern Languages
Music (Comprehensive Music/ Music Education, Music Performance•)
Musical Theatre†
Nonprofit Studies†
Nursing

Occupational Therapy (6-year B.A./M.S. dual-degree)∞
Philosophical Theology√
Philosophy•
Physical Therapy (6-year B.S./D.P.T. dual-degree)∞
Physician Assistant (6-year B.S./M.S. dual-degree)∞
Physics (B.A. or B.S.)•
Political Science•
Pre-Dental*
Pre-Law*
Pre-Medical*
Pre-Optometry*
Pre-Veterinary*
Psychology (B.A. or B.S.)•
Public Relations
Religion•
Russian†
Russian and East European Studies†√
Secondary Education (optional integration with special education)
Social and Behavioral Sciences
Social Work•
Sociology•
Spanish•
Special Education (integrated with early childhood, elementary, and secondary education)
Speech Language Pathology (6-year with Bachelors in Education or Psychology)∞
Sport Management•
Supply Chain Management√
Theatre and Performance•
Web Design√
Women and Gender Studies†
Writing†
Undecided

• Minor also available
† Minor only
√ Certificate program only
‡ Certificate program also available
§ Dual-degree program with New Jersey Institute of Technology
∞ Seton Hall dual-degree program
* Pre-professional programs (students must also select a major)

Campus Facilities

Seton Hall places a strong emphasis on the use of state-of-the-art technology, facilities, and support services to aid in its students' development. Many investments have been made to the campus infrastructure, including the recent construction of a new academic classroom building, new residence hall space, a new parking deck, a Dunkin' Donuts, and a new recreation and fitness center. In addition, the campus boasts a state-of-the-art research library complete with a computerized catalog and 200 computer terminals. The Science and Technology Center is home to state-of-the-future biology and chemistry labs, an atrium, and auditorium, as well as an observatory and greenhouse.

The campus also offers many unique learning labs, such as a Mock Trading Room, Patient Simulation Laboratory, Market Research Center, a student-run radio station (ranked the number-one noncommercial radio station by the National Association of Broadcasters), and Sport Polling Center. All incoming students are provided a new, fully loaded laptop computer.

Costs

Seton Hall offers a flat-tuition rate for students taking between 12 and 18 credit hours. The 2018–19 tuition and fees were $42,470. Room and board costs vary depending on meal plans; however, the average rate is $14,500.

Financial Aid

Paying for college is a major investment. Seton Hall University has been rated as one of the best schools in the nation for return on investment and is committed to providing students with the resources needed to make their dreams a reality. The University gives over $96 million in aid each year; 98 percent of students receive some form of financial aid, and 97 percent receive scholarships or grants directly from the University. Most scholarships are automatically awarded upon admission and do not require separate applications. However, there are also several special scholarships for which students can apply; more information on those is available online at www.shu.edu/go/scholarships. Seton Hall also provides need-based aid to eligible students who complete the Free Application for Federal Student Aid (FAFSA) form by November 1.

Student Organizations and Activities

On campus, Seton Hall leaders learn to put their ideas into action; discover something new; become part of a community; and build trust, spirit, and lasting friendships. Extracurricular activities abound, with over 130 clubs and organizations, twenty-two Greek societies, fourteen Division 1 Big East athletic teams, and extensive club and intramural sports. Students can audition for one of the many theater productions each year; broadcast at the number-one ranked college radio station in the nation, WSOU-FM, which attracts more than 120,000 listeners a week from the NYC area; be part of the Brownson Speech and Debate team, which has been ranked among the top 20 college and university forensic teams for years; or write for one of three student newspapers. More than two thirds of Seton Hall students participate in clubs and organizations and over 50 percent participate in club or intramural sports.

Admissions Process

Seton Hall takes a holistic approach to reviewing applications for admission, considering academic performance in high school, grades and the rigor of the curriculum, and SAT and/or ACT scores. These are essential indicators of a potential student's ability to succeed at Seton Hall. A personal essay, recommendations, extracurricular activities, and interest in the University are also considerations. Students can apply using the Common Application or the Seton Hall application, located on the admission.shu.edu website.

The typical student who entered Seton Hall last year had an average GPA of 3.6 (B+), an average SAT score of 1230 and/or an average ACT score of 26.

Application and Information

Potential students are encouraged to visit Seton Hall in person. Tours are offered Mondays through Fridays at 10 a.m. and 2 p.m. and on Saturdays at 10 a.m., noon, and 2 p.m. Open houses are offered in mid-October, mid-November, mid-February, and late April. Visits can be scheduled online at www.shu.edu/visiting

For more information, prospective students should contact:

Office of Undergraduate Admissions
Seton Hall University
400 South Orange Avenue
South Orange, New Jersey 07079
Phone: 800-THE-HALL (843-4255; toll-free)
E-mail: thehall@shu.edu
Website: http://www.admissions.shu.edu

Students enjoy a spring day on the University Green, the scenic pathway located at the heart of Seton Hall's campus.

SIMPSON COLLEGE

INDIANOLA, IOWA

SIMPSON COLLEGE

The College

Founded in 1860, Simpson College produces successful students by combining the best of a liberal arts education with outstanding career preparation and extracurricular programs. With 1,300 full-time students and a student to faculty ratio of 15:1, students have the opportunity to work closely with their professors. Simpson's faculty members are as dedicated to their fields of study as they are to teaching—and it shows in the classroom. When this type of dedication and passion is combined with well-prepared and motivated students, the potential for success is unlimited.

The campus is located just minutes from Iowa's capital city, Des Moines, which was recently ranked as the top city for business and careers. The proximity to Des Moines allows Simpson students to take advantage of an abundance of internship opportunities. Whether working with Fortune 500 companies, spending time in an elementary school, or gaining resume-building experiences in a medical field, students learn to push their own boundaries. Simpson's excellent internship program gives students an advantage in today's competitive job market.

Simpson's beautiful, tree-lined campus in Indianola provides small-town friendliness and safety, while the campus facilities are continually enhanced and updated for academic and recreational opportunities. Within the last ten years, multimillion-dollar projects include the renovation and expansion of Blank Performing Arts Center, renovation of outdoor athletic facilities, the addition of a stunning new student center, and a $6-million expansion and renovation of the Simpson Athletic Complex and Steven Johnson Fitness Center.

Simpson's 4-4-1 academic calendar includes a May Term that provides students with unique learning opportunities in the classroom, an internship setting, or while studying abroad. Throughout the year, students take advantage of Simpson's innovative Engaged Citizenship Curriculum. This curriculum allows students to gain skills and experiences valued most by employers while choosing classes that interest them.

Extracurricular activities at Simpson are designed to supplement and reinforce the academic programs and contribute to a total learning experience. Activities range from an award-winning music program to nationally recognized NCAA Division III athletic teams. Students have the opportunity to participate in student government, campus publications, religious life, music, theater, departmental clubs, and various other organizations. Simpson competes in 19 intercollegiate sports and has an extensive intramural program. Simpson has eight Greek chapters on campus, including three national fraternities, one local fraternity, and four national sororities; each with their own house.

Location

Simpson is located in Indianola, a residential community with a population of 14,400. Indianola is 12 miles south of Des Moines, with easy access to Interstates 35 and 80. The Des Moines International Airport is 20 minutes from campus. Indianola is host to nationally known events including the Des Moines Metropolitan Opera and the National Balloon Classic. The vibrant, small-town community has many choices for entertainment and recreation including Lake Ahquabi State Park, Summerset Trail, and unique restaurants and shops within walking distance of campus. Indianola's proximity to Des Moines gives students plenty of distinct advantages. Within minutes, students are right in the heart of some of the best entertainment and employment options Iowa and the Midwest have to offer.

Majors and Degrees

Simpson College grants Bachelor of Arts and Bachelor of Music degrees. Majors include accounting, actuarial science, applied philosophy, biochemistry, biology, business management, chemistry, computer information systems, computer science, criminal justice, data analytics, data science, economics, education (elementary and secondary), English, environmental science, forensic science/biochemistry, graphic design, health and exercise science, health services leadership, history, human services, interactive media, interdisciplinary studies, international management, international relations, management information systems, marketing communication, mathematics, multimedia journalism, music, music education, music performance, neuroscience, philosophy, physical education, physics, political science, psychology, religion, social justice, sociology, Spanish, sport administration, sport communication, and theater arts.

Simpson also offers pre-professional programs in athletic training, chiropractic, dentistry, engineering, law, medicine, nursing, occupational therapy, optometry, pharmacy, physical therapy, theology/ministry, and veterinary medicine. Concentration areas such as early childhood education and ethics are available, as well as many additional minors, including women's studies, human resources management, Latin American studies, and coaching endorsements.

Academic Programs

Simpson College operates on a 4-4-1 academic calendar. The first semester starts in late August and ends in mid-December; the second semester starts in mid-January and ends in late April. A three-week session takes place during the month of May. During this period, students participate in a field experience/internship, study abroad, or take a course on campus with a hands-on focus.

The First-Year Program is an extensive program of orientation, team building, mentoring, community service, advising, and course work structured to help new students adapt to their first year of college. The program begins with orientation and continues throughout the academic year. The academic component of the First-Year Program is the Simpson Colloquium, a joint classroom and advising concept that is unique among first-year programs. These courses are small in size—no more than 18 first-year students each—and all are taught by each student's faculty adviser.

With Simpson's Engaged Citizenship Curriculum, students delve deeper in their courses and focus more on projects that provide hands-on understanding of the subject matter. These courses allow students to work closely and build strong relationships with faculty members, one of the hallmarks of a Simpson education. The curriculum encourages students to take advantage of Simpson's community partnerships, hold internships, study abroad, or conduct independent research. It was developed in response to research that indicates future employers are looking for effective communicators, innovators, and problem solvers. Simpson is on the forefront of providing the kind of experiential, liberal arts education that college graduates need to succeed in their careers and achieve fulfillment in their lives.

Off-Campus Programs

Simpson provides many opportunities for studying abroad, with the choice of a semester-long program or a three-week May Term. Simpson's semester-long, faculty-led study abroad programs include England, Thailand, Tahiti, Australia, and Chile. Students also have the opportunity for semester study-abroad programs in France, Spain, Italy, and more locations.

In addition, 10 to 15 travel courses are offered each May Term. Recent destinations include Africa, Central America, Great Britain, France, Greece, Ireland, New Zealand, the Galapagos Islands, Brazil, Argentina, and Scandinavia. May Term study abroad courses are led by Simpson faculty members and give students the opportunity to experience a different culture while gaining a stronger global perspective. Over 40 percent of students travel abroad during their time at Simpson.

The Capitol Hill Internship Program (CHIP) provides students with the opportunity to spend either the fall or spring semester in Washington, D.C. Past participants have had various experiences including interning for members of Congress, the Smithsonian Institution, the Republican National Committee, the Justice Department, CNN, the Australian Embassy, and FOX News.

Academic Facilities

Simpson has a wireless campus network with high-speed Internet access. There are numerous computer labs throughout campus where students can use standard office suite applications or specialized, discipline-specific applications.

The Carver Science Center, named after Simpson's most distinguished alumnus George Washington Carver, provides state-of-the-art research facilities, computer labs, a cadaver lab, and classrooms.

The Henry H. and Thomas H. McNeill Hall houses classrooms for business management, accounting, health services leadership, and economics.

The Amy Robertson Music Center is home to Simpson's acclaimed music department and contains the Sven and Mildred Lekberg Recital Hall, ten studios, twenty-two practice rooms, a music computer lab, and the band rehearsal room. The Salsbury Wing includes a choral rehearsal room, a classroom, and studios.

Dunn Library, a modern academic learning resource center, contains over 175,000 books, periodicals, videos/DVDs, and CDs. Many resources (print and online) can be located from the library website. Additional materials for research can be obtained through a national interlibrary loan network. The Center for Academic Resources is also located in Dunn Library, which provides free academic support services to all students.

The A. H. and Theo Blank Performing Arts Center underwent a multimillion-dollar expansion and renovation in 2011. The center accommodates Simpson's well-known programs in theater arts and opera. It includes the magnificent 500-seat Pote Theatre, with both proscenium and hydraulically controlled thrust stages, a studio theater, the Barborka Gallery, technical facilities, and shops and classrooms.

Wallace Hall, named to the National Register of Historic Places, contains facilities for education, sociology, and applied social science.

Mary Berry Hall houses the psychology department which includes six labs, a control room for observation and data processing, and an animal care space. In addition, the building is home to humanities classrooms, a language lab, faculty offices, and the Farnham Art Galleries.

The Gaumer Center contains offices for multimedia communication and provides space for the college newspaper, *The Simpsonian*, and radio station KSTM.

Faculty

Simpson offers one professor for every 15 students. Simpson's faculty members serve as academic advisers as well as teachers. Their commitment goes beyond the classroom as they often attend college plays, operas, and athletic events, reinforcing their sincere interest in the lives of the students and their ultimate success.

Costs

Tuition and fees for 2019-20 are $ 40,666; room charges are $ 4,276; and board is $ 4,544. These figures do not include books, music fees, or personal expenses.

Financial Aid

Simpson College is dedicated to making it financially feasible for qualified students to experience the advantages of a Simpson education. In fact, 100 percent of full-time Simpson students receive financial assistance. Generous gifts from alumni, trustees, and friends of the College—in addition to state and federal student aid programs—make this opportunity possible. Simpson offers financial assistance on both a need and non-need basis. Need is determined by filing the Free Application for Federal Student Aid.

Financial assistance granted on a non-need basis includes generous academic scholarships (awarded on the basis of prior academic records) and talent scholarships (available in theater, music, art, and speech/debate). The talent scholarships are determined by audition/portfolio or application.

In addition, specific scholarships such as the John C. Culver Fellowship, the Iowa History Center Scholarship, the George Washington Carver Fellowship, the Interfaith Fellowship, and the Wesley Service Scholarship can be obtained through application.

Admission Requirements

In the holistic review of applications, a strong academic record is essential. Applications are acted upon by an admissions committee, which is elected by the faculty. These faculty members consider the college-preparatory courses taken and the grades received in those courses (transcripts and cumulative GPA), standardized test scores (ACT and/or SAT) as well as optional information (e.g. recommendations or personal statements/essays).Transfer applicants are accepted on the basis of successful completion of academic work at an accredited college or university.

Application and Information

Applications are accepted on a rolling basis beginning in early fall and continuing on a space-available basis. Simpson's rolling admission policy allows flexibility; however, early application is recommended.

Application information can be found at www.simpson.edu/apply.

For additional information or to obtain application materials, students should contact:

Office of Admissions
Simpson College
701 North C Street
Indianola, Iowa 50125
Phone: 515-961-1624
800-362-2454 Ext. 1624
E-mail: admiss@simpson.edu
Website: http://www.simpson.edu
http://www.facebook.com/simpsoncollege
http://twitter.com/simpsoncollege
http://www.youtube.com/simpsonweb
http://instagram.com/simpsoncollege

SKIDMORE COLLEGE

SARATOGA SPRINGS, NEW YORK

SKIDMORE COLLEGE

The College

Skidmore College is an independent liberal arts college of 2,500 students from more than 40 states and nearly 70 countries that prides itself on its creative approaches to just about everything. Hence the college's belief that "Creative Thought Matters." About 60 percent of the student body is female and 40 percent male, with 22 percent being domestic students of color, 11 percent international students, and 13 percent first-generation students.

Students enjoy a full schedule of intellectual, cultural, and social activities, such as lectures, visiting scholars in residence, art exhibits, concerts, and dance and theater performances. There are approximately 120 student clubs and organizations, including a newspaper, radio and TV stations, ethnic and cultural associations, art and literary journals, a student-run EMS program, and a volunteer network. There are no fraternities or sororities. A strong NCAA Division III intercollegiate sports program for men and women—19 teams in all—includes baseball, basketball, field hockey, golf, ice hockey, lacrosse, riding, rowing, soccer, softball, swimming and diving, tennis, and volleyball. Skidmore competes in the Liberty League, which also includes Bard, Clarkson, Hobart and William Smith, Ithaca, Rensselaer Polytechnic Institute, Rochester Institute of Technology, St. Lawrence, Union, and Vassar. The college has programs in intramural and club sports, health, fitness, and wellness.

Skidmore's campus includes more than 50 buildings. The Williamson Sports and Recreation Complex has a pool and diving well, racquet-sport courts, basketball and volleyball courts, several intramural gyms, three dance studios, a weight room, a fitness center, and a human performance laboratory. Adjacent to the complex are Wachenheim Field, a small stadium with an artificial turf field for soccer, lacrosse, and intramurals, and a 400-meter all-weather track; softball and field hockey turf fields; and the lighted Wenger Tennis Courts. The Frances Young Tang Teaching Museum and Art Gallery, unique in its interdisciplinary approach to exhibits and programming, opened in 2000.

The more than 1,000-acre campus, 300 acres of which consists of the recreation- and research-rich North Woods, has been recently upgraded with renovations to athletics, dining, and residential facilities. Skidmore's newest academic building is the Zankel Music Center, featuring a spectacular 600-seat recital hall and state-of-the art recording studio. In addition, the Sussman Village Apartments, opened in 2013 for upperclassmen, feature "green" apartments that use geothermal heating and cooling systems. In 2018, the college broke ground for construction of the first phase of the new Center for Integrated Sciences.

Location

Saratoga Springs, 30 miles north of Albany, New York's state capital, is perennially short-listed as one of the most interesting and vibrant small cities in the U.S. Famed for health, history, and horses—its mineral waters, Revolutionary War battlefield, and the nation's oldest thoroughbred racetrack—Saratoga is renowned as an arts and cultural destination. In recent years, *Travel + Leisure* named Saratoga Springs America's seventh-best college town and USA Today named it the seventh-best main street in the U.S. The Saratoga Performing Arts Center is summer home to the New York City Ballet, Philadelphia Orchestra, and Opera Saratoga, and is a performing venue for top rock and jazz musicians. Downtown is just a 10-minute walk from Skidmore and is brimming with galleries, clubs, shops, coffeehouses, and restaurants. Its location near the foothills of the Adirondack Mountains puts an abundance of recreational opportunities—ski areas, parks, lakes, and mountains from New York, Vermont, and Massachusetts—within an hour's drive. Boston, New York City, and Montreal are each approximately 180 miles from the campus.

Majors and Degrees

Skidmore grants degrees in 43 academic disciplines, including a Bachelor of Arts degree in American studies, anthropology, art history, Asian studies, biology, chemistry, classics, computer science, economics, English, environmental science, environmental studies, gender studies, geosciences, history, international affairs, mathematics, music, neuroscience, philosophy, physics, political science, psychology, religious studies, sociology, and world languages and literatures (French, German, and Spanish). The Bachelor of Science degree is granted in business, dance, education studies, health and human physiological sciences, social work, studio art, and theater. There are seven interdepartmental majors, business-French and political science-Spanish being two examples. A self-determined major is also available. Most majors have corresponding minors. Minors are also available in arts administration, Chinese, intergroup relations, Italian, Japanese, Latin American and Latinix studies, media and film studies, and statistics. In keeping with the college's creative spirit and the realities of the marketplace, about half of Skidmore students choose a second major or minor.

Through partnerships with other institutions, Skidmore offers enhanced program/degree offerings. These include 4+1 M.B.A. programs with Rochester Institute of Technology, and Clarkson University Graduate School; the Whitman M.B.A. Advantage program with Syracuse University; 4+1 M.S.A. and M.S.F. programs with Syracuse; dual-degree programs in engineering with Clarkson, Dartmouth College, and Rensselaer Polytechnic Institute; an M.S. in accountancy with Wake Forest University; dual-degree programs in physical therapy and occupational therapy with Sage Graduate School; an M.S. in Teaching with Clarkson; and a 4+1 nursing program (New York University School of Nursing). Skidmore also has certification programs in teaching and social work and preprofessional programs in law and medicine/health professions.

Academic Programs

The Skidmore journey begins with the First-Year Experience, which introduces students to the rigorous interdisciplinary academic program and overall approach to learning and connects them with a faculty adviser/mentor. Talented but economically disadvantaged students accepted into the Opportunity Program (Higher Education Opportunity Program and Academic Opportunity Program) participate in a month-long summer program. Some 250 students are members of Skidmore's Periclean Honors Forum on the basis of their academic achievement and aspirations, leadership qualities, and civic commitment.

Generally, students choose a major by the end of sophomore year. They are also expected to take one to two courses in both quantitative reasoning and expository writing, and at least one course of the following: natural science, social science, arts, humanities, and culture-centered inquiry. There is plenty of academic support through Student Academic Services. In their junior and senior years, students often add value to their courses of study through faculty-student collaborative research (academic year and summer program), internships (many funded and for credit), volunteerism, service-learning, and off-campus study.

Off-Campus Programs

About 60 percent of Skidmore's students spend a semester or year off campus. In addition to Skidmore programs in England, France, New Zealand, and Spain, students can access approximately 120 international programs through the college's Approved Programs structure, including programs in Africa, Asia, Europe, Latin America, and Australia. All academic majors and minors can be accommodated and transfer credits are guaranteed for students studying on an Approved Program. Financial aid is transferable to most off-campus study programs. Annually, some 25 percent of the student body members engage in research with a faculty mentor, including nearly 100 in the summer student-faculty research program. The college also offers a Washington Semester (internship in conjunction with American University) and a semester at the Marine Biological Laboratory in Woods Hole, Massachusetts.

Academic Facilities

Skidmore's 1,000-acre campus is comprised of more than 50 buildings. The newest academic building, the Arthur Zankel Music Center, features a spectacular 600-seat recital hall and a state-of-the-art recording studio. Skidmore's visual and performing arts space includes the Saisselin Art Center, with studios and the Schick Art Gallery; the Janet Kinghorn Bernhard Theater, with a seating capacity of 350, and an experimental black box theater; and the Dance Center. The Frances Young Tang Teaching Museum and Art Gallery provides a focal point for cross-disciplinary study through the visual arts. The Dana Science Center offers state-of-the-art teaching and research space, including a microscopy center. Dana links the College's science departments to the Mathematics and Computer Science departments in neighboring Harder Hall, which features a Linux lab with more than 20 workstations for advanced computer science projects. In 2018, the college broke ground for construction of the first phase of the new Center for Integrated Sciences.

Costs

In 2017–18, tuition and fees were $52,446, a double dorm room was $8,278, and board was $5,726.

Financial Aid

Skidmore annually provides approximately $45 million in financial aid. The average 2018–19 first-year aid package was $50,200 and ranged from $2,000 to $65,000; 44 percent of students receive need-based grants; 50 percent receive some form of financial aid; and 50 percent are given the opportunity to work on campus. Average postcollege student debt (just under $23,000) is well below the national average. Students interested in applying for admission are encouraged to do so regardless of their intention to seek financial aid. The FAFSA, a copy of the federal income tax form, and the CSS Profile must be filed each year. The College hosts an annual Filene Music Scholarship Competition to award four to six $60,000 ($15,000 per year) scholarships on the basis of musical ability without regard to financial need. Twelve to fourteen $15,000 Porter-Wachenheim Science and Mathematics scholarships ($60,000 over four years) are also awarded annually. The Skidmore Scholars in Science and Mathematics program provides up to eight S3M scholars with demonstrated financial need annual financial-aid packages with no loan component in the first two years and with reduced loans in years three and four.

Faculty

Skidmore has more than 300 full-time faculty members, 87 percent of whom hold a doctorate or the highest degree in their field. The student-to-faculty ratio is about 8:1 and the average class size is 16. Although actively engaged in research and publication in their individual fields, Skidmore faculty members regard teaching as their primary commitment. All students have faculty advisers who assist them in selecting courses and in designing individual academic programs.

Student Government

Students at Skidmore play an active role in college governance. Through the Student Government Association (SGA) and membership on a number of major college committees, they participate in academic and social life. The SGA operates under the authority granted by the Board of Trustees and is dedicated to democratic self-government and responsible citizenship. Elected faculty members and student representatives serve on the All-College Council, the Academic Integrity Board, and the Social Integrity Board. Broad concerns of the SGA include educational policy, elections, social and student events, first-year orientation, student publications, and student clubs and organizations.

Admission Requirements

Those seeking admission to Skidmore's first-year class should complete a secondary school curriculum that includes at least 16 credits in college-preparatory courses. The Admissions Committee is also pleased to consider applications from qualified high school juniors who plan to accelerate and enter college early. Applicants typically have completed 4 years of English, 4 years of a foreign language, 4 years of mathematics, 4 years of social studies, and 3 to 4 years of laboratory science. Applicants must provide a secondary school transcript, letters of recommendation from two teachers of academic subjects, and a report from their guidance counselor. Although Skidmore is test optional (some exceptions for international and home-schooled students), students who wish to can submit their standardized test scores (SAT with writing or ACT with writing). A campus visit and interview are also recommended.

Through its participation in the Higher Education Opportunity Program, Skidmore enrolls capable, energetic, and ambitious New York state residents who, because of their academic and financial situations, would not otherwise gain admission to the College under traditional requirements. Skidmore's Academic Opportunity Program (AOP) recruits similar students who reside outside of New York. The programs are collectively referred to as the Opportunity Program.

Application and Information

Applicants for admission are requested to complete the Common Application—online at www.commonapp.org—and submit it with a $65 fee or request a fee waiver from their adviser. They may also apply through the Coalition for Access, Affordability, and Success, online at www.coalitionforcollegeaccess.org. All information should be postmarked by January 15. Applications from Early Decision candidates should be submitted by November 15 for the Round I Early Decision plan or by January 15 for the Round II Early Decision plan. Transfer candidates are urged to apply by April 1 for the fall term and by November 1 for the spring term. In addition to a high school transcript, transfer candidates are required to submit, by the appropriate deadlines, an official transcript of all college-level work completed, recommendations from two professors, and a statement regarding personal and academic standing from the dean of students at the current college. International students are given special attention throughout the admissions process. Applicants whose first language is not English are encouraged to submit the results of the Test of English as a Foreign Language (TOEFL). There are a limited number of need-based financial aid awards available for outstanding international students.

Mary Lou W. Bates
Vice President and Dean of Admissions and Financial Aid
Skidmore College
815 North Broadway
Saratoga Springs, New York 12866
Phone: 518-580-5570
800-867-6007 (toll-free)
E-mail: admissions@skidmore.edu
Website: www.skidmore.edu
www.facebook.com/SkidmoreCollege
http://twitter.com/skidmorecollege
https://www.instagram.com/skidmorecollege
https://www.pinterest.com/skidmorecollege
www.skidmore.edu/admissions/visit/youvisit.php#virtualtour
www.skidmore.edu/videos/ www.youtube.com/skidmorecollege

Students chat, with Haupt Pond and the southeastern corner of campus in the distance.

SOUTHERN METHODIST UNIVERSITY
DALLAS, TEXAS

SMU.

The University

Southern Methodist University (SMU) is a nationally ranked comprehensive research university in the dynamic city of Dallas. SMU's alumni, faculty, and 11,000-plus students in seven degree-granting schools demonstrate an enterprising spirit as they lead change in their professions, communities, and the world.

SMU celebrates diversity, with students from across the United States and nearly 90 nations, as well as a variety of ethnic, socioeconomic, and religious backgrounds. Sixty-five percent of SMU first-year students come from outside Texas. Fall 2017 undergraduate enrollment included 27 percent of students from diverse ethnic backgrounds.

Students can choose from more than 100 majors and 85 minors. One in five SMU students opts to pursue a double major. Students can customize their education by combining a major in the humanities or sciences with another in engineering, business or the arts for a dual degree. According to the Center for World University Rankings 2017, SMU is in the top 0.5 percent of world universities.

SMU hosts more than 400 performances, concerts, and exhibits on campus during the school year. The Tate Lecture Series brings world-changers and experts to campus. Recent speakers have included Condoleezza Rice, Robert Edsel, Scott Kelly, and Brandon Stanton.

Location

SMU students benefit from the University's proximity to the heart of Dallas, which is home to amazing restaurants, a world-renowned arts district, exciting nightlife, and professional sports.

SMU's location in Dallas—home to more than 20 Fortune 500 companies—offers students abundant internship opportunities. Dallas is also ranked number one for jobs by *Forbes* in 2017. The Dallas area is home to companies such as American Airlines, AT&T, Texas Instruments, Toyota, Southwest Airlines, and ExxonMobil. Ninety-three percent of May 2017 SMU graduates were employed or in graduate/professional school six months after graduation.

Dallas-Fort Worth is the nation's fourth-largest metropolitan area and home to about 7 million residents. Dallas offers top-tier museums and performance facilities, including the AT&T Performing Arts Center, Meyerson Symphony Center, Dallas Museum of Art, Nasher Sculpture Center, Perot Museum of Nature and Science, and SMU's Meadows Museum. The Dallas area is home to the Dallas Cowboys, Dallas Mavericks, Dallas Stars, Texas Rangers, FC Dallas, Lone Star Park, Texas Motor Speedway and professional golf tournaments.

Dallas-Fort Worth International Airport offers service to 149 domestic destinations—including access to every major city in the continental U.S. within four hours—and 57 international destinations. Dallas Love Field, home to Southwest Airlines, serves more than 42,000 passengers daily.

Majors and Degrees

SMU offers strong undergraduate, graduate, and professional programs through seven schools.

The **Dedman College of Humanities and Sciences** is SMU's largest and most diverse academic unit. It is home to the humanities and social, natural, and mathematical sciences—disciplines that are the core of higher education. Undergraduate students in Dedman College may major and minor in more than 50 programs. Dedman College offers 18 master's programs and 15 doctoral programs, plus numerous interdisciplinary programs.

The **Cox School of Business** equips students with the knowledge, skills, and experience needed to become business leaders. Major publications, including *Bloomberg Businessweek, The Economist, Poets&Quants,* and *Forbes*, rank SMU Cox among the top business schools nationally and globally. Degrees offered by the Cox School include: Bachelor of Business Administration with majors in accounting, finance, financial consulting, general business, management, marketing, and real estate finance; Full-Time, Fast Track Professional, and Executive Master of Business Administration; and master's degrees in accounting, business analytics, finance, management,and sport management (in partnership with the Simmons School).

The **Lyle School of Engineering**, ranked among the top 5 percent of schools for highest-paid computer science and engineering graduates by College Factual 2019, prepares today's engineering students to be tomorrow's innovators equipped with both technical and leadership skills. Degree programs offered include bachelor's, master's, and doctoral degrees through the departments of Civil and Environmental Engineering; Computer Science and Engineering; Electrical Engineering; Engineering Management, Information and Systems; Mechanical Engineering; Multidisciplinary Studies; and dual- and joint-degree programs with other schools on campus, such as the Cox School of Business.

The **Meadows School of the Arts** prepares students to lead professional careers in the arts and communications and provides opportunities for all SMU students to grow in appreciation of the arts. A leader in innovative community engagement programs, Meadows challenges students to make a difference locally and globally by developing connections between arts entrepreneurship and social change. The School offers minors and bachelor's and master's degrees through 11 divisions: Temerlin Advertising Institute, Art, Art History (also offering a Ph.D.), Arts Management and Arts Entrepreneurship, Corporate Communication and Public Affairs, Creative Computation, Dance, Film and Media Arts, Journalism, Music, and Theatre.

The **Annette Caldwell Simmons School of Education and Human Development** prepares exemplary professionals and advances knowledge through evidence-based research. Undergraduate programs include a major and three different concentrations in applied physiology and sport management and a major in educational studies. The school offers three doctoral programs, about 10 master's degrees, and a number of graduate professional-preparation programs. Its academic departments include Teaching and Learning, Applied Physiology and Wellness, Dispute Resolution and Counseling, Education Policy and Leadership, and Liberal Studies.

Students at SMU can also opt to focus on specialized studies through degree-track programs such as pre-law, pre-health, physical therapy, and biomedical research.

SMU's undergraduate curriculum is complemented by the nationally recognized **Dedman School of Law**, offering a personalized legal education in a community of distinguished scholars, and **Perkins School of Theology**, which prepares women and men for faithful leadership in vital Christian ministry.

Academic Programs

Students benefit from small classes and opportunities for research, leadership development, and unique learning experiences on campus and around the world. Undergraduate students participate in scholarly research, civic engagement, professional internships, and creative activity related to education goals.

SMU faculty and students conduct research in the U.S. and worldwide in the sciences, engineering, education, arts, humanities, and business. Examples include natural hazards, water quality, cyber security, data analytics, learning disabilities, human performance, immigration, and the search for dark matter, as well as treatments for cancer, neurodegenerative diseases, diabetes, anxiety, and depression.

Off-Campus Programs

Students can expand their horizons with SMU Abroad's more than 150 programs in 50-plus countries to study for a semester, a summer, or a year. The unique SMU-in-Taos program brings history, science, and art to life at SMU's spectacular campus in Northern New Mexico.

Academic Facilities

SMU's campus includes 134 buildings featuring state-of-the-art teaching and learning facilities and equipment.

SMU's eight libraries house the largest private collection of research materials in the Southwest, with more than four million volumes.

The Meadows Museum houses one of the largest and most comprehensive collections of Spanish art outside Spain. A partnership with Madrid's Prado Museum includes the loan of major paintings from the Prado and an internship exchange.

SMU is also home to the George W. Bush Presidential Library and Museum. This is the first presidential library to share the campus of a private university.

Estimated Costs

For the 2018-19 academic year, undergraduate tuition and fees was $54,492; average housing and dining was $16,950.

Financial Aid

In addition to providing a valuable education with lifelong benefits, SMU partners with families to manage the cost of that education. Besides academic scholarships and customized financial aid packages for eligible students, SMU offers several payment plans. Three out of four SMU undergraduate students receive some form of financial assistance from the University, including academic or need-based aid. According to *Forbes* 2017 Best Value Colleges ranking, SMU is one of only 300 schools nationwide that are worth the investment. Competitive academic scholarships include the President's Scholars Program, the Nancy Ann and Ray L. Hunt Leadership Scholars Program, and scholarships offered by SMU's individual schools.

Faculty

SMU has 1,204 full- and part-time faculty members, and more than 80 percent of full-time faculty hold a Ph.D. or the highest degree in their field. The undergraduate student-to-faculty ratio is 11-to-1.

Student Life

Approximately 3,200 undergraduate and graduate students live on campus in 11 Residential Commons and six upperclass/graduate communities. The Residential Commons enable all first- and second-year students to live on campus and include on-site classes, social activities, and Faculty in Residence.

Students can make their mark, meet new people, and develop leadership skills through nearly 200 clubs and organizations spanning a variety of activities. They can also get involved in student government, campus programming, or community service. Annually, nearly 2,500 undergraduate volunteers make a difference through approximately 70 nonprofit agencies. Students also participate in Alternative Breaks national service projects. Other options for students include joining a religious or multicultural group, or getting involved in Greek life.

SMU has 17 NCAA Division I athletics programs, including the Mustang football team, which has played in four recent bowl games. Mustang spirit and traditions make for memories that will last a lifetime.

Students can stay in shape at the Dedman Center for Lifetime Sports with the latest health and fitness equipment. Students interested in sports can opt to participate in one or more of the 18 intramurals, such as flag football, basketball, and softball, as well as 15 club sports, including lacrosse, baseball, and hockey.

Admission Requirements

SMU carefully considers each application with the goal of adding dimension to its diverse, ambitious community of scholars. The strongest applications are not always those with the greatest number of accomplishments, but those that resonate with authenticity and passion.

Prospective students need to submit a completed application (either SMU's online application; The Common Application; ApplyTexas; or My Coalition for College Application for first-year undergraduate applicants), the completed Early Decision agreement form (if applying Early Decision), a $60 nonrefundable application fee, an official high school transcript, official SAT or ACT scores—SMU does not require the SAT optional essay or the ACT writing test (students graduating outside of the U.S. and music, theatre, dance, studio art, and film B.F.A. applicants are not required to submit test scores), a personal essay, a counselor recommendation (required), a teacher recommendation (optional), an extracurricular resume (optional), and a Home School supplement (if applicable). Students applying for dance, music, theatre, art, or film programs should also review audition and portfolio requirements. As of August 1, 2019 - students interested in majoring in any of the majors within the Cox School of Business should visit www.smu.edu/cox/Degrees-and-Programs/BBA/admissions to view information on Cox Business Direct Admission.

The Early Action (nonbinding) and Early Decision I (binding) deadline is November 1. The Regular Decision (nonbinding) and Early Decision II (binding) deadline is January 15.

Application and Information

The best way for students to get a feel for SMU is to visit. SMU offers many structured visits, such as Mustang Days and Academic Spotlights, where prospective students can meet current students, talk with academic representatives, and tour campus. Prospective students can also attend an information session, speak with an admission counselor, and tour on a weekday or selected Saturday. More information is available at smu.edu/visit.

For more information, prospective students should contact:
SMU Undergraduate Admission
Southern Methodist University
6425 Boaz Lane
P.O. Box 750100
Dallas, Texas 75275
Phone: 214-768-2058
800-323-0672 (toll-free)
E-mail: ugadmission@smu.edu
Website: smu.edu/admission

SOUTHERN NEW HAMPSHIRE UNIVERSITY

MANCHESTER, NEW HAMPSHIRE

Southern New Hampshire University

The University

At Southern New Hampshire University (SNHU), student success is the number-one priority. This sense of dedication to helping students achieve their education and career goals can be seen across the entire institution.

U.S. News and World Report has consistently ranked SNHU among the country's most innovative universities. Last year, the publication ranked SNHU as the most innovative regional Tier 1 University in the northern United States—an impressive achievement for a school that is committed to consistently reinventing the way that education is delivered and received.

Academic programs are created with the real world in mind, so students are prepared to launch successful careers when they graduate. Classes are taught by highly credentialed faculty who have professional experience and remain current in their fields. Academic and personal support is readily available, both inside and outside the classroom. With small class sizes, students never feel like just a name or a number, and are able to get to know their professors. Students in need of help will find that faculty and staff are quick to rally around them and work toward furthering their understanding and success. With more than 50 undergraduate programs (in addition to more than 60 graduate programs), students can have meaningful experiences that will better prepare them for the real world in a wide range of fields.

SNHU is always looking to improve and provide state-of-the-art facilities that enhance the student experience. A new science and technology building opened in the fall of 2017, featuring a wind tunnel, robotics lab, machine shop, and more. Other recent additions to campus include the Gustafson Center, home to SNHU's Admission and Career Development departments, an athletic stadium, and two new residence halls. A second science and technology building is slated to open in early 2020.

Students can get involved with over 70 student-run clubs and organizations at SNHU, or even start their own. We are proud to be the first school in the state to offer and sponsor scholarships for competitive varsity esports. We are currently fielding teams to compete in the esports of Fortnite, Overwatch, League of Legends, and Hearthstone.

Intercollegiate teams compete in the Northeast-10 Conference of the NCAA's Division II, and available sports include baseball, men's and women's basketball, cheerleading, men's and women's cross-country, men's golf, ice hockey, men's and women's lacrosse, men's and women's soccer, softball, men's and women's tennis, women's track and field, and women's volleyball. Intramural sports are also extremely popular. SNHU's powerful athletic teams have earned honors from the NCAA and *USA Today* for high grades and 100 percent graduation rates. Athletic facilities include an indoor, 25-meter competition-size swimming pool, a racquetball court, an aerobic studio, and more. The university also recently finished construction of a brand-new athletic complex.

The Wellness Center provides short-term health care, health education, and counseling services for students, and develops a robust schedule of events around issues ranging from bullying and domestic violence prevention to nutrition and physical fitness. In addition, students with disabilities will find that SNHU ensures that all buildings and facilities on campus are handicapped-accessible.

The Career and Professional Development Center provides assistance with resume development, letter writing, company research, networking, and informational interviewing, in addition to facilitating internships and job opportunities. Lifetime counseling and career services are available to both current students and alumni.

Location

SNHU is conveniently located just five minutes from downtown Manchester, New Hampshire's largest city, and has been named one of the top college towns in the country. Public transportation is available, and students may keep cars on campus beginning in their freshman year. The mountains, beaches, and Boston are all just an hour away. CQ Press has repeatedly named New Hampshire one of the nation's most livable states.

Majors and Degrees

SNHU's academics are comprised of the School of Arts and Sciences, the School of Business, the School of Education, and the College of Engineering, Technology, and Aeronautics. The university offers associate, bachelors, masters, and doctoral degrees. Undergraduate programs provide students with a strong general education foundation and the knowledge and skills they need to succeed in their careers.

The College of Engineering, Technology, and Aeronautics reflects the increased demand for graduates in STEM fields. SNHU has recently launched several new majors in these fields, including mechanical engineering, aeronautical engineering, computer science, information technologies, electrical and computer engineering, air traffic management, and construction management. Most recently, SNHU launched aviation operations and management, which brings a college flight program back to New Hampshire and allows students the opportunity to pursue their dream of becoming a commercial airline pilot. Once complete, the new science and technology building will provide additional resources in support of these programs.

The School of Arts and Sciences offers degrees in communication, creative writing, English language and literature, environmental science, game art and development, game programming and development, graphic design and media arts, history, justice studies, law and politics (pre-J.D. option), mathematics, psychology, and sociology. In addition, SNHU added a new biology major in 2018 to better serve those students seeking to enter the health and biological research fields.

The School of Business majors include accounting, accounting and finance, business administration, business analytics, economics, fashion merchandising and management, hospitality business, hospitality management, marketing, operations and project management, sport management, and technical management. SNHU also offers a unique Degree in Three track which is available for most programs in the School of Business. Through Degree in Three, students are able to earn their degree in three years through a blend of traditional academics and real-world experience. The goal of the program is to foster and enhance effective communication, critical thinking, and teamwork. The program enables students to save more than $40,000 in tuition and room and board; take a traditional course load of five classes per semester; graduate in six semesters with no night, weekend, or summer courses; secure internships and participate in community events; and pursue interests—such as graduate school, employment, or travelling abroad—instead of their fourth year.

The School of Education majors include early childhood education, elementary education (with optional certification in general special education), English education, middle school mathematics education, middle school science education, music education, secondary mathematics education, social studies education, and special education.

Off-Campus Programs

Southern New Hampshire University excels at mixing academic theory with practical experience both inside and outside of the classroom. Undergraduates participate in off-campus cooperative education experiences and internships, which can earn them up to 12 academic credits. Such opportunities are based on a student's major and career goals, and are typically undertaken during a student's junior or senior year. Students can work with faculty members and the Career and Professional Development Center to find appropriate assignments.

Students also work with real-world off-campus partners in their courses. For example, marketing students have created media campaigns for area businesses, while education students assist local teachers in their classrooms. SNHU graduates are always in demand because businesses know they have been prepared to contribute both on the job and in their communities.

At SNHU, students are able to go beyond the campus and enjoy opportunities for studying abroad at a number of partnering institutions in countries around the world. In terms of tuition and room and board, studying abroad costs no more than living on campus and SNHU will even pick up the tab for a student's flight (up to $1,000) and the full cost of travel health insurance. All of the credits and grades earned overseas at a partner university will apply directly towards an SNHU degree.

Costs

For the 2018–19 academic year, undergraduate tuition cost $31,136. For on-campus residents, the average room and board cost was $12,278. Students should plan to budget funds for books, supplies, travel, and personal expenses. In an effort to continue to remain an affordable private university option for as many students as possible, SNHU has frozen tuition for the 2019–20 academic year. This marks the fourth time in six academic years that SNHU has not increased campus tuition.

Financial Aid

A private university education can and should be affordable, and SNHU operates on the belief that college should change students' lives—not break the bank. That's why students with high school GPAs of 2.5 and higher can earn up to $20,000 in academic scholarships in addition to generous financial aid packages. More than 90 percent of the students at SNHU receive some type of financial aid, which may include need-based grants, academic and merit scholarships, and loans. SNHU also participates in the Federal Work-Study Program and the Federal Supplemental Educational Opportunity Grant Program. The school is also eligible under the Federal Stafford Student Loan Program and the Federal Pell Grant Program. Aid applicants should complete the Free Application for Federal Student Aid (FAFSA) by the priority deadline of March 15. Student Financial Services can provide the appropriate forms, or students can go online to http://www.fafsa.ed.gov. Academic, athletic, and leadership scholarships are also available for students who qualify.

Faculty

SNHU has more than 128 full-time faculty members and over 200 part-time instructors, with a student-faculty ratio of 14:1. A majority of the full-time faculty members at the university hold a Ph.D. or the equivalent degree in their area of expertise.

Programs at SNHU blend theory with practice to stimulate students' professional development and personal growth. Faculty members bring extensive academic, work, travel, and life experiences to their classrooms. Although their primary goal is teaching, faculty members remain current in their disciplines. Outside the classroom, faculty members are management consultants, CPAs, analysts, small-business owners, economists, accountants, marketing professionals, engineers, entrepreneurs, innkeepers, chefs, world travelers, artists, poets, novelists, psychologists, and much more.

Student Government

The Student Government Association is led by 25 students, including five officers, who represent all of the students at SNHU. Its primary function is to represent the student body in campus affairs and to distribute student activity funds. One student is appointed to represent the student body on the Board of Trustees. Students are also appointed to most other standing committees, including the Dining Services Committee, Residence Life Committee, Public Safety Committee, the Curriculum Advisory Committee, and the Library Committee.

Admission Requirements

Applicants for admission are evaluated individually on the basis of academic credentials and personal characteristics. When reviewing applicants, primary emphasis is placed on a student's academic record, as demonstrated by the quality and level of college-preparatory course work and achievement attained. Most successful candidates admitted to SNHU present a program of study consisting of 16 college-preparatory courses, including 4 years of English, 3 or more years of mathematics (up through successful completion of algebra II), 2 or more years of science, and 2 or more years of social science. Separate consideration is given to admission decisions for transfer, nontraditional, international, and Bradley Three-Year Honors Program in Business applicants.

Application and Information

Applicants for undergraduate day programs must submit an application (via the Common Application), college essay, $40 application fee, official high school transcript, and one letter of recommendation from a school counselor or teacher. SNHU is a test-optional institution and SAT/ACT scores are not required.

Freshman applicants can apply before November 15 to be considered for the early action deadline. SNHU operates on a rolling admission basis; however, the priority application deadline is February 1. Admission and scholarship decisions are made within 30 days of receiving all required admission materials.

For more information about Southern New Hampshire University, students should contact:

Office of Admission
Southern New Hampshire University
2500 North River Road
Manchester, New Hampshire 03106-1045
Phone: 603-645-9611
Fax: 603-645-9693
E-mail: admission@snhu.edu
Website: http://www.snhu.edu
http://www.facebook.com/snhuoncampus
http://www.twitter.com/snhuoncampus

COLLEGE CLOSE-UPS

STATE UNIVERSITY OF NEW YORK AT OSWEGO

OSWEGO, NEW YORK

The University

Founded in 1861, SUNY Oswego is one of 13 comprehensive colleges in the 64-campus State University of New York (SUNY) system with an excellent academic reputation and a commitment to teaching, learning, research, and service. Inspired by a shared commitment to excellence and the desire to transcend traditional higher education boundaries, SUNY Oswego provides a transformative experience to a diverse student body. Total enrollment, including part-time and graduate students, is approximately 8,000 students including 7,000 undergraduates. More than 110 liberal arts and career-oriented programs are offered through the College of Liberal Arts and Sciences; School of Business; School of Communication, Media, and the Arts; and School of Education.

Located on 700 acres on the southern shore of Lake Ontario, the spacious tree-lined campus consists of over 50 academic and residential buildings. Twelve residence halls and The Village townhouse complex offer a variety of on-campus housing opportunities. More than 200 registered extracurricular organizations cover a wide range of social, academic, cultural, and intellectual interests. Theater, art, film, music, dance, and discussion events fill the campus cultural calendar throughout the school year as well. There are 24 NCAA Division III intercollegiate sports for men and women, along with a full complement of competitive club sports and intramural athletics.

SUNY Oswego receives more than 14,000 applications for some 2,000 freshman and transfer openings each fall. It has been recognized by a number of authoritative guides for its outstanding academic opportunities and high academic standards. In recent years, SUNY Oswego has been cited for excellence and selectivity in *U.S. News & World Report's Top Regional Universities in the North* and *Best Colleges Guide, Colleges of Distinction,* and in both the Princeton Review's *Best Northeastern Colleges* and their *Best Value Colleges.*

Over the past 20 years, SUNY Oswego has invested more than $900 million in academic, residential, and infrastructure enhancements to better support the mission of the college and improve the experience of its students. Recently completed projects include the comprehensive $49 million renewal of Park and Wilber Halls for the School of Education; a $53 million renovation of Tyler Hall—a 100,000-square foot visual and performing arts building—that now provides art, theatre, and music students access to digital-age instructional tools and program delivery; the $118-million Richard S. Shineman Center for Science, Engineering, and Innovation; a new Biological Field Station lab facility and contemporary, sustainable renovations to Scales Hall and Waterbury Hall—two of four lakeside residential halls on the Oswego campus.

Location

With a population of nearly 18,000, the city of Oswego is a modest-sized, friendly upstate New York community. It is the country's oldest freshwater port and one of the leading ports on the Great Lakes and St. Lawrence Seaway. The city and its surrounding area are known for summer and winter recreation, including camping, boating, sailing, fishing, tennis, golf, ice skating, alpine and cross-country skiing, snowboarding, and sledding. The campus is conveniently located 35 miles northwest of Syracuse and 65 miles east of Rochester. Students traveling by rail or air may utilize bus service to Oswego through the Regional Transportation Center located adjacent to one of the largest malls in the northeast, Destiny USA in Syracuse.

Majors and Degrees

SUNY Oswego awards the Bachelor of Arts (B.A.), Bachelor of Science (B.S.), and Bachelor of Fine Arts (B.F.A.) degrees.

Through the College of Liberal Arts and Sciences, students can earn a baccalaureate degree in American studies; anthropology; applied mathematics; applied mathematical economics; biochemistry; biology; chemistry; cinema and screen studies; cognitive science; computer science; creative writing; criminal justice; economics; electrical and computer engineering; English; French; gender and women's studies; geochemistry; geology; German; global and international studies; history; human development; information science; language and international trade; linguistics; mathematics; meteorology; philosophy; philosophy, politics, and economics; philosophy-psychology; physics; political science; psychology; public justice; sociology; software engineering; Spanish; and zoology.

The School of Business offers B.S. degree programs in accounting; business administration; finance; human resource management; marketing; operations management and information systems; and risk management and insurance. The globally respected Association for the Advancement of Collegiate Schools of Business International (AACSB) extended, in fall 2018, the accreditation of SUNY Oswego's School of Business for five years, following a rigorous Continuous Improvement Review. The AACSB commended Oswego's School of Business —first AACSB-accredited in 2002—for a variety of strengths, innovations, and unique features, and specifically noted high levels of student satisfaction with faculty and staff, advisement, internship supervision, business-based student organizations, and other applied-learning opportunities.

The School of Communication, Media, and the Arts offers baccalaureate degree programs in art; broadcasting and mass communication; communication and social interaction; graphic design; journalism; music; public relations; and theater.

The School of Education offers B.S. degree programs in adolescence education; career and technical educator preparation; childhood education; teaching English to speakers of other languages (TESOL); technology education; technology management; and wellness management.

In addition, four innovative five-year combined bachelor's and master's programs are available: a bachelor's degree in accounting with an M.B.A., a bachelor's in psychology with an M.B.A., a bachelor's in psychology with a master's in human computer interaction, and a bachelor's in broadcasting and mass communication with an M.B.A.

Cooperative programs include a 3+3 program leading to a B.S./D.P.T. in physical therapy from SUNY Upstate Medical University; and a 3+4 pre-optometry program leading to a bachelor's in chemistry from Oswego and an O.D. in optometry from SUNY College of Optometry.

Academic Programs

Oswego offers students a broad range of courses in the liberal arts and in pre-professional and professional studies. In addition to core courses within a major, all students must satisfy general education requirements designed to strengthen basic writing and analytical proficiency, give students awareness of their cultural heritage, and provide a level of literacy in the social and behavioral sciences, natural sciences, and humanities.

Before arriving on campus, students are assigned an advisor who specializes in their academic major. Advisors assist students with academic, personal, and career concerns, and collaborate in scheduling courses needed for graduation. The college has a strong reputation for working with undeclared students and helping them to discover and apply their education passions.

Students may be selected for the college's honors program, which provides a challenging academic experience for high achievers regardless of major.

Off-Campus Programs

Opportunities exist for students to broaden their knowledge of other countries by participating in one of 80 different summer or semester overseas academic programs offered. This includes options in short study-abroad quarter courses offering an intensive curriculum followed by a one-to-two-week experience in a foreign country.

SUNY Oswego provides many opportunities for students to engage in experiential education through internships, undergraduate research, and service learning. Internships and other field experiences are available for students from all disciplines through EXCEL: Experiential Courses and Engaged Learning. In addition, a formalized cooperative education program (co-op) is available to students from over 25 major areas. Each year, more than 1,000 Oswego students participate in internships, co-ops, and service-learning activities on campus, in the local area, and throughout the world.

Academic Facilities

Penfield Library is a high-tech information center supporting the curriculum, teaching, and research of SUNY Oswego. Through Interlibrary Loan, Penfield can provide additional materials from libraries all over the world.

Campus-wide computer technology service professionals support students in their classroom, residence, and Internet activities. Wireless access is available throughout the campus. The campus maintains hundreds of Mac and Windows-based computers.

Adjacent to the campus, the college maintains the 330-acre Rice Creek Field Station, with its $5.5-million modern, 7,200-square-foot lab facility which opened its doors in the fall of 2013. The facility has two lab/classrooms, a lecture room, and exhibit areas with an indoor viewing gallery, providing a unique vista of the creek and pond. College classes and community education programs are regularly held at the field station, which ranks among the five most extensively used facilities of its kind in the country.

Tyler Hall, Oswego's newly renovated fine arts center, has an art gallery that features annual traveling exhibitions, locally produced theme exhibitions, and the best work of students and faculty members. Tyler Hall's Waterman Theatre hosts student plays, musical performances, and productions by internationally renowned traveling artists. Other new facilities support musical performances and audio production opportunities.

The WRVO Stations, the college's 50,000-watt public radio outlet, provides outstanding on-campus internship opportunities. Communication Department facilities also include two new all-digital television studios, a modern radio lab, and two new journalism labs in Lanigan Hall. Student-run TV and radio stations and the college newspaper are located in the Marano Campus Center facilities.

Costs

Tuition for 2018–19 was $3,435 per semester for New York State residents and $8,325 per semester for nonresidents. Room and board charges were approximately $7,214 per semester for entering students, depending on the meal plan, and additional fees totaled approximately $1,570 per year. SUNY Oswego guarantees that a student's initial first-year costs for room and board will be frozen for up to four consecutive years.

Financial Aid

Need-based financial assistance consists of grants, loans, and part-time employment. Oswego offers more than $84 million in aid to its students annually. Students interested in financial aid must file a Free Application for Federal Student Aid (FAFSA). New York State residents also need to file an application for the state's Tuition Assistance Program (TAP).

Oswego offers a very generous merit scholarship program. Students receive more than $6.5 million annually in merit scholarships and approximately 45 percent of first-year students receive one. The average four-year renewable scholarship is more than $3,000 per year. Through New York State's Excelsior Scholarship program, a large number of New York students are also eligible for free tuition at SUNY Oswego. For scholarship qualifications and details, visit http://www.oswego.edu/admissions/scholarships.

Faculty

With approximately 88 percent of SUNY Oswego faculty holding doctoral or other terminal degrees, students can be assured of the opportunity for an outstanding undergraduate education. The student-faculty ratio is approximately 17:1. While dedicated to teaching first and foremost, Oswego's faculty members are also actively engaged in research—often in partnership with undergraduate students.

Admission Requirements

Admission to SUNY Oswego is competitive, with high school average, academic program, and standardized test scores being the most important criteria for applicants. Special talents such as artistic, musical, athletic, and creative writing skills are also considered. The Committee on Admissions accepts results of either the ACT or the SAT. A campus admissions visit is encouraged.

Transfer students in good standing are encouraged to apply for admission. The average GPA for entering transfer students is 3.0.

Application and Information

Oswego accepts both The Common Application and the SUNY Application for admission. Both applications are available online at http://www.oswego.edu/apply. Oswego evaluates applications as they are completed and as space remains available. Applications completed by November 15 will be considered for Early Action. Early Action applicants will be notified of our decision by December 15. Applications completed by January 15 for the fall term or October 15 for the spring term are ensured equal consideration. Applications received after those dates are welcomed, although considered as space remains available. Regular admission applicants for the fall term will receive their decision beginning January 15, and spring applicants will receive their decision beginning November 15.

Prospective students and their parents are encouraged to visit the campus to participate in a student-guided tour and speak with an admissions counselor. Visits can be scheduled online at www.oswego.edu/admissions. Interested candidates can also call the Office of Admissions in advance to schedule a visit.

For further information, students should contact:

Office of Admissions
229 Sheldon Hall
SUNY Oswego
Oswego, New York 13126
Phone: 315-312-2250
Fax: 315-312-3260
E-mail: admiss@oswego.edu
Website: http://www.oswego.edu/admissions

SUNY Oswego is located on 700+ acres on the southern shore of Lake Ontario.

STOCKTON UNIVERSITY
GALLOWAY, NEW JERSEY

STOCKTON UNIVERSITY

The University

Thinking translates into doing at Stockton. Students gain hands-on experience in Nursing, Exercise Science, Occupational Therapy or Physical Therapy in state-of-the-art facilities on campus; use cutting-edge technology to preserve historic underwater wreck sites or analyze the seafloor's ecosystems at Stockton's Marine Field Station; study artistic techniques firsthand through a partnership with the Noyes Museum of Art or at the Philadelphia Museum of Art; or bask in the beautiful, 1,600-acre campus in the Pinelands National Reserve just minutes from the ocean, a perfect setting for Stockton's nationally renowned Environmental and Marine Science programs.

Stockton students engage with Fulbright Scholars, Guggenheim Fellows, and Pulitzer-awarded authors. Small classes are guided by professors who care as much about teaching as research, allowing for discussion, debate, and discovery in the classroom and beyond.

Founded in 1969, Stockton offers extensive service-learning opportunities and has become an international leader in alternative energy research and conservation efforts.

In 2015, Stockton celebrated a new designation and name change to Stockton University. The University offers bachelor's, master's, and doctoral degree programs designed to challenge the brightest students, providing many of the academic, technological, and cultural advantages of a large university, but with the communal spirit typical of smaller colleges.

Stockton enrolls over 9,600 students from New Jersey, the Mid-Atlantic states, and foreign countries, providing unique educational programs with a curriculum focused on developing the students' analytic and creative capabilities through the encouragement of individually planned courses of study.

The Stockton experience is enhanced with 200-plus ways to get involved with clubs, organizations, and activities. In addition to extensive intramural and club sports, NCAA Division III sports teams offered include men's baseball, basketball, lacrosse, and soccer, women's basketball, cross country, field hockey, lacrosse, soccer, softball, tennis, and volleyball, and men's and women's cross-country and track and field.

Stockton provides on-campus housing for more than 4,000 students in traditional residence halls, apartments, campus-owned facilities, and at the Residential Complex at the new Stockton University Atlantic City. All complexes are furnished and air conditioned, with cable TV and Internet. Others choose to live off campus in nearby apartment complexes or winter rentals in one of the local shore towns.

Beyond its undergraduate programs, Stockton offers the following graduate degrees: Doctor of Nursing Practice, Doctor of Physical Therapy, and Doctor of Education in Organizational Leadership; Master of Arts in American Studies, Counseling, Criminal Justice, Education, Holocaust & Genocide Studies, and Instructional Technology; Master of Business Administration; Master of Science in Communication Disorders, Data Science and Strategic Analytics, Nursing, and Occupational Therapy; Master of Social Work; and a Professional Science Master's in Environmental Science. Certificate and endorsement programs are offered in Administration and Leadership, Adult Gerontology Primary Care Nurse Practitioner, American Studies, Bilingual/Bicultural Education, Data Science, Energy, ESL (English as a second language), Family Nurse Practitioner, Forensic Science, Forensic Psychology, Genocide Prevention, Geographic Information Systems, Gerontology, Homeland Security, Learning Disabilities Teacher Consultant, Middle School Endorsement, New Jersey Standard Supervisor Endorsement, Preschool–Grade 3 Endorsement, Reading Specialist, Special Education, and Student Assistance Coordinator.

Stockton University is accredited by the Commission on Higher Education of the Middle States Association of Colleges and Schools. In addition, the School of Business is accredited by the Association to Advance Collegiate Schools of Business, the Social Work program is accredited by the Council on Social Work Education; teacher education is approved by the New Jersey Department of Education, the National Association of State Directors of Teacher Education and Certification, and the Teacher Education Accreditation Council; nursing is accredited by the New Jersey Board of Nursing and the Commission on Collegiate Nursing Education; chemistry is accredited by the American Chemical Society; physical therapy is accredited by the Commission on Accreditation in Physical Therapy Education of the American Physical Therapy Association; environmental health is accredited by the National Environmental Health Sciences and Protection Accreditation Council; occupational therapy is accredited by the Accreditation Council for Occupational Therapy Education of the American Occupational Therapy Association; communication disorders is accredited by the Council on Academic Accreditation in Audiology and Speech-Language Pathology; the Biochemistry and Molecular Biology Program is accredited by the American Society for biochemistry and molecular biology, and criminal justice is accredited by the Academy of Criminal Justice Sciences.

Location

Stockton's main campus is located in Galloway, New Jersey, nestled in the environmentally protected Pinelands National Reserve, just minutes west of Atlantic City, an hour from Philadelphia, and two hours from New York City. Courses are also offered online and at the Atlantic City, Hammonton, Manahawkin, and Woodbine locations. Collaboration with the Sam Azeez Museum of Woodbine Heritage and the Noyes Museum of Art provides enriching exhibitions and educational programs. The new Stockton University Atlantic City , which includes an Academic Center and Residential Complex overlooking the Boardwalk, will allow Stockton to grow and support its surrounding communities as well as expand the hospitality and tourism management studies, organizational leadership, business studies, social work, and community leadership snf civic engagement programs.

Majors and Degrees

The Bachelor of Arts, Bachelor of Fine Arts and Bachelor of Science degrees are offered in studies in the arts (visual and performing), Africana studies, biochemistry/molecular biology, biology, business studies (accounting, business analytics, finance, financial planning, management, marketing), chemistry, communication studies, computer information systems, computer science, computing, criminal justice (forensic psychology/investigation, homeland security), economics, education, environmental science, exercise science, geology, health science, historical studies, hospitality and tourism management studies, languages and culture studies, liberal studies, literature, marine science, mathematics, nursing, philosophy and religion, physics, political science, psychology, public health, social work, sociology and anthropology, studio art, and sustainability.

Stockton also offers pre-professional preparation in dentistry, law, medicine, pharmacy, veterinary medicine, communication disorders (speech therapy), occupational therapy, physical therapy, and physician assistant studies, with the master's degree in Occupational Therapy, Communication Disorders, and Doctorate in Physical Therapy completed at Stockton. The university also has an accelerated seven-year dual-degree articulation agreements with Rowan School of Osteopathic Medicine; an accelerated dual-degree program in pharmaceutical engineering with New Jersey Institute of Technology;

a five-year BS-MSPA that combines a B.S. in Health Science from Stockton with a master's in Physician Assistant Studies from Thomas Jefferson University; and five-year, dual-degree programs with New Jersey Institute of Technology, Rowan University and Rutgers University for engineering. In addition, students can graduate from Stockton with a Bachelor of Science degree in Biochemistry/Molecular Biology or Biology and finish their Doctor of Pharmacy degree through the Ernest Mario School of Pharmacy at Rutgers University.

Academic Programs

To earn a baccalaureate degree from Stockton, a student must satisfactorily complete a minimum of 128 semester credits. Degree programs include a combination of general studies and major studies. Bachelor of Arts students must earn 64 credits in general studies; Bachelor of Science students must earn 48. General studies courses are cross-disciplinary courses designed to introduce students to all major areas of the curriculum and to the intellectual skills necessary for success in college. Students must select courses from each major curricular area. The only required courses within general studies are basic studies (up to three); students may be exempt from these courses based on testing. Bachelor of Arts students must earn 64 credits in major studies; Bachelor of Science students must earn 80. Requirements are carefully structured and emphasize sequences of specific courses.

Stockton students have the opportunity to influence what and how they learn. The preceptorial system enables students to work closely with a faculty-staff preceptor in planning and evaluating courses and in exploring career paths.

Off-Campus Programs

Off-campus experiences for credit are a requirement for most programs, namely in the form of internships, research projects, and field studies. Stockton sends more students to the Washington Internship Program than any other college or university outside the Washington, D.C., area.

Study abroad, Semester at Sea, and an honors program provide additional opportunities.

The Career Center as well as academic offices coordinate off-campus internships; education abroad is coordinated by the Office of Global Engagement.

Academic Facilities

Stockton's campuses in Galloway and Atlantic City serve as living-learning centers, with academic, recreational, and living spaces mixed to promote interaction among students, faculty, and staff. Facilities include interactive and electronic classrooms, an extensive library containing the Sara & Sam Schoffer Holocaust Resource Center, an art gallery, and performing arts center. New academic facilities in 2018 included a 58,000 square-foot addition to the current Unified Science Center as well as a new 38,000 square-foot Health Sciences Center.

Costs

Costs for the 2018–19 academic year were $13,979 for in-state students and $21,106 for out-of-state students (flat-rate tuition up to 40 credits per year, fees); on-campus housing and board were $12,326 (double-occupancy residence room, Ultimate meal plan). Books, supplies, transportation, and personal items are extra. Costs are subject to change.

Financial Aid

Financial aid is available as scholarships, grants, loans, and work-study. Need-based financial aid is awarded according to student and family need. Students seeking financial aid should file the Free Application for Federal Student Aid (FAFSA) as soon as possible after October 1. Stockton offers aggressive and generous merit-based aid awards to academically talented freshman and transfer students based on standardized test scores, grade point average, high school class rank and college-level performance.

Faculty

Stockton's faculty represent highly diverse academic, training, and social backgrounds, with 92 percent holding terminal degrees in their field. Faculty members work closely with students through individualized research opportunities, and share social, recreational, and cultural programs with students and staff. This arrangement supports the exceptional rapport and learning relationships among students and faculty members.

Student Government

The Stockton University Student Senate consists of 27 student members. The advisory council is made up of one faculty member and two staff members. Student senators hold office for one year. The Student Senate reviews and makes recommendations on budgets of funded student organizations and acts as the official representative of the student body.

Admission Requirements

Stockton operates on rolling admission. Fall admission deadline is May 1 for most freshmen, with special program deadlines posted on the university's website. Transfer deadline for fall admission is July 1. Spring (January) admission deadline for all students is December 1. Students may apply for admission to the fall or spring term and are notified of the decision as soon as their application file is completed and has been reviewed. Some freshman applicants must submit ACT and/or SAT scores. All students must submit official transcripts from all educational institutions attended. Admission is selective.

Armed Services veterans and those who have been away from formal education for some time are encouraged to apply. Stockton makes no distinction between part- and full-time students in offering admission.

Stockton offers special admission to a limited number of New Jersey students from educationally and financially disadvantaged backgrounds. Students wishing to explore this opportunity should contact the Office of Admissions.

Application and Information

For more information, contact:
Chief Enrollment Management Officer
Stockton University
101 Vera King Farris Drive
Galloway, New Jersey 08205-9441
Phone: 609-652-4261
Fax: 609-626-5541
E-mail: admissions@stockton.edu
Website: Facebook.com/StocktonUniversity
Twitter.com/@Stockton_edu
Instagram.com/stocktonuniversity

Stockton University is ranked among the top public universities in the Northeast. Students can choose to live and learn on the main campus in the Pinelands National Reserve and at a new coastal residential campus just steps from the beach and Boardwalk in Atlantic City. Learn about our more than 160 undergraduate and graduate programs at Stockton.edu.

COLLEGE CLOSE-UPS

TEMPLE UNIVERSITY
PHILADELPHIA, PENNSYLVANIA

Temple University

The University

Temple University attracts some of the most diverse, driven and motivated minds from across the nation and around the world. These students and faculty bring the university to life and move Temple forward and upward in academics, athletics, research and the arts. Powering Temple's ascent are innovative approaches to admissions and affordability; a campus transformation; plentiful creative and research opportunities; rigorous academic programs; an indelible bond with the city of Philadelphia; and groundbreaking work in science, research and technology.

Temple is home to about 40,000 students, is the thirty-first largest public, four-year institution in the United States and offers more than 570 academic programs in 17 schools and colleges, on eight campuses, including locations in Japan and Italy.

More than 3,800 distinguished faculty members; five professional schools; and dozens of renowned programs make Temple an academic powerhouse. Students enjoy the advantages and atmosphere of a large urban, public research university with the individualized attention that comes from a 14:1 student-to-faculty ratio.

The majority of first-year students live on campus, where they are steps away from classes; a state-of-the-art TECH Center; the library; fitness and recreation facilities; dining options such as cafés, dining halls and food trucks; and the many arts, cultural, sports and scholarly events that happen daily at Temple and throughout the city.

By living and learning in an urban environment, Temple students are well prepared for the world. Employers laud Owls for their tenacity, teamwork and talent. Students also have access to an immense alumni network 332,000 strong for guidance, job opportunities and mentoring.

Location

Each of Temple's distinct campuses has its own personality and environment, from urban to suburban to international. Temple's Main Campus is located just 1.5 miles from the center of Philadelphia, one of the largest cities on the East Coast. Philadelphia is among the most walkable cities in the U.S.—meaning students can easily access all the city has to offer, including more than 100 museums, a thriving restaurant scene, numerous athletic events, and the largest urban landscaped park in the country. The professional world is also right outside Temple's door: There are thousands of opportunities for hands-on learning and internships in the Philadelphia area, and the University's more than 100,000 alumni in the region love to hire Temple graduates.

Temple's other seven campuses include a location in Tokyo—the largest and oldest American university in Japan—and another in Rome, Italy. Temple University Harrisburg is located in the heart of Pennsylvania's capital city. The University's campus in Ambler, Pennsylvania, is the hub of the University's environmental programs and home to a 187-acre arboretum that serves as a living laboratory. In addition to Main Campus, Temple's Philadelphia campuses are the Health Sciences Center just north of Main Campus, and the Center City and Podiatric Medicine campuses, both a short subway ride away in downtown Philadelphia.

Majors and Degrees

Temple offers more than 160 undergraduate degree programs, making it easy for students to follow, or discover, their passions. Students who need time to decide on a major can explore their interests through the University Studies program. Those who would like to accelerate their education can apply to one of Temple's many dual-degree programs.

The Tyler School of Art offers a B.F.A. with concentrations in ceramics, glass, fibers and materials studies, graphic and interactive design, metals/jewelry/CAD-CAM, painting, photography, printmaking, and sculpture (all concentrations available with entrepreneurial studies); a B.A. in art history, art therapy, and visual studies; and a B.S. in art education. Tyler's architecture program confers a B.S. in historic preservation, architecture (pre-professional), and facilities management. B.S. programs are offered in community development and in horticulture and landscape architecture.

The Fox School of Business offers a B.B.A. in accounting; actuarial science; business management; economics; entrepreneurship and innovation management; finance; financial planning; human resource management; international business; legal studies; management information systems; marketing, real estate, risk management and insurance, and supply chain management. The school also offers a B.S. in statistical science and data analytics.

The College of Education offers a B.A. in adult and organizational development and a B.S. in career and technical education, early childhood–elementary education, human development and community engagement, middle-grades education (4–8), and secondary education combined with a second major or subject area.

The College of Engineering offers a B.S. in bioengineering; civil engineering; construction engineering technology; electrical engineering; engineering (general program); engineering technology; environmental engineering; industrial and systems engineering; and mechanical engineering.

The College of Liberal Arts offers a B.A. in Africology and African American studies; American studies; anthropology; Asian studies; Chinese; classics; criminal justice; economics; English; environmental studies; French; gender, sexuality, and women's studies; geography and urban studies; German language and cultural studies; global studies; history; interdisciplinary German studies; interdisciplinary liberal arts; Italian; Jewish studies; Latin American studies; liberal studies; mathematical economics; neuroscience: systems, behaviors, and plasticity; philosophy; political science; psychology; religion; sociology; and Spanish. Temple University Japan offers a B.A. in general studies; international affairs; Japanese; and psychological studies.

The Klein College of Media and Communication offers a B.A. in advertising, communication and social influence, communication studies, journalism, media studies and production, and public relations.

The Boyer College of Music and Dance offers a B.S. in music and music technology; and a B.M. in jazz studies composition, jazz studies performance (instrumental or vocal); composition; music education, music education with jazz studies component; music history (instrumental or vocal); theory; music therapy, music therapy with jazz studies component, performance (instrumental or vocal); and piano pedagogy. A B.F.A. is offered in dance.

The College of Public Health offers a B.S. in exercise and sport science; health information management; health professions; kinesiology; nursing; public health; recreational therapy; speech, language, and hearing science.

The College of Science and Technology offers a B.A. in biology; chemistry; computer science; geology; information science and technology; mathematical economics; mathematics; natural sciences; and physics. The college also offers a B.S. in applied mathematics; biochemistry; biology; biology with teaching; biophysics; chemistry; chemistry with teaching; computer science; computer science and physics; data science; Earth and space science with teaching; environmental science; general science with teaching; geology; information science and technology; mathematics; mathematics and computer science with teaching; mathematics with teaching; mathematics and computer science; mathematics and physics; natural sciences; neuroscience: cellular and molecular; pharmaceutical sciences; physics; and physics with teaching.

The School of Social Work offers the B.S.W. degree.

The School of Theater, Film, and Media Arts offers a B.A. in film and media arts; and theater as well as a B.F.A. in film and media arts; and musical theater.

The School of Sport Tourism and Hospitality Management offers a B.S. in sport and recreation management and in tourism and hospitality management.

Academic Programs

Students are attracted to Temple because of its diversity and quality of academic programs: More than 570 are offered, including more than 160 undergraduate degree programs. The University provides all of the resources and opportunities of a large, world-class research institution and the individual attention of a small college—with a 14:1 student-to-faculty ratio.

All students complete the General Education curriculum, a cross-section of courses that focuses on making connections locally and globally and looks at cutting-edge issues from multiple angles. Flexibility in coursework offers each student a unique and transformative experience.

Some students pursue common interests in Living and Learning Communities. Academically qualified students take on extra intellectual challenges through the Honors Program. Temple's study abroad programs offer opportunities to take learning around the world.

The Diamond Research Scholars program provides students with the opportunity to engage in a focused, mentored research or creative arts project. TUteach allows students to graduate with a bachelor of science in a math or science field and the qualifications to earn a middle or high school teaching certificate. Through various special academic programs, students can work directly with renowned faculty and present at professional conferences, publish in peer-reviewed journals, and premiere music and dance at venues around the globe.

And to keep students on track academically, Fly in 4 was established. It's a program unique to Temple and helps students create academic plans to ensure they graduate in four years to limit debt. If students meet all of the programs obligations and are still unable to graduate in four years, Temple pays for the remaining coursework.

Academic Facilities

Whether in a high-tech classroom or the University's Science Education and Research Center (SERC), Temple students learn in world-class facilities. At SERC, which is home to 68 research and teaching labs and leading-edge technologies, students work with faculty on real-world projects, making the connection between understanding science and putting advanced research techniques into practice.

At the TECH Center—among the largest student computer labs in the country—students can collaborate in breakout rooms, edit video in a specialized lab, get assistance from the 24-hour help desk, or work on one of 700 computers. There are more than 100 other computer labs on campus and 90 percent of classrooms are smart classrooms.

Costs

Typical tuition and fees for the 2018–19 academic year were $19,618 for Pennsylvania residents and $33,058 for out-of-state residents (tuition rates vary by major). Room and board on Main Campus for the academic year were about $11,916.

Financial Aid

Temple offers a multitude of options to help make college more affordable. A variety of scholarships, grants, loans, and work-study programs are available: 70 percent of first-year students receive need-based financial aid, and Temple awards more than $100 million in scholarships each year. Four-year academic merit scholarships for talented freshmen range from $2,000 to full tuition, and several include summer stipends for research, internships, and study abroad.

Most incoming freshmen—more than 90 percent—commit to Temple's Fly in 4 program, an innovative plan which helps students limit their debt and enter the workforce sooner by graduating in four years. The program also offers 500 need-based grants per entering class to help reduce the need for students to work for pay while studying. Based on the Free Application for Federal Student Aid (FAFSA), eligible students receive $4,000 per year.

Faculty

Students at Temple learn from and collaborate with faculty at the forefront of their fields—winners of prestigious teaching and research awards, scientists doing groundbreaking research, and working artists who exhibit all over the world.

Temple faculty members are also known for their practical experience—a marketing class may be led by a successful entrepreneur; music lessons by a member of the Philadelphia Orchestra. Marine biologists, newspaper editors, published authors, practicing architects, and healthcare professionals all bring their expertise to the classroom.

And the roster of outstanding faculty members is growing. Renowned faculty join Temple from leading universities and research centers including Princeton University, MIT, and the Cleveland Clinic.

Admission Requirements

Temple's admissions process is holistic; every aspect of the student's academic history is considered. Typically, students have a B+ average or better in a strong college-prep curriculum in grades 9–12. For students submitting test scores, the average SAT score in 2018 was 1237, and the average ACT composite was 27. Temple Option is an admissions path for determined and tenacious students who have the ability to succeed in college but may not perform well on standardized tests. When students apply with Temple Option, they show their potential by answering open-ended questions rather than submitting SAT or ACT scores.

For freshman admissions, high school grades (quality of courses and grade trends), standardized test scores or Temple Option responses, and other factors are considered. Temple uses a sliding scale rather than absolute cutoffs. Students self-report their high school transcripts online through TUportal once they apply. Official standardized test scores must be sent directly to the admissions office. SAT subject tests and personal interviews are not required.

The application fee is $55; most students apply online through Temple or the Common Application.

Temple offers rolling admissions and early action decision plans for the fall semester. Those interested in early action must submit a completed application by November 1 and will receive notification by mid-January. The rolling admissions deadline is February 1; freshman decisions begin in early fall.

Applicants are considered transfer students if they have taken 15 or more college-level credits after high school. If this is not the case, they should apply as freshman students. In admissions decisions, careful consideration is given to the quality of a student's program, number of credits earned, and GPA. The mean GPA for new transfer students is 3.15 (on a 4.0 scale). The architecture, nursing, and pharmacy programs have higher minimum GPA requirements. For most programs, transfer students must complete the application process by June 1 for the fall semester or by November 1 for the spring semester. The fall priority deadline for the health information management and nursing programs is February 1. SAT or ACT scores are not required if an applicant has earned at least 15 college-level credits.

Application and Information

A completed file contains an application form accompanied by a nonrefundable application fee, a secondary-school transcript (sent by the student's school), and SAT or ACT scores (sent directly by the testing agencies) or responses to the Temple Option questions.

For additional information, students may contact:

Office of Undergraduate Admissions
Temple University
Philadelphia, Pennsylvania 19122-6096
United States
Phone: 215-204-7200
888-340-2222 (toll-free)
E-mail: askanowl@temple.edu
Website: nextstop.temple.edu
Facebook: facebook.com/TempleU
Twitter: @admissionsTU
Instagram: @admissionsTU
Snapchat: @admissionsTU

At Temple University, students get a full campus experience—complete with state-of-the-art facilities and labs, and bountiful, green social spaces—while being in the heart of a destination city.

JEFFERSON
(Philadelphia University + Thomas Jefferson University)
PHILADELPHIA, PENNSYLVANIA

Jefferson
Philadelphia University +
Thomas Jefferson University
HOME OF SIDNEY KIMMEL MEDICAL COLLEGE

The University

Jefferson (Philadelphia University + Thomas Jefferson University) is a comprehensive national university with nine colleges and three schools, offering bachelor's, master's and doctoral degrees, and a history of prominence dating back to 1824. Yet Jefferson maintains an intimate campus community with 2,800 undergraduates on its East Falls Campus.

At Jefferson, personal attention and professionally oriented curricula are cornerstones. From the moment students enroll, they have a network of resources to help them transition to a university environment, find academic support, and facilitate their personal and professional development. These benefits, together with an emphasis on quality, professional education, are the reasons why the school brings out the best in every student.

The Jefferson, East Falls Campus student body is academically, geographically, culturally, and economically diverse. The campus has 2,800 full- and part-time students from 47 states and 34 countries. More than 90 percent of Jefferson freshmen live in one of its residence halls. Class sizes average 18 students, allowing for lively discussions and fostering relationships between and among its students and its experienced and dedicated faculty. From day one, students are treated like professionals. They work on class projects alongside students from a variety of majors outside their own, mirroring what happens in the real world. At Jefferson, it's known as Nexus Learning.

Jefferson has established a phenomenal record of career success for its graduates; its career placement rate in major-related jobs has consistently been above 90 percent, within a few months of graduation, for more than twenty years. Ninety-five percent of Jefferson's 2018 graduates are working in their disciplines or have been accepted to the graduate school of their choice.

Jefferson offers many chances for its students to get involved outside of the classroom—from clubs and student-run organizations to campus-wide community service projects, from Open Mic nights to resume writing workshops—learning is integrated in all the University does.

In addition, Jefferson is a member of the CACC conference at the NCAA Division II level for the following sports: men's baseball, basketball, cross-country/track, golf, soccer, and tennis, and women's basketball, cross-country/track, golf, lacrosse, rowing, soccer, softball, tennis, and volleyball. An extensive intramural sports program is also available to all students.

Jefferson is a private institution of higher learning, fully accredited by the Middle States Association of Colleges and Schools.

Location

Jefferson (Philadelphia University + Thomas Jefferson University) East Falls Campus is located 15 minutes northwest of Center City Philadelphia, a rich and vibrant city in Pennsylvania. The 52 buildings on the University's 100-acre campus range from historic Victorian mansions to contemporary classroom, library, and residential facilities. Jefferson offers the best of both worlds: a beautiful campus with tree-lined walkways, spacious lawns, and classical architecture, just minutes away from its extended classroom—one the nation's most exciting and lively cities, filled with entertainment, cultural events, and more than 300 years of American history.

Majors and Degrees

Jefferson, East Falls offers more than 50 undergraduate and graduate degree programs leading to the Bachelor of Science, Bachelor of Architecture, Bachelor of Science in Engineering, Bachelor of Landscape Architecture, master's degrees, and doctoral degrees.

Jefferson's most popular degrees include fashion, architecture, engineering, health sciences, landscape architecture, textiles, digital media, fashion merchandising and management, marketing, physician assistant studies, business, psychology, and biology.

Academic Programs

Through a unique blend of liberal and specialized education with an interdisciplinary focus, the University prepares students for today's complex, global workplace. The University achieves this by focusing on innovation, innovative thinking and an award-winning Nexus Learning approach—active, collaborative learning that is connected to the real world and infused with the liberal arts.

Study-abroad and internship opportunities are available for fall, spring, and summer semesters at locations all around the world. Along with an exciting and memorable experience, students may receive credit for courses and positions that apply directly to their challenging, professional-oriented curricula.

Costs

For the 2018–19 academic year, tuition totals $39,495 and the general fee is $1,006. Room rates range from $6,295 to $9,285, depending on style of accommodations; meal plans range from $2,425 to $7,170. Books and supplies are estimated at $1,000. Costs are subject to change.

Financial Aid

Jefferson is committed to making a high-quality, professional education affordable for every qualified student. If meeting educational costs is a concern, applicants are encouraged to apply for financial aid, regardless of family financial circumstances. More than 90 percent of students receive aid in the form of grants, loans, campus employment and/or scholarships. Merit, need-based, and athletic scholarships are available. More information on scholarship opportunities is available on the University's website at http://eastfalls.jefferson.edu/financialaid/undergraduate/scholarships/.

Admission Requirements

To be considered for admission to Jefferson, first-year applicants must submit:

- $40 nonrefundable application fee
- Official high school transcript(s)
- SAT and/or ACT scores. The code for the SAT is 2666 and the ACT is 3668.
- Letter of recommendation from a teacher or counselor who can speak to academic preparation and college readiness. An academic recommendation form is available to download from the University's website.
- Essay of at least 250 words.

Jefferson does not require a portfolio review for first-year applicants. If an applicant has some college-level coursework, a portfolio review may be required to assess transferable credit.

Application and Information

Jefferson has an Early Action deadline of November 1 and a Regular Decision deadline of March 1.

The Admissions Committee begins reviewing applications for fall terms in October and for spring terms in June. The Admissions Committee will review applications for a given term until all programs are filled. Some academic programs, as well as on-campus housing, may have limited capacity and may close earlier than others. For this reason, students are encouraged to apply early in the academic year prior to their desired enrollment term. After submitting all required application materials, applicants can expect to receive their admissions decision within 4 to 6 weeks.

The Admissions Committee reviews each candidate's application by examining a variety of factors, including high school and/or college academic performance, standardized test scores (SAT and/or ACT), counselor or teacher recommendation, and application essay. Involvement in extracurricular activities, volunteer or work experience relevant to a candidate's chosen major, and the level of the candidate's academic curriculum are also considered. Jefferson has a customized admissions application and also accepts the Common Application. To apply online to Jefferson as an undergraduate student, complete the Jefferson Online Application or Common Application.

Prospective students are encouraged to visit Jefferson. There are several types of visit opportunities available.

For more information, contact:

Office of Admissions
Jefferson (Philadelphia University + Thomas Jefferson University)
4201 Henry Avenue
Philadelphia, Pennsylvania 19144
Phone: 215-951-2800
E-mail: admissions@PhilaU.edu
Website: http://eastfalls.jefferson.edu/undergrad/

TRINE UNIVERSITY
ANGOLA, INDIANA

The University

Trine University has a reputation for producing in-demand work-ready graduates, proven by Trine's 99.4 percent job placement rate over the past five years. Career opportunities are one reason students choose Trine, along with its well-maintained campus, welcoming community, and opportunities to excel.

Students can expect a well-rounded college experience with challenging courses taught by engaged, experienced faculty members, eager to help students succeed. Small class size and a 15:1 student-to-faculty ratio foster personalized attention and optimal classroom performance.

Trine is private, independent, and coeducational, offering associate, baccalaureate, master's and doctoral degrees to students in about 35 programs, including engineering, mathematics, forensic science, pre–physical therapy, business, education, psychology, exercise science, criminal justice and sport management.

Trine has invested more than $155 million in campus upgrades since 2000. In fall 2017, the university opened the Thunder Ice Arena, home to its new men's and women's hockey teams as well as student and community activities. The new MTI Center, including basketball courts, a six-lane bowling alley, and esports arena, began hosting athletic, student and entertainment events in January 2018. A new residence hall opened in fall 2018 helps meet the housing needs of a growing student body.

Recognized as Indiana's fastest-growing private college over the past several years, Trine has 5,074 students, with more than 2,200 main campus undergraduates.

The Trine student body breaks down as follows:

- Academic averages for the freshman class include a 3.47 GPA, 1119 SAT, and 24 ACT. Eighteen percent were in the top 10 percent of their high school graduating class and 46 percent were in the top 25 percent.
- Students represent 35 states and 24 countries.
- Engineering is the most popular program, with 46 percent of students enrolled.
- More than 900 students are involved in NCAA Division III athletics.

The 450-acre campus offers an inviting, safe, vibrant atmosphere that complements the seriousness and determination with which Trine students pursue academic goals. Trine has more than 60 academic, cultural, service, and Greek organizations and 34 intercollegiate teams.

Trine is a member of National Collegiate Athletic Association (NCAA) Division III and the Michigan Intercollegiate Athletic Association (MIAA), the nation's oldest athletic conference. The NCAA hockey teams are members of the Northern Collegiate Hockey Association. Men's sports include baseball, basketball, bowling, cross country, esports, football, golf, hockey, lacrosse, soccer, tennis, track, volleyball and wrestling. Women's sports include basketball, bowling, cross country, esports, golf, hockey, lacrosse, soccer, softball, synchronized and figure skating, tennis, track, triathlon and volleyball. Many students also participate on intramural sports teams.

Trine students excel on the field and in and out of the classroom.

- Chemical engineering seniors have won the American Institute of Chemical Engineers national individual design competition six times and the national design safety award numerous times.
- Trine's Tau Alpha Omicron chapter of the American Criminal Justice Association annually wins regional and national awards for marksmanship, crime scene investigation, and physical agility.
- In 2017, Trine's softball team made history by earning its second trip to the NCAA Division III National Championships. The team has appeared in the NCAA postseason every year since 2008, hosting its first Super Regional championship in 2016.
- Trine's women's basketball and football teams have won the MIAA Conference championship and advanced to the NCAA Division III tournament each of the last two seasons.
- Trine's track and field program has sent at least two participants to national championship meets since the 2013–14 season, with an All-American honoree in every indoor and outdoor season since that date.
- During 2017-18, 56 Thunder student-athletes were recognized on all-conference teams. Trine boasted 157 student-athletes on the MIAA honor roll for having above a 3.5 grade-point average and lettering in a varsity sport.

Location

Trine is in Angola, the heart of northeast Indiana's scenic lake resort region, halfway between Chicago and Cleveland. Just a 45-minute drive from Indiana's second-largest city, Fort Wayne, Trine offers the safety and ease of a small-town environment, near some of the nation's most vital cities.

Majors and Degrees

The Allen School of Engineering & Technology awards Bachelor of Science degrees in biomedical, chemical and bioprocess, civil, electrical and mechanical engineering and design engineering technology.

The Ketner School of Business awards Bachelor of Science in business administration degrees with majors in accounting, business administration, golf management, management, marketing, and sport management. Associate's degrees are offered in accounting and business administration.

The Franks School of Education awards Bachelor of Science degrees in elementary, English, health and physical, mathematics, science, and social studies education. Dual licensure in special education/mild intervention is available with many of these majors.

The Jannen School of Arts and Sciences awards Bachelor of Arts degrees with majors in communication, English, general arts and sciences, and general studies (pre-legal and self-designated), and Bachelor of Science degrees with majors in criminal justice, mathematics and psychology. Associate's degrees are offered in arts, criminal justice and general studies.

The Rinker-Ross School of Health Sciences offers Bachelor of Science degrees in biochemistry, biology, chemistry, exercise science, forensic science, and sport and recreation; and pre–physician assistant, pre–physical therapy, and pre-medical professional tracks, as well as Master of Physician Assistant Studies and Doctor of Physical Therapy degrees. Rinker-Ross offers an associate's degree in science, with an Associate of Science in surgical technology planned for fall 2019.

The School of Computing, launching in 2019, will encompass current Trine programs in computer and software engineering as well as a revitalized computer science and information technology major.

The College of Graduate and Professional Studies awards associate's, bachelor's and master's degrees in 18 online programs. Graduate programs include a Master of Business Administration and Master of Science degrees in leadership, criminal justice, engineering management, and information studies.

Academic Programs

Students learn from professionals with advanced degrees and industry expertise, and get hands-on experience in laboratories stocked with state-of-the-art equipment. About 90 percent of Trine students complete an internship, co-op, or other experiential learning.

Trine University is accredited by the Higher Learning Commission and a member of the North Central Association (www.hlcommission.org; phone: 312-263-0456). Trine's programs in chemical engineering, civil engineering, computer engineering, electrical engineering, and mechanical engineering are accredited by the Engineering Accreditation Commission of ABET (111 Market Place, Suite 1050, Baltimore, Maryland 21202-4012; phone: 410-347-7700). All teacher preparation programs are accredited by the Council for the Accreditation of Educator Preparation (www.caepnet.org) and the Indiana Department Education/Office of Educator Licensing and Development (www.doe.ingov/licensing). The Ketner School of Business, Bachelor of Science in business administration program is accredited by the Accreditation Council for Business Schools and Programs (www.acbsp.org). Associate degree programs in accounting and business administration are also accredited.

The Doctor of Physical Therapy Program at Trine University is accredited by the Commission on Accreditation in Physical Therapy Education (CAPTE), 1111 North Fairfax Street, Alexandria, Virginia, 22314; phone: 703-706-3245; e-mail: accreditation@apta.org; website: http://capteonline.org).

The Accreditation Review Commission on Education for the Physician Assistant (ARC-PA) has granted Accreditation-Provisional status to the Trine University Physician Assistant Program. Accreditation-Provisional is an accreditation status granted when the plans and resource allocation, if fully implemented as planned, of a proposed program that has not yet enrolled students appear to demonstrate the program's ability to meet the ARC-PA Standards or when a program holding Accreditation-Provisional status appears to demonstrate continued progress in complying with the Standards as it prepares for the graduation of the first class (cohort) of students. Accreditation-Provisional does not ensure any subsequent accreditation status. It is limited to no more than five years from matriculation of the first class.

Enhanced Learning

Trine's Innovation One provides opportunities for students to work with business and industry. Innovation One, located in the Jim and Joan Bock Center for Innovation and Biomedical Engineering, provides expertise and services to businesses, organizations and schools to meet respective needs and goals, connecting business, industry and the community with the creativity, brainpower and enthusiasm of Trine University.

Off-Campus Programs

Trine's Career Services works with diverse companies to provide co-op and internship opportunities. Semesters of classroom study alternate with professional work experience, which can give students a competitive edge in the job market and offset college expenses. Often, co-ops and internships launch careers as they lead to full-time employment.

Academic Facilities

The John G. Best Hall of Science, home of the Rinker-Ross School of Health Sciences, contains classrooms and science laboratories. A $6.6 million, 26,000-square-foot addition opened in January 2017, housing seven laboratories, twelve offices and group study spaces.

The Jim and Joan Bock Center for Innovation and Biomedical Engineering houses laboratories to support the Allen School of Engineering & Technology and Innovation One. Experiential learning for students in all majors is also available through i1.

The Thomas L. Fawick Hall of Engineering, home to the Allen School of Engineering & Technology, features classrooms and laboratories, providing student access to technology from day one.

The Perry T. Ford Memorial Building, home of the Ketner School of Business, boasts technology-rich classrooms and a design that mimics a contemporary business setting.

The T. Furth Center for Performing Arts is home to Trine's music program and the Ryan Concert Hall is the venue for a variety of concerts, which include university instrumental and vocal ensembles, as well as nationally known entertainers like the Oak Ridge Boys, Michael Bolton, Wynonna Judd, Three Dog Night, Amy Grant, America, Kenny Rogers, and The Guess Who.

The Rick L. and Vicki L. James University Center is the hub for student activity, including a library stocked with computers, Fabiani Theatre, WEAX radio station, student health center, and the Whitney Commons dining hall.

William D. Shambaugh Hall, home of the Franks School of Education, offers a juvenile literature and school curriculum collection, kits, and audio-visual resource materials, as well as workspace and materials to support education students. An updated state-of-the-art classroom space features six digital screens, screen-casting software, enhanced wireless capabilities, new lighting, a large interactive screen, new seating options, new carpet and a new wall color scheme.

The Charles and Nancy Taylor Hall of Humanities houses the Department of Humanities & Communication as well as classrooms, the Wells Gallery, the Humanities Institute, the Fine Arts Library, and Wells Theater, home of the university's drama club.

Costs

Tuition for the academic year (two semesters) in 2019-20 is $32,330 ($34,880 for engineering). Room and standard meal plan (19 meals per week) for the academic year cost $11,110 (double occupancy).

Financial Aid

Financial aid may be awarded in the form of scholarships, grants, loans, or campus employment. Trine requires the Free Application for Federal Student Aid (FAFSA) and recommends submission by March 1.

Trine stands out in this area because:

- Ninety-four percent of undergraduate students receive some form of financial aid.
- More than $31 million is awarded in institutional aid.
- Average financial aid per student is $33,046.
- The school has been recognized for graduating students with the least amount of debt.

Faculty

Trine has 114 full-time faculty members; most have doctoral degrees and professional experience.

Student Government

The student senate is organized to provide funding and formulate policies for campus organizations. Each class elects representatives to the senate.

Admission Requirements

Graduation from an approved high school or equivalent preparation is required for admission. Selection is made without regard to race, religion, or gender. Applicants are required to take the ACT or SAT prior to approval for admission. Applicants' high school grade point average and class rank are also important factors.

Graduates of community or junior colleges and students who have attended other colleges and universities are eligible for transfer. Counselors work closely with those who wish to transfer to ensure a smooth transition to Trine. Credit may be allowed in subjects that parallel Trine programs, provided the student earned a C or better in the course.

Application and Information

Trine University's online application is free and available at trine.edu. The university admits applicants on the basis of scholastic achievement and academic potential. Admission decisions are made on a rolling basis. Applicants are notified of their status within two weeks of receipt of their application, high school record and test scores. Transfer students must also submit an official copy of their college transcript(s).

Interested students and their parents are encouraged to visit the campus. Contact the Office of Admission to make arrangements.

For additional information, students should call or write:

Office of Admission
Trine University
One University Avenue
Angola, Indiana 46703-1764
Phone: 260-665-4100
800-347-4878
E-mail: admit@trine.edu
Website: trine.edu
facebook.com/trineadmissions
youtube/trineuniversity

Trine University provides a safe, comfortable environment for learning and intellectual growth as well as for athletics and diverse activities.

UNITED STATES MERCHANT MARINE ACADEMY
KINGS POINT, NEW YORK

The Academy

The United States Merchant Marine Academy is a federal service academy that educates and trains students for careers as licensed Merchant Marine officers, who serve America's marine transportation and defense needs. With 95 percent of the world's products transported over water, these leaders are vital to the effective operation of our merchant fleet for both commercial and military transport during war and peace.

The Academy is known for providing rigorous education and training. In fact, its bachelor degree program contains more credit hours than programs in any other federal service academy. This challenging coursework is augmented by the Academy's Sea Year experience, which affords midshipmen (students) the opportunity to acquire hands-on, real-world experiences aboard working commercial vessels sailing to ports around the world. Midshipmen who master this demanding curriculum earn three credentials: a Bachelor of Science degree, a United States Coast Guard license, and an officer's commission in the United States armed forces.

All midshipmen, in return for attendance in the academy's four-year program at taxpayer expense, must serve five years in the maritime industry or on active duty as an officer in the armed forces. Commissions may be obtained in the U.S. Army, U.S. Marine Corps, U.S. Navy, U.S. Air Force, or U.S. Coast Guard. Service as an officer on active duty in the National Oceanic and Atmospheric Administration (NOAA) is also acceptable. If graduates choose the maritime industry, they have a U.S. Navy Reserve obligation of eight years. Graduates must also maintain a current (valid) license as either a Third Mate or Third Assistant Engineer (or higher) for six years after graduation.

The Academy's Regiment of Midshipmen numbers approximately 950 young men and women who represent every state of the Union as well as U.S. Trust Territories and Possessions. The size of the student body contributes to a true sense of camaraderie among the members of the Regiment and permits the Academy to maintain an excellent student-teacher ratio.

The U.S. Merchant Marine Academy is accredited by the Middle States Commission on Higher Education (MSCHE), 3624 Market Street, Philadelphia, Pennsylvania 19104, 267-284-5000, http://www.msche.org. Both the Marine Engineering Systems and Marine Engineering & Shipyard Management curricula are accredited by the Accreditation Board for Engineering and Technology (ABET), 111 Market Place, Suite 1050, Baltimore MD 21202-4012, http://www.abet.org.

Location

The U.S. Merchant Marine Academy is located in Kings Point, New York in the northeastern region of the United States. It's situated on Long Island's "Gold Coast" neighborhood and provides a stunning view of New York City's skyline.

The academy's 82-acre campus features the beautiful American Merchant Marine Museum, a swimming pool along the waterfront, numerous academic buildings including Gibbs Hall, with its state-of-the-art engineering and science laboratories, Yocum Sailing Center, and an interfaith chapel.

Degree Programs

A sound college education is the foundation for every profession in our society and the mariner's profession is no exception. The academic curriculum at the Academy provides each midshipman with the broad college education required for a Bachelor of Science degree, a U. S. Coast Guard License as Merchant Marine Officer, and a Commission as Ensign in the Navy Reserve.

As part of the Bachelor of Science curriculum, midshipmen complete core courses, courses in their majors, and elective courses as well as hands-on experience at sea. Core courses provide in-depth knowledge in the following academic and professional areas: comparative literature and history, English, leadership and ethics, mathematics, and naval science.

The Academy offers the following five majors:

- Marine Transportation—emphasizes nautical science and maritime business management.
- Maritime Logistics and Security—emphasizes nautical science, managing complex maritime and intermodal supply chains, security challenges facing the marine transportation system.
- Marine Engineering—emphasizes shipboard engineering operations.
- Marine Engineering Systems—emphasizes design of shipboard systems and machinery.
- Marine Engineering and Shipyard Management—emphasizes the management of shipyards, and the production and repair of marine vehicles.

The Academy challenges its midshipmen intellectually and physically. Freshman students make the transition from high school graduate to Academy midshipman. In their first few months, they learn many new terms, the quality of endurance, how to perform under pressure, and most importantly, how to successfully manage time. During sophomore year, and again during junior year, midshipmen are sent to sea for practical shipboard training amounting to nearly 300 days. Aboard ship, sailing the trade routes of the world, they learn the value of self-reliance and initiative as they gain firsthand experience in the mariner's environment. In senior year, they fine-tune the skills learned in the classroom and at sea as they prepare to enter the professional world.

Career Opportunities

Graduates of the U.S. Merchant Marine Academy are fully equipped to take advantage of the many career opportunities that await them. They typically serve at sea or ashore as Merchant Marine officers or as commissioned officers in the armed forces.

Employers are eager to hire them because of their exemplary character, hands-on experience, leadership and problem-solving skills, professional expertise, and self-discipline. Nearly 100 percent of the Academy's graduates secure well-paying jobs within three to six months of graduation.

Students acquire the tools to achieve long-term career success. A Standard and Poor's report ranked the US. Merchant Marine Academy eighteenth among the top 550 colleges and universities whose alumni include directors of U.S. companies, presidents, and vice presidents (in proportion to total number of graduates).

Facilities

The campus includes multiple buildings, state-of-the-art classrooms and labs, dining facilities, recently renovated barracks (dorms), and recreational and physical fitness buildings. There are also extensive waterfront facilities and activities.

The Academy library is dedicated to providing information and services to further the education process at Kings Point by offering resources in a variety of formats from traditional to high tech. Easy access to resources quickly provides the reference, research, and reading material needed to support the curriculum.

Costs and Financial Aid

The federal government covers the cost of tuition, books, room, board, and uniforms. Midshipmen pay for an Academy-approved personal laptop, activity fees, licensing fees, personal and transportation expenses, and personal services (such as tailoring, laundry, personal grooming, etc.).

The Academy doesn't offer traditional institutional aid such as scholarships. However, all students, no matter their income levels, are eligible for federal financial aid. They can also seek scholarships from private sources.

Faculty

Faculty members are highly skilled scholars, mentors, and leaders. They help create a supportive, stimulating, and rigorous learning environment where students can reach their full potential.

Student Life

The Academy's 950 midshipmen lead regimented yet interesting and enjoyable lives. During the academic year, they follow a daily schedule Monday through Friday which includes meal times, room inspections, classes, athletics, and study time. On Friday afternoons and Saturday mornings they participate in inspections and regimental parades.

Midshipmen have access to more than 40 registered student organizations that host a variety of events and programs. They can also take on leadership roles such as campus activities board member, morale or diversity training officer, or petty officer. USMMA has 27 varsity and intramural sports available, including basketball, baseball, cross-country, football, lacrosse, swimming, track and field, volleyball, and wresting.

There are also plenty of opportunities to venture off campus to enjoy the culture of New York City (which is only 20 minutes away) and Long Island.

Admission Requirements

To be eligible to enter the Academy, candidates must be at least 17 years of age and no older than 24; be a citizen of the United States; meet the physical, security, suitability, and character requirements necessary for commission in the U.S. Navy Reserve; obtain a Congressional nomination to the Academy; submit a completed application; and qualify scholastically.

Candidates should pursue studies in high school that will prepare them for the Academy's rigorous program. Candidates must have satisfactorily completed their high school education at an accredited secondary school or its equivalent. They must have earned at least 16 units of credit: 4 units must be in English; 3 units in mathematics (from algebra, trigonometry, pre-calculus, and/or calculus); and 1 unit in physics or chemistry with a laboratory. The Academy strongly recommends that candidates take four years of mathematics and both physics and chemistry. Courses in mechanical drawing and machine shop are also desirable.

All candidates are required to take either the SAT or ACT test. The current minimum qualifying scores for the SAT Reasoning Test are 29 Reading and 580 for Math. The current minimum qualifying scores for the ACT are 23 English and 24 Math; applicants must also achieve a minimum composite score of 23. Each of the three minimum scores must be achieved individually in order to meet the Academy's minimum test score requirements.

Satisfactory completion of the Candidate Fitness Assessment (CFA) is required for admission. Passing results must be received in the Admissions Office by the February 1 application deadline. The CFA is a test of strength, agility, speed and endurance. The examination may be administered by a J/ROTC instructor, physical education teacher, coach, or any commissioned/noncommissioned officer other than a parent/guardian.

Candidates must be nominated to the Academy by a U.S. Representative or Senator. The ideal time for a candidate to apply for a nomination is in May of junior year in high school.

Application and Information

Students may begin applying to the Academy on May 1 of their junior year of high school. The application deadline is February 1 of the year they wish to enter the Academy. U.S. candidates for admission to the Academy must apply online; however, all required documents must be received in the Admissions Office by February 1.

For more information, prospective candidates may contact:
Admissions Office
United States Merchant Marine Academy
300 Steamboat Road
Kings Point, New York 11024
United States
Phone: 866-546-4778
Fax: 516-773-5390
E-mail: admissions@usmma.edu
Website: https://www.usmma.edu/

UNIVERSITY OF CALIFORNIA SAN DIEGO

UC San Diego

SAN DIEGO, CALIFORNIA

The University

The University of California San Diego—one of the world's top public research universities—is defined by a culture of risk-taking, collaboration, and innovation. Established in 1960, UC San Diego has been shaped by exceptional scholars who aren't afraid to look deeper, challenge expectations, and transform conventional wisdom in order to make our world better. Our founders had one criterion—to be distinctive—and bold experimentation has been the norm since day one.

The 1,200-acre campus is located on a sunny cliff overlooking the Pacific Ocean in the La Jolla neighborhood of San Diego, Calif.—the heart of one of the most densely concentrated innovation hubs in the nation. The campus is consistently ranked among the top 10 best public universities in the nation and top 15 in the world for research, teaching, public service, and post-graduation career prospects.

The university is organized into six undergraduate residential colleges, five academic divisions—Arts and Humanities, Biological Sciences, Jacobs School of Engineering, Physical Sciences, and Social Sciences—and five professional and graduate schools, including the Rady School of Management, School of Global Policy and Strategy, School of Medicine, Scripps Institution of Oceanography/School of Marine Sciences, and Skaggs School of Pharmacy and Pharmaceutical Sciences.

Over the last 50 years, 16 Nobel laureates have taught on campus. Over 160 current faculty are members of one or more of the prestigious national academies, while numerous others have garnered such awards as the McArthur Fellowship, National Medal of Science, Pulitzer Prize, Fields Medal, and Academy Award.

The university's 190,000 alumni are making an impact, including Kate Rubins, NASA astronaut who recently conducted human health studies in space; Nathan East, one of the most recorded bassists in history; DJ Patil, who is unleashing data to transform how we solve the world's biggest problems; and Albert Lin, a high-tech tomb hunter using laser imaging across the globe.

UC San Diego is committed to achieving inclusive excellence. Through innovative programs and life-changing scholarships, the campus offers access to higher education for students from all backgrounds, including first generation students and those from underserved communities. The university was recently ranked fourth in the nation for providing access to low-income students by *The New York Times*. In addition, UC San Diego graduates the largest percentage of women with STEM degrees, and has been named one of the top 10 most LGBTQ-friendly public universities.

Students are invited to engage in open dialogue, develop leadership skills, and learn about social issues at six campus community centers. In addition, students can take part in numerous cultural events and celebrations of diversity, from Raza Awareness Week to the annual UC San Diego Powwow and Martin Luther King Jr. Parade and Day of Service.

Majors and Degrees

The campus offers more than 100 undergraduate degree programs spanning five academic divisions, as well as master's and doctoral degree programs in 60 academic departments. A complete list of undergraduate degree programs can be found at http://ucsd.edu/academics-detail.html.

Academic Programs

UC San Diego's academic programs, taught by highly regarded scholars, prepare students to stand out and lead change. All UC San Diego undergraduates can find their community thanks to the college system, patterned after the small-college feel of Cambridge and Oxford. Each of the university's six colleges have distinct neighborhoods, residence facilities, staff, traditions, and general education requirements. Every UC San Diego undergraduate is assigned to one of six colleges when they are admitted to UC San Diego; furthermore, college assignments are not based on major. Students may select from the full range of available majors regardless of college assignment.

A student-centered university, UC San Diego offers supplemental learning, tutoring, and career development programs to equip students to thrive academically. Through services offered at the Teaching + Learning Commons, students develop transferable skills, participate in peer-facilitated study groups, and are matched with experiential learning projects.

In addition, nearly a dozen makerspaces and incubators offer resources, training, and mentorship opportunities to help students launch their big ideas. At The Basement, students gain business guidance and funding ideas from alumni and industry mentors. For hands-on projects, the EnVision Arts and Engineering Maker Studio contains tools to design, fabricate, and prototype, including 3-D printers, welding stations, and laser cutters.

Students apply their learning outside the classroom through faculty-mentored research, service learning projects, study abroad and professional internships. Undergraduates can explore opportunities through the Research Experience and Applied Learning Portal, get matched with real-world training opportunities through the Academic Internship Program, and become immersed in the culture of another country through the Study Abroad Office.

Costs

For the 2019–20 academic years, tuition and fees for California residents is $14,429; nonresidents pay a supplemental tuition of $28,992. The estimated cost of on-campus housing and meals is $14,304. Books and supplies are estimated at $1,138.

Financial Aid

For prospective students and their families, budgeting, costs and how to pay for college can seem complicated. UC San Diego offers information and advising to help students understand the big picture and the bottom line. Students may utilize a wide array of grants, loans, scholarships, veteran's benefits, work-study, and other means to finance their education.

Student Life

Life at UC San Diego is far from ordinary. In 2018, UC San Diego was ranked first nationally among "Top 10 Surf Colleges" by *Surfer* magazine. The campus features a competitive surf team, classes on the physics of surfing as well as opportunities to learn how to ride the salty swells.

When students aren't immersed in the sea, they unwind at one of dozens of campuswide events, including Triton Fest, a month-long fall kickoff experience that has featured a haunted trail, go-kart racing, and outdoor movie night; Winter Game Fest, the largest student-run gaming festival on the West Coast; and the Sun God Festival, a day-long carnival and concert.

The university features nearly 500 student organizations on campus, ranging from academic-focused and pre-professional groups to social and cultural clubs as well as spiritual and service groups. There are also more than 40 Greek organizations focused on academic excellence, service and leadership. In addition, UC San Diego students are very active in their community through a number of co-curricular community service programs; more than 70 student organizations have a primary focus on service. On average, nearly 20,000 UC San Diego students complete more than 3 million hours of change-making community service each year.

UC San Diego's Triton Athletics includes 23 intercollegiate sports teams, which have garnered 30 national championship titles. The university is reclassifying into NCAA Division I, and will begin a full Big West Conference competitive slate in the 2020–21 academic year. Facilities include a 5,000-seat arena, ballpark, aquatic center with two Olympic-sized pools, and a state-of-the-art athletic performance center. Students can also take part in dozens of sports clubs and intramural leagues, choose from hundreds of recreation classes, and venture into the wild with the campus's Outback Adventures.

Within the six residential colleges, students bond over shared classes and annual events, from the summertime watermelon drop—a fruity physics experiment—to the 1960s-inspired Muirstock concert and the annual chocolate festival. In addition, transfer students find community in the Village Apartments, comprised of 13 buildings dedicated to transfer student housing, including two high rises with ocean views; while graduate students have the option to reside in one of six housing communities on or nearby campus, with amenities for couples and students with children.

UC San Diego is an ever-evolving campus, with big transformational plans over the next five years to accommodate the growing needs of the university. New construction includes the arrival of light rail transit in 2021; the Torrey Pines Living and Learning Neighborhood, a mixed-use community with student housing and state-of-the-art academic facilities; and an Innovation and Design Center, a hub for creativity, collaboration, and entrepreneurship.

Admission Requirements

UC San Diego looks for students at the freshman level who are well-prepared to succeed in a rigorous and challenging academic setting. Admission is highly competitive and applicants must exceed the minimum requirements. Every application, including the personal insight questions, is reviewed by a minimum of two individuals.

In addition to the 14 factors that are detailed on the University of California admissions website, freshman applicants must earn a high school diploma (or equivalent); complete a rigorous array of college preparatory classes with a C grade or better (detailed on the university's website); earn a GPA of 3.0 or better (California residents) or 3.4 or better (nonresidents); submit scores from either ACT Plus Writing, SAT Reasoning Test with critical reading, math, and writing; answers to UC San Diego's Personal Insight Questions; and a portfolio for students who want to major in history, literature, music, philosophy, theatre and dance, and visual arts. Meeting these requirements does not guarantee admission. Students admitted to UC San Diego exceed UC admission requirements.

Application and Information

The University of California application (available online) must be submitted by November 30. In December, applicants will receive an email that confirms receipt of their application. In January, applicants will receive instructions on how to log into UC San Diego's application status portal. The FAFSA or California Dream Act application must be filed by March 2. Freshman admission decisions will be posted by the end of March.

UC San Diego receives more than 90,000 freshman applications each year. Successful applicants must exceed minimum UC admission requirements. Enrollment goals are established annually. The campus does not select students on the basis of academic major or choice of UC San Diego undergraduate college.

For more information, prospective students may contact:

Office of Admissions
University of California San Diego
9500 Gilman Drive
La Jolla, California 92093
Phone: 858-534-4831
Fax: 858-534-5629
E-mail: admissionsreply@ucsd.edu
Website: www.ucsd.edu

UC San Diego Geisel Library

COLLEGE CLOSE-UPS

UNIVERSITY OF COLORADO BOULDER

BOULDER, COLORADO

University of Colorado Boulder

The University

The University of Colorado Boulder (CU Boulder) is a dynamic community of scholars and learners situated on one of the most spectacular college campuses in the country. CU Boulder is one of thirty-four U.S. public institutions belonging to the prestigious Association of American Universities (AAU) and has an established reputation for world-class teaching, research, and service to the global society.

At the cornerstone of the university experience are CU Boulder's innovative academic programs, hands-on opportunities, and rigorous coursework that will prepare students for a complex global society. Within the supportive learning community, students will interact with world-renowned faculty—which include Nobel laureates, MacArthur "genius grant" fellows, U.S. Professor of the Year awardees and National Medal of Science winners—who listen, question and help students refine their ideas to develop a broad understanding of the world, strong leadership skills and an enhanced ability to think critically.

CU Boulder offers more than 110 undergraduate and graduate programs; 84 bachelor's majors; 34 concurrent bachelor's/master's degree programs; more than 30 minors and 29 certificate programs; 11 research institutes and nearly 90 research centers. More than 2,000 undergraduate students are directly involved in faculty research.

With hands-on experience, world-class education and the ability to think critically, globally and creatively, CU Boulder graduates benefit from a strong salary potential, high employment rates and the opportunity to find and excel in a career they are passionate about.

Location

Students at CU Boulder get to live in spectacular surroundings and learn in a campus environment of extraordinary opportunities.

The city of Boulder is a fitting home for this institution. It's known as the number-one place for entrepreneurs (Livability,2017), the number one mid-sized metro area in the nation (Amer. Institute for Economic Research, 2017) and the top metro area for female entrepreneurship (Fast Company, 2015). Ranked the number-one college town in America (American Institute of Economic Research, 2017) and smartest city in America (Bloomberg, 2017), Boulder is known as one of the best places to live because of its beautiful setting, its 45,000 acres of open space, and its lively atmosphere.

Home to approximately 100,000 residents, Boulder has a mild, dry climate with more than 300 days of sunshine per year. Over 300 miles of bike lanes, bike paths, bike routes, designated shoulders and paths in and around Boulder, as well as a convenient bus system, provide excellent options for getting around town.

Majors and Degrees

CU Boulder has eight colleges, schools and programs. Amongst them, CU Boulder offers more than 3,900 academic courses across 150 fields of study, enabling students to create an academic experience that is unique.

College of Arts and Sciences: The oldest and largest college at CU Boulder and intellectual core of the university, conducting research, scholarship, creative work and education in more than 60 fields. CU Boulder's research generates new knowledge, solving some of the world's most critical problems. The College offers 50 majors, 25 minors and 10 certificate programs; there are 10 different residential academic programs available to students during their first year of studies.

College of Engineering and Applied Science: The top-ranked engineering programs in Colorado and the entire Rocky Mountain region are found in this college, with a full range of degree programs that emphasize hands-on, active learning and a tradition of research excellence. Engineers Without Borders began at CU in 2000, and has since grown to 206 chapters in 34 countries.

College of Media, Communication and Information (CMCI): Students learn and prepare to be leaders in the ever-changing information society. CMCI students and faculty think across boundaries, innovate around emerging problems and create culture that transcends convention. CU offers six student media outlets and six affiliated centers and labs.

College of Music: CU Boulder is the home of one of the country's top public music programs. A talented and active faculty of musicians, composers and scholars teach an impressive series of programs, ranging from performance to music theory. The college offers 7 degree plans and more than 23 fields of study. The College of Music's library contains more than 150,000 volumes, scores, recordings and periodicals.

Leeds School of Business: Students can earn undergraduate, master's and doctoral degrees from the top-ranked Colorado business school, also one of the best business schools in the Rocky Mountain and Midwest regions. Leeds has several points of pride: 88 percent of internships are paid; 92 percent of 2016 graduates were in a job within three months of graduation; and about 200 students annually take part in the Leeds First-Year Global Experience program (offered in 11 countries); and 8 global initiative programs give students the opportunity to travel and learn about international business.

School of Education: CU Boulder is a proud national leader in the field of education, working professionally with colleagues and communities to deliver outstanding undergraduate and graduate programs for classroom teachers and future scholars alike. More than half of the college's alumni teach in Colorado public schools. Students log many hours of field experience and in turn, 98.5 percent of teacher licensure graduates are employed or in graduate school within a year.

Program in Environmental Design (ENVD): This program fosters an innovative interdisciplinary education to prepare students for practice and advanced study in numerous design-based fields, as well as to apply design thinking to a variety of other possible careers. ENVD houses a state-of-the-art design fabrication lab that includes woodworking tools, metal welding and shaping equipment.

Preprofessional Study Programs in Health and Law: These programs prepare undergraduate students for future advanced education in their field of interest through specialized advising, resources and networking opportunities—all of which help to determine if it is the right fit.

Academic Programs

CU Boulder offers students a wealth of opportunities to engage in hands-on learning and scholarly research in fields as diverse as literature and biology. Programs include the Undergraduate Research Opportunities Program, which funds research projects and scholarly and creative work; the Engineering Active Learning Program, which gives students the chance to gain hands-on engineering experience while forging professional connections through internships; the Biological Sciences Initiative Scholars in STEM Undergraduate Research, which helps students gain research experience as paid research assistants; and the Herbst Program of Humanities for engineering students, a unique program that encourages engineering students to develop thinking skills that incorporate humanities disciplines.

A group of programs, referred to as Top Scholars, is designed to enhance the educational opportunities for high-achieving students who are seeking the challenge of becoming more critical and analytical thinkers.

The CU LEAD Alliance and Scholarship Program is a set of academic learning. LEAD stands for Leadership, Excellence, Achievement and Diversity, and the students, faculty and staff in these communities work together to help students from diverse and underrepresented backgrounds succeed at CU Boulder.

Off-Campus Programs

Studying abroad is a unique opportunity for students to learn from other cultures, enhance their resumes, travel the world and grow as individuals. Education Abroad gives students the chance to earn academic credit while taking classes in another country. The Education Abroad Office administers 400 CU Boulder sponsored programs in 64 countries. More than 1,300 students study through CU Boulder programs annually.

Costs

Estimated tuition, fees, on-campus housing (double room), and meals (19 per week) for the 2018–19 academic year for Colorado residents ranges from $28,750 to $34,054, based on course of study. The totals for nonresidents ranges from $53,504 to $56,802, based on course of study.

In April 2016, the University of Colorado Board of Regents approved a four-year guarantee of tuition and mandatory fee costs for undergraduate resident and nonresident students. The purpose of this guarantee is to provide financial predictability for students and families to understand the required costs each year. The CU Boulder Guarantee will allow students and families to understand not just first-year tuition and mandatory fee costs, but the cost of fees throughout four years of study.

Financial Aid

Approximately 17,500 undergraduate students received over $305 million in federal, state and university aid in 2017–18. Of that total, almost $185 million was in the form of grants, scholarships and work-study. Prospective students are encouraged to complete the Free Application for Federal Student Aid (FAFSA) by February 15 to ensure full consideration for limited funds. The FAFSA is available starting October 1 and must be completed each year. Incoming students are automatically considered for some scholarships, but more are available via the CU Boulder Scholarship Application between October 1 and February 15.

Faculty

CU Boulder and its nationally and internationally ranked faculty have built a global reputation for outstanding teaching, research and creative work across more than 150 academic fields. CU Boulder faculty members are leaders in their fields, but are also dedicated to working closely with undergraduate students. Among faculty members, there are: the 2004 and 2013 National Professor of the Year; 5 Nobel Laureates; 9 recipients of MacArthur Fellowships (also known as the "genius grant"); 19 Rhodes Scholars; 89 faculty who are part of the National Academies of Science, Arts and Sciences, Engineering, or Education; and more than 100 Fulbright fellows. The student to faculty ratio is 18:1.

Student Life

Estimated CU Boulder's inclusive community offers many ways to get involved and make lifelong friends. CU Boulder has one of the most active college campuses in the nation, where recreation, sports and student groups play a key role in the campus experience. More than 3,500 students are enrolled in Residential Academic Programs and Living and Learning communities. CU Boulder has 33 competitive club sports, including crew, hockey, snowboarding and swimming, while 12+ intramural sports provide opportunity for campus competition in sports like broomball, inner-tube water polo and flag football.

Students also have the opportunity to serve the greater good through volunteerism and civic engagement, whether it's around the world or across the street. More than 6,000 students serve each year through the CU Boulder Volunteer Resource Center.

Admission Requirements

CU Boulder's mission is to enroll an incoming class of highly qualified, intellectually curious and actively involved students who have demonstrated high levels of maturity and personal integrity as well as a commitment to serving their communities. While admission is competitive, applicants will be considered on an individual basis relative to a prediction of academic success in the college to which they apply.

The primary factor in admission decisions is academic achievement: classroom performance in core academic and prerequisite courses, the rigor of those courses and the best combination of scores on the SAT or ACT.

While academics and test scores play a large role in admission decisions, secondary factors, such as school and community involvement, also help assess the overall qualities of an applicant.

Application and Information

Materials needed for application include the online application, a $50 application fee, a personal essay and writing supplement, a letter of recommendation, high school transcript or equivalency and SAT or ACT scores. The Early Action deadline is November 15 and the Regular Decision deadline is January 15.

Office of Admissions
University of Colorado at Boulder
552 UCB
Boulder, Colorado 80309
Phone: 303-492-6301
Fax: 303-492-7115
E-mail: admissions@colorado.edu
Website: http://www.colorado.edu

UNIVERSITY OF DENVER

DENVER, COLORADO

The University

Since its founding in 1864, the University of Denver (DU) has grown into one of the West's premier private universities. As the oldest private university in the Rocky Mountain region, the University is home to not only a top-ranked undergraduate program, but also to a number of world-renowned research centers and professional programs, including the Josef Korbel School of International Studies, the Sturm College of Law, the Daniel Felix Ritchie School of Engineering & Computer Science and the Daniels College of Business. A student-centered research university with a liberal arts philosophy, DU develops knowledge in students through classroom academics, hands-on educational experiences and global learning adventures, putting students on the path toward lives and careers that will shape the world.

The DU community brings together 5,801 traditional undergraduate students and 6,151 graduate students from 50 states and over 80 countries. In an environment that prizes innovation, cross-disciplinary study, and adventurous learning partnerships, students embark on a personalized educational journey inspired and framed by a spirit of exploration and openness. Whatever their backgrounds and majors, DU students are engaged and active, taking advantage of the region's many recreational and cultural opportunities—everything from world-class skiing and white-water rafting to award-winning professional theater at the Denver Center for the Performing Arts and alternative music shows at Red Rocks Amphitheatre. On campus, students attend performances at the three-venue Newman Center for the Performing Arts and cheer for the 17 varsity teams that compete in NCAA Division I Athletics at the Ritchie Center for Sports & Wellness. DU has claimed many athletic successes over the years including eight national hockey titles, one lacrosse title, several All-American gymnasts and 24 national championship skiing titles.

The University of Denver is accredited by the Higher Learning Commission. The Carnegie Foundation classifies the University of Denver as a Doctoral/ Research University–Extensive.

Location

The University of Denver is built to inspire. Nestled in the Denver metro area, the 130 acre campus is located just eight miles from bustling downtown Denver and 30 minutes from the Rocky Mountains. With 300 days of sunshine and beautiful views year-round, this is a place students are excited to call home. DU's tree-shaded campus is surrounded by pleasant urban neighborhoods offering coffee shops, retail stores, and diverse restaurants. The institution is located along a light-rail line and major bus lines, providing access to the city's arts districts, shopping centers, sports arenas, and an extensive network of parks. DU students can ride all public transportation for free, using their University-supplied CollegePass smart cards.

Majors and Degrees

Whether a student already has a career in mind or they're just exploring what moves them, DU has a program that will inspire them to make their mark. There are over 100 areas of study available to undergrads, and students can further match degrees with their passions with a minor or a concentration. Areas of study include the arts, business, computer science, engineering, humanities, international studies, mathematics, natural sciences, and social sciences. Students who are interested in pre-professional programs can choose from law, medical, dental, and veterinary programs that prepare them for professional study beyond their undergraduate degree.

In addition, the University offers 4+1 and 3+2 dual-degree programs that allow students to complete both a bachelor's and master's degree in five years or less. These dual-degree programs are offered in education, social work, computer science, engineering, accounting, art history, international studies, public policy, and geographic information science. There is also a six-year B.A. or B.S./J.D. program in conjunction with DU's Sturm College of Law.

Academic Programs

Undergraduate programs at the University operate on the quarter system and emphasize experiential, dynamic, and cross-disciplinary learning, providing students with the culture and tools to create a positive impact and make meaningful, lasting contributions to their communities and professions. The University will work with students to help them discover the programs they want to build their future around. Start with liberal arts coursework as well as major-related classes, then blend formal degree programs with professional education to launch an inspiring career. These foundational courses in mathematics and computer science, the arts and humanities, natural sciences, and social sciences (DU's Common Curriculum) ensures students have a wide base of knowledge upon graduation.

First-year students also enroll in a First-Year Seminar. Limited to a small cohort of around 20 students, these seminars focus on a topic that reflects the professor's research interests. This professor, who serves as a mentor throughout the student's first year, introduces the class to university-level work and inquiry, while also advising students on everything from time management to University procedures. The seminar is complemented by a two-quarter writing sequence that trains students to conduct research, construct arguments, and write persuasively for the academic setting. The University's emphasis on writing continues throughout the next three years, with upper-division writing-intensive classes across the disciplines. By the time they graduate, DU students have developed the communication skills that are essential for career success.

A DU education takes students out of the classroom and into communities where they can learn by making an impact. The academic programs incorporate real-world learning, connecting students with the professional environments they'll strive toward after graduation. Because the University believes in the value of hands-on learning, students are encouraged to collaborate with faculty members and peers on research projects and creative endeavors. Through the Partners in Scholarship (PinS) program, DU sponsors student work through grants that fund field studies, research trips, and special materials. At year's end, students share their research and findings at a special symposium for their peers.

Thanks to opportunities like these, the University's academic programs earn high marks from students. In the 2018 National Survey of Student Engagement (NSSE), first-year students and seniors at over 500 participating U.S. colleges and universities reported their satisfaction with their own campus. National results revealed that DU students reported significantly higher levels of satisfaction than the average of students at all other participating mid-size private schools for involvement in collaborative learning, quantitative reasoning, reflective and integrative learning, interaction with faculty members, and the quality of interactions on campus.

Global Opportunities

Studying abroad is an important part of the DU experience—a chance to immerse students in a new perspective and use that knowledge and understanding to strengthen their studies, their community and their career. The Office of International Education guides students through the entire process, from finding a program that meets their needs and goals, to applying, to working to ensure any health or safety concerns are addressed.

With more than 150 DU Partner Programs offered in over 50 countries, DU students find experiences that advance their current academic work and passions. The Cherrington Global Scholars program helps offset some of the significant costs of studying abroad on these programs, like roundtrip airfare and visa fees.

On average, just over 72 percent of all DU students participate, ranking the University 4th in the nation for the percentage of students studying abroad.

In addition to academics, students explore and surround themselves with new cultures and ideas while making connections with locals and other program participants. Prior to departure, students develop cross-cultural communication skills that help them maximize these experiences abroad in a required Exploring Global Citizenship course.

Academic Facilities

The University has invested hundreds of millions of dollars in new buildings and learning centers to ensure that students can prepare for the challenges awaiting them after graduation. These include the Robert and Judi Newman Center for the Performing Arts, home to the University's celebrated Lamont School of Music and host to a performing arts series known for its adventurous offerings; the Knoebel School of Hospitality Management, home to a full-production kitchen, a beverage-management center, a 120-person dining hall, a student-run coffee shop, and a student-faculty-staff commons; and the Anderson Academic Commons, which serves as the library and hub of the University with a central campus location, multimedia software support services, and a full complement of individual and group study areas and rooms. DU recently opened the Daniel Felix Ritchie School of Engineering and Computer Science, which allows dramatic expansion of both current programming and new STEM initiatives, including the Knoebel Center for the Study of Aging as well as the Sie Complex, part of the Korbel School of International Studies. Both facilities make use of state-of-the-art tools to enhance the ability of students to gain the knowledge and skills needed to excel in their careers.

With a state-of-the-art fitness center, a natatorium, a field house, two ice arenas, a gymnastics venue, a lacrosse stadium, a soccer stadium, and a tennis pavilion, the Ritchie Center for Sports and Wellness brings students and members of the Denver community together to exercise, try new sports, and cheer on the Pioneer athletic teams to victory.

Three new physical spaces are currently under construction as well —a Community Commons that brings the entire DU community together; a first-year residence hall that builds a sense of community from day one; and a Pioneer Career Achievement Center that connects students to DU's 140,000+ global alumni.

Cost of Attendance

For the 2019–20 academic year, tuition will be $51,336, fees are estimated at $1,179, and on-campus room and board costs are $13,437, for a total of $65,952. Because the University of Denver is a private institution, costs are the same for in-state and out-of-state students.

Financial Aid

The University of Denver offers two types of financial assistance to students: need-based aid, which includes scholarships, grants, loans, and work-study based on financial need; and merit-based awards, which include scholarships based on merit or special talent. Each year, the Financial Aid office awards over $156.6 million in need- and merit-based assistance to undergraduate students. About 84% of full-time DU undergraduates receive some form of financial assistance.

To recognize achievement in the classroom, the sports arena, leadership, and in music, theatre, and art, the University sponsors a number of merit- and talent-based scholarships. Although the requirements vary from scholarship to scholarship, most are renewable each year if the student maintains a specified minimum GPA. More information regarding scholarships can be found at http://www.du.edu/financialaid.

Need-based financial aid is computed using a number of factors, including family income, assets, size, and the number of family members attending college at the same time. DU utilizes both the CSS Profile and the Free Application for Federal Student Aid (FAFSA) to determine need-based aid. Need-based awards generally combine scholarships, grants, loans, and work-study opportunities from a variety of federal, state, and institutional sources. The financial aid offer may also include any competitive scholarships the student has been awarded at the point of admission. To help determine how much need- and merit-based aid might be available to a prospective student and his or her family, DU offers access to a comprehensive net price calculator, found at www.du.edu/estimator.

The priority deadline for applying for financial aid is November 15 for Early Action and Early Decision I applicants, and February 1 for Regular Decision and Early Decision II applicants. Because some financial aid funds are limited, students who complete their financial aid applications in a timely manner are more likely to maximize financial aid resources. Students who simultaneously complete both their application checklist as well as their financial aid applications will receive notification of both their admission decision and need-based award package (a student's financial aid package cannot be determined until they are officially admitted to DU). More information on applying for financial aid at DU is available at http://www.du.edu/financialaid.

Faculty

DU professors teach more than 99% of undergraduate courses, ensuring students work closely with faculty members and the intensity of the learning environment is maximized. The average class size is 22 students; 80% of undergraduate classes have fewer than 30 students and 95% of classes have fewer than 50 students.

Committed teachers, innovative researchers, and prolific publishers, University of Denver professors often include undergraduate students in their research projects and fieldwork. It is not uncommon for an undergraduate student to share publication credit with a professor or to participate in groundbreaking research with tangible, transformational benefits for humankind.

Student Government

At the University of Denver, the student population is represented by the Undergraduate Student Government (USG), whose elected representatives participate in the University's legislative process and communicate student interests to the administration. In addition, USG oversees the allocation of the student activities fee and the licensing of DU's 150-plus student organizations. In the past few years this group has worked extensively on matters ranging from sustainability to diversity and academic affairs to spirit on campus.

USG includes senators from each major, each geographic area (on-campus, off-campus), and each class (senior, junior, etc.). The USG Executive Board includes an advisor, graduate advisor, president, vice president, and a cabinet of members.

Admission Requirements

Admission to the University of Denver is selective. Students are evaluated individually on the basis of their academic record, test scores (when submitted, as DU recently became test-optional), essay, and recommendations. In making its admission decisions, the University seeks to foster an academic community of geographically, ethnically, and economically diverse learners. The admission committee seeks students who are committed to integrity, innovation, inclusiveness, leadership, academic excellence, and community engagement.

Applicants are required to submit either the Common Application or the DU Pioneer Application—both are posted on the DU website. In addition, applicants are required to submit their high school transcripts, an essay, and a high school counselor recommendation. If students wish to submit an ACT or SAT test score, that score will also be evaluated. Students may submit a teacher recommendation and/or a ZeeMee profile, although neither are required.

Application and Information

The University of Denver offers four application programs for first-year domestic students seeking fall quarter admission. Early Action (deadline of November 1) is a nonbinding program leading to an admission decision in mid-December. Early Decision I (also a November 1 deadline) is a binding program leading to an admission decision in early December. Regular Decision and Early Decision II (deadline of January 15 for both), which are nonbinding and binding respectively, are the final admission programs for fall quarter consideration. Regular Decision applicants and Early Decision II applicants receive their admission decision in early March.

To learn more about the University of Denver, students should contact:

Undergraduate Admission
University of Denver
2197 South University Boulevard
Denver, Colorado, 80208-9401
United States
Phone: 303-871-2036
E-mail: admission@du.edu
Website: http://www.du.edu/admission
http://www.youtube.com/uofdenver
http://www.facebook.com/uofdenveradmission
http://twitter.com/uofdenver

University of Denver

UNIVERSITY OF DUBUQUE

DUBUQUE, IOWA

UNIVERSITY *of* DUBUQUE

A Tradition of Professional and Theological Training

The University of Dubuque (UD) is a private, Presbyterian professional university that combines a broad study of liberal arts with hands-on experience. Students gain specialized knowledge and master particular skills within their major. Students develop critical abilities that serve them well in adapting to a changing world.

Located about 175 miles from Chicago, the University has been known throughout its 166-year history as a place of hope, opportunity, and promise for students coming from regional, national, and international locations.

UD is one of the most diverse campuses in the Midwest, representing students from 43 states and 22 countries. It is a college of community where Christian commitment, intellectual integrity, and academic excellence are the basis for learning. Students can adjust their mix of liberal arts and professional training in ways that suit their learning styles and that help achieve both personal and professional goals. More information is available online at http://www.dbq.edu/campuslife/officeofstudentlife.

Campus Setting and Surrounding Area

Situated on the Mississippi River where the borders of Wisconsin, Illinois, and Iowa meet, UD is located in Iowa's first city, Dubuque. This central location puts UD students within easy driving distance of cities such as Chicago, Illinois; Des Moines, Iowa; Madison, Wisconsin; and Rochester, Minnesota.

A lively cultural scene, Dubuque is home to the National Mississippi River Museum and Aquarium, the Dubuque Museum of Art, the Grand Opera House, the Dubuque Symphony Orchestra, and a variety of shops, restaurants, and event venues. The city boasts miles of trails for walking, hiking, biking, downhill and cross country skiing opportunities, and many Mississippi waterway and byway activities.

Surrounded by comfortable green spaces within a historic city, UD students enjoy the benefits of modern facilities. Since 1998, the University has invested over $300 million into new construction and renovations that integrate contemporary green spaces within historic architecture.

Required Freshman Courses

The first-year curriculum orients students into the rigor of upper-level course work, while building a community of new friends through the experiences they share with their peers. With the support of an enthusiastic community, new UD students are challenged to build upon their gifts through academic inquiry, social interactions, and spiritual exploration as they discover their place within a diverse campus community. Students and faculty together explore topics that influence global cultures within the context of the University's Christian tradition.

Undergraduate and Graduate Degrees at a Glance

The University of Dubuque developed Diamond, an education model that focuses all classroom learning around four key principles: academics, stewardship, vocation, and community and character. These features of Diamond set the standards for committed faculty and staff involvement, exciting and relevant course content, and inspirational spiritual guidance. Diamond helps students reach their full potential by promoting an environment that is student centered and individually focused. Students are prepared to manage change by building confidence, developing flexibility, and encouraging critical thinking.

The University's 14 departments outline the academic programs found within each area as well as options for interdisciplinary majors. UD also has options for individually designed majors and minors through consultation with academic advisers.

Undergraduate degrees within the Bachelor of Arts area of study include: criminal justice; dance; English; fine and performing arts; liberal studies; music; psychology; religious studies; sociology; sports marketing and management; and theatre.

Undergraduate degrees within the Bachelor of Business Administration field of study include: accounting, business administration, computer information systems, computer information technology, human resource management, and marketing.

Undergraduate degrees within the Bachelor of Science program include: aviation management; biology; communication; digital art and design; chemistry; digital forensics; elementary education; environmental science; flight operations; human health science; mathematics; natural and applied science; secondary education; nursing; pre-professional health science; philosophy; physical education; psychology; sociology; teacher education; and wellness and exercise science.

Graduates are eligible for certification where applicable. For example, the Bachelor of Science degree in Flight Operations is centered on a Pilot Training School certified under FAA 14 CFR Part 141, and prepares students for FAA certification (licensing) and ratings.

All students who complete the UD Teacher Education Program are eligible to apply for an Iowa Initial Teacher License.

Students who graduate with their Bachelor of Science in Nursing are eligible to take the licensure exam NCLEX (National Council [of State Boards of Nursing] Licensure Examination) to become registered nurses.

The University of Dubuque's academic strengths support and align with several prominent needs for graduate education both in the region and globally. Offered in a traditional semester-long course format, courses are taught by both University of Dubuque faculty as well as subject matter experts who are currently in the work world. Degrees include: Master of Arts in Communication, Master of Business Administration, Accelerated Adult MBA and MAC Degree (LIFE), Master in Physician Assistant Studies, and a Master of Arts in Christian Leadership.

The MBA degree gives students advanced business acumen with courses that integrate communication and knowledge management, finance, human capital, organizational management, and business strategy and modeling.

Research Fellowships

The Joseph and Linda Chlapaty Summer Research Fellowship and The Butler Fellowship are two examples of the research opportunities available to UD students. These fellowships help prepare undergraduate students for their postgraduate pursuits, no matter their discipline of study. Each year, over 30 upperclassmen are awarded a fellowship to conduct research over the course of a summer. The University of Dubuque works hard to ensure that these awards cover the costs of research supplies and travel, giving students free reign to explore and inquire within their area of study.

Heeding the Call to Theological Education and Service

The University of Dubuque Theological Seminary (UDTS), a seminary of the Presbyterian Church (U.S.A), is a vibrant and growing ecumenical community, with students and faculty from the Presbyterian Church (U.S.A), the United Methodist Church, the United Church of Christ, the Reformed Church of America, and a number of other denominations and cultures.

The seminary offers a variety of degrees in both residential and distance formats, along with unique programming options. UDTS is the only seminary in the Presbyterian Church (U.S.A) that is accredited by ATS to provide distance education programs, and is the only seminary that is part of a larger university.

UDTS offers three master's degrees: the Master of Divinity and the Master of Arts in Mission and Discipleship, in both residential and distance formats, and together with the larger university, the Master of Arts in Mission and Discipleship program which is offered completely online via distance education. Cooperative programs with the University include the 3/3, and 3/2 programs, along with the Young Adult Ministry Scholars (YAMS) program, which allows students to engage in ministry with young adults while earning either a Master of Divinity or Master of Arts in Mission and Discipleship at the same time. The YAMS program is a 100 percent tuition remission program.

Success Center Provides Every Kind of Help

The University's Academic Success Center connects students with the resources to achieve both academic and personal goals.

Services include individual tutoring, writing, disability accommodations, testing services, academic probation support services, English learning labs, math learning labs, peer-assisted learning study groups, and athletic study tables.

Student Life and Community Service

UD has four traditional residence halls and six apartment-style buildings for undergraduate students living on campus. Townhouses are available for seminary and graduate students.

Activities and events planned by over 60 clubs and organizations supplement students' academic life with valuable experience, fun, and friendship. Out-of-classroom programs provide opportunities for vocational growth, leadership training, community service, and personal development. Greek life also thrives at UD through numerous sororities and fraternities.

UD has been recognized nationally for its history of community service throughout the years. Students participate in service projects they plan both in the classroom and through co-curricular programs, fraternities or sororities, and in campus ministry.

Study Abroad Opportunities

UD Study-Abroad programs bring both long-term (semester) and short-term international experience to students. Students return, even from short study trips, with new knowledge about foreign societies and world viewpoints.

Costs

Tuition (based on a full academic year): $34,070; full-time student fees: $1,440; room and board: $9,780; room only: $4,860.

Academic and Career Guidance, Financial Aid, and ROTC

The University provides academic advising services that empower students to make informed decisions about their academic and professional aspirations. At the beginning of their first year, each student is assigned a Director of Advising who helps them plan their course schedules and enter the University with a platform for success. The University's Center for Vocation and Civic Engagement helps students direct their strengths to real-world experiences outside the college setting. The Center's staff guides students to discover their unique strengths and gifts, providing them with insight into their chosen vocation and directing them toward appropriate internships, potential employers, and possible graduate schools.

Eighty-five percent of UD's students receive financial assistance through scholarships, awards and grants, loans, or work-study programs.

An Army Reserve Officers' Training Corps (ROTC) program is available along with associated merit-based scholarships.

Faculty

UD faculty totals 216. The student-to-faculty ratio is 14:1.

Application Information

All applicants must submit their complete high school transcripts, an essay or personal statement, two letters of recommendation, and a $25 application fee. An average high school GPA of 2.5 is required for first-year students to be regularly admitted. UD offers rolling admissions.

For further information, prospective students should contact:

Robert D. Broshous
Associate Vice President and Dean of Admission
University of Dubuque
2000 University Avenue
Dubuque, Iowa 52001-5009
Phone: 563-589-3199
Fax: 563-589-3690
E-mail: admissns@dbq.edu
Website: http://www.dbq.edu

Heritage Center, the University's fine and performing arts, worship, and campus center, opened in May 2013.

UNIVERSITY OF LYNCHBURG FORMERLY LYNCHBURG COLLEGE

LYNCHBURG, VIRGINIA

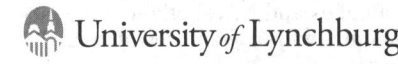

University *of* Lynchburg

The College

The University of Lynchburg is a vibrant learning community where students are empowered to discover their abilities and passions, connect with professors and the community, and achieve more than they dreamed possible. Formerly known as Lynchburg College (LC), a name change to the University of Lynchburg went into effect in the fall of 2018. In claiming its university status, Lynchburg remains committed to its student-centered approach to instruction and has expanded on its institutional priority for active, engaged, and relevant learning opportunities across disciplines and throughout the University's curricula.

A fully accredited, coeducational, residential university affiliated with the Christian Church (Disciples of Christ), The University of Lynchburg offers 50 undergraduate majors, 60 minors, and 14 pre-professional programs, all supported by a strong liberal arts foundation. The University's graduate studies program includes three doctoral degrees and 14 master's programs. The University of Lynchburg is nationally recognized by such publications as The Princeton Review's The Best 384 Colleges: 2019 edition, *U.S. News & World Report* (Best Regional Universities category and Best Colleges for Veterans in the South), and the John Templeton Foundation's Honor Roll of Character-Building Colleges. Lynchburg is one of the 40 colleges and universities featured in Loren Pope's *Colleges That Change Lives*.

The University of Lynchburg is home to 2,800 undergraduate and graduate students, representing 38 states and 19 foreign countries. The University community is largely residential with 75 percent of the full-time undergraduate student body living on campus.

Located in the heart of Lynchburg, Virginia on 250 acres, the beautifully landscaped campus is a showplace. Set against a backdrop of the majestic Blue Ridge Mountains, the campus comprises more than 40 buildings, many of Georgian-style architecture. Buildings form an elliptical pattern with Hopwood Hall at the east end of campus and Snidow Chapel at the west end, symbolically linking the principles of faith and reason, the vision of Dr. Josephus Hopwood, the University's founder. The Drysdale Student Center is the hub for student activities with dining options, fitness room, club and student organization meeting space, the Campus Store, and Veterans Center.

The University community is a busy place, with a wide variety of activities including service and honor organizations, such as the national Bonner Leader Program; more than 100 clubs and organizations; 12 fraternities and sororities; and opportunities to participate in dramatic productions, student publications, religious activities, and musical performances. The Outdoor Leadership Program provides adventure-based leadership and team-building opportunities for individuals and groups. Community service (www.lynchburg.edu/volunteering-and-service) is a distinguishing feature of University of Lynchburg students, staff, and faculty, who last year contributed more than 70,000 volunteer hours to the community. The University has been on the President's Higher Education Community Service Honor Roll for the past seven years.

The University of Lynchburg encourages students to develop and maintain a sustainable lifestyle and supports sustainability initiatives on campus that include recycling, climate commitment, a community bike project, energy upgrades, and free bus rides for students.

The intercollegiate athletic program (www.lynchburgsports.com/landing/index) provides opportunities for men and women to compete in 21 sports in the NCAA Division III and the Old Dominion Athletic Conference (ODAC). In 2014, Lynchburg's women's soccer team won the NCAA Division III championship, bringing home the first team national championship in the history of the institution. Lynchburg students can also play a variety of intramural and club sports. The Turner Athletic Facility includes exercise and fitness areas, a dance studio, and one of the top exercise physiology labs in Virginia.

Shellenberger Field, named for Lynchburg's legendary soccer coach, is state-of-the-art with artificial turf, an eight-lane track, night lighting, and a 3,000-spectator capacity stadium with chair and bleacher seating. The field hosts men's and women's soccer, lacrosse, track and field, field hockey, and intramural and club sports. Moon Field is home to Lynchburg's softball team and the track and field events of javelin, hammer, shot put, and discus. Fox Field is one of the best baseball fields in the ODAC, with batting cages, a press box, and seating for up to 1,000 spectators.

Location

The University of Lynchburg (www.lynchburg.edu) is located in central Virginia, 100 miles from Richmond, Virginia, 180 miles southwest of Washington, D.C., and 50 miles east of Roanoke. Air, bus, and railroad transportation place Lynchburg within easy reach of any urban center. Greater Lynchburg is a growing business and industrial center with a population of more than 240,000. The city is noted for its climate, culture, historic landmarks, and proximity to the Blue Ridge Mountains.

Majors and Degrees

The University of Lynchburg offers the bachelor of arts degree in: accounting, art (graphic design or studio art), athletic training, business administration, communication studies (convergent journalism, social influence, electronic media or public relations), economics (financial or general), English (literature or writing), French, history, international relations, liberal arts studies, management, marketing, music (instrumental or vocal education, instrumental or vocal performance), philosophy, political science, religious studies, sociology (cultural studies, deviance and crime, human services), Spanish, sports management, and theater. The Bachelor of Science degree is offered in: biology, biomedical science, chemistry, computer science, environmental science, exercise physiology, health promotion, human development and learning (elementary education or special education), mathematics, nursing, physics, and psychology. More information is available at www.lynchburg.edu/majors-and-minors.

Pre-professional and professional courses are available in art therapy, dentistry, engineering, forestry and wildlife management, law, library science, medicine, ministry and ministry-related occupations, museum studies, occupational therapy, optometry, pharmacy, physical therapy, and veterinary medicine.

Academic Programs

To be eligible for a degree, a student must complete at least 124 semester hours of college-level academic work with a grade point average of at least 2.0 or higher on all work undertaken in the major field.

The curriculum at the University of Lynchburg is divided into two general areas: general education requirements and the major, providing students with breadth and depth of study. General education requirements are selected from the broad disciplines of world literature, fine arts, philosophy, religious studies, mathematics, history, social science, laboratory science, foreign languages, and health and movement science. Additional hours are available for students to explore coursework in free elective hours of their choice or students may devote their free elective hours to a minor.

The University's Westover Honors Program (www.lynchburg.edu/academics/westover-honors-program) is designed to attract, stimulate, challenge, and fulfill academically gifted students through a challenging curriculum that promotes intellectual curiosity and independent thinking and places strong emphasis on creative problem solving.

Off-Campus Programs

Lynchburg students are encouraged to engage in foreign-study programs, particularly Lynchburg's study-abroad program (www.lynchburg.edu/study-abroad).

More than 1,000 internships (www.lynchburg.edu/career-services) are available locally, nationally, and internationally, and are integral parts of a Lynchburg education. As members of the Tri-College Consortium of Virginia, Lynchburg College, Randolph College, and Sweet Briar College maintain cooperative relationships for sharing facilities and offerings.

Academic Facilities

The University of Lynchburg has 23 computer labs with both PCs and Macs. New students may bring a computer of their own or utilize one of the many available on campus. All students are assigned an e-mail account and have access to the internet. All residence hall rooms are wired for network access and the intranet, which serves the University community. Wireless internet access is available in most areas of the campus.

The University has several active learning classrooms where students can write on the walls, collaborate in the cloud with the help of Chromecast-enabled monitors, and easily rearrange the room thanks to wheeled tables and chairs.

The Hobbs-Sigler Science Center provides an outstanding learning environment for students studying biology, chemistry, physics, biomedical sciences, environmental science, psychology, mathematics, and computer science. A cadaver lab, cutting-edge research labs, online weather station, GIS and remote sensing software, and digitizer are just some of the learning tools available. This facility is also used during the summer by the Virginia Governor's School for Math and Science to provide programming for selected high school students.

Schewel Hall, a $12-million classroom and laboratory facility, houses the School of Business and Economics, the Communication Studies program, foreign languages, and performing arts. This 67,000 square-foot facility includes technology-based classrooms, computer laboratories, and specialized teaching-learning settings, including a model stock exchange room, a digital darkroom, and a multimedia development center with television and recording studios. Sydnor Performance Hall provides an excellent venue for concerts, lectures, and other programs, with seating for 250 people.

The Daura Gallery (www.lynchburg.edu/daura-gallery) is the major repository of more than 1,000 works of Pierre Daura, the Catalan-American artist for whom the Gallery is named. Each year, The Daura Gallery features traveling exhibitions throughout the academic year and is the site for the Senior Art Show where selected student works are exhibited.

The Claytor Nature Study Center located on nearly 500 acres in nearby Bedford County provides an outdoor classroom and laboratory for hands-on, field-based environmental study and research. Donated to the institution by the late A. Boyd Claytor III, a member of the Lynchburg Board of Trustees, the property features lakes, woodlands, wetlands, grasslands, rare plants, formal gardens, a primitive campground, and three miles of hiking trails. The land is now managed for environmental conservation and restoration through agreements with the Virginia Outdoors Foundation and the USDA's Natural Resources Conservation Service. The A. Boyd Claytor III Education and Research Facility, a 7,700 square-foot multipurpose building, offers Lynchburg students and regional K–12 students and teachers an ideal location for learning with seminar, laboratory, classroom, conference, and retreat space.

The Belk Astronomical Observatory sits at one of the highest points of the Claytor Center property (approximately 960 feet above sea level) and is one of the most publicly accessible dark sky observatories in Virginia. The observatory features an RC Optical Systems 20-inch (0.51 meter) Truss Ritchey-Chrétien telescope with a 177-square-foot dome housing, and an observation deck equipped with 12 piers for mounting smaller telescopes. The control room is equipped with instrumentation that allows Lynchburg to conduct extensive stellar and planetary research and pursue astronomical research with other regional colleges and universities.

The Chandler Eco-Lodge, a 16-bed facility at Claytor, provides overnight accommodations for students and researchers who wish to study outside the classroom. The 2,100 square-foot lodge is built with energy-efficiency and low-impact design and includes a constructed wetland to handle wastewater.

Costs

Total charges for resident students for the 2019–20 session are $52,140: $38,720 tuition, $11,450 room and board, and $970 student fees (www.lynchburg.edu/undergraduate-admission/tuition-fees).

Financial Aid

The University of Lynchburg administers a financial aid program of more than $40 million annually. These resources are awarded to students for meritorious achievement and/or for demonstrated need. The University of Lynchburg offers academic scholarships (www.lynchburg.edu/financial-aid/scholarships) that range from $10,000 to $22,000 and are based on performance and accomplishments at the high school or community university level. In addition, the University offers scholarship competitions with awards ranging from $1,000 to $5,000, which are awarded in conjunction with other academic scholarships. The competitions are based upon academic performance, leadership, community service and talent. These awards are renewable each year until the student graduates, as long as the recipient maintains a qualifying minimum academic average each year. Students are identified to receive these scholarships through the admission application; no separate application is necessary. Free early aid estimates are available for students. More than 98 percent of last year's entering class received academic and/or need-based financial aid. The average amount of aid received was $37,000.

To determine eligibility for need-based financial aid, the student should complete the Free Application for Federal Student Aid (FAFSA), which may be obtained at most high schools and at the University. The FAFSA results determine the student's eligibility for federally funded grants and loans and other support such as work-study opportunities. In addition, students from Virginia are eligible to apply for the Virginia Tuition Assistance grant.

Faculty

The University of Lynchburg's faculty members are outstanding scholars who are leaders in their disciplines. Of the 190 full-time members, 83 percent hold the doctorate or terminal degree in their fields. The student-faculty ratio is 11:1, which allows for personal attention and student-faculty collaborative research, both of which are essential to the Lynchburg experience. While Lynchburg faculty are involved in various research and writing projects, University policy requires that teaching is to be their top priority.

Admission Requirements

A candidate for admission to the University of Lynchburg (www.lynchburg.edu/undergraduate-admission) should be a graduate of an approved secondary school with a minimum of 16 academic units or the equivalent, as shown by examination. It is required that the academic work include major emphases in the areas of English, foreign language, social science, natural sciences, and mathematics. An applicant must demonstrate above-average academic ability in all areas of study, as admission is competitive. In support of the record, a student must present satisfactory scores on the ACT or SAT (critical reading and math scores are used to determine admission decisions and merit scholarship awards). It is recommended that all students have a personal interview and visit the campus beginning the spring semester of their junior year or during their senior year. Enrollment Office hours during the academic year are 9 a.m. to 5 p.m. Monday through Friday and 10 a.m. to noon on Saturday during the academic year.

Application and Information

The University operates on an early semester calendar. The first semester begins in late August and ends before Christmas, and the second semester runs from mid-January to early May. An optional winter term abroad is also offered.

Early decision admission applications must be received by November 15 (www.lynchburg.edu/undergraduate-admission/freshman-application-steps); notification of acceptance is made by December 15. All other applications are processed on a rolling admissions basis. Applicants are notified of the status of their application usually within two to four weeks of the date their application file is completed.

For information, students should contact:

Sharon Walters-Bower, Director of Admissions
The University of Lynchburg
1501 Lakeside Drive
Lynchburg, Virginia 24501
Phone: 434-544-8300
800-426-8101 (toll-free)
Fax: 434-544-8653
E-mail: admissions@lynchburg.edu
Website: http://www.lynchburg.edu

The iconic LOVEworks sculpture at the University of Lynchburg serves as a visible reminder of the University's commitment to embracing all people and to our past as Lynchburg College (LC).

UNIVERSITY OF MAINE

ORONO, MAINE

1865 THE UNIVERSITY OF MAINE

The University

The University of Maine (UMaine) offers the extensive academic opportunities expected from a major research university, with the close-knit feel of a small college. The University of Maine is Maine's Flagship University, offering the most comprehensive academic experience in the state. There are over 100 majors and academic programs, 75 master's degree programs, and 35 doctoral programs. All majors benefit from a strong foundation in the liberal arts. Top students are invited to join the Honors College, one of the country's oldest and most prestigious honors colleges in the nation. UMaine is also the state's only public research university, housing facilities with an international reputation for excellence. UMaine students have extraordinary opportunities to gain real-world experience through research and experiential learning. Undergraduates have the opportunity to collaborate with faculty, conduct fieldwork, and participate in internships around the world. Wildlife ecology majors learn about animal behavior by working in the field with wildlife biologists and black bear cubs. Many engineering students secure co-ops that typically lead to employment immediately after graduation. Education majors have the opportunity to take advantage of urban, rural, and international student-teaching opportunities. There are over 200 student organizations, such as the student investment club that manages a $3.5-million real-money portfolio, Greek Life, Division I athletics, and many more.

Location

There's no place like Maine. UMaine students are surrounded by the great outdoors and have ample opportunity to explore everything the state has to offer. Orono is nestled between the Stillwater and Penobscot rivers. The campus has a traditional New England feel with ivy-covered brick buildings, towering pines, and beautiful fall foliage. Some of the best skiing in the Northeast is within easy driving distance. Beautiful tourist attractions such as Bar Harbor, Acadia National Park, Baxter State Park, and the northern terminus of the Appalachian Trail are just a short drive from campus. The University of Maine is 10 minutes from the city of Bangor, Maine's third-largest city, with its own international airport.

Majors and Degrees

UMaine offers over 100 majors and programs across six colleges at the undergraduate level: the College of Education and Human Development; College of Engineering; College of Liberal Arts and Sciences; College of Natural Sciences, Forestry, and Agriculture; the Maine Business School; and the Honors College. In addition, UMaine offers the Explorations program, designed to help undecided students identify a major across the vast academic opportunities available and find the best fit for a degree program. The Division of Lifelong Learning offers online classes, Summer University, Winter Session, and distance-learning opportunities for students who need a flexible class schedule.

Academic Programs

UMaine provides a comprehensive academic and student experience, yielding graduates who are well-educated, well-adjusted, and well-prepared to succeed after graduation and assume leadership roles within their respective careers. The University seeks to foster excellence and innovation through inspired, dedicated teaching by ensuring there is a constant discovery of new knowledge for students. In addition to their major or concentration within their degree programs, University of Maine students benefit from a solid liberal arts foundation. Students develop and refine the qualities needed to fully engage with the world around them, regardless of their academic discipline.

Undergraduate research is a major component of the learning atmosphere. The University of Maine offers students true hands-on research experience, as early as their first year on campus. UMaine is the state's largest research university, providing rich and diverse opportunities for undergraduates to publish findings, travel the globe, and work alongside UMaine's world-class scholars and researchers. The Center for Undergraduate Research connects students with faculty projects applicable to their academic interests and future careers. The abundance of research opportunities also provides students with great mentoring connections between faculty and students that carry benefits beyond the classroom. The skills students develop through research creates applicants who are much more competitive in the workplace and graduate school.

Campus Programs

Students will get a full and enriching college experience at UMaine. The University of Maine hosts many on-campus programs and opportunities for students to explore and meet new people. There are over 200 clubs and organizations for students to get involved in, such as Greek Life, Woodsmen's Team, Robotics Club, Spanish Club, and more. The Campus Activities Board also puts on free events during the school year, including movies, karaoke, game nights, and astronomy shows. Students can join an athletic team or cheer the UMaine Black Bears Division I teams to victory for free during the year.

There are many ways to explore Maine off campus as well through outdoor recreation, music and food festivals, museums, and much more. Bangor, a 10-minute drive from campus, hosts Summer Concerts in the Park, the American Folk Festival, and a state fair.

Through UMaine study-abroad programs, students explore globally while enhancing their education by taking courses, researching or volunteering. UMaine students have traveled to China to study emerging financial markets, to Italy to learn about Renaissance art history, to Turkey to study film, and to Brazil to look at our world's diverse ecosystem.

Academic Facilities

The University of Maine is home to state-of-the-art research facilities, classrooms, and teaching laboratories. Fogler Library is the state's largest library and located in the heart of campus. It houses more than 1.4 million volumes, 1.6 million microforms, and 2.3 million U.S. and Canadian government publications. It's also the archive of papers written by famous UMaine Alumnus Stephen King. Students have access to UMaine's new Capital Markets Training Laboratory with state-of-the-art technology and 12 Bloomberg Terminals that provide hands-on learning in finance. The Virtual Environment and Multimodal Interaction Laboratory (VEMI) is a research facility that combines fully immersive virtual reality with augmented reality technologies in an integrated research and development environment. Students from all interests and majors collaborate in VEMI Lab research in areas such as aging, vision impairment, and virtual realities. The new, multi-million-dollar Innovative Media Research and Commercialization Center (IMRC) and the Wyeth Family Studio Art Center contain facilities for training, research, development, and commercialization. Students have access to many different labs, such as a fabrication studio, electronics lab, audio and video production labs, 3-D printing and design, and prototype production.

The University of Maine is also a cultural hub. It is home to the region's premier performing arts center, the Collins Center for the Arts, as well as several museums and galleries.

Costs

For the 2019–20 academic year, tuition for in-state undergraduate students is estimated at $9,000, and $29,310 for out-of-state residents. Canadian residents and students who qualify for the New England Regional Program (NEBHE) will pay an estimated $14,400 for tuition. The average credit load for full-time students is 15 credit hours per semester or 30 credit hours for the academic year. Required university fees are estimated at $2,438 per year for a full-time student. These fees include a variety of healthcare services and admission to cultural, recreational, and athletic events. Books and supplies cost, on average, about $1,000, and room and board estimated cost is $13,254 for one academic year.

Financial Aid

UMaine requires all financial aid applicants to file the Free Application for Federal Student Aid (FAFSA). The priority deadline to apply for aid is March 1. Awards usually consist of a combination of several types of aid, ranging from grants and scholarships to work-study jobs and student loans. Students are encouraged to apply by the Early Action deadline of December 1 to ensure admission in selective academic programs and receive merit scholarships based on high school achievement, as demonstrated by high school rank, grade point average, and standardized test results (SAT and ACT). Additional information on application deadlines and merit scholarships is available online at go.umaine.edu.

Faculty

UMaine is known for its beautiful and vast campus, large student body, and family atmosphere. Students will get to know each other quickly, but even more importantly, so will their professors. UMaine's professors have an open-door policy and encourage students to meet with them outside of class. Undergraduate classes are taught by professors, and many faculty go on to be academic and professional mentors for their students. Students have the opportunity to work alongside UMaine's renowned scholars and scientists in research and other academic ventures.

Student Government

Student Government, Inc. is the independent representative body for UMaine's undergraduate students. An elected president, vice president, and vice president of financial affairs direct and coordinate student clubs and programs at the University of Maine. Student Government works closely with the Office of the Vice President for Student Life and appoints 200 student representatives to various university committees. These students assist with the planning and implementation of residence hall programs, student discipline, athletics, and cultural activities on campus.

Admission Requirements

Admission to the University of Maine is a highly competitive and selective process. Successful applicants hold high scholastic achievement, intellectual curiosity, and extracurricular involvement that promise success at the University of Maine. The holistic selection process looks at the strength of the high school curriculum, grades received, class rank, counselor recommendation, and SAT or ACT scores for admission consideration. Additional information such as essays and community involvement may help the admissions committee evaluate student applications. UMaine recognizes advanced work completed in secondary schools in Advanced Placement tests, honors, or higher education courses. Students who pass examinations may be exempt from certain courses at UMaine.

Application and Information

Applicants may submit electronic or paper versions of the Common Application, the University of Maine Mobile Application, or the ApplyMaine Application. Required documents for all applicants include official high school or college transcripts, counselor recommendations, and SAT or ACT scores. Students above the age of 20 do not need to submit SAT or ACT test scores. Students are encouraged to apply by December 1 to ensure admission in selective academic programs and receive merit scholarship–based application review. More information on application deadlines and merit scholarships can be found on the University's website at go.umaine.edu. Applications and all supporting documents (i.e., SAT or ACT scores, transcripts, essays, etc.) should be sent to UMS Processing, P.O. Box 412, Bangor, ME 04402-0412.

For additional information on the application process, prospective students can contact the Office of Admissions at 207-581-1561 or umaineadmissions@maine.edu.

Office of Admissions
5713 Chadbourne Hall
University of Maine
Orono, Maine 04469-5713
Phone: 207-581-1561
Fax: 207-581-1213
E-mail: umaineadmissions@maine.edu
Website: go.umaine.edu
facebook.com/UMaineAdmissions
twitter.com@GoUMaine
instagram.com@university.of.maine
linkedin.com/edu/school?id=18586
pinterest.com/GoUMaine/

The Mall is the heart of the University of Maine campus.

UNIVERSITY OF NEW HAVEN

WEST HAVEN, CONNECTICUT

University of New Haven

The University

The University of New Haven's mission is to prepare career-ready graduates for meaningful roles in today's global economy and to nurture the pursuit of lifelong learning. Founded in 1920, the University of New Haven is a private, independent institution focused on combining experience-based learning with liberal arts and sciences. The University is committed to student success through educational innovation, continuous improvement in career and professional education, and support of scholarship and personal development. The main campus moved to its present location in West Haven in 1960 and has since rapidly expanded its programs, facilities, and faculty, attracting a student body that now stands at over 6,800—including the current enrollment of 4,700 full-time undergraduates.

The University is fully accredited by the New England Association of Schools and Colleges (NEASC). Individual programs, departments, and schools hold various forms of national and professional accreditations, including the American Bar Association, American Dental Association, Forensic Science Education Programs Accreditation Commission, National Association of Schools of Art and Design, and the Association to Advance Collegiate Schools of Business. In addition, seven of the University of New Haven's bachelor's degree programs—chemical, civil, electrical, computer, industrial and systems, mechanical engineering, and computer science—are fully accredited by the Engineering Accreditation Commission of the Accreditation Board for Engineering and Technology, Inc. (EAC/ABET).

The main campus is in West Haven, Connecticut, on a hillside close to Long Island Sound. The main campus houses five academic colleges: the College of Arts and Sciences, the College of Business, the Tagliatela College of Engineering, the Henry C. Lee College of Criminal Justice and Forensic Sciences, and the School of Health Sciences. The University of New Haven also operates three satellite campuses: a graduate business campus in Orange, Connecticut; the M.S. National Security campus in Albuquerque, New Mexico; and an international campus in Prato, Italy. Following the addition of the Graduate School in 1969, New Haven College was designated a university. Over thirty-five master's degree programs attract full- and part-time graduate students, while just over 100 associate and bachelor's degree programs are available to entering first year and transfer students in a great variety of academic disciplines.

Other main campus buildings include the Marvin K. Peterson Library, the Henry C. Lee Institute of Forensic Science, the Bayer Hall admissions building, the Campus Bookstore, new residence halls and apartments, and Bartels Hall, the campus center, which houses one of the dining facilities and student activities. Across the street from main campus is the Dental Hygiene Clinic and North Hall, which houses the arson investigation labs. The Charger Gymnasium, blue and gold turf of the football stadium, and athletic fields are located on the North Campus, just two short blocks from Maxcy Hall, the historic main administration building.

The University of New Haven has one of the most respected and successful NCAA Division II athletics programs in the country, with Charger teams combining to make over 120 post-season tournament appearances. The University is a member of the Northeast-10 Conference, one of the most prestigious and celebrated conferences in the nation. The University of New Haven and its student athletes have won numerous conference, regional, and national awards, both athletically and academically. The University offers seventeen varsity sports: men's baseball, basketball, cross-country, football, soccer, indoor and outdoor track and field; and women's basketball, cross-country, field hockey, lacrosse, soccer, softball, tennis, indoor and outdoor track and field, and volleyball.

Over 65 percent of the full-time undergraduate students live on campus in thirteen residence halls. More than 200 clubs and organizations are available to students. Included are student chapters of professional societies, religious organizations, social groups, special-interest clubs, student councils, cultural groups, and fraternities and sororities.

Location

West Haven is contiguous to New Haven. There are theaters that attract star performers from the entertainment world, a harbor and beaches, fine restaurants, museums, and galleries in the area. Numerous social and cultural programs are presented by the many colleges and universities in the area. New Haven is served by a local airport and major railroads, and its location at the junction of two interstate highways places the University of New Haven within easy driving distance of New York, Boston, Cape Cod, and the ski areas of New England.

Majors and Degrees

The College of Arts and Sciences offers a Bachelor of Arts degree in art, communication, English, global studies, history, international development and diplomacy, marine affairs, mathematics, music, music and sound recording, music industry, political science, theater, and psychology; a Bachelor of Fine Arts degree in graphic design and interior design; and a Bachelor of Science degree in biology, communication, genetics and biotechnology, dental hygiene, environmental science, legal studies, marine biology, mathematics, music and sound recording, and nutrition and dietetics.

The College of Business offers the Bachelor of Science degree in accounting, business analytics, business management, economics, finance, hospitality and tourism management, international business, marketing, and sport management. In addition, the College of Business offers a fast-track 3+1 study program allowing academically strong students the opportunity to earn a Bachelor of Science degree in business and a Master of Business Administration (M.B.A.) in only four years.

The Tagliatela College of Engineering offers a Bachelor of Science degree in chemical engineering, chemistry, civil engineering, computer engineering, computer science, cyber security and networks, electrical engineering, general engineering, industrial and systems engineering, and mechanical engineering.

The Henry C. Lee College of Criminal Justice and Forensic Sciences offers a Bachelor of Science degree in criminal justice, fire science, forensic science, homeland security and emergency management, and national security.

The School of Health Sciences offers a Bachelor of Science degree in dental hygiene, nutrition and dietetics, health sciences, and paramedicine.

Academic Programs

The University of New Haven offers a broad range of programs in both liberal arts, sciences, and professional areas. Experiential learning is emphasized, and there are diverse and numerous opportunities for internships, cooperative education, independent study, and industrial projects. Professional experiences are required for graduation in a number of degree programs. The

University provides student-support services including the Accessibility Resources Center, Center for Student Success, Career Development, and a Center for Learning Resources, offering tutoring service open to all students.

The undergraduate division operates on a 4-1-4 calendar. Credit is given for successful scores on International Baccalaureate and Advanced Placement examinations. The University Honors Program provides outstanding study opportunities for high-achieving students. The residency requirement for all degrees is 30 credit hours.

The University of New Haven believes that all students pursuing a bachelor's degree should develop a common set of skills; its goal is to prepare all graduates for the complex lives they will lead in a changing world. This can best be done through the University Core Curriculum, which consists of a minimum of 40 credit hours in nine basic competencies.

Academic Facilities

The Marvin K. Peterson Library contains more than 400,000 volumes in hard copy and provides access to about 20,000 electronic books and 20,000 e-journals from the library website and Voyager online catalog. Databases are available on a wide variety of subjects, with a focus on business, criminal justice/forensic science, engineering, and psychology, as well as general arts and sciences. Through interlibrary loan services, the University community has access to the holdings of more than 8,650 other libraries. The building also includes study and social spaces on the upper levels.

The communication program allows students to utilize professional equipment and software in the Laurel Vlock Center for Convergent Media, as well as on-campus field and studio production labs, editing labs, a fully equipped television studio, and an award-winning radio station (WNHU 88.7 FM).

The University's Marine Biology students benefit from the brand-new 6,000 square-foot Marine Sciences Center built on the historic site of New Haven's Canal Dock shipping pier. The facility is built on a floating dock and features state-of-the-art marine research and teaching labs, a large wet lab, boathouse, and direct waterfront access.

The Tagliatela College of Engineering features labs with state-of-the-art hardware and software, including a Solar Testing and Training laboratory and University Makerspace. The University's cross-disciplinary cyber security and networks program allows students to experience virtual reality technology in the Cyber Forensics Research and Education Lab. Facilities for the internationally recognized forensic science and criminal justice programs were expanded with the addition of a Crime Scene Training House. This unique learning space allows faculty to replicate crime scenes and then use cameras to monitor each room as students independently process the scene from start to finish.

Costs

Full-time undergraduate tuition for the 2018–19 academic year, including all fees, is $39,270; room and board costs total $16,320.

Financial Aid

The University of New Haven offers a comprehensive financial aid program that includes University resources as well as state, federal, and private-aid programs. Approximately 95 percent of full-time undergraduate students receive some form of assistance. Students receive federal aid through the Federal Pell Grant, Federal Supplemental Educational Opportunity Grant, Federal Work-Study, Federal Direct Student Loan, and Federal Direct PLUS loan programs. The University also administers programs sponsored by the state of Connecticut for Connecticut residents attending the University. Some students also qualify for financial aid from other states and from private companies, organizations, and foundations.

Faculty

The University of New Haven prides itself that the majority of its full-time faculty members (more than 90 percent) hold terminal degrees in their disciplines. No classes are taught by teaching assistants. Faculty are available for students to meet with for advisement as well as collaborate with on undergraduate research. There are over 270 full-time and 400 part-time faculty members, making the student-faculty ratio 16:1.

Student Government

The Undergraduate Student Government Association supervises annual expenditures by undergraduate clubs and organizations, directs liaison committees, supports student publications and the student-operated FM radio station, and schedules cultural and social events. Student representatives are elected annually to the University's Board of Governors.

Admission Requirements

To be eligible for admission, one must be a high school graduate or present evidence of equivalent preparation and have submitted all necessary application documents for consideration. The admissions decision is based on an applicant's high school transcript, SAT or ACT scores, letter(s) of recommendation, and personal essay. The transfer admissions decision is based on an applicant's college transcript(s) and personal essay. Out-of-state residents are considered for admission on the same basis as in-state residents. The University of New Haven does not discriminate on the basis of age, color, sex, religion, race, sexual orientation, national origin, or disability in admission or treatment of students, administration or distribution of financial aid, or recruitment of employees.

Application and Information

To apply to the University of New Haven, one must submit a completed application via the Common Application (with $50 fee), official records of all academic enrollment, SAT or ACT results, a letter of recommendation (from an academic source), and a personal essay (250–650 words). International students are required to demonstrate proficiency in English and provide documentation of financial support. Applications are considered on a rolling admissions basis with the opportunity to apply for early action, early decision, and regular decision.

For more information, contact:

Office of Undergraduate Admissions
University of New Haven
300 Boston Post Road
West Haven, Connecticut 06516
Phone: 203-932-7319
E-mail: admissions@newhaven.edu
Website: http://www.newhaven.edu

Maxcy Hall on the campus of the University of New Haven.

COLLEGE CLOSE-UPS

UNIVERSITY OF PITTSBURGH AT BRADFORD

BRADFORD, PENNSYLVANIA

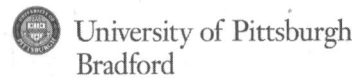

University of Pittsburgh Bradford

BEYOND SUCCESS

The University

The University of Pittsburgh at Bradford (Pitt-Bradford) can take students beyond. Students will go beyond smart by having real-world experiences that will take them beyond the intellectual aspects of college and give them the skills they need to succeed; beyond fun by participating in an active student life, a friendly residence-life environment, excellent athletic and cultural facilities, and a wide range of recreational opportunities; beyond borders by being exposed to the world through many study-abroad opportunities; beyond expectations by having a college experience that can transform them; and beyond success by achieving a life that has impact and one in which they are happy, healthy, productive members of society.

At Pitt-Bradford, students live and learn on a safe, intimate campus, where they receive individual and personalized attention from committed professors who work at their side. In addition, students earn a degree from the University of Pittsburgh, which commands respect around the world.

Students can work out in a state-of-the-art fitness center or swim in the six-lane swimming pool in the Richard E. and Ruth McDowell Sport and Fitness Center. The building also houses facilities for intercollegiate and intramural athletic events.

The Frame-Westerberg Commons offers a place to eat, gather, and participate in campus life. The building houses the dining hall, where students can help themselves to a wide assortment of meals; a bookstore, which features an after-hours convenience store; offices for many student clubs and organizations; and areas to read or relax.

There are more than sixty clubs and organizations, from the campus radio station and newspaper to academic clubs, honor societies, and fraternities and sororities. Pitt-Bradford competes in Division III of the NCAA and fields seven men's teams in baseball, basketball, golf, soccer, swimming, tennis, and wrestling, and seven women's teams in basketball, bowling, soccer, softball, swimming, tennis, and volleyball. Pitt-Bradford also has an ice hockey club sport and an esports club team.

Location

Pitt-Bradford encompasses 319 acres in the foothills of the Allegheny Mountains, only steps from the Allegheny National Forest. Pitt-Bradford also is a short drive from larger cities such as Buffalo, New York (80 miles north); Pittsburgh (160 miles southeast); and Erie, Pennsylvania (90 miles west). Pitt-Bradford can also be reached easily by car and plane.

At Pitt-Bradford, students have many opportunities to participate in co-curricular opportunities in the region, including cross-country and downhill skiing, snowboarding, snowshoeing, ice skating, biking, fishing, hiking, and hunting.

Majors and Degrees

Students may pursue four-year degrees in accounting, applied mathematics; athletic training; biology; biology education 7–12; broadcast communications; business, computer and information technology K–12; business management; chemistry; chemistry education 7–12; communications, computer information systems and technology; criminal justice; early level education PreK–4; economics; energy science and technology; English; English education 7–12; environmental studies; exercise science; general studies; health and physical education K–12; history/political science; hospitality management; interdisciplinary arts; international affairs; mathematics education 7–12; nursing; physical sciences; psychology; radiological science; social studies education 7–12; sociology; sport and recreation management; and writing.

Pitt-Bradford also offers associate degrees in engineering science, information systems, liberal studies, nursing (RN), and petroleum technology.

Students may also study engineering for up to two years at Pitt-Bradford and then complete a program at the Oakland campus in bioengineering, chemical and petroleum engineering, civil and environmental engineering, electrical and computer engineering, industrial engineering, materials science and engineering, or mechanical engineering.

Pitt-Bradford also offers programs for students to continue their studies in many of the University of Pittsburgh's graduate and professional programs such as medicine, dentistry, and law.

Pitt-Bradford also offers the first two years of study leading to the doctorate in pharmacy. Students must complete the program at the Oakland campus, where admission is competitive. The Pittsburgh School of Pharmacy pre-admits some qualified high school seniors, pending completion of the first two years of the pre-professional program at Pitt-Bradford.

The University also has an agreement with Lake Erie College of Osteopathic Medicine (LECOM), which allows qualifying students to continue their education in medicine at LECOM after their third year at Pitt-Bradford. Students who have successfully completed their first year of medical school classes at LECOM will receive their bachelor's degree from Pitt-Bradford. They will then continue at LECOM to finish their medical studies.

Academic Programs

The academic programs stress critical-thinking and communication skills and encourage hands-on learning through field experience, internships, and faculty-student collaboration on research. A Pitt-Bradford bachelor's degree requires 120–128 credit hours (requirements differ slightly among programs). Students need to complete between 60 and 70 credit hours to earn an associate degree.

The accounting major prepares students for the workplace, which has a growing need for accountants. The major also prepares students to earn a master's degree in either professional accountancy or business administration. They'll also develop skills in the virtual reality lab.

The biology program prepares students for careers in health-related professions, education, and research; technical positions in governmental agencies; and careers with food, pharmaceutical, chemical, and biotechnology companies. Most students interested in medicine, dentistry, optometry, pharmacy, osteopathy, physical therapy, occupational therapy, podiatry, chiropractic medicine, veterinary medicine, preclinical dietetics and nutrition, and a variety of careers in health and rehabilitation sciences are biology majors.

Students who choose to major in broadcast communications, English or writing are able to work on the award-winning student newspaper, *The Source;* broadcast over the college radio station, WDRQ; and publish original works in the award-winning student literary magazine, *Baily's Beads.* Students also have access to an all-digital television studio and two digital radio facilities.

Students who choose a major in computer information systems and technology will get a broad IT background and gain hands-on lab experiences. Students will learn programming applications, network development, systems design and analysis, web technologies, multimedia applications, database development, and systems administration. They'll also develop skills in the virtual reality lab.

In the criminal justice program, students are able to intern with local and regional police departments, county court and probation offices, and a federal prison. State-of-the-art crime-scene investigatory tools enable students to work a crime scene using many of the same tools as professional law enforcement agents. In the Crime Scene Investigation (CSI) House students can process simulated crime scenes and collect evidence just like the pros.

An education major prepares a student for a career as a teacher in a world of rapid political, economic, scientific, and cultural change. The Education Department seeks to graduate students who have general knowledge and specific content knowledge, as well as sound theory and practice.

The nursing program at Pitt-Bradford offers an Associate of Science degree that can be completed in two years and a Bachelor of Science in Nursing degree that requires two additional years. Students may commence this program upon completion of the associate degree.

In psychology, students gain knowledge in the scientific and theoretical aspects of psychology as well as the application of this knowledge. The major prepares students for graduate work in psychology and related disciplines and for employment in social service agencies, mental health centers, industries, and not-for-profit and governmental agencies.

Students may relocate to another University of Pittsburgh campus to complete academic programs not offered at Pitt-Bradford, but they may earn no more than 70 credits before transferring. All students in the arts and sciences may relocate, provided they are in good standing. Engineering students may relocate if they maintain a grade point average of at least 3.0.

Academic Facilities

In addition to the T. Edward and Tullah Hanley Library on campus, Pitt-Bradford students have online access to the entire University of Pittsburgh library system.

Blaisdell Hall, the fine arts and communication arts building, houses the art, communication arts, interdisciplinary arts, theater, and music programs and features state-of-the-art equipment. Students can find a computer graphics lab, two art studios, a music/theater rehearsal hall, and a radio and television studio. The building also houses a multipurpose theater and serves as the cultural center for the region by housing plays, concerts, lectures, and other arts-related events.

Fisher Hall houses the science programs, such as biology, chemistry, engineering, engineering science and technology, petroleum technology, and physics. The science labs are filled with up-to-date scientific equipment, enabling students to perform a variety of experiments. The building also has two computer-aided learning centers and, on the roof, a campus greenhouse.

In Swarts Hall, students take courses in business, education, sociology, anthropology, psychology, history/political science, languages, English, writing, and criminal justice. The building also houses a nursing suite and multimedia classrooms that can turn a typical class into an audio and visual experience.

There is more to the Richard E. and Ruth McDowell Sport and Fitness Center than sports. The building also houses the athletic training, exercise science, and sport and recreation management programs, along with a human performance lab and an athletic training room.

In the Ceramic Studio, students get their hands dirty—literally. Students have sixteen motorized pottery wheels, a manual kick wheel, a work table, and a kiln to help turn slabs of clay into art.

Costs

For 2018–19, tuition for full-time students was $6,470 per fifteen-week term for Pennsylvania residents and $12,092 for nonresidents. Nursing tuition was $8,289 per term for Pennsylvania residents and $15,419 for nonresidents. Room and board expenses were $4,666 per term. Other costs include an activity fee of $100 per term, a wellness fee of $75 per term, a parking and transportation fee of $40 per term, and a computer fee of $175 per term. Books and supplies cost approximately $500 per term.

Financial Aid

Pitt-Bradford believes that the cost of a college education should not be a deterrent to any student regardless of family financial circumstances. Nearly 99 percent of students who apply for assistance receive some form of financial aid, including grants, scholarships, loans and work-study opportunities administered through the Financial Aid Office. During 2018–19, the average financial aid award was roughly $19,903 for Pennsylvania students and $26,076 for out-of-state students. All aid applicants must submit the Free Application for Federal Student Aid (FAFSA) by March 1 to receive priority consideration. Pennsylvania residents who complete the FAFSA by March 1 are also eligible for Pennsylvania Higher Education Assistance Agency (PHEAA) grants. Students who live outside of Pennsylvania should contact their state agency to learn more about the prerequisites for grants.

The University awards merit-based scholarships to those who demonstrate exceptional academic achievement. The University ROTC program is another possible source of aid. The University encourages veterans to contact the VA about educational benefits.

To learn more about financial assistance, students should contact the Financial Aid Office or visit the financial aid website at http://www.upb.pitt.edu/financialaid.

Faculty

Pitt-Bradford's 96 full-time faculty members hold doctorates and master's degrees from some of the most prestigious universities in the nation, including Cornell, Harvard, Stanford, and the University of Pittsburgh. Teaching is the primary activity of the faculty, and personal attention is emphasized in the classroom. Faculty members welcome the chance to meet with their students and know them by name. The student-faculty ratio is 15:1.

Student Government

Because Pitt-Bradford is a personalized campus, opportunities for leadership abound. Many students become campus leaders as early as their sophomore year. Regardless of students' background or interests, most find many places to become involved at Pitt-Bradford.

The Student Activities Council schedules comedy performances, lectures, art exhibits, movies, and trips to such cities as Toronto, Niagara Falls, Cooperstown, and New York City.

Admission Requirements

The Admissions Committee considers three primary factors in evaluating an applicant's ability to succeed in college work: the high school record, the results of standardized tests (SAT or ACT), and the high school's recommendations. In addition, personal qualifications, extracurricular activities, and potential to contribute to the college community may be taken into consideration.

Application and Information

Pitt-Bradford has a rolling admissions program, and students may apply at any time. All candidates are notified as soon as action is taken on their application.

Candidates for admission should complete and return the paper application with a nonrefundable $45 fee. However, students can apply online at no charge. Students must also submit an official copy of their high school record and scores from either the SAT or ACT. In addition to fulfilling the above requirements, transfer applicants must submit all official college transcripts and must have a minimum cumulative grade point average of 2.0.

The Office of Admissions welcomes campus visits by students and their families; such visits help students arrive at a final decision about Pitt-Bradford. Interviews and tours are scheduled Monday through Friday, 9 a.m. to 3 p.m., and on selected Saturdays. Arrangements can be made by contacting the Office of Admissions or by going online to http://www.upb.pitt.edu/visit.

For application forms, catalogs, and further information, students should contact:

Office of Admissions
University of Pittsburgh at Bradford
300 Campus Drive
Bradford, Pennsylvania 16701-2898
Phone: 814-362-7555
800-872-1787 (toll-free)
Website: http://www.upb.pitt.edu
http://www.facebook.com/PittBradford
https://twitter.com/PittBradford
http://www.instagram.com/upittbradford

UNIVERSITY OF SAN FRANCISCO
SAN FRANCISCO, CALIFORNIA

UNIVERSITY OF SAN FRANCISCO
CHANGE THE WORLD FROM HERE

The University

The University of San Francisco—a private, Jesuit university—reflects the diverse and dynamic city that surrounds it. USF provides students from all backgrounds an education that is intensely personalized, intellectually inspiring, and designed expressly to help them change the world for the better.

USF enrolls 6,745 undergraduate and 4,293 graduate students, offers more than 100 undergraduate and graduate degree programs, and boasts a network of over 110,000 alumni who live in all 50 states, six U.S. territories, and 135 countries. The school's campus, in the geographic heart of San Francisco, puts students right in the middle of everything San Francisco has to offer.

USF is one of the most diverse university campuses in the United States. Living and learning in a community that comprises students from 50 states and 98 countries is a unique opportunity. USF guarantees two semesters of housing to all first-time, first-year students who enroll for the fall semester. Approximately 90 percent of incoming first-years live on campus. Any new student who is not a first-time, first-year student may apply for housing and will be assigned housing based on space availability.

The University offers five on-campus residence halls, one on-campus house, two off-campus residence halls, and one on-campus apartment-style residence. Housing for first-time first-year students is in Gillson, Hayes-Healy, Lone Mountain, and Fromm. Housing for upper-division students under the age of 21 is in Toler. Pedro Arrupe, 12 blocks from campus, offers housing for upper-division students of all ages. Housing for upper-division students ages 21+ is in Loyola Village (apartment-style living). Fulton House, a single-family home and cottage, is reserved for specific graduate student populations. St. Anne, in the Inner Sunset district, houses law students. Each residence hall has laundry facilities, study rooms/spaces, community kitchens, television lounges, and 24-hour front desk staff (except St. Anne and Fulton House, which do not have desk operations).

University Center, in the heart of campus, is home to the USF bookstore, Center for Academic and Student Achievement, Career Services Center, and the Cultural Centers, which bring students together to increase their understanding and embrace their roles as members of a diverse local and global community.

The Koret Health and Recreation Center provides facilities for court games, weight training, massage, personal training, and various aquatic activities in an Olympic-size pool. Spin, yoga, and Pilates mat are just some of the free classes offered at Koret. Outdoor adventures include horseback riding, skiing/snowboarding, and sea kayaking. Intramural and club sports include basketball, soccer, flag football, sailing, table tennis, karate, lacrosse, rugby, water polo, Ultimate (Frisbee), and volleyball. NCAA Division I sports include baseball, basketball, cross-country, golf, soccer, tennis, track and field, and women's volleyball and sand volleyball.

Dining venues are located all over campus. The Market Café in University Center offers a food court with a variety of choices, including global and vegetarian options. Other dining options include Wolf & Kettle Café, Crossroads Café, and Kendrick Café in the School of Law.

Location

USF's 55-acre campus is located in the center of one of the world's most dynamic cities, just minutes from the Financial District, Golden Gate Park, Fisherman's Wharf, and the Pacific Ocean. Students take advantage of the opportunities available in San Francisco including concerts, museums, theater, dining, the ballet, opera, and major sporting events. The city also offers a wide range of research, community involvement, internship, and employment opportunities.

Majors and Degrees

The College of Arts and Sciences offers both B.A. and B.S. degrees. The School of Management offers B.S. and B.S.B.A. degrees. The School of Nursing and Health Professions offers a direct-entry, four-year B.S. in Nursing for qualified high school and transfer applicants. Major programs include accounting, advertising, architecture and community design, art history/arts management, Asian studies, biology, chemistry, communication studies, comparative literature and culture, computer science, critical diversity studies, data science, design, economics, English, entrepreneurship and innovation, environmental science, environmental studies, finance, fine arts, French studies, history, hospitality management, international business, international studies, Japanese studies, kinesiology, Latin American studies, marketing, management, mathematics, media studies, nursing, performing arts and social justice, philosophy, physics, politics, psychology, sociology, Spanish, theology and religious studies, and urban studies.

USF offers 71 minors and special programs, including astronomy; African studies; Asia Pacific studies; Black Achievement Success and Engagement (BASE) program; Catholic studies and social thought; ethnic studies; film studies; Honors College; Jewish studies and social justice; Latin@/Chican@ studies; Middle Eastern studies; neuroscience; 4+3 dual degrees in law, premedical, and other pre-professional health studies; public relations; an undergraduate and a five-year dual-degree teacher preparation program that results in teacher certification at the elementary or secondary level; and the School of Management honors cohort program.

Academic Programs

The University of San Francisco offers a well-rounded education that prepares students not only for successful careers but also for fulfilling lives. A baccalaureate degree is issued upon the successful completion of a 128-credit curriculum consisting of 44 credits in core requirements chosen from six specified categories, with the remainder of credits being taken as part of major requirements and electives. The academic year is based on two semesters, with summer sessions and a winter intersession also available. USF101, a 1-unit course available to first-semester undergraduates, helps students learn about USF's Jesuit mission, join the campus community, navigate the university's academic requirements and resources, and map their individual paths to graduation.

USF accepts Advanced Placement (AP) credits, as certified by the College Board's Advanced Placement Program exams; the International Baccalaureate program courses; and the College-Level Examination Program (CLEP). Students in the College of Arts and Sciences may earn a bachelor's degree in three years with a combination of Advanced Placement credits and an academically rigorous schedule.

The USF Pre-Professional Health Committee serves to guide and recommend students to medical and dental professional schools as well as to schools for pharmacy, optometry, veterinary medicine, and podiatry. A student may complete the premedical or other pre–health science requirements as part of, or in addition to, the requirements of an academic major. The Pre-Professional Health Committee assists students with the application process, collects and mails recommendations to professional schools, conducts interviews in preparation for application, and endorses approved candidates via a committee letter of recommendation sent to all professional schools selected by the student.

The St. Ignatius Institute offers a core curriculum based on the great books of Western civilization. Any undergraduate student, regardless of major, may take Institute courses to meet core curriculum requirements. The University also offers Army ROTC, which offers scholarships for qualified applicants and continuing students.

Off-Campus Programs

The USF Center for Global Education offers over 100 semester-long programs including exchange programs with Jesuit and Catholic-affiliated universities in Argentina, Australia, Brazil, Chile, China, Colombia, Ecuador, England, France, Greece, Ireland, Japan, Korea, Mexico, Netherlands, Peru, Philippines, Spain, Taiwan, Turkey, and

Uruguay. The Center also offers internship-specific programs in a broad range of fields including arts, business, hospitality, international relations, plus field study programs focused on global issues such as sustainable development, public health, human rights, and climate change.

Because all USF students are encouraged to be civically and politically engaged, the Leo T. McCarthy Center for Public Service and the Common Good creates partnerships between local communities and USF. Students participate in community engaged learning to understand community organizing, advocacy, policy, power, and privilege and to change the world in ways both small and large.

Academic Facilities

USF students have access to Gleeson Library's 2.2 million holdings and to Lo Schiavo Center for Science and Innovation, which houses a digital lecture hall; spaces for collaborative learning; and labs for chemistry, toxicology, advanced biotechnology, and mathematics. Cowell Hall, the base for nursing classes and the Nursing Skills Laboratory, includes the Instructional Media Center. Malloy Hall, headquarters for the School of Management, houses a computer lab and special seminar rooms. Kalmanovitz Hall houses all programs in the humanities and social sciences and features state-of-the-art classrooms, a rooftop sculpture garden, and 17 laboratories for language, writing, media, and psychology. The 281 Masonic building is home to the Performing Arts and Social Justice department, the first program in the nation that trains young artists to create a humane and just society through their craft. The Presentation Theater and Lone Mountain Studio Theater offer space for theatrical productions and guest speakers.

Costs

Tuition and fees for the 2018–19 school year were $48,066. Room and board were $14,830 for the academic year.

Financial Aid

A variety of financial aid programs are available at the University, including scholarships, grants, loans, and campus employment. Domestic students who wish to be considered for financial aid must file the Free Application for Federal Student Aid (FAFSA) and College Scholarship Service Profile (CSS) by February 15. More than two thirds of all USF students receive some type of financial aid. In addition to need-based financial aid, the University has a generous academic scholarship program based on the applicant's high school record and test scores. Eligible students are identified during the admission process and can apply as early action, early decision, or regular action applicants. Scholarship recipients are expected to maintain a competitive GPA while enrolled at USF.

Faculty

The University has 1,184 full- and part-time faculty members; 95.6 percent of full-time faculty hold doctoral or terminal degrees in the fields they teach. USF fosters a close relationship between students and faculty members. This is reflected in the small classes (fewer than 25 students), the low student-to-faculty ratio (13:1), and the faculty members' availability for advising. The central focus of faculty is on classroom teaching and working with students on research. Classes are not taught by student teachers or teachers' assistants.

Student Clubs and Organizations

Undergraduates participate in over 100 student associations, including fraternities and sororities, honor societies, student media, performing arts groups, and culturally focused clubs. Annual events sponsored by student organizations range from Campus Movie Fest to theater productions and cultural events such as Black Cultural Dinner, Barrio Fiesta, Lu'au, Culturescape, and Dia de la Mujer. Students also participate in Campus Activities Board–sponsored events including Fright Night, Holiday Roller Rink, Donaroo Spring Concert, Spring Carnival, and Late Nights at Crossroads.

All undergraduates are members of the Associated Students of the University of San Francisco (ASUSF). ASUSF Senate is the official representative body of undergraduate students at USF, composed of an executive board and student senators. The ASUSF government has three functions: to represent the official student viewpoint, to recommend policies, and to fund activities and services.

Admission Requirements

The University seeks students who are sincerely interested in pursuing a well-rounded education and who hope to make a positive difference in the world. The admission process is selective, and each application is reviewed individually. To enhance the quality and diversity of its student body, USF welcomes men and women of all races, nationalities, and religious beliefs—or no religious belief—to apply. Eligibility is based on high school course work and GPA, the application essay, an academic recommendation, extracurricular involvement, and test scores. Domestic applicants are required to submit SAT or ACT test scores. International applicants are required to submit TOEFL or IELTS test scores; however, if an international applicant submits sufficient SAT or ACT test scores, the TOEFL or IELTS may be waived.

Application and Information

A completed application includes the application form, the application fee, a personal essay, all academic transcripts, standardized test scores, and one letter of recommendation. For the fall semester, the application deadlines are: November 1 for early action and early decision (freshmen), January 15 for regular decision (freshmen), and March 1 (transfers).

Inquiries should be addressed to:

Office of Admission
University of San Francisco
2130 Fulton Street
San Francisco, California 94117-1080
Phone: 415-422-6563
800-CALL-USF (toll-free outside California)
Fax: 415-422-2217
E-mail: admission@usfca.edu
Website: http://www.usfca.edu
http://www.facebook.com/University.of.San.Francisco
http://twitter.com/USFCA
http://www.youtube.com/usfcalifornia

THE UNIVERSITY OF TULSA

TULSA, OKLAHOMA

THE UNIVERSITY *of* TULSA

The University

The University of Tulsa (TU) is a private, comprehensive degree-granting university that provides high-quality education in the arts, humanities, sciences, engineering, business, education, applied health sciences, and law. Fully accredited by the North Central Association of Colleges and Universities, TU comprises the Kendall College of Arts and Sciences, the Collins College of Business, the College of Engineering and Natural Sciences, the Oxley College of Health Sciences, the College of Law, and a Graduate School.

The university is an NCAA Division IA participant currently in the American Athletic Conference. TU, which maintains a covenant relationship with the Presbyterian Church (U.S.A.), is a force for good locally, through its True Blue Neighbors initiatives (with more than 78,000 volunteer hours per year), as well as through various student programs that include projects such as producing assistive devices for locally disabled people and working on international projects that provide self-sustaining sources of energy and hot water.

TU's 11:1 student-faculty ratio, average class size of 20, and emphasis on individual attention anchor an educational culture where students receive both rigorous challenges and comprehensive support. In 2017, TU graduates had a 95 percent placement rate in full-time jobs or graduate/professional schools.

Extracurricular opportunities include intramural sports, special interest clubs, preprofessional organizations, national fraternities and sororities, community service organizations, student government, departmental honorary groups, and campus ministries.

Total fall 2018 enrollment was 4,412, with 3,297 undergraduates and 1,115 graduate and law students. The ratio of men to women is 56:44, 25 percent of the students are multicultural, and 17 percent international. TU's diverse student population comes from Oklahoma, 42 states and the District of Columbia, and 66 countries.

Location

TU is a 220-acre residential campus in midtown Tulsa, Oklahoma. Tulsa's prominent industries include energy, telecommunications, technology, data processing, manufacturing, health care, aerospace, transportation, and education, all of which provide TU students with opportunities for internships and employment after graduation. The Tulsa metropolitan area has about 500,000 residents. Cultural assets include the Performing Arts Center, BOK Center (venue for popular entertainers), acclaimed ballet and opera companies, a symphony, Philbrook Museum, Gilcrease Museum, Brady Arts District, and cultural festivals. Professional sports in Tulsa include baseball and hockey. The River Parks system provides facilities for outdoor activities with jogging and biking trails; Guthrie Green is a popular arts, music, and food truck destination; and the new Gathering Place Park (2018) is a vibrant, inclusive space designed to bring Tulsans of all ages and backgrounds together.

Majors and Degrees

The Kendall College of Arts and Sciences grants the Bachelor of Arts, Bachelor of Fine Arts, Bachelor of Music, Bachelor of Music Education, and Bachelor of Science degrees with majors in anthropology, art, art history, arts management, arts & sciences & law (accelerated master's), Chinese studies, creative writing, deaf education, earth and environmental sciences, economics, education, English, environmental policy, film studies, French, German, history, media studies, music, musical theatre, organizational studies, philosophy, political science, psychology, religion, Russian studies, sociology, Spanish, theatre, women's and gender studies, and self-designed majors.

The Collins College of Business awards the Bachelor of Science in Business Administration degree in accounting (accelerated master's), business administration (accelerated master's), computer information systems, economics, energy management, finance, management, and marketing; and a Bachelor of Science in international business and language. Certificate programs are available in accounting, finance, management information systems, not-for-profit administration, and sports administration. Management majors may choose specializations in business law, entrepreneurship and family business management, or human resource management. The college is home to several specialized centers, including the Energy Management Program, Family Owned Business Institute, the Genave King Rogers Center for Business Law, and the Williams Risk Management Center.

The Oxley College of Health Sciences offers the Bachelor of Science degree in nursing, athletic training (accelerated master's), exercise and sport science, and speech-language pathology.

The College of Engineering and Natural Sciences offers the Bachelor of Arts degree in biology, earth & environmental sciences, and physics; and the Bachelor of Science degree in applied mathematics, biochemistry, biogeosciences, biological science (options in pre-medicine, pre-dentistry, and pre–veterinary science), chemical engineering, chemistry, computer science, computer simulation and gaming, cyber security, electrical and computer engineering, electrical engineering, engineering physics, geology, geophysics, geosciences, information technology, mathematics, mechanical engineering, petroleum engineering, and physics. The college features state-of-the-art research facilities for all majors. Since 1995, more than 60 TU engineering students have received the prestigious Barry M. Goldwater Scholarship, the nation's premier award for undergraduate students in engineering, math, or science; and 67 National Science Foundation fellowships.

Minors are available in major fields of study, as well as advertising; African American studies; ancient Greek; bioinformatics; biomedical engineering; business administration; business analytics; Chinese; coaching; computational sciences; creative writing; cyber security; dance; digital studies; early intervention; energy and environmental resources management; energy business; film scoring; geology; healthcare informatics; high performance computing; innovation and entrepreneurship; international business; Latin; law, policy and social justice; linguistics; medieval and early modern studies; Portuguese; Russian; and sport management.

Academic Programs

The Tulsa Curriculum links a broad, humanities-based core and writing-across-the-curriculum approach for all students with a highly flexible group of majors, minors, concentrations, and certificate programs. TU students can receive an education that is well-rounded, in-depth, and uniquely personalized. Candidates for graduation must complete at least 124 semester hours of course work, with more hours required of engineering and business administration majors.

The Honors Program engages students in a critical examination of the major epochs and ideas of Western thought and culture through careful study of primary texts. The acclaimed Tulsa Undergraduate Research Challenge (TURC) program combines advanced research in most disciplines, scholarship, and community service.

The TU Institute for Information Security is developing defenses against cyber-attacks and comprised infrastructure. The center supports the university's National Security Agency (NSA)–accredited certificate program in information assurance, a curriculum that integrates information security with computer law and policy issues. TU has been designated a Center of Excellence in information assurance by the NSA and is one of six pioneer institutions selected by the National Science Foundation for the Federal Cyber Service Initiative (Cyber Corps).

Air Force ROTC is available through a satellite program.

Qualified students may receive credit through Advanced Placement testing. Students who complete the International Baccalaureate diploma can receive up to 30 college credit hours.

The University of Tulsa operates on a semester calendar. The fall term begins in late August and the spring term in mid-January.

Off-Campus Programs

The university is supportive of study-abroad and internship experiences. The Center for Global Education helps students locate the perfect program, whether for TU credit or as an intern or volunteer. Students choose from hundreds of opportunities offered around the world through a direct exchange with an international university, an affiliate-sponsored program, or as part of a faculty-led course. Internship opportunities are also available in Tulsa and throughout the nation.

Academic Facilities

TU's libraries, historic McFarlin Library and Mabee Legal Information Center, house more than 4 million items. McFarlin holdings include over 990,000 volumes, 680,000 titles, 450,000 e-books, 54,000 electronic periodicals, 9,900 videos, and 11,900 recordings. McFarlin's special collections rare book holdings number over 125,000 volumes and are internationally recognized, particularly for holdings of Native American history and law, along with nineteenth- and twentieth-century Irish, English, and American literature. McFarlin is home to the papers of 2001 Nobel Laureate V. S. Naipaul. The 12,000 square-foot Academic Technology Center annex was dedicated in 2009, adding computer labs, a coffee shop, and restored reading rooms.

The College of Engineering and Natural Sciences added J. Newton Rayzor Hall, a $14-million home for the Tandy School of Computer Science and Department of Electrical Engineering with 24 integrated classrooms and state-of-the-art teaching/research laboratories; and Stephenson Hall, the 38,600 square-foot home for the Department of Mechanical Engineering and McDougall School of Petroleum Engineering. The university's flagship Keplinger Hall is undergoing renovation. Additional research facilities are housed at Tulsa's North Campus where government- and industry-funded research consortia explore innovations and solve problems faced by the petroleum industry while fostering student learning.

Helmerich Hall, which houses the Collins College of Business, includes innovative learning spaces such as the Williams Students Services Center and Studio Blue. The Williams Risk Management Center combines the latest in trading-floor technology and advanced study in risk management theories and techniques.

The Roxana Rózsa and Robert Eugene Lorton Performance Center houses the School of Music and the Department of Film Studies. The 77,000 square-foot facility includes a 600-seat concert hall, specialized rehearsal and practice rooms, and a film production suite with postproduction editing and scoring capabilities.

The Oxley College of Health Sciences moved is located in downtown Tulsa, occupying 50,000 square feet of the building at 1215 South Boulder. To accommodate travel between the main campus and the college, the university operates continuous shuttle routes for students, faculty, and staff. Oxley expands TU's downtown presence, which also includes the Henry Zarrow Center for Art and Education in the Tulsa Arts District.

The Donald W. Reynolds Center is the campus arena and convocation center, home for TU basketball and volleyball, and includes cutting-edge facilities for video editing and training.

The Allen Chapman Student Union offers dining options and meeting spaces. Meals and snacks are also available in the Pat Case Dining Center, the Collins Fitness Center, and the McFarlin Library Café.

The 29,000 square-foot Case Athletic Complex is home to the Golden Hurricane football program and adjoins the H. A. Chapman Stadium where players enjoy one of the nation's elite college football training and playing environments.

The university's 34-acre sports and recreation complex features a 64,000 square-foot fitness center, the Michael Case Tennis Center, track, NCAA soccer and softball fields, and intramural fields.

TU manages the city's Gilcrease Museum, home to the world's largest collection of art and artifacts of the American West. The two entities have expanded into the Tulsa Arts District to open the Henry Zarrow Center for Art and Education, providing classes and studio space. In 2014, the university opened the Helmerich Center for American Research at Gilcrease Museum to house the museum's library and archive. Visiting faculty, students, and scholars from around the world visit the 25,000 square-foot facility to conduct research and present symposia on their research topics.

Costs

For 2019-20, the typical cost for students living on campus is $41,698 for tuition, $11,450 for room and board, and fees of $1,025. Additional miscellaneous expenses (including books) average about $4,500 per year.

Financial Aid

In 2018, 96 percent of entering students received some form of financial aid (including grants, scholarships, work-study, and loans). TU offers a limited number of highly competitive Presidential Scholarships that cover full tuition, room, and board. All applicants may be considered for a range of University scholarships based on academic merit. Performance scholarships are available in music and theater by audition. The University of Tulsa participates in National Merit and National Achievement Scholarship Corporation's Finalist program and the National Hispanic Scholar Program. Applicants for aid should submit the Free Application for Federal Student Aid (FAFSA) by January 15 for priority consideration.

Faculty

The University has 355 full-time faculty members, with 94 percent having earned the highest degree in their field of study. The faculty is primarily a teaching faculty, although most of its members are also involved in funded research or publishing activities.

Admission Requirements

The University of Tulsa seeks students whose academic background indicates potential for success in the university's rigorous academic environment. Performance in high school college-preparatory subjects and scores on the SAT or ACT are key factors in the admission evaluation, but each applicant is reviewed holistically. Each applicant's counselor recommendation; extracurricular activities; and indicators of leadership, creativity, and focus are all taken into consideration. Campus visits and interviews are highly recommended but not required.

Application and Information

TU has a nonbinding, early action freshman admission plan with an application deadline of November 1. Decisions are mailed within five weeks. Applications received after November 1 are reviewed under a rolling admission process with notifications made on an ongoing basis in early January.

An application, high school transcript, ACT or SAT score results, and a guidance counselor recommendation are required. TU accepts the Common Application or its own online or paper application form. TU adheres to the national Candidate's Reply Date of May 1.

For more information, students should contact:

Office of Undergraduate Admission
The University of Tulsa
800 South Tucker Drive
Tulsa, Oklahoma 74104-3189
Phone: 918-631-2307 (in Tulsa)
800-331-3050 (toll-free)
Fax: 918-631-5008
E-mail: admission@utulsa.edu
Website: https://admission.utulsa.edu

Bayless Plaza is home to the iconic Kendall Bell.

UTICA COLLEGE

UTICA, NEW YORK

UTICA COLLEGE

The College

A private, independent college founded in 1946, Utica College (UC) is known for its excellent academic programs, outstanding faculty, personal attention, and diverse student population. The hallmarks of Utica College's academic programs are the integration of liberal and professional studies and a strong emphasis on internships, research, and other experiential learning opportunities, but UC is best known for the close, personal relationship students have with both faculty and staff members. More than 4,000 undergraduate and graduate students attend UC, including students from a wide variety of socioeconomic and cultural backgrounds. While most students come from New York, New England, and the middle Atlantic states, students are drawn to UC from all parts of the United States, and there is a growing international student population.

Utica College offers a broad selection of undergraduate majors, minors, and special programs, as well as graduate programs in rapidly growing professions such as cybersecurity, financial crime, physical therapy, and health care administration. UC also offers a robust selection of study-abroad opportunities as well as pre-professional programs and an honors program.

In fall of 2016, Utica College ushered in a new era for college affordability, reducing the cost of undergraduate tuition and fees by 42 percent for all new and returning students in the on-campus undergraduate program. The 2018–19 published price of tuition and fees is $20,832, and when the average room and board of $11,248 is added in, the approximate total cost of attendance is $32,080 per year, before financial aid.

Located in a suburban residential area of Utica, New York, Utica College's modern, 128-acre campus offers excellent learning, living, and recreational facilities. Half of UC's students live on campus in residence halls that feature a variety of housing options, modern amenities, and lounges for studying or relaxing with friends. Freshmen primarily live in North and South Halls, which offer double- and triple-occupancy rooms. Dining options on campus satisfy a wide variety of tastes, including American and international cuisines, vegetarian meals, a large salad bar, and lighter fare such as burgers and pizza. Students enjoy a range of dining venues on campus, from the main dining commons in Strebel Student Center, which recently underwent a $4 million overhaul, to convenient cafes in the Library and academic buildings, plus customizable Mexican entrees at Tres Habaneros, located in the Pioneer Cafe.

Whether students live on or off campus, they can take advantage of more than eighty student organizations, focusing on community service, music, theater, and politics as well as fraternities, sororities, and major-related clubs that provide opportunities for students to organize academic and career-related events. Students can write for the student newspaper, work at the College's radio station, submit entries for the literary magazine, or work on the yearbook. Students also have the opportunity to enjoy lectures, concerts, poetry readings, art exhibits, plays, and nationally recognized speakers.

Utica College offers twenty-six NCAA Division III varsity sports, including men's baseball, basketball, cross-country, football, golf, ice hockey, lacrosse, soccer, swimming and diving, tennis, and track and field; and women's basketball, cross-country, field hockey, golf, ice hockey, lacrosse, soccer, softball, swimming and diving, tennis, track and field, volleyball, and water polo. UC also offers club sports and a wide variety of intramural opportunities. Utica College is a member of the Empire 8 Athletic Conference and the United Collegiate Hockey Conference. Nearly a third of all UC students participate in at least one Division III intercollegiate sport, and more than 45 percent are active in intramural or nonvarsity club sports.

Athletic facilities include the 1,200-seat multisport Gaetano Stadium with a state-of-the-art field turf synthetic grass playing surface; the Clark Athletic Center, which contains a large gymnasium, racquetball courts, a swimming pool, saunas, a 6,400-square-foot free-weight room and fully equipped fitness facility, and the Todd and Jen Hutton Sports and Recreation Center, a 135,000-square-foot multi-sport dome that is one of the largest facilities of its kind in North America. Ice hockey games are played at the recently upgraded Adirondack Bank Center, a 4,000-seat arena in downtown Utica featuring pro-style hockey locker rooms and training facilities.

Location

The city of Utica is located in the heart of the historic Mohawk Valley in the center of New York State. Just 90 miles west of Albany and 50 miles east of Syracuse, Utica has a thriving arts community, beautiful parks, and expanding shopping centers featuring national retailers. Utica College is conveniently located just 10 minutes from the nearest bus and Amtrak station, and only 50 miles east of Hancock International Airport in Syracuse. There are numerous recreational facilities, including a municipal ski slope and an excellent golf course less than a mile from the Utica College campus. Other nearby recreational opportunities include tennis, swimming, boating, hiking, and camping.

Academic Programs

Utica College offers undergraduate degree programs in accounting, animal behavior, biochemistry, biology, business economics and finance, business management, chemistry, communication and media, computer science, construction management, criminal intelligence analysis, criminal justice, cybersecurity and information assurance, diet and nutrition, economics, English, foreign language, fraud and financial crime investigation, French, geoscience, government and politics, health care management, health studies, history, international studies, liberal studies, mathematics, neuroscience, nursing (traditional, RN to B.S.N., and accelerated), occupational therapy, philosophy, physical therapy, physics, psychobiology, psychology, psychology–child life, public relations, sociology and anthropology, Spanish, sports management, teacher education, therapeutic recreation, and wellness and adventure education. Pre-professional programs include dentistry, law, medicine, optometry, podiatry, and veterinary medicine.

Occupational therapy and physical therapy majors earn a bachelor's degree in health studies with direct entry into UC's graduate programs, as long as academic requirements are met. Utica College offers a master's degree in occupational therapy and a doctorate in physical therapy (D.P.T.).

A complete list of programs, including undergraduate minors, can be found online at www.utica.edu/programs.

For those students who are undecided, professionals in the Center for Student Success and the Center for Career and Professional Development facilitate exploratory programs, academic advising, and career counseling.

Utica College offers the Higher Education Opportunity Program (HEOP), the Collegiate Science and Technology Entry Program (CSTEP), and Summer Institute, which serves as an academic bridge between high school and college.

Off-Campus Programs

UC's study-abroad programs give students opportunities to widen their global perspectives through exchange programs with universities in Spain, Italy, Poland, Finland, Hungary, Peru, Scotland, and Wales, as well as American College in Dublin, Ireland, among other options. Special study-abroad opportunities include the College's annual forensic anthropology field school in Albania as well as learning experiences in London and elsewhere.

Students are encouraged to complete internships and field placements to gain professional experience with businesses and organizations while they are earning college credit. Utica College's cooperative education program allows students to earn money while gaining professional experience.

Academic Facilities

The Frank E. Gannett Memorial Library includes a collection of some 172,000 volumes, 800 serial subscriptions, hundreds of online journals, and other resources, as well as the Kelly Teaching and Learning Center, which contains the College's Writing and Math Centers. Located on the lower level of the library are the Media Center, computer labs, the Edith Langley Barrett Fine Art Gallery, and a large concourse—the site of special events, such as musical recitals, receptions, and guest lectures.

Along with smart classrooms and faculty offices, UC's main academic complex features advanced new laboratories for biology, chemistry, and zoology. F. Eugene Romano Hall provides state-of-the-art classroom, laboratory, and clinical space, as well as learning technology for students in the health sciences. The Economic Crime, Justice Studies, and Cybersecurity Building supports cutting-edge research and advanced learning at both the undergraduate and graduate levels in these very dynamic disciplines. In 2019, the College opened Thurston Hall, providing modern facilities for its growing construction management program. The Professor Raymond Simon Convergence Media Center features a high-definition broadcast facility, control room, and edit suite. Located in the heart of Utica's revitalized downtown financial district, the recently completed Robert Brvenik Center for Business Education features a fully functional trading room with live stock ticker, smart classrooms, a large student lounge, and other resources to support students enrolled in the college's business and economics programs.

In addition to wireless Internet available across campus, Utica College maintains computer laboratories with both Windows and Macintosh computers.

Costs

In the fall of 2016, Utica College's "Bold Move For Tomorrow" affordability initiative took effect, reducing the tuition price by 42 percent, with a substantial reduction in room and board costs. For 2018–19, tuition is $20,832. Average room and board costs are $11,248. Student activity and technology fees will total $550. Books and supplies average $1,400 per year.

Financial Aid

Keeping quality, private education affordable is central to Utica College's mission. More than 90 percent of UC freshmen typically receive financial aid. The College also awards numerous merit scholarships.

Almost every federal and state financial aid program is available through Utica College, including New York State's Enhanced Tuition Award. Students apply for institutional and governmental financial aid by filing the Free Application for Federal Student Aid (FAFSA).

Faculty

Utica College's faculty is diverse, energetic, accomplished, and devoted to their students. The vast majority of faculty members have earned their Ph.D. or other terminal degree, and while many are involved in research, the primary focus of faculty members is teaching. The typical class size is 20 students, the student-faculty ratio is 11:1, and all faculty members are involved in assisting students with their academic planning.

Student Government

One of Utica College's strongest traditions is student participation in the College's governance structure. Students may serve on a number of student governing bodies, and students also serve on all standing committees of the College.

Admission Requirements

Utica College admits students who can best benefit from the educational opportunities the College offers. The Admission Committee gives each application individual attention, and the potential for a student's success at UC is measured primarily by an evaluation of past academic performance, scholastic ability, and personal characteristics. Freshman applicants must have completed 16 academic units, including 4 years of English. Students should follow a college-preparatory program, including 3 units of mathematics, 3 units of science, 2 units of foreign language, and 3 units of social studies.

Application and Information

Students may apply for fall, spring, or summer admission. Materials required include a completed Utica College application form, official high school or college transcripts, one letter of recommendation, a personal statement, and a $40 application fee. Utica College is test-optional and therefore does not require SAT or ACT scores, with the exception of the programs listed below. A personal interview for all applications is strongly suggested.

Occupational therapy, physical therapy, nursing, and joint health professions program applicants must submit SAT or ACT scores. International students must complete the international student application form. The application fee is waived for students who apply to HEOP or CSTEP; however, SAT or ACT scores are required to be considered for either program.

The College offers three admissions programs: early decision, early action, and rolling admissions.

Additional admissions information can be found online at http://www.utica.edu/admissions.

Inquiries should be sent to:

Office of Undergraduate Admissions
Utica College
1600 Burrstone Road
Utica, New York 13502-4892
Phone: 315-792-3006
800-782-8884 (toll-free)
E-mail: admiss@utica.edu
Website: http://www.utica.edu
http://www.facebook.com/UticaCollegeAdmissions
http://twitter.com/uticacollege

Utica College's newest academic building, Thurston Hall, features state-of-the-art learning facilities, laboratories, and gathering spaces to support students and faculty in UC's growing Construction Management program.

VANDERBILT UNIVERSITY

NASHVILLE, TENNESSEE

VANDERBILT UNIVERSITY

The University

In 1873, on the heels of the Civil War, "Commodore" Cornelius Vanderbilt gave $1 million to the university that now bears his name, with the hope that it would "contribute to strengthening the ties which should exist between all sections of our common country." Since then, Vanderbilt has consistently enrolled highly talented students and challenged them daily to expand their intellectual horizons in an inclusive environment based on open inquiry and respect. Vanderbilt's comprehensive interdisciplinary approach to education allows students to pursue a wide array of academic and curricular interests outside of their main focus of study, and the University's Opportunity Vanderbilt financial aid program ensures that Vanderbilt is often cited among the country's best values.

Consistently ranked among the top 20 universities in the country by *U.S. News & World Report,* Vanderbilt is a private research university that features ten schools including four undergraduate schools. Each year, 1,600 first-year students join the University, bringing the total undergraduate population to approximately 6,900 students. Vanderbilt students come from across the country and around the world, and represent a rich diversity of backgrounds. Among undergraduates, 8.8 percent are international students, 41 percent are minority students, and 65 percent receive some type of financial assistance.

Vanderbilt's 7:1 student-faculty ratio gives students access to faculty members of prominence in every area of academic study. More than 50 percent of undergraduates collaborate with professors on research spanning almost every academic field, including natural and social sciences, humanities, engineering, and education. Faculty members share their perspectives as instructors and advisers with the goal of providing a challenging, comprehensive education that encourages broad perspectives and critical thinking.

A park-like campus located in the heart of Nashville, Vanderbilt offers a top-ranked residential experience for its undergraduates, nearly all of whom live on campus all four years. First-year students live and learn on The Martha Rivers Ingram Commons, a collection of ten residence halls, or Houses, clustered along one side of campus. The Ingram Commons incorporates more than just bricks and mortar. Faculty members—including the dean of The Commons and faculty heads of house—and their families live there, facilitating easy and meaningful interactions between students and professors. Frequent educational and social programming at The Commons invites students and faculty to explore current events and social issues. After their first year, students have many housing options, including apartment-style living and residential colleges, which include E. Bronson Ingram, opened in 2018.

Vanderbilt students take full advantage of student life in over 430 student organizations, a full range of study-abroad programs, Division I Athletics, and a variety of internship opportunities.

Location

Vanderbilt University is located in Nashville, the capital of Tennessee. Ranked one of the Best U.S. Cities to Visit in 2019 by *Smarter Travel*, Nashville boasts a rich mosaic of cultures, vibrant arts, business, health, and technology sectors, and an array of recreational opportunities. Nashville hosts thousands of live concerts each year in every conceivable genre and is recognized as a top college city in America and an excellent location for businesses. Nashville's booming cultural scene, striking natural beauty, and thriving economy attract people from around the world.

Majors and Degrees

College of Arts and Science: African American and Diaspora Studies; American Studies; Anthropology; Art; Asian Studies; Biochemistry and Chemical Biology; Biological Sciences; Chemistry; Cinema and Media Arts; Classical and Mediterranean Studies; Communication of Science and Technology; Communication Studies; Earth and Environmental Sciences; Ecology, Evolution, and Organismal Biology; Economics; Economics and History; English; Environmental Sociology; European Studies; French; French and European Studies; German Studies; German and European Studies; History; History of Art; Italian and European Studies; Jewish Studies; Latin American Studies; Latino and Latina Studies; Law, History, and Society; Mathematics; Medicine, Health, and Society; Molecular and Cellular Biology; Neuroscience; Philosophy; Physics; Political Science; Psychology; Public Policy Studies; Religious Studies; Russian; Russian, East European, and European Studies; Sociology; Spanish; Spanish and European Studies; Spanish and Portuguese; Spanish, Portuguese, and European Studies; Theatre; and Women's and Gender Studies.

Blair School of Music: Composition; Integrated Studies; Integrated Studies/Teacher Education; and Performance.

School of Engineering: Biomedical Engineering; Chemical Engineering; Civil Engineering; Computer Engineering; Computer Science; Electrical Engineering; Engineering Science; and Mechanical Engineering.

Peabody College of Education and Human Development: Child Development; Child Studies; Cognitive Studies; Early Childhood and Elementary Education; Human and Organizational Development; Secondary Education; and Special Education.

Graduate/Professional Schools: Divinity School; Graduate School; Law School; Owen Graduate School of Management; Peabody College of Education and Human Development; School of Engineering; School of Medicine; and School of Nursing.

Pre-professional advising is available for undergraduate students interested in pursuing graduate degrees in architecture, business, law, or health professions.

Academic Programs

Students apply for admission to one of four undergraduate schools: the College of Arts and Science, the School of Engineering, Peabody College of Education and Human Development, or the Blair School of Music. In all four schools, honors programs and opportunities for research, independent study, and internships are available. Thirty-two percent of undergraduate students pursue double majors within or across the four undergraduate schools, and 55 percent add an optional minor.

The College of Arts and Science offers a wide spectrum of courses in the humanities, social sciences, and natural sciences, and has majors and minors in approximately 50 departments and interdisciplinary areas. Students in A&S achieve both breadth and depth in their education by satisfying a set of liberal arts and science courses through AXLE (Achieving eXcellence in Liberal Education), and by completing at least one major.

The Blair School of Music offers conservatory-level music training in a strong liberal arts environment. Vanderbilt is one of only four top-twenty universities in the nation to offer an accredited undergraduate school of music, and the only one whose school of music is solely for undergraduates. The curriculum combines intensive musical training with liberal arts studies and students take approximately one-third of their courses outside of the music school. The Blair School also offers a music minor and a wide variety of courses, private instruction, and performing organizations for non-majors.

For more than 125 years, the School of Engineering has educated engineers for practice in industry, government, consulting, teaching, and research careers. In addition to technical courses, each student's program includes a rich complement of course work in the humanities and social sciences, resulting in a balanced foundation for future achievement and the assumption of leadership roles in their chosen fields. All programs leading to a Bachelor of Engineering degree are ABET-accredited, and students can earn a Bachelor of Science degree while majoring in Computer Science or Engineering Science.

Ranked one of the top eight graduate schools of education (according to *U.S. News & World Report*) for twenty consecutive years, Peabody College offers degree programs in education and human development. The degree reflects a strong liberal arts foundation combined with a solid program of pre-professional courses and a multitude of internship and practicum opportunities. All undergraduates must complete requirements in communications, the humanities, mathematics, the natural sciences, and the social sciences. Moreover, students have an abundance of field experiences throughout their four years.

Regardless of school or major, the academic experience at Vanderbilt goes well beyond the traditional classroom. Across all four undergraduate schools, students engage in hands-on learning that complements and furthers their academic experience at Vanderbilt. Immersion Vanderbilt provides students with the opportunity to pursue their passions and cultivate intellectual interests by calling for each undergraduate to undertake an intensive learning experience in and beyond the classroom, culminating in the creation of a final project. Students will engage in a civic and professional, creative expression, international, or research immersion experience.

Off-Campus Programs

Study-abroad programs allow students to immerse themselves in languages and cultures around the world. Vanderbilt offers more than 120 programs in countries such as Argentina, Australia, Austria, Chile, China, Cuba, Czech Republic, Denmark, the Dominican Republic, Egypt, England, France, Israel, Italy, Japan, Russia, Singapore, South Africa, and Spain. In these Vanderbilt-approved programs, students receive direct credit for their courses, and the cost of tuition is usually the same as for study on campus in Nashville. In addition, any scholarships, grants, or loans a student has been awarded apply to Vanderbilt study-abroad programs. Students may also participate in programs sponsored by other universities by working with an adviser.

Academic Facilities

The newest academic facilities on campus are the Engineering and Science Building and the adjacent Innovation Pavilion. The Engineering and Science Building is a 230,000 square-foot, seven-story teaching and research building designed to foster project teamwork and promote interdisciplinary research. Next door in the Innovation Pavilion is the Wond'ry, Vanderbilt's new epicenter for innovation and entrepreneurship. Through collaborative work environments, maker spaces, and curricular programming, the Wond'ry is the place where abstract ideas are transformed into concrete realities that will make differences in people's lives.

Costs

The estimated costs for 2019–20 include: tuition, $50,788; housing, $11,044; meals, $5,866; books and supplies, $1,294; student activities and recreation fee, $1,272; personal expenses allowance, $2,874; first-year experience fee, $836; new student transcript fee, $100; engineering lab fee*, $800; and engineering laptop allowance*, $1,600. Travel allowances are variable. *The engineering laptop allowance and laboratory fee apply to engineering students only. First-year engineering students are required to either purchase a laptop from Vanderbilt or provide their own computer that meets published requirements.

Financial Aid

Through Opportunity Vanderbilt, the University makes three important commitments reflecting a strong dedication to making a Vanderbilt education possible: Vanderbilt is need-blind for all U.S. citizens and eligible non-citizens; Vanderbilt meets 100 percent of demonstrated need for all admitted students; and Vanderbilt's financial aid packages do not include loans. Also, there are no income cutoffs that limit eligibility. These three commitments combined place Vanderbilt among a small number of universities to adopt such progressive policies. Need-based aid is awarded according to the evaluation of the FAFSA and the CSS/Financial Aid PROFILE.

Vanderbilt also awards merit-based scholarships to selected first-year applicants who demonstrate exceptional accomplishment and intellectual promise. Three signature scholarships comprise the majority of these honor scholarships: the Ingram Scholarship Program, the Cornelius Vanderbilt Scholarship, and the Chancellor's Scholarship. To be considered for the Cornelius Vanderbilt Scholarship, a separate application is required. To be considered for the Ingram or Chancellor's Scholarship, a separate application is strongly encouraged.

In the 2018–19 school year, 65 percent of Vanderbilt undergraduates received some type of financial assistance.

Faculty

Vanderbilt University has 975 full-time instructional faculty members. All undergraduate faculty members teach undergraduate students and many also serve as research mentors and academic advisers. A low student-faculty ratio provides for an intimate academic experience between students and professors who are recognized nationally and worldwide for their research. Ninety-two percent of classes have fewer than 50 students.

Student Government

The Vanderbilt Student Government (VSG) provides students with an opportunity to participate actively in maintaining a high quality of life on campus. It works with student organizations to bring nationally prominent speakers to campus and provides an interesting and diverse array of programming throughout the year. A vital part of life at Vanderbilt is the honor system, governed entirely by students through representatives on the Honor Council. Each year, a senior is selected as a Young Alumni Trustee of the University's Board of Trust.

Admission Requirements

Vanderbilt uses a holistic admissions process—there are no cutoffs based on standardized testing or grade point averages. The Admissions Committee evaluates students' academic records, test scores (either the SAT or ACT is required), extracurricular involvement, counselor and teacher recommendations, and personal essay. Applicants to the Blair School of Music are required to submit a separate application and a prescreening video, and selected applicants are invited to an on-campus audition.

Vanderbilt seeks students with high standards of scholarship and character. Most competitive applicants have a strong academic profile—including excellent grades in the context of a rigorous course load, strong test scores, and positive academic letters of recommendation. In addition, most successful applicants demonstrate significant levels of engagement and leadership outside the classroom.

Application and Information

Students whose first choice is Vanderbilt may apply under one of Vanderbilt's early decision plans. Applications are due by November 1 for Early Decision I and by January 1 for Early Decision II; notification is made by mid-December for Early Decision I and by mid-February for Early Decision II. Regular Decision applications are due January 1 and admission decisions are available by late March. The priority application deadline for students seeking transfer admission is March 15 for the following fall semester entry.

Office of Undergraduate Admissions
Vanderbilt University
2305 West End Avenue
Nashville, Tennessee 37203-1727
Phone: 615-322-2561
800-288-0432 (toll-free)
E-mail: admissions@vanderbilt.edu
Website: admissions.vanderbilt.edu
facebook.com/vanderbiltadmissions
twitter.com/vanderbiltu
instagram.com/vanderbiltadmissions

Kirkland Hall, Vanderbilt's oldest and most historic building.

WESTMONT COLLEGE
SANTA BARBARA, CALIFORNIA

WESTMONT

The College

Westmont College helps students unite both spirit and mind through a liberal arts education that offers rigorous training in every area of human knowledge and fosters a deep love of God. The college's nationally ranked program focuses entirely on undergraduates, and helps them develop deep relationships by living in a residential Christian community. Westmont professors lead semesters on four continents to help students develop a global perspective.

Learning at Westmont extends beyond the classroom as students participate in a variety of student clubs, activities and service projects. Athletes can compete with a Warrior team or play for a club sport or intramural league. Musicians have the opportunity to perform with accomplished choirs and instrumental groups, the theater program stages classic plays and an exciting Fringe Festival, and art students study in beautifully designed studios and exhibit artwork in the Westmont Ridley-Tree Museum of Art. Other possibilities include the student newspaper, literary magazine, or yearbook; intercultural clubs and political organizations; or volunteer opportunities in the community. Chapel, an integral part of a Westmont education, features inspiring speakers who encourage students to grow in their faith. Attendance is required three days a week.

Westmont's Office of Career Planning and Calling helps students discover their strengths and weaknesses, then prepare for a career by facilitating internships. Westmont's professors and classes also provide preparation for graduate school; Westmont alumni have attended some of the finest universities in the world, such as UCLA, Stanford, Harvard, Yale, Princeton, Cambridge, the University of Chicago, and others.

The college's 1,200 students come from more than 30 states and 16 countries, with the highest percentage from California. About 61 percent are women, 34 percent are students of color, and 2 percent are international students. Ninety-five percent of students live in the six residence halls on campus or the apartment complex off campus.

Westmont belongs to the National Association of Intercollegiate Athletics and the Golden State Athletic Conference and competes in intercollegiate sports for men and women in basketball, cross-country, golf, soccer, tennis, and track and field and in baseball (men) and swimming and volleyball (women). Club teams for men include polo, rugby, soccer, volleyball, Ultimate (Frisbee), and golf; women's club teams are polo, cheer, and golf. Both men and women can participate in intramural sports.

Location

Located in scenic Santa Barbara, Westmont's 111-acre wooded campus lies between the Santa Ynez Mountains and the Pacific Ocean. Students enjoy the beach and mountain trails year-round. The local community offers a wealth of culture, including museums, theaters, libraries, concerts, lectures, and historic sites.

Majors and Degrees

Westmont awards Bachelor of Arts (B.A.) and Bachelor of Science (B.S.) degrees in more than 100 academic majors, minors, and programs: alternative major, art, art history, biology, chemistry, communication studies, computer science, economics and business, data analytics, education, engineering, engineering physics, English, English and modern languages, European studies, French, history, kinesiology, liberal studies, mathematics, music, philosophy, physics, political science, psychology, religious studies, social science, sociology and anthropology, Spanish, and theater arts. The California Commission for Teacher Preparation and Licensing accredits the teacher-preparation program, and students may qualify for either the single-subject or the multiple-subject credential. Pre-professional programs include athletic training, dentistry, engineering, law, medicine, ministry and missionary studies, pharmacy, physical therapy, and veterinary studies. Westmont awaits approval for a Bachelor of Music program.

Academic Programs

All majors and programs of study feature thought-provoking and inspiring ways to integrate belief, thought, and action to reach a deeper, more accurate understanding of the world and achieve a wider impact. Professors demand critical thinking and encourage exploration of the world of ideas through a wide range of opportunities and organizations. For example, students consider issues of science and religion through the Pascal Society and attend lectures in the humanities sponsored by the Erasmus Society. At Westmont, an exclusively undergraduate college, students can engage in significant research projects in the sciences and all disciplines by assisting professors in their scholarly work and completing independent study. Professors, staff members, and alumni seek to help students grow through their questions toward an ever-deeper faith.

Global Education

Westmont professors lead the college's global education programs, including **Europe Semester**, which offers the broadest geographical scope. **England Semester** combines travel and residential study of literature in the British Isles. At **Westmont in Cairo** students live in a developing world megalopolis at the heart of the Islamic world. **Westmont in Jerusalem** lets students explore the ancient world of Jesus and modern Israel-Palestine. Through **Westmont in Mexico**, students gain skills for effective cross-cultural living and improve their Spanish-speaking skills. **Westmont in East Asia** takes participants to Seoul, Shanghai, and Singapore to learn about globalization, culture, society, and Christianity. **Westmont in Northern Europe** features extended stays in London, Berlin, and Northern Ireland and focuses on conflict and peace-making. **Global Health: Uganda** gives medical and public-health-related majors an international field placement at a local organization in Uganda. Students can take part in a meaningful internship during **Westmont in San Francisco** and grapple with big questions while staying in a historic mansion in a vibrant area of the city. The **Summer Session in Singapore** combines academic study, an internship, and some travel in the region. At **Westmont Downtown**, participants live in downtown Santa Barbara, study social entrepreneurship, and spend 20 hours a week in a significant internship. Westmont's membership in the Christian College Consortium (CCC) lets students explore additional opportunities and programs led by other colleges, such as language and cultural study in places such as France, Spain, and Latin America; a Washington Semester in the nation's capital; and the Consortium Visitor Program, in which students spend a semester at another of the CCC's 13 campuses.

Academic Facilities

Westmont's newest buildings include the Global Leadership Center, Adams Center for the Visual Arts, which features the Westmont Ridley-Tree Museum of Art, Winter Hall for Science and Mathematics, and the Westmont Observatory with the powerful Keck Telescope. The tri-level Roger John Voskuyl Library, named for Westmont's third president, provides resources and services that support the teaching and research needs of faculty, staff, students, and the surrounding community. The library collections include 237,000 books, media items, music scores, and microforms; 300 print periodical titles; 105 online databases with access to 12,000 online periodicals; and access to additional resources through the Gold Coast Library Network, Camino, and Interlibrary Loan Services. Westmont's network consists of both wired and wireless components. Wireless coverage extends to all campus buildings and most outdoor areas, with a total Internet bandwidth of 135 Mb/s. Students obtain Google Apps accounts through Westmont, providing email, a calendar, document sharing, and 4 GB of storage per student. The college provides a computer lab with 27 dual-platform iMacs located on the main floor of the library. Westmont's Learning Commons, a 21st-century space in the library, brings together library, technology, and other campus services in an environment that fosters collaborative and creative work and social interaction. Voskuyl Library also houses departments that provide student support services: Academic Advising and Disability Services, Internship Programs, Writer's Corner, and Information Technology. Porter Theatre contains state-of-the-art equipment for dramatic productions and concerts, including the Black Box Theatre. Mericos H. Whittier Science Building and Winter Hall for Science and Mathematics house the college's science program and equipment, including an ultracentrifuge, a liquid scintillation counter for measuring radioactivity, physiographic units, and other equipment for advanced physiological studies.

Costs

Tuition and fees for 2018–19 were $45,410, and room and board for the academic year are $14,646. The cost of books and personal expenses are estimated at $3,000.

Financial Aid

Westmont provides generous financial aid and encourages all students to apply regardless of their financial resources. Ninety-five percent of students receive some form of financial assistance. Westmont offers awards worth 85 percent of tuition through the Augustinian Scholars Program to 60 students each year, available only to first-year applicants who apply via nonbinding early action. A select group of these applicants participate in a formal competition on campus; interested students should contact the Office of Admissions for more information. Other merit awards in the financial aid program—President's, Ruth Kerr, Wallace L. Emerson, and Founders Scholarships and the Warrior Academic Award—range from $15,000 to $25,000. Transfer students may be eligible for scholarships ranging from $9,000 to $15,000, offered to students with impressive academic achievement. Westmont also gives awards to those who demonstrate strength in art, music, theater arts, dance, cultural diversity, and athletics. After submitting the Free Application for Federal Student Aid (FAFSA), students may be eligible for state grants, aid from federal programs, institutional grants, loans, and work-study programs.

Faculty

One of Westmont's highest priorities is attracting and retaining Christian teachers and scholars with outstanding credentials and a love for students. Students get to know professors personally and will likely spend time with them outside of class. The college's 96 full-time and 58 part-time professors are dedicated to integrating faith and learning and being actively involved in the lives of students. The student-faculty ratio is 11:1; the average class size is 17. Ninety-eight percent of tenure-track faculty members hold a terminal degree. Professors are committed to teaching at the undergraduate level and advise either incoming first-year students or majors in their department. Although teaching is their primary scholarly activity, many professors engage in research, write books, and publish articles in leading journals and periodicals.

Student Government

The Westmont College Student Association (WCSA) is a self-governing body. Students elect WCSA representatives, who are responsible for organizing social, cultural, and educational activities. They actively participate as voting members on most faculty committees, and allocate the student budget to various clubs and organizations. Westmont Student Ministries, another student-managed organization, organizes a range of outreach programs and ministries on and off campus.

Admission Requirements

Westmont selects candidates for admission from prospective students who demonstrate their preparation for the academic stimulation and spiritual vitality central to Westmont's character. All applicants must submit one academic letter of recommendation, official high school or college transcripts, and official SAT or ACT scores. A pastoral/character reference is optional. An interview is strongly encouraged. For transfer students from an accredited two- or four-year college or university or a Bible college or university that is accredited by the American Association of Bible Colleges, the evaluation is based on achievement in solid, transferable course work; an assessment of the personal areas covered by the application (as stated above); and the quality of the written responses. High school records must also be submitted by transfer students having completed fewer than 24 semester units or 36 quarter units.

Application and Information

Students may enroll at Westmont at the beginning of either the fall or spring semester. The college offers an early-action plan. High school seniors interested in applying Early Action 1 must submit an application by October 15, and those interested in applying Early Action 2 must submit an application by November 1. Notifications are mailed by December 1 and January 1, respectively. The priority deadline for regular decision is January 15 for first-year applicants and March 15 for transfers. Notifications are mailed on a rolling basis. Applications should be submitted online via the Common Application or the Westmont Application. No application fee is required. The Office of Admission encourages prospective students to complete the application process as early as possible.

Visitors are welcome any time. Guests may stay overnight in the residence halls, attend classes and chapel, speak with professors or coaches, audition for a music program, share a portfolio with the art department, interview with an admissions counselor, and eat meals with Westmont students. Several Preview Day events are held each semester. Westmont seeks to enroll a well-rounded and varied first-year class while creating a dynamic and culturally and traditionally diverse community of learners possessing a variety of attributes, accomplishments, backgrounds, and interests.

For more information regarding admissions students should contact:

Office of Admission
Westmont College
955 La Paz Road
Santa Barbara, California 93108
Phone: 800-777-9011 (toll-free)
Fax: 805-565-6234
E-mail: admissions@westmont.edu
Website: http://www.westmont.edu/
http://www.facebook.com/westmont
http://twitter.com/westmontnews

Discover a premiere liberal arts college on one of the most beautiful college campuses in the country.

COLLEGE CLOSE-UPS

WEST VIRGINIA WESLEYAN COLLEGE

BUCKHANNON, WEST VIRGINIA

WEST VIRGINIA WESLEYAN

The College

Here, you're Home. West Virginia Wesleyan is a private four-year co-educational residential college that is affiliated with The United Methodist Church. West Virginia Wesleyan creates a unique learning environment enabling our students to develop the skills, values, relationships, and perspective needed for them to obtain employment, enhance their careers, and demonstrate leadership throughout their lives. Wesleyan graduates are well prepared to be successful and respected citizens in a rapidly changing world. 97% of the class of 2017 graduates attained a job in their field or attended graduate school within 6 months of graduation (with 85% of the class reporting). The College has an enrollment of 1,250 undergraduate students from thirty-five states and twenty-one countries. The average class size is 19 and the student-faculty ratio is 13:1. Each fall, West Virginia Wesleyan enrolls approximately 325 freshmen and 25 transfers. Fifty percent of students originate from out-of-state. Approximately 24 percent of the students are minority or international students. More than 80 percent of students live on campus, and housing is required for all four years of study. Housing options include residence halls, suites, on-campus apartments, and campus-adjacent residence units.

Among the many services available to students is the Learning Center, which provides comprehensive learning resources for all students, as well as robust services for students with diagnosed learning differences and is one of the foremost programs of its type in the country.

In addition to challenging academic curriculum and innovative technology, Wesleyan offers a balanced and comprehensive student-life program. Co-curricular activities include twenty-one NCAA Division II varsity sports, intramurals, and outdoor recreation adventures. More than seventy campus organizations include vocal and instrumental musical ensembles, theatre arts, dance, community service, clubs, special interest groups, Greek life, and spiritual and religious life programming. On-campus media opportunities include a campus radio station, student newspaper, and yearbook. The student-run Bobcat Entertainment Board schedules cultural and social entertainment every week during the academic year.

Location

Situated in the foothills of the Allegheny Mountains, Wesleyan's picturesque 100-acre campus is located in the historic town of Buckhannon, West Virginia. Buckhannon is located two hours south of Pittsburgh, Pennsylvania, and 90 minutes north of Charleston, West Virginia. It is easily accessible by interstate highways. Buckhannon has been included in Norman Crampton's book, The Top 100 Best Small Towns in America and The 120 Best College Towns in America. Students are drawn to the attractive and friendly setting and the many restaurants, social events, and outdoor adventures available within a short distance from campus.

Majors and Degrees

The College awards Bachelor of Arts, Bachelor of Science, Bachelor of Science in Nursing, and Bachelor of Music Education degrees, in addition to a number of master's-level degrees. Majors include: accounting, art, arts administration, athletic training, biology, business administration, five-year bachelor's + master's in business administration, chemistry, Christian formation, communication studies, computer information science, computer science, criminal justice, economics, education (combined elementary/secondary, elementary, or secondary), engineering 3-2, English (literature, education, or writing), environmental science, environmental studies, exercise science, gender studies, graphic design, history, international business, international studies, management, marketing, mathematics, music (applied or theory), music education, musical theatre, nursing, painting and drawing, philosophy, physics, political science, psychology, public relations, religion, sociology, sport business, and theatre arts.

Preprofessional study programs are offered in dentistry, law, medicine, optometry, pharmacy, physical therapy, and veterinary medicine. The degrees are determined by the content of the student's program.

West Virginia Wesleyan also offers the following graduate degrees: Master of Science in Athletic Training, Master of Business Administration, Master of Fine Arts in Creative Writing, and Doctor of Nursing Practice (DNP).

Academic Programs

Students are required to complete 120 credit hours of course work to become eligible for graduation. Approximately one third of those hours are taken in a student's major, one third in the general studies curriculum requirement, and one third in electives. The general studies and elective courses are taken to develop and enhance a student's worldview. Wesleyan operates on a traditional semester system. The optional May Term is a three-week intensive period of study giving students the opportunity to earn three credit hours. International travel opportunities are popular options during May Term.

The honors program is offered for superior students who meet the specific requirements and are willing to commit themselves to a rigorous and enriching curriculum that affirms the highest ideals of a liberal arts institution. Challenging classes and cultural outings are an integral part of the honors program and are offered throughout the academic year. Advanced credit is available for students who achieve required scores on Advanced Placement exams, International Baccalaureate exams, and CLEP tests. New students are assigned a faculty adviser who assists with course selection and student concerns. All first-year students are required to successfully complete a four-hour First Year Seminar course. In addition to helping students adapt to college life, the First Year Seminar courses are topical and apply credit toward a general studies requirement.

Off-Campus Programs

Study abroad is highly encouraged and is an important part of the Wesleyan student's experience. In the recent past, students have studied in such countries as Australia, Austria, Bolivia, Bulgaria, England, Ireland, Italy, Kenya, Korea, Spain, and Wales, but there are several other countries in which students may study. Internships are required for many majors and highly encouraged for others. They are available locally, as well as in cities such as Pittsburgh, New York, Washington, D.C., and others around the globe. These off-campus opportunities can be taken for a complete semester, during the May Term, or during the summer.

Academic Facilities

Wesleyan's twenty-four buildings, including eleven modern residence hall units, house some of the most impressive facilities in the region. Residence hall facilities include Fleming Hall, which was completely remodeled in 2008; Dunn Hall, a new residence hall that opened to students in 2011; and Doney Hall (single rooms) that opened in 2013. Other recent campus construction includes the Virginia Thomas Law Center for the Performing Arts and the Reemsnyder Research Center for the sciences. A brand-new wellness center with Nautilus equipment, full cardio theater, separate workout rooms, and locker room facilities opened in 2012. In 2014 the College opened a new Welcome Center and over the last five years have remodeled major academic classroom through funding received from a Title III grant program. This $10-million grant also provides for a Student Success Center and Center for Teaching and Learning, providing Wesleyan unparalleled support services.

The Annie Merner Pfeiffer Library houses more than 105,000 volumes, 700 periodicals, and 10,000 media materials. More than 220 million additional resources worldwide can be accessed through a number of online databases from students' own residence halls 24 hours a day. Located in the center of the campus is Wesley Chapel, the largest sanctuary in West Virginia, and the Martin Religious Center. The library will re-open in Fall 2019 after undergoing a 2-million-dollar renovation making it the academic hub of campus and an unrivaled student-centered space.

The Benedum Campus and Community Center houses a convenience store, bookstore, swimming pool, the Cat's Claw restaurant, the campus radio station, and student services offices.

The Rockefeller Health and Physical Education Center includes a main gymnasium that seats 3,700, an intramural gymnasium, weight-training rooms, and an indoor Astroturf training and recreational area. Other key campus buildings include Christopher Hall of Science and the adjacent Reemsnyder Research Center, which houses state-of-the-art laboratories and classrooms to complement the Christopher's planetarium, herbarium, and greenhouse; Loar Hall, which includes a 165-seat recital hall and state-of-the-art computer music lab; Middleton Hall, which houses the department of nursing; Haymond Hall of Science; and the Lynch-Raine Administration Building.

Costs

The College's 2019-20 tuition and fees will be $31,944 and room and board will be $9,298. Wesleyan offers numerous interest-free payment plans.

Financial Aid

Wesleyan allocates nearly $15 million each year to help supplement the financial needs of students and their families. Merit scholarships are available for students who demonstrate excellence in the classroom, as well as those who demonstrate talent in the arts and athletics. Scholarship opportunities are available for students who have a strong commitment to community service and for those who have a comprehensive co-curricular resume. A variety of need-based programs are also available, including government grants and loans, institutional grants, and student employment. All students and their families should file the Free Application for Federal Student Aid by February 15. The institutional code for West Virginia Wesleyan is 003830.

Faculty

The faculty members at Wesleyan have a primary goal of teaching and advising. More than 80 percent of the full-time faculty members hold the highest degree in their respective fields. With a 13:1 student-faculty ratio, classes are small, and personal attention is evident in all departments. Not only are faculty members teachers and advisers, but they are also mentors and friends.

Student Government

The Student Senate is structured to encourage and promote student participation. The four peer-elected officers are elected by their respective classes or representative student organizations. Student Senate meets biweekly, along with faculty members, administration, and staff members, and is recognized as the driving force behind many initiatives and decisions on campus.

Admission Requirements

Wesleyan seeks students who have proven academic credentials, combined with achievements and talents that enhance the quality of life on campus. Students are selected by the Office of Admission on the basis of their high school transcripts, college entrance exam results, letters of recommendation, campus interviews, and other supportive information. All applicants must take the SAT or ACT and submit secondary school transcripts from all schools attended, along with the application for admission. Candidates are considered on an individual basis without regard to race, color, national origin, sex, sexual orientation, age, disability, or religious affiliation. Essays and campus interviews are strongly encouraged and may be required in some instances.

Transfer students from accredited institutions are considered for admission. All official college transcripts must be submitted, along with high school transcripts and college entrance exam results.

Applicants who complete their secondary education through an alternative program (e.g., home schooling) must present evidence that they have been adequately prepared for college work to be considered for admission. SAT or ACT results are also required.

Application and Information

Applicants must submit an application for admission, official transcripts, and ACT or SAT scores. The application review period opens each year on September 1. Applying online is free of charge at www.wvwc.edu. Wesleyan is also a Common Application school and applicants may apply free of charge there as well. A paper application is also available. Admission decisions are made on a rolling basis, and students are notified within three weeks of receipt of all required documents.
The preferred application deadline is March 1 for the fall semester, and December 1 for the spring semester. Applicants who wish to be considered for merit scholarships must apply before March 1. Interviews, campus tours, faculty and staff appointments, and class visits are encouraged and may be arranged through the Office of Admission.
For additional information, students should contact admissions@wvwc.edu and:

Office of Admission
West Virginia Wesleyan College
59 College Avenue
Buckhannon, West Virginia 26201
Phone: 304-473-8510
Admissions@wvwc.edu
www.wvwc.edu

The Central Campus Green is one of many outdoor gathering spaces where students meet, study, and pass through on their way to classes and co-curricular activities.

WHEATON COLLEGE
WHEATON, ILLINOIS

Wheaton College
For Christ and His Kingdom

The College

Ranked by *U.S. News & World Report* as one of the nation's top liberal arts colleges, Wheaton College attracts exceptional students from all fifty states and as many as ninety countries. An interdenominational Christian liberal arts college, Wheaton takes the pursuit of faith and learning seriously. In addition to upholding an academically rigorous curriculum, Wheaton is committed to being a community that fearlessly pursues God's truth; invests in developing whole, well-rounded students; and prepares its graduates to lead lives that make a difference in the world.

The student body at Wheaton College consists of approximately 2,400 undergraduates (including 150+ students in the Conservatory of Music), approximately 80 percent of which come from outside Illinois.

Wheaton College's nearly 160-year history demonstrates the benefits of stable leadership in private Christian higher education—it has had only 8 presidents since it was founded in 1860. Wheaton has been faithful to its original precepts, and its legacy is shown in the lives of its graduates. Many distinguished graduate schools currently enroll Wheaton graduates, including Notre Dame, Princeton, SMU, Yale, and the Universities of Chicago and Missouri–Kansas City; several of the Big Ten music schools; and the A.R.T./MXAT Institute for Advanced Theater Training at Harvard. Wheaton alumni also excel in a wealth of endeavors around the world, with many holding positions in business and finance, government and foreign service, teaching, ministry, law, medicine, and the arts. Wheaton graduates actively contribute to their communities and churches, and no matter what position they hold, they strive to make a difference in the world around them.

Wheaton offers a rich, life-changing education, with graduates trained for life, not just jobs. Students are taught to think, reason, and express themselves effectively. They are equipped to attain knowledge and measure it against the truth of God's word, understand the importance of service, and value faith that embraces both theological accuracy and actively living it out. Developing strong, life-long relationships—with classmates, professors, and Jesus Christ—is a priority. Graduates are well-positioned for whatever they want to pursue and prepared to face the challenges of life. The Wheaton experience is distinctive, and living and learning at Wheaton is extraordinary. As a visiting lecturer recently observed, "I was so impressed by the enthusiasm of the Wheaton students to shape the world, and to make it a better place. And they are approaching this goal in practical ways. Some colleges are full of dour cynics. Wheaton is the opposite—brimming with optimists!"

Location

Wheaton's 80-acre campus is located in a residential suburb (population 55,000) 25 miles west of Chicago. The educational and cultural features of the Chicago metropolitan area are easily accessible by train and regularly visited by students.

Majors and Degrees

Wheaton grants the Bachelor of Arts and Bachelor of Science degrees and, through the Wheaton Conservatory of Music, the Bachelor of Music and Bachelor of Music Education degrees.

The following majors are available in the arts and sciences: anthropology, applied health science, archaeology, art, biblical and theological studies, biology, business/economics, chemistry, Christian education and ministry, classical languages (Greek, Hebrew, Latin), communication, computer science, economics, education, English, environmental studies, geology, history, interdisciplinary studies, international relations, mathematics, modern languages (Chinese, French, German, and Spanish), music, philosophy, physics, political science, psychology, sociology, and urban studies.

The Wheaton Conservatory of Music offers a full range of professional music majors, including composition, education, history/literature, performance, music with elective studies in an outside field, and music with an emphasis in a music-related field (such as media/film music, pedagogy, conducting, and collaborative piano). Students seeking these professional music degrees are accepted directly into the program by audition.

An on-campus program in military science leads to a commission in the U.S. Army at graduation. In addition to the majors offered, Wheaton has programs leading to teacher certification and to athletic training certification as well as programs preparing students for careers in business, health professions, law, and ministry.

Academic Programs

Because of the College's strong commitment to developing effective servant/leaders for society worldwide and the church, there is a particularly strong integration of faith and learning in all degree programs. A new general education curriculum, Christ at the Core, implemented in fall '16, brings a well-rounded, Christ-centered academic experience while allowing increased freedom and flexibility among cohorts.

Students must demonstrate core competencies (either by examination or by taking prescribed courses) as essential skills for the pursuit of knowledge: First Year Writing, Modern and Classical Languages, Oral Communication and Wellness.

SHARED CORE classes foster developmental learning with special attention to integrating faith with learning.

THEMATIC CORE courses allow students to shape their own learning experience to their intellectual needs and vocational calling through the many creative course offerings within ten multidisciplinary themes. A student may be granted advanced placement or college credit on the basis of examination (including SAT Subject Tests, AP, or IB).

Wheaton offers ten natural science majors—applied health science, biology, chemistry, computer science, environmental studies, geology, liberal arts engineering, liberal arts nursing, mathematics, and physics—in six academic departments. Also, 3-2 programs are offered in engineering and nursing, alongside a five-year cooperative engineering program with Illinois Institute of Technology and other engineering schools. The Wheaton faculty members engage the study of science authoritatively, enthusiastically, and creatively in the classrooms and laboratories and beyond the campus. They are creative and offer more than two dozen general education courses in the natural sciences as well as the majors listed above. The programming includes the use of state-of-the-art technologies and techniques on the main Wheaton campus, cutting edge geological and biological studies in a large science station in the scientifically rich area of the Black Hills of South Dakota, and marine biology studies in Belize.

Off-Campus Programs

Wheaton offers a variety of off-campus opportunities to enhance students' programs of study. The Wheaton Passage program is a popular pre-orientation experience available to new students at the College's Northwoods Campus in the wilderness of northern Wisconsin, or the Urban track available to students wishing to experience time in Chicago prior to transitioning to Wheaton. Another program, Human Needs and Global Resources (HNGR), combines classroom study with a six-month, field-based, service-learning internship in the Global South. A similar program in urban studies, Wheaton in Chicago, focuses on urban issues in U.S. cities and includes a semester living in College-owned housing in urban Chicago.

The Aequitas Program in Urban Leadership provides $20,000 in merit scholarships, additional funded study opportunities, and a challenging and supportive cohort experience to 10-12 outstanding students from many different majors.

Other special summer programs for credit include field study at the Wheaton College Science Station in the Black Hills of South Dakota; working with youth at HoneyRock Camp; interdisciplinary study in East Asia; the study of English literature in England; language study in France, Germany, and Spain; the Wheaton in the Holy Lands program, involving biblical and archaeological studies; the Arts in London program, which includes course work in music, theater, and art; and an international study program based in England and the Netherlands, offering courses in economics, political science, and psychology. Wheaton is a member of the Council of Christian Colleges and Universities, based in Washington, D.C. The council's activities increase students' learning opportunities by bringing special programs to campus and by providing off-campus study.

Off-campus programs include American Studies in Washington, D.C.; the Washington Journalism Center in Washington, D.C.; the Los Angeles Film Studies Center; the Contemporary Music Center in Martha's Vineyard; Latin American Studies in Costa Rica; Middle East Studies in Cairo; the Australia Studies Center; China Studies Program; the Scholar's Semester in Oxford; Russia Studies Program; and Uganda Studies Program. Wheaton is also affiliated with the International Sustainable Development Studies Institute in Chiang Mai, Thailand. In addition, Wheaton's membership in the Christian College Consortium allows students a semester of study at one of the other twelve consortium colleges in the CCCU.

Academic Facilities

A new Welcome Center housing undergraduate admissions and the new Armerding Center for Music and the Arts opened in Fall 2017, with the new Concert Hall to follow during the 2019-2020 school year.

An $80-million science and mathematics facility opened in Fall 2010. The 128,000-square-feet of space includes eight teaching labs and research space designed to promote collaborative teacher-student research.

In 2009, an $11 million renovation of Adams Hall added art gallery and studio space. Edman Chapel, often the venue for concerts by world-class musicians, has undergone a $9 million renovation that added rehearsal space, including a large rehearsal room named for alum John Nelson, former conductor of Ensemble Orchestral de Paris.

In 2008, Wheaton's Memorial Student Center reopened after an extensive renovation to house the Wheaton Center for Faith, Politics and Economics. The facility provides classroom, research, and public discussion space geared toward the study of economics, politics, and values in business, government, and ministry. Other recent additions to campus facilities include the Todd Beamer Student Center (2004); the Wade Center (2001), which houses the books and papers of seven British authors, including C. S. Lewis and J. R. R. Tolkien; and the Chrouser Sports Complex (2000).

Costs

Tuition for the 2019-20 is $37,700; room and board are $10,510. The Wheaton Fund (supported by alumni, parents, and friends of Wheaton) subsidizes what would be the actual cost of tuition by nearly a third.

Financial Aid

Realizing that a private college education is a sizable investment, Wheaton is committed to providing the necessary need-based financial aid so students can attend. Last year Wheaton awarded over $34 million in grants and scholarships.

For first-time, full-time freshman who have financial need and were awarded any financial aid, the average amount of need-based scholarship or grant awarded for 2018-19 was $27,000.

The Center for Vocation and Career helps students to secure part-time jobs, as well as future employment, including Canvas to engage sophomores, employer recruiting, job fairs, professional development, and Wheaton in Network (WiN) alumni networking resources for upperclass students.

Faculty

Ninety-four percent of Wheaton's 222 full-time faculty members hold terminal degrees. The professors' primary commitment as educators and advisers is enriched by their considerable research, publishing, and artistic activities. In addition, the professors are active Christians who strive to show how a profound commitment to God's word structures a vision of all of life, including intellectual life. They are dedicated to honoring a Christian perspective and to modeling Christ's love to their students.

All undergraduate courses are taught by faculty members.

To ensure a rich range of perspectives and expertise, every department at Wheaton has at least 3 full-time professors, and most have 5 to 10. The student-faculty ratio is 10:1.

Student Government

Student Government ensures a student voice in institutional affairs and provides a wide range of opportunities to develop leadership abilities. Student Government's vision is "To further the educational, spiritual, and relational development of the Wheaton College community as elected servant leaders representing student initiative, concern, creativity, and enthusiasm."

Besides Student Government, there are over forty academic, cultural, social justice, and entertainment student groups on campus. In addition, the Office of Christian Outreach provides opportunities for student ministry through student-run mission trips and ministries in urban and suburban Chicago.

Admission Requirements

Wheaton is a selective college that seeks to enroll students who evidence a vital Christian experience, high moral character, personal integrity, social concern, strong academic ability and motivation, and the desire to pursue Christian higher education as defined in the aims and objectives of the College. These qualities are evaluated by consideration of each applicant's academic record, autobiographical essays, test scores, recommendations, optional interview, and participation in extracurricular activities. For students applying to the Conservatory of Music, strong consideration is given to the evaluation of the required audition.

Applicants must have a high school diploma or the equivalent, and at the time of graduation should have completed a college-preparatory curriculum with a minimum of 18 acceptable units.

Satisfactory scores on the SAT or on the ACT examination are required of all applicants to the freshman class. The middle 50 percent range of scores for those admitted is 27–32 (ACT) and 1220–1440 composite score on the SAT.

Application and Information

An application packet, complete with detailed instructions and requirements, can be obtained from the Admissions Office or online. For early action (nonbinding), students seeking admission in the fall term should apply to either the College of Arts and Sciences or the Conservatory of Music by November 1. The regular action deadline is January 10; the transfer application deadline is March 1. An admissions counselor can provide more information about Wheaton in general or the application process in particular.

Further information is available from:

Admissions Office
Wheaton College
501 College Avenue
Wheaton, Illinois 60187
Phone: 630-752-5005
800-222-2419
E-mail: admissions@wheaton.edu
Website: wheaton.edu
wheaton.edu/connect

Historic Blanchard Hall overlooks Wheaton's front of campus.

WHITTIER COLLEGE

WHITTIER, CALIFORNIA

The College

Whittier College is a private, four-year liberal arts college located in Whittier, California. The school—which has an enrollment of 1,700 students—offers small class sizes, personalized degree programs, and ample opportunities for real-world learning experiences.

Whittier has earned a reputation for providing a high-quality liberal arts education. The Princeton Review recently named Whittier as one of the country's best institutions for undergraduate education, and it included Whittier in the 2019 edition of "The Best 384 Colleges." Whittier is also among 200 schools listed in "Colleges of Distinction," a national college guidebook that showcases colleges that offer engaged students, great teaching, a vibrant community, and successful outcomes.

Whittier takes on the liberal arts in a distinctly West Coast way—with a fresh eye toward how ideas intersect across disciplines. The College places an emphasis on providing students with a truly interdisciplinary liberal arts education. Whittier students are encouraged to think critically and to learn about other perspectives and cultures through cross-curricular courses and experiential learning activities such as internships and study-abroad opportunities.

The value of a Whittier College education lies in Whittier's core mission: to prepare students from diverse backgrounds for success in a complex global society. Whittier's approach to education produces graduates with skills that are highly valued by employers and graduate schools alike.

With a low faculty-to-student ratio, Whittier students receive the one-on-one attention that helps them stay focused and on-track. Because there are no impacted majors or programs, students can choose their major freely without the stress of competing for a spot.

Eighty-nine percent of Whittier graduates complete their degree in four years. With access to hundreds of semester courses and an interim term, Whittier students can fulfill major requirements without delays.

Whittier College is accredited by the Western Association of Schools and Colleges (WASC).

Location

Whittier College is located in the heart of Southern California, between the vibrant city of Los Angeles and scenic Orange County. Whittier students and professors take full advantage of the region's incomparable geography, culture, and industry, and use it as an extended classroom.

Southern California offers a wide array of recreation, entertainment, educational, and professional opportunities. The region is home to many of the nation's and the world's leading cultural and industry influencers. Hollywood's production studios, Anaheim's theme parks, and the South Bay's aerospace industry are all a short drive from Whittier College.

Just a few blocks from the College, Uptown Whittier boasts cafes and restaurants, a movie theater, a farmer's market, and dozens more shops for students to explore and enjoy.

Majors and Degrees

Students at Whittier College may choose from 30 majors, 37 minors, and 3 pre-professional programs, including anthropology, history, mathematics, political science, economics, English, and business administration. Programs of study include: anthropology, art (art history, studio art, or digital art and design), biochemistry, biology, business administration (accounting, finance, international business, management, or marketing concentrations), chemistry, child development, Chinese, economics (business economics, general distributive, or pre-professional economics options), engineering 3-2 (chemistry, mathematics, physics, or science and letters options), English (creative writing emphasis available), environmental science (environmental studies or environmental science tracks), French, global and cultural studies (culture, geographical area, issues, or national/transnational institutions options), health sciences (pre-med, pre-vet, or pre-pharm), history, kinesiology and nutrition science (pre–physical therapy or sports management emphasis), mathematics (teaching credential emphasis available), mathematics–business, music, applied philosophy, philosophy, physics (astronomy emphasis available), political science (international relations track available), pre-law, pre-therapy (physical, occupational, or recreational), psychology, religious studies, social work, sociology, Spanish, and theatre and communication arts (design and technology or performance emphasis).

Whittier College also provides students with opportunities to pursue self-designed majors through its Whittier Scholars Program (WSP). WSP students work closely with faculty members to develop a highly personalized course of study in specific areas of interest. This program culminates in the research, presentation, and defense of senior projects. Approximately 12 percent of Whittier students participate in WSP.

Academic Programs

In addition to completing the required course work for their major, all Whittier students are required to complete six hours of course work each in the areas of natural science, social science, fine arts, and humanities. The College's paired classes help students see the interconnectedness of ideas. Students take at least two paired classes while at Whittier, and in these classes they explore subjects that intersect in provocative ways.

All Whittier College students are required to complete several specialized courses designed to help them improve and refine their writing skills. The required writing course work begins with a first-year writing seminar and culminates in a paper-in-the-major, which each student completes during his or her senior year of study. The paper-in-the-major, which is developed with the guidance of a faculty member, is often used as a writing sample by students applying to graduate programs.

Whittier provides a wide range of services and programs designed to help new students adjust to college life. All first-year students participate in a linked class, two courses that are taken together during the first semester. These small classes of no more than 16 students help to create a common intellectual experience. In addition, each student is assigned a faculty mentor to provide advising and mentoring during their first semester. They also have a peer mentor who connects them to the College.

First-year students also live in close proximity; they are placed in three residence halls, forming a residential community. Resident Advisers in these communities will intentionally coordinate programs that will assist students in their transition to college. Additional activities, such as orientation and pre-orientation, also play a key role in ensuring student success.

Off-Campus Programs

Because Whittier College is located within driving distance to Los Angeles and Orange County, students have access to a wide range of internships with companies in industries ranging from entertainment to business. Whittier students have completed internships with Sony Pictures, Merrill Lynch, the J. Paul Getty Museum, EMI Music Publishing, New Line Cinema, First Heritage Bank, Southern California Edison, and the U.S. Department of Education.

Students may also choose to gain hands-on work experience through one of Whittier's many partnerships with community and government organizations such as the Boys and Girls Club of Whittier. Students in fields such as education, child psychology, and social work can participate in work-study programs at Broadoaks Children's School, Whittier's private, nonprofit demonstration school.

Whittier College provides many opportunities for students interested in learning about other cultures. Each student may choose to spend a semester, a year, or a summer living and studying in a variety of locations around the world. Whittier also offers several study-abroad opportunities through its faculty-led JanTerm and MayTerm programs. Past and upcoming study-abroad opportunities include a course on managing multinational corporations in Mexico; a study of Islamic culture in Morocco; an examination of race, religion, and gender in South America; and an anthropology course in Tanzania. Whittier's Global Poet Scholarship (GPS) gives every student $2,000 to study abroad.

Academic Facilities

The campus boasts an eclectic mix of historic architecture and state-of-the art amenities including a 400-seat performing arts center, an art gallery, an outdoor amphitheater, a recently upgraded library, a 7,000-seat sports stadium with a new track and field, and a beautiful aquatics center. The College also opened a new Science & Learning Center in fall 2016.

Costs

For the 2019–20 academic year, tuition is $48,924 with fees of $590. The cost of a double room is $7,896 and the 15-weekly meal plan is $6,258.

Financial Aid

Scholarships and financial aid are available, and over 90 percent of Whittier students receive a combination of grants, scholarships, and loans. More than $8.5 million in aid was awarded to Whittier students in 2018–19. Students will automatically be considered for a wide range of academic awards when they apply. In addition, there are talent scholarships in art, music, and theater that students can pursue without having to major or even minor in those academic disciplines.

Faculty

At Whittier, professors, students, and staff support each other and come together to share in the thrill of discovery, the joy of learning, and the gratification that comes with contributing to society. Students work with professors and staff to tap into their unique abilities, talents, and aspirations. Together, they design a complete college experience that combines academics, internships, fellowships, and service learning.

The College's full-time faculty numbers 130. The average class size is 19, with a student-faculty ratio of 12:1.

Student Life

Students interested in getting involved in extracurricular activities can choose from a wide variety of options. Whittier is home to nearly 100 academic, cultural, political, and general-interest clubs and organizations, as well as several service-oriented fraternities and sororities, called societies at Whittier. The school also has a student newspaper, yearbook, literary magazine, video production studio, and radio station. Through the Leadership Experience and Programs (LEAP) Office, there are opportunities for involvement in student government, community service, and a number of programs dedicated to helping students develop their leadership skills.

Whittier is home to 22 intercollegiate sports teams, including men's and women's basketball, cross-country, track and field, swimming and diving, water polo, soccer, lacrosse, golf, and tennis. Whittier also offers men's baseball and football and women's volleyball and softball.

Admission Requirements

Students interested in applying to Whittier College must submit a completed application (available at www.commonapp.org), a $50 application fee, transcripts, SAT I or ACT scores (test optional for students with a cumulative GPA of 3.0 and higher), a personal statement/essay, counselor evaluation, and letter of recommendation from a current or former teacher. Students interested in transferring to Whittier from another college or university must also submit college transcripts and letters of recommendation from two former or current professors.

Application and Information

Students are encouraged to apply early to ensure consideration for the fullest range of scholarship opportunities. Applications are reviewed on a rolling basis as they are completed.

The application filing date for Early Action candidates (nonbinding early deadline) is November 15. The priority application filing date for Regular Decision candidates is February 1 and the deadline for financial aid applicants to file the Free Application for Federal Student Aid (FAFSA) and for California Residents to apply for the Cal Grant Program is March 2.

Whittier College Admission Office
13406 East Philadelphia Street
P.O. Box 634
Whittier, California 90608
United States
Phone: 562-907-4238
888-200-0369 (toll-free)
Fax: 562-907-4870
E-mail: admissions@whittier.edu
Website: https://www.whittier.edu
https://www.facebook.com/WhittierCollege
https://www.instagram.com/whittiercollege
https://twitter.com/whittiercollege

WILKES UNIVERSITY
WILKES-BARRE, PENNSYLVANIA

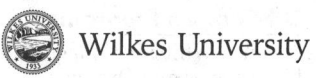

Wilkes University

The University

Wilkes University offers the opportunities of a large university and the personal attention of a small institution. Its unique program mix and variety of extracurricular activities let students build their educational experience to suit their goals and interests.

Students may notice something unexpected: professors genuinely interested in their thoughts and aspirations. All Wilkes students have opportunities to gain real-world experience, whether starting a business, conducting research, or using high-tech instruments that even graduate students at other institutions rarely touch.

Located at the foothills of the Pocono Mountains, along the shore of the Susquehanna River and within walking distance of downtown Wilkes-Barre, Pennsylvania, Wilkes University is a private, comprehensive institution with more than 2,500 undergraduate students.

The University includes the College of Arts, Humanities, and Social Sciences; the College of Science and Engineering; the Nesbitt School of Pharmacy; the Passan School of Nursing; the Sidhu School of Business and Leadership; the School of Education; and University College (for undecided students). Wilkes offers bachelor's and master's degrees in the humanities, social and natural sciences, engineering, business administration, nursing, and education as well as the Master of Fine Arts, Doctor of Pharmacy, Doctor of Education, and Doctor of Nursing Practice degrees.

The Wilkes campus features a parklike quadrangle surrounded by modern classroom buildings and historic nineteenth-century mansions that have been restored as student residences and academic buildings. Facilities include the Cohen Science Center, a sports and conference center, a financial trading room, a new media and communication center, and new engineering facilities with state-of-the-art laboratories.

Programs provide students with a liberal arts foundation that cultivates independent thinking and prepares them for professional life or for graduate or professional school. Academic advising integrated with career planning is stressed, and hands-on experiences are provided in laboratory, internship, and cooperative education settings. Free tutorial services are available to all students.

The University is accredited by the Middle States Association of Colleges and Schools and has specialized accreditation in the sciences, engineering, nursing, education, and business. Ninety-six percent of students are employed or attending graduate/professional school within one year of receiving their degrees.

First-year students enrolling prior to May 1 are guaranteed housing, and all students may have cars on campus. Campus housing is available for all four years. Residence halls include modern, multifloor buildings and historic mansions.

Student activities complement academic life. Intercollegiate athletics encompass 23 Division III sports, including swimming and women's and men's ice hockey. About 100 clubs and organizations recognize student achievement and provide opportunities for leadership development, professional growth, and community service. The award-winning e-mentor program links current students with incoming freshmen to ease the transition to college life.

Location

Wilkes-Barre is a medium-sized city of about 43,000. Nearby recreational facilities include Pocono Mountain ski resorts; PNC Field, home of a Triple A baseball team; the Mohegan Sun Arena, home to a professional hockey team; golf courses; state parks; tennis courts; and harness racing.

The University is located in the historic district, which features a performing arts center, the Wilkes University/King's College Barnes and Noble bookstore, a fourteen-screen movie complex, and numerous shops and restaurants. Other offerings include art galleries, ethnic and community festivals, and libraries and museums. The city is approximately 2 hours from New York City and Philadelphia.

Wilkes-Barre lies near the intersection of Interstates 80, 81, and 476 and within 6 hours of Washington, D.C. and Boston. The Wilkes-Barre/Scranton International Airport is about 20 minutes from campus.

Majors and Degrees

Wilkes University offers Bachelor of Arts, Bachelor of Fine Arts, Bachelor of Business Administration, and Bachelor of Science degrees, as well as a guaranteed-seat Doctor of Pharmacy program. Majors offered are: accounting; applied and engineering sciences; biochemistry; biology; chemistry; communication studies; computer information systems; computer science; corporate finance; criminology; digital design and media art; earth and environmental sciences; electrical engineering; education (elementary and early childhood, middle-level, secondary with a subject-area major, and special education certification); engineering management; English; entrepreneurship; environmental engineering; financial investments; geology; history; hospitality leadership; international studies; management; marketing; mathematics; mechanical engineering; medical laboratory sciences; musical theatre; neuroscience; nursing; philosophy; physics; political science; psychology; public administration; sociology; Spanish; sports management; supply chain management; theatre arts; and theatre design and technology. Wilkes also offers the six-year guaranteed-seat pharmacy program, a pharmacy/M.B.A. dual degree program, a five-year B.A./M.B.A. in industrial/organizational psychology, and a 4+1 B.S./M.S. in bioengineering.

Premedical and prelaw preparation programs are strong. Other preprofessional programs include dentistry, occupational therapy, optometry, physical therapy, physician assistant, podiatry, and veterinary science. A full-time director of health sciences and student success advises students who wish to continue study in a professional health-care field. The University offers an affiliated program in medicine with the Penn State College of Medicine at Hershey; in optometry with the Pennsylvania College of Optometry and the State University of New York (SUNY) College of Optometry; in podiatry with Temple University School of Podiatric Medicine; in occupational therapy with Temple University; in physical therapy with Drexel University, Temple University, and Widener University; and in medical technology/medical laboratory sciences with Robert Packer Hospital.

Academic Programs

Through a rigorous curriculum that emphasizes hands-on experience, Wilkes helps prepare students in all majors to adapt to a technologically and socially evolving world. To graduate, students must complete a core curriculum from 120 to 136 credits, depending on their major.

At Wilkes, we help translate your ambition into reality. Our Center for Career Development and Internships can help you clarify goals, assess skills, and find the internship experiences that will build your resume and launch your career. Services include internship and career fairs, career coaching, resume assistance, practice interviews, career development workshops and networking opportunities.

The University operates on a dual-semester calendar, with optional summer sessions and a January intersession. Advanced Placement test credits, College Level Examination Program (CLEP) credits, and International Baccalaureate (I.B.) credits are accepted.

Off-Campus Programs

A cooperative education (internship) program is available to all students, with credit applicable in most majors. Many government offices and private businesses in northeastern Pennsylvania, as well as in New York City, Philadelphia, Harrisburg, and Washington, D.C., employ Wilkes students. A study-abroad adviser works with interested students, placing them in the situation best suited to their academic pursuits. Students have recently attended programs in Costa Rica, England, Spain, Tanzania, and Uganda.

Academic Facilities

Wilkes University recently invested $100 million in campus upgrades. The new Mark Engineering Center has cutting-edge flex labs, additive manufacturing, 3-D visualization and high-performance computing; the Cohen Science Center boasts four floors of state-of-the-art laboratories designed for interdisciplinary research and study; the Karambelas Media and Communication Center is equipped with a professional television studio and radio station; the Sidhu School of Business offers a trading room with an electronic stock ticker, and even has a Starbuck's in the lobby. In addition, the newly renovated Farley Library is one of the largest resource libraries in the region, the NeuroTraining and Research Center is utilized by the campus community to enhance academic, athletic and artistic performance, and the Darte Performing Arts Center contains a 500-set theatre, a 45-seat black box theatre and a dance studio.

Costs

For the 2018–19 academic year, tuition is $34,454 per year, and room and board are $14,682. Fees are $1,740 annually.

Financial Aid

Financial aid is available to students who demonstrate quality academic ability and/or financial need, as verified by the Free Application for Federal Student Aid (FAFSA). Merit-based and need-based aid is available for qualified students. Scholarships ranging from $13,000 to $19,000 per year are available to students based on academic ability, regardless of financial need. Approximately 90 percent of students receive some type of financial assistance.

Faculty

Wilkes University has a nationally recruited full-time faculty of 193 members, approximately 91 percent of whom have earned Ph.D.'s or terminal degrees in their chosen field. Faculty evaluation criteria emphasize teaching excellence and effective advising, while recognizing continued scholarly activities. The student-faculty ratio is 13:1.

Admission Requirements

SAT or ACT scores are required. In cases where a student has taken the examination more than once, scores from the highest testing in each category are used. Freshman applicants should either have completed or be in the process of completing a college-preparatory course of study, including 3 to 4 years of mathematics, social studies, science, and English. Additional courses should be elected in academic subjects according to individual interests. Acceptable electives include foreign language and computing, among others. Students who have not followed this pattern may still qualify for admission if there is other strong evidence of preparation for college work. Letters of recommendation are not required but may be submitted. Students intending to pursue a major in pharmacy should have completed algebra I and II, geometry, and trigonometry prior to enrollment. Students intending to major in nursing should have completed courses in biology and chemistry. An audition is required for all prospective musical theatre and theatre arts students. Transfer students must submit a transcript from every college previously attended.

Wilkes University is an Equal Opportunity/Affirmative Action institution. No applicant shall be denied admission to the University because of race, color, gender, religion, national or ethnic origin, sexual orientation, or handicap.

Application and Information

Applications for admission should be completed early in the senior year of secondary school. Applications are reviewed after all of the student's credentials have been received. Notification of the University's decision reaches the student two to four weeks after the application file is complete. Priority deadline for all applications is March 1; applications for the Guaranteed Seat Pharmacy Program must be received by February 1. Other health science programs may have additional deadlines.

Contact the Admissions Office for more information.

Admissions Office
Wilkes University
84 West South Street
Wilkes-Barre, Pennsylvania 18766
Phone: 570-408-4400
800-945-5378 Ext. 4400 (toll-free)
Website: http://www.wilkes.edu

Wilkes University is currently in the midst of a $100 million campus improvement initiative.

WORCESTER POLYTECHNIC INSTITUTE
WORCESTER, MASSACHUSETTS

WPI

The University

Following its founding motto of "Theory and Practice," Worcester Polytechnic Institute (WPI) offers a distinct project-based curriculum that prepares students to take on the world's great challenges. Students take rigorous classes and also complete distinctive hands-on projects that address real issues in communities across the globe. In addition, small classes, one-on-one interaction with professors, non-punitive grading, and a spirit of innovation and teamwork encourage students to think creatively, collaborate across disciplines, and put their ideas into practice.

WPI has been widely recognized for its research-based academic programs and the success of its graduates. It is consistently ranked among the top national universities by *U.S. News & World Report* and The Princeton Review. According to the National Association of Colleges and Employers, the starting salaries of WPI graduates are 34 percent higher than those of many other college graduates. WPI was also ranked fifteenth in the nation for return on investment by *Forbes* and seventh by CNBC for colleges where students go on to earn the most money.

Top-tier employers seek out WPI graduates for their real-world experience and their ability to work collaboratively. More than 90 percent are in full-time jobs or attending graduate school within several months of graduation. Students are recruited by leading organizations such as Amazon Robotics, Pfizer, General Electric, Fidelity Investments, Johnson & Johnson, and Tesla. Each year, WPI graduates are accepted at many prestigious graduate schools, including MIT, Yale, Johns Hopkins, and Tufts University Medical School.

While many students attend WPI for its top-notch engineering and science programs, about 20 percent of students enter undeclared. WPI encourages students to explore their passions first and foremost. The university provides a comprehensive academic advising program and many academic support services, including a robust career services center, top-ranked in The Princeton Review's list for job and career services.

Location

With its beautiful architecture and grassy quad, WPI provides a traditional New England campus situated on 95 acres in a hilltop residential neighborhood. Students stop and chat with faculty members on tree-lined paths, study by the fountain in Reunion Plaza, grab a coffee at the Rubin Campus Center, and watch live entertainment at the Goat's Head restaurant.

Home to nine colleges and universities and more than 38,000 college students, Worcester is a true college town. NPR called Worcester "the New 'It' Town" as the fastest growing small city in America. Late-night diners, clubs, museums, concert venues, and theaters are just minutes from WPI. Boston is less than an hour away by commuter rail, and major attractions in the region, including New York City and Cape Cod, are easily accessible.

Majors and Degrees

WPI offers Bachelor of Science (B.S.) and Bachelor of Art (B.A.) degrees, and a combined B.S./M.S. program that enables students to complete a master's degree in four or five years. Students may major in various STEM disciplines, as well as subjects in the humanities and arts, social sciences, and business. They may also design their own majors or choose from interdisciplinary programs such as interactive media and game development, bioinformatics and computational biology, and robotics engineering (WPI's was the first undergraduate program in robotics in the nation). Additional information is available online at wpi.edu/academics.

WPI also offers preprofessional programs in dentistry, law, medicine, and veterinary medicine (wpi.edu/+prehealth). The university also offers teacher licensure (wpi.edu/+teach).

Academic Programs

Most students take three courses during each of the four 7-week terms (two in fall and two in spring). Classes aim to provide a balance between academic content and hands-on projects and group work. WPI's academic program also encourages collaboration, not competition—students can get grades of A, B, C, or no credit, but do not receive failing grades.

Regardless of their majors, all students must meet a humanities and arts requirement that encourages them to broaden their thinking and explore new areas of performance, creativity, and culture by taking courses in disciplines such as music, art, theatre, foreign language, history, and literature.

Paid internships and co-ops are available to advance education and earn income. Hundreds of opportunities are available each year with global companies such as Boston Scientific, ExxonMobil, General Electric, and SpaceX.

WPI Projects Program

Projects are at the heart of the WPI curriculum. All students complete a junior-year project in which they work with a team to address a real-world problem at the intersection of science, technology, and society—from designing bicycle paths in WPI's hometown of Worcester to creating an ambulance dispatch system in Venice. As seniors, students undertake an intensive capstone project related to their major field of study.

Through WPI's Global Projects Program, over 75 percent of undergraduates complete at least one project off campus at the more than 45 project centers around the world. Students immerse themselves in other cultures while working to solve real-world problems in partnership with organizational sponsors. The experience is on WPI—each undergraduate receives a one-time global scholarship of $5,000 to help cover the costs of studying abroad.

Students, alumni, and employers praise WPI's project model for helping students develop professional and personal skills including strategically managing projects, problem solving, teamwork, communication, and leadership abilities, as well as increased global awareness and enriched personal lives. Additional information is available at admissions.wpi.edu/+global.

Academic Facilities

There are many teaching, research, and project facilities available to undergraduates at WPI.

The brand-new Foisie Innovation Studio is a state-of-the-art innovation space suited for WPI's distinctive hands-on collaborative problem solving. The Studio contains a robotics lab, high-tech classrooms, and makerspaces. The Center for Innovation and Entrepreneurship helps students find paths to commercialization for their projects.

In addition, undergraduates have access to more than 40 cutting-edge research centers, laboratories, including two atomic-force microscopes, medical imaging laboratories, a fire science laboratory, a laser holography lab, a computer music lab, a satellite navigation lab, and a research library.

The Life Sciences and Bioengineering Center at Gateway Park is a modern 130,000 sq. ft. facility for research and teaching in biology and biotechnology, biomedical engineering, chemistry and biochemistry, and chemical engineering.

WPI also has an exceptional computer and networking infrastructure, including hundreds of computers in open-access 24/7 labs, powerful UNIX workstations, access to specialized scientific and engineering software, and a campus-wide high-speed data network.

Costs

For 2017–18, full-time tuition for first-year undergraduates was $49,860. Room and board charges were $14,774.

Financial Aid

Approximately 92 percent of students at WPI receive financial assistance in the form of need- and merit-based aid. Need-based aid includes financial aid packages, on-campus jobs, and loan programs. WPI has one of the nation's best loan repayment rates, a marker of its graduates' return on investment. More information is available from WPI's Office of Student Aid & Financial Literacy at wpi.edu/+finaid.

All accepted students are automatically considered for academic scholarships based upon academic performance, leadership, extracurricular involvement, and community service. More information is available at wpi.edu/+scholarships.

Faculty

WPI's full- and part-time faculty members are passionate teachers as well as committed researchers and scholars with world-class credentials. They are leading contributors to the fields of bioengineering, cybersecurity, robotics, energy and sustainability, materials science, and more. Sixteen members of the current faculty are Fulbright Scholars and more than 30 have won the CAREER Award, the National Science Foundation's most prestigious honor for young faculty members.

With a 13:1 student-faculty ratio, WPI facilitates small classes where students have ample opportunity to join discussions, work in teams, and interact with professors. The *Wall Street Journal* ranks WPI as number one in "Faculty That Best Combine Scholarly Research and Classroom Instruction," the National Survey of Student Engagement ranks the Institute as number one for student-faculty interaction, and the *U.S. News & World Report* ranks WPI as one of the top 50 colleges among national universities for faculty resources, including salary, class size, and student-faculty ratio.

Student Activities

Students work hard at WPI and play hard too—undergraduates at all levels take part in more than 225 clubs and organizations, ranging from music and theater ensembles to cultural and religious organizations, community service clubs, and professional groups. Every year, WPI students perform over 35,000 hours of community service.

WPI "Gets Greek Life Right," according to BestCollegesOnline.com—more than 30 percent of students participate in one of the 19 fraternities and sororities on campus. The Student Government Association gives a voice to undergraduates within WPI's close-knit community.

More than 80 percent of students are involved in sports programs, including 20 varsity (NCAA Division III) athletics teams and numerous club and intramural sports. Students also work out at the university's state-of-the art sports and recreation center, one of the finest university athletic facilities in the Northeast, featuring a four-court gymnasium, indoor jogging track, racquetball and squash courts, and competition pool. The Rec Center is also a reflection of WPI's commitment to support the environment with its green design and sustainable attributes.

Admission Requirements

WPI has high standards for applicants and looks for more than just outstanding academic performance. They take care to admit students who will thrive at the university. These students tend to be creative and curious; like to work in teams; are comfortable making their own decisions; love math and science but feel just as passionate about literature, music, movies, and the arts; and are ready to make a positive impact on the world around them.

As a test-optional university, applicants are not required to submit SAT or ACT scores. WPI will accept scores if they are sent, but admission decisions will not be influenced by the exclusion of standardized test scores. Full admissions requirements can be found at admissions.wpi.edu.

Application and Information

The Common Application is the only way to apply to WPI. The deadline for Early Action round 1 is November 1, with notification by December 20. The deadline for Early Action round 2 is January 1, with notification by February 10. The regular decision deadline is February 1, with notification by April 1. More information is available at wpi.edu/+apply.

Students are encouraged to visit the WPI campus to learn more about the university, see its facilities, and hear firsthand about the WPI experience. Many students call the campus visit the most influential decision on determining their fit at WPI. Students may also view a VR-enabled virtual tour at wpi.edu/+tour.

To schedule a visit or request more information, students should contact:

Undergraduate Admissions
Bartlett Center
Worcester Polytechnic Institute
100 Institute Road
Worcester, Massachusetts 01609-2280
Phone: 508-831-5286
Fax: 508-831-5875
E-mail: admissions@wpi.edu
Website: admissions.wpi.edu
Facebook: facebook.com/WPI
Instagram: instagram.com/WPI
Twitter: twitter.com/WPI

WPI is situated on a 95-acre campus, 40 miles west of Boston in a residential section of Worcester, Massachusetts, the second largest city in New England and home to nine colleges.

Indexes

Majors

ACCOUNTING
Adams State U (CO)
Adelphi U (NY)
Alabama State U (AL)
Albion Coll (MI)
Albright Coll (PA)
Alfred U (NY)
American Public U System (WV)
American U (DC)
Angelo State U (TX)
Appalachian State U (NC)
Arkansas Tech U (AR)
Assumption Coll (MA)
Auburn U (AL)
Auburn U at Montgomery (AL)
Aurora U (IL)
Austin Peay State U (TN)
Averett U (VA)
Avila U (MO)
Babson Coll (MA)
Baker U (KS)
Baldwin Wallace U (OH)
Baruch Coll of the City U of New York (NY)
Baylor U (TX)
Bellarmine U (KY)
Benedictine U (IL)
Bentley U (MA)
Berkeley Coll–New York City Campus (NY)
Berkeley Coll–Woodland Park Campus (NJ)
Blackburn Coll (IL)
Boston Coll (MA)
Boston U (MA)
Bowling Green State U (OH)
Bradley U (IL)
Brenau U (GA)
Bridgewater State U (MA)
Bryant U (RI)
Buena Vista U (IA)
Butler U (IN)
Caldwell U (NJ)
California Lutheran U (CA)
California State U, Fullerton (CA)
California State U, Long Beach (CA)
California State U, Northridge (CA)
California State U, San Bernardino (CA)
California State U, San Marcos (CA)
California U of Pennsylvania (PA)
Calumet Coll of Saint Joseph (IN)
Calvin Coll (MI)
Cameron U (OK)
Campbellsville U (KY)
Canisius Coll (NY)
Carson-Newman U (TN)
Carthage Coll (WI)
The Catholic U of America (DC)
Cedarville U (OH)
Centenary Coll of Louisiana (LA)
Central Connecticut State U (CT)
Central Michigan U (MI)
Central State U (OH)
Central Washington U (WA)
Champlain Coll (VT)
Christian Brothers U (TN)
Christopher Newport U (VA)
Claremont McKenna Coll (CA)
Clarion U of Pennsylvania (PA)
Coastal Carolina U (SC)
The Coll at Brockport, State U of New York (NY)
Coll of Charleston (SC)
The Coll of Idaho (ID)
Coll of Saint Benedict (MN)
The Coll of Saint Rose (NY)
The Coll of St. Scholastica (MN)
Coll of Staten Island of the City U of New York (NY)
Coll of the Holy Cross (MA)
Coll of the Ozarks (MO)
The Coll of William and Mary (VA)
Colorado State U–Pueblo (CO)
Columbia Coll (MO)
Concordia U Chicago (IL)
Creighton U (NE)
Culver-Stockton Coll (MO)
Curry Coll (MA)
Dakota State U (SD)
Dallas Baptist U (TX)
Davenport U, Grand Rapids (MI)
Delta State U (MS)
DePaul U (IL)
Dominican U (IL)
Drake U (IA)
Drury U (MO)
Duquesne U (PA)
East Carolina U (NC)
Eastern Illinois U (IL)
Eastern Mennonite U (VA)
Eastern Washington U (WA)
East Stroudsburg U of Pennsylvania (PA)
East Tennessee State U (TN)
East Texas Baptist U (TX)
Elizabeth City State U (NC)
Emmanuel Coll (MA)
Endicott Coll (MA)
Excelsior Coll (NY)
Fairfield U (CT)
Fayetteville State U (NC)
Fitchburg State U (MA)
Florida Ag and Mech U (FL)
Florida Atlantic U (FL)
Florida Southern Coll (FL)
Fordham U (NY)
Fort Lewis Coll (CO)
Framingham State U (MA)
Franklin Pierce U (NH)
Furman U (SC)
Geneva Coll (PA)
George Mason U (VA)
Georgetown Coll (KY)
Georgia Coll & State U (GA)
Georgia Southern U (GA)
Georgia State U (GA)
Gonzaga U (WA)
Gordon Coll (MA)
Goshen Coll (IN)
Graceland U (IA)
Grand Valley State U (MI)
Greenville U (IL)
Grove City Coll (PA)
Gwynedd Mercy U (PA)
Hamline U (MN)
Harding U (AR)
Hardin-Simmons U (TX)
Hartwick Coll (NY)
High Point U (NC)
Hillsdale Coll (MI)
Hofstra U (NY)
Hood Coll (MD)
Hult Intl Business School (United Kingdom)
Hunter Coll of the City U of New York (NY)
Idaho State U (ID)
Illinois Coll (IL)
Immaculata U (PA)
Indiana State U (IN)
Indiana U of Pennsylvania (PA)
Inter American U of Puerto Rico, Aguadilla Campus (PR)
Inter American U of Puerto Rico, Barranquitas Campus (PR)
Inter American U of Puerto Rico, Bayamón Campus (PR)
Inter American U of Puerto Rico, Fajardo Campus (PR)
Inter American U of Puerto Rico, San Germán Campus (PR)
Iona Coll (NY)
Iowa State U of Science and Technology (IA)
Ithaca Coll (NY)
Jackson State U (MS)
Jacksonville U (FL)
Judson U (IL)
Juniata Coll (PA)
Kansas Wesleyan U (KS)
Kean U (NJ)
Kennesaw State U (GA)
King's Coll (PA)
Kuyper Coll (MI)
LaGrange Coll (GA)
Lamar U (TX)
La Salle U (PA)
Lasell Coll (MA)
La Sierra U (CA)
Lawrence Technological U (MI)
Lebanon Valley Coll (PA)
Lee U (TN)
LeTourneau U (TX)
Liberty U (VA)
Limestone Coll (SC)
Lindenwood U (MO)
Linfield Coll (OR)
Lipscomb U (TN)
Lock Haven U of Pennsylvania (PA)
Loras Coll (IA)
Louisiana Coll (LA)
Louisiana State U and A&M Coll (LA)
Loyola Marymount U (CA)
Loyola U Chicago (IL)
Loyola U New Orleans (LA)
Lubbock Christian U (TX)
Lycoming Coll (PA)
Madonna U (MI)
Manchester U (IN)
Manhattan Coll (NY)
Manhattanville Coll (NY)
Mansfield U of Pennsylvania (PA)
Marian U (IN)
Marist Coll (NY)
Marquette U (WI)
Marshall U (WV)
Marymount California U (CA)
Maryville U of Saint Louis (MO)
Marywood U (PA)
Massachusetts Coll of Liberal Arts (MA)
McNeese State U (LA)
Mercer U, Macon (GA)
Mercy Coll (NY)
Merrimack Coll (MA)
Messiah Coll (PA)
Miami U (OH)
Miami U Hamilton (OH)
Michigan State U (MI)
Middle Tennessee State U (TN)
Milligan Coll (TN)
Millikin U (IL)
Millsaps Coll (MS)
Minnesota State U Moorhead (MN)
Missouri Baptist U (MO)
Molloy Coll (NY)
Montclair State U (NJ)
Mount Marty Coll (SD)
Mount St. Joseph U (OH)
Mount Saint Mary Coll (NY)
Murray State U (KY)
Muskingum U (OH)
National U (CA)
Nazareth Coll of Rochester (NY)
New England Coll (NH)
New Jersey City U (NJ)
New York U (NY)
Nichols Coll (MA)
North Carolina State U (NC)
Northeastern State U (OK)
Northern Illinois U (IL)
Northern Kentucky U (KY)
Northern State U (SD)
Northwest Christian U (OR)
Northwestern Oklahoma State U (OK)
Northwest Missouri State U (MO)
Northwood U, Michigan Campus (MI)
Oglethorpe U (GA)
Ohio Dominican U (OH)
The Ohio State U (OH)
Ohio U (OH)
Ohio Wesleyan U (OH)
Oklahoma Baptist U (OK)
Oklahoma Christian U (OK)
Oklahoma State U (OK)
Old Dominion U (VA)
Ottawa U (KS)
Ouachita Baptist U (AR)
Pace U (NY)
Pace U, Pleasantville Campus (NY)
Palm Beach Atlantic U (FL)
Pepperdine U, Malibu (CA)
Pfeiffer U (NC)
Point Loma Nazarene U (CA)
Point U (GA)
Portland State U (OR)
Prairie View A&M U (TX)
Providence Coll (RI)
Purdue U (IN)
Purdue U Northwest (IN)
Queens Coll of the City U of New York (NY)
Queens U of Charlotte (NC)
Radford U (VA)
Randolph-Macon Coll (VA)
Redeemer U Coll (ON, Canada)
Regent U (VA)
Regis U (CO)
Reinhardt U (GA)
Rhode Island Coll (RI)
Rider U (NJ)
Rochester Coll (MI)
Rochester Inst of Technology (NY)
Rockford U (IL)
Rocky Mountain Coll (MT)
Sacred Heart U (CT)
The Sage Colls (NY)
Saginaw Valley State U (MI)
Saint Anselm Coll (NH)
Saint Francis U (PA)
St. John Fisher Coll (NY)
Saint John's U (MN)
St. Joseph's Coll, Long Island Campus (NY)
St. Joseph's Coll, New York (NY)
Saint Joseph's U (PA)
Saint Leo U (FL)
Saint Louis U (MO)
Saint Martin's U (WA)
St. Mary's U (TX)
Saint Mary's U of Minnesota (MN)
St. Norbert Coll (WI)
Saint Vincent Coll (PA)
Salisbury U (MD)
Salve Regina U (RI)
Samford U (AL)
San Diego State U (CA)
San Francisco State U (CA)
San Jose State U (CA)
Scripps Coll (CA)
Seattle U (WA)
Seton Hill U (PA)
Southeastern Louisiana U (LA)
Southeastern U (FL)
Southeast Missouri State U (MO)
Southern Arkansas U–Magnolia (AR)
Southern Illinois U Carbondale (IL)
Southern Illinois U Edwardsville (IL)
Southern U and Ag and Mech Coll (LA)
Southwest Baptist U (MO)
Spring Hill Coll (AL)
State U of New York at Fredonia (NY)
State U of New York at Plattsburgh (NY)
State U of New York Coll at Geneseo (NY)
Stetson U (FL)
Stonehill Coll (MA)
Sullivan U (KY)
Syracuse U (NY)
Taylor U (IN)
Temple U (PA)
Texas A&M Intl U (TX)
Texas A&M U–Central Texas (TX)
Texas Christian U (TX)
Texas Lutheran U (TX)
Texas Tech U (TX)
Texas Woman's U (TX)
Tiffin U (OH)
Towson U (MD)
Trevecca Nazarene U (TN)
Trinity Christian Coll (IL)
Truman State U (MO)
Tulane U (LA)
Union Coll (KY)
Université de Sherbrooke (QC, Canada)
U at Buffalo, the State U of New York (NY)
U of Arkansas (AR)
U of Central Arkansas (AR)
U of Central Florida (FL)
U of Dayton (OH)
U of Detroit Mercy (MI)
The U of Findlay (OH)
U of Florida (FL)
U of Georgia (GA)
U of Guam (GU)
U of Hawaii at Manoa (HI)
U of Houston (TX)
U of Houston–Clear Lake (TX)
U of Houston–Downtown (TX)
U of Idaho (ID)
U of Illinois at Springfield (IL)
U of Kentucky (KY)
U of La Verne (CA)
U of Louisville (KY)
U of Lynchburg (VA)
U of Maine (ME)
U of Maine at Presque Isle (ME)
U of Mary Hardin-Baylor (TX)
U of Maryland, Coll Park (MD)
U of Maryland Eastern Shore (MD)
U of Maryland U Coll (MD)
U of Massachusetts Amherst (MA)
U of Massachusetts Dartmouth (MA)
U of Memphis (TN)
U of Michigan–Dearborn (MI)
U of Minnesota, Duluth (MN)
U of Minnesota, Twin Cities Campus (MN)
U of Missouri (MO)
U of Montevallo (AL)
U of Mount Union (OH)
U of Nebraska–Lincoln (NE)
U of Nevada, Las Vegas (NV)
U of Nevada, Reno (NV)
U of New Haven (CT)
U of North Carolina at Asheville (NC)
The U of North Carolina at Charlotte (NC)
The U of North Carolina at Greensboro (NC)
The U of North Carolina at Pembroke (NC)
U of North Dakota (ND)
U of Northern Iowa (IA)
U of North Florida (FL)
U of Northwestern–St. Paul (MN)
U of Notre Dame (IN)
U of Oregon (OR)
U of Pennsylvania (PA)
U of Pittsburgh (PA)
U of Pittsburgh at Bradford (PA)
U of Providence (MT)
U of Puerto Rico–Bayamón (PR)
U of Regina (SK, Canada)
U of Richmond (VA)
U of Saint Francis (IN)
U of Saint Mary (KS)
U of St. Thomas (MN)
U of St. Thomas (TX)
U of San Diego (CA)
U of San Francisco (CA)
U of Sioux Falls (SD)
U of South Alabama (AL)
U of South Carolina (SC)
U of South Dakota (SD)
U of Southern Indiana (IN)
U of South Florida (FL)
U of South Florida Sarasota-Manatee (FL)
The U of Tampa (FL)
The U of Tennessee (TN)
The U of Tennessee at Martin (TN)
The U of Texas at Austin (TX)
The U of Texas at El Paso (TX)
The U of Texas of the Permian Basin (TX)
The U of Texas Rio Grande Valley (TX)
U of the Incarnate Word (TX)
The U of Toledo (OH)
The U of Tulsa (OK)
U of Washington (WA)
U of Washington, Bothell (WA)
U of Washington, Tacoma (WA)
The U of West Alabama (AL)

U of West Georgia (GA)
U of Wisconsin–Eau Claire (WI)
U of Wisconsin–La Crosse (WI)
U of Wisconsin–Milwaukee (WI)
U of Wisconsin–River Falls (WI)
U of Wisconsin–Superior (WI)
U of Wyoming (WY)
Utah State U (UT)
Utah Valley U (UT)
Utica Coll (NY)
Valparaiso U (IN)
Vanguard U of Southern California (CA)
Virginia Commonwealth U (VA)
Virginia Polytechnic Inst and State U (VA)
Wartburg Coll (IA)
Washington & Jefferson Coll (PA)
Washington State U (WA)
Washington State U–Tri-Cities (WA)
Washington State U–Vancouver (WA)
Washington U in St. Louis (MO)
Waynesburg U (PA)
Weber State U (UT)
Wesleyan Coll (GA)
West Chester U of Pennsylvania (PA)
Western Connecticut State U (CT)
Western Illinois U (IL)
Western Kentucky U (KY)
Western State Colorado U (CO)
Western Washington U (WA)
West Virginia U Inst of Technology (WV)
Whitworth U (WA)
Widener U (PA)
Wilkes U (PA)
William Jewell Coll (MO)
Wofford Coll (SC)
Woodbury U (CA)
Wright State U–Lake Campus (OH)
Youngstown State U (OH)

ACCOUNTING AND BUSINESS/MANAGEMENT
Babson Coll (MA)
Bryant U (RI)
Canisius Coll (NY)
East Carolina U (NC)
Mercy Coll (NY)
Northwest Christian U (OR)
Rocky Mountain Coll (MT)
U of Providence (MT)
Washington and Lee U (VA)

ACCOUNTING AND COMPUTER SCIENCE
Grove City Coll (PA)

ACCOUNTING AND FINANCE
Albright Coll (PA)
Babson Coll (MA)
Bentley U (MA)
Bethel U (MN)
Bridgewater State U (MA)
Bucknell U (PA)
Clarkson U (NY)
DEREE - The American Coll of Greece (Greece)
Drake U (IA)
Eastern U (PA)
Fordham U (NY)
Granite State Coll (NH)
Hiram Coll (OH)
Saint Francis U (PA)
U of North Dakota (ND)

ACCOUNTING RELATED
Bentley U (MA)
Gwynedd Mercy U (PA)
Maryville U of Saint Louis (MO)
McDaniel Coll (MD)
Rocky Mountain Coll (MT)
Southwest Baptist U (MO)

ACOUSTICS
Columbia Coll Chicago (IL)

ACTING
Acad of Art U (CA)
Averett U (VA)
Baldwin Wallace U (OH)
Baylor U (TX)
Boston U (MA)
Bradley U (IL)
Brenau U (GA)
California State U, Long Beach (CA)
Central Michigan U (MI)
Central Washington U (WA)
Coll of the Ozarks (MO)
Columbia Coll Chicago (IL)
DePaul U (IL)
Drake U (IA)
Emerson Coll (MA)
Florida Southern Coll (FL)
Hofstra U (NY)
Ithaca Coll (NY)
Kean U (NJ)
Liberty U (VA)
Lindenwood U (MO)
Lipscomb U (TN)
Marymount Manhattan Coll (NY)
Michigan State U (MI)
Minnesota State U Moorhead (MN)
Ohio U (OH)
Pace U (NY)
Pepperdine U, Malibu (CA)
Purdue U (IN)
Regent U (VA)
Rhode Island Coll (RI)
Seton Hill U (PA)
Syracuse U (NY)
Temple U (PA)
Texas Christian U (TX)
Towson U (MD)
U of Maryland, Baltimore County (MD)
U of Nevada, Las Vegas (NV)
U of Northern Iowa (IA)
U of Regina (SK, Canada)
The U of Texas at Austin (TX)
U of Washington (WA)
Whitworth U (WA)

ACTUARIAL SCIENCE
Alfred U (NY)
Appalachian State U (NC)
Assumption Coll (MA)
Aurora U (IL)
Baruch Coll of the City U of New York (NY)
Bellarmine U (KY)
Bentley U (MA)
Bowling Green State U (OH)
Bradley U (IL)
Bryant U (RI)
Butler U (IN)
Calvin Coll (MI)
Carnegie Mellon U (PA)
Central Michigan U (MI)
Central Washington U (WA)
DePaul U (IL)
Drake U (IA)
Georgia State U (GA)
Hartwick Coll (NY)
High Point U (NC)
Indiana U Northwest (IN)
Indiana U South Bend (IN)
Lebanon Valley Coll (PA)
Lycoming Coll (PA)
Maryville U of Saint Louis (MO)
Messiah Coll (PA)
Michigan State U (MI)
Minnesota State U Moorhead (MN)
New York U (NY)
The Ohio State U (OH)
Ohio U (OH)
Purdue U (IN)
Queens Coll of the City U of New York (NY)
Roanoke Coll (VA)
Saint Joseph's U (PA)
Saint Mary's U of Minnesota (MN)
Temple U (PA)
Texas Christian U (TX)
U of Central Florida (FL)
U of Maine at Farmington (ME)
U of Nebraska–Lincoln (NE)
U of Pennsylvania (PA)
U of Regina (SK, Canada)
U of St. Thomas (MN)
U of Wisconsin–Milwaukee (WI)
Valparaiso U (IN)
Wartburg Coll (IA)

ADMINISTRATIVE ASSISTANT AND SECRETARIAL SCIENCE
Idaho State U (ID)
Weber State U (UT)

ADULT AND CONTINUING EDUCATION
Auburn U (AL)
Eastern Illinois U (IL)
Eastern Washington U (WA)
Louisiana State U and A&M Coll (LA)
U of Regina (SK, Canada)

ADULT DEVELOPMENT AND AGING
Madonna U (MI)
Rhode Island Coll (RI)

ADULT HEALTH NURSING
King U (TN)
Worcester State U (MA)

ADVERTISING
Adams State U (CO)
Appalachian State U (NC)
Boston U (MA)
Bowling Green State U (OH)
Bradley U (IL)
California State U, Fullerton (CA)
Central Michigan U (MI)
The Coll of St. Scholastica (MN)
Columbia Coll Chicago (IL)
Drake U (IA)
Emerson Coll (MA)
Fashion Inst of Technology (NY)
Grand Valley State U (MI)
Harding U (AR)
Iona Coll (NY)
Iowa State U of Science and Technology (IA)
Lamar U (TX)
Lee U (TN)
Loyola U Chicago (IL)
Marquette U (WI)
Michigan State U (MI)
Minnesota State U Moorhead (MN)
Murray State U (KY)
Northwest Missouri State U (MO)
Oklahoma Christian U (OK)
Pace U (NY)
Pace U, Pleasantville Campus (NY)
Pepperdine U, Malibu (CA)
Portland State U (OR)
Rider U (NJ)
Rochester Inst of Technology (NY)
San Diego State U (CA)
San Jose State U (CA)
Syracuse U (NY)
Temple U (PA)
Texas Christian U (TX)
Texas Tech U (TX)
U of Central Florida (FL)
U of Florida (FL)
U of Georgia (GA)
U of Houston (TX)
U of Idaho (ID)
U of Oregon (OR)
U of San Francisco (CA)
U of South Carolina (SC)
U of Southern Indiana (IN)
The U of Tennessee (TN)
The U of Texas at Austin (TX)
Washington State U (WA)
Washington U in St. Louis (MO)
Waynesburg U (PA)
Wesleyan Coll (GA)
Western Kentucky U (KY)
Widener U (PA)
Youngstown State U (OH)

AERONAUTICAL/AEROSPACE ENGINEERING TECHNOLOGY
American Public U System (WV)
Bowling Green State U (OH)
Embry-Riddle Aeronautical U–Worldwide (FL)
Idaho State U (ID)
LeTourneau U (TX)
Purdue U (IN)
Utah State U (UT)

AERONAUTICS/AVIATION/AEROSPACE SCIENCE AND TECHNOLOGY
Averett U (VA)
Bowling Green State U (OH)
Bridgewater State U (MA)
Delta State U (MS)
Elizabeth City State U (NC)
Embry-Riddle Aeronautical U–Daytona (FL)
Embry-Riddle Aeronautical U–Prescott (AZ)
Embry-Riddle Aeronautical U–Worldwide (FL)
Indiana State U (IN)
LeTourneau U (TX)
Liberty U (VA)
Middle Tennessee State U (TN)
The Ohio State U (OH)
Ohio U (OH)
Oklahoma State U (OK)
Purdue U (IN)
Saint Louis U (MO)
San Jose State U (CA)
Texas Lutheran U (TX)
U of Maryland Eastern Shore (MD)
U of Memphis (TN)
Vaughn Coll of Aeronautics and Technology (NY)

AEROSPACE, AERONAUTICAL AND ASTRONAUTICAL/SPACE ENGINEERING
Auburn U (AL)
California Polytechnic State U, San Luis Obispo (CA)
California State U, Long Beach (CA)
Clarkson U (NY)
Embry-Riddle Aeronautical U–Daytona (FL)
Embry-Riddle Aeronautical U–Prescott (AZ)
Iowa State U of Science and Technology (IA)
Massachusetts Inst of Technology (MA)
North Carolina State U (NC)
The Ohio State U (OH)
Oklahoma State U (OK)
Purdue U (IN)
Rochester Inst of Technology (NY)
Saint Louis U (MO)
San Diego State U (CA)
San Jose State U (CA)
Syracuse U (NY)
U at Buffalo, the State U of New York (NY)
U of California, Davis (CA)
U of California, Irvine (CA)
U of California, Los Angeles (CA)
U of Central Florida (FL)
U of Florida (FL)
U of Maryland, Coll Park (MD)
U of Michigan (MI)
U of Minnesota, Twin Cities Campus (MN)
U of Notre Dame (IN)
The U of Tennessee (TN)
The U of Texas at Austin (TX)
U of Virginia (VA)
U of Washington (WA)
Utah State U (UT)
Virginia Polytechnic Inst and State U (VA)
West Virginia U Inst of Technology (WV)
Worcester Polytechnic Inst (MA)

AEROSPACE GROUND EQUIPMENT TECHNOLOGY
Liberty U (VA)

AEROSPACE PHYSIOLOGY AND MEDICINE
Embry-Riddle Aeronautical U–Daytona (FL)

AFRICAN AMERICAN/BLACK STUDIES
American U (DC)
Berea Coll (KY)
Bowling Green State U (OH)
Brandeis U (MA)
California State U, Fullerton (CA)
California State U, Long Beach (CA)
California State U, Los Angeles (CA)
California State U, Northridge (CA)
Claremont McKenna Coll (CA)
The Coll at Brockport, State U of New York (NY)
Coll of Charleston (SC)
Coll of Staten Island of the City U of New York (NY)
The Coll of William and Mary (VA)
Columbia U (NY)
Cornell U (NY)
Dartmouth Coll (NH)
DePaul U (IL)
Dominican U (IL)
Drew U (NJ)
Earlham Coll (IN)
East Carolina U (NC)
Eastern Illinois U (IL)
Florida Ag and Mech U (FL)
Fordham U (NY)
Georgia State U (GA)
Hamilton Coll (NY)
Harvard U (MA)
Hunter Coll of the City U of New York (NY)
Indiana State U (IN)
Indiana U Bloomington (IN)
Indiana U Northwest (IN)
Indiana U–Purdue U Indianapolis (IN)
Johns Hopkins U (MD)
Knox Coll (IL)
Lake Forest Coll (IL)
Loyola Marymount U (CA)
Loyola U Chicago (IL)
Marquette U (WI)
Mercer U, Macon (GA)
Miami U (OH)
Middle Tennessee State U (TN)
New York U (NY)
Northwestern U (IL)
Occidental Coll (CA)
The Ohio State U (OH)
Ohio U (OH)
Ohio Wesleyan U (OH)
Old Dominion U (VA)
Pitzer Coll (CA)
Portland State U (OR)
Princeton U (NJ)
Purdue U (IN)
Queens Coll of the City U of New York (NY)
Rhode Island Coll (RI)
Saint Louis U (MO)
San Diego State U (CA)
San Francisco State U (CA)
Sonoma State U (CA)
Southern Illinois U Carbondale (IL)
State U of New York Coll at Geneseo (NY)
Syracuse U (NY)
Temple U (PA)
U at Buffalo, the State U of New York (NY)
U of California, Davis (CA)
U of California, Irvine (CA)
U of California, Los Angeles (CA)
U of California, Riverside (CA)
U of Central Arkansas (AR)
U of Florida (FL)
U of Georgia (GA)
U of Houston (TX)
U of Louisville (KY)
U of Maryland, Baltimore County (MD)
U of Maryland, Coll Park (MD)
U of Massachusetts Amherst (MA)
U of Massachusetts Boston (MA)
U of Memphis (TN)
U of Michigan (MI)
U of Michigan–Dearborn (MI)
U of Minnesota, Twin Cities Campus (MN)
U of Nevada, Las Vegas (NV)
U of New Mexico (NM)
The U of North Carolina at Chapel Hill (NC)
The U of North Carolina at Charlotte (NC)
The U of North Carolina at Greensboro (NC)
U of Northern Colorado (CO)
U of Notre Dame (IN)
U of Pennsylvania (PA)
U of Pittsburgh (PA)
U of Puget Sound (WA)
U of South Carolina (SC)
U of South Florida (FL)
The U of Texas at Austin (TX)
The U of Toledo (OH)
U of Virginia (VA)
U of Wisconsin–Milwaukee (WI)
U of Wyoming (WY)
Virginia Commonwealth U (VA)
Washington U in St. Louis (MO)
Wesleyan U (CT)
Wheaton Coll (MA)

AFRICAN LANGUAGES
U of California, Los Angeles (CA)

AFRICAN STUDIES
Agnes Scott Coll (GA)

Bowling Green State U (OH)
Central Michigan U (MI)
Coll of the Holy Cross (MA)
Columbia U (NY)
Connecticut Coll (CT)
Davidson Coll (NC)
Dickinson Coll (PA)
Haverford Coll (PA)
Hofstra U (NY)
Kennesaw State U (GA)
Middlebury Coll (VT)
Northwestern U (IL)
Ohio U (OH)
Portland State U (OR)
Sarah Lawrence Coll (NY)
Tulane U (LA)
Union Coll (NY)
U of Chicago (IL)
U of Pennsylvania (PA)
U of Richmond (VA)
Vassar Coll (NY)
Washington U in St. Louis (MO)
Willamette U (OR)

AGRIBUSINESS
Adams State U (CO)
American U of Beirut (Lebanon)
Angelo State U (TX)
Arkansas Tech U (AR)
Colorado State U (CO)
Delaware Valley U (PA)
Florida Ag and Mech U (FL)
Greenville U (IL)
Iowa State U of Science and Technology (IA)
Middle Tennessee State U (TN)
North Carolina State U (NC)
Northwest Missouri State U (MO)
Southeast Missouri State U (MO)
U of Arkansas (AR)
U of Georgia (GA)
U of Idaho (ID)
The U of Tennessee at Martin (TN)
U of Wisconsin–River Falls (WI)
U of Wyoming (WY)
Vermont Tech Coll (VT)
Washington State U (WA)

AGRICULTURAL AND EXTENSION EDUCATION
North Carolina State U (NC)
Northwestern Oklahoma State U (OK)
The Ohio State U (OH)
U of Arkansas (AR)
The U of Tennessee (TN)

AGRICULTURAL AND FOOD PRODUCTS PROCESSING
Angelo State U (TX)
Morningside Coll (IA)
The Ohio State U (OH)
U of Nebraska–Lincoln (NE)
Washington State U (WA)

AGRICULTURAL AND HORTICULTURAL PLANT BREEDING
Washington State U (WA)

AGRICULTURAL BUSINESS AND MANAGEMENT
California Polytechnic State U, San Luis Obispo (CA)
California State U, Chico (CA)
Coll of the Ozarks (MO)
Florida Southern Coll (FL)
Graceland U (IA)
Iowa State U of Science and Technology (IA)
Louisiana State U and A&M Coll (LA)
Michigan State U (MI)
Oklahoma State U (OK)
Purdue U (IN)
Southern Arkansas U–Magnolia (AR)
Texas Tech U (TX)
U of Maryland Eastern Shore (MD)
U of Missouri (MO)
U of Nebraska–Lincoln (NE)
The U of Tennessee (TN)
The U of Tennessee at Martin (TN)
Utah State U (UT)

AGRICULTURAL BUSINESS AND MANAGEMENT RELATED
U of California, Davis (CA)
U of Minnesota, Twin Cities Campus (MN)
Utah State U (UT)

AGRICULTURAL BUSINESS TECHNOLOGY
Auburn U (AL)

AGRICULTURAL COMMUNICATION/ JOURNALISM
Auburn U (AL)
California Polytechnic State U, San Luis Obispo (CA)
Oklahoma State U (OK)
Purdue U (IN)
Texas Tech U (TX)
U of Georgia (GA)
U of Idaho (ID)
U of Nebraska–Lincoln (NE)
U of Wyoming (WY)

AGRICULTURAL ECONOMICS
Auburn U (AL)
Colorado State U (CO)
Cornell U (NY)
The Ohio State U (OH)
Oklahoma State U (OK)
Purdue U (IN)
Southern Illinois U Carbondale (IL)
Southern U and Ag and Mech Coll (LA)
Texas Tech U (TX)
U of Florida (FL)
U of Georgia (GA)
U of Idaho (ID)
U of Kentucky (KY)
U of Maryland, Coll Park (MD)
U of Nebraska–Lincoln (NE)
Utah State U (UT)
Virginia Polytechnic Inst and State U (VA)

AGRICULTURAL ENGINEERING
Auburn U (AL)
California Polytechnic State U, San Luis Obispo (CA)
Cornell U (NY)
Florida Ag and Mech U (FL)
Iowa State U of Science and Technology (IA)
Michigan State U (MI)
North Carolina State U (NC)
The Ohio State U (OH)
Oklahoma State U (OK)
Purdue U (IN)
U of California, Los Angeles (CA)
U of Georgia (GA)
U of Hawaii at Manoa (HI)
U of Kentucky (KY)
U of Maryland, Coll Park (MD)
U of Minnesota, Twin Cities Campus (MN)
U of Nebraska–Lincoln (NE)
The U of Tennessee (TN)
U of Wisconsin–River Falls (WI)
Utah State U (UT)

AGRICULTURAL MECHANIZATION
California Polytechnic State U, San Luis Obispo (CA)
Iowa State U of Science and Technology (IA)
North Carolina State U (NC)
Purdue U (IN)
U of Idaho (ID)
U of Missouri (MO)
U of Nebraska–Lincoln (NE)

AGRICULTURAL PRODUCTION
Washington State U (WA)

AGRICULTURAL PUBLIC SERVICES RELATED
Oklahoma State U (OK)
U of Kentucky (KY)

AGRICULTURAL TEACHER EDUCATION
Arkansas Tech U (AR)
Auburn U (AL)
California Polytechnic State U, San Luis Obispo (CA)
Central State U (OH)
Coll of the Ozarks (MO)
Colorado State U (CO)
Iowa State U of Science and Technology (IA)
Michigan State U (MI)
North Carolina State U (NC)
Northwest Missouri State U (MO)
The Ohio State U (OH)
Oklahoma State U (OK)
Purdue U (IN)
Southeast Missouri State U (MO)
Southern Arkansas U–Magnolia (AR)
Southern U and Ag and Mech Coll (LA)
U of Florida (FL)
U of Georgia (GA)
U of Idaho (ID)
U of Minnesota, Twin Cities Campus (MN)
U of Missouri (MO)
U of Nebraska–Lincoln (NE)
U of Wisconsin–River Falls (WI)
U of Wyoming (WY)
Utah State U (UT)
Washington State U (WA)

AGRICULTURE
American U of Beirut (Lebanon)
Angelo State U (TX)
Auburn U (AL)
Austin Peay State U (TN)
Berea Coll (KY)
Cameron U (OK)
Cornell U (NY)
Florida Ag and Mech U (FL)
McNeese State U (LA)
North Carolina State U (NC)
Northwestern Oklahoma State U (OK)
Northwest Missouri State U (MO)
Prairie View A&M U (TX)
Purdue U (IN)
Southern Arkansas U–Magnolia (AR)
Southern Illinois U Carbondale (IL)
Texas Tech U (TX)
Truman State U (MO)
U of Georgia (GA)
U of Guam (GU)
U of Maine at Presque Isle (ME)
U of Maryland, Coll Park (MD)
U of Maryland Eastern Shore (MD)
U of Missouri (MO)
U of Nebraska–Lincoln (NE)
U of Nevada, Reno (NV)
The U of Tennessee at Martin (TN)
U of Vermont (VT)
U of Wisconsin–River Falls (WI)
Utah State U (UT)
Washington State U (WA)
Western Illinois U (IL)
Western Kentucky U (KY)

AGRICULTURE AND AGRICULTURE OPERATIONS RELATED
Emmanuel Coll (GA)
Murray State U (KY)
The Ohio State U (OH)
U of California, Davis (CA)
U of Kentucky (KY)
U of Nebraska–Lincoln (NE)

AGROECOLOGY AND SUSTAINABLE AGRICULTURE
Central State U (OH)
Delaware Valley U (PA)
The Evergreen State Coll (WA)
Goshen Coll (IN)
Maharishi U of Management (IA)
Purdue U (IN)
U of Idaho (ID)
U of Maine (ME)
U of Massachusetts Amherst (MA)
U of New Hampshire (NH)
U of Wyoming (WY)
Washington State U (WA)

AGRONOMY AND CROP SCIENCE
Auburn U (AL)
California Polytechnic State U, San Luis Obispo (CA)
Coll of the Ozarks (MO)
Delaware Valley U (PA)
Iowa State U of Science and Technology (IA)
North Carolina State U (NC)
Northwest Missouri State U (MO)
Purdue U (IN)
U of Arkansas (AR)
U of Idaho (ID)
U of Kentucky (KY)
U of Nebraska–Lincoln (NE)
U of Vermont (VT)
U of Wisconsin–River Falls (WI)
Utah State U (UT)
Virginia Polytechnic Inst and State U (VA)
Washington State U (WA)

AIR AND SPACE OPERATIONS TECHNOLOGY
Embry-Riddle Aeronautical U–Daytona (FL)

AIRCRAFT POWERPLANT TECHNOLOGY
Embry-Riddle Aeronautical U–Worldwide (FL)
Idaho State U (ID)

AIRFRAME MECHANICS AND AIRCRAFT MAINTENANCE TECHNOLOGY
Vaughn Coll of Aeronautics and Technology (NY)

AIRLINE PILOT AND FLIGHT CREW
Auburn U (AL)
Austin Peay State U (TN)
Baylor U (TX)
Bridgewater State U (MA)
Central Washington U (WA)
Delta State U (MS)
Embry-Riddle Aeronautical U–Daytona (FL)
Embry-Riddle Aeronautical U–Prescott (AZ)
Farmingdale State Coll (NY)
Indiana State U (IN)
Jacksonville U (FL)
LeTourneau U (TX)
Purdue U (IN)
Rocky Mountain Coll (MT)
Texas A&M U–Central Texas (TX)
U of North Dakota (ND)
Utah Valley U (UT)

AIR TRAFFIC CONTROL
Embry-Riddle Aeronautical U–Daytona (FL)
Embry-Riddle Aeronautical U–Prescott (AZ)
LeTourneau U (TX)
U of North Dakota (ND)

AIR TRANSPORTATION RELATED
Inter American U of Puerto Rico, Bayamón Campus (PR)
U of North Dakota (ND)

ALLIED HEALTH AND MEDICAL ASSISTING SERVICES RELATED
Cedarville U (OH)
The Ohio State U (OH)
The Ohio State U at Lima (OH)
U of Vermont (VT)
Widener U (PA)

ALLIED HEALTH DIAGNOSTIC, INTERVENTION, AND TREATMENT PROFESSIONS RELATED
Hofstra U (NY)
Immaculata U (PA)
Millersville U of Pennsylvania (PA)
Point Loma Nazarene U (CA)
Sacred Heart U (CT)
The U of North Carolina at Charlotte (NC)
Weber State U (UT)

AMERICAN GOVERNMENT AND POLITICS
Bridgewater State U (MA)
Emmanuel Coll (MA)
Fitchburg State U (MA)
La Salle U (PA)
Oklahoma Christian U (OK)

AMERICAN HISTORY
Bryant U (RI)
Florida Coll (FL)
Morningside Coll (IA)
Sarah Lawrence Coll (NY)
U of Washington, Tacoma (WA)

AMERICAN INDIAN/NATIVE AMERICAN STUDIES
Central Michigan U (MI)
Colgate U (NY)
Dartmouth Coll (NH)
The Evergreen State Coll (WA)
Fort Lewis Coll (CO)
Humboldt State U (CA)
Northeastern State U (OK)
Portland State U (OR)
San Diego State U (CA)
San Francisco State U (CA)
Sonoma State U (CA)
U of California, Davis (CA)
U of California, Los Angeles (CA)
U of California, Riverside (CA)
U of Hawaii at Manoa (HI)
U of Minnesota, Duluth (MN)
U of Minnesota, Morris (MN)
U of Minnesota, Twin Cities Campus (MN)
U of New Mexico (NM)
The U of North Carolina at Pembroke (NC)
U of North Dakota (ND)
U of Regina (SK, Canada)
U of South Dakota (SD)
U of Washington (WA)
U of Wisconsin–Eau Claire (WI)
U of Wyoming (WY)

AMERICAN LITERATURE
Bryant U (RI)
U of California, Los Angeles (CA)
Washington U in St. Louis (MO)
Whittier Coll (CA)

AMERICAN NATIVE/NATIVE AMERICAN EDUCATION
The Coll of St. Scholastica (MN)
Northeastern State U (OK)
U of Regina (SK, Canada)

AMERICAN NATIVE/NATIVE AMERICAN LANGUAGES
U of Minnesota, Twin Cities Campus (MN)
U of Regina (SK, Canada)

AMERICAN SIGN LANGUAGE (ASL)
Lamar U (TX)
Liberty U (VA)
Madonna U (MI)
Rochester Inst of Technology (NY)
U of Houston (TX)
U of Wisconsin–Milwaukee (WI)
Utah Valley U (UT)

AMERICAN STUDIES
Albright Coll (PA)
American U (DC)
Austin Coll (TX)
Baylor U (TX)
Bethany Lutheran Coll (MN)
Boston U (MA)
Bowling Green State U (OH)
Brandeis U (MA)
Bryant U (RI)
California State U, Fullerton (CA)
California State U, Long Beach (CA)
California State U, San Bernardino (CA)
Christopher Newport U (VA)
Claremont McKenna Coll (CA)
Coll of Coastal Georgia (GA)
Coll of Staten Island of the City U of New York (NY)
The Coll of William and Mary (VA)
Columbia U (NY)
Connecticut Coll (CT)
Cornell U (NY)
Creighton U (NE)
DePaul U (IL)
Dickinson Coll (PA)
Dominican U (IL)
Eckerd Coll (FL)
Emmanuel Coll (MA)
Fairfield U (CT)
Fordham U (NY)
Georgetown Coll (KY)
Hamilton Coll (NY)
Hillsdale Coll (MI)
Hofstra U (NY)
Indiana U Bloomington (IN)
Knox Coll (IL)
Lake Forest Coll (IL)
La Salle U (PA)

Lesley U (MA)
Lipscomb U (TN)
Lycoming Coll (PA)
Manhattanville Coll (NY)
Marist Coll (NY)
Miami U (OH)
Miami U Hamilton (OH)
Middlebury Coll (VT)
Nazareth Coll of Rochester (NY)
Northwestern U (IL)
Occidental Coll (CA)
Oglethorpe U (GA)
Oklahoma State U (OK)
Pace U (NY)
Pace U, Pleasantville Campus (NY)
Pitzer Coll (CA)
Providence Coll (RI)
Purdue U (IN)
Queens Coll of the City U of New York (NY)
Rider U (NJ)
Rollins Coll (FL)
St. John Fisher Coll (NY)
Saint Louis U (MO)
St. Olaf Coll (MN)
Salve Regina U (RI)
San Francisco State U (CA)
Scripps Coll (CA)
Skidmore Coll (NY)
State U of New York Coll at Geneseo (NY)
Stetson U (FL)
Stonehill Coll (MA)
Temple U (PA)
Towson U (MD)
Tulane U (LA)
Union Coll (NY)
U at Buffalo, the State U of New York (NY)
U of California, Davis (CA)
U of Hawaii at Manoa (HI)
U of Kentucky (KY)
U of Maryland, Baltimore County (MD)
U of Maryland, Coll Park (MD)
U of Massachusetts Boston (MA)
U of Massachusetts Lowell (MA)
U of Michigan (MI)
U of Minnesota, Twin Cities Campus (MN)
U of New Mexico (NM)
The U of North Carolina at Chapel Hill (NC)
U of Notre Dame (IN)
U of Pennsylvania (PA)
U of Richmond (VA)
U of South Florida (FL)
The U of Texas at Austin (TX)
The U of the South (TN)
The U of Toledo (OH)
U of Washington, Bothell (WA)
U of Washington, Tacoma (WA)
U of Wyoming (WY)
Ursinus Coll (PA)
Utah State U (UT)
Valparaiso U (IN)
Vassar Coll (NY)
Washington U in St. Louis (MO)
Wesleyan U (CT)
Western Connecticut State U (CT)
Western Washington U (WA)
Wheaton Coll (MA)
Whitworth U (WA)
Williams Coll (MA)

ANALYTICAL CHEMISTRY
West Chester U of Pennsylvania (PA)

ANATOMY
Bryant U (RI)
Tulane U (LA)

ANCIENT/CLASSICAL GREEK
Baylor U (TX)
Boston U (MA)
California State U, Long Beach (CA)
Canisius Coll (NY)
Colgate U (NY)
Duquesne U (PA)
Hampden-Sydney Coll (VA)
Hillsdale Coll (MI)
Hunter Coll of the City U of New York (NY)
Indiana U Bloomington (IN)
Knox Coll (IL)
Loyola U Chicago (IL)
Loyola U New Orleans (LA)
Queens Coll of the City U of New York (NY)
Randolph-Macon Coll (VA)
Rice U (TX)
St. Olaf Coll (MN)
Samford U (AL)
Sarah Lawrence Coll (NY)
Southwestern U (TX)
U of California, Los Angeles (CA)
U of Michigan (MI)
The U of North Carolina at Greensboro (NC)
U of Notre Dame (IN)
U of Richmond (VA)
The U of Texas at Austin (TX)
The U of the South (TN)
U of Vermont (VT)
U of Washington (WA)
Wabash Coll (IN)
Washington U in St. Louis (MO)

ANCIENT NEAR EASTERN AND BIBLICAL LANGUAGES
Baylor U (TX)
Carson-Newman U (TN)
Concordia U Irvine (CA)
Geneva Coll (PA)
Oklahoma Baptist U (OK)
Ouachita Baptist U (AR)
Toccoa Falls Coll (GA)
U of Washington (WA)

ANCIENT STUDIES
Boston U (MA)
Columbia U (NY)
Creighton U (NE)
Dartmouth Coll (NH)
Eckerd Coll (FL)
Fordham U (NY)
Loyola Marymount U (CA)
Ohio Wesleyan U (OH)
Purdue U (IN)
Rollins Coll (FL)
Saint Joseph's U (PA)
St. Olaf Coll (MN)
U of Maryland, Baltimore County (MD)
U of Michigan (MI)
U of Nebraska–Lincoln (NE)
U of Richmond (VA)
The U of Texas at Austin (TX)
Washington U in St. Louis (MO)
Wheaton Coll (MA)

ANIMAL-ASSISTED THERAPY
Aurora U (IL)
Averett U (VA)

ANIMAL BEHAVIOR AND ETHOLOGY
Bucknell U (PA)
Canisius Coll (NY)
Indiana U Bloomington (IN)

ANIMAL GENETICS
Ohio Wesleyan U (OH)

ANIMAL HEALTH
U of Georgia (GA)

ANIMAL/LIVESTOCK HUSBANDRY AND PRODUCTION
Delaware Valley U (PA)

ANIMAL PHYSIOLOGY
Sonoma State U (CA)
Utah State U (UT)

ANIMAL SCIENCES
Angelo State U (TX)
Auburn U (AL)
California Polytechnic State U, San Luis Obispo (CA)
California State U, Chico (CA)
Coll of the Ozarks (MO)
Colorado State U (CO)
Cornell U (NY)
Delaware Valley U (PA)
Iowa State U of Science and Technology (IA)
Louisiana State U and A&M Coll (LA)
Lubbock Christian U (TX)
Michigan State U (MI)
Middle Tennessee State U (TN)
North Carolina State U (NC)
Northwest Missouri State U (MO)
The Ohio State U (OH)
Oklahoma State U (OK)
Purdue U (IN)
Southern Illinois U Carbondale (IL)
Texas Tech U (TX)
U of Arkansas (AR)
U of California, Davis (CA)
The U of Findlay (OH)
U of Florida (FL)
U of Georgia (GA)
U of Hawaii at Manoa (HI)
U of Idaho (ID)
U of Kentucky (KY)
U of Maine (ME)
U of Maryland, Coll Park (MD)
U of Massachusetts Amherst (MA)
U of Minnesota, Twin Cities Campus (MN)
U of Missouri (MO)
U of Nebraska–Lincoln (NE)
U of New Hampshire (NH)
The U of Tennessee (TN)
U of Vermont (VT)
U of Wisconsin–River Falls (WI)
U of Wyoming (WY)
Utah State U (UT)
Virginia Polytechnic Inst and State U (VA)
Washington State U (WA)

ANIMAL SCIENCES RELATED
Delaware Valley U (PA)
Southern U and Ag and Mech Coll (LA)
U of California, Davis (CA)

ANIMAL TRAINING
Saint Francis U (PA)

ANIMATION, INTERACTIVE TECHNOLOGY, VIDEO GRAPHICS AND SPECIAL EFFECTS
Acad of Art U (CA)
Bradley U (IL)
Buena Vista U (IA)
Cleveland Inst of Art (OH)
Columbia Coll Chicago (IL)
Davenport U, Grand Rapids (MI)
DePaul U (IL)
DigiPen Inst of Technology (WA)
Drury U (MO)
East Tennessee State U (TN)
Fashion Inst of Technology (NY)
George Mason U (VA)
Lawrence Technological U (MI)
Loyola Marymount U (CA)
Middle Tennessee State U (TN)
New England Inst of Technology (RI)
Pennsylvania Coll of Art & Design (PA)
Regent U (VA)
Rochester Inst of Technology (NY)
Savannah Coll of Art and Design (GA)
State U of New York Coll of Technology at Alfred (NY)
U of Idaho (ID)
U of Northwestern–St. Paul (MN)
The U of Tampa (FL)
U of the Incarnate Word (TX)

ANTHROPOLOGY
Adelphi U (NY)
Agnes Scott Coll (GA)
Albion Coll (MI)
Albright Coll (PA)
American U (DC)
Antioch Coll, Yellow Springs (OH)
Appalachian State U (NC)
Auburn U (AL)
Austin Coll (TX)
Baylor U (TX)
Beloit Coll (WI)
Boston U (MA)
Brandeis U (MA)
Bridgewater State U (MA)
Bucknell U (PA)
Butler U (IN)
California State U, Bakersfield (CA)
California State U, Chico (CA)
California State U, Fullerton (CA)
California State U, Long Beach (CA)
California State U, Los Angeles (CA)
California State U, Northridge (CA)
California State U, San Bernardino (CA)
California State U, San Marcos (CA)
California U of Pennsylvania (PA)
The Catholic U of America (DC)
Central Connecticut State U (CT)
Central Michigan U (MI)
Central Washington U (WA)
Clarion U of Pennsylvania (PA)
Coastal Carolina U (SC)
Colgate U (NY)
The Coll at Brockport, State U of New York (NY)
Coll of Charleston (SC)
The Coll of Idaho (ID)
Coll of the Holy Cross (MA)
The Coll of William and Mary (VA)
The Colorado Coll (CO)
Colorado State U (CO)
Columbia U (NY)
Connecticut Coll (CT)
Cornell Coll (IA)
Cornell U (NY)
Dartmouth Coll (NH)
Davidson Coll (NC)
DePaul U (IL)
Dickinson Coll (PA)
Drake U (IA)
Drew U (NJ)
East Carolina U (NC)
Eastern Washington U (WA)
East Tennessee State U (TN)
Eckerd Coll (FL)
Florida Atlantic U (FL)
Fordham U (NY)
Fort Lewis Coll (CO)
Franklin Pierce U (NH)
Furman U (SC)
George Mason U (VA)
Georgia Southern U (GA)
Georgia State U (GA)
Grand Valley State U (MI)
Hamilton Coll (NY)
Hamline U (MN)
Hanover Coll (IN)
Hartwick Coll (NY)
Harvard U (MA)
Haverford Coll (PA)
Hofstra U (NY)
Humboldt State U (CA)
Hunter Coll of the City U of New York (NY)
Idaho State U (ID)
Indiana U Bloomington (IN)
Indiana U Northwest (IN)
Indiana U of Pennsylvania (PA)
Indiana U–Purdue U Indianapolis (IN)
Indiana U South Bend (IN)
Inter American U of Puerto Rico, San Germán Campus (PR)
Iowa State U of Science and Technology (IA)
Ithaca Coll (NY)
Johns Hopkins U (MD)
Kennesaw State U (GA)
Lafayette Coll (PA)
Lake Forest Coll (IL)
Lawrence U (WI)
Lee U (TN)
Lindenwood U (MO)
Linfield Coll (OR)
Louisiana State U and A&M Coll (LA)
Loyola U Chicago (IL)
Macalester Coll (MN)
Marquette U (WI)
Massachusetts Inst of Technology (MA)
Miami U (OH)
Miami U Hamilton (OH)
Michigan State U (MI)
Middlebury Coll (VT)
Middle Tennessee State U (TN)
Millersville U of Pennsylvania (PA)
Minnesota State U Moorhead (MN)
Montclair State U (NJ)
Muskingum U (OH)
Nazareth Coll of Rochester (NY)
New Coll of Florida (FL)
New York U (NY)
North Carolina State U (NC)
Northern Illinois U (IL)
Northern Kentucky U (KY)
Northwestern U (IL)
The Ohio State U (OH)
Ohio U (OH)
Oklahoma Baptist U (OK)
Pacific Lutheran U (WA)
Pitzer Coll (CA)
Portland State U (OR)
Princeton U (NJ)
Purchase Coll, State U of New York (NY)
Purdue U (IN)
Queens Coll of the City U of New York (NY)
Radford U (VA)
Rhode Island Coll (RI)
Rhodes Coll (TN)
Rice U (TX)
Rollins Coll (FL)
St. John Fisher Coll (NY)
Saint Louis U (MO)
Saint Martin's U (WA)
St. Mary's Coll of Maryland (MD)
Saint Vincent Coll (PA)
San Diego State U (CA)
San Francisco State U (CA)
San Jose State U (CA)
Sarah Lawrence Coll (NY)
Scripps Coll (CA)
Seattle U (WA)
Skidmore Coll (NY)
Sonoma State U (CA)
Southern Illinois U Carbondale (IL)
Southern Illinois U Edwardsville (IL)
Southwestern U (TX)
State U of New York at Plattsburgh (NY)
State U of New York Coll at Geneseo (NY)
State U of New York Coll at Potsdam (NY)
Sweet Briar Coll (VA)
Syracuse U (NY)
Temple U (PA)
Texas Christian U (TX)
Texas Tech U (TX)
Tulane U (LA)
Union Coll (NY)
U at Buffalo, the State U of New York (NY)
U of Arkansas (AR)
U of California, Davis (CA)
U of California, Irvine (CA)
U of California, Los Angeles (CA)
U of California, Merced (CA)
U of California, Riverside (CA)
U of California, Santa Cruz (CA)
U of Central Florida (FL)
U of Chicago (IL)
U of Colorado Denver (CO)
U of Florida (FL)
U of Georgia (GA)
U of Guam (GU)
U of Hawaii at Manoa (HI)
U of Houston (TX)
U of Houston–Clear Lake (TX)
U of Idaho (ID)
U of Kentucky (KY)
U of La Verne (CA)
U of Louisville (KY)
U of Maine (ME)
U of Maryland, Baltimore County (MD)
U of Maryland, Coll Park (MD)
U of Massachusetts Amherst (MA)
U of Massachusetts Boston (MA)
U of Memphis (TN)
U of Michigan (MI)
U of Michigan–Dearborn (MI)
U of Minnesota, Duluth (MN)
U of Minnesota, Morris (MN)
U of Minnesota, Twin Cities Campus (MN)
U of Missouri (MO)
U of Nebraska–Lincoln (NE)
U of Nevada, Las Vegas (NV)
U of Nevada, Reno (NV)
U of New Hampshire (NH)
U of New Mexico (NM)
U of North Carolina at Asheville (NC)
The U of North Carolina at Chapel Hill (NC)
The U of North Carolina at Charlotte (NC)
The U of North Carolina at Greensboro (NC)
U of North Dakota (ND)
U of Northern Colorado (CO)

U of Northern Iowa (IA)
U of North Florida (FL)
U of Notre Dame (IN)
U of Oregon (OR)
U of Pennsylvania (PA)
U of Pittsburgh (PA)
U of Regina (SK, Canada)
U of Richmond (VA)
U of San Diego (CA)
U of South Alabama (AL)
U of South Carolina (SC)
U of South Dakota (SD)
U of Southern Indiana (IN)
U of South Florida (FL)
The U of Tennessee (TN)
The U of Texas at Austin (TX)
The U of Texas at El Paso (TX)
The U of Texas Rio Grande Valley (TX)
The U of the South (TN)
The U of Toledo (OH)
The U of Tulsa (OK)
U of Vermont (VT)
U of Virginia (VA)
U of Washington (WA)
U of West Georgia (GA)
U of Wisconsin–Milwaukee (WI)
U of Wyoming (WY)
Utah State U (UT)
Vanguard U of Southern California (CA)
Vassar Coll (NY)
Virginia Commonwealth U (VA)
Washington State U (WA)
Washington State U–Vancouver (WA)
Washington U in St. Louis (MO)
Weber State U (UT)
Wesleyan U (CT)
West Chester U of Pennsylvania (PA)
Western Connecticut State U (CT)
Western Illinois U (IL)
Western Kentucky U (KY)
Western State Colorado U (CO)
Western Washington U (WA)
Westmont Coll (CA)
Wheaton Coll (IL)
Wheaton Coll (MA)
Whittier Coll (CA)
Widener U (PA)
Willamette U (OR)
Williams Coll (MA)
Wright State U–Lake Campus (OH)
Youngstown State U (OH)

ANTHROPOLOGY RELATED
Bridgewater State U (MA)
Butler U (IN)
U of Michigan (MI)
Western Washington U (WA)

APPAREL AND ACCESSORIES MARKETING
Woodbury U (CA)

APPAREL AND TEXTILE MANUFACTURING
Acad of Art U (CA)
Fashion Inst of Technology (NY)
FIDM/Fashion Inst of Design & Merchandising, Los Angeles Campus (CA)
Michigan State U (MI)

APPAREL AND TEXTILE MARKETING MANAGEMENT
Acad of Art U (CA)
Auburn U (AL)
Central Washington U (WA)
Colorado State U (CO)
Savannah Coll of Art and Design (GA)
U of Nebraska–Lincoln (NE)
U of the Incarnate Word (TX)

APPAREL AND TEXTILES
Acad of Art U (CA)
Appalachian State U (NC)
Auburn U (AL)
Bowling Green State U (OH)
California State U, Long Beach (CA)
East Carolina U (NC)
Framingham State U (MA)
Georgia Southern U (GA)
Indiana State U (IN)
Indiana U Bloomington (IN)
Iowa State U of Science and Technology (IA)
Lamar U (TX)
Liberty U (VA)
Lipscomb U (TN)
Louisiana State U and A&M Coll (LA)
Michigan State U (MI)
Middle Tennessee State U (TN)
Northern Illinois U (IL)
The Ohio State U (OH)
Ohio U (OH)
Rhode Island School of Design (RI)
Southern Illinois U Carbondale (IL)
U of Arkansas (AR)
U of California, Davis (CA)
U of Hawaii at Manoa (HI)
U of Idaho (ID)
U of Kentucky (KY)
U of Minnesota, Twin Cities Campus (MN)
U of Missouri (MO)
U of Nebraska–Lincoln (NE)
The U of North Carolina at Greensboro (NC)
U of Northern Iowa (IA)
The U of Texas at Austin (TX)
Virginia Polytechnic Inst and State U (VA)
Washington State U (WA)
Western Kentucky U (KY)

APPAREL AND TEXTILES RELATED
Savannah Coll of Art and Design (GA)

APPLIED AND PROFESSIONAL ETHICS
Carnegie Mellon U (PA)
Carson-Newman U (TN)

APPLIED BEHAVIOR ANALYSIS
Capilano U (BC, Canada)
Saint Joseph's U (PA)

APPLIED ECONOMICS
Bowling Green State U (OH)
Bryant U (RI)
Farmingdale State Coll (NY)
Ithaca Coll (NY)
U of Dayton (OH)
U of Massachusetts Amherst (MA)
U of Minnesota, Twin Cities Campus (MN)
U of Northern Iowa (IA)
U of San Francisco (CA)
Ursinus Coll (PA)
Wabash Coll (IN)

APPLIED HORTICULTURE/ HORTICULTURE OPERATIONS
Colorado State U (CO)
Farmingdale State Coll (NY)
North Carolina State U (NC)
U of Maine (ME)
U of Massachusetts Amherst (MA)

APPLIED LINGUISTICS
Caldwell U (NJ)
Johnson U Florida (FL)
Portland State U (OR)
U of Idaho (ID)

APPLIED MATHEMATICS
American U (DC)
American U of Beirut (Lebanon)
Auburn U (AL)
Baldwin Wallace U (OH)
Baylor U (TX)
Brandeis U (MA)
Bryant U (RI)
California State U, Fullerton (CA)
California State U, Long Beach (CA)
Central Michigan U (MI)
Christopher Newport U (VA)
Clarkson U (NY)
Coastal Carolina U (SC)
Colgate U (NY)
The Coll of Idaho (ID)
Columbia U (NY)
Endicott Coll (MA)
Farmingdale State Coll (NY)
Fitchburg State U (MA)
Geneva Coll (PA)
Hampden-Sydney Coll (VA)
Harvard U (MA)
Hillsdale Coll (MI)
Humboldt State U (CA)
Indiana U South Bend (IN)
Inter American U of Puerto Rico, San Germán Campus (PR)
Iona Coll (NY)
Johns Hopkins U (MD)
Kennesaw State U (GA)
King U (TN)
La Salle U (PA)
Lasell Coll (MA)
Lee U (TN)
Lipscomb U (TN)
Loyola Marymount U (CA)
Marist Coll (NY)
Maryville U of Saint Louis (MO)
Millsaps Coll (MS)
New Coll of Florida (FL)
New Jersey Inst of Technology (NJ)
North Carolina State U (NC)
Northwestern U (IL)
Ohio U (OH)
Purdue U (IN)
Rice U (TX)
Saginaw Valley State U (MI)
San Diego State U (CA)
San Francisco State U (CA)
San Jose State U (CA)
Sonoma State U (CA)
Southeastern U (FL)
State U of New York Coll at Geneseo (NY)
Syracuse U (NY)
Taylor U (IN)
Temple U (PA)
Trevecca Nazarene U (TN)
U at Buffalo, the State U of New York (NY)
U of California, Davis (CA)
U of California, Los Angeles (CA)
U of California, Merced (CA)
The U of Findlay (OH)
U of Houston–Downtown (TX)
U of Idaho (ID)
U of Massachusetts Lowell (MA)
U of New Hampshire (NH)
U of New Haven (CT)
The U of North Carolina at Chapel Hill (NC)
U of North Florida (FL)
U of Northwestern–St. Paul (MN)
U of Pittsburgh (PA)
U of Pittsburgh at Bradford (PA)
U of Saint Mary (KS)
U of Sioux Falls (SD)
U of South Carolina Aiken (SC)
The U of Texas at El Paso (TX)
The U of Tulsa (OK)
U of Wisconsin–Milwaukee (WI)
Washington State U (WA)
Washington State U–Vancouver (WA)
Washington U in St. Louis (MO)
Weber State U (UT)
Wesleyan Coll (GA)
Western Washington U (WA)
Wheaton Coll (IL)

APPLIED MATHEMATICS RELATED
Averett U (VA)
Berea Coll (KY)
Bucknell U (PA)
Inter American U of Puerto Rico, Bayamón Campus (PR)
Louisiana Coll (LA)
Merrimack Coll (MA)
Mount St. Joseph U (OH)
The Ohio State U (OH)
Temple U (PA)
U of Michigan–Dearborn (MI)
U of Washington (WA)
U of Wisconsin–Milwaukee (WI)
Whitworth U (WA)
Willamette U (OR)

APPLIED PSYCHOLOGY
Bryant U (RI)
Carson-Newman U (TN)
Christian Brothers U (TN)
Embry-Riddle Aeronautical U–Daytona (FL)
Farmingdale State Coll (NY)
Gwynedd Mercy U (PA)
Judson U (IL)
Kansas Wesleyan U (KS)
Loyola U Chicago (IL)
Miami U (OH)
New York U (NY)
Pace U (NY)
Pace U, Pleasantville Campus (NY)
U of Saint Mary (KS)

AQUACULTURE
Auburn U (AL)

AQUATIC BIOLOGY/ LIMNOLOGY
State U of New York Coll of Environmental Science and Forestry (NY)
Stetson U (FL)
U of South Carolina (SC)

ARABIC
American U (DC)
Baylor U (TX)
California U of Pennsylvania (PA)
Dartmouth Coll (NH)
DePaul U (IL)
Lebanese American U (Lebanon)
Michigan State U (MI)
Middlebury Coll (VT)
Montclair State U (NJ)
The Ohio State U (OH)
Portland State U (OR)
U of California, Los Angeles (CA)
U of Georgia (GA)
U of Maryland, Coll Park (MD)
U of Notre Dame (IN)
The U of Texas at Austin (TX)
Washington U in St. Louis (MO)
Western Kentucky U (KY)

ARCHEOLOGY
American U of Beirut (Lebanon)
Boston U (MA)
Bridgewater State U (MA)
Coll of Charleston (SC)
Columbia U (NY)
Cornell Coll (IA)
Cornell U (NY)
Dickinson Coll (PA)
Hamilton Coll (NY)
Haverford Coll (PA)
Hunter Coll of the City U of New York (NY)
Johns Hopkins U (MD)
Lycoming Coll (PA)
New York U (NY)
State U of New York Coll at Potsdam (NY)
U of Missouri (MO)
The U of North Carolina at Chapel Hill (NC)
The U of Texas at Austin (TX)
U of Wisconsin–La Crosse (WI)
Washington U in St. Louis (MO)
Wesleyan U (CT)
Western Washington U (WA)
Wheaton Coll (IL)

ARCHITECTURAL AND BUILDING SCIENCES
Carnegie Mellon U (PA)
Iowa State U of Science and Technology (IA)
Lawrence Technological U (MI)
Oklahoma State U (OK)
Rhode Island School of Design (RI)
Savannah Coll of Art and Design (GA)
State U of New York Coll of Technology at Delhi (NY)
Syracuse U (NY)
Temple U (PA)
U of Massachusetts Amherst (MA)
Washington U in St. Louis (MO)

ARCHITECTURAL DRAFTING AND CAD/CADD
Acad of Art U (CA)

ARCHITECTURAL ENGINEERING
Auburn U (AL)
California Polytechnic State U, San Luis Obispo (CA)
Lawrence Technological U (MI)
Oklahoma State U (OK)
U of Detroit Mercy (MI)
U of Nebraska–Lincoln (NE)
The U of Texas at Austin (TX)
U of Wyoming (WY)
Worcester Polytechnic Inst (MA)

ARCHITECTURAL ENGINEERING TECHNOLOGY
Farmingdale State Coll (NY)
Fitchburg State U (MA)
Indiana U–Purdue U Indianapolis (IN)
New England Inst of Technology (RI)
Purdue U (IN)
State U of New York Coll of Technology at Alfred (NY)
Vermont Tech Coll (VT)
Washington U in St. Louis (MO)

ARCHITECTURAL HISTORY AND CRITICISM
Boston U (MA)
Coll of the Holy Cross (MA)
Cornell U (NY)
DePaul U (IL)
Miami U Hamilton (OH)
Savannah Coll of Art and Design (GA)
Syracuse U (NY)
U of San Diego (CA)
U of Virginia (VA)

ARCHITECTURAL TECHNOLOGY
Indiana State U (IN)
Washington U in St. Louis (MO)
Western Kentucky U (KY)

ARCHITECTURE
Acad of Art U (CA)
American U of Beirut (Lebanon)
Auburn U (AL)
California Polytechnic State U, San Luis Obispo (CA)
Carnegie Mellon U (PA)
The Catholic U of America (DC)
Columbia U (NY)
Cornell Coll (IA)
Cornell U (NY)
Drury U (MO)
Dunwoody Coll of Technology (MN)
Florida Ag and Mech U (FL)
Florida Atlantic U (FL)
Inter American U of Puerto Rico, San Germán Campus (PR)
Ithaca Coll (NY)
Judson U (IL)
Kean U (NJ)
Kennesaw State U (GA)
Lebanese American U (Lebanon)
Louisiana State U and A&M Coll (LA)
Marywood U (PA)
Massachusetts Inst of Technology (MA)
Miami U (OH)
Miami U Hamilton (OH)
Middlebury Coll (VT)
New Jersey Inst of Technology (NJ)
North Carolina State U (NC)
The Ohio State U (OH)
Portland State U (OR)
Prairie View A&M U (TX)
Princeton U (NJ)
Rice U (TX)
Sarah Lawrence Coll (NY)
Southern Illinois U Carbondale (IL)
Southern U and Ag and Mech Coll (LA)
State U of New York Coll of Technology at Alfred (NY)
Texas Tech U (TX)
Tulane U (LA)
U at Buffalo, the State U of New York (NY)
U of Arkansas (AR)
U of California, Los Angeles (CA)
U of Central Florida (FL)
U of Colorado Denver (CO)
U of Detroit Mercy (MI)
U of Florida (FL)
U of Hawaii at Manoa (HI)
U of Houston (TX)
U of Idaho (ID)
U of Kentucky (KY)
U of Maryland, Coll Park (MD)
U of Memphis (TN)
U of Michigan (MI)
U of Minnesota, Twin Cities Campus (MN)
U of Nebraska–Lincoln (NE)
U of Nevada, Las Vegas (NV)
U of New Mexico (NM)
The U of North Carolina at Charlotte (NC)
U of Notre Dame (IN)

U of Oregon (OR)
U of Pennsylvania (PA)
U of Pittsburgh (PA)
U of San Francisco (CA)
The U of Tennessee (TN)
The U of Texas at Austin (TX)
U of Virginia (VA)
U of Washington (WA)
U of Wisconsin–Milwaukee (WI)
Virginia Polytechnic Inst and State U (VA)
Washington State U (WA)
Washington U in St. Louis (MO)
Woodbury U (CA)

ARCHITECTURE RELATED
Connecticut Coll (CT)
Drury U (MO)
Lipscomb U (TN)
New Jersey Inst of Technology (NJ)
Washington U in St. Louis (MO)

AREA STUDIES RELATED
Boston U (MA)
Bridgewater State U (MA)
Colgate U (NY)
Hofstra U (NY)
Lake Forest Coll (IL)
Lycoming Coll (PA)
Millersville U of Pennsylvania (PA)
New York U (NY)
Northeastern State U (OK)
Northwestern U (IL)
U of Michigan–Dearborn (MI)
U of Missouri (MO)
U of Pittsburgh (PA)
U of Richmond (VA)
U of San Francisco (CA)
U of Virginia (VA)
U of Washington (WA)
Utah State U (UT)
Virginia Commonwealth U (VA)
Washington U in St. Louis (MO)
Williams Coll (MA)

ARMY ROTC/MILITARY SCIENCE
Iowa State U of Science and Technology (IA)

ARMY ROTC, MILITARY SCIENCE AND OPERATIONS RELATED
Western Kentucky U (KY)

ART
Alabama State U (AL)
Albion Coll (MI)
Albright Coll (PA)
Alfred U (NY)
Alverno Coll (WI)
Appalachian State U (NC)
Arkansas Tech U (AR)
Auburn U at Montgomery (AL)
Austin Coll (TX)
Austin Peay State U (TN)
Averett U (VA)
Avila U (MO)
Baldwin Wallace U (OH)
Barton Coll (NC)
Baylor U (TX)
Berea Coll (KY)
Bethel U (MN)
Blackburn Coll (IL)
Bowling Green State U (OH)
Bradley U (IL)
Bucknell U (PA)
Buena Vista U (IA)
Caldwell U (NJ)
California Lutheran U (CA)
California State U, Bakersfield (CA)
California State U, Chico (CA)
California State U, Fullerton (CA)
California State U, Long Beach (CA)
California State U, Los Angeles (CA)
California State U, Monterey Bay (CA)
California State U, Northridge (CA)
California State U, San Bernardino (CA)
California U of Pennsylvania (PA)
Calvin Coll (MI)
Cameron U (OK)
Campbellsville U (KY)
Carnegie Mellon U (PA)
Carson-Newman U (TN)
The Catholic U of America (DC)
Centenary Coll of Louisiana (LA)
Central Connecticut State U (CT)
Central Michigan U (MI)
Central State U (OH)
Central Washington U (WA)
Clarion U of Pennsylvania (PA)
Colgate U (NY)
The Coll at Brockport, State U of New York (NY)
The Coll of Idaho (ID)
Coll of Saint Benedict (MN)
Coll of Saint Mary (NE)
The Coll of St. Scholastica (MN)
The Coll of William and Mary (VA)
Columbia Coll (MO)
Concordia U Chicago (IL)
Concordia U Irvine (CA)
Cornell Coll (IA)
Creighton U (NE)
Culver-Stockton Coll (MO)
Dallas Baptist U (TX)
Davidson Coll (NC)
DePaul U (IL)
Dickinson Coll (PA)
Drake U (IA)
Earlham Coll (IN)
Eastern Illinois U (IL)
Eastern Mennonite U (VA)
Eastern Oregon U (OR)
East Tennessee State U (TN)
The Evergreen State Coll (WA)
Fayetteville State U (NC)
Florida Atlantic U (FL)
Fort Lewis Coll (CO)
Framingham State U (MA)
Georgia Coll & State U (GA)
Georgia Southern U (GA)
Gonzaga U (WA)
Gordon Coll (MA)
Goshen Coll (IN)
Graceland U (IA)
Greenville U (IL)
Hanover Coll (IN)
Hartwick Coll (NY)
Haverford Coll (PA)
Hillsdale Coll (MI)
Hollins U (VA)
Hood Coll (MD)
Humboldt State U (CA)
Hunter Coll of the City U of New York (NY)
Idaho State U (ID)
Illinois Coll (IL)
Indiana State U (IN)
Indiana U Bloomington (IN)
Indiana U East (IN)
Indiana U Kokomo (IN)
Indiana U of Pennsylvania (PA)
Indiana U South Bend (IN)
Indiana U Southeast (IN)
Inter American U of Puerto Rico, San Germán Campus (PR)
Ithaca Coll (NY)
Jacksonville U (FL)
Judson U (IL)
Kalamazoo Coll (MI)
Kean U (NJ)
Kennesaw State U (GA)
Lafayette Coll (PA)
Lake Forest Coll (IL)
La Sierra U (CA)
Lebanon Valley Coll (PA)
Lesley U (MA)
Linfield Coll (OR)
Lock Haven U of Pennsylvania (PA)
Lycoming Coll (PA)
Macalester Coll (MN)
Manchester U (IN)
Marian U (IN)
Marshall U (WV)
Maryland Inst Coll of Art (MD)
Marymount Manhattan Coll (NY)
Massachusetts Coll of Liberal Arts (MA)
McDaniel Coll (MD)
McNeese State U (LA)
Mercer U, Macon (GA)
Miami U (OH)
Miami U Hamilton (OH)
Michigan State U (MI)
Middle Tennessee State U (TN)
Millersville U of Pennsylvania (PA)
Minnesota State U Moorhead (MN)
Montclair State U (NJ)
Mount St. Joseph U (OH)
Muskingum U (OH)
Nazareth Coll of Rochester (NY)
New England Coll (NH)
New Jersey City U (NJ)
New Jersey Inst of Technology (NJ)
Northeastern State U (OK)
Northern Illinois U (IL)
Northern State U (SD)
Northwestern U (IL)
Oakland City U (IN)
Occidental Coll (CA)
Oglethorpe U (GA)
Ohio Dominican U (OH)
The Ohio State U (OH)
Ohio U (OH)
Oklahoma Baptist U (OK)
Oklahoma Christian U (OK)
Oklahoma State U (OK)
Old Dominion U (VA)
Ottawa U (KS)
Pepperdine U, Malibu (CA)
Piedmont Coll (GA)
Portland State U (OR)
Providence Coll (RI)
Purchase Coll, State U of New York (NY)
Radford U (VA)
Redeemer U Coll (ON, Canada)
Regis U (CO)
Rhodes Coll (TN)
Rice U (TX)
Rider U (NJ)
Roanoke Coll (VA)
Rockford U (IL)
Rocky Mountain Coll (MT)
Rollins Coll (FL)
Sacred Heart U (CT)
Saginaw Valley State U (MI)
Saint Anselm Coll (NH)
Saint John's U (MN)
Saint Joseph's U (PA)
St. Mary's Coll of Maryland (MD)
St. Norbert Coll (WI)
St. Olaf Coll (MN)
Salisbury U (MD)
San Diego State U (CA)
San Francisco State U (CA)
San Jose State U (CA)
Savannah Coll of Art and Design (GA)
Scripps Coll (CA)
Skidmore Coll (NY)
Sonoma State U (CA)
Southeastern Louisiana U (LA)
Southeast Missouri State U (MO)
Southern Arkansas U–Magnolia (AR)
Southern Illinois U Carbondale (IL)
Southern Illinois U Edwardsville (IL)
Southwest Baptist U (MO)
State U of New York at Fredonia (NY)
State U of New York at Plattsburgh (NY)
Stetson U (FL)
Taylor U (IN)
Texas Lutheran U (TX)
Texas Tech U (TX)
Texas Woman's U (TX)
Tiffin U (OH)
Towson U (MD)
Truman State U (MO)
Tulane U (LA)
U at Buffalo, the State U of New York (NY)
U of Arkansas (AR)
U of California, Los Angeles (CA)
U of California, Riverside (CA)
U of California, Santa Cruz (CA)
U of Central Arkansas (AR)
U of Central Florida (FL)
U of Dallas (TX)
The U of Findlay (OH)
U of Georgia (GA)
U of Hawaii at Manoa (HI)
U of Houston (TX)
U of Idaho (ID)
U of La Verne (CA)
U of Lynchburg (VA)
U of Maine at Farmington (ME)
U of Maine at Machias (ME)
U of Maine at Presque Isle (ME)
U of Massachusetts Boston (MA)
U of Memphis (TN)
U of Michigan (MI)
U of Minnesota, Duluth (MN)
U of Minnesota, Twin Cities Campus (MN)
U of Missouri (MO)
U of Montevallo (AL)
U of Mount Union (OH)
U of Nevada, Las Vegas (NV)
U of Nevada, Reno (NV)
U of New Hampshire (NH)
U of New Mexico (NM)
U of North Carolina at Asheville (NC)
The U of North Carolina at Greensboro (NC)
U of North Dakota (ND)
U of Northern Iowa (IA)
U of North Florida (FL)
U of Oregon (OR)
U of Providence (MT)
U of Puget Sound (WA)
U of Saint Mary (KS)
U of San Diego (CA)
U of Sioux Falls (SD)
U of South Alabama (AL)
U of South Dakota (SD)
U of Southern Indiana (IN)
U of South Florida (FL)
The U of Tampa (FL)
The U of Texas of the Permian Basin (TX)
The U of Texas Rio Grande Valley (TX)
U of the Incarnate Word (TX)
The U of Toledo (OH)
U of Virginia (VA)
U of Washington (WA)
U of West Georgia (GA)
U of Wisconsin–Eau Claire (WI)
U of Wisconsin–La Crosse (WI)
U of Wisconsin–Milwaukee (WI)
U of Wisconsin–River Falls (WI)
U of Wyoming (WY)
Ursinus Coll (PA)
Utah State U (UT)
Valley City State U (ND)
Valparaiso U (IN)
Virginia Polytechnic Inst and State U (VA)
Wabash Coll (IN)
Wartburg Coll (IA)
Washington & Jefferson Coll (PA)
Washington U in St. Louis (MO)
Waynesburg U (PA)
Weber State U (UT)
Western Connecticut State U (CT)
Western Illinois U (IL)
Western Washington U (WA)
Westmont Coll (CA)
West Virginia State U (WV)
Wheaton Coll (IL)
Whittier Coll (CA)
Whitworth U (WA)
Willamette U (OR)
Williams Coll (MA)
Winthrop U (SC)
Wright State U–Lake Campus (OH)
Youngstown State U (OH)

ART HISTORY, CRITICISM AND CONSERVATION
Acad of Art U (CA)
Adams State U (CO)
Adelphi U (NY)
Agnes Scott Coll (GA)
Albion Coll (MI)
Alfred U (NY)
American U (DC)
Baker U (KS)
Baylor U (TX)
Beloit Coll (WI)
Boston Coll (MA)
Boston U (MA)
Bowling Green State U (OH)
Bradley U (IL)
Brandeis U (MA)
Bridgewater State U (MA)
Bucknell U (PA)
California State U, Fullerton (CA)
California State U, Long Beach (CA)
Carthage Coll (WI)
The Catholic U of America (DC)
Clark U (MA)
Coastal Carolina U (SC)
Coll of Charleston (SC)
Coll of the Holy Cross (MA)
The Coll of William and Mary (VA)
The Colorado Coll (CO)
Columbia Coll Chicago (IL)
Columbia U (NY)
Connecticut Coll (CT)
Cornell Coll (IA)
Cornell U (NY)
Creighton U (NE)
Dartmouth Coll (NH)
DePaul U (IL)
DEREE - The American Coll of Greece (Greece)
Dominican U (IL)
Drake U (IA)
Drew U (NJ)
Drury U (MO)
Duquesne U (PA)
Eastern Washington U (WA)
Fairfield U (CT)
Florida Southern Coll (FL)
Fordham U (NY)
Furman U (SC)
George Mason U (VA)
Grand Valley State U (MI)
Hamilton Coll (NY)
Hamline U (MN)
Hanover Coll (IN)
Hartwick Coll (NY)
Harvard U (MA)
Haverford Coll (PA)
Hofstra U (NY)
Hollins U (VA)
Holy Apostles Coll and Sem (CT)
Humboldt State U (CA)
Hunter Coll of the City U of New York (NY)
Indiana U Bloomington (IN)
Indiana U–Purdue U Indianapolis (IN)
Ithaca Coll (NY)
Jacksonville U (FL)
John Cabot U (Italy)
Johns Hopkins U (MD)
Juniata Coll (PA)
Kalamazoo Coll (MI)
Kennesaw State U (GA)
Knox Coll (IL)
Lake Forest Coll (IL)
La Salle U (PA)
Lawrence U (WI)
Lewis & Clark Coll (OR)
Lindenwood U (MO)
Loyola Marymount U (CA)
Loyola U Chicago (IL)
Lycoming Coll (PA)
Manhattanville Coll (NY)
Mansfield U of Pennsylvania (PA)
Marist Coll (NY)
Maryland Inst Coll of Art (MD)
Marymount Manhattan Coll (NY)
McDaniel Coll (MD)
Merrimack Coll (MA)
Messiah Coll (PA)
Miami U (OH)
Michigan State U (MI)
Middlebury Coll (VT)
Millsaps Coll (MS)
Mills Coll (CA)
Minnesota State U Moorhead (MN)
Nazareth Coll of Rochester (NY)
New Coll of Florida (FL)
New York U (NY)
North Carolina State U (NC)
Northern Illinois U (IL)
Northwestern U (IL)
Oglethorpe U (GA)
The Ohio State U (OH)
Ohio U (OH)
Ohio Wesleyan U (OH)
Old Dominion U (VA)
Pace U (NY)
Pacific Lutheran U (WA)
Pepperdine U, Malibu (CA)
Portland State U (OR)
Princeton U (NJ)
Providence Coll (RI)
Purchase Coll, State U of New York (NY)
Purdue U (IN)
Queens Coll of the City U of New York (NY)
Queens U of Charlotte (NC)
Randolph Coll (VA)
Randolph-Macon Coll (VA)
Regis U (CO)
Rhode Island Coll (RI)
Rice U (TX)
Roanoke Coll (VA)
Rockford U (IL)
Rollins Coll (FL)
Saint Louis U (MO)

St. Mary's Coll of Maryland (MD)
St. Olaf Coll (MN)
Saint Vincent Coll (PA)
Salve Regina U (RI)
San Diego State U (CA)
San Jose State U (CA)
Sarah Lawrence Coll (NY)
Savannah Coll of Art and Design (GA)
Scripps Coll (CA)
Seattle U (WA)
Seton Hill U (PA)
Skidmore Coll (NY)
Sonoma State U (CA)
Southwestern U (TX)
State U of New York at Fredonia (NY)
State U of New York Coll at Geneseo (NY)
Stetson U (FL)
Sweet Briar Coll (VA)
Syracuse U (NY)
Temple U (PA)
Texas Christian U (TX)
Towson U (MD)
Tulane U (LA)
U at Buffalo, the State U of New York (NY)
U of Arkansas (AR)
U of California, Davis (CA)
U of California, Irvine (CA)
U of California, Los Angeles (CA)
U of California, Riverside (CA)
U of California, Santa Cruz (CA)
U of Chicago (IL)
U of Dallas (TX)
U of Dayton (OH)
U of Florida (FL)
U of Georgia (GA)
U of Houston (TX)
U of Kentucky (KY)
U of La Verne (CA)
U of Louisville (KY)
U of Maine (ME)
U of Maryland, Coll Park (MD)
U of Massachusetts Amherst (MA)
U of Massachusetts Dartmouth (MA)
U of Memphis (TN)
U of Michigan (MI)
U of Michigan–Dearborn (MI)
U of Minnesota, Duluth (MN)
U of Minnesota, Morris (MN)
U of Minnesota, Twin Cities Campus (MN)
U of Nebraska–Lincoln (NE)
U of Nevada, Las Vegas (NV)
U of Nevada, Reno (NV)
U of New Mexico (NM)
U of North Carolina at Asheville (NC)
The U of North Carolina at Chapel Hill (NC)
The U of North Carolina at Charlotte (NC)
U of Northern Iowa (IA)
U of North Florida (FL)
U of Notre Dame (IN)
U of Oregon (OR)
U of Pennsylvania (PA)
U of Pittsburgh (PA)
U of Regina (SK, Canada)
U of Richmond (VA)
U of Saint Francis (IN)
U of St. Thomas (MN)
U of San Diego (CA)
U of San Francisco (CA)
U of South Carolina (SC)
U of South Florida (FL)
The U of Tennessee (TN)
The U of Texas at Austin (TX)
The U of the South (TN)
The U of Toledo (OH)
The U of Tulsa (OK)
U of Vermont (VT)
U of Washington (WA)
U of Wisconsin–Milwaukee (WI)
U of Wisconsin–Superior (WI)
U of Wyoming (WY)
Vassar Coll (NY)
Virginia Commonwealth U (VA)
Washington and Lee U (VA)
Washington U in St. Louis (MO)
Wesleyan U (CT)
Western Kentucky U (KY)
Western Washington U (WA)
Wheaton Coll (MA)
Whitworth U (WA)
Willamette U (OR)
Williams Coll (MA)
Winthrop U (SC)
Wofford Coll (SC)
Wright State U–Lake Campus (OH)
Youngstown State U (OH)

ARTIFICIAL INTELLIGENCE
Indiana U Bloomington (IN)

ARTS, ENTERTAINMENT, AND MEDIA MANAGEMENT
Albright Coll (PA)
Butler U (IN)
Champlain Coll (VT)
Columbia Coll Chicago (IL)
Dean Coll (MA)
Drury U (MO)
Judson U (IL)
Kansas Wesleyan U (KS)
Loyola U New Orleans (LA)
National U (CA)
State U of New York at Fredonia (NY)
U of Central Florida (FL)
The U of Findlay (OH)
U of Kentucky (KY)
The U of Tulsa (OK)

ARTS, ENTERTAINMENT, AND MEDIA MANAGEMENT RELATED
Delta State U (MS)
Loyola U New Orleans (LA)
Wesleyan Coll (GA)

ART TEACHER EDUCATION
Acad of Art U (CA)
Adams State U (CO)
Adelphi U (NY)
Albright Coll (PA)
Alfred U (NY)
Alverno Coll (WI)
Appalachian State U (NC)
Arkansas Tech U (AR)
Averett U (VA)
Baker U (KS)
Baylor U (TX)
Beloit Coll (WI)
Bethany Lutheran Coll (MN)
Bethel U (MN)
Boston U (MA)
Bowling Green State U (OH)
Bradley U (IL)
Bridgewater State U (MA)
Buena Vista U (IA)
California Lutheran U (CA)
California State U, Long Beach (CA)
Calvin Coll (MI)
Campbellsville U (KY)
Carson-Newman U (TN)
Central Connecticut State U (CT)
Central Michigan U (MI)
Central State U (OH)
Coll of Saint Mary (NE)
Coll of the Ozarks (MO)
Concordia U Chicago (IL)
Culver-Stockton Coll (MO)
DePaul U (IL)
East Carolina U (NC)
Eastern Washington U (WA)
Escuela de Artes Plasticas y Diseño de Puerto Rico (PR)
Fayetteville State U (NC)
Florida Southern Coll (FL)
Georgia Southern U (GA)
Georgia State U (GA)
Goshen Coll (IN)
Graceland U (IA)
Grand Valley State U (MI)
Harding U (AR)
Hardin-Simmons U (TX)
Hofstra U (NY)
Humboldt State U (CA)
Indiana State U (IN)
Indiana U Bloomington (IN)
Indiana U–Purdue U Indianapolis (IN)
Indiana U South Bend (IN)
Inter American U of Puerto Rico, San Germán Campus (PR)
Ithaca Coll (NY)
Jacksonville U (FL)
Kennesaw State U (GA)
Lee U (TN)
Lipscomb U (TN)
Louisiana Coll (LA)
Lubbock Christian U (TX)
Manchester U (IN)
Manhattanville Coll (NY)
Maryland Inst Coll of Art (MD)
Maryville U of Saint Louis (MO)
Marywood U (PA)
Messiah Coll (PA)
Miami U (OH)
Miami U Hamilton (OH)
Michigan State U (MI)
Middle Tennessee State U (TN)
Millikin U (IL)
Minnesota State U Moorhead (MN)
Molloy Coll (NY)
Morningside Coll (IA)
Mount St. Joseph U (OH)
Muskingum U (OH)
Nazareth Coll of Rochester (NY)
New Jersey City U (NJ)
Northeastern State U (OK)
Northern Illinois U (IL)
Northern State U (SD)
Northwest Missouri State U (MO)
Ohio Dominican U (OH)
The Ohio State U (OH)
Ohio Wesleyan U (OH)
Ottawa U (KS)
Ouachita Baptist U (AR)
Palm Beach Atlantic U (FL)
Piedmont Coll (GA)
Point Loma Nazarene U (CA)
Purdue U (IN)
Queens Coll of the City U of New York (NY)
Rhode Island Coll (RI)
Rocky Mountain Coll (MT)
Saginaw Valley State U (MI)
Saint Joseph's U (PA)
St. Mary's U (TX)
Saint Vincent Coll (PA)
Seton Hill U (PA)
Southeast Missouri State U (MO)
Southern Arkansas U–Magnolia (AR)
Southern U and Ag and Mech Coll (LA)
Southwest Baptist U (MO)
State U of New York Coll at Potsdam (NY)
Syracuse U (NY)
Taylor U (IN)
Temple U (PA)
Texas Christian U (TX)
Texas Lutheran U (TX)
Towson U (MD)
Trinity Christian Coll (IL)
U of Dayton (OH)
The U of Findlay (OH)
U of Florida (FL)
U of Kentucky (KY)
U of Maine (ME)
U of Mary Hardin-Baylor (TX)
U of Maryland, Coll Park (MD)
U of Maryland Eastern Shore (MD)
U of Massachusetts Dartmouth (MA)
U of Minnesota, Duluth (MN)
U of New Mexico (NM)
The U of North Carolina at Greensboro (NC)
The U of North Carolina at Pembroke (NC)
U of North Florida (FL)
U of Northwestern–St. Paul (MN)
U of Providence (MT)
U of Regina (SK, Canada)
U of Saint Francis (IN)
U of Sioux Falls (SD)
U of South Carolina (SC)
U of South Dakota (SD)
U of Vermont (VT)
U of Wisconsin–Milwaukee (WI)
U of Wisconsin–River Falls (WI)
U of Wisconsin–Superior (WI)
Utah Valley U (UT)
Valley City State U (ND)
Valparaiso U (IN)
Virginia Commonwealth U (VA)
Wartburg Coll (IA)
Washington & Jefferson Coll (PA)
Washington U in St. Louis (MO)
Weber State U (UT)
Western Washington U (WA)
Westmont Coll (CA)
Whitworth U (WA)
Youngstown State U (OH)

ART THERAPY
Alverno Coll (WI)
Bowling Green State U (OH)
Concordia U Chicago (IL)
Emmanuel Coll (MA)
Harding U (AR)
Kansas Wesleyan U (KS)
Lesley U (MA)
Lipscomb U (TN)
Marywood U (PA)
Millikin U (IL)
Nazareth Coll of Rochester (NY)
Seton Hill U (PA)
Taylor U (IN)
Trinity Christian Coll (IL)
U of Saint Francis (IN)
The U of Tampa (FL)
U of Wisconsin–Superior (WI)

ASIAN AMERICAN STUDIES
California State U, Fullerton (CA)
California State U, Long Beach (CA)
California State U, Los Angeles (CA)
California State U, Northridge (CA)
Pitzer Coll (CA)
San Francisco State U (CA)
Scripps Coll (CA)
U of California, Davis (CA)
U of California, Irvine (CA)
U of California, Los Angeles (CA)
U of California, Riverside (CA)

ASIAN HISTORY
Sarah Lawrence Coll (NY)
U of Washington, Tacoma (WA)

ASIAN STUDIES
American U (DC)
Austin Coll (TX)
Baylor U (TX)
Berea Coll (KY)
Boston U (MA)
Bowling Green State U (OH)
California State U, Chico (CA)
California State U, Long Beach (CA)
Calvin Coll (MI)
Carthage Coll (WI)
Claremont McKenna Coll (CA)
Clark U (MA)
Colgate U (NY)
Coll of Saint Benedict (MN)
Coll of the Holy Cross (MA)
The Colorado Coll (CO)
Cornell U (NY)
Dartmouth Coll (NH)
Furman U (SC)
Gonzaga U (WA)
Hamilton Coll (NY)
Indiana U of Pennsylvania (PA)
Kean U (NJ)
Kennesaw State U (GA)
Knox Coll (IL)
Lake Forest Coll (IL)
Lewis & Clark Coll (OR)
Loyola Marymount U (CA)
Macalester Coll (MN)
McDaniel Coll (MD)
Nazareth Coll of Rochester (NY)
Northwestern U (IL)
Ohio U (OH)
Old Dominion U (VA)
Pace U (NY)
Pepperdine U, Malibu (CA)
Purdue U (IN)
Randolph-Macon Coll (VA)
Rice U (TX)
Rollins Coll (FL)
Saint John's U (MN)
Saint Joseph's U (PA)
St. Mary's Coll of Maryland (MD)
St. Olaf Coll (MN)
San Diego State U (CA)
Sarah Lawrence Coll (NY)
Scripps Coll (CA)
Seattle U (WA)
Skidmore Coll (NY)
Temple U (PA)
Tulane U (LA)
Union Coll (NY)
U at Buffalo, the State U of New York (NY)
U of California, Riverside (CA)
U of Hawaii at Manoa (HI)
U of Louisville (KY)
U of Maryland, Baltimore County (MD)
U of Maryland U Coll (MD)
U of Massachusetts Boston (MA)
U of Michigan (MI)
U of Nevada, Las Vegas (NV)
U of New Mexico (NM)
The U of North Carolina at Chapel Hill (NC)
U of Northern Colorado (CO)
U of Oregon (OR)
U of Richmond (VA)
U of San Francisco (CA)
The U of Texas at Austin (TX)
The U of the South (TN)
The U of Toledo (OH)
U of Vermont (VT)
U of Washington (WA)
Utah State U (UT)
Vassar Coll (NY)
Washington State U (WA)
Washington U in St. Louis (MO)
Western Kentucky U (KY)
Willamette U (OR)
Williams Coll (MA)

ASIAN STUDIES (EAST)
Austin Coll (TX)
Boston U (MA)
Brandeis U (MA)
Bucknell U (PA)
Central Michigan U (MI)
Columbia U (NY)
Connecticut Coll (CT)
Davidson Coll (NC)
DePaul U (IL)
Dickinson Coll (PA)
Grand Valley State U (MI)
Harvard U (MA)
Haverford Coll (PA)
Hofstra U (NY)
Indiana U Bloomington (IN)
Johns Hopkins U (MD)
Kalamazoo Coll (MI)
Lawrence U (WI)
Miami U (OH)
Middlebury Coll (VT)
Minnesota State U Moorhead (MN)
New York U (NY)
Occidental Coll (CA)
Ohio Wesleyan U (OH)
Portland State U (OR)
Princeton U (NJ)
Queens Coll of the City U of New York (NY)
U of California, Davis (CA)
U of California, Irvine (CA)
U of Pennsylvania (PA)
Ursinus Coll (PA)
Valparaiso U (IN)
Washington U in St. Louis (MO)
Wesleyan U (CT)
Western Washington U (WA)
Willamette U (OR)

ASIAN STUDIES (SOUTH)
Indiana U Bloomington (IN)
Middlebury Coll (VT)
U of Pennsylvania (PA)
U of Washington (WA)

ASIAN STUDIES (SOUTHEAST)
U of Washington (WA)

ASIAN STUDIES (URAL-ALTAIC AND CENTRAL)
Indiana U Bloomington (IN)

ASTRONOMY
Baylor U (TX)
Boston U (MA)
Central Michigan U (MI)
Columbia U (NY)
Cornell U (NY)
Dartmouth Coll (NH)
Drake U (IA)
Embry-Riddle Aeronautical U–Prescott (AZ)
George Mason U (VA)
Haverford Coll (PA)
Indiana U Bloomington (IN)
Lycoming Coll (PA)
Northwestern U (IL)
The Ohio State U (OH)
Ohio Wesleyan U (OH)
Rice U (TX)
San Diego State U (CA)
San Francisco State U (CA)

Stonehill Coll (MA)
Union Coll (NY)
U of Chicago (IL)
U of Florida (FL)
U of Georgia (GA)
U of Hawaii at Manoa (HI)
U of Maryland, Coll Park (MD)
U of Massachusetts Amherst (MA)
U of Michigan (MI)
U of Pittsburgh (PA)
The U of Texas at Austin (TX)
The U of Toledo (OH)
U of Virginia (VA)
U of Washington (WA)
Valparaiso U (IN)
Vassar Coll (NY)
Wesleyan U (CT)
Williams Coll (MA)
Youngstown State U (OH)

ASTRONOMY AND ASTROPHYSICS RELATED
Butler U (IN)
Coll of Charleston (SC)
Embry-Riddle Aeronautical U–Daytona (FL)
Harvard U (MA)
Texas Christian U (TX)
U of Wyoming (WY)
Wheaton Coll (MA)

ASTROPHYSICS
Agnes Scott Coll (GA)
Baylor U (TX)
Boston U (MA)
California Inst of Technology (CA)
Carnegie Mellon U (PA)
Colgate U (NY)
Columbia U (NY)
Haverford Coll (PA)
Lycoming Coll (PA)
Michigan State U (MI)
Ohio U (OH)
Ohio Wesleyan U (OH)
Princeton U (NJ)
Rice U (TX)
San Francisco State U (CA)
U of California, Los Angeles (CA)
U of California, Santa Cruz (CA)
U of Hawaii at Manoa (HI)
U of Minnesota, Twin Cities Campus (MN)
U of New Mexico (NM)
Williams Coll (MA)

ATHLETIC TRAINING
Alfred U (NY)
Averett U (VA)
Baldwin Wallace U (OH)
Bethel Coll (KS)
Bethel U (MN)
Boston U (MA)
Bowling Green State U (OH)
Bridgewater State U (MA)
Buena Vista U (IA)
California State U, Fullerton (CA)
California State U, Long Beach (CA)
California State U, Northridge (CA)
California U of Pennsylvania (PA)
Canisius Coll (NY)
Carthage Coll (WI)
Cedarville U (OH)
Central Connecticut State U (CT)
Central Michigan U (MI)
The Coll at Brockport, State U of New York (NY)
Colorado State U–Pueblo (CO)
Concordia U Irvine (CA)
Culver-Stockton Coll (MO)
Duquesne U (PA)
East Carolina U (NC)
Eastern Illinois U (IL)
Eastern U (PA)
Eastern Washington U (WA)
East Stroudsburg U of Pennsylvania (PA)
East Texas Baptist U (TX)
Endicott Coll (MA)
Georgetown Coll (KY)
Georgia Coll & State U (GA)
Georgia Southern U (GA)
Grand Valley State U (MI)
Harding U (AR)
Hardin-Simmons U (TX)
Hofstra U (NY)
Indiana State U (IN)
Indiana U Bloomington (IN)
Iowa State U of Science and Technology (IA)
Ithaca Coll (NY)
Kean U (NJ)
King's Coll (PA)
Lasell Coll (MA)
Lee U (TN)
Liberty U (VA)
Limestone Coll (SC)
Loras Coll (IA)
Lubbock Christian U (TX)
Manchester U (IN)
Marist Coll (NY)
Marquette U (WI)
Marshall U (WV)
Marywood U (PA)
Massachusetts Coll of Liberal Arts (MA)
Messiah Coll (PA)
Miami U (OH)
Miami U Hamilton (OH)
Michigan State U (MI)
Middle Tennessee State U (TN)
Millikin U (IL)
Minnesota State U Moorhead (MN)
Montclair State U (NJ)
Mount St. Joseph U (OH)
Muskingum U (OH)
Northern Illinois U (IL)
Northern Kentucky U (KY)
The Ohio State U (OH)
Ohio U (OH)
Oklahoma Baptist U (OK)
Palm Beach Atlantic U (FL)
Piedmont Coll (GA)
Radford U (VA)
Sacred Heart U (CT)
Saginaw Valley State U (MI)
Salisbury U (MD)
San Diego State U (CA)
Southeastern Louisiana U (LA)
Southeast Missouri State U (MO)
Southern Arkansas U–Magnolia (AR)
Southwest Baptist U (MO)
Tabor Coll (KS)
Texas Christian U (TX)
Texas Lutheran U (TX)
Tiffin U (OH)
Towson U (MD)
U of Central Florida (FL)
U of Florida (FL)
U of Georgia (GA)
U of Lynchburg (VA)
U of Maine (ME)
U of Michigan (MI)
U of Minnesota, Duluth (MN)
U of Nebraska–Lincoln (NE)
U of Nevada, Las Vegas (NV)
U of New Hampshire (NH)
The U of North Carolina at Pembroke (NC)
U of North Dakota (ND)
U of Northern Colorado (CO)
U of Northern Iowa (IA)
U of North Florida (FL)
U of Pittsburgh at Bradford (PA)
The U of Tampa (FL)
The U of Texas at Austin (TX)
The U of Texas of the Permian Basin (TX)
U of the Incarnate Word (TX)
The U of Tulsa (OK)
U of Vermont (VT)
The U of West Alabama (AL)
U of Wisconsin–Eau Claire (WI)
U of Wisconsin–La Crosse (WI)
U of Wisconsin–Milwaukee (WI)
Valley City State U (ND)
Vanguard U of Southern California (CA)
Washington State U (WA)
Weber State U (UT)
West Chester U of Pennsylvania (PA)
Winthrop U (SC)
Wright State U–Lake Campus (OH)
Youngstown State U (OH)

ATMOSPHERIC SCIENCES AND METEOROLOGY
The Coll at Brockport, State U of New York (NY)
Cornell U (NY)
Embry-Riddle Aeronautical U–Daytona (FL)
Embry-Riddle Aeronautical U–Prescott (AZ)
George Mason U (VA)
Jackson State U (MS)
Millersville U of Pennsylvania (PA)
North Carolina State U (NC)
Northern Illinois U (IL)
The Ohio State U (OH)
Ohio U (OH)
Purdue U (IN)
Saint Louis U (MO)
San Jose State U (CA)
State U of New York Maritime Coll (NY)
U of California, Davis (CA)
U of Georgia (GA)
U of Louisville (KY)
U of Michigan (MI)
U of Missouri (MO)
U of Nebraska–Lincoln (NE)
U of Nevada, Reno (NV)
U of North Carolina at Asheville (NC)
U of North Dakota (ND)
U of Washington (WA)
Valparaiso U (IN)
Western Connecticut State U (CT)

ATMOSPHERIC SCIENCES AND METEOROLOGY RELATED
East Carolina U (NC)
Indiana U Bloomington (IN)
U of California, Los Angeles (CA)

ATOMIC/MOLECULAR PHYSICS
San Diego State U (CA)

AUDIOLOGY
California State U, Long Beach (CA)
Northwestern U (IL)
The Ohio State U (OH)
Queens Coll of the City U of New York (NY)
U of Montevallo (AL)

AUDIOLOGY AND SPEECH-LANGUAGE PATHOLOGY
Adelphi U (NY)
Auburn U (AL)
Auburn U at Montgomery (AL)
Boston U (MA)
Bowling Green State U (OH)
California State U, Long Beach (CA)
Calvin Coll (MI)
The Coll of Idaho (ID)
The Coll of Saint Rose (NY)
Delta State U (MS)
East Carolina U (NC)
Emerson Coll (MA)
Hardin-Simmons U (TX)
Hofstra U (NY)
Hunter Coll of the City U of New York (NY)
Idaho State U (ID)
Indiana State U (IN)
Indiana U Bloomington (IN)
Indiana U of Pennsylvania (PA)
Iona Coll (NY)
Ithaca Coll (NY)
Louisiana State U and A&M Coll (LA)
Marymount Manhattan Coll (NY)
Marywood U (PA)
Mercy Coll (NY)
Miami U (OH)
Miami U Hamilton (OH)
Middle Tennessee State U (TN)
Minnesota State U Moorhead (MN)
Murray State U (KY)
Nazareth Coll of Rochester (NY)
New York U (NY)
Northeastern State U (OK)
Northwestern U (IL)
Ohio U (OH)
Old Dominion U (VA)
Purdue U (IN)
Southeastern Louisiana U (LA)
Southern Illinois U Edwardsville (IL)
Southern U and Ag and Mech Coll (LA)
State U of New York at Fredonia (NY)
Temple U (PA)
Towson U (MD)
U at Buffalo, the State U of New York (NY)
U of Arkansas (AR)
U of Central Arkansas (AR)
U of Central Florida (FL)
U of Florida (FL)
U of Kentucky (KY)
U of Minnesota, Twin Cities Campus (MN)
U of New Mexico (NM)
The U of North Carolina at Greensboro (NC)
U of Northern Colorado (CO)
U of Pittsburgh (PA)
U of South Florida (FL)
The U of Tennessee (TN)
The U of Texas at El Paso (TX)
The U of Tulsa (OK)
U of Virginia (VA)
U of Wisconsin–Milwaukee (WI)
U of Wyoming (WY)
Utah State U (UT)
Washington State U (WA)
Washington State U–Spokane (WA)
West Chester U of Pennsylvania (PA)

AUDITING
Babson Coll (MA)
Bradley U (IL)
Davenport U, Grand Rapids (MI)
Inter American U of Puerto Rico, Bayamón Campus (PR)
State U of New York Coll of Technology at Delhi (NY)

AUTOBODY/COLLISION AND REPAIR TECHNOLOGY
Idaho State U (ID)

AUTOMATION ENGINEER TECHNOLOGY
Millersville U of Pennsylvania (PA)
State U of New York Coll of Technology at Delhi (NY)

AUTOMOBILE/AUTOMOTIVE MECHANICS TECHNOLOGY
Idaho State U (ID)
New England Inst of Technology (RI)

AUTOMOTIVE ENGINEERING TECHNOLOGY
Colorado State U–Pueblo (CO)
Indiana State U (IN)
Southern Illinois U Carbondale (IL)
Weber State U (UT)
Western Washington U (WA)

AVIATION/AIRWAY MANAGEMENT
Auburn U (AL)
Averett U (VA)
Baylor U (TX)
Bridgewater State U (MA)
California State U, Los Angeles (CA)
Central Washington U (WA)
Embry-Riddle Aeronautical U–Worldwide (FL)
Farmingdale State Coll (NY)
Indiana State U (IN)
Inter American U of Puerto Rico, Bayamón Campus (PR)
Jacksonville U (FL)
LeTourneau U (TX)
Liberty U (VA)
Marywood U (PA)
The Ohio State U (OH)
Ohio U (OH)
Rocky Mountain Coll (MT)
Southern Illinois U Carbondale (IL)
Texas A&M U–Central Texas (TX)
U of North Dakota (ND)
Vaughn Coll of Aeronautics and Technology (NY)
West Virginia U Inst of Technology (WV)

AVIONICS MAINTENANCE TECHNOLOGY
Southern Illinois U Carbondale (IL)
Vaughn Coll of Aeronautics and Technology (NY)

AYURVEDIC MEDICINE
Maharishi U of Management (IA)

BALLET
Indiana U Bloomington (IN)
Marymount Manhattan Coll (NY)
Texas Christian U (TX)

BANKING AND FINANCIAL SUPPORT SERVICES
Buena Vista U (IA)
Hardin-Simmons U (TX)
Northern State U (SD)
U of Nebraska–Lincoln (NE)
U of North Florida (FL)
U of the Incarnate Word (TX)
Youngstown State U (OH)

BEHAVIORAL ASPECTS OF HEALTH
Point U (GA)
Taylor U (IN)
U of Houston–Downtown (TX)
U of Massachusetts Dartmouth (MA)
The U of Texas at Austin (TX)
U of Vermont (VT)

BEHAVIORAL SCIENCES
Central Washington U (WA)
Columbia Southern U (AL)
Concordia U Irvine (CA)
Duquesne U (PA)
East Texas Baptist U (TX)
Gwynedd Mercy U (PA)
Inter American U of Puerto Rico, San Germán Campus (PR)
Johns Hopkins U (MD)
Missouri Baptist U (MO)
Purdue U Northwest (IN)
Rider U (NJ)
Rochester Coll (MI)
San Jose State U (CA)
Tabor Coll (KS)
Trevecca Nazarene U (TN)
U of Houston–Clear Lake (TX)
U of Maine at Machias (ME)
U of West Georgia (GA)
Widener U (PA)

BIBLICAL STUDIES
Bethel U (MN)
Calvin Coll (MI)
Campbellsville U (KY)
Canisius Coll (NY)
Carson-Newman U (TN)
Cedarville U (OH)
Coll of the Ozarks (MO)
Covenant Coll (GA)
Dallas Baptist U (TX)
Dallas Christian Coll (TX)
Eastern Mennonite U (VA)
Eastern U (PA)
Florida Coll (FL)
Geneva Coll (PA)
Goshen Coll (IN)
Harding U (AR)
Hardin-Simmons U (TX)
Johnson U Florida (FL)
Judson U (IL)
Kuyper Coll (MI)
Lancaster Bible Coll (PA)
Lee U (TN)
LeTourneau U (TX)
Liberty U (VA)
Lincoln Christian U (IL)
Lipscomb U (TN)
Louisiana Coll (LA)
Lubbock Christian U (TX)
Messiah Coll (PA)
Milligan Coll (TN)
Northwest Christian U (OR)
Oklahoma Baptist U (OK)
Oklahoma Christian U (OK)
Ouachita Baptist U (AR)
Palm Beach Atlantic U (FL)
Point U (GA)
Redeemer U Coll (ON, Canada)
Rochester Coll (MI)
Shiloh U (IA)
Southeastern U (FL)
Southwest Baptist U (MO)
Taylor U (IN)
Theological U of the Caribbean (PR)
Toccoa Falls Coll (GA)
Trinity Christian Coll (IL)
Tyndale U Coll & Sem (ON, Canada)
The U of Findlay (OH)

U of Minnesota, Twin Cities Campus (MN)
U of Northwestern–St. Paul (MN)
Vanguard U of Southern California (CA)
Waynesburg U (PA)
Wheaton Coll (IL)
Whitworth U (WA)

BILINGUAL AND MULTILINGUAL EDUCATION
Boston U (MA)
Calvin Coll (MI)
Canisius Coll (NY)
Loyola U Chicago (IL)
Queens Coll of the City U of New York (NY)
Texas A&M Intl U (TX)
Texas Christian U (TX)
The U of Findlay (OH)
U of Guam (GU)
U of Regina (SK, Canada)
U of Wisconsin–Milwaukee (WI)
Western Illinois U (IL)

BIOCHEMICAL ENGINEERING
Christian Brothers U (TN)
U of Georgia (GA)

BIOCHEMISTRY
Adams State U (CO)
Adelphi U (NY)
Agnes Scott Coll (GA)
Albion Coll (MI)
Albright Coll (PA)
Allegheny Coll (PA)
American U (DC)
Auburn U (AL)
Austin Coll (TX)
Baker U (KS)
Baylor U (TX)
Beloit Coll (WI)
Bethany Lutheran Coll (MN)
Boston Coll (MA)
Bowling Green State U (OH)
Bradley U (IL)
Brandeis U (MA)
Bridgewater Coll (VA)
Bridgewater State U (MA)
Bryant U (RI)
Bucknell U (PA)
Buena Vista U (IA)
Butler U (IN)
California Lutheran U (CA)
California Polytechnic State U, San Luis Obispo (CA)
California State U, Chico (CA)
California State U, Fullerton (CA)
California State U, Long Beach (CA)
California State U, Los Angeles (CA)
California State U, Northridge (CA)
California State U, San Marcos (CA)
Calvin Coll (MI)
Canisius Coll (NY)
Carson-Newman U (TN)
The Catholic U of America (DC)
Centenary Coll of Louisiana (LA)
Central Connecticut State U (CT)
Central Michigan U (MI)
Central Washington U (WA)
Christian Brothers U (TN)
Christopher Newport U (VA)
Claremont McKenna Coll (CA)
Coastal Carolina U (SC)
Colgate U (NY)
The Coll at Brockport, State U of New York (NY)
Coll of Saint Benedict (MN)
The Coll of Saint Rose (NY)
The Coll of St. Scholastica (MN)
Coll of Staten Island of the City U of New York (NY)
The Colorado Coll (CO)
Colorado State U (CO)
Columbia U (NY)
Connecticut Coll (CT)
Cornell Coll (IA)
Curry Coll (MA)
Dartmouth Coll (NH)
DePaul U (IL)
Dominican U (IL)
Drake U (IA)
Drew U (NJ)
Drury U (MO)
Duquesne U (PA)
Earlham Coll (IN)
East Carolina U (NC)
Eastern Mennonite U (VA)
Eastern U (PA)
East Stroudsburg U of Pennsylvania (PA)
Eckerd Coll (FL)
Emmanuel Coll (MA)
Fairfield U (CT)
Fort Lewis Coll (CO)
Framingham State U (MA)
Geneva Coll (PA)
Georgetown Coll (KY)
Gonzaga U (WA)
Gordon Coll (MA)
Grand Valley State U (MI)
Grove City Coll (PA)
Hamilton Coll (NY)
Hamline U (MN)
Hanover Coll (IN)
Harding U (AR)
Hartwick Coll (NY)
Harvard U (MA)
Haverford Coll (PA)
High Point U (NC)
Hillsdale Coll (MI)
Hiram Coll (OH)
Hofstra U (NY)
Hood Coll (MD)
Humboldt State U (CA)
Idaho State U (ID)
Indiana U Bloomington (IN)
Indiana U East (IN)
Indiana U Kokomo (IN)
Indiana U Northwest (IN)
Indiana U of Pennsylvania (PA)
Indiana U South Bend (IN)
Iona Coll (NY)
Iowa State U of Science and Technology (IA)
Ithaca Coll (NY)
Judson U (IL)
Juniata Coll (PA)
Kennesaw State U (GA)
King U (TN)
Knox Coll (IL)
Lafayette Coll (PA)
LaGrange Coll (GA)
Lamar U (TX)
La Salle U (PA)
La Sierra U (CA)
Lawrence Technological U (MI)
Lawrence U (WI)
Lee U (TN)
Lewis & Clark Coll (OR)
Liberty U (VA)
Lipscomb U (TN)
Loras Coll (IA)
Louisiana State U and A&M Coll (LA)
Loyola Marymount U (CA)
Loyola U Chicago (IL)
Loyola U New Orleans (LA)
Lubbock Christian U (TX)
Lycoming Coll (PA)
Madonna U (MI)
Manchester U (IN)
Manhattan Coll (NY)
Manhattanville Coll (NY)
Mansfield U of Pennsylvania (PA)
Marist Coll (NY)
Marymount U (VA)
Maryville U of Saint Louis (MO)
Mercer U, Macon (GA)
Merrimack Coll (MA)
Messiah Coll (PA)
Miami U (OH)
Miami U Hamilton (OH)
Michigan State U (MI)
Middlebury Coll (VT)
Millsaps Coll (MS)
Mills Coll (CA)
Missouri Baptist U (MO)
Montclair State U (NJ)
Mount St. Joseph U (OH)
Nazareth Coll of Rochester (NY)
New Jersey Inst of Technology (NJ)
New York U (NY)
North Carolina State U (NC)
Northwestern U (IL)
Occidental Coll (CA)
The Ohio State U (OH)
Oklahoma Baptist U (OK)
Oklahoma Christian U (OK)
Oklahoma State U (OK)
Old Dominion U (VA)
Pace U (NY)
Pace U, Pleasantville Campus (NY)
Pitzer Coll (CA)
Point Loma Nazarene U (CA)
Portland State U (OR)
Providence Coll (RI)
Purchase Coll, State U of New York (NY)
Purdue U (IN)
Queens U of Charlotte (NC)
Redeemer U Coll (ON, Canada)
Regis U (CO)
Rhode Island Coll (RI)
Rice U (TX)
Rider U (NJ)
Roanoke Coll (VA)
Rochester Inst of Technology (NY)
Rockford U (IL)
Rollins Coll (FL)
Sacred Heart U (CT)
The Sage Colls (NY)
Saginaw Valley State U (MI)
Saint Anselm Coll (NH)
Saint Francis U (PA)
Saint John's U (MN)
Saint Joseph's U (PA)
Saint Louis U (MO)
St. Mary's Coll of Maryland (MD)
St. Mary's U (TX)
Saint Mary's U of Minnesota (MN)
Saint Vincent Coll (PA)
Samford U (AL)
San Francisco State U (CA)
San Jose State U (CA)
Scripps Coll (CA)
Seattle U (WA)
Seton Hill U (PA)
Southwestern U (TX)
Spring Hill Coll (AL)
State U of New York at Fredonia (NY)
State U of New York at Plattsburgh (NY)
State U of New York Coll at Geneseo (NY)
State U of New York Coll at Potsdam (NY)
State U of New York Coll of Environmental Science and Forestry (NY)
Stetson U (FL)
Stevens Inst of Technology (NJ)
Stockton U (NJ)
Stonehill Coll (MA)
Syracuse U (NY)
Tabor Coll (KS)
Taylor U (IN)
Temple U (PA)
Texas Christian U (TX)
Texas Tech U (TX)
Texas Woman's U (TX)
Trinity Christian Coll (IL)
Tulane U (LA)
Union Coll (NY)
Université de Sherbrooke (QC, Canada)
U at Buffalo, the State U of New York (NY)
U of California, Los Angeles (CA)
U of California, Riverside (CA)
U of Dallas (TX)
U of Dayton (OH)
U of Detroit Mercy (MI)
U of Hawaii at Manoa (HI)
U of Houston (TX)
U of Idaho (ID)
U of Illinois at Springfield (IL)
U of Maine (ME)
U of Mary Hardin-Baylor (TX)
U of Maryland, Coll Park (MD)
U of Maryland Eastern Shore (MD)
U of Massachusetts Boston (MA)
U of Michigan (MI)
U of Michigan–Dearborn (MI)
U of Minnesota, Duluth (MN)
U of Minnesota, Twin Cities Campus (MN)
U of Missouri (MO)
U of Mount Union (OH)
U of Nebraska–Lincoln (NE)
U of Nevada, Las Vegas (NV)
U of Nevada, Reno (NV)
U of New Mexico (NM)
The U of North Carolina at Greensboro (NC)
U of Northern Iowa (IA)
U of Northwestern–St. Paul (MN)
U of Notre Dame (IN)
U of Oregon (OR)
U of Pennsylvania (PA)
U of Puget Sound (WA)
U of Regina (SK, Canada)
U of St. Thomas (MN)
U of St. Thomas (TX)
U of San Diego (CA)
U of Southern Indiana (IN)
The U of Tampa (FL)
The U of Texas at Austin (TX)
U of the Incarnate Word (TX)
The U of the South (TN)
The U of Toledo (OH)
The U of Tulsa (OK)
U of Vermont (VT)
U of Washington (WA)
U of Washington, Bothell (WA)
U of Wisconsin–La Crosse (WI)
U of Wisconsin–Milwaukee (WI)
Ursinus Coll (PA)
Valparaiso U (IN)
Vanguard U of Southern California (CA)
Vassar Coll (NY)
Virginia Polytechnic Inst and State U (VA)
Wabash Coll (IN)
Wartburg Coll (IA)
Washington & Jefferson Coll (PA)
Washington and Lee U (VA)
Washington State U (WA)
Washington U in St. Louis (MO)
Weber State U (UT)
West Chester U of Pennsylvania (PA)
Western Kentucky U (KY)
Western Washington U (WA)
Wheaton Coll (MA)
Whittier Coll (CA)
Whitworth U (WA)
Widener U (PA)
Wilkes U (PA)
William Jewell Coll (MO)
Worcester Polytechnic Inst (MA)
Wright State U–Lake Campus (OH)
Youngstown State U (OH)

BIOCHEMISTRY AND MOLECULAR BIOLOGY
Bellarmine U (KY)
Benedictine U (IL)
Boston U (MA)
California State U, Long Beach (CA)
Coll of the Ozarks (MO)
Connecticut Coll (CT)
Dickinson Coll (PA)
The Evergreen State Coll (WA)
Florida Southern Coll (FL)
Hampden-Sydney Coll (VA)
Harding U (AR)
Hardin-Simmons U (TX)
Lake Forest Coll (IL)
Lebanon Valley Coll (PA)
Linfield Coll (OR)
Marquette U (WI)
Michigan State U (MI)
Middlebury Coll (VT)
Minnesota State U Moorhead (MN)
Purdue U (IN)
Rhodes Coll (TN)
Salve Regina U (RI)
U of California, Irvine (CA)
U of Georgia (GA)
U of Maryland, Baltimore County (MD)
U of Massachusetts Amherst (MA)
U of Minnesota, Duluth (MN)
U of New Hampshire (NH)
U of Regina (SK, Canada)

BIOCHEMISTRY, BIOPHYSICS AND MOLECULAR BIOLOGY RELATED
Blackburn Coll (IL)
Indiana U Kokomo (IN)
St. Mary's U (TX)
Towson U (MD)

BIOENGINEERING AND BIOMEDICAL ENGINEERING
Alabama State U (AL)
Alfred U (NY)
Boston U (MA)
Bucknell U (PA)
California Inst of Technology (CA)
California Polytechnic State U, San Luis Obispo (CA)
California State U, Long Beach (CA)
The Catholic U of America (DC)
Central Michigan U (MI)
Colorado School of Mines (CO)
Colorado State U (CO)
Columbia U (NY)
Dartmouth Coll (NH)
Duquesne U (PA)
Endicott Coll (MA)
Fairfield U (CT)
Florida Ag and Mech U (FL)
George Mason U (VA)
Harding U (AR)
Harvard U (MA)
Hofstra U (NY)
Indiana U–Purdue U Indianapolis (IN)
Johns Hopkins U (MD)
Lawrence Technological U (MI)
LeTourneau U (TX)
Louisiana State U and A&M Coll (LA)
Loyola U Chicago (IL)
Marquette U (WI)
Marshall U (WV)
Massachusetts Inst of Technology (MA)
Messiah Coll (PA)
Miami U (OH)
New Jersey Inst of Technology (NJ)
New York U (NY)
North Carolina State U (NC)
Northwestern U (IL)
The Ohio State U (OH)
Purdue U (IN)
Rice U (TX)
Rochester Inst of Technology (NY)
Saint Louis U (MO)
State U of New York Coll of Environmental Science and Forestry (NY)
Stevens Inst of Technology (NJ)
Syracuse U (NY)
Temple U (PA)
Tulane U (LA)
Union Coll (NY)
U at Buffalo, the State U of New York (NY)
U of Arkansas (AR)
U of California, Davis (CA)
U of California, Irvine (CA)
U of California, Merced (CA)
U of California, Riverside (CA)
U of California, Santa Cruz (CA)
U of Colorado Denver (CO)
U of Florida (FL)
U of Houston (TX)
U of Louisville (KY)
U of Maine (ME)
U of Massachusetts Amherst (MA)
U of Massachusetts Dartmouth (MA)
U of Massachusetts Lowell (MA)
U of Memphis (TN)
U of Michigan (MI)
U of Michigan–Dearborn (MI)
U of Minnesota, Twin Cities Campus (MN)
U of Mount Union (OH)
U of Nevada, Reno (NV)
U of New Hampshire (NH)
The U of North Carolina at Chapel Hill (NC)
U of Pennsylvania (PA)
U of Pittsburgh (PA)
U of South Carolina (SC)
U of South Dakota (SD)
The U of Tennessee (TN)
The U of Texas at Austin (TX)
The U of Toledo (OH)
U of Vermont (VT)
U of Virginia (VA)
U of Washington (WA)
Valparaiso U (IN)
Virginia Commonwealth U (VA)
Washington State U (WA)
Washington U in St. Louis (MO)
West Chester U of Pennsylvania (PA)
Widener U (PA)
Worcester Polytechnic Inst (MA)
Wright State U–Lake Campus (OH)

BIOETHICS/MEDICAL ETHICS
U of Richmond (VA)

MAJORS LISTING

BIOINFORMATICS
Baylor U (TX)
California State U, San Bernardino (CA)
Davenport U, Grand Rapids (MI)
Inter American U of Puerto Rico, Bayamón Campus (PR)
Iowa State U of Science and Technology (IA)
Lebanese American U (Lebanon)
Loyola U Chicago (IL)
Marquette U (WI)
New Jersey Inst of Technology (NJ)
Portland State U (OR)
Rochester Inst of Technology (NY)
Saint Vincent Coll (PA)
Trinity Christian Coll (IL)
U at Buffalo, the State U of New York (NY)
U of California, Santa Cruz (CA)
U of Maryland, Baltimore County (MD)
U of Memphis (TN)
U of Pennsylvania (PA)
U of Pittsburgh (PA)
U of St. Thomas (TX)
Virginia Commonwealth U (VA)
Wheaton Coll (MA)
Whitworth U (WA)
Worcester State U (MA)

BIOLOGICAL AND BIOMEDICAL SCIENCES RELATED
Baptist Coll of Health Sciences (TN)
Bethel U (MN)
Boston U (MA)
Central Michigan U (MI)
Central Washington U (WA)
Christopher Newport U (VA)
Cornell U (NY)
Dakota State U (SD)
Grand Valley State U (MI)
Indiana U Bloomington (IN)
Indiana U East (IN)
Rochester Inst of Technology (NY)
The Sage Colls (NY)
San Jose State U (CA)
State U of New York Coll of Environmental Science and Forestry (NY)
Trevecca Nazarene U (TN)
Union Coll (NY)
U of Maryland U Coll (MD)
U of Michigan (MI)
U of New Hampshire (NH)
U of North Dakota (ND)
U of Puerto Rico–Bayamón (PR)
Utah State U (UT)
Washington U in St. Louis (MO)

BIOLOGICAL AND PHYSICAL SCIENCES
Adelphi U (NY)
Alfred U (NY)
Averett U (VA)
Baker U (KS)
Baldwin Wallace U (OH)
Calumet Coll of Saint Joseph (IN)
Calvin Coll (MI)
Clarion U of Pennsylvania (PA)
Concordia U Chicago (IL)
Covenant Coll (GA)
Delta State U (MS)
Dominican U (IL)
East Stroudsburg U of Pennsylvania (PA)
The Evergreen State Coll (WA)
Fordham U (NY)
Indiana U Kokomo (IN)
Indiana U of Pennsylvania (PA)
Indiana U–Purdue U Indianapolis (IN)
Johns Hopkins U (MD)
King's Coll (PA)
Lawrence U (WI)
Mansfield U of Pennsylvania (PA)
Maryville U of Saint Louis (MO)
Michigan State U (MI)
Middle Tennessee State U (TN)
Northwestern U (IL)
Northwest Missouri State U (MO)
Portland State U (OR)
Purdue U (IN)
Rockford U (IL)
Saint Anselm Coll (NH)
St. Norbert Coll (WI)
San Francisco State U (CA)
Southern Arkansas U–Magnolia (AR)
State U of New York at Fredonia (NY)
Texas Tech U (TX)
Union Coll (NY)
U of Georgia (GA)
U of Houston–Downtown (TX)
U of Massachusetts Amherst (MA)
U of Northern Iowa (IA)
U of Notre Dame (IN)
U of Oregon (OR)
U of Pittsburgh (PA)
U of Puget Sound (WA)
U of Regina (SK, Canada)
U of Southern Indiana (IN)
U of South Florida (FL)
The U of West Alabama (AL)
U of Wisconsin–Superior (WI)
Vanguard U of Southern California (CA)
Virginia Commonwealth U (VA)
Washington State U (WA)
Washington State U–Tri-Cities (WA)
Washington U in St. Louis (MO)
Wesleyan U (CT)
Western Washington U (WA)

BIOLOGICAL/BIOSYSTEMS ENGINEERING
Auburn U (AL)
U of Arkansas (AR)
U of Florida (FL)
U of Georgia (GA)
U of Idaho (ID)
U of Nebraska–Lincoln (NE)

BIOLOGY/BIOLOGICAL SCIENCES
Acadia U (NS, Canada)
Adams State U (CO)
Adelphi U (NY)
Agnes Scott Coll (GA)
Alabama State U (AL)
Albion Coll (MI)
Albright Coll (PA)
Alfred U (NY)
Allegheny Coll (PA)
Alverno Coll (WI)
American U (DC)
Angelo State U (TX)
Appalachian State U (NC)
Arkansas Tech U (AR)
Assumption Coll (MA)
Auburn U (AL)
Auburn U at Montgomery (AL)
Aurora U (IL)
Austin Coll (TX)
Austin Peay State U (TN)
Averett U (VA)
Avila U (MO)
Baker U (KS)
Baldwin Wallace U (OH)
Barton Coll (NC)
Baylor U (TX)
Bellarmine U (KY)
Beloit Coll (WI)
Benedictine U (IL)
Bennett Coll (NC)
Berea Coll (KY)
Bethany Lutheran Coll (MN)
Bethel Coll (KS)
Bethel U (MN)
Blackburn Coll (IL)
Boston Coll (MA)
Boston U (MA)
Bowling Green State U (OH)
Bradley U (IL)
Brandeis U (MA)
Brenau U (GA)
Bridgewater Coll (VA)
Bridgewater State U (MA)
Bryant U (RI)
Bryn Athyn Coll of the New Church (PA)
Bucknell U (PA)
Buena Vista U (IA)
Butler U (IN)
Caldwell U (NJ)
California Inst of Technology (CA)
California Lutheran U (CA)
California Polytechnic State U, San Luis Obispo (CA)
California State U, Bakersfield (CA)
California State U, Chico (CA)
California State U, Fullerton (CA)
California State U, Long Beach (CA)
California State U, Los Angeles (CA)
California State U, Monterey Bay (CA)
California State U, Northridge (CA)
California State U, San Bernardino (CA)
California State U, San Marcos (CA)
California U of Pennsylvania (PA)
Calvin Coll (MI)
Cameron U (OK)
Campbellsville U (KY)
Canisius Coll (NY)
Carnegie Mellon U (PA)
Carson-Newman U (TN)
Carthage Coll (WI)
The Catholic U of America (DC)
Cedarville U (OH)
Centenary Coll of Louisiana (LA)
Central Connecticut State U (CT)
Central Michigan U (MI)
Central State U (OH)
Central Washington U (WA)
Christian Brothers U (TN)
Christopher Newport U (VA)
Claremont McKenna Coll (CA)
Clarion U of Pennsylvania (PA)
Clarkson U (NY)
Clark U (MA)
Coastal Carolina U (SC)
Colgate U (NY)
The Coll at Brockport, State U of New York (NY)
Coll of Charleston (SC)
Coll of Coastal Georgia (GA)
The Coll of Idaho (ID)
Coll of Saint Benedict (MN)
Coll of Saint Mary (NE)
The Coll of Saint Rose (NY)
The Coll of St. Scholastica (MN)
Coll of Staten Island of the City U of New York (NY)
Coll of the Holy Cross (MA)
The Coll of William and Mary (VA)
Colorado State U (CO)
Colorado State U–Pueblo (CO)
Columbia Coll (MO)
Columbia U (NY)
Concordia U Chicago (IL)
Concordia U Irvine (CA)
Connecticut Coll (CT)
Cornell Coll (IA)
Cornell U (NY)
Covenant Coll (GA)
Creighton U (NE)
Culver-Stockton Coll (MO)
Curry Coll (MA)
Dallas Baptist U (TX)
Dartmouth Coll (NH)
Davidson Coll (NC)
Dean Coll (MA)
Delaware Valley U (PA)
Delta State U (MS)
DePaul U (IL)
Dickinson Coll (PA)
Dominican U (IL)
Drake U (IA)
Drew U (NJ)
Drury U (MO)
Duquesne U (PA)
Earlham Coll (IN)
East Carolina U (NC)
Eastern Illinois U (IL)
Eastern Mennonite U (VA)
Eastern Oregon U (OR)
Eastern U (PA)
Eastern Washington U (WA)
East Stroudsburg U of Pennsylvania (PA)
East Tennessee State U (TN)
East Texas Baptist U (TX)
Eckerd Coll (FL)
Elizabeth City State U (NC)
Emmanuel Coll (GA)
Emmanuel Coll (MA)
The Evergreen State Coll (WA)
Excelsior Coll (NY)
Fairfield U (CT)
Farmingdale State Coll (NY)
Fayetteville State U (NC)
Fitchburg State U (MA)
Florida Ag and Mech U (FL)
Florida Atlantic U (FL)
Florida Southern Coll (FL)
Fordham U (NY)
Framingham State U (MA)
Franklin Pierce U (NH)
Furman U (SC)
Geneva Coll (PA)
George Mason U (VA)
Georgetown Coll (KY)
Georgia Coll & State U (GA)
Georgia Southern U (GA)
Georgia State U (GA)
Gonzaga U (WA)
Gordon Coll (MA)
Goshen Coll (IN)
Graceland U (IA)
Grand Valley State U (MI)
Greenville U (IL)
Grove City Coll (PA)
Gwynedd Mercy U (PA)
Hamilton Coll (NY)
Hamline U (MN)
Hampden-Sydney Coll (VA)
Hanover Coll (IN)
Harding U (AR)
Hardin-Simmons U (TX)
Hartwick Coll (NY)
Harvard U (MA)
Haverford Coll (PA)
High Point U (NC)
Hillsdale Coll (MI)
Hiram Coll (OH)
Hofstra U (NY)
Hollins U (VA)
Hood Coll (MD)
Humboldt State U (CA)
Hunter Coll of the City U of New York (NY)
Idaho State U (ID)
Illinois Coll (IL)
Immaculata U (PA)
Indiana State U (IN)
Indiana U Bloomington (IN)
Indiana U East (IN)
Indiana U Kokomo (IN)
Indiana U Northwest (IN)
Indiana U of Pennsylvania (PA)
Indiana U–Purdue U Indianapolis (IN)
Indiana U South Bend (IN)
Indiana U Southeast (IN)
Inter American U of Puerto Rico, Aguadilla Campus (PR)
Inter American U of Puerto Rico, Barranquitas Campus (PR)
Inter American U of Puerto Rico, Bayamón Campus (PR)
Inter American U of Puerto Rico, Fajardo Campus (PR)
Inter American U of Puerto Rico, San Germán Campus (PR)
Iona Coll (NY)
Iowa State U of Science and Technology (IA)
Ithaca Coll (NY)
Jackson State U (MS)
Jacksonville U (FL)
Johns Hopkins U (MD)
Johnson C. Smith U (NC)
Judson U (IL)
Juniata Coll (PA)
Kalamazoo Coll (MI)
Kansas Wesleyan U (KS)
Kean U (NJ)
Kennesaw State U (GA)
King's Coll (PA)
King U (TN)
Knox Coll (IL)
Lafayette Coll (PA)
LaGrange Coll (GA)
Lake Forest Coll (IL)
Lamar U (TX)
La Salle U (PA)
Lasell Coll (MA)
La Sierra U (CA)
Lawrence U (WI)
Lebanese American U (Lebanon)
Lebanon Valley Coll (PA)
Lees-McRae Coll (NC)
Lee U (TN)
LeTourneau U (TX)
Lewis & Clark Coll (OR)
Liberty U (VA)
Life U (GA)
Limestone Coll (SC)
Lindenwood U (MO)
Linfield Coll (OR)
Lipscomb U (TN)
Lock Haven U of Pennsylvania (PA)
Loras Coll (IA)
Louisiana Coll (LA)
Louisiana State U and A&M Coll (LA)
Loyola Marymount U (CA)
Loyola U Chicago (IL)
Loyola U New Orleans (LA)
Lubbock Christian U (TX)
Lycoming Coll (PA)
Macalester Coll (MN)
Madonna U (MI)
Manchester U (IN)
Manhattan Coll (NY)
Manhattanville Coll (NY)
Mansfield U of Pennsylvania (PA)
Marian U (IN)
Marist Coll (NY)
Marquette U (WI)
Marshall U (WV)
Marymount California U (CA)
Marymount Manhattan Coll (NY)
Marymount U (VA)
Maryville U of Saint Louis (MO)
Marywood U (PA)
Massachusetts Coll of Liberal Arts (MA)
Massachusetts Inst of Technology (MA)
McDaniel Coll (MD)
McNeese State U (LA)
Mercer U, Macon (GA)
Mercy Coll (NY)
Mercy Coll of Ohio (OH)
Merrimack Coll (MA)
Messiah Coll (PA)
Miami U (OH)
Michigan State U (MI)
Middlebury Coll (VT)
Middle Tennessee State U (TN)
Millersville U of Pennsylvania (PA)
Milligan Coll (TN)
Millikin U (IL)
Millsaps Coll (MS)
Mills Coll (CA)
Minnesota State U Moorhead (MN)
Missouri Baptist U (MO)
Molloy Coll (NY)
Montclair State U (NJ)
Morningside Coll (IA)
Mount Marty Coll (SD)
Mount St. Joseph U (OH)
Mount Saint Mary Coll (NY)
Murray State U (KY)
National U (CA)
Nazareth Coll of Rochester (NY)
New Coll of Florida (FL)
New England Coll (NH)
New Jersey City U (NJ)
New Jersey Inst of Technology (NJ)
New York U (NY)
North Carolina State U (NC)
Northeastern State U (OK)
Northern Illinois U (IL)
Northern Kentucky U (KY)
Northern State U (SD)
Northwest Christian U (OR)
Northwestern Oklahoma State U (OK)
Northwestern U (IL)
Northwest Missouri State U (MO)
Oakland City U (IN)
Occidental Coll (CA)
Oglethorpe U (GA)
Ohio Dominican U (OH)
The Ohio State U (OH)
The Ohio State U at Lima (OH)
The Ohio State U at Marion (OH)
Ohio U (OH)
Ohio Wesleyan U (OH)
Oklahoma Baptist U (OK)
Oklahoma Christian U (OK)
Oklahoma State U (OK)
Old Dominion U (VA)
Ottawa U (KS)
Ouachita Baptist U (AR)
Pace U (NY)
Pace U, Pleasantville Campus (NY)
Pacific Lutheran U (WA)
Palm Beach Atlantic U (FL)
Pepperdine U, Malibu (CA)
Pfeiffer U (NC)
Piedmont Coll (GA)
Pitzer Coll (CA)
Point Loma Nazarene U (CA)
Point U (GA)
Portland State U (OR)
Prairie View A&M U (TX)

Providence Coll (RI)
Purchase Coll, State U of New York (NY)
Purdue U (IN)
Purdue U Northwest (IN)
Queens Coll of the City U of New York (NY)
Queens U of Charlotte (NC)
Radford U (VA)
Randolph Coll (VA)
Randolph-Macon Coll (VA)
Redeemer U Coll (ON, Canada)
Regis U (CO)
Reinhardt U (GA)
Rhode Island Coll (RI)
Rhodes Coll (TN)
Rice U (TX)
Rider U (NJ)
Roanoke Coll (VA)
Rochester Coll (MI)
Rochester Inst of Technology (NY)
Rockford U (IL)
Rocky Mountain Coll (MT)
Rollins Coll (FL)
Sacred Heart U (CT)
The Sage Colls (NY)
Saginaw Valley State U (MI)
Saint Anselm Coll (NH)
Saint Francis U (PA)
St. John Fisher Coll (NY)
Saint John's U (MN)
St. Joseph's Coll, Long Island Campus (NY)
St. Joseph's Coll, New York (NY)
Saint Joseph's U (PA)
Saint Leo U (FL)
Saint Louis U (MO)
Saint Martin's U (WA)
St. Mary's Coll of Maryland (MD)
St. Mary's U (TX)
Saint Mary's U of Minnesota (MN)
St. Norbert Coll (WI)
St. Olaf Coll (MN)
Saint Vincent Coll (PA)
Salisbury U (MD)
Salve Regina U (RI)
Samford U (AL)
San Diego State U (CA)
San Francisco State U (CA)
San Jose State U (CA)
Sarah Lawrence Coll (NY)
Scripps Coll (CA)
Seattle U (WA)
Seton Hill U (PA)
Skidmore Coll (NY)
Sonoma State U (CA)
Southeastern Louisiana U (LA)
Southeastern U (FL)
Southeast Missouri State U (MO)
Southern Arkansas U–Magnolia (AR)
Southern Illinois U Carbondale (IL)
Southern Illinois U Edwardsville (IL)
Southern U and Ag and Mech Coll (LA)
Southwest Baptist U (MO)
Southwestern U (TX)
Spring Hill Coll (AL)
State U of New York at Fredonia (NY)
State U of New York at Plattsburgh (NY)
State U of New York Coll at Geneseo (NY)
State U of New York Coll at Potsdam (NY)
Stetson U (FL)
Stevens Inst of Technology (NJ)
Stockton U (NJ)
Stonehill Coll (MA)
Sweet Briar Coll (VA)
Syracuse U (NY)
Tabor Coll (KS)
Taylor U (IN)
Temple U (PA)
Texas A&M Intl U (TX)
Texas A&M U–Central Texas (TX)
Texas Christian U (TX)
Texas Lutheran U (TX)
Texas Tech U (TX)
Texas Woman's U (TX)
Toccoa Falls Coll (GA)
Towson U (MD)
Trevecca Nazarene U (TN)
Trinity Christian Coll (IL)
Truman State U (MO)
Tulane U (LA)
Union Coll (KY)
Union Coll (NY)
Université de Sherbrooke (QC, Canada)
U at Buffalo, the State U of New York (NY)
U of Arkansas (AR)
U of California, Davis (CA)
U of California, Irvine (CA)
U of California, Los Angeles (CA)
U of California, Merced (CA)
U of California, Riverside (CA)
U of California, Santa Cruz (CA)
U of Central Arkansas (AR)
U of Central Florida (FL)
U of Chicago (IL)
U of Colorado Denver (CO)
U of Dallas (TX)
U of Dayton (OH)
U of Detroit Mercy (MI)
The U of Findlay (OH)
U of Florida (FL)
U of Georgia (GA)
U of Guam (GU)
U of Hawaii at Manoa (HI)
U of Houston (TX)
U of Houston–Clear Lake (TX)
U of Houston–Downtown (TX)
U of Idaho (ID)
U of Illinois at Springfield (IL)
U of Kentucky (KY)
U of La Verne (CA)
U of Louisville (KY)
U of Lynchburg (VA)
U of Maine (ME)
U of Maine at Farmington (ME)
U of Maine at Machias (ME)
U of Maine at Presque Isle (ME)
U of Mary Hardin-Baylor (TX)
U of Maryland, Baltimore County (MD)
U of Maryland, Coll Park (MD)
U of Maryland Eastern Shore (MD)
U of Massachusetts Amherst (MA)
U of Massachusetts Boston (MA)
U of Massachusetts Dartmouth (MA)
U of Massachusetts Lowell (MA)
U of Memphis (TN)
U of Michigan (MI)
U of Michigan–Dearborn (MI)
U of Minnesota, Duluth (MN)
U of Minnesota, Morris (MN)
U of Minnesota, Twin Cities Campus (MN)
U of Missouri (MO)
U of Montevallo (AL)
U of Mount Union (OH)
U of Nebraska–Lincoln (NE)
U of Nevada, Las Vegas (NV)
U of Nevada, Reno (NV)
U of New Hampshire (NH)
U of New Haven (CT)
U of New Mexico (NM)
U of North Carolina at Asheville (NC)
The U of North Carolina at Chapel Hill (NC)
The U of North Carolina at Charlotte (NC)
The U of North Carolina at Greensboro (NC)
The U of North Carolina at Pembroke (NC)
U of North Dakota (ND)
U of Northern Colorado (CO)
U of Northern Iowa (IA)
U of North Florida (FL)
U of Northwestern–St. Paul (MN)
U of Notre Dame (IN)
U of Oregon (OR)
U of Pennsylvania (PA)
U of Pittsburgh (PA)
U of Pittsburgh at Bradford (PA)
U of Providence (MT)
U of Puerto Rico–Bayamón (PR)
U of Puget Sound (WA)
U of Regina (SK, Canada)
U of Richmond (VA)
U of Saint Francis (IN)
U of Saint Mary (KS)
U of St. Thomas (MN)
U of St. Thomas (TX)
U of San Diego (CA)
U of San Francisco (CA)
U of Sioux Falls (SD)
U of South Alabama (AL)
U of South Carolina (SC)
U of South Carolina Aiken (SC)
U of South Dakota (SD)
U of Southern Indiana (IN)
U of South Florida (FL)
U of South Florida Sarasota-Manatee (FL)
The U of Tampa (FL)
The U of Tennessee (TN)
The U of Tennessee at Martin (TN)
The U of Texas at Austin (TX)
The U of Texas at El Paso (TX)
The U of Texas of the Permian Basin (TX)
The U of Texas Rio Grande Valley (TX)
U of the Incarnate Word (TX)
The U of the South (TN)
The U of Toledo (OH)
The U of Tulsa (OK)
U of Vermont (VT)
U of Virginia (VA)
U of Washington (WA)
U of Washington, Bothell (WA)
The U of West Alabama (AL)
U of West Georgia (GA)
U of Wisconsin–Eau Claire (WI)
U of Wisconsin–La Crosse (WI)
U of Wisconsin–Milwaukee (WI)
U of Wisconsin–River Falls (WI)
U of Wisconsin–Superior (WI)
U of Wyoming (WY)
Ursinus Coll (PA)
Utah State U (UT)
Utah Valley U (UT)
Utica Coll (NY)
Valley City State U (ND)
Valparaiso U (IN)
Vanguard U of Southern California (CA)
Vassar Coll (NY)
Virginia Commonwealth U (VA)
Virginia Polytechnic Inst and State U (VA)
Wabash Coll (IN)
Wartburg Coll (IA)
Washington & Jefferson Coll (PA)
Washington and Lee U (VA)
Washington State U (WA)
Washington State U–Tri-Cities (WA)
Washington State U–Vancouver (WA)
Washington U in St. Louis (MO)
Waynesburg U (PA)
Wesleyan Coll (GA)
Wesleyan U (CT)
West Chester U of Pennsylvania (PA)
Western Connecticut State U (CT)
Western Illinois U (IL)
Western Kentucky U (KY)
Western State Colorado U (CO)
Western Washington U (WA)
Westmont Coll (CA)
West Virginia State U (WV)
West Virginia U Inst of Technology (WV)
Wheaton Coll (IL)
Wheaton Coll (MA)
Whittier Coll (CA)
Whitworth U (WA)
Widener U (PA)
Wilkes U (PA)
Willamette U (OR)
William Jewell Coll (MO)
Williams Coll (MA)
Winthrop U (SC)
Wofford Coll (SC)
Worcester Polytechnic Inst (MA)
Worcester State U (MA)
Youngstown State U (OH)

BIOLOGY/BIOTECHNOLOGY LABORATORY TECHNICIAN
Davenport U, Grand Rapids (MI)
State U of New York at Fredonia (NY)

BIOLOGY TEACHER EDUCATION
Adams State U (CO)
Albion Coll (MI)
Arkansas Tech U (AR)
Baylor U (TX)
Bowling Green State U (OH)
Bradley U (IL)
Bridgewater State U (MA)
Buena Vista U (IA)
California State U, Long Beach (CA)
Calvin Coll (MI)
Campbellsville U (KY)
Canisius Coll (NY)
Cedarville U (OH)
Central Michigan U (MI)
Central State U (OH)
Central Washington U (WA)
Coll of Saint Mary (NE)
The Coll of Saint Rose (NY)
Coll of Staten Island of the City U of New York (NY)
Coll of the Ozarks (MO)
Concordia U Chicago (IL)
Culver-Stockton Coll (MO)
Dakota State U (SD)
Daytona State Coll (FL)
Eastern Washington U (WA)
East Texas Baptist U (TX)
Fitchburg State U (MA)
Florida Southern Coll (FL)
Fort Lewis Coll (CO)
Goshen Coll (IN)
Grand Valley State U (MI)
Greenville U (IL)
Grove City Coll (PA)
Gwynedd Mercy U (PA)
Harding U (AR)
Hofstra U (NY)
Hunter Coll of the City U of New York (NY)
Immaculata U (PA)
Indiana U Bloomington (IN)
Indiana U Northwest (IN)
Indiana U South Bend (IN)
Indiana U Southeast (IN)
Inter American U of Puerto Rico, Aguadilla Campus (PR)
Inter American U of Puerto Rico, Barranquitas Campus (PR)
Inter American U of Puerto Rico, San Germán Campus (PR)
Iona Coll (NY)
Ithaca Coll (NY)
Juniata Coll (PA)
Kansas Wesleyan U (KS)
Kennesaw State U (GA)
Lee U (TN)
Lipscomb U (TN)
Louisiana Coll (LA)
Madonna U (MI)
Manchester U (IN)
Manhattanville Coll (NY)
Marist Coll (NY)
Marywood U (PA)
Merrimack Coll (MA)
Messiah Coll (PA)
Michigan State U (MI)
Millikin U (IL)
Minnesota State U Moorhead (MN)
Morningside Coll (IA)
Nazareth Coll of Rochester (NY)
Northern State U (SD)
Northwest Missouri State U (MO)
Oakland City U (IN)
Ohio Dominican U (OH)
Ohio Wesleyan U (OH)
Pace U (NY)
Pace U, Pleasantville Campus (NY)
Palm Beach Atlantic U (FL)
Providence Coll (RI)
Queens Coll of the City U of New York (NY)
Reinhardt U (GA)
Rocky Mountain Coll (MT)
Saginaw Valley State U (MI)
Saint Francis U (PA)
St. John Fisher Coll (NY)
St. Joseph's Coll, Long Island Campus (NY)
St. Joseph's Coll, New York (NY)
Saint Joseph's U (PA)
Saint Mary's U of Minnesota (MN)
Salve Regina U (RI)
Seattle U (WA)
Seton Hill U (PA)
Southeastern U (FL)
Southern U and Ag and Mech Coll (LA)
Southwest Baptist U (MO)
Spring Hill Coll (AL)
State U of New York Coll at Potsdam (NY)
Syracuse U (NY)
Taylor U (IN)
Trevecca Nazarene U (TN)
Trinity Christian Coll (IL)
Union Coll (KY)
U of California, Irvine (CA)
The U of Findlay (OH)
U of Maine (ME)
U of Maine at Farmington (ME)
U of Maine at Machias (ME)
U of Mary Hardin-Baylor (TX)
U of Maryland, Baltimore County (MD)
U of Nebraska–Lincoln (NE)
U of Providence (MT)
U of Regina (SK, Canada)
U of Sioux Falls (SD)
U of South Dakota (SD)
U of Wisconsin–Superior (WI)
Utah State U (UT)
Utah Valley U (UT)
Utica Coll (NY)
Valley City State U (ND)
Valparaiso U (IN)
Washington U in St. Louis (MO)
Waynesburg U (PA)
Weber State U (UT)
Western Washington U (WA)
Widener U (PA)
Youngstown State U (OH)

BIOMATHEMATICS, BIOINFORMATICS, AND COMPUTATIONAL BIOLOGY RELATED
La Sierra U (CA)
U of California, Los Angeles (CA)
Washington U in St. Louis (MO)
Worcester Polytechnic Inst (MA)

BIOMEDICAL SCIENCES
AdventHealth U (FL)
Alverno Coll (WI)
Antioch Coll, Yellow Springs (OH)
Auburn U (AL)
Bradley U (IL)
Bridgewater State U (MA)
Central Michigan U (MI)
Central Washington U (WA)
Christian Brothers U (TN)
Coll of the Ozarks (MO)
Colorado State U (CO)
Fitchburg State U (MA)
Georgetown Coll (KY)
Hiram Coll (OH)
La Sierra U (CA)
Liberty U (VA)
Madonna U (MI)
Marist Coll (NY)
Marquette U (WI)
Marymount Manhattan Coll (NY)
Maryville U of Saint Louis (MO)
Michigan State U (MI)
Minnesota State U Moorhead (MN)
The Ohio State U (OH)
Ouachita Baptist U (AR)
Rochester Inst of Technology (NY)
Saint Leo U (FL)
State U of New York at Fredonia (NY)
State U of New York at Plattsburgh (NY)
U at Buffalo, the State U of New York (NY)
U of California, Riverside (CA)
U of California, Santa Cruz (CA)
U of Central Florida (FL)
U of Colorado Denver (CO)
U of Lynchburg (VA)
U of Minnesota, Duluth (MN)
U of New Hampshire (NH)
U of Northern Iowa (IA)
U of Pennsylvania (PA)
U of Saint Mary (KS)
U of South Alabama (AL)
U of South Carolina Aiken (SC)
U of South Dakota (SD)
U of South Florida (FL)
The U of Texas Rio Grande Valley (TX)
U of Washington, Tacoma (WA)
Washington State U (WA)

BIOMEDICAL TECHNOLOGY
Indiana U–Purdue U Indianapolis (IN)

BIOMETRY/BIOMETRICS
Carnegie Mellon U (PA)

MAJORS LISTING

Cornell U (NY)

BIOPHYSICS
Brandeis U (MA)
Claremont McKenna Coll (CA)
Columbia U (NY)
Haverford Coll (PA)
Iowa State U of Science and Technology (IA)
Johns Hopkins U (MD)
La Sierra U (CA)
Lipscomb U (TN)
Loyola U Chicago (IL)
Loyola U New Orleans (LA)
Marquette U (WI)
Miami U (OH)
New Jersey Inst of Technology (NJ)
Ouachita Baptist U (AR)
Pitzer Coll (CA)
Regent U (VA)
Scripps Coll (CA)
State U of New York Coll at Geneseo (NY)
Syracuse U (NY)
Temple U (PA)
U at Buffalo, the State U of New York (NY)
U of California, Los Angeles (CA)
U of Michigan (MI)
U of Pennsylvania (PA)
U of San Diego (CA)
U of Southern Indiana (IN)
Washington & Jefferson Coll (PA)
Washington U in St. Louis (MO)
Whitworth U (WA)

BIOPSYCHOLOGY
Bucknell U (PA)
Carnegie Mellon U (PA)
Geneva Coll (PA)
Grand Valley State U (MI)
Immaculata U (PA)
Liberty U (VA)
Life U (GA)
Messiah Coll (PA)
Morningside Coll (IA)
New Coll of Florida (FL)
Oglethorpe U (GA)
Ohio Dominican U (OH)
Rider U (NJ)
Spring Hill Coll (AL)
Washington U in St. Louis (MO)

BIOSTATISTICS
Emmanuel Coll (MA)
Indiana U–Purdue U Indianapolis (IN)
Saint Louis U (MO)
Tulane U (LA)
The U of North Carolina at Chapel Hill (NC)

BIOTECHNOLOGY
Auburn U (AL)
California State U, San Marcos (CA)
Colorado State U (CO)
Eastern Illinois U (IL)
East Stroudsburg U of Pennsylvania (PA)
Endicott Coll (MA)
Fitchburg State U (MA)
Florida Southern Coll (FL)
Hunter Coll of the City U of New York (NY)
Indiana U Bloomington (IN)
Indiana U East (IN)
Indiana U–Purdue U Indianapolis (IN)
Inter American U of Puerto Rico, Aguadilla Campus (PR)
Inter American U of Puerto Rico, Barranquitas Campus (PR)
Inter American U of Puerto Rico, Bayamón Campus (PR)
Liberty U (VA)
Manhattan Coll (NY)
Marywood U (PA)
Massachusetts Coll of Liberal Arts (MA)
Missouri Baptist U (MO)
Rochester Inst of Technology (NY)
State U of New York Coll of Environmental Science and Forestry (NY)
Syracuse U (NY)
U at Buffalo, the State U of New York (NY)
U of California, Davis (CA)
U of Central Florida (FL)
U of Georgia (GA)
U of Hawaii at Manoa (HI)
U of Houston (TX)
U of Houston–Downtown (TX)
U of Idaho (ID)
U of Kentucky (KY)
U of Maryland, Baltimore County (MD)
U of Nevada, Reno (NV)
The U of North Carolina at Pembroke (NC)
U of Wisconsin–River Falls (WI)
Utah Valley U (UT)
Western Kentucky U (KY)
Worcester State U (MA)

BOTANY/PLANT BIOLOGY
Auburn U (AL)
California State U, Long Beach (CA)
Connecticut Coll (CT)
Humboldt State U (CA)
Miami U (OH)
Michigan State U (MI)
North Carolina State U (NC)
Ohio U (OH)
Ohio Wesleyan U (OH)
Oklahoma State U (OK)
Purdue U (IN)
San Francisco State U (CA)
Sonoma State U (CA)
Southern Illinois U Carbondale (IL)
U of California, Davis (CA)
U of California, Riverside (CA)
U of Florida (FL)
U of Georgia (GA)
U of Hawaii at Manoa (HI)
U of Maine (ME)
U of Nebraska–Lincoln (NE)
U of Providence (MT)
U of Vermont (VT)
U of Washington (WA)
U of Wyoming (WY)
Utah State U (UT)
Utah Valley U (UT)
Weber State U (UT)

BOTANY/PLANT BIOLOGY RELATED
Miami U Hamilton (OH)
U of Hawaii at Manoa (HI)
U of Minnesota, Twin Cities Campus (MN)

BRASS INSTRUMENTS
Liberty U (VA)
Youngstown State U (OH)

BROADCAST JOURNALISM
Auburn U (AL)
Bowling Green State U (OH)
California State U, Long Beach (CA)
Cameron U (OK)
Central State U (OH)
Central Washington U (WA)
The Coll at Brockport, State U of New York (NY)
Concordia U Chicago (IL)
Drake U (IA)
Emerson Coll (MA)
Gonzaga U (WA)
Goshen Coll (IN)
Harding U (AR)
Humboldt State U (CA)
Ithaca Coll (NY)
Johnson U Florida (FL)
Manchester U (IN)
Marywood U (PA)
Massachusetts Coll of Liberal Arts (MA)
Minnesota State U Moorhead (MN)
Northern Kentucky U (KY)
Ohio Wesleyan U (OH)
Oklahoma Christian U (OK)
Syracuse U (NY)
Trevecca Nazarene U (TN)
U of Nebraska–Lincoln (NE)
U of South Carolina (SC)
The U of Texas at El Paso (TX)
Wartburg Coll (IA)
Washington State U (WA)
Western Kentucky U (KY)
Youngstown State U (OH)

BUILDING/CONSTRUCTION FINISHING, MANAGEMENT, AND INSPECTION RELATED
California State U, Long Beach (CA)

BUILDING CONSTRUCTION TECHNOLOGY
Université de Sherbrooke (QC, Canada)

BUSINESS ADMINISTRATION AND MANAGEMENT
Acadia U (NS, Canada)
Adams State U (CO)
Adelphi U (NY)
Agnes Scott Coll (GA)
Alabama State U (AL)
Albion Coll (MI)
Albright Coll (PA)
Alfred U (NY)
Alverno Coll (WI)
American Public U System (WV)
American U (DC)
American U in Bulgaria (Bulgaria)
Angelo State U (TX)
Appalachian State U (NC)
Arkansas Tech U (AR)
Assumption Coll (MA)
Auburn U (AL)
Auburn U at Montgomery (AL)
Aurora U (IL)
Austin Coll (TX)
Austin Peay State U (TN)
Avila U (MO)
Babson Coll (MA)
Baldwin Wallace U (OH)
Barton Coll (NC)
Baruch Coll of the City U of New York (NY)
Baylor U (TX)
Bellarmine U (KY)
Bennett Coll (NC)
Bentley U (MA)
Berea Coll (KY)
Berkeley Coll–New York City Campus (NY)
Berkeley Coll–White Plains Campus (NY)
Berkeley Coll–Woodland Park Campus (NJ)
Bethany Lutheran Coll (MN)
Bethel U (MN)
Boston Coll (MA)
Boston U (MA)
Bowling Green State U (OH)
Bradley U (IL)
Brandman U (CA)
Brenau U (GA)
Bridgewater Coll (VA)
Bridgewater State U (MA)
Bryant U (RI)
Bucknell U (PA)
Buena Vista U (IA)
Caldwell U (NJ)
California Lutheran U (CA)
California Polytechnic State U, San Luis Obispo (CA)
California State U, Bakersfield (CA)
California State U, Fullerton (CA)
California State U, Long Beach (CA)
California State U, Los Angeles (CA)
California State U, Monterey Bay (CA)
California State U, Northridge (CA)
California State U, San Bernardino (CA)
California State U, San Marcos (CA)
California U of Pennsylvania (PA)
Calumet Coll of Saint Joseph (IN)
Calvin Coll (MI)
Cameron U (OK)
Campbellsville U (KY)
Canisius Coll (NY)
Capilano U (BC, Canada)
Carnegie Mellon U (PA)
Carson-Newman U (TN)
Carthage Coll (WI)
The Catholic U of America (DC)
Cedarville U (OH)
Centenary Coll of Louisiana (LA)
Central Connecticut State U (CT)
Central Michigan U (MI)
Central Washington U (WA)
Champlain Coll (VT)
Christian Brothers U (TN)
Christopher Newport U (VA)
Clarion U of Pennsylvania (PA)
Clarkson U (NY)
Clark U (MA)
Coastal Carolina U (SC)
The Coll at Brockport, State U of New York (NY)
Coll of Charleston (SC)
Coll of Coastal Georgia (GA)
The Coll of Idaho (ID)
Coll of Saint Benedict (MN)
Coll of Saint Mary (NE)
The Coll of Saint Rose (NY)
The Coll of St. Scholastica (MN)
Coll of the Ozarks (MO)
The Coll of William and Mary (VA)
Colorado State U (CO)
Columbia Coll (MO)
Columbia Southern U (AL)
Concordia U Chicago (IL)
Concordia U Irvine (CA)
Creighton U (NE)
Culver-Stockton Coll (MO)
Curry Coll (MA)
Dakota State U (SD)
Dallas Baptist U (TX)
Dallas Christian Coll (TX)
Davenport U, Grand Rapids (MI)
Dean Coll (MA)
Delaware Valley U (PA)
Delta State U (MS)
DePaul U (IL)
DEREE - The American Coll of Greece (Greece)
Dominican U (IL)
Drake U (IA)
Drew U (NJ)
Drury U (MO)
Dunwoody Coll of Technology (MN)
Earlham Coll (IN)
East Carolina U (NC)
Eastern Illinois U (IL)
Eastern Mennonite U (VA)
Eastern U (PA)
Eastern Washington U (WA)
East Stroudsburg U of Pennsylvania (PA)
East Tennessee State U (TN)
East Texas Baptist U (TX)
Eckerd Coll (FL)
Elizabeth City State U (NC)
Embry-Riddle Aeronautical U–Worldwide (FL)
Emmanuel Coll (MA)
Endicott Coll (MA)
Excelsior Coll (NY)
Fairfield U (CT)
Farmingdale State Coll (NY)
Fayetteville State U (NC)
Fitchburg State U (MA)
Florida Ag and Mech U (FL)
Florida Atlantic U (FL)
Florida Coll (FL)
Florida Southern Coll (FL)
Fordham U (NY)
Fort Lewis Coll (CO)
Franklin Pierce U (NH)
Furman U (SC)
Geneva Coll (PA)
George Mason U (VA)
Georgetown Coll (KY)
Georgia Coll & State U (GA)
Georgia Southern U (GA)
Georgia State U (GA)
Gonzaga U (WA)
Gordon Coll (MA)
Graceland U (IA)
Granite State Coll (NH)
Greenville U (IL)
Grove City Coll (PA)
Hamline U (MN)
Harding U (AR)
Hardin-Simmons U (TX)
Hartwick Coll (NY)
High Point U (NC)
Hiram Coll (OH)
Hofstra U (NY)
Hood Coll (MD)
Hult Intl Business School (United Kingdom)
Humboldt State U (CA)
Idaho State U (ID)
Illinois Coll (IL)
Immaculata U (PA)
Indiana State U (IN)
Indiana U East (IN)
Indiana U Kokomo (IN)
Indiana U Northwest (IN)
Indiana U of Pennsylvania (PA)
Indiana U South Bend (IN)
Indiana U Southeast (IN)
Inter American U of Puerto Rico, Aguadilla Campus (PR)
Inter American U of Puerto Rico, Fajardo Campus (PR)
Inter American U of Puerto Rico, San Germán Campus (PR)
Iona Coll (NY)
Ithaca Coll (NY)
Jackson State U (MS)
Jacksonville U (FL)
John Cabot U (Italy)
Johnson C. Smith U (NC)
Johnson U Florida (FL)
Judson U (IL)
Juniata Coll (PA)
Kansas Wesleyan U (KS)
Kean U (NJ)
Kennesaw State U (GA)
King's Coll (PA)
King U (TN)
Knox Coll (IL)
Kuyper Coll (MI)
LaGrange Coll (GA)
Lancaster Bible Coll (PA)
La Salle U (PA)
Lasell Coll (MA)
La Sierra U (CA)
Lawrence Technological U (MI)
Lebanese American U (Lebanon)
Lebanon Valley Coll (PA)
Lees-McRae Coll (NC)
Lee U (TN)
Lesley U (MA)
LeTourneau U (TX)
Liberty U (VA)
Limestone Coll (SC)
Lindenwood U (MO)
Linfield Coll (OR)
Lipscomb U (TN)
Lock Haven U of Pennsylvania (PA)
Loras Coll (IA)
Louisiana Coll (LA)
Louisiana State U and A&M Coll (LA)
Loyola U Chicago (IL)
Loyola U New Orleans (LA)
Lubbock Christian U (TX)
Lycoming Coll (PA)
Madonna U (MI)
Maharishi U of Management (IA)
Manchester U (IN)
Manhattanville Coll (NY)
Mansfield U of Pennsylvania (PA)
Marian U (IN)
Marist Coll (NY)
Marquette U (WI)
Marshall U (WV)
Marymount California U (CA)
Marymount Manhattan Coll (NY)
Marymount U (VA)
Maryville U of Saint Louis (MO)
Marywood U (PA)
Massachusetts Coll of Liberal Arts (MA)
McDaniel Coll (MD)
McNeese State U (LA)
Mercy Coll (NY)
Merrimack Coll (MA)
Messenger Coll (TX)
Messiah Coll (PA)
Miami U (OH)
Michigan State U (MI)
Middle Tennessee State U (TN)
Millersville U of Pennsylvania (PA)
Milligan Coll (TN)
Millikin U (IL)
Millsaps Coll (MS)
Minnesota State U Moorhead (MN)
Missouri Baptist U (MO)
Molloy Coll (NY)
Montclair State U (NJ)
Morningside Coll (IA)
Mount Marty Coll (SD)
Mount St. Joseph U (OH)
Mount Saint Mary Coll (NY)
Murray State U (KY)
Muskingum U (OH)
National Paralegal Coll (AZ)
National U (CA)
Nazareth Coll of Rochester (NY)
New England Coll (NH)

New England Inst of Technology (RI)
New Jersey City U (NJ)
New Jersey Inst of Technology (NJ)
Nichols Coll (MA)
North Carolina State U (NC)
Northeastern State U (OK)
Northern Illinois U (IL)
Northern Kentucky U (KY)
Northern State U (SD)
Northwest Christian U (OR)
Northwestern Oklahoma State U (OK)
Northwest Missouri State U (MO)
Northwood U, Michigan Campus (MI)
Oakland City U (IN)
Oglethorpe U (GA)
Ohio Dominican U (OH)
The Ohio State U (OH)
The Ohio State U at Lima (OH)
The Ohio State U at Mansfield (OH)
The Ohio State U at Marion (OH)
The Ohio State U at Newark (OH)
Ohio U (OH)
Ohio Wesleyan U (OH)
Oklahoma Christian U (OK)
Oklahoma State U (OK)
Old Dominion U (VA)
Ottawa U (KS)
Ouachita Baptist U (AR)
Pace U (NY)
Pacific Lutheran U (WA)
Palm Beach Atlantic U (FL)
Pepperdine U, Malibu (CA)
Pfeiffer U (NC)
Piedmont Coll (GA)
Point Loma Nazarene U (CA)
Point U (GA)
Portland State U (OR)
Potomac State Coll of West Virginia U (WV)
Prairie View A&M U (TX)
Providence Coll (RI)
Purdue U (IN)
Purdue U Northwest (IN)
Queens U of Charlotte (NC)
Radford U (VA)
Redeemer U Coll (ON, Canada)
Regent U (VA)
Regis U (CO)
Reinhardt U (GA)
Rhode Island Coll (RI)
Rhodes Coll (TN)
Rice U (TX)
Rider U (NJ)
Roanoke Coll (VA)
Rochester Coll (MI)
Rochester Inst of Technology (NY)
Rockford U (IL)
Rocky Mountain Coll (MT)
Rollins Coll (FL)
Sacred Heart U (CT)
The Sage Colls (NY)
Saginaw Valley State U (MI)
Saint Francis U (PA)
St. John Fisher Coll (NY)
Saint John's U (MN)
St. Joseph's Coll, Long Island Campus (NY)
St. Joseph's Coll, New York (NY)
Saint Joseph's U (PA)
Saint Leo U (FL)
Saint Louis U (MO)
Saint Martin's U (WA)
St. Mary's U (TX)
St. Norbert Coll (WI)
Saint Vincent Coll (PA)
Salisbury U (MD)
Salve Regina U (RI)
Samford U (AL)
San Diego State U (CA)
San Francisco State U (CA)
San Jose State U (CA)
Seattle U (WA)
Seton Hill U (PA)
Sonoma State U (CA)
Southeastern Louisiana U (LA)
Southeastern U (FL)
Southeast Missouri State U (MO)
Southern Arkansas U–Magnolia (AR)
Southern Illinois U Carbondale (IL)
Southern Illinois U Edwardsville (IL)
Southern U and Ag and Mech Coll (LA)
Southwest Baptist U (MO)
Spring Hill Coll (AL)
State U of New York at Fredonia (NY)
State U of New York at Plattsburgh (NY)
State U of New York Coll at Geneseo (NY)
State U of New York Coll at Potsdam (NY)
State U of New York Coll of Technology at Alfred (NY)
State U of New York Coll of Technology at Delhi (NY)
Stetson U (FL)
Stevens Inst of Technology (NJ)
Stockton U (NJ)
Stonehill Coll (MA)
Sullivan U (KY)
Syracuse U (NY)
Taylor U (IN)
Texas A&M Intl U (TX)
Texas A&M U–Central Texas (TX)
Texas Lutheran U (TX)
Texas Tech U (TX)
Texas Woman's U (TX)
Tiffin U (OH)
Toccoa Falls Coll (GA)
Towson U (MD)
Trevecca Nazarene U (TN)
Truman State U (MO)
Tulane U (LA)
Union Coll (KY)
Université de Sherbrooke (QC, Canada)
U at Buffalo, the State U of New York (NY)
U of Arkansas (AR)
U of California, Irvine (CA)
U of California, Merced (CA)
U of California, Riverside (CA)
U of Central Arkansas (AR)
U of Central Florida (FL)
U of Colorado Denver (CO)
U of Dallas (TX)
U of Detroit Mercy (MI)
The U of Findlay (OH)
U of Florida (FL)
U of Georgia (GA)
U of Guam (GU)
U of Hawaii at Manoa (HI)
U of Houston (TX)
U of Houston–Clear Lake (TX)
U of Houston–Downtown (TX)
U of Idaho (ID)
U of Illinois at Springfield (IL)
U of La Verne (CA)
U of Lynchburg (VA)
U of Maine (ME)
U of Maine at Machias (ME)
U of Mary Hardin-Baylor (TX)
U of Maryland Eastern Shore (MD)
U of Maryland U Coll (MD)
U of Massachusetts Amherst (MA)
U of Massachusetts Boston (MA)
U of Massachusetts Dartmouth (MA)
U of Massachusetts Lowell (MA)
U of Memphis (TN)
U of Michigan (MI)
U of Michigan–Dearborn (MI)
U of Minnesota, Duluth (MN)
U of Minnesota, Morris (MN)
U of Montevallo (AL)
U of Mount Union (OH)
U of Nebraska–Lincoln (NE)
U of Nevada, Las Vegas (NV)
U of Nevada, Reno (NV)
U of New Hampshire (NH)
U of New Haven (CT)
U of New Mexico (NM)
U of North Carolina at Asheville (NC)
The U of North Carolina at Chapel Hill (NC)
The U of North Carolina at Charlotte (NC)
The U of North Carolina at Greensboro (NC)
The U of North Carolina at Pembroke (NC)
U of North Dakota (ND)
U of Northern Colorado (CO)
U of Northern Iowa (IA)
U of North Florida (FL)
U of Northwestern–St. Paul (MN)
U of Pennsylvania (PA)
U of Pittsburgh at Bradford (PA)
U of Providence (MT)
U of Puget Sound (WA)
U of Regina (SK, Canada)
U of Richmond (VA)
U of Saint Francis (IN)
U of Saint Mary (KS)
U of St. Thomas (MN)
U of St. Thomas (TX)
U of San Diego (CA)
U of San Francisco (CA)
U of Sioux Falls (SD)
U of South Alabama (AL)
U of South Carolina (SC)
U of South Carolina Aiken (SC)
U of South Dakota (SD)
U of Southern Indiana (IN)
U of South Florida (FL)
U of South Florida Sarasota-Manatee (FL)
The U of Tampa (FL)
The U of Tennessee (TN)
The U of Tennessee at Martin (TN)
The U of Texas at Austin (TX)
The U of Texas at El Paso (TX)
The U of Texas of the Permian Basin (TX)
The U of Texas Rio Grande Valley (TX)
U of the Incarnate Word (TX)
The U of Toledo (OH)
The U of Tulsa (OK)
U of Vermont (VT)
U of Washington (WA)
U of Washington, Bothell (WA)
U of Washington, Tacoma (WA)
The U of West Alabama (AL)
U of West Georgia (GA)
U of Wisconsin–Eau Claire (WI)
U of Wisconsin–La Crosse (WI)
U of Wisconsin–River Falls (WI)
U of Wisconsin–Superior (WI)
U of Wyoming (WY)
Utah State U (UT)
Utah Valley U (UT)
Utica Coll (NY)
Valley City State U (ND)
Vanguard U of Southern California (CA)
Vermont Tech Coll (VT)
Virginia Polytechnic Inst and State U (VA)
Wartburg Coll (IA)
Washington and Lee U (VA)
Washington State U (WA)
Washington State U–Spokane (WA)
Washington State U–Tri-Cities (WA)
Washington State U–Vancouver (WA)
Washington U in St. Louis (MO)
Waynesburg U (PA)
Weber State U (UT)
Wesleyan Coll (GA)
West Chester U of Pennsylvania (PA)
Western Connecticut State U (CT)
Western Illinois U (IL)
Western Kentucky U (KY)
Western State Colorado U (CO)
Western Washington U (WA)
West Virginia State U (WV)
West Virginia U Inst of Technology (WV)
Wheaton Coll (MA)
Whittier Coll (CA)
Whitworth U (WA)
Widener U (PA)
Wilkes U (PA)
William Jewell Coll (MO)
Winthrop U (SC)
Woodbury U (CA)
Worcester State U (MA)
Youngstown State U (OH)

BUSINESS ADMINISTRATION, MANAGEMENT AND OPERATIONS RELATED
Adams State U (CO)
Alverno Coll (WI)
Austin Coll (TX)
Babson Coll (MA)
Benedictine U (IL)
Bentley U (MA)
Blackburn Coll (IL)
Bowling Green State U (OH)
California State U, San Bernardino (CA)
Calumet Coll of Saint Joseph (IN)
Carnegie Mellon U (PA)
Central Michigan U (MI)
Central Washington U (WA)
Coll of Central Florida (FL)
Davenport U, Grand Rapids (MI)
Daytona State Coll (FL)
Eastern Oregon U (OR)
Embry-Riddle Aeronautical U–Daytona (FL)
Embry-Riddle Aeronautical U–Prescott (AZ)
Embry-Riddle Aeronautical U–Worldwide (FL)
Hofstra U (NY)
Jacksonville U (FL)
Judson U (IL)
Limestone Coll (SC)
Lincoln Christian U (IL)
Mercer U, Macon (GA)
Miami U Hamilton (OH)
Millikin U (IL)
Missouri Baptist U (MO)
Rider U (NJ)
San Jose State U (CA)
Spring Hill Coll (AL)
Texas Tech U (TX)
Trinity Christian Coll (IL)
U of Houston–Clear Lake (TX)
U of Illinois at Springfield (IL)
U of Louisville (KY)
U of Maine at Farmington (ME)
U of Maryland, Baltimore County (MD)
U of Maryland U Coll (MD)
U of Pennsylvania (PA)
U of Puerto Rico–Bayamón (PR)
U of Wyoming (WY)
Washington U in St. Louis (MO)
Waynesburg U (PA)
Widener U (PA)

BUSINESS AUTOMATION/ TECHNOLOGY/DATA ENTRY
The U of Tampa (FL)

BUSINESS/COMMERCE
Adams State U (CO)
Alverno Coll (WI)
American Coll of Thessaloniki (Greece)
Auburn U at Montgomery (AL)
Austin Coll (TX)
Avila U (MO)
Baker U (KS)
Baylor U (TX)
Bellarmine U (KY)
Bentley U (MA)
Bethel Coll (KS)
Bowling Green State U (OH)
Brandeis U (MA)
Brenau U (GA)
Bryn Athyn Coll of the New Church (PA)
Bucknell U (PA)
California U of Pennsylvania (PA)
Canisius Coll (NY)
The Catholic U of America (DC)
Central State U (OH)
Champlain Coll (VT)
Christian Brothers U (TN)
Coll of Central Florida (FL)
Coll of Coastal Georgia (GA)
Coll of Staten Island of the City U of New York (NY)
Colorado State U–Pueblo (CO)
Columbia Central U, Caguas (PR)
Columbia Central U, Yauco (PR)
Columbia Coll (MO)
Covenant Coll (GA)
Davenport U, Grand Rapids (MI)
Delta State U (MS)
Drake U (IA)
Earlham Coll (IN)
East Texas Baptist U (TX)
The Evergreen State Coll (WA)
Excelsior Coll (NY)
Framingham State U (MA)
Goshen Coll (IN)
Grand Valley State U (MI)
Hofstra U (NY)
Hollins U (VA)
Hult Intl Business School (United Kingdom)
Idaho State U (ID)
Indiana State U (IN)
Indiana U Bloomington (IN)
Indiana U Kokomo (IN)
Indiana U Northwest (IN)
Indiana U of Pennsylvania (PA)
Indiana U–Purdue U Indianapolis (IN)
Indiana U South Bend (IN)
Indiana U Southeast (IN)
Ithaca Coll (NY)
Jacksonville U (FL)
Juniata Coll (PA)
Kalamazoo Coll (MI)
Lamar U (TX)
La Salle U (PA)
La Sierra U (CA)
LIM Coll (NY)
Limestone Coll (SC)
Louisiana Coll (LA)
Loyola U New Orleans (LA)
Manchester U (IN)
Marymount Manhattan Coll (NY)
Maryville U of Saint Louis (MO)
Massachusetts Inst of Technology (MA)
Mercer U, Macon (GA)
Miami U Hamilton (OH)
Murray State U (KY)
New York U (NY)
Nichols Coll (MA)
Northern Kentucky U (KY)
Northwest Christian U (OR)
The Ohio State U (OH)
The Ohio State U at Lima (OH)
The Ohio State U at Mansfield (OH)
The Ohio State U at Marion (OH)
The Ohio State U at Newark (OH)
Ohio Wesleyan U (OH)
Oklahoma Christian U (OK)
Pace U (NY)
Pace U, Pleasantville Campus (NY)
Purdue U Northwest (IN)
Randolph Coll (VA)
Randolph-Macon Coll (VA)
Rochester Inst of Technology (NY)
Saginaw Valley State U (MI)
Saint Anselm Coll (NH)
Saint Vincent Coll (PA)
Seattle U (WA)
Skidmore Coll (NY)
Southeastern U (FL)
Southern Arkansas U–Magnolia (AR)
Southwestern U (TX)
Sullivan U (KY)
Tabor Coll (KS)
Temple U (PA)
Texas Tech U (TX)
Texas Woman's U (TX)
Trinity Christian Coll (IL)
Tyndale U Coll & Sem (ON, Canada)
U of Arkansas (AR)
U of Central Florida (FL)
U of Georgia (GA)
U of Hawaii at Manoa (HI)
U of Houston–Clear Lake (TX)
U of Houston–Downtown (TX)
U of Kentucky (KY)
U of Maryland, Coll Park (MD)
U of Massachusetts Dartmouth (MA)
U of Nevada, Reno (NV)
U of Notre Dame (IN)
U of Oregon (OR)
U of Pittsburgh (PA)
U of Puget Sound (WA)
U of Regina (SK, Canada)
U of Saint Francis (IN)
U of South Alabama (AL)
U of South Dakota (SD)
U of South Florida (FL)
U of South Florida Sarasota-Manatee (FL)
The U of Texas at Austin (TX)
The U of Tulsa (OK)
U of Virginia (VA)
U of Wisconsin–Milwaukee (WI)
Utah State U (UT)
Virginia Commonwealth U (VA)
Washington & Jefferson Coll (PA)
Washington U in St. Louis (MO)
Westmont Coll (CA)
West Virginia U Inst of Technology (WV)
Worcester Polytechnic Inst (MA)
Worcester State U (MA)
Wright State U–Lake Campus (OH)

Youngstown State U (OH)

BUSINESS/CORPORATE COMMUNICATIONS
Babson Coll (MA)
Baruch Coll of the City U of New York (NY)
Bentley U (MA)
Bryant U (RI)
Capilano U (BC, Canada)
Christian Brothers U (TN)
Concordia U Chicago (IL)
Duquesne U (PA)
Lycoming Coll (PA)
Marquette U (WI)
Morningside Coll (IA)
National U (CA)
Nichols Coll (MA)
Point Loma Nazarene U (CA)
Saint Leo U (FL)
Stevens Inst of Technology (NJ)
Trinity Christian Coll (IL)
U of Houston (TX)
U of Wisconsin–River Falls (WI)

BUSINESS FAMILY AND CONSUMER SCIENCES/ HUMAN SCIENCES
U of Houston (TX)
Virginia Polytechnic Inst and State U (VA)

BUSINESS, MANAGEMENT, AND MARKETING RELATED
Adelphi U (NY)
American U (DC)
Benedictine U (IL)
Bentley U (MA)
Bowling Green State U (OH)
Bradley U (IL)
Bridgewater State U (MA)
Duquesne U (PA)
Eastern U (PA)
FIDM/Fashion Inst of Design & Merchandising, Los Angeles Campus (CA)
Hofstra U (NY)
Loyola U Chicago (IL)
Messiah Coll (PA)
New Jersey Inst of Technology (NJ)
New York U (NY)
Northwest Christian U (OR)
Saint Anselm Coll (NH)
Saint Mary's U of Minnesota (MN)
Seton Hill U (PA)
Skidmore Coll (NY)
State U of New York Coll of Technology at Alfred (NY)
State U of New York Coll of Technology at Delhi (NY)
State U of New York Maritime Coll (NY)
Trevecca Nazarene U (TN)
Utica Coll (NY)
Worcester Polytechnic Inst (MA)

BUSINESS/MANAGERIAL ECONOMICS
Allegheny Coll (PA)
Arkansas Tech U (AR)
Auburn U (AL)
Baruch Coll of the City U of New York (NY)
Baylor U (TX)
Beloit Coll (WI)
Benedictine U (IL)
Bentley U (MA)
Boston Coll (MA)
Bowling Green State U (OH)
Bradley U (IL)
Bryant U (RI)
California Inst of Technology (CA)
California State U, Fullerton (CA)
California State U, Long Beach (CA)
Campbellsville U (KY)
Canisius Coll (NY)
Carson-Newman U (TN)
Cedarville U (OH)
Central Washington U (WA)
Clarion U of Pennsylvania (PA)
Coastal Carolina U (SC)
The Coll of Saint Rose (NY)
Colorado State U–Pueblo (CO)
DePaul U (IL)
Duquesne U (PA)
Eastern Washington U (WA)
East Tennessee State U (TN)
Fort Lewis Coll (CO)
Georgetown Coll (KY)
Georgia Coll & State U (GA)
Georgia Southern U (GA)
Georgia State U (GA)
Grand Valley State U (MI)
Grove City Coll (PA)
Hampden-Sydney Coll (VA)
Hofstra U (NY)
Illinois Coll (IL)
Inter American U of Puerto Rico, Bayamón Campus (PR)
Inter American U of Puerto Rico, San Germán Campus (PR)
Iowa State U of Science and Technology (IA)
Ithaca Coll (NY)
Jackson State U (MS)
Kennesaw State U (GA)
Lake Forest Coll (IL)
Lamar U (TX)
Limestone Coll (SC)
Lipscomb U (TN)
Louisiana Coll (LA)
Louisiana State U and A&M Coll (LA)
Loyola U Chicago (IL)
Loyola U New Orleans (LA)
Marquette U (WI)
Marshall U (WV)
Marymount Manhattan Coll (NY)
Miami U (OH)
Miami U Hamilton (OH)
Middle Tennessee State U (TN)
Molloy Coll (NY)
New York U (NY)
Nichols Coll (MA)
North Carolina State U (NC)
Northern Kentucky U (KY)
Northwest Missouri State U (MO)
Northwood U, Michigan Campus (MI)
Oglethorpe U (GA)
The Ohio State U (OH)
Ohio U (OH)
Ohio Wesleyan U (OH)
Oklahoma State U (OK)
Old Dominion U (VA)
Ottawa U (KS)
Pace U (NY)
Pace U, Pleasantville Campus (NY)
Pfeiffer U (NC)
Point Loma Nazarene U (CA)
Rider U (NJ)
Saginaw Valley State U (MI)
Saint Anselm Coll (NH)
Saint Louis U (MO)
Salisbury U (MD)
Samford U (AL)
Seattle U (WA)
Sonoma State U (CA)
Southern Illinois U Carbondale (IL)
Southern U and Ag and Mech Coll (LA)
Spring Hill Coll (AL)
State U of New York Coll at Potsdam (NY)
Stetson U (FL)
Taylor U (IN)
Union Coll (NY)
U of Arkansas (AR)
U of California, Irvine (CA)
U of California, Los Angeles (CA)
U of California, Riverside (CA)
U of California, Santa Cruz (CA)
U of Central Florida (FL)
U of Dayton (OH)
U of Georgia (GA)
U of Idaho (ID)
U of Kentucky (KY)
U of Louisville (KY)
U of Maine at Farmington (ME)
U of Mary Hardin-Baylor (TX)
U of Massachusetts Amherst (MA)
U of Memphis (TN)
U of Nebraska–Lincoln (NE)
U of Nevada, Reno (NV)
The U of North Carolina at Charlotte (NC)
The U of North Carolina at Greensboro (NC)
U of North Dakota (ND)
U of North Florida (FL)
U of San Diego (CA)
U of South Carolina (SC)
The U of Tennessee (TN)
The U of Tennessee at Martin (TN)
The U of Texas of the Permian Basin (TX)
U of the Incarnate Word (TX)
U of West Georgia (GA)
U of Wyoming (WY)
Utica Coll (NY)
Virginia Commonwealth U (VA)
Virginia Polytechnic Inst and State U (VA)
Washington U in St. Louis (MO)
Weber State U (UT)
West Chester U of Pennsylvania (PA)
Western Illinois U (IL)
Western Kentucky U (KY)
Westmont Coll (CA)
Wheaton Coll (IL)
Widener U (PA)
Wofford Coll (SC)
Wright State U–Lake Campus (OH)
Youngstown State U (OH)

BUSINESS STATISTICS
Baruch Coll of the City U of New York (NY)
Baylor U (TX)
Hofstra U (NY)
Loyola U New Orleans (LA)
Marian U (IN)
Maryville U of Saint Louis (MO)
New York U (NY)
U of New Haven (CT)
The U of Tennessee (TN)
The U of Tulsa (OK)

BUSINESS TEACHER EDUCATION
Adams State U (CO)
Arkansas Tech U (AR)
Auburn U (AL)
Avila U (MO)
Baylor U (TX)
Bowling Green State U (OH)
Buena Vista U (IA)
Campbellsville U (KY)
Canisius Coll (NY)
Carson-Newman U (TN)
Coll of Saint Mary (NE)
Dakota State U (SD)
Eastern Washington U (WA)
Emmanuel Coll (GA)
Fayetteville State U (NC)
Goshen Coll (IN)
Gwynedd Mercy U (PA)
Hofstra U (NY)
Immaculata U (PA)
Indiana State U (IN)
Lee U (TN)
Louisiana Coll (LA)
Middle Tennessee State U (TN)
Missouri Baptist U (MO)
Nazareth Coll of Rochester (NY)
Northwest Missouri State U (MO)
Oakland City U (IN)
Ohio Wesleyan U (OH)
Rider U (NJ)
Saint Vincent Coll (PA)
Southern Arkansas U–Magnolia (AR)
Trevecca Nazarene U (TN)
Trinity Christian Coll (IL)
U of Maine at Machias (ME)
U of Maryland Eastern Shore (MD)
U of Minnesota, Twin Cities Campus (MN)
U of Nebraska–Lincoln (NE)
U of Northern Iowa (IA)
U of Regina (SK, Canada)
Utah State U (UT)
Utah Valley U (UT)
Utica Coll (NY)
Valley City State U (ND)
Weber State U (UT)
Western Kentucky U (KY)

CAD/CADD DRAFTING/ DESIGN TECHNOLOGY
Acad of Art U (CA)
Idaho State U (ID)
Murray State U (KY)

CANADIAN STUDIES
Acadia U (NS, Canada)
Université Sainte-Anne (NS, Canada)
U of Washington (WA)
Western Washington U (WA)

CARDIOVASCULAR TECHNOLOGY
Piedmont Coll (GA)
Saint Mary's U of Minnesota (MN)
Weber State U (UT)

CARIBBEAN STUDIES
Hofstra U (NY)
Northwestern U (IL)

CELL AND MOLECULAR BIOLOGY
Adams State U (CO)
Bradley U (IL)
Bridgewater State U (MA)
Bryant U (RI)
Bucknell U (PA)
Cedarville U (OH)
Central Washington U (WA)
Christopher Newport U (VA)
The Colorado Coll (CO)
Fort Lewis Coll (CO)
Grand Valley State U (MI)
Harvard U (MA)
Johns Hopkins U (MD)
Limestone Coll (SC)
Loyola U New Orleans (LA)
Marymount U (VA)
Minnesota State U Moorhead (MN)
Northeastern State U (OK)
Ohio U (OH)
Purdue U (IN)
Sacred Heart U (CT)
Seattle U (WA)
Texas Tech U (TX)
Université Sainte-Anne (NS, Canada)
U of California, Irvine (CA)
U of California, Los Angeles (CA)
U of California, Santa Cruz (CA)
U of Hawaii at Manoa (HI)
U of Michigan (MI)
U of Puget Sound (WA)
U of Regina (SK, Canada)
U of St. Thomas (TX)
U of Washington (WA)
Western Washington U (WA)

CELL BIOLOGY AND ANATOMICAL SCIENCES RELATED
Tulane U (LA)
U of Mary Hardin-Baylor (TX)

CELL BIOLOGY AND ANATOMY
Dallas Baptist U (TX)

CELL BIOLOGY AND HISTOLOGY
Beloit Coll (WI)
California State U, Long Beach (CA)
California State U, San Marcos (CA)
The Coll of Saint Rose (NY)
Humboldt State U (CA)
Johns Hopkins U (MD)
Mansfield U of Pennsylvania (PA)
Northwestern U (IL)
San Francisco State U (CA)
Sonoma State U (CA)
Tulane U (LA)
U of California, Davis (CA)
U of Georgia (GA)
U of Minnesota, Twin Cities Campus (MN)

CELTIC LANGUAGES
U of Notre Dame (IN)

CERAMIC ARTS AND CERAMICS
Adams State U (CO)
Alfred U (NY)
Bowling Green State U (OH)
Bradley U (IL)
California State U, Long Beach (CA)
Central Washington U (WA)
Cleveland Inst of Art (OH)
Coll of the Ozarks (MO)
Columbia Coll (MO)
Hofstra U (NY)
Inter American U of Puerto Rico, San Germán Campus (PR)
Maryland Inst Coll of Art (MD)
Marywood U (PA)
Rhode Island Coll (RI)
Rhode Island School of Design (RI)
Rochester Inst of Technology (NY)
Seton Hill U (PA)
Syracuse U (NY)
Temple U (PA)
Texas Christian U (TX)
U of Dallas (TX)
U of Massachusetts Dartmouth (MA)
U of Michigan (MI)
U of Oregon (OR)
U of Regina (SK, Canada)
U of Washington (WA)
Washington U in St. Louis (MO)

CERAMIC SCIENCES AND ENGINEERING
Alfred U (NY)

CHEMICAL AND BIOMOLECULAR ENGINEERING
Johns Hopkins U (MD)
Massachusetts Inst of Technology (MA)
New York U (NY)
U of Chicago (IL)
U of Washington (WA)

CHEMICAL ENGINEERING
American U of Beirut (Lebanon)
Auburn U (AL)
Bucknell U (PA)
California Inst of Technology (CA)
California State U, Long Beach (CA)
Calvin Coll (MI)
Carnegie Mellon U (PA)
Christian Brothers U (TN)
Clarkson U (NY)
Colorado School of Mines (CO)
Colorado State U (CO)
Columbia U (NY)
Cornell U (NY)
Florida Ag and Mech U (FL)
Iowa State U of Science and Technology (IA)
Johns Hopkins U (MD)
Lafayette Coll (PA)
Lamar U (TX)
Louisiana State U and A&M Coll (LA)
Manhattan Coll (NY)
Massachusetts Inst of Technology (MA)
Miami U (OH)
Michigan State U (MI)
New Jersey Inst of Technology (NJ)
New York U (NY)
North Carolina State U (NC)
Northwestern U (IL)
The Ohio State U (OH)
Ohio U (OH)
Oklahoma State U (OK)
Pace U (NY)
Prairie View A&M U (TX)
Princeton U (NJ)
Purdue U (IN)
Rice U (TX)
Rochester Inst of Technology (NY)
San Jose State U (CA)
Stevens Inst of Technology (NJ)
Syracuse U (NY)
Texas Tech U (TX)
Tulane U (LA)
Université de Sherbrooke (QC, Canada)
U at Buffalo, the State U of New York (NY)
U of Arkansas (AR)
U of California, Davis (CA)
U of California, Irvine (CA)
U of California, Los Angeles (CA)
U of California, Riverside (CA)
U of Dayton (OH)
U of Florida (FL)
U of Houston (TX)
U of Idaho (ID)
U of Kentucky (KY)
U of Louisville (KY)
U of Maine (ME)
U of Maryland, Baltimore County (MD)
U of Maryland, Coll Park (MD)
U of Massachusetts Amherst (MA)
U of Massachusetts Lowell (MA)
U of Michigan (MI)
U of Minnesota, Duluth (MN)

U of Minnesota, Twin Cities Campus (MN)
U of Missouri (MO)
U of Nebraska–Lincoln (NE)
U of Nevada, Reno (NV)
U of New Hampshire (NH)
U of New Haven (CT)
U of New Mexico (NM)
U of North Dakota (ND)
U of Notre Dame (IN)
U of Pennsylvania (PA)
U of Pittsburgh (PA)
U of South Alabama (AL)
U of South Carolina (SC)
U of South Florida (FL)
The U of Tennessee (TN)
The U of Texas at Austin (TX)
The U of Texas of the Permian Basin (TX)
The U of Toledo (OH)
The U of Tulsa (OK)
U of Virginia (VA)
U of Washington (WA)
U of Wyoming (WY)
Virginia Commonwealth U (VA)
Virginia Polytechnic Inst and State U (VA)
Washington State U (WA)
Washington U in St. Louis (MO)
West Virginia U Inst of Technology (WV)
Widener U (PA)
Worcester Polytechnic Inst (MA)
Youngstown State U (OH)

CHEMICAL PHYSICS
Adams State U (CO)
Columbia U (NY)
Hamilton Coll (NY)
Harvard U (MA)
Michigan State U (MI)
Saginaw Valley State U (MI)

CHEMICAL TECHNOLOGY
U of Regina (SK, Canada)

CHEMISTRY
Acadia U (NS, Canada)
Adams State U (CO)
Adelphi U (NY)
Agnes Scott Coll (GA)
Alabama State U (AL)
Albion Coll (MI)
Albright Coll (PA)
Alfred U (NY)
Allegheny Coll (PA)
Alverno Coll (WI)
American U (DC)
American U of Beirut (Lebanon)
Angelo State U (TX)
Appalachian State U (NC)
Arkansas Tech U (AR)
Assumption Coll (MA)
Auburn U (AL)
Auburn U at Montgomery (AL)
Aurora U (IL)
Austin Coll (TX)
Austin Peay State U (TN)
Averett U (VA)
Baker U (KS)
Baldwin Wallace U (OH)
Barton Coll (NC)
Baylor U (TX)
Bellarmine U (KY)
Beloit Coll (WI)
Benedictine U (IL)
Bennett Coll (NC)
Berea Coll (KY)
Bethany Lutheran Coll (MN)
Bethel Coll (KS)
Bethel U (MN)
Blackburn Coll (IL)
Boston Coll (MA)
Boston U (MA)
Bowling Green State U (OH)
Bradley U (IL)
Brandeis U (MA)
Bridgewater Coll (VA)
Bridgewater State U (MA)
Bucknell U (PA)
Buena Vista U (IA)
Butler U (IN)
Caldwell U (NJ)
California Inst of Technology (CA)
California Lutheran U (CA)
California Polytechnic State U, San Luis Obispo (CA)
California State U, Bakersfield (CA)
California State U, Chico (CA)
California State U, Fullerton (CA)
California State U, Long Beach (CA)
California State U, Los Angeles (CA)
California State U, Northridge (CA)
California State U, San Bernardino (CA)
California State U, San Marcos (CA)
California U of Pennsylvania (PA)
Calvin Coll (MI)
Cameron U (OK)
Campbellsville U (KY)
Canisius Coll (NY)
Carnegie Mellon U (PA)
Carson-Newman U (TN)
Carthage Coll (WI)
The Catholic U of America (DC)
Cedarville U (OH)
Centenary Coll of Louisiana (LA)
Central Connecticut State U (CT)
Central Michigan U (MI)
Central State U (OH)
Central Washington U (WA)
Christian Brothers U (TN)
Christopher Newport U (VA)
Claremont McKenna Coll (CA)
Clarion U of Pennsylvania (PA)
Clarkson U (NY)
Clark U (MA)
Coastal Carolina U (SC)
Colgate U (NY)
The Coll at Brockport, State U of New York (NY)
Coll of Charleston (SC)
The Coll of Idaho (ID)
Coll of Saint Benedict (MN)
Coll of Saint Mary (NE)
The Coll of Saint Rose (NY)
The Coll of St. Scholastica (MN)
Coll of Staten Island of the City U of New York (NY)
Coll of the Holy Cross (MA)
Coll of the Ozarks (MO)
The Coll of William and Mary (VA)
The Colorado Coll (CO)
Colorado School of Mines (CO)
Colorado State U (CO)
Colorado State U–Pueblo (CO)
Columbia Coll (MO)
Columbia U (NY)
Concordia U Chicago (IL)
Concordia U Irvine (CA)
Connecticut Coll (CT)
Cornell Coll (IA)
Cornell U (NY)
Covenant Coll (GA)
Creighton U (NE)
Culver-Stockton Coll (MO)
Dartmouth Coll (NH)
Davidson Coll (NC)
Delaware Valley U (PA)
Delta State U (MS)
DePaul U (IL)
Dickinson Coll (PA)
Dominican U (IL)
Drake U (IA)
Drew U (NJ)
Drury U (MO)
Duquesne U (PA)
Earlham Coll (IN)
East Carolina U (NC)
Eastern Illinois U (IL)
Eastern Mennonite U (VA)
Eastern U (PA)
Eastern Washington U (WA)
East Stroudsburg U of Pennsylvania (PA)
East Tennessee State U (TN)
East Texas Baptist U (TX)
Eckerd Coll (FL)
Elizabeth City State U (NC)
Emmanuel Coll (MA)
Fairfield U (CT)
Fayetteville State U (NC)
Fitchburg State U (MA)
Florida Ag and Mech U (FL)
Florida Atlantic U (FL)
Florida Southern Coll (FL)
Fordham U (NY)
Fort Lewis Coll (CO)
Framingham State U (MA)
Furman U (SC)
Geneva Coll (PA)
George Mason U (VA)
Georgetown Coll (KY)
Georgia Coll & State U (GA)
Georgia Southern U (GA)
Georgia State U (GA)
Gonzaga U (WA)
Gordon Coll (MA)
Goshen Coll (IN)
Graceland U (IA)
Grand Valley State U (MI)
Greenville U (IL)
Grove City Coll (PA)
Hamilton Coll (NY)
Hamline U (MN)
Hampden-Sydney Coll (VA)
Hanover Coll (IN)
Harding U (AR)
Hardin-Simmons U (TX)
Hartwick Coll (NY)
Harvard U (MA)
Haverford Coll (PA)
High Point U (NC)
Hillsdale Coll (MI)
Hiram Coll (OH)
Hofstra U (NY)
Hollins U (VA)
Hood Coll (MD)
Humboldt State U (CA)
Hunter Coll of the City U of New York (NY)
Idaho State U (ID)
Illinois Coll (IL)
Immaculata U (PA)
Indiana State U (IN)
Indiana U Bloomington (IN)
Indiana U Kokomo (IN)
Indiana U Northwest (IN)
Indiana U of Pennsylvania (PA)
Indiana U–Purdue U Indianapolis (IN)
Indiana U South Bend (IN)
Indiana U Southeast (IN)
Inter American U of Puerto Rico, San Germán Campus (PR)
Iona Coll (NY)
Iowa State U of Science and Technology (IA)
Ithaca Coll (NY)
Jackson State U (MS)
Jacksonville U (FL)
Johns Hopkins U (MD)
Johnson C. Smith U (NC)
Judson U (IL)
Juniata Coll (PA)
Kalamazoo Coll (MI)
Kansas Wesleyan U (KS)
Kean U (NJ)
Kennesaw State U (GA)
King's Coll (PA)
King U (TN)
Knox Coll (IL)
Lafayette Coll (PA)
LaGrange Coll (GA)
Lake Forest Coll (IL)
Lamar U (TX)
La Salle U (PA)
La Sierra U (CA)
Lawrence Technological U (MI)
Lawrence U (WI)
Lebanese American U (Lebanon)
Lebanon Valley Coll (PA)
Lee U (TN)
LeTourneau U (TX)
Lewis & Clark Coll (OR)
Liberty U (VA)
Limestone Coll (SC)
Lindenwood U (MO)
Linfield Coll (OR)
Lipscomb U (TN)
Lock Haven U of Pennsylvania (PA)
Loras Coll (IA)
Louisiana Coll (LA)
Louisiana State U and A&M Coll (LA)
Loyola Marymount U (CA)
Loyola U Chicago (IL)
Loyola U New Orleans (LA)
Lubbock Christian U (TX)
Lycoming Coll (PA)
Macalester Coll (MN)
Madonna U (MI)
Manchester U (IN)
Manhattan Coll (NY)
Manhattanville Coll (NY)
Mansfield U of Pennsylvania (PA)
Marian U (IN)
Marist Coll (NY)
Marquette U (WI)
Marshall U (WV)
Maryville U of Saint Louis (MO)
Massachusetts Coll of Liberal Arts (MA)
Massachusetts Inst of Technology (MA)
McDaniel Coll (MD)
McNeese State U (LA)
Mercer U, Macon (GA)
Merrimack Coll (MA)
Messiah Coll (PA)
Miami U (OH)
Miami U Hamilton (OH)
Michigan State U (MI)
Middlebury Coll (VT)
Middle Tennessee State U (TN)
Millersville U of Pennsylvania (PA)
Milligan Coll (TN)
Millikin U (IL)
Millsaps Coll (MS)
Mills Coll (CA)
Minnesota State U Moorhead (MN)
Missouri Baptist U (MO)
Montclair State U (NJ)
Morningside Coll (IA)
Mount Marty Coll (SD)
Mount St. Joseph U (OH)
Mount Saint Mary Coll (NY)
Murray State U (KY)
Muskingum U (OH)
Nazareth Coll of Rochester (NY)
New Coll of Florida (FL)
New Jersey City U (NJ)
New Jersey Inst of Technology (NJ)
New York U (NY)
North Carolina State U (NC)
Northeastern State U (OK)
Northern Illinois U (IL)
Northern Kentucky U (KY)
Northern State U (SD)
Northwestern Oklahoma State U (OK)
Northwestern U (IL)
Northwest Missouri State U (MO)
Occidental Coll (CA)
Oglethorpe U (GA)
Ohio Dominican U (OH)
The Ohio State U (OH)
Ohio U (OH)
Ohio Wesleyan U (OH)
Oklahoma Baptist U (OK)
Oklahoma Christian U (OK)
Oklahoma State U (OK)
Old Dominion U (VA)
Ouachita Baptist U (AR)
Pace U (NY)
Pace U, Pleasantville Campus (NY)
Pacific Lutheran U (WA)
Pepperdine U, Malibu (CA)
Pfeiffer U (NC)
Piedmont Coll (GA)
Pitzer Coll (CA)
Point Loma Nazarene U (CA)
Portland State U (OR)
Prairie View A&M U (TX)
Princeton U (NJ)
Providence Coll (RI)
Purchase Coll, State U of New York (NY)
Purdue U (IN)
Purdue U Northwest (IN)
Queens Coll of the City U of New York (NY)
Queens U of Charlotte (NC)
Radford U (VA)
Randolph Coll (VA)
Randolph-Macon Coll (VA)
Redeemer U Coll (ON, Canada)
Regis U (CO)
Rhode Island Coll (RI)
Rhodes Coll (TN)
Rice U (TX)
Rider U (NJ)
Roanoke Coll (VA)
Rochester Inst of Technology (NY)
Rockford U (IL)
Rocky Mountain Coll (MT)
Rollins Coll (FL)
Sacred Heart U (CT)
The Sage Colls (NY)
Saginaw Valley State U (MI)
Saint Anselm Coll (NH)
Saint Francis U (PA)
St. John Fisher Coll (NY)
Saint John's U (MN)
St. Joseph's Coll, Long Island Campus (NY)
St. Joseph's Coll, New York (NY)
Saint Joseph's U (PA)
Saint Louis U (MO)
Saint Martin's U (WA)
St. Mary's Coll of Maryland (MD)
St. Mary's U (TX)
Saint Mary's U of Minnesota (MN)
St. Norbert Coll (WI)
St. Olaf Coll (MN)
Saint Vincent Coll (PA)
Salisbury U (MD)
Salve Regina U (RI)
Samford U (AL)
San Diego State U (CA)
San Francisco State U (CA)
San Jose State U (CA)
Sarah Lawrence Coll (NY)
Scripps Coll (CA)
Seattle U (WA)
Seton Hill U (PA)
Skidmore Coll (NY)
Sonoma State U (CA)
Southeastern Louisiana U (LA)
Southeast Missouri State U (MO)
Southern Arkansas U–Magnolia (AR)
Southern Illinois U Carbondale (IL)
Southern Illinois U Edwardsville (IL)
Southern U and Ag and Mech Coll (LA)
Southwest Baptist U (MO)
Southwestern U (TX)
Spring Hill Coll (AL)
State U of New York at Fredonia (NY)
State U of New York at Plattsburgh (NY)
State U of New York Coll at Geneseo (NY)
State U of New York Coll at Potsdam (NY)
State U of New York Coll of Environmental Science and Forestry (NY)
Stetson U (FL)
Stevens Inst of Technology (NJ)
Stockton U (NJ)
Stonehill Coll (MA)
Sweet Briar Coll (VA)
Syracuse U (NY)
Tabor Coll (KS)
Taylor U (IN)
Temple U (PA)
Texas A&M Intl U (TX)
Texas Christian U (TX)
Texas Lutheran U (TX)
Texas Tech U (TX)
Texas Woman's U (TX)
Towson U (MD)
Trevecca Nazarene U (TN)
Trinity Christian Coll (IL)
Truman State U (MO)
Tulane U (LA)
Union Coll (KY)
Union Coll (NY)
Université de Sherbrooke (QC, Canada)
U at Buffalo, the State U of New York (NY)
U of Arkansas (AR)
U of California, Davis (CA)
U of California, Irvine (CA)
U of California, Los Angeles (CA)
U of California, Merced (CA)
U of California, Riverside (CA)
U of California, Santa Cruz (CA)
U of Central Arkansas (AR)
U of Central Florida (FL)
U of Chicago (IL)
U of Colorado Denver (CO)
U of Dallas (TX)
U of Dayton (OH)
U of Detroit Mercy (MI)
The U of Findlay (OH)
U of Florida (FL)
U of Georgia (GA)
U of Guam (GU)
U of Hawaii at Manoa (HI)
U of Houston (TX)
U of Houston–Clear Lake (TX)
U of Houston–Downtown (TX)
U of Idaho (ID)
U of Illinois at Springfield (IL)
U of Kentucky (KY)
U of La Verne (CA)
U of Louisville (KY)

U of Lynchburg (VA)
U of Maine (ME)
U of Mary Hardin-Baylor (TX)
U of Maryland, Baltimore County (MD)
U of Maryland, Coll Park (MD)
U of Maryland Eastern Shore (MD)
U of Massachusetts Amherst (MA)
U of Massachusetts Boston (MA)
U of Massachusetts Dartmouth (MA)
U of Massachusetts Lowell (MA)
U of Memphis (TN)
U of Michigan (MI)
U of Michigan–Dearborn (MI)
U of Minnesota, Duluth (MN)
U of Minnesota, Morris (MN)
U of Minnesota, Twin Cities Campus (MN)
U of Missouri (MO)
U of Montevallo (AL)
U of Mount Union (OH)
U of Nebraska–Lincoln (NE)
U of Nevada, Las Vegas (NV)
U of New Hampshire (NH)
U of New Haven (CT)
U of New Mexico (NM)
U of North Carolina at Asheville (NC)
The U of North Carolina at Chapel Hill (NC)
The U of North Carolina at Charlotte (NC)
The U of North Carolina at Greensboro (NC)
The U of North Carolina at Pembroke (NC)
U of North Dakota (ND)
U of Northern Colorado (CO)
U of Northern Iowa (IA)
U of North Florida (FL)
U of Notre Dame (IN)
U of Oregon (OR)
U of Pennsylvania (PA)
U of Pittsburgh (PA)
U of Pittsburgh at Bradford (PA)
U of Providence (MT)
U of Puget Sound (WA)
U of Regina (SK, Canada)
U of Richmond (VA)
U of Saint Francis (IN)
U of Saint Mary (KS)
U of St. Thomas (MN)
U of St. Thomas (TX)
U of San Diego (CA)
U of San Francisco (CA)
U of Sioux Falls (SD)
U of South Alabama (AL)
U of South Carolina (SC)
U of South Carolina Aiken (SC)
U of South Dakota (SD)
U of Southern Indiana (IN)
U of South Florida (FL)
The U of Tampa (FL)
The U of Tennessee (TN)
The U of Tennessee at Martin (TN)
The U of Texas at Austin (TX)
The U of Texas at El Paso (TX)
The U of Texas of the Permian Basin (TX)
The U of Texas Rio Grande Valley (TX)
U of the Incarnate Word (TX)
The U of the South (TN)
The U of Toledo (OH)
The U of Tulsa (OK)
U of Vermont (VT)
U of Virginia (VA)
U of Washington (WA)
U of Washington, Bothell (WA)
The U of West Alabama (AL)
U of West Georgia (GA)
U of Wisconsin–Eau Claire (WI)
U of Wisconsin–La Crosse (WI)
U of Wisconsin–Milwaukee (WI)
U of Wisconsin–River Falls (WI)
U of Wisconsin–Superior (WI)
U of Wyoming (WY)
Ursinus Coll (PA)
Utah State U (UT)
Utah Valley U (UT)
Utica Coll (NY)
Valley City State U (ND)
Valparaiso U (IN)
Vanguard U of Southern California (CA)
Vassar Coll (NY)
Virginia Commonwealth U (VA)
Virginia Polytechnic Inst and State U (VA)
Wabash Coll (IN)
Wartburg Coll (IA)
Washington & Jefferson Coll (PA)
Washington and Lee U (VA)
Washington State U (WA)
Washington U in St. Louis (MO)
Waynesburg U (PA)
Weber State U (UT)
Wesleyan Coll (GA)
Wesleyan U (CT)
West Chester U of Pennsylvania (PA)
Western Connecticut State U (CT)
Western Illinois U (IL)
Western Kentucky U (KY)
Western State Colorado U (CO)
Western Washington U (WA)
Westmont Coll (CA)
West Virginia State U (WV)
West Virginia U Inst of Technology (WV)
Wheaton Coll (IL)
Wheaton Coll (MA)
Whittier Coll (CA)
Whitworth U (WA)
Widener U (PA)
Wilkes U (PA)
Willamette U (OR)
William Jewell Coll (MO)
Williams Coll (MA)
Winthrop U (SC)
Wofford Coll (SC)
Worcester Polytechnic Inst (MA)
Worcester State U (MA)
Youngstown State U (OH)

CHEMISTRY RELATED
Boston U (MA)
Bridgewater Coll (VA)
Bridgewater State U (MA)
Carnegie Mellon U (PA)
Coll of Charleston (SC)
Dartmouth Coll (NH)
Duquesne U (PA)
Eastern Oregon U (OR)
Eastern U (PA)
East Stroudsburg U of Pennsylvania (PA)
Harvard U (MA)
Inter American U of Puerto Rico, Bayamón Campus (PR)
Kansas Wesleyan U (KS)
LeTourneau U (TX)
Mercer U, Macon (GA)
Mount St. Joseph U (OH)
Palm Beach Atlantic U (FL)
Saginaw Valley State U (MI)
Saint Anselm Coll (NH)
Saint Vincent Coll (PA)
Taylor U (IN)
Union Coll (KY)
U at Buffalo, the State U of New York (NY)
U of Chicago (IL)
U of Notre Dame (IN)
U of Wisconsin–Eau Claire (WI)
U of Wisconsin–Milwaukee (WI)
Washington U in St. Louis (MO)
Western Illinois U (IL)

CHEMISTRY TEACHER EDUCATION
Adams State U (CO)
Albion Coll (MI)
Arkansas Tech U (AR)
Baylor U (TX)
Boston U (MA)
Bowling Green State U (OH)
Bradley U (IL)
Buena Vista U (IA)
Calvin Coll (MI)
Campbellsville U (KY)
Canisius Coll (NY)
Cedarville U (OH)
Central Michigan U (MI)
Central State U (OH)
Central Washington U (WA)
Coll of Saint Mary (NE)
Coll of Staten Island of the City U of New York (NY)
Coll of the Ozarks (MO)
Concordia U Chicago (IL)
Daytona State Coll (FL)
Eastern Washington U (WA)
Fort Lewis Coll (CO)
Geneva Coll (PA)
Goshen Coll (IN)
Grand Valley State U (MI)
Greenville U (IL)
Grove City Coll (PA)
Hofstra U (NY)
Immaculata U (PA)
Indiana U Bloomington (IN)
Indiana U Northwest (IN)
Indiana U South Bend (IN)
Inter American U of Puerto Rico, San Germán Campus (PR)
Ithaca Coll (NY)
Juniata Coll (PA)
Kansas Wesleyan U (KS)
Lee U (TN)
Lipscomb U (TN)
Louisiana Coll (LA)
Madonna U (MI)
Manchester U (IN)
Manhattanville Coll (NY)
Marist Coll (NY)
Martin Luther Coll (MN)
Merrimack Coll (MA)
Messiah Coll (PA)
Miami U Hamilton (OH)
Michigan State U (MI)
Millikin U (IL)
Minnesota State U Moorhead (MN)
Morningside Coll (IA)
Mount Marty Coll (SD)
Nazareth Coll of Rochester (NY)
New York U (NY)
Northern State U (SD)
Northwest Missouri State U (MO)
Ohio Dominican U (OH)
Ohio Wesleyan U (OH)
Pace U (NY)
Pace U, Pleasantville Campus (NY)
Pepperdine U, Malibu (CA)
Providence Coll (RI)
Queens Coll of the City U of New York (NY)
Rhode Island Coll (RI)
Saginaw Valley State U (MI)
Saint Francis U (PA)
St. John Fisher Coll (NY)
St. Joseph's Coll, Long Island Campus (NY)
St. Joseph's Coll, New York (NY)
Saint Joseph's U (PA)
Saint Mary's U of Minnesota (MN)
Seattle U (WA)
Seton Hill U (PA)
Southern U and Ag and Mech Coll (LA)
Southwest Baptist U (MO)
State U of New York Coll at Potsdam (NY)
Syracuse U (NY)
Taylor U (IN)
Trevecca Nazarene U (TN)
Trinity Christian Coll (IL)
Union Coll (KY)
U of Maine (ME)
U of Maine at Farmington (ME)
U of Mary Hardin-Baylor (TX)
U of Maryland, Baltimore County (MD)
U of Michigan–Dearborn (MI)
U of Nebraska–Lincoln (NE)
U of Providence (MT)
U of Regina (SK, Canada)
U of St. Thomas (MN)
U of Sioux Falls (SD)
U of Wisconsin–Superior (WI)
Utah State U (UT)
Utah Valley U (UT)
Utica Coll (NY)
Valley City State U (ND)
Valparaiso U (IN)
Washington U in St. Louis (MO)
Waynesburg U (PA)
Weber State U (UT)
Western Washington U (WA)
Widener U (PA)

CHILD-CARE AND SUPPORT SERVICES MANAGEMENT
Framingham State U (MA)
Idaho State U (ID)
Manor Coll (PA)
Seton Hill U (PA)
Texas Tech U (TX)
The U of Texas Rio Grande Valley (TX)

CHILD DEVELOPMENT
Appalachian State U (NC)
Auburn U (AL)
Bowling Green State U (OH)
California State U, Long Beach (CA)
California State U, Northridge (CA)
Cameron U (OK)
Carson-Newman U (TN)
Central Michigan U (MI)
Coll of the Ozarks (MO)
Eastern Washington U (WA)
East Tennessee State U (TN)
Harding U (AR)
Humboldt State U (CA)
Kuyper Coll (MI)
Lesley U (MA)
Madonna U (MI)
Manor Coll (PA)
Michigan State U (MI)
Missouri Baptist U (MO)
Oklahoma Christian U (OK)
Point Loma Nazarene U (CA)
Point U (GA)
Portland State U (OR)
Seton Hill U (PA)
Texas Tech U (TX)
Texas Woman's U (TX)
U of Houston–Clear Lake (TX)
U of La Verne (CA)
U of Saint Mary (KS)
U of Virginia (VA)
Weber State U (UT)
Whittier Coll (CA)
Youngstown State U (OH)

CHILDREN'S AND ADOLESCENT LITERATURE
Central Michigan U (MI)

CHINESE
Beloit Coll (WI)
Boston U (MA)
Bryant U (RI)
California State U, Long Beach (CA)
California State U, Los Angeles (CA)
Calvin Coll (MI)
Carthage Coll (WI)
Colgate U (NY)
Coll of the Holy Cross (MA)
Davidson Coll (NC)
Hamilton Coll (NY)
Hofstra U (NY)
Hunter Coll of the City U of New York (NY)
Lawrence U (WI)
Macalester Coll (MN)
Messiah Coll (PA)
Michigan State U (MI)
Middlebury Coll (VT)
Nazareth Coll of Rochester (NY)
New Coll of Florida (FL)
Occidental Coll (CA)
The Ohio State U (OH)
Portland State U (OR)
Queens Coll of the City U of New York (NY)
St. Olaf Coll (MN)
San Francisco State U (CA)
San Jose State U (CA)
Sarah Lawrence Coll (NY)
Scripps Coll (CA)
Temple U (PA)
Union Coll (NY)
U of California, Davis (CA)
U of California, Los Angeles (CA)
U of Hawaii at Manoa (HI)
U of Houston (TX)
U of Kentucky (KY)
U of Maryland, Coll Park (MD)
U of Massachusetts Amherst (MA)
U of Notre Dame (IN)
U of Oregon (OR)
U of Pittsburgh (PA)
U of Puget Sound (WA)
U of Regina (SK, Canada)
U of Vermont (VT)
U of Washington (WA)
Vassar Coll (NY)
Washington State U (WA)
Washington U in St. Louis (MO)
Western Kentucky U (KY)
Western Washington U (WA)
Wheaton Coll (IL)
Whittier Coll (CA)
Williams Coll (MA)
Wofford Coll (SC)

CHINESE STUDIES
The Coll of William and Mary (VA)
DePaul U (IL)
Drew U (NJ)
Furman U (SC)
Pacific Lutheran U (WA)
U of California, Irvine (CA)
U of Minnesota, Duluth (MN)
U of North Dakota (ND)
U of Richmond (VA)
The U of Tulsa (OK)
U of Washington (WA)
Willamette U (OR)

CHRISTIAN STUDIES
Canisius Coll (NY)
The Coll of St. Scholastica (MN)
Coll of the Holy Cross (MA)
Gordon Coll (MA)
Hardin-Simmons U (TX)
Hillsdale Coll (MI)
Lee U (TN)
Liberty U (VA)
Louisiana Coll (LA)
Loyola U Chicago (IL)
Loyola U New Orleans (LA)
Marian U (IN)
Messenger Coll (TX)
Missouri Baptist U (MO)
Oklahoma Baptist U (OK)
Ouachita Baptist U (AR)
Point Loma Nazarene U (CA)
Roanoke Coll (VA)
Saint Mary's U of Minnesota (MN)
Stonehill Coll (MA)
Tabor Coll (KS)
Toccoa Falls Coll (GA)
U of Mary Hardin-Baylor (TX)
Whitworth U (WA)

CINEMATOGRAPHY AND FILM/VIDEO PRODUCTION
Acad of Art U (CA)
American U (DC)
California State U, Long Beach (CA)
California State U, Northridge (CA)
Capilano U (BC, Canada)
Central Washington U (WA)
Columbia Coll Chicago (IL)
DePaul U (IL)
Eastern Washington U (WA)
Emerson Coll (MA)
The Evergreen State Coll (WA)
Fashion Inst of Technology (NY)
FIDM/Fashion Inst of Design & Merchandising, Los Angeles Campus (CA)
Fitchburg State U (MA)
George Mason U (VA)
Goshen Coll (IN)
High Point U (NC)
Humboldt State U (CA)
Hunter Coll of the City U of New York (NY)
Ithaca Coll (NY)
John Paul the Great Catholic U (CA)
Kuyper Coll (MI)
La Sierra U (CA)
Lee U (TN)
Liberty U (VA)
Lindenwood U (MO)
Loyola Marymount U (CA)
Loyola U New Orleans (LA)
Maharishi U of Management (IA)
Marymount Manhattan Coll (NY)
Messiah Coll (PA)
Montclair State U (NJ)
New England Inst of Technology (RI)
New York U (NY)
Occidental Coll (CA)
Ohio U (OH)
Pace U, Pleasantville Campus (NY)
Palm Beach Atlantic U (FL)
Purchase Coll, State U of New York (NY)
Regent U (VA)
Rochester Inst of Technology (NY)
Sarah Lawrence Coll (NY)
Savannah Coll of Art and Design (GA)
Southeastern U (FL)
Southern Illinois U Carbondale (IL)
Syracuse U (NY)

Taylor U (IN)
Temple U (PA)
U of California, Riverside (CA)
U of Central Florida (FL)
U of North Carolina School of the Arts (NC)
U of Regina (SK, Canada)
Vanguard U of Southern California (CA)
Virginia Commonwealth U (VA)
Woodbury U (CA)

CITY/URBAN, COMMUNITY AND REGIONAL PLANNING
Appalachian State U (NC)
Bridgewater State U (MA)
California Polytechnic State U, San Luis Obispo (CA)
Cornell U (NY)
East Carolina U (NC)
Eastern Washington U (WA)
Florida Atlantic U (FL)
Indiana U of Pennsylvania (PA)
Iowa State U of Science and Technology (IA)
Jacksonville U (FL)
Massachusetts Inst of Technology (MA)
Miami U (OH)
Miami U Hamilton (OH)
Michigan State U (MI)
The Ohio State U (OH)
Portland State U (OR)
Salisbury U (MD)
Temple U (PA)
U of California, Davis (CA)
U of New Hampshire (NH)
U of Virginia (VA)
U of Washington (WA)
West Chester U of Pennsylvania (PA)

CIVIL ENGINEERING
American U of Beirut (Lebanon)
Angelo State U (TX)
Auburn U (AL)
Bradley U (IL)
Bucknell U (PA)
California Polytechnic State U, San Luis Obispo (CA)
California State U, Chico (CA)
California State U, Long Beach (CA)
California State U, Los Angeles (CA)
California State U, Northridge (CA)
Calvin Coll (MI)
Carnegie Mellon U (PA)
The Catholic U of America (DC)
Central Connecticut State U (CT)
Christian Brothers U (TN)
Clarkson U (NY)
Colorado School of Mines (CO)
Colorado State U (CO)
Columbia U (NY)
Cornell U (NY)
Florida Ag and Mech U (FL)
Florida Atlantic U (FL)
George Mason U (VA)
Georgia Southern U (GA)
Gonzaga U (WA)
Hofstra U (NY)
Idaho State U (ID)
Iowa State U of Science and Technology (IA)
Jackson State U (MS)
Johns Hopkins U (MD)
Kennesaw State U (GA)
King's Coll (PA)
Lafayette Coll (PA)
Lamar U (TX)
Lawrence Technological U (MI)
Lebanese American U (Lebanon)
LeTourneau U (TX)
Lipscomb U (TN)
Louisiana State U and A&M Coll (LA)
Loyola Marymount U (CA)
Manhattan Coll (NY)
Marquette U (WI)
Massachusetts Inst of Technology (MA)
Merrimack Coll (MA)
Messiah Coll (PA)
Michigan State U (MI)
New Jersey Inst of Technology (NJ)
New York U (NY)
North Carolina State U (NC)
Northwestern U (IL)
The Ohio State U (OH)
Ohio U (OH)
Oklahoma State U (OK)
Old Dominion U (VA)
Portland State U (OR)
Prairie View A&M U (TX)
Princeton U (NJ)
Purdue U (IN)
Purdue U Northwest (IN)
Rice U (TX)
Saint Louis U (MO)
Saint Martin's U (WA)
San Diego State U (CA)
San Francisco State U (CA)
San Jose State U (CA)
Seattle U (WA)
Southern Illinois U Carbondale (IL)
Southern Illinois U Edwardsville (IL)
Southern U and Ag and Mech Coll (LA)
Stevens Inst of Technology (NJ)
Syracuse U (NY)
Temple U (PA)
Texas Tech U (TX)
Université de Sherbrooke (QC, Canada)
U at Buffalo, the State U of New York (NY)
U of Arkansas (AR)
U of California, Davis (CA)
U of California, Irvine (CA)
U of California, Los Angeles (CA)
U of Central Florida (FL)
U of Colorado Denver (CO)
U of Dayton (OH)
U of Detroit Mercy (MI)
U of Florida (FL)
U of Georgia (GA)
U of Hawaii at Manoa (HI)
U of Houston (TX)
U of Idaho (ID)
U of Kentucky (KY)
U of Louisville (KY)
U of Maine (ME)
U of Maryland, Coll Park (MD)
U of Massachusetts Amherst (MA)
U of Massachusetts Dartmouth (MA)
U of Massachusetts Lowell (MA)
U of Memphis (TN)
U of Michigan (MI)
U of Minnesota, Duluth (MN)
U of Minnesota, Twin Cities Campus (MN)
U of Missouri (MO)
U of Mount Union (OH)
U of Nebraska–Lincoln (NE)
U of Nevada, Las Vegas (NV)
U of Nevada, Reno (NV)
U of New Hampshire (NH)
U of New Haven (CT)
U of New Mexico (NM)
The U of North Carolina at Charlotte (NC)
U of North Dakota (ND)
U of North Florida (FL)
U of Notre Dame (IN)
U of Pittsburgh (PA)
U of South Alabama (AL)
U of South Carolina (SC)
U of South Florida (FL)
The U of Tennessee (TN)
The U of Texas at Austin (TX)
The U of Texas at El Paso (TX)
The U of Texas Rio Grande Valley (TX)
The U of Toledo (OH)
U of Vermont (VT)
U of Virginia (VA)
U of Washington (WA)
U of Wisconsin–Milwaukee (WI)
U of Wyoming (WY)
Utah State U (UT)
Valparaiso U (IN)
Virginia Polytechnic Inst and State U (VA)
Washington State U (WA)
Washington State U–Tri-Cities (WA)
Western Kentucky U (KY)
West Virginia U Inst of Technology (WV)
Widener U (PA)
William Jewell Coll (MO)
Worcester Polytechnic Inst (MA)
Youngstown State U (OH)

CIVIL ENGINEERING RELATED
California Polytechnic State U, San Luis Obispo (CA)
Embry-Riddle Aeronautical U–Daytona (FL)

CIVIL ENGINEERING TECHNOLOGY
Cedarville U (OH)
Colorado State U–Pueblo (CO)
Idaho State U (ID)
Indiana State U (IN)
Murray State U (KY)
Rochester Inst of Technology (NY)
U of Houston–Downtown (TX)
U of Maine (ME)
U of Maryland Eastern Shore (MD)
U of Massachusetts Lowell (MA)
The U of North Carolina at Charlotte (NC)
Youngstown State U (OH)

CLASSICAL, ANCIENT MEDITERRANEAN AND NEAR EASTERN STUDIES AND ARCHAEOLOGY
Baylor U (TX)
Butler U (IN)
Calvin Coll (MI)
Colgate U (NY)
Hanover Coll (IN)
Kalamazoo Coll (MI)
Lycoming Coll (PA)
Randolph-Macon Coll (VA)
Saint Anselm Coll (NH)
Syracuse U (NY)
U of California, Davis (CA)
U of California, Los Angeles (CA)
U of Michigan (MI)
U of St. Thomas (MN)

CLASSICS AND CLASSICAL LANGUAGES
Acadia U (NS, Canada)
Agnes Scott Coll (GA)
Austin Coll (TX)
Baylor U (TX)
Beloit Coll (WI)
Boston Coll (MA)
Boston U (MA)
Bowling Green State U (OH)
Brandeis U (MA)
Bucknell U (PA)
Carthage Coll (WI)
The Catholic U of America (DC)
Christopher Newport U (VA)
Claremont McKenna Coll (CA)
Clark U (MA)
Colgate U (NY)
Coll of Charleston (SC)
Coll of Saint Benedict (MN)
Coll of the Holy Cross (MA)
The Coll of William and Mary (VA)
The Colorado Coll (CO)
Columbia U (NY)
Connecticut Coll (CT)
Cornell Coll (IA)
Cornell U (NY)
Creighton U (NE)
Dartmouth Coll (NH)
Davidson Coll (NC)
Dickinson Coll (PA)
Drew U (NJ)
Duquesne U (PA)
Earlham Coll (IN)
The Evergreen State Coll (WA)
Fordham U (NY)
Furman U (SC)
Grand Valley State U (MI)
Hamilton Coll (NY)
Hampden-Sydney Coll (VA)
Hanover Coll (IN)
Harvard U (MA)
Haverford Coll (PA)
Hillsdale Coll (MI)
Hofstra U (NY)
Hollins U (VA)
Hunter Coll of the City U of New York (NY)
Indiana U Bloomington (IN)
John Cabot U (Italy)
Johns Hopkins U (MD)
Knox Coll (IL)
Lawrence U (WI)
Lewis & Clark Coll (OR)
Loyola U Chicago (IL)
Macalester Coll (MN)
Manhattan Coll (NY)
Marquette U (WI)
Mercer U, Macon (GA)
Miami U (OH)
Miami U Hamilton (OH)
Middlebury Coll (VT)
Millsaps Coll (MS)
Montclair State U (NJ)
New York U (NY)
Northwestern U (IL)
The Ohio State U (OH)
Ohio U (OH)
Ohio Wesleyan U (OH)
Pitzer Coll (CA)
Princeton U (NJ)
Queens Coll of the City U of New York (NY)
Randolph Coll (VA)
Randolph-Macon Coll (VA)
Rice U (TX)
Rockford U (IL)
Saint Anselm Coll (NH)
Saint John's U (MN)
Saint Joseph's U (PA)
Saint Louis U (MO)
St. Olaf Coll (MN)
Samford U (AL)
San Diego State U (CA)
San Francisco State U (CA)
Scripps Coll (CA)
Skidmore Coll (NY)
Southwestern U (TX)
Sweet Briar Coll (VA)
Syracuse U (NY)
Temple U (PA)
Texas Tech U (TX)
Truman State U (MO)
Tulane U (LA)
Union Coll (NY)
U at Buffalo, the State U of New York (NY)
U of Arkansas (AR)
U of California, Irvine (CA)
U of California, Santa Cruz (CA)
U of Chicago (IL)
U of Dallas (TX)
U of Florida (FL)
U of Georgia (GA)
U of Hawaii at Manoa (HI)
U of Kentucky (KY)
U of Maryland, Coll Park (MD)
U of Massachusetts Amherst (MA)
U of Massachusetts Boston (MA)
U of Michigan (MI)
U of Minnesota, Twin Cities Campus (MN)
U of Missouri (MO)
U of Nebraska–Lincoln (NE)
U of New Hampshire (NH)
U of New Mexico (NM)
U of North Carolina at Asheville (NC)
The U of North Carolina at Chapel Hill (NC)
The U of North Carolina at Greensboro (NC)
U of North Dakota (ND)
U of Notre Dame (IN)
U of Oregon (OR)
U of Pennsylvania (PA)
U of Pittsburgh (PA)
U of Puget Sound (WA)
U of St. Thomas (MN)
U of South Carolina (SC)
U of South Florida (FL)
The U of Tennessee (TN)
The U of Texas at Austin (TX)
The U of the South (TN)
U of Vermont (VT)
U of Virginia (VA)
U of Washington (WA)
U of Wisconsin–Milwaukee (WI)
Valparaiso U (IN)
Vassar Coll (NY)
Wabash Coll (IN)
Washington and Lee U (VA)
Washington U in St. Louis (MO)
Wesleyan U (CT)
Willamette U (OR)
Williams Coll (MA)

CLASSICS AND CLASSICAL LANGUAGES RELATED
Austin Coll (TX)
California State U, Long Beach (CA)
Eckerd Coll (FL)
Gonzaga U (WA)
Lee U (TN)
Loyola U New Orleans (LA)
Marquette U (WI)
New Coll of Florida (FL)
Ohio U (OH)
Providence Coll (RI)
Tulane U (LA)
U of California, Los Angeles (CA)
Wheaton Coll (IL)
Wheaton Coll (MA)

CLINICAL LABORATORY SCIENCE/MEDICAL TECHNOLOGY
Arkansas Tech U (AR)
Auburn U (AL)
Austin Peay State U (TN)
Baylor U (TX)
Bellarmine U (KY)
Benedictine U (IL)
Blackburn Coll (IL)
Bowling Green State U (OH)
Bradley U (IL)
Caldwell U (NJ)
Campbellsville U (KY)
Canisius Coll (NY)
The Catholic U of America (DC)
Clarion U of Pennsylvania (PA)
The Coll at Brockport, State U of New York (NY)
Coll of Saint Mary (NE)
The Coll of Saint Rose (NY)
Coll of Staten Island of the City U of New York (NY)
Coll of the Ozarks (MO)
DePaul U (IL)
East Carolina U (NC)
Eastern Illinois U (IL)
Eastern Mennonite U (VA)
East Stroudsburg U of Pennsylvania (PA)
Farmingdale State Coll (NY)
Florida Southern Coll (FL)
George Mason U (VA)
Hartwick Coll (NY)
Idaho State U (ID)
Illinois Coll (IL)
Indiana State U (IN)
Indiana U of Pennsylvania (PA)
Indiana U–Purdue U Indianapolis (IN)
Indiana U South Bend (IN)
Indiana U Southeast (IN)
Inter American U of Puerto Rico, San Germán Campus (PR)
Jacksonville U (FL)
Kean U (NJ)
King's Coll (PA)
Lebanon Valley Coll (PA)
Louisiana Coll (LA)
Manchester U (IN)
Mansfield U of Pennsylvania (PA)
Marian U (IN)
Marist Coll (NY)
Marquette U (WI)
Marshall U (WV)
Maryville U of Saint Louis (MO)
Marywood U (PA)
McNeese State U (LA)
Mercy Coll (NY)
Miami U (OH)
Miami U Hamilton (OH)
Michigan State U (MI)
Morningside Coll (IA)
Mount Marty Coll (SD)
Muskingum U (OH)
National U (CA)
Nazareth Coll of Rochester (NY)
Northeastern State U (OK)
Northern Illinois U (IL)
Northern State U (SD)
Northwest Missouri State U (MO)
The Ohio State U (OH)
Oklahoma Christian U (OK)
Old Dominion U (VA)
Purdue U (IN)
Purdue U Northwest (IN)
Rochester Inst of Technology (NY)
Saginaw Valley State U (MI)
Saint Francis U (PA)
St. Joseph's Coll, Long Island Campus (NY)
St. Joseph's Coll, New York (NY)
Saint Louis U (MO)
Saint Mary's U of Minnesota (MN)
Salisbury U (MD)

Salve Regina U (RI)
Seton Hill U (PA)
Southeast Missouri State U (MO)
Southern Arkansas U–Magnolia (AR)
Southwest Baptist U (MO)
State U of New York at Fredonia (NY)
State U of New York at Plattsburgh (NY)
Sullivan U (KY)
Texas Woman's U (TX)
U at Buffalo, the State U of New York (NY)
U of Central Florida (FL)
The U of Findlay (OH)
U of Hawaii at Manoa (HI)
U of Illinois at Springfield (IL)
U of Kentucky (KY)
U of Maine (ME)
U of Massachusetts Dartmouth (MA)
U of Massachusetts Lowell (MA)
U of Mount Union (OH)
The U of North Carolina at Chapel Hill (NC)
U of North Dakota (ND)
U of Regina (SK, Canada)
U of Saint Francis (IN)
U of Sioux Falls (SD)
U of South Dakota (SD)
U of South Florida (FL)
The U of Tennessee (TN)
The U of Texas at Austin (TX)
The U of Texas at El Paso (TX)
The U of Texas Rio Grande Valley (TX)
The U of Toledo (OH)
U of Vermont (VT)
U of Washington (WA)
U of Wisconsin–La Crosse (WI)
U of Wisconsin–Milwaukee (WI)
U of Wyoming (WY)
Utah State U (UT)
Valley City State U (ND)
Virginia Commonwealth U (VA)
Wartburg Coll (IA)
Western Connecticut State U (CT)
Western Illinois U (IL)
Western Kentucky U (KY)
Wilkes U (PA)
Wright State U–Lake Campus (OH)
Youngstown State U (OH)

CLINICAL/MEDICAL LABORATORY ASSISTANT
Baptist Coll of Health Sciences (TN)

CLINICAL/MEDICAL LABORATORY SCIENCE AND ALLIED PROFESSIONS RELATED
Allen Coll (IA)
Auburn U (AL)
The Coll of Idaho (ID)
East Texas Baptist U (TX)
Gwynedd Mercy U (PA)
Hunter Coll of the City U of New York (NY)
New Jersey Inst of Technology (NJ)
Saint Louis U (MO)
U of Idaho (ID)
U of Massachusetts Lowell (MA)
U of Minnesota, Twin Cities Campus (MN)
U of Saint Mary (KS)

CLINICAL/MEDICAL LABORATORY TECHNOLOGY
Auburn U (AL)
Auburn U at Montgomery (AL)
Boston U (MA)
Rhode Island Coll (RI)
U of New Mexico (NM)
Weber State U (UT)

CLINICAL NURSE SPECIALIST
LeTourneau U (TX)

CLINICAL NUTRITION
La Salle U (PA)
Life U (GA)
Southern Illinois U Edwardsville (IL)
U of North Dakota (ND)

CLINICAL PSYCHOLOGY
Redeemer U Coll (ON, Canada)
U of Mary Hardin-Baylor (TX)

COGNITIVE PSYCHOLOGY AND PSYCHOLINGUISTICS
Dartmouth Coll (NH)
Fitchburg State U (MA)
Northwestern U (IL)
Scripps Coll (CA)
Tulane U (LA)
Vassar Coll (NY)
Washington U in St. Louis (MO)

COGNITIVE SCIENCE
Carnegie Mellon U (PA)
Indiana U Bloomington (IN)
Johns Hopkins U (MD)
Loyola U New Orleans (LA)
Massachusetts Inst of Technology (MA)
Millsaps Coll (MS)
Occidental Coll (CA)
Sarah Lawrence Coll (NY)
U of California, Irvine (CA)
U of California, Los Angeles (CA)
U of California, Merced (CA)
U of California, Santa Cruz (CA)
U of Georgia (GA)
U of Michigan (MI)
U of Pennsylvania (PA)
U of Richmond (VA)
Virginia Polytechnic Inst and State U (VA)
Washington U in St. Louis (MO)

COLLEGE STUDENT COUNSELING AND PERSONNEL SERVICES
Bowling Green State U (OH)

COMMERCIAL AND ADVERTISING ART
Acad of Art U (CA)
Bethel Coll (KS)
Bowling Green State U (OH)
Buena Vista U (IA)
California State U, Long Beach (CA)
California U of Pennsylvania (PA)
Carson-Newman U (TN)
Clark U (MA)
The Coll of Saint Rose (NY)
Columbia Coll Chicago (IL)
Dallas Baptist U (TX)
Dominican U (IL)
Drake U (IA)
Fashion Inst of Technology (NY)
Jacksonville U (FL)
Lipscomb U (TN)
Lycoming Coll (PA)
Marymount Manhattan Coll (NY)
Mercy Coll (NY)
Miami U (OH)
Millikin U (IL)
Minnesota State U Moorhead (MN)
New York U (NY)
Oklahoma Christian U (OK)
Pennsylvania Coll of Art & Design (PA)
Portland State U (OR)
Purchase Coll, State U of New York (NY)
Rochester Inst of Technology (NY)
St. Norbert Coll (WI)
Seattle U (WA)
Seton Hill U (PA)
Southwest Baptist U (MO)
State U of New York at Fredonia (NY)
Syracuse U (NY)
U of Maryland Eastern Shore (MD)
U of Minnesota, Duluth (MN)
The U of Tennessee (TN)
The U of Texas at El Paso (TX)
Wartburg Coll (IA)
Washington U in St. Louis (MO)
Waynesburg U (PA)
Woodbury U (CA)

COMMERCIAL PHOTOGRAPHY
Appalachian State U (NC)
Dallas Baptist U (TX)
Fashion Inst of Technology (NY)
Framingham State U (MA)
Rochester Inst of Technology (NY)

COMMUNICATION
Albion Coll (MI)
Albright Coll (PA)
Averett U (VA)
Bethany Lutheran Coll (MN)
Bethel U (MN)
Blackburn Coll (IL)
Boston Coll (MA)
Boston U (MA)
Bradley U (IL)
Brenau U (GA)
California State U, Northridge (CA)
Carthage Coll (WI)
Centenary Coll of Louisiana (LA)
Central Washington U (WA)
Coll of the Ozarks (MO)
Columbia Coll Chicago (IL)
Concordia U Irvine (CA)
Cornell U (NY)
DePaul U (IL)
DEREE - The American Coll of Greece (Greece)
Drury U (MO)
Eastern Illinois U (IL)
Florida Coll (FL)
Fordham U (NY)
Geneva Coll (PA)
Gonzaga U (WA)
Goshen Coll (IN)
High Point U (NC)
Hiram Coll (OH)
John Cabot U (Italy)
Kansas Wesleyan U (KS)
Lake Forest Coll (IL)
Lamar U (TX)
La Salle U (PA)
Lasell Coll (MA)
Lebanese American U (Lebanon)
Liberty U (VA)
Limestone Coll (SC)
Lincoln Christian U (IL)
Lycoming Coll (PA)
Marist Coll (NY)
Marquette U (WI)
Marymount Manhattan Coll (NY)
Marymount U (VA)
Massachusetts Coll of Liberal Arts (MA)
Miami U (OH)
Michigan State U (MI)
Milligan Coll (TN)
Northwest Christian U (OR)
Northwest Missouri State U (MO)
Oakland City U (IN)
Oglethorpe U (GA)
Ouachita Baptist U (AR)
Pepperdine U, Malibu (CA)
Portland State U (OR)
Purchase Coll, State U of New York (NY)
Purdue U (IN)
Queens U of Charlotte (NC)
Randolph-Macon Coll (VA)
Regent U (VA)
Reinhardt U (GA)
Roanoke Coll (VA)
Sacred Heart U (CT)
Saint Anselm Coll (NH)
St. John Fisher Coll (NY)
Saint Joseph's U (PA)
Saint Louis U (MO)
Saint Martin's U (WA)
Southeastern U (FL)
Spring Hill Coll (AL)
Stetson U (FL)
Taylor U (IN)
Toccoa Falls Coll (GA)
Towson U (MD)
U of Houston–Clear Lake (TX)
U of Illinois at Springfield (IL)
U of Maine (ME)
U of Mary Hardin-Baylor (TX)
U of Massachusetts Amherst (MA)
U of Massachusetts Boston (MA)
U of Mount Union (OH)
U of North Dakota (ND)
U of Saint Francis (IN)
U of San Diego (CA)
The U of Tampa (FL)
The U of Tennessee at Martin (TN)
The U of Texas of the Permian Basin (TX)
U of Wisconsin–Eau Claire (WI)
Valparaiso U (IN)
Wesleyan Coll (GA)
Whitworth U (WA)
Woodbury U (CA)
Youngstown State U (OH)

COMMUNICATION AND JOURNALISM RELATED
Auburn U (AL)
Benedictine U (IL)
Boston U (MA)
Bowling Green State U (OH)
Buena Vista U (IA)
California Lutheran U (CA)
Endicott Coll (MA)
Farmingdale State Coll (NY)
Immaculata U (PA)
Madonna U (MI)
Manhattanville Coll (NY)
Marquette U (WI)
Merrimack Coll (MA)
The Ohio State U (OH)
Oklahoma Christian U (OK)
Pepperdine U, Malibu (CA)
Sacred Heart U (CT)
Trevecca Nazarene U (TN)
U of Guam (GU)
U of Minnesota, Duluth (MN)
U of Minnesota, Twin Cities Campus (MN)
Valparaiso U (IN)
Virginia Polytechnic Inst and State U (VA)
Washington U in St. Louis (MO)
Western Illinois U (IL)

COMMUNICATION AND MEDIA RELATED
Acad of Art U (CA)
Adelphi U (NY)
Auburn U (AL)
Austin Coll (TX)
Butler U (IN)
Cameron U (OK)
Canisius Coll (NY)
Carthage Coll (WI)
The Coll of Saint Rose (NY)
Curry Coll (MA)
DePaul U (IL)
Georgetown Coll (KY)
Granite State Coll (NH)
Greenville U (IL)
Hood Coll (MD)
Judson U (IL)
Kennesaw State U (GA)
King's Coll (PA)
King U (TN)
Lasell Coll (MA)
Lees-McRae Coll (NC)
Loyola U Chicago (IL)
Lycoming Coll (PA)
Marquette U (WI)
Marymount Manhattan Coll (NY)
Milligan Coll (TN)
Missouri Baptist U (MO)
Molloy Coll (NY)
Montclair State U (NJ)
New Jersey Inst of Technology (NJ)
New York U (NY)
Northwestern U (IL)
Pace U (NY)
Pace U, Pleasantville Campus (NY)
Pitzer Coll (CA)
Reinhardt U (GA)
Rochester Inst of Technology (NY)
Rollins Coll (FL)
Saint Francis U (PA)
Salve Regina U (RI)
Université de Sherbrooke (QC, Canada)
U of Oregon (OR)
The U of West Alabama (AL)
Washington & Jefferson Coll (PA)

COMMUNICATION DISORDERS SCIENCES AND SERVICES RELATED
Marquette U (WI)
Ouachita Baptist U (AR)
U of New Hampshire (NH)

COMMUNICATION SCIENCES AND DISORDERS
Appalachian State U (NC)
Auburn U (AL)
Baldwin Wallace U (OH)
Baylor U (TX)
Bowling Green State U (OH)
Bridgewater State U (MA)
Butler U (IN)
California State U, Chico (CA)
California State U, Fullerton (CA)
California State U, Long Beach (CA)
California State U, Los Angeles (CA)
California State U, Northridge (CA)
California U of Pennsylvania (PA)
Central Michigan U (MI)
Eastern Illinois U (IL)
Emerson Coll (MA)
Harding U (AR)
Ithaca Coll (NY)
Jacksonville U (FL)
Lamar U (TX)
La Salle U (PA)
Lebanon Valley Coll (PA)
Maryville U of Saint Louis (MO)
Northern Illinois U (IL)
Northwestern U (IL)
Pace U (NY)
Portland State U (OR)
Queens Coll of the City U of New York (NY)
Radford U (VA)
Rhode Island Coll (RI)
Saint Louis U (MO)
Samford U (AL)
San Diego State U (CA)
San Francisco State U (CA)
San Jose State U (CA)
Southeastern U (FL)
Southeast Missouri State U (MO)
Southern Illinois U Carbondale (IL)
State U of New York at Fredonia (NY)
Syracuse U (NY)
Texas A&M Intl U (TX)
Texas Woman's U (TX)
Truman State U (MO)
U of Georgia (GA)
U of Houston (TX)
U of Maine (ME)
U of Maryland, Coll Park (MD)
U of Massachusetts Amherst (MA)
U of Minnesota, Duluth (MN)
U of North Dakota (ND)
U of Oregon (OR)
U of South Alabama (AL)
U of South Dakota (SD)
U of South Florida Sarasota-Manatee (FL)
The U of Texas at Austin (TX)
The U of Texas Rio Grande Valley (TX)
U of Vermont (VT)
U of Wisconsin–Eau Claire (WI)
U of Wisconsin–River Falls (WI)
Western Illinois U (IL)
Western Kentucky U (KY)
Western Washington U (WA)
Winthrop U (SC)
Worcester State U (MA)

COMMUNICATIONS TECHNOLOGIES AND SUPPORT SERVICES RELATED
Alverno Coll (WI)
Framingham State U (MA)
Lesley U (MA)
Trinity Christian Coll (IL)

COMMUNICATIONS TECHNOLOGY
East Stroudsburg U of Pennsylvania (PA)
Inter American U of Puerto Rico, Bayamón Campus (PR)
Messiah Coll (PA)

COMMUNITY HEALTH AND PREVENTIVE MEDICINE
Bowling Green State U (OH)
Canisius Coll (NY)
George Mason U (VA)
Georgia Coll & State U (GA)
Hofstra U (NY)
Indiana U Bloomington (IN)
Mansfield U of Pennsylvania (PA)
Murray State U (KY)
National U (CA)
Portland State U (OR)
U of Florida (FL)
U of La Verne (CA)
U of Maryland, Coll Park (MD)
U of the Incarnate Word (TX)
U of Wisconsin–Eau Claire (WI)
U of Wisconsin–La Crosse (WI)
Western Kentucky U (KY)

COMMUNITY HEALTH SERVICES COUNSELING
Canisius Coll (NY)

Central Michigan U (MI)
Eastern Washington U (WA)
Indiana State U (IN)
Johnson C. Smith U (NC)
Massachusetts Coll of Liberal Arts (MA)
Ohio U (OH)
Rhode Island Coll (RI)
U of Central Arkansas (AR)
U of Maine at Farmington (ME)
U of Massachusetts Lowell (MA)
U of Pennsylvania (PA)
Western Connecticut State U (CT)
Western Washington U (WA)
Whitworth U (WA)
Worcester State U (MA)
Wright State U–Lake Campus (OH)
Youngstown State U (OH)

COMMUNITY ORGANIZATION AND ADVOCACY
Acadia U (NS, Canada)
Allegheny Coll (PA)
Alverno Coll (WI)
Bryant U (RI)
Central Michigan U (MI)
Madonna U (MI)
Nazareth Coll of Rochester (NY)
New York U (NY)
Northwestern U (IL)
Providence Coll (RI)
Saint Louis U (MO)
Southern Arkansas U–Magnolia (AR)
U of California, Santa Cruz (CA)
U of Massachusetts Boston (MA)
West Virginia U Inst of Technology (WV)

COMMUNITY PSYCHOLOGY
Northwestern U (IL)
U of Washington, Bothell (WA)

COMPARATIVE LITERATURE
Beloit Coll (WI)
Boston U (MA)
Brandeis U (MA)
California State U, Fullerton (CA)
California State U, Long Beach (CA)
Clark U (MA)
Coll of the Holy Cross (MA)
The Colorado Coll (CO)
Columbia U (NY)
Cornell U (NY)
Dartmouth Coll (NH)
Eckerd Coll (FL)
Fordham U (NY)
Harvard U (MA)
Haverford Coll (PA)
Hillsdale Coll (MI)
Hofstra U (NY)
Hunter Coll of the City U of New York (NY)
Indiana U Bloomington (IN)
Inter American U of Puerto Rico, San Germán Campus (PR)
Lycoming Coll (PA)
Manchester U (IN)
Middlebury Coll (VT)
New York U (NY)
Northwestern U (IL)
The Ohio State U (OH)
Ohio Wesleyan U (OH)
Princeton U (NJ)
Purdue U (IN)
Queens Coll of the City U of New York (NY)
Rockford U (IL)
San Diego State U (CA)
San Francisco State U (CA)
Sarah Lawrence Coll (NY)
Sonoma State U (CA)
State U of New York Coll at Geneseo (NY)
U of California, Davis (CA)
U of California, Irvine (CA)
U of California, Los Angeles (CA)
U of California, Merced (CA)
U of California, Santa Cruz (CA)
U of Chicago (IL)
U of Georgia (GA)
U of Massachusetts Amherst (MA)
U of Michigan (MI)
U of Minnesota, Twin Cities Campus (MN)
U of New Mexico (NM)
U of Oregon (OR)
U of Pennsylvania (PA)
U of St. Thomas (MN)
U of San Francisco (CA)
U of South Carolina (SC)
U of Virginia (VA)
U of Washington (WA)
U of Wisconsin–Milwaukee (WI)
Washington U in St. Louis (MO)
Willamette U (OR)
Williams Coll (MA)

COMPUTATIONAL AND APPLIED MATHEMATICS
American Public U System (WV)
Bryant U (RI)
Maryville U of Saint Louis (MO)
Purdue U (IN)
U of Notre Dame (IN)
Virginia Polytechnic Inst and State U (VA)
William Jewell Coll (MO)

COMPUTATIONAL BIOLOGY
Lipscomb U (TN)
Massachusetts Inst of Technology (MA)

COMPUTATIONAL MATHEMATICS
California Inst of Technology (CA)
Carnegie Mellon U (PA)
Christopher Newport U (VA)
Coll of Saint Benedict (MN)
Embry-Riddle Aeronautical U–Daytona (FL)
Loyola U New Orleans (LA)
Marquette U (WI)
Michigan State U (MI)
The Ohio State U (OH)
Rochester Inst of Technology (NY)
Saint John's U (MN)
Southwestern U (TX)
U of California, Davis (CA)
U of California, Los Angeles (CA)
U of Washington (WA)

COMPUTATIONAL SCIENCE
American U (DC)
Canisius Coll (NY)
Colorado State U (CO)
Hood Coll (MD)
Mercer U, Macon (GA)
Temple U (PA)
U of Michigan–Dearborn (MI)
U of Wisconsin–River Falls (WI)
Washington State U (WA)
Washington State U–Vancouver (WA)

COMPUTER AND INFORMATION SCIENCES
Adelphi U (NY)
Albright Coll (PA)
Alverno Coll (WI)
American U (DC)
American U in Bulgaria (Bulgaria)
Angelo State U (TX)
Arkansas Tech U (AR)
Assumption Coll (MA)
Auburn U (AL)
Avila U (MO)
Bellarmine U (KY)
Bennett Coll (NC)
Bentley U (MA)
Berea Coll (KY)
Bethel U (MN)
Boston Coll (MA)
Bowling Green State U (OH)
Bradley U (IL)
Brandman U (CA)
Bryant U (RI)
Bucknell U (PA)
Butler U (IN)
Caldwell U (NJ)
California Lutheran U (CA)
California U of Pennsylvania (PA)
Carthage Coll (WI)
The Catholic U of America (DC)
Central Connecticut State U (CT)
Champlain Coll (VT)
Clarion U of Pennsylvania (PA)
Coastal Carolina U (SC)
The Coll at Brockport, State U of New York (NY)
Coll of Charleston (SC)
The Coll of St. Scholastica (MN)
The Coll of William and Mary (VA)
Colorado State U (CO)
Concordia U Chicago (IL)
Cornell U (NY)
Covenant Coll (GA)
Curry Coll (MA)
Dakota State U (SD)
Dallas Baptist U (TX)
Davidson Coll (NC)
DEREE - The American Coll of Greece (Greece)
Eastern Oregon U (OR)
Eastern Washington U (WA)
East Stroudsburg U of Pennsylvania (PA)
East Tennessee State U (TN)
Emmanuel Coll (GA)
The Evergreen State Coll (WA)
Fairfield U (CT)
Fitchburg State U (MA)
Florida Ag and Mech U (FL)
Florida Atlantic U (FL)
Fordham U (NY)
Framingham State U (MA)
Geneva Coll (PA)
George Mason U (VA)
Georgia Southern U (GA)
Georgia State U (GA)
Graceland U (IA)
Grand Valley State U (MI)
Greenville U (IL)
Gwynedd Mercy U (PA)
Hamilton Coll (NY)
Hartwick Coll (NY)
Hiram Coll (OH)
Indiana State U (IN)
Indiana U of Pennsylvania (PA)
Inter American U of Puerto Rico, Fajardo Campus (PR)
Ithaca Coll (NY)
Jackson State U (MS)
Jacksonville U (FL)
Johns Hopkins U (MD)
Johnson C. Smith U (NC)
Judson U (IL)
Juniata Coll (PA)
Kalamazoo Coll (MI)
Kean U (NJ)
Kennesaw State U (GA)
King's Coll (PA)
Lamar U (TX)
La Salle U (PA)
Lebanon Valley Coll (PA)
Liberty U (VA)
Lindenwood U (MO)
Lock Haven U of Pennsylvania (PA)
Loyola Marymount U (CA)
Loyola U Chicago (IL)
Loyola U New Orleans (LA)
Lubbock Christian U (TX)
Macalester Coll (MN)
Manor Coll (PA)
Mansfield U of Pennsylvania (PA)
Marist Coll (NY)
Marquette U (WI)
Marshall U (WV)
Massachusetts Coll of Liberal Arts (MA)
McDaniel Coll (MD)
Mercy Coll (NY)
Miami U (OH)
Michigan State U (MI)
Millersville U of Pennsylvania (PA)
Milligan Coll (TN)
Mills Coll (CA)
Molloy Coll (NY)
Montclair State U (NJ)
Mount St. Joseph U (OH)
New England Coll (NH)
New England Inst of Technology (RI)
New Jersey City U (NJ)
New Jersey Inst of Technology (NJ)
New York U (NY)
Northern Kentucky U (KY)
Northwestern U (IL)
Northwest Missouri State U (MO)
Northwood U, Michigan Campus (MI)
Occidental Coll (CA)
The Ohio State U (OH)
Ohio U (OH)
Oklahoma Baptist U (OK)
Oklahoma State U (OK)
Old Dominion U (VA)
Pace U (NY)
Pace U, Pleasantville Campus (NY)
Palm Beach Atlantic U (FL)
Portland State U (OR)
Prairie View A&M U (TX)
Regis U (CO)
Rhode Island Coll (RI)
Rice U (TX)
Rider U (NJ)
Rochester Inst of Technology (NY)
Rollins Coll (FL)
Sacred Heart U (CT)
Saginaw Valley State U (MI)
St. John Fisher Coll (NY)
Saint Leo U (FL)
Saint Louis U (MO)
St. Mary's Coll of Maryland (MD)
St. Mary's U (TX)
St. Norbert Coll (WI)
Saint Vincent Coll (PA)
Salisbury U (MD)
Skidmore Coll (NY)
Southeast Missouri State U (MO)
Southern Arkansas U–Magnolia (AR)
Southern Illinois U Edwardsville (IL)
Southwest Baptist U (MO)
Southwestern U (TX)
Spring Hill Coll (AL)
State U of New York at Plattsburgh (NY)
State U of New York Coll at Potsdam (NY)
Stetson U (FL)
Stockton U (NJ)
Syracuse U (NY)
Temple U (PA)
Texas A&M U–Central Texas (TX)
Texas Christian U (TX)
Texas Tech U (TX)
Texas Woman's U (TX)
Tiffin U (OH)
Trinity Christian Coll (IL)
Truman State U (MO)
Tulane U (LA)
Union Coll (NY)
U of Arkansas (AR)
U of California, Irvine (CA)
U of California, Los Angeles (CA)
U of Central Arkansas (AR)
U of Central Florida (FL)
U of Colorado Denver (CO)
U of Dayton (OH)
The U of Findlay (OH)
U of Florida (FL)
U of Hawaii at Manoa (HI)
U of Houston (TX)
U of Houston–Clear Lake (TX)
U of Houston–Downtown (TX)
U of Kentucky (KY)
U of La Verne (CA)
U of Mary Hardin-Baylor (TX)
U of Maryland Eastern Shore (MD)
U of Maryland U Coll (MD)
U of Massachusetts Boston (MA)
U of Massachusetts Dartmouth (MA)
U of Michigan (MI)
U of Michigan–Dearborn (MI)
U of Missouri (MO)
U of Nebraska–Lincoln (NE)
U of Nevada, Reno (NV)
U of New Hampshire (NH)
U of New Haven (CT)
U of New Mexico (NM)
U of North Dakota (ND)
U of North Florida (FL)
U of Notre Dame (IN)
U of Oregon (OR)
U of Providence (MT)
U of Puerto Rico–Bayamón (PR)
U of Puget Sound (WA)
U of Richmond (VA)
U of Saint Mary (KS)
U of San Francisco (CA)
U of South Carolina (SC)
U of South Carolina Aiken (SC)
U of South Dakota (SD)
U of Southern Indiana (IN)
U of South Florida (FL)
The U of Tampa (FL)
The U of Texas at Austin (TX)
The U of Texas of the Permian Basin (TX)
U of the Incarnate Word (TX)
U of Virginia (VA)
U of Washington, Bothell (WA)
U of Washington, Tacoma (WA)
U of West Georgia (GA)
U of Wisconsin–Eau Claire (WI)
U of Wisconsin–La Crosse (WI)
U of Wisconsin–Milwaukee (WI)
U of Wisconsin–River Falls (WI)
Utah State U (UT)
Utica Coll (NY)
Valley City State U (ND)
Vassar Coll (NY)
Virginia Commonwealth U (VA)
Virginia Polytechnic Inst and State U (VA)
Wartburg Coll (IA)
Washington State U (WA)
Washington State U–Tri-Cities (WA)
Washington U in St. Louis (MO)
Waynesburg U (PA)
Weber State U (UT)
West Chester U of Pennsylvania (PA)
Western Illinois U (IL)
Western Kentucky U (KY)
Western Washington U (WA)
Westmont Coll (CA)
West Virginia U Inst of Technology (WV)
Widener U (PA)
Wilkes U (PA)
Willamette U (OR)
Winthrop U (SC)
Worcester State U (MA)
Wright State U–Lake Campus (OH)
Youngstown State U (OH)

COMPUTER AND INFORMATION SCIENCES AND SUPPORT SERVICES RELATED
Amridge U (AL)
Coll of Staten Island of the City U of New York (NY)
DePaul U (IL)
Hofstra U (NY)
Limestone Coll (SC)
Marshall U (WV)
New York U (NY)
U of Northern Iowa (IA)
U of Notre Dame (IN)
U of Pittsburgh (PA)
U of Providence (MT)
U of Washington, Bothell (WA)
Utah State U (UT)
Washington U in St. Louis (MO)

COMPUTER AND INFORMATION SCIENCES RELATED
Buena Vista U (IA)
California State U, Monterey Bay (CA)
Carnegie Mellon U (PA)
Coll of Charleston (SC)
The Colorado Coll (CO)
Eastern Illinois U (IL)
Gwynedd Mercy U (PA)
Hofstra U (NY)
Limestone Coll (SC)
Miami U Hamilton (OH)
Northern Kentucky U (KY)
Taylor U (IN)
Temple U (PA)
Université de Sherbrooke (QC, Canada)
U of New Haven (CT)
U of Northern Iowa (IA)
U of Providence (MT)

COMPUTER AND INFORMATION SYSTEMS SECURITY
American Public U System (WV)
Arkansas Tech U (AR)
Assumption Coll (MA)
Aurora U (IL)
Bentley U (MA)
Central Connecticut State U (CT)
Central Washington U (WA)
Columbia Southern U (AL)
Dakota State U (SD)
Davenport U, Grand Rapids (MI)
DePaul U (IL)
East Stroudsburg U of Pennsylvania (PA)
Excelsior Coll (NY)
Fort Lewis Coll (CO)
Hofstra U (NY)
Immaculata U (PA)
Iona Coll (NY)
Kennesaw State U (GA)
LeTourneau U (TX)
Limestone Coll (SC)

Lindenwood U (MO)
Lipscomb U (TN)
Loyola U Chicago (IL)
Marshall U (WV)
Marywood U (PA)
Mercy Coll (NY)
Messiah Coll (PA)
Northwest Missouri State U (MO)
Old Dominion U (VA)
Point U (GA)
Radford U (VA)
Randolph-Macon Coll (VA)
Rochester Inst of Technology (NY)
Sacred Heart U (CT)
Saint Francis U (PA)
Saint Leo U (FL)
Southeast Missouri State U (MO)
State U of New York Coll of Technology at Alfred (NY)
Stevens Inst of Technology (NJ)
Sullivan U (KY)
Syracuse U (NY)
Taylor U (IN)
U of Illinois at Springfield (IL)
U of Maine at Presque Isle (ME)
U of Maryland U Coll (MD)
U of Michigan–Dearborn (MI)
U of Providence (MT)
U of St. Thomas (MN)
The U of Tampa (FL)
The U of Tulsa (OK)
Western Illinois U (IL)
Western Washington U (WA)

COMPUTER ENGINEERING

Arkansas Tech U (AR)
Auburn U (AL)
Bellarmine U (KY)
Bethel U (MN)
Boston U (MA)
Bowling Green State U (OH)
Bradley U (IL)
Bucknell U (PA)
California Polytechnic State U, San Luis Obispo (CA)
California State U, Chico (CA)
California State U, Fullerton (CA)
California State U, Long Beach (CA)
California State U, Northridge (CA)
California State U, San Bernardino (CA)
Cedarville U (OH)
Central Michigan U (MI)
Christian Brothers U (TN)
Christopher Newport U (VA)
Clarkson U (NY)
Colorado State U (CO)
Columbia U (NY)
DigiPen Inst of Technology (WA)
Embry-Riddle Aeronautical U–Daytona (FL)
Embry-Riddle Aeronautical U–Prescott (AZ)
Fairfield U (CT)
Florida Ag and Mech U (FL)
Florida Atlantic U (FL)
Fort Lewis Coll (CO)
George Mason U (VA)
Gonzaga U (WA)
Grand Valley State U (MI)
Hanover Coll (IN)
Harding U (AR)
Hofstra U (NY)
Indiana U–Purdue U Indianapolis (IN)
Inter American U of Puerto Rico, Bayamón Campus (PR)
Iowa State U of Science and Technology (IA)
Jackson State U (MS)
Johns Hopkins U (MD)
Johnson C. Smith U (NC)
Lawrence Technological U (MI)
Lebanese American U (Lebanon)
LeTourneau U (TX)
Liberty U (VA)
Lipscomb U (TN)
Louisiana State U and A&M Coll (LA)
Loyola U Chicago (IL)
Manhattan Coll (NY)
Marquette U (WI)
Merrimack Coll (MA)
Miami U (OH)
Miami U Hamilton (OH)
Michigan State U (MI)
New Jersey Inst of Technology (NJ)
New York U (NY)
North Carolina State U (NC)
Northwestern U (IL)
The Ohio State U (OH)
Oklahoma Christian U (OK)
Oklahoma State U (OK)
Old Dominion U (VA)
Portland State U (OR)
Prairie View A&M U (TX)
Purdue U (IN)
Purdue U Northwest (IN)
Regent U (VA)
Rice U (TX)
Rochester Inst of Technology (NY)
Sacred Heart U (CT)
Saint Louis U (MO)
St. Mary's U (TX)
San Diego State U (CA)
San Francisco State U (CA)
San Jose State U (CA)
Southern Illinois U Carbondale (IL)
Southern Illinois U Edwardsville (IL)
Stevens Inst of Technology (NJ)
Syracuse U (NY)
Taylor U (IN)
Texas Tech U (TX)
Université de Sherbrooke (QC, Canada)
U at Buffalo, the State U of New York (NY)
U of Arkansas (AR)
U of California, Irvine (CA)
U of California, Los Angeles (CA)
U of California, Merced (CA)
U of California, Riverside (CA)
U of California, Santa Cruz (CA)
U of Central Florida (FL)
U of Dayton (OH)
U of Florida (FL)
U of Georgia (GA)
U of Houston (TX)
U of Houston–Clear Lake (TX)
U of Idaho (ID)
U of Kentucky (KY)
U of Louisville (KY)
U of Maine (ME)
U of Maryland, Baltimore County (MD)
U of Maryland, Coll Park (MD)
U of Massachusetts Amherst (MA)
U of Massachusetts Boston (MA)
U of Massachusetts Dartmouth (MA)
U of Massachusetts Lowell (MA)
U of Memphis (TN)
U of Michigan (MI)
U of Michigan–Dearborn (MI)
U of Minnesota, Twin Cities Campus (MN)
U of Missouri (MO)
U of Mount Union (OH)
U of Nebraska–Lincoln (NE)
U of Nevada, Las Vegas (NV)
U of Nevada, Reno (NV)
U of New Hampshire (NH)
U of New Haven (CT)
U of New Mexico (NM)
The U of North Carolina at Charlotte (NC)
U of Notre Dame (IN)
U of Pennsylvania (PA)
U of Pittsburgh (PA)
U of St. Thomas (MN)
U of South Alabama (AL)
U of South Carolina (SC)
U of South Florida (FL)
The U of Tennessee (TN)
The U of Texas Rio Grande Valley (TX)
The U of Toledo (OH)
The U of Tulsa (OK)
U of Virginia (VA)
U of Washington (WA)
U of Washington, Bothell (WA)
U of Wisconsin–Milwaukee (WI)
U of Wyoming (WY)
Utah State U (UT)
Valparaiso U (IN)
Virginia Commonwealth U (VA)
Virginia Polytechnic Inst and State U (VA)
Washington State U (WA)
Washington U in St. Louis (MO)
Weber State U (UT)
West Virginia U Inst of Technology (WV)
Wright State U–Lake Campus (OH)

COMPUTER ENGINEERING RELATED

Auburn U (AL)
U of California, Santa Cruz (CA)
U of Massachusetts Dartmouth (MA)

COMPUTER ENGINEERING TECHNOLOGIES RELATED

Inter American U of Puerto Rico, Bayamón Campus (PR)

COMPUTER ENGINEERING TECHNOLOGY

California State U, Long Beach (CA)
California U of Pennsylvania (PA)
Central Connecticut State U (CT)
Central Washington U (WA)
Farmingdale State Coll (NY)
Indiana State U (IN)
Indiana U–Purdue U Indianapolis (IN)
Kennesaw State U (GA)
LeTourneau U (TX)
Prairie View A&M U (TX)
Rochester Inst of Technology (NY)
State U of New York Coll of Technology at Alfred (NY)
U of Dayton (OH)
U of Houston (TX)
U of Houston–Downtown (TX)
U of Memphis (TN)
Utah State U (UT)
Vermont Tech Coll (VT)

COMPUTER GRAPHICS

Acad of Art U (CA)
Champlain Coll (VT)
Clarkson U (NY)
Dakota State U (SD)
DePaul U (IL)
Purdue U (IN)
Purdue U Northwest (IN)
Rochester Inst of Technology (NY)
State U of New York at Fredonia (NY)
U of Houston (TX)
U of Mary Hardin-Baylor (TX)
U of Pennsylvania (PA)
Whitworth U (WA)

COMPUTER HARDWARE ENGINEERING

Auburn U (AL)
Utah Valley U (UT)

COMPUTER/INFORMATION TECHNOLOGY SERVICES ADMINISTRATION RELATED

Berkeley Coll–New York City Campus (NY)
Berkeley Coll–Woodland Park Campus (NJ)
Limestone Coll (SC)
Marywood U (PA)
St. Joseph's Coll, Long Island Campus (NY)
St. Joseph's Coll, New York (NY)
U at Buffalo, the State U of New York (NY)
U of California, Santa Cruz (CA)
The U of Findlay (OH)
U of Guam (GU)
U of Maryland, Baltimore County (MD)
U of Northern Iowa (IA)
U of Providence (MT)
Washington U in St. Louis (MO)

COMPUTER PROGRAMMING

Champlain Coll (VT)
Columbia Coll Chicago (IL)
Davenport U, Grand Rapids (MI)
DePaul U (IL)
Farmingdale State Coll (NY)
Hardin-Simmons U (TX)
Inter American U of Puerto Rico, San Germán Campus (PR)
La Salle U (PA)
Limestone Coll (SC)
New England Inst of Technology (RI)
Southeast Missouri State U (MO)
Université de Sherbrooke (QC, Canada)
U of Michigan–Dearborn (MI)
U of Mount Union (OH)
U of Providence (MT)
Western State Colorado U (CO)
Youngstown State U (OH)

COMPUTER PROGRAMMING RELATED

Curry Coll (MA)

COMPUTER PROGRAMMING (SPECIFIC APPLICATIONS)

Acad of Art U (CA)
DePaul U (IL)
DigiPen Inst of Technology (WA)
Jacksonville U (FL)
Kennesaw State U (GA)
State U of New York Coll of Technology at Alfred (NY)
U of Washington, Bothell (WA)

COMPUTER SCIENCE

Acadia U (NS, Canada)
Adams State U (CO)
Alabama State U (AL)
Albright Coll (PA)
Allegheny Coll (PA)
American Coll of Thessaloniki (Greece)
American U of Beirut (Lebanon)
Appalachian State U (NC)
Auburn U at Montgomery (AL)
Aurora U (IL)
Austin Coll (TX)
Austin Peay State U (TN)
Baker U (KS)
Baldwin Wallace U (OH)
Baylor U (TX)
Beloit Coll (WI)
Benedictine U (IL)
Bethany Lutheran Coll (MN)
Bethel Coll (KS)
Blackburn Coll (IL)
Boston Coll (MA)
Boston U (MA)
Bradley U (IL)
Brandeis U (MA)
Bridgewater Coll (VA)
Bridgewater State U (MA)
Buena Vista U (IA)
California Inst of Technology (CA)
California Lutheran U (CA)
California Polytechnic State U, San Luis Obispo (CA)
California State U, Bakersfield (CA)
California State U, Chico (CA)
California State U, Fullerton (CA)
California State U, Long Beach (CA)
California State U, Los Angeles (CA)
California State U, Northridge (CA)
California State U, San Bernardino (CA)
California State U, San Marcos (CA)
Calvin Coll (MI)
Cameron U (OK)
Canisius Coll (NY)
Carnegie Mellon U (PA)
Carson-Newman U (TN)
Carthage Coll (WI)
The Catholic U of America (DC)
Cedarville U (OH)
Central Michigan U (MI)
Central State U (OH)
Central Washington U (WA)
Champlain Coll (VT)
Christian Brothers U (TN)
Christopher Newport U (VA)
Clarkson U (NY)
Clark U (MA)
Colgate U (NY)
Coll of Saint Benedict (MN)
The Coll of Saint Rose (NY)
Coll of Staten Island of the City U of New York (NY)
Coll of the Holy Cross (MA)
Coll of the Ozarks (MO)
Colorado School of Mines (CO)
Columbia Coll (MO)
Columbia U (NY)
Connecticut Coll (CT)
Cornell Coll (IA)
Cornell U (NY)
Creighton U (NE)
Dallas Baptist U (TX)
Dartmouth Coll (NH)
DePaul U (IL)
Dickinson Coll (PA)
DigiPen Inst of Technology (WA)
Dominican U (IL)
Drake U (IA)
Drew U (NJ)
Duquesne U (PA)
Earlham Coll (IN)
East Carolina U (NC)
Eastern Illinois U (IL)
Eastern Mennonite U (VA)
Eastern U (PA)
Eckerd Coll (FL)
Elizabeth City State U (NC)
Embry-Riddle Aeronautical U–Daytona (FL)
Endicott Coll (MA)
Fayetteville State U (NC)
Fitchburg State U (MA)
Florida Southern Coll (FL)
Furman U (SC)
George Mason U (VA)
Georgia Coll & State U (GA)
Georgia State U (GA)
Gonzaga U (WA)
Gordon Coll (MA)
Goshen Coll (IN)
Grove City Coll (PA)
Hampden-Sydney Coll (VA)
Hanover Coll (IN)
Harding U (AR)
Harvard U (MA)
Haverford Coll (PA)
High Point U (NC)
Hiram Coll (OH)
Hofstra U (NY)
Hood Coll (MD)
Humboldt State U (CA)
Hunter Coll of the City U of New York (NY)
Idaho State U (ID)
Illinois Coll (IL)
Indiana U Bloomington (IN)
Indiana U Kokomo (IN)
Indiana U Northwest (IN)
Indiana U–Purdue U Indianapolis (IN)
Indiana U South Bend (IN)
Indiana U Southeast (IN)
Inter American U of Puerto Rico, Aguadilla Campus (PR)
Inter American U of Puerto Rico, Barranquitas Campus (PR)
Inter American U of Puerto Rico, Bayamón Campus (PR)
Inter American U of Puerto Rico, San Germán Campus (PR)
Iona Coll (NY)
Iowa State U of Science and Technology (IA)
Ithaca Coll (NY)
Kennesaw State U (GA)
King's Coll (PA)
Knox Coll (IL)
Lafayette Coll (PA)
Lake Forest Coll (IL)
La Salle U (PA)
La Sierra U (CA)
Lawrence Technological U (MI)
Lebanese American U (Lebanon)
LeTourneau U (TX)
Lewis & Clark Coll (OR)
Limestone Coll (SC)
Lindenwood U (MO)
Linfield Coll (OR)
Lipscomb U (TN)
Loras Coll (IA)
Louisiana Coll (LA)
Louisiana State U and A&M Coll (LA)
Madonna U (MI)
Maharishi U of Management (IA)
Manchester U (IN)
Manhattan Coll (NY)
Manhattanville Coll (NY)
Mansfield U of Pennsylvania (PA)
Marian U (IN)
Marist Coll (NY)
Marywood U (PA)
Massachusetts Coll of Liberal Arts (MA)
Massachusetts Inst of Technology (MA)
McNeese State U (LA)
Mercer U, Macon (GA)
Mercy Coll (NY)
Merrimack Coll (MA)

Messiah Coll (PA)
Miami U Hamilton (OH)
Middlebury Coll (VT)
Middle Tennessee State U (TN)
Milligan Coll (TN)
Millsaps Coll (MS)
Mills Coll (CA)
Minnesota State U Moorhead (MN)
Mount St. Joseph U (OH)
Murray State U (KY)
Muskingum U (OH)
National U (CA)
New Coll of Florida (FL)
New England Inst of Technology (RI)
New Jersey Inst of Technology (NJ)
North Carolina State U (NC)
Northeastern State U (OK)
Northern Illinois U (IL)
Northwestern Oklahoma State U (OK)
Northwestern U (IL)
Ohio Dominican U (OH)
Ohio U (OH)
Ohio Wesleyan U (OH)
Oklahoma Baptist U (OK)
Oklahoma Christian U (OK)
Ouachita Baptist U (AR)
Pace U (NY)
Pace U, Pleasantville Campus (NY)
Pacific Lutheran U (WA)
Palm Beach Atlantic U (FL)
Portland State U (OR)
Prairie View A&M U (TX)
Princeton U (NJ)
Providence Coll (RI)
Purdue U (IN)
Purdue U Northwest (IN)
Queens Coll of the City U of New York (NY)
Radford U (VA)
Randolph-Macon Coll (VA)
Regent U (VA)
Regis U (CO)
Renton Tech Coll (WA)
Rhode Island Coll (RI)
Rhodes Coll (TN)
Rider U (NJ)
Roanoke Coll (VA)
Rochester Inst of Technology (NY)
Rockford U (IL)
Rocky Mountain Coll (MT)
Saginaw Valley State U (MI)
Saint Anselm Coll (NH)
Saint Francis U (PA)
Saint John's U (MN)
Saint Louis U (MO)
Saint Martin's U (WA)
St. Mary's U (TX)
Saint Mary's U of Minnesota (MN)
St. Norbert Coll (WI)
St. Olaf Coll (MN)
Samford U (AL)
San Diego State U (CA)
San Francisco State U (CA)
San Jose State U (CA)
Sarah Lawrence Coll (NY)
Scripps Coll (CA)
Seattle U (WA)
Seton Hill U (PA)
Sonoma State U (CA)
Southeastern Louisiana U (LA)
Southern Illinois U Carbondale (IL)
Southern Illinois U Edwardsville (IL)
Southern U and Ag and Mech Coll (LA)
Southwest Baptist U (MO)
State U of New York at Fredonia (NY)
State U of New York Coll at Potsdam (NY)
Stetson U (FL)
Stevens Inst of Technology (NJ)
Stockton U (NJ)
Stonehill Coll (MA)
Taylor U (IN)
Texas Lutheran U (TX)
Tiffin U (OH)
Towson U (MD)
Trinity Christian Coll (IL)
Tulane U (LA)
Université de Sherbrooke (QC, Canada)
U at Buffalo, the State U of New York (NY)
U of Arkansas (AR)
U of California, Irvine (CA)
U of California, Riverside (CA)
U of California, Santa Cruz (CA)
U of Chicago (IL)
U of Dallas (TX)
U of Dayton (OH)
U of Detroit Mercy (MI)
The U of Findlay (OH)
U of Georgia (GA)
U of Guam (GU)
U of Hawaii at Manoa (HI)
U of Houston–Clear Lake (TX)
U of Idaho (ID)
U of Illinois at Springfield (IL)
U of La Verne (CA)
U of Lynchburg (VA)
U of Maine (ME)
U of Maine at Farmington (ME)
U of Mary Hardin-Baylor (TX)
U of Maryland, Baltimore County (MD)
U of Maryland, Coll Park (MD)
U of Massachusetts Amherst (MA)
U of Massachusetts Lowell (MA)
U of Memphis (TN)
U of Minnesota, Duluth (MN)
U of Minnesota, Morris (MN)
U of Minnesota, Twin Cities Campus (MN)
U of Nevada, Las Vegas (NV)
U of Nevada, Reno (NV)
U of New Haven (CT)
U of North Carolina at Asheville (NC)
The U of North Carolina at Chapel Hill (NC)
The U of North Carolina at Charlotte (NC)
The U of North Carolina at Greensboro (NC)
The U of North Carolina at Pembroke (NC)
U of Northern Iowa (IA)
U of Northwestern–St. Paul (MN)
U of Pittsburgh (PA)
U of Pittsburgh at Bradford (PA)
U of Providence (MT)
U of Puget Sound (WA)
U of Regina (SK, Canada)
U of St. Thomas (MN)
U of St. Thomas (TX)
U of San Diego (CA)
U of San Francisco (CA)
U of Sioux Falls (SD)
U of South Alabama (AL)
U of Southern Indiana (IN)
The U of Tennessee (TN)
The U of Tennessee at Martin (TN)
The U of Texas at El Paso (TX)
The U of Texas Rio Grande Valley (TX)
The U of the South (TN)
The U of Tulsa (OK)
U of Vermont (VT)
U of Washington (WA)
U of Washington, Bothell (WA)
U of Wisconsin–Milwaukee (WI)
U of Wisconsin–River Falls (WI)
U of Wisconsin–Superior (WI)
U of Wyoming (WY)
Ursinus Coll (PA)
Utah Valley U (UT)
Valparaiso U (IN)
Virginia Polytechnic Inst and State U (VA)
Wartburg Coll (IA)
Washington and Lee U (VA)
Washington State U (WA)
Washington State U–Tri-Cities (WA)
Washington State U–Vancouver (WA)
Washington U in St. Louis (MO)
Weber State U (UT)
Wesleyan U (CT)
Western Connecticut State U (CT)
Westmont Coll (CA)
West Virginia State U (WV)
West Virginia U Inst of Technology (WV)
Wheaton Coll (IL)
Wheaton Coll (MA)
Whitworth U (WA)
Widener U (PA)
Willamette U (OR)
Williams Coll (MA)
Wofford Coll (SC)
Worcester Polytechnic Inst (MA)
Youngstown State U (OH)

COMPUTER SOFTWARE AND MEDIA APPLICATIONS RELATED
Acad of Art U (CA)
Champlain Coll (VT)
Coll of Charleston (SC)
DePaul U (IL)
Duquesne U (PA)
LeTourneau U (TX)
Limestone Coll (SC)
Loyola U Chicago (IL)
Northwest Christian U (OR)
Pace U, Pleasantville Campus (NY)
U of Providence (MT)
Worcester Polytechnic Inst (MA)

COMPUTER SOFTWARE ENGINEERING
Auburn U (AL)
Aurora U (IL)
Baldwin Wallace U (OH)
Bethel U (MN)
Bowling Green State U (OH)
Clarkson U (NY)
DigiPen Inst of Technology (WA)
Dunwoody Coll of Technology (MN)
Embry-Riddle Aeronautical U–Daytona (FL)
Embry-Riddle Aeronautical U–Prescott (AZ)
Fairfield U (CT)
Iowa State U of Science and Technology (IA)
Kennesaw State U (GA)
Lawrence Technological U (MI)
Loyola U Chicago (IL)
Manchester U (IN)
Miami U (OH)
Ohio Dominican U (OH)
Point Loma Nazarene U (CA)
Rochester Inst of Technology (NY)
St. Mary's U (TX)
Stevens Inst of Technology (NJ)
U of California, Irvine (CA)
U of Detroit Mercy (MI)
U of Massachusetts Dartmouth (MA)
U of Nebraska–Lincoln (NE)
U of Northern Colorado (CO)
U of Regina (SK, Canada)
Utah Valley U (UT)
Valley City State U (ND)
Vermont Tech Coll (VT)
Washington State U (WA)

COMPUTER SOFTWARE TECHNOLOGY
Farmingdale State Coll (NY)

COMPUTER SYSTEMS ANALYSIS
Arkansas Tech U (AR)
Austin Peay State U (TN)
Buena Vista U (IA)
California Polytechnic State U, San Luis Obispo (CA)
Calvin Coll (MI)
Davenport U, Grand Rapids (MI)
Dunwoody Coll of Technology (MN)
Lindenwood U (MO)
Miami U Hamilton (OH)
Purdue U Northwest (IN)
Rochester Inst of Technology (NY)
Saginaw Valley State U (MI)
State U of New York at Plattsburgh (NY)
Texas Christian U (TX)
Tiffin U (OH)
U of Houston (TX)
U of Illinois at Springfield (IL)
U of Minnesota, Twin Cities Campus (MN)
U of North Dakota (ND)
U of Providence (MT)
U of Vermont (VT)
U of Washington, Bothell (WA)
West Virginia U Inst of Technology (WV)

COMPUTER SYSTEMS NETWORKING AND TELECOMMUNICATIONS
Baldwin Wallace U (OH)
Champlain Coll (VT)
Davenport U, Grand Rapids (MI)
DePaul U (IL)
Idaho State U (ID)
Inter American U of Puerto Rico, Aguadilla Campus (PR)
Inter American U of Puerto Rico, Bayamón Campus (PR)
Iona Coll (NY)
Kean U (NJ)
Lindenwood U (MO)
Northwestern Oklahoma State U (OK)
Ohio U (OH)
Rochester Inst of Technology (NY)
Tiffin U (OH)
U of Minnesota, Duluth (MN)
U of Minnesota, Twin Cities Campus (MN)
The U of North Carolina at Greensboro (NC)
U of Pennsylvania (PA)
U of Providence (MT)
Utah Valley U (UT)
Weber State U (UT)

COMPUTER TEACHER EDUCATION
Arkansas Tech U (AR)
Baylor U (TX)
Bowling Green State U (OH)
Buena Vista U (IA)
Concordia U Chicago (IL)
Dakota State U (SD)
Dallas Baptist U (TX)
Grand Valley State U (MI)
Michigan State U (MI)
Southern U and Ag and Mech Coll (LA)
U of Nebraska–Lincoln (NE)
Utica Coll (NY)

COMPUTER TECHNOLOGY/ COMPUTER SYSTEMS TECHNOLOGY
Excelsior Coll (NY)
Florida Atlantic U (FL)
New England Inst of Technology (RI)
Point Loma Nazarene U (CA)

CONDENSED MATTER AND MATERIALS PHYSICS
Kansas Wesleyan U (KS)

CONDUCTING
Ithaca Coll (NY)

CONSERVATION BIOLOGY
Boston U (MA)
Bryant U (RI)
Grove City Coll (PA)
Seattle U (WA)
State U of New York Coll of Environmental Science and Forestry (NY)
U of Idaho (ID)

CONSTRUCTION ENGINEERING
American U of Beirut (Lebanon)
Bowling Green State U (OH)
Bradley U (IL)
California State U, Long Beach (CA)
Iowa State U of Science and Technology (IA)
Kennesaw State U (GA)
Lamar U (TX)
Marquette U (WI)
National U (CA)
New York U (NY)
North Carolina State U (NC)
Purdue U (IN)
Texas Tech U (TX)
U of Nebraska–Lincoln (NE)
U of New Mexico (NM)
Washington State U (WA)

CONSTRUCTION ENGINEERING TECHNOLOGY
Bowling Green State U (OH)
Bradley U (IL)
California State U, Chico (CA)
California State U, Long Beach (CA)
Central Michigan U (MI)
Colorado State U (CO)
Farmingdale State Coll (NY)
Fitchburg State U (MA)
Florida Ag and Mech U (FL)
Georgia Southern U (GA)
Michigan State U (MI)
Oklahoma State U (OK)
Prairie View A&M U (TX)
Purdue U Northwest (IN)
San Diego State U (CA)
Southern Illinois U Edwardsville (IL)
Temple U (PA)
U of Florida (FL)
U of Houston (TX)
U of Nebraska–Lincoln (NE)
U of North Florida (FL)
The U of Toledo (OH)
Western Kentucky U (KY)

CONSTRUCTION MANAGEMENT
Appalachian State U (NC)
California State U, Northridge (CA)
Central Connecticut State U (CT)
Central Washington U (WA)
Colorado State U–Pueblo (CO)
Dunwoody Coll of Technology (MN)
Eastern Illinois U (IL)
Indiana State U (IN)
Kennesaw State U (GA)
Lawrence Technological U (MI)
Louisiana State U and A&M Coll (LA)
Michigan State U (MI)
Middle Tennessee State U (TN)
Minnesota State U Moorhead (MN)
National U (CA)
New England Inst of Technology (RI)
Northern Kentucky U (KY)
State U of New York Coll of Environmental Science and Forestry (NY)
State U of New York Coll of Technology at Alfred (NY)
State U of New York Coll of Technology at Delhi (NY)
U of Minnesota, Twin Cities Campus (MN)
U of Nevada, Las Vegas (NV)
U of Northern Iowa (IA)
Utah Valley U (UT)
Vermont Tech Coll (VT)
Virginia Polytechnic Inst and State U (VA)
Washington State U (WA)
Weber State U (UT)
Western Illinois U (IL)
West Virginia U Inst of Technology (WV)

CONSTRUCTION TRADES
Utica Coll (NY)

CONSUMER ECONOMICS
U of Georgia (GA)
The U of Tennessee (TN)

CONSUMER MERCHANDISING/ RETAILING MANAGEMENT
Acad of Art U (CA)
Bradley U (IL)
Purdue U (IN)
San Francisco State U (CA)
Savannah Coll of Art and Design (GA)
Syracuse U (NY)
U of Memphis (TN)

CONSUMER SERVICES AND ADVOCACY
Carson-Newman U (TN)

CORRECTIONS
Adams State U (CO)
Bowling Green State U (OH)
Hardin-Simmons U (TX)
Lee U (TN)
Southeast Missouri State U (MO)
Tiffin U (OH)
U of New Mexico (NM)
U of Pittsburgh (PA)
U of Providence (MT)
Youngstown State U (OH)

CORRECTIONS ADMINISTRATION
U of Providence (MT)

CORRECTIONS AND CRIMINAL JUSTICE RELATED
Averett U (VA)
Cameron U (OK)
Cedarville U (OH)
Gwynedd Mercy U (PA)

Inter American U of Puerto Rico, Aguadilla Campus (PR)
Limestone Coll (SC)
Muskingum U (OH)
Regis U (CO)
Saint Mary's U of Minnesota (MN)
U of Providence (MT)

COSTUME DESIGN
Acad of Art U (CA)
Albright Coll (PA)
Brenau U (GA)
FIDM/Fashion Inst of Design & Merchandising, Los Angeles Campus (CA)
Marymount Manhattan Coll (NY)

COUNSELING PSYCHOLOGY
Averett U (VA)
Avila U (MO)
Delaware Valley U (PA)
Eastern Washington U (WA)
Emmanuel Coll (MA)
Fort Lewis Coll (CO)
Geneva Coll (PA)
Lesley U (MA)
Morningside Coll (IA)
Northwestern U (IL)
Point U (GA)
Saint Leo U (FL)
Toccoa Falls Coll (GA)
U of Chicago (IL)

COUNSELOR EDUCATION/ SCHOOL COUNSELING AND GUIDANCE
Bowling Green State U (OH)
Lancaster Bible Coll (PA)
Université de Sherbrooke (QC, Canada)
U of South Dakota (SD)

CRAFTS, FOLK ART AND ARTISANRY
Bowling Green State U (OH)
Bridgewater State U (MA)
Rochester Inst of Technology (NY)
Virginia Commonwealth U (VA)

CREATIVE WRITING
Adams State U (CO)
Agnes Scott Coll (GA)
Albion Coll (MI)
Arkansas Tech U (AR)
Austin Coll (TX)
Baldwin Wallace U (OH)
Beloit Coll (WI)
Blackburn Coll (IL)
Bowling Green State U (OH)
Bradley U (IL)
Brandeis U (MA)
Bridgewater State U (MA)
Bucknell U (PA)
Butler U (IN)
California State U, Long Beach (CA)
Canisius Coll (NY)
Carnegie Mellon U (PA)
Carson-Newman U (TN)
Central Michigan U (MI)
Central Washington U (WA)
Christian Brothers U (TN)
The Coll of Idaho (ID)
The Colorado Coll (CO)
Columbia Coll Chicago (IL)
Columbia U (NY)
Cornell Coll (IA)
Dartmouth Coll (NH)
Drew U (NJ)
Eckerd Coll (FL)
Emerson Coll (MA)
Florida Southern Coll (FL)
Franklin Pierce U (NH)
George Mason U (VA)
Hamilton Coll (NY)
Hamline U (MN)
Hartwick Coll (NY)
Hiram Coll (OH)
Hofstra U (NY)
Hollins U (VA)
Ithaca Coll (NY)
Johns Hopkins U (MD)
Knox Coll (IL)
Lebanon Valley Coll (PA)
Lee U (TN)
Linfield Coll (OR)
Loras Coll (IA)
Loyola U New Orleans (LA)
Lubbock Christian U (TX)
Lycoming Coll (PA)
Marymount Manhattan Coll (NY)
Massachusetts Coll of Liberal Arts (MA)
Massachusetts Inst of Technology (MA)
Mercer U, Macon (GA)
Miami U (OH)
Miami U Hamilton (OH)
Mount St. Joseph U (OH)
Murray State U (KY)
New England Coll (NH)
Northeastern State U (OK)
Ohio U (OH)
Ohio Wesleyan U (OH)
Oklahoma Christian U (OK)
Pepperdine U, Malibu (CA)
Portland State U (OR)
Providence Coll (RI)
Purchase Coll, State U of New York (NY)
Purdue U (IN)
Queens U of Charlotte (NC)
Randolph Coll (VA)
Redeemer U Coll (ON, Canada)
Reinhardt U (GA)
Rhode Island Coll (RI)
Roanoke Coll (VA)
Rocky Mountain Coll (MT)
Saginaw Valley State U (MI)
San Francisco State U (CA)
Sarah Lawrence Coll (NY)
Seattle U (WA)
Seton Hill U (PA)
Southeastern U (FL)
State U of New York at Plattsburgh (NY)
State U of New York Coll at Potsdam (NY)
Sweet Briar Coll (VA)
Texas Christian U (TX)
Truman State U (MO)
U of California, Riverside (CA)
U of Chicago (IL)
The U of Findlay (OH)
U of Houston (TX)
U of Idaho (ID)
U of La Verne (CA)
U of Maine at Farmington (ME)
U of Michigan (MI)
U of Pittsburgh at Bradford (PA)
U of Providence (MT)
U of Puget Sound (WA)
U of Regina (SK, Canada)
U of St. Thomas (MN)
The U of Texas at El Paso (TX)
Valparaiso U (IN)
Washington U in St. Louis (MO)
Waynesburg U (PA)
Weber State U (UT)
Western Washington U (WA)
Wheaton Coll (MA)

CRIMINALISTICS AND CRIMINAL SCIENCE
Alabama State U (AL)
Saint Leo U (FL)
Seattle U (WA)
Tiffin U (OH)
Weber State U (UT)

CRIMINAL JUSTICE/LAW ENFORCEMENT ADMINISTRATION
Adams State U (CO)
Alfred U (NY)
Austin Peay State U (TN)
Averett U (VA)
Berkeley Coll–New York City Campus (NY)
Berkeley Coll–White Plains Campus (NY)
Berkeley Coll–Woodland Park Campus (NJ)
Blackburn Coll (IL)
Bowling Green State U (OH)
Bradley U (IL)
California Lutheran U (CA)
California State U, Bakersfield (CA)
California State U, Long Beach (CA)
Campbellsville U (KY)
Canisius Coll (NY)
Carthage Coll (WI)
Clarion U of Pennsylvania (PA)
The Coll of Saint Rose (NY)
Columbia Coll (MO)
Culver-Stockton Coll (MO)
Delaware Valley U (PA)
East Tennessee State U (TN)
East Texas Baptist U (TX)
Emmanuel Coll (GA)
Excelsior Coll (NY)
Fayetteville State U (NC)
Franklin Pierce U (NH)
Georgia Coll & State U (GA)
Grand Valley State U (MI)
Greenville U (IL)
Hartwick Coll (NY)
Indiana U East (IN)
Iona Coll (NY)
Kansas Wesleyan U (KS)
Kean U (NJ)
Lees-McRae Coll (NC)
Limestone Coll (SC)
Lock Haven U of Pennsylvania (PA)
Lubbock Christian U (TX)
Manor Coll (PA)
Mansfield U of Pennsylvania (PA)
Marist Coll (NY)
Marymount California U (CA)
Marymount U (VA)
Marywood U (PA)
Mercy Coll (NY)
Merrimack Coll (MA)
Miami U (OH)
Michigan State U (MI)
Middle Tennessee State U (TN)
Millikin U (IL)
Muskingum U (OH)
National U (CA)
New England Coll (NH)
New England Inst of Technology (RI)
Nichols Coll (MA)
Northeastern State U (OK)
Pace U (NY)
Pace U, Pleasantville Campus (NY)
Pfeiffer U (NC)
Piedmont Coll (GA)
Portland State U (OR)
Regent U (VA)
Rochester Inst of Technology (NY)
St. Joseph's Coll, Long Island Campus (NY)
St. Joseph's Coll, New York (NY)
St. Mary's U (TX)
Salve Regina U (RI)
San Francisco State U (CA)
Sonoma State U (CA)
Southwest Baptist U (MO)
State U of New York at Fredonia (NY)
Texas A&M U–Central Texas (TX)
Tiffin U (OH)
Toccoa Falls Coll (GA)
Trevecca Nazarene U (TN)
Trinity Christian Coll (IL)
Union Coll (KY)
U of Colorado Denver (CO)
U of Dayton (OH)
The U of Findlay (OH)
U of Georgia (GA)
U of Guam (GU)
U of Louisville (KY)
U of Maine at Presque Isle (ME)
U of Mary Hardin-Baylor (TX)
U of Massachusetts Lowell (MA)
U of Memphis (TN)
U of New Haven (CT)
U of Northern Iowa (IA)
U of Pittsburgh at Bradford (PA)
U of Providence (MT)
U of Regina (SK, Canada)
U of South Alabama (AL)
U of South Carolina (SC)
U of South Dakota (SD)
The U of Tennessee at Martin (TN)
The U of Texas at El Paso (TX)
U of the Incarnate Word (TX)
Utah Valley U (UT)
Utica Coll (NY)
Virginia Commonwealth U (VA)
Waynesburg U (PA)
Western Illinois U (IL)
West Virginia U Inst of Technology (WV)
Widener U (PA)
Youngstown State U (OH)

CRIMINAL JUSTICE/POLICE SCIENCE
Bowling Green State U (OH)
Columbia Southern U (AL)
Eastern Illinois U (IL)
George Mason U (VA)
Gwynedd Mercy U (PA)
Idaho State U (ID)
Inter American U of Puerto Rico, San Germán Campus (PR)
Manor Coll (PA)
Middle Tennessee State U (TN)
Northwestern Oklahoma State U (OK)
Oklahoma Baptist U (OK)
Southern U and Ag and Mech Coll (LA)
Texas A&M Intl U (TX)
U of Providence (MT)
U of Regina (SK, Canada)
U of Washington, Tacoma (WA)
Washington State U (WA)
Washington State U–Vancouver (WA)
Weber State U (UT)
Western Connecticut State U (CT)

CRIMINAL JUSTICE/SAFETY
Adelphi U (NY)
Alabama State U (AL)
American Public U System (WV)
American U (DC)
Angelo State U (TX)
Appalachian State U (NC)
Arkansas Tech U (AR)
Auburn U at Montgomery (AL)
Aurora U (IL)
Baldwin Wallace U (OH)
Barton Coll (NC)
Bellarmine U (KY)
Benedictine U (IL)
Boston U (MA)
Bowling Green State U (OH)
Brandman U (CA)
Bridgewater State U (MA)
Buena Vista U (IA)
Caldwell U (NJ)
California State U, Chico (CA)
California State U, Fullerton (CA)
California State U, Los Angeles (CA)
California State U, San Bernardino (CA)
California U of Pennsylvania (PA)
Calumet Coll of Saint Joseph (IN)
Central State U (OH)
Central Washington U (WA)
Champlain Coll (VT)
The Coll at Brockport, State U of New York (NY)
Coll of Coastal Georgia (GA)
Coll of the Ozarks (MO)
Curry Coll (MA)
Dallas Baptist U (TX)
Davenport U, Grand Rapids (MI)
Dean Coll (MA)
Delta State U (MS)
East Carolina U (NC)
East Stroudsburg U of Pennsylvania (PA)
Elizabeth City State U (NC)
Endicott Coll (MA)
Fitchburg State U (MA)
Florida Ag and Mech U (FL)
Florida Atlantic U (FL)
Georgia State U (GA)
Graceland U (IA)
Granite State Coll (NH)
Harding U (AR)
Hardin-Simmons U (TX)
High Point U (NC)
Hood Coll (MD)
Immaculata U (PA)
Indiana U Bloomington (IN)
Indiana U Kokomo (IN)
Indiana U Northwest (IN)
Indiana U–Purdue U Indianapolis (IN)
Indiana U South Bend (IN)
Indiana U Southeast (IN)
Inter American U of Puerto Rico, Fajardo Campus (PR)
Iowa State U of Science and Technology (IA)
Jackson State U (MS)
Kennesaw State U (GA)
King's Coll (PA)
King U (TN)
Lamar U (TX)
La Salle U (PA)
La Sierra U (CA)
Liberty U (VA)
Limestone Coll (SC)
Lindenwood U (MO)
Lipscomb U (TN)
Loras Coll (IA)
Louisiana Coll (LA)
Loyola U Chicago (IL)
Lycoming Coll (PA)
Madonna U (MI)
Manchester U (IN)
Marshall U (WV)
McNeese State U (LA)
Michigan State U (MI)
Minnesota State U Moorhead (MN)
Missouri Baptist U (MO)
Molloy Coll (NY)
Mount Marty Coll (SD)
Murray State U (KY)
New Jersey City U (NJ)
Nichols Coll (MA)
Northern Kentucky U (KY)
Northern State U (SD)
Oakland City U (IN)
Oklahoma Christian U (OK)
Point U (GA)
Potomac State Coll of West Virginia U (WV)
Prairie View A&M U (TX)
Radford U (VA)
Rhode Island Coll (RI)
Rider U (NJ)
Roanoke Coll (VA)
Rochester Inst of Technology (NY)
Sacred Heart U (CT)
Saginaw Valley State U (MI)
Saint Anselm Coll (NH)
Saint Leo U (FL)
Saint Louis U (MO)
Saint Martin's U (WA)
San Diego State U (CA)
San Jose State U (CA)
Seattle U (WA)
Seton Hill U (PA)
Southeastern Louisiana U (LA)
Southeastern U (FL)
Southern Arkansas U–Magnolia (AR)
Southern Illinois U Edwardsville (IL)
Southern U and Ag and Mech Coll (LA)
State U of New York at Plattsburgh (NY)
State U of New York Coll at Potsdam (NY)
State U of New York Coll of Technology at Delhi (NY)
Sullivan U (KY)
Temple U (PA)
Texas Christian U (TX)
Texas Woman's U (TX)
Truman State U (MO)
U of Arkansas (AR)
U of Central Florida (FL)
U of Detroit Mercy (MI)
U of Houston–Downtown (TX)
U of Illinois at Springfield (IL)
U of Maryland U Coll (MD)
U of Massachusetts Boston (MA)
U of Michigan–Dearborn (MI)
U of Mount Union (OH)
U of Nevada, Las Vegas (NV)
The U of North Carolina at Charlotte (NC)
The U of North Carolina at Pembroke (NC)
U of North Dakota (ND)
U of Northern Colorado (CO)
U of North Florida (FL)
U of Northwestern–St. Paul (MN)
U of Providence (MT)
U of Regina (SK, Canada)
U of Richmond (VA)
U of Saint Francis (IN)
U of South Dakota (SD)
U of Southern Indiana (IN)
The U of Texas of the Permian Basin (TX)
The U of Texas Rio Grande Valley (TX)
U of the Incarnate Word (TX)
The U of Toledo (OH)
U of Wisconsin–Eau Claire (WI)
U of Wisconsin–Milwaukee (WI)
U of Wisconsin–Superior (WI)
U of Wyoming (WY)
Weber State U (UT)

West Chester U of Pennsylvania (PA)
West Virginia State U (WV)
Woodbury U (CA)
Worcester State U (MA)
Youngstown State U (OH)

CRIMINOLOGY
Adams State U (CO)
Albright Coll (PA)
Assumption Coll (MA)
Auburn U (AL)
Avila U (MO)
Butler U (IN)
California State U, San Marcos (CA)
Central Connecticut State U (CT)
Colorado State U–Pueblo (CO)
Concordia U Chicago (IL)
DePaul U (IL)
Dominican U (IL)
Drury U (MO)
Eastern U (PA)
Eastern Washington U (WA)
Emmanuel Coll (MA)
Florida Southern Coll (FL)
Fort Lewis Coll (CO)
Framingham State U (MA)
Geneva Coll (PA)
Gonzaga U (WA)
Hamline U (MN)
Hofstra U (NY)
Humboldt State U (CA)
Indiana State U (IN)
Indiana U of Pennsylvania (PA)
Johnson C. Smith U (NC)
Lasell Coll (MA)
Lebanon Valley Coll (PA)
Lees-McRae Coll (NC)
Lee U (TN)
LeTourneau U (TX)
Loyola U New Orleans (LA)
Lycoming Coll (PA)
Marquette U (WI)
Maryville U of Saint Louis (MO)
Mercer U, Macon (GA)
Mount St. Joseph U (OH)
Mount Saint Mary Coll (NY)
North Carolina State U (NC)
Ohio Dominican U (OH)
The Ohio State U (OH)
The Ohio State U at Mansfield (OH)
The Ohio State U at Marion (OH)
Ohio U (OH)
Old Dominion U (VA)
Randolph-Macon Coll (VA)
Regis U (CO)
St. John Fisher Coll (NY)
Saint Joseph's U (PA)
St. Mary's U (TX)
Saint Vincent Coll (PA)
Spring Hill Coll (AL)
Stockton U (NJ)
Stonehill Coll (MA)
Tabor Coll (KS)
U at Buffalo, the State U of New York (NY)
U of California, Irvine (CA)
U of Florida (FL)
U of Houston–Clear Lake (TX)
U of La Verne (CA)
U of Lynchburg (VA)
U of Maryland, Coll Park (MD)
U of Massachusetts Dartmouth (MA)
U of Memphis (TN)
U of Minnesota, Duluth (MN)
U of Minnesota, Twin Cities Campus (MN)
U of Nevada, Reno (NV)
U of New Hampshire (NH)
U of Northern Iowa (IA)
U of Saint Mary (KS)
U of St. Thomas (MN)
U of St. Thomas (TX)
U of Sioux Falls (SD)
U of South Florida (FL)
U of South Florida Sarasota-Manatee (FL)
The U of Tampa (FL)
The U of Texas of the Permian Basin (TX)
U of West Georgia (GA)
U of Wisconsin–River Falls (WI)
Valparaiso U (IN)
Western Kentucky U (KY)
Wilkes U (PA)
Wright State U–Lake Campus (OH)

CRISIS/EMERGENCY/DISASTER MANAGEMENT
Adelphi U (NY)
American Public U System (WV)
Arapahoe Comm Coll (CO)
Arkansas Tech U (AR)
Elizabeth City State U (NC)
Embry-Riddle Aeronautical U–Worldwide (FL)
Immaculata U (PA)
Kansas Wesleyan U (KS)
Lee U (TN)
Northwest Missouri State U (MO)
Saint Louis U (MO)
Southeast Missouri State U (MO)
Truckee Meadows Comm Coll (NV)
U of Central Florida (FL)
U of New Haven (CT)
U of Northern Iowa (IA)

CRITICAL INFRASTRUCTURE PROTECTION
Drury U (MO)
Excelsior Coll (NY)
George Mason U (VA)
Idaho State U (ID)
Indiana State U (IN)

CROP PRODUCTION
U of Idaho (ID)

CULINARY ARTS
Coll of the Ozarks (MO)
Inter American U of Puerto Rico, Barranquitas Campus (PR)
State U of New York Coll of Technology at Delhi (NY)

CULINARY ARTS RELATED
U of Nevada, Las Vegas (NV)

CULINARY SCIENCE
Texas Woman's U (TX)

CULTURAL ANTHROPOLOGY
Creighton U (NE)
Stonehill Coll (MA)

CULTURAL STUDIES/ CRITICAL THEORY AND ANALYSIS
American Public U System (WV)
Bryant U (RI)
Excelsior Coll (NY)
Occidental Coll (CA)
Rollins Coll (FL)
Samford U (AL)
The U of Tampa (FL)
Western Kentucky U (KY)
Willamette U (OR)

CURRICULUM AND INSTRUCTION
Curry Coll (MA)
Eastern Washington U (WA)
Franklin Pierce U (NH)
Lasell Coll (MA)
U of South Dakota (SD)
Utah State U (UT)

CUSTOMER SERVICE MANAGEMENT
Ohio U (OH)

CYBER/COMPUTER FORENSICS AND COUNTERTERRORISM
Champlain Coll (VT)
Christian Brothers U (TN)
The Coll of Saint Rose (NY)
Davenport U, Grand Rapids (MI)
Embry-Riddle Aeronautical U–Prescott (AZ)
Excelsior Coll (NY)
Farmingdale State Coll (NY)
Kansas Wesleyan U (KS)
National U (CA)
Northeastern State U (OK)
Regent U (VA)
Sullivan U (KY)
Tiffin U (OH)
U of the Incarnate Word (TX)

CYBER/ELECTRONIC OPERATIONS AND WARFARE
Excelsior Coll (NY)
LeTourneau U (TX)
Maryville U of Saint Louis (MO)

CYTOTECHNOLOGY
Illinois Coll (IL)
Indiana U–Purdue U Indianapolis (IN)
Marshall U (WV)
Saint Mary's U of Minnesota (MN)
State U of New York at Plattsburgh (NY)

DAIRY SCIENCE
California Polytechnic State U, San Luis Obispo (CA)
Delaware Valley U (PA)
Iowa State U of Science and Technology (IA)
U of Georgia (GA)
U of New Hampshire (NH)
U of Wisconsin–River Falls (WI)
Utah State U (UT)
Virginia Polytechnic Inst and State U (VA)

DANCE
Adelphi U (NY)
Agnes Scott Coll (GA)
Alabama State U (AL)
American U (DC)
Appalachian State U (NC)
Baldwin Wallace U (OH)
Beloit Coll (WI)
Bowling Green State U (OH)
Brenau U (GA)
Butler U (IN)
California State U, Fullerton (CA)
California State U, Long Beach (CA)
The Coll at Brockport, State U of New York (NY)
Coll of Charleston (SC)
The Colorado Coll (CO)
Colorado State U (CO)
Columbia Coll Chicago (IL)
Columbia U (NY)
Connecticut Coll (CT)
Dean Coll (MA)
Dickinson Coll (PA)
East Carolina U (NC)
Florida Southern Coll (FL)
Fordham U (NY)
George Mason U (VA)
Gonzaga U (WA)
Grand Valley State U (MI)
Hamilton Coll (NY)
High Point U (NC)
Hofstra U (NY)
Hollins U (VA)
Hunter Coll of the City U of New York (NY)
Idaho State U (ID)
Indiana U Bloomington (IN)
Jacksonville U (FL)
The Juilliard School (NY)
Kennesaw State U (GA)
Lindenwood U (MO)
Loyola Marymount U (CA)
Loyola U Chicago (IL)
Madonna U (MI)
Manhattanville Coll (NY)
Marymount Manhattan Coll (NY)
Messiah Coll (PA)
Middlebury Coll (VT)
Mills Coll (CA)
Montclair State U (NJ)
Nazareth Coll of Rochester (NY)
New York U (NY)
Northwestern U (IL)
The Ohio State U (OH)
Ohio U (OH)
Pace U (NY)
Palm Beach Atlantic U (FL)
Purchase Coll, State U of New York (NY)
Radford U (VA)
Randolph Coll (VA)
Rhode Island Coll (RI)
Rider U (NJ)
Rockford U (IL)
St. Olaf Coll (MN)
San Diego State U (CA)
San Francisco State U (CA)
San Jose State U (CA)
Sarah Lawrence Coll (NY)
Scripps Coll (CA)
Seton Hill U (PA)
Skidmore Coll (NY)
State U of New York at Fredonia (NY)
State U of New York Coll at Potsdam (NY)
Sweet Briar Coll (VA)
Temple U (PA)
Texas Christian U (TX)
Texas Tech U (TX)
Texas Woman's U (TX)
Towson U (MD)
Tulane U (LA)
U at Buffalo, the State U of New York (NY)
U of California, Irvine (CA)
U of California, Los Angeles (CA)
U of Florida (FL)
U of Georgia (GA)
U of Hawaii at Manoa (HI)
U of Houston (TX)
U of Idaho (ID)
U of Kentucky (KY)
U of Maryland, Baltimore County (MD)
U of Maryland, Coll Park (MD)
U of Massachusetts Amherst (MA)
U of Michigan (MI)
U of Minnesota, Twin Cities Campus (MN)
U of Nebraska–Lincoln (NE)
U of Nevada, Las Vegas (NV)
U of Nevada, Reno (NV)
U of New Mexico (NM)
The U of North Carolina at Charlotte (NC)
The U of North Carolina at Greensboro (NC)
U of North Carolina School of the Arts (NC)
U of Oregon (OR)
U of Richmond (VA)
U of Saint Francis (IN)
U of St. Thomas (TX)
U of South Carolina (SC)
U of South Florida (FL)
The U of Tampa (FL)
The U of Texas at Austin (TX)
The U of Texas Rio Grande Valley (TX)
U of Washington (WA)
U of Wisconsin–Milwaukee (WI)
Ursinus Coll (PA)
Utah State U (UT)
Utah Valley U (UT)
Virginia Commonwealth U (VA)
Washington U in St. Louis (MO)
Weber State U (UT)
Wesleyan U (CT)
Western Kentucky U (KY)
Western Washington U (WA)
Winthrop U (SC)
Wright State U–Lake Campus (OH)

DANCE RELATED
California State U, Long Beach (CA)
Marymount Manhattan Coll (NY)
Youngstown State U (OH)

DANISH
U of Washington (WA)

DATA MODELING/ WAREHOUSING AND DATABASE ADMINISTRATION
Bryant U (RI)
Central Washington U (WA)
Champlain Coll (VT)
Eastern U (PA)
Limestone Coll (SC)
Marist Coll (NY)
Northwest Missouri State U (MO)
Rochester Inst of Technology (NY)
U of Michigan (MI)

DATA PROCESSING AND DATA PROCESSING TECHNOLOGY
California State U, San Marcos (CA)
Campbellsville U (KY)
U of Northwestern–St. Paul (MN)
U of San Francisco (CA)
Wesleyan Coll (GA)

DEAF STUDIES
California State U, Northridge (CA)
Coll of the Holy Cross (MA)
Columbia Coll Chicago (IL)
Towson U (MD)

DENTAL HYGIENE
Creighton U (NE)
Eastern Washington U (WA)
East Tennessee State U (TN)
Farmingdale State Coll (NY)
Georgia Highlands Coll (GA)
Idaho State U (ID)
Indiana U Northwest (IN)
Indiana U–Purdue U Indianapolis (IN)
Indiana U South Bend (IN)
New York U (NY)
The Ohio State U (OH)
Old Dominion U (VA)
Pueblo Comm Coll (CO)
Rhode Island Coll (RI)
Southern Illinois U Carbondale (IL)
Texas Woman's U (TX)
Tyler Jr Coll (TX)
U of Detroit Mercy (MI)
U of Hawaii at Manoa (HI)
U of Louisville (KY)
U of Michigan (MI)
U of Minnesota, Twin Cities Campus (MN)
U of New Haven (CT)
U of New Mexico (NM)
The U of North Carolina at Chapel Hill (NC)
U of South Dakota (SD)
U of Southern Indiana (IN)
U of Washington (WA)
U of Wyoming (WY)
Utah Valley U (UT)
Vermont Tech Coll (VT)
Virginia Commonwealth U (VA)
Weber State U (UT)
Western Kentucky U (KY)
Youngstown State U (OH)

DENTAL SERVICES AND ALLIED PROFESSIONS RELATED
Indiana U–Purdue U Indianapolis (IN)

DESIGN AND APPLIED ARTS RELATED
Alverno Coll (WI)
Auburn U (AL)
Butler U (IN)
Carnegie Mellon U (PA)
Farmingdale State Coll (NY)
Fashion Inst of Technology (NY)
Harding U (AR)
Hiram Coll (OH)
Hofstra U (NY)
Inter American U of Puerto Rico, San Germán Campus (PR)
Mansfield U of Pennsylvania (PA)
Maryland Inst Coll of Art (MD)
Marymount Manhattan Coll (NY)
Merrimack Coll (MA)
Montclair State U (NJ)
Portland State U (OR)
State U of New York at Fredonia (NY)
U of California, Los Angeles (CA)
The U of Findlay (OH)
U of Oregon (OR)
Virginia Commonwealth U (VA)
Washington U in St. Louis (MO)

DESIGN AND VISUAL COMMUNICATIONS
American U (DC)
Auburn U (AL)
Barton Coll (NC)
Bellarmine U (KY)
Bowling Green State U (OH)
Bryant U (RI)
California State U, Chico (CA)
California State U, Monterey Bay (CA)
Capilano U (BC, Canada)
Carnegie Mellon U (PA)
Cedarville U (OH)
Central Connecticut State U (CT)
Coll of the Ozarks (MO)
Endicott Coll (MA)
Escuela de Artes Plasticas y Diseño de Puerto Rico (PR)
Farmingdale State Coll (NY)
FIDM/Fashion Inst of Design & Merchandising, Los Angeles Campus (CA)
Graceland U (IA)
Indiana U Bloomington (IN)

Iowa State U of Science and Technology (IA)
Kean U (NJ)
Lawrence Technological U (MI)
Lees-McRae Coll (NC)
LIM Coll (NY)
Loyola U Chicago (IL)
Loyola U New Orleans (LA)
Lubbock Christian U (TX)
Madonna U (MI)
Maryland Inst Coll of Art (MD)
Marymount Manhattan Coll (NY)
Marymount U (VA)
Millersville U of Pennsylvania (PA)
Mount St. Joseph U (OH)
Muskingum U (OH)
Nazareth Coll of Rochester (NY)
North Carolina State U (NC)
Northwest Coll of Art & Design (WA)
The Ohio State U (OH)
Purdue U (IN)
Radford U (VA)
Rochester Inst of Technology (NY)
Saginaw Valley State U (MI)
San Francisco State U (CA)
Savannah Coll of Art and Design (GA)
Southern Illinois U Carbondale (IL)
Syracuse U (NY)
Texas Christian U (TX)
U of Arkansas (AR)
U of Dayton (OH)
U of Mary Hardin-Baylor (TX)
U of Maryland, Baltimore County (MD)
U of Notre Dame (IN)
U of Saint Francis (IN)
U of San Francisco (CA)
The U of Texas at Austin (TX)
U of Washington (WA)
Utah Valley U (UT)
Washington U in St. Louis (MO)
Western Washington U (WA)

DESKTOP PUBLISHING AND DIGITAL IMAGING DESIGN
New England Inst of Technology (RI)
Rochester Inst of Technology (NY)

DEVELOPMENTAL AND CHILD PSYCHOLOGY
Boston Coll (MA)
Brandman U (CA)
Bridgewater State U (MA)
California State U, Bakersfield (CA)
Carson-Newman U (TN)
Eastern Washington U (WA)
East Texas Baptist U (TX)
Emmanuel Coll (MA)
Fitchburg State U (MA)
LeTourneau U (TX)
Mills Coll (CA)
Saint Leo U (FL)
Sonoma State U (CA)
Texas Christian U (TX)
U of Detroit Mercy (MI)
U of Minnesota, Twin Cities Campus (MN)
U of Saint Francis (IN)
Utica Coll (NY)
Western Washington U (WA)

DEVELOPMENT ECONOMICS AND INTERNATIONAL DEVELOPMENT
Calvin Coll (MI)
Clark U (MA)
Eastern Mennonite U (VA)
Messiah Coll (PA)
Point Loma Nazarene U (CA)
Stetson U (FL)
U of California, Los Angeles (CA)
U of Dayton (OH)
U of Richmond (VA)
U of St. Thomas (TX)
U of Vermont (VT)
Williams Coll (MA)

DIAGNOSTIC MEDICAL SONOGRAPHY AND ULTRASOUND TECHNOLOGY
AdventHealth U (FL)
Allen Coll (IA)
Baptist Coll of Health Sciences (TN)
Benedictine U (IL)
Grand Valley State U (MI)
Nebraska Methodist Coll (NE)
Rhode Island Coll (RI)
Rochester Inst of Technology (NY)
Seattle U (WA)
The U of Findlay (OH)
Weber State U (UT)

DIESEL MECHANICS TECHNOLOGY
Idaho State U (ID)

DIETETICS
Acadia U (NS, Canada)
Appalachian State U (NC)
Bowling Green State U (OH)
Bradley U (IL)
California Polytechnic State U, San Luis Obispo (CA)
California State U, Long Beach (CA)
California State U, San Bernardino (CA)
Carson-Newman U (TN)
Central Michigan U (MI)
Central Washington U (WA)
Coll of the Ozarks (MO)
Dominican U (IL)
East Carolina U (NC)
Georgia State U (GA)
Harding U (AR)
Idaho State U (ID)
Immaculata U (PA)
Indiana State U (IN)
Iowa State U of Science and Technology (IA)
Lebanese American U (Lebanon)
Life U (GA)
Lipscomb U (TN)
Mansfield U of Pennsylvania (PA)
Marshall U (WV)
Marywood U (PA)
Messiah Coll (PA)
Miami U (OH)
Miami U Hamilton (OH)
Michigan State U (MI)
Northeastern State U (OK)
Northern Illinois U (IL)
Northwest Missouri State U (MO)
The Ohio State U (OH)
Ouachita Baptist U (AR)
Point Loma Nazarene U (CA)
Purdue U (IN)
Queens Coll of the City U of New York (NY)
Saint Louis U (MO)
San Francisco State U (CA)
Seton Hill U (PA)
Texas Christian U (TX)
Texas Tech U (TX)
U of Arkansas (AR)
U of Dayton (OH)
U of Florida (FL)
U of Georgia (GA)
U of New Haven (CT)
U of North Dakota (ND)
U of Northern Colorado (CO)
U of North Florida (FL)
U of Pittsburgh (PA)
U of Vermont (VT)
West Chester U of Pennsylvania (PA)
Western Illinois U (IL)
Youngstown State U (OH)

DIETETICS AND CLINICAL NUTRITION SERVICES RELATED
Bowling Green State U (OH)
Madonna U (MI)
Texas Christian U (TX)

DIGITAL ARTS
Acad of Art U (CA)
Albright Coll (PA)
Antioch Coll, Yellow Springs (OH)
Austin Coll (TX)
Blackburn Coll (IL)
Bowling Green State U (OH)
Champlain Coll (VT)
Concordia U Chicago (IL)
Delta State U (MS)
Escuela de Artes Plasticas y Diseño de Puerto Rico (PR)
Florida Southern Coll (FL)
Fordham U (NY)
Greenville U (IL)
Hamline U (MN)
Kansas Wesleyan U (KS)
Kennesaw State U (GA)
King U (TN)
La Salle U (PA)
Linfield Coll (OR)
Lipscomb U (TN)
Lubbock Christian U (TX)
Manchester U (IN)
Marymount California U (CA)
Marymount Manhattan Coll (NY)
Minnesota State U Moorhead (MN)
Pennsylvania Coll of Art & Design (PA)
Point Loma Nazarene U (CA)
Rhode Island Coll (RI)
Stetson U (FL)
Tiffin U (OH)
Trinity Christian Coll (IL)
U of Central Florida (FL)
U of Florida (FL)
U of Kentucky (KY)
U of Massachusetts Dartmouth (MA)
U of New Mexico (NM)
U of North Carolina at Asheville (NC)
U of Puget Sound (WA)
U of Saint Francis (IN)
The U of Tampa (FL)
The U of Toledo (OH)
Wartburg Coll (IA)

DIGITAL COMMUNICATION AND MEDIA/MULTIMEDIA
Acad of Art U (CA)
Albright Coll (PA)
Baldwin Wallace U (OH)
Baylor U (TX)
Bethany Lutheran Coll (MN)
Bowling Green State U (OH)
Bradley U (IL)
Bryant U (RI)
Buena Vista U (IA)
Butler U (IN)
California Lutheran U (CA)
Calvin Coll (MI)
Canisius Coll (NY)
Carson-Newman U (TN)
Cedarville U (OH)
Central Washington U (WA)
Columbia Coll Chicago (IL)
Dallas Baptist U (TX)
Eastern Illinois U (IL)
Eastern Mennonite U (VA)
Endicott Coll (MA)
The Evergreen State Coll (WA)
Fitchburg State U (MA)
Florida Atlantic U (FL)
Fordham U (NY)
Georgia Southern U (GA)
Grand Valley State U (MI)
Granite State Coll (NH)
Harding U (AR)
High Point U (NC)
Indiana U Bloomington (IN)
Indiana U Kokomo (IN)
Indiana U–Purdue U Indianapolis (IN)
Indiana U South Bend (IN)
Kuyper Coll (MI)
Lawrence Technological U (MI)
Lebanon Valley Coll (PA)
Lee U (TN)
Liberty U (VA)
Limestone Coll (SC)
Loyola U Chicago (IL)
Loyola U New Orleans (LA)
Lycoming Coll (PA)
Manhattanville Coll (NY)
Marquette U (WI)
Marymount California U (CA)
Maryville U of Saint Louis (MO)
Marywood U (PA)
Messiah Coll (PA)
Miami U (OH)
Middle Tennessee State U (TN)
Minnesota State U Moorhead (MN)
Muskingum U (OH)
National U (CA)
New York U (NY)
Northwood U, Michigan Campus (MI)
Ohio U (OH)
Reinhardt U (GA)
Rochester Inst of Technology (NY)
Saginaw Valley State U (MI)
Saint Francis U (PA)
St. John Fisher Coll (NY)
San Diego State U (CA)
Savannah Coll of Art and Design (GA)
Seattle U (WA)
Southeastern U (FL)
State U of New York at Plattsburgh (NY)
Texas Tech U (TX)
Tiffin U (OH)
Trevecca Nazarene U (TN)
U of Detroit Mercy (MI)
U of Georgia (GA)
U of Idaho (ID)
U of Maine (ME)
U of Mount Union (OH)
U of Northern Iowa (IA)
The U of Tampa (FL)
U of the Incarnate Word (TX)
Valparaiso U (IN)
Washington State U (WA)
Washington State U–Tri-Cities (WA)
Washington State U–Vancouver (WA)
Wilkes U (PA)
William Jewell Coll (MO)

DIRECTING AND THEATRICAL PRODUCTION
Averett U (VA)
Baldwin Wallace U (OH)
Boston U (MA)
Bradley U (IL)
California State U, Long Beach (CA)
Columbia Coll Chicago (IL)
Drake U (IA)
Hofstra U (NY)
Lipscomb U (TN)
Marymount Manhattan Coll (NY)
Pace U (NY)
Pepperdine U, Malibu (CA)
Rider U (NJ)
Rochester Coll (MI)
Texas Christian U (TX)
U of Chicago (IL)
U of Washington (WA)
Whitworth U (WA)

DISABILITY STUDIES
Aurora U (IL)

DISPUTE RESOLUTION
Life U (GA)

DIVINITY/MINISTRY
Carson-Newman U (TN)
Johnson U Florida (FL)
Judson U (IL)
Kansas Wesleyan U (KS)
Messenger Coll (TX)
Milligan Coll (TN)
Oklahoma Baptist U (OK)
Regent U (VA)
Rochester Coll (MI)
Shiloh U (IA)
Southeastern U (FL)
Toccoa Falls Coll (GA)
Trevecca Nazarene U (TN)
Tyndale U Coll & Sem (ON, Canada)

DOCUMENTARY PRODUCTION
Columbia Coll Chicago (IL)
Ithaca Coll (NY)

DRAFTING AND DESIGN TECHNOLOGY
Acad of Art U (CA)
East Carolina U (NC)

DRAFTING/DESIGN ENGINEERING TECHNOLOGIES RELATED
Central Michigan U (MI)
Weber State U (UT)

DRAMA AND DANCE TEACHER EDUCATION
Adams State U (CO)
Austin Coll (TX)
Bridgewater State U (MA)
Central Connecticut State U (CT)
Central Washington U (WA)
Coll of the Ozarks (MO)
East Carolina U (NC)
East Texas Baptist U (TX)
Emerson Coll (MA)
Hardin-Simmons U (TX)
Hofstra U (NY)
Jacksonville U (FL)
Lees-McRae Coll (NC)
Lee U (TN)
Lipscomb U (TN)
Lubbock Christian U (TX)
Missouri Baptist U (MO)
Montclair State U (NJ)
Ohio Wesleyan U (OH)
Piedmont Coll (GA)
State U of New York Coll at Potsdam (NY)
Trevecca Nazarene U (TN)
U of Regina (SK, Canada)
U of South Dakota (SD)
Utah Valley U (UT)
Valparaiso U (IN)
Washington U in St. Louis (MO)
Weber State U (UT)

DRAMATIC/THEATER ARTS
Acadia U (NS, Canada)
Adelphi U (NY)
Agnes Scott Coll (GA)
Alabama State U (AL)
Albion Coll (MI)
Albright Coll (PA)
Alfred U (NY)
Allegheny Coll (PA)
American U (DC)
Angelo State U (TX)
Appalachian State U (NC)
Auburn U (AL)
Austin Peay State U (TN)
Averett U (VA)
Avila U (MO)
Baker U (KS)
Barton Coll (NC)
Baylor U (TX)
Bellarmine U (KY)
Beloit Coll (WI)
Berea Coll (KY)
Bethany Lutheran Coll (MN)
Blackburn Coll (IL)
Boston Coll (MA)
Boston U (MA)
Bowling Green State U (OH)
Bradley U (IL)
Brandeis U (MA)
Brenau U (GA)
Bridgewater Coll (VA)
Bridgewater State U (MA)
Bucknell U (PA)
Butler U (IN)
California Lutheran U (CA)
California Polytechnic State U, San Luis Obispo (CA)
California State U, Bakersfield (CA)
California State U, Fullerton (CA)
California State U, Long Beach (CA)
California State U, Los Angeles (CA)
California State U, Northridge (CA)
California State U, San Bernardino (CA)
California U of Pennsylvania (PA)
Carnegie Mellon U (PA)
Carson-Newman U (TN)
Carthage Coll (WI)
The Catholic U of America (DC)
Cedarville U (OH)
Centenary Coll of Louisiana (LA)
Central Connecticut State U (CT)
Christopher Newport U (VA)
Claremont McKenna Coll (CA)
Clark U (MA)
Coastal Carolina U (SC)
Colgate U (NY)
The Coll at Brockport, State U of New York (NY)
Coll of Charleston (SC)
The Coll of Idaho (ID)
Coll of Saint Benedict (MN)
Coll of Staten Island of the City U of New York (NY)
Coll of the Holy Cross (MA)
Coll of the Ozarks (MO)
The Coll of William and Mary (VA)
The Colorado Coll (CO)
Colorado State U (CO)
Columbia Coll Chicago (IL)
Columbia U (NY)
Concordia U Chicago (IL)
Concordia U Irvine (CA)
Connecticut Coll (CT)
Cornell Coll (IA)

Cornell U (NY)
Covenant Coll (GA)
Creighton U (NE)
Culver-Stockton Coll (MO)
Dartmouth Coll (NH)
Davidson Coll (NC)
Dean Coll (MA)
DePaul U (IL)
Dickinson Coll (PA)
Dominican U (IL)
Drake U (IA)
Drew U (NJ)
Drury U (MO)
Duquesne U (PA)
Earlham Coll (IN)
East Carolina U (NC)
Eastern Illinois U (IL)
Eastern Oregon U (OR)
Eastern Washington U (WA)
East Stroudsburg U of Pennsylvania (PA)
East Tennessee State U (TN)
East Texas Baptist U (TX)
Eckerd Coll (FL)
Emerson Coll (MA)
The Evergreen State Coll (WA)
Fairfield U (CT)
Fitchburg State U (MA)
Florida Ag and Mech U (FL)
Florida Atlantic U (FL)
Florida Southern Coll (FL)
Fordham U (NY)
Fort Lewis Coll (CO)
Furman U (SC)
George Mason U (VA)
Georgetown Coll (KY)
Georgia Coll & State U (GA)
Georgia Southern U (GA)
Gonzaga U (WA)
Gordon Coll (MA)
Goshen Coll (IN)
Hamilton Coll (NY)
Hamline U (MN)
Hanover Coll (IN)
Harding U (AR)
Hardin-Simmons U (TX)
Hartwick Coll (NY)
High Point U (NC)
Hillsdale Coll (MI)
Hofstra U (NY)
Hollins U (VA)
Humboldt State U (CA)
Hunter Coll of the City U of New York (NY)
Idaho State U (ID)
Illinois Coll (IL)
Indiana State U (IN)
Indiana U Bloomington (IN)
Indiana U Northwest (IN)
Indiana U of Pennsylvania (PA)
Indiana U South Bend (IN)
Ithaca Coll (NY)
Jacksonville U (FL)
The Juilliard School (NY)
Juniata Coll (PA)
Kalamazoo Coll (MI)
Kansas Wesleyan U (KS)
Kean U (NJ)
Kennesaw State U (GA)
King's Coll (PA)
King U (TN)
Knox Coll (IL)
Lafayette Coll (PA)
LaGrange Coll (GA)
Lake Forest Coll (IL)
Lamar U (TX)
Lawrence U (WI)
Lees-McRae Coll (NC)
Lewis & Clark Coll (OR)
Liberty U (VA)
Limestone Coll (SC)
Lindenwood U (MO)
Linfield Coll (OR)
Lipscomb U (TN)
Louisiana Coll (LA)
Louisiana State U and A&M Coll (LA)
Loyola Marymount U (CA)
Loyola U Chicago (IL)
Loyola U New Orleans (LA)
Lycoming Coll (PA)
Manchester U (IN)
Marquette U (WI)
Marymount Manhattan Coll (NY)
Marywood U (PA)
Massachusetts Inst of Technology (MA)
McDaniel Coll (MD)
Mercer U, Macon (GA)
Merrimack Coll (MA)
Messiah Coll (PA)
Miami U (OH)
Michigan State U (MI)
Middlebury Coll (VT)
Middle Tennessee State U (TN)
Millikin U (IL)
Mills Coll (CA)
Minnesota State U Moorhead (MN)
Missouri Baptist U (MO)
Molloy Coll (NY)
Montclair State U (NJ)
Morningside Coll (IA)
Murray State U (KY)
Muskingum U (OH)
Nazareth Coll of Rochester (NY)
New Coll of Florida (FL)
New England Coll (NH)
New York U (NY)
Northeastern State U (OK)
Northern Illinois U (IL)
Northern Kentucky U (KY)
Northern State U (SD)
Northwestern U (IL)
Northwest Missouri State U (MO)
Occidental Coll (CA)
Oglethorpe U (GA)
The Ohio State U (OH)
The Ohio State U at Lima (OH)
Ohio U (OH)
Ohio Wesleyan U (OH)
Oklahoma Baptist U (OK)
Oklahoma Christian U (OK)
Oklahoma State U (OK)
Old Dominion U (VA)
Ottawa U (KS)
Ouachita Baptist U (AR)
Pacific Lutheran U (WA)
Palm Beach Atlantic U (FL)
Pepperdine U, Malibu (CA)
Piedmont Coll (GA)
Portland State U (OR)
Prairie View A&M U (TX)
Providence Coll (RI)
Purchase Coll, State U of New York (NY)
Purdue U (IN)
Queens Coll of the City U of New York (NY)
Radford U (VA)
Randolph Coll (VA)
Randolph-Macon Coll (VA)
Redeemer U Coll (ON, Canada)
Rhode Island Coll (RI)
Rhodes Coll (TN)
Roanoke Coll (VA)
Rochester Coll (MI)
Rockford U (IL)
Rocky Mountain Coll (MT)
Sacred Heart U (CT)
The Sage Colls (NY)
Saginaw Valley State U (MI)
Saint John's U (MN)
Saint Louis U (MO)
Saint Martin's U (WA)
St. Mary's Coll of Maryland (MD)
Saint Mary's U of Minnesota (MN)
St. Norbert Coll (WI)
St. Olaf Coll (MN)
Salisbury U (MD)
Salve Regina U (RI)
Samford U (AL)
San Diego State U (CA)
San Francisco State U (CA)
San Jose State U (CA)
Sarah Lawrence Coll (NY)
Savannah Coll of Art and Design (GA)
Scripps Coll (CA)
Seattle U (WA)
Seton Hill U (PA)
Skidmore Coll (NY)
Sonoma State U (CA)
Southeast Missouri State U (MO)
Southern Arkansas U–Magnolia (AR)
Southern Illinois U Carbondale (IL)
Southern Illinois U Edwardsville (IL)
Southern U and Ag and Mech Coll (LA)
Southwest Baptist U (MO)
Southwestern U (TX)
Spring Hill Coll (AL)
State U of New York at Fredonia (NY)
State U of New York at Plattsburgh (NY)
State U of New York Coll at Geneseo (NY)
State U of New York Coll at Potsdam (NY)
Stetson U (FL)
Sweet Briar Coll (VA)
Syracuse U (NY)
Tabor Coll (KS)
Taylor U (IN)
Texas Christian U (TX)
Texas Lutheran U (TX)
Texas Tech U (TX)
Texas Woman's U (TX)
Towson U (MD)
Trevecca Nazarene U (TN)
Truman State U (MO)
Tulane U (LA)
U at Buffalo, the State U of New York (NY)
U of Arkansas (AR)
U of California, Irvine (CA)
U of California, Los Angeles (CA)
U of California, Riverside (CA)
U of California, Santa Cruz (CA)
U of Central Arkansas (AR)
U of Central Florida (FL)
U of Colorado Denver (CO)
U of Dallas (TX)
U of Dayton (OH)
U of Detroit Mercy (MI)
The U of Findlay (OH)
U of Florida (FL)
U of Georgia (GA)
U of Hawaii at Manoa (HI)
U of Houston (TX)
U of Idaho (ID)
U of Illinois at Springfield (IL)
U of Kentucky (KY)
U of La Verne (CA)
U of Louisville (KY)
U of Lynchburg (VA)
U of Maine (ME)
U of Maryland, Baltimore County (MD)
U of Maryland, Coll Park (MD)
U of Massachusetts Amherst (MA)
U of Massachusetts Boston (MA)
U of Memphis (TN)
U of Michigan (MI)
U of Minnesota, Duluth (MN)
U of Minnesota, Morris (MN)
U of Minnesota, Twin Cities Campus (MN)
U of Missouri (MO)
U of Montevallo (AL)
U of Mount Union (OH)
U of Nebraska–Lincoln (NE)
U of Nevada, Las Vegas (NV)
U of Nevada, Reno (NV)
U of New Hampshire (NH)
U of New Mexico (NM)
U of North Carolina at Asheville (NC)
The U of North Carolina at Chapel Hill (NC)
The U of North Carolina at Charlotte (NC)
The U of North Carolina at Greensboro (NC)
The U of North Carolina at Pembroke (NC)
U of North Carolina School of the Arts (NC)
U of North Dakota (ND)
U of Northern Colorado (CO)
U of Northern Iowa (IA)
U of Northwestern–St. Paul (MN)
U of Notre Dame (IN)
U of Oregon (OR)
U of Pennsylvania (PA)
U of Pittsburgh (PA)
U of Puget Sound (WA)
U of Regina (SK, Canada)
U of Richmond (VA)
U of Saint Mary (KS)
U of St. Thomas (TX)
U of San Diego (CA)
U of Sioux Falls (SD)
U of South Alabama (AL)
U of South Carolina (SC)
U of South Dakota (SD)
U of Southern Indiana (IN)
U of South Florida (FL)
The U of Tampa (FL)
The U of Tennessee (TN)
The U of Texas at Austin (TX)
The U of Texas at El Paso (TX)
The U of Texas Rio Grande Valley (TX)
U of the Incarnate Word (TX)
The U of the South (TN)
The U of Toledo (OH)
The U of Tulsa (OK)
U of Vermont (VT)
U of Virginia (VA)
U of Washington (WA)
U of West Georgia (GA)
U of Wisconsin–Eau Claire (WI)
U of Wisconsin–La Crosse (WI)
U of Wisconsin–Milwaukee (WI)
U of Wisconsin–River Falls (WI)
U of Wyoming (WY)
Ursinus Coll (PA)
Utah State U (UT)
Utah Valley U (UT)
Valparaiso U (IN)
Vanguard U of Southern California (CA)
Vassar Coll (NY)
Virginia Commonwealth U (VA)
Virginia Polytechnic Inst and State U (VA)
Wabash Coll (IN)
Washington and Lee U (VA)
Washington U in St. Louis (MO)
Weber State U (UT)
Wesleyan Coll (GA)
Wesleyan U (CT)
West Chester U of Pennsylvania (PA)
Western Connecticut State U (CT)
Western Illinois U (IL)
Western Kentucky U (KY)
Western Washington U (WA)
Westmont Coll (CA)
Whittier Coll (CA)
Whitworth U (WA)
Wilkes U (PA)
Willamette U (OR)
William Jewell Coll (MO)
Williams Coll (MA)
Winthrop U (SC)
Wofford Coll (SC)
Wright State U–Lake Campus (OH)
Youngstown State U (OH)

DRAMATIC/THEATER ARTS AND STAGECRAFT RELATED
Adams State U (CO)
Columbia Coll Chicago (IL)
DePaul U (IL)
Drake U (IA)
Fayetteville State U (NC)
Indiana U South Bend (IN)
Lee U (TN)
Macalester Coll (MN)
Pepperdine U, Malibu (CA)
Seton Hill U (PA)
Southern Illinois U Carbondale (IL)
Syracuse U (NY)
U of Northern Colorado (CO)
Western Kentucky U (KY)
Wheaton Coll (MA)

DRAWING
Adams State U (CO)
Bowling Green State U (OH)
Bradley U (IL)
California State U, Long Beach (CA)
Carson-Newman U (TN)
Central Washington U (WA)
Cleveland Inst of Art (OH)
Drake U (IA)
Georgia State U (GA)
Inter American U of Puerto Rico, San Germán Campus (PR)
Maryland Inst Coll of Art (MD)
New England Coll (NH)
Portland State U (OR)
Seton Hill U (PA)
Sonoma State U (CA)
State U of New York at Fredonia (NY)
U of Massachusetts Dartmouth (MA)
U of Michigan (MI)
U of Regina (SK, Canada)
Washington U in St. Louis (MO)

EARLY CHILDHOOD EDUCATION
Adams State U (CO)
Alabama State U (AL)
Auburn U (AL)
Baldwin Wallace U (OH)
Barton Coll (NC)
Baylor U (TX)
Boston U (MA)
Bradley U (IL)
Brandman U (CA)
Bridgewater State U (MA)
Bucknell U (PA)
Butler U (IN)
California State U, Chico (CA)
California State U, Los Angeles (CA)
California State U, San Bernardino (CA)
California State U, San Marcos (CA)
California U of Pennsylvania (PA)
Calvin Coll (MI)
Cameron U (OK)
Capilano U (BC, Canada)
Carson-Newman U (TN)
The Catholic U of America (DC)
Cedarville U (OH)
Central Connecticut State U (CT)
Central Michigan U (MI)
Central State U (OH)
Central Washington U (WA)
Champlain Coll (VT)
Christian Brothers U (TN)
Clarion U of Pennsylvania (PA)
Coastal Carolina U (SC)
Coll of Central Florida (FL)
Coll of Charleston (SC)
Coll of Coastal Georgia (GA)
The Coll of Saint Rose (NY)
Coll of the Ozarks (MO)
Colorado State U (CO)
Colorado State U–Pueblo (CO)
Concordia U Chicago (IL)
Curry Coll (MA)
Dean Coll (MA)
DePaul U (IL)
Dominican U (IL)
Duquesne U (PA)
Eastern Oregon U (OR)
Eastern U (PA)
Eastern Washington U (WA)
East Stroudsburg U of Pennsylvania (PA)
Endicott Coll (MA)
Fayetteville State U (NC)
Fitchburg State U (MA)
Florida Ag and Mech U (FL)
Florida Atlantic U (FL)
Fort Lewis Coll (CO)
Framingham State U (MA)
Georgia Coll & State U (GA)
Gordon Coll (MA)
Granite State Coll (NH)
Grove City Coll (PA)
Harding U (AR)
Hardin-Simmons U (TX)
Hiram Coll (OH)
Hofstra U (NY)
Hood Coll (MD)
Idaho State U (ID)
Illinois Coll (IL)
Indiana U Bloomington (IN)
Indiana U Kokomo (IN)
Indiana U of Pennsylvania (PA)
Inter American U of Puerto Rico, San Germán Campus (PR)
Iona Coll (NY)
Iowa State U of Science and Technology (IA)
Judson U (IL)
Kennesaw State U (GA)
King's Coll (PA)
Lancaster Bible Coll (PA)
La Salle U (PA)
Lasell Coll (MA)
Lebanon Valley Coll (PA)
Lees-McRae Coll (NC)
Lee U (TN)
Liberty U (VA)
Limestone Coll (SC)
Lindenwood U (MO)
Lock Haven U of Pennsylvania (PA)
Louisiana State U and A&M Coll (LA)
Loyola U Chicago (IL)
Lubbock Christian U (TX)

Madonna U (MI)
Martin Luther Coll (MN)
Marywood U (PA)
McNeese State U (LA)
Mercy Coll (NY)
Merrimack Coll (MA)
Messiah Coll (PA)
Miami U (OH)
Miami U Hamilton (OH)
Michigan State U (MI)
Middle Tennessee State U (TN)
Millersville U of Pennsylvania (PA)
Milligan Coll (TN)
Millikin U (IL)
Minnesota State U Moorhead (MN)
Missouri Baptist U (MO)
Mount St. Joseph U (OH)
Mount Saint Mary Coll (NY)
Murray State U (KY)
Muskingum U (OH)
National U (CA)
New Jersey City U (NJ)
New York U (NY)
Northeastern State U (OK)
Northern Illinois U (IL)
Northwest Christian U (OR)
Northwestern Oklahoma State U (OK)
Oakland City U (IN)
Ohio Dominican U (OH)
Ohio U (OH)
Ohio Wesleyan U (OH)
Oklahoma Baptist U (OK)
Oklahoma Christian U (OK)
Ouachita Baptist U (AR)
Point U (GA)
Purdue U (IN)
Purdue U Northwest (IN)
Regent U (VA)
Rhode Island Coll (RI)
Rochester Coll (MI)
Rockford U (IL)
Saint Vincent Coll (PA)
Salisbury U (MD)
Salve Regina U (RI)
San Diego State U (CA)
San Francisco State U (CA)
Southeastern Louisiana U (LA)
Southeastern U (FL)
Southern Arkansas U–Magnolia (AR)
Southern Illinois U Carbondale (IL)
Southern Illinois U Edwardsville (IL)
Southern U and Ag and Mech Coll (LA)
Southwest Baptist U (MO)
Spring Hill Coll (AL)
State U of New York Coll at Geneseo (NY)
State U of New York Coll at Potsdam (NY)
Stonehill Coll (MA)
Texas Christian U (TX)
Towson U (MD)
Trevecca Nazarene U (TN)
U of Central Florida (FL)
U of Dayton (OH)
U of Georgia (GA)
U of Hawaii at Manoa (HI)
U of Kentucky (KY)
U of Maine at Farmington (ME)
U of Massachusetts Boston (MA)
U of Michigan–Dearborn (MI)
U of Missouri (MO)
U of Mount Union (OH)
U of Nevada, Las Vegas (NV)
U of New Mexico (NM)
The U of North Carolina at Chapel Hill (NC)
The U of North Carolina at Greensboro (NC)
U of North Dakota (ND)
U of Northern Colorado (CO)
U of North Florida (FL)
U of Northwestern–St. Paul (MN)
U of Regina (SK, Canada)
U of South Alabama (AL)
U of South Carolina Aiken (SC)
U of Southern Indiana (IN)
U of South Florida (FL)
The U of Tulsa (OK)
U of Vermont (VT)
U of Wisconsin–Milwaukee (WI)
U of Wisconsin–River Falls (WI)
Weber State U (UT)
West Chester U of Pennsylvania (PA)
Western Kentucky U (KY)
Western Washington U (WA)
Wheaton Coll (MA)
Widener U (PA)
Worcester State U (MA)
Wright State U–Lake Campus (OH)
Youngstown State U (OH)

EARTH SCIENCE EDUCATION
Albion Coll (MI)
Calvin Coll (MI)
Central Michigan U (MI)
Coll of Staten Island of the City U of New York (NY)
Minnesota State U Moorhead (MN)
Pace U (NY)
Pace U, Pleasantville Campus (NY)
Queens Coll of the City U of New York (NY)
State U of New York Coll at Potsdam (NY)
Syracuse U (NY)
U of Maine at Farmington (ME)
Western Washington U (WA)

EAST ASIAN LANGUAGES
Austin Coll (TX)
Columbia U (NY)
Eckerd Coll (FL)
Indiana U Bloomington (IN)
U of Georgia (GA)
U of Pennsylvania (PA)
U of Puget Sound (WA)
Washington and Lee U (VA)

EAST ASIAN LANGUAGES RELATED
Boston U (MA)
Dartmouth Coll (NH)
Northwestern U (IL)
U of Chicago (IL)
U of Florida (FL)
U of Minnesota, Twin Cities Campus (MN)
Washington U in St. Louis (MO)

ECOLOGY
Beloit Coll (WI)
Bryant U (RI)
California State U, Long Beach (CA)
California State U, San Marcos (CA)
Central Washington U (WA)
Christian Brothers U (TN)
Clark U (MA)
Coll of the Ozarks (MO)
Colorado State U (CO)
Columbia U (NY)
The Evergreen State Coll (WA)
Fort Lewis Coll (CO)
Georgetown Coll (KY)
Iowa State U of Science and Technology (IA)
Manchester U (IN)
Molloy Coll (NY)
New York U (NY)
Northern State U (SD)
Northwestern U (IL)
Ohio U (OH)
Oklahoma State U (OK)
Rice U (TX)
Salisbury U (MD)
San Diego State U (CA)
San Francisco State U (CA)
Sonoma State U (CA)
State U of New York at Plattsburgh (NY)
Tulane U (LA)
Université de Sherbrooke (QC, Canada)
U of California, Los Angeles (CA)
U of California, Santa Cruz (CA)
U of Georgia (GA)
U of Maine at Machias (ME)
U of Maryland, Coll Park (MD)
U of Minnesota, Twin Cities Campus (MN)
U of Northern Iowa (IA)
U of Pittsburgh (PA)
Utah State U (UT)
Washington U in St. Louis (MO)

ECOLOGY AND EVOLUTIONARY BIOLOGY
Angelo State U (TX)
Bradley U (IL)
The Colorado Coll (CO)
Loyola U New Orleans (LA)
Minnesota State U Moorhead (MN)
Princeton U (NJ)
Purdue U (IN)
U of California, Irvine (CA)
U of Michigan (MI)
U of Pittsburgh (PA)

ECOLOGY, EVOLUTION, SYSTEMATICS AND POPULATION BIOLOGY RELATED
Hofstra U (NY)
U of California, Davis (CA)
U of Regina (SK, Canada)
U of Washington (WA)

E-COMMERCE
Limestone Coll (SC)
Maryville U of Saint Louis (MO)
Seattle U (WA)
Southern U and Ag and Mech Coll (LA)
Trevecca Nazarene U (TN)
U of La Verne (CA)
U of Pennsylvania (PA)
U of the Incarnate Word (TX)
The U of Toledo (OH)
Winthrop U (SC)

ECONOMETRICS AND QUANTITATIVE ECONOMICS
American U (DC)
Baldwin Wallace U (OH)
Bryant U (RI)
Bucknell U (PA)
Carnegie Mellon U (PA)
Clarkson U (NY)
Colgate U (NY)
The Colorado Coll (CO)
Columbia U (NY)
Dickinson Coll (PA)
Hampden-Sydney Coll (VA)
High Point U (NC)
Hofstra U (NY)
Ithaca Coll (NY)
Lake Forest Coll (IL)
Macalester Coll (MN)
Marquette U (WI)
Massachusetts Inst of Technology (MA)
Miami U Hamilton (OH)
New York U (NY)
Providence Coll (RI)
Purdue U (IN)
U of California, Irvine (CA)
U of Chicago (IL)
U of Dayton (OH)
U of Minnesota, Twin Cities Campus (MN)
U of Northern Iowa (IA)
U of Richmond (VA)
U of San Francisco (CA)
The U of West Alabama (AL)
Washington U in St. Louis (MO)
Weber State U (UT)
Wesleyan U (CT)
Western Kentucky U (KY)
Williams Coll (MA)
Youngstown State U (OH)

ECONOMICS
Acadia U (NS, Canada)
Adams State U (CO)
Adelphi U (NY)
Agnes Scott Coll (GA)
Albion Coll (MI)
Albright Coll (PA)
Allegheny Coll (PA)
American U (DC)
American U in Bulgaria (Bulgaria)
American U of Beirut (Lebanon)
Appalachian State U (NC)
Assumption Coll (MA)
Auburn U (AL)
Auburn U at Montgomery (AL)
Austin Coll (TX)
Babson Coll (MA)
Baker U (KS)
Baldwin Wallace U (OH)
Baruch Coll of the City U of New York (NY)
Baylor U (TX)
Bellarmine U (KY)
Beloit Coll (WI)
Benedictine U (IL)
Berea Coll (KY)
Bethel U (MN)
Boston Coll (MA)
Boston U (MA)
Bowling Green State U (OH)
Bradley U (IL)
Brandeis U (MA)
Bridgewater Coll (VA)
Bridgewater State U (MA)
Bryant U (RI)
Bucknell U (PA)
Butler U (IN)
Caldwell U (NJ)
California Inst of Technology (CA)
California Lutheran U (CA)
California Polytechnic State U, San Luis Obispo (CA)
California State U, Bakersfield (CA)
California State U, Chico (CA)
California State U, Fullerton (CA)
California State U, Long Beach (CA)
California State U, Los Angeles (CA)
California State U, Northridge (CA)
California State U, San Bernardino (CA)
California State U, San Marcos (CA)
Calvin Coll (MI)
Campbellsville U (KY)
Canisius Coll (NY)
Carnegie Mellon U (PA)
Carthage Coll (WI)
The Catholic U of America (DC)
Centenary Coll of Louisiana (LA)
Central Connecticut State U (CT)
Central Michigan U (MI)
Central Washington U (WA)
Christopher Newport U (VA)
Claremont McKenna Coll (CA)
Clarion U of Pennsylvania (PA)
Clark U (MA)
Coastal Carolina U (SC)
Colgate U (NY)
Coll of Charleston (SC)
Coll of Saint Benedict (MN)
Coll of Staten Island of the City U of New York (NY)
Coll of the Holy Cross (MA)
The Coll of William and Mary (VA)
The Colorado Coll (CO)
Colorado School of Mines (CO)
Colorado State U (CO)
Columbia U (NY)
Concordia U Irvine (CA)
Connecticut Coll (CT)
Cornell Coll (IA)
Cornell U (NY)
Creighton U (NE)
Dartmouth Coll (NH)
Davidson Coll (NC)
DePaul U (IL)
DEREE - The American Coll of Greece (Greece)
Dickinson Coll (PA)
Dominican U (IL)
Drew U (NJ)
Drury U (MO)
Duquesne U (PA)
Earlham Coll (IN)
East Carolina U (NC)
Eastern Illinois U (IL)
Eastern Mennonite U (VA)
Eastern Oregon U (OR)
Eastern Washington U (WA)
East Stroudsburg U of Pennsylvania (PA)
East Tennessee State U (TN)
Eckerd Coll (FL)
Emmanuel Coll (MA)
Fairfield U (CT)
Fitchburg State U (MA)
Florida Ag and Mech U (FL)
Florida Atlantic U (FL)
Florida Southern Coll (FL)
Fordham U (NY)
Fort Lewis Coll (CO)
Framingham State U (MA)
Furman U (SC)
George Mason U (VA)
Georgia Southern U (GA)
Georgia State U (GA)
Gonzaga U (WA)
Gordon Coll (MA)
Graceland U (IA)
Grand Valley State U (MI)
Grove City Coll (PA)
Hamilton Coll (NY)
Hamline U (MN)
Hampden-Sydney Coll (VA)
Hanover Coll (IN)
Harding U (AR)
Hardin-Simmons U (TX)
Hartwick Coll (NY)
Harvard U (MA)
Haverford Coll (PA)
Hillsdale Coll (MI)
Hofstra U (NY)
Hollins U (VA)
Hood Coll (MD)
Humboldt State U (CA)
Hunter Coll of the City U of New York (NY)
Idaho State U (ID)
Illinois Coll (IL)
Indiana State U (IN)
Indiana U Bloomington (IN)
Indiana U Northwest (IN)
Indiana U of Pennsylvania (PA)
Indiana U–Purdue U Indianapolis (IN)
Indiana U South Bend (IN)
Indiana U Southeast (IN)
Inter American U of Puerto Rico, San Germán Campus (PR)
Iona Coll (NY)
Iowa State U of Science and Technology (IA)
Ithaca Coll (NY)
Jacksonville U (FL)
John Cabot U (Italy)
Johns Hopkins U (MD)
Johnson C. Smith U (NC)
Juniata Coll (PA)
Kalamazoo Coll (MI)
Kean U (NJ)
King's Coll (PA)
Knox Coll (IL)
Lafayette Coll (PA)
La Salle U (PA)
La Sierra U (CA)
Lawrence U (WI)
Lebanese American U (Lebanon)
Lebanon Valley Coll (PA)
Lewis & Clark Coll (OR)
Limestone Coll (SC)
Lindenwood U (MO)
Linfield Coll (OR)
Loras Coll (IA)
Louisiana State U and A&M Coll (LA)
Loyola Marymount U (CA)
Loyola U New Orleans (LA)
Lubbock Christian U (TX)
Lycoming Coll (PA)
Manchester U (IN)
Manhattan Coll (NY)
Manhattanville Coll (NY)
Marist Coll (NY)
Marquette U (WI)
Marshall U (WV)
Marymount U (VA)
McDaniel Coll (MD)
Mercer U, Macon (GA)
Merrimack Coll (MA)
Messiah Coll (PA)
Miami U (OH)
Miami U Hamilton (OH)
Michigan State U (MI)
Middlebury Coll (VT)
Middle Tennessee State U (TN)
Millersville U of Pennsylvania (PA)
Milligan Coll (TN)
Millsaps Coll (MS)
Mills Coll (CA)
Minnesota State U Moorhead (MN)
Montclair State U (NJ)
Murray State U (KY)
Muskingum U (OH)
Nazareth Coll of Rochester (NY)
New Coll of Florida (FL)
New Jersey City U (NJ)
New York U (NY)
Nichols Coll (MA)
Northern Illinois U (IL)
Northern State U (SD)
Northwestern U (IL)
Northwest Missouri State U (MO)
Occidental Coll (CA)
Oglethorpe U (GA)
Ohio Dominican U (OH)
The Ohio State U (OH)
Ohio U (OH)
Ohio Wesleyan U (OH)
Oklahoma State U (OK)

Old Dominion U (VA)
Pace U (NY)
Pace U, Pleasantville Campus (NY)
Pacific Lutheran U (WA)
Pepperdine U, Malibu (CA)
Pitzer Coll (CA)
Portland State U (OR)
Princeton U (NJ)
Providence Coll (RI)
Purchase Coll, State U of New York (NY)
Queens Coll of the City U of New York (NY)
Radford U (VA)
Randolph Coll (VA)
Randolph-Macon Coll (VA)
Regis U (CO)
Rhode Island Coll (RI)
Rhodes Coll (TN)
Rice U (TX)
Rider U (NJ)
Roanoke Coll (VA)
Rochester Inst of Technology (NY)
Rockford U (IL)
Rollins Coll (FL)
Sacred Heart U (CT)
Saginaw Valley State U (MI)
Saint Anselm Coll (NH)
Saint Francis U (PA)
St. John Fisher Coll (NY)
Saint John's U (MN)
St. Joseph's Coll, Long Island Campus (NY)
St. Joseph's Coll, New York (NY)
Saint Joseph's U (PA)
Saint Leo U (FL)
St. Mary's Coll of Maryland (MD)
St. Mary's U (TX)
St. Norbert Coll (WI)
St. Olaf Coll (MN)
Saint Vincent Coll (PA)
Salisbury U (MD)
Salve Regina U (RI)
Samford U (AL)
San Diego State U (CA)
San Francisco State U (CA)
San Jose State U (CA)
Sarah Lawrence Coll (NY)
Scripps Coll (CA)
Seattle U (WA)
Seton Hill U (PA)
Skidmore Coll (NY)
Sonoma State U (CA)
Southeast Missouri State U (MO)
Southern Illinois U Carbondale (IL)
Southern Illinois U Edwardsville (IL)
Southwestern U (TX)
State U of New York at Fredonia (NY)
State U of New York Coll at Geneseo (NY)
State U of New York Coll at Potsdam (NY)
Stetson U (FL)
Stockton U (NJ)
Stonehill Coll (MA)
Sweet Briar Coll (VA)
Syracuse U (NY)
Temple U (PA)
Texas Christian U (TX)
Texas Lutheran U (TX)
Texas Tech U (TX)
Towson U (MD)
Truman State U (MO)
Tulane U (LA)
Union Coll (NY)
Université de Sherbrooke (QC, Canada)
U at Buffalo, the State U of New York (NY)
U of Arkansas (AR)
U of California, Davis (CA)
U of California, Irvine (CA)
U of California, Los Angeles (CA)
U of California, Merced (CA)
U of California, Riverside (CA)
U of California, Santa Cruz (CA)
U of Central Arkansas (AR)
U of Central Florida (FL)
U of Colorado Denver (CO)
U of Dallas (TX)
U of Dayton (OH)
U of Detroit Mercy (MI)
The U of Findlay (OH)
U of Florida (FL)
U of Georgia (GA)
U of Hawaii at Manoa (HI)
U of Houston (TX)
U of Idaho (ID)
U of Illinois at Springfield (IL)
U of Kentucky (KY)
U of La Verne (CA)
U of Louisville (KY)
U of Lynchburg (VA)
U of Maine (ME)
U of Maryland, Baltimore County (MD)
U of Maryland, Coll Park (MD)
U of Massachusetts Amherst (MA)
U of Massachusetts Boston (MA)
U of Massachusetts Dartmouth (MA)
U of Massachusetts Lowell (MA)
U of Memphis (TN)
U of Michigan (MI)
U of Michigan–Dearborn (MI)
U of Minnesota, Duluth (MN)
U of Minnesota, Morris (MN)
U of Minnesota, Twin Cities Campus (MN)
U of Missouri (MO)
U of Mount Union (OH)
U of Nebraska–Lincoln (NE)
U of Nevada, Las Vegas (NV)
U of New Hampshire (NH)
U of New Haven (CT)
U of New Mexico (NM)
U of North Carolina at Asheville (NC)
The U of North Carolina at Chapel Hill (NC)
The U of North Carolina at Greensboro (NC)
U of North Dakota (ND)
U of Northern Colorado (CO)
U of Northern Iowa (IA)
U of North Florida (FL)
U of Notre Dame (IN)
U of Oregon (OR)
U of Pennsylvania (PA)
U of Pittsburgh (PA)
U of Pittsburgh at Bradford (PA)
U of Puget Sound (WA)
U of Regina (SK, Canada)
U of Richmond (VA)
U of St. Thomas (MN)
U of St. Thomas (TX)
U of San Diego (CA)
U of San Francisco (CA)
U of South Carolina (SC)
U of South Dakota (SD)
U of Southern Indiana (IN)
U of South Florida (FL)
The U of Tampa (FL)
The U of Tennessee (TN)
The U of Texas at Austin (TX)
The U of Texas at El Paso (TX)
The U of Texas Rio Grande Valley (TX)
The U of the South (TN)
The U of Toledo (OH)
The U of Tulsa (OK)
U of Vermont (VT)
U of Virginia (VA)
U of Washington (WA)
U of West Georgia (GA)
U of Wisconsin–Eau Claire (WI)
U of Wisconsin–La Crosse (WI)
U of Wisconsin–Milwaukee (WI)
U of Wisconsin–River Falls (WI)
U of Wisconsin–Superior (WI)
Utah State U (UT)
Utah Valley U (UT)
Utica Coll (NY)
Valparaiso U (IN)
Vassar Coll (NY)
Virginia Polytechnic Inst and State U (VA)
Wabash Coll (IN)
Wartburg Coll (IA)
Washington & Jefferson Coll (PA)
Washington and Lee U (VA)
Washington State U (WA)
Washington U in St. Louis (MO)
Weber State U (UT)
Wesleyan Coll (GA)
Western Connecticut State U (CT)
Western Illinois U (IL)
Western Kentucky U (KY)
Western State Colorado U (CO)
Western Washington U (WA)
Westmont Coll (CA)
West Virginia State U (WV)
Wheaton Coll (IL)
Wheaton Coll (MA)
Whittier Coll (CA)
Whitworth U (WA)
Widener U (PA)
Willamette U (OR)
William Jewell Coll (MO)
Winthrop U (SC)
Wofford Coll (SC)
Worcester Polytechnic Inst (MA)
Worcester State U (MA)
Wright State U–Lake Campus (OH)
Youngstown State U (OH)

ECONOMICS RELATED
Central Washington U (WA)
The Colorado Coll (CO)
Lindenwood U (MO)
Regis U (CO)
U of Detroit Mercy (MI)
U of Maine (ME)
U of Minnesota, Duluth (MN)
U of Regina (SK, Canada)
U of Richmond (VA)
U of San Francisco (CA)
Valparaiso U (IN)
Washington & Jefferson Coll (PA)
Western Washington U (WA)

EDUCATION
Acadia U (NS, Canada)
Alverno Coll (WI)
Auburn U (AL)
Avila U (MO)
Baylor U (TX)
Beloit Coll (WI)
Berea Coll (KY)
Bethany Lutheran Coll (MN)
Boston U (MA)
Bowling Green State U (OH)
Bradley U (IL)
Brandeis U (MA)
Brenau U (GA)
Bucknell U (PA)
Canisius Coll (NY)
Carson-Newman U (TN)
The Catholic U of America (DC)
Central Washington U (WA)
Christian Brothers U (TN)
Clark U (MA)
Colgate U (NY)
Coll of Saint Mary (NE)
The Colorado Coll (CO)
Columbia U (NY)
Concordia U Chicago (IL)
Curry Coll (MA)
Dallas Christian Coll (TX)
Dominican U (IL)
Duquesne U (PA)
Eastern Washington U (WA)
East Texas Baptist U (TX)
The Evergreen State Coll (WA)
Fitchburg State U (MA)
Franklin Pierce U (NH)
Furman U (SC)
Goshen Coll (IN)
Gwynedd Mercy U (PA)
Haverford Coll (PA)
Hiram Coll (OH)
Humboldt State U (CA)
Illinois Coll (IL)
Inter American U of Puerto Rico, Barranquitas Campus (PR)
Inter American U of Puerto Rico, San Germán Campus (PR)
Jacksonville U (FL)
Juniata Coll (PA)
LaGrange Coll (GA)
Lake Forest Coll (IL)
Lancaster Bible Coll (PA)
Lebanese American U (Lebanon)
Lesley U (MA)
Liberty U (VA)
Limestone Coll (SC)
Lindenwood U (MO)
Lipscomb U (TN)
Lycoming Coll (PA)
Macalester Coll (MN)
Manchester U (IN)
Manhattan Coll (NY)
Manhattanville Coll (NY)
Mansfield U of Pennsylvania (PA)
Marian U (IN)
Massachusetts Coll of Liberal Arts (MA)
Merrimack Coll (MA)
Miami U (OH)
Michigan State U (MI)
Millsaps Coll (MS)
Missouri Baptist U (MO)
Mount Marty Coll (SD)
Mount St. Joseph U (OH)
Muskingum U (OH)
Nazareth Coll of Rochester (NY)
New England Coll (NH)
North Carolina State U (NC)
Northern Illinois U (IL)
Northwestern U (IL)
Ohio Dominican U (OH)
The Ohio State U (OH)
Ohio Wesleyan U (OH)
Oklahoma Baptist U (OK)
Pacific Lutheran U (WA)
Pfeiffer U (NC)
Piedmont Coll (GA)
Purdue U (IN)
Redeemer U Coll (ON, Canada)
Regent U (VA)
Regis U (CO)
Rhodes Coll (TN)
Rockford U (IL)
Saginaw Valley State U (MI)
Saint Francis U (PA)
Saint Louis U (MO)
Saint Martin's U (WA)
Skidmore Coll (NY)
Southeastern U (FL)
Southwestern U (TX)
State U of New York at Fredonia (NY)
State U of New York Coll at Geneseo (NY)
Stetson U (FL)
Stonehill Coll (MA)
Syracuse U (NY)
Tabor Coll (KS)
Taylor U (IN)
Texas Lutheran U (TX)
Tiffin U (OH)
Trinity Christian Coll (IL)
Union Coll (KY)
Université de Sherbrooke (QC, Canada)
Université Sainte-Anne (NS, Canada)
U of Arkansas (AR)
U of California, Irvine (CA)
U of Colorado Denver (CO)
U of Dallas (TX)
U of Detroit Mercy (MI)
U of Hawaii at Manoa (HI)
U of Maine at Machias (ME)
U of Massachusetts Amherst (MA)
U of Massachusetts Boston (MA)
U of Michigan–Dearborn (MI)
U of Minnesota, Duluth (MN)
U of Missouri (MO)
U of Nevada, Las Vegas (NV)
U of Oregon (OR)
U of Regina (SK, Canada)
U of Saint Francis (IN)
U of Saint Mary (KS)
U of South Dakota (SD)
The U of Tulsa (OK)
U of Vermont (VT)
U of Washington, Bothell (WA)
U of Washington, Tacoma (WA)
U of Wisconsin–Milwaukee (WI)
Ursinus Coll (PA)
Vanguard U of Southern California (CA)
Vassar Coll (NY)
Washington & Jefferson Coll (PA)
Washington U in St. Louis (MO)
Westmont Coll (CA)
Whitworth U (WA)
Wilkes U (PA)
Youngstown State U (OH)

EDUCATIONAL ADMINISTRATION AND SUPERVISION RELATED
Canisius Coll (NY)

EDUCATIONAL ASSESSMENT, EVALUATION, AND RESEARCH RELATED
Blackburn Coll (IL)

EDUCATIONAL, INSTRUCTIONAL, AND CURRICULUM SUPERVISION
Canisius Coll (NY)
Millikin U (IL)
Saint Joseph's U (PA)

EDUCATIONAL/ INSTRUCTIONAL TECHNOLOGY
Acad of Art U (CA)
Bowling Green State U (OH)
Bridgewater State U (MA)
Canisius Coll (NY)
Eastern Washington U (WA)
Jackson State U (MS)
Rhode Island Coll (RI)
U of Michigan–Dearborn (MI)
Widener U (PA)

EDUCATIONAL LEADERSHIP AND ADMINISTRATION
Avila U (MO)
Bradley U (IL)
Canisius Coll (NY)
Eastern Washington U (WA)

EDUCATIONAL PSYCHOLOGY
Saint Vincent Coll (PA)
U of Pittsburgh (PA)

EDUCATIONAL STATISTICS AND RESEARCH METHODS
Bucknell U (PA)

EDUCATION (MULTIPLE LEVELS)
Adams State U (CO)
Assumption Coll (MA)
Austin Peay State U (TN)
Averett U (VA)
Bowling Green State U (OH)
Canisius Coll (NY)
Coll of Charleston (SC)
Coll of Saint Mary (NE)
The Coll of Saint Rose (NY)
The Coll of St. Scholastica (MN)
Columbia U (NY)
Concordia U Chicago (IL)
DePaul U (IL)
Dominican U (IL)
Eastern Washington U (WA)
Florida Southern Coll (FL)
Geneva Coll (PA)
Georgetown Coll (KY)
Grove City Coll (PA)
Gwynedd Mercy U (PA)
Hamline U (MN)
Harding U (AR)
Hofstra U (NY)
Illinois Coll (IL)
Ithaca Coll (NY)
Lindenwood U (MO)
Manchester U (IN)
Manhattan Coll (NY)
Merrimack Coll (MA)
Miami U Hamilton (OH)
Middle Tennessee State U (TN)
Missouri Baptist U (MO)
Molloy Coll (NY)
Mount Saint Mary Coll (NY)
New England Coll (NH)
Ohio Wesleyan U (OH)
Piedmont Coll (GA)
Redeemer U Coll (ON, Canada)
Samford U (AL)
Stockton U (NJ)
Texas Lutheran U (TX)
U of Central Florida (FL)
U of Louisville (KY)
U of Memphis (TN)
U of Minnesota, Duluth (MN)
U of Nebraska–Lincoln (NE)
U of Providence (MT)
U of Puerto Rico–Bayamón (PR)
The U of Tennessee at Martin (TN)
The U of Toledo (OH)
The U of West Alabama (AL)
Utah State U (UT)
Washington U in St. Louis (MO)
Western Kentucky U (KY)
William Jewell Coll (MO)

EDUCATION RELATED
Blackburn Coll (IL)
Bowling Green State U (OH)
DePaul U (IL)
Eastern Oregon U (OR)
Indiana U Bloomington (IN)
Jackson State U (MS)
Lancaster Bible Coll (PA)
Lee U (TN)
Northwest Missouri State U (MO)
Piedmont Coll (GA)
Saginaw Valley State U (MI)
Saint Mary's U of Minnesota (MN)

Towson U (MD)
U of Maine at Presque Isle (ME)
U of Minnesota, Duluth (MN)
U of Minnesota, Twin Cities Campus (MN)
U of Nevada, Reno (NV)
U of Northern Iowa (IA)
U of South Alabama (AL)
U of Washington (WA)

EDUCATION (SPECIFIC LEVELS AND METHODS) RELATED
Appalachian State U (NC)
Inter American U of Puerto Rico, San Germán Campus (PR)
Roanoke Coll (VA)
U of Lynchburg (VA)
U of Northwestern–St. Paul (MN)
Washington U in St. Louis (MO)

EDUCATION (SPECIFIC SUBJECT AREAS) RELATED
Appalachian State U (NC)
Averett U (VA)
Avila U (MO)
Baylor U (TX)
Bowling Green State U (OH)
Graceland U (IA)
Indiana U Bloomington (IN)
Knox Coll (IL)
Madonna U (MI)
Marywood U (PA)
Murray State U (KY)
Northwest Missouri State U (MO)
Old Dominion U (VA)
Piedmont Coll (GA)
U of Kentucky (KY)
U of Minnesota, Duluth (MN)
U of Nebraska–Lincoln (NE)
U of Regina (SK, Canada)
U of Wisconsin–Eau Claire (WI)
Utah State U (UT)
Wartburg Coll (IA)
Weber State U (UT)

ELECTRICAL AND ELECTRONIC ENGINEERING TECHNOLOGIES RELATED
Excelsior Coll (NY)
LeTourneau U (TX)
Rochester Inst of Technology (NY)
Southern Illinois U Carbondale (IL)
Vaughn Coll of Aeronautics and Technology (NY)
West Virginia U Inst of Technology (WV)

ELECTRICAL AND ELECTRONICS ENGINEERING
American Public U System (WV)
Arkansas Tech U (AR)
Auburn U (AL)
Baylor U (TX)
Bethel U (MN)
Boston U (MA)
Bradley U (IL)
Bucknell U (PA)
California Inst of Technology (CA)
California Polytechnic State U, San Luis Obispo (CA)
California State U, Chico (CA)
California State U, Fullerton (CA)
California State U, Long Beach (CA)
California State U, Los Angeles (CA)
California State U, Northridge (CA)
Calvin Coll (MI)
Carnegie Mellon U (PA)
The Catholic U of America (DC)
Cedarville U (OH)
Central Michigan U (MI)
Christian Brothers U (TN)
Christopher Newport U (VA)
Clarkson U (NY)
Coll of Staten Island of the City U of New York (NY)
Colorado School of Mines (CO)
Colorado State U (CO)
Columbia U (NY)
Cornell U (NY)
Dominican U (IL)
Dunwoody Coll of Technology (MN)
Eastern Washington U (WA)
Embry-Riddle Aeronautical U–Daytona (FL)
Embry-Riddle Aeronautical U–Prescott (AZ)
Fairfield U (CT)
Florida Ag and Mech U (FL)
Florida Atlantic U (FL)
Franklin W. Olin Coll of Eng (MA)
George Mason U (VA)
Georgia Southern U (GA)
Gonzaga U (WA)
Grand Valley State U (MI)
Grove City Coll (PA)
Hanover Coll (IN)
Harding U (AR)
Hofstra U (NY)
Idaho State U (ID)
Indiana U–Purdue U Indianapolis (IN)
Inter American U of Puerto Rico, Bayamón Campus (PR)
Iowa State U of Science and Technology (IA)
Jackson State U (MS)
Jacksonville U (FL)
Johns Hopkins U (MD)
Kennesaw State U (GA)
Lafayette Coll (PA)
Lamar U (TX)
Lawrence Technological U (MI)
Lebanese American U (Lebanon)
LeTourneau U (TX)
Liberty U (VA)
Louisiana State U and A&M Coll (LA)
Loyola Marymount U (CA)
Manhattan Coll (NY)
Marquette U (WI)
Marshall U (WV)
Massachusetts Inst of Technology (MA)
Merrimack Coll (MA)
Messiah Coll (PA)
Miami U (OH)
Michigan State U (MI)
Milligan Coll (TN)
National U (CA)
New England Inst of Technology (RI)
New Jersey Inst of Technology (NJ)
New York U (NY)
North Carolina State U (NC)
Northern Illinois U (IL)
Northwestern U (IL)
The Ohio State U (OH)
Ohio U (OH)
Oklahoma Christian U (OK)
Oklahoma State U (OK)
Old Dominion U (VA)
Portland State U (OR)
Prairie View A&M U (TX)
Princeton U (NJ)
Purdue U (IN)
Purdue U Northwest (IN)
Rice U (TX)
Rochester Inst of Technology (NY)
Saginaw Valley State U (MI)
Saint Louis U (MO)
St. Mary's U (TX)
San Diego State U (CA)
San Francisco State U (CA)
San Jose State U (CA)
Seattle U (WA)
Southern Illinois U Carbondale (IL)
Southern Illinois U Edwardsville (IL)
Southern U and Ag and Mech Coll (LA)
State U of New York Maritime Coll (NY)
Stevens Inst of Technology (NJ)
Syracuse U (NY)
Temple U (PA)
Texas Tech U (TX)
Tulane U (LA)
Union Coll (NY)
Université de Sherbrooke (QC, Canada)
U at Buffalo, the State U of New York (NY)
U of Arkansas (AR)
U of California, Davis (CA)
U of California, Irvine (CA)
U of California, Los Angeles (CA)
U of California, Riverside (CA)
U of California, Santa Cruz (CA)
U of Central Florida (FL)
U of Colorado Denver (CO)
U of Dayton (OH)
U of Detroit Mercy (MI)
U of Florida (FL)
U of Georgia (GA)
U of Hawaii at Manoa (HI)
U of Houston (TX)
U of Idaho (ID)
U of Kentucky (KY)
U of Louisville (KY)
U of Maine (ME)
U of Maryland, Coll Park (MD)
U of Massachusetts Amherst (MA)
U of Massachusetts Boston (MA)
U of Massachusetts Dartmouth (MA)
U of Massachusetts Lowell (MA)
U of Memphis (TN)
U of Michigan (MI)
U of Michigan–Dearborn (MI)
U of Minnesota, Duluth (MN)
U of Minnesota, Twin Cities Campus (MN)
U of Missouri (MO)
U of Mount Union (OH)
U of Nebraska–Lincoln (NE)
U of Nevada, Las Vegas (NV)
U of Nevada, Reno (NV)
U of New Hampshire (NH)
U of New Haven (CT)
U of New Mexico (NM)
The U of North Carolina at Charlotte (NC)
U of North Dakota (ND)
U of North Florida (FL)
U of Notre Dame (IN)
U of Pennsylvania (PA)
U of Pittsburgh (PA)
U of Regina (SK, Canada)
U of St. Thomas (MN)
U of San Diego (CA)
U of South Alabama (AL)
U of South Carolina (SC)
U of South Florida (FL)
The U of Tennessee (TN)
The U of Texas at El Paso (TX)
The U of Texas of the Permian Basin (TX)
The U of Texas Rio Grande Valley (TX)
The U of Toledo (OH)
The U of Tulsa (OK)
U of Vermont (VT)
U of Virginia (VA)
U of Washington (WA)
U of Washington, Bothell (WA)
U of Washington, Tacoma (WA)
U of Wisconsin–Milwaukee (WI)
U of Wyoming (WY)
Utah State U (UT)
Valparaiso U (IN)
Virginia Commonwealth U (VA)
Virginia Polytechnic Inst and State U (VA)
Washington State U (WA)
Washington State U–Tri-Cities (WA)
Washington State U–Vancouver (WA)
Washington U in St. Louis (MO)
Weber State U (UT)
Western Kentucky U (KY)
Western Washington U (WA)
West Virginia U Inst of Technology (WV)
Widener U (PA)
Wilkes U (PA)
Worcester Polytechnic Inst (MA)
Wright State U–Lake Campus (OH)
Youngstown State U (OH)

ELECTRICAL, ELECTRONIC AND COMMUNICATIONS ENGINEERING TECHNOLOGY
Bowling Green State U (OH)
California State U, Long Beach (CA)
California U of Pennsylvania (PA)
Carnegie Mellon U (PA)
Central Connecticut State U (CT)
Central Washington U (WA)
Farmingdale State Coll (NY)
Fitchburg State U (MA)
Florida Ag and Mech U (FL)
Idaho State U (ID)
Indiana State U (IN)
Indiana U–Purdue U Indianapolis (IN)
Inter American U of Puerto Rico, Aguadilla Campus (PR)
Inter American U of Puerto Rico, San Germán Campus (PR)
Kennesaw State U (GA)
LeTourneau U (TX)
Middle Tennessee State U (TN)
Northern Kentucky U (KY)
Oklahoma State U (OK)
Prairie View A&M U (TX)
Purdue U (IN)
Purdue U Northwest (IN)
Southern U and Ag and Mech Coll (LA)
State U of New York Coll of Technology at Alfred (NY)
U of Dayton (OH)
U of Houston (TX)
U of Maine (ME)
U of Massachusetts Lowell (MA)
U of Memphis (TN)
The U of North Carolina at Charlotte (NC)
U of Puerto Rico–Bayamón (PR)
Vaughn Coll of Aeronautics and Technology (NY)
Vermont Tech Coll (VT)
Weber State U (UT)
Youngstown State U (OH)

ELECTRICAL, ELECTRONICS AND COMMUNICATIONS ENGINEERING RELATED
Marquette U (WI)
Vaughn Coll of Aeronautics and Technology (NY)

ELECTROMECHANICAL AND INSTRUMENTATION AND MAINTENANCE TECHNOLOGIES RELATED
Excelsior Coll (NY)

ELECTROMECHANICAL ENGINEERING
Hanover Coll (IN)

ELECTROMECHANICAL TECHNOLOGY
Excelsior Coll (NY)
Miami U Hamilton (OH)
Murray State U (KY)
Purdue U Northwest (IN)
Rochester Inst of Technology (NY)
U of Northern Iowa (IA)
The U of Toledo (OH)
Vermont Tech Coll (VT)

ELEMENTARY AND MIDDLE SCHOOL ADMINISTRATION/ PRINCIPALSHIP
The Ohio State U (OH)

ELEMENTARY EDUCATION
Acadia U (NS, Canada)
Alabama State U (AL)
Alfred U (NY)
Alverno Coll (WI)
American U (DC)
Appalachian State U (NC)
Arkansas Tech U (AR)
Auburn U (AL)
Auburn U at Montgomery (AL)
Aurora U (IL)
Austin Coll (TX)
Avila U (MO)
Baker U (KS)
Barton Coll (NC)
Baylor U (TX)
Bellarmine U (KY)
Beloit Coll (WI)
Benedictine U (IL)
Bennett Coll (NC)
Bethany Lutheran Coll (MN)
Bethel Coll (KS)
Bethel U (MN)
Blackburn Coll (IL)
Boston Coll (MA)
Boston U (MA)
Bowling Green State U (OH)
Bradley U (IL)
Brenau U (GA)
Bridgewater State U (MA)
Bryn Athyn Coll of the New Church (PA)
Bucknell U (PA)
Buena Vista U (IA)
Butler U (IN)
Caldwell U (NJ)
Calumet Coll of Saint Joseph (IN)
Calvin Coll (MI)
Cameron U (OK)
Campbellsville U (KY)
Carson-Newman U (TN)
Carthage Coll (WI)
The Catholic U of America (DC)
Centenary Coll of Louisiana (LA)
Central Connecticut State U (CT)
Central Michigan U (MI)
Central Washington U (WA)
Champlain Coll (VT)
Clark U (MA)
Coastal Carolina U (SC)
Coll of Charleston (SC)
Coll of Saint Benedict (MN)
Coll of Saint Mary (NE)
The Coll of Saint Rose (NY)
The Coll of St. Scholastica (MN)
Coll of Staten Island of the City U of New York (NY)
Coll of the Ozarks (MO)
Concordia U Chicago (IL)
Cornell Coll (IA)
Covenant Coll (GA)
Creighton U (NE)
Culver-Stockton Coll (MO)
Curry Coll (MA)
Dakota State U (SD)
Dallas Baptist U (TX)
Daytona State Coll (FL)
Delta State U (MS)
DePaul U (IL)
Dominican U (IL)
Drake U (IA)
Drury U (MO)
East Carolina U (NC)
Eastern Illinois U (IL)
East Texas Baptist U (TX)
Elizabeth City State U (NC)
Emmanuel Coll (GA)
Emmanuel Coll (MA)
Endicott Coll (MA)
Fayetteville State U (NC)
Fitchburg State U (MA)
Florida Ag and Mech U (FL)
Florida Atlantic U (FL)
Florida Coll (FL)
Florida Southern Coll (FL)
Fort Lewis Coll (CO)
Framingham State U (MA)
Franklin Pierce U (NH)
Furman U (SC)
Geneva Coll (PA)
Georgetown Coll (KY)
Georgia Southern U (GA)
Gonzaga U (WA)
Gordon Coll (MA)
Goshen Coll (IN)
Graceland U (IA)
Grand Valley State U (MI)
Greenville U (IL)
Hamline U (MN)
Hanover Coll (IN)
Harding U (AR)
High Point U (NC)
Hofstra U (NY)
Humboldt State U (CA)
Hunter Coll of the City U of New York (NY)
Idaho State U (ID)
Illinois Coll (IL)
Indiana State U (IN)
Indiana U Bloomington (IN)
Indiana U East (IN)
Indiana U Kokomo (IN)
Indiana U Northwest (IN)
Indiana U–Purdue U Indianapolis (IN)
Indiana U South Bend (IN)
Indiana U Southeast (IN)
Inter American U of Puerto Rico, Aguadilla Campus (PR)
Inter American U of Puerto Rico, Fajardo Campus (PR)
Inter American U of Puerto Rico, San Germán Campus (PR)
Iona Coll (NY)
Iowa State U of Science and Technology (IA)
Jackson State U (MS)
Jacksonville U (FL)
Johnson U Florida (FL)
Judson U (IL)
Kansas Wesleyan U (KS)
Kean U (NJ)
Kennesaw State U (GA)
King's Coll (PA)
Knox Coll (IL)
Kuyper Coll (MI)

LaGrange Coll (GA)
Lancaster Bible Coll (PA)
Lasell Coll (MA)
La Sierra U (CA)
Lees-McRae Coll (NC)
Lee U (TN)
Lesley U (MA)
LeTourneau U (TX)
Liberty U (VA)
Limestone Coll (SC)
Lindenwood U (MO)
Linfield Coll (OR)
Lipscomb U (TN)
Loras Coll (IA)
Louisiana Coll (LA)
Louisiana State U and A&M Coll (LA)
Loyola U Chicago (IL)
Madonna U (MI)
Manchester U (IN)
Manhattan Coll (NY)
Manhattanville Coll (NY)
Mansfield U of Pennsylvania (PA)
Marian U (IN)
Marquette U (WI)
Marshall U (WV)
Martin Luther Coll (MN)
Marymount U (VA)
Maryville U of Saint Louis (MO)
Marywood U (PA)
McDaniel Coll (MD)
McNeese State U (LA)
Mercer U, Macon (GA)
Merrimack Coll (MA)
Messiah Coll (PA)
Michigan State U (MI)
Middlebury Coll (VT)
Millikin U (IL)
Minnesota State U Moorhead (MN)
Missouri Baptist U (MO)
Molloy Coll (NY)
Morningside Coll (IA)
Mount Marty Coll (SD)
Murray State U (KY)
National U (CA)
Nazareth Coll of Rochester (NY)
New England Coll (NH)
New Jersey City U (NJ)
New York U (NY)
North Carolina State U (NC)
Northeastern State U (OK)
Northern Illinois U (IL)
Northern Kentucky U (KY)
Northern State U (SD)
Northwest Christian U (OR)
Northwestern Oklahoma State U (OK)
Oakland City U (IN)
The Ohio State U (OH)
The Ohio State U at Lima (OH)
The Ohio State U at Mansfield (OH)
The Ohio State U at Marion (OH)
The Ohio State U at Newark (OH)
Ohio Wesleyan U (OH)
Oklahoma Baptist U (OK)
Oklahoma Christian U (OK)
Oklahoma State U (OK)
Ottawa U (KS)
Pace U (NY)
Pace U, Pleasantville Campus (NY)
Palm Beach Atlantic U (FL)
Pfeiffer U (NC)
Point Loma Nazarene U (CA)
Purdue U (IN)
Purdue U Northwest (IN)
Queens Coll of the City U of New York (NY)
Queens U of Charlotte (NC)
Redeemer U Coll (ON, Canada)
Regis U (CO)
Reinhardt U (GA)
Rhode Island Coll (RI)
Rider U (NJ)
Roanoke Coll (VA)
Rochester Coll (MI)
Rockford U (IL)
Rocky Mountain Coll (MT)
Rollins Coll (FL)
The Sage Colls (NY)
Saginaw Valley State U (MI)
Saint Anselm Coll (NH)
Saint Francis U (PA)
St. John Fisher Coll (NY)
Saint John's U (MN)
St. Joseph's Coll, Long Island Campus (NY)
St. Joseph's Coll, New York (NY)
Saint Joseph's U (PA)
Saint Leo U (FL)
Saint Martin's U (WA)
Saint Mary's U of Minnesota (MN)
St. Norbert Coll (WI)
Salisbury U (MD)
Salve Regina U (RI)
Seton Hill U (PA)
Skidmore Coll (NY)
Southeastern Louisiana U (LA)
Southeastern U (FL)
Southeast Missouri State U (MO)
Southern Illinois U Carbondale (IL)
Southern Illinois U Edwardsville (IL)
Southern U and Ag and Mech Coll (LA)
Southwest Baptist U (MO)
Spring Hill Coll (AL)
State U of New York at Fredonia (NY)
State U of New York at Plattsburgh (NY)
State U of New York Coll at Geneseo (NY)
State U of New York Coll at Potsdam (NY)
Stetson U (FL)
Stonehill Coll (MA)
Tabor Coll (KS)
Taylor U (IN)
Temple U (PA)
Texas Christian U (TX)
Texas Lutheran U (TX)
Toccoa Falls Coll (GA)
Towson U (MD)
Trevecca Nazarene U (TN)
Trinity Christian Coll (IL)
Union Coll (KY)
Université de Sherbrooke (QC, Canada)
Université Sainte-Anne (NS, Canada)
U of Arkansas (AR)
U of Central Florida (FL)
U of Detroit Mercy (MI)
The U of Findlay (OH)
U of Florida (FL)
U of Guam (GU)
U of Hawaii at Manoa (HI)
U of Idaho (ID)
U of Illinois at Springfield (IL)
U of Kentucky (KY)
U of Louisville (KY)
U of Lynchburg (VA)
U of Maine (ME)
U of Maine at Farmington (ME)
U of Maine at Machias (ME)
U of Maine at Presque Isle (ME)
U of Mary Hardin-Baylor (TX)
U of Maryland, Coll Park (MD)
U of Michigan (MI)
U of Minnesota, Morris (MN)
U of Minnesota, Twin Cities Campus (MN)
U of Missouri (MO)
U of Montevallo (AL)
U of Nebraska–Lincoln (NE)
U of Nevada, Las Vegas (NV)
U of Nevada, Reno (NV)
U of New Mexico (NM)
The U of North Carolina at Chapel Hill (NC)
The U of North Carolina at Charlotte (NC)
The U of North Carolina at Greensboro (NC)
The U of North Carolina at Pembroke (NC)
U of North Dakota (ND)
U of Northern Colorado (CO)
U of Northern Iowa (IA)
U of North Florida (FL)
U of Northwestern–St. Paul (MN)
U of Pennsylvania (PA)
U of Pittsburgh at Bradford (PA)
U of Providence (MT)
U of Regina (SK, Canada)
U of Saint Francis (IN)
U of Saint Mary (KS)
U of Sioux Falls (SD)
U of South Alabama (AL)
U of South Carolina (SC)
U of South Carolina Aiken (SC)
U of South Dakota (SD)
U of Southern Indiana (IN)
U of South Florida (FL)
U of South Florida Sarasota-Manatee (FL)
The U of Tampa (FL)
U of the Incarnate Word (TX)
The U of Tulsa (OK)
U of Vermont (VT)
U of West Georgia (GA)
U of Wisconsin–Eau Claire (WI)
U of Wisconsin–La Crosse (WI)
U of Wisconsin–Milwaukee (WI)
U of Wisconsin–River Falls (WI)
U of Wisconsin–Superior (WI)
U of Wyoming (WY)
Utah State U (UT)
Utah Valley U (UT)
Utica Coll (NY)
Valley City State U (ND)
Valparaiso U (IN)
Vanguard U of Southern California (CA)
Wartburg Coll (IA)
Washington State U (WA)
Washington State U–Tri-Cities (WA)
Washington State U–Vancouver (WA)
Washington U in St. Louis (MO)
Waynesburg U (PA)
Weber State U (UT)
Wesleyan Coll (GA)
Western Connecticut State U (CT)
Western Illinois U (IL)
Western Kentucky U (KY)
Western State Colorado U (CO)
Western Washington U (WA)
Westmont Coll (CA)
West Virginia State U (WV)
Wheaton Coll (IL)
Wheaton Coll (MA)
Whitworth U (WA)
Widener U (PA)
Wilkes U (PA)
William Jewell Coll (MO)
Winthrop U (SC)
Worcester State U (MA)
Wright State U–Lake Campus (OH)
Youngstown State U (OH)

EMERGENCY MEDICAL TECHNOLOGY (EMT PARAMEDIC)

Central Washington U (WA)
Columbia Southern U (AL)
Concordia U Chicago (IL)
Creighton U (NE)
Franklin Pierce U (NH)
U of Maryland, Baltimore County (MD)
U of New Haven (CT)
U of New Mexico (NM)
U of Sioux Falls (SD)
U of South Alabama (AL)
U of Washington (WA)

ENERGY MANAGEMENT AND SYSTEMS TECHNOLOGY

Creighton U (NE)
Excelsior Coll (NY)
Fitchburg State U (MA)
Idaho State U (ID)
Vermont Tech Coll (VT)

ENGINEERING

Albion Coll (MI)
Auburn U (AL)
Aurora U (IL)
Baldwin Wallace U (OH)
Baylor U (TX)
Beloit Coll (WI)
Boston U (MA)
Bradley U (IL)
California Inst of Technology (CA)
California State U, Long Beach (CA)
California State U, Los Angeles (CA)
Calvin Coll (MI)
Carthage Coll (WI)
The Catholic U of America (DC)
Clarkson U (NY)
Clark U (MA)
Coll of Staten Island of the City U of New York (NY)
Coll of the Ozarks (MO)
Colorado School of Mines (CO)
Cornell Coll (IA)
Cornell U (NY)
Dartmouth Coll (NH)
Dominican U (IL)
East Carolina U (NC)
Eastern Mennonite U (VA)
Endicott Coll (MA)
Framingham State U (MA)
Franklin W. Olin Coll of Eng (MA)
Geneva Coll (PA)
Gonzaga U (WA)
Hanover Coll (IN)
Harvard U (MA)
Indiana State U (IN)
Indiana U Bloomington (IN)
Indiana U–Purdue U Indianapolis (IN)
Inter American U of Puerto Rico, San Germán Campus (PR)
Jacksonville U (FL)
Johns Hopkins U (MD)
Juniata Coll (PA)
Lafayette Coll (PA)
LaGrange Coll (GA)
LeTourneau U (TX)
Manchester U (IN)
Manhattan Coll (NY)
Marian U (IN)
Marshall U (WV)
McNeese State U (LA)
Mercer U, Macon (GA)
Messiah Coll (PA)
Miami U (OH)
Michigan State U (MI)
North Carolina State U (NC)
Northwestern U (IL)
Oglethorpe U (GA)
Oklahoma Christian U (OK)
Old Dominion U (VA)
Ottawa U (KS)
Pacific Lutheran U (WA)
Princeton U (NJ)
Purdue U Northwest (IN)
Rochester Inst of Technology (NY)
Saginaw Valley State U (MI)
Saint Anselm Coll (NH)
Saint Francis U (PA)
Saint Louis U (MO)
Saint Vincent Coll (PA)
San Diego State U (CA)
San Jose State U (CA)
Seattle U (WA)
Temple U (PA)
Texas Christian U (TX)
U of California, Irvine (CA)
U of Detroit Mercy (MI)
U of Hawaii at Manoa (HI)
U of Mary Hardin-Baylor (TX)
U of Michigan (MI)
U of Nebraska–Lincoln (NE)
U of Nevada, Las Vegas (NV)
U of New Haven (CT)
U of North Carolina at Asheville (NC)
U of Northwestern–St. Paul (MN)
U of Regina (SK, Canada)
U of San Diego (CA)
U of Southern Indiana (IN)
The U of Tennessee at Martin (TN)
U of the Incarnate Word (TX)
U of Vermont (VT)
U of Virginia (VA)
Vaughn Coll of Aeronautics and Technology (NY)
Washington and Lee U (VA)
Washington U in St. Louis (MO)
Western Illinois U (IL)
Whitworth U (WA)
Widener U (PA)
Wilkes U (PA)
Youngstown State U (OH)

ENGINEERING DESIGN

Earlham Coll (IN)

ENGINEERING FIELDS RELATED

California State U, Chico (CA)

ENGINEERING/INDUSTRIAL MANAGEMENT

Bowling Green State U (OH)
California State U, Long Beach (CA)
Christian Brothers U (TN)
Clarkson U (NY)
Fort Lewis Coll (CO)
Iowa State U of Science and Technology (IA)
Kennesaw State U (GA)
Mercer U, Macon (GA)
Miami U (OH)
Miami U Hamilton (OH)
Middle Tennessee State U (TN)
Pitzer Coll (CA)
Purdue U (IN)
Purdue U Northwest (IN)
Saginaw Valley State U (MI)
St. Mary's U (TX)
Stevens Inst of Technology (NJ)
U of Northwestern–St. Paul (MN)
U of the Incarnate Word (TX)
Widener U (PA)
Wilkes U (PA)

ENGINEERING MECHANICS

Columbia U (NY)
Johns Hopkins U (MD)
Virginia Polytechnic Inst and State U (VA)

ENGINEERING PHYSICS/ APPLIED PHYSICS

Adams State U (CO)
Arkansas Tech U (AR)
Austin Peay State U (TN)
California Inst of Technology (CA)
Central Washington U (WA)
Christian Brothers U (TN)
Colorado School of Mines (CO)
Columbia U (NY)
Cornell U (NY)
Dartmouth Coll (NH)
Embry-Riddle Aeronautical U–Daytona (FL)
Fordham U (NY)
Fort Lewis Coll (CO)
Goshen Coll (IN)
Hamline U (MN)
Hampden-Sydney Coll (VA)
Jacksonville U (FL)
Juniata Coll (PA)
Kansas Wesleyan U (KS)
LeTourneau U (TX)
Linfield Coll (OR)
Loras Coll (IA)
Loyola Marymount U (CA)
Miami U (OH)
Miami U Hamilton (OH)
Minnesota State U Moorhead (MN)
Morningside Coll (IA)
Murray State U (KY)
New York U (NY)
Northeastern State U (OK)
The Ohio State U (OH)
Piedmont Coll (GA)
Point Loma Nazarene U (CA)
Providence Coll (RI)
Randolph Coll (VA)
Randolph-Macon Coll (VA)
Saint Louis U (MO)
Saint Mary's U of Minnesota (MN)
Samford U (AL)
Southeast Missouri State U (MO)
Stevens Inst of Technology (NJ)
Taylor U (IN)
Trevecca Nazarene U (TN)
U at Buffalo, the State U of New York (NY)
U of Maine (ME)
U of Massachusetts Boston (MA)
U of Michigan (MI)
U of Minnesota, Duluth (MN)
U of Nevada, Reno (NV)
U of New Hampshire (NH)
U of Pittsburgh (PA)
U of St. Thomas (TX)
The U of Tulsa (OK)
Westmont Coll (CA)
Whittier Coll (CA)
Whitworth U (WA)
Worcester Polytechnic Inst (MA)

ENGINEERING RELATED

Agnes Scott Coll (GA)
Alfred U (NY)
Auburn U (AL)
California State U, Chico (CA)
California State U, Long Beach (CA)
Claremont McKenna Coll (CA)
The Coll of Idaho (ID)
Colorado State U–Pueblo (CO)
Eastern Illinois U (IL)
Indiana U–Purdue U Indianapolis (IN)
Madonna U (MI)
Maryville U of Saint Louis (MO)

Massachusetts Maritime Acad (MA)
Michigan State U (MI)
New York U (NY)
Northwestern U (IL)
The Ohio State U (OH)
Ohio Wesleyan U (OH)
Purdue U (IN)
Rochester Inst of Technology (NY)
Stevens Inst of Technology (NJ)
U of California, Davis (CA)
U of Maryland, Coll Park (MD)
U of New Hampshire (NH)
U of Pennsylvania (PA)
U of Washington (WA)
Washington U in St. Louis (MO)
Waynesburg U (PA)
Wheaton Coll (IL)

ENGINEERING-RELATED TECHNOLOGIES
Rochester Inst of Technology (NY)

ENGINEERING SCIENCE
Benedictine U (IL)
Bethany Lutheran Coll (MN)
Bethel U (MN)
California Polytechnic State U, San Luis Obispo (CA)
Coastal Carolina U (SC)
Colorado State U (CO)
Cornell Coll (IA)
Hanover Coll (IN)
Hofstra U (NY)
Muskingum U (OH)
New Jersey Inst of Technology (NJ)
Northwestern U (IL)
Ohio Wesleyan U (OH)
Piedmont Coll (GA)
St. Mary's U (TX)
Sonoma State U (CA)
Sweet Briar Coll (VA)
Tulane U (LA)
U of Michigan (MI)
U of New Mexico (NM)
U of Pittsburgh (PA)
U of Pittsburgh at Bradford (PA)
U of South Carolina (SC)
Wartburg Coll (IA)
Washington and Lee U (VA)
Wright State U–Lake Campus (OH)

ENGINEERING TECHNOLOGIES AND ENGINEERING RELATED
Bowling Green State U (OH)
Daytona State Coll (FL)
East Carolina U (NC)
Eastern Washington U (WA)
Elizabeth City State U (NC)
Excelsior Coll (NY)
Northeastern State U (OK)
Northern Kentucky U (KY)
Old Dominion U (VA)
The U of North Carolina at Charlotte (NC)
The U of West Alabama (AL)

ENGINEERING TECHNOLOGY
Austin Peay State U (TN)
California State U, Long Beach (CA)
Eastern Illinois U (IL)
East Tennessee State U (TN)
Indiana State U (IN)
Kennesaw State U (GA)
Lawrence Technological U (MI)
Miami U (OH)
Miami U Hamilton (OH)
Middle Tennessee State U (TN)
New Jersey Inst of Technology (NJ)
Northern Illinois U (IL)
Southeastern Louisiana U (LA)
Southeast Missouri State U (MO)
Southern Illinois U Carbondale (IL)
Temple U (PA)
U of Memphis (TN)
The U of Texas Rio Grande Valley (TX)
The U of West Alabama (AL)
Western Illinois U (IL)
West Virginia U Inst of Technology (WV)
Youngstown State U (OH)

ENGLISH
Acadia U (NS, Canada)
Adams State U (CO)
Adelphi U (NY)
Agnes Scott Coll (GA)
Alabama State U (AL)
Albion Coll (MI)
Albright Coll (PA)
Alfred U (NY)
Allegheny Coll (PA)
Alverno Coll (WI)
American Coll of Thessaloniki (Greece)
American Public U System (WV)
Angelo State U (TX)
Appalachian State U (NC)
Arkansas Tech U (AR)
Assumption Coll (MA)
Auburn U (AL)
Auburn U at Montgomery (AL)
Aurora U (IL)
Austin Coll (TX)
Austin Peay State U (TN)
Averett U (VA)
Avila U (MO)
Baker U (KS)
Baldwin Wallace U (OH)
Barton Coll (NC)
Baruch Coll of the City U of New York (NY)
Baylor U (TX)
Bellarmine U (KY)
Beloit Coll (WI)
Benedictine U (IL)
Bennett Coll (NC)
Bentley U (MA)
Berea Coll (KY)
Bethany Lutheran Coll (MN)
Bethel Coll (KS)
Bethel U (MN)
Blackburn Coll (IL)
Boston Coll (MA)
Boston U (MA)
Bowling Green State U (OH)
Bradley U (IL)
Brandeis U (MA)
Brenau U (GA)
Bridgewater Coll (VA)
Bridgewater State U (MA)
Bryant U (RI)
Bryn Athyn Coll of the New Church (PA)
Bucknell U (PA)
Buena Vista U (IA)
Butler U (IN)
Caldwell U (NJ)
California Inst of Technology (CA)
California Lutheran U (CA)
California Polytechnic State U, San Luis Obispo (CA)
California State U, Bakersfield (CA)
California State U, Chico (CA)
California State U, Fullerton (CA)
California State U, Long Beach (CA)
California State U, Los Angeles (CA)
California State U, Northridge (CA)
California State U, San Bernardino (CA)
California State U, San Marcos (CA)
California U of Pennsylvania (PA)
Calumet Coll of Saint Joseph (IN)
Calvin Coll (MI)
Cameron U (OK)
Campbellsville U (KY)
Canisius Coll (NY)
Carnegie Mellon U (PA)
Carson-Newman U (TN)
Carthage Coll (WI)
The Catholic U of America (DC)
Cedarville U (OH)
Centenary Coll of Louisiana (LA)
Central Connecticut State U (CT)
Central Michigan U (MI)
Central State U (OH)
Central Washington U (WA)
Christian Brothers U (TN)
Christopher Newport U (VA)
Claremont McKenna Coll (CA)
Clarion U of Pennsylvania (PA)
Clark U (MA)
Coastal Carolina U (SC)
Colgate U (NY)
The Coll at Brockport, State U of New York (NY)
Coll of Charleston (SC)
The Coll of Idaho (ID)
Coll of Saint Benedict (MN)
Coll of Saint Mary (NE)
The Coll of Saint Rose (NY)
The Coll of St. Scholastica (MN)
Coll of Staten Island of the City U of New York (NY)
Coll of the Holy Cross (MA)
Coll of the Ozarks (MO)
The Coll of William and Mary (VA)
The Colorado Coll (CO)
Colorado State U (CO)
Colorado State U–Pueblo (CO)
Columbia Coll (MO)
Columbia Coll Chicago (IL)
Columbia U (NY)
Concordia U Chicago (IL)
Concordia U Irvine (CA)
Connecticut Coll (CT)
Cornell Coll (IA)
Cornell U (NY)
Covenant Coll (GA)
Creighton U (NE)
Culver-Stockton Coll (MO)
Curry Coll (MA)
Dallas Baptist U (TX)
Dartmouth Coll (NH)
Davidson Coll (NC)
Dean Coll (MA)
Delaware Valley U (PA)
Delta State U (MS)
DePaul U (IL)
DEREE - The American Coll of Greece (Greece)
Dickinson Coll (PA)
Dominican U (IL)
Drake U (IA)
Drew U (NJ)
Drury U (MO)
Duquesne U (PA)
East Carolina U (NC)
Eastern Illinois U (IL)
Eastern Mennonite U (VA)
Eastern Oregon U (OR)
Eastern Washington U (WA)
East Tennessee State U (TN)
East Texas Baptist U (TX)
Eckerd Coll (FL)
Elizabeth City State U (NC)
Emmanuel Coll (GA)
Emmanuel Coll (MA)
Endicott Coll (MA)
The Evergreen State Coll (WA)
Fairfield U (CT)
Fayetteville State U (NC)
Fitchburg State U (MA)
Florida Ag and Mech U (FL)
Florida Atlantic U (FL)
Fordham U (NY)
Fort Lewis Coll (CO)
Framingham State U (MA)
Franklin Pierce U (NH)
Furman U (SC)
Geneva Coll (PA)
George Mason U (VA)
Georgetown Coll (KY)
Georgia Coll & State U (GA)
Georgia Southern U (GA)
Georgia State U (GA)
Gonzaga U (WA)
Gordon Coll (MA)
Goshen Coll (IN)
Graceland U (IA)
Grand Valley State U (MI)
Granite State Coll (NH)
Greenville U (IL)
Gwynedd Mercy U (PA)
Hamline U (MN)
Hampden-Sydney Coll (VA)
Hanover Coll (IN)
Harding U (AR)
Hardin-Simmons U (TX)
Hartwick Coll (NY)
Harvard U (MA)
Haverford Coll (PA)
High Point U (NC)
Hillsdale Coll (MI)
Hiram Coll (OH)
Hofstra U (NY)
Hollins U (VA)
Hood Coll (MD)
Humboldt State U (CA)
Hunter Coll of the City U of New York (NY)
Idaho State U (ID)
Illinois Coll (IL)
Immaculata U (PA)
Indiana State U (IN)
Indiana U Bloomington (IN)
Indiana U East (IN)
Indiana U Kokomo (IN)
Indiana U Northwest (IN)
Indiana U of Pennsylvania (PA)
Indiana U–Purdue U Indianapolis (IN)
Indiana U South Bend (IN)
Indiana U Southeast (IN)
Inter American U of Puerto Rico, San Germán Campus (PR)
Iona Coll (NY)
Iowa State U of Science and Technology (IA)
Ithaca Coll (NY)
Jackson State U (MS)
Jacksonville U (FL)
Johns Hopkins U (MD)
Johnson C. Smith U (NC)
Judson U (IL)
Juniata Coll (PA)
Kalamazoo Coll (MI)
Kansas Wesleyan U (KS)
Kean U (NJ)
Kennesaw State U (GA)
King's Coll (PA)
King U (TN)
Knox Coll (IL)
Lafayette Coll (PA)
LaGrange Coll (GA)
Lake Forest Coll (IL)
Lamar U (TX)
La Salle U (PA)
Lasell Coll (MA)
La Sierra U (CA)
Lawrence Technological U (MI)
Lawrence U (WI)
Lebanese American U (Lebanon)
Lebanon Valley Coll (PA)
Lees-McRae Coll (NC)
Lee U (TN)
Lesley U (MA)
LeTourneau U (TX)
Lewis & Clark Coll (OR)
Liberty U (VA)
Limestone Coll (SC)
Lindenwood U (MO)
Lipscomb U (TN)
Lock Haven U of Pennsylvania (PA)
Loras Coll (IA)
Louisiana Coll (LA)
Louisiana State U and A&M Coll (LA)
Loyola Marymount U (CA)
Loyola U Chicago (IL)
Lycoming Coll (PA)
Macalester Coll (MN)
Madonna U (MI)
Maharishi U of Management (IA)
Manchester U (IN)
Manhattan Coll (NY)
Manhattanville Coll (NY)
Mansfield U of Pennsylvania (PA)
Marian U (IN)
Marist Coll (NY)
Marquette U (WI)
Marshall U (WV)
Marymount Manhattan Coll (NY)
Marymount U (VA)
Maryville U of Saint Louis (MO)
Marywood U (PA)
Massachusetts Coll of Liberal Arts (MA)
Massachusetts Inst of Technology (MA)
McDaniel Coll (MD)
McNeese State U (LA)
Mercer U, Macon (GA)
Mercy Coll (NY)
Merrimack Coll (MA)
Messiah Coll (PA)
Miami U (OH)
Miami U Hamilton (OH)
Michigan State U (MI)
Middle Tennessee State U (TN)
Millersville U of Pennsylvania (PA)
Milligan Coll (TN)
Millikin U (IL)
Millsaps Coll (MS)
Mills Coll (CA)
Minnesota State U Moorhead (MN)
Missouri Baptist U (MO)
Molloy Coll (NY)
Montclair State U (NJ)
Morningside Coll (IA)
Mount Marty Coll (SD)
Mount St. Joseph U (OH)
Mount Saint Mary Coll (NY)
Murray State U (KY)
Muskingum U (OH)
National U (CA)
Nazareth Coll of Rochester (NY)
New Coll of Florida (FL)
New Jersey City U (NJ)
New York U (NY)
Nichols Coll (MA)
North Carolina State U (NC)
Northeastern State U (OK)
Northern Illinois U (IL)
Northern Kentucky U (KY)
Northern State U (SD)
Northwest Christian U (OR)
Northwestern Oklahoma State U (OK)
Northwestern U (IL)
Northwest Missouri State U (MO)
Oakland City U (IN)
Occidental Coll (CA)
Oglethorpe U (GA)
Ohio Dominican U (OH)
The Ohio State U (OH)
The Ohio State U at Lima (OH)
The Ohio State U at Mansfield (OH)
The Ohio State U at Marion (OH)
The Ohio State U at Newark (OH)
Ohio U (OH)
Ohio Wesleyan U (OH)
Oklahoma Christian U (OK)
Oklahoma State U (OK)
Old Dominion U (VA)
Ottawa U (KS)
Ouachita Baptist U (AR)
Pace U (NY)
Pace U, Pleasantville Campus (NY)
Pacific Lutheran U (WA)
Palm Beach Atlantic U (FL)
Pepperdine U, Malibu (CA)
Pfeiffer U (NC)
Piedmont Coll (GA)
Point Loma Nazarene U (CA)
Point U (GA)
Portland State U (OR)
Prairie View A&M U (TX)
Princeton U (NJ)
Providence Coll (RI)
Purdue U (IN)
Purdue U Northwest (IN)
Queens Coll of the City U of New York (NY)
Radford U (VA)
Randolph Coll (VA)
Randolph-Macon Coll (VA)
Redeemer U Coll (ON, Canada)
Regent U (VA)
Regis U (CO)
Reinhardt U (GA)
Rhode Island Coll (RI)
Rhodes Coll (TN)
Rice U (TX)
Rider U (NJ)
Roanoke Coll (VA)
Rochester Coll (MI)
Rockford U (IL)
Rocky Mountain Coll (MT)
Rollins Coll (FL)
Sacred Heart U (CT)
The Sage Colls (NY)
Saginaw Valley State U (MI)
Saint Anselm Coll (NH)
Saint Francis U (PA)
St. John Fisher Coll (NY)
Saint John's U (MN)
St. Joseph's Coll, Long Island Campus (NY)
St. Joseph's Coll, New York (NY)
Saint Joseph's U (PA)
Saint Leo U (FL)
Saint Louis U (MO)
Saint Martin's U (WA)
St. Mary's Coll of Maryland (MD)
St. Mary's U (TX)
St. Norbert Coll (WI)
St. Olaf Coll (MN)
Saint Vincent Coll (PA)
Salisbury U (MD)
Salve Regina U (RI)
Samford U (AL)
San Diego State U (CA)
San Francisco State U (CA)
San Jose State U (CA)
Scripps Coll (CA)
Seattle U (WA)
Seton Hill U (PA)
Skidmore Coll (NY)
Sonoma State U (CA)
Southeastern Louisiana U (LA)

Southeastern U (FL)
Southeast Missouri State U (MO)
Southern Arkansas U–Magnolia (AR)
Southern Illinois U Carbondale (IL)
Southern Illinois U Edwardsville (IL)
Southern U and Ag and Mech Coll (LA)
Southwest Baptist U (MO)
Southwestern U (TX)
Spring Hill Coll (AL)
State U of New York at Fredonia (NY)
State U of New York at Plattsburgh (NY)
State U of New York Coll at Geneseo (NY)
State U of New York Coll at Potsdam (NY)
Stetson U (FL)
Stockton U (NJ)
Stonehill Coll (MA)
Sweet Briar Coll (VA)
Syracuse U (NY)
Tabor Coll (KS)
Taylor U (IN)
Temple U (PA)
Texas A&M Intl U (TX)
Texas A&M U–Central Texas (TX)
Texas Christian U (TX)
Texas Lutheran U (TX)
Texas Tech U (TX)
Texas Woman's U (TX)
Tiffin U (OH)
Toccoa Falls Coll (GA)
Towson U (MD)
Trevecca Nazarene U (TN)
Trinity Christian Coll (IL)
Truman State U (MO)
Tulane U (LA)
Tyndale U Coll & Sem (ON, Canada)
Union Coll (KY)
Union Coll (NY)
Université de Sherbrooke (QC, Canada)
Université Sainte-Anne (NS, Canada)
U at Buffalo, the State U of New York (NY)
U of Arkansas (AR)
U of California, Davis (CA)
U of California, Irvine (CA)
U of California, Los Angeles (CA)
U of California, Merced (CA)
U of California, Riverside (CA)
U of Central Arkansas (AR)
U of Central Florida (FL)
U of Chicago (IL)
U of Colorado Denver (CO)
U of Dallas (TX)
U of Dayton (OH)
U of Detroit Mercy (MI)
U of Florida (FL)
U of Georgia (GA)
U of Guam (GU)
U of Hawaii at Manoa (HI)
U of Houston (TX)
U of Houston–Clear Lake (TX)
U of Houston–Downtown (TX)
U of Idaho (ID)
U of Illinois at Springfield (IL)
U of Kentucky (KY)
U of La Verne (CA)
U of Louisville (KY)
U of Lynchburg (VA)
U of Maine (ME)
U of Maine at Farmington (ME)
U of Maine at Machias (ME)
U of Maine at Presque Isle (ME)
U of Mary Hardin-Baylor (TX)
U of Maryland, Baltimore County (MD)
U of Maryland, Coll Park (MD)
U of Maryland Eastern Shore (MD)
U of Maryland U Coll (MD)
U of Massachusetts Amherst (MA)
U of Massachusetts Boston (MA)
U of Massachusetts Dartmouth (MA)
U of Massachusetts Lowell (MA)
U of Memphis (TN)
U of Michigan (MI)
U of Michigan–Dearborn (MI)
U of Minnesota, Duluth (MN)
U of Minnesota, Morris (MN)
U of Minnesota, Twin Cities Campus (MN)
U of Missouri (MO)
U of Montevallo (AL)
U of Mount Union (OH)
U of Nebraska–Lincoln (NE)
U of Nevada, Las Vegas (NV)
U of Nevada, Reno (NV)
U of New Hampshire (NH)
U of New Haven (CT)
U of New Mexico (NM)
U of North Carolina at Asheville (NC)
The U of North Carolina at Chapel Hill (NC)
The U of North Carolina at Charlotte (NC)
The U of North Carolina at Greensboro (NC)
The U of North Carolina at Pembroke (NC)
U of North Dakota (ND)
U of Northern Colorado (CO)
U of Northern Iowa (IA)
U of North Florida (FL)
U of Northwestern–St. Paul (MN)
U of Notre Dame (IN)
U of Oregon (OR)
U of Pennsylvania (PA)
U of Pittsburgh at Bradford (PA)
U of Providence (MT)
U of Puget Sound (WA)
U of Regina (SK, Canada)
U of Richmond (VA)
U of Saint Francis (IN)
U of Saint Mary (KS)
U of St. Thomas (MN)
U of St. Thomas (TX)
U of San Diego (CA)
U of San Francisco (CA)
U of Sioux Falls (SD)
U of South Alabama (AL)
U of South Carolina (SC)
U of South Carolina Aiken (SC)
U of South Dakota (SD)
U of Southern Indiana (IN)
U of South Florida (FL)
U of South Florida Sarasota-Manatee (FL)
The U of Tampa (FL)
The U of Tennessee (TN)
The U of Tennessee at Martin (TN)
The U of Texas at Austin (TX)
The U of Texas at El Paso (TX)
The U of Texas of the Permian Basin (TX)
The U of Texas Rio Grande Valley (TX)
U of the Incarnate Word (TX)
The U of the South (TN)
The U of Toledo (OH)
The U of Tulsa (OK)
U of Vermont (VT)
U of Virginia (VA)
U of Washington (WA)
The U of West Alabama (AL)
U of West Georgia (GA)
U of Wisconsin–Eau Claire (WI)
U of Wisconsin–La Crosse (WI)
U of Wisconsin–Milwaukee (WI)
U of Wisconsin–River Falls (WI)
U of Wisconsin–Superior (WI)
U of Wyoming (WY)
Ursinus Coll (PA)
Utah State U (UT)
Utah Valley U (UT)
Utica Coll (NY)
Valley City State U (ND)
Valparaiso U (IN)
Vanguard U of Southern California (CA)
Vassar Coll (NY)
Virginia Commonwealth U (VA)
Virginia Polytechnic Inst and State U (VA)
Wabash Coll (IN)
Wartburg Coll (IA)
Washington & Jefferson Coll (PA)
Washington and Lee U (VA)
Washington State U (WA)
Washington State U–Tri-Cities (WA)
Washington State U–Vancouver (WA)
Washington U in St. Louis (MO)
Waynesburg U (PA)
Weber State U (UT)
Wesleyan Coll (GA)
Wesleyan U (CT)
West Chester U of Pennsylvania (PA)
Western Connecticut State U (CT)
Western Illinois U (IL)
Western Kentucky U (KY)
Western State Colorado U (CO)
Western Washington U (WA)
Westmont Coll (CA)
West Virginia State U (WV)
Wheaton Coll (IL)
Wheaton Coll (MA)
Whittier Coll (CA)
Whitworth U (WA)
Widener U (PA)
Wilkes U (PA)
Willamette U (OR)
William Jewell Coll (MO)
Williams Coll (MA)
Winthrop U (SC)
Wofford Coll (SC)
Worcester State U (MA)
Wright State U–Lake Campus (OH)
Youngstown State U (OH)

ENGLISH AS A SECOND/ FOREIGN LANGUAGE (TEACHING)

American U (DC)
Bethel U (MN)
Calvin Coll (MI)
The Catholic U of America (DC)
Eastern Washington U (WA)
Goshen Coll (IN)
Inter American U of Puerto Rico, Aguadilla Campus (PR)
Inter American U of Puerto Rico, Barranquitas Campus (PR)
Inter American U of Puerto Rico, Fajardo Campus (PR)
Inter American U of Puerto Rico, San Germán Campus (PR)
Lee U (TN)
Liberty U (VA)
Minnesota State U Moorhead (MN)
Molloy Coll (NY)
The Ohio State U (OH)
Oklahoma Christian U (OK)
Queens Coll of the City U of New York (NY)
Salisbury U (MD)
The U of Findlay (OH)
U of Guam (GU)
U of Hawaii at Manoa (HI)
U of Northern Iowa (IA)
U of Northwestern–St. Paul (MN)
U of Wisconsin–Milwaukee (WI)
U of Wisconsin–River Falls (WI)

ENGLISH LANGUAGE AND LITERATURE RELATED

Dakota State U (SD)
Earlham Coll (IN)
Eastern U (PA)
Emmanuel Coll (MA)
Fort Lewis Coll (CO)
Harvard U (MA)
Hofstra U (NY)
John Cabot U (Italy)
Loyola U New Orleans (LA)
Middlebury Coll (VT)
Ohio U (OH)
Pitzer Coll (CA)
Saint Leo U (FL)
Saint Mary's U of Minnesota (MN)
Southeastern U (FL)
State U of New York Coll at Potsdam (NY)
U of Michigan (MI)
U of Pennsylvania (PA)
U of Providence (MT)
Washington U in St. Louis (MO)
Wesleyan U (CT)
Western Kentucky U (KY)

ENGLISH/LANGUAGE ARTS TEACHER EDUCATION

Adams State U (CO)
Albion Coll (MI)
Alverno Coll (WI)
Appalachian State U (NC)
Arkansas Tech U (AR)
Auburn U (AL)
Averett U (VA)
Baylor U (TX)
Bethany Lutheran Coll (MN)
Bethel U (MN)
Blackburn Coll (IL)
Boston U (MA)
Bowling Green State U (OH)
Bradley U (IL)
Bridgewater State U (MA)
Buena Vista U (IA)
California State U, Long Beach (CA)
Cameron U (OK)
Campbellsville U (KY)
Canisius Coll (NY)
The Catholic U of America (DC)
Cedarville U (OH)
Central Michigan U (MI)
Central State U (OH)
Central Washington U (WA)
Christian Brothers U (TN)
Coll of Saint Mary (NE)
The Coll of Saint Rose (NY)
Coll of Staten Island of the City U of New York (NY)
Coll of the Ozarks (MO)
Concordia U Chicago (IL)
Covenant Coll (GA)
Culver-Stockton Coll (MO)
Dakota State U (SD)
Dallas Baptist U (TX)
Delta State U (MS)
Duquesne U (PA)
East Carolina U (NC)
Eastern Washington U (WA)
East Texas Baptist U (TX)
Emmanuel Coll (GA)
Fitchburg State U (MA)
Florida Ag and Mech U (FL)
Florida Atlantic U (FL)
Florida Southern Coll (FL)
Fort Lewis Coll (CO)
Goshen Coll (IN)
Grand Valley State U (MI)
Granite State Coll (NH)
Greenville U (IL)
Grove City Coll (PA)
Harding U (AR)
Hardin-Simmons U (TX)
Hiram Coll (OH)
Hofstra U (NY)
Immaculata U (PA)
Indiana U Bloomington (IN)
Indiana U Northwest (IN)
Indiana U–Purdue U Indianapolis (IN)
Indiana U South Bend (IN)
Inter American U of Puerto Rico, San Germán Campus (PR)
Iona Coll (NY)
Ithaca Coll (NY)
Juniata Coll (PA)
Kansas Wesleyan U (KS)
Kennesaw State U (GA)
Lee U (TN)
LeTourneau U (TX)
Limestone Coll (SC)
Lipscomb U (TN)
Louisiana Coll (LA)
Madonna U (MI)
Manchester U (IN)
Manhattanville Coll (NY)
Marist Coll (NY)
Martin Luther Coll (MN)
Marywood U (PA)
Merrimack Coll (MA)
Messiah Coll (PA)
Miami U (OH)
Miami U Hamilton (OH)
Millikin U (IL)
Minnesota State U Moorhead (MN)
Morningside Coll (IA)
Mount Marty Coll (SD)
National U (CA)
Nazareth Coll of Rochester (NY)
Northeastern State U (OK)
Northern State U (SD)
Northwestern Oklahoma State U (OK)
Northwest Missouri State U (MO)
Oakland City U (IN)
Ohio Dominican U (OH)
The Ohio State U (OH)
Oklahoma Baptist U (OK)
Oklahoma Christian U (OK)
Pace U (NY)
Pace U, Pleasantville Campus (NY)
Palm Beach Atlantic U (FL)
Pepperdine U, Malibu (CA)
Piedmont Coll (GA)
Providence Coll (RI)
Purdue U (IN)
Queens Coll of the City U of New York (NY)
Reinhardt U (GA)
Rhode Island Coll (RI)
Rocky Mountain Coll (MT)
Saginaw Valley State U (MI)
Saint Francis U (PA)
St. John Fisher Coll (NY)
St. Joseph's Coll, Long Island Campus (NY)
St. Joseph's Coll, New York (NY)
Saint Joseph's U (PA)
Saint Mary's U of Minnesota (MN)
Salve Regina U (RI)
Seton Hill U (PA)
Southeastern Louisiana U (LA)
Southeastern U (FL)
Southeast Missouri State U (MO)
Southern U and Ag and Mech Coll (LA)
Southwest Baptist U (MO)
Spring Hill Coll (AL)
State U of New York Coll at Potsdam (NY)
Syracuse U (NY)
Taylor U (IN)
Temple U (PA)
Texas Christian U (TX)
Tiffin U (OH)
Toccoa Falls Coll (GA)
Trevecca Nazarene U (TN)
Trinity Christian Coll (IL)
Union Coll (KY)
The U of Findlay (OH)
U of Georgia (GA)
U of Idaho (ID)
U of Maine (ME)
U of Maine at Farmington (ME)
U of Maine at Machias (ME)
U of Mary Hardin-Baylor (TX)
The U of North Carolina at Greensboro (NC)
The U of North Carolina at Pembroke (NC)
U of Northwestern–St. Paul (MN)
U of Providence (MT)
U of Regina (SK, Canada)
U of St. Thomas (MN)
U of Sioux Falls (SD)
U of South Dakota (SD)
U of South Florida (FL)
U of Vermont (VT)
U of Wisconsin–Milwaukee (WI)
U of Wisconsin–Superior (WI)
Utah Valley U (UT)
Utica Coll (NY)
Valley City State U (ND)
Valparaiso U (IN)
Washington U in St. Louis (MO)
Waynesburg U (PA)
Weber State U (UT)
Westmont Coll (CA)
Widener U (PA)
Youngstown State U (OH)

ENGLISH LITERATURE (BRITISH AND COMMONWEALTH)

Hunter Coll of the City U of New York (NY)
New York U (NY)
Pace U (NY)
Purchase Coll, State U of New York (NY)
U of Pittsburgh (PA)
Washington U in St. Louis (MO)
Whittier Coll (CA)

ENTOMOLOGY

Cornell U (NY)
Michigan State U (MI)
The Ohio State U (OH)
Oklahoma State U (OK)
Purdue U (IN)
U of California, Davis (CA)
U of California, Riverside (CA)
U of Florida (FL)
U of Georgia (GA)
U of Idaho (ID)
U of Nebraska–Lincoln (NE)
Utah State U (UT)

ENTREPRENEURIAL AND SMALL BUSINESS RELATED

Babson Coll (MA)
Fashion Inst of Technology (NY)
Fort Lewis Coll (CO)

Lipscomb U (TN)
Loyola U Chicago (IL)
U of St. Thomas (MN)

ENTREPRENEURSHIP
American Public U System (WV)
Auburn U at Montgomery (AL)
Avila U (MO)
Babson Coll (MA)
Baruch Coll of the City U of New York (NY)
Baylor U (TX)
Boston Coll (MA)
Bradley U (IL)
Bryant U (RI)
Buena Vista U (IA)
Butler U (IN)
California State U, Fullerton (CA)
Canisius Coll (NY)
Carnegie Mellon U (PA)
Central Michigan U (MI)
Clarkson U (NY)
Columbia Coll (MO)
Dallas Baptist U (TX)
Davenport U, Grand Rapids (MI)
DEREE - The American Coll of Greece (Greece)
Duquesne U (PA)
Eastern U (PA)
Emerson Coll (MA)
Endicott Coll (MA)
Grand Valley State U (MI)
Grove City Coll (PA)
High Point U (NC)
Hofstra U (NY)
Hult Intl Business School (United Kingdom)
Inter American U of Puerto Rico, Aguadilla Campus (PR)
Inter American U of Puerto Rico, Barranquitas Campus (PR)
Inter American U of Puerto Rico, Bayamón Campus (PR)
Inter American U of Puerto Rico, San Germán Campus (PR)
Iowa State U of Science and Technology (IA)
Jackson State U (MS)
Jacksonville U (FL)
John Paul the Great Catholic U (CA)
Juniata Coll (PA)
Kennesaw State U (GA)
Lamar U (TX)
Lasell Coll (MA)
Lindenwood U (MO)
Lipscomb U (TN)
Louisiana State U and A&M Coll (LA)
Loyola Marymount U (CA)
Maharishi U of Management (IA)
Marquette U (WI)
Marymount Manhattan Coll (NY)
Mercer U, Macon (GA)
Mercy Coll (NY)
Middle Tennessee State U (TN)
Millikin U (IL)
Northeastern State U (OK)
Northern Kentucky U (KY)
Northwood U, Michigan Campus (MI)
Oklahoma State U (OK)
Pace U (NY)
Pace U, Pleasantville Campus (NY)
Point Loma Nazarene U (CA)
Purdue U Northwest (IN)
Rider U (NJ)
Rochester Coll (MI)
Rollins Coll (FL)
Saint Louis U (MO)
St. Mary's U (TX)
Saint Mary's U of Minnesota (MN)
Samford U (AL)
Seton Hill U (PA)
Stetson U (FL)
Syracuse U (NY)
Temple U (PA)
Texas Christian U (TX)
Trinity Christian Coll (IL)
U of Central Arkansas (AR)
U of Dayton (OH)
U of Hawaii at Manoa (HI)
U of Houston (TX)
U of Maine at Machias (ME)
U of Minnesota, Duluth (MN)
U of Nevada, Las Vegas (NV)
The U of North Carolina at Greensboro (NC)
The U of North Carolina at Pembroke (NC)
U of North Dakota (ND)
U of Regina (SK, Canada)
U of St. Thomas (MN)
U of San Francisco (CA)
U of Sioux Falls (SD)
U of South Dakota (SD)
The U of Tampa (FL)
The U of Texas Rio Grande Valley (TX)
The U of Toledo (OH)
U of Vermont (VT)
U of Washington (WA)
Washington State U (WA)
Washington U in St. Louis (MO)
Waynesburg U (PA)
Western Kentucky U (KY)
Wilkes U (PA)

ENVIRONMENTAL BIOLOGY
Beloit Coll (WI)
Blackburn Coll (IL)
Boston U (MA)
Bridgewater State U (MA)
Central Washington U (WA)
Christopher Newport U (VA)
Columbia U (NY)
East Stroudsburg U of Pennsylvania (PA)
Fitchburg State U (MA)
Fort Lewis Coll (CO)
Franklin Pierce U (NH)
Greenville U (IL)
Humboldt State U (CA)
Inter American U of Puerto Rico, Bayamón Campus (PR)
Iona Coll (NY)
Kuyper Coll (MI)
Liberty U (VA)
Lindenwood U (MO)
Manchester U (IN)
Michigan State U (MI)
Saint Mary's U of Minnesota (MN)
State U of New York Coll of Environmental Science and Forestry (NY)
Tulane U (LA)
Université Sainte-Anne (NS, Canada)
U of Dayton (OH)
U of Regina (SK, Canada)
Washington U in St. Louis (MO)

ENVIRONMENTAL CHEMISTRY
Beloit Coll (WI)
Central Washington U (WA)
Lawrence Technological U (MI)
Queens U of Charlotte (NC)
Rhode Island Coll (RI)

ENVIRONMENTAL DESIGN/ ARCHITECTURE
Auburn U (AL)
Bowling Green State U (OH)
Cornell U (NY)
Delaware Valley U (PA)
Florida Atlantic U (FL)
Maryland Inst Coll of Art (MD)
Marywood U (PA)
North Carolina State U (NC)
U at Buffalo, the State U of New York (NY)
U of Hawaii at Manoa (HI)
U of Houston (TX)
U of Massachusetts Amherst (MA)
U of Memphis (TN)
U of Minnesota, Twin Cities Campus (MN)
U of New Mexico (NM)
U of Pennsylvania (PA)

ENVIRONMENTAL EDUCATION
Sonoma State U (CA)
U of Maine at Machias (ME)

ENVIRONMENTAL ENGINEERING TECHNOLOGY
Appalachian State U (NC)
Bowling Green State U (OH)
California State U, Long Beach (CA)
Michigan State U (MI)
North Carolina State U (NC)
The U of Findlay (OH)

ENVIRONMENTAL/ ENVIRONMENTAL HEALTH ENGINEERING
Bucknell U (PA)
California Inst of Technology (CA)
California Polytechnic State U, San Luis Obispo (CA)
Central State U (OH)
Clarkson U (NY)
Colorado School of Mines (CO)
Colorado State U (CO)
Columbia U (NY)
Connecticut Coll (CT)
Humboldt State U (CA)
Indiana U of Pennsylvania (PA)
Johns Hopkins U (MD)
Kennesaw State U (GA)
Lafayette Coll (PA)
Louisiana State U and A&M Coll (LA)
Loyola U Chicago (IL)
Manhattan Coll (NY)
Marquette U (WI)
Massachusetts Inst of Technology (MA)
New Jersey Inst of Technology (NJ)
North Carolina State U (NC)
Northwestern U (IL)
The Ohio State U (OH)
Portland State U (OR)
Purdue U (IN)
Rice U (TX)
Saint Francis U (PA)
San Diego State U (CA)
Seattle U (WA)
State U of New York Coll of Environmental Science and Forestry (NY)
Stevens Inst of Technology (NJ)
Syracuse U (NY)
Taylor U (IN)
Temple U (PA)
Texas Tech U (TX)
Tulane U (LA)
U at Buffalo, the State U of New York (NY)
U of California, Irvine (CA)
U of California, Merced (CA)
U of California, Riverside (CA)
U of Central Florida (FL)
U of Florida (FL)
U of Georgia (GA)
U of Massachusetts Lowell (MA)
U of Michigan (MI)
U of Minnesota, Twin Cities Campus (MN)
U of Nevada, Reno (NV)
U of New Hampshire (NH)
U of North Dakota (ND)
U of Notre Dame (IN)
U of Pennsylvania (PA)
U of Pittsburgh (PA)
U of Regina (SK, Canada)
The U of Toledo (OH)
U of Vermont (VT)
U of Washington (WA)
Utah State U (UT)
Wilkes U (PA)
Worcester Polytechnic Inst (MA)

ENVIRONMENTAL HEALTH
American U of Beirut (Lebanon)
Baylor U (TX)
Bowling Green State U (OH)
California State U, Northridge (CA)
Central Michigan U (MI)
Colorado State U (CO)
East Carolina U (NC)
East Tennessee State U (TN)
Indiana U Bloomington (IN)
Ohio U (OH)
Old Dominion U (VA)
Rhode Island Coll (RI)
State U of New York Coll of Environmental Science and Forestry (NY)
U of Georgia (GA)
U of Massachusetts Lowell (MA)
The U of North Carolina at Chapel Hill (NC)
U of Regina (SK, Canada)
U of Saint Francis (IN)
U of Washington (WA)
West Chester U of Pennsylvania (PA)
Western Kentucky U (KY)
Willamette U (OR)

ENVIRONMENTAL SCIENCE
Albion Coll (MI)
Albright Coll (PA)
Alverno Coll (WI)
American Public U System (WV)
American U (DC)
Antioch Coll, Yellow Springs (OH)
Appalachian State U (NC)
Arkansas Tech U (AR)
Assumption Coll (MA)
Auburn U (AL)
Auburn U at Montgomery (AL)
Averett U (VA)
Baldwin Wallace U (OH)
Baylor U (TX)
Bellarmine U (KY)
Benedictine U (IL)
Bethel U (MN)
Boston U (MA)
Bradley U (IL)
Bridgewater Coll (VA)
Bryant U (RI)
Bucknell U (PA)
Buena Vista U (IA)
California Lutheran U (CA)
California State U, Long Beach (CA)
California State U, Monterey Bay (CA)
California U of Pennsylvania (PA)
Calvin Coll (MI)
Canisius Coll (NY)
Carthage Coll (WI)
Cedarville U (OH)
Central Michigan U (MI)
Central Washington U (WA)
Clarion U of Pennsylvania (PA)
Clarkson U (NY)
Colgate U (NY)
The Coll at Brockport, State U of New York (NY)
The Colorado Coll (CO)
Colorado State U (CO)
Columbia Coll (MO)
Columbia U (NY)
Creighton U (NE)
Dallas Baptist U (TX)
Delaware Valley U (PA)
DePaul U (IL)
Dickinson Coll (PA)
Dominican U (IL)
Drake U (IA)
Duquesne U (PA)
Earlham Coll (IN)
Eastern U (PA)
Eastern Washington U (WA)
Endicott Coll (MA)
The Evergreen State Coll (WA)
Florida Ag and Mech U (FL)
Fordham U (NY)
Framingham State U (MA)
Geneva Coll (PA)
George Mason U (VA)
Georgia Coll & State U (GA)
Goshen Coll (IN)
Hardin-Simmons U (TX)
Hartwick Coll (NY)
Hollins U (VA)
Humboldt State U (CA)
Hunter Coll of the City U of New York (NY)
Idaho State U (ID)
Indiana U Bloomington (IN)
Indiana U–Purdue U Indianapolis (IN)
Inter American U of Puerto Rico, Aguadilla Campus (PR)
Inter American U of Puerto Rico, Barranquitas Campus (PR)
Inter American U of Puerto Rico, Bayamón Campus (PR)
Inter American U of Puerto Rico, San Germán Campus (PR)
Iowa State U of Science and Technology (IA)
Johns Hopkins U (MD)
Juniata Coll (PA)
Kennesaw State U (GA)
King's Coll (PA)
Knox Coll (IL)
Lamar U (TX)
La Salle U (PA)
La Sierra U (CA)
Lebanon Valley Coll (PA)
Linfield Coll (OR)
Lipscomb U (TN)
Louisiana State U and A&M Coll (LA)
Loyola Marymount U (CA)
Loyola U Chicago (IL)
Loyola U New Orleans (LA)
Madonna U (MI)
Marshall U (WV)
Maryville U of Saint Louis (MO)
Marywood U (PA)
Massachusetts Coll of Liberal Arts (MA)
Massachusetts Maritime Acad (MA)
Merrimack Coll (MA)
Miami U (OH)
Miami U Hamilton (OH)
Michigan State U (MI)
Mills Coll (CA)
Muskingum U (OH)
Nazareth Coll of Rochester (NY)
New England Coll (NH)
New Jersey Inst of Technology (NJ)
North Carolina State U (NC)
Northern Kentucky U (KY)
Northwestern U (IL)
Ohio Dominican U (OH)
The Ohio State U (OH)
Oklahoma State U (OK)
Pace U (NY)
Pace U, Pleasantville Campus (NY)
Pfeiffer U (NC)
Piedmont Coll (GA)
Point Loma Nazarene U (CA)
Portland State U (OR)
Queens Coll of the City U of New York (NY)
Queens U of Charlotte (NC)
Randolph Coll (VA)
Regis U (CO)
Rhodes Coll (TN)
Rider U (NJ)
Rochester Inst of Technology (NY)
Rocky Mountain Coll (MT)
Saint Francis U (PA)
Saint Joseph's U (PA)
Saint Louis U (MO)
St. Mary's U (TX)
St. Norbert Coll (WI)
Saint Vincent Coll (PA)
Salisbury U (MD)
Samford U (AL)
San Diego State U (CA)
San Francisco State U (CA)
Scripps Coll (CA)
Seattle U (WA)
Skidmore Coll (NY)
Southeast Missouri State U (MO)
Southern Illinois U Edwardsville (IL)
State U of New York at Plattsburgh (NY)
State U of New York Coll of Environmental Science and Forestry (NY)
Stetson U (FL)
Stonehill Coll (MA)
Sweet Briar Coll (VA)
Taylor U (IN)
Temple U (PA)
Texas Christian U (TX)
Trinity Christian Coll (IL)
U of Arkansas (AR)
U of California, Irvine (CA)
U of California, Los Angeles (CA)
U of California, Riverside (CA)
U of Florida (FL)
U of Georgia (GA)
U of Hawaii at Manoa (HI)
U of Houston (TX)
U of Houston–Clear Lake (TX)
U of Idaho (ID)
U of Lynchburg (VA)
U of Maine (ME)
U of Maine at Farmington (ME)
U of Maine at Presque Isle (ME)
U of Maryland, Baltimore County (MD)
U of Maryland, Coll Park (MD)
U of Massachusetts Amherst (MA)
U of Massachusetts Boston (MA)
U of Massachusetts Lowell (MA)
U of Michigan–Dearborn (MI)
U of Minnesota, Duluth (MN)
U of Minnesota, Morris (MN)
U of Minnesota, Twin Cities Campus (MN)
U of Mount Union (OH)

U of Nevada, Reno (NV)
U of New Hampshire (NH)
U of New Haven (CT)
U of New Mexico (NM)
The U of North Carolina at Chapel Hill (NC)
The U of North Carolina at Pembroke (NC)
U of Northern Iowa (IA)
U of Notre Dame (IN)
U of Oregon (OR)
U of Saint Francis (IN)
U of St. Thomas (MN)
U of San Diego (CA)
U of San Francisco (CA)
U of South Carolina (SC)
U of Southern Indiana (IN)
U of South Florida (FL)
The U of Texas Rio Grande Valley (TX)
U of the Incarnate Word (TX)
The U of Toledo (OH)
U of Vermont (VT)
U of Virginia (VA)
U of Washington (WA)
U of Washington, Bothell (WA)
U of Washington, Tacoma (WA)
U of Wisconsin–Milwaukee (WI)
U of Wisconsin–Superior (WI)
Utah Valley U (UT)
Valley City State U (ND)
Valparaiso U (IN)
Vassar Coll (NY)
Wartburg Coll (IA)
Washington & Jefferson Coll (PA)
Washington State U (WA)
Washington State U–Tri-Cities (WA)
Washington State U–Vancouver (WA)
Washington U in St. Louis (MO)
Western Washington U (WA)
Wheaton Coll (IL)
Wheaton Coll (MA)
Whittier Coll (CA)
Willamette U (OR)
Williams Coll (MA)
Winthrop U (SC)
Worcester State U (MA)
Wright State U–Lake Campus (OH)
Youngstown State U (OH)

ENVIRONMENTAL STUDIES
Acadia U (NS, Canada)
Adelphi U (NY)
Albion Coll (MI)
Albright Coll (PA)
Alfred U (NY)
American U (DC)
Appalachian State U (NC)
Austin Coll (TX)
Baylor U (TX)
Bellarmine U (KY)
Beloit Coll (WI)
Bethel U (MN)
Blackburn Coll (IL)
Boston Coll (MA)
Bowling Green State U (OH)
Brandeis U (MA)
Bryant U (RI)
Bucknell U (PA)
California State U, Monterey Bay (CA)
California State U, San Marcos (CA)
California U of Pennsylvania (PA)
Calvin Coll (MI)
Canisius Coll (NY)
Central Michigan U (MI)
Central Washington U (WA)
Champlain Coll (VT)
Christopher Newport U (VA)
Claremont McKenna Coll (CA)
Colgate U (NY)
Coll of Coastal Georgia (GA)
The Coll of Idaho (ID)
Coll of Saint Benedict (MN)
The Coll of St. Scholastica (MN)
Coll of the Holy Cross (MA)
The Colorado Coll (CO)
Columbia Southern U (AL)
Columbia U (NY)
Connecticut Coll (CT)
Cornell Coll (IA)
Dartmouth Coll (NH)
Davidson Coll (NC)
DEREE - The American Coll of Greece (Greece)
Dickinson Coll (PA)
Drake U (IA)
Drew U (NJ)
Earlham Coll (IN)
Eastern Mennonite U (VA)
Eckerd Coll (FL)
The Evergreen State Coll (WA)
Excelsior Coll (NY)
Fairfield U (CT)
Florida Ag and Mech U (FL)
Florida Southern Coll (FL)
Fordham U (NY)
Fort Lewis Coll (CO)
Framingham State U (MA)
Franklin Pierce U (NH)
Furman U (SC)
Gonzaga U (WA)
Hamilton Coll (NY)
Hamline U (MN)
Harvard U (MA)
Hiram Coll (OH)
Hofstra U (NY)
Hollins U (VA)
Hood Coll (MD)
Humboldt State U (CA)
Illinois Coll (IL)
Indiana U Bloomington (IN)
Indiana U South Bend (IN)
Indiana U Southeast (IN)
Inter American U of Puerto Rico, San Germán Campus (PR)
Iona Coll (NY)
Iowa State U of Science and Technology (IA)
Ithaca Coll (NY)
Jacksonville U (FL)
Johns Hopkins U (MD)
Juniata Coll (PA)
Kansas Wesleyan U (KS)
King's Coll (PA)
Knox Coll (IL)
Lake Forest Coll (IL)
Lasell Coll (MA)
Lawrence U (WI)
Lesley U (MA)
Lewis & Clark Coll (OR)
Linfield Coll (OR)
Loyola Marymount U (CA)
Loyola U Chicago (IL)
Loyola U New Orleans (LA)
Macalester Coll (MN)
Maharishi U of Management (IA)
Manchester U (IN)
Manhattanville Coll (NY)
Mansfield U of Pennsylvania (PA)
Marquette U (WI)
Marymount Manhattan Coll (NY)
Maryville U of Saint Louis (MO)
Massachusetts Coll of Liberal Arts (MA)
McDaniel Coll (MD)
Merrimack Coll (MA)
Miami U Hamilton (OH)
Michigan State U (MI)
Middlebury Coll (VT)
Millikin U (IL)
Mills Coll (CA)
Minnesota State U Moorhead (MN)
Muskingum U (OH)
New Coll of Florida (FL)
New York U (NY)
Northern Illinois U (IL)
Northwestern U (IL)
Occidental Coll (CA)
Ohio U (OH)
Ohio Wesleyan U (OH)
Ouachita Baptist U (AR)
Pace U (NY)
Pace U, Pleasantville Campus (NY)
Pacific Lutheran U (WA)
Pfeiffer U (NC)
Pitzer Coll (CA)
Portland State U (OR)
Purchase Coll, State U of New York (NY)
Queens Coll of the City U of New York (NY)
Queens U of Charlotte (NC)
Randolph Coll (VA)
Randolph-Macon Coll (VA)
Redeemer U Coll (ON, Canada)
Regis U (CO)
Rhode Island Coll (RI)
Roanoke Coll (VA)
Rocky Mountain Coll (MT)
Rollins Coll (FL)
Saint Anselm Coll (NH)
Saint Francis U (PA)
Saint John's U (MN)
Saint Louis U (MO)
Saint Martin's U (WA)
St. Mary's Coll of Maryland (MD)
St. Olaf Coll (MN)
Saint Vincent Coll (PA)
Salve Regina U (RI)
San Diego State U (CA)
San Francisco State U (CA)
San Jose State U (CA)
Seattle U (WA)
Skidmore Coll (NY)
Sonoma State U (CA)
Southwestern U (TX)
State U of New York at Plattsburgh (NY)
State U of New York Coll at Potsdam (NY)
State U of New York Coll of Environmental Science and Forestry (NY)
Stockton U (NJ)
Stonehill Coll (MA)
Syracuse U (NY)
Temple U (PA)
Tulane U (LA)
Université de Sherbrooke (QC, Canada)
U of California, Davis (CA)
U of California, Irvine (CA)
U of California, Santa Cruz (CA)
U of Central Florida (FL)
U of Chicago (IL)
U of Illinois at Springfield (IL)
U of Kentucky (KY)
U of Lynchburg (VA)
U of Maine at Farmington (ME)
U of Maine at Machias (ME)
U of Maine at Presque Isle (ME)
U of Maryland, Baltimore County (MD)
U of Michigan (MI)
U of Michigan–Dearborn (MI)
U of Minnesota, Duluth (MN)
U of Minnesota, Morris (MN)
U of Nebraska–Lincoln (NE)
U of Nevada, Las Vegas (NV)
U of North Carolina at Asheville (NC)
The U of North Carolina at Chapel Hill (NC)
The U of North Carolina at Pembroke (NC)
U of North Dakota (ND)
U of Oregon (OR)
U of Pennsylvania (PA)
U of Pittsburgh at Bradford (PA)
U of Puget Sound (WA)
U of Regina (SK, Canada)
U of Richmond (VA)
U of St. Thomas (MN)
U of San Francisco (CA)
U of Southern Indiana (IN)
The U of Tampa (FL)
The U of the South (TN)
The U of Toledo (OH)
The U of Tulsa (OK)
U of Vermont (VT)
U of Washington (WA)
U of Washington, Bothell (WA)
U of Washington, Tacoma (WA)
U of Wyoming (WY)
Ursinus Coll (PA)
Vassar Coll (NY)
Virginia Commonwealth U (VA)
Virginia Polytechnic Inst and State U (VA)
Washington & Jefferson Coll (PA)
Washington and Lee U (VA)
Washington U in St. Louis (MO)
Waynesburg U (PA)
Wesleyan Coll (GA)
Wesleyan U (CT)
Western State Colorado U (CO)
Western Washington U (WA)
Whittier Coll (CA)
Widener U (PA)
Williams Coll (MA)
Winthrop U (SC)
Wofford Coll (SC)

ENVIRONMENTAL TOXICOLOGY
Bryant U (RI)
Clarkson U (NY)
U of California, Davis (CA)

EPIDEMIOLOGY
Indiana U Bloomington (IN)

EQUESTRIAN STUDIES
Averett U (VA)
Colorado State U (CO)
Delaware Valley U (PA)
Rocky Mountain Coll (MT)
Savannah Coll of Art and Design (GA)
The U of Findlay (OH)

ETHICS
Bridgewater State U (MA)
Drake U (IA)
Millikin U (IL)
Southeastern Baptist Theological Sem (NC)
Syracuse U (NY)
U of Washington, Bothell (WA)

ETHNIC, CULTURAL MINORITY, GENDER, AND GROUP STUDIES RELATED
Albion Coll (MI)
Allegheny Coll (PA)
American U (DC)
Beloit Coll (WI)
Bethel U (MN)
Bowling Green State U (OH)
California Polytechnic State U, San Luis Obispo (CA)
California State U, Chico (CA)
California State U, Los Angeles (CA)
Central Michigan U (MI)
Christian Brothers U (TN)
The Colorado Coll (CO)
Colorado State U (CO)
Columbia Coll Chicago (IL)
Cornell Coll (IA)
Davidson Coll (NC)
The Evergreen State Coll (WA)
Humboldt State U (CA)
Indiana U Bloomington (IN)
Indiana U South Bend (IN)
Kalamazoo Coll (MI)
Lawrence U (WI)
Miami U Hamilton (OH)
Mills Coll (CA)
New Coll of Florida (FL)
New York U (NY)
The Ohio State U (OH)
Pitzer Coll (CA)
Portland State U (OR)
San Diego State U (CA)
Sarah Lawrence Coll (NY)
Skidmore Coll (NY)
Stonehill Coll (MA)
U at Buffalo, the State U of New York (NY)
U of California, Irvine (CA)
U of California, Riverside (CA)
U of Chicago (IL)
U of Dayton (OH)
U of Hawaii at Manoa (HI)
U of Houston (TX)
U of Kentucky (KY)
U of Minnesota, Duluth (MN)
U of Nebraska–Lincoln (NE)
U of Pittsburgh (PA)
U of Washington, Tacoma (WA)
Washington State U (WA)
Washington U in St. Louis (MO)
Wesleyan U (CT)
Western Kentucky U (KY)
Williams Coll (MA)

ETHNIC STUDIES
Columbia U (NY)
Messiah Coll (PA)
Queens Coll of the City U of New York (NY)
St. Olaf Coll (MN)
Sarah Lawrence Coll (NY)
U of California, Santa Cruz (CA)
U of Colorado Denver (CO)
U of Oregon (OR)
U of San Diego (CA)
The U of Texas at Austin (TX)
Willamette U (OR)

EUROPEAN HISTORY
Sarah Lawrence Coll (NY)
U of Idaho (ID)
U of Washington, Tacoma (WA)

EUROPEAN STUDIES
American U in Bulgaria (Bulgaria)
Boston U (MA)
Bowling Green State U (OH)
Brandeis U (MA)
Canisius Coll (NY)
Central Michigan U (MI)
Coll of Saint Benedict (MN)
Georgetown Coll (KY)
Gonzaga U (WA)
Hillsdale Coll (MI)
Loyola Marymount U (CA)
Middlebury Coll (VT)
Millsaps Coll (MS)
New York U (NY)
Ohio U (OH)
Pepperdine U, Malibu (CA)
Portland State U (OR)
Saint John's U (MN)
San Diego State U (CA)
Scripps Coll (CA)
U of California, Irvine (CA)
U of California, Los Angeles (CA)
The U of North Carolina at Chapel Hill (NC)
U of Northern Colorado (CO)
U of Richmond (VA)
U of South Carolina (SC)
The U of Texas at Austin (TX)
U of Vermont (VT)
U of Washington (WA)
Washington U in St. Louis (MO)

EUROPEAN STUDIES (WESTERN)
Seattle U (WA)
Willamette U (OR)

EVOLUTIONARY BIOLOGY
Columbia U (NY)
Harvard U (MA)
Rice U (TX)
Tulane U (LA)

EXECUTIVE ASSISTANT/ EXECUTIVE SECRETARY
Bowling Green State U (OH)
U of Puerto Rico–Bayamón (PR)

EXERCISE PHYSIOLOGY
Auburn U (AL)
Baldwin Wallace U (OH)
Baylor U (TX)
Central Washington U (WA)
Coll of Charleston (SC)
The Coll of St. Scholastica (MN)
Creighton U (NE)
East Carolina U (NC)
Fitchburg State U (MA)
Florida Southern Coll (FL)
Gonzaga U (WA)
Gordon Coll (MA)
Marquette U (WI)
Merrimack Coll (MA)
Miami U Hamilton (OH)
Northwest Christian U (OR)
Ohio U (OH)
Pfeiffer U (NC)
Saint Francis U (PA)
Skidmore Coll (NY)
State U of New York Coll at Potsdam (NY)
Taylor U (IN)
Texas A&M U–Central Texas (TX)
U at Buffalo, the State U of New York (NY)
U of California, Davis (CA)
U of California, Irvine (CA)
U of Dayton (OH)
U of Florida (FL)
U of Lynchburg (VA)
U of Massachusetts Amherst (MA)
U of Minnesota, Twin Cities Campus (MN)
The U of Toledo (OH)
U of Wisconsin–Superior (WI)
Ursinus Coll (PA)
Washington State U (WA)
Washington State U–Spokane (WA)

EXPERIMENTAL PSYCHOLOGY
Brandeis U (MA)
Purdue U (IN)
Redeemer U Coll (ON, Canada)
Saint Leo U (FL)
Tiffin U (OH)
U of Chicago (IL)

U of Mary Hardin-Baylor (TX)
U of Michigan (MI)
U of South Carolina (SC)
Washington U in St. Louis (MO)

FACILITIES PLANNING AND MANAGEMENT
New England Inst of Technology (RI)

FAMILY AND COMMUNITY SERVICES
Auburn U (AL)
Bowling Green State U (OH)
East Carolina U (NC)
Harding U (AR)
Iowa State U of Science and Technology (IA)
Merrimack Coll (MA)
Messiah Coll (PA)
Michigan State U (MI)
Oklahoma Baptist U (OK)
Oklahoma Christian U (OK)
Ouachita Baptist U (AR)
Texas Tech U (TX)
Toccoa Falls Coll (GA)
U of Florida (FL)
U of Maryland, Coll Park (MD)
U of Northern Iowa (IA)
Youngstown State U (OH)

FAMILY AND CONSUMER ECONOMICS RELATED
Bowling Green State U (OH)
Carson-Newman U (TN)
U of Hawaii at Manoa (HI)
U of Minnesota, Twin Cities Campus (MN)
U of Nebraska–Lincoln (NE)
U of Northern Iowa (IA)
Utah State U (UT)

FAMILY AND CONSUMER SCIENCES/HOME ECONOMICS TEACHER EDUCATION
Baylor U (TX)
Bowling Green State U (OH)
Bradley U (IL)
Carson-Newman U (TN)
Central Washington U (WA)
East Carolina U (NC)
Harding U (AR)
Messiah Coll (PA)
Ohio U (OH)
Queens Coll of the City U of New York (NY)
Seton Hill U (PA)
Southeast Missouri State U (MO)
U of Georgia (GA)
Utah State U (UT)
Virginia Polytechnic Inst and State U (VA)
Western Kentucky U (KY)
Winthrop U (SC)

FAMILY AND CONSUMER SCIENCES/HUMAN SCIENCES
Auburn U (AL)
Baylor U (TX)
Berea Coll (KY)
Bowling Green State U (OH)
Bradley U (IL)
Bridgewater Coll (VA)
California State U, Long Beach (CA)
California State U, Northridge (CA)
Carson-Newman U (TN)
Central Washington U (WA)
Colorado State U (CO)
Delta State U (MS)
Eastern Illinois U (IL)
East Tennessee State U (TN)
Harding U (AR)
Idaho State U (ID)
Indiana U of Pennsylvania (PA)
Iowa State U of Science and Technology (IA)
Liberty U (VA)
Lipscomb U (TN)
Madonna U (MI)
Miami U (OH)
Montclair State U (NJ)
Northeastern State U (OK)
Prairie View A&M U (TX)
Purdue U (IN)
Queens Coll of the City U of New York (NY)
San Francisco State U (CA)
Seton Hill U (PA)
Southeastern Louisiana U (LA)
Southeast Missouri State U (MO)
Southern U and Ag and Mech Coll (LA)
Texas Tech U (TX)
Texas Woman's U (TX)
U of Arkansas (AR)
U of Central Arkansas (AR)
U of Kentucky (KY)
U of Montevallo (AL)
U of New Mexico (NM)
The U of Tennessee at Martin (TN)
U of Wyoming (WY)
Washington State U (WA)
Youngstown State U (OH)

FAMILY AND CONSUMER SCIENCES/HUMAN SCIENCES COMMUNICATION
U of Georgia (GA)

FAMILY AND CONSUMER SCIENCES/HUMAN SCIENCES RELATED
Auburn U (AL)
California State U, Long Beach (CA)

FAMILY PRACTICE NURSING
Grand Valley State U (MI)
Michigan State U (MI)
Pace U (NY)
Pace U, Pleasantville Campus (NY)

FAMILY PSYCHOLOGY
Kansas Wesleyan U (KS)

FAMILY RESOURCE MANAGEMENT
Iowa State U of Science and Technology (IA)
Middle Tennessee State U (TN)
The Ohio State U (OH)
Ohio U (OH)
Texas Tech U (TX)
U of Georgia (GA)

FAMILY SYSTEMS
Bowling Green State U (OH)
Central Michigan U (MI)
Central Washington U (WA)
Lipscomb U (TN)
Lubbock Christian U (TX)
Towson U (MD)
Weber State U (UT)

FARM AND RANCH MANAGEMENT
Iowa State U of Science and Technology (IA)
Purdue U (IN)
Texas Christian U (TX)

FASHION AND FABRIC CONSULTING
Acad of Art U (CA)
U of Houston–Downtown (TX)

FASHION/APPAREL DESIGN
Acad of Art U (CA)
Albright Coll (PA)
Baylor U (TX)
Bowling Green State U (OH)
Brenau U (GA)
Carson-Newman U (TN)
Columbia Coll Chicago (IL)
Dominican U (IL)
Escuela de Artes Plasticas y Diseño de Puerto Rico (PR)
Fashion Inst of Technology (NY)
FIDM/Fashion Inst of Design & Merchandising, Los Angeles Campus (CA)
Indiana U Bloomington (IN)
Jacksonville U (FL)
Lasell Coll (MA)
Lebanese American U (Lebanon)
Marist Coll (NY)
Marymount U (VA)
Michigan State U (MI)
Montclair State U (NJ)
Purdue U (IN)
Savannah Coll of Art and Design (GA)
Syracuse U (NY)
Texas Tech U (TX)
Texas Woman's U (TX)
U of the Incarnate Word (TX)
Virginia Commonwealth U (VA)
Washington U in St. Louis (MO)
Woodbury U (CA)

FASHION MERCHANDISING
Acad of Art U (CA)
Albright Coll (PA)
Baylor U (TX)
Berkeley Coll–New York City Campus (NY)
Berkeley Coll–White Plains Campus (NY)
Berkeley Coll–Woodland Park Campus (NJ)
Bowling Green State U (OH)
Brenau U (GA)
California State U, Long Beach (CA)
Carson-Newman U (TN)
Central Michigan U (MI)
Dominican U (IL)
Fashion Inst of Technology (NY)
Harding U (AR)
Immaculata U (PA)
Indiana U of Pennsylvania (PA)
Lasell Coll (MA)
LIM Coll (NY)
Lipscomb U (TN)
Marist Coll (NY)
Marymount Manhattan Coll (NY)
Marymount U (VA)
Northwood U, Michigan Campus (MI)
Sacred Heart U (CT)
Texas Christian U (TX)
Texas Tech U (TX)
Texas Woman's U (TX)
U of Georgia (GA)
Utah State U (UT)
Western Illinois U (IL)
Youngstown State U (OH)

FIBER, TEXTILE AND WEAVING ARTS
Adams State U (CO)
Bowling Green State U (OH)
California State U, Long Beach (CA)
Cornell U (NY)
Maryland Inst Coll of Art (MD)
Rhode Island School of Design (RI)
Savannah Coll of Art and Design (GA)
Syracuse U (NY)
Temple U (PA)
U of Massachusetts Dartmouth (MA)
U of Michigan (MI)
U of Oregon (OR)

FILIPINO/TAGALOG
U of Hawaii at Manoa (HI)

FILM/CINEMA/VIDEO STUDIES
Baldwin Wallace U (OH)
Boston Coll (MA)
Boston U (MA)
Bowling Green State U (OH)
Brandeis U (MA)
California State U, Long Beach (CA)
California State U, Northridge (CA)
Carson-Newman U (TN)
Central Washington U (WA)
Champlain Coll (VT)
Claremont McKenna Coll (CA)
Clark U (MA)
Colgate U (NY)
Coll of Staten Island of the City U of New York (NY)
Coll of the Holy Cross (MA)
The Colorado Coll (CO)
Columbia U (NY)
Connecticut Coll (CT)
Cornell U (NY)
Dartmouth Coll (NH)
Dominican U (IL)
Eastern Washington U (WA)
Eckerd Coll (FL)
Emerson Coll (MA)
The Evergreen State Coll (WA)
Fashion Inst of Technology (NY)
Florida Southern Coll (FL)
Fordham U (NY)
Georgia State U (GA)
Grand Valley State U (MI)
Hamilton Coll (NY)
Hunter Coll of the City U of New York (NY)
Ithaca Coll (NY)
Jacksonville U (FL)
Johns Hopkins U (MD)
Lafayette Coll (PA)
La Sierra U (CA)
Lawrence U (WI)
Lipscomb U (TN)
Loyola Marymount U (CA)
Lycoming Coll (PA)
Maryland Inst Coll of Art (MD)
Marymount Manhattan Coll (NY)
McDaniel Coll (MD)
Miami U (OH)
Michigan State U (MI)
Middlebury Coll (VT)
Minnesota State U Moorhead (MN)
National U (CA)
New York U (NY)
Northwestern U (IL)
The Ohio State U (OH)
Pace U (NY)
Pace U, Pleasantville Campus (NY)
Pepperdine U, Malibu (CA)
Purdue U (IN)
Queens Coll of the City U of New York (NY)
Rhode Island Coll (RI)
San Francisco State U (CA)
Sarah Lawrence Coll (NY)
Seattle U (WA)
State U of New York at Fredonia (NY)
U at Buffalo, the State U of New York (NY)
U of California, Davis (CA)
U of California, Irvine (CA)
U of California, Los Angeles (CA)
U of California, Riverside (CA)
U of Chicago (IL)
U of Georgia (GA)
U of Idaho (ID)
U of Mary Hardin-Baylor (TX)
U of Maryland, Coll Park (MD)
U of Michigan (MI)
U of Nebraska–Lincoln (NE)
U of Nevada, Las Vegas (NV)
U of New Mexico (NM)
U of Oregon (OR)
U of Pennsylvania (PA)
U of Pittsburgh (PA)
U of Regina (SK, Canada)
U of Richmond (VA)
The U of Tampa (FL)
The U of Toledo (OH)
The U of Tulsa (OK)
U of Vermont (VT)
U of Washington (WA)
U of Wisconsin–Milwaukee (WI)
Vassar Coll (NY)
Washington U in St. Louis (MO)
Wesleyan U (CT)
Wheaton Coll (MA)
Wright State U–Lake Campus (OH)

FILM/VIDEO AND PHOTOGRAPHIC ARTS RELATED
Fairfield U (CT)
Hollins U (VA)
Louisiana State U and A&M Coll (LA)
Maryland Inst Coll of Art (MD)
The Ohio State U (OH)
Portland State U (OR)
Rhode Island School of Design (RI)
Saint Joseph's U (PA)
U of California, Santa Cruz (CA)
U of Minnesota, Twin Cities Campus (MN)
Woodbury U (CA)

FINANCE
Adams State U (CO)
Adelphi U (NY)
Alabama State U (AL)
Albion Coll (MI)
Albright Coll (PA)
Alfred U (NY)
American U (DC)
Angelo State U (TX)
Appalachian State U (NC)
Auburn U (AL)
Auburn U at Montgomery (AL)
Aurora U (IL)
Austin Coll (TX)
Austin Peay State U (TN)
Avila U (MO)
Babson Coll (MA)
Baldwin Wallace U (OH)
Baruch Coll of the City U of New York (NY)
Baylor U (TX)
Bellarmine U (KY)
Benedictine U (IL)
Bentley U (MA)
Boston Coll (MA)
Bowling Green State U (OH)
Bradley U (IL)
Bridgewater State U (MA)
Bryant U (RI)
Butler U (IN)
California State U, Bakersfield (CA)
California State U, Long Beach (CA)
California State U, Northridge (CA)
California State U, San Marcos (CA)
California U of Pennsylvania (PA)
Calvin Coll (MI)
Canisius Coll (NY)
Carnegie Mellon U (PA)
Carthage Coll (WI)
The Catholic U of America (DC)
Cedarville U (OH)
Central Connecticut State U (CT)
Central Michigan U (MI)
Central Washington U (WA)
Champlain Coll (VT)
Christopher Newport U (VA)
Clarion U of Pennsylvania (PA)
Coastal Carolina U (SC)
The Coll at Brockport, State U of New York (NY)
Coll of Charleston (SC)
The Coll of Saint Rose (NY)
The Coll of St. Scholastica (MN)
The Coll of William and Mary (VA)
Columbia Coll (MO)
Creighton U (NE)
Culver-Stockton Coll (MO)
Dakota State U (SD)
Dallas Baptist U (TX)
Davenport U, Grand Rapids (MI)
Delta State U (MS)
DePaul U (IL)
DEREE - The American Coll of Greece (Greece)
Dominican U (IL)
Drake U (IA)
Drury U (MO)
Duquesne U (PA)
East Carolina U (NC)
Eastern Illinois U (IL)
Eastern Washington U (WA)
East Tennessee State U (TN)
Emmanuel Coll (MA)
Endicott Coll (MA)
Fairfield U (CT)
Fayetteville State U (NC)
Fitchburg State U (MA)
Florida Atlantic U (FL)
Fordham U (NY)
Fort Lewis Coll (CO)
Framingham State U (MA)
Franklin Pierce U (NH)
George Mason U (VA)
Georgetown Coll (KY)
Georgia Southern U (GA)
Georgia State U (GA)
Gonzaga U (WA)
Gordon Coll (MA)
Grand Valley State U (MI)
Grove City Coll (PA)
Hamline U (MN)
Harding U (AR)
Hardin-Simmons U (TX)
High Point U (NC)
Hillsdale Coll (MI)
Hofstra U (NY)
Hult Intl Business School (United Kingdom)
Idaho State U (ID)
Illinois Coll (IL)
Immaculata U (PA)
Indiana State U (IN)
Indiana U of Pennsylvania (PA)
Inter American U of Puerto Rico, Bayamón Campus (PR)
Inter American U of Puerto Rico, San Germán Campus (PR)
Iona Coll (NY)
Ithaca Coll (NY)
Jackson State U (MS)
Jacksonville U (FL)
Juniata Coll (PA)
Kean U (NJ)

Kennesaw State U (GA)
King's Coll (PA)
Lake Forest Coll (IL)
Lamar U (TX)
La Salle U (PA)
Lasell Coll (MA)
La Sierra U (CA)
Lawrence Technological U (MI)
Lebanon Valley Coll (PA)
LeTourneau U (TX)
Lindenwood U (MO)
Linfield Coll (OR)
Loras Coll (IA)
Louisiana State U and A&M Coll (LA)
Loyola Marymount U (CA)
Loyola U Chicago (IL)
Loyola U New Orleans (LA)
Lubbock Christian U (TX)
Manchester U (IN)
Manhattan Coll (NY)
Manhattanville Coll (NY)
Marian U (IN)
Marquette U (WI)
Marshall U (WV)
Marymount Manhattan Coll (NY)
McNeese State U (LA)
Mercer U, Macon (GA)
Merrimack Coll (MA)
Messiah Coll (PA)
Miami U (OH)
Miami U Hamilton (OH)
Michigan State U (MI)
Middle Tennessee State U (TN)
Minnesota State U Moorhead (MN)
Molloy Coll (NY)
Mount St. Joseph U (OH)
Murray State U (KY)
National U (CA)
Nazareth Coll of Rochester (NY)
New England Coll (NH)
New Jersey City U (NJ)
New York U (NY)
Nichols Coll (MA)
Northeastern State U (OK)
Northern Illinois U (IL)
Northern Kentucky U (KY)
Northern State U (SD)
Northwest Missouri State U (MO)
Northwood U, Michigan Campus (MI)
Ohio Dominican U (OH)
The Ohio State U (OH)
Ohio U (OH)
Oklahoma Baptist U (OK)
Oklahoma Christian U (OK)
Oklahoma State U (OK)
Old Dominion U (VA)
Ottawa U (KS)
Pace U (NY)
Pace U, Pleasantville Campus (NY)
Palm Beach Atlantic U (FL)
Pepperdine U, Malibu (CA)
Point Loma Nazarene U (CA)
Portland State U (OR)
Prairie View A&M U (TX)
Providence Coll (RI)
Purdue U (IN)
Purdue U Northwest (IN)
Queens Coll of the City U of New York (NY)
Queens U of Charlotte (NC)
Radford U (VA)
Regis U (CO)
Rhode Island Coll (RI)
Rider U (NJ)
Rochester Inst of Technology (NY)
Rockford U (IL)
Sacred Heart U (CT)
Saginaw Valley State U (MI)
Saint Anselm Coll (NH)
Saint Francis U (PA)
St. John Fisher Coll (NY)
Saint Joseph's U (PA)
Saint Louis U (MO)
St. Mary's U (TX)
Saint Mary's U of Minnesota (MN)
Saint Vincent Coll (PA)
Salisbury U (MD)
Salve Regina U (RI)
Samford U (AL)
San Diego State U (CA)
San Francisco State U (CA)
San Jose State U (CA)
Seattle U (WA)
Southeastern Louisiana U (LA)
Southeastern U (FL)
Southeast Missouri State U (MO)
Southern Illinois U Carbondale (IL)
Southern U and Ag and Mech Coll (LA)
Southwest Baptist U (MO)
State U of New York at Fredonia (NY)
State U of New York at Plattsburgh (NY)
Stetson U (FL)
Stonehill Coll (MA)
Syracuse U (NY)
Taylor U (IN)
Temple U (PA)
Texas A&M Intl U (TX)
Texas A&M U–Central Texas (TX)
Texas Christian U (TX)
Texas Lutheran U (TX)
Texas Tech U (TX)
Texas Woman's U (TX)
Tiffin U (OH)
Trinity Christian Coll (IL)
Tulane U (LA)
Université de Sherbrooke (QC, Canada)
U of Arkansas (AR)
U of Central Arkansas (AR)
U of Central Florida (FL)
U of Dayton (OH)
The U of Findlay (OH)
U of Florida (FL)
U of Georgia (GA)
U of Hawaii at Manoa (HI)
U of Houston (TX)
U of Houston–Clear Lake (TX)
U of Houston–Downtown (TX)
U of Idaho (ID)
U of Kentucky (KY)
U of Louisville (KY)
U of Maine (ME)
U of Mary Hardin-Baylor (TX)
U of Maryland, Coll Park (MD)
U of Maryland U Coll (MD)
U of Massachusetts Amherst (MA)
U of Massachusetts Dartmouth (MA)
U of Memphis (TN)
U of Michigan–Dearborn (MI)
U of Minnesota, Duluth (MN)
U of Minnesota, Twin Cities Campus (MN)
U of Montevallo (AL)
U of Mount Union (OH)
U of Nebraska–Lincoln (NE)
U of Nevada, Las Vegas (NV)
U of Nevada, Reno (NV)
U of New Haven (CT)
The U of North Carolina at Charlotte (NC)
The U of North Carolina at Greensboro (NC)
U of North Dakota (ND)
U of Northern Iowa (IA)
U of North Florida (FL)
U of Northwestern–St. Paul (MN)
U of Notre Dame (IN)
U of Pennsylvania (PA)
U of Pittsburgh (PA)
U of Puerto Rico–Bayamón (PR)
U of Regina (SK, Canada)
U of Saint Francis (IN)
U of St. Thomas (MN)
U of St. Thomas (TX)
U of San Diego (CA)
U of San Francisco (CA)
U of South Alabama (AL)
U of South Carolina (SC)
U of South Dakota (SD)
U of Southern Indiana (IN)
U of South Florida (FL)
U of South Florida Sarasota-Manatee (FL)
The U of Tampa (FL)
The U of Tennessee (TN)
The U of Tennessee at Martin (TN)
The U of Texas at Austin (TX)
The U of Texas at El Paso (TX)
The U of Texas of the Permian Basin (TX)
The U of Texas Rio Grande Valley (TX)
U of the Incarnate Word (TX)
The U of Toledo (OH)
The U of Tulsa (OK)
U of Washington (WA)
U of Washington, Tacoma (WA)
The U of West Alabama (AL)
U of West Georgia (GA)
U of Wisconsin–Eau Claire (WI)
U of Wisconsin–La Crosse (WI)
U of Wisconsin–Milwaukee (WI)
U of Wyoming (WY)
Utah State U (UT)
Utah Valley U (UT)
Valparaiso U (IN)
Vanguard U of Southern California (CA)
Virginia Polytechnic Inst and State U (VA)
Wartburg Coll (IA)
Washington State U (WA)
Washington State U–Vancouver (WA)
Washington U in St. Louis (MO)
Waynesburg U (PA)
Weber State U (UT)
West Chester U of Pennsylvania (PA)
Western Connecticut State U (CT)
Western Illinois U (IL)
Western Kentucky U (KY)
Western Washington U (WA)
Whitworth U (WA)
Wilkes U (PA)
Wofford Coll (SC)
Wright State U–Lake Campus (OH)
Youngstown State U (OH)

FINANCE AND FINANCIAL MANAGEMENT SERVICES RELATED

Babson Coll (MA)
Brenau U (GA)
Hofstra U (NY)
Point U (GA)
San Jose State U (CA)
U of Northern Iowa (IA)
The U of Tampa (FL)
Virginia Commonwealth U (VA)

FINANCIAL FORENSICS AND FRAUD INVESTIGATION

Champlain Coll (VT)
Embry-Riddle Aeronautical U–Prescott (AZ)

FINANCIAL MATHEMATICS

American U (DC)
Blackburn Coll (IL)
Carnegie Mellon U (PA)
Hofstra U (NY)
Knox Coll (IL)
Lee U (TN)
LeTourneau U (TX)
Massachusetts Inst of Technology (MA)
Mount St. Joseph U (OH)
Purdue U (IN)
Southwest Baptist U (MO)
Stevens Inst of Technology (NJ)
U of California, Los Angeles (CA)
U of Kentucky (KY)
U of Mount Union (OH)

FINANCIAL PLANNING AND SERVICES

Baylor U (TX)
Berkeley Coll–New York City Campus (NY)
Berkeley Coll–Woodland Park Campus (NJ)
Bryant U (RI)
Central Michigan U (MI)
The Coll of Saint Rose (NY)
Maryville U of Saint Louis (MO)
Marywood U (PA)
Merrimack Coll (MA)
Purdue U (IN)
Saint Joseph's U (PA)
St. Mary's U (TX)
San Diego State U (CA)
State U of New York Coll of Technology at Alfred (NY)
Temple U (PA)
U of Minnesota, Duluth (MN)
Utah Valley U (UT)
Widener U (PA)
Youngstown State U (OH)

FINE AND STUDIO ARTS MANAGEMENT

Albright Coll (PA)
Baldwin Wallace U (OH)
Bellarmine U (KY)
Buena Vista U (IA)
Butler U (IN)
Coll of Charleston (SC)
The Coll of Idaho (ID)
Columbia Coll Chicago (IL)
Concordia U Chicago (IL)
Culver-Stockton Coll (MO)
DePaul U (IL)
Fashion Inst of Technology (NY)
Indiana U Bloomington (IN)
Ithaca Coll (NY)
Lasell Coll (MA)
Lipscomb U (TN)
Maryland Inst Coll of Art (MD)
Marywood U (PA)
Massachusetts Coll of Liberal Arts (MA)
Messiah Coll (PA)
Miami U (OH)
North Carolina State U (NC)
Pfeiffer U (NC)
Purchase Coll, State U of New York (NY)
Queens U of Charlotte (NC)
Randolph-Macon Coll (VA)
Rider U (NJ)
Saint Vincent Coll (PA)
Seton Hill U (PA)
Spring Hill Coll (AL)
State U of New York at Fredonia (NY)
Syracuse U (NY)
The U of North Carolina at Greensboro (NC)
U of Oregon (OR)
The U of Tulsa (OK)
Waynesburg U (PA)
Whitworth U (WA)

FINE ARTS RELATED

Acad of Art U (CA)
Adelphi U (NY)
Alfred U (NY)
Allegheny Coll (PA)
Benedictine U (IL)
Bowling Green State U (OH)
Bryn Athyn Coll of the New Church (PA)
California State U, Long Beach (CA)
Cleveland Inst of Art (OH)
The Coll of Saint Rose (NY)
Columbia Coll Chicago (IL)
Covenant Coll (GA)
Excelsior Coll (NY)
Fordham U (NY)
Jacksonville U (FL)
Kansas Wesleyan U (KS)
Madonna U (MI)
Manhattanville Coll (NY)
Maryland Inst Coll of Art (MD)
New York U (NY)
The Ohio State U (OH)
Purchase Coll, State U of New York (NY)
Rhode Island School of Design (RI)
Seattle U (WA)
Seton Hill U (PA)
Skidmore Coll (NY)
Stevens Inst of Technology (NJ)
Temple U (PA)
U of California, Los Angeles (CA)
U of Guam (GU)
U of Maryland, Baltimore County (MD)
U of Massachusetts Lowell (MA)
U of Michigan (MI)
U of New Haven (CT)
U of Regina (SK, Canada)
U of Washington (WA)
U of Wisconsin–Milwaukee (WI)
U of Wisconsin–River Falls (WI)
U of Wisconsin–Superior (WI)
Widener U (PA)

FINE/STUDIO ARTS

Acad of Art U (CA)
Agnes Scott Coll (GA)
Albion Coll (MI)
Albright Coll (PA)
Alfred U (NY)
Allegheny Coll (PA)
American U (DC)
Angelo State U (TX)
Antioch Coll, Yellow Springs (OH)
Appalachian State U (NC)
Arkansas Tech U (AR)
Auburn U (AL)
Baker U (KS)
Baldwin Wallace U (OH)
Barton Coll (NC)
Baylor U (TX)
Bellarmine U (KY)
Beloit Coll (WI)
Benedictine U (IL)
Bethany Lutheran Coll (MN)
Bethel Coll (KS)
Bethel U (MN)
Boston Coll (MA)
Bowling Green State U (OH)
Bradley U (IL)
Brandeis U (MA)
Brenau U (GA)
Bridgewater Coll (VA)
Bridgewater State U (MA)
Bucknell U (PA)
Caldwell U (NJ)
California Polytechnic State U, San Luis Obispo (CA)
California State U, Fullerton (CA)
California State U, Long Beach (CA)
California U of Pennsylvania (PA)
Calvin Coll (MI)
Carthage Coll (WI)
Cedarville U (OH)
Centenary Coll of Louisiana (LA)
Central Michigan U (MI)
Central Washington U (WA)
Christian Brothers U (TN)
Christopher Newport U (VA)
Clark U (MA)
Coastal Carolina U (SC)
Coll of Charleston (SC)
The Coll of Idaho (ID)
Coll of Staten Island of the City U of New York (NY)
Coll of the Holy Cross (MA)
The Colorado Coll (CO)
Colorado State U (CO)
Colorado State U–Pueblo (CO)
Columbia Coll Chicago (IL)
Connecticut Coll (CT)
Cornell U (NY)
Creighton U (NE)
Culver-Stockton Coll (MO)
Curry Coll (MA)
Dartmouth Coll (NH)
Dominican U (IL)
Drake U (IA)
Drew U (NJ)
Drury U (MO)
East Carolina U (NC)
Eastern Washington U (WA)
Emmanuel Coll (MA)
Endicott Coll (MA)
The Evergreen State Coll (WA)
Fairfield U (CT)
Fashion Inst of Technology (NY)
Florida Ag and Mech U (FL)
Florida Southern Coll (FL)
Furman U (SC)
Georgetown Coll (KY)
Georgia Southern U (GA)
Gordon Coll (MA)
Hamilton Coll (NY)
Hamline U (MN)
Hampden-Sydney Coll (VA)
Harding U (AR)
Hardin-Simmons U (TX)
High Point U (NC)
Hofstra U (NY)
Humboldt State U (CA)
Hunter Coll of the City U of New York (NY)
Indiana State U (IN)
Indiana U Bloomington (IN)
Indiana U Kokomo (IN)
Indiana U Northwest (IN)
Indiana U of Pennsylvania (PA)
Indiana U–Purdue U Indianapolis (IN)
Indiana U South Bend (IN)
Indiana U Southeast (IN)
Ithaca Coll (NY)
Jacksonville U (FL)
Judson U (IL)
Juniata Coll (PA)
Kean U (NJ)
Knox Coll (IL)
Lafayette Coll (PA)
Lamar U (TX)
La Sierra U (CA)
Lebanese American U (Lebanon)
Lee U (TN)
Lewis & Clark Coll (OR)

Liberty U (VA)
Limestone Coll (SC)
Linfield Coll (OR)
Lipscomb U (TN)
Lock Haven U of Pennsylvania (PA)
Louisiana Coll (LA)
Louisiana State U and A&M Coll (LA)
Loyola Marymount U (CA)
Loyola U Chicago (IL)
Loyola U New Orleans (LA)
Lubbock Christian U (TX)
Maharishi U of Management (IA)
Manchester U (IN)
Manhattanville Coll (NY)
Marist Coll (NY)
Maryland Inst Coll of Art (MD)
Marymount Manhattan Coll (NY)
Marymount U (VA)
Maryville U of Saint Louis (MO)
Messiah Coll (PA)
Michigan State U (MI)
Middlebury Coll (VT)
Millikin U (IL)
Millsaps Coll (MS)
Mills Coll (CA)
Molloy Coll (NY)
Morningside Coll (IA)
Mount St. Joseph U (OH)
Murray State U (KY)
Nazareth Coll of Rochester (NY)
New Coll of Florida (FL)
New England Coll (NH)
New York U (NY)
Northern Illinois U (IL)
Northern Kentucky U (KY)
Northern State U (SD)
Northwest Missouri State U (MO)
Oglethorpe U (GA)
Ohio U (OH)
Ohio Wesleyan U (OH)
Oklahoma Baptist U (OK)
Ouachita Baptist U (AR)
Pace U (NY)
Palm Beach Atlantic U (FL)
Pennsylvania Acad of the Fine Arts (PA)
Pennsylvania Coll of Art & Design (PA)
Piedmont Coll (GA)
Pitzer Coll (CA)
Purdue U (IN)
Queens Coll of the City U of New York (NY)
Queens U of Charlotte (NC)
Randolph Coll (VA)
Randolph-Macon Coll (VA)
Rice U (TX)
Rochester Inst of Technology (NY)
The Sage Colls (NY)
Saginaw Valley State U (MI)
St. Joseph's Coll, Long Island Campus (NY)
Saint Louis U (MO)
St. Mary's Coll of Maryland (MD)
Saint Mary's U of Minnesota (MN)
Saint Vincent Coll (PA)
Salisbury U (MD)
Salve Regina U (RI)
Samford U (AL)
San Diego State U (CA)
San Jose State U (CA)
Sarah Lawrence Coll (NY)
Scripps Coll (CA)
Seattle U (WA)
Seton Hill U (PA)
Sonoma State U (CA)
Southern Arkansas U–Magnolia (AR)
Southern Illinois U Carbondale (IL)
Southern U and Ag and Mech Coll (LA)
Southwestern U (TX)
Spring Hill Coll (AL)
State U of New York at Fredonia (NY)
Stockton U (NJ)
Stonehill Coll (MA)
Sweet Briar Coll (VA)
Syracuse U (NY)
Tabor Coll (KS)
Taylor U (IN)
Texas A&M Intl U (TX)
Texas Christian U (TX)
Towson U (MD)
Trinity Christian Coll (IL)
Truman State U (MO)
Tulane U (LA)
Union Coll (NY)
U at Buffalo, the State U of New York (NY)
U of California, Davis (CA)
U of California, Irvine (CA)
U of California, Riverside (CA)
U of Central Florida (FL)
U of Colorado Denver (CO)
U of Dallas (TX)
U of Dayton (OH)
U of Florida (FL)
U of Georgia (GA)
U of Houston–Clear Lake (TX)
U of Idaho (ID)
U of Illinois at Springfield (IL)
U of Kentucky (KY)
U of La Verne (CA)
U of Louisville (KY)
U of Maine (ME)
U of Maine at Presque Isle (ME)
U of Mary Hardin-Baylor (TX)
U of Maryland, Coll Park (MD)
U of Massachusetts Amherst (MA)
U of Minnesota, Duluth (MN)
U of Minnesota, Morris (MN)
U of Nebraska–Lincoln (NE)
U of New Hampshire (NH)
U of North Carolina at Asheville (NC)
The U of North Carolina at Chapel Hill (NC)
The U of North Carolina at Charlotte (NC)
The U of North Carolina at Greensboro (NC)
The U of North Carolina at Pembroke (NC)
U of Northern Colorado (CO)
U of Northern Iowa (IA)
U of North Florida (FL)
U of Northwestern–St. Paul (MN)
U of Notre Dame (IN)
U of Oregon (OR)
U of Pennsylvania (PA)
U of Pittsburgh (PA)
U of Providence (MT)
U of Regina (SK, Canada)
U of Richmond (VA)
U of Saint Francis (IN)
U of St. Thomas (TX)
U of San Francisco (CA)
U of South Carolina (SC)
U of South Carolina Aiken (SC)
U of South Florida (FL)
The U of Tennessee (TN)
The U of Texas at Austin (TX)
U of the Incarnate Word (TX)
The U of the South (TN)
The U of Tulsa (OK)
U of Vermont (VT)
Vassar Coll (NY)
Washington and Lee U (VA)
Washington State U (WA)
Washington State U–Tri-Cities (WA)
Washington U in St. Louis (MO)
Wesleyan Coll (GA)
Wesleyan U (CT)
West Chester U of Pennsylvania (PA)
Western Illinois U (IL)
Western Kentucky U (KY)
Western State Colorado U (CO)
Wheaton Coll (MA)
Whitworth U (WA)
Willamette U (OR)
Wright State U–Lake Campus (OH)
Youngstown State U (OH)

FIRE PREVENTION AND SAFETY TECHNOLOGY
Oklahoma State U (OK)
U of New Haven (CT)

FIRE PROTECTION RELATED
U of New Haven (CT)

FIRE SCIENCE/FIREFIGHTING
American Public U System (WV)
Columbia Southern U (AL)
Idaho State U (ID)
Madonna U (MI)
New Jersey City U (NJ)
Providence Coll (RI)
U of Florida (FL)
Utah Valley U (UT)

FIRE SERVICES ADMINISTRATION
Bowling Green State U (OH)
California State U, Los Angeles (CA)
Colorado State U (CO)
Columbia Southern U (AL)
Eastern Oregon U (OR)
Fayetteville State U (NC)
Liberty U (VA)
Southern Illinois U Carbondale (IL)
Western Illinois U (IL)

FISHING AND FISHERIES SCIENCES AND MANAGEMENT
Humboldt State U (CA)
Mansfield U of Pennsylvania (PA)
Michigan State U (MI)
Purdue U (IN)
U of Idaho (ID)
U of Minnesota, Twin Cities Campus (MN)

FLIGHT INSTRUCTION
U of North Dakota (ND)

FOLKLORE
Indiana U Bloomington (IN)
U of Oregon (OR)

FOODS AND NUTRITION RELATED
California State U, Long Beach (CA)
U of Minnesota, Twin Cities Campus (MN)
Utah State U (UT)

FOOD SCIENCE
Acadia U (NS, Canada)
Auburn U (AL)
California Polytechnic State U, San Luis Obispo (CA)
Cornell U (NY)
Delaware Valley U (PA)
Dominican U (IL)
Florida Ag and Mech U (FL)
Framingham State U (MA)
Iowa State U of Science and Technology (IA)
Michigan State U (MI)
North Carolina State U (NC)
The Ohio State U (OH)
Oklahoma State U (OK)
Purdue U (IN)
San Jose State U (CA)
Texas Tech U (TX)
U of Arkansas (AR)
U of California, Davis (CA)
U of Florida (FL)
U of Georgia (GA)
U of Idaho (ID)
U of Kentucky (KY)
U of Maine (ME)
U of Maryland, Coll Park (MD)
U of Massachusetts Amherst (MA)
U of Minnesota, Twin Cities Campus (MN)
U of Missouri (MO)
U of Nebraska–Lincoln (NE)
The U of Tennessee (TN)
U of Wisconsin–River Falls (WI)
Virginia Polytechnic Inst and State U (VA)
Washington State U (WA)

FOOD SCIENCE AND TECHNOLOGY RELATED
Appalachian State U (NC)
Middle Tennessee State U (TN)
Saint Francis U (PA)
Virginia Polytechnic Inst and State U (VA)

FOOD SERVICE AND DINING ROOM MANAGEMENT
Michigan State U (MI)

FOOD SERVICE SYSTEMS ADMINISTRATION
Dominican U (IL)
Lamar U (TX)
Lipscomb U (TN)
The Ohio State U (OH)
Ohio U (OH)
Point Loma Nazarene U (CA)
Rochester Inst of Technology (NY)

FOODS, NUTRITION, AND WELLNESS
Acadia U (NS, Canada)
Auburn U (AL)
Benedictine U (IL)
Bowling Green State U (OH)
Bradley U (IL)
Carson-Newman U (TN)
Dominican U (IL)
Framingham State U (MA)
Georgia Southern U (GA)
Hunter Coll of the City U of New York (NY)
Indiana State U (IN)
Indiana U of Pennsylvania (PA)
Ithaca Coll (NY)
Life U (GA)
Madonna U (MI)
Middle Tennessee State U (TN)
Montclair State U (NJ)
Murray State U (KY)
New York U (NY)
Ohio U (OH)
Oklahoma State U (OK)
Point Loma Nazarene U (CA)
Prairie View A&M U (TX)
Radford U (VA)
Samford U (AL)
Syracuse U (NY)
Texas Woman's U (TX)
U of Arkansas (AR)
U of Georgia (GA)
U of Idaho (ID)
U of Kentucky (KY)
U of Missouri (MO)
U of Nebraska–Lincoln (NE)
U of New Mexico (NM)
The U of North Carolina at Chapel Hill (NC)
The U of Tennessee (TN)
Virginia Polytechnic Inst and State U (VA)
Washington State U (WA)
Western Illinois U (IL)
Youngstown State U (OH)

FOOD TECHNOLOGY AND PROCESSING
California State U, Los Angeles (CA)
Central Michigan U (MI)
Regis U (CO)

FOREIGN LANGUAGES AND LITERATURES
Alfred U (NY)
Arkansas Tech U (AR)
Auburn U (AL)
Auburn U at Montgomery (AL)
Austin Peay State U (TN)
California Polytechnic State U, San Luis Obispo (CA)
Cameron U (OK)
Coastal Carolina U (SC)
Colorado State U (CO)
Colorado State U–Pueblo (CO)
Covenant Coll (GA)
Duquesne U (PA)
East Carolina U (NC)
Eastern Illinois U (IL)
East Tennessee State U (TN)
The Evergreen State Coll (WA)
Framingham State U (MA)
George Mason U (VA)
Georgia Coll & State U (GA)
Gordon Coll (MA)
Hamilton Coll (NY)
Jackson State U (MS)
Juniata Coll (PA)
Knox Coll (IL)
Lamar U (TX)
Lewis & Clark Coll (OR)
Lock Haven U of Pennsylvania (PA)
Louisiana Coll (LA)
Lycoming Coll (PA)
Manchester U (IN)
Marshall U (WV)
Massachusetts Inst of Technology (MA)
Middle Tennessee State U (TN)
Millersville U of Pennsylvania (PA)
New York U (NY)
North Carolina State U (NC)
Old Dominion U (VA)
Pace U (NY)
Piedmont Coll (GA)
Purdue U Northwest (IN)
Radford U (VA)
St. Mary's Coll of Maryland (MD)
Scripps Coll (CA)
Southern Illinois U Carbondale (IL)
Southern Illinois U Edwardsville (IL)
Stockton U (NJ)
Stonehill Coll (MA)
Syracuse U (NY)
Texas Tech U (TX)
Towson U (MD)
Tulane U (LA)
Union Coll (NY)
U of California, Riverside (CA)
U of California, Santa Cruz (CA)
U of Central Arkansas (AR)
U of Dayton (OH)
U of Florida (FL)
U of Houston (TX)
U of Idaho (ID)
U of Maryland, Baltimore County (MD)
U of Massachusetts Lowell (MA)
U of Memphis (TN)
U of Minnesota, Twin Cities Campus (MN)
U of Montevallo (AL)
U of New Mexico (NM)
The U of North Carolina at Chapel Hill (NC)
The U of North Carolina at Greensboro (NC)
U of North Dakota (ND)
U of Northern Colorado (CO)
U of South Alabama (AL)
U of South Florida (FL)
The U of Tennessee (TN)
U of Wisconsin–River Falls (WI)
Utica Coll (NY)
Virginia Commonwealth U (VA)
West Chester U of Pennsylvania (PA)
Western Illinois U (IL)
Western Washington U (WA)
Widener U (PA)
Winthrop U (SC)
Youngstown State U (OH)

FOREIGN LANGUAGES RELATED
Averett U (VA)
Framingham State U (MA)
Georgia Southern U (GA)
Indiana State U (IN)
Kennesaw State U (GA)
Miami U (OH)
Murray State U (KY)
New York U (NY)
Occidental Coll (CA)
Purchase Coll, State U of New York (NY)
U of California, Los Angeles (CA)
U of Hawaii at Manoa (HI)
U of Washington (WA)
U of West Georgia (GA)

FOREIGN LANGUAGE TEACHER EDUCATION
Arkansas Tech U (AR)
Auburn U (AL)
Baylor U (TX)
Boston U (MA)
Bowling Green State U (OH)
Calvin Coll (MI)
Coll of Staten Island of the City U of New York (NY)
DePaul U (IL)
Florida Southern Coll (FL)
Grand Valley State U (MI)
Hofstra U (NY)
Iona Coll (NY)
Manchester U (IN)
Messiah Coll (PA)
Miami U (OH)
Nazareth Coll of Rochester (NY)
New York U (NY)
The Ohio State U (OH)
Ohio Wesleyan U (OH)
Pace U, Pleasantville Campus (NY)
Piedmont Coll (GA)
Providence Coll (RI)
Queens Coll of the City U of New York (NY)
Rhode Island Coll (RI)
Saint Francis U (PA)
Seton Hill U (PA)
Southeast Missouri State U (MO)
State U of New York at Plattsburgh (NY)

Temple U (PA)
U of Dayton (OH)
The U of Findlay (OH)
U of Georgia (GA)
U of Maine (ME)
U of Mary Hardin-Baylor (TX)
U of Minnesota, Duluth (MN)
U of Nebraska–Lincoln (NE)
U of South Dakota (SD)
U of South Florida (FL)
U of Vermont (VT)
U of Wisconsin–Milwaukee (WI)
Valparaiso U (IN)
Youngstown State U (OH)

FORENSIC CHEMISTRY
Alabama State U (AL)
Bowling Green State U (OH)
Emmanuel Coll (MA)
Lamar U (TX)
LeTourneau U (TX)
Loyola U New Orleans (LA)
Maryville U of Saint Louis (MO)
Missouri Baptist U (MO)
Palm Beach Atlantic U (FL)
U of Saint Francis (IN)

FORENSIC PSYCHOLOGY
Canisius Coll (NY)
The Coll of Saint Rose (NY)
Embry-Riddle Aeronautical U–Prescott (AZ)
Northwest Christian U (OR)
Oklahoma Baptist U (OK)
Tiffin U (OH)
U of New Haven (CT)

FORENSIC SCIENCE AND TECHNOLOGY
American Public U System (WV)
Bryant U (RI)
Cedarville U (OH)
The Coll of Saint Rose (NY)
Columbia Coll (MO)
Embry-Riddle Aeronautical U–Prescott (AZ)
Farmingdale State Coll (NY)
Fayetteville State U (NC)
George Mason U (VA)
Hofstra U (NY)
Indiana U–Purdue U Indianapolis (IN)
Inter American U of Puerto Rico, Aguadilla Campus (PR)
Inter American U of Puerto Rico, Barranquitas Campus (PR)
Inter American U of Puerto Rico, Bayamón Campus (PR)
King U (TN)
Lasell Coll (MA)
Liberty U (VA)
Loyola U Chicago (IL)
Madonna U (MI)
Miami U (OH)
Middle Tennessee State U (TN)
Mount Marty Coll (SD)
Pace U (NY)
Piedmont Coll (GA)
Saint Francis U (PA)
Saint Louis U (MO)
St. Mary's U (TX)
Seton Hill U (PA)
State U of New York Coll of Technology at Alfred (NY)
Syracuse U (NY)
Tiffin U (OH)
Towson U (MD)
U of Central Florida (FL)
The U of Findlay (OH)
U of Maryland U Coll (MD)
U of Nebraska–Lincoln (NE)
U of New Haven (CT)
U of North Dakota (ND)
U of Pittsburgh at Bradford (PA)
U of Providence (MT)
The U of Tampa (FL)
Utah Valley U (UT)
Virginia Commonwealth U (VA)
Waynesburg U (PA)
Weber State U (UT)
West Virginia U Inst of Technology (WV)
Youngstown State U (OH)

FOREST/FOREST RESOURCES MANAGEMENT
North Carolina State U (NC)
State U of New York Coll of Environmental Science and Forestry (NY)
U of Idaho (ID)
U of Nevada, Reno (NV)

FORESTRY
Beloit Coll (WI)
California Polytechnic State U, San Luis Obispo (CA)
Colorado State U (CO)
Humboldt State U (CA)
Michigan State U (MI)
Purdue U (IN)
Southern Illinois U Carbondale (IL)
State U of New York Coll of Environmental Science and Forestry (NY)
U of Florida (FL)
U of Georgia (GA)
U of Idaho (ID)
U of Maine (ME)
U of New Hampshire (NH)
The U of Tennessee (TN)
U of Vermont (VT)
Utah State U (UT)
Virginia Polytechnic Inst and State U (VA)
Washington State U (WA)

FORESTRY RELATED
Auburn U (AL)
Northwest Missouri State U (MO)
State U of New York Coll of Environmental Science and Forestry (NY)
U of Minnesota, Twin Cities Campus (MN)
Utah State U (UT)

FOREST SCIENCES AND BIOLOGY
Auburn U (AL)
Colorado State U (CO)
Iowa State U of Science and Technology (IA)
State U of New York Coll of Environmental Science and Forestry (NY)
U of Idaho (ID)
U of Kentucky (KY)
The U of the South (TN)

FRANCHISING
Northwood U, Michigan Campus (MI)

FRENCH
Acadia U (NS, Canada)
Adelphi U (NY)
Agnes Scott Coll (GA)
Albion Coll (MI)
Albright Coll (PA)
Allegheny Coll (PA)
American U (DC)
Auburn U (AL)
Austin Coll (TX)
Baker U (KS)
Baldwin Wallace U (OH)
Baylor U (TX)
Beloit Coll (WI)
Berea Coll (KY)
Boston Coll (MA)
Boston U (MA)
Bowling Green State U (OH)
Bradley U (IL)
Bridgewater Coll (VA)
Bryant U (RI)
Bucknell U (PA)
Butler U (IN)
California Lutheran U (CA)
California State U, Chico (CA)
California State U, Fullerton (CA)
California State U, Long Beach (CA)
California State U, Los Angeles (CA)
California State U, Northridge (CA)
California State U, San Bernardino (CA)
Calvin Coll (MI)
Carthage Coll (WI)
The Catholic U of America (DC)
Centenary Coll of Louisiana (LA)
Central Connecticut State U (CT)
Central Michigan U (MI)
Central Washington U (WA)
Christopher Newport U (VA)
Claremont McKenna Coll (CA)
Clark U (MA)
Colgate U (NY)
The Coll at Brockport, State U of New York (NY)
Coll of Charleston (SC)
Coll of Coastal Georgia (GA)
Coll of Saint Benedict (MN)
Coll of the Holy Cross (MA)
The Coll of William and Mary (VA)
The Colorado Coll (CO)
Columbia U (NY)
Connecticut Coll (CT)
Cornell Coll (IA)
Cornell U (NY)
Creighton U (NE)
Dartmouth Coll (NH)
Davidson Coll (NC)
DePaul U (IL)
Dickinson Coll (PA)
Dominican U (IL)
Drew U (NJ)
Drury U (MO)
Earlham Coll (IN)
Eastern Washington U (WA)
Eckerd Coll (FL)
Fairfield U (CT)
Florida Atlantic U (FL)
Fordham U (NY)
Furman U (SC)
Georgia State U (GA)
Gonzaga U (WA)
Gordon Coll (MA)
Grand Valley State U (MI)
Grove City Coll (PA)
Hamilton Coll (NY)
Hampden-Sydney Coll (VA)
Hanover Coll (IN)
Harding U (AR)
Hartwick Coll (NY)
Haverford Coll (PA)
High Point U (NC)
Hillsdale Coll (MI)
Hofstra U (NY)
Hollins U (VA)
Hood Coll (MD)
Humboldt State U (CA)
Hunter Coll of the City U of New York (NY)
Idaho State U (ID)
Illinois Coll (IL)
Indiana U Bloomington (IN)
Indiana U Northwest (IN)
Indiana U–Purdue U Indianapolis (IN)
Indiana U South Bend (IN)
Indiana U Southeast (IN)
Iona Coll (NY)
Ithaca Coll (NY)
Jacksonville U (FL)
Johns Hopkins U (MD)
Johnson C. Smith U (NC)
Juniata Coll (PA)
Kalamazoo Coll (MI)
King's Coll (PA)
Knox Coll (IL)
Lafayette Coll (PA)
Lake Forest Coll (IL)
Lawrence U (WI)
Lebanon Valley Coll (PA)
Lee U (TN)
Lewis & Clark Coll (OR)
Lindenwood U (MO)
Linfield Coll (OR)
Lipscomb U (TN)
Louisiana Coll (LA)
Louisiana State U and A&M Coll (LA)
Loyola Marymount U (CA)
Loyola U Chicago (IL)
Loyola U New Orleans (LA)
Lycoming Coll (PA)
Macalester Coll (MN)
Manchester U (IN)
Manhattan Coll (NY)
Marist Coll (NY)
Marquette U (WI)
McDaniel Coll (MD)
Mercer U, Macon (GA)
Merrimack Coll (MA)
Messiah Coll (PA)
Miami U (OH)
Miami U Hamilton (OH)
Michigan State U (MI)
Middlebury Coll (VT)
Montclair State U (NJ)
Muskingum U (OH)
Nazareth Coll of Rochester (NY)
New Coll of Florida (FL)
New York U (NY)
North Carolina State U (NC)
Northern Illinois U (IL)
Northern Kentucky U (KY)
Northwestern U (IL)
Occidental Coll (CA)
Oglethorpe U (GA)
The Ohio State U (OH)
Ohio U (OH)
Ohio Wesleyan U (OH)
Oklahoma State U (OK)
Pacific Lutheran U (WA)
Pepperdine U, Malibu (CA)
Point Loma Nazarene U (CA)
Portland State U (OR)
Princeton U (NJ)
Providence Coll (RI)
Purdue U (IN)
Queens Coll of the City U of New York (NY)
Queens U of Charlotte (NC)
Randolph Coll (VA)
Randolph-Macon Coll (VA)
Redeemer U Coll (ON, Canada)
Regis U (CO)
Rhode Island Coll (RI)
Rhodes Coll (TN)
Rice U (TX)
Rider U (NJ)
Roanoke Coll (VA)
Rockford U (IL)
Saginaw Valley State U (MI)
Saint Anselm Coll (NH)
St. John Fisher Coll (NY)
Saint John's U (MN)
Saint Joseph's U (PA)
Saint Louis U (MO)
St. Norbert Coll (WI)
St. Olaf Coll (MN)
Saint Vincent Coll (PA)
Salisbury U (MD)
Salve Regina U (RI)
Samford U (AL)
San Diego State U (CA)
San Francisco State U (CA)
San Jose State U (CA)
Sarah Lawrence Coll (NY)
Scripps Coll (CA)
Seattle U (WA)
Skidmore Coll (NY)
Sonoma State U (CA)
Southern U and Ag and Mech Coll (LA)
Southwestern U (TX)
State U of New York at Fredonia (NY)
State U of New York at Plattsburgh (NY)
State U of New York Coll at Geneseo (NY)
State U of New York Coll at Potsdam (NY)
Stetson U (FL)
Stonehill Coll (MA)
Syracuse U (NY)
Temple U (PA)
Texas Christian U (TX)
Texas Tech U (TX)
Truman State U (MO)
Tulane U (LA)
Union Coll (NY)
Université de Sherbrooke (QC, Canada)
Université Sainte-Anne (NS, Canada)
U at Buffalo, the State U of New York (NY)
U of Arkansas (AR)
U of California, Davis (CA)
U of California, Irvine (CA)
U of California, Los Angeles (CA)
U of California, Riverside (CA)
U of Central Arkansas (AR)
U of Central Florida (FL)
U of Colorado Denver (CO)
U of Dallas (TX)
U of Dayton (OH)
U of Florida (FL)
U of Georgia (GA)
U of Hawaii at Manoa (HI)
U of Houston (TX)
U of Idaho (ID)
U of Kentucky (KY)
U of La Verne (CA)
U of Louisville (KY)
U of Lynchburg (VA)
U of Maine (ME)
U of Maryland, Coll Park (MD)
U of Massachusetts Amherst (MA)
U of Massachusetts Boston (MA)
U of Massachusetts Dartmouth (MA)
U of Michigan (MI)
U of Michigan–Dearborn (MI)
U of Minnesota, Duluth (MN)
U of Minnesota, Morris (MN)
U of Minnesota, Twin Cities Campus (MN)
U of Mount Union (OH)
U of Nebraska–Lincoln (NE)
U of Nevada, Las Vegas (NV)
U of Nevada, Reno (NV)
U of New Hampshire (NH)
U of New Mexico (NM)
U of North Carolina at Asheville (NC)
The U of North Carolina at Charlotte (NC)
U of North Dakota (ND)
U of Notre Dame (IN)
U of Oregon (OR)
U of Pennsylvania (PA)
U of Pittsburgh (PA)
U of Puget Sound (WA)
U of Regina (SK, Canada)
U of Richmond (VA)
U of St. Thomas (MN)
U of St. Thomas (TX)
U of San Diego (CA)
U of San Francisco (CA)
U of South Carolina (SC)
U of South Dakota (SD)
U of Southern Indiana (IN)
U of South Florida (FL)
The U of Tennessee (TN)
The U of Texas at Austin (TX)
The U of Texas at El Paso (TX)
The U of the South (TN)
The U of Toledo (OH)
The U of Tulsa (OK)
U of Vermont (VT)
U of Virginia (VA)
U of Washington (WA)
U of Wisconsin–Eau Claire (WI)
U of Wisconsin–La Crosse (WI)
U of Wisconsin–Milwaukee (WI)
U of Wyoming (WY)
Ursinus Coll (PA)
Utah State U (UT)
Valparaiso U (IN)
Vassar Coll (NY)
Virginia Polytechnic Inst and State U (VA)
Wabash Coll (IN)
Washington & Jefferson Coll (PA)
Washington and Lee U (VA)
Washington State U (WA)
Washington U in St. Louis (MO)
Weber State U (UT)
West Chester U of Pennsylvania (PA)
Western Kentucky U (KY)
Western Washington U (WA)
Westmont Coll (CA)
Wheaton Coll (IL)
Whittier Coll (CA)
Whitworth U (WA)
Widener U (PA)
Willamette U (OR)
Williams Coll (MA)
Wofford Coll (SC)
Wright State U–Lake Campus (OH)

FRENCH AS A SECOND/ FOREIGN LANGUAGE (TEACHING)
Saginaw Valley State U (MI)
U of Wisconsin–Milwaukee (WI)

FRENCH LANGUAGE TEACHER EDUCATION
Albion Coll (MI)
Auburn U (AL)
Austin Coll (TX)
California Lutheran U (CA)
Calvin Coll (MI)
Canisius Coll (NY)
The Catholic U of America (DC)
Central Michigan U (MI)
Central Washington U (WA)
Eastern Washington U (WA)
Grand Valley State U (MI)
Grove City Coll (PA)

Harding U (AR)
Hofstra U (NY)
Indiana U South Bend (IN)
Iona Coll (NY)
Ithaca Coll (NY)
Juniata Coll (PA)
Lee U (TN)
Lipscomb U (TN)
Louisiana Coll (LA)
Manchester U (IN)
Manhattanville Coll (NY)
Marist Coll (NY)
Merrimack Coll (MA)
Messiah Coll (PA)
Miami U (OH)
Miami U Hamilton (OH)
Michigan State U (MI)
New York U (NY)
Ohio U (OH)
Ohio Wesleyan U (OH)
Providence Coll (RI)
Queens Coll of the City U of New York (NY)
Rhode Island Coll (RI)
St. John Fisher Coll (NY)
Saint Joseph's U (PA)
Salve Regina U (RI)
Southern U and Ag and Mech Coll (LA)
State U of New York Coll at Potsdam (NY)
Université Sainte-Anne (NS, Canada)
U of Maine (ME)
U of Nebraska–Lincoln (NE)
U of Regina (SK, Canada)
U of St. Thomas (MN)
U of South Dakota (SD)
Valparaiso U (IN)
Washington U in St. Louis (MO)
Weber State U (UT)
Western Washington U (WA)
Whitworth U (WA)
Widener U (PA)

FRENCH STUDIES
American U (DC)
Brandeis U (MA)
The Colorado Coll (CO)
Columbia U (NY)
Fordham U (NY)
Lewis & Clark Coll (OR)
Linfield Coll (OR)
Manhattanville Coll (NY)
Mills Coll (CA)
Rhode Island Coll (RI)
Saint Joseph's U (PA)
Skidmore Coll (NY)
U of New Hampshire (NH)
U of North Florida (FL)
Wesleyan U (CT)
Wheaton Coll (MA)

FUNERAL SERVICE AND MORTUARY SCIENCE
Southern Illinois U Carbondale (IL)
U of Minnesota, Twin Cities Campus (MN)

FURNITURE DESIGN AND MANUFACTURING
Rhode Island School of Design (RI)

GAME AND INTERACTIVE MEDIA DESIGN
Acad of Art U (CA)
Albright Coll (PA)
Arkansas Tech U (AR)
Bradley U (IL)
Champlain Coll (VT)
Cleveland Inst of Art (OH)
Columbia Coll Chicago (IL)
Dakota State U (SD)
DePaul U (IL)
Drury U (MO)
Embry-Riddle Aeronautical U–Prescott (AZ)
Fitchburg State U (MA)
Florida Southern Coll (FL)
High Point U (NC)
Indiana U Bloomington (IN)
Inter American U of Puerto Rico, Barranquitas Campus (PR)
Inter American U of Puerto Rico, Bayamón Campus (PR)
Kennesaw State U (GA)
Marist Coll (NY)
Maryland Inst Coll of Art (MD)
New England Inst of Technology (RI)
Oklahoma Christian U (OK)
Rochester Inst of Technology (NY)
Sacred Heart U (CT)
Sarah Lawrence Coll (NY)
Savannah Coll of Art and Design (GA)
Southern Arkansas U–Magnolia (AR)
State U of New York Coll of Technology at Alfred (NY)
U of California, Irvine (CA)
U of California, Santa Cruz (CA)
U of Saint Francis (IN)
Woodbury U (CA)
Worcester Polytechnic Inst (MA)

GAY/LESBIAN STUDIES
Bryant U (RI)
Cornell U (NY)
Mills Coll (CA)
Sarah Lawrence Coll (NY)

GENERAL STUDIES
Alfred U (NY)
American Public U System (WV)
Austin Coll (TX)
Austin Peay State U (TN)
Brenau U (GA)
California State U, San Bernardino (CA)
California State U, San Marcos (CA)
Calumet Coll of Saint Joseph (IN)
Cameron U (OK)
The Catholic U of America (DC)
Champlain Coll (VT)
Clarion U of Pennsylvania (PA)
Coll of the Ozarks (MO)
Columbia Coll (MO)
Columbia Coll Chicago (IL)
Concordia U Chicago (IL)
Cornell U (NY)
Dean Coll (MA)
Delta State U (MS)
DePaul U (IL)
Earlham Coll (IN)
East Carolina U (NC)
East Tennessee State U (TN)
Fairfield U (CT)
George Mason U (VA)
Georgia Southern U (GA)
Granite State Coll (NH)
Harding U (AR)
Humboldt State U (CA)
Idaho State U (ID)
Indiana State U (IN)
Jacksonville U (FL)
Kansas Wesleyan U (KS)
LaGrange Coll (GA)
Lamar U (TX)
La Salle U (PA)
Lasell Coll (MA)
La Sierra U (CA)
Liberty U (VA)
Lincoln Christian U (IL)
Lipscomb U (TN)
Louisiana Coll (LA)
Loyola U Chicago (IL)
Madonna U (MI)
Marshall U (WV)
Marywood U (PA)
McNeese State U (LA)
Middle Tennessee State U (TN)
Missouri Baptist U (MO)
Molloy Coll (NY)
Mount Marty Coll (SD)
Mount St. Joseph U (OH)
Murray State U (KY)
National U (CA)
New Jersey Inst of Technology (NJ)
New York U (NY)
Northeastern State U (OK)
Northwestern Oklahoma State U (OK)
Northwestern U (IL)
Oakland City U (IN)
Ohio Wesleyan U (OH)
Oklahoma State U (OK)
Palm Beach Atlantic U (FL)
Point U (GA)
Providence Coll (RI)
Sacred Heart U (CT)
Saginaw Valley State U (MI)
Saint Louis U (MO)
San Diego State U (CA)
Seton Hill U (PA)
Southeastern Louisiana U (LA)
Southeastern U (FL)
Southeast Missouri State U (MO)
Southern Arkansas U–Magnolia (AR)
Spring Hill Coll (AL)
State U of New York at Plattsburgh (NY)
State U of New York Coll of Technology at Alfred (NY)
State U of New York Maritime Coll (NY)
Texas Christian U (TX)
Texas Tech U (TX)
Texas Woman's U (TX)
Tiffin U (OH)
Toccoa Falls Coll (GA)
Trevecca Nazarene U (TN)
Union Coll (KY)
U of Central Florida (FL)
U of Dayton (OH)
U of Idaho (ID)
U of Kentucky (KY)
U of La Verne (CA)
U of Maine at Machias (ME)
U of Mary Hardin-Baylor (TX)
U of Massachusetts Amherst (MA)
U of Memphis (TN)
U of Michigan (MI)
U of Michigan–Dearborn (MI)
U of Missouri (MO)
U of Nevada, Reno (NV)
U of New Mexico (NM)
U of North Dakota (ND)
U of Northern Iowa (IA)
U of St. Thomas (TX)
U of South Dakota (SD)
U of South Florida (FL)
U of South Florida Sarasota-Manatee (FL)
The U of Tampa (FL)
The U of Toledo (OH)
U of Washington (WA)
U of Washington, Bothell (WA)
U of Washington, Tacoma (WA)
Valley City State U (ND)
Western Kentucky U (KY)
West Virginia State U (WV)
West Virginia U Inst of Technology (WV)
Whitworth U (WA)
Widener U (PA)
Worcester State U (MA)
Youngstown State U (OH)

GENETICS
Iowa State U of Science and Technology (IA)
North Carolina State U (NC)
Ohio Wesleyan U (OH)
Purdue U (IN)
U of California, Davis (CA)
U of California, Irvine (CA)
U of Georgia (GA)
U of New Hampshire (NH)
Washington State U (WA)

GENOME SCIENCES/ GENOMICS
U of New Haven (CT)

GEOCHEMISTRY
Bowling Green State U (OH)
Bridgewater State U (MA)
California Inst of Technology (CA)
Grand Valley State U (MI)
State U of New York Coll at Geneseo (NY)
Washington U in St. Louis (MO)

GEOGRAPHIC INFORMATION SCIENCE AND CARTOGRAPHY
Auburn U at Montgomery (AL)
Central Michigan U (MI)
Central Washington U (WA)
DePaul U (IL)
Farmingdale State Coll (NY)
Hofstra U (NY)
Kennesaw State U (GA)
Michigan State U (MI)
Northwest Missouri State U (MO)
The Ohio State U (OH)
Oklahoma State U (OK)
Radford U (VA)
U at Buffalo, the State U of New York (NY)
U of Maryland, Coll Park (MD)
U of Oregon (OR)
U of Regina (SK, Canada)
U of Wisconsin–Eau Claire (WI)
Western Kentucky U (KY)

GEOGRAPHY
Adams State U (CO)
Appalachian State U (NC)
Auburn U (AL)
Boston U (MA)
Bowling Green State U (OH)
Bridgewater State U (MA)
Bucknell U (PA)
California State U, Chico (CA)
California State U, Fullerton (CA)
California State U, Long Beach (CA)
California State U, Los Angeles (CA)
California State U, Northridge (CA)
California State U, San Bernardino (CA)
California U of Pennsylvania (PA)
Calvin Coll (MI)
Carthage Coll (WI)
Central Connecticut State U (CT)
Central Michigan U (MI)
Central Washington U (WA)
Clark U (MA)
Colgate U (NY)
Coll of Staten Island of the City U of New York (NY)
Colorado State U (CO)
Concordia U Chicago (IL)
Dartmouth Coll (NH)
DePaul U (IL)
East Carolina U (NC)
Eastern Illinois U (IL)
Eastern Washington U (WA)
East Tennessee State U (TN)
Fayetteville State U (NC)
Fitchburg State U (MA)
Florida Atlantic U (FL)
Framingham State U (MA)
George Mason U (VA)
Georgia Coll & State U (GA)
Georgia Southern U (GA)
Georgia State U (GA)
Grand Valley State U (MI)
Hofstra U (NY)
Humboldt State U (CA)
Hunter Coll of the City U of New York (NY)
Indiana State U (IN)
Indiana U Bloomington (IN)
Indiana U of Pennsylvania (PA)
Indiana U–Purdue U Indianapolis (IN)
Indiana U Southeast (IN)
Jacksonville U (FL)
Johns Hopkins U (MD)
Kennesaw State U (GA)
Louisiana State U and A&M Coll (LA)
Macalester Coll (MN)
Marshall U (WV)
Miami U (OH)
Miami U Hamilton (OH)
Michigan State U (MI)
Middlebury Coll (VT)
Millersville U of Pennsylvania (PA)
Montclair State U (NJ)
Northeastern State U (OK)
Northern Illinois U (IL)
Northern Kentucky U (KY)
Northwestern U (IL)
Northwest Missouri State U (MO)
The Ohio State U (OH)
Ohio U (OH)
Ohio Wesleyan U (OH)
Oklahoma State U (OK)
Old Dominion U (VA)
Portland State U (OR)
Rhode Island Coll (RI)
Rocky Mountain Coll (MT)
Saginaw Valley State U (MI)
Salisbury U (MD)
Samford U (AL)
San Diego State U (CA)
San Francisco State U (CA)
San Jose State U (CA)
Sarah Lawrence Coll (NY)
Sonoma State U (CA)
Southern Illinois U Carbondale (IL)
Southern Illinois U Edwardsville (IL)
State U of New York at Plattsburgh (NY)
State U of New York Coll at Geneseo (NY)
Syracuse U (NY)
Taylor U (IN)
Texas Christian U (TX)
Texas Tech U (TX)
Towson U (MD)
U at Buffalo, the State U of New York (NY)
U of Arkansas (AR)
U of California, Los Angeles (CA)
U of Central Arkansas (AR)
U of Chicago (IL)
U of Colorado Denver (CO)
U of Florida (FL)
U of Georgia (GA)
U of Hawaii at Manoa (HI)
U of Houston–Clear Lake (TX)
U of Idaho (ID)
U of Kentucky (KY)
U of Louisville (KY)
U of Maine at Farmington (ME)
U of Massachusetts Amherst (MA)
U of Memphis (TN)
U of Minnesota, Duluth (MN)
U of Minnesota, Twin Cities Campus (MN)
U of Missouri (MO)
U of Nebraska–Lincoln (NE)
U of Nevada, Reno (NV)
U of New Hampshire (NH)
U of New Mexico (NM)
The U of North Carolina at Chapel Hill (NC)
The U of North Carolina at Charlotte (NC)
The U of North Carolina at Greensboro (NC)
U of North Dakota (ND)
U of Northern Colorado (CO)
U of Northern Iowa (IA)
U of Oregon (OR)
U of Regina (SK, Canada)
U of Richmond (VA)
U of St. Thomas (MN)
U of South Alabama (AL)
U of South Carolina (SC)
U of South Florida (FL)
The U of Tennessee (TN)
The U of Texas at Austin (TX)
The U of Toledo (OH)
U of Vermont (VT)
U of Washington (WA)
U of West Georgia (GA)
U of Wisconsin–Eau Claire (WI)
U of Wisconsin–La Crosse (WI)
U of Wisconsin–Milwaukee (WI)
U of Wisconsin–River Falls (WI)
U of Wyoming (WY)
Utah State U (UT)
Valparaiso U (IN)
Vassar Coll (NY)
Virginia Polytechnic Inst and State U (VA)
Weber State U (UT)
West Chester U of Pennsylvania (PA)
Western Illinois U (IL)
Western Kentucky U (KY)
Western Washington U (WA)
Worcester State U (MA)
Wright State U–Lake Campus (OH)
Youngstown State U (OH)

GEOGRAPHY RELATED
Arkansas Tech U (AR)
Bridgewater State U (MA)
Central Washington U (WA)
Ohio U (OH)
Temple U (PA)
U of California, Los Angeles (CA)

GEOGRAPHY TEACHER EDUCATION
Calvin Coll (MI)
Grand Valley State U (MI)
Michigan State U (MI)
Rhode Island Coll (RI)
Valparaiso U (IN)
Weber State U (UT)

GEOLOGICAL AND EARTH SCIENCES/GEOSCIENCES RELATED
Allegheny Coll (PA)
Boston U (MA)

Bridgewater State U (MA)
California State U, Chico (CA)
California State U, Fullerton (CA)
Cedarville U (OH)
Central Washington U (WA)
Eckerd Coll (FL)
Hamilton Coll (NY)
Minnesota State U Moorhead (MN)
Muskingum U (OH)
Old Dominion U (VA)
Rocky Mountain Coll (MT)
Salisbury U (MD)
San Jose State U (CA)
Texas Christian U (TX)
Towson U (MD)
Union Coll (NY)
U at Buffalo, the State U of New York (NY)
U of Pittsburgh (PA)
U of Washington (WA)
U of Wyoming (WY)
Utica Coll (NY)

GEOLOGICAL/GEOPHYSICAL ENGINEERING
Colorado School of Mines (CO)
New Jersey Inst of Technology (NJ)
U of California, Los Angeles (CA)
U of Michigan (MI)
U of Minnesota, Twin Cities Campus (MN)
U of Nevada, Reno (NV)
U of North Dakota (ND)

GEOLOGY/EARTH SCIENCE
Acadia U (NS, Canada)
Adams State U (CO)
Albion Coll (MI)
Alfred U (NY)
Allegheny Coll (PA)
Angelo State U (TX)
Appalachian State U (NC)
Arkansas Tech U (AR)
Auburn U (AL)
Austin Peay State U (TN)
Baylor U (TX)
Beloit Coll (WI)
Boston Coll (MA)
Boston U (MA)
Bowling Green State U (OH)
Bridgewater State U (MA)
Bucknell U (PA)
California Inst of Technology (CA)
California Lutheran U (CA)
California Polytechnic State U, San Luis Obispo (CA)
California State U, Bakersfield (CA)
California State U, Chico (CA)
California State U, Fullerton (CA)
California State U, Long Beach (CA)
California State U, Los Angeles (CA)
California State U, Northridge (CA)
California State U, San Bernardino (CA)
California U of Pennsylvania (PA)
Calvin Coll (MI)
Cedarville U (OH)
Centenary Coll of Louisiana (LA)
Central Connecticut State U (CT)
Central Michigan U (MI)
Central Washington U (WA)
Clarion U of Pennsylvania (PA)
Clark U (MA)
Colgate U (NY)
The Coll at Brockport, State U of New York (NY)
Coll of Charleston (SC)
Coll of Staten Island of the City U of New York (NY)
The Coll of William and Mary (VA)
The Colorado Coll (CO)
Colorado State U (CO)
Columbia U (NY)
Concordia U Chicago (IL)
Cornell Coll (IA)
Dartmouth Coll (NH)
Dickinson Coll (PA)
Earlham Coll (IN)
East Carolina U (NC)
Eastern Illinois U (IL)
Eastern Washington U (WA)
East Stroudsburg U of Pennsylvania (PA)
East Tennessee State U (TN)
Florida Atlantic U (FL)
Fort Lewis Coll (CO)
Framingham State U (MA)
George Mason U (VA)
Georgia Southern U (GA)
Georgia State U (GA)
Hamilton Coll (NY)
Hanover Coll (IN)
Hardin-Simmons U (TX)
Hartwick Coll (NY)
Harvard U (MA)
Haverford Coll (PA)
Hofstra U (NY)
Humboldt State U (CA)
Idaho State U (ID)
Indiana State U (IN)
Indiana U Bloomington (IN)
Indiana U Northwest (IN)
Indiana U of Pennsylvania (PA)
Indiana U–Purdue U Indianapolis (IN)
Jackson State U (MS)
Johns Hopkins U (MD)
Juniata Coll (PA)
Kean U (NJ)
Lafayette Coll (PA)
Lamar U (TX)
Lawrence U (WI)
Lock Haven U of Pennsylvania (PA)
Louisiana State U and A&M Coll (LA)
Macalester Coll (MN)
Marshall U (WV)
Massachusetts Inst of Technology (MA)
Miami U (OH)
Miami U Hamilton (OH)
Michigan State U (MI)
Middlebury Coll (VT)
Middle Tennessee State U (TN)
Millersville U of Pennsylvania (PA)
Millsaps Coll (MS)
Montclair State U (NJ)
Murray State U (KY)
Muskingum U (OH)
New Jersey City U (NJ)
North Carolina State U (NC)
Northern Illinois U (IL)
Northern Kentucky U (KY)
Northwestern U (IL)
Northwest Missouri State U (MO)
Occidental Coll (CA)
The Ohio State U (OH)
Ohio U (OH)
Ohio Wesleyan U (OH)
Oklahoma State U (OK)
Pacific Lutheran U (WA)
Piedmont Coll (GA)
Portland State U (OR)
Princeton U (NJ)
Purdue U (IN)
Queens Coll of the City U of New York (NY)
Radford U (VA)
Rice U (TX)
Rider U (NJ)
Rocky Mountain Coll (MT)
Saint Louis U (MO)
St. Norbert Coll (WI)
San Diego State U (CA)
San Francisco State U (CA)
San Jose State U (CA)
Scripps Coll (CA)
Skidmore Coll (NY)
Sonoma State U (CA)
Southern Illinois U Carbondale (IL)
State U of New York at Fredonia (NY)
State U of New York at Plattsburgh (NY)
State U of New York Coll at Geneseo (NY)
Stockton U (NJ)
Syracuse U (NY)
Temple U (PA)
Texas Christian U (TX)
Texas Tech U (TX)
Towson U (MD)
Tulane U (LA)
Union Coll (NY)
U at Buffalo, the State U of New York (NY)
U of Arkansas (AR)
U of California, Davis (CA)
U of California, Irvine (CA)
U of California, Los Angeles (CA)
U of California, Merced (CA)
U of California, Riverside (CA)
U of California, Santa Cruz (CA)
U of Dayton (OH)
U of Florida (FL)
U of Georgia (GA)
U of Hawaii at Manoa (HI)
U of Houston (TX)
U of Houston–Downtown (TX)
U of Idaho (ID)
U of Kentucky (KY)
U of Maine (ME)
U of Maine at Farmington (ME)
U of Maryland, Coll Park (MD)
U of Massachusetts Amherst (MA)
U of Massachusetts Boston (MA)
U of Memphis (TN)
U of Michigan (MI)
U of Michigan–Dearborn (MI)
U of Minnesota, Duluth (MN)
U of Minnesota, Morris (MN)
U of Minnesota, Twin Cities Campus (MN)
U of Missouri (MO)
U of Mount Union (OH)
U of Nebraska–Lincoln (NE)
U of Nevada, Las Vegas (NV)
U of Nevada, Reno (NV)
U of New Hampshire (NH)
U of New Mexico (NM)
The U of North Carolina at Chapel Hill (NC)
The U of North Carolina at Charlotte (NC)
U of North Dakota (ND)
U of Northern Colorado (CO)
U of Northern Iowa (IA)
U of Oregon (OR)
U of Pennsylvania (PA)
U of Pittsburgh (PA)
U of Puget Sound (WA)
U of Regina (SK, Canada)
U of St. Thomas (MN)
U of South Alabama (AL)
U of South Carolina (SC)
U of South Dakota (SD)
U of Southern Indiana (IN)
U of South Florida (FL)
The U of Tennessee (TN)
The U of Tennessee at Martin (TN)
The U of Texas at Austin (TX)
The U of Texas at El Paso (TX)
The U of Texas of the Permian Basin (TX)
The U of the South (TN)
The U of Toledo (OH)
The U of Tulsa (OK)
U of Vermont (VT)
U of Washington (WA)
U of West Georgia (GA)
U of Wisconsin–Eau Claire (WI)
U of Wisconsin–Milwaukee (WI)
U of Wisconsin–River Falls (WI)
U of Wyoming (WY)
Utah State U (UT)
Utah Valley U (UT)
Vassar Coll (NY)
Virginia Polytechnic Inst and State U (VA)
Washington and Lee U (VA)
Washington State U (WA)
Washington State U–Tri-Cities (WA)
Washington State U–Vancouver (WA)
Washington U in St. Louis (MO)
Weber State U (UT)
West Chester U of Pennsylvania (PA)
Western Connecticut State U (CT)
Western Illinois U (IL)
Western Kentucky U (KY)
Western State Colorado U (CO)
Western Washington U (WA)
Wheaton Coll (IL)
Wilkes U (PA)
Williams Coll (MA)
Youngstown State U (OH)

GEOPHYSICS AND SEISMOLOGY
Baylor U (TX)
Boston Coll (MA)
Boston U (MA)
Bowling Green State U (OH)
California Inst of Technology (CA)
Rice U (TX)
Saint Louis U (MO)
State U of New York Coll at Geneseo (NY)
U of California, Los Angeles (CA)
U of California, Riverside (CA)
U of Chicago (IL)
U of Houston (TX)
U of Nevada, Reno (NV)
U of South Carolina (SC)
The U of Texas at Austin (TX)
The U of Texas at El Paso (TX)
The U of Tulsa (OK)
U of Washington (WA)
Washington U in St. Louis (MO)
Western Washington U (WA)

GERMAN
Agnes Scott Coll (GA)
Albion Coll (MI)
American U (DC)
Auburn U (AL)
Austin Coll (TX)
Baker U (KS)
Baldwin Wallace U (OH)
Baylor U (TX)
Beloit Coll (WI)
Berea Coll (KY)
Boston Coll (MA)
Boston U (MA)
Bowling Green State U (OH)
Bucknell U (PA)
Butler U (IN)
California Lutheran U (CA)
California State U, Chico (CA)
California State U, Long Beach (CA)
Calvin Coll (MI)
Carthage Coll (WI)
The Catholic U of America (DC)
Central Connecticut State U (CT)
Central Michigan U (MI)
Central Washington U (WA)
Christopher Newport U (VA)
Colgate U (NY)
Coll of Charleston (SC)
Coll of Saint Benedict (MN)
Coll of the Holy Cross (MA)
The Coll of William and Mary (VA)
The Colorado Coll (CO)
Columbia U (NY)
Cornell Coll (IA)
Cornell U (NY)
Creighton U (NE)
Dartmouth Coll (NH)
Davidson Coll (NC)
DePaul U (IL)
Dickinson Coll (PA)
Drew U (NJ)
Earlham Coll (IN)
Fairfield U (CT)
Fordham U (NY)
Furman U (SC)
Georgia State U (GA)
Gordon Coll (MA)
Hamline U (MN)
Hampden-Sydney Coll (VA)
Harvard U (MA)
Haverford Coll (PA)
Hillsdale Coll (MI)
Hofstra U (NY)
Hood Coll (MD)
Hunter Coll of the City U of New York (NY)
Idaho State U (ID)
Illinois Coll (IL)
Indiana U–Purdue U Indianapolis (IN)
Indiana U South Bend (IN)
Indiana U Southeast (IN)
Ithaca Coll (NY)
Johns Hopkins U (MD)
Juniata Coll (PA)
Kalamazoo Coll (MI)
Knox Coll (IL)
Lafayette Coll (PA)
Lawrence U (WI)
Lebanon Valley Coll (PA)
Lewis & Clark Coll (OR)
Linfield Coll (OR)
Lipscomb U (TN)
Lycoming Coll (PA)
Macalester Coll (MN)
Marquette U (WI)
McDaniel Coll (MD)
Mercer U, Macon (GA)
Messiah Coll (PA)
Miami U (OH)
Miami U Hamilton (OH)
Michigan State U (MI)
Middlebury Coll (VT)
Montclair State U (NJ)
Muskingum U (OH)
Nazareth Coll of Rochester (NY)
New Coll of Florida (FL)
New York U (NY)
Northern Illinois U (IL)
Northern Kentucky U (KY)
Northern State U (SD)
Northwestern U (IL)
The Ohio State U (OH)
Ohio U (OH)
Ohio Wesleyan U (OH)
Oklahoma State U (OK)
Pacific Lutheran U (WA)
Pepperdine U, Malibu (CA)
Portland State U (OR)
Princeton U (NJ)
Purdue U (IN)
Queens Coll of the City U of New York (NY)
Randolph-Macon Coll (VA)
Rhodes Coll (TN)
Rice U (TX)
Rider U (NJ)
Saint John's U (MN)
Saint Joseph's U (PA)
Saint Louis U (MO)
St. Norbert Coll (WI)
St. Olaf Coll (MN)
Samford U (AL)
San Diego State U (CA)
San Francisco State U (CA)
Sarah Lawrence Coll (NY)
Scripps Coll (CA)
Skidmore Coll (NY)
Southwestern U (TX)
Stetson U (FL)
Syracuse U (NY)
Temple U (PA)
Texas Christian U (TX)
Texas Tech U (TX)
Truman State U (MO)
Tulane U (LA)
Union Coll (NY)
U at Buffalo, the State U of New York (NY)
U of Arkansas (AR)
U of California, Davis (CA)
U of California, Los Angeles (CA)
U of Chicago (IL)
U of Dallas (TX)
U of Dayton (OH)
U of Florida (FL)
U of Georgia (GA)
U of Hawaii at Manoa (HI)
U of Kentucky (KY)
U of Maryland, Coll Park (MD)
U of Michigan (MI)
U of Minnesota, Duluth (MN)
U of Missouri (MO)
U of Mount Union (OH)
U of Nebraska–Lincoln (NE)
U of Nevada, Las Vegas (NV)
U of New Hampshire (NH)
U of New Mexico (NM)
U of North Carolina at Asheville (NC)
The U of North Carolina at Charlotte (NC)
U of North Dakota (ND)
U of Notre Dame (IN)
U of Oregon (OR)
U of Pennsylvania (PA)
U of Pittsburgh (PA)
U of Puget Sound (WA)
U of Regina (SK, Canada)
U of St. Thomas (MN)
U of South Carolina (SC)
U of South Dakota (SD)
U of Southern Indiana (IN)
U of South Florida (FL)
The U of Tennessee (TN)
The U of Texas at Austin (TX)
The U of the South (TN)
The U of Toledo (OH)
The U of Tulsa (OK)
U of Vermont (VT)
U of Virginia (VA)
U of Wisconsin–La Crosse (WI)
U of Wyoming (WY)
Ursinus Coll (PA)
Utah State U (UT)
Valparaiso U (IN)
Vassar Coll (NY)
Virginia Polytechnic Inst and State U (VA)
Wabash Coll (IN)

Wartburg Coll (IA)
Washington & Jefferson Coll (PA)
Washington and Lee U (VA)
Washington State U (WA)
Washington U in St. Louis (MO)
Weber State U (UT)
Western Kentucky U (KY)
Western Washington U (WA)
Wheaton Coll (IL)
Wheaton Coll (MA)
Willamette U (OR)
Williams Coll (MA)
Wofford Coll (SC)
Wright State U–Lake Campus (OH)

GERMANIC LANGUAGES
Columbia U (NY)
Grand Valley State U (MI)
Indiana U Bloomington (IN)
Jacksonville U (FL)
U of Washington (WA)
U of Wisconsin–Eau Claire (WI)
U of Wisconsin–Milwaukee (WI)
Washington U in St. Louis (MO)

GERMANIC LANGUAGES RELATED
Calvin Coll (MI)
U of Minnesota, Twin Cities Campus (MN)

GERMAN LANGUAGE TEACHER EDUCATION
Albion Coll (MI)
Auburn U (AL)
California Lutheran U (CA)
Calvin Coll (MI)
Canisius Coll (NY)
The Catholic U of America (DC)
Grand Valley State U (MI)
Hofstra U (NY)
Hunter Coll of the City U of New York (NY)
Indiana U South Bend (IN)
Ithaca Coll (NY)
Messiah Coll (PA)
Miami U (OH)
Miami U Hamilton (OH)
Michigan State U (MI)
Ohio U (OH)
Ohio Wesleyan U (OH)
Queens Coll of the City U of New York (NY)
Saint Joseph's U (PA)
U of Nebraska–Lincoln (NE)
U of St. Thomas (MN)
U of South Dakota (SD)
U of Wisconsin–Milwaukee (WI)
Valparaiso U (IN)
Washington U in St. Louis (MO)
Weber State U (UT)
Western Washington U (WA)

GERMAN STUDIES
American U (DC)
Brandeis U (MA)
Columbia U (NY)
Connecticut Coll (CT)
Cornell U (NY)
Fordham U (NY)
Hamilton Coll (NY)
Ithaca Coll (NY)
Linfield Coll (OR)
North Carolina State U (NC)
Temple U (PA)
U of California, Irvine (CA)
U of California, Riverside (CA)
U of Massachusetts Amherst (MA)
U of Minnesota, Morris (MN)
U of Pittsburgh (PA)
U of Richmond (VA)
Wesleyan U (CT)
Wheaton Coll (MA)

GERONTOLOGY
Alfred U (NY)
Barton Coll (NC)
Bowling Green State U (OH)
California U of Pennsylvania (PA)
Gwynedd Mercy U (PA)
Ithaca Coll (NY)
Madonna U (MI)
Miami U (OH)
Miami U Hamilton (OH)
Minnesota State U Moorhead (MN)
Regent U (VA)
San Diego State U (CA)
U of Maryland U Coll (MD)
U of Massachusetts Boston (MA)
U of Northern Iowa (IA)
U of Regina (SK, Canada)
U of South Florida (FL)
Weber State U (UT)
Youngstown State U (OH)

GOLF COURSE OPERATION AND GROUNDS MANAGEMENT
U of the Incarnate Word (TX)

GRAPHIC AND PRINTING EQUIPMENT OPERATION/ PRODUCTION
Western Illinois U (IL)

GRAPHIC COMMUNICATIONS
Bradley U (IL)
California Polytechnic State U, San Luis Obispo (CA)
California State U, Los Angeles (CA)
Eastern Washington U (WA)
Fort Lewis Coll (CO)
Kuyper Coll (MI)
Murray State U (KY)
New England Inst of Technology (RI)
Rochester Inst of Technology (NY)
The U of Findlay (OH)
U of Maryland U Coll (MD)
U of Northern Iowa (IA)

GRAPHIC COMMUNICATIONS RELATED
Bowling Green State U (OH)

GRAPHIC DESIGN
Acad of Art U (CA)
Adams State U (CO)
American U (DC)
American U of Beirut (Lebanon)
Appalachian State U (NC)
Arkansas Tech U (AR)
Assumption Coll (MA)
Auburn U (AL)
Aurora U (IL)
Baldwin Wallace U (OH)
Benedictine U (IL)
Berkeley Coll–Woodland Park Campus (NJ)
Bethany Lutheran Coll (MN)
Bethel U (MN)
Boston U (MA)
Bradley U (IL)
Bridgewater State U (MA)
Caldwell U (NJ)
California State U, Long Beach (CA)
California U of Pennsylvania (PA)
Calvin Coll (MI)
Carson-Newman U (TN)
Carthage Coll (WI)
Cedarville U (OH)
Central Michigan U (MI)
Central Washington U (WA)
Champlain Coll (VT)
Cleveland Inst of Art (OH)
Coastal Carolina U (SC)
Coll of the Ozarks (MO)
Columbia Coll (MO)
Columbia Coll Chicago (IL)
Concordia U Irvine (CA)
Creative Center (NE)
Creighton U (NE)
Culver-Stockton Coll (MO)
Curry Coll (MA)
Dallas Baptist U (TX)
DePaul U (IL)
DEREE - The American Coll of Greece (Greece)
Drake U (IA)
Eastern Washington U (WA)
Elizabeth City State U (NC)
Emmanuel Coll (MA)
Endicott Coll (MA)
Fashion Inst of Technology (NY)
FIDM/Fashion Inst of Design & Merchandising, Los Angeles Campus (CA)
Fitchburg State U (MA)
Florida Ag and Mech U (FL)
Georgia Southern U (GA)
Harding U (AR)
Hardin-Simmons U (TX)
High Point U (NC)
Inter American U of Puerto Rico, Aguadilla Campus (PR)
Inter American U of Puerto Rico, San Germán Campus (PR)
Iowa State U of Science and Technology (IA)
Judson U (IL)
Kansas Wesleyan U (KS)
Lamar U (TX)
Lasell Coll (MA)
La Sierra U (CA)
Lebanese American U (Lebanon)
Liberty U (VA)
Limestone Coll (SC)
Louisiana Coll (LA)
Madonna U (MI)
Mansfield U of Pennsylvania (PA)
Maryland Inst Coll of Art (MD)
Marymount Manhattan Coll (NY)
Maryville U of Saint Louis (MO)
Marywood U (PA)
Mercer U, Macon (GA)
Messiah Coll (PA)
Miami U Hamilton (OH)
Michigan State U (MI)
Milligan Coll (TN)
Minnesota State U Moorhead (MN)
Montclair State U (NJ)
Morningside Coll (IA)
Mount St. Joseph U (OH)
North Carolina State U (NC)
Northern State U (SD)
Ohio U (OH)
Oklahoma Baptist U (OK)
Ouachita Baptist U (AR)
Palm Beach Atlantic U (FL)
Pennsylvania Coll of Art & Design (PA)
Point Loma Nazarene U (CA)
Portland State U (OR)
Prairie View A&M U (TX)
Queens Coll of the City U of New York (NY)
Queens U of Charlotte (NC)
Regent U (VA)
Rhode Island Coll (RI)
Rhode Island School of Design (RI)
Rider U (NJ)
Rochester Inst of Technology (NY)
The Sage Colls (NY)
Saginaw Valley State U (MI)
Saint Mary's U of Minnesota (MN)
St. Norbert Coll (WI)
Saint Vincent Coll (PA)
Samford U (AL)
San Diego State U (CA)
San Jose State U (CA)
Southeastern U (FL)
Spring Hill Coll (AL)
State U of New York Coll of Technology at Alfred (NY)
Stonehill Coll (MA)
Tabor Coll (KS)
Taylor U (IN)
Temple U (PA)
Texas Christian U (TX)
Trinity Christian Coll (IL)
U of Dayton (OH)
U of Florida (FL)
U of Houston (TX)
U of Mary Hardin-Baylor (TX)
U of Massachusetts Dartmouth (MA)
U of Michigan (MI)
U of Minnesota, Twin Cities Campus (MN)
U of Nebraska–Lincoln (NE)
U of Nevada, Las Vegas (NV)
U of New Haven (CT)
U of North Dakota (ND)
U of Northern Iowa (IA)
U of Northwestern–St. Paul (MN)
The U of Tampa (FL)
U of the Incarnate Word (TX)
Virginia Commonwealth U (VA)
Washington U in St. Louis (MO)
Weber State U (UT)
Whitworth U (WA)
Youngstown State U (OH)

HEALTH AND MEDICAL ADMINISTRATIVE SERVICES RELATED
Brenau U (GA)
Eastern Oregon U (OR)
Indiana U East (IN)
Indiana U Kokomo (IN)
Indiana U Northwest (IN)
Indiana U South Bend (IN)
Indiana U Southeast (IN)
Manor Coll (PA)
U of Detroit Mercy (MI)

HEALTH AND PHYSICAL EDUCATION/FITNESS
Adelphi U (NY)
Austin Peay State U (TN)
Averett U (VA)
Baker U (KS)
Baldwin Wallace U (OH)
Barton Coll (NC)
Baylor U (TX)
Berea Coll (KY)
Bethel Coll (KS)
Blackburn Coll (IL)
Bridgewater Coll (VA)
California Polytechnic State U, San Luis Obispo (CA)
California State U, Chico (CA)
California State U, Fullerton (CA)
California State U, Los Angeles (CA)
California State U, Monterey Bay (CA)
California State U, San Bernardino (CA)
California State U, San Marcos (CA)
Cameron U (OK)
Coll of the Ozarks (MO)
The Coll of William and Mary (VA)
Concordia U Irvine (CA)
Dallas Baptist U (TX)
Eastern Oregon U (OR)
Eastern Washington U (WA)
East Tennessee State U (TN)
East Texas Baptist U (TX)
Florida Ag and Mech U (FL)
Graceland U (IA)
Hanover Coll (IN)
Hillsdale Coll (MI)
Humboldt State U (CA)
Indiana U Bloomington (IN)
Indiana U of Pennsylvania (PA)
Ithaca Coll (NY)
Jacksonville U (FL)
Johnson U Florida (FL)
King U (TN)
La Sierra U (CA)
Lee U (TN)
Liberty U (VA)
Lindenwood U (MO)
Linfield Coll (OR)
Louisiana Coll (LA)
Lubbock Christian U (TX)
Marian U (IN)
Marywood U (PA)
McDaniel Coll (MD)
Middle Tennessee State U (TN)
Milligan Coll (TN)
Minnesota State U Moorhead (MN)
Muskingum U (OH)
New England Coll (NH)
Northern Illinois U (IL)
Northern State U (SD)
Oakland City U (IN)
The Ohio State U (OH)
Ohio U (OH)
Oklahoma Baptist U (OK)
Palm Beach Atlantic U (FL)
Point Loma Nazarene U (CA)
Randolph Coll (VA)
Redeemer U Coll (ON, Canada)
Rhode Island Coll (RI)
Rocky Mountain Coll (MT)
San Diego State U (CA)
San Jose State U (CA)
Southeast Missouri State U (MO)
Southwest Baptist U (MO)
Syracuse U (NY)
Tabor Coll (KS)
Texas Christian U (TX)
Truman State U (MO)
U of Arkansas (AR)
The U of Findlay (OH)
U of Georgia (GA)
U of Guam (GU)
U of Hawaii at Manoa (HI)
U of Louisville (KY)
U of Lynchburg (VA)
U of Maine at Presque Isle (ME)
U of Massachusetts Boston (MA)
U of Michigan (MI)
U of Montevallo (AL)
The U of North Carolina at Chapel Hill (NC)
The U of North Carolina at Charlotte (NC)
The U of North Carolina at Pembroke (NC)
U of Northern Iowa (IA)
U of Providence (MT)
U of Regina (SK, Canada)
U of St. Thomas (MN)
The U of Tampa (FL)
The U of Tennessee at Martin (TN)
U of Wisconsin–Superior (WI)
Utah Valley U (UT)
Valley City State U (ND)
Valparaiso U (IN)
Vanguard U of Southern California (CA)
Weber State U (UT)
West Chester U of Pennsylvania (PA)
West Virginia State U (WV)
Whittier Coll (CA)
Youngstown State U (OH)

HEALTH AND PHYSICAL EDUCATION RELATED
Adelphi U (NY)
Averett U (VA)
Avila U (MO)
Bowling Green State U (OH)
Bridgewater State U (MA)
California State U, Long Beach (CA)
Cornell Coll (IA)
East Carolina U (NC)
Ithaca Coll (NY)
La Sierra U (CA)
Limestone Coll (SC)
Lock Haven U of Pennsylvania (PA)
Mount Marty Coll (SD)
Texas Lutheran U (TX)
U of Wisconsin–Superior (WI)
Weber State U (UT)

HEALTH AND WELLNESS
Bowling Green State U (OH)
Canisius Coll (NY)
Creighton U (NE)
Culver-Stockton Coll (MO)
Farmingdale State Coll (NY)
Georgetown Coll (KY)
Granite State Coll (NH)
Indiana U Kokomo (IN)
Indiana U South Bend (IN)
Lamar U (TX)
Maryville U of Saint Louis (MO)
Missouri Baptist U (MO)
Mount St. Joseph U (OH)
Northwest Missouri State U (MO)
The Ohio State U (OH)
Point Loma Nazarene U (CA)
Prairie View A&M U (TX)
Purdue U (IN)
Rhode Island Coll (RI)
Texas Woman's U (TX)
Towson U (MD)
Tulane U (LA)
Union Coll (KY)
U of Houston (TX)
U of Nevada, Reno (NV)
U of Saint Francis (IN)
The U of Texas Rio Grande Valley (TX)
U of Vermont (VT)
U of West Georgia (GA)
U of Wisconsin–La Crosse (WI)
U of Wisconsin–River Falls (WI)
U of Wisconsin–Superior (WI)

HEALTH COMMUNICATION
Bethany Lutheran Coll (MN)
Calvin Coll (MI)
Eastern Illinois U (IL)
Grand Valley State U (MI)
Juniata Coll (PA)
Miami U (OH)
Northern Kentucky U (KY)
San Diego State U (CA)
Southeast Missouri State U (MO)
Trinity Christian Coll (IL)
U of Houston (TX)

HEALTH/HEALTH-CARE ADMINISTRATION
Adams State U (CO)
AdventHealth U (FL)
Appalachian State U (NC)
Auburn U (AL)
Baldwin Wallace U (OH)

Baptist Coll of Health Sciences (TN)
Barton Coll (NC)
Bellarmine U (KY)
Benedictine U (IL)
Berkeley Coll–New York City Campus (NY)
Berkeley Coll–White Plains Campus (NY)
Berkeley Coll–Woodland Park Campus (NJ)
Bowling Green State U (OH)
Brenau U (GA)
Butler U (IN)
Caldwell U (NJ)
California State U, Long Beach (CA)
Central Michigan U (MI)
Coastal Carolina U (SC)
The Coll at Brockport, State U of New York (NY)
Columbia Coll (MO)
Columbia Southern U (AL)
Concordia U Chicago (IL)
Concordia U Irvine (CA)
Creighton U (NE)
Culver-Stockton Coll (MO)
Dallas Baptist U (TX)
Davenport U, Grand Rapids (MI)
Delta State U (MS)
DEREE - The American Coll of Greece (Greece)
East Carolina U (NC)
Eastern Illinois U (IL)
Eastern Washington U (WA)
Fayetteville State U (NC)
Florida Ag and Mech U (FL)
Florida Atlantic U (FL)
Florida Southern Coll (FL)
Georgetown Coll (KY)
Georgia Highlands Coll (GA)
Granite State Coll (NH)
Harding U (AR)
Idaho State U (ID)
Immaculata U (PA)
Indiana U–Purdue U Indianapolis (IN)
Iona Coll (NY)
Ithaca Coll (NY)
Jackson State U (MS)
Juniata Coll (PA)
King U (TN)
La Sierra U (CA)
Lebanon Valley Coll (PA)
Lee U (TN)
LeTourneau U (TX)
Liberty U (VA)
Limestone Coll (SC)
Lindenwood U (MO)
Loyola U Chicago (IL)
Madonna U (MI)
Manor Coll (PA)
Maria Coll (NY)
Marywood U (PA)
Mercy Coll of Ohio (OH)
Minnesota State U Moorhead (MN)
Missouri Baptist U (MO)
Muskingum U (OH)
National U (CA)
Nebraska Methodist Coll (NE)
New England Coll (NH)
New England Inst of Technology (RI)
Northwood U, Michigan Campus (MI)
Ohio U (OH)
Piedmont Coll (GA)
Point U (GA)
Providence Coll (RI)
Regent U (VA)
Regis U (CO)
Rhode Island Coll (RI)
Saint Leo U (FL)
Saint Louis U (MO)
Salve Regina U (RI)
San Jose State U (CA)
Southeast Missouri State U (MO)
Southern Illinois U Carbondale (IL)
State U of New York Coll of Technology at Alfred (NY)
Stonehill Coll (MA)
Tiffin U (OH)
Towson U (MD)
Trevecca Nazarene U (TN)
Tyler Jr Coll (TX)
U of Central Florida (FL)
U of Houston–Clear Lake (TX)
U of Kentucky (KY)
U of La Verne (CA)
U of Maryland U Coll (MD)
U of Massachusetts Dartmouth (MA)
U of Minnesota, Duluth (MN)
U of Minnesota, Twin Cities Campus (MN)
U of Nevada, Las Vegas (NV)
U of New Hampshire (NH)
The U of North Carolina at Chapel Hill (NC)
The U of North Carolina at Charlotte (NC)
U of North Florida (FL)
U of Pennsylvania (PA)
U of Providence (MT)
U of Saint Francis (IN)
U of Sioux Falls (SD)
U of Southern Indiana (IN)
U of South Florida (FL)
U of Virginia (VA)
U of Wisconsin–Eau Claire (WI)
Valparaiso U (IN)
Washington U in St. Louis (MO)
Waynesburg U (PA)
Weber State U (UT)
Western Illinois U (IL)
Western Kentucky U (KY)
West Virginia U Inst of Technology (WV)

HEALTH INFORMATION/MEDICAL RECORDS ADMINISTRATION
Alabama State U (AL)
American Public U System (WV)
Arkansas Tech U (AR)
Bowling Green State U (OH)
Coll of Coastal Georgia (GA)
The Coll of St. Scholastica (MN)
Dakota State U (SD)
Davenport U, Grand Rapids (MI)
Duquesne U (PA)
East Carolina U (NC)
Eastern Washington U (WA)
Florida Ag and Mech U (FL)
Grand Valley State U (MI)
Granite State Coll (NH)
Gwynedd Mercy U (PA)
Indiana U Northwest (IN)
Indiana U–Purdue U Indianapolis (IN)
Indiana U Southeast (IN)
Kean U (NJ)
The Ohio State U (OH)
Regis U (CO)
Saint Louis U (MO)
Samford U (AL)
Trevecca Nazarene U (TN)
U of Central Florida (FL)
U of Detroit Mercy (MI)
U of Maine at Farmington (ME)
U of Pittsburgh (PA)
U of Southern Indiana (IN)
The U of Toledo (OH)
U of Washington (WA)
U of Wisconsin–La Crosse (WI)
Weber State U (UT)
Western Kentucky U (KY)

HEALTH INFORMATION/MEDICAL RECORDS TECHNOLOGY
Excelsior Coll (NY)
Idaho State U (ID)
U of Saint Mary (KS)

HEALTH/MEDICAL PHYSICS
California State U, Northridge (CA)
Creighton U (NE)
U of Nevada, Las Vegas (NV)

HEALTH/MEDICAL PREPARATORY PROGRAMS RELATED
Aurora U (IL)
Avila U (MO)
Baylor U (TX)
Benedictine U (IL)
Blackburn Coll (IL)
Duquesne U (PA)
Grove City Coll (PA)
Hofstra U (NY)
Ithaca Coll (NY)
Kansas Wesleyan U (KS)
Lee U (TN)
Lipscomb U (TN)
Lock Haven U of Pennsylvania (PA)
Louisiana Coll (LA)
Lubbock Christian U (TX)
Madonna U (MI)
Marshall U (WV)
Maryville U of Saint Louis (MO)
Mercer U, Macon (GA)
Mount Marty Coll (SD)
Northern Illinois U (IL)
Saginaw Valley State U (MI)
Seattle U (WA)
The U of Findlay (OH)
U of Regina (SK, Canada)
U of South Alabama (AL)
Utica Coll (NY)
Valley City State U (ND)
Weber State U (UT)
Western Washington U (WA)

HEALTH/MEDICAL PSYCHOLOGY
Averett U (VA)
Bridgewater State U (MA)
Greenville U (IL)
Kansas Wesleyan U (KS)
U of Mary Hardin-Baylor (TX)

HEALTH POLICY ANALYSIS
Brandeis U (MA)
Rider U (NJ)

HEALTH PROFESSIONS RELATED
American Public U System (WV)
Baldwin Wallace U (OH)
Boston U (MA)
Bowling Green State U (OH)
Bradley U (IL)
California State U, Long Beach (CA)
California State U, Los Angeles (CA)
Coll of Coastal Georgia (GA)
Cornell U (NY)
Curry Coll (MA)
DePaul U (IL)
East Tennessee State U (TN)
Furman U (SC)
George Mason U (VA)
Grand Valley State U (MI)
King's Coll (PA)
Lock Haven U of Pennsylvania (PA)
Manchester U (IN)
Maryville U of Saint Louis (MO)
Marywood U (PA)
Mercy Coll (NY)
Merrimack Coll (MA)
Molloy Coll (NY)
Muskingum U (OH)
New Jersey City U (NJ)
New York U (NY)
Northeastern State U (OK)
Old Dominion U (VA)
Purdue U (IN)
The Sage Colls (NY)
St. Joseph's Coll, Long Island Campus (NY)
St. Joseph's Coll, New York (NY)
Saint Joseph's U (PA)
San Francisco State U (CA)
Sonoma State U (CA)
U of Central Arkansas (AR)
U of Maryland, Baltimore County (MD)
U of New Hampshire (NH)
U of Northern Iowa (IA)
U of Pennsylvania (PA)
U of Pittsburgh (PA)
The U of Texas at El Paso (TX)
Washington U in St. Louis (MO)
Weber State U (UT)
West Virginia State U (WV)
Worcester State U (MA)
Youngstown State U (OH)

HEALTH SERVICES ADMINISTRATION
Alfred U (NY)
Bentley U (MA)
Indiana U Northwest (IN)
Indiana U–Purdue U Indianapolis (IN)
Indiana U South Bend (IN)
McNeese State U (LA)
Northeastern State U (OK)
Rider U (NJ)
Southeastern Louisiana U (LA)
U of Detroit Mercy (MI)
U of San Francisco (CA)
U of Washington, Tacoma (WA)

HEALTH SERVICES/ALLIED HEALTH/HEALTH SCIENCES
AdventHealth U (FL)
Albion Coll (MI)
Angelo State U (TX)
Assumption Coll (MA)
Boston U (MA)
Bradley U (IL)
Butler U (IN)
California State U, Chico (CA)
California State U, Fullerton (CA)
California State U, Los Angeles (CA)
California State U, Northridge (CA)
California State U, San Bernardino (CA)
California U of Pennsylvania (PA)
Canisius Coll (NY)
Clarion U of Pennsylvania (PA)
The Coll at Brockport, State U of New York (NY)
The Coll of Idaho (ID)
The Coll of St. Scholastica (MN)
Coll of the Ozarks (MO)
DePaul U (IL)
East Texas Baptist U (TX)
The Evergreen State Coll (WA)
Florida Ag and Mech U (FL)
Fort Lewis Coll (CO)
Georgia Southern U (GA)
Graceland U (IA)
Granite State Coll (NH)
Hofstra U (NY)
Idaho State U (ID)
Lasell Coll (MA)
Lee U (TN)
Madonna U (MI)
Maria Coll (NY)
Marian U (IN)
Marymount U (VA)
Marywood U (PA)
Massachusetts Coll of Liberal Arts (MA)
Mercy Coll (NY)
Mercy Coll of Ohio (OH)
Merrimack Coll (MA)
Messiah Coll (PA)
Milligan Coll (TN)
National U (CA)
Nebraska Methodist Coll (NE)
Northern Kentucky U (KY)
Pace U (NY)
Pace U, Pleasantville Campus (NY)
Piedmont Coll (GA)
Purdue U Northwest (IN)
Queens U of Charlotte (NC)
Radford U (VA)
Rhode Island Coll (RI)
Rider U (NJ)
Rochester Coll (MI)
The Sage Colls (NY)
Saginaw Valley State U (MI)
Saint Louis U (MO)
St. Luke's Coll (IA)
San Jose State U (CA)
Southeast Missouri State U (MO)
Spring Hill Coll (AL)
State U of New York Coll of Technology at Alfred (NY)
Stetson U (FL)
Stockton U (NJ)
Stonehill Coll (MA)
Taylor U (IN)
Texas Woman's U (TX)
Towson U (MD)
U of Central Florida (FL)
U of Florida (FL)
U of Kentucky (KY)
U of New Haven (CT)
U of Northern Colorado (CO)
U of North Florida (FL)
U of South Dakota (SD)
U of South Florida (FL)
The U of Tampa (FL)
The U of Texas Rio Grande Valley (TX)
U of the Incarnate Word (TX)
U of Washington, Bothell (WA)
The U of West Alabama (AL)
Valparaiso U (IN)
Washington U in St. Louis (MO)
West Chester U of Pennsylvania (PA)
Western Kentucky U (KY)
Wheaton Coll (IL)
Whitworth U (WA)
Widener U (PA)
Youngstown State U (OH)

HEALTH TEACHER EDUCATION
Alverno Coll (WI)
Auburn U (AL)
Averett U (VA)
Bethel U (MN)
Bowling Green State U (OH)
Bridgewater State U (MA)
Campbellsville U (KY)
Central Michigan U (MI)
Central State U (OH)
The Coll at Brockport, State U of New York (NY)
Eastern Illinois U (IL)
Eastern Washington U (WA)
East Stroudsburg U of Pennsylvania (PA)
George Mason U (VA)
Grand Valley State U (MI)
Harding U (AR)
Hofstra U (NY)
Hunter Coll of the City U of New York (NY)
Idaho State U (ID)
Indiana U Bloomington (IN)
Inter American U of Puerto Rico, San Germán Campus (PR)
Ithaca Coll (NY)
Kansas Wesleyan U (KS)
Lee U (TN)
Linfield Coll (OR)
Miami U Hamilton (OH)
Michigan State U (MI)
Minnesota State U Moorhead (MN)
Missouri Baptist U (MO)
Montclair State U (NJ)
Murray State U (KY)
National U (CA)
Northern Illinois U (IL)
Northwestern Oklahoma State U (OK)
Ohio Wesleyan U (OH)
Portland State U (OR)
Rhode Island Coll (RI)
Salisbury U (MD)
Southwest Baptist U (MO)
Union Coll (KY)
The U of Findlay (OH)
U of Kentucky (KY)
U of Maine at Farmington (ME)
U of Mount Union (OH)
U of Nevada, Las Vegas (NV)
U of New Mexico (NM)
U of Northwestern–St. Paul (MN)
U of Providence (MT)
U of Regina (SK, Canada)
U of South Dakota (SD)
U of Wisconsin–La Crosse (WI)
Utah State U (UT)
Utah Valley U (UT)
Valley City State U (ND)
Virginia Commonwealth U (VA)
Washington State U (WA)
Western Connecticut State U (CT)
Youngstown State U (OH)

HEBREW
Baruch Coll of the City U of New York (NY)
Hofstra U (NY)
Hunter Coll of the City U of New York (NY)
New York U (NY)
The Ohio State U (OH)
Queens Coll of the City U of New York (NY)
The U of Texas at Austin (TX)
Washington U in St. Louis (MO)

HIGHER EDUCATION/HIGHER EDUCATION ADMINISTRATION
Geneva Coll (PA)

HISPANIC-AMERICAN, PUERTO RICAN, AND MEXICAN-AMERICAN/CHICANO STUDIES
Boston Coll (MA)
Bowling Green State U (OH)
California State U, Fullerton (CA)
California State U, Long Beach (CA)
California State U, Los Angeles (CA)

California State U, Northridge (CA)
Claremont McKenna Coll (CA)
The Colorado Coll (CO)
Columbia U (NY)
Dartmouth Coll (NH)
Hunter Coll of the City U of New York (NY)
Loyola Marymount U (CA)
Mills Coll (CA)
Pepperdine U, Malibu (CA)
Pitzer Coll (CA)
San Diego State U (CA)
San Francisco State U (CA)
Scripps Coll (CA)
Sonoma State U (CA)
Tulane U (LA)
U of California, Davis (CA)
U of California, Irvine (CA)
U of California, Riverside (CA)
U of California, Santa Cruz (CA)
U of Michigan (MI)
U of Minnesota, Twin Cities Campus (MN)
U of New Mexico (NM)
U of Northern Colorado (CO)
The U of Texas at Austin (TX)
The U of Texas at El Paso (TX)
The U of Texas Rio Grande Valley (TX)
Wheaton Coll (MA)

HISPANIC AND LATIN AMERICAN LANGUAGES
Boston U (MA)
Hamilton Coll (NY)
Loyola U New Orleans (LA)
Molloy Coll (NY)
Pacific Lutheran U (WA)
Purdue U (IN)
U of California, Merced (CA)
U of Washington, Tacoma (WA)

HISTORIC PRESERVATION AND CONSERVATION
Coll of Charleston (SC)
Salve Regina U (RI)
Savannah Coll of Art and Design (GA)
Southeast Missouri State U (MO)
Temple U (PA)

HISTORY
Acadia U (NS, Canada)
Adams State U (CO)
Adelphi U (NY)
Agnes Scott Coll (GA)
Alabama State U (AL)
Albion Coll (MI)
Albright Coll (PA)
Alfred U (NY)
Allegheny Coll (PA)
Alverno Coll (WI)
American Public U System (WV)
American U (DC)
American U in Bulgaria (Bulgaria)
American U of Beirut (Lebanon)
Angelo State U (TX)
Antioch Coll, Yellow Springs (OH)
Appalachian State U (NC)
Arkansas Tech U (AR)
Assumption Coll (MA)
Auburn U (AL)
Auburn U at Montgomery (AL)
Aurora U (IL)
Austin Coll (TX)
Austin Peay State U (TN)
Averett U (VA)
Avila U (MO)
Baker U (KS)
Baldwin Wallace U (OH)
Barton Coll (NC)
Baruch Coll of the City U of New York (NY)
Baylor U (TX)
Bellarmine U (KY)
Beloit Coll (WI)
Benedictine U (IL)
Bentley U (MA)
Berea Coll (KY)
Bethany Lutheran Coll (MN)
Bethel Coll (KS)
Bethel U (MN)
Blackburn Coll (IL)
Boston Coll (MA)
Boston U (MA)
Bowling Green State U (OH)
Bradley U (IL)
Brandeis U (MA)
Brenau U (GA)
Bridgewater Coll (VA)
Bridgewater State U (MA)
Bryant U (RI)
Bucknell U (PA)
Buena Vista U (IA)
Butler U (IN)
Caldwell U (NJ)
California Inst of Technology (CA)
California Lutheran U (CA)
California Polytechnic State U, San Luis Obispo (CA)
California State U, Bakersfield (CA)
California State U, Chico (CA)
California State U, Fullerton (CA)
California State U, Long Beach (CA)
California State U, Los Angeles (CA)
California State U, Northridge (CA)
California State U, San Bernardino (CA)
California State U, San Marcos (CA)
California U of Pennsylvania (PA)
Calvin Coll (MI)
Cameron U (OK)
Campbellsville U (KY)
Canisius Coll (NY)
Carson-Newman U (TN)
Carthage Coll (WI)
The Catholic U of America (DC)
Cedarville U (OH)
Centenary Coll of Louisiana (LA)
Central Connecticut State U (CT)
Central Michigan U (MI)
Central State U (OH)
Central Washington U (WA)
Christian Brothers U (TN)
Christopher Newport U (VA)
Claremont McKenna Coll (CA)
Clarion U of Pennsylvania (PA)
Clarkson U (NY)
Clark U (MA)
Coastal Carolina U (SC)
Colgate U (NY)
The Coll at Brockport, State U of New York (NY)
Coll of Charleston (SC)
The Coll of Idaho (ID)
Coll of Saint Benedict (MN)
The Coll of Saint Rose (NY)
The Coll of St. Scholastica (MN)
Coll of Staten Island of the City U of New York (NY)
Coll of the Holy Cross (MA)
Coll of the Ozarks (MO)
The Coll of William and Mary (VA)
The Colorado Coll (CO)
Colorado State U (CO)
Colorado State U–Pueblo (CO)
Columbia Coll (MO)
Columbia U (NY)
Concordia U Chicago (IL)
Concordia U Irvine (CA)
Connecticut Coll (CT)
Cornell Coll (IA)
Cornell U (NY)
Covenant Coll (GA)
Creighton U (NE)
Culver-Stockton Coll (MO)
Dallas Baptist U (TX)
Dartmouth Coll (NH)
Davidson Coll (NC)
Dean Coll (MA)
Delta State U (MS)
DePaul U (IL)
DEREE - The American Coll of Greece (Greece)
Dickinson Coll (PA)
Dominican U (IL)
Drake U (IA)
Drew U (NJ)
Duquesne U (PA)
Earlham Coll (IN)
East Carolina U (NC)
Eastern Illinois U (IL)
Eastern Mennonite U (VA)
Eastern Oregon U (OR)
Eastern U (PA)
Eastern Washington U (WA)
East Stroudsburg U of Pennsylvania (PA)
East Tennessee State U (TN)
East Texas Baptist U (TX)
Eckerd Coll (FL)
Elizabeth City State U (NC)
Emmanuel Coll (MA)
Endicott Coll (MA)
Excelsior Coll (NY)
Fairfield U (CT)
Fayetteville State U (NC)
Fitchburg State U (MA)
Florida Ag and Mech U (FL)
Florida Atlantic U (FL)
Florida Coll (FL)
Florida Southern Coll (FL)
Fordham U (NY)
Fort Lewis Coll (CO)
Framingham State U (MA)
Franklin Pierce U (NH)
Furman U (SC)
Geneva Coll (PA)
George Mason U (VA)
Georgetown Coll (KY)
Georgia Coll & State U (GA)
Georgia Southern U (GA)
Georgia State U (GA)
Gonzaga U (WA)
Gordon Coll (MA)
Goshen Coll (IN)
Graceland U (IA)
Grand Valley State U (MI)
Granite State Coll (NH)
Greenville U (IL)
Grove City Coll (PA)
Gwynedd Mercy U (PA)
Hamilton Coll (NY)
Hamline U (MN)
Hampden-Sydney Coll (VA)
Hanover Coll (IN)
Harding U (AR)
Hardin-Simmons U (TX)
Hartwick Coll (NY)
Harvard U (MA)
Haverford Coll (PA)
High Point U (NC)
Hillsdale Coll (MI)
Hiram Coll (OH)
Hofstra U (NY)
Hollins U (VA)
Hood Coll (MD)
Humboldt State U (CA)
Hunter Coll of the City U of New York (NY)
Idaho State U (ID)
Illinois Coll (IL)
Immaculata U (PA)
Indiana State U (IN)
Indiana U Bloomington (IN)
Indiana U East (IN)
Indiana U Kokomo (IN)
Indiana U Northwest (IN)
Indiana U of Pennsylvania (PA)
Indiana U–Purdue U Indianapolis (IN)
Indiana U South Bend (IN)
Indiana U Southeast (IN)
Inter American U of Puerto Rico, San Germán Campus (PR)
Iona Coll (NY)
Iowa State U of Science and Technology (IA)
Ithaca Coll (NY)
Jackson State U (MS)
Jacksonville U (FL)
John Cabot U (Italy)
Johns Hopkins U (MD)
Johnson C. Smith U (NC)
Judson U (IL)
Juniata Coll (PA)
Kalamazoo Coll (MI)
Kansas Wesleyan U (KS)
Kean U (NJ)
Kennesaw State U (GA)
King's Coll (PA)
King U (TN)
Knox Coll (IL)
Lafayette Coll (PA)
LaGrange Coll (GA)
Lake Forest Coll (IL)
Lamar U (TX)
La Salle U (PA)
Lasell Coll (MA)
La Sierra U (CA)
Lawrence U (WI)
Lebanese American U (Lebanon)
Lebanon Valley Coll (PA)
Lees-McRae Coll (NC)
Lee U (TN)
Lewis & Clark Coll (OR)
Liberty U (VA)
Limestone Coll (SC)
Lindenwood U (MO)
Linfield Coll (OR)
Lipscomb U (TN)
Lock Haven U of Pennsylvania (PA)
Loras Coll (IA)
Louisiana Coll (LA)
Louisiana State U and A&M Coll (LA)
Loyola Marymount U (CA)
Loyola U Chicago (IL)
Loyola U New Orleans (LA)
Lubbock Christian U (TX)
Lycoming Coll (PA)
Macalester Coll (MN)
Madonna U (MI)
Manchester U (IN)
Manhattan Coll (NY)
Manhattanville Coll (NY)
Mansfield U of Pennsylvania (PA)
Marian U (IN)
Marist Coll (NY)
Marquette U (WI)
Marshall U (WV)
Marymount U (VA)
Maryville U of Saint Louis (MO)
Marywood U (PA)
Massachusetts Coll of Liberal Arts (MA)
Massachusetts Inst of Technology (MA)
McDaniel Coll (MD)
McNeese State U (LA)
Mercer U, Macon (GA)
Mercy Coll (NY)
Merrimack Coll (MA)
Messiah Coll (PA)
Miami U (OH)
Miami U Hamilton (OH)
Michigan State U (MI)
Middlebury Coll (VT)
Middle Tennessee State U (TN)
Millersville U of Pennsylvania (PA)
Milligan Coll (TN)
Millikin U (IL)
Millsaps Coll (MS)
Mills Coll (CA)
Minnesota State U Moorhead (MN)
Missouri Baptist U (MO)
Molloy Coll (NY)
Montclair State U (NJ)
Morningside Coll (IA)
Mount Marty Coll (SD)
Mount St. Joseph U (OH)
Mount Saint Mary Coll (NY)
Murray State U (KY)
Muskingum U (OH)
National U (CA)
Nazareth Coll of Rochester (NY)
New Coll of Florida (FL)
New England Coll (NH)
New Jersey City U (NJ)
New Jersey Inst of Technology (NJ)
New York U (NY)
Nichols Coll (MA)
North Carolina State U (NC)
Northeastern State U (OK)
Northern Illinois U (IL)
Northern Kentucky U (KY)
Northern State U (SD)
Northwest Christian U (OR)
Northwestern Oklahoma State U (OK)
Northwestern U (IL)
Northwest Missouri State U (MO)
Oakland City U (IN)
Occidental Coll (CA)
Oglethorpe U (GA)
Ohio Dominican U (OH)
The Ohio State U (OH)
The Ohio State U at Lima (OH)
The Ohio State U at Mansfield (OH)
The Ohio State U at Marion (OH)
The Ohio State U at Newark (OH)
Ohio U (OH)
Ohio Wesleyan U (OH)
Oklahoma Baptist U (OK)
Oklahoma Christian U (OK)
Oklahoma State U (OK)
Old Dominion U (VA)
Ottawa U (KS)
Ouachita Baptist U (AR)
Pace U (NY)
Pace U, Pleasantville Campus (NY)
Pacific Lutheran U (WA)
Palm Beach Atlantic U (FL)
Pepperdine U, Malibu (CA)
Pfeiffer U (NC)
Piedmont Coll (GA)
Pitzer Coll (CA)
Point Loma Nazarene U (CA)
Point U (GA)
Portland State U (OR)
Prairie View A&M U (TX)
Princeton U (NJ)
Providence Coll (RI)
Purchase Coll, State U of New York (NY)
Purdue U (IN)
Purdue U Northwest (IN)
Queens Coll of the City U of New York (NY)
Queens U of Charlotte (NC)
Radford U (VA)
Randolph Coll (VA)
Randolph-Macon Coll (VA)
Redeemer U Coll (ON, Canada)
Regent U (VA)
Regis U (CO)
Reinhardt U (GA)
Rhode Island Coll (RI)
Rhodes Coll (TN)
Rice U (TX)
Rider U (NJ)
Roanoke Coll (VA)
Rockford U (IL)
Rocky Mountain Coll (MT)
Rollins Coll (FL)
Sacred Heart U (CT)
The Sage Colls (NY)
Saginaw Valley State U (MI)
Saint Anselm Coll (NH)
Saint Francis U (PA)
St. John Fisher Coll (NY)
Saint John's U (MN)
St. Joseph's Coll, Long Island Campus (NY)
St. Joseph's Coll, New York (NY)
Saint Joseph's U (PA)
Saint Leo U (FL)
Saint Louis U (MO)
Saint Martin's U (WA)
St. Mary's Coll of Maryland (MD)
St. Mary's U (TX)
Saint Mary's U of Minnesota (MN)
St. Norbert Coll (WI)
St. Olaf Coll (MN)
Saint Vincent Coll (PA)
Salisbury U (MD)
Salve Regina U (RI)
Samford U (AL)
San Diego State U (CA)
San Francisco State U (CA)
San Jose State U (CA)
Sarah Lawrence Coll (NY)
Scripps Coll (CA)
Seattle U (WA)
Seton Hill U (PA)
Skidmore Coll (NY)
Sonoma State U (CA)
Southeastern Louisiana U (LA)
Southeast Missouri State U (MO)
Southern Arkansas U–Magnolia (AR)
Southern Illinois U Carbondale (IL)
Southern Illinois U Edwardsville (IL)
Southern U and Ag and Mech Coll (LA)
Southwest Baptist U (MO)
Southwestern U (TX)
Spring Hill Coll (AL)
State U of New York at Fredonia (NY)
State U of New York at Plattsburgh (NY)
State U of New York Coll at Geneseo (NY)
State U of New York Coll at Potsdam (NY)
Stetson U (FL)
Stevens Inst of Technology (NJ)
Stockton U (NJ)
Stonehill Coll (MA)
Sweet Briar Coll (VA)
Syracuse U (NY)
Tabor Coll (KS)
Taylor U (IN)
Temple U (PA)
Texas A&M Intl U (TX)
Texas A&M U–Central Texas (TX)
Texas Christian U (TX)
Texas Lutheran U (TX)
Texas Tech U (TX)
Texas Woman's U (TX)
Tiffin U (OH)

Toccoa Falls Coll (GA)
Towson U (MD)
Trevecca Nazarene U (TN)
Trinity Christian Coll (IL)
Truman State U (MO)
Tulane U (LA)
Tyndale U Coll & Sem (ON, Canada)
Union Coll (KY)
Union Coll (NY)
Université de Sherbrooke (QC, Canada)
Université Sainte-Anne (NS, Canada)
U at Buffalo, the State U of New York (NY)
U of Arkansas (AR)
U of California, Davis (CA)
U of California, Irvine (CA)
U of California, Los Angeles (CA)
U of California, Merced (CA)
U of California, Riverside (CA)
U of California, Santa Cruz (CA)
U of Central Arkansas (AR)
U of Central Florida (FL)
U of Chicago (IL)
U of Colorado Denver (CO)
U of Dallas (TX)
U of Dayton (OH)
U of Detroit Mercy (MI)
The U of Findlay (OH)
U of Florida (FL)
U of Georgia (GA)
U of Guam (GU)
U of Hawaii at Manoa (HI)
U of Houston (TX)
U of Houston–Clear Lake (TX)
U of Houston–Downtown (TX)
U of Idaho (ID)
U of Illinois at Springfield (IL)
U of Kentucky (KY)
U of La Verne (CA)
U of Louisville (KY)
U of Lynchburg (VA)
U of Maine (ME)
U of Maine at Farmington (ME)
U of Maine at Machias (ME)
U of Maine at Presque Isle (ME)
U of Mary Hardin-Baylor (TX)
U of Maryland, Baltimore County (MD)
U of Maryland, Coll Park (MD)
U of Maryland Eastern Shore (MD)
U of Maryland U Coll (MD)
U of Massachusetts Amherst (MA)
U of Massachusetts Boston (MA)
U of Massachusetts Dartmouth (MA)
U of Massachusetts Lowell (MA)
U of Memphis (TN)
U of Michigan (MI)
U of Michigan–Dearborn (MI)
U of Minnesota, Duluth (MN)
U of Minnesota, Morris (MN)
U of Minnesota, Twin Cities Campus (MN)
U of Missouri (MO)
U of Montevallo (AL)
U of Mount Union (OH)
U of Nebraska–Lincoln (NE)
U of Nevada, Las Vegas (NV)
U of Nevada, Reno (NV)
U of New Hampshire (NH)
U of New Haven (CT)
U of New Mexico (NM)
U of North Carolina at Asheville (NC)
The U of North Carolina at Chapel Hill (NC)
The U of North Carolina at Charlotte (NC)
The U of North Carolina at Greensboro (NC)
The U of North Carolina at Pembroke (NC)
U of North Dakota (ND)
U of Northern Colorado (CO)
U of Northern Iowa (IA)
U of North Florida (FL)
U of Northwestern–St. Paul (MN)
U of Notre Dame (IN)
U of Oregon (OR)
U of Pennsylvania (PA)
U of Pittsburgh (PA)
U of Providence (MT)
U of Puget Sound (WA)
U of Regina (SK, Canada)
U of Richmond (VA)
U of Saint Francis (IN)
U of Saint Mary (KS)
U of St. Thomas (MN)
U of St. Thomas (TX)
U of San Diego (CA)
U of San Francisco (CA)
U of Sioux Falls (SD)
U of South Alabama (AL)
U of South Carolina (SC)
U of South Carolina Aiken (SC)
U of South Dakota (SD)
U of Southern Indiana (IN)
U of South Florida (FL)
U of South Florida Sarasota-Manatee (FL)
The U of Tampa (FL)
The U of Tennessee (TN)
The U of Tennessee at Martin (TN)
The U of Texas at Austin (TX)
The U of Texas at El Paso (TX)
The U of Texas of the Permian Basin (TX)
The U of Texas Rio Grande Valley (TX)
U of the Incarnate Word (TX)
The U of the South (TN)
The U of Toledo (OH)
The U of Tulsa (OK)
U of Vermont (VT)
U of Virginia (VA)
U of Washington (WA)
U of Washington, Tacoma (WA)
The U of West Alabama (AL)
U of West Georgia (GA)
U of Wisconsin–Eau Claire (WI)
U of Wisconsin–La Crosse (WI)
U of Wisconsin–Milwaukee (WI)
U of Wisconsin–River Falls (WI)
U of Wisconsin–Superior (WI)
U of Wyoming (WY)
Ursinus Coll (PA)
Utah State U (UT)
Utah Valley U (UT)
Utica Coll (NY)
Valley City State U (ND)
Valparaiso U (IN)
Vanguard U of Southern California (CA)
Vassar Coll (NY)
Virginia Commonwealth U (VA)
Virginia Polytechnic Inst and State U (VA)
Wabash Coll (IN)
Wartburg Coll (IA)
Washington & Jefferson Coll (PA)
Washington and Lee U (VA)
Washington State U (WA)
Washington State U–Tri-Cities (WA)
Washington State U–Vancouver (WA)
Washington U in St. Louis (MO)
Waynesburg U (PA)
Weber State U (UT)
Wesleyan Coll (GA)
Wesleyan U (CT)
West Chester U of Pennsylvania (PA)
Western Connecticut State U (CT)
Western Illinois U (IL)
Western Kentucky U (KY)
Western State Colorado U (CO)
Western Washington U (WA)
Westmont Coll (CA)
West Virginia State U (WV)
West Virginia U Inst of Technology (WV)
Wheaton Coll (IL)
Wheaton Coll (MA)
Whittier Coll (CA)
Whitworth U (WA)
Widener U (PA)
Wilkes U (PA)
Willamette U (OR)
William Jewell Coll (MO)
Williams Coll (MA)
Winthrop U (SC)
Wofford Coll (SC)
Woodbury U (CA)
Worcester State U (MA)
Youngstown State U (OH)

HISTORY AND PHILOSOPHY OF SCIENCE AND TECHNOLOGY

California Inst of Technology (CA)
Harvard U (MA)
Johns Hopkins U (MD)
Michigan State U (MI)
U of Chicago (IL)
U of Pennsylvania (PA)
U of Pittsburgh (PA)
U of Washington (WA)

HISTORY RELATED

Bentley U (MA)
Bridgewater Coll (VA)
Bridgewater State U (MA)
Bryn Athyn Coll of the New Church (PA)
Carnegie Mellon U (PA)
Harvard U (MA)
Indiana U Kokomo (IN)
Juniata Coll (PA)
Lebanon Valley Coll (PA)
LeTourneau U (TX)
Marquette U (WI)
The Ohio State U (OH)
Purdue U Northwest (IN)
Regent U (VA)
Saint Mary's U of Minnesota (MN)
Sarah Lawrence Coll (NY)
U of Washington (WA)
U of Washington, Tacoma (WA)

HISTORY TEACHER EDUCATION

Albion Coll (MI)
Appalachian State U (NC)
Auburn U (AL)
Bowling Green State U (OH)
Bradley U (IL)
Buena Vista U (IA)
California Lutheran U (CA)
Calvin Coll (MI)
Campbellsville U (KY)
The Catholic U of America (DC)
Central Michigan U (MI)
Central Washington U (WA)
Christian Brothers U (TN)
Coll of Staten Island of the City U of New York (NY)
Coll of the Ozarks (MO)
Concordia U Chicago (IL)
Covenant Coll (GA)
Culver-Stockton Coll (MO)
Dallas Baptist U (TX)
East Texas Baptist U (TX)
Fitchburg State U (MA)
Florida Southern Coll (FL)
Geneva Coll (PA)
Grand Valley State U (MI)
Greenville U (IL)
Gwynedd Mercy U (PA)
Hardin-Simmons U (TX)
Inter American U of Puerto Rico, San Germán Campus (PR)
Ithaca Coll (NY)
Kansas Wesleyan U (KS)
Lee U (TN)
LeTourneau U (TX)
Lipscomb U (TN)
Manchester U (IN)
Merrimack Coll (MA)
Michigan State U (MI)
Morningside Coll (IA)
Mount Marty Coll (SD)
Nazareth Coll of Rochester (NY)
Northern State U (SD)
Oakland City U (IN)
Ohio Wesleyan U (OH)
Piedmont Coll (GA)
Providence Coll (RI)
Rhode Island Coll (RI)
Rocky Mountain Coll (MT)
Saginaw Valley State U (MI)
Saint Francis U (PA)
St. John Fisher Coll (NY)
Saint Joseph's U (PA)
Salve Regina U (RI)
Spring Hill Coll (AL)
Texas Lutheran U (TX)
Tiffin U (OH)
Toccoa Falls Coll (GA)
Trevecca Nazarene U (TN)
Trinity Christian Coll (IL)
U of Maine (ME)
U of Maine at Machias (ME)
U of Mary Hardin-Baylor (TX)
U of Providence (MT)
U of Sioux Falls (SD)
U of South Dakota (SD)
U of Wisconsin–Superior (WI)
Utah Valley U (UT)
Utica Coll (NY)
Valley City State U (ND)
Valparaiso U (IN)
Wartburg Coll (IA)
Washington U in St. Louis (MO)
Weber State U (UT)
Western Washington U (WA)
Widener U (PA)

HOMELAND SECURITY

American Public U System (WV)
Angelo State U (TX)
Columbia Southern U (AL)
Embry-Riddle Aeronautical U–Daytona (FL)
Embry-Riddle Aeronautical U–Worldwide (FL)
Excelsior Coll (NY)
Mercy Coll (NY)
National U (CA)
Northeastern State U (OK)
Regent U (VA)
Saint Leo U (FL)
Tulane U (LA)
U of New Hampshire (NH)

HOMELAND SECURITY, LAW ENFORCEMENT, FIREFIGHTING AND PROTECTIVE SERVICES RELATED

Florida Atlantic U (FL)
Idaho State U (ID)
Madonna U (MI)
Massachusetts Maritime Acad (MA)
Northwestern Oklahoma State U (OK)
Tiffin U (OH)
Union Coll (KY)
The U of West Alabama (AL)
Virginia Commonwealth U (VA)

HORSE HUSBANDRY/EQUINE SCIENCE AND MANAGEMENT

Averett U (VA)
Delaware Valley U (PA)
U of Kentucky (KY)
U of New Hampshire (NH)

HORTICULTURAL SCIENCE

Auburn U (AL)
Coll of the Ozarks (MO)
Colorado State U (CO)
Delaware Valley U (PA)
Iowa State U of Science and Technology (IA)
Michigan State U (MI)
North Carolina State U (NC)
Northwest Missouri State U (MO)
Oklahoma State U (OK)
Purdue U (IN)
Temple U (PA)
U of Florida (FL)
U of Georgia (GA)
U of Idaho (ID)
U of Nebraska–Lincoln (NE)
U of Vermont (VT)
U of Wisconsin–River Falls (WI)
Utah State U (UT)
Virginia Polytechnic Inst and State U (VA)

HOSPITAL AND HEALTH-CARE FACILITIES ADMINISTRATION

Avila U (MO)
Champlain Coll (VT)
Ithaca Coll (NY)
St. Joseph's Coll, Long Island Campus (NY)
St. Joseph's Coll, New York (NY)
Saint Joseph's U (PA)
Tiffin U (OH)
U of South Dakota (SD)
The U of Toledo (OH)
U of Wisconsin–Milwaukee (WI)
Youngstown State U (OH)

HOSPITALITY ADMINISTRATION

American Public U System (WV)
Appalachian State U (NC)
Arkansas Tech U (AR)
Auburn U (AL)
Boston U (MA)
Bowling Green State U (OH)
Central Connecticut State U (CT)
Central Michigan U (MI)
Coll of Charleston (SC)
Coll of Coastal Georgia (GA)
Coll of the Ozarks (MO)
Columbia Southern U (AL)
Dallas Baptist U (TX)
DePaul U (IL)
East Carolina U (NC)
East Stroudsburg U of Pennsylvania (PA)
Endicott Coll (MA)
Florida Atlantic U (FL)
Framingham State U (MA)
Georgia State U (GA)
Grand Valley State U (MI)
Granite State Coll (NH)
Indiana U Kokomo (IN)
Indiana U of Pennsylvania (PA)
Iowa State U of Science and Technology (IA)
Lasell Coll (MA)
Lebanese American U (Lebanon)
Madonna U (MI)
Marywood U (PA)
Michigan State U (MI)
Montclair State U (NJ)
Nichols Coll (MA)
Northwood U, Michigan Campus (MI)
Oklahoma State U (OK)
Purdue U Northwest (IN)
Rochester Inst of Technology (NY)
St. Joseph's Coll, Long Island Campus (NY)
St. Joseph's Coll, New York (NY)
Saint Leo U (FL)
San Diego State U (CA)
San Francisco State U (CA)
San Jose State U (CA)
Seton Hill U (PA)
Southeastern U (FL)
State U of New York Coll of Technology at Delhi (NY)
Stockton U (NJ)
Sullivan U (KY)
Syracuse U (NY)
Temple U (PA)
Tiffin U (OH)
U of Central Florida (FL)
The U of Findlay (OH)
U of Georgia (GA)
U of Kentucky (KY)
U of Massachusetts Amherst (MA)
U of Memphis (TN)
U of Nebraska–Lincoln (NE)
U of Nevada, Las Vegas (NV)
U of New Hampshire (NH)
U of New Haven (CT)
The U of North Carolina at Greensboro (NC)
U of Pittsburgh at Bradford (PA)
U of San Francisco (CA)
U of South Alabama (AL)
U of South Carolina (SC)
U of South Florida Sarasota-Manatee (FL)
The U of Texas Rio Grande Valley (TX)
Utah Valley U (UT)
Washington State U (WA)
Washington State U–Tri-Cities (WA)
Washington State U–Vancouver (WA)
Western Illinois U (IL)
Western Kentucky U (KY)
Wilkes U (PA)
Youngstown State U (OH)

HOSPITALITY ADMINISTRATION RELATED

Auburn U (AL)
California State U, Fullerton (CA)
DEREE - The American Coll of Greece (Greece)
Southern Illinois U Carbondale (IL)
U of Central Florida (FL)
U of Nevada, Las Vegas (NV)
Widener U (PA)

HOSPITALITY AND RECREATION MARKETING

Rochester Inst of Technology (NY)
Saint Joseph's U (PA)
Tyndale U Coll & Sem (ON, Canada)

HOTEL/MOTEL ADMINISTRATION

Auburn U (AL)

California State U, Long Beach (CA)
Cornell U (NY)
Grand Valley State U (MI)
Inter American U of Puerto Rico, Aguadilla Campus (PR)
New York U (NY)
The Ohio State U (OH)
Pace U (NY)
Purdue U (IN)
Rochester Inst of Technology (NY)
Sacred Heart U (CT)
State U of New York Coll of Technology at Delhi (NY)
Texas Tech U (TX)
U of Houston (TX)
U of Maine at Machias (ME)
U of Memphis (TN)
U of Missouri (MO)
U of New Haven (CT)
The U of Tennessee (TN)
Virginia Polytechnic Inst and State U (VA)
Washington State U (WA)
Widener U (PA)

HOTEL, MOTEL, AND RESTAURANT MANAGEMENT
Endicott Coll (MA)

HOUSING AND HUMAN ENVIRONMENTS
Harding U (AR)
Ohio U (OH)
U of Georgia (GA)
U of Minnesota, Twin Cities Campus (MN)
U of Missouri (MO)
Utah State U (UT)

HUMAN BIOLOGY
Baker U (KS)
Hamline U (MN)
Indiana U–Purdue U Indianapolis (IN)
Johns Hopkins U (MD)
Pitzer Coll (CA)
Scripps Coll (CA)
U of California, Irvine (CA)
U of California, Los Angeles (CA)
U of Saint Mary (KS)

HUMAN COMPUTER INTERACTION
DigiPen Inst of Technology (WA)
Savannah Coll of Art and Design (GA)
Whitworth U (WA)
Woodbury U (CA)

HUMAN DEVELOPMENT AND FAMILY STUDIES
Auburn U (AL)
Baylor U (TX)
Bowling Green State U (OH)
California State U, Long Beach (CA)
California State U, San Bernardino (CA)
California State U, San Marcos (CA)
Colorado State U (CO)
Connecticut Coll (CT)
Cornell U (NY)
Eckerd Coll (FL)
George Mason U (VA)
Georgia Southern U (GA)
Indiana State U (IN)
Indiana U of Pennsylvania (PA)
Lamar U (TX)
Lesley U (MA)
Liberty U (VA)
Louisiana State U and A&M Coll (LA)
Michigan State U (MI)
Montclair State U (NJ)
Northern Illinois U (IL)
The Ohio State U (OH)
Ohio U (OH)
Oklahoma State U (OK)
Purdue U (IN)
Purdue U Northwest (IN)
Rockford U (IL)
St. Joseph's Coll, Long Island Campus (NY)
St. Joseph's Coll, New York (NY)
Samford U (AL)
State U of New York at Plattsburgh (NY)
Syracuse U (NY)
Temple U (PA)
Texas Tech U (TX)
Texas Woman's U (TX)
U of Arkansas (AR)
U of California, Davis (CA)
U of Colorado Denver (CO)
U of Georgia (GA)
U of Houston (TX)
U of Idaho (ID)
U of Maine (ME)
U of Memphis (TN)
U of Missouri (MO)
U of Mount Union (OH)
U of Nevada, Reno (NV)
U of New Hampshire (NH)
U of New Mexico (NM)
The U of North Carolina at Greensboro (NC)
U of St. Thomas (MN)
The U of Tennessee (TN)
The U of Texas at Austin (TX)
The U of Texas of the Permian Basin (TX)
U of Vermont (VT)
Utah State U (UT)
Vanguard U of Southern California (CA)
Virginia Polytechnic Inst and State U (VA)
Washington State U (WA)
Washington State U–Vancouver (WA)
Youngstown State U (OH)

HUMAN DEVELOPMENT AND FAMILY STUDIES RELATED
Auburn U (AL)
Bowling Green State U (OH)
Harding U (AR)
LaGrange Coll (GA)
Merrimack Coll (MA)
Point U (GA)
Portland State U (OR)
Winthrop U (SC)

HUMANITIES
Adelphi U (NY)
Baylor U (TX)
Benedictine U (IL)
Bucknell U (PA)
California State U, Chico (CA)
California State U, Monterey Bay (CA)
California State U, Northridge (CA)
California State U, San Bernardino (CA)
Clarkson U (NY)
Coastal Carolina U (SC)
Colgate U (NY)
Coll of Saint Mary (NE)
The Coll of St. Scholastica (MN)
Concordia U Irvine (CA)
Eastern Washington U (WA)
Eckerd Coll (FL)
The Evergreen State Coll (WA)
Excelsior Coll (NY)
Florida Southern Coll (FL)
Fordham U (NY)
Harding U (AR)
Holy Apostles Coll and Sem (CT)
Hunter Coll of the City U of New York (NY)
Indiana U East (IN)
Indiana U Kokomo (IN)
Jacksonville U (FL)
John Cabot U (Italy)
John Paul the Great Catholic U (CA)
Juniata Coll (PA)
Lasell Coll (MA)
Lawrence Technological U (MI)
Lee U (TN)
Lesley U (MA)
Loyola Marymount U (CA)
Lubbock Christian U (TX)
Marshall U (WV)
Marymount Manhattan Coll (NY)
Michigan State U (MI)
Milligan Coll (TN)
Montclair State U (NJ)
Muskingum U (OH)
New Coll of Florida (FL)
New York U (NY)
Northwestern U (IL)
Oakland City U (IN)
The Ohio State U (OH)
Ohio Wesleyan U (OH)
Oklahoma Baptist U (OK)
Point U (GA)
Portland State U (OR)
Providence Coll (RI)
Purchase Coll, State U of New York (NY)
Purdue U (IN)
Rockford U (IL)
Rollins Coll (FL)
The Sage Colls (NY)
St. Norbert Coll (WI)
San Diego State U (CA)
San Francisco State U (CA)
San Jose State U (CA)
Scripps Coll (CA)
Seattle U (WA)
Stevens Inst of Technology (NJ)
Union Coll (NY)
U of California, Irvine (CA)
U of California, Riverside (CA)
U of Central Florida (FL)
U of Chicago (IL)
U of Houston–Clear Lake (TX)
U of Houston–Downtown (TX)
U of Louisville (KY)
U of Massachusetts Amherst (MA)
U of Michigan (MI)
U of Michigan–Dearborn (MI)
U of New Mexico (NM)
U of Northern Iowa (IA)
U of Oregon (OR)
U of Pennsylvania (PA)
U of Pittsburgh (PA)
U of Regina (SK, Canada)
U of Richmond (VA)
U of San Diego (CA)
U of South Florida (FL)
The U of Texas at Austin (TX)
The U of Texas of the Permian Basin (TX)
U of Washington (WA)
U of Washington, Bothell (WA)
U of Washington, Tacoma (WA)
U of Wyoming (WY)
Valparaiso U (IN)
Wabash Coll (IN)
Washington State U (WA)
Washington State U–Tri-Cities (WA)
Washington State U–Vancouver (WA)
Washington U in St. Louis (MO)
Wesleyan U (CT)
Western Washington U (WA)
Widener U (PA)
Willamette U (OR)
Wofford Coll (SC)
Worcester Polytechnic Inst (MA)

HUMAN NUTRITION
Baylor U (TX)
Bridgewater Coll (VA)
Central Washington U (WA)
The Ohio State U (OH)
Rochester Inst of Technology (NY)
Syracuse U (NY)
U of Dayton (OH)
U of Houston (TX)
U of Kentucky (KY)
Utica Coll (NY)
Weber State U (UT)

HUMAN RESOURCES DEVELOPMENT
Blackburn Coll (IL)
Bryant U (RI)
Limestone Coll (SC)
Northern Kentucky U (KY)
U of Arkansas (AR)
U of Houston (TX)
U of Wisconsin–Milwaukee (WI)

HUMAN RESOURCES MANAGEMENT
Auburn U (AL)
Auburn U at Montgomery (AL)
Avila U (MO)
Baldwin Wallace U (OH)
Baruch Coll of the City U of New York (NY)
Baylor U (TX)
Boston Coll (MA)
Bowling Green State U (OH)
Bradley U (IL)
Brenau U (GA)
Bryant U (RI)
Buena Vista U (IA)
California State U, Long Beach (CA)
California U of Pennsylvania (PA)
Calvin Coll (MI)
Canisius Coll (NY)
The Catholic U of America (DC)
Central Michigan U (MI)
Central Washington U (WA)
The Coll of Saint Rose (NY)
Columbia Coll (MO)
Columbia Southern U (AL)
Cornell Coll (IA)
Davenport U, Grand Rapids (MI)
Eastern Washington U (WA)
Granite State Coll (NH)
Gwynedd Mercy U (PA)
Idaho State U (ID)
Immaculata U (PA)
Indiana State U (IN)
Indiana U of Pennsylvania (PA)
Inter American U of Puerto Rico, Aguadilla Campus (PR)
Inter American U of Puerto Rico, Barranquitas Campus (PR)
Inter American U of Puerto Rico, Bayamón Campus (PR)
Inter American U of Puerto Rico, Fajardo Campus (PR)
Inter American U of Puerto Rico, San Germán Campus (PR)
Juniata Coll (PA)
King's Coll (PA)
Lamar U (TX)
La Salle U (PA)
La Sierra U (CA)
Limestone Coll (SC)
Lindenwood U (MO)
Lipscomb U (TN)
Loyola U Chicago (IL)
Madonna U (MI)
Mansfield U of Pennsylvania (PA)
Marquette U (WI)
Marymount Manhattan Coll (NY)
Mercer U, Macon (GA)
Merrimack Coll (MA)
Michigan State U (MI)
Nazareth Coll of Rochester (NY)
Nichols Coll (MA)
Oglethorpe U (GA)
The Ohio State U (OH)
Ohio U (OH)
Pace U (NY)
Pace U, Pleasantville Campus (NY)
Portland State U (OR)
Purdue U Northwest (IN)
Regent U (VA)
Regis U (CO)
Rhode Island Coll (RI)
Saint Francis U (PA)
St. Joseph's Coll, Long Island Campus (NY)
St. Joseph's Coll, New York (NY)
Saint Joseph's U (PA)
Saint Mary's U of Minnesota (MN)
San Diego State U (CA)
San Jose State U (CA)
Seton Hill U (PA)
State U of New York Coll of Technology at Alfred (NY)
State U of New York Coll of Technology at Delhi (NY)
Sullivan U (KY)
Temple U (PA)
Texas A&M U–Central Texas (TX)
Texas Woman's U (TX)
Tiffin U (OH)
Trinity Christian Coll (IL)
The U of Findlay (OH)
U of Hawaii at Manoa (HI)
U of Idaho (ID)
U of Lynchburg (VA)
U of Maryland U Coll (MD)
U of Michigan–Dearborn (MI)
U of Minnesota, Duluth (MN)
U of Minnesota, Twin Cities Campus (MN)
The U of North Carolina at Chapel Hill (NC)
U of North Dakota (ND)
U of Pennsylvania (PA)
U of Regina (SK, Canada)
U of St. Thomas (MN)
The U of Tennessee (TN)
U of the Incarnate Word (TX)
The U of Toledo (OH)
U of Washington (WA)
Utah State U (UT)
Washington U in St. Louis (MO)
Weber State U (UT)
Western Illinois U (IL)
Wright State U–Lake Campus (OH)
Youngstown State U (OH)

HUMAN RESOURCES MANAGEMENT AND SERVICES RELATED
Grand Valley State U (MI)
Immaculata U (PA)
Miami U Hamilton (OH)
Michigan State U (MI)
Oakland City U (IN)
U of Mount Union (OH)
U of Pittsburgh (PA)
Widener U (PA)

HUMAN SERVICES
California State U, Fullerton (CA)
California State U, Monterey Bay (CA)
California State U, San Bernardino (CA)
Calumet Coll of Saint Joseph (IN)
Carson-Newman U (TN)
Central Washington U (WA)
Columbia Coll (MO)
Dominican U (IL)
East Tennessee State U (TN)
Emmanuel Coll (MA)
Fitchburg State U (MA)
Geneva Coll (PA)
Granite State Coll (NH)
Gwynedd Mercy U (PA)
Hardin-Simmons U (TX)
Judson U (IL)
Kennesaw State U (GA)
Lasell Coll (MA)
Lees-McRae Coll (NC)
Lesley U (MA)
LeTourneau U (TX)
Liberty U (VA)
Loyola U Chicago (IL)
Mercer U, Macon (GA)
Missouri Baptist U (MO)
Mount Marty Coll (SD)
Mount Saint Mary Coll (NY)
Northern Illinois U (IL)
Ohio U (OH)
Ottawa U (KS)
Pfeiffer U (NC)
Queens U of Charlotte (NC)
St. Joseph's Coll, Long Island Campus (NY)
St. Joseph's Coll, New York (NY)
Saint Mary's U of Minnesota (MN)
Seton Hill U (PA)
Southeastern U (FL)
Syracuse U (NY)
Towson U (MD)
Tyndale U Coll & Sem (ON, Canada)
U of Maine at Machias (ME)
U of Massachusetts Boston (MA)
U of Minnesota, Morris (MN)
U of Nevada, Las Vegas (NV)
U of Oregon (OR)
U of Providence (MT)
U of South Florida (FL)
Valley City State U (ND)
Waynesburg U (PA)
Western Washington U (WA)

HYDROLOGY AND WATER RESOURCES SCIENCE
The Coll at Brockport, State U of New York (NY)
U of California, Davis (CA)
U of Idaho (ID)
The U of Texas at Austin (TX)

ILLUSTRATION
Acad of Art U (CA)
California State U, Long Beach (CA)
Cleveland Inst of Art (OH)
Columbia Coll Chicago (IL)
Fashion Inst of Technology (NY)
Maryland Inst Coll of Art (MD)
Marywood U (PA)
Pennsylvania Coll of Art & Design (PA)
Rhode Island School of Design (RI)
Rochester Inst of Technology (NY)
Savannah Coll of Art and Design (GA)
Syracuse U (NY)

U of Massachusetts Dartmouth (MA)
U of Michigan (MI)
U of New Haven (CT)
Virginia Commonwealth U (VA)
Washington U in St. Louis (MO)

INDUSTRIAL AND ORGANIZATIONAL PSYCHOLOGY
Avila U (MO)
Baldwin Wallace U (OH)
Baruch Coll of the City U of New York (NY)
Bridgewater State U (MA)
Concordia U Irvine (CA)
Embry-Riddle Aeronautical U–Prescott (AZ)
Excelsior Coll (NY)
Fitchburg State U (MA)
Fort Lewis Coll (CO)
Ithaca Coll (NY)
Maryville U of Saint Louis (MO)
Marywood U (PA)
Middle Tennessee State U (TN)
Morningside Coll (IA)
Pepperdine U, Malibu (CA)
Washington U in St. Louis (MO)

INDUSTRIAL AND PHYSICAL PHARMACY AND COSMETIC SCIENCES
The U of Toledo (OH)

INDUSTRIAL AND PRODUCT DESIGN
Acad of Art U (CA)
Appalachian State U (NC)
Auburn U (AL)
California State U, Long Beach (CA)
Carnegie Mellon U (PA)
Cedarville U (OH)
Cleveland Inst of Art (OH)
Escuela de Artes Plasticas y Diseño de Puerto Rico (PR)
Fashion Inst of Technology (NY)
FIDM/Fashion Inst of Design & Merchandising, Los Angeles Campus (CA)
Iowa State U of Science and Technology (IA)
Kean U (NJ)
Lawrence Technological U (MI)
Lebanon Valley Coll (PA)
Maryland Inst Coll of Art (MD)
Montclair State U (NJ)
New Jersey Inst of Technology (NJ)
North Carolina State U (NC)
The Ohio State U (OH)
Purdue U (IN)
Rhode Island School of Design (RI)
Rochester Inst of Technology (NY)
San Francisco State U (CA)
San Jose State U (CA)
Savannah Coll of Art and Design (GA)
Syracuse U (NY)
U of Houston (TX)
U of Michigan (MI)
U of Minnesota, Twin Cities Campus (MN)
U of Washington (WA)
Virginia Polytechnic Inst and State U (VA)
Western Washington U (WA)

INDUSTRIAL ENGINEERING
American U of Beirut (Lebanon)
Auburn U (AL)
Bradley U (IL)
California Polytechnic State U, San Luis Obispo (CA)
California State U, Long Beach (CA)
Colorado State U–Pueblo (CO)
Columbia U (NY)
Florida Ag and Mech U (FL)
Hofstra U (NY)
Inter American U of Puerto Rico, Bayamón Campus (PR)
Iowa State U of Science and Technology (IA)
Lamar U (TX)
Lawrence Technological U (MI)
Lebanese American U (Lebanon)
Liberty U (VA)
Louisiana State U and A&M Coll (LA)
New Jersey Inst of Technology (NJ)
North Carolina State U (NC)
Northern Illinois U (IL)
Northwestern U (IL)
The Ohio State U (OH)
Ohio U (OH)
Oklahoma State U (OK)
Purdue U (IN)
Rochester Inst of Technology (NY)
St. Mary's U (TX)
San Jose State U (CA)
Southern Illinois U Edwardsville (IL)
State U of New York Maritime Coll (NY)
Temple U (PA)
Texas Tech U (TX)
U at Buffalo, the State U of New York (NY)
U of Arkansas (AR)
U of Central Florida (FL)
U of Dayton (OH)
U of Houston (TX)
U of Louisville (KY)
U of Massachusetts Amherst (MA)
U of Michigan (MI)
U of Michigan–Dearborn (MI)
U of Minnesota, Duluth (MN)
U of Minnesota, Twin Cities Campus (MN)
U of Missouri (MO)
U of New Haven (CT)
U of Pittsburgh (PA)
U of Regina (SK, Canada)
U of San Diego (CA)
U of South Carolina Aiken (SC)
U of South Florida (FL)
The U of Tennessee (TN)
The U of Texas at El Paso (TX)
U of Vermont (VT)
U of Washington (WA)
U of Wisconsin–Milwaukee (WI)
Virginia Polytechnic Inst and State U (VA)
Worcester Polytechnic Inst (MA)
Youngstown State U (OH)

INDUSTRIAL PRODUCTION TECHNOLOGIES RELATED
Bowling Green State U (OH)
California U of Pennsylvania (PA)
Central Washington U (WA)
Kennesaw State U (GA)
Millersville U of Pennsylvania (PA)
Northwest Missouri State U (MO)
Saginaw Valley State U (MI)

INDUSTRIAL SAFETY TECHNOLOGY
Central Washington U (WA)
Mansfield U of Pennsylvania (PA)
Northeastern State U (OK)
U of Houston–Downtown (TX)

INDUSTRIAL TECHNOLOGY
Bowling Green State U (OH)
California Polytechnic State U, San Luis Obispo (CA)
California State U, Long Beach (CA)
California State U, Los Angeles (CA)
Central Connecticut State U (CT)
Central State U (OH)
Central Washington U (WA)
Clarion U of Pennsylvania (PA)
East Carolina U (NC)
Eastern Illinois U (IL)
Farmingdale State Coll (NY)
Fitchburg State U (MA)
Indiana State U (IN)
Iowa State U of Science and Technology (IA)
Jackson State U (MS)
Lamar U (TX)
Millersville U of Pennsylvania (PA)
Ohio U (OH)
Purdue U (IN)
Southeastern Louisiana U (LA)
Southeast Missouri State U (MO)
Southern Illinois U Carbondale (IL)
U of Dayton (OH)
U of Idaho (ID)
U of Massachusetts Lowell (MA)
U of North Dakota (ND)
U of Northern Iowa (IA)
The U of Texas of the Permian Basin (TX)
Vincennes U (IN)
Western Kentucky U (KY)
West Virginia U Inst of Technology (WV)

INFORMATICS
Allegheny Coll (PA)
American Coll of Thessaloniki (Greece)
Assumption Coll (MA)
Dominican U (IL)
Indiana U Bloomington (IN)
Indiana U East (IN)
Indiana U Kokomo (IN)
Indiana U Northwest (IN)
Indiana U–Purdue U Indianapolis (IN)
Indiana U South Bend (IN)
Indiana U Southeast (IN)
Liberty U (VA)
Texas Woman's U (TX)
U at Buffalo, the State U of New York (NY)
U of California, Irvine (CA)
U of Massachusetts Amherst (MA)
U of Michigan (MI)
U of Washington (WA)

INFORMATION RESOURCES MANAGEMENT
Juniata Coll (PA)
Lawrence Technological U (MI)
Lipscomb U (TN)
Lubbock Christian U (TX)
Michigan State U (MI)
U of California, Irvine (CA)
U of Wisconsin–Eau Claire (WI)

INFORMATION SCIENCE/ STUDIES
Adelphi U (NY)
Alabama State U (AL)
Albright Coll (PA)
Averett U (VA)
Baruch Coll of the City U of New York (NY)
Benedictine U (IL)
Bentley U (MA)
Bowling Green State U (OH)
Bradley U (IL)
California Inst of Technology (CA)
California Lutheran U (CA)
California State U, Northridge (CA)
Campbellsville U (KY)
Carson-Newman U (TN)
Christian Brothers U (TN)
Christopher Newport U (VA)
Clarion U of Pennsylvania (PA)
Coastal Carolina U (SC)
The Coll at Brockport, State U of New York (NY)
Coll of Charleston (SC)
Coll of Staten Island of the City U of New York (NY)
Colorado State U (CO)
Colorado State U–Pueblo (CO)
Columbia U (NY)
Dakota State U (SD)
Davenport U, Grand Rapids (MI)
DePaul U (IL)
East Carolina U (NC)
Excelsior Coll (NY)
Fordham U (NY)
Georgia Southern U (GA)
Goshen Coll (IN)
Grand Valley State U (MI)
Idaho State U (ID)
Illinois Coll (IL)
Inter American U of Puerto Rico, San Germán Campus (PR)
Jacksonville U (FL)
Kennesaw State U (GA)
La Sierra U (CA)
LeTourneau U (TX)
Limestone Coll (SC)
Lipscomb U (TN)
Mansfield U of Pennsylvania (PA)
Mercer U, Macon (GA)
Mercy Coll (NY)
Minnesota State U Moorhead (MN)
Molloy Coll (NY)
Murray State U (KY)
New Jersey Inst of Technology (NJ)
Northern Kentucky U (KY)
Northwestern Oklahoma State U (OK)
Northwestern U (IL)
Oklahoma Baptist U (OK)
Oklahoma Christian U (OK)
Ottawa U (KS)
Pace U (NY)
Portland State U (OR)
Radford U (VA)
The Sage Colls (NY)
St. Joseph's Coll, Long Island Campus (NY)
St. Joseph's Coll, New York (NY)
Saint Joseph's U (PA)
St. Mary's U (TX)
Salisbury U (MD)
San Francisco State U (CA)
Southern Illinois U Carbondale (IL)
State U of New York at Fredonia (NY)
Stockton U (NJ)
Syracuse U (NY)
Texas A&M Intl U (TX)
Texas Lutheran U (TX)
Texas Tech U (TX)
Towson U (MD)
Tulane U (LA)
Université de Sherbrooke (QC, Canada)
U of Houston (TX)
U of Kentucky (KY)
U of Mary Hardin-Baylor (TX)
U of Maryland, Baltimore County (MD)
U of Maryland, Coll Park (MD)
U of Maryland U Coll (MD)
U of Massachusetts Lowell (MA)
U of Michigan (MI)
U of Nevada, Las Vegas (NV)
The U of North Carolina at Chapel Hill (NC)
The U of North Carolina at Greensboro (NC)
U of Northwestern–St. Paul (MN)
U of Pittsburgh (PA)
U of Providence (MT)
U of St. Thomas (MN)
U of South Alabama (AL)
U of South Carolina (SC)
U of South Florida (FL)
The U of Texas at El Paso (TX)
The U of Texas of the Permian Basin (TX)
The U of Toledo (OH)
The U of Tulsa (OK)
U of Washington, Bothell (WA)
U of Wisconsin–Milwaukee (WI)
Utah State U (UT)
Utah Valley U (UT)
Virginia Commonwealth U (VA)
Virginia Polytechnic Inst and State U (VA)
Weber State U (UT)
Widener U (PA)
Wilkes U (PA)

INFORMATION TECHNOLOGY
American Public U System (WV)
Arkansas Tech U (AR)
Austin Peay State U (TN)
Baylor U (TX)
Bradley U (IL)
Bryant U (RI)
Buena Vista U (IA)
Caldwell U (NJ)
California State U, Fullerton (CA)
California State U, Los Angeles (CA)
California State U, San Bernardino (CA)
Cameron U (OK)
Central Michigan U (MI)
Central Washington U (WA)
Christopher Newport U (VA)
Coastal Carolina U (SC)
The Coll of Saint Rose (NY)
Coll of the Ozarks (MO)
Columbia Southern U (AL)
Cornell U (NY)
Daytona State Coll (FL)
DePaul U (IL)
DEREE - The American Coll of Greece (Greece)
Duquesne U (PA)
East Carolina U (NC)
Florida Ag and Mech U (FL)
Furman U (SC)
George Mason U (VA)
Georgia Southern U (GA)
Granite State Coll (NH)
Harding U (AR)
Indiana State U (IN)
Indiana U–Purdue U Indianapolis (IN)
Inter American U of Puerto Rico, Bayamón Campus (PR)
Johnson C. Smith U (NC)
Juniata Coll (PA)
Kansas Wesleyan U (KS)
Kennesaw State U (GA)
King U (TN)
La Salle U (PA)
Lasell Coll (MA)
La Sierra U (CA)
Lawrence Technological U (MI)
Lee U (TN)
Liberty U (VA)
Life U (GA)
Limestone Coll (SC)
Lindenwood U (MO)
Lipscomb U (TN)
Loyola U Chicago (IL)
Marist Coll (NY)
Marquette U (WI)
Marymount U (VA)
Merrimack Coll (MA)
Miami U (OH)
Missouri Baptist U (MO)
Montclair State U (NJ)
Mount Saint Mary Coll (NY)
Murray State U (KY)
New England Inst of Technology (RI)
New Jersey Inst of Technology (NJ)
New York U (NY)
Northern Kentucky U (KY)
Oklahoma State U (OK)
Ottawa U (KS)
Point Loma Nazarene U (CA)
Purdue U (IN)
Purdue U Northwest (IN)
Regent U (VA)
Regis U (CO)
Rochester Inst of Technology (NY)
Sacred Heart U (CT)
Saint Martin's U (WA)
San Diego State U (CA)
Southeastern Louisiana U (LA)
State U of New York at Plattsburgh (NY)
Stockton U (NJ)
Sullivan U (KY)
Temple U (PA)
Texas Christian U (TX)
Tiffin U (OH)
Towson U (MD)
Trevecca Nazarene U (TN)
Université de Sherbrooke (QC, Canada)
U of Central Florida (FL)
U of Houston–Clear Lake (TX)
U of La Verne (CA)
U of Massachusetts Boston (MA)
U of New Hampshire (NH)
The U of North Carolina at Pembroke (NC)
U of Providence (MT)
U of San Francisco (CA)
U of Sioux Falls (SD)
U of South Alabama (AL)
U of South Florida (FL)
U of South Florida Sarasota-Manatee (FL)
The U of Toledo (OH)
The U of Tulsa (OK)
U of Washington (WA)
U of Washington, Tacoma (WA)
Vanguard U of Southern California (CA)
Vermont Tech Coll (VT)
Washington & Jefferson Coll (PA)
Western Illinois U (IL)
Western Kentucky U (KY)
Youngstown State U (OH)

INFORMATION TECHNOLOGY PROJECT MANAGEMENT
American Public U System (WV)
Davenport U, Grand Rapids (MI)
Michigan State U (MI)
National U (CA)
Pace U (NY)
Pace U, Pleasantville Campus (NY)

INSURANCE
Appalachian State U (NC)
Baylor U (TX)
Bowling Green State U (OH)
Butler U (IN)

Georgia State U (GA)
Idaho State U (ID)
Indiana State U (IN)
Northwood U, Michigan Campus (MI)
Ohio Dominican U (OH)
The Ohio State U (OH)
Saint Joseph's U (PA)
Temple U (PA)
U of Central Arkansas (AR)
U of Georgia (GA)
U of Houston–Downtown (TX)
U of Minnesota, Twin Cities Campus (MN)
U of Mount Union (OH)
U of Pennsylvania (PA)
U of Saint Francis (IN)
U of South Carolina (SC)
U of South Florida Sarasota-Manatee (FL)

INTELLIGENCE
Coastal Carolina U (SC)
Excelsior Coll (NY)
Indiana State U (IN)

INTERCULTURAL/ MULTICULTURAL AND DIVERSITY STUDIES
Bryant U (RI)
The Evergreen State Coll (WA)
Judson U (IL)
Macalester Coll (MN)
Pitzer Coll (CA)
Sarah Lawrence Coll (NY)
Southeastern U (FL)
Trevecca Nazarene U (TN)
U of Regina (SK, Canada)
U of the Incarnate Word (TX)
Vanguard U of Southern California (CA)
Wofford Coll (SC)
Wright State U–Lake Campus (OH)

INTERDISCIPLINARY STUDIES
Agnes Scott Coll (GA)
Alfred U (NY)
Auburn U (AL)
Auburn U at Montgomery (AL)
Averett U (VA)
Beloit Coll (WI)
Blackburn Coll (IL)
Boston Coll (MA)
Brandman U (CA)
Bryn Athyn Coll of the New Church (PA)
Bucknell U (PA)
California Lutheran U (CA)
California State U, Bakersfield (CA)
California State U, Long Beach (CA)
Calvin Coll (MI)
Carson-Newman U (TN)
Centenary Coll of Louisiana (LA)
Christian Brothers U (TN)
Clark U (MA)
Coll of Coastal Georgia (GA)
The Coll of William and Mary (VA)
Connecticut Coll (CT)
Cornell Coll (IA)
Eastern Oregon U (OR)
East Stroudsburg U of Pennsylvania (PA)
Eckerd Coll (FL)
Elizabeth City State U (NC)
Embry-Riddle Aeronautical U–Daytona (FL)
Embry-Riddle Aeronautical U–Prescott (AZ)
Emerson Coll (MA)
FIDM/Fashion Inst of Design & Merchandising, Los Angeles Campus (CA)
Florida Ag and Mech U (FL)
Geneva Coll (PA)
Goshen Coll (IN)
Hamilton Coll (NY)
Hollins U (VA)
Illinois Coll (IL)
Indiana U Bloomington (IN)
Indiana U East (IN)
Indiana U Kokomo (IN)
Indiana U Northwest (IN)
Indiana U–Purdue U Indianapolis (IN)
Indiana U South Bend (IN)
Indiana U Southeast (IN)
Inter American U of Puerto Rico, Barranquitas Campus (PR)
Ithaca Coll (NY)
Jacksonville U (FL)
Johns Hopkins U (MD)
Kuyper Coll (MI)
Lees-McRae Coll (NC)
Liberty U (VA)
Life U (GA)
Lipscomb U (TN)
Loyola U New Orleans (LA)
Maharishi U of Management (IA)
Marist Coll (NY)
Marymount Manhattan Coll (NY)
Massachusetts Coll of Liberal Arts (MA)
Merrimack Coll (MA)
Millersville U of Pennsylvania (PA)
Mills Coll (CA)
Minnesota State U Moorhead (MN)
Mount Saint Mary Coll (NY)
National U (CA)
Northwestern U (IL)
Oglethorpe U (GA)
Ohio Dominican U (OH)
Oklahoma Baptist U (OK)
Ouachita Baptist U (AR)
Piedmont Coll (GA)
Purdue U Northwest (IN)
Queens Coll of the City U of New York (NY)
Rhode Island Coll (RI)
Rhodes Coll (TN)
Roanoke Coll (VA)
Rochester Inst of Technology (NY)
Sacred Heart U (CT)
Shiloh U (IA)
Sonoma State U (CA)
Southern Illinois U Edwardsville (IL)
State U of New York at Fredonia (NY)
Sweet Briar Coll (VA)
Syracuse U (NY)
Texas Christian U (TX)
Towson U (MD)
Union Coll (KY)
Université de Sherbrooke (QC, Canada)
U of Arkansas (AR)
U of Central Florida (FL)
U of Kentucky (KY)
U of Lynchburg (VA)
U of Memphis (TN)
U of Minnesota, Duluth (MN)
U of New Mexico (NM)
U of North Dakota (ND)
U of North Florida (FL)
U of Puget Sound (WA)
U of Saint Francis (IN)
U of Saint Mary (KS)
U of San Francisco (CA)
U of Sioux Falls (SD)
U of South Alabama (AL)
The U of Tennessee at Martin (TN)
The U of Toledo (OH)
The U of Tulsa (OK)
U of Washington, Tacoma (WA)
The U of West Alabama (AL)
U of West Georgia (GA)
Vanguard U of Southern California (CA)
Vassar Coll (NY)
Virginia Polytechnic Inst and State U (VA)
Wesleyan Coll (GA)
Western Illinois U (IL)
Western Washington U (WA)
Whitworth U (WA)

INTERIOR ARCHITECTURE
Auburn U (AL)
Bowling Green State U (OH)
Colorado State U (CO)
Indiana State U (IN)
Lawrence Technological U (MI)
Lebanese American U (Lebanon)
Louisiana State U and A&M Coll (LA)
Miami U (OH)
Syracuse U (NY)
Texas Tech U (TX)
U of Houston (TX)
U of Nebraska–Lincoln (NE)
U of Nevada, Las Vegas (NV)
U of Oregon (OR)
Woodbury U (CA)

INTERIOR DESIGN
Acad of Art U (CA)
Appalachian State U (NC)
Auburn U (AL)
Baylor U (TX)
Berkeley Coll–Woodland Park Campus (NJ)
California State U, Long Beach (CA)
Carson-Newman U (TN)
Cleveland Inst of Art (OH)
Colorado State U (CO)
Columbia Coll Chicago (IL)
Dunwoody Coll of Technology (MN)
East Carolina U (NC)
East Tennessee State U (TN)
Endicott Coll (MA)
Fashion Inst of Technology (NY)
FIDM/Fashion Inst of Design & Merchandising, Los Angeles Campus (CA)
Georgia Southern U (GA)
Harding U (AR)
High Point U (NC)
Indiana U Bloomington (IN)
Indiana U of Pennsylvania (PA)
Indiana U–Purdue U Indianapolis (IN)
Iowa State U of Science and Technology (IA)
Judson U (IL)
Kean U (NJ)
Lebanese American U (Lebanon)
Liberty U (VA)
Marist Coll (NY)
Maryland Inst Coll of Art (MD)
Marymount U (VA)
Maryville U of Saint Louis (MO)
Marywood U (PA)
Miami U Hamilton (OH)
Michigan State U (MI)
Middle Tennessee State U (TN)
New England Inst of Technology (RI)
New Jersey Inst of Technology (NJ)
The Ohio State U (OH)
Oklahoma Christian U (OK)
Oklahoma State U (OK)
Purdue U (IN)
Queens U of Charlotte (NC)
Rochester Inst of Technology (NY)
The Sage Colls (NY)
Samford U (AL)
San Diego State U (CA)
San Francisco State U (CA)
San Jose State U (CA)
Savannah Coll of Art and Design (GA)
Southern Illinois U Carbondale (IL)
Texas Christian U (TX)
U of Arkansas (AR)
U of Central Arkansas (AR)
U of Florida (FL)
U of Idaho (ID)
U of Kentucky (KY)
U of Memphis (TN)
U of Minnesota, Twin Cities Campus (MN)
U of New Haven (CT)
The U of North Carolina at Greensboro (NC)
U of Northern Iowa (IA)
The U of Tennessee (TN)
The U of Texas at Austin (TX)
U of the Incarnate Word (TX)
Utah State U (UT)
Virginia Commonwealth U (VA)
Virginia Polytechnic Inst and State U (VA)
Washington State U (WA)
Washington State U–Spokane (WA)
Weber State U (UT)

INTERMEDIA/MULTIMEDIA
Calumet Coll of Saint Joseph (IN)
Columbia Coll Chicago (IL)
Emerson Coll (MA)
The Evergreen State Coll (WA)
Indiana U of Pennsylvania (PA)
Jacksonville U (FL)
Marist Coll (NY)
Maryland Inst Coll of Art (MD)
Mills Coll (CA)
Rochester Inst of Technology (NY)
State U of New York at Fredonia (NY)
State U of New York Coll of Technology at Alfred (NY)
U of Maine at Farmington (ME)
U of Oregon (OR)
U of Regina (SK, Canada)
U of the Incarnate Word (TX)
The U of Toledo (OH)
Weber State U (UT)

INTERNATIONAL AGRICULTURE
Coll of the Ozarks (MO)
Cornell U (NY)
Iowa State U of Science and Technology (IA)
U of California, Davis (CA)
Utah State U (UT)

INTERNATIONAL AND COMPARATIVE EDUCATION
Avila U (MO)

INTERNATIONAL AND INTERCULTURAL COMMUNICATION
DePaul U (IL)
Johnson U Florida (FL)
Linfield Coll (OR)
Pepperdine U, Malibu (CA)

INTERNATIONAL BUSINESS/ TRADE/COMMERCE
Adams State U (CO)
Alverno Coll (WI)
Angelo State U (TX)
Appalachian State U (NC)
Assumption Coll (MA)
Auburn U (AL)
Auburn U at Montgomery (AL)
Austin Coll (TX)
Avila U (MO)
Babson Coll (MA)
Baker U (KS)
Baldwin Wallace U (OH)
Baruch Coll of the City U of New York (NY)
Baylor U (TX)
Benedictine U (IL)
Berkeley Coll–New York City Campus (NY)
Berkeley Coll–Woodland Park Campus (NJ)
Bowling Green State U (OH)
Bradley U (IL)
Bridgewater State U (MA)
Bryant U (RI)
Bucknell U (PA)
Butler U (IN)
Caldwell U (NJ)
California State U, Fullerton (CA)
California State U, Long Beach (CA)
California State U, San Marcos (CA)
Canisius Coll (NY)
Carnegie Mellon U (PA)
The Catholic U of America (DC)
Cedarville U (OH)
Central Michigan U (MI)
Champlain Coll (VT)
Clarion U of Pennsylvania (PA)
The Coll at Brockport, State U of New York (NY)
Coll of Charleston (SC)
The Coll of Idaho (ID)
Columbia Coll (MO)
Cornell Coll (IA)
Creighton U (NE)
Davenport U, Grand Rapids (MI)
DEREE - The American Coll of Greece (Greece)
Dickinson Coll (PA)
Dominican U (IL)
Drake U (IA)
Duquesne U (PA)
Eastern Mennonite U (VA)
Eastern U (PA)
Eckerd Coll (FL)
Embry-Riddle Aeronautical U–Prescott (AZ)
Endicott Coll (MA)
Fairfield U (CT)
Farmingdale State Coll (NY)
Florida Atlantic U (FL)
Fordham U (NY)
Fort Lewis Coll (CO)
Framingham State U (MA)
Georgia Southern U (GA)
Gonzaga U (WA)
Grand Valley State U (MI)
Grove City Coll (PA)
Hamline U (MN)
Harding U (AR)
High Point U (NC)
Hillsdale Coll (MI)
Hofstra U (NY)
Indiana U of Pennsylvania (PA)
Iona Coll (NY)
Iowa State U of Science and Technology (IA)
Ithaca Coll (NY)
Jacksonville U (FL)
John Cabot U (Italy)
Juniata Coll (PA)
Kean U (NJ)
Kennesaw State U (GA)
King's Coll (PA)
La Salle U (PA)
Lasell Coll (MA)
Lebanon Valley Coll (PA)
LIM Coll (NY)
Lindenwood U (MO)
Linfield Coll (OR)
Lipscomb U (TN)
Louisiana State U and A&M Coll (LA)
Loyola U Chicago (IL)
Loyola U New Orleans (LA)
Madonna U (MI)
Mansfield U of Pennsylvania (PA)
Marshall U (WV)
Marymount Manhattan Coll (NY)
Maryville U of Saint Louis (MO)
Marywood U (PA)
Massachusetts Coll of Liberal Arts (MA)
Massachusetts Maritime Acad (MA)
Mercer U, Macon (GA)
Merrimack Coll (MA)
Messiah Coll (PA)
Millikin U (IL)
Muskingum U (OH)
Nazareth Coll of Rochester (NY)
New Jersey Inst of Technology (NJ)
New York U (NY)
Nichols Coll (MA)
Northeastern State U (OK)
Northern State U (SD)
Northwest Christian U (OR)
Northwest Missouri State U (MO)
Northwood U, Michigan Campus (MI)
The Ohio State U (OH)
Ohio U (OH)
Ohio Wesleyan U (OH)
Oklahoma Baptist U (OK)
Oklahoma State U (OK)
Pace U (NY)
Pace U, Pleasantville Campus (NY)
Palm Beach Atlantic U (FL)
Pepperdine U, Malibu (CA)
Pfeiffer U (NC)
Queens Coll of the City U of New York (NY)
Rhode Island Coll (RI)
Rhodes Coll (TN)
Rider U (NJ)
Rochester Inst of Technology (NY)
Rollins Coll (FL)
Saginaw Valley State U (MI)
Saint Anselm Coll (NH)
Saint Joseph's U (PA)
Saint Louis U (MO)
St. Mary's U (TX)
Saint Mary's U of Minnesota (MN)
St. Norbert Coll (WI)
Saint Vincent Coll (PA)
Salisbury U (MD)
San Diego State U (CA)
San Francisco State U (CA)
San Jose State U (CA)
Seattle U (WA)
Seton Hill U (PA)
Southeastern U (FL)
Southeast Missouri State U (MO)
Southwest Baptist U (MO)
Spring Hill Coll (AL)
State U of New York at Plattsburgh (NY)
Stetson U (FL)
Stonehill Coll (MA)
Taylor U (IN)
Temple U (PA)
Texas Christian U (TX)
Texas Tech U (TX)

Tiffin U (OH)
Trevecca Nazarene U (TN)
U at Buffalo, the State U of New York (NY)
U of Arkansas (AR)
U of Dayton (OH)
The U of Findlay (OH)
U of Hawaii at Manoa (HI)
U of Houston–Downtown (TX)
U of La Verne (CA)
U of Mary Hardin-Baylor (TX)
U of Maryland, Coll Park (MD)
U of Memphis (TN)
U of Minnesota, Twin Cities Campus (MN)
U of Nebraska–Lincoln (NE)
U of Nevada, Las Vegas (NV)
U of Nevada, Reno (NV)
U of New Haven (CT)
The U of North Carolina at Charlotte (NC)
The U of North Carolina at Greensboro (NC)
U of North Florida (FL)
U of Northwestern–St. Paul (MN)
U of Pennsylvania (PA)
U of Pittsburgh (PA)
U of Puget Sound (WA)
U of Regina (SK, Canada)
U of St. Thomas (MN)
U of San Diego (CA)
U of San Francisco (CA)
U of South Alabama (AL)
U of South Carolina (SC)
U of South Florida (FL)
The U of Tampa (FL)
The U of Texas Rio Grande Valley (TX)
U of the Incarnate Word (TX)
The U of Toledo (OH)
The U of Tulsa (OK)
U of Wisconsin–Eau Claire (WI)
U of Wisconsin–La Crosse (WI)
U of Wisconsin–Superior (WI)
Utica Coll (NY)
Valparaiso U (IN)
Vanguard U of Southern California (CA)
Wartburg Coll (IA)
Washington & Jefferson Coll (PA)
Washington State U (WA)
Washington U in St. Louis (MO)
Waynesburg U (PA)
Wesleyan Coll (GA)
West Chester U of Pennsylvania (PA)
Western Kentucky U (KY)
Western Washington U (WA)
Widener U (PA)

INTERNATIONAL ECONOMICS
Albion Coll (MI)
Austin Coll (TX)
Bryant U (RI)
Carthage Coll (WI)
The Coll of Idaho (ID)
The Colorado Coll (CO)
Fitchburg State U (MA)
Georgia State U (GA)
La Salle U (PA)
Rhodes Coll (TN)
Rockford U (IL)
Salve Regina U (RI)
Texas Christian U (TX)
Texas Tech U (TX)
U of California, Santa Cruz (CA)
U of Puget Sound (WA)
U of Richmond (VA)
U of West Georgia (GA)
Valparaiso U (IN)
Washington U in St. Louis (MO)
Weber State U (UT)
Youngstown State U (OH)

INTERNATIONAL FINANCE
Babson Coll (MA)
Bryant U (RI)
The Catholic U of America (DC)
Texas Christian U (TX)
Washington U in St. Louis (MO)

INTERNATIONAL/GLOBAL STUDIES
Adelphi U (NY)
Albion Coll (MI)
Alfred U (NY)
American Public U System (WV)
Appalachian State U (NC)
Arkansas Tech U (AR)
Assumption Coll (MA)
Baker U (KS)
Baldwin Wallace U (OH)
Benedictine U (IL)
Bentley U (MA)
Boston Coll (MA)
Bowling Green State U (OH)
Brandeis U (MA)
Bryant U (RI)
California Lutheran U (CA)
Carnegie Mellon U (PA)
Cedarville U (OH)
Central Connecticut State U (CT)
Coll of Charleston (SC)
The Coll of St. Scholastica (MN)
Coll of Staten Island of the City U of New York (NY)
Coll of the Holy Cross (MA)
Colorado State U (CO)
Concordia U Irvine (CA)
Culver-Stockton Coll (MO)
East Texas Baptist U (TX)
Emmanuel Coll (MA)
Endicott Coll (MA)
The Evergreen State Coll (WA)
Framingham State U (MA)
Georgetown Coll (KY)
Graceland U (IA)
Grand Valley State U (MI)
Greenville U (IL)
Hamline U (MN)
Hanover Coll (IN)
Harding U (AR)
Hartwick Coll (NY)
Hiram Coll (OH)
Hofstra U (NY)
Hood Coll (MD)
Humboldt State U (CA)
Juniata Coll (PA)
Kean U (NJ)
Knox Coll (IL)
Lasell Coll (MA)
La Sierra U (CA)
Lawrence U (WI)
Lebanon Valley Coll (PA)
Lee U (TN)
LeTourneau U (TX)
Liberty U (VA)
Linfield Coll (OR)
Louisiana State U and A&M Coll (LA)
Lycoming Coll (PA)
Macalester Coll (MN)
Manchester U (IN)
Manhattanville Coll (NY)
Marymount Manhattan Coll (NY)
Maryville U of Saint Louis (MO)
Mercer U, Macon (GA)
Merrimack Coll (MA)
Miami U (OH)
Miami U Hamilton (OH)
Michigan State U (MI)
Middle Tennessee State U (TN)
Minnesota State U Moorhead (MN)
Morningside Coll (IA)
National U (CA)
New Coll of Florida (FL)
New York U (NY)
North Carolina State U (NC)
The Ohio State U (OH)
Oklahoma State U (OK)
Pace U, Pleasantville Campus (NY)
Pacific Lutheran U (WA)
Pepperdine U, Malibu (CA)
Pitzer Coll (CA)
Point Loma Nazarene U (CA)
Portland State U (OR)
Providence Coll (RI)
Randolph Coll (VA)
Regent U (VA)
Rhode Island Coll (RI)
Rockford U (IL)
Saginaw Valley State U (MI)
Saint Leo U (FL)
Saint Mary's U of Minnesota (MN)
St. Norbert Coll (WI)
Salisbury U (MD)
Salve Regina U (RI)
Samford U (AL)
Sarah Lawrence Coll (NY)
Scripps Coll (CA)
Seattle U (WA)
Southeast Missouri State U (MO)
Southern Illinois U Edwardsville (IL)
State U of New York Coll at Potsdam (NY)
Tabor Coll (KS)
Temple U (PA)
Texas Tech U (TX)
U of California, Irvine (CA)
U of California, Los Angeles (CA)
U of California, Riverside (CA)
U of Central Arkansas (AR)
U of Central Florida (FL)
U of Colorado Denver (CO)
U of Dayton (OH)
U of Florida (FL)
U of Illinois at Springfield (IL)
U of Kentucky (KY)
U of Maine at Farmington (ME)
U of Maryland, Baltimore County (MD)
U of Michigan (MI)
U of Nebraska–Lincoln (NE)
U of New Haven (CT)
U of New Mexico (NM)
The U of North Carolina at Charlotte (NC)
U of North Dakota (ND)
U of Northern Colorado (CO)
U of Northern Iowa (IA)
U of North Florida (FL)
U of Notre Dame (IN)
U of Oregon (OR)
U of Pennsylvania (PA)
U of Regina (SK, Canada)
U of South Alabama (AL)
U of South Dakota (SD)
The U of Tampa (FL)
The U of Texas at Austin (TX)
The U of the South (TN)
U of Vermont (VT)
U of Washington, Bothell (WA)
U of Washington, Tacoma (WA)
U of Wisconsin–Milwaukee (WI)
U of Wyoming (WY)
Valparaiso U (IN)
Virginia Polytechnic Inst and State U (VA)
Washington & Jefferson Coll (PA)
West Virginia State U (WV)
Whittier Coll (CA)
Willamette U (OR)
Wright State U–Lake Campus (OH)

INTERNATIONAL MARKETING
Bryant U (RI)
Fashion Inst of Technology (NY)
Oklahoma Baptist U (OK)
Pace U, Pleasantville Campus (NY)
Texas Christian U (TX)
U of Northern Iowa (IA)

INTERNATIONAL POLICY ANALYSIS
Waynesburg U (PA)

INTERNATIONAL PUBLIC HEALTH
Allegheny Coll (PA)
American U (DC)
La Sierra U (CA)
Mercer U, Macon (GA)

INTERNATIONAL RELATIONS AND AFFAIRS
Agnes Scott Coll (GA)
Albright Coll (PA)
Allegheny Coll (PA)
Alverno Coll (WI)
American Coll of Thessaloniki (Greece)
American U (DC)
Austin Coll (TX)
Baylor U (TX)
Beloit Coll (WI)
Benedictine U (IL)
Bethel U (MN)
Boston U (MA)
Bowling Green State U (OH)
Bradley U (IL)
Bridgewater Coll (VA)
Bridgewater State U (MA)
Bryant U (RI)
Bucknell U (PA)
Butler U (IN)
California Lutheran U (CA)
California State U, Chico (CA)
California State U, Long Beach (CA)
California State U, Monterey Bay (CA)
California State U, San Marcos (CA)
Calvin Coll (MI)
Canisius Coll (NY)
Carnegie Mellon U (PA)
Central Michigan U (MI)
Claremont McKenna Coll (CA)
Clark U (MA)
Colgate U (NY)
The Coll at Brockport, State U of New York (NY)
The Coll of Idaho (ID)
The Coll of William and Mary (VA)
Connecticut Coll (CT)
Cornell Coll (IA)
Creighton U (NE)
DePaul U (IL)
DEREE - The American Coll of Greece (Greece)
Dickinson Coll (PA)
Dominican U (IL)
Drake U (IA)
Drew U (NJ)
Duquesne U (PA)
Earlham Coll (IN)
Eastern Washington U (WA)
East Tennessee State U (TN)
Eckerd Coll (FL)
Embry-Riddle Aeronautical U–Prescott (AZ)
Emmanuel Coll (MA)
Excelsior Coll (NY)
Fairfield U (CT)
Fitchburg State U (MA)
Fordham U (NY)
George Mason U (VA)
Georgia Southern U (GA)
Gonzaga U (WA)
Gordon Coll (MA)
Grand Valley State U (MI)
Hamilton Coll (NY)
Hampden-Sydney Coll (VA)
High Point U (NC)
Hollins U (VA)
Idaho State U (ID)
Illinois Coll (IL)
Immaculata U (PA)
Indiana U Bloomington (IN)
Indiana U East (IN)
Indiana U of Pennsylvania (PA)
Indiana U–Purdue U Indianapolis (IN)
Indiana U Southeast (IN)
Iona Coll (NY)
Jacksonville U (FL)
John Cabot U (Italy)
Johns Hopkins U (MD)
Juniata Coll (PA)
Kalamazoo Coll (MI)
Kennesaw State U (GA)
Knox Coll (IL)
Lafayette Coll (PA)
Lake Forest Coll (IL)
Lebanese American U (Lebanon)
Lewis & Clark Coll (OR)
Liberty U (VA)
Lindenwood U (MO)
Linfield Coll (OR)
Lock Haven U of Pennsylvania (PA)
Loras Coll (IA)
Loyola Marymount U (CA)
Loyola U Chicago (IL)
Manhattan Coll (NY)
Marquette U (WI)
Marshall U (WV)
Marymount Manhattan Coll (NY)
Mercer U, Macon (GA)
Mercy Coll (NY)
Miami U (OH)
Michigan State U (MI)
Middlebury Coll (VT)
Middle Tennessee State U (TN)
Mills Coll (CA)
Morningside Coll (IA)
Murray State U (KY)
Muskingum U (OH)
Nazareth Coll of Rochester (NY)
New York U (NY)
Northern Kentucky U (KY)
Northwestern U (IL)
Occidental Coll (CA)
Oglethorpe U (GA)
The Ohio State U (OH)
Ohio U (OH)
Ohio Wesleyan U (OH)
Oklahoma Baptist U (OK)
Old Dominion U (VA)
Portland State U (OR)
Queens U of Charlotte (NC)
Randolph-Macon Coll (VA)
Redeemer U Coll (ON, Canada)
Rider U (NJ)
Roanoke Coll (VA)
Rochester Inst of Technology (NY)
Rollins Coll (FL)
Saginaw Valley State U (MI)
Saint Anselm Coll (NH)
St. John Fisher Coll (NY)
Saint Joseph's U (PA)
Saint Louis U (MO)
St. Mary's U (TX)
St. Norbert Coll (WI)
Samford U (AL)
San Diego State U (CA)
San Francisco State U (CA)
Sarah Lawrence Coll (NY)
Seton Hill U (PA)
Skidmore Coll (NY)
Sonoma State U (CA)
Southwestern U (TX)
Spring Hill Coll (AL)
State U of New York Coll at Geneseo (NY)
Stetson U (FL)
Sweet Briar Coll (VA)
Syracuse U (NY)
Taylor U (IN)
Texas Christian U (TX)
Tiffin U (OH)
Towson U (MD)
Tulane U (LA)
U of Arkansas (AR)
U of California, Davis (CA)
U of Chicago (IL)
U of Georgia (GA)
U of Idaho (ID)
U of La Verne (CA)
U of Lynchburg (VA)
U of Maine (ME)
U of Massachusetts Boston (MA)
U of Memphis (TN)
U of Minnesota, Duluth (MN)
U of Minnesota, Twin Cities Campus (MN)
U of Mount Union (OH)
U of Nevada, Reno (NV)
U of New Hampshire (NH)
U of Pennsylvania (PA)
U of Pittsburgh at Bradford (PA)
U of Puget Sound (WA)
U of Richmond (VA)
U of St. Thomas (MN)
U of St. Thomas (TX)
U of San Diego (CA)
U of San Francisco (CA)
U of South Carolina (SC)
U of Southern Indiana (IN)
U of South Florida (FL)
The U of Tennessee at Martin (TN)
U of the Incarnate Word (TX)
The U of Toledo (OH)
U of Virginia (VA)
U of West Georgia (GA)
U of Wisconsin–River Falls (WI)
Ursinus Coll (PA)
Utica Coll (NY)
Valparaiso U (IN)
Vassar Coll (NY)
Virginia Polytechnic Inst and State U (VA)
Wartburg Coll (IA)
Washington State U (WA)
Washington U in St. Louis (MO)
Western Kentucky U (KY)
Wheaton Coll (IL)
Wheaton Coll (MA)
Whitworth U (WA)
Widener U (PA)
Wilkes U (PA)
William Jewell Coll (MO)
Worcester Polytechnic Inst (MA)

INTERNATIONAL RELATIONS AND NATIONAL SECURITY RELATED
Indiana U Bloomington (IN)
King U (TN)
Middlebury Coll (VT)
San Diego State U (CA)
U of Mount Union (OH)
Virginia Polytechnic Inst and State U (VA)

INVESTMENTS AND SECURITIES
Babson Coll (MA)
Marymount Manhattan Coll (NY)
U of Nebraska–Lincoln (NE)
U of North Dakota (ND)
U of Northern Iowa (IA)

IRANIAN LANGUAGES
U of Maryland, Coll Park (MD)

ISLAMIC STUDIES
Boston Coll (MA)
Connecticut Coll (CT)
DePaul U (IL)
The Ohio State U (OH)
Sarah Lawrence Coll (NY)
The U of Texas at Austin (TX)
U of Washington (WA)
Washington U in St. Louis (MO)

ITALIAN
Boston Coll (MA)
California State U, Long Beach (CA)
Central Connecticut State U (CT)
Coll of Staten Island of the City U of New York (NY)
Coll of the Holy Cross (MA)
The Colorado Coll (CO)
Columbia U (NY)
Cornell U (NY)
Dartmouth Coll (NH)
DePaul U (IL)
Dominican U (IL)
Drew U (NJ)
Fairfield U (CT)
Fordham U (NY)
Gonzaga U (WA)
Haverford Coll (PA)
Hofstra U (NY)
Hunter Coll of the City U of New York (NY)
Indiana U Bloomington (IN)
Iona Coll (NY)
Ithaca Coll (NY)
Johns Hopkins U (MD)
Loyola U Chicago (IL)
Marist Coll (NY)
Middlebury Coll (VT)
Montclair State U (NJ)
Nazareth Coll of Rochester (NY)
New York U (NY)
Northwestern U (IL)
The Ohio State U (OH)
Pepperdine U, Malibu (CA)
Providence Coll (RI)
Queens Coll of the City U of New York (NY)
Saint Joseph's U (PA)
Saint Louis U (MO)
San Francisco State U (CA)
Sarah Lawrence Coll (NY)
Scripps Coll (CA)
Syracuse U (NY)
Temple U (PA)
Tulane U (LA)
U at Buffalo, the State U of New York (NY)
U of California, Davis (CA)
U of California, Los Angeles (CA)
U of Dallas (TX)
U of Houston (TX)
U of Maryland, Coll Park (MD)
U of Massachusetts Amherst (MA)
U of Massachusetts Boston (MA)
U of Michigan (MI)
U of Minnesota, Twin Cities Campus (MN)
U of New Hampshire (NH)
U of Notre Dame (IN)
U of Oregon (OR)
U of Pennsylvania (PA)
U of Pittsburgh (PA)
U of San Francisco (CA)
U of South Florida (FL)
The U of Tennessee (TN)
The U of Texas at Austin (TX)
U of Virginia (VA)
U of Washington (WA)
U of Wisconsin–Milwaukee (WI)
Vassar Coll (NY)
Washington U in St. Louis (MO)
Youngstown State U (OH)

ITALIAN STUDIES
Boston U (MA)
The Colorado Coll (CO)
Columbia U (NY)
Connecticut Coll (CT)
Dickinson Coll (PA)
Fordham U (NY)
John Cabot U (Italy)
Merrimack Coll (MA)
Miami U (OH)
The Ohio State U (OH)
Purdue U (IN)
Saint Joseph's U (PA)
Scripps Coll (CA)
Tulane U (LA)
U of California, Santa Cruz (CA)
U of Richmond (VA)
U of San Diego (CA)
U of Vermont (VT)
Wesleyan U (CT)
Wheaton Coll (MA)

JAPANESE
Beloit Coll (WI)
Boston U (MA)
California State U, Fullerton (CA)
California State U, Long Beach (CA)
California State U, Los Angeles (CA)
California State U, Monterey Bay (CA)
Calvin Coll (MI)
Carthage Coll (WI)
Central Washington U (WA)
Colgate U (NY)
Dartmouth Coll (NH)
Earlham Coll (IN)
Hofstra U (NY)
Linfield Coll (OR)
Macalester Coll (MN)
Michigan State U (MI)
Middlebury Coll (VT)
Murray State U (KY)
Occidental Coll (CA)
The Ohio State U (OH)
Portland State U (OR)
Purdue U (IN)
St. Olaf Coll (MN)
San Diego State U (CA)
San Francisco State U (CA)
San Jose State U (CA)
Sarah Lawrence Coll (NY)
Scripps Coll (CA)
Temple U (PA)
U of California, Davis (CA)
U of California, Irvine (CA)
U of California, Los Angeles (CA)
The U of Findlay (OH)
U of Hawaii at Manoa (HI)
U of Kentucky (KY)
U of Maryland, Coll Park (MD)
U of Massachusetts Amherst (MA)
U of Mount Union (OH)
The U of North Carolina at Charlotte (NC)
U of Notre Dame (IN)
U of Oregon (OR)
U of Pittsburgh (PA)
U of Puget Sound (WA)
U of Regina (SK, Canada)
U of San Francisco (CA)
U of Vermont (VT)
U of Washington (WA)
Vassar Coll (NY)
Washington State U (WA)
Washington U in St. Louis (MO)
Western Washington U (WA)
Williams Coll (MA)

JAPANESE STUDIES
Earlham Coll (IN)
Hofstra U (NY)
Linfield Coll (OR)
U of Washington (WA)
Willamette U (OR)

JAZZ/JAZZ STUDIES
Butler U (IN)
Capilano U (BC, Canada)
Central State U (OH)
Central Washington U (WA)
Columbia U (NY)
DePaul U (IL)
Drake U (IA)
Hofstra U (NY)
Ithaca Coll (NY)
Jacksonville U (FL)
Limestone Coll (SC)
Loyola U New Orleans (LA)
Michigan State U (MI)
Minnesota State U Moorhead (MN)
Northwestern U (IL)
The Ohio State U (OH)
Temple U (PA)
U of Maryland, Baltimore County (MD)
U of Michigan (MI)
U of North Carolina at Asheville (NC)
U of Northern Iowa (IA)
U of North Florida (FL)
U of Oregon (OR)
The U of Texas at Austin (TX)
U of Washington (WA)
Whitworth U (WA)
Youngstown State U (OH)

JEWISH/JUDAIC STUDIES
American U (DC)
California State U, Northridge (CA)
Clark U (MA)
Coll of Charleston (SC)
Dickinson Coll (PA)
Florida Atlantic U (FL)
Hofstra U (NY)
Hunter Coll of the City U of New York (NY)
Indiana U Bloomington (IN)
The Ohio State U (OH)
Portland State U (OR)
Purdue U (IN)
Queens Coll of the City U of New York (NY)
San Diego State U (CA)
San Francisco State U (CA)
Sarah Lawrence Coll (NY)
Scripps Coll (CA)
Syracuse U (NY)
Temple U (PA)
Tulane U (LA)
U at Buffalo, the State U of New York (NY)
U of California, Los Angeles (CA)
U of California, Santa Cruz (CA)
U of Chicago (IL)
U of Florida (FL)
U of Maryland, Coll Park (MD)
U of Massachusetts Amherst (MA)
U of Michigan (MI)
U of Minnesota, Twin Cities Campus (MN)
U of Oregon (OR)
U of Pennsylvania (PA)
The U of Texas at Austin (TX)
U of Washington (WA)
U of Wisconsin–Milwaukee (WI)
Vassar Coll (NY)
Washington U in St. Louis (MO)

JOURNALISM
Acad of Art U (CA)
Albright Coll (PA)
American U (DC)
Angelo State U (TX)
Appalachian State U (NC)
Arkansas Tech U (AR)
Auburn U (AL)
Averett U (VA)
Baruch Coll of the City U of New York (NY)
Baylor U (TX)
Bethel U (MN)
Boston U (MA)
Bowling Green State U (OH)
Bradley U (IL)
Butler U (IN)
California Lutheran U (CA)
California Polytechnic State U, San Luis Obispo (CA)
California State U, Chico (CA)
California State U, Fullerton (CA)
California State U, Long Beach (CA)
California State U, Northridge (CA)
Campbellsville U (KY)
Canisius Coll (NY)
Cedarville U (OH)
Central Connecticut State U (CT)
Central Michigan U (MI)
Central State U (OH)
Central Washington U (WA)
The Coll of St. Scholastica (MN)
Coll of the Ozarks (MO)
Colorado State U (CO)
Columbia Coll Chicago (IL)
Concordia U Chicago (IL)
Creighton U (NE)
DePaul U (IL)
Dominican U (IL)
Drake U (IA)
Drury U (MO)
Duquesne U (PA)
Eastern Illinois U (IL)
Eastern Washington U (WA)
Emerson Coll (MA)
Florida Ag and Mech U (FL)
Fordham U (NY)
Fort Lewis Coll (CO)
Franklin Pierce U (NH)
Georgia Coll & State U (GA)
Georgia Southern U (GA)
Georgia State U (GA)
Gonzaga U (WA)
Goshen Coll (IN)
Grand Valley State U (MI)
Harding U (AR)
High Point U (NC)
Hofstra U (NY)
Humboldt State U (CA)
Indiana U Bloomington (IN)
Indiana U of Pennsylvania (PA)
Indiana U–Purdue U Indianapolis (IN)
Indiana U Southeast (IN)
Iona Coll (NY)
Iowa State U of Science and Technology (IA)
Ithaca Coll (NY)
Kennesaw State U (GA)
Lebanese American U (Lebanon)
Liberty U (VA)
Lindenwood U (MO)
Louisiana Coll (LA)
Loyola Marymount U (CA)
Loyola U Chicago (IL)
Loyola U New Orleans (LA)
Lubbock Christian U (TX)
Madonna U (MI)
Marquette U (WI)
Marshall U (WV)
Marymount Manhattan Coll (NY)
Massachusetts Coll of Liberal Arts (MA)
Mercer U, Macon (GA)
Messiah Coll (PA)
Miami U (OH)
Miami U Hamilton (OH)
Michigan State U (MI)
Middle Tennessee State U (TN)
Montclair State U (NJ)
Murray State U (KY)
Muskingum U (OH)
New England Coll (NH)
New York U (NY)
Northeastern State U (OK)
Northern Illinois U (IL)
Northern Kentucky U (KY)
Northwestern U (IL)
The Ohio State U (OH)
Ohio U (OH)
Ohio Wesleyan U (OH)
Oklahoma Baptist U (OK)
Oklahoma Christian U (OK)
Pace U, Pleasantville Campus (NY)
Palm Beach Atlantic U (FL)
Pepperdine U, Malibu (CA)
Pfeiffer U (NC)
Point Loma Nazarene U (CA)
Purchase Coll, State U of New York (NY)
Radford U (VA)
Rider U (NJ)
Rochester Inst of Technology (NY)
St. Joseph's Coll, Long Island Campus (NY)
St. Joseph's Coll, New York (NY)
Samford U (AL)
San Diego State U (CA)
San Francisco State U (CA)
San Jose State U (CA)
Seattle U (WA)
Seton Hill U (PA)
Southeastern U (FL)
Southern Arkansas U–Magnolia (AR)
Southern Illinois U Carbondale (IL)
Spring Hill Coll (AL)
State U of New York at Plattsburgh (NY)
Syracuse U (NY)
Taylor U (IN)
Temple U (PA)
Texas Christian U (TX)
Texas Tech U (TX)
Tiffin U (OH)
Trevecca Nazarene U (TN)
U of Arkansas (AR)
U of Central Arkansas (AR)
U of Central Florida (FL)
The U of Findlay (OH)
U of Florida (FL)
U of Georgia (GA)
U of Hawaii at Manoa (HI)
U of Houston (TX)
U of Idaho (ID)
U of Kentucky (KY)
U of La Verne (CA)
U of Maine (ME)
U of Maryland, Coll Park (MD)
U of Massachusetts Amherst (MA)
U of Memphis (TN)
U of Minnesota, Duluth (MN)
U of Minnesota, Twin Cities Campus (MN)
U of Missouri (MO)
U of Nevada, Reno (NV)
U of New Mexico (NM)
The U of North Carolina at Chapel Hill (NC)
U of Northern Colorado (CO)
U of Oregon (OR)
U of Regina (SK, Canada)
U of Richmond (VA)
U of South Carolina (SC)
U of Southern Indiana (IN)
The U of Tennessee (TN)
The U of Texas at Austin (TX)
The U of Texas at El Paso (TX)
U of the Incarnate Word (TX)
U of Washington (WA)
U of West Georgia (GA)
U of Wisconsin–Eau Claire (WI)
U of Wisconsin–River Falls (WI)
U of Wyoming (WY)
Utah State U (UT)
Utica Coll (NY)
Wartburg Coll (IA)
Washington and Lee U (VA)
Washington State U (WA)
Washington U in St. Louis (MO)
Waynesburg U (PA)
Weber State U (UT)
Western Kentucky U (KY)
Western Washington U (WA)
Whitworth U (WA)
Youngstown State U (OH)

JOURNALISM RELATED
Benedictine U (IL)
Bennett Coll (NC)
Bowling Green State U (OH)
California State U, Long Beach (CA)
Fairfield U (CT)
Marymount Manhattan Coll (NY)
Missouri Baptist U (MO)
Oklahoma State U (OK)
Queens U of Charlotte (NC)
Syracuse U (NY)
Taylor U (IN)
U of California, Irvine (CA)
U of Nebraska–Lincoln (NE)
Western Washington U (WA)

JUVENILE CORRECTIONS
Prairie View A&M U (TX)

KEYBOARD INSTRUMENTS
Acadia U (NS, Canada)
Baldwin Wallace U (OH)
Boston U (MA)
Bowling Green State U (OH)
Campbellsville U (KY)
Carson-Newman U (TN)
The Catholic U of America (DC)
Central Washington U (WA)
Coll of the Ozarks (MO)
Dallas Baptist U (TX)
Drake U (IA)
Hardin-Simmons U (TX)
Ithaca Coll (NY)
Jacksonville U (FL)
Liberty U (VA)
Lipscomb U (TN)
Madonna U (MI)
New York U (NY)
Northwestern U (IL)
Ohio U (OH)
Ouachita Baptist U (AR)
Palm Beach Atlantic U (FL)
Point Loma Nazarene U (CA)
Rider U (NJ)

Samford U (AL)
Southeastern U (FL)
State U of New York at Fredonia (NY)
Stetson U (FL)
Syracuse U (NY)
Texas Christian U (TX)
The U of Tulsa (OK)
U of Washington (WA)
Valparaiso U (IN)
Weber State U (UT)
Willamette U (OR)
Youngstown State U (OH)

KINDERGARTEN/PRESCHOOL EDUCATION
Baylor U (TX)
Bowling Green State U (OH)
Bucknell U (PA)
California Polytechnic State U, San Luis Obispo (CA)
California U of Pennsylvania (PA)
Carson-Newman U (TN)
Central Connecticut State U (CT)
East Carolina U (NC)
Eastern Illinois U (IL)
Elizabeth City State U (NC)
Georgia State U (GA)
Hunter Coll of the City U of New York (NY)
Inter American U of Puerto Rico, Aguadilla Campus (PR)
Inter American U of Puerto Rico, San Germán Campus (PR)
Kean U (NJ)
Lees-McRae Coll (NC)
Lesley U (MA)
Mansfield U of Pennsylvania (PA)
Marshall U (WV)
Michigan State U (MI)
New Jersey City U (NJ)
Northern Kentucky U (KY)
Northwestern Oklahoma State U (OK)
Ohio Wesleyan U (OH)
Oklahoma Baptist U (OK)
Oklahoma Christian U (OK)
Piedmont Coll (GA)
State U of New York at Fredonia (NY)
Université de Sherbrooke (QC, Canada)
U of Arkansas (AR)
U of Maine at Farmington (ME)
U of Maryland, Coll Park (MD)
U of Minnesota, Duluth (MN)
U of Minnesota, Twin Cities Campus (MN)
The U of North Carolina at Charlotte (NC)
The U of North Carolina at Pembroke (NC)
U of Northern Iowa (IA)
U of Providence (MT)
U of Regina (SK, Canada)
The U of Toledo (OH)
Utah State U (UT)
Wartburg Coll (IA)
Widener U (PA)

KINESIOLOGY AND EXERCISE SCIENCE
Acadia U (NS, Canada)
Adams State U (CO)
Adelphi U (NY)
Albion Coll (MI)
Angelo State U (TX)
Appalachian State U (NC)
Auburn U at Montgomery (AL)
Aurora U (IL)
Avila U (MO)
Baker U (KS)
Barton Coll (NC)
Baylor U (TX)
Bellarmine U (KY)
Bethel U (MN)
Brenau U (GA)
Bridgewater State U (MA)
California Lutheran U (CA)
California State U, Chico (CA)
California State U, Long Beach (CA)
California State U, Los Angeles (CA)
California State U, Northridge (CA)
California State U, San Marcos (CA)
California U of Pennsylvania (PA)
Calvin Coll (MI)
Carson-Newman U (TN)
Carthage Coll (WI)
Cedarville U (OH)
Central Connecticut State U (CT)
Central Michigan U (MI)
Central State U (OH)
Central Washington U (WA)
Coastal Carolina U (SC)
The Coll at Brockport, State U of New York (NY)
The Coll of Idaho (ID)
Coll of Saint Mary (NE)
The Coll of William and Mary (VA)
Colorado State U (CO)
Colorado State U–Pueblo (CO)
Concordia U Chicago (IL)
Cornell Coll (IA)
Dakota State U (SD)
Dean Coll (MA)
DePaul U (IL)
Eastern Illinois U (IL)
Eastern U (PA)
Eastern Washington U (WA)
East Stroudsburg U of Pennsylvania (PA)
East Texas Baptist U (TX)
Elizabeth City State U (NC)
Emmanuel Coll (GA)
Endicott Coll (MA)
Fitchburg State U (MA)
Florida Atlantic U (FL)
George Mason U (VA)
Georgetown Coll (KY)
Georgia Coll & State U (GA)
Georgia Southern U (GA)
Gonzaga U (WA)
Goshen Coll (IN)
Grand Valley State U (MI)
Greenville U (IL)
Grove City Coll (PA)
Hamline U (MN)
Hanover Coll (IN)
Harding U (AR)
Hardin-Simmons U (TX)
High Point U (NC)
Hillsdale Coll (MI)
Hiram Coll (OH)
Humboldt State U (CA)
Immaculata U (PA)
Indiana State U (IN)
Indiana U Bloomington (IN)
Indiana U–Purdue U Indianapolis (IN)
Iowa State U of Science and Technology (IA)
Ithaca Coll (NY)
Jacksonville U (FL)
Kansas Wesleyan U (KS)
Kennesaw State U (GA)
King's Coll (PA)
King U (TN)
Kuyper Coll (MI)
LaGrange Coll (GA)
Lamar U (TX)
Lasell Coll (MA)
La Sierra U (CA)
Lebanon Valley Coll (PA)
Lee U (TN)
LeTourneau U (TX)
Liberty U (VA)
Life U (GA)
Lindenwood U (MO)
Linfield Coll (OR)
Lipscomb U (TN)
Loras Coll (IA)
Louisiana Coll (LA)
Madonna U (MI)
Manchester U (IN)
Marian U (IN)
Marshall U (WV)
Maryville U of Saint Louis (MO)
McDaniel Coll (MD)
McNeese State U (LA)
Mercy Coll (NY)
Miami U (OH)
Michigan State U (MI)
Middle Tennessee State U (TN)
Minnesota State U Moorhead (MN)
Missouri Baptist U (MO)
Montclair State U (NJ)
Mount Marty Coll (SD)
Murray State U (KY)
Northeastern State U (OK)
Occidental Coll (CA)
Ohio Dominican U (OH)
The Ohio State U (OH)
Oklahoma Baptist U (OK)
Oklahoma State U (OK)
Ottawa U (KS)
Ouachita Baptist U (AR)
Pacific Lutheran U (WA)
Palm Beach Atlantic U (FL)
Pepperdine U, Malibu (CA)
Piedmont Coll (GA)
Point U (GA)
Prairie View A&M U (TX)
Purdue U (IN)
Queens Coll of the City U of New York (NY)
Redeemer U Coll (ON, Canada)
Regis U (CO)
Rice U (TX)
Roanoke Coll (VA)
Rockford U (IL)
Rocky Mountain Coll (MT)
Saginaw Valley State U (MI)
Saint Louis U (MO)
Saint Martin's U (WA)
St. Mary's U (TX)
St. Olaf Coll (MN)
Salisbury U (MD)
San Diego State U (CA)
San Francisco State U (CA)
Seattle U (WA)
Seton Hill U (PA)
Sonoma State U (CA)
Southeastern Louisiana U (LA)
Southeastern U (FL)
Southern Arkansas U–Magnolia (AR)
Southern Illinois U Carbondale (IL)
Southern Illinois U Edwardsville (IL)
Southwest Baptist U (MO)
Southwestern U (TX)
State U of New York at Fredonia (NY)
Stockton U (NJ)
Syracuse U (NY)
Tabor Coll (KS)
Taylor U (IN)
Temple U (PA)
Texas A&M Intl U (TX)
Texas Lutheran U (TX)
Texas Tech U (TX)
Texas Woman's U (TX)
Towson U (MD)
Trinity Christian Coll (IL)
Truman State U (MO)
Union Coll (KY)
Université de Sherbrooke (QC, Canada)
U of Central Arkansas (AR)
U of Dayton (OH)
U of Georgia (GA)
U of Hawaii at Manoa (HI)
U of Houston (TX)
U of Houston–Clear Lake (TX)
U of Idaho (ID)
U of Illinois at Springfield (IL)
U of La Verne (CA)
U of Mary Hardin-Baylor (TX)
U of Maryland, Coll Park (MD)
U of Memphis (TN)
U of Michigan (MI)
U of Minnesota, Duluth (MN)
U of Mount Union (OH)
U of Nevada, Las Vegas (NV)
U of New Hampshire (NH)
The U of North Carolina at Greensboro (NC)
U of North Dakota (ND)
U of Northern Colorado (CO)
U of Northwestern–St. Paul (MN)
U of Pittsburgh at Bradford (PA)
U of Puget Sound (WA)
U of Regina (SK, Canada)
U of Saint Mary (KS)
U of San Francisco (CA)
U of Sioux Falls (SD)
U of South Carolina (SC)
U of South Carolina Aiken (SC)
U of Southern Indiana (IN)
The U of Tennessee (TN)
The U of Texas at Austin (TX)
The U of Texas of the Permian Basin (TX)
The U of Texas Rio Grande Valley (TX)
U of the Incarnate Word (TX)
The U of Toledo (OH)
The U of Tulsa (OK)
U of Vermont (VT)
U of Virginia (VA)
The U of West Alabama (AL)
U of Wisconsin–Eau Claire (WI)
U of Wisconsin–La Crosse (WI)
U of Wisconsin–Milwaukee (WI)
U of Wyoming (WY)
Valparaiso U (IN)
Vanguard U of Southern California (CA)
Wartburg Coll (IA)
Washington State U (WA)
Waynesburg U (PA)
Western Illinois U (IL)
Western Kentucky U (KY)
Western State Colorado U (CO)
Western Washington U (WA)
Westmont Coll (CA)
Whittier Coll (CA)
Whitworth U (WA)
Willamette U (OR)
Winthrop U (SC)
Wright State U–Lake Campus (OH)
Youngstown State U (OH)

KINESIOTHERAPY
Boston U (MA)
Bridgewater State U (MA)
California State U, Long Beach (CA)

KNOWLEDGE MANAGEMENT
Framingham State U (MA)
Saint Joseph's U (PA)
Syracuse U (NY)

KOREAN
The Ohio State U (OH)
U of California, Irvine (CA)
U of California, Los Angeles (CA)
U of Hawaii at Manoa (HI)
U of Washington (WA)

KOREAN STUDIES
U of Washington (WA)

LABOR AND INDUSTRIAL RELATIONS
Baruch Coll of the City U of New York (NY)
Bowling Green State U (OH)
Clarion U of Pennsylvania (PA)
Cornell U (NY)
New York U (NY)
Rider U (NJ)
San Francisco State U (CA)
State U of New York at Fredonia (NY)
U of Massachusetts Boston (MA)
U of Minnesota, Twin Cities Campus (MN)

LABOR STUDIES
Hofstra U (NY)
Indiana U Bloomington (IN)
Indiana U Northwest (IN)
Indiana U–Purdue U Indianapolis (IN)
Indiana U South Bend (IN)
Queens Coll of the City U of New York (NY)

LANDSCAPE ARCHITECTURE
Acad of Art U (CA)
American U of Beirut (Lebanon)
California Polytechnic State U, San Luis Obispo (CA)
Colorado State U (CO)
Cornell U (NY)
Delaware Valley U (PA)
Iowa State U of Science and Technology (IA)
Louisiana State U and A&M Coll (LA)
Michigan State U (MI)
The Ohio State U (OH)
Oklahoma State U (OK)
Purdue U (IN)
State U of New York Coll of Environmental Science and Forestry (NY)
Temple U (PA)
Texas Tech U (TX)
U of Arkansas (AR)
U of California, Davis (CA)
U of Florida (FL)
U of Georgia (GA)
U of Idaho (ID)
U of Kentucky (KY)
U of Maryland, Coll Park (MD)
U of Massachusetts Amherst (MA)
U of Nebraska–Lincoln (NE)
U of Nevada, Las Vegas (NV)
U of Oregon (OR)
U of Washington (WA)
Utah State U (UT)
Virginia Polytechnic Inst and State U (VA)
Washington State U (WA)

LANDSCAPING AND GROUNDSKEEPING
Delaware Valley U (PA)
Oklahoma State U (OK)
U of Nebraska–Lincoln (NE)
Washington State U (WA)

LAND USE PLANNING AND MANAGEMENT
California State U, Bakersfield (CA)
Central Michigan U (MI)

LANGUAGE INTERPRETATION AND TRANSLATION
Lebanese American U (Lebanon)
The U of Texas Rio Grande Valley (TX)

LASER AND OPTICAL ENGINEERING
Stonehill Coll (MA)
U of Central Florida (FL)

LATIN
Acadia U (NS, Canada)
Austin Coll (TX)
Baylor U (TX)
Boston U (MA)
Bowling Green State U (OH)
Canisius Coll (NY)
The Catholic U of America (DC)
Colgate U (NY)
Dartmouth Coll (NH)
Duquesne U (PA)
Furman U (SC)
Hampden-Sydney Coll (VA)
Haverford Coll (PA)
Hillsdale Coll (MI)
Hofstra U (NY)
Hunter Coll of the City U of New York (NY)
Knox Coll (IL)
Loyola U Chicago (IL)
Loyola U New Orleans (LA)
Mercer U, Macon (GA)
Miami U Hamilton (OH)
Montclair State U (NJ)
New York U (NY)
Queens Coll of the City U of New York (NY)
Randolph-Macon Coll (VA)
Rice U (TX)
Rockford U (IL)
St. Olaf Coll (MN)
Samford U (AL)
Sarah Lawrence Coll (NY)
Southwestern U (TX)
Tulane U (LA)
U of California, Los Angeles (CA)
U of Michigan (MI)
U of New Hampshire (NH)
U of Richmond (VA)
U of St. Thomas (MN)
The U of Texas at Austin (TX)
The U of the South (TN)
U of Vermont (VT)
U of Washington (WA)
Wabash Coll (IN)
Washington U in St. Louis (MO)
Wright State U–Lake Campus (OH)

LATIN AMERICAN AND CARIBBEAN STUDIES
Coll of Charleston (SC)
Linfield Coll (OR)
Rollins Coll (FL)
Union Coll (NY)
U of Georgia (GA)
U of Michigan (MI)
U of Vermont (VT)
U of Wisconsin–Milwaukee (WI)

LATIN AMERICAN STUDIES
Adelphi U (NY)
Albion Coll (MI)
Albright Coll (PA)
Alverno Coll (WI)
American U (DC)
Assumption Coll (MA)
Baylor U (TX)

Boston U (MA)
Bowling Green State U (OH)
Brandeis U (MA)
Bucknell U (PA)
California State U, Fullerton (CA)
California State U, Los Angeles (CA)
California State U, Northridge (CA)
Canisius Coll (NY)
Central Michigan U (MI)
Colgate U (NY)
Coll of the Holy Cross (MA)
The Coll of William and Mary (VA)
Columbia U (NY)
Connecticut Coll (CT)
Cornell Coll (IA)
Dartmouth Coll (NH)
Davidson Coll (NC)
DePaul U (IL)
Dickinson Coll (PA)
Earlham Coll (IN)
Fordham U (NY)
George Mason U (VA)
Gonzaga U (WA)
Haverford Coll (PA)
Hofstra U (NY)
Hood Coll (MD)
Hunter Coll of the City U of New York (NY)
Johns Hopkins U (MD)
Knox Coll (IL)
Lake Forest Coll (IL)
Macalester Coll (MN)
Marquette U (WI)
Miami U (OH)
Middlebury Coll (VT)
Millsaps Coll (MS)
New York U (NY)
Occidental Coll (CA)
Ohio U (OH)
Ohio Wesleyan U (OH)
Pace U (NY)
Pepperdine U, Malibu (CA)
Portland State U (OR)
Purchase Coll, State U of New York (NY)
Queens Coll of the City U of New York (NY)
Rhode Island Coll (RI)
Rhodes Coll (TN)
Rice U (TX)
Saint Louis U (MO)
St. Olaf Coll (MN)
Samford U (AL)
San Diego State U (CA)
Sarah Lawrence Coll (NY)
Scripps Coll (CA)
Southwestern U (TX)
State U of New York at Plattsburgh (NY)
Syracuse U (NY)
Temple U (PA)
Tulane U (LA)
U of California, Los Angeles (CA)
U of California, Riverside (CA)
U of Central Florida (FL)
U of Chicago (IL)
U of Idaho (ID)
U of Kentucky (KY)
U of Louisville (KY)
U of Minnesota, Duluth (MN)
U of Minnesota, Morris (MN)
U of Nebraska–Lincoln (NE)
U of Nevada, Las Vegas (NV)
U of New Mexico (NM)
The U of North Carolina at Chapel Hill (NC)
The U of North Carolina at Charlotte (NC)
U of Oregon (OR)
U of Pennsylvania (PA)
U of Richmond (VA)
U of San Francisco (CA)
U of South Carolina (SC)
The U of Texas at Austin (TX)
U of Washington (WA)
U of Wisconsin–Eau Claire (WI)
Valparaiso U (IN)
Vassar Coll (NY)
Washington U in St. Louis (MO)
Wesleyan U (CT)
Western Washington U (WA)
Whittier Coll (CA)
Willamette U (OR)

LATIN TEACHER EDUCATION
Boston U (MA)
Duquesne U (PA)
Miami U (OH)
Miami U Hamilton (OH)
Ohio Wesleyan U (OH)
Queens Coll of the City U of New York (NY)
Valparaiso U (IN)

LAY MINISTRY
Bethel U (MN)
Liberty U (VA)
Point Loma Nazarene U (CA)
Saint Mary's U of Minnesota (MN)
Trevecca Nazarene U (TN)
Trinity Christian Coll (IL)
U of Saint Francis (IN)
U of St. Thomas (MN)

LEARNING SCIENCES
Purdue U (IN)

LEGAL ASSISTANT/ PARALEGAL
Boston U (MA)
Brandman U (CA)
Capilano U (BC, Canada)
Champlain Coll (VT)
Clarion U of Pennsylvania (PA)
Coll of Saint Mary (NE)
Davenport U, Grand Rapids (MI)
Grand Valley State U (MI)
Hamline U (MN)
Idaho State U (ID)
Indiana U–Purdue U Indianapolis (IN)
Liberty U (VA)
Loyola U Chicago (IL)
Madonna U (MI)
Maryville U of Saint Louis (MO)
Mercy Coll (NY)
Minnesota State U Moorhead (MN)
Mount St. Joseph U (OH)
National U (CA)
Regent U (VA)
Southern Illinois U Carbondale (IL)
Sullivan U (KY)
Texas Woman's U (TX)
Tiffin U (OH)
Tulane U (LA)
U of Central Florida (FL)
U of Houston–Clear Lake (TX)
U of La Verne (CA)
U of Providence (MT)
Western Kentucky U (KY)

LEGAL PROFESSIONS AND STUDIES RELATED
Berkeley Coll–New York City Campus (NY)
Berkeley Coll–Woodland Park Campus (NJ)
Brenau U (GA)
California U of Pennsylvania (PA)
Georgia Southern U (GA)
Maryville U of Saint Louis (MO)
Montclair State U (NJ)
New Jersey Inst of Technology (NJ)
Syracuse U (NY)
Temple U (PA)
Tulane U (LA)
U of Nebraska–Lincoln (NE)
U of Pennsylvania (PA)
The U of Tulsa (OK)
U of Wisconsin–Superior (WI)

LEGAL STUDIES
Adams State U (CO)
American Public U System (WV)
American U (DC)
Auburn U (AL)
Bethany Lutheran Coll (MN)
Blackburn Coll (IL)
Brandman U (CA)
Bridgewater State U (MA)
Central Michigan U (MI)
Culver-Stockton Coll (MO)
Dickinson Coll (PA)
Dominican U (IL)
Hamline U (MN)
Harding U (AR)
Lasell Coll (MA)
Lipscomb U (TN)
Mercy Coll (NY)
Mount St. Joseph U (OH)
National Paralegal Coll (AZ)
Nazareth Coll of Rochester (NY)
Northeastern State U (OK)
Northwestern U (IL)
St. John Fisher Coll (NY)
Saint Joseph's U (PA)
Samford U (AL)
Scripps Coll (CA)
Southeastern U (FL)
State U of New York at Fredonia (NY)
Université de Sherbrooke (QC, Canada)
U of California, Santa Cruz (CA)
U of Central Florida (FL)
U of Detroit Mercy (MI)
U of Illinois at Springfield (IL)
U of La Verne (CA)
U of Maryland U Coll (MD)
U of Massachusetts Amherst (MA)
U of New Haven (CT)
U of Pittsburgh (PA)
U of Washington (WA)
U of Washington, Tacoma (WA)

LIBERAL ARTS AND SCIENCES AND HUMANITIES RELATED
Antioch Coll, Yellow Springs (OH)
Auburn U (AL)
Butler U (IN)
California Polytechnic State U, San Luis Obispo (CA)
Coll of Charleston (SC)
Coll of Saint Mary (NE)
The Colorado Coll (CO)
Duquesne U (PA)
Eastern U (PA)
Fairfield U (CT)
Florida Atlantic U (FL)
George Mason U (VA)
Georgia Coll & State U (GA)
Graceland U (IA)
Hofstra U (NY)
Indiana U Bloomington (IN)
Indiana U East (IN)
Indiana U Kokomo (IN)
Indiana U Northwest (IN)
Indiana U–Purdue U Indianapolis (IN)
Indiana U South Bend (IN)
Indiana U Southeast (IN)
Kansas Wesleyan U (KS)
La Sierra U (CA)
Lewis & Clark Coll (OR)
Marymount California U (CA)
Missouri Baptist U (MO)
Molloy Coll (NY)
Montclair State U (NJ)
New York U (NY)
North Carolina State U (NC)
Ohio U (OH)
Pepperdine U, Malibu (CA)
Saint Anselm Coll (NH)
Seattle U (WA)
Tulane U (LA)
U of California, Los Angeles (CA)
U of Maine at Farmington (ME)
U of Maryland U Coll (MD)
U of Massachusetts Amherst (MA)
U of Michigan–Dearborn (MI)
U of Wisconsin–Milwaukee (WI)
Vassar Coll (NY)
Western Illinois U (IL)
West Virginia U Inst of Technology (WV)
Worcester Polytechnic Inst (MA)

LIBERAL ARTS AND SCIENCES/LIBERAL STUDIES
Adams State U (CO)
Albion Coll (MI)
Alverno Coll (WI)
American U (DC)
Appalachian State U (NC)
Aurora U (IL)
Averett U (VA)
Barton Coll (NC)
Baruch Coll of the City U of New York (NY)
Bellarmine U (KY)
Bentley U (MA)
Bethany Lutheran Coll (MN)
Boston U (MA)
Bowling Green State U (OH)
Bradley U (IL)
Brandman U (CA)
Brenau U (GA)
Bridgewater Coll (VA)
California Lutheran U (CA)
California Polytechnic State U, San Luis Obispo (CA)
California State U, Bakersfield (CA)
California State U, Chico (CA)
California State U, Fullerton (CA)
California State U, Long Beach (CA)
California State U, Los Angeles (CA)
California State U, Monterey Bay (CA)
California State U, Northridge (CA)
California State U, San Bernardino (CA)
California State U, San Marcos (CA)
California U of Pennsylvania (PA)
Canisius Coll (NY)
Capilano U (BC, Canada)
Carnegie Mellon U (PA)
Carson-Newman U (TN)
The Catholic U of America (DC)
Cedarville U (OH)
Central Michigan U (MI)
Champlain Coll (VT)
Christian Brothers U (TN)
Clarkson U (NY)
Coastal Carolina U (SC)
The Coll at Brockport, State U of New York (NY)
The Coll of Saint Rose (NY)
The Coll of St. Scholastica (MN)
Colorado State U (CO)
Colorado State U–Pueblo (CO)
Concordia U Irvine (CA)
Cornell Coll (IA)
Culver-Stockton Coll (MO)
Curry Coll (MA)
Dakota State U (SD)
Dean Coll (MA)
Duquesne U (PA)
East Carolina U (NC)
Eastern Illinois U (IL)
Eastern Mennonite U (VA)
East Tennessee State U (TN)
Emmanuel Coll (MA)
Endicott Coll (MA)
The Evergreen State Coll (WA)
Excelsior Coll (NY)
Fayetteville State U (NC)
Fitchburg State U (MA)
Florida Atlantic U (FL)
Florida Coll (FL)
Framingham State U (MA)
Franklin Pierce U (NH)
George Mason U (VA)
Grand Valley State U (MI)
Granite State Coll (NH)
Greenville U (IL)
Harvard U (MA)
Hofstra U (NY)
Humboldt State U (CA)
Illinois Coll (IL)
Immaculata U (PA)
Indiana State U (IN)
Indiana U Bloomington (IN)
Indiana U of Pennsylvania (PA)
Indiana U Southeast (IN)
Iona Coll (NY)
Iowa State U of Science and Technology (IA)
Ithaca Coll (NY)
Jacksonville U (FL)
Juniata Coll (PA)
Knox Coll (IL)
La Sierra U (CA)
Lee U (TN)
Lesley U (MA)
Liberty U (VA)
Limestone Coll (SC)
Lock Haven U of Pennsylvania (PA)
Loras Coll (IA)
Louisiana State U and A&M Coll (LA)
Loyola Marymount U (CA)
Loyola U Chicago (IL)
Manchester U (IN)
Manhattan Coll (NY)
Manhattanville Coll (NY)
Manor Coll (PA)
Mansfield U of Pennsylvania (PA)
Maria Coll (NY)
Marymount California U (CA)
Marymount Manhattan Coll (NY)
Marymount U (VA)
Maryville U of Saint Louis (MO)
Massachusetts Coll of Liberal Arts (MA)
Massachusetts Inst of Technology (MA)
McNeese State U (LA)
Mercer U, Macon (GA)
Mercy Coll (NY)
Merrimack Coll (MA)
Miami U (OH)
Middlebury Coll (VT)
Middle Tennessee State U (TN)
Mount Marty Coll (SD)
Mount St. Joseph U (OH)
Murray State U (KY)
New York U (NY)
North Carolina State U (NC)
Northern Illinois U (IL)
Northern Kentucky U (KY)
Northern State U (SD)
Northwest Christian U (OR)
Northwestern U (IL)
Northwest Missouri State U (MO)
Oklahoma Christian U (OK)
Oklahoma State U (OK)
Pace U (NY)
Pace U, Pleasantville Campus (NY)
Pepperdine U, Malibu (CA)
Point Loma Nazarene U (CA)
Portland State U (OR)
Providence Coll (RI)
Purchase Coll, State U of New York (NY)
Purdue U Northwest (IN)
Queens Coll of the City U of New York (NY)
Regis U (CO)
Reinhardt U (GA)
Rhode Island Coll (RI)
Rider U (NJ)
Sacred Heart U (CT)
The Sage Colls (NY)
St. John Fisher Coll (NY)
St. John's Coll (MD)
St. John's Coll (NM)
St. Joseph's Coll, Long Island Campus (NY)
St. Joseph's Coll, New York (NY)
Saint Joseph's U (PA)
St. Olaf Coll (MN)
Saint Vincent Coll (PA)
Salisbury U (MD)
Salve Regina U (RI)
San Diego State U (CA)
San Francisco State U (CA)
San Jose State U (CA)
Sarah Lawrence Coll (NY)
Seattle U (WA)
Skidmore Coll (NY)
Soka U of America (CA)
Sonoma State U (CA)
Southern Illinois U Carbondale (IL)
Southern Illinois U Edwardsville (IL)
Spring Hill Coll (AL)
State U of New York at Fredonia (NY)
Stevens Inst of Technology (NJ)
Stockton U (NJ)
Sweet Briar Coll (VA)
Syracuse U (NY)
Temple U (PA)
Texas A&M U–Central Texas (TX)
Texas Tech U (TX)
Tulane U (LA)
Tyndale U Coll & Sem (ON, Canada)
Union Coll (KY)
Union Coll (NY)
U of California, Riverside (CA)
U of Detroit Mercy (MI)
U of Hawaii at Manoa (HI)
U of Houston (TX)
U of Illinois at Springfield (IL)
U of Kentucky (KY)
U of La Verne (CA)
U of Louisville (KY)
U of Maine (ME)
U of Maine at Farmington (ME)
U of Maine at Presque Isle (ME)
U of Massachusetts Dartmouth (MA)
U of Massachusetts Lowell (MA)
U of Memphis (TN)
U of Michigan–Dearborn (MI)
U of Nebraska–Lincoln (NE)
U of Nevada, Las Vegas (NV)
U of New Haven (CT)
U of New Mexico (NM)
U of North Carolina at Asheville (NC)
The U of North Carolina at Chapel Hill (NC)

The U of North Carolina at Charlotte (NC)
The U of North Carolina at Greensboro (NC)
U of Northern Iowa (IA)
U of Notre Dame (IN)
U of Pennsylvania (PA)
U of Pittsburgh at Bradford (PA)
U of Regina (SK, Canada)
U of Saint Francis (IN)
U of Saint Mary (KS)
U of St. Thomas (TX)
U of San Diego (CA)
U of South Carolina (SC)
U of South Carolina Aiken (SC)
U of South Dakota (SD)
U of Southern Indiana (IN)
The U of Tampa (FL)
The U of Texas at Austin (TX)
U of the Incarnate Word (TX)
The U of Toledo (OH)
The U of Tulsa (OK)
U of Vermont (VT)
U of Virginia (VA)
U of Wisconsin–Eau Claire (WI)
Utah State U (UT)
Utica Coll (NY)
Washington State U (WA)
Washington U in St. Louis (MO)
Weber State U (UT)
West Chester U of Pennsylvania (PA)
Western Connecticut State U (CT)
Western Illinois U (IL)
Westmont Coll (CA)
Whittier Coll (CA)
Wilkes U (PA)
Willamette U (OR)
William Jewell Coll (MO)

LIBRARY SCIENCE RELATED
U of Providence (MT)

LINGUISTIC AND COMPARATIVE LANGUAGE STUDIES RELATED
Appalachian State U (NC)
Boston U (MA)
U of California, Los Angeles (CA)
U of Kentucky (KY)

LINGUISTICS
Baylor U (TX)
Bethel U (MN)
Boston Coll (MA)
Boston U (MA)
Brandeis U (MA)
Bucknell U (PA)
California State U, Fullerton (CA)
California State U, Monterey Bay (CA)
California State U, Northridge (CA)
Calvin Coll (MI)
Carnegie Mellon U (PA)
Carson-Newman U (TN)
Cedarville U (OH)
The Coll of William and Mary (VA)
Columbia U (NY)
Cornell U (NY)
Dartmouth Coll (NH)
Earlham Coll (IN)
Florida Atlantic U (FL)
Georgia State U (GA)
Gordon Coll (MA)
Harvard U (MA)
Hofstra U (NY)
Indiana U Bloomington (IN)
Iowa State U of Science and Technology (IA)
Lawrence U (WI)
Macalester Coll (MN)
Massachusetts Inst of Technology (MA)
Miami U (OH)
Miami U Hamilton (OH)
Michigan State U (MI)
Montclair State U (NJ)
New York U (NY)
Northwestern U (IL)
The Ohio State U (OH)
Ohio U (OH)
Pitzer Coll (CA)
Portland State U (OR)
Purdue U (IN)
Queens Coll of the City U of New York (NY)
Regis U (CO)
Rice U (TX)
Saint Joseph's U (PA)
San Diego State U (CA)
San Jose State U (CA)
Scripps Coll (CA)
Southern Illinois U Carbondale (IL)
Syracuse U (NY)
Truman State U (MO)
Tulane U (LA)
U at Buffalo, the State U of New York (NY)
U of California, Davis (CA)
U of California, Irvine (CA)
U of California, Los Angeles (CA)
U of California, Riverside (CA)
U of California, Santa Cruz (CA)
U of Chicago (IL)
U of Florida (FL)
U of Georgia (GA)
U of Houston (TX)
U of Kentucky (KY)
U of Maryland, Coll Park (MD)
U of Massachusetts Amherst (MA)
U of Michigan (MI)
U of Minnesota, Duluth (MN)
U of Minnesota, Twin Cities Campus (MN)
U of Missouri (MO)
U of Nevada, Las Vegas (NV)
U of New Hampshire (NH)
U of New Mexico (NM)
The U of North Carolina at Chapel Hill (NC)
U of Oregon (OR)
U of Pennsylvania (PA)
U of Pittsburgh (PA)
U of Regina (SK, Canada)
The U of Texas at Austin (TX)
The U of Texas at El Paso (TX)
U of Vermont (VT)
U of Washington (WA)
U of Wisconsin–Milwaukee (WI)
Washington State U (WA)
Washington U in St. Louis (MO)
Western Washington U (WA)

LITERATURE
American U (DC)
Antioch Coll, Yellow Springs (OH)
Bradley U (IL)
Bryant U (RI)
Calvin Coll (MI)
Carson-Newman U (TN)
Excelsior Coll (NY)
Florida Southern Coll (FL)
Grove City Coll (PA)
Hamilton Coll (NY)
Linfield Coll (OR)
Lipscomb U (TN)
Loyola U New Orleans (LA)
Lubbock Christian U (TX)
Marymount Manhattan Coll (NY)
Massachusetts Coll of Liberal Arts (MA)
New Coll of Florida (FL)
New York U (NY)
Occidental Coll (CA)
Saint Mary's U of Minnesota (MN)
Sarah Lawrence Coll (NY)
Stevens Inst of Technology (NJ)
The U of Findlay (OH)
Washington U in St. Louis (MO)
Whitworth U (WA)

LITERATURE RELATED
Marymount Manhattan Coll (NY)

LIVESTOCK MANAGEMENT
The Ohio State U (OH)

LOGIC
Carnegie Mellon U (PA)
U of Pennsylvania (PA)

LOGISTICS, MATERIALS, AND SUPPLY CHAIN MANAGEMENT
American Public U System (WV)
Appalachian State U (NC)
Auburn U (AL)
Baylor U (TX)
Bowling Green State U (OH)
Bradley U (IL)
Bryant U (RI)
Central Michigan U (MI)
Central Washington U (WA)
Clarkson U (NY)
Coll of Charleston (SC)
DEREE - The American Coll of Greece (Greece)
Duquesne U (PA)
Embry-Riddle Aeronautical U–Worldwide (FL)
Florida Ag and Mech U (FL)
Georgia Highlands Coll (GA)
Georgia Southern U (GA)
Grand Valley State U (MI)
Hofstra U (NY)
Kennesaw State U (GA)
Michigan State U (MI)
Minnesota State U Moorhead (MN)
Murray State U (KY)
Northeastern State U (OK)
Northwood U, Michigan Campus (MI)
The Ohio State U (OH)
Portland State U (OR)
Rider U (NJ)
Southeastern Louisiana U (LA)
Syracuse U (NY)
Temple U (PA)
Texas Christian U (TX)
Texas Tech U (TX)
Tiffin U (OH)
Truckee Meadows Comm Coll (NV)
U of Arkansas (AR)
The U of Findlay (OH)
U of Maryland, Coll Park (MD)
U of Massachusetts Amherst (MA)
U of Memphis (TN)
U of Michigan–Dearborn (MI)
U of Nebraska–Lincoln (NE)
U of Northern Iowa (IA)
U of Pittsburgh (PA)
U of Puerto Rico–Bayamón (PR)
The U of Tennessee (TN)
The U of Texas at Austin (TX)
The U of Texas Rio Grande Valley (TX)
The U of Toledo (OH)
U of Washington (WA)
U of Wisconsin–Superior (WI)
Valparaiso U (IN)
Weber State U (UT)
Western Illinois U (IL)
Wilkes U (PA)
Wright State U–Lake Campus (OH)

LONG TERM CARE ADMINISTRATION
Bellarmine U (KY)
Bowling Green State U (OH)
Maryville U of Saint Louis (MO)
Weber State U (UT)

MACHINE TOOL TECHNOLOGY
Idaho State U (ID)

MAGNETIC RESONANCE IMAGING (MRI) TECHNOLOGY
Allen Coll (IA)
Saint Louis U (MO)
Weber State U (UT)

MANAGEMENT INFORMATION SYSTEMS
Adams State U (CO)
Angelo State U (TX)
Appalachian State U (NC)
Auburn U (AL)
Avila U (MO)
Babson Coll (MA)
Baruch Coll of the City U of New York (NY)
Baylor U (TX)
Boston Coll (MA)
Bowling Green State U (OH)
Bradley U (IL)
Bridgewater Coll (VA)
Bridgewater State U (MA)
Bryant U (RI)
Butler U (IN)
California State U, Long Beach (CA)
Canisius Coll (NY)
Carson-Newman U (TN)
Cedarville U (OH)
Central Connecticut State U (CT)
Central Michigan U (MI)
Central Washington U (WA)
Clarkson U (NY)
Columbia Coll (MO)
Concordia U Chicago (IL)
Dallas Baptist U (TX)
Delta State U (MS)
DePaul U (IL)
DEREE - The American Coll of Greece (Greece)
East Carolina U (NC)
Eastern Washington U (WA)
Fairfield U (CT)
Fayetteville State U (NC)
Florida Atlantic U (FL)
Georgia Southern U (GA)
Gonzaga U (WA)
Greenville U (IL)
Hardin-Simmons U (TX)
Hofstra U (NY)
Illinois Coll (IL)
Immaculata U (PA)
Indiana State U (IN)
Indiana U of Pennsylvania (PA)
Inter American U of Puerto Rico, Aguadilla Campus (PR)
Inter American U of Puerto Rico, Barranquitas Campus (PR)
Iona Coll (NY)
Jacksonville U (FL)
Lamar U (TX)
Liberty U (VA)
Linfield Coll (OR)
Loras Coll (IA)
Loyola Marymount U (CA)
Loyola U Chicago (IL)
Madonna U (MI)
Marshall U (WV)
Maryville U of Saint Louis (MO)
Massachusetts Coll of Liberal Arts (MA)
Miami U (OH)
Middle Tennessee State U (TN)
Millikin U (IL)
National U (CA)
Northeastern State U (OK)
Northern Kentucky U (KY)
Northern State U (SD)
Northwest Missouri State U (MO)
Northwood U, Michigan Campus (MI)
The Ohio State U (OH)
Ohio U (OH)
Oklahoma Baptist U (OK)
Old Dominion U (VA)
Pfeiffer U (NC)
Point Loma Nazarene U (CA)
Prairie View A&M U (TX)
Regent U (VA)
Rhode Island Coll (RI)
Rochester Inst of Technology (NY)
Rockford U (IL)
Saint Francis U (PA)
Saint Joseph's U (PA)
Saint Louis U (MO)
Seton Hill U (PA)
State U of New York at Plattsburgh (NY)
Stetson U (FL)
Texas A&M Intl U (TX)
U of Central Arkansas (AR)
U of Dayton (OH)
U of Georgia (GA)
U of Hawaii at Manoa (HI)
U of Houston (TX)
U of Houston–Downtown (TX)
U of Idaho (ID)
U of Louisville (KY)
U of Mary Hardin-Baylor (TX)
U of Massachusetts Dartmouth (MA)
U of Memphis (TN)
U of Michigan–Dearborn (MI)
U of Nevada, Las Vegas (NV)
U of Northern Iowa (IA)
U of Northwestern–St. Paul (MN)
U of Notre Dame (IN)
U of Pennsylvania (PA)
U of Puget Sound (WA)
U of Saint Francis (IN)
U of South Florida (FL)
The U of Tennessee at Martin (TN)
The U of Texas at Austin (TX)
The U of Texas Rio Grande Valley (TX)
U of the Incarnate Word (TX)
The U of Tulsa (OK)
U of Washington (WA)
The U of West Alabama (AL)
U of West Georgia (GA)
U of Wisconsin–Eau Claire (WI)
U of Wisconsin–La Crosse (WI)
U of Wisconsin–Milwaukee (WI)
Valley City State U (ND)
Washington State U (WA)
Washington State U–Vancouver (WA)
Weber State U (UT)
Western Connecticut State U (CT)
Western Kentucky U (KY)
Western Washington U (WA)
Worcester Polytechnic Inst (MA)
Wright State U–Lake Campus (OH)
Youngstown State U (OH)

MANAGEMENT INFORMATION SYSTEMS AND SERVICES RELATED
Bowling Green State U (OH)
Temple U (PA)
Tiffin U (OH)
U of Pittsburgh (PA)
Widener U (PA)

MANAGEMENT SCIENCE
Auburn U (AL)
Averett U (VA)
Bridgewater State U (MA)
California State U, Northridge (CA)
The Catholic U of America (DC)
Creighton U (NE)
DePaul U (IL)
Drake U (IA)
Duquesne U (PA)
Eastern Illinois U (IL)
Fitchburg State U (MA)
Grand Valley State U (MI)
Hamline U (MN)
Hardin-Simmons U (TX)
Jacksonville U (FL)
La Salle U (PA)
Loras Coll (IA)
Louisiana State U and A&M Coll (LA)
Manhattan Coll (NY)
Manor Coll (PA)
Minnesota State U Moorhead (MN)
New York U (NY)
Northern Illinois U (IL)
Oklahoma Baptist U (OK)
Pitzer Coll (CA)
Point Loma Nazarene U (CA)
Portland State U (OR)
Regent U (VA)
Rider U (NJ)
Rocky Mountain Coll (MT)
Saint Louis U (MO)
Saint Mary's U of Minnesota (MN)
Salve Regina U (RI)
Southern Illinois U Carbondale (IL)
Stonehill Coll (MA)
U of Arkansas (AR)
U of California, Merced (CA)
U of Florida (FL)
U of Kentucky (KY)
U of Maryland, Coll Park (MD)
U of Memphis (TN)
U of New Hampshire (NH)
U of Notre Dame (IN)
U of Providence (MT)
U of South Carolina (SC)
U of Washington, Bothell (WA)
U of Washington, Tacoma (WA)
U of Wyoming (WY)
Valparaiso U (IN)
Vaughn Coll of Aeronautics and Technology (NY)
Virginia Polytechnic Inst and State U (VA)
Western Kentucky U (KY)

MANAGEMENT SCIENCES AND QUANTITATIVE METHODS RELATED
Arkansas Tech U (AR)
Baruch Coll of the City U of New York (NY)
Canisius Coll (NY)
Cornell Coll (IA)
George Mason U (VA)
Indiana State U (IN)
Juniata Coll (PA)
Massachusetts Inst of Technology (MA)
Mercer U, Macon (GA)
Miami U (OH)
New York U (NY)
Pace U (NY)
Purdue U (IN)
Purdue U Northwest (IN)
Rider U (NJ)
U of Pennsylvania (PA)
U of South Dakota (SD)

MANUFACTURING ENGINEERING
Boston U (MA)
Bradley U (IL)
California Polytechnic State U, San Luis Obispo (CA)
California State U, Northridge (CA)
Central State U (OH)
Dunwoody Coll of Technology (MN)
Georgia Southern U (GA)
Grand Valley State U (MI)
Hofstra U (NY)
Miami U (OH)
National U (CA)
New Jersey Inst of Technology (NJ)
Northwestern U (IL)
Savannah Coll of Art and Design (GA)
U of Detroit Mercy (MI)
U of Michigan–Dearborn (MI)
U of Southern Indiana (IN)
The U of Texas Rio Grande Valley (TX)
U of Wisconsin–Milwaukee (WI)
Western Washington U (WA)
Youngstown State U (OH)

MANUFACTURING ENGINEERING TECHNOLOGY
Bradley U (IL)
California State U, Long Beach (CA)
Central Connecticut State U (CT)
Central Michigan U (MI)
Central Washington U (WA)
East Carolina U (NC)
Farmingdale State Coll (NY)
Fitchburg State U (MA)
Idaho State U (ID)
Indiana State U (IN)
Millersville U of Pennsylvania (PA)
Murray State U (KY)
Northern Kentucky U (KY)
Purdue U (IN)
Rochester Inst of Technology (NY)
Sullivan U (KY)
U of Dayton (OH)
U of Memphis (TN)
U of Northern Iowa (IA)
U of Southern Indiana (IN)
Weber State U (UT)
Western Kentucky U (KY)

MARINE BIOLOGY AND BIOLOGICAL OCEANOGRAPHY
Alabama State U (AL)
Auburn U (AL)
Boston U (MA)
California State U, Long Beach (CA)
Coastal Carolina U (SC)
Coll of Charleston (SC)
East Stroudsburg U of Pennsylvania (PA)
Eckerd Coll (FL)
Florida Southern Coll (FL)
Humboldt State U (CA)
Jacksonville U (FL)
Loyola U New Orleans (LA)
Montclair State U (NJ)
New Coll of Florida (FL)
Northwest Missouri State U (MO)
Rollins Coll (FL)
Sacred Heart U (CT)
Saint Francis U (PA)
Samford U (AL)
San Francisco State U (CA)
San Jose State U (CA)
Sonoma State U (CA)
Spring Hill Coll (AL)
Stockton U (NJ)
U of California, Los Angeles (CA)
U of California, Santa Cruz (CA)
U of Hawaii at Manoa (HI)
U of Maine at Machias (ME)
U of New Haven (CT)
U of Oregon (OR)
U of South Carolina (SC)
The U of Tampa (FL)
The U of Texas Rio Grande Valley (TX)
U of Washington (WA)
The U of West Alabama (AL)
Waynesburg U (PA)
Western Washington U (WA)

MARINE SCIENCE/MERCHANT MARINE OFFICER
Massachusetts Maritime Acad (MA)
State U of New York Maritime Coll (NY)
U of South Carolina (SC)

MARINE SCIENCES
California State U, Monterey Bay (CA)
Goshen Coll (IN)
Rider U (NJ)
U of Maine (ME)

MARITIME STUDIES
DEREE - The American Coll of Greece (Greece)

MARKETING/MARKETING MANAGEMENT
Adams State U (CO)
Adelphi U (NY)
Alabama State U (AL)
Albright Coll (PA)
Alfred U (NY)
American Public U System (WV)
Angelo State U (TX)
Appalachian State U (NC)
Arkansas Tech U (AR)
Assumption Coll (MA)
Auburn U (AL)
Auburn U at Montgomery (AL)
Aurora U (IL)
Austin Peay State U (TN)
Averett U (VA)
Avila U (MO)
Babson Coll (MA)
Baldwin Wallace U (OH)
Baylor U (TX)
Benedictine U (IL)
Bentley U (MA)
Berkeley Coll–New York City Campus (NY)
Berkeley Coll–White Plains Campus (NY)
Berkeley Coll–Woodland Park Campus (NJ)
Blackburn Coll (IL)
Boston Coll (MA)
Bowling Green State U (OH)
Bradley U (IL)
Brenau U (GA)
Bridgewater State U (MA)
Bryant U (RI)
Bucknell U (PA)
Buena Vista U (IA)
Butler U (IN)
Caldwell U (NJ)
California Lutheran U (CA)
California State U, Fullerton (CA)
California State U, Long Beach (CA)
California State U, Northridge (CA)
California State U, San Marcos (CA)
California U of Pennsylvania (PA)
Calvin Coll (MI)
Campbellsville U (KY)
Canisius Coll (NY)
Carnegie Mellon U (PA)
Carson-Newman U (TN)
Carthage Coll (WI)
The Catholic U of America (DC)
Cedarville U (OH)
Central Connecticut State U (CT)
Central Michigan U (MI)
Central Washington U (WA)
Champlain Coll (VT)
Christopher Newport U (VA)
Clarion U of Pennsylvania (PA)
Coastal Carolina U (SC)
The Coll at Brockport, State U of New York (NY)
Coll of Charleston (SC)
The Coll of Saint Rose (NY)
The Coll of St. Scholastica (MN)
Coll of the Ozarks (MO)
The Coll of William and Mary (VA)
Columbia Coll (MO)
Columbia Coll Chicago (IL)
Columbia Southern U (AL)
Concordia U Chicago (IL)
Creighton U (NE)
Culver-Stockton Coll (MO)
Dakota State U (SD)
Dallas Baptist U (TX)
Davenport U, Grand Rapids (MI)
Dean Coll (MA)
Delta State U (MS)
DePaul U (IL)
DEREE - The American Coll of Greece (Greece)
Dominican U (IL)
Drake U (IA)
Drury U (MO)
Duquesne U (PA)
East Carolina U (NC)
Eastern Illinois U (IL)
Eastern Mennonite U (VA)
Eastern Washington U (WA)
East Stroudsburg U of Pennsylvania (PA)
East Tennessee State U (TN)
East Texas Baptist U (TX)
Emerson Coll (MA)
Emmanuel Coll (MA)
Endicott Coll (MA)
Fairfield U (CT)
Fayetteville State U (NC)
FIDM/Fashion Inst of Design & Merchandising, Los Angeles Campus (CA)
Fitchburg State U (MA)
Florida Atlantic U (FL)
Fordham U (NY)
Fort Lewis Coll (CO)
Framingham State U (MA)
Franklin Pierce U (NH)
George Mason U (VA)
Georgetown Coll (KY)
Georgia Coll & State U (GA)
Georgia Southern U (GA)
Georgia State U (GA)
Gonzaga U (WA)
Goshen Coll (IN)
Grand Valley State U (MI)
Granite State Coll (NH)
Greenville U (IL)
Grove City Coll (PA)
Hamline U (MN)
Harding U (AR)
Hardin-Simmons U (TX)
High Point U (NC)
Hillsdale Coll (MI)
Hiram Coll (OH)
Hofstra U (NY)
Hult Intl Business School (United Kingdom)
Idaho State U (ID)
Immaculata U (PA)
Indiana State U (IN)
Indiana U of Pennsylvania (PA)
Inter American U of Puerto Rico, Aguadilla Campus (PR)
Inter American U of Puerto Rico, Bayamón Campus (PR)
Inter American U of Puerto Rico, Fajardo Campus (PR)
Inter American U of Puerto Rico, San Germán Campus (PR)
Iona Coll (NY)
Iowa State U of Science and Technology (IA)
Ithaca Coll (NY)
Jackson State U (MS)
Jacksonville U (FL)
John Cabot U (Italy)
Judson U (IL)
Juniata Coll (PA)
Kansas Wesleyan U (KS)
Kean U (NJ)
Kennesaw State U (GA)
King's Coll (PA)
Lamar U (TX)
La Salle U (PA)
Lasell Coll (MA)
La Sierra U (CA)
LeTourneau U (TX)
LIM Coll (NY)
Limestone Coll (SC)
Lindenwood U (MO)
Linfield Coll (OR)
Lipscomb U (TN)
Loras Coll (IA)
Louisiana State U and A&M Coll (LA)
Loyola Marymount U (CA)
Loyola U Chicago (IL)
Loyola U New Orleans (LA)
Lubbock Christian U (TX)
Madonna U (MI)
Manchester U (IN)
Manhattan Coll (NY)
Manhattanville Coll (NY)
Mansfield U of Pennsylvania (PA)
Marian U (IN)
Marquette U (WI)
Marshall U (WV)
Marymount Manhattan Coll (NY)
Maryville U of Saint Louis (MO)
Marywood U (PA)
Massachusetts Coll of Liberal Arts (MA)
McNeese State U (LA)
Mercer U, Macon (GA)
Mercy Coll (NY)
Merrimack Coll (MA)
Messiah Coll (PA)
Miami U (OH)
Michigan State U (MI)
Middle Tennessee State U (TN)
Millikin U (IL)
Missouri Baptist U (MO)
Molloy Coll (NY)
Murray State U (KY)
Muskingum U (OH)
Nazareth Coll of Rochester (NY)
New England Coll (NH)
New York U (NY)
Nichols Coll (MA)
Northeastern State U (OK)
Northern Illinois U (IL)
Northern Kentucky U (KY)
Northern State U (SD)
Northwest Christian U (OR)
Northwest Missouri State U (MO)
Northwood U, Michigan Campus (MI)
The Ohio State U (OH)
Ohio U (OH)
Oklahoma Baptist U (OK)
Oklahoma Christian U (OK)
Oklahoma State U (OK)
Old Dominion U (VA)
Ottawa U (KS)
Pace U (NY)
Pace U, Pleasantville Campus (NY)
Palm Beach Atlantic U (FL)
Pfeiffer U (NC)
Point Loma Nazarene U (CA)
Point U (GA)
Portland State U (OR)
Prairie View A&M U (TX)
Providence Coll (RI)
Purdue U (IN)
Purdue U Northwest (IN)
Radford U (VA)
Redeemer U Coll (ON, Canada)
Regent U (VA)
Regis U (CO)
Rhode Island Coll (RI)
Rider U (NJ)
Rochester Inst of Technology (NY)
Rockford U (IL)
Sacred Heart U (CT)
Saginaw Valley State U (MI)
Saint Francis U (PA)
St. Joseph's Coll, Long Island Campus (NY)
St. Joseph's Coll, New York (NY)
Saint Joseph's U (PA)
Saint Leo U (FL)
Saint Louis U (MO)
St. Mary's U (TX)
Saint Mary's U of Minnesota (MN)
Saint Vincent Coll (PA)
Salisbury U (MD)
Salve Regina U (RI)
Samford U (AL)
San Diego State U (CA)
San Francisco State U (CA)
San Jose State U (CA)
Seattle U (WA)
Seton Hill U (PA)
Southeastern Louisiana U (LA)
Southeastern U (FL)
Southeast Missouri State U (MO)
Southern Illinois U Carbondale (IL)
Southern U and Ag and Mech Coll (LA)
Southwest Baptist U (MO)
Spring Hill Coll (AL)
State U of New York at Fredonia (NY)
State U of New York at Plattsburgh (NY)
Stetson U (FL)
Stonehill Coll (MA)
Syracuse U (NY)
Taylor U (IN)
Temple U (PA)
Texas A&M U–Central Texas (TX)
Texas Christian U (TX)
Texas Tech U (TX)
Texas Woman's U (TX)
Tiffin U (OH)
Trevecca Nazarene U (TN)
Trinity Christian Coll (IL)
Tulane U (LA)
Union Coll (KY)
Université de Sherbrooke (QC, Canada)
U of Arkansas (AR)
U of Central Arkansas (AR)
U of Central Florida (FL)
U of Dayton (OH)
The U of Findlay (OH)
U of Florida (FL)
U of Georgia (GA)
U of Hawaii at Manoa (HI)
U of Houston (TX)
U of Houston–Clear Lake (TX)
U of Houston–Downtown (TX)
U of Idaho (ID)
U of Kentucky (KY)
U of La Verne (CA)
U of Louisville (KY)
U of Lynchburg (VA)
U of Maine (ME)
U of Maine at Machias (ME)
U of Mary Hardin-Baylor (TX)
U of Maryland, Coll Park (MD)
U of Maryland U Coll (MD)
U of Massachusetts Amherst (MA)
U of Massachusetts Dartmouth (MA)
U of Memphis (TN)
U of Michigan–Dearborn (MI)
U of Minnesota, Duluth (MN)
U of Minnesota, Twin Cities Campus (MN)
U of Montevallo (AL)
U of Mount Union (OH)
U of Nebraska–Lincoln (NE)
U of Nevada, Las Vegas (NV)
U of Nevada, Reno (NV)
U of New Haven (CT)
The U of North Carolina at Charlotte (NC)
U of North Dakota (ND)
U of Northern Iowa (IA)
U of North Florida (FL)
U of Northwestern–St. Paul (MN)
U of Notre Dame (IN)
U of Pennsylvania (PA)
U of Pittsburgh (PA)
U of Providence (MT)
U of Puerto Rico–Bayamón (PR)
U of Regina (SK, Canada)
U of Saint Francis (IN)
U of St. Thomas (MN)
U of St. Thomas (TX)
U of San Diego (CA)
U of San Francisco (CA)
U of South Alabama (AL)
U of South Carolina (SC)
U of South Dakota (SD)
U of Southern Indiana (IN)
U of South Florida (FL)
U of South Florida Sarasota-Manatee (FL)
The U of Tampa (FL)
The U of Tennessee (TN)
The U of Tennessee at Martin (TN)
The U of Texas at Austin (TX)
The U of Texas at El Paso (TX)
The U of Texas of the Permian Basin (TX)
The U of Texas Rio Grande Valley (TX)
U of the Incarnate Word (TX)
The U of Toledo (OH)
The U of Tulsa (OK)
U of Washington (WA)
U of Washington, Bothell (WA)
U of Washington, Tacoma (WA)
The U of West Alabama (AL)
U of West Georgia (GA)
U of Wisconsin–Eau Claire (WI)
U of Wisconsin–La Crosse (WI)
U of Wisconsin–Milwaukee (WI)
U of Wisconsin–Superior (WI)
U of Wyoming (WY)
Utah State U (UT)
Utah Valley U (UT)
Valparaiso U (IN)
Vanguard U of Southern California (CA)

Virginia Commonwealth U (VA)
Virginia Polytechnic Inst and State U (VA)
Wartburg Coll (IA)
Washington State U (WA)
Washington State U–Vancouver (WA)
Washington U in St. Louis (MO)
Waynesburg U (PA)
Weber State U (UT)
Western Connecticut State U (CT)
Western Illinois U (IL)
Western Kentucky U (KY)
Western Washington U (WA)
Whitworth U (WA)
Widener U (PA)
Wilkes U (PA)
Woodbury U (CA)
Wright State U–Lake Campus (OH)
Youngstown State U (OH)

MARKETING RELATED
Babson Coll (MA)
Bowling Green State U (OH)
Duquesne U (PA)
Eastern U (PA)
Mercer U, Macon (GA)
Miami U Hamilton (OH)
Mount St. Joseph U (OH)
Northwood U, Michigan Campus (MI)
Point U (GA)
Saginaw Valley State U (MI)
U of Michigan–Dearborn (MI)
U of Minnesota, Duluth (MN)
U of South Florida (FL)
Washington U in St. Louis (MO)

MARKETING RESEARCH
Bowling Green State U (OH)
Bryant U (RI)
Fashion Inst of Technology (NY)
Ithaca Coll (NY)
Lawrence Technological U (MI)

MARRIAGE AND FAMILY THERAPY/COUNSELING
Johnson U Florida (FL)
Oklahoma Baptist U (OK)

MASSAGE THERAPY
Idaho State U (ID)

MASS COMMUNICATION/ MEDIA
Adams State U (CO)
American U (DC)
American U in Bulgaria (Bulgaria)
Auburn U (AL)
Austin Coll (TX)
Austin Peay State U (TN)
Baker U (KS)
Baldwin Wallace U (OH)
Barton Coll (NC)
Beloit Coll (WI)
Bentley U (MA)
Berea Coll (KY)
Bethel Coll (KS)
Bethel U (MN)
Brandman U (CA)
Brenau U (GA)
Bridgewater Coll (VA)
Bryant U (RI)
Buena Vista U (IA)
California Lutheran U (CA)
California State U, Bakersfield (CA)
California State U, Long Beach (CA)
California State U, San Marcos (CA)
Calvin Coll (MI)
Campbellsville U (KY)
Carson-Newman U (TN)
Central Connecticut State U (CT)
Central Michigan U (MI)
Clark U (MA)
Colorado State U–Pueblo (CO)
Culver-Stockton Coll (MO)
Dean Coll (MA)
Delaware Valley U (PA)
DePaul U (IL)
Drake U (IA)
Drew U (NJ)
East Tennessee State U (TN)
East Texas Baptist U (TX)
Emerson Coll (MA)
Emmanuel Coll (GA)
Endicott Coll (MA)
The Evergreen State Coll (WA)
Florida Southern Coll (FL)
Franklin Pierce U (NH)
Greenville U (IL)
Hanover Coll (IN)
Hofstra U (NY)
Hollins U (VA)
Hunter Coll of the City U of New York (NY)
Illinois Coll (IL)
Indiana U Bloomington (IN)
Iona Coll (NY)
Ithaca Coll (NY)
Jackson State U (MS)
Jacksonville U (FL)
Johnson C. Smith U (NC)
Kuyper Coll (MI)
LeTourneau U (TX)
Linfield Coll (OR)
Lipscomb U (TN)
Lock Haven U of Pennsylvania (PA)
Loras Coll (IA)
Louisiana Coll (LA)
Louisiana State U and A&M Coll (LA)
Lubbock Christian U (TX)
Macalester Coll (MN)
Manchester U (IN)
Mansfield U of Pennsylvania (PA)
Marist Coll (NY)
Marquette U (WI)
Marymount Manhattan Coll (NY)
Maryville U of Saint Louis (MO)
Massachusetts Inst of Technology (MA)
McNeese State U (LA)
Mercer U, Macon (GA)
Mercy Coll (NY)
Miami U (OH)
Miami U Hamilton (OH)
Michigan State U (MI)
Middle Tennessee State U (TN)
Mount Saint Mary Coll (NY)
Muskingum U (OH)
New England Coll (NH)
Northwestern Oklahoma State U (OK)
Oglethorpe U (GA)
Oklahoma Baptist U (OK)
Oklahoma Christian U (OK)
Ottawa U (KS)
Ouachita Baptist U (AR)
Pace U (NY)
Palm Beach Atlantic U (FL)
Piedmont Coll (GA)
Point Loma Nazarene U (CA)
Queens Coll of the City U of New York (NY)
Rhode Island Coll (RI)
Rochester Coll (MI)
St. Norbert Coll (WI)
Scripps Coll (CA)
Sonoma State U (CA)
Southeastern U (FL)
Southern Illinois U Edwardsville (IL)
Southern U and Ag and Mech Coll (LA)
State U of New York at Fredonia (NY)
Temple U (PA)
Texas Tech U (TX)
Towson U (MD)
Trevecca Nazarene U (TN)
Tulane U (LA)
Union Coll (KY)
U of Houston (TX)
U of Maine (ME)
U of Mary Hardin-Baylor (TX)
U of Maryland, Baltimore County (MD)
U of Memphis (TN)
U of Michigan–Dearborn (MI)
U of Nevada, Las Vegas (NV)
U of New Mexico (NM)
U of North Carolina at Asheville (NC)
The U of North Carolina at Chapel Hill (NC)
The U of North Carolina at Greensboro (NC)
The U of North Carolina at Pembroke (NC)
U of Northern Iowa (IA)
U of North Florida (FL)
U of Pittsburgh (PA)
U of San Francisco (CA)
U of Sioux Falls (SD)
U of South Dakota (SD)
U of Southern Indiana (IN)
U of South Florida (FL)
The U of Texas Rio Grande Valley (TX)
U of the Incarnate Word (TX)
U of Washington, Bothell (WA)
U of Washington, Tacoma (WA)
U of Wisconsin–Eau Claire (WI)
U of Wisconsin–Milwaukee (WI)
U of Wisconsin–Superior (WI)
Ursinus Coll (PA)
Vassar Coll (NY)
Virginia Commonwealth U (VA)
Wartburg Coll (IA)
Washington State U (WA)
Widener U (PA)
Winthrop U (SC)
Worcester State U (MA)

MATERIALS ENGINEERING
Alfred U (NY)
Auburn U (AL)
California Inst of Technology (CA)
California Polytechnic State U, San Luis Obispo (CA)
California State U, Long Beach (CA)
Columbia U (NY)
Cornell U (NY)
Iowa State U of Science and Technology (IA)
Johns Hopkins U (MD)
Massachusetts Inst of Technology (MA)
Michigan State U (MI)
North Carolina State U (NC)
Northwestern U (IL)
The Ohio State U (OH)
Purdue U (IN)
Rice U (TX)
San Jose State U (CA)
U of California, Davis (CA)
U of California, Irvine (CA)
U of California, Los Angeles (CA)
U of California, Merced (CA)
U of Florida (FL)
U of Idaho (ID)
U of Kentucky (KY)
U of Maryland, Coll Park (MD)
U of Michigan (MI)
U of Minnesota, Twin Cities Campus (MN)
U of Pennsylvania (PA)
U of Pittsburgh (PA)
The U of Tennessee (TN)
U of Washington (WA)
U of Wisconsin–Eau Claire (WI)
U of Wisconsin–Milwaukee (WI)
Virginia Polytechnic Inst and State U (VA)
Washington State U (WA)
Wright State U–Lake Campus (OH)

MATERIALS SCIENCE
Carnegie Mellon U (PA)
Columbia U (NY)
Johns Hopkins U (MD)
Linfield Coll (OR)
Northwestern U (IL)
Rice U (TX)
U of California, Los Angeles (CA)
U of California, Riverside (CA)
U of Pennsylvania (PA)
U of Wisconsin–Eau Claire (WI)

MATHEMATICAL BIOLOGY
Averett U (VA)
LeTourneau U (TX)
U of Houston (TX)
U of Idaho (ID)
U of Pittsburgh (PA)

MATHEMATICAL STATISTICS AND PROBABILITY
Albion Coll (MI)
Bryant U (RI)
Calvin Coll (MI)
Carnegie Mellon U (PA)
High Point U (NC)
Marquette U (WI)
Purdue U (IN)
U of the Incarnate Word (TX)

MATHEMATICS
Acadia U (NS, Canada)
Adams State U (CO)
Adelphi U (NY)
Agnes Scott Coll (GA)
Alabama State U (AL)
Albion Coll (MI)
Albright Coll (PA)
Alfred U (NY)
Allegheny Coll (PA)
Alverno Coll (WI)
American U (DC)
American U in Bulgaria (Bulgaria)
American U of Beirut (Lebanon)
Angelo State U (TX)
Appalachian State U (NC)
Arkansas Tech U (AR)
Assumption Coll (MA)
Auburn U (AL)
Auburn U at Montgomery (AL)
Aurora U (IL)
Austin Coll (TX)
Austin Peay State U (TN)
Averett U (VA)
Avila U (MO)
Baker U (KS)
Baldwin Wallace U (OH)
Barton Coll (NC)
Baruch Coll of the City U of New York (NY)
Baylor U (TX)
Bellarmine U (KY)
Beloit Coll (WI)
Benedictine U (IL)
Bennett Coll (NC)
Bentley U (MA)
Berea Coll (KY)
Bethany Lutheran Coll (MN)
Bethel Coll (KS)
Bethel U (MN)
Blackburn Coll (IL)
Boston Coll (MA)
Boston U (MA)
Bowling Green State U (OH)
Bradley U (IL)
Brandeis U (MA)
Bridgewater Coll (VA)
Bridgewater State U (MA)
Bucknell U (PA)
Buena Vista U (IA)
Butler U (IN)
Caldwell U (NJ)
California Inst of Technology (CA)
California Lutheran U (CA)
California Polytechnic State U, San Luis Obispo (CA)
California State U, Bakersfield (CA)
California State U, Chico (CA)
California State U, Fullerton (CA)
California State U, Long Beach (CA)
California State U, Los Angeles (CA)
California State U, Monterey Bay (CA)
California State U, Northridge (CA)
California State U, San Bernardino (CA)
California State U, San Marcos (CA)
California U of Pennsylvania (PA)
Calvin Coll (MI)
Cameron U (OK)
Campbellsville U (KY)
Carnegie Mellon U (PA)
Carson-Newman U (TN)
Carthage Coll (WI)
The Catholic U of America (DC)
Cedarville U (OH)
Centenary Coll of Louisiana (LA)
Central Connecticut State U (CT)
Central Michigan U (MI)
Central State U (OH)
Central Washington U (WA)
Christian Brothers U (TN)
Christopher Newport U (VA)
Claremont McKenna Coll (CA)
Clarion U of Pennsylvania (PA)
Clarkson U (NY)
Clark U (MA)
Colgate U (NY)
The Coll at Brockport, State U of New York (NY)
Coll of Charleston (SC)
Coll of Coastal Georgia (GA)
The Coll of Idaho (ID)
Coll of Saint Benedict (MN)
Coll of Saint Mary (NE)
The Coll of Saint Rose (NY)
The Coll of St. Scholastica (MN)
Coll of Staten Island of the City U of New York (NY)
Coll of the Holy Cross (MA)
Coll of the Ozarks (MO)
The Coll of William and Mary (VA)
The Colorado Coll (CO)
Colorado School of Mines (CO)
Colorado State U (CO)
Colorado State U–Pueblo (CO)
Columbia Coll (MO)
Columbia U (NY)
Concordia U Chicago (IL)
Concordia U Irvine (CA)
Connecticut Coll (CT)
Cornell Coll (IA)
Cornell U (NY)
Covenant Coll (GA)
Creighton U (NE)
Culver-Stockton Coll (MO)
Dallas Baptist U (TX)
Dartmouth Coll (NH)
Davidson Coll (NC)
Delta State U (MS)
DePaul U (IL)
Dickinson Coll (PA)
Dominican U (IL)
Drake U (IA)
Drew U (NJ)
Duquesne U (PA)
Earlham Coll (IN)
East Carolina U (NC)
Eastern Illinois U (IL)
Eastern Mennonite U (VA)
Eastern Oregon U (OR)
Eastern U (PA)
Eastern Washington U (WA)
East Stroudsburg U of Pennsylvania (PA)
East Tennessee State U (TN)
East Texas Baptist U (TX)
Eckerd Coll (FL)
Elizabeth City State U (NC)
Emmanuel Coll (GA)
Emmanuel Coll (MA)
Endicott Coll (MA)
Fairfield U (CT)
Fayetteville State U (NC)
Fitchburg State U (MA)
Florida Ag and Mech U (FL)
Florida Atlantic U (FL)
Florida Southern Coll (FL)
Fordham U (NY)
Fort Lewis Coll (CO)
Framingham State U (MA)
Furman U (SC)
George Mason U (VA)
Georgetown Coll (KY)
Georgia Coll & State U (GA)
Georgia Southern U (GA)
Georgia State U (GA)
Gonzaga U (WA)
Gordon Coll (MA)
Goshen Coll (IN)
Graceland U (IA)
Grand Valley State U (MI)
Greenville U (IL)
Grove City Coll (PA)
Gwynedd Mercy U (PA)
Hamilton Coll (NY)
Hamline U (MN)
Hampden-Sydney Coll (VA)
Hanover Coll (IN)
Harding U (AR)
Hardin-Simmons U (TX)
Hartwick Coll (NY)
Harvard U (MA)
Haverford Coll (PA)
High Point U (NC)
Hillsdale Coll (MI)
Hofstra U (NY)
Hollins U (VA)
Hood Coll (MD)
Humboldt State U (CA)
Hunter Coll of the City U of New York (NY)
Idaho State U (ID)
Illinois Coll (IL)
Indiana State U (IN)
Indiana U Bloomington (IN)
Indiana U East (IN)
Indiana U Kokomo (IN)
Indiana U Northwest (IN)
Indiana U of Pennsylvania (PA)
Indiana U–Purdue U Indianapolis (IN)
Indiana U South Bend (IN)
Indiana U Southeast (IN)

Inter American U of Puerto Rico, Bayamón Campus (PR)
Inter American U of Puerto Rico, San Germán Campus (PR)
Iona Coll (NY)
Iowa State U of Science and Technology (IA)
Ithaca Coll (NY)
Jackson State U (MS)
Jacksonville U (FL)
Johns Hopkins U (MD)
Johnson C. Smith U (NC)
Judson U (IL)
Juniata Coll (PA)
Kalamazoo Coll (MI)
Kansas Wesleyan U (KS)
Kean U (NJ)
Kennesaw State U (GA)
King's Coll (PA)
King U (TN)
Knox Coll (IL)
Lafayette Coll (PA)
LaGrange Coll (GA)
Lake Forest Coll (IL)
Lamar U (TX)
La Salle U (PA)
La Sierra U (CA)
Lawrence Technological U (MI)
Lawrence U (WI)
Lebanese American U (Lebanon)
Lebanon Valley Coll (PA)
Lee U (TN)
LeTourneau U (TX)
Lewis & Clark Coll (OR)
Liberty U (VA)
Limestone Coll (SC)
Lindenwood U (MO)
Linfield Coll (OR)
Lipscomb U (TN)
Lock Haven U of Pennsylvania (PA)
Loras Coll (IA)
Louisiana Coll (LA)
Louisiana State U and A&M Coll (LA)
Loyola Marymount U (CA)
Loyola U Chicago (IL)
Loyola U New Orleans (LA)
Lubbock Christian U (TX)
Lycoming Coll (PA)
Macalester Coll (MN)
Madonna U (MI)
Maharishi U of Management (IA)
Manchester U (IN)
Manhattan Coll (NY)
Manhattanville Coll (NY)
Mansfield U of Pennsylvania (PA)
Marian U (IN)
Marist Coll (NY)
Marquette U (WI)
Marshall U (WV)
Marymount U (VA)
Maryville U of Saint Louis (MO)
Marywood U (PA)
Massachusetts Coll of Liberal Arts (MA)
Massachusetts Inst of Technology (MA)
McDaniel Coll (MD)
McNeese State U (LA)
Mercer U, Macon (GA)
Mercy Coll (NY)
Merrimack Coll (MA)
Messiah Coll (PA)
Miami U (OH)
Miami U Hamilton (OH)
Michigan State U (MI)
Middlebury Coll (VT)
Middle Tennessee State U (TN)
Millersville U of Pennsylvania (PA)
Milligan Coll (TN)
Millikin U (IL)
Millsaps Coll (MS)
Mills Coll (CA)
Minnesota State U Moorhead (MN)
Missouri Baptist U (MO)
Molloy Coll (NY)
Montclair State U (NJ)
Morningside Coll (IA)
Mount Marty Coll (SD)
Mount St. Joseph U (OH)
Mount Saint Mary Coll (NY)
Murray State U (KY)
Muskingum U (OH)
National U (CA)
Nazareth Coll of Rochester (NY)
New Coll of Florida (FL)
New Jersey City U (NJ)
New Jersey Inst of Technology (NJ)
New York U (NY)
Nichols Coll (MA)
North Carolina State U (NC)
Northeastern State U (OK)
Northern Illinois U (IL)
Northern Kentucky U (KY)
Northern State U (SD)
Northwest Christian U (OR)
Northwestern Oklahoma State U (OK)
Northwestern U (IL)
Northwest Missouri State U (MO)
Oakland City U (IN)
Occidental Coll (CA)
Oglethorpe U (GA)
Ohio Dominican U (OH)
The Ohio State U (OH)
Ohio U (OH)
Ohio Wesleyan U (OH)
Oklahoma Baptist U (OK)
Oklahoma Christian U (OK)
Oklahoma State U (OK)
Old Dominion U (VA)
Ottawa U (KS)
Ouachita Baptist U (AR)
Pace U (NY)
Pace U, Pleasantville Campus (NY)
Pacific Lutheran U (WA)
Palm Beach Atlantic U (FL)
Pepperdine U, Malibu (CA)
Pfeiffer U (NC)
Piedmont Coll (GA)
Pitzer Coll (CA)
Point Loma Nazarene U (CA)
Portland State U (OR)
Prairie View A&M U (TX)
Princeton U (NJ)
Providence Coll (RI)
Purdue U (IN)
Purdue U Northwest (IN)
Queens Coll of the City U of New York (NY)
Queens U of Charlotte (NC)
Radford U (VA)
Randolph Coll (VA)
Randolph-Macon Coll (VA)
Redeemer U Coll (ON, Canada)
Regent U (VA)
Regis U (CO)
Reinhardt U (GA)
Rhode Island Coll (RI)
Rhodes Coll (TN)
Rice U (TX)
Rider U (NJ)
Roanoke Coll (VA)
Rochester Inst of Technology (NY)
Rockford U (IL)
Rocky Mountain Coll (MT)
Rollins Coll (FL)
Sacred Heart U (CT)
Saginaw Valley State U (MI)
Saint Anselm Coll (NH)
Saint Francis U (PA)
St. John Fisher Coll (NY)
Saint John's U (MN)
St. Joseph's Coll, Long Island Campus (NY)
St. Joseph's Coll, New York (NY)
Saint Joseph's U (PA)
Saint Leo U (FL)
Saint Louis U (MO)
Saint Martin's U (WA)
St. Mary's Coll of Maryland (MD)
St. Mary's U (TX)
Saint Mary's U of Minnesota (MN)
St. Norbert Coll (WI)
St. Olaf Coll (MN)
Saint Vincent Coll (PA)
Salisbury U (MD)
Salve Regina U (RI)
Samford U (AL)
San Diego State U (CA)
San Francisco State U (CA)
San Jose State U (CA)
Sarah Lawrence Coll (NY)
Scripps Coll (CA)
Seattle U (WA)
Seton Hill U (PA)
Skidmore Coll (NY)
Sonoma State U (CA)
Southeastern Louisiana U (LA)
Southeastern U (FL)
Southeast Missouri State U (MO)
Southern Arkansas U–Magnolia (AR)
Southern Illinois U Carbondale (IL)
Southern Illinois U Edwardsville (IL)
Southern U and Ag and Mech Coll (LA)
Southwest Baptist U (MO)
Southwestern U (TX)
Spring Hill Coll (AL)
State U of New York at Fredonia (NY)
State U of New York at Plattsburgh (NY)
State U of New York Coll at Geneseo (NY)
State U of New York Coll at Potsdam (NY)
Stetson U (FL)
Stevens Inst of Technology (NJ)
Stockton U (NJ)
Stonehill Coll (MA)
Sweet Briar Coll (VA)
Syracuse U (NY)
Tabor Coll (KS)
Taylor U (IN)
Temple U (PA)
Texas A&M Intl U (TX)
Texas A&M U–Central Texas (TX)
Texas Christian U (TX)
Texas Lutheran U (TX)
Texas Tech U (TX)
Texas Woman's U (TX)
Towson U (MD)
Trevecca Nazarene U (TN)
Trinity Christian Coll (IL)
Truman State U (MO)
Tulane U (LA)
Union Coll (KY)
Union Coll (NY)
Université de Sherbrooke (QC, Canada)
U at Buffalo, the State U of New York (NY)
U of Arkansas (AR)
U of California, Davis (CA)
U of California, Irvine (CA)
U of California, Los Angeles (CA)
U of California, Riverside (CA)
U of California, Santa Cruz (CA)
U of Central Arkansas (AR)
U of Central Florida (FL)
U of Chicago (IL)
U of Colorado Denver (CO)
U of Dallas (TX)
U of Dayton (OH)
U of Detroit Mercy (MI)
The U of Findlay (OH)
U of Florida (FL)
U of Georgia (GA)
U of Guam (GU)
U of Hawaii at Manoa (HI)
U of Houston (TX)
U of Houston–Clear Lake (TX)
U of Houston–Downtown (TX)
U of Idaho (ID)
U of Illinois at Springfield (IL)
U of Kentucky (KY)
U of La Verne (CA)
U of Louisville (KY)
U of Lynchburg (VA)
U of Maine (ME)
U of Maine at Farmington (ME)
U of Maine at Presque Isle (ME)
U of Mary Hardin-Baylor (TX)
U of Maryland, Baltimore County (MD)
U of Maryland, Coll Park (MD)
U of Maryland Eastern Shore (MD)
U of Massachusetts Amherst (MA)
U of Massachusetts Boston (MA)
U of Massachusetts Dartmouth (MA)
U of Massachusetts Lowell (MA)
U of Memphis (TN)
U of Michigan (MI)
U of Michigan–Dearborn (MI)
U of Minnesota, Duluth (MN)
U of Minnesota, Morris (MN)
U of Minnesota, Twin Cities Campus (MN)
U of Missouri (MO)
U of Montevallo (AL)
U of Mount Union (OH)
U of Nebraska–Lincoln (NE)
U of Nevada, Las Vegas (NV)
U of Nevada, Reno (NV)
U of New Hampshire (NH)
U of New Haven (CT)
U of New Mexico (NM)
U of North Carolina at Asheville (NC)
The U of North Carolina at Chapel Hill (NC)
The U of North Carolina at Charlotte (NC)
The U of North Carolina at Greensboro (NC)
The U of North Carolina at Pembroke (NC)
U of North Dakota (ND)
U of Northern Colorado (CO)
U of Northern Iowa (IA)
U of North Florida (FL)
U of Northwestern–St. Paul (MN)
U of Notre Dame (IN)
U of Oregon (OR)
U of Pennsylvania (PA)
U of Pittsburgh (PA)
U of Providence (MT)
U of Puget Sound (WA)
U of Regina (SK, Canada)
U of Richmond (VA)
U of Saint Francis (IN)
U of Saint Mary (KS)
U of St. Thomas (MN)
U of St. Thomas (TX)
U of San Diego (CA)
U of San Francisco (CA)
U of Sioux Falls (SD)
U of South Carolina (SC)
U of South Dakota (SD)
U of Southern Indiana (IN)
U of South Florida (FL)
The U of Tampa (FL)
The U of Tennessee (TN)
The U of Tennessee at Martin (TN)
The U of Texas at Austin (TX)
The U of Texas at El Paso (TX)
The U of Texas of the Permian Basin (TX)
The U of Texas Rio Grande Valley (TX)
U of the Incarnate Word (TX)
The U of the South (TN)
The U of Toledo (OH)
The U of Tulsa (OK)
U of Vermont (VT)
U of Virginia (VA)
U of Washington (WA)
U of Washington, Bothell (WA)
The U of West Alabama (AL)
U of West Georgia (GA)
U of Wisconsin–Eau Claire (WI)
U of Wisconsin–La Crosse (WI)
U of Wisconsin–Milwaukee (WI)
U of Wisconsin–River Falls (WI)
U of Wisconsin–Superior (WI)
U of Wyoming (WY)
Ursinus Coll (PA)
Utah State U (UT)
Utah Valley U (UT)
Utica Coll (NY)
Valley City State U (ND)
Valparaiso U (IN)
Vanguard U of Southern California (CA)
Vassar Coll (NY)
Virginia Commonwealth U (VA)
Virginia Polytechnic Inst and State U (VA)
Wabash Coll (IN)
Wartburg Coll (IA)
Washington & Jefferson Coll (PA)
Washington and Lee U (VA)
Washington State U (WA)
Washington State U–Tri-Cities (WA)
Washington U in St. Louis (MO)
Waynesburg U (PA)
Weber State U (UT)
Wesleyan Coll (GA)
Wesleyan U (CT)
West Chester U of Pennsylvania (PA)
Western Connecticut State U (CT)
Western Illinois U (IL)
Western Kentucky U (KY)
Western State Colorado U (CO)
Western Washington U (WA)
Westmont Coll (CA)
West Virginia State U (WV)
West Virginia U Inst of Technology (WV)
Wheaton Coll (IL)
Wheaton Coll (MA)
Whittier Coll (CA)
Whitworth U (WA)
Widener U (PA)
Wilkes U (PA)
Willamette U (OR)
William Jewell Coll (MO)
Williams Coll (MA)
Winthrop U (SC)
Wofford Coll (SC)
Worcester Polytechnic Inst (MA)
Worcester State U (MA)
Wright State U–Lake Campus (OH)
Youngstown State U (OH)

MATHEMATICS AND COMPUTER SCIENCE

Albright Coll (PA)
Calvin Coll (MI)
Christian Brothers U (TN)
Clarkson U (NY)
Colgate U (NY)
The Colorado Coll (CO)
Columbia U (NY)
DePaul U (IL)
Dominican U (IL)
Eastern Illinois U (IL)
George Mason U (VA)
Hampden-Sydney Coll (VA)
Hofstra U (NY)
Immaculata U (PA)
Ithaca Coll (NY)
Lawrence Technological U (MI)
Lawrence U (WI)
LeTourneau U (TX)
Lewis & Clark Coll (OR)
Loyola U Chicago (IL)
Manchester U (IN)
Massachusetts Inst of Technology (MA)
Palm Beach Atlantic U (FL)
Pepperdine U, Malibu (CA)
Pfeiffer U (NC)
Purdue U (IN)
Redeemer U Coll (ON, Canada)
Rochester Inst of Technology (NY)
Temple U (PA)
U of California, Irvine (CA)
The U of Findlay (OH)
U of Kentucky (KY)
U of Massachusetts Amherst (MA)
U of Massachusetts Dartmouth (MA)
U of Michigan–Dearborn (MI)
U of Oregon (OR)
U of Regina (SK, Canada)
The U of Tampa (FL)
The U of Texas at Austin (TX)
U of Vermont (VT)
Valparaiso U (IN)
Washington U in St. Louis (MO)
Western Washington U (WA)
Wheaton Coll (MA)

MATHEMATICS AND STATISTICS

Canisius Coll (NY)
Dakota State U (SD)
The Evergreen State Coll (WA)
Florida Southern Coll (FL)
Graceland U (IA)
Southeastern U (FL)
U of Houston–Downtown (TX)
U of Notre Dame (IN)
U of South Alabama (AL)
U of Washington, Tacoma (WA)
Western Washington U (WA)

MATHEMATICS AND STATISTICS RELATED

Carnegie Mellon U (PA)
Fordham U (NY)
Hofstra U (NY)
Miami U Hamilton (OH)
New York U (NY)
Pitzer Coll (CA)
Purchase Coll, State U of New York (NY)
St. Joseph's Coll, Long Island Campus (NY)
St. Joseph's Coll, New York (NY)
Tulane U (LA)
The U of North Carolina at Charlotte (NC)
U of Notre Dame (IN)
U of Pittsburgh (PA)
U of Regina (SK, Canada)
Worcester Polytechnic Inst (MA)

MATHEMATICS RELATED
Agnes Scott Coll (GA)
Carnegie Mellon U (PA)
Louisiana Coll (LA)
Piedmont Coll (GA)
Reinhardt U (GA)
Seton Hill U (PA)
Temple U (PA)
U of California, Los Angeles (CA)
U of Pittsburgh (PA)
U of Washington (WA)
Wheaton Coll (MA)

MATHEMATICS TEACHER EDUCATION
Adams State U (CO)
Albion Coll (MI)
Arkansas Tech U (AR)
Auburn U (AL)
Averett U (VA)
Baylor U (TX)
Bethany Lutheran Coll (MN)
Bethel U (MN)
Blackburn Coll (IL)
Boston U (MA)
Bowling Green State U (OH)
Bradley U (IL)
Buena Vista U (IA)
California Lutheran U (CA)
California State U, Long Beach (CA)
Calvin Coll (MI)
Campbellsville U (KY)
Canisius Coll (NY)
The Catholic U of America (DC)
Cedarville U (OH)
Central Michigan U (MI)
Central State U (OH)
Central Washington U (WA)
Christian Brothers U (TN)
Coll of Saint Mary (NE)
The Coll of Saint Rose (NY)
Coll of Staten Island of the City U of New York (NY)
Coll of the Ozarks (MO)
Concordia U Chicago (IL)
Covenant Coll (GA)
Culver-Stockton Coll (MO)
Curry Coll (MA)
Dakota State U (SD)
Daytona State Coll (FL)
Delta State U (MS)
Duquesne U (PA)
East Carolina U (NC)
Eastern Washington U (WA)
East Texas Baptist U (TX)
Emmanuel Coll (GA)
Fitchburg State U (MA)
Florida Ag and Mech U (FL)
Florida Atlantic U (FL)
Florida Southern Coll (FL)
Geneva Coll (PA)
Goshen Coll (IN)
Grand Valley State U (MI)
Granite State Coll (NH)
Greenville U (IL)
Grove City Coll (PA)
Gwynedd Mercy U (PA)
Harding U (AR)
Hardin-Simmons U (TX)
Hofstra U (NY)
Hunter Coll of the City U of New York (NY)
Indiana U Bloomington (IN)
Indiana U Northwest (IN)
Indiana U South Bend (IN)
Indiana U Southeast (IN)
Inter American U of Puerto Rico, San Germán Campus (PR)
Iona Coll (NY)
Ithaca Coll (NY)
Jackson State U (MS)
Juniata Coll (PA)
Kansas Wesleyan U (KS)
Lee U (TN)
LeTourneau U (TX)
Limestone Coll (SC)
Lipscomb U (TN)
Louisiana Coll (LA)
Loyola U Chicago (IL)
Madonna U (MI)
Manchester U (IN)
Manhattanville Coll (NY)
Marist Coll (NY)
Marquette U (WI)
Martin Luther Coll (MN)
Marywood U (PA)
Merrimack Coll (MA)
Messiah Coll (PA)
Miami U (OH)
Miami U Hamilton (OH)
Michigan State U (MI)
Millikin U (IL)
Minnesota State U Moorhead (MN)
Morningside Coll (IA)
Mount Marty Coll (SD)
National U (CA)
Nazareth Coll of Rochester (NY)
New York U (NY)
North Carolina State U (NC)
Northeastern State U (OK)
Northern State U (SD)
Northwestern Oklahoma State U (OK)
Northwestern U (IL)
Northwest Missouri State U (MO)
Oakland City U (IN)
Ohio Dominican U (OH)
Ohio Wesleyan U (OH)
Oklahoma Baptist U (OK)
Oklahoma Christian U (OK)
Pace U (NY)
Pace U, Pleasantville Campus (NY)
Palm Beach Atlantic U (FL)
Pepperdine U, Malibu (CA)
Piedmont Coll (GA)
Providence Coll (RI)
Queens Coll of the City U of New York (NY)
Regis U (CO)
Reinhardt U (GA)
Rhode Island Coll (RI)
Rocky Mountain Coll (MT)
Saginaw Valley State U (MI)
Saint Francis U (PA)
St. John Fisher Coll (NY)
St. Joseph's Coll, Long Island Campus (NY)
St. Joseph's Coll, New York (NY)
Saint Joseph's U (PA)
Saint Mary's U of Minnesota (MN)
Salve Regina U (RI)
Seattle U (WA)
Seton Hill U (PA)
Southeastern Louisiana U (LA)
Southeastern U (FL)
Southeast Missouri State U (MO)
Southern U and Ag and Mech Coll (LA)
Southwest Baptist U (MO)
Spring Hill Coll (AL)
State U of New York Coll at Potsdam (NY)
Syracuse U (NY)
Taylor U (IN)
Temple U (PA)
Texas Christian U (TX)
Texas Lutheran U (TX)
Trevecca Nazarene U (TN)
Trinity Christian Coll (IL)
Union Coll (KY)
U of Detroit Mercy (MI)
The U of Findlay (OH)
U of Georgia (GA)
U of Maine (ME)
U of Maine at Farmington (ME)
U of Maine at Machias (ME)
U of Mary Hardin-Baylor (TX)
U of Michigan–Dearborn (MI)
U of Minnesota, Duluth (MN)
U of Nebraska–Lincoln (NE)
U of New Hampshire (NH)
The U of North Carolina at Pembroke (NC)
U of Northern Iowa (IA)
U of North Florida (FL)
U of Northwestern–St. Paul (MN)
U of Providence (MT)
U of Regina (SK, Canada)
U of St. Thomas (MN)
U of Sioux Falls (SD)
U of South Dakota (SD)
U of South Florida (FL)
The U of Tulsa (OK)
U of Vermont (VT)
U of Wisconsin–Milwaukee (WI)
U of Wisconsin–Superior (WI)
Utah State U (UT)
Utah Valley U (UT)
Utica Coll (NY)
Valley City State U (ND)
Valparaiso U (IN)
Vincennes U (IN)
Wartburg Coll (IA)
Washington U in St. Louis (MO)
Waynesburg U (PA)
Weber State U (UT)
Western Washington U (WA)
Westmont Coll (CA)
Whitworth U (WA)
Widener U (PA)
Youngstown State U (OH)

MECHANICAL DRAFTING AND CAD/CADD
Indiana U–Purdue U Indianapolis (IN)

MECHANICAL ENGINEERING
Alfred U (NY)
American U of Beirut (Lebanon)
Arkansas Tech U (AR)
Auburn U (AL)
Baylor U (TX)
Bethel Coll (KS)
Boston U (MA)
Bradley U (IL)
Bucknell U (PA)
California Inst of Technology (CA)
California Polytechnic State U, San Luis Obispo (CA)
California State U, Chico (CA)
California State U, Fullerton (CA)
California State U, Long Beach (CA)
California State U, Los Angeles (CA)
California State U, Northridge (CA)
Calvin Coll (MI)
Carnegie Mellon U (PA)
The Catholic U of America (DC)
Cedarville U (OH)
Central Connecticut State U (CT)
Central Michigan U (MI)
Christian Brothers U (TN)
Clarkson U (NY)
Colorado School of Mines (CO)
Colorado State U (CO)
Columbia U (NY)
Cornell U (NY)
Dunwoody Coll of Technology (MN)
Eastern Washington U (WA)
Embry-Riddle Aeronautical U–Daytona (FL)
Embry-Riddle Aeronautical U–Prescott (AZ)
Fairfield U (CT)
Florida Ag and Mech U (FL)
Florida Atlantic U (FL)
Franklin W. Olin Coll of Eng (MA)
George Mason U (VA)
Georgia Southern U (GA)
Gonzaga U (WA)
Grand Valley State U (MI)
Grove City Coll (PA)
Hanover Coll (IN)
Harding U (AR)
Hofstra U (NY)
Idaho State U (ID)
Indiana U–Purdue U Indianapolis (IN)
Inter American U of Puerto Rico, Bayamón Campus (PR)
Iowa State U of Science and Technology (IA)
Jacksonville U (FL)
Johns Hopkins U (MD)
Kennesaw State U (GA)
King's Coll (PA)
Lafayette Coll (PA)
Lamar U (TX)
Lawrence Technological U (MI)
Lebanese American U (Lebanon)
LeTourneau U (TX)
Liberty U (VA)
Lipscomb U (TN)
Louisiana State U and A&M Coll (LA)
Loyola Marymount U (CA)
Manhattan Coll (NY)
Marquette U (WI)
Marshall U (WV)
Massachusetts Inst of Technology (MA)
Merrimack Coll (MA)
Messiah Coll (PA)
Miami U (OH)
Michigan State U (MI)
Milligan Coll (TN)
New England Inst of Technology (RI)
New Jersey Inst of Technology (NJ)
New York U (NY)
North Carolina State U (NC)
Northern Illinois U (IL)
Northwestern U (IL)
The Ohio State U (OH)
Ohio U (OH)
Oklahoma Christian U (OK)
Oklahoma State U (OK)
Old Dominion U (VA)
Portland State U (OR)
Prairie View A&M U (TX)
Princeton U (NJ)
Purdue U (IN)
Purdue U Northwest (IN)
Rice U (TX)
Rochester Inst of Technology (NY)
Saginaw Valley State U (MI)
Saint Louis U (MO)
Saint Martin's U (WA)
St. Mary's U (TX)
San Diego State U (CA)
San Francisco State U (CA)
San Jose State U (CA)
Seattle U (WA)
Southern Illinois U Carbondale (IL)
Southern Illinois U Edwardsville (IL)
Southern U and Ag and Mech Coll (LA)
State U of New York Maritime Coll (NY)
Stevens Inst of Technology (NJ)
Syracuse U (NY)
Temple U (PA)
Texas Tech U (TX)
Union Coll (NY)
Université de Sherbrooke (QC, Canada)
U at Buffalo, the State U of New York (NY)
U of Arkansas (AR)
U of California, Davis (CA)
U of California, Irvine (CA)
U of California, Los Angeles (CA)
U of California, Merced (CA)
U of California, Riverside (CA)
U of Central Florida (FL)
U of Colorado Denver (CO)
U of Dayton (OH)
U of Florida (FL)
U of Georgia (GA)
U of Hawaii at Manoa (HI)
U of Houston (TX)
U of Houston–Clear Lake (TX)
U of Idaho (ID)
U of Kentucky (KY)
U of Louisville (KY)
U of Maine (ME)
U of Maryland, Baltimore County (MD)
U of Maryland, Coll Park (MD)
U of Massachusetts Amherst (MA)
U of Massachusetts Dartmouth (MA)
U of Massachusetts Lowell (MA)
U of Memphis (TN)
U of Michigan (MI)
U of Michigan–Dearborn (MI)
U of Minnesota, Duluth (MN)
U of Minnesota, Twin Cities Campus (MN)
U of Missouri (MO)
U of Mount Union (OH)
U of Nebraska–Lincoln (NE)
U of Nevada, Las Vegas (NV)
U of Nevada, Reno (NV)
U of New Hampshire (NH)
U of New Haven (CT)
U of New Mexico (NM)
The U of North Carolina at Charlotte (NC)
U of North Dakota (ND)
U of North Florida (FL)
U of Notre Dame (IN)
U of Pennsylvania (PA)
U of Pittsburgh (PA)
U of St. Thomas (MN)
U of San Diego (CA)
U of South Alabama (AL)
U of South Carolina (SC)
U of Southern Indiana (IN)
U of South Florida (FL)
The U of Tennessee (TN)
The U of Texas at Austin (TX)
The U of Texas at El Paso (TX)
The U of Texas of the Permian Basin (TX)
The U of Texas Rio Grande Valley (TX)
The U of Toledo (OH)
The U of Tulsa (OK)
U of Vermont (VT)
U of Virginia (VA)
U of Washington (WA)
U of Washington, Bothell (WA)
U of Wisconsin–Milwaukee (WI)
U of Wyoming (WY)
Utah State U (UT)
Valparaiso U (IN)
Vaughn Coll of Aeronautics and Technology (NY)
Virginia Commonwealth U (VA)
Virginia Polytechnic Inst and State U (VA)
Washington State U (WA)
Washington State U–Tri-Cities (WA)
Washington State U–Vancouver (WA)
Washington U in St. Louis (MO)
Western Illinois U (IL)
Western Kentucky U (KY)
Westmont Coll (CA)
West Virginia U Inst of Technology (WV)
Widener U (PA)
Wilkes U (PA)
Worcester Polytechnic Inst (MA)
Wright State U–Lake Campus (OH)
Youngstown State U (OH)

MECHANICAL ENGINEERING/ MECHANICAL TECHNOLOGY
Bowling Green State U (OH)
California State U, Long Beach (CA)
Central Connecticut State U (CT)
Central Michigan U (MI)
Central Washington U (WA)
Eastern Washington U (WA)
Farmingdale State Coll (NY)
Idaho State U (ID)
Kennesaw State U (GA)
LeTourneau U (TX)
Miami U Hamilton (OH)
Oklahoma State U (OK)
Purdue U Northwest (IN)
State U of New York Coll of Technology at Alfred (NY)
Texas A&M U–Central Texas (TX)
U of Dayton (OH)
U of Houston (TX)
U of Maine (ME)
The U of North Carolina at Charlotte (NC)
The U of Toledo (OH)
Weber State U (UT)
Youngstown State U (OH)

MECHANICAL ENGINEERING TECHNOLOGIES RELATED
Indiana State U (IN)
Indiana U–Purdue U Indianapolis (IN)
LeTourneau U (TX)
Purdue U Northwest (IN)
U of Massachusetts Lowell (MA)
Vaughn Coll of Aeronautics and Technology (NY)

MECHANICS AND REPAIR
Idaho State U (ID)

MECHATRONICS, ROBOTICS, AND AUTOMATION ENGINEERING
California U of Pennsylvania (PA)
Lawrence Technological U (MI)
Lebanese American U (Lebanon)
Middle Tennessee State U (TN)
Southern Illinois U Edwardsville (IL)
U of Detroit Mercy (MI)
U of Michigan–Dearborn (MI)
U of Washington (WA)
Widener U (PA)
Worcester Polytechnic Inst (MA)

MEDICAL ANTHROPOLOGY
Creighton U (NE)
Lycoming Coll (PA)
The Ohio State U (OH)
Washington U in St. Louis (MO)

MEDICAL/CLINICAL ASSISTANT
Idaho State U (ID)

MEDICAL/HEALTH MANAGEMENT AND CLINICAL ASSISTANT
Davenport U, Grand Rapids (MI)
Nebraska Methodist Coll (NE)
Rider U (NJ)

MEDICAL ILLUSTRATION
Cleveland Inst of Art (OH)
Iowa State U of Science and Technology (IA)
Rochester Inst of Technology (NY)

MEDICAL INFORMATICS
Idaho State U (ID)
Indiana U–Purdue U Indianapolis (IN)
King U (TN)
LeTourneau U (TX)
Northern Kentucky U (KY)
State U of New York at Plattsburgh (NY)
Texas Woman's U (TX)
U of South Alabama (AL)

MEDICAL MICROBIOLOGY AND BACTERIOLOGY
Adams State U (CO)
Auburn U (AL)
Bowling Green State U (OH)
California Polytechnic State U, San Luis Obispo (CA)
Ohio Wesleyan U (OH)
San Francisco State U (CA)
Sonoma State U (CA)
Université de Sherbrooke (QC, Canada)
U of Florida (FL)
U of Minnesota, Twin Cities Campus (MN)
U of South Florida (FL)
Utah State U (UT)

MEDICAL OFFICE MANAGEMENT
Manor Coll (PA)

MEDICAL RADIOLOGIC TECHNOLOGY
Averett U (VA)
Avila U (MO)
Baptist Coll of Health Sciences (TN)
Bellarmine U (KY)
California State U, Long Beach (CA)
Clarion U of Pennsylvania (PA)
Grand Valley State U (MI)
Gwynedd Mercy U (PA)
Idaho State U (ID)
Indiana U Kokomo (IN)
Indiana U Northwest (IN)
Indiana U–Purdue U Indianapolis (IN)
Indiana U South Bend (IN)
Inter American U of Puerto Rico, San Germán Campus (PR)
Mount Marty Coll (SD)
National U (CA)
Northern Kentucky U (KY)
The Ohio State U (OH)
Saint Louis U (MO)
Southern Illinois U Carbondale (IL)
U of Nevada, Las Vegas (NV)
U of New Mexico (NM)
The U of North Carolina at Chapel Hill (NC)
U of Sioux Falls (SD)
U of Southern Indiana (IN)
U of Vermont (VT)
U of Wisconsin–La Crosse (WI)
Weber State U (UT)

MEDICINAL AND PHARMACEUTICAL CHEMISTRY
U of Dayton (OH)
U of Michigan (MI)

MEDIEVAL AND RENAISSANCE STUDIES
The Catholic U of America (DC)
Coll of the Holy Cross (MA)
The Coll of William and Mary (VA)
Columbia U (NY)
Cornell Coll (IA)
Dickinson Coll (PA)
Fordham U (NY)
Hanover Coll (IN)
Lycoming Coll (PA)
New Coll of Florida (FL)
New York U (NY)
The Ohio State U (OH)
Ohio Wesleyan U (OH)
Purdue U (IN)
Saint Louis U (MO)
St. Olaf Coll (MN)
Tulane U (LA)
U of Chicago (IL)
U of Michigan (MI)
U of Minnesota, Morris (MN)
U of Nebraska–Lincoln (NE)
U of Notre Dame (IN)
U of Oregon (OR)
U of Regina (SK, Canada)
The U of the South (TN)
Vassar Coll (NY)
Washington and Lee U (VA)

MEETING AND EVENT PLANNING
Central Michigan U (MI)
Coll of the Ozarks (MO)
High Point U (NC)
Iowa State U of Science and Technology (IA)
Lasell Coll (MA)
U of Central Florida (FL)

MENTAL AND SOCIAL HEALTH SERVICES AND ALLIED PROFESSIONS RELATED
Clarion U of Pennsylvania (PA)
New England Inst of Technology (RI)
Northern Kentucky U (KY)
Old Dominion U (VA)

MENTAL HEALTH COUNSELING
Canisius Coll (NY)
Iona Coll (NY)

MERCHANDISING, SALES, AND MARKETING OPERATIONS RELATED (GENERAL)
Georgia State U (GA)
High Point U (NC)
Washington U in St. Louis (MO)

MERCHANDISING, SALES, AND MARKETING OPERATIONS RELATED (SPECIALIZED)
Baylor U (TX)
Fashion Inst of Technology (NY)
Graceland U (IA)
High Point U (NC)

METAL AND JEWELRY ARTS
Acad of Art U (CA)
Adams State U (CO)
Bowling Green State U (OH)
California State U, Long Beach (CA)
Central Washington U (WA)
Cleveland Inst of Art (OH)
Hofstra U (NY)
Rhode Island Coll (RI)
Rhode Island School of Design (RI)
Rochester Inst of Technology (NY)
Savannah Coll of Art and Design (GA)
Seton Hill U (PA)
Syracuse U (NY)
Temple U (PA)
U of Massachusetts Dartmouth (MA)
U of Michigan (MI)
U of Oregon (OR)

METALLURGICAL ENGINEERING
Colorado School of Mines (CO)
LeTourneau U (TX)
U of Nevada, Reno (NV)
The U of Texas at El Paso (TX)

METEOROLOGY
Central Michigan U (MI)
Coll of Charleston (SC)
Iowa State U of Science and Technology (IA)
U of Hawaii at Manoa (HI)
The U of North Carolina at Charlotte (NC)
U of South Alabama (AL)
U of the Incarnate Word (TX)
U of Wisconsin–Milwaukee (WI)
Virginia Polytechnic Inst and State U (VA)
Western Illinois U (IL)
Western Kentucky U (KY)

MICROBIOLOGICAL SCIENCES AND IMMUNOLOGY RELATED
U of California, Los Angeles (CA)

MICROBIOLOGY
Auburn U (AL)
Bowling Green State U (OH)
California State U, Chico (CA)
California State U, Long Beach (CA)
California State U, Los Angeles (CA)
Central Washington U (WA)
Colorado State U (CO)
Concordia U Chicago (IL)
Idaho State U (ID)
Indiana U Bloomington (IN)
Inter American U of Puerto Rico, Aguadilla Campus (PR)
Inter American U of Puerto Rico, Bayamón Campus (PR)
Inter American U of Puerto Rico, San Germán Campus (PR)
Iowa State U of Science and Technology (IA)
Louisiana State U and A&M Coll (LA)
Miami U (OH)
Miami U Hamilton (OH)
Michigan State U (MI)
North Carolina State U (NC)
The Ohio State U (OH)
Ohio U (OH)
Oklahoma State U (OK)
San Diego State U (CA)
Southern Illinois U Carbondale (IL)
Texas Tech U (TX)
U of California, Davis (CA)
U of Georgia (GA)
U of Hawaii at Manoa (HI)
U of Idaho (ID)
U of Maine (ME)
U of Maryland, Coll Park (MD)
U of Massachusetts Amherst (MA)
U of Michigan (MI)
U of Michigan–Dearborn (MI)
U of Nebraska–Lincoln (NE)
U of Pittsburgh (PA)
U of Vermont (VT)
U of Washington (WA)
U of Wisconsin–La Crosse (WI)
U of Wisconsin–Milwaukee (WI)
U of Wyoming (WY)
Washington State U (WA)
Washington U in St. Louis (MO)
Weber State U (UT)

MICROBIOLOGY AND IMMUNOLOGY
Purdue U (IN)
U of California, Irvine (CA)
U of Nevada, Reno (NV)

MIDDLE/NEAR EASTERN AND SEMITIC LANGUAGES
Indiana U Bloomington (IN)
Pepperdine U, Malibu (CA)
U of Pennsylvania (PA)

MIDDLE/NEAR EASTERN AND SEMITIC LANGUAGES RELATED
Boston U (MA)
U of Chicago (IL)
U of Michigan (MI)
U of Washington (WA)

MIDDLE SCHOOL EDUCATION
Alverno Coll (WI)
Appalachian State U (NC)
Arkansas Tech U (AR)
Austin Coll (TX)
Avila U (MO)
Baker U (KS)
Baldwin Wallace U (OH)
Barton Coll (NC)
Bellarmine U (KY)
Berea Coll (KY)
Bowling Green State U (OH)
Brenau U (GA)
California U of Pennsylvania (PA)
Carson-Newman U (TN)
Cedarville U (OH)
Central State U (OH)
Champlain Coll (VT)
Clark U (MA)
Coastal Carolina U (SC)
Coll of Charleston (SC)
Coll of Coastal Georgia (GA)
DePaul U (IL)
Duquesne U (PA)
East Carolina U (NC)
Eastern Illinois U (IL)
Eastern U (PA)
East Stroudsburg U of Pennsylvania (PA)
Emmanuel Coll (GA)
Fayetteville State U (NC)
Fitchburg State U (MA)
Georgia Coll & State U (GA)
Georgia Southern U (GA)
Gordon Coll (MA)
Grand Valley State U (MI)
Granite State Coll (NH)
Grove City Coll (PA)
Harding U (AR)
High Point U (NC)
Hiram Coll (OH)
Indiana U of Pennsylvania (PA)
Ithaca Coll (NY)
Kennesaw State U (GA)
La Salle U (PA)
Lee U (TN)
Lesley U (MA)
Lindenwood U (MO)
Lipscomb U (TN)
Lock Haven U of Pennsylvania (PA)
Lubbock Christian U (TX)
Manchester U (IN)
Manhattan Coll (NY)
Maryville U of Saint Louis (MO)
Mercer U, Macon (GA)
Merrimack Coll (MA)
Messiah Coll (PA)
Miami U (OH)
Michigan State U (MI)
Millersville U of Pennsylvania (PA)
Millikin U (IL)
Missouri Baptist U (MO)
Mount St. Joseph U (OH)
Murray State U (KY)
Muskingum U (OH)
North Carolina State U (NC)
Northern Kentucky U (KY)
Northwest Christian U (OR)
Northwest Missouri State U (MO)
Ohio Dominican U (OH)
The Ohio State U (OH)
The Ohio State U at Lima (OH)
The Ohio State U at Mansfield (OH)
The Ohio State U at Marion (OH)
The Ohio State U at Newark (OH)
Ohio Wesleyan U (OH)
Ouachita Baptist U (AR)
Piedmont Coll (GA)
Point U (GA)
Reinhardt U (GA)
Saint Leo U (FL)
Saint Vincent Coll (PA)
Southeastern Louisiana U (LA)
Southeast Missouri State U (MO)
Southern Arkansas U–Magnolia (AR)
Southern Illinois U Edwardsville (IL)
Southern U and Ag and Mech Coll (LA)
Southwest Baptist U (MO)
Temple U (PA)
Texas Lutheran U (TX)
Toccoa Falls Coll (GA)
Towson U (MD)
Trinity Christian Coll (IL)
U of Dayton (OH)
The U of Findlay (OH)
U of Georgia (GA)
U of Kentucky (KY)
U of Maryland, Baltimore County (MD)
U of Maryland, Coll Park (MD)
U of Minnesota, Duluth (MN)
U of Missouri (MO)
U of Mount Union (OH)
The U of North Carolina at Chapel Hill (NC)
The U of North Carolina at Charlotte (NC)
The U of North Carolina at Greensboro (NC)
The U of North Carolina at Pembroke (NC)
U of North Dakota (ND)
U of Northern Iowa (IA)
U of North Florida (FL)
U of Providence (MT)
U of Regina (SK, Canada)
U of St. Thomas (MN)
U of Sioux Falls (SD)
U of South Carolina (SC)
U of South Carolina Aiken (SC)
U of Vermont (VT)
U of Wisconsin–Milwaukee (WI)
Valparaiso U (IN)
Washington U in St. Louis (MO)
West Chester U of Pennsylvania (PA)
Western Illinois U (IL)
Western Kentucky U (KY)
Wilkes U (PA)
Wright State U–Lake Campus (OH)
Youngstown State U (OH)

MILITARY AND STRATEGIC LEADERSHIP
Excelsior Coll (NY)

MILITARY HISTORY
American Public U System (WV)
Marquette U (WI)

MILITARY STUDIES
American Public U System (WV)
Excelsior Coll (NY)

MINING AND MINERAL ENGINEERING
Colorado School of Mines (CO)
Southern Illinois U Carbondale (IL)
U of Kentucky (KY)
U of Nevada, Reno (NV)
Virginia Polytechnic Inst and State U (VA)

MISSIONARY STUDIES AND MISSIOLOGY
Carson-Newman U (TN)
Cedarville U (OH)
Dallas Baptist U (TX)
Eastern U (PA)
Geneva Coll (PA)
Harding U (AR)
Johnson U Florida (FL)
Lancaster Bible Coll (PA)
Lee U (TN)
LeTourneau U (TX)
Lincoln Christian U (IL)
Lipscomb U (TN)
Lubbock Christian U (TX)
Milligan Coll (TN)
Northwest Christian U (OR)
Oklahoma Christian U (OK)
Ouachita Baptist U (AR)
Palm Beach Atlantic U (FL)
Samford U (AL)
Southeastern U (FL)
Southwest Baptist U (MO)
Toccoa Falls Coll (GA)
U of Northwestern–St. Paul (MN)
Vanguard U of Southern California (CA)

MODELING, VIRTUAL ENVIRONMENTS AND SIMULATION
Acad of Art U (CA)
Albright Coll (PA)
DigiPen Inst of Technology (WA)
Rider U (NJ)

MODERN GREEK
Furman U (SC)
The Ohio State U (OH)
Tulane U (LA)
U of Michigan (MI)
Wright State U–Lake Campus (OH)

MODERN LANGUAGES
Beloit Coll (WI)
Clark U (MA)
The Coll of William and Mary (VA)
Cornell Coll (IA)
Nazareth Coll of Rochester (NY)
Purchase Coll, State U of New York (NY)
Washington U in St. Louis (MO)
Westmont Coll (CA)
Widener U (PA)

MOLECULAR BIOCHEMISTRY
Bryant U (RI)
Clarkson U (NY)
U of California, Davis (CA)
U of California, Santa Cruz (CA)
U of Richmond (VA)
Wesleyan U (CT)

MOLECULAR BIOLOGY
Alverno Coll (WI)
Assumption Coll (MA)
Auburn U (AL)
Beloit Coll (WI)
Blackburn Coll (IL)
Boston U (MA)
California Lutheran U (CA)
Central Connecticut State U (CT)
Claremont McKenna Coll (CA)
Clarion U of Pennsylvania (PA)
Clark U (MA)
Colgate U (NY)
Dartmouth Coll (NH)
Goshen Coll (IN)
Grove City Coll (PA)
Humboldt State U (CA)
Johns Hopkins U (MD)
Lawrence Technological U (MI)
Messiah Coll (PA)
Millikin U (IL)
Montclair State U (NJ)
Muskingum U (OH)
Northwestern U (IL)
Pitzer Coll (CA)
Princeton U (NJ)
Rollins Coll (FL)
San Francisco State U (CA)
San Jose State U (CA)
Scripps Coll (CA)
Stetson U (FL)
Tulane U (LA)
U of California, Santa Cruz (CA)
U of Idaho (ID)
U of Maine (ME)
U of Michigan (MI)
U of North Dakota (ND)
U of Pittsburgh (PA)
U of Vermont (VT)
U of Wisconsin–Eau Claire (WI)
U of Wyoming (WY)
William Jewell Coll (MO)

MOLECULAR GENETICS
Michigan State U (MI)
The Ohio State U (OH)

MOVEMENT THERAPY AND MOVEMENT EDUCATION
Texas Christian U (TX)

MULTICULTURAL EDUCATION
Fort Lewis Coll (CO)

MULTI/INTERDISCIPLINARY STUDIES RELATED
Adams State U (CO)
Adelphi U (NY)
Agnes Scott Coll (GA)
Alabama State U (AL)
Albion Coll (MI)
Allegheny Coll (PA)
Alverno Coll (WI)
American U (DC)
Angelo State U (TX)
Arkansas Tech U (AR)
Austin Coll (TX)
Baldwin Wallace U (OH)
Barton Coll (NC)
Baylor U (TX)
Bellarmine U (KY)
Bennett Coll (NC)
Bentley U (MA)
Berea Coll (KY)
Bethel U (MN)
Boston U (MA)
Bowling Green State U (OH)
Brandeis U (MA)
Bucknell U (PA)
Buena Vista U (IA)
Caldwell U (NJ)
California Inst of Technology (CA)
California Lutheran U (CA)
California Polytechnic State U, San Luis Obispo (CA)
California State U, Long Beach (CA)
California State U, Los Angeles (CA)
California State U, Monterey Bay (CA)
California State U, San Bernardino (CA)
California State U, San Marcos (CA)
Cameron U (OK)
Cedarville U (OH)
Central Connecticut State U (CT)
Central Washington U (WA)
Christopher Newport U (VA)
Claremont McKenna Coll (CA)
Clarkson U (NY)
Coll of Charleston (SC)
The Coll of Idaho (ID)
The Coll of William and Mary (VA)
The Colorado Coll (CO)
Columbia Coll Chicago (IL)
Cornell Coll (IA)
Covenant Coll (GA)
Curry Coll (MA)
Dallas Baptist U (TX)
Dallas Christian Coll (TX)
Dartmouth Coll (NH)
Davidson Coll (NC)
Delaware Valley U (PA)
Delta State U (MS)
Earlham Coll (IN)
Eastern Illinois U (IL)
Eastern Mennonite U (VA)
Eastern Washington U (WA)
East Tennessee State U (TN)
East Texas Baptist U (TX)
Embry-Riddle Aeronautical U–Prescott (AZ)
Emmanuel Coll (MA)
The Evergreen State Coll (WA)
Florida Southern Coll (FL)
Fordham U (NY)
Framingham State U (MA)
Georgia State U (GA)
Granite State Coll (NH)
Greenville U (IL)
Hamline U (MN)
High Point U (NC)
Hood Coll (MD)
Humboldt State U (CA)
Idaho State U (ID)
Immaculata U (PA)
Indiana State U (IN)
Indiana U–Purdue U Indianapolis (IN)
Indiana U Southeast (IN)
Inter American U of Puerto Rico, Aguadilla Campus (PR)
Ithaca Coll (NY)
Jackson State U (MS)
Jacksonville U (FL)
Johnson C. Smith U (NC)
Juniata Coll (PA)
Kalamazoo Coll (MI)
Kennesaw State U (GA)
King U (TN)
Lamar U (TX)
Lasell Coll (MA)
Lawrence U (WI)
Lebanon Valley Coll (PA)
LeTourneau U (TX)
Liberty U (VA)
Louisiana Coll (LA)
Louisiana State U and A&M Coll (LA)
Loyola Marymount U (CA)
Loyola U Chicago (IL)
Loyola U New Orleans (LA)
Lycoming Coll (PA)
Macalester Coll (MN)
Manchester U (IN)
Manhattan Coll (NY)
Marquette U (WI)
McDaniel Coll (MD)
Mercer U, Macon (GA)
Messiah Coll (PA)
Miami U (OH)
Miami U Hamilton (OH)
Michigan State U (MI)
Middle Tennessee State U (TN)
Millikin U (IL)
Millsaps Coll (MS)
Minnesota State U Moorhead (MN)
Missouri Baptist U (MO)
Montclair State U (NJ)
Northeastern State U (OK)
Northern Illinois U (IL)
Northwest Christian U (OR)
Northwestern Oklahoma State U (OK)
Northwestern U (IL)
The Ohio State U (OH)
Ohio Wesleyan U (OH)
Old Dominion U (VA)
Pace U (NY)
Palm Beach Atlantic U (FL)
Pepperdine U, Malibu (CA)
Prairie View A&M U (TX)
Princeton U (NJ)
Radford U (VA)
Regis U (CO)
Rice U (TX)
Rochester Coll (MI)
Rollins Coll (FL)
Saginaw Valley State U (MI)
Saint Anselm Coll (NH)
Saint Martin's U (WA)
St. Mary's Coll of Maryland (MD)
Salisbury U (MD)
San Diego State U (CA)
San Francisco State U (CA)
San Jose State U (CA)
Scripps Coll (CA)
Sonoma State U (CA)
Southeastern U (FL)
Southeast Missouri State U (MO)
Southern Arkansas U–Magnolia (AR)
Southern Illinois U Carbondale (IL)
State U of New York Maritime Coll (NY)
Stevens Inst of Technology (NJ)
Stonehill Coll (MA)
Syracuse U (NY)
Taylor U (IN)
Temple U (PA)
Texas A&M U–Central Texas (TX)
Texas Tech U (TX)
Texas Woman's U (TX)
Towson U (MD)
Trevecca Nazarene U (TN)
Truman State U (MO)
Tulane U (LA)
U at Buffalo, the State U of New York (NY)
U of California, Davis (CA)
U of California, Irvine (CA)
U of California, Los Angeles (CA)
U of California, Merced (CA)
U of Colorado Denver (CO)
U of Dallas (TX)
U of Florida (FL)
U of Houston (TX)
U of Houston–Clear Lake (TX)
U of Houston–Downtown (TX)
U of Idaho (ID)
U of Kentucky (KY)
U of Maine (ME)
U of Maine at Farmington (ME)
U of Maryland, Baltimore County (MD)
U of Maryland, Coll Park (MD)
U of Maryland U Coll (MD)
U of Massachusetts Amherst (MA)
U of Massachusetts Boston (MA)
U of Massachusetts Dartmouth (MA)
U of Memphis (TN)
U of Michigan (MI)
U of Michigan–Dearborn (MI)
U of Minnesota, Duluth (MN)
U of Minnesota, Morris (MN)
U of Minnesota, Twin Cities Campus (MN)
U of Montevallo (AL)
U of Nevada, Las Vegas (NV)
U of New Hampshire (NH)
The U of North Carolina at Greensboro (NC)
The U of North Carolina at Pembroke (NC)
U of North Dakota (ND)
U of Northern Colorado (CO)
U of Northwestern–St. Paul (MN)
U of Pittsburgh (PA)
U of Richmond (VA)
U of South Dakota (SD)
The U of Tennessee (TN)
The U of Tennessee at Martin (TN)
The U of Texas of the Permian Basin (TX)
The U of Texas Rio Grande Valley (TX)
The U of the South (TN)
U of Virginia (VA)
U of Washington, Bothell (WA)
U of Washington, Tacoma (WA)
The U of West Alabama (AL)
U of Wisconsin–Milwaukee (WI)
U of Wisconsin–River Falls (WI)
U of Wisconsin–Superior (WI)
U of Wyoming (WY)
Ursinus Coll (PA)
Utah State U (UT)
Utah Valley U (UT)
Valparaiso U (IN)
Vassar Coll (NY)
Virginia Commonwealth U (VA)
Washington & Jefferson Coll (PA)
Washington and Lee U (VA)
Washington State U (WA)
Washington U in St. Louis (MO)
Waynesburg U (PA)
Western Kentucky U (KY)
Western Washington U (WA)
West Virginia U Inst of Technology (WV)
Wheaton Coll (IL)
Wheaton Coll (MA)
Wilkes U (PA)
William Jewell Coll (MO)
Williams Coll (MA)
Woodbury U (CA)
Wright State U–Lake Campus (OH)

MUSEUM STUDIES
Beloit Coll (WI)
Central Washington U (WA)
The Colorado Coll (CO)
Juniata Coll (PA)
Middlebury Coll (VT)
Randolph Coll (VA)
U of Saint Francis (IN)

MUSIC
Acadia U (NS, Canada)
Adams State U (CO)
Adelphi U (NY)
Agnes Scott Coll (GA)
Alabama State U (AL)
Albion Coll (MI)
Allegheny Coll (PA)
Alverno Coll (WI)
American U (DC)
Angelo State U (TX)
Arkansas Tech U (AR)
Assumption Coll (MA)
Auburn U (AL)
Aurora U (IL)
Austin Coll (TX)
Austin Peay State U (TN)
Averett U (VA)
Avila U (MO)
Baker U (KS)
Baldwin Wallace U (OH)
Baruch Coll of the City U of New York (NY)
Baylor U (TX)
Bellarmine U (KY)
Benedictine U (IL)
Bennett Coll (NC)
Berea Coll (KY)
Bethany Lutheran Coll (MN)
Bethel U (MN)
Blackburn Coll (IL)
Boston Coll (MA)
Boston U (MA)
Bowling Green State U (OH)
Bradley U (IL)
Brandeis U (MA)
Brenau U (GA)
Bridgewater State U (MA)
Bucknell U (PA)
Butler U (IN)
Caldwell U (NJ)
California Lutheran U (CA)
California Polytechnic State U, San Luis Obispo (CA)
California State U, Bakersfield (CA)
California State U, Chico (CA)
California State U, Fullerton (CA)
California State U, Long Beach (CA)
California State U, Los Angeles (CA)
California State U, Monterey Bay (CA)
California State U, Northridge (CA)
California State U, San Bernardino (CA)
California State U, San Marcos (CA)
Calvin Coll (MI)
Cameron U (OK)
Campbellsville U (KY)
Capilano U (BC, Canada)
Carson-Newman U (TN)
Carthage Coll (WI)
The Catholic U of America (DC)
Cedarville U (OH)
Centenary Coll of Louisiana (LA)
Central Connecticut State U (CT)
Central Michigan U (MI)
Central Washington U (WA)
Clark U (MA)
Coastal Carolina U (SC)
Colgate U (NY)
Coll of Charleston (SC)
The Coll of Idaho (ID)
Coll of Saint Benedict (MN)
The Coll of Saint Rose (NY)
Coll of Staten Island of the City U of New York (NY)
Coll of the Holy Cross (MA)
Coll of the Ozarks (MO)
The Coll of William and Mary (VA)
The Colorado Coll (CO)
Colorado State U (CO)
Colorado State U–Pueblo (CO)
Columbia Coll (MO)
Columbia Coll Chicago (IL)
Columbia U (NY)
Concordia U Chicago (IL)
Connecticut Coll (CT)
Cornell Coll (IA)
Cornell U (NY)
Covenant Coll (GA)
Creighton U (NE)
Culver-Stockton Coll (MO)
Dallas Baptist U (TX)
Dartmouth Coll (NH)
Davidson Coll (NC)
Delta State U (MS)
DePaul U (IL)
DEREE - The American Coll of Greece (Greece)
Dickinson Coll (PA)
Dominican U (IL)
Drake U (IA)
Drew U (NJ)
Drury U (MO)
Duquesne U (PA)
Earlham Coll (IN)
East Carolina U (NC)
Eastern Illinois U (IL)
Eastern Mennonite U (VA)
Eastern Oregon U (OR)
Eastern U (PA)
Eastern Washington U (WA)
East Tennessee State U (TN)
East Texas Baptist U (TX)
Eckerd Coll (FL)
Elizabeth City State U (NC)
Emmanuel Coll (GA)
Fairfield U (CT)
Fayetteville State U (NC)
Florida Ag and Mech U (FL)
Florida Atlantic U (FL)
Florida Coll (FL)
Florida Southern Coll (FL)
Fordham U (NY)
Fort Lewis Coll (CO)
Franklin Pierce U (NH)
Furman U (SC)
Geneva Coll (PA)
Georgia Coll & State U (GA)
Georgia Southern U (GA)
Gordon Coll (MA)
Goshen Coll (IN)
Grand Valley State U (MI)
Greenville U (IL)
Grove City Coll (PA)
Hamilton Coll (NY)
Hamline U (MN)
Hanover Coll (IN)
Harding U (AR)
Hardin-Simmons U (TX)
Hartwick Coll (NY)
Harvard U (MA)
Haverford Coll (PA)
High Point U (NC)
Hillsdale Coll (MI)
Hofstra U (NY)
Hollins U (VA)
Hood Coll (MD)
Humboldt State U (CA)
Hunter Coll of the City U of New York (NY)
Idaho State U (ID)
Illinois Coll (IL)
Immaculata U (PA)

Indiana State U (IN)
Indiana U of Pennsylvania (PA)
Indiana U South Bend (IN)
Indiana U Southeast (IN)
Inter American U of Puerto Rico, San Germán Campus (PR)
Iowa State U of Science and Technology (IA)
Ithaca Coll (NY)
Jacksonville U (FL)
Johns Hopkins U (MD)
Johnson C. Smith U (NC)
The Juilliard School (NY)
Kalamazoo Coll (MI)
Kansas Wesleyan U (KS)
Kean U (NJ)
Kennesaw State U (GA)
King U (TN)
Knox Coll (IL)
Lafayette Coll (PA)
LaGrange Coll (GA)
Lake Forest Coll (IL)
Lamar U (TX)
La Sierra U (CA)
Lawrence U (WI)
Lee U (TN)
Liberty U (VA)
Limestone Coll (SC)
Lindenwood U (MO)
Linfield Coll (OR)
Lipscomb U (TN)
Lock Haven U of Pennsylvania (PA)
Loras Coll (IA)
Louisiana Coll (LA)
Louisiana State U and A&M Coll (LA)
Loyola Marymount U (CA)
Loyola U Chicago (IL)
Loyola U New Orleans (LA)
Lubbock Christian U (TX)
Lycoming Coll (PA)
Macalester Coll (MN)
Madonna U (MI)
Manchester U (IN)
Manhattanville Coll (NY)
Mansfield U of Pennsylvania (PA)
Marian U (IN)
Massachusetts Coll of Liberal Arts (MA)
Massachusetts Inst of Technology (MA)
McDaniel Coll (MD)
Mercer U, Macon (GA)
Messiah Coll (PA)
Miami U (OH)
Miami U Hamilton (OH)
Michigan State U (MI)
Middlebury Coll (VT)
Middle Tennessee State U (TN)
Millersville U of Pennsylvania (PA)
Milligan Coll (TN)
Millikin U (IL)
Millsaps Coll (MS)
Mills Coll (CA)
Minnesota State U Moorhead (MN)
Missouri Baptist U (MO)
Molloy Coll (NY)
Montclair State U (NJ)
Morningside Coll (IA)
Mount St. Joseph U (OH)
Murray State U (KY)
Muskingum U (OH)
Nazareth Coll of Rochester (NY)
New Coll of Florida (FL)
New Jersey City U (NJ)
New York U (NY)
Northeastern State U (OK)
Northern Illinois U (IL)
Northern Kentucky U (KY)
Northern State U (SD)
Northwestern Oklahoma State U (OK)
Northwestern U (IL)
Northwest Missouri State U (MO)
Oakland City U (IN)
Occidental Coll (CA)
The Ohio State U (OH)
Ohio Wesleyan U (OH)
Oklahoma Baptist U (OK)
Oklahoma Christian U (OK)
Oklahoma State U (OK)
Ottawa U (KS)
Ouachita Baptist U (AR)
Pacific Lutheran U (WA)
Palm Beach Atlantic U (FL)
Pepperdine U, Malibu (CA)
Pfeiffer U (NC)
Piedmont Coll (GA)
Point Loma Nazarene U (CA)
Point U (GA)
Portland State U (OR)
Prairie View A&M U (TX)
Princeton U (NJ)
Providence Coll (RI)
Purchase Coll, State U of New York (NY)
Queens U of Charlotte (NC)
Radford U (VA)
Randolph-Macon Coll (VA)
Redeemer U Coll (ON, Canada)
Reinhardt U (GA)
Rhode Island Coll (RI)
Rhodes Coll (TN)
Rice U (TX)
Rider U (NJ)
Roanoke Coll (VA)
Rockford U (IL)
Rocky Mountain Coll (MT)
Rollins Coll (FL)
Saginaw Valley State U (MI)
Saint John's U (MN)
Saint Joseph's U (PA)
Saint Louis U (MO)
Saint Martin's U (WA)
St. Mary's Coll of Maryland (MD)
St. Mary's U (TX)
Saint Mary's U of Minnesota (MN)
St. Norbert Coll (WI)
St. Olaf Coll (MN)
Saint Vincent Coll (PA)
Salisbury U (MD)
Salve Regina U (RI)
Samford U (AL)
San Diego State U (CA)
San Francisco State U (CA)
San Jose State U (CA)
Sarah Lawrence Coll (NY)
Scripps Coll (CA)
Seattle U (WA)
Seton Hill U (PA)
Sonoma State U (CA)
Southeast Missouri State U (MO)
Southern Arkansas U–Magnolia (AR)
Southern Illinois U Carbondale (IL)
Southern Illinois U Edwardsville (IL)
Southwest Baptist U (MO)
Southwestern U (TX)
State U of New York at Fredonia (NY)
State U of New York at Plattsburgh (NY)
State U of New York Coll at Geneseo (NY)
State U of New York Coll at Potsdam (NY)
Stetson U (FL)
Sweet Briar Coll (VA)
Syracuse U (NY)
Taylor U (IN)
Temple U (PA)
Texas A&M Intl U (TX)
Texas A&M U–Central Texas (TX)
Texas Christian U (TX)
Texas Lutheran U (TX)
Texas Tech U (TX)
Texas Woman's U (TX)
Tiffin U (OH)
Toccoa Falls Coll (GA)
Towson U (MD)
Trinity Christian Coll (IL)
Truman State U (MO)
Tulane U (LA)
Union Coll (KY)
Université de Sherbrooke (QC, Canada)
U at Buffalo, the State U of New York (NY)
U of California, Davis (CA)
U of California, Irvine (CA)
U of California, Los Angeles (CA)
U of California, Riverside (CA)
U of California, Santa Cruz (CA)
U of Chicago (IL)
U of Colorado Denver (CO)
U of Dayton (OH)
U of Florida (FL)
U of Georgia (GA)
U of Hawaii at Manoa (HI)
U of Houston (TX)
U of La Verne (CA)
U of Louisville (KY)
U of Lynchburg (VA)
U of Maine (ME)
U of Maine at Farmington (ME)
U of Maine at Machias (ME)
U of Mary Hardin-Baylor (TX)
U of Maryland, Baltimore County (MD)
U of Maryland, Coll Park (MD)
U of Massachusetts Amherst (MA)
U of Massachusetts Boston (MA)
U of Massachusetts Dartmouth (MA)
U of Massachusetts Lowell (MA)
U of Memphis (TN)
U of Michigan (MI)
U of Minnesota, Duluth (MN)
U of Minnesota, Morris (MN)
U of Minnesota, Twin Cities Campus (MN)
U of Missouri (MO)
U of Montevallo (AL)
U of Mount Union (OH)
U of Nebraska–Lincoln (NE)
U of Nevada, Las Vegas (NV)
U of Nevada, Reno (NV)
U of New Hampshire (NH)
U of New Haven (CT)
U of North Carolina at Asheville (NC)
The U of North Carolina at Chapel Hill (NC)
The U of North Carolina at Charlotte (NC)
The U of North Carolina at Greensboro (NC)
The U of North Carolina at Pembroke (NC)
U of North Dakota (ND)
U of Northern Colorado (CO)
U of Northern Iowa (IA)
U of Northwestern–St. Paul (MN)
U of Notre Dame (IN)
U of Oregon (OR)
U of Pennsylvania (PA)
U of Pittsburgh (PA)
U of Puget Sound (WA)
U of Regina (SK, Canada)
U of Richmond (VA)
U of St. Thomas (MN)
U of St. Thomas (TX)
U of San Diego (CA)
U of Sioux Falls (SD)
U of South Alabama (AL)
U of South Carolina (SC)
U of South Dakota (SD)
The U of Tampa (FL)
The U of Tennessee (TN)
The U of Tennessee at Martin (TN)
The U of Texas at Austin (TX)
The U of Texas at El Paso (TX)
The U of Texas of the Permian Basin (TX)
U of the Incarnate Word (TX)
The U of the South (TN)
The U of Toledo (OH)
The U of Tulsa (OK)
U of Vermont (VT)
U of Virginia (VA)
U of Washington (WA)
The U of West Alabama (AL)
U of Wisconsin–Eau Claire (WI)
U of Wisconsin–La Crosse (WI)
U of Wisconsin–Milwaukee (WI)
U of Wisconsin–River Falls (WI)
U of Wisconsin–Superior (WI)
U of Wyoming (WY)
Utah State U (UT)
Utah Valley U (UT)
Valley City State U (ND)
Valparaiso U (IN)
Vanguard U of Southern California (CA)
Vassar Coll (NY)
Virginia Polytechnic Inst and State U (VA)
Wabash Coll (IN)
Wartburg Coll (IA)
Washington & Jefferson Coll (PA)
Washington and Lee U (VA)
Washington State U (WA)
Washington U in St. Louis (MO)
Weber State U (UT)
Wesleyan Coll (GA)
West Chester U of Pennsylvania (PA)
Western Connecticut State U (CT)
Western State Colorado U (CO)
Western Washington U (WA)
Westmont Coll (CA)
Wheaton Coll (IL)
Wheaton Coll (MA)
Whittier Coll (CA)
Whitworth U (WA)
Willamette U (OR)
William Jewell Coll (MO)
Williams Coll (MA)
Winthrop U (SC)
Wright State U–Lake Campus (OH)
Youngstown State U (OH)

MUSICAL THEATER
American U (DC)
Aurora U (IL)
Averett U (VA)
Blackburn Coll (IL)
Brenau U (GA)
Carthage Coll (WI)
Central Michigan U (MI)
Central Washington U (WA)
Columbia Coll Chicago (IL)
Cornell Coll (IA)
Creighton U (NE)
Culver-Stockton Coll (MO)
Dean Coll (MA)
Florida Southern Coll (FL)
Indiana U Bloomington (IN)
Ithaca Coll (NY)
Kansas Wesleyan U (KS)
LaGrange Coll (GA)
Lees-McRae Coll (NC)
Limestone Coll (SC)
Lindenwood U (MO)
Louisiana Coll (LA)
Loyola U New Orleans (LA)
Marywood U (PA)
Messiah Coll (PA)
Milligan Coll (TN)
Millikin U (IL)
Minnesota State U Moorhead (MN)
Missouri Baptist U (MO)
Ouachita Baptist U (AR)
Pace U (NY)
Rhode Island Coll (RI)
Samford U (AL)
Sweet Briar Coll (VA)
Syracuse U (NY)
Taylor U (IN)
Texas Christian U (TX)
U at Buffalo, the State U of New York (NY)
U of California, Irvine (CA)
U of Michigan (MI)
U of North Dakota (ND)
The U of Tampa (FL)
Weber State U (UT)
William Jewell Coll (MO)

MUSIC HISTORY, LITERATURE, AND THEORY
American U (DC)
Baldwin Wallace U (OH)
Baylor U (TX)
Bowling Green State U (OH)
Bridgewater Coll (VA)
Bucknell U (PA)
California State U, Long Beach (CA)
Calvin Coll (MI)
The Catholic U of America (DC)
Hofstra U (NY)
Jacksonville U (FL)
Liberty U (VA)
Nazareth Coll of Rochester (NY)
Northwestern U (IL)
The Ohio State U (OH)
Ouachita Baptist U (AR)
Randolph Coll (VA)
Rice U (TX)
Rider U (NJ)
Skidmore Coll (NY)
Southwestern U (TX)
State U of New York at Fredonia (NY)
Syracuse U (NY)
Temple U (PA)
U of California, Los Angeles (CA)
U of Kentucky (KY)
U of Michigan (MI)
U of Regina (SK, Canada)
U of Washington (WA)
Ursinus Coll (PA)
Washington U in St. Louis (MO)
Western Washington U (WA)
Wheaton Coll (IL)
Wright State U–Lake Campus (OH)
Youngstown State U (OH)

MUSIC MANAGEMENT
Albright Coll (PA)
Appalachian State U (NC)
Bradley U (IL)
Buena Vista U (IA)
Columbia Coll Chicago (IL)
Dallas Baptist U (TX)
DePaul U (IL)
Drake U (IA)
Florida Atlantic U (FL)
Florida Southern Coll (FL)
Geneva Coll (PA)
Greenville U (IL)
Grove City Coll (PA)
Hardin-Simmons U (TX)
Hofstra U (NY)
Jacksonville U (FL)
Judson U (IL)
Lamar U (TX)
Lebanon Valley Coll (PA)
Lee U (TN)
Liberty U (VA)
Lindenwood U (MO)
Loyola U New Orleans (LA)
Lubbock Christian U (TX)
Madonna U (MI)
Mansfield U of Pennsylvania (PA)
Messiah Coll (PA)
Middle Tennessee State U (TN)
Missouri Baptist U (MO)
Murray State U (KY)
Nazareth Coll of Rochester (NY)
Northwest Christian U (OR)
Southeastern U (FL)
State U of New York at Fredonia (NY)
State U of New York Coll at Potsdam (NY)
Syracuse U (NY)
Trevecca Nazarene U (TN)
U of Idaho (ID)
U of Memphis (TN)
U of New Haven (CT)
U of Puget Sound (WA)
U of the Incarnate Word (TX)

MUSICOLOGY AND ETHNOMUSICOLOGY
Boston U (MA)
Bowling Green State U (OH)
East Tennessee State U (TN)
Liberty U (VA)
Northwestern U (IL)
U of California, Los Angeles (CA)

MUSIC PEDAGOGY
Baylor U (TX)
Cedarville U (OH)
Ithaca Coll (NY)
Liberty U (VA)
Michigan State U (MI)
Temple U (PA)
U of Maryland, Baltimore County (MD)
Weber State U (UT)
Wheaton Coll (IL)
Whitworth U (WA)
Willamette U (OR)

MUSIC PERFORMANCE
Adams State U (CO)
Albion Coll (MI)
Appalachian State U (NC)
Avila U (MO)
Baldwin Wallace U (OH)
Baylor U (TX)
Bethel U (MN)
Boston U (MA)
Bowling Green State U (OH)
Bradley U (IL)
Bucknell U (PA)
Buena Vista U (IA)
Butler U (IN)
California State U, Fullerton (CA)
California State U, Long Beach (CA)
California State U, Los Angeles (CA)
Calvin Coll (MI)
Carnegie Mellon U (PA)
Carson-Newman U (TN)
The Catholic U of America (DC)
Cedarville U (OH)
Central State U (OH)
Central Washington U (WA)
Christopher Newport U (VA)
The Coll of Saint Rose (NY)
The Coll of St. Scholastica (MN)

Columbia Coll Chicago (IL)
Concordia U Chicago (IL)
Covenant Coll (GA)
DePaul U (IL)
Drake U (IA)
Duquesne U (PA)
Florida Southern Coll (FL)
Fort Lewis Coll (CO)
George Mason U (VA)
Georgia State U (GA)
Gonzaga U (WA)
Gordon Coll (MA)
Graceland U (IA)
Grove City Coll (PA)
Hamline U (MN)
Hofstra U (NY)
Idaho State U (ID)
Indiana State U (IN)
Indiana U Bloomington (IN)
Indiana U of Pennsylvania (PA)
Indiana U South Bend (IN)
Ithaca Coll (NY)
Jackson State U (MS)
Jacksonville U (FL)
Johnson C. Smith U (NC)
Judson U (IL)
The Juilliard School (NY)
Kansas Wesleyan U (KS)
Kean U (NJ)
Kennesaw State U (GA)
LaGrange Coll (GA)
La Sierra U (CA)
Lawrence U (WI)
Lebanon Valley Coll (PA)
Lee U (TN)
Liberty U (VA)
Limestone Coll (SC)
Lipscomb U (TN)
Louisiana State U and A&M Coll (LA)
Loyola U New Orleans (LA)
Madonna U (MI)
Manchester U (IN)
Mansfield U of Pennsylvania (PA)
Marian U (IN)
Marywood U (PA)
McNeese State U (LA)
Mercer U, Macon (GA)
Messiah Coll (PA)
Miami U (OH)
Michigan State U (MI)
Millikin U (IL)
Missouri Baptist U (MO)
Montclair State U (NJ)
Morningside Coll (IA)
Nazareth Coll of Rochester (NY)
New York U (NY)
Northern Illinois U (IL)
Northwestern U (IL)
The Ohio State U (OH)
Ohio U (OH)
Ohio Wesleyan U (OH)
Oklahoma Baptist U (OK)
Old Dominion U (VA)
Ouachita Baptist U (AR)
Palm Beach Atlantic U (FL)
Piedmont Coll (GA)
Point Loma Nazarene U (CA)
Portland State U (OR)
Purchase Coll, State U of New York (NY)
Queens Coll of the City U of New York (NY)
Randolph Coll (VA)
Rhode Island Coll (RI)
Rice U (TX)
Rochester Coll (MI)
Rockford U (IL)
Rocky Mountain Coll (MT)
Saint Mary's U of Minnesota (MN)
St. Olaf Coll (MN)
Saint Vincent Coll (PA)
Samford U (AL)
San Diego State U (CA)
San Francisco State U (CA)
San Jose State U (CA)
Seton Hill U (PA)
Southeastern Louisiana U (LA)
Southeastern U (FL)
Southern U and Ag and Mech Coll (LA)
Southwestern U (TX)
State U of New York Coll at Potsdam (NY)
Stetson U (FL)
Syracuse U (NY)
Taylor U (IN)
Temple U (PA)
Texas Christian U (TX)
Toccoa Falls Coll (GA)
Trevecca Nazarene U (TN)
Truman State U (MO)
Tulane U (LA)
U at Buffalo, the State U of New York (NY)
U of Arkansas (AR)
U of California, Irvine (CA)
U of Central Arkansas (AR)
U of Central Florida (FL)
U of Dayton (OH)
U of Georgia (GA)
U of Houston (TX)
U of Idaho (ID)
U of Kentucky (KY)
U of Maine (ME)
U of Mary Hardin-Baylor (TX)
U of Maryland, Baltimore County (MD)
U of Maryland, Coll Park (MD)
U of Massachusetts Amherst (MA)
U of Massachusetts Lowell (MA)
U of Michigan (MI)
U of Minnesota, Duluth (MN)
U of Nevada, Reno (NV)
U of New Mexico (NM)
The U of North Carolina at Chapel Hill (NC)
The U of North Carolina at Greensboro (NC)
The U of North Carolina at Pembroke (NC)
U of North Carolina School of the Arts (NC)
U of North Dakota (ND)
U of Northern Iowa (IA)
U of North Florida (FL)
U of Northwestern–St. Paul (MN)
U of Oregon (OR)
U of Puget Sound (WA)
U of St. Thomas (MN)
U of South Dakota (SD)
U of South Florida (FL)
The U of Tampa (FL)
The U of Texas at Austin (TX)
The U of Tulsa (OK)
U of Vermont (VT)
U of Washington (WA)
U of West Georgia (GA)
U of Wisconsin–Superior (WI)
U of Wyoming (WY)
Utah Valley U (UT)
Valparaiso U (IN)
Vanguard U of Southern California (CA)
Virginia Commonwealth U (VA)
Wartburg Coll (IA)
Washington State U (WA)
Weber State U (UT)
West Chester U of Pennsylvania (PA)
Western Connecticut State U (CT)
Western Illinois U (IL)
Western Kentucky U (KY)
Western Washington U (WA)
West Virginia State U (WV)
Wheaton Coll (IL)
Whitworth U (WA)
Willamette U (OR)
William Jewell Coll (MO)
Wright State U–Lake Campus (OH)
Youngstown State U (OH)

MUSIC RELATED

Acad of Art U (CA)
Alverno Coll (WI)
Bellarmine U (KY)
Bethel Coll (KS)
Bowling Green State U (OH)
Carnegie Mellon U (PA)
Coll of the Ozarks (MO)
Columbia Coll Chicago (IL)
Concordia U Irvine (CA)
DePaul U (IL)
Duquesne U (PA)
Greenville U (IL)
Grove City Coll (PA)
Indiana U Bloomington (IN)
Indiana U South Bend (IN)
Jacksonville U (FL)
Lipscomb U (TN)
Mercer U, Macon (GA)
Messiah Coll (PA)
Murray State U (KY)
Northwestern U (IL)
Palm Beach Atlantic U (FL)
Pepperdine U, Malibu (CA)
Saint Mary's U of Minnesota (MN)
Tiffin U (OH)
Trevecca Nazarene U (TN)
Trinity Christian Coll (IL)
U of California, Riverside (CA)
U of Memphis (TN)
U of Minnesota, Duluth (MN)
U of North Carolina at Asheville (NC)
U of Northern Iowa (IA)
The U of Tennessee at Martin (TN)
The U of Tulsa (OK)
U of Washington (WA)
Valparaiso U (IN)
Wesleyan U (CT)
Western Illinois U (IL)
Western Kentucky U (KY)
Wheaton Coll (IL)
Whitworth U (WA)

MUSIC TEACHER EDUCATION

Acadia U (NS, Canada)
Adams State U (CO)
Adelphi U (NY)
Alabama State U (AL)
Albion Coll (MI)
Appalachian State U (NC)
Arkansas Tech U (AR)
Auburn U (AL)
Baker U (KS)
Baldwin Wallace U (OH)
Baylor U (TX)
Beloit Coll (WI)
Benedictine U (IL)
Bethel U (MN)
Boston U (MA)
Bowling Green State U (OH)
Bradley U (IL)
Brenau U (GA)
Bridgewater State U (MA)
Bucknell U (PA)
Buena Vista U (IA)
Butler U (IN)
California Lutheran U (CA)
California State U, Fullerton (CA)
Cameron U (OK)
Campbellsville U (KY)
Carson-Newman U (TN)
Carthage Coll (WI)
Cedarville U (OH)
Centenary Coll of Louisiana (LA)
Central Connecticut State U (CT)
Central Michigan U (MI)
Central State U (OH)
Central Washington U (WA)
The Coll of Saint Rose (NY)
Coll of the Ozarks (MO)
Concordia U Chicago (IL)
Cornell Coll (IA)
Culver-Stockton Coll (MO)
Dallas Baptist U (TX)
Delta State U (MS)
DePaul U (IL)
Drake U (IA)
Duquesne U (PA)
East Carolina U (NC)
Eastern Washington U (WA)
East Texas Baptist U (TX)
Emmanuel Coll (GA)
Florida Ag and Mech U (FL)
Florida Atlantic U (FL)
Florida Southern Coll (FL)
Fort Lewis Coll (CO)
Furman U (SC)
Geneva Coll (PA)
Georgia Coll & State U (GA)
Georgia Southern U (GA)
Gonzaga U (WA)
Gordon Coll (MA)
Goshen Coll (IN)
Grand Valley State U (MI)
Greenville U (IL)
Grove City Coll (PA)
Harding U (AR)
Hardin-Simmons U (TX)
Hartwick Coll (NY)
Hofstra U (NY)
Humboldt State U (CA)
Idaho State U (ID)
Immaculata U (PA)
Indiana U Bloomington (IN)
Indiana U South Bend (IN)
Inter American U of Puerto Rico, San Germán Campus (PR)
Ithaca Coll (NY)
Jackson State U (MS)
Jacksonville U (FL)
Kansas Wesleyan U (KS)
Kean U (NJ)
Kennesaw State U (GA)
King U (TN)
LaGrange Coll (GA)
Lancaster Bible Coll (PA)
La Sierra U (CA)
Lawrence U (WI)
Lebanon Valley Coll (PA)
Lee U (TN)
Limestone Coll (SC)
Lindenwood U (MO)
Lipscomb U (TN)
Loras Coll (IA)
Louisiana Coll (LA)
Louisiana State U and A&M Coll (LA)
Loyola U New Orleans (LA)
Lubbock Christian U (TX)
Madonna U (MI)
Manchester U (IN)
Manhattanville Coll (NY)
Mansfield U of Pennsylvania (PA)
Marian U (IN)
Martin Luther Coll (MN)
Marywood U (PA)
Mercer U, Macon (GA)
Messiah Coll (PA)
Miami U (OH)
Miami U Hamilton (OH)
Michigan State U (MI)
Milligan Coll (TN)
Millikin U (IL)
Minnesota State U Moorhead (MN)
Missouri Baptist U (MO)
Molloy Coll (NY)
Morningside Coll (IA)
Muskingum U (OH)
Nazareth Coll of Rochester (NY)
New Jersey City U (NJ)
New York U (NY)
Northeastern State U (OK)
Northern Kentucky U (KY)
Northern State U (SD)
Northwestern Oklahoma State U (OK)
Northwestern U (IL)
Northwest Missouri State U (MO)
The Ohio State U (OH)
Ohio Wesleyan U (OH)
Oklahoma Baptist U (OK)
Oklahoma Christian U (OK)
Oklahoma State U (OK)
Ouachita Baptist U (AR)
Pacific Lutheran U (WA)
Palm Beach Atlantic U (FL)
Pepperdine U, Malibu (CA)
Pfeiffer U (NC)
Piedmont Coll (GA)
Point Loma Nazarene U (CA)
Providence Coll (RI)
Queens Coll of the City U of New York (NY)
Reinhardt U (GA)
Rhode Island Coll (RI)
Rider U (NJ)
Rocky Mountain Coll (MT)
Saginaw Valley State U (MI)
Saint Mary's U of Minnesota (MN)
St. Norbert Coll (WI)
St. Olaf Coll (MN)
Salve Regina U (RI)
Samford U (AL)
San Diego State U (CA)
Seton Hill U (PA)
Sonoma State U (CA)
Southeastern U (FL)
Southeast Missouri State U (MO)
Southern Arkansas U–Magnolia (AR)
Southern U and Ag and Mech Coll (LA)
Southwest Baptist U (MO)
State U of New York at Fredonia (NY)
State U of New York Coll at Potsdam (NY)
Stetson U (FL)
Syracuse U (NY)
Tabor Coll (KS)
Taylor U (IN)
Temple U (PA)
Texas Christian U (TX)
Texas Lutheran U (TX)
Toccoa Falls Coll (GA)
Towson U (MD)
Trevecca Nazarene U (TN)
Trinity Christian Coll (IL)
U of Dayton (OH)
U of Florida (FL)
U of Georgia (GA)
U of Idaho (ID)
U of Kentucky (KY)
U of Louisville (KY)
U of Lynchburg (VA)
U of Maine (ME)
U of Mary Hardin-Baylor (TX)
U of Maryland, Coll Park (MD)
U of Michigan (MI)
U of Minnesota, Duluth (MN)
U of Minnesota, Twin Cities Campus (MN)
U of Mount Union (OH)
U of Nebraska–Lincoln (NE)
U of Nevada, Reno (NV)
U of New Mexico (NM)
The U of North Carolina at Greensboro (NC)
The U of North Carolina at Pembroke (NC)
U of North Dakota (ND)
U of Northern Colorado (CO)
U of Northern Iowa (IA)
U of North Florida (FL)
U of Northwestern–St. Paul (MN)
U of Oregon (OR)
U of Puget Sound (WA)
U of Regina (SK, Canada)
U of St. Thomas (MN)
U of St. Thomas (TX)
U of Sioux Falls (SD)
U of South Carolina (SC)
U of South Carolina Aiken (SC)
U of South Dakota (SD)
U of South Florida (FL)
The U of Tampa (FL)
U of the Incarnate Word (TX)
The U of Tulsa (OK)
U of Vermont (VT)
U of Washington (WA)
U of Wisconsin–Milwaukee (WI)
U of Wisconsin–River Falls (WI)
U of Wisconsin–Superior (WI)
U of Wyoming (WY)
Utah State U (UT)
Utah Valley U (UT)
Valley City State U (ND)
Valparaiso U (IN)
Vanguard U of Southern California (CA)
Wartburg Coll (IA)
Weber State U (UT)
Western Connecticut State U (CT)
Western Washington U (WA)
Wheaton Coll (IL)
Whitworth U (WA)
Winthrop U (SC)
Wright State U–Lake Campus (OH)
Youngstown State U (OH)

MUSIC TECHNOLOGY

American U (DC)
California U of Pennsylvania (PA)
Carnegie Mellon U (PA)
Columbia Coll Chicago (IL)
Connecticut Coll (CT)
Culver-Stockton Coll (MO)
Indiana U–Purdue U Indianapolis (IN)
LaGrange Coll (GA)
La Sierra U (CA)
Lebanon Valley Coll (PA)
Loyola U New Orleans (LA)
Mercy Coll (NY)
Millersville U of Pennsylvania (PA)
Northwest Christian U (OR)
Stetson U (FL)
Stevens Inst of Technology (NJ)
Syracuse U (NY)
U of Maryland, Baltimore County (MD)
U of Michigan (MI)
U of New Haven (CT)
U of North Carolina at Asheville (NC)
U of Northern Iowa (IA)
U of Saint Francis (IN)
The U of Texas at Austin (TX)
Utah Valley U (UT)

MUSIC THEORY AND COMPOSITION

Acad of Art U (CA)

Adams State U (CO)
Baldwin Wallace U (OH)
Baylor U (TX)
Boston U (MA)
Bowling Green State U (OH)
Bradley U (IL)
Bucknell U (PA)
Butler U (IN)
California State U, Long Beach (CA)
Calvin Coll (MI)
Carnegie Mellon U (PA)
Carson-Newman U (TN)
The Catholic U of America (DC)
Cedarville U (OH)
Central Michigan U (MI)
Central Washington U (WA)
Coll of the Ozarks (MO)
Columbia Coll Chicago (IL)
Concordia U Chicago (IL)
Dallas Baptist U (TX)
DePaul U (IL)
DigiPen Inst of Technology (WA)
Hardin-Simmons U (TX)
Hofstra U (NY)
Ithaca Coll (NY)
Jacksonville U (FL)
Lawrence U (WI)
Lewis & Clark Coll (OR)
Lipscomb U (TN)
Loyola U New Orleans (LA)
Madonna U (MI)
Manchester U (IN)
Michigan State U (MI)
Northwest Christian U (OR)
Northwestern U (IL)
The Ohio State U (OH)
Ohio U (OH)
Oklahoma Baptist U (OK)
Ouachita Baptist U (AR)
Palm Beach Atlantic U (FL)
Pepperdine U, Malibu (CA)
Point Loma Nazarene U (CA)
Purchase Coll, State U of New York (NY)
Rice U (TX)
Rider U (NJ)
St. Olaf Coll (MN)
Samford U (AL)
Southwestern U (TX)
Stetson U (FL)
Syracuse U (NY)
Taylor U (IN)
Temple U (PA)
Texas Christian U (TX)
Trevecca Nazarene U (TN)
Tulane U (LA)
U of Dayton (OH)
U of Georgia (GA)
U of Idaho (ID)
U of Maryland, Baltimore County (MD)
U of Michigan (MI)
U of Minnesota, Duluth (MN)
U of Northern Iowa (IA)
U of Northwestern–St. Paul (MN)
U of Oregon (OR)
U of Regina (SK, Canada)
The U of Texas at Austin (TX)
The U of Tulsa (OK)
U of Washington (WA)
Valparaiso U (IN)
Wartburg Coll (IA)
Washington State U (WA)
Washington U in St. Louis (MO)
Western Connecticut State U (CT)
Western Washington U (WA)
Wheaton Coll (IL)
Whitworth U (WA)
Willamette U (OR)
Youngstown State U (OH)

MUSIC THERAPY
Alverno Coll (WI)
Appalachian State U (NC)
Baldwin Wallace U (OH)
Capilano U (BC, Canada)
Drury U (MO)
Duquesne U (PA)
Georgia Coll & State U (GA)
Immaculata U (PA)
Indiana U–Purdue U Indianapolis (IN)
Loyola U New Orleans (LA)
Maryville U of Saint Louis (MO)
Marywood U (PA)
Molloy Coll (NY)
Montclair State U (NJ)
Nazareth Coll of Rochester (NY)
Queens U of Charlotte (NC)
Seton Hill U (PA)
State U of New York at Fredonia (NY)
Temple U (PA)
Texas Woman's U (TX)
U of Dayton (OH)
U of Georgia (GA)
U of Louisville (KY)
U of Minnesota, Twin Cities Campus (MN)
U of North Dakota (ND)
U of the Incarnate Word (TX)
Utah State U (UT)
Wartburg Coll (IA)

NANOTECHNOLOGY
Excelsior Coll (NY)
Virginia Polytechnic Inst and State U (VA)

NATIONAL SECURITY POLICY
Angelo State U (TX)
Baldwin Wallace U (OH)
Excelsior Coll (NY)
U of New Haven (CT)

NATURAL RESOURCE ECONOMICS
Baldwin Wallace U (OH)
Juniata Coll (PA)
Michigan State U (MI)
U of New Hampshire (NH)
The U of Tennessee (TN)

NATURAL RESOURCE RECREATION AND TOURISM
Auburn U (AL)
U of Georgia (GA)
U of Idaho (ID)
U of Vermont (VT)

NATURAL RESOURCES AND CONSERVATION RELATED
Bowling Green State U (OH)
California Polytechnic State U, San Luis Obispo (CA)
Juniata Coll (PA)
U of California, Davis (CA)
Utah State U (UT)

NATURAL RESOURCES/ CONSERVATION
Central Michigan U (MI)
Colorado State U (CO)
Colorado State U–Pueblo (CO)
Cornell U (NY)
The Evergreen State Coll (WA)
Grand Valley State U (MI)
Humboldt State U (CA)
Lubbock Christian U (TX)
Manchester U (IN)
Muskingum U (OH)
North Carolina State U (NC)
The Ohio State U (OH)
Purdue U (IN)
Texas Tech U (TX)
Towson U (MD)
U of California, Davis (CA)
U of Kentucky (KY)
U of Maryland, Coll Park (MD)
U of Maryland U Coll (MD)
U of Massachusetts Amherst (MA)
U of Michigan (MI)
U of Michigan–Dearborn (MI)
U of Nebraska–Lincoln (NE)
U of New Hampshire (NH)
The U of the South (TN)
U of Vermont (VT)
U of Wisconsin–River Falls (WI)
Washington State U (WA)
Washington U in St. Louis (MO)

NATURAL RESOURCES/ CONSERVATION RELATED
Miami U (OH)

NATURAL RESOURCES LAW ENFORCEMENT AND PROTECTIVE SERVICES
Texas Tech U (TX)

NATURAL RESOURCES MANAGEMENT AND POLICY
Angelo State U (TX)
Auburn U (AL)
Bowling Green State U (OH)
Bryant U (RI)
Clark U (MA)
Humboldt State U (CA)
Louisiana State U and A&M Coll (LA)
Marist Coll (NY)
North Carolina State U (NC)
The Ohio State U (OH)
Rochester Inst of Technology (NY)
State U of New York Coll of Environmental Science and Forestry (NY)
U of Hawaii at Manoa (HI)
U of La Verne (CA)
U of Nebraska–Lincoln (NE)
U of New Haven (CT)
The U of Tennessee at Martin (TN)
Washington U in St. Louis (MO)

NATURAL RESOURCES MANAGEMENT AND POLICY RELATED
Humboldt State U (CA)
The Ohio State U (OH)
Western Washington U (WA)

NATURAL SCIENCES
American Public U System (WV)
Bethel Coll (KS)
California State U, Los Angeles (CA)
Calvin Coll (MI)
Carthage Coll (WI)
Christian Brothers U (TN)
Colgate U (NY)
Coll of Saint Benedict (MN)
Coll of Saint Mary (NE)
Colorado State U (CO)
Concordia U Chicago (IL)
Dallas Baptist U (TX)
Dominican U (IL)
The Evergreen State Coll (WA)
Excelsior Coll (NY)
Fordham U (NY)
Hofstra U (NY)
Humboldt State U (CA)
Indiana U East (IN)
Inter American U of Puerto Rico, Aguadilla Campus (PR)
Inter American U of Puerto Rico, San Germán Campus (PR)
Johns Hopkins U (MD)
Judson U (IL)
Juniata Coll (PA)
Lesley U (MA)
Loyola Marymount U (CA)
Madonna U (MI)
Mount St. Joseph U (OH)
Mount Saint Mary Coll (NY)
New Coll of Florida (FL)
Oklahoma Baptist U (OK)
Pepperdine U, Malibu (CA)
Saint John's U (MN)
Saint Vincent Coll (PA)
San Jose State U (CA)
State U of New York Coll at Geneseo (NY)
State U of New York Coll at Potsdam (NY)
Temple U (PA)
U of California, Santa Cruz (CA)
U of Detroit Mercy (MI)
U of La Verne (CA)
U of Pennsylvania (PA)
U of Puget Sound (WA)
U of Washington (WA)
Washington U in St. Louis (MO)

NAVAL ARCHITECTURE AND MARINE ENGINEERING
Massachusetts Maritime Acad (MA)
State U of New York Maritime Coll (NY)
Stevens Inst of Technology (NJ)
U of Michigan (MI)

NAVY/MARINE CORPS ROTC/ NAVAL SCIENCE
Iowa State U of Science and Technology (IA)

NEAR AND MIDDLE EASTERN STUDIES
American U (DC)
Boston U (MA)
Brandeis U (MA)
Central Michigan U (MI)
Claremont McKenna Coll (CA)
Colgate U (NY)
Coll of the Holy Cross (MA)
Columbia U (NY)
Cornell U (NY)
Dartmouth Coll (NH)
Dickinson Coll (PA)
Fordham U (NY)
Harvard U (MA)
Hood Coll (MD)
Johns Hopkins U (MD)
Manhattanville Coll (NY)
McDaniel Coll (MD)
Middlebury Coll (VT)
New York U (NY)
Portland State U (OR)
Princeton U (NJ)
Queens Coll of the City U of New York (NY)
Sarah Lawrence Coll (NY)
Scripps Coll (CA)
Syracuse U (NY)
U of California, Riverside (CA)
U of Massachusetts Amherst (MA)
U of Michigan (MI)
U of Richmond (VA)
The U of Texas at Austin (TX)
The U of Toledo (OH)
Washington U in St. Louis (MO)
Williams Coll (MA)

NETWORK AND SYSTEM ADMINISTRATION
Central Connecticut State U (CT)
Champlain Coll (VT)
Columbia Central U, Caguas (PR)
Kansas Wesleyan U (KS)
Point U (GA)
Regis U (CO)
Rochester Inst of Technology (NY)
U of Providence (MT)

NEUROBIOLOGY AND ANATOMY
Harvard U (MA)
Purdue U (IN)
U of California, Davis (CA)
U of California, Irvine (CA)
U of Washington (WA)

NEUROBIOLOGY AND BEHAVIOR
Fitchburg State U (MA)
La Sierra U (CA)

NEUROBIOLOGY AND NEUROSCIENCES RELATED
Carnegie Mellon U (PA)
Wesleyan Coll (GA)

NEUROSCIENCE
Adelphi U (NY)
Agnes Scott Coll (GA)
Allegheny Coll (PA)
American U (DC)
Assumption Coll (MA)
Auburn U (AL)
Baldwin Wallace U (OH)
Baylor U (TX)
Boston Coll (MA)
Boston U (MA)
Bowling Green State U (OH)
Brandeis U (MA)
Bucknell U (PA)
California Inst of Technology (CA)
Carnegie Mellon U (PA)
Carthage Coll (WI)
Centenary Coll of Louisiana (LA)
Central Michigan U (MI)
Christopher Newport U (VA)
Claremont McKenna Coll (CA)
Clark U (MA)
Colgate U (NY)
The Coll of William and Mary (VA)
The Colorado Coll (CO)
Colorado State U (CO)
Columbia U (NY)
Connecticut Coll (CT)
Creighton U (NE)
DePaul U (IL)
Dickinson Coll (PA)
Dominican U (IL)
Drake U (IA)
Drew U (NJ)
Drury U (MO)
Earlham Coll (IN)
Eastern Illinois U (IL)
Emmanuel Coll (MA)
Fordham U (NY)
Furman U (SC)
George Mason U (VA)
Georgia State U (GA)
Grand Valley State U (MI)
Grove City Coll (PA)
Hamilton Coll (NY)
Hamline U (MN)
High Point U (NC)
Hiram Coll (OH)
Hofstra U (NY)
Indiana U Bloomington (IN)
Indiana U–Purdue U Indianapolis (IN)
Indiana U Southeast (IN)
Johns Hopkins U (MD)
Juniata Coll (PA)
King's Coll (PA)
King U (TN)
Knox Coll (IL)
Lake Forest Coll (IL)
La Sierra U (CA)
Lawrence U (WI)
Lebanon Valley Coll (PA)
Loras Coll (IA)
Lycoming Coll (PA)
Macalester Coll (MN)
Marymount Manhattan Coll (NY)
Massachusetts Inst of Technology (MA)
Mercer U, Macon (GA)
Miami U (OH)
Michigan State U (MI)
Middlebury Coll (VT)
Mount St. Joseph U (OH)
Muskingum U (OH)
New York U (NY)
Northern Kentucky U (KY)
Northwestern U (IL)
The Ohio State U (OH)
Ohio U (OH)
Ohio Wesleyan U (OH)
Pitzer Coll (CA)
Princeton U (NJ)
Randolph-Macon Coll (VA)
Regis U (CO)
Rhodes Coll (TN)
Rice U (TX)
Sacred Heart U (CT)
Saginaw Valley State U (MI)
Saint Anselm Coll (NH)
Saint Louis U (MO)
Scripps Coll (CA)
Skidmore Coll (NY)
State U of New York Coll at Geneseo (NY)
Stonehill Coll (MA)
Syracuse U (NY)
Temple U (PA)
Texas Christian U (TX)
Tulane U (LA)
Union Coll (NY)
U of California, Riverside (CA)
U of California, Santa Cruz (CA)
U of Chicago (IL)
U of Kentucky (KY)
U of Michigan (MI)
U of Minnesota, Twin Cities Campus (MN)
U of Mount Union (OH)
U of Nevada, Reno (NV)
U of New Hampshire (NH)
The U of North Carolina at Chapel Hill (NC)
U of Notre Dame (IN)
U of Pennsylvania (PA)
U of Pittsburgh (PA)
U of St. Thomas (MN)
U of San Diego (CA)
The U of Texas at Austin (TX)
The U of the South (TN)
U of Vermont (VT)
U of Wisconsin–Eau Claire (WI)
U of Wisconsin–River Falls (WI)
Ursinus Coll (PA)
Virginia Polytechnic Inst and State U (VA)
Wartburg Coll (IA)
Washington & Jefferson Coll (PA)
Washington and Lee U (VA)
Washington State U (WA)
Washington State U–Vancouver (WA)
Washington U in St. Louis (MO)
Western Washington U (WA)
Westmont Coll (CA)
Wheaton Coll (MA)
Wilkes U (PA)
Willamette U (OR)

NONPROFIT MANAGEMENT
Austin Coll (TX)
Austin Peay State U (TN)
Bryant U (RI)
Concordia U Chicago (IL)
Concordia U Irvine (CA)
Duquesne U (PA)
Granite State Coll (NH)
Hardin-Simmons U (TX)
High Point U (NC)
Johnson U Florida (FL)
LaGrange Coll (GA)
LeTourneau U (TX)
Marymount Manhattan Coll (NY)
Mercy Coll (NY)
Morningside Coll (IA)
Point Loma Nazarene U (CA)
Southeastern U (FL)
Tiffin U (OH)
Toccoa Falls Coll (GA)
Trevecca Nazarene U (TN)
U of Central Florida (FL)
U of Minnesota, Twin Cities Campus (MN)
William Jewell Coll (MO)

NORWEGIAN
Pacific Lutheran U (WA)
St. Olaf Coll (MN)
U of North Dakota (ND)
U of Washington (WA)

NUCLEAR AND INDUSTRIAL RADIOLOGIC TECHNOLOGIES RELATED
Manhattan Coll (NY)

NUCLEAR ENGINEERING
Idaho State U (ID)
Massachusetts Inst of Technology (MA)
North Carolina State U (NC)
Purdue U (IN)
U of Florida (FL)
U of Massachusetts Lowell (MA)
U of Michigan (MI)
U of New Mexico (NM)
The U of Tennessee (TN)

NUCLEAR ENGINEERING TECHNOLOGY
Excelsior Coll (NY)
Idaho State U (ID)

NUCLEAR MEDICAL TECHNOLOGY
AdventHealth U (FL)
Baptist Coll of Health Sciences (TN)
Benedictine U (IL)
Indiana U of Pennsylvania (PA)
Indiana U–Purdue U Indianapolis (IN)
Manhattan Coll (NY)
Molloy Coll (NY)
Old Dominion U (VA)
Rhode Island Coll (RI)
Saint Louis U (MO)
Saint Mary's U of Minnesota (MN)
U at Buffalo, the State U of New York (NY)
The U of Findlay (OH)
U of Nevada, Las Vegas (NV)
U of the Incarnate Word (TX)
U of Wisconsin–La Crosse (WI)
Weber State U (UT)

NUCLEAR/NUCLEAR POWER TECHNOLOGY
Excelsior Coll (NY)

NUCLEAR PHYSICS
Arkansas Tech U (AR)

NURSING ADMINISTRATION
Northwest Christian U (OR)

NURSING EDUCATION
Bradley U (IL)

NURSING PRACTICE
Brenau U (GA)
Christian Brothers U (TN)
Eastern U (PA)
Lebanese American U (Lebanon)
Michigan State U (MI)

NURSING SCIENCE
Averett U (VA)
Carson-Newman U (TN)
Duquesne U (PA)
Inter American U of Puerto Rico, Barranquitas Campus (PR)
Kean U (NJ)
Millersville U of Pennsylvania (PA)
New Jersey City U (NJ)
Rochester Coll (MI)
U of California, Irvine (CA)
U of Providence (MT)

NUTRITION SCIENCES
Auburn U (AL)
Boston U (MA)
Bowling Green State U (OH)
California State U, Los Angeles (CA)
Canisius Coll (NY)
Central Washington U (WA)
Coll of Saint Benedict (MN)
Colorado State U (CO)
Cornell U (NY)
Farmingdale State Coll (NY)
Huntington U of Health Sciences (TN)
Iowa State U of Science and Technology (IA)
La Salle U (PA)
Lebanese American U (Lebanon)
Louisiana State U and A&M Coll (LA)
Merrimack Coll (MA)
Michigan State U (MI)
New York U (NY)
North Carolina State U (NC)
The Ohio State U (OH)
Pepperdine U, Malibu (CA)
Purdue U (IN)
The Sage Colls (NY)
Saint John's U (MN)
San Diego State U (CA)
Southern Illinois U Carbondale (IL)
Syracuse U (NY)
Texas Tech U (TX)
Texas Woman's U (TX)
U of California, Davis (CA)
U of Florida (FL)
U of Georgia (GA)
U of Hawaii at Manoa (HI)
U of Massachusetts Amherst (MA)
U of Massachusetts Lowell (MA)
U of Minnesota, Twin Cities Campus (MN)
U of Nevada, Las Vegas (NV)
U of Nevada, Reno (NV)
U of New Hampshire (NH)
The U of North Carolina at Greensboro (NC)
U of Northern Colorado (CO)
U of Saint Francis (IN)
U of Southern Indiana (IN)
The U of Texas Rio Grande Valley (TX)
U of the Incarnate Word (TX)
U of Vermont (VT)
U of Wisconsin–Milwaukee (WI)

OCCUPATIONAL HEALTH AND INDUSTRIAL HYGIENE
Grand Valley State U (MI)
Ohio U (OH)

OCCUPATIONAL SAFETY AND HEALTH TECHNOLOGY
Central Washington U (WA)
Columbia Southern U (AL)
Embry-Riddle Aeronautical U–Daytona (FL)
Embry-Riddle Aeronautical U–Worldwide (FL)
Grand Valley State U (MI)
Indiana State U (IN)
Indiana U of Pennsylvania (PA)
Marshall U (WV)
Millersville U of Pennsylvania (PA)
Murray State U (KY)
Rochester Inst of Technology (NY)
Southeastern Louisiana U (LA)
Southwest Baptist U (MO)

OCCUPATIONAL THERAPIST ASSISTANT
Idaho State U (ID)

OCCUPATIONAL THERAPY
Alabama State U (AL)
Calvin Coll (MI)
Carthage Coll (WI)
Duquesne U (PA)
Eastern Washington U (WA)
Grand Valley State U (MI)
Illinois Coll (IL)
Ithaca Coll (NY)
Louisiana Coll (LA)
Nazareth Coll of Rochester (NY)
New York U (NY)
Saginaw Valley State U (MI)
Saint Francis U (PA)
Saint Louis U (MO)
Saint Vincent Coll (PA)
San Jose State U (CA)
Towson U (MD)
Université de Sherbrooke (QC, Canada)
U at Buffalo, the State U of New York (NY)
U of New Hampshire (NH)
U of Southern Indiana (IN)
U of Wisconsin–Milwaukee (WI)
Wartburg Coll (IA)
Worcester State U (MA)

OCEAN ENGINEERING
California State U, Long Beach (CA)
Florida Atlantic U (FL)
U of New Hampshire (NH)
Virginia Polytechnic Inst and State U (VA)

OCEANOGRAPHY (CHEMICAL AND PHYSICAL)
Humboldt State U (CA)
Louisiana State U and A&M Coll (LA)
Millersville U of Pennsylvania (PA)
North Carolina State U (NC)
U of Michigan (MI)
U of South Carolina (SC)
U of Washington (WA)

OFFICE MANAGEMENT
Adams State U (CO)
Babson Coll (MA)
Bowling Green State U (OH)
Inter American U of Puerto Rico, Aguadilla Campus (PR)
Inter American U of Puerto Rico, Barranquitas Campus (PR)
Inter American U of Puerto Rico, Bayamón Campus (PR)
Inter American U of Puerto Rico, Fajardo Campus (PR)
Inter American U of Puerto Rico, San Germán Campus (PR)
Loyola U Chicago (IL)
Miami U Hamilton (OH)
Point Loma Nazarene U (CA)
Rider U (NJ)
Southwest Baptist U (MO)
U of Maine at Machias (ME)
U of South Carolina (SC)

OPERATIONS MANAGEMENT
Auburn U (AL)
Avila U (MO)
Babson Coll (MA)
Boston Coll (MA)
Bowling Green State U (OH)
Brenau U (GA)
California State U, Long Beach (CA)
Carnegie Mellon U (PA)
Central Connecticut State U (CT)
Fort Lewis Coll (CO)
Gonzaga U (WA)
Grand Valley State U (MI)
Granite State Coll (NH)
Indiana U–Purdue U Indianapolis (IN)
Inter American U of Puerto Rico, Bayamón Campus (PR)
Lamar U (TX)
Loyola U Chicago (IL)
Miami U (OH)
Minnesota State U Moorhead (MN)
Northeastern State U (OK)
Northern Illinois U (IL)
Oakland City U (IN)
The Ohio State U (OH)
Point U (GA)
Rhode Island Coll (RI)
Saginaw Valley State U (MI)
San Diego State U (CA)
U of Dayton (OH)
U of Houston (TX)
U of Massachusetts Dartmouth (MA)
U of Minnesota, Twin Cities Campus (MN)
The U of North Carolina at Charlotte (NC)
U of North Dakota (ND)
U of Pennsylvania (PA)
U of St. Thomas (MN)
U of Southern Indiana (IN)
U of Wisconsin–Milwaukee (WI)
Utah State U (UT)
Utah Valley U (UT)
Washington State U (WA)
Washington State U–Tri-Cities (WA)
Washington State U–Vancouver (WA)
Washington U in St. Louis (MO)
Western Washington U (WA)
Widener U (PA)
Youngstown State U (OH)

OPERATIONS RESEARCH
Babson Coll (MA)
Bowling Green State U (OH)
Bryant U (RI)
California State U, Fullerton (CA)
Canisius Coll (NY)
Columbia U (NY)
Cornell U (NY)
New York U (NY)
Princeton U (NJ)
U of Washington (WA)

OPTICAL SCIENCES
Albright Coll (PA)
The Ohio State U (OH)
Saginaw Valley State U (MI)

ORGANIZATIONAL BEHAVIOR
Benedictine U (IL)
Bowling Green State U (OH)
The Coll of St. Scholastica (MN)
Eastern Mennonite U (VA)
Greenville U (IL)
High Point U (NC)
Indiana U Bloomington (IN)
Manhattan Coll (NY)
Mount St. Joseph U (OH)
National U (CA)
Northern Kentucky U (KY)
Northwestern U (IL)
Oglethorpe U (GA)
Palm Beach Atlantic U (FL)
Pitzer Coll (CA)
Rider U (NJ)
Saint Joseph's U (PA)
Saint Louis U (MO)
Scripps Coll (CA)
U of Michigan (MI)
U of Richmond (VA)
U of the Incarnate Word (TX)
The U of Toledo (OH)
The U of Tulsa (OK)

ORGANIZATIONAL COMMUNICATION
Assumption Coll (MA)
Bradley U (IL)
Buena Vista U (IA)
Butler U (IN)
Calvin Coll (MI)
DePaul U (IL)
East Texas Baptist U (TX)
Emmanuel Coll (GA)
Florida Coll (FL)
Florida Southern Coll (FL)
Idaho State U (ID)
Lindenwood U (MO)
Lubbock Christian U (TX)
Murray State U (KY)
Muskingum U (OH)
Nichols Coll (MA)
Northwest Missouri State U (MO)
Pepperdine U, Malibu (CA)
Pfeiffer U (NC)
Southeast Missouri State U (MO)
Temple U (PA)
Trevecca Nazarene U (TN)
U of Idaho (ID)
U of Mount Union (OH)
The U of Texas at Austin (TX)
Weber State U (UT)
Western Kentucky U (KY)

ORGANIZATIONAL LEADERSHIP
Alverno Coll (WI)
Auburn U at Montgomery (AL)
Averett U (VA)
Avila U (MO)
Blackburn Coll (IL)
Boston Coll (MA)
Bradley U (IL)
Brandman U (CA)
Brenau U (GA)
Bryant U (RI)
Central Washington U (WA)
Columbia Southern U (AL)
Creighton U (NE)
Davenport U, Grand Rapids (MI)
Eastern U (PA)
East Texas Baptist U (TX)
Graceland U (IA)
La Salle U (PA)
Lincoln Christian U (IL)
Lipscomb U (TN)
Lubbock Christian U (TX)
Marquette U (WI)
Marymount Manhattan Coll (NY)
Missouri Baptist U (MO)
National U (CA)
Ottawa U (KS)
Point U (GA)
Providence Coll (RI)
Purdue U (IN)
Regent U (VA)
Rochester Coll (MI)
Saint Louis U (MO)
Salve Regina U (RI)
Samford U (AL)
Seattle U (WA)
Southeastern Louisiana U (LA)
Southeastern U (FL)
Spring Hill Coll (AL)
Syracuse U (NY)
Toccoa Falls Coll (GA)
U of Dayton (OH)
U of Houston (TX)
U of La Verne (CA)
U of Maine at Farmington (ME)
U of Mary Hardin-Baylor (TX)
U of Northern Iowa (IA)
U of South Dakota (SD)
U of West Georgia (GA)
Western Kentucky U (KY)
Wright State U–Lake Campus (OH)

ORNAMENTAL HORTICULTURE
Delaware Valley U (PA)
U of Arkansas (AR)

ORTHOTICS/PROSTHETICS
U of Washington (WA)

OUTDOOR EDUCATION
Liberty U (VA)
Messiah Coll (PA)
Toccoa Falls Coll (GA)
Weber State U (UT)

PACIFIC AREA/PACIFIC RIM STUDIES
Central Washington U (WA)
U of Guam (GU)
U of Hawaii at Manoa (HI)

PACKAGING SCIENCE
Indiana State U (IN)
Michigan State U (MI)

PAINTING
Adams State U (CO)
Boston U (MA)
Bowling Green State U (OH)
Bradley U (IL)
California State U, Long Beach (CA)
Carson-Newman U (TN)
Central Washington U (WA)
Cleveland Inst of Art (OH)
Coll of the Ozarks (MO)
Columbia Coll (MO)
Drake U (IA)
Escuela de Artes Plasticas y Diseño de Puerto Rico (PR)
Harding U (AR)
Hofstra U (NY)
Inter American U of Puerto Rico, San Germán Campus (PR)
Maryland Inst Coll of Art (MD)
Marywood U (PA)
Rhode Island Coll (RI)
Rhode Island School of Design (RI)
Rochester Inst of Technology (NY)
Savannah Coll of Art and Design (GA)
Seton Hill U (PA)

Syracuse U (NY)
Temple U (PA)
Texas Christian U (TX)
U of Dallas (TX)
U of Houston (TX)
U of Massachusetts Dartmouth (MA)
U of Oregon (OR)
U of Puget Sound (WA)
U of Regina (SK, Canada)
The U of Tampa (FL)
U of Washington (WA)
Virginia Commonwealth U (VA)
Washington U in St. Louis (MO)
Youngstown State U (OH)

PALEONTOLOGY
Bowling Green State U (OH)

PALLIATIVE CARE NURSING
Madonna U (MI)

PAPER SCIENCE AND ENGINEERING
State U of New York Coll of Environmental Science and Forestry (NY)

PARASITOLOGY
Bowling Green State U (OH)

PARKS, RECREATION AND LEISURE
Aurora U (IL)
Baker U (KS)
Bowling Green State U (OH)
Bridgewater State U (MA)
California Polytechnic State U, San Luis Obispo (CA)
California State U, Chico (CA)
California State U, Long Beach (CA)
California State U, Northridge (CA)
Central Michigan U (MI)
Central State U (OH)
Dean Coll (MA)
East Carolina U (NC)
Eastern Washington U (WA)
Fort Lewis Coll (CO)
Georgia Coll & State U (GA)
Georgia Southern U (GA)
Gordon Coll (MA)
Humboldt State U (CA)
Indiana U Bloomington (IN)
Ithaca Coll (NY)
Limestone Coll (SC)
Lindenwood U (MO)
Manchester U (IN)
Messiah Coll (PA)
Michigan State U (MI)
New England Coll (NH)
Ohio U (OH)
Oklahoma Baptist U (OK)
Oklahoma State U (OK)
Radford U (VA)
Rhode Island Coll (RI)
Salisbury U (MD)
San Diego State U (CA)
San Francisco State U (CA)
San Jose State U (CA)
Southeast Missouri State U (MO)
Southern Illinois U Carbondale (IL)
Southwest Baptist U (MO)
U of Arkansas (AR)
U of Maine at Machias (ME)
U of Minnesota, Duluth (MN)
U of Minnesota, Twin Cities Campus (MN)
U of Missouri (MO)
U of Nevada, Las Vegas (NV)
The U of North Carolina at Greensboro (NC)
U of Northern Iowa (IA)
U of South Alabama (AL)
U of South Dakota (SD)
Utah State U (UT)
Western State Colorado U (CO)
Western Washington U (WA)

PARKS, RECREATION AND LEISURE FACILITIES MANAGEMENT
Alabama State U (AL)
Appalachian State U (NC)
Arkansas Tech U (AR)
California U of Pennsylvania (PA)
Central Michigan U (MI)
Central Washington U (WA)
The Coll at Brockport, State U of New York (NY)
Coll of the Ozarks (MO)
Colorado State U (CO)
Eastern Illinois U (IL)
Eastern Washington U (WA)
East Stroudsburg U of Pennsylvania (PA)
Franklin Pierce U (NH)
Humboldt State U (CA)
Indiana State U (IN)
Kean U (NJ)
Lock Haven U of Pennsylvania (PA)
Marshall U (WV)
Middle Tennessee State U (TN)
Mount Marty Coll (SD)
New England Coll (NH)
New York U (NY)
North Carolina State U (NC)
Northwest Missouri State U (MO)
Old Dominion U (VA)
St. Joseph's Coll, Long Island Campus (NY)
St. Joseph's Coll, New York (NY)
State U of New York Coll of Technology at Delhi (NY)
Trinity Christian Coll (IL)
U of Florida (FL)
U of Idaho (ID)
U of Maine (ME)
U of Maine at Machias (ME)
U of New Hampshire (NH)
U of North Dakota (ND)
U of Northern Colorado (CO)
U of West Georgia (GA)
U of Wisconsin–La Crosse (WI)
Western Illinois U (IL)
Western Kentucky U (KY)
West Virginia State U (WV)

PARKS, RECREATION, LEISURE, AND FITNESS STUDIES RELATED
New England Coll (NH)
Ottawa U (KS)
Trinity Christian Coll (IL)
Utah State U (UT)

PASTORAL COUNSELING AND SPECIALIZED MINISTRIES RELATED
Judson U (IL)
Lancaster Bible Coll (PA)
Lee U (TN)
Lipscomb U (TN)
Madonna U (MI)
Messenger Coll (TX)
Ouachita Baptist U (AR)
U of Dallas (TX)

PASTORAL STUDIES/ COUNSELING
Campbellsville U (KY)
Dominican U (IL)
Duquesne U (PA)
Emmanuel Coll (GA)
Greenville U (IL)
Johnson U Florida (FL)
Lancaster Bible Coll (PA)
Lee U (TN)
Liberty U (VA)
Loyola U Chicago (IL)
Marian U (IN)
Messenger Coll (TX)
Mount St. Joseph U (OH)
Northwest Christian U (OR)
Ouachita Baptist U (AR)
Providence Coll (RI)
Southwest Baptist U (MO)
Taylor U (IN)
Theological U of the Caribbean (PR)
Tyndale U Coll & Sem (ON, Canada)
U of Mary Hardin-Baylor (TX)
U of Saint Mary (KS)
U of the Incarnate Word (TX)
Vanguard U of Southern California (CA)

PEACE STUDIES AND CONFLICT RESOLUTION
Berea Coll (KY)
Bethel U (MN)
Butler U (IN)
Clark U (MA)
Colgate U (NY)
Coll of Saint Benedict (MN)
The Coll of St. Scholastica (MN)
Creighton U (NE)
DePaul U (IL)
Earlham Coll (IN)
Eastern Mennonite U (VA)
Embry-Riddle Aeronautical U–Daytona (FL)
George Mason U (VA)
Goshen Coll (IN)
Hamline U (MN)
Haverford Coll (PA)
Juniata Coll (PA)
Manchester U (IN)
Manhattan Coll (NY)
Marquette U (WI)
Messiah Coll (PA)
Nazareth Coll of Rochester (NY)
Pace U (NY)
Portland State U (OR)
Regis U (CO)
Saint Anselm Coll (NH)
Saint John's U (MN)
Salisbury U (MD)
U of Massachusetts Lowell (MA)
The U of North Carolina at Chapel Hill (NC)
The U of North Carolina at Greensboro (NC)
U of St. Thomas (MN)
Wartburg Coll (IA)
Whitworth U (WA)
Willamette U (OR)

PEDIATRIC NURSING
Youngstown State U (OH)

PERCUSSION INSTRUMENTS
Acadia U (NS, Canada)
Central Washington U (WA)
Northwestern U (IL)
Oklahoma Christian U (OK)
State U of New York at Fredonia (NY)
Syracuse U (NY)
U of Washington (WA)
Youngstown State U (OH)

PERSONALITY PSYCHOLOGY
Pace U, Pleasantville Campus (NY)

PETROLEUM ENGINEERING
Colorado School of Mines (CO)
Lebanese American U (Lebanon)
Louisiana State U and A&M Coll (LA)
Saint Francis U (PA)
Texas Tech U (TX)
U of Houston (TX)
U of North Dakota (ND)
U of Regina (SK, Canada)
The U of Texas at Austin (TX)
The U of Texas of the Permian Basin (TX)
The U of Tulsa (OK)
U of Wyoming (WY)

PETROLEUM TECHNOLOGY
Muskingum U (OH)

PHARMACEUTICAL SCIENCES
Cedarville U (OH)
Duquesne U (PA)
Lebanese American U (Lebanon)
Samford U (AL)
U of California, Irvine (CA)
U of Georgia (GA)
U of Michigan (MI)
U of Pittsburgh (PA)

PHARMACEUTICS AND DRUG DESIGN
Purdue U (IN)
Temple U (PA)
The U of Toledo (OH)
West Chester U of Pennsylvania (PA)

PHARMACOLOGY
Université de Sherbrooke (QC, Canada)

PHARMACOLOGY AND TOXICOLOGY
U at Buffalo, the State U of New York (NY)

PHARMACOLOGY AND TOXICOLOGY RELATED
U at Buffalo, the State U of New York (NY)

PHARMACY
Butler U (IN)
The Coll of Idaho (ID)
Drake U (IA)
Manchester U (IN)
The Ohio State U (OH)
Regis U (CO)
Saint Vincent Coll (PA)
The U of Toledo (OH)
Washington State U (WA)
Washington State U–Spokane (WA)

PHARMACY ADMINISTRATION AND PHARMACY POLICY AND REGULATORY AFFAIRS
Drake U (IA)
U of Michigan (MI)

PHARMACY, PHARMACEUTICAL SCIENCES, AND ADMINISTRATION RELATED
Alverno Coll (WI)
Duquesne U (PA)
Florida Ag and Mech U (FL)
St. John Fisher Coll (NY)

PHARMACY TECHNICIAN
Columbia Central U, Caguas (PR)

PHILOSOPHY
Acadia U (NS, Canada)
Adelphi U (NY)
Agnes Scott Coll (GA)
Albion Coll (MI)
Albright Coll (PA)
Alfred U (NY)
Allegheny Coll (PA)
Alverno Coll (WI)
American U (DC)
American U of Beirut (Lebanon)
Angelo State U (TX)
Antioch Coll, Yellow Springs (OH)
Appalachian State U (NC)
Assumption Coll (MA)
Auburn U (AL)
Austin Coll (TX)
Austin Peay State U (TN)
Baker U (KS)
Baldwin Wallace U (OH)
Baruch Coll of the City U of New York (NY)
Baylor U (TX)
Bellarmine U (KY)
Beloit Coll (WI)
Benedictine U (IL)
Bentley U (MA)
Berea Coll (KY)
Bethel U (MN)
Boston Coll (MA)
Boston U (MA)
Bowling Green State U (OH)
Bradley U (IL)
Brandeis U (MA)
Bridgewater State U (MA)
Bucknell U (PA)
Butler U (IN)
California Inst of Technology (CA)
California Lutheran U (CA)
California Polytechnic State U, San Luis Obispo (CA)
California State U, Bakersfield (CA)
California State U, Chico (CA)
California State U, Fullerton (CA)
California State U, Long Beach (CA)
California State U, Los Angeles (CA)
California State U, Northridge (CA)
California State U, San Bernardino (CA)
Calvin Coll (MI)
Canisius Coll (NY)
Carnegie Mellon U (PA)
Carson-Newman U (TN)
Carthage Coll (WI)
The Catholic U of America (DC)
Centenary Coll of Louisiana (LA)
Central Connecticut State U (CT)
Central Michigan U (MI)
Christopher Newport U (VA)
Claremont McKenna Coll (CA)
Clarion U of Pennsylvania (PA)
Clark U (MA)
Coastal Carolina U (SC)
Colgate U (NY)
The Coll at Brockport, State U of New York (NY)
Coll of Charleston (SC)
The Coll of Idaho (ID)
Coll of Saint Benedict (MN)
The Coll of St. Scholastica (MN)
Coll of Staten Island of the City U of New York (NY)
Coll of the Holy Cross (MA)
The Coll of William and Mary (VA)
The Colorado Coll (CO)
Colorado State U (CO)
Columbia Coll (MO)
Columbia U (NY)
Concordia U Chicago (IL)
Connecticut Coll (CT)
Cornell Coll (IA)
Cornell U (NY)
Covenant Coll (GA)
Creighton U (NE)
Curry Coll (MA)
Dallas Baptist U (TX)
Dartmouth Coll (NH)
Davidson Coll (NC)
DePaul U (IL)
DEREE - The American Coll of Greece (Greece)
Dickinson Coll (PA)
Dominican U (IL)
Drake U (IA)
Drew U (NJ)
Drury U (MO)
Duquesne U (PA)
Earlham Coll (IN)
East Carolina U (NC)
Eastern Illinois U (IL)
Eastern U (PA)
Eastern Washington U (WA)
East Stroudsburg U of Pennsylvania (PA)
East Tennessee State U (TN)
Eckerd Coll (FL)
Emmanuel Coll (MA)
The Evergreen State Coll (WA)
Fairfield U (CT)
Florida Atlantic U (FL)
Florida Southern Coll (FL)
Fordham U (NY)
Fort Lewis Coll (CO)
Furman U (SC)
Geneva Coll (PA)
George Mason U (VA)
Georgetown Coll (KY)
Georgia Coll & State U (GA)
Georgia Southern U (GA)
Georgia State U (GA)
Gonzaga U (WA)
Gordon Coll (MA)
Grand Valley State U (MI)
Greenville U (IL)
Grove City Coll (PA)
Gwynedd Mercy U (PA)
Hamilton Coll (NY)
Hamline U (MN)
Hampden-Sydney Coll (VA)
Hanover Coll (IN)
Hardin-Simmons U (TX)
Hartwick Coll (NY)
Harvard U (MA)
Haverford Coll (PA)
High Point U (NC)
Hillsdale Coll (MI)
Hofstra U (NY)
Hollins U (VA)
Holy Apostles Coll and Sem (CT)
Hood Coll (MD)
Humboldt State U (CA)
Hunter Coll of the City U of New York (NY)
Idaho State U (ID)
Illinois Coll (IL)
Indiana State U (IN)
Indiana U Bloomington (IN)
Indiana U Northwest (IN)
Indiana U of Pennsylvania (PA)
Indiana U–Purdue U Indianapolis (IN)
Indiana U South Bend (IN)
Indiana U Southeast (IN)
Iona Coll (NY)
Iowa State U of Science and Technology (IA)
Ithaca Coll (NY)
Jacksonville U (FL)
Johns Hopkins U (MD)
Juniata Coll (PA)
Kalamazoo Coll (MI)

Kansas Wesleyan U (KS)
Kennesaw State U (GA)
King's Coll (PA)
King U (TN)
Knox Coll (IL)
Lafayette Coll (PA)
Lake Forest Coll (IL)
La Salle U (PA)
Lawrence U (WI)
Lebanese American U (Lebanon)
Lebanon Valley Coll (PA)
Lewis & Clark Coll (OR)
Liberty U (VA)
Lincoln Christian U (IL)
Lindenwood U (MO)
Linfield Coll (OR)
Lipscomb U (TN)
Loras Coll (IA)
Louisiana State U and A&M Coll (LA)
Loyola Marymount U (CA)
Loyola U Chicago (IL)
Loyola U New Orleans (LA)
Lycoming Coll (PA)
Macalester Coll (MN)
Manchester U (IN)
Manhattan Coll (NY)
Manhattanville Coll (NY)
Mansfield U of Pennsylvania (PA)
Marian U (IN)
Marist Coll (NY)
Marquette U (WI)
Marymount Manhattan Coll (NY)
Marymount U (VA)
Marywood U (PA)
Massachusetts Coll of Liberal Arts (MA)
Massachusetts Inst of Technology (MA)
McDaniel Coll (MD)
Mercer U, Macon (GA)
Merrimack Coll (MA)
Messiah Coll (PA)
Miami U (OH)
Miami U Hamilton (OH)
Michigan State U (MI)
Middlebury Coll (VT)
Middle Tennessee State U (TN)
Millersville U of Pennsylvania (PA)
Millikin U (IL)
Millsaps Coll (MS)
Mills Coll (CA)
Minnesota State U Moorhead (MN)
Molloy Coll (NY)
Montclair State U (NJ)
Morningside Coll (IA)
Muskingum U (OH)
Nazareth Coll of Rochester (NY)
New Coll of Florida (FL)
New England Coll (NH)
New Jersey City U (NJ)
New York U (NY)
North Carolina State U (NC)
Northern Illinois U (IL)
Northern Kentucky U (KY)
Northwestern U (IL)
Northwest Missouri State U (MO)
Occidental Coll (CA)
Oglethorpe U (GA)
Ohio Dominican U (OH)
The Ohio State U (OH)
Ohio U (OH)
Ohio Wesleyan U (OH)
Oklahoma Baptist U (OK)
Oklahoma State U (OK)
Old Dominion U (VA)
Ouachita Baptist U (AR)
Pacific Lutheran U (WA)
Palm Beach Atlantic U (FL)
Pepperdine U, Malibu (CA)
Piedmont Coll (GA)
Pitzer Coll (CA)
Point Loma Nazarene U (CA)
Portland State U (OR)
Princeton U (NJ)
Providence Coll (RI)
Purchase Coll, State U of New York (NY)
Purdue U (IN)
Purdue U Northwest (IN)
Queens Coll of the City U of New York (NY)
Queens U of Charlotte (NC)
Randolph Coll (VA)
Randolph-Macon Coll (VA)
Redeemer U Coll (ON, Canada)
Regis U (CO)
Rhode Island Coll (RI)
Rhodes Coll (TN)
Rice U (TX)
Rider U (NJ)
Roanoke Coll (VA)
Rochester Inst of Technology (NY)
Rockford U (IL)
Rollins Coll (FL)
Sacred Heart U (CT)
Saint Anselm Coll (NH)
Saint Francis U (PA)
St. John Fisher Coll (NY)
Saint John's U (MN)
Saint Joseph's U (PA)
Saint Louis U (MO)
St. Mary's Coll of Maryland (MD)
St. Mary's U (TX)
Saint Mary's U of Minnesota (MN)
St. Norbert Coll (WI)
St. Olaf Coll (MN)
Saint Vincent Coll (PA)
Salisbury U (MD)
Salve Regina U (RI)
Samford U (AL)
San Diego State U (CA)
San Francisco State U (CA)
San Jose State U (CA)
Sarah Lawrence Coll (NY)
Scripps Coll (CA)
Seattle U (WA)
Skidmore Coll (NY)
Sonoma State U (CA)
Southeast Missouri State U (MO)
Southern Illinois U Carbondale (IL)
Southern Illinois U Edwardsville (IL)
Southwestern U (TX)
Spring Hill Coll (AL)
State U of New York at Fredonia (NY)
State U of New York at Plattsburgh (NY)
State U of New York Coll at Geneseo (NY)
State U of New York Coll at Potsdam (NY)
Stetson U (FL)
Stonehill Coll (MA)
Sweet Briar Coll (VA)
Syracuse U (NY)
Taylor U (IN)
Temple U (PA)
Texas Christian U (TX)
Texas Lutheran U (TX)
Texas Tech U (TX)
Toccoa Falls Coll (GA)
Towson U (MD)
Trinity Christian Coll (IL)
Tulane U (LA)
Tyndale U Coll & Sem (ON, Canada)
Union Coll (NY)
Université de Sherbrooke (QC, Canada)
U at Buffalo, the State U of New York (NY)
U of Arkansas (AR)
U of California, Davis (CA)
U of California, Irvine (CA)
U of California, Los Angeles (CA)
U of California, Riverside (CA)
U of California, Santa Cruz (CA)
U of Central Arkansas (AR)
U of Central Florida (FL)
U of Chicago (IL)
U of Colorado Denver (CO)
U of Dallas (TX)
U of Dayton (OH)
U of Detroit Mercy (MI)
The U of Findlay (OH)
U of Florida (FL)
U of Georgia (GA)
U of Guam (GU)
U of Hawaii at Manoa (HI)
U of Houston (TX)
U of Houston–Downtown (TX)
U of Idaho (ID)
U of Illinois at Springfield (IL)
U of Kentucky (KY)
U of La Verne (CA)
U of Louisville (KY)
U of Lynchburg (VA)
U of Maine (ME)
U of Maryland, Baltimore County (MD)
U of Maryland, Coll Park (MD)
U of Massachusetts Amherst (MA)
U of Massachusetts Boston (MA)
U of Massachusetts Dartmouth (MA)
U of Massachusetts Lowell (MA)
U of Memphis (TN)
U of Michigan (MI)
U of Michigan–Dearborn (MI)
U of Minnesota, Duluth (MN)
U of Minnesota, Morris (MN)
U of Minnesota, Twin Cities Campus (MN)
U of Missouri (MO)
U of Mount Union (OH)
U of Nebraska–Lincoln (NE)
U of Nevada, Las Vegas (NV)
U of Nevada, Reno (NV)
U of New Hampshire (NH)
U of New Mexico (NM)
U of North Carolina at Asheville (NC)
The U of North Carolina at Chapel Hill (NC)
The U of North Carolina at Charlotte (NC)
The U of North Carolina at Greensboro (NC)
U of North Dakota (ND)
U of Northern Colorado (CO)
U of Northern Iowa (IA)
U of North Florida (FL)
U of Northwestern–St. Paul (MN)
U of Notre Dame (IN)
U of Oregon (OR)
U of Pennsylvania (PA)
U of Pittsburgh (PA)
U of Puget Sound (WA)
U of Regina (SK, Canada)
U of Richmond (VA)
U of Saint Francis (IN)
U of St. Thomas (MN)
U of St. Thomas (TX)
U of San Diego (CA)
U of San Francisco (CA)
U of South Alabama (AL)
U of South Carolina (SC)
U of South Dakota (SD)
U of Southern Indiana (IN)
U of South Florida (FL)
The U of Tampa (FL)
The U of Tennessee (TN)
The U of Tennessee at Martin (TN)
The U of Texas at Austin (TX)
The U of Texas at El Paso (TX)
The U of Texas Rio Grande Valley (TX)
U of the Incarnate Word (TX)
The U of the South (TN)
The U of Toledo (OH)
The U of Tulsa (OK)
U of Vermont (VT)
U of Virginia (VA)
U of Washington (WA)
U of West Georgia (GA)
U of Wisconsin–Eau Claire (WI)
U of Wisconsin–La Crosse (WI)
U of Wisconsin–Milwaukee (WI)
U of Wyoming (WY)
Ursinus Coll (PA)
Utah State U (UT)
Utah Valley U (UT)
Utica Coll (NY)
Valparaiso U (IN)
Vassar Coll (NY)
Virginia Commonwealth U (VA)
Virginia Polytechnic Inst and State U (VA)
Wabash Coll (IN)
Wartburg Coll (IA)
Washington & Jefferson Coll (PA)
Washington and Lee U (VA)
Washington State U (WA)
Washington U in St. Louis (MO)
Weber State U (UT)
Wesleyan U (CT)
West Chester U of Pennsylvania (PA)
Western Washington U (WA)
Westmont Coll (CA)
Wheaton Coll (IL)
Wheaton Coll (MA)
Whittier Coll (CA)
Whitworth U (WA)
Wilkes U (PA)
Willamette U (OR)
William Jewell Coll (MO)
Williams Coll (MA)
Wofford Coll (SC)
Wright State U–Lake Campus (OH)
Youngstown State U (OH)

PHILOSOPHY AND RELIGIOUS STUDIES
Barton Coll (NC)
Central Washington U (WA)
Christian Brothers U (TN)
Colgate U (NY)
Hillsdale Coll (MI)
LaGrange Coll (GA)
Marist Coll (NY)
Marymount Manhattan Coll (NY)
Muskingum U (OH)
Pace U (NY)
Pace U, Pleasantville Campus (NY)
Point Loma Nazarene U (CA)
St. Joseph's Coll, Long Island Campus (NY)
Samford U (AL)
Stockton U (NJ)
U of Maine at Farmington (ME)
U of North Dakota (ND)

PHILOSOPHY AND RELIGIOUS STUDIES RELATED
Bridgewater Coll (VA)
Butler U (IN)
Covenant Coll (GA)
Florida Ag and Mech U (FL)
Millsaps Coll (MS)
Ouachita Baptist U (AR)
Radford U (VA)
Rocky Mountain Coll (MT)
San Francisco State U (CA)
Truman State U (MO)
The U of North Carolina at Pembroke (NC)
U of Notre Dame (IN)
Washington U in St. Louis (MO)
William Jewell Coll (MO)
Winthrop U (SC)

PHILOSOPHY RELATED
Butler U (IN)
Coll of Staten Island of the City U of New York (NY)
Loyola U New Orleans (LA)
U of Massachusetts Boston (MA)
U of Pennsylvania (PA)
Washington U in St. Louis (MO)

PHOTOGRAPHIC AND FILM/VIDEO TECHNOLOGY
Coll of the Ozarks (MO)
Rochester Inst of Technology (NY)

PHOTOGRAPHY
Adams State U (CO)
Bowling Green State U (OH)
Bradley U (IL)
Bridgewater State U (MA)
California State U, Long Beach (CA)
Carson-Newman U (TN)
Central Washington U (WA)
Cleveland Inst of Art (OH)
Columbia Coll (MO)
Columbia Coll Chicago (IL)
Dominican U (IL)
Eastern Mennonite U (VA)
Endicott Coll (MA)
Fitchburg State U (MA)
Grand Valley State U (MI)
Hofstra U (NY)
Inter American U of Puerto Rico, San Germán Campus (PR)
Ithaca Coll (NY)
Judson U (IL)
Kansas Wesleyan U (KS)
Lindenwood U (MO)
Maryland Inst Coll of Art (MD)
Marymount Manhattan Coll (NY)
Marywood U (PA)
Morningside Coll (IA)
New York U (NY)
Pennsylvania Coll of Art & Design (PA)
Purchase Coll, State U of New York (NY)
Purdue U (IN)
Rhode Island Coll (RI)
Rhode Island School of Design (RI)
Savannah Coll of Art and Design (GA)
Seattle U (WA)
Syracuse U (NY)
Temple U (PA)
Texas Christian U (TX)
U of Central Florida (FL)
U of Dayton (OH)
U of Houston (TX)
U of La Verne (CA)
U of Massachusetts Dartmouth (MA)
U of Oregon (OR)
U of Washington (WA)
Virginia Commonwealth U (VA)
Washington U in St. Louis (MO)
Weber State U (UT)
Youngstown State U (OH)

PHOTOJOURNALISM
Barton Coll (NC)
Bradley U (IL)
Central Michigan U (MI)
Columbia Coll Chicago (IL)
Minnesota State U Moorhead (MN)
Ohio U (OH)
Point Loma Nazarene U (CA)
Rochester Inst of Technology (NY)
Syracuse U (NY)
Western Kentucky U (KY)

PHYSICAL AND BIOLOGICAL ANTHROPOLOGY
U of Washington (WA)

PHYSICAL CHEMISTRY
LeTourneau U (TX)
Rice U (TX)
Whitworth U (WA)

PHYSICAL EDUCATION TEACHING AND COACHING
Adams State U (CO)
Adelphi U (NY)
Alabama State U (AL)
Appalachian State U (NC)
Arkansas Tech U (AR)
Auburn U (AL)
Aurora U (IL)
Austin Coll (TX)
Baylor U (TX)
Benedictine U (IL)
Bethel U (MN)
Blackburn Coll (IL)
Boston U (MA)
Bowling Green State U (OH)
Bridgewater State U (MA)
Buena Vista U (IA)
California Lutheran U (CA)
California State U, Bakersfield (CA)
California State U, Long Beach (CA)
Calvin Coll (MI)
Campbellsville U (KY)
Canisius Coll (NY)
Carson-Newman U (TN)
Carthage Coll (WI)
Cedarville U (OH)
Central Connecticut State U (CT)
Central Michigan U (MI)
Central State U (OH)
Central Washington U (WA)
Coastal Carolina U (SC)
The Coll at Brockport, State U of New York (NY)
Coll of Charleston (SC)
The Coll of Idaho (ID)
Coll of the Ozarks (MO)
Concordia U Chicago (IL)
Cornell Coll (IA)
Culver-Stockton Coll (MO)
Dakota State U (SD)
Dallas Baptist U (TX)
Delta State U (MS)
DePaul U (IL)
East Carolina U (NC)
East Stroudsburg U of Pennsylvania (PA)
East Texas Baptist U (TX)
Elizabeth City State U (NC)
Fayetteville State U (NC)
Fort Lewis Coll (CO)
George Mason U (VA)
Georgia Southern U (GA)
Georgia State U (GA)
Gonzaga U (WA)
Goshen Coll (IN)
Grand Valley State U (MI)
Greenville U (IL)
Hardin-Simmons U (TX)
High Point U (NC)
Hofstra U (NY)
Humboldt State U (CA)

Hunter Coll of the City U of New York (NY)
Idaho State U (ID)
Illinois Coll (IL)
Indiana State U (IN)
Inter American U of Puerto Rico, Aguadilla Campus (PR)
Inter American U of Puerto Rico, San Germán Campus (PR)
Ithaca Coll (NY)
Jackson State U (MS)
Jacksonville U (FL)
Judson U (IL)
Kean U (NJ)
Kennesaw State U (GA)
Lancaster Bible Coll (PA)
Lees-McRae Coll (NC)
LeTourneau U (TX)
Limestone Coll (SC)
Lindenwood U (MO)
Linfield Coll (OR)
Lipscomb U (TN)
Louisiana Coll (LA)
Louisiana State U and A&M Coll (LA)
Lubbock Christian U (TX)
Madonna U (MI)
Manchester U (IN)
Manhattan Coll (NY)
Marshall U (WV)
Martin Luther Coll (MN)
Marywood U (PA)
McNeese State U (LA)
Messiah Coll (PA)
Miami U Hamilton (OH)
Michigan State U (MI)
Millikin U (IL)
Minnesota State U Moorhead (MN)
Missouri Baptist U (MO)
Montclair State U (NJ)
Muskingum U (OH)
New England Coll (NH)
Northeastern State U (OK)
Northern Illinois U (IL)
Northern Kentucky U (KY)
Northern State U (SD)
Northwestern Oklahoma State U (OK)
Northwest Missouri State U (MO)
Oakland City U (IN)
The Ohio State U (OH)
Oklahoma Baptist U (OK)
Oklahoma Christian U (OK)
Oklahoma State U (OK)
Old Dominion U (VA)
Ottawa U (KS)
Ouachita Baptist U (AR)
Palm Beach Atlantic U (FL)
Pepperdine U, Malibu (CA)
Pfeiffer U (NC)
Purdue U (IN)
Queens Coll of the City U of New York (NY)
Radford U (VA)
Redeemer U Coll (ON, Canada)
Rhode Island Coll (RI)
Roanoke Coll (VA)
Rockford U (IL)
Rocky Mountain Coll (MT)
The Sage Colls (NY)
Saginaw Valley State U (MI)
Salisbury U (MD)
San Francisco State U (CA)
Sonoma State U (CA)
Southeastern Louisiana U (LA)
Southeast Missouri State U (MO)
Southern Arkansas U–Magnolia (AR)
Southern U and Ag and Mech Coll (LA)
Southwest Baptist U (MO)
Syracuse U (NY)
Tabor Coll (KS)
Taylor U (IN)
Texas Christian U (TX)
Texas Lutheran U (TX)
Towson U (MD)
Trevecca Nazarene U (TN)
Trinity Christian Coll (IL)
Union Coll (KY)
Université de Sherbrooke (QC, Canada)
U of Central Florida (FL)
U of Guam (GU)
U of Idaho (ID)
U of Kentucky (KY)
U of La Verne (CA)
U of Maine (ME)
U of Maine at Presque Isle (ME)
U of Mary Hardin-Baylor (TX)
U of Maryland, Coll Park (MD)
U of Memphis (TN)
U of Minnesota, Duluth (MN)
U of Mount Union (OH)
U of Nebraska–Lincoln (NE)
U of New Mexico (NM)
The U of North Carolina at Greensboro (NC)
The U of North Carolina at Pembroke (NC)
U of Northern Iowa (IA)
U of North Florida (FL)
U of Northwestern–St. Paul (MN)
U of Pittsburgh (PA)
U of Pittsburgh at Bradford (PA)
U of Providence (MT)
U of Regina (SK, Canada)
U of St. Thomas (MN)
U of South Alabama (AL)
U of South Carolina (SC)
U of Southern Indiana (IN)
U of South Florida (FL)
The U of Tampa (FL)
U of the Incarnate Word (TX)
U of Vermont (VT)
The U of West Alabama (AL)
U of West Georgia (GA)
U of Wisconsin–River Falls (WI)
U of Wisconsin–Superior (WI)
U of Wyoming (WY)
Utah State U (UT)
Utah Valley U (UT)
Valley City State U (ND)
Valparaiso U (IN)
Vanguard U of Southern California (CA)
Wartburg Coll (IA)
Weber State U (UT)
Western Illinois U (IL)
Western Kentucky U (KY)
Western Washington U (WA)
Westmont Coll (CA)
West Virginia U Inst of Technology (WV)
Winthrop U (SC)
Wright State U–Lake Campus (OH)
Youngstown State U (OH)

PHYSICAL FITNESS TECHNICIAN
Averett U (VA)
Clarion U of Pennsylvania (PA)
Pepperdine U, Malibu (CA)
Trevecca Nazarene U (TN)

PHYSICAL SCIENCES
Arkansas Tech U (AR)
Calvin Coll (MI)
Colgate U (NY)
The Coll of St. Scholastica (MN)
Concordia U Chicago (IL)
Dakota State U (SD)
The Evergreen State Coll (WA)
Graceland U (IA)
La Sierra U (CA)
Michigan State U (MI)
Purdue U Northwest (IN)
Queens Coll of the City U of New York (NY)
Saint Vincent Coll (PA)
Salisbury U (MD)
San Diego State U (CA)
San Francisco State U (CA)
Seattle U (WA)
U of California, Riverside (CA)
U of California, Santa Cruz (CA)
U of Dayton (OH)
U of Maryland, Coll Park (MD)
U of North Dakota (ND)
U of Pittsburgh (PA)
U of Pittsburgh at Bradford (PA)
U of Wyoming (WY)
Washington State U (WA)
Washington State U–Tri-Cities (WA)
Wesleyan U (CT)
Western Kentucky U (KY)
Worcester State U (MA)
Wright State U–Lake Campus (OH)
Youngstown State U (OH)

PHYSICAL SCIENCES RELATED
Bowling Green State U (OH)
Covenant Coll (GA)
Rochester Inst of Technology (NY)
Saginaw Valley State U (MI)
Temple U (PA)
Union Coll (NY)
U of California, Davis (CA)
The U of North Carolina at Chapel Hill (NC)

PHYSICAL THERAPY
Bellarmine U (KY)
Bowling Green State U (OH)
Dominican U (IL)
Duquesne U (PA)
Grand Valley State U (MI)
Ithaca Coll (NY)
Loyola U Chicago (IL)
Maryville U of Saint Louis (MO)
Muskingum U (OH)
Nazareth Coll of Rochester (NY)
New York U (NY)
Saint Francis U (PA)
Saint Vincent Coll (PA)
Vanguard U of Southern California (CA)

PHYSICAL THERAPY TECHNOLOGY
Idaho State U (ID)

PHYSICIAN ASSISTANT
Brenau U (GA)
Butler U (IN)
Duquesne U (PA)
Grand Valley State U (MI)
Rochester Inst of Technology (NY)
Saint Francis U (PA)
Saint Mary's U of Minnesota (MN)
Saint Vincent Coll (PA)
Seton Hill U (PA)
Southern Illinois U Carbondale (IL)
U of Kentucky (KY)
U of South Dakota (SD)
U of Washington (WA)

PHYSICS
Acadia U (NS, Canada)
Adams State U (CO)
Adelphi U (NY)
Agnes Scott Coll (GA)
Alabama State U (AL)
Albion Coll (MI)
Albright Coll (PA)
Alfred U (NY)
Allegheny Coll (PA)
American U (DC)
American U of Beirut (Lebanon)
Angelo State U (TX)
Appalachian State U (NC)
Arkansas Tech U (AR)
Auburn U (AL)
Austin Coll (TX)
Austin Peay State U (TN)
Baker U (KS)
Baldwin Wallace U (OH)
Baylor U (TX)
Bellarmine U (KY)
Beloit Coll (WI)
Benedictine U (IL)
Berea Coll (KY)
Bethel U (MN)
Boston Coll (MA)
Boston U (MA)
Bowling Green State U (OH)
Bradley U (IL)
Brandeis U (MA)
Bridgewater Coll (VA)
Bridgewater State U (MA)
Bucknell U (PA)
Buena Vista U (IA)
Butler U (IN)
California Inst of Technology (CA)
California Lutheran U (CA)
California Polytechnic State U, San Luis Obispo (CA)
California State U, Bakersfield (CA)
California State U, Chico (CA)
California State U, Fullerton (CA)
California State U, Long Beach (CA)
California State U, Los Angeles (CA)
California State U, Northridge (CA)
California State U, San Bernardino (CA)
California U of Pennsylvania (PA)
Calvin Coll (MI)
Cameron U (OK)
Canisius Coll (NY)
Carnegie Mellon U (PA)
Carson-Newman U (TN)
Carthage Coll (WI)
The Catholic U of America (DC)
Cedarville U (OH)
Central Connecticut State U (CT)
Central Michigan U (MI)
Central Washington U (WA)
Christian Brothers U (TN)
Claremont McKenna Coll (CA)
Clarion U of Pennsylvania (PA)
Clarkson U (NY)
Clark U (MA)
Coastal Carolina U (SC)
Colgate U (NY)
The Coll at Brockport, State U of New York (NY)
Coll of Charleston (SC)
The Coll of Idaho (ID)
Coll of Saint Benedict (MN)
Coll of Staten Island of the City U of New York (NY)
Coll of the Holy Cross (MA)
The Coll of William and Mary (VA)
The Colorado Coll (CO)
Colorado State U (CO)
Colorado State U–Pueblo (CO)
Columbia U (NY)
Concordia U Irvine (CA)
Connecticut Coll (CT)
Cornell Coll (IA)
Cornell U (NY)
Covenant Coll (GA)
Creighton U (NE)
Dartmouth Coll (NH)
Davidson Coll (NC)
DePaul U (IL)
Dickinson Coll (PA)
Drake U (IA)
Drew U (NJ)
Drury U (MO)
Duquesne U (PA)
Earlham Coll (IN)
East Carolina U (NC)
Eastern Illinois U (IL)
Eastern Washington U (WA)
East Stroudsburg U of Pennsylvania (PA)
East Tennessee State U (TN)
Eckerd Coll (FL)
Fairfield U (CT)
Florida Ag and Mech U (FL)
Florida Atlantic U (FL)
Fordham U (NY)
Furman U (SC)
Geneva Coll (PA)
George Mason U (VA)
Georgetown Coll (KY)
Georgia Coll & State U (GA)
Georgia Southern U (GA)
Georgia State U (GA)
Gonzaga U (WA)
Gordon Coll (MA)
Goshen Coll (IN)
Grand Valley State U (MI)
Greenville U (IL)
Grove City Coll (PA)
Hamilton Coll (NY)
Hamline U (MN)
Hampden-Sydney Coll (VA)
Hanover Coll (IN)
Harding U (AR)
Hardin-Simmons U (TX)
Hartwick Coll (NY)
Harvard U (MA)
Haverford Coll (PA)
High Point U (NC)
Hillsdale Coll (MI)
Hiram Coll (OH)
Hofstra U (NY)
Humboldt State U (CA)
Hunter Coll of the City U of New York (NY)
Idaho State U (ID)
Illinois Coll (IL)
Indiana State U (IN)
Indiana U Bloomington (IN)
Indiana U of Pennsylvania (PA)
Indiana U–Purdue U Indianapolis (IN)
Indiana U South Bend (IN)
Indiana U Southeast (IN)
Iona Coll (NY)
Iowa State U of Science and Technology (IA)
Ithaca Coll (NY)
Jackson State U (MS)
Jacksonville U (FL)
Johns Hopkins U (MD)
Juniata Coll (PA)
Kalamazoo Coll (MI)
Kansas Wesleyan U (KS)
Kennesaw State U (GA)
King U (TN)
Knox Coll (IL)
Lafayette Coll (PA)
Lake Forest Coll (IL)
Lamar U (TX)
La Sierra U (CA)
Lawrence Technological U (MI)
Lawrence U (WI)
Lebanon Valley Coll (PA)
Lewis & Clark Coll (OR)
Linfield Coll (OR)
Lipscomb U (TN)
Lock Haven U of Pennsylvania (PA)
Louisiana State U and A&M Coll (LA)
Loyola Marymount U (CA)
Loyola U Chicago (IL)
Loyola U New Orleans (LA)
Lycoming Coll (PA)
Macalester Coll (MN)
Manchester U (IN)
Manhattan Coll (NY)
Marquette U (WI)
Marshall U (WV)
Massachusetts Coll of Liberal Arts (MA)
Massachusetts Inst of Technology (MA)
McDaniel Coll (MD)
Mercer U, Macon (GA)
Merrimack Coll (MA)
Messiah Coll (PA)
Miami U (OH)
Miami U Hamilton (OH)
Michigan State U (MI)
Middlebury Coll (VT)
Middle Tennessee State U (TN)
Millersville U of Pennsylvania (PA)
Millikin U (IL)
Millsaps Coll (MS)
Minnesota State U Moorhead (MN)
Montclair State U (NJ)
Morningside Coll (IA)
Murray State U (KY)
Muskingum U (OH)
New Coll of Florida (FL)
New Jersey City U (NJ)
New Jersey Inst of Technology (NJ)
New York U (NY)
North Carolina State U (NC)
Northern Illinois U (IL)
Northern Kentucky U (KY)
Northwestern U (IL)
Occidental Coll (CA)
Oglethorpe U (GA)
The Ohio State U (OH)
Ohio U (OH)
Ohio Wesleyan U (OH)
Oklahoma Baptist U (OK)
Oklahoma State U (OK)
Old Dominion U (VA)
Ouachita Baptist U (AR)
Pace U, Pleasantville Campus (NY)
Pacific Lutheran U (WA)
Pepperdine U, Malibu (CA)
Piedmont Coll (GA)
Pitzer Coll (CA)
Point Loma Nazarene U (CA)
Portland State U (OR)
Princeton U (NJ)
Purdue U (IN)
Purdue U Northwest (IN)
Queens Coll of the City U of New York (NY)
Radford U (VA)
Randolph Coll (VA)
Randolph-Macon Coll (VA)
Regis U (CO)
Rhode Island Coll (RI)
Rhodes Coll (TN)
Rice U (TX)
Roanoke Coll (VA)
Rocky Mountain Coll (MT)
Rollins Coll (FL)
Saginaw Valley State U (MI)
Saint Anselm Coll (NH)
St. John Fisher Coll (NY)
Saint John's U (MN)
Saint Joseph's U (PA)
Saint Louis U (MO)
St. Mary's Coll of Maryland (MD)

St. Mary's U (TX)
Saint Mary's U of Minnesota (MN)
St. Norbert Coll (WI)
St. Olaf Coll (MN)
Saint Vincent Coll (PA)
Salisbury U (MD)
Samford U (AL)
San Diego State U (CA)
San Francisco State U (CA)
San Jose State U (CA)
Sarah Lawrence Coll (NY)
Scripps Coll (CA)
Seattle U (WA)
Skidmore Coll (NY)
Sonoma State U (CA)
Southeastern Louisiana U (LA)
Southeast Missouri State U (MO)
Southern Arkansas U–Magnolia (AR)
Southern Illinois U Carbondale (IL)
Southern Illinois U Edwardsville (IL)
Southern U and Ag and Mech Coll (LA)
Southwestern U (TX)
State U of New York at Fredonia (NY)
State U of New York at Plattsburgh (NY)
State U of New York Coll at Geneseo (NY)
State U of New York Coll at Potsdam (NY)
Stetson U (FL)
Stevens Inst of Technology (NJ)
Stockton U (NJ)
Stonehill Coll (MA)
Syracuse U (NY)
Taylor U (IN)
Temple U (PA)
Texas Christian U (TX)
Texas Lutheran U (TX)
Texas Tech U (TX)
Towson U (MD)
Trevecca Nazarene U (TN)
Truman State U (MO)
Tulane U (LA)
Union Coll (NY)
Université de Sherbrooke (QC, Canada)
U at Buffalo, the State U of New York (NY)
U of Arkansas (AR)
U of California, Davis (CA)
U of California, Irvine (CA)
U of California, Los Angeles (CA)
U of California, Merced (CA)
U of California, Riverside (CA)
U of California, Santa Cruz (CA)
U of Central Arkansas (AR)
U of Central Florida (FL)
U of Chicago (IL)
U of Colorado Denver (CO)
U of Dallas (TX)
U of Dayton (OH)
U of Florida (FL)
U of Georgia (GA)
U of Hawaii at Manoa (HI)
U of Houston (TX)
U of Houston–Clear Lake (TX)
U of Idaho (ID)
U of Kentucky (KY)
U of La Verne (CA)
U of Louisville (KY)
U of Lynchburg (VA)
U of Maine (ME)
U of Maryland, Baltimore County (MD)
U of Maryland, Coll Park (MD)
U of Massachusetts Amherst (MA)
U of Massachusetts Boston (MA)
U of Massachusetts Dartmouth (MA)
U of Massachusetts Lowell (MA)
U of Memphis (TN)
U of Michigan (MI)
U of Michigan–Dearborn (MI)
U of Minnesota, Duluth (MN)
U of Minnesota, Morris (MN)
U of Minnesota, Twin Cities Campus (MN)
U of Missouri (MO)
U of Mount Union (OH)
U of Nebraska–Lincoln (NE)
U of Nevada, Las Vegas (NV)
U of Nevada, Reno (NV)
U of New Hampshire (NH)
U of New Mexico (NM)
U of North Carolina at Asheville (NC)
The U of North Carolina at Chapel Hill (NC)
The U of North Carolina at Charlotte (NC)
The U of North Carolina at Greensboro (NC)
The U of North Carolina at Pembroke (NC)
U of North Dakota (ND)
U of Northern Colorado (CO)
U of Northern Iowa (IA)
U of North Florida (FL)
U of Notre Dame (IN)
U of Oregon (OR)
U of Pennsylvania (PA)
U of Pittsburgh (PA)
U of Puget Sound (WA)
U of Regina (SK, Canada)
U of Richmond (VA)
U of St. Thomas (MN)
U of St. Thomas (TX)
U of San Diego (CA)
U of San Francisco (CA)
U of South Alabama (AL)
U of South Carolina (SC)
U of South Dakota (SD)
U of South Florida (FL)
The U of Tampa (FL)
The U of Tennessee (TN)
The U of Texas at Austin (TX)
The U of Texas at El Paso (TX)
The U of Texas Rio Grande Valley (TX)
The U of the South (TN)
The U of Toledo (OH)
The U of Tulsa (OK)
U of Vermont (VT)
U of Virginia (VA)
U of Washington (WA)
U of West Georgia (GA)
U of Wisconsin–Eau Claire (WI)
U of Wisconsin–La Crosse (WI)
U of Wisconsin–Milwaukee (WI)
U of Wisconsin–River Falls (WI)
U of Wyoming (WY)
Ursinus Coll (PA)
Utah State U (UT)
Utah Valley U (UT)
Utica Coll (NY)
Valparaiso U (IN)
Vassar Coll (NY)
Virginia Commonwealth U (VA)
Virginia Polytechnic Inst and State U (VA)
Wabash Coll (IN)
Wartburg Coll (IA)
Washington & Jefferson Coll (PA)
Washington and Lee U (VA)
Washington State U (WA)
Washington U in St. Louis (MO)
Weber State U (UT)
Wesleyan U (CT)
West Chester U of Pennsylvania (PA)
Western Illinois U (IL)
Western Kentucky U (KY)
Western Washington U (WA)
Westmont Coll (CA)
Wheaton Coll (IL)
Wheaton Coll (MA)
Whittier Coll (CA)
Whitworth U (WA)
Widener U (PA)
Wilkes U (PA)
Willamette U (OR)
William Jewell Coll (MO)
Williams Coll (MA)
Wofford Coll (SC)
Worcester Polytechnic Inst (MA)
Wright State U–Lake Campus (OH)
Youngstown State U (OH)

PHYSICS RELATED
Albion Coll (MI)
Bridgewater Coll (VA)
Bridgewater State U (MA)
Buena Vista U (IA)
California State U, San Marcos (CA)
Christopher Newport U (VA)
Coll of Saint Benedict (MN)
Embry-Riddle Aeronautical U–Daytona (FL)
Embry-Riddle Aeronautical U–Prescott (AZ)
Fort Lewis Coll (CO)
Lawrence Technological U (MI)
Saint John's U (MN)
Saint Mary's U of Minnesota (MN)
Southern Arkansas U–Magnolia (AR)
Southwestern U (TX)
U of California, Davis (CA)
U of California, Irvine (CA)
U of Dayton (OH)
U of Notre Dame (IN)
U of Regina (SK, Canada)

PHYSICS TEACHER EDUCATION
Albion Coll (MI)
Arkansas Tech U (AR)
Auburn U (AL)
Bowling Green State U (OH)
Bradley U (IL)
Buena Vista U (IA)
Canisius Coll (NY)
Cedarville U (OH)
Central Michigan U (MI)
Coll of Staten Island of the City U of New York (NY)
Daytona State Coll (FL)
Eastern Washington U (WA)
Goshen Coll (IN)
Grand Valley State U (MI)
Greenville U (IL)
Grove City Coll (PA)
Hofstra U (NY)
Indiana U Bloomington (IN)
Indiana U South Bend (IN)
Ithaca Coll (NY)
Juniata Coll (PA)
Kansas Wesleyan U (KS)
Kennesaw State U (GA)
Lipscomb U (TN)
Madonna U (MI)
Manchester U (IN)
Martin Luther Coll (MN)
Merrimack Coll (MA)
Messiah Coll (PA)
Miami U Hamilton (OH)
Michigan State U (MI)
Minnesota State U Moorhead (MN)
Morningside Coll (IA)
Muskingum U (OH)
Ohio Wesleyan U (OH)
Providence Coll (RI)
Queens Coll of the City U of New York (NY)
Randolph Coll (VA)
Rhode Island Coll (RI)
Saginaw Valley State U (MI)
St. John Fisher Coll (NY)
Saint Joseph's U (PA)
Saint Mary's U of Minnesota (MN)
Saint Vincent Coll (PA)
Seattle U (WA)
Southern U and Ag and Mech Coll (LA)
State U of New York Coll at Potsdam (NY)
Syracuse U (NY)
Taylor U (IN)
Trevecca Nazarene U (TN)
U of Maine at Farmington (ME)
U of Maryland, Baltimore County (MD)
U of Nebraska–Lincoln (NE)
U of Regina (SK, Canada)
U of St. Thomas (MN)
U of South Dakota (SD)
Utah State U (UT)
Utica Coll (NY)
Valparaiso U (IN)
Washington U in St. Louis (MO)
Weber State U (UT)

PHYSIOLOGICAL PSYCHOLOGY/ PSYCHOBIOLOGY
Albright Coll (PA)
Averett U (VA)
Florida Atlantic U (FL)
La Sierra U (CA)
Mills Coll (CA)
Pace U, Pleasantville Campus (NY)
Rochester Coll (MI)
U of California, Los Angeles (CA)
U of Colorado Denver (CO)
U of Michigan (MI)
Vassar Coll (NY)
Wesleyan U (CT)

PHYSIOLOGY
Boston U (MA)
California State U, Long Beach (CA)
California State U, San Marcos (CA)
Emmanuel Coll (MA)
Fort Lewis Coll (CO)
Marquette U (WI)
Michigan State U (MI)
Oklahoma Baptist U (OK)
Oklahoma State U (OK)
Southern Illinois U Carbondale (IL)
Taylor U (IN)
U of California, Los Angeles (CA)
U of Minnesota, Twin Cities Campus (MN)
U of Oregon (OR)
U of Washington (WA)
U of Wyoming (WY)

PLANETARY ASTRONOMY AND SCIENCE
California Inst of Technology (CA)
Stonehill Coll (MA)

PLANT GENETICS
Purdue U (IN)

PLANT NURSERY MANAGEMENT
Washington State U (WA)

PLANT PATHOLOGY/ PHYTOPATHOLOGY
The Ohio State U (OH)

PLANT PROTECTION AND INTEGRATED PEST MANAGEMENT
U of Hawaii at Manoa (HI)
Washington State U (WA)

PLANT SCIENCES
Auburn U (AL)
Cornell U (NY)
Louisiana State U and A&M Coll (LA)
Middle Tennessee State U (TN)
The Ohio State U (OH)
Southern Illinois U Carbondale (IL)
Texas Tech U (TX)
U of California, Santa Cruz (CA)
U of Florida (FL)
U of Maryland, Coll Park (MD)
U of Massachusetts Amherst (MA)
U of Minnesota, Twin Cities Campus (MN)
U of Missouri (MO)
The U of Tennessee (TN)
Utah State U (UT)
Washington State U (WA)

PLANT SCIENCES RELATED
Auburn U (AL)
U of Hawaii at Manoa (HI)
Utah State U (UT)

PLASTICS AND POLYMER ENGINEERING TECHNOLOGY
Weber State U (UT)

PLAYWRITING AND SCREENWRITING
Acad of Art U (CA)
Central Washington U (WA)
Columbia Coll Chicago (IL)
DePaul U (IL)
Emerson Coll (MA)
Judson U (IL)
La Sierra U (CA)
Loyola Marymount U (CA)
Marymount Manhattan Coll (NY)
Ohio U (OH)
Purchase Coll, State U of New York (NY)
Savannah Coll of Art and Design (GA)

POLISH
U of Michigan (MI)
U of Pittsburgh (PA)

POLITICAL COMMUNICATION
Emerson Coll (MA)
Florida Southern Coll (FL)
Regent U (VA)
U of Washington (WA)
Weber State U (UT)

POLITICAL ECONOMY
Antioch Coll, Yellow Springs (OH)
Bryant U (RI)
Eastern Oregon U (OR)
The Evergreen State Coll (WA)
Hillsdale Coll (MI)
La Salle U (PA)
Rhodes Coll (TN)
Rollins Coll (FL)
Sarah Lawrence Coll (NY)
U of Washington, Bothell (WA)
U of Washington, Tacoma (WA)
Williams Coll (MA)

POLITICAL SCIENCE AND GOVERNMENT
Acadia U (NS, Canada)
Adams State U (CO)
Adelphi U (NY)
Agnes Scott Coll (GA)
Alabama State U (AL)
Albion Coll (MI)
Albright Coll (PA)
Alfred U (NY)
Allegheny Coll (PA)
Alverno Coll (WI)
American Public U System (WV)
American U (DC)
Angelo State U (TX)
Appalachian State U (NC)
Arkansas Tech U (AR)
Assumption Coll (MA)
Auburn U (AL)
Auburn U at Montgomery (AL)
Aurora U (IL)
Austin Coll (TX)
Austin Peay State U (TN)
Averett U (VA)
Avila U (MO)
Baldwin Wallace U (OH)
Barton Coll (NC)
Baruch Coll of the City U of New York (NY)
Baylor U (TX)
Bellarmine U (KY)
Beloit Coll (WI)
Benedictine U (IL)
Bennett Coll (NC)
Berea Coll (KY)
Bethel U (MN)
Blackburn Coll (IL)
Boston Coll (MA)
Boston U (MA)
Bowling Green State U (OH)
Bradley U (IL)
Bridgewater Coll (VA)
Bridgewater State U (MA)
Bryant U (RI)
Bucknell U (PA)
Buena Vista U (IA)
Butler U (IN)
Caldwell U (NJ)
California Inst of Technology (CA)
California Lutheran U (CA)
California Polytechnic State U, San Luis Obispo (CA)
California State U, Bakersfield (CA)
California State U, Chico (CA)
California State U, Fullerton (CA)
California State U, Long Beach (CA)
California State U, Los Angeles (CA)
California State U, Northridge (CA)
California State U, San Bernardino (CA)
California State U, San Marcos (CA)
California U of Pennsylvania (PA)
Calvin Coll (MI)
Cameron U (OK)
Campbellsville U (KY)
Canisius Coll (NY)
Carson-Newman U (TN)
Carthage Coll (WI)
The Catholic U of America (DC)
Cedarville U (OH)
Centenary Coll of Louisiana (LA)
Central Connecticut State U (CT)
Central Michigan U (MI)
Central State U (OH)
Central Washington U (WA)
Christopher Newport U (VA)
Claremont McKenna Coll (CA)
Clarion U of Pennsylvania (PA)
Clarkson U (NY)
Clark U (MA)

Coastal Carolina U (SC)
Colgate U (NY)
The Coll at Brockport, State U of New York (NY)
Coll of Charleston (SC)
The Coll of Idaho (ID)
Coll of Saint Benedict (MN)
The Coll of Saint Rose (NY)
Coll of Staten Island of the City U of New York (NY)
Coll of the Holy Cross (MA)
The Coll of William and Mary (VA)
The Colorado Coll (CO)
Colorado State U (CO)
Colorado State U–Pueblo (CO)
Columbia Coll (MO)
Columbia U (NY)
Concordia U Chicago (IL)
Concordia U Irvine (CA)
Connecticut Coll (CT)
Cornell Coll (IA)
Cornell U (NY)
Creighton U (NE)
Culver-Stockton Coll (MO)
Dallas Baptist U (TX)
Dartmouth Coll (NH)
Davidson Coll (NC)
DePaul U (IL)
Dickinson Coll (PA)
Dominican U (IL)
Drake U (IA)
Drew U (NJ)
Drury U (MO)
Duquesne U (PA)
Earlham Coll (IN)
East Carolina U (NC)
Eastern Illinois U (IL)
Eastern U (PA)
Eastern Washington U (WA)
East Stroudsburg U of Pennsylvania (PA)
East Tennessee State U (TN)
East Texas Baptist U (TX)
Eckerd Coll (FL)
Elizabeth City State U (NC)
Emmanuel Coll (MA)
Endicott Coll (MA)
The Evergreen State Coll (WA)
Fairfield U (CT)
Fayetteville State U (NC)
Fitchburg State U (MA)
Florida Ag and Mech U (FL)
Florida Atlantic U (FL)
Florida Southern Coll (FL)
Fordham U (NY)
Fort Lewis Coll (CO)
Framingham State U (MA)
Franklin Pierce U (NH)
Furman U (SC)
Geneva Coll (PA)
Georgetown Coll (KY)
Georgia Coll & State U (GA)
Georgia Southern U (GA)
Georgia State U (GA)
Gonzaga U (WA)
Gordon Coll (MA)
Grand Valley State U (MI)
Grove City Coll (PA)
Hamilton Coll (NY)
Hamline U (MN)
Hampden-Sydney Coll (VA)
Hanover Coll (IN)
Harding U (AR)
Hardin-Simmons U (TX)
Hartwick Coll (NY)
Harvard U (MA)
Haverford Coll (PA)
High Point U (NC)
Hillsdale Coll (MI)
Hiram Coll (OH)
Hofstra U (NY)
Hollins U (VA)
Hood Coll (MD)
Humboldt State U (CA)
Hunter Coll of the City U of New York (NY)
Idaho State U (ID)
Illinois Coll (IL)
Indiana State U (IN)
Indiana U Bloomington (IN)
Indiana U East (IN)
Indiana U Northwest (IN)
Indiana U of Pennsylvania (PA)
Indiana U–Purdue U Indianapolis (IN)
Indiana U South Bend (IN)
Indiana U Southeast (IN)
Inter American U of Puerto Rico, San Germán Campus (PR)
Iona Coll (NY)
Iowa State U of Science and Technology (IA)
Ithaca Coll (NY)
Jackson State U (MS)
Jacksonville U (FL)
John Cabot U (Italy)
Johns Hopkins U (MD)
Johnson C. Smith U (NC)
Juniata Coll (PA)
Kalamazoo Coll (MI)
Kean U (NJ)
Kennesaw State U (GA)
King's Coll (PA)
King U (TN)
Knox Coll (IL)
Lafayette Coll (PA)
LaGrange Coll (GA)
Lake Forest Coll (IL)
Lamar U (TX)
La Salle U (PA)
Lawrence U (WI)
Lebanese American U (Lebanon)
Lebanon Valley Coll (PA)
Lee U (TN)
LeTourneau U (TX)
Lewis & Clark Coll (OR)
Liberty U (VA)
Lindenwood U (MO)
Linfield Coll (OR)
Lipscomb U (TN)
Lock Haven U of Pennsylvania (PA)
Loras Coll (IA)
Louisiana State U and A&M Coll (LA)
Loyola Marymount U (CA)
Loyola U Chicago (IL)
Loyola U New Orleans (LA)
Lycoming Coll (PA)
Macalester Coll (MN)
Madonna U (MI)
Manchester U (IN)
Manhattan Coll (NY)
Manhattanville Coll (NY)
Mansfield U of Pennsylvania (PA)
Marian U (IN)
Marist Coll (NY)
Marquette U (WI)
Marshall U (WV)
Marymount Manhattan Coll (NY)
Marymount U (VA)
Massachusetts Coll of Liberal Arts (MA)
Massachusetts Inst of Technology (MA)
McNeese State U (LA)
Mercer U, Macon (GA)
Mercy Coll (NY)
Merrimack Coll (MA)
Messiah Coll (PA)
Miami U (OH)
Miami U Hamilton (OH)
Michigan State U (MI)
Middlebury Coll (VT)
Middle Tennessee State U (TN)
Millersville U of Pennsylvania (PA)
Milligan Coll (TN)
Millikin U (IL)
Millsaps Coll (MS)
Mills Coll (CA)
Minnesota State U Moorhead (MN)
Molloy Coll (NY)
Montclair State U (NJ)
Morningside Coll (IA)
Mount Saint Mary Coll (NY)
Murray State U (KY)
Muskingum U (OH)
National U (CA)
Nazareth Coll of Rochester (NY)
New Coll of Florida (FL)
New England Coll (NH)
New Jersey City U (NJ)
New York U (NY)
North Carolina State U (NC)
Northeastern State U (OK)
Northern Illinois U (IL)
Northern Kentucky U (KY)
Northern State U (SD)
Northwestern Oklahoma State U (OK)
Northwestern U (IL)
Northwest Missouri State U (MO)
Occidental Coll (CA)
Oglethorpe U (GA)
Ohio Dominican U (OH)
The Ohio State U (OH)
Ohio U (OH)
Ohio Wesleyan U (OH)
Oklahoma Baptist U (OK)
Oklahoma State U (OK)
Old Dominion U (VA)
Ouachita Baptist U (AR)
Pace U (NY)
Pace U, Pleasantville Campus (NY)
Pacific Lutheran U (WA)
Palm Beach Atlantic U (FL)
Pepperdine U, Malibu (CA)
Piedmont Coll (GA)
Pitzer Coll (CA)
Point Loma Nazarene U (CA)
Portland State U (OR)
Prairie View A&M U (TX)
Princeton U (NJ)
Providence Coll (RI)
Purchase Coll, State U of New York (NY)
Purdue U (IN)
Purdue U Northwest (IN)
Queens Coll of the City U of New York (NY)
Queens U of Charlotte (NC)
Radford U (VA)
Randolph Coll (VA)
Randolph-Macon Coll (VA)
Redeemer U Coll (ON, Canada)
Regis U (CO)
Reinhardt U (GA)
Rhode Island Coll (RI)
Rhodes Coll (TN)
Rice U (TX)
Rider U (NJ)
Roanoke Coll (VA)
Rochester Inst of Technology (NY)
Rockford U (IL)
Rocky Mountain Coll (MT)
Rollins Coll (FL)
Sacred Heart U (CT)
Saginaw Valley State U (MI)
Saint Anselm Coll (NH)
Saint Francis U (PA)
St. John Fisher Coll (NY)
Saint John's U (MN)
St. Joseph's Coll, Long Island Campus (NY)
St. Joseph's Coll, New York (NY)
Saint Joseph's U (PA)
Saint Leo U (FL)
Saint Louis U (MO)
Saint Martin's U (WA)
St. Mary's Coll of Maryland (MD)
St. Mary's U (TX)
St. Norbert Coll (WI)
St. Olaf Coll (MN)
Saint Vincent Coll (PA)
Salisbury U (MD)
Salve Regina U (RI)
Samford U (AL)
San Diego State U (CA)
San Francisco State U (CA)
San Jose State U (CA)
Sarah Lawrence Coll (NY)
Scripps Coll (CA)
Seattle U (WA)
Seton Hill U (PA)
Skidmore Coll (NY)
Sonoma State U (CA)
Southeastern Louisiana U (LA)
Southeastern U (FL)
Southeast Missouri State U (MO)
Southern Illinois U Carbondale (IL)
Southern Illinois U Edwardsville (IL)
Southern U and Ag and Mech Coll (LA)
Southwest Baptist U (MO)
Southwestern U (TX)
Spring Hill Coll (AL)
State U of New York at Fredonia (NY)
State U of New York at Plattsburgh (NY)
State U of New York Coll at Geneseo (NY)
State U of New York Coll at Potsdam (NY)
Stetson U (FL)
Stockton U (NJ)
Stonehill Coll (MA)
Sweet Briar Coll (VA)
Syracuse U (NY)
Taylor U (IN)
Temple U (PA)
Texas A&M U–Central Texas (TX)
Texas Christian U (TX)
Texas Lutheran U (TX)
Texas Tech U (TX)
Texas Woman's U (TX)
Towson U (MD)
Truman State U (MO)
Tulane U (LA)
Union Coll (NY)
Université de Sherbrooke (QC, Canada)
U at Buffalo, the State U of New York (NY)
U of Arkansas (AR)
U of California, Davis (CA)
U of California, Irvine (CA)
U of California, Los Angeles (CA)
U of California, Merced (CA)
U of California, Riverside (CA)
U of California, Santa Cruz (CA)
U of Central Arkansas (AR)
U of Central Florida (FL)
U of Chicago (IL)
U of Colorado Denver (CO)
U of Dallas (TX)
U of Dayton (OH)
U of Detroit Mercy (MI)
The U of Findlay (OH)
U of Florida (FL)
U of Georgia (GA)
U of Guam (GU)
U of Hawaii at Manoa (HI)
U of Houston (TX)
U of Houston–Downtown (TX)
U of Idaho (ID)
U of Illinois at Springfield (IL)
U of Kentucky (KY)
U of La Verne (CA)
U of Louisville (KY)
U of Lynchburg (VA)
U of Maine (ME)
U of Maine at Farmington (ME)
U of Maine at Presque Isle (ME)
U of Mary Hardin-Baylor (TX)
U of Maryland, Baltimore County (MD)
U of Maryland, Coll Park (MD)
U of Maryland U Coll (MD)
U of Massachusetts Amherst (MA)
U of Massachusetts Boston (MA)
U of Massachusetts Dartmouth (MA)
U of Massachusetts Lowell (MA)
U of Memphis (TN)
U of Michigan (MI)
U of Michigan–Dearborn (MI)
U of Minnesota, Duluth (MN)
U of Minnesota, Morris (MN)
U of Minnesota, Twin Cities Campus (MN)
U of Missouri (MO)
U of Montevallo (AL)
U of Mount Union (OH)
U of Nebraska–Lincoln (NE)
U of Nevada, Las Vegas (NV)
U of Nevada, Reno (NV)
U of New Hampshire (NH)
U of New Haven (CT)
U of New Mexico (NM)
U of North Carolina at Asheville (NC)
The U of North Carolina at Chapel Hill (NC)
The U of North Carolina at Charlotte (NC)
The U of North Carolina at Greensboro (NC)
The U of North Carolina at Pembroke (NC)
U of North Dakota (ND)
U of Northern Colorado (CO)
U of Northern Iowa (IA)
U of North Florida (FL)
U of Notre Dame (IN)
U of Oregon (OR)
U of Pennsylvania (PA)
U of Pittsburgh (PA)
U of Pittsburgh at Bradford (PA)
U of Puget Sound (WA)
U of Regina (SK, Canada)
U of Richmond (VA)
U of Saint Francis (IN)
U of Saint Mary (KS)
U of St. Thomas (MN)
U of St. Thomas (TX)
U of San Diego (CA)
U of San Francisco (CA)
U of South Alabama (AL)
U of South Carolina (SC)
U of South Carolina Aiken (SC)
U of South Dakota (SD)
U of Southern Indiana (IN)
U of South Florida (FL)
The U of Tampa (FL)
The U of Tennessee (TN)
The U of Tennessee at Martin (TN)
The U of Texas at Austin (TX)
The U of Texas at El Paso (TX)
The U of Texas of the Permian Basin (TX)
The U of Texas Rio Grande Valley (TX)
U of the Incarnate Word (TX)
The U of the South (TN)
The U of Toledo (OH)
The U of Tulsa (OK)
U of Vermont (VT)
U of Virginia (VA)
U of Washington (WA)
U of West Georgia (GA)
U of Wisconsin–Eau Claire (WI)
U of Wisconsin–La Crosse (WI)
U of Wisconsin–Milwaukee (WI)
U of Wisconsin–River Falls (WI)
U of Wyoming (WY)
Ursinus Coll (PA)
Utah State U (UT)
Utah Valley U (UT)
Utica Coll (NY)
Valparaiso U (IN)
Vanguard U of Southern California (CA)
Vassar Coll (NY)
Virginia Commonwealth U (VA)
Virginia Polytechnic Inst and State U (VA)
Wabash Coll (IN)
Wartburg Coll (IA)
Washington & Jefferson Coll (PA)
Washington and Lee U (VA)
Washington State U (WA)
Washington U in St. Louis (MO)
Weber State U (UT)
Wesleyan U (CT)
West Chester U of Pennsylvania (PA)
Western Connecticut State U (CT)
Western Illinois U (IL)
Western Kentucky U (KY)
Western State Colorado U (CO)
Western Washington U (WA)
Westmont Coll (CA)
West Virginia State U (WV)
West Virginia U Inst of Technology (WV)
Wheaton Coll (IL)
Wheaton Coll (MA)
Whittier Coll (CA)
Whitworth U (WA)
Widener U (PA)
Wilkes U (PA)
Willamette U (OR)
William Jewell Coll (MO)
Williams Coll (MA)
Winthrop U (SC)
Wofford Coll (SC)
Woodbury U (CA)
Wright State U–Lake Campus (OH)
Youngstown State U (OH)

POLITICAL SCIENCE AND GOVERNMENT RELATED

American U in Bulgaria (Bulgaria)
Blackburn Coll (IL)
Brandeis U (MA)
Buena Vista U (IA)
George Mason U (VA)
Georgetown Coll (KY)
LeTourneau U (TX)
McDaniel Coll (MD)
Pitzer Coll (CA)
Saint Mary's U of Minnesota (MN)
U of California, Davis (CA)
U of Northern Iowa (IA)
U of Washington (WA)
Wesleyan Coll (GA)

POLYMER/PLASTICS ENGINEERING

Auburn U (AL)
U of Massachusetts Lowell (MA)
Western Washington U (WA)

POPULATION BIOLOGY

Providence Coll (RI)

PORTUGUESE
Columbia U (NY)
Indiana U Bloomington (IN)
The Ohio State U (OH)
Queens Coll of the City U of New York (NY)
Rhode Island Coll (RI)
Tulane U (LA)
U of California, Los Angeles (CA)
U of Florida (FL)
U of Massachusetts Amherst (MA)
U of Massachusetts Dartmouth (MA)
U of New Mexico (NM)
The U of Texas at Austin (TX)

POULTRY SCIENCE
Auburn U (AL)
North Carolina State U (NC)
U of Arkansas (AR)
U of Georgia (GA)
Virginia Polytechnic Inst and State U (VA)

PRE-CHIROPRACTIC
Millikin U (IL)
U of Regina (SK, Canada)
U of Sioux Falls (SD)

PRE-DENTISTRY STUDIES
Acadia U (NS, Canada)
Albright Coll (PA)
American U (DC)
Auburn U (AL)
Baldwin Wallace U (OH)
Boston U (MA)
Bowling Green State U (OH)
Bradley U (IL)
Calvin Coll (MI)
Campbellsville U (KY)
Carthage Coll (WI)
Clark U (MA)
Concordia U Chicago (IL)
Drake U (IA)
Fordham U (NY)
Franklin Pierce U (NH)
Furman U (SC)
Grand Valley State U (MI)
Hamline U (MN)
Hofstra U (NY)
Illinois Coll (IL)
King's Coll (PA)
Limestone Coll (SC)
Lindenwood U (MO)
Lipscomb U (TN)
Lubbock Christian U (TX)
Madonna U (MI)
Manchester U (IN)
Maryville U of Saint Louis (MO)
Millikin U (IL)
Muskingum U (OH)
Nazareth Coll of Rochester (NY)
Northwestern Oklahoma State U (OK)
Oglethorpe U (GA)
Ohio Wesleyan U (OH)
Ouachita Baptist U (AR)
Rhode Island Coll (RI)
Rochester Inst of Technology (NY)
Rockford U (IL)
Saginaw Valley State U (MI)
Saint Anselm Coll (NH)
Saint Francis U (PA)
Sonoma State U (CA)
State U of New York Coll at Geneseo (NY)
State U of New York Coll of Environmental Science and Forestry (NY)
Stetson U (FL)
Syracuse U (NY)
U of Dayton (OH)
U of Maryland, Coll Park (MD)
U of Nebraska–Lincoln (NE)
U of Regina (SK, Canada)
U of Sioux Falls (SD)
The U of Tampa (FL)
Utah State U (UT)
Utica Coll (NY)
Washington U in St. Louis (MO)
Waynesburg U (PA)
Westmont Coll (CA)
Whitworth U (WA)
Widener U (PA)
Youngstown State U (OH)

PRE-ENGINEERING
Baldwin Wallace U (OH)
Canisius Coll (NY)
Drake U (IA)
Hamline U (MN)
Inter American U of Puerto Rico, Aguadilla Campus (PR)
Inter American U of Puerto Rico, San Germán Campus (PR)
Louisiana Coll (LA)
Ouachita Baptist U (AR)
Providence Coll (RI)
Scripps Coll (CA)
Spring Hill Coll (AL)
Ursinus Coll (PA)
Waynesburg U (PA)

PRE-LAW STUDIES
Acadia U (NS, Canada)
Albright Coll (PA)
Auburn U (AL)
Babson Coll (MA)
Baylor U (TX)
Bowling Green State U (OH)
Bryant U (RI)
Buena Vista U (IA)
Calvin Coll (MI)
Campbellsville U (KY)
Carthage Coll (WI)
Cedarville U (OH)
Champlain Coll (VT)
Clark U (MA)
The Coll of Saint Rose (NY)
Concordia U Chicago (IL)
Dominican U (IL)
Drake U (IA)
Emmanuel Coll (GA)
Fordham U (NY)
Franklin Pierce U (NH)
Furman U (SC)
Hamline U (MN)
Hartwick Coll (NY)
Hofstra U (NY)
Illinois Coll (IL)
Ithaca Coll (NY)
Judson U (IL)
King's Coll (PA)
Liberty U (VA)
Limestone Coll (SC)
Lindenwood U (MO)
Lipscomb U (TN)
Louisiana Coll (LA)
Madonna U (MI)
Manchester U (IN)
Mansfield U of Pennsylvania (PA)
Massachusetts Coll of Liberal Arts (MA)
Michigan State U (MI)
Millikin U (IL)
Muskingum U (OH)
National U (CA)
Nazareth Coll of Rochester (NY)
Northwestern Oklahoma State U (OK)
Oglethorpe U (GA)
Ohio Wesleyan U (OH)
Oklahoma Christian U (OK)
Ouachita Baptist U (AR)
Palm Beach Atlantic U (FL)
Rhode Island Coll (RI)
Rochester Inst of Technology (NY)
Rockford U (IL)
Saginaw Valley State U (MI)
Saint Anselm Coll (NH)
Saint Francis U (PA)
Seton Hill U (PA)
Sonoma State U (CA)
State U of New York at Fredonia (NY)
State U of New York Coll at Geneseo (NY)
State U of New York Coll of Environmental Science and Forestry (NY)
Stetson U (FL)
Syracuse U (NY)
The U of Findlay (OH)
U of Maryland, Coll Park (MD)
U of Regina (SK, Canada)
U of Sioux Falls (SD)
The U of Tampa (FL)
Utah State U (UT)
Utica Coll (NY)
Waynesburg U (PA)
Westmont Coll (CA)
Whittier Coll (CA)
Whitworth U (WA)
Youngstown State U (OH)

PREMEDICAL STUDIES
Acadia U (NS, Canada)
Albright Coll (PA)
American U (DC)
Auburn U (AL)
Averett U (VA)
Avila U (MO)
Baldwin Wallace U (OH)
Boston U (MA)
Bowling Green State U (OH)
Bradley U (IL)
Bryant U (RI)
Calvin Coll (MI)
Campbellsville U (KY)
Carthage Coll (WI)
Clark U (MA)
Concordia U Chicago (IL)
Dominican U (IL)
Drake U (IA)
Fordham U (NY)
Franklin Pierce U (NH)
Furman U (SC)
Hamline U (MN)
Hartwick Coll (NY)
Hofstra U (NY)
Illinois Coll (IL)
Ithaca Coll (NY)
King's Coll (PA)
La Salle U (PA)
Limestone Coll (SC)
Lindenwood U (MO)
Lipscomb U (TN)
Lubbock Christian U (TX)
Madonna U (MI)
Manchester U (IN)
Maryville U of Saint Louis (MO)
Massachusetts Coll of Liberal Arts (MA)
Mercer U, Macon (GA)
Miami U (OH)
Michigan State U (MI)
Millikin U (IL)
Mount St. Joseph U (OH)
Muskingum U (OH)
Nazareth Coll of Rochester (NY)
Northwestern Oklahoma State U (OK)
Northwestern U (IL)
Oglethorpe U (GA)
Ohio Wesleyan U (OH)
Ouachita Baptist U (AR)
Rhode Island Coll (RI)
Rochester Inst of Technology (NY)
Rockford U (IL)
Saginaw Valley State U (MI)
Saint Anselm Coll (NH)
Saint Francis U (PA)
Samford U (AL)
Sarah Lawrence Coll (NY)
Sonoma State U (CA)
State U of New York at Fredonia (NY)
State U of New York Coll at Geneseo (NY)
State U of New York Coll of Environmental Science and Forestry (NY)
Stetson U (FL)
Syracuse U (NY)
Texas Lutheran U (TX)
Université de Sherbrooke (QC, Canada)
U of Arkansas (AR)
U of Dayton (OH)
U of Maine at Machias (ME)
U of Nebraska–Lincoln (NE)
U of Notre Dame (IN)
U of Regina (SK, Canada)
U of Sioux Falls (SD)
The U of Tampa (FL)
U of Wisconsin–Milwaukee (WI)
U of Wisconsin–Superior (WI)
Utah State U (UT)
Utica Coll (NY)
Vanguard U of Southern California (CA)
Washington U in St. Louis (MO)
Waynesburg U (PA)
West Chester U of Pennsylvania (PA)
Westmont Coll (CA)
Whittier Coll (CA)
Whitworth U (WA)
Widener U (PA)
Youngstown State U (OH)

PRENURSING STUDIES
Averett U (VA)
Baylor U (TX)
California State U, Fullerton (CA)
Central Washington U (WA)
The Coll of Idaho (ID)
Concordia U Chicago (IL)
Hardin-Simmons U (TX)
Jacksonville U (FL)
La Salle U (PA)
Limestone Coll (SC)
Lindenwood U (MO)
Lipscomb U (TN)
Lubbock Christian U (TX)
Madonna U (MI)
Mount St. Joseph U (OH)
Ouachita Baptist U (AR)
Seattle U (WA)
U of Northwestern–St. Paul (MN)

PRE-OCCUPATIONAL THERAPY
Bradley U (IL)
Gwynedd Mercy U (PA)
Lubbock Christian U (TX)
Millikin U (IL)
Pace U (NY)
Trevecca Nazarene U (TN)
U of Regina (SK, Canada)

PRE-OPTOMETRY
Calvin Coll (MI)
Madonna U (MI)
Millikin U (IL)
Pace U (NY)
Rhode Island Coll (RI)
U of Regina (SK, Canada)

PRE-PHARMACY STUDIES
Auburn U (AL)
Baldwin Wallace U (OH)
Benedictine U (IL)
Butler U (IN)
Calvin Coll (MI)
Dominican U (IL)
Emmanuel Coll (GA)
Hamline U (MN)
King's Coll (PA)
Limestone Coll (SC)
Lipscomb U (TN)
Louisiana Coll (LA)
Lubbock Christian U (TX)
Manchester U (IN)
Millikin U (IL)
Muskingum U (OH)
Ouachita Baptist U (AR)
U of Nebraska–Lincoln (NE)
U of Regina (SK, Canada)
U of the Incarnate Word (TX)
Washington U in St. Louis (MO)
Westmont Coll (CA)
Youngstown State U (OH)

PRE-PHYSICAL THERAPY
Bradley U (IL)
Calvin Coll (MI)
Hamline U (MN)
Kansas Wesleyan U (KS)
Lubbock Christian U (TX)
Massachusetts Coll of Liberal Arts (MA)
Merrimack Coll (MA)
Millikin U (IL)
Mount St. Joseph U (OH)
Pace U (NY)
Rockford U (IL)
Saint Mary's U of Minnesota (MN)
Trevecca Nazarene U (TN)
U of Dayton (OH)
The U of Findlay (OH)
U of Kentucky (KY)
U of Mary Hardin-Baylor (TX)
U of Regina (SK, Canada)
U of Sioux Falls (SD)
Western Washington U (WA)

PRE-THEOLOGY/PRE-MINISTERIAL STUDIES
Calvin Coll (MI)
Concordia U Chicago (IL)
Geneva Coll (PA)
Lee U (TN)
Manchester U (IN)
Martin Luther Coll (MN)
Ohio Wesleyan U (OH)
Tabor Coll (KS)
U of Dallas (TX)
U of Northwestern–St. Paul (MN)
Waynesburg U (PA)
Westmont Coll (CA)

PRE-VETERINARY STUDIES
Acadia U (NS, Canada)
Albright Coll (PA)
American U (DC)
Auburn U (AL)
Baldwin Wallace U (OH)
Bradley U (IL)
Calvin Coll (MI)
Campbellsville U (KY)
Carthage Coll (WI)
Clark U (MA)
Drake U (IA)
Fordham U (NY)
Franklin Pierce U (NH)
Furman U (SC)
Grand Valley State U (MI)
Hamline U (MN)
Hartwick Coll (NY)
Hofstra U (NY)
Illinois Coll (IL)
King's Coll (PA)
Limestone Coll (SC)
Lindenwood U (MO)
Lipscomb U (TN)
Lubbock Christian U (TX)
Madonna U (MI)
Manchester U (IN)
Maryville U of Saint Louis (MO)
Mercy Coll (NY)
Michigan State U (MI)
Millikin U (IL)
Muskingum U (OH)
Nazareth Coll of Rochester (NY)
Northwest Missouri State U (MO)
Oglethorpe U (GA)
Ohio Wesleyan U (OH)
Ouachita Baptist U (AR)
Purdue U Northwest (IN)
Rhode Island Coll (RI)
Rochester Inst of Technology (NY)
Rockford U (IL)
Saint Francis U (PA)
Sonoma State U (CA)
State U of New York at Fredonia (NY)
State U of New York Coll at Geneseo (NY)
State U of New York Coll of Environmental Science and Forestry (NY)
Stetson U (FL)
Syracuse U (NY)
The U of Findlay (OH)
U of Maryland, Coll Park (MD)
U of Massachusetts Amherst (MA)
U of Nebraska–Lincoln (NE)
U of Nevada, Reno (NV)
U of Regina (SK, Canada)
U of Sioux Falls (SD)
The U of Tampa (FL)
Utah State U (UT)
Utica Coll (NY)
Washington U in St. Louis (MO)
Waynesburg U (PA)
Westmont Coll (CA)
Whitworth U (WA)
Widener U (PA)
Youngstown State U (OH)

PRINTING MANAGEMENT
Rochester Inst of Technology (NY)
U of Minnesota, Duluth (MN)

PRINTMAKING
Adams State U (CO)
Boston U (MA)
Bowling Green State U (OH)
Bradley U (IL)
California State U, Long Beach (CA)
Cleveland Inst of Art (OH)
Columbia Coll (MO)
Drake U (IA)
Escuela de Artes Plasticas y Diseño de Puerto Rico (PR)
Inter American U of Puerto Rico, San Germán Campus (PR)
Maryland Inst Coll of Art (MD)
Purchase Coll, State U of New York (NY)
Rhode Island Coll (RI)
Rhode Island School of Design (RI)
Savannah Coll of Art and Design (GA)
Seton Hill U (PA)
Sonoma State U (CA)

MAJORS LISTING

Syracuse U (NY)
Temple U (PA)
Texas Christian U (TX)
U of Dallas (TX)
U of Massachusetts Dartmouth (MA)
U of Michigan (MI)
U of Oregon (OR)
U of Puget Sound (WA)
U of Regina (SK, Canada)
The U of Texas at El Paso (TX)
Washington U in St. Louis (MO)
Youngstown State U (OH)

PROFESSIONAL, TECHNICAL, BUSINESS, AND SCIENTIFIC WRITING
Albion Coll (MI)
Baylor U (TX)
Blackburn Coll (IL)
Bowling Green State U (OH)
Carnegie Mellon U (PA)
Cedarville U (OH)
Eastern Washington U (WA)
Excelsior Coll (NY)
Fitchburg State U (MA)
Immaculata U (PA)
Juniata Coll (PA)
Lubbock Christian U (TX)
Madonna U (MI)
Massachusetts Coll of Liberal Arts (MA)
Miami U (OH)
Miami U Hamilton (OH)
Michigan State U (MI)
New Jersey Inst of Technology (NJ)
Purdue U (IN)
Saginaw Valley State U (MI)
Saint Leo U (FL)
San Francisco State U (CA)
Savannah Coll of Art and Design (GA)
Taylor U (IN)
Texas Tech U (TX)
U of Houston–Downtown (TX)
U of Northwestern–St. Paul (MN)
U of South Dakota (SD)
U of South Florida Sarasota-Manatee (FL)
U of Washington (WA)
Valparaiso U (IN)
Weber State U (UT)
Winthrop U (SC)
Woodbury U (CA)
Youngstown State U (OH)

PROJECT MANAGEMENT
Bryant U (RI)
Coll of Charleston (SC)
Davenport U, Grand Rapids (MI)
Embry-Riddle Aeronautical U–Worldwide (FL)
Minnesota State U Moorhead (MN)
Saint Louis U (MO)
U of the Incarnate Word (TX)

PROTECTIVE SERVICES OPERATIONS
Embry-Riddle Aeronautical U–Worldwide (FL)

PSYCHIATRIC/MENTAL HEALTH SERVICES TECHNOLOGY
Columbia Southern U (AL)

PSYCHOLOGY
Acadia U (NS, Canada)
Adams State U (CO)
Adelphi U (NY)
Agnes Scott Coll (GA)
Alabama State U (AL)
Albion Coll (MI)
Albright Coll (PA)
Alfred U (NY)
Allegheny Coll (PA)
Alverno Coll (WI)
American Coll of Thessaloniki (Greece)
American Public U System (WV)
American U (DC)
American U of Beirut (Lebanon)
Angelo State U (TX)
Antioch Coll, Yellow Springs (OH)
Appalachian State U (NC)
Arkansas Tech U (AR)
Assumption Coll (MA)
Auburn U (AL)
Auburn U at Montgomery (AL)
Aurora U (IL)
Austin Coll (TX)
Austin Peay State U (TN)
Averett U (VA)
Avila U (MO)
Baker U (KS)
Baldwin Wallace U (OH)
Barton Coll (NC)
Baruch Coll of the City U of New York (NY)
Baylor U (TX)
Bellarmine U (KY)
Beloit Coll (WI)
Benedictine U (IL)
Bennett Coll (NC)
Berea Coll (KY)
Bethany Lutheran Coll (MN)
Bethel Coll (KS)
Bethel U (MN)
Blackburn Coll (IL)
Boston Coll (MA)
Boston U (MA)
Bowling Green State U (OH)
Bradley U (IL)
Brandman U (CA)
Brenau U (GA)
Bridgewater Coll (VA)
Bridgewater State U (MA)
Bryant U (RI)
Bryn Athyn Coll of the New Church (PA)
Bucknell U (PA)
Buena Vista U (IA)
Butler U (IN)
Caldwell U (NJ)
California Lutheran U (CA)
California Polytechnic State U, San Luis Obispo (CA)
California State U, Bakersfield (CA)
California State U, Chico (CA)
California State U, Fullerton (CA)
California State U, Long Beach (CA)
California State U, Los Angeles (CA)
California State U, Monterey Bay (CA)
California State U, Northridge (CA)
California State U, San Bernardino (CA)
California State U, San Marcos (CA)
California U of Pennsylvania (PA)
Calumet Coll of Saint Joseph (IN)
Calvin Coll (MI)
Cameron U (OK)
Campbellsville U (KY)
Canisius Coll (NY)
Carnegie Mellon U (PA)
Carson-Newman U (TN)
Carthage Coll (WI)
The Catholic U of America (DC)
Cedarville U (OH)
Centenary Coll of Louisiana (LA)
Central Connecticut State U (CT)
Central Michigan U (MI)
Central State U (OH)
Central Washington U (WA)
Champlain Coll (VT)
Christian Brothers U (TN)
Christopher Newport U (VA)
Claremont McKenna Coll (CA)
Clarion U of Pennsylvania (PA)
Clarkson U (NY)
Clark U (MA)
Coastal Carolina U (SC)
Colgate U (NY)
The Coll at Brockport, State U of New York (NY)
Coll of Charleston (SC)
Coll of Coastal Georgia (GA)
The Coll of Idaho (ID)
Coll of Saint Benedict (MN)
Coll of Saint Mary (NE)
The Coll of Saint Rose (NY)
The Coll of St. Scholastica (MN)
Coll of Staten Island of the City U of New York (NY)
Coll of the Holy Cross (MA)
Coll of the Ozarks (MO)
The Coll of William and Mary (VA)
The Colorado Coll (CO)
Colorado State U (CO)
Colorado State U–Pueblo (CO)
Columbia Coll (MO)
Columbia U (NY)
Concordia U Chicago (IL)
Concordia U Irvine (CA)
Connecticut Coll (CT)
Cornell Coll (IA)
Cornell U (NY)
Covenant Coll (GA)
Culver-Stockton Coll (MO)
Curry Coll (MA)
Dallas Baptist U (TX)
Dallas Christian Coll (TX)
Dartmouth Coll (NH)
Davidson Coll (NC)
Dean Coll (MA)
Delta State U (MS)
DePaul U (IL)
DEREE - The American Coll of Greece (Greece)
Dickinson Coll (PA)
Dominican U (IL)
Drake U (IA)
Drew U (NJ)
Duquesne U (PA)
Earlham Coll (IN)
East Carolina U (NC)
Eastern Illinois U (IL)
Eastern Mennonite U (VA)
Eastern Oregon U (OR)
Eastern U (PA)
Eastern Washington U (WA)
East Stroudsburg U of Pennsylvania (PA)
East Tennessee State U (TN)
East Texas Baptist U (TX)
Eckerd Coll (FL)
Elizabeth City State U (NC)
Emmanuel Coll (GA)
Emmanuel Coll (MA)
Endicott Coll (MA)
The Evergreen State Coll (WA)
Excelsior Coll (NY)
Fairfield U (CT)
Fayetteville State U (NC)
Fitchburg State U (MA)
Florida Ag and Mech U (FL)
Florida Atlantic U (FL)
Florida Southern Coll (FL)
Fordham U (NY)
Fort Lewis Coll (CO)
Framingham State U (MA)
Franklin Pierce U (NH)
Furman U (SC)
Geneva Coll (PA)
George Mason U (VA)
Georgetown Coll (KY)
Georgia Southern U (GA)
Georgia State U (GA)
Gonzaga U (WA)
Gordon Coll (MA)
Goshen Coll (IN)
Graceland U (IA)
Grand Valley State U (MI)
Granite State Coll (NH)
Greenville U (IL)
Grove City Coll (PA)
Gwynedd Mercy U (PA)
Hamilton Coll (NY)
Hamline U (MN)
Hampden-Sydney Coll (VA)
Hanover Coll (IN)
Harding U (AR)
Hardin-Simmons U (TX)
Hartwick Coll (NY)
Harvard U (MA)
Haverford Coll (PA)
High Point U (NC)
Hillsdale Coll (MI)
Hiram Coll (OH)
Hofstra U (NY)
Hollins U (VA)
Hood Coll (MD)
Humboldt State U (CA)
Hunter Coll of the City U of New York (NY)
Idaho State U (ID)
Illinois Coll (IL)
Immaculata U (PA)
Indiana State U (IN)
Indiana U East (IN)
Indiana U Kokomo (IN)
Indiana U Northwest (IN)
Indiana U of Pennsylvania (PA)
Indiana U–Purdue U Indianapolis (IN)
Indiana U South Bend (IN)
Indiana U Southeast (IN)
Inter American U of Puerto Rico, Aguadilla Campus (PR)
Inter American U of Puerto Rico, Fajardo Campus (PR)
Inter American U of Puerto Rico, San Germán Campus (PR)
Iona Coll (NY)
Iowa State U of Science and Technology (IA)
Ithaca Coll (NY)
Jackson State U (MS)
Jacksonville U (FL)
Johns Hopkins U (MD)
Johnson C. Smith U (NC)
Judson U (IL)
Juniata Coll (PA)
Kalamazoo Coll (MI)
Kansas Wesleyan U (KS)
Kean U (NJ)
Kennesaw State U (GA)
King's Coll (PA)
King U (TN)
Kuyper Coll (MI)
Lafayette Coll (PA)
LaGrange Coll (GA)
Lamar U (TX)
La Salle U (PA)
Lasell Coll (MA)
La Sierra U (CA)
Lawrence Technological U (MI)
Lawrence U (WI)
Lebanese American U (Lebanon)
Lebanon Valley Coll (PA)
Lees-McRae Coll (NC)
Lee U (TN)
LeTourneau U (TX)
Lewis & Clark Coll (OR)
Liberty U (VA)
Life U (GA)
Limestone Coll (SC)
Lincoln Christian U (IL)
Lindenwood U (MO)
Linfield Coll (OR)
Lipscomb U (TN)
Lock Haven U of Pennsylvania (PA)
Loras Coll (IA)
Louisiana Coll (LA)
Louisiana State U and A&M Coll (LA)
Loyola Marymount U (CA)
Loyola U Chicago (IL)
Lubbock Christian U (TX)
Lycoming Coll (PA)
Madonna U (MI)
Manchester U (IN)
Manhattan Coll (NY)
Manhattanville Coll (NY)
Mansfield U of Pennsylvania (PA)
Maria Coll (NY)
Marian U (IN)
Marist Coll (NY)
Marquette U (WI)
Marshall U (WV)
Marymount California U (CA)
Marymount Manhattan Coll (NY)
Marymount U (VA)
Maryville U of Saint Louis (MO)
Marywood U (PA)
Massachusetts Coll of Liberal Arts (MA)
McDaniel Coll (MD)
McNeese State U (LA)
Mercer U, Macon (GA)
Mercy Coll (NY)
Merrimack Coll (MA)
Messiah Coll (PA)
Miami U (OH)
Miami U Hamilton (OH)
Michigan State U (MI)
Middlebury Coll (VT)
Middle Tennessee State U (TN)
Millersville U of Pennsylvania (PA)
Milligan Coll (TN)
Millikin U (IL)
Millsaps Coll (MS)
Mills Coll (CA)
Minnesota State U Moorhead (MN)
Missouri Baptist U (MO)
Molloy Coll (NY)
Montclair State U (NJ)
Morningside Coll (IA)
Mount Marty Coll (SD)
Mount St. Joseph U (OH)
Mount Saint Mary Coll (NY)
Muskingum U (OH)
National U (CA)
Nazareth Coll of Rochester (NY)
New Coll of Florida (FL)
New England Coll (NH)
New Jersey City U (NJ)
New York U (NY)
Nichols Coll (MA)
North Carolina State U (NC)
Northern Illinois U (IL)
Northern Kentucky U (KY)
Northern State U (SD)
Northwest Christian U (OR)
Northwestern Oklahoma State U (OK)
Northwestern U (IL)
Northwest Missouri State U (MO)
Oakland City U (IN)
Occidental Coll (CA)
Oglethorpe U (GA)
Ohio Dominican U (OH)
The Ohio State U (OH)
The Ohio State U at Lima (OH)
The Ohio State U at Mansfield (OH)
The Ohio State U at Marion (OH)
The Ohio State U at Newark (OH)
Ohio U (OH)
Ohio Wesleyan U (OH)
Oklahoma Baptist U (OK)
Oklahoma Christian U (OK)
Oklahoma State U (OK)
Old Dominion U (VA)
Ottawa U (KS)
Ouachita Baptist U (AR)
Pace U (NY)
Pace U, Pleasantville Campus (NY)
Pacific Lutheran U (WA)
Palm Beach Atlantic U (FL)
Pepperdine U, Malibu (CA)
Pfeiffer U (NC)
Piedmont Coll (GA)
Pitzer Coll (CA)
Point Loma Nazarene U (CA)
Point U (GA)
Portland State U (OR)
Prairie View A&M U (TX)
Princeton U (NJ)
Providence Coll (RI)
Purchase Coll, State U of New York (NY)
Purdue U Northwest (IN)
Queens Coll of the City U of New York (NY)
Queens U of Charlotte (NC)
Radford U (VA)
Randolph Coll (VA)
Randolph-Macon Coll (VA)
Redeemer U Coll (ON, Canada)
Regent U (VA)
Regis U (CO)
Reinhardt U (GA)
Rhode Island Coll (RI)
Rhodes Coll (TN)
Rice U (TX)
Rider U (NJ)
Roanoke Coll (VA)
Rochester Coll (MI)
Rochester Inst of Technology (NY)
Rockford U (IL)
Rocky Mountain Coll (MT)
Rollins Coll (FL)
Sacred Heart U (CT)
The Sage Colls (NY)
Saginaw Valley State U (MI)
Saint Anselm Coll (NH)
Saint Francis U (PA)
St. John Fisher Coll (NY)
Saint John's U (MN)
St. Joseph's Coll, Long Island Campus (NY)
St. Joseph's Coll, New York (NY)
Saint Joseph's U (PA)
Saint Leo U (FL)
Saint Louis U (MO)
Saint Martin's U (WA)
St. Mary's Coll of Maryland (MD)
St. Mary's U (TX)
Saint Mary's U of Minnesota (MN)
St. Norbert Coll (WI)
St. Olaf Coll (MN)
Saint Vincent Coll (PA)
Salisbury U (MD)
Salve Regina U (RI)
Samford U (AL)
San Diego State U (CA)
San Francisco State U (CA)
San Jose State U (CA)
Sarah Lawrence Coll (NY)
Scripps Coll (CA)
Seattle U (WA)
Seton Hill U (PA)
Skidmore Coll (NY)

Sonoma State U (CA)
Southeastern Louisiana U (LA)
Southeastern U (FL)
Southeast Missouri State U (MO)
Southern Arkansas U–Magnolia (AR)
Southern Illinois U Carbondale (IL)
Southern Illinois U Edwardsville (IL)
Southern U and Ag and Mech Coll (LA)
Southwest Baptist U (MO)
Southwestern U (TX)
Spring Hill Coll (AL)
State U of New York at Fredonia (NY)
State U of New York at Plattsburgh (NY)
State U of New York Coll at Geneseo (NY)
State U of New York Coll at Potsdam (NY)
Stetson U (FL)
Stockton U (NJ)
Stonehill Coll (MA)
Sweet Briar Coll (VA)
Syracuse U (NY)
Tabor Coll (KS)
Taylor U (IN)
Temple U (PA)
Texas A&M Intl U (TX)
Texas A&M U–Central Texas (TX)
Texas Christian U (TX)
Texas Lutheran U (TX)
Texas Tech U (TX)
Texas Woman's U (TX)
Tiffin U (OH)
Towson U (MD)
Trevecca Nazarene U (TN)
Trinity Christian Coll (IL)
Truman State U (MO)
Tulane U (LA)
Tyndale U Coll & Sem (ON, Canada)
Union Coll (KY)
Union Coll (NY)
Université de Sherbrooke (QC, Canada)
U at Buffalo, the State U of New York (NY)
U of Arkansas (AR)
U of California, Davis (CA)
U of California, Irvine (CA)
U of California, Los Angeles (CA)
U of California, Merced (CA)
U of California, Riverside (CA)
U of California, Santa Cruz (CA)
U of Central Arkansas (AR)
U of Central Florida (FL)
U of Colorado Denver (CO)
U of Dallas (TX)
U of Dayton (OH)
U of Detroit Mercy (MI)
The U of Findlay (OH)
U of Florida (FL)
U of Georgia (GA)
U of Guam (GU)
U of Hawaii at Manoa (HI)
U of Houston (TX)
U of Houston–Clear Lake (TX)
U of Houston–Downtown (TX)
U of Idaho (ID)
U of Illinois at Springfield (IL)
U of Kentucky (KY)
U of La Verne (CA)
U of Louisville (KY)
U of Lynchburg (VA)
U of Maine (ME)
U of Maine at Farmington (ME)
U of Maine at Machias (ME)
U of Maine at Presque Isle (ME)
U of Maryland, Baltimore County (MD)
U of Maryland, Coll Park (MD)
U of Maryland U Coll (MD)
U of Massachusetts Amherst (MA)
U of Massachusetts Boston (MA)
U of Massachusetts Dartmouth (MA)
U of Massachusetts Lowell (MA)
U of Memphis (TN)
U of Michigan–Dearborn (MI)
U of Minnesota, Duluth (MN)
U of Minnesota, Morris (MN)
U of Minnesota, Twin Cities Campus (MN)
U of Missouri (MO)
U of Montevallo (AL)
U of Mount Union (OH)
U of Nebraska–Lincoln (NE)
U of Nevada, Las Vegas (NV)
U of Nevada, Reno (NV)
U of New Hampshire (NH)
U of New Haven (CT)
U of New Mexico (NM)
U of North Carolina at Asheville (NC)
The U of North Carolina at Chapel Hill (NC)
The U of North Carolina at Charlotte (NC)
The U of North Carolina at Greensboro (NC)
The U of North Carolina at Pembroke (NC)
U of North Dakota (ND)
U of Northern Colorado (CO)
U of Northern Iowa (IA)
U of North Florida (FL)
U of Northwestern–St. Paul (MN)
U of Notre Dame (IN)
U of Oregon (OR)
U of Pennsylvania (PA)
U of Pittsburgh (PA)
U of Pittsburgh at Bradford (PA)
U of Providence (MT)
U of Puget Sound (WA)
U of Regina (SK, Canada)
U of Richmond (VA)
U of Saint Mary (KS)
U of St. Thomas (MN)
U of St. Thomas (TX)
U of San Diego (CA)
U of San Francisco (CA)
U of Sioux Falls (SD)
U of South Alabama (AL)
U of South Carolina Aiken (SC)
U of South Dakota (SD)
U of Southern Indiana (IN)
U of South Florida (FL)
U of South Florida Sarasota-Manatee (FL)
The U of Tampa (FL)
The U of Tennessee (TN)
The U of Tennessee at Martin (TN)
The U of Texas at Austin (TX)
The U of Texas at El Paso (TX)
The U of Texas of the Permian Basin (TX)
The U of Texas Rio Grande Valley (TX)
U of the Incarnate Word (TX)
The U of the South (TN)
The U of Toledo (OH)
The U of Tulsa (OK)
U of Vermont (VT)
U of Virginia (VA)
U of Washington (WA)
U of Washington, Tacoma (WA)
The U of West Alabama (AL)
U of West Georgia (GA)
U of Wisconsin–Eau Claire (WI)
U of Wisconsin–La Crosse (WI)
U of Wisconsin–Milwaukee (WI)
U of Wisconsin–River Falls (WI)
U of Wisconsin–Superior (WI)
U of Wyoming (WY)
Ursinus Coll (PA)
Utah State U (UT)
Utah Valley U (UT)
Utica Coll (NY)
Valley City State U (ND)
Valparaiso U (IN)
Vanguard U of Southern California (CA)
Virginia Commonwealth U (VA)
Virginia Polytechnic Inst and State U (VA)
Wabash Coll (IN)
Wartburg Coll (IA)
Washington & Jefferson Coll (PA)
Washington State U (WA)
Washington State U–Tri-Cities (WA)
Washington State U–Vancouver (WA)
Washington U in St. Louis (MO)
Waynesburg U (PA)
Weber State U (UT)
Wesleyan Coll (GA)
Wesleyan U (CT)
West Chester U of Pennsylvania (PA)
Western Connecticut State U (CT)
Western Illinois U (IL)
Western Kentucky U (KY)
Western State Colorado U (CO)
Western Washington U (WA)
Westmont Coll (CA)
West Virginia State U (WV)
West Virginia U Inst of Technology (WV)
Wheaton Coll (IL)
Wheaton Coll (MA)
Whittier Coll (CA)
Whitworth U (WA)
Widener U (PA)
Wilkes U (PA)
Willamette U (OR)
William James Coll (MA)
William Jewell Coll (MO)
Williams Coll (MA)
Winthrop U (SC)
Wofford Coll (SC)
Woodbury U (CA)
Worcester Polytechnic Inst (MA)
Worcester State U (MA)
Wright State U–Lake Campus (OH)
Youngstown State U (OH)

PSYCHOLOGY RELATED
Adams State U (CO)
Buena Vista U (IA)
Butler U (IN)
Canisius Coll (NY)
Kansas Wesleyan U (KS)
Kean U (NJ)
Marist Coll (NY)
National U (CA)
Palm Beach Atlantic U (FL)
San Jose State U (CA)
Tiffin U (OH)
Washington U in St. Louis (MO)

PSYCHOLOGY TEACHER EDUCATION
Albion Coll (MI)
California Lutheran U (CA)
Lee U (TN)
Ohio Wesleyan U (OH)
Rocky Mountain Coll (MT)
Valparaiso U (IN)
Weber State U (UT)
Widener U (PA)

PUBLIC ADMINISTRATION
American U of Beirut (Lebanon)
Auburn U (AL)
Baldwin Wallace U (OH)
Baruch Coll of the City U of New York (NY)
Baylor U (TX)
Blackburn Coll (IL)
Bowling Green State U (OH)
Buena Vista U (IA)
California Lutheran U (CA)
California State U, Bakersfield (CA)
California State U, Chico (CA)
California State U, Fullerton (CA)
Columbia Coll (MO)
Eastern Oregon U (OR)
Eastern Washington U (WA)
The Evergreen State Coll (WA)
Florida Atlantic U (FL)
George Mason U (VA)
Grand Valley State U (MI)
Harding U (AR)
Indiana U Bloomington (IN)
Indiana U Kokomo (IN)
Indiana U Northwest (IN)
Indiana U–Purdue U Indianapolis (IN)
Iowa State U of Science and Technology (IA)
Jacksonville U (FL)
Kean U (NJ)
La Salle U (PA)
Lee U (TN)
Liberty U (VA)
Lindenwood U (MO)
Lipscomb U (TN)
Louisiana Coll (LA)
Manor Coll (PA)
Miami U (OH)
Miami U Hamilton (OH)
Millsaps Coll (MS)
Muskingum U (OH)
National U (CA)
New York U (NY)
The Ohio State U (OH)
Ohio Wesleyan U (OH)
Regent U (VA)
Regis U (CO)
Rhode Island Coll (RI)
Saginaw Valley State U (MI)
Saint Francis U (PA)
Samford U (AL)
San Diego State U (CA)
Seattle U (WA)
Syracuse U (NY)
U of Central Arkansas (AR)
U of Central Florida (FL)
U of Guam (GU)
U of Houston–Clear Lake (TX)
U of Illinois at Springfield (IL)
U of La Verne (CA)
U of Maryland U Coll (MD)
U of Massachusetts Dartmouth (MA)
U of Nevada, Las Vegas (NV)
The U of North Carolina at Pembroke (NC)
U of North Dakota (ND)
U of Northern Iowa (IA)
U of Oregon (OR)
U of Pittsburgh (PA)
The U of Tennessee (TN)
U of Wisconsin–La Crosse (WI)
Wilkes U (PA)

PUBLIC ADMINISTRATION AND SOCIAL SERVICE PROFESSIONS RELATED
Coll of Coastal Georgia (GA)
The Evergreen State Coll (WA)
New York U (NY)
San Diego State U (CA)
Trevecca Nazarene U (TN)
U of Colorado Denver (CO)
U of Detroit Mercy (MI)

PUBLIC/APPLIED HISTORY
Arkansas Tech U (AR)
Baldwin Wallace U (OH)
Bryant U (RI)
Central Michigan U (MI)
Ouachita Baptist U (AR)
Rhode Island Coll (RI)

PUBLIC HEALTH
Agnes Scott Coll (GA)
Albright Coll (PA)
Allen Coll (IA)
American Public U System (WV)
American U (DC)
Appalachian State U (NC)
Austin Coll (TX)
Baker U (KS)
Baldwin Wallace U (OH)
Bowling Green State U (OH)
Caldwell U (NJ)
California State U, Long Beach (CA)
California State U, Los Angeles (CA)
Calvin Coll (MI)
Central Washington U (WA)
The Coll of Saint Rose (NY)
Curry Coll (MA)
East Stroudsburg U of Pennsylvania (PA)
East Tennessee State U (TN)
Excelsior Coll (NY)
Fairfield U (CT)
Fort Lewis Coll (CO)
Franklin Pierce U (NH)
Hartwick Coll (NY)
Hiram Coll (OH)
Hunter Coll of the City U of New York (NY)
Indiana U of Pennsylvania (PA)
Indiana U–Purdue U Indianapolis (IN)
Ithaca Coll (NY)
Johns Hopkins U (MD)
La Salle U (PA)
Marian U (IN)
Marshall U (WV)
Marymount Manhattan Coll (NY)
Mercer U, Macon (GA)
Merrimack Coll (MA)
Miami U (OH)
Montclair State U (NJ)
Muskingum U (OH)
New York U (NY)
The Ohio State U (OH)
Ohio U (OH)
Old Dominion U (VA)
Point U (GA)
Portland State U (OR)
Roanoke Coll (VA)
Saint Francis U (PA)
St. John Fisher Coll (NY)
Saint Louis U (MO)
Samford U (AL)
San Diego State U (CA)
Syracuse U (NY)
Tabor Coll (KS)
U at Buffalo, the State U of New York (NY)
U of Arkansas (AR)
U of California, Merced (CA)
U of Colorado Denver (CO)
U of Florida (FL)
U of Hawaii at Manoa (HI)
U of Kentucky (KY)
U of Louisville (KY)
U of Massachusetts Amherst (MA)
U of Massachusetts Lowell (MA)
U of Nevada, Las Vegas (NV)
The U of North Carolina at Charlotte (NC)
U of South Florida (FL)
The U of Tampa (FL)
The U of Texas at Austin (TX)
U of Washington (WA)
Valparaiso U (IN)
Wartburg Coll (IA)
Weber State U (UT)
Youngstown State U (OH)

PUBLIC HEALTH EDUCATION AND PROMOTION
American U (DC)
Barton Coll (NC)
Baylor U (TX)
California State U, Long Beach (CA)
Central Washington U (WA)
Coastal Carolina U (SC)
Coll of Charleston (SC)
Drew U (NJ)
East Carolina U (NC)
Eastern Washington U (WA)
Excelsior Coll (NY)
Georgia Southern U (GA)
Ithaca Coll (NY)
Kennesaw State U (GA)
Liberty U (VA)
Oklahoma State U (OK)
Purdue U (IN)
Queens U of Charlotte (NC)
Rhode Island Coll (RI)
Southeastern Louisiana U (LA)
Southern Illinois U Edwardsville (IL)
Taylor U (IN)
Temple U (PA)
U of Georgia (GA)
U of Lynchburg (VA)
U of Michigan–Dearborn (MI)
U of Minnesota, Duluth (MN)
U of Mount Union (OH)
U of North Carolina at Asheville (NC)
The U of North Carolina at Greensboro (NC)
U of North Dakota (ND)
U of St. Thomas (MN)
The U of Texas at Austin (TX)
The U of Toledo (OH)
U of Washington (WA)
Weber State U (UT)
West Chester U of Pennsylvania (PA)
Western Illinois U (IL)

PUBLIC HEALTH RELATED
Baptist Coll of Health Sciences (TN)
Indiana U Bloomington (IN)
Stockton U (NJ)
U of California, Irvine (CA)
U of Maryland, Coll Park (MD)
U of Michigan (MI)
U of South Carolina (SC)
Utah State U (UT)

PUBLIC POLICY ANALYSIS
Albion Coll (MI)
Bentley U (MA)
Bryant U (RI)
Carnegie Mellon U (PA)
Central Washington U (WA)
The Coll of William and Mary (VA)
Cornell U (NY)
Dallas Baptist U (TX)
DePaul U (IL)

Georgia State U (GA)
Hamilton Coll (NY)
Hofstra U (NY)
Jacksonville U (FL)
Massachusetts Coll of Liberal Arts (MA)
Mercer U, Macon (GA)
Michigan State U (MI)
Mills Coll (CA)
Muskingum U (OH)
New Coll of Florida (FL)
Northwestern U (IL)
The Ohio State U (OH)
Princeton U (NJ)
Rice U (TX)
Rochester Inst of Technology (NY)
St. Mary's Coll of Maryland (MD)
Saint Vincent Coll (PA)
Sarah Lawrence Coll (NY)
Scripps Coll (CA)
Trevecca Nazarene U (TN)
U of California, Riverside (CA)
U of Chicago (IL)
U of Illinois at Springfield (IL)
U of Maryland, Coll Park (MD)
U of Michigan (MI)
The U of North Carolina at Chapel Hill (NC)
U of Pennsylvania (PA)
U of Virginia (VA)
Virginia Polytechnic Inst and State U (VA)
Washington & Jefferson Coll (PA)
Washington State U (WA)
Washington State U–Vancouver (WA)

PUBLIC RELATIONS, ADVERTISING, AND APPLIED COMMUNICATION
Albright Coll (PA)
Bradley U (IL)
Butler U (IN)
Carthage Coll (WI)
Central Connecticut State U (CT)
Coll of the Ozarks (MO)
Dallas Baptist U (TX)
Endicott Coll (MA)
Florida Southern Coll (FL)
Goshen Coll (IN)
Kansas Wesleyan U (KS)
Kennesaw State U (GA)
Louisiana Coll (LA)
Loyola U New Orleans (LA)
Marymount Manhattan Coll (NY)
Massachusetts Coll of Liberal Arts (MA)
Messiah Coll (PA)
Minnesota State U Moorhead (MN)
Mount Saint Mary Coll (NY)
Muskingum U (OH)
National U (CA)
Oglethorpe U (GA)
Ohio Dominican U (OH)
Pepperdine U, Malibu (CA)
Rhode Island Coll (RI)
Seattle U (WA)
Southeastern U (FL)
Taylor U (IN)
Texas Christian U (TX)
U of Central Arkansas (AR)
The U of Findlay (OH)
U of Kentucky (KY)
U of Mount Union (OH)
U of Nebraska–Lincoln (NE)
The U of Tampa (FL)
Wartburg Coll (IA)
Washington State U (WA)
Washington State U–Vancouver (WA)
Washington U in St. Louis (MO)
William Jewell Coll (MO)

PUBLIC RELATIONS, ADVERTISING, AND APPLIED COMMUNICATION RELATED
Buena Vista U (IA)
Butler U (IN)
California Lutheran U (CA)
Columbia Coll (MO)
DePaul U (IL)
Duquesne U (PA)
East Texas Baptist U (TX)
Fairfield U (CT)
La Sierra U (CA)
Lipscomb U (TN)
Loyola U Chicago (IL)
Marywood U (PA)
Muskingum U (OH)
Oklahoma State U (OK)
Pepperdine U, Malibu (CA)
Rochester Inst of Technology (NY)
Saint Mary's U of Minnesota (MN)
Spring Hill Coll (AL)
Temple U (PA)
Tulane U (LA)
U of Central Arkansas (AR)
The U of Tampa (FL)
U of Vermont (VT)
Virginia Polytechnic Inst and State U (VA)
Weber State U (UT)

PUBLIC RELATIONS/IMAGE MANAGEMENT
Appalachian State U (NC)
Auburn U (AL)
Avila U (MO)
Baldwin Wallace U (OH)
Boston U (MA)
Bowling Green State U (OH)
Bradley U (IL)
Buena Vista U (IA)
California Lutheran U (CA)
California State U, Fullerton (CA)
California State U, Long Beach (CA)
Central Michigan U (MI)
Central Washington U (WA)
Columbia Coll Chicago (IL)
Dominican U (IL)
Drake U (IA)
Eastern Illinois U (IL)
Emerson Coll (MA)
Florida Ag and Mech U (FL)
Georgia Southern U (GA)
Gonzaga U (WA)
Greenville U (IL)
Harding U (AR)
Hofstra U (NY)
Hood Coll (MD)
Iona Coll (NY)
Iowa State U of Science and Technology (IA)
Ithaca Coll (NY)
La Salle U (PA)
Lee U (TN)
Lipscomb U (TN)
Loras Coll (IA)
Manchester U (IN)
Mansfield U of Pennsylvania (PA)
Marquette U (WI)
Miami U (OH)
Minnesota State U Moorhead (MN)
Missouri Baptist U (MO)
Murray State U (KY)
New England Coll (NH)
Northern Kentucky U (KY)
Oklahoma Christian U (OK)
Palm Beach Atlantic U (FL)
Rider U (NJ)
Rochester Inst of Technology (NY)
San Diego State U (CA)
San Jose State U (CA)
Southwest Baptist U (MO)
State U of New York at Plattsburgh (NY)
Syracuse U (NY)
Taylor U (IN)
Temple U (PA)
Texas Christian U (TX)
Texas Tech U (TX)
Tiffin U (OH)
U of Florida (FL)
U of Georgia (GA)
U of Houston (TX)
U of Idaho (ID)
U of Memphis (TN)
U of Northern Iowa (IA)
U of Northwestern–St. Paul (MN)
U of Oregon (OR)
U of South Carolina (SC)
The U of Tennessee (TN)
The U of Texas at Austin (TX)
Utica Coll (NY)
Wartburg Coll (IA)
Washington and Lee U (VA)
Washington State U (WA)
Weber State U (UT)
Western Kentucky U (KY)
Winthrop U (SC)

PUBLISHING
Emerson Coll (MA)
Rochester Inst of Technology (NY)

PURCHASING, PROCUREMENT/ ACQUISITIONS AND CONTRACTS MANAGEMENT
Central Michigan U (MI)
U of Houston–Downtown (TX)

QUALITY CONTROL AND SAFETY TECHNOLOGIES RELATED
Madonna U (MI)

QUALITY CONTROL TECHNOLOGY
Bowling Green State U (OH)
California State U, Long Beach (CA)
San Jose State U (CA)

RADIATION PROTECTION/ HEALTH PHYSICS TECHNOLOGY
Indiana U–Purdue U Indianapolis (IN)

RADIO AND TELEVISION
Appalachian State U (NC)
Auburn U (AL)
Boston U (MA)
Bowling Green State U (OH)
Bradley U (IL)
Butler U (IN)
California State U, Fullerton (CA)
California State U, Long Beach (CA)
California State U, Los Angeles (CA)
California State U, Monterey Bay (CA)
Columbia Coll Chicago (IL)
Drake U (IA)
Emerson Coll (MA)
Franklin Pierce U (NH)
Grand Valley State U (MI)
Hofstra U (NY)
Iona Coll (NY)
Ithaca Coll (NY)
La Sierra U (CA)
Lebanese American U (Lebanon)
Missouri Baptist U (MO)
Montclair State U (NJ)
Murray State U (KY)
Northwestern U (IL)
Ohio U (OH)
Oklahoma Christian U (OK)
Palm Beach Atlantic U (FL)
Pepperdine U, Malibu (CA)
Rider U (NJ)
San Diego State U (CA)
San Francisco State U (CA)
San Jose State U (CA)
Savannah Coll of Art and Design (GA)
Southeastern U (FL)
Southern Illinois U Carbondale (IL)
State U of New York at Fredonia (NY)
State U of New York at Plattsburgh (NY)
Syracuse U (NY)
Temple U (PA)
Texas Tech U (TX)
U of Central Florida (FL)
U of Dayton (OH)
U of Florida (FL)
U of Houston (TX)
U of Kentucky (KY)
U of La Verne (CA)
U of Montevallo (AL)
U of Northwestern–St. Paul (MN)
U of Pittsburgh at Bradford (PA)
U of Southern Indiana (IN)
The U of Texas at Austin (TX)
U of the Incarnate Word (TX)
Vanguard U of Southern California (CA)
Wartburg Coll (IA)
Waynesburg U (PA)
Western Kentucky U (KY)
Youngstown State U (OH)

RADIO AND TELEVISION BROADCASTING TECHNOLOGY
Coll of the Ozarks (MO)
Emerson Coll (MA)
New England Inst of Technology (RI)
New York U (NY)
Worcester State U (MA)

RADIOLOGIC TECHNOLOGY/ SCIENCE
AdventHealth U (FL)
Austin Peay State U (TN)
Baptist Coll of Health Sciences (TN)
Gwynedd Mercy U (PA)
Indiana U Northwest (IN)
Inter American U of Puerto Rico, Aguadilla Campus (PR)
Inter American U of Puerto Rico, Barranquitas Campus (PR)
Inter American U of Puerto Rico, San Germán Campus (PR)
Manhattan Coll (NY)
Marshall U (WV)
McNeese State U (LA)
Nebraska Methodist Coll (NE)
Northern Kentucky U (KY)
Northwest Missouri State U (MO)
Pueblo Comm Coll (CO)
Rhode Island Coll (RI)
Sacred Heart U (CT)
U of Pittsburgh at Bradford (PA)
U of South Alabama (AL)
U of Southern Indiana (IN)
Virginia Commonwealth U (VA)
Weber State U (UT)
Widener U (PA)

RADIOLOGIST ASSISTANT
Weber State U (UT)

RADIO, TELEVISION, AND DIGITAL COMMUNICATION RELATED
Central Michigan U (MI)
Champlain Coll (VT)
Dallas Baptist U (TX)
Drake U (IA)
Emerson Coll (MA)
Hofstra U (NY)
Louisiana Coll (LA)
Madonna U (MI)
Marquette U (WI)
San Francisco State U (CA)
Spring Hill Coll (AL)
Texas Christian U (TX)
Towson U (MD)

RANGE SCIENCE AND MANAGEMENT
Colorado State U (CO)
Humboldt State U (CA)
U of Idaho (ID)
U of Nebraska–Lincoln (NE)
U of Nevada, Reno (NV)
U of Wyoming (WY)
Utah State U (UT)
Washington State U (WA)

READING TEACHER EDUCATION
Baylor U (TX)
Canisius Coll (NY)
Concordia U Chicago (IL)
Dallas Baptist U (TX)
Eastern Washington U (WA)
Grand Valley State U (MI)
Harding U (AR)
Michigan State U (MI)
U of Michigan–Dearborn (MI)
U of Providence (MT)

REAL ESTATE
Baruch Coll of the City U of New York (NY)
Baylor U (TX)
Bowling Green State U (OH)
Central Michigan U (MI)
Clarion U of Pennsylvania (PA)
Coll of Charleston (SC)
DePaul U (IL)
Florida Atlantic U (FL)
Georgia State U (GA)
Marquette U (WI)
New York U (NY)
The Ohio State U (OH)
Portland State U (OR)
San Diego State U (CA)
Syracuse U (NY)
Temple U (PA)
Texas Christian U (TX)
U of Central Florida (FL)
U of Florida (FL)
U of Georgia (GA)
U of Nevada, Las Vegas (NV)
U of Northern Iowa (IA)
U of Pennsylvania (PA)
U of St. Thomas (MN)
U of San Diego (CA)
U of South Carolina (SC)
U of West Georgia (GA)
U of Wisconsin–Milwaukee (WI)
Virginia Commonwealth U (VA)
Virginia Polytechnic Inst and State U (VA)

RECORDING ARTS TECHNOLOGY
Acad of Art U (CA)
American U (DC)
Butler U (IN)
Columbia Coll Chicago (IL)
Greenville U (IL)
Indiana U Bloomington (IN)
Ithaca Coll (NY)
Kuyper Coll (MI)
Loyola Marymount U (CA)
Minnesota State U Moorhead (MN)
New England Inst of Technology (RI)
Portland State U (OR)
Savannah Coll of Art and Design (GA)
State U of New York at Fredonia (NY)

REGIONAL STUDIES
The Colorado Coll (CO)
Columbia U (NY)
Linfield Coll (OR)
Mercer U, Macon (GA)
U of Regina (SK, Canada)
Washington U in St. Louis (MO)

REGISTERED NURSING, NURSING ADMINISTRATION, NURSING RESEARCH AND CLINICAL NURSING RELATED
Columbia Central U, Caguas (PR)
Indiana State U (IN)
Indiana U Bloomington (IN)
Indiana U East (IN)
Indiana U Kokomo (IN)
Indiana U Northwest (IN)
Indiana U–Purdue U Indianapolis (IN)
Indiana U South Bend (IN)
Indiana U Southeast (IN)
Jacksonville U (FL)
Molloy Coll (NY)
Tabor Coll (KS)
Union Coll (KY)
U of California, Los Angeles (CA)
U of Massachusetts Dartmouth (MA)
U of Saint Mary (KS)
Vincennes U (IN)
Wheaton Coll (IL)

REGISTERED NURSING/ REGISTERED NURSE
Adams State U (CO)
Adelphi U (NY)
AdventHealth U (FL)
Allen Coll (IA)
Alverno Coll (WI)
American U of Beirut (Lebanon)
Angelo State U (TX)
Appalachian State U (NC)
Arkansas Tech U (AR)
Assumption Coll (MA)
Auburn U (AL)
Auburn U at Montgomery (AL)
Aurora U (IL)
Austin Comm Coll District (TX)
Austin Peay State U (TN)
Avila U (MO)
Baker U (KS)
Baldwin Wallace U (OH)
Baptist Coll of Health Sciences (TN)
Barton Coll (NC)
Baylor U (TX)
Bellarmine U (KY)
Benedictine U (IL)
Berea Coll (KY)
Berkeley Coll–Woodland Park Campus (NJ)
Bethany Lutheran Coll (MN)
Bethel Coll (KS)
Bethel U (MN)
Boston Coll (MA)
Bowling Green State U (OH)
Bradley U (IL)
Brandman U (CA)
Caldwell U (NJ)

California State U, Bakersfield (CA)
California State U, Chico (CA)
California State U, Long Beach (CA)
California State U, Los Angeles (CA)
California State U, Monterey Bay (CA)
California State U, Northridge (CA)
California State U, San Bernardino (CA)
California State U, San Marcos (CA)
California U of Pennsylvania (PA)
Calvin Coll (MI)
Campbellsville U (KY)
Carson-Newman U (TN)
Carthage Coll (WI)
The Catholic U of America (DC)
Cedarville U (OH)
Central Connecticut State U (CT)
Clarion U of Pennsylvania (PA)
Coastal Carolina U (SC)
The Coll at Brockport, State U of New York (NY)
Coll of Central Florida (FL)
Coll of Coastal Georgia (GA)
Coll of Saint Benedict (MN)
Coll of Saint Mary (NE)
The Coll of St. Scholastica (MN)
Coll of Staten Island of the City U of New York (NY)
Coll of the Ozarks (MO)
Colorado State U–Pueblo (CO)
Concordia U Irvine (CA)
Creighton U (NE)
Culver-Stockton Coll (MO)
Curry Coll (MA)
Davenport U, Grand Rapids (MI)
Daytona State Coll (FL)
Delta State U (MS)
DePaul U (IL)
Dominican U (IL)
Duquesne U (PA)
East Carolina U (NC)
Eastern Illinois U (IL)
Eastern Mennonite U (VA)
Eastern U (PA)
Eastern Washington U (WA)
East Stroudsburg U of Pennsylvania (PA)
East Tennessee State U (TN)
East Texas Baptist U (TX)
Endicott Coll (MA)
Excelsior Coll (NY)
Fairfield U (CT)
Farmingdale State Coll (NY)
Fayetteville State U (NC)
Fitchburg State U (MA)
Florida Ag and Mech U (FL)
Florida Atlantic U (FL)
Florida Southern Coll (FL)
Framingham State U (MA)
George Mason U (VA)
Georgia Coll & State U (GA)
Georgia Highlands Coll (GA)
Georgia Southern U (GA)
Georgia State U (GA)
Gonzaga U (WA)
Goshen Coll (IN)
Graceland U (IA)
Granite State Coll (NH)
Gwynedd Mercy U (PA)
Harding U (AR)
Hardin-Simmons U (TX)
Hartwick Coll (NY)
Hiram Coll (OH)
Hood Coll (MD)
Hunter Coll of the City U of New York (NY)
Idaho State U (ID)
Immaculata U (PA)
Indiana State U (IN)
Indiana U Bloomington (IN)
Indiana U East (IN)
Indiana U Kokomo (IN)
Indiana U Northwest (IN)
Indiana U of Pennsylvania (PA)
Indiana U–Purdue U Indianapolis (IN)
Indiana U South Bend (IN)
Indiana U Southeast (IN)
Inter American U of Puerto Rico, Aguadilla Campus (PR)
Inter American U of Puerto Rico, Bayamón Campus (PR)
Inter American U of Puerto Rico, San Germán Campus (PR)
Iowa State U of Science and Technology (IA)
Jacksonville U (FL)
Kansas Wesleyan U (KS)
Kennesaw State U (GA)
King's Coll (PA)
LaGrange Coll (GA)
Lamar U (TX)
La Salle U (PA)
Lawrence Technological U (MI)
Lees-McRae Coll (NC)
Lee U (TN)
Liberty U (VA)
Limestone Coll (SC)
Linfield Coll (OR)
Lipscomb U (TN)
Lock Haven U of Pennsylvania (PA)
Louisiana Coll (LA)
Loyola U Chicago (IL)
Loyola U New Orleans (LA)
Lubbock Christian U (TX)
Madonna U (MI)
Mansfield U of Pennsylvania (PA)
Maria Coll (NY)
Marian U (IN)
Marquette U (WI)
Marshall U (WV)
Marymount U (VA)
Maryville U of Saint Louis (MO)
Marywood U (PA)
McNeese State U (LA)
Mercer U, Macon (GA)
Mercy Coll (NY)
Mercy Coll of Ohio (OH)
Messiah Coll (PA)
Michigan State U (MI)
Middle Tennessee State U (TN)
Milligan Coll (TN)
Millikin U (IL)
Minnesota State U Moorhead (MN)
Missouri Baptist U (MO)
Molloy Coll (NY)
Montclair State U (NJ)
Morningside Coll (IA)
Mount Carmel Coll of Nursing (OH)
Mount Marty Coll (SD)
Mount St. Joseph U (OH)
Mount Saint Mary Coll (NY)
Murray State U (KY)
Muskingum U (OH)
National U (CA)
Nazareth Coll of Rochester (NY)
Nebraska Methodist Coll (NE)
New England Inst of Technology (RI)
New York U (NY)
Northeastern State U (OK)
Northern Illinois U (IL)
Northern Kentucky U (KY)
Northwestern Oklahoma State U (OK)
Northwest Missouri State U (MO)
The Ohio State U (OH)
The Ohio State U at Marion (OH)
The Ohio State U at Newark (OH)
Ohio U (OH)
Oklahoma Baptist U (OK)
Oklahoma Christian U (OK)
Oklahoma State U (OK)
Old Dominion U (VA)
Pace U (NY)
Pace U, Pleasantville Campus (NY)
Pacific Lutheran U (WA)
Palm Beach Atlantic U (FL)
Pfeiffer U (NC)
Piedmont Coll (GA)
Point Loma Nazarene U (CA)
Potomac State Coll of West Virginia U (WV)
Prairie View A&M U (TX)
Purdue U (IN)
Purdue U Northwest (IN)
Queens U of Charlotte (NC)
Radford U (VA)
Regent U (VA)
Regis U (CO)
Rhode Island Coll (RI)
Rider U (NJ)
Rockford U (IL)
Sacred Heart U (CT)
The Sage Colls (NY)
Saginaw Valley State U (MI)
Saint Francis U (PA)
St. John Fisher Coll (NY)
Saint John's U (MN)
St. Joseph's Coll, Long Island Campus (NY)
St. Joseph's Coll, New York (NY)
Saint Louis U (MO)
St. Luke's Coll (IA)
Saint Martin's U (WA)
St. Olaf Coll (MN)
Salisbury U (MD)
Salve Regina U (RI)
Samford U (AL)
San Diego State U (CA)
San Francisco State U (CA)
San Jose State U (CA)
Seattle U (WA)
Sonoma State U (CA)
Southeastern Louisiana U (LA)
Southeastern U (FL)
Southeast Missouri State U (MO)
Southern Arkansas U–Magnolia (AR)
Southern Illinois U Edwardsville (IL)
Southern U and Ag and Mech Coll (LA)
Southwest Baptist U (MO)
Spring Hill Coll (AL)
State U of New York at Plattsburgh (NY)
State U of New York Coll of Technology at Alfred (NY)
State U of New York Coll of Technology at Delhi (NY)
Stockton U (NJ)
Sullivan U (KY)
Temple U (PA)
Texas A&M Intl U (TX)
Texas A&M U–Central Texas (TX)
Texas Christian U (TX)
Texas Lutheran U (TX)
Texas Woman's U (TX)
Toccoa Falls Coll (GA)
Towson U (MD)
Trevecca Nazarene U (TN)
Trinity Christian Coll (IL)
Truman State U (MO)
Union Coll (KY)
Université de Sherbrooke (QC, Canada)
U at Buffalo, the State U of New York (NY)
U of Arkansas (AR)
U of Central Arkansas (AR)
U of Central Florida (FL)
U of Colorado Denver (CO)
U of Detroit Mercy (MI)
The U of Findlay (OH)
U of Florida (FL)
U of Guam (GU)
U of Hawaii at Manoa (HI)
U of Houston (TX)
U of Houston–Clear Lake (TX)
U of Houston–Downtown (TX)
U of Kentucky (KY)
U of Louisville (KY)
U of Lynchburg (VA)
U of Maine (ME)
U of Mary Hardin-Baylor (TX)
U of Maryland U Coll (MD)
U of Massachusetts Amherst (MA)
U of Massachusetts Boston (MA)
U of Massachusetts Lowell (MA)
U of Memphis (TN)
U of Michigan (MI)
U of Minnesota, Twin Cities Campus (MN)
U of Missouri (MO)
U of Mount Union (OH)
U of Nevada, Las Vegas (NV)
U of Nevada, Reno (NV)
U of New Hampshire (NH)
U of New Mexico (NM)
The U of North Carolina at Chapel Hill (NC)
The U of North Carolina at Charlotte (NC)
The U of North Carolina at Greensboro (NC)
The U of North Carolina at Pembroke (NC)
U of North Dakota (ND)
U of Northern Colorado (CO)
U of North Florida (FL)
U of Northwestern–St. Paul (MN)
U of Pennsylvania (PA)
U of Pittsburgh (PA)
U of Pittsburgh at Bradford (PA)
U of Regina (SK, Canada)
U of Saint Francis (IN)
U of Saint Mary (KS)
U of St. Thomas (TX)
U of San Francisco (CA)
U of Sioux Falls (SD)
U of South Alabama (AL)
U of South Carolina (SC)
U of South Carolina Aiken (SC)
U of South Dakota (SD)
U of Southern Indiana (IN)
U of South Florida (FL)
The U of Tampa (FL)
The U of Tennessee (TN)
The U of Tennessee at Martin (TN)
The U of Texas at Austin (TX)
The U of Texas of the Permian Basin (TX)
The U of Texas Rio Grande Valley (TX)
U of the Incarnate Word (TX)
The U of Tulsa (OK)
U of Vermont (VT)
U of Virginia (VA)
U of Washington (WA)
U of Washington, Bothell (WA)
U of Washington, Tacoma (WA)
U of West Georgia (GA)
U of Wisconsin–Eau Claire (WI)
U of Wisconsin–Milwaukee (WI)
U of Wyoming (WY)
Utah Valley U (UT)
Utica Coll (NY)
Valparaiso U (IN)
Vanguard U of Southern California (CA)
Virginia Commonwealth U (VA)
Washington State U (WA)
Washington State U–Spokane (WA)
Washington State U–Tri-Cities (WA)
Washington State U–Vancouver (WA)
Waynesburg U (PA)
Weber State U (UT)
Wesleyan Coll (GA)
West Chester U of Pennsylvania (PA)
Western Connecticut State U (CT)
Western Illinois U (IL)
Western Kentucky U (KY)
Western Washington U (WA)
West Virginia U Inst of Technology (WV)
Whitworth U (WA)
Widener U (PA)
Wilkes U (PA)
William Jewell Coll (MO)
Worcester State U (MA)
Wright State U–Lake Campus (OH)
Youngstown State U (OH)

REHABILITATION AND THERAPEUTIC PROFESSIONS RELATED

Alabama State U (AL)
Assumption Coll (MA)
Boston U (MA)
Coll of Saint Mary (NE)
East Stroudsburg U of Pennsylvania (PA)
Indiana U of Pennsylvania (PA)
Ithaca Coll (NY)
Lock Haven U of Pennsylvania (PA)
Southern Illinois U Carbondale (IL)
Southern U and Ag and Mech Coll (LA)
U of Massachusetts Lowell (MA)

REHABILITATION SCIENCE

Arkansas Tech U (AR)
Boston U (MA)
George Mason U (VA)
Marshall U (WV)
New England Inst of Technology (RI)
U of Maine at Farmington (ME)
U of North Dakota (ND)
U of Pittsburgh (PA)
The U of Texas Rio Grande Valley (TX)
U of the Incarnate Word (TX)

RELIGIOUS EDUCATION

Campbellsville U (KY)
Cedarville U (OH)
Concordia U Chicago (IL)
Concordia U Irvine (CA)
Dallas Baptist U (TX)
Florida Coll (FL)
Harding U (AR)
Inter American U of Puerto Rico, Fajardo Campus (PR)
Lancaster Bible Coll (PA)
Lee U (TN)
Louisiana Coll (LA)
Loyola U Chicago (IL)
Loyola U New Orleans (LA)
Marian U (IN)
Messiah Coll (PA)
Muskingum U (OH)
Oklahoma Christian U (OK)
Pfeiffer U (NC)
Saint Mary's U of Minnesota (MN)
Southwest Baptist U (MO)
Taylor U (IN)
Theological U of the Caribbean (PR)
Toccoa Falls Coll (GA)
Tyndale U Coll & Sem (ON, Canada)
U of Dayton (OH)
The U of Findlay (OH)
Vanguard U of Southern California (CA)
Wheaton Coll (IL)

RELIGIOUS/SACRED MUSIC

Baylor U (TX)
Bowling Green State U (OH)
Campbellsville U (KY)
Carson-Newman U (TN)
Coll of the Ozarks (MO)
Concordia U Chicago (IL)
Drake U (IA)
East Texas Baptist U (TX)
Emmanuel Coll (GA)
Greenville U (IL)
Hardin-Simmons U (TX)
Johnson U Florida (FL)
Judson U (IL)
Lancaster Bible Coll (PA)
Lee U (TN)
LeTourneau U (TX)
Liberty U (VA)
Madonna U (MI)
Marian U (IN)
Milligan Coll (TN)
Missouri Baptist U (MO)
Northwest Christian U (OR)
Oakland City U (IN)
Oklahoma Baptist U (OK)
Ouachita Baptist U (AR)
Pfeiffer U (NC)
Point Loma Nazarene U (CA)
Rider U (NJ)
St. Olaf Coll (MN)
Samford U (AL)
Seton Hill U (PA)
Southeastern U (FL)
Texas Christian U (TX)
Trevecca Nazarene U (TN)
U of Mary Hardin-Baylor (TX)
U of Sioux Falls (SD)
Wartburg Coll (IA)

RELIGIOUS STUDIES

Agnes Scott Coll (GA)
Albion Coll (MI)
Albright Coll (PA)
Allegheny Coll (PA)
Alverno Coll (WI)
American U (DC)
Appalachian State U (NC)
Austin Coll (TX)
Averett U (VA)
Avila U (MO)
Baker U (KS)
Baldwin Wallace U (OH)
Baruch Coll of the City U of New York (NY)
Baylor U (TX)
Beloit Coll (WI)
Berea Coll (KY)
Bethany Lutheran Coll (MN)
Bethel Coll (KS)
Boston U (MA)
Bradley U (IL)
Bryn Athyn Coll of the New Church (PA)
Bucknell U (PA)
Butler U (IN)
California Lutheran U (CA)
California State U, Bakersfield (CA)
California State U, Fullerton (CA)

California State U, Long Beach (CA)
California State U, Northridge (CA)
Calvin Coll (MI)
Campbellsville U (KY)
Canisius Coll (NY)
Carson-Newman U (TN)
Carthage Coll (WI)
The Catholic U of America (DC)
Centenary Coll of Louisiana (LA)
Central Michigan U (MI)
Central Washington U (WA)
Claremont McKenna Coll (CA)
Colgate U (NY)
Coll of Charleston (SC)
The Coll of Idaho (ID)
The Coll of St. Scholastica (MN)
Coll of the Holy Cross (MA)
The Coll of William and Mary (VA)
The Colorado Coll (CO)
Columbia U (NY)
Concordia U Chicago (IL)
Concordia U Irvine (CA)
Connecticut Coll (CT)
Cornell Coll (IA)
Cornell U (NY)
Culver-Stockton Coll (MO)
Dartmouth Coll (NH)
Davidson Coll (NC)
DePaul U (IL)
Dickinson Coll (PA)
Drake U (IA)
Drew U (NJ)
Drury U (MO)
Earlham Coll (IN)
Eckerd Coll (FL)
Emmanuel Coll (MA)
The Evergreen State Coll (WA)
Fairfield U (CT)
Florida Southern Coll (FL)
Fordham U (NY)
Furman U (SC)
George Mason U (VA)
Georgetown Coll (KY)
Georgia State U (GA)
Gonzaga U (WA)
Goshen Coll (IN)
Greenville U (IL)
Grove City Coll (PA)
Hamilton Coll (NY)
Hamline U (MN)
Hampden-Sydney Coll (VA)
Hartwick Coll (NY)
Harvard U (MA)
Haverford Coll (PA)
High Point U (NC)
Hillsdale Coll (MI)
Hofstra U (NY)
Hollins U (VA)
Holy Apostles Coll and Sem (CT)
Hood Coll (MD)
Humboldt State U (CA)
Hunter Coll of the City U of New York (NY)
Illinois Coll (IL)
Indiana U Bloomington (IN)
Indiana U of Pennsylvania (PA)
Indiana U–Purdue U Indianapolis (IN)
Inter American U of Puerto Rico, Aguadilla Campus (PR)
Iona Coll (NY)
Iowa State U of Science and Technology (IA)
Johnson U Florida (FL)
Juniata Coll (PA)
Kalamazoo Coll (MI)
King U (TN)
Lafayette Coll (PA)
LaGrange Coll (GA)
Lake Forest Coll (IL)
La Salle U (PA)
La Sierra U (CA)
Lawrence U (WI)
Lebanon Valley Coll (PA)
Lees-McRae Coll (NC)
Lewis & Clark Coll (OR)
Liberty U (VA)
Linfield Coll (OR)
Loras Coll (IA)
Loyola U New Orleans (LA)
Lycoming Coll (PA)
Macalester Coll (MN)
Madonna U (MI)
Manchester U (IN)
Manhattan Coll (NY)
Manhattanville Coll (NY)
Marist Coll (NY)
Marymount U (VA)
Marywood U (PA)
McDaniel Coll (MD)
Mercer U, Macon (GA)
Merrimack Coll (MA)
Miami U (OH)
Michigan State U (MI)
Middlebury Coll (VT)
Millsaps Coll (MS)
Molloy Coll (NY)
Montclair State U (NJ)
Morningside Coll (IA)
Mount Marty Coll (SD)
Mount St. Joseph U (OH)
Muskingum U (OH)
Nazareth Coll of Rochester (NY)
New Coll of Florida (FL)
New York U (NY)
North Carolina State U (NC)
Northwestern U (IL)
Oakland City U (IN)
Occidental Coll (CA)
The Ohio State U (OH)
Ohio U (OH)
Ohio Wesleyan U (OH)
Oklahoma Baptist U (OK)
Oklahoma Christian U (OK)
Ottawa U (KS)
Pacific Lutheran U (WA)
Pepperdine U, Malibu (CA)
Pfeiffer U (NC)
Piedmont Coll (GA)
Pitzer Coll (CA)
Portland State U (OR)
Princeton U (NJ)
Providence Coll (RI)
Purdue U (IN)
Queens Coll of the City U of New York (NY)
Queens U of Charlotte (NC)
Randolph Coll (VA)
Randolph-Macon Coll (VA)
Redeemer U Coll (ON, Canada)
Regis U (CO)
Reinhardt U (GA)
Rhodes Coll (TN)
Rice U (TX)
Roanoke Coll (VA)
Rollins Coll (FL)
Sacred Heart U (CT)
Saint Francis U (PA)
St. John Fisher Coll (NY)
Saint Joseph's U (PA)
Saint Leo U (FL)
Saint Martin's U (WA)
St. Mary's Coll of Maryland (MD)
St. Norbert Coll (WI)
St. Olaf Coll (MN)
Salve Regina U (RI)
Samford U (AL)
San Diego State U (CA)
San Jose State U (CA)
Sarah Lawrence Coll (NY)
Scripps Coll (CA)
Seattle U (WA)
Seton Hill U (PA)
Skidmore Coll (NY)
Southwest Baptist U (MO)
Southwestern U (TX)
Spring Hill Coll (AL)
Stetson U (FL)
Stonehill Coll (MA)
Syracuse U (NY)
Temple U (PA)
Texas Christian U (TX)
Towson U (MD)
Trevecca Nazarene U (TN)
Tulane U (LA)
Union Coll (KY)
Union Coll (NY)
U of California, Davis (CA)
U of California, Irvine (CA)
U of California, Los Angeles (CA)
U of California, Riverside (CA)
U of Central Arkansas (AR)
U of Central Florida (FL)
U of Dayton (OH)
U of Detroit Mercy (MI)
U of Florida (FL)
U of Georgia (GA)
U of Hawaii at Manoa (HI)
U of Houston (TX)
U of La Verne (CA)
U of Lynchburg (VA)
U of Michigan (MI)
U of Minnesota, Twin Cities Campus (MN)
U of Missouri (MO)
U of Mount Union (OH)
U of New Mexico (NM)
U of North Carolina at Asheville (NC)
The U of North Carolina at Chapel Hill (NC)
The U of North Carolina at Charlotte (NC)
The U of North Carolina at Greensboro (NC)
U of Northern Iowa (IA)
U of North Florida (FL)
U of Oregon (OR)
U of Pennsylvania (PA)
U of Pittsburgh (PA)
U of Providence (MT)
U of Puget Sound (WA)
U of Regina (SK, Canada)
U of Richmond (VA)
U of St. Thomas (MN)
U of San Diego (CA)
U of South Carolina (SC)
U of South Florida (FL)
The U of Tennessee (TN)
The U of Texas at Austin (TX)
U of the Incarnate Word (TX)
The U of the South (TN)
The U of Toledo (OH)
The U of Tulsa (OK)
U of Vermont (VT)
U of Virginia (VA)
U of Washington (WA)
U of Wisconsin–Eau Claire (WI)
U of Wisconsin–Milwaukee (WI)
U of Wyoming (WY)
Ursinus Coll (PA)
Vanguard U of Southern California (CA)
Vassar Coll (NY)
Virginia Commonwealth U (VA)
Wabash Coll (IN)
Wartburg Coll (IA)
Washington and Lee U (VA)
Washington State U (WA)
Washington U in St. Louis (MO)
Wesleyan Coll (GA)
Wesleyan U (CT)
Western Kentucky U (KY)
Western Washington U (WA)
Westmont Coll (CA)
Wheaton Coll (MA)
Whittier Coll (CA)
Whitworth U (WA)
Willamette U (OR)
Williams Coll (MA)
Wofford Coll (SC)
Wright State U–Lake Campus (OH)
Youngstown State U (OH)

RELIGIOUS STUDIES RELATED
Agnes Scott Coll (GA)
Bryn Athyn Coll of the New Church (PA)
Grand Valley State U (MI)
Louisiana Coll (LA)

RESEARCH AND EXPERIMENTAL PSYCHOLOGY RELATED
Colgate U (NY)
Creighton U (NE)
Georgia Coll & State U (GA)
Indiana U Bloomington (IN)
Knox Coll (IL)
Lake Forest Coll (IL)
Loyola U New Orleans (LA)
Macalester Coll (MN)
Murray State U (KY)
Northeastern State U (OK)
Vassar Coll (NY)
Washington and Lee U (VA)

RESEARCH METHODOLOGY AND QUANTITATIVE METHODS
Bryant U (RI)

RESORT MANAGEMENT
Coastal Carolina U (SC)
Lasell Coll (MA)
Rochester Inst of Technology (NY)

RESPIRATORY CARE THERAPY
Baptist Coll of Health Sciences (TN)
Bellarmine U (KY)
Bowling Green State U (OH)
Canisius Coll (NY)
Dakota State U (SD)
Florida Ag and Mech U (FL)
Georgia State U (GA)
Gwynedd Mercy U (PA)
Indiana U of Pennsylvania (PA)
Indiana U–Purdue U Indianapolis (IN)
Liberty U (VA)
Marshall U (WV)
Marywood U (PA)
Molloy Coll (NY)
Nebraska Methodist Coll (NE)
Northern Kentucky U (KY)
The Ohio State U (OH)
Salisbury U (MD)
Samford U (AL)
The U of North Carolina at Charlotte (NC)
U of South Alabama (AL)
U of Southern Indiana (IN)
The U of Toledo (OH)
Weber State U (UT)
Youngstown State U (OH)

RESPIRATORY THERAPY TECHNICIAN
Rhode Island Coll (RI)

RESTAURANT, CULINARY, AND CATERING MANAGEMENT
Bowling Green State U (OH)
Delaware Valley U (PA)

RESTAURANT/FOOD SERVICES MANAGEMENT
Central Washington U (WA)
Colorado State U (CO)
Kennesaw State U (GA)
Rochester Inst of Technology (NY)
U of Central Florida (FL)
U of Nevada, Las Vegas (NV)

RETAILING
American Public U System (WV)
Bowling Green State U (OH)
Central Washington U (WA)
Lamar U (TX)
U of Minnesota, Twin Cities Campus (MN)
U of South Carolina (SC)

RETAIL MANAGEMENT
U of Arkansas (AR)

RHETORIC AND COMPOSITION
Auburn U (AL)
Bowling Green State U (OH)
California State U, Fullerton (CA)
California State U, Long Beach (CA)
California State U, Los Angeles (CA)
Calvin Coll (MI)
Carson-Newman U (TN)
Carthage Coll (WI)
Coll of Saint Benedict (MN)
Cornell Coll (IA)
DePaul U (IL)
Drake U (IA)
Duquesne U (PA)
East Tennessee State U (TN)
East Texas Baptist U (TX)
Emerson Coll (MA)
George Mason U (VA)
Georgia Coll & State U (GA)
Georgia Southern U (GA)
Humboldt State U (CA)
Illinois Coll (IL)
Ithaca Coll (NY)
Jackson State U (MS)
Lipscomb U (TN)
Manchester U (IN)
Marshall U (WV)
Northern State U (SD)
Northwestern Oklahoma State U (OK)
Northwestern U (IL)
Oglethorpe U (GA)
Ohio U (OH)
Oklahoma Baptist U (OK)
Oklahoma Christian U (OK)
Old Dominion U (VA)
Ouachita Baptist U (AR)
Portland State U (OR)
Rider U (NJ)
Saint John's U (MN)
St. Joseph's Coll, Long Island Campus (NY)
St. Joseph's Coll, New York (NY)
Southern U and Ag and Mech Coll (LA)
State U of New York Coll at Potsdam (NY)
Texas Tech U (TX)
U of Central Florida (FL)
U of Kentucky (KY)
U of Minnesota, Morris (MN)
U of Minnesota, Twin Cities Campus (MN)
U of Montevallo (AL)
U of New Mexico (NM)
U of Pittsburgh (PA)
U of Puget Sound (WA)
U of Richmond (VA)
U of South Dakota (SD)
Utah State U (UT)
Wabash Coll (IN)
West Chester U of Pennsylvania (PA)
Willamette U (OR)
Youngstown State U (OH)

RHETORIC AND COMPOSITION/WRITING RELATED
Pepperdine U, Malibu (CA)
Syracuse U (NY)

ROBOTICS TECHNOLOGY
Central Connecticut State U (CT)
Idaho State U (ID)
Indiana State U (IN)
Université de Sherbrooke (QC, Canada)

ROMANCE LANGUAGES
Beloit Coll (WI)
Dartmouth Coll (NH)
Harvard U (MA)
Haverford Coll (PA)
Hunter Coll of the City U of New York (NY)
Johns Hopkins U (MD)
Loyola Marymount U (CA)
Merrimack Coll (MA)
Rockford U (IL)
Samford U (AL)
Truman State U (MO)
U of Georgia (GA)
U of Maryland, Coll Park (MD)
U of Michigan (MI)
U of Notre Dame (IN)
U of Oregon (OR)
U of Washington (WA)
Washington and Lee U (VA)
Washington U in St. Louis (MO)

ROMANCE LANGUAGES RELATED
Boston U (MA)
The Ohio State U (OH)
U of Chicago (IL)
U of Maine (ME)
U of Nevada, Las Vegas (NV)
The U of North Carolina at Chapel Hill (NC)
U of Pennsylvania (PA)
Wesleyan U (CT)

RUSSIAN
American U (DC)
Baylor U (TX)
Beloit Coll (WI)
Boston Coll (MA)
Boston U (MA)
Bowling Green State U (OH)
Bucknell U (PA)
Central Washington U (WA)
Coll of the Holy Cross (MA)
Columbia U (NY)
Cornell Coll (IA)
Cornell U (NY)
Dartmouth Coll (NH)
Dickinson Coll (PA)
Haverford Coll (PA)
Hofstra U (NY)
Hunter Coll of the City U of New York (NY)
Juniata Coll (PA)
Lawrence U (WI)
Macalester Coll (MN)
Miami U Hamilton (OH)
Michigan State U (MI)
Middlebury Coll (VT)

New Coll of Florida (FL)
New York U (NY)
The Ohio State U (OH)
Ohio U (OH)
Portland State U (OR)
Purdue U (IN)
Queens Coll of the City U of New York (NY)
Saint Louis U (MO)
St. Olaf Coll (MN)
San Diego State U (CA)
Sarah Lawrence Coll (NY)
Scripps Coll (CA)
Syracuse U (NY)
Tulane U (LA)
U of California, Davis (CA)
U of California, Los Angeles (CA)
U of Florida (FL)
U of Georgia (GA)
U of Hawaii at Manoa (HI)
U of Kentucky (KY)
U of Maryland, Coll Park (MD)
U of Michigan (MI)
U of Minnesota, Twin Cities Campus (MN)
U of Missouri (MO)
U of Nebraska–Lincoln (NE)
U of New Hampshire (NH)
U of Notre Dame (IN)
U of Pennsylvania (PA)
U of Pittsburgh (PA)
U of South Carolina (SC)
U of South Florida (FL)
The U of Tennessee (TN)
The U of the South (TN)
U of Vermont (VT)
U of Washington (WA)
U of Wisconsin–Milwaukee (WI)
U of Wyoming (WY)
Vassar Coll (NY)
Virginia Polytechnic Inst and State U (VA)
Washington State U (WA)
Wheaton Coll (MA)
Willamette U (OR)
Williams Coll (MA)

RUSSIAN, CENTRAL EUROPEAN, EAST EUROPEAN AND EURASIAN STUDIES
Colgate U (NY)
Coll of the Holy Cross (MA)
Miami U (OH)
Portland State U (OR)
San Diego State U (CA)
Washington U in St. Louis (MO)

RUSSIAN STUDIES
American U (DC)
Boston Coll (MA)
Bowling Green State U (OH)
Brandeis U (MA)
The Colorado Coll (CO)
Columbia U (NY)
Cornell Coll (IA)
Dartmouth Coll (NH)
George Mason U (VA)
Grand Valley State U (MI)
Hamilton Coll (NY)
Lafayette Coll (PA)
Lawrence U (WI)
Middlebury Coll (VT)
Rhodes Coll (TN)
St. Olaf Coll (MN)
Stetson U (FL)
Syracuse U (NY)
Texas Tech U (TX)
Tulane U (LA)
U of California, Los Angeles (CA)
U of California, Riverside (CA)
U of Maryland, Coll Park (MD)
U of Massachusetts Amherst (MA)
U of Michigan (MI)
U of Missouri (MO)
U of Oregon (OR)
U of Richmond (VA)
The U of Texas at Austin (TX)
The U of Tulsa (OK)
U of Vermont (VT)
Washington and Lee U (VA)
Washington U in St. Louis (MO)
Wesleyan U (CT)
Wheaton Coll (MA)

SALES AND MARKETING/ MARKETING AND DISTRIBUTION TEACHER EDUCATION
Bowling Green State U (OH)
Central Washington U (WA)
Fayetteville State U (NC)
North Carolina State U (NC)
Utah State U (UT)

SALES, DISTRIBUTION, AND MARKETING OPERATIONS
Avila U (MO)
Babson Coll (MA)
Baylor U (TX)
Bentley U (MA)
Bowling Green State U (OH)
Harding U (AR)
Kennesaw State U (GA)
New York U (NY)
Seton Hill U (PA)
U of Houston (TX)
U of Memphis (TN)
U of Minnesota, Twin Cities Campus (MN)
U of Pennsylvania (PA)
West Chester U of Pennsylvania (PA)

SANSKRIT AND CLASSICAL INDIAN LANGUAGES
Harvard U (MA)

SCANDINAVIAN STUDIES
U of California, Los Angeles (CA)
U of Washington (WA)

SCHOOL LIBRARIAN/SCHOOL LIBRARY MEDIA
The Coll of St. Scholastica (MN)
U of Providence (MT)

SCHOOL PSYCHOLOGY
Alverno Coll (WI)
Eastern Washington U (WA)
Kansas Wesleyan U (KS)

SCIENCE TEACHER EDUCATION
Adams State U (CO)
Albion Coll (MI)
Alverno Coll (WI)
Arkansas Tech U (AR)
Auburn U (AL)
Baylor U (TX)
Blackburn Coll (IL)
Boston U (MA)
Bowling Green State U (OH)
Bradley U (IL)
Buena Vista U (IA)
California Lutheran U (CA)
Calvin Coll (MI)
Campbellsville U (KY)
Canisius Coll (NY)
Cedarville U (OH)
Central Michigan U (MI)
Central Washington U (WA)
Christian Brothers U (TN)
Coll of Saint Mary (NE)
Concordia U Chicago (IL)
Covenant Coll (GA)
Dallas Baptist U (TX)
Daytona State Coll (FL)
East Carolina U (NC)
Eastern Illinois U (IL)
Eastern Washington U (WA)
Florida Ag and Mech U (FL)
Florida Atlantic U (FL)
Goshen Coll (IN)
Grand Valley State U (MI)
Harding U (AR)
Hardin-Simmons U (TX)
Hofstra U (NY)
Hunter Coll of the City U of New York (NY)
Immaculata U (PA)
Indiana State U (IN)
Indiana U South Bend (IN)
Inter American U of Puerto Rico, San Germán Campus (PR)
Ithaca Coll (NY)
Juniata Coll (PA)
LeTourneau U (TX)
Loyola U Chicago (IL)
Madonna U (MI)
Manchester U (IN)
Marquette U (WI)
Martin Luther Coll (MN)
Marywood U (PA)
Merrimack Coll (MA)
Miami U (OH)
Miami U Hamilton (OH)
Michigan State U (MI)
Missouri Baptist U (MO)
Morningside Coll (IA)
New York U (NY)
North Carolina State U (NC)
Northeastern State U (OK)
Northwestern Oklahoma State U (OK)
Northwest Missouri State U (MO)
Ohio Dominican U (OH)
Oklahoma Baptist U (OK)
Oklahoma Christian U (OK)
Ouachita Baptist U (AR)
Pfeiffer U (NC)
Piedmont Coll (GA)
Rhode Island Coll (RI)
Rider U (NJ)
Rocky Mountain Coll (MT)
Saginaw Valley State U (MI)
Saint Francis U (PA)
Southeast Missouri State U (MO)
Southern Illinois U Edwardsville (IL)
Southern U and Ag and Mech Coll (LA)
Southwest Baptist U (MO)
State U of New York at Fredonia (NY)
Temple U (PA)
Texas Christian U (TX)
Tiffin U (OH)
U of Central Arkansas (AR)
U of Dayton (OH)
The U of Findlay (OH)
U of Georgia (GA)
U of Kentucky (KY)
U of Maine (ME)
U of Maine at Machias (ME)
U of Mary Hardin-Baylor (TX)
U of Michigan–Dearborn (MI)
U of Minnesota, Duluth (MN)
U of Nebraska–Lincoln (NE)
U of Nevada, Las Vegas (NV)
The U of North Carolina at Pembroke (NC)
U of North Dakota (ND)
U of North Florida (FL)
U of Notre Dame (IN)
U of Providence (MT)
U of Regina (SK, Canada)
U of St. Thomas (MN)
U of South Dakota (SD)
U of South Florida (FL)
U of Vermont (VT)
U of Wisconsin–Eau Claire (WI)
U of Wisconsin–La Crosse (WI)
U of Wisconsin–Milwaukee (WI)
U of Wisconsin–River Falls (WI)
Utah State U (UT)
Utah Valley U (UT)
Valparaiso U (IN)
Vincennes U (IN)
Washington U in St. Louis (MO)
Waynesburg U (PA)
Weber State U (UT)
Western Washington U (WA)
Widener U (PA)
Wright State U–Lake Campus (OH)
Youngstown State U (OH)

SCIENCE TECHNOLOGIES
Baylor U (TX)
Excelsior Coll (NY)

SCIENCE TECHNOLOGIES RELATED
Bridgewater State U (MA)
Delta State U (MS)
Excelsior Coll (NY)
Kean U (NJ)
Madonna U (MI)
North Carolina State U (NC)

SCIENCE, TECHNOLOGY AND SOCIETY
Butler U (IN)
Carnegie Mellon U (PA)
Claremont McKenna Coll (CA)
Cornell U (NY)
Farmingdale State Coll (NY)
Massachusetts Inst of Technology (MA)
New Jersey Inst of Technology (NJ)
North Carolina State U (NC)
Northwestern U (IL)
Pitzer Coll (CA)
Scripps Coll (CA)
Texas Tech U (TX)
U of Puget Sound (WA)
U of Washington, Bothell (WA)
Vassar Coll (NY)
Washington U in St. Louis (MO)
Wesleyan U (CT)
Worcester Polytechnic Inst (MA)

SCULPTURE
Boston U (MA)
Bowling Green State U (OH)
Bradley U (IL)
California State U, Long Beach (CA)
Central Washington U (WA)
Cleveland Inst of Art (OH)
Dominican U (IL)
Drake U (IA)
Escuela de Artes Plasticas y Diseño de Puerto Rico (PR)
Inter American U of Puerto Rico, San Germán Campus (PR)
Maryland Inst Coll of Art (MD)
Marywood U (PA)
Portland State U (OR)
Rhode Island Coll (RI)
Rhode Island School of Design (RI)
Rochester Inst of Technology (NY)
Savannah Coll of Art and Design (GA)
Seton Hill U (PA)
Sonoma State U (CA)
Syracuse U (NY)
Temple U (PA)
Texas Christian U (TX)
U of Dallas (TX)
U of Houston (TX)
U of Massachusetts Dartmouth (MA)
U of Michigan (MI)
U of Oregon (OR)
U of Puget Sound (WA)
U of Regina (SK, Canada)
U of Washington (WA)
Virginia Commonwealth U (VA)
Washington U in St. Louis (MO)

SECONDARY EDUCATION
Acadia U (NS, Canada)
Alabama State U (AL)
Albright Coll (PA)
Alverno Coll (WI)
American U (DC)
Auburn U (AL)
Auburn U at Montgomery (AL)
Aurora U (IL)
Austin Coll (TX)
Baker U (KS)
Baylor U (TX)
Bellarmine U (KY)
Beloit Coll (WI)
Blackburn Coll (IL)
Boston Coll (MA)
Bradley U (IL)
Bridgewater State U (MA)
Bucknell U (PA)
Butler U (IN)
Caldwell U (NJ)
Calvin Coll (MI)
Campbellsville U (KY)
Canisius Coll (NY)
Carson-Newman U (TN)
Carthage Coll (WI)
The Catholic U of America (DC)
Champlain Coll (VT)
Clark U (MA)
Coll of Charleston (SC)
Coll of Saint Mary (NE)
Concordia U Chicago (IL)
Cornell Coll (IA)
Delaware Valley U (PA)
DePaul U (IL)
Dominican U (IL)
Drake U (IA)
Emmanuel Coll (MA)
Endicott Coll (MA)
Fitchburg State U (MA)
Florida Ag and Mech U (FL)
Fort Lewis Coll (CO)
Franklin Pierce U (NH)
Furman U (SC)
Gonzaga U (WA)
Gordon Coll (MA)
Goshen Coll (IN)
Grand Valley State U (MI)
Granite State Coll (NH)
Hamline U (MN)
Harding U (AR)
High Point U (NC)
Hofstra U (NY)
Hunter Coll of the City U of New York (NY)
Idaho State U (ID)
Illinois Coll (IL)
Indiana U Bloomington (IN)
Indiana U East (IN)
Indiana U Kokomo (IN)
Indiana U Northwest (IN)
Indiana U South Bend (IN)
Indiana U Southeast (IN)
Inter American U of Puerto Rico, Barranquitas Campus (PR)
Inter American U of Puerto Rico, San Germán Campus (PR)
Iona Coll (NY)
Ithaca Coll (NY)
Judson U (IL)
Kansas Wesleyan U (KS)
Knox Coll (IL)
Kuyper Coll (MI)
La Salle U (PA)
Lasell Coll (MA)
Lesley U (MA)
LeTourneau U (TX)
Lock Haven U of Pennsylvania (PA)
Loyola U Chicago (IL)
Lubbock Christian U (TX)
Manchester U (IN)
Manhattanville Coll (NY)
Mansfield U of Pennsylvania (PA)
Marian U (IN)
Marquette U (WI)
Marshall U (WV)
Mercy Coll (NY)
Merrimack Coll (MA)
Michigan State U (MI)
Middlebury Coll (VT)
Missouri Baptist U (MO)
Molloy Coll (NY)
Mount Marty Coll (SD)
Mount Saint Mary Coll (NY)
National U (CA)
Nazareth Coll of Rochester (NY)
New England Coll (NH)
Northern Kentucky U (KY)
Northwest Christian U (OR)
Northwestern Oklahoma State U (OK)
Northwestern U (IL)
Ohio U (OH)
Ohio Wesleyan U (OH)
Oklahoma Christian U (OK)
Oklahoma State U (OK)
Ouachita Baptist U (AR)
Piedmont Coll (GA)
Point U (GA)
Providence Coll (RI)
Rhode Island Coll (RI)
Rider U (NJ)
Rochester Coll (MI)
Rockford U (IL)
Rocky Mountain Coll (MT)
Saint Anselm Coll (NH)
Saint Francis U (PA)
Saint Joseph's U (PA)
Saint Leo U (FL)
Saint Martin's U (WA)
Salve Regina U (RI)
Samford U (AL)
Southern U and Ag and Mech Coll (LA)
Spring Hill Coll (AL)
State U of New York at Fredonia (NY)
Stonehill Coll (MA)
Tabor Coll (KS)
Taylor U (IN)
Texas Christian U (TX)
Toccoa Falls Coll (GA)
Université de Sherbrooke (QC, Canada)
Université Sainte-Anne (NS, Canada)
U of Arkansas (AR)
U of Central Florida (FL)
U of Dayton (OH)
U of Detroit Mercy (MI)
U of Guam (GU)
U of Hawaii at Manoa (HI)
U of Idaho (ID)
U of Maine (ME)
U of Maine at Farmington (ME)
U of Maine at Presque Isle (ME)
U of Maryland, Coll Park (MD)

U of Michigan (MI)
U of Missouri (MO)
U of Nevada, Las Vegas (NV)
U of New Mexico (NM)
U of North Dakota (ND)
U of North Florida (FL)
U of Pittsburgh at Bradford (PA)
U of Providence (MT)
U of Regina (SK, Canada)
U of Sioux Falls (SD)
U of South Alabama (AL)
U of South Carolina Aiken (SC)
U of South Dakota (SD)
The U of Tampa (FL)
The U of Toledo (OH)
U of Vermont (VT)
U of Wyoming (WY)
Utah State U (UT)
Utica Coll (NY)
Valparaiso U (IN)
Vanguard U of Southern California (CA)
Virginia Polytechnic Inst and State U (VA)
Wartburg Coll (IA)
Washington U in St. Louis (MO)
Waynesburg U (PA)
Western Connecticut State U (CT)
Westmont Coll (CA)
West Virginia State U (WV)
Wheaton Coll (IL)
Wheaton Coll (MA)
Whitworth U (WA)
William Jewell Coll (MO)
Youngstown State U (OH)

SECURITIES SERVICES ADMINISTRATION
American Public U System (WV)
Dean Coll (MA)
Saint Louis U (MO)
Vincennes U (IN)

SELLING SKILLS AND SALES
Bradley U (IL)
High Point U (NC)
Manchester U (IN)
Purdue U (IN)
Stetson U (FL)
U of Memphis (TN)
Weber State U (UT)

SIGN LANGUAGE INTERPRETATION AND TRANSLATION
Columbia Coll Chicago (IL)
Framingham State U (MA)
Goshen Coll (IN)
Idaho State U (ID)
Indiana U–Purdue U Indianapolis (IN)
Madonna U (MI)
Rochester Inst of Technology (NY)
U of Louisville (KY)
U of New Mexico (NM)
U of Northern Colorado (CO)
U of North Florida (FL)
U of Wisconsin–Milwaukee (WI)

SLAVIC LANGUAGES
Boston Coll (MA)
Columbia U (NY)
Harvard U (MA)
Indiana U Bloomington (IN)
Northwestern U (IL)
Princeton U (NJ)
U of California, Los Angeles (CA)
U of Chicago (IL)
U of Virginia (VA)
U of Washington (WA)

SLAVIC STUDIES
Baylor U (TX)
Columbia U (NY)
Connecticut Coll (CT)
Northwestern U (IL)

SMALL BUSINESS ADMINISTRATION
Adams State U (CO)
Avila U (MO)
Babson Coll (MA)
Bradley U (IL)
Carson-Newman U (TN)
Florida Southern Coll (FL)
Ohio Wesleyan U (OH)
Rocky Mountain Coll (MT)
Saint Joseph's U (PA)
U of Michigan–Dearborn (MI)

SOCIAL AND PHILOSOPHICAL FOUNDATIONS OF EDUCATION
Dickinson Coll (PA)
Eastern Washington U (WA)
High Point U (NC)
Northwestern U (IL)
U of California, Riverside (CA)
Washington U in St. Louis (MO)

SOCIAL PSYCHOLOGY
Clarion U of Pennsylvania (PA)
Florida Atlantic U (FL)
Grand Valley State U (MI)
Maryville U of Saint Louis (MO)
Northwest Missouri State U (MO)
U of California, Irvine (CA)

SOCIAL SCIENCES
Adelphi U (NY)
American U (DC)
Benedictine U (IL)
Bethany Lutheran Coll (MN)
Bethel U (MN)
Bowling Green State U (OH)
Brandman U (CA)
Caldwell U (NJ)
California Lutheran U (CA)
California State U, Monterey Bay (CA)
California State U, San Bernardino (CA)
California State U, San Marcos (CA)
California U of Pennsylvania (PA)
Calvin Coll (MI)
Campbellsville U (KY)
Canisius Coll (NY)
Carthage Coll (WI)
Central Connecticut State U (CT)
Central Michigan U (MI)
Central Washington U (WA)
Clarkson U (NY)
Colgate U (NY)
The Coll of St. Scholastica (MN)
Colorado State U–Pueblo (CO)
Delta State U (MS)
Eastern Mennonite U (VA)
Excelsior Coll (NY)
Florida Atlantic U (FL)
Florida Southern Coll (FL)
Granite State Coll (NH)
Harding U (AR)
Harvard U (MA)
Holy Apostles Coll and Sem (CT)
Humboldt State U (CA)
Indiana U Southeast (IN)
Ithaca Coll (NY)
Jacksonville U (FL)
La Salle U (PA)
Lesley U (MA)
Liberty U (VA)
Lock Haven U of Pennsylvania (PA)
Loyola U New Orleans (LA)
Manchester U (IN)
Manhattanville Coll (NY)
Mansfield U of Pennsylvania (PA)
Marywood U (PA)
Mercy Coll (NY)
Michigan State U (MI)
Missouri Baptist U (MO)
Mount Saint Mary Coll (NY)
National U (CA)
Nazareth Coll of Rochester (NY)
New Coll of Florida (FL)
New York U (NY)
Northern Kentucky U (KY)
Northwestern Oklahoma State U (OK)
The Ohio State U (OH)
Oklahoma Baptist U (OK)
Pace U (NY)
Pace U, Pleasantville Campus (NY)
Palm Beach Atlantic U (FL)
Pfeiffer U (NC)
Piedmont Coll (GA)
Portland State U (OR)
Providence Coll (RI)
Radford U (VA)
Rockford U (IL)
The Sage Colls (NY)
St. Joseph's Coll, Long Island Campus (NY)
St. Joseph's Coll, New York (NY)
Salisbury U (MD)
San Diego State U (CA)
San Jose State U (CA)
Southeast Missouri State U (MO)
Southern Arkansas U–Magnolia (AR)
Southern Illinois U Carbondale (IL)
Spring Hill Coll (AL)
Stetson U (FL)
Stevens Inst of Technology (NJ)
Towson U (MD)
Tulane U (LA)
Union Coll (NY)
U at Buffalo, the State U of New York (NY)
U of California, Irvine (CA)
U of Central Florida (FL)
U of Dallas (TX)
U of Detroit Mercy (MI)
U of Houston–Downtown (TX)
U of La Verne (CA)
U of Maryland U Coll (MD)
U of Massachusetts Boston (MA)
U of Michigan (MI)
U of Michigan–Dearborn (MI)
U of Montevallo (AL)
U of Nevada, Las Vegas (NV)
U of North Dakota (ND)
U of Oregon (OR)
U of Pennsylvania (PA)
U of Pittsburgh (PA)
U of Pittsburgh at Bradford (PA)
U of Providence (MT)
U of Regina (SK, Canada)
U of St. Thomas (MN)
U of Sioux Falls (SD)
U of South Florida (FL)
U of South Florida Sarasota-Manatee (FL)
The U of Texas Rio Grande Valley (TX)
U of Washington (WA)
U of Wisconsin–Superior (WI)
U of Wyoming (WY)
Utica Coll (NY)
Valley City State U (ND)
Valparaiso U (IN)
Wartburg Coll (IA)
Washington State U (WA)
Washington State U–Tri-Cities (WA)
Washington State U–Vancouver (WA)
Washington U in St. Louis (MO)
Waynesburg U (PA)
Western Connecticut State U (CT)
Western Kentucky U (KY)
Westmont Coll (CA)
Whittier Coll (CA)
Widener U (PA)

SOCIAL SCIENCES RELATED
Boston U (MA)
Bowling Green State U (OH)
California Polytechnic State U, San Luis Obispo (CA)
Central Michigan U (MI)
Clarion U of Pennsylvania (PA)
The Coll of Idaho (ID)
Coll of Staten Island of the City U of New York (NY)
Covenant Coll (GA)
Curry Coll (MA)
Eastern Oregon U (OR)
The Evergreen State Coll (WA)
Hamline U (MN)
Indiana U of Pennsylvania (PA)
Kalamazoo Coll (MI)
Knox Coll (IL)
Marywood U (PA)
Millersville U of Pennsylvania (PA)
New York U (NY)
Northwestern U (IL)
Ouachita Baptist U (AR)
Pace U (NY)
Purchase Coll, State U of New York (NY)
Queens Coll of the City U of New York (NY)
Randolph-Macon Coll (VA)
Skidmore Coll (NY)
Towson U (MD)
U of Chicago (IL)
U of La Verne (CA)
U of Maine at Presque Isle (ME)
U of Massachusetts Amherst (MA)
U of Pittsburgh (PA)
U of Regina (SK, Canada)
U of Washington, Tacoma (WA)
Washington U in St. Louis (MO)
Wesleyan U (CT)
Williams Coll (MA)

SOCIAL SCIENCE TEACHER EDUCATION
Auburn U (AL)
Baylor U (TX)
Blackburn Coll (IL)
Bowling Green State U (OH)
Buena Vista U (IA)
California Lutheran U (CA)
Campbellsville U (KY)
Central Washington U (WA)
Coll of Saint Mary (NE)
The Coll of St. Scholastica (MN)
Concordia U Chicago (IL)
Delta State U (MS)
Eastern Illinois U (IL)
Eastern Washington U (WA)
Emmanuel Coll (GA)
Fayetteville State U (NC)
Florida Ag and Mech U (FL)
Florida Atlantic U (FL)
Florida Southern Coll (FL)
Jackson State U (MS)
Manchester U (IN)
Mansfield U of Pennsylvania (PA)
Marywood U (PA)
Michigan State U (MI)
Millikin U (IL)
Northwest Missouri State U (MO)
Ohio Dominican U (OH)
Rhode Island Coll (RI)
Saginaw Valley State U (MI)
Saint Mary's U of Minnesota (MN)
Southeastern U (FL)
Southwest Baptist U (MO)
U of Detroit Mercy (MI)
U of Maine at Farmington (ME)
U of Maine at Machias (ME)
U of Nebraska–Lincoln (NE)
The U of North Carolina at Greensboro (NC)
U of North Dakota (ND)
U of Northern Iowa (IA)
U of Providence (MT)
U of South Dakota (SD)
U of South Florida (FL)
U of Wisconsin–River Falls (WI)
Utica Coll (NY)
Valley City State U (ND)
Valparaiso U (IN)
Wartburg Coll (IA)
Washington U in St. Louis (MO)
Weber State U (UT)
Western Washington U (WA)
Westmont Coll (CA)
Youngstown State U (OH)

SOCIAL STUDIES TEACHER EDUCATION
Adams State U (CO)
Alverno Coll (WI)
Arkansas Tech U (AR)
Averett U (VA)
Barton Coll (NC)
Baylor U (TX)
Bethany Lutheran Coll (MN)
Bethel U (MN)
Blackburn Coll (IL)
Boston U (MA)
Bowling Green State U (OH)
Bradley U (IL)
Calvin Coll (MI)
Cameron U (OK)
Campbellsville U (KY)
Canisius Coll (NY)
Cedarville U (OH)
Central Michigan U (MI)
Central State U (OH)
The Coll of Saint Rose (NY)
Duquesne U (PA)
East Carolina U (NC)
Eastern Washington U (WA)
East Texas Baptist U (TX)
Geneva Coll (PA)
Goshen Coll (IN)
Grand Valley State U (MI)
Granite State Coll (NH)
Grove City Coll (PA)
Harding U (AR)
Hardin-Simmons U (TX)
Hiram Coll (OH)
Hofstra U (NY)
Immaculata U (PA)
Indiana State U (IN)
Indiana U Bloomington (IN)
Indiana U Northwest (IN)
Indiana U–Purdue U Indianapolis (IN)
Indiana U South Bend (IN)
Indiana U Southeast (IN)
Inter American U of Puerto Rico, San Germán Campus (PR)
Iona Coll (NY)
Ithaca Coll (NY)
Juniata Coll (PA)
Kennesaw State U (GA)
LeTourneau U (TX)
Louisiana Coll (LA)
Madonna U (MI)
Manchester U (IN)
Manhattanville Coll (NY)
Mansfield U of Pennsylvania (PA)
Marist Coll (NY)
Martin Luther Coll (MN)
Merrimack Coll (MA)
Messiah Coll (PA)
Miami U (OH)
Miami U Hamilton (OH)
Michigan State U (MI)
Minnesota State U Moorhead (MN)
Nazareth Coll of Rochester (NY)
New York U (NY)
Northeastern State U (OK)
Ohio Wesleyan U (OH)
Oklahoma Baptist U (OK)
Oklahoma Christian U (OK)
Ouachita Baptist U (AR)
Pace U (NY)
Pace U, Pleasantville Campus (NY)
Pfeiffer U (NC)
Purdue U (IN)
Queens Coll of the City U of New York (NY)
Rocky Mountain Coll (MT)
Saint Francis U (PA)
St. John Fisher Coll (NY)
St. Joseph's Coll, Long Island Campus (NY)
St. Joseph's Coll, New York (NY)
St. Olaf Coll (MN)
Southeastern Louisiana U (LA)
Southeast Missouri State U (MO)
Southern U and Ag and Mech Coll (LA)
Spring Hill Coll (AL)
State U of New York Coll at Potsdam (NY)
Syracuse U (NY)
Taylor U (IN)
Temple U (PA)
Texas Christian U (TX)
Texas Lutheran U (TX)
Union Coll (KY)
U of Detroit Mercy (MI)
The U of Findlay (OH)
U of Georgia (GA)
U of Kentucky (KY)
U of Maine (ME)
U of Michigan–Dearborn (MI)
U of Minnesota, Duluth (MN)
The U of North Carolina at Greensboro (NC)
The U of North Carolina at Pembroke (NC)
U of North Dakota (ND)
U of Northern Colorado (CO)
U of Northwestern–St. Paul (MN)
U of Providence (MT)
U of Regina (SK, Canada)
U of St. Thomas (MN)
U of Vermont (VT)
U of Wisconsin–Eau Claire (WI)
U of Wisconsin–La Crosse (WI)
U of Wisconsin–Milwaukee (WI)
U of Wisconsin–Superior (WI)
Utah State U (UT)
Utica Coll (NY)
Washington U in St. Louis (MO)
Waynesburg U (PA)
Weber State U (UT)
Western Washington U (WA)
Widener U (PA)
Youngstown State U (OH)

SOCIAL WORK
Adams State U (CO)
Adelphi U (NY)
Alabama State U (AL)
Alverno Coll (WI)
Angelo State U (TX)
Appalachian State U (NC)
Auburn U (AL)
Aurora U (IL)

Austin Peay State U (TN)
Avila U (MO)
Barton Coll (NC)
Baylor U (TX)
Bennett Coll (NC)
Bethel Coll (KS)
Bethel U (MN)
Bowling Green State U (OH)
Bradley U (IL)
Brandman U (CA)
Bridgewater State U (MA)
Buena Vista U (IA)
California State U, Long Beach (CA)
California State U, Los Angeles (CA)
California State U, San Bernardino (CA)
California U of Pennsylvania (PA)
Calvin Coll (MI)
Campbellsville U (KY)
Carthage Coll (WI)
The Catholic U of America (DC)
Cedarville U (OH)
Central Connecticut State U (CT)
Central Michigan U (MI)
Central State U (OH)
Champlain Coll (VT)
Christopher Newport U (VA)
The Coll at Brockport, State U of New York (NY)
The Coll of Saint Rose (NY)
The Coll of St. Scholastica (MN)
Coll of Staten Island of the City U of New York (NY)
Coll of the Ozarks (MO)
Colorado State U (CO)
Colorado State U–Pueblo (CO)
Concordia U Chicago (IL)
Creighton U (NE)
Delta State U (MS)
East Carolina U (NC)
Eastern Mennonite U (VA)
Eastern U (PA)
Eastern Washington U (WA)
East Stroudsburg U of Pennsylvania (PA)
East Tennessee State U (TN)
Elizabeth City State U (NC)
Fairfield U (CT)
Fayetteville State U (NC)
Florida Ag and Mech U (FL)
Florida Atlantic U (FL)
Fordham U (NY)
Franklin Pierce U (NH)
George Mason U (VA)
Georgia State U (GA)
Gordon Coll (MA)
Goshen Coll (IN)
Grand Valley State U (MI)
Greenville U (IL)
Grove City Coll (PA)
Gwynedd Mercy U (PA)
Harding U (AR)
Hardin-Simmons U (TX)
Hood Coll (MD)
Humboldt State U (CA)
Idaho State U (ID)
Indiana State U (IN)
Indiana U Bloomington (IN)
Indiana U East (IN)
Indiana U Northwest (IN)
Indiana U–Purdue U Indianapolis (IN)
Indiana U South Bend (IN)
Inter American U of Puerto Rico, Aguadilla Campus (PR)
Inter American U of Puerto Rico, Fajardo Campus (PR)
Iona Coll (NY)
Jackson State U (MS)
Johnson C. Smith U (NC)
Juniata Coll (PA)
Kuyper Coll (MI)
Lamar U (TX)
Lancaster Bible Coll (PA)
La Salle U (PA)
La Sierra U (CA)
Lebanese American U (Lebanon)
Liberty U (VA)
Limestone Coll (SC)
Lindenwood U (MO)
Lipscomb U (TN)
Lock Haven U of Pennsylvania (PA)
Loras Coll (IA)
Louisiana Coll (LA)
Louisiana State U and A&M Coll (LA)
Loyola U Chicago (IL)
Lubbock Christian U (TX)
Madonna U (MI)
Manchester U (IN)
Mansfield U of Pennsylvania (PA)
Marian U (IN)
Marist Coll (NY)
Marshall U (WV)
Marywood U (PA)
McDaniel Coll (MD)
Mercy Coll (NY)
Messiah Coll (PA)
Miami U (OH)
Michigan State U (MI)
Middle Tennessee State U (TN)
Millersville U of Pennsylvania (PA)
Milligan Coll (TN)
Millikin U (IL)
Minnesota State U Moorhead (MN)
Molloy Coll (NY)
Montclair State U (NJ)
Mount St. Joseph U (OH)
Murray State U (KY)
Nazareth Coll of Rochester (NY)
New York U (NY)
North Carolina State U (NC)
Northeastern State U (OK)
Northern Kentucky U (KY)
Northwestern Oklahoma State U (OK)
Oglethorpe U (GA)
Ohio Dominican U (OH)
The Ohio State U (OH)
The Ohio State U at Lima (OH)
The Ohio State U at Mansfield (OH)
The Ohio State U at Marion (OH)
The Ohio State U at Newark (OH)
Ohio U (OH)
Pacific Lutheran U (WA)
Point Loma Nazarene U (CA)
Point U (GA)
Portland State U (OR)
Prairie View A&M U (TX)
Providence Coll (RI)
Purdue U Northwest (IN)
Radford U (VA)
Redeemer U Coll (ON, Canada)
Rhode Island Coll (RI)
Sacred Heart U (CT)
Saginaw Valley State U (MI)
Saint Anselm Coll (NH)
Saint Francis U (PA)
Saint Leo U (FL)
Saint Louis U (MO)
Saint Martin's U (WA)
St. Olaf Coll (MN)
Salisbury U (MD)
Salve Regina U (RI)
San Diego State U (CA)
San Francisco State U (CA)
San Jose State U (CA)
Seattle U (WA)
Seton Hill U (PA)
Skidmore Coll (NY)
Southeastern Louisiana U (LA)
Southeastern U (FL)
Southeast Missouri State U (MO)
Southern Arkansas U–Magnolia (AR)
Southern Illinois U Carbondale (IL)
Southern Illinois U Edwardsville (IL)
Southern U and Ag and Mech Coll (LA)
Southwest Baptist U (MO)
State U of New York at Fredonia (NY)
State U of New York at Plattsburgh (NY)
Stockton U (NJ)
Syracuse U (NY)
Tabor Coll (KS)
Taylor U (IN)
Temple U (PA)
Texas A&M U–Central Texas (TX)
Texas Christian U (TX)
Texas Tech U (TX)
Texas Woman's U (TX)
Trevecca Nazarene U (TN)
Trinity Christian Coll (IL)
Université de Sherbrooke (QC, Canada)
U of Arkansas (AR)
U of Central Florida (FL)
U of Detroit Mercy (MI)
The U of Findlay (OH)
U of Georgia (GA)
U of Guam (GU)
U of Hawaii at Manoa (HI)
U of Houston–Clear Lake (TX)
U of Houston–Downtown (TX)
U of Illinois at Springfield (IL)
U of Kentucky (KY)
U of Louisville (KY)
U of Maine (ME)
U of Maine at Presque Isle (ME)
U of Mary Hardin-Baylor (TX)
U of Maryland, Baltimore County (MD)
U of Memphis (TN)
U of Minnesota, Duluth (MN)
U of Missouri (MO)
U of Montevallo (AL)
U of Nevada, Las Vegas (NV)
U of Nevada, Reno (NV)
U of New Hampshire (NH)
The U of North Carolina at Charlotte (NC)
The U of North Carolina at Greensboro (NC)
The U of North Carolina at Pembroke (NC)
U of North Dakota (ND)
U of Northern Iowa (IA)
U of North Florida (FL)
U of Pittsburgh (PA)
U of Regina (SK, Canada)
U of Saint Francis (IN)
U of St. Thomas (MN)
U of Sioux Falls (SD)
U of South Alabama (AL)
U of South Carolina (SC)
U of South Dakota (SD)
U of Southern Indiana (IN)
U of South Florida (FL)
The U of Tennessee (TN)
The U of Tennessee at Martin (TN)
The U of Texas at Austin (TX)
The U of Texas at El Paso (TX)
The U of Texas of the Permian Basin (TX)
The U of Texas Rio Grande Valley (TX)
The U of Toledo (OH)
U of Vermont (VT)
U of Washington (WA)
U of Washington, Tacoma (WA)
U of Wisconsin–Eau Claire (WI)
U of Wisconsin–Milwaukee (WI)
U of Wisconsin–River Falls (WI)
U of Wisconsin–Superior (WI)
U of Wyoming (WY)
Utah State U (UT)
Utah Valley U (UT)
Valparaiso U (IN)
Virginia Commonwealth U (VA)
Wartburg Coll (IA)
Weber State U (UT)
West Chester U of Pennsylvania (PA)
Western Connecticut State U (CT)
Western Illinois U (IL)
Western Kentucky U (KY)
West Virginia State U (WV)
Whittier Coll (CA)
Widener U (PA)
Winthrop U (SC)
Wright State U–Lake Campus (OH)
Youngstown State U (OH)

SOCIAL WORK RELATED

Davenport U, Grand Rapids (MI)
Eastern Washington U (WA)
King U (TN)
Marquette U (WI)
Miami U Hamilton (OH)
Southeastern U (FL)

SOCIOLOGY

Acadia U (NS, Canada)
Adelphi U (NY)
Agnes Scott Coll (GA)
Albion Coll (MI)
Albright Coll (PA)
Alfred U (NY)
Alverno Coll (WI)
American Public U System (WV)
American U (DC)
Angelo State U (TX)
Appalachian State U (NC)
Arkansas Tech U (AR)
Assumption Coll (MA)
Auburn U (AL)
Auburn U at Montgomery (AL)
Aurora U (IL)
Austin Coll (TX)
Austin Peay State U (TN)
Averett U (VA)
Avila U (MO)
Baker U (KS)
Baldwin Wallace U (OH)
Baruch Coll of the City U of New York (NY)
Baylor U (TX)
Bellarmine U (KY)
Beloit Coll (WI)
Benedictine U (IL)
Berea Coll (KY)
Boston Coll (MA)
Boston U (MA)
Bowling Green State U (OH)
Bradley U (IL)
Brandeis U (MA)
Brandman U (CA)
Bridgewater Coll (VA)
Bridgewater State U (MA)
Bryant U (RI)
Bucknell U (PA)
Buena Vista U (IA)
Butler U (IN)
Caldwell U (NJ)
California Lutheran U (CA)
California Polytechnic State U, San Luis Obispo (CA)
California State U, Bakersfield (CA)
California State U, Fullerton (CA)
California State U, Long Beach (CA)
California State U, Los Angeles (CA)
California State U, Northridge (CA)
California State U, San Bernardino (CA)
California State U, San Marcos (CA)
Calvin Coll (MI)
Cameron U (OK)
Campbellsville U (KY)
Canisius Coll (NY)
Carson-Newman U (TN)
Carthage Coll (WI)
The Catholic U of America (DC)
Centenary Coll of Louisiana (LA)
Central Connecticut State U (CT)
Central Michigan U (MI)
Central State U (OH)
Central Washington U (WA)
Christopher Newport U (VA)
Clarion U of Pennsylvania (PA)
Clarkson U (NY)
Clark U (MA)
Coastal Carolina U (SC)
Colgate U (NY)
The Coll at Brockport, State U of New York (NY)
Coll of Charleston (SC)
Coll of Saint Benedict (MN)
Coll of the Holy Cross (MA)
Coll of the Ozarks (MO)
The Coll of William and Mary (VA)
The Colorado Coll (CO)
Colorado State U (CO)
Colorado State U–Pueblo (CO)
Columbia Coll (MO)
Columbia U (NY)
Concordia U Chicago (IL)
Connecticut Coll (CT)
Cornell Coll (IA)
Cornell U (NY)
Covenant Coll (GA)
Creighton U (NE)
Curry Coll (MA)
Dallas Baptist U (TX)
Dartmouth Coll (NH)
Davidson Coll (NC)
Dean Coll (MA)
DePaul U (IL)
DEREE - The American Coll of Greece (Greece)
Dickinson Coll (PA)
Dominican U (IL)
Drake U (IA)
Drew U (NJ)
Duquesne U (PA)
East Carolina U (NC)
Eastern Illinois U (IL)
Eastern Mennonite U (VA)
Eastern U (PA)
Eastern Washington U (WA)
East Stroudsburg U of Pennsylvania (PA)
East Tennessee State U (TN)
East Texas Baptist U (TX)
Eckerd Coll (FL)
Elizabeth City State U (NC)
Emmanuel Coll (MA)
The Evergreen State Coll (WA)
Excelsior Coll (NY)
Fairfield U (CT)
Fayetteville State U (NC)
Fitchburg State U (MA)
Florida Ag and Mech U (FL)
Florida Atlantic U (FL)
Fordham U (NY)
Fort Lewis Coll (CO)
Framingham State U (MA)
Franklin Pierce U (NH)
Furman U (SC)
Geneva Coll (PA)
George Mason U (VA)
Georgetown Coll (KY)
Georgia Coll & State U (GA)
Georgia Southern U (GA)
Georgia State U (GA)
Gonzaga U (WA)
Gordon Coll (MA)
Goshen Coll (IN)
Graceland U (IA)
Grand Valley State U (MI)
Greenville U (IL)
Grove City Coll (PA)
Hamilton Coll (NY)
Hamline U (MN)
Hanover Coll (IN)
Hardin-Simmons U (TX)
Hartwick Coll (NY)
Harvard U (MA)
Haverford Coll (PA)
Hillsdale Coll (MI)
Hiram Coll (OH)
Hofstra U (NY)
Hollins U (VA)
Hood Coll (MD)
Humboldt State U (CA)
Hunter Coll of the City U of New York (NY)
Idaho State U (ID)
Illinois Coll (IL)
Immaculata U (PA)
Indiana U Bloomington (IN)
Indiana U East (IN)
Indiana U Kokomo (IN)
Indiana U Northwest (IN)
Indiana U of Pennsylvania (PA)
Indiana U–Purdue U Indianapolis (IN)
Indiana U South Bend (IN)
Indiana U Southeast (IN)
Inter American U of Puerto Rico, San Germán Campus (PR)
Iona Coll (NY)
Iowa State U of Science and Technology (IA)
Ithaca Coll (NY)
Jackson State U (MS)
Jacksonville U (FL)
Johns Hopkins U (MD)
Juniata Coll (PA)
Kansas Wesleyan U (KS)
Kean U (NJ)
Kennesaw State U (GA)
King's Coll (PA)
Lafayette Coll (PA)
LaGrange Coll (GA)
Lake Forest Coll (IL)
Lamar U (TX)
La Salle U (PA)
Lasell Coll (MA)
Lebanon Valley Coll (PA)
Lee U (TN)
Lindenwood U (MO)
Linfield Coll (OR)
Lock Haven U of Pennsylvania (PA)
Loras Coll (IA)
Louisiana State U and A&M Coll (LA)
Loyola Marymount U (CA)
Loyola U Chicago (IL)
Loyola U New Orleans (LA)
Lycoming Coll (PA)
Macalester Coll (MN)
Madonna U (MI)
Manchester U (IN)
Manhattan Coll (NY)
Manhattanville Coll (NY)
Marian U (IN)

Marquette U (WI)
Marshall U (WV)
Marymount Manhattan Coll (NY)
Marymount U (VA)
Maryville U of Saint Louis (MO)
Marywood U (PA)
Massachusetts Coll of Liberal Arts (MA)
McDaniel Coll (MD)
McNeese State U (LA)
Mercer U, Macon (GA)
Mercy Coll (NY)
Merrimack Coll (MA)
Messiah Coll (PA)
Miami U (OH)
Miami U Hamilton (OH)
Michigan State U (MI)
Middlebury Coll (VT)
Middle Tennessee State U (TN)
Millersville U of Pennsylvania (PA)
Milligan Coll (TN)
Millikin U (IL)
Mills Coll (CA)
Minnesota State U Moorhead (MN)
Molloy Coll (NY)
Montclair State U (NJ)
Mount St. Joseph U (OH)
Mount Saint Mary Coll (NY)
Murray State U (KY)
Muskingum U (OH)
National U (CA)
Nazareth Coll of Rochester (NY)
New Coll of Florida (FL)
New England Coll (NH)
New Jersey City U (NJ)
New York U (NY)
North Carolina State U (NC)
Northeastern State U (OK)
Northern Illinois U (IL)
Northern Kentucky U (KY)
Northern State U (SD)
Northwestern Oklahoma State U (OK)
Northwestern U (IL)
Occidental Coll (CA)
Oglethorpe U (GA)
Ohio Dominican U (OH)
The Ohio State U (OH)
The Ohio State U at Mansfield (OH)
The Ohio State U at Marion (OH)
Ohio U (OH)
Ohio Wesleyan U (OH)
Oklahoma Baptist U (OK)
Oklahoma State U (OK)
Old Dominion U (VA)
Ottawa U (KS)
Ouachita Baptist U (AR)
Pacific Lutheran U (WA)
Pepperdine U, Malibu (CA)
Piedmont Coll (GA)
Pitzer Coll (CA)
Point Loma Nazarene U (CA)
Point U (GA)
Portland State U (OR)
Prairie View A&M U (TX)
Princeton U (NJ)
Providence Coll (RI)
Purchase Coll, State U of New York (NY)
Purdue U (IN)
Purdue U Northwest (IN)
Queens Coll of the City U of New York (NY)
Queens U of Charlotte (NC)
Radford U (VA)
Randolph Coll (VA)
Randolph-Macon Coll (VA)
Regis U (CO)
Reinhardt U (GA)
Rhode Island Coll (RI)
Rice U (TX)
Rider U (NJ)
Roanoke Coll (VA)
Rockford U (IL)
Rocky Mountain Coll (MT)
Rollins Coll (FL)
Sacred Heart U (CT)
The Sage Colls (NY)
Saginaw Valley State U (MI)
Saint Anselm Coll (NH)
Saint Francis U (PA)
St. John Fisher Coll (NY)
Saint John's U (MN)
St. Joseph's Coll, Long Island Campus (NY)
St. Joseph's Coll, New York (NY)
Saint Joseph's U (PA)
Saint Leo U (FL)
Saint Louis U (MO)
St. Mary's Coll of Maryland (MD)
St. Mary's U (TX)
Saint Mary's U of Minnesota (MN)
St. Norbert Coll (WI)
Saint Vincent Coll (PA)
Salisbury U (MD)
Salve Regina U (RI)
Samford U (AL)
San Diego State U (CA)
San Francisco State U (CA)
San Jose State U (CA)
Sarah Lawrence Coll (NY)
Scripps Coll (CA)
Seattle U (WA)
Seton Hill U (PA)
Skidmore Coll (NY)
Sonoma State U (CA)
Southeastern Louisiana U (LA)
Southern Illinois U Carbondale (IL)
Southern Illinois U Edwardsville (IL)
Southern U and Ag and Mech Coll (LA)
Southwest Baptist U (MO)
Southwestern U (TX)
Spring Hill Coll (AL)
State U of New York at Fredonia (NY)
State U of New York at Plattsburgh (NY)
State U of New York Coll at Geneseo (NY)
State U of New York Coll at Potsdam (NY)
Stetson U (FL)
Stockton U (NJ)
Stonehill Coll (MA)
Syracuse U (NY)
Taylor U (IN)
Temple U (PA)
Texas A&M Intl U (TX)
Texas A&M U–Central Texas (TX)
Texas Christian U (TX)
Texas Lutheran U (TX)
Texas Tech U (TX)
Texas Woman's U (TX)
Trevecca Nazarene U (TN)
Truman State U (MO)
Tulane U (LA)
Union Coll (KY)
Union Coll (NY)
U at Buffalo, the State U of New York (NY)
U of Arkansas (AR)
U of California, Davis (CA)
U of California, Irvine (CA)
U of California, Los Angeles (CA)
U of California, Merced (CA)
U of California, Riverside (CA)
U of California, Santa Cruz (CA)
U of Central Arkansas (AR)
U of Central Florida (FL)
U of Chicago (IL)
U of Colorado Denver (CO)
U of Dayton (OH)
U of Detroit Mercy (MI)
U of Florida (FL)
U of Georgia (GA)
U of Guam (GU)
U of Hawaii at Manoa (HI)
U of Houston (TX)
U of Houston–Clear Lake (TX)
U of Houston–Downtown (TX)
U of Idaho (ID)
U of Kentucky (KY)
U of La Verne (CA)
U of Louisville (KY)
U of Lynchburg (VA)
U of Maine (ME)
U of Mary Hardin-Baylor (TX)
U of Maryland, Baltimore County (MD)
U of Maryland, Coll Park (MD)
U of Maryland Eastern Shore (MD)
U of Massachusetts Amherst (MA)
U of Massachusetts Boston (MA)
U of Massachusetts Dartmouth (MA)
U of Massachusetts Lowell (MA)
U of Memphis (TN)
U of Michigan (MI)
U of Michigan–Dearborn (MI)
U of Minnesota, Duluth (MN)
U of Minnesota, Morris (MN)
U of Minnesota, Twin Cities Campus (MN)
U of Missouri (MO)
U of Montevallo (AL)
U of Mount Union (OH)
U of Nebraska–Lincoln (NE)
U of Nevada, Las Vegas (NV)
U of Nevada, Reno (NV)
U of New Hampshire (NH)
U of New Mexico (NM)
U of North Carolina at Asheville (NC)
The U of North Carolina at Chapel Hill (NC)
The U of North Carolina at Charlotte (NC)
The U of North Carolina at Greensboro (NC)
The U of North Carolina at Pembroke (NC)
U of North Dakota (ND)
U of Northern Colorado (CO)
U of Northern Iowa (IA)
U of North Florida (FL)
U of Notre Dame (IN)
U of Oregon (OR)
U of Pennsylvania (PA)
U of Pittsburgh (PA)
U of Pittsburgh at Bradford (PA)
U of Providence (MT)
U of Puget Sound (WA)
U of Regina (SK, Canada)
U of Richmond (VA)
U of Saint Francis (IN)
U of St. Thomas (MN)
U of San Diego (CA)
U of San Francisco (CA)
U of Sioux Falls (SD)
U of South Alabama (AL)
U of South Carolina (SC)
U of South Carolina Aiken (SC)
U of South Dakota (SD)
U of Southern Indiana (IN)
U of South Florida (FL)
The U of Tampa (FL)
The U of Tennessee (TN)
The U of Tennessee at Martin (TN)
The U of Texas at Austin (TX)
The U of Texas at El Paso (TX)
The U of Texas of the Permian Basin (TX)
The U of Texas Rio Grande Valley (TX)
U of the Incarnate Word (TX)
The U of Toledo (OH)
The U of Tulsa (OK)
U of Vermont (VT)
U of Virginia (VA)
U of Washington (WA)
The U of West Alabama (AL)
U of West Georgia (GA)
U of Wisconsin–Eau Claire (WI)
U of Wisconsin–La Crosse (WI)
U of Wisconsin–Milwaukee (WI)
U of Wisconsin–River Falls (WI)
U of Wyoming (WY)
Utah State U (UT)
Utica Coll (NY)
Valparaiso U (IN)
Vanguard U of Southern California (CA)
Vassar Coll (NY)
Virginia Commonwealth U (VA)
Virginia Polytechnic Inst and State U (VA)
Wartburg Coll (IA)
Washington & Jefferson Coll (PA)
Washington State U (WA)
Washington State U–Vancouver (WA)
Washington U in St. Louis (MO)
Waynesburg U (PA)
Weber State U (UT)
Wesleyan U (CT)
West Chester U of Pennsylvania (PA)
Western Connecticut State U (CT)
Western Illinois U (IL)
Western Kentucky U (KY)
Western State Colorado U (CO)
Western Washington U (WA)
Westmont Coll (CA)
West Virginia State U (WV)
Wheaton Coll (IL)
Wheaton Coll (MA)
Whittier Coll (CA)
Whitworth U (WA)
Widener U (PA)
Wilkes U (PA)
Willamette U (OR)
Williams Coll (MA)
Winthrop U (SC)
Wofford Coll (SC)
Worcester State U (MA)
Wright State U–Lake Campus (OH)
Youngstown State U (OH)

SOCIOLOGY AND ANTHROPOLOGY

Albion Coll (MI)
American U of Beirut (Lebanon)
Coll of Staten Island of the City U of New York (NY)
Earlham Coll (IN)
Fairfield U (CT)
High Point U (NC)
Lewis & Clark Coll (OR)
Lycoming Coll (PA)
Middlebury Coll (VT)
Millsaps Coll (MS)
Pace U (NY)
Rochester Inst of Technology (NY)
St. Olaf Coll (MN)
Taylor U (IN)
U of Illinois at Springfield (IL)
U of Maine at Farmington (ME)
U of Massachusetts Dartmouth (MA)
U of Puget Sound (WA)
Ursinus Coll (PA)
Washington and Lee U (VA)
Wofford Coll (SC)

SOIL CHEMISTRY AND PHYSICS

The U of Tennessee (TN)

SOIL SCIENCE AND AGRONOMY

California Polytechnic State U, San Luis Obispo (CA)
Colorado State U (CO)
Michigan State U (MI)
Oklahoma State U (OK)
Purdue U (IN)
U of California, Davis (CA)
U of Florida (FL)
U of Georgia (GA)
U of Nebraska–Lincoln (NE)
Utah State U (UT)

SOIL SCIENCES RELATED

North Carolina State U (NC)
U of Hawaii at Manoa (HI)
U of Idaho (ID)

SOUTH ASIAN LANGUAGES

Northwestern U (IL)
U of Chicago (IL)
U of Washington (WA)

SOUTHEAST ASIAN LANGUAGES

Harvard U (MA)

SPANISH

Adams State U (CO)
Adelphi U (NY)
Agnes Scott Coll (GA)
Albion Coll (MI)
Albright Coll (PA)
Alfred U (NY)
Allegheny Coll (PA)
American U (DC)
Angelo State U (TX)
Assumption Coll (MA)
Auburn U (AL)
Aurora U (IL)
Austin Coll (TX)
Baker U (KS)
Baldwin Wallace U (OH)
Barton Coll (NC)
Baruch Coll of the City U of New York (NY)
Baylor U (TX)
Bellarmine U (KY)
Beloit Coll (WI)
Benedictine U (IL)
Bentley U (MA)
Berea Coll (KY)
Bethel U (MN)
Blackburn Coll (IL)
Boston Coll (MA)
Boston U (MA)
Bowling Green State U (OH)
Bradley U (IL)
Bridgewater Coll (VA)
Bridgewater State U (MA)
Bryant U (RI)
Bucknell U (PA)
Buena Vista U (IA)
Butler U (IN)
Caldwell U (NJ)
California Lutheran U (CA)
California State U, Bakersfield (CA)
California State U, Fullerton (CA)
California State U, Long Beach (CA)
California State U, Los Angeles (CA)
California State U, Monterey Bay (CA)
California State U, Northridge (CA)
California State U, San Bernardino (CA)
California State U, San Marcos (CA)
Calvin Coll (MI)
Canisius Coll (NY)
Carson-Newman U (TN)
Carthage Coll (WI)
The Catholic U of America (DC)
Cedarville U (OH)
Central Connecticut State U (CT)
Central Michigan U (MI)
Central Washington U (WA)
Christopher Newport U (VA)
Claremont McKenna Coll (CA)
Clark U (MA)
Colgate U (NY)
The Coll at Brockport, State U of New York (NY)
Coll of Charleston (SC)
Coll of Coastal Georgia (GA)
The Coll of Idaho (ID)
Coll of Saint Benedict (MN)
The Coll of St. Scholastica (MN)
Coll of Staten Island of the City U of New York (NY)
Coll of the Holy Cross (MA)
Coll of the Ozarks (MO)
The Colorado Coll (CO)
Columbia U (NY)
Concordia U Chicago (IL)
Connecticut Coll (CT)
Cornell Coll (IA)
Cornell U (NY)
Creighton U (NE)
Dallas Baptist U (TX)
Dartmouth Coll (NH)
Davidson Coll (NC)
DePaul U (IL)
Dickinson Coll (PA)
Dominican U (IL)
Drew U (NJ)
Drury U (MO)
Duquesne U (PA)
Earlham Coll (IN)
Eastern Mennonite U (VA)
Eastern U (PA)
Eastern Washington U (WA)
East Stroudsburg U of Pennsylvania (PA)
Eckerd Coll (FL)
Emmanuel Coll (MA)
Fairfield U (CT)
Fayetteville State U (NC)
Florida Atlantic U (FL)
Florida Southern Coll (FL)
Fordham U (NY)
Fort Lewis Coll (CO)
Framingham State U (MA)
Furman U (SC)
Georgetown Coll (KY)
Georgia State U (GA)
Gonzaga U (WA)
Gordon Coll (MA)
Goshen Coll (IN)
Graceland U (IA)
Grand Valley State U (MI)
Greenville U (IL)
Grove City Coll (PA)
Hamline U (MN)
Hampden-Sydney Coll (VA)
Hanover Coll (IN)
Harding U (AR)
Hardin-Simmons U (TX)
Hartwick Coll (NY)
Haverford Coll (PA)
High Point U (NC)
Hillsdale Coll (MI)
Hofstra U (NY)
Hollins U (VA)

Hood Coll (MD)
Humboldt State U (CA)
Hunter Coll of the City U of New York (NY)
Idaho State U (ID)
Illinois Coll (IL)
Indiana U Bloomington (IN)
Indiana U East (IN)
Indiana U Northwest (IN)
Indiana U of Pennsylvania (PA)
Indiana U–Purdue U Indianapolis (IN)
Indiana U South Bend (IN)
Indiana U Southeast (IN)
Iona Coll (NY)
Ithaca Coll (NY)
Jacksonville U (FL)
Johns Hopkins U (MD)
Johnson C. Smith U (NC)
Juniata Coll (PA)
Kalamazoo Coll (MI)
Kean U (NJ)
King's Coll (PA)
King U (TN)
Knox Coll (IL)
Lafayette Coll (PA)
LaGrange Coll (GA)
Lake Forest Coll (IL)
La Salle U (PA)
La Sierra U (CA)
Lawrence U (WI)
Lebanon Valley Coll (PA)
Lee U (TN)
Lewis & Clark Coll (OR)
Liberty U (VA)
Lindenwood U (MO)
Linfield Coll (OR)
Lipscomb U (TN)
Loras Coll (IA)
Louisiana State U and A&M Coll (LA)
Loyola Marymount U (CA)
Loyola U Chicago (IL)
Loyola U New Orleans (LA)
Lycoming Coll (PA)
Macalester Coll (MN)
Madonna U (MI)
Manchester U (IN)
Manhattan Coll (NY)
Manhattanville Coll (NY)
Marian U (IN)
Marist Coll (NY)
Marquette U (WI)
Marywood U (PA)
McDaniel Coll (MD)
Mercer U, Macon (GA)
Mercy Coll (NY)
Merrimack Coll (MA)
Messiah Coll (PA)
Miami U (OH)
Miami U Hamilton (OH)
Michigan State U (MI)
Middlebury Coll (VT)
Milligan Coll (TN)
Millikin U (IL)
Millsaps Coll (MS)
Mills Coll (CA)
Minnesota State U Moorhead (MN)
Montclair State U (NJ)
Morningside Coll (IA)
Mount Saint Mary Coll (NY)
Murray State U (KY)
Muskingum U (OH)
National U (CA)
Nazareth Coll of Rochester (NY)
New Coll of Florida (FL)
New Jersey City U (NJ)
New York U (NY)
North Carolina State U (NC)
Northeastern State U (OK)
Northern Illinois U (IL)
Northern Kentucky U (KY)
Northern State U (SD)
Northwest Christian U (OR)
Northwestern U (IL)
Northwest Missouri State U (MO)
Occidental Coll (CA)
Oglethorpe U (GA)
The Ohio State U (OH)
Ohio U (OH)
Ohio Wesleyan U (OH)
Oklahoma Baptist U (OK)
Oklahoma Christian U (OK)
Oklahoma State U (OK)
Ouachita Baptist U (AR)
Pace U (NY)
Pace U, Pleasantville Campus (NY)
Pepperdine U, Malibu (CA)
Pitzer Coll (CA)
Point Loma Nazarene U (CA)
Portland State U (OR)
Princeton U (NJ)
Providence Coll (RI)
Queens Coll of the City U of New York (NY)
Queens U of Charlotte (NC)
Randolph Coll (VA)
Randolph-Macon Coll (VA)
Regis U (CO)
Reinhardt U (GA)
Rhode Island Coll (RI)
Rhodes Coll (TN)
Rice U (TX)
Rider U (NJ)
Roanoke Coll (VA)
Rockford U (IL)
Rollins Coll (FL)
Sacred Heart U (CT)
Saginaw Valley State U (MI)
Saint Anselm Coll (NH)
Saint Francis U (PA)
St. John Fisher Coll (NY)
Saint John's U (MN)
St. Joseph's Coll, Long Island Campus (NY)
St. Joseph's Coll, New York (NY)
Saint Joseph's U (PA)
Saint Louis U (MO)
St. Mary's U (TX)
Saint Mary's U of Minnesota (MN)
St. Norbert Coll (WI)
St. Olaf Coll (MN)
Saint Vincent Coll (PA)
Salisbury U (MD)
Salve Regina U (RI)
Samford U (AL)
San Diego State U (CA)
San Francisco State U (CA)
San Jose State U (CA)
Sarah Lawrence Coll (NY)
Scripps Coll (CA)
Seattle U (WA)
Seton Hill U (PA)
Skidmore Coll (NY)
Sonoma State U (CA)
Southeastern Louisiana U (LA)
Southern Arkansas U–Magnolia (AR)
Southern U and Ag and Mech Coll (LA)
Southwest Baptist U (MO)
Southwestern U (TX)
Spring Hill Coll (AL)
State U of New York at Fredonia (NY)
State U of New York at Plattsburgh (NY)
State U of New York Coll at Geneseo (NY)
State U of New York Coll at Potsdam (NY)
Stetson U (FL)
Stonehill Coll (MA)
Syracuse U (NY)
Taylor U (IN)
Temple U (PA)
Texas A&M Intl U (TX)
Texas Christian U (TX)
Texas Lutheran U (TX)
Texas Tech U (TX)
Trinity Christian Coll (IL)
Truman State U (MO)
Tulane U (LA)
Union Coll (NY)
U at Buffalo, the State U of New York (NY)
U of Arkansas (AR)
U of California, Davis (CA)
U of California, Irvine (CA)
U of California, Los Angeles (CA)
U of California, Riverside (CA)
U of California, Santa Cruz (CA)
U of Central Arkansas (AR)
U of Central Florida (FL)
U of Colorado Denver (CO)
U of Dallas (TX)
U of Dayton (OH)
The U of Findlay (OH)
U of Florida (FL)
U of Georgia (GA)
U of Hawaii at Manoa (HI)
U of Houston (TX)
U of Houston–Downtown (TX)
U of Idaho (ID)
U of Kentucky (KY)
U of La Verne (CA)
U of Louisville (KY)
U of Lynchburg (VA)
U of Maine (ME)
U of Mary Hardin-Baylor (TX)
U of Maryland, Coll Park (MD)
U of Massachusetts Amherst (MA)
U of Massachusetts Boston (MA)
U of Massachusetts Dartmouth (MA)
U of Michigan (MI)
U of Michigan–Dearborn (MI)
U of Minnesota, Duluth (MN)
U of Minnesota, Morris (MN)
U of Minnesota, Twin Cities Campus (MN)
U of Mount Union (OH)
U of Nebraska–Lincoln (NE)
U of Nevada, Las Vegas (NV)
U of Nevada, Reno (NV)
U of New Hampshire (NH)
U of New Mexico (NM)
U of North Carolina at Asheville (NC)
The U of North Carolina at Charlotte (NC)
The U of North Carolina at Pembroke (NC)
U of North Dakota (ND)
U of Northern Colorado (CO)
U of Northern Iowa (IA)
U of North Florida (FL)
U of Northwestern–St. Paul (MN)
U of Notre Dame (IN)
U of Oregon (OR)
U of Pennsylvania (PA)
U of Pittsburgh (PA)
U of Puget Sound (WA)
U of Regina (SK, Canada)
U of Richmond (VA)
U of St. Thomas (MN)
U of St. Thomas (TX)
U of San Diego (CA)
U of San Francisco (CA)
U of Sioux Falls (SD)
U of South Carolina (SC)
U of South Dakota (SD)
U of Southern Indiana (IN)
U of South Florida (FL)
The U of Tampa (FL)
The U of Tennessee (TN)
The U of Tennessee at Martin (TN)
The U of Texas at Austin (TX)
The U of Texas at El Paso (TX)
The U of Texas of the Permian Basin (TX)
The U of Texas Rio Grande Valley (TX)
U of the Incarnate Word (TX)
The U of the South (TN)
The U of Toledo (OH)
The U of Tulsa (OK)
U of Vermont (VT)
U of Virginia (VA)
U of Washington (WA)
U of Wisconsin–Eau Claire (WI)
U of Wisconsin–La Crosse (WI)
U of Wisconsin–Milwaukee (WI)
U of Wyoming (WY)
Ursinus Coll (PA)
Utah State U (UT)
Utah Valley U (UT)
Valley City State U (ND)
Valparaiso U (IN)
Vassar Coll (NY)
Virginia Polytechnic Inst and State U (VA)
Wabash Coll (IN)
Wartburg Coll (IA)
Washington & Jefferson Coll (PA)
Washington and Lee U (VA)
Washington State U (WA)
Washington U in St. Louis (MO)
Weber State U (UT)
Wesleyan Coll (GA)
West Chester U of Pennsylvania (PA)
Western Connecticut State U (CT)
Western Kentucky U (KY)
Western State Colorado U (CO)
Western Washington U (WA)
Westmont Coll (CA)
Wheaton Coll (IL)
Whittier Coll (CA)
Whitworth U (WA)
Widener U (PA)
Wilkes U (PA)
Willamette U (OR)
William Jewell Coll (MO)
Williams Coll (MA)
Wofford Coll (SC)
Worcester State U (MA)
Youngstown State U (OH)

SPANISH AND IBERIAN STUDIES

Austin Coll (TX)
Brandeis U (MA)
Columbia U (NY)
Fordham U (NY)
New York U (NY)
Wabash Coll (IN)
Wesleyan U (CT)

SPANISH LANGUAGE TEACHER EDUCATION

Adams State U (CO)
Albion Coll (MI)
Auburn U (AL)
Aurora U (IL)
Baylor U (TX)
Bethel U (MN)
Blackburn Coll (IL)
Buena Vista U (IA)
California Lutheran U (CA)
Calvin Coll (MI)
Canisius Coll (NY)
The Catholic U of America (DC)
Cedarville U (OH)
Central Michigan U (MI)
Central Washington U (WA)
Coll of Saint Mary (NE)
Coll of Staten Island of the City U of New York (NY)
Coll of the Ozarks (MO)
Eastern Washington U (WA)
Fort Lewis Coll (CO)
Goshen Coll (IN)
Grand Valley State U (MI)
Greenville U (IL)
Grove City Coll (PA)
Harding U (AR)
Hardin-Simmons U (TX)
Hofstra U (NY)
Indiana U–Purdue U Indianapolis (IN)
Indiana U South Bend (IN)
Inter American U of Puerto Rico, Aguadilla Campus (PR)
Inter American U of Puerto Rico, Barranquitas Campus (PR)
Inter American U of Puerto Rico, San Germán Campus (PR)
Iona Coll (NY)
Ithaca Coll (NY)
Juniata Coll (PA)
Lee U (TN)
Lipscomb U (TN)
Louisiana Coll (LA)
Lubbock Christian U (TX)
Manchester U (IN)
Manhattanville Coll (NY)
Marist Coll (NY)
Martin Luther Coll (MN)
Marywood U (PA)
Merrimack Coll (MA)
Messiah Coll (PA)
Miami U (OH)
Miami U Hamilton (OH)
Michigan State U (MI)
Minnesota State U Moorhead (MN)
Morningside Coll (IA)
New York U (NY)
Northeastern State U (OK)
Northern State U (SD)
Northwest Missouri State U (MO)
Ohio U (OH)
Ohio Wesleyan U (OH)
Oklahoma Baptist U (OK)
Pace U (NY)
Providence Coll (RI)
Queens Coll of the City U of New York (NY)
Rhode Island Coll (RI)
Saginaw Valley State U (MI)
St. John Fisher Coll (NY)
St. Joseph's Coll, Long Island Campus (NY)
St. Joseph's Coll, New York (NY)
Saint Joseph's U (PA)
Saint Mary's U of Minnesota (MN)
Salve Regina U (RI)
Southern U and Ag and Mech Coll (LA)
Spring Hill Coll (AL)
State U of New York Coll at Potsdam (NY)
Syracuse U (NY)
Taylor U (IN)
Trinity Christian Coll (IL)
The U of Findlay (OH)
U of Maine (ME)
U of Mary Hardin-Baylor (TX)
U of Nebraska–Lincoln (NE)
U of Nevada, Las Vegas (NV)
U of Northwestern–St. Paul (MN)
U of St. Thomas (MN)
U of Sioux Falls (SD)
U of South Dakota (SD)
U of Wisconsin–Milwaukee (WI)
Utah Valley U (UT)
Valparaiso U (IN)
Washington U in St. Louis (MO)
Weber State U (UT)
Western Washington U (WA)
Whitworth U (WA)
Widener U (PA)
Youngstown State U (OH)

SPECIAL EDUCATION

Adams State U (CO)
Alabama State U (AL)
Auburn U (AL)
Auburn U at Montgomery (AL)
Aurora U (IL)
Austin Peay State U (TN)
Avila U (MO)
Barton Coll (NC)
Baylor U (TX)
Bellarmine U (KY)
Benedictine U (IL)
Bennett Coll (NC)
Bethany Lutheran Coll (MN)
Boston U (MA)
Bowling Green State U (OH)
Bridgewater State U (MA)
Buena Vista U (IA)
Calvin Coll (MI)
Carson-Newman U (TN)
Carthage Coll (WI)
Cedarville U (OH)
Central State U (OH)
Central Washington U (WA)
Christian Brothers U (TN)
Coastal Carolina U (SC)
The Coll at Brockport, State U of New York (NY)
Coll of Charleston (SC)
The Coll of Saint Rose (NY)
Concordia U Chicago (IL)
Curry Coll (MA)
Dallas Baptist U (TX)
Daytona State Coll (FL)
DePaul U (IL)
East Carolina U (NC)
Eastern Illinois U (IL)
Eastern Washington U (WA)
East Tennessee State U (TN)
Elizabeth City State U (NC)
Fitchburg State U (MA)
Florida Atlantic U (FL)
Geneva Coll (PA)
Georgia Coll & State U (GA)
Georgia Southern U (GA)
Gonzaga U (WA)
Goshen Coll (IN)
Grand Valley State U (MI)
Greenville U (IL)
Grove City Coll (PA)
High Point U (NC)
Idaho State U (ID)
Indiana State U (IN)
Indiana U Bloomington (IN)
Indiana U of Pennsylvania (PA)
Indiana U South Bend (IN)
Indiana U Southeast (IN)
Inter American U of Puerto Rico, Barranquitas Campus (PR)
Inter American U of Puerto Rico, Fajardo Campus (PR)
Inter American U of Puerto Rico, San Germán Campus (PR)
Jackson State U (MS)
Jacksonville U (FL)
Lebanon Valley Coll (PA)
Lee U (TN)
Lesley U (MA)
Liberty U (VA)
Lindenwood U (MO)
Lipscomb U (TN)
Loyola U Chicago (IL)

Manchester U (IN)
Manhattan Coll (NY)
Mansfield U of Pennsylvania (PA)
Marian U (IN)
Martin Luther Coll (MN)
Marymount U (VA)
Marywood U (PA)
Merrimack Coll (MA)
Miami U (OH)
Miami U Hamilton (OH)
Michigan State U (MI)
Middle Tennessee State U (TN)
Millersville U of Pennsylvania (PA)
Minnesota State U Moorhead (MN)
Morningside Coll (IA)
Mount Marty Coll (SD)
Mount St. Joseph U (OH)
Murray State U (KY)
Muskingum U (OH)
National U (CA)
Nazareth Coll of Rochester (NY)
New England Coll (NH)
New Jersey City U (NJ)
New York U (NY)
Northern Kentucky U (KY)
Northern State U (SD)
Northwestern Oklahoma State U (OK)
Oakland City U (IN)
Ohio Dominican U (OH)
The Ohio State U (OH)
Ohio U (OH)
Oklahoma Baptist U (OK)
Pace U (NY)
Pace U, Pleasantville Campus (NY)
Pfeiffer U (NC)
Portland State U (OR)
Providence Coll (RI)
Rhode Island Coll (RI)
Rockford U (IL)
Saginaw Valley State U (MI)
Saint Francis U (PA)
St. John Fisher Coll (NY)
St. Joseph's Coll, Long Island Campus (NY)
St. Joseph's Coll, New York (NY)
Saint Martin's U (WA)
Salve Regina U (RI)
San Jose State U (CA)
Southeastern Louisiana U (LA)
Southeastern U (FL)
Southeast Missouri State U (MO)
Southern Illinois U Carbondale (IL)
Southern Illinois U Edwardsville (IL)
Southern U and Ag and Mech Coll (LA)
State U of New York Coll at Geneseo (NY)
Stonehill Coll (MA)
Texas A&M Intl U (TX)
Texas Christian U (TX)
Towson U (MD)
Trevecca Nazarene U (TN)
Trinity Christian Coll (IL)
Université de Sherbrooke (QC, Canada)
U of Arkansas (AR)
U of Central Arkansas (AR)
U of Central Florida (FL)
U of Dayton (OH)
U of Detroit Mercy (MI)
The U of Findlay (OH)
U of Florida (FL)
U of Georgia (GA)
U of Hawaii at Manoa (HI)
U of Kentucky (KY)
U of Maine at Farmington (ME)
U of Maryland, Coll Park (MD)
U of Memphis (TN)
U of Michigan–Dearborn (MI)
U of Minnesota, Twin Cities Campus (MN)
U of Mount Union (OH)
U of Nevada, Las Vegas (NV)
U of New Mexico (NM)
The U of North Carolina at Charlotte (NC)
The U of North Carolina at Greensboro (NC)
The U of North Carolina at Pembroke (NC)
U of Northern Colorado (CO)
U of North Florida (FL)
U of Providence (MT)
U of Saint Francis (IN)
U of South Alabama (AL)
U of South Carolina Aiken (SC)
U of South Dakota (SD)
U of South Florida (FL)
The U of Tennessee (TN)
The U of Toledo (OH)
The U of West Alabama (AL)
U of West Georgia (GA)
U of Wisconsin–Eau Claire (WI)
U of Wisconsin–Milwaukee (WI)
U of Wyoming (WY)
Utah State U (UT)
Vincennes U (IN)
Waynesburg U (PA)
Weber State U (UT)
West Chester U of Pennsylvania (PA)
Western Illinois U (IL)
Western Kentucky U (KY)
Western Washington U (WA)
Whitworth U (WA)
Widener U (PA)
Winthrop U (SC)
Youngstown State U (OH)

SPECIAL EDUCATION–EARLY CHILDHOOD
Aurora U (IL)
Bowling Green State U (OH)
Canisius Coll (NY)
Clarion U of Pennsylvania (PA)
Eastern Washington U (WA)
East Stroudsburg U of Pennsylvania (PA)
Harding U (AR)
Indiana U of Pennsylvania (PA)
Inter American U of Puerto Rico, Aguadilla Campus (PR)
Judson U (IL)
Juniata Coll (PA)
Lee U (TN)
Lindenwood U (MO)
Lock Haven U of Pennsylvania (PA)
Missouri Baptist U (MO)
State U of New York Coll at Geneseo (NY)
Syracuse U (NY)
U of Maine at Farmington (ME)
U of Mount Union (OH)
U of Vermont (VT)
U of Wisconsin–Milwaukee (WI)
Western Washington U (WA)
Youngstown State U (OH)

SPECIAL EDUCATION–ELEMENTARY SCHOOL
Canisius Coll (NY)
Granite State Coll (NH)
La Salle U (PA)
Lee U (TN)
Molloy Coll (NY)
Rhode Island Coll (RI)
Syracuse U (NY)
Towson U (MD)
U of Massachusetts Lowell (MA)
U of Mount Union (OH)
U of Wisconsin–Milwaukee (WI)
U of Wyoming (WY)
Weber State U (UT)

SPECIAL EDUCATION–GIFTED AND TALENTED
Canisius Coll (NY)
Grand Valley State U (MI)
U of Providence (MT)

SPECIAL EDUCATION–INDIVIDUALS WHO ARE DEVELOPMENTALLY DELAYED
Millikin U (IL)

SPECIAL EDUCATION–INDIVIDUALS WITH EMOTIONAL DISTURBANCES
Central Michigan U (MI)
Grand Valley State U (MI)
Morningside Coll (IA)
U of Detroit Mercy (MI)

SPECIAL EDUCATION–INDIVIDUALS WITH HEARING IMPAIRMENTS
Barton Coll (NC)
Boston U (MA)
Bowling Green State U (OH)
Canisius Coll (NY)
Grand Valley State U (MI)
Michigan State U (MI)
Texas Christian U (TX)
The U of North Carolina at Greensboro (NC)
U of North Florida (FL)
The U of Tulsa (OK)
Utah Valley U (UT)

SPECIAL EDUCATION–INDIVIDUALS WITH INTELLECTUAL DISABILITIES
Bowling Green State U (OH)
Brenau U (GA)
Central Michigan U (MI)
Grand Valley State U (MI)
Manchester U (IN)
Morningside Coll (IA)

SPECIAL EDUCATION–INDIVIDUALS WITH MULTIPLE DISABILITIES
AdventHealth U (FL)
Bowling Green State U (OH)
Bradley U (IL)
Central Michigan U (MI)
Grand Valley State U (MI)
Lee U (TN)
Missouri Baptist U (MO)
Northwest Missouri State U (MO)
Wright State U–Lake Campus (OH)

SPECIAL EDUCATION–INDIVIDUALS WITH ORTHOPEDIC AND OTHER PHYSICAL HEALTH IMPAIRMENTS
Grand Valley State U (MI)
U of Puerto Rico–Bayamón (PR)

SPECIAL EDUCATION–INDIVIDUALS WITH SPECIFIC LEARNING DISABILITIES
Appalachian State U (NC)
Baldwin Wallace U (OH)
Bowling Green State U (OH)
Bradley U (IL)
Canisius Coll (NY)
Judson U (IL)
Michigan State U (MI)
Northeastern State U (OK)
Northwestern U (IL)
U of Detroit Mercy (MI)

SPECIAL EDUCATION–INDIVIDUALS WITH SPEECH/LANGUAGE IMPAIRMENTS
Baylor U (TX)
Emerson Coll (MA)
Ithaca Coll (NY)
Pace U (NY)
The U of Toledo (OH)

SPECIAL EDUCATION–JUNIOR HIGH/MIDDLE SCHOOL
East Stroudsburg U of Pennsylvania (PA)
La Salle U (PA)
U of Wisconsin–Milwaukee (WI)

SPECIAL EDUCATION RELATED
Auburn U (AL)
Bowling Green State U (OH)
Brenau U (GA)
Canisius Coll (NY)
Clarion U of Pennsylvania (PA)
Dakota State U (SD)
East Carolina U (NC)
Hood Coll (MD)
Kean U (NJ)
Lee U (TN)
Purdue U (IN)
U of Missouri (MO)
U of Nebraska–Lincoln (NE)
The U of North Carolina at Charlotte (NC)
U of Southern Indiana (IN)

SPECIAL EDUCATION–SECONDARY SCHOOL
Canisius Coll (NY)
Lee U (TN)
Molloy Coll (NY)
Rhode Island Coll (RI)
U of Wisconsin–Milwaukee (WI)

SPECIAL PRODUCTS MARKETING
Central Washington U (WA)
Dominican U (IL)
Fashion Inst of Technology (NY)
Rochester Inst of Technology (NY)
Saint Joseph's U (PA)

SPEECH COMMUNICATION AND RHETORIC
Alabama State U (AL)
Albright Coll (PA)
Alfred U (NY)
Allegheny Coll (PA)
Alverno Coll (WI)
American U (DC)
Appalachian State U (NC)
Arkansas Tech U (AR)
Auburn U at Montgomery (AL)
Aurora U (IL)
Austin Coll (TX)
Avila U (MO)
Baldwin Wallace U (OH)
Baylor U (TX)
Bellarmine U (KY)
Benedictine U (IL)
Blackburn Coll (IL)
Bowling Green State U (OH)
Bridgewater State U (MA)
Bryant U (RI)
Buena Vista U (IA)
Caldwell U (NJ)
California Polytechnic State U, San Luis Obispo (CA)
California State U, Fullerton (CA)
California State U, San Marcos (CA)
California U of Pennsylvania (PA)
Calvin Coll (MI)
Carthage Coll (WI)
The Catholic U of America (DC)
Cedarville U (OH)
Central Michigan U (MI)
Champlain Coll (VT)
Christopher Newport U (VA)
Clarkson U (NY)
Coastal Carolina U (SC)
The Coll at Brockport, State U of New York (NY)
Coll of Charleston (SC)
The Coll of St. Scholastica (MN)
Coll of Staten Island of the City U of New York (NY)
Colorado State U (CO)
Columbia Coll (MO)
Concordia U Chicago (IL)
Creighton U (NE)
Culver-Stockton Coll (MO)
Dallas Baptist U (TX)
DePaul U (IL)
Dominican U (IL)
Duquesne U (PA)
East Carolina U (NC)
Eastern Oregon U (OR)
Eastern U (PA)
Eastern Washington U (WA)
Eckerd Coll (FL)
Elizabeth City State U (NC)
Embry-Riddle Aeronautical U–Daytona (FL)
Embry-Riddle Aeronautical U–Worldwide (FL)
Emerson Coll (MA)
Emmanuel Coll (MA)
Excelsior Coll (NY)
Fairfield U (CT)
Fayetteville State U (NC)
Fitchburg State U (MA)
Florida Atlantic U (FL)
Furman U (SC)
Georgia State U (GA)
Gordon Coll (MA)
Graceland U (IA)
Greenville U (IL)
Grove City Coll (PA)
Gwynedd Mercy U (PA)
Hamline U (MN)
Harding U (AR)
Hardin-Simmons U (TX)
Hillsdale Coll (MI)
Hofstra U (NY)
Indiana State U (IN)
Indiana U Bloomington (IN)
Indiana U East (IN)
Indiana U Kokomo (IN)
Indiana U Northwest (IN)
Indiana U of Pennsylvania (PA)
Indiana U–Purdue U Indianapolis (IN)
Indiana U South Bend (IN)
Indiana U Southeast (IN)
Iona Coll (NY)
Iowa State U of Science and Technology (IA)
Judson U (IL)
Juniata Coll (PA)
Kansas Wesleyan U (KS)
Kean U (NJ)
Kennesaw State U (GA)
Kuyper Coll (MI)
La Sierra U (CA)
Lawrence Technological U (MI)
Lee U (TN)
Lewis & Clark Coll (OR)
Liberty U (VA)
Lindenwood U (MO)
Linfield Coll (OR)
Louisiana Coll (LA)
Louisiana State U and A&M Coll (LA)
Loyola Marymount U (CA)
Loyola U Chicago (IL)
Lycoming Coll (PA)
Manchester U (IN)
Manhattanville Coll (NY)
Mansfield U of Pennsylvania (PA)
Marian U (IN)
Marymount Manhattan Coll (NY)
McDaniel Coll (MD)
Mercer U, Macon (GA)
Messiah Coll (PA)
Miami U Hamilton (OH)
Michigan State U (MI)
Millersville U of Pennsylvania (PA)
Millikin U (IL)
Millsaps Coll (MS)
Minnesota State U Moorhead (MN)
Molloy Coll (NY)
Montclair State U (NJ)
Mount St. Joseph U (OH)
Muskingum U (OH)
Nazareth Coll of Rochester (NY)
New York U (NY)
North Carolina State U (NC)
Northeastern State U (OK)
Northern Illinois U (IL)
Northern Kentucky U (KY)
Northwest Christian U (OR)
Northwestern U (IL)
Northwest Missouri State U (MO)
Oglethorpe U (GA)
The Ohio State U (OH)
Ohio U (OH)
Oklahoma Baptist U (OK)
Ottawa U (KS)
Ouachita Baptist U (AR)
Pace U, Pleasantville Campus (NY)
Palm Beach Atlantic U (FL)
Pepperdine U, Malibu (CA)
Pfeiffer U (NC)
Point Loma Nazarene U (CA)
Prairie View A&M U (TX)
Purchase Coll, State U of New York (NY)
Purdue U Northwest (IN)
Radford U (VA)
Randolph Coll (VA)
Regis U (CO)
Rhode Island Coll (RI)
Rider U (NJ)
Rochester Inst of Technology (NY)
Rocky Mountain Coll (MT)
Sacred Heart U (CT)
Saginaw Valley State U (MI)
Saint Anselm Coll (NH)
Saint Joseph's U (PA)
St. Mary's U (TX)
St. Norbert Coll (WI)
Saint Vincent Coll (PA)
Salisbury U (MD)
Samford U (AL)
San Diego State U (CA)
San Francisco State U (CA)
Seattle U (WA)
Seton Hill U (PA)
Sonoma State U (CA)
Southeastern Louisiana U (LA)
Southeast Missouri State U (MO)
Southern Illinois U Edwardsville (IL)
Southern U and Ag and Mech Coll (LA)
Southwest Baptist U (MO)
Southwestern U (TX)
State U of New York at Plattsburgh (NY)
State U of New York Coll at Potsdam (NY)
Stockton U (NJ)
Stonehill Coll (MA)
Syracuse U (NY)
Tabor Coll (KS)

Taylor U (IN)
Texas Christian U (TX)
Texas Lutheran U (TX)
Trevecca Nazarene U (TN)
Trinity Christian Coll (IL)
Truman State U (MO)
U at Buffalo, the State U of New York (NY)
U of Arkansas (AR)
U of California, Davis (CA)
U of Central Florida (FL)
U of Colorado Denver (CO)
U of Dayton (OH)
U of Detroit Mercy (MI)
U of Georgia (GA)
U of Hawaii at Manoa (HI)
U of Houston (TX)
U of Kentucky (KY)
U of La Verne (CA)
U of Louisville (KY)
U of Lynchburg (VA)
U of Mary Hardin-Baylor (TX)
U of Maryland, Coll Park (MD)
U of Maryland U Coll (MD)
U of Memphis (TN)
U of Michigan (MI)
U of Michigan–Dearborn (MI)
U of Minnesota, Duluth (MN)
U of Nebraska–Lincoln (NE)
U of Nevada, Las Vegas (NV)
U of Nevada, Reno (NV)
U of New Hampshire (NH)
U of New Haven (CT)
The U of North Carolina at Chapel Hill (NC)
The U of North Carolina at Charlotte (NC)
The U of North Carolina at Greensboro (NC)
U of Northern Colorado (CO)
U of Northern Iowa (IA)
U of Northwestern–St. Paul (MN)
U of Pennsylvania (PA)
U of Puget Sound (WA)
U of St. Thomas (TX)
U of San Francisco (CA)
U of Sioux Falls (SD)
U of South Alabama (AL)
U of South Carolina Aiken (SC)
U of South Dakota (SD)
U of South Florida (FL)
The U of Tennessee (TN)
The U of Texas at Austin (TX)
The U of Texas Rio Grande Valley (TX)
U of the Incarnate Word (TX)
The U of Toledo (OH)
The U of Tulsa (OK)
U of Washington (WA)
U of Wisconsin–La Crosse (WI)
U of Wisconsin–Milwaukee (WI)
U of Wisconsin–River Falls (WI)
U of Wisconsin–Superior (WI)
U of Wyoming (WY)
Utica Coll (NY)
Valley City State U (ND)
Vanguard U of Southern California (CA)
Virginia Polytechnic Inst and State U (VA)
Washington U in St. Louis (MO)
Waynesburg U (PA)
Weber State U (UT)
West Chester U of Pennsylvania (PA)
Western Connecticut State U (CT)
Western Illinois U (IL)
Western Kentucky U (KY)
Western State Colorado U (CO)
Western Washington U (WA)
Westmont Coll (CA)
West Virginia State U (WV)
Wheaton Coll (IL)
Whitworth U (WA)
Wilkes U (PA)
Willamette U (OR)
William Jewell Coll (MO)
Worcester State U (MA)
Wright State U–Lake Campus (OH)
Youngstown State U (OH)

SPEECH-LANGUAGE PATHOLOGY
Clarion U of Pennsylvania (PA)
Duquesne U (PA)
Eastern Washington U (WA)
East Stroudsburg U of Pennsylvania (PA)
Emerson Coll (MA)
Geneva Coll (PA)
Grand Valley State U (MI)
Harding U (AR)
Inter American U of Puerto Rico, Aguadilla Campus (PR)
Inter American U of Puerto Rico, Fajardo Campus (PR)
Jackson State U (MS)
Lebanon Valley Coll (PA)
Marshall U (WV)
Marymount Manhattan Coll (NY)
Maryville U of Saint Louis (MO)
Miami U Hamilton (OH)
Molloy Coll (NY)
Nazareth Coll of Rochester (NY)
Northwestern U (IL)
Oklahoma State U (OK)
Sacred Heart U (CT)
San Diego State U (CA)
Texas Christian U (TX)
Trinity Christian Coll (IL)
U of Montevallo (AL)
U of Nebraska–Lincoln (NE)
U of Nevada, Reno (NV)
U of Northern Iowa (IA)
U of West Georgia (GA)

SPEECH TEACHER EDUCATION
Albion Coll (MI)
Arkansas Tech U (AR)
Austin Coll (TX)
Bowling Green State U (OH)
Buena Vista U (IA)
Central Michigan U (MI)
Culver-Stockton Coll (MO)
Dallas Baptist U (TX)
East Texas Baptist U (TX)
Harding U (AR)
Kansas Wesleyan U (KS)
Lee U (TN)
Saginaw Valley State U (MI)
Southwest Baptist U (MO)
Trevecca Nazarene U (TN)
U of Mary Hardin-Baylor (TX)
The U of North Carolina at Greensboro (NC)
U of Sioux Falls (SD)
U of South Dakota (SD)
William Jewell Coll (MO)

SPORT AND FITNESS ADMINISTRATION/ MANAGEMENT
Adelphi U (NY)
American Public U System (WV)
Aurora U (IL)
Averett U (VA)
Baker U (KS)
Baldwin Wallace U (OH)
Barton Coll (NC)
Bellarmine U (KY)
Blackburn Coll (IL)
Bowling Green State U (OH)
Bridgewater State U (MA)
Buena Vista U (IA)
Caldwell U (NJ)
California U of Pennsylvania (PA)
Calvin Coll (MI)
Canisius Coll (NY)
Carthage Coll (WI)
Cedarville U (OH)
Central Michigan U (MI)
Clarion U of Pennsylvania (PA)
Coastal Carolina U (SC)
The Coll at Brockport, State U of New York (NY)
The Coll of Idaho (ID)
Columbia Coll (MO)
Columbia Coll Chicago (IL)
Concordia U Chicago (IL)
Culver-Stockton Coll (MO)
Dallas Baptist U (TX)
Davenport U, Grand Rapids (MI)
Dean Coll (MA)
DEREE - The American Coll of Greece (Greece)
Eastern Illinois U (IL)
Eastern Mennonite U (VA)
East Stroudsburg U of Pennsylvania (PA)
East Tennessee State U (TN)
East Texas Baptist U (TX)
Emmanuel Coll (GA)
Emmanuel Coll (MA)
Endicott Coll (MA)
Farmingdale State Coll (NY)
Fitchburg State U (MA)
Florida Southern Coll (FL)
Fort Lewis Coll (CO)
Franklin Pierce U (NH)
Geneva Coll (PA)
Georgetown Coll (KY)
Georgia Southern U (GA)
Gonzaga U (WA)
Goshen Coll (IN)
Graceland U (IA)
Grand Valley State U (MI)
Greenville U (IL)
Harding U (AR)
Hardin-Simmons U (TX)
High Point U (NC)
Hillsdale Coll (MI)
Hiram Coll (OH)
Indiana State U (IN)
Indiana U Kokomo (IN)
Ithaca Coll (NY)
Jacksonville U (FL)
Johnson C. Smith U (NC)
Judson U (IL)
Kansas Wesleyan U (KS)
Kennesaw State U (GA)
King U (TN)
Lamar U (TX)
Lasell Coll (MA)
La Sierra U (CA)
Lees-McRae Coll (NC)
Lee U (TN)
LeTourneau U (TX)
Liberty U (VA)
Limestone Coll (SC)
Lindenwood U (MO)
Linfield Coll (OR)
Lipscomb U (TN)
Lock Haven U of Pennsylvania (PA)
Loras Coll (IA)
Louisiana State U and A&M Coll (LA)
Lubbock Christian U (TX)
Madonna U (MI)
Manchester U (IN)
Manor Coll (PA)
Maryville U of Saint Louis (MO)
Merrimack Coll (MA)
Messiah Coll (PA)
Miami U (OH)
Millikin U (IL)
Missouri Baptist U (MO)
Mount St. Joseph U (OH)
Muskingum U (OH)
New England Coll (NH)
Nichols Coll (MA)
North Carolina State U (NC)
Northern Kentucky U (KY)
Northern State U (SD)
Northwood U, Michigan Campus (MI)
Ohio Dominican U (OH)
The Ohio State U (OH)
Oklahoma Baptist U (OK)
Oklahoma Christian U (OK)
Oklahoma State U (OK)
Old Dominion U (VA)
Pepperdine U, Malibu (CA)
Pfeiffer U (NC)
Piedmont Coll (GA)
Purdue U Northwest (IN)
Queens U of Charlotte (NC)
Radford U (VA)
Reinhardt U (GA)
Rice U (TX)
Rider U (NJ)
Roanoke Coll (VA)
Rochester Coll (MI)
Rockford U (IL)
Rocky Mountain Coll (MT)
Saginaw Valley State U (MI)
St. John Fisher Coll (NY)
Saint Leo U (FL)
Saint Louis U (MO)
Samford U (AL)
Seton Hill U (PA)
Southeastern Louisiana U (LA)
Southeastern U (FL)
Southeast Missouri State U (MO)
Southern Illinois U Carbondale (IL)
Southwest Baptist U (MO)
State U of New York Coll of Technology at Alfred (NY)
Stetson U (FL)
Syracuse U (NY)
Taylor U (IN)
Temple U (PA)
Texas Lutheran U (TX)
Texas Tech U (TX)
Tiffin U (OH)
Toccoa Falls Coll (GA)
Towson U (MD)
Trevecca Nazarene U (TN)
Union Coll (KY)
U of Dayton (OH)
The U of Findlay (OH)
U of Florida (FL)
U of Georgia (GA)
U of Houston (TX)
U of Louisville (KY)
U of Lynchburg (VA)
U of Mary Hardin-Baylor (TX)
U of Massachusetts Amherst (MA)
U of Memphis (TN)
U of Michigan (MI)
U of Minnesota, Morris (MN)
U of Minnesota, Twin Cities Campus (MN)
U of Mount Union (OH)
U of New Haven (CT)
U of North Florida (FL)
U of Pittsburgh at Bradford (PA)
U of Regina (SK, Canada)
U of Saint Mary (KS)
U of Sioux Falls (SD)
U of South Carolina (SC)
U of Southern Indiana (IN)
The U of Tampa (FL)
The U of Tennessee (TN)
U of the Incarnate Word (TX)
The U of Tulsa (OK)
The U of West Alabama (AL)
Valparaiso U (IN)
Wartburg Coll (IA)
Washington State U (WA)
Widener U (PA)
Winthrop U (SC)

SPORTS COMMUNICATION
Bradley U (IL)
Bryant U (RI)
Butler U (IN)
Culver-Stockton Coll (MO)
Duquesne U (PA)
East Texas Baptist U (TX)
Emerson Coll (MA)
Florida Southern Coll (FL)
High Point U (NC)
LeTourneau U (TX)
Louisiana Coll (LA)
Muskingum U (OH)
Oklahoma State U (OK)
Piedmont Coll (GA)
Rider U (NJ)
U of Nebraska–Lincoln (NE)
Youngstown State U (OH)

SPORTS STUDIES
Bryant U (RI)
Canisius Coll (NY)
Hillsdale Coll (MI)
Inter American U of Puerto Rico, San Germán Campus (PR)
Lubbock Christian U (TX)
Manhattanville Coll (NY)
National U (CA)
Ottawa U (KS)
Texas Christian U (TX)
U of Saint Mary (KS)
Western Kentucky U (KY)

STATISTICS
American U (DC)
American U of Beirut (Lebanon)
Baruch Coll of the City U of New York (NY)
Baylor U (TX)
Bowling Green State U (OH)
California Polytechnic State U, San Luis Obispo (CA)
California State U, Fullerton (CA)
California State U, Long Beach (CA)
California U of Pennsylvania (PA)
Carnegie Mellon U (PA)
Central Michigan U (MI)
Colorado School of Mines (CO)
Colorado State U (CO)
Columbia U (NY)
Cornell U (NY)
George Mason U (VA)
Grand Valley State U (MI)
Harvard U (MA)
Hunter Coll of the City U of New York (NY)
Idaho State U (ID)
Indiana U Bloomington (IN)
Iowa State U of Science and Technology (IA)
Jackson State U (MS)
LeTourneau U (TX)
Loyola U Chicago (IL)
Miami U (OH)
Miami U Hamilton (OH)
Michigan State U (MI)
North Carolina State U (NC)
Northern Kentucky U (KY)
Northwestern U (IL)
The Ohio State U (OH)
Ohio Wesleyan U (OH)
Oklahoma State U (OK)
Rice U (TX)
Rochester Inst of Technology (NY)
St. John Fisher Coll (NY)
San Diego State U (CA)
San Francisco State U (CA)
Sonoma State U (CA)
Temple U (PA)
Truman State U (MO)
U at Buffalo, the State U of New York (NY)
U of California, Davis (CA)
U of California, Los Angeles (CA)
U of California, Riverside (CA)
U of Central Florida (FL)
U of Chicago (IL)
U of Florida (FL)
U of Georgia (GA)
U of Idaho (ID)
U of Maine (ME)
U of Maryland, Baltimore County (MD)
U of Michigan (MI)
U of Michigan–Dearborn (MI)
U of Minnesota, Duluth (MN)
U of Minnesota, Morris (MN)
U of Minnesota, Twin Cities Campus (MN)
U of Missouri (MO)
U of New Mexico (NM)
U of North Florida (FL)
U of Pennsylvania (PA)
U of Pittsburgh (PA)
U of Regina (SK, Canada)
U of St. Thomas (MN)
U of South Carolina (SC)
U of South Florida (FL)
The U of Tennessee (TN)
The U of Texas Rio Grande Valley (TX)
U of Vermont (VT)
U of Washington (WA)
U of Wisconsin–La Crosse (WI)
U of Wyoming (WY)
Utah State U (UT)
Valparaiso U (IN)
Virginia Polytechnic Inst and State U (VA)
Washington U in St. Louis (MO)
Williams Coll (MA)
Wright State U–Lake Campus (OH)

STATISTICS RELATED
U of New Hampshire (NH)
U of Northern Iowa (IA)

STRATEGIC INTELLIGENCE
Dakota State U (SD)

STRINGED INSTRUMENTS
Acadia U (NS, Canada)
Boston U (MA)
Carnegie Mellon U (PA)
Central Washington U (WA)
Liberty U (VA)
Northwestern U (IL)
Seattle U (WA)
State U of New York at Fredonia (NY)
Stetson U (FL)
Syracuse U (NY)
Texas Christian U (TX)
U of Washington (WA)
Willamette U (OR)
Youngstown State U (OH)

STRUCTURAL BIOLOGY
Indiana U Bloomington (IN)

STRUCTURAL ENGINEERING
U of Central Florida (FL)

SUBSTANCE ABUSE/ ADDICTION COUNSELING
The Coll at Brockport, State U of New York (NY)
Kansas Wesleyan U (KS)
Rhode Island Coll (RI)
Tiffin U (OH)
Union Coll (KY)
U of Central Arkansas (AR)
U of Detroit Mercy (MI)
U of Providence (MT)
U of South Dakota (SD)
The U of Texas Rio Grande Valley (TX)

SURVEYING ENGINEERING
Florida Atlantic U (FL)

SURVEYING TECHNOLOGY
East Tennessee State U (TN)
Idaho State U (ID)
Kennesaw State U (GA)
State U of New York Coll of Technology at Alfred (NY)
U of Florida (FL)
U of Maine (ME)
Utah Valley U (UT)

SUSTAINABILITY STUDIES
Albion Coll (MI)
Allegheny Coll (PA)
Aurora U (IL)
Bentley U (MA)
Columbia U (NY)
Creighton U (NE)
The Evergreen State Coll (WA)
Furman U (SC)
George Mason U (VA)
Goshen Coll (IN)
Hartwick Coll (NY)
Hofstra U (NY)
Jacksonville U (FL)
Kean U (NJ)
Lipscomb U (TN)
Maharishi U of Management (IA)
Maryville U of Saint Louis (MO)
Messiah Coll (PA)
Miami U (OH)
Montclair State U (NJ)
St. John Fisher Coll (NY)
State U of New York Coll of Environmental Science and Forestry (NY)
Stockton U (NJ)
Taylor U (IN)
Toccoa Falls Coll (GA)
U of California, Riverside (CA)
U of Florida (FL)
U of Louisville (KY)
U of New Hampshire (NH)
U of New Haven (CT)
U of Northern Colorado (CO)
U of South Dakota (SD)
The U of Texas at Austin (TX)
The U of Texas Rio Grande Valley (TX)
The U of the South (TN)
U of Wisconsin–River Falls (WI)
U of Wisconsin–Superior (WI)
Washington U in St. Louis (MO)
Western Washington U (WA)
Worcester Polytechnic Inst (MA)

SWEDISH
U of Washington (WA)

SYSTEM, NETWORKING, AND LAN/WAN MANAGEMENT
Central Washington U (WA)
Dakota State U (SD)
Rochester Inst of Technology (NY)
State U of New York Coll of Technology at Alfred (NY)
U of Providence (MT)

SYSTEMS ENGINEERING
George Mason U (VA)
Kennesaw State U (GA)
Massachusetts Maritime Acad (MA)
Providence Coll (RI)
Regent U (VA)
Rochester Inst of Technology (NY)
Stevens Inst of Technology (NJ)
Taylor U (IN)
Texas A&M Intl U (TX)
U of Florida (FL)
The U of North Carolina at Charlotte (NC)
U of Pennsylvania (PA)
U of Virginia (VA)
U of Wyoming (WY)
Washington U in St. Louis (MO)

SYSTEMS SCIENCE AND THEORY
Boston U (MA)
Carnegie Mellon U (PA)
Marshall U (WV)
Purdue U (IN)
Syracuse U (NY)
U of Wyoming (WY)
Washington U in St. Louis (MO)

TAXATION
Grand Valley State U (MI)

TEACHER ASSISTANT/AIDE
Blackburn Coll (IL)

TECHNICAL AND SCIENTIFIC COMMUNICATION
Indiana U–Purdue U Indianapolis (IN)
Mercer U, Macon (GA)
Washington State U (WA)
Worcester Polytechnic Inst (MA)

TECHNICAL TEACHER EDUCATION
Auburn U (AL)
Bowling Green State U (OH)
Central Washington U (WA)
Coll of the Ozarks (MO)
Eastern Illinois U (IL)
The Ohio State U (OH)
Oklahoma State U (OK)
U of Arkansas (AR)
U of Idaho (ID)
U of Kentucky (KY)
Utah State U (UT)
Valley City State U (ND)
West Virginia U Inst of Technology (WV)
Wright State U–Lake Campus (OH)

TECHNOLOGY/INDUSTRIAL ARTS TEACHER EDUCATION
Berea Coll (KY)
Bowling Green State U (OH)
Central Connecticut State U (CT)
Fitchburg State U (MA)
Indiana State U (IN)
Jackson State U (MS)
Lindenwood U (MO)
Middle Tennessee State U (TN)
North Carolina State U (NC)
Purdue U (IN)
Rhode Island Coll (RI)
Southeast Missouri State U (MO)
U of New Mexico (NM)
U of Northern Iowa (IA)
U of Wyoming (WY)
Utah State U (UT)
Valley City State U (ND)

TELECOMMUNICATIONS TECHNOLOGY
Canisius Coll (NY)
Farmingdale State Coll (NY)
Lawrence Technological U (MI)
Pace U (NY)
Pace U, Pleasantville Campus (NY)
Rochester Inst of Technology (NY)

TEXTILE SCIENCE
Michigan State U (MI)
U of Nebraska–Lincoln (NE)

TEXTILE SCIENCES AND ENGINEERING
Auburn U (AL)
North Carolina State U (NC)

THEATER DESIGN AND TECHNOLOGY
Averett U (VA)
Baldwin Wallace U (OH)
Baylor U (TX)
Boston U (MA)
Brenau U (GA)
Central Washington U (WA)
Columbia Coll Chicago (IL)
DePaul U (IL)
Emerson Coll (MA)
Fitchburg State U (MA)
Florida Southern Coll (FL)
Ithaca Coll (NY)
Kean U (NJ)
Lindenwood U (MO)
Lipscomb U (TN)
Marymount Manhattan Coll (NY)
Millikin U (IL)
Nazareth Coll of Rochester (NY)
New Jersey Inst of Technology (NJ)
Pepperdine U, Malibu (CA)
Piedmont Coll (GA)
Purchase Coll, State U of New York (NY)
Purdue U (IN)
Rhode Island Coll (RI)
Rocky Mountain Coll (MT)
Savannah Coll of Art and Design (GA)
Seton Hill U (PA)
Syracuse U (NY)
Texas Christian U (TX)
U of Michigan (MI)
U of Nevada, Las Vegas (NV)
U of New Mexico (NM)
U of North Carolina School of the Arts (NC)
U of Northern Iowa (IA)
U of Regina (SK, Canada)
Vanguard U of Southern California (CA)
Wilkes U (PA)
Wright State U–Lake Campus (OH)

THEATER LITERATURE, HISTORY AND CRITICISM
Averett U (VA)
Buena Vista U (IA)
DePaul U (IL)
Marymount Manhattan Coll (NY)
Northwestern U (IL)
Sarah Lawrence Coll (NY)
U of Washington (WA)
Washington U in St. Louis (MO)

THEATER/THEATER ARTS MANAGEMENT
Albright Coll (PA)
Buena Vista U (IA)
Columbia Coll Chicago (IL)
DEREE - The American Coll of Greece (Greece)
Graceland U (IA)
Ithaca Coll (NY)
Marymount Manhattan Coll (NY)
Massachusetts Coll of Liberal Arts (MA)
Messiah Coll (PA)
Miami U Hamilton (OH)
Michigan State U (MI)
Nazareth Coll of Rochester (NY)
Oglethorpe U (GA)
Ohio U (OH)
Pace U (NY)
Regent U (VA)
Rockford U (IL)
Seton Hill U (PA)
U of New Haven (CT)
U of Regina (SK, Canada)

THEOLOGICAL AND MINISTERIAL STUDIES RELATED
East Texas Baptist U (TX)
Grove City Coll (PA)
Hardin-Simmons U (TX)
Lincoln Christian U (IL)
Lubbock Christian U (TX)
Marquette U (WI)
Providence Coll (RI)
U of Northwestern–St. Paul (MN)
Whitworth U (WA)

THEOLOGY
Assumption Coll (MA)
Bellarmine U (KY)
Benedictine U (IL)
Boston Coll (MA)
Caldwell U (NJ)
California Lutheran U (CA)
Calvin Coll (MI)
Coll of Saint Benedict (MN)
Coll of Saint Mary (NE)
Concordia U Chicago (IL)
Concordia U Irvine (CA)
Creighton U (NE)
Dominican U (IL)
Duquesne U (PA)
Eastern Mennonite U (VA)
Eastern U (PA)
Hanover Coll (IN)
Hardin-Simmons U (TX)
Holy Apostles Coll and Sem (CT)
Immaculata U (PA)
King's Coll (PA)
Kuyper Coll (MI)
Lee U (TN)
LeTourneau U (TX)
Liberty U (VA)
Louisiana Coll (LA)
Loyola Marymount U (CA)
Loyola U Chicago (IL)
Marian U (IN)
Marquette U (WI)
Ohio Dominican U (OH)
Ouachita Baptist U (AR)
Palm Beach Atlantic U (FL)
Point Loma Nazarene U (CA)
Providence Coll (RI)
Redeemer U Coll (ON, Canada)
Saint Anselm Coll (NH)
Saint John's U (MN)
Saint Louis U (MO)
St. Mary's U (TX)
Saint Mary's U of Minnesota (MN)
Saint Vincent Coll (PA)
Southwest Baptist U (MO)
Stonehill Coll (MA)
Texas Lutheran U (TX)
Trinity Christian Coll (IL)
U of Chicago (IL)
U of Dallas (TX)
U of Notre Dame (IN)
U of Providence (MT)
U of Saint Francis (IN)
U of Saint Mary (KS)
U of St. Thomas (TX)
U of San Francisco (CA)
U of Sioux Falls (SD)
Valparaiso U (IN)
Vanguard U of Southern California (CA)
Whitworth U (WA)

THEOLOGY AND RELIGIOUS VOCATIONS RELATED
Cedarville U (OH)
Lee U (TN)
LeTourneau U (TX)
Martin Luther Coll (MN)
Missouri Baptist U (MO)
Northwest Christian U (OR)
Ouachita Baptist U (AR)
Trevecca Nazarene U (TN)
Trinity Christian Coll (IL)

THEORETICAL AND MATHEMATICAL PHYSICS
Carnegie Mellon U (PA)
U at Buffalo, the State U of New York (NY)

THERAPEUTIC RECREATION
Aurora U (IL)
Calvin Coll (MI)
Central Michigan U (MI)
East Carolina U (NC)
Eastern Washington U (WA)
Grand Valley State U (MI)
Ithaca Coll (NY)
Kean U (NJ)
Southern U and Ag and Mech Coll (LA)
Temple U (PA)
The U of Toledo (OH)
U of Wisconsin–La Crosse (WI)
U of Wisconsin–Milwaukee (WI)
Utica Coll (NY)

TOOL AND DIE TECHNOLOGY
Utah State U (UT)

TOURISM AND TRAVEL SERVICES MANAGEMENT
Bowling Green State U (OH)
Capilano U (BC, Canada)
Central Washington U (WA)
Fort Lewis Coll (CO)
George Mason U (VA)
Indiana U–Purdue U Indianapolis (IN)
Northeastern State U (OK)
U of Hawaii at Manoa (HI)
U of Maine at Machias (ME)
U of South Carolina (SC)

TOURISM AND TRAVEL SERVICES MARKETING
Rochester Inst of Technology (NY)

TOURISM PROMOTION
Bowling Green State U (OH)

TOXICOLOGY
Nazareth Coll of Rochester (NY)

TRADE AND INDUSTRIAL TEACHER EDUCATION
Auburn U (AL)
Bowling Green State U (OH)
California State U, Long Beach (CA)
California State U, San Bernardino (CA)
Central Washington U (WA)
Fitchburg State U (MA)
Florida Ag and Mech U (FL)
Indiana State U (IN)
Indiana U of Pennsylvania (PA)
Lindenwood U (MO)
Southern Illinois U Carbondale (IL)
Temple U (PA)
U of Central Florida (FL)
U of Louisville (KY)
U of Nebraska–Lincoln (NE)
U of Wyoming (WY)

TRANSPORTATION AND MATERIALS MOVING RELATED
U of Wisconsin–Superior (WI)

TRANSPORTATION/MOBILITY MANAGEMENT
Bridgewater State U (MA)
Bryant U (RI)
LeTourneau U (TX)
U of North Florida (FL)
U of Pennsylvania (PA)

TURF AND TURFGRASS MANAGEMENT
Delaware Valley U (PA)
North Carolina State U (NC)
Purdue U (IN)
U of Georgia (GA)
U of Massachusetts Amherst (MA)
U of Nebraska–Lincoln (NE)
Washington State U (WA)

TURKISH
The U of Texas at Austin (TX)

URALIC LANGUAGES
U of Washington (WA)

URBAN EDUCATION AND LEADERSHIP
U of Nevada, Las Vegas (NV)
U of Wisconsin–Milwaukee (WI)

URBAN FORESTRY
Southern U and Ag and Mech Coll (LA)
U of California, Davis (CA)

URBAN MINISTRY
Greenville U (IL)
Redeemer U Coll (ON, Canada)
Tabor Coll (KS)

URBAN STUDIES/AFFAIRS
Albright Coll (PA)
Boston U (MA)
California State U, Northridge (CA)
Canisius Coll (NY)
Coll of Charleston (SC)
Columbia U (NY)
Fordham U (NY)
Furman U (SC)
Haverford Coll (PA)
Hunter Coll of the City U of New York (NY)
Jackson State U (MS)
Lipscomb U (TN)
Loyola Marymount U (CA)
Loyola U Chicago (IL)
Manhattan Coll (NY)
New Coll of Florida (FL)
New Jersey City U (NJ)
New York U (NY)
Northwestern U (IL)
Oglethorpe U (GA)
Ohio U (OH)
Ohio Wesleyan U (OH)
Portland State U (OR)
Queens Coll of the City U of New York (NY)
Rhodes Coll (TN)
San Diego State U (CA)
San Francisco State U (CA)
Sarah Lawrence Coll (NY)
Towson U (MD)
U of California, Irvine (CA)

U of Michigan–Dearborn (MI)
U of Minnesota, Twin Cities Campus (MN)
U of Pennsylvania (PA)
U of Pittsburgh (PA)
U of San Francisco (CA)
The U of Texas at Austin (TX)
The U of Toledo (OH)
U of Washington, Tacoma (WA)
Vassar Coll (NY)
Virginia Commonwealth U (VA)
Virginia Polytechnic Inst and State U (VA)
Washington U in St. Louis (MO)
Wheaton Coll (IL)
Worcester State U (MA)
Wright State U–Lake Campus (OH)

VEHICLE AND VEHICLE PARTS AND ACCESSORIES MARKETING
Northwood U, Michigan Campus (MI)

VETERINARY/ANIMAL HEALTH TECHNOLOGY
Michigan State U (MI)
Murray State U (KY)
Purdue U (IN)
U of Massachusetts Amherst (MA)
U of Nebraska–Lincoln (NE)

VISION SCIENCE/ PHYSIOLOGICAL OPTICS
Indiana U Bloomington (IN)
Providence Coll (RI)
U of the Incarnate Word (TX)

VISUAL AND PERFORMING ARTS
Antioch Coll, Yellow Springs (OH)
Austin Coll (TX)
Bennett Coll (NC)
Blackburn Coll (IL)
Boston U (MA)
Bucknell U (PA)
California State U, San Marcos (CA)
Capilano U (BC, Canada)
Centenary Coll of Louisiana (LA)
Champlain Coll (VT)
Columbia U (NY)
Delta State U (MS)
DEREE - The American Coll of Greece (Greece)
Eckerd Coll (FL)
Emerson Coll (MA)
The Evergreen State Coll (WA)
Fayetteville State U (NC)
George Mason U (VA)
Harvard U (MA)
Hiram Coll (OH)
Indiana U of Pennsylvania (PA)
Inter American U of Puerto Rico, San Germán Campus (PR)
Iowa State U of Science and Technology (IA)
Ithaca Coll (NY)
Jackson State U (MS)
Jacksonville U (FL)
Johnson C. Smith U (NC)
Kansas Wesleyan U (KS)
Kennesaw State U (GA)
LaGrange Coll (GA)
Lebanese American U (Lebanon)
Lees-McRae Coll (NC)
Louisiana Coll (LA)
Manhattanville Coll (NY)
Marshall U (WV)
Maryland Inst Coll of Art (MD)
Massachusetts Coll of Liberal Arts (MA)
Milligan Coll (TN)
Mount Marty Coll (SD)
New York U (NY)
Northwestern U (IL)
Oklahoma State U (OK)
Point Loma Nazarene U (CA)
Purchase Coll, State U of New York (NY)
Saint Joseph's U (PA)
San Jose State U (CA)
Sarah Lawrence Coll (NY)
Southeastern U (FL)
Southeast Missouri State U (MO)
Stockton U (NJ)
Stonehill Coll (MA)
Temple U (PA)
U of California, Irvine (CA)
U of Dayton (OH)
U of Houston–Downtown (TX)
U of Maine at Farmington (ME)
U of Maine at Machias (ME)
U of Massachusetts Dartmouth (MA)
U of Pennsylvania (PA)
U of Puget Sound (WA)
U of Regina (SK, Canada)
U of Saint Mary (KS)
U of San Francisco (CA)
U of South Dakota (SD)
The U of Tennessee at Martin (TN)
Vassar Coll (NY)
Western Washington U (WA)
Worcester State U (MA)
Youngstown State U (OH)

VISUAL AND PERFORMING ARTS RELATED
Adelphi U (NY)
Baldwin Wallace U (OH)
Cameron U (OK)
Clark U (MA)
Cornell U (NY)
Endicott Coll (MA)
Millikin U (IL)
New York U (NY)
Purchase Coll, State U of New York (NY)
Rice U (TX)
Samford U (AL)
Seton Hill U (PA)
State U of New York Coll at Geneseo (NY)
U of California, Davis (CA)
U of California, Los Angeles (CA)
U of Chicago (IL)
U of Michigan (MI)
U of South Florida (FL)
U of Washington (WA)
U of Washington, Bothell (WA)

VITICULTURE AND ENOLOGY
California Polytechnic State U, San Luis Obispo (CA)
Cornell U (NY)
Washington State U (WA)
Washington State U–Tri-Cities (WA)

VOCATIONAL REHABILITATION COUNSELING
Bowling Green State U (OH)
East Carolina U (NC)
Maryville U of Saint Louis (MO)
Southern U and Ag and Mech Coll (LA)
Wright State U–Lake Campus (OH)

VOICE AND OPERA
Acadia U (NS, Canada)
Baldwin Wallace U (OH)
Bowling Green State U (OH)
Bucknell U (PA)
California State U, Long Beach (CA)
Calvin Coll (MI)
Campbellsville U (KY)
Carnegie Mellon U (PA)
Carson-Newman U (TN)
The Catholic U of America (DC)
Central Washington U (WA)
Coll of the Ozarks (MO)
Drake U (IA)
Furman U (SC)
Ithaca Coll (NY)
Jacksonville U (FL)
Liberty U (VA)
Lipscomb U (TN)
Loyola U Chicago (IL)
Loyola U New Orleans (LA)
Madonna U (MI)
Northwestern U (IL)
Ohio U (OH)
Oklahoma Baptist U (OK)
Oklahoma Christian U (OK)
Ouachita Baptist U (AR)
Palm Beach Atlantic U (FL)
Point Loma Nazarene U (CA)
Rider U (NJ)
Samford U (AL)
Southeastern U (FL)
State U of New York at Fredonia (NY)
Stetson U (FL)
Syracuse U (NY)
Texas Christian U (TX)
U of Idaho (ID)
The U of Tulsa (OK)
U of Washington (WA)
U of Wisconsin–Superior (WI)
Valparaiso U (IN)
Washington U in St. Louis (MO)
Weber State U (UT)
Whitworth U (WA)
Willamette U (OR)
Youngstown State U (OH)

WATER QUALITY AND WASTEWATER TREATMENT MANAGEMENT AND RECYCLING TECHNOLOGY
Virginia Polytechnic Inst and State U (VA)

WATER RESOURCES ENGINEERING
Central State U (OH)
U of Nevada, Reno (NV)

WATER, WETLANDS, AND MARINE RESOURCES MANAGEMENT
Colorado State U (CO)

WEB/MULTIMEDIA MANAGEMENT AND WEBMASTER
Georgia Coll & State U (GA)
Limestone Coll (SC)
Pepperdine U, Malibu (CA)
Rochester Inst of Technology (NY)
Saint Leo U (FL)
State U of New York Coll of Technology at Alfred (NY)
Trevecca Nazarene U (TN)
U of Providence (MT)

WEB PAGE, DIGITAL/ MULTIMEDIA AND INFORMATION RESOURCES DESIGN
Acad of Art U (CA)
Albright Coll (PA)
Cedarville U (OH)
Central Connecticut State U (CT)
Central Washington U (WA)
Davenport U, Grand Rapids (MI)
Duquesne U (PA)
Graceland U (IA)
Gwynedd Mercy U (PA)
Harding U (AR)
Immaculata U (PA)
Iona Coll (NY)
Juniata Coll (PA)
Limestone Coll (SC)
Lindenwood U (MO)
Lipscomb U (TN)
Louisiana Coll (LA)
Mount St. Joseph U (OH)
New England Inst of Technology (RI)
Northwest Missouri State U (MO)
Rochester Inst of Technology (NY)
Seattle U (WA)
Trevecca Nazarene U (TN)
Tulane U (LA)
The U of Findlay (OH)
U of Mount Union (OH)
U of Providence (MT)
U of Washington, Bothell (WA)
Utah Valley U (UT)
Weber State U (UT)

WELDING ENGINEERING TECHNOLOGY
LeTourneau U (TX)
Weber State U (UT)

WELDING TECHNOLOGY
Idaho State U (ID)

WILDLIFE BIOLOGY
Adams State U (CO)
Colorado State U (CO)
Lees-McRae Coll (NC)
Liberty U (VA)
Ohio U (OH)
State U of New York Coll of Environmental Science and Forestry (NY)
U of Vermont (VT)
U of Wyoming (WY)

WILDLIFE, FISH AND WILDLANDS SCIENCE AND MANAGEMENT
Arkansas Tech U (AR)
Auburn U (AL)
Coll of the Ozarks (MO)
Delaware Valley U (PA)
Humboldt State U (CA)
McNeese State U (LA)
Michigan State U (MI)
Murray State U (KY)
Northwest Missouri State U (MO)
U of Florida (FL)
U of Georgia (GA)
U of Idaho (ID)
U of Maine (ME)
U of Nevada, Reno (NV)
U of New Hampshire (NH)
The U of Tennessee (TN)
Utah State U (UT)
Valley City State U (ND)
Washington State U (WA)

WOMEN'S STUDIES
Agnes Scott Coll (GA)
Albion Coll (MI)
Albright Coll (PA)
Alverno Coll (WI)
American U (DC)
Appalachian State U (NC)
Austin Coll (TX)
Berea Coll (KY)
Bowling Green State U (OH)
Brandeis U (MA)
Bryant U (RI)
Bucknell U (PA)
Butler U (IN)
California State U, Fullerton (CA)
California State U, Long Beach (CA)
California State U, Northridge (CA)
California State U, San Marcos (CA)
Canisius Coll (NY)
Central Michigan U (MI)
Clark U (MA)
Colgate U (NY)
The Coll at Brockport, State U of New York (NY)
Coll of Charleston (SC)
Coll of Saint Benedict (MN)
The Coll of St. Scholastica (MN)
Coll of the Holy Cross (MA)
The Coll of William and Mary (VA)
The Colorado Coll (CO)
Colorado State U (CO)
Columbia U (NY)
Concordia U Chicago (IL)
Connecticut Coll (CT)
Cornell Coll (IA)
Dartmouth Coll (NH)
DePaul U (IL)
Dickinson Coll (PA)
Dominican U (IL)
Drew U (NJ)
Duquesne U (PA)
Earlham Coll (IN)
Eastern Washington U (WA)
East Tennessee State U (TN)
Eckerd Coll (FL)
Fordham U (NY)
Fort Lewis Coll (CO)
Georgia Southern U (GA)
Georgia State U (GA)
Grand Valley State U (MI)
Hamilton Coll (NY)
Hamline U (MN)
Harvard U (MA)
Hofstra U (NY)
Hollins U (VA)
Hunter Coll of the City U of New York (NY)
Knox Coll (IL)
Lafayette Coll (PA)
Loyola Marymount U (CA)
Loyola U Chicago (IL)
Macalester Coll (MN)
Manchester U (IN)
Marquette U (WI)
Mercer U, Macon (GA)
Merrimack Coll (MA)
Miami U (OH)
Michigan State U (MI)
Middlebury Coll (VT)
Minnesota State U Moorhead (MN)
Montclair State U (NJ)
Nazareth Coll of Rochester (NY)
New Jersey City U (NJ)
North Carolina State U (NC)
Northwestern U (IL)
The Ohio State U (OH)
Ohio U (OH)
Ohio Wesleyan U (OH)
Old Dominion U (VA)
Pace U (NY)
Pacific Lutheran U (WA)
Portland State U (OR)
Providence Coll (RI)
Purchase Coll, State U of New York (NY)
Purdue U (IN)
Queens Coll of the City U of New York (NY)
Randolph-Macon Coll (VA)
Regis U (CO)
Rhode Island Coll (RI)
Rice U (TX)
Saint John's U (MN)
Saint Louis U (MO)
St. Olaf Coll (MN)
San Diego State U (CA)
San Francisco State U (CA)
Scripps Coll (CA)
Seattle U (WA)
Sonoma State U (CA)
Southwestern U (TX)
State U of New York at Fredonia (NY)
State U of New York at Plattsburgh (NY)
State U of New York Coll at Geneseo (NY)
State U of New York Coll at Potsdam (NY)
Syracuse U (NY)
Temple U (PA)
Towson U (MD)
Tulane U (LA)
U of California, Davis (CA)
U of California, Riverside (CA)
U of California, Santa Cruz (CA)
U of Dayton (OH)
U of Florida (FL)
U of Georgia (GA)
U of Hawaii at Manoa (HI)
U of Houston–Clear Lake (TX)
U of Louisville (KY)
U of Maine (ME)
U of Maryland, Baltimore County (MD)
U of Maryland, Coll Park (MD)
U of Massachusetts Amherst (MA)
U of Massachusetts Boston (MA)
U of Massachusetts Dartmouth (MA)
U of Michigan (MI)
U of Michigan–Dearborn (MI)
U of Minnesota, Duluth (MN)
U of Minnesota, Morris (MN)
U of Minnesota, Twin Cities Campus (MN)
U of Nebraska–Lincoln (NE)
U of Nevada, Las Vegas (NV)
U of Nevada, Reno (NV)
U of New Hampshire (NH)
U of New Mexico (NM)
U of North Carolina at Asheville (NC)
The U of North Carolina at Chapel Hill (NC)
The U of North Carolina at Greensboro (NC)
U of Notre Dame (IN)
U of Oregon (OR)
U of Pennsylvania (PA)
U of Pittsburgh (PA)
U of Regina (SK, Canada)
U of Richmond (VA)
U of St. Thomas (MN)
U of South Carolina (SC)
U of South Florida (FL)
The U of Texas at Austin (TX)
The U of the South (TN)
The U of Toledo (OH)
The U of Tulsa (OK)
U of Vermont (VT)
U of Washington (WA)
U of Wisconsin–Eau Claire (WI)
U of Wisconsin–La Crosse (WI)
U of Wisconsin–Milwaukee (WI)
U of Wyoming (WY)
Vassar Coll (NY)
Virginia Commonwealth U (VA)
Washington & Jefferson Coll (PA)
Washington State U (WA)

Washington U in St. Louis (MO)
Wesleyan Coll (GA)
West Chester U of Pennsylvania (PA)
Wheaton Coll (MA)
Willamette U (OR)
Williams Coll (MA)

WOOD SCIENCE AND WOOD PRODUCTS/PULP AND PAPER TECHNOLOGY
North Carolina State U (NC)
Purdue U (IN)
U of Idaho (ID)

WOODWIND INSTRUMENTS
Acadia U (NS, Canada)
Northwestern U (IL)
Oklahoma Christian U (OK)
State U of New York at Fredonia (NY)
U of Michigan (MI)
Youngstown State U (OH)

WOODWORKING
Rochester Inst of Technology (NY)

WORK AND FAMILY STUDIES
Miami U Hamilton (OH)

WRITING
Aurora U (IL)
Baylor U (TX)
Bridgewater Coll (VA)
Calvin Coll (MI)
Canisius Coll (NY)
Central Washington U (WA)
Champlain Coll (VT)
Eastern Mennonite U (VA)
Fort Lewis Coll (CO)
Geneva Coll (PA)
Georgia Southern U (GA)
Goshen Coll (IN)
Grand Valley State U (MI)
High Point U (NC)
Kansas Wesleyan U (KS)
Lipscomb U (TN)
Lubbock Christian U (TX)
Madonna U (MI)
Marquette U (WI)
Massachusetts Coll of Liberal Arts (MA)
Miami U Hamilton (OH)
Northwest Missouri State U (MO)
Point Loma Nazarene U (CA)
Queens U of Charlotte (NC)
San Diego State U (CA)
Sarah Lawrence Coll (NY)
Spring Hill Coll (AL)
State U of New York Coll at Potsdam (NY)
U of Central Arkansas (AR)
U of Colorado Denver (CO)
The U of Findlay (OH)
U of Mount Union (OH)
U of Providence (MT)
The U of Tampa (FL)
The U of Texas at Austin (TX)
U of Washington, Tacoma (WA)
U of Wisconsin–Superior (WI)
Whitworth U (WA)

YOUTH MINISTRY
Carson-Newman U (TN)
Cedarville U (OH)
Eastern U (PA)
Florida Southern Coll (FL)
Geneva Coll (PA)
Gordon Coll (MA)
Greenville U (IL)
Harding U (AR)
Judson U (IL)
King U (TN)
Lancaster Bible Coll (PA)
Lee U (TN)
LeTourneau U (TX)
Liberty U (VA)
Lincoln Christian U (IL)
Lipscomb U (TN)
Lubbock Christian U (TX)
Milligan Coll (TN)
Northwest Christian U (OR)
Pfeiffer U (NC)
Point Loma Nazarene U (CA)
Redeemer U Coll (ON, Canada)
Rochester Coll (MI)
Southeastern U (FL)
Taylor U (IN)
Toccoa Falls Coll (GA)
Trevecca Nazarene U (TN)
Trinity Christian Coll (IL)
U of Northwestern–St. Paul (MN)
U of Sioux Falls (SD)
Vanguard U of Southern California (CA)

YOUTH SERVICES
Boston U (MA)
Montclair State U (NJ)
Murray State U (KY)
Rhode Island Coll (RI)
Samford U (AL)

ZOOLOGY/ANIMAL BIOLOGY
Auburn U (AL)
California State U, Long Beach (CA)
Canisius Coll (NY)
Colorado State U (CO)
Delaware Valley U (PA)
The Evergreen State Coll (WA)
Humboldt State U (CA)
Liberty U (VA)
Miami U (OH)
Miami U Hamilton (OH)
Michigan State U (MI)
Muskingum U (OH)
North Carolina State U (NC)
The Ohio State U (OH)
The Ohio State U at Lima (OH)
Ohio U (OH)
Ohio Wesleyan U (OH)
Oklahoma State U (OK)
San Diego State U (CA)
San Francisco State U (CA)
Sonoma State U (CA)
Southern Illinois U Carbondale (IL)
Texas Tech U (TX)
U of California, Davis (CA)
U of Florida (FL)
U of Hawaii at Manoa (HI)
U of Maine (ME)
U of New Hampshire (NH)
U of Vermont (VT)
U of Wyoming (WY)
Utah State U (UT)
Washington State U (WA)
Weber State U (UT)

Entrance Difficulty

This index groups colleges by their own assessment of their entrance difficulty level. The colleges were asked to select the level that most closely corresponds to their entrance difficulty, according to the guidelines below. Institutions for which high school class rank and/or standardized test scores do not apply as admission criteria were asked to select the level that best indicates their entrance difficulty as compared to other institutions.

MOST DIFFICULT

More than 75 percent of the freshmen were in the top 10 percent of their high school class and scored over 1310 on the SAT (critical reading and mathematical combined) or over 29 on the ACT (composite); about 30 percent or fewer of the applicants were accepted.

Brandeis U (MA)
Bucknell U (PA)
California Inst of Technology (CA)
Carnegie Mellon U (PA)
Claremont McKenna Coll (CA)
Colgate U (NY)
The Coll of William and Mary (VA)
Columbia U (NY)
Cornell U (NY)
Dartmouth Coll (NH)
Franklin W. Olin Coll of Eng (MA)
Harvard U (MA)
Haverford Coll (PA)
Hillsdale Coll (MI)
The Juilliard School (NY)
Massachusetts Inst of Technology (MA)
Middlebury Coll (VT)
Northwestern U (IL)
Princeton U (NJ)
Rice U (TX)
Soka U of America (CA)
U of Chicago (IL)
U of Notre Dame (IN)
U of Pennsylvania (PA)
Washington and Lee U (VA)
Washington U in St. Louis (MO)
Wesleyan U (CT)
Williams Coll (MA)

VERY DIFFICULT

More than 50 percent of the freshmen were in the top 10 percent of their high school class and scored over 1230 on the SAT or over 26 on the ACT; about 60 percent or fewer applicants were accepted.

Allegheny Coll (PA)
American U (DC)
American U in Bulgaria (Bulgaria)
Babson Coll (MA)
Baruch Coll of the City U of New York (NY)
Bentley U (MA)
Boston Coll (MA)
Boston U (MA)
Clarkson U (NY)
Coll of the Holy Cross (MA)
The Colorado Coll (CO)
Colorado School of Mines (CO)
Connecticut Coll (CT)
Davidson Coll (NC)
Dickinson Coll (PA)
Earlham Coll (IN)
Emerson Coll (MA)
Fairfield U (CT)
Fordham U (NY)
Hamilton Coll (NY)
Kalamazoo Coll (MI)
Knox Coll (IL)
Lafayette Coll (PA)
Lawrence U (WI)
Lewis & Clark Coll (OR)
Macalester Coll (MN)
Marist Coll (NY)
Maryland Inst Coll of Art (MD)
New Coll of Florida (FL)
New York U (NY)
North Carolina State U (NC)
Occidental Coll (CA)
Oglethorpe U (GA)
The Ohio State U (OH)
Ohio Wesleyan U (OH)
Pepperdine U, Malibu (CA)
Pitzer Coll (CA)
Queens Coll of the City U of New York (NY)
Rhodes Coll (TN)
St. John's Coll (MD)
St. John's Coll (NM)
Saint Louis U (MO)
St. Olaf Coll (MN)
San Diego State U (CA)
San Jose State U (CA)
Sarah Lawrence Coll (NY)
Scripps Coll (CA)
Skidmore Coll (NY)
Southwestern U (TX)
State U of New York Coll of Environmental Science and Forestry (NY)
State U of New York Maritime Coll (NY)
Stevens Inst of Technology (NJ)
Stockton U (NJ)
Stonehill Coll (MA)
Syracuse U (NY)
Texas Christian U (TX)
Tulane U (LA)
Union Coll (NY)
U of California, Davis (CA)
U of California, Irvine (CA)
U of California, Los Angeles (CA)
U of California, Riverside (CA)
U of California, Santa Cruz (CA)
U of Florida (FL)
U of Michigan (MI)
The U of North Carolina at Chapel Hill (NC)
U of Pittsburgh (PA)
U of Puerto Rico–Bayamón (PR)
U of Richmond (VA)
U of San Diego (CA)
The U of the South (TN)
The U of Tulsa (OK)
U of Virginia (VA)
U of Washington (WA)
Vassar Coll (NY)
Washington & Jefferson Coll (PA)
Wheaton Coll (IL)
Wheaton Coll (MA)
Willamette U (OR)
Wofford Coll (SC)
Worcester Polytechnic Inst (MA)

MODERATELY DIFFICULT

More than 75 percent of the freshmen were in the top half of their high school class and scored over 1010 on the SAT or over 18 on the ACT; about 85 percent or fewer of the applicants were accepted.

Acadia U (NS, Canada)
Adams State U (CO)
Adelphi U (NY)
Agnes Scott Coll (GA)
Albright Coll (PA)
Alfred U (NY)
Allen Coll (IA)
Alverno Coll (WI)
Angelo State U (TX)
Antioch Coll, Yellow Springs (OH)
Appalachian State U (NC)
Arkansas Tech U (AR)
Assumption Coll (MA)
Auburn U (AL)
Auburn U at Montgomery (AL)
Aurora U (IL)
Austin Coll (TX)
Austin Peay State U (TN)
Averett U (VA)
Baker U (KS)
Baldwin Wallace U (OH)
Baptist Coll of Health Sciences (TN)
Baylor U (TX)
Bellarmine U (KY)
Benedictine U (IL)
Berea Coll (KY)
Bethany Lutheran Coll (MN)
Bethel Coll (KS)
Bethel U (MN)
Blackburn Coll (IL)
Bowling Green State U (OH)
Bradley U (IL)
Brenau U (GA)
Bridgewater Coll (VA)
Bridgewater State U (MA)
Bryant U (RI)
Buena Vista U (IA)
Butler U (IN)
Caldwell U (NJ)
California Lutheran U (CA)
California Polytechnic State U, San Luis Obispo (CA)
California State U, Chico (CA)
California State U, Fullerton (CA)
California State U, Long Beach (CA)
California State U, Los Angeles (CA)
California State U, Monterey Bay (CA)
California State U, Northridge (CA)
California State U, San Bernardino (CA)
California State U, San Marcos (CA)
California U of Pennsylvania (PA)
Calvin Coll (MI)
Campbellsville U (KY)
Canisius Coll (NY)
Carson-Newman U (TN)
Carthage Coll (WI)
The Catholic U of America (DC)
Cedarville U (OH)
Centenary Coll of Louisiana (LA)
Central Connecticut State U (CT)
Central Michigan U (MI)
Central Washington U (WA)
Champlain Coll (VT)
Christian Brothers U (TN)
Christopher Newport U (VA)
Clark U (MA)
Cleveland Inst of Art (OH)
Coastal Carolina U (SC)
The Coll at Brockport, State U of New York (NY)
Coll of Charleston (SC)
The Coll of Idaho (ID)
Coll of Saint Benedict (MN)
The Coll of Saint Rose (NY)
The Coll of St. Scholastica (MN)
Coll of the Ozarks (MO)
Colorado State U (CO)
Concordia U Chicago (IL)
Concordia U Irvine (CA)
Cornell Coll (IA)
Covenant Coll (GA)
Creighton U (NE)
Culver-Stockton Coll (MO)
Curry Coll (MA)
Dakota State U (SD)
Dallas Baptist U (TX)
Dallas Christian Coll (TX)
Dean Coll (MA)
DePaul U (IL)
DEREE - The American Coll of Greece (Greece)
Dominican U (IL)
Drake U (IA)
Drew U (NJ)
Drury U (MO)

INDEXES

Duquesne U (PA)
East Carolina U (NC)
Eastern Illinois U (IL)
Eastern Mennonite U (VA)
Eastern U (PA)
East Stroudsburg U of Pennsylvania (PA)
East Tennessee State U (TN)
East Texas Baptist U (TX)
Eckerd Coll (FL)
Elizabeth City State U (NC)
Embry-Riddle Aeronautical U–Daytona (FL)
Embry-Riddle Aeronautical U–Prescott (AZ)
Endicott Coll (MA)
Escuela de Artes Plasticas y Diseño de Puerto Rico (PR)
The Evergreen State Coll (WA)
Farmingdale State Coll (NY)
Fashion Inst of Technology (NY)
FIDM/Fashion Inst of Design & Merchandising, Los Angeles Campus (CA)
Fitchburg State U (MA)
Florida Ag and Mech U (FL)
Florida Atlantic U (FL)
Florida Coll (FL)
Florida Southern Coll (FL)
Fort Lewis Coll (CO)
Framingham State U (MA)
Furman U (SC)
Geneva Coll (PA)
George Mason U (VA)
Georgetown Coll (KY)
Georgia Coll & State U (GA)
Georgia Southern U (GA)
Georgia State U (GA)
Gonzaga U (WA)
Gordon Coll (MA)
Goshen Coll (IN)
Graceland U (IA)
Grand Valley State U (MI)
Greenville U (IL)
Grove City Coll (PA)
Gwynedd Mercy U (PA)
Hamline U (MN)
Hampden-Sydney Coll (VA)
Hanover Coll (IN)
Harding U (AR)
Hardin-Simmons U (TX)
Hartwick Coll (NY)
High Point U (NC)
Hiram Coll (OH)
Hofstra U (NY)
Hollins U (VA)
Hood Coll (MD)
Hult Intl Business School (United Kingdom)
Hunter Coll of the City U of New York (NY)
Illinois Coll (IL)
Immaculata U (PA)
Indiana State U (IN)
Indiana U Bloomington (IN)
Indiana U East (IN)
Indiana U–Purdue U Indianapolis (IN)
Indiana U South Bend (IN)
Inter American U of Puerto Rico, Aguadilla Campus (PR)
Inter American U of Puerto Rico, Fajardo Campus (PR)
Inter American U of Puerto Rico, San Germán Campus (PR)
Iona Coll (NY)
Iowa State U of Science and Technology (IA)
Ithaca Coll (NY)
Jacksonville U (FL)
John Paul the Great Catholic U (CA)
Johnson C. Smith U (NC)
Judson U (IL)
Juniata Coll (PA)
Kansas Wesleyan U (KS)
Kean U (NJ)
Kennesaw State U (GA)
King's Coll (PA)
King U (TN)
Kuyper Coll (MI)
LaGrange Coll (GA)
Lake Forest Coll (IL)
La Salle U (PA)
Lasell Coll (MA)
Lawrence Technological U (MI)
Lebanese American U (Lebanon)
Lebanon Valley Coll (PA)
Lee U (TN)
LeTourneau U (TX)
Lincoln Christian U (IL)
Lindenwood U (MO)
Linfield Coll (OR)
Lipscomb U (TN)
Lock Haven U of Pennsylvania (PA)
Loras Coll (IA)
Louisiana Coll (LA)
Louisiana State U and A&M Coll (LA)
Loyola U Chicago (IL)
Loyola U New Orleans (LA)
Lubbock Christian U (TX)
Lycoming Coll (PA)
Madonna U (MI)
Maharishi U of Management (IA)
Manchester U (IN)
Manhattan Coll (NY)
Mansfield U of Pennsylvania (PA)
Marian U (IN)
Marquette U (WI)
Marshall U (WV)
Martin Luther Coll (MN)
Marymount Manhattan Coll (NY)
Marymount U (VA)
Maryville U of Saint Louis (MO)
Marywood U (PA)
Massachusetts Coll of Liberal Arts (MA)
Massachusetts Maritime Acad (MA)
McDaniel Coll (MD)
McNeese State U (LA)
Mercer U, Macon (GA)
Mercy Coll (NY)
Mercy Coll of Ohio (OH)
Merrimack Coll (MA)
Messenger Coll (TX)
Messiah Coll (PA)
Miami U (OH)
Michigan State U (MI)
Middle Tennessee State U (TN)
Millersville U of Pennsylvania (PA)
Milligan Coll (TN)
Millikin U (IL)
Millsaps Coll (MS)
Mills Coll (CA)
Minnesota State U Moorhead (MN)
Missouri Baptist U (MO)
Molloy Coll (NY)
Montclair State U (NJ)
Morningside Coll (IA)
Mount Carmel Coll of Nursing (OH)
Mount Saint Mary Coll (NY)
Murray State U (KY)
Muskingum U (OH)
Nebraska Methodist Coll (NE)
New Jersey City U (NJ)
New Jersey Inst of Technology (NJ)
Northeastern State U (OK)
Northern Illinois U (IL)
Northern Kentucky U (KY)
Northwestern Oklahoma State U (OK)
Northwest Missouri State U (MO)
Northwood U, Michigan Campus (MI)
Ohio Dominican U (OH)
Ohio U (OH)
Oklahoma Baptist U (OK)
Oklahoma Christian U (OK)
Oklahoma State U (OK)
Old Dominion U (VA)
Ottawa U (KS)
Ouachita Baptist U (AR)
Pace U (NY)
Pace U, Pleasantville Campus (NY)
Pacific Lutheran U (WA)
Palm Beach Atlantic U (FL)
Pennsylvania Coll of Art & Design (PA)
Pfeiffer U (NC)
Piedmont Coll (GA)
Point Loma Nazarene U (CA)
Point U (GA)
Portland State U (OR)
Prairie View A&M U (TX)
Providence Coll (RI)
Purchase Coll, State U of New York (NY)
Purdue U (IN)
Purdue U Northwest (IN)
Queens U of Charlotte (NC)
Randolph Coll (VA)
Randolph-Macon Coll (VA)
Regis U (CO)
Reinhardt U (GA)
Rhode Island Coll (RI)
Rider U (NJ)
Roanoke Coll (VA)
Rochester Inst of Technology (NY)
Rocky Mountain Coll (MT)
Rollins Coll (FL)
Sacred Heart U (CT)
The Sage Colls (NY)
Saginaw Valley State U (MI)
Saint Anselm Coll (NH)
Saint Francis U (PA)
St. John Fisher Coll (NY)
Saint John's U (MN)
St. Joseph's Coll, Long Island Campus (NY)
St. Joseph's Coll, New York (NY)
Saint Joseph's U (PA)
Saint Leo U (FL)
Saint Martin's U (WA)
St. Mary's Coll of Maryland (MD)
St. Mary's U (TX)
Saint Mary's U of Minnesota (MN)
St. Norbert Coll (WI)
Saint Vincent Coll (PA)
Salisbury U (MD)
Samford U (AL)
San Francisco State U (CA)
Savannah Coll of Art and Design (GA)
Seattle U (WA)
Seton Hill U (PA)
Sonoma State U (CA)
Southeastern Louisiana U (LA)
Southeast Missouri State U (MO)
Southern Arkansas U–Magnolia (AR)
Southern Illinois U Carbondale (IL)
Southern Illinois U Edwardsville (IL)
Southern U and Ag and Mech Coll (LA)
Southwest Baptist U (MO)
Spring Hill Coll (AL)
State U of New York at Fredonia (NY)
State U of New York at Plattsburgh (NY)
State U of New York Coll at Geneseo (NY)
State U of New York Coll at Potsdam (NY)
State U of New York Coll of Technology at Alfred (NY)
State U of New York Coll of Technology at Delhi (NY)
Stetson U (FL)
Tabor Coll (KS)
Taylor U (IN)
Temple U (PA)
Texas A&M Intl U (TX)
Texas Lutheran U (TX)
Texas Tech U (TX)
Texas Woman's U (TX)
Tiffin U (OH)
Toccoa Falls Coll (GA)
Towson U (MD)
Trevecca Nazarene U (TN)
Trinity Christian Coll (IL)
Truman State U (MO)
Tyndale U Coll & Sem (ON, Canada)
Union Coll (KY)
Université de Sherbrooke (QC, Canada)
Université Sainte-Anne (NS, Canada)
U at Buffalo, the State U of New York (NY)
U of Arkansas (AR)
U of California, Merced (CA)
U of Central Arkansas (AR)
U of Central Florida (FL)
U of Colorado Denver (CO)
U of Dallas (TX)
U of Dayton (OH)
U of Detroit Mercy (MI)
The U of Findlay (OH)
U of Georgia (GA)
U of Hawaii at Manoa (HI)
U of Houston (TX)
U of Idaho (ID)
U of Illinois at Springfield (IL)
U of Kentucky (KY)
U of La Verne (CA)

U of Louisville (KY)
U of Lynchburg (VA)
U of Maine (ME)
U of Maine at Farmington (ME)
U of Maine at Machias (ME)
U of Mary Hardin-Baylor (TX)
U of Maryland, Baltimore County (MD)
U of Maryland, Coll Park (MD)
U of Maryland Eastern Shore (MD)
U of Massachusetts Amherst (MA)
U of Massachusetts Boston (MA)
U of Massachusetts Dartmouth (MA)
U of Massachusetts Lowell (MA)
U of Memphis (TN)
U of Michigan–Dearborn (MI)
U of Minnesota, Duluth (MN)
U of Minnesota, Morris (MN)
U of Minnesota, Twin Cities Campus (MN)
U of Missouri (MO)
U of Montevallo (AL)
U of Mount Union (OH)
U of Nebraska–Lincoln (NE)
U of Nevada, Las Vegas (NV)
U of Nevada, Reno (NV)
U of New Hampshire (NH)
U of New Haven (CT)
U of New Mexico (NM)
U of North Carolina at Asheville (NC)
The U of North Carolina at Charlotte (NC)
The U of North Carolina at Greensboro (NC)
The U of North Carolina at Pembroke (NC)
U of Northern Colorado (CO)
U of Northern Iowa (IA)
U of North Florida (FL)
U of Northwestern–St. Paul (MN)
U of Oregon (OR)
U of Puget Sound (WA)
U of Saint Mary (KS)
U of St. Thomas (MN)
U of St. Thomas (TX)
U of San Francisco (CA)
U of Sioux Falls (SD)
U of South Alabama (AL)
U of South Carolina (SC)
U of South Carolina Aiken (SC)
U of South Dakota (SD)
U of Southern Indiana (IN)
U of South Florida Sarasota-Manatee (FL)
The U of Tampa (FL)
The U of Tennessee (TN)
The U of Tennessee at Martin (TN)
The U of Texas at Austin (TX)
The U of Texas of the Permian Basin (TX)
U of Vermont (VT)
U of Washington, Bothell (WA)
U of Washington, Tacoma (WA)
U of West Georgia (GA)
U of Wisconsin–Eau Claire (WI)
U of Wisconsin–La Crosse (WI)
U of Wisconsin–Milwaukee (WI)
U of Wisconsin–River Falls (WI)
U of Wyoming (WY)
Ursinus Coll (PA)
Utah State U (UT)
Utica Coll (NY)
Valparaiso U (IN)
Vanguard U of Southern California (CA)
Vaughn Coll of Aeronautics and Technology (NY)
Vermont Tech Coll (VT)
Virginia Polytechnic Inst and State U (VA)
Wabash Coll (IN)
Wartburg Coll (IA)
Washington State U (WA)
Washington State U–Spokane (WA)
Washington State U–Tri-Cities (WA)
Washington State U–Vancouver (WA)
Waynesburg U (PA)
Wesleyan Coll (GA)
West Chester U of Pennsylvania (PA)
Western Connecticut State U (CT)
Western Illinois U (IL)
Western State Colorado U (CO)
Western Washington U (WA)
Westmont Coll (CA)
Whittier Coll (CA)
Whitworth U (WA)
Widener U (PA)
Wilkes U (PA)
William Jewell Coll (MO)
Winthrop U (SC)
Woodbury U (CA)
Worcester State U (MA)

MINIMALLY DIFFICULT

Most freshmen were not in the top half of their high school class and scored somewhat below 1010 on the SAT or below 19 on the ACT; up to 95 percent of the applicants were accepted.

AdventHealth U (FL)
Alabama State U (AL)
American Coll of Thessaloniki (Greece)
Amridge U (AL)
Avila U (MO)
Barton Coll (NC)
Bennett Coll (NC)
Berkeley Coll–New York City Campus (NY)
Berkeley Coll–White Plains Campus (NY)
Berkeley Coll–Woodland Park Campus (NJ)
Bryn Athyn Coll of the New Church (PA)
Central State U (OH)
Clarion U of Pennsylvania (PA)
Coll of Coastal Georgia (GA)
Coll of Saint Mary (NE)
Colorado State U–Pueblo (CO)
Columbia Central U, Yauco (PR)
Columbia Coll (MO)
Columbia Coll Chicago (IL)
Davenport U, Grand Rapids (MI)
Delaware Valley U (PA)
DigiPen Inst of Technology (WA)
Dunwoody Coll of Technology (MN)
Eastern Oregon U (OR)
Embry-Riddle Aeronautical U–Worldwide (FL)
Emmanuel Coll (GA)
Fayetteville State U (NC)
Franklin Pierce U (NH)
Humboldt State U (CA)
Idaho State U (ID)
Indiana U Kokomo (IN)
Indiana U Northwest (IN)
Indiana U of Pennsylvania (PA)
Indiana U Southeast (IN)
Jackson State U (MS)
Johnson U Florida (FL)
Lamar U (TX)
Lancaster Bible Coll (PA)
La Sierra U (CA)
Lees-McRae Coll (NC)
Liberty U (VA)
Life U (GA)
Limestone Coll (SC)
Manhattanville Coll (NY)
Manor Coll (PA)
Maria Coll (NY)
Marymount California U (CA)
Mount Marty Coll (SD)
Mount St. Joseph U (OH)
New England Coll (NH)
New England Inst of Technology (RI)
Nichols Coll (MA)
Northern State U (SD)
Northwest Christian U (OR)
Oakland City U (IN)
Radford U (VA)
Regent U (VA)
Rochester Coll (MI)
Rockford U (IL)
St. Luke's Coll (IA)
Southeastern U (FL)
Sullivan U (KY)
Sweet Briar Coll (VA)
U of Houston–Clear Lake (TX)
U of Maine at Presque Isle (ME)
U of North Dakota (ND)
U of Pittsburgh at Bradford (PA)
U of Regina (SK, Canada)
U of South Carolina Union (SC)
The U of Texas at El Paso (TX)
U of the Incarnate Word (TX)
The U of West Alabama (AL)
U of Wisconsin–Superior (WI)
Western Kentucky U (KY)
West Virginia State U (WV)
West Virginia U Inst of Technology (WV)
Wright State U–Lake Campus (OH)
Youngstown State U (OH)

NONCOMPETITIVE

Virtually all applicants were accepted regardless of high school rank or test scores.

Acad of Art U (CA)
American Public U System (WV)
Arapahoe Comm Coll (CO)
Austin Comm Coll District (TX)
Calumet Coll of Saint Joseph (IN)
Cameron U (OK)
Capilano U (BC, Canada)
Coll of Central Florida (FL)
Coll of Staten Island of the City U of New York (NY)
Columbia Central U, Caguas (PR)
Columbia Southern U (AL)
Daytona State Coll (FL)
Delta State U (MS)
Georgia Highlands Coll (GA)
Granite State Coll (NH)
Holy Apostles Coll and Sem (CT)
Huntington U of Health Sciences (TN)
Miami U Hamilton (OH)
National U (CA)
The Ohio State U at Lima (OH)
The Ohio State U at Mansfield (OH)
The Ohio State U at Marion (OH)
The Ohio State U at Newark (OH)
Potomac State Coll of West Virginia U (WV)
Pueblo Comm Coll (CO)
Renton Tech Coll (WA)
Shiloh U (IA)
Southeastern Baptist Theological Sem (NC)
Truckee Meadows Comm Coll (NV)
Tyler Jr Coll (TX)
U of Guam (GU)
U of Houston–Downtown (TX)
U of Maryland U Coll (MD)
U of Providence (MT)
U of Saint Francis (IN)
The U of Texas Rio Grande Valley (TX)
The U of Toledo (OH)
Valley City State U (ND)
Vincennes U (IN)
Weber State U (UT)

Cost Ranges

LESS THAN $2000

Colleges with No Room and Board or with Room Only
The U of North Carolina at Pembroke (NC)

$2000–$3999

Colleges with No Room and Board or with Room Only
Truckee Meadows Comm Coll (NV)

$4000–$5999

Colleges with No Room and Board or with Room Only
Columbia Southern U (AL)
Pueblo Comm Coll (CO)
Shiloh U (IA)

$6000–$7999

Colleges with No Room and Board or with Room Only
Granite State Coll (NH)
Huntington U of Health Sciences (TN)
New Coll of Florida (FL)

Colleges with Room and Board
Berea Coll (KY)
Theological U of the Caribbean (PR)

$8000–$9999

Colleges with No Room and Board or with Room Only
California State U, Fullerton (CA)
U of Houston–Downtown (TX)

Colleges with Room and Board
Coll of the Ozarks (MO)
Union Coll (KY)
U of Guam (GU)

$10,000–$11,999

Colleges with No Room and Board or with Room Only
U of Houston–Clear Lake (TX) **(room only)**

$12,000–$13,999

Colleges with No Room and Board or with Room Only
National U (CA)

Colleges with Room and Board
Central Connecticut State U (CT)
Elizabeth City State U (NC)
Sweet Briar Coll (VA)

$14,000–$15,999

Colleges with No Room and Board or with Room Only
Baptist Coll of Health Sciences (TN) **(room only)**
DEREE - The American Coll of Greece (Greece)

Colleges with Room and Board
American U in Bulgaria (Bulgaria)
Auburn U at Montgomery (AL)
Inter American U of Puerto Rico, Bayamón Campus (PR)
Marian U (IN)
U of Wyoming (WY)

$16,000–$17,999

Colleges with No Room and Board or with Room Only
Colorado School of Mines (CO)

Colleges with Room and Board
Angelo State U (TX)
Columbia Central U, Caguas (PR)
Florida Ag and Mech U (FL)
Florida Atlantic U (FL)
Messenger Coll (TX)
Texas A&M Intl U (TX)
U of Maine at Presque Isle (ME)
U of West Georgia (GA)

$18,000–$19,999

Colleges with No Room and Board or with Room Only
Northwest Coll of Art & Design (WA)

Colleges with Room and Board
California State U, Los Angeles (CA)
California State U, San Marcos (CA)
Prairie View A&M U (TX)
Texas Woman's U (TX)
U of Maryland Eastern Shore (MD)
U of North Carolina School of the Arts (NC)
U of South Florida (FL)

$20,000–$24,999

Colleges with No Room and Board or with Room Only
AdventHealth U (FL) **(room only)**
Calumet Coll of Saint Joseph (IN)
St. Luke's Coll (IA)
Texas A&M U–Central Texas (TX)

Colleges with Room and Board
Bridgewater State U (MA)
Central Washington U (WA)
Colorado State U (CO)
Colorado State U–Pueblo (CO)
Eastern Washington U (WA)
Framingham State U (MA)
Humboldt State U (CA)
Johnson U Florida (FL)
Maharishi U of Management (IA)
Manor Coll (PA)
Martin Luther Coll (MN)
North Carolina State U (NC)
Portland State U (OR)
Purdue U (IN)
San Francisco State U (CA)
Southern Illinois U Edwardsville (IL)
State U of New York at Plattsburgh (NY)
State U of New York Coll of Technology at Alfred (NY)
Towson U (MD)
U of Hawaii at Manoa (HI)
U of Houston (TX)
U of Illinois at Springfield (IL)
U of Louisville (KY)
The U of North Carolina at Chapel Hill (NC)
U of Northern Colorado (CO)
U of Wisconsin–Milwaukee (WI)
Western Connecticut State U (CT)
Western State Colorado U (CO)
West Virginia State U (WV)

$25,000–$29,999

Colleges with No Room and Board or with Room Only
Columbia Coll Chicago (IL)
Creative Center (NE)
Mount Carmel Coll of Nursing (OH) **(room only)**
Pennsylvania Coll of Art & Design (PA)

Colleges with Room and Board
Allen Coll (IA)
Avila U (MO)
Coll of Saint Mary (NE)
Dunwoody Coll of Technology (MN)
Emmanuel Coll (GA)
Grove City Coll (PA)
Lee U (TN)
Lindenwood U (MO)
Nebraska Methodist Coll (NE)
Point U (GA)
Regent U (VA)
San Diego State U (CA)
U of Michigan (MI)
U of Sioux Falls (SD)
Vermont Tech Coll (VT)

$30,000 AND OVER

Colleges with No Room and Board or with Room Only
Benedictine U (IL)
DigiPen Inst of Technology (WA) **(room only)**
FIDM/Fashion Inst of Design & Merchandising, Los Angeles Campus (CA)
Iona Coll (NY)
John Paul the Great Catholic U (CA) **(room only)**
Palm Beach Atlantic U (FL) **(room only)**
Pennsylvania Acad of the Fine Arts (PA) **(room only)**
The Sage Colls (NY)
St. John Fisher Coll (NY)

Colleges with Room and Board
Acad of Art U (CA)
Agnes Scott Coll (GA)
Albion Coll (MI)
Albright Coll (PA)
Alfred U (NY)
Allegheny Coll (PA)
American U (DC)
Antioch Coll, Yellow Springs (OH)
Assumption Coll (MA)
Aurora U (IL)
Austin Coll (TX)
Babson Coll (MA)
Baker U (KS)
Baldwin Wallace U (OH)
Barton Coll (NC)
Baylor U (TX)
Bellarmine U (KY)
Bentley U (MA)
Bethany Lutheran Coll (MN)
Bethel Coll (KS)
Bethel U (MN)
Blackburn Coll (IL)
Boston U (MA)
Brandeis U (MA)
Brenau U (GA)
Bridgewater Coll (VA)

Bryant U (RI)
Bucknell U (PA)
Buena Vista U (IA)
Butler U (IN)
Caldwell U (NJ)
California Inst of Technology (CA)
California Lutheran U (CA)
Calvin Coll (MI)
Campbellsville U (KY)
Canisius Coll (NY)
Carnegie Mellon U (PA)
Carson-Newman U (TN)
Carthage Coll (WI)
The Catholic U of America (DC)
Cedarville U (OH)
Centenary Coll of Louisiana (LA)
Champlain Coll (VT)
Claremont McKenna Coll (CA)
Clarkson U (NY)
Clark U (MA)
Cleveland Inst of Art (OH)
Colgate U (NY)
The Coll of Idaho (ID)
The Coll of Saint Rose (NY)
The Coll of St. Scholastica (MN)
Coll of the Holy Cross (MA)
The Colorado Coll (CO)
Concordia U Chicago (IL)
Concordia U Irvine (CA)
Cornell Coll (IA)
Covenant Coll (GA)
Creighton U (NE)
Culver-Stockton Coll (MO)
Curry Coll (MA)
Dallas Baptist U (TX)
Dartmouth Coll (NH)
Davidson Coll (NC)
Dean Coll (MA)
Delaware Valley U (PA)
Dickinson Coll (PA)
Dominican U (IL)
Drury U (MO)
Duquesne U (PA)
Earlham Coll (IN)
Eastern U (PA)
East Texas Baptist U (TX)
Embry-Riddle Aeronautical U–Daytona (FL)
Embry-Riddle Aeronautical U–Prescott (AZ)
Emerson Coll (MA)
Emmanuel Coll (MA)
Endicott Coll (MA)
Franklin Pierce U (NH)
Franklin W. Olin Coll of Eng (MA)
Geneva Coll (PA)
Georgetown Coll (KY)
Gonzaga U (WA)
Gordon Coll (MA)
Goshen Coll (IN)
Graceland U (IA)
Greenville U (IL)
Gwynedd Mercy U (PA)
Hamilton Coll (NY)
Hamline U (MN)
Hampden-Sydney Coll (VA)
Hanover Coll (IN)
Hardin-Simmons U (TX)
Hartwick Coll (NY)
Hiram Coll (OH)
Hollins U (VA)
Hood Coll (MD)
Hult Intl Business School (United Kingdom)
Immaculata U (PA)
Ithaca Coll (NY)
Jacksonville U (FL)
John Cabot U (Italy)
Judson U (IL)
The Juilliard School (NY)
Juniata Coll (PA)
Kalamazoo Coll (MI)
Kansas Wesleyan U (KS)
Keystone Coll (PA)
King's Coll (PA)
King U (TN)
Knox Coll (IL)
Lafayette Coll (PA)
Lake Forest Coll (IL)
Lasell Coll (MA)
La Sierra U (CA)
Lawrence U (WI)
Lebanon Valley Coll (PA)
Lees-McRae Coll (NC)
Lesley U (MA)
LeTourneau U (TX)
Liberty U (VA)
LIM Coll (NY)
Limestone Coll (SC)
Linfield Coll (OR)
Lipscomb U (TN)
Loras Coll (IA)
Loyola U Chicago (IL)
Loyola U New Orleans (LA)
Lubbock Christian U (TX)
Lycoming Coll (PA)
Macalester Coll (MN)
Madonna U (MI)
Manchester U (IN)
Manhattanville Coll (NY)
Marist Coll (NY)
Marymount Manhattan Coll (NY)
Maryville U of Saint Louis (MO)
Marywood U (PA)
Massachusetts Inst of Technology (MA)
Messiah Coll (PA)
Middlebury Coll (VT)
Milligan Coll (TN)
Millikin U (IL)
Millsaps Coll (MS)
Missouri Baptist U (MO)
Morningside Coll (IA)
Mount Marty Coll (SD)
Muskingum U (OH)
Nazareth Coll of Rochester (NY)
New England Coll (NH)
New England Inst of Technology (RI)
New Jersey Inst of Technology (NJ)
Nichols Coll (MA)
Northwest Christian U (OR)
Oakland City U (IN)
Occidental Coll (CA)
Oglethorpe U (GA)
Ohio Dominican U (OH)
Oklahoma Baptist U (OK)
Oklahoma Christian U (OK)
Ouachita Baptist U (AR)
Pace U (NY)
Pacific Lutheran U (WA)
Piedmont Coll (GA)
Princeton U (NJ)
Providence Coll (RI)
Randolph Coll (VA)
Randolph-Macon Coll (VA)
Reinhardt U (GA)
Rhode Island School of Design (RI)
Rhodes Coll (TN)
Rice U (TX)
Rider U (NJ)
Roanoke Coll (VA)
Rochester Coll (MI)
Rocky Mountain Coll (MT)
Saint Anselm Coll (NH)
Saint Francis U (PA)
St. John's Coll (MD)
St. John's Coll (NM)
Saint Joseph's U (PA)
Saint Leo U (FL)
Saint Louis U (MO)
Saint Martin's U (WA)
St. Mary's U (TX)
Saint Mary's U of Minnesota (MN)
St. Norbert Coll (WI)
Salve Regina U (RI)
Samford U (AL)
Savannah Coll of Art and Design (GA)
Seattle U (WA)
Seton Hill U (PA)
Soka U of America (CA)
Southeastern U (FL)
Southwest Baptist U (MO)
Southwestern U (TX)
Stetson U (FL)
Stevens Inst of Technology (NJ)
Tabor Coll (KS)
Taylor U (IN)
Texas Christian U (TX)
Tiffin U (OH)
Toccoa Falls Coll (GA)
Trevecca Nazarene U (TN)
Trinity Christian Coll (IL)
Tulane U (LA)
U of Dallas (TX)
U of Dayton (OH)
U of Detroit Mercy (MI)
The U of Findlay (OH)
U of La Verne (CA)
U of Mount Union (OH)
U of Northwestern–St. Paul (MN)
U of Pennsylvania (PA)
U of Providence (MT)
U of Puget Sound (WA)
U of Richmond (VA)
U of Saint Francis (IN)
U of Saint Mary (KS)
U of St. Thomas (MN)
U of St. Thomas (TX)
U of San Diego (CA)
U of San Francisco (CA)
U of the Incarnate Word (TX)
The U of the South (TN)
The U of Tulsa (OK)
Ursinus Coll (PA)
Valparaiso U (IN)
Vanguard U of Southern California (CA)
Vaughn Coll of Aeronautics and Technology (NY)
Wabash Coll (IN)
Wartburg Coll (IA)
Washington U in St. Louis (MO)
Waynesburg U (PA)
Wesleyan Coll (GA)
Wesleyan U (CT)
Westmont Coll (CA)
Wheaton Coll (IL)
Wheaton Coll (MA)
Whitworth U (WA)
Widener U (PA)
Willamette U (OR)
William Jewell Coll (MO)
Williams Coll (MA)
Wofford Coll (SC)
Woodbury U (CA)

Advertisers Index

INDEXES

Alphabetical Listing of Colleges and Universities

INDEXES

INDEXES

INDEXES

INDEXES

INDEXES

INDEXES

INDEXES

INDEXES

INDEXES

Geographic Listing of Close-Ups

NOTES

NOTES

NOTES

NOTES

NOTES

NOTES

NOTES

NOTES

NOTES

NOTES

NOTES

NOTES

In contrast, the gradiental/distributive view of the brain suggests that the brain—especially in contextually rich, meaningful, real-lifelike settings—is extremely active and that the activity shifts over time as the new learnings are used and committed to long-term memory. As seen in the graphic on the previous page, the frontal lobe is active when the cognitive task is new (the brain is naive), row (a). Frontal activation drops with task familiarization, row (b). The frontal lobes become partially activated again when a somewhat different task is introduced (similar to a known one but not identical to it). These right to left, front to back, and top to bottom shifts illustrate the widespread involvement of the brain in learning and the significant physiological activity and growth/change that is the process of learning, a process unique to each brain with a timeline that cannot be dictated by bureaucratic needs.

Brain Organization and the ITI Definition of Learning

Perhaps the most fascinating aspect of Goldberg's gradiental model with its shifts from right to left frontal, from front to back, and neocortex to older structures is that it provides a physiological explanation for Leslie Hart's definition of learning as a two-step process (see graphic in next column). To assist teachers in planning curriculum and instructional strategies, we have broken each of those steps into two phases. The correspondence is striking.

Admittedly, these are broad brush strokes but knowing that different parts of the brain must be engaged to move learning from an initial "Aha" to long-term memory of how to *use* the knowledge or skill gives us a larger view of learning. It allows us to key in to what sensory and motor input students need, what practice *using* the knowledge or skill will move the learning from new to practiced, and the time it takes to make those physiological shifts in the brain. Suddenly, "covering" content and relying on paper-pencil tests to indicate mastery can be seen as the useless strategies that they are.

New definition of learning	***Brain activity when learning something new***
▪ **Step One: Pattern-Seeking**	
Identifying patterns..................................	Primarily right frontal lobes shifting to
Making meaning/understanding................	Primarily left frontal lobes
▪ **Step Two: Program-Building**	
Able to use learning with support..............	Shift from front toward back of brain
Ability to use the learning becomes automatic and part of long-term memory.......	Shift to back and lower/older brain structures

The Program Cycle

This chapter addresses the second step of learning—developing programs for using what is understood.

The basic cycle in using programs is:

Step 1. Evaluate the situation or need (detect and identify the pattern or patterns). For example, is it a birthday, graduation, holiday, costume, or office party? (Each demands certain consideration, appropriate dress, gift, contribution to the potluck, etc.) Ah, it's a birthday party.

Step 2. In response to the incoming patterns, select the most appropriate program from those stored. For example, because it's a birthday party you prepare to RSVP, buy a present, wear party clothes, and eat a skimpy breakfast and lunch because you know there will be cake and ice cream.

Step 3. Implement the program. For example, you execute your plans by going to the party and having a great time.

As illustrated in the previous example, the first step in the learning process is detecting pattern. Once a situation has been analyzed, and if action is required, the brain scans its repertoire of stored programs, selecting the one that is most appropriate or calling forth two or more and using them in fresh combinations.

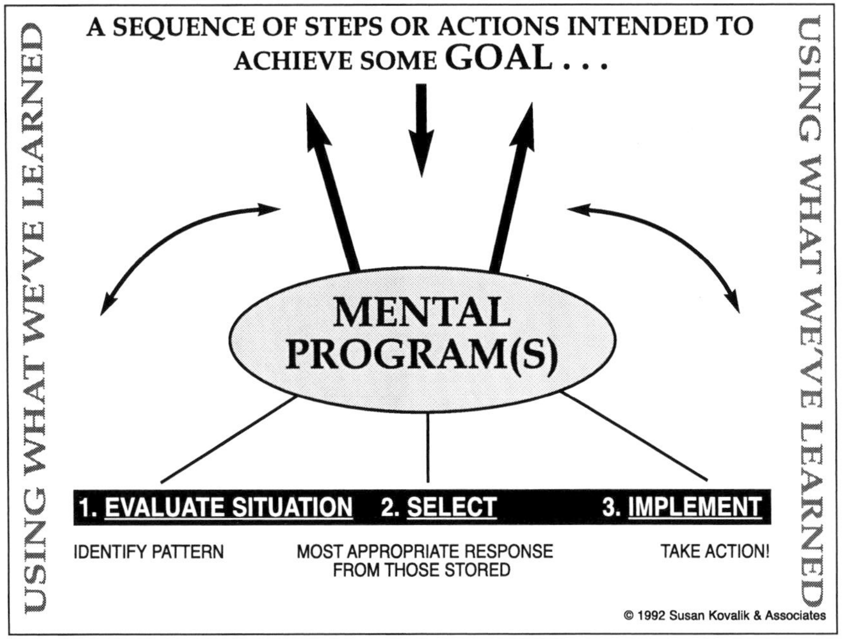

Towards a positive end, such capacity to "use old programs in fresh combinations" underlies what we call creativity.[4]

Used negatively, this evaluate—select—implement process is seen in the case of the student who repeatedly misbehaves. Wanting to attract the teacher's attention, this student reaches into his/her mental bag of programs and, as unconsciously as the driver arriving at the wrong parking lot, automatically pulls out a behavior that will attract attention. Unfortunately, the behavior also makes the teacher furious. In such students' mental bag of programs, there are too many of the "wrong" behaviors/programs and too few of the "right" ones, i.e., ones that get the attention of the teacher but without the anger.

Equally somber is the child-grown-adult who has no program for using multiplication for real-world applications such as computing mortgage payments or figuring the real cost of an item he/she let ride on the VISA charge card. Unpleasant consequences flow from lack of appropriate mental programs.

Successful implementation of a mental program is its own reward, accompanied by feelings of accomplishment and increased satisfaction. Aborting a mental program that doesn't work is emotionally unsettling because it leaves us unsure of what to do next and decreases our sense of self confidence.[5] When orchestrating your curriculum, provide the time and experiences that allow youngsters to master new information and add it to prior knowledge in a meaningful way, thereby creating new mental programs.

Hart, in fact, defines learning as "the acquisition of useful programs."[6] "Learning," such as getting an A on a paper/pencil test, which does not result in acquisition of a mental program is not learning from Hart's perspective because it doesn't stick. Hart points out that information that does not become part of a program is usually unretrievable. For example, recall your sophomore college days and the traditional western civilization class. The characteristics of this stunning experience: yearlong, 99.9 percent lecture, and an enormously fat textbook. For the mid-term and final exams, you used the ubiquitous blue book. Weeks later when the blue book was graded and returned, you glanced inside. To your total shock, there were paragraphs of stuff you didn't even recognize—never heard of before! A classic example of information that never became part of a program and, thus, is unretrievable and often unrecognizable, even a bare three weeks later. In other words, most information that we use is embedded in programs; the corollary is: information that is not used is also not retrievable and, if truth be told, was probably never "learned" in the first place. Thus, "covering information" is a colossal waste of time for both students and teachers.

The implications for the classroom of the 21st century are obvious—students must master concepts and skills with depth of understanding and use what they understand. We in turn need to present less content and give students time to "use" the information again and again in varying settings until the information is recallable in a usable form, i.e., a behavior, a program.

It should be noted that programs and subskills are not identical and have little in common. A program, while it can be enormously complex, such as driving a car, is a sequence for accomplishing some end—a goal, objective, or outcome—an end with meaning to the learner. Subskills, such as the blend *ch* or the short *i* are not a sequence for accomplishing some end; they are experienced as isolated, fragmented pieces. In contrast, the program to be attained is the act of reading—an insight young students can easily miss.

To reinforce the difference between pattern-seeking (making meaning of input) and program building (using what is learned), consider diapering a baby. Everyone recognizes the patterns diaper and baby; But, as Diane Keaton makes clear in the movie, *Baby Boom,* not everyone can diaper a moving baby. The same is true with returning a rental car. Everyone knows what the words *car, return, rental,* and *airport* mean. But not everyone has a mental program of the steps for *returning a rental car to an airport.*

Because this discussion of building programs and wiring knowledge and skills into long-term memory is so critical to what we as teachers do in the classroom, we are providing here part of Hart's description of program building from his book *Human Brain and Human Learning.*

Second Fundamental of Learning: We Live by Programs*

Extraction of patterns—identifying and making meaning of them—constitutes the first of two steps in learning. But plainly enough, we do not live by sitting in an armchair and detecting patterns. We live by doing, by action. Thus, the second step in learning is the development of mental programs to use what we know, i.e., the patterns we have come to understand. Step two in learning is defined as "the acquisition of useful programs.

The Mystery of Behavior

For thousands of years, back to the dim origins of humans, behavior has seemed largely a mystery. What people did seemed utterly haphazard, unpredictable, and unexplainable.

Teachers have long struggled with the behavior of their charges, often to the degree that class management threatens to push instruction into a secondary function. Even corporate personnel specialists confess to being frequently surprised and baffled by the behavior of workers, for all the "motivation" that pay and prospects of advancement would seem to offer. More than half of marriages in the United States go astray; the inability of spouses to understand each other, even after years of intimacy, stands out. At any gathering of parents, the difficulties of comprehending the strange worlds children inhabit take a prominent place in the discussions.

However, in the last four decades and more, researchers studying the brain and several other disciplines have made progress on many fronts. When their findings are brought together and unified, our understanding of human behavior can take a great leap. This opens the door to revolutionary advances in education and gives us the chance to catch up, at least somewhat, with the discoveries resulting from the dazzling and often upsetting advances in technology.

The Basis of Behavior: Programs

The key to understanding human behavior is the realization that we act very largely by programs. The word programs need not alarm us with visions of robots. It means simply a fixed sequence for accomplishing some intended objective. In other words, we act to carry out some purpose, some personal, individual, and usually self-selected purpose—the exact opposite of robot behavior.

Suppose, for example, that I wish to telephone my dentist. I pick up the phone, push the buttons in a certain order, and put the receiver to my ear to wait for the call to go through. I have executed a program for making a phone call. Should I call him again tomorrow, I will go through just about the same procedure.

* Text in this font, from here to page 5.9, indicates excerpt from *Human Brain and Human Learning* by Leslie A. Hart. Used with permission of the publisher.

Should I wish to phone a local store, I may have to use an additional program to find the number. I get the phone book, look up the listing, then dial—a variation of the program I used to call my dentist.

If now I want to visit the store, I must implement a longer program. I go to my car, take out my keys, find the right one, unlock the door, open it, get in, put the key in the ignition switch, fasten the seat belt, turn the switch and start the engine, release the parking brake, put the car in gear, press the accelerator pedal—just to start on my trip. To get there in my accustomed way I go through a series of dozens of steps, including the right choices of turns at street intersections. Yet I can "reel off" this program with the greatest of ease, hardly giving any attention to what comes next, much as I can put a cassette in a player and have the tape reel off a musical or other program.

Clearly, one of the reasons for our huge brain is that as humans we need and use a great number of programs to carry on our complex activities—thousands of times as many as the most intelligent of other animals. Exactly how that is achieved remains unknown, although the progress of researchers in the neurosciences suggests that we may have a good start toward understanding the neuronal, chemical, and molecular mechanisms involved within another few years.[7]

The Source of Programs

Present knowledge makes clear that programs can be acquired in two distinct ways: transmitted with the genes or learned after birth. As a general rule, the more brainpower an animal has, the more it learns after birth. The more neocortex or new brain it possesses, the greater the relative reliance on after-birth learning. We see once more why the laboratory rat and other small experimental animals can shed so little light on human learning: Their programs are largely species wisdom, transmitted genetically, while humans use the splendid new brain to do most learning after birth, over many years.

No aspect of being human appears more dominant than this incessant accumulation of programs. The process, of course, is most rapid in the earlier years then gradually tapers off. But since we live in a world that changes constantly, we are under far greater pressure than our forebears to continue to learn, to continue acquiring new programs. The man of 75 who is given a video tape recorder to honor that birthday must master some new programs to operate his new machine. A few centuries ago the programs acquired by age 25 would pretty well see one through a full life; today much of what is learned by age 25 will become obsolete. Failure to keep on learning can prove restrictive, costly, or embarrassing.

How Programs Work

To carry on activities, one must constantly select a program from those that are stored in the brain and implement it—put it into use.[8] Even to walk across the room, one must use an extremely complex program involving many of the body's 600-plus muscles and the shifting of weight from one side to the other as the feet alternate in moving forward. The program has to be repeated every two paces, with continual fine adjustments to change direction or to pick up and carry articles. To walk, one program is used; to go up stairs, another; to go down stairs, a third. To take a stroll outside one may have to use programs for going uphill, downhill, crossing rough ground, jumping over a puddle, or running a few steps to avoid traffic. Each time, the program in use has to be switched off and another selected and switched on. The brain does this so smoothly that we ordinarily are not aware of the switches being thrown, but this is the main key to our present insight into behavior.

If I am getting dressed in the morning and open a drawer full of shirts, I must make a conscious selection of which I will wear. After I have made that choice, opening up the shirt, putting it on, and buttoning it up "runs off" as a kind of automatic program to which I don't have to give any conscious attention unless something goes wrong—I find a button missing—and interferes.

Which shirt will I select? It depends on a perception of the pattern I will be dealing with. If I am going to a business meeting, I select a dress shirt; if I plan to make some repairs, I choose a work shirt; if I plan to exercise, I choose another type of shirt. Even more subtle patterns may influence me: I may want a conservative dress shirt for the meeting or a brighter one if the meeting will become a celebration with old friends. Though the decision may be trivial, I cannot act until some decision is made. (Following fixed habits or rituals, where possible, avoids decisions and so may seem more "comfortable.")

In much the same way, we select the most appropriate program from those stored in the brain to deal with what is happening at the time. For example, seeing stairs ahead, I select a going-up-stairs program. Having accidentally jostled somebody, I choose an offering-apology program. Facing an arithmetical problem, I tap my division program. Meeting a neighbor, I select a greeting program, complete with smile, nod, and suitable words.

The Program Implementation Cycle

In each of the above examples, a basic cycle is plainly in use. One must:

1. Evaluate the situation or need (detect and identify the pattern or patterns being dealt with).
2. Select the most appropriate program from those stored.
3. Implement the program selected.

Human behavior looked at in these terms may hardly seem simple but such a perspective provides more penetrating insight.

Key Observations

For educators, viewing behavior as a function of the program implementation cycle significantly expands our ability to observe and analyze student behavior during the learning process. Key observations include:

1. Unless the learner can reasonably and accurately evaluate the need or problem at hand (that is, detect and identify the patterns involved), the cycle goes astray at the outset. The student simply does not know what to do.

   A familiar example is the student trying to cope with an arithmetic problem couched in words. Unable to detect the pertinent pattern, the student flounders, wondering whether to add, or divide, or give up entirely. Another example is spelling of longer words. Lacking any sense of the structure or pattern of the word, the student tries to simply remember the order of the letters—perhaps producing some weird versions.[9]

2. People can access and use only those programs they already possess. However much one may be coerced or urged, or motivated or rewarded, there is no way to perform the program unless it has already been stored. He or she does not know how to do it. No program, no ability to perform the needed action.

   There is no way to force a person to ride a bicycle, or play Chopin on the piano, or write a scientific paper, if those programs have not previously been acquired. That many other people can do these things has no bearing. Yet in almost any classroom, at any level, this principle is ignored. On the playground, one may hear a child being called "clumsy" or "poorly coordinated" when the real difficulty is that the child has not yet learned certain programs. In homes, parents scold children; in businesses, bosses scold employees—all in the same futile way for the same futile reason. If the program has not been acquired, the solution is to acquire it, not in criticizing, labeling, or giving a poor mark, practices that prove devastating to learners.

3. A student cannot implement a program unless given the chance to do so.

   A test question might ask, "How can you verify the correct spelling of a word?" The answer intended is, "Look it up in a dictionary." A student who gives that answer, we must note, is not using that program. Rather, he or she is using a program for answering a question on a test. So commonly are tests used in instruction that this all-important difference may be overlooked; students may pass tests yet often be unable to carry out the programs themselves—a complaint loudly uttered today. Similarly, if students are always directed to use certain programs, there is no way to know whether they can detect the pattern, have a program to select, and can implement it. Rather, they are implementing programs for following directions. Such "learning" may prove fictitious.

As I indicated earlier, a program always has a goal, an objective—it is an activity to achieve some intended outcome. What happens if the program selected and implemented does not work?

When Programs Don't Work

During the program implementation cycle, the brain asks, "What pattern am I dealing with; what program should I choose to deal with it?" The most appropriate program is then implemented. Usually it will work. If it aborts, the brain must recycle—pattern detection, program selection, implementation. Let's say that I have taken out my keys to open the car door. I insert the key but it won't turn—the program aborts. I must now go through the three-step cycle again: reevaluate the situation, select another program that seems appropriate, and implement that. Perhaps I have the wrong key, in which case I recycle to find the right one and try again. Perhaps the lock has jammed, so I recycle to the unusual program of going around to the opposite door.

Aborting Programs Is Disturbing

Aborting a program always causes some degree of emotional shift because the failure of a program to work is in general disturbing and threatening, especially when no workable alternative program can be found. The degree to which programs usually work when implemented to achieve the intended goal serves as a direct, continuous measure of how well one has "made sense of the world," how competent we generally are. Programs should work. When they do, confidence in oneself increases; when too often they don't, confidence diminishes.[10]

Impact on Self-Confidence. Teachers have long sensed that self-image and the belief that one can successfully learn is important to self-concept and, in turn, to learning. Brain research now concurs. An individual's confidence rises or falls when programs do or do not work. We can see, too, that children whose parents or teachers have over-directed their activities and over-stressed second-person estimates of achievement, may mistrust their own ability to evaluate situations and select appropriate programs.[11]

This program view of behavior, I submit, is consistent both with present scientific understandings of the brain, and with what we can clearly see—once we know where to look—in the normal functioning of children, other adults, and ourselves. True, we cannot see into another person's brain to observe what pattern-detecting abilities and programs have been established there. However, we can see with new insights what happens when that person is allowed to use what he or she considers the most appropriate program—or when the individual has none to apply, or can't identify the pertinent pattern to begin with.

Acquisition of Useful Programs

The word useful in "acquisition of useful programs" deserves attention. Primarily, it means useful to the individual who will possess the program—in that person's view, rather than in someone else's view or to satisfy some supposed social or other standard. While it is true that one can be coerced into acquiring a program and may use it under duress, such programs are likely to become unused as soon as the duress ceases, if good mental health prevails. If use of the forced program does continue, it usually will signify either superstitious ritual, with anxiety that something dreadful will occur if it is not used, or the inappropriate behavior that goes under the common name of neurosis. Inherently, the use of a freely learned program satisfies; that of a coerced program brings back the old fears under which it was built. We see this in mild form when people do arithmetic with obvious pain and reluctance and, in more serious degree, when individuals who have been forced to learn a musical instrument well cannot bear to play before an audience in later life.

Transfer of Learning

In a far wider sense, useful conveys the possibilities of transfer of learning, which can greatly increase the speed of new learning. For example, a program for roller skating can readily transfer to ice skating; one for using a typewriter keyboard can easily be extended to using a computer keyboard which then can serve as a mental anchor for learning new information about the computer. The ability to transfer some of these behavioral building blocks, adapting and adjusting them to new needs, explains why some individuals can master a new task far more rapidly than others who lack the programs to transfer, or who in some cases may not yet have recognized the similarity of pattern involved which leads to and permits transfer.

Source of Creativity

The capacity to use old programs in fresh combinations seems to underlie what we call creativity. Greater sensitivity to pattern similarities facilitates the transfer. While I would doubt that sensitivity can be directly taught, it seems probable that it can be facilitated.

The Power of Programs

The implications for education of the program concept of behavior—evaluate, select, implement program cycle—are stupendous, bringing not only fresh insights into human behavior but also generating some major guidelines for improving learning achievement.

To summarize:

1. We live by programs, switching on one after another, selecting from those that have been acquired and stored in the brain.
2. As humans, we are far more dependent on programs acquired by the tens of thousands after birth, in contrast to animals that rely more on programs genetically transmitted.
3. A program is a fixed sequence for accomplishing some end—a goal, objective, or outcome. Our human nature makes the working of a program pleasurable; the concept of some after-the-event "reward" is neither necessary or valid. However, feedback is essential to establish that the program did work more or less as intended.
4. We can use only those programs that have already been built and stored. What programs another person has, or many people have, has no bearing. If a person does not possess a program, efforts to force its use are absurd.

5. We routinely use a three-step cycle: evaluate the situation (involving pattern detection and recognition), select the program that seems most appropriate from our store, and implement it.
6. The abortion of a program—upon its failure to work—calls for recycling. When a high proportion of self-selected programs work well, confidence rises; when too many programs are aborted, confidence is reduced and the learner may become far less able to self-select programs.
7. Although laboriously built, fully acquired programs have an automatic quality that can easily lead one to forget that other individuals may not have acquired these programs.
8. Learning can be defined as the acquisition of useful programs.
9. Learning progress can be properly evaluated only by observing undirected behavior.[12] Questioning and testing dealing primarily with information can reveal little. It shows only poorly what individuals can do.
10. Effective transfer of learning depends on using established programs in new applications and combinations. (Skill in putting together new combinations may equal "creativity.") The learner who can adapt established programs to new tasks, by seeing similarities of patterns involved, learns much more rapidly than one who cannot.
11. In general, if we regard human learning and behavior in terms of continually asking "What program is being used?", sharp new insights can be gained, and many confusions avoided.

When extracting patterns and building programs, specific information may be helpful to the task or even required. But, this does not imply that there is necessarily any great virtue in "stuffing the head with facts."

It can be handy to carry in memory certain information that will be frequently used. For example, we may store the phone numbers of a dozen people we often contact so we don't have to look them up each time. If patterns are involved, such information is much more easily remembered as when one knows that Tim, Linda, and Vance all work in the same office, and can be reached through its main number, at hours when that office will be open.

In our real world today, there exists vastly more information than can be memorized and it tends to change or obsolete rapidly, so that trusting memory can be treacherous.

A better strategy than trying to collect facts is to possess programs for finding various information—knowing what reference books are available and how to use them, or where to obtain help. But until specific information is linked to need for pattern or program, it serves little purpose. When such needs exist, learners typically "gobble up" information at an astonishing rate because they see it has immediate and meaningful application.

Translating Brain Research into Action Using the Nine Bodybrain-Compatible Elements

Of the four principles of learning gleaned from recent brain research, the redefinition of learning is the most revolutionary. As mentioned earlier, our billion dollar a year testing industry stops far short of measuring learning by this new definition. So, too, do all the traditional tools teachers have inherited, with the possible exception of rote memorization. That schools teach until students can use what they learn in practical, real-world ways—and remember what they've learned years later—is a wholly new expectation. It is long overdue but nevertheless a bit unnerving.

Bodybrain-Compatible Elements

- *Movement*
- *Meaningful Content*
- *Immediate Feedback*
- *Mastery*
- *Adequate Time*
- *Enriched Environment*
- *Choices*
- *Collaboration*
- *Absence of Threat/ Nurturing Reflective Thinking*

Where to start? Right here, with lots of commonsense.

First, what do we want students to understand? Look at this from a parent's point of view. Ask them. Survey your own life's lessons. What do you wish you had understood much earlier in life before the lessons got so expensive? Better interpersonal skills, a better understanding of interest and financing, auto mechanics for drivers, savings from conserving (electricity, water, recycling garbage, and so forth), gourmet cooking on a budget, how to create and stick to a budget, investment strategies, tips on child rearing. Probably these and much, much more.

Also, look at what's worth knowing from your students' point of view. Every generation faces its unique challenges as well as those that plague us all. What are those special challenges facing your students? What knowledge and skills would help them most?

The answers to these questions will help you focus your curriculum on what's important to know and be able to do.

The question that will help you revamp your instructional strategies is "What do we want them to do with what they understand?" Whatever that is, students must begin to do it. That doing will transform your classroom.

Movement

Because it is the movement centers of the brain that sequence thinking, it is essential that movement—doing—be part of learning from beginning to end, from the conception of curriculum content to instruction to assessing outcomes. Said more strongly, restriction of movement and all forms of passivity restrict learning. So, whether such active learning is a personal preference or not, we owe it to our students to make learning in our classroom the active, joyful process that it naturally is.

USING *MOVEMENT* TO ENHANCE PROGRAM BUILDING

Curriculum Development

- Develop inquiries that ask that students ***use*** what they understand in real-world ways and situations. Make sure your inquiries clearly state what students are to **do** with what they understand.
- Provide the real-world tools and materials needed to produce the product called for in the inquiry.
- Design inquiries that ask students to act out the sequence of steps or processes inherent in the key point.
- Always include inquiries that require use of bodily-kinesthetic intelligence for solving problems and producing products.

USING *MOVEMENT* TO ENHANCE PROGRAM BUILDING

Instructional Strategies

- During direct instruction, checking for understanding, and groupwork, include as many forms of the dramatic arts as you can; for example, role playing, miming, simulations, planned and impromptu skits, impersonations (of people and machines), and so forth.

- Reduce, if not eliminate, worksheets until the end of the learning process so that students learn how to describe what they have done linguistically. This is important not only to test-taking but also being able to acquire additional information through reading.

- Assign moment activities not just for the sake of movement but to activate the bodily-kinesthetic intelligence.

Meaningful Content

Just as beauty is in the eyes of the beholder, so too is meaningfulness in the eyes of the learner. The brain is ruthless in its judgments about what is worth sending to long-term memory versus what will simply fade away from short-term memory. Its most important criterion is whether something is meaningful to the learner, something that is useful, that will be called upon again.

USING *MEANINGFUL CONTENT* TO ENHANCE PROGRAM BUILDING

Curriculum Development

- Ensure that your *being there* locations allow for doing, not just looking, and that those responsible for hosting the visit are prepared for students to actively research the key points—ask questions, compare answers, delve into behind-the-scenes information, and so forth.

- Make sure your inquiries ask students to apply the key point to situations that are part of students' current world as well as future situations.

- Ask students to write inquiries for your key points that apply the concept or skill to their lives. Select those that best relate to students' current experiences and assign them to students for homework which they can share with parents and siblings, for groupwork which will give them more perspective, and for individual work which will provide reflection time.

Instructional Strategies

- Provide adequate time for students to reflect on what they're learning—how it applies to their lives now and in the future, to their community and the world.

- Require journal writing every day; include at least one assignment that asks students to reflect on what they've learned today and two ways they can apply it during the coming week.

- Involve students in self-assessment processes.

Immediate Feedback

Creating programs, especially accurate ones, is impossible without feedback. Assembling sensory input into understandable pieces then wholes, training the muscles to use what is understood—at every step along the way our learning is a set of approximations under refinement.

The best feedback is that built into the learning situation and materials—inherent, immediate, consistent. For example, learning to ride a bike, play a saxophone, use a hand lens or microscope, match yesterday's colors for painting in oils or water color, and so on. In each case, learners knows immediately if they have successfully performed the action. No one needs to tell them.

The most hazardous kind of feedback for learners to rely on is teacher feedback. Why? Because it is external not internal, and therefore can't be replicated by the learner, and because it is rarely immediate due to the demands on the teacher by other learners. Grading papers overnight, even by the end of the day, does little to help a learner develop accurate programs. To be useful, feedback must come at the time the learner is engaged in using the knowledge or skill. This axiom is urgent when learner and new material meet.

This discussion brings up some interesting observations about homework. From a brain research point of view, it is clearly a mistake to assign a page of division problems if students have not yet mastered division because it is likely that they will get as much practice doing division wrong as they will doing it right. This only serves to deepen the confusion and makes reteaching more difficult the next day. On the other hand, if students have already mastered division, why should we burden them with a page of busywork? In our opinion, homework should consist primarily of students applying concepts and skills to real-life situations around the home and neighborhood through meaningful projects.

Because some learners need more feedback and thus more time to learn a particular concept or skill, homework assignments are a way to vary the time and number of practices.

USING *IMMEDIATE FEEDBACK* TO ENHANCE PROGRAM BUILDING

Curriculum Development

- For every inquiry you develop for students, think through what means and level of feedback students will receive in the process. Will the situation and materials provide the needed feedback? If not, can Learning Clubs do an adequate job or are all the members at ground zero relative to the concept or skill to be learned? How available are you as teacher? Can you shift your role to guide on the side so that you can freely roam and provide sufficient feedback to all?

- If adequate feedback can't come from the learning situation and materials of the inquiry, make sure the forms of feedback vary, as they do in real life. Among the choices, include inquiries that:
  - Require students to develop rubrics for self assessment and to practice the 3Cs of assessment.
  - Require Learning Club members to provide feedback to each other. Have students assess both the quality of the feedback received and what they learned in the process of analyzing and providing the feedback.

- Develop long-term projects such as the Yearlong Research Project, social/political action projects, service projects, Kids Vote America, and so forth.

USING *IMMEDIATE FEEDBACK* TO ENHANCE PROGRAM BUILDING

Instructional Strategies

- Ask students frequently, on a scale of 1-10, how well they think they will remember what they are learning 10 years from now. If less than 9.5, ask them what it would take for them to wire the knowledge/skill into their long-term memory. Follow up on those suggestions by having them write their own inquiries and then follow up on those inquiries. Assign those you approve of to be done as homework or in-class assignments. Your goal here is for students to learn to become responsible for their learning outcomes. If you've chosen your content well, they will willingly take up this responsibility.

- Commit yourself to effective first teaching goals and strategies. Intend to make your first lesson so effective that additional teaching or, heaven forbid, re-teaching/remedial teaching is unnecessary. Guided practice allows you to ensure that early learning is correct and sufficient to override previously-held misconceptions.

- Develop a deep repertoire of feedback strategies, such as ask three-before-me (three students before the teacher), peer response, self-assessment with rubrics and the 3Cs, target talk, coaching by knowledgeable peers and experts, teaching a younger buddy (through the act of teaching, they discover what is not well understood), and so forth.

Mastery

Mastery and an accurate program wired into long-term memory are one and the same thing. They are the outer and inner manifestations of each other.

To help students reach mastery, see the recommendations for curriculum development and instructional strategies for the other eight bodybrain-compatible elements discussed in this chapter.

Adequate Time

Those who liken the brain to a computer fail to appreciate the true biological nature of the brain. While it may take nanoseconds to switch from 0 to 1 and back again, the gist of learning in computers, learning in the brain requires physiological growth of neurons, dendrites, axons, and time for mylination to occur. Such growth takes time.[13] Wish as we may, wish as we might, there are no short cuts except going at it as if we understood how the brain works. That would call for teaching it well once, guiding practice of application in varying circumstances (not just rote memorization), and having students use it—without birdwalking—until the physiological process is completed and learning has been hard-wired into long-term memory. Teaching the concept and skill of division in a single, uninterrupted day is a perfect example of adequate time in action. Please see the video, *Divide and Conquer: A Concept in a Day,** by Martha Kaufeldt. Division Day has been replicated in schools and districts across the country over the past 15 years; the results are always the same. Mastery for all students that day and a program wired into long-term memory that doesn't slip away over time.

USING *ADEQUATE TIME* TO ENHANCE PROGRAM BUILDING

Curriculum Development

- Use your *being there* locations to naturally integrate content and skills. Thus, a one-hour writing assignment about their favorite ecosystem equals two hours of learning because language arts and science are both used simultaneously. This helps free time for practicing basic skills, such as writing, math, speaking, and so forth, without ever losing focus on the study of ecosystems. Similarly, if the focus were on math, you could explore the math possibilities at your current *being there* plus revisit earlier sites while maintaining focus on math.

- Develop, and have your students (from grade three and up) help you develop, lots of inquiries—more than you think you'll need. For substantive concepts, that means a dozen or more. For significant knowledge key points, perhaps five to eight inquiries. There is no magical number of inquiries that are needed. The richness of the sensory input, extent of prior related experience, degree of personal interest, all affect the speed and depth of learning.

USING *ADEQUATE TIME* TO ENHANCE PROGRAM BUILDING

Instructional Strategies

- Eliminate pull-out programs. Invest your resources in more effective instructional strategies and improved curriculum in each classroom.

- Eliminate rigid schedules; use time flexibly. Make the schedule from day to day fit the learning. On some days, science is the focus all day with skills hitchhiking along as a means to practice a concept or significant knowledge.

- Take advantage of teachable moments.

- Teach students to assess their progress toward building a program. Have them assess where they are almost hourly:

Step One: Recognizes the pattern

Understands the pattern

Step Two: Can apply/use what they understand with assistance

Can apply/use what they understand without assistance and almost automatically

Enriched Environment

With the goal of developing programs in mind, any discussion of enriched environment will have to bury the "rich for the sake of richness" idea. Planning for an enriched environment is a calculated process, not an artistic fling. Every item you allow through the doors must relate directly to the concepts and skills being studied for the month. Further, most of the items should allow learners to handle and do something with them as they practice applying what they understand.

USING *ENRICHED ENVIRONMENT* TO ENHANCE PROGRAM BUILDING

Curriculum Development

- Give each item that you bring in the acid test: Is it needed for an inquiry or for direct instruction? If not, don't bring it. There is a huge difference between interesting things and related things. Stick with those things that are conceptually related and significant to acquiring an understanding of the concept.

Instructional Strategies

- Plan your immersion environment to not just look good but to be user friendly.
- When experts visit the classroom, ask them to bring items that students can handle and do something with. Look-and-admire items are nifty but from the bodybrain learning partnership's point of view, nowhere near as powerful.
- Invite students to contribute to the immersion environment. Their items can be kept in a guest corner, available for only a couple of days.

* Available through Books for Educators.

Choices

Because every brain is different—in wiring, in prior experiences, in interests—every student goes about using what they understand differently. For example, remedial readers use reading skills much more fully if they get to choose the content—car magazines or fashion magazines, spy novels or *Ranger Rick*, sports magazines or *National Geographic*. This is true for all learners. If we can see ourselves in the action, we are more able to learn and remember something.

USING *CHOICES* TO ENHANCE PROGRAM BUILDING

Curriculum Development

- When developing inquiries, make sure that there are some for each intelligence so that students can choose their level of difficulty. If the content is unfamiliar, allow them to begin with their intelligence of strength. As they become more adept at using the knowledge or skill of the key point, encourage them to use inquiries calling for intelligences that are less developed.
- Encourage students to develop inquiries that would allow them to apply the key point in an arena of personal interest.

Instructional Strategies

- Encourage students to expand their interests, to develop hobbies, and to explore careers. Use those interests as examples for concepts and skills you are teaching.

Collaboration

The number one cause of passivity in the classroom is being stuck in the role of listener. As listener, there is no chance to check one's thoughts for understanding, to explore possibilities, or to try out how to use something. Collaboration pulls the learner out of passivity and thrusts him/her into using what is learned through conversation, joint problem solving, and the work of carrying out a project. In effect, collaboration multiplies the number of teachers in the room, increases the amount of practice applying key points, and increases the level of challenge.

USING *COLLABORATION* TO ENHANCE PROGRAM BUILDING

Curriculum Development

- Design inquiries that can't be done by any one member of the Learning Club working alone. Increasing the challenge and making real the need for each member to participate forces students to dig deeper and seek connections and relationships that would otherwise remain hidden.

Instructional Strategies

- Don't fly by the seat of your pants when framing collaborative tasks. The potential of collaboration to cement learning into long-term memory is too great to be handled casually. Be purposeful and on target. See *Designing Groupwork* by Elizabeth Cohen.

Absence of Threat/ Nurturing Reflective Thinking

Although absence of threat is listed last, it should be understood from reading previous chapters of this book that it must be teachers' first and continuing consideration and that, for this discussion of program building, it is accepted here as a given. Academic learning is all but impossible without an atmosphere of no threat. But absence of threat is only the beginning of the emotional continuum. In-depth learning begins to occur when the learning environment nurtures reflective thinking.

USING *REFLECTIVE THINKING* TO ENHANCE PATTERN SEEKING

Curriculum Development

- Create inquiries requiring students to practice what they understand on their own—through homework, individual projects, and the Yearlong Research Project. Require them to personalize/adapt an inquiry to an area of special interest to them.

Instructional Strategies

- Create a daily journal entry assignment: How does/could this concept or skill apply to your personal life?

Notes

1 To grasp the significance of Hart's conceptualization and definition of learning as a two-part process, consider for a moment what is required of a student taking a typical standardized test with its multiple choice and true-false items. With both kinds of test items, the right answer is present. The student has only to detect the answer (pattern) that is most familiar (a process usually accompanied by a small niggling in the back of the brain that says, "Hey, we've heard of that one before!" "Familiar" doesn't represent understanding of the concept inherent in the test question; ability to apply in a real-life setting is clearly light years away. Thus, in essence, the multi-billion dollar testing juggernaut assesses only the first half of the first stage of learning. To push this realization further, consider the Friday quiz, also typically weighted heavily toward multiple choice and true-false items. Sometimes 80% is accepted as indication of mastery; sometimes it is considered sufficient to just record the letter grades, A-F, and then the whole class moves on to the next topic.

If America is disappointed in the student outcomes of its public schools, it must examine what definition of "learning" is serving as the basis for the design and implementation of its curriculum and instructional practices. If Hart's two-part definition of learning were adopted, outcomes would—and do—soar because it forces profound and radical change at the very core of the business of teaching-learning. See Leslie A. Hart, *Human Brain and Human Learning* (Covington, WA: Books for Educators, 1999), 166.

2 Hart, *Human Brain and Human Learning*, 156-157.

3 John J. Ratey, *A User's Guide to the Brain: Perception, Attention, and the Four Theaters of the Brain* (New York: Pantheon Books, 2001), 21.

4 Hart, *Human Brain and Human Learning*, 166-167.

5 Ibid., 167.

6 Ibid., 161.

7 Recent research suggests that memory storage is not restricted to the brain only but is a bodybrain function (see Chapter 5). However, until researchers can provide a clear, detailed picture of how this functions, we will continue to refer to the brain as the location for storing programs.

8 Dr. Jose M. R. Delgad has stated this as: "To act is to choose one motor pattern from among the many available possibilities and inhibitions are continually acting to suppress inappropriate or socially unacceptable activities." See "Intracerebral Mechanisms and Future Education" in *New York State Education* (February, 1968), 17.

9 James Doran, director of Algonquin Reading Camp, Rhinelander, Wisconsin, has demonstrated to me a simple, quick technique for giving students a sense of pattern that produces startling gains in their competency in spelling. His brain-compatible methods also produce large, rapid gains in reading.

For truly surprising gains in reading, see *The Auditory Discrimination in Depth (ADD)* and the *Visualizing and Verbalizing for Improved Comprehension* programs by Lindamood-Bell. For information, contact the Lindamood-Bell Reading Processes Center, San Luis Obispo, California 800-233-8756.

10 Self-esteem or self-concept programs have long had a questionable base, primarily a "touchy-feely" approach aimed at "feeling good about yourself" as a result of others' telling you that you are a "good person" (sometimes in the face of evidence to the contrary). Current brain research tells a different story about the brain's producing and receiving its own opiate-like molecules as a response to mental programs that work, to a sense of competence in handling the world. See Candace Pert, Ph.D.,

Molecules of Emotion: Why You Feel the Way You Feel (New York: Scribner, 1997); Stanley I. Greenspan, M.D. with Beryl Lieff Benderly, *The Growth of the Mind and the Endangered Origins of Intelligence* (New York: Addison-Wesley Publishing Company, 1997), 104; and Robert Sylwester, "The Neurobiology of Self-Esteem and Aggression" in *Educational Leadership* (February, 1997, Volume 54, No. 5), 75-78.

11 Parents might well ask if this over-emphasis on valuing of performance by a second person might not also contribute to the extraordinary power of peer groups and peer pressure during the teen years (and beyond). See Alfie Kohn, *Punished by Rewards: The Trouble with Gold Stars, Incentive Plans, A's, Praise, and Other Bribes* (Boston: Houghton Mifflin, 1993) and *Beyond Discipline: From Compliance to Community* (Alexandria, VA: ASCD, 1996).

12 Teachers "driving" a conventional class and initiating most activity have little chance to observe what students do on their own. In good "open," Montessori, or similar settings, teachers can readily become observers because they have time and can be more detached. Students feel relaxed and absorbed in their work rather than on guard against criticism or a bad mark.

13 We speak here of academic learning. Some kinds of life-and-death experiences cause the brain to grow dendrites instantly, ready to assess the situation and respond during the incident. Academic learning, however, must travel a slower learning route.

Part B

Implementing Stage 1: Getting Started

Because the ITI model is so all-encompassing—providing a single framework for viewing the entire range of curriculum development and instructional strategies needed to translate current brain research into the classroom—it is essential that teachers avoid trying to do it all the first year. Full implementation of the ITI model is a three- to five-year effort. The experience of thousands of ITI teachers can be distilled into several pieces of hard-won advice:

1) Start at the beginning.
2) Do first what brain research says needs to be done first. Don't jump ahead to the things you most like to do, such as integrating curriculum, when you're just starting Stage 1.
3) Do thoroughly and well those parts that you begin with before moving onward. Drips and drabs aren't sufficient to make for real change in outcomes. Make an agreement with yourself to move through any discomfort you might experience rather than to avoid it.
4) Consciously maintain practices from prior stages as you begin a new stage of implementation.
5) Be kind to yourself and enjoy the journey as you go!

As you proceed, know that the ITI model has many resources to support you. One of the most valuable is *ITI Classroom Stages of Implementation* by Karen D. Olsen and Susan Kovalik and its companion *ITI Schoolwide Stages of Implementation.* The rest of this book is organized around the stages of classroom implementation. Each goal or benchmark for curriculum and instructional strategies is accompanied by practical how-to suggestions for achieving that goal.

Part B addresses Stage 1 of the *ITI Classroom Stages of Implementation*—where and how to begin. Chapter 7 describes what to do before students arrive; Chapter 8 addresses what to do the first day of school, and Chapter 9 discusses what needs to be accomplished before moving on to Stage 2. The criteria for assessing Step 1—making the environment bodybrain compatible—is applied 100% of the day.

Part C discusses Stage 2 of the *ITI Classroom Stages of Implementation*—entry level for making curriculum bodybrain compatible—and what needs to be accomplished before moving on to further improving curriculum. The criteria for implementing Stage 2 is applied only for that portion of the day, week, or year for which the teacher has developed bodybrain-compatible curriculum using the ITI model.

Part D provides practical steps for working toward total curriculum integration as described in Stages 3-5.

ITI Classroom Stages of Implementation was distilled from the experiences of more than 500 teachers who implemented the ITI model over a 10-year period while improving science education in the Mid-California Science Improvement Program. The stages were designed to provide a road map for teachers and their coaches. The Stages have continued to evolve over the intervening years. Much hard-earned wisdom is packed into these descriptions of curriculum, instructional strategies, expectations, and indicators.

> **Guidelines**
>
> *The stages described in ITI Classroom Stages of Implementation are:*
>
> - *Stage 1: Entry level for making the learning environment bodybrain compatible*
> - *Stage 2: Entry level for making curriculum bodybrain compatible*
> - *Stages 3-5: Advanced levels of curriculum work to refine and expand integrated curriculum*

The stages of implementation are an invaluable guide. They help clarify pictures of end goals as well as next steps. They are also a useful tool to assess progress toward implementing a bodybrain-compatible learning environment individually and as a group.

ITI Classroom Stages of Implementation

Entry level for making the learning environment bodybrain compatible

Stage 1.1

Before School

CURRICULUM

- Gets a class list of students with phone numbers and addresses.
- Becomes familiar with state and district health/environment standards. Posts these standards in a class binder to share with parents and students (as age appropriate).
- Learns about and prepares to teach students to recognize and fix conditions in their environment that are unhealthful, not aesthetically pleasing, and/or cluttered.
- Becomes familiar with state and district curriculum standards and assessment practices.
- Selects *being there* locations that best match the curriculum to be taught.
- Selects a professional and/or peer coach(es) who can/will support his/her implementation of a bodybrain-compatible teaching/learning environment. Establishes a schedule for meeting frequently.

INSTRUCTIONAL STRATEGIES

- Before school starts, sends each student a postcard or letter of welcome to class; introduces self to students and tells them a little about what they will be learning.
- With other adults at the school (custodial, cafeteria, transportation, and office staff and classroom aide, and parents) has taken the necessary steps to identify and fix environmental problems in the classroom.
- Visits potential *being there* locations that could provide real-world experiences for the concepts/skills of the standards.
- Establishes/updates list of promising guest speakers and topics.
- Creates and maintains a healthful, aesthetically pleasing, and uncluttered classroom:
  - Healthful—free of toxins, clean, well lighted, well ventilated with fresh air, ambient temperature, pleasant smelling (the smell of freshness, not of artificial odors), and safe
  - Aesthetically pleasing (calming colors and music, living plants, and well laid out for multiple uses)
  - Uncluttered yet reflects what is being learned.
- Arranges seating in clusters with easy access to work tools.

ITI Classroom Stages of Implementation

Entry level for making the learning environment bodybrain compatible

Stage 1.2

First Day of School and Thereafter

CURRICULUM

- The bodybrain-compatible element of absence of threat and nurturing reflective thinking is taught as an important and on-going part of the curriculum. Such curriculum contains the following five areas:

  1) The Lifelong Guidelines, including the LIFESKILLS

INSTRUCTIONAL STRATEGIES

- Models the Lifelong Guidelines and LIFESKILLS as the basis for his/her classroom leadership and management. Leads rather than controls; inspires rather than manipulates. Creates/maintains an atmosphere that is participatory rather than dictatorial.
- Uses target talk and teachable moments daily to reinforce and extend student understanding and practice of the Lifelong Guidelines and LIFESKILLS.
- Systematically introduces the meaning and importance of each of the Lifelong Guidelines and selected LIFESKILLS through formal lessons (key points and inquiries) and the context of classroom life. The Lifelong Guidelines and selected LIFESKILLS (as age appropriate) are posted and readable from a distance.
- Bases "discipline" on helping students develop the personal and social skills and behaviors needed to successfully practice the Lifelong Guidelines/LIFESKILLS rather than on a system of externally imposed rewards and punishments.

CURRICULUM

  2) The power of emotions to enhance or impede learning and performance

INSTRUCTIONAL STRATEGIES

- Formally introduces age-appropriate lessons about the power of emotion to drive attention and learning. The role of emotion is discussed daily in multiple ways, such as during reflective thinking questions, Town Hall Meetings, and teacher feedback to individual students as well as during planned lessons.
- Provides consistency and emotional security for students:
  - Greets students at the door at the beginning and ending of every day.
  - Uses agendas every day to provide focus for learning, to enable students to direct their own learning, and to encourage learning ways to manage time.
  - Uses written procedures for all frequently occurring events/activities to provide consistency, continuity, and emotional security for students. Visuals include graphics as well as words.
- Frequently uses collaborative learning, as appropriate, to extend and deepen learning and to create a sense of community.
- An "Australia" in the classroom provides a place and time to help students bring their emotions and behavior back under control.

ITI Classroom Stages of Implementation

Stage 1.2

First Day of School and Thereafter-continued

CURRICULUM	INSTRUCTIONAL STRATEGIES
3) The important role of movement in academic learning	• Models and teaches students about using movement to enhance learning. • Uses movement to enhance learning. Provides daily movement sessions to energize, calm, and assist in understanding and remembering key points and inquiries. Uses such resources as *Brain Gym* and teacher-designed movement activities that grow naturally from curriculum content. • Includes movement and other bodily-kinesthetic action in direct instruction of key points as well as in follow-up activities and inquiries.
4) Personal and social skills for collaboration	• Models and formally teaches the personal and social skills needed to work collaboratively. • Organizes students into Learning Clubs. Teaches how and when to use various group processes (such as leading, supporting, listening, encouraging, sharing, "3-before-me," and so forth). • Leads students in activities, including Town Hall Meeting and Acknowledgement Box, that are appropriate for each stage of group development—developing a sense of belonging, creating common ground, and taking action. The resulting sense of community serves as the basis for achieving high academic performance as well as enhancing personal and social growth. • Uses collaborative learning to achieve specific goals daily.

ITI Classroom Stages of Implementation

Stage 1.2

First Day of School and Thereafter *-continued*

CURRICULUM

5) How to nurture and utilize reflective thinking

INSTRUCTIONAL STRATEGIES

- Uses a calm voice, synchronizes his/her heart-brain coherence, and stays emotionally centered.
- Provides a variety of processes and structures throughout the day which enhance students' reflective thinking, such as wait time, journal writing, reflecting on the daily agenda (beginning and end of the day), making choices that allow students to direct their learning, forecasting how to take on a learning task, reflecting on what one has learned academically, the process of collaborative work (before, during, and after and asking about content, social, and personal outcomes), providing adequate time for students to complete assignments, and strategies to help students refocus.

ITI Classroom Stages of Implementation

Entry level for making the learning environment bodybrain compatible

Stage 1.3

What to Accomplish Before Moving On

CURRICULUM

- The concept of multiple intelligences—defined as problem-solving and product-producing capabilities—is taught to students early in the year. It is also used in developing inquiries and is a frequent, on-going topic for reflective thinking about the process and product of collaborative work.

INSTRUCTIONAL STRATEGIES

- Includes real-life experiences—*being there*, immersion, hands-on materials, and visiting resource people—to supplement classroom instruction and provide rich input for each of the multiple intelligences.
- Is learning how to provide students with multiple ways to understand, solve problems, produce products, and demonstrate what they understand through:
  - Use of the multiple intelligences as a guide when lesson planning, selecting instructional strategies, and developing/selecting inquiries and other assignments for students, including homework
  - Use of the multiple intelligences during direct instruction of key points and other instructional strategies
  - Flexibility in allocating time for students to complete their work
  - Student choice of tasks, materials, and processes used for completing projects whenever appropriate
- Has mastered the instructional skills identified in Stage 1.2 and continues to use them daily:
  - Modeling of the Lifelong Guidelines and LIFESKILLS
  - Target talk
  - "Discipline" based on using the Lifelong Guidelines & LIFESKILLS
  - Daily agenda
  - Written procedures
  - Models movement to enhance learning and uses it with students to energize and calm
  - Collaboration to enhance personal and social growth and increase achievement (Stage 3 of building a sense of community, Taking Action, has been achieved)
  - Calm voice, heart-brain coherence, and emotionally centered
  - Nurturing reflective thinking through numerous strategies

ITI Classroom Stages of Implementation

Stage 1.3

Accomplish Before Moving On -continued

CURRICULUM

- Meets frequently with a professional or peer coach who supports the implementation of a bodybrain-compatible teaching/learning environment for students.

INSTRUCTIONAL STRATEGIES

- Is developing a variety of instructional strategies to ensure students can identify/ understand *patterns* and develop *programs* for using what they understand understand and wire them into long-term memory. Such instructional strategies include:
  - Modeling how to be a lifelong learner and participating citizen
  - Expanded and deepened use of movement to enhance learning
  - Direct instruction, usually limited to 16 minutes per hour
  - Nurturing reflective thinking
  - Graphic organizers
  - Discussion
  - Literature
  - Songs
  - Video clips, great artwork, and photographs
  - Journal writing to enhance social and personal growth and academic learning
  - Celebrations of Learning
- Designs time frames for ITI integrated curriculum to fit the content rather than a rigid daily schedule; is learning to adjust time frames to best accommodate needed instructional strategies and to give students adequate time to complete their work.

Note: Stage 1 of implementing ITI begins not with themes or integration but with the brain research relevant to creating a bodybrain-compatible environment in which learning can occur.

Although a bodybrain-compatible learning environment cannot be fully realized until curriculum becomes bodybrain compatible, curricular changes have little impact if the learning environment is not consistent with how the brain learns. Therefore, implementors are advised to proceed slowly with curriculum development until significant strides toward maintaining a bodybrain-compatible learning environment are achieved.

Stage 1, entry level into a bodybrain-compatible environment, is to be applied to the classroom 100% of the time unless specified otherwise. Note that this stage is broken into three parts in order to give teachers greater focus on where and how to begin.

Chapter 6: What to Do Before Students Arrive

ITI Classroom Stages of Implementation

Stage 1.1

Entry level for making the learning environment bodybrain compatible

Before School

CURRICULUM

- Gets a class list of students with phone numbers and addresses.
- Becomes familiar with state and district health/environment standards. Posts these standards in a class binder to share with parents and students (as age appropriate).
- Learns about and prepares to teach students to recognize and fix conditions in their environment that are unhealthful, not aesthetically pleasing, and/or cluttered.
- Becomes familiar with state and district curriculum standards and assessment practices.
- Selects *being there* locations that best match the curriculum to be taught.

INSTRUCTIONAL STRATEGIES

- Before school starts, sends each student a postcard or letter of welcome to class; introduces self to students and tells them a little about what they will be learning.
- With other adults at the school (custodial, cafeteria, transportation, and office staff, classroom aide, and parents) have taken the necessary steps to identify and fix environmental problems in the classroom.
- Visits potential *being there* locations that could provide real-world experiences for the concepts/skills of the standards.
- Establishes/updates list of promising guest speakers and topics.

Before School

ITI Classroom Stages of Implementation

Entry level for making the learning environment bodybrain compatible

Stage 1.1

CURRICULUM

INSTRUCTIONAL STRATEGIES

- Creates and maintains a healthful, aesthetically pleasing, and uncluttered classroom:
  - Healthful
    - free of toxins
    - clean
    - well-lighted
    - well-ventilated with fresh air
    - ambient temperature
    - pleasant smelling (the smell of freshness, not of artificial odors)
    - safe
  - Aesthetically pleasing (calming colors and music, living plants, and well laid out for multiple uses)
  - Uncluttered yet reflects what is being learned.

- Seating is arranged in clusters with easy access to work tools

- Selects a professional and/or peer coach(s) who can support implementation of a bodybrain-compatible teaching/learning environment. Establishes a schedule for meeting frequently.

Getting Started . . . First Impressions

Where and how do you begin your program improvement efforts? Start with brain research firmly in mind. Your number one goal is to make your classroom a bodybrain-compatible environment. Once that is in place—for you as well as for your students—powerful learning will occur.

Much of the foundation work for Stage 1 occurs before the school year even begins. Take seriously what architects have known for centuries: form dictates function, and the behaviors that drive it. Students come to typical classrooms with "school behaviors," a reaction to bureaucratic institutionalism. These school behaviors are often far from the polite behaviors expected when they visit a friend's house and want to earn the right to come again. A change in the environment (form) will makes changes in students' perception of school and thus their behavior in school.

First Impressions

As any substitute teacher or Dale Carnegie workshop presenter can testify, first impressions mean a great deal, making the kind of long-term relationships in a classroom easier to build or poisoning them from the beginning. To get your year off to a good start, take the time to invest in a positive, strong first impression. Send each student a postcard or letter before they arrive; this will predispose them to look forward to and enjoy their first day of school and every day thereafter.

For a mailing list, ask the school secretary if she could print out a set of labels for you. Share with students how excited you are to meet them and what they can expect—what you will study the first month (and more if appropriate) and the *being there* experiences they can look forward to. Following this personal invitation, the first day of school is more like a reunion than a first meeting. You've set the tone and are off to a good start.

First Things First . . . Making the Environment Safe

Reading up on environmental hazards may not at first seem like requisite reading for teachers. But times have changed. The staggering increases in special ed students and classifications of disabilities has led many researchers to believe the causes go beyond genetics; many environmental toxins, especially neurotoxins, are known culprits. Become familiar with your district and state health/environmental standards and the resources referred to in this chapter. The actions you take to free your classroom of toxins may well be your most important gift to students this year.

Find out if your school has a functional committee responsible for investigating and resolving environmental issues. Ask to join the committee and encourage others to attend its meetings. Share what you have learned and ask for copies of the research the committee has operated on in the past. Collect this information in a format you can share with students and parents. Keep it handy for ready reference.

Prepare to Teach Students

The key to identifying and resolving environmental hazards is to educate, educate, educate. And that includes students. Prepare age-appropriate curriculum to present to your students. Extend your lessons into homework assignments so students can apply what they learn to other indoor environments.

In this dawning of the 21st century, knowledge of chemical hazards is no longer solely the domain of chemists. For our own health and welfare, we must become knowledgeable about our exposures and risks. We must learn to look out for ourselves and learn how to take action to correct unacceptable risks to our health and well-being.

The Classroom Is Healthful

Negative "messages" from the environment often set off behaviors that impede student learning and frustrate teachers. For example, a dirty, ill-kempt classroom tells occupants that they aren't valued; if no one cares, why should students?

And, as life in the 21st century becomes more technology-based, our environment—indoor and outdoor—is becoming increasingly more chemical-laden. Forty years ago, healthful was defined as clean, an absence of dirt.

Today, the definition of healthful must include the invisible as well as the visible—the presence of toxic off-gassing. We must look at the dark side of noise-snuffing carpets, energy conservation measures dictating that heating/cooling systems restrict inflow of fresh air and windows be sealed shut, high-tech machines that spew gases (copiers, laser printers, and more), art and science chemicals, the ubiquitous and potent cleaning compounds, and the effects of poor maintenance (allergens, toxic molds, and chemicals). We must take a new look at our classrooms and school campuses using a 21st century awareness of healthful. We must inform ourselves and take responsibility for acting upon our knowledge.

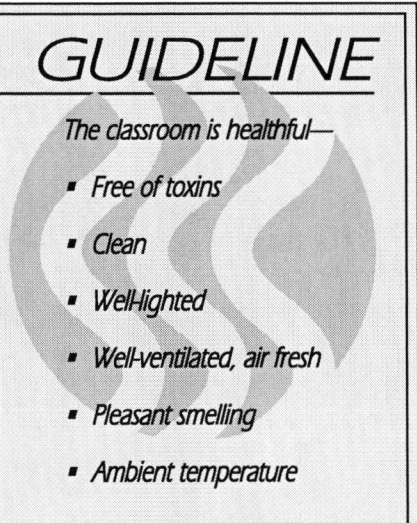

> **GUIDELINE**
>
> *The classroom is healthful—*
>
> - *Free of toxins*
> - *Clean*
> - *Well-lighted*
> - *Well-ventilated, air fresh*
> - *Pleasant smelling*
> - *Ambient temperature*

Free of Toxins

A growing body of evidence makes it clear that unhealthy environments can and do cause serious learning and health problems for students and staff alike. Learning and behavior problems include: headaches, fatigue, weakness, exhaustion, listlessness; depression, easy crying; moodiness, anger, confusion; excessive talking, explosive speech, stuttering, slurred speech; inattentiveness, disruptive behavior, impulsiveness; nervousness, irritability, agitation; a short attention span, inability to concentrate; memory loss, learning problems; numbness and/or tingling of face, hands, arms; dizziness, clumsiness; restless legs, finger tapping, tremors, tics; excessive fatigue, nightmares; hyperactivity, wild unrestrained behavior, and increased sensitivity to odors, light, sound, temperature, touch and pain.[1]

> **Self Check**
>
> ***When toxins are eliminated:***
>
> - There is a decrease in hyperactivity, absenteeism, complaints of feeling ill, and trips to the nurse's office.
> - Behavior at home and school is congruent.
> - There is an overall sense of well-being for students and staff.

Medical problems resulting from major, long-term toxic exposure include measurable abnormalities in the blood, nervous and immune systems, and in the brain. These health effects can be permanent, including later reproductive problems, or can even cascade into "spreading syndrome," a condition in which previously tolerated chemicals become intolerable. In serious "sick building" situations, Norma Miller, editor of *The Healthy School Handbook: Conquering the Sick Building Syndrome and Other Environmental Hazards In and Around Your School,* suggests that 80 percent of those who become sick get better in six to 12 months; 15 percent do not improve; and five percent may become worse in spite of therapy, moving into spreading syndrome, their health forever compromised and their future in jeopardy.[2]

These are shocking statistics. Unfortunately, there are many scientific and medical studies that suggest that a significant portion of misbehavior, learning problems, and even the dramatic increases in special education enrollments and classifications, such as A.D.D., may be a result of chemical poisoning. Creating and maintaining a healthful environment must become the number one priority of teachers, administrators, school boards, and parents.

A sage comment about education is, "If you think education is expensive, try ignorance." Likewise, if we think environmental issues are too expensive to face, we are not looking at the exponential increase in costs of rising special education enrollments and lifelong damage to student and adult health.

At a research conference at Texas Woman's University to establish ecological guidelines for a healthful school building, 60 environmental specialists from 26 states and two other countries gathered to share concerns about construction and maintenance of healthful school buildings. The top ten major areas, listed in order of importance, are:[3]

1. Heating, cooling, and ventilation
2. Pest controls
3. Cleaning products
4. Chemicals
5. Fragrances
6. Site selection
7. Lighting
8. Remodeling the school building
9. Floors
10. Art supplies

The pervasiveness of toxins suggested by this list is hair-raising. The symptoms caused by the chemicals involved reads like a Who's Who of reasons why students are sent to the principal's office. For a list of particularly toxic chemicals, their location, and symptoms, see page 7.4.

Pesticides. Pesticides are not harmless. They are intended to kill target organisms. Even in small quantities in larger animals, they can poison. Many believe that the mushrooming numbers of children with learning problems is attributable to the increase in toxins in the environment. According to Norma Miller, "Classroom environments can be extremely volatile sites, constantly off-gassing pesticides that have been applied repeatedly for years in the same routine fashion. The general application of pesticides fails to address those micro-environments where insects actually live. Instead, poisons are placed within the confines of the classroom, making it possibly the most toxic place a child will spend time during his or her entire life."[4]

As Norma Miller points out, most school systems don't have a policy that specifically addresses issues surrounding pesticide use. She recommends that such a policy include:

- "Establishment of specific contractual amendments that will attract vendors capable of delivering services to contract specification. Policies that have allowed for low-bid acceptance as the norm should be modified. A stringent policy of bid acceptance that emphasizes value for dollars spent based on a 60% technical and 40% value standard will better serve both the contractor and the school system.
- Discontinuance of the practice of routine spraying.
- Reduction of pesticide use, targeting specific amounts (percentages) over a given period of time. Not many school systems are equipped to move from one approach to another overnight. It is important, therefore, that time constraints be imposed, and that appropriate scheduling be followed when the practice of routine spraying is discontinued.

Chemical	Where It Is Found	What It Does
Benzene	Adhesives, anthraquinone colors, art class, auto exhaust, cigarette smoke, degreaser/solvent, eggs, fossil fuel, fungicide, gasoline, glue, paint, paint stripper, plastics, room deodorizers, solvents, spot removing products, synthetic fibers, tobacco, smoke, VOCs*, water, wood finish	**Cause of cancer. Immunotoxic.** Anorexia, aplastic anemia, blurred vision, bone marrow and central nervous system depression, chromosomal abnormalities, dermatitis, disorientation, drowsiness, drunken behavior, euphoria, irritation of eyes and gastrointestinal and respiratory tracts, fatigue, headache, leukemia, leukopenia, lightheadedness, loss of appetite, multiple myeloma, pancytopenia, paralysis, polyneuritis, reproductive hazard
Toluene	Adhesives, carpets, classrooms, cleaners, composite wood products, room deodorizers, floor tile, fossil fuel, fuel additive, gasoline, furniture, glue, insulation, lacquer, liquid paper/white out, paint, paint thinner and stripper, petroleum products, polyethylene, polyurethane wood finish, printing materials, solvents, tobacco smoke, varnish, wallcoverings, water	**Cause of cancer. Narcotic.** Brain malfunction, central nervous system damage, depression, disorientation, irritation of eyes, lung, nose, and skin, fatigue, hoarseness, irritability, kidney, liver and spleen damage, loss of coordination, bone marrow suppression, reproductive hazard, and, with prolonged exposure, permanent neurological damage
Methylene chloride	Adhesives, classrooms, coffee, epoxy, furniture, glue, paint, paint remover, pharmaceuticals, phenolic thermosetting resins, wallcoverings	**Suspected carcinogen. Mutagen.** Bronchitis, central nervous system and heart damage, irritation of eyes, lung, and skin, metabolizes to carbon monoxide in blood, pulmonary edema or lung fluid
Trichloroethane	Art class, duplicating fluid, vinyl floor tile, VOCs, degreaser/solvent, dry cleaning fluid, fumigants, insecticides, insulators, paint, solvent, water	**Cause of cancer.** Dizziness, headaches, possible liver damage

* VOC = volatile organic compounds

Taken from *The Healthy School Handbook: Conquering the Sick Building Syndrome and Other Environmental Hazards In and Around Your School*, Norma L. Miller, Ed.D., Editor, page 9.

- Determining that staff members understand the pesticide regulations and the reasons for them. Staff members who apply pesticides either should be state-certified or should practice under the guidance of certified applicators. Anyone who violates pesticide regulations during the application of a pesticide, especially by applying a pesticide prohibited by the policies of the system or state, should face disciplinary action. Contractors who send in workers without proper documentation should be dismissed.
- Notification of all concerned when pesticide application is scheduled.
- Documentation of all chemically sensitive students, teachers, and other persons who are involved in the daily function of the building.
- Providing when requested full disclosure of the materials used by both the school system and its contractors.
- Establishment of standards for pesticide use. It should be determined which pesticide will have the least negative impact on human beings and which areas will be acceptable for the application of the pesticide."[5]

From *The Healthy School Handbook: Conquering the Sick Building Syndrome and Other Environmental Hazards In and Around Your School* by Norma L. Miller, Editor. Washington, DC: National Education Association, 1995, p. 228.

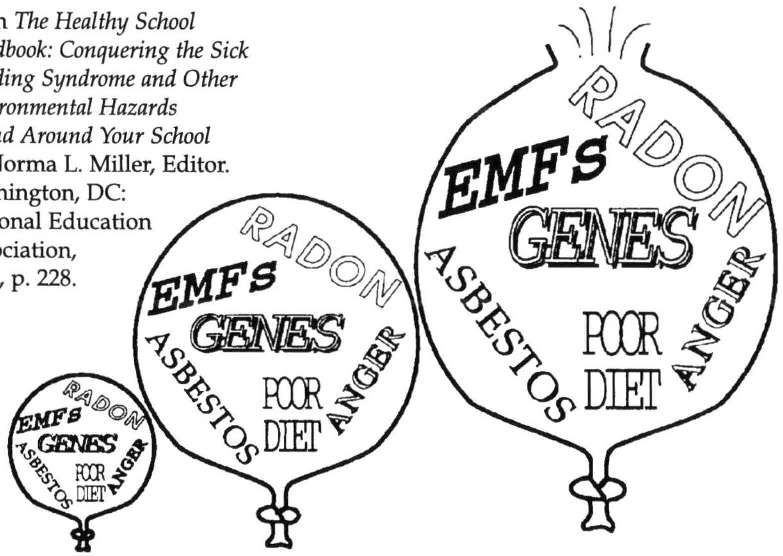

How to Locate and Eliminate Toxins

- Get educated. Two resources to begin with are: *The Healthy School Handbook: Conquering the Sick Building Syndrome and Other Environmental Hazards In and Around Your School* by Norma Miller and *Talking Dirty with the Queen of Clean* by Linda Cobb (New York: Simon & Schuster, 1998).
- Know your students' allergies before the first day of school and make sure that the materials, live animals, and *being there* locations will not trigger an allergic or asthmatic attack.
- Give colleagues and students the benefit of the doubt when they tell you they don't feel well at school but okay at home. Listen to their complaints and take action.
- Create a school committee composed of staff and parents to investigate complaints. Set policies and procedures to determine priorities for eliminating toxins. Budget resources each year to handle situations as they arise.
- Set and closely monitor school policies for chemical use for pests, weed treatments, and cleaning—which, how, when.
- Where possible, enlist the assistance of students to help identify and solve problems.
- Recognize that this is a community problem and the community deserves to know the extent of the problems their children face. Enlist the support of parents and community—time and talents as well as money donations.

Cumulative Effects. The dangers of one-time exposure are considerable enough but the real problem that educators must face is the accumulated effects of multiple toxins. The figure on the previous page illustrates the total-body-load theory of human disease and ill-health. No single factor is the complete culprit but each factor adds a burden to the body's adaptive capacity; disease develops when the body's ability to adapt has been exceeded.

The Classroom Is Clean

Clean is clean. It is the clean you make your house when special guests are coming. It means absence of dirt. It means shiny windows, beautiful ceilings and walls with good paint and no water stains, gleaming floors/carpets unstained and free of dust, molds, and other allergens. It means desks without last year's fingerprints, art project mishaps, and gum. It means clean.

Somehow we've come to accept a second-rate standard for cleanliness in our schools. Whether we like it or not, the degree of cleanliness signals clearly how much we value our guests and ourselves. If we want students to choose to be in our classrooms, we need to let them know by our deeds that they're welcome and valued. Nothing you do can mask a dirty environment or mute its messages to students, parents, and colleagues. A dirty environment clearly signals that there are no standards here, people have to be here, and are powerless to change their situation. These are all the wrong messages for a school to telegraph to its students.

If you think we're over-reacting here, guess again. Children love cleanliness and classy surroundings (think Disneyland standards). Standards of cleanliness, tidiness, "classiness," and professionalism do matter.

Making the Most of Resources. Although insufficient resources for proper maintenance and repairs is the rule rather than the exception, before you campaign for an increase in your maintenance budget, analyze what is or is not happening now. It is always possible to make better use of what we have. The most frequent culprit is lack of agreed-upon policies and procedures—an overall plan of the priorities. Or, the plan is written but unknown to most and followed by few.

Here are some questions to ask:

- Exactly what cleaning is done daily? What are the standards?
- How do day-to-day procedures build in time for non-daily, rotational needs such as washing windows, sanitizing desks, washing walls, cleaning carpets, and so forth?
- Who should be notified when things are not done according to the plan? When first reports aren't responded to, what is the follow-up process?

Often maintenance staffs are not under the direct supervision of the principal or, even worse, the their needs and priorities are theirs alone. They are said to run the school. If so, make some changes. Create a maintenance/repairs advisory committee composed of teachers, parents, community members (especially those who have earned good reputations for supervising high quality maintenance and repair services), the principal, and the maintenance staff. Put the cards on the table. Hammer out agreements and priorities. Politics must be made to bow to the health needs of children.

Recruit and Delegate. For the most part, teaching is a solitary act. But the issue of a healthful environment is too important to allow isolate to dictate what happens. If your school administration doesn't insist on clean and won't assign anyone to help you, recruit help from parents and students. Don't be bashful. They have as much a vested interest in the classroom as you do.

Need tissues in the classroom but it's not in your school's budget? No soap in the bathroom? Ask for donations. Bathrooms superficially cleaned and a health hazard? Let parents press for higher standards. This is their school for their children.

Also, recruit students for tasks similar to those chores they would perform at home. If you want the maintenance staff to perform more of the major cleaning projects such as window washing, cleaning walls, sanitizing desks, etc., then make the students responsible for cleaning up their own daily messes . . . just as they are responsible for them at home so that their parents can spend their time on real cleaning and repair tasks.

Getting Started. As we know from cleaning our own home—and keeping it clean—cleaning is difficult if our space is cluttered. To get your space really clean, you may first have to conquer clutter (see discussion on page 8.14). Before attempting to clean, remove clutter—all of it. If possible, move everything but the furniture out into the hall. Then, scrub, sanitize, paint. Scrutinize the carpet. If it's not cleanable to acceptable health (not just visual) standards, have it removed immediately; if cleanable, get it cleaned immediately using as chemical-free a process as possible.

Before you move anything back in, make sure that it is absolutely essential to what you are studying this year. If not, don't let it through the door. Keep visible only those things that will be used this month; store things needed for the rest of the year in cupboards that have doors (or solid colored curtains) and thus can be kept out of sight.

Items that will not be used this year should be removed from your classroom. Recycle (give them to teachers who can use them), give them away, throw them away, or store them off-site. Then, clean the room and everything in it. Make floors and walls and everything within sanitary as well as tidy.

Don't stop until the room meets your standards for your own home . . . you know . . . if your future mother-in-law were coming to visit for the first time. Now that's clean!

Don't Overlook the Restrooms. The bathrooms your students regularly use are a big part of maintaining a healthful environment.

If your bathrooms are frequently trashed by students, perhaps students are expressing their discontent about the lack of cleanliness and the inadequate supplies (no toilet paper or soap or towels). If you want to turn things around, hold a bathroom celebration on the weekend. Invite parents and students to the party. Deep clean, paint, and decorate the bathroom. Make it look as much like yours at home (or what you'd like yours to look like!). Add a touch of wallpaper or special paint for color and class. Post relevant LIFESKILLS and procedures where necessary but don't make it look like a military camp. And add a sign telling users how to report a problem, e.g., "If you find something wrong in this bathroom, come to room X to report it. Thank you for helping us keep our bathroom clean."

Also take note of in-classroom sinks and drinking fountains. Not only should they be visually clean but also they must be kept sanitary.

Hanging in There. To maintain this new standard of clean, talk with your custodian. Share your intentions and standards for your classroom. Ask what you can do to help achieve and maintain your goals. Pride is a powerful motivator. Help both of you to be proud of your classroom.

Tell your maintenance person what allergies you and your students have. Together select cleaning products for use in your classroom. Choose those that don't leave toxic fumes; naphtha, creosol, lye, formaldehyde in disinfectants and ammonia, ethanol, or chlorine bleach in scouring powders are particularly bad. For nontoxic alternatives, see *Talking Dirty with the Queen of Clean* by Linda Cobb. See also the discussion of pollutants and ventilation, pages 8.10-8.12.

Mastering the Art of Clean

- Make the most of your resources by ensuring there are daily procedures both for day-to-day cleaning and for larger jobs, parts of which need to be done each day to ensure they are completed as expected.
- Make sure that the daily procedures are performed as expected.
- Involve parents and the community in maintenance issues. It is their school and their children. Ask their advice, recruit their assistance, and delegate tasks.
- Involve students; help them become responsible for cleaning up their own daily messes so that maintenance staff can address larger cleaning issues.
- In your own classroom, raise the bar. Insist on standards of cleanliness at least as high as those you maintain at home.
- Before school starts, find out what allergies your students have. Plan materials and resources accordingly.
- Pay attention to the bathrooms.
- Schoolwide, create a maintenance/repairs advisory committee of teachers, parents, community members, the principal, and the school maintenance staff. Hammer out agreements about standards and priorities within current resources and determine if additional resources are needed, where, and why.

Self Check

The Classroom Is Clean

Clean to meet the evaluative yardstick of our senses:

- Visual—no dust bunnies, streaks and smears, discoloration, dullness/lack of shine; nothing broken or mis-functioning; no clutter (no furniture, resources, materials not in current use)
- Smell—no odor, no allergens/antigens such as molds, bacteria, dust. Air filters are cleaned every two months or more often as needed; carpeting is deep-cleaned twice a year and removed when it can no longer be cleaned to standards. Air purifiers are installed in each classroom that needs one.
- Touch—no stickiness or roughness (from dried materials on surfaces or from scraps and cracks)
- Sanitation—absenteeism due to illness by school contagion less than one percent

The Classroom Is Well-lighted

Lighting in schools has been examined from various points of view over the past 50 years. Sufficient light to easily read a book, see work on one's desk, and see the board have long been the accepted standards for classroom lighting. More recently, energy conservation issues have prevailed. Aesthetics is also a consideration. However, recent research goes beyond these typical issues and makes it clear that light—amount, intensity, and color spectrum—has a profound effect on people of all ages, not just children. For those new to the body of research about the effects of light on physical, emotional, and brain function, the findings are quite startling. The implications for teaching and learning are huge.

Effects of Lighting on Physical and Emotional Health. John Ott, pioneer and giant in the study of the effects of light on humans, believes that "humans are photosynthetic," that full-spectrum light acts as the ignition switch for all human biological functions: "The light-mediated process known as photosynthesis in plants is, in my opinion, the same thing as metabolism in humans."[6] According to Fritz Hollwich, M.D., "Light is a primal element of life. Artificial light may be an optic substitute but is by no means equivalent to nature's light in physiological terms."[7] Light from the sun synchronizes most body functions; its absence or imbalance can cause a reduction in our physiological, emotional, and intellectual functioning.[8]

Light not only permits us to see but, through its stimulation of the pineal and hypothalamus glands, also affects virtually every function of the body. The spectral properties of sunlight are fundamental to the:

- Endocrine system, biological clock, immune system, circulatory system, respiratory system, and sexual development
- Ability to control stress and fatigue
- Healthy functioning of the nervous system[9]

Most of us spend the majority of our waking hours drenched in light whose spectral characteristics differ markedly from those of sunlight. Artificial sources of light fail to duplicate the full spectrum of natural sunlight which casts a broad, continuous rainbow of colors.[10]

Most indoor artificial light tends to be weak in strength and density and distorted in terms of color.[11] One component of natural light, which we rarely receive indoors, is ultraviolet light. It is virtually absent from incandescent lighting, shielded in standard fluorescent tubes, and blocked by normal window pane glass and eyeglass lenses. According to Faber Birren in *Light, Color, and Environment,* UV stimulates blood circulation, lowers blood pressure, prevents rickets, increases protein metabolism, decreases fatigue, stimulates glandular activity, stimulates white blood cell activity, increases the release of endorphins, and enhances the production of vitamin D, thereby increasing the absorption of calcium and phosphorus.[12]

According to Richard J. Wurtman, M.D., 16 hours of artificial lighting provides less physical and emotional benefit than one hour of natural lighting.[13] Prolonged exposure to artificial lighting has been associated with:

- Irritability, eyestrain, headaches, fatigue
- Hyperactivity, allergies, frequent minor illnesses
- Inability to concentrate, vision problems
- Susceptibility to osteoporosis and rickets
- Increased incidence of dental cavities
- Changes in heart rate, blood pressure, electrical brain wave patterns, hormonal secretions, and body rhythms
- Depression/Seasonal Affective Disorder, alcoholism, suicide (the third leading cause of death for young adults), weight gain, anxiety, and insomnia.[14]

In short, natural sunlight is a key ingredient in maintaining our health and mental acuity for learning—*a vital nutrient.* Lack of sufficient light affects many children and adults so much that their behavior, learning, and performance are significantly impaired.[15]

Effects of Lighting on Brain Function and Achievement. Modern indoor life, with its radical changes in the amount, intensity, and color spectrum of our lighting, challenges our brain in many ways that make learning more difficult for all of us. The difficulties arise indirectly from physical symptoms described previously, and directly, due to actual changes in brain waves and disturbances in producing various neurotransmitters.

Studies show surprisingly strong effects of lighting on brain function. For example, lack of natural light from the sun results in:

- Increased incidence of anxiety and irritability, an inability to tolerate stress, difficulty in getting started in the morning, crying spells, and an overall decrease in activity levels, specifically in the fall semester[16]
- Overeating, oversleeping, and sluggishness[17]
- Increased absenteeism (more than double)[18]
- Lower achievement scores[19]

Given the billions of dollars spent on public education each year, it makes no sense to "stack the cards against educational success by ignoring issues of polluted light."[20]

Using Light to Improve Learning & Performance

- Conduct a thorough analysis of the light in your classroom and other areas where students spend a lot of time. Check for:
  - Amount of lighting for near and far work (the old-fashioned measurement of whether a student can see his/her work at desk and board)
  - Intensity (high enough to prevent eye strain but without glare)
  - Color spectrum (the color spectrum matches natural sunlight).
- Remove the omnipresent, blue-spectrum fluorescent tubes; substitute full-spectrum tubes that mimic natural sunshine. Replace or repair lights that hum.
- Add incandescent lighting to special reading areas and the teacher's desk.
- Install/Repair window treatments that block the glare of direct sun but allow sunlight in (shades that mount at the bottom of the window and pull up are often more useable than those that hang from the top).
- During design and renovation of schools, insist on windows in every classroom and all offices, full spectrum fluorescent lights, and separate switches for each bank of lighting.
- Consider visual needs and sensitivities of students when drawing up student seating assignments.
- Keep exposure to computer screens, videos, and TV to a minimum.[21]

Self Check

Well-Lighted Classroom

- Lighting includes natural sunlight supplemented by full spectrum and incandescent light; lighting is cheerful but without harshness or glare.
- Burned out elements are repaired in a timely manner or, in overly bright areas, rearranged to pair them with working elements.
- Winter depression (SAD) is minimal. Students are cheerful and healthy.

Well-Ventilated

The two most essential fuels for the brain are glucose and oxygen. Proper diet supplies the first. Fresh air provides the second. Without fresh air—oxygen—learning is impossible. Fresh air means an absence of neurotoxins and biological allergens/antigens such as molds, bacteria, viruses, dust mites, dust, pollens, and so forth.

The importance of fresh air to a healthful environment can't be overemphasized. Most of the pollutants discussed earlier off-gas into the air and thus become a ventilation/fresh air problem. For example, all of the issues in the top 10 most serious indoor sources of pollution identified in the Texas Woman's University study (see page 8.3) except lighting impinge on air quality—adequate oxygen and absence of toxins. Thus, the adequacy of a school's ventilation system should be the first system analyzed and have first call on resources.

The authors have yet to see a large building whose HVAC (heating, ventilation, and air conditioning) system really works, i.e., provides a pleasant environment (good air quality and appropriate temperature) for everyone year round.

Before the advent of so many chemicals, the biggest challenges to air quality were the products of human bodies—carbon dioxide, moisture, odors. Now, like cleanliness, we need to recognize a 21st century definition of well-ventilated: complete absence of toxins and full presence of fresh oxygen, pleasant smelling (the absence of odor), and a constant, appropriate temperature.

For an excellent discussion of current challenges for ventilation and toxin removal, see *The Healthy School Handbook: Conquering the Sick Building Syndrome and Other Environmental Hazards In and Around Your School* by Norma Miller, often cited in this chapter, and her videotape, *Environmentally Sick Schools – What You WANT and NEED to Know: A Guide for Parents and Teachers.*

Providing oxygen—fresh air with no neurotoxins and allergens—to the brain is the most important contribution to learning that educators and taxpayers can make. The formula is a simple one: "No oxygen, no learning."

Improving Ventilation and Providing Fresh Air

- Listen to those who complain about poor air and not feeling well. They are your "canaries"—your indicators of air quality.
- Check the intake and outflow points of your system(s) to make sure that outflow from the ventilation system and any other outflow points do not feed dirty air into the "fresh air" intake.
- If you have windows that open, open them (monitor when the outside might be unsafe). Your goal is to have fresh air at head height. Make a point of asking yourself, "How's the air in here right now?" Ask this question at least once every hour. Does it smell of body odor, is the air stale, do students look alert yet calm?
- Insist on the maximum percentage of fresh air exchange allowed by law in your state. Reducing fresh air intake to conserve energy is absurd—far less expensive than lost learning due to inattention caused by low oxygen levels to the brain and or the presence of neurotoxins and allergens. If the allowed exchange rate is inadequate, lobby your legislature for exemptions for those schools that can prove a need for more fresh air intake. If your school is located in an area of high outdoor pollution, widen your political action focus.

Improving Ventilation and Providing Fresh Air *continued*

- Thoroughly clean the system, including duct work, each year before school starts. Replace the air filters at least every two months. Add purifying systems to areas of high concentrations of chemicals or classrooms whose students or teacher is particularly sensitive to poor ventilation.
- Given the rate of introduction of new chemicals into the environment, analyze the chemical composition of every item that comes onto the campus, from construction materials to cleaning agents, computers to book print, white board markers to science and art supplies, particularly items brought on to the campus in large quantities.
- Eliminate artificial fertilizers, pesticides, or herbicides from playgrounds and athletic fields because these chemicals are tracked in and can build up in high concentrations.
- When designing or remodeling a single story building, compare the long-range costs (purchase, maintenance, and repair) of a heat pump HVAC unit for each classroom versus the large, centralized unit. Individual units over time are often more cost-effective, not to mention pleasant, because each classroom can have the temperature the occupants want, contaminants from elsewhere in the building spread less readily, and each room has access to fresh, high-oxygen outside air.

Self Check

Well Ventilated

- All exhaust vents are properly separated from intake vents.
- Filters fit and are free from dirt, molds, and bacteria. Duct work is also clean and free from contaminants.
- Air purifying machines have been installed in each classroom where needed.
- Water leaks are fixed immediately; pockets of mold and bacteria have been eliminated; all drain traps contain water to decrease sewer gas.
- Buses run their engines only when in motion.
- An Integrated Pest Control System has replaced all routine pesticide/insecticide treatments.

Pleasant Smelling

The most pleasant-smelling environment is one that has no particular smell, just a sense of air that is fresh and well-oxygenated. That means absence of smell from cleaning chemicals, body odor, mold from air conditioners and other sources, stale air, dust, old books with mites, and so forth.

Use of potpourri and air fresheners on a regular basis is not desirable because some of your students may be allergic to them. On an occasional basis, to heighten an immersion or hands-on experience, adding an odor can be very useful, provided of course that no student has an allergic reaction to the fragrance used.

When adding a smell to the classroom, use natural rather than artificial sources, such as natural oils from real plants.

Ambient Temperature

A steady, reliable temperature of 68 degrees in the winter and 76 degrees in the summer helps students stay focused on learning. Yet few centralized systems can deliver. Our recommendation is careful monitoring of windows that open and, whenever possible, a separate HVAC unit for each classroom.

Safe

That our public schools provide a safe environment is assumed, at least a minimal level of care. But the truth is that delayed maintenance and repairs often present real safety hazards. Examples include: an electrical supply inadequate to the demands of the classroom, broken or missing plates for electric plugs and switches, furniture that is ill-fitting, unsteady, chipped, cracked, or splintery. Other hazards include tears in the carpet, loose throw rugs, coats and boots on the floor due to lack of hangers, and so forth. The list goes on.

Unfortunately, timely maintenance is a common budget-cutting target. School board members and administrators need your support and input as they address competing priorities.

Safety First

- Take a fresh look at your classroom. As you come through the door, crouch down to the height of your students. Slowly survey the room. What safety hazards do you see?
- Run your hand over and around the edges of the furniture. Fix any rough or sharp edges and surfaces.
- Make sure written procedures for handling toxic chemicals are in place and known to staff.
- Make sure written procedures for handling each classroom pet are posted and used by students.

Aesthetically Pleasing

Aesthetics is defined as the study or theory of beauty and of the psychological responses to it. It is the branch of philosophy dealing with art, its creative sources, its forms, and its effects. While this is more inclusive than necessary for our purposes here, the sense of rigor is important to the classroom. That is to say, the scientific research behind the physiological, mental, and emotional impact of color and other elements of design, versus interior design based on personal preference or tradition, is critical. By basing classroom design on research findings, we can create classrooms that nurture reflective thinking for the highest possible percentage of our students.

For a workaday definition of aesthetics, we will focus on two areas: art and design. Art is usually thought of in terms of line, shape or form, value, texture, and color. Design is often thought of in terms of space, color, composition, different materials and techniques, and purpose or use.

Our ultimate criteria of acceptability and excellence in these areas is not how chic or groovy or cool a classroom may look but rather how well it nurtures reflective thinking. Questions to ask under each category of art and design include the following:

Purpose in Design. To what extent do the elements allow you to implement the bodybrain-compatible elements to best advantage? For example, does the form of the room allow such functions as Learning Clubs, Community Circle, and other group projects? For intrapersonal space and time, a time-alone space (often call an "Australia")? For movement, immersion and hands-on-of-the-real-thing, and ready access to needed resources, materials, and tools? Does it provide an attractive entry that provides transition into the room?

Space. Is there a sense of spaciousness yet a location for every purpose and a place for everything and everything in its place without clutter and crowding? Does the layout allow for flow and freedom to move about? Has all unnecessary furniture been removed? Is the teacher's desk in an inconspicuous place?

Color. There is plenty of hard data about the physiological, emotional, and mental effects of color. To ignore it when designing and remodeling schools and even a single classroom is to squander public resources. There is great power in color. We need to learn to harness it as a way to enhance learning. For example, intense reds, yellows, and oranges over-stimulate students, making it difficult for them to focus on learning; the incidence of discipline problems is high. Other colors, especially the cool colors, greens and blues, are soothing and calming, inviting reflection and introspection.

As color emits its effects on students every minute of every day, it should be considered one of our strongest instructional allies. Accordingly, color should be selected with great care.[22]

Historically, elementary schools have used either institutional colors such as drab greens and grays or the ubiquitous white, or they have used bright, vivid colors such as red, orange, and yellow. Recent color research would have us avoid both extremes. Recommended colors for classrooms that enhance intellectual work include the following:[23]

- For preschool and elementary grades, light salmon, soft warm yellow, pale yellow-orange, coral, and peach. For example, such combinations as light salmon walls and forest green floors
- For upper grade and secondary classrooms, beige, pale or light green, and blue-green; where students face one direction, side and back walls in beige, sandstone, or light tan with front wall in medium tones of gold, terra-cotta, green, or blue
- For libraries, pale or light green (creates a passive effect that enhances concentration)

If we want to nurture reflective thinking, we should choose the colors that most enhance it.

Like any well-decorated five-star hotel, color schemes should consist of a basic color and not more than two or three accent colors on the walls. Multiple patterns, such as bears around one bulletin board and crayons or geometric patterns around another, are a violation of every good design principle. If you wouldn't do something in your own living room, rethink it for the classroom. Somehow we've developed some strange traditions for color and interior decoration for school classrooms.

The design principles of understated and simple elegance are as important for the classroom as they are for the board room of a multinational corporation.

Color and light go together. Color should not allow glare and should maximize the visual appeal of the classroom.

Texture. Because classrooms must be so utilitarian, they often consist of one smooth artificial surface after another. Very boring to the eye. Plants, a fabric-covered couch or wooden rocker, desk lamps with fabric window shades, and a handwoven rug or ceramic floor tile all help add texture and eye appeal to the classroom. Conversely, limit the number of doorless/curtainless shelves; their "stuff," be it book spines or piles of papers, provides the kind of texture that amounts to clutter.

Line. What lines catch the eye? Rows of desks/tables that make the room appear long and skinny? Chaotic lines from haphazard arrangement of chairs, bookcases, and such? Consider a three-to-four- inch-wide, solid-accent color strip around the room about three to four feet from the ceiling. This draws the ceiling down, making the room more kid-sized and gives the eye a line to follow to view the room from one end to the other.

Value. Could a visitor entering your room identify what you and your students value in the learning process? What you are currently studying? What is your focus?

Cluttered Classroom Illustration
by Sue Pearson, *associate*, Susan Kovalik and Associates

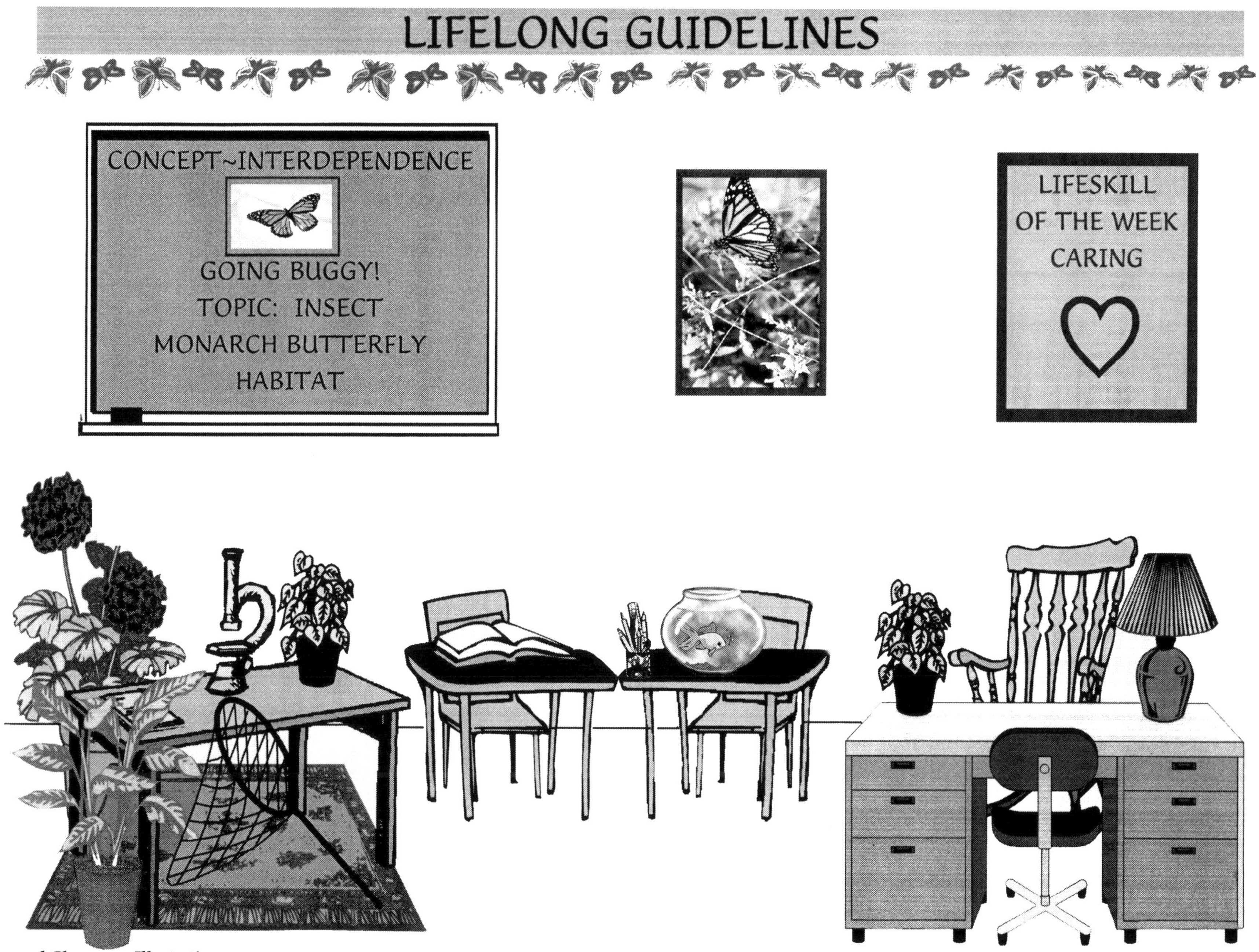

Focused Classroom Illustration
by Sue Pearson, *associate*, Susan Kovalik and Associates

Uncluttered, Yet Reflects What Is Being Learned

Somewhere along the line, we have confused an enriched environment with a cluttered environment. If we don't have things hanging from the ceiling, floor to ceiling word walls, student work from the last month(s), bulletin boards in multicolors (even 3-D), and more, then we feel we don't have an enriched environment. Unfortunately, the very students who have the most difficulty focusing on learning are the ones most distracted and most likely to experience sensory overload in the midst of clutter.

However, architectural and interior designers of 5-Star hotels are under no such illusions. Their goal is to make people feel welcome and relaxed, not distracted and over-stimulated.

The goal of ITI is an uncluttered but rich environment. The theme wall sets the itinerary for the month and where that fits within the yearlong theme. Print and non-print material support the content being learned. An uncluttered, well-designed room significantly improves student and teacher performance and enjoyment. It's well worth the effort. (See classroom designs on pages 6.16 -6.19 and the video *One Day Makeover for Your ITI Classroom* with Dottie Brown.)

Seating Is Arranged in Clusters with Easy Access to Work Tools

Of all the images of school that bespeak a mindless bureaucracy at work, rows of desks bolted to the floor in rigid rows win the academy award. No talking, do your own work, keep your eyes to yourself. A recipe for restricting sensory input and brain activity.

In the bodybrain-compatible classroom, students need flexible seating to fit the nature of their work. If possible, trade your desks for tables and chairs.

The size of the clusters—two to five students—will depend upon the collaborative skill of your students. If you think your students will have difficulty handling participation in a group of five, begin with two (or, if need be, a committee of one) and work upward.

Become Familiar with State and District Curriculum Standards and Assessment Practices

No matter what your tools—textbooks or teacher written curriculum—allow state/district standards to frame what is expected of your students. Within this frame, dedicate yourself to making the content as conceptual and engaging as possible.

Select "Being There" Locations

That *being there* experiences greatly enhance learning is hardly a new notion. It is confirmed by our own experiences as learners, by educational research from John Dewey to the present day, and by current brain research. And yet, we ignore our wisdom day after day. We complain that "it's not in the budget" or "I don't have time" or "my kids couldn't handle such a trip." However, the school grounds and neighborhood only need shoes that can go a-walkin" or a public transportation bus pass; study trips need not be expensive or distant. *Being there* study trips are a powerful use of time, promoting far more learning than the same amount of seat time; and kids can and will rise to the occasion and the opportunity to learn something exciting.

Matching the curriculum with real-world experiences that demonstrate how and why that learning is important is key to creating a bodybrain-compatible learning environment.

Before you take students, visit the locations yourself. See them through the eyes of your students. Ask yourself how well the people at these locations (workers and visitors) demonstrate the concepts and skills of your state standards. For more discussion about selecting and using *being there* locations, see Chapter 12.

Guest Speakers

Guest speakers are a great way to introduce and extend the excitement generated by *being there* study trips. They provide that critical context for students—who uses these concepts and skills, how, and why.

If your guest speakers represent famous persons or periods in history, have them come in dress and role play the issues of the time.

Teacher Meets Frequently with a Professional or Peer Coach

As you plan for students, remember to plan for your own needs. Set aside the necessary resources, especially time, to ensure that you have opportunities to meet frequently with a professional or peer coach who has mastered the ITI model in his/her own classroom and can support your implementation of a bodybrain-compatible learning environment.

Support is critical to your success. Make sure you get needed assistance through both formal and informal venues.

Finding a Coach

Insist on frequent, at least monthly, support from a coach who has implemented the ITI model at Stage 3 or higher. While peer coaching (two peers at nearly the same level of implementation) can work, the process is agonizingly slow. The blind leading the blind, both strangers to the landscape, is too costly in terms of time, effort, and lost opportunities.

In addition to your coach, find a colleague who is committed to implementing the ITI model and who is willing to share deeply about professional issues and growth. The combination of a coach and a partner is very powerful. Ask the coach to work with the two of you as a team. Triads are also a good size for coaching.

Implementing As Team Member or Solo

Analyze where your peers are. What knowledge and commitment to bodybrain-compatible education do they share? Whether you are to implement solo or as a member of a team is critical to your planning.

As any parent knows, consistency is critical when it comes to behavior guidelines. So it is with the Lifelong Guidelines and LIFESKILLS of Stage One. Schoolwide implementation as a team effort is clearly the best way to go, the more so with older students. But students will respond to consistent use of the Lifelong Guidelines and LIFESKILLS in their classroom. The solo approach does work for students but, as with most tasks, working alone is harder.

ITI schools that use the Lifelong Guidelines and LIFESKILLS begin implementing them in a variety of ways. Some just dive right in! The staff agrees that these behaviors will help expedite the learning process by providing absence of threat for the students and nurturing reflective thinking. The school wants such social and behavioral guidelines, they want them now, and they also want them schoolwide.

Other sites reach schoolwide consensus more slowly. They often begin with initiating schoolwide discussions, hold book talks around key ITI books and then bring in ITI trainings (e.g., the Lifelong Guidelines and LIFESKILLS PowerPack provided by Susan Kovalik & Associates) and other opportunities for the staff to practice and learn brain research-based strategies.

In other schools, teams of teachers begin using Lifelong Guidelines and LIFESKILLS in their classrooms, using the resources of the team for support and maintaining an ongoing dialogue with other colleagues about the progress of their students.

Implementation moves more quickly and is more rewarding if others at your school have adopted the Lifelong Guidelines and LIFESKILLS as their model for interacting with students. But never overlook the power of one—a single teacher leading the way.

Whatever your situation, you can start now. Start in your own classroom and let the Lifelong Guidelines and LIFESKILLS grow from there. They have a way of taking on a life of their own as students, parents, and other staff embrace their use.

The Advantages of Implementing Schoolwide

Agreeing to implement the Lifelong Guidelines and LIFESKILLS schoolwide has many advantages. First, there is a common vocabulary that, over time, builds a commonly shared belief system about how children learn and how adults should treat students and each other, a necessary building block for developing a sense of community. Second, consistency from class to class results in more rapid change in student and adult behavior. Last, the "spill-over" factor is high: The students will take the desired behaviors into other areas of their lives outside school—at home and in group situations such as neighborhood play, sports, scouts, and so forth. With everyone involved at the same time, there is an opportunity to build common understandings and buy-in very quickly.

Team Implementation

Implementation by a small group (grade level or team) is harder because students receive mixed messages about the importance of using the Lifelong Guidelines and LIFESKILLS as community-building strategies by those outside the team which interfere with the learning process. In addition, lack of consistency—between the classroom and other locations within the school—makes the process slower, especially for students having behavior problems.

Solo Implementation

If you are doing this alone, you will have to work hard to create an alternative culture on campus, one which your students will see as viable and valuable. The process of implementation at the classroom level is, however, the same whether implementing solo, as a team, or schoolwide. In general: Start the first day of school, work intensively during the first four to five weeks, and reinforce daily thereafter.

Notes

1 Norma Miller, ed., *The Healthy School Handbook: Conquering the Sick Building Syndrome and Other Environmental Hazards In and Around Your School* (Washington, DC: NEA Professional Library, 1995), 5.

2 Miller, *Healthy School Handbook*, 23.

3 Ibid., 64

4 Ibid., 244.

5 Ibid., 247-248.

6 John Ott, photobiologist and trailblazing researcher as quoted in Miller, *Healthy School Handbook*, 203.

7 Miller, *Healthy School Handbook*, 195. See also Fritz Hollwich, M.D., *The Influence of Ocular Light Perception on Metabolism in Man and Animals.*

8 Miller, *Healthy School Handbook*, 196.

9 Ibid.

10 There are numerous books and articles that catalog the detrimental effects on health and brain wiring in children who spend too much time in front of computer and TV/video screens. See also Miller, Chapter 10, especially pages 195-206.

11 Ibid., 197.

12 Faber Birren as quoted in Miller, *Healthy School Handbook*, 208.

13 Richard J. Wurtman quote in Miller, *Healthy School Handbook*, 197.

14 Miller, *Healthy School Handbook*, 196.
Seasonal Affective Disorder (SAD) is a common companion, if not a major source, of childhood and adult depression. It is believed that winter's feeble light rays, some 70% weaker in intensity and duration than summer sunlight, are responsible for the deep depression experienced by 5% of the population and for the less serious *winter blahs* familiar to some 30-40% of the population. This is significant because the pineal gland, "the light meter and conductor that orchestrates our body clocks, plays a vital role in every aspect of human function, regulating reproduction, growth, body temperature, blood pressure, motor activity, sleep, tumor growth, mood immune function, and even longevity. And, interestingly, the *activity of the pineal gland is governed by environmental light.*"

Dr. Thomas A. Wehr of National Institute for Mental Health believes that SAD has "a tremendous impact on children's ability to function in school. They start out the school year fairly strong, thinking they will enjoy it. In November, it starts to fall apart. They sleep 12 hours a day. They're not creative. They've lost the spark. Those with winter depression are slowed down." Miller, *Healthy School Handbook*, 212-213.

15 "Energy- and money-saving concerns have created classroom lighting conditions that foster the 'sunlight starvation syndrome.' The light distribution in our schools tends to be so deficient in most parts of the natural spectrum that we may just be fighting an uphill battle, attempting to teach students in 'the twilight zone.' It's time to acknowledge that light is a *cooperating teacher* in every classroom." Miller, *Healthy School Handbook*, 196-197.

16 Miller, *Healthy School Handbook*, 213.

17 Ubell as quoted by Miller, *Healthy School Handbook*, 213.

18 Wohlfart as quoted by Miller, *Healthy School Handbook*, 209.

19 Dozens of studies detail increased achievement when typical fluorescent tubes are replaced by full spectrum tubes or natural sunlight. See Miller, *Healthy School Handbook*, Chapter 10.

20 Miller, *Healthy School Handbook*, 213.

21 Jane M. Healy, Ph.D., *Failure to Connect: How Computers Affect Our Children's Minds* (New York: Touchstone, 1998).

22 We highly recommend Frank H. and Rudolf H. Mahnke, *Color and Light in Man-Made Environments* (New York: John Wiley & Sons, 1993).

23 Frank and Rudolf Mahnke are deeply committed to color and design based on hard science rather than on personal preferences and style, as color has specific physiological effects on humans that are universal rather than culture dependent.

Chapter 7: What to Do the First Day of School & Beyond

First Day of School and Beyond

ITI Classroom Stages of Implementation **Stage 1.2**

Entry level for making the learning environment bodybrain compatible

CURRICULUM

- The bodybrain-compatible element of absence of threat and nurturing reflective thinking is taught as an important and ongoing part of the curriculum. Such curriculum contains the following five areas:

  1) The Lifelong Guidelines, including the LIFESKILLS

INSTRUCTIONAL STRATEGIES

- Models the Lifelong Guidelines and LIFESKILLS as the basis for his/her classroom leadership and management. Leads rather than controls; inspires rather than manipulates. Creates/maintains an atmosphere that is participatory rather than dictatorial.
- Uses target talk and teachable moments daily to reinforce and extend student understanding and practice of the Lifelong Guidelines and LIFESKILLS.
- Systematically introduces the meaning and importance of each of the Lifelong Guidelines and selected LIFESKILLS through formal lessons (key points and inquiries) and the context of classroom life. The Lifelong Guidelines and selected LIFESKILLS (as age appropriate) are posted and readable from a distance.
- Bases "discipline" on helping students develop the personal and social skills and behaviors needed to successfully practice the Lifelong Guidelines/LIFESKILLS rather than on a system of externally imposed rewards and punishments.

ITI Classroom Stages of Implementation **Stage 1.2**

First Day of School and Beyond *-continued*

CURRICULUM

2) The power of emotions to enhance or impede learning and performance

INSTRUCTIONAL STRATEGIES

- Formally introduces age-appropriate lessons about the power of emotion to drive attention and learning. The role of emotion (positive and negative) is discussed daily in multiple ways, such as during reflective thinking questions, Town Hall Meetings, and teacher feedback to individual students as well as during planned lessons.
- Provides consistency and emotional security for students:
  - Greets students at the door at the beginning of every day; says goodbye at the end of the every day.
  - Uses agendas every day to provide focus for learning, to enable students to direct their own learning, and to encourage learning ways to manage time.
  - Uses written procedures for all frequently occurring events/activities to provide consistency, continuity, and emotional security for students. Visuals include graphics as well as words.
- Frequently uses collaborative learning, as appropriate, to extend and deepen learning and to create a sense of community.
- An "Australia" in the classroom provides a place and time to help students bring their emotions and behavior back under control.

---

3) The important role of movement to enhance academic learning

- Models and teaches students about using movement to enhance learning
- Uses movement to enhance learning. Provides daily movement sessions to energize, calm, and assist in understanding and remembering key points and inquiries. Uses such resources as *Brain Gym* and teacher-designed movement activities that grow naturally from curriculum content.
- Includes movement and other bodily-kinesthetic action during instruction of key points as well as in follow-up activities and inquiries.

ITI Classroom Stages of Implementation **Stage 1.2**

First Day of School and Beyond -continued

CURRICULUM	INSTRUCTIONAL STRATEGIES
4) Personal and social skills for collaboration	• Models and formally teaches the personal and social skills needed to work collaboratively. • Organizes students into Learning Clubs. Teaches how and when to use various group processes (such as leading, supporting, listening, encouraging, sharing, and "3-before-me," etc.). • Leads students in activities, such as Town Hall Meeting and Acknowledgement Box, that are appropriate for each of the three stages of group development—developing a sense of inclusion/belonging, creating common ground, and taking action. The resulting sense of community serves as the basis for achieving high academic performance. • Uses collaborative learning to achieve specific goals daily.
5) How to nurture and utilize reflective thinking	• Uses a calm voice, synchronizes his/her heart-brain coherence, and stays emotionally centered. • Provides a variety of processes and structures throughout the day which enhance students' reflective thinking, such as wait time, journal writing, reflecting on the daily agenda (beginning and end of the day), making choices that allow students to direct their learning, forecasting how to take on a learning task, reflecting on what one has learned academically, the process of collaborative work (before, during, and after and asking about content, social, and personal outcomes), providing adequate time for students to complete assignments, and strategies to help students refocus.
	• Meets frequently with a professional or peer coach who supports his/her implementation of a bodybrain-compatible teaching/learning environment.

Making the Most of Anticipation

The big day has arrived. You are ready and the students are full of anticipation. For sheer exuberance and excitement, nothing beats the first day of school. Kindergartners have been talking about school for months. Their mothers are full of anticipation and dread simultaneously. First graders "can't wait." Who is my teacher? What kind of person is she/he? Will my teacher like me? Will I like her? Will my classmates like me? Will I like them? Even upper grade students have geared up their curiosity about what it will be like this year. "Will any of my friends be in my class with me?" "What will my teacher be like?" "Will school be fun?" The excitement is contagious.

Capitalize on this openness of students. They are their most hopeful the first day of school and the most willing to join the teacher in creating an extraordinary year for themselves.

Leadership Versus Managing the Classroom

For teachers, this is your most powerful moment. As any self-improvement, Dale-Carnegie kind of course will tell you, first impressions are powerful and lasting. And, as any substitute knows, we have 60 seconds in which to establish who we are and what we're about, that our classroom isn't about typical school with worksheets and boredom, anxiety and dread.

The first day of school is a social event of importance; treat it that way. Model what your parents taught you about being a host/hostess. Follow the same procedures you would if you were inviting yet-to-be-met guests to your home.

Few of us like to be managed; we'd rather be led by a leader who possesses both vision and common sense and who, above all, keeps our best interests at heart—collectively and individually. The ITI approach to the issue of classroom management and discipline is to be proactive—to lead rather than control, to inspire rather than manipulate. Thus, the leadership you display on the first day must be your finest in the classroom for the entire year. Even before the first day of school, there are several leadership steps that will make your first moments together go smoothly.

The Invitation. First, send a written invitation to your students—a real note through the U.S. mail.[1] Welcome them, tell them how pleased you are that they will be coming to your classroom, that you look forward to spending the year with them. Tell them something about yourself and what you have planned for them. Give the date for your classroom's Back to School Night; ask that they invite their family.

The Greeting. Greet your students as you would greet guests coming to your house. Greet them at the door. Shake each one's hand. Exchange a word of welcome with them. Tell each one you're glad he/she came and that you're looking forward to the year. Let your work in preparing the room for them tell them that they are important to you. Point out the posted procedures[2] for arriving to class and help each student understand and follow them. As students pass by, give each a piece of puzzle that they will use to find their fellow Learning Club members.[3] Plan to greet students at the door each and every day.

Settling In. As you would at a sit-down dinner, invite them to find their name tag, where to put their personal belongings, what they can do to settle in and feel comfortable.[4] Preparation says that you care, you value their coming.

Introductions—Developing a Sense of Inclusion/Belonging. Once students have settled into their assigned seat, give them an inclusion activity with fellow members of their Learning Club to help them get to know each other.[5] At the dinner table, this is the equivalent of the host or hostess introducing each guest by providing a key piece of information about them and directing the conversation along those lines until comfort levels have been established and conversation takes on a life of its own.

Absence of Threat and Nurturing Reflective Thinking

The bodybrain-compatible element of absence of threat and nurturing reflective thinking should be taught as an important and on-going part of the curriculum. The first of the five areas is the Lifelong Guidelines, including the LIFESKILLS.

Even young students are capable of understanding basic concepts from brain research. For content, review Chapter 1 and the curriculum examples at the back of this chapter.

There are numerous ways to implement absence of threat and nurture reflective thinking. Key among these are: modeling the Lifelong Guidelines and LIFESKILLS; using target talk; teaching the meaning and importance of each Lifelong Guideline and selected LIFESKILLS to represent Personal Best; using written procedures, daily agendas, and calm voice; and collaborative learning.

The Lifelong Guidelines and LIFESKILLS

Implementation of the Lifelong Guidelines and LIFESKILLS must be the first thing on your agenda the first day of school and the highest priority thereafter. Use both planned curriculum and teachable moments that occur. These guidelines are the basis of your leadership of the classroom and the foundation for students' academic success.

Modeling

The single most powerful instructional strategy—regardless of what you are teaching—is modeling. As you already know, "Do what I do" is always more powerful than "Do what I say."

However, consistent modeling of the values and beliefs of a lifelong learner and a contributing citizen—core goals of the ITI model—are more easily said than done. Be prepared for some self-evaluation.

For example, when preparing to teach the Lifelong Guidelines and LIFESKILLS, reflect on your own conduct and be open to fine tuning anything less than perfect manners, attitudes, and conduct. Muster the courage to make appropriate changes. Model for your students how to make changes in long-standing patterns of behavior. Remember, modeling isn't about being perfect, it's about showing others how to be the best human being possible—imperfect perhaps, but always improving and always willing to make amends for mistakes.

To model is to commit to making one's outer and inner life—words and actions—congruent and consistent. Learn how to discuss with your students those times when you fall short. Modeling is not about being perfect but about continually improving.

Do As I Do. As teachers, we are some of the most powerful role models in the lives of our students. They study us carefully, whether they appear to or not. They watch to see if we offer up only "token" lessons about being a learner or productive citizen, or if we truly believe that such skills are important social and behavioral guidelines for *all* to follow—at home and elsewhere. Take time to visualize exactly the kind of person you want to be and what you want mirrored in your students' behaviors. Then, define and write down strategies that will achieve these personal goals. Remember, you're on stage and actions always speak louder than words.

Modeling of the Lifelong Guidelines/ LIFESKILLS is a daily priority. What students see in their teacher is that the guidelines are not rules to be blindly followed in the classroom but rather they are guidelines for succeeding in life. Your high expectations of yourself and for your students create an environment in which students can internalize responsibility for their behavior. By the end of Stage 1.3, "discipline" programs that depend on external control and rewards should be eliminated. Teacher and students should be operating with the Lifelong Guidelines and LIFESKILLS as guidelines to behaviors that enable us to succeed in life, not as "rules" to be resisted. We strongly urge you to jump ahead to Chapters 8 and 9.

It should be noted, however, that full use of the Lifelong Guidelines/LIFESKILLS hinges on engaging content based in *being there* experiences. With that in mind, teachers should look forward to Stage 2 with relish. Stage 2 enhances all that you have strived for in Stage 1; conversely, continuance of Stage 1 instructional strategies makes Stage 2 possible.

Target Talk

The second most powerful strategy for teaching skills and behaviors such as the Lifelong Guidelines and LIFESKILLS is to acknowledge their use as they occur, taking advantage of the teachable moment—when appropriate behaviors or skills are demonstrated and deserve comment or should be used and the consequences need to be discussed. These spontaneous moments occur naturally and can be more powerful than preplanned lessons. Target talk* provides your students an opportunity to understand what the behavior or skill looks like, sounds like, and feels like, and does not look, sound, or feel like, in varying situations. Such on-the-spot feedback helps build shared understanding of the Lifelong Guidelines and LIFESKILLS as a common language to discuss the behaviors that go with them. You'll be surprised how quickly your students, regardless of age, will make target talk comments about the behavior of others . . . and you. Be prepared!

The Goal of Target Talk. As Pat Belvel** points out, misbehavior is a teaching opportunity. It is a symptom that students don't know enough of the appropriate behaviors and/or know too many of the wrong behaviors. She developed "target talk" as a teaching tool to provide clear pictures of expected behaviors. As adapted for use in the ITI model, it is extremely effective for teaching students desirable behaviors and skills such as the Lifelong Guidelines and LIFESKILLS.

Additional pictures of what a behavior or skill does and doesn't look, sound, and feel like are essential, especially when that behavior or skill is conceptually rich and its application to real life is complex. Mastering the Lifelong Guidelines and LIFESKILLS is a lifelong pursuit. For example, the attributes of truthfulness are not only complex but often subtle; frequently, the difference between truthful and tactless depends on circumstance. Be patient.

Students need lots of opportunities for guided practice and heaps of patience by the teacher—the ability to apply many of the nuances come with experience and maturity. Learning to apply behaviors, attitudes, and/or skills, such as the Lifelong Guidelines and LIFESKILLS, is a lifetime endeavor, a work in progress. Have patience, knowing that social and self-awareness don't spring full blown but unfold over time. Continue the dialogue of target talk on a daily basis so that it becomes part of the fabric of classroom life.

How to Use Target Talk. Target talk is simple to use if you leave behind any habits of lavishing praise for behavior or overusing/misusing "I statements." For example, saying "I like the way [John] is using his time while he waits for . . . ." is a bondage statement that may control behavior for the moment but keeps the focus on pleasing the teacher rather than on students developing their own sense of what's right or wrong, appropriate or inappro-

* Because target talk and modeling are the two most powerful ways to teach the Lifelong Guidelines and LIFESKILLS, both strategies must be fully mastered, i.e., become second nature, automatic.

** Pat Belvel, TCI Consulting of San Jose, CA, specializes in trainings on classroom management and peer coaching.

priate. Target talk helps students develop responsibility for their behavior.

Target Talk in Three Steps. The three steps of target talk are short and to the point. For example:

- First, use the student's name. "Mike, . . ."
- Second, label the Lifelong Guideline/LIFESKILL that the student is using. "Mike, you were using the Lifelong Guideline of Active Listening. . ."
- Third, identify the action. "Mike, you were using the Lifelong Guideline of Active Listening when you faced the speaker, looked interested, and were able to tell in your own words what the speaker meant."

With these three steps, verbal feedback is quick and easy. The same steps should be used for short written acknowledgements—from the teacher and from other students. Written acknowledgements are important because they provide a long-lasting communication, a treasured note that can be referred to again and again. An easy device for capturing such written comments is the Acknowledgement Box (see below).

Avoid Value Judgment. Target talk is best without value judgment. As the Sergeant in the TV series *Dragnet* would say, "Just the facts, ma'am." The facts are ***who***, ***what*** Lifelong Guideline or LIFESKILL was demonstrated, and ***how*** it was used. Such clear statements provide immediate feedback about use of the desired behaviors. Students see the Lifelong Guidelines and LIFESKILLS in action and make their own judgments about how useful they are. This independent analysis is critical to building character traits, values, and attitudes—and their related behaviors—that will last a lifetime.

Acknowledgements Box. Comments for the Acknowledgments Box can be written by both teacher* and students, signed or anonymous. They should be brief, nonjudgmental, and follow the three-step format described above: "I want to acknowledge Jack for using the Lifelong Guideline of No Put-Downs when he gave me useful feedback about grammar and spelling on my thank-you letter to the Governor." Whenever you have a spare moment during the day, such as when getting ready to move on to a new activity, simply pull three or four acknowledgements from the box and read them aloud to the class. Students are always eager to hear positive things others have to say about them.

Remember, the purpose of giving and receiving acknowledgments** is to encourage your students to reflect on their behavior and build their own internal dialogue about it. They will soon begin to feel the acknowledgement inside because they themselves said so, not the teacher, not another student; the student's own perspective then becomes the motivator and guide of behavior. This decreases the power of peer pressure now and later.

Using Target Talk to Correct Misbehavior. Target talk is a potent teaching tool to deal with misbehavior and it is easy to use. First ask "What happened here?" Then, "What Lifelong Guidelines and/or LIFESKILLS didn't you use?" Lastly, "What Lifelong Guidelines and/or LIFESKILLS could you have used to have prevented this situation?" Remember to remain neutral in tone. This is the teaching phase of correcting misbehavior. And always make sure students understand how their misbehavior affected that person and how it made that person feel. Strengthening students' awareness of how their behavior affects others is a critical step in helping them internalize the Lifelong Guidelines and LIFESKILLS.

The consequences phase—sometimes referred to as the punishment—should always be in proportion to the gravity of the act. For example, if serious physical or emotional harm occurred, the consequences should be grave. Likewise, don't overreact if the

* Teachers should take care to ensure that no student is left out. Anonymous acknowledgements written by the teacher can ensure that all students receive an acknowledgement each week.

** Acknowledgements differ from compliments in subtle but powerful ways. Compliments arise from the speaker having applied his/her criteria for what's good or commendable. Acknowledgements are a way of applying generally accepted criteria for behavior, such as the Lifelong Guidelines and LIFESKILLS. The goal is to redirect students from relying on external standards to relying on internal ones.

misbehavior was irritating but didn't cause injury or damage. Also, if the misbehavior occurs due to unclear expectations, such as lack of procedures that spell out the expected personal and social behaviors (see page 21.11-21.12), point the finger back to yourself. Such misbehavior is hardly the student's fault and it's a teaching opportunity.

Any consequences should also be related to the situation in which the misbehavior took place. For example, if serious misbehavior took place on the playground, the student should not be allowed to be on the playground with others for a specified period and/or under specified conditions. If the misbehavior was bad language or teasing another student in class, perhaps suspension of a classroom privilege would suffice. If the misbehavior was hitting and hurting someone, a class meeting is in order and serious consequences applied.

Before jumping to consequences, always discuss with the student the impact of his/her behavior on the other person(s). Make sure the student understands and has some emotional feel for what that person suffered. And, always ask the misbehaving student how he/she could "clean it up" or make amends with the wounded party and what consequences would help him/her to remember not to do such things again. Often students are harder on themselves than adults would be.

If the student's recommended solution is sufficient, apply it. If the impact of the misbehavior is serious, such as hitting someone or damaging their property, additional consequences are appropriate.

If such conversations between you and a student fail to curb the behavior, add an audience—the injured student plus whoever else was present; if necessary, add all of the members of his/her Learning Club or even the entire class. However, do so only after you have created a sense of community in the classroom—a community in which that student is fully a member. In our experience, the only students who continue to misbehave are those who feel no connection to others and therefore feel they have nothing to lose by misbehaving. Students want to belong, they want to matter, they want to be loved and respected. When they are included, when they belong, they value what their peers think.

Systematically Introduce Meaning and Importance of Each Lifelong Guideline

Teachers should never make assumptions about what understandings students bring to school. This is particularly true in the realm of the Lifelong Guidelines and LIFESKILLS. From America's diversity come multiple points of view and beliefs about what is appropriate behavior, about what makes for a sense of community. It is the job of the teacher to create a common set of understandings, the basis for a common culture in the classroom, a shared sense of community, which in turn becomes the foundation for high academic achievement.

Chapters 9 and 10 discuss the Lifelong Guidelines and LIFESKILLS and ways to begin systematically introducing the meaning and importance of each.

Teaching the Lifelong Guidelines. Although we adults might think of curriculum as the stuff of state standards and textbooks, for students, curriculum is what we ask them to do and how we ask them to do it. Where we might think curriculum hasn't begun until the textbooks have been passed out, students see curriculum in the way the bus driver treats them, how (or if) and principal greets them at the door of the school, and what the teacher says from the moment students see him/her.

Put your best foot forward. Make sure that the first things communicated to students are the most important things. They want to know that their teacher is someone they can like and respect, that their classmates will be their friends—the kind you keep for life—and that what they'll study is important and useful in the real world.

Our advice is to keep the textbooks and other traditional materials on the shelf during the first week of school. Focus full time on the curriculum content described for Stage 1 of the *ITI Classroom Stages of Implementation.* Also see the schedule for the first day of school beginning on page 18 of this chapter

Basis for "Discipline"

Perhaps one of the most disconcerting implications of brain research is that conventional "discipline" programs—those that depend upon externally imposed rewards and punishments—are brain antagonistic. They are inconsistent with both brain research, as discussed in Part A of this book, and sociological research, as illustrated in Alfie Kohn's book, *Punished by Rewards: The Trouble with Gold Stars, Incentive Plans, A's, Praise, and Other Bribes.*

Such discipline programs are also inconsistent with the central goal of a democratic society—the development of a citizenry willing to commit to nurturing a society that works for all.

[Note: If your school requires schoolwide adherence to a particular disciplinary program and process that is brain antagonistic, make sure that you talk with your principal about how you intend to use the Lifelong Guidelines and LIFESKILLS in a brain-compatible way. Get his/her agreement about how you will proceed.]

The Power of Emotions to Enhance/ Impede Learning and Performance

Although the Prussian roots of our educational system have taught us that discipline and cerebral function define both the goals and the processes of public education, brain research tells us a different story (review Chapter 2). As we now know, emotion drives attention which drives learning, memory, and almost everything else. If we want students to learn and remember, we must learn how to create a learning environment which uses the power of emotion in positive and effective ways.

Teaching Students About Absence of Threat and Nurturing Reflective Thinking

Because the purpose of your being together is learning, tell your students that you want them to understand how their brain works. Make models,[6] introduce the role of emotion in learning and performing. Start the first day of school and teach an aspect of how our brains work each day for the first month; after that, use every teachable moment to reinforce what they've learned and to help them learn to apply it in practical ways.

How much you choose to teach students about how their brain learns depends on their age. It is our experience that students K-6 can grasp the concepts; it is the vocabulary that may need adjusting. And yet, don't underestimate them! Just as kindergartners love the sound of big words, such as the names of dinosaurs, they can pick up on many of the brain terms, cerebral cortex, molecules of emotion, limbic system, frontal lobes, and so forth.

The Role of Emotions in Learning and Performing. The content about the pivotal role of emotions in learning and performing is presented in Chapter 2; for examples of key points and inquiries for first and fourth grades, see Chapters 15 and 16.

In truth, we *cannot control* our emotions, nor the feelings they produce. Feelings are our bodybrain's way of letting us know what's going on inside.[7] But we ***can* control our *responses* to our feelings.** This is a critical distinction for students to understand and a critical choice to make every time an emotion comes up. Because we feel something doesn't mean we have to act on it. For example, everyone gets angry, even furious, from time to time but we can choose to **not act** on that anger. Likewise, everyone feels jealous from time to time but we don't have to attack or undermine the person we envy. Model having control over your responses and include it as a topic during class meetings and other appropriate forums.

Also discuss with students how their emotions filter their perceptions of what's going on around them. For example, the person with a negative outlook on life tends to see all the things that are wrong or not good enough while the person with a positive view sees what's good.

The Lifelong Guidelines and LIFESKILLS. Teaching ***and using on a daily basis*** the Lifelong Guidelines and LIFESKILLS is the heart of Stage 1 of implementation and is the ongoing foundation for all later stages of implementation. They provide a set of standards for behavior by students, staff, and parents. They set the expectations and tone for all interactions that occur every school day—adult-adult, student-adult, and student-student. Chapters 9 and 10 explain the Lifelong Guidelines and LIFESKILLS and how to teach them. We also highly recommend *Tools for Citizenship and Life: Using the ITI Lifelong Guidelines and LIFESKILLS in Your Classroom* by Sue Pearson. With a separate chapter for each of the Guidelines and LIFESKILLS, it describes why and how to practice the guideline/skill, what it looks like in the real world, what it looks like in school, 500 inquiries (whole group and small group/individual), signs of success, suggested literature (by grade spans: primary, intermediate, and middle/high school), and sample family letters.

The Lifelong Guidelines and LIFESKILLS form the fabric of your classroom. They are always front and center, always a topic of the teachable moment when student behavior is particularly conducive to learning and citizenship as well as when it goes awry.

For the first day of school, introduce students to target talk and the Acknowledgements Box.[8]

Daily Agendas

Once students have settled in and met the members of their Learning Club, introduce the daily agenda. Like written procedures, the daily agenda is a key element in your classroom leadership. Posted for all to see through the day, it continues to put forth your intentions for the day—what students will do and the key pieces that you will do. It is also an important means of teaching time management skills to students. As each task is completed, check it off your classroom agenda and have each student learn to check it off the agenda they copy down each morning upon entering the classroom.

Keep in mind that the agenda is not a time schedule. The only times written on it are for special events for which students can't be late, such as the bus for a study trip, class photo appointment, and so forth. The agenda is a mindmap of the important tasks of the day from the students' point of view. It is not the same outline as for lesson planning.

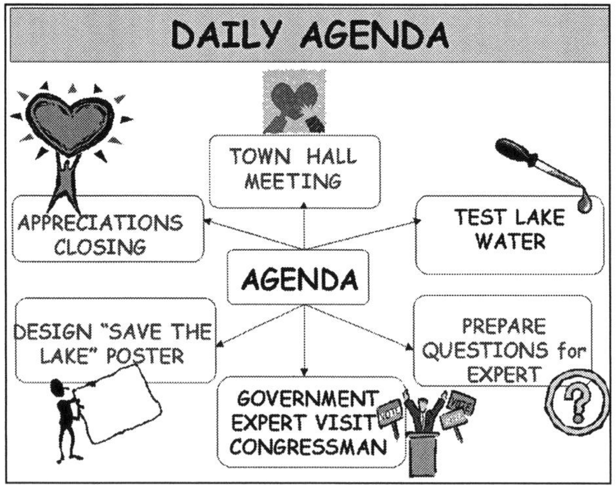

Completion of a daily agenda is occasion for a mini-celebration and the LIFESKILL of Pride.

Be sure to include on your first agenda the date for your classroom's Back to School Night. [Note: We strongly recommend that you hold your Back to School Night for your classroom during the first or second week of school—even if the rest of the school holds one later.]

Written Procedures

Written procedures are a multi-purpose instructional strategy. They are a systematic and unambiguous way to describe for students the personal and social skills they need to be successful as a learner and team player in your classroom and beyond. They are also a primary tool for extending your classroom leadership during times when students are working independently or in groups.

Procedures are not "rules." They are descriptions of the personal and social behaviors students need to perform well during a learning project, such during group work or independent study, or during a social interaction such as entering the classroom, transitioning to lunch or school assembly, or going to the office. Also, procedures are **not** the directions for completing an assignment, such as "Spend 10 minutes on this problem. First draw a graphic illustrating the problem, then show your work to arrive at the answer." Procedures are the personal and social behaviors needed to perform a task successfully. See examples on this and the next page and on pages 7.19-21.

Think your procedures through carefully; involve students in developing them. Most importantly, be 100 percent consistent in having students adhere to them. These are guides for success—now and in the future—the stuff useful habits of mind are made of.

Use written procedures for all frequently occurring events/activities to provide consistency, continuity, and emotional security for students. Include graphics as well as words; visuals help students learn and remember the steps, especially younger students.

Before the first day of school, have the written procedures described here ready to go. Others can be developed later with the participation of students. For the first day, have written procedures for the following:

- Morning entering the classroom
- Leaving at the end of the day

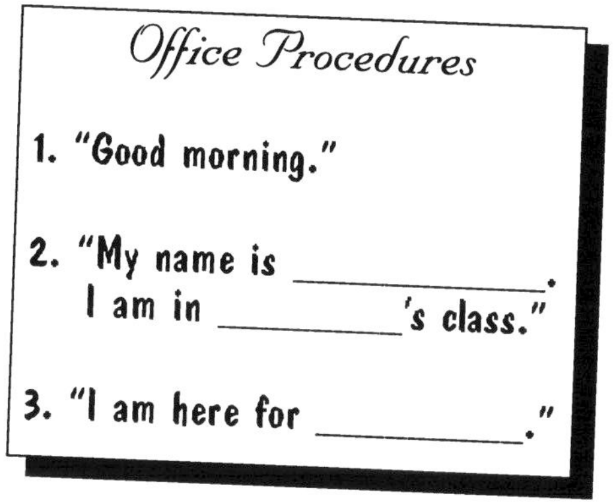
Office Procedures
1. "Good morning."
2. "My name is ________.
I am in ________'s class."
3. "I am here for ________."

Good Morning!
1. Greet Mrs. Kay with a handshake
2. Hang up your coat, hat & pack
3. Put homework & notes in basket
4. Check tools
5. Greet learning club members
6. Work on Journal

Group Work PROCEDURE
1. Cooperate
2. Soft voice
3. Take turns talking
4. See 3 before me
5. Share ideas
6. Do your personal best
7. Clean up

Quiet Place
1. One person
2. Sh-h-h-h
3. Turn timer

- Leaving and re-entering during the day for regular events, such as recess and special subjects, and for special events, such as schoolwide assemblies
- Lunch room procedures
- Learning Club
- Town Hall Meeting
- Quiet time

The Role of Movement in Enhancing Academic Learning

Few among us consider ourselves movement specialists. We haven't mastered movement and exercise for ourselves much less our students. There are clear reasons in our minds why we chose not to become a P.E. specialist. Are we striking a familiar chord here? If so, rest assured that what we are talking about with movement here is a far cry from such discussions.

The motivation behind movement as a critical bodybrain-compatible element in the ITI model is not movement for the sake of movement or exercise because it's good for you but rather because movement is critical to the functioning of the brain and therefore to learning. And it's not just any movement, it is the kind of movement associated with using what is learned and also movement to reset students' emotional states to a level appropriate to the next activity. This can include the typical letting off steam as well as focusing the brain for learning, reenergizing for a shift to a new topic of learning, or simply relaxing and taking a break.

Movement and Emotion. Because emotion drives attention and all other aspects of learning, the emotional states of students are critical to your success as a teacher (and to your students' successes as learners). Thus, you must learn to teach students how to handle their emotional life so they can maximize their learning.

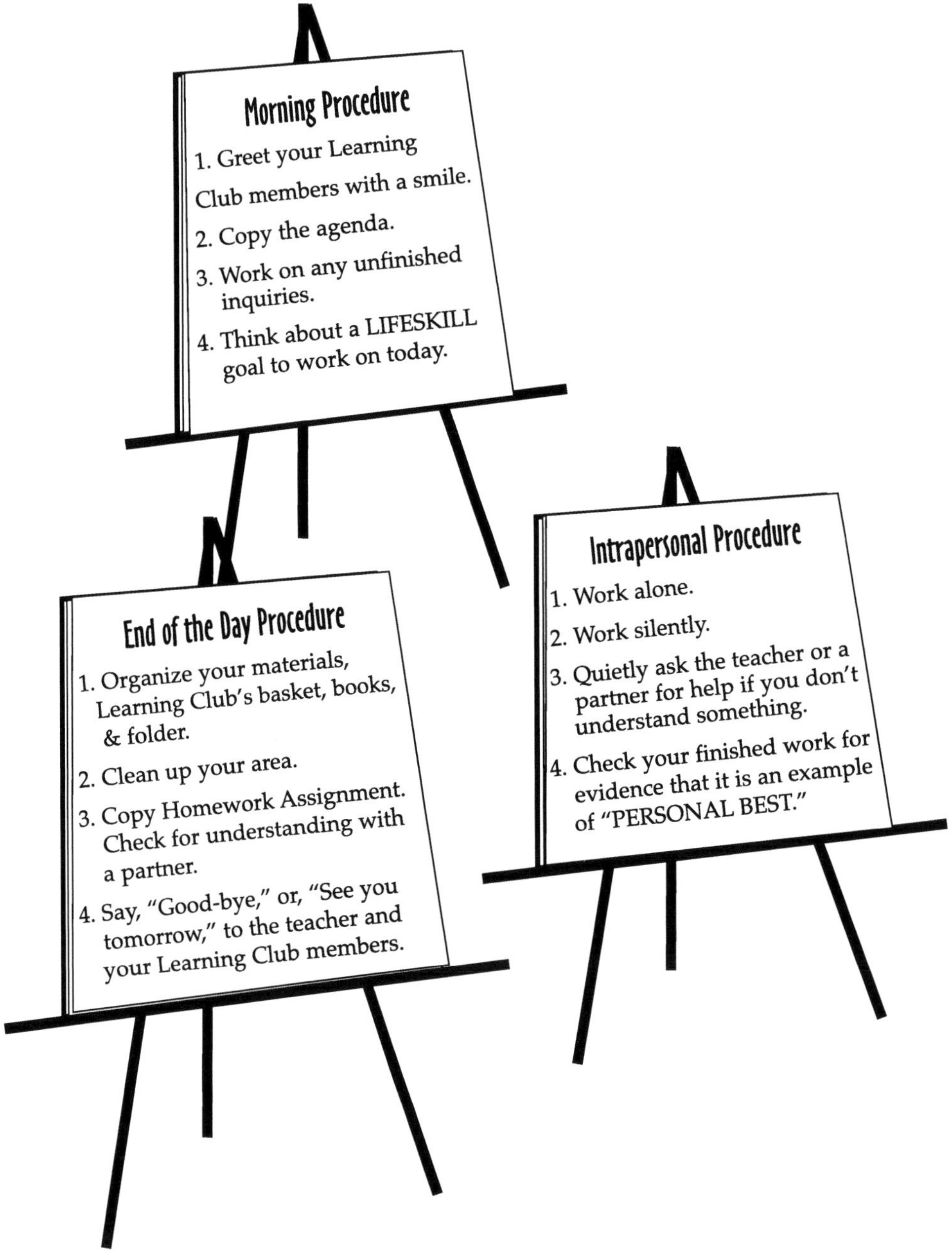
Morning Procedure
1. Greet your Learning Club members with a smile.
2. Copy the agenda.
3. Work on any unfinished inquiries.
4. Think about a LIFESKILL goal to work on today.
End of the Day Procedure
1. Organize your materials, Learning Club's basket, books, & folder.
2. Clean up your area.
3. Copy Homework Assignment. Check for understanding with a partner.
4. Say, "Good-bye," or, "See you tomorrow," to the teacher and your Learning Club members.
Intrapersonal Procedure
1. Work alone.
2. Work silently.
3. Quietly ask the teacher or a partner for help if you don't understand something.
4. Check your finished work for evidence that it is an example of "PERSONAL BEST."

We all know there are times that we feel so keyed up we can't concentrate or so listless that we can't get going. It's the same for our students. There are times when we need to help them slow themselves down and times when we need to help them speed themselves up. Movement can do both.

When and how? Well, some of those times are predictable; others are serendipitous.

Planning for Movement. Because movement is so key to optimum functioning of the bodybrain learning partnership, it should be planned for as carefully as for the 3 Rs. Plan carefully for the predictable moments and be prepared for the unpredictable moments.

Predictable Moments. The predictable moments when movement is helpful include coming back to the classroom after recesses, lunch, and schoolwide events; changing activities, especially from a high-energy task to a low-energy one or vice versa; or in the middle of a long task such as test-taking or working on a challenging inquiry. Movement facilitates smooth transitions and a flow from one activity to the next.

For such predictable moments, develop movement activities that grow out of subject content.

Unpredictable Moments. Although when unpredictable moments may occur may be a surprise, that they will occur is virtually guaranteed. So, develop a handful of movement routines that you can do at a moment's notice. For example, if you see glazed eyes that signal little learning is taking place, shift gears and energize with simple stretches, deep breathing, or Brain Gym movements. Such activities may have nothing to do with the content of the theme but they will get the job done.

Resources. Good resources for these activities include:

- *Emotion: Gatekeeper to Performance* with Dr. Candace Pert, Susan Kovalik, and Carla Hannaford (30-minute video)
- *Let's Get Moving: Movement in the Classroom* by Diane Berry (95-minute video and booklet)
- *Hands on: How to Use Brain Gym in the Classroom* by Isabel Cohen and Marcell Goldsmith

Things to Avoid. Resist the urge to stifle movement, even irritating and distracting movement. Instead, redirect it. Highly bodily-kinesthetic students simply can't keep still and even if they could it would shut down their most powerful intelligence for learning. Redirect, redirect, redirect. For example, for those who can't keep their hands still or to themselves, give them a spongy, squishy ball to manipulate; the ground rule is that they can handle it any time they want or feel they need to, as long as they don't bother others.

For students who constantly pop up and walk around, seat them in the back of the room and allow them to move around whenever they feel they need to, as long as they don't bother others.

What you're dealing with in these instances is not short-term behavior problems but students who need to develop lifelong strategies for handling themselves in appropriate ways—ways that enhance their ability to learn and to be considerate of other's needs.

Personal and Social Skills for Collaboration

The personal and social skills for collaboration are the skills that make our lives work. They are the basis for making and keeping friends, getting along with co-workers, and, most importantly, maintaining a loving and healthy family. They are also the interpersonal skills that widen and deepen our resources for learning throughout our lives. Knowing this, don't lose patience and give up on what might at first seem like a waste of time.

Furthermore, the power of collaborative learning—academically as well as socially and personally—is perhaps the most well documented and compelling area of educational practice. The difference in the quality and depth of learning that occurs once a sense of community or class family has been achieved is phenomenal—believable only when you've experienced it. Be patient. Keep at it.

Model the Personal and Social Skills Needed to Work Collaboratively

Because our popular media so enshrines competition and the necessity of being #1, many students not only have few personal and social skills to collaborate, they don't value collaboration. It's for dweebs, not successful folk.

Nor is the field of education noteworthy for a collaborative tradition. "Go to your room, shut the door, and do whatever you want to do" is the time-worn approach to teaching.

Against such a backdrop, consistent modeling is essential. Students must be able to see, hear, and feel collaboration and its power to enhance not only academic learning and performance but joy and satisfaction in one's personal life.

Modeling in the Classroom. To model collaboration, teachers must shift their role from sage on the stage to guide on the side, from autocratic disciplinarian to a leader who invites students into helping design the learning environment. Teachers must also model their citizenship skills in the way they work with colleagues to improve the school's program and environment.

Resources. The most important personal and social skills for collaboration are included in the Lifelong Guidelines and LIFESKILLS. Useful resources for modeling collaborative skills are:

- Chapters 9 and 10
- Curriculum and instructional strategies for collaboration discussed in detail in Chapters 1-5 as one of the nine bodybrain-compatible elements of the ITI model
- *Tools for Citizenship and Life: Using the Lifelong Guidelines & LIFESKILLS in the Classroom* by Sue Pearson

Teach the Personal and Social Skills Needed to Work Collaboratively

Given the diversity in student backgrounds, no teacher can assume that students come with the personal and social skills needed to work collaboratively. Plan to start from scratch and teach every element through each of the stages of group development. Furthermore, don't assume that the adults at your school—teachers, classified staff, and parents—possess a common view of what these skills are and how to practice them. We strongly recommend that you:

- Begin with teaching the Lifelong Guidelines/LIFESKILLS and build a comprehensive and uniform understanding, among adults and students, of what each of those behaviors looks, sounds, and feels like (and does not look, sound, or feel like).
- Understand that written procedures are part of a larger picture, not just a short cut to better behavior in the short run.

Resources. Resources for teaching students the personal and social skills needed for powerful collaboration include:

- *Designing Groupwork: Strategies for the Heterogeneous Classroom* by Elizabeth Cohen
- *Cooperative Learning, All Grades* by Spencer Kagan and Kagan's *Smart Cards: Cooperative Learning* which summarizes 56 cooperative structures.

Organize Students into Learning Clubs

Every group of students brings to collaborating their own unique blend of personal and social skills, or lack of, and their own preferences for collaborative structures. Thus, while Learning Clubs of four students may be ideal, you may need to begin with pairs and work your way methodically and carefully to your desired number. As you proceed, remember that the goal of collaboration is singular: To create a sense of community that enhances each student's academic achievement. In the process, you will also enhance social and personal growth.

Resources. Resources include those cited above for collaboration plus how to structure a Town Hall Meeting (see pages 9. 7-9).

Living Citizenship

Citizenship is not learned by true-false or multiple choice questions. It must be learned by doing. Ongoing Town Hall Meetings are a critical part of that experience in the ITI classroom. See Chapter 9, Getting Started with the Lifelong Guidelines and LIFESKILLS.

Lead Students in Activities Appropriate for Each Stage of Group Development

Group development and a sense of community don't happen by accident, nor are they simply a product of time. They must be worked on daily. Luckily, there is a blueprint. Most experts in group development recognize at least three stages, each with its predictable behaviors and process needs. See pages 9.2-6 for an ITI model version of these three stages.

As you proceed, keep in mind the three levels of community-building. Make sure the strategies you select don't require a greater sense of community than the stage your students are actually in at the moment.

The most common error is selecting an activity that requires coming to a decision or vote—handling the pressures of persuasion, the influence of higher social status, and the desire to control—before students have developed the trust and leadership-followership skills to handle such processes. The second biggest error is not letting student truly engage in meaningful group projects once they have developed the skills to do so.

Analyze your favorite collaborative strategies according to the stage of community building you are working on.

Creating a Sense of Belonging—Activities that help build a sense of inclusion ask participants to do a task together, such as mill to music, share a favorite hobby, what they like most in a friend, or create a visual using a T-shirt outline that shares something about where they were born, their family members, etc.—all for the purpose of getting to know others and letting others get to know you.

Daily use of the Lifelong Guidelines and LIFESKILLS is essential for creating an environment that welcomes everyone to become a part of the group and ensures that each person feels they belong.

Acceptance of who we are and of differences is an essential condition during these activities. Inclusion activities must be safe interactions with no potential criticism of performance or test of status in the group.

Inclusion activities should **not** ask individuals to share something they might consider personal or private, such as the origin of their name, where their ancestors came from, what jobs their parents hold, whether they live in a house or an apartment, and so forth.

These activities also do **not** ask that a product be created that can be judged or evaluated, such as a group project made by a study group. Nor do these activities ask members to vote on or agree to something, a process that requires some boundary bumping and use of persuasion and personal influence that comes from social status in the group—all part of the next stage in developing community, creating common ground.

Brainstorming activities protected by the DOVE rule which prohibits judging the ideas offered are good ways to meld curriculum content with this stage of group building.

List your favorite activities for creating a sense of belonging for ready reference.

Creating Common Ground—Creating a sense of common ground is essential for effective work as a citizen. Activities that create common ground must elicit an appreciation for members' strengths and capabilities and engender mutual respect so that the exercise of creating common ground is not a competition but a give-and-take interaction, through which students learn to handle and temper the pressures of persuasion (facile verbal skills), the influence that comes from higher social status, and desire to control. In this stage, students learn how to transition from leader to follower, follower to leader smoothly as appropriate to the task at hand and in response to the ever-changing roles among the group (assigned or self-assigned) rather than to ego or power. At its core, this stage of group development means that you listen respectfully when I speak and I listen respectfully when you talk, with the intent of understanding each other. We see value in each other and are willing to work cooperatively with each other.

Activities to develop this stage require high levels of trust among team members; clearly, a strong sense of inclusion must be built before embarking on the task of creating common ground.

This is the stage when students learn to trust in the power of the group and let go of the need to control while at the same time learning how to be a leader in a democratic setting—using persuasion, influence, and power in a positive way for the benefit of the group rather than to be self-serving. And, conversely, become willing to allow others to lead.

Activities for this stage include building a group project, making decisions about what group project to undertake and how to proceed, solving problems facing the class or a Learning Club, and so forth. In the early stages, tasks should be teacher-generated and involve emotionally-neutral tasks, gradually evolving into .

This stage can take quite a while, depending upon the personal and social skills of students.

List your favorite activities for creating common ground for ready reference.

Taking Action—Taking action to improve the well-being of the community as a whole and the individuals within it requires **and further develops** group cohesion and a deep sense of respect, trust, and affection in the group. With the goal of growing responsible citizens, the activities chosen for this stage should be genuine tasks worthy of citizen activity. Celebrations of Learning and Social/Political Action Projects are idea. Start with small but meaningful projects, which will likely be largely teacher directed, and then let students' commitment to building a better world for themselves and others take over the planning and execution of activities.

List your favorite activities for preparing students to take action for ready reference.

How to Nurture and Utilize Reflective Thinking

Reflective thinking is the basis for many skills, personal and academic. Personally, it enables us to check our anger, think before we burst out with a comment we'll later regret, put ourselves in other people's shoes, etc. Academically it allows us to guide ourselves through alternative approaches to solving a problem, explore how we might need a skill or concept in the future, imagine how things might fit together, plan alternative courses of action, etc.

Calm Voice

A voice of calm is the voice of someone who picks his/her words carefully. Repetition of directions and expectations soon begins to reflect impatience. Daily agendas and written procedures do much to allow teachers to speak calmly because there is no need to repeat directions or scold when students don't comply with the teacher's expectations. Save your voice and your students' willingness to listen for the important things.

Processes and Structures

There are many ways to help students develop reflective thinking as a habit of mind. For example, wait time, journal writing, reflecting on the daily agenda (beginning and end of the day), making choices that allow students to direct their learning, forecasting how to take on a learning task, reflecting on what one learned academically, the process of collaborative work (before, during, and after and asking about content, social, and personal outcomes), providing adequate time for students to complete assignments, and strategies to help students refocus.

Nurturing reflective thinking should be a daily, even hourly, endeavor.

Schedule and Lesson Plan for the First Day of School

As any parent, or author, knows, it's risky to offer advice; it unerringly finds its way to that person's stubborn streak, however small and well hidden that streak might be. So, with apologies in advance, we offer some great ideas from a gifted teacher and associate of Susan Kovalik & Associates, Sue Pearson. Pick and choose as you like but our best advice is to make a trusting leap and try Sue's recommendations. Do everything. By Christmas, you'll find yourself weeks ahead of where you usually are.

The first daily schedule and lesson plan is for primary grades, the second for intermediate grades.

Primary Grades—Schedule for the First Day of School

8:30	ARRIVAL
8:45	STANDARD TASKS
9:00	INTRODUCTIONS/INCLUSION
9:15	DAILY AGENDA
9:30	MOVEMENT/SNACK/BATHROOM
9:45	KEY POINTS & INQUIRIES ABOUT COMMUNITY
11:00	MOVEMENT/MUSIC
11:15	DIRECT INSTRUCTION/INQUIRIES
11:50	LUNCH ROOM PROCEDURES
12:00	LUNCH
12:30	STORY/REST TIME
1:15	DIRECT INSTRUCTION/INQUIRIES
1:45	MOVEMENT
2:00	NURTURING REFLECTIVE THINKING
2:15	REVIEW COMMUNITY, BRAIN MODEL, BRAIN SONG
2:30	LEARNING CLUB CLOSURE
2:45	LEAVING PROCEDURES/DISMISSAL

Primary Grades—Lesson Plan for the First Day of School

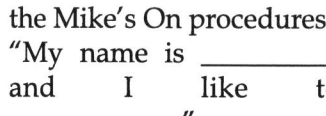

➢Note to Teacher: Your goal is quality of experience, not quantity of information; be sure to provide adequate time for each inclusion activity and key point. These key points need extensive development using literature, discussion, reflection, journaling, and real-life experiences.

Morning Procedures
1. Greet Miss Lee with a hug or handshake.
2. Say hello to your Learning Club.
3. Work in your journal.
Notes
4. Expect a great day!

8:30 ARRIVAL: Await students at the classroom door; welcome them with a handshake, "high five," or a hug. Give each student a "puzzle piece" (see Puzzle Inclusion Activity at the end of this lesson plan). Make sure each student reads and follows the "Morning Procedures."

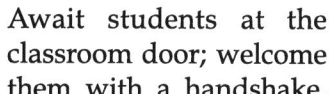

8:45 STANDARD SCHOOL TASKS: Allow time for opening ceremonies (pledge of allegiance, songs, and so forth) and for standard school procedures such as taking attendance and lunch count, collecting notes, and performing any other tasks required by your school district.

9:00 INTRODUCTIONS: Introduce yourself. Share some hobbies, interests, and family information. Introduce "Mike's On" procedures. Then, within each Learning Club, have each student introduce him/herself to members of the Learning Club using the Mike's On procedures : "My name is ________ and I like to ________."

➢ This symbol indicates a note to the teacher.

1. One person holds the "mike" & shares.
2. Share name & interests in about 2 minutes.

4. Pass the microphone to another.

➢Note to Teacher: Walk around the room offering support for the shyer students and to ensure that no one student in a group monopolizes the time. Allow students a few minutes to exchange information.

9:15 DAILY AGENDA: Tell the students that an agenda—the plan for the day—will be posted every morning on the board (overhead, flannel board, white board) and that it is their responsibility to copy it in their spiral notebook.

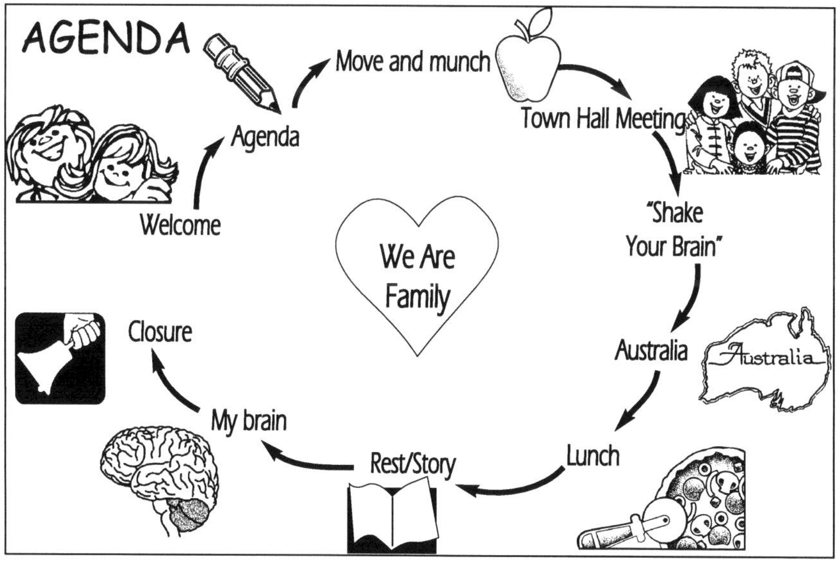

Move and munch

Rest/Story

We Are Family

Explain each part of the agenda, why it will be used every day, and how it will benefit both students and teacher. Invite students to predict the written words by observing the accompanying graphics. Allow them sufficient time to copy the agenda, words, and graphics. As the day unfolds, check off each item on the agenda as it is completed. Have the students do the same on their own agendas. Explain that the agenda is a time management and organizational tool and that it will be used every day. Any items not completed will be assigned as homework or done the next day.

9:30 MOVEMENT/SNACK/QUIET TIME/RESTROOM

➤You may wish to introduce the following movement activities from *Brain Gym* by Paul E. and Gail E. Dennison: Lazy 8s, Thinking Cap, and Hook-ups. Also see *Hands on: How to Use Brain Gym in the Classroom* by Isabel Cohen and Marcell Goldstein.

Quiet Time Procedure
1. Find your personal space. Stay there during quiet time.
2. Listen to music. No talking.
3. Read a book, write, or draw.

For snack, use the "3 before sugar rule" to judge the snacks. Permit students to bring only those items whose top three ingredients are not sugar or another form of sweetener.

2. One at a time.
3. Wash hands.

4. Come right back.

Play quiet, instrumental music, approximately 50-60 beats per minute. Ask students to use only their 12-inch voice while talking with each other.

9:45 KEY POINTS & INQUIRIES ABOUT COMMUNITY

Conceptual Key Point—

A spirit of community doesn't just happen in a neighborhood or classroom because people live or work in the same area. Each member—young and old—must take responsibility for creating and enhancing a sense of community throughout each day, month, and year. Creating a sense of community is a three-step process:

- Developing a sense of inclusion or belonging
- Creating common ground, and
- Taking action

Our beginning point for step 1, developing a sense of inclusion, is using the Lifelong Guidelines and LIFESKILLS:

- TRUSTWORTHINESS
- TRUTHFULNESS
- ACTIVE LISTENING
- NO PUT-DOWNS
- PERSONAL BEST/LIFESKILLS

Inquiry for Direct Instruction—

Think about your best friend; recall three things that you like best about him/her. Share those qualities with the class. Discuss with your Learning Club what your best friend has taught you about the Lifelong Guidelines. Share with your Learning Club which Lifelong Guideline you most appreciate your best friend using when you're together.

Record student responses on the board and group their responses as best you can. Then have students compare the list they generated to the Lifelong Guidelines.

Inquiry for Whole Class Discussion—

Identify the three most common qualities your Learning Club values in best friends. Have the recorder for your Learning Club read these to the rest of the class.

Skill Key Point—

Present the procedures for the community circle. They should replicate some of these examples:

> **TOWN HALL MEETING**
> **Procedures**
> 1. Come to the meeting area when your Learning Club is called.
> 2. Find a place on the rug (oval, line, etc.) to sit. Sit where you can see everyone and everyone can see you.
> 3. Sit comfortably in your own personal space.
> 4. Remember to use the Lifelong Guidelines throughout Town Hall Meeting time.
> 5. When you hear the chimes, it's time to use Active Listening.

A simplified version of these procedures for primary grades can be sung to the tune of "Supercalifragilisticexpialidocious." Those words are: "Push in chair, walk quietly, and sit in listening shape. Come and make a circle at our favorite gathering place." Then repeat.

Introduce the chimes as a reminder to "actively listen." Ask the students to name the tool and parts (chimes, mallet) and to observe how the hammer is used to gently strike the metal rods. Ask them to identify the number of tones the chimes can make (one per metal rod/cylinder). Instruct them to show active listening (you/me, ears, eyes, heart, and undivided attention) when they hear the chimes. From here on, use the chimes as one of the strategies to call for active listening from the students.

[For more information about how to conduct a Town Hall Meeting, see Appendix E.]

Conceptual Key Point—

In a community, people come together to create a safe place to live and work. In order for our class community to be safe for everyone, there are certain guidelines that community members must be willing to follow. When problems occur, people talk together to solve them in peaceful and fair ways.

Topics for Whole Class Discussion—

- What guidelines would make our community a safe place to learn? Hint: Think about what we learned about our best friends.
- Discuss student answers to the above question and the Lifelong Guidelines as acceptable behaviors for our classroom community. Get agreement which Lifelong Guidelines and LIFESKILLS the students want to begin with.
- Recite Lifelong Guideline Pledge:*

  "I am Trustworthy, Truthful, and an Active Listener, too.
  I will do my Personal Best and give No Put-Downs to you!"

Significant Knowledge Key Point—

Our brains will help us learn many new things this year. When our brains feel safe and are protected from danger, they learn and remember more information. We, as a community, can all help each other's brains by practicing certain safety rules and learning ways to solve our problems. In our classroom, we will all work hard to build a community based on using the Lifelong Guidelines and the LIFESKILLS. The Lifelong Guidelines are the behaviors we will use with each other so that we can be successful in school and life.

Tips for Direct Instruction About the Lifelong Guidelines-

- Lead a general discussion on each Lifelong Guideline. Record what students think each guideline means on a classroom wall where everyone can see and refer to them.

* This pledge is just an example. We recommend you involve your students in developing your own once students have a full understanding of the Lifelong Guidelines.

- Teach a sign for "Active Listening" that can be used immediately, such as American Sign Language or hand in the air with fingers spread apart to represent the five elements of active listening—you, eyes, ears, heart, and undivided attention.

- Provide examples of working together, such as "Community Jobs." Introduce these community jobs; use real-world terms when possible, e.g., horticulturist (plant care-taker), messenger (delivers materials to the office), personal trainer (in charge of recess equipment). Brainstorm the performance standards for each of these jobs. Choose volunteers to demonstrate/pantomime the task being done incorrectly and then correctly. Invite the students to describe one more job that they feel is needed in the classroom.

Inquiries for Choice — For Learning Clubs or Individuals

1. Illustrate at least five people other than your family (or for young students, within the family) upon whom you depend for food, safety, and services each week. Describe to your Learning Club what at least two of these people do for you and why that's important. Identify one person the group has in common and be ready to share your information with the class.

2. Identify at least five community services that you and your family depend on to stay healthy and safe. Record your finding on the T-chart under the following headings: HEALTH, SAFETY, CONVENIENCE, FUN.

3. Write a story or draw a picture that shares a time when you cooperated with another person and it helped both of you. Share your product and explain what happened as a result of your cooperation.

4. Brainstorm with your Learning Club two or more ways you will work to build a community using the Lifelong Guidelines of Trustworthiness, Truthfulness, Active Listening, No Put-Downs, and Personal Best. Prepare your ideas for class sharing time.

5. In your journal, write about a time or draw a picture of a time you used one of the Lifelong Guidelines. Explain your choice to a partner.

11:00 MOVEMENT/MUSIC

Teach one of the brain songs (e.g., "Shake Your Brain" by Red Grammer on the CD *Teaching Peace* or one of those listed at the end of this lesson plan). Allow the students to create movements that demonstrate the meaning of the lyrics. Practice the song twice. Afterwards, provide reflection time asking questions such as: How did this song make you feel? Which motions will be the easiest for you to remember? What changes do you notice in your feelings? Does anyone know another brain song that the class could sing later in the week?

11:15 DIRECT INSTRUCTION

Significant Knowledge Key Point—

Our brains will help us learn many new things this year. When we feel safe and are protected from danger, our brain learns and remembers more. As a community, we can all help each other feel safe by following certain agreements. Agreements to use the Lifelong Guidelines and the LIFESKILLS will help us get to know and respect one another so that we can be better learners.

➤Direct Instruction with these materials: A copy of *Franklin Goes to School* by Paulette Bourgeois or *Chrysanthemum* by Kevin Henkes plus a chart paper and colored markers (blue, green, red, black).

Anticipatory Set: Ask questions such as: Did anyone feel a little nervous about coming to school today? What made you feel nervous ? How did your body let you know it was nervous? What did you do to try to feel less worried? Were any of you excited?

What feelings did you have? Share a personal story of your own first day at school. Explain that you have a story where the main character shares some of their same feelings.

Direct Instruction: Read aloud the book you chose. Ask the students to do a "thumbs up" when they have the same feelings that Franklin (or the character in your book) does. Use a "thumbs down" when they have different feelings. Obviously, there will be some story parts when there will be "thumbs up" and "thumbs down" simultaneously depending on each student's individual experiences and personal feelings. Ask questions that focus on feelings. For example, how did you feel on your first day of kindergarten? How did your family help you prepare for school? Do you still feel nervous or excited when school is starting? Why do you suppose you feel that way?

Acknowledge that each of us can and does have different reactions to things and that our reactions change over time. By asking questions such as these, you also provide an opening for you to share your own childhood recollections of school as well as an opportunity to share your excitement as the teacher of this class! Participate in the discussion as well as supervise it. Let your students know who you are.

Inquiry –

Compare your feelings about the first day of school with Franklin from the story *Franklin Goes to School.* Tell your partner how your feelings and Franklin's are alike. Share how your feelings are different than Franklin's. Listen to your partner's feelings. Explain your feelings about school to your classmates when the teacher invites you to share.

Skill Key Point: Using a T-chart –

There are many kinds of T-charts. The common element is that they have two or more columns which allow us to compare or contrast information about a topic. Two T-charts we will use often are the KWL and LSF (see pages 22.8 and 22.9).

T-Chart of My Feelings Before School

LOOKS LIKE	*SOUNDS LIKE*	*FEELS LIKE*
smiling	"I can't wait to go!"	happy
crying	"I'm scared!"	nervous
laughing	"It will be fun."	good
unhappy face	"I don't want to go!"	scared

Review some of the answers offered by the students. Emphasize the variety of feelings that were shared. Suggest that the class revisit the chart in one week for another check on feelings and any changes that may occur.

11:50 LUNCH PROCEDURE

Go To Lunch Procedure

1. Clean work area.
2. Get your coat & lunch.

3. Line up at the door and stand quietly.
4. Proceed to cafeteria.

12:00 LUNCH/RECESS

Rest Time Procedure

1. Find your quiet space and stay there during rest time.
2. May listen to music. No talking.
3. If you don't feel sleepy, take a toy with you and play quietly.

12:30 REST TIME/ STORY TIME

Younger students may require a short rest time after lunch for the first few days until they are back into the routine of school. This is an excellent time to play some quiet, classical music with 40-60 beats per minute which helps to regulate the heartbeat after strenuous activity.

12:45 DIRECT INSTRUCTION

Significant Knowledge Key Point (continued)—

Our brains will help us learn many new things this year. When we feel safe, our brains learn and remember more. As a kind of community, we can all help each other feel safe by following certain agreements. By agreeing to use the Lifelong Guidelines and the LIFESKILLS, we will get to know and respect one another so that we can be better learners.

Story: *Alexander and the Terrible, Horrible, No-Good, Very Bad Day* by Judith Viorst

Predictable story: Invite students to repeat chorus whenever it appears: "It was a terrible, horrible, no-good, very bad day."

Judith Viorst's story centers on a young boy, Alexander, for whom everything is going wrong. His response? "I'm going to Australia!" Use Alexander's experiences as an introduction for your class's own personal "Australia," a small corner of the room where the students can visit to relax, refocus and reflect. Lead the students to this special area.

The following items are suggested for Australia

- Some type of chair (rocking, Adirondack, stuffed, bean bag, large pillows)
- Procedures for visiting Australia
- Small table covered with cloth
- Lamp
- Quiet timer such as an executive-style oil drip timer (up to about 10 minutes)
- Headset with classical music tapes in basket ~ optional
- Stress relief "squeeze ball"
- Small class photo or inspirational quotation in a frame. Invite students to visit "Australia," a "safe" place for the brain to reflect and the heart to heal. A comfortable place in the classroom with a rocking chair, Adirondack lawn chair, bean bag, pillows, or cushions. Teaching strategy: Tell each student to write his/her name on a small piece of paper. Pull names out, one at a time, for visits to Australia on this first day, thereby preventing a rush to Australia.

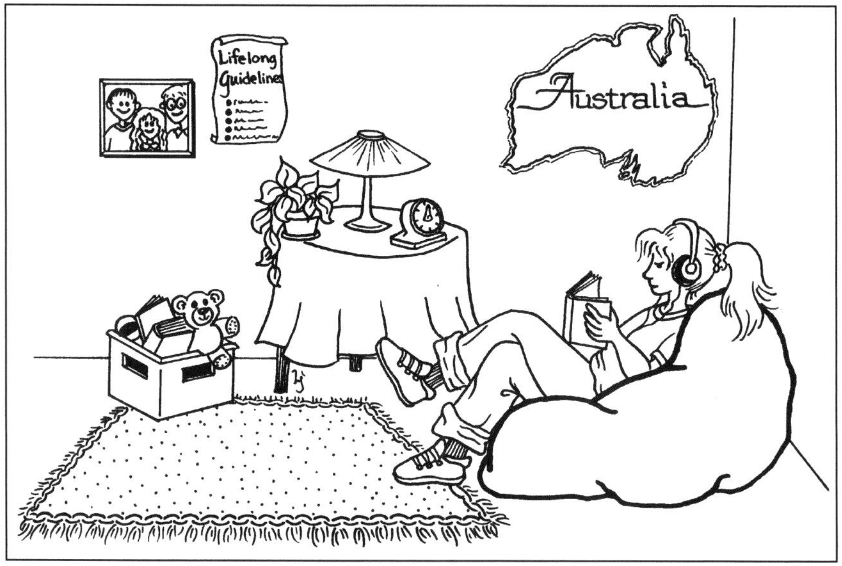

Demonstrate the use of any special items (e.g., timer, headset). Write procedures for using Australia with the students. Choose two or more students to demonstrate the procedures.

Inquiry—

Draw a picture of a "safe place" you go to when you are feeling sad, mad, angry, or stressed. Share this special place with your teacher. Add it to your "My Special Place" Book. ("My Special

Place Book" can be as simple as a binder with plastic sleeves. Slip each drawing into one of the sleeves and add a title page.)

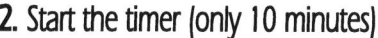

"Australia" Procedure

1. Wait your turn. One person at a time.
2. Start the timer (only 10 minutes).
3. Put items back in their place.
4. Return to your seat when time is up.

1:15 MOVEMENT

The activities from *Brain Gym* can be repeated with simple aerobics added.

1:45 DISCOVERY INQUIRIES

Conceptual Key Point –

Learning is the result of a partnership between our brain and our body. Our brain talks to our body and our body talks to our brain. The number one topic of conversation is our emotions. How we feel affects how we learn.

Significant Knowledge Key Point –

The heart and brain tend to match each other. If your heart is racing, you brain is also in a high state of emotional override. If your heart slows, your brain calms down and more fully engages the thinking part of the brain.

Inquiry –

Have students discuss with a partner:

–What emotions are you feeling now?

–Can you feel your heart beating? How many times per minute is it beating? (Have students count for 15 seconds and then multiply by four.)

–How fast is your brain working?

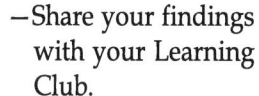

–How can you calm yourself (after getting excited or running around) to get ready for learning?

–Share your findings with your Learning Club.

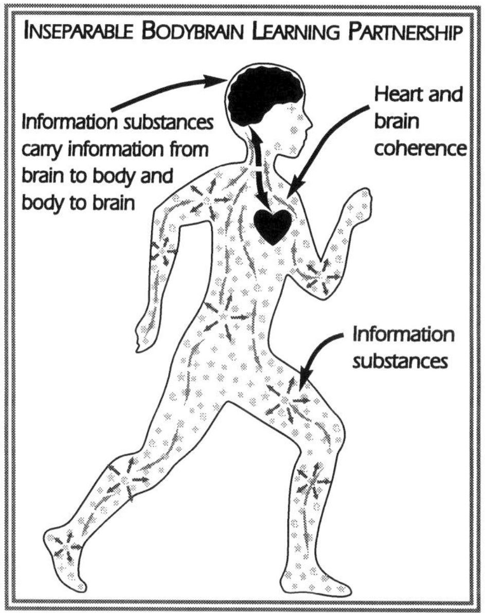

Today is but an introduction to these ideas. Continue studying about the impact of emotions for 15 minutes a day over the next two weeks and into the school year.

2:00 REFLECTIVE THINKING: Quiet Time with Music

Many students need time alone to think while their brains begin to integrate new information. Build this into each day. Suggest that your students reflect on their experiences today.

Inquiry –

Take time to calm your heart and brain. When your heart and brain are both calm, think about your day. Discuss the following questions with your Learning Club, then have your recorder share two of the most memorable things with the class.

- What have you learned today that you want to share with your family?
- What would you like to remember forever?

2:15 REVIEW KEY POINTS OF THE DAY

Guide a review of "What makes a community?" and "How brains work best when people feel safe and why." Sing the song "Shake Your Brain." Invite two or more students to model the movement/motions for the rest of the class.

2:30 CLOSURE: Learning Club

Review the sign(s) for "Active Listening." Teach the students to use the "Mike's On" procedure (a defunct microphone or look-alike item should be a standard item in each Learning Club basket of materials). Start with one student in each group (wearing the most red, blue, green, etc.) who will share. Question: What one word describes how you feel right now? Proceed around the group until each student has shared (right to pass is always an option).

2:45 LEAVING PROCEDURES

Introduce "end-of-the-day procedures" for the students to complete before leaving the classroom.

End of Day Procedure

1. Clean your area.
2. Help others straighten up.
3. Put items in your pack.
4. Say goodbye to others.
5. Share 1 thing you learned.

2:55 DISMISSAL

Be present at the door to share a "good-bye" handshake, hug, or "high five" with each student as he/she leaves.

TEACHER'S OVERVIEW OF THE FIRST DAY OF SCHOOL for INTERMEDIATE GRADES

8:30	ARRIVAL
8:45	STANDARD SCHOOL TASKS
9:00	INTRODUCTIONS
9:15	DAILY AGENDA
9:30	INCLUSION ACTIVITY
10:00	DISCOVERY INQUIRIES
10:20	REFLECTIVE THINKING
10:30	MOVEMENT/SNACK/RESTROOM
10:45	CONCEPTUAL KEY POINT
11:00	WHOLE CLASS INQUIRY
11:15	MOVEMENT/MUSIC
11:30	TOWN HALL MEETING
12:00	LUNCH PROCEDURES/LUNCH
12:45	REVIEW MORNING
1:00	INQUIRY
1:45	RECESS
2:00	KEY POINT/INQUIRY
2:45	SIGNIFICANT KNOWLEDGE KEY POINT
3:15	PLEDGE/LEARNING CLUB CLOSURE
3:30	DISMISSAL

Intermediate Grades—Lesson Plan for the First Day of School

➤Note to Teacher: Your goal is quality of experience, not quantity of information; be sure to provide adequate time for each inclusion activity and key point. These key points need extensive development using literature, discussion, reflection, journaling, and real-life experiences.

8:30 ARRIVAL: Await students at the classroom door; welcome them with a handshake, "high five," or a hug. Give each student a "puzzle piece" (see My Piece of the Puzzle directions that follow). Make sure each student reads and follows the "Morning Procedures." Tell them to look for procedures every morning.

Morning Procedures

1. *Be Friendly*: Greet Mr. Smith with a handshake or hug.
2. *Be responsible*: Hang coat/sweater on the hook by your name.
3. *Be organized*: Remove school materials from your pack.
4. Place pack by your coat and take school materials with you.
5. Sit where you see your name.
6. *Be caring*: Greet 3 or more students with a big "Hello!"
7. *Be ready*: Copy the agenda.

8:45 STANDARD SCHOOL TASKS: Allow time for opening ceremonies (Pledge of Allegiance, songs, and so forth) and for standard school procedures such as taking attendance and lunch count, collecting notes, and performing any other tasks required by your school district.

9:00 INTRODUCTIONS: Introduce yourself. Share some hobbies, interests, and family information. Introduce "Mike's On" procedures. Then, within each Learning Club, have each student introduce him/herself to members of the Learning Club using the Mike's On procedures : "My name is __________ and I like to ____________."

➤Note to Teacher: Walk around the room offering support for the shyer students and to ensure that no one student in a group monopolizes the time. Allow students a few minutes to exchange information.

"Mike's On" Procedure

1. Take the mike from the basket.
2. Follow directions for who goes first. Only one at a time.
3. Pass the mike by handing to the next person.
4. Actively listen to the person holding the mike.
5. Last person to share returns the mike to the basket.

9:15 DAILY AGENDA: Tell the students that an agenda— the plan for the day—will be posted every morning on the board (overhead, flannel board, white board) and that it is their responsibility to copy it in their spiral notebook.

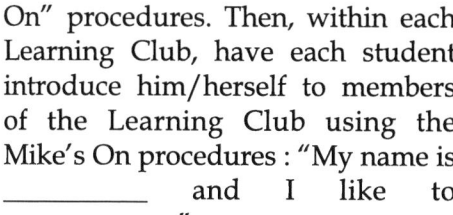

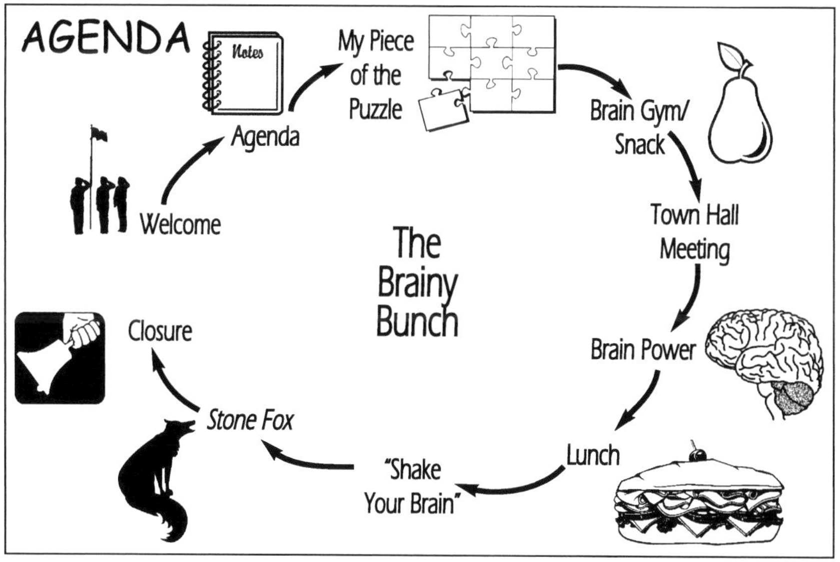

➤ This symbol indicates a note to the teacher.

Explain each part of the agenda, why it will be used every day, and how it will benefit both students and teacher. Allow students sufficient time to copy the agenda, words, and graphics. As the day unfolds, check off each item on the agenda as it is completed. Have the students do the same on their own agendas. Explain that the agenda is a time management and organizational tool and that it will be used every day. Any items not completed will be assigned as homework or done the next day.

9:30 **INCLUSION ACTIVITY:** "My Piece of the Puzzle"

➤Check to ensure that every student received a puzzle piece as he/she entered the room. Then, post the "My Piece of the Puzzle" Inquiry so all can easily see it.

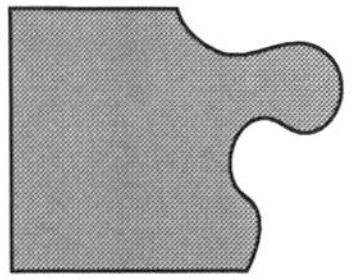

"My Piece of the Puzzle" Inquiry

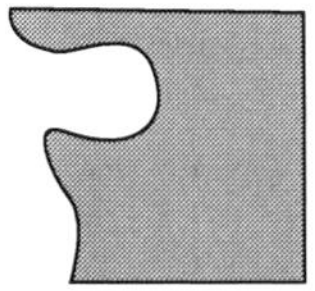

1. When the music starts, stand up, push in your chair, take your puzzle piece, and walk around the room.
2. Without talking, find puzzle pieces that fit with yours. When you find a match, stay with that person. Continue to find students with other pieces that fit with yours.
3. When you have all the pieces that fit together to make a rectangle, send a messenger to the teacher for a piece of oaktag paper.
4. Working together, paste all the pieces on the oaktag paper to make a completed jigsaw puzzle.
5. Choose a name for your Learning Club and print it with a dark marker at the top of your poster.
6. Hang the poster on our "Getting to Know You" bulletin board.

➤***Directions for preparing "My Piece of the Puzzle"—***

For each group, gather up one piece of 9"x 12" construction paper and one piece of 12"x 18" oaktag (make sure the paper and oaktag are of different colors), and one black marker.

1. Right before school begins, use your class list and divide the students into groups or what ITI calls "Learning Clubs."

2. Determine how many students will sit together and where the location of the groups will be. (For example, five students in a group: Group 1 near the door, Group 2 by the teacher's desk, Group 3 next to the classroom library, Group 4 by the windows, and Group 5 near the overhead.)

3. Using one piece of construction paper start with the first group. Divide the paper into puzzle pieces, one for each student in the group. Using the marker, write one student's name on each piece. Make the patterns of the cut unique for each group.

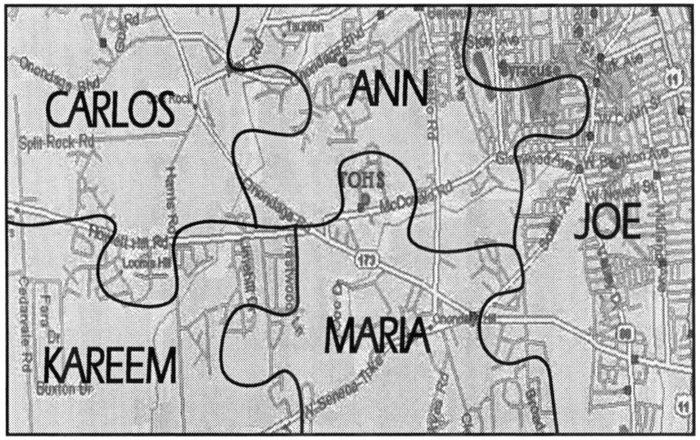

4. Repeat this pattern for each individual group until done.

5. Cut out the pieces.

6. Be ready to hand each student his/her own piece upon entering the classroom.

➤Give the students parameters for selecting a name for their Learning Club, such as a name that represents powerful learners or the power of the brain.

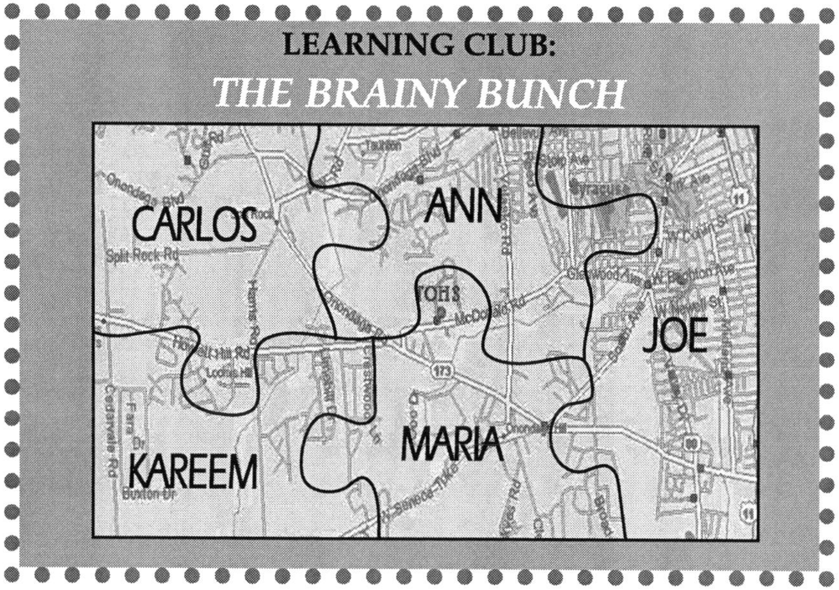

Inquiry –

After completing the puzzle, each Learning Club conducts a "Spotlight" interview of each of its members. Each student is asked two questions by each member of the group to learn more about his/her hobbies, interests, and family.

Reflective Thinking Inquiry –

As a Learning Club, reflect on this set of activities to build a sense of belonging. Ask questions such as: What did you like best about this activity and why? What was the most difficult part for you? The easiest part? What would you do differently next time to learn more about each other?

➤Tell the students that membership in the Learning Clubs will change often (about once a month) and will also start with inclusion activities that are fun. For example: a variety of codes, word searches, several clues on index cards to lead the students to find the other members of a new Learning Club. The purpose is to give them opportunities to get to know each other well and to practice using the LIFESKILL of Friendship – making and keeping friends.

10:00 DISCOVERY INQUIRIES

Conceptual Key Point –

Learning is the result of a partnership between our brain and our body. Our brain talks to our body and our body talks to our brain. The number one topic of conversation is our emotions. How we feel affects how we learn.

Significant Knowledge Key Point –

The heart and brain tend to match each other. If your heart is racing, your brain is also in high gear. If your heart slows, your brain calms down.

Inquiry –

Have students discuss with a partner:

– What emotions are you feeling now?

– Can you feel your heart beating? How many times per minute is it beating? (Have students count for 15 seconds and then multiply by four.)

– How fast is your brain working?

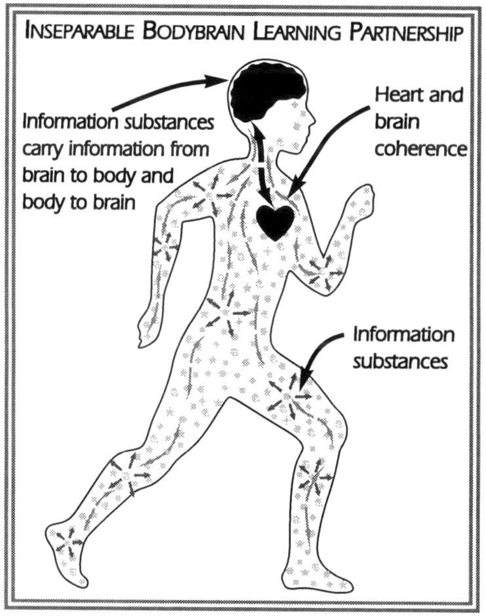

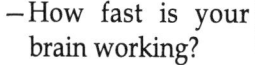

–How can you calm yourself (after getting excited or running around) to get ready for learning?

–Share your findings with your Learning Club.

Today is but an introduction to these ideas. Continue studying about the impact on emotions for fifteen minutes a day over the next two weeks and revisit it throughout the school year.

10:20 REFLECTIVE THINKING: Quiet Time with Music

Many students need time alone to think while their brains begin to integrate new information. Build this into each day. Suggest that your students reflect on their experiences today.

Inquiry–

Take time to calm your heart and brain. When your heart and brain are both calm, think about your day. Discuss the following questions with your Learning Club, then have your recorder share two of the most memorable things with the class.

- What have you learned today that you want to share with your family?
- What would you like to remember forever?

10:30 MOVEMENT/ SNACK/RESTROOM BREAK

Allow the students to create movements that demonstrate the meaning of the lyrics to at least two Lifelong Guideline/ LIFESKILLS songs (see back of book for songs by Jeff Pedersen and Judy Eacker.

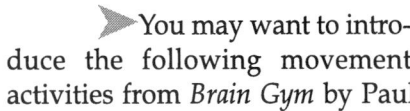

Restroom Procedure

1. Quietly signal the teacher.
2. Wash hands.
3. Come right back.

You may want to introduce the following movement activities from *Brain Gym* by Paul E. and Gail E. Dennison: Lazy 8s, Thinking Cap, and Hook-ups. Also see the book and video, *How to Make Learning a Moving Experience* by Jean Bladyes. Preview the video so you will have an appropriate activity to show to the students.

Snack Time Procedure

1. Clear off desk or table.
2. Get your snack.
3. Join your group.
4. Eat quietly.
5. Clean up when done.

Snack time can include quiet music playing, students talking with Learning Club members, etc. Just add what you want to the snack time procedures.

10:45 CONCEPTUAL KEY POINT

Conceptual Key Point: Community

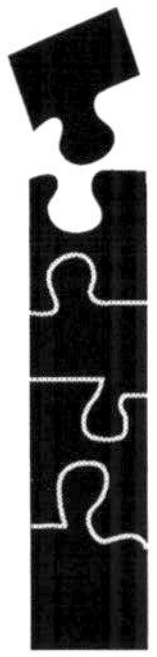

A spirit of community doesn't just happen in a neighborhood or classroom because people live or work in the same area. Each member–young and old–must take responsibility for creating and enhancing a sense of community throughout each day, month, and year. Creating a sense of community is a three-step process:

- Developing a sense of inclusion or belonging
- Creating common ground, and
- Taking action

Our beginning point for step 1, developing a sense of inclusion, is using the Lifelong Guidelines and LIFESKILLS:

- TRUSTWORTHINESS
- TRUTHFULNESS
- ACTIVE LISTENING
- NO PUT-DOWNS
- PERSONAL BEST/LIFESKILLS

Whole Class Inquiry –

Think back over your school experiences. Choose the year you feel you were an enthusiastic, successful learner. Using pencil or fine point markers, create a mindmap sharing five or more reasons you feel that the class supported your needs as a learner. Share the results with your fellow Learning Club members during Round Robin (sharing information in a clockwise way in the group).

See *Cooperative Learning* by Spencer Kagan. Bring your mindmap to the Town Hall Meeting later in the morning.

11:15 MOVEMENT/MUSIC

This is an opportunity to move around the room, either in a structured way (exercises) or non-structured (explore the classroom and find out where materials are located as you listen to the music). This is a good time to introduce the Lifelong Guidelines songs with the video *Spread Your Wings* by Jeff Pedersen.

11:30 KEY POINT / TOWN HALL / T-CHART

Introduce the chimes as an "active listening" tool. Teach the other signals that you plan to use when students need to be active listeners, such as American Sign Language for "to listen" or hand in the air with fingers spread apart to represent the five elements of the Chinese Tang symbol—you/me, eyes, ears, heart, and undivided attention.)* Also see *Spread Your Wings: the Life-long Guidelines* by Jeff Pedersen, CD and video which has a

* The Chinese symbol is an excellent visual because it contains all the important elements for active listening. See *TRIBES: A New Way of Being Together* by Jeanne Gibbs.

song for each of the Lifelong Guidelines. Creating new lyrics for common melodies is also a fun activity.

Significant Knowledge Key Point–

Step 2 in building a sense of community is creating common ground. Through this process, we discover and come to respect each others' strengths and gifts and become willing to lead and to accept the leadership of others to maximize the capabilities of the community.

Discuss the concept of community: Guide the students through a discussion of community. Utilizing their real-life stories, literature, and other topics, draw out a definition of community.

- Invite the students to share information from their mindmaps about characteristics of classrooms in which they were successful learners.
- Write the attributes on a chart tablet either in list or mindmap form. Use this information as a lead-in to adopting the Lifelong Guidelines (and LIFESKILLS) as acceptable behaviors for everyone (adults included), to use in the classroom. Using the Lifelong Guidelines will build community and promote successful learning.
- Introduce each of the Lifelong Guidelines and assess the students' understandings of these concepts by having them record their ideas on a chart.
- Decide as a group which Lifelong Guideline to first focus on. (Hint: No Put-Downs is especially critical in intermediate grades and secondary schools.)

This is a good time to show video clips of TV shows that use put-downs continuously.

Town Hall Meeting Inquiry

For more information about how to conduct a Town Hall Meeting, see Appendix E.

TOWN HALL MEETING

Procedures

1. Come to the meeting area when your Learning Club is called.
2. Find a place on the rug (circle, line, etc.) to sit. Sit where you can see everyone and everyone can see you.
3. Identify and sit comfortably in your own personal space.
4. Remember to use the Lifelong Guidelines throughout the Town Hall Meeting.
5. When you hear the chimes, it is time to use active listening.

➤ MATERIALS: The individual handouts of Lifelong Guidelines and LIFESKILLS, plus chart paper, and markers.

Lifelong Guidelines—

Create a T-Chart using the Lifelong Guideline the students have selected as their starting point. Use a large chart tablet so you can collect information for all of the Lifelong Guidelines/ LIFESKILLS in one place. Ideas can be added throughout the school year. Following is an example of how such a chart might look:

T-Chart with Put-Downs

LOOKS LIKE	*SOUNDS LIKE*	*FEELS LIKE*
arms crossed	You can't play with us!	left out
laughing at clothing	Where'd you get that old thing?	humiliation
laughing at answer	"You sure are stupid!"	hurt
no one noticing	"Who's she/he?"	isolation

➤ For the second day of school, plan on doing a second version of this chart so that it looks like the following chart.

T-Chart with NO Put-Downs

LOOKS LIKE	*SOUNDS LIKE*	*FEELS LIKE*
Students greeting each other	Hi! How are you today? Want to play at recess?	welcome
High fives!	Great job! You mastered the 7 times tables.	capable
Someone waving	"Maria, come join us."	belonging

Additional ideas can be put on the chart as students notice them in literature, common experiences, newspaper articles, biographies, and real-life adventures.

12:00 LUNCH PROCEDURES/ LUNCH

12:45 REVIEW MORNING

Circle up by birthday and share with two other persons what you learned from this morning. Check the agenda and cross off the items that have been accomplished. Discuss why the procedures will help the students.

1:00 INQUIRY

Design a poster on 12" x 18" paper that encourages our school community to eliminate put-downs and use put-ups in their place.

Go to Lunch Procedure

1. Clean up your work area.
2. Get your coat & lunch.

3. Line up at the door and stand quietly.

4. Proceed to cafeteria.

Using pencil, write a catchy heading and add drawings that illustrate your suggestions. Print your name in the lower right hand corner and ask a partner to check your work for any areas that may need improvement. Color your poster when you know that you have done your personal best. Share the poster and ideas with your Learning Club. Hang your work in the hallway with any other posters from the class. Complete your work before class starts tomorrow.

1:45 RECESS

2:00 KEY POINT/INQUIRY

Significant Knowledge Key Point

Step 3 in creating a sense of community is taking action. Communities are dynamic; they are either vibrant and growing or diminishing and dying. Maintaining community requires taking actions that nurture and expand the well-being of the group.

MATERIALS: One copy (or class set) of *Stone Fox* by John Reynolds Gardiner. This story:

- Is written at a third/fourth grade reading level but revered by students in grades 2-8 (regardless of students' reading level)
- Includes each Lifelong Guideline and LIFESKILL (great for beginning of the year introductions)
- Grabs the emotions (read this story before you use it with the students; it is emotionally compelling)
- Develops the concepts of community/survival
- Focuses on problem-solving skills
- Centers on a non-traditional family (grandpa and grandson)
- Is only ten chapters long (short enough to complete in one or two weeks).

While this book is a favorite, there are many others (*My Side of the Mountain, Where the Red Fern Grows, Charlotte's Web,* or a personal choice) that provide a basis for developing the concept of community, Lifelong Guidelines, and LIFESKILLS through literature.

Pre-reading strategies:

- Locate your state in relation to Wyoming on a U.S. map. Determine if any students have visited Wyoming.
- Determine what kind of pets, if any, the students have at home. Lead a discussion of the kinds of "jobs" dogs do.
- Discuss the Husky as a canine breed—where and why the breed was developed.
- Have students write in their journals their predictions for why the book is titled *Stone Fox* and what they think the story plot will be.
- Review strategies for decoding new words.

Reading: Chapters 1 and 2 can be read aloud by the teacher, individually by each student, with a partner, or in the Learning Club.

Inquiry —

Develop a mindmap that focuses on Lifelong Guideline/LIFESKILLS used by the three main characters (you may include an animal as well as humans) in the first two chapters of *Stone Fox.* Choose two of your favorite characters; for each, identify two Lifelong Guidelines and/or LIFESKILLS used by each character uses. Write that word on a line; include the page number where this example can be found. Defend your choices with your

Learning Club during inquiry share time. For example:

Little Willy and Grandpa used the LIFESKILL of Sense of Humor when they. . . .

2:45 CONCEPTUAL KEY POINT REVIEW - TOWN HALL MEETING

Guide your discussion with the following ideas:

- Ask students to review the information from their mindmaps and the T-chart created in the morning.
- Present the LIFESKILL of Cooperation as a goal for Learning Club projects/inquiries. Brainstorm attributes of the LIFESKILL of Cooperation. Ask the students to locate the word in class dictionaries to be sure of the definition.
- Invite the students to reflect on an activity/ situation/inquiry when they have been part of a collaborative group. Provide time for a "popcorn" share (strategy where group members may "pop" out their answers in any order providing they still follow the Lifelong Guideline of Active Listening.
- Practice writing "Popcorn Procedures" together (students and teacher).

End-of-Day Procedure

1. Organize the items in your area.
2. Help others straighten up the Learning Club materials.
3. Put important items in your pack.
4. Say goodbye to others.

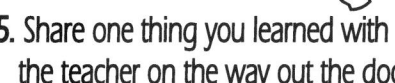

5. Share one thing you learned with the teacher on the way out the door.

3:15 PLEDGE/LEARNING CLUB CLOSURE

Inquiry

With your Learning Club members, create a Lifelong Guidelines Pledge. Use rhyme or free verse, including the names of the Lifelong Guidelines and the word "community." Motions/ Signing may also be included. Share this pledge tomorrow during Town Hall Meeting.*

3:30 DISMISSAL

Meeting with a Coach

As discussed in Chapter 7, pages 7.18-7.19, coaching on a regular basis is critically important. If you don't already have a coach assigned to you by the end of the first day of school, don't hesitate. Ask for one. Schedule yourself to meet for an hour or two every two weeks if at all possible. Again, frequent small amounts of time are more productive than all day twice a year. Also find a peer coach to work with you and join you when you meet with your professional coach.

* During the next Town Hall Meeting, students can continue to discuss or, if they desire, develop additional versions of a class pledge.Or, the best parts of each pledge can be combined to make a unique verse.Once they have agreed upon a pledge they feel best expresses the principles they want for their classroom community, they should recite it after the Pledge of Allegiance.

Notes

1 The invitation should be a personal note. It needn't be lengthy or detailed. The important message is that you're inviting them to share a wonderful year with you.

2 For examples of procedures, see Chapter 21, pp. 21.5-21.6.

3 For a description of this community building process, see Chapter 9, pages 9.2-8.

4 If you live in a northern climate requiring lots of heavy clothing or if your classroom has nowhere to hang coats and carry bags, your procedures should be detailed. Also, when elements of the classroom are new, consider an invitation to explore the classroom for 2-5 minutes before they sit down.

5 Developing a sense of inclusion/belonging is a critical first step in any classroom. See pages 9.2-8.

6 Although the triune brain theory has largely been eclipsed by for a larger view of how emotion affects learning, there is still value in teaching students (adjusted for the age of your students, of course) about their brain and its functions; for example, brain stem and cerebellum, limbic system, and cerebral cortex.

7 Antonio Damasio, *Looking for Spinoza: Joy, Sorrow, and the Feeling Brain.* (New York: Harcourt, 2003), 85..

8 For more information about the Acknowledgements Box, see pp. 7.7-8.

9 We strongly recommend you hold Back to School Night for your classroom during the first or second week of school—even if the rest of the school holds one later.

Notes to Myself

Chapter 8: The Lifelong Guidelines and LIFESKILLS

The Lifelong Guidelines and LIFESKILLS

The Lifelong Guidelines are a result of asking the question: "What qualities do you want in a lifelong partner?" Conversely, these Lifelong Guidelines also ask you to consider what qualities you should possess to make someone want to spend a lifetime with you. Also, what qualities would you hope a stranger on the street would have? A neighbor? However you ask the question, under whatever the circumstances or length of time of interaction, these five qualities come out high on the list. They form the foundation for positive, valued relationships and make learning joyous and powerful. They are also the keystone to good classroom leadership and, more than instructional strategy, help eliminate threat and enhance reflective thinking. The Lifelong Guidelines must become internalized. They shape the culture of the classroom.

An invaluable tool for teaching the Lifelong Guidelines and LIFESKILLS is *Tools for Citizenship and Life: Using the ITI LIfelong Guidelines and LIFESKILLS in Your Classroom* by Sue Pearson. With a separate chapter for each of the Guidelines and LIFESKILLS, it describes why and how to practice the guideline/skill, what it looks like in the real world, what it looks like in school, more than 500 inquiries (whole group and small group/individual), signs of success, suggested literature (by grade spans: primary, intermediate, and middle/high school), and sample family letters.

For a discussion of the Lifelong Guidelines, see the following excerpt from *Tools for Citizenship & Life: Using the ITI Lifelong Guidelines and LIFESKILLS in Your Classroom,* pages 10.2-10.16.

Lifelong Guidelines

TRUSTWORTHINESS: To act in a manner that makes one worthy of trust and confidence

TRUTHFULNESS: To act with personal responsibility and mental accountability

ACTIVE LISTENING: To listen attentively and with the intention of understanding

NO PUT-DOWNS: To never use words, actions, and/or body language that degrade, humiliate, or dishonor others

PERSONAL BEST: To do one's best given the circumstances and available resources

TRUSTWORTHINESS:

To act in a manner that makes one worthy of trust and confidence

What Is Trustworthiness?

If we were artists commissioned to paint a masterpiece representing the Lifelong Guideline of Trustworthiness, we would choose for our model a mother rocking her infant child, the baby's eyes intently studying her mother's face, a tiny hand reaching up to touch her mother's cheek. The purest form of trust in life is child to mother. The parent provides food when the child is hungry, warmth when cold and comfort when hurt. This relationship between mother and baby is a child's first experience with trustworthiness.

Yet we know there are other pictures in which food is late or lacking, comfort is in short supply, and warmth is missing. What do such babies begin to learn about trustworthiness? They learn that "people in my world are not reliable." Such early experiences with family and caretakers impair a child's ability to have confidence in other people.

Trustworthiness: An Umbrella in Stormy Weather. Trustworthi-ness, identified by specific attributes such as reliability and dependability, is vital because it is an umbrella under which we protect ourselves from stormy weather. Each one of us needs at least one such umbrella for protection—if not a trustworthy friend, at least a parent or close family member with whom we can talk and know that our words will go no further. We need to trust that those close to us will adhere to the Lifelong Guidelines and LIFESKILLS. Likewise, we need to be the umbrella of protection for other people by providing confidentiality, steadiness, and support during those occasional drizzles, steady rains, and torrential downpours that life presents.

Trustworthiness Is a Double-Sided Coin. But trustworthiness is more than an umbrella in stormy weather for us as we seek out those who are trustworthy, safe, and comfortable to be with. Trustworthiness is a double-sided coin, a two-way street. It isn't just what we receive; we in turn must be trustworthy for others. Students must be taught that they can't expect the gift of trustworthiness from others if they are not trustworthy in return.

The Lifelong Guideline of Trustworthiness requires that parents and teachers teach both sides of Trustworthiness—how to give it and how to receive it. To do so, we must teach children the signposts for recognizing this characteristic in others. Who really deserves their trust so others don't take advantage of them? How do they extend their trust so that relationships of all levels can deepen and enrich their lives?

Why Practice Trustworthiness?

The Lifelong Guideline of Trustworthiness forms the basis of relationships—effective working partnerships, close friendships, healthy family bonds, and the long-lasting intimate relationship of husband and wife. If people can't trust us, they don't want to be around us—it's too risky. The lower the level of trustworthiness, the more distant people remain. And, because few pursuits in life are solitary, most goals require the participation of others. If we are to succeed in our goals, we must become trustworthy people.

For Staff. The higher the stakes become, the more crucial trustworthiness becomes. Designing seal rings for the space shuttle booster rocket, problem-solving safety design issues on the Boeing aircraft assembly line, doing customer service in a small business whose owner has just invested his entire life savings into his business are examples of everyday work environments in which our trustworthiness and ability to work as a team can have life-and-death or life-changing impact.

Can your colleagues feel secure that you are dependable (the job gets done), consistent (high quality of work), and reliable (follows directions and meets deadlines)? Does your word have credibility? Does your supervisor have confidence that you'll complete a task he/she assigns or keep confidential information secure?

As our trust-building skills improve, we are more likely to be included in upper-level planning and decision making. Such involvement is a key element in satisfaction in the workplace.

For Students. Close relationships of any kind, including teacher-student and student-student, cannot exist without trustworthiness. It is the cornerstone of respect and liking. One can love someone without liking and respecting him /her—a common burden of children abused by their parents. Trustworthiness is also the source of one's sense of security, safety, and confidence.

A key ingredient in the Lifelong Guideline of Trustworthiness is emotional consistency—that the student knows the teacher cares about him/her and that the teacher's emotional and physical behaviors are consistent with that love, that no matter what happens, the student knows he/she will be fairly treated.

When students feel safe and secure in the classroom, learning becomes paramount because the bodybrain can focus on learning. The atmosphere in the classroom, instead of tense and suspicious, is calm and steady. The teacher can be relied on to keep her word when students share problems. Consistency is the standard for student and teacher actions, both in application and outcome.

For Families. When a teacher is known to be trustworthy, relationships with students' families will flourish. A teacher who consistently and fairly applies rules and consequences wins respect from both students and adults. Family members recognize that we are working with them, not against them, in the education of their child. Generally, the more we know and understand about a child's circumstances, the greater the possibility that the teacher can provide emotional support, which in turn will promote academic learning. The parent-teacher relationship exudes confidentiality, whether relating to family or school concerns; this raises the level of trustworthiness for all involved, leading to additional exchanges of pertinent information.

Note: The only time a teacher must divulge confidential information from a student is when some form of abuse is apparent. Many states have laws requiring that this information be disclosed, and indeed, the penalties are severe if they're not reported. A student sharing this type of information is crying out for help and trusting that we will provide guidance, backing, and support.

How Do You Practice Trustworthiness?

We practice being trustworthy by not abusing others' trust; we don't share confidences, ignore deadlines, spread rumors, talk behind backs, lie, cheat, steal, or exhibit any of the other behaviors that would abuse trust.

The beginnings of trustworthiness lie deep within our childhood experiences. As infants, was food consistently there when we felt the pangs of hunger? Were we changed when wet and uncomfortable, rocked when ill, comforted when frightened? If the answers to these questions are yes, then we trusted our caretaker. On the other hand, were we left to wonder if food would come or if someone would take care of us when we were ill or frightened? Did our caretakers keep their word? Did they model good judgment and integrity? Clearly, the development of trust and trustworthiness in the classroom comes more quickly for some students than for others. Whatever it takes, however, it is our job as educators to develop future citizens who are trustworthy and who are capable of trusting those who have earned their trust.

Making Wise Choices. Trustworthiness is the result of making wise choices over time—some wise, others not so wise. The ability to do so, however, isn't automatic. It takes practice, in the midst of which we make mistakes—lots of them! For instance, when sent to deliver a message, does the student attend to the task at hand or slowly meander through the hallways disrupting other learners by waving in classroom windows? Do you remember some of these situations from your own childhood experiences? One friend shares a secret with another, who promises not to tell. The two are part of a trust-building pact. Did the secret get told as soon as another warm body was in sight or remain private? Remember going to a friend's house and promising to return home by dinner time? Were you at your place at the dinner table or nowhere to be seen? Remember finding money around the house or at school? Did you search for the owner or pocket the cash? These are all examples of early trust-building opportunities.

At school, does a trip to the bathroom take a few minutes or is it necessary to dispatch an escort to accompany the unreliable student back to class? Can the child be trusted to complete her own work and not to copy someone else's work? Will the child tell the truth even though negative consequences may result? Does the student return forms and homework on time, turn in "found" objects and money, work hard to eliminate put-downs from his vocabulary, and do his personal best consistently?

As adults, every action we take, every deed we accomplish, every word we utter, creates the person others see us to be. People either believe us or they don't. Building trust is a definitive example of actions speaking louder than words because all of the good intentions and promises in the world cannot compensate for jobs undone, deadlines ignored, secrets revealed, and promises broken. Therefore, tell the truth, work to your personal best, keep your word, exceed expectations—be a person viewed as reliable, dependable, and believable.

Building a Reputation Takes Time. A reputation of trustworthiness is earned slowly since it is based on a collection of positive experiences among people over time. Consistency, reliability, and honest actions all typify a person who is worthy of our trust. The same is true for each of us. Our actions and reactions will be watched for awhile, before we are known to be trustworthy.

Adults must recognize that trustworthiness develops in stages. Expectations of trustworthiness for five-year olds should be more basic than expectations for fifteen-year olds. Students must understand that each time trust is broken, it takes longer to be restored; sometimes trust can be irrevocably broken.

TRUTHFULNESS:

To be honest about things and feelings with oneself and others

What Is Truthfulness?

Truthfulness has many aspects; its complexity unfolds as students mature. It is a difficult Lifelong Guideline to practice. Its attributes are complex and often depend on circumstances. The definition of truthfulness that follows is the result of brainstorming by a class of teachers and administrators at U.C. Davis, California.

"To be truthful means being honest about things and feelings . . . being honest with ourselves and with others. Being truthful is not always easy because truth is not absolute (black and white) and two seemingly contradictory statements could both be true depending upon the perspectives of the observers (for example, the blind men discovering the elephant). It takes courage to be truthful because others may disagree.

"Being truthful requires good judgment about:

- What to say (possible risk to our source of information)
- When to say it (in private or before others)
- To whom to say it (to the person responsible for the problem/situation or as a complaint to anyone who will listen)
- How to say it (with sensitivity and tact or intended to hurt)[1]

"Truthfulness is a critical building block for human relationships and therefore has significant consequences, both short-term and long-term, for each of us."[2]

Preserving the Truth. Preserving the truth depends on each one of us refusing to exaggerate, change, or vary the facts we share. This requires careful observation and clear thinking as we perceive and analyze a situation; it also requires precise communication when sharing.

Whether it's the policeman asking, "What happened here? Which driver caused the accident and how?" or the parent asking, "How did this happen? Who started this?" the situation calls for the truth. How well did we observe the incident? Do we stick to the facts or make inferences that may or may not be true? Are we committed to telling the truth despite consequences?

Why Practice Truthfulness?

Most people to believe what they hear (especially from someone they know or from someone who is supposed to be trustworthy) unless the information is proven to be inaccurate. After that, the informant's word is not as good as it used to be; people listen with a sense of disbelief or the feeling that they should check another source. Recall the story from Aesop's Fables about the boy who cried wolf. The boy lied so many times about the wolf being after the sheep that when the wolf really did attack, none of the villagers responded to his cries for help. If we aren't truthful at all times, people—especially family and friends—will be suspicious when we share stories; they'll want proof or verification from other sources. The greater the number of lies and careless statements that pass through our lips, the more corroboration our listeners will need.

It is important, sometimes even a matter of life or death, that people believe us. Nothing is as precious as our reputation that we say what we mean and mean what we say. Truthfulness is the bedrock of trustworthiness.

Effective Relationships Rely on Truthfulness. Based on a survey of more than 15,000 people, 88 percent chose honesty as the key trait of effective leadership.[3] Honest people have credibility; credible leaders gain the trust and confidence of their followers. They keep their promises and follow through on their commitments. In contrast, people who consistently lie are shunned, have few friends, and have fewer options for well-paying employment.

In personal relationships, if we can't be trusted to tell the truth even with insignificant information, how can anyone believe that our important ideas are true? By always telling the truth, friends, family, and co-workers will believe what we say. We become respected and valued members of our families and communities.

When the Lifelong Guidelines of Truthfulness and Trustworthiness are present, a sense of community develops. Then, all members are less likely to be dishonest because each is genuinely cherished for who he/she is. When we belong, we have something to lose if we break the norms of our group. When we belong, there is no need to create some persona bigger and better than in real life.

Benefits to Telling the Truth. According to Dr. Abraham Kryger, D.M.D., M.D., there are real benefits to telling the truth. Among them are: greater success/personal expertise, an increased sense of grounding/confidence, less anxiety/worry/guilt, increased ability to deal with crises/breakdowns, improved problem-solving abilities, improved interpersonal relationships, greater emotional health/control of one's emotions, increased ability to influence others, better sleep, better health, increased ability to think well/reason soundly, less need to control, good humor, and greater self-expression and self-satisfaction.[4] Do those sound like qualities you'd like in your life? Truth—and its dark twin, lies—drive world events, nudge the fall of civilizations, and sculpt our lives like no other character trait.

Consequences of Not Telling the Truth. There are also consequences that result from not telling the truth. Some of these consequences according to Dr. Kryger are: more frequent failures/frustrations in life, being distrusted by others, lack of self-esteem/self-confidence, dysfunctional interpersonal relationships, inability to self-correct, and stress of many kinds. Almost all types of human stress can be traced to not telling the truth at one level or another.[5]

How Do You Practice Truthfulness?

Always tell the truth! It was Mark Twain who said, "If you tell the truth, you don't have to remember anything."[6] It is easier to remember what really happened, what words were really spoken than to try to recall a made-up story or a distorted version. You also practice the Lifelong Guideline of Truthfulness by telling the entire truth immediately rather than telling the story a little bit at a time until finally the whole truth emerges. Credibility is easy to destroy with some simple untruths told in a moment to either create a better impression, deny involvement, or refuse to acknowledge that an incident has occurred. As a teacher, you're on stage; be honest with your class. Remember, what you do is more important than what you say you do!

Recognize That There are Barriers to Telling the Truth. When teaching students about the Lifelong Guideline of Truthfulness, we must admit to ourselves and to them that there are formidable barriers to telling the truth in our society. Perhaps the biggest is refusing to accept that it is possible to tell the truth. A widespread but false belief held by many is that it isn't humanly possible to tell the truth. That is just a handy excuse that absolves us of the need to question our lack of truthfulness.

A second powerful barrier is fear of consequences if we tell the truth. For example, the boss firing us, someone close to us may losing respect for us, people may retaliate if we challenge their belief system, or we may not know how to disagree with a friend whose "truth" is far different from our own.[7]

Practice, Practice. Have students share stories and repeat information as accurately as possible. Teach them to write terms and facts on paper so they can refer to them if needed. Show them the importance of being willing to recheck any data that seem to lack credibility by going back to the source of the information. Teach students many problem-solving strategies; when logical, natural choices are available, a student is less likely to lie. Avoid setting a trap for a student, as when you already know the answer but ask the question anyway. All you accomplish is catching him/her in a falsehood. Why not catch someone when telling the truth and thus reinforce the desired, rather than the negative, behavior?

Seek Workplaces and Friendships That Value Truthfulness. Telling the truth isn't always easy. Often, telling parents, friends, the boss, and co-workers the truth brings unpleasant consequences. However, telling a lie under these circumstances almost always has far-reaching consequences, often of greater severity than if we simply spoke the truth up front and accepted the consequences, as unpleasant as they might be. Once we're caught lying, people lose faith and confidence in us. In work relationships and with friends, this is devastating.[8]

One final caution. Sometimes people in power will ask for our honest opinion about plans, choices, and situations. If the level of trust in that business or organization is high, we feel comfortable in sharing our thoughts. If it's low, our risk is much greater, particularly if our true beliefs are not what the person in power wants to hear. Rather than be part of a lie that will have unwanted consequences for us and others, we should look for work settings where truthfulness is truly valued. During interviews, ask questions that will reveal the level of truthfulness in that culture. By gathering as much information as possible before accepting a position, we can make more informed decisions.

ACTIVE LISTENING:

To listen with the intention of understanding what the speaker intends to communicate[9]

What Is Active Listening?

Hearing is an inactive, involuntary process that occurs when the ears pick up sound waves being transmitted by some kind of vibration and forward them to the brain. Listening, however, is an active, voluntary process which includes recognizing, and intending to understand the messages received. Listening requires participation, patience, energy, and the **intention** to "get it"—not just what the speaker says but what he/she intends to communicate.

To actively listen, the brain must be physiologically active. Not only must it perceive the sounds correctly but it must also compare words to emotional nuances for consistency, then convert words into images that can be analyzed, compared, and stored for future reference. This is an extremely active process requiring neural wiring that, unfortunately, one out of four students hasn't developed by the time he/she starts school.[10] However, such wiring can easily be developed in the classroom. For more information about how to create the needed wiring, contact Lindamood-Bell Learning Processes Center, San Luis Obispo, California, (800) 233-1819.

Most people listen passively. That means the sound acts on them—enters their ears—but they don't actively and consciously participate in the process; they don't exert effort in order to listen and attend to what they are hearing. An example is listening to a book on tape while driving or a music CD while cleaning the house. In contrast, active listening is far more complex.

A wonderful metaphor for active listening, and an excellent way to teach it to students, is illustrated in the TANG, a Chinese character for "to listen"—to listen with our eyes, ears, heart, and give undivided attention.[11] If we do so, we are truly acting upon our intention to understand what the speaker intends to communicate.

The active listener is more than a receiver. In many ways, he assists the speaker to deliver his/her message by providing encouragement, such as attentive body posture, full eye contact, positive body signals, and multi-tiered acknowledgements, such as "Mmm; uhuh; yes; I understand; I agree; yes, interesting; I heard something about that yesterday . . . tell me more." The listener is saying to the speaker, "Your ideas and message are important to me and to others in the room. I will listen while you communicate with me and then I will ask questions if I disagree or don't understand. Above all, I respect your opinions and your right to speak." And, eventually, "I understand what you are trying to tell me."

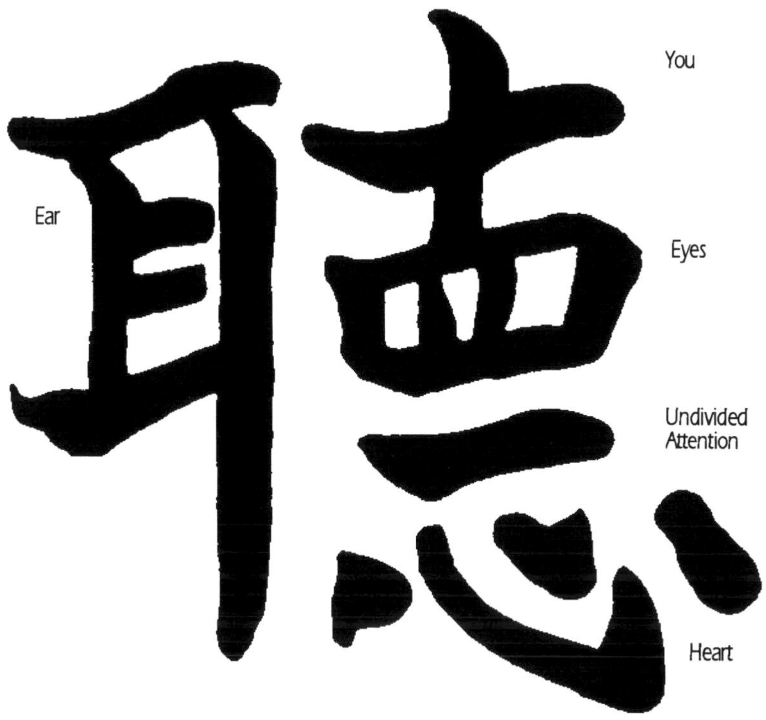

Why Practice Active Listening?

Active listening is critical because it is the doorway to understanding. Whether in social settings, at work, or with family and friends, not getting it can cause serious problems. At best, it is embarrassing and makes us feel like outsiders. All too often it is also costly in our relationships with others and expensive for our employers when we misinterpret instructions. Furthermore, it is difficult to be successful in life if we are not taking in accurate information about the world and how it works.

On a daily basis, our sense of hearing collects a wide range of information that we need to protect ourselves and to enhance our problem solving. What might happen, for instance, if a jogger, wearing headphones and listening to music, is crossing the street against the walk sign and can't hear a persistent honking horn? Or, if a worried parent is unable to focus on the doctor's directions for the baby's medicine and care? Wouldn't you feel sad if you missed your plane to Disney World because you didn't hear the final boarding call? Since one of the ways we stay safe and make informed decisions includes listening to sounds collected from the real world, isn't it common sense to concentrate on what we hear?

Unlike reading, we can't regulate the pace of someone else's speech, replaying it again to check an unfamiliar word. Thus, we may miss important information reported to us and respond in a peculiar way. To immediately understand what we hear, it's crucial that we perfect the skill of listening well. We can only talk intelligently about a topic when we can grasp what is said to us. To be able to listen well gives us confidence when communicating with others. Listening in the real world is an everyday skill.

Spotlight on Brain Research. Most educators don't realize that active listening—turning words into mental images that can be processed and stored in short- and long-term memory—requires neural wiring that over 25 percent of the population does not have or has not developed sufficiently to succeed in school. Nanci Bell, author of *Visualizing and Verbalizing for Improved Language Comprehension,* describes typical symptoms of oral language processing difficulty, any one of which would increase difficulty and frustration in learning as well as in social settings. Unfortunately, most people who have difficulty with language processing display more than one of these symptoms. It is a sobering list:[12]

"1. *Individuals may frequently not understand jokes.* Language humor depends on imagery, whereas sight humor (pie in face) does not and is more easily understood. Almost everyone gets sight gags but not everyone gets language-based humor.

2. *Individuals may not understand concepts of cause and effect.* To process cause and effect relationships you must be able to process a gestalt from which to judge an effect.

3. *Individuals may not respond to explanations given in language.* If a student's performance needs correcting, a "talking to" may be only partially understood or not understood at all because the student is connecting to only a part of the oral explanation.

4. *Individuals may ask and re-ask questions that have already been answered.* The individual hears the answer but is unable to process and connect to the given information and will therefore ask the same question again, only phrased differently. Such individuals are often not aware that they are asking the same question over and over, only with modified language.

5. *Individuals may not grasp the main idea or inferences from television shows or movies, although they may get a few details.* Individuals may seem to miss concepts or nuances from movies they've seen. In discussions with them, they don't interpret the movie or story sequence well.

6. *Individuals may lose attention quickly in conversation or lectures.* Students who are unable to connect to the gestalt of language will find that in a few minutes, often less, they are "lost" and may drift away mentally and/or physically.

7. *Individuals may have weakness in auditory memory and in following directions.* These symptoms may be severe and labeled as aphasia[13] . . . [or] be subtle weaknesses that cause others to suspect lack of intelligence or lack of motivation. In fact, individuals with these symptoms will frequently doubt their intelligence."

Ms. Bell also points to a link between listening difficulties and oral language expression:

"The oral language comprehension weakness is often accompanied by an oral language expression weakness. Individuals experience difficulty organizing their verbalizing and expressing themselves easily and fluently or they are verbal but scattered, relating information out of sequence. For example, a student on academic probation, with severely impaired auditory and reading comprehension, frequently interjected irrelevant comments in conversation. His comments were disjointed both unto themselves and to the topic. Consequently, he was often viewed as mentally disabled."[14]

Every teacher can list students who have exhibited these frustrating symptoms. There is more to being an active listener than most people realize.

How Do You Practice Active Listening?

If these listening difficulties sound familiar, you owe it to yourself and your students to read Nanci Bell's book. Use it as a teacher's manual with your entire class every day for 30 minutes for at least six weeks. You'll be astounded at the transformation in academic capability of individual students and the class as a whole.

Once the necessary neural wiring is in place, more traditional classroom strategies for teaching students to pay closer attention, try harder, focus more, and so forth, can be used with greater success.

Proficient listening requires the neural wiring to process language plus the social skills our society has come to expect of listeners. There are many ways for students to practice these social-based listening techniques.

Using the Chinese Symbol for Listening. The Chinese symbol which depicts "to listen" as an act involving ears, eyes, heart, and undivided attention[15] is a good place to start. It offers a handy visual and helps turn intention into tangible action. Listening with intention helps the listener "hear" with an open mind and rid him/herself of any preconcieved notions that would corrupt the speaker's message. Many poor listeners get so involved in the speaker's style of delivery or their judgments about the speaker that they miss the message. Listening with ears, eyes, heart, undivided attention, and with the intention to receive the intended message are keys to active listening.

Social Expectations

In Western culture, certain behaviors are expected of a good listener, including "attending skills" and "follow-up skills." Attending skills include not interrupting the speaker, listening for what he/she intends to say rather than what we want or think he/she will say, holding eye contact, using open body language, and offering some encouraging responses ("Wow!" "Then what happened?" "Really?") and actions (nodding, smiling).

Personal Behaviors. To form a more accurate impression of a speaker's intended message, we must pay constant, careful attention. When we lose our concentration, we also lose much of the information. There are a number of ways to help ourselves focus on listening and collecting information.

- Limit distractions. Change places to promote concentration.
- Look at the speaker. Observe body language (open versus closed), listen to the tone of voice (pitch, quality, and timbre), and note facial expressions as clues to emotions. In many instances, the medium is the message—most of the message is communicated non-verbally.[16]
- Focus your attention on the meaning of the words; use signals (head nodding, smiles) to indicate you understand.
- Create pictures in your mind of what you're hearing.
- Visualize how this information fits with what you already know and what it means to you. Expect to act upon what you hear.

NO PUT-DOWNS:

To not use words, actions, and/or body language to degrade, humiliate, or dishonor others

What Are Put-Downs?

Put-downs are words and body language that imply, "I am better than you. I have more money than you, I am smarter than you, I have more options than you." The objective is to elevate the speaker's social standing and power. By creating a laugh at someone else's expense, the speaker gains power in the situation by controlling the behavior of others and undermining relationships of those in the audience have with the targeted person. Put-downs are also a way of avoiding the real issues of the moment. They often reveal unconscious feelings of jealousy, anger, fear, or inadequacy. Whether from one person or a group, the goal of put-downs is always the same—humiliation, power, control, and increased social status.

The body language of put-downs—actions and body movements, such as rolling the eyes, tapping the forehead, caricaturing, and so forth—are honed to an art in sitcoms and other popular media in our society. They are every bit as powerful as words.

Sometimes put-downs affect us more deeply than usual. For example, when they're spoken by people we like and trust or by people we want to like us, the results are devastating. We feel betrayed. If the people whose opinion we so value express something negative about us, then it must really be so. Also, if the comments are aimed at a sensitive area (e.g., physical changes during puberty, being overweight or underweight, being an immigrant with beginning English skills), students often feel shame about something over which they have little or no control. Similarly, when we receive put-downs in front of our peers, the humiliation and shame deepen as we lose face.

Why Practice No Put-Downs?

Put-downs among adults produce a lack of trust which is extremely detrimental to an educational agency, especially when it trickles down to influence students' attitudes and behaviors. If a staff is to pursue efforts to improve the school program, put-downs must be eliminated. To be open to learning is to be vulnerable. We're open to snickers when we make mistakes or admit we can't answer a question. Every student should be able to approach new opportunities and learning experiences without dreading verbal abuse.

When we refuse to allow put-downs in the classroom, we're teaching respect for all people, ideas, and situations. We're building a positive emotional climate in our classroom so that our students feel comfortable enough to risk an answer, offer a thought, and try some new skill without worrying about mocking remarks or gestures. This is particularly important for children in the middle position of sibling birth order whose skills and knowledge can't match their older sibling but who don't have the safety of being the baby. Prohibiting the use of disparaging remarks is akin to constructing an invisible shield that protects and nurtures.

How Do You Practice It?

To change a negative habit to a more positive one, we first must recognize the negative behavior. Thus, we must teach students to recognize put-downs and become sensitive to their effects despite their pervasiveness in our mass media and society. Many students look on the word plays of put-downs as a form of humor, overlooking that it's at the expense of others.

Next, we must create an action plan to eliminate put-downs and encourage respect for others.

Recognizing the Need to Change. Select a video clip ripe with put-downs. Have your students identify and count the put-downs they hear and see. Discuss with your students how they would feel if they were on the receiving end of these put-downs. Next, focus on comments heard in the classroom and school common areas. Ask your students to observe the participants. Who is handing out the put-downs? Who is the brunt of the put-downs? Who has power and social position and who doesn't? Refer to Glasser's needs list: belonging, power, fun, and freedom.[17] Which of these fundamental human needs is the speaker missing? If put-downs occur in your classroom, what's missing from your classroom environment? Look for patterns that demand change and then, with your students' help, create an action plan.

The Importance of Modeling. Creating an environment free of put-downs requires constant modeling by all adults. The entire school staff (administrators, teachers, aides, custodial workers, cafeteria staff, and parent volunteers) need to understand their role as role models for students. A "Do as I say but not as I do" atmosphere doesn't work. Post the Lifelong Guidelines/LIFESKILLS around the school for all to see and follow. Initiate discussions about the harmful effects of put-downs. If a put-down is heard, deal with it immediately using a calm, rational manner before the situation escalates.

Taking Responsibility for Eliminating Put-Downs. Everyone plays a part in eliminating put-downs. To begin cleansing your classroom of put-downs, eliminate the put-down banter that is passed off as humor. Recall a comment that had dual interpretations and then the speaker quickly said, "Just kidding!"—but you never knew the intent for sure. As the saying goes, "Many a true word is said in jest." Second, agree on a "cancel" signal. Whenever someone says a put-down, other family members simply say, "Cancel." The hurt is canceled, the power play is canceled.

PERSONAL BEST

One's best possible performance given the time and resources available

What Is Personal Best?

For those using the ITI model, the Lifelong Guideline of Personal Best is defined by the 18 LIFESKILLS defined here. To pursue one's personal best means working to develop and strengthen each LIFESKILL.

Quality work is never an accident; it is always the result of combining clear goals, high standards, knowledge and skills, and genuine effort. It represents the wisest choice among many options matched with commitment, perseverance, and wise use of time, talents, and resources. There is no one way to achieve a sense of fulfillment, but doing one's personal best on a consistent basis is the best road we know to reach that end.

The Lifelong Guideline of Personal Best is not about treats, rewards, or bonuses; it's about a deep sense of personal satisfaction for a job well done, mastering a skill, or making a contribution.

Personal Best Is Not a Fixed Standard. Personal Best is not about perfectionism. Personal Best is the result of our consistent pursuit of a moving target within an ever-changing terrain. Our performance in the same activity looks different over time. As our competence grows, our performance improves. As the tools, time, and resources available to us improve, our performance improves.

For example, while supporting your family (emotionally, financially, and physically), you might take up jogging. You try hard to improve your running technique but you struggle to complete the course. You're doing your personal best in both areas—family life and jogging—but your jogging skill and capabilities in no way compare to those of a professional athlete who devotes full focus and

LIFESKILLS

CARING: To feel and show concern for others

COMMON SENSE: To use good judgment

COOPERATION: To work together toward a common goal or purpose

COURAGE: To act according to one's beliefs despite fear of adverse consequences

CURIOSITY: A desire to investigate and seek understanding of one's world

EFFORT: To do your best

FLEXIBILITY: To be willing to alter plans when necessary

FRIENDSHIP: To make and keep a friend through mutual trust and caring

INITIATIVE: To do something, of one's own free will, because it needs to be done

INTEGRITY: To act according to a sense of what's right and wrong

ORGANIZATION: To plan, arrange, and implement in an orderly way; to keep things orderly and ready to use

PATIENCE: To wait calmly for someone or something

PERSEVERANCE: To keep at it

PRIDE: Satisfaction from doing one's personal best

PROBLEM SOLVING: To create solutions to difficult situations and everyday problems

RESOURCEFULNESS: To respond to challenges and opportunities in innovative and creative ways

RESPONSIBILITY: To respond when appropriate; to be accountable for one's actions

SENSE OF HUMOR: To laugh and be playful without harming others

time to his/her athletic pursuits. Personal Best is using the utmost effort possible and striving for a heightened stage of excellence. This may or may not translate into being Number 1, the winner, the hero; in the real world, such status is rare. But all of us can achieve our personal best.

The Lifelong Guideline of Personal Best is one's best possible performance at the time, under the circumstances of the moment, and using the tools, time, knowledge/skill, and resources available at the moment. This, of course, takes into account the LIFESKILL of Resourcefulness!

Personal Best Is a Mindset. What drives you to do your personal best? The most important element is a clear vision of your goals and personal performance standards and love of what you are doing. When such vision and love are united, you want to do your best! The secret about goals is to make them personal—to focus on your performance, not on the status or glamour of the project, job, or assignment. Athletes strive to surpass their previous personal accomplishments. This provides a vision that pushes them to constantly improve. Then, love the process of working toward your goals, celebrating each step toward your vision.

Doing one's personal best is a way of life, not an isolated incident.

Why Practice Personal Best?

Aristotle wrote, "We are what we repeatedly do. Excellence, then, is not an act, but a habit."[18] The Lifelong Guideline of Personal Best is transferable from one sector of life to another—in family and social life, in one's job, in religious experiences, and in recreational activities. You can't work on excellence in one area and not have it show up in other areas. But the converse is also true: Refusing to do your personal best in one area will show up as laziness or avoidance in other areas.

Some people start out by thinking, "Doing my personal best is too difficult! I'll have to work really hard." But think of the opposite—do you really want to work toward personal worst or mediocrity? You may have to expend the same amount of effort to achieve less. Does that make sense? Self-respect—and the respect of others—depends heavily upon performing consistently at our personal best.

How Do You Practice It?

As we're sure the Army has discovered, the slogan "Be all that you can be!" is far more easily said than done. Not that it is a mystery. But to achieve our personal best requires a broad range of personal and social skills that need to be learned early and practiced daily until they become dependable habits of mind rather than now-and-then skills we pull up when we get in a pinch.

The Lifelong Guideline of Personal Best is defined by 18 LIFESKILLS as shown on this page. To the surprise of many, children seem to have an intuitive grasp of the LIFESKILLS. The word and concept of "perseverance," for example, is no hurdle at all for kindergarteners. And they seem delighted to be let in on the secret of how to succeed at things—when they want something, they know how to go about getting it. What a wonderful gift so early in life. One might say that the road to success in life is paved with 23 yellow bricks: the 18 LIFESKILLS and five Lifelong Guidelines.

In addition to keeping our feet on the yellow brick road, we must also:

- Identify a vision, set personal goals.
- Continuously self-evaluate in order to improve as needed (attitude, performance, or goal-setting) and to revise or completely redesign our plans as needed.
- Welcome suggestions from others who have different perspectives and who may have unique experiences to share.
- Understand that we will make mistakes but that we can turn them into life lessons; realize that we have discovered a way ***not*** to do something and must fine tune our thinking. Thomas Edison discovered over 2,000 ways not to make the light bulb before he found a way that worked.[19] We should expect to refine our methods, thinking, and techniques—any variation that might improve us or our product. We can feel pride in our heart when all of these LIFESKILL efforts combine as one and provide us with the experience of doing our personal best.

Does this sound like a recipe for adults only? Not true. Even five year olds can set a vision of what they would like to be when they grow up although it ften changes weekly. At five, many of the skills children learn have feedback built into the learning event; they don't have to ask, "Teacher, is this right?" They are able to judge for themselves. As for welcoming suggestions from others, they are used to getting plenty of advice from grown ups! And when it comes to learning from mistakes, young children do it with much more grace than adults do.

Can children younger than five learn these aspects of doing the Lifelong Guideline of Personal Best? In their own age-appropriate ways, absolutely! It may in fact be more difficult for high school students and adults to learn the Lifelong Guideline of Personal Best because they must first shed old attitudes and habits of mind.

A Reminder

Most of pages 8.9-16 is excerpted from *Tools for Citizenship & Life: Using the ITI Lifelong Guidelines & LIFESKILLS in Your Classroom* by Sue Pearson (see order information at the back of this book). The book also provides a separate chapter for each LIFESKILL that discusses what the LIFESKILL is, why it is important, and how to practice it. Most importantly, the book contains 500 inquiries, activities ready-to-go for teaching and student practice of each Lifelong Guideline and LIFESKILL. It also recommends high quality literature books whose characters illustrate the Lifelong Guidelines and LIFESKILLS—successes and possible life consequences if they are not used. We strongly recommend this book to you. It will make your first day of school and succeeding weeks much, much easier.

Notes

1 Karen D. Olsen, instructor, extension course in brain-compatible learning at the University of California, Davis, 1993.

2 James M.Kouzes and Barry Z. Posner, *The Leadership Challenge* (San Francisco, CA: Jossey-Bass, Inc.), 21-22.

3 Dr. Abraham Kryger, D.M.D., M.D., *Benefits of Telling the Truth.* (http:www. wellnessmd.com/tellingtruth.html). See also Bill Moyer, *The Truth About Lies,* videotape, 1987.

4 The lie detector test is based on physiological evidence of the body's reaction to lying—more rapid pulse and rise in blood pressure. Also see *The Orman Health Letter* published monthly by TRO Productions, Inc., Baltimore, M.D., and http://www.wellnessmd.com/tellingtruth.html

5 Kryger, "Benefits of".

6 Mark Twain, *Notebook,* 1984.

7 Kryger, "Benefits of".

8 Ibid.

9 This definition of listening comes from an *est* communication workshop developed by Werner Earhart in the 1970s. Earhart believed that communication is an act of intention: The listener must intend to "get" what the speaker intends to say; the speaker must intend to speak the truth about what he/she thinks and feels.

10 Not surprisingly, the more hours spent in front of a television, the less time spent developing language. See Nanci Bell, *Visualizing and Verbaliz-ing for Improved Language Comprehension (Palo Alto, CA: Gander Publishing, 1991),*. 21.

11 For a discussion of the meaning of the Chinese symbol for "to listen," see Jeanne Gibbs, *TRIBES: A New Way of Learning and Being Together* (Windsor, CA: CenterSource Systems, LLC, 2001), 93-94.

12 Bell, *Visualizing and Verbalizing,* xxi.

13 Aphasia is the loss of one's ability to speak or understand spoken or written language due to disease or injury of the brain.

14 Bell, *Visualizing and Verbalizing,* xxi.

15 Gibbs, *TRIBES,* p. 93-94. The book also provides many ready-to-go activities for students to practice active listening.

16 "The Importance of Effective Communication," (Northeastern University, College of Business Administration, October, 1999. http://www.cba.neu.edu/~ewertheim/ interper/commun.htm).

17 William, Glasser, M.D. *Choice Theory: A New Psychology of Personal Freedom,* (New York: HarperPerennial, 1998), 31-41.

18 Aristotle, *Nicomachean Ethics,* 350 BC., (W.D. Ross, translator, *The Internet Classics Archives/Works by Aristotle,* http://classics.mit.edu/Browse/browse-Aristotle.html).

19 Jack Canfield and Mark Victor, *A 2nd Helping of Chicken Soup for the Soul: 101 More Stories to Open the Heart and Rekindle the Spirit* (Deerfield Beach, Florida: Health Communications, Inc., 1995), 253. See also *Thomas Alva Edison Home Page,* (http://www.thomasedison.com)

Chapter 9: Getting Started with the Lifelong Guidelines and LIFESKILLS

Three Purposes of Ongoing Use of the Lifelong Guidelines/LIFESKILLS

The Lifelong Guidelines and LIFESKILLS provide the basis for three important functions of a bodybrain-compatible learning environment:

- They are the agreed-upon behaviors for all and thus replace the *rules* of traditional "discipline" programs.
- They provide a safe environment for creating and maintaining a sense of community
- They describe the behaviors of civil discourse which are the foundation of citizenship

The Lifelong Guidelines/LIFESKILLS As Agreed-Upon Behaviors

The difference between agreed-upon behaviors and rules is not subtle; it is the difference between behavior that is internally motivated and monitored versus behavior that is externally imposed and controlled—and therefore typically resisted. Your goal is to have students who commit themselves to living the Lifelong Guidelines and LIFESKILLS because they make their lives work, not because they're what the teacher makes them do.

Most of this chapter is about how to teach the Lifelong Guidelines/LIFESKILLS in a way that enables students to understand their power to make their lives work—in the classroom today and, more importantly, now and later in life. See pages 9.9 through the end of the chapter.

Creating a Community of Learners Through the Lifelong Guidelines/LIFESKILLS

Because creating and maintaining a community of learners is such a powerful engine for improving academic performance, it should be your number one goal beginning the first day of school and every day thereafter.

In the ITI model, creating community occurs in three stages:

- Developing a sense of belonging
- Creating common ground
- Taking action

Developing a Sense of Belonging

The need to belong is just that—a psychological imperative, not a luxury.[1] Once it is taken care of, students can direct their attention to other matters of importance in the classroom. All five Lifelong Guidelines plus the LIFESKILLS, particularly Caring, Cooperation, and Friendship, provide a useful foundation for creating a safe environment in which a sense of belonging can develop.*

* Although time spent developing a sense of community may initially seem to be an unaffordable luxury in the face of today's curriculum demands, the many school shootings and tragedies tell us otherwise. Common descriptors of such students include: he never belonged, he was a loner who kept to himself, he was never accepted, he was different, he was an outcast, he was teased/bullied, no one had any idea that he was struggling with so many problems . . . he was just a quiet kid that kept to himself.

If we want to belong to a group, we must in turn be willing to extend an invitation to others to be included. This sense of reciprocity helps override the in-group, out-group, us versus them mentality of cliques and gangs. It builds the foundation for tolerating diversity and accepting differences. It is the basis for respect and self-respect.

Willingness to include others is modeled by the teacher in the welcome letter to students before school starts, by standing at the door every morning to give a personal good morning (more than a polite hello, this includes an emotional check-in), and saying farewell at the end of the day (with a thank you for a good day and looking forward to seeing you tomorrow). This willingness to be inclusive, rather than exclusive, is modeled throughout the day in equitable and appropriate treatment of students—no favorites, none ignored or addressed with short temper, all accepted as full members of the group. This equity and respect of others is also put forth as a clear expectation of each student and his/her treatment of others.

The LIFESKILL of Friendship is multifaceted; learning it begins the first day of class. We must teach students the importance of being inclusive in our relationships with others, to understand that a close friendship with one person does not mean we can't also have a close friendship with another or several others. Opening ourselves up to multiple close friendships is not a sign of disloyalty or an indication that one of the friendships is less valuable to us. Instead, it may be an indication of many personal interests, hobbies, personality comfort zone, or proximity (neighborhood or groups we belong to that meet weekly).

At this first stage of community development, students need lots of interaction to get to know each other and practice the Lifelong Guidelines—Trustworthiness, Truthfulness, Active Listening, No Put-Downs, and Personal Best. They need opportunities to explore life's perennial questions: Who are we? What will we do together? How will we treat each other? Will I be safe? Will I be allowed to be myself? All of such discovery requires that students move beyond stereotypes to see each classmate as an individual yet as a member of their classroom and Learning Club and to understand and appreciate each other's gifts and talents. This stage of building a community of learners parallels the formin' stage, the first of four stages described by Bruce Wayne Tuckman, a pioneer in group development, in 1965.[2] Tuckman's descriptions of group development are widely used in business and governmental settings as well as in education.

Developing a sense of belonging is built over time through many shared activities that add meaning to students' lives. Be aware that you will need many such activities because this stage must be nurtured throughout the school year. It is not something initially achieved and then left behind; it must be reinforced and nurtured all year long, becoming stronger over time in order to support work that challenges the group because it surfaces disagreements, demands resolution of problems, and necessitates compromise.

Building Community
• Developing a Sense of Belonging
• Creating Common Ground
• Taking Action

Plan activities daily for the first month of school no matter the grade level. Continue at least weekly the remainder of the school year (more frequently if you have new students joining your class). When your students start to wrangle with each other, you'll know it's time to bring out more activities and do some reteaching.

Don't try to reinvent the wheel; there are excellent, ready-made resources. We recommend you own a copy of the following: *Cooperative Learning* and a set of *SmartCards* both by Spencer Kagan. There are also many on-line resources. Using Google, search keywords such as professional development activities, team building activities, inclusion activities, and ice breakers. You will find many activities in the public domain that can be used in any way you choose without copyright infringement.

See examples of how to weave these activities into the first day of school in Chapter 7, beginning on page 7.18 for primary grades and page 7.26 for intermediate grades.

Keep in mind that this stage may take days or months depending upon factors such as the following:

- The level of personal and social skills your students bring to the classroom
- Student turnover in your class
- The amount of group disruption due to extensive pullout programming
- The consistency of your modeling and expectations
- The focus you give to community development (frequency and intensity of initial teaching/practice, reteaching, use of the teachable moment, and so forth)

Whatever the challenges, **do not** succumb to the urge to move on before this stage is solidly in place.

Students Are Showing Signs of Developing a Sense of Belonging When They

- Know each other's names
- Are participating members of their Learning Club
- Are actively listened to when they speak and actively listen when others speak
- Feel free to speak up during class and Town Hall Meetings

- Enjoy coming to school and indicate they like their classmates and teacher
- Use the Lifelong Guidelines and LIFESKILLS with others and expect others to use them in school interactions
- Refrain from Put-Downs and readily and sincerely give appreciations of others
- Are willing to work with a new study partner or group
- Welcome and immediately include new students and visitors into their Learning Club and the class
- Know and appreciate the strengths of each individual in the class
- Are sensitive to what is happening to others in the class and consistently use the LIFESKILLS of Caring and Friendship so that there are no loners or isolated students

Students Need More Practice Developing a Sense of Belonging When They

- Do not feel free to speak up or share ideas during Learning Club, class, and/or Town Hall Meetings
- Do not actively participate in Learning Club and class activities
- Do not use the Lifelong Guidelines and LIFESKILLS in classroom interactions
- Do not actively listen to others
- Do not welcome new students and visitors into their Learning Club and class
- Put others down
- Treat people preferentially; have special buddies and exclude others from membership in their circle of friends
- Notice someone alone and do nothing to invite him/her to join in (classroom, playground, cafeteria)
- Don't create a sense of inclusion for new students and other visitors
- Don't offer help and directions to a visitor on campus

Creating Common Ground

To create common ground, you must help students to:

- Create and maintain the conditions that make it safe to disagree
- Understand that it is okay to hold differing opinions
- Realize that it is equally okay to change one's mind without it being considered a sign of weakness or of losing face

Just as we expect citizens in our melting pot of nationalities, races, creeds, religions, socioeconomic status, and languages to work together to make our democratic government work, so we expect it in the classroom. Just realize in advance that this takes lots of practice, patience, and perseverance—all guided by a high level of intention that common ground can and will be achieved.

This is the stormin' stage described by Tuckman,[3] characterized by challenging the leadership (yours and the group's), experimenting with power and how to wield it, sticking to a position out of pride and refusal to back down before one's peers, learning when and how to lead and when and how to follow, etc. Conflict at this stage, and in life, is inevitable. Your goal must be to help students learn effective skills and strategies to navigate through conflict rather than to minimize or shrink from it.

In this stage of creating community, students must make a commitment to community—Spock's mantra (of Star Trek), "the good of the many outweighs the needs of a few." They must also transition from following the Lifelong Guidelines/LIFESKILLS as agreed-upon behaviors to using the Lifelong Guidelines/LIFESKILLS as foundation stones with which to build their lives.

Even with daily work on this stage, expect that it will take time for students to internalize the processes. There are no magic formulas. Use your common sense, your knowledge of developmental levels of students (primary, intermediate, middle school, high school), and your knowledge of this particular group of students. What you're creating is an experience of what is possible when people commit themselves to work together to accomplish tasks that make a difference in the world. Citizenship succeeds or fails at this step in community building—in a classroom, a homeowners' association, or a city council.

The depth of coming to know and respect others while creating common ground helps open up a grasp of the richness of the wider world and a curiosity to explore it. The sooner students discover that there is more than one valid point of view to consider, the sooner they can begin to appreciate and participate in the role of informed citizen.

For resources supporting the developing of this stage, see those mentioned on page 9.3 plus the discussion of conducting a Town Hall Meeting that follows.

Students Are Showing Signs of Creating Common Ground When They

- Are willing to remind each other to use the Lifelong Guidelines and LIFESKILLS
- Feel free to express their opinions in their Learning Club and the classroom
- Feel free to disagree and yet are willing to change their position when the facts warrant it or when the majority votes for another position
- Focus on the facts and merits of an issue, not on the person who advocates it
- Look forward to solving problems and making decisions because they are confident in the group's (Learning Club and class) ability to do so and feel safe during the process
- Are willing to iron out differences for the good of the group rather than press for a win-lose solution
- Have developed skills to resolve conflicts one-on-one or through more formal means such as mediation and Town Hall Meetings
- Are comfortable with being the leader for a project yet willing to allow and support someone else to lead when that person has been assigned that responsibility by the group

Students Need More Practice Creating Common Ground When They

- Refuse to listen to classmates who are trying to remind them to use the Lifelong Guidelines and LIFESKILLS
- Continue arguing for their position because they don't want to give in even when it is not the solution or course of action voted on by the group
- Refuse to support the action agreed to by the group because it wasn't their idea
- Argue positions based on who advocates it rather than on its facts and merits
- Cause disruptions so the group can't reach agreement or bring an issue to a vote
- Have to win at all costs and neglect to think of the good of the group
- Undermine implementation of an agreed-upon course of action

Taking Action

Taking Action is the use of community to achieve academically—individually and as a group—and to perform any number of tasks, especially social/political action projects that emerge from studying the curriculum.[4] As Herbert Spencer, English philosopher noted: "The great aim of education is not knowledge, but action."[5]

The goals of this stage of group development are to:

- Strengthen the sense of belonging through working together to accomplish an agreed-upon task
- Give students practice in applying the personal and social skills needed to create and maintain common ground
- Provide practice using the concepts and skills of our curriculum in real-world situations
- Give students practice in using the levers of our democratic society to change for the common good

Teaching students how and when and why they should Take Action is the ultimate purpose of public education, the reason we have tax payer-supported free education in this country.[6] That we should have taught them the basic skills at high levels is a given. That they should understand the concepts and issues before them is a given. That there has been rigor and high expectations is a given. Thomas Jefferson understood that a democratic society was and continues to be dependent upon public education for all, public education that understands and remains true to its mission to create an informed, participating citizenry.

Students Are Showing Signs of Taking Action When They

- Help develop inquiries for curriculum content and select those that most challenge their ability to apply the concepts and skills to real-world situations
- Invite classmates to join them in self-generated projects
- Take responsibility for helping set the agenda and conduct Town Hall Meetings
- Understand the need to give and serve others in the community and larger world (citizens acting individually and in groups)
- Generate ideas for Social/Political Action Projects
- Carry the majority of the responsibility for planning and carrying out Social/Political Action Projects
- Self-organize within their Learning Club to take on projects to improve the school and community and to help those less fortunate

Students Need More Practice Taking Action When They

- Need frequent reminders to use the Lifelong Guidelines/LIFESKILLS
- Remain unfocused; do not take charge of their own learning; are content to let time slip by; don't set personal or group learning goals
- Need to be motivated or prodded by their teacher to work on their projects
- Wait for their teacher to select and plan Social/Political Action Projects
- Don't understand the need to help improve their school or community or to help those less fortunate than they

Putting It All Together: Implementing The Lifelong Guidelines Through Town Hall Meetings

As stated before, the Lifelong Guidelines and LIFESKILLS are not meant to be the basis for a rule-based discipline program; they are the ingredients necessary to build a community of learners. They are for everyone—a common language for agreed-upon behaviors of all staff (certified and classified), students, and parents. They solve the mystery of how to be successful in the classroom, the school, and in life. Their use is a tangible commitment to creating a sense of group—a community of learners—a prerequisite to improving academic outcomes. They are both context and vehicle for practicing citizenship in the classroom through Town Hall Meetings.

Why Town Hall Meetings

Community does not happen accidentally or overnight. Both teacher and students must share this goal and be intentional about developing it. Getting together in formal and informal ways in order to get to know one another better and solve problems facing the group is as old as time and critical to the democratic processes of our society.

The commonsense core of group-building is this: You can't build a sense of community if you don't get together and act like a community. Town Hall Meetings provide opportunities to teach students how to become involved, informed citizens. The Lifelong Guidelines and LIFESKILLS provide the context for being together (the behaviors and skills that allow community to develop) and, often, the agenda items for the meeting (the behaviors not being followed that cause problems among members of the group).

The purposes for calling a Town Hall Meeting are to:

- Nurture ongoing community building at each stage of group development through a variety of agendas such as:
  - Selected activities at each stage of group development
  - Sharing acknowledgements
  - Celebrating accomplishments
  - Introducing a new student to the classroom
  - Planning and carrying out Social/Political Action Projects
- Solve problems affecting the entire class
- Develop or revise written procedures and other guidelines or rubrics to create greater student self-direction in learning and self-governance of the classroom
- Make decisions about class projects
- Learn the necessary skills to lead and participate in formal meetings
- Experience firsthand the civics lessons described in the state/district curriculum standards[7]

Town Hall Meetings as a Vehicle for Group Development

Not all activities to create a community of learners occur in Town Hall Meetings. However, an important goal of every Town Hall Meeting is to further develop a sense of community. Therefore, always make sure that the task you ask of students in a Town Hall Meeting is clearly articulated, appropriate for the age of your students, and suitable for the stage of community development at the moment. For example, don't expect students to handle the pressurse of persuasion or influence based in social standing and still come to agreement on something before you've built a sense of belonging and they've learned to work through conflict to create common ground. (Refer to pages 9.2-6.)

How to Start

For the first two weeks of school, Town Hall Meetings should be conducted every day, led by the teacher. However, as student skill develops, students may request a meeting and may co-chair selected meetings as appropriate.

After two weeks, evaluate your students' progress. Do they need more experience with Town Hall Meetings to master the personal and social skills needed? Or is the need for group problem solving a daily occurrence? If so, continue meeting frequently, daily if needed. As students become more adept at creating common ground, try scheduling Town Hall Meetings just twice a week, adding additional meetings as needed.

Let agendas for meetings emerge from the needs of the classroom. For example:

- Build a sense of community
- Implement the Lifelong Guidelines/LIFESKILLS
- Develop/revise written procedures for guiding personal and group behaviors (such as morning entry or end of day procedures)
- Share acknowledgments
- Solve behavior problems that affect the class

Teach Students Strategies for Coping and Cleaning Things Up

Living the Lifelong Guidelines and LIFESKILLS requires two key strategies: Coping when others don't follow the Lifelong Guidelines and LIFESKILLS and cleaning things up when we (students and teacher) don't follow them.

Coping Strategies

Strategies for coping:[8] include

- Ignore it.
- Walk away or do hook-ups (see *Brain Gym*).
- Go to another activity.
- Talk it out.
- Use an "I" message. I feel ____ when _____. I need ____.
- Go back and try again.
- Apologize if needed.
- Tell him/her/them to stop.
- Stop to cool off.
- Count from 1 to 25 to cool off.
- Take 10 deep breaths and release them slowly.

- Problem-solve with a friend or with your Learning Club.
- Add the issue to a Town Hall Meeting agenda.
- Draw a picture to show what happened; share it with someone.
- Write about the incident in your journal.
- Do a "freeze frame" (see *HeartMath Solutions*).

Strategies for Cleaning Things Up

Strategies for cleaning things up include:

- Make sure you understand how you made the person feel when you didn't follow the Lifelong Guidelines and LIFESKILLS.
- Apologize with more than a simple "I'm sorry." Be specific. Restate the harm that you did, such as hurt their feelings, humiliated them in front of others, bruised their arm, or broke something.
- Ask what you can do to repair the harm and what you can do to make it up to them. If it's within reason and appropriate to the damage inflicted, do it without delay and do it sincerely.
- Learn from your mistakes. Ask yourself why you did what you did. Was it to feel important? To avoid looking weak or less than perfect? To avoid consequences for earlier misbehavior? Remember, whittling away at others never makes us feel better about ourselves. Figure out how to meet your own needs. That is your responsibility, something no one else can do for you.

Reflective thinking so that we understand why we did what we did and how it affected the other person is critical to learning to change and master our behavior—to have emotions but not be run by them. Never underestimate the importance of questions that cause students to reflect on their internal thoughts and reactions to external events. It is the examined life that Socrates so prized.

See discussions of reflective thinking on pages 1.25, 2.7-8, 3.16-17, 4.21-23, 5.17, and 10.12-13.

How to Teach the Lifelong Guidelines and LIFESKILLS

There are innumerable ways to begin using the Lifelong Guidelines and LIFESKILLS. This chapter contains advice from those who have gone before you as described in *Tools for Citizenship and Life*[9] by Sue Pearson. We highly recommend you own your own copy of this book and use it daily.

To get off to a good start, plan thoroughly before you begin. Some steps are mechanical, such as setting and sticking to an organized schedule and using a variety of instructional strategies to teach, reteach, and reinforce (see Chapters 10 and 14). Other steps will require personal transitions. Be open to the power that the Lifelong Guidelines and LIFESKILLS can have in your life and in that of your students. Your most rewarding and satisfying years of teaching are just around the corner!

Consider the following planning steps:

- Take time to reflect; do a self-evaluation of your own understanding and practice of the Lifelong Guidelines and LIFESKILLS; set personal goals for improving.
- Start with the Lifelong Guidelines; begin the first day of school.

- Create a schedule for teaching and implementing the Lifelong Guidelines and LIFESKILLS for the first four to five weeks; know what you want to teach and the activities the students will do each day.
- Teach the Lifelong Guidelines/LIFESKILLS through weekly (daily in the early weeks of the year) literature selections that you read aloud to the class and for other reading assignments.
- Use graphic organizers to make the behaviors associated with the Lifelong Guidelines and LIFESKILLS.
- Use real-world events and to capture the teachable moment.

Take Time to Reflect

Before you begin, take time to assess your own personal understanding of the Lifelong Guidelines and LIFESKILLS.

The Importance of Self-Evaluation. Evaluate yourself in relation to each of the Lifelong Guidelines and the LIFESKILLS. Which ones are strengths for you? Are some "just okay?" Are some not as strong as they need to be? Remember, these behavior guidelines are something you must live and model, not just teach about.

If you're like co-author Karen Olsen, some will make you squirm. Organization? Karen had to jump up from the computer and start organizing and cleaning her house. You can't just talk about the Lifelong Guidelines and LIFESKILLS, you have to live them! (See the discussion about modeling in Chapter 10.)

Bring It Home. The classroom is your living room and students need to feel welcome. As you reflect on your own use of the Lifelong Guidelines and LIFESKILLS as a teacher, it often helps to picture how you would want your own children, nieces and nephews, or grandchildren treated; then, commit yourself to treating other people's children that same way. The quality and nature of the connections between the teacher and his/her students, and among students, are the basis for all else in the classroom, especially academic learning. Model the behaviors you would show to honored guests visiting your home and business—behaviors that exemplify the Lifelong Guidelines of Trustworthiness, Truthfulness, Active Listening, No Put-Downs, and Personal Best defined by the LIFESKILLS.

Start with the Lifelong Guidelines the First Day of School

What usually works best is to introduce all five Lifelong Guidelines at once as a collection of behaviors to enhance learning and being together for everyone. Then, go back and teach each Lifelong Guideline in-depth using the instructional strategies described in Chapters 7, 10, and 14.

Enhancing the Physical Environment. The physical environment sends a continuous message to students. So, design it with care. Choose a focal point in the classroom/school to display[1] the Lifelong Guidelines and LIFESKILLS* for immediate reference. The back of the room, for instance, is not a handy place. Until everyone is totally familiar and comfortable with the Lifelong Guidelines, daily visual reminders will help in recognizing and identifying expectations. With the terms and definitions posted, it's easier to remember to use target talk (see Chapter 21) as a reinforcement strategy. Some teachers also prepare copies of the Lifelong Guidelines (and later, the LIFESKILLS) for every student to place in his/her binder or notebook. Providing copies for parents helps to provide a basis for common vocabulary between the home and school and allows for reinforcement and connections outside of the school day.

Parent/Family Involvement. Parents want to know what is happening in the classroom. The Lifelong Guidelines and LIFESKILLS are easy to share with parents and readily understandable.

Whether you're part of a schoolwide effort or working alone in your classroom, it's important to keep family members informed of the behaviors that are expected in class.

A newsletter is one vehicle for building understanding of the Guidelines. First, send a general introduction to all the Lifelong Guidelines and LIFESKILLS (see the sample letters at the end of this chapter). In future issues, offer more information about the specific activities students will be doing.

For parents who want to reinforce the Lifelong Guidelines and LIFESKILLS at home, we recommend the parent version of *Tools for Citizenship and Life: Using the Lifelong Guidelines and LIFESKILLS in Your Classroom* called *Character Begins at Home: Using the ITI Lifelong Guidelines and LIFESKILLS in Your Home* by Sue Pearson and Karen D. Olsen. These two books work as companions to nurture the home-school partnership.

Create a Schedule

Good teaching is not an accident. You must have a month-long plan that tells you what to do from day to day. The following plans are recommended by numerous ITI practitioners and associates of Susan Kovalik & Associates. Adopt or adapt to fit the needs of your students.

Plan #1: One a Week. The "one a week" plan is a popular one with ITI teachers. Its strength is that it allows you to focus in depth on one Lifelong Guideline (and later on, one LIFESKILL) at a time. This is particularly important with younger students.

- Week One—Trustworthiness
- Week Two—Truthfulness
- Week Three—Active Listening
- Week Four—No Put-Downs
- Week Five—Personal Best

The following outline offers suggestions for teaching and providing practice for the Lifelong Guideline each day during each of the five weeks. For example, for the first week focusing on the Lifelong Guideline of Trustworthiness:

- Monday—definition of the Lifelong Guideline of Trustworthiness illustrated through literature and song
- Tuesday—video segment showing both use and lack of use of Trustworthiness plus discussion and role playing
- Wednesday—song, T-chart, and literature illustrating Trustworthiness
- Thursday—role playing and literature illustrating Trustworthiness
- Friday—song, role playing, and journal writing illustrating Trustworthiness

For the second week focusing on the Lifelong Guideline of Truthfulness, you could use the same combination of teaching strategies as shown above or change them as you see fit. Likewise, for the third, fourth, and fifth weeks focus on the remaining Lifelong Guidelines of Active Listening, No Put-Downs, and Personal Best. Follow the suggestions or feel free to change them according to your intuition.

For descriptions of the teaching strategies referred to above, see Chapter 10.

Plan #2: One a Day and Repeat. The "one a day and repeat" plan is also easy to use. Designed by Joy Raboli, it allows students to see where they are going by the end of the first week. This is useful for older students from upper elementary through high school. You decide based on your own students' needs, learning patterns, and temperament.

Under this plan, set aside a small portion of each day to develop a deeper understanding of the Lifelong Guidelines. The time of day isn't important, although most teachers prefer to have a set schedule so they are sure to teach them each day. This plan focuses on a particular Lifelong Guideline each day of the week and repeats the week throughout the month.

- Monday—Trustworthiness
- Tuesday—Truthfulness
- Wednesday—Active Listening
- Thursday—No Put-Downs
- Friday—Personal Best

For example, a schedule for Plan #2 might look like this:

LIFELONG GUIDELINES
TRUSTWORTHINESS TRUTHFULNESS
ACTIVE LISTENING NO PUT-DOWNS
PERSONAL BEST

WEEK	Mon	Tue	Wed	Thu	Fri
	DAY ONE TRUSTWORTHINESS	**DAY TWO TRUTHFULNESS**	**DAY THREE ACTIVE LISTENING**	**DAY FOUR NO PUT-DOWNS**	**DAY FIVE PERSONAL BEST**
ONE	**TRUSTWORTHINESS** Define~Story~Discuss	**TRUTHFULNESS** Define~Story~Discuss	**ACTIVE LISTENING** Define~Story~Discuss	**NO PUT-DOWNS** Define~Story~Discuss	**PERSONAL BEST** Define~Story~Discuss
TWO	**TRUSTWORTHINESS** Video~Tally~Graph	**TRUTHFULNESS** Video~Tally~Graph	**ACTIVE LISTENING** Video~Tally~Graph	**NO PUT-DOWNS** Video~Tally~Graph	**PERSONAL BEST** Video~Tally~Graph
THREE	**TRUSTWORTHINESS** T-chart~Role Play~Real Life	**TRUTHFULNESS** T-chart~Role Play~Real Life	**ACTIVE LISTENING** T-chart~Role Play~Real Life	**NO PUT-DOWNS** T-chart~Role Play~Real Life	**PERSONAL BEST** T-chart~Role Play~Real Life
FOUR	**TRUSTWORTHINESS** Creative Writing~Journal	**TRUTHFULNESS** Creative Writing~Journal	**ACTIVE LISTENING** Creative Writing~Journal	**NO PUT-DOWNS** Creative Writing~Journal	**PERSONAL BEST** Creative Writing~Journal
	The Bears on Hemlock Mountain, The Velveteen Rabbit, The Secret Garden	*Berenstein Bears Tell the Truth, Sam, Bangs and Moonshine, Pinocchio*	*3 Little Pigs-Wolf's Point of View, Charlotte's Web, Horton Hears a Who*	*Ugly Duckling, Ira Sleeps Over, Crow Boy, Whipping Boy, Charlie Brown books*	*Amazing Grace, Stone Fox, The Giving Tree, The Three Little Pigs, Brave Irene*

Plan #3: Your Choice. A few teachers have asked why they even have to have a plan for introducing and teaching the Lifelong Guidelines and LIFESKILLS. They have felt that it should just be taught naturally, whenever the circumstances are appropriate. We, too, believe in teaching them in the most natural way possible during the teachable moment. But, we also know that current curricular demands have a way of pushing the best of intentions aside. The result, all too often, is that focus is lost and so are the lessons to be learned.

Communicating with Parents / Families

Whichever schedule for incorporating the Lifelong Guidelines and LIFESKILLS you adopt/adapt, be sure you communicate to families what you are doing, how, when, and why. The letters to parents on pages 10.9 and 10.10 can help open a teacher-parent dialogue about first the Lifelong Guidelines and then later the LIFESKILLS.

Literature

There are innumerable ways to use literature to introduce, reteach, or reinforce the Lifelong Guidelines and LIFESKILLS. Here are but a few. Remember to think of changes you would make for your own students and your literary choices. The examples here are for teaching a Lifelong Guideline or LIFESKILL. (See *Tools for Citizenship and Life: Using the ITI Lifelong Guidelines and LIFESKILLS in Your Classroom.)*

- Character Web: Read a book that exemplifies one of the Lifelong Guidelines or LIFESKILLS. Write the name of one main character in the center of a piece of chart tablet paper. Draw a circle around the name. Add rays coming out from the circle, similar to a child's drawing of the sun. (For very young students, consider using a felt story board with images rather than words.) Have your students identify a Lifelong Guideline or LIFESKILL that this storybook character used to solve problems and reach his/her goals. Write the target word on the ray and the action below the ray. For example, based on *Charlotte's Web,* put the name Wilbur in the center circle. Add a ray; above it write Perseverance; under the ray write the descriptors of action from the text, e.g., "He thought and thought until he created a plan to help save his friend Charlotte, the spider." (See an example of such a character web on the next page.)
- Identify three Lifelong Guidelines or LIFESKILLS that were used to solve a problem in the story. Identify two Lifelong Guidelines or LIFESKILLS that were not used and thus contributed to problems.
- Read a traditional story such as *The Three Little Pigs.* Rewrite the ending as if the pigs had used the Lifelong Guideline of Personal Best to solve their problem with the wolf.
- After reading a biography or autobiography, label three or more Lifelong Guidelines or LIFESKILLS that the person used well. Link them to actions from the book. Next, invite members of your Learning Club to share their experiences in developing these same Lifelong Guidelines or LIFESKILLS. Using a Venn diagram, identify the behaviors associated with the selected LIFESKILLS that the book character and your learning-club members have in common and which behaviors are different. Again using a Venn diagram, compare two LIFESKILLS you use to do your personal best with those used by a character in the story.
- After completing several stories, play "Who Am I?" Choose a character from a previously read book. Share the Lifelong Guidelines/LIFESKILLS used along with one or two related actions to carry out the Lifelong Guidelines/LIFESKILLS. Invite other students who have read the book to guess who the character is.
- Compare three LIFESKILLS used by two well-known people. Select people from different time periods and settings such as Madame Curie and Rosa Parks. List three LIFESKILL strengths they have in common. List three weaknesses that each one has. Discuss whether or not the LIFESKILLS are unique to the time period/setting of the story.
- Find local newspaper articles describing problems that are occurring because people didn't use the Lifelong Guidelines/LIFESKILLS. Read the articles with your students and have them determine which Lifelong Guideline or LIFESKILL was or wasn't used. Ask students to share their thinking with other members of their Learning Club.

Hopefully these few ideas will have you thinking in many different directions. Perhaps you remember a favorite biography and think, "Of course, why didn't I ever mention perseverance when we read about Thomas Edison or Rosa Parks?" Or, perhaps you recall a link to humor using *Charlotte's Web*? How about the courage shown in *The True Story of Ruby Bridges*? Eventually, you'll wonder why you ever thought it would be hard to make connections. They'll be popping up everywhere!

A character web for *Charlotte's Web* could look like that on the next page.

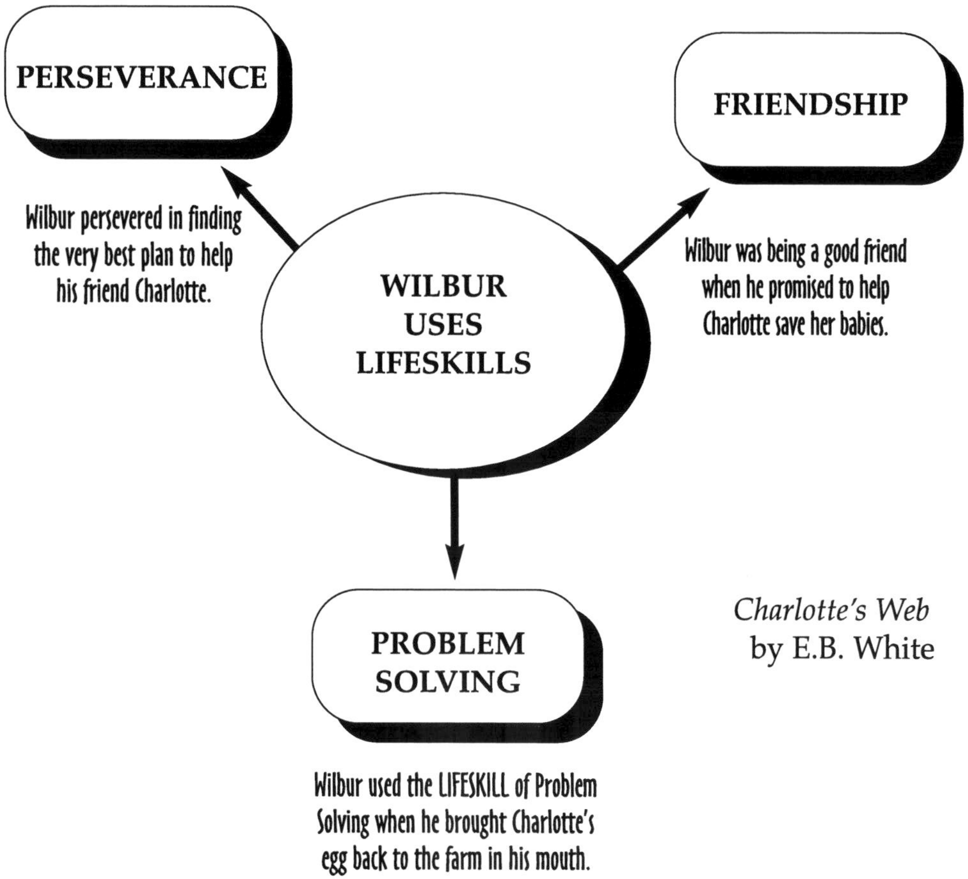

Graphic Organizers

There are many kinds of graphic organizers; each has its purpose. Students should learn how to use all of them, a task they can do very easily if their use is modeled by the teacher during direct instruction and required by those inquiries for which they are particularly useful.

T-Charts are an excellent graphic organizer to help introduce, reteach, or reinforce a Lifelong Guideline or LIFESKILL.

Kinds of T-Charts. There are many kinds of T-charts. The common element is that they have two or more columns which allow students to compare or contrast information about a topic. The two most common T-charts are the LSF chart (looks, sounds, feels like) show on the next page and the KWL (know, want to know, have learned) chart (see Chapter 10).

The LSF T-chart asks students to analyze a concept or skill for relevant attributes—what something looks like, sounds like, and feels like and then what it does not look, sound, and feel like. The simple and more comprehensive versions of such T-charts are illustrated here using the Lifelong Guideline of Trustworthiness.

How to Use T-Charts. Using a large chart tablet, write the name of the concept or skill across the top of the page; select two or more attributes that will help students focus on key aspects of the concept or skill. Create and name these columns. By adding a comparison of what something is to what it isn't, students can more easily develop a broader and deeper understanding of what they are learning.

Then, ask students to think of personal experiences at school or situations from stories they have read that will fit into each category. Allow them sufficient time to think to fill in the spaces with minimal prompting. Let them use their own words (for younger students, draw simple pictures to illustrate the meaning). Once students can connect new learning to previous personal experiences, learning speeds up significantly. As for the Lifelong Guidelines and LIFESKILLS, students' intuitive understanding of them is often surprising.

Save the T-chart(s) and add to the columns daily throughout the first week of study and weekly thereafter as students identify more attributes. The more pictures students have for a concept or skill, the more adept they will become in applying them in real-world settings and the more likely the concept/skill will become wired into long-term memory.

Use Real-World Happenings to Capture the Teachable Moment

The real power in teaching the Lifelong Guidelines and LIFESKILLS comes from making them part of daily living. This means using real-world happenings to capture the teachable moment rather than depending on an occasional, carefully prepared or canned lesson.

For a discussion of daily teaching strategies that will allow you to capture the teachable moment, see target talk.

The curriculum content of the teachable moment lies right at your finger tips—your own experiences with school as a child and your students' current and past experiences with school. For older students, include current events from community, nation, and world.

Teacher's Childhood Experiences at School. Since students love hearing stories of their teacher's experiences, begin by telling about your own learning experiences in school. When did you feel safe enough in school to take a risk? What things happened that kept you from being the best student you could be? What mistakes do you still regret? What were your most embarrassing moments? Use your LIFESKILL of Sense of Humor. Avoid becoming preachy. Let children know that, for all of us, our lives are a work in

TRUSTWORTHINESS

Looks Like	*Sounds Like*	*Feels Like*
students sharing ideas	"I've got something to share!"	safety
people working together	"Will you teach me how to do that?"	comfortable
student running an errand	"Please take this to Mrs. X down the street."	I'm trusted
students helping one another	"Would you help me?" "Yes."	friendliness
student turning in found object	"I found this. It belongs to someone else."	honesty

TRUSTWORTHINESS

Looks Like	*Sounds Like*	*Feels Like*	*Doesn't Look Like*	*Doesn't Sound Like*	*Doesn't Feel Like*
going on an errand alone	"You can do it!	special	someone supervising you	"I know you can't get there without getting into trouble."	sarcastic
borrowing a library book	"I know you will take good care of it."	honored	losing a library book	"I think somebody stole it!"	distrust
finding money	"Thank you for bringing the money to the lost and found."	trusted	pocketing found money	"Finders keepers! Losers weepers!"	suspicion
going to a friend's house	"Be home on time."	someone depends on me	sneaking out of the house	"I wouldn't do that. Trust me!"	lying

progress and that the Lifelong Guidelines and LIFESKILLS are lifelong pursuits.

Invite students to share examples of situations when they have felt safe and comfortable enough for learning to take place. Ask for examples of behaviors that prohibit or limit learning for them. Provide time for small groups to create a mindmap or other visual organizer detailing conditions that promote learning for everyone. Then present the Lifelong Guidelines (or later, the LIFESKILLS) and suggest that the Learning Clubs organize their responses to match up with a Lifelong Guideline/LIFESKILL. For example, if one Learning Club's mindmap has, "It helps us when people listen to our ideas," this would support the Lifelong Guideline of Active Listening. Another group may have, "When people speak respectfully to us, we can concentrate on learning," and might decide that this links to the Lifelong Guideline of No Put-Downs. After all of the positive learning behaviors have been categorized, agree that these guidelines will be part of classroom life.

Students' Experiences at School. From a student perspective, a school day is full of experiences—good and bad. Use these events and interactions at school as the context for discussing the Lifelong Guidelines and LIFESKILLS. During Town Hall Meetings, invite the students to share some of the problems they have experienced during school, past and present, that kept them from concentrating on learning, e.g., fights on the playground, name calling, use of put-downs, a bully who frightened them, and friends telling lies.

Current Events. For older students, a discussion of current issues in the news can lead into the Lifelong Guidelines and LIFESKILLS. Pose pertinent questions to promote analysis of what Lifelong Guidelines or LIFESKILLS helped the people to solve the problem or accomplish what they did. And what Lifelong Guidelines and LIFESKILLS didn't the people use that landed them in the predicament described in the news articles. What characteristics in people do the students admire?

Are these the only lessons that teach about the Lifelong Guidelines? No. There are many more. Our purpose is to offer some beginning points. Go back to your own roots and experiences for hooks that will help you make the Lifelong Guidelines and LIFESKILLS memorable and part of the fabric of classroom life.

It Starts with Staff

Implementing the Lifelong Guidelines and LIFESKILLS must begin with the adults on campus—all staff, not just teachers and classroom aides. This means bus drivers, coaches, cafeteria personnel, maintenance staff, parent volunteers, and visitors. Everyone. To get each one on the same page, generate a T-chart just as you would with students. The T-charts on the next page were generated by teachers and administrators at a Summer Institute[10] training. The differences between what should be and what should not be make a drastic difference in community. The Lifelong Guidelines and LIFESKILLS are something everyone does. "Do what I say, not what I do" has never worked and never will.

LIFELONG GUIDELINE—

Trustworthiness

Looks Like:	***Sounds Like:***	***Feels Like:***
communal resources	addressing issues directly	equality
whole staff collaboration, professional mutual respect	sharing useful information	team effort productive
laughter	sharing ideas/curriculum	safety, family
living up to responsibilities; keeping one's word	adequate time to discuss differences	support is dependable

Behaviors Should No Longer Look, Sound, or Feel Like:
▪rumors ▪favoritism ▪missing materials ▪frequent absences ▪terrified new teachers ▪competition ▪power struggles ▪put downs of children ▪fear of failure ▪betrayal ▪empty promises ▪gossip

LIFELONG GUIDELINE—

Truthfulness

Looks Like:	Sounds Like:	Feels Like:
eye contact	ownership by using "I" statements	safe, non-threatening
active listening	open communication	respectful
cohesiveness, okay to disagree	verbal reinforcement, compliments	opinion is valued
calmness	constructive feedback	validating, supportive

Behaviors Should No Longer Look, Sound, or Feel Like:
▪withholding ▪dishonesty ▪deceit ▪gossip ▪cliques ▪labeling others

LIFELONG GUIDELINE—

Active Listening

Looks Like:	Sounds Like:	Feels Like:
eye contact	respectful silence awareness on speaker	non-judgmental
open body language	collegial, refreshing, connected	energized
nodding, smile	respond with respect, calm voices	respectful, trusting
focused attention	one voice at a time	positive atmosphere

Behaviors Should No Longer Look, Sound, or Feel Like:
▪misunderstood ▪rude interruptions ▪feelings of inequality ▪excluded ▪isolation ▪anger ▪frustration

LIFELONG GUIDELINE—

No Put-Downs

Looks Like:	Sounds Like:	Feels Like:
energized gatherings	authentic conversations	supportive/understanding of peers
cooperation	no blaming someone else	loyalty to those not present
collaboration	appreciating input	willing to risk
a well functioning community	willing to hear other perspectives	safe teaching and learning environment

Behaviors Should No Longer Look, Sound, or Feel Like:
▪sarcasm ▪personal attacks ▪insults ▪demeaning ▪power trips ▪prejudice

LIFELONG GUIDELINE—

Personal Best

Looks Like:	Sounds Like:	Feels Like:
professional appearance	open communication willingness to share	relaxed
self-confidence	comments of appreciation	positive, warmth
organized	open to others' perspectives	team pride
walk the LIFESKILL talk	talk the LIFESKILLS talk	contagious atmosphere of excellence

Behaviors Should No Longer Look, Sound, or Feel Like:
▪negative, unwillingness to improve ▪blaming others for problems ▪sloppy ▪refusal ▪apathy

When to Teach the LIFESKILLS

Remember that the LIFESKILLS are not separate from the Lifelong Guidelines; they define the Lifelong Guideline of Personal Best. Begin teaching the LIFESKILLS only when you are ready to teach the Lifelong Guideline of Personal Best.

To teach the LIFESKILLS, use the same approaches that worked well for you when teaching the Lifelong Guidelines. Remember that developing habits of mind and heart take time. Master the instructional strategies described in Chapters 12 and 13 so they are readily available for daily use. Above all, have fun with your students. Learning values and appropriate behaviors may be serious business but it need not be joyless! Enjoy watching your students (and yourself!) grow.

Date ________________________

Letters to Parents

Dear Family,

Who doesn't want to have a sense of community whether it be in the neighborhood, an organization, a church, or workplace? Community is that sense of belonging one feels when many hearts and minds come together to work toward a common goal and live by a common set of behavioral standards.

In our classroom, we will follow the Lifelong Guidelines of:

- TRUSTWORTHINESS
- TRUTHFULNESS
- ACTIVE LISTENING
- NO PUT-DOWNS
- PERSONAL BEST

These five Lifelong Guidelines are the agreed upon behaviors for our classroom—what behaviors to expect from ourselves and others. They are the social outcomes we set for the community. They also ensure that all students are in an environment that encourages exploring, discovering, and learning.

These behaviors contribute to a sense of workability in life, not only in our classroom now, but also as adults.

Sometime during the sixth century B.C., Lao-Tzu (a name meaning "old sage") wrote:

"The journey of a thousand miles begins with a single step."

As we venture into learning and living each guideline, I invite you to join us on our journey and provide an important supportive role in the development of our classroom community. We will keep you up-to-date with our progress through letters, newsletters and projects.

Sincerely,

Your child's teacher

Date ________________________

Dear Family,

Our class has been working hard to learn to live by the Lifelong Guidelines in our classroom community. Our efforts will continue throughout the year as we attach new meanings and deeper understandings of their application. At this time, we are ready to progress from group standards and expectations, the Lifelong Guidelines, to those that are more individual, the LIFESKILLS.

The fifth Lifelong Guideline, "PERSONAL BEST," is defined by 18 LIFESKILLS:

CARING	FLEXIBILITY	PERSEVERANCE
COMMON SENSE	FRIENDSHIP	PRIDE
COOPERATION	INITIATIVE	PROBLEM SOLVING
COURAGE	INTEGRITY	RESOURCEFULNESS
CURIOSITY	ORGANIZATION	RESPONSIBILITY
EFFORT	PATIENCE	SENSE OF HUMOR

The Lifelong Guidelines and LIFESKILLS will be introduced in our community one at a time. This will assure that all students arrive at common understandings of the meanings of each and how to practice them.

Margaret Mead, a famous anthropologist, provides an inspiring quote to spark our journey:

> "Never doubt that a small group of thoughtful,
> committed people can change the world.
> Indeed, it is the only thing that ever has."

Once again, we invite you to learn with us as we venture forth in creating our classroom community.

Sincerely,

Your child's teacher

Notes

1 William Glasser, *Control Theory in the Classroom* (New York: Harper & Row, Perennial Library, 1986). According to Glasser, there are four needs that must be met in the classroom (beyond survival): To belong and love, to gain power, to be free, and to have fun.

2 In 1965, Bruce Wayne Tuckman published his now famous article on group development entitled "Developmental Sequence in Small Groups." (*Psychological Bulletin*, 63, 384-399). The article was reprinted in *Group Facilitiation: A Research and Applications Journal* - Number 3 (Spring 2001). It is also available at http://www.dennislearningcenter.osu.edu. He describes four stages and their characteristics: formin', stormin', normin', and performin'. Most current discussions of group development parallel these stages. In the ITI version of building community, Tuckman's last two stages are grouped together. Hence, the three stages of developing community described in this book are: Developing a sense of belonging, creating common ground, and taking action.

3 Tuckman hoped that if people understood the stages that groups naturally progress through, they could work more effectively together and reach optimum functioning more quickly. Many groups, however, fail to break thrugh the stormin' stage.

4 In a democratic society, taking action to preserve our democratic system is not an option. If we pay attention to the process of group development, we can learn to take action in ways that strengthen, not weaken, the glue that holds us together.

5 Hert Spencer, 1820-1903. Quote taken from "Education Quotes-The Quotation Page": http://www.quotationspage.com/subjects/education/

6 See Carl Glickman, *Renewing America's Schools* (San Francisco, CA: Jossey-Bass, 1993) for a powerful discussion of the purpose of public education in America and a call to action to fulfill that purpose.

7 Because creating an informed citizenry is the reason we provide free public education, you will find many state curriculum standards that apply to Town Hall Meetings. For example:

National Standards for Language Arts—K-12

NL-ENG. K-12.4 Communication Skills—Students adjust their use of spoken, written, and visual language (e.g., conventions, style, vocabulary) to communicate effectively with a variety of audiences and for different purposes.

NL-ENG. K-12.7—Students conduct research on issues and interests by generating ideas and questions, and by posing problems. They gather, evaluate, and synthesize data from a variety of sources (e.g., print and non-print texts, artifacts, people) to communicate their discoveries in ways that suit their purpose and audience.

NL-ENG. K-12 Developing Research Skills—Students use a variety of technological and information resources (e.g., libraries, databases, computer networks, video) to gather and synthesize information and to create and communicate knowledge.

NL-ENG. K-12 Applying Language Skills—Students use spoken, written, and visual language to accomplish their own purposes (e.g., for learning, enjoyment, persuasion, and the exchange of information).

National Standards for Civics and Government—K-4

NSS-C.K-4.1 What is government?

NSS-C.K-4.2 Values and principles of democracy

NSS-C K-4.3 Principles of democracy

NSS-C.K-4.5 Roles of the citizen

National Standards for Civics and Government—Grades 5-12

NSS-C.5-8.1; 9-12.1—Civic life, politics, and government

NSS-C.5-8.2; 9-12.2—Foundations of the political system

NSS-C.5-8.3; 9-12.3—Principles of democracy

NSS-C.5-8.5; 9-12.5—Roles of the citizen

8 List developed by Sue Pearson, associate of Susan Kovalik & Associates.

9 This book plus posters of the Lifelong Guidelines/LIFESKILLS and their definitions are available through Books for Educators (see order forms at the back of this book).

10 Summer Institutes are sponsored by Susan Kovalik & Associates. They are designed to provide an overview of the ITI model for teachers, administrators, board members, parents, and community members. For more information, or for a free brochure, call Susan Kovalik & Associates or visit their Web site at http://www.kovalik.com.

Chapter 10: What to Accomplish Before Moving to Stage 2

ITI Classroom Stages of Implementation **Stage 1.3**

Entry level for making the learning environment bodybrain compatible

What to Accomplish Before Moving On

CURRICULUM

- Formally teaches the concept of multiple intelligences (defined as problem-solving and product-producing capabilities) and the capabilities and gifts of each intelligence; includes discussion of the intelligences as a frequent, ongoing topic for reflective thinking during collaborative work.

INSTRUCTIONAL STRATEGIES

- Includes real-life experiences—*being there*, immersion, hands-on materials, and visiting resource people—to supplement classroom instruction and provide rich input for each of the multiple intelligences.
- Is learning how to provide students with multiple ways to understand, solve problems, produce products, and demonstrate what they understand through:
  - Use of the multiple intelligences as a guide when lesson planning, selecting instructional strategies, and developing assignments for students, including homework
  - Use of the multiple intelligences when developing / selecting inquiries
  - Use of the multiple intelligences during direct instruction of key points and other instructional strategies
  - Flexibility in allocating time for students to complete their work
  - Student choice of tasks, materials, and processes used for completing projects whenever appropriate

ITI Classroom Stages of Implementation **Stage 1.3**

Entry level for making the learning environment bodybrain compatible

Accomplish Before Moving On *—continued*

CURRICULUM

INSTRUCTIONAL STRATEGIES

- Has mastered the instructional skills identified in Stage 1.2 and continues to use them daily:
  - Modeling of the Lifelong Guidelines and LIFESKILLS
  - Target talk
  - "Discipline" based on using the Lifelong Guidelines & LIFESKILLS
  - Daily agenda
  - Written procedures
  - Models movement to enhance learning and uses it with students to energize and calm
  - Collaboration to enhance personal and social growth and increase achievement (Stage 3 of building a sense of community, Taking Action, has been achieved)
  - Calm voice, heart-brain coherence, and emotionally centered
  - Nurturing reflective thinking through numerous strategies

ITI Classroom Stages of Implementation

Entry level for making the learning environment bodybrain compatible

Stage 1.3

Accomplish Before Moving On *—continued*

CURRICULUM

INSTRUCTIONAL STRATEGIES

- Is developing a variety of instructional strategies to ensure students can identify/understand *patterns* and develop *programs* for using what they understand understand and wire them into long-term memory. Such instructional strategies include:
  - Modeling how to be a lifelong learner and participating citizen
  - Expanded and deepened use of movement to enhance learning
  - Direct instruction, usually limited to 16 minutes per hour
  - Nurturing reflective thinking
  - Graphic organizers
  - Discussion
  - Literature
  - Songs
  - Video clips, great artwork, and photographs
  - Journal writing to enhance social and personal growth and academic learning
  - Celebrations of Learning

- Designs time frames for ITI integrated curriculum to fit the content rather than a rigid daily schedule; is learning to adjust time frames to best accommodate needed instructional strategies and to give students adequate time to complete their work

- Meets frequently with a professional or peer coach who supports the implementation of a bodybrain-compatible learning environment for students.

Working with the Multiple Intelligences

Of the areas of brain research discussed in Part A of this book, none are more immediately experienceable than the multiple intelligences. Just look around you at the range of occupations of extended family and close friends. For example, the contractor who can estimate time, materials, and costs within minutes; the businesswoman who at a glance can identify an emerging pattern in monthly financial reports; the newspaper reporter who can cut to the chase and write a pithy, accurate story under a deadline of minutes, not hours; the mother who awakens from a dead sleep because she can "hear" that something is wrong with her infant five rooms away; the interior designer who can see different hues within a color that the rest of us see simply as off-white; the musician who sees mathematical perfections and chord progressions in music that others of us describe merely as something we either like or don't like but can't tell you why; the junior high student who finds her dissection kit, an out-of-character Christmas present, an irresistible introduction to the world of the animal kingdom in her yard and the discovery of a lifelong occupation as science teacher. Well, you get the picture. Each of these occupations activates a different part of the brain.

The goal of the ITI teacher is to create Renaissance minds—students who are proficient in using all the intelligences to solve problems and produce products. Such multi-faceted people are invaluable employees, friends, and family members. Perhaps most importantly, these are people with a wide range of interests, abilities, and satisfactions.They are people who have joined the ranks of lifelong learners and capable, committed citizens.

Unfortunately, traditional education primarily builds on only one of these areas, linguistic intelligence. Math is typically taught as a talk-about-it set of arithmetic skills done on worksheets. Few of us receive any real music or art training through the public school system; mostly we dabble and experience art as a form of self-expression rather than as a set of specific skills. Science is typically a drawn-out exercise in vocabulary with little practical application, mostly through textbooks and their inevitable end-of-the-chapter questions limited to Bloom's knowledge and comprehension levels. History/social studies is taught as a linguistic survey of knowledge rather than as a way of thinking or as a lens to analyze events.

Perhaps most egregious of all, students that are not high in linguistic intelligence, approximately 80 percent of the population, leave school feeling inadequate. As dropouts, pushouts, or squeakbys, they doubt their ability to learn; yet, when using the intelligences they're strong in, they are powerful learners and valuable community members.

Multiple Intelligences As Curriculum Content

Introducing students to the multiple intelligences is a way to open doors to the reality that, in fact, all students can learn, all students can succeed but they will go about it differently. Luckily, students have an intuitive grasp of the multiple intelligences. For many students, having language to talk about the multiple intelligences often provides immediate relief for the years they may have felt inadequate in the classroom.

There are three ways to proceed: First, teach the multiple intelligences as curriculum content. Expect all students to recognize, understand, and maximize their gifts and learning strengths and to understand how to build other areas of intelligence. Invite them into the challenge of becoming Renaissance minds.

Second, alter your instructional strategies and curriculum development processes to create a learning environment conducive to learning in multiple ways. Mastery of each of the instructional strategies identified in Stages 1.2 and 1.3 is a good beginning.

Third, after a short introduction of the multiple intelligences, rely on teachable moments frequent questions for reflective thinking about collaborative work. For example, have students reflect on what intelligence(s) they'll need to accomplish a learning task, individually and as a Learning Club. After the task is completed, ask students to reflect on what they learned about the multiple intelligences—their own and others'—that they used to tackle and complete the task. Always ask what they learned from each other; acknowledge multiple intelligences using target talk and as a regular concluding activity in Learning Club. The best way to strengthen an area of weakness is to see it modeled, talk about it, and then practice it in a supportive environment.

Multiple Intelligences Through Real-Life Experiences.

Including the multiple intelligences in your instructional strategies is easier than you might think. The two most effective ways are to provide *being there* experiences for students—study trips to locations that best illustrate the concepts and skills you want your students to learn—and to bring resource people to the classroom.

Being There. Any slice of life illustrates the multiple intelligences because the world is multidimensional. Except for assembly lines, real work requires a range of capabilities to move a job from beginning to end. Let students see for themselves how important it is to become as well-rounded as they can.

Analyze the intelligences required for each task and assignment. Make it an ongoing topic for reflecting about collaborative work. Keep the topic of multiple intelligences alive through teachable moments.

Resource People. If possible, have resource people come dressed in the clothes typical of their occupation or role in history and surrounded by as many immersion and hands-on-of-the-real-thing tools as possible. Briefly explain the multiple intelligences to each resource person. Ask that they refer to the intelligences required to do their work. Have them explain the activities in their youth that allowed them to develop such intelligences. This personalization of key figures encourages students and provides an example of a life map they might draw from for their own growth and development.

Have resource people take the students through at least one activity using some of the hands-on items used during their presentation.

Providing Multiple Ways to Think and Perform

For too long, school has predominantly been an experience of lecture, reading, recitation—processes and products of linguistic intelligence. If we're committed to ensuring that all kids can learn, we must significantly reduce our reliance on linguistic intelligence, using it to supplement, not lead, instructional approaches. We must provide students ample opportunities to learn and perform using all the intelligences. Our goal should be a classroom that uses nonlinguistic intelligences at least 50 percent of the time.

Use of the Multiple Intelligences As a Guide to Classroom Life. Stage 1.3 introduces teaching the multiples intelligences to students, explores how students can use their strengths to understand the content and skills of their curriculum, and then how students can use what they understand in real-world ways. Full implementation of the multiple intelligences occurs in curriculum development in Stage 2.

Stage 1.3 also invites you as teacher to begin to explore your own strengths in intelligences other than linguistic. Because we teach the way we learn, we must first become aware of our own intelligences and consciously work to strengthen and use each of them. Only then can we help our students to grow in all intelligences.

Don't be afraid to invite students into this exploration process. The sage on the stage is a lonely role and will only slow your progress. Invite them to join you in thinking through how the knowledge and skills of your curriculum are used in real life at the *being there* location you have chosen. Create assignments that ask them to perform a task that is typical of the *being there* location. These real-world uses **always** involve multiple intelligences, usually two or more simultaneously. Use these contexts or scenarios to help you expand your instructional strategies and assignments to utilize all the intelligences.

One last reminder: Collaborative tasks are excellent structures for eliciting many intelligences at once. However, don't forget to provide students ample intrapersonal time—time to explore and think things through on their own and time to reflect on what each has learned through journal writing and planning projects.

Flexibility in Allocating Time. Because no two brains are alike in how they process or in what prior experiences they bring, each student will need different amounts of time to seek patterns and develop ment programs. "Less is more" is the best piece of advice we can give ourselves. Avoid "covering" material; focus on less content but take learning to application and mastery and long-term memory. [See the two part definition of learning below.]

Part one : **Input stage: Pattern detection** consists of:

- Identifying or recognizing the pattern and
- Making meaning of the pattern including its relationship to other patterns.

and

Part two: **Output stage: Program building** consists of:

- Learning to apply what is learned, at first experimentally and consciously, and then,
- After practice, wiring it up into long-term memory and applying what is learned with the almost automatic ease and skill of the expert.

We suspect that one of the enduring attractions of a solely linguistic approach to teaching is that a teacher can describe content faster than he/she can lead students through discovery processes or collaborative assignments. Thus, the false impression arises that more learning takes place through lecture and other applications of linguistic intelligence. However, as we well know from our own college days, high test scores, even on essay exams, don't necessarily translate into long-term memory. Most of us can recall shockingly little of our college content and probably even less from high school.

We recommend that you mount the new definition of learning that emerges from brain research on your desk to serve as a daily reminder of your purpose as teacher.

There are many ways to provide time; none are new but must be implemented with the intention of improving the likelihood that students will **learn** as defined above.

- During direct instruction, use such techniques as wait time, think-pair-share, check with your Learning Club, 3 Before Me, and so forth.
- During collaborative work, use the techniques described in Elizabeth Cohen's *Designing Groupwork* and Spencer Kagan's *Cooperative Learning* and *SmartCards*. Especially important is rotating leadership and other specific roles so as to give each student ample opportunity to talk about and process what they are learning.
- For complex or large tasks, create frequent progress checks and adjust time as needed.

For additional advice on how to implement the multiple intelligences in Stage 1.3, revisit Chapter 3. For advice on how to use the multiple intelligences when developing curriculum, see Chapters 16 and 17.

Choices. Providing choice is more than a nice-thing-to-do option, it is a bodybrain learning partnership imperative. To make school a success for everyone, we **must** provide choices that invite all of the multiple intelligences to come out to play. This can be done in many, many ways, such as during direct instruction, the materials and supplies we provide for students to use, the nature of the assignments, projects, and homework we assign, the use of collaboration, flexibility in time allocations, and, yes, how we assess/test students.

Student choices of tasks, materials, and processes to complete projects is bodybrain-compatible on a number of levels. Psychologically, choice is an important part of William Glasser's theory about what makes people tick. He identifies four essential human needs—to belong and to love, to have freedom, to gain power, and have fun.[1] When appropriate, choice of task, materials, and processes for completing projects helps meet the last three of Glasser's needs:

- Choosing something that coincides with a special personal interest, such as writing an essay about a personal passion such as cars or horses, makes learning more **fun**.
- Choosing among alternatives, such as which intelligence to use to show that we understand something rather than always having to take a paper and pencil test, gives us **freedom** in how we go about learning.
- Choosing materials and projects that allow us to be successful gives us a sense of **power**.

Also, for many students, being able to select the tools they will use for a task is highly motivating and elicits a burst of interest and keen attention to the task. However, that same set of supplies and materials may be new to others and thus a complete distraction. Just as birds must learn the fine points of flying, each of us must learn to make the most of our bodybrain partnership. Allowing students to choose their supplies and materials is an important step toward becoming a self-directed learner capable of maximizing the likelihood that they will master new learning.

Mastery and Continued Use of Instructional Strategies in Stage 1.2

All of the instructional strategies identified in Stage 1.2 are continued on a daily basis and the teacher has developed a mental program for using them on a moment's notice. These strategies include:

- Modeling of the Lifelong Guidelines/LIFESKILLS
- Target talk
- "Discipline" based on using the Lifelong Guidelines & LIFESKILLS
- Daily agenda and written procedures
- Movement to enhance learning
- Collaboration
- Calm voice, heart-brain coherence, and emotional centeredness
- Nurturing reflective thinking

Developing a Variety of Other Instructional Strategies

Stage 1.3 is also the time to launch additional instructional strategies in preparation for Stage 2 and entry into making curriculum bodybrain compatible. The strategies for Stage 1.3 include:

- Modeling how to be a lifelong learner and participating citizen
- Expanded and deepened use of movement to enhance learning
- Direct instruction, usually limited to 16 minutes per hour.

- Nurturing reflective thinking
- Graphic organizers
- Discussion
- Literature
- Songs
- Video clips, great artwork, and photographs
- Journal writing to enhance social and personal growth and academic learning
- Celebrations of Learning

Modeling Being a Lifelong Learner and Participating Citizen

The single most powerful instructional strategy—regardless of what you are teaching—is modeling. As you already know, "Do what I do" is always more powerful than "Do what I say."

If you're not sure what you're modeling as a lifelong learner and participating citizen, do a self assessment and also ask a colleague whose opinion you value. Here are some questions to ask.

Do you read daily? For how many minutes? Do you read multiple genre, e.g., magazines, newspapers, professional literature, fiction, nonfiction, poetry? Do you read more than one book at a time? Do you talk about what you're reading with others—family, friends, colleagues, your students? Are you passionate about learning something new? Do you express wonder and awe? Are you enthusiastic about students' work to plan and carry out a Celebration of Learning or is it just one more item in your lesson plan book?

Are you registered to vote? Do you vote in every election at your precinct? Do you eagerly apply what students are learning to current events in the school, community, nation, and world (as age appropriate)? Do you donate regularly to a charity or two? Do you volunteer to help those less fortunate? Do you share with students how you live your life so that you make a difference? Do you engage in supporting students' Social/Political Action projects with enthusiasm and spirit or as just another job to be done?

If you have answered no to any of the above questions, you might want to consider the fact that you are working at cross purposes with yourself. On the one hand, you are working hard to educate the nation's young; on the other hand you are demonstrating to them that someone other than they will take up the responsibility to somehow make the world a better place, help those less fortunate, and preserve our democratic way of life.

Movement

Brain research makes it very clear that movement plays a key role in the learning process. There is a strong connection between movement and emotion and the part of the brain that controls physical movement also helps sequence thinking. Movement in the classroom is not a luxury, it's a necessity.

Movement to enhance emotional receptivity to learning is a daily consideration. As you approach Stage 2, the role of movement to help students let off steam and to reenergize and refocus must expand and to enhance learning and memory of concepts and skills.

Movement and Content. Movement should be implicit in learning, that is, most learning involves, or should involve, application to real-world situation. So the more completely we base our curriculum in being there locations, the more doing we can build into our students' day. Similarly, the more we teach to the brain-based definition of learning—continuing to develop mental programs to use what is learned and wiring it into long-term memory—the more movement we need from students. Allow and encourage them to use their bodies to increase sensory input, practice ways to use what they understand, and to hard-wire learning into long-term memory. For example, make study trips truly exploratory not just look and see. Develop role-playing plots and actions that illustrate the concepts and skills to be learned.

Movement as a mnemonic is also very powerful. Hand jives, dance steps,whole-body movements/postures, finger tapping rhythms—all involve additional areas of the brain in the recall process. The important thing is having the movements grow out of the content rather than trying to fit predesigned movements to content. Students are wonderfully creative when it comes to making up movements. Invite them in creating movements, then pick the best one(s) for the class to use.

Resources. Good resources for these activities include:

- *Stage 2 of the ITI Stages of Implementation: Intelligence Is a Function of Experience* (video, 14 minutes)
- *ITI in the Urban Middle School* by Nicole McNeil-Miller (video, 15 minutes)
- *Multiple Intelligences and the Second Language Learner* by Jo Gusman (video, 40 minutes)
- *Smart Moves: Why Learning Is Not All in Your Head* by Carla Hannaford

See also Chapter 2 and pages 1.22, 2.13, 3.21, 4.15, and 5.10.

Direct Instruction

Many people define direct instruction as lecture. Lecture has its place but it is a limited one. It is the driest version of direct instruction which typically provides little sensory input beyond hearing and seeing the speaker. Lecture is but a small part of good direct instruction.

There are many models for direct instruction. Perhaps the most widely known is the ITIP model (Instructional Theory into Practice) created by Dr. Madeline Hunter of UCLA (University of California, Los Angeles). We briefly describe an ITI adaptation[2] of it here as an example of deliberate, intentional steps to foster learning. Any solid model well implemented will serve the purpose for ITI.

The steps proposed by Madeline Hunter were a result of her research into what effective teachers do. However, she always cautioned people not to make it a static formula and not to believe that every step must be used every time the teacher chooses to use direct instruction as the most appropriate strategy. She acknowledged that teaching is heavily contextual and that only the teacher, with full knowledge of the subject matter and his/her students, can know what is best done at any one moment.

What Is Direct Instruction? Direct doesn't mean boring. It does mean focused, clear, interactive, well paced, and readily understandable by students. According to Linda Jordan, ITI Associate and Assistant Professor at Hope College, School of Education, in Holland, Michigan, direct instruction is:

- A teaching method through which the teacher maintains a highly structured environment for teaching specific concepts and skills

- A process that enables the teacher to maximize student engagement and time spent on task.

- Is characterized by teacher direction on an academic focus followed up with student practice and application.

When Is Direct Instruction Effective? Direct instruction is effective when other means to discover and explore are insufficient or frustratingly inefficient.

Direct Instruction in the ITI Model. The Hunter ITIP model was widely promoted by states and districts during the 1970s and it resurfaces whenever educators look for a training model for direct instruction. We believe it is a very valuable tool. What follows is an ITI version of ITIP.

By direct instruction in the ITI model, we mean an orchestrated presentation by the teacher that is limited to 11-16 minutes per hour and that is accompanied by full sensory input to as many of the 19 senses as possible when working within an immersion environment.

Direct instruction should be looked at not as an end in itself—the way to teach—but rather as the catalyst to student work on inquiries. Direct instruction can lead the way or follow a discovery process. It can be most powerful during the teachable moment when students are already fully engaged in their work and hungry for more answers.

Steps in Planning and Conducting Direct Instruction. The steps in planning and conducting direct instruction are simple and straight forward. Each has a basis in brain research.

Anticipatory Set. The anticipatory set works at two levels:

- It creates an emotional hook or bridge to the new learning. In the words of Dr. Robert Sylwester, "Emotion drives attention which drives learning, memory, problem solving, and just about everything else."[3]

- It accesses prior experiences by illustrating how, where, and why this concept or skill is used in real life and how students might use it. This starts the pattern-seeking, meaning-making operation of the brain—looking for related patterns in its memory banks, a beginning place for processing incoming data.

Anticipatory sets common in the ITI model are:

- Being there experiences
- The ITI Discovery Process
- Visit by an expert
- A hands-on-of-the-real-thing activity
- An inclusion activity which asks students to recall an experience common to all classmates

The goal of an anticipatory set is to get students motivated, curious, excited about the concept or skill, and aware of how the concept or skill is used in real life.

Learning Objective The learning objective in an ITI classroom is the key point to be learned. For grades 2 and up, the key point should be written and posted—on the wall or in their notebooks. For K-1, the key point is usually represented by a pictorial mindmap that students who cannot yet read can understand.

This key point, a sentence or two, tells students specifically what is expected of them, what they are to learn.

Purpose or Rationale. Purpose or rationale is always answered by how, where, and why this concept or skill is important to know and be able to do in real life. No students should be told by a teacher, as one of the authors was in her high school algebra and trig classes, "I don't know when and where you would use this. Just learn it." In the ITI classroom, purpose or rationale should be part of the anticipatory set. Apply it to your students' lives and the *being there* experiences you've selected.

Input. This is the teacher's opportunity to give his/her best shot at making the patterns in the concept or skill meaningful, useful, and memorable. This is the "teaching" part. Will you provide a *being there* experience, immersion experience, demonstration using hand-on-of-the-real thing, a structured discovery process? Will you engage students in a set of questions for discussion by Learning Clubs or partners?

Remember, just as curriculum development is a pattern-enhancing activity, so too is the input part of your lesson. Your input should be planned to make pattern seeking by students inescapable. Think about what you are teaching from the students' point of view:

- What information do they need (don't bury them);
- What are the patterns/programs or components of the task (analyze the tasks but don't splinter it into a zillion meaningless pieces)
- What order do I teach those components in, which will be picked up effortlessly through the *being there* experience?
- What teaching strategies should I use?

Modeling. Choose a whole-class inquiry that asks students to use the knowledge or skill of the key point. Carry out the inquiry, or first part of it, as a model, showing students what they need to do and how. Again, make sure that the inquiry requires application to real life; include as many of the multiple intelligences as possible.

Check for Understanding. During modeling, ask questions to test student understanding. Use collaborative structures, such as check with a partner, or think-pair-share and, for individual response, allow plenty of think time. Check to see who agrees or disagrees. Most importantly, urge students to talk about what they think they understand and how they would use it.

Checking for understanding is to ensure that the end of Step 1 in learning—understanding the pattern(s)—is completed (see Chapter 4, especially pages 4.1-4.2).

Guided Practice. After modeling and checking for understanding, select another inquiry for students to complete collaboratively, either whole Learning Club or pairs. As they work, circulate among the groups, checking for accuracy and completeness of understanding. The key to providing guided practice is immediate feedback.

If misconceptions appear or if students aren't getting it, use the teachable moment to reteach an individual or the class; of course, use a different way using different examples.

Guided practice is the beginning of Step 2 of the new definition of learning—applying what is understood to the real world (see Chapter 5, especially pages 5.1-5.2) Don't move on until understanding is accurate and sufficient to complete other related inquiries, first in collaborative settings and, eventually, alone.

Independent Practice. Select an inquiry for individual or partner work. Again, make sure that the inquiry reflects real-life use of the concept or skill.

Independent practice ensures that each student can apply the concept or skill to real life and that they are wiring this learning into long-term memory.

Students should be given several inquiries at this stage. Hard wiring comes from applying knowledge and skills over time. The teacher must use his/her best judgment about whether students have developed a program for using the knowledge and skills and if it will be retained years into the future.

Working independently gives students time to reflect on the depth and breadth of their understanding (or lack of) and their ability to apply their knowledge. With this information, they can begin to direct their own learning.

Closure. Closure to a lesson does not equal completion of wiring into long-term memory. However, the strength of the closure will likely determine whether students will persevere through sufficient practice to commit a concept or skill to long-term memory.

One of the most powerful elements of closure is time for reflective thinking. Ways to nurture reflective thinking include journal writing, personal think time (in writing) before sharing with a partner, writing a thank you note to the visiting expert listing the things learned/appreciated, writing a paragraph to parents describing what the student as learned and how it can be applied immediately in their life, creating a graphic organizer that represents what they learned, writing additional inquiries that the student thinks would help create long-term memory of the key point, and so forth.

Teachers also need closure and time for reflective thinking. For the teacher's sake, there must be reflection time to recap the key point and to clarify and check again that students learned the key point as intended. Do you move on to another key point or do you plan additional inquiries for the students to practice until the information/skill gets wired into long-term memory?

An Analogy. A useful analogy for direct instruction is teaching someone to bake bread. Linda Jordan describes this as follows:

Steps in Direction Instruction	**Baking Bread Analogy**
Anticipatory set	The aroma brings you in
Stating the key point (objective)	The recipe
Stating the rationale/purpose	What are we cooking? For whom?
Input	Choosing the ingredients
Modeling	Showing how bread is baked
Checking for understanding	Tasting the bread
Guided practice	Give them the recipe and help as needed
Independent practice	New baker takes over kitchen
Closure	Reflect on how to improve the product next time

Although Hunter's instructional model predates brain research on this subject, her instincts were right on target.

Elements of ITIP Model	**The ITI Definition of Learning**
Anticipatory set	Identifying or recognizing the pattern
Stating the key point	↓
Stating the rationale/purpose	
Input	Making meaning of the pattern
Modeling	↓
Checking for understanding	
Guided practice	Learning to apply/use what is understood (a program)
Independent practice	↓
Closure	
	Stored in long-term memory

Nurturing Reflective Thinking

Life in the 21st century is anything but conducive to reflective thinking and becoming more difficult by the year. Students come to us with a revved up sense of time while more demands are heaped upon us from year to year. The pressures seem endless. But brain research and our common sense tell us that reflective thinking is a essential—personally as well as academically.

Thinking about information and skills—deciding how they relate to our lives or those we admire, thinking about how something new relates to what we already understand, wondering about how we could ever use something—gives the brain an opportunity to process them in numerous locations of the brain, enriching our understanding and increasing the likelihood that it will become retrievable.

Nurturing reflective thinking is more a habit of mind than a specific instructional strategy, more an intention to do so than a silver bullet from our bag of instructional strategies. There are a variety of processes and structures to nurture reflective thinking, old and new.

For example, wait time, journal writing, reflecting on the daily agenda (beginning and end of the day), making choices that allow students to direct their learning, forecasting how to take on a learning task, reflecting on what one learned academically, the process of collaborative work (before, during, and after and asking about content, social, and personal outcomes), providing adequate time for students to complete assignments, strategies to help students refocus, making detailed drawings of an object, homework assignments that require action to apply something to real-world settings, the Three-Before-Me rule, action-oriented individual projects, and much more.

As you approach Stage 2, intensify your focus on academic reflections while continuing to include inner musings.

To keep journal writing vital and vigorous, add an element of audience. For selected journal writings, assign or let students choose a real person to write to. Encourage them to actually mail some of these "letters." Of course, one of those people could be the student him/herself. From time to time, announce in advance a journal entry that you will respond to. A good rule of thumb is that you will write back as much as they write to you.

Vary the assignments, the point of view, and the content. Encourage students to use their journal writing to explore their own thoughts and feelings and to reflect on how their new knowledge and skills can/will apply to their life in the future.

To invigorate learning from the product and process of group and individual work, give students time and, in the beginning, the questions to reflect on prior to work, during work, and after. Creating a reliable "voice in the back of the head" that helps us learn from the past and operate more intelligently in the future is the heart of becoming a successful lifelong learner as well as a successful student in the classroom.

When it comes to reflecting on personal work, make sure you include homework. For more information, see pages 1.27, 2.8-12, 3.15-16, 4.23-24, and 5.16.

Graphic Organizers

Graphic organizers are important learning tools because they can show the rich relationships that exist among concepts, ideas, and elements. Although this is very important for all students, it is especially critical for students high in spatial intelligence and those who have difficulty seeing the whole picture (see Appendix A). No other instructional process can illustrate such relationships as clearly or efficiently.

Kinds of Graphic Organizers. There are various kinds of graphic organizers:

- Pictorial representations of content, such as mindmaps, flow charts, time lines, story boards, and so forth
- Illustrations of important interrelationships, such as more complex mindmaps, webs, bridges, and so on
- Data formats that invite comparisons of quantities or qualities, such as those from the fields of science and mathematics (axis graphs, bar charts, Venn diagrams, pie charts, etc.)

Why Use Graphic Organizers. The strength of graphic organizers is that they record information in ways that make information more understandable by focusing our attention and enabling us to see relationships which in turn pushes us to see a bigger picture. They also bring up questions that would never have occurred to us. The pursuit of answers to such questions happily leads us further into the concepts, into ways to apply them in similar and differing situations.

Examples of Graphic Organizers. Some graphic organizers deal with precise comparisons and relationships such as the axis graph and bar charts; these work well when dealing with quantities. Others illustrate interrelationships of many facets of many items such as mindmapping and Venn diagrams; these work well when dealing with qualitative aspects such as the attributes of concepts. Others simply transform information from words to pictures.

The KWL T-chart is developed over time. It is used to record what students already **know** about a concept or skill before you begin instruction and what they **want to know** about it. This is important information. Not only does it pique students' interest but it also helps the teacher know if their are any misconceptions that need to be corrected and what examples of a concept hold the most interest for students. Over time, once a week, students add on what they have **learned.**

Choose the form of graphic organizer that would best assist the reader to perceive and interpret the data that you most want him/her to analyze and understand. Useful, and easy to use, graphic organizers include:

- Bar graphs and pie charts assist the observer to compare quantities of numerous items.
- Axis graphs assist in observing for directions or trends in the quantitative interaction of two things. They also indicates how much of which of two ingredients must be increased or decreased in order to reach a desired goal.
- Venn diagrams assist the observer in comparing two entities for differences and similarities.
- Column charts simply separate out the data by designated characteristics (e.g., bookkeeping formats and decision-making formats such as P.M.I. or plus, minus, and interesting/neutral effect).
- Mindmaps are capable of presenting a large amount of data and, most importantly, showing the interrelationships among that data. Because it is a visual format, it gives the brain more clues for analyzing relationships and remembering the big idea and its relevant details.

For more information, see *Visual Tools for Constructing Knowledge* by David Hyerle, ASCD.

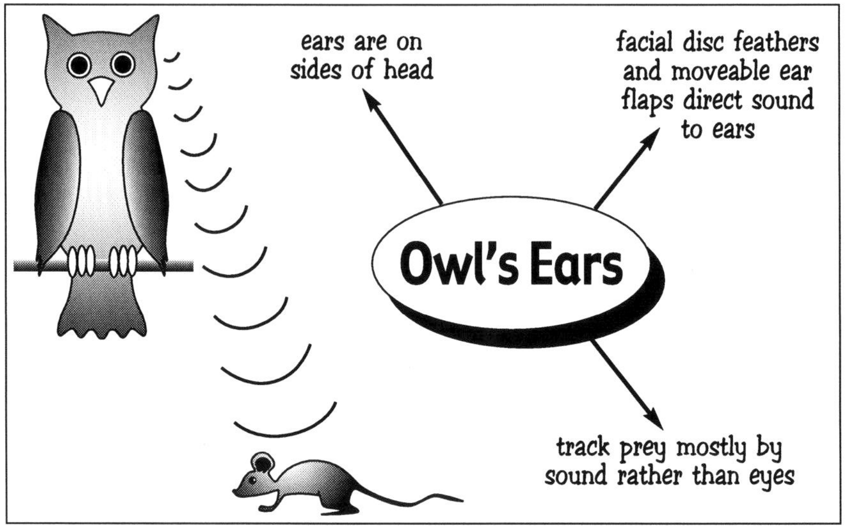

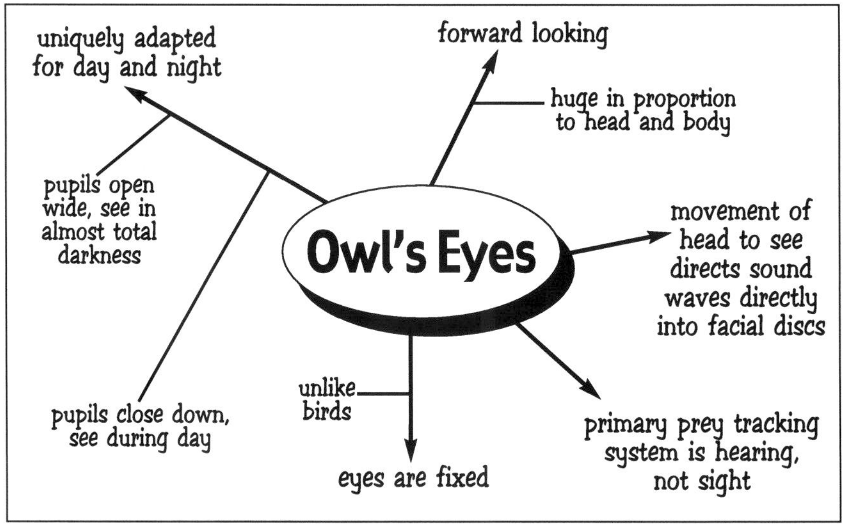

The graphic organizers above are examples of mindmaps for key points—for primary grades and for intermediate. The mindmap on the next page is yet another example of how visuals can help a learner to remember information. Color adds another dimension, especially for those high in spatial intelligence.

For an example of T-Charts, see page 10.16.

Discussion

Discussion is powerful because it gives students multiple opportunities to turn an idea over in their minds, to try it out for size, to sharpen meaning by exploring the boundaries of what something is and isn't, and to see how it applies to the world they live in and the world of the *being there* location. Often, we're not sure what we really think about something until we hear ourselves talk about it. Discussion helps uncover misconceptions about things, misconceptions we can't correct until we realize they're there.[4]

As any professional facilitator will tell you, there is an art and science to framing questions that generate rich discussion. This in contrast to questions that lead to a single, correct answer.

Go on line and pick up a synopsis of how to lead discussions that fits your situation. An excellent resource is Jamie McKenzie's "The Question Mark" at http://questioning.org

A few commonsense rules to keep in mind:

- Discussion is most powerful when it occurs immediately after the trigger event.
- Give students a window on what discussion looks like. Take them to see "discussion" in action, at school board meetings, city council meetings, PTA meetings, and so forth.
- Involve students in developing written procedures for different kinds of discussion, from informal classroom discussions to formal Town Hall Meetings.

An excellent resource for structuring discussions and other forms of groupwork is *Cooperative Learning* by Spencer Kagan. Also see the discussion of Town Hall Meetings on page 9.7-8.

The KWL T-chart is developed over time. It is used to record what students already **know** about a concept or skill before you

Know	*What to Know*	*Have Learned*
students sharing ideas	"I'd like to share something."	safety
people working together	"Will you teach me how to do that?"	comfortable
student running an errand	"Please take this to Mrs. X down the hall."	I'm trusted
students helping one another	"Would you help me?" "Yes."	friendliness
student turning in found object	"I found this. It belongs to someone else."	honesty

TRUSTWORTHINESS

Looks Like	*Sounds Like*	*Feels Like*	*Doesn't Look Like*	*Doesn't Sound Like*	*Doesn't Feel Like*
going on an errand alone	"You can do it!	special	someone supervising you	"I know you can't get there without getting into trouble."	sarcastic
borrowing a library book	"I know you will take good care of it."	honored	losing a library book	"I think somebody stole it!"	distrust
finding money	"Thank you for bringing the money to the lost and found."	trusted	pocketing found money	"Finders keepers! Losers weepers!"	suspicion
going to a friend's house	"Be home on time."	someone depends on me	sneaking out of the house	"I wouldn't do that. Trust me!"	lying

begin instruction and what they **want to know** about it. This is important information. Not only does it pique students' interest but it also helps the teacher know if their are any misconceptions that need to be corrected and what examples of a concept hold the most interest for students. Over time, once a week, students add on what they have **learned.**

Literature

There is nothing better than a great story to pique students' interest and curiosity and, in the process, to teach a meaningful lesson. For your daily focus or story time with students, select a story rich with examples of what you want to teach, such as the Lifelong Guideline or LIFESKILL you are currently focusing on, on what addresses an important incident/situation from the day, or on the concept or skill you are teaching. Which stories offer strong examples of Trustworthiness? Truthfulness? Active Listening? Integrity? Which teach the destructiveness of Put-Downs? Which support development of Personal Best or Resourcefulness? Select emotion grabbers such as *Chrysanthemum* by Kevin Henkes, *Leo, the Late Bloomer* by Robert Kraus, *Charlotte's Web* by E. B. White, *Stone Fox* by John Reynolds Gardiner, *Shiloh* by Phyllis Reynolds Naylor, *My Side of the Mountain* by Jean Craighead George, and *Where the Red Fern Grows* by Wilson

Rawls. The strong characterizations created by the various authors make youth and adults identify with the characters, giving a vicarious but intense experience with the dilemmas faced in the stories.

Selecting Books. Always have a good story going for students. Invite them into other worlds, other possibilities for their yet-to-be-seen futures. Find a good children's librarian at your school or local library or even at a child-oriented bookstore. Ask what kids select to read and select from those kid-tested book list, then use your personal experiences and judgment to determine which stories are good choices for your own students, both in content and age appropriateness.

Pre-Reading Student Books Is Important. It is important that you read each story before you read it aloud to your students. First, you will want to determine if the story content and language are consistent with what you want your students to experience. Such previews allow you to sidestep objectionable language, skip parts that students might find upsetting, determine if the content and language are appropriate for your students, and to consider its fit with your students' life experiences.

By pre-reading you also familiarize yourself with the story and find comfortable discussion spots and those places in the plot that will most effectively highlight the importance of a concept, skill, or behavior you want to teach and connect to your students' experiences. It also allows you to add a bit of drama to your reading.

This same care needs to be given to books that you assign to the class. Just because a book is on the school's literature list doesn't mean it would be a good match for your students.

Songs

Songs are a wonderful teaching device and, along with storytelling, the best mnemonic available. They combine the power of memorable melody and the rhythm and rhyme of poetry and significantly increase the likelihood that what is learned will become stored in long-term memory. They also provide powerful hooks for

Pride, Great Pride

(to the tune of
Ain't She Sweet?)

Pride, great pride
Feel it way down deep inside.
When you just can't rest
Until you do your best,
Feel that PRIDE.

Mastery,
Just remember "CCC"
When it's correct, complete,
And comprehensive
How proud you'll be.

When you've got pride
You'll aim much higher.
That little spark
Becomes a fire.

Pride, great pride
Feel it way down deep inside.
When you just can't rest
Until you do your best,
Feel that pride!

© Jean Spanko

Used by written permission
from Jean Spanko.

Resourcefulness

(to the tune of *This Old Man*)

When you face problems tough,
Resourcefulness will be enough
Look around for answers,
Change your point of view.
Great ideas will come to you.

Keep your mind focused well;
Stay away from folks that tell you
That "This won't work,
we tried it once before."
Show those people out the door.

If you fail, don't give in
Try your first ideas again.
The solution may be
Just a step away.
Be resourceful every day.

When you're stumped, you can ask
Trusted friends to share your task.
They can listen well
And dream along with you...
Give a different point of view.

Think in ways new and strange.
There's a world that you can
change.
Be resourceful and you'll
See the answer clear.
All the world will stand and cheer.

© Jean Spanko

retrieving memories. To test this power, think of your favorite song and the vividness of memories that reappear every time you hear it. Every chunk, topic, of ITI integrated curriculum you develop should have its own "theme" song.

Some songs come ready made, perfect words to a catchy melody. But don't be afraid to write your own lyrics to familiar melodies in order to capture the content you are teaching, be it science, math, art, or P.E. Students delight in this creative task.

Singing is fun and something that all can do; musical talent and training are not required (but desirable!). Make curriculum-based songs a hallmark of your classroom.

Some examples of content lyrics to famous tunes appear on the next page.

Video Clips, Great Artwork, and Photographs

Art has often been called the window to our inner life. Certainly it carries and preserves the images of our civilization. Images grip us and speak to us on many levels; truly, a picture is worth a thousand words.

When using video clips, be sure you select just the clip that introduces or reteaches or tests the concept or skill of your curriculum. Don't play the entire segment from the point of view of the video; just the segment that hits your goal. Don't allow the tail to wag the dog.

When choosing great art or photographs, enlist the watchful eyes of your nearest librarian. Show her/him your curriculum and ask for recommendations. To display your art piece or photograph, clear a space on the wall, at least 10′ x 10′. Leave the wall bare so that it doesn't compete with the art. This is especially important with students who are easily distracted.

Journal Writing

Journal writing is an excellent device to help students reflect on what they are learning or thinking about a topic. With no one looking over their shoulder or judging their words, they can reflect on what they truly think and feel. Since writing is thinking on paper, the very act of writing requires students to sort through their thoughts, reflect on their feelings, and organize their ideas.

Journal writing provides opportunities for students to reflect, respond, react, and reply to a wide variety of ideas, comments, and stories. It is a powerful instructional tool. Use it daily to offer students chances to revisit, review, and renew previous beliefs and thoughts and to compare them to new ones. It is particularly useful to provide adequate time to reflect about their experiences relating to the Lifelong Guidelines and LIFESKILLS.

A simple strategy for journal writing is to have students write in their journal every day. Once a week, have them indicate the one or two things they want you to respond to (which you should do in writing in their journal for them to keep). This addition of a real audience makes the journal more than an academic exercise and establishes the standard for writing—what real people use in the real world.

Note: A journal differs from a diary which primarily records day to day occurrences. Journals reflect one's personal journey. Periodically you should invite students to write something to you, something that you will respond to. Rule of thumb: Write as much back as the student writes to you. This encourages length and depth in their writing.

Although reading student writing can sometimes be overwhelming due to the sheer volume of it, keep in mind that "writing is the inking of our thinking"—it's as close as we can get to seeing what goes on in the students' heads.

Celebrations of Learning

As the saying goes, "All work and no play makes Jack a dull boy." The same goes for Jill and for teachers and parents as well. Celebrating successes, big and small, is very, very important. Such celebrations provide markers for our progress, announce to us and others that we have hit a new milestone and, very importantly, that we have left some old behaviors and beliefs behind.

Change, for students and adults, is not about adding new crusts to our outer layers but about truly leaving behind some old behaviors and beliefs that no longer serve us and are no longer appropriate to who we are becoming.

Celebrating to Internalize Change. Leaving old behaviors and beliefs behind is obviously a critical part of learning to live the Lifelong Guidelines and LIFESKILLS. And the way to do so—with grace and the support of those we live with—is to celebrate those milestones. In the ITI model, we call these Celebrations of Learning. Be they markers of small accomplishments or large, they are public and full of hard-won pride. They are not, however, "I/we are #1" or "Student of the week" episodes. They are a way to share with others what one has learned; they state one's intent to continue moving forward. In the case of students and staff, this means moving forward together.

Part one : **Input stage: Pattern detection** consists of:

- Identifying or recognizing the pattern and
- Making meaning of the pattern including its relationship to other patterns.

and

Part two: **Output stage: Program building** consists of:

- Learning to apply what is learned, at first experimentally and consciously, and then,
- After practice and wiring it up into long-term memory, applying what is learned with the almost automatic ease and skill of the expert.

In Stage 1, Celebrations of Learning focus heavily on the Lifelong Guidelines/LIFESKILLS. By the end of Stage 1.3, Celebrations of Learning should also include curriculum content.

Celebrating, Not Rewarding. Do not confuse celebrating with giving rewards. There is a world of difference between a deep sense of personal satisfaction and an ice cream cone. As discussed on page 17.3, external rewards extinguish the very behavior for which the reward was given. In contrast, celebrations in the ITI model stoke an internal sense of pride and satisfaction; they are public acknowledgments of a student's (or teacher's) growth that he/she has already internally acknowledged and values. Celebrating as a group allows each individual to acknowledge and value the same accomplishment by others.

Celebrating Growth in Using the Lifelong Guidelines. Because internalizing and consistently using the Lifelong Guidelines and LIFESKILLS are key to academic growth, on-going celebrations of growth in these behaviors are an important investment in future academic achievement and in creating future citizens.

There are many ways to celebrate growth toward learning to apply the Lifelong Guidelines and LIFESKILLS. These are starters for you:

- A LIFESKILLS Fair for Parents, a special evening during which your students plan LIFESKILL "booths"—demonstrations of what his/her favorite LIFESKILL means and how to use it. Students can work as a learning club, in partners, or individually.
- A LIFESKILL Day planned for the entire class during which students, as members of a small group of 2-5 students, carry

out their plans to practice that Lifelong Guideline or LIFESKILL for the entire day (or whatever time period is chosen). Projects can be carried out on campus (Caring and Friendship with younger buddies, reading to them, helping them learn to use the library), at a nearby public park (Effort and Cooperation, clean up projects, trail restoration), or at a museum or aquarium (Curiosity, a behind the scenes tour). The possibilities are endless. On return to class, have each group give a 3-5 minute presentation of how the LIFESKILL of the day helped make that day special for them—more interesting, more fun, more friendships.

Taking time to acknowledge students' success in implementing the Lifelong Guidelines and LIFESKILLS helps students experience that deep sense of personal satisfaction that comes from doing one's best, contributing to the group, doing something because it's the right thing to do. These celebrations provide the initial external feedback that promotes an internal sense of pride—earned and deserved.

Celebrating Academic Growth. Academic growth is often considered an invisible activity made manifest only by tests and grades. Nonsense! There are many ways to make academic growth visible, tangible, experienceable—something always appreciated by parents and essential to students in their journey to becoming self-directed, lifelong learners.

Celebrations of Learning are one of the best ways. For a full discussion of using Celebrations of Learning to acknowledge and celebrate academic learning, see Chapter 21.

Flexible Time Frames

Inadequate time is the 21st century's foremost stressor. Those of us caught up in it don't need brain research to remind us that rigid time schedules loyal to the needs of bureaucracy rather than the needs of individual learners are killers. They frustrate learning and performance of students and staff alike.

Although freighted with tradition, there is not a shred of brain research to support the typical time schedule allocating set amounts of time per subject each day. Indeed, a growing and convincing body of evidence suggests that such schedules are counterproductive. Students need time to engage, explore, try out, master, and commit concepts and skills to long-term memory. Time frames should flex with the needs at the moment. Fortunately, integrating subject content through *being there* experiences enables us to make time frames longer, such as all afternoon or two-thirds of the morning. Sheltering a significant block of time during each day or each week ensures adequate time to focus, explore in depth, and practice the use of new mental programs.

When planning time frames, keep in mind the new, bodybrain-compatible definition of learning as a two-step process summarized below. (Also see Chapters 4 and 5).

As a rule of thumb, time frames should be planned to ensure that each of the four steps of learning described above can be accomplished by students. If so, future study and practice can add depth and increase expertise.

The effects of inadequate time can be very detrimental. For example, a student studying a new math skill only gets a peremptory swipe at it and, as a result, does not "get" it. The coinciding emotional message is often, "I'm not good at math," or, "I don't like math", or both. The next time the concept/skill is presented, it comes freighted with negative emotional baggage. So, not only does the student start from ground zero academically but the task is made all the more difficult by negative emotions.

Meeting Frequently with a Coach

Goals to work on for you and your coach include ensuring that you master all of the elements initiated during Stage 1.2 and continue using them on a daily basis and that you work systematically to accomplish each of the curricular and instructional strategies of Stage 1.3. Go for mastery of one thing at a time rather than jumping into everything at once. Be kind to yourself!

Also, find tools that support you. A "must have" tool is *Your Personal Guide to Implementing ITI* by Karen D. Olsen. It describes five stages of implementation starting with what to do before school starts, the first day and beyond, what to accomplish before moving to Stage 2, beginning stages of integrating curriculum, etc. Each stage describes what to do for curriculum development and for instructional strategies. In addition it describes what the classroom will look like and feel like as students join in, called "The Dance," and when students begin to internalize what is happening, called "Taking Flight." These pictures provide a needed road map to direct you and also provide a means of assessing progress. The document is intended to be used with your coach. No secrets, both of you on the same page.

Notes

1 William Glasser, M.D. *Quality School: Managing Students Without Coercion, The.* New York: HarperCollins, 1998. Also see William Glasser, M.D. *Control Theory in the Classroom, revised* New York: Perennial Library, 2001.

2 This description of ITIP applied to the ITI model was developed by Linda Jordan, an associate trainer for Susan Kovalik & Associates and Assistant Professor at Hope College, School of Education, Holland, Michigan.

3. Dr. Robert Sylwester, "The Role of the Arts in Brain Development and Maintenance." (An unpublished paper). See also *A Celebration of Neurons: An Educator's Guide to the Human Brain.* (Alexandria, VA: ASCD, 1995), especially Chapter 4.

4 "A Private Universe" is a fascinating window on interviews with Harvard University students on their graduation day. The question put to them is "Explain the reason for the seasons." Even those who had taken astronomy classes gave the "Hot, baby, hot" explanation: When the sun gets closer, our season gets warmer. It is a powerful illustration of the power of misconceptions to override subsequent learning. Instructional strategies such as discussion and collaboration work are excellent tools for rooting out and correct stubborn misconceptions.

Notes to Myself

Chapter 11: Dealing with Challenging Behaviors

It's Not Just Your Imagination

With 30 students in a classroom—each one with unique brain wiring and prior experience—behavior which disrupts learning is as inevitable as death and taxes. Toxins in the environment, prescribed and recreational drugs, shattered families, stressful living that leaves little time to connect with family members, violence in society and inside our schools—all these and more contribute to changes in brain wiring. And, make no mistake, behavior is neurologically driven.[1]

How to respond? Many teacher behaviors make the situation worse. Some "fix" the problem in the moment but do nothing to keep it from reoccurring. Some dramatically improve the situation in ways that have long-term ability to reduce or eliminate problem behavior.

Searching for Solutions: Balancing Old Beliefs and New Science

There are many schools of thought about how to handle challenging behaviors. Some are home grown, such as "Spare the rod, spoil the child." Others seem to seep from the woodwork of our schools, such as "Don't smile until Thanksgiving." Behavioral psychologists, the Skinnerian model of punishments and rewards, have had a strong influence on education. Consequently, candy and detention, carrot and stick are the premise of many "classroom management" programs. However, whatever our roots and our current beliefs about behavior and how to handle it, we owe it to our students, and ourselves, to take a fresh look at the issue and come to a balanced perspective—a 21st century combination of the best of old beliefs and the best from brain research.

This new perspective must be a blend of behavioral science, psychology/sociology, and brain research. First let us dig up our deeply held beliefs, examine them in the light of the 21st century, and integrate their best elements for today's challenges.

The most useful application of new brain research to the classroom that we have found is the work of Dr. Sigurd Zielke. Through his intensive work over the years with adjudicated teens, crisis residency centers, and research study, he has put together a program that can help teachers see with new eyes those students whose behaviors place them at risk.[2]

Taking a Fresh Look at Challenging Behaviors in the Classroom

The first step in dealing with the challenge of extreme behavior in the classroom is to examine what our deeply held beliefs are and where they came from. For the most part, new teachers arrive steeped in theories and assumptions from the schools of behaviorism and psychology (cognitive-rational) but with precious little information about what brain research has to say about behavior.

Perspectives on Classroom Leadership

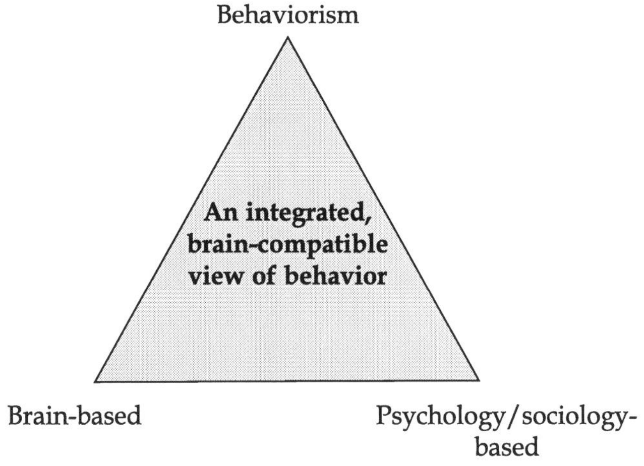

© Zielke & Zielke, 2004

Behaviorism. The school of behaviorism, whose best known proponent was Dr. B. F. Skinner, was built on the stimulus-response view of human behavior. Provide the proper stimulus—either a reward or a punishment—and you can evoke the desired response. The reward and punishment approaches to classroom management combine M&Ms and other "carrots" plus punishments, creating highly controlling environments in which all authority and judgment is held by the adults.

Psychology-Based Approaches. Psychology-based approaches focus on creating a need-fulfilling environment and interactions. Examples include those centered on Maslow's hierarchy of needs, Glasser's choice theory (the need to belong/love, gain power, have freedom, and have fun)[3], and Gossen's restitution (make amends/clean up what you did).[4]

Brain-Based View of Behavior. Looking at behavior from a brain research perspective requires that we shift our thinking from behavior as a set of choices to be manipulated or redirected to behavior as being neurologically driven, a mix of genes and childhood experiences, what Dr. Bob Sylwester calls the "genes and jeans" from our parents/primary caregivers.

This is not a fatalistic view of behavior, that you are your wiring, but it suggests that much misbehavior is beyond a child's ability to correct simply by choosing to do so.

Taking an Integrated, Brain-Compatible View of Behavior

Brain research suggests that, while the behaviorist approach is effective and even necessary in the short run, it is counter-productive in the long run.[5] Unfortunately, most preservice training does not take us beyond this short-term approach to help us develop strategies for the long haul.

Brain research also suggests that the psychological/sociological approaches can be valuable immediately and in the long run, but they don't provide the tools to delve deeply enough into the extremely challenging behavior of individual students to help them change the mental wiring that produces their at-risk behavior.

For most of us, this message is unsettling to say the least. Didn't we grow up in a system that embraced such notions and strategies? Didn't these assumptions go unchallenged through our teacher prep classes? For most of us, the answer is a yes. And no doubt we hear them woven into political debate and even family get-togethers, a reflection of generationally held beliefs.

What we need is to balance these outlooks, working from within the triangle, using an integrated approach that allows us to make commonsense choices as we move through our day, interacting in ways most effective for each student.

What is needed is consistent teacher-student and student-student interaction in a bodybrain-compatible environment that builds new neurological pathways that produce the kinds of behaviors that allow the student to be successful academically and socially.

Analyzing the Problem: One Size Does NOT Fit All

There are many barriers to analyzing behavior problems. The most significant is that most serious misbehavior needs one-on-one intervention which is often impossible to achieve given that we operate in a group setting—usually 25-35 students. The most common mistake is designing a behavior management program for the entire class when only a few students need the intervention.

As you analyze student behavior, focus on each individual.

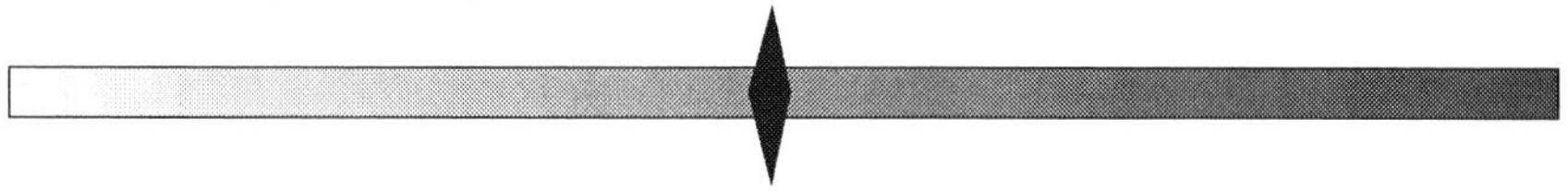

On one end of the spectrum, misbehavior can be described as mild and episodic, the result of being disengaged from the curriculum or unclear about procedures or expectations. Or, the student may just be reacting to/following the lead of a more disruptive classmate. Resolution of these problems is entirely under the control of the classroom teacher and requires orchestrating the environment primarily by using group structures and processes.

On the other end of the spectrum, misbehavior can be described as severe and chronic, disruptive to everyone, fed by brain dysfunction and/or severe, repeated trauma. Resolving these problems requires orchestrating the environment using group structures and processes AND one-on-one interventions.

Once you've analyzed the degree of severity of misbehavior for each student, determine how well the group solution—your Lifelong Guideline/LIFESKILLS-based, classroom-wide leadership program—will handle these misbehaviors. Will it suffice or do you need to add one-on-one interventions?

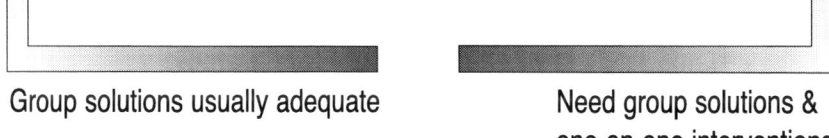

For group solutions, the first step is developing a sense of belonging. (See the description of how to build a sense of community in Chapters 9 and 7.) This is a critical drive for humans; when thwarted, it creates a major disturbance in a child's growth and development, even in learning as the child's attention to his/her world is overridden by the search for connection with a primary caregiver and others. Antisocial behavior is but a natural manifestation of this wiring in search of completion. (For a fascinating discussion of this neurological drive to connect to others, see *Hardwired to Connect: The New Scientific Case for Authoritative Communities . . . A Report to the Nation from the Commission on Children at Risk.*[3]

Getting Real: My Part in the Problem

Before you begin to analyze individual students to "see what's wrong," first analyze how you orchestrate your environment—curriculum, instruction, and group structures and processes. You may well find that there are things you are doing and not doing that make student behaviors worse, not better. In other words, are you adding fuel to the fire? Before you begin to plan one-on-one interventions or class-wide fixes, first throw away the combustibles.

Teacher's Belief System. How you view challenging behavior is critically important. Teachers who have trouble with "classroom management" tend to take misbehavior personally—a deliberate attempt by students to bedevil their teacher; it's an aggravation, something to be controlled and eliminated. Teachers with the greatest success with misbehavior view it as a teaching opportunity. Simply put, a student has too many of the wrong behaviors or too few correct behaviors or perhaps can't tell when to use the appropriate behaviors.[7] In any case, it's a learning opportunity for the student, not a major disruption in the teacher's day.

If you feel the heat of frustration or anger, students will stoke it for you. To succeed, you must remain calm and centered.

Lack of Personal Relationship Between Teacher and Student. If students don't feel they have a relationship with their teacher, they have nothing to lose by causing the teacher grief, so why not misbehave? And, besides, pushing the teacher's buttons and watching his/her veins pop out on the neck is a fun thing to do!

If students have nothing to lose by misbehaving, the incentive is to misbehave, show off, get a laugh. Eliminate this incentive by establishing a relationship with them that makes them identify with your situation.

Lack of a Sense of Community in the Classroom. Learning new correct behaviors and when to apply them is most efficiently acquired through imitating the behaviors of the group. When fully a member of the group, the incentive is to behave within the norms of the group.

Failure to Provide for Student Needs. According to Glasser, there are four essential needs a classroom must provide: to belong and to love, to gain power, to be free, and to have fun. Teachers ignore these at their peril.[8]

Instructional strategies and curriculum must be adjusted to ensure that they respond to these needs.

Lack of Emotional and Procedural Consistency. For students trying hard to keep a rein on their behavior, the anxiety caused by unpredictable events or a teacher's mood swings can be the straw that breaks their control. Teachers must model the Lifelong Guidelines/LIFESKILLS at all times and use agendas and written procedures every day to provide a sense of predictability, and thus of safety and security.

Lack of Engaging Curriculum. Re-evaluate your curriculum. Avoid curriculum that is boring because it's too easy or irrelevant to students' lives, too difficult because it requires skills that students don't have, or age-inappropriate (students can't understand it and must therefore resort to memorization). Such content is unengaging and no trickery of instructional strategies can overcome its deficits.

Overuse of Lecture and Worksheets. Limited instructional strategies is also a significant source of boredom and increased distractibility as the brain is always on the prowl for sensory input. Also, instructional strategies can help meet or thwart students' needs to gain power and be free (be self-directed) as well as have fun.

Teaching As a Contact Sport

Old approaches to dealing with students attempt to minimize or insulate emotion during human interaction, thus reducing friction. In contrast, the new, integrated view of working with students promotes the opposite. Dr. Zielke refers to teaching as a "contact sport" requiring that the teacher keep bumping the child's boundaries so as to nudge him/her toward experiences and responses that help with this rewiring. The idea here is not to eliminate conflict but to help students learn how to learn from it and deal with it in productive ways.

During this "contact sport," teachers need tools from the fields of behaviorism and psychology/sociology but they must keep their eye on brain research, using it to set the vision of where they are going, what tools to use along the way, and when to use those tools or abandon them.

Solutions

The best antidote for misbehavior is building a sense of community. The Lifelong Guidelines/LIFESKILLS—modeling them, formally teaching them, reteaching them, reinforcing them moment-by-moment through target talk—provide an excellent vehicle for boundary bumping in a supportive and nurturing environment.

Second, create an environment with absence of threat. Review Chapters 2 and 7.

Third, stay centered. Students delight in pushing adults' buttons. It's a big energy rush for them—power and fun. Zielke points out why by showing four quadrants of student misbehavior juxtaposed against related quadrants of adult response. When teacher behavior enters the same agressive quadrant as the student's behavior, the situation becomes explosive. If the teacher enters one of the passive quadrants, the students take over. The more a teacher

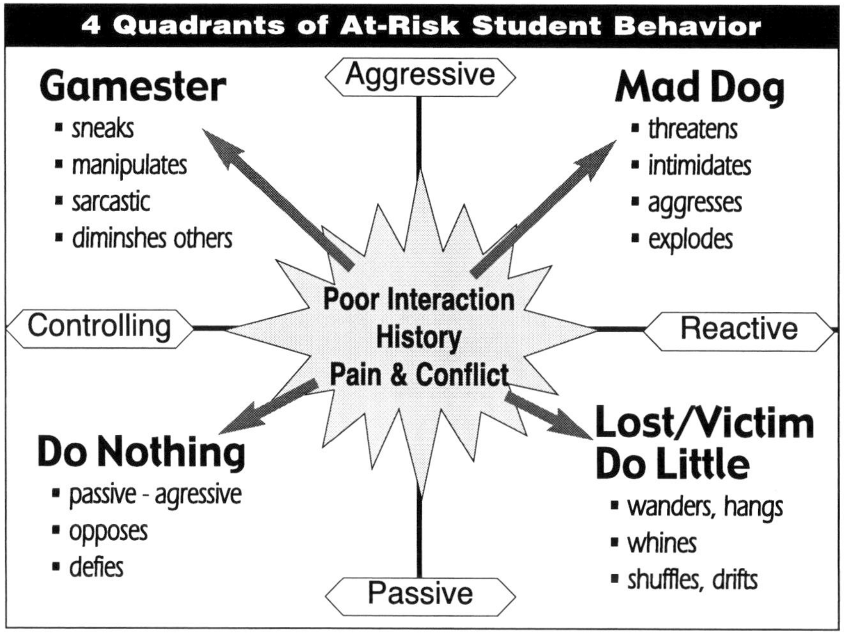

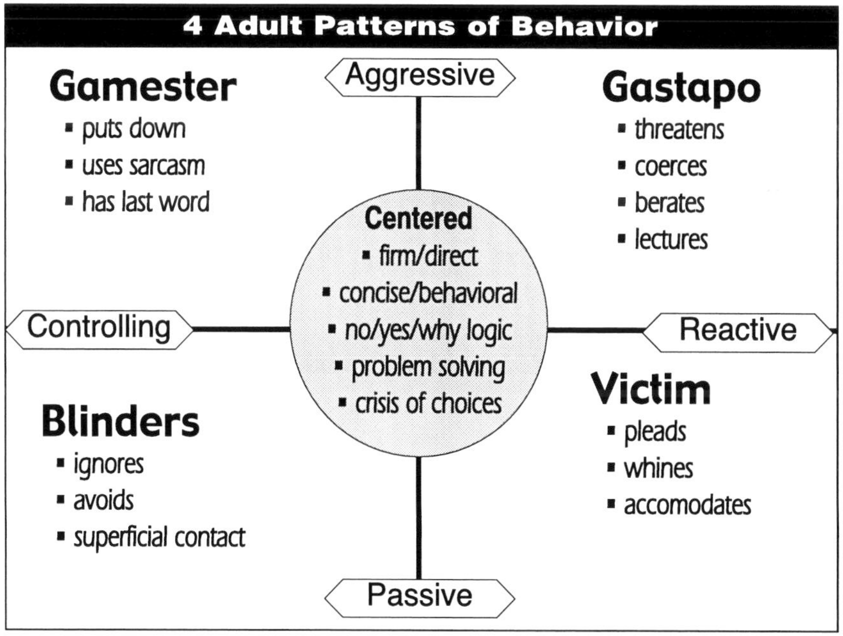

interacts from the center, the greater the ability to pull students from the outer edges of their quadrants into the middle.

If teachers allow themselves to stray from an emotional set pointing away from centeredness, the fireworks begin.

Silver Lining

However difficult behavior problems can become, your silver lining is this: Humans are hardwired to connect with others—to be loved and cared for and to love and care for others.[9] This is a biological imperative. However unreachable a student may seem, inside him/her is a powerful, neurological drive to connect. With this knowledge, we must commit ourselves to establishing a personal relationship with each student through which to model healthy interactions with others and help each become capable of creating healthy connections with others.[10]

Notes

1 Sigurd Zielke, Ph.D. "An Introduction to Neurobehavioral-Developmental & Social Classroom Management," a presentation to Susan Kovalik & Associates on January 20-22, 2005.

2 Dr. Zielke is currently producing books and a videotape about his work which will be available through Books for Educators by 2006. We strongly recommend his publications. They are the best tools for dealing with challenging behavior that we have seen in over 30 years.

3 William Glasser, M.D. *Quality School: Managing Students Without Coercion, The.* (New York: HarperCollins, 1998). Also see William Glasser, M.D. *Control Theory in the Classroom, revised,* (New York: Perennial Library, 2001).

4 Diane Gossen, *Restitution: Restructuring School Discipline,* (New York: Perennial Library, 1986). This book offers a process to redirect the individual, leading away from traditional methods of discipline towards a more research-based approach.

5 Every field of endeavor—from business to education—has studies that indicate that long-term, external manipulation of behavior doesn't work; it squashes the development of internal motivation and intrinsic drive to perform at high levels. For example, employers complain that employees develop a "what's in it for me" attitude about every work assignment, even the basic work load, never mind the over-and-above performance levels that they wish to encourage with rewards. In the classroom, students want to "negotiate" the minimum.

Even the external imposition of rewards is deadly. Alfie Kohn, *Punished by Rewards: The Trouble with Gold Stars, Incentive Plans, A's, Praise, and Other Bribes,* (Boston: Houghton Mifflin, 1993).

6 *Hardwired to Connect.* A collaborative work by the Commission of Children at Risk. (New York: sponsored by YMCA of the USA, Dartmouth Medical School, Institute for American Values, 2003).

7 Pat Belvel, TCI Consulting of San Jose, CA, specializes in trainings on classroom management and peer coaching.

8 Glasser, *Control Theory.*

9 *Hardwired to Connect.*

10 Connection to another is real. The Lifelong Guidelines and LIFESKILLS must become part of who we are, not things we ask of students in order to control their behavior. Likewise, the classroom can't become a community of learners until every student internalizes the Lifelong Guidelines and LIFESKILLS.

Part C

Implementing Stage 2: First Steps to Integrating Curriculum

Part C, Chapters 12 through 15, describes how to implement Stage 2 of the *ITI Classroom Stages of Implementation*—beginning steps in making curriculum brain compatible. It assumes that you have made significant progress in implementing Stage 1 to make the learning environment bodybrain compatible.

How to Use Stage 2

Whereas Stage 1 applies to the classroom 100% of the time, Stage 2 should be applied only to that portion of the day, week, or year for which teachers have developed curriculum using the ITI model. **The goal for Stage 2 is to implement *quality* bodybrain-compatible learning. Quality is more important than quantity.** *Keep working at Stage 2* **until at least 10-15 percent of the curriculum** for the total year is bodybrain compatible.

The time frames and content that teachers select to begin implementation of their bodybrain-compatible curriculum vary widely. Typically teachers begin where they feel they will be the most successful and expand from there. Whatever the starting point, however modest or bold, these descriptors at this stage apply only during the time when a teacher is implementing his/her bodybrain-compatible curriculum.

The actions that teachers must take, for curriculum and instructional strategies for Stage 2, are outlined on the following pages.

As a rule of thumb, Stage 2 should be completed within one year, two at most.

Curriculum Goals for Stage 2

Your primary curriculum development goals for Stage 2 of the *ITI Classroom Stages of Implementation* are to develop curriculum that:

- Fits how the brain learns
- Is based in *being there* locations
- Starts with an important concept that can integrate subject areas and basic skills together in ways students experience in their own lives

As you proceed, look for a concept(s) that helps pull together what the people at the *being there* site need to understand and be able to do AND the content from your state/district standards.

Also, note that integration should begin at home. Be sure you integrate areas ***within*** a subject area, such as physical, earth, and life sciences and technology and history, geography, civics, and economics, plus sociology/psychology and other windows on understanding man.

When integrating basic skills, let the circumstances of the *bieng there* location invite the skills into the curriculum in a natural way; ask yourself what the people there must be able to do.

Chapter 11 discusses developing curriculum based on *being there* experiences. Chapter 12 describes how to write integrated curriculum. Chapter 13 examines how to start organizing your curriculum.

ITI Classroom Stages of Implementation

Stage 2

Entry level for making curriculum bodybrain compatible

Entry Level into Integrating Curriculum

CURRICULUM	INSTRUCTIONAL STRATEGIES
• Bases curriculum on a physical location that students can and do frequently experience through *being there* study trips. • Chooses at least four *being there* locations that will provide real-life experiences with the selected concepts and skills.	• Takes students to each *being there* location at the beginning of study as well as at the end and in between as needed for students to see concepts in action.
• Selects the most powerful, intrinsically engaging concepts and skills captured by the overlapping answers to two questions: – What do people need to understand and be able to do at this site? (Includes workers, visitors, and users/consumers.) – What content and skills from my curriculum standards describe what one needs to understand and be able to do at this site?	• Teaches concepts and skills through the lives of those at the *being there* location rather than through the perspective of textbooks. Utilizes onsite interviews, visiting resource people, situational role playing, and other instructional strategies that make the concepts and skills come alive for students. • Integrates skills from other content areas whenever necessary to provide the tools students need to accomplish their learning tasks. Integration of curricular areas through team planning with colleagues is natural, not forced. Content and skills are organized to reflect the combinations of knowledge and skills needed by people working at/using the *being there* location.
• States clearly and succinctly each concept students are to understand. Determines what significant knowledge about the concept students must understand in order to achieve a deep understanding of the concept.	• Posts the key point(s) being studied on the theme bulletin board or in student binders. For younger students, includes visual symbols to help convey the meaning of the content. • Uses a variety of instructional strategies, each selected to best teach students the concept, significant knowledge, or skill at hand.
• For every concept, significant knowledge, and skill (key point) to be taught, provides sufficient related activities (inquiries) typical of those performed at the *being there* location to enable students to practice until the concepts, knowledge, and skills are wired into long-term memory.	• Provides each student ample time to complete sufficient inquiries to master the key points. Ensures that students are allowed to work through their strengths (multiple intelligences) through the first three stages of learning (see the New Definition of Learning, page 5.3).

ITI Classroom Stages of Implementation **Stage 2**

Entry Level into Integrating Curriculum - continued

Entry level for making curriculum bodybrain compatible

CURRICULUM	INSTRUCTIONAL STRATEGIES
• Provides students with choices and multiple opportunities for real-world application through daily inquiries that also allow multiple ways of solving problems and producing products.	• Regularly provides choices honoring both personal interests and the multiple intelligences through activities/inquiries and other means.
• Integrates curriculum by using a concept to pull together content and skills from multiple subject areas. This organizing concept is the theme unifying study for the year. • For at least two chunks of integrated curriculum during the year, includes a Social/Political Action Project and concludes with a Celebration of Learning.	• Displays the theme on the wall along with immersion items to heighten student interest and elicit memories of prior experiences with the topic being studied. • Uses Social/Political Action Projects and Celebrations of Learning to provide real-world contexts for learning and using knowledge and skills, to provide real audiences for practicing/developing language arts and math skills, and to provide students opportunities to practice responsible citizenship.
	• Completes writing curriculum (key points and inquiries) before beginning to plan lessons.

Note: The goal of Stage 2 is to develop and implement integrated curriculum for 10-15% of the year.

ITI Classroom Stages of Implementation **Stage 2**

Entry level for making curriculum bodybrain compatible

Entry Level into Integrating Curriculum - continued

CURRICULUM

INSTRUCTIONAL STRATEGIES

- Expertly uses all the instructional strategies identified in Stages 1.2 and 1.3 everyday, throughout the day for both ITI integrated curriculum time and for other curriculum as well.
- Expertly selects strategies for ITI integrated curriculum time that ensure that students reach mastery, i.e., that students identify/understand patterns and develop programs for using what they understand in real-world ways. Such instructional strategies include those in Stages 1.2 and 1.3 plus the following:
  - Modeling being a lifelong learner and participating citizen.
  - Movement to help students identify and understand patterns and sequences of events/processes, and to build mental programs for using concepts and skills, retaining them in long-term memory.
  - Collaboration, the content for which is specially designed so that no one student can complete an inquiry by him/herself. Collaborative work sessions include identifying in advance the Lifelong Guidelines and LIFESKILLS that will be necessary to successfully complete an assignment plus reflective thinking at the end of the work. Whenever possible, the structure and roles within the collaborative group are an extension of the content to be learned, such as roles of people in a court room (judge, jury, legal stenographer, and so forth).
  - Knowledge of temperament, used during instruction and when designing inquiries in ways that speed up and deepen learning.

ITI Classroom Stages of Implementation

Stage 2

Entry level for making curriculum bodybrain compatible

Entry Level into Integrating Curriculum - continued

CURRICULUM	INSTRUCTIONAL STRATEGIES
• Chooses at least four *being there* locations that will provide real-life experiences with the selected concepts and skills.	• Instructional strategies for introducing and reteaching concepts and skills of the ITI integrated curriculum: – *Being there* experiences which are enhanced and deepened through lead-up activities, assignments during bus rides, focused follow-up activities including return trips to the *being there* location, visits by resource people, immersion and simulations, personalized homework assignments, and so forth. – Teaching concepts and skills through the lives of those at the *being there* location rather than through the perspective of textbooks. Utilizes on-site interviews, visiting resource people, situational role playing, and other instructional strategies that make the concepts and skills come alive for students. Includes role playing to help students learn to apply concepts and skills and to build C.U.E. (creative, useful, emotional) into the teacher's instructional strategies and inquiries. – The ITI Discovery Process as a frequent alternative to direct instruction and an important means of helping students learn how to learn.
• For at least two chunks of integrated curriculum during the year, includes a social/political action project and concludes with a celebration of learning. • Meets frequently with a professional or peer coach who supports the implementation of a bodybrain-compatible learning environment for students.	• Expertly uses instructional strategies for enhancing wiring into long-term memory and for assessment: – Clear performance criteria for students through inquiries and rubrics that describe the performance levels expected of them. These statements of expectation are written and do not require explanation from the teacher. – Social/political action projects that grow naturally out of students' study at a *being there* location (or from a current event/situation in school, community, nation, or world) and that provide students practice in using the democratic processes of our government and society and in contributing to others. – Celebrations of learning that heighten emotional involvement in applying the key points and help wire learning into long-term memory.

Chapter 12: Developing Curriculum Based on a Being There Experience

ITI Classroom Stages of Implementation **Stage 2**

Entry level for making curriculum bodybrain compatible

CURRICULUM

- Bases curriculum on a physical location that students can and do frequently experience through *being there* study trips.
- Chooses at least four *being there* locations that will provide real-life experiences with the selected concepts and skills.

INSTRUCTIONAL STRATEGIES

- Takes students to each *being there* location at the beginning of study as well as at the end and in between as needed for students to see concepts in action.

- Selects the most powerful, intrinsically engaging concepts and skills captured by the overlapping answers to two questions:
  - What do people need to understand and be able to do at this site? (Includes workers, visitors, and users/consumers.)
  - What content and skills from my curriculum standards describe what one needs to understand and be able to do at this site?

- Teaches concepts and skills through the lives of those at the *being there* location rather than through the perspective of textbooks. Utilizes on-site interviews, visiting resource people, situational role playing, and other instructional strategies that make the concepts and skills come alive for students.
- Integrates skills from other content areas whenever necessary to provide the tools students need to accomplish their learning tasks. Integration of curricular areas through team planning with colleagues is natural, not forced. Content and skills are organized to reflect the combinations of knowledge and skills needed by people working at/using the *being there* location.

Anchoring Curriculum in Real-Life Locations

In our opinion, the two most convincing areas of brain research are: 1) the importance of emotion and movement in the bodybrain learning partnership[1] and 2) the need—the absolute requirement—for full sensory input to the brain through all 19 senses.[2]

For teachers, this means that content must be meaningful and mentally and physically engaging and that the amount of sensory input must be vastly increased over that of the traditional tools of textbooks, worksheets, lectures, and an occasional video or Internet scan. Anchoring curriculum and instruction in *being there* locations meets both requirements handily. Don't teach from a book, teach from the real world—a backyard, a mall, a park in the neighborhood, a grocery store. Teach from real places where real people go to meet their needs—as shoppers, business people, people looking for a place to play, relax, or be entertained.

Some readers may complain that their district doesn't allow money for field trips. We're not talking about *field trips* or end-of-the year *travel rewards*. We are talking about **study** trips designed in accordance with brain research findings about how the human brain learns. Is there a difference? You bet! Is it doable? Affordable? Absolutely, ***if*** we choose locations near the school that we and our students can revisit frequently by walking or by taking a short ride on public transportation.

Are we talking about throwing away textbooks? No. But we are suggesting that textbooks be used as one of many resources, not as ***the*** curriculum and paramount instructional tool.

Are we talking about ignoring state standards? Absolutely not. Standards adopted by the district tell us what we as teachers are expected to teach our students. We owe our students a curriculum with no gaps and no repetitions as they progress from grade to grade. Curriculum standards, be they district adopted, state driven, or school generated, are an essential foundation for good curriculum planning at the classroom level.

Anchoring curriculum in real-life locations gives students clear pictures of **what we want them to understand** and **what we want them to do with what they understand** because they can see how and when people use such knowledge and skills. The richness of these pictures also allows students to make connections both to other locations and among other content areas.

Examples of Engaging Being There Locations

Look for sites that are immediately accessible—a walking trip of 15 minutes or less. First look for sites on campus, such as the cafeteria, bus barn, or maintenance center. Next, branch out into the neighborhood within walking distance. Then, look for sites that can be reached by inexpensive public transportation.

Be creative. The most intriguing study trips are often the ones right under our noses—locations where we have gone innumerable times but never thought to take a behind-the-scenes look, such as grocery stores, malls, our own school cafeteria or bus system. Examples: [3]

Kindergarten: School yard, backyard of a nearby home (for the natural world and for hobbies), nearby pond or creek, manmade pond on the school grounds, nearby park, nearby empty lot, pet store, and animals living in or visiting the classroom.

First grade: Any of the above locations plus underground aspects of those locations, local habitats that are rich in animal and plant life, farm, garden (on the school grounds or nearby home), larger bodies of water such as lakes, rivers, ocean, and a zoo, aquarium, or pet store.

Second grade: Any of the above locations plus natural history museums, taxidermy shop, construction and repair shops where a variety of tools are used, and local businesses.

Third grade: Any of the above locations plus nearby road cuts that expose changes, fast or slow, in landscape, before and after flood scenes, a variety of construction projects that illustrate new building and remodeling, recycling operations from pick-up to remanufacturing to resale, and lots of in-classroom and neighborhood illustrations of life cycles, physical science cycles, machines, and so forth. Also, community landmarks, businesses (grocery store, mall, mom-and-pop stores of any kind), and city agencies and resources such as police, fire, and medical hospitals, clinics, etc. And, don't forget observation of daily weather and the nighttime sky.

Fourth grade: Any of the above locations plus those a little farther afield, including state agencies and state historical sites or their replications.

Fifth grade: Any of the above from the perspective of systems or change and sites of national significance.

Sixth grade: Any of the above observed with a specific perspective based in a concept from state standards that would integrate both science and history/social studies.

How to Bring Together Real-Life Locations and Curriculum Standards

Just as a magnet attracts metal shards, a *being there* experience helps attract important concepts and skills from your state standards/district-adopted curriculum. At this stage of your implementation, allow this magnetic quality of *being there* locations to do your curriculum integration and development work for you. Rather than trying to chase down various curriculum pieces, allow the intrinsically interesting aspects of the *being there* location and the most important points from your curriculum standards to simply pull together, a natural fit of related patterns. Curriculum for this stage of implementation should be intriguing and enjoyable to both you and your students. Remember, this is your entry into integrated curriculum. Make it fun. Give yourself the best chance at succeeding.

Ask these two pivotal questions when developing curriculum based on a *being there* location:

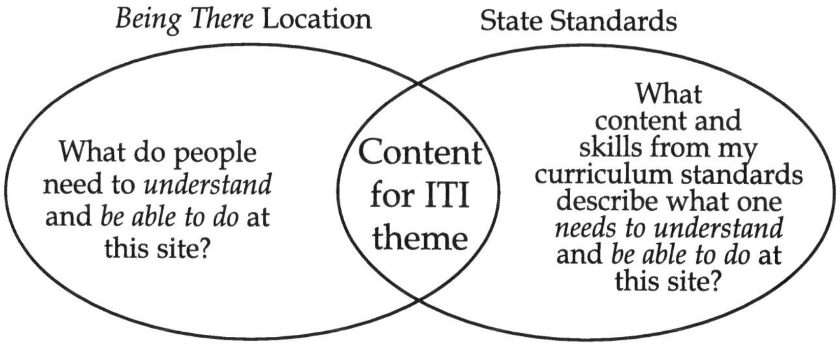

The answers to these two questions help you analyze your real-life location and your curriculum standards so that you can:

- Extract what is most meaningful and important for students to learn and then select and organize the most engaging, relevant concepts and skills from your state standards.
- Create a basis for authentic assessment (see Chapter 23) by building in real-life standards and expectations for what a capable person should understand and be able to do at this location.

The answers to these two questions give you the content for your curriculum. Curriculum development in the ITI model requires an eye for the practical and lots of common sense; it is not a theoretical exercise.

Older students enjoy exploring the question, "How would this location and its operation be different if people really understood the content and skills we are learning?" This question

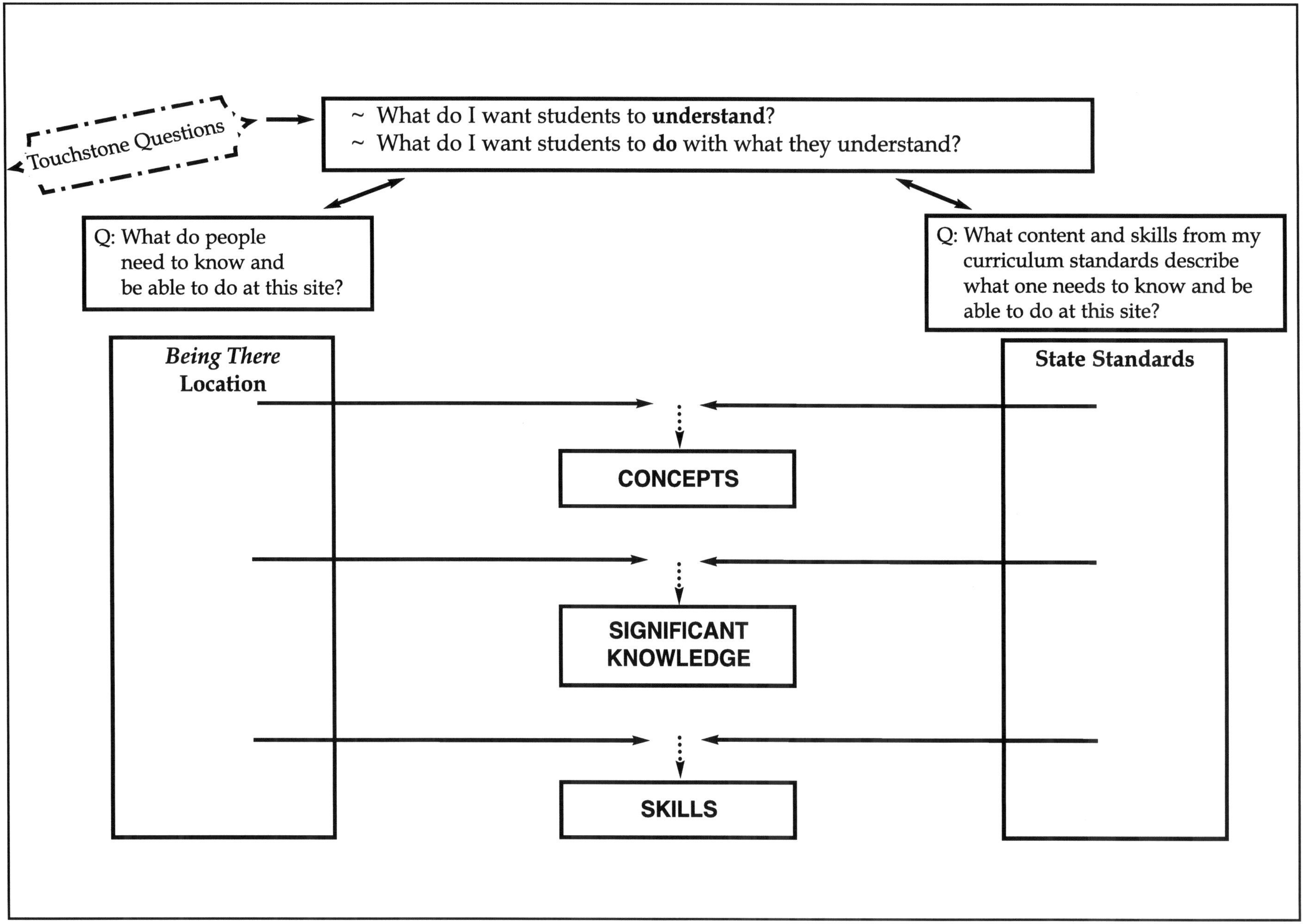
Touchstone Questions
~ What do I want students to **understand**?
~ What do I want students to **do** with what they understand?
Q: What do people need to know and be able to do at this site?
Q: What content and skills from my curriculum standards describe what one needs to know and be able to do at this site?
Being There Location
State Standards
CONCEPTS
SIGNIFICANT KNOWLEDGE
SKILLS

allows/forces the teacher and students to "think outside the box" and look afresh at the question, "What's worth teaching/learning?"

Choosing a physical location as the anchor for curriculum is critical to the ITI model for several reasons:

- The best way to ensure that students quickly grasp an accurate and comprehensive understanding of the concepts and skills of the curriculum is to allow them to experience those concepts in their real-world contexts.
- Once students understand concepts in one location, they can generalize them to other locations and use them to make predictions about events past and future. *This speeds up and deepens the pace of future learning.*
- Each of us must understand how our community works to become an informed citizen.

Guidelines for Selecting Being There Locations

Selecting physical locations upon which to build your curriculum is the most critical curricular decision you will make for the year. Like any builder, choose your site with care. The more solid the foundation, the more empowering your curriculum can be.

Before selecting a physical location, do your homework. Think through the following steps.

Step 1: Analyze the Potential of a Site to Teach What Your Students Need to Learn

Remember, you are not developing curriculum for separate subjects which must have a designated amount of seat time per day. Let the locations integrate the aspects of a subject area naturally. For example, don't just focus on the biological aspects of a location; examine your *being there* location in its full science context, including technology and physical and earth science. Or, when looking at the historical aspects, include today's problems created by similar social, economic, and governmental forces. Then, if halfway through the year or semester one area needs more study, concentrate on it during your last *being there* experience or address it during the gaps between your chunks of integrated curriculum. Remember, let the world integrate your curriculum naturally.

Also, focus on the fact that real life is all around you. A location need not be far afield to be powerful. Consider first your school campus, the immediate neighborhood accessible on foot, and then those locations that you can access via public transportation. Avoid the traditional "field trip" location that is too expensive to visit more than once.

For example, consider the common grocery store. Been there a million times? Of course. But have you ever been behind the scenes and looked at it from a business perspective? Would you be amazed to discover that the typical profit margin for grocery stores is two to three cents on the dollar? Ever wonder how many items change price? When? How often? The possibilities for study are unlimited: profit/loss, employer/employee relationships, the demographics of the clientele/producer, legal restrictions, health inspections, competition, energy costs, OSHA requirements, and so forth.

Step 2: Visit the Site

First, go to each location with new eyes. Pretend you've never been there before. Get curious! Look everything over from a fresh perspective. Look behind the scenes. Imagine what others see—those who work there, those who come there to shop, visit, enjoy. What do these folks need to know to perform their roles well? What do visitors need to know to get the best value for their dollar, to make the wisest decisions, to avoid being taken advantage of, or to enjoy it most fully? Here's an interesting challenge: How would the location and its operations be different if people fully understood the content and skills you plan to teach your students?Second, interview people—those who create the environment (employees and owners) and those who come here (clients/customers and sightseers). Skip past the knowledge and comprehension questions of Bloom's Taxonomy and dive right into the levels of application, analysis, evaluation, and synthesis. That's where the fun and engagement are! Ask the interviewees why they choose to work or shop here. What about this place makes them proud to work/visit here?

Third, put yourself in your students' shoes. What is gripping about this location? What would bring you back again and again?

Step 3: Expand Your Knowledge Base

Solid curriculum can't be developed from information off the top of one's head and our typical curriculum tools are limited; state standards/district curriculum offer an outline, textbooks provide only summary, superficial information. Expect to become a learner. Open yourself up to the joy of discovery. Don't expect to have all the answers. Long gone is the era when what you knew by age 25 would carry you through a lifetime. Learning how to learn and learning to embrace the necessity for learning with enjoyment are the demands of our time. Model this and let your excitement and passion transfer to your students.

Pursue concepts that you believe will allow students to unlock meaning in other settings. Ask yourself several questions: What can be generalized and what can be used to predict events or happenings in other locations? From the students' points of view, what's useful? What are the most empowering concepts and skills you can help them understand?

Keep in mind that the availability of resources is an important consideration when you select a location. You should expect to have at least 50 resources in your room, such as books (e.g., *Eye Witness, Usbourne* series), magazines, print of all kinds written at a range of reading levels (including children's books that provide clear explanations and lots of visuals), plus multi-media options which capitalize on today's technologies (Internet, video, encyclopedias on CD, and so forth). And, very importantly, real things for hands-on exploration.

STEP 4: Revisit Your Curriculum

However small or large this chunk of curriculum for the *being there* experience, is it as conceptual as you can make it? (See discussion in Chapter 11 and Part C.) Have you prioritized the content so students will have time to *understand* and learn to *apply* the most important concepts, significant knowledge, and skills? Are your curriculum choices solid and acceptable to your supervisors? Can you explain them thoroughly to the parents? If so, you are ready to begin developing key points and inquiries.

Integration Made Easy

The usual way to prepare to integrate curriculum is to take the prescribed content of traditional subject areas, schedule them one at a time, and then search for ways to make them come alive for your students. In contrast, ITI curriculum makes integration easy and natural by allowing *being there* locations to make curriculum match the world we see when we look out the window, walk down the street, and window shop in the mall. Science is everywhere we look, the results of history and social interaction are unavoidable, the arts are everywhere we turn, and all are going on together.

Integrating Subject Content and Basic Skills

If you're still on the fence, not yet ready to base your curriculum in *being there* locations, consider this: *Being there* locations are the great mixer—not only blending together subject areas but also content with skills, in natural and engaging ways.

Be assured that the basic skills—basic and universally essential—can be taught using any location where they are used in real life. Any location drips with numbers; all you have to do is decide what mathematic functions and concepts you want to apply to those numbers.

Use the numbers built into your physical location to make algebra and geometry, as well as basic math, come alive—how far, how long, how tall, how wide, how much, what volume, what angle, which direction, how many years since, how much per square foot/mile, and so forth. Keep a running list of numerical data inherent in each *being there* location. When test-practice time comes, have students use data from these lists instead of that from dull worksheets so students can create their own problems demanding skills they are studying. Make geometry and algebra come alive.

Reading? Writing? Oh my, yes. *Being there* locations offer students something real to read about and a real audience to write to. Have students communicate their discoveries and thank resource people who helped them learn.

For a comprehensive discussion of how to integrate the basic skills, see Chapter 18.

Being there locations also bring together all the other subject areas in a natural, effortless way—science, social studies, the arts, and so on. Almost any mixture of natural and man-made settings will demonstrate the concepts, significant knowledge, and skills you have chosen from your state standards to include in your integrated curriculum. As for history/social studies, just add people to your location and you will have a window through which to view human nature past, present, or future. All other content areas can be similarly accessed.

Integration and Assessment

Anchoring curriculum content in the real world also allows us to develop assessment that mirrors performance standards that students and teachers encounter in their everyday lives. For example, we write a letter with perfect grammar and spelling because we want a real person to take our opinion seriously; we want to calculate math problems accurately when the answers impact our personal lives.

For more information about assessment, see Chapter 19.

Self Check

Ideal *being there* locations:

- Capture student, and teacher, interest and enthusiasm in order to sustain willingness to learn over time, leading students to eagerly ask and pursue questions.
- Provide a powerful illustration of how the concepts and skills are used—why, how, when, by whom.
- Provide maximum sensory input (using as many of the 19 senses as possible).
- Invite authentic use of the concepts and skills you have selected from your state/district curriculum standards.
- Are readily accessible (time and expense) so that the class can visit regularly, allowing for in-depth exploration.
- Have significant carry-over potential, i.e., if students come to understand this setting well (the scientific and technological aspects as well as the historical and social science concepts that drove the setting's creation and continuance), they will be able to immediately understand a great deal about other similar settings.
- Become a prototype for learning ***how*** to learn about the real world.

Notes

1 See Chapter 2 for an in-depth discussion of the power and role of emotion and movement to effect learning and performance.

2 See Chapter 1 for a discussion of sensory input and its importance to learning.

3 Karen D. Olsen, *Science Continuum of Concepts For Grades K-6* (Covington, WA: Books for Educators, 1995).

Chapter 13: Tools for Developing Integrated Curriculum

ITI Classroom Stages of Implementation **Stage 2**

Entry level for making curriculum bodybrain compatible

CURRICULUM	INSTRUCTIONAL STRATEGIES
• States clearly and succinctly each concept students are to understand. Determines what significant knowledge about the concept students must understand in order to achieve a deep understanding of the concept.	• Posts the key point(s) being studied on the theme bulletin board or in student binders. For younger students, includes visual symbols to help convey the meaning of the content.
• For every concept, significant knowledge, and skill (key point) to be taught, provides sufficient related activities (inquiries) typical of those performed at the *being there* location to enable students to practice until the concepts, knowledge, and skills are wired into long-term memory.	• Provides each student ample time to complete sufficient inquiries to master the key points. Ensures that students are allowed to work through their strengths (multiple intelligences) through the first three stages of learning (see the New Definition of Learning, page 5.3).
• Provides students with choices and multiple opportunities for real-world application through daily inquiries that also allow multiple ways of solving problems and producing products.	• Regularly provides choices honoring both personal interests and the multiple intelligences through activities/inquiries and other means.
	• Completes writing curriculum before beginning to lesson plans.

Tips for Developing Curriculum for Stage 2

Since the goal of Stage 2 is to develop curriculum for only 10-15% of the school year, select *being there* experiences and content that you consider most engaging to students and that most interest you as well. Don't start with the "dry" stuff in your state standards; pull out the enlivening concepts that are best illustrated at the *being there* location. All else builds on these decisions.

Don't worry about how to integrate. That's the easy part. As discussed in the previous chapter, simply allow the context of the *being there* experience to integrate your subject areas and skills naturally—as you see it in real life at the *being there* location.

The hardest part about developing integrated curriculum is being clear about what you want students to understand and what you want them to do with it. This is different from a generalized question about what you want students to *know.* Such vagueness often leads us into a sea of factoids—details, dates, and definitions—and we quickly end up drowning in a soup of overwhelming possibilities.

Again, begin by asking yourself what jumps out at you as the big idea, the most important concept, the most needed skills at this location. Then, look through your state standards and identify the concepts and skills that are a good match. State what you want students to understand clearly and crisply—preferably as a single sentence. Never use more than three or four sentences for each idea. Keep it short, simple, and clear. These are key points.

Next, think through what you want students to be able to do with what they understand and how they can practice applying those concepts and skills in the context of the *being there* experience or a simulation of it. These are inquiries.

One concept and a handful of significant knowledge and skill key points with inquiries attached will get you through a mini-theme lasting half days for a week or more.

Have we made this sound too easy? Well, the mechanics aren't that difficult. Again, the hard part is getting clear on what *exactly* you want students to understand and *exactly* what you want them to do with it.

Always start with a concept, something that students can carry with them to unlock meaning in new situations, something generalizable and transferable. Then add on from there. Once you're clear about the concepts and skills and how students will use them in real-world ways, the actual process of writing them down on paper is an easy writing task, much like writing one short paragraph at a time.

Just as business admonishes us to think outside the box, it is helpful to think beyond the usual questions about what may be on the test. Instead, ask what students need to know to understand their world and what skills they need to act on it.

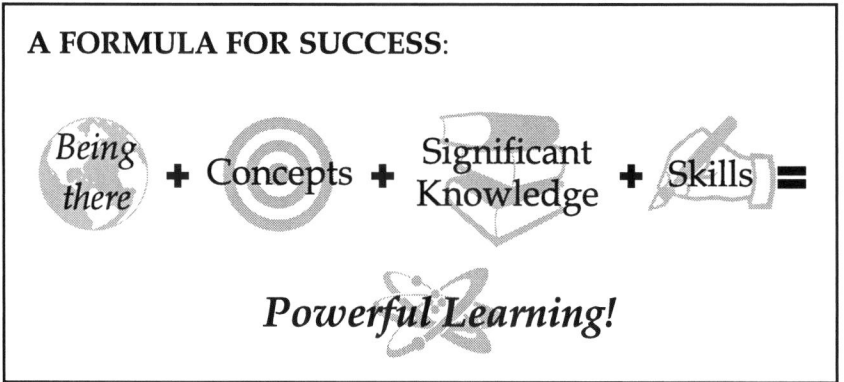

A FORMULA FOR SUCCESS:

Being there + Concepts + Significant Knowledge + Skills =

Powerful Learning!

Making Curriculum Fit the Brain

The purpose in writing your own curriculum is to make it more powerful for students. Otherwise, why bother? To make it more powerful, curriculum should be developed to fit how the brain learns (review brain research presented in Chapters 4 and 5—the brain as pattern seeker and meaning maker and learning as the acquisition of mental programs). Powerful, bodybrain-compatible curriculum:

- Builds on local *being there* experiences that provide maximum sensory input, engage the body in learning, and level the playing field for students who lack prior experience with the concepts and skills to be learned.
- Is conceptual
- Carries the learner through the four steps of the ITI brain-based definition of learning (see below)
- Is tailored to your specific students' interests, needs, and ways of learning in ways that unleash positive emotions and deepen commitment to learning.

Definition of Learning

Part One—**Input stage: Pattern detection** consists of first identifying or recognizing the pattern and then making meaning of the pattern, including its relationship to other patterns.

and

Part Two—**Output stage: Program building** consists of learning to apply what is learned, at first experimentally and consciously, and then, after practice and wiring it into long-term memory, applying what is learned with the almost automatic ease and skill of the expert.

Tools for Writing Curriculum for Stage 2

Once you have selected the most engaging concepts and skills based on the overlap between your *being there* location and your curriculum standards as described in Chapter 12, you are ready to begin writing your curriculum. Curriculum writing is made much easier if you ask yourself two questions:

- ***What do I want my students to understand?***

  This question helps you focus on what you want to teach—the concepts and skills identified during your work in Chapter 12. It also requires that you write clear and specific statements of what you want students to understand.

  These statements are your ***key points***. (See pages 13.6-8).

- ***What do I want students to be able to do with what they understand?***

  This question helps you figure out ways students can apply what you are teaching in real-world—and thus memorable—ways, beginning with uses at the *being there* location and then generalizing to other situations. This is the step that ensures mastery and long-term memory, gives you a solid foundation for authentic assessmen, and ensures success - yours as a teacher and your students' as learners.

  These statements are your ***inquiries***. (See pages 13.11-13)

Key Points: What I Want My Students to Understand

The most important thing to say about key points is this: Make them as conceptual as you can. Avoid writing down a string of factoids. Factoids are good for playing Jeopardy but aren't useful in real life.

Conceptual Key Points

Go for big ideas/concepts that will engage your students. Use the GUTS criteria to guide you:

G = generalizable—a principle or conclusion that can be used to explain specifics; pulls idea into general use

U = understandable by students this age

T = transferable to new locations/situations

S = succinct and clear

Generalizable. "Teacher, why is this important? What's this good for?" All students deserve curriculum that answers these questions. In our mind, it's curriculum that can be generalized to a big idea or concept that explains an important aspect of our world and that can be transferred to similar but different situations. Such curriculum empowers students and makes teachers more effective and efficient.

Always ask yourself what you want your students to understand and why.

To write powerful curriculum, you must be willing to do some independent research and to learn to play the Bump Up game.

Research Is a Must. One can't extract concepts out of district/state curriculum standards or a textbook without a solid knowledge base. Writing factoids? That's easy; they are everywhere. But conceptual statements that can be generalized and applied in similar but different situations require a knowledge base beyond that which is needed to teach from published curriculum tools and curriculum frameworks.

A good beginning place for research is the information available at the *being there* location, such as brochures, pamphlets, booklets, magazines, and books. Next, follow up on any references found in these sources. Then, branch out. Visit the Internet as well as your library and media center.

Your goal is to obtain enough knowledge to write key points that can be generalized and transferred.

Bumping Up. The Bump Up game is a search for big ideas/concepts to organize, ideas that give meaning to what we expect our students to learn. Here are some examples of the Bump Up game applied to information found in a brochure on dog worms—research for a *being there* visit to a vet's office. Let's assume that the relevant state standards you have chosen are about parasites.

As you read through this brochure about parasites, you find lots of information about worms, especially heartworms. However, you want to make the information as transferable as possible so that students who have a pet other than a dog can also relate to the problem. Ultimately, your students should be able to transfer some of the knowledge about parasites in dogs to parasites in other animals, including humans.

Your task is to "bump up" the contents of the brochure to make it more conceptual. Begin by checking your state standards. Are there relevant concepts about parasites? If so, you're ready to write key points. If not, you will need to extract concepts from the brochure using your knowledge of parasites.

The brochure about heartworms on the next page is typical of information sources we run across in our day-to-day lives—specific information about a specific topic. Unfortunately, such information often does not help us generalize to other situations. For example, suppose we have a cat in the house. What does this brochure tell us about taking care of our cat to ensure against parasites? Not much. But, with more research, we can state the important concepts rather than just restating these specifics; our students can then learn a great deal that they can transfer to other situations now and in the future. They can know something about cats, rabbits, hamsters, and any other pet they may choose. Concepts provide post office boxes in the brain to which new information can be sent for comparison, add-on, updating, etc. This makes learning more efficient.

For example, look at the heartworm brochure on the next two pages. Facts and factoids abound. The challenge is to recognize what is really important for students to understand and be able to use. First pull out the concepts; then look for significant knowledge necessary to build a conceptual understanding of internal parasites that is sufficient to help one become a competent pet owner and apply the concept of parasitism more broadly to other species, including humans. Select those facts that help students more fully understand our concept about parasites.

As you can see, the details stated in the "facts and factoids" column, although interesting, can't be generalized or transferred. Their use ends with dogs and, if one doesn't own a dog, the information is largely forgettable. However, when bumped up to a conceptual statement about parasites, the learner can acquire an understanding that has wide application.

Where heartworm disease comes from...

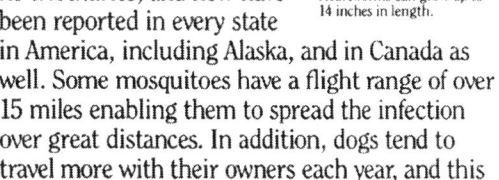

Mosquitoes transmit heartworm disease.

Mosquitoes transmit heartworm disease by biting an infected dog, then passing the infection on to other dogs they bite. Developing heartworms migrate to the dog's heart, where they can grow up to 14 inches in length as they mature. If not removed, they can cause permanent heart and lung damage and even death. But you may not see any signs before it's too late. And once diagnosed, the treatment for heartworm disease can be dangerous and costly.

How it spreads....

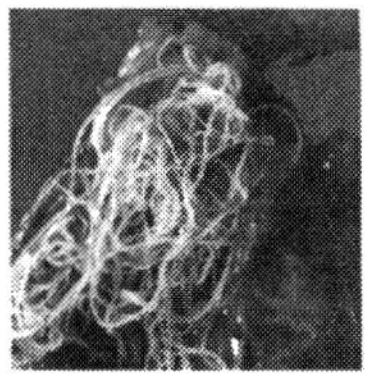

Heartworms can grow up to 14 inches in length.

Heartworm infections are common along the Atlantic and Gulf coasts and the Mississippi River Valley and its tributaries, and now have been reported in every state in America, including Alaska, and in Canada as well. Some mosquitoes have a flight range of over 15 miles enabling them to spread the infection over great distances. In addition, dogs tend to travel more with their owners each year, and this also can increase the spread of heartworm disease.

When the weather begins to turn cold, mosquitoes often try to find protected areas such as inside your home or doghouse. So even dogs kept mainly indoors can become infected. They are also at risk when taken for walks or released in the yard.

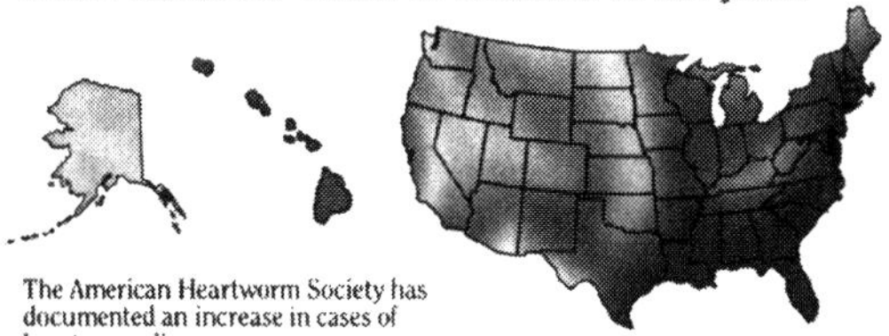

The American Heartworm Society has documented an increase in cases of heartworm disease.

Heartworms aren't the only threat to your dog

Roundworms (Ascarids) and Hookworms: There are two important species of ascarids and hookworms that commonly infect all dogs. These intestinal parasites can cause poor growth—and even death. Dogs of all ages are at risk, but puppies are particularly vulnerable. Your veterinarian can diagnose these infections in your dog by examining a fecal sample to determine if eggs are present.

Puppies are often born with roundworms (Ascarids)...

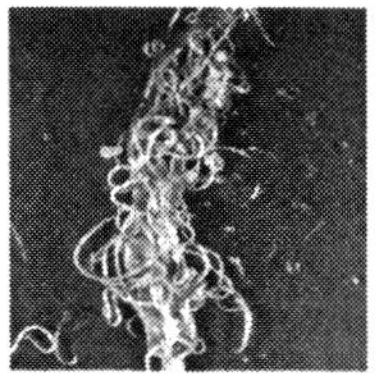

Roundworms (ascarids) *Toxocara canis*

Many puppies are born with roundworms, which they contract from their mothers before birth. These worms can also be passed in egg form through a dog's feces. Roundworms live and grow in a dog's intestines, and can reach lengths of up to 7 inches. Dogs suffering from a heavy roundworm infection appear potbellied, have a dull coat, and may experience vomiting and diarrhea. Lung damage, pneumonia, and liver damage may also occur.

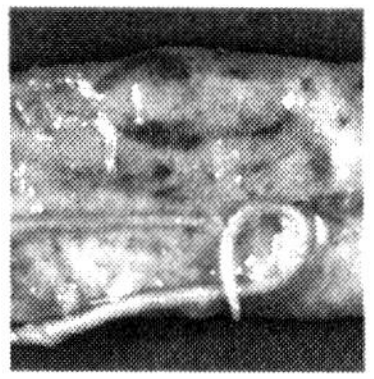

Roundworm (ascarids) *Toxascaris leonina*

Hookworm can be fatal...

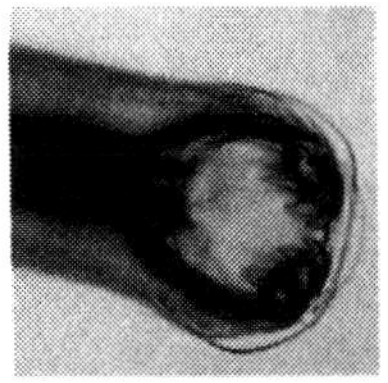

Hookworm
Ancylostoma caninum

Hookworms are also common in puppies. If left untreated, heavy infections can cause a puppy's death within weeks.

Hookworms can be passed through the mother's milk, or in egg form via the feces. Infection can also occur as the result of larvae penetrating the skin (causing a local rash), after which they migrate via the bloodstream to the intestines. Hookworms can cause diarrhea, severe anemia, and weakness. Dogs may also lose weight due to the bloodsucking of hookworms.

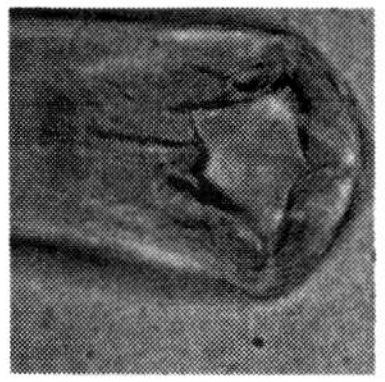

Hookworm
Uncinaria stenocephala

Taken from "To protect your dog . . . Ask for heartworm preventive that has a heart." Heartgard [30]

Note: **Some concepts are global** enough that they provide an **umbrella for study across subject areas.** For example: "Prevention is the best cure." This concept can be applied to history (the importance of resolving conflicts which escalate into war); to economics (controlling theft in a business before the business runs out of money or controlling inflation in the stock market to prevent deep, long-lasting depressions or failure to make and enforce laws controlling large corporations, e.g., Enron, WorldCom, Savings & Loans, and so forth); to geography (the value of taking steps to avoid catastrophic floods); to sociology (the end cost of restricting access to quality education by the poor, such as larger prison populations and higher recidivism rates), and so forth.

Playing the Bump Up Game

From These Facts & Factoids and a Knowledge Base . . .

- Heartworms in dogs are transmitted by mosquitoes.
- Roundworms in puppies and dogs can be contracted before birth and through feces.
- Hookworms in puppies and adult dogs can be passed through the mother's milk or via feces in egg form; the larvae can also penetrate the skin.
- Treatments to kill heartworms can sometimes lead to death because the remains of the heartworms drift into the lungs and cause potentially fatal blood clots.
- Mosquitoes, some of which have a flight range of 15 miles, have carried heartworms to all 50 states and Canada.

Come These Conceptual Key Points:

- Because internal parasites have evolved such a wide array of methods of reproduction and acquiring access to a host, all animals can have them, including pets and humans. Parasites harm and even cause the death of their host if untreated.
- Prevention is the best cure.

Parasitic behavior is also a concept that can be applied across subject areas. In addition to biological applications such as pet ownership, commercial animal husbandry, dangers within our food supply system, and personal health, parasitism is a useful concept through which to study areas of economics (extorting lunch money from younger students and anti-trust behavior of large corporations such as Microsoft and Enron) and sociology (co-dependency, organized crime, and imperialism).

Some concepts, however, provide a **quality study base only within one subject area** such as study of the *methods* by which parasites reproduce. Although not generalizable across subject areas, it nonetheless is a concept that opens the door to a lifetime of study in biology and is very generalizable and transferable across species, including humans.

Understandable. Curriculum content for students must be understandable by students at their age. (For more information on age-appropriate curriculum, see Appendix B). The test for age-appropriateness is this: **If students**—even after a *being there* experience and lots of hands-on-of-the-real-thing input—**still must resort to memorization, *then the content is not age-appropriate.*** Examples include atoms and molecules for third graders, photosynthesis for sixth graders, and so forth. Such content sounds good to politicians and the public but confuse students (and convince them they can't learn science) and frustrate their teacher.

Transferable. The power of conceptual curriculum is that it can be transferred to new locations/situations. If students understand the idea of habitat in the rain forest, for example, they will also understand the principles of habitat in a desert. They don't have to start from scratch learning about deserts, they already know quite a bit.

Succinct and Clear. As George Bernard Shaw once wrote, apologizng to a friend: "I'm sorry this is so long; I didn't have time to write a short letter." Writing clear, concise, succinct key points demands the best writing skills you possess and requires mental discipline. This is a time for the Lifelong Guideline of Personal Best!

Significant Knowledge Key Points

If a concept is new to students, it should be accompanied by knowledge key points that help students understand the concept. For example, the significant knowledge key points below help students understand the conceptual key points stated on the previous page:

- Worm infestations can occur in dogs at any age—from before birth through adulthood—and can occur in a variety of ways: via mother's milk, infected mosquitoes, eggs in feces, the mother before birth, and larvae penetrating the skin.

- The three most common parasites in dogs—heartworms, roundworms, and hookworms—are dangerous not only because they rob nutrients from their host but because their presence can cause permanent damage to heart, lungs, and liver and, if untreated, death. For example, heartworms can grow up to 14 inches long and roundworms up to 7 inches.

- The presence of some internal parasites is often hard to detect until serious damage to the host, even death, has occurred. Therefore, prevention is the best and safest treatment for parasites. Learn about the parasites that are typical to the areas where your dog lives and visits, test your pet as recommended by a veterinarian, and treat accordingly.

These knowledge key points about parasites in dogs help students understand the concept of parasites in a real-world way. This combination of concepts and significant knowledge allows students to achieve competence both for taking tests and operating in the real world; and, it makes learning about parasites affecting cats or even people more efficient, taking but a fraction of the time to learn compared to a first exposure to learning about parasites in dogs. Teaching conceptually—starting with a concept followed by the significant knowledge needed to understand the concept—not only deepens learning but it also makes your teaching time efficient as well as effective.

Skill Key Points

To understand a concept in real-world ways, students may need specific skills. Often these skills are not directly related to the concept; they are basic skills—math, writing, speaking, and so forth. Make sure you identify them and teach them so your students can succeed in using what they understand from the conceptual and significant knowledge key points. Other skills are unique to the context of the application of what we know.

The following skill key points include the need for math skills as well as for pet ownership:

- Precise measurement of dosages of medication (for dogs and humans) is important because an overdose can be lethal and an inadequate dose can be ineffective in treating the problem. Most dosages for humans and animals are now measured using the metric system, in milliliters (ml) or cubic centimeters (cc) rather than ounces because measuring in milliliters or cubic centimeters provides a more accurate and reliable measurement of small quantities. For example, one fluid ounce equals 30 milliliters; five centimeters is about one teaspoon. Because the measurements on the syringe or bottle of medication may differ from the prescription, one must be able to convert measurements from US to metric and vice versa.

- Recommended dosages indicate how many cc's or ml's to administer per x pounds of an animal's weight. To calculate the correct dose for an animal: First, carefully weigh the animal. Second, divide the animal's weight by the number of pounds indicated in the recommended dosage (for example, 10 pounds per one cc of medicine). Third, multiply this number times the number of cc's or ml's to be administered.

- Shots for a dog are usually delivered in the loose skin at the top of the neck and shoulders by first pulling up the loose skin and then inserting the needle sideways so as to avoid hitting the spine or muscle.

> Recommended dosage:
> 5 cc per 10 pounds of animal
> 1) Fido weighs 70 pounds
> 2) Divide 70 by 10 = 7 doses
> 3) Multiple 7 times 5cc's = 35cc's

- Some medications are given to dogs orally. Put the medication in a food morsel. Hold the dog's mouth open, insert the food far back in the mouth, and hold the dog's mouth closed until it swallows.

To summarize, always lead with a concept, then add information necessary to understand the concept. When skills are needed, state them simply and succinctly, just the way you want students to remember them.

Self Check

All my key points:

- Are based in *being there* locations
- Are a marriage between what the people that work at and use that location need to understand and be able to do **AND** content from my state/district standards

My conceptual key points meet the GUTS criteria:

G = generalizable—a principle or conclusion that can be used to explain specifics; pulls idea into general use

U = understandable by students this age

T = transferable to new locations/situations

S = succinct and clear

Inquiries: What I Want My Students to Be Able to Do with What They Understand

Once you have stated what you want your students to understand as conceptually as possible and included significant knowledge and skills, think through ways students can apply these understandings in real-world ways. Go back to your *being there* location and watch how these concepts and skills are applied by the people who work and visit there. Then, keeping in mind the age of your students and what is appropriate for their stage of mental development, start writing these applications down on paper. Jot down as many as you see and others that come to mind. You are now ready to write inquiries.

The ABC Rules for Writing Inquiries

As you write inquiries, keep the following rules in mind:

- Always start with the action in mind.* What are students to do? How can they practice applying what they understand to real-world situations?
- Be specific with your directions so that students can see the outcome or finished product in their mind's eye. What is the inquiry asking them to do?
- Connect to the key point. Will doing this inquiry help students both understand and be able to apply the concept, significant knowledge, or skill described in the key point? Never select an activity just because it is fun or clever or cute. If it doesn't help students understand and practice the key point, throw it out. Learning is serious business; stay focused on what you want students to understand and what you want them to do with what they understand.
- Don't stop writing until you have enough inquiries for each key point to take students through mastery to long-term memory.

* For action verbs, see the Inquiry Builder chart on page 13.10. Decide which of the multiple intelligences you want students to use (listed along the left of the chart from top to bottom) and the kind of performance you want them to engage in (Bloom's taxonomy along the top of the chart from left to right). Start your directions to students using this verb. [Note: We have revised the order of Bloom's Taxonomy to better fit how the brain learns.]

Providing Choice

One of the biggest benefits of developing your own curriculum is the opportunity to build in choices for students. Choices allow them to learn through the intelligences in which they are strong while working on those less developed. They also allow them to expand interests and to deepen motivation to learn. Inquiries are your major means of providing meaningful choice; fortunately, it's easy to do. Simply refer to the Inquiry Builder Chart on the next page. Select action words from each segment of the chart and you will be able to write inquiries that meet the multiple intelligences and levels of application.

The inquiries about parasites on page 13.10 are examples of how a teacher can use inquiries to build in choices for students. The initials after each inquiry indicate which intelligence is needed to carry out the task. Also, some inquiries require collaboration, while others require individual work.

Another important way to build in choices is to invite students, third grade and up, to develop inquiries for your key points. A good starter question is, "What examples of this concept (skill) have you seen today?" Gather up these inquiries and then decide which you would like to offer to the class, Learning Club, or individuals to choose to do.

Inquiry Builder

Starting Point with being there experience

Ending Point for test preparation

← Bloom's Taxonomy (adapted) →

MULTIPLE INTELLIGENCES	Application	Analysis	Evaluation	Synthesis	Comprehension	Knowledge
Logical/ Mathematical	▪apply ▪solve ▪convert ▪expand ▪schedule ▪sequence ▪organize	▪question ▪solve ▪inventory ▪compare ▪distinguish ▪differentiate	▪estimate ▪measure ▪choose ▪predict ▪judge ▪select ▪assess ▪value ▪rate ▪review	▪design ▪infer ▪classify ▪hypothesize ▪prepare ▪formulate ▪propose	▪describe ▪calculate ▪identify ▪explain ▪retell ▪recognize ▪sequence ▪organize	▪label ▪name
Linguistic	▪apply ▪teach ▪translate ▪interview ▪communicate	▪analyze ▪debate ▪criticize ▪discuss ▪question ▪investigate ▪interpret	▪critique ▪interpret ▪discuss ▪rate ▪relate ▪probe ▪judge ▪justify	▪compose ▪rewrite ▪propose ▪infer ▪adapt ▪debate ▪impersonate ▪produce	▪review ▪describe ▪discuss ▪express ▪report ▪explain ▪restate	▪name ▪tell ▪label ▪recall ▪define ▪record ▪narrate ▪list ▪memorize
Spatial	▪diagram ▪exhibit ▪translate ▪teach ▪illustrate ▪make ▪apply ▪chart ▪summarize ▪graph	▪disassemble ▪differentiate ▪diagram ▪distinguish	▪predict ▪estimate ▪measure ▪judge	▪formulate ▪plan ▪propose ▪arrange ▪design ▪organize ▪restructure	▪locate ▪sort ▪identify ▪compare ▪describe ▪illustrate ▪recognize ▪relate parts	▪interpret ▪adapt ▪draw ▪match ▪sketch
Bodily/ Kinesthetic	▪apply ▪rhythm ▪dramatize ▪mime ▪operate ▪(teach) ▪(demonstrate) ▪(practice)	▪interpret ▪disassemble ▪experiment ▪diagram ▪(inventory)	▪rehearse ▪(measure) ▪(debate)	▪convey emotion ▪tell a story ▪(invent) ▪(assemble) ▪(design) ▪(construct) ▪(arrange) ▪(prepare) ▪(classify)	▪perform ▪(locate)	▪imitate ▪play
Musical	▪perform (solo or group) ▪harmonize ▪(express) ▪rhythm ▪synchronize ▪(characterize)	▪interpret ▪analyze ▪(compare)	▪interpret ▪critique ▪(characterize)	▪create a variation ▪improvise ▪(express) ▪(convey emotion) ▪(symbolize) ▪compose ▪(tell a story) ▪transpose	▪imitate ▪rehearse	▪recite

( ) = could have this quality if so designed.

Examples of Inquiries with Key Points

Examples of inquiries for the key points about parasites could include the following.

Conceptual Key Point #1: Because internal parasites have evolved such a wide array of methods for acquiring access to a host and for reproducing, all animals are host to internal parasites—including pets and humans. Parasites harm and even cause the death of their host if untreated.

Inquiries for Conceptual Key Point #1:

1) Working in pairs for five minutes, write down as much information as you can about parasites that you have learned from your own pets and pets owned by your friends and neighbors. Share this information with the class during the next inquiry. (L)*

2) As a class, add as much information as you can to the KW columns of a KWL chart about parasites. (L, LM)

3) As a Learning Club, select a parasite to research that often infects humans. Using the Internet or media center, discover at least one method by which this parasite accesses its host, when the parasite was first discovered and named, and the treatments commonly used over time. Illustrate the life cycle of the parasite on a poster board; make a timeline representing the years when the parasite was discovered and the treatments used for it over time. Present your findings to the class. After your presentation, post your information for a class Gallery Walk. (L, LM, S, BK)

4) After each Learning Club has presented its findings, take a Gallery Walk with your Learning Club. Compare your research findings with that of other Learning Clubs. (BK, LM, L)

* These symbols at the end of each inquiry refer to the multiple intelligences; see the Inquiry Builder Chart on the previous page.

5) As a class, add more information to the KW** columns of the KWL chart about parasites. (L, LM)

6) As a Learning Club, plan a visit to a veterinarian's office. List five things that you would like the vet to show or explain to you about parasites that infect dogs. (L, LM)

Significant Knowledge Key Point #1: Worm infestations can occur in dogs at any age—from before birth through adult—and can occur in a variety of ways: via mother's milk, infected mosquitoes, eggs in feces, the mother before birth, and larvae penetrating the skin.

Inquiries for Significant Knowledge Key Point #1:

Before going to the vet's office:

1) As a Learning Club, choose one of the three most common worms that infect dogs—heartworms, roundworms, or hookworms. Using the Internet or media center, create an illustration on poster board of that worm's life cycle; indicate each stage during which this parasite accesses its host and how the parasite does so. Make a life-sized clay model of your worm and the organ it attacks. Describe the treatments commonly used to treat such infestations. Present your Learning Club's findings, illustration, and models to another class. (L, S, BK)

2) Select a dog owned by a member of your Learning Club or a neighbor. Estimate the dog's weight. Based on this weight, compute how much of the following medicines should be administered to this dog or puppy (or kitten). (L, LM) [See Math Skill Key Point #1.]

   For roundworms, one cc of Pyramtel Paomate per 10 pounds of body weight

   For hookworms, one cc of Pyramtel Paomate per 10 pounds of body weight

** KW charts are used for brainstorming **w**hat students **k**now and what they **w**ant to know.

3) Working in pairs, select four breeds of dogs that interest you. Visit a website to discover the average adult weight of these dog breeds. Compute how much of the medication for heartworms, round worms, and hookworms should be administered to each of these breeds. (L, LM)

Math Skill Key Point #1: Recommended dosages indicate how many cc's or ml's to administer per x pounds of an animal's weight. Use the following three steps to calculate the correct dose for an animal: First, carefully weigh the animal. Second, divide the animal's weight by the number of pounds indicated in the recommended dosage (for example, 10 pounds per one cc of medicine). Third, multiply this number times the number of cc's or ml's to be administered.

Recommended dosage:
5 cc per 10 pounds of animal
1) Fido weighs 70 pounds
2) Divide 70 by 10 = 7 doses
3) Multiple 7 times 5cc's = 35cc's

At the vet's office:

1) As a Learning Club, interview the owner of a dog brought to the vet's office. List the reasons why the owner thought his/her pet might have worms. Next, interview the vet to determine his/her diagnosis. Prepare to present your findings to the class when you return from the vet's office. (L)

2) Observe the vet examining a dog for possible worm infestation. If the vet prescribes treatment for worms, compute the amount of the dose to be administered. Check your computations against the vet's. Observe the vet giving the prescribed treatment. (L, LM)

Back at the classroom:

1) As a Learning Club, decide which member will bring one dog and which will bring one cat. Assign those members to bring that pet to the Classroom Vet Clinic Day. (L)

2) On Classroom Vet Clinic Day, weigh your Learning Club's two pets on an accurate scale before the vet arrives. Ask the vet to explain his/her reasons for diagnosing of the presence or absence of parasites in each animal. Check with your Learning Club; do you agree or do you have more questions? Also ask the vet why he/she chose that particular method of treatment. Then, calculate the correct dose for each pet. Ask the vet to check your calculations. Watch the vet closely as he/she administers that treatment. (L, LM)

3) Write a personal thank you letter to the vet for allowing your class to visit his/her vet clinic and for coming to the classroom for Classroom Vet Clinic Day. Share with him/her three things you learned about parasites that most fascinated you. (L)

Language Arts Skill Key Point #1: A letter is a form of written communication that expresses personal thoughts, experiences, or feelings, requests information, services, or products. There are three types of letters, each with a slightly different structure.

1) The **personal letter**, often called a friendly letter, is an informal communication, usually written to a close friend or relative. Personal letters can be handwritten or typed. The structure of a friendly letter includes the following:
   - Date
   - Greeting
   - Body
   - Closing
   - Signature

Personal letters include thank you notes, letters of condolence, regret, or apology, notes of congratulations, letters to catch the recipient up to date or inquire about his/her life, and so forth. Email communications are also a version of a friendly letter. However, the date is usually left out because the software records the date.

A personal letter

February 29, 2004

Dear Mom,

[Body of letter]

Love,

Karen

The widespread use of the computer and Internet is altering the way we communicate. Today, virtually all business and most personal letters are produced on the computer, rarely handwritten. As a result, a handwritten personal letter is a special occurrence and is appreciated by most people as a special effort to communicate, a special touch.

2) A **business letter** is written from one business or organization to another business or organization. Its purpose is to request information, to discuss a problem or situation, or propose ways the two entities can cooperate together. Because it is written on behalf of one's business or organization, it is the most formal letter. Both its language and its structure are more formal than in a friendly letter.

A business letter includes:

- Date
- Heading (name and address of the recipient)
- Formal salutation (usually followed by a colon instead of a comma)
- Body
- Closing
- Signature
- Name, title, and address of sender

February 29, 2004

Ms. Joy Hands,
Customer Service Manager
Books for Educators, Inc.
17051 SE 272nd Street, Suite 18
Covington, WA 98042

Dear Ms. Hands:

[Body of Letter]

Sincerely,

Jack Paperback
Mr. Jack Paperback, President
Paperback Press
131 West Lane
Corporate City, CA 98000

A business letter

Business letters are usually typed. When sent via email, it is often scanned and sent as an attachment so that the letterhead and signature can be conveyed to the receiver. Like a fax, this electronically conveyed letter constitutes a legally binding document.

If both sender and recipient know each other, are of similar rank in the organization, and are on good terms, the salutation often uses the person's first name followed by a comma. For example: Dear Judy,
The sender then also signs only his/her first name.

3) A **personal business letter** is a combination of a friendly and business letter. It is written to a business from a person representing him/herself, not the business he/she works for; it is therefore slightly less formal than the business letter but not as chummy or familiar as the personal letter. Common uses of a personal business letter are to thank the company or to register a complaint, to send an

appreciation to a member of the company for superior service, or to acknowledge something the company or someone working for the company has done.

A personal business letter has the same seven parts as a business letter: date, heading; recipient's name, title, and address; salutation; body; closing; signature; and sender's name and address (see format for a business letter on the next page). A personal business letter is also usually typed.

February 29, 2004

Ms. Joy Hands,
Customer Service Manager
Books for Educators, Inc.
17051 SE 272nd Street, Suite 18
Covington, WA 98042

Dear Judy,

[Body of Letter]

Sincerely,

Jack
Mr. Jack Paperback, President
Paperback Press
131 West Lane
Corporate City, CA 98000

A personal business letter

In a personal business letter, the salutation usually uses the person's first name followed by a comma (not a colon). The sender also signs only his/her first name.

Inquiries for Skill Key Point #2:

- As a Learning Club, create movements to represent each part of the three kinds of letters. Use the same movement for the same part if found in all three types of letters. Create additional movements for any new part not found in the other types of letters. Create a chant to accompany the movements that explains each part of each type of letter. Teach the movements and chant to the class. (BK, L, M)

- Brainstorm at least six situations that would require that a letter be written. Include the name of the person (classmate, guest teacher, or business) to whom the letter should be written. Put your scenario in the bag your teacher passes around the room. Then, draw a scenario out of the bag. Determine the type of letter you need to write and the structures you will need in the letter. List the things you would want to say. Write the letter. Have a member of your Learning Club review your letter for correctness of format. (BK, L, LM)

- As a Learning Club, select a community problem or issue that you think needs action. Determine the type of letter to use and follow its structure. Write a letter to the editor of your local newspaper expressing your concern and giving your recommendations for resolving this issue. (L)

- Create a PowerPoint presentation showing the different parts of all three types of letters. Each slide should include a title, a description of each type of letter, criteria for determining when and why to select one of the types of letters, and a short sample letter for each with the parts labeled. Show your presentation to the class. (L, S, M)

- Compare the similarities and differences among the three types of letters. Illustrate your analysis using a graphic organizer and explain your findings to at least two other classmates. (LM, L)

- As a Learning Club, analyze the model of each of three letters shown on the overhead projector. Identify the elements of each letter and determine which of the three types of letters each is. Share your responses with the class; be prepared to defend your answers. (LM, L)

- As a Learning Club, write a business letter to thank the vet for allowing your class to visit the clinic. Include how he/she helped you learn about parasites and prevention. Swap letters with another Learning Club; edit theirs for format, formal language, and clarity. When you get your letter back, make any necessary corrections. Hang your letter on the wall for a Gallery Walk. Prepare a perfect copy to be sent to the vet. Address the envelope and ask your teacher to mail it. (S, L)

- Write a personal letter to the vet thanking him/her for providing a pet clinic in your classroom. Share about the knowledge and skills you most valued and describe three things you learned about parasites and their treatment and prevention. Have a member of your Learning Club review your letter. Make any necessary corrections and place it in the mailbag to be mailed to the vet. (L)

Significant Knowledge Key Point #2: The three most common parasites in dogs—heartworms, roundworms, and hookworms—are dangerous not only because they rob nutrients from their host but because their presence can cause permanent damage to heart, lungs, liver, and intestines and can, if untreated, death. For example, heartworms can grow up to 14 inches long and roundworms 7 inches.

Inquiries for Significant Knowledge Key Point #2:

1) As a Learning Club, select a common pet parasite; research it. Write words to a familiar song that would inform dog owners about this common parasite, how it acquires access to its host, the damage it causes, how to to treat it, and how to prevent it. Perform the song for another class. (L, BK)

2) As a Learning Club, research common parasites that infect humans. Complete a KWL chart based on your research. After the doctor speaks to the class and you have had a chance to ask questions, review your KWL chart. Update it, adding information and correcting any misconceptions you had. Rewrite your chart and present it to the class. (L, S, LM)

3) With your Learning Club, select a familiar tune and write lyrics that will teach pet owners important information about worm infestations and how to take good care of their pet. Videotape the performance; send it to the vet so that he/she can create a check-out library for his/her clients. (L, M, S)

4) Create a 3-minute video that presents information about worm infestations and how it applies to pets. Show the video to another class. Give a copy to the vet whose clinic you visited as a thank you. (L, S)

Conceptual Key Point #2: The best and safest treatment for parasites is prevention.

Inquiries for Conceptual Key Point #2:

- Write a short paragraph or chant describing the damage that a 14 inches long heartworm can do to a dog's heart. Include why such damage is permanent and why treatment can cause death. Read/perform your paragraph/chant to your Learning Club. (L)

- As a Learning Club, select your favorite paragraph or rap song performed to you. Perform it for the class (choral reading of the paragraph or group performance of the rap song). (L, BK)

- Select the dog-infesting parasite that most concerns you. Develop a "Parasite Prevention for Your Pet" pamphlet for owners that describes the parasite, how it gains access to its host, the damage it causes, and the best means to prevent and treat it. Use illustrations, graphics, maps, and other graphic organizers whenever possible. Make it informative and colorful. Have your Learning Club check your pamphlet for accuracy. Make 10 copies and have your teacher deliver them to the vet's office to be shared with pet owners. (L, S, LM)

Significant Knowledge Key Point #3: The presence of some internal parasites is often hard to detect until serious damage to the host, even death, has occurred. Therefore, prevention is the best and safest treatment for parasites. Regular tests as recommended by a veterinarian help determine if parasites are present. Also, learn what parasites are typical to the areas your dog lives in and visits and how to treat your dog accordingly.

- Homework Assignment: Interview two neighbors who are dog owners. Use a Venn diagram to record similarities and differences in the places their dog has lived and visited during the last year. Based on this information, prescribe a preventative treatment for the dog. If the treatment includes medication, compute the amount of medication the dog needs. Show your math work to determine this dosage. (BK, S, L, LM)

- Social/Political Action: Plan and carry out a Pet Parasite Prevention Clinic for all the students at your school (grades 4 and up) who have a dog. (LM, L, BK, S)

Self Check

My inquiries:

- Directly relate to a key point
- Meet the ABC rules for writing inquiries
  - A = Always starts with the action in mind
  - B = Be specific, clear, and unambiguous
  - C = Connects to the key point
- Include actions needed at the *being there* locations and similar real-world locations
- Give students sufficient practice in applying a concept or skill to allow them to use it with proficiency and to wire it into long-term memory

Words of Advice

From the thousands of teachers who precede you on your journey into integrated ITI curriculum, please heed two pieces of advice:

Start Small. Start small . . . an integrated half day or two here and there, then a week of integrated half days. Small chunks of integrated curriculum that are well planned, well implemented, and occur frequently are more productive than a few large, overwhelming chunks because they are better teachers. A small-amount-frequently approach allows a teacher the best opportunity to practice how to write and teach from integrated, location-based curriculum versus textbooks and worksheets and, very importantly, to learn from successes and failures. Quality is far more important than quantity during Stage 2.

Complete Writing Curriculum Before Starting to Lesson Plan. To maintain your focus on what you want students to understand and be able to do with what they understand, complete your curriculum work **before** you begin to think about how you will teach the curriculum. We can guarantee you that if you try to do both simultaneously, your curriculum will suffer.

Self Check

My curriculum:

- Is based in *being there* locations
- Is a marriage between what the people that work and use that location need to understand and be able to do **AND** content from my state/district standards
- Starts with an important concept
- Integrates at least two subject areas, such as science and math
- Integrates at least one basic skill area
- Constitutes approximately 10-15% of my year

Notes to Myself

Chapter 14: Integrating Curriculum Through Concepts

ITI Classroom Stages of Implementation **Stage 2**

Entry level for making curriculum bodybrain compatible

CURRICULUM	INSTRUCTIONAL STRATEGIES
• Integrates curriculum by using a concept to pull together content and skills from multiple subject areas. This organizing concept is the theme unifying study for the year.	• Displays the mindmap of the curriculum on the wall along with immersion items to heighten student interest and elicit memories of prior experiences with the topic being studied.
• For at least two chunks of integrated curriculum during the year, includes a Social/Political Action Project and concludes with a Celebration of Learning.	• Uses Social/Political Action Projects and Celebrations of Learning to provide real-world contexts for learning and using knowledge and skills, to provide real audiences for practicing/developing language arts and math skills, and to provide students opportunities to practice responsible citizenship.

Creating Curriculum

The hallmark and heart of curriculum for the ITI model is that it is based in *being there* locations and that it uses a concept to integrate content and skills from multiple subject areas. Chapter 12 describes how to base curriculum in *being there* locations. This chapter outlines how to use concepts to integrate and organize your curriculum.

Concept = Power

Concept = 1. A general notion or idea

2. An idea of something formed by mentally combining all its characteristics or particulars; a construct[1]

In the world of our biological brain, patterns are neural food. They are what our brain seeks and from which it makes meaning. Concepts are rich, powerful patterns for the brain, useful in unlocking meaning around us and much easier to store in long-term memory than curriculum fragments and factoids. To learn fragments and factoids, students mostly resort to memorization; in contrast, concepts allow students to leapfrog from today's lesson to yesterday's personal experience to tomorrow's situations in life. Concepts are powerful curriculum builders.

Concepts: Curriculum Structures Without Borders

Concepts travel. They don't stay where we last put them, such as in science or art. They know no curriculum borders. They are not stopped by time or space. That's why they are so good at integrating curriculum.

Example #1: Consider this statement: "A system is a collection of things and processes (and often people) that interact to perform some function." Clearly this invites an exploration of science—ecosystems, mechanical engineering, and so forth. But it is also a powerful lens through which to view civics: "Our democratic government is a collection of things (laws, government bodies, and citizens) and processes (those described in or allowed by laws). Our federal constitution, including its Bill of Rights, sets the boundaries of our government. Democratic governments are rule-based systems of government rather than power- or people-based forms, such as dictatorships, oligarchies, monarchies, and theocracies."

Economics? Yes. Supply and demand are two interacting components of the capitalist system. Art? Of course. The Munsell Color Wheel is a system of analyzing color combinations and intensity of hue. The potential for integration goes on and on.

Example #2: Consider the rich exploration that could come from study through a related concept: "To study a system one must define its boundaries." For example, in science, a watershed can't be studied if its boundaries aren't established.

History/social studies: Our federal constitution, including its Bill of Rights, sets the boundaries of our government. Laws considered outside this boundary are considered unconstitutional and are set aside or repealed. (Without such boundaries, there would be chaos.)

Boundary lines could also be drawn to include philosophical precursors to our constitution such as the Declaration of Independence, the writings of Thomas Paine, and the constitution of the Iroquois Confederation.

Example #3: Consider the further depth and power from studying another related concept: "Thinking about things as systems means looking for how every part relates to others. Most systems, living and non-living, are made up of smaller parts that, when put together, can do things the parts couldn't do by themselves."

This is a powerful lens through which to study the danger of extinction of animals and plants—together they create a self-sustaining ecosystem but if missing a partner perhaps they will die.

In history/social studies: "Our constitution establishes a system with three parts or subsystems: executive, legislative, and judicial. They are designed to provide checks and balances to preserve a balance of power."

Concepts are like computer worms. Once they infect your hard drive, they never stop moving; once they lodge in your brain, your brain keeps extending the patterns, using them to make sense of more and more of the external world.

Getting Started

Once you have selected your *being there* locations and the concept(s) you want to teach, decide how you want to start organizing your curriculum. Do you want to start small and proceed one step at a time or do you want to start with a yearlong theme in mind? In either case, remember that your goal during Stage 2 of Implementation is only 10-15% of curriculum for the entire year. This modest start allows you to learn from your experiences and master the science and art of developing integrated, thematic curriculum before you begin Stage 3.

Starting Small . . . One Step at a Time

A topic is the the smallest piece of an integrated ITI theme. So starting small means starting with one *being there* location and selecting a conceptual key point that is well illustrated by the location, engaging to your students, and in important aspect of your state standards.

Around this nucleus, determine what you want students to understand (key points) and be able to do (inquiries). How to write key points and inquiries is discussed in Chapter 12.

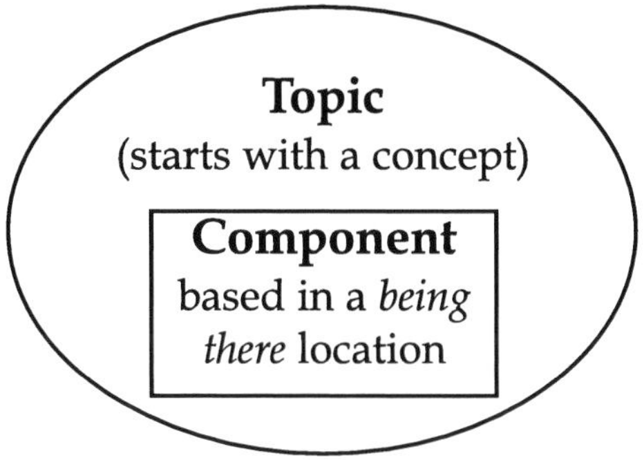

This first topic, a part of a compnent, is often designed for one to three half-days. It is big enough to take you through the tools for building an ITI theme but small enough that you can get started with relatively short lead-up time. How long a topic lasts depends on your purpose and planning. The curriculum starting on page 14.6 is designed for 10-12 half days.

Starting Small: An Example of One Small Chunk of Curriculum forFirst Grade

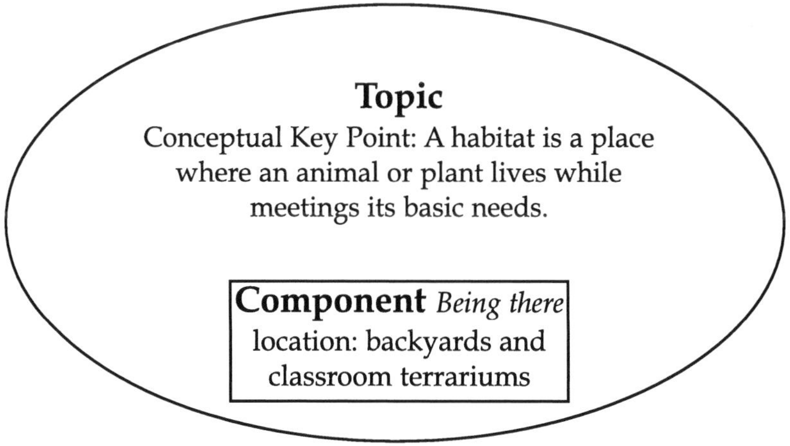

You choose the time frames; the ITI theme structure will work with time spans long or short, full days or partial. However, be aware that curriculum often takes on a life of its own; be prepared to follow the teachable moments. Feel free to extend or shorten any topic as best serves students and your responsibilities for curriculum content.

Focusing on a single component/topic at a time is a good beginning point for teachers working alone or those who find it easier to work from details to big picture rather than from big picture to details. It allows you to master three critical ITI theme strategies - basing curriculum in *being there* locations, starting with concepts, and integrating content and skills. As you master these strategies, you will be ready to delve into the power of concepts to create memorable patterns for the brain.

Stepping Out

To reach the goal of Stage 2—having 15% of your year's curriculum be integrated and thematic—you will need to take the next step in curriculum development: Writing curriculum for more than one topic per component and its *being there* location. This next step allows you to explore the richness of the real world by focusing on another aspect of the *being there* location, yet one still related to the concept of the component.

For example, if the *being there* location is a local watershed, the topics might be "Watersheds: An Irreversible System" and "We All Live Downstream." In this example, the concept of the component is systems. You could, however, choose as a concept habitats, all things are connected, change, or many others. Because each topic is related to the concept of the component, the topics are thus related to each other. This conceptual pattern established by the concept for the component serves as the force that pulls together or integrates all the subject content and skills for all topics.

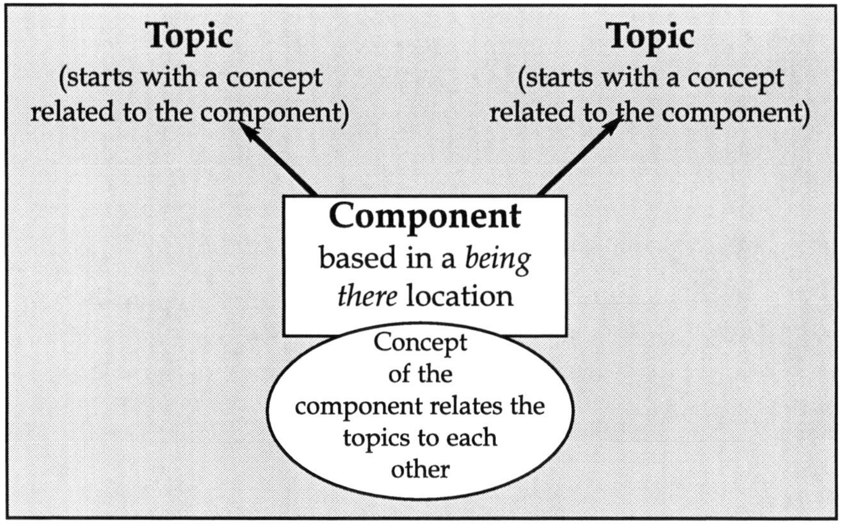

Stepping Out: An Example of a Component with Two Topics for Fifth Grade

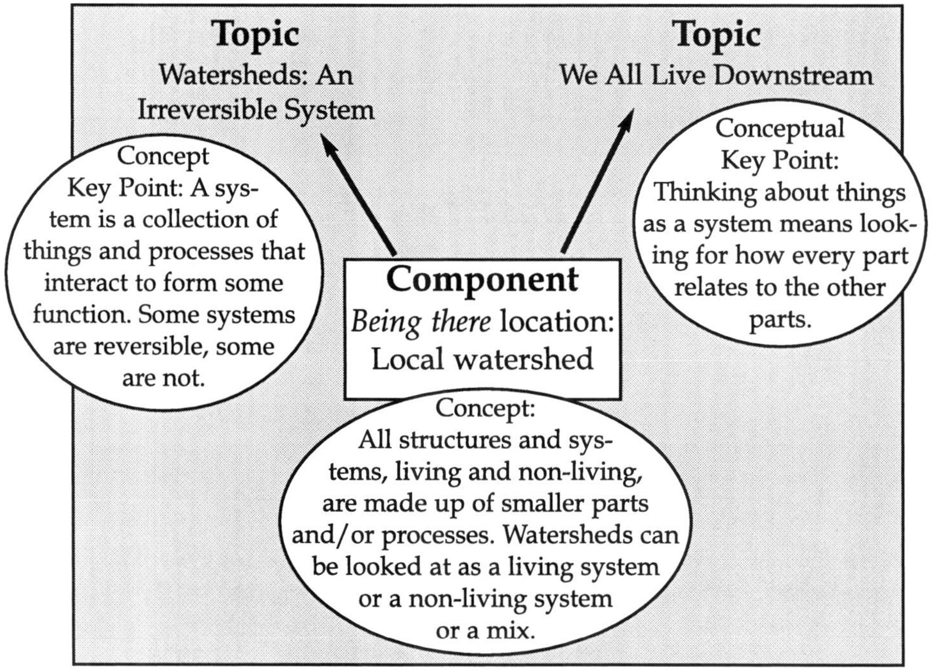

Starting with the End in Mind

As shown in the mindmap on this page, your first yearlong theme can start out small—a topic related to the organizing concept of the theme—and then graduate to the level of a yearlong theme by the end of the year, a component with three to four topics. We strongly recommend this "progressive dinner" approach. It allows you to do small amounts of curriculum frequently while experimenting with conceptual connections that integrate chunks of curriculum.

Like the topic developed on page 14.3, the first component shown here has but one topic. However, that topic/component, and each that follows, is not built on an isolated, stand alone concept; it is related to the organizing concept for the theme.

The number of topics per component then increases. Each topic has at least one conceptual (transferable/generalizable) key point plus related significant knowledge and skill key points and their inquiries (refer to Chapter 13).

Progressive Dinner Approach to Developing a Yearlong Theme

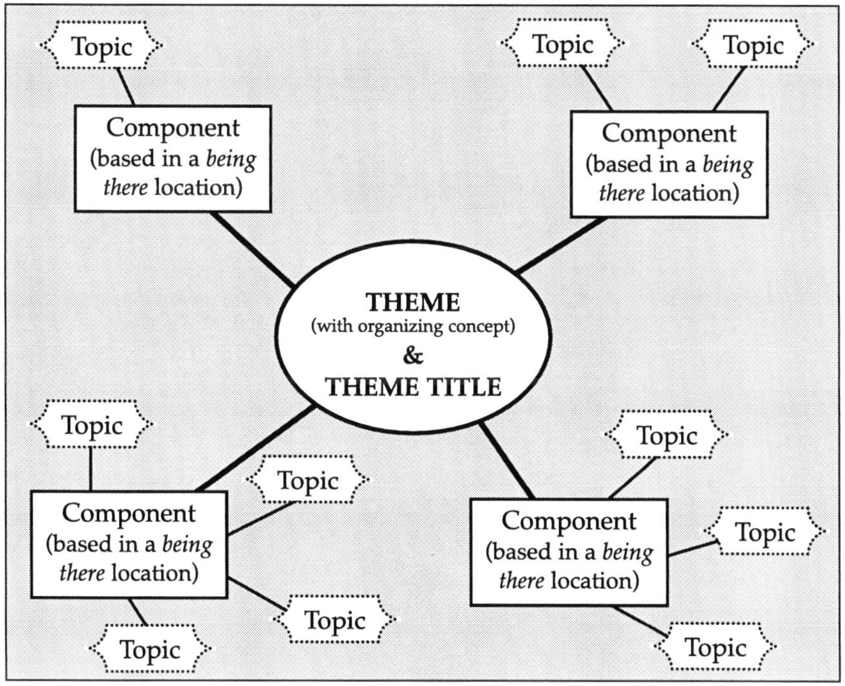

Starting with a skeletal yearlong theme allows you to start small but use the tools for building a yearlong theme, especially an organizing concept to web together all the content and skills for the year and finding a kid-grabbing title that stirs up student enthusiasm, conveys the essence of the concept, and is memorable.

For example, if habitats is the organizing concept for your theme, then the *being there* location for the components can be various kinds of habitats such as underground, airborne, pond/lake, tidepools, creek/river, or watershed. Choose those that can be easily visited by your students and readily turned into an immersion experience in the classroom or on the school grounds. Topics for each component then focus on various aspects of the component's concept. For an underground habitat, for example, study animals in the food web or ways they locate and get food.

What's important is ensuring that the pattern or conceptual relationship between the theme and each component and between each component and its topics is obvious to students. The greater the conceptual webbing of the theme, the more connections students can make. This quickens and deepens learning and makes efficient use of instructional time. This makes the content easier for the students to understand. It also integrates your content and skills in a natural way that students can recognize as they look out the window, walk down the street, visit a mall, or relax with Mother Nature.

Mastering the tools for developing a yearlong theme now will save you time when you begin Stage 3. For more information about the yearlong theme, see Chapter 18.

Sample Curriculum

Beginning on the next page is curriculum developed for 1-3 weeks depending on how much time is devoted to it each day. Notice how each chunk of curriculum begins with a concept which is explored through the significant knowledge needed to understand that concept. Basic skills are practiced, or taught and practiced, in relationship to inquiries, the "doing" part of the curriculum.

Organizing Concept: Form dictates function; function demands form.

Theme Rationale: Understanding the relationship between physical characteristics and use helps students to understand how the world around them operates and instructs their ability to invent or design objects in order to solve problems and make our world a better place.

How Did You Do That?

Find the Way

- Tools for Life - Lifelong Guidelines (citizenship)/LIFESKILLS
- Leading the Way (mapping)
- Hand Tools (designing, using, changing, inventing)

Concept: Form and Function

***Being There* Locations:** School, Neighborhood

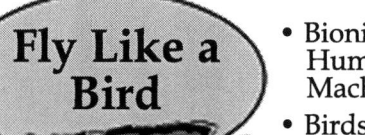

Fly Like a Bird

- Bionic Me – similarities of Human Body and Simple Machines
- Birds: Wings, Beaks, & Eyes (animal body parts/functions)
- Similarities of Animal Bodies & Hand Tools

Concept: Form and Function

***Being There* Locations:** Zoo, Pet Store

Travel Like a Plant

- Plant and Soil Characteristics
- Dig It! (hand tools and modern technology)
- Stems that Bend (weather and adaptations for protection)

Concept: Form and Function

***Being There* Locations:** School Garden, Neighborhood

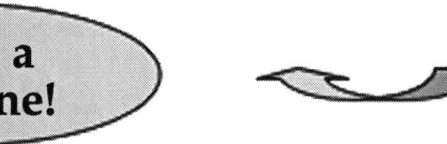

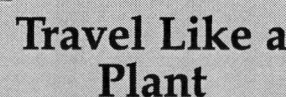

Build a Machine!

- Inventions Convention (non-living things, magnetism)
- Innovative Mechanical Devices
- Our Community Environment (community service, research)

Concept: Form and Function

***Being There* Locations:** Museum, City Hall

Sample Curriculum

Curriculum Team, Susan Kovail & Associates ©2005

Adapted from Brenda Russell, Model Teaching Week Curriculum, Appropriate for 2nd–4th Grade

Organizing Concept for the Yearlong Theme: Form dictates function; function demands form.

Yearlong Theme Kid-Grabbing Title: How Did You Do That?

Component Kid-Grabbing Title: Fly Like a Bird

Concept for Component: Form and Function

Being There Locations for the Component: State Park, Bird Viewing Preserve, Playground

Guest Speakers for the Component: State Park Rangers, Naturalist, Audubon Member

Conceptual Key Point for the Component:

Form dictates function is a rule based on observation of nature and has led to man-made designs and inventions. This means that the shape of something and what it is made of determines how it can be used and what it can do. Conversely, a task or function to be done requires a particular form to be possible or efficiently or effectively done.

Guided Practice Inquiries:

1. With your Learning Club, describe the physical characteristics you have that allow you to meet your basic needs. Create a list of the physical characteristics and what each does and what basic need it helps you to meet. Compare your list to the list of at least one other Learning Club. (BK, LM, L)
2. As a Learning Club, observe the animals in the two classroom habitats. Create a T-chart for each animal showing the physical characteristics (form) that allow the animal to meet each of its basic needs (function). In the left column list the basic need to be met and in the right column, the physical characteristic used to meet the basic need. On the back of your T-Chart, create an illustration that shows at least one physical characteristic (form) of one of the animals and write a brief summary describing how this characteristic helps this animal meet its basic needs (function). (BK, LM, LS)

Inquiries:

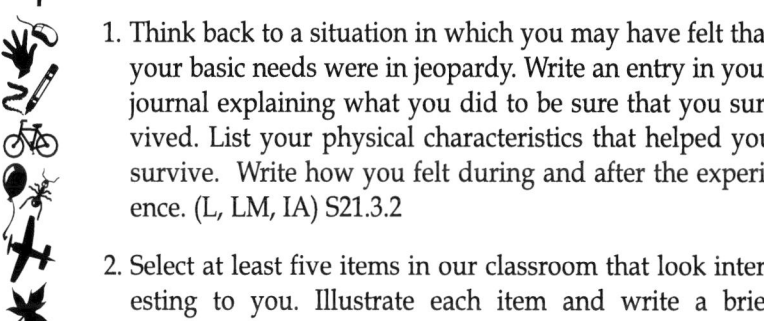

1. Think back to a situation in which you may have felt that your basic needs were in jeopardy. Write an entry in your journal explaining what you did to be sure that you survived. List your physical characteristics that helped you survive. Write how you felt during and after the experience. (L, LM, IA) S21.3.2
2. Select at least five items in our classroom that look interesting to you. Illustrate each item and write a brief description of the attributes (form) of each item. On a Post-It Note, describe the use (function) of each item. With your Learning Club, pantomime the form and function of at least one of your items. Record in your science journal at least one other item that is similar in form or function to one you chose. Example: pencil, long and narrow; similar to a pen, both are used to write.
3. Make a poster showing how you do something that helps you survive. Include both words and illustrations on your poster showing your understanding of form and function. Explain your poster to your Learning Club. (L, LM, S)
4. Observe and list in your journal any birds and other animals you see while on a nature walk. Record and illustrate

in your journal and explain to a partner the different birds and animals seen, the different body parts, and how each part was used. (N, S, L) S4.21

5. With your Learning Club, brainstorm and name at least five characteristics of birds or other animals that help them meet their basic needs and at least three other details you would like to know about birds or other animals and how they survive. Have your recorder write the results on lined paper, compare your results with other Learning Clubs, and create a final list for a class research project. (L)

6. With at least two other students, select four or more pictures of animals from the cards on the resource table. Create a four-column chart. Write the name of one of the pictured animals at the top of each column. List the characteristics the animal uses to meet its basic needs in the column below the name of the animal. Share your chart with another student. (S, L, LM, N)

7. With a partner, choose two of your favorite animal cartoon characters and write a short paragraph for each one naming their body parts and describing how each part helps the animal meet its basic needs. Read your paragraphs to another pair of students for feedback. (LM, L, N)

Topic: Birds - Wings, Beaks and Eyes

Significant Knowledge Key Point #1:

One of the most important physical characteristics (form) of birds is their wings. The function of a bird's wing is to lift it in flight. Wings allow birds to get around effectively in the environment to find food, water, shelter, a mate, and protection. Birds' wings are covered with feathers that function to smooth the wing surface to create the air flow that is necessary for flight. Not all birds fly in the same way. Some birds soar for hours without flapping a wing while other birds might flap their wings over 70 times a second as they hover, fly forward, or even backwards. Many birds can be identified by these flight patterns. These flight patterns have been developed to help them meet their basic needs. SCI 6.3.3, 8.3.2, 9.3.2, 15.3.2, 15.4.2

Guided Practice Inquiries:

1. Mimic various birds' wing movements after the teacher demonstrates each one. With a partner, use the Wing Beat Chart as a guide to practice flapping as a hawk, crow, chickadee, robin, starling, pigeon, and hummingbird. One person should keep the time while the other person flaps. Take turns. Try to flap in time with each of the birds on the chart. Discuss how your arms feel when you finish flapping like a particular bird. Try to identify the bird your partner is mimicking and predict how the wing-beat patterns impact at least two birds' flight. Record your observations in your science journal. (L, S, BK, N) Math 1.3.1, 1.4.2, 1.3.3, 1.4.3, 3.3.6, 5.3.1, 5.4.1

2. Study the illustration your teacher has placed on the overhead projector/computer screen. Working with a partner, discuss, compare,. and contrast the illustration of the bird's wing to your own arm. Using your arms, show your partner how a bird's wing works. Write a paragraph describing a bird's wing in your science journal. (L, BK, N)

Inquiries:

1. Make a model of a bird's wing with pipe cleaners and feathers. Be ready to explain how the wing (form) helps the bird fly (function). (L, S, N)

2. Write either a story or a movie scene* that describes a situation where a bird must use its flying abilities (form) to escape from danger (function). Include details about how the bird's wing works, its flight patterns and the environment that it lives in. (L, N) R5.3.3, 5.4.3 (*See Language Arts Skill Key Point #1)

3. Write a haiku poem* about a specific bird. Use your previous experiences with the Wing Beat inquiry to describe the bird and the way it flies. Illustrate your poem and add it to our class book to be donated to a local children's hospital. (L, S) (*See Language Arts Skill Key Point #2)

4. Using the pictures of birds and airplanes in your packet, complete a Venn Diagram* that shows how the form of a plane and a bird are alike and different. Describe in your Science Journal how each part of a bird and each part of a plane affects their flight. (S, LM, L) (*See Math Skill Key Point #1)

5. With your Learning Club research at least five birds of your choice. Design a bar graph that shows the speed each bird flies. Describe the special attributes of at least two birds' wings noting what impact each bird's wings (form) has on the bird's flight capabilities (function). (Differentiation: Research the flight speed of at least three birds, calculate the time it would take each bird to fly 50 miles, 100 miles and 135 miles.) (S, LM, L)

Significant Knowledge Key Point #2:

Birds are the only animals in the world with feathers. The form of the feather determines its use. Contour feathers, which are found on the bird's body, wings, and tail, are stiff and have barbs that lock them together so they can push air for flight. Contour feathers also provide camouflage (coloring that blends in with a bird's typical environment). Down feathers, which are fluffier, softer, and lie close to a bird's body under the contour feathers, help provide warmth and protection from the weather.

Guided Practice Inquiries:

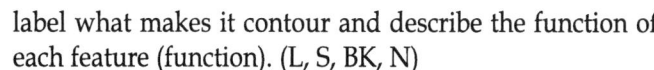

1. Observe the large contour feather on the screen. Notice how the barbs stick out from the shaft with tiny barbules that grow from each. Illustrate a contour feather (form); label what makes it contour and describe the function of each feature (function). (L, S, BK, N)

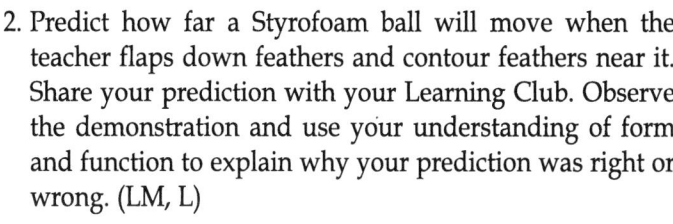

2. Predict how far a Styrofoam ball will move when the teacher flaps down feathers and contour feathers near it. Share your prediction with your Learning Club. Observe the demonstration and use your understanding of form and function to explain why your prediction was right or wrong. (LM, L)

3. With your Learning Club, select from among the different environments shown on the overhead/computer the one that best matches the bird you have been given. Be prepared to share why you made your choice, based on the physical features of the bird. Describe how the physical features (form) of at least three of these birds influence the survival (function) of the bird in this environment. (S, L)

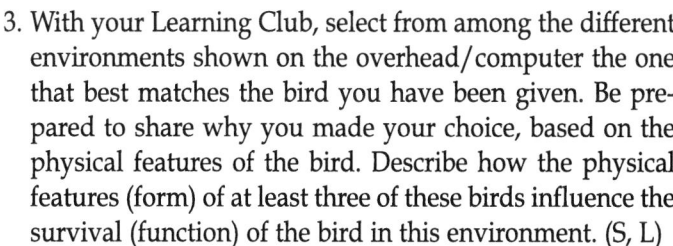

4. List and illustrate at least one human-made product that mimics the form of the contour feather. Describe its function. Discuss your observations with your Learning Club. (L, S, BK, N)

Inquiries:

1. Select and observe a contour feather and a down feather. Draw a picture of each, label what kind of feather it is and describe the special features and function of each of the feathers. (L, S, BK, N)

2. With your Learning Club, sort your bag of feathers into two groups: contour and down. Record a list of attributes of each kind of feather. Compare your list to others' and edit yours to your personal best. Record at least five important feather words in your personal dictionary. (S, BK, N)

3. Use the Internet to research the form and function of your favorite bird's feathers. Describe such attributes as color, size, and special features of your bird's feathers. Illustrate

one contour and one down feather from your bird. Draw a picture of the kind of environment that would help camouflage your bird. Save this work for a future project. (L, S, BK, N) R 11.3.2, 11.3.5, 11.4.5, 5.3.1, 5.4.1

4. Explain the function of each kind of feather (contour and down) to one other person so that he/she understands how the feathers help the bird move and survive. (L, S, N)

5. Write a poem or song of at least two verses about the two different kinds of feathers (contour and down). Explain how birds use these feathers. (L, BK, N, M)

6. Explain, in writing, why down feathers won't help a bird fly and contour feathers do. (LM, L)

7. With your Learning Club draw and color a bird that will be camouflaged in the environment given to you. Explain to a partner how camouflage helps protect a bird. (S, LM, L)

Significant Knowledge Key Point #3:

Each species of bird has a special beak adapted for gathering its food and preparing it for eating. Knowing what a bird's beak looks like helps predict what it will eat and how it will eat it. Knowing what birds eat helps us predict what their beaks look like.

Guided Practice Inquiries:

1. Visit each of the eight different feeding stations. Try to "eat" the food with each of the three different "beaks." Record which beak works best for each type of food. (L, S, BK, N) SCI 22.3.1, 22.3.3, R 4.3.6, 4.4.6, 4.3.4, 4.4.4

2. View the Eyewitness video "Birds" to observe different bird beak forms and their functions. Discuss with your Learning Club the physical characteristics (form) of four or more different bird beaks and what they allowed the bird to do (function). Share with the class. (BK, LM, L)

3. Use your prior experience to help you describe at least one kind of bird with each of the beak examples you see in the feeding stations. Describe the kinds of food for which this sort of beak is best suited. Explain why the other beaks would not function in specific environments such as grass, mud, water, and trees. (L, S, BK, N) SCI 22.3.1, 22.3.3, R 4.3.6, 4.4.6, 4.3.4, 4.4.4

Inquiries:

1. Observe pictures of five or more birds and their beaks. Make a list of different beak types and the kind of food you think the bird eats based on the beak type. Describe the kind of environment this bird must live in to find the food for which its beak is best suited. Create a beak/food game that will challenge your peers. Include at least five birds and their beaks. Write the directions for playing your game. Ask two members of your Learning Club to play the game and give you feedback on the directions and the game. (L, N)

2. Illustrate a poster of at least three different types (form) of bird beaks and the jobs for which they are best suited. Print the job (function) the beak does under the picture of each one. (L, S, N)

3. From clay create a bird beak and a model of the food that it might eat. Display your beak with a written description telling how the beak (form) impacts what the bird can eat (function). (S, BK, N) SCI 20.3.1

4. Write a poem or a song about at least three different kinds of bird beaks describing how they are different and how they are used. (L, BK, M, N)

5. With your Learning Club, create and perform a skit about bird beaks and the different ways they are used. Include at least four of the different beaks in your skit. (L, BK, M, S, N)

Significant Knowledge Key Point #4:

What a bird must do to find food and escape predators determines where the eyes are placed on the head. Most birds have eyes on the sides of their heads allowing each eye to focus on a different image (monocular vision). This allows the bird to see a different view with each eye and gives a broader range of vision. Birds of prey, like people, have forward facing eyes, fixed in their heads, which allow them to focus on a single image with both eyes at the same time (binocular vision).

Guided Practice Inquiries:

1. Make an eye patch with a small piece of black paper and a piece of yarn. Adjust it so that it will fit on your head like a pirate's eye patch. When all your classmates are ready, play "Fowl Ball" with them. With a partner, talk about how you felt while playing the game. Be ready to share how this experience helped you understand monocular vision. (S, BK, N)

2. With your Learning Club, discuss the bird pictures that the teacher shows from the overhead/computer. Create a T-Chart to record whether they have monocular vision or binocular vision. List the name of the bird under the category in which it belongs. Compare your T-Chart with those of another Learning Club, and edit yours for accuracy. (L, N) SCI 2.3.2

Inquiries:

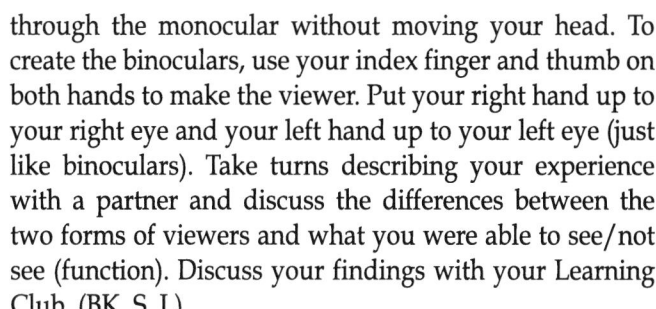

1. Create a monocular viewer and a binocular viewer using your hands. For the monocular, use your right hand to make a circle with your index finger and thumb. Shut your right eye, place your right hand circle on your left eye, and look straight ahead with your left eye. Stand next to a partner and take turns describing all that you see through the monocular without moving your head. To create the binoculars, use your index finger and thumb on both hands to make the viewer. Put your right hand up to your right eye and your left hand up to your left eye (just like binoculars). Take turns describing your experience with a partner and discuss the differences between the two forms of viewers and what you were able to see/not see (function). Discuss your findings with your Learning Club. (BK, S, L)

2. Working with a partner, create two T-Charts labeled Monocular Vision and Binocular Vision. Record the advantages and disadvantages of each kind of vision. Compare and edit to complete your charts with those of another Learning Club. (L, S)

3. Choose a bird with either monocular or binocular vision. Imagine what you could see if you were that bird. Write a paragraph that describes the form and function of that bird's vision. (L)

4. Working alone, divide a group of bird picture cards into two piles. Label one pile monocular vision and the other binocular vision. Record your findings in your science journal. (L, LM)

5. With your Learning Club, create a skit demonstrating monocular and binocular vision and how birds use each kind of vision to get their food and escape predators. (BK, L)

Language Arts Skill Key Point #1:

A scene in a movie is a unit of related actions that take place at a single location. Full-length television shows, animated cartoons, and movies are made by editing together a series of selected small units or scenes.

Guided Practice Inquiries:

1. With your Learning Club, watch a short video clip. Determine three or more different scenes that were in the clip. Discuss the criteria you used to select the scenes. Share your group's conclusions with the class and how watching the clip or the process helped you understand a movie scene. (BK, L, S, LM)

2. With your Learning Club, recreate a short scene from a movie or television show that you have seen. Present to the class and have the class determine if your small product was or was not a "scene." (BK, L)

Inquiries:

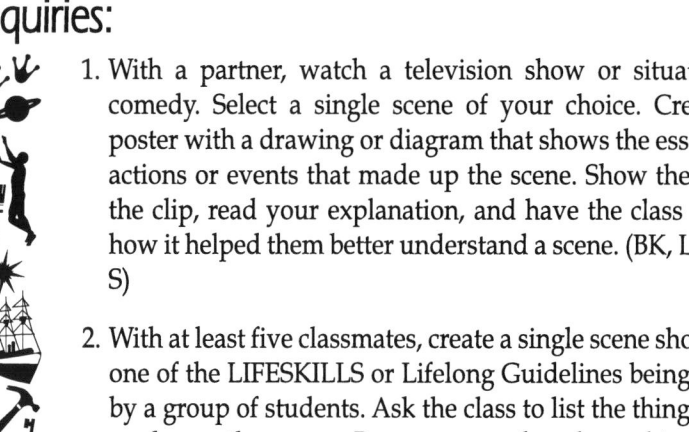

1. With a partner, watch a television show or situational comedy. Select a single scene of your choice. Create a poster with a drawing or diagram that shows the essential actions or events that made up the scene. Show the class the clip, read your explanation, and have the class share how it helped them better understand a scene. (BK, LM, L, S)

2. With at least five classmates, create a single scene showing one of the LIFESKILLS or Lifelong Guidelines being used by a group of students. Ask the class to list the things that made up the scene. Process as a class how this scene helped everyone gain a better understanding of a movie scene. (BK, LM, L)

3. Clip three or more cartoon strips from a local newspaper or go on the Internet to www.comics.com, and print out a cartoon. With your Learning Club discuss and be able to explain how each frame of the strip can be the same thing as a single scene in a move or play. Cut out one frame and paste the remaining frames back together. Share with the class how the cartoon changed when one scene or frame was removed. (BK, LM, L, S)

4. Bring in a DVD of an appropriate film or cartoon. Select and show one of the scenes deleted in the editing process before the film was released. With your Learning Club, discuss and share at least one reason why the scene was deleted. Process why filming one scene at a time is important to the final product. (BK, LM, L, S)

5. With your Learning Club, compile a written list of plays, ice shows, television shows, cartoons, and movies. Each member selects a scene he/she remembers from one of the items and shares the highlights. The Learning Club selects one to share with the class. Include why it was chosen and how it is an example of a scene. (L, LM)

Language Arts Skill Key Point #2:

Haiku poetry allows us to express our feelings through a three-line poem. The first line has five syllables, the second line has seven syllables, and the third line has five syllables. R 9.3.4, 9.4.4

Guided Practice Inquiries:

1. With your group read and share together the sample haiku poems the teacher provides. Using the Internet or research books, find one other example of haiku poetry. Share it with the class. (L, N)

2. With the class write a haiku poem that describes the class. Plan a movement for each line. (L, BK)

Inquiries:

1. Choose one haiku poem from those shared. Write a paragraph telling what the poem means to you. (L, N)

2. Write a haiku poem about a bird that we have observed. Share it with your group. (L, N)

3. Write a modified haiku poem by adding a fourth line with five syllables. Illustrate your poem. (L, LM, N)

4. Write a haiku poem that explains or compares binocular and monocular vision. (L, LM, N)

5. Write a haiku poem that explains form and function. (LM, L, N)

Math Skill Key Point #1:

A Venn diagram is a graphic organizer made of at least two overlapping circles. It can be used to compare two or more attributes to see how they are similar and how they are different. Shared attributes are written in the area where the two circles overlap. R 6.3.2, 6.4.2

Guided Practice Inquiries:

1. Make a class Venn diagram comparing the heights of students. (L, S)

2. With a partner make a Venn diagram using similar and different attributes of something you choose. (L, S)

Inquiries:

1. Using all of the LIFESKILLS and Lifelong Guidelines, make a Venn diagram comparing our class community to a bird's community. After you decide which Lifelong Guidelines and LIFESKILLS describe the behaviors of both yourself and birds, compare your Venn Diagram with a member of your Learning Club. (L, S, N)

2. Create a Venn diagram question that will compare humans and birds. Write the attributes to be compared above each circle and ask your partner to complete the Venn Diagram. (L, S, N)

3. Make a Venn diagram to compare monocular vision and binocular vision. Compare directions eyes are facing and the number of images one sees. (L, S, N)

4. Make a Venn diagram to compare your arms to a bird's wings. (L, S, N)

5. Make a Venn diagram to compare how a bird meets its basic need for survival to how you meet your basic need for survival. (S, L, N)

Social/Political Action Inquiries or Celebrations of Learning:

1. With a partner, research the National Audubon web site to find information regarding the national annual bird count done in the United States. Find out the procedures for a person volunteering to be one of the counters in your area. Create a chart showing the procedures an individual must follow to be one of the volunteers. Present the information to the class. Create a list of volunteers and follow the procedures so all can become annual counters. (BK, LM, S, L)

2. Do an Internet search for the web site of your state's Department of Natural Resources. Search throughout the site to determine if there are any endangered or threatened bird species in your area. Choose one as a focus for a class project to inform the community of the bird and why it is endangered or threatened. Include at least three suggestions for what people can do to help the species get removed from the endangered or threatened list. (BK, LM, L, N)

3. With a group of classmates, go on a walking tour of an area near your school or home. Determine the species of birds that live or feed in that area. Create a plan to help improve or maintain the area so the birds that live there will be able to find food and shelter. Share your plan with at least two other groups. Have them critique the plan and give you feedback. (BK, N, LM, L)

Standards/Benchmarks for the Content Addressed in this Topic:

Reading

2.3.3 & 2.4.3	Summarizing, paraphrasing, drawing conclusions
2.4.4	Note taking, outlining, summarizing
4.3.4 & 4.4.4	Drawing conclusions
4.3.6 & 4.4.6.	Read & follow directions
5.3.1 & 5.4.1	Locate sources for research
5.3.2 & 5.4.2	Writing letters
5.3.3 & 5.4.3	Writing narrative stories
6.3.2 & 6.4.2	Organize ideas with graphic organizers
6.3.3 & 6.4.3	Write compositions with paragraphs
6.3.4 & 6.4.4	Revise drafts
6.3.5 & 6.4.5	Edit for Standard English
6.3.7 & 6.4.7	Share writing with others
8.3.2 & 8.4.2	Listen to connect prior experiences
9.3.2 & 9.4.2	Public speaking
9.3.4 & 9.4.4	Poetry
10.3.1	Speak and listen in group discussions
11.3.2	Use variety of media for research
11.3.5, 11.4.5	Present research findings

Math

1.3.1 & 1.4.1	Addition and subtraction facts
1.3.2 & 1.4.2	Operations with regrouping
3.3.6	Identify elapsed time
5.3.1 & 5.4.1	Collect & organize data

Science

2.3.2	Sort & classify objects
6.3.2 & 6.4.2	Investigate, compare, & contrast identifiable characteristics of plants and animals
6.3.3	Investigate & describe how plants and animals require certain conditions to survive
8.3.2	Investigate & describe how some living things are alike in appearance and behavior; others are not
9.3.2	Explain how particular features of plants & animals help them live in different kinds of places
15.3.2, 15.4.2	Identify & describe variables that affect the survival of organisms within an ecosystem
18.3.1	Use science as a process that involves observing & asking questions
18.3.2, 18.4.2	Scientific observation
18.4.4	Exchange scientific observation & ideas
20.3.1	Compare a model with what it represents
21.3.1	Ask questions & investigate to get answers
21.3.2	Record observations in a journal
22.3.1	Follow verbal & written directions
22.3.2	Create illustrations, graphs, charts
22.3.3	Cooperate & contribute ideas within a group
24.3.3	Identify & gather tools & materials needed in an investigation

Resources:

Teacher:

Print–

Braus, Judy. Ranger Rick's Nature Scope: Birds, Birds, Birds, Washington, D.C.: National Wildlife Federation, 1992.

Hume, Rob. Birdwatching. New York: Random House, 1992.

National Audubon Society First Field Guide: Birds. New York: Chanticleer Press, 1998.

Stokes, Donald & Lillia. Stokes Field Guide to Birds. Boston: Little, Brown and Company, 1996.

Web Sites–

www.audubon.org/states/nv

www.nbii.gov/education.birds.html

Video–

Eyewitness Videos: Birds, Sight, Flight (available from Amazon.com)

Student:

Print–

Hume, Rob. Birdwatching. New York: Random House, 1992.

National Audubon Society First Field Guide: Birds. New York: Chanticleer Press, 1998.

Stokes, Donald & Lillia. Stokes Field Guide to Birds. Boston: Little, Brown and Company, 1996.

Literature–

Avi. Poppy. New York: HarperCollins Publishers, Inc., 1994.

Cannon, Janell. Stellaluna, San Diego: Harcourt Brace & Co., 1992.

Yolen, Jane. Owl Moon, New York: Scholastic, Inc., 1987.

Video–
Eyewitness Videos: Birds, Sight, Flight (available from Amazon.com)
National Audubon Society, Owl Up Close, Nature Science Network, Inc., Carrboro, NC, 1991.
Bluebirds Up Close, Nature Science Network, Inc., Carrboro, NC, 1991.
Hawks Up Close, Nature Science Network, Inc., Carrboro, NC, 1991.
Hummingbirds Up Close, Nature Science Network, Inc., Carrboro, NC, 1991.
Cardinals Up Close, Nature Science Network, Inc., Carrboro, NC, 1991.

Websites–
www.audubon.org/states/nv
www.surfbirds.com
www.cityofhenderson.com
www.springmountainranch.com
www.birds.cornell.edu
www.dnr.state
www.library.thinkquest.org
www.nbii.gov/education.birds.html
www.erin.utoronto.ca/~w3bio325/325lab1.html

Music–
"Land of the Loon" by Dan Gibson and John Herberman from Solitudes
"Piano Songbirds" by Dan Gibson and John Herberman from Solitudes (http://www.somersetent.com/WebMusic/cdmshow.wws)

Artifacts/Models–
1. A collection of bird figures. Some with "chirping" are available from National Geographic.
2. Bird feathers collected on a bird walk

Guest Speaker–
Naturalist from local zoo who specializes in birds

Lesson Design– SK&A Team © 2005

Anticipatory Set-
Read orally the first chapter of Poppy by Avi. Discuss the owl's feeding habits.

Inclusion Activity-
Each Learning Club will try to open and eat a walnut without using a nutcracker and share strategies they used with the class.

Lesson Objective-
Significant Knowledge Key Point #3 Each species of bird has a special beak adapted for gathering its food and preparing it for eating. Knowing what a bird's beak looks like helps predict what it will eat and how it will eat it. Knowing what birds eat helps us predict what their beaks look like.

Rationale/Purpose: To help students see the application of form and function in nature

Input

Guided Practice Inquiries:

1. Visit each of the eight different feeding stations. Try to "eat" the food with each of the three different "beaks." Record which beak works best for each type of food. (L, S, BK, N) SCI 22.3.1, 22.3.3, R 4.3.6, 4.4.6, 4.3.4, 4.4.4

2. View the Eyewitness video "Birds" to observe different bird beak forms and their functions. Discuss with your Learning Club the physical characteristics (form) of four or more different bird beaks and what they allowed the bird to do (function). Share with the class. (BK, LM, L)

Modeling: Demonstrate each of the feeding stations to show what will be done at each station and how the tools are to be used.

Checking for Understanding: Teacher will circulate and question each Learning Club about the feeding stations and their observations. (All levels of Bloom's)

3. Use your prior experience to help you describe at least one kind of bird with each of the beak examples you see in the feeding stations. Describe the kinds of food for which this sort of beak is best suited. Explain why the other beaks would not function in specific environments such as grass, mud, water, and trees. (L, S, BK, N) SCI 22.3.1, 22.3.3, R 4.3.6, 4.4.6, 4.3.4, 4.4.4

Independent Practice:

Inquiries:

1. Observe pictures of five or more birds and their beaks. Make a list of different beak types and the kind of food you think the bird eats based on the beak type. Describe

the kind of environment this bird must live in to find the food for which its beak is best suited. Create a beak/food game that will challenge your peers. Include at least five birds and their beaks. Write the directions for playing your game. Ask two members of your Learning Club to play the game and give you feedback on the directions and the game. (L, N)

2. Illustrate a poster of at least three different types of bird beaks and the jobs for which they are best suited. Print the job the beak does under the picture of each one. (L, S, N)

Closure: Learning Clubs process the feeding activity by completing their "Fill the Bill" record sheet. Learning Clubs share their sheets with the class. The class plans the next learning activity based on the consensus of the group.

Instructional Strategies:

- Learning Clubs
- Group Roles
- Direct Instruction
- Brainstorming
- Demonstrations
- Bird Walk
- Pairs
- Internet
- Models

Implementation Tips

Teaching from key points and inquiries based on a *being there* location is considerably different from teaching from textbooks and worksheets. Our advice to you is this:

- Start early in the year, October at the latest, to give yourself maximum time between components—time to learn from experience before starting another curriculum chunk and time to do your personal best when planning and implementing the next component. Remember, doing small amounts of curriculum frequently is a much better learning experience than attempting a few large chunks.
- Keep your focus on the two main goals of Stage 2 curriculum:
  - Developing curriculum based on a *being there* location
  - Starting with a concept which can integrate content within and among subjects and skills and making all curriculum as conceptual as possible
- However you start, be sure you always post your theme on the wall for students to see. Add immersion items to your theme wall. For second grade students and up, also post your key points as you go. For the benefit of students who are high in spatial intelligence but not in linguistic intelligence, use graphics to represent the content. Remember, you want your theme to focus students' attention on what is to be studied and to connect it with what they have previously studied and will study in the future.

Notes

1 *Webster's New Universal Unabridged Dictionary.* (New York: Barnes & Noble, 1996).

Chapter 15: Instructional Strategies for Stage 2

Stage 2 Instructional Strategies

ITI Classroom Stages of Implementation
Entry level to making curriculum and instruction bodybrain compatible

Stage 2

CURRICULUM	INSTRUCTIONAL STRATEGIES
	• Expertly uses all the instructional strategies identified in Stages 1.2 and 1.3 everyday, throughout the day for both ITI integrated curriculum time and for other curriculum as well.
	• Expertly selects strategies for ITI integrated curriculum time that ensure that students reach mastery, i.e., that students identify/understand patterns and develop programs for using what they understand in real-world ways. Such instructional strategies include those in Stages 1.2 and 1.3 plus the following: – Modeling being a lifelong learner and participating citizen. – Movement to help students identify and understand patterns and sequences of events/processes, and to build mental programs for using concepts and skills, retaining them in long-term memory. – Collaboration, the content for which is specially designed so that no one student can complete an inquiry alone. Collaborative work sessions include identifying in advance the Lifelong Guidelines and LIFESKILLS necessary to successfully complete an assignment plus reflective thinking at the end of the work. Whenever possible, the structure and roles within the collaborative group are an extension of the content to be learned, such as roles of people in a court room (judge, jury, legal stenographer, and so forth).

ITI Classroom Stages of Implementation **Stage 2**

Entry level for making the learning environment bodybrain compatible

CURRICULUM	INSTRUCTIONAL STRATEGIES
	– Knowledge of temperament, used during instruction and when designing inquiries in ways that speed up and deepen learning.
• Chooses at least four *being there* locations that will provide real-life experiences with the selected concepts and skills.	• Instructional strategies for introducing and reteaching concepts and skills of the ITI integrated curriculum: – *Being there* experiences which are enhanced and deepened through lead up-activities, assignments during bus rides, focused follow-up activities including return trips to the *being there* location, visits by resource people, immersion and simulations, personalized homework assignments, and so forth. – Teaching concepts and skills through the lives of those at the *being there* location rather than through the perspective of textbooks. Utilizes on-site interviews, visiting resource people, situational role playing, and other instructional strategies that make the concepts and skills come alive for students. Includes role playing to help students learn to apply concepts and skills and to build C.U.E. (creative, useful, emotional) into the teacher's instructional strategies and inquiries. – The ITI Discovery Process as a frequent alternative to direct instruction and an important means of helping students learn how to learn.
• Includes a Social/Political Action Project and concludes with a Celebration of Learning for at least two chunks of integrated curriculum during the year. • Meets frequently with a professional or peer coach who supports the implementation of a bodybrain-compatible learning environment for students.	• Expertly uses instructional strategies for enhancing wiring into long-term memory and assessment: – Clear performance criteria for students through inquiries and rubrics that describe the performance levels expected of them. These statements of expectation are written and do not require explanation from the teacher. – Celebrations of Learning that heighten emotional involvement in applying the key points and help wire learning into long-term memory. – Social/Political Action Projects that grow naturally out of students' study at a *being there* location (or from a current event/situation in school, community, nation, or world) and that provide students practice in using the democratic processes of our government and society and in contributing to others.

Improving Instructional Strategies: The Challenge

Before you can profit from powerful curriculum, there are two prerequisites: You must provide a bodybrain-compatible environment (discussed in Stage 1 of implementation) and you must possess expertise at a variety of instructional strategies.

Why? Because the day is long for elementary school students. From their point of view, variety in instructional strategies from hour to hour is a must, not a luxury. Limited instructional strategies leads to monotony, putting both students and teacher at risk. Lecture, textbook reading assignments, and worksheets can't be sustained all day long. Students won't sit still for it; they couldn't even if they wanted to. Movement and full engagement of the sensory system is the biological nature of young students. When students tire of their teacher's limited instructional strategies and leadership, they take over the class themselves and the tug-of-war begins.

We believe that improving instructional strategies should be the first priority during Stage 2 and should garner 80 percent of the staff development and support resources. Our schools won't improve until every teacher can and does effectively use a wide variety of instructional strategies.

Stage 2 is a clarion call to you to deepen and master a wide variety of instructional strategies, a foundation for your continuing work to improve curriculum.

Using a Variety of Instructional Strategies

Instructional strategies must vary and they must increasingly become a natural extension of the content to be learned, not pre-designed, publisher-provided activities. At Stage 2, instructional strategies used during Stages 1.2 and 1.3 must deepen and be crafted to best deliver the content at hand. This represents an important shift from Stage 1 in which movement to enhance learning, for example, focused mostly on movement which help students reset their emotions. Then, the content of these movements was unimportant as long as they achieved the goal of energizing or relaxing students. However, in Stage 2, movements must also be crafted to help deliver the content to be learned. Whether teacher-made or student-made, these movements must help students understand, use, and store the content of the current key points in long-term memory.

In similar fashion, the songs and literature used during Stage 2 must help students understand, use, and remember the content of the key points. If your favorite songs and literature don't help teach your key points, they must be left behind. Collaborative learning activities must also pass this acid test; the structure of roles within the Learning Clubs should help teach the content of the day's/week's key points.

In short, your use of instructional strategies in Stages 2 and beyond must be designed to deliver the content you are teaching. To do so, your use of each strategy must deepen and become a natural outgrowth of your content—the best possible way to teach the content of the moment.

Connecting Instructional Strategies to Content

For Stage 2 and beyond, it is essential that you extend and deepen your use of strategies so that they become more content driven than formula. Implement them not only during the ITI integrated curriculum but all day every day.

Movement to Enhance Learning

In Stage 1, movement mostly centered on ways to energize and calm students. In Stage 2 and beyond, your use of movement must connect to and grow out of the curriculum you are teaching—the key points and inquiries of your ITI integrated curriculum. Examples: body mapping to learn the continents of the world, steps of the scientific thinking process, body movements to form the letters of the alphabet, and so forth.

Movement should be daily, sometimes even hourly, so that students not strong in linguistic intelligence (approximately 80% of our students) have another avenue through which to learn and remember.

Content for Movement. Your first goal in using movement is to integrate movement with the content being studied. Encourage students to use their bodies to increase sensory input, practice ways to use what they understand, and hard-wire learning into long-term memory. For example, make study trips truly exploratory not just look and see. Develop hand jives and whole-body movement routines as mnemonic devices. Develop role-playing plots and actions that illustrate the concepts and skills to be learned. Create dance routines based on the concepts or skills. Add movement to songs. Be creative. Above all, have fun!

Once you get started, the ideas will flow. Don't be afraid to involve students. Invite them to write inquiries to develop explorations, hand jives, role-playing scenarios, dance routines, songs, and so on.

To get you started, the following resources provide pictures that will stir your imagination:*

- *Stage 2 of the ITI Stages of Implementation: Intelligence Is a Function of Experience* (video, 14 minutes)
- *ITI in the Urban Middle School* by Nicole McNeil-Miller (video, 15 minutes)
- *Multiple Intelligences and the Second Language Learner* by Jo Gusman (video, 40 minutes)

For more information about movement to enhance learning, see pages 1.20-21, 2.13-14, 3.21-22, 4.15-16, and 5.10-11.

The motivation behind movement, a critical bodybrain-compatible element in the ITI model, is not movement for the sake of movement or exercise because it's good for you but because movement is critical to the functioning of the brain and therefore to learning. It's not just any movement, it is the kind of movement associated with using what is learned as well as to reset students' emotional states to a level appropriate to the next activity. This can include the letting off steam as well as focusing the brain for learning, reenergizing for a shift to a new topic of learning, or simply relaxing and taking a break.

Collaboration

Collaboration is far too rich a topic to adequately address here. For specific strategies, see *Designing Groupwork* by Elizabeth Cohen and *Cooperative Learning* by Spencer Kagan. In addition, make sure that:

- Students receive formal instruction in the personal and social skills necessary to make collaboration work

- The content of collaborative inquiries is specifically designed so that no one student can complete an inquiry by him/herself, thus forcing full participation by each student.[1]
- Collaborative work begins with an analysis of the Lifelong Guidelines/LIFESKILLS needed and ends with reflective thinking questions about the process and content of the collaborative work.

Also, from Stage 2 on, the structures of collaboration—especially the roles assigned within Learning Clubs—should be an extension of the content currently being studied in the component or topic. For example, instead of the usual roles of chair, recorder, timer, supporter, etc., the roles should be those inherent in the key points for the week(s), such as judge, prosecutor, defender, jury; or, labor and management negotiators, consumers, and public opinion experts.

The roles in collaboration groups should be as natural and fluid as those in real life. Collaboration is a means of extending and deepening student experience with content and skills. Collaboration is not an end goal; creating a sense of community is a means to greater academic achievement and practice in citizenship.

For more information about collaboration, see pages 7.15-7.18 plus 1.18-1.19, 2.14-2.15, 3.17-3.18, 4.25, and 5.16. For a wonderful discussion about how to develop curriculum for collaborative work, see *Designing Groupwork: Strategies for the Heterogeneous Classroom, Second Edition* by Elizabeth Cohen.

Providing for Temperament

"He's been like this since the day he was born . . . all smiles and easy going," "I knew she'd be interested in this job because as a child she was always intrigued by such things." Such comments recognize that many of our personality preferences are innate, part of who we are. Accommodating such personality traits, rather than resisting them, makes life in the classroom much more productive for both teacher and students.

What Makes Us Tick? Temperament, factors of one's personality, strongly impact the learning process, affecting:

- How we take in information
- How we organize during learning and applying learning
- What we value when making decisions
- Our orientation to others

We are born with these preferences or temperaments. The place we call home—where we feel most comfortable on the sliding scale for each of these four areas of behavior—remains relatively unchanged throughout life.

The Power of Temperament. The power of temperament upon school participation and achievement is enormous. First, we should stop expecting everyone to be like us; we need to begin to understand and appreciate our differences and learn how to make them an asset, rather than an irritant, in the daunting task of succeeding in life.[2]

Second, we must keep foremost in our minds that powerful learning (greatest depth, speed, ability to apply) occurs when students operate consistently with their mental wirings. Thus, we must recommit ourselves to the idea that schools must remold themselves to fit children rather than expecting children to fit schools. For a discussion of personality preferences and how to make them work for you through the nine bodybrain-compatible elements, see Appendix A.

Instructional Strategies for Introducing and Reteaching

To get the most power out of your ITI integrated curriculum, you must master three more instructional strategies:

- Using *being there* experiences as the basis for both curriculum and instruction
- Teaching concepts and skills through the lives of those at the *being there* location
- The ITI Discovery Process

Using Being There Experiences

As you spend more time studying each *being there* location, allow the *being there* experience to push you into more real-life application of concepts and skills. Abandon workbooks and worksheets; rely more on practice of skills and concepts using the situations at the *being there* location. For example, teach/practice math using interesting situations at the site, such as profit/loss, costs of running a business, computing taxes, number of people who come and go, etc. Examine law making and enforcement, historical comparisons of then and now, and so forth. Invite students, third grade and up, to write inquiries from which you select those that offer challenge for both individual and group work.

Be creative. Be real. Give students a window into the real world; help them understand what goes on behind the scenes so they better understand what they see and hear.

Teaching Through the Lives of Those at the Being There Location

Children are extremely adept at learning by imitation. Develop inquiries that require them to become someone at the *being there* location—a business owner, clerk, customer, customer service rep, biologist, water treatment engineer, college student.

Use role playing frequently. Each time a student plays a person at the *being there* location, it broadens his/her horizons. If you can imagine it, you can do it. If they can imagine themselves doing many different roles, they can also imagine more career possibilities.

Role playing is also highly appealing to those in the audience; there is action to watch, dialogue to hear, and a story line to follow. The emotional impact makes it easier for students to see connections to real life.

Role playing is especially powerful for teaching concepts that students have difficulty learning because they are abstract or because students hold misconceptions.[3]

Role playing can be formal—with time allowed to prepare and rehearse an assigned scenario—or spontaneous. Both are powerful. Role playing is especially effective for teaching students alternative responses.

Be playful. And be rigorous. Know that for many students, hearing about something is seldom as powerful as seeing it. And, because education is about giving students options in life, what better way than to have them experience those options now through role playing in the safe environment of your classroom.

The ITI Discovery Process

The ITI Discovery Process is designed to encourage curiosity and initiative—key LIFESKILLS for becoming a lifelong learner and a contributing citizen. It is an opportunity to present students with an object, specimen, or problem and let them discover both the questions and the answers. This process is exciting and allows Learning Clubs to orchestrate their own learning. It is used most effectively when the Lifelong Guidelines and the LIFESKILLS are in place.

The steps in the Discovery Process are:

1. Stimulating curiosity
2. Setting standards and expectations
3. Providing lead-up time
4. Orchestrating the exploration
5. Providing small group follow-up time
6. Capturing the teachable moment
7. Assessing student learning
8. Creating long-term memories through outreach

Curiosity, the Great Motivator. When to use the Discovery Process? Whenever you introduce a firsthand item—a specimen (owl pellets, worm farms, kiwi fruit), something unusual (starfish, oak galls, nests, etc.), something about which you want to pique student interest.

The Discovery Process takes full advantage of a child's natural curiosity. It is an opportunity to explore both the questions and answers, to explore connections between prior experiences and new, fact and fiction, to lead one's own learning.

In the ITI model, the Discovery Process is usually a Learning Club activity. In the spirit of two heads are better than one, working together usually uncovers the most patterns and the richest, most complex connections.

Step 1—Stimulating Curiosity. This is your chance to open the doors to wonder and awe for your students and a chance for them to experience being active, self-directed learners. This isn't direct instruction time, it's a time to pose "what ifs," and drop amazing facts. Have fun! Get excited yourself! Tell your students that they are going to have a most amazing time.

Step 2—Setting Standards and Expectations. Setting standards and expectations for behavior and performance is critical. In addition to the everyday expectations to use the Lifelong Guidelines and LIFESKILLS, clearly establish standards and expectations specific to the nature of the event.

In ten minutes or less:

- Identify the necessary procedures for working with a specimen (live or otherwise).
- Discuss use of exploratory tools, procedures, or other special equipment they will use.
- Review what teamwork looks and sounds like and does **not** look and sound like.

It's critical that the teacher is an enthusiastic leader. Yes, handle the snake, touch the shark, open the owl pellet, reach for the worms, and watch the live owl with fascination.

A KWL T-chart (see Chapter 10) is an effective tool to help students focus their thoughts. For the *K* column, have them list what they already know; in *W* column, list what they want to know. This discussion helps them set their expectations and begin to develop strategies for exploring. Afterwards, in the third column, have them list what they learned.

Step 3—Providing Lead-Up Time. Before beginning the Discovery Process, students need time to assimilate what they have heard, seen, and experienced during Steps 1 and 2. This should be done both individually and as a group. Provide time for students to discuss their mindmaps, share something from their personal experience, ask themselves, "Where does this fit into my knowledge/experience base?" and so forth. This is the time to communicate, a time during which students must actively and purposefully manipulate information to extract as much meaning from it as possible so that information is accurately stored in the brain.

The internal dialogue that occurs in answer to the question "How does this affect me?" is critical to activating the brain's attention mechanisms and decision to store something in long-term memory.

During this settling in, getting comfortable period, students might be sketching a specimen, comparing pictures with the real thing, hypothesizing about what they're going to discover, or sharing their personal experiences related to the lesson. This is their motivational lead-up for what they are about to do. For many students, this is the time to overcome fears and apprehensions about the unknown, e.g. a scary-looking owl. Not everyone is ready to jump in when the teacher says, "Go." Lead-up time is invaluable even if only ten minutes.

During lead-up time, decisions must be made about who's responsible for each group task. For example, "I'll be the recorder." "John draws well; he can sketch the parts." "Who wants to label?"

Sometimes it's appropriate for the teacher to select who will do specific jobs. This guarantees that students have an opportunity to practice various roles exercising leadership and responsibility. An efficient way to identify who does what is to assign every student in the group a number. All the teacher has to do is say, "For today, number 1 is the recorder, number 3 is the organizer, and number 5 is the facilitator," and so on. Another way is to post job assignments identifying specific jobs (one for each member of the group) that can be rotated. Possible roles are:

- Facilitator—sees that each group member has the opportunity to share ideas; reviews ground rules (if any) and initiates the discussion; helps restart discussion when things bog down
- Inquisitor—asks at least two questions about the subject/topic to reveal the big idea
- Connector—looks for and shares connections between the topic and personal experiences
- Illustrator—draws a picture of the most important elements of the topic
- Summarizer/recorder—summarizes discussions to clarify content or how to proceed; records events, procedures, conclusions for the group
- Reporter—reads the instructions or information aloud and reports the outcomes
- Organizer—makes sure the work area is organized and clean
- Quieter—notices when the teacher signals for active listening

Equal opportunity to experience responsibility and leadership is a cornerstone commitment in an ITI classroom. Giving job responsibilities does not, however, mean that only one or two students "do" the activity, work with firsthand materials, and so on. Everyone is a learner, all must participate in the activity. The jobs assigned to the group are in addition to the job of learning as individuals.

Step 4—The Exploration. The students are mentally ready to proceed. Let them explore, guide when it is necessary, help them interpret what they find. Shift your role from sage on the stage to guide on the side.

Step 5—Providing Small Group Follow-Up. Can you remember how important it seemed to you when a teacher gave you positive, instructive feedback? Remember how good it felt and how pleased you were that he/she noticed you personally? Such feedback is critical, yet finding time to interact with students more frequently is difficult. Usually students who receive most of our time are those with behavior problems or special needs. To solve this dilemma, limit the time allotted for direct instruction, suggest students ask each other for help ("Ask Three Before Me"), and then take this purloined time to purposefully circulate during the groupwork activity.

"Purposefully circulate" means that you will especially target groups and individuals to reteach, redirect, and/or reenergize. This is the teacher's time to observe, listen, and analyze student responses and to give immediate feedback. This is also a perfect opportunity to acknowledge the use of the Lifelong Guidelines, especially Personal Best as defined by the LIFESKILLS.

Step 6—Capturing the Teachable Moment. The teachable moment is when the student's curiosity is sparked and the teacher can enhance learning by drawing on his/her own knowledge base. It is an opportunity for the teacher to model being an active and competent learner. Taking advantage of teachable moments requires a broad knowledge base, willingness to extend learning on the spur of the moment, or even digress when appropriate.

In this information age, we're both frustrated and excited by the bombardment of knowledge all around us. To find time to increase your knowledge base, take 20 minutes a day (10 in the morning and 10 in the afternoon or evening) to read about the concepts, significant knowledge, and skills of your theme. Read books, magazines, newsletters, audio cassettes, professional journals, and any other materials that relate. When you are an ITI teacher, your theme will help you assimilate information and hold it organizationally in your mind. Teachers must be active learners committed to mastering how to use information and skills, not just talk about them.

Remembering how good it feels to learn—reliving the feeling each day—enables us to recognize when learning is actually taking place in the classroom and to capture the teachable moment.

Step 7—Assessing Learning. Because the Discovery Process is so multidimensional, assessment should be so also. In addition to checking for context, we should assess the strength of our students' emotional involvement in learning. How students feel about learning determines whether that learning will get wired into long-term memory.

Assessing Emotional Impact. Assessing the emotional impact of a lesson is just as important as assessing content. Feelings while learning something new become the attitudes we hold for the rest of our lives. How often have we heard, "I wasn't good in that when I went to school, so I'm not surprised my child isn't doing well either," or "I've never liked math or science or reading."

A daily journal is one way students can express their emotional responses to what they're learning. After a vigorous lesson such as dissecting owl pellets, it's imperative to allow students to ponder how they feel about what they learned and how this experience will affect learning in the future. Never discount your students' feelings; acknowledge that feelings are a part of being alive and, more importantly, they are the gate keeper to the cognitive domain. Everyone has emotions; unguided or ignored emotions usually hinder learning rather than assist.

If an activity has generated feelings of indignation, outrage, or heightened personal interest and concern, it is time for political action, a time to write letters to the editor, school board, planning commission, Save-the-Whales committee, a chemical company, the President of the United States, local businesses, Sierra Club, and the like. Learning and internalizing information are not enough in today's society. Individuals must realize they have a right and a responsibility to become involved and that their opinions and concerns need to be heard.

Taking action on social issues imparts a sense of importance to lessons learned at school. It provides a real-world context in which to fully explore concepts and skills and gives an audience (and a reason) for exercising a wide range of communication skills.

Assessing Academic Learning. The current "authentic assessment"[4] movement is a pleasant breath of spring across the educational landscape. Brushing aside contrived, trivial standardized assessments, Grant Wiggins, Fred Newmann, and other authentic assessment leaders admonish us to measure ability to use knowledge—producing knowledge rather than reproducing it. Thus the phrase "authentic expressions of knowledge."

In the ITI model we speak of mastery/competence in terms of performance. There's a large gap between knowing about, and selecting choice *A, B, C,* or *D* and being able to apply information to a real-life situation. Measuring the ability to use what we know is what authentic assessment is all about.

The exploration phase of the Discovery Process is just the beginning and should lead onward to specific demonstrations of what is learned during the Discovery Process. See Chapter 16 for a discussion of assessment in the ITI model.

Step 8—Creating Long-term Memories Through Outreach. Outreach is the purposeful connection of classroom activity to someone or something outside the classroom—a way of applying lessons to reality.[5] Outreach can be planned by contacting a resource person or it can be spontaneous such as when students suggest a course of action. Outreach asks the question, "Knowing this information leads me where or to whom?" To have knowledge and skills is to be responsible. Does it demand we take action? In a democracy, if we don't take action to correct problems or social ills, who will? Perhaps the students want to share with other classes or schools, produce a videotape, invite someone in to answer questions, start an information center, or set up a display at the local library or school district office. Educating others is a major responsibility of us all. Outreach demands application of what is studied. It may have long-range effects or short-term impact, but it is an important classroom activity, one which gently prods both the students and the teacher into looking at content in an active, meaningful way.

When looking at outreach, called "political or social action" in the ITI model, we should use the language arts skills of reading, writing, listening and speaking. Outreach activities provide real audiences and a clear sense of purpose. What better environment in which to master these skills? In students' minds it becomes clear that these skills are a means to an important end—the ability to cope in the real world.

The best tools we know to assist you in planning outreach is *Kid's Guide to Social Action: How to Solve the Social Problems You Choose—And Turn Creative Thinking into Positive Action* and *The Kid's Guide to Service Projects: Over 500 Service Ideas for Young People Who Want to Make a Difference,* both by Barbara A. Lewis. These books are filled with practical suggestions for getting involved and vignettes of student political action from around the country. They will assist your students with form, content, addresses, procedures, and presentations. They are comprehensive and written as user's guides. *Enriching Curriculum Through Service Learning,* edited by C.W. Kinsley and K. McPherson, is another fine resource.

Enjoy the moment. Your students certainly will!

Instructional Strategies for Long-Term Memory & Assessment

If students don't wire curriculum content into their long-term memory, the brain does a short-term memory dump and nothing remains except an emotional memory of whether they enjoyed the subject/skill or disliked it and a grade, even an *A,* on a test paper. We have wasted their time and ours. This is an important idea from brain research. It explains why spiral curricula, in which students are exposed to different parts of something each year with the expectation that they will add up at the end, don't work. And, it underscores the wisdom of "less is more," why covering content results in little long-term memory.

To revisit Chapter 1, learning is the result of real—observable and measurable—physiological growth/change in the brain. If we are to take students to long-term memory, we need to provide curriculum which is highly engaging, a task that *being there* experiences do well, and we must carry out instructional strategies that heighten and prolong the engagement.

Clear Performance Criteria

The beauty of inquiries that call for applying concepts and skills to situations at the *being there* location is that the tasks are real to students and they can readily see that real-world standards should apply. Rather than resistance to classroom "stuff," they can readily accept that performance standards are just how it is and if you want to succeed in life, get to it. For example, students grumble about grammar rules but they will work diligently on a letter to the mayor to make a good impression and thus increase the likelihood that their request will be taken seriously.

Whenever possible, let students discover what the real-world standards are for themselves. Younger students can interview people at the *being there* location; older students can also visit websites, especially those connected to professions such as unions, construction codes, work performance evaluation criteria, and rubrics of all kinds, scoring tools that list criteria for a piece of work. A useful website for school related rubrics is http://rubistar.4teachers.org

For information about how to make your inquiries better assessment tools, see Chapter 19.

Celebrations of Learning

Celebrations of Learning are a unique kind of party. They are events that make public what students have learned, give them a showcase for proving it, and let them bask in the delight of an important accomplishment. The audiences are real—parents and other students. The LIFESKILL of Pride is real.

Celebrations of Learning can come before or after a Social/Political Action Project and can be an integral part or completely independent. It all depends upon what you want to achieve and whether the content has taken on a life of its own (which frequently happens!). So, you may change your mind as you work through the component or topic of study.

For more information about conducting Celebrations of Learning, see Chapters 7 and 10.

Social/Political Action Projects

Social/Political Action Projects are at the heart of the ITI model for three reasons:

- They are the most powerful combination of curriculum and instruction you can devise
- They create an informed, involved citizenry—the ultimate purpose of public education
- They teach students how to become a lifelong learner

For more information about Social/Political Action Projects, see Chapter 21.

Notes

1 Elizabeth G. Cohen, *Designing Groupwork: Strategies for the Heterogeneous Classroom, Second Edition* (New York: Teachers College Press, 1994), 64-65. When no one person could easily do a task alone, members find it necessary to exchange ideas. Elizabeth Cohen calls this kind of collaboration an "equal exchange model." Cohen points out that "if only one person can do the task alone, then there is no motivation for a free exchange of ideas; the only issue is whether the person who know how to do the job will help those that don't." Cohen refers to this kind of interaction as a "limited exchange model of working together." Studies show a significant difference in performance levels of high thinking skills between these two kinds of collaborative work.

2 Keirsey & Bates

3 "A Private Universe" is a fascinating window on interviews with Harvard University students on their graduation day. The question put to them is "Explain the reason for the seasons." Even those who had taken astronomy classes gave the "Hot, baby, hot" explanation: When the sun gets closer, our season gets warmer. It is a powerful illustration of the power of misconceptions to override subsequent learning. Instructional strategies such as discussion and collaboration work are excellent tools for rooting out and correct stubborn misconceptions.

4 Fred Newman, one of the primary leaders of the authentic assessment movement, states, "The idea of authentic achievement requires students to engage in disciplined inquiry to produce knowledge that has value in their lives beyond simply proving their competence in school."

5 The power of outreach experiences to cement learning is well documented through a plethora of studies. Sarah S. Pearson, *Finding Common Ground: Service Learning and Education Reform, A Survey of 28 Leading School Reform Models* (Washington, DC: American Youth Policy Forum, 2002), 72-75.

Part D

Implementing Stage 3: Next Steps into Integrated Curriculum

Curriculum Development: Opportunity and Challenge

As discussed in Chapter 12, the purpose of writing your own curriculum is to make it more powerful for students by:

- Capturing the power of local *being there* experiences to engage the bodybrain learning partnership and naturally integrate all content and skills
- Providing pattern-rich content for the brain's inherent pattern-seeking nature
- Providing a vehicle for tailoring curriculum to **your** students' specific interests, needs, and ways of learning in ways that help students build mental programs and wire them into long-term memory.

These are the opportunities. The challenges lie in the fact that *teacher-made curriculum is better than publisher-developed curriculum **only if it is**.*

To ensure that your curriculum is more powerful than canned curriculum available off the shelf, it must be developed to fit how the brain learns. Recall the brain research presented in Chapters 4 and 5—the brain as pattern seeker and meaning maker and learning as the acquisition of mental programs.

The Goals of Curriculum Development

The crucial curriculum development goals for Stages 2 were to master the art of basing content and skills in a *being there* location and making curriculum more conceptual. Maintain these building blocks.

The curriculum development goals for Stage 3 and beyond are to master writing curriculum that:

- Enhances students' ability—through key points, yearlong theme, and *being there* experiences—to detect and understand patterns
- Promotes—through inquiries and *being there* experiences—development of mental programs to use in real-world ways what students understand

Stage 3 requires that you deepen your understanding of how to make the glove fit the hand—how to make curriculum fit the brain. This chapter will explore how to make key points and inquiries that better fit your students.

ITI Classroom Stages of Implementation **Stage 3**

Entry level for making curriculum bodybrain compatible

Entry Level into Integrating Curriculum

CURRICULUM

- Maintains, expands, and deepens all the aspects of integrated curriculum described in Stage 2.
- Develops key points that enhance students' ability to identify patterns and make meaning.
- Uses science as either the core or a prominent part of curriculum integration because science is everywhere and in everything; it explains how the universe works and thus provides universal concepts for integrating content; understanding science and technology is also vital to the role of citizenship in the 21st century.
- Includes in the curriculum many of the elements that appear as a natural part or extension of the *being there* focus, e.g., science, technology, history/social studies, fine arts, as well as mathematics, reading, writing, and oral expression. Integration of content is natural, not contrived.
- Prominently displays the theme on the wall so it can serve as the framework for teaching and learning. Bases at least 25-35 percent of instruction during the school year upon the bodybrain-compatible curriculum developed for this theme.
- Provides practice in citizenship through inquiries and other Social/Political Action Projects that are natural outgrowths of *being there* experiences and other related study.
- Ensures that content is age-appropriate.

INSTRUCTIONAL STRATEGIES

- Ensures that the primary sensory input provided to supplement and extend *being there* experiences is immersion and hands-on-of-the-real-thing.
- Varies instructional strategies and chooses the most effective methods for the particular content at hand, e.g., direct instruction and ITI discovery processes, collaboration and personal study time, mindmapping, organizing materials, and cross-age/multi-age interaction.
- Supports the theme with multiple, varied, and rich resources. Resource people and experts are regular visitors to the classroom. Visits to off-campus learning sites are frequent and serve as the organizers for the curriculum being studied.
- Regularly provides choices through inquiries and other means.
- Allows adequate time for students to complete their work.
- Provides sufficient inquiries for each key point to ensure mastery and development of mental programs to use the concepts and skills of the key points. Ensures that the inquiry provide students with choices and multiple opportunities for real-world applications and multiple ways to solve problems and produce products. Some inquiries are designed specifically to provide realistic opportunities for students to practice citizenship, e.g., Social/Political Action Projects, community service, and special classroom and schoolwide events.
- Effectively uses collaboration to enhance learning for academic and social growth.
- Concludes each significant chunk of integrated curriculum with a Celebration of Learning.

Notes to Myself

Chapter 16: Making Curriculum More Conceptual: Key Points

Improving a school is neither simple nor easy. Your journey to Stage 3 has likely taken 2-3 years. But don't become discouraged. As the saying goes, "If the task were easy, someone else would already have done it for you." Congratulate yourself for a long, hard job done well and know that the full payoff for your efforts lies in Stage 3 and beyond. Here, students bloom and dreams become reality. You will see achievement levels soar, the projects that students eagerly engage in will amaze you, and you will enjoy teaching more than you ever thought possible. Stage 3 is where you want to be. Enjoy this segment of your journey!

The Challenge

The challenge at Stage 3 is to make your key points more conceptual. To do so, you will need to:

- Revisit key points and what they are supposed to do
- Continue to base your key points in *being there* locations. Let the experience of the location unfold naturally, integrating the science, mathematics, technology, history/social studies, fine arts, reading, writing, and oral expression as you see it happening.
- Make science either the core or a prominent part of your curriculum. Use its universal concepts to integrate all subjects and skills. (See the concepts on pages 16.5-16.6.)
- Look with new eyes at everyday locations and select concepts that will enhance responsible citizenship. Stretch yourself to find a few powerful concepts that will explain a lot of things instead of collecting a lot of content under many organizers.
- Improve the quality of your key points

Revisit Key Points

Good key points enhance students' capacity to extract meaningful patterns and develop useful mental programs. Good key points help students build larger, more abstract conceptualizations and generalizations about the world. Knowledge is power.

Key Point Defined

A key point is a clear, concise statement of what you want students to understand and be able to apply. A key point presents a pattern—usually a collection of related patterns—that when taken together add up to something worth knowing, something that can be used in real life. For example, sharp pointed ears, a long tail, and a meow sound are attributes or parts of the pattern called cat. Two metal objects pulling toward each other in absence of an outside force such as a push or gravity suggests one of the metal pieces is a magnet. Or, here comes Calvin home from school and Hobbes is stalking through the house. You guessed it. Whooosh! An overly exuberant tiger knocks Calvin flat. We live our lives by identifying and interpreting such patterns.

From the humor that makes our day (Calvin and Hobbes) to the minute-by-minute conversations that make up the fabric of our lives, from job training to learning parenting and relationship skills, detecting and understanding patterns is the brain's way of making meaning of our world. It follows then that *we should view curriculum development—and the lesson planning that follows—as **a pattern-enhancing activity.** Your job is to write curriculum that makes recognizing and understanding patterns engaging, even gripping, and totally unavoidable.* In other words, all students can and will master each key point.

Curriculum As a Pattern-Enhancing Activity

Patterns are everywhere.[1] Our job is to enhance students' ability to identify and understand them.

For example, suppose we want students to understand the following science concept: "Interactions among animals and plants to meet the need for food within a habitat are called a 'food chain' or 'food web.'" There are at least four large and fairly complex patterns essential to understanding this idea—interactions, need for food (different ways plants and animals take in food), habitat, and food chain/food web. Once these four patterns are understood, students can begin to grasp the significance of the concept or pattern represented by the concept.

The Pattern Called "Need for Food." Students should understand that plants have various ways to take in food, such as through the roots, the air, ingesting meat (Venus fly traps), making their own food through photosynthesis, and so forth. They also should understand that animals have an even greater variety of ways to take in food and what "food" is needed varies tremendously among species. Pulling in prior knowledge or previously understood patterns, speeds up and enriches the learning process.

The Pattern Called "Interactions." Plants and animals don't take in food in isolation. Interaction implies give and take. Exploring the ways plants and animals interact (who eats whom/what, who assists whom by doing what) to have food available, to find it and to take it in lays the foundation for understanding a habitat and the interdependence of its inhabitants. Animals and plants can interact in hundreds of ways. Things are becoming interesting!

The Pattern Called "Habitat." The concept or pattern of habitat—all who live in this location—tells us what to include in our food web. The garden, the neighborhood, the city, an old oak tree—all create unique and diverse habitats. Theory can become experience at a *being there* location.

The Pattern Called "Food Chain/Food Web." Pulling forward what students already understand about chains—bicycle chains, key chains, and figures of speech—deepens and speeds their learning. For example, chains are only as strong as their weakest link or the chain of events drove everyone onward. Lose a link and the chain becomes too short to do its job (the loss of one animal may cause one or more animals or plants in the habitat to die off).

Once students understand the idea of a food chain, they'll also understand the complexity of a food web—multiple overlapping chains. In a very short time, their understanding of this concept can become very rich, broad, and forever memorable, all through connecting previous smaller patterns with new ones and finally creating one large pattern to capture the concept.

Once these four large and complex patterns are understood, they provide post office boxes in the brain where new information can be sent to and added to quickly and effortlessly.

Collectively, key points constitute the common core of knowledge and skills that all students are to understand and be able to apply.

Three Kinds of Key Points

The ITI model uses three kinds of key points:

- **Conceptual** key points are those that capture big ideas that apply worldwide; they are universal truths about how the world works. They can be generalized and transferred to multiple settings
- **Significant knowledge** key points provide information necessary to understand the concept locally where it can be directly experienced at *being there* locations
- **Skill** key points describe those basic skills needed to explore and utilize the big ideas.

Why three kinds of key points? Early in the development of the ITI model, there was just one kind of key point. We learned two lessons. First, when content is truly integrated, even students didn't recognize they were learning math or how to write a paragraph. Designating skill points as such helps teachers communicate to students, parents, peers, and supervisors that skills are being taught and learned, which ones, and when. Second, we learned that teacher's key points tended to mirror the district's/school's curriculum which, until the recent state standards movement, consisted primarily of factoids. Factoids deaden interest; concepts intrigue and challenge.

Continue to Base Curriculum in Being There Locations

When we think back over the enormous volume of information we ourselves covered during high school and college and the almost equally enormous volume of information we no longer remember, we should be more humble and honest about curriculum planning for today's students. If covering volumes of details—dates, definitions, names of famous people, and other fill-in-the-blank items—didn't stick with us, why do we pass it on? Especially when brain research clearly tells us why it doesn't work.

If you search for one strategy that would most satisfy the demands of the brain, it is this—basing curriculum in *being there* locations, letting the real world integrate content and skills as it naturally occurs, and visiting that site often (before, during, and at the end of study). The importance and power of this strategy cannot be over emphasized.

Science As Core

Although science may not be your favorite subject, its universal, what-makes-the-world-tick concepts are far and away the versatile set of concepts to engage students and to readily integrate content at a *being there* location. Our advice to you, based on coaching thousands of teachers through curriculum development, is to make science the core of your planning.

Why are we so keen on focusing on science? Because science is the great equalizer. The differences in student backgrounds in science are the least whereas the differences in student background in language arts are the greatest. Also, students love to explore their world—its objects, what they can do, how they are made, and why. This is science.

Science is also far and away the subject that elicits the most sensory input. As we have learned from brain research, the greater the sensory input, the greater the physiological change in brain; the greater the physiological change, the greater the learning.

For a user-friendly list of science concepts by grade level, see *Science Continuum of Concepts for Grades K-6* (for more information, see the order form at the back of this book). The main science idea for each grade level K-6 appears on the next page. Many of these concepts could be carried through high school.

Stretch Yourself—Find a Few Powerful Concepts That Will Enhance Citizenship

Look with new eyes at everyday locations and select concepts that will enhance responsible citizenship. Stretch yourself to find a few powerful concepts that will explain a lot of things instead of collecting a lot of content under many organizers.

Carefully pick through your standards to identify concepts and to "chunk up" ideas to make them more conceptual. This chunking up process is vital, the only way to eliminate factoids which are largely devoid of patterns and thus appear meaningless to the students.

What makes a concept powerful? It's universal—it explains a great deal about many things—and it can be directly experienced (seen and touched). The main science idea for each grade level of the *Science Continuum* is a powerful concept for integrating all subjects. For example:

Kindergarten: People can learn about things around them by observing them carefully—what they are made of, how they are put together, what they do, and how they are similar and different. Observing and comparing similarities and differences is a key way to help interpret and understand our world. Often we can learn even more about these things if we do something to them and note what happens.

First grade: All living things, including humans, have basic needs (food, water, air, protection from weather, disease, and predators, and to reproduce). A habitat is the place where the animal or plant lives while meeting these needs.

Second grade: The physical characteristics of animals and plants vary greatly and determine what they can do and how they do it to meet their needs. Similarly, the physical characteristics of non-living things vary greatly and determine what changes can occur in them and how they can be used.

Third grade: Things are changing around us all the time. Change can occur in a variety of ways (reversible, irreversible; controllable, not controllable; steady or repetitive and thus fairly predictable or not steady or repetitive and thus unpredictable) and for different reasons. The rate and size of change may not be observable with human senses; we need tools to measure such change. Change can be helpful, harmful, or neutral.

Fourth grade: Plants and animals interact with each other and their environment in ways that allow them to meet their basic needs. Keep in mind that humans are animals.

Fifth grade: All structures and systems, living and non-living, are made up of smaller parts and/or processes.

Sixth grade: Both living and non-living systems have situations in which they change in some way and other situations in which they remain essentially unchanged or constant. Why situations in such systems change and why they remain constant can be explained in terms of particular variables. Much change in our world is human-made; some is intended and some inadvertent.

How Conceptual Key Points Drive the Curriculum:

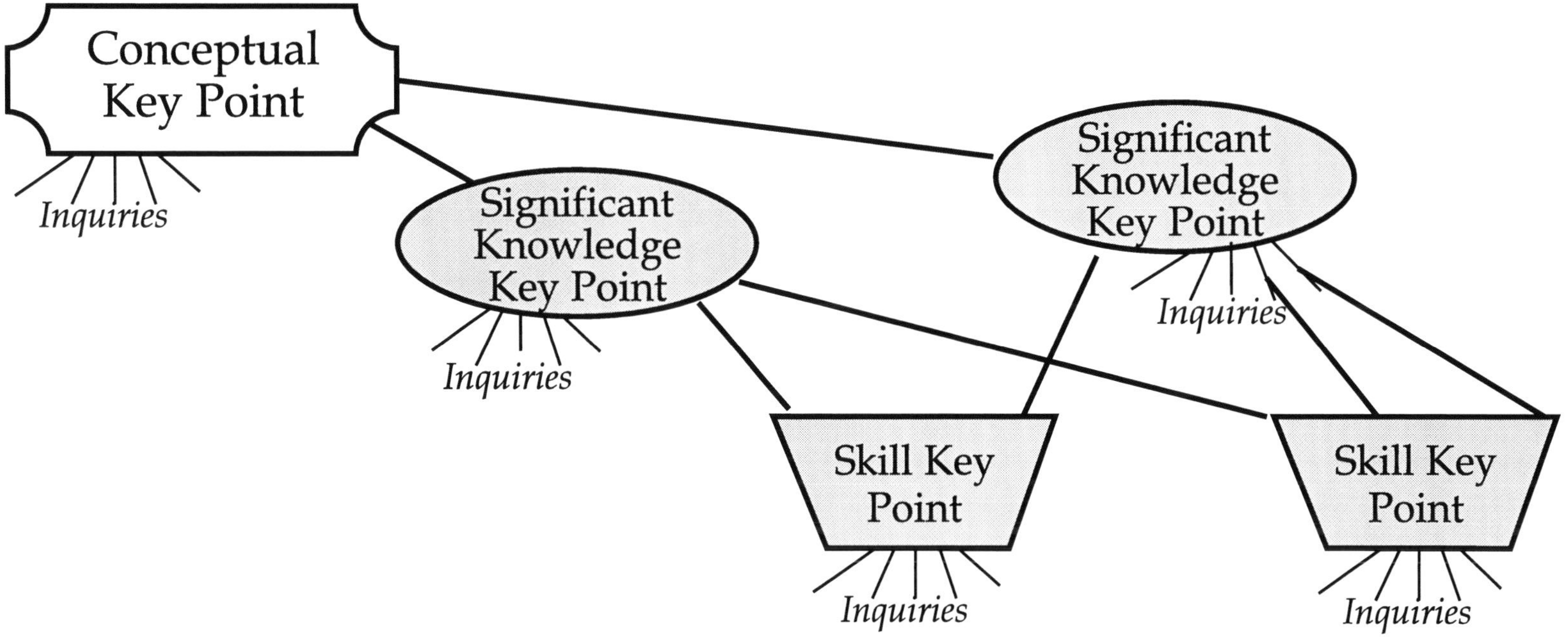

Improve the Quality of Your Key Points

Just as students have to learn and practice how to write in different genres, such as essay, short story, journaling, technical writing, poetry, etc., so must teachers. Writing key points is definitely a different genre—part essay, part technical writing, and part revelation of one's soul (or at least your prior life's experiences and knowledge base).

Guidelines for Improving

Here are some guidelines—the S.T.U.D.E.N.T.S. rule—to help you improve your key points:

S = Be succinct and clear, simple but not simplistic.

Learn to cut to the chase to say exactly what you wanted to say, no more and no less. Keep a copy of Strunk and White's pithy little book on how to be pithy.

GUIDELINES FOR WRITING KEY POINTS

STUDENTS —

S = *Succinct* and clear, ***simple*** but not simplistic

T = ***Tied*** to real-world situations

U = ***Universal*** concepts that naturally integrate all subjects and skills at a *being there* location

D = ***Designed*** for students

E = Understandable by ***every*** student (age-appropriate)

N = ***NOT*** lesson planning

T = Worthy of the ***time*** of teacher and students

S = Tight connection between ***significant*** knowledge key points and conceptual key points

T = Tie your key point to real-world situations.

Select concepts and skills from your state/district standards that students see illustrated at their *being there* locations. Context is very important to the brain when seeking patterns. Context enables students to see what something is and what it is not in addition to how and when it is used and why. The understandings reached are **always** deeper and broader than when the concept or skill is taught in the classroom isolated from its real-world context.

U = Look for universal concepts that will naturally integrate all subjects and skills at a being there location.

Today's future citizens face challenges ever so much bigger than we did. Yesterday's curriculum with its overload of factoids must be replaced with curriculum that allows students to make more connections, see bigger pictures.

Factoids are statements of fact that offer little potential for detecting patterns because they represent such a small dot of life and thus offer few attributes for students to grab on to. Factoids rarely make it past short-term memory processing. A week after the test, all is forgotten. Unfortunately, most textbooks consist primarily of factoids and thus are difficult to learn from. Their content is watered down, written in short, simple sentences for low readability, and summarized so briefly as to be cryptic and seemingly unrelated to real life or student experiences. Most curriculum—state standards as well as district level—has traditionally been over-weighted with factoids. Examples: weekly vocabulary-building lists in English classes that do not relate to concurrent areas of study, definitions in science that students have no prior or current experience with, and strings of historical dates for which students have little context.

D = Design the key point for students.

State exactly what you want them to understand so they can use that concept or skill. State it just as you want it remembered, just as they will retrieve it to use it in the real world. Avoid starting with " The student will. . . ." For example, don't say "The student will understand why civilizations fail." State that "Civilizations fail for five main reasons which are . . . ."

E = Be sure the content is age appropriate so that every student can understand it.

Be aware that much content in today's curriculum standards, while it may impress the public, is not age appropriate. For example, compare the table of contents of your science textbook with the concepts in the *Science Continuum of Concepts*. You'll find many concepts should be moved upward to later grades when students' brains are organized to process the content, not just memorize it. See discussion of age appropriateness in Appendix B.

N = Writing key points is not lesson planning.

Always complete writing key points and inquiries before you begin to lesson plan.

For example, a skill key point about journal writing might look like this: "Journal writing helps us clarify our thoughts, make connections, summarize things to help us remember them, and/or sort through our emotions."

However, mixed in with lesson planning or advice to yourself, it could well end up like: "Journal writing is a learning tool based on the ideas that students write to learn. Students are actively engaged in using the journals to write about topics of personal interest, to note their observations, to imagine, to wonder and to connect new information with things they already know."

The above key point fails on several key criteria: First, it does not state clearly what students are to understand and remember nor is it concise. It also treats students as third persons not present for or part of the conversation. Writing key points and lesson planning at the same time ALWAYS distorts the key points.

T = Make sure what you write is worth the time spent on it—yours and your students.

For all the criticism of textbooks and related worksheets, homespun curriculum is no better if it is more of the same and doesn't fit how the brain learns. As you gather information about your components and topics, you become more knowledgeable about the world around you and thus better able to craft your key points. Spend your time well.

S = Tighten up the connection between significant knowledge key points and conceptual key point.

Make sure the significant knowledge key points are what students need to know to understand how the conceptual key point applies locally at their *being there* location and elsewhere in their area. Resist the temptation to toss in tidbits that, although interesting in themselves, don't actively contribute to understanding the conceptual key point.

For examples of good key points, see Chapter 14.

Notes

1 See the discussion of pattern seeking and making meaning as the first stage of the new, brain-based definition of learning in Chapter 4.

Chapter 17: Making Curriculum More Memorable: Inquiries

When you look back on your years as a student, how many teachers come to mind for positive reasons? How many names can you remember? How many made a difference in your life? Why? What did they do that made their class so memorable? Because of who they were? Because of what they did and what they had you do?

Reading textbooks and answering the questions at the end of the chapter or plodding through ditto after ditto probably didn't register, except negatively. This we know. The antidote to poor learning is action. And that is what inquiries do. They frame the action students will take to explore and use concepts and skills until the learning becomes wired into long-term memory.

Well-written inquiries make every day memorable. Parents know when their children are learning because there is an answer to the question, "What'd you do in school today?" The children chatter endlessly. They were excited about learning and they remember it well enough to regale their parents hours later.

The Not-So-Secret Ingredients for Making Things Memorable

The list of not-so-secret ingredients for making things memorable is not a long one:

- Revisit what inquiries are and what they're supposed to do
- Maintain a sense of community that supports learning and nurtures reflective learning
- Connect to prior experience, knowledge, and skills
- Allow students to see and practice applying concepts and skills in a real-world context so critical details are available for ready reference, especially the *being there* location on which the curriculum is based

- Offer opportunities to apply concepts and skills to areas of learners' interest
- Provide choices so students may use their intelligence of strength to explore concepts and skills in order to arrive at an accurate understanding; then, encourage them to use their less developed intelligences as they wire learning into long-term memory.
- Improve the quality of your inquiries

Revisit Inquiries

The purpose of inquiries is to add action to learning so that students can achieve an accurate understanding, develop mental programs for using concepts and skills, and wire learning into long-term memory. Inquiries complete step two of the new definition of learning. (See Chapter 4 for a discussion of learning as the acquisition of new programs.)

LEARNING IS A TWO-STEP PROCESS

- Detecting and understanding patterns—a process through which our brain creates meaning
- Developing meaningful mental programs to use what is understood and to store it in long-term memory—the capacity to use what is understood, first with assistance and then almost automatically

Inquiries Defined

Inquiries, a key curriculum development structure in the ITI model, are activities that enable students to understand and apply the concept, skill, or significant knowledge of a key point. The primary purpose of inquiries is to enable students to develop mental programs to apply the key point in real-world situations. They make learning active and memorable. They answer the question: *What do you want students to do with what they understand?*

What Makes a Good Inquiry?

We owe it to our students to prepare them for their most important role—informed, active citizenship.

If we can't come up with a real-world use of a key point, then one of two things is true: The information or skill is in fact not key and teaching it would be a waste of student and teacher time ***or*** our own knowledge base is insufficient. In either case, expect the writing of inquiries to dredge up some surprises and some questions that may not be comfortable to answer. What you will discover, and what thousands of ITI teachers before you have discovered, is that much of our traditional curriculum is brain antagonistic. If our intent is to implement the best of what we know about recent brain research, we must make our curriculum bodybrain-compatible. For most states, the state standards developed during the late 1990s are a step in the right direction.

A test of curriculum: How can students apply the following concepts? How can the knowledge empower students? How can they use them in real-world situations? If you cannot answer these questions,you cannot write powerful inquiries. For example, the following are typical concepts from state standards. While they may seem abstract and distant from students' lives as they are stated, inquiries, such as those on the next page, can bring them home and make them real.

- When warmer things are put with cooler ones, the warm ones lose heat and the cool ones gain heat until they are all the same temperature. A warmer object can warm a cooler one by contact or at a distance.
- There are three ways in which heat can go into or out of something.
  Conduction is the transfer of heat from one thing to another by direct touching, such as a frying pan sitting on top of an electric stove or the heating element in an electric water heater .
  Convection is the transfer of heat through moving air currents such as in the circulating air in forced air furnaces or cold air entering the house through cracks around poorly insulated windows and doors.
  Radiation is the transfer of energy through light such as the heat generated by an electric light bulb, a computer, or warmth from the sun.
- We can affect these heat transfer processes by using insulation, materials that are poor conductors of heat.[1]

Very real applications for the concepts on the above key points include the following:

- Analyze your home (house or apartment) identifying all the ways the family attempts to stabilize temperature by adding heat via conduction, convection, radiation, and insulating against heat loss. Analyze incidental/accidental ways by which heat is added and lost. Determine how effective/adequate the attempts to insulate are. List three ways insulation could be made more effective; estimate savings over a 10-year period and 30-year period.
- Record your information on a chart or poster. Share your findings with an adult family member and record his/her response. Share what you have learned about the heat loss and gain to your Learning Club.
- Compare your home to a friend's home. Determine which home is easier to keep stabilized and which is more economical. Record in your journal at least three reasons to explain your conclusion.

Would you be interested in this issue if we told you that you could save from $40,000 to $70,000 over a lifetime plus keep the coastal inter-tie system from brown-out or going down altogether? And be more comfortable in your home? Such applications satisfy us that we have some concepts worth learning, that we're on the right track. So, now we can develop inquiries that will help students understand and apply these concepts in real-life, in memorable ways.

Maintain a Sense of Community

As previously discussed, there is a wealth of research confirming the power of a sense of community to promote not only personal and social growth but academic achievement as well. Nurture this sense of community daily; take its temperature every week. The emotional climate in your classroom is either deepening or it is fading; it is either focused on learning or it is sliding into becoming a social club. Make sure your curriculum has a receptive audience when it arrives in the classroom.

See building a learning community in Chapter 9.

Connect to Prior Experience

Learning is far more efficient and powerful when the brain already has a "post office address" established in the brain where new learning can be processed and added on to. This allows the brain to compare patterns, a rapid way to reach new understandings of a new *being there* location or a new idea.

Make sure you develop inquiries that ask students to compare prior experience to new experiences.

Allow Students to See & Apply in Real-World Contexts

A picture really is worth a thousand words. Don't reply on lecture and reading assignments to explain what you want students to learn—show them and let them apply content in real and meaningful ways. Write inquiries that let them experience first-hand the real-world standards of performance, the joys and the frustrations. Give them a window on life that they can study and master . . . one window at a time.

Offer Opportunities to Apply in Areas of Learners' Interests

Since conceptual key points, and basic skills, apply worldwide, there are many settings in which to study how to use them. Whenever possible, give students choices about the context in which they are studied. If a student is fascinated with cars, let him/her apply geometry to map reading and trip planning. Or let a student captivated by trains use them as a vehicle for studying geography. For a student fascinated by statistics and baseball, let her put the two together. And so forth.

The more conceptual your curriculum, the most opportunity there is to build in student interests.

Provide Choices in Intelligence Strengths & Weaknesses

Traditionally, our schools cater to those high in linguistic intelligence. For the majority who are not, who have other strengths when taking in information, solving problems, and producing products, our failure to provide a balanced instructional program is a serious barrier to their success. Allow students to see concepts and skills in action in *being there* settings and apply what they understand in those settings—not on a paper and pencil test. This significantly levels the playing field.

Write enough inquiries to allow all students to operate from their strengths while they strengthen their less developed intelligences. Visit the *being there* location as often as you can, at least in the beginning of study, the middle, and the end.

Invite your students into the process of writing inquiries. From third grade and up, they do a wonderful job. Just teach them the ABC Guidelines and give them the a copy of the Inquiry Builder chart (see Chapter 14). Then, you choose those you want students to consider.

For examples of inquiries addressing the multiple intelligences, see the video *I Can Divide and Conquer,* which depicts 50 third through fifth graders mastering division in a single day, and *Mission Addition,* which shows first graders mastering their addition facts in one week.

Improve the Quality of Your Inquiries

To improve the quality of your inquiries, build in more action and greater use of the *being there* location. Use the ABC Guidelines and the Inquiry Builder chart. Consider labeling each inquiry, noting what intelligence(s) is required, so that you know in advance the kinds of choices you are offering.

Most importantly, remember that less is more. Stick with a concept or basic skill until students have developed a mental program for applying it at the *being there* location and through social/political action. Don't move on until students have wired it into long-term memory. If you have chosen powerful concepts that apply around the globe as well as in the backyard, the time will be well spent.

A well-written inquiry can also be used as an assessment tool. (See Chapter 19).

Notes to Myself

Chapter 18: Integrating Basic Skills

Misconception About Integrating Basic Skills

There are two misconceptions about integrating basic skills. One is that the ITI model is fine for the content areas, such as science and social studies, but not for teaching the basic skills—reading, writing, and arithmetic. This is not true. The ITI model does, however, recommend that these basic skills are best taught as a means to an end, not as an end in themselves, that they be taught with and through engaging subject content.

The second common misconception is that the basic skills are the sole domain of first and second grade teachers and language arts and math specialist. Other teachers are thus exempt from any responsibility to teach or reinforce basic skills. Wrong. It is everyone's responsibility in public education to ensure that our citizens are literate and fully capable of engaging in the significant debates of the day. It is everyone's responsibility to ensure that our citizens can make informed judgments about both policy and funding issues, the environment, and who their leaders should be.

Teaching the Basic Skills Is Serious Business

Although test scores across the nation strongly suggest that we must change how we teach the 3Rs, experience suggests that we shouldn't burn our bridges until we are on solid footing on the other side.[1] Before you abandon the old reading program and leap to a new approach, make sure you are well trained in the new before you stop teaching the old. In other words, make sure that you have rigorous training in the new approaches so students can achieve at least as much as before. This is not a time for leap of faith. The futures of your students hang in the balance. Become fully prepared before you leap.

Thus, our advice about beginning to integrate the basic skills with content is to first use the high-interest *being there* and immersion experiences of the theme to *practice* applying basic skills in real-world situation. Then, when you're trained and prepared, begin to teach basic skills through the theme.

This chapter describes five ways to integrate the basic skills in the context of other subjects and real life:

- Full integration of all subjects and skills in the "Classroom of the 21st Century" (see pages 18.2-10)
- An integrated day to teach a basic skill—division—in a single day (see pages "A Concept-in-a-Day," 18.11-14.
- How to anchor math in real life (see *'Anchor' Math*, pages 18.14-16.
- A list of 50+ real writing experiences that can be used to practice or teach writing skills (see pages 18.17)
- How to organize a yearlong research project (see page 18.18)

Reason & Purpose Accelerate Reading*

Skills are taught in the Integrated Thematic Instruction classroom but they do not drive the curriculum. Content drives the curriculum and skills are taught as they relate to the content, as their usefulness becomes apparent. Before public education took hold in this country, many young boys were apprenticed to skilled workers in a variety of fields. This is a perfect example of the power of relevant context for learning skills. As they learned a trade, boys learned all the skills associated with that trade, and there was never a doubt as to why?

Skills only have meaning within the larger context of their usefulness. When they are useful, they are learned. Children do not learn to speak because adults want them to; children learn to speak because it is useful. This is true of adults as well; we know it from our own experience. I took five years of Spanish while attending public schools, but it wasn't until I moved to an ethnically diverse area that I needed to know Spanish. Suddenly it became useful; there was a reason to learn a second language. Reason and purpose accelerate learning.

Thus, skills are taught in the brain-compatible classroom, but only within the context of the content of the integrated theme. The difference is that skills do not drive the curriculum. Instead, they are placed within a meaningful framework. For example, learning the sound "a" in isolation has no meaning without the larger context of a word. The word "heel" only has meaning within the larger context of a sentence because the "heel" of a shoe is different from the "heel" who broke last night's date. Likewise, learning how to compute the area of rectangles has no meaning without the context of a useful application such as "How many cans of this color paint do we need for this part of the room?"

* Pages 18.2-10 are taken directly from the ITI book, *Classroom of the 21st Century* by Robert Ellingsen. The book documents Robert's classroom application of the ITI model as a framework for integrating all basic skills and content areas. Used with the written permission of the publisher.

Without the context of the theme, the mastery of the skill becomes meaningless. The question invariably will be asked, "Why?" and "Because I told you so" is not a satisfactory answer.

So how does one make something like computing the area of rectangles useful within a theme? I teach the skill within a meaningful framework. Each year my class performs a Shakespearean play. As part of our preparation, the class designs and paints stage flats of scenery for our performance. Each of the five flats are 4′ by 8′ and the students need to construct scale drawings of their set design. Students find the area formula a useful tool as they construct their own three-dimensional, miniature sets. Frank Smith states that "learning is incidental."[2] Learning takes place within the course of everyday, real activities. It is within the context of this real activity—building a stage set—that students learn the geometric concept of area.

Reading

You learn by doing. A child does not learn to speak by learning about speaking; a child learns to speak by speaking. So, first and foremost, when teaching reading, let students read. And since usefulness is a prime motivator, what the students read must relate to the topic being explored in some meaningful way. Sara Zimet notes that conventional "reading texts emphasize skill, and reading is taught for the sake of the skill itself [whereas] we need to shift our emphasis from 'reading to learn to read' to 'reading about something meaningful while learning to read.' By emphasizing the process to the exclusion of meaningful ideas, we sacrifice the raison d'etre for learning to read."[3]

Children's fantasies and realities are so much more exciting than the boring words and scenes of most basal reading texts. For this reason my method has been to use children's novels to teach reading. As I plan my year theme, I brainstorm possibilities for the reading component. During the PATHFINDERS component of my theme, the novel I selected was *My Side of the Mountain*[4] by Jean George. It is the story of a boy who ventures into the wilderness and learns to survive without the trappings of modern life—a perfect fit with our study of Lewis and Clark and the other pathfinders of history.

All students should have equal access to rich, significant literature. Oftentimes educators separate their poor readers from their good readers. And where are these poor readers placed? Into a basal text that is even more simplistic and contrived than the one from which they were pulled, thereby compounding their difficulty in searching for meaning. **ALL students should have an enriched curriculum.**

All students of all abilities in my classroom read *My Side of the Mountain*, some with ease, some with difficulty, but all with fascination and enjoyment. Each day a selection is assigned. Students make the free choice of whether to read silently, with a partner, or orally in a group. The only requirement is that they meet with the teacher at least once a week for an oral reading check. When students are entrusted with the power to make their own choices, they tend to self-select the appropriate placement given their ability. My poorer readers chose to meet with me daily. But when they came to reading group, they were joined by other students making the choice to read orally, a heterogeneous group full of good reading models. Why do we put poor readers only with poor readers? Who will model correct reading behaviors for them?

Heterogeneous reading groups, in addition to being academically sound, have the extra benefit of building self-esteem. There is no "dumb group." It builds the sense that "we're all in this together" and encourages understanding and acceptance of individual differences.

Granted, there are students who can legitimately benefit from extra help. I do think moving to a more enriched curriculum will eliminate the need for some diagnostic/prescriptive services, but not all. What about those students? They do need extra help but that help should be **offered within the bounds of the curriculum**

and tied closely to the theme of their classroom experience. And the single most meaningful place for a child is with the classroom teacher. Pull-out programs should be avoided at all cost. I propose, instead, a **pull-in program** where specialists work with students within a self-contained, safe, supportive classroom. Logistics can be a problem to overcome but we need to do what is best for kids, not what is most convenient for the bureaucracy.

Comprehension. The best way to learn to read is to read. But there is more to reading than correctly decoding words. The Spanish alphabet is phonetically regular and I have learned my sounds well. I can go into many classrooms, pick up a Spanish reader and pronounce word after word with only the slightest Anglo accent. But am I reading? Correctly calling words with no understanding is not reading, and phonics, while a helpful tool, is only that—a tool for correct decoding. Phonics does not concern itself with understanding. How is comprehension addressed in the ITI classroom? Not with worksheets.

I propose to involve students more actively in the comprehension process. Once more I find Bloom's Taxonomy to be an amazing aid in this respect—simple to use, but powerful. Daily, after reading period, the class comes together for a discussion of the day's selection. A copy of Bloom's Taxonomy is placed on the overhead and the class uses this to discuss the story. This copy is the only comprehension worksheet the students receive during the year. At first, the teacher may use it to ask questions, but, with practice, students become quite adept at generating the questions and at knowing the level at which they are being asked to think. This is metacognition at its best—knowing how to learn and knowing when you are doing it.

Once a week I obtain a written record of their work by having learning teams brainstorm questions, present them to the class, and choose a specified number to answer. Students then write the questions and answers neatly, in complete sentences, and with correct spelling and capitalization—a much more active approach than that elicited by most commercially produced worksheets. How, you might ask, do students complete a neat and grammatically correct paper? First, they are held accountable for it. Expectations are everything. Second, in the absence of worksheets, students have many more opportunities for real writing; the worksheet doesn't do the writing for them. And finally, no one is left without support. Students have their cooperative learning team to assist them and the teacher, as part of the learning team, is constantly circling the room, encouraging and giving **immediate feedback.**

Reading Skills. Although teaching the skills of reading can sometimes be frustrating and tedious, we must accept that these skills are there to support reading. However, if a skill does not directly aid a student in decoding and comprehending of a passage, then its viability needs to be seriously questioned. Skills for the sake of skills—because it's in the workbook—is a grave mistake. For example, I have clear and painful memories of trying to teach students how to identify accent marks in words with a program that even went so far as to differentiate between primary and secondary accents. The irony, of course, is that the students could already read the words. Nevertheless, they failed in that all-important skill: the fine distinctions in stress. The question remains: "Was the skill useful?" And a further question continues to haunt us: "How many of these workbook skills, which consume such a large part of a student's learning time, are necessary to produce successful and lifelong readers?" Teaching skills is not teaching reading; reading teaches reading—the practice of extracting meaning from print. Skills can be a useful aid, but only within a larger context, and only when they are useful. They are not an end in themselves.

When skills are taught when they make the most sense—when they are needed to understand something—they are learned more easily and are more readily wired into long-term memory. For example, teaching students how to use an index when they begin their research projects and find using an index a helpful way to locate information; time lines are taught as students study historical events; and outlining is taught as students write research papers. Workbooks, which present skills in an arbitrary fashion, are both unnecessary and unproductive.

Parts of Speech. We all teach them. Apparently students never learn them--why else do we ALL teach them? My class is introduced to parts of speech during our GEOGRAPHY component. As students study our state, they find one location for each letter of the alphabet, plot it on a grid, compute miles and kilometers from our location, and use that location in an ABC book. This provides ample opportunity for work in a wide variety of skills: alphabetical order, map skills, and mathematical computations. Students then write their own ABC books, using a pattern established in the *Oregon ABC Book*: "Adrian Albright, the adorable actress, anticipates acclaim in Ashland's amphitheater."[5] Children identify proper nouns for people and places, adjectives to describe the nouns, verbs to state the action, and adverbs to describe the verbs. And all this is done within the context of their own writing, about locations they have studied in their home state. This is the teachable moment, that point in time when students are most in tune with the learning. Why? Because it is useful, it is creative, and it is emotional—there is a healthy dose of fun as students stretch their imaginations.

As I developed the skill component of the reading program, I found that the skills are repeated in a cycle. Of the thirty skills taught in the intermediate level of the Houghton-Mifflin reading series, twenty-one are taught at two grade levels, and an amazing seventeen are taught at all three grade levels. Why, then, must students be placed in ability groups, forever labeled, with no chance for reprieve, when all levels are working on the same skills?

In the ITI classroom, skills are introduced in the large group, students work on the skill only until they have mastered it, and students continue working on that skill until it is mastered. There is no low group, middle group, or high group. Instead there is a guide word group, a syllabification group, etc. Within these temporary, flexible groups are students with a wide range of achievement levels, all of whom need practice with the same skill. Once again, the "we're all in this together" attitude is developed. Artificial demarcations convenient to the authorities are torn down and students work in heterogeneous settings.

Vocabulary. Vocabulary development is an ongoing process. In a meaningful classroom environment it happens continuously at an informal level, just as children originally learn the spoken language. "All children except the most severely deprived or handicapped acquire a vocabulary of over 10,000 words during the first four or five years of their lives. At the age of four they are adding to their vocabulary at the rate of twenty new words a day. By seven this rate may have increased to nearly thirty words. . . . By late adolescence the average vocabulary is at least 50,000 words."[6] How is this done? Not by worksheets, not by looking words up in the dictionary, not by formal instruction. It is done because the brain is the organ for learning; it will learn what is useful. The 50,000 words children pick up by adolescence are words they find to be useful.

The key to formal vocabulary instruction is to make it useful and meaningful to the student. The obvious method in an ITI classroom is to closely tie vocabulary instruction to the theme.

Current events are an integral part of the brain-compatible classroom because the brain-compatible classroom focuses on the real world. Knowledge of current events is essential for the politically active populace of a democracy. The brain-compatible classroom is the classroom that prepares students to take on this role as active citizens.

OREGON TODAY is the name given to the current events strand of our curriculum. Each morning one student is responsible for sharing an article related to the theme. That article then becomes part of our classroom collection folder where all articles are filed and classified. Once a week an article is chosen to be the class' reading selection for the day. Learning teams read, mindmap, and discuss the article. They are also responsible for choosing the one word that interests them most. Learning teams share their word with the class and the class then has five new vocabulary words, one word per learning team. These words are entered into the students' personal dictionaries and onto our Oregon Today vocabulary chart for continual reinforcement. Whenever a student finds that word in any other reading, a star is added to the chart. A very simple approach but, tied to the theme, it becomes meaningful. And the probability that the word is learned and stored increases.

Writing

A pattern is forming: children learn to speak by speaking and to read by reading. Little wonder, then, that children learn to write by writing. That is not to say that merely writing, with no skill instruction, will produce literate citizens. But we do know that heavy doses of skill instruction, separated from the meaningful context of real writing, do not work. The literate student must write every day. And that writing must have purpose and an audience.

The journal approach to daily writing is an exceptional example of real writing assignments. Students keep a notebook full of their own musing: dreams, concerns, and questions, a daily record of their lives. This is real writing in its truest sense because it is student-centered and student-directed. There are no contrived topics or arbitrary limits on length. Writing is useful because it becomes a vehicle by which children connect with the outside world, taking what is within and giving it form and substance.

I have had much success with this method, yet I know that not all teachers have. When I've compared notes with my colleagues for whom it hasn't worked, I find one noticeable difference: I write back to the author—not just a few sprinklings of "great" or "good point," but written feedback of significant length and meaning. If a child writes to me about his/her pets, I write about my pets. If a child writes about favorite foods, I write about mine. The journal becomes a dialogue between us; it establishes rapport. Finally, it provides a meaningful context within which to place skill instruction.

I recommend several different approaches to writing. Journals are but one component of the writing program, writing folders are another. Journals are daily jottings. The writing folder is for long-term story development and is worked on every day during WRITERS' WORKSHOP, a time when students learn the writing process: pre-writing, rough draft, revision, editing, and publishing. Children use the skills developed during writers' workshop to develop their own creative writing. Works in progress are filed in the writing folder until that time the student determines the piece is ready for publication. Occasionally specific assignments are given if they fit the theme, but more often students are engaged in constructing stories from their own imaginations. Many states have ongoing summer institutes where teachers learn the writing process. The key is that the teacher also becomes a writer and models for the class his own ongoing work. My students assisted me in writing my story "Reggie at the Bat." The students, in a sense, become apprenticed to the teacher as author.

Teaching Writing Skills

The daily journal and the writing folder provide the structure for direct instruction of skills. They are the blueprint. Once they are in place, the skills, which are the building materials, can be used to construct literacy. But where would they be placed with no blueprint as a guide? Teaching skills such as capitalization and noun/verb agreement, apart from any meaningful writing, is like giving the carpenter the 2′ x 4′s and asking him/her to build a house without a plan. The product would be a haphazard, rickety construction, destined to come tumbling down and ill-fitting the needs of its inhabitants.

Once the framework of real writing is in place, skill instruction can proceed. A variety of methods can be used. Basal English series offer pages of practice, and there is nothing wrong with their occasional use as need dictates. But why go through the book cover to cover? Why let the textbook publisher dictate the curriculum when it is the classroom teacher who is the educational expert? It is the teacher who, having student writing in hand, can diagnose and prescribe skill instruction appropriate to the needs of each particular group of writers.

If, in their writing, students are writing conversations, and writing them incorrectly, then that is the teachable moment—the appropriate time to teach the correct use of quotation marks. If certain words are consistently misspelled, then they become a part of that student's spelling list. If letters are continually formed illegibly, then handwriting instruction is called for.

The theme itself may provide opportune times to address particular skills. During our Shakespeare unit, the class play is *A Midsummer Night's Dream.* This is the perfect opportunity to introduce apostrophes. The play's title becomes a meaningful "hook" on which to attach the skill instruction.

To ensure that skill instruction proceeds at a systematic pace I have a daily editing practice modeled after the DAILY ORAL LANGUAGE series (D.O.L.). Admittedly, the name is a bit misleading. A more accurate title might be DAILY WRITTEN LANGUAGE, as the editing task is with paper and pencil. The program's title stems from the fact that once the written editing assignment is complete, it is processed orally.

A short selection, full of errors, is placed on the board most mornings when students enter the classroom. They know from the posted daily agenda that their first task is to edit this selection. Once again, cooperation is encouraged. Later in the morning the class meets together and orally processes the passage, finally recopying a fully corrected final version. This happens over time until the majority of the class has mastered the skill and can independently write a perfect copy the first time. New writing skills are then introduced, taken from common errors occurring in journals and writing folders. Those students who still have not mastered the original skill continue to meet with me during Writers' Workshop.

Math

For five years I had avoided integrating mathematics. I was tied to the text, my own math anxiety holding me back. Finally, I had no choice if I wanted a fully integrated classroom—math was the only subject still on the outside. What I found, to my amazement, was that math is the simplest of all skill areas to integrate. All that is needed is statistics, real-life numbers to work with. How lucky! Statistics are everywhere!

Cobblestone magazine is a history magazine for young people. In September, 1980, the entire issue was devoted to Lewis and Clark. It became our "basal text" for the week, the base of study for all subjects, including math. It is a rich source of statistics about the Lewis and Clark expedition. Those below are only a small sampling of the statistics available, providing many opportunities for real world "story problems." But, given the full immersion of the students into reliving the Lewis and Clark expedition, they become more than mere "story problems"; they become real-life applications.

Available Statistics:

- Lewis and Clark started their journey up the Missouri River on May 14, 1804.
- The entire central basin of North America was purchased from the French for four cents an acre, or a total of $15,000,000.
- A Scotsman named Alexander Mackenzie had published an account of the same region in 1793.
- The Great Falls were a series of five large waterfalls that stretched over 15 miles on the Missouri River.
- From beginning to end, the walk over the Rocky Mountains took three-and-a-half months.
- On their return trip, Lewis and Clark separated for six weeks to explore different regions.
- Lewis and Clark returned to St. Louis on September 23, 1806.

Problems to Be Solved Based on the Available Statistics:

- How many years ago did Lewis and Clark begin exploring the Louisiana Purchase?

- How many acres of land did Thomas Jefferson purchase from France?
- Approximately how many miles were between each of the Great Falls of the Missouri River?
- Assuming that all months are thirty days long, how many days did it take Lewis and Clark to cross the Rocky Mountains?
- Using your previous answer, how many weeks did it take Lewis and Clark to cross the Rocky Mountains?
- How many days were Lewis and Clark separated during their trip?
- 30 days have September, April, June, and November. All the rest have 31, excepting February, which has 28. Knowing this, what was the total number of days of the Lewis and Clark expedition?

This last problem is the most difficult of all. Very few of my fourth graders answered it correctly at first. But I've never seen such excitement, motivation, and problem-solving strategies as when students attempt it.

Problems such as these form the core of THEME MATH, a term I use with students to distinguish it from other components of the math program. Theme math uses **real-world** problems closely tied to the content. Students attack these problems with more motivation than the artificial problems of basal series. The interest is built in; the students have some curiosity to find out more about whom and what they have been studying.

The amount of thinking involved is awesome when compared to a basal text. Students need to identify the problem, find the data necessary to solve the problem, identify the operation needed to solve the problem, and then finally compute the answer. What's more, the statistics are not conveniently listed for them as they are for you here. Students search for them within the context of the historical narrative.

Theme math is a prime motivator for students to learn mathematical skills. Suddenly there is a reason for memorizing those basic facts, to KNOW—**to really know** everything about the Lewis and Clark expedition. In addition, theme math is an excellent way to build conceptual understanding of the four operations (addition, subtraction, multiplication, and division). Students develop a sense of what addition looks like, how it "feels" and sounds compared to the other operations. *And all the while they are working in the realm of the real world, with real numbers*—**APPLICATION!**

It is essential that the teacher understand the purpose of theme math. It is to build ***conceptual understanding***, not to drill on memorization of facts and computations. Students who have not memorized their multiplication facts are still capable of understanding the concept of multiplication. *Memorization of facts should not be a prerequisite to opportunities for applying concepts.* If anything, building the concepts should come first, giving the student the meaningful framework before the individual skill bits are put into place.

Math Skills. Mathematical computation is an essential life skill. Theme math does not replace that. But it does enhance computation by giving it meaning and purpose. Computation is still addressed. In fact, within this meaningful context of the theme, computation is learned much more readily.

DAILY ORAL MATH (D.O.M.) is one way to reinforce math skills. Similar to daily oral language (the daily drill in written language), it is a short and sweet math review. Alternating with D.O.L., it may consist of four problems reviewing the four operations, or it may be other math skills more closely aligned with the day's thematic activities. Skills such as a review of the formula for computing area during our Shakespearean set design, or using a scale of miles to compute distance during our GEOGRAPHY component can be reinforced during D.O.M. The daily agenda points out that this is one of the first tasks to be completed. Later in the day, student volunteers solve the problems for the class, modeling correct form and computation.

Day in the Life Of

So how does it all come together? How does the teacher orchestrate all the various elements of a brain-compatible classroom? The ITI model is truly unique in that it draws from a wide variety of excellent approaches and sources and synthesizes them into a coherent, seamless whole. Language experience is an excellent approach to teaching reading, but what about math? The university sponsored writing projects teach writing in a brain-compatible way, but what about social studies? Math Their Way is an experiential and hands-on approach to mathematics instruction, but what about science? The ITI approach seeks to break down these artificial walls between curricular areas, take the best from each, and infuse brain-compatible instruction into all subjects for a truly integrated whole. And it does so with a profound respect for the professional expertise of the classroom teacher.

Flexibility is the key word in planning a fully integrated day, week, month, or year. School schedules are arbitrary demarcations of time and **are highly brain-antagonistic.** Lessons should not be forced into the artificial constraints of a set time period; **the content should determine the schedule.** The self-contained classroom offers the greatest opportunity for fully integrating subject areas.

I hesitate to share specifics of a daily schedule because the model will find a unique implementation in every classroom. **The power of the model lies in its adaptability to individual teaching styles.** The graphic on this page is my plan for the week. Such a plan could take many forms. This picture of a typical day in the life of a brain-compatible classroom starts a schedule for flexible frameworks to be altered as content dictates. My 9:00 A.M. starting time and a 3:30 P.M. closing time made it possible for me to think of the instructional day as being divided into four blocks: two morning periods and two afternoon periods.

I recommend that you begin the day with the theme. It provides students with a focal point for the day's activities. In a classroom not yet fully integrated, this would mean beginning the day with the content area on which the theme is based, e.g., a classroom whose theme is "Entomology" would begin the day with science. The benefit of the fully integrated classroom is that all subjects relate to the theme and the day may begin with whatever subject area makes the most sense within the context of the day's topic. What the teacher organizes is a blend of common elements which maintain a sense of stability and comfort for students, intermixed with a daily flow of ever-changing events and topics—a miniature slice of real life. Here is an example:

Generally, I begin my day[7] with a language arts block. When students enter the classroom, they are greeted by me personally, a daily agenda detailing exactly what will occur that day, and back-

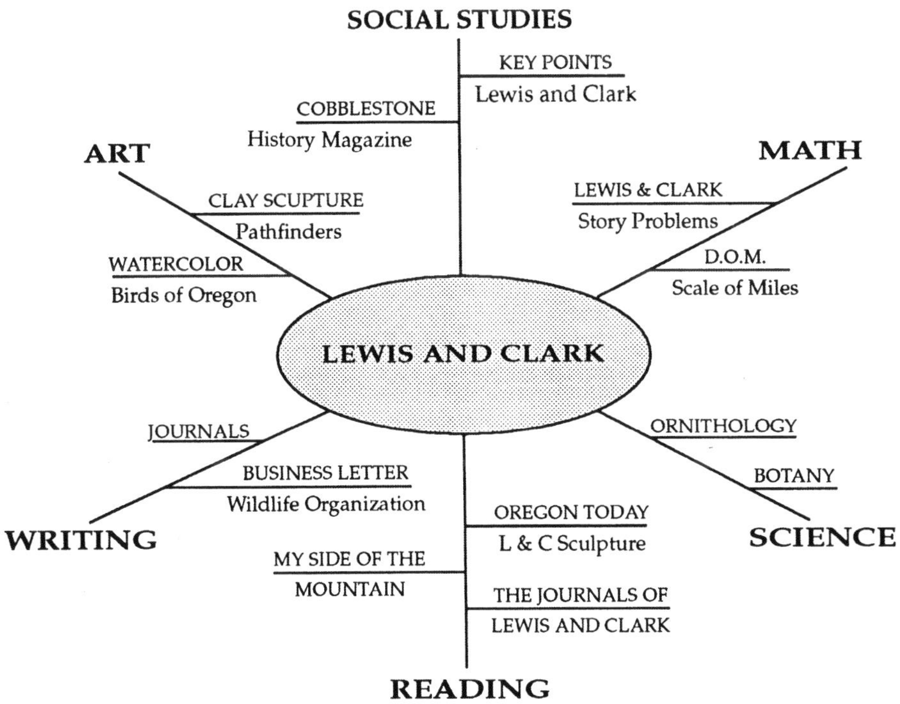

ground music playing softly to enhance thinking. The rule is quiet study as students begin their tasks: DAILY ORAL LANGUAGE and/or DAILY ORAL MATH to review skills, then on to silent and/or oral reading of the day's selection, followed by independent work with ongoing INQUIRY projects. At some point I bring the class together for stretching, aerobics, and relaxation—important techniques which help focus students' bodies and minds on the topic for the day. This is followed by a discussion of the day's reading based on Bloom's Taxonomy and a large group discussion and correction of the skills review. Finally, during OREGON TODAY, the current events article for the day is shared.

The second morning block is reserved for science and social studies. This is when students receive and work with the key points of instruction. Lecture, reading, discussion, films, experiments, and inquiries all receive equal emphasis as conceptual understanding of the major thematic components is built. Each day sees a different focus. Perhaps a lecture and reading on the key points early in the week, moving toward more interactive pursuits by the end of the week, with possible closure of the week, topic, or entire component by Friday.

The first afternoon block is reserved for mathematics. This is equally divided between THEME MATH for concept building and MATH GROUPS for computation practice. Oftentimes the week begins and ends with THEME MATH to provide a frame within which the rest of math instruction is placed.

The final afternoon block returns to language arts. A skill is introduced or reinforced with the large group. This is followed by a large group WRITERS' WORKSHOP where works in progress are shared and elements of good writing are discussed. Students then move on to independent writing time, engaging in real writing activities such as JOURNAL, letters, and creative writing of their own choice. During this independent time the teacher is free to confer with individuals and/or conduct SKILLSHOPS, the small, temporary, and flexible skill groups.

What about other subject areas such as art, music, and computers? They all find a place in the schedule as appropriate. Sketching and watercolor techniques are taught when the day's reading concerns that subject, e.g., Sam's sketching of his falcon. Students work with clay after reading and discussing a newspaper article about a local sculptor and his Lewis and Clark statues. Pioneer songs and instruments are used to prepare for the class' Oregon Trail adventure. Computers are used during the writing process as students edit and publish their work. Computers are also used when software exists that enhances understanding of the topic, such as the Oregon Trail or Pathfinders simulation games. Everything fits. It's just a new fit. In the traditional classroom, content is made to fit the schedule; in the ITI classroom, **the schedule is made to fit the content.**

A self-contained, heterogeneous classroom is a superior design for the ITI classroom. There are fewer interruptions to fragment the day, the sense of belonging is more fully developed, and students aren't segregated according to ability. Because the mathematical problems are selected mostly with an eye to their meaningfulness, assignments and group collaboration guidelines are set up to ensure that all students, of varying degrees of ability, experience success. Problems are solved within the learning team and calculators are allowed.

Orchestrating a Concept-in-a-Day: Long Division*

It is estimated that it takes two years and three months for students to learn long division. The division facts are introduced in the third grade, the algorithm is introduced in the fourth grade, and again in the fifth and sixth grades. From year to year, the same instructional pattern, even into the basic math courses in junior and senior high—the teacher does a problem on the board, the class does a number of "practice" problems at their desks, and then students are responsible for completing ten to twenty problems for homework.

While attending a week-long Susan Kovalik Model Teaching Program, Martha Kaufeldt was challenged to address this problem by orchestrating the learning environment and curriculum in such a way that it would be possible to INTRODUCE and have the students achieve MASTERY of the CONCEPT AND COMPUTATION OF LONG DIVISION **IN A SINGLE DAY!**

Martha's work pioneered the notion of teaching a major concept in a single day. Since her Long Division Day in 1986, thousands of students across the country have been able to master division in a single day using this approach.

Here is her story.

* The description of orchestrating a concept in a day, pages 20.11-20.14, is a summary of Martha Kaufeldt's experience as described in her book *I Can Divide and Conquer: A Concept in a Day!*, a teachers' handbook for implementing Division Day in their own classroom. The book is a companion to the videotape of the same name published by Susan Kovalik & Associates. See the order form at the back of this book.

For the first three months of school, my thirty-three fourth and fifth grade students worked on sharpening their accuracy in addition, subtraction, and multiplication. Division facts were memorized by rote. Seventeen other fifth and sixth grade students in our school were recommended by their teachers as students who had mastered the skills of multiplication but had failed to master division.

The day before Division Day all fifty students met. I led them verbally through some relaxation techniques and also asked them to see their own success in learning long division. They all took a pretest in division and were given encouraging words about what would happen the next day.

Overview of the Day's Activities

Theme for the day: I CAN DIVIDE AND CONQUER!

In planning the day, I knew I had to address several important areas: how to ensure positive performance, the format for each activity station, and methods of orchestrating learning.

Elements Used to Program Positive Performance

- Students saw their success
- Each student received a "goodie" box with pencil, slate, and name tag
- Students were divided into groups of five. Group building activities included adopting a famous mathematician who would serve as the group mascot for the day
- Incentives were given at every other station
- Mini-stickers were given to anyone who ASKED FOR HELP
- Direct instruction was limited to 11-16 minutes per hour
- Group work was provided at each station (45 minutes)

- Relaxation periods were provided throughout the day
- Lunch was provided by parents. Pizza was divided into different numbers of slices
- Each student earned an "I CAN DIVIDE AND CONQUER" badge and a certificate at the end of the day
- Warm, loving, enthusiastic adult leaders were always available

Format at Each Station

To simplify training of volunteers and to ensure students had the opportunity to think through each activity, the format for each station was the same: tell, show, solve, and check. Each process is written as a direction to the adult responsible for a station.

Tell

- Read problem aloud—(every student)
- Discuss what the problem is asking or describing. Have students restate in own words
- Point out (ask students to identify) DIVIDEND and DIVISOR
- Ask students to close eyes while you help them visualize the problem. Use a soothing voice while using lots of descriptive words. Ask students to see themselves in the picture, doing the sorting or dividing
- Draw students' attention to manipulatives they will be using, e.g., beads, beans, etc. Point out that they are substitutes for the real thing

Show

Have students work out the problem with the manipulatives. If possible, each student should have his/her own set of manipulatives. If not, work it out cooperatively. Have students:

- Repeat the problem two or more times if necessary until they can confidently show the problem
- Identify quotient and remainders, if any (have a special place for the "remainder" to be placed)

Solve

As each student solves a problem, have them:

- Demonstrate how a problem is written as a number sentence
- Identify terms
- Begin a step-by-step approach to the algorithm.—divide, multiply, subtract, bring down—and frequently relate their computation to what has been done with manipulatives
- Have students work out problem on graph paper for accuracy
- Ask each to turn to his/her partner and ask the partner to explain the problem in "MATH SPEAK"

Check

- Demonstrate how to check by multiplying and adding remainder
- If there is time, make variations of the problem and ask students to solve
- Write a comment in each student passport if you feel student has mastered that problem

- If the student needs more help, continue working, or ask the student to come back at free-choice time, or direct student to a roving helper
- Repeat center to next group. Give incentive rewards to students in second center

Methods of Orchestrating Learning

Because our Divide and Conquer Day was just that, a single day, I needed to vary the ways to help students learn. My strategies included:

- Using the Library Media Center with assistance from the Media Specialist
- Providing 26 different learning stations, each with concrete examples to illustrate concepts
- Providing choices at those stations students were allowed to choose among
- Adhering to two management standards for the day: No Put-Downs and Active Listening
- Providing a snack station (items such as graham crackers and juice that are set up by parents)
- Having students work through recesses and taking breaks as needed
- Organizing students into groups of five
- Recruiting and training at least 15 adults to help: parents, aides, student teachers, and community volunteers
- Soliciting additional money—mini-grants and parent donations

Maximizing Input to the Brain

Each segment of the day was designed to maximize input to the brain. Every activity and presentation appealed to a variety of intelligences. In addition, students were allowed to make selections that would best assist them.

The problem to be solved was presented on the bulletin board and in the student handbook. Students used manipulatives to SEE the problem.

Every station leader explained each problem. Students in turn explained the problem using Math Speak. A hand-jive was developed for the mathematical algorithm of division—first you divide, then multiple, subtract, and bring it (the remainder) down.

Each of the 26 stations used different sets of manipulatives. Most were common classroom items as well as shells, buttons, small cars, and dominoes.

Kinesthetic activities included Division P.E., Division Drama, Division Art, Division Music, and a hand jive—a set of hand motions representing the algorithm of division: divide (hand clap), multiply (bring your hands together in the form of an X and tap them twice), subtract (with lower arms pointing upward and hands at shoulder height, bend fingers at knuckle keeping fingers flat and parallel to the floor; rotate wrists outward in flipping motion), bring it (the remainder) down (form a fist and pull downward).

Choices

Choices for students included art, music or drama stations, flexible breaks when needed, and more help on a one-to-one basis. Feeling that they were in control of their learning truly empowered students to feel that they "conquered division."

Outcomes

At the end of the *seven hour day* (yes, they came early and stayed late!), students received a certificate and a badge.

The post-test was given the following day. Some students improved as much as 150 percent. All mastered single digit division. Post-tests given three months later showed continued improvement and retention. Students have shared with me that they felt this was one of the most important days in their lives!

To see how brain research can be used to teach a single concept and how to apply it to mastery—and to long-term memory—see Martha's video and book of the same name: *I Can Divide and Conquer.* Available through Books for Educators.

"Anchor" Math*

Not only did Leslie Hart coin the term "brain-compatible," he has also given us ways to "anchor" math to real-life experiences of children. His book, *Anchor Math: An Informal Book for All Who Teach Elementary Math and Want to Greatly Increase Student Achievement,* is a treasure trove of wonderfully simple but instantly doable ways of making numbers and mathematics real to students.

Hart illustrates how to teach math in ways that create "mental programs." For a starting point, Hart says that it may be helpful, or at least intriguing, to think of math languages in three clusters.

Three Levels of Math Language

Practical Math

"Practical" math help us deal with the mostly concrete world of here and now, including all of our daily transactions, ordering, physical work, current data, etc. Examples: spent $144.75 for clothes, poured 12 cubic yards of concrete, produced 12,000 widgets, have 322 patients in the hospital.

Projective Math

"Projective" math helps us deal with what should, or could, or might happen. You plan out a trip, or work out estimates for a new business, or figure out how fast a rocket will likely be traveling within four minutes after launch, or how many cases of measles could occur within the next two years.

* Pages 18.14-18 of this chapter are excerpted from *Anchor Math: An Informal Book for All Who Teach Elementary Math and Want to Greatly Increase Student Achievement* written by Leslie Hart and published by Books for Educators (see order form at the back of this book).

Investigative Math

"Investigative" math helps us dig out significant concepts by using mathematical techniques, e.g., trends and relationships, limits, and interactions. We might analyze election results to see the role played by racial concerns or gain some insight into an intricate chemical reaction. Included would be "game" math, essentially playing with numbers or mathematical elements for no immediate, "real" purpose.

Our purpose, or need, would determine which kind of math we do. Outside of classrooms, nobody does math without some purpose in mind. (That should make us think about some things we do in classrooms.)

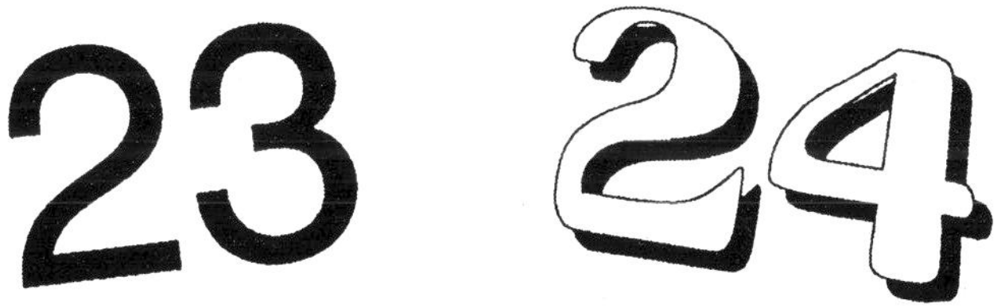

THE CONCEPT OF "n-NESS"

Let us assume that a particular student is able to

- Name the digit . . . "five"
- Write the digit
- Count off objects to match the digit

It still may be true that the student does not have the sense of that number, a sense that we can call "five-ness." This sense of number constitutes one of the main foundational elements of grasping math and being able to do or interpret math with ease and confidence. Some people like to say that the student "feels" the number—which is all right if you like that expression.

Another way to put it is to say that the student has acquired a sense of "shape" for that number and a direct approach, not a "counting" approach.

For instance, if the student hears "five" and then counts one-two-three-four-five, that is a slow and cumbersome way, as compared with directly feeling "five-ness."

This sense of "n-ness" can readily be encouraged and developed by the teacher . . . and, as we shall see, it can be applied not only to the digits but to many numbers as they are "anchored." (The term "anchor" will be explained soon.)

Suppose we ask a 10-year-old student: "What is the difference between numbers 23 and 24?" One student may reply, "24 is one more than 23." That is correct but not the reply we are seeking.

Another student says, "Oh, they are very different! 23 is a stiff, awkward number while 24 is wonderful—it can be the hours in a day, or two dozen, or 4 x 6, or 3 x 8. . . . I can do all sorts of things with it." We can exult, "Ah, this student has really learned the "anchor" math way; this student feels the number." Numbers have shapes and characters and personalities, much as do people. Math becomes much more interesting and easier to do when "the numbers come alive!"

INTRODUCING "FLEXING"

We can use the problems of scanty three-ness to illustrate a simple technique for exploring numbers and patterns to which I'll attach the name "flexing." If you don't care for that term for this activity, use another or create your own. The idea is simple: *push the number, or pattern, or quantity around* in all the ways you can think of.

To flex 3, for example, you pose the question to students: how many ways can you arrange 3 markers? (The markers can be plastic chips, coins, beans, bottle caps or pebbles, or marks on paper or chalkboard. It's a good idea to vary the markers so that the patterns become attached to the number, not to the markers.)

On this page are some of the arrangements possible for 3. For higher numbers, the variations increase.

Flexing has several purposes that enhance math learning. To begin with, of course, experience with three-ness can be greatly expanded. Of major general importance is encouraging students to *explore* on their own and as a member of a little team and at times and in ways hinted at or prompted by the teacher. Most of the time there should be no rules—anything goes. (For example, the counters can be stacked up; who said no?) At other times restraints can be imposed for the moment: the markers must be put in one dimension (or two or three), or must stay within a 2-inch square or other figure given (or must touch), and so on.

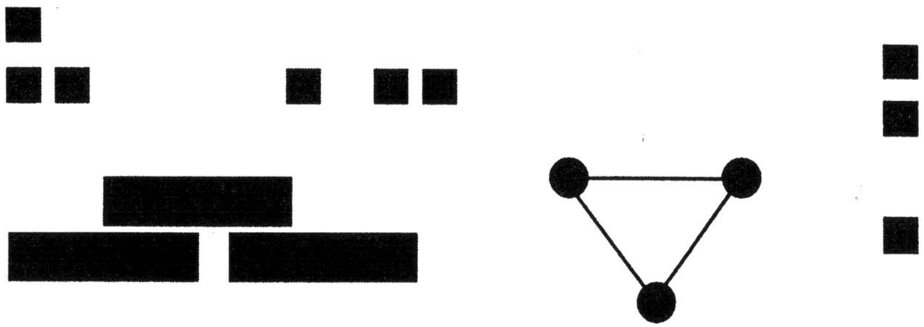

Flex . . . and find patterns.

Such exploration contrasts with sitting meekly in place and doing only what one is told. Youngsters have a strong, genetic drive to *explore*—as we can plainly see by watching any normal toddler. Allowed to explore, learners find math far more interesting, even absorbing. But we can go beyond that benefit, major as it is. In the conventional math schoolroom, numbers push children around. Many become a little gun-shy as they find the numbers given to them to deal with often overpower or intimidate them. In addition, they probably tremble before the "right answer," which must be obtained on penalty of some kind of disapproval or low mark. What a difference when we begin early on to show students that ***they*** can push numbers! And that, in many instances in math, there is no simple, right, carved-in-stone answer, or at least none that can be found without substantial investigation. When we set students free and "empower" them, they become almost different people. Further, they begin building understanding—from experience—of when a simple calculated answer will do and when it will not. That usually makes them much better at calculating when it is required because they acquire a feeling of confidence that lets their brains work at their best.

One more benefit may be discerned. Flexing gives room for a *creative* approach, as strict calculating does not. So, some students, who might otherwise be considered on the "dumb" side, suddenly show unexpected ability. This can help teachers abstain from judgments about students which are too quick and easy—and perhaps from making unneeded judgments at all.

Get into the act yourself. Can you suggest any flexes of 3 not shown here? Here's a sample of a hint: overlap.

Why do we all need to learn arithmetic? There's a good solid answer to that question: so that we can *measure*. That's what this math is for—measuring. We need to measure how much things cost, how much they weigh, how far away or big something is, how long a trip takes, how many watts a light bulb draws, where on the dial a favorite radio station will come in, our body temperature and much, much more.

To see Hart's vision of making math accessible to students, see *Anchor Math: An Informal Book for All Who Teach Elementary Math and Want to Greatly Increase Student Achievement*. Available through Books for Educators. See the back of this book.

Real Writing Experiences

Too many traditional writing assignments lack meaning and purpose—a topic of little interest to students and no real audience (except the teacher's and his/her grade book). Again, using brain research as home plate, no meaning, no engagement. The second most disliked assignment, following closely on the heels of fear of speaking before one's peers, is writing. And yet, the skill of expressing oneself in written form in a variety of circumstances is very important, allowing us to influence people and events.

How do we turn the tide? Often the writing experiences assigned to students are either creative writing or essays. In between these extremes are at least fifty real experiences that we may use in our lifetime.

Real-Life Writing Products

For writing to be meaningful and engaging, rather than contrived and boring, there must be a real purpose and a real audience. The list of writing products below illustrate the possibilities for meaningful writing assignments.

Letters to:
- relative
- friend
- pen pal
- editor of a paper
- association
- service club
- congratulate
- farewell
- complaint
- resignation

Letters of:
- sympathy
- recommendation
- protest
- regret
- apology
- independence
- civil rights
- peace

Speech:
- sales pitch
- sermon
- state of the nation address
- inauguration
- judicial decision
- nomination for office
- political campaign

Newspaper article for:
- front page story
- editorial
- advertisement
- obituary
- movie review
- sports story
- advice column

How-to manuals:
- operate a specific piece of equipment (bicycle, skateboard, Nintendo, VCR)
- survival (wilderness, on the subway, when visiting a foreign country)
- airline safety instructions

Writing for an audience:
- monologue
- dialogue
- poetry
- eulogy
- interview
- (ten questions to ask a famous person)
- recipe
- menu
- dictionary
- encyclopedia entry

Writing for social/political action to:
- president of the U.S.
- federal or state legislative representative
- governor
- mayor
- city council
- school board

Special issues such as:
- declaration of war
- declaration of independence
- civil rights
- environmental protection

Advertisement for:
- school lunch program
- yearbook
- magazine
- newspaper
- television
- books or movies

Invitation to:
- party (be specific)
- dinner
- weekend outing
- conference (boy scout, girl scout, 4-H, etc.)
- join an organization

The Personal Writing Binder

Encourage each student to have a writing binder with the student's own best examples of how to write, address, and respond to a variety of situations. In addition to the final product, all drafts preceding the final copy are included; these edited pages are good reminders of WHY something is done and the writing/editing skills he/she has developed.

This binder can be added to year by year so that a worthwhile reference will always be at your students' fingertips.

The Yearlong Research Project

Research is the ability to gather, analyze, organize, and eventually synthesize information about a topic. In the ITI classroom, we invite students of all ages to keep a yearlong collection binder filled with data about a topic of their choosing from within the yearlong theme. Their challenge: to become an expert on that topic.

By the end of the second week of school, all students select a topic for their yearlong research project. Two students may choose the same topic. What's important is that each student has content that fires their interest.

To help facilitate information gathering, ask parents to send their old magazines and newspapers to class. Provide at least 45 minutes a week for students to seek, read, and organize information. In addition, have at least 20 different addresses where students can write for information, such as those in the yellow pages of your phone book, the *Encyclopedia of Associations* at your public library, and so forth).

As they collect information, have the students:

- Highlight important points
- Create a mindmap of three new facts learned from each article
- Begin to organize the information into categories, such as letters sent and received, pictures (of projects, locations, people visited), audio or video interviews, and so forth. Eventually they will organize the information into a document with a table of contents, an index, a summation or executive summary of what was learned, and explanation of the most important content behind the summary.
- Share with a younger buddy every two weeks what they are learning
- By the end of the year, identify and invite to class their favorite resource person
- As a culminating activity, present the highlights of their research through a 10-minute multimedia presentation

The most important lessons from the yearlong research project are:

- Developing an awareness of what it means to truly know something about a topic, to become expert at it ("to know when you know and know when you don't know")
- Spawning a hobby or vocation and paving the way for lifelong interests
- Learning the necessary research skills to find, collect, organize, and synthesize information

Notes

1 During a mammoth school improvement effort in California during the mid and late 1970s called Early Childhood Education (ECE), the State Department of Education was pulled up short with a devastating discovery, one borne out by reform programs around the country. Whenever significant change is asked of teachers, the test scores of one-fourth of the teachers—or one-fourth of the schools—experience a drop in test scores for the first year or two before moving back upward and eventually surpassing the original benchmarks. This back sliding occurred primarily when teachers were ill-prepared to succeed with the new tools and methods but had been coaxed into leaving the old behind.

2 Frank Smith, *Insult to Intelligence: The Bureaucratic Invasion of Our Classrooms*, (New York: Arbor House, 1986).

3 Sara Goodman Zimet, *What Children Read in School*, (New York: Grune and Stratton, 1976).

4 Jean Craighead George, *My Side of the Mountain*, (New York: Penguin USA, 2000).

5 Susan Torrence and Leslie Polansky, *Oregon ABC Book*, (T.P. Publications, 1983).

6 Smith, *Insult to Intelligence.*

7 This structure for organizing the day was developed by Robert Ellingsen, over a five-year period. It is offered here as a beginning point, not a model. Structure for the day should ensure that the basic skills are included on a daily basis but should also flow with the content and encourage full integration.

Notes to Myself

Chapter 19: Assessing Competence Vs. Grading

The goal of the ITI model—and the innate drive of the human mind—is mastery. Mastery, not in the sense of "mastery learning" of each of 834 discrete skills of reading, but rather mastery as in competence: capacity, sufficiency; possession of required skill, knowledge, qualification; sufficient means for a modest livelihood. Not only has the student mastered a skill or a concept but he/she knows when and how to apply it in the real world in similar but varying circumstances. It has been incorporated into a mental program for storage in long-term memory (see Leslie Hart's discussion of programs, Chapter 5). Such mastery and competence is at the heart of positive self-concept; it gives a sense of empowerment and ability to direct one's life; it is the brain's innate search for meaning.

In contrast, assessing students' progress traditionally means sorting and grading and creating bell curves. Such reduction to comparative numbers via true-false and multiple choice formats is affordable but tests only the first stage of learning—pattern detection (see Chapter 4). Whether students can use what they understand in meaningful, real-world situations that would enhance their futures is considered too costly and messy to assess. These simple and simplistic formats compare one student with another rather than plumb the depth of student knowledge. Pitting students against each other causes stress for students and redirecting them from intrinsic rewards to external rewards. In too many instances, it also creates either low self-esteem or a sense of false assurance.

From a teacher perspective, the demands of standardized testing distort our views of what's valuable for students to know by forcing us to test what's easy to assess rather than what's important to know and be able to do as future citizens.[1]

There is yet another, more crucial reason why traditional evaluation and grading is brain-antagonistic; it totally ignores how learning takes place. As Leslie Hart, pioneer in applying brain research to education, states: "Learning is the acquisition of useful programs."[2] In contrast, selecting A, B, C, or D on a multiple choice exam or choosing between true/false options based on a tiny niggling that we've heard of one of the choices before, doesn't indicate understanding nor is it enough to create a mental program for long-term memory. And, as Hart points out, information that does not become embedded in a mental program is information that is irretrievable.[3]

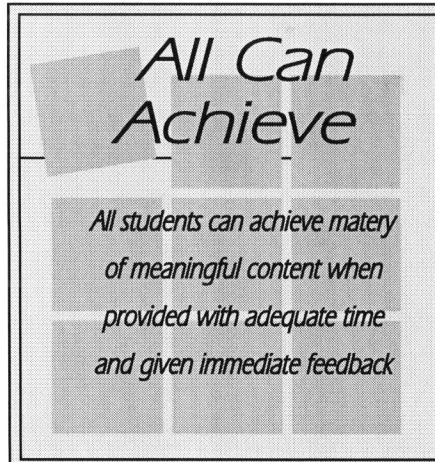

All Can Achieve

All students can achieve matery of meaningful content when provided with adequate time and given immediate feedback

Before we go on, check with your own experience. Do you recall your college days, cramming all night for your essay exam in your sophomore World Civilizations class? Mountains of data with little or no application to real life. By the time the Blue Book essays were returned, there was stuff in yours that you had never heard of before! Even the handwriting looked strange. Surely, you said to yourself, this must be someone else's! But, sadly, it was yours . . . what a waste of time, money, and effort.

Even in more active forms of classroom assessment, doing something once or twice does not a program make. Thus, even an "A" on a true/false or multiple choice test can mean little in terms of long-term memory. And grades of less than an "A" usually mean that the learner, at the time, still harbored uncertainty or misunderstandings. Such tentative feelings indicate that an accurate mental program had not been put in place and thus he/she remembers little or nothing six weeks later. This is the basis for teachers' common complaint: "I taught them but they didn't learn."

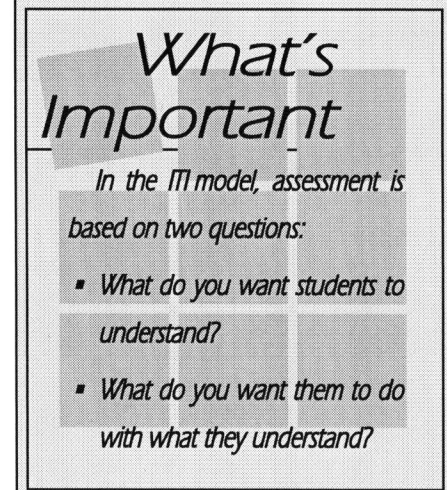

> **What's Important**
>
> *In the ITI model, assessment is based on two questions:*
>
> - *What do you want students to understand?*
> - *What do you want them to do with what they understand?*

In life outside of the classroom, the difference between mastery and the bell curve is stark. In the real world, a "C" or even a "B" is wholly insufficient. Who would want to fly in an airplane that had been serviced by a mechanic who had just passed skill tests with a "C-"? Would you? Certainly not! How about just a little leak left behind by your plumber? Is that OK with you? No!

In such situations what really matters is mastery. It is a cruel lie to tell students that a "B" or "C" is OK. The simple but painful truth is that a grade of "B" or "C" represents failure to achieve mastery. To come close to mastery but not succeed is, in the long run, no better than an "F" or never having taken the class at all.

All of this may sound unduly harsh, even spiteful. But if we are honest with ourselves, the evidence of students failing to become competent is all around us.

New Perspectives About Assessment

Two trends offer some hope: application of current brain research (the major topic of this book) and authentic assessment, often referred to as performance-based assessment. Both require massive changes in curriculum content and structure, in the means of assessing student learning, and in attitudes—of teachers, students, and the system.

Brain research and the ITI model ask two simple but powerful questions about assessing our students' learning:

> - **What do we want students to understand?** (As defined in the key points)
> - **What do we want them to do with what they understand?** (As described in the inquiries)

Similarly, two valuable ideas from the authentic assessment movement are:

- Use real-life settings and real-world levels of expectation[4]
- Assess what's worth assessing rather than what's easy to assess

Renata and Geoffrey Caine, two authors committed to helping educators apply brain research, propose using at least four relevant indicators for determining mastery:[5]

Real–World Tests of Mastery

- The ability to use the language of the discipline or subject in complex situations and in social interaction
- The ability to perform appropriately in unanticipated situations
- The ability to solve real problems using the skills and concepts
- The ability to show, explain, or teach the idea or skill to another person who has a real need to know

These approaches to assessing mastery focus on competence in real life rather than performances on artificial tasks found only in school. Unfortunately, all too often, there is no change in the curriculum against which student outcomes are assessed. Authentic assessment of unauthentic curriculum results in more work for staff but little change for students. Likewise, creating brain-compatible assessment processes to assess brain-antagonistic curriculum is a waste of time and energy and money.

This chapter discusses several tools for evaluating student learning that are bodybrain-compatible and satisfy district requirements for accountability.

Using the Tools at Hand

In an ITI classroom, there is no need to invent or buy tests or assessment instruments beyond what the teacher has already created when implementing the ITI model. To answer the ITI assessment questions—what do you want students to understand and what do you want them to do with it—requires no special tools or instruments. They are already built in.

Your Curriculum

Authentic assessment of unauthentic curriculum is simply not possible. Thus, your first step must be to ensure that the curriculum you ask students to master and yourself to assess is, in fact, authentic. In ITI that means that the curriculum must be conceptually stated rather than a collection of factoids, be based in the real world, and be age-appropriate.

Authentic Assessment

Authentic assessment of unauthentic curriculum is an oxymoron, resulting in more work for staff but little change for students.

The Role of Key Points in Assessment. Key points state clearly what's worth learning and, therefore, what's worth assessing (see Chapter 14). They provide the base for instructional planning, they serve as an official communique to parents and peers about curriculum content and expectations, and they can record what is being taught and learned in your classroom. By giving key points to students up front (except when conducting a discovery process), you put students in the driver's seat, able to take the initiative and self-direct their learning. Key points are the perfect focus for assessment tools and procedures.

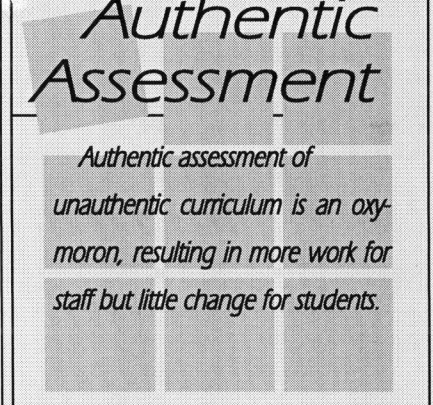

Your first assessment task, therefore, occurs early in curriculum planning—how you translate your district/school's curriculum and state standards into key points. Are they conceptual? Are they based in the real world? Are they meaningful enough to be transferred into long-term memory? If yes, developing key points and inquiries that lead to meaningful assessment is a much easier task.

The Role of Inquiries in Assessment. Inquiries require the kinds of observable actions from students that allow a teacher—and parents and the student—to determine whether the student has accurate understanding of a key point (concept or skill), can use it in real-world contexts, and has wired this capability into long-term memory. Mastery has occurred when students can apply the concept/skill in ways described by the Caines on the previous page. Such a level of mastery ensures that the concept/skill has been wired into long-term memory, precisely the point of schooling.

Rubrics

Rubrics are another useful assessment tool because they specifically describe the attributes of a successful product. There are many excellent sources of commonly needed rubrics available through state and national curriculum organizations. They are also relatively easy to construct. Involve your students in the process to increase skills for self-assessment.

Be Patient

Learning doesn't happen overnight. Recall Leslie Hart's definition of learning as a two-step process: the extraction from confusion of meaningful patterns and then the development of mental programs for using what is understood. These physiological changes in the brain take time. Jumping to assessment before both steps are complete is an utter waste of time and is even cruel.

Thus, before you start formal assessment, use your best judgment to determine if formal assessment is warranted or still premature. To decide if a student is ready for assessment, look over each completed inquiry. Here are possible questions to ask:

- How many inquiries has the student successfully completed?
- Do these inquiries represent all the multiple intelligences or just his/her favorite?
- Do these inquiries call for real-world performances assessed with real-world expectations and standards?
- Have these inquiries provided the student with enough practice to ensure that the knowledge/skills are wired into long-term memory?

> **Inquiries**
>
> *Inquiries are ready-made performance-based assessment tools. All that one needs to add to the inquiries are criteria to guide professional judgement regarding how well students have learned.*

The chart on the following page will help you determine how fully and deeply the student has applied and practiced a concept or skill. Simply write the number of each completed inquiry in the box that best characterizes the intelligence(s) required for the task and the level of Bloom's Taxonomy called for. Has the linguistically strong student stayed in his/her safe harbor of linguistic tasks? Or, did the student have little choice in selecting such inquiries because there were too few inquiries to choose from or most called on linguistic intelligence? Or, did the student complete inquiries at only one or two levels of Bloom's Taxonomy, typically knowledge and comprehension?

When the student shows mastery in applying a concept or skill to real-world situations (at least four similar but different) and has wired it into long-term memory, only then considered it mastered.

Ensuring Mastery

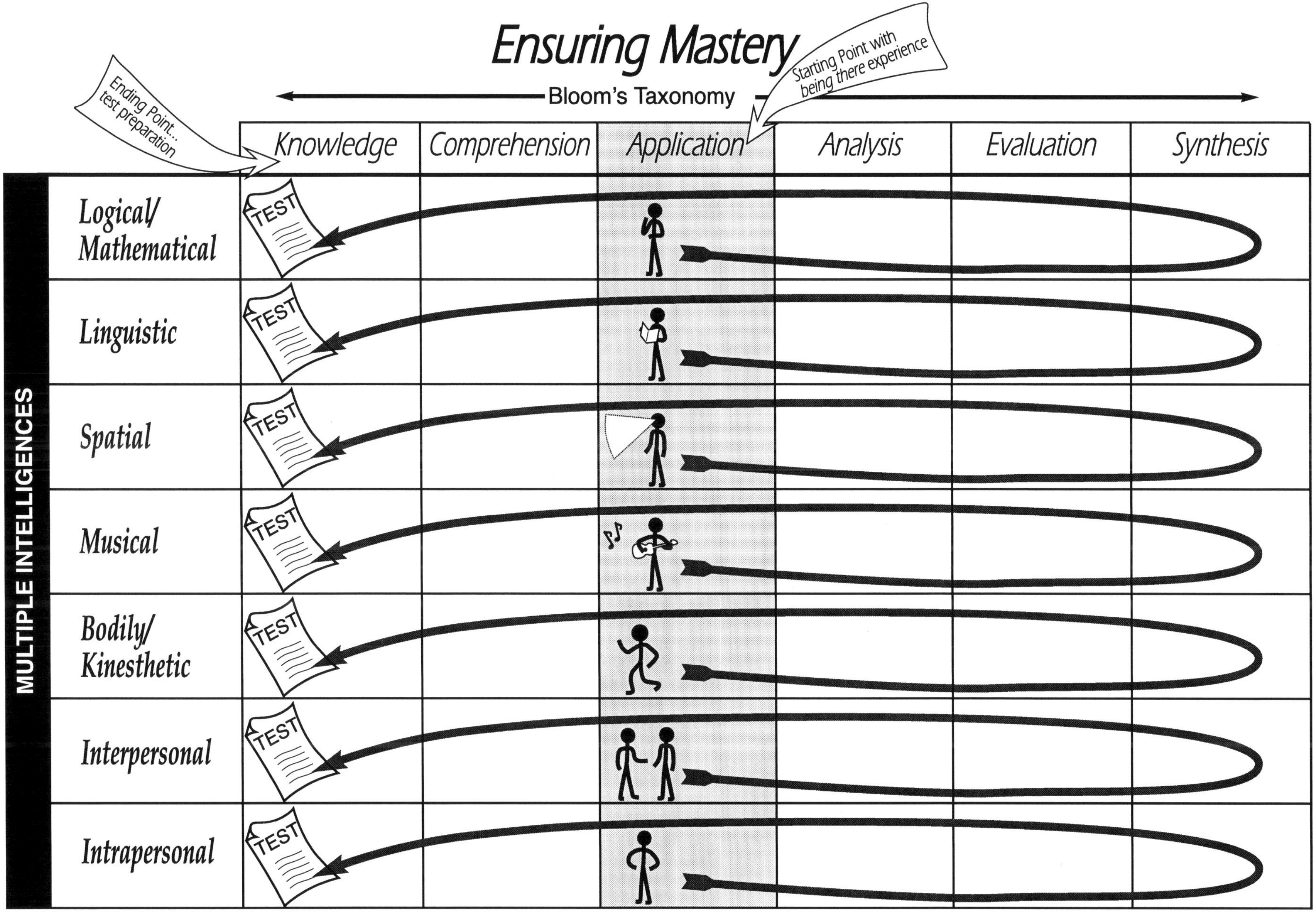
Starting Point with being there experience
Bloom's Taxonomy
Ending Point... test preparation
Knowledge
Comprehension
Application
Analysis
Evaluation
Synthesis
MULTIPLE INTELLIGENCES
Logical/ Mathematical
Linguistic
Spatial
Musical
Bodily/ Kinesthetic
Interpersonal
Intrapersonal
TEST

The "Ensuring Mastery" chart is a useful tool both when developing inquiries and when determining readiness for assessment. The more varied the input and more diverse the application and practice, the more likely it is that long-term memory will occur.

Determining "Yes" or "No"

The primary purpose of assessment is to improve teaching and learning. Although we believe that a well-trained, experienced teacher can determine whether learning has or has not taken place—a task they have been performing for centuries—the ITI model offers two kinds of criteria to help you make a yes/no decision:

- The 3Cs of Assessment
- Tweaked* Inquiries

These two tools lead to a clear yes/no judgment and also help to determine follow-up teaching needs when the answer isn't a firm "yes." For example, a "no" can mean anything from a student's understanding that is incomplete or even inaccurate to a student's ability to apply a concept or skill but it is not yet part of his/her long-term memory (e.g., the student still uses crutches such as speech notes, occasionally rereads the directions, etc.). "No" can also mean the inquiry was poorly written or age-inappropriate.

It's time to stop behaving, albeit under pressure, as if the end goal of schooling is correct answers on tests. Instead, we should be acting as if our lives depended upon ensuring that students have the knowledge and skills to be successful, contributing members of society.

* The verb "tweak" goes back to the early 1600s. Over time it has come to mean to fine tune, adjust, modify, and perfect. We offer it here with a bit of tongue-in-cheek humor to lighten your day and to make the point that even good inquiries usually need some additional fine tuning to serve the purpose of assessment and evaluation.

The 3Cs of Assessment

The 3Cs of assessment are correct, complete, and comprehensive.

These criteria are used by both students and their teachers in assessing day-to-day work. They are tools that help students focus on real-world standards of performance.

The 3Cs of Assessment

- **Correct**—conforming to fact or truth; free from error; accurate
- **Complete**—having all parts or elements
- **Comprehensive**—of large scope; inclusive; extensive mental range or grasp

Here is how the 3Cs apply to the task of washing a car:

Correct—The outside of the car has been washed and rinsed.

Complete—The outside has been washed and rinsed; windows have been wiped inside and out.

Comprehensive—The outside has been washed and rinsed; windows have been wiped inside and out; mats have been washed and the floor has been vacuumed; "stuff" has been cleared, the trunk has been organized, and receipts have been collected.

Another example from everyday life, doing the dishes:

Correct—Dishes are in the dishwasher

Complete—Dishes are in the dishwasher; pots and pans are washed and put away

Comprehensive—Dishes are in the dishwasher; pots and pans have been washed and put away; the stove and counter area has been wiped, the table cleaned and place mats shaken; the sink is scrubbed; floor is swept and the garbage taken out

For a classroom example, consider the assignment to define "egg":

Correct—Female cell of reproduction

Complete—Female cell of reproduction in all species, large and small, delicate and robust; can vary in size and color

Comprehensive—Female cell of reproduction across all species, large and small, delicate and robust; can vary in size and color; can develop inside and outside of the body. Can have different size, shape, and strength of shell, i.e., from very hard, ostrich, to very delicate, frog; can be fertilized in a petri dish; can be harvested and frozen for future use

It's estimated that 80% of parent wrangling with their children over "unfinished" work and 80% of poor work in the classroom is due to lack of understanding or misunderstanding between adult and child about the criteria for judging performance. A discussion with a child about what the 3Cs would look like when applied to a particular task will greatly increase the quality of the performance and the satisfaction of all involved.

The 3Cs can be used to judge mastery for any activity when it is clearly defined.

The Tweaked Inquiry

Inquiries are ready-made performance-based assessment tools. While not all inquiries need to carry the burden of formal assessment, all require observable action of students.

For classroom purposes, assessment should help improve the teaching-learning process. For that, applying the 3Cs to students' performance on an inquiry plus drawing on teacher experience analyzing student projects are usually adequate to determine mastery.

However, for more formal assessment purposes and when communicating with parents and colleagues, inquiries may need to be tweaked to make judgment less subjective and more objective, i.e., three people assessing the same performance would agree. To build in objectivity, ensure that all the needed assessment elements are clearly there—**who** will know and be able to apply **what**, **how well**, **how** measured, and **when**. Thus, the goal of tweaking is to make the yes/no (mastered or not mastered) assessment determinations less of a subjective leap and more obviously based on criteria understandable to students and parents. Add/Strengthen any missing elements that would help guide your professional judgment regarding how well students have learned, i.e., whether their patterns are correct and a mental program has been built. Procedures and examples for tweaking follow.

The Elements of Successful Assessment

Successful assessment is relatively straightforward. It must answer the basic question: **Who** will do **what, how well,** as measured by **what,** and **when**?

Elements of a measurable test item:

- **Who**—all students (not just the "good" students)
- **What** students should do/know and be able to apply (the concept or skill described in the key point)
- **How**—as described in the inquiry

- **How well**—framed by the inquiries with rubrics and inquiries judged according to the "3 Cs" of mastery
- **When**—as described in the inquiry (e.g., within the next 10 minutes, by the end of the day, by tomorrow morning, by the end of the week or month. When is often understood and may not need to be stated.)

How to Tweak an Inquiry

- First, select two or three inquiries which you feel would be the best real-world application of the content or skill you want to assess. Make sure that reading ability or a particular intelligence is not a fundamental prerequisite to succeeding.
- Analyze these inquiries to determine the intelligence(s) which the performance requires (see discussion of seven intelligences in Chapter 3).
- Avoid inquiries whose prerequisite skills might interfere with accurate assessment of the content or skills being examined. For example, inability to write short essay might preclude the student from expressing their mastery of a concept or skill.
- Take time to craft the inquiries; build in real-world contexts and situations. Inquiries which reflect only linguistic or logical/mathematical intelligences or inquiries that are busywork with no real-world application (or for other reasons are just not brain-compatible) are useless as assessment tools. (For discussion of inquiries, and particularly writing inquiries using the seven intelligences, see Chapter 19.)

Together, key points and inquiries provide the basic assessment tools. How to handle the remaining two elements, who and when, is quite clear in a brain-compatible learning environment. All students can achieve mastery of meaningful content when provided with adequate time and given immediate feedback (either by the learning materials/situation itself or by the teacher).

Examples of Tweaking

Here are some examples of key points and inquiries and how to tweak them to make yes/no decisions about mastery more objective and clear cut for you, students, and parents. It isn't difficult.

Example from Typical Fifth Grade Curriculum:

Conceptual Key Point: A system is a collection of parts and processes that interact to perform some function. Many things can be looked at as a system or as part of a system. To study a system, one must define its boundaries and parts.[6]

Inquiries:

1) In your Learning Club, analyze a bicycle. Experiment with drawing boundaries which would define a system within the bicycle. Draw the boundary of at least five different systems; record your findings and explain why you chose the boundary you did for each system. Share your findings with at least one other Learning Club.
2) Select one of the systems identified in Inquiry #1 above. Analyze the structures and describe the parts and processes that interact to perform some function. Identify the function performed. Record your findings in your science notebook. Share your findings with other members of your Learning Club.
3) Based on what your Learning Club now knows about parts and processes of structures and systems, complete a KWL (now <u>k</u>now, <u>w</u>ant to learn, <u>l</u>earned during study) chart for your

Learning Club. Contribute your group's ideas to the creation of a KWL chart for the class.

First, step: Analyze these three inquiries. Which one is the best real-world application of the content or skill you want to assess? We would choose the first one.

Second step: Ask yourself if the action required by the inquiry is a real-world test of understanding and being able to apply the conceptual key point. Answer: Mostly yes but the action required needs tweaking. For example, the "what" is incomplete. Add "Describe the parts and processes of the system you chose and the functions these parts and processes create."

Would this inquiry as written tell you if each member of the Learning Club understood and could apply it? Answer: Probably not. Tweak it by making it an individual task.

Does this inquiry provide a time frame for completion? No.

So, once tweaked, the inquiry would look like this:

"Working alone, analyze a bicycle. Sketch the bicycle. Experiment with drawing boundaries which would define a system within the bicycle. Draw the boundary of at least five different systems. Describe in your science journal why you chose each boundary.

Then, select one of five systems and diagram its parts and processes. Describe on the diagram the functions that those parts and processes perform together. Add this diagram to your science journal.

Complete your work by the end of the day. Before submitting your journal to the teacher to review, look over your work. Analyze it using the 3Cs of Assessment. If improvements need to be made, ask your teacher for extra time."

As tweaked, this inquiry now allows you to answer the question who will do what, how will they do it, how well must they do it, and when or in the time allowed:

- **Who**—a particular student working alone
- **What** the learner will do/know and be able to apply—how to define boundaries of a system
- **How**—by analyzing and identifying five systems of a bicycle and describing the parts and processes of one of those systems and the function the parts and processes create
- **How well**—framed by the inquiries and judged according to the "3Cs" of mastery
- **When**—by the end of the day plus additional time as discussed with the teacher

You now have an assessment tool that would allow you to say quite objectively, "Yes, the student understands and can apply this concept."

Final question: Has the student truly mastered this concept, that is, is it part of his/her long-term memory? Understanding and applying are the beginning steps. But, in your professional judgment, has the student developed a mental program for long-term memory? If in doubt, ask the student to select his/her favorite toy (must have moving parts). Have him/her do the same inquiry but substitute this toy for the bicycle. Still in doubt, you select a toy or machine and have him/her do the same inquiry again. To repeat Leslie Hart: "Learning is the acquisition of useful programs." Programs are anchored in long-term memory.

Transitioning to Mastery

For older students who have mastered the system, substituting procedures to assess mastery/competence for grading based on seat time and quizzes is not a minor event. For many students, particularly the higher achieving, the major motivation is how many points are needed to get a desirable grade or how many pages, exactly, does the essay have to be? A class with only two grades, mastery or no credit can come as a real shock. Have to think? Do one's personal best when mediocre will pull the desired grade? Students may resist the changes.

So, be prepared. Think through concrete steps for transitioning students. Here are some tried and true methods. But remember, these are transition steps* on the way to full bodybrain-compatibility. Don't get stuck on them. Your ultimate goal is an assessment system with only two possibilities—mastery (a grade of A if you have to use letter grades) or no credit (an incomplete). Using assessment tools based on the key points of curriculum and measured by hand-crafted inquiries keeps teachers and students focused on mastery every day. Again, the goal is to acquire useful mental programs.

Introduce the 3Cs

After ensuring that your key points and inquiries are well crafted, introduce the 3Cs. Begin using the criterion "correct" first. Any assignment that does not meet this criterion is returned to the student, repeatedly if necessary, until the work is correct.

After a week or so, and with some forewarning, add the criteria of complete and comprehensive—but only after you have taught the notion to students with multiple, clear examples.

During this transition to inquiries demanding real-life application and real-life standards of workmanship, you may feel that adapting your old "points for grades" system is needed. If so, don't forget that it is a transition stage. Truly brain-compatible assessment is much further down the road.

* Ann Ross, Associate, Susan Kovalik & Associates, was the first ITI teacher to develop a comprehensive system for weaning students off the external rewards/punishments of grades and into a more internally-driven appreciation for learning and mastery. Thank you, Ann, for your ideas.

A Point System for Transitioning to Personal Best

If your students are firmly attached to a point system, shift what you give points for. Award points for completing inquiries written to Bloom's taxonomy with performance judged using the 3Cs. For example:

Knowledge	1 point
Comprehension	2 points
Application	5 points
Analysis	6 points
Evaluation	8 points
Synthesis	9 points

Students will soon realize that taking a short cut, doing the more time-consuming but more interesting inquiries gives them more points. Furthermore, using the 3Cs to judge performance rather than looking for the "right answer" moves them toward ownership of their work and taking more responsibility for their own learning.

Remember, however, giving points is a transitional ploy only. Leave it behind as quickly as you can. (For a stunning discussion of the problems created by external rewards, see *Punished by Rewards: the Trouble with Gold Stars, Incentive Plans, A's, Praise, and Other Bribes* by Alfie Kohn.[7])

Becoming Responsible for One's Own Learning

Becoming a lifelong learner requires taking responsibility for one's learning—seeking it and keeping at it until mastery is achieved. A first step is giving students the game card—a chart which lists every key point for each component. An abbreviated version of the key points listed on the bulletin board or illustrated in your curriculum mindmap is fine. This should be a permanent part of each student's notebook and a key part of his/her assessment portfolio.

Students should be responsible for selecting and conducting demonstrations of their mastery. This helps students develop an appreciation for what it means to know something in depth as contrasted with realizing that their knowledge is superficial.

Again, assessment in the ITI model is based on mastery. Feedback is given on a mastered/passed or not-yet-mastered/no-credit-yet basis, **not** on a pass/fail basis. Timelines should be flexible. Mastering a key point the last day of school should count as much as mastering it in the first week. Mastery is mastery.

Assessment in Group Settings

Another transitional issue to face is that of individual vs. group, competition vs. collaboration. Some students may initially resist the idea of receiving the same number of points each member of the group received. High-achieving students will complain that their grades will be pulled down, that other students will "cheat" or copy from their work. High-achieving students may in fact hog the task and low achieving students may be intimidated and withdraw from participation. Until a sense of community is reached and such differences melt away, base assessment of individual mastery primarily on individual inquiries. Extra points can be given for contributing to successful collaboration.

Again, this is a transitional approach only. For help in developing curriculum appropriate for groupwork and for equalizing social status, see *Designing Groupwork* by Elizabeth Cohen.

Death of the "Right" Answer

Yet another transition, for students and teacher, is a shift away from the teacher as the authority to the individual learner as the person responsible for figuring things out. In real life, there is no 40 hour-a-week person who follows us about shouldering the responsibility for ensuring that the information we encounter is trustworthy or pointing out that we really didn't get it when our boss explained a new procedure. A hallmark of the lifelong learner is determining what information is reliable and whether or not we truly understand it.

Accordingly, you will want students to develop their own resources for making such determinations. One useful classroom rule which handles the spontaneous, short-term questions, is "Ask Three Before Me"; students may not ask the teacher a question until they have first asked three other students.

To handle the need for immediate feedback without you providing the right answer, have Learning Club members assess each other's inquiry using the 3Cs of assessment. Each member initials the inquiry and returns it to the student who requested feedback. Only after reworking the inquiry and making all necessary corrections does the work go to the teacher for feedback. It is easy for the teacher to quickly look at the student's binder and determine if the inquiry satisfies the 3Cs. If not, a note is written next to the inquiry asking the student to rethink or redo it. Students can redo the inquiry or select a different one. Again this is their choice. But the message is clear: What matters in real life is mastery, competence.

Initially, frustration for older students may be high. They may wallow in disbelief or even anger. Teachers need to be patient and maintain their high expectations. By midway through the year, almost all students will have accepted the process as the way things are done in this classroom. Although some students may take longer to adjust, refuse to lower your expectations; eventually all of the students will come to understand the importance of mastery in your classroom and especially for their lives.

As shifts in these attitudes begin to occur and alternatives to traditional assessment gain credence, the door will open to yet more bodybrain-compatible assessment practices, e.g., no points for inquiries completed, only a check-off on key points mastered. Eventually, the internal student motivator becomes the satisfaction of mastery itself and the confidence of knowing one is a competent problem-solver which is a necessary ingredient for a contributing member of society.

This shift to internal motivation is greatly aided by implementation of the Lifelong Guideline of Personal Best as defined by the LIFESKILLS (see Chapters 9 and 10). Again, the goal of the ITI classroom is mastery with all students receiving an "A."

The Mechanics of Keeping Track

The mechanics of tracking progress toward mastery can take on a life of its own. The end result is almost always a far less bodybrain-compatible atmosphere than we had intended and we begin to have that cheerless feeling of being embedded in mindless requirements.

To help counteract the bureaucratic tug of the system, keep in mind the nine elements of bodybrain-compatibility. For example, adequate time demands that there is no reason a teacher should close the grade book on students just because one grading period has ended and another begun. Our goal should be mastery, whenever it occurs. Continue working with those individuals even while moving on with the class to the next component. Again, the expectation of the teacher and the clear message to students is MASTERY!

If students are involved in keeping track of their progress toward mastery of the key points and in daily work on inquiries, they can stay focused on their work; the teacher needn't nag. Even better, if the curriculum for your next component is based in the real world, students will see additional examples of the key points they are still working on.

Keeping Track of What's Important

The mechanics of using key points as the main assessment tools in the classroom are surprisingly easy. The teacher simply converts his/her grade book into a record of each student's mastery of key points. Key points are listed across the top, students' names along the left. A simple check can suffice or a teacher may choose to record the date and the number of the inquiry used as the assessment tool. The discussions that will ensue around what it means to "know that you know" and "know that you don't know" will be invaluable for students as they begin to piece together what it means to become a lifelong learner and responsible citizen.

Keep a chart showing each student's progress toward mastering each key point. A simple chart will suffice—students' names from top to bottom of page on the left and number of the key point from left to right along the top. Indicate the date each key point is mastered. Note: mastery is mastery; either the key point is mastered or is not yet mastered. No grade is given, only a date when mastered. Such a chart shows at a glance which key points a student needs help with. This can be done through cooperative learning groups or one-to-one contact with the teacher. This process is repeated until every student masters all key points for a component. Students really become interested in how they are progressing and want to master every key point. If the component ends with any student still having key points to master, the teacher should continue to provide support for individual students through using Learning Club partners, cross-age tutors, and other resources until mastery has been achieved. The expectation is for mastery by all students.

Use spiral notebooks. Have students use a spiral notebook in which they keep a record of every key point, the mindmap (their notes) of direct instruction, the inquiries they have completed, and the research they conduct. This helps students gather all the things they need under one cover. Unlike three-ring binders, contents don't get lost.

Note: Be sure student buy the spiral notebooks that come three-hole punched so they can be stored in a notebook binder. It helps students organize their papers or assignments. It provides an easier way for teachers to keep track of student inquiries for checking purposes. If work is generated on a separate sheet of paper, it can be stapled onto a page in the spiral notebook.

A Most Important Reminder

Consistent with the multiple intelligences, students should be allowed to demonstrate mastery in a variety of ways rather than being limited only to linguistic processes such as reading and checking a box, writing, or oral presentations. We must stay focused on whether the student understands the key points, can apply them in real-life settings, and has created programs for the skills or concepts connected with them. The means of expressing mastery through an inquiry should not be a simultaneous test of linguistic ability. Therefore, be sure to select inquiries that require solving problems/producing products from all of the multiple intelligences.

Guidelines for Assessment

- Only assess what's important to know and **be able to do**. Be authentic.
- Align assessment with the two-step definition of learning (see Chapters 4 and 5). Focus on what students can **do** with what they understand **and** whether it has become wired into long-term memory.
- Help students learn to assess their own mastery using the 3Cs and self-made and other rubrics.

Alternative Assessments

Social/Political Action Projects

Social and political action projects—midway into study or as a culminating activity—put learning to the test. They require students to apply what they have learned to personal use in the real world. What we know from brain research is that locking knowledge and skill into long-term memory takes practice—multiple uses in varying situations. Test

While taking tests is usually performed from short-term memory, social and political action projects immerse students in complex projects that extend over time, thus giving rich, engaging practice that ensures mastery and long-term memory storage of a wide range of skills and knowledge.

Celebrations of Learning as Assessment Tools

Celebrations can take a variety of forms, allowing you to assess student learning—academic and behavioral. And, in the process, they further deepen that learning. For more information about celebrations of learning, see Chapter 17, pages 17.3-17.6.

Notes

1 The traditional curriculum of our public schools is bodybrain-antagonistic in numerous ways:

- It consists primarily of factoids rather than concepts
- Its tools (textbooks and workbooks/sheets) are heavily dependent on linguistic intelligence
- It was codified over a 100 years ago before we had brain research to inform us
- The times and how we live have changed significantly; so should our content

2 See *Human Brain and Human Learning* by Leslie Hart, a brilliant and user-friendly examination of brain research applied to school settings.

3 Hart's insistence that learning be defined as a mental program for using what we understand is a revolutionary idea, especially in the world of assessment and evaluation. See Chapter 5.

4 Fred Newman, one of the primary leaders of the authentic assessment movement, states, "The idea of authentic achievement requires students to engage in disciplined inquiry to produce knowledge that has value in their lives beyond simply proving their competence in school."

5 Renata and Geoffrey Caine, *Making Connections: Teaching and Learning and the Human Brain*, p. 156.

6 This conceptual key point was taken from *Science Continuum of Science Concepts, K-6* by Karen D. Olsen (Covington, WA: Center for the Future of Public Education, 1995), p. 40.

7 Alfie Kohn, *Punished by Rewards: The Trouble with Gold Stars, Incentive Plans, A's, Praise, and Other Bribes.*

Part E

Implementing Stages 4-5: Working Toward Total Integration

Implementing Stages 4-5

Stages 4 and 5 build upon continued implementation of earlier stages. The bodybrain-compatible learning environment created in Stage 1 has been well established and is consistently nurtured and maintained *all day* and the tools for developing bodybrain-compatible curriculum from Stage 2 are consistently and effectively used *during the time targeted for implementing ITI curriculum.*

Stage 3 builds on a yearlong theme and emphasizes Social/Political Action Projects as training for citizenship. ITI curriculum also continues. Stage 3 is also the first time that a basic skill area is expected to be taught as well as practiced through the high interest area of the ITI theme. Using the curriculum of the theme to practice and teach the basic skills increases through the stages until full integration is achieved.

Stage 4 adds the richness of a microsociety for citizenship training and for increasing performance. ITI curriculum is to be implemented at least 50% of the time.

Stage 5 emphasizes schoolwide implementation, creating multi-age classrooms (preferably a three-year span) and/or using looping patterns by which students stay with the same teacher two to three years, and fully integrated use of technology. Fully integrated curriculum is implemented at least 90% of the time. (Note that Stage 5 does not expect that 100% of the day be organized by the yearlong theme. It is likely that there will be content areas that a district/school will insist be taught in a specified way that cannot be integrated into the theme. This is political reality; accept it as is. Implementing a truly bodybrain-compatible learning environment for 90% of the day is an enormous gift to your students and an extraordinary achievement by you as a top-flight master teacher.)

ITI Classroom Stages of Implementation **Stage 4-5**

Creating an Integrated Curriculum

CURRICULUM

- All aspects of ITI integrated curriculum described in Stages 1-3 are maintained, expanded, and deepened.
- A yearlong theme, prominently displayed on the wall for both students and teacher, serves as the framework for content development. On average, more than 50-90 percent of instruction during the school year is based upon bodybrain-compatible curriculum developed for this theme.
- Curriculum content, as expressed in the key points, enhances pattern-seeking, making it easier for students to perceive and understand the most important ideas and concepts in the curriculum. Inquiries are designed to help students make connections to the real world, to practice using the concepts and skills of the key points, and to develop mental programs and store them for long-term memory. Inquiries that provide experiences in citizenship, such as social/political action activities and collaborative grouping practices, occur weekly.
- The content of the theme is consistently used as a high interest area for applying the skills/knowledge in at least one basic skill area (e.g., math, reading, writing).
- Curriculum for collaborative assignments is specifically designed for group work.

INSTRUCTIONAL STRATEGIES

- Immersion and hands-on-of-the-real-thing are the primary input used to supplement and extend *being there* experiences.
- All instructional time during the theme is based upon the progression of

> *Sensory input from being there*
> *EXPERIENCE → CONCEPT → LANGUAGE → APPLICATION TO REAL WORLD → LONG-TERM MEMORY*

rather than the traditional progression of

> *LANGUAGE → → → CONCEPT → → → APPLICATION*

- Collaboration is used daily whenever it will enhance pattern seeking and program building.
- Time is allocated in accordance with the nature of the tasks and student and teacher need for adequate time; such time allocations are made in recognition of the need to develop programs for using knowledge and skills in real-world contexts.
- Peers and cross-age tutors substantially increase teaching and practice time for students in areas of individual need.

Stage 4

Citizenship & Integration of Basic Skills Through a Micro-Community

CURRICULUM

- The integrated curriculum serves as the framework for content development and implementation for teaching at least two areas of basic skills (e.g., math, reading, writing, oral expression, second and primary language acquisition) and is used for applying all the basic skills. The theme is the basis for 90% of the day/year. Key points and inquiries effectively enhance pattern seeking and program building.
- The development and practice of citizenship continues to be a central focus of curriculum. A schoolwide, ongoing microsociety provides realistic and believable experiences in the governing and commerce of our democratic society. These experiences are used to learn and practice the basic skills.

INSTRUCTIONAL STRATEGIES

- Basic skills taught are taught within the integrated theme and the micro-community as a means to an end, not as an end in themselves. Thus, while the teacher utilizes specific techniques for teaching the basic skills on a daily basis, student's primary focus is on the meaningful content which the basic skills help unlock.
- The teacher takes advantage of the power of what Frank Smith calls "incidental learning," especially during micro-community time, to build mental programs applying the basic skills.
- Students use technology as a natural extension of their senses to explore and learn.

Schoolwide Implementation

CURRICULUM

- The integrated curriculum serves as the framework for content development and implementation for all basic skills and content 90% of the day/year. Key points and inquiries effectively enhance pattern seeking and program building.
- The curriculum of the district provides each teacher with pattern-enhancing tools for curriculum planning.
- Bodybrain-compatible curriculum is implemented schoolwide, providing consistency for students as they move through the school.
- The curricular elements of Stages 1 and 4 are maintained and deepened, especially the focus on citizenship through social/political action and micro-community.
- All basic skills are taught and practiced through the other subject areas.

INSTRUCTIONAL STRATEGIES

- All instructional strategies identified in Stages 1 through 4 are in place and effectively used 100 percent of the time.
- Students have the same teacher for two or more consecutive years (due either to multi-aging or the teacher moving with the students).
- Technology in the classroom allows teachers and students full access to databases and communication systems throughout the country and the world. It is used to extend, not replace, *being there* experiences which provide a starting point for understanding and applying concepts and skills in real-world situations.

Notes to Myself

Chapter 20: Full Integration—More Time, More Quality

More Time

At last count, there are not enough minutes in the day to meet all the demands of state and federal requirements. Once you add up the minimum minutes for reading, language, math, aerobic exercise, etc., there simply are enough minutes in the typical school day to do each of them. This is a problem multitasking can't solve. Integrating will. An hour of integrated curriculum can easily buy you 40 minutes of science, 10 minutes of math, 25 minutes of reading, 10 minutes of writing (journal reflections and recording findings), five minutes of art, five minutes of history/social studies, and five minutes of music—all depending on the kinds of inquiries that students engage in.

How is it possible to get 100 minutes of study packed into one hour? Easy. Review the sample curriculum on pages 14.7-14.13. Notice how many skills and content areas are woven into each inquiry. For an example, analyze inquiry #2 on page 14.7:

2. Select at least five items in our classroom that look interesting to you. Illustrate each item and write a brief description of the attributes (form) of each item. On a Post-It note, describe the use (function) of each item. With your Learning Club, pantomime the form and function of at least one of your items. Record in your science journal at least one other item that is similar in form or function to one you chose. Example: pencil, long and narrow; similar to a pen, both are used to write with.

This inquiry calls for art (the illustration would be done as a simple line drawing or using a specific technique recently taught by the art teacher) for 5-7 minutes, writing for 5-10 minutes, oral language (to plan the pantomime) for 7-10 minutes, pantomiming (drama) for 5-8 minutes, and more writing for 3-5 minutes. Students would also be getting 20-30 minutes of science. In this 25-40 time slot, students would be getting 45-70 minutes of curriculum content and skills.

As you read through the sample curriculum, notice the extent of integration—subject areas and skills—that the inquiries require. The time you spend writing inquiries to ensure you address all the multiple intelligences and levels of Bloom's Taxonomy pay you back in time saved—your time teaching and providing practice time in multiple subjects and skills and student time in learning.

Integration is the gift of time that keeps on giving.

More Quality

The foremost challenge in fully integrating your curriculum is quality. Your curriculum must be better than publisher-generated textbooks with their workbooks and black-line masters. This is particularly important as you increase the amount of time for integrated curriculum to 50 percent for Stage 4 and 90 percent for Stage 5.

Quality integrated curriculum:

- Enhances pattern seeking
- Provides enough opportunities to apply concepts and skills in real-world ways to ensure development of long-term memory
- Avoids the compulsion to "cover" content

Enhancing Pattern-Seeking

Curriculum development is a pattern-enhancing activity. To enhance pattern:

- Eliminate factoids
- Make your key points as conceptual as possible
- Choose organizing concepts for the yearlong theme that have enough depth to unfold throughout the year

Eliminate Factoids. Because factoids are devoid of pattern and are so small they don't explain much about how the world works, they carry little meaning and are thus extremely difficult for students to learn. As a result, students must resort to memorization with few hooks to assist with retrieval.

If your state standards are lean on concepts and fat on factoids, you must build a bridge for your students. Sweep all the factoids into a pile and begin to sort. What are the concepts that would make these tidbits of knowledge meaningful and understandable? In what settings, besides Jeopardy, would they be useful? State these concepts and identify the settings. Teach from these. Let the factoids tag along. Never lead with them.

Make Your Key Points As Conceptual As Possible. Master the game of bumping up. Also search for the most universal statement in order to increase students' ability to generalize to other ideas and transfer to other settings and applications.

Select Organizing Concepts That Are Rich in Pattern. Select organizing concepts for the yearlong theme that are rich in patterns and have power of organize a year's worth of content and skills.

For example: discovery can help ***organize*** a theme, that is, all the content is about discovery of different kinds by different people in different locales. But, discovery as a concept is one-dimensional. Once you're used the dictionary to define it—the act or process of discovering; something discovered; to make sight or knowledge of something for the first time—there is nothing about the concept as a concept to pursue. What would follow are examples of discoveries made, factoids organized by chronology or country or time period or nationality. Discovery is an example of a concept that has little power to create a pattern for the discoveries that follow to help make them memorable and retrievable.

On the other hand, concepts such as systems, change, form and function, and interdependence in a habitat are each a nest of related concepts that can be explored for a year, even a lifetime. Each related or subconcept enriches and interconnects what came before and what will come after.

For example, see the conceptual map for systems on the next page. The concept is mapped as if it were the basis for a yearlong theme with components and topics. Unlike discovery, systems is rich and very multi-dimensional, perfect for enhancing and interconnecting pattern seeking in ways that expand meaning and make content more memorable and more retrievable. It is a fertile concept for grades 5 and up.

Concept mapping is one way to obtain strong patterns for students. Another is selecting a well-known entity whose pattern is instantly recognized by students, whose pieces spin off the organizing concept is predictable, natural ways. An example is the theme, "We, the People," whose monthly components are the goals of our government expressed in the preamble of our constitution. Recite that sentence and an entire year pops to mind. Again, easy to add on to and easy to recall. A compelling pattern. The glue here is obvious and embedded in the organizing concept of the theme. This theme is also appropriate for grades 5 and up.

Organizing concepts for lower grades are less abstract and more experiential but still conceptual. For example, a theme for first grade could be built on the main science idea for first grade: "All living things, including humans, have basic needs—for food, water, air, protection (from weather, disease, and predators), and reproduction. A habitat is the place where the animal or plant lives while meeting these needs." Because the ways that animals and plants go about meeting their needs varies dramatically, and therefore how they are interdependent can be surprising, this concept works well for an entire year. The components could be different habitats, different homes, in which those needs get met in different ways. See the theme on page 20.5

Rule of thumb: The more content you have to integrate—the bigger the percentage of yearly content—the more powerful the organizing glue must be. Your goal should be greater pattern enhancement as you move from stage to stage. Thus, while discovery may be adequate to organize a week or two of integrated curriculum, it is weak glue for 50 percent of a year. Likewise, themes which have a different concept for each component with some connection back to the organizing concept are not untypical themes for Stages 2 and early Stage 3, and work when integrated curriculum amounts to only 10-25 percent of the year; at this stage, the components are largely isolated islands of curriculum, separated by time and lots of typical curriculum.

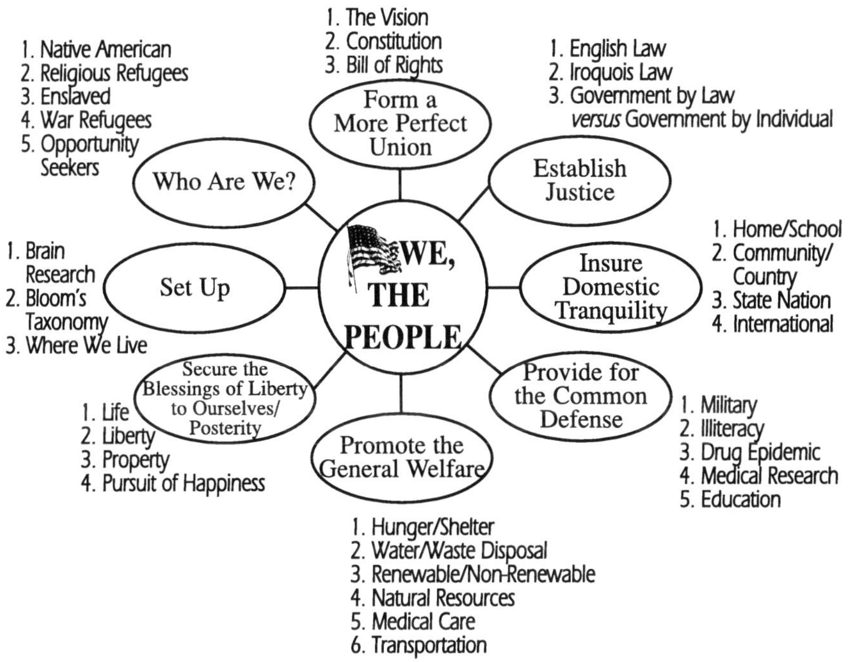

Organizing concept: The goals of democracy are to promote the common good, not the benefit of the few.

Rationale: Democracy can not be sustained if its people do not understand, support, and exercise the responsibilities as well as the rights of democracy on a daily basis.

CONCEPTUAL MAP

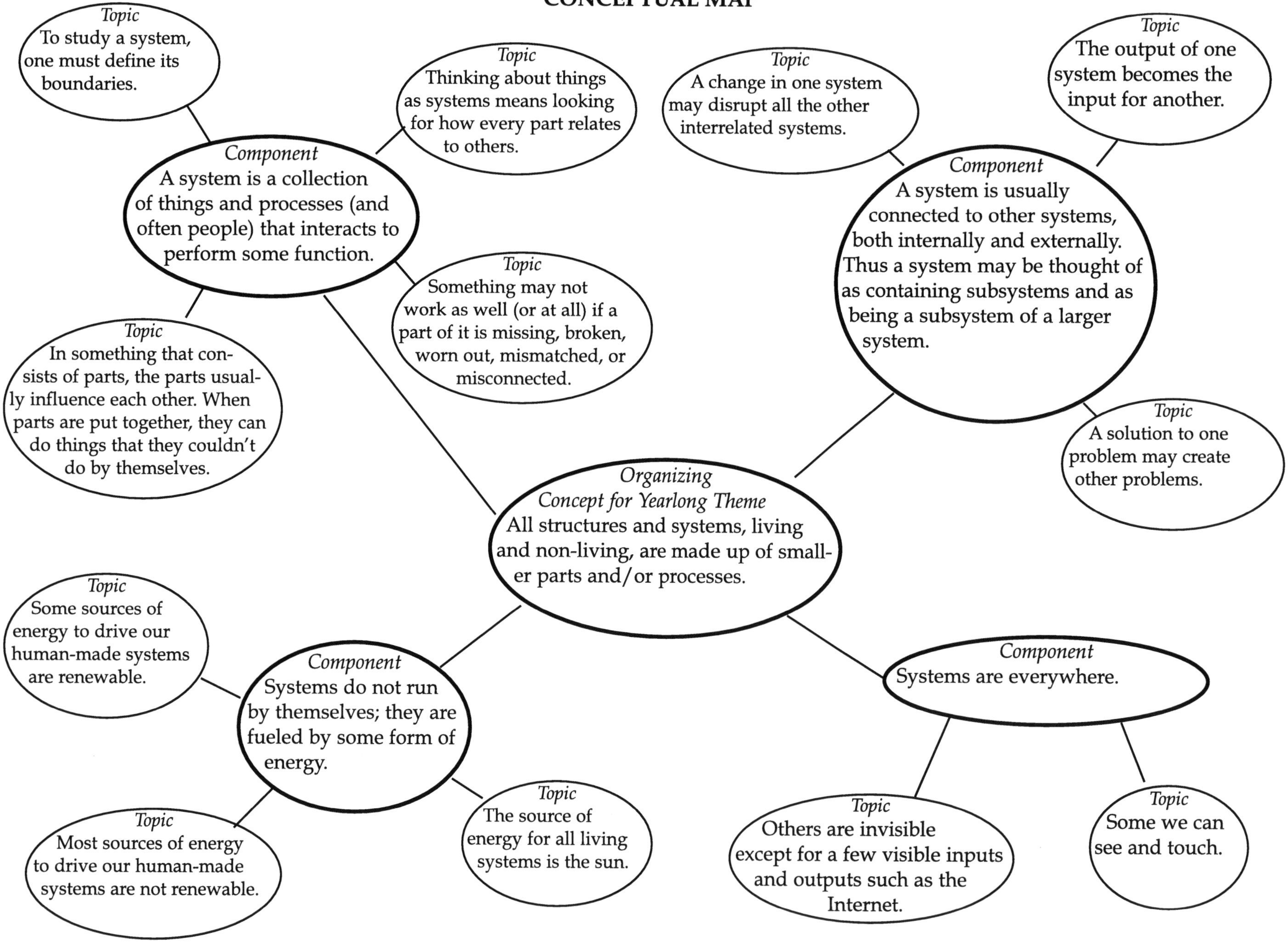
Organizing Concept for Yearlong Theme
All structures and systems, living and non-living, are made up of smaller parts and/or processes.
Component
A system is a collection of things and processes (and often people) that interacts to perform some function.
Topic
To study a system, one must define its boundaries.
Topic
Thinking about things as systems means looking for how every part relates to others.
Topic
Something may not work as well (or at all) if a part of it is missing, broken, worn out, mismatched, or misconnected.
Topic
In something that consists of parts, the parts usually influence each other. When parts are put together, they can do things that they couldn't do by themselves.
Component
A system is usually connected to other systems, both internally and externally. Thus a system may be thought of as containing subsystems and as being a subsystem of a larger system.
Topic
A change in one system may disrupt all the other interrelated systems.
Topic
The output of one system becomes the input for another.
Topic
A solution to one problem may create other problems.
Component
Systems do not run by themselves; they are fueled by some form of energy.
Topic
Some sources of energy to drive our human-made systems are renewable.
Topic
Most sources of energy to drive our human-made systems are not renewable.
Topic
The source of energy for all living systems is the sun.
Component
Systems are everywhere.
Topic
Others are invisible except for a few visible inputs and outputs such as the Internet.
Topic
Some we can see and touch.

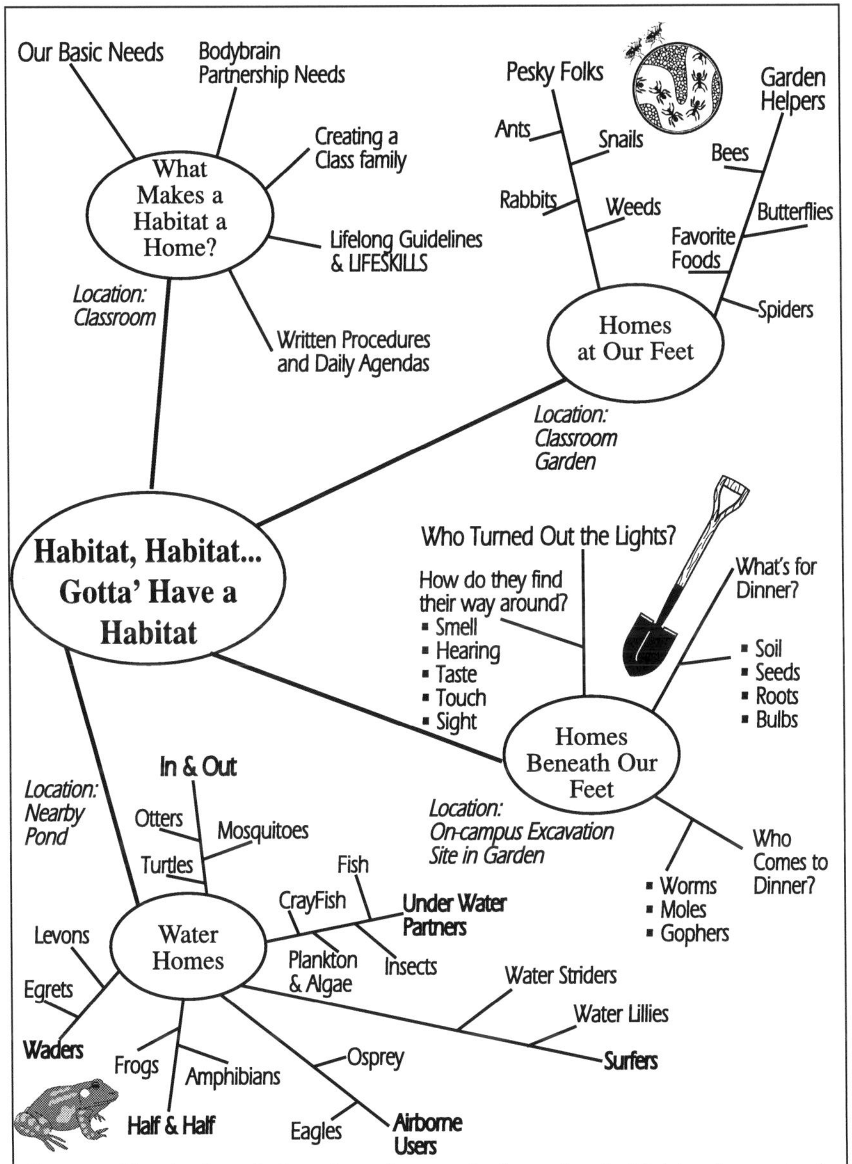

Concept: All animals and plants have the same basic needs; a habitat is where animals and plants interact with each other and their environment to meet their needs.
Rationale: Understanding how animals & plants meet their needs in different nearly habitats will enable them to predict needs in other habitats and become stewards of our world.
Rationale: Understanding the diversity of ways animals meet common needs enables students to understand the complexities of stewardship.

Practice Concepts and Skills in Real-World Contexts

The hallmark of the the ITI model is basing curriculum in *being there* experiences. This is common sense and brain research combined. We learn what we need to in order to accomplish something important to us; it is easier to learn something we can see in action than something that is only talked about. Review Chapter 12 for a discussion of basing curriculum in *being there* locations.

Suggestions:

- Base your curriculum on science concepts. They are observable and directly experienceable. Transferring them into other content areas makes those areas less abstract.
- After guided practice of a basic skill, provide practice through inquiries, celebrations of learning, and social/political action projects. Eliminate worksheets as practice tools.
- Teach basic skills as tools to better understand and communicate about important ideas rather than as ends in themselves. Spend more time teaching these skills within the context of inquiries calling for action rather than during set time periods of the day (because X number of minutes of such instruction is required).
- Ensure that homework requires application of concepts to real-world situations around the home and neighborhood; embed skill practice into these assignments.

Avoid the Compulsion to "Cover" Content

A pound of common sense is worth a ton of "shoulds." When you examine your curriculum, keep asking yourself why? Why is this important? Is this worth teaching/learning? Would this help students understand the world of today and tomorrow? How, where, under what circumstances could this be useful in the real world?

If you can't come up with compelling answers to these questions, allocate such content to the end of the year, knowing full well that there is already too much content to teach and that this content will fall by the wayside. We call this selective abandonment. Since there is too much to teach, make sure what you leave behind is most deserving of being left behind. In other words, first things first. Put the most important things first and teach them to mastery and long-term memory. Don't feel bedeviled by what you can't control, in this case, limited time coupled with unrealistic expectations.

Tips to help put the most important things first include:

- Consider organizing and teaching history around concepts rather than chronologically. In a chronological study of U.S. history, for example, few students ever get to the Vietnam War and its related civil unrest or the Gulf War or the conundrums surrounding the invasion of Iraq.

- Teach basic skills to mastery in a concentrated way. For example, long division in a day, multiplication in a week, punctuation in half day spurts (apostrophes one time, colons and semi-colons another).

Chapter 21: Citizenship Through Social/Political Action and Micro-Community

Preparing students to become participating citizens in our democratic society is a core value of the ITI model. It can and should be done in small and big ways on a daily basis. Two of the most effective ways are involving students in social/political action projects and creating a micro-community which gives students a *being there* experience of community life. While Social/Political Action Projects begin in Stage 3 and progressively deepen through Stages 4 and 5, micro-community begins at Stage 4.

Social/Political Action Projects

Social/Political Action Projects are central to the ITI model and its core goal of growing responsible citizens and for providing students opportunities to apply concepts, knowledge, and skills in real-world ways.

From Knowledge to Action

Social/Political action is a call to action, moving from knowing about to doing something that matters. A project can occur midway into study of a topic or be a culminating activity. It can grow organically out of students' experiences studying the theme and its *being there* experiences. It's what students find important and compelling. It might take the form of lobbying the city council for a stoplight at the school, pressing the EPA or local governmental entity to complete a toxic clean up, urging other students not to eat tuna that doesn't carry the dolphin-friendly symbol, picketing the superintendent's office to get the kindergarten toilets fixed and the restroom reopened, replanting mangrove forests, working in a soup kitchen, visiting the elderly, ensuring that homeless children get school supplies, launching an anti-drug campaign at school, and so forth. In the process of such projects, young citizens discover the levers of our democratic system, learn the personal skills to make their opinions heard and considered, and develop the courage and perseverance to press on until problems get resolved. They also develop a commitment to give back to society through service projects, governmental internships, voter responsibility, etc.

Social/Political Action Projects are usually undertaken as an entire class although Learning Clubs could take on separate parts of a class project. There are no hard and fast rules here, just the intent to have students engage in something meaningful and experience the deep sense of satisfaction that comes from making a contribution to the world and helping make it a better place.

Resources

Resources to assist you and your students to identify, plan, and carry out social/political action projects include: *The Kids' Guide to Service Projects: Over 500 Service Ideas for Young People Who Want to Make a Difference* and *The Kids Guide to Social Action: How to Solve the Social Problems You Choose – And Turn Creative Thinking into Positive Action* both by Barbara A. Lewis and *Enriching Curriculum Through Service Learning* edited by C.W. Kinsley and K. McPherson. For ideas about community service projects, also contact Sarah Pearson, American Youth Policy Forum, 1836 Jefferson Place, WE, Washington, D.C., 20036, aypf@aypf.org, 202/775-9731.

Behaviors of Responsible Citizenship

Responsible citizens:

- Participate in community dialog; are informed voters
- Treat others with respect and courtesy
- Obey the law; work through the system to change those laws they believe are unfair or wrong
- Practice conservation
- Maintain a positive work ethic; develop the personal and social skills to be financially self sufficient
- Take responsibility for personal health
- Are committed to family and do their part to make the family a successful unit
- Are tolerant of religious, racial, ethnic, gender, and age differences

Remember the Lifelong Guidelines/LIFESKILLS

The Lifelong Guidelines/LIFESKILLS should be an integral part of any Social/Political Action Project. They describe the personal and social skills your students need to take action about a problem or societal issue. This is particularly true if the nature of the topic and the community's position about it result in contentious debate, such as supporting the Endangered Species Act and the spotted owl in a classroom located in the heart of logging country or reacting to the discovery of water registering in the unhealthy range several times a week during a visit to the local water treatment plant. Students should not be told that they can't work on issues of consequence just because there will be consequences that affect someone or some business in their community. The idea behind democracy is, as Star Trek's Spock comments, "The needs of the many outweigh the needs of the few."

Social/Political Action Projects As Assessment Tools

What we know from brain research is that wiring knowledge and skill into long-term memory takes practice – multiple uses in varying situations. While test taking is usually performed from short-term memory, Social/Political Action Projects immerse students in complex projects that extend over time, thus giving rich, engaging practice that ensures mastery and creates long-term memory of a wide range of skills and knowledge.

Self Check

Social/Political Action

- The call to action is genuine, a project chosen by students.
- The project is a natural outgrowth of the experiences of the theme.
- The project is a sincere contribution to improving the life of others.
- The work of the project will require a wide range of knowledge and skills, including basic skills as well as social and personal skills. The standards for this work are those of the real world. For example, a letter must be perfect in spelling and grammar, a speech must be informative and delivered with conviction and presence, the information presented must be accurate and fair, appointments must be scheduled and kept as agreed, and so forth.
- Social/Political Action Projects are conducted at least two to three times a year.

A Micro-Community

Despite the innumerable achievements of our technological era, we must rank as a major shortcoming our failure to involve children in our adult world. Most children have not a clue what their parents do for a living and thus are learning precious few of the skills necessary to build a successful life.

The reasons are many: It's unsafe for children to roam about the neighborhood as they could 50 years ago; more people are employees, not entrepreneurs or owners of mom-and-pop operations that involved the children from an early age onward; and many jobs have become fantastically specialized so that even if children did accompany their parents to work, they could not understand what their parent was doing. And yet, the challenges facing future citizens continue to mushroom.

A powerful antidote to these conditions is a micro-community on campus—a microcosm of American life, replete with city council, sheriff, court system, bank, currency system, post office, newspaper, radio and TV stations, recycling center, class and individual businesses, and more. All student run. A micro-community not as an add-on, something done after school or on special days, but a fully integrated, daily ingredient in the vibrant life of the school.

Francie Summers, a truly gifted administrator in Las Vegas, Nevada, and her hard-working, capable staff have demonstrated the power of such a micro-community at two schools. Her current campus, Edith Gareheim Elementary, a K-5 school, is a great illustration of the power of a micro-community to not only induct the young into the roles of citizenship but also to dramatically increase academic performance.

The Power of a Micro-Community

"Our Title I school serves children and families from poverty. ITI works for our students because it makes them feel worthy as individuals. It unleashes their natural curiosity in such a way that learning makes sense and the world around them is understandable. They know they can make positive changes in their world and be productive, responsible citizens. ITI is powerful and changes the lives of children and the adults who work with them."
—Terri Patterson, Principal , Sul Ross Elementary, Waco, Texas

"ITI has had a dramatic impact on students, staff, and the community during the eleven years I have served as principal at two micro-community schools. The students have acquired the knowledge to be successful in school and in life; staff have felt empowered as professionals and are excited about teaching. The communities have been exceedingly supportive because they have reaped the benefits as we 'grew responsible citizens'."
—Francie Summers, Principal, Edith Gareheim Elementary, Las Vegas, Nevada

Another fully-developed micro-community was created at Sul Ross Elementary, Waco, Texas, by an equally talented staff with principal Terri Patterson. It, too, experienced sharp increases in academic performance and, quite impressively, with a high minority, very low-income student population.

Key features of these two micro-community models include:

- Using the Lifelong Guidelines and LIFESKILLS to shape the culture and define the way we treat others
- Replication of essential elements of community life such as daily mail delivery, a banking system (training provided by a bank), an in-house monetary system capable of exchanging real dollars for "Gareheim Gold," a newspaper and TV station, stores open daily for such necessities as extra pencils and pens, special paper, snacks, a recycling service, and more
- Governmental services such as a court system that convenes weekly or more often if needed, a city council that legislates the rules of behavior for its citizens, local EPA, business license bureau, and so forth
- Class and individual businesses which operate every week, some daily. "Going to Town Day," which occurs three to four times a year, provides a sales outlet for all businesses and a breathless exchange of Gareheim Gold in a fast-paced, two-hour period. Prospective business owners must mull through an approvable business plan, buy a business license, arrange for advertising over the schoolwide intercom or student-run TV station and newspaper, and rent retail space
- Engagement in city projects of importance, such as the fifth grade developing an architectural plan to turn an empty lot across the street from the school into a city park (the plan was accepted by the local authorities and became a reality)
- Community participation through volunteerism, monetary donations, and business partnerships
- Participation of parents and younger siblings

The richer the micro-community, the more real it is to students. The more real it seems, the more fully they embrace participating in it. The micro-community creates a real need to know, making learning deeper and more comprehensive. See *Jacobsonville:: An ITI Micro-Society,* a 30-minute video of the model used at Gareheim School, Las Vegas, Nevada.

Self Check

A Micro-Community

- The micro-community is seamlessly woven into the life of the school. Students participate in some aspect of the micro-community on a daily basis.
- Every student participates in his/her class business (recycling program, convenience store) or schoolwide project (post office, newspaper, TV station, a bank). In addition, many students also run a business in partnership or as sole proprietor.
- Although students are aware that theirs is a micro-community of their own making, they value being a member and realize that they are learning invaluable business and citizenship skills.
- Students understand the importance of learning to use what they learn—from the Lifelong Guidelines to academic concepts and skills to everyday common sense.
- Staff use the high-interest experiences of the micro-community as a proving ground for students to apply basic skills. For example, every business must calculate its expenses and percentage of profit/loss.
- The micro-community is student run; staff serve as guide on the side, not sage on the stage.

Part F

Living with Change: Personal & Group Tools, School Structures

Living with Change

At least in its rhetoric, every school in America is committed to improving its program for students. The schools that go beyond rhetoric are those that have a realistic picture of the challenges of change, have developed the personal and group tools for living with it, and have committed themselves to move forward together on an agreed upon path.

Chapter 22 describes personal tools needed for the journey. Included is advice by William Bridges about transitions necessary for change and a variety of personal tools you will need along your journey. Also included is a discussion of some group tools that will help you and your colleagues become best allies, not enemies, as you pursue profound change in your school.

Chapter 23 describes several structural changes that support change. In other words, how to begin to reshape your school's bureaucratic structures so they support, not thwart, your change efforts.

We dedicate this part of the book to those courageous educators who have committed their lives to making our schools a place where all children thrive and all adults enjoy a professional, challenging, and humane work environment that feeds their souls and enlivens their workday. May every reader of this book join your ranks and contribute to the mission.

Chapter 22: Personal Tools for Living with Change

Given the size of the gap between traditional schools, modeled on the Prussian system of the 1840s, and the way they must become to be bodybrain-compatible, the degree of change needed is truly enormous. A school cannot make the jump in one leap but a clear picture of the landing site can make first steps more purposeful. We hope that the following discussion of change processes will provide some of the needed brush strokes to reveal a landscape for the future.

Transition Versus Change

William Bridges, in his book *Managing Transitions: Making the Most of Change,* points out that, "It isn't the changes that do you in, it's the transitions."[1]

Change Is External

Change, he says, is situational: reassignment to a new grade level or subject area, new team structure or roles, changes in homework policies, different vision by new principal or incoming superintendent or school board, the start of double or triple length instruction periods, converting from dependency on textbooks to developing curriculum based on a physical location, and so forth.

Change occurs in external behavior and events.

Transition Is Internal

In contrast, transition is "the psychological process people go through to come to terms with the new situation."[2] Transitions require that we change our personal programs that attach us to old behaviors and actions and that interfere with being able or willing to carry out new behaviors. For example, in order to design instructional strategies that support the bodybrain learning partnership, we might have to toss out decade-old lesson plans, be willing to start from zero and stumble like a novice over an aspect of something that in the past earned us praise and recognition for our expertise.

To choose transition is to choose to reinvent ourself as an educator and as a person, after which change is remarkably easy. Again, "Change is external, transition is internal."[3]

No Transition, No Change

Bridges cautions us that change can't work unless transition occurs. To understand how profound this comment is, think back to your school's last big change effort that went nowhere. The school plan was totally revamped after an extensive needs assessment that included faculty and student involvement. Good ideas were written on the page, complete with detailed calendar and who was to do what. Yet, six months later . . . nothing. No behaviors changed, no new actions were taken. Things remained as before. Why? Because transition—internal shifts—did not occur.

Transition Begins with Endings

Bridges maintains that transition is very different from change. The starting point for change is the outcome to be implemented. The starting point for transition is the ending that you must make in order to leave the old situation, actions, and attitudes behind—the old beliefs, the old reality, and the old identity you had before the change can take place.[4] For example, letting go of textbooks as our curriculum, rigid time schedules, teaching as a solitary act. And, yes, letting go of our established place as "experts."

Four Levels of Transition and Change

Living with change is neither easy nor comfortable. But it can become interesting rather than irritating, a helpful friend rather than a feared foe, if we better understand the personal and group dynamics that accompany it.

There are four levels of transition and change:[5]

- Personal transitions
- Personal learning curve changes
- Group transitions
- Institutional change

Personal Transition

According to Bridges, **"Nothing so undermines organizational change as the failure to think through who will have to let go of what when change occurs."**[6] Ask yourself what endings you need to complete. What beliefs or attitudes or facets of your identity are incompatible with or competes with the new action to be implemented; whatever that is, it must be left behind.

Transition starts with an ending. We begin with letting go of many things, some of which are simply habit, some that we dearly cherish. But letting go need not be a funeral. Some things we are glad to be rid of. Others things served us well and were successful for their time and use, so celebrate them. Thank them for their service and then step forward with a sense of adventure and high hopes, not with regret. Transition and change are swirling dance partners. Enjoy the dance.

Because there is much about our traditional model to let go of and so many vested participants (staff, parents, and even students from intermediate grades and up) who must make the transition, it is unlikely that we will make the transition in one year or even two; three to five years is more likely. Be patient but be thorough. The challenge in school reform is that we cannot fully succeed in creating a bodybrain-compatible learning environment for students until our fellow travellers join us.

Personal Learning Curve Changes

Typical of the journey to transform one's school is the urge to do everything at once. If it's a good idea to end up with a restructured school, let's restructure it now. If it's a good idea to put everyone in teams to best integrate curriculum, let's require team teaching now. This "Let's start where we want to end up" action plan is a recipe for disaster. In our opinion, it is the foremost reason why school reform efforts fail. Restructuring before staff have the skills to succeed has never worked and never will.

So. . . we beg of you: Start at the beginning; start from where you are. Start with a focus on Stage 1. *Make it your personal goal to complete Stage 1 in one year.*

Stage 2 is also primarily a personal learning curve challenge, especially mastering the instructional strategies described in Stages 1 and 2. By the end of Stage 2, you should be working in close collaboration with colleagues to develop the best curriculum for your students that you can and the best instructional strategies for delivering that curriculum.

Levels of Use. Our journey through transitions and change often feels like an out-of-control roller coaster ride and that "the harder we work, the behinder we get." Understanding Levels of Use can reduce our distress and help us capture a sense of our progress.

Developed by Gene Hall, Susan Loucks, and others at the University of Texas in the mid-1970s, the Levels of Use (see next page) describe the levels of implementation people go through when implementing something new.

When using these levels, remember three things:[7]

- They are not a one-way street; for example, each time you add a new strategy to your collaborative approaches, you go back to Level 0.
- "Skipping" levels does not occur. With luck, one can speed through a stage; with even more luck, one can achieve level 5 and beyond. But there are no guarantees.
- These levels apply to specific subskills, not to a teacher generally, or how a teacher may teach a particular subject area, or to an instructional strategy. It applies to a specific subskill within a curricular or instructional area. For example, the ability to utilize cooperative learning during science experiments or to structure clear roles and responsibilities for each group member. Do not apply this scale on a gestalt level, e.g., saying that as an elementary school teacher, a teacher is at the level of non-use; or, as a teacher of reading, he/she is at preparation. Apply Levels of Use only to a particular subskill.

For more information on using Levels of Use, see Chapter 5, *Making Bodybrain-Compatible Education a Reality: Coaching for the ITI Model* by Karen D. Olsen.

Levels of Use[8]

Level	Indices
0 - Non-use	No action being taken. It is not part of the teacher's conversation; if it is, questions indicate a significant lack of understanding or misunderstanding.
1 - Orientation	Teacher is just acquiring information and is exploring, or will soon explore, its potential impact on self and classroom operation. At the last stages of this level, teacher faces the critical decision to implement the skill/task or to turn away. Major consideration: Will there be adequate support?
	Major decision point
2 - Preparation	Teacher is preparing to use it and is thus finding out more about it, gathering the necessary resources (materials, management structures, personal skills/knowledge, support, time, etc.). A difficult stage.
3 - Mechanical Use	Teacher's focus is on the day-to-day doing of it and is attempting to master the tasks in a step-by-step process. Typically the "system" at this level is less than its parts and often the whole is not clearly envisioned.
4 - Routine Use	Use is stabilized. The few changes the teacher makes are made in response to the needs of the implementor rather than of the students. This is a fairly comfortable stage; little preparation is needed to sustain the implementation.

Level	Indices
4 - Routine Use (continued)	Teacher gives little thought of improving use of the skill/task or of its consequences for students. At the last stage of this level, teacher faces a critical decision to make changes in the program to make it work better for students or to stay stuck in a comfort zone. Major consideration: Will the increased benefit to students be worth the effort?
	major decision point
5 - Refinement	Teacher changes implementation to increase both long- and short-term results for students (groups and individuals); work to make changes is limited to own students in own classroom only.
6 - Integration/ collaboration	Teacher has made all the refinements possible working alone in his/her classroom at the refinement level and now makes deliberate efforts to collaborate with others to achieve broader changes, a collective impact across several classrooms or even schoolwide.
7 - Renewal	Teacher has made all the refinements and integrations possible and now seeks more effective alternatives—new approaches/systems/goals for self and school. In the latter stages, the teacher faces the decision to abandon the old system (or significant parts of it) and adopt/adapt the new or to fall back to an earlier stage such as routine use. If the decision is to go forward with the new, the next stop is "non-use" and the cycle begins anew.

Applying Levels of Use: The Bread Baking Story[9]

Level 0—NON-USE

Barbara notices that when I visit her house, I always go straight to the bread box and help myself to her homemade bread. She concludes, given my obvious interest in bread and her information regarding nutritional superiority of natural vs. wonder bread puff, that I should learn to bake bread. At her first suggestion I begin to ask questions such as, "Well, can I cook it in the microwave? Or how about on top of the stove? I'm always in a hurry."

Clues: Questions about "cooking" the bread in the microwave oven or on top of the stove indicate significant lack of understanding (dare I say misunderstanding?) of how bread is baked and, clearly, non-use of the skill called baking bread.

Level 1—ORIENTATION

Barbara begins to talk with me about the merits of home-baked bread: taste (That one I'm clear on!), nutrition (I'm not impressed), texture (I still like to wad up my bread into a tight round ball from time to time), dinner guests are pleased and impressed with warm-from-the-oven home-baked bread (my friends know better than to come to my house if they're hungry). "Barbara, how long does homemade bread last? Is it still tasty after 3-4 days (I travel a lot during the week)."

"Do you have a simple recipe? Like a 4-H cookbook type recipe . . . you know, one for kids, nice and simple, fail-safe." Barbara says "yes" twice. I say, "I want to do it. If you'll give me a recipe and any other information you think I might need right now, I'll begin this weekend. First stop, shopping; I have none of the things that this recipe calls for."

Clues: I'm willing to acquire information and I'm considering its impact on my operation (such as it is!). However, notice that in the early stages of this level I haven't yet made a decision to bake my own bread. I'm just shopping for information (and enjoying Barbara's bread in the process!). During my shopping, I reveal what motivates me. Barbara is thus able to determine what information (knowledge, skill, or motivation) will move me forward to the next level of use. In the last stage of this level, I make the critical step – deciding to implement. Barbara loads me up with "stuff" and I go merrily on my way.

Level 2—PREPARATION

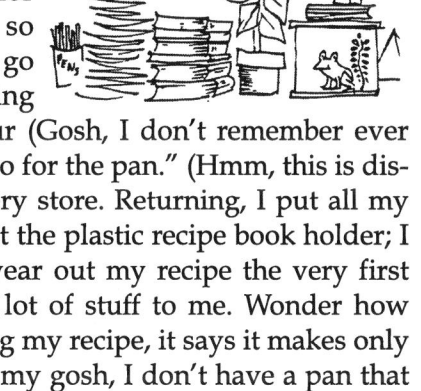

Saturday morning, the big day, I take out my 4-H recipe and read the reminder list at the top for ingredients I'll need (So far, so good). Firmly grasping the list, I go to my cupboards. "Oh, oh, no baking soda, no yeast, no pre-sifted flour (Gosh, I don't remember ever seeing them at the store), no Crisco for the pan." (Hmm, this is disheartening.) Off I go to the grocery store. Returning, I put all my ingredients on the counter, get out the plastic recipe book holder; I don't want to smudge up and wear out my recipe the very first time. (Say, this sure looks like a lot of stuff to me. Wonder how many loaves it makes.) Rechecking my recipe, it says it makes only one (One!) loaf 6" x 4" x 4". (Oh, my gosh, I don't have a pan that size!) Back to the store I go. My Saturday is not going smoothly. (Where is that Barbara, anyway? Easy for her to say!! Where is she when I need her?) Shucks, I'm out of time. I'll have to wait until next Saturday.

Clues: I am struggling! And, I'm looking for help. I don't have the materials I need, time is a problem, there is no recognizable management of anything here.

Level 3—MECHANICAL USE

Sparing my reader the gory details, it is now 10 consecutive Saturdays and eight loaves later (it took two Saturdays to get organized). I now have the ingredients (no trip to the store is necessary); I've gotten the task down to 2 1/2 hours; however, I'm still using the plastic recipe holder to protect the recipe because I still read and reread and reread the recipe each step of the way. I'm also trying to figure out how to speed things up a bit and to ferret out how to eliminate the burning on the bottom (On the top is OK; makes for crunchy crust). Oh, well, finicky is for cats.

Clues: It does happen! The stuff gets mixed up to the correct proportions and it does come out of the oven within the approximate time; however, it's a bit black on the top and bottom. My response: "I can do it, but it's a lot of work and the result doesn't quite match my pictures."

Level 4—ROUTINE USE

At last! I can whip it up in 30 minutes and have mastered the recipe." (I don't have to use the plastic holder anymore; reading it once is enough). And my loaves aren't black on the bottom or the top!! Funny thing though, there is always as much of the loaf left when I get home on Friday as when I left Sunday evening.

Barbara asks how my housemates like the bread. "My housemates?" I ask blankly. "What about them?" (Barbara knows there are three of us at the house.) "Hmm, well, they don't seem to eat much of it, just me, I guess." Barbara asks why. "I don't know; I'll ask." (Barbara knows!) "Maybe they'd like sesame seeds or something on it."

Clues: From my perspective things are going just fine. Little effort is needed to do the job now. But so far I've not thought much about others' responses. As I begin to think about how what I'm doing works for others, I'm brought toe to toe with an important decision, in fact, a critical turning point. From this point forward, am I willing to direct my attention to how my efforts work for those around me? Finally, I decide to find out why others don't eat my bread and commit myself to do something about it.

Level 5—REFINEMENT

So I begin my quest to discover why it is that people in my household don't eat my bread. The information is specific and concrete, i.e., useful but decidedly discouraging. I consider whether it is worth it to me to make the effort to make the changes necessary to have it work better for them. So I ask them, "Well, what if I add sesame seeds or raisins or something like that?" I go back to Barbara (my trusted mentor) and ask her for other (still relatively simple but tasty) recipes I might try. She's delighted (Darn her!). I come home with several that include the special things to meet the finicky tastebuds of my household. Dawns the Saturday. This time, in my foresight, I have acquired the right ingredients. I'm ready. I even risk not using the plastic recipe holder (I'm getting good at this stuff!). In less than two hours and a quarter, wonderful smelling, terrific looking, and wow-tasting bread (two loaves this time) pop from the oven, sporting some new ingredients and experimental toppings. Wow! Tasty bread!

CLUES: I am in pursuit of information about how I can make the bread better for others and I am committed to doing so. Notice that my skill in preparing for the new changes is much more advanced than when I first entered the preparation level. (Almost any change, however seemingly slight, will push one back to earlier levels of implementation but, usually, the trip back to the refinement level goes much more quickly than the first journey.)

Level 6—INTEGRATION/COLLABORATION

Am I pleased and confident! I've worked out all the bugs (forgive the computer language reference) in the recipes Barbara has given me, experimented and even made some changes on my own. But my household is demanding and they want more and better! I become the instigator in setting up a bread baking support group—The International Order of Bread Bakers! We share and share, talk and talk. Our first Recipe Swap Meet is wildly successful (and wild). We are now challenging the time-honored kitchen wisdoms about baking bread. In our collective search for the Better Loaf, we all make significant changes in our individual baking practices.

Clues: Having exhausted my individual resources for adapting my bread baking program, I have gotten together with others to share ideas and solutions. In doing so, I am able to make further changes in my baking to improve the outcome of my labors for the recipients.

Level 7—RENEWAL

After months of collaborating and making changes based on our collective work, we have uncovered a major AH, HA! "There must be a better mousetrap!" My helpful household makes a suggestion: "Forget the bread. How about croissants?" (Oh, no!!!) Visions of my terrible shopping trips, plastic recipe holder, reading, re-reading, and re-re-reading the recipe, and black top and bottom pass before my eyes. I groan out loud. Can I really bear to go back to the level of non-use again and work painstakingly and painfully down through the levels of implementation again? "No, no, no, and NO!" (But I do like croissants!)

CLUES: At this stage I have great skill and expertise in bread baking. I can adapt or make up recipes at will (and are they delicious!). But there is a cloud on the horizon—this just isn't enough anymore. I'm becoming restive. And, yes, bread baking has suddenly become insufficient—there must be something better. I search high and low for the better loaf.

At the later stages of this level, you can easily recognize a dangerous person! Finally, with great relish, I decide to abandon the old bread baking routines and leap into croissant baking. And, if I can convince my fellow international friends of the wonderment of croissants, there will be a whole-lotta' baking going on and the entire bunch of us will go back to the stage of non-use—baking croissants is, after all, a new task. The decision to shift to croissants is a major one, not unlike adoption of a new continuum or new textbook or restructuring the curriculum. However, since there is considerable carryover to some of the related skills and knowledge, this journey will be much easier. Better yet, I have a clear picture (with trained taste buds as well) of what a baker of dough does and needs.

The dog days we complain about are usually times we realize we've gone back to zero in a number of areas. The half-empty glass explanation is that the reform model our school has adopted doesn't work. The half-full glass explanation is that we are making progress but have just added a new element to an instructional strategy that has temporarily taken us back to Level 0.

Also, knowing where you are helps you plan what staff development content you need to move yourself forward. For example, the inservice content should answer these questions:

Level	Content Needs to Address:
0	What's in this for me? What/how would it improve things for students and for me?
1	How does this work? What exactly do I have to do? Convince me that it's a good idea and doable (Where's the support?) Convince me to say, "Yes, I will do this."
2	Having decided to do this, lay it on me! Give me all the details I need—materials, management structures, knowledge and skills, etc.
3	Come coach me. Watch what I do and tell me what to fix/ where I can improve? Why do I seem to be working so hard and getting so little result? Why aren't I getting better results from/with my students?
4	What? Make changes . . . and go back to zero! Convince me that ____ (the "it" you're doing at Level 4) can result in higher outcomes for students and that this would be worth the effort to make these changes.
5	Explain what those changes would be and help me figure out how to do them.
6	Let's get together and share. We need time together.
7	We've exhausted the possibilities of our current approach. We need to search for a better mousetrap. Who/what can help us?

The Levels of Use is an invaluable tool when learning something new or making significant changes in something familiar. It is value free, merely descriptive. It explains our sense of frustration with taking two steps forward and, when things change just a bit, taking one or two steps backward (to orientation or mechanical use).

Group Transition and Change

However extra-ordinary a teacher may be, he/she is only one person. Providing a world-class education to all students requires a concerted and cohesive effort of each and every staff member. No exceptions. Group change requires the transition stage at a group level—going through whatever psychological processes the group as a group must go through to come to terms with the new demands for improving the school—to reinvent the group as a cohesive staff dedicated to working together to create the best possible education for for all students.

This means that the current social groups must dissolve and new groupings committed to getting real work done must be formed. Any serious attempt to implement curriculum models 2-4 require a healthy and productive group environment. You and your colleagues must be willing to apply to yourselves all that you have learned about nurturing collaborative work capacity in your students. Leadership must be revolving, group success is more important than individual ego and social standing. There must be unanimous commitment to doing one's Personal Best when working on the task to be accomplished, etc.

Group change and development must begin with personal and group transitions. Each individual must answer the question, "What must be left behind?" Are there old grudges or slights that must be set aside? Are there lingering resentments about who has played what roles in the past or who got recognition that was not truly deserved? Are there hurt feelings that have never been resolved? Is there anger about events or words that were unfair?

And so forth. If so, transition must occur . . . things need to be left behind, individually and as a group.

Some staff environments are so toxic that an experienced group leader will be needed to help people work through the morass. And not just for one session but on an on-going basis until the environment becomes healthy and productive. Remember, adults can't give to students what they don't themselves have. A healthy and productive group environment is essential.

Know Your Goal—Collegial, not Congenial

As you move through group change, know that your goal is a collegial environment, not a congenial one. This distinction is vital. This professional-social polarization is addressed by Carl Glickman, in his book *Renewing America's Schools: A Guide for School-Based Action*. He describes the dilemma in terms of collegial versus congenial.[10]

"*Congenial* schools are characterized by an open, social climate for adults. Communications are friendly, and teachers, parents, caretakers, and principals easily socialize with one another. Faculty meetings are pleasant, holiday parties are great, refreshments at meetings are plentiful, and faculty members spend time together away from school (aerobics on Thursday night, stress-management workshops. Members describe their school as a nice place where everyone gets along well.

"*Collegial* schools are characterized by purposeful, adult-level interactions focused on the teaching and learning of students. People do not necessarily socialize with one another, but they respect their differences of opinion about education. Mutual professional respect comes from the belief that everyone has the students' interest in mind. The result of such respect is seen in school meetings, where the school community members debate, disagree, and argue before educational decisions are made. Even in the hottest of debates, people's professional respect for others supersedes personal discomfort. People believe that differences will be resolved and that students will benefit. Social satisfaction is a by-product of professional engagement and resolution, of seeing how students benefit, and of the personal regard in which adults hold one another. They become colleagues in the deep sense of being able to work and play together, and each side of the relationship strengthens the other. Being collegial means being willing to move beyond the social facade of communication, to discuss conflicting ideas and issues with candor, sensitivity, and respect. For many schools, the first job is to move from being conventional to being congenial, but the big job for public education is to become collegial, so that social satisfaction is derived mainly from the benefits derived from efforts on behalf of students."

Conventional	Congenial	Collegial
__Isolated	__________Social	__________Professional respect; personal caring as a by-product of work
Individual teacher's autonomy	Individual teacher's autonomy	Collective autonomy
School seen as physical site for work	Pleasant and open climate for adults	Purposeful conflicts, resolution on behalf of students

Paint the Picture for All to See—The Four P's

According to William Bridges, to make a new beginning, people need four things:[11]

- The purpose—each person can explain the basic logic behind what is to be implemented
- The picture—each can see a clear picture of how what to be implemented will look and feel

- The plan—a step-by-step plan for implementing the new thing, how to get started, how to proceed
- A part to play—a role for each person that allows him or her to be part of the phasing in and full implementation of the new thing

This is especially true when the change to be made is a group task, such as implementing the ITI model.

Transitions from old to new can be hastened by helping people shape new, specific behaviors for implementing the new changes. Many ITI teams use the following, or an adaptation of it, to frame their work together.

Expectations for Working Together

Failure to become an effective group has many causes. One of the most common reasons is the group's failure to meet the unspoken needs of individual members. Meeting needs is hard enough when we know about them; it's virtually impossible if they remain unknown.

Use this worksheet to elicit the typically unspoken needs of the group's individual members. Each person completes the form and shares it with the group. For example:

Personal Needs

Purpose:
To make more effective use of my time

Picture:
That everyone arrives on time
& everyone shares the load

Plan:
To make work assignments clear

Part to Play:
To do my Personal Best to complete my tasks as promised and on time

Professional Needs

Purpose:
To improve my groupwork skills
To plan curriculum as quickly as possible

Picture:
To "walk the talk" of the Lifelong Guidelines and LIFESKILLS

Plan:
To divide up the curriculum work to save time and to share ideas (produce the best curriculum)

Part to Play:
To complete the Group Work Tasks form for each task and complete tasks as written

Group Agreements for Specific Work Tasks

Date____________

Name of Project______________________________________

Name______________________________________

- Tasks I agree to do to make this project successful/complete

______________________________________Date__________

______________________________________Date__________

- Research I agree to do and share with my group

______________________________________Date__________

______________________________________Date__________

- Materials I agree to make/bring to help complete this project

______________________________________Date__________

______________________________________Date__________

Lifelong Guidelines/LIFESKILLS we agree to use during our work together: ______________________________________

____

Deadline for project completion: ________________

Questions for Self- and Group-Monitoring

The most difficult aspect of group work is giving feedback to a group member who isn't keeping his/her agreements for group behavior or who is not doing his/her part on group tasks. John Champion, former superintendent, gives us a clean, nonjudgmental, non-confrontation way to bring a member back on board. It is a simple question, one whose exact wording is agreed to in advance:

- We agreed that (identify agreement)__________________.
- I see the following behaviors________________________.
- Help me to understand how these behaviors are consistent with our agreements.

These questions, agreed on in advance, make it more comfortable for group members to confront and be confronted about behavior that is inconsistent with necessary group agreements. Agreeing how to disagree provides a safe environment for working together.

Impact of Temperament

During any transition and efforts to change, it is critical that we remember who we are so that we make the most of our strengths and compensate for our weaknesses. No one needs to be Hercules, no one needs to be an Einstein, but all of us need to be effective team players.

We are not robots, we are not alike, we cannot expect others to think like we do or to value what we do in the same way. Thus, when working in teams to plan curriculum, we must keep in mind our personality preferences/temperament. We recommend that you revisit Chapter 6 frequently, especially pp. 6.1-6—how we take in information and what we value when we make decisions.

Taking in Information. While working with a partner or partners, do recall that, although the end result is the same, "sensors" and "intuitors" go about taking in information very differently. Be patient with each other. One way is not better than another and remember that dual perspectives will produce the best curriculum.

Expect that you will likely choose different starting points. Sensors will likely choose to begin with state standards; intuitors will likely want to begin with the big idea and concepts of the theme. *To resolve these preferences, our advice is that you both agree to start with a physical location.* Go visit it. Then pull forth the state standards and ideas for an organizing concept.

The bottom line is that, no matter what beginning point you might choose, decisions in one area will make you revisit the others. Planning is not linear, one way from beginning to end.

Making Decisions. Deciding what and what not to include in your curriculum is not as easy as it sounds. First of all, there is too much stuff included in state standards and other district-adopted curriculum. Teaching it all to mastery is not possible. Even covering it all is impossible.

Second, each teacher arrives at the table with his/her own set of favorite activities and topics. The LIFESKILL of Flexibility and willingness to compromise is essential.

Understand that "thinkers" are making decisions primarily based on objective, logical considerations about what content best fits in the overlapping area of the Venn circles:

"Feelers," on the other hand, base their decisions primarily on subjective input, perhaps valuing tradition at the school ("the curriculum we've always done before") and empathizing with team mates who agonize over throwing out a favorite unit.

Introvert, Extrovert. No discussion about personality preferences is complete without considering our orientation to others. Extroverts gain energy during committee meetings and think out loud. They are the first to interject a thought while thinking out loud and may be blunt or even offensive.

In contrast, introverts often leave committee meetings feelings drained and unwilling to return. Due to the time necessary to rethink and edit their comments, they often don't get a chance to talk and become frustrated. They may also complain at the ongoing insensitivity of extroverts and their lack of active listening.

Lifestyle. Since much of the work to change a school depends on schoolwide implementation, and similar results by everyone, it is important to stay vigilant about lifestyle—the way we like life to unfold. Those at the "judging" end of the scale—who like organization, closure—may delay implementation until the plan is specific, detailed, and clear. Those on the "perceiving" end of the scale—who just want to get started and often consider waiting for details to be foot dragging—may accuse their colleague of sabotage.

Remember to make plans specific enough for the judgers and beginning dates near enough to convince the perceivers that action will occur.

Honoring and Respecting Each Other

Clearly, a book similar to *Men Are from Mars, Women Are from Venus* could be written here!

In the heat of disagreements and irritations, it's important to remember that two heads are better than one, not just because the collective I.Q. is boosted, but also because perspectives are multiplied. And although pulling together multiple perspectives may be, and usually is, frustrating and time consuming in the short run, it's better in the long run. It will be more thoroughly thought through and will offer students, whose personality preferences differ markedly from their teacher, a curriculum that allows them to be the learners they are.

In the end, everyone wins. But, in the meanwhile, we must remember to honor and respect each others gifts. We strongly recommend that a staff development session be devoted to taking the Keirsey-Bates temperament test and a discussion of what it means for working together. See Appendix A for the reference to *Please Understand Me: Temperament Character intelligence.*

Notes

1 William Bridges, *Managing Transitions: Making the Most of Change* (California: Addison-Wesley Publishing Company, Inc., 1991), 3.

2 Ibid., p. 3.

3 Ibid.

4 Ibid.

5 Ibid,

6 Ibid.

7 Karen.D. Olsen, *Making Bodybrain-Compatible Education a Reality: Coaching for the ITI Model* (Covington, WA: Books for Educators, 1999), 82.

8 Adapted from Gene Hall, et al, by Karen D. Olsen, *The California Mentor Teacher: Owners' Manual* (Covington, WA: Books for Educators, 1999), 68.

9 Olsen, *The California Mentor Teacher Role*, 71-78.

10 Carl Glickman, *Renewing America's Schools: A Guide to School-Based Action* (San Francisco: Jossey-Bass Publishers, 1993), 22-23.

11 Bridges, *Managing Transitions*, 55-60.

Chapter 23: Structural Tools

Our traditional graded system is a bureaucratic device born of administrative convenience. However, if we are to create body-brain-compatible learning environments, we must abandon age-grading, departmentalized, fragmented structures in favor of those that put teachers and students in humane, personal settings. While there are numerous ways to do so, many of which can be combined, the following deserve consideration.

The Year Round School

In the ever-shifting world of synaptic connections, there is one undisputable truth: Use it or lose it. Use those connections that allow us to read, to compute, to name the capitals of each state or to lose them.

During the years when federal programs for low achieving students required fall and spring testing, every Chapter 1 director knew that the subsequent fall test scores of returning students would be lower than those of the previous spring. The students didn't continue using their academic synaptic connections and they were lost. The lesson from this is clear: The students who most need public education are least well served by a long summer break.

Consider changing the school calendar so that every 35-45 days there is a two week break. That's not long enough for students to lose their learning and just long enough for staff to rest up and have some joint planning time and/or inservice training.

The Multi-Graded Classroom

Multi-aged classrooms is certainly not a new idea. In fact, it started as a necessity in sparsely populated areas—the little red school house, grades 1-8 in one room. It's being done now by innovative schools that want to increase the quality and outcomes of learning for their students. It's power to enhance student learning is well documented by John Goodlad in his book *The Multigrade Classroom.* Every educator truly interested in improving student outcomes should read this book.

Co-author Karen Olsen attended a one-room school with grades 1-8, for eight years. From a student perspective there are many advantages. Those she most values as an adult include:

- Learning the skills to be both leaders and followers
- Opportunities to teach others—a benchmark noting progress—which increases one's own understanding. This is in marked contrast to the common perception of low achievers in age-graded structures who always feel inadequate compared to their classmates and rarely get opportunities to see how much they have accomplished. In addition, the ego of the very bright students is held in check as they interact with older students and see what they have yet to learn.

- More one-on-one learning opportunities than are possible when there is only one teacher in the room
- When learning from older, more knowledgeable students, finding out what they used the information for and why they valued it enough to want to pass it on
- Discovering the need for genuine collaboration among all age levels (a simple game of baseball wasn't possible unless the entire student body was on the field)
- Mentors to teach me skills and knowledge in an area of personal interest
- Tolerance of different abilities and interests. As a result of our experiences in school, we expected differences and we respected them. (Could it be that our near phobia of "isms" is an outgrowth of the training in sameness that occurs in our schools? Same age, same books, same instructional processes, etc. Ageism, classism, racism, ethnicism, sexism . . . all are expressions of distrust and fear of differences.)
- Passing through adolescence as if it were no big deal (there were only a handful of us)
- Time and space for small group interactions (because there were older students to serve as leaders and teachers) and for intrapersonal time when we wanted
- Opportunities to do everything—drama, singing, writing for the newspaper, etc., and an expectation that we all could and would try them all
- Lack of stress. What wasn't learned this year would be picked up next year. Intellectual growth spurts didn't have to arrive by a certain month or year.

For the teacher, the advantages were also numerous and powerful:

- A great environment for learning to live, acquiring social skills and personal skills such as the LIFESKILLS
- An effective structure in which to meet individual needs and interests by increasing the number of available teachers, tutors, and mentors
- An effective structure for integrating all subjects and skills (wide range of materials allows all students to study the same unit)
- An easier structure for action-based, project-focused teaching because complex, real-life projects that capture student interest can be readily done with multiple levels of skills and interests
- Makes orchestrating genuine, significant schoolwide and community projects easier because older students can anchor many of the subcommittees
- Lots of opportunities to redirect most potential discipline problems by giving older students leadership responsibilities for significant tasks
- Easy to convey to young learners the use of basic skills and high performance standards (modeled by older students)
- No lost time at the beginning of the year teaching classroom norms and procedures (half to two-thirds of the class already know them and help teach and enforce them on your behalf)

As you might guess, the above lists could go on and on. The significant idea here is that the multigrade structure provides instructional opportunities for teachers and students that just aren't possible in an age-graded setting.

Looping

In the instructional structure called "looping," teachers follow their students from one grade to the next for at least two years (better, three or four) and then loop back to begin again with new students. This structure assists both teachers and students to build a self-sustaining community. It eliminates the need to enter school each fall with the dreaded task of spending the first five to six weeks getting to know each other, assessing academic and social skills, and reviewing the skills and concepts learned the previous year. Instead, teachers and students are free to continue where they left off when school ended the previous year. The practice of looping is used in many schools across the United States and is the accepted practice of ITI teachers in Bratislava, Slovakia, where teachers have the same students from grades one to four and from five to eight.

Leaping

Similar to looping, teachers using the leaping structure follow their students from the last year of middle school into their first year in high school or from the last year of elementary into the first year of middle school. This has all of the benefits of looping plus the added benefit of easing the transition from middle school to traditional high school environment or elementary school to middle school.

Notes to Myself

Appendices

A: Temperament

B: Age Appropriateness

C: Study Trips

D: Communicating with Parents

Appendix A: Temperament

What Makes Us Tick?

When it comes to explaining temperament or personality types, brain research is in its infancy. However, the need to understand and deal with temperament and personality in the classroom is immediate and ongoing and *very* important to life in the classroom. Therefore, until brain research can provide guidance, we continue to recommend that teachers consider the work of psychologist Carl Jung and those who have updated his work and made it a practical tool, especially the teams of Myers-Briggs and, more recently, Keirsey-Bates.*

> **Intelligence**
>
> *"Each person is a unique bundle of relatively stable 'personality traits' overlaid by more temporary emotional states and colored by ever-shifting moods and feelings."*
>
> *William Poole,*
> *The Heart of Healing, 1993*

* This line of work, based in early 20th century observations of behavior, is described by Dr. Robert Sylwester as "essentially oriented around *mind* and not *brain* research." For now, however, it is the most useful information we've found when working with temperament of both students and staff. Easy to understand and apply, it is one more window through which learners can view how they go about learning, yet one more step toward becoming self-directed, lifelong learners.[1]

Temperament types or personality preferences[2] strongly impact the learning process by affecting four important areas:

- How learners take in information
- How they organize during learning and when applying learning
- What they value when making decisions
- How they orient to others

We are born with these temperament types. The place we call home—where we feel most comfortable on each of these four areas of behavior—remains relatively unchanged throughout life.

However, preferences are just that—preferences. They are preferred ways of behaving but one is not stuck at any one place along a scale. To the contrary, anyone can slide along the scales if and when he/she chooses. All it takes is the desire to do so, practice to acquire the skills needed to operate from another point along the continuums, and then willingness to be a bit uncomfortable as we leave "home."

> **Lifelong Traits**
>
> *Although born with these personality preferences, we can learn to shift our behavior along the four temperament scales. This is a critical skill when operating in the real world where things are as they are, not as we'd like them to be.*

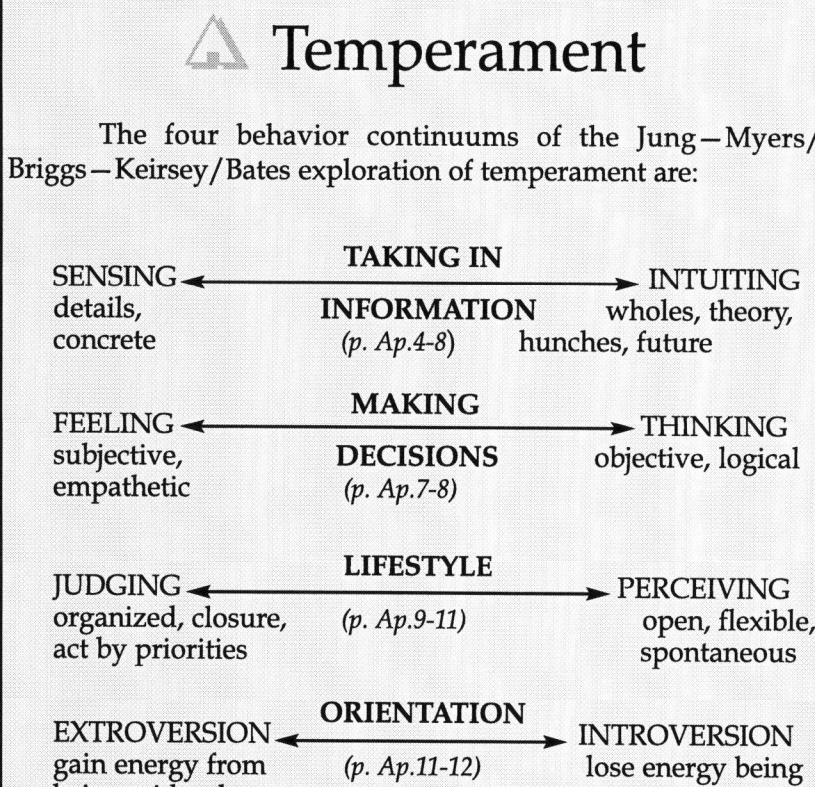

For more information, see *Please Understand Me: Character and Temperament Types* by David Keirsey and Marilyn Bates whose work is based upon that of Carl Jung and the team of Meyers and Briggs. It is an extraordinarily readable, practical book. Give yourself the gift of reading about the self inside, hidden beneath the classroom roles of teacher and student. See also www.keirsey.com. Because temperament theory is used widely in the corporate world, there are numerous magazines and newsletters dedicated to this subject.

Give students, grades three and up, the Keirsey-Bates temperament survey the first week of school. Explain the behaviors typical of the ends of each continuum or scale below plus:

Temperament

The four behavior continuums of the Jung—Myers/Briggs—Keirsey/Bates exploration of temperament are:

TAKING IN INFORMATION *(p. Ap.4-8)*

SENSING ←→ INTUITING
details, concrete — wholes, theory, hunches, future

MAKING DECISIONS *(p. Ap.7-8)*

FEELING ←→ THINKING
subjective, empathetic — objective, logical

LIFESTYLE *(p. Ap.9-11)*

JUDGING ←→ PERCEIVING
organized, closure, act by priorities — open, flexible, spontaneous

ORIENTATION *(p. Ap.11-12)*

EXTROVERSION ←→ INTROVERSION
gain energy from being with others — lose energy being with others

- Where they are on the scales
- Where the members of their Learning Club are on the scales
- That they can learn to slide along the scales when it's important to them to work successfully with another

Taking In Information[3]

Knowing how we and our students take in information is critical both to teaching content and guiding behavior. Differences in this area are at the root of most friction, exasperation and, occasionally, complete inability to get along with family, friends, co-workers, students. Never mind differences in values or interests; if the information we receive isn't what the speaker intended, communication and relationships quickly roll downhill. How we take in information can alter the incoming message, especially if our way of taking in information differs considerably from that of the speaker.

It is important to note that this aspect of temperament describes the internal "wiring" of the mind—*how it works* when it acquires sensory input and munches it about to make meaning of it, to relate it to prior learning, to make it meaningful, to apply it. This is different from the issue of how one acquires information or

TAKE IN

SENSING———————————————**INTUITIVE**

details, concrete — **INFORMATION** — wholes, theory, hunches, future

brings it in from outside. ***At issue here is what the brain does with what it gathers and the form it prefers it in as it does so.***

Sensing

Those who prefer to learn via details and concrete input, called sensors, learn by dealing with what can be seen, heard, touched, or otherwise directly experienced. Figuratively, they're from Missouri, the "show me" state. They learn by gathering details, collecting them one after the other, and fitting them together until they snap into place, into a pattern that makes sense. This is much like putting together a puzzle without knowing what the framework or picture is ahead of time. Most of us are this kind of learner—75 percent of the population.[4]

Sensors on the very end of the continuum need assistance in seeing and applying the big picture—the parts in relationship to the whole and to each other. They often have difficulty dealing with two or more competing ideas or ideas that are not fully compatible. Ambiguity is unsettling to them. Sensors learn best by being allowed to interact with the real world, not textbooks which are an abstraction of the real world and so fragmented that the pieces never add up. The real world helps them see how the pieces fit together.

Intuiting

In contrast, intuitors are sometimes referred to as the "big W" people—*whole notion*. They prefer to begin with the big picture—a framework or theory to give meaning to the pieces. Intuitors want to know the theory or the why behind a thing before they get into the details about it; they work well going from theory to application. They are "what if" people, preferring to deal with the possible rather than the details of the actual; they deal in hunches, the future, and the abstract. Often they are very impatient with details and consider the typical school curriculum quite boring.

It is important to note, however, that the end result for both sensors and intuitors is the same—a full understanding of the concept and the particulars. What differs is the route and, at times, the speed, in reaching the destination. One kind of learner is not smarter than another. Just different.

Why is this discussion about ways of taking in information important? Because it tells us a great deal about how to write curriculum—both key points and inquiries.

Implications for Sensors. Realizing these differences is critically important when designing instructional settings and processes for students to experience in a bodybrain-compatible classroom. When comparing and organizing, the sensor generally tends to work with smaller pieces. At first glance, our traditional curriculum would seem ideal for these students—small pieces for learners who prefer pieces. Unfortunately, the pieces of the curriculum, e.g., 847 skills for reading, are so small that they don't add up, they don't make sense.

SENSORS

Curriculum Development and Instructional Strategies

- Develop key points that are concepts rather than factoids.
- Always teach concepts and skills in the context of real-life uses familiar to students. Focus on the why and the how. Check for understanding of the big picture as you go.
- Revisit your *being there* location numerous times, going more in-depth and more big-picture each time. Focus on how people use the concepts and skills of your curriculum to be intelligent users/participants at that location.
- Lead with inquiries based on the middle levels of Bloom's Taxonomy—application. Then progress to the upper levels—analysis, evaluation, and synthesis. Finish with comprehension and knowledge—the form of most tests.

When information is presented via second-hand sources, which it typically is, perceiving meaning is even harder. Worse yet for the sensor is information presented via symbolic sources; learning becomes nearly impossible for most sensors. It's not surprising to find that, of those students who drop out of school before completing the 8th grade, 99.6 percent of them are sensors.[6] A truly shocking statistic! The typical curriculum does not help the sensor develop the capacity to see how the pieces of the curriculum and their world come together. It fails to give sensors a big picture of what's going on and why it's important—crucial triggers that tell the brain to store something in long-term memory.

Implications for Intuitors. Since most of the curriculum and instructional tools of the traditional classroom are fragmented and piecemeal, intuitors are frustrated and bored much of the time. Extreme intuitors, like the extreme sensor, often act out their frustration. These are the curriculum-induced behavior problem students in our schools—the under achievers, students we know could and should be doing much better than they are.[7]

INTUITORS

Curriculum Development and Instructional Strategies

- Develop key points that are conceptual rather than factoid.
- Always teach concepts and skills in the context of real-life uses familiar to students. Focus on how the theory is applied and the details of how it is done.
- Early in your direct instruction, explain the theory behind what is being studied so that the details make sense and have a post office box in the brain.
- Lead with inquiries based on the middle levels of Bloom's Taxonomy—application. Then progress to the upper levels—analysis, evaluation, and synthesis. Finish program-building practice with comprehension and knowledge—the form of most standardized tests.

Bloom's Taxonomy and How Students Take in Information.

As discussed in Chapter 13, Bloom's taxonomy is a key resource when writing inquiries because it focuses on actions to be taken. Although not truly hierarchical (higher representing "better" thinking), the different levels do require different mixes of "pieces and wholes" thinking—taking in and processing input like a sensor or like an intuitor. Thus, temperament and Bloom's Taxonomy complement each other. When overlaid, they sharpen our understanding of how to help students learn more effectively. The chart below illustrates the nature of pieces-to-wholes mental processing required by curriculum developed at each level of Bloom's Taxonomy: K=knowledge, C=comprehension, AP=application, AN=analysis, E=evaluation, S=synthesis.[5]

TAKE IN

SENSING————————————————INTUITIVE

INFORMATION

K C AP AN E S

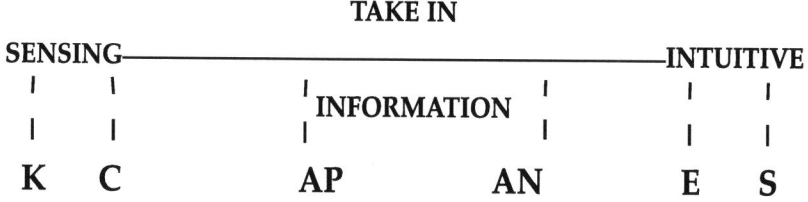

For example, intuitive learners prefer working on inquiries that require them to apply, analyze, evaluate, and synthesize information. They typically find inquiries written for knowledge and comprehension quite boring. Sensors, on the other hand, are often frustrated with inquiries written at the evaluation and synthesis levels and are more comfortable with knowledge and comprehension questions.

Given these differences, we recommend that you begin your curriculum writing and lesson planning with a focus on application. This directs your thinking to how the concept or skill to be taught is demonstrated at the *being there* location and provides a common entry point for both sensors and intuitors.

Our job as teachers is to help students spread their wings to become proficient learners from all kinds of input in all kinds of settings. Further study should challenge both sensors and intuitors, giving all students ample practice in every level of Blooms' Taxonomy and ensuring a mix to enhance their problem-solving/product-producing capabilities as adults. (For a discussion of how to use Bloom's taxonomy in curriculum development, see pages 13.9-10.)

Decision Making [8]

Effective decision-making is a bedrock skill for lifelong learning. Among many important decisions is the recurring "Do I want to learn this, or not?" "Will mastering this concept/skill move me toward my goals?" "What are my goals as a learner?" "What do I want to specialize in when I grow up?" "What's my answer to peer pressure to use drugs?" And on and on.

The decision-making scale described by Keirsey and Bates examines what people value as they perceive and weigh facts, events, circumstances, their own thoughts and feelings, and those of others, to make a decision. Because decision making is a skill so fundamental to success in life, we must give our students the gift of learning about themselves and others.

DECISION

FEELING————————————————**THINKING**

subjective, empathetic **MAKING** objective, logical

Feeling

Those at the feeling end of the scale strongly value *how the decision will affect others,* more so than the logic or principle(s) or the cold, hard facts involved. As a consequence, their decisions tend to be subjective and empathetic. For example, if a "feeling" police officer stopped a car for rolling through a stop sign enroute to the hospital delivery room, he would likely conclude that, under the circumstances, allowing the nervous young father to get the soon-to-be mother in labor to the hospital as quickly as possible was more important than applying the usual consequences for the stop sign infraction. He might even escort them to the hospital.

FEELERS

Curriculum Development and instructional strategies

- Because the willingness to learn is the learner's choice, remember to provide inspirational pep talks when engaging students in new lines of inquiry. Focus on feelings.
- Guide student reflection on how they felt about working together and how successful they were in sliding along the scale to increase the potential for group success. Ask "How did you feel about ______?" kinds of questions. Use reflective thinking questions following collaborative work to focus their attention on what they value when they make decisions and how they felt during the activity.
- When disciplining the feeling student, always point out how his/her actions made the other person feel.
- When studying literature or history or conducting a class meeting, make sure that you point out the emotional issues and themes, the angst of the situation.

Thinking

The "thinking" decision-makers *value the objective, logical elements*. If the principle is x then the choice of y is obvious and not to be distorted by extraneous circumstances or the reactions of the people involved. Thus, a thinking police officer observing the same stop sign infraction would likely conclude that labor pains do not necessarily signal imminent birth and that the safety of others as well as the mother-to-be and child is of paramount importance. The nervous husband should receive a ticket *and* be monitored for several blocks to ensure that he doesn't speed or run another stop sign.

Life in a Bureaucracy. It is not difficult to imagine the reactions of feelers and thinkers making decisions together in our public school bureaucracy which tends to zigzag between extremes and non-action. For example, zero tolerance drug/weapon policies violate the feelers sense of justice when a bystander is swept up in a dragnet because he/she is a friend of one of the offenders and thus was in the wrong place at the wrong time.

On the other hand, thinkers are driven to distraction when the system turns a blind eye to instances of bad behavior because of political pressure, lethargy of individual staff not wanting to bother applying the consequences, or the issues don't show up on the system's radar screen even though it bugs students. Some inconsistencies in decision making are part of human behavior and teacher judgment about individual differences. However, when students participate in pull-out programs and must deal with multiple teachers, all of whom decide procedures and behavior differently, students become frustrated. The solution lies not in having more rules but in opening up the dialogue about the importance of decisions and how each of us weigh the alternatives.

Life in a Learning Club. Collaborative work can really strain relationships if students aren't aware of temperament. For example, thinkers often object when procedures aren't being followed properly. A rule is a rule. Feelers often react to the nature and circumstances of an issue and the perceived fairness, regardless of the rules. Needless to say, groupwork goes much more smoothly for students and teacher if students are taught this information about decision-making early in the year as part of group development and LIFESKILLS.

THINKERS

Curriculum Development and Instructional Strategies

- Because the willingness to learn is the learner's choice/decision, remember to provide convincing arguments and "what if" explorations when engaging students in new lines of inquiry.
- Guide students to reflect on how temperament helped or hindered group work and how successful they were in sliding along the scale to accomplish the task. Ask "What/how well did you think about ______?" kinds of questions. Use reflective thinking questions[9] following collaborative work to focus students' attention on what they value when they make decisions.
- When disciplining the thinking student, always point out the consequences of his/her actions. Ask "what if" questions such as "What if you were Jack and someone did that to you?" "What if Jack had fallen a little harder and broken his arm?" "What would it take for you to control your temper a little bit more?"
- When studying literature or history or conducting a class meeting, make sure that you point out the "what if" questions. For example, what if others had joined in the same behavior, would the society/class/family collapse?

Lifestyle[10]

Lifestyle refers to how people like to organize their lives—not lifestyle as in living high on the hog. On one end of the scale are people who live life by judging—not in the sense of good or bad but rather by decree or judgment, e.g., in Camelot, by decree of the king, it only snows between certain hours during certain months of the year. Camelot is a very orderly, predictable world.

On the other end of the scale are the spontaneous folk who attend to what's happening right now, not five minutes ago, not in response to agreed upon priorities (unless that's what's going on now). These people are open, flexible, and tolerate ambiguity.

LIFESTYLE

JUDGING————————————PERCEIVING

organized, closure, priorities — open, flexible, spontaneous

In any group setting, it is essential to value the qualities on the other end of the lifestyle scale (and anywhere along it). A healthy tension between demand for organization and attention to the events and demands of the moment almost always produces a better result, a better mouse trap, greater learning for students, and better curriculum and instructional programs by teachers.

Judging

The judging person likes a great deal of organization and closure, avoids surprises and ambiguity, and prefers clear priorities. These are the makers (and doers!) of to-do lists, people who set and work toward priorities, and who are adamant about closure and nailing down loose ends. The judging person is the one to announce in a loud voice during a meeting, "Well, what's the decision here? We've wasted 25 minutes and no decision has been made! For heaven's sake, let's stop the jawing and make a decision before more time is wasted!" Ambiguity is intolerable, closure (even if the decision is a bad one) is highly valued. Also, judgers do not like surprises in their world. They plan carefully to make things run smoothly and predictably.

Perceiving

Perceivers, on the other hand, literally perceive their environment *right now,* take in new information, perceive the essence of what's happening now—minute-by-minute and then respond to the "right now" situation. Forget the to-do lists and last week's priorities. The moment is now!

Perceivers are frequently described as open, flexible, spontaneous. And those are the nice words to describe them! Colleagues who are in supervisory or close teaming roles with the perceiver often use other, not-so-kind descriptions! For example, deadline for a perceiver means "It's almost time to start." A loose end, not a problem; it's never too late to rethink an issue or change one's course of action. Ambiguity? No worries. Handle things as they come up; just improvise a little. Got a fire to put out, a crisis to handle? Here is your person! Spontaneity is the hallmark of the perceiver.

Working Together. For the judger and perceiver to work together—as team teachers or as students in a cooperative learning group—is assuredly a strain. For example, imagine traveling together . . . the judging person, in pre-terrorist times, was likely to insist upon arriving at the airport at least an hour in advance, pre-paid ticket with pre-assigned seating designation in hand. In contrast, the perceiver was likely to cut arrival time down to the very last minute—no ticket and, not unlikely, no reservation. He/she was the last passenger to enter the plane, giving a slight leap to clear the widening gap as the jetway was pulling back.

In classroom settings, the perceiving student is an anomaly, a square peg that the highly routinized bureaucracy tries to jam into a round hole. Spontaneity? This is **the** schedule. Flexibility? You may choose the odd-numbered questions for homework or the even-numbered ones. Distracted by the real world outside the window? None of that. Get back to your work.

> ## Lifelong Traits
>
> *Although born with our temperament, we can learn to shift our behavior along the four temperament scales. This is a critical skill when operating in the real world where things are as they are, not as we'd like them.*

Although approximately 38 percent of the general population is an SP personality, a combination of sensing and perceiving, only two percent of teachers are SP types. This means that few SP children will ever have an SP teacher who understands and can appreciate their temperament type.

JUDGERS

Curriculum Development and Instructional Strategies

- Realize that being a judger is innate. Ambiguity and unmade decisions are genuinely unsettling and even upsetting. Judgers appreciate and expect directions to be clear and well thought through. Changing directions makes them uncomfortable.
- Be organized. Have an agenda every day and follow it. When you deviate, do so for a good reason and explain why and how you will handle the change, such as when undone tasks will get finished.
- Develop and use written procedures. When many parts of the day are predictable, judgers can then begin to handle small amounts of ambiguity and develop their tolerance for doing so over time.
- Develop inquiries that are clear and unambiguous about what is to be done and what the final product is to look like.
- Judgers often have their own schemes for organizing and may resist the teacher's method. When possible, invite students to come up with ways of organizing, tackling problem solving or producing a product. However, be watchful for the students who insist there is only one good way to do things. Help those students develop more flexibility, to operate based on the circumstances of the moment rather than on a fixed view of the world.

PERCEIVERS

Curriculum Development and Instructional Strategies

- Realize that the rules and essence of bureaucracy create an especially difficult environment for perceivers. Just getting by from minute-to-minute is a strain. Provide moments of relief through humor, guide bird walks gently back to the topic rather than just interrupting and scolding, allow choices, and most of all, appreciate the differences instead of becoming annoyed by them.
- Realize that being a perceiver is not a temporary disability. It is a personality preference from birth onward and it is part of who that person is. The role of education is to expand students' options in life rather than punish them because who they are is frequently and, to a bureaucracy, fundamentally irritating. Therefore, teach perceivers to use their perceiving tendencies to good advantage and to recognize when those tendencies are a disadvantage and how to slide along the scale when circumstances call for it. Teach them the LIFESKILL of Perseverance and encourage them to take responsibility for completing a final product before moving on to the next thing.
- Ensure that choice is available and then help the perceiver to complete the chosen inquiries/tasks.
- Whenever possible, assign perceivers jobs and inquiries that have some unpredictability to them, that call for flexibility and resourcefulness.

Orientation to Self and Others[11]

Extroversion and introversion are two commonly known qualities. Much of the folk wisdom about them is accurate enough to be useful. Not so well known, however, is the energy flow that occurs.

Extroversion

Extroverts gain energy from being with others. For example, when completely fatigued, extroverts go where there are people such as to a party—arriving early and going home late, returning refreshed and frisky. They literally absorb energy from others. Thus, many introverts find it exhausting to be around a highly extroverted person.

Introversion

Introverts, on the other hand, lose energy when around other people. When tired, a party or any grouping of people is the last place introverts want to go. They instead prefer to go off to a quiet place alone and re-energize from the inside out. It is important to note, however, that introverts can behave like an extrovert. Many introverts can socialize and dramatize along with the best of the extroverts. Many have jobs that require a high degree of extrovertive behavior. However, the energy cost to an introvert for such jobs is very high, the basis of burn-out for many.

EXTROVERTS

Curriculum Development and Instructional Strategies

- As teacher, master the ability to gear up and gear down your energy flow to match that of individual students and groups. Model it for students; teach them how to do it.
- Understand that extroverts think out loud and need talking time to learn. Develop a tolerance for "busy noise" when students are talking yet still on task.
- Make sure you build in group interaction time (even groups of two). Include inquiries that call for group work. Vary the nature of the activities to best fit extroverts at times and introverts at others. For example, a steady diet of cooperative learning assignments is as deadly for introverts as an unvarying lecture is for extroverts.
- Provide quiet time for extroverts to learn to appreciate their own company. Teach them to use their inner voice as a learning partner, to talk themselves through things on their own, especially when solving problems and producing products.

INTROVERTS

Curriculum Development and Instructional Strategies

- As teacher, master the ability to gear up and gear down your energy flow to match that of individual students and groups. Model it for students; teach them how to do it.
- Active learning requires huge amounts of mental energy that can easily be drained away when introverts interact with others. Classrooms that are out of control or that overuse cooperative learning or have lots of conflict (student-student and student-teacher) can become incapacitating for introverts, stealing the energy they need for learning. Use your classroom leadership to create an environment that doesn't rob energy from introverts. Include choices that call for individual work, work in teams of two rather than five, and so forth. Create quiet corners where introverted students can go during the day to reenergize themselves.
- Teach introverts how to participate in groupwork without becoming uncomfortable and drained of energy.
- Make sure you have a balance of introvert-extrovert activities. For introverts, reflection time and journal writing, SSR reading time, individual projects, and working in pairs rather than as a learning club. For extroverts, collaboration, collaboration, collaboration—with as many people as possible!

The Impact of Personality

The impact of personality on school participation and achievement is enormous. We should stop expecting everyone to be like us; we need to begin to understand and appreciate our differences and learn how to make them an asset, rather than an irritant, in the daunting task of succeeding in life.[12]

In addition, we must keep foremost in our minds that powerful learning (greatest depth, speed, ability to apply) occurs when learners are able to operate consistent with their mental wirings. Schools must remold themselves to fit children rather than expect children to change how they learn to fit how schools teach. For example, although 38 percent of the general population are a combination of sensor and perceiver (SP), only two percent of teachers are that temperament type. On the other hand, 56 percent of teachers (compared to only 38 percent in the population at large) are sensor-judgers (SJ).[13] Thus, it is rare for SP students ever to have an SP teacher, someone who understands them. On the other hand, SJ students have many teachers whose temperament matches theirs; school is a relatively comfortable experience for them.

> *We must recommit ourselves to the idea that schools must remold themselves to fit children rather than expect children to change how they learn to fit how schools teach.*

Most shocking of all, 75-90 percent of at-risk students are SP personalities. They are not "drop outs," they are "push outs." The system is simply too structured, too rigid, too boring, too oppressive.[14] While SJ students have less than a four percent chance of drop outs, SP students have a 34 percent chance of dropping out. This means that SP students are nine times as likely to become casualties of the system and for no other reason than their temperament, the temperament they were born with.

Notes

1 Robert Sylwester, Emeritus Professor of Education, University of Oregon. Letter to the authors, August 4, 2003. In the world of brain research, "brain" and "mind" are definitely not interchangeable. Brain research is the stuff of physiology, the biology that can be seen and measured. Mind is explored through observable behaviors.

2 David Keirsey and Marilyn Bates. *Please Understand Me: Character and Temperament Type.* California: Prometheus Nemesis Book Co., 1984. Although an undated version is available, we prefer this book because of its brevity and clarity.

3 Keirsey and Bates, pp. 16-19.

4 Keirsey and Bates, p. 160.

5 Olsen, Karen D. *Making Bodybrain-Compatible Education a Reality: Coaching for the ITI Model.* (Covington, Washington: Books for Educators, 1999), Chapter 7.

6 Keirsey and Bates, p. 160.

7 It's not just the students who "act out" when the curriculum is boring and/or the instructional strategies don't fit how they learn. Think of your colleagues during inservice trainings. Sensors are driven to distraction by theories (which they tend to call "ivory tower notions"). A successful inservice for them is one with a minimum of theory and a maximum of practicality—specifics and step-by-step how-tos.
Intuitors, on the other hand, are often insulted by step-by-step how-tos, especially those that are highly detailed and, to them, obvious once they understand the theory or general principles behind the details. They chafe at presentations that do not give them the theory or framework first and then allow them to figure out the details. It just "doesn't make sense"if they have no frame of reference from which to judge the value or usefulness of the specifics.

The lesson here is that we teach the way we learn but if we want all children to learn from us, we must teach as intuitor **and** sensor.

8 Keirsey and Bates, pp. 20-22. Please note that the use of "feeling" in this discussion does not at all parallel the use of feeling and emotion used in brain research, such as in the work of Antonio Damasio and others examining the emotional system of the brain.

9 Students cannot become self-directed learners until they master the art of reflective thinking, reflecting not only on things after the fact (learning from what they have just done) but also anticipating what is to come (applying previous experiences to the task at hand).

Feelers must learn to keep in mind the facts and the outcomes, not just feelings during the process. Thinkers must learn to keep in mind how people around them feel about the process of an activity and how they feel about the outcome.

Good leaders keep track of both, which enables them to lead a wide spectrum of people, not just those like themselves. While most areas of leadership capability seem to be unconscious, this area can become conscious and thus utilized by students (and adults) on a minute-by-minute basis until it becomes a habit of mind.

10 Keirsey and Bates, pp. 22-24.

11 Keirsey and Bates, pp. 14-16.

12 Keirsey and Bates, p. 97.

13 Keirsey and Bates, p. 160.

14 Karen Olsen, An unpublished, study-based survey of more than 100 district administrators in California responsible for reporting and combatting their district's dropout rate, 1985.

Appendix B: Age Appropriateness

Age-Appropriateness

A young child's brain is not just a "junior" version of the adult brain, an adult brain with less information in it. It processes differently. The human brain unfolds in predictable developmental stages. Each stage is like an ever more complex template laid over the top of the previous one. At each of these stages, the brain is capable of more complex thinking, comparing, and analyzing. Incoming information that requires a level of processing not yet acquired by the brain results in lack of understanding, inability to "get it." When things are "ungettable," students give up and resort to memorization. Over time, when too many things are "ungettable," students slowly learn not to try to understand but merely to memorize and parrot back.

This is a serious issue because it undermines the student's confidence in self as a learner as well as teachers' expectations for student outcomes. Worse, it absolutely kills the joy of learning.

Following is a brief overview of developmental stages based on the work of Larry Lowery, as reflected in presentations to administrators and teachers of the Mid-California Science Improvement Program (MCSIP) and in his book, *Thinking and Learning: Matching Developmental Stages with Curriculum and Instruction.**

* Used with written permission of the publisher, Books for Educators.

Age Three to First Grade:

Comparing the Known to the Unknown

During this stage of life, children learn to understand more words (and the concepts behind them) than they will for the rest of their lives. The child does this through one-to-one correspondences, putting two objects together on the basis of a single property and learning from these comparisons more than was known before. According to Lowery, the child constructs fundamental concepts about the physical world and its properties (similarity and difference comparisons based on size, shape, color, texture, etc.), about ordinal and cardinal numbers (one-to-one correspondence of varying degrees), about all measures (comparison of known to unknown), and about the use of symbols to stand for meaning (word recognitions).[1]

The major mode of operation at this stage is trial and error. Often, adults mistakenly try to "help" the child in an attempt to reduce or eliminate error or reprimand the child for making an error. This is unfortunate, because the important point here is that the child learns from the situation in either case—erroneous or correct. Whether putting puzzle shapes into the wrong space, learning to dress oneself and getting the shoes on the wrong feet, or falling off a tricycle. For the child, a "no" provides as much information as a "yes."

An important characteristic of this stage is that the child does not yet have the ability to group objects using more than one property simultaneously.[2] For example, pairings made on the basis of size, color, shape, texture, speed, using one property or characteristic to pair them. The three- to six-year-old may also arrange objects by chaining, i.e., the third object in the chain shares an important characteristic with the second object (which was initially chosen to pair with the first object) based on a different characteristic:

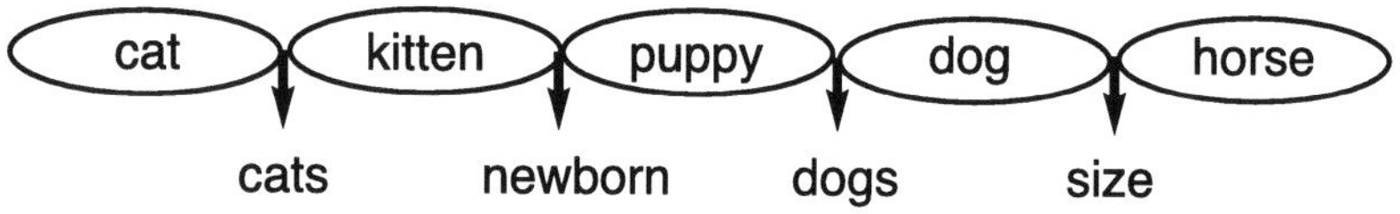

This stage is variously described as: ability to put two objects together on the basis of a single property[3] or learning by one-to-one correspondence. Piaget's description: *pre-operational stage.*

If you take the time to put this information to use and analyze your district's scope and sequence or current textbooks, you're in for a genuine shock and complete surprise. You will find that there is a high percentage of material that is wholly inappropriate. Examples of age-inappropriate topics from a popular, state-adopted science textbook for first grade include: earth as it looks from space, landforms around the world, how water shapes the land, air, and much more!

Second Grade to Third Grade:

Putting Things Together, Taking Things Apart

At this stage a child develops the capability to group all objects in a set on the basis of one common attribute (as compared to putting only two objects together on the basis of a single property). This capacity begins at about age six (late) and is established for most youngsters by age eight.

According to Lowery, "for the first time the student's mental construct is comprehensive and has a rationale or logic to it. . . . Simple rules can be understood and generated by the student if given the opportunity."[4]

At this stage students do less trial and error exploration and are more thoughtful about the actions they impose upon their environment; they create an internal mental structure of those manipulations.[5] An important aspect of students' actions is the rearrangement of the materials with which they work. Students also have the capacity to do things in reverse direction without distorting the concept, e.g., 3 + 2 = 5; 5 - 2 = 3. This is one of the powerful aspects of thinking at this stage.[6]

From an adult's perspective, there is a correct and an incorrect way to put things together or take them apart; the child at variance is thus seen as having done the job "incorrectly." Rather than just judging the task, however, adults should also examine the reason why the student chose that particular response and then focus on the quality of the understanding that is revealed in the answers given.

This stage is variously described as: ability to put all objects together on the basis of a consistent, single property rationale or putting things together and returning things to the way they were.[7] Piaget's term: early concrete operations.

Again, examples of age-inappropriate content from a popular science textbook include the following. For second graders: prehistoric animals and climate changes creating extinction, matter, magnets, light waves, heat transfer, air and air in water, rotation of the earth. For third graders: photosynthesis, particles in matter, changes in matter, forces (gravity, magnetism), energy (work, earth core, earthquakes), forces which shape the land (weathering, water, wind), tilt of the earth produces weather changes, and the solar system. Such topics require an ability to think abstractly which is not possible until the pre-frontal lobes are developed.

Fourth Grade to Sixth Grade:

Simultaneous Ideas

At about age eight to ten, children develop the capacity to mentally coordinate two or more properties or concepts at a time. According to Lowery, when this capacity is in place—which may occur as early as age eight or as late as age ten—students can comprehend place value in math, the need for controlling variables in a science experiment, the use of similes and multiple themes in literature, and can begin to understand the relationships that exist in free trade in social studies.[8] According to Lowery, "as with earlier capabilities, this new one integrates with those preceding it much like a new map of greater abstraction that can be overlaid upon other layers of maps."[9]

At this stage, students enjoy puns and can easily learn about homonyms. In their writing they shift to using multiple descriptors: "an old, bent, tired man." They shift from trial and error thinking to contemplating the effects of comparing two or more situations under different situations.[10] Arrangement of objects now indicates the intersection of multiple properties.

Piaget refers to this stage as late concrete operations; Lowery's term is simultaneity of ideas.

Examples of age-inappropriate content from the same popular science textbook (distributed 1985) are mind boggling. For fourth grade: heat as particle activity, how fossils are formed, ocean floor, causes of tides, ocean currents around the world. For fifth grade: atoms, elements, compounds, molecules, chemical bonding; nuclear fusion; light energy waves; and many other topics which should be moved to junior and senior high. For sixth grade: virtually all areas should be moved to junior and mostly senior high levels.

The irony here is that, for all of America's glorification of youth and childhood, our traditional school curriculum treats elementary students as young adults. Yet for our young adults—high school students—the curriculum for the non-college bound is a rerun of what students were given in elementary school and, thus, is unchallenging and often boring.

So, what does all this mean for an ITI classroom? It means that the closer the curriculum is to the real world, the more likely it will be age-appropriate rather than abstract and calling for mental processing students don't yet possess.

Note: The idea of age-appropriateness is certainly not new. Montessori, Piaget, and countless others have addressed the issue quite clearly. Yet, it just gets pushed aside by tradition when textbooks and state frameworks are being created. A glance through textbooks from the past several decades shows tradition at its most mindless and blind adherence to "the way we've always done it."

The purpose of looking at what is appropriate at each age level is to make thoughtful decisions for less is more. Notice, in particular, the age at which each capacity comes into place. And bear in mind that there will be some students on both ends of each predicted age group. If the mental scaffolding doesn't exist for learning a particular concept, content must be changed to match the stage of intellectual development of individual students. Because some students can understand something doesn't mean that all students at that age can, nor does it mean that such students are less capable.

Notes

1 Lawrence F. Lowery, Thinking and Learning: Matching Developmental Stages with Curriculum and Instruction, (Covington, WA: Books for Educators, 1993), p. 2.

2 Lowery, op. cit., p. 20.

3 Lowery, op. cit., p. 18.

4 Lowery, op. cit., p. 31.

5 Lowery, op. cit., p. 33.

6 Lowery, op. cit., p. 34.

7 Lowery, op. cit., p. 36.

8 Lowery, op. cit., p. 41.

9 Lowery, op. cit., p. 37.

10Lowery, op. cit., p. 41.

Appendix C: Organizing Study Trips

Getting the Most Out of Your Being There Study Trips[1]

Being there study trips are a powerful way to introduce curriculum because they provide a full sensory input to the brain, create an emotional experience, and provide real-world application of concepts and skills. Through a combination of exploration (individual and group) and mediation[2] (guided tour with interpretation), they level the playing field, giving students with no prior experience an opportunity to catch up with more advantaged peers. Study trips are a key strategy in applying brain research to the classroom; therefore, they are not to be used as rewards, nor should students be left behind as a punishment.

To ensure that your *being there* visitation is more than a motivational tool or fun fling, you need detailed planning and a range of instructional strategies not called for when relying on textbooks and worksheets.

Begin Before You Start

A successful study trip to a *being there* location starts before you leave the classroom. Make sure you have completed the curriculum planning work outlined in Chapter 12 before you begin planning the study trip. As you plan your study trip, keep in mind these two questions as you proceed:

- What do people (workers and visitors) need to know and be able to do at this location in order to work at/use this site effectively?
- What are the most important concepts and skills from my curriculum standards that describe what people need to know and be able to do at this site?

Preplanning

Although logistics and paperwork may not make the heart sing, they do help ensure that your study trip goes off without a hitch. Complete several weeks before the study trip:

- Once the site has been chosen, get permission from your principal and district office. Inform the students and parents well in advance.
- Visit the study trip location to finalize what you want the person (tour guide, docent, store manager, etc.) to explain/show your students. Give him/her a copy of the Lifelong Guidelines and LIFESKILLS and your concept and key points.

- As you tour the site together, be clear what you want him/her to focus on with your students. Often tour guides have their own agenda and want guests to see or tour parts of the site that are not applicable to your concept/key points. Don't go there! Insist that he/she stick to your concept/key points. You are not asking for the usual tour. Leave other content for later trips.

- Meet the tour guide; share your on-site inquiries and ask for ways to improve them. If possible, also share your follow-up inquiries, especially the social/political action inquiries. Get feedback on their accuracy and appropriateness. Send the final version of the inquiries to the guide before you arrive with students.

- Ask the guide if it is possible to break the students into smaller groups. One with the guide, the other with you (or another guide) for exploration. (It is almost impossible to hear and stay on task when standing in the back of a pack of 25+ students.)

- Fill out the necessary paperwork to request a bus.

- Find out about procedures for bus drop off, parking, and pick up.

- Meet with the person in charge of students' medication (school nurse or school secretary). Know clearly who gets what, when, and how to dispense them on the trip. Do not delegate this job; keep this responsibility yourself.

- Organize materials and emergency plans.

- Assemble your clipboard and have it ready to pick up as you board the bus. Information, in addition to what you give students and chaperones for their clipboards, should include:
  ~ Class list and emergency numbers for school and parents
  ~ Student allergies
  ~ Schedule for site and contact person's phone number
  ~ Bus garage phone number
  ~ Notes about the site from your pre-visit
  ~ Blank paper for questions and notes

- Prepare content and logistics for a parent training.

Training Chaperones

Hopefully this is not the first training you have done for parents because it's best to begin training them on how to help out in your classroom and go on study trips the first week of school. Offer the training several times on different days and times, such as after school, evenings, or even a Saturday morning.

If you cannot get enough parents, recruit qualified candidates wherever you can find them, college students, grandparents, neighbors, friends, classroom aides from other classrooms, etc.

Areas to cover during the training include:

- Confidentiality—after the trip, do not talk about students, parents, or other chaperones or what you may have heard them say.

- Role—they are here to **coach** students, to ask questions rather than give answers. Tell them they can answer questions only with a question. For example:
  ~ What do you think?
  ~ How could you find the answer to that question?
  ~ What do you see or notice that is different or the same?

~ What do you hear, smell?

~ What is that like?

~ Why do you ask that?

~ Does anyone know the answer to that?

~ Good question. Let's write that down and we will ask the tour guide or the teacher.

- Expectations—chaperones should expect students and other adults to behave in accordance with the Lifelong Guidelines and LIFESKILLS. Remind them that this study trip is not a reward but a serious and central piece to the curriculum of the classroom. (This might be a good time to share some brain research information with them.) Give parents a copy of any additional behavior guidelines and procedures for this particular study trip.
- Target talk—describe how to use target talk to guide and support students.
- Curriculum—explain what students will be studying. Give them copies of the concept/key points. Also give them copies of all assignments—blank and completed—so that the parents have the answers in advance and feel confident about the content students are to learn.
- Procedures—go over the procedures for the study trip. Remember, most parents have only experienced trips for fun; they need to develop a new mental program for what an ITI *being there* study trip is. Typical procedures for all chaperones include:

1. Arrive 30 minutes before the trip to be trained, review procedures for the trip, and learn about any last-minute changes.
2. Keep ALL of your students with you at all times; if one has to go to the bathroom, you all go together, including you the parents!
3. Don't purchase anything for the students, including food, trinkets, or souvenirs.
4. Don't bring any children/students not enrolled in the class.
5. Work with your assigned group only; do not join up with another group so the adults can chat. Students have been placed in small groups for a reason—the opportunity to communicate with you.
6. Don't smoke, eat, or drink (even coffee.) You may have a student snack when the students have theirs (if one is provided).
7. Sit with your student group on the bus.
8. Bring the fanny pack or backpack and materials provided by the teacher (see list that follows). Don't hesitate to contact the teacher in person or via cell phone (in your pack) if you need to. If students are not using the Lifelong Guidelines/LIFESKILLS or you have an emergency, let the teacher know ASAP.
9. Be on time. Know the time you are to meet with tour guides and the time and sites for any rendezvous during the tour and for departure.
10. Have fun! Enjoy the opportunity to spend some time with your son or daughter and his/her friends.

Equipment for Chaperones. Equip your chaperones with the tools and supplies they might need. These items help make their responsibilities concrete and give them confidence that they can handle the job. Ask a local store or other business to provide fanny- or backpacks for the chaperones. This is an opportunity for local businesses to offer support in a tangible way. Get one for each chaperone (about six).

Include the following items in the packs:

- Cell phone (borrow from teachers, parents, friends, etc., so that every chaperone has one)

- Your teacher's cell phone number
- Kleenex tissue
- Band-aids
- Rubber/latex gloves
- Extra pens/pencils
- Camera (optional)
- A clipboard with the same contents as the students' clipboards plus the following:
  - ~ Procedures and responsibilities for chaperones
  - ~ Names of students in his/her group
  - ~ Times his/her group is to meet with the tour guide, for departure, etc.
  - ~ Filled-in version of student worksheets

Preparing Your Students

Prepare your students for the *being there* location they are about to visit. Tell them where they will be going and explain why you have chosen this site and how it relates to the curriculum. This does not mean that all the content must be taught before they go; that is an old picture of "field trips." Prepare them by:

- Explaining what they are going to see and how it fits in with what they will be studying—the theme on the wall
- Brainstorming the questions they want to ask of those who work at and use the location
- Engaging them in a discussion of the Lifelong Guidelines and LIFESKILLS they will need to use
- Inviting students to help you write procedures for all to follow
- Creating a bus trip assignment that students will do when going to and returning from the site. Relate these to what students will be studying on site; explain it thoroughly so they know what to do without having to ask a lot of questions once on the bus
- Asking them to predict what they think they might see at such a *being there* location; keep these responses so that students can test these assumptions when they return

Equipment for Students. Each student should have a clipboard that includes the following items:

- Pencil attached with a string
- Lifelong Guidelines and LIFESKILLS laminated and taped to the back of the clipboard
- Procedures for the bus and when at the *being there* location
- Assignments for the bus (to and from) and on site
- Blank paper for recording questions and illustrations
- Names of the chaperones

The Day Before the Study Trip

The day before the study trip, double-check your arrangements:

- Review your procedures.
- Call the site to confirm the visit time and your expectations for the tour.
- Call the bus garage to confirm when the bus will arrive at school for departure and when it will return to the school after the study trip.
- Call the chaperones to confirm their assignment and the time they are to arrive. Remind them how important it is that they are on time.

- Form student groups (about 4-5 students per parent/ adult chaperone). Unless there is an overriding reason for not doing so, keep students in their Learning Clubs.
- Assign a chaperone to each group. Invite student input; some students do and some do not want their parent as a chaperone for their group.
[Note: Do NOT assign yourself as a chaperone for a group; you need to be the leader of the total group. Your job is to ensure that each group functions well to maximize learning and to be available to handle an illness, accident, or difficulty a student or chaperone might have.]
- If you do not have an active parent group to act as chaperones on a study trip, consider asking local businesses if they would allow their employees to volunteer. You could also ask grandparents, senior citizens, or even the teacher aides from other classrooms. Remember, you need one chaperone per Learning Club.

30 Minutes Before the Study Trip

Just before getting on the bus, meet with parents and with students to review expectations and duties.

With Chaperones. Review the important points with parents. This serves both as a reminder and as a confidence booster. Review the following:

- Standard procedures
- Student assignments (on the bus and at the site)
- How to use target talk for the Lifelong Guidelines and LIFESKILLS
- Any questions about the trip or curriculum content
- The contents of the chaperone backpack

Have chaperones come to the classroom (stand at the back of the room) during your final review with students.

With Students. Before leaving for the bus:

- Introduce the chaperones.
- Review the site procedures (use chart)—
  - ~ Use the Lifelong Guidelines and LIFESKILLS
  - ~ Focus on the LIFESKILL of Curiosity
  - ~ Stay with your group and follow the directions of your group's chaperone
  - ~ Represent yourself and your school in a positive way.
- Hand out the study trip clipboard.
- Answer any questions about what's to be studied.
- Make a final count of the total number of students going on the trip. Have each chaperone count—and remember!—the number of students in his/her group. Have each chaperone say out loud to the class how many students are in his/her group; as they do so, add the numbers on the board to make sure they equal the count for the total class.

For Yourself. Don't forget *your* clipboard as you board the bus! And, make sure you count the students as they board.

The Bus Trip

Don't allow bus time to deteriorate into a bus driver's nightmare. Once students lose their focus, it is harder to refocus them when you arrive at the *being there* site.

Here are some suggestions for setting up expectations for travel to and from the *being there* site:

Getting on the Bus

Start off on the right foot.

- Introduce the bus driver by name and tell students about the Lifelong Guidelines and LIFESKILLS the bus driver will be using to drive them safely to the *being there* location.
- Introduce the chaperones to the bus driver.
- Review the bus procedures (use chart).
  - ~ Sit with someone from your Learning Club (if uneven numbers, sit with your group's chaperone). Sit as near to your chaperone as possible.
  - ~ Stay in your seat.
  - ~ Talk quietly with your seat mate.
  - ~ Use the Lifelong Guideline of Active Listening and the LIFESKILL of Responsibility at all times.
  - ~ Do the bus assignment with your seat partner.
- Review the bus assignment and answer questions about how to complete it.
- Count students (and chaperones!) twice—once using a total student count and once asking each chaperone to give a count of the students in his/her group.

Traveling To the Site

Give students an assignment(s) that will last the length of the drive. This forces students to direct their attention to the world outside the bus and bridges your pre-departure orientation and the visitation. Make sure that the assignment relates to the site to be visited.

Here are some examples for bus time activities while traveling to the site:

- Reading through the field guide and developing at least three questions to ask the guide (the field guide must be developed in advance).
- A visual scavenger hunt for items that students think can also be found at the site.
- A variation of an acrostic (a series of lines or verses in which the first, last, or other particular letters when taken in order spell out a word, phrase, etc.) For example:

  L — lake, laundromat, ladies' restroom

  A — aquatic center, airport, arena, airplane

  N — nursery, neighborhood

  D — dog, donut shop

  F — factory, fence

  I — ice, inlet, iron, ice cream parlor

  L — light, leaf

  L — lawn, lip

~ List and tally items for an acrostic based on the name of the *being there* location.

~ List and tally names for an acrostic based on commercial signs or a key concept to be studied at the *being there* location.

~ List and tally names for an acrostic based on a category of items chosen by students (the acrostic must be based on the name of a concept to be studied at the *being there* location).

Returning from the Site

Make sure you have everyone—students and adults! Count students (and chaperones!) twice—once using a total student count and once asking each chaperone to give a count of the students in his/her group. Then, don't lose momentum. Again have an assignment(s) that lasts the duration of the bus drive. This time, have them look for examples of something they learned at the *being there* site. Examples include:

- Sit with a member of your Learning Club. Review your notes in your field guide. Complete writing down your findings. Compare notes with your partner. Add any information that he/she gathered that you did not. If you have any blank spaces, discuss with someone sitting across the aisle from you to add to your notes. Complete all items in the study guide.
- With your partner, list the Lifelong Guidelines and LIFESKILLS your bus driver used on this trip. Write an Acknowledgment thanking him/her for supporting your study trip. Be specific. Give your note to the bus driver as you get off the bus. Also tell him/her thank you in person.
- With your partner, write a thank you note to your chaperone. Be sure to mention specifically what you most appreciated about his/her support during the *being there* visit.
- As you exit the bus, check for belongings.

Teacher Roles/Responsibilities On Site

- Organize the groups. Make sure each chaperone has collected his/her students and they are ready to begin. Check that chaperones and students have their clipboards with them. Make sure each chaperone has his/her backpack.
- Touch base with each group at least once during the trip. Check on the chaperone and provide needed assistance and support. Offer expertise.
- Check on target kids.
- Keep the tour guide on target (time and content).
- Point out Lifelong Guidelines/LIFESKILLS as they occur.
- Provide a time for snacks, drinks, and bathroom breaks.
- Report any accidents to the manager at the site and, on your return, to your principal.
- Follow time schedule.

After the Study Trip

To make sure that you squeeze every ounce of value from your study trip, don't pass up an opportunity to have students review in their minds what they experienced.

On Your Return

This is a chance to demonstrate the LIFESKILLS of Organization and Initiative for your students.

- As students reenter the classroom, have them remove their papers from the study trip clipboards and put them on their desks. Then, have them sharpen the clipboard pencils and put the clipboards back in the box ready for the next study trip.

- Brainstorm things about the tour guide that you most appreciated learning. If possible, include chaperones in this activity. Have students write personal thank you notes to the guide(s), chaperones, and/or bus drivers.

While the experience is still fresh in their minds (students and chaperones), debrief the *being there* experience.

- What did they learn? What most impressed/surprised them? What did they learn that they can use this week in the classroom? Outside of school? What did they learn about the concept being studied?
- How did the procedures work? Should any changes be made before the next *being there* study trip?
- What were the highlights, surprises, disappointments? If we were to do the same study trip again, what changes would we make? And so forth. Preface the discussion with the request that people (students and chaperones) use the Lifelong Guideline of Truthfulness and the LIFESKILLS, including Caring.

Follow-Up Strategies

To carry the momentum of student enthusiasm from the *being there* experience back into the classroom, choose your most engaging instructional strategies:

- Bring in resource people to further explain what they do at the *being there* site and why it is important.
- Base your direct instruction on examples from the common experience of the study trip.
- Involve students in role-playing activities so they can explore why the concepts and skills of your curriculum are important and how and when they might use them.
- Engage students in both structured and unstructured discussion.
- Structure Discovery Processes that will carry them deeper into the concepts.
- Invite students to select and pursue their own independent study which extends and deepens the concepts and skills of the curriculum.
- Revisit the site.

Notes

1 These recommendations for planning and conducting a study trip are adapted from the work of Linda Jordan and Sue Pearson, associates of Susan Kovalik & Associates.

2 As most teachers already know, students may or may not come away from a study trip having learned what the teacher intended. Mediation—structuring what students focus on, process, and practice using—is essential.

Appendix D: Communicating with Parents

Communicating with Parents

Communication with parents and guardians is a completely understated, largely overlooked opportunity for teachers, yet it is one of our most powerful sources of support. Introduce yourself to your parents even before school starts. Let them know that your classroom will be a special experience for their child. Don't wait for the traditional Back-to-School Night in October; it is entirely too late in the fall to serve as a tool for creating an anticipatory set.

Welcome Letter to Students

Begin by sending a letter to their child welcoming him/her to your classroom. In this letter include a personal greeting expressing that you're looking forward to meeting him/her, your commitment to making this year the best ever, and an outline of your plans for the year—the *being there* experiences, the theme, and why you're excited about the year. Also include a request that the child invite his/her parents/guardians to attend a Back to School night held the very first week of school—Thursday night.

Back to School Night

If the first week seems too soon, consider this reality: substitute teachers have less than 60 seconds to establish themselves with students. Four days is more than enough to capture your students' attention and hearts. And, the sooner you communicate with parents, the less time for assumptions or misunderstandings. Your ITI program may be new and different from what they have known in the past, so capture their attention and spread your enthusiasm in the same way you do with your students. Remember, parents are the first and foremost teachers in the children's lives.

At Back to School night, provide a comprehensive information packet such as the one described here. For parents/guardians unable to attend, send the packet home with their child the next day.

Dear Parents/Guardians,

The ITI model (Integrated Thematic Instruction) is an innovative and proven method of implementing in the classroom what we know from current brain research. It also integrates skills and content in real-life ways.

The following pages will introduce you to many of the concepts, terms, and resources which will be used in your child's classroom this year. I am looking forward to working with you to create an extraordinary year for your child.

CONTENTS OF THE PARENT INFORMATION PACKET

1. Recommended Books
2. A Week in the Life of My Child
3. The Power of Emotion in Learning and Performance
4. Lifelong Guidelines/LIFESKILLS
5. Food and its Effects on Learning
6. Yearlong Theme
7. Public Library
8. Research Project
9. Mindmapping
10. Homework
11. Letter to Parents
12. Possible Family Study Trips (aka Study Adventures)
13. Contacting the Teacher

1. Recommended Books for Parents to Read

Character Begins at Home: Family Tools for Teaching Character at Home by Karen D. Olsen and Sue Pearson.

Simple, enjoyable activities with hundreds of ideas for nurturing character through the Lifelong Guidelines and LIFESKILLS. Understanding a common language at home and at school helps children develop the social skills of respect and responsible citizenship.

Human Brain and Human Learning by Leslie Hart.

The most significant book on "brain-compatible" education (a term coined by this author). His examples of how learning goes astray inside schools will remind all readers of their own experiences as children. This is the foundation book for Integrated Thematic Instruction, which is based on brain-compatible learning.

Seven Kinds of Smarts: Identifying and Developing Your Many Intelligences by Thomas Armstrong.

Armstrong, a leader in translating the multiple intelligences into practical applications at school and home, provides a clear, understandable overview of the theory of multiple intelligences, as well as a 40-item assessment inventory, and everyday examples.

Punished By Rewards: The Trouble with Gold Stars, Incentive Plans, A's, Praise, & Other Bribes by Alfie Kohn

The more we use artificial inducements to motivate children, the more they lose interest in what we're bribing them to do. Offer practical strategies for parents to minimize bribing children to do a job.

The Over-Scheduled Child by Alvin Rosenfeld and Nicole Wise

This book provides choices to the nonstop pressures of overscheduling academic, social, and athletics. The authors offer clear steps to attack this rampant phenomenon of micromanaging every detail of a child's life, thereby encouraging healthier and happier children, and revitalizing the parenting experience.

The Ritalin Nation: Transformation of Human Consciousness by Richard DeGrandpre

The author attributes the disturbing prevalence of inattention and hyperactivity in children to the larger psychological consequences of living in a rapid-fire culture. Practical guidelines for charting a hopeful future and moving away from sensory addiction.

Magic Trees of the Mind: How to Nurture Your Child's Intelligence, Creativity, and Healthy Emotions from Birth Through Adolescence by Marion Diamond and Janet Hopson

Interaction with resources, new experiences, and rich sensory input greatly affects learning. This fascinating book explains how parents and teachers are literally building children's brains.

Boys and Girls Learn Differently by Michael Gurian.

An explanation of how learning is affected by the fundamental differences between boys and girls–and what can be done about it. Provides information on brain development, strategies, and tips beginning with preschool through high school.

Teaching Children to Love by Doc Lew Childre.

This book provides a wide range of 80 games and fun activities for developing emotional intelligence while increasing learning performance. Helps children make positive and wise choices.

Kid's Guide to Working Out Conflicts by Naomi Drew, MA.

This tremendous resource tells how to keep cool, stay safe, and get along by taking a closer look at common forms of conflict, reasons behind them, and positive ways to handle tough situations. Offers tips for countering bullying and dealing with difficult people.

Homework and Kids by William Haggart and Christine Juhasz.

This wonderful parent's guide helps to identify how each child learns by discovering their learning styles. You can ensure their success by guiding them through new approaches for completing homework assignments and gaining knowledge.

2. A Week in the Life of My Child

The grid on the next page is for recording the activities of your child for one week. This is useful for you and your child so that you can get a picture of your child's "education" when outside of school. Remember, you are your child's first teacher. Seeing exactly where and on what your child spends his/her time is the beginning step in examining how you might play a more powerful supportive role with your child this year. Also, I would be happy to discuss your child's schedule with you and its possible impact on your child's learning.

The time chart is broken into four sections to help you capture a full 24-hour day overview of seven consecutive days. Record the adult and peer influences your child experiences each day. How much support time are you able to give your child. The more detailed your information, the more valuable it will be.

3. Current Brain Research

The ITI model is based upon the findings of brain research from the past 25 years. Gleaned from many fields and supported by research made possible by high tech instruments such as CAT scans, PET scans, MRI, and fMRI, we can now literally watch a brain in action. For 25 years, the research has provided very consistent findings which are summarized in the ITI model as:

- Intelligence is a function of experiences which cause physiological growth in the brain. Genetics plays a lesser role than generally believed and high levels of sensory input is more important than usually recognized.
- Learning is the result of an inseparable partnership of brain and body. Emotion is the gatekeeper to learning

	Monday	Tuesday	Wednesday	Thursday	Friday	Saturday	Sunday
BEFORE SCHOOL							
AT SCHOOL							
AFTER SCHOOL							
AFTER DINNER							

and performance and movement is key to optimal brain function.

- We have at least seven intelligences. An intelligence is defined as a problem-solving and/or product-producing capability. Each of the intelligences functions from a different part of the brain.
- The brain extracts and creates meaning through a pattern-seeking process. It is not logical and sequential when making meaning (however, it can be very logical and sequential when it is ***using*** information that it has learned).
- Most useful information is embedded in mental programs; information that does not become embedded in a program for using it in real-world applications is largely forgotten.

Because of these findings, the ITI classroom is dedicated to providing a learning environment with the following bodybrain-compatible elements:

- Absence of threat/ Nurturing reflective thinking
- Meaningful content
- Movement to enhance learning
- Enriched environment
- Choices
- Adequate time
- Collaboration
- Immediate feedback
- Mastery and the ability to use concepts and skills in real life

Each of these concepts about how the brain works and the bodybrain-compatible elements will be discussed at parent night and in home-school communications throughout the year. We will be spending a great deal of time at the beginning of the year on the role of emotion in learning and how to create an environment notable for absence of threat and enhancing reflective thinking. These are key elements of my classroom management and approach to discipline. Also, these are important areas of a strong home-school partnership. I look forward to working with you to help your child learn and grow.

4. Lifelong Guidelines & LIFESKILLS

Our classroom is practicing Lifelong Guidelines and LIFESKILLS (the definition of Personal Best). These differ from regular school rules because they apply to all age groups (adults and children) and in all situations. They form the basis for agreement between teacher and students, and among the students, about behavior and expectations (social and academic). I encourage you to learn about them (ask your child!) and I ask that you reinforce them at home.

Lifelong Guidelines

TRUSTWORTHINESS: To act in a manner that makes one worthy of trust and confidence

TRUTHFULNESS: To act with personal responsibility and mental accountability

ACTIVE LISTENING: To listen attentively and with the intention of understanding

NO PUT-DOWNS: To never use words, actions, and/or body language that degrade, humiliate, or dishonor others

PERSONAL BEST: To do one's best given the circumstances and available resources

LIFESKILLS

CARING: To feel and show concern for others

COMMON SENSE: To use good judgment

COOPERATION: To work together toward a common goal or purpose

COURAGE: To act according to one's beliefs despite fear of adverse consequences

CURIOSITY: A desire to investigate and seek understanding of one's world

EFFORT: To do your best

FLEXIBILITY: To be willing to alter plans when necessary

FRIENDSHIP: To make and keep a friend through mutual trust and caring

INITIATIVE: To do something, of one's own free will, because it needs to be done

INTEGRITY: To act according to a sense of what's right and wrong

ORGANIZATION: To plan, arrange, and implement in an orderly way; to keep things orderly and ready to use

PATIENCE: To wait calmly for someone or something

PERSEVERANCE: To keep at it

PRIDE: Satisfaction from doing one's personal best

PROBLEM SOLVING: To create solutions to difficult situations and everyday problems

RESOURCEFULNESS: To respond to challenges and opportunities in innovative and creative ways

RESPONSIBILITY: To respond when appropriate; to be accountable for one's actions

SENSE OF HUMOR: To laugh and be playful without harming others

5. Food & Its Effects on Learning

There are three books, all very readable, which offer some sound advice and suggestions for feeding children in a healthy manner. I recommend them as a beginning point in understanding the powerful influence food (especially junk food) has upon the chemistry of the brain and, therefore, its ability to learn.

Good For Me! by Marilyn Burns

This is a great book to read with your child. There are also many "things to do" that families will find fun and informational. A quick look at the table of contents gives you an idea of the excitement of this book: Biting In, What's the Use of Food, Anyway?; You Can Hurt Your Stomach's Feelings; The Fizz in Your Diet; The National Meal in a Bun; The Ice Cream Story; Learning to Read Labels; and, Will an Apple a Day Keep the Doctor Away?

Food For Healthy Kids by Dr. Lendon Smith

This provides a thorough look at food, behavior, allergies, and addictions from ages pre-birth to adulthood. Chapter headings include: Hyperactivity and Tension at All Ages; Sugar Cravings—Foods and Moods; Sleep Problems—Foods for Restless Children. Recipes for over a hundred healthy and tasty meals for children are included.

The Body's Many Cries for Water by F. Batmanghelidj, M.D.

Hydration also has a big effect on how the brain functions. Make sure your child drinks at least eight glasses of water a day. Sodas are not a water source; they contain chemicals that cause the body to use its water reserves to dilute and eliminate those chemicals. Numerous health and behavior problems are being attributed to dehydration. See www. watercure.com

6. Yearlong Theme, Key Points, and Inquiries

The basis for Integrated Thematic Instruction is the brain research of the past twenty years. The model was designed to best fit the brain's natural way of learning.

Yearlong Theme and Key Points

Because brain research tells us that the brain learns through seeking out understandable patterns, our curriculum is designed to enhance students' ability to detect and make meaning of patterns. The staff has worked hard at making our key points conceptual because concepts are big patterns and to organize our content around a single, yearlong theme through which all content and basic skills are taught. This is a dramatic departure from the fragmented day during which each subject is taught separately.

Examples of Key Points.

Key points are statements of what is most essential for students to learn—the essential core of knowledge and skills in each of the subject areas included in our yearlong theme. Key points are identified for each day, week, month, and year. They are the content every student needs to learn and be able to apply.

An example of a ***conceptual key point*** is: In our complex world we use increasingly more and complicated sources of power and machines to help meet our daily needs. Many tools and machines that help us do our work are powered with electricity. Electricity powers machines that help make our homes light at night, keep us warm in the winter or cool in the summer, keep our food cold so that it won't spoil, as well as many other uses. Electrical energy occurs naturally or can be generated and controlled by man.

An example of a ***significant knowledge key point*** that supports the conceptual key point is: In order for an electrical current to flow, it must have an uninterrupted conducting path. This is called an electric circuit. There are two kinds of electric circuits. A series circuit has only one electrical path, and any break in the path will interrupt the flow of electricity (for example old-fashioned Christmas tree lights). A parallel circuit has multiple paths. A break in one path will not interrupt the flow of electricity in the other paths (for example a string of lights that remain on when one bulb burns out). Knowing the properties, advantages and disadvantages of each kind of circuit can help us to understand why an appliance may or may not work, make decisions about energy conservation and create more complex electrical environments.

A Yearlong Theme. The purpose of the yearlong theme is to provide an umbrella pattern under which everything fits in a way that shows relationships among ideas and thus makes smaller ideas more memorable and retrievable.

The yearlong theme for our classroom is shown below. As you can see, the topics that we will be studying are varied and exciting.

Paste a copy of your yearlong theme here

so that parents can know what's coming next.

Inquiries

Inquiries are the activities your child will do to "learn" the concepts and skills identified in the key points. Inquiries require the application of reading, writing, computing, and best of all, thinking!

The intent is to better provide your child with the capabilities that come with understanding at the level of application and the ability to solve problems in the real world versus rely on rote memorization. The two questions I kept in mind as I was developing curriculum for this year were:

- What do I want students to understand?
- What do I want them to be able to do with what they understand?

These two questions will lead us into higher expectations for student performance, especially in the area of basic skills — reading, writing, and 'rithmetic—because they are basic to doing something in the world outside of the classroom. I look forward to sharing with you the key points and inquiries your child will be studying.

In developing inquiries for both work in class and homework for this class, I have also utilized the conceptual framework of Howard Gardner as presented in his book, *Frames of Mind: Theory of Multiple Intelligences*. Gardner defines intelligence as a "problem-solving and/or product-producing capability" rather than an I.Q. number. He says that we are all born with at least seven different, each one operating from a different location in the brain. Each of us develops a propensity for using one or more capabilities in our everyday lives. In the classroom, my goal is to help your child develop all of these areas of intelligence because all are necessary to succeed in life beyond our school years.

Here are some inquiries written for the key points mentioned above. They illustrate the range of problem-solving and product-producing capabilities that can be tapped and nurtured. They are examples of the types of activities your child will be involved in during our course of study.

1. *Design* and *build* a series or parallel circuit that will light each room in your Learning Club's "house." *Discuss* your plan for wiring your house with each other before you begin. *Propose* to each other how the materials will be used and how the electricity will flow through the house.

2. *Diagram* the wiring in your house. *Label* the electrical parts. *Describe* the circuit. *Determine* if it is a series or parallel circuit and *explain* why.

3. *Create* a flow chart that describes what you know about the flow of electricity through a circuit to make something work. *Read* the article "Relay Race" about telegraphs and discuss the sequence of events in the story as well as the sequence of events that enables a message to travel from the sender in one end of the country to the receiver in the other end of the country. *Illustrate* and *describe* the sequence in a step book.

4. By yourself or with a partner, use the measurements for your Learning Club's house to *calculate* the length of wire you will need to complete the circuit of electricity in your house. *Share* your results with the rest of your Learning Club. *Compare* your results with the others in your Learning Club and together *determine* the total length of wire you will need.

INQUIRIES FOR ASSESSMENT:

1. *Design* and *build* a model for an invention that uses electricity to meet a need that could help make life easier in some way or solve an everyday problem. *Diagram* your invention and how it should work. *Write* a brief explanation of how the invention is helpful and

how it should work. If your invention does not work as you planned it after you build it, *analyze* why you think it did not work and record your analysis in your journal. Be sure to use all of our key points for the week in your invention and your explanations.

2. Edit your research paper first by yourself, then with a partner. Use the rubric to be sure you have included or corrected everything. Rewrite it in its final form. Read it to a partner. Be ready to present it to the class.

As you can see, the inquiries ask students to apply what they are learning to real-world situations. This deepens their understanding, makes learning more memorable, and significantly increases the likelihood that they will remember the knowledge and skills years later. Our assessment inquiries are especially good tests of ability to use knowledge and skills.

To help make this year as rich an experience as possible, I would appreciate any and all support from parents, e.g., serving as a resource person in the classroom, providing materials, generating ideas for possible class study trips, assistance with study trips, etc.

7. The Public Library

Our public library should become your child's favorite place to find information and have questions answered. According to an article published by Northwest Airlines, "There are more than 115,000 libraries serving the American public; libraries employ over 300,000 people and spend almost $3 billion per year on materials and services—less than a dollar a month for every man, woman and child in the United States. America's public libraries circulate more than one billion items per year—everything from books to computer software to children's toys, games, audio cassettes, videotapes, art prints, and films."

It is ironic that some libraries are closing for lack of support in this country. It is the last "free" source of information available to all, regardless of income or education, and deserves to be used and supported. Interestingly, even during a recession, libraries which are heavily used and strongly supported by their communities are never cut from the budget. Libraries which close are eliminated more because public use is limited, not because public funds are limited. Support your library!

The public library is your closest and easiest vehicle to adventure. And, it's free. If your child does not already have his/her own library card, apply for one immediately. We have application cards available at Parent Night. Set a goal of visiting the library twice a week. Teach your child how to browse through the library and how to use the card catalog (or computerized system!).

Check the schedule for special events for children. Most libraries provide a surprisingly wide array of cultural events for children.

Lastly, teach your child how to read public transportation schedules and how to use public transportation. When your child is old enough, teach him/her to go alone. Going to the library will become as typical an adult behavior as turning on TV to watch the news.

8. Yearlong Research Project

As part of the Integrated Thematic Instruction model, each child is requested to choose a topic of interest that relates to our theme and to conduct a yearlong research project. Information can be gleaned from the newspaper, magazines, encyclopedias, and museum pamphlets, at all readability levels designed for both children and adults. This is your child's chance to develop practical, everyday information-gathering skills and discover life-long interests.

Resources are as near as the yellow pages of your phone book and Internet and as far away as those listed in the *Encyclopedia of Associations*, a remarkable publication available through your public library. It contains over 30,000 addresses of public and private organizations that have been formed to "get the word out"—information on all subjects. Writing letters to request free information provides a real audience for your child's writing skills. And when the information arrives in the child's mailbox with his/her name on it . . . well, of course, it will be high interest reading material!

The research project articles should be kept in a three-ring binder. Each article is read, highlighted, and at least three facts that your child thinks are interesting or important are mindmapped; the information is then added to the binder which can be easily reorganized as time goes on. Copies of letters sent and answered belong in the binder. At the appropriate time during the year, the teacher will ask for the expertise of your child to be presented to the class. This is the beginning of a lifelong habit of collecting, analyzing, synthesizing, and using information.

The long-term research project is the best "homework" you can do with your child. It provides a point of discussion and analysis. The end products are pride in accomplishing a significant task, deep knowledge, and lifelong learning skills.

9. Mindmapping

This year your child will be introduced to a concept called mindmapping—a way of visually representing how concepts and ideas related to each other. Pictures, as well as colors, enhance long-term memory, and retrieval. Mindmapping is a skill and, like other skills, it demands practice in order to do it well. Learn and practice it along with your child. It is a powerful study skill.

Recommended book: *Mapping Inner Space: Learning and Teaching Mind Mapping* by Nancy Margulies.

10. Homework

Homework is best assigned when it has meaning and purpose (from the learner's perspective. It should support and expand the skills, content, and concepts that were presented in the class. It will supplement what has gone on in the classroom that day—something which could not be done at school, either for lack of time or materials necessary to do the job well.

Do not expect your child to bring home "dittos" or "worksheets." Such drills too often kill the joy of learning, and, worst of all, seldom enhance learning. The intent of homework in this class is to give your child practice in using knowledge and skills in everyday life and at real-world standards for acceptability and excellence.

The best homework is the time you spend with your child reading, answering and posing questions, and investigating areas and concepts that will generate a sense of purpose for what your child is learning in the classroom.

11. Letter to Parents

Because your participation in your child's education is so critical to his/her progress this year, I will send you a letter at least twice a month. The letter will keep you up-to-date with happenings in the classroom—what we are currently studying, how you can support your child in mastering the key points for the month, what you might do to assist your child in learning how to apply what he/she is learning to real life (in your home, neighborhood, community), and, lastly, how you might assist the class as a whole—in the classroom or on a study trip.

The letter will typically follow the outline below:

Dear Parents,

We are into our ___ component of this year's theme, and our weekly topics for this month will include:

1.

2.

3.

4.

This week we will be working on inquiries for these key points in our content study:

1.

2.

3.

Our key points in the basic skills area (reading, writing, and mathematics) are:

1.

2.

3.

I invite you to assist your child in understanding those inquiries your child has selected to work on (or that I may have assigned), which support the key points. In particular, I invite you to help your child apply this information to real-life situations.

Your continuing to work with your child on his/her year-long research project is appreciated and makes the efforts all the more worthwhile.

Our resource person for this month (week) will be __________________. If you have any additional suggestions regarding resources, especially non-print ones, please let us know.

Our next study trip:____________________________

Our next learning celebration event: _____________

These are special days. Please mark them on your family calendar.

12. Possible Family Study Adventures within a 50-Mile Radius

Parents are not only the first teachers of their children but also the most important. Schools are but a supplement to the educating process of the parents. Your modeling of lifelong learning is the most important gift you can give your child. Make a list of all the possible educational locations within a 50-mile radius of your home (for small towns, increase the radius to 75 or 100 miles; rural areas, 100–300 miles). For example:

- Parks and historical sites
- Museums
- Cultural centers
- Natural environments: lakes, rivers, mountains, oceans, etc.
- Neighboring cities
- Plays and concerts
- Fairs
- Other

Set as your goal at least one study adventure every four weeks. Remember, intelligence is a function of experience. The more experiences children have, the greater is their ability to make connections.

13. Contacting Your Child's Teacher

If you need to contact me, please feel free to call the school and leave a message with the school secretary.

I appreciate your willingness to spend quality time with your child, investing in the role of "first teacher," modeling the behaviors and values of lifelong learners and contributing members of society. Do know that I will be doing everything possible in the classroom to support those goals for your child and I am looking forward to forming a close working partnership with you so that together we can ensure that your child fulfills his/her capabilities.

Sincerely,

Your Child's Teacher

Glossary
Bibliography
Index

Glossary

3Cs of Assessment

A set of criteria for assessing student work used by both students and teachers. The Cs stand for: Correct—conforming to fact or truth, free from error; accurate; Complete—having all parts or elements; the assignment is done to the defined specifications; Comprehensive—of large scope, inclusive, extensive mental range or grasp; reflects multiple points of view, thorough.

Absence of Threat/Nurturing Reflective Thinking

One of the nine Bodybrain-Compatible Elements of the ITI model. See Chapters 1-5.

Adequate Time

One of the nine Bodybrain-Compatible Elements of the ITI model. See Chapters 1-5.

Age-Appropriate

Concepts and/or facts which are understandable (versus memorizable) by students, given the current degree of development of the brain. These biological stages of thinking and learning gained attention through the work of Piaget.

Assessment/Evaluation

A process by which student achievement is assessed. In an ITI classroom the expectation is for mastery of key points by all students on an "A/no credit yet" basis.

"Australia"

A small corner of the room where the students can go to relax, refocus, and reflect. Used to assist students who are highly upset—angry or sad—to reset their emotions so they can return to learning.

Being There

The most powerful input to the brain is being in a real world location that activates all 19 senses, thereby significantly increasing learning (pattern identification and program building).

Bloom's Taxonomy

A model by Benjamin Bloom, et al, originally designed for developing questioning strategies for college exams. In the ITI model, the process verbs characterizing each level are used to develop inquiries.

Bodybrain-Compatible Elements

These are nine conditions that enhance and support powerful learning, the basis for the ITI model. They are: Absence of Threat/Nurturing Reflective Thinking, Meaningful Content, Movement to Enhance Learning, Enriched Environment, Choices, Adequate Time, Collaboration, Immediate Feedback, and Mastery/Application.

Bodybrain Learning Partnership

One of the five concepts from brain research upon which the ITI model is based. Includes emotions as the gatekeeper to learning and performance and movement to enhance learning.

Brain-Compatible Learning

Coined by Leslie A. Hart in his book *Human Brain and Human Learning,* it is a key goal of the Kovalik ITI model. A brain-compatible environment is one which allows the brain to work as it naturally, and thus most powerfully, works. Recent brain research has updated this term to "bodybrain-compatible" learning.

Celebrations of Learning

An activity to not only acknowledge accomplishments but to also practice using the knowledge and skills mastered through demonstrating and teaching others, particularly parents.

Choices

One of the nine Bodybrain-Compatible Elements of the ITI model. See Chapters 1-5.

Collaboration

One of the nine Bodybrain-Compatible Elements of the ITI model. See Chapters 1-5.

Common Core of Knowledge

Defined in the ITI model to mean those concepts, significant knowledge, and skills all students are expected to master and that are considered essential to success in life (school and adulthood) and to sustain a democracy and participate in our high-tech society.

Component

An integral structure of the ITI model based on a *being there* location. In a yearlong theme, components are related to the organizing concept of the yearlong theme; components, a framework designed for approximately one month of study is broken into topics, important aspects of the concept for the *being there* location.

Emotion As Gatekeeper to Learning and Performance

One of the two aspects of bodybrain learning partnership, a brain research concepts upon which the ITI model is based. See Chapter 2.

C.U.E.

An acronym describing the three ways information can be presented in order for the learner to readily retrieve it. The "C" stands for creative, the "U" for useful and the "E" for emotional bridge.

Direct Instruction

The 11 to 16 minutes of teacher presentation of a key point which provides the focus of the classroom activities; direct instruction is only one way of orchestrating key points.

Enriched Environment

One of the nine Bodybrain-Compatible Elements of the ITI model. See Chapters 1-5.

Hands-On Experience

A term describing two levels of sensory input: hands-on of the real thing and hands-on of something symbolic or representative of a real thing. Hands-on of symbolic or representational things provides significantly less sensory input, and thus less stimulation of the brain, than does interacting with the real thing.

Group Development—3 Stages of

In the ITI model, group development and creating community occurs in three stages: Developing a sense of belonging, Creating common ground, and Taking action. The end result is a sense of community that increases academic learning as well as enhances personal and social growth. See Chapter 9.

Immediate Feedback

One of the nine Bodybrain-Compatible Elements of the ITI model. See Chapters 1-5.

Immersion

An environment that simulates as richly as possible the real-life environment being studied, e.g., transforming a classroom into wetlands or a pond or a period of history, allowing students to experience or role-play as if they were actually there.

Input, Types of

1. *Being there*, physically being in the real world environment; 2. Immersion—full simulation of the real world environment, includes many real world things; 3. Hands-on of the real thing, (e.g., frog); 4. Hands-on of representation (e.g., plastic model of a frog); 5. Second-hand—pictorial representation, written word (e.g., pictures, videos, or stories about frogs); and 6. Symbolic—mathematics, phonics, grammar (scientific definition of a frog)

Inquiries

A key curriculum development structure in the ITI model, inquiries are activities that enable students to understand and apply the concept, skill, or significant knowledge of a key point. The primary purpose of inquiries is to enable students to develop mental programs for applying, in real-world situations, the key point and wiring such knowledge and skills into long-term memory. Inquiries make learning active and memorable.

Inquiry Builder
A chart that organizes the process verbs of Bloom's Taxonomy of Cognitive Objectives according to five of Howard Gardner's seven intelligences

Inseparable Bodybrain Learning Partnership
Current brain research indicates that the limbic system is part of a larger emotional system involving "information substances" produced and received throughout the body. In other words, the brain talks to the body and the body talks back to the brain. Learning is the result of an inseparable bodybrain partnership.

Instructional Strategies
A variety of instructional strategies are critical to implementing the ITI model at each stage.
For Stage 1.2—list them
For Stage 1.3—
For Stage 2 and Beyond—

Integrated
Combining or coordinating separate elements so as to provide a harmonious interrelated whole (as defined by *Webster's Encyclopedia Unabridged Dictionary of the English Language* 1996).

ITI (Integrated Thematic Instruction)
The name given to a bodybrain-compatible, fully integrated instructional model developed by Susan Kovalik. It is a comprehensive model that translates the best of what we know about learning from current brain research into effective teaching strategies and meaningful curriculum.

Key Point
Essential concept, skill, or significant knowledge all students are expected to master (know and be able to use). The primary purpose of key points is to enhance students' ability to detect pattern, i.e., to readily identify the collection of attributes that is essential for understanding the concept, skill, or significant idea of the key point. They also provide a clear focus for the teacher for instructional planning and for orchestration of learning.

Learning, a Two-Step Process
Defined by Leslie Hart as a two-part process: 1. Detecting and understanding patterns—a process through which our brain creates meaning. 2. Developing meaningful mental programs to use what is understood and to store it in long-term memory—the capacity to use what is understood first with assistance and then almost automatically.

Learning Clubs
Learning Clubs are collaborative student groups, the composition of which may change monthly to every six weeks. Getting to know others well accelerates learning, prevenets cliques, and increases opportunities for growth. Learning how to get to know others, and be comfortable doing so, is a critical personal/social skill. For Stage 1 and beyond — see Chapter 7.

Lifelong Guidelines
The parameters for classroom/schoolwide interactions with other students and staff. They are TRUSTWORTHINESS, TRUTHFULNESS, ACTIVE LISTENING, NO PUT-DOWNS, and PERSONAL BEST.

LIFESKILLS
The 18 LIFESKILLS are the day-to-day definition of the Lifelong Guideline of Personal Best. The LIFESKILLS are the personal/social parameters for everyone—students and adults. They include: Integrity, Initiative, Flexibility, Perseverance, Organization, Sense of Humor, Effort, Common Sense, Resourcefulness, Problem-Solving, Responsibility, Patience, Friendship, Curiosity, Cooperation, Caring, Courage, and Pride.

Mastery
One of the nine Bodybrain-Compatible Elements of the ITI model; see Chapters 1-6. Mastery in the ITI model means completion of both steps in the new definition of learning (see Chapters 4 and 5); it means being able to apply what is understood in real-world ways and practicing how to use that skill or knowledge until it becomes wired into long-term memory.

Meaningful Content
One of the nine Bodybrain-Compatible Elements of the ITI model. See Chapters 1-6.

Mindmapping
A way to visually represent information, usually as a web or cluster around the main idea with symbols and colors, rather than in traditional outline form.

Movement to Enhance Learning
One of the two aspects of bodybrain learning partnership, a brain research concepts upon which the ITI model is based. See Chapter 2.

Multiple Intelligences
Defined by Howard Gardner as "problem-solving or product-producing capabilities." The first seven intelligences identified by Gardner are: logical-mathematical, linguistic, spatial, bodily-kinesthetic, musical, intrapersonal, and interpersonal. Humans are born with all the intelligences but will develop each according to family and cultural preference, demands of one's environment, and the individual's inclinations and experiences. Gardner has subsequently added an eighth intelligence, naturalist. The multiple intelligences are a key ingredient of inquiries.

Pattern Seeking
A key concept of bodybrain-compatibility; describes the means by which the brain makes meaning from incoming sensory input.

Procedures, Written
Written procedures are an important classroom leadership strategy in the ITI model. They state the social and personal behaviors are expected for commonly occurring events, such as entering and leaving the room, lunchroom behaviors, and so forth. By describing what social and personal behaviors are expected, these procedures allow students to be successful.

Program Building
A key concept of brain-compatibility describing how the brain stores and uses what it learns. It is defined as "a personal goal achieved by a sequence of steps or actions" which becomes stored in the brain for later retrieval when an action is required. Every goal we accomplish is due to implementation of a program or programs.

Social/Political Action
An integral part of the ITI model which provides students a vehicle for applying what they learn to real-world problems. It assists students in becoming contributing citizens. Begin in Stage 2.

Symbolic Input
The most difficult way for the brain to grasp new information such as phonics, grammar, and algebraic equations.

Temperament or Personality Preferences
Based on the work of Carl Jung, Myers and Briggs, and Keirsey and Bates, these four behavior scales strongly affect learning. The behavior areas are: taking in information (sensor or intuitor), decision making (feeling or thinking), lifestyle (judging or perceiving), and orientation to others (extrovert and introvert)

Target Talk
A key instructional tool to teach the Lifelong Guidelines/LIFESKILLS. Labels a behavior in context without value judgment.

Topics
A curriculum development structure of the ITI model for dividing each component into important topics or areas of the concept for the component's *being there* experience. In the yearlong theme, topics are planned for approximately one week.

Yearlong Research Projects
Topics students choose during the first two weeks of school to become the "expert" on for the class. Students research their project throughout the year and present it to the entire class (and others students as well).

Yearlong Theme
The yearlong theme is the central organizer for integrated curriculum in the ITI model. It is a concept that organizes all the concepts, significant knowledge, and skills to be learned during the theme. It is represented by a kid-grabbing title.

Bibliography

ABC News Prime Time. *"Your Child's Brain"* with Diane Sawyer. January 25, 1995.

Ackerman, Diane. *An Alchemy of Mind: The Marvel and Mystery of the Brain.* New York: Scribner, 2004.

Armstrong, Thomas. *In Their Own Way*. Los Angeles: Tarcher Press, 1987.

Armstrong, Thomas. *7 Kinds of Smart: Identifying and Developing Your Multiple Intelligences*. New York: Penguin Putnam, 1999.

Beane, James A. *A Middle School Curriculum: From Rhetoric to Reality,* second edition. Westerville, Ohio: National Middle School Association, 1993.

Bell, Nanci. *Visualizing and Verbalizing for Improved Comprehension: A Teacher's Manual*. San Luis Obispo, CA: Gander Educational Publishing, 1991.

Belvel, Pat. TCI Consulting in Classroom Management and Peer Coaching, 1990.

Brady, Marion. *What's Worth Teaching? Selecting, Organizing, and Integrating Knowledge*. Covington, WA: Books for Educators, 1989.

Caine, Renata and Geoffrey. *Making Connections: Teaching and the Human Brain*. California: Addison-Wesley, 1994.

Calvin, William H. *How Brains Think: Evolving Intelligence, Then and Now*. New York: BasicBooks, 1996.

Calvin, William H. *"The Mind's Big Bang and Mirroring,"* unpublished manuscript. Seattle, WA: University of Washington, 2000.

Childre, Doc. *Freeze Frame: One Minute Stress Management.* Boulder Creek, CA: Planetary Publications, 1998.

Childre, Doc and Martin, Howard with Beech, Donna. *The HeartMath Solution*. San Francisco: Harper, 2000.

Cohen, Elizabeth. *Designing Groupwork: Strategies for the Heterogeneous Classroom*, Second Edition. New York: Teachers College Press, 1994.

Cohen, Isabel and Marcelle Goldsmith. *Hands On: How to Use Brain Gym in the Classroom.; A Practical Photo Manual for Educators, Parents, and Learners.*Ventura, CA: Edu-Kinesthetics, Inc., 2003.

Csikszentmihalyi, Mihaley. *Flow: The Psychology of Optimal Experience*. New York: Harper, 1990.

Cytowic, Richard E. *The Man who Tasted Shapes: A Bizarre Medical Mystery Offers Revolutionary Insights into Emotions, Reasoning, and Consciousness*. New York: Tarcher/Putnam, 1993.

Damasio, Antonio. *Descartes' Error: Emotion, Reason, and the Human Brain*. New York: G. P. Putnam Sons, 1994.

Damasio, Antonio. *Looking for Spinoza: Joy, Sorrow, and the Feeling Brain*. New York: Harcourt, 2003.

Damasio, Antonio. *"Thinking about Emotion,"* presentation at Emotional Intelligence, Education, and the Brain: A Symposium. Chicago, IL: December 5, 1997.

Diamond, Marion and Hopson, Janet. *Magic Trees of the Mind: How to Nurture Your Child's Intelligence, Creativity, and Healthy Emotions from Birth Through Adolescence*. New York: Penguin, 1998.

Gallese, Vittorio and Goldman, Alvin. "Mirror Neurons and the Simulation Theory of Mind-Reading" in *Trends in Cognitive Sciences*, Vol. 2, 1998.

Gardner, Howard. *Frames of Mind: Theory of Multiple Intelligences*. New York: Basic Books, 1983.

Gardner, Howard. *Intelligence Reframed: Multiple Intelligences for the 21st Century*. New York: Basic Books, 1999.

Gibbs, Jeanne. *Discovering Gifts in Middle School: Learning in a Caring Culture Called Tribes*. Windsor, California: CenterSource Systems, LLC, 2001.

Gibbs, Jeanne. *TRIBES: A New Way of Learning and Being Together*. Windsor, California: CenterSource Systems, LLC, 2001.

Glasser, William, M.D. *Control Theory in the Classroom*. New York: Perennial Library, 1986.

Goldberg, Elkhonon. *The Executive Brain: Frontal Lobes and the Civilized Mind*. Oxford: University Press, 2001.

Goldberg, Elkhonon. *The Wisdom Paradox: How Your Mind Can Grow Stronger As Your Brain Grows Older*. New York, NY: Gotham Books/Division of Penquin Books, 2005.

Gopnik, A., A. Meltzoff, and Patricia Kuhl. *The Scientist in the Crib: Minds, Brains, and How Children Learn*. New York: William Morrow and Company, 1999.

Gossen, Diane. *Restitution: Restructuring School Disclipline*. Chapel Hill, NC: New View Publications, 1996.

Greenspan, Stanley I. with Beryl Lieff Benderly. *The Growth of the Mind and the Endangered Origins of Intelligence*. New York: Addison-Wesley Publishing Company, 1997.

Hannaford, Carla. *Smart Moves: Why Learning Is Not All in Your Head*. Alexander, North Carolina: Great Ocean, 1995.

Hardwired to Connect. A collaborative work by the Commission of Children at Risk. New York: sponsored by YMCA of the USA, Dartmouth Medical School, Institute for American Values, 2003.

Hart, Leslie A. *Human Brain and Human Learning*. Covington, WA: Books for Educators, Inc., 1999.

Hawkins, Jeff with Sandra Blakeslee. *On Intelligence: How a New Understanding of the Brain Will Lead to the Creation of Truly Intelligent Machines*. New York: Times Books/Henry Holt and Company, 2004.

Healy, Jane. *Endangered Minds: Why Children Don't Think – and What We Can Do About It*. New York: Simon & Schuster, 1990.

Healy, Jane. *Failure to Connect: How Computers Affect Our Children's Minds – And What We Can Do About It*. New York: Simon & Schuster, 1998.

Hermann, Ned. *The Creative Brain*. North Carolina: Brain Books, 1990.

Hyerle, David. *Visual Tools for Constructing Knowledge* . Alexandria, VA: Association for Supervision & Curriculum Development, 1996

Kagan, Spencer. *Cooperative Learning*. San Clemente, CA Kagan, 1994.

Kagan, Spencer. *SmartCards*. San Juan Capistrano, CA, Kagan, 2003

Kaufelt, Martha Miller. *I Can Divide and Conquer: a Concept in a Day*. Covington, WA: Books for Educators, 1987.

Keirsey, David. *Please Understand Me II: Temperament Character Intelligence*. Del Mar, CA: Prometheus Nemesis Book Company, 1998.

Kinsey, C.W. and McPhearson, K, editors. *Enriching Curriculum Through Service Learning*. Alexandria, VA: Association for Supervision and Curriculum Development, 1995.

Kohn, Alfie. *Punished by Rewards: The Trouble with Gold Stars, Incentive Plans, A's, Praise, and Other Bribes*. Boston: Houghton Mifflin, 1993.

Kovalik, Susan. *Integrated Thematic Instruction: The Model*, third edition. Covington, WA: Susan Kovalik and Associates, 1997.

Kovalik, Susan J. & Olsen, Karen. *Kid's Eye View of Science: A Teacher's Handbook for Implementing and Integrated Thematic Approach to Science, K-6*. Covington, WA: Books For Educators, Inc., 1994.

LeDoux, Joseph. *"The Emotional Brain,"* presentation at Emotional Intelligence, Education, and the Brain: A Symposium. Chicago, IL: December 5, 1997.

LeDoux, Joseph E. *The Emotional Brain: The Mysterious Underpinnings of Emotional Life*. New York: Simon and Schuster, 1996.

Lewis, Barbara A. *Kid's Guide to Social Action: How to Solve the Social Problems YOU CHOOSE – and Turn Creative Thinking into Positive Action*. Minneapolis, MN: Free Spirit Publishing, 1981.

Lewis, Barbara A. *Kid's Guide to Service Projects: Over 500 Service Ideas for Young People who Want to Make a Difference*. Minneapolis, MN: Free Spirit Publishing, 1995.

Lewis, Thomas. *A General Theory of Love*. New York: Random House, 2000.

Lowery, Lawrence F. *Thinking and Learning: Matching Developmental Stages With Curriculum and Instruction*. Kent, Washington: Books for Educators, Inc., 1995.

Mahnke, Frand H and Rudolf H. Mahnke. *Color and Light in Man-Made Environments*. New York: John Wiley & Sons, Inc., 1993.

Margulies, Nancy. *Mapping Inner Space: Learning and Teaching Visual Mapping*. Tucson, AZ: Zephyr Press, 2002.

Miller, Norma, ed. *The Healthy School Handbook: Conquering the Sick Building Syndrome and Other Environmental Hazards In and Around Your School*. Washington, DC: NEA Professional Library, 1995.

Motluk, Alison. "Read My Mind" in *New Scientist*, Jan. 27, 2001.

Olsen, Karen D. *Making Bodybrain-Compatible Education a Reality: Coaching for the ITI Model*. Covington, Washington: Books for Educators, 1999.

Olsen, Karen D. *Science Continuum of Concepts, K-6*. Covington, WA: Center for the Future of Public Education, 1995.

Pearson, Sarah S. *Finding Common Ground: Service Learning and Education Reform*. Washington, D.C.: American Youth Policy Forum, 2002.

Pert, Candace. *Molecules of Emotion: Why You Feel the Way You Feel*. New York: Scribner, 1997.

Ramachandran, V. S. *Mirror Neurons and Imitation Learning As the Driving Force Behind "The Great Leap Forward" in Human Evolution*. www.edge.org/documents/archive/edge69.html

Ratey, John J. *A User's Guide to the Brain: Perception, Attention, and the Four Theaters of the Brain*. New York: Pantheon Books, 2001.

Rivlin, Robert and Gravelle, Karen. *Deciphering Your Senses*. New York: Simon and Schuster, 1984.

Rizzolatti, Giacomo and Arbib, Michael. "Language Within Our Grasp" in *Trends in Neurosciences*, Vol. 21, 1998.

Samples, Bob. *Open Mind, Whole Mind*. California: Jalmar Press, 1987.

Simon, H.erbert, *The Sciences of the Artificial*, Cambridge, MA: MIT Press, 1996.

Smith, Frank. *Insult to Intelligence: The Bureaucratic Invasion of Our Classrooms*. New York: Arbor House Publishing Company, 1986.

Smith, Frank. *to Think*. New York: Teachers College Press, 1990.

Sylwester, Robert. *A Celebration of Neurons: An Educator's Guide to the Human Brain*. Alexandria, VA: ASCD, 1995.

Sylwester, Robert. *How to Explain a Brain: An Educator's Handbook of Brain Terms and Cognitive Processes.* Thousand Oaks, CA: Corwin Press, 2005.

Zielke, Dr. Sigurd. "An Introduction to Neurobehavioral-Developmental & Social Classroom Management," a presentation to Susan Kovalik & Associates, January20-22, 2005.

Index

Catalog of RESOURCES

Catalog of RESOURCES

Exceeding Expectations:
A User's Guide to Implementing Brain Research in the Classroom, Third Edition by Susan Kovalik and Karen D. Olsen.. $34.95

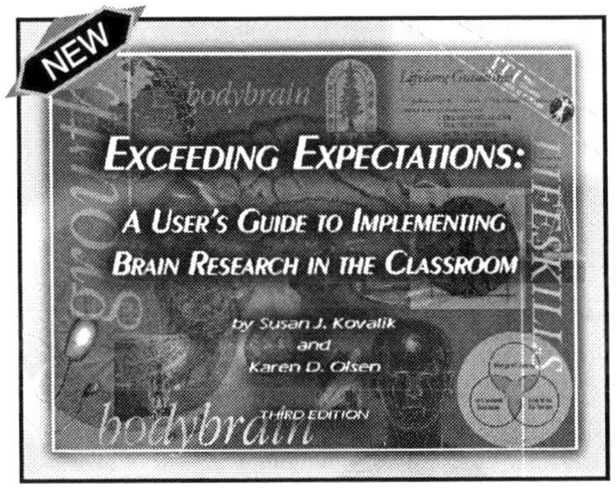

The new revised edition is an absolute essential resource for any educator. The first edition replaced the book entitled, *ITI: The Model.* This expanded edition is the most comprehensive book available on integration for grades K-6. It describes clearly and succinctly the brain research base which makes ITI (Integrated Thematic Instruction) so powerful for students, and provides practical step-by-step explanations of how to create a bodybrain-compatible classroom. Learn how to develop and implement a yearlong theme as a structure for integrating all basic skills and content areas. Loaded with curriculum examples, implementation tips, starting points, and timelines. Comprehensive, practical, and insightful. *(480 pages)*
Includes *Your Personal Handbook for Implementing the ITI Model.*

Tools For Citizenship & Life: Using the ITI Lifelong Guidelines & LIFESKILLS in Your Classroom

by Sue Pearson.. $27.50

Here is the book you've been waiting to have at your fingertips! For each of the Lifelong Guidelines and LIFESKILLS, you get the description, why to practice it, how to practice it, what it looks like in the real world, what it looks like in school, inquiries to develop, signs of success, and links to related literature to use with students grades K-8. Includes the newest LIFESKILL, resourcefulness. *(365 pgs.)*

Character Begins at Home: Using the ITI Lifelong Guidelines & LIFESKILLS in Your Classroom

by Sue Pearson and Karen D. Olsen.............................. $14.95

Here are hundreds of ideas for nurturing children's characters through the Lifelong Guidelines and LIFESKILLS using simple, enjoyable activities at home. Children and youth benefit by hearing and using a common language at home and at school as they develop the social skills of respect and responsible citizenship. Great idea for building family/community support!

LIFESKILLS: Creating a Class Family

(17 min. video).. $29.95

Research conclusively shows that learning is accelerated when a sense of community is established in the classroom. Join Joy Raboli and Karen Janik and their 60 fifth and sixth graders for a look at what a multi-age class family looks like and how to create one in your own classroom.

Lifelong Guidelines and LIFESKILLS

A wall poster set.. $39.95

The ITI Lifelong Guidelines call for trustworthiness, truthfulness, active listening, no put-downs, and personal best. What is personal best? The LIFESKILLS poster set provides colorful definitions and examples. Set includes a Lifelong Guidelines poster, a Personal Best Clubhouse poster (18" x 22 1/2"), and posters for each of the 18 LIFESKILLS (8 1/2" x 11"). LIFESKILLS include such traits as cooperation, caring, responsibility, initiative, and problem-solving. Artwork by Gwen Pribble is whimsical, action-oriented, and multi-ethnic. Ideal for incorporating character education.
Also available in Spanish.

LIFESKILLS (compact disc).............................. $17.95
LIFESKILLS (songbook)................................... $6.50
by Judy and Russ Eacker

Music is a wonderful way to introduce the LIFESKILLS, which can become a partner in creating a trusting environment that enhances learning. These original tunes and lyrics are whimsical and memorable. Lyrics booklet includes all 17 songs and has large print ideal for making sing-along copies or overhead transparencies. Created by R&J Productions. Each sold separately.

LIFESKILLS Notecards

Susan Kovalik & Associates.................. $16.95

These lovely notecards with a garden motif each feature a separate LIFESKILL on a cream background. Use them to write to friends or family, or thank a student or co-worker for good use of a LIFESKILL! Set of eighteen on high quality paper with matching envelopes, suitable for framing.

LIFESKILLS Activity Cards, set of 18

Susan Kovalik & Associates.............................$29.95

These new 8 1/2" x 11" cards are a terrific resource for teachers and students. On the front, information is provided for direct instruction in the LIFESKILLS while offering the middle grade students the opportunity to select from a variety of activities on the back. Full color graphics on durable card stock will hold up for repeated use. Order the set of 18, or individually at $2.50 each.

Stage 1 of the ITI Stages of Implementation:

First Things First

(17 min. video)... $29.95

In this video, Joy Raboli takes you through the first steps of setting up an ITI classroom, illustrating each aspect of Stage 1 of the ITI Rubric. Covering the physical layout of the room, beginning curriculum and instructional strategies, how to invite parents into the program, and what you can expect students to accomplish, this is a video that will answer your practical questions.

Lifelong Guidelines & LIFESKILLS Mug

Susan Kovalik & Associates...................................... $6.00

Like the popular posters you have in your classroom, these mugs offer a daily reminder of the Lifelong Guidelines and LIFESKILLS with an added bonus —you can fill them up with your favorite beverage! These commuter mugs are insulated and easily fit in your vehicle's cupholders.

A One-Day Makeover for Your ITI Classroom

(14 min. video)... $21.95

Join veteran ITI teacher/administrator, Dottie Brown, as she transforms a stark classroom into a bodybrain-compatible learning space. Listen and watch as she analyzes the function for each space and decides how to arrange furniture to meet that need. See the simple strategies she uses so that the classroom promotes cooperation, looks beautiful, is calming and focused, and reflects the topic under study. She did it in one day and so can you!

Your Personal Handbook for Implementing the ITI Model

by Karen D. Olsen..(5 or more only $7.00) $9.95

Whether you are implementing ITI alone or traveling the ITI road with colleagues and a coach, you will find this guide an indispensable companion. Following the ITI Sages of Implementation, the handbook provides descriptors of what to do, what it looks like when students collaborate with their teacher - "the dance" - and what it looks like when students internalize ITI and "take flight". It is an excellent self-coaching guide and an invaluable communication tool when working with a coach. (45 pages). Specify whether you need ELEMENTARY or SECONDARY when ordering.

The ITI Schoolwide Rubric:

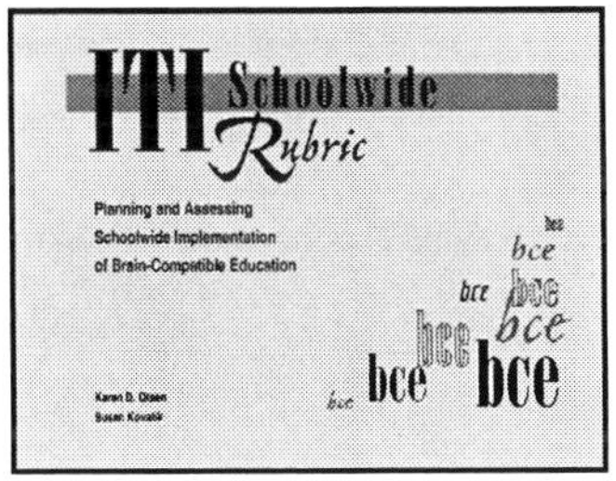

Assessing Schoolwide Implementation of Brain-Compatible Education

by Karen D. Olsen and Susan Kovalik............. $7.50

The *ITI Schoolwide Rubric* is designed to provide both road signs and mileage markers along the road to implementing ITI in an entire school. It describes five stages of training and achievement plus the governance necessary schoolwide in order to provide individual classroom teachers with the support they need and deserve as they work to implement ITI for their students. Includes expected outcomes and their likely indicators. *(56 pages)*

Stage 2 of the ITI Stages of Implementation:

Intelligence is a Function of Experience

(14 min. video).. .... $29.95

Intelligence is a function of experience! Schools need to be able to equalize student experiences in order to increase understanding of content. Follow these 2nd through 8th graders as they engage in a variety of experiences both in and out of the classroom. With a high level of cooperation and commitment to purpose, these students are learning to be responsible, productive citizens.

Mission Addition: Mastery through Integration

Susan Kovalik & Associates.........................VHS or DVD $49.95

Can your students master their addition skills in a concentrated period of time? Follow 85 second-graders for two days as they are taught five new learning strategies to enhance their ability to add. Using the ITI model, you will see how to layer your teaching techniques through art, music, drama, and physical movement. Watch as these students build their confidence in math by learning strategies to master addition. (18 minutes)

Sign On with the Lifelong Guidelines and LIFESKILLS through American Sign language

Susan Kovalik & Associates.....................VHS or DVD $49.95

In today's ever changing society, learning a new language can be fun, exciting, and valuable. In "Sign On," you will join students from the Colorado School for the Deaf and the Blind as they teach your class the gift of American Sign Language. Watch as the children demonstrate how to sign the Lifelong Guidelines and LIFESKILLS with accuracy. Soon your students will be on their way to learning a new language. (22 minutes)

The Spyglass Series

by Susan Kovalik & Associates

VHS or DVD format .... $21.95 each

Series in VHS or DVD $89.95

These innovative video resources are the perfect tool for portraying the ITI model in action. Available in VHS or DVD format, there are five titles: Agenda, Being There, Community Circle, Enriched Environment, and Writing Procedures. Each presentation presents an overview of the subject and how to implement the techniques to create the ultimate learning environment where academic achievement can increase. Real-life demonstrations by SK&A Associates interacting with the classroom students.

I Can Divide and Conquer:
A Concept in a Day by Martha M. Kaufeldt
(55 min. video & 76-page handbook).. $29.95

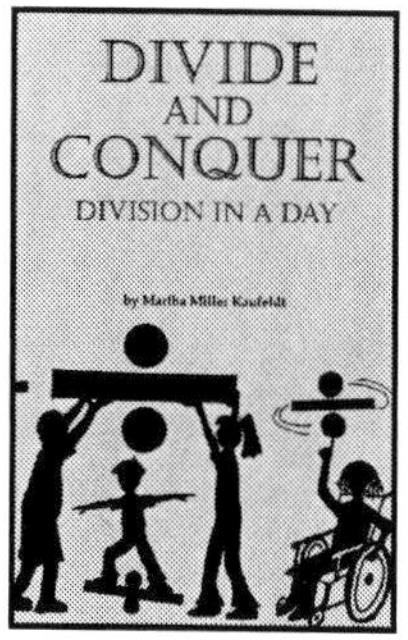

When the learning environment is brain-compatible, something as "hard" as long division—concept and computation—can be mastered in a single day. Follow a fourth grade teacher as she takes fifty fourth, fifth, and sixth graders through an unforgettable day of conquering long division.

Classroom of the 21st Century
(50 min. video).. $29.95

Observe an ITI fourth grade classroom where all curriculum content and skills are orchestrated around a yearlong theme. Hear students speak for the power of the model.

Thinking and Learning: Matching Developmental Stages with Curriculum and Instruction
by Dr. Larry Lowery.. $9.95

A concise description of the evolving thinking processes of children, this is a handy tool at school and district levels for examining curriculum content and determining what is age-appropriate for our students and, thus, understandable (rather than memorizable). You'll see why textbooks are wildly inappropriate in many areas! *(98 pages)*

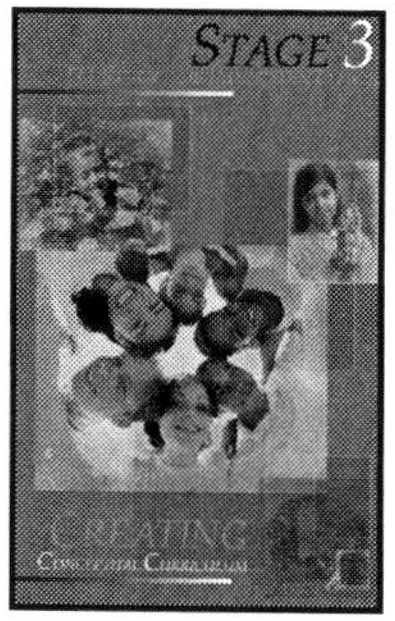

Stage 3 of the ITI Stages of Implementation:
Creating Conceptual Curriculum
(25 min. video).. $29.95

Join Joy Raboli and Karen Janik to see how a conceptual curriculum is powerful, meaningful, and allows students to predict and generalize. In this video, 5th and 6th grade students learn from guest speakers, "being there" experiences, and skill integration. Watch as they internalize the meaning of responsibility for one's own learning. This is ITI in action!

Jacobsonville: An ITI Micro Society
(30 min. video).. $39.95

Learners have long asked their teachers, "When am I ever going to use this?" Follow students and teachers as they unfold a comprehensive micro-society. In this ITI K-5 school, using information and skills is the goal. From a city government with elected officials to commerce with postal and banking services and a variety of small businesses, students negotiate the business trail (complete with business permits, design, production, marketing, business space rental, and profit margin calculations). A "must see" video!

Making Bodybrain-Compatible Education a Reality:
Coaching for the ITI Model
by Karen D. Olsen.. $21.95

Even champions rely on their coaches. This book helps you prepare to be a top-notch ITI coach. It introduces a coaching model designed specifically for ITI coaches that is based on the ITI stages of implementation. *(214 pages)*

Human Brain and Human Learning
by Leslie A. Hart
(3rd Edition, 2002).. $15.95

Orchestrating learning that is bodybrain-compatible must be the foundation for what goes on in the classroom. Hart brilliantly explains the biology of learning related to classroom practice and allows the reader to "see" what is necessary for real reform efforts to succeed. The reader comes to appreciate how the brain makes meaning through pattern recognition, prepares to act through mental programs, and responds to emotion. *(402 pages)*

The Kid's Guide to Social Action:
How to Solve the Social Problems You Choose—and Turn Creative Thinking into Positive Action

by Barbara A. Lewis.. $18.95

Here is an extraordinary source for exploring life beyond the classroom. It provides step-by-step examples of how to initiate and carry out social action projects. Students learn to write letters, create surveys, get TV coverage, and lobby their legislators. Fabulous integration of the language arts skills, social studies, and real life! *(211 pages)*

Science Continuum of Concepts, K-6

by Karen D. Olsen.. $7.95

ITI teachers are encouraged to use science as the basis for all content integration. This amazing K-6 guide identifies the developmentally appropriate conceptual key points, recommended field trips, and expected student performance for each grade level. It is an essential tool for writing integrated curriculum and for making science come alive for students. *(53 pages)*

Lifelines: Songs of Character

(45 min. CD)... $17.95

Jeff Pedersen's original songs add vitality to the school day while reinforcing the LIFESKILLS of perseverance, caring, initiative, curiosity, friendship, sense of humor, and effort. Use the joy and power of music to bring a deeper meaning of these LIFESKILLS to your students. Lyrics for each song are included.

What's Worth Teaching?
Selecting, Organizing, and Integrating Knowledge

by Marion Brady.. $9.95

Brady provides a workable framework for analyzing deficits of traditional curriculum and for creating curriculum appropriate for the 21st century. According to Brady, "The proper subject matter of education is reality." It should be demonstrably applicable to daily experience, universal, and equally valid for every student, as well as being integrated and part of a coherent conceptual structure. This is a "must-read" book for teachers and administrators, grades 7-12. *(147 pages)*

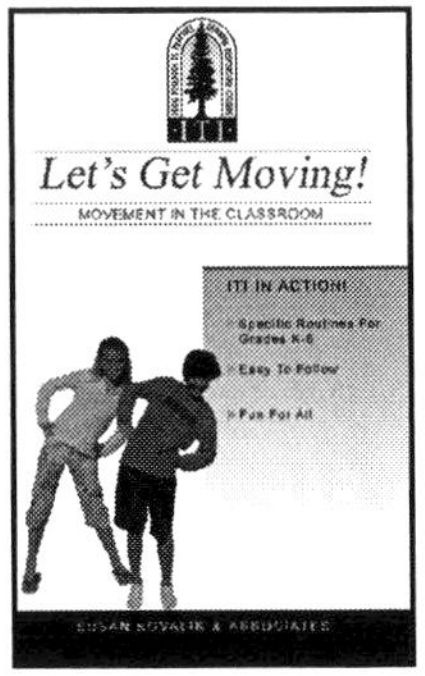

Let's Get Moving:
Movement in the Classroom

(95 min. video with manual).. $19.95

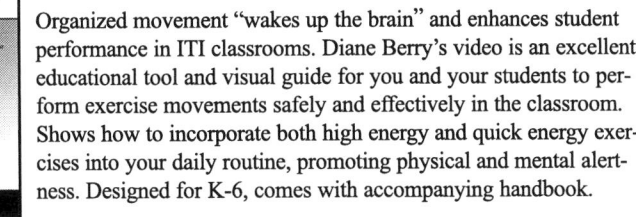

Organized movement "wakes up the brain" and enhances student performance in ITI classrooms. Diane Berry's video is an excellent educational tool and visual guide for you and your students to perform exercise movements safely and effectively in the classroom. Shows how to incorporate both high energy and quick energy exercises into your daily routine, promoting physical and mental alertness. Designed for K-6, comes with accompanying handbook.

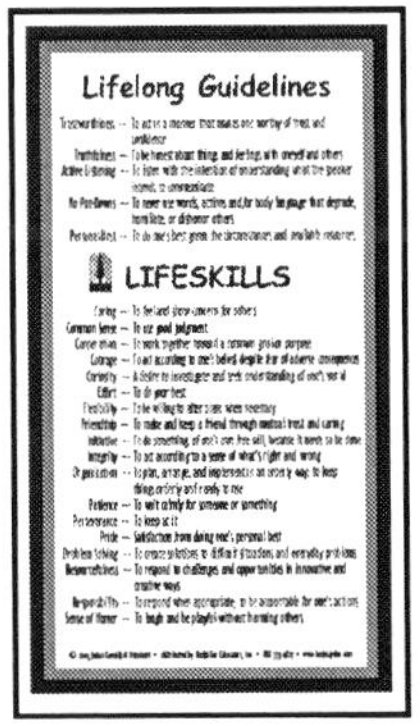

LifeGuide Poster

Susan Kovalik & Associates...$10.00

If you like our LIFESKILLS magnets, you'll love the LifeGuide Poster! The poster lists the five Lifelong Guidelines and the eighteen LIFESKILLS along with their definitions all on one handy poster. This easy to read poster measures 18" x 22 1/2". Display it in the hallway, office, lunchroom, home, or classroom.

It's Not About Math, It's About Life

by Kari Simmons Kling..$24.95

Was math a difficult subject for you when you were in school? Is math the subject area you have the most difficulty integrating? Math is everywhere! Opportunities for helping children find math skills in the world around them are endless. Learn from an expert how to base math instruction and practice on real-life places, such as in the classroom, at home, at a grocery store, or other familiar events and situations. Includes math skills taught at each grade level, K-6, and tips for assessment. (221 pages)

The Kid's Guide to Service Projects

Over 500 Service Ideas for Young People Who Want to Make a Difference

by Barbara A. Lewis... $16.95

Kids. . . pick any topic that interests you, whether it be animals, environment, crime, politics, or another. Use this resource to guide you to simple service projects you can do or to larger projects that may involve groups or communities. With the guidance of this wonderful handbook, you can start making a difference today! *(175 pages)*

Mapping Inner Space: Learning and Teaching Mind Mapping

by Nancy Margulies....................................... $34.95

Recipient of the 1992 Susan Kovalik Gold Medal Award for best student resource, this delightfully useful and powerful book is for both adults and children, the experienced mind mapper as well as the first-timer. It will assist students and teachers in using "a revolutionary system for pouring ideas onto paper." Includes many colorful examples. *(123 pages)*

"Anchor" Math: The Brain-Compatible Approach to Learning

by Leslie A. Hart.. $14.95

This book is for teachers who find that students respond to math as if it were of another world and had nothing to do with them. It is an informative book for all who teach elementary math and want to greatly increase student achievement. It explores the ways of "anchoring" math to the real world as perceived and processed by a student's mind. A follow-up book to *Human Brain and Human Learning*, it discusses how to teach math in a brain-compatible way. Perceptive, fresh, challenging. Just the tool needed to breathe real life into math and significantly increase student learning. *(148 pages)*

Transformations:

Leadership For Bodybrain-Compatible Learning

Contributing Editor Jane McGeehan $9.95

Is your school or district investigating or in beginning stages of implementing ITI? What are the steps to creating and sustaining ITI? All persons in leadership positions would benefit from this book. Beginning with a succinct overview of ITI, subsequent chapters share the real experiences of leaders who have implemented ITI along with the lessons they have learned about what works and what doesn't work. Practical strategies include implementation at all grade levels, fund-raising, parent involvement, district-wide implementation, handling special interest groups, support agencies, and ideas for assessment. (269 pages)

ORDER FORM

Books for Educators, Inc.
33506 10th Place S. • Federal Way, WA 98003
Call toll free! 888-777-9827
E-mail: books4@oz.net • Internet: www.books4educ.com
Hours: M-Th, 6:00AM-4:30PM, Pacific Time • Closed Fridays

Organization: ____________________

Name: ____________________

Street Address: ____________________

City: ____________ State: ____ Zip: ______

Phone: (   ) ____________

E-mail: ____________

Payment Method: ❑ Payment Enclosed — check # ________
❑ Visa or MasterCard

Credit Card # ____________ Exp. Date: ______

Authorizing Signature: ____________

Please Fax or Mail Authorized Purchase Orders

Prices subject to change without notice

FREE Shipping with 25 or More of Same Title

Does not apply to *RUSH* Service

Shipping via UPS: Please specify preferred shipping option below

Regular Service–
Prices listed below.

❑ Regular Ground UPS

$0 - $49.99............. $6.00
$50 - $99.99............. $7.00
$100 - $499.99.......... 7% of order
$500 and above........ 5% of order

RUSH Service Options–
Please call for current rates.

❑ 3–Day Service
❑ 2–Day Service
❑ 1–Day Service

Add shipping Charge to Order ➜

QTY	TITLE/DESCRIPTION	PRICE	TOTAL

SUBTOTAL	
WA Residents Only Add 8.8% (.088) Sales Tax	
Shipping	

Thank you! **TOTAL** ______

ORDER FORM

Books for Educators, Inc.
33506 10th Place S. • Federal Way, WA 98003
Call toll free! 888-777-9827
E-mail: books4@oz.net • Internet: www.books4educ.com
Hours: M-Th, 6:00AM-4:30PM, Pacific Time • Closed Fridays

Organization: ______________________

Name: ______________________

Street Address: ______________________

City: ______________ State: ____ Zip: ________

Phone: (   ) ______________

E-mail: ______________

Payment Method: ❑ Payment Enclosed — check # ________
❑ Visa or MasterCard

Credit Card # ______________ Exp. Date: ________

Authorizing Signature: ______________________

Please Fax or Mail Authorized Purchase Orders

Prices subject to change without notice

FREE Shipping with 25 or More of Same Title

Does not apply to *RUSH* Service

Shipping via UPS: Please specify preferred shipping option below

Regular Service–
Prices listed below.

❑ Regular Ground UPS

$0 - $49.99............. $6.00
$50 - $99.99............. $7.00
$100 - $499.99.......... 7% of order
$500 and above........ 5% of order

RUSH Service Options–
Please call for current rates.

❑ 3–Day Service
❑ 2–Day Service
❑ 1–Day Service

Add shipping Charge to Order ➔

QTY	TITLE/DESCRIPTION	PRICE	TOTAL

SUBTOTAL	
WA Residents Only Add 8.8% (.088) Sales Tax	
Shipping	

Thank you! **TOTAL** ______

ORDER FORM

Books for Educators, Inc.
33506 10th Place S. • Federal Way, WA 98003
Call toll free! 888-777-9827
E-mail: books4@oz.net • Internet: www.books4educ.com
Hours: M-Th, 6:00AM-4:30PM, Pacific Time • Closed Fridays

Organization: ____________________

Name: ____________________

Street Address: ____________________

City: ____________ State: ____ Zip: ________

Phone: (   ) ____________

E-mail: ____________

Payment Method: ❑ Payment Enclosed — check # ________
❑ Visa or MasterCard

Credit Card # ________________ Exp. Date: ______

Authorizing Signature: ____________________

Please Fax or Mail Authorized Purchase Orders

Prices subject to change without notice

FREE Shipping with 25 or More of Same Title

Does not apply to *RUSH* Service

Shipping via UPS: Please specify preferred shipping option below

Regular Service–
Prices listed below.

❑ Regular Ground UPS

$0 - $49.99............. $6.00
$50 - $99.99............. $7.00
$100 - $499.99.......... 7% of order
$500 and above........ 5% of order

RUSH Service Options–
Please call for current rates.

❑ 3–Day Service
❑ 2–Day Service
❑ 1–Day Service

Add shipping Charge to Order ➜

QTY	TITLE/DESCRIPTION	PRICE	TOTAL

SUBTOTAL

WA Residents Only Add 8.8% (.088) Sales Tax

Shipping

Thank you!

TOTAL

ORDER FORM

Books for Educators, Inc.
33506 10th Place S. • Federal Way, WA 98003
Call toll free! 888-777-9827
E-mail: books4@oz.net • Internet: www.books4educ.com
Hours: M-Th, 6:00AM-4:30PM, Pacific Time • Closed Fridays

Organization: ______________________

Name: ______________________

Street Address: ______________________

City: ______________ State: ____ Zip: ________

Phone: (   ) ____________

E-mail: ____________

Payment Method: ❑ Payment Enclosed — check # ________
❑ Visa or MasterCard

Credit Card # ______________ Exp. Date: ______

Authorizing Signature: ______________

Please Fax or Mail Authorized Purchase Orders

Prices subject to change without notice

FREE Shipping with 25 or More of Same Title

Does not apply to *RUSH* Service

Shipping via UPS: Please specify preferred shipping option below

Regular Service–
Prices listed below.

❑ Regular Ground UPS

$0 - $49.99............. $6.00
$50 - $99.99............. $7.00
$100 - $499.99.......... 7% of order
$500 and above........ 5% of order

RUSH Service Options–
Please call for current rates.

❑ 3–Day Service
❑ 2–Day Service
❑ 1–Day Service

Add shipping Charge to Order ➜

QTY	TITLE/DESCRIPTION	PRICE	TOTAL

SUBTOTAL	
WA Residents Only Add 8.8% (.088) Sales Tax	
Shipping	
TOTAL	

Thank you!